Legalease is a leading independent publisher of information for law firms and their clients. Established in 1987, Legalease is the publisher of *The Legal 500* series which today provides analysis and information on law firms in over 85 countries around the world through *The Legal 500 Europe, Middle East & Africa, The UK Legal 500* and *The Asia Pacific Legal 500*. Legalease is the publisher of *Legal Business* magazine, *The In-House Lawyer* magazine, *Tax Business, Lex, The Practical Lawyer, Employment Law Journal, Trusts and Estates Law & Tax Journal, Property Law Journal, Family Law Journal, Personal Injury Law Journal* and *Wills and Trusts Law Reports*. Legalease runs the leading legal website – **www.legal500.com** – where visitors are able to access many of our publications and find information regarding international commercial legal developments. The site has nearly 500,000 users a month. Additionally, Legalease runs conferences and events for the legal profession and offers bespoke research services.

The LEGAL 500

JOHN PRITCHARD

EUROPE
MIDDLE
EAST &
AFRICA

Published annually by Legalease, Kensington Square House, 12-14 Ansdell Street, London W8 5BN
Phone: +44 20 7396 9292, Fax: +44 20 7396 9300

Printed and bound by LegoPrint SpA. Lavis, Italy

First published 1991
Sixteenth edition 2006

ISBN 1 903927 56 0

Enquiries about inclusion in the directory sections of *The Legal 500 Europe, Middle East & Africa* should be directed to Catherine Wallen; enquiries about the editorial sections should be addressed to Mairead Keohane.

Further copies can be ordered from our subscriptions department
Phone: +44 20 7396 5688, Fax: +44 20 7396 9302,
e-mail: subscriptions@legalease.co.uk

CONTENTS

From the publisher

We are pleased to send you a copy of *The Legal 500 Europe, Middle East & Africa*.

However one looks at today's market, one thing is clear: the international market for commercial lawyers' services continues to grow. Much has changed in the 16 years since we first started commentating on this region of the world: for instance, clients' demands on their law firms; the way in which law firms operate as businesses; and the international strategies of those independent and international law firms. However, what has not changed is that clients and lawyers will always need quality service and advice from outside their own jurisdiction. This book provides our research as a starting point for all readers when identifying the firms they should be talking to.

We hope that you will find the book useful in making contact with lawyers throughout these regions. We are committed to providing our readers with fair and accurate reporting and analysis. As always, we welcome your feedback on our research and we extend our heartfelt thanks to everyone who has helped on this project.

John Pritchard

INTRODUCTION
How to use this book

The Legal 500 Europe, Middle East & Africa is a guide to commercial law firms in Europe, the Middle East and Africa. Countries throughout Western, Central, and Eastern Europe are included, as are Bahrain, Egypt, Iran, Israel, Jordan, Kuwait, Lebanon, Oman, Qatar, Saudi Arabia, Syria and the UAE; Algeria, Ghana, Kenya, Libya, Morocco, Nigeria, South Africa and Tunisia.

Each chapter falls into two distinct parts: the editorial section and the directory section. The editorial section is a mixture of factual information and commentary. This commentary consists of a general review of which firms do what types of work, and which firms are generally reckoned by their peers to have a 'good name' within the national, and international, legal community. The editorial is based largely on the combined opinions of the many lawyers and law firm clients who co-operated in the research in each country. Accordingly, it is important to appreciate that the editorial lists should not be taken as a definitive statement on law firms, but rather as a starting point for discussion.

All editorial comments and listings are completely independent and no firm has been able to secure its inclusion within the editorial sections through payment.

The directory section for each country is made up of professional cards based on information supplied by the firms and approved by them prior to publication.

THE EDITORIAL

The editorial sections consist largely of our own opinions. The views expressed represent the opinions of the editors, with no assumption of legal liability or responsibility for mistakes or inaccuracies. The research for the editorial is based on the combined opinions of the many lawyers interviewed in each jurisdiction, commentary from clients and analysis of deals or contentious issues reported. It is important to note that the editorial is therefore a subjective overview based on systematic research.

Once again, in this edition we have included a table showing the largest firms, according to the number of lawyers in the firm, in each particular country (except Liechtenstein, Syria and the African countries). As always, we rely on the integrity of the firms to supply the correct figures. British and American readers should note that there are relatively few really large continental firms (with more than 50 lawyers, for example) and that many of the leading firms within particular areas of practice will be found to be comparatively small. Many of the larger offices today are those of the international firms of UK or US origin.

In certain jurisdictions some of the larger firms will dominate several categories of work. The research is not, however, limited to these firms only; smaller firms and specialist boutique practices are included where appropriate.

The tables of recommendations are divided into groups: firms are listed in groups in order of priority, and alphabetically within groups. Furthermore, the firms have been sorted alphabetically by using the first name or initial of the firm and not by terms such as *Advokatfirmaet* or *Law Office*. Sole practitioners are listed in the same way as firms, alphabetically by initial or first name.

Readers should also note the differences between local Bar regulations within different jurisdictions. In a number of countries, the local Bar rules on advertising and publicity are a matter of delicacy. In such jurisdictions, no comments have been made with regard to the expertise of particular firms. Instead, lists have been made of firms known to be involved in commercial work – with the proviso that no significance should be attached to the inclusion or non-inclusion of a firm. It should not be inferred in such cases that one firm is 'better' than another; the tables serve only as an indication of suitability.

✪ This symbol in the tables denotes that a law firm has a professional card at the end of that chapter.

England and Wales, Scotland, Guernsey, Jersey, and the Isle of Man

The editorial for England and Wales, Scotland and Offshore Britain (ie Guernsey, Isle of Man, and Jersey) is a digest of the information contained in ***The Legal 500 (2005 UK edition)***. However, we have requested details of the number of lawyers in each firm in order to bring the size tables for these areas in line with those in the rest of the book. As always, we rely on the integrity of the firms to supply the correct figures.

THE DIRECTORY

The directory sections of the book contain professional cards placed by firms within each jurisdiction. The full-page professional cards have profiles based on information provided by the participating firms. These profiles, having been approved by the firms prior to publication, are completely separate and different from the editorial. The professional cards are designed for use by lawyers and clients in different jurisdictions.

We should also emphasise that taking an entry in the directory section does not necessarily mean that a firm will be mentioned in the editorial section.

Within the directory sections, firms are listed in alphabetical order within each town. Thus, in Spain, for example, the listing for firms in Barcelona will precede that for firms in Madrid. As mentioned above, the alphabetical listing uses the first name or initial of the firm and not generic terms such as *Advokatfirmaet* or *Law Office*.

Firm names: There is often a surprising amount of confusion about the correct name for a law firm. To the outsider, it can often be difficult to identify the correct firm. In some jurisdictions, it is virtually mandatory to include the names of all partners within the full firm name. Thus the retirement of an individual partner can result in a change in the firm name. Similarly, some firms operate as the local offices of major international practices, such as *Baker & McKenzie*. In certain jurisdictions, the correct name of the parent firm can be used; in other jurisdictions local Bar rules mean that the foreign name cannot be used. Thus, it is not always easy to identify whether a firm is independent or the local office of an international practice.

A further complication is that local tradition may require that a phrase such as *Law Office of...* (or equivalent) has to be used at the beginning of the name of the firm. Thus many firms in Italy begin with *Studio Legale*; similarly, in Sweden many firms start with the title *Advokatfirman*. All of this means that some care has to be taken in identifying particular firms.

Addresses of firms: We list only one address for each firm within a particular city. This is for reasons of space and simplicity (as well as clarity). Many firms have more than one office, however, and these are listed under '**Other offices**' (see below).

Phone numbers: Most firms will, of course, have many phone lines and several different phone numbers. For reasons of space and clarity, we have restricted ourselves to the main phone number.

All phone numbers are quoted in their international form. Thus we have included the country code in a firm's telephone number (for use when dialling that number from outside the country – the relevant international dialling-out code has to be inserted in place of the + sign).

Fax numbers: Once again, we have quoted only one fax number (despite the fact that many firms will have more than one fax line). It should also be noted that some countries continue to use phrases such as telefax and telecopier when referring to fax machines.

Languages: The languages spoken in the office are generally listed alphabetically – the native language is not usually included (for example, a German firm in Germany would not include German as one of the languages spoken). However, for bilingual or trilingual countries all the native languages spoken in that country may be listed. Additionally, we do include mention of local language capability for firms' foreign offices.

Other offices: Many firms have other offices; these are generally listed in alphabetical order. Some firms have indicated that particular offices are 'associated' offices, and we have marked those with an asterisk (*). However, many of these other offices are not, in practice, genuine offices. Instead, they may amount to a correspondent relationship with a local firm, or merely the displaying of a nameplate in another law firm's office. These are also denoted by *.

Number of lawyers: Most firms have supplied us with the total number of lawyers in the firm and, where applicable, the total number at the office which appears on the professional card. The definition of 'lawyers' includes partners, assistants, associates, attorneys, solicitors, and so on; it does not include consultants, paralegals, trainees, and notaries. (It should be noted, however, that in some countries the title of lawyer cannot be assumed when the person is employed by someone else; for example a *Rechtsanwalt* in Austria.)

However, it is important not to place too much emphasis on these figures. Firstly, a few firms have refused to supply this information and, secondly, we would repeat the point that the size of a firm will often not be a significant factor. There are many very small firms in most countries that are strong within particular areas of law.

Categories of work: Each professional card lists categories of work that the firm undertakes (generally with the name of the person to be contacted for each category).

WHO'S WHO IN THE LAW

Professional contacts: In this section we include biographies of selected partners and contacts in the firms. The information has been provided by the firms themselves. Please note that the partners listed for each firm do not necessarily represent the whole of the partnership. For the total number of lawyers in a firm, please refer to the firm's professional card.

INDEX OF PROFESSIONAL CARDS

Each professional card is listed at the back of the book alphabetically by firm name, followed by the location and the page number on which the professional card appears.

ALGERIA

Population	32.5 million
Number of lawyers	n/a
Professional title	Advocate
Currency	Algerian Dinar
Index	
Corporate and commercial	12
Country index	5

Against a background of years of civil war and perennial political instability, Algeria is experiencing a significant improvement in its fortunes, including increased stability in its government. The country has suffered with the civil war in the north of the country, but the government is now bringing the situation under control with a recent general amnesty marking an attempt by the government to draw a line under the civil law.

Abdelaziz Bouteflika has been president since 1999 and, when re-elected with a landslide victory in 2004 (widely regarded internationally as free and fair), kick-started plans for national reconciliation and business-friendly economic reform. However, long-term problems include major unemployment (higher than 25%), housing shortages, government corruption, and political violence from Islamic fundamentalists. The consolidation of civilian rule is thought to be likely within the next two years as Bouteflika strengthens his position and accelerates economic deregulation and foreign investment.

Algeria is, however, gaining economic momentum and is slowly opening up to the West, with its extensive reserves of oil and gas proving a strong magnet. The performance of crude oil prices is good and the level of external debt is being well managed internally.

The relationship between the state and the economy is intertwined, with the economy decided to a major degree by the prevailing political situation.

But in 2004, poor relations between the privately owned press and the government worsened as several papers campaigned against President Bouteflika's re-election bid and suffered serious consequences after his resounding victory. There is a continued problem of journalists being hounded by police and the courts and there remains little impartiality in the state-owned media.

BILLING

Various billing methods are employed, including hourly rates, a percentage of transaction or dispute value (result-determined) and lump sums. The method is agreed in advance.

MARKETING

The rules of the Algerian Bar prohibit law firms from local advertising. As a result, few Algerian law firms have websites of any substance.

ECONOMY

Algeria is experiencing a significant economic upturn with strong oil and natural gas export revenues, further encouraged by recent discoveries of new oil fields. Algeria is close to the European market and Europe's need of oil and natural gas is an immense advantage for the country. At present, 95% of Algeria's exports are destined for European countries.

The government's economic programme is focusing on structural reforms, and in early 2005 the IMF praised the government's progress, highlighting the fact that prevailing high oil prices are an opportunity for Algeria to make strides in implementing reforms. Algeria assumed a two-year seat on the UN Security Council in early 2004 and is also hoping to join the WTO.

After many years of economic isolation, Algeria is slowly opening up in terms of international business, with progress being made in the government's privatisation programme. Algeria boasts the world's second-largest gas exports and is fourteenth in oil reserves; the hydrocarbons sector is the backbone of the country's economy. Algeria's other main industries of mining, chemicals and cement production, together with gas, are all to be privatised under government plans, although few privatisations have been successful so far. Privatisation projects are also planned for Algeria's airlines, the water and agricultural sectors and transport.

The 2006 Finance Bill was approved in 2005 with Algeria's government declaring that the country needed to open up its financial sector to international insurance groups to raise standards of living, accelerate the privatisation process and increase foreign investment opportunities. In addition, the new and markedly liberal Hydrocarbons Law was published in July 2005 in a move towards increasing investment in the sector. The government has indicated that the political route ahead for privatisations is clear and its target date for completing the privatisation programme, is 2009.

Algeria has huge tourist potential, not least because of its Mediterranean coastline, and is making concerted efforts to develop this. The government held a tourism festival in December 2004 in an attempt to attract both investors and tourists.

Algeria's banking system is undergoing major change but there are practical obstacles to investing in the country including its need of modernisation and 'legacy' of bureaucracy relating to business and investment rules and regulations. The government has announced plans to privatise some of the public banks as a first step to reforming the banking and financial industry and make it conform to international standards.

The postal and telecommunications sectors have been marked by major growth over the last two years but despite a boom in Algeria's mobile market, it remains behind its neighbours in terms of penetration and the fixed-line market remains poor in terms of competition, marked by high prices for consumers. That said, the privatisation of Algérie Télécom is expected to be fairly imminent.

LEGAL MARKET

There is currently no real specialisation by lawyers in Algeria with the exception of some maritime lawyers. There are few recommended business lawyers, a problem recognised by foreign firms who sometimes require local expertise. It is thought this is partly due to the fact that most lawyers study abroad before returning to set up a practice in Algeria. In addition, legal education in Algeria is only available in Arabic.

The first and only foreign law firm to establish an office in Algeria is French firm **Gide Loyrette Nouel** which opened at the end of 2003, headed by Samy Laghouati. US firm **Thompson & Knight LLP** has an associated office in Algiers and tax specialist **KPMG** also operates in Algeria.

Denton Wilde Sapte has no official presence in the country, but has previously advised on a number of matters in the oil and energy sectors – a past client is British Gas. Foreign firms may appear in Algerian courts if they belong to one of the 20 countries to have signed an agreement with Algeria. Generally, foreign firms adopt informal agreements with local firms where necessary.

Norton Rose acts for a wide variety of regional and international clients in the oil and gas, telecoms, tobacco, energy and utilities, shipping and financial services sectors. The firm recently advised Black & Veatch, the international contractor in relation to a multi-stage flash sea water desalination facility in Dem Arzew, and advised British American Tobacco on its joint venture between BAT UK and an Algerian tobacco company. Other notable clients include Enel, Eni and Petrofac Resources International Limited.

Herbert Smith LLP has an Algerian lawyer in its Paris office from which the Africa practice is based. It boasts strong mining and energy capability, with clients including the Gold Mines of Algeria, and has a major practice in relation to infrastructure work. The firm recently advised Burlington Resources International on Algerian unitisation agreements, BHP Billiton on the aborted potential refinancing of its Algerian hydrocarbon assets by Société Générale on limited recourse project financing, and Shell International in relation to an LNG sale and purchase agreement. It also advised the Algerian Ministry of Telecommunications on the financing, acquisition and launching of a telecommunications satellite. **Herbert Smith LLP** also counts the following among its clients: BHP Petroleum, Devon Energy, Anadarko and France Télécom.

Lovells represents clients in the oil, gas and energy sectors. The firm acted for Statoil in its acquisition from BP of interests in the In Salah and In Amenas projects in Algeria. Partner David Moss has wide experience of upstream and downstream energy work in Algeria.

US firm **Thompson & Knight LLP** has an associated office in Algiers headed by Hassan Yassine. Established locally for more than 80 years, the firm has a strong focus on the energy sector.

White & Case remains active in Algeria and recently advised in relation to the Algerian telecoms financing for Orascom.

CORPORATE AND COMMERCIAL

CORPORATE AND COMMERCIAL
Aidoud Law Firm
Ben Abderrahmane (Dr) & Partners, Law Office of
Bouchaib Law Firm ✪
Ghellal & Mekerba
Law Office Yamina Kebir
Abu-Ghazaleh Intellectual Property
Gide Loyrette Nouel ✪
Guerrouche Mouloud MG Avocats
Mustapha Rouabah
Saba & Co
Samir Hamouda Cabinet d'Avocats
Sator Cabinet
Thompson & Knights LLP

Firms are listed A-Z in tiers which are ranked in order of priority
✪ Indicates firm displays contact details at the end of this chapter.

Three-partner **Aidoud Law Firm** is led by reputable name partner Mamoun Aidoud, who is renowned for his commercial activities, and takes frequent referrals from major international law firms. The firm, which keeps current client names confidential, specialises in corporate and commercial, banking and foreign direct investment, and recently advised major US corporations in relation to investment in Algeria. It also advised on Algerian telecoms law in relation to a telecoms licence. Past clients include British Telecom, the European Investment Bank, BAE Systems (Québec), US company Northrop Grumman and BP.

Law Office of Dr. Ben Abderrahmane & Partners is based in Paris but has four offices in Africa including one in Algeria. The Algiers office specialises mainly in corporate and commercial law.

Bouchaib Law Firm has built up a strong general practice in the ten years since it was established. The firm has two offices, one in Algiers and one in Medea and specialises in dispute resolution, contract and employment law. It has good contacts with the Algerian administration, including the Ministry of Finance.

Ghellal & Mekerba is a twelve-lawyer firm, highly regarded as perhaps Algeria's leading firm for international trade contracts, company and commercial work, and natural resources. The practice benefits from experience in international commercial arbitration, particularly in the construction and energy sectors. The firm also specialises in maritime and shipping law, privatisation and projects and handles cross-border disputes in the domestic courts. It has also forged close contacts with major law firms internationally.

Law Office Yamina Kebir is unusual in being a predominantly English-speaking firm, and has good links with international firms for referrals. The practice specialises in corporate and commercial finance and investments and intellectual property, led by Yamina Kebir, reputed for her expertise in corporate legal practice. The majority of clients are multinational corporations but the office also advises local companies. In 2005, the firm advised an international corporation in a major acquisition and was counsel to Orascom Telecom Holdings in relation to the financing of a major investment in Algeria.

Abu-Ghazaleh Intellectual Property has a number of Middle East offices, including one in Algiers, specialising in intellectual property registration.

Parisian firm **Gide Loyrette Nouel** opened its doors in Algiers at the end of 2003 and is growing rapidly with eight lawyers, currently headed by Samy Laghouati, a member of the Paris Bar. The firm has recently been joined by Djamila Annad, an expert in the hydrocarbons sector with ten years' experience in the management of Sonatrach. The firm advises the Ministry of Participation and Investment Promotion in relation to the government's privatisation programme, and advised the government on structural law reform in the telecommunications sector. It is also advising AIG Infrastructure Fund LLC on the largest AIM transaction in Algeria to date. Other notable clients include Lafarge SA and international food products company Lesaffre SA and the firm's practice also covers M&A, banking and finance, business law and taxation.

Guerrouche Mouloud MG Avocats is a reputable firm with five lawyers and is recommended for its corporate and commercial practice. The firm also has a maritime and shipping practice.

The three-partner **Mustapha Rouabah** is experienced in the privatisation sector, particularly in telecommunications. Name partner Mustapha Hamdane has a reputation in the domestic legal market and beyond for his experience and expertise in IP and telecoms. The practice also has a strong company and commercial practice and has experience in dispute resolution, and boasts membership of the International Committee of Commercial Arbitration. **Saba & Co** has a strong intellectual property practice in Africa and Asia and its lawyers have frequently contributed to the drafting of laws and to reform committees. Its office in Algiers advises on matters generally relating to designs, patents and trade marks.

Four-partner **Cabinet d'Avocats Samir Hamouda** is now 20 years old and is led by name partner Samir Hamouda, described by peers as 'a good lawyer'. The team acts as local counsel for **KPMG** and **Landwell Global**. The firm essentially advises national and international companies and has advised on the first GSM private licence in Algeria, in relation to privatisation operations including in the cement sector, and on an investment project in the pharmaceutical field. The firm has also recently advised in relation to joint ventures and major banking and investment transactions and is well-known for its expertise in IP and trade marks, and the tourist sector.

Cabinet Sator specialises in trade marks and patents and is well-known for its corporate practice.

US-based **Thompson & Knight LLP** has decades of experience in the region and runs a good international energy practice.

BOUCHAIB LAW FIRM

35 RUE BOUAMAMA
BELFORT
EL HARRACH
ALGIERS

Telephone: +213 61 55 21 42
Fax: +213 21 82 47 70
E-mail: adbouchaib@yahoo.fr

Other offices
Medea

Number of lawyers 5

Contact
Mr Adnane Bouchaib (abouchaib@yahoo.fr)

CATEGORIES OF WORK

- Intellectual property (registration of patents and trade marks among others)
- Health law
- Commercial law
- Mining law
- Corporate law
- Maritime law
- Vessel registration
- Banking law
- Insurance
- Labour law
- Civil law
- Criminal law
- Environmental law
- International law
- Immigration
- Trusts and private foundations
- Privatisations, government contracts and public bids
- Financial law
- Communications law
- Litigation of commercial, civil and criminal matters
- Real estate

GIDE LOYRETTE NOUEL

8 RUE LAROUSSI AMROUNE
LES GLYCINES
16035 ALGIERS

Telephone: +213 21 23 94 94
Fax: +213 21 23 92 73
E-mail: gln.algiers@gide.com
Website: www.gide.com

Other offices
Beijing, Belgrade, Brussels, Bucharest, Budapest, Casablanca, Hanoi, Istanbul, London, Moscow, New York, Paris, Prague, Riyadh, Shanghai, Tunis, Warsaw

Number of lawyers 586
at this office 8

Contact
Samy Laghouati (laghouati@gide.com)

CATEGORIES OF WORK

- Banking and finance law
- Corporate law
- Mergers and acquisitions
- Telecommunications law
- Economic law
- Exchange control
- Taxation
- Capital markets
- Employment law
- Real estate
- Project finance
- Energy

BOUCHAIB LAW FIRM

ROUTE DE L'AGHOUTE
QUARTIER TAHTOUH
MEDEA

Telephone: +213 25 58 72 88
Fax: +213 21 82 47 70
E-mail: adbouchaib@yahoo.fr

Other offices
Algiers

Number of lawyers 5

Contact
Mr Adnane Bouchaib (abouchaib@yahoo.fr)

CATEGORIES OF WORK

Intellectual property (registration of patents and trademarks among others)

Health law

Commercial law

Mining law

Corporate law

Maritime law

Vessel registration

Banking law

Insurance

Labour law

Civil law

Criminal law

Environmental law

International law

Immigration

Trusts and private foundations

Privatisations, Government contracts and public bids

Financial law

Communications law

Litigation of commercial, civil and criminal matters

Real estate

AUSTRIA

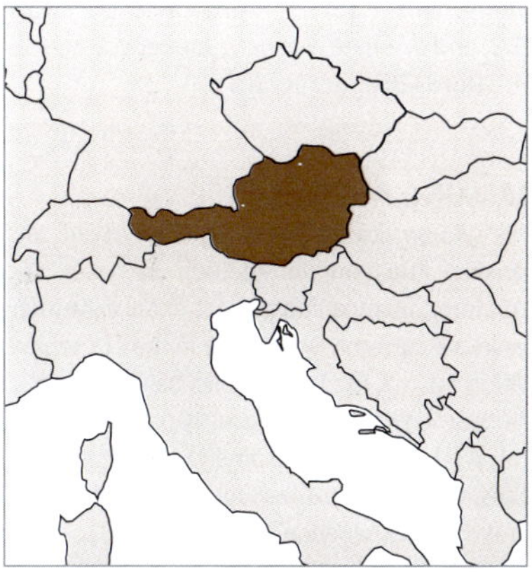

Population	8.1 million
Number of lawyers	4,100
Professional title	Rechtsanwält Rechtsanwältin
Currency	Euro (€)

Index

Austria is a small country which is an EU member and benefits from its location in the centre of Europe, sitting on the key Danube trade route and acting as a bridge between Western Europe and Eastern Europe and the Middle East. It borders with Germany, the Czech Republic, Slovakia, Hungary, Slovenia, Italy, Switzerland and Liechtenstein. Germany is the most important Austrian trading partner, followed by Italy and the neighbouring former Eastern bloc states. Austrian businesses regard the latter as their home market, and trade with these countries is becoming increasingly important following the accession to the EU of the Czech Republic, Hungary, Slovakia and Slovenia, and with Bulgaria, Romania, Croatia and Turkey on the membership candidate list. Austria is a federal republic with nine autonomous provinces, of which Vienna is the wealthiest. The government is a coalition between the far-right, populist, anti-immigration Freedom Party of Austria and the dominant conservative Austrian People's Party, led by Chancellor Wolfgang Schussel. The President is Social Democrat Heinz Fischer.

BILLING

Billing rates are governed by the Austrian Lawyers' Scale of Fees Act. The Austrian Bar Association also issues guidelines on fees. Most foreign clients are billed on an hourly basis to spare them the intricacies of the Act. Fixed-fee lump sums are popular in litigation, but if a party agrees to pay more than the rate, the additional fees are not recoverable from the losing party. Contingency or success-related fees are prohibited, but a fixed percentage of the claim can be negotiated as a bonus in advance.

MARKETING

Austrian lawyers are now able to publish a client's name with the client's approval. Increasingly, commercial law firms are appointing in-house marketing professionals.

IN-HOUSE LAWYERS

Many medium-sized Austrian companies do not have in-house lawyers, but will instead employ a person with a legal education who also has responsibility for areas such as insurance, property or human resources. However the larger companies, particularly banks, now have significant in-house teams of up to 30 lawyers.

ECONOMY

Austria, with its well-developed market economy and high standard of living, is closely tied to other EU economies, especially Germany's. Membership of the EU (since 1995) has drawn an influx of foreign investors attracted by Austria's access to the single European market and proximity to the new EU economies. Austrian companies are increasingly investing into the Central and Eastern Europe (CEE) region as far as Turkey and the Ukraine.

The Austrian economy has recently turned up, with estimated GDP for 2005 at 2.1% compared to 1.9% in 2004, and employment currently at a record high. A plethora of mid-sized M&A deals is now taking place in the market, though not many major takeovers are yet closing.

However, the M&A climate is increasingly positive. In 2004 a major acquisition – Swisscom's takeover of Telekom Austria – fell through for reasons that were widely perceived to be political. In 2005, however, the politically controversial acquisition of the Vienna Stock Exchange (VSE)-listed VA Technology AG (VA Tech) by Siemens AG – there was widespread opposition to a German company becoming a major shareholder in VA Tech, with potential job losses in Austria – was ultimately successful.

Projects, including public private partnerships (PPPs) – innovative for the Austrian market – are also finally coming to fruition, although most are still at the tender and procurement stage.

In Austria's regional markets upper Austria, dominated by Linz and the border with Germany, is one of the most successful economically, with a heavyweight industrial base and an influx of highly qualified workers from Germany.

Austria's main exports are machinery, metals, paper, textiles, food and livestock. The energy sector is becoming increasingly important, though it is still very concentrated. The jurisdiction is popular as a location for structuring international M&A transactions, and is a notable international arbitration centre.

Austrian takeover law will be changed in 2006 to introduce a fixed threshold of 30%.

LEGAL MARKET

The largest firms in Austria – whose sizes are currently under 100 lawyers within the country – believe that there is still substantial room for growth to the size of Sweden and the Netherlands,

The largest firms

1	Wolf Theiss	96
2	Schönherr	71
3	Freshfields Bruckhaus Deringer	61
4	Dorda Brugger Jordis	60
5	DLA Weiss-Tessbach	53
6	CHSH Cerha Hempel Spiegelfeld Hlawati	51
7	Binder Grösswang Attorneys-at-Law	50
8	Saxinger Chalupsky Weber & Partner Rechtsanwälte GmbH	49
9	CMS Reich-Rohrwig Hainz	45
10	Baier Lambert	30
11	Baker & McKenzie	28
12	Fellner Wratzfeld & Partner Rechtsanwälte GmbH	27
	Karasek Wietrzyk Rechtsanwälte GmbH	27
14	Lansky, Ganzger & Partner Rechtsanwälte GmbH	26
15	Hausmaninger Kletter Rechtsanwälte GmbH	25
16	Preslmayr Attorneys at Law	24
17	Haslinger/Nagele & Partner Rechtsanwälte GmbH	23
18	Graf, Maxl & Pitkowitz Rechtsanwälte GMBH	22
19	Fiebinger, Polak, Leon & Partner Rechtsanwälte	21
	enwc attorneys at law Eiselsberg Natlacen Walderdorff Cancola	21
21	Herbst Vavrovsky Kinsky Rechtsanwälte GmbH	20
	Kunz Schima Wallentin Rechtsanwälte Keg	20
23	Brauneis, Klauser & Prändl	17
24	Greiter Pegger Kofler & Partners	16
	Siemer-Siegl-Füreder & Partner, Rechtsanwälte	16

These figures represent the total number of lawyers in this country only, and have been supplied by the firms themselves. The figures should be accurate as at 1 January 2006.

where law firms can be four times this size. The largest firms are also growing substantially through offices in their home market of the CEE region.

Legal academics in Austria are much more active in the market than those in Anglo-American jurisdictions, often taking the role – played by UK barristers – of providing expert opinions to law firms. 'Junior partner' in Austria is a term which applies to any lawyer who is five years' qualified and has passed the Rechtsanwälte Bar exam, with only equity partners having the seniority which is normally associated with the term 'partner'.

The leading heavyweight corporate law firms in Austria are: **Wolf Theiss**, a firm with a particularly strong reputation in the banking sector, and which has only been established for 11 years; **Freshfields Bruckhaus Deringer**, a firm which has made important strides internationally since it merged with the UK-based giant in 2000; and **Schönherr**, a very old and well-established firm which has the leading corporate practice in Austria. Of all the law firms in Austria, only **Freshfields Bruckhaus Deringer** is an integrated part of a global law firm giant, and a wave of international tie-ups is unlikely to take place in the near future.

Other firms with ties to international firms or networks include **CMS Reich-Rohrwig Hainz**, **Haarmann Hügel** – which is a co-operation, to all intents and purposes a merger, with the international network of Germany-based **Haarmann Hemmelrath** – and **DLA Weiss-Tessbach**, whose market position is strengthening and recovering. Leading dispute resolution practice **Baier Lambert** has an association with **Eversheds LLP**. **Baker & McKenzie** is perceived by the market to be primarily a local firm, though it is increasingly handling international work. US-based **Skadden, Arps, Slate, Meagher & Flom LLP** has a very small greenfield operation in Vienna, which handles exclusively international work.

Some of the most successful local firms, such as **Binder Grösswang Attorneys-at-Law**, **CHSH Cerha Hempel Spiegelfeld Hlawati** and **Dorda Brugger Jordis**, have no formal international links.

In 2005, well-known banking and M&A firm *Hausmaninger Herbst Rechtsanwälte* split to become **Hausmaninger Kletter Rechtsanwälte GmbH** and **Herbst Vavrovsky Kinsky Rechtsanwälte GmbH**. The latter achieved its new form through merger with the Salzburg-based firm *Vavrovsky*, and consequently has a Salzburg office.

Several new firms were also established in 2005. **AVIA Law Group** is a regional corporate practice formed by the merger of *Wolczik Knotek Winalek*, which had offices in Baden and Klagenfurt, with a Vienna office established by Claudio Arturo, formerly a partner with **Petsch, Frosch & Klein**, together with a small Vienna firm. **Dr Alexandra Knell** is an employment boutique established by a former member of the employment team at **Dorda Brugger Jordis**. **Dietrich Majoros Marchl Rechtsanwälte** is a corporate practice founded by three lawyers from **Lansky, Ganzger & Partner Rechtsanwälte GmbH**. **Schwarz Schönherr Rechtsanwälte OEG** is an IP boutique founded by Georg Schönherr, formerly a name partner and head of IP with **Engin-Deniz Reimitz Hafner Rechtsanwälte KEG**, and Winfried Schwarz, formerly a partner with **Dorda Brugger Jordis**.

BANKING AND FINANCE

This section covers loans, regulatory work and banking litigation, in addition to asset and structured finance and project finance. Austrian banks are currently very active in the CEE region. Within Austria, the larger banks have substantial in-house legal teams, and usually prefer to handle loan work, including in some cases cross-border loans, in-house. However, the best banking law firms have experience in advising on complex loans. Project finance is currently a very active area for lawyers (see **Economic environment** and **Corporate and M&A** sections). On the structured finance side, there has been a considerable amount of activity in property-linked securitisation, and recent legislative changes have facilitated transactions by reducing their previously inherent risks relating to taxation and regulation.

Binder Grösswang Attorneys-At-Law has a particularly strong reputation for financing work and tax-driven structures. It set up an innovative asset-backed securities (ABS) programme for Investkredit Bank AG, the first such programme governed by Austrian law and tailor-made for medium-sized companies. It also advised Raiffeisen Leasing on a structured financing sale and lease-back of a wind farm. In addition, it advises national banks such as Bank Austria Creditanstalt AG, the largest Austrian bank and a subsidiary of Germany-based HVB Bank Biochim AD (HVB), and international banks such as Merill Lynch on syndicated loan agreements and their respective security packages. On the project finance side, it has been representing the banks of one of the consortia bidding for the motorway project (see also **Corporate and M&A** section). Christian Klausegger and Stefan Tiefenthaler, whom clients describe as 'excellent', are recommended for structured finance, and Tibor Fabian for project finance. Name partner Michael Binder handles regulatory and contentious banking.

The Vienna office of **Freshfields Bruckhaus Deringer** benefits from its integration into the firm's international banking team. The Vienna office has a strong securitisation practice, and was involved in drafting the legislation described

BANKING AND FINANCE

BINDER GRÖSSWANG ATTORNEYS-AT-LAW ✪
FRESHFIELDS BRUCKHAUS DERINGER
SCHÖNHERR ✪
WOLF THEISS ✪

CHSH Cerha Hempel Spiegelfeld Hlawati ✪
DLA Weiss-Tessbach ✪
Dorda Brugger Jordis ✪

Dallmann & Juranek
Saxinger Chalupsky Weber & Partner Rechtsanwälte GmbH ✪

CMS Reich-Rohrwig Hainz ✪
enwc attorneys at law Eiselsberg Natlacen Walderdorff Cancola ✪
Fellner Wratzfeld & Partner Rechtsanwälte GmbH ✪
Fiebinger, Polak, Leon & Partner Rechtsanwälte ✪
Haarmann Hügel ✪
Hauser Partners Rechtsanwälte GmbH ✪
Hausmaninger Kletter Rechtsanwälte GmbH ✪
Herbst Vavrovsky Kinsky Rechtsanwälte GmbH ✪
Karasek Wietrzyk Rechtsanwälte GmbH
Ortner Pöch Foramitti
Preslmayr Attorneys at Law ✪

ARNOLD Rechtsanwalts-Partnerschaft
Baier Lambert ✪
Baker & McKenzie ✪
Brandl & Talos Rechtsanwälte GmbH ✪
Brauneis, Klauser & Prändl ✪
Graf, Maxl & Pitkowitz Rechtsanwälte GMBH ✪
Griss & Partner
Hasch & Partner Anwaltsgesellschaft mbH
Kunz Schima Wallentin Rechtsanwälte Keg ✪
Neudorfer Rechtsanwälte ✪
Skadden, Arps, Slate, Meagher & Flom LLP

Alix Frank Rechtsanwälte GmbH
AVIA Law Group
bmp Rechtsanwälte
Barnert Egermann Illigasch Rechtsanwälte OEG
Eckert & Fries Rechtsanwälte GmbH
Greiter Pegger Kofler & Partners ✪
Haslinger/Nagele & Partner Rechtsanwälte GmbH ✪
Held Berdnik Astner & Partner, Rechtsanwälte
Lansky, Ganzger & Partner Rechtsanwälte GmbH
Lovells in association with Mondl, Trummer, Thomas & Partner Rechtsanwälte GmbH
Zirngibl Langwieser

Firms are listed A-Z in tiers which are ranked in order of priority
✪ *Indicates firm displays contact details at the end of this chapter.*

above. It advised on a public leasing securitisation worth €425m by Bank Austria Creditanstalt Leasing, and acted as transaction counsel on an asset-backed commercial paper securitisation of auto lease and loan receivables of Porsche Bank, arranged by ABN Amro. Loan work includes advising Sappi on a €600m revolving facility. Friedrich Jergitsch is recommended for asset and structured finance, and Maria Th. Pflügl for general banking work and for project finance. Clients express their 'absolute satisfaction'.

Schönherr, best known in the market as the leading corporate law firm, is very strong on structured finance and acquisition finance transactions. The firm acted as Austrian counsel to arrangers Barclays Capital and Citigroup in relation to a €750m syndicated loan to Verbund, the energy group; at the time of closing, the transaction was the largest-ever syndicated loan granted to an Austrian group. It also advised arranger HVB on a €200m revolving securitisation of sale and lease-back receivables of car rental company Sixt, and advised Goldman Sachs as one of the bidders in the tender sale of a portfolio of NPLs by an Austrian bank. Martin Ebner is recommended for securities work, and Christoph Lindinger for project finance.

Wolf Theiss, which has a market-leading reputation for banking law, has recently been handling a considerable amount of work relating to the structuring of financial products. It advised Deutsche Bank on a €250m financing for the Vienna-based Donau Bank, and advised a consortium of ABN Amro, CIBC and BNP Paribas on the financing and security structure for the €1.3bn refinancing of the Yellow Brick Road/Mediatel Group. In relation to project finance, Andreas Schmid advised a consortium, which included Siemens AG Germany and Siemens AG Austria, on the €500m financing of a toll road system in the Czech Republic. Markus Heidinger – who is strong on debt finance – is recommended.

CHSH Cerha Hempel Spiegelfeld Hlawati's Peter Knobl has a regulatory and loans practice, and is also specialised in high-end fund work. He advised Sal. Oppenheim on its €500m future structure for Austrian offerings, and also advised JP Morgan on a €1.5bn multi-currency revolving securities Repo facility agreement. Volker Glas handles project finance, while dispute resolution head Irene Welser has a good reputation for banking litigation. Clients say they are 'quite satisfied'.

DLA Weiss-Tessbach is particularly strong in project finance, but has also been building up its reputation for general banking work. It has been handling a €100m monetisation transaction, and also advising an Austrian investment group on a synthetic loan provided by an international bank and involving a share swap transaction. In relation to regulatory matters, it has handled an international group restructuring of an Austrian banking group, which was extremely innovative for Austria. Martin Geiger is recommended for structured finance, Stefan Eder for project finance, and Ivo Deskovic for regulatory matters.

Dorda Brugger Jordis was retained by the IFC to advise the Bosnian Ministry of Finance on the privatisation of government-owned bank participations. It also acted as Austrian counsel to the senior and mezzanine lenders in the €261m acquisition financing of the Bulgarian Telecommunications Company. Tibor Varga is recommended for project finance and structured finance.

Dallmann & Juranek has a good reputation for project finance, and has been advising a major European financial institution on the €300m refinancing of a real estate investment portfolio with assets in several CEE jurisdictions. It has also been advising investment bankers on issues of capital. Armin Dallman has a good reputation for structured finance.

At **Saxinger Chalupsky Weber & Partner Rechtsanwälte GmbH**, Franz Mittendorfer handles project finance, and has been advising some European investment banks in relation to the financing of the motorway project. Stefan Weber handles regulatory work and structured finance, including work on ABS structures and tier 1 structures.

CMS Reich-Rohrwig Hainz has been advising Bank Austria on the financings, worth €20m each, of two office buildings in Belgrade. Peter Huber handles project finance.

enwc attorneys at law Eiselsberg Natlacen Walderdorff Cancola's banking clients include Italian bank San Paolo IML, Bank Austria Real Estate GmbH and GE Commercial Finance Fleet Service. Dieter Natlacen handles banking work.

At **Fellner Wratzfeld & Partner Rechtsanwälte GmbH**, corporate partner Markus Fellner is well known for his project finance work, and the firm also has a regulatory practice.

Fiebinger, Polak, Leon & Partner Rechtsanwälte also has project finance as a core focus. Peter Polak is the specialist here.

Haarmann Hügel has a banking practice focused on cross-border loans and regulatory work. The team advised VB Investmentbank AG on a €110m syndicated loan transaction in the Czech Republic. Robert Leuthner handles loan work, while leading competition partner Rainer Roniger advises banks on regulatory matters.

Hauser Partners Rechtsanwälte GmbH has been advising one of the world's largest banks on the refinancing of loans relating to a senior €1bn financing and a €70m mezzanine financing. Kordula Fleiss is recommended.

Hausmaninger Kletter Rechtsanwälte GmbH's Christian Hausmaninger enjoys an excellent reputation for banking work, and was described by one market commentator as an 'extremely savvy guy'. His firm recently advised the State of Lower Austria on one of the largest securitisation transactions ever to take place in Austria.

Herbst Vavrovsky Kinsky Rechtsanwälte GmbH's Wolfgang Schwackhöfer advised Westdeutsche Landesbank on a US$25m international container financing transaction. Philipp Kinsky has a strong reputation in public securities offerings, while Christoph Herbst has a solid regulatory practice.

Karasek Wietrzyk Rechtsanwälte GmbH has been advising an Austrian company on the refinancing of a group through a €500m offshore financing vehicle. Otto Dietrich is recommended, and Gerold Wietryzk for securities.

Ortner Pöch Foramitti has a strong reputation for regulatory work, where Heinz Rindler is recommended. Marie Helen Pichler has a hedge funds practice.

Preslmayr Attorneys at Law acts for foreign, mainly US-based, venture capital (VC) funds that are active in Austria. It also advises foreign companies seeking financing or the arranging of securities in Austria.

CAPITAL MARKETS

In 2005 there were some substantial capital increases of Austrian listed companies on the equity capital markets. The debt capital markets have also been active; in Austria it is common in smaller offerings for one law firm to advise both the issuer and the underwriter.

CHSH Cerha Hempel Spiegelfeld Hlawati has a reputation for innovative work on the Austrian capital markets. This recently included work on the first pre-IPO bond of a public entity in Austria, advising HSBC Bank Plc as lead manager and bookrunner on the issue of €500 pre-IPO exchangeable notes of Kärtner Landesholding into shares of Hypo Alpe-Adria-Bank. The team also advised Böhler-Uddeholm on a €235m rights offering and, in relation to debt, advised Telekom Austria on a €1bn drawdown under its EMTN programme and the listing of these bonds on the VSE. Edith Hlawati, whom clients describe as 'extremely experienced', has a market-leading reputation, and Albert Birkner is also highly regarded. Volker Glas is recommended for debt transactions.

Dorda Brugger Jordis advised on one of the largest Austrian debt capital markets transactions ever – which was also Austria's first successful combined share capital increase and convertible bond issue – advising underwriters Deutsche Bank, Erste Bank and Merrill Lynch on the €1.2bn offering and issue by Austrian giant OMV Akiengesellschaft AG (OMV). It also advised on the complex first IPO of a Delaware-based company listing in Austria, the IPO of Christ Water Technology AG, and on the IPO in Austria by capital increase of Century Casinos Inc. Andreas Mayr has a market-leading reputation, while Tibor Varga is also recommended for debt.

Saxinger Chalupsky Weber & Partner Rechtsanwälte GmbH's Stefan Weber has a market-leading reputation. He acted for OMV on the deal described above. He also advised Merrill Lynch as underwriters of the €1.1bn IPO of Raiffeisen International Bank Holding AG, the largest IPO ever in Austria. In addition, he acted for Deustche Bank as underwriters of convertible bonds worth €250m issued by voestalpine AG, handled an MTN programme worth €10bn for the Austrian Railways, and handled the VSE €70m flotation of Slovakia-based Sky Europe.

CAPITAL MARKETS

CHSH CERHA HEMPEL SPIEGELFELD HLAWATI ✪
DORDA BRUGGER JORDIS ✪
SAXINGER CHALUPSKY WEBER & PARTNER RECHTSANWÄLTE GMBH ✪
WOLF THEISS ✪

Binder Grösswang Attorneys-at-Law ✪
Freshfields Bruckhaus Deringer
Schönherr ✪

Brandl & Talos Rechtsanwälte GmbH ✪
CMS Reich-Rohrwig Hainz ✪
Dallmann & Juranek
Ortner Pöch Foramitti

Barnert Egermann Illigasch Rechtsanwälte OEG
DLA Weiss-Tessbach ✪
Haarmann Hügel ✪
Hasch & Partner Anwaltsgesellschaft mbH
Hauser Partners Rechtsanwälte GmbH ✪
Hausmaninger Kletter Rechtsanwälte GmbH ✪
Herbst Vavrovsky Kinsky Rechtsanwälte GmbH ✪
Karasek Wietrzyk Rechtsanwälte GmbH

Firms are listed A-Z in tiers which are ranked in order of priority
✪ Indicates firm displays contact details at the end of this chapter.

Wolf Theiss is the only Austrian firm to have a market-leading practice for banking, finance and capital markets. It advised the issuer and the parent company on the IPO of Raiffeisen, described above. On the debt side, it advised Erste Bank as lead manager of the supplementary €300m capital bond issue of WIENER STAEDISCHE Allgemeine Versicherung Aktiengeselschaft. Richard Wolf is recommended for equity work and Christian Temmel for debt, while Markus Heidinger focuses on the introduction into Austria and tax structuring of new products from Frankfurt, London and Luxembourg.

Binder Grösswang Attorneys-At-Law has worked on some significant MTN programmes in the debt capital markets, where clients include a significant proportion of the Austrian banking market, notably Investcredit and Bank Austria. Tibor Fabian is recommended.

Freshfields Bruckhaus Deringer is active in advising international investment banks on the Austrian capital markets, where its Frankfurt office is also highly visible. The Vienna office advised Bank Austria on its Luxembourg MTN programme. In relation to equity, it advised Austrian biotechnology business Intercell and its core shareholders and investors on the company's VSE IPO. Maria Th. Pflügl is recommended.

Schönherr has a strong practice in the field of public takeovers, and has been advising on prospective changes to Austrian takeover law. It advised the issuer on the first Eurobond of a major Romanian issuer, the €500m debut London Stock Exchange listing of Banca Commerciala Romana. It also advised the underwriters of a VSE €228m secondary offering by AGRANA beteiligungs AG, and the managers of a €150m tier 1 issue by Bank Austria. Peter Feyl is recommended.

Brandl & Talos Rechtsanwälte GmbH is a banking and capital markets boutique which is increasingly building a reputation in the financial services sector. It advises VSE-listed BETandWIN.com Interactive Entertainment AG on the issuance of its bonds and, recently, on the IPO of spin-off Betbull plc. It also advises AIG Financial Services AG on the structuring and placement of complex financial products on the Austrian market, and the VSE listing of securities. Thomas Talos handles equity work while Ernst Brandl, formerly chief legal counsel to the Austrian Securities Agency, handles financial products and is described by one client as 'one of the profoundest experts on regulatory capital markets law in Austria'. Clients also say the team is 'top notch' and has a 'brilliant combination of skill, wit, commitment and common sense'.

CMS Reich-Rohrwig Hainz's new equity partner Martin Zuffer has a good reputation for debt capital markets work, and a client list which includes Raiffeisen and Erste Bank. He also advised the underwriters in relation to the public offering and VSE listing of the €100m corporate bond of A-TEC INDUSTRIES AG. One client said: 'We particularly like the tough stance which this firm is taking with auditors'.

Dallmann & Juranek has a strong debt practice, and has been advising the Austrian underwriter on one of the first genuinely Austro-Hungarian offerings, involving bonds worth €150m and HUF200m, the highest Hungarian Forint bond ever issued. It also advised the underwriters and issuers of bonds, both worth €70m, by Austrian companies. Thomas Zivny is recommended.

Ortner Pöch Foramitti's Peter Pöch has a well-regarded bond practice, and advises the Republic of Austria, the largest issuer in the country.

CENTRAL AND EASTERN EUROPE

This section focuses on corporate work in CEE, but also covers Austrian firms providing real estate, banking and capital markets, dispute resolution and EU and competition law advice to companies with interests in these jurisdictions. Austrian, and increasingly German, companies consider the CEE region to be their home market, and are currently

CENTRAL AND EASTERN EUROPE

DLA WEISS-TESSBACH ✪
FRESHFIELDS BRUCKHAUS DERINGER
SCHÖNHERR ✪
WOLF THEISS ✪

CHSH Cerha Hempel Spiegelfeld Hlawati ✪
CMS Reich-Rohrwig Hainz ✪
Dorda Brugger Jordis ✪
enwc attorneys at law Eiselsberg Natlacen Walderdorff Cancola ✪
Haarmann Hügel ✪

Baier Lambert ✪
Fiebinger, Polak, Leon & Partner Rechtsanwälte ✪
Gassauer-Fleissner Rechtsanwälte ✪
Griss & Partner
Hasch & Partner Anwaltsgesellschaft mbH
Haslinger/Nagele & Partner Rechtsanwälte GmbH ✪
Hauser Partners Rechtsanwälte GmbH ✪
Karasek Wietrzyk Rechtsanwälte GmbH
Saxinger Chalupsky Weber & Partner Rechtsanwälte GmbH ✪
Zeiner & Zeiner

Firms are listed A-Z in tiers which are ranked in order of priority
✪ Indicates firm displays contact details at the end of this chapter.

investing heavily in the region. Bratislava, for example, is only 35 minutes by car from Vienna. The areas of greatest interest to Austrian law firms are currently in the south-east; Bulgaria, Macedonia, Romania, Turkey and the Ukraine. Macedonia is in the process of privatising its banking and electricity industries, Turkish companies are investing heavily in Bulgaria and Romania, Romanian banks are starting to develop sophisticated financial products, while Western investors going into the Ukraine prefer to do so via Vienna rather via Moscow.

The corporate practice at **DLA Weiss-Tessbach** is strongest in CEE, a region on which it has a longstanding focus. The firm has offices in Bratislava, Budapest, Prague, Zagreb and Sarajevo. Out of Vienna, the firm has been advising on a major privatisation of an airport in Central Europe. The team has been joined by Oskar Winkler, recruited from **CHSH Cerha Hempel Spiegelfeld Hlawati**, who will head the firm's insurance working group in CEE. Winkler's work at his previous firm includes advising international insurance company Allianz on the establishment of a major Hungarian subsidiary.

Freshfields Bruckhaus Deringer has access to a world-wide network with offices in Moscow, Bratislava and Budapest, and Vienna partner Willibald Plesser is the network's managing partner for CEE. The Vienna office focuses on foreign investment transactions in CEE. It advised RZB on an M&A transaction for the purchase by Raiffeisen International of shares in the Ukrainian Aval-Bank, and advised EnBW on the privatisation of the Bucharest electricity distribution company EMS.

Schönherr has a network of offices in south-eastern Europe and in the former Yugoslavia states – Bucharest, Ljubljana, Zagreb and Belgrade – and has just opened a new office in Kiev. Recent work handled out of Vienna includes the first Romanian Eurobond issued by a bank. This was a landmark transaction for the south-eastern European region. Christoph Lindinger is recommended.

Wolf Theiss is arguably the leading Austrian firm in CEE. It has offices in Prague, Belgrade, Bratislava, Ljubljana and Tirana, and has just opened new offices in Sarajevo and Bucharest. It has recruited as head of the Bucharest office a US-qualified partner, Bryan Jardine, from **Squire, Sanders & Dempsey**. Together with the highly regarded, Vienna-based Horst Ebhardt, whom clients praise for his 'high-quality service', Jardine led a team which advised Bank Austria on the acquisition of the Romanian Banka Commerciala 'Ion Tiriac' SA. The Vienna office has also recruited US-qualified partner David Ayres, formerly the senior partner of the Munich office of **Wilmer Cutler Pickering Hale and Dorr LLP**, who will focus on capital markets work in CEE.

CMS Reich-Rohrwig Hainz has offices in Belgrade, Bratislava, Prague, Sofia and Zagreb. It advised on a major foreign investment in Bulgaria, acting for Telekom Austria AG in relation to its €1.6bn acquisition of the largest mobile operator in Bulgaria, MobilTel AD. This was one of the 20 largest telecommunication transactions world-wide in 2005. Real estate clients speak highly of the firm's work in the CEE region, saying the lawyers are 'very efficient workers with profound know-how'. Peter Huber and Gregor Famira are recommended.

CHSH Cerha Hempel Spiegelfeld Hlawati has a Budapest office and a newly opened office in Bucharest. Best known in the region for its commercial property advice, corporate partner Benedikt Spiegelfeld is increasingly expanding the CEE practice into M&A work. The team advised Rail Cargo Austria on the privatisation of the Slovak Rail Company, and Vienna airport operator Flughafen Wien on the privatisation of airports at Bratislava and Kosice.

Dorda Brugger Jordis has a network of best friends in the CEE region, which aims to offer a 'one-stop-shop' service in Vienna. It has been acting for leading Austrian energy company Verbund in several transactions in CEE, and also acted as Austrian counsel for the major car supplier Miba AG in relation to the establishment of a €60m greenfield project in Slovakia.

enwc attorneys at law Eiselsberg Natlacen Walderdorff Cancola has offices in Budapest, Bratislava, Brno, Prague and Warsaw, which handle dispute resolution in addition to corporate work. It advised a US-based group, which is active worldwide, on merger control matters related to the acquisition of a significant Australian target with several subsidiaries in CEE countries. From Vienna, the team co-ordinated the merger control issues for this client across Europe. Raimund Cancola is recommended.

Haarmann Hügel's co-operation with **Haarmann Hemmelrath** gives it access to offices in Budapest, Bucharest, Moscow, Prague and Warsaw. In co-operation with its partner's Paris and London offices, it advised M-Tel Holding GmbH, the Austrian majority shareholder of Bulgarian mobile communications operator Mobiltel AD, on the takeover of Mobitel by the Telekom Austria Group.

Baier Lambert has a network of relationship firms in CEE, and a relationship with **Eversheds LLP**, which also has associated firms in Budapest and Sofia. Magda Svoboda-Mascher recently advised on the restructuring of a major supermarket chain in the Czech Republic, while Erhard Böhm advised on two large investments in Russia and Romania.

Fiebinger, Polak, Leon & Partner Rechtsanwälte has particular experience in advising the life sciences industry in CEE.

Gassauer-Fleissner Rechtsanwälte also has a CEE network, and its Vienna corporate department has recently been conducting due diligence related to the prospective acquisition of parcel courier companies in Bulgaria and the Czech Republic.

Hasch & Partner Anwaltsgesellschaft mbH has an office in Prague, and a close co-operation with a local firm in Zagreb. It has recently been handling M&A work in the Czech Republic, a jurisdiction in which Alexander Hasch is dual qualified.

Haslinger/Nagele & Partner Rechtsanwälte GmbH has offices in Bratislava and Prague. The Bratislava office is headed by Bernhard Hager, a specialist in waste shipment law. From Vienna, the firm has been involved in the acquisition by the largest Austrian window producer of a company in Bratislava.

Hauser Partners Rechtsanwälte GmbH has a Bratislava office. The firm has been advising leading Hungarian paper manufacturer Mondi Business Paper Hungary on the sale of a mill, and representing a leading Slovakian company in relation to the sale of a majority stake in a subsidiary to a major international company.

Karasek Wietrzyk Rechtsanwälte GmbH has been developing a CEE practice which focuses on Bulgaria, Romania and Turkey. The firm's lawyers include native speakers of Bulgarian and Turkish, and it has close links to the Turkish Embassy in Vienna, and a representative office in Bucharest. The firm, which has a strong energy practice, has been advising on a US$80m energy project in Bulgaria. Otto Dietrich is recommended.

Saxinger Chalupsky Weber & Partner Rechtsanwälte GmbH has an office in Prague, and a strong practice in the CEE energy sector.

Zeiner & Zeiner has an office in Prague, and is acting from Vienna for Bulgarian clients with holdings in Austria. The firm also has a strong trade marks practice in CEE, where clients include an Austrian mobile phone company.

CORPORATE AND M&A

In addition to general corporate and commercial work, this section covers private equity, energy and the corporate aspects of infrastructure work. The M&A and venture capital (VC) markets in Austrian are currently reviving. The most controversial deal of the year was Siemens AG's €950m acquisition of the listed VA Tech. Also, the €1.3bn acquisition by T-Mobile and Deutsche Telecom of the Austrian mobile phone services provider tele.ring from Western Wireless International was one of the largest Austrian M&A deals in the market so far. On the infrastructure side, the major Austrian project in the market – currently at the bidding stage – is the €3bn construction of a motorway from Vienna to the Czech border (the motorway project).

The Vienna office of **Freshfields Bruckhaus Deringer** has been involved in the largest-ever cross-border bank merger in Europe, advising UniCredit on the acquisition of HVB and its direct Austrian subsidiary Bank Austria and its indirect Polish subsidiary BHP, a deal involving a combined market capitalisation of around €45bn. This work included representing UniCredit at the Austrian Takeover Commission in relation to the first share-for-share offer ever made under Austrian takeover law. The team also advised Western Wireless International on the Austrian law aspects of the major deal described above. The office has a strong energy practice, and has been advising the Austrian gas group RAG on a JV for the construction and start-up of the second-largest gas storage facility in Central Europe. Clients appreciate the office's 'profound project management skills, which are highly appreciated when dealing with foreign corporate projects'. Willibald Plesser is recommended.

Schönherr is particularly strong in representing foreign companies investing into Austria. In 2005 it was involved in two out of the three public takeovers in the Austrian market. It advised Siemens on its acquisition of VA Tech (described above) and a subsequent squeeze out and delisting. This complex transaction involved lobbying by the firm, after the Austria's Takeover Commission initially blocked the transaction, then shortened the pricing period and allowed a second round. The team also advised ÖVAG Österreichische Volksbanken AG (Volksbanken) on the €800m takeover of listed bank Investkredit. In relation to private transactions, it advised Dublin-based building group CRH on the acquisition of Quester GmbH. It has also been involved in unbundlings in the energy sector, and advised a consortium bidding for the motorway project. Christian Herbst and Sascha Hödl, who handled the Siemens lobbying, are recommended.

CORPORATE AND M&A

FRESHFIELDS BRUCKHAUS DERINGER
SCHÖNHERR ✪
WOLF THEISS ✪

Binder Grösswang Attorneys-at-Law ✪
CHSH Cerha Hempel Spiegelfeld Hlawati ✪
Dorda Brugger Jordis ✪

Baker & McKenzie ✪
CMS Reich-Rohrwig Hainz ✪
DLA Weiss-Tessbach ✪
Fellner Wratzfeld & Partner Rechtsanwälte GmbH ✪
Fiebinger, Polak, Leon & Partner Rechtsanwälte ✪
Haarmann Hügel ✪
Hauser Partners Rechtsanwälte GmbH ✪
Saxinger Chalupsky Weber & Partner Rechtsanwälte GmbH ✪
Skadden, Arps, Slate, Meagher & Flom LLP

Baier Lambert ✪
Brauneis, Klauser & Prändl ✪
enwc attorneys at law Eiselsberg Natlacen Walderdorff Cancola ✪
Gassauer-Fleissner Rechtsanwälte ✪
Hausmaninger Kletter Rechtsanwälte GmbH ✪
Karasek Wietrzyk Rechtsanwälte GmbH
Kunz Schima Wallentin Rechtsanwälte Keg ✪
Ortner Pöch Foramitti
Preslmayr Attorneys at Law ✪

Alix Frank Rechtsanwälte GmbH
ARNOLD Rechtsanwalts-Partnerschaft
Brandl & Talos Rechtsanwälte GmbH ✪
Draxler & Partner Rechtsanwälte
Eckert & Fries Rechtsanwälte GmbH
Foglar-Deinhardstein KEG ✪
Graf, Maxl & Pitkowitz Rechtsanwälte GMBH ✪
Greiter Pegger Kofler & Partners ✪
Griss & Partner
Hasch & Partner Anwaltsgesellschaft mbH
Haslinger/Nagele & Partner Rechtsanwälte GmbH ✪
Herbst Vavrovsky Kinsky Rechtsanwälte GmbH ✪
Lovells in association with Mondl, Trummer, Thomas & Partner Rechtsanwälte GmbH
Neudorfer Rechtsanwälte ✪
Petsch, Frosch & Klein
Sattler & Schanda
Siemer-Siegl-Füreder & Partner, Rechtsanwälte ✪

Continued

Wolf Theiss, which has strong banking and CEE practices, advised Bank Austria and HVB on the purchase of 99% of the shares in Bulgaria's Hebros Bank from the Charlemagne Group. It also advised Macquarie Bank Ltd on the Austrian law aspects of the €1.1bn acquisition of European phone directory business the Yellow Brick Road Group. On the infrastructure side, Peter Oberlechner is advising the Hochtief consortium on its €1bn bid for the privatisation of Budapest Airport. Christian Hoenig is recommended, as is Horst Ebhardt for banking M&A.

Binder Grösswang Attorneys-at-Law is a smaller firm, but one that is specialised in the corporate and banking sectors. It advised HVB in relation to its acquisition by UniCredit, and advised Investkredit in relation to its takeover by Volksbanken, in the deals described above. The firm also advised KNP on its unsuccessful bid for tele.ring, and the Herold company, the Austrian member of the Yellow Brick Road Group, on its acquisition by Macquarie. Michael Kutschera, who is highly recommended, has a strong energy practice, and Michael Binder is also well-regarded. Clients say they are 'very satisfied with the level of expertise and the professionalism'. One international lawyer commented: 'I would certainly recommend using this law firm for any size of deal.'

CHSH Cerha Hempel Spiegelfeld Hlawati is an Austrian leader in capital markets, and a consequent market-leader on public takeovers. It advised UBS and Bank Austria on the €1.3bn takeover of UniCredit, described above and in the CEE section. It also advised EnBW Energie Baden-Würtenberg on the €840m acquisition of a 30% stake in EVN. Capital markets guru and managing partner Edith Hlawati has a reputation as an outstanding lawyer on very high-value transactions. Benedikt Spiegelfeld and Albert Birkner are also well regarded.

Dorda Brugger Jordis is strong in the private equity sector, and has been advising an Austrian private equity fund in relation to five acquisitions in CEE. The well-regarded Walter Brugger advised on the €600m demerger of the industrial water proceeding division of BWT, a transaction with important elements in the capital markets, where the firm is strong. It is also strong in the energy sector, with Verbund being a key client. Christian Dorda is recommended, and Martin Brodey is also well-regarded by clients, who praise him for being 'pragmatic, easy to work with and smart', 'very professional and expedient' and for showing 'great sensitivity to timing'.

Baker & McKenzie has been involved in a €30m transaction in Romania, the largest in this jurisdiction in 2005. Christoph Kerres heads the corporate department, while Gerhard Eichberger has a VC practice. One client commented: 'Dr Kerres has excellent negotiation skills and an unusually high capacity for strategic thinking. Within the network of **Baker & McKenzie**, the firm also finds astonishingly strong international support'.

CMS Reich-Rohrwig Hainz advised Polaris, the US-listed automotive producer, on the €68m acquisition of a 25% participation in Austria-listed KTM Power Sport. Clients say the firm is 'among Austria's top M&A lawyers' and 'excellent', and praise Peter Huber and new equity partner Günther Hanslik for a 'truly outstanding job'. Johannes Reich-Rohrwig is also very well known in the market.

DLA Weiss-Tessbach in strong on corporate work in CEE, and has this year been recovering its old reputation as a corporate heavyweight by advising in the deal of the year, acting as Austrian counsel to T-Mobile and Deutsche Telecom in relation to the acquisition of tele.ring, with the London office of **Clifford Chance** advising on the international aspects of the deal. On the infrastructure side, the firm is advising an Austro-German consortium bidding for the motorway project. Ivo Deskovic is recommended for corporate work, and Stefan Eder for infrastructure.

Fellner Wratzfeld & Partner Rechtsanwälte GmbH has an excellent reputation as a corporate firm, and Gregor Schett has a strong energy practice. Name partner Markus Fellner is also well-regarded.

Fiebinger, Polak, Leon & Partner Rechtsanwälte has a speciality in acting for pharmaceutical and life sciences clients, where Peter Polak is recommended. The firm also has a strong energy practice.

Haarmann Hügel advised Österreichische Volksbanken Aktiengeselschaft in connection with block trades and a public tender offer worth €800m for Investcredit. The teams of Hanns Hügel – a very well known corporate lawyer in Austria, who works from a small office of the firm outside Vienna – and Vienna-based Florian Gibitz, worked together on this transaction.

Hauser Partners Rechtsanwälte GmbH's Wulf Gordian Hauser is one of the leading corporate finance lawyers in Austria, and has recently been appointed to Austria's Takeover Commission, on which he is the only corporate lawyer. He recently handled the Austrian aspects of the €400m sale of a majority stake in eastern European mobile telephone provider Serbian Mobtel to an Austrian consortium.

Vienna-based **Saxinger Chalupsky Weber & Partner Rechtsanwälte GmbH** has offices in Graz and Linz, giving it strong regional coverage in Austria. Capital markets partner Stefan Weber is also well regarded for corporate work, and has recently been handling a bank acquisition. The team has advised the IMMOFINANZ-group on the €100m acquisition of real estate company ESG Villach, and also advised on the purchase, with option arrangement, of a 25% share worth €80m in KTM Power Sports AG by Polaris Industries Inc.

Skadden, Arps, Slate, Meagher & Flom LLP handles work which is 100% cross-border, advising international corporates that are investing in Austria. The small Austrian operation of a US-firm, it is headed by Rainer Wachter, who is US but not Austrian qualified. Philip Wahl, who is of-counsel and handles corporate work, is Austrian qualified.

Baier Lambert is particularly strong in the banking and insurance sectors. Michael Böhme handles insurance work, while Arthur Wolff has extensive knowledge of Chinese law. Andreas Alzinger recently advised on the Europe-wide restructuring of one of the world's largest suppliers to the automotive industry.

Brauneis, Klauser & Prändl advised Taiwan-based BenQ Mobile Holding, which acquired the Siemens mobile phone business, on the establishment of its complete corporate structure in Austria, Switzerland, and eight CEE countries. It also advised a global Swiss bank on the establishment of a tax-driven JV, comprising a capital investment of over €2bn, with a mid-sized German bank in Austria. Arno Brauneis has an excellent reputation.

enwc attorneys at law Eiselsberg Natlacen Walderdorff Cancola has a strong reputation for M&A. The firm advised Schneider SA on the establishment of a JV company in Austria which was to become a holding company for the business's worldwide operations. Raimund Cancola is recommended.

Gassauer-Fleissner Rechtsanwälte's Hanno Schatzmann is developing an excellent reputation. He recently advised the Austrian subsidiaries of an international supplier of electrical equipment on the restructuring of a €2.5bn loan.

Hausmaninger Kletter Rechtsanwälte GmbH advised Victory Beteiligungs AG on its acquisition of a 20% state in VA Tech, and on its subsequent plans to launch a public takeover of VA Tech together with Siemens, and then on the sale of this stake to Siemens, which allowed Siemens to launch the takeover offer for VA Tech described above. Clients say they are 'extremely satisfied' with the work of Christian Hausmaninger. The firm has recruited Robert Bachner from **Schönher,r** who is also very highly regarded by clients. One client who followed him to his new firm said that he was 'the best I have experienced in cross- border transactions'.

Karasek Wietrzyk Rechtsanwälte GmbH has a focus on the energy sector, where Thomas Rabl is the expert. His team has been advising Austrian natural gas companies on organisational restructuring subsequent to unbundling. He has also been developing an environmental impact assessment practice in the energy sector. Wolfgang Brandstetter is one of Austria's leading corporate crime lawyers.

Kunz Schima Wallentin Rechtsanwälte Keg's Matthias Göschke has a specialism in succession planning, while Veronika Kozak is a specialist on the aviation industry, and Peter Kunz has a niche in advising private hospitals.

Ortner Pöch Foramitti is a banking firm that specialises in finance transactions. Michael Krassnigg and Heinz Rindler are recommended.

Preslmayr Attorneys at Law has been handling the merger of Austrian bank Bawag with PSK. The corporate team also acts for Shell and for private equity funds from the US, Switzerland and Scandinavia. The firm enjoys an excellent reputation with international in-house lawyers, and Martin Preslmayr is recommended.

Arnold Rechtsanwalts-Partnerschaft is best known as a tax firm, and consequently has good restructuring expertise. Wolf-Dieter Arnold has been advising on the acquisition of state-owned social building company WBG by BWS and Bawag.

Brandl & Talos Rechtsanwälte GmbH handles a significant amount of VC work. Clients describe corporate partner Thomas Talos as being 'of outstanding quality, an excellent negotiator with a very sharp mind and splendid common sense'. He advised Motion Media Plc in connection with its €49m merger with a Graz-based technology company. The firm is also advising Austria-listed BETandWIM.com on preliminary discussions with Ongame e-solutions AB and its shareholders regarding a potential substantial acquisition.

Eckert & Fries Rechtsanwälte GmbH is a corporate law boutique based in Baden, an industrial area close to Vienna. It advised Austria-listed Böhler Uddeholm AG on the acquisition of Germany-based Buderus Edelstahl AG, and on the acquisition of Sweden-based Avesta Welding AB. It also has a strong private equity practice. Vitus Eckert is recommended.

Graf, Maxl & Pitkowitz Rechtsanwälte GMBH handles commercial work in Austria for one of the

CORPORATE AND M&A Continued

AVIA Law Group
bmp Rechtsanwälte
Barnert Egermann Illigasch Rechtsanwälte OEG
Dallmann & Juranek
Deissenberger & Partners
Dietrich Majoros Marchl Rechtsanwälte
Held Berdnik Astner & Partner, Rechtsanwälte
Höhne, In der Maur & Partner Rechtsanwälte GmbH
Jakobljevich, Grave & Vetter
Kaan Cronenberg & Partners
Kammerlander, Piaty, Mueller-Mezin, Schoeller
Kosch & Partner
Lansky, Ganzger & Partner Rechtsanwälte GmbH
MMag Gustav Walzel
Pallauf Pullmann Meißnitzer & Partner, Rechtsanwälte OEG
Renate Weinberger (Dr), Rechtsanwaltskanzlei
Schramm Öhler Rechtsanwälte ✪
Zeiner & Zeiner
Zirngibl Langwieser

Firms are listed A-Z in tiers which are ranked in order of priority
✪ Indicates firm displays contact details at the end of this chapter.

largest Danish industrial conglomerates, and has also been advising a US client on the acquisition of key players in the Austrian internet market. Otto Waechter is recommended for infrastructure, where clients describe him as 'a pleasure to work with'. Ferdinand Graf is also much liked by clients.

Graz-based **Griss & Partner** acts for a substantial share of the local industry and local subsidiaries of foreign companies. It has been advising a car engine developer on the acquisition of the development division of a German industry group, and advised the largest hotel group in Graz on a complete restructuring. One international client said: 'Despite the fact that the firm is not located in Vienna, the quality of legal work is at least equal to that of Vienna firms.'

Hasch & Partner Anwaltsgesellschaft mbH has a focus on VC. Corporate clients include Beko Holding AG and Gericom.

Haslinger/Nagele & Partner Rechtsanwälte GmbH is based in Linz, with an office in Vienna. There are corporate partners in both offices, but the focus of the heavyweight corporate work is on Linz. The team has recently been advising on a merger involving one of Austria's largest construction companies. Its corporate clients include state-owned construction company ASFINAG, and some major banks and paper industry clients.

Herbst Vavrovsky Kinsky Rechtsanwälte GmbH's Christoph Herbst, who is well known for his work in the field of public and administrative law, advised Land Burgenland on the prospective sale of Bank Burgenland. The firm also has a strong VC practice, and advises a number of international private equity funds.

At **Sattler & Schanda**, Reinhard Schanda is increasingly developing a reputation as an energy specialist. The firm acts as the representative office in Austria of leading German energy law firm **Becker Büttner Held, Rechtsanwälte Wirtschaftsprüfer Steuerberater**. Recent work includes advising companies in the energy intensive production industry on the purchase of electricity and natural gas.

Siemer-Siegl-Füreder & Partner, Rechtsanwälte's Hannes Füreder is active in the field of sports sponsorship agreements. Markus Fellner is also recommended, and has been advising Canada-based CCL Inc on the acquisition of shares in an Austrian company. Clients describe him as 'energetic and capable'.

AVIA Law Group's Vienna-based corporate partner Claudio Arturo was formerly with **Petsch, Frosch & Klein**, a firm well know for its Italian expertise, and he continues to advise Austrian companies with interests in Italy. He has also advised Boehringer-Ingelheim Austria on work in CEE. The firm has an office in Klagenfurt, which is close geographically to Italy, and an office-sharing and co-operation agreement with a Milan firm. It also has an office in Baden, an industrial area close to Vienna, from which it advises some large industrial companies. Clients describe the firm as 'professional and competent'.

Barnert Egermann Illigasch Rechtsanwälte OEG has been advising the Russia-based Sibneft Group on the establishment of a new trading entity in Austria, and advising on the sale of Villas Hungaria, a member of the group of a public Austrian company. Michael Barnert has a strong energy practice, and has been advising e&t Energie Handesgesellschaft mbH and Austria Ferngas Gesellschaft mbH. Clients describe the firm as 'efficient'.

Dietrich Majoros Marchl Rechtsanwälte's corporate partner Claus Marchl often works together with sole practitioner **MMag Gustav Walzel** on corporate matters, and have recently done so to advise a large Austrian company on a cross-border JV.

Sole practitioner **MMag Gustav Walzel** has been advising on the implementation of one of the largest corporate restructurings ever to take place in Austria. He has also advised on the structure for an Austro-German JV.

Zeiner & Zeiner acts for a number of international companies in relation to their Austrian subsidiaries. These include Johnson & Johnson and the largest French cosmetics retailers, for whom it handles international holdings out of Austria.

DISPUTE RESOLUTION

Vienna is one of the most important arbitration centres in Europe, with a popular central location that is increasingly used by Polish and Czech companies. On the litigation side, the Austrian Ministry of Justice is currently working to modify the country's civil procedure laws to allow formal class actions. In all but the largest and most specialised firms, it is usual to find corporate lawyers handling a mix of non-contentious work and litigation or arbitration.

Andreas Reiner of **Andreas Reiner & Partner** is Austria's highest-profile arbitrator. He has a worldwide practice, arbitrating many cases that have no link to Austria. He focuses on cases involving public international law, with parties who are states, state-owned companies and entities involved in privatisations. Christian Aschauer handles arbitration-related litigation, challenging or defending arbitration awards.

Baier Lambert has an outstanding practice in arbitration, and one of the largest arbitration teams, headed by Anton Baier, who has been handling a number of public infrastructure construction disputes worth several US$100m. Erhard Boehm is also a highly experienced arbitrator, and has been advising on disputes in the Turkish telecommunications sector and the crude oil industry of Khazakstan. The firm is also strong in domestic litigation, and Marie-Therese Trofaier has recently qualified as a mediator.

DISPUTE RESOLUTION

ANDREAS REINER & PARTNER
BAIER LAMBERT ⭘
CHSH CERHA HEMPEL SPIEGELFELD HLAWATI ⭘
FRESHFIELDS BRUCKHAUS DERINGER
SCHÖNHERR ⭘
WOLF THEISS ⭘

Brauneis, Klauser & Prändl ⭘
Dorda Brugger Jordis ⭘
Fiebinger, Polak, Leon & Partner Rechtsanwälte ⭘
Karasek Wietrzyk Rechtsanwälte GmbH

Baker & McKenzie ⭘
Binder Grösswang Attorneys-at-Law ⭘
CMS Reich-Rohrwig Hainz ⭘
DLA Weiss-Tessbach ⭘
Draxler & Partner Rechtsanwälte
Engin-Deniz Reimitz Hafner Rechtsanwälte KEG
Greiter Pegger Kofler & Partners ⭘
Griss & Partner
Haarmann Hügel ⭘
Haslinger/Nagele & Partner Rechtsanwälte GmbH ⭘
Hauser Partners Rechtsanwälte GmbH ⭘
Preslmayr Attorneys at Law ⭘
Sattler & Schanda
Siemer-Siegl-Füreder & Partner, Rechtsanwälte ⭘

AVIA Law Group
ARNOLD Rechtsanwalts-Partnerschaft
Burgstaller & Preyer Rechtsanwälten GmbH
Deissenberger & Partners
enwc attorneys at law Eiselsberg Natlacen Walderdorff Cancola ⭘
Gassauer-Fleissner Rechtsanwälte ⭘
Graf, Maxl & Pitkowitz Rechtsanwälte GMBH ⭘
Hasch & Partner Anwaltsgesellschaft mbH
Hausmaninger Kletter Rechtsanwälte GmbH ⭘
Lansky, Ganzger & Partner Rechtsanwälte GmbH
Neudorfer Rechtsanwälte ⭘
Ortner Pöch Foramitti
Pallauf Pullmann Meißnitzer & Partner, Rechtsanwälte OEG
Petsch, Frosch & Klein
Saxinger Chalupsky Weber & Partner Rechtsanwälte GmbH ⭘
Zandl: Grundei Rechtsanwälte
Zeiner & Zeiner

Firms are listed A-Z in tiers which are ranked in order of priority
⭘ Indicates firm displays contact details at the end of this chapter.

CHSH Cerha Hempel Spiegelfeld Hlawati has a discrete contentious business department. Irene Welser focuses on litigation, and has recently successfully represented Vienna Airport Security Services Gmbh in a €68m procurement-related dispute. Corporate partner Benedikt Spiegelfeld arbitrates commercial disputes, and has recently been representing the claimant in a challenge to an arbitral award. Felix Stortecky is a mediator, while Angela Zaffalon speaks Italian. Prof Welser's clients say that: 'All tasks were fulfilled in a timely, efficient and highly successful manner. Through its international network the firm was able to handle international matters in a similarly successful way.'

Freshfields Bruckhaus Deringer also has a distinct litigation department, and holds a leading position in international arbitration, including M&A-related arbitration. The group, headed by Günther Horvath, has been advising a Kosovan cement and construction materials manufacturer. Thomas Kustor is recommended for litigation and Jenny Power for arbitration. EU partner Axel Reidlinger has been handling some complex disputes involving issues of administrative law, while Thomas Kustor has been advising two major insurers in litigation and arbitration.

Schönherr's Hellwig Torggler is a leading and very well regarded arbitrator, and also handles mediations. He has recently arbitrated international disputes relating to the laying of an offshore pipeline, and a JV concerning the telecommunications network of an Eastern European country. The firm has a distinct litigation group headed by Gerold Zeiler, which has been handling disputes involving parties from the US, Russia and the Middle East.

Wolf Theiss also has a very large litigation practice group, consisting of highly specialised lawyers who are full-time litigators. Bettina Knötzl and Andreas Theiss successfully defended Salzburger Sparkasse Bank AG, part of the Erste Bank group, against a claim by 3240 claimants, resulting in a settlement with a substantial reduction of the initial amount claimed. This was the largest-ever piece of civil litigation in Austria, and was seen as a test case about the viability of introducing class actions in the country. Christoph Liebscher has been chairing a US$230m ICC arbitration between Motorola and Turkish telecommunications operator Telsim. Clients recommend Dr Theiss and Dr Liebscher for the 'highest service standards', and one added: 'Wolf Theiss have the best contacts in the judiciary and the Supreme Court.'

Brauneis, Klauser & Prändl's Alexander Klauser heads the strong litigation team. Klauser is advising the Austrian Ministry of Justice on the drafting of its new class action bill. In advance of the new legislation and under the existing civil procedure rules, he has also developed a new form of combined litigation or 'Austrian-style class action', representing individuals and SMEs in multi-party claims against banks. In addition, he successfully advised Austria's largest consumer organisation, VKI, in a dispute with the European Commission over access to documents relating to a highly sensitive Austrian banking cartel case, resulting in the Commission's decision not to grant access being declared nul and void by the Court of First Instance. Arno Brauneis handles arbitration matters.

Dorda Brugger Jordis has a dedicated litigation department, headed by Florian Kremslehner, which has been handling an increasing amount of litigation in the field of directors' and officers' liability insurance. Kremslehner also has a focus on banking litigation, and has been advising the Austrian Ministry of Finance on a dispute concerning state liability for the negligent supervision of banks. The firm is also strong in arbitration, where Christoph Stippl has been advising a major Eastern European telecommunications operator on a dispute involving several €100m. Christian Dorda has been mediating a major corporate dispute. Clients praise the team's 'knowledge, experience and professionalism'. One added: 'We require bilingual partners and knowledge of international law, and in relation to this the performance of the firm is excellent.'

Fiebinger, Polak, Leon & Partner Rechtsanwälte's Rudolf Fiebinger has a reputation as a good and tough litigator, and clients also appreciate the firm's skills in complex international arbitration proceedings.

Karasek Wietrzyk Rechtsanwälte GmbH has particular expertise in property litigation and construction arbitration. Georg Karasek is a leading construction arbitrator and also handles litigation including, recently, acting for a consortium of construction companies in a €3.6m dispute with a railway company. Thomas Frad, who also arbitrates, has been representing Gletscherbahnen Kaprun AG in connection with a major ski train disaster involving claims of €35m. Thomas Rabl handles administrative law disputes, and the firm also has expertise in disputes in the energy field.

In the lower tier, it is worth noting that **Binder Grösswang Attorneys-at-Law**'s partner Christian Klausegger is now focusing on dispute resolution. Clients say he has 'good skills in court and excellent legal instincts', and one added: 'He is also experienced in German law, so I really recommend him for German clients'.

EU AND COMPETITION

With the new EU member states dealing with EU matters for the first time, Austrian law firms are positioning themselves as the regional specialists for advice in this area. They are also grappling with the new Austrian competition law, which came into effect on 1 January 2006 and covers the first Austrian cartel leniency system ever adopted. In addition to EU and competition law, this section also covers public procurement law, which in Austria has traditionally been handled by competition lawyers. All the larger law firms now have a public procurement expert, and there are some prominent boutiques and practices specialised in the field. With most of Austria's PPP projects currently in the procurement stage, this is a busy area of work for many firms.

Freshfields Bruckhaus Deringer's Axel Reidlinger has an outstanding reputation, and heads a specialised team with a focus on advice related to M&A or IP and IT driven transactions. The team has been representing Austrian utility

EU AND COMPETITION

FRESHFIELDS BRUCKHAUS DERINGER
HAARMANN HÜGEL ✪
SCHÖNHERR ✪

Binder Grösswang Attorneys-at-Law ✪
CMS Reich-Rohrwig Hainz ✪
DLA Weiss-Tessbach ✪
Dorda Brugger Jordis ✪
Schramm Öhler Rechtsanwälte ✪
Siemer-Siegl-Füreder & Partner, Rechtsanwälte ✪
Wolf Theiss ✪

Brauneis, Klauser & Prändl ✪
CHSH Cerha Hempel Spiegelfeld Hlawati ✪
enwc attorneys at law Eiselsberg Natlacen Walderdorff Cancola ✪
Fiebinger, Polak, Leon & Partner Rechtsanwälte ✪
Georg Legat (Dr)
Graf, Maxl & Pitkowitz Rechtsanwälte GMBH ✪
Hauser Partners Rechtsanwälte GmbH ✪
Hausmaninger Kletter Rechtsanwälte GmbH ✪
Heid Schiefer Rechsanwälte Gmbh
Karasek Wietrzyk Rechtsanwälte GmbH
Preslmayr Attorneys at Law ✪
Schwartz und Huber-Medek Rechtsanwälte OEG

AVIA Law Group
Alix Frank Rechtsanwälte GmbH
ARNOLD Rechtsanwalts-Partnerschaft
Dietrich Majoros Marchl Rechtsanwälte
Fellner Wratzfeld & Partner Rechtsanwälte GmbH ✪
Gassauer-Fleissner Rechtsanwälte ✪
Greiter Pegger Kofler & Partners ✪
Griss & Partner
Gugerbauer & Partner Rechtsanwälte KEG
Hasch & Partner Anwaltsgesellschaft mbH
Haslinger/Nagele & Partner Rechtsanwälte GmbH ✪
Held Berdnik Astner & Partner, Rechtsanwälte
Höhne, In der Maur & Partner Rechtsanwälte GmbH
Lansky, Ganzger & Partner Rechtsanwälte GmbH
Ortner Pöch Foramitti
Saxinger Chalupsky Weber & Partner Rechtsanwälte GmbH ✪
Wiltschek Rechtsanwälte
Zeiner & Zeiner

Firms are listed A-Z in tiers which are ranked in order of priority
✪ Indicates firm displays contact details at the end of this chapter.

company EVN in a merger control case relating to the acquisition of a majority share in a gas company. It also handles regulatory issues for some major Austrian and international energy players, including advising BEAG on the unbundling of its electricity network. The office also has a public procurement team, which has been advising a bidder consortium in relation to the motorway project. Competition clients describe themselves as 'very satisfied', and one added: 'There are just a few law firms in Austria that could compete with **Freshfields** for issues that deal with the new EU regulatory framework'.

Haarmann Hügel's Rainer Roniger is a market leader for multi-jurisdictional work, and his partner Astrid Ablasser is also well regarded. The team advised the Österresichische Volksbanken Aktiengesellschaft, the fifth-largest bank in Austria, on national and EU merger control proceedings relating to its public tender offer for Investkredit. It also advised a major Austrian group with international operations on proceedings, involving major cartel issues, before Austria's Takeover Commission, and is involved in a European Court of Justice banking cartel case. Christian Schneider has a public procurement practice, and has been advising the local government of the Austrian State of Corinthia on the establishment of local area networks.

Schönherr's Hanno Wollmann enjoys a superb reputation for merger control work, and has been handling the lion's share of phase two merger control proceedings at the Austrian cartel court. He is frequently instructed on the competition aspects of major corporate transactions. Banking partner Peter Feyl also advised on the cartel aspects of Siemens' acquisition of VA Tech. Christian Schmelz handles public procurement and regulatory matters including, recently, advising on a €800m public sector fund raising via swap and other loan derivatives.

Binder Grösswang Attorneys-at-Law has been advising Bank Austria in a major competition law dispute with Erste Bank and other savings banks before the Austrian cartel court, including a complaint lodged with the European Commission. It also advised Royal KPN NV on the competition law aspects of its bid for tele.ring. Competition partner Raoul Hoffer acts for a large number of energy suppliers, particularly in relation to regulatory matters and unbundling. Clients say he 'knows how to handle big cases' and has experience comparable to that at City of London law firms.

CMS Reich-Rohrwig Hainz's Bernst Elsner is specialised in pubic procurement work. He has been advising Swietelsky Baugesellschaft on an extremely complex €70m PPP-related procurement, and Leyrer + Graf Baugesellschaft on the PPP-related procurement of funds for a public swimming pool. He also has a solid practice in competition and merger control, including handling some major proceedings related to market abuse. Partner Daniela Karollus-Bruner has been advising a new client, VC fund Industrikapital, on merger control filings.

DLA Weiss-Tessbach has recruited Claudia Vartian, formerly with **CHSH Cerha Hempel Spiegelfeld Hlawati**, to head its working group for competition law in the CEE region. She is known for her merger control and telecommunications industry expertise, and since her arrival has been handling merger negotiations relating to a major telecommunications acquisition. Together with Max Becker, she has also advised a world leading Austrian producer of cartons in relation to merger control filings in the CEE region. The team has also recruited senior associate Philipp Götzl, who focuses on public procurement, from *Schwarz & Götzl Rechtsanwälte*.

Dorda Brugger Jordis has been advising Verbund on merger control proceedings relating to a JV in excess of €1bn, one of the largest in Austria. It also advises a major international gas supplier on energy law, some of which advice is at the forefront of gas regulation development in Austria and Europe. Stephan Polster heads the team, and competition clients praise international M&A head Martin Brodey as being 'among the top-five competition lawyers in Austria'. The firm also has a public procurement practice. Walter Brugger is recommended.

Schramm Öhler Rechtsanwälte is a leading public procurement boutique, highly specialised and highly regarded. Johannes Schramm and Matthias Öhler have been advising the Österresichische Bundesbahnen on a €300m public tendering procedure, and advising a university college on an innovative PFI project. Georg Zellhofer advises on state aid, and has also recently advised a 100% subsidiary of the Austrian Republic on a privatisation. One client said: 'We can highly recommend the firm not only in public procurement but also in the field of antitrust law.'

Siemer-Siegl-Füreder & Partner, Rechtsanwälte also has a strong public procurement practice headed by Michael Breitenfeld. He has been advising the Vienna Harbour, the largest goods distribution centre in the east of Austria, on the tender of a new storage hall. Clients also speak of 'highly qualified teams' in competition law, where the practice is headed by Markus Fellner.

Wolf Theiss focuses on merger control and cartel law, where it has a substantial practice. Katja Tautscher has been advising on the Austrian merger notification of the Lancaster Group Austria GmbH, with respect to a US$800m acquisition.

In the third tier, **CHSH Cerha Hempel Spiegelfeld Hlawati** has lost corporate and competition partner Claudine Vartian to **DLA Weiss-Tessbach**. However, it has recruited two lawyers from **Lansky, Ganzger & Partner Rechtsanwälte GmbH** into its already strong public procurement team, which is headed by dispute resolution expert Irene Welser. She has successfully represented Vienna Airport Security Services GmbH in €68m procurement proceedings, the largest Austrian service contract ever.

Also in the third tier, **Karasek Wietrzyk Rechtsanwälte GmbH** has recruited Katharina Hahnl, a public procurement specialist with an academic background.

EMPLOYMENT

Labour law is highly regulated in Austria, and there is consequently some well-developed legal expertise in the country in relation to contentious employment matters, including mediation.

Leading labour and employment boutique **Burgstaller & Preyer Rechtsanwälten GmbH** has strong clients in the telecommunications, IT, pharmaceutical, transport and banking sectors. The recent focus of the firm's work has been advising on the reduction of workforces, closing of plants, transfer of groups of employees out of Austria, outsourcing of IT and the transfer of pension entitlements. Helmut Preyer and Gerald Burgstaller are recommended.

CMS Reich-Rohrwig Hainz's Bernhard Hainz is one of the leading employment lawyers in Austria. Hainz recently advised Austria's largest bank, BA-CA Austria Creditanstalt, on proceedings relating to company pensions and the employer's liability for stock market rights, and won a pitch for the *CMS Group* to act for MONDI Europe-wide on labour law matters. Christoph Wolf, whose clients include Telekom Austria, has a corporate-focused employment practice, and has been advising the Austrian railways, ÖBB, on restructuring-related matters.

Kunz Schima Wallentin Rechtsanwälte Keg's market leading employment department is headed by the renowned Georg Schima, whose clients include Bank Austria.

DLA Weiss-Tessbach moves up a tier due to its recent recruitment of a new head of its labour law working group, Franz Marhold. He was formerly the full-time chairman of the Institute for Employment Law and Social Law at the law faculty in Graz, a position which he continues to hold. He brings with him some blue-chip corporate clients, and his focus is on non-contentious work including, recently, advising an Austrian lotteries and casinos operator on the establishment of an early retirement scheme combined with a severance payment scheme.

Dorda Brugger Jordis's Thomas Angermair has an excellent reputation and heads a growing team, which has some major clients in the pharmaceutical industry and is strong on HR-related restructuring programmes. Clients for whom it has recently acted on restructuring matters include concrete producer Cemex. Angermair also acts as a mediator for

EMPLOYMENT

BURGSTALLER & PREYER RECHTSANWÄLTEN GMBH
CMS REICH-ROHRWIG HAINZ ✪
KUNZ SCHIMA WALLENTIN RECHTSANWÄLTE KEG ✪

DLA Weiss-Tessbach ✪
Dorda Brugger Jordis ✪
Draxler & Partner Rechtsanwälte
Zandl: Grundei Rechtsanwälte

CHSH Cerha Hempel Spiegelfeld Hlawati ✪
enwc attorneys at law Eiselsberg Natlacen Walderdorff Cancola ✪
Fellner Wratzfeld & Partner Rechtsanwälte GmbH ✪
Freshfields Bruckhaus Deringer
Gassauer-Fleissner Rechtsanwälte ✪
Graf, Maxl & Pitkowitz Rechtsanwälte GMBH ✪
Neudorfer Rechtsanwälte ✪
Preslmayr Attorneys at Law ✪
Schönherr ✪
Siemer-Siegl-Füreder & Partner, Rechtsanwälte ✪

Alexandra Knell (Dr)
Baker & McKenzie ✪
Binder Grösswang Attorneys-at-Law ✪
Brauneis, Klauser & Prändl ✪
Dietrich Majoros Marchl Rechtsanwälte
Fiebinger, Polak, Leon & Partner Rechtsanwälte ✪
Greiter Pegger Kofler & Partners ✪
Hasch & Partner Anwaltsgesellschaft mbH
Saxinger Chalupsky Weber & Partner Rechtsanwälte GmbH ✪
Wolf Theiss ✪

Firms are listed A-Z in tiers which are ranked in order of priority
✪ Indicates firm displays contact details at the end of this chapter.

employment-related disputes. Partner Alexandra Knell has now left to set up her own boutique, **Dr Alexandra Knell**, described below. Walter Brugger is praised by employment clients for his 'personality, his very hard working style and his flexibility'.

Draxler & Partner Rechtsanwälte has been advising ÖBB in relation to a major labour law dispute. Peter Stock is well known for his work on collective labour agreements, outsourcing and pensions.

Zandl: Grundei Rechtsanwälte has particular expertise in advising on employers' insurance. Andreas Grundei is recommended.

CHSH Cerha Hempel Spiegelfeld Hlawati's labour law clients include McDonald's, the Vienna Airport Authority and Prada. Julian Feichtinger is recommended.

enwc attorneys at law Eiselsberg Natlacen Walderdorff Cancola advises major clients from the food and drink and retail sectors.

Fellner Wratzfeld & Partner Rechtsanwälte GmbH has a strong reputation in the corporate field. Kurt Wratzfeld is known for his employment advice to public companies.

Freshfields Bruckhaus Deringer's employment law practice has a focus on advisory work related to multinational M&A transactions. The team has recently been involved in restructuring transactions in the logistics sector, and in model litigation relating to company pension schemes. Stefan Köck is recommended.

Graf, Maxl & Pitkowitz Rechtsanwälte GMBH moves up a tier due to the high regard in which Jakob Widner is held by international clients. One of these commented: 'Jakob is definitely one of Austria's more knowledgeable employment lawyers. As he is also admitted to practise law in the state of New York, it is helpful to have someone like him as a legal advisor when it comes to communicating the Austrian world of industrial relations to our affiliates and corporate officers.'

Preslmayr Attorneys at Law's Andrea Futterknecht has left the firm, but it has recruited Barbara Kurz to replace her. She often works closely with the firm's IT specialist Rainer Knyrim on employment-related data protection issues.

Schönherr's litigation partner Gerold Zeiler heads the firm's employment law practice, which has been advising a Germany-based multinational group in the chemical industry on the transfer of part of its Austrian business to Slovakia.

Siemer-Siegl-Füreder & Partner, Rechtsanwälte has been advising a subsidiary of a world-leading inspection, verification, testing and certification company on employment law matters relating to the acquisition of a privatised company.

In the fourth tier, name partner Alexandra Knell at **Dr Alexandra Knell** was formerly a partner with **Dorda Brugger Jordis**, and has now established her own practice. Her clients include Austrian newspaper *Wiener Zeitung*, two pharmaceutical companies, and a private university.

IT AND TELECOMMUNICATIONS

BAIER LAMBERT ✪
BRAUNEIS, KLAUSER & PRÄNDL ✪
FRESHFIELDS BRUCKHAUS DERINGER
GASSAUER-FLEISSNER RECHTSANWÄLTE ✪
HÖHNE, IN DER MAUR & PARTNER RECHTSANWÄLTE GMBH

Alix Frank Rechtsanwälte GmbH
ARNOLD Rechtsanwalts-Partnerschaft
Binder Grösswang Attorneys-at-Law ✪
CHSH Cerha Hempel Spiegelfeld Hlawati ✪
DLA Weiss-Tessbach ✪
Dallmann & Juranek
Dorda Brugger Jordis ✪
enwc attorneys at law Eiselsberg Natlacen Walderdorff Cancola ✪
Engin-Deniz Reimitz Hafner Rechtsanwälte KEG
Fiebinger, Polak, Leon & Partner Rechtsanwälte ✪
Meinhard Ciresa (DDr)
Preslmayr Attorneys at Law ✪
Sattler & Schanda
Saxinger Chalupsky Weber & Partner Rechtsanwälte GmbH ✪
Schönherr ✪
Wolf Theiss ✪

Fellner Wratzfeld & Partner Rechtsanwälte GmbH ✪
Graf, Maxl & Pitkowitz Rechtsanwälte GMBH ✪
Greiter Pegger Kofler & Partners ✪
Haarmann Hügel ✪
Hasch & Partner Anwaltsgesellschaft mbH
Hauser Partners Rechtsanwälte GmbH ✪
Karasek Wietrzyk Rechtsanwälte GmbH
Kunz Schima Wallentin Rechtsanwälte Keg ✪
Ortner Pöch Foramitti
Schmidt, Kornfeld, Wukoschitz, Windhager
Schwarz Schönherr Rechtsanwälte OEG
Siemer-Siegl-Füreder & Partner, Rechtsanwälte ✪

Firms are listed A-Z in tiers which are ranked in order of priority
✪ Indicates firm displays contact details at the end of this chapter.

The Austrian IT market is currently in a slump, with only the largest companies investing in outsourcing or the development of personnel in the IT arena. The telecommunications sector, however, is recovering after its 2003 slump, and several firms have significant expertise in this field.

Baier Lambert is a leader in computer and internet law, particularly on regulatory issues. Georg Röhsner advises the largest publishing house in Austria on all internet-related legal issues, and advises the Austrian subsidiary of a large UK telecommunications company on regulatory matters. Arnold Wolf is also very well regarded in the market, particularly on licensing matters.

Brauneis, Klauser & Prändl has a market-leading IT lawyer in Felix Prändl, whose clients include Oracle, Veritas and the Austrian regulatory authority for telecommunications and broadcasting. He recently advised Hewlett-Packard as bidder for a multi-million euro project aimed at redesigning the entire IT-structure of the Austrian financial administration. Corporate partner Arno Brauneis advises telecommunications companies, particularly on the setting up of fixed lines, and has some major Scandinavian clients. Bernhard Girsch has been advising an international internet games provider.

Freshfields Bruckhaus Deringer wins its place in this tier due to the strength of its telecommunications practice. One telecommunications client commented: 'There are only one or two other firms in Austria that could support a communications company like ourselves in such a broad way'. Competition partner Alex Reidlinger and IP partner Cristof Pöchhacker advise on IT and telecommunications matters, and have recently recruited telecommunications lawyers at a junior level. In relation to IT, the team has been focusing on technology licensing and outsourcing transactions involving Eastern European jurisdictions. In relation to telecommunications, the team acted for Western Wireless in the sale of the Austrian mobile network operator tele.ring to T-Mobile Austria. Telecommunications clients also appreciate the quality of the firm' associates. The team has also been involved in e-commerce matters, in relation to which it is permanent counsel in Austria to Microsoft.

Gassauer-Fleissner Rechtsanwälte's Michael Wolner has an impressive track record for major outsourcing projects, in relation to which he has recently won as a new client one of the largest outsourcing companies in continental Europe, for work which includes advice on bank licensing matters. His team, which works closely with the firm's corporate lawyers, has also been handling a significant amount of hi-tech licensing, and some e-commerce work. In addition, Wolner has recently litigated a number of cases, including two matters involving a large failed ERP implementation project.

Höhne, In der Maur & Partner Rechtsanwälte GmbH has an outstanding IT practice, with a reputation for advising internet service providers. The team also advises some major telecommunications providers.

Alix Frank Rechtsanwälte GmbH is strong on licensing and outsourcing, and on domain name disputes. Stephan Novotny and Franz Heidinger are recommended.

Arnold Rechtsanwalts-Partnerschaft has been advising a leading software corporation on licence agreements concerning SAP-based add-ons, and clients include two major worldwide computer producers. The firm also has telecommunications experience. Nikolaus Arnold is recommended.

Binder Grösswang Attorneys-At-Law's junior partner Isabell Lichtenstrasser heads the IT team, which is strong in the telecommunications sector, where it acts on regulatory matters for Tele2UTA, the largest alternative telecommunications company in Austria. Telecommunications clients also appreciate the 'quality' of the work done by litigation head Christian Klausegger.

CHSH Cerha Hempel Spiegelfeld Hlawati acts for Telekom Austria, whom it has recently advised on a major project involving the restructuring of its wireless business.

DLA Weiss-Tessbach has been advising Austrian and international private equity investors on the sale of their shareholdings in a large Austrian internet platform, and advising Austrian subsidiaries of US-based companies on compliance with Austrian data protection regulations.

Dallmann & Juranek has a reputation in the banking field, and name partner Johannes Juranek advises banks, publishers and insurance companies on licensing and contracts for tailor-made software. He has been advising a major Austrian bank on the IT-integration of new subsidiaries, and advising an insurance company on one of the largest IT projects in Europe.

Dorda Brugger Jordis has lost Winfried Schwarz. However it retains a good reputation for commercial and telecommunications law.

enwc attorneys at law Eiselsberg Natlacen Walderdorff Cancola advises one of the global players in telecommunications equipment, and provides ongoing advice on IT matters to Nokia in Austria.

Engin-Deniz Reimitz Hafner Rechtsanwälte KEG's Christian Reimitz handles software and contractual work, and IT-related litigation.

Fiebinger, Polak, Leon & Partner Rechtsanwälte's Constantin Kletzer has strong experience in advising on the IT aspects of corporate transactions.

Sattler & Schanda's Reinhard Schanda is an expert on copyright law relating to IT.

Saxinger Chalupsky Weber & Partner Rechtsanwälte GmbH is another banking firm with a reputation for advising banks on the outsourcing of their IT departments. The team has also recently handled significant distribution work relating to data protection in the banking industry. Dietmar Huemer is recommended.

Schönherr's Peter Madl has a good reputation, and is praised by clients for his 'in-depth industry knowledge'. Christian Hauer is also very well known. The team has been advising leading Austrian insurance group Wiener Städtische on the sale and lease-back of its SAP-based insurance software to a special purpose vehicle, a major IT project for Austria.

Wolf Theiss has a leading corporate practice which advises IT and telecommunications clients. Georg Kresbach, who has been advising Sony Europe in relation to an internet platform for the downloading of music, is praised by clients for his 'legal expertise, high verbal quality, speed and above all excellence in execution'.

At **Fellner Wratzfeld & Partner Rechtsanwälte GmbH**, Sabine Fehringer has a good reputation for outsourcing.

INSOLVENCY AND CORPORATE RECOVERY

Some smaller Austrian law firms have outstanding reputations as court-appointed receivers, while the larger corporate practices advise banks and companies on insolvencies and often choose not to act as receivers because of conflicts.

Brauneis, Klauser & Prändl acts as an insolvency administrator. Alexander Klauser, who also has strong experience in out-of-court restructurings, is involved in one of the largest insolvency proceedings ongoing in Austria, representing US and Dutch subsidiaries of the Babcock Borsig Power Group in litigation against the receiver of the group's Austrian subsidiary, Austrian Energy. It has favourably settled its clients' claims.

Graf, Maxl & Pitkowitz Rechtsanwälte GMBH's team has been advising a financial investor in connection with the disencumberment of Vienna-based Augarten Porzellan, and has also advised an Austrian real estate investor in connection with the enforcement of damages in Austria against a US-based parent company. Clients say that the firm 'reacts quickly and precisely, with a client-oriented response, and is never satisfied with second best'. Alexander Isola is recommended.

Held Berdnik Astner & Partner, Rechtsanwälte is an insolvency boutique whose partners are all well-known receivers. The firm was

INSOLVENCY AND CORPORATE RECOVERY

BRAUNEIS, KLAUSER & PRÄNDL ✪
GRAF, MAXL & PITKOWITZ RECHTSANWÄLTE GMBH ✪
HELD BERDNIK ASTNER & PARTNER, RECHTSANWÄLTE
KOSCH & PARTNER
PRESLMAYR ATTORNEYS AT LAW ✪
SCHULYOK UNGER & PARTNER RECHTSANWÄLTE OEG

Abel & Abel
Baier Lambert ✪
CHSH Cerha Hempel Spiegelfeld Hlawati ✪
CMS Reich-Rohrwig Hainz ✪
enwc attorneys at law Eiselsberg Natlacen Walderdorff Cancola ✪
Freshfields Bruckhaus Deringer
Haslinger/Nagele & Partner Rechtsanwälte GmbH ✪
Saxinger Chalupsky Weber & Partner Rechtsanwälte GmbH ✪
Wolf Theiss ✪

DLA Weiss-Tessbach ✪
Dorda Brugger Jordis ✪
Fellner Wratzfeld & Partner Rechtsanwälte GmbH ✪
Hasch & Partner Anwaltsgesellschaft mbH
Herbst Vavrovsky Kinsky Rechtsanwälte GmbH ✪
Kunz Schima Wallentin Rechtsanwälte Keg ✪
Lansky, Ganzger & Partner Rechtsanwälte GmbH
Neudorfer Rechtsanwälte ✪
Sattler & Schanda
Schönherr ✪
Siemer-Siegl-Füreder & Partner, Rechtsanwälte ✪

Firms are listed A-Z in tiers which are ranked in order of priority
✪ *Indicates firm displays contact details at the end of this chapter.*

recently involved as administrator in an energy-sector bankruptcy. Bernhard Astner has an excellent reputation.

Kosch & Partner is another firm of receivers with a market-leading reputation and a focus on the Lower Austria market. Clients speak very highly of Gerhard Schilcher.

Preslmayr Attorneys at Law's Florian Gehmacher advises banks in relation to insolvency and restructuring cases, while Matthias Schmidt is also very active in the firm's insolvency practice, and was recently appointed as the Austrian receiver of food retailer Subway.

Schulyok Unger & Partner Rechtsanwälte OEG is known for its advice to banks in insolvency proceedings and also works as a debtors' counsel and as an official receiver.

Abel & Abel is a boutique with some well-regarded receivers on the team.

Baier Lambert's Andreas Alzinger recently acted as the receiver in a major bankruptcy in the Austrian food sector, and is advising on the bankruptcy of a large Austrian printing house.

CHSH Cerha Hempel Spiegelfeld Hlawati has a leading finance practice, and is consequently also strong on restructuring. Litigation partner Irene Welser has been representing the bankruptcy receiver of Parmalat in a large-scale dispute against an Austrian bank. Creditors advised in connection with insolvency proceedings include Thyssen Krupp AG, Telekom Austria, and Dubai-based SPS.

enwc attorneys at law Eiselsberg Natlacen Walderdorff Cancola has a practice advising creditors, while **Freshfields Bruckhaus Deringer** also advises major creditors and assists large companies with restructurings. It has recently advised a consortium of international lending banks, represented by Bank of America Securities Ltd as agent, in the €175m bankruptcy of an Austrian group. Banking partners Maria Th. Pflügl and Friedrich Jergitsch are recommended.

Haslinger/Nagele & Partner Rechtsanwälte GmbH has been advising a large motor industry component supplier on its insolvency. It also recently acted for a bankrupt Austrian construction company.

Saxinger Chalupsky Weber & Partner Rechtsanwälte GmbH's insolvency practice benefits from its ties with the firm's excellent banking team.

Wolf Theiss has a market-leading banking practice. Eva Spiegel, who works in the dispute resolution group, has been advising a number of major creditors in relation to the insolvency of Austrian financial services group AMIS.

INTELLECTUAL PROPERTY AND MEDIA

Austrian intellectual property (IP) lawyers have traditionally also handled unfair competition matters, and that area of law is consequently covered in this section. Austria has a very active generics market, and a handful of law firms have excellent patents practices. In Austria patent attorneys are a separate profession. They practice on their own or in small firms, and need to be employed for the registration of patents. Experienced clients can instruct patent attorneys directly. Patent attorneys cannot, however, appear in court without a lawyer. Sohn Pauvloy is the largest and leading firm of patent attorneys. Both Peter Pauvloy and Helmut Hohn are highly regarded, handling a considerable amount of international business. Kopecky & Schwarz is the other main firm of patent attorneys, with an excellent reputation for litigation. Sole practitioner Dr Thomas Haffner also has a good reputation. It is common for counterfeiters from the East to use Austria as an entry point into Europe, and product piracy advice is therefore very important. In the media industry, Austria's radio broadcasting market has now been liberalised.

Dr Michel Walter is Austria's leading copyright boutique. Michel Walter acts for some prominent artists and international clients. He is a university professor, and was described by one market commentator as 'head and shoulders above anyone else'. Felix Daum has a particular niche in piracy matters, while Albrecht Haller specialises in multimedia and internet-related IP law.

Schönherr is the only full-service corporate Austrian firm with a leading reputation for IP. Guido Kucsko, who focuses on patents and also has a good reputation for copyright, is praised by clients for 'exceptional services and always maintaining high professional standards'. Christian Hauer, who is best known for trade mark and unfair competition work, is also very highly regarded, and the team is respected for product piracy work. Clients include Microsoft, Red Bull and some major pharmaceutical companies.

Wiltschek Rechtsanwälte is the boutique of Lothar Wiltschek, widely acknowledged to be one of Austria's leading patent litigators. He has been representing a major pharmaceutical company in parallel import litigation which is also subject to European Court of Justice proceedings. Wiltschek also has an excellent reputation for unfair competition work, and a soft IP practice. On the media side, he has been advising broadcasting companies on licensing procedures. Ernst Tremmel provides EU and competition law support to the practice. Trade marks lawyer Stephanie Heine-Geldern has now left the firm.

Gassauer-Fleissner Rechtsanwälte has the largest specialised patent litigation team in Austria, comprising three equity partners, and led by the very highly regarded Christian Gassauer-Fleissner. He acts for four out of the ten largest pharmaceutical companies worldwide, and has been handling some landmark disputes between pharmaceutical companies and generic companies in Austria's 'Swiss-type claims'. He has also been recently involved in a test case involving the infringement of a software patent. The trade marks practice is led by Barbara Kucher, who also handles anti-counterfeiting work for some major French clients. Michael Wolner handles trade marks

INTELLECTUAL PROPERTY AND MEDIA

MICHEL WALTER (DR)
SCHÖNHERR ✪
WILTSCHEK RECHTSANWÄLTE

Gassauer-Fleissner Rechtsanwälte ✪

---

enwc attorneys at law Eiselsberg Natlacen Walderdorff Cancola ✪
Fiebinger, Polak, Leon & Partner Rechtsanwälte ✪
Freshfields Bruckhaus Deringer
Höhne, In der Maur & Partner Rechtsanwälte GmbH
Kunz Schima Wallentin Rechtsanwälte Keg ✪
Meinhard Ciresa (DDr)
Sattler & Schanda
Schwarz Schönherr Rechtsanwälte OEG
Zeiner & Zeiner

Baier Lambert ✪
CHSH Cerha Hempel Spiegelfeld Hlawati ✪
CMS Reich-Rohrwig Hainz ✪
DLA Weiss-Tessbach ✪
Dorda Brugger Jordis ✪
Engin-Deniz Reimitz Hafner Rechtsanwälte KEG
Griss & Partner
Haslinger/Nagele & Partner Rechtsanwälte GmbH ✪
Lansky, Ganzger & Partner Rechtsanwälte GmbH
Saxinger Chalupsky Weber & Partner Rechtsanwälte GmbH ✪
Schmidt, Kornfeld, Wukoschitz, Windhager
Wolf Theiss ✪

AVIA Law Group
Binder Grösswang Attorneys-at-Law ✪
Brauneis, Klauser & Prändl ✪
Dallmann & Juranek
Foglar-Deinhardstein KEG ✪
Greiter Pegger Kofler & Partners ✪
Haarmann Hügel ✪
Kammerlander, Piaty, Mueller-Mezin, Schoeller
Lovells in association with Mondl, Trummer, Thomas & Partner Rechtsanwälte GmbH
Ortner Pöch Foramitti
Petsch, Frosch & Klein
Siemer-Siegl-Füreder & Partner, Rechtsanwälte ✪

Firms are listed A-Z in tiers which are ranked in order of priority
✪ Indicates firm displays contact details at the end of this chapter.

including, recently, litigation relating to the infringement of a figurative trade mark in the cigarette industry. The team also handles domain name litigation and unfair competition, and Wolner has been handling copyright work for a leading Austrian institution in the field of classical music. On the media side, the team advises a UK-listed advertising company in Austria.

enwc attorneys at law Eiselsberg Natlacen Walderdorff Cancola has a strong practice in the protection of luxury goods from product piracy. The firm provides ongoing advice on IT matters to Nokia in Austria.

Fiebinger, Polak, Leon & Partner Rechtsanwälte has a focus on media law. Christoph Leon works in the newspaper and radio sectors, and regularly acts for one of the largest Austrian newspaper groups. Peter Polak has been for ten years chief counsel to the Austrian publishers' association. The firm also has an IP practice with patent litigation capability.

Freshfields Bruckhaus Deringer's Christof Pöchhacker has recently been appointed as managing partner of the office, but continues to handle client work in the IP field, where he has a strong reputation for trade mark matters. His team has been advising gM Tabak on trade mark and unfair competition proceedings against BAT British American Tobacco and, on the transactional side, advising Scientific Games on the IP aspects of an Austrian acquisition. Competition partner Axel Reidlinger has a solid media law practice, and acted for Medicur, part of the Raiffeisen Group, in relation to an investment in the infrastructure subsidiary of the public Austrian broadcasting corporation.

Höhne, In der Maur & Partner Rechtsanwälte GmbH is a leading media law firm. Georg Streit acts for the largest Austrian private radio station and some major private television stations, in addition to large media companies, publishing houses and political parties. Thomas Höhne handles IP work, including copyright matters for film companies and unfair competition matters.

Kunz Schima Wallentin Rechtsanwälte Keg's Thomas Wallentin has a leading reputation for IP work in the film and television industries.

DDr Meinhard Ciresa has been handling copyright litigation against Volkswagen, and trade mark litigation against Swiss Post on behalf of the Austrian post office regarding the trade-marking of the colour yellow. In addition, he has recently handled unfair competition lawsuits against Novartis. Clients describe him as 'very quick off the mark'.

Sattler & Schanda has a well-respected practitioner in Reinhard Schanda, who is an expert in trade marks, where he focuses on litigation.

Schwarz Schönherr Rechtsanwälte OEG is a new boutique which has been founded by Georg Schönherr, formerly a name partner and head of IP with **Engin-Deniz Reimitz Hafner Rechtsanwälte KEG**, and Winfried Schwarz, formerly a partner with **Dorda Brugger Jordis**. Schönherr, who brings with him a team of junior lawyers with trade marks expertise, is known as a patent litigator. Whilst at his previous firm, he handled two important patent infringement cases for the Hexal Group, part of the Sandoz group, in the 'Swiss-type claims' described above. Schwarz focuses on copyright law. Whilst at his previous firm, he represented the rights owner, in a matter related to the infringement of copyright in furniture, in asserting its rights against the largest chain of Austrian supermarket. In relation to media, he advised a software producer on media monitoring relating to television broadcasting. Clients following these lawyers to the new firm say the team is 'very competent and very reliable', and one added that Schönherr is 'very efficient, prompt and experienced'.

Zeiner & Zeiner is a trade marks litigation boutique, with a focus on EU trade marks and a Spanish office in Alicante for the purpose of filing such trade marks. Hans Georg Zeiner heads a substantial team in Vienna, which has been handling a hearing in Luxembourg for a German company with Austrian subsidiaries. The office also handles patent registration.

In the lower tier, **CMS Reich-Rohrwig Hainz**'s competition partner Daniela Karollus-Bruner has a strong practice in the film industry, while **Haarmann Hügel** wins its new ranking thanks to the recruitment of Meinhard Novak, who has particular experience in unfair competition.

PRIVATE CLIENT

Austria's private clients include some major family owned industrial companies, many of which are increasingly attracting the interest of international investment banks. Private client work is therefore considered an important area of practice to Austria's top commercial law firms, and there is some excellent advice on offer. Austrian law allows for the establishment of the private foundation, an entity that is mid-way between a company and a trust.

Dorda Brugger Jordis' Theresa Jordis is described by clients as being 'at the highest level'. She has a strong name for private client work in Austria, is a member of the supervisory boards of Erste Bank and Generali, and has strong connections to the car supply, paper and textile industries.

enwc Attorneys at Law Eiselsberg Natlacen Walderdorff Cancola has a leading private client practice. Founding partner Maximilian Eiselsberg is known as an outstanding specialist who is particularly strong on private foundations.

Hasch & Partner Anwaltsgesellschaft mbH moves up a tier as it is one of the few firms with experience in litigation involving private foundations. In addition, Alexander Hasch and Gerhard Hochedlinger both have leading practices in the field of private foundations.

Jakobljevich, Grave & Vetter is Austria's leading boutique private client law firm. Jörg Jakobljevich and Christian Grave enjoy outstanding reputations. Grave sits on the board of directors of many private foundations. He is frequently instructed by foreign clients to advise on family foundations – with similar structures to Austrian private foundations –in jurisdictions such as Germany, Switzerland and the Netherlands.

Schönherr is a market-leading corporate firm, whose partner Hellwig Torggler was one of the pioneers of Austrian private foundation law. Torggler is a tax expert and enjoys an excellent reputation.

Arnold Rechtsanwalts-Partnerschaft's Nikolaus Arnold is a tax expert who regularly advises private foundations.

Baker & McKenzie's Christoph Kerres is a strong M&A lawyer who also has a significant private client practice. He has been conducting a large mediation of a dispute within a prominent Austrian family, with assets at stake worth US$2bn.

CHSH Cerha Hempel Spiegelfeld Hlawati acts for many leading families with interests in Austrian and foreign industry.

PRIVATE CLIENT

DORDA BRUGGER JORDIS ✪
ENWC ATTORNEYS AT LAW EISELSBERG NATLACEN WALDERDORFF CANCOLA ✪
HASCH & PARTNER ANWALTSGESELLSCHAFT MBH
JAKOBLJEVICH, GRAVE & VETTER
SCHÖNHERR ✪

ARNOLD Rechtsanwalts-Partnerschaft
Baker & McKenzie ✪
CHSH Cerha Hempel Spiegelfeld Hlawati ✪
Freshfields Bruckhaus Deringer
Greiter Pegger Kofler & Partners ✪
Griss & Partner
Haarmann Hügel ✪
Siemer-Siegl-Füreder & Partner, Rechtsanwälte ✪

Brauneis, Klauser & Prändl ✪
DLA Weiss-Tessbach ✪
Draxler & Partner Rechtsanwälte
Eckert & Fries Rechtsanwälte GmbH
Gassauer-Fleissner Rechtsanwälte ✪
Haslinger/Nagele & Partner Rechtsanwälte GmbH ✪
Hauser Partners Rechtsanwälte GmbH ✪
Karasek Wietrzyk Rechtsanwälte GmbH
Saxinger Chalupsky Weber & Partner Rechtsanwälte GmbH ✪

Firms are listed A-Z in tiers which are ranked in order of priority
✪ *Indicates firm displays contact details at the end of this chapter.*

Freshfields Bruckhaus Deringer brings its international experience in advising investment banks to bear on its private client work. Tax lawyer Michael Sedlaczek has experience in designing tax efficient capital investment products for private clients.

Greiter Pegger Kofler & Partners has a good reputation for advising on private foundations. Ivo Greiter is recommended.

Griss & Partner's Peter Griss, who is based in Graz, has been advising a large real estate fund, and has substantial experience in handling industry holdings and private foundations.

Haarmann Hügel's leading corporate partner, Hanns Hügel, also has an excellent reputation for private client work.

Siemer-Siegl-Füreder & Partner, Rechtsanwälte is particularly strong in property advice to private clients, and on sponsorship agreements. It has been advising a client who sold shares in one of Austria's largest producers of mineral waters on the reinvestment of the proceeds of the transaction, and the restructuring of assets. Mario Schiavon is recommended for estate planning, and Hannes Füreder for the corporate structuring of private wealth.

REAL ESTATE AND CONSTRUCTION

When selecting a law firm it is often important to look at the quality of environmental law advice on offer, as Austria also has extremely strict regulations for the protection of the environment.

CHSH Cerha Hempel Spiegelfeld Hlawati has Austria's leading real estate practice. The team is led by Alfred Nemetschke. He advised one of Bankhaus Wölbern's investment companies on the €150m acquisition of the technical centre of BA-CA. His partner Walter Anderl advised the listed Hungarian company Immoeast on the €210m acquisition of a chain of shopping centres.

Karasek Wietrzyk Rechtsanwälte GmbH's Georg Karasek is Austria's leading construction law advisor and arbitrator. He is advising several companies working on the construction of a new underground line in Vienna, and advising a consortium of construction companies in relation to the execution of tunnel projects worth a total of €180m. He has also been advising one of Austria's major energy companies on a tender related to a biomass power plant, and handles property litigation. Thomas Frad also handles construction work, and the firm has an environmental impact assessment practice.

Wolf Theiss' well-regarded Peter Oberlechner advised Warburg-Henderson Kapitalanlagegesellschaft für Imobilien mbH on the €60m acquisition of a shopping centre. On the construction side, he also advised McArthur/Glen on the €21m construction and financing of an enlargement to a designer outlet centre. Construction partner Georg Kresbach is also much liked by clients, who describe him as 'well-informed, quick and efficient'.

CMS Reich-Rohrwig Hainz's Nikolaus Weselik has a well-regarded real estate practice and considerable expertise in construction-related litigation. His team advised Bilfinger & Berger on the refurbishment of a Salzburg hotel. Clients speak highly of the real estate financing advice provided by Günther Hanslik.

REAL ESTATE AND CONSTRUCTION

CHSH CERHA HEMPEL SPIEGELFELD HLAWATI ✪
KARASEK WIETRZYK RECHTSANWÄLTE GMBH
WOLF THEISS ✪

CMS Reich-Rohrwig Hainz ✪
DLA Weiss-Tessbach ✪
Dorda Brugger Jordis ✪
Freshfields Bruckhaus Deringer
Schönherr ✪
Siemer-Siegl-Füreder & Partner, Rechtsanwälte ✪

Alix Frank Rechtsanwälte GmbH
AVIA Law Group
Baier Lambert ✪
Binder Grösswang Attorneys-at-Law ✪
Brauneis, Klauser & Prändl ✪
enwc attorneys at law Eiselsberg Natlacen Walderdorff Cancola ✪
Fiebinger, Polak, Leon & Partner Rechtsanwälte ✪
Gassauer-Fleissner Rechtsanwälte ✪
Haarmann Hügel ✪
Neudorfer Rechtsanwälte ✪
Saxinger Chalupsky Weber & Partner Rechtsanwälte GmbH ✪
Schwartz und Huber-Medek Rechtsanwälte OEG

Deissenberger & Partners
Eckert & Fries Rechtsanwälte GmbH
Griss & Partner
Hasch & Partner Anwaltsgesellschaft mbH
Hausmaninger Kletter Rechtsanwälte GmbH ✪
Held Berdnik Astner & Partner, Rechtsanwälte
Herbst Vavrovsky Kinsky Rechtsanwälte GmbH ✪
Höhne, In der Maur & Partner Rechtsanwälte GmbH
Kaan Cronenberg & Partners
Kammerlander, Piaty, Mueller-Mezin, Schoeller
Lansky, Ganzger & Partner Rechtsanwälte GmbH
Lovells in association with Mondl, Trummer, Thomas & Partner Rechtsanwälte GmbH
Sattler & Schanda
Zirngibl Langwieser

Firms are listed A-Z in tiers which are ranked in order of priority
✪ Indicates firm displays contact details at the end of this chapter.

DLA Weiss-Tessbach's Gerhard Benn-Ibler has a good reputation for construction arbitration. His team has been advising an international investor and owner of one of Austria's largest office buildings on issues of construction law, landlord and tenant law, and financing. Clients also appreciate the firm's specialised house administration business.

Dorda Brugger Jordis advised Bundesimmobiliengesellschaft mbH, the privatisation and holding company for real estate of the Republic of Austria, on the privatisation of a majority interest in a property in Vienna. Stefan Artner is recommended by clients, who say that he is 'absolutely brilliant, and never gets tired of explaining the smallest details of an ongoing case with practicality and patience'.

Freshfields Bruckhaus Deringer's team is headed by Georg Bahn, who is praised by clients for his 'experience and knowledge in dealing with complex projects, and ability to handle deals under time pressure'. His team advised Austrian real estate developer Projekta Bauvorbereitungs GmbH on a major arbitration. In relation to construction, Thomas Kustor's team has been advising the Austrian subsidiary of a major French construction company in a dispute. The environmental group is headed by Paul Luiki, who has been advising Austria Metall AG on a contaminated site.

Schönherr is advising Brau Union and Heineken on the €238m sale of its real estate division. Department head Peter Madl is praised by clients for his 'high level of professionalism'. The firm also has an environmental practice, headed by Christian Schmelz, which has been advising on plant licensing, and environmental impact assessments in the automotive and energy sectors.

Siemer-Siegl-Füreder & Partner, Rechtsanwälte has been advising a client on the purchase of a forestry estate from the Republic of Austria, and advising Siemens on the leasing of a power plant and office site worth €23m. Reinhard Bruner is recommended. One international client commented: 'The advice and assistance was delivered in a manner that took into consideration our lack of familiarity with Austrian practice'.

In the third tier, two firms which have been increasing the amount of real estate work that they handle are **enwc attorneys at law Eiselsberg Natlacen Walderdorff Cancola**, where Thomas Brandstätter has been advising a real estate fund organised by one of the largest Austrian banks, and **Gassauer-Fleissner Rechtsanwälte**, where Klaus Fischer and Christian Gassauer-Fleissner have advised the developer of one of the largest and most successful office developments in Vienna.

In the fourth tier, Graz-based **Griss & Partner**, ranked here for the first time, has a strong environmental practice. Peter Griss and Edwin Mächler are advising on a large environmental liability case relating to pollution, following a real estate acquisition.

TAX

The Austrian tax system – with its low corporate tax rate of 25% – makes it a beneficial jurisdiction to international companies, and a popular one with international banks developing structured products. Only the law firms with the largest tax practices have lawyers focusing exclusively on tax work. It is more common for the corporate partners to advise on corporate restructuring and tax-driven finance structures. There are now a number of dual-qualified tax advisors and lawyers working within law firms.

Arnold Rechtsanwalts-Partnerschaft is Austria's leading tax litigation practice, and also handles tax-structuring matters. It is currently handling cases concerning the taxation of zero bonds, with the amount in dispute being several €100m, and an energy tax refund case involving a €300m claim. Wolf-Dieter Arnold is recommended, and is well known as the Austrian specialist on stamp duty.

Freshfields Bruckhaus Deringer is Austria's leading corporate tax practice. It has been advising UniCredit on its acquisition of the HVB group, work which shows that its six-lawyer team is now competing in the league of Austria's Big Four accounting firms. Michael Sedlaczek and Claus Staringer are recommended, and advise many US and German investment banks.

CHSH Cerha Hempel Spiegelfeld Hlawati has hired a new partner, Clemens Hasenauer, formerly a key player in the tax department at **Haarmann Hügel**, and a new tax consultant. The team focuses on tax structuring related to M&A, financial products, and capital markets prospectuses. Banking partner Peter Knobl has a good reputation for tax-related structured finance matters.

Dorda Brugger Jordis's tax work is mainly carried out by the banking partners. They have been representing Austrian banks before the Austrian tax authority in matters concerning their alleged liability for withholding tax in relation to zero coupon bonds. Clients say that the lawyers advising on tax 'always take an effective and cost-conscious approach'.

Haarmann Hügel is part of the international **Haarmann Hemmelrath** network, which has a leading international tax practice. The bulk of the tax work in Austria is handled by Hanns Hügel, who has an outstanding reputation as a corporate lawyer. Corporate partner Florian Gibitz also advises on tax. Their recent work includes advising Novartis on the restructuring of its Austrian group, and advising the Shell group on an international restructuring. Clemens Hasenauer has now left the firm.

At **Wolf Theiss**, the tax group has been advising some major institutional investors on the tax basis for capital markets transactions. Christian Hoenig, who advised Macquarie on the Austrian law aspects of the financing of the acquisition of the Yellow Brick Road Group, is recommended for tax advice.

Brauneis, Klauser & Prändl has a co-operation with Deloitte & Touche, and a significant proportion of its corporate and commercial work is tax driven.

CMS Reich-Rohrwig Hainz wins its place in this tier thanks to the recruitment of tax consultant Beate Wallner from a Big Four accounting firm. She has been advising a major European group on EU infringement proceedings relating to tobacco tax. The tax group is headed by corporate partner Johannes Reich-Rohrwig, who has been advising Casinos Austria on the tax-driven restructuring of a JV.

Karasek Wietrzyk Rechtsanwälte GmbH has a close relationship with Ernst & Young. Partner Gerold Wietrzyk, who is dual-qualified as a lawyer and a tax advisor, focuses on corporate support work in the tax field, particularly corporate advice on tax-driven structures.

Schönherr moves up a tier due to a solid reputation in the field and the recruitment of tax advisor Paul Doralt from KPMG, where he worked in the Vienna and New York offices. Hellwig Torggler heads the team, which advised BNP Paribas on the tax structuring of a major securitisation transaction in Austria.

TAX

ARNOLD RECHTSANWALTS-PARTNERSCHAFT
FRESHFIELDS BRUCKHAUS DERINGER

CHSH Cerha Hempel Spiegelfeld Hlawati ✪
Dorda Brugger Jordis ✪
Haarmann Hügel ✪
Wolf Theiss ✪

Brauneis, Klauser & Prändl ✪
CMS Reich-Rohrwig Hainz ✪
Karasek Wietrzyk Rechtsanwälte GmbH
Schönherr ✪

---

bmp Rechtsanwälte
Baker & McKenzie ✪
Binder Grösswang Attorneys-at-Law ✪
DLA Weiss-Tessbach ✪
enwc attorneys at law Eiselsberg Natlacen Walderdorff Cancola ✪
Greiter Pegger Kofler & Partners ✪
Hauser Partners Rechtsanwälte GmbH ✪
Hausmaninger Kletter Rechtsanwälte GmbH ✪
MMag Gustav Walzel
Saxinger Chalupsky Weber & Partner Rechtsanwälte GmbH ✪
SchneideR'S Rechtsanwalts-KEG
Siemer-Siegl-Füreder & Partner, Rechtsanwälte ✪

Firms are listed A-Z in tiers which are ranked in order of priority
✪ *Indicates firm displays contact details at the end of this chapter.*

BINDER GRÖSSWANG ATTORNEYS-AT-LAW

KAISERJÄGERSTRASSE 1
6020 INNSBRUCK

Telephone: +43 512 57 99 73
Fax: +43 512 57 99 738
E-mail: tirol@bgnet.at
Website: www.bgnet.at

Languages
Croatian, English, French, German, Italian, Spanish

Other offices
Vienna

Number of lawyers 50
at this office 6

CATEGORIES OF WORK

Banking and finance
Tibor Fabian, Stefan Tiefenthaler

Banking regulatory and investment funds
Michael Binder

Capital markets
Michael Binder, Florian Khol

Competition, public procurement
Raoul Hoffer, Johannes Barbist

Corporate and commercial
Michael Binder, Ivo Rungg

Dispute resolution, arbitration
Christian Klausegger, Michael Kutschera

Energy, deregulation
Raoul Hoffer

Intellectual property
Ivo Rungg, Hellmut Buchroithner

Labour law
Horst Lukanec

M&A
Thomas Schirmer, Michael Kutschera

Real estate
Tibor Fabian

Structured finance, project finance
Tibor Fabian, Stefan Tiefenthaler

Tax
Andreas Hable, Michael Binder

GREITER PEGGER KOFLER & PARTNERS

MARIA-THERESIEN-STRASSE 24
6020 INNSBRUCK 158

Telephone: +43 512 57 18 11
Fax: +43 512 58 49 25
E-mail: info@greiter.lawfirm.at
Website: www.greiter.lawfirm.at

Languages
English, French, German, Italian

Number of lawyers 16

CATEGORIES OF WORK

Personal injury

Companies, corporations

Banking, securities and finance

Mergers and acquisitions

Competition, antitrust

Commercial law (general)

Employment, labour

Tax

Insurance

Intellectual property, trade marks

Commercial agency/distribution agreements

Real property

Inheritance

Environment

Establishment of companies, subsidiaries

HASLINGER/NAGELE & PARTNER RECHTSANWÄLTE GMBH

ROSEGGERSTRASSE 58
4020 LINZ

Telephone: +43 732 78 43 310
Fax: +43 732 77 43 31
E-mail: office@haslinger-nagele.com
Website: www.haslinger-nagele.com

Languages
Czech, English, French, German

Other offices
Bratislava, Prague, Vienna

Number of lawyers 25
at this office 14

Contacts
Dr Norbert Nagele, Dr Klaus Haslinger, Dr Christoph Szep, Mag Thomas Kurz, Dr Wilhelm Bergthaler, Dr Dietmar Lux, Mag Karin Lindner, Mag Martin Oder, Mag Martin Stempkowski, Mag Martin Niederhuber, Mag Bernhard Hager, Mag Lukas Leszkovics

CATEGORIES OF WORK

Commercial and corporate law
Dr Nagele, Dr Szep, Dr Lux

Banking and finance
Dr Lux, Mag Leszkovics

Mergers and acquisitions
Dr Nagele, Dr Szep, Dr Lux

Commercial property, real estate
Mag Lindner, Mag Hager

Insolvency, corporate restructuring
Mag Kurz, Mag Lindner

Energy and natural resources
Mag Oder, Mag Stempkowski, Mag Hager

Competition law and intellectual property
Dr Haslinger, Mag Stempkowski

Antitrust
Mag Stempkowski, Mag Oder

Environment
Dr Bergthaler, Mag Niederhuber, Mag Hager

Labour and employment
Mag Lindner, Mag Leszkovics

Dispute resolution, litigation and international arbitration
Dr Lux

BAIER LAMBERT

KÄRNTNERRING 12
1010 VIENNA

Telephone: +43 1 515 50
Fax: +43 1 515 50 50
E-mail: office@baierlambert.com
Website: www.baierlambert.com

Languages
Czech, English, French, German

Number of lawyers 30

Contact
Dr Erhard Böhm

CATEGORIES OF WORK

Banking

Litigation and arbitration

Company and commercial law

Mergers and acquisitions

Central and Eastern European law

Real estate and property law

EU law

Telecommunications

Energy and natural resources

Distribution and agency

Franchising law

Capital markets

Intellectual property

Insolvency and restructuring

International transactions

Employment and labour law

BAKER & McKENZIE

KERRES & DIWOK RECHTSANWÄLTE GMBH

SCHUBERTRING 2
1010 VIENNA

Telephone: +43 1 516 60
Fax: +43 1 516 60 60
E-mail: vienna.info@bakernet.com
Website: www.bakernet.com

Languages
English, French, German, Hungarian, Italian, Polish, Spanish

Other offices
The member firms of Baker & McKenzie International, a Swiss Verein, have 70 offices in 38 countries around the world. For a complete list, please visit www.bakernet.com.

Number of lawyers 3,300+
at this office 20+

Contacts
Christoph Kerres, Georg Diwok

CATEGORIES OF WORK

- **Antitrust**
- **Banking and finance**
- **Capital markets**
- **Corporate and commercial**
- **Dispute resolution**
- **Employment**
- **Information technology**
- **Intellectual property**
- **Mergers and acquisitions**
- **Private foundations and trust**
- **Public law, environmental and energy law**
- **Regulatory and compliance**
- **Real estate**
- **Tax**
- **Telecoms**

THE FIRM

Baker & McKenzie has provided sophisticated legal advice and services to many of the world's most dynamic and global organisations for more than 50 years. With a network of more than 3,300 locally qualified, internationally experienced lawyers in 38 countries, the firm has the knowledge and resources to deliver the broad scope of quality legal services required to respond effectively to both international and local needs – consistently, confidently and with a sensitivity for cultural, social and legal practice differences. Baker & McKenzie has been established in Europe for 40 years, having opened its first European offices in 1957. Since then, the European and Middle Eastern network has grown to 29 offices, giving it unparalled geographical coverage.

Since February 2003, the firm is represented in Vienna with more than 20 lawyers. Being one of the leading Austrian law firms, it advises both national and international companies from a variety of industrial sectors in all areas of private and public commercial law. The firm offers clients advice combining comprehensive expertise in national and European law with international experience, enhanced by access to the resources of its worldwide organisation.

AREAS OF PRACTICE

Baker & McKenzie advises multinational enterprises, large Austrian companies, medium-sized enterprises, banks and insurance companies, as well as institutions and entities under public law in all questions of Austrian, European and banking and finance, corporate and commercial law, labour law, intellectual property, private foundations and tax law. Furthermore the firm handles litigation and arbitration matters. Baker & McKenzie co-ordinates its core practice areas on local, regional and multinational teams of specialists. Utilising a global practice group structure and groundbreaking technology, coupled with a personal, detailed understanding of a client's specific business, Baker & McKenzie is able to organise its extensive resources to provide focused and strategic counsel to clients.

Baker & McKenzie is a Swiss Verein with member law firms around the world.

BINDER GRÖSSWANG ATTORNEYS-AT-LAW

STERNGASSE 13
1010 VIENNA

Telephone: +43 1 534 80
Fax: +43 1 534 808
E-mail: bg@bgnet.at
Website: www.bgnet.at

Languages
Croatian, English, French, German, Italian, Spanish

Other offices
Innsbruck

Number of lawyers 50
at this office 44

CATEGORIES OF WORK

Banking and finance
Tibor Fabian,
Stefan Tiefenthaler

Banking regulatory and investment funds
Michael Binder

Capital markets
Michael Binder, Florian Khol

Competition, public procurement
Raoul Hoffer, Johannes Barbist

Corporate and commercial
Michael Binder, Ivo Rungg

Dispute resolution, arbitration
Christian Klausegger,
Michael Kutschera

Energy, deregulation
Raoul Hoffer

Intellectual property
Ivo Rungg, Hellmut Buchroithner

Labour law
Horst Lukanec

M&A
Thomas Schirmer, Michael Kutschera

Real estate
Tibor Fabian

Structured finance, project finance
Tibor Fabian, Stefan Tiefenthaler

Tax
Andreas Hable, Michael Binder

THE FIRM

Binder Grösswang is one of the leading law firms in Austria, with offices in Vienna and Innsbruck. The members of the team aspire to meet client's needs on an outstanding level by pooling both individual experience and the collective know-how of the firm.

The firm consists of 22 partners and approximately 30 associates. Committed to the highest level of legal expertise, the firm advises major Austrian corporate, banking and industry clients. Binder Grösswang has established a strong international competence in various areas during the last four decades.

From its Innsbruck office, the firm aims to meet the needs of enterprises doing business in the western parts of Austria by giving on-the-spot counsel. As the office consists of local lawyers, the economic circumstances of the region are well known and a close connection to clients is guaranteed. Moreover, this office assists the firm's presence in the economic areas of northern Italy and southern Germany because of its geographical location.

AREAS OF PRACTICE

The major areas of the firm's practice are M&A, banking and finance and dispute resolution, as well as competition and public procurement. Over the last few years, Binder Grösswang has also developed a strong reputation for practice in capital markets, structured finance and project finance, labour law, real estate and intellectual property.

BRANDL & TALOS RECHTSANWÄLTE GMBH

MARIAHILFER STRASSE 116
1070 VIENNA

Telephone: +43 1 522 5700
Fax: +43 1 522 5701
E-mail: brandl@btp.at
Website: www.btp.at

Languages
English

Number of lawyers 8

International groupings
International Masters of Gaming Law (IMGL); Alternative Investment Forum Austria (AIFA); Austrian Society for Bank Research

CATEGORIES OF WORK

Capital markets law
Ernst Brandl, Thomas Talos

Banking and finance
Ernst Brandl, Thomas Talos

Corporate, M&A
Thomas Talos, Christopher Schrank

Gaming law
Thomas Talos, Christopher Schrank

BRAUNEIS KLAUSER PRÄNDL
RECHTSANWÄLTE GMBH

BAUERNMARKT 2
1010 WIEN

Telephone: +43 1 532 12 10 0
Fax: +43 1 532 12 10 20
E-mail: viennalaw@bkp.at
Website: www.bkp.at

Languages
Bulgarian, English, French, German, Italian

Number of lawyers 17

CATEGORIES OF WORK

EU and competition law
Dr Alexander Klauser,
Dr Bernhard Girsch

IT and telecommunications law
Dr Felix Prändl,
Dr Arno Brauneis

Intellectual property
Dr Arno Brauneis,
Dr Bernhard Girsch

International distribution law
Dr Arno Brauneis

Companies, corporations, tax
Dr Felix Prändl,
Mag Brigitte Sammer

Mergers and acquisitions
Dr Felix Prändl,
Mag Stefan Geppert

Real estate
Dr Arno Brauneis, Dr Orlin Radinsky

Insolvency
Dr Alexander Klauser,
Mag Barbara Pogacar

Litigation and arbitration
Dr Alexander Klauser

Banking law and securities
Mag Stefan Geppert

Labour and employment
Dr Arno Brauneis, Dr Orlin Radinsky

CHSH CERHA HEMPEL SPIEGELFELD HLAWATI

PARKRING 2
1010 WIEN

Telephone: +43 1 514 35 0
Fax: +43 1 514 35 35
E-mail: office@chsh.at
Website: www.chsh.at

Languages
Croatian, Danish, English, French, German, Hungarian, Italian, Polish, Romanian, Russian, Spanish

Other offices
Brussels, Bucharest, Budapest

Number of lawyers 76
at this office 51

CATEGORIES OF WORK

Mergers and acquisitions
Edith Hlawati, Benedikt Spiegelfeld

Banking
Edith Hlawati, Peter Knobl

Capital markets
Edith Hlawati, Volker Glas

Companies, corporations
Albert Birkner

Arbitration and litigation
Irene Welser, Peter Vcelouch

Commercial law (contracts)
Benedikt Spiegelfeld, Irene Welser

Franchising and distribution
Benedikt Spiegelfeld

Information technology
Volker Glas

Real estate, construction, building
Alfred Nemetschke, Walter Anderl

Competition, antitrust, IP
Julian Feichtinger

Privatisation, telecommunications
Edith Hlawati

Labour law
Irene Welser, Julian Feichtinger

Eastern Europe
Alfred Nemetschke, Johannes Aehrenthal

Regulation, administrative, constitutional law
Peter Lewisch

Energy
Benedikt Spiegelfeld, Albert Birkner

Tax
Clemens Hasenauer

CMS REICH-ROHRWIG HAINZ

EBENDORFERSTRASSE 3
1010 WIEN

Telephone: +43 1 404 43 0
Fax: +43 1 404 43 90 00
E-mail: vienna@cms-rrh.com
Website: www.cms-rrh.com

Languages
Bulgarian, Chinese, Croatian, Czech, English, French, German, Russian, Serbian, Slovakian, Slovenian, Spanish

Other offices
Belgrade, Bratislava, Brussels, Prague, Sofia, Zagreb

Number of lawyers 71
at this office 45

Contacts
Bernt Elsner, Peter Huber

Member
CMS Alliance of major European law firms; World Law Group

CATEGORIES OF WORK

Banking and finance
Peter Huber, Martin Zuffer

Capital markets
Martin Zuffer

Central and Eastern Europe
Peter Huber

Commercial property, real estate and construction
Nikolaus Weselik, Egon Engin-Deniz

Competition and EU
Bernt Elsner

Corporate and commercial
Johannes Reich-Rohrwig, Peter Huber

Dispute resolution
Johannes Reich-Rohrwig, Daniela Karollus-Bruner

Energy and national resources
Daniela Karollus-Bruner, Günther Hanslik

Public procurement, regulatory
Bernt Elsner, Robert Keisler

Tax
Johannes Reich-Rohrwig, Beate Wallner

Infrastructure
Peter Huber, Nikolaus Weselik

Insolvency and corporate restructuring
Johannes Reich-Rohrwig, Nikolaus Weselik

Intellectual property, media
Egon Engin-Deniz

Labour and employment
Bernhard Hainz, Andreas Tinhofer

M&A, transactions
Peter Huber, Günther Hanslik

Medical law
Christoph Wolf

DLA WEISS-TESSBACH

ROTENTURMSTRASSE 13
1010 WIEN

Telephone: +43 1 531 78 0
Fax: +43 1 533 52 52
E-mail: vienna@dlapiper.com
Website: www.dlapiper.com

Languages
Bosnian, Croatian, Czech, English, French, German, Hungarian, Italian, Polish, Russian, Slovak

Other offices
Belgium, Bosnia-Herzegovina, China, Croatia, Czech Republic, Denmark*, Egypt*, France, Georgia, Germany, Hong Kong, Hungary, Italy, Japan, Netherlands, Norway*, Poland*, Russia, Singapore*, Slovakia, South Africa*, Spain, Sweden*, Thailand, UK, Ukraine, United Arab Emirates, US

Number of lawyers 3,100
at this office 50

Contacts
Stefan Eder, Ivo Deskovic

Member
DLA Piper Group

CATEGORIES OF WORK

General corporate
Wieland Schmid-Schmidsfelden

Commercial (general) and contract
Ivo Deskovic

Competition
Claudine Vartian

Project finance, financing
Stefan Eder

EU law
Max Becker

Eastern Europe
Stefan Eder

Litigation
Ivo Deskovic

Banking
Stefan Eder

Intellectual property
Alexander Cizek

Property, real estate
Gerhard Benn-Ibler

Mergers and acquisitions
Wieland Schmid-Schmidsfelden

Environmental
Ivo Deskovic

Labour
Franz Marhold

Telecoms, IT
Ivo Deskovic

Public procurement
Ivo Deskovic

THE FIRM

DLA Weiss-Tessbach was established in 1878 in Austria and is one of the longest-established law firms in the country. Since 1989, the firm has undergone a dynamic expansion across Central and Eastern Europe, growing from 15 to 100 lawyers and from one to seven offices. DLA Weiss-Tessbach will continue to expand in the Central and Eastern European region as countries adjust to EU membership.

DLA Weiss-Tessbach is part of DLA Piper Rudnick Gray Cary, one of the leading global legal services providers with approximately 3,100 lawyers in 58 offices across 22 countries. The organisation is committed to building long-term relationships with its clients and supports their strategic and operational needs, both locally and internationally.

AREAS OF PRACTICE

The firm has strengthened its core areas of expertise (commercial and corporate, M&A, banking and finance, general commercial law, real estate) and advises its clients as a full-service firm in all relevant areas of business law, including administrative law, employment law, IT and telecoms, technology, intellectual property, venture capital and capital markets.

DLA Weiss-Tessbach has well-established relations with clients of various backgrounds. The firm advises medium-sized enterprises as well as leading (often publicly listed) international and domestic industrial groups, service providers, banks and other financial institutions and individuals.

DLA Weiss-Tessbach has established a particular reputation for its ability to handle cases in international cross-border contexts. The firm is renowned for its expertise in the structuring and implementation of projects and transactions in Austria, as well as in Central and Eastern Europe. It carefully monitors the ongoing developments in the Central and Eastern European region with the aim of combining the needs of the constantly changing international legal market and industry, whilst also upholding the high standard of service that the firm has always been able to offer to its clients.

DORDA BRUGGER JORDIS

DR KARL LUEGER-RING 10
1010 VIENNA

Telephone: +43 1 533 47 95
Fax: +43 1 533 47 97
E-mail: office@dbj.at
Website: www.dbj.at

Languages
English, French, German, Italian, Spanish

Number of lawyers 60

Contacts
Christian Dorda, Martin Brodey

CATEGORIES OF WORK

Arbitration
Christian Dorda, Florian Kremslehner

Banking and finance
Andreas Zahradnik, Tibor Varga

Capital markets
Andreas W Mayr, Andreas Zahradnik

Central and Eastern Europe
Martin Brodey, Christian Dorda

Competition and antitrust
Stephan Polster, Walter Brugger

Corporate and commercial
Christoph Brogyányi, Walter Brugger

IT, IP and media
Axel Anderl

Labour
Thomas Angermair

Litigation
Florian Kremslehner,
Thomas Angermair

M&A and privatisations
Christian Dorda, Martin Brodey

Private client
Theresa Jordis

Project finance
Tibor Varga

Public procurement and administrative law
Stefan Günther

Real estate and construction
Stefan Artner

Restructuring and insolvency
Andreas Zahradnik

Tax
Tibor Varga

Telecoms, energy and liberalised markets
Stephan Polster, Martin Brodey

THE FIRM

Dorda Brugger Jordis is a leading law firm in Austria, specialising in commercial law and international business transactions. Clients range from large international corporations and their Austrian subsidiaries to large and medium-sized Austrian business entities (banks, industrial and commercial enterprises). The firm also has links with large accountancy firms and has built up a strong and effective network of contacts worldwide. Dorda Brugger Jordis is renowned for quick, thorough and reliable legal services, both nationally and internationally.

For projects in Central and Eastern Europe, Dorda Brugger Jordis has adopted the *Best Friends* programme, a close co-operation with independent top-tier law firms in CEE countries. All the law firms participating in Dorda Brugger Jordis' *Best Friends* network share the same high standards of quality and provide in-depth regional expertise. Clients currently have access to know-how from leading law firms in the following countries: Bosnia and Herzegovina, Bulgaria, Croatia, Czech Republic, Hungary, Poland, Romania, Serbia, Slovakia and Slovenia.

AREAS OF PRACTICE

Dorda Brugger Jordis' activities focus on corporate and tax law, M&A, banking and finance, competition, CEE projects, real estate, employment, intellectual property, arbitration and litigation, EU law, public procurement, private clients, telecoms, IT, energy, restructuring and insolvency.

e|n|w|c ATTORNEYS AT LAW

EISELSBERG NATLACEN WALDERDORFF CANCOLA

SCHWARZENBERGPLATZ 7
1030 VIENNA

Telephone: +43 1 716 55
Fax: +43 1 716 55 99
E-mail: wien@enwc.com
Website: www.enwc.com

Languages
Czech, English, French, Hungarian, Italian, Polish, Slovak, Turkish

Other offices
Bratislava, Brno, Budapest, Prague, Warsaw

Number of lawyers 47
at this office 25

Contacts
Dr Maximilan Eiselsberg, Dr Raimund Cancola

CATEGORIES OF WORK

Corporate and commercial law	EU and competition
Banking and finance	Labour and employment
Private client	Intellectual property
Central and Eastern Europe	Telecommunications
Tax	Litigation and arbitration
Commercial property	Real estate
Capital markets	Construction and building

THE FIRM

e|n|w|c is one of Austria's leading law firms, and has offices in Vienna, Budapest, Prague, Brno, Bratislava and Warsaw. The firm's main areas of practice are commercial law and private client.

The firm was founded by Dr Maximilian Eiselsberg and Dr Dieter Natlacen in 1986. In 1991 it merged with the practices of Dr Erich Schwinner and Dr Georg Walderdorff, attorneys at law, and in 1993 Dr Raimund Cancola became a partner, and the firm's name now became Eiselsberg Natlacen Walderdorff Cancola. Today e|n|w|c has more than 45 lawyers at work, and advises major Austrian and international companies in the commercial, industrial, service, banking and insurance sectors.

The legal staff at e|n|w|c are highly trained commercial lawyers with international experience whose expertise covers every aspect of business law. By operating in specialist teams the firm is able to provide first-class service in all areas of law, despite the growing complexity of the legal issues facing its clients.

AREAS OF PRACTICE:

e|n|w|c advises its clients on the following fields of law: administrative law, agency agreements, antitrust law, arbitration, banking law, capital market law, collection, commercial law, competition law, construction, contracts, contract law, copyright, corporate law, distribution law, energy law, European law, franchising, industrial property protection, ITT law, labour law, litigation, media law, mergers and acquisitions, patent law, private client, private foundations, probate and wills, procurement law, real estate law, takeover law, tax law, tenancy law, trade law, trade mark and design protection, unfair competition.

Good advice is not just a question of legal expertise. What matters most of all to its clients is the firm's understanding of the business they are in.

e|n|w|c has extensive experience of the following industries: agriculture and forestry, automotive distribution, banking, insurance, financial services, leasing and credit insurance, clothing, construction, direct selling, energy, food and beverages, information technology and telecommunications, mining and quarrying, postal services, pulp and paper, real estate development, transport and logistics, and wood processing.

FELLNER WRATZFELD & PARTNER

RECHTSANWÄLTE – ATTORNEYS AT LAW

SCHOTTENRING 12
1010 VIENNA

Telephone: +43 1 537 70
Fax: +43 1 537 70 70
E-mail: office@fwp.at
Website: www.fwp.at

Languages
English, French, German

Number of lawyers 27

CATEGORIES OF WORK

Mergers and acquisitions
Markus Fellner

Antitrust and competition
Markus Fellner

Real estate
Markus Kajaba, Michael Achleitner

Public law, environment
Michael Hecht, Markus Kajaba

Employment, labour
Kurt Wratzfeld

Telecoms
Sabine Fehringer, Michael Hecht

Trade marks, intellectual property
Sabine Fehringer

Media, unfair competition
Sabine Fehringer

Banking, securities and finance
Markus Fellner, Michael Hecht

Companies and corporations
Markus Fellner, Gregor Schett

Arbitration and litigation
Kurt Wratzfeld

Agricultural, food, drugs
Michael Hecht

IP, IT
Sabine Fehringer

Damage/product liability, insurance
Kurt Wratzfeld

Trusts and foundations, inheritance
Markus Fellner, Kurt Wratzfeld

Tax
Markus Fellner

Public sector
Michael Hecht

Energy
Gregor Schett

FIEBINGER, POLAK, LEON & PARTNER RECHTSANWÄLTE

AM GETREIDEMARKT 1
1060 VIENNA

Telephone: +43 1 58 25 80
Fax: +43 1 58 25 82
Email: fplp@fplp.at
Website: www.fplp.at

Languages
English, French, German, Italian, Spanish

Number of lawyers 21

CATEGORIES OF WORK

Administrative law
M Maurer-Kollenz

Antitrust law
M Gudenus, P Polak

Banking and capital markets
B Ortner, P Polak

Competition law
C Leon, R Fiebinger

Corporate law and M&A
P Polak, B Ortner

Financing/cross-border transactions
P Polak, B Ortner

Distribution
B Ortner, M Gudenus

Employment and benefits
B Ortner, R Fiebinger

Energy law
P Polak, M Gudenus

EU law
M Gudenus

Intellectual property
C Leon, C Kletzer

International arbitration/litigation
R Fiebinger, C Leon

IT, e-commerce and telecoms
B Ortner

Media law
C Leon, R Fiebinger

Pharmaceuticals
C Kletzer

Private foundations
C Leon

Public procurement
P Polak

Real estate law
M Maurer-Kollenz, S Kirchdorfer

FOGLAR-DEINHARDSTEIN KEG

PLANKENGASSE 7
1010 VIENNA

Telephone: +43 1 512 15 71
Fax: +43 1 513 43 42
E-mail: office@fdblawyers.com
Website: www.fdblawyers.com

Languages
English, French, German, Spanish

Number of lawyers 9

CATEGORIES OF WORK

Mergers and acquisitions
Dr Foglar-Deinhardstein, Mag Hoffmann

Commercial and company law
Dr Foglar-Deinhardstein, Mag Hoffmann

EU and antitrust law
Mag Görg

Competition law
Mag Hoffmann, Mag Görg

Intellectual property
Dr Ankershofen, Mag Görg

Litigation
Dr Ankershofen, Dr Trauttenberg

Arbitration
Dr Foglar-Deinhardstein

Banking and finance
Dr Foglar-Deinhardstein

Real estate and construction, public procurement
Mag Hinteregger, Dr Trauttenberg

Employment
Mag Hinteregger, Dr Ankershofen

Telecommunications
Dr Foglar-Deinhardstein, Mag Görg

Environmental
Mag Hinteregger

Food and drugs
Dr Ankershofen

Administrative
Mag Hoffmann, Mag Hinteregger

Product liability
Mag Hinteregger, Dr Ankershofen

Tax law
Mag Hoffmann

GASSAUER-FLEISSNER
RECHTSANWÄLTE GmbH

WALLNERSTRASSE 4
1010 WIEN

Telephone: +43 1 205 20 60
Fax: +43 1 205 20 62 07
E-mail: office@gassauer.at
Website: www.gassauer.at

Languages
English, French, German, Italian, Portuguese, Spanish

Other offices
Salzburg

Number of lawyers 13

CATEGORIES OF WORK

M&A, corporate

IP/IT

Labour law

Private client

Public law

Real estate

Competition law

Distribution and agency

Public procurement

State aid

GRAF, MAXL & PITKOWITZ GMBH

ATTORNEYS AT LAW

STADIONGASSE 2
1010 WIEN

Telephone: +43 1 401 17
Fax: +43 1 401 17 40
E-mail: office@gmp.at
Website: www.gmp.at

Languages
English, French, German, Russian

Other offices
Graz

Number of lawyers 22

Contact
Dr Nikolaus Pitkowitz MBL-HSG

CATEGORIES OF WORK

Corporate and commercial
All partners

Mergers and acquisitions
Martin Maxl, Ferdinand Graf

Intellectual property
Ferdinand Graf

Unfair competition
Ferdinand Graf

Antitrust
Ferdinand Graf, Martin Maxl

Media
Nikolaus Pitkowitz

Real estate
Nikolaus Pitkowitz

Eastern Europe (joint venture and privatisation)
Nikolaus Pitkowitz

Infrastructure
Otto Waechter

Telecoms
Ferdinand Graf, Otto Waechter

Arbitration
Nikolaus Pitkowitz

Litigation
Nikolaus Pitkowitz

Food law
Martin Maxl

Distribution law
Martin Maxl

Insolvency and restructuring
Alexander Isola

Project finance
Otto Waechter

Public procurement
Otto Waechter

Labour and employment law
Jakob Widner

HAARMANN HÜGEL

ARES-TOWER
DONAU-CITY-STRASSE 11
1220 VIENNA

Telephone: +43 1 260 50 0
Fax: +43 1 260 50 13 3
Website: www.haarmannhuegel.com
www.hugelaw.com

Languages
English, French, German, Italian, Spanish

Other offices
Brussels

Number of lawyers 32

CATEGORIES OF WORK

Commercial law (general)
Univ Prof Dr Hanns F Hügel, Mag Dominik Leiter

Company law, M&A
Univ Prof Dr Hanns F Hügel, Dr Florian Gibitz

Tax law
Univ Prof Dr Hanns F Hügel, Dr Florian Gibitz

Banking and finance
Dr Florian Gibitz, Mag Robert Leuthner

Labour law
Mag Dominik Leiter

Competition – antitrust, distribution law
Dr Rainer Roniger, Dr Astrid Ablasser

Litigation
Mag Dominik Leiter, Dr Meinhard Novak

EU law, public procurement, energy
Dr Rainer Roniger, DDr Christian Schneider

Real estate
Mag Dominik Leiter

Intellectual property law, media law
Mag Dominik Leiter, Dr Meinhard Novak

Public law, environment
DDr Christian Schneider

Capital markets
Univ Prof Dr Hanns F Hügel, Mag Robert Leuthner

HAUSER PARTNERS RECHTSANWÄLTE GMBH

RECHTSANWALTSKANZLEI, ATTORNEYS AT LAW PC

SEILERSTÄTTE 18–20
1010 VIENNA

Telephone: +43 1 512 29 00 14
Fax: +43 1 513 77 42
E-mail: hauser@hauserpartners.com
Website: www.hauserpartners .com

Languages
Czech, English, French, German

Other offices
Bratislava, Vaduz

Number of lawyers 9

Contacts
Dr Wulf Gordian Hauser LLM
(admitted in Austria, New York, Washington DC, Liechtenstein, and Slovakia),
Dr Kordula Fleiß
(admitted in Austria and Slovakia),
Mag Peter Blaschke (admitted in Austria),
Mag Veronika Grögerova
(admitted in Czech Republic)

CATEGORIES OF WORK

Mergers and acquisitions

Corporate and commercial

Banking and finance

International commercial arbitration and litigation

Antitrust and competition

Commercial real estate

International transactions and joint ventures

Capital markets and takeovers

Foreign investment in Austria and central and eastern Europe

Distribution and agency

Labour

Foundations and trusts

HAUSMANINGER KLETTER RECHTSANWÄLTE GMBH

FRANZ JOSEFS-KAI 3
1010 VIENNA

Telephone: +43 1 513 95 40
Fax: +43 1 513 95 40 12
E-mail: office@hhw.at
Website: www.hhw.at

Languages
English, French, German, Italian

Number of lawyers 20

CATEGORIES OF WORK

Banking and finance
Christian Hausmaninger, Robert Bachner

Commercial and company law
Christian Hausmaninger, Mark Kletter

Mergers and acquisitions
Christian Hausmaninger, Mark Kletter

EU and merger control
Mark Kletter

Arbitration
Christian Hausmaninger

Corporate governance
Christian Hausmaninger, Mark Kletter

Litigation
Robert Leitner

Capital markets
Christian Hausmaninger, Manfred Ketzer

PPP and project finance
Robert Bachner

Labour law
Robert Leitner

Competition and media law
Mark Kletter

Real estate
Mark Kletter, Robert Bachner

HERBST VAVROVSKY KINSKY RECHTSANWÄLTE GMBH

DR KARL LUEGER-PLATZ 5
1010 VIENNA

Telephone: +43 1 904 21 80 0
Fax: +43 1 904 21 80 21 0
E-mail: office@hvk.at
Website: www.hvk.at

Languages
English, French, German, Italian

Other offices
Salzburg

Number of lawyers 20
at this office 17

CATEGORIES OF WORK

Banking and finance
Christoph Herbst, Philipp Kinsky

Capital markets
Philipp Kinsky

Corporate law
Nikolaus Vavrovsky, Wolfgang Schwackhöfer

Mergers and aquisitions
Christoph Herbst, Wolfgang Schwackhöfer

Antitrust
Christoph Herbst, Sonja Hebenstreit

Private equity and venture capital
Philipp Kinsky, Wolfgang Schwackhöfer

Litigation and arbitration
Karl Ludwig Vavrovsky, Jürgen Zouplna

Reorganisation and insolvency
Karl Ludwig Vavrovsky, Nikolaus Vavrovsky

Real estate and construction
Karl Ludwig Vavrovsky, Nikolaus Vavrovsky

Property finance
Nikolaus Vavrovsky

Labour law
Jürgen Zouplna

IP, IT and life sciences
Sonja Hebenstreit

KRAFT & WINTERNITZ

NIBELUNGENGASSE 11
1010 WIEN

Telephone: +43 1 587 16 60
Fax: +43 1 586 31 17
E-mail: office@kwlaw.at
Website: www.kwlaw.at

Languages
English, French, Italian, Spanish

Number of lawyers 15

CATEGORIES OF WORK

Agency and distribution
Mr Kraft, Mr Beer

Banking, securities and finance
Mr Winternitz, Mr Aigner

Capital markets
Mr Winternitz, Mr Beer

Commercial and company law
Mr Kraft, Ms Mayer-Wilderhofer

Insurance, real estate
Mr Kraft, Mr Aigner

Intellectual property
Mr Kraft, Mr Steinmair

Litigation
Mr Beer, Mr Perschler

Unfair competition
Mr Winternitz, Mr Steinmair

Medical law
Mr Perschler

Debt collection
Mr Kraft, Mr Beer

Transportation
Ms Mayer-Wilderhofer, Mr Steinmair

Private client
Mr Winternitz, Ms Mayer-Wilderhofer

Internet/information technology
Mr Beer, Mr Steinmair

Labour/social law
Mr Kraft, Mr Steinmair

KUNZ SCHIMA WALLENTIN, member of ius laboris

RECHTSANWÄLTE KEG

PORZELLANGASSE 4
1090 VIENNA

Telephone: +43 1 313 74
Fax: +43 1 313 74 80
E-mail: office@ksw.at
Website: www.ksw.at

Languages
English, French, German, Italian

Number of lawyers 20

Contacts
Dr Peter Kunz, Dr Thomas Wallentin

Member
ius laboris, International Employment Law, Pensions and Employee Benefits Alliance

CATEGORIES OF WORK

Antitrust
Dr Thomas Wallentin, Dr Peter Kunz

Commercial and business
Dr Eberhard Wallentin, Dr Peter Kunz

Corporate
Dr Peter Kunz, Dr Georg Schima

Hospital and healthcare
Dr Peter Kunz, Dr Christian Gepart

Intellectual property, copyright, trade marks
Dr Thomas Wallentin

Insolvency
Dr Eberhard Wallentin

Internet and e-commerce
Dr Thomas Wallentin

Labour and employment
Dr Georg Schima,
Mag Birgit Vogt-Majarek

Real estate
Dr Peter Kunz, Mag Wolfgang Friedl

Succession planning
Dr Eberhard Wallentin,
Dr Matthias Göschke

Tax
Dr Eberhard Wallentin,
Dr Matthias Göschke

Mergers and acquisitions
Dr Peter Kunz, Mag Wolfgang Friedl

NEUDORFER RECHTSANWÄLTE

ESSLINGGASSE 9
1010 VIENNA

Telephone: +43 1 536 50
Fax: +43 1 536 50 12
E-mail: officewien@aaa–law.at
Website: www.aaa–law.at/wien

Languages
Croatian, English, German, Italian, Spanish

Other offices
Bratislava, Graz*, Innsbruck*, Salzburg*

Number of lawyers 15

Member
In association with Kaan Cronenberg & Partner (Graz); Pallauf Pullmann Meissnitzer & Partner (Salzburg); Knoflach Söllner Kroker (Innsbruck); – AAA Austrian Advocates Alliance

International groupings
IAG International; DIRO Eine Europäische Rechtanwaltsorganisation; CLG Commercial Law Group

CATEGORIES OF WORK

Arbitration
Wolfgang Hahnkamper

Banking and finance, capital markets and securities
Helmut Neudorfer, Michael Steiner

Mergers and acquisitions
Wolfgang Hahnkamper,
Michael Steiner

Distribution, trade agencies and franchising
Wolfgang Hahnkamper

Antitrust, unfair competition
Stephan Probst

Liability and insurance
Wolfgang Zacherl

Employment and labour
Wolfgang Hahnkamper

EU law, tenders
Michael Steiner

Insolvency and corporate recovery
Christof Stapf, Michael Neuhauser

Debt collection
Wolfgang Zacherl, Stefan Jahns

Property and agriculture
Stephan Probst

Food and drug law
Michael Neuhauser

Foundations, inheritance and wills (private client)
Helmut Neudorfer

Media
Stephan Probst

Commercial litigation
(all partners)

IP, patent and trade mark, licensing and copyright
Helmut Neudorfer

PRESLMAYR ATTORNEYS AT LAW

DR KARL LUEGER-RING 12
1010 VIENNA

Telephone: +43 1 533 16 95
Fax: +43 1 535 56 86
E-mail: office@preslmayr.at
Website: www.preslmayr.at

Languages
English, French, German, Italian

Number of lawyers 22

Member
TAGlaw; ICC

CATEGORIES OF WORK

Companies, corporations
Dr Rainer Herzig,
Dr Martin Bartlmä

Mergers and acquisitions
Dr Martin Preslmayr, Dr Karl Preslmayr

Venture capital, private equity
Dr Martin Preslmayr, Mag Peter Resch

Antitrust and competition
Mag Dieter Hauck, Dr Rainer Herzig

EU law
Mag Dieter Hauck, Dr Rainer Herzig

Banking, securities, finance
Dr Karl Preslmayr,
Dr Florian Gehmacher

Public procurement
Mag Dieter Hauck, Dr Raimund Madl

Contract
Dr Karl Preslmayr, Mag Erland Pirker

Telecommunications
Mag Dieter Hauck, Dr Rainer Knyrim

Advertising
Dr Rainer Herzig, Dr Karl Preslmayr

Arbitration and litigation
Dr Karl Preslmayr, Dr Martin Preslmayr

Insolvency
Dr Florian Gehmacher,
Dr Matthias Schmidt

Food and drug law
Dr Rainer Herzig

Employment, labour
Dr Barbara Kurz, Dr Karl Preslmayr

Trade marks, intellectual property
Dr Rainer Herzig, Dr Karl Preslmayr

Data protection
Dr Rainer Knyrim

SCHRAMM ÖHLER RECHTSANWÄLTE

BARTENSTEINGASSE 2
1010 WIEN

Telephone: +43 1 409 76 09
Fax: +43 1 409 76 09 30
E-mail: kanzlei@schramm-oehler.at
Website: www.schramm-oehler.at

Languages
English, French, German

Number of lawyers 10

CATEGORIES OF WORK

Public procurement
Dr Johannes Schramm,
Dr Matthias Öhler

Privatisation
Dr Johannes Schramm,
Dr Georg Zellhofer

Subsidies
Dr Georg Zellhofer

EC law and competition
Dr Georg Zellhofer,
Dr Johannes Schramm

Administrative law
Dr Johannes Schramm
Dr Matthias Öhler

Contracts and commercial
Dr Matthias Öhler
Mag Gregor Stickler

Corporate
Dr Johannes Schramm
Mag Gregor Stickler

SAXINGER CHALUPSKY WEBER & PARTNERS
RECHTSANWÄLTE GMBH

RATHAUSPLATZ 4
1010 VIENNA

Telephone: +43 1 427 20 00
Fax: +43 1 427 20 10
E-mail: vienna@scwp.at
Website: www.scwp.at

Languages
Czech, English, French, German, Italian, Russian, Spanish

Other offices
Graz, Linz, Pilsen, Prague, Wels

Number of lawyers 51
at this office 12

CATEGORIES OF WORK

Administrative law
Markus Nußbaumer, Franz Waldl

Antitrust
Wolfgang Lauss, Karl Weinhäupl

Arbitration
Eduard Saxinger

Banking and secured financing
Stefan Weber, Franz Mittendorfer

Capital markets
Stefan Weber

Commercial and company law
Gerald Schmidsberger

Corporate law
Wolfgang Lauss, Gerald Schmidsberger

Energy and environmental law
Markus Nußbaumer, Franz Waldl

EU and competition law
Stefan Weber, Karl Weinhäupl

Insolvency and restructurings
Ernst Chalupsky, Alexander Anderle

Labour and industrial relations
Johannes Blätterbinder, Alois Hutterer

Litigation and dispute resolution
Eduard Saxinger, Daniela Witt-Dörring, Hella Ranner

Mergers and acquisitions
Wolfgang Lauss, Gerald Schmidsberger

Tax law
Werner Minihold

Intellectual property
Peter Baumann, Maximilian Gumpoldsberger

Public private partnerships
Franz Mittendorfer, Stefan Weber

Public procurement
Maria Lang, Dietmar Huemer

Real estate and construction
Franz Mittendorfer, Daniela Witt-Dörring

THE FIRM
Saxinger Chalupsky Weber & Partners is one of the leading Austrian law firms. Its lawyers are highly specialised and committed to the highest standards of legal service and proficiency.

The firm resulted from a merger of three leading Austrian firms, the roots of which date back to 1919. On the basis of its long-standing tradition, Saxinger Chalupsky Weber & Partners offers legal services in all areas of law relevant to businesses. Through its offices in Vienna, Linz, Wels and Graz, as well as Prague and Pilsen, the firm is in the unique position to directly cover the most important Austrian and Czech industrial regions, locally connected to the relevant authorities.

The firm's approach is creative and pragmatic, helping its clients to assess and effectively manage legal risks and to find practical solutions in the relevant legal, business and, when necessary, political environments.

Saxinger Chalupsky Weber & Partners has extensive experience in the legal management of projects in Austria and in foreign jurisdictions. Partners of the firm have authored numerous articles and books on domestic and international business law, and they teach in leading European law schools. They are regularly consulted by the Austrian legislature on legislative matters.

AREAS OF PRACTICE
Partners of Saxinger Chalupsky Weber & Partners are leading experts in their areas of law. Saxinger Chalupsky Weber & Partners provides legal services in all areas of law relevant to businesses and, in particular, when clearance with public authorities is necessary. Services range from general advice on legal matters to conducting complex national and international transactions.

In addition to their experience in Austria, the firm's lawyers have practised, studied or trained abroad. Their areas of specialisation include corporate and commercial matters, mergers and acquisitions involving special financial structures and multi-jurisdictional issues, corporate finance, securities (public offerings), banking and financial services, energy law, production facilities and business permits, environmental law, insolvency, inward investments, privatisation projects, litigation and arbitration

Saxinger Chalupsky Weber & Partners advises Austrian and foreign, large and medium-sized, public and private companies, as well as Austrian and international governments and governmental organisations.

The firm's partners have a wide range of experience in providing legal advice in the implementation of cross-border transactions, as well as in the structuring and legal co-ordination of companies' activities in foreign countries. Through its network of excellent partner firms, Saxinger Chalupsky Weber & Partners regularly assists clients in their business strategies throughout Central and Eastern Europe.

International companies who operate businesses or branches or provide services directly in Austria can rely on comprehensive legal services through the firm's offices in Austria's primary industrial regions.

SCHÖNHERR

TUCHLAUBEN 17
1010 WIEN

Telephone: +43 1 53 43 70
Fax: +43 1 53 43 76 100
E-mail: office@schoenherr.at
Website: www.schoenherr.at

Languages
English, French, Italian

Other offices
Belgrade, Brussels, Bucharest, Kyiv, Ljubljana, Sofia, Zagreb (co-operation office)

Number of lawyers 130
at this office 75

CATEGORIES OF WORK

Antitrust and competition
Hanno Wollmann

Public law, regulatory
Christian Schmelz

Companies, corporations, tax
Hellwig Torggler, Peter Feyl

Corporate reorganisations
Stephan Frotz, Peter Konwitschka

Mergers and acquisitions
Christian Herbst, Christoph Lindinger

EU law
Hanno Wollmann

Banking, securities and finance
Peter Feyl, Stephan Frotz

Real estate, construction
Peter Madl, Thomas Wenger

Contract and commercial law
Peter Madl, Thomas Wenger

Employment, labour
Gerold Zeiler

Media, unfair competition
Guido Kucsko, Christian Hauer

Tax
Peter Feyl

Trade marks, intellectual property
Christian Hauer, Guido Kucsko

Arbitration and litigation
Hellwig Torggler, Gerold Zeiler

THE FIRM

Schönherr Rechtsanwälte was founded in 1950 and is one of the leading law firms in Austria. It is also among Austria's largest law firms with 25 partners and over 70 other fee-earners. The firm has offices in Vienna, Brussels, Belgrade, Bucharest, Kyiv, Ljubljana, Sofia and Zagreb (co-operation office).

AREAS OF PRACTICE

The firm is a full-service commercial and corporate law firm covering all areas of corporate, civil and commercial law. Principal areas include corporate, banking, international transactions, (cross-border) M&A, takeovers, privatisations, capital markets, intellectual property, unfair competition, antitrust, public, including environmental law, labour law, EU law, media, information technology, telecoms, energy, commercial litigation and arbitration.

The firm serves international and Austrian corporate clients ranging from US-based and international corporations and their Austrian subsidiaries, large and medium-sized enterprises to governmental agencies. Clients come from the financial, industrial and service sectors including banking, insurance, information technology, media, food, pharmaceuticals, energy, construction, automotive, and paper and packaging.

The firm's first priority is to provide top quality efficient and responsive legal work to its international and Austrian clients.

SIEMER-SIEGL-FÜREDER & PARTNER

DOMINIKANERBASTEI 10
1010 WIEN

Telephone: + 43 1 512 14 45
Fax: + 43 1 513 79 84
E-mail: office@ra-siefur.at
Website: www.ra-siefur.at

Languages
English, French, Italian, Japanese

Number of lawyers 16

Contacts
Hannes Füreder, Markus Fellner

Member
MERITAS

CATEGORIES OF WORK

Corporate and commercial, mergers and acquisitions
Hannes Füreder, Markus Fellner

Procurement law, PPP, privatisation, government business
Michael Breitenfeld, Astrid Edlinger

Tax
Hannes Füreder

Dispute resolution, litigation and arbitration
Heinrich Siegl, Markus Fellner

Unfair competition
Heinrich Siegl, Reinhard Brunar

Commercial property, real estate and construction
Reinhard Brunar, Mario Schiavon

Aviation law
Hannes Füreder, Gerald Gries

Private clients and trusts
Hannes Füreder, Mario Schiavon

Banking and finance
Hannes Füreder, Mario Schiavon

Competition and EU
Markus Fellner, Michael Breitenfeld

Distribution, franchise and commercial agents
Markus Fellner, Hannes Füreder

Insolvency, corporate restructuring
Heinrich Siegl, Hannes Füreder

Employment (labour law)
Hannes Füreder, Gerald Gries

IT and e-commerce, intellectual property and media
Reinhard Brunar

Pharmaceutical/biotechnology law
Heinrich Siegl, Gerald Gries

WOLF THEISS
ATTORNEYS AT LAW

SCHUBERTRING 6
1010 VIENNA

Telephone: +43 1 515 10
Fax: +43 1 515 10 25
E-mail: wien@wolftheiss.com
Website: www.wolftheiss.com

Languages
Albanian, Bosnian, Croatian, Czech, English, French, German, Hungarian, Italian, Spanish, Slovenian, Slovak, Romanian

Other offices
Belgrade, Bratislava, Bucharest, Ljubljana, Prague, Sarajevo, Tirana, Zagreb

Number of lawyers 161
at this office 97

Contacts
Markus Heidinger (managing partner), Horst Ebhardt (senior partner)

CATEGORIES OF WORK

Antitrust, competition, merger control
Peter Oberlechner, Katja Tautscher

Arbitration, litigation, mediation
Christoph Liebscher, Bettina Knoetzl

Banking, capital markets, securities, project finance, investment funds
Markus Heidinger, Nikolaus Paul

Contracts and commercial
Manfred Essletzbichler, Bettina Knoetzl

Corporate and M&A
Martin Abram, Horst Ebhardt

Eastern Europe
Horst Ebhardt, Peter Oberlechner

Employment and labour
Ralf Peschek, Matthias Unterrieder

Insolvency
Bettina Knoetzl, Eva Spiegel

Insurance
Kurt Retter, Andreas Theiss

IT and IP
Bettina Knoetzl, Georg Kresbach

Public law, public entities, and infrastructure
Manfred Essletzbichler, Christian Hoenig

Real estate, construction and leasing
Gabriele Etzl, Georg Kresbach

Tax
Christian Hoenig, Niklas Schmidt

Telecoms and energy
Christian Hoenig, Peter Oberlechner

THE FIRM

Wolf Theiss was founded in 1957 in Vienna, and today is one of the leading law firms in the CEE/SEE region. Over the past few years the firm has experienced extraordinarily dynamic growth, both domestically and internationally.

Wolf Theiss has established a network of nine offices* in Albania, Austria, Bosnia and Herzegovina, Croatia, the Czech Republic, Romania, Serbia and Montenegro, Slovakia and Slovenia. In 2005 alone, Wolf Theiss opened two new offices, in Bucharest and Sarajevo. The firm also regularly assists its clients with projects in Bulgaria, Hungary, Macedonia, Moldova, Poland, Turkey and Ukraine, in co-operation with local attorneys.

The firm's dynamic growth is also refelcted in its increase in personnal. At present, Wolf Theiss employs over 350 individuals at nine locations – compare this to 30 employees in one office, Vienna, ten years ago and the growth is apparent.

*The firm's operations in the various locations are set up in compliance with local law and the Bar rules requirements which include the form of co-operation with independent local attorneys.

BAHRAIN

Population	754,000
Number of lawyers	n/a
Professional title	Advocate
Currency	Bahraini dinar (BD))

Index

The largely desert Kingdom of Bahrain is an archipelago of low-lying islands in the Arabian Gulf, linked by road and causeway to the eastern shore of Saudi Arabia. Shia Muslims make up the majority of the population, although approximately one third of Bahrain's population are expatriate workers.

Bahrain has been ruled by the al-Khalifah dynasty for over 200 years. The current emir, Sheikh Hamad bin Isa al-Khalifah, inherited the throne from his father in 1999, and since coming to power has initiated sweeping political and economic reforms. A referendum in February 2001 saw strong backing for proposals under which the country would become a democratic constitutional monarchy, with an independent judiciary and elected lower chamber of parliament. Parliamentary elections – the country's first for nearly 30 years – took place towards the end of that same year, although a boycott by the Shi'ite groups meant that Sunni Islamists captured most of the seats in the lower house. The king responded by appointing secular MPs to the upper house, which met with criticism. In 2005, thousands of Bahrainis staged protests to demand a fully elected parliament.

Bahrain's good relationship with the US has now extended to the signing in September 2004 of a bilateral free-trade agreement.

BILLING

Associates charge between €150 and €300 per hour, while clients should expect to pay between €300 to €500 for a partner. Capped or fixed-fee arrangements are popular amongst local clients.

MARKETING

All of the international firms have websites, as well as individual email addresses for their partners and associates. Local firms still lag behind in this respect, although a few do now have websites and their use of email continues to grow.

IN-HOUSE LAWYERS

In-house lawyers are commonly found in large financial institutions and banks. Other commercial entities operating in Bahrain tend to instruct firms rather than employ their own lawyers.

ECONOMY

As the first Gulf state to discover oil, Bahrain was the first to benefit from oil revenues. Its reserves, however, are minimal and these days the country limits itself to oil refining and export, which make up approximately 60% of revenue.

Forced to diversify into other sectors, Bahrain transformed itself into a financial hub for the region. With its strategic location between East and West time zones, the country attracts a wealth of foreign investment, underpinned by government incentives and legislation; foreigners can now own up to 100% of business and, in certain areas including the capital, Manama, 100% of land and property. The Bahrain Financial Harbour, expected to be open for business within a year, will add weight to Bahrain's existing chain of financial institutions, which number approximately 400 to date. Despite increased competition from Dubai, Bahrain retains its crown as the region's banking and finance hotspot, generating excellent returns for investors.

The government's plan to increase foreign investment includes downsizing public-sector ownership, with a number of projects being sold off, such as the Al Hidd power and water station. Other sectors are also targeted for privatisation; Batelco has lost its monopoly over telecommunications, whilst the country's airline, Gulf Air, is next in line for a private-sector buy out. The success of the government's privatisation programme can be seen in the recent financial closure of Bahrain's first independent power project, the award-winning Al-Ezzel project. The government, with increasing help from foreign investors, is now focusing its spending on other sectors, such as infrastructure, commercial and residential projects. The tourism sector is also a targeted growth area, with the Al Areen project making good progress, and Dubai International Properties' Salam Beach Resort and Spa project recently launched.

LEGAL MARKET

The Bahrain legal market has suffered over recent years, mainly due to the increasing attractiveness of Dubai as a business centre for the Middle East. Several firms have now closed their Bahrain offices, with some now preferring Dubai. However, Bahrain remains well established in the banking sector.

The largest firms

1	Haya Rashed Al Khalifa Attorneys at Law & Legal Consultants	14
2	Al Mahmood & Zu'Bi	9
	Norton Rose	9
	Qays H. Zu'bi, Attorneys & Legal Consultants	9
5	Trowers & Hamlins	7
6	Hassan Radhi & Associates	5
	Taqi & Mohammad Ahmed	5
8	Ali Al Jabal Law Office	4
9	Abu-Ghazaleh Legal	2
	Baker & McKenzie	2

These figures represent the total number of lawyers in this country only, and have been supplied by the firms themselves. The figures should be accurate as at 1 January 2006.

Norton Rose has a long-established presence in Bahrain, being one of the pioneering international firms to open an office there, and building tremendous strength in almost every practice area over its 25 years of experience in the country. The management of the practice was recently taken over by Dominic Harvey, a banking and projects specialist from the London office, following the retirement of Carol Roberts in April 2005.

Baker & McKenzie enjoys a celebrated global banking and project finance practice, and its ubiquity in the Gulf region is no exception. Its Bahrain branch opened in 1999 as the latest addition to its collection of Middle Eastern offices; the larger Riyadh office is geographically nearby and works very closely in conjunction with the Bahrain office.

Towers & Hamlins' endeavours in getting to grips with the local markets in the Middle East have paid off; the firm benefits from a strong network of regional offices and associations with several local firms throughout the Middle East to offer a combination of local and international expertise.

Local firms of note include **Al Mahmood & Zu'Bi**, **Hassan Radhi & Associates**, **Haya Rashed Al Khalifa Attorneys at Law & Legal Consultants** and **Taqi & Mohammad Ahmed**, all of which are considered useful local counsel by international firms. Having recently lost former **Clifford Chance** partner Chris Johnstone and a number of other lawyers, **Qays H. Zu'bi, Attorneys & Legal Consultants** is gradually rebuilding itself and has recruited a number of new assistants.

Among the most prominent foreign firms working in Bahrain without an office are **Clifford Chance**, **Allen & Overy LLP** and **Freshfields Bruckhaus Deringer**. **Clifford Chance** recently acted as counsel to the lead manager in respect of a US$60m Sukuk listed on the Bahrain Stock Exchange. **Allen & Overy LLP** is currently advising on the property financing for a new shopping mall, while **Freshfields Bruckhaus Deringer** recently completed its advice to the government in respect of Bahrain's first IPP project. **Clyde & Co** is also noteworthy for its advice on commercial agency and distribution arrangements in the country. All four firms operate from offices in the UAE. Meanwhile, **White & Case** can frequently be found advising the Bahraini government on various matters in the country, such as the reform of the telecommunications sector.

BANKING AND FINANCE

According to clients, **Baker & McKenzie**'s 'professional' integrated Saudi and Bahrain team is doing an 'excellent job' under partner Ian Siddell, who oversees the Manama branch. The team recently advised Arab Banking Corporation in connection with a US$153m term loan and revolving credit facility for the development of a steel plant in Bahrain. Other matters in the last 12 months include advising on a US$600m loan facility and a US$140m receivable and finance facility to Samba Financial Group.

BANKING AND FINANCE

BAKER & McKENZIE
NORTON ROSE

Trowers & Hamlins

Al Mahmood & Zu'Bi
Haya Rashed Al Khalifa Attorneys at Law & Legal Consultants ✪

Hassan Radhi & Associates
Qays H. Zu'bi, Attorneys & Legal Consultants ✪
Taqi & Mohammad Ahmed

Firms are listed A-Z in tiers which are ranked in order of priority
✪ Indicates firm displays contact details at the end of this chapter.

Market-leading **Norton Rose** offers 'first-class quality of service, efficiency, and project management skills', with one client noting a marked improvement in resource management since the arrival of new managing partner, Dominic Harvey, from London's prestigious banking and projects team. Gulf International Bank called on the firm three times in 2005 for significant financing matters, which include a US$800m senior term debt facility for its expansion. Other recent conventional banking work includes advising BNP Paribas as arranger of an ECA-backed facility to the Kingdom of Bahrain.

Regional banking and finance partner Neale Downes and the rest of the team at **Trowers & Hamlins** are 'very competent attorneys' and 'prompt in their feedback and support'. Its conventional banking arm covers asset-backed and asset-based financing, syndicated lending, project finance and acquisition finance, with names such as HSBC, GIB, Arab Bank, Standard Chartered and Gulf Finance House on its books. In 2005 the firm was appointed to the panel of Citibank in Bahrain for advice on a range of facilities. It also advised regular client Global Investment House in relation to a US$500m pre-IPO private equity fund.

According to clients, **Al Mahmood & Zu'Bi**'s Ma'awia Nayal and Hugh Stokes are 'very competent attorneys, particularly with regard to local laws and regulations'. The team is local counsel of choice for many international firms.

For a local angle on banking matters, **Haya Rashed Al Khalifa Attorneys at Law & Legal Consultants** is highly recommended, and the practice enjoys good relations with a number of top-drawer international firms. Local counsel on some major transactions for clients such as BNP Paribas, HSBC, Arab Banking Corporation and Gulf Finance House, significant matters in 2005 include advising the multi-party financiers on the US$1.2bn BAPCO financing, which combined a number of financing techniques. Managing partner Sheikha Haya Al Khalifa is described as 'very decent and reasonable'.

Under new associates Phillip Sacks and Naveen Thakur, **Qays H. Zu'bi, Attorneys & Legal Consultants**' recent work includes advising in relation to private placements and IPO transactions, on foreign exchange transactions for a leading American bank, and on the sale of structured notes by a French insurance company.

In Jalila Sayed, **Hassan Radhi & Associates** has an 'extremely capable' banking lawyer, while new entrant to our tables **Taqi & Mohammad Ahmed** garners similar levels of praise.

CORPORATE AND M&A

The ongoing privatisation of many commercial sectors in Bahrain has led to an increased call for expert legal direction on incorporation of foreign companies, and disposal of government interests in certain industries. Corporate finance transactions, IPOs and investment funds are lucrative and abundant areas of work for firms.

Growing from five to eleven lawyers during 2005, **Norton Rose**'s skills in all corporate areas, including IPOs, investment funds, and private equity, secure its place in the top tier. For private equity funds, the team recently advised clients Ithmar Management Partners, Atlas Investment Group and National Technology and Enterprises Company (Kuwait). Meanwhile the firm's growing focus on Islamic products and investment schemes for its corporate clients includes advising Kuwait Finance House on setting up the Durrat Al Bahrain Investment Fund; and acting for Bags Holdings in the establishment of a shari'ah-compliant commodity trading fund.

A favourite of many international firms for local advice, **Al Mahmood & Zu'Bi**'s 'commercially minded' managing partner, Mr Zu'Bi, is extremely well regarded, while the 'bright and charming' Hugh Stokes is 'worth his weight in gold'.

Hassan Radhi & Associates is deemed a 'very competent' local firm, with Jalila Sayed particularly recommended. In addition to its broad commercial practice, the firm has provided regulatory advice to government departments engaging in international deals.

Towers & Hamlins has a great name for its corporate and commercial advice to local entities, particularly in respect of their investments, joint ventures and IPOs, with office head Dominic O'Neil specialising in private equity. The firm's regular clients include IDB Infrastructure Fund, which focuses on private-sector projects such as power, petrochemicals, and telecoms. Since the fund was established in December 2001, the firm has helped it invest approximately US$400m throughout the region and beyond. Ongoing work includes advising Bahrain Financial Harbour Holding Co on the legal structure for ownership of interests in its mixed-use development, and advising on the restructuring of a Bahraini business, which involved the country's first IPO of a family trading house. A strong focus on telecommunications is attracting increasing numbers of clients in the sector.

CORPORATE AND M&A

NORTON ROSE

Al Mahmood & Zu'Bi
Hassan Radhi & Associates
Towers & Hamlins

Baker & McKenzie
Haya Rashed Al Khalifa Attorneys at Law & Legal Consultants ✪
Qays H. Zu'bi, Attorneys & Legal Consultants ✪
Taqi & Mohammad Ahmed

Firms are listed A-Z in tiers which are ranked in order of priority
✪ *Indicates firm displays contact details at the end of this chapter.*

Clients of regional giant **Baker & McKenzie** note the firm's 'strong local presence' across Saudi Arabia and Bahrain, supported by its experts in London. In the last year the team has acted on a number of IPOs, corporate restructurings, private equity transactions and mergers and acquisitions.

Clients of **Haya Rashed Al Khalifa Attorneys at Law & Legal Consultants**' excellent assistant Nabeel Saeed describe him as 'a person who understands his work and has a flair for producing quality deliverables'. The firm's expertise includes capital markets, private equity and collective investment schemes, with the team recently acting for Gulf Finance House in the creation of the US$400m Al Basha'er Equity Fund. Clients for general corporate and commercial work include the BMA, Bahrain Financial Harbour and Al Areen Resort and Development. The firm is respected for its work in relation to privatisation and the establishment of free zones, from a local perspective.

Having mutually dissolved its formal relationship with **Clifford Chance**, **Qays H. Zu'bi, Attorneys & Legal Consultants** is steadily building its relationships with other international firms. Recent matters for the team include advice pertaining to the inception of a Gulf-based financial reference business, and, on behalf of a local projects company, helping to negotiate the management of executive apartments with Marriott Hotels. The firm represented the respective bidders in the privatisation of the Mina Salman Port, and the Al Hidd power plant.

Taqi & Mohammad Ahmed is considered a good all-round firm, with a particular flair for labour law issues.

DISPUTE RESOLUTION

International firms wishing to represent clients in local courts must employ a lawyer of Bahraini origin for this purpose. These regulations over rights of audience mean that local firms continue to dominate in litigation whilst the international firms are better known for their banking and corporate transactions.

DISPUTE RESOLUTION

AL MAHMOOD & ZU'BI
HASSAN RADHI & ASSOCIATES
HAYA RASHED AL KHALIFA ATTORNEYS AT LAW & LEGAL CONSULTANTS ✪

Norton Rose
Qays H. Zu'bi, Attorneys & Legal Consultants ✪
Towers & Hamlins

Firms are listed A-Z in tiers which are ranked in order of priority
✪ *Indicates firm displays contact details at the end of this chapter.*

Educated in England, Jordanian-born Hatim Zu'Bi is founder and senior partner of **Al Mahmood & Zu'Bi**. An experienced arbitrator, he is held in high esteem as a local 'mover-shaker'. Fellow partner Hamid Abdulrahman Al Mahmood is a former member of Bahrain's legislative assembly, while the firm's very highly thought-of UK solicitor Hugh Stokes has over 25 years of experience advising on issues of Bahraini law.

Hassan Radhi & Associates sports a fantastic track record for disputes. Name partner Hassan Radhi is a prolific and highly respected individual in the country who has acted on many high-profile disputes on behalf of leading international clients. Experience includes acting as arbitrator in the highly contentious talks surrounding the potential formation of an independent journalists' trade union.

According to clients, **Haya Rashed Al Khalifa Attorneys at Law & Legal Consultants** has been 'revitalised' since the return of its founding partner, experienced arbitrator Sheikha Haya Al Khalifa, from her position as Bahraini Ambassador to France. The firm has an excellent reputation for litigation, particularly employment-related disputes, with over 20 years of experience in the field. It acted on behalf of the government of Bahrain in relation to the high-profile Hawar Island International Court of Arbitration dispute, and represented the Bahrain defence force in the biggest international arbitration in Bahrain's history. Rashid Bo-Ghammar is an expert in corporate and commercial litigation, including insurance. The firm was recently appointed legal adviser to Bahraini Telecommunications Regulatory Authority for local legal and arbitration matters.

Norton Rose's dispute resolution division recently passed into the hands of Antony Dutton, described by clients as 'very cool, assured, helpful and professional'. Assistant Sarah Roach is also credited as 'excellent'. Via its successful representation of the appellant in *Shamil Bank of Bahrain v Beximco Pharmaceutical and others*, the team can claim responsibility for helping to establish the leading case on applicable law relating to Islamic finance transactions, ratified in 2005 when the defendant's leave to appeal was refused.

A range of domestic and international disputes at **Qays H. Zu'bi, Attorneys & Legal Consultants** includes acting on behalf of a telecoms client in recent commercial litigation involving both Bahraini and UK law. Qays Zu'Bi heads the practice.

In new partner and former **Norton Rose** star Abdullah Mutawi, **Trowers & Hamlins** has gained considerable arbitration expertise. Among various issues since his induction, he has acted for Bahrain National Insurance and Medgulf in relation to disputes concerning blanket bond policies.

ISLAMIC FINANCE

The demand for shari'ah-compliant products and services means that the Islamic finance market is growing increasingly diverse, and many financial undertakings now contain Islamic tranches.

A clear forerunner in the development of Islamic bonds, and a dab hand at integrating Islamic and conventional funds, **Norton Rose** boasts two full-time Islamic finance specialists. In 2005, overseen by Mohammed Paracha who is very widely recognised for his expertise in Islamic financial products, Emirates Telecommunications Corporation instructed the team in the US$2.1bn Islamic bridge finance facility for its purchase of a 26% stake in Pakistan Telecommunication Corporation. The Bahrain Monetary Agency sought advice in respect of its US$250m ijarah sukuk issue, whilst meanwhile, instructions have been rolling in from Riyad Bank, Liquidity Management Centre and Arab Investment Company. Significantly, the team has also been acting in relation to the Islamic financing of the Bahrain Financial Harbour and Bahrain World Trade Centre developments.

Boasting a cross-office team in Manama and Riyadh, **Baker & McKenzie** is an experienced Islamic finance player, and many of its banking and projects transactions contain Islamic tranches, including the project financing of the Aluminium Bahrain plant expansion. It also recently advised on a US$27m sukuk securitisation in Saudi Arabia, and BNP Paribas on two separate murabaha facilities to Kuwait-based companies.

Trowers & Hamlins' banking expert Neale Downes acts on many Islamic finance matters, recently advising retainer client Arab Bank on two separate secured transactions to a large Saudi Arabian corporate. Another highlight was advising Global Investment House (GIH) on a US$500m pre-IPO fund and a US$100m GCC real estate fund, in addition to supporting GIH in its ongoing investment in a Saudi healthcare group. The firm acted for the borrower in relation to the US$30m Islamic tranche of the Bahrain World Trade Centre financing, and has been appointed to advise the joint venture partners on the financing of the recently announced US$900m, wholly Islamic financed Bahrain Bay development.

ISLAMIC FINANCE

NORTON ROSE

Baker & McKenzie
Trowers & Hamlins

Haya Rashed Al Khalifa Attorneys at Law & Legal Consultants ✪
Qays H. Zu'bi, Attorneys & Legal Consultants ✪

Firms are listed A-Z in tiers which are ranked in order of priority
✪ Indicates firm displays contact details at the end of this chapter.

Haya Rashed Al Khalifa Attorneys at Law & Legal Consultants' Nabeel Saeed, previously legal counsel to Gulf Finance House, is a seasoned and 'well-connected' Islamic finance expert who, clients say, can deliver 'quick and effective solutions'. Recent transactions include acting as local counsel in relation to the Bahrain Financial Harbour's US$1.3bn Islamic sukuk, and acting for the lenders in relation to a US$330m ijara Islamic leave facility as part of the finance package for the US$1.2bn BAPCO financing.

Islamic funds and bond issues have been keeping **Qays H. Zu'bi, Attorneys & Legal Consultants**' Islamic experts busy in recent months. Instructions include assisting a leading local investment bank in setting up two shari'ah-compliant investment funds.

PROJECT FINANCE

Project finance in Bahrain is abundant, and is largely concerned with the development of the Bahrain Financial Harbour and Bahrain World Trade Centre, as well as the construction of petrochemicals facilities.

Baker & McKenzie has a world-class Middle East projects practice, and can be found acting on many of the major deals throughout the region. In 2005 it advised on the structured financing of a US$1.1bn integrated petrochemicals facility, while more recently it assisted in the provision of a US$330m facility to finance the expansion of a fertiliser plant in Jubail, Saudi Arabia. Ian Siddell and Julie Alexander are highly recommended individuals.

Under new managing partner and projects expert Dominic Harvey, **Norton Rose** focuses largely on Saudi Arabian-based power and petrochemicals facilities, and was recently appointed to act for the successful bidders in connection with the Rabigh power generation and desalination plant. Meanwhile, the sponsors of a similar project in Abu Dhabi have sought advice from the team. Closer to home, the team has been advising Aluminium Bahrain on its US$1.55bn Line 5 expansion; BNP Paribas and HSBC on multi-sourced facilities for its low sulphur diesel production project; and Kuwait Finance House on the development of an IWPP and chemical production plant in the country.

PROJECT FINANCE

BAKER & McKENZIE
NORTON ROSE

Trowers & Hamlins

Al Mahmood & Zu'Bi
Hassan Radhi & Associates
Haya Rashed Al Khalifa Attorneys at Law & Legal Consultants ✪
Qays H. Zu'bi, Attorneys & Legal Consultants ✪

Firms are listed A-Z in tiers which are ranked in order of priority
✪ Indicates firm displays contact details at the end of this chapter.

Dominic O'Neil's team at **Towers & Hamlins** assisted in raising finance for the US$300m Riffa Gulf Club development and the US$950m Bahrain Business Bay project on behalf of Arcapita Bank. It also recently advised Kuwait Finance House in relation to the US$2bn joint venture 'Diyaar Al Muharraq' land reclamation project.

Haya Rashed Al Khalifa Attorneys at Law & Legal Consultants is highly regarded by peers, getting involved at a local level in many of the country's top-drawer projects; the firm is currently advising on the financing, construction, development and sale of the Bahrain Financial Harbour Project. The team's advice in relation to the US$1.2bn BAPCO financing includes advising a consortium of banks on local law issues.

Qays H. Zu'bi, Attorneys & Legal Consultants has worked on a number of projects in the region, adding strengthening layers to its relationships with international firms such as **White & Case**, **Richards Butler** and **Taylor Wessing**. Recently the firm's attentions have been largely directed towards the development of a large residential and commercial complex, including the formation of the project company, a special vehicle for raising funds through the offering of shares, and the drafting of various commercial contracts, including design, engineering and construction.

Other local firms active in the field are **Al Mahmood & Zu'Bi** and **Hassan Radhi & Associates**, both of which garner copious plaudits.

HAYA RASHED AL KHALIFA
ATTORNEYS AT LAW & LEGAL CONSULTANTS

1ST FLOOR, BAHRAIN DEVELOPMENT BANK BUILDING
PO BOX 1188, DIPLOMATIC AREA
MANAMA

Telephone: +973 17 537 771
Fax: +973 17 537 117
E-mail: info@hraklf.com
Website: www.hraklf.com

Languages
Arabic, English, Farsi, French

Other offices
Al Khobar (Saudia Arabia)

Number of lawyers 14
at this office 11

Contacts
Haya Rashed Al Khalifa, Rashid Bo-Ghammar, Nabeel Saeed

Member
International Bar Association; ICC Arbitration Centre (court member); GCC Arbitration Centre

CATEGORIES OF WORK

Arbitration	Investment funds
Banking	Intellectual property
Capital markets and private equity	Islamic finance structures
Construction and major projects	Joint ventures
Corporate and commercial	Labour and employment
Distribution and licensing	Litigation
Family and criminal law	Privatisation
Franchise and agencies	Securities
Insurance	Telecommunications

QAYS H. ZU'BI, ATTORNEYS & LEGAL CONSULTANTS

12TH FLOOR, AL JASRAH TOWER
BLDG 95, ROAD 1702
AREA 317, DIPLOMATIC AREA
PO BOX 2397
MANAMA

Telephone: +973 17 538 600
Fax: +973 17 532 342
E-mail: qzubi@qayszubilaw.com
Website: www.qayszubilaw.com

Languages
Arabic, English, French

Other offices
Dubai, Manama

Number of lawyers 11

Member
International Bar Association; AIPPI; GCC Commercial Arbitration Centre

CATEGORIES OF WORK

Banking
Qays H Zu'bi, Grahame Nelson

Construction
Qays H Zu'bi, Phillip Sacks

Telecommunications
Qays H Zu'bi, Grahame Nelson

Investment funds
Qays H Zu'bi, Naveen Thakur

Islamic finance structures
Qays H Zu'bi, Naveen Thakur

Distribution and licensing
Qays H Zu'bi, Mamoon Eltayeb

Mergers and acquisitions
Qays H Zu'bi, Grahame Nelson

Company listing and formation
Qays H Zu'bi, Maaria Ashraf

Intellectual property
Qays H Zu'bi, Grahame Nelson

Securities
Qays H Zu'bi, Naveen Thakur

Joint ventures
Qays H Zu'bi, Foutoun Alami

Insurance
Qays H Zu'bi, Grahame Nelson

Infrastructure
Qays H Zu'bi, Phillip Sacks

Procurement and tenders
Qays H Zu'bi, Grahame Nelson

Franchise and agencies
Qays H Zu'bi, Mamoon Eltayeb

Labour and employment
Qays H Zu'bi, Mamoon Eltayeb

Litigation and arbitration
Qays H Zu'bi, Mamoon Eltayeb

BELGIUM

Population	10.4 million
Number of lawyers	13,050
Professional title	Avocat; Advocaat
Currency	Euro (€)

Index

A historical setting for battles between European powers, Belgium has been referred to as the 'cockpit of Europe'. The fact that its capital city Brussels now serves as the embryonic 'capital' of the European Union (EU) gives the description contemporary relevance, hosting as it does the headquarters of the European Commission and most sessions of the European Parliament.

Bordered by France, Germany, the Netherlands and Luxembourg, the country is both culturally and linguistically divided. Flemish is the language of Flanders to the north, whilst the inhabitants of southern Wallonia speak French, and a German-speaking minority lives towards the east. Such diversity is reflected in Belgium's complex system of government, which is structured on three levels: the federal state, the three language communities and the three regions of Flanders, Wallonia and Brussels-Capital.

The Federal Government has responsibility for foreign affairs, defence, economic management, social welfare and the supervision of taxation by regional authorities. The community governments promote language, culture and education, and the regional governments manage mostly land and property-based issues such as housing and transportation. Titular Head of State King Albert II plays a ceremonial and symbolic role in the nation.

Economically, Belgium is located at the heart of one of the world's most highly industrialised regions. The country was the first in Europe to undergo an industrial revolution, and has developed a sophisticated infrastructure of ports, canals, railways and highways to integrate with its neighbours. As a founding member of the European Community, it strongly supports an extension of powers to the EU institutions, and replaced the Belgian Franc with the Euro in 2002. With few natural resources the industrial sector tends to import substantial quantities of raw materials and semi-finished goods that are further processed and re-exported, making its economy strongly dependant on foreign trade. Most of the traditional industries are represented, including steel, textiles, refining, chemicals, food-processing, pharmaceuticals, automobiles, electronics and machinery fabrication. Despite such a heavy industrial component, services account for a significant proportion of GDP.

BILLING

The presence of the European Commission in Brussels acts as a magnet for international law firms, most of which practise competition, regulatory or other aspects of EU law on behalf of clients who may or may not have business interests in Belgium. As such, two distinct legal markets co-exist in the city, with costs and billing methods varying between Belgian and international firms, and between Belgian and EU law matters. The fact that many of the foreign firms also have domestic lawyers to advise on Belgian law further complicates the picture. On average, top-level local advice can be sourced for a maximum of around €350, with rates for EU work significantly higher and indeed closer to what they would be in London, Paris or Frankfurt.

MARKETING

Belgium's 29 Bars share a restrictive approach to advertising, with Brussels lawyers generally having to adhere to both the French and Belgian Bar rules, which restrict all forms of active marketing. Brochures and websites have to be approved by the local Bar, and lawyers are prohibited from mentioning client names in response to press enquiries.

IN-HOUSE LAWYERS

In-house lawyers are often referred to as *juristes* in French, a term used to describe legal professionals not fully-qualified as *avocats*. Most of the larger companies employ significant teams of *juristes* to handle day-to-day corporate house-keeping and some litigation in the lower courts. In-house lawyers can make written submissions to the higher courts, but are not members of the Bar. Major litigation, or difficult corporate deals, will require the services of an experienced lawyer.

LIMITING LIABILITY

Professional indemnity rules vary a great deal between individual Bars in Belgium, to the extent that some Bars do not require it at all. The Brussels Bar Association has an insurance policy, which members can subscribe to, usually as part of their annual Bar Council subscription fee. The premium is roughly €175. In Brussels, individual claims under the professional indemnity insurance cover are capped at a certain level, but policies can vary

The largest firms

1	Linklaters De Bandt	152
2	Allen & Overy LLP	144
3	Lawfort	120
	Liedekerke Wolters Waelbroeck Kirkpatrick	120
5	Stibbe	108
6	elegis - Buyle Dieryck Maingain	107
7	Loyens	106
8	Eubelius	90
9	Laga	89
10	NautaDutilh	81
11	DLA Piper Rudnick Gray Cary	80
12	Baker & McKenzie	77
	Freshfields Bruckhaus Deringer	77
14	Monard - D'Hulst	66
15	Claeys & Engels, member of ius laboris	60
	Janson Baugniet	60
17	Van Bael & Bellis	58
18	Van Eeckhoutte, Taquet & Clesse	57
19	Cleary, Gottlieb, Steen & Hamilton LLP	51
	Clifford Chance	51
21	Altius (in cooperation with Tiberghien)	50
	CMS DeBacker	50
	Simont Braun	50
24	Lontings & Partners	43
	Tiberghien (in cooperation with Altius)	43

These figures represent the total number of lawyers in this country only, and have been supplied by the firms themselves. The figures should be accurate as at 1 January 2006.

in the amount and extent of cover. Some policies do not cover fraud and misappropriation of funds, and the excess can vary a great deal. Clients should check the policies if instructing a firm in an unfamiliar town.

A, B AND C LIST

Belgium's list system relates to the standing of individual lawyers, their rights of audience in court, and which individuals can advise on Belgian law.

Most Belgian lawyers are on the A list, which is for practising Belgian lawyers who are entitled to give advice on Belgian law and have full rights of audience in all courts except the Court of Cassation.

Non-Belgian lawyers can register on the B list, and can only advise on Belgian law in conjunction with an A-list lawyer. The activities of B-list lawyers are subject to the control of the Belgian Bar.

The C list is similar to the B list, but is a common list between the French and Flemish Bars in Brussels. Foreign lawyers are allowed to register, but the list has become increasingly unpopular.

However, Belgium is the heart of the EU and European law provides for the free movement of workers between member states. As such, lawyers from other member states must be admitted to the A list, but have to pass aptitude tests in practice areas where their training is different to that in Belgium. Unsurprisingly, these exams are difficult and few have passed.

COURT STRUCTURE

Belgium's legal system is closely modelled on that of the French Republic, and is organised according to specialisation and territorial jurisdiction. In civil law matters, the first court stage is one of the 27 courts of first instance, and the next stage up is one of the five courts of appeal, each of which has its own territorial jurisdiction. Finally, the highest domestic court before the European Court of Justice is the Court of Cassation, or Supreme Court, which hears appeals on issues of law or procedure only.

Only 20 lawyers in Belgium have rights of audience in the Court of Cassation, appointed by Royal Decree. Some of those individuals are listed in the **Dispute resolution** section of this chapter.

LEGAL MARKET

A combination of geographical factors, cultural differences and the unique political landscape of Brussels all contribute towards a legal market that is notoriously difficult to characterise. Insofar as there is a coherent narrative, it revolves around the distinction between firms who are there to advise on Belgian law and those primarily concerned with EU matters. But within these categories there are further differences, such as the various Flemish, French-speaking and Benelux firms domestically, and the pan-European nature of competition law practices, where many lawyers divide their time equally between Brussels and their home jurisdictions.

A further complication has been the establishment of domestic practices by many of the international firms. Apart from global players such as the UK's Magic Circle, who would have been expected to set up shop regardless of the EU scenario, this phenomenon has partly occurred because after originally envisaging themselves as EU boutiques, commercial imperatives have made it necessary for firms to hire local lawyers. However, in these instances it is generally the case that domestic and EU practitioners operate independently from each other, and for the purposes of this chapter we maintain that distinction.

The size of the Belgian economy means that the majority of corporate transactions would be classed as 'mid-market' in larger jurisdictions. Though a handful of purely domestic big-ticket deals take place every year, many have a multi-jurisdictional element and are worked on in tandem with lawyers from other countries. Consequently, when it comes to assessing domestic market share, the gap between the global elite and local players is not as wide as the prominence given to a few headline transactions might suggest.

Nevertheless, there is no disputing the fact that **Linklaters De Bandt** and **Allen & Overy LLP** dominate the full-service domestic market. Both were created as a result of mergers between members of the Magic Circle and leading Belgian outfits *De Bandt van Hecke Lagae & Loesch* and *Loeff Claeys Verbeke*. Whether on the corporate or finance side of the table, the pair is almost ever present when it comes to Belgium's biggest mandates.

Clifford Chance and **Freshfields Bruckhaus Deringer** also have significant domestic practices, though unlike the bigger two, whose size requires them to maintain a mid-market presence, their efforts are mainly concentrated at the bulge-bracket end of the scale. In both cases success has been achieved by targeted lateral hiring as opposed to all-out merger. Elsewhere, **Cleary, Gottlieb, Steen & Hamilton LLP**'s representation of Telenet in its recent IPO is further evidence of the firm's continued emergence from its historical roots as a public sector adviser, and **Eubelius** is perhaps the only remaining Belgian independent that is able to consistently punch at the highest level.

DLA Piper Rudnick Gray Cary certainly has ambitions to enter the top tier, as its recent acquisition of 35 lawyers from the dissolved *Coudert Brothers LLP – Coppens, Van Ommeslaghe & Faurès* amply demonstrates. Undoubtedly the most significant event of the past few years, the move makes sense on many levels. Firstly, it gives what was predominantly a Flemish practice exposure to more French-speaking clients. Moreover, esteemed figures such as Pierre Van Ommeslagh enhance the firm's profile amongst the political and economic establishment. But perhaps of greatest long-term significance is the fact that superb dispute resolution and corporate capabilities have now been grafted onto leading administrative, real estate and technology departments. That said, the fact that the cream of the former *Coudert* Belgian corporate team decided to join **Dechert LLP**, and the cultural challenges that integration will no doubt present, means that at least for now there are as many questions as answers.

Of the rest, **Loyens**' staggering growth suggests that comparisons in some quarters with the old *De Bandt* are not wholly wide of the mark, **Stibbe** has recovered some of its former élan under the strategic direction brought by Olivier Clevenbergh, and **NautaDutilh** remains synonymous with quality at every level. All three are Benelux firms, and in respect of purely domestic players both **Laga** and **Monard – D'Hulst** have good national coverage.

When it comes to EU law, **Cleary, Gottlieb, Steen & Hamilton LLP** is almost universally recognised as simply the best. Much of this reputation stems from the role that former partners played in drafting the relevant provisions of the Treaty of Rome, and the head-start this inevitably gave to following generations. More recently **Freshfields Bruckhaus Deringer** has come to be accepted as pretty much the US firm's equal. Its status as a corporate heavyweight has certainly helped in this regard, and the increased emphasis on compliance at member state-level bodes well for the future, particularly given the market-leading nature of its competition practices in other major jurisdictions.

Most of Europe's premier firms are well-represented, with multi-jurisdictional merger clearance work, and the behavioural issues that dominant players throw up, an influential factor. **Clifford Chance** and **Linklaters** compete with other City firms as well as Continental peers such as **Gleiss Lutz** and **Gide Loyrette Nouel**. Moreover, the economic muscle of US corporates ensures a strong showing from the US contingent, with **Latham & Watkins LLP**, **Jones Day** and **Wilmer Cutler Pickering Hale and Dorr LLP** all members of a group of about fifteen international firms that can claim to have a sizeable Brussels-based practice consistently doing work of the highest calibre across the whole gamut of EU-related work.

AVIATION

AVIATION

ALLEN & OVERY LLP ✪
BIRD & BIRD ✪

DLA Piper Rudnick Gray Cary ✪
Dechert LLP ✪
Freshfields Bruckhaus Deringer
Liedekerke Wolters Waelbroeck Kirkpatrick ✪
NautaDutilh
Verhaegen Walravens ✪

Firms are listed A-Z in tiers which are ranked in order of priority
✪ Indicates firm displays contact details at the end of this chapter.

Werner Eyskens advises on aviation contracts, aircraft financing and leasing, air carriers' liability and related regulatory aspects at **Allen & Overy LLP**. The firm represents Delta Air Lines and Saudi Arabian Airlines on noise emission limitation infringements around Brussels Airport, as well as domestic carrier VLM Airlines.

Catherine Erkelens' influence within the international aviation community is reflected in the work of **Bird & Bird**, which successfully represented the Board of Airline Representatives in a landmark case contesting the legality of a tax on all airlines flying into Brussels National Airport. In another landmark matter the firm won high-profile litigation for 27 airlines where it was ruled that the 'Passenger Service Charge' is not commissionable.

In its capacity as administrator and collector of Sabena, **DLA Piper Rudnick Gray Cary** concluded the sale of Sabena Technics to TAT Industries Group. The practice also advises air traffic controller Belgocontrol in respect of night-flights around Brussels Airport. Christian Van Buggenhout and Ilse Van de Mierop are recommended.

At **Dechert LLP** Richard Temko advises banks and lessors on aviation finance matters, and aviation clients on corporate and regulatory issues. Recent highlights include acting on the acquisition of a fractional leasehold interest in a business jet and related civil law and regulatory issues.

NautaDutilh receives client praise for being 'very professional in every respect, punctual to deadlines and helpful in explaining documents in a way that laymen can easily understand'. The firm advises SN Brussels Airlines, and acted for Jet Airways in respect of its start-up activities in Belgium.

Verhaegen Walravens acts for Virgin Express against the trustees of Sabena in connection with the bankruptcy of Belgium's former flag carrier. The firm undertakes the full range of aviation work including passenger claims, noise abatement regulations, aircraft finance and employment.

Also recommended are **Freshfields Bruckhaus Deringer**, whose asset finance practice advises airlines, lenders, lessors and manufacturers, and Marc Godfroid at **Liedekerke Wolters Waelbroeck Kirkpatrick**.

BANKING, FINANCE AND CAPITAL MARKETS

ALLEN & OVERY LLP ✪
CLIFFORD CHANCE
FRESHFIELDS BRUCKHAUS DERINGER
LINKLATERS DE BANDT ✪

BAKER & McKENZIE ✪
CLEARY, GOTTLIEB, STEEN & HAMILTON LLP ✪

Altius (in cooperation with Tiberghien) ✪
DLA Piper Rudnick Gray Cary ✪
Dechert LLP ✪
Eubelius ✪
Jones Day ✪
Liedekerke Wolters Waelbroeck Kirkpatrick ✪
Loyens ✪
NautaDutilh
Simont Braun ✪
Stibbe ✪
White & Case LLP Avocats Advocaten

Berwin Leighton Paisner LLP
Bird & Bird ✪
CMS DeBacker ✪
elegis – Buyle Dieryck Maingain ✪
Eversheds
Hunton & Williams LLP ✪
Laga ✪
Lawfort ✪
Lontings & Partners ✪
Monard – D'Hulst ✪
Simmons & Simmons ✪
Verhaegen Walravens ✪
Willkie Farr & Gallagher LLP ✪

Firms are listed A-Z in tiers which are ranked in order of priority
✪ Indicates firm displays contact details at the end of this chapter.

BANKING, FINANCE AND CAPITAL MARKETS

Allen & Overy LLP built on its leading position in acquisition finance by advising Macquarie Bank on the financing aspects of its acquisition of 70% of the privatised Brussels International Airport. The firm has also developed its securitisation and regulatory capabilities, whilst on the capital markets side involvement on the Galapagos and Punch Graphics IPOs illustrates the benefits of local market knowledge working in concert with an international network. Peter Bienenstock is the key contact.

Yves Herinckx leads a finance team at **Clifford Chance** which continues to act on the largest and most complex mandates for banks and borrowers in a variety of syndicated loans, acquisition finance, project finance and debt capital markets transactions. In respect of equity capital markets, Laurent Legein is advising the underwriters in the IPO of Elia System Operator.

Banking and finance lawyers at **Freshfields Bruckhaus Deringer** are well versed in applying innovative international techniques to Belgian structures. Ivan Peeters leads an asset finance and securitisation team renowned for expertise in cross-border sale and lease-back transactions. In respect of capital markets the firm advised Eurodisney on its rights offering and additional listing on Euronext Brussels, as well as on its further delisting. Chris Sunt is recommended.

François De Bauw heads up a fine capital markets team at **Linklaters de Bandt** which acted for InBev on its mandatory public tender offer for AmBev further to both companies' merger. Advising RHJ International on its €1.5bn listing on Euronext Brussels was another recent highlight. On the banking side Jacques Richelle is described as 'having the ability to cover off all the obscure angles that a lawyer of lesser standing might miss'.

Baker & McKenzie is praised for 'outstanding' levels of service by more than one client, and capped one of its best-ever years for capital markets work by representing the selling shareholders in the Telenet IPO. Banking partner Antoine De Raeve, respected in the market as a 'good deal attorney', led a team which advised KBC Bank in connection with the financing of the cross-border acquisition by 3i of the Aviapartner group of companies.

'If you really have a problem in Belgium you go to him', says one client of **Cleary, Gottlieb, Steen & Hamilton LLP** rainmaker Jan Meyers. The firm, which has longstanding connections with the Belgian Government, was involved in a €539m secondary offering of 5.3% of Belgacom's shares, and advised Telenet in connection with its IPO.

ALTIUS (in cooperation with Tiberghien)'s Johan De Bruycker has a good local reputation and marshals a team which acts for a wide range of domestic and international banking clients. The firm recently represented Bayerische Hypo-und Vereinsbank in relation to the financing of the LBO of Six Flags Europe by Palaman.

The acquisition of a team from *Coudert Brothers LLP – Coppens, Van Ommeslaghe & Faurès*, including partners Jean-Michel Detry and Yves Tavernier, should enhance the standing of **DLA Piper Rudnick Gray Cary**. 'Knowledgeable and professional' departmental head Yves Brosens acted for Barclays Bank on the financing of a new Marriott Hotel being constructed in Ghent.

The demise of *Coudert Brothers LLP – Coppens, Van Ommeslaghe & Faurès* also led to the arrival of corporate finance expertise at **Dechert LLP** in the shape of Eric Deltour and René Gonne. Both join Richard Temko, who has over 30 years' experience in the Belgian asset-based finance and leasing market.

2005 saw **Eubelius** represent Belgian electricity transmission operator Elia on its IPO and admission to trading on Euronext Brussels, and the firm is currently advising IT company Zetes on its IPO.

Thierry Buytaert is the key contact at **Jones Day**, which recently represented the Lubrizol/Noveon Group as the borrower in a five-year €250m corporate financing by a lending group led by ABN Amro.

Jan Vincent Lindemans is a key figure at **Liedekerke Wolters Waelbroeck Kirkpatrick**, which recently assisted USB in setting up the refinancing of an existing syndicated loan secured by a number of security interests for the three Belgian entities of the Quadrant group.

Loyens has vast experience acting for both borrowers and lenders, and recently advised a Spanish bank on a €25m secured loan facility in relation to the acquisition and refinancing of a major hotel group in Brussels. Grégoire Jakhian and Wilfred Goris are well respected, and both represented a US bank in reorganising its corporate structure in Belgium.

Benoit Feron, Dirk Van Gerven and the 'excellent' Marc van der Haegen are respected names at **NautaDutilh**, which advises the Belgian Government in connection with the securitisation of its tax receivables. The firm also acted for Zenitel with respect to the public offering of new shares for the amount of €25m as a result of a capital increase.

The recruitment of Vanessa Marquette as a partner from **Freshfields Bruckhaus Deringer** provides **Simont Braun** with greater securitisation expertise. Lucien Simont leads a five-partner department that recently advised a French Group in connection with a public offer of securities in Belgium to be listed on Euronext.

Jan Peeters' securitisation practice at **Stibbe** acted for Rosy Blue in a tap issue under the whole business (diamonds) securitisation programme. Assisting Arkimedes in the public offering of shares and bonds in the ARKimedes fund was a recent capital markets highlight.

'They are proactive, quick, come up with good ideas and use their network efficiently, which optimises the value of their services', says one client of **White & Case LLP Avocats Advocaten**. The 'precise' Stefan Odeurs heads a practice which acted for BNP Paribas, CCF, ING Belgium and KBC Bank as mandated lead arrangers of a €690m multi-currency revolving credit facility agreement for Agfa-Gevaert, which was one of the largest facilities of the year involving a Belgian-listed company.

We also recommend: Harold Wouters at **Berwin Leighton Paisner LLP**; Paul Hermant at **Bird & Bird**; Catherine Houssa at **CMS DeBacker**; Jean-Pierre Buyle at **elegis – Buyle Dieryck Maingain**; Philippe Delsaut at **Eversheds**; Herve Cogels at **Hunton & Williams LLP**; **Laga**, where Werner Van Lembergen recently arrived from **Freshfields Bruckhaus Deringer** to head up the banking and finance team; Marc Vandemeulebroeke and Koen Vanderheyden, who both work in **Lawfort**'s financial services team; Vincent Dirckx at **Lontings & Partners**; Peter Rooryck at **Monard – D'Hulst**; France Wilmet at **Simmons & Simmons**; Emmanuel Roger France at **Verhaegen Walravens**; and Xavier Dieux at **Willkie Farr & Gallagher LLP**.

CORPORATE AND M&A
Antwerp

ALLEN & OVERY LLP ✪
LINKLATERS DE BANDT

Baker & McKenzie ✪
DLA Piper Rudnick Gray Cary
elegis – Buyle Dieryck Maingain ✪
elegis – Huybrechts Engels Craen & partners ✪
Lawfort
Loyens
Van de Vijver Van Clemen

Firms are listed A-Z in tiers which are ranked in order of priority
✪ Indicates firm displays contact details at the end of this chapter.

CORPORATE AND M&A
Antwerp

Allen & Overy LLP managing partner Wim Dejonghe is currently advising the Telindus Group on the public offer by Belgacom to acquire the entire issued share capital of Telindus, which is the first hostile takeover in the country for years. The firm is also representing United Services Group on its €585m friendly public takeover bid for Solvus.

Jean-Pierre Blumberg of **Linklaters de Bandt** is another managing partner who discharges his functions from Antwerp. He leads a local team comprising a further partner and 13 associates. Last year was notable for advising Indian pharmaceutical company Matrix Laboratories on its acquisition of a controlling stake in Docpharma, and subsequent launch of a mandatory public takeover bid for the remaining shares.

Jan Cerfontaine is the mainstream corporate partner at **Baker & McKenzie**, and Koen De Winter is the local contact for the firm's commercial contracts group, which undertakes work for the likes of ConocoPhillips and Saatchi & Saatchi.

Dirk Caestecker is the key contact at **DLA Piper Rudnick Gray Cary**, where he practises in most areas of corporate law, particularly acquisitions and group reorganisations involving mergers, de-mergers, equity and asset-based transactions, contributions of branch operations and public offerings.

Hugo Callens is the key contact at **elegis – Buyle Dieryck Maingain**, where he specialises in corporate and commercial, construction, real estate and customs law. The firm has a very close relationship with **elegis – Huybrechts Engels Craen & partners**.

Lawfort has 24 lawyers in Antwerp, many of whom undertake commercial and distribution instructions on both a contentious and non-contentious basis. Olivier Van Fraeyenhoven and Wilfried Van Looveren are the key contacts.

Martine De Roeck manages the Antwerp outpost of **Loyens**, which can call upon the services of over 20 lawyers dealing mainly with corporate and tax matters. The office has a particular focus on port, transport and customs law, and Saskia Lust leads a specialised private client team.

Kurt Faes is the key contact at **Van de Vijver Van Clemen**, which has recently assisted clients such as Alcopa, Skytanking and Select Interim on various acquisitions. The firm also has commercial contracts and corporate house-keeping capabilities.

CORPORATE AND M&A
Brussels

Following its appointment to the 3i legal panel **Allen & Overy LLP** recently advised the private equity house on its acquisition of AviaPartner. The firm also landed a role on KBC Bank/Almanij merger, acting for two of the controlling shareholders in the latter, and represented Goldman Sachs and KBC Securities in their capacity as financial advisers to the board of Electrabel on the public takeover bid by Suez. Dirk Meeus heads the group, and Pierre-Olivier Mahieu is also recommended, having led a team which advised Centrica on its successful £252m bid with Gaz de France for a stake in Belgian energy company SPE.

Led by the 'impeccable' Jean-Marie Nelissen Grade **Linklaters de Bandt** continues to be involved in the majority of high-profile transactions that take place in Belgium, such as acting for Suez in respect of its public tender offer for Electrabel, and Umicore on its partial split. The team also worked with the Antwerp office in acting for KBC Bank and Insurance on its €15.6bn merger with Almanij to create one of the top-ten banks in Euroland. Paul Van Hooghten and Eric Pottier are also recommended in a team praised by clients for having 'a good combination of Belgian skills with international knowledge'.

Jean-Louis Joris and the hugely respected Jan Meyers are leading figures at the 'extremely deal-minded' **Cleary, Gottlieb, Steen & Hamilton LLP**, where according to one client the 'ratio of very high quality is probably the highest in the sector'. The firm counselled Electrabel in connection with Suez's public takeover offer, and represents La Poste in its negotiations for a strategic partnership. Historical client the Belgian Government recently required advice, along with institutional investors, on the sale of a 70% interest in Brussels International Airport Company (BIAC) to Macquarie for €745m.

Laurent Legein is the key personality at **Clifford Chance**, which acted for Goldman Sachs in the KBC Bank/Almanij merger, and the shareholders in the sale of Aviapartner to 3i. The firm also advised Publi-Gas in the acquisition of an additional stake in Distrigas and Fluxys.

Eubelius remains the pick of the Belgian independents for corporate and M&A work, as manifested by its representation of Electrabel's board in the public tender offer by Suez, and its advisory role to Almanij in the merger with KBC Bank. The firm is also acting for Belgacom in its hostile takeover bid for Telindus. The 'always available' Hans Gilliams receives plaudits for producing 'excellent-quality work'.

Heavyweight competition, tax and finance capabilities form the backdrop to **Freshfields Bruckhaus Deringer**'s developing corporate practice, where Chris Sunt is highly regarded by peers. Acting for Gaz de France on its joint acquisition with Centrica of a 51% shareholding in SPE, as well as BIAC on the Belgian Government's sale of its 70% stake to Macquarie, demonstrate the firm's status as a genuine competitor for Belgium's biggest deals.

CORPORATE AND M&A
Brussels

ALLEN & OVERY LLP ✪
LINKLATERS DE BANDT ✪

Cleary, Gottlieb, Steen & Hamilton LLP ✪
Clifford Chance
Eubelius ✪
Freshfields Bruckhaus Deringer

Altius (in cooperation with Tiberghien) ✪
Ashurst ✪
Baker & McKenzie ✪
DLA Piper Rudnick Gray Cary ✪
Liedekerke Wolters Waelbroeck Kirkpatrick ✪
Loyens ✪
NautaDutilh
Stibbe ✪
White & Case LLP Avocats Advocaten

Bird & Bird ✪
CMS DeBacker ✪
Dechert LLP ✪
Jones Day ✪
Laga
Lawfort ✪
Lontings & Partners ✪
Monard – D'Hulst ✪
Simmons & Simmons ✪
Simont Braun ✪
Van Bael & Bellis ✪

Berwin Leighton Paisner LLP
Crowell & Moring ✪
elegis – Buyle Dieryck Maingain ✪
Eversheds
Hunton & Williams LLP ✪
Marx, Van Ranst, Vermeersch & Partners ✪
Olislaegers & De Creus
Van Olmen & Wynant
Verhaegen Walravens ✪
Weil, Gotshal & Manges LLP
Wilmer Cutler Pickering Hale and Dorr LLP ✪

Firms are listed A-Z in tiers which are ranked in order of priority
✪ Indicates firm displays contact details at the end of this chapter.

'They fully understand our business, know what we expect and are able to think ahead', notes one client of **ALTIUS (in cooperation with Tiberghien)**, which also receives praise for the quality of its assistants as well as partners. The firm, which is renowned for M&A expertise, recently represented the Delhaize Group in relation to its €165m acquisition of the Cash Fresh supermarket group. Johan De Bruycker is recommended.

Carl Meyntjens continues to attract high-quality mandates at **Ashurst**, particularly in the M&A, corporate finance and private equity arenas. Last year was notable for advising Royal Bank of Scotland in connection with the buy-out of the Bureau Van Dijk Group, and Candover on the leveraged management buy-out of UCB's films business.

Koen Vanhaerents is praised as an 'excellent lawyer' who is 'good on negotiations and speedy in response' at **Baker & McKenzie**. The firm, which holds its own in size as well as quality, undertakes a healthy amount of work for KBC Private Equity, whom it recently advised in the management buy-out of Pizza Holding Company, which operates the Pizza Hut franchise in Belgium.

The arrival of four partners from *Coudert Brothers LLP – Coppens, Van Ommeslaghe & Faurès*, including Francis Goffin and Lemaire Herman, bulks up a department at **DLA Piper Rudnick Gray Cary** which could already call upon established names such as Koen De Maeyer and Erwin Simons, who is praised by one client for 'exceeding expectations'. Apart from localised activity, the firm undertakes a significant amount of work in the Democratic Republic of Congo in the fields of mining, energy, trade, health and real estate.

Philippe Malherbe and Christel Van den Eynden are both recommended at **Liedekerke Wolters Waelbroeck Kirkpatrick**, an 'efficient' firm which provides 'sound advice', according to one international client. The practice acted on behalf of the South African Bidvest Group in respect of its acquisition of Benelux foodservice supplier Deli XL. Corporate real estate is a particular strength.

Roel Nieuwdorp and Grégoire Jakhian are leading lights at **Loyens**, a terrific Benelux firm which frequently appears at the higher end of the domestic market as well as on cross-border transactions. Acting for a major international company in its acquisition of a Belgian industrial equipment manufacturing company was one of many M&A deals the firm was mandated on over the past year.

NautaDutilh's Peter Callens is singled out for praise as an 'on the ball' and 'independent' advisor who is willing to 'stand up and try to persuade clients to do things his way'. A major highlight of last year involved advising Docpharma on the sale of a controlling interest to Matrix Laboratories of India, where Dirk Van Gerven took the lead.

Olivier Clevenbergh and Jan Peeters remain the leading lights at **Stibbe**, where Mark Fyon recently assisted Ripplewood in its €900m acquisition of the Honsel Group, as well as being involved in the subsequent restructuring of the Honsel shareholding with a view to the listing of RHJI, Honsel's controller post-acquisition. The firm also has a first-class distribution law practice.

Toyota Industries is amongst one of several important client gains for the 'extremely well-equipped' **White & Case LLP Avocats Advocaten** over the past year, for whom the firm acted on its purchase of a range of subsidiaries of Toyota Tsusho across Europe. The firm has particular expertise in public M&A and private equity. The 'pragmatic' Thierry Lohest, Stefan Odeurs and Gisèle Rosselle have all previously practised at some of Belgium's heavyweight corporate firms.

Corporate litigation is an area where **Bird & Bird** excels, as demonstrated by the firm's representation of Schneider Electric in a case brought by the Brussels public prosecutor's office and minority shareholders relating to alleged undervalued public takeover bids launched in the 1990s. In the M&A sphere, advising the shareholders of Unda in the sale of their controlling stake to Boiron Group was a notable recent transaction.

At **CMS DeBacker**, Jean-François Goffin and Margareta Bresseleers are both experienced corporate lawyers. Carl Leermakers heads the M&A team and Jean-Marie De Backer specialises in restructuring, public investments, privatisations and public-private partnerships, particularly in the fields of steel and aeronautics.

The recruitment of what amounted to the cream of *Coudert Brothers LLP – Coppens, Van Ommeslaghe & Faurès'* corporate, securities and M&A team has significantly strengthened **Dechert LLP**'s hand amongst the firm's existing and potential clients. Amongst the four new partners are René Gonne and Eric Deltour, the latter of whom is a leader in cross-border M&A and private equity.

Fujitsu Consulting and Solvay are amongst Howard Liebman's clients at **Jones Day**. Luc Houben recently represented PepsiCo in connection with the US$750m redemption of General Mills' 40.5% interest in its Belgian Snack Ventures Europe joint venture.

Hilde Laga is the key figure at **Laga**, which retains close links with its former alliance partner Deloitte. With five offices around the country the firm has a good position in the domestic mid to upper-market, and partner Thomas Denys recently led a team acting for Betafence in the post-acquisition corporate restructuring and debt push down of the Betafence group. Formerly known as *Laga & Philippe*, Denis Philippe has now left to set up **Philippe & Partners**.

Having merged with *Bertouille & Partners* **Lawfort** can call upon the collective skills of Stephane Bertouille, Katrin De Saedeleir, Marie Evrard, Koen Selleslags and Philippe Van Den Broecke for corporate law. A further three partners undertake commercial and distribution work. M&A and private equity are key areas of activity for the firm.

'Straight to the point advice' is the hallmark of **Lontings & Partners**, a firm which regularly gains referral opportunities from City and Wall Street players. Last year was notable for assisting German printing inks manufacturer Siegwerk Druckfarben in connection with the Belgian aspects of its acquisition of the worldwide packaging division of Sicpa Holding.

Ortwin Carron and Peter Rooryck are the key Brussels contacts at **Monard – D'Hulst**, which also has offices in Kortrijk and Hasselt, where Erik Monard is based. The firm acts as general corporate and commercial counsel to large and mid-sized corporations, and frequently advises on commercial contracts, international group structuring and distribution matters. A major M&A highlight involved representing the seller in the sale of Cash Fresh to Delhaize.

Four partners handle corporate, M&A and commercial work at **Simmons & Simmons**, including Anthony Orr, Frank De Paepe and Leo Peeters. Over the past year the firm has been involved in the acquisition of a Belgian telecoms operator and the sale by a French multinational of a consultancy business.

Ten lawyers conduct M&A at **Simont Braun** including departmental head Sandrine Hirsch. During the past year the firm acted for a Belgian insurance company in the acquisition of the life and non-life insurance business of a Swiss insurance group in Belgium and Luxembourg. Significant acquisitions in the banking and real estate sectors have also been advised upon in the recent past.

Pascal Faes is recommended at **Van Bael & Bellis**, which undertakes the full array of instructions including commercial agreements, advisory work, corporate bookkeeping and strategic advice. Steven De Schrijver excels on IT-related mandates, where he recently assisted Ordina in the acquisition of Recyfin.

The Brussels branch of **Berwin Leighton Paisner LLP** does an 'excellent job' as a corporate finance and private equity boutique that undertakes a healthy amount of mid-sized M&A. Harold Wouters is a niche specialist in the biomass field, particularly with respect to joint venture and asset-backed financing issues.

Emmanuel Gybels is the key figure at **Crowell & Moring**, where he advises national and multinational companies on cross-border transactions including M&A, as well as assisting clients in establishing, monitoring and restructuring their European presence. New technologies are a particular focus for the firm.

Eversheds undertakes the Belgian aspects in respect of much of the firm's global transactional work, such as its representation of Dana Corporation in the sale of its automotive after-market businesses to Affinia Group. Philippe Delsaut and Koen Devos are the respective corporate and commercial contacts.

Hunton & Williams LLP focuses on cross-border transactions for multinationals, and also advises on commercial agreements including agency, distribution, franchising, licensing and equipment leasing contracts. Herve Cogels mans the fort.

Name partners Nicole Van Ranst and Kristoffel Vermeersche undertake corporate work at **Marx, Van Ranst, Vermeersch & Partners**, which undertakes a fair amount of domestic M&A as well as assisting international clients and law firms in the Belgian aspects of cross-border acquisitions.

Michael Olislaegers is the leading personality at **Olislaegers & De Creus**, which has a *groupement* arrangement with **Steptoe & Johnson LLP** whereby it acts as the US firm's in-house Belgian law practice. Blue-chip Belgian enterprises and the local subsidiaries of multinational companies make up much of the corporate client base.

Stanislas De Peuter at **Weil, Gotshal & Manges LLP** undertakes a good deal of M&A and private equity work, much of which has a real estate object.

Wilmer Cutler Pickering Hale and Dorr LLP's profile in EU-related work has started to translate into significant domestic instructions, where Karel Daele has recently joined with a team from **Freshfields Bruckhaus Deringer**. The firm advised Amer Sports Group from Finland on the takeover of Belgian company Luxilon.

We also recommend: Jean-Pierre Buyle at **elegis – Buyle Dieryck Maingain**; Luc Wynant at **Van Olmen & Wynant** for private equity; and Jacques Verhaegen at **Verhaegen Walravens**.

DISPUTE RESOLUTION

Only 20 lawyers can litigate in Belgium's highest court, the Court of Cassation (Supreme Court). They are hand-picked by the King of Belgium, and spread amongst several firms. As this court only hears appeals on issues of law and procedure, it should not be considered the sole indicator of a firm's dispute resolution capabilities.

Allen & Overy LLP continues to represent the former parent companies of Swissair in their epic defence of claims brought by the Belgian Government and the Sabena estate. The firm is also involved in a high-profile CERA arbitration in which a minority group of shareholders has launched a claim for winding up the holding company controlling one of the major Belgian banks. Koen Van den Broeck leads the department, and Luc Demeyere is an experienced arbitrator and mediator.

Niche dispute resolution firm **Hanotiau & Van Den Berg** can call upon the skills of Supreme Court lawyer Paul Lefebvre, Bernard Hanotiau, who has been involved in international arbitrations as both arbitrator and counsel, Albert Jan Van Den Berg and Pascal Hollander, who has mediation experience.

The 'excellent' **Linklaters de Bandt** is the choice of Belgium's biggest companies for high-stakes litigation, an example of which is its

DISPUTE RESOLUTION

ALLEN & OVERY LLP ✪
HANOTIAU & VAN DEN BERG ✪
LINKLATERS DE BANDT ✪
STIBBE ✪

Baker & McKenzie ✪
DLA Piper Rudnick Gray Cary ✪
Freshfields Bruckhaus Deringer
Liedekerke Wolters Waelbroeck Kirkpatrick ✪
Lontings & Partners ✪
NautaDutilh
Van Bael & Bellis ✪
White & Case LLP Avocats Advocaten

Altius (in cooperation with Tiberghien) ✪
CMS DeBacker ✪
Clifford Chance
Dal & Veldekens
De Schrijver, Van de Gehuchte, Messiaen *Ghent, Kortrijk*
elegis – Buyle Dieryck Maingain ✪
Eubelius ✪
Eversheds
Janson Baugniet ✪
Jones Day ✪
Laga ✪
Loyens ✪
Olislaegers & De Creus
Simmons & Simmons ✪
Verhaegen Walravens ✪
Wilmer Cutler Pickering Hale and Dorr LLP ✪

Firms are listed A-Z in tiers which are ranked in order of priority
✪ Indicates firm displays contact details at the end of this chapter.

representation of the Electrabel/De Nul joint venture in its claim against the Belgian Government for annulling the necessary permits for the construction and operation of a wind farm in the North Sea. Johan Verbist leads a three-partner practice with particular expertise in corporate, restructuring and financial litigation.

Akzo, Interbrew and Thomas Cook have all instructed **Stibbe** over the past year, the latter with respect to arbitration and judicial proceedings concerning the failed takeover of City Bird. Jean-Pierre Fierens leads a department which can also call upon the skills of Supreme Court lawyers Ludovic De Gryse and Bruno Maes.

Four partners can handle dispute resolution at **Baker & McKenzie** in Brussels, including Pierre Sculier and Mia Declercq. The firm is experienced in most areas of commercial litigation.

In addition to the Supreme Court practices of Pierre Van Ommeslaghe and Isabelle Heenen, **DLA Piper Rudnick Gray Cary** can call upon the skills of André Faurès, who is an arbitrator of world repute. All three have been recruited as of counsel from *Coudert Brothers LLP – Coppens, Van Ommeslaghe & Faurès*. Charles Price has left the firm and joined **Cruyplants Eloy Wagemans & Partners**

Klaus Heinemann is a key figure at **Freshfields Bruckhaus Deringer**, which handles a good volume of disputes work for Belgian and international clients. British Nuclear Fuels and ClearChannel are both clients.

'We appreciate their business-oriented approach, rapid response times and high level of lawyering skills,' says one client of **Liedekerke Wolters Waelbroeck Kirkpatrick**. Aimery de Schoutheete and Joe Sepulchre are leading personalities in a firm that undertakes a wide range of disputes work, including a recent case involving an international treaty dispute which was adjudicated by the Permanent Court of Arbitration in The Hague.

Lontings & Partners recently acted for an international joint venture entity in €90m construction litigation against Fina Antwerp Olefins, where it worked alongside UK construction luminaries **Pinsent Masons**. Hugo Keulers' vast experience of the insurance sector leads to plenty of contentious opportunities.

NautaDutilh is currently acting for the Ukranian Government in a case involving the attachment of an Antropov aircraft which is grounded at Brussels National Airport. François Tulkens is recommended for his expertise on constitutional and administrative law.

Van Bael & Bellis's Catherine Longeval is praised by one client for being a lawyer of the 'highest calibre'. The firm has a great deal of experience in the pharmaceutical sector. Intellectual property and Belgian competition matters are a particular strength.

Financial institutions are a regular source of work for **White & Case LLP Avocats Advocaten**, which recently acted for Merrill Lynch in a suit relating to a major property development in Brussels being rented by the Belgian State, a case which raised political as well as legal issues. Thierry Bosly leads the team.

We also recommend: Christophe Ronse at **ALTIUS (in cooperation with Tiberghien)**; Luc Depré at **CMS DeBacker**; Sébastien Ryelandt at **Clifford Chance**; Patrick Van Leynseele at **Dal & Veldekens**; **De Schrijver, Van de Gehuchte, Messiaen**; Jean-Pierre Buyle at **elegis – Buyle Dieryck Maingain**; Ludo Cornelis at **Eubelius**; Koen Devos at **Eversheds**; Jean-Jacques Van Raemdonck at **Janson Baugniet**; Geoffroy de Foestraets at **Jones Day**; Bart De Moor at **Laga**; Geert Bogaert at **Loyens**; Frank Roose at **Olislaegers & De Creus**; Frank De Paepe at **Simmons & Simmons**; Philip Walravens at **Verhaegen Walravens**; and Karel Daele at **Wilmer Cutler Pickering Hale and Dorr LLP**.

ENVIRONMENT

ALLEN & OVERY LLP ✪
DLA PIPER RUDNICK GRAY CARY ✪
STIBBE ✪

Haumont Scholasse & Partners
Liedekerke Wolters Waelbroeck Kirkpatrick ✪
Linklaters De Bandt ✪
NautaDutilh

Baker & McKenzie ✪
Hunton & Williams LLP ✪
Laga ✪
Lawfort ✪
Lontings & Partners ✪
Monard – D'Hulst *Kortrijk* ✪
Ryckbost & Ryckbost *Ostende*

Firms are listed A-Z in tiers which are ranked in order of priority
✪ Indicates firm displays contact details at the end of this chapter.

ENVIRONMENT

Readers should cross-refer with the **EU regulatory** section later in the chapter, for firms with expertise in EU environmental law.

Gauthier van Thuyne specialises in contaminated land, waste and environmental liability issues at **Allen & Overy LLP**. The firm recently advised Borealis on emission allowances and permits relating to the construction of its combined heat and power plant. On the contentious side Delta and Saudi Arabian Airlines instructed the firm on noise litigation against the Brussels Instituut voor Milieubeheer concerning noise around Brussels National Airport.

The 'very professional' Bob Martens heads a team at **DLA Piper Rudnick Gray Cary** that includes leading waste and soil pollution lawyer Dominique Devos and town planning expert Els Empereur. The last year has witnessed the firm's involvement in PPP advice as well as brownfield development and regeneration projects.

The Region of Brussels and Harbour of Antwerp are both clients of **Stibbe**, where Jan Bouckaert is a constitutional and administrative law specialist with a particular focus on zoning and planning, who also drafts laws and regulatory texts for public authorities. Monique Kestemont-Soumeryn deals with environmental and town planning, expropriation, public office and education. Both are experienced litigators.

Land, property and environment boutique **Haumont Scholasse & Partners** can call upon the skills of ten partners, including Francis Haumont and Michel Scholasse. The firm undertakes work relating to town planning, public procurement, expropriation, commercial sites and environmental tax.

Dirk Lindemans and Bernard Deltour are recommended at **Liedekerke Wolters Waelbroeck Kirkpatrick**, which receives client praise for having 'a rapid understanding of the problems put forward'. Much of the firm's work has a contentious element, with particular strengths in the soil pollution arena.

In addition to transactional support work **Linklaters De Bandt** has a significant stand-alone capability. The firm acted for UMICORE on the negotiation and implementation of a long-term agreement with the Flemish Government and Flemish environmental authority OVAM on the programming, financing and execution of soil contamination remediation in the Flanders region. Francis Van Nuffel and the 'responsive, knowledgeable and proactive' Lieve Swartenbroux are commended.

NautaDutilh recently took on **Linklaters De Bandt**'s vastly experienced head of environmental and administrative law Patrick Peeters. The firm counselled RTL TVi in connection with obtaining building and environmental permits for several sites, and advised the government of the Brussels-Capital Region on air-traffic noise nuisance. François Tulkens is praised by one client for knowing 'everything about Belgian environmental law'.

Baker & McKenzie offers the full range of environmental services, including the defence of clients before the criminal courts. Jean-François Vandenberghe is the key contact in Brussels, which specialises in transactional work, and Pascal Mallien handles contentious matters from Antwerp.

Professor Lucas Bergkamp is the key contact at **Hunton & Williams LLP**, a firm praised for its 'competence, professionalism and teamwork'. Multinational companies receive advice in all areas of environmental compliance, permitting and enforcement and occupational health and safety, including the impact of such laws on business transactions.

Stora Enso is a key client of **Lontings & Partners** and recently instructed the firm in its dispute with OVAM concerning the incineration of paper sludge in a cogeneration plant.

We also recommend: Dirk Van Heuven at **Laga**; Ciska Servais at **Lawfort**; Xavier D'Hulst at **Monard – D'Hulst** and Donatienne Ryckbost at niche Ostende practice **Ryckbost & Ryckbost**.

FRAUD AND WHITE-COLLAR CRIME

Christian Van Buggenhout leads a team at **DLA Piper Rudnick Gray Cary** which now includes Pierre Van Ommeslaghe and Isabelle Heenen, who joined as of counsel from *Coudert Brothers LLP – Coppens, Van Ommeslaghe & Faurès*.

Raf Verstraeten acts as both defence counsel as well as representing victims at **Eubelius**. Tax and customs fraud, insider trading, anti-money laundering and misuse of corporate goods and funds are all covered. Ludo Cornelis handles civil matters.

Linklaters de Bandt's head of litigation Johan Verbist also leads the white-collar crime team of **Linklaters** worldwide, and regularly handles high-profile criminal cases.

Two associates assist partner Hans Van Bavel at **Stibbe**, which covers all aspects of company related criminal law. The team is experienced in serious fraud, tax fraud, employee fraud and intellectual property espionage.

FRAUD AND WHITE-COLLAR CRIME

DLA PIPER RUDNICK GRAY CARY ✪
EUBELIUS ✪
LINKLATERS DE BANDT ✪
STIBBE ✪

Allen & Overy LLP ✪
Dumon Sablon & Vanheeswijck
elegis – Buyle Dieryck Maingain ✪
Hanotiau & van den Berg ✪
Johan Scheers
Lontings & Partners ✪
Monard – D'Hulst ✪
Simont Braun ✪
Vanderveeren & Associés
Verhaegen Walravens ✪

Firms are listed A-Z in tiers which are ranked in order of priority
✪ *Indicates firm displays contact details at the end of this chapter.*

Senior associate Jurgen Egger specialises in economic criminal litigation at **Allen & Overy LLP**, including tax fraud, anti-money laundering and asset tracing matters.

Tax boutique **Dumon Sablon & Vanheeswijck** advises on tax fraud, customs fraud and the application of money laundering legislation. Johan Dumon, Stefan Sablon and Luc Vanheeswijck are all experienced practitioners.

Johan Scheers specialises in all matters relating to financial criminal law including tax and asset offences, anti-money laundering and white-collar crime.

Over the past year **Lontings & Partners** has advised clients in relation to VAT fraud, anti-money laundering and infringements of anti-racism legislation.

We also recommend: **elegis – Buyle Dieryck Maingain**'s Jean-Pierre Buyle; Paul Lefebvre at **Hanotiau & van den Berg**; Reinhold Tournicourt at **Monard – D'Hulst**; **Simont Braun**'s Jean-Francois Terlinden; Emmanuel Roger France at **Verhaegen Walravens**; and Pascal Vanderveeren of **Vanderveeren & Associés**.

INFORMATION TECHNOLOGY

Filip Van Elsen leads a 12-strong team at **Allen & Overy LLP** that has undertaken several cross-border data protection projects for the likes of SWIFT and Toyota. The firm recently represented Inbev in the outsourcing of its IT and telecommunications services, which involved 28 jurisdictions and was the largest such transaction in the Belgian private sector.

Bird & Bird has developed strong relationships with international clients such as BT, whom it recently advised on its network and voice telecommunications services outsourcing agreement with Inbev. The firm also works for domestic companies and the Belgian Government on major IT projects relating to e-government and general IT contracting. Catherine Erkelens leads the team.

Steven De Keyser has a heavyweight reputation for large scale IT projects and outsourcing at **DLA Piper Rudnick Gray Cary**, whilst of-counsel Patrick Van Eecke assists multinationals on e-commerce matters, and senior associate Kristof De Vulder is singled out as 'an outstanding bright young lawyer'. The firm advises eBay in respect of online sales.

During the past year **Baker & McKenzie** has represented one client in the implementation of a worldwide data management outsourcing solution, and has also assisted in the review of a company's privacy policy. Daniel Fesler and Koen De Winter are recommended.

Jones Day's Alexandre Verheyden is recommended for contentious work, where he is representing Telenet in several matters following its termination rate increase, and Base in connection with a claim against Belgacom Mobile for breach of competitive rules.

Tanguy Van Overstraeten leads **Linklaters De Bandt**'s technology, media and telecommunications practice, which covers data protection, e-business, computer security, outsourcing and other transactions.

Erik Valgaeren is the key contact at **Stibbe**, which recently assisted Electrabel on the drafting and negotiating of an agreement with respect to the installation of a new ICT platform for customer data management.

Steven De Schrijver is praised for 'putting in the hours' and being 'committed to getting the deal across the line' at **Van Bael & Bellis**. In addition to a steady stream of acquisition work the firm regularly advises on contractual matters and recently conducted a data protection risk assessment for Eisai's entire European business.

Wilmer Cutler Pickering Hale and Dorr LLP's practice has expanded into the commercial

INFORMATION TECHNOLOGY

ALLEN & OVERY LLP ✪
BIRD & BIRD ✪
DLA PIPER RUDNICK GRAY CARY ✪

Baker & McKenzie ✪
Jones Day ✪
Linklaters De Bandt ✪
Stibbe ✪
Van Bael & Bellis ✪
Wilmer Cutler Pickering Hale and Dorr LLP ✪

Crowell & Moring ✪
Hunton & Williams LLP ✪
Lawfort ✪
Loyens ✪
Verhaegen Walravens ✪
White & Case LLP Avocats Advocaten

Firms are listed A-Z in tiers which are ranked in order of priority
✪ *Indicates firm displays contact details at the end of this chapter.*

arena from a strong antitrust and regulatory base. The firm's particular focus is on the mobile communications sector and broadband, where it acts for some terrific clients.

Also recommended are: Thomas De Meese at **Crowell & Moring**; Christopher Kuner, a data protection expert at **Hunton & Williams LLP**; Jos Dumortier at **Lawfort**; Benoit Van Asbroeck at **Loyens**; Jacques Verhaegen at **Verhaegen Walravens**; and Rolf Olofsson at **White & Case LLP Avocats Advocaten**.

INTELLECTUAL PROPERTY

Acting for EURid on the launch of the .eu top-level domain name demonstrates **Allen & Overy LLP**'s stand-alone capabilities, and indeed the IP practice plays an important role in channelling corporate work to the firm. On the contentious side Sony BMG received advice on various copyright claims, and Innogenetics was counselled on patent infringement procedures. Filip Van Elsen and Geert Glas are the leading partners, with the latter praised by clients for his 'pragmatism' and 'availability'.

Paul Maeyaert leads the line at **ALTIUS (in cooperation with Tiberghien)**, assisted by a team including Christophe Ronse, who is an expert in the pharmaceutical and biotechnological fields and has experience of numerous patent infringement matters. The firm's anti-counterfeiting task force represents the likes of Imperial Tobacco, Nintendo and adidas.

High-profile and technically complex patent litigation is where **Bird & Bird** excels. The firm recently represented stent developer Medinol on an infringement matter which raised interesting questions on double patenting and the doctrine of equivalents, and in respect of trade marks Electrolux received advice on a cancellation action. Bruno Vandermeulen is the key contact. Clients praise the firm's 'innovative approach'.

Linklaters de Bandt recently lost the services of Carl De Meyer to **Howrey LLP**, but can call upon the skills of Jean-Christophe Troussel, a figure renowned for his 'business-orientated' and 'proactive' approach. The firm advised Mars on its dispute with an opponent regarding the trade dress of its Maltesers brand. Up-and-coming associate Pieter Van Den Broecke is praised for his 'excellent knowledge' and 'clear and precise advice'.

'I've used IP counsel all over the world and they are as responsive as anybody else', says one client of **NautaDutilh**. The firm assists BMW and Rolls-Royce in cases involving infringement of their trade marks on the internet, and represents Boston Scientific in cross-border patent litigation. Both Philippe Péters and Florence Verhoestraete are praised for being 'extremely good and easy to deal with'.

Benoit Michaux's arrival from **DLA Piper Rudnick Gray Cary** has enhanced an already superb team at **Simont Braun**, which can call

INTELLECTUAL PROPERTY

ALLEN & OVERY LLP ✪
ALTIUS (IN COOPERATION WITH TIBERGHIEN) ✪
BIRD & BIRD ✪
LINKLATERS DE BANDT ✪
NAUTADUTILH
SIMONT BRAUN ✪

Covington & Burling ✪
Crowell & Moring ✪
DLA Piper Rudnick Gray Cary ✪
Stibbe ✪

Baker & McKenzie ✪
Howrey LLP ✪
Jones Day ✪
Marx, Van Ranst, Vermeersch & Partners ✪
Van Bael & Bellis ✪

---

elegis – Buyle Dieryck Maingain ✪
Lawfort ✪
Liedekerke Wolters Waelbroeck Kirkpatrick ✪
Van de Vijver Van Clemen *Ghent*

Firms are listed A-Z in tiers which are ranked in order of priority
✪ *Indicates firm displays contact details at the end of this chapter.*

upon the skills of five partners including Emmanuel Cornu and Eric De Gryse. The firm is conducting a test case regarding contributory infringement in a patent dispute between two elevator manufacturers, and in the international sphere it is currently defending the interests of a US artist in a copyright infringement matter.

Though much of **Covington & Burling**'s work is focussed on the EU arena the firm is also active domestically, and is a good choice for litigation, particularly with respect to the enforcement of IP rights in new media. Alain Strowel is a leading copyright lawyer.

Complex patent litigation in the pharmaceutical sector is the forte of **Crowell & Moring**, where the excellent Kristof Roox has been involved in a number of cases concerning parallel litigation in several jurisdictions. The firm also acts for media and entertainment clients, particularly on the copyright aspects of digital television.

Benoit Michaux's departure to **Simont Braun** means that Alois Puts now leads the practice at **DLA Piper Rudnick Gray Cary**. The firm recently advised publishing company Kluwer on a copyright infringement matter, and has in-depth experience of anti-counterfeiting, trade mark and patent litigation.

Three partners practise IP at **Stibbe** including Ludovic De Gryse, who concentrates on arbitration and procedures before the Supreme Court, and Erik Valgaeren for technology matters.

Baker & McKenzie's Koen De Winter leads the practice from Antwerp, and Pierre Sculier is the key contact in Brussels. The firm advises clients in both contentious and non-contentious matters including patents, copyright, trade marks, trade names, domain names, advertising and trade practices.

The recruitment of Carl De Meyer provides **Howrey LLP**'s fledgling practice with a 'great IP all rounder'. The former **Linklaters De Bandt** man is popular with clients for being a 'good stand-up litigator who is respected by everyone he works with'.

Mireille Buydens at **Jones Day** is praised for her 'years of experience and knowledge' and having 'a good feel for the way things are going to fly'. The firm currently represents Danone in a trade practices dispute against Unilever.

Peter Marx and Herman Croux are the leading figures at **Marx, Van Ranst, Vermeersch & Partners**. Much of the firm's work is for media and entertainment clients active in the television, motion pictures, music, advertising and sports fields.

Peter L'Ecluse and Catherine Longeval are the key contacts at **Van Bael & Bellis**, which is currently representing a large pharmaceutical group in complex patent litigation against generic competitors. The firm regularly acts before customs authorities to obtain the seizure of counterfeit goods imported into the EU.

Also recommended are: Daniel De Jaeger at **elegis – Buyle Dieryck Maingain**; Annick Mottet Haugaard at **Lawfort**; Martine Demeur at **Liedekerke Wolters Waelbroeck Kirkpatrick**; and Karen Ongena at **Van De Vijver Van Clemen**.

LABOUR AND EMPLOYMENT

Claeys & Engels, member of ius laboris' roots can be traced back to *Loeff Claeys Verbeke* and *De Bandt van Hecke Lagae & Loesch*, the domestic merger partners of **Allen & Overy LLP** and **Linklaters**, where name partners Thierry Claeys and Chris Engels used to practise. The firm is indisputably Belgium's premier employment law adviser, with 15 partners making up a boutique practice offering the full range of services concerning human resources and personnel policy. Individual, collective and European employment law, as well as the criminal aspects of labour law are covered.

Pieter De Koster heads a team at **Allen & Overy LLP** which covers all aspects of human resources, pension and compensation policies in the advisory and contentious spheres. Equal treatment, outsourcing, pensions and privacy are all developing practice areas, reflecting the department's proactive and client-focussed ethos. Advising Hilton International on intricate litigation involving its pay systems, which has ramifications throughout the leisure industry, was a notable recent highlight.

Five partners, including the respected Véronique Pertry, handle employment matters at **Lawfort**, which incorporates labour law, social security and

LABOUR AND EMPLOYMENT

CLAEYS & ENGELS, MEMBER OF IUS LABORIS ✪

ALLEN & OVERY LLP ✪
LAWFORT ✪
LIEDEKERKE WOLTERS WAELBROECK KIRKPATRICK ✪
LINKLATERS DE BANDT ✪
LONTINGS & PARTNERS ✪
LOYENS ✪
VAN EECKHOUTTE, TAQUET & CLESSE

Baker & McKenzie ✪
Bird & Bird ✪
DLA Piper Rudnick Gray Cary ✪
Eversheds
Freshfields Bruckhaus Deringer
Laga ✪
Marx, Van Ranst, Vermeersch & Partners ✪
NautaDutilh
Stibbe ✪
Van Bael & Bellis ✪

Altius (in cooperation with Tiberghien) ✪
CMS DeBacker ✪
De Schrijver, Van de Gehuchte, Messiaen *Ghent*
Monard – D'Hulst Hasselt ✪
Simmons & Simmons ✪
Van Olmen & Wynant

Firms are listed A-Z in tiers which are ranked in order of priority
✪ Indicates firm displays contact details at the end of this chapter.

pensions capabilities. The firm is renowned for advising on reorganisations and restructurings, international employment and optimisation of salary structures, as well as having particular expertise advising the public sector. Stefan Nerinckx is recommended for e-migration matters.

Liedekerke Wolters Waelbroeck Kirkpatrick is praised by one client for providing an 'extensive quality of advice that analyses all aspects of a problem'. Multinational companies make up a large slice of the department's client base, with Aimery de Schoutheete recently advising one in a series of disputes against the Belgian Office of Social Security.

The 'outstanding' Luc Vanaverbeke is praised for his 'good judgement' at **Linklaters De Bandt**. High-calibre corporate support work is a constant, with employment advice recently supplied in connection with Electrabel's IPO and numerous transactional mandates. In terms of stand-alone work, the firm is advising Ford on discrimination litigation involving 40 ex-employees.

Alexander Vandenbergen and Jan Hofkens lead a department at **Lontings & Partners** that continues to impress in the quality and range of its instructions. Pensions-wise the firm is something of a leader, as demonstrated by its assistance to the Belgian communes in the sale of energy company SPE to a consortium made up of Centrica and Gaz de France. Advising Belgacom chairman Theo Dilissen in negotiating his departure package with Real Software was another recent highlight.

Jean-Louis Davain's arrival from **Claeys & Engels, member of ius laboris** has strengthened the hand of **Loyens**, particularly with respect to his considerable expertise in international mobility issues, share-based plans, present and deferred compensation structures, professional status and end-of-career planning. Christian Willems, who recently advised on a multinational's termination of several top executives' employment contracts, is also recommended.

Van Eeckhoutte, Taquet & Clesse is a 50-lawyer firm that has a core focus on labour law with offices in Brussels, Liege and Ghent. Complex employment matters are a particular forte.

Three partners handle employment work at **Baker & McKenzie**, including practice head François Gabriel. In addition to a healthy stream of transaction-related mandates the firm also advises on corporate restructurings and collective lay-offs, and is praised for 'focussing not only on laws but also on practices and risk assessment'.

Bird & Bird leans towards company reorganisation, employee IP and new workplace rights issues, on a stand-alone as well as support basis. The firm recently advised Servisair/GlobeGround on the social aspects of ceasing operations at Brussels International Airport, including union and government negotiations.

Bruno Blanpain left **DLA Piper Rudnick Gray Cary** to join **Marx, Van Ranst, Vermeersch & Partners**, though the practice has strengthened its numbers with several associate appointments. Over the past year the firm has been busy advising clients on new remuneration structures, company restructurings, cross-border employment matters and various high-profile disputes. Eddy Lievens leads the practice.

Company restructuring is the major expertise at **Eversheds**, where Stefan Corbanie heads the department. The firm handles day-to-day employment advice to Belgian and international clients, and in respect of multi-jurisdictional matters often takes on a project management role.

Continental Airlines, ING Bank and P&O are all employment clients at **Freshfields Bruckhaus Deringer**, which advises on the individual and collective employment aspects of M&A and corporate restructurings, as well as offering stand-alone advice.

Five partners and nine associates comprise **Laga**'s national department, including Tim Baart and Ilse Govaert in Diegem. The firm represents Kenwood Electronics in labour and social security-related litigation, in addition to advising the company on various non-contentious matters.

Bruno Blanpain's arrival from **DLA Piper Rudnick Gray Cary** has added to **Marx, Van Ranst, Vermeersch & Partners**' capabilities, where he joins Rafael Claes and a further four assistants. The firm, which also houses a business immigration team, has been involved in various restructurings, remuneration exercises and disputes over the past year.

Philippe François is the key figure at **NautaDutilh**, a firm praised by one client for making predictions that 'practically always come true'. Last year was notable for involvement in several transactional pieces of work, including employment-related advice to TAT Industries following its acquisition of Sabena Technics.

Jean-Philippe Cordier has taken over the helm at **Stibbe** following his arrival from **Van Eeckhoutte, Taquet & Clesse**, which along with several associate-level appointments brings the number of employment fee-earners to nine. The firm assisted Struik Foods in its dispute with unions raised by the employment of Polish workers in Belgium.

'We have tried other firms but we never got half as good advice,' says one client of **Van Bael & Bellis**, which assists clients with respect to collective redundancies, plant closures, transfers of undertakings and most other aspects of individual and collective employment law.

We also recommend: Sylvie Dubois at **ALTIUS (in cooperation with Tiberghien)**; Stanislas van Wassenhove at **CMS DeBacker**; Luk De Schrijver at **De Schrijver, Van de Gehuchte, Messiaen**; Piet Carlier at **Monard – D'Hulst**; Marcel Houben at **Simmons & Simmons**; and Chris Van Olmen at **Van Olmen & Wynant**.

MEDIA AND ENTERTAINMENT

Allen & Overy LLP's brand of 'thorough, prompt, extensive and correct' advice ensures a good following amongst Belgium's leading media companies, such as Vlaamse Media Maatschappij and De Persgroep – all the more impressive at a time of consolidation within the industry. With regards to international players the firm advised 20th Century Fox on the sales of new releases and catalogue titles by Belgian distributors, not to mention Warner Bros on various matters. Geert Glas and Filip van Elsen are the leading lawyers.

Advising MGM on the Belgian aspects of the worldwide merger between MGM Home Entertainment and Sony Pictures was the main transactional highlight for **Bird & Bird** last year. The firm also advises on regulatory and compliance matters, and recently assisted advertising management services company Macstrat on the renegotiation of its contract with a leading Belgian magazine.

Dirk Vandermeersch is the key figure at **Cleary, Gottlieb, Steen & Hamilton LLP**, which recently counselled Belgian newspaper publisher VUM Media in connection with the acquisition of Uitgeversbedrijf Tijd by De Persgroep and Rossel & Cie. The firm also advised the same client in its

MEDIA AND ENTERTAINMENT

ALLEN & OVERY LLP ✪

Bird & Bird ✪
Cleary, Gottlieb, Steen & Hamilton LLP ✪
DLA Piper Rudnick Gray Cary ✪
Marx, Van Ranst, Vermeersch & Partners ✪
NautaDutilh

Crowell & Moring ✪
Jones Day ✪
Loyens ✪
Van de Vijver Van Clemen *Antwerp*

Firms are listed A-Z in tiers which are ranked in order of priority
✪ *Indicates firm displays contact details at the end of this chapter.*

complaint against VMMa and De Persgroep before Belgium's competition authorities and courts in respect of abuse of dominant position.

Much of **DLA Piper Rudnick Gray Cary**'s work has an IP flavour, and in this respect Benoit Michaux's departure to **Simont Braun** has been compensated for by the arrival of Alois Puts from *Coudert Brothers LLP – Coppens, Van Ommeslaghe & Faurès*, who handles general media and entertainment matters along with Steven De Keyser.

Marx, Van Ranst, Vermeersch & Partners advises a host of broadcasters, production companies, record labels, publishers, managers, sports agencies and performing arts companies, as well as some high-profile actors and musicians. Peter Marx and Herman Croux are the leading figures.

NautaDutilh undertakes a fair degree of IP-related work as well as handling an interesting array of instructions across the board. The firm successfully represented the Belgian Premier League in a case where Telenet argued that it was entitled to a right of pre-emption to acquire the broadcasting rights for the League's competition after the League had auctioned its rights to Belgacom. Peter Callens and Fabienne Brison are recommended.

We also recommend: Thomas De Meese at **Crowell & Moring**; Geoffroy de Foestraets at **Jones Day**; Benoit Van Asbroeck at **Loyens**; and Christiaan Lesaffer at **Van De Vijver Van Clemen**.

REAL ESTATE

ALLEN & OVERY LLP ✪
BAKER & McKENZIE ✪
DLA PIPER RUDNICK GRAY CARY ✪
LIEDEKERKE WOLTERS WAELBROECK KIRKPATRICK ✪
LINKLATERS DE BANDT ✪
STIBBE ✪

CMS DeBacker ✪
Clifford Chance
Freshfields Bruckhaus Deringer
Laga ✪
Lawfort ✪
Lontings & Partners ✪
Loyens ✪
NautaDutilh

Firms are listed A-Z in tiers which are ranked in order of priority
✪ *Indicates firm displays contact details at the end of this chapter.*

REAL ESTATE

Daniel Gillet heads a real estate practice at **Allen & Overy LLP** that offers clients an integrated service in property development, investment and financing. The firm is retained by leading fund manager AXA REIM on a number of investments, and last year advised Bank of Ireland on transactions amounting to €140m. Retail client Foruminvest is currently receiving assistance on the development of three major shopping centres.

Dominique Lechien is the leading figure at **Baker & McKenzie**, where foreign investors are a key source of work. The firm recently advised a Spanish group in the acquisition of two Belgian companies that collectively own the Dorint Hotel, as well as a German fund in the acquisition of an office building located in Brussels.

DLA Piper Rudnick Gray Cary is particularly active on the regeneration side, where it currently acts for developers on several major projects. The firm has also been notably active on the deals front over the past year, including representing the Vastned Group on the acquisition of two real estate companies, and Intervest Retail on the sale of a portfolio of ten retail shops. 'I consider Dirk Caestecker and his real estate team as the number one in Belgium,' asserts one client.

Close co-operation with the firm's planning, tax and corporate teams means that 15 lawyers are involved in real estate matters at **Liedekerke Wolters Waelbroeck Kirkpatrick**, including the respected Yves Delacroix. The firm is a preferred advisor of IKEA, and acts for BEFIMMO, Belgian's second-largest real estate investment trust, in all of its investment and management work.

'I can't find anyone better than them, they make the deals happen,' says one client of **Linklaters De Bandt**, a firm praised in other quarters for 'offering a higher quality of service than others we have come across'. Jacques Périlleux leads a team which had a co-ordinating role over Deutsche Bank's sale and leaseback of 51 properties over nine European jurisdictions.

Four partners handle property matters at **Stibbe**, including France Maussion and Rudy Nauwelaerts, the latter of whom is described as 'still one of the best' by a leading client. The firm is particularly strong in infrastructure, where it is currently advising the City of Antwerp on various PPP projects. Slough Estates is another key client which is currently receiving assistance in relation to the further development of landmark business parks.

Corporate real estate is a major practice area at **CMS DeBacker**. Over the past year the firm has been involved in financings, acquisitions, disposals, developments and leasing instructions.

Thierry Blockerye leads the tax and real estate practice at **Clifford Chance**, which acts for a number of German funds including Deka and Degi. The firm recently represented Fortress in the sale of its Belgian real estate companies portfolio.

Klaus Heinemann is the key figure at **Freshfields Bruckhaus Deringer**, which recently acted for Mable Commercial Funding on the sale of Brussels' Le Méridien hotel. Ivan Peeters pitches in on the financing side.

Benoit Nibelle is a real estate tax specialist at **Laga**, which recently assisted with the restructuring of a holding and real estate company by means of a partial de-merger.

François de Montpellier is the key contact at **Lawfort**, which undertakes a fair amount of projects-related work in addition to a healthy stream of transactional matters.

Lontings & Partners recently carried out a corporate due diligence of around 20 real estate asset-holding companies belonging to Mercator Verzekeringen. Wouter Neven is the contact partner.

Loyens undertakes a high volume of real estate work in most areas, including purchases and sales, litigation, financing and projects. One of last year's highlights involved advising on the acquisition of multiple stores for a client.

Cofinimmo is a key client of **NautaDutilh**, which recently advised the leading real estate investment fund on the acquisition of property company North Galaxy, owner of two major Brussels office buildings.

SHIPPING AND TRANSPORT

Fransen Advocaten is a four-partner, nine-lawyer firm based in Antwerp. Specialising in maritime matters, senior partner Wim Fransen is a former President of the Belgian Maritime Law Association, and Tom Luyten is also recommended. The practice acts for owners, carriers and P&I clubs.

Kegels & Co Advocaten has capabilities in maritime, inland waters and road and air carriage. Tony Kegels is a good choice for insurance-related work, André Kegels represents P&I clubs, and Dirk Noels is the key dry-side contact.

Maritime, transport and insurance practice **Roosendaal Keyzer** completes the trio of leading Antwerp firms. Frank Roosendaal, Luc Keyzer and Gerald Straatman are all experienced practitioners of good local standing.

Lawyers from **Allen & Overy LLP**'s litigation, finance and commercial teams all pitch in on transport-related instructions, such as advising Levi Strauss on its freight-forwarding, sea, air and road transport contracts for the shipment of goods from Asia to Europe. Antwerp associate

SHIPPING AND TRANSPORT

FRANSEN ADVOCATEN *Antwerp*
KEGELS & CO ADVOCATEN ✪ *Antwerp*
ROOSENDAAL KEYZER *Antwerp*

Allen & Overy LLP ✪
AntwerpLaw Attorneys *Antwerp*
DLA Piper Rudnick Gray Cary ✪
elegis – Buyle Dieryck Maingain ✪ *Antwerp*
Liedekerke Wolters Waelbroeck Kirkpatrick ✪
Stibbe ✪
Van Aerde & Partners *Bruges*
Van de Vijver Van Clemen *Antwerp*
Van Doosselaere Advocaten *Antwerp*
Verhaegen Walravens ✪
Wijffels, Geuens, De Paep *Antwerp*

Firms are listed A-Z in tiers which are ranked in order of priority
✪ *Indicates firm displays contact details at the end of this chapter.*

Axel Craeybeckx is an experienced maritime and shipping lawyer.

AntwerpLaw Attorneys undertakes the full range of transport-related work, including admiralty, marine insurance, road, rail, air and inland navigation matters. Dirk De Beule and insurance expert Patricia Leers are both recommended.

Clive Van Aerde is the key figure at **Van Aerde & Partners** in Bruges. Over the past year the firm has been involved in ship arrests, disputes concerning the commission owed to ship brokers, damage and loss of containers stowed on the decks of container vessels, and infringements of laws with respect to fishing at sea.

Peter Van de Vijver and Ingrid Van Clemen are the key contacts at **Van de Vijver Van Clemen**, which counts the Ghent Port Authority and German shipowner Hamburg Sud as clients.

Verhaegen Walravens has substantial experience in road transport and railway matters. The firm represents Luxembourg National Railways for all cases relating to Belgium, as well as Thalys, the operator of the Paris-Brussels high-speed train.

We also recommend: Koen De Maeyer at **DLA Piper Rudnick Gray Cary**; Christian Dieryck and Paul Verguts at **elegis – Buyle Dieryck Maingain**; Marc Godfroid at **Liedekerke Wolters Waelbroeck Kirkpatrick**; Walter Verstrepen at **Stibbe**; Luc Maes at **Van Doosselaere Advocaten**; and Luc Wijffels at **Wijffels, Geuens, De Paep**.

TAX

Alain Huyghe and Philippe Lion are the key contacts at **Baker & McKenzie**, which was recently involved in the pre-IPO restructuring of the Telenet Group, and acted for Monsanto on the tax due diligence of the European affiliates of Seminis in the framework of an acquisition.

TAX

BAKER & McKENZIE ✪
FRESHFIELDS BRUCKHAUS DERINGER
LIEDEKERKE WOLTERS WAELBROECK KIRKPATRICK ✪
LINKLATERS DE BANDT ✪
LOYENS ✪
TIBERGHIEN (IN COOPERATION WITH ALTIUS) ✪

Afschrift ✪
Allen & Overy LLP ✪
Clifford Chance
Dumon Sablon & Vanheeswijck
Monard – D'Hulst ✪
NautaDutilh
Stibbe ✪

CMS DeBacker ✪
DLA Piper Rudnick Gray Cary ✪
Eubelius ✪
Jones Day ✪
Laga ✪
Lontings & Partners ✪

Firms are listed A-Z in tiers which are ranked in order of priority
✪ *Indicates firm displays contact details at the end of this chapter.*

Freshfields Bruckhaus Deringer has a significant stand-alone practice advising on transactional work, financial products, investigations and litigation. Already an advisor to the Belgian Government and Minister of Finance, the firm has recently been appointed as special advisor to the Flemish Administration. Representing Alcatel Bell in its successful litigation concerning Belgian stock options was a highlight of the past year. Axel Haelterman leads a team rated by one investment banker as 'consistently very good'.

Liedekerke Wolters Waelbroeck Kirkpatrick has advised on the tax aspects of company reorganisations, acquisitions of real estate companies and various investments in the Belgian Tax Shelter for the movie industry. On the contentious side the firm recently appeared before the Supreme Court regarding the construction of the General Anti-avoidance rule. Daniel Garabedian and John Kirkpatrick are leading figures.

Big-ticket transactional work served up by the corporate and finance teams at **Linklaters de Bandt** ensures a top-tier billing for its tax partners. The Brazilian MTO of InBev, Johnson & Johnson's acquisition of Guidant, Suez's tender offer on Electrabel's outstanding listed shares and the merger of KBC Bank and Alamanij have all required significant tax advice. Ivo Onkelinx leads a six-partner team renowned for its competence in 'highly technical and sensitive tax issues'.

'They are the best for this kind of sophisticated work, which requires a thorough knowledge of the local environment,' says one client of **Loyens**. Christian Chéruy and Enrico Schoonvliet are the leading lawyers in a department which recently assisted GE in restructuring part of its Belgian business, Deutsche Bank on new financial products for the Belgian market and Orange in restructuring some of its Nordic operations.

Independent tax boutique **Tiberghien (in cooperation with ALTIUS)** has an operational relationship with **ALTIUS (in cooperation with Tiberghien)** whereby the latter refers its tax work to the firm in return for reciprocal non-tax arrangements. In addition to corporate work the practice undertakes tax and estate planning for high-net-worth individuals and wealthy families.

Tax boutique **Afschrift** undertakes the full gamut of tax-related advice, including tax planning, litigation and corporate support. Leading partner Thierry Afschrift sits as a deputy judge at the Court of Appeal and is also a founder member of the Tax Management School in Brussels.

Allen & Overy LLP's work is largely concentrated on M&A and finance-related matters. Patrick Smet leads a team of nine fee-earners which recently assisted Macquarie Bank on the tax structuring of the acquisition and financing of a majority stake in Brussels Airport, and Centrica on the tax structuring of its acquisition of a majority stake (together with Gaz de France) in SPE.

Clifford Chance's Thierry Blockerye is renowned for his expertise in real estate tax issues, and over the past year the firm has been involved in numerous transactions for various clients including some German real estate funds.

Dumon Sablon & Vanheeswijck is a 22-lawyer tax boutique which works mainly for Belgian enterprises as well as some international clients. Johan Dumon, Luc Vanheeswijk and Stefan Sablon are all recommended.

The sizeable tax practice at **Monard – D'Hulst** encompasses nine partners including tax litigators and lawyers involved in structuring, estate planning and transactional work. Work is spread across Brussels, Hasselt and Kortrijk.

NautaDutilh is a good choice for the taxation of financial instruments. The firm recently advised ING in setting up an incentive product related to stock options, which required the filing of a ruling request that was approved by the appropriate tax authorities. The 'proactive, enthusiastic and creative' Patrick della Faille is recommended, as is the 'experienced, calm and prudent' Benoit Malvaux.

Stibbe undertakes a significant amount of work for US clients, and was recently instructed by a multinational in respect of its wage tax and social security in Belgium. Werner Heyvaert heads the group after his arrival from **NautaDutilh**, and he works alongside the respected Jacques Malherbe.

We also recommend: Eric De Plaen at **CMS DeBacker**; Marc De Munter at **DLA Piper Rudnick**

Gray Cary; Philippe Hinnekens at **Eubelius**; Howard Liebman at **Jones Day**; Benoit Nibelle at **Laga**; and Alain Claes at **Lontings & Partners**.

EU AND COMPETITION

Competition: According to one client, **Cleary, Gottlieb, Steen & Hamilton LLP**'s world-class competition team is 'a cut above everybody I have ever used', and the similarly high regard in which its US practice is held gives it the edge over most Brussels rivals. Complex mergers with a transatlantic connection are a common feature, with last year's advice to Verizon on its acquisition of MCI, where Maurits Dolmans, James Modrall and John Temple Lang all advised, a notable recent example. Elsewhere the firm counselled RealNetworks in its successful complaint against Microsoft, Romano Subiotto represented Alrosa in the Commission's investigation into its rough diamonds trade agreement with De Beers, and Nicholas Levy acted for Coca-Cola in the settlement of the Commission's five-year long Article 82 investigation. Antoine Winckler and Robbert Snelders are other respected names in a team which 'rarely fumbles in terms of getting right at the issue quickly'.

'If things get really tough and you need to get a lot of work done in a short period of time, they have the critical mass to deal with it', says one client of **Freshfields Bruckhaus Deringer**, which is comfortably the pick of the European practices. With 14 Brussels-based partners, the firm has the resources to match anyone, particularly on the merger side, where Dr Frank Montag advised Goldman Sachs on its €1.3bn acquisition of the energy and telecoms cable business of Pirelli, and the 'excellent' Andrew Renshaw represented Alcan on the Commission's approval of the creation and spin-off of Novelis. Amongst the rest, John Davies was involved in PepsiCo's complaints regarding Coca-Cola's alleged abuse of a dominant position, and the 'superlative' Rachel Brandenburger counselled Carnival in relation to a third-party appeal before the Court of First Instance (CFI) regarding the Commission's approval of the Carnival/P&O Princess Cruises transaction. Along with others, David Broomhall and Onno Brouwer spend a significant amount of time on cartel matters, and in state aid, expert Dr Michael Schütte advised Dutch brewery Bavaria on the Commission's investigation in relation to Holland Malt.

Simon Baxter and Tony Reeves are heavyweight partners in an 'insanely responsive' team at **Clifford Chance**, which is also praised by clients for having 'top-level connections in the Commission'. Martin Bechtold was involved in advising Oracle on its hostile takeover bid of PeopleSoft, one of the largest IT sector mergers ever, as well as Kone in the Commission's investigation into an alleged cartel in the elevator industry. The firm is currently representing the Software and Information Industry Association as an intervener in Microsoft's appeal against the Commission's Article 82 decision against it, where Thomas Vinje, who is described as 'without peer' in the EU IP field, is the lead partner.

In advising Johnson & Johnson on its acquisition of Guidant, St Gobain on its hostile takeover bid for BPB, and PeopleSoft on its defence of Oracle's hostile takeover bid, **Linklaters** has been involved in some of the highest-profile merger cases of recent years. Alec Burnside and Gerwin Van Gerven jointly head the team, with the latter currently acting for Vodafone on Article 82 proceedings alleging excessive pricing of the company's UK wholesale roaming services. Wolfgang Deselaers and the 'excellent case handler' Johan Ysewyn are also recommended.

Four partners at **Allen & Overy LLP**, including Michel Struys and Dirk Arts, are former judicial assistants at the European Court of Justice (ECJ) and CFI, making this one of the best-connected teams in Brussels. Transactional work over the past year included advising Centrica on the antitrust aspects of its joint bid with Gaz de France for a stake in Société Publique d'Electricité, whereas advising engineering company IMI in relation to cartel investigations in the copper tubing sector was a behavioural highlight. David Harrison has returned to London to take up a position at **Berwin Leighton Paisner LLP**, leaving the 'well-networked' Michael Reynolds as the department's leading figure.

Both Julian Ellison and Matthew Hall are described as 'very capable' at **Ashurst**, whose top-notch merger control practice acted for Tetra Laval before the ECJ in its historic confirmation of the CFI's annulment and criticism of the Commission's decision in the company's merger with Sidel. The firm's litigation reputation is demonstrated by its representation of the Commission in the seven Lombard Club Cartel cases before the CFI, and in the state aid field P&O is a regular source of work.

In advising Pernod Ricard during its public bid to acquire Allied Domecq, **Gide Loyrette Nouel** was involved in one of last year's headline transactions. Merger control apart, the firm is advising a French bank in a cartel investigation regarding the country's bank card payment system, and represents France Télécom before the CFI in its application for annulment of the Commission's decisions regarding the package of financial measures decided by the French State. Antoine Gosset-Grainville and Stéphane Hautbourg, the latter of whom has 'the ability to deliver innovative solutions in complex and sensitive matters', are both recommended.

Gleiss Lutz's formidable reputation is in large part due to its longstanding Brussels presence stretching back 40 years. The firm has excellent capabilities in merger control, state aid and behavioural matters, and has recently been involved in the citric acid, tubes and carbon brush

COMPETITION

CLEARY, GOTTLIEB, STEEN & HAMILTON LLP ✪
FRESHFIELDS BRUCKHAUS DERINGER

CLIFFORD CHANCE
LINKLATERS ✪

ALLEN & OVERY LLP ✪
ASHURST ✪
GIDE LOYRETTE NOUEL ✪
GLEISS LUTZ ✪
JONES DAY ✪
LATHAM & WATKINS LLP
LOVELLS ✪
SKADDEN, ARPS, SLATE, MEAGHER & FLOM LLP
SLAUGHTER AND MAY ✪
VAN BAEL & BELLIS ✪
WHITE & CASE LLP AVOCATS ADVOCATEN

WILMER CUTLER PICKERING HALE AND DORR LLP ✪

Arnold & Porter LLP ✪
Baker & McKenzie ✪
Crosby & Co Law Firm ✪
DLA Piper Rudnick Gray Cary ✪
Gibson, Dunn & Crutcher LLP
Hengeler Mueller ✪
Herbert Smith LLP ✪
Hogan & Hartson L.L.P. ✪
Howrey LLP ✪
McDermott Will & Emery/Stanbrook LLP ✪
Norton Rose
O'Melveny & Myers LLP ✪
Shearman & Sterling LLP
Sidley Austin Brown & Wood LLP ✪
Squire, Sanders & Dempsey L.L.P. ✪
Steptoe & Johnson LLP ✪

Bird & Bird ✪
Bredin Prat ✪
Covington & Burling ✪
Crowell & Moring ✪
Dechert LLP ✪
Eversheds
Haarmann Hügel ✪
Heuking Kühn Lüer Wojtek ✪
Kemmler Rapp Böhlke
Mayer, Brown, Rowe & Maw LLP ✪
Morrison & Foerster LLP ✪
NautaDutilh
SJ Berwin LLP ✪
Simmons & Simmons ✪
Stibbe ✪
Taylor Wessing ✪
Uría Menéndez
Weil, Gotshal & Manges LLP

Firms are listed A-Z in tiers which are ranked in order of priority
✪ Indicates firm displays contact details at the end of this chapter.

cartel matters. Simon Hirsbrunner and Dr Ulrich Soltész are the leading figures.

Bernard Amory is a leading personality in **Jones Day**'s terrific practice, which continues to defend MM02 plc in Article 82 proceedings regarding roaming charges, and also acts for Apple Computer in its defence of antitrust complaints regarding iTune and iPod, as well as BT on various acquisitions. Away from the telecoms arena the firm represented Procter & Gamble on its acquisition of Gillette, and Vincent Brophy advised FIFA and MasterCard in the Commission's investigation on their alleged anti-competitive arrangements for the World Cup.

'They know everything that goes on in the corridors of the Commission,' says one client of **Latham & Watkins LLP**. The firm, which has a national presence across the US, is advising Reebok on its combination with adidas-Salomon both within the EU and beyond. Behaviourally, the practice represents Groupement des Cartes Bancaires and coordinates the defence of ten large retail banks in the payment card sector cartel case. Dr Andreas Weitbrecht leads a team of all the nationalities where many of the partners divide their time between Brussels and other jurisdictions.

Philip Collins recently left **Lovells** to become chairman at the UK's Office of Fair Trading, though the firm can still call upon considerable talent, particularly in the shape of Christopher Thomas, described by one client as 'the complete package', who assisted Novell in securing the rejection of Microsoft's attempt to suspend the Commission's interoperability remedy. Tom McQuail recently advised a competitor in connection with the Phase II investigation of Johnson & Johnson's takeover of Guidant, and Matthew Levitt represented Royal P&O Nedlloyd in obtaining merger clearances for its acquisition by AP Moller Maersk. Jacques Derenne is a good choice for state aid work, and Ciara Kennedy-Loest for procurement.

Merger control is where **Skadden, Arps, Slate, Meagher & Flom LLP** excels, with the Wall Street firm undertaking a phenomenal amount of work in the area. Recent highlights include advising Cendant in its US$1.13bn acquisition of Gulliver Travel Associates and OctopusTravel.com, as well as Guidant in its US$23.9bn purchase by Johnson & Johnson. James Venit is the most recognisable partner.

'Technical excellence' and 'outstanding effectiveness' are the hallmarks of **Slaughter and May**, which recently advised Gillette on its merger with Procter & Gamble, and BAE Systems on the unconditional clearance granted by the Commission in relation to its acquisition of Alvis. John Boyce is praised for being 'very good on the practical interpretation of complex laws'. As part of its 'best-friends' strategy, the firm has close ties with the competition practices of other independent European practices, so as to enable the provision of co-ordinated advice to clients covering leading jurisdictions. **Hengeler Mueller**, **Bredin Prat**, and **Uría Menéndez** are all participants, with both **Slaughter and May** and **Uría Menéndez** forming an integrated team acting for Cemex on a public bid for RMC, which received clearance from the Commission.

The enormous reputation enjoyed by Jean-François Bellis and Ivo Van Bael contributes to the standing of **Van Bael & Bellis**, a measure of which is the firm's continued representation of Microsoft in its Article 82 proceedings, specifically with respect to the alleged tying of Windows Media Player with Windows PC operating systems. State aid and merger control apart, the firm has exceptional experience in cartel cases, where it represents Nippon Steel in a proceeding involving alleged market-sharing among steel tube producers, and UCB in its appeal before the CFI seeking the annulment of the Commission's decision in the Choline Chloride cartel case.

White & Case LLP Avocats Advocaten's reputation as a serious Brussels litigator is reflected in its continuing reputation of Microsoft with respect to its Article 82 proceedings, an instruction which has raised the firm's profile and calibre of work. Apart from Ian Forrester, who is recognised by peers as an expert on the pharmaceuticals industry, Alastair Sutton, Mark Powell, Jacquelyn MacLennan and Pontus Lindfelt are experienced practitioners. The firm represents Norske Skog in cartel investigations into the paper and pulp industry.

Wilmer Cutler Pickering Hale and Dorr LLP is noted for the strength of its telecoms practice, and was co-counsel to Oracle in relation to its hostile bid for PeopleSoft, which received approval following a 15-month investigation. In respect of litigation, having intervened in an appeal before the CFI against a Commission decision which rejected objections against FIFA's players' agents' regulations, the firm represents FIFA before the ECJ following an appeal by the unsuccessful complainant. Thomas Mueller, John Ratliff, Marco Bronckers and Christian Duvernoy are all recommended.

The 'very smart' Marleen Van Kerckhove spearheads **Arnold & Porter LLP**'s competition team, which has recently added to its ranks in the shape of Luc Gyselen, formerly of the Commission. Tim Frazer, who divides his time between Brussels and London, is commended by one client for 'combining a deep intellect with a consummately practical approach – an absolutely fantastic lawyer'.

Baker & McKenzie's European network makes it a good choice for cartel work, and the firm recently assisted one client in a multi-jurisdictional dawn raid and submission of multiple simultaneous leniency applications at EU and national level. Fiona Carlin is the key contact who has experience in cartels, merger control, distribution and licensing agreements. Nina Niejahr is a state aid specialist.

Boutique outfit **Crosby & Co Law Firm** has established a number of bilateral relationships with UK regional law firms, with Scott Crosby, Ursula O'Dwyer and Jane Golding recommended for litigation, state aid and merger control respectively. The firm is advising Impala, the European association of independent music companies, in its appeal against the Commission's decision to approve the merger of Sony and BMG – the first 'third-party' appeal of a merger in the entertainment sector.

DLA Piper Rudnick Gray Cary has recently taken on Jean Naslin from **Gide Loyrette Nouel** as well as Bertold Bar-Bouyssière from *Coudert Brothers LLP – Coppens, Van Ommeslaghe & Faurès*, the latter of whom brings to the firm a significant amount of German experience and is described by clients as 'very well-organised, devoted and methodical'. David Cox leads a team praised generally for 'rapidly grasping esoteric technical issues, and incorporating their implications into legal drafts'.

Gibson, Dunn & Crutcher LLP's Peter Alexiadis is a communications expert of world repute, as demonstrated by his representation of MCI in its victory before the CFI in an appeal against the Commission's prohibition decision with respect to the proposed merger between MCI/WorldCom and Sprint. David Wood is commended for his expertise in the financial services, media and hi-tech sectors.

Herbert Smith LLP recently lost the services of Stephen Kinsella, who has joined **Sidley Austin Brown & Wood LLP**, though Craig Pouncey and Veronica Roberts are both well-respected practitioners praised for providing 'sensible and commercial advice'. The firm represented Time Warner in relation to the EU merger aspects of its proposal to acquire ContentGuard jointly with Microsoft, and advised Fortune Brands on its acquisition of a number of major spirits and wine brands from Pernod Ricard. Away from mergers M-Real has instructed the team on the Commission's investigation into alleged co-operation between competitors in fine paper.

Hogan & Hartson L.L.P. undertakes significant transatlantic competition work for major international clients such as Ford, whom it recently represented in relation to the EU and international antitrust aspects of its increase in shareholding in Mazda and in the sale of Hertz. Catriona Hatton leads the team, and George Metaxas is recommended for communications matters.

At **Howrey LLP**, both Trevor Soames and Howard Rosenblatt advised Xerox in relation to the Phase II investigation of the proposed joint acquisition by Microsoft and Time Warner of ContentGuard. The breadth of the firm's work is demonstrated by its representation of Intel in the Commission's Article 82 investigation, as well as Olympic Airways in a state aid matter.

'High-quality', 'excellent in all regards' and 'first-rate' are how clients describe the services of

McDermott Will & Emery/Stanbrook LLP. The recent link-up between the US firm and one of Brussels' most revered EU boutiques gives clients access to the considerable advocacy skills of Clive Stanbrook QC, a figure held in extremely high regard by peers. Representing Lockheed Martin in opposing the Boeing McDonnell Douglas merger before the Commission was a notable recent highlight.

John Cook's departure to **O'Melveny & Myers LLP** leaves Jürgen Werner as the resident partner at **Norton Rose**, though clients praise Marc Waha as a 'business-minded, straight-to-the-point and brilliant lawyer'. The firm is currently acting for easyJet in its ECJ challenge against the Commission's decision to clear the Air France/KLM merger, and represents HSBC with respect to the Commission's sectoral inquiry into retail banking.

O'Melveny & Myers LLP's Brussels outpost is predominantly made up of Riccardo Celli's former team at **Norton Rose**, including John Cook who has now joined the practice as of-counsel. The firm undertakes a lot of work for Honeywell International, whom it recently represented in relation to its public bid to acquire Novar. Acting for Advanced Micro Devices on its complaint against Intel for abuse of dominant position in the market for x86-microprocessors is a good example of non-merger activity. Clients praise the firm for providing 'on-the-mark' advice.

Antitrust lawyers in **Shearman & Sterling LLP**'s German, London and Paris offices work closely together with a three-partner team in Brussels, making it well-equipped to handle complex multi-jurisdictional cases. Moreover, a combined US/EU capability means that it is regularly instructed by clients to advise on competition matters on both sides of the Atlantic, such as securing Phase II clearance for Siemens' acquisition of VA Tech. On the behavioural side the firm advised Paramount in the Commission's investigation into aspects of the pay-TV sector.

Sidley Austin Brown & Wood LLP's nascent competition practice was launched with the recruitment of two lawyers of longstanding Brussels repute: Stephen Kinsella, who heads the team after arriving from **Herbert Smith LLP**; and Stephen Spinks, formerly global co-head of *Coudert Brothers'* antitrust group. The firm is currently acting for the Fédération Internationale de l'Automobile on various matters relating to the sale of media rights.

Squire, Sanders & Dempsey L.L.P. managing partner Brian Hartnett has recently represented clients in a graphite electrodes cartel investigation, a Euro Exchange Rate cartel investigation and an abuse of market power investigation. He has also been involved in significant mergers involving the telecommunications, chemicals manufacturing and global market research industries.

At **Steptoe & Johnson LLP** the tech-savvy Kees Kuilwijk receives plaudits for being 'one of the few lawyers that goes to the trouble of getting to know his clients inside out'. Over the past year the firm has represented a number of companies on Article 81 and 82 issues, as well as merger notifications at both EU and national levels.

Hi-tech companies remain a focal point for **Bird & Bird**, which has sound litigation capabilities and has been advising Dun & Bradstreet on a number of merger control notifications. Japanese-speaking Wilko van Weert is the key contact.

Lawyers at **Covington & Burling** have particular expertise in dealing with the interface between IP and competition law and the structuring of pan-European distribution and licensing arrangements, as well as in-depth experience of several hi-tech industries. David Hull and Georg Berrisch are the key figures in a team which advised a major US publishing house on its proposed acquisition of a European publishing outlet.

Crowell & Moring recently took on Dr Werner Berg from **Gleiss Lutz**, who brings to the table experience of complex remedy issues and second-phase procedures in the merger control arena. Berg also advises on horizontal co-operation, vertical agreements and dominance issues, and has a particular focus on life sciences, pharmaceuticals and the chemical industry.

The recruitment of Pierre Louis from *Coudert Brothers LLP – Coppens, Van Ommeslaghe & Faurès* has added to **Dechert LLP**'s ranks over the past year, which could already call upon the skills of Isabelle Rahman. In addition to a number of merger control matters, the firm continues to defend a leading US chemical supplier in a Commission cartel investigation.

John Grayston is the key contact at **Eversheds**, which excels in state aid matters, particularly acting for aid donors in regeneration, universities and research establishments. The firm has recently secured many of the major instructions arising out of the UK, such as the London Olympics, and advises on the state aid implications of collaborative research, IP licensing, incubation and business support facilities and the financing of spin out companies.

Dr Rainer Roniger and Martina Maier are the resident partners at **Haarmann Hügel**, which undertakes a large amount of EU and multinational merger control work, and recently advised JP Morgan with respect to several intended transactions within the banking sector.

Led by Gabrielle Williamson, **Heuking Kühn Lüer Wojtek** is currently acting for a transport company in European merger notifications, and various other clients in antitrust enforcement actions.

EU boutique **Kemmler Rapp Böhlke** can call upon the skills of Barbara Rapp, Rainer Bierwagen and Alexander Böhlke, who is recommended for litigation.

Kiran Desai holds the fort at **Mayer, Brown, Rowe & Maw LLP**, which is currently advising ICI on its appeal to the CFI against the Commission's decision that it abused a dominant position contrary to Article 82. Merger-wise the firm represented LBO France on its acquisition of Terral, which involved competition filings across the world.

Morrison & Foerster LLP is renowned for its hi-tech expertise, and led by Christopher Norall the firm recently represented Hitachi on the merger control aspects of its acquisition of the hard disc drive business of IBM, as well as Thomson on its acquisition of a minority stake in ContentGuard.

Charles van Sasse van Ysselt heads **NautaDutilh**'s EU and competition law practice, and in addition to merger control filings he has defended cartel respondents in the agricultural, energy, financial services, media, paper and packaging industries.

At **SJ Berwin LLP** Ramon Garcia Gallardo is advising Portuguese electricity operator EDP on its action for annulment of the Commission's prohibition of its acquisition (with Eni) of GDP, the incumbent gas operator in Portugal.

Simmons & Simmons' Marco Slotboom is active in several cartel investigations, such as representing Vermeer Infrastructure in the bitumen sector, amongst other matters. Merger-wise, the firm advised TPV Technology on the EU and multinational merger control aspects of the acquisition of Philips' computer monitor business.

Peter Wytinck is the key contact at **Stibbe**, which is assisting the Flemish Region before the Commission regarding a number of state aid files, including the PPP project for Deurne Airport.

Taylor Wessing's recent recruitment of Marc Picat from **Lawfort** provides the firm with a respected local figure to sit at the hub of a competition practice with partners operating from London, Paris and Germany. Healthcare, life sciences and technology matters are a particular focus.

Jon Filipek is the resident partner at **Weil, Gotshal & Manges LLP**, which was recently involved in the appeal of a Commission state aid decision in the airline sector.

Other recommended EU lawyers are: Jacques Bourgeois at **Akin Gump Strauss Hauer & Feld**; Julie Nazerali at **Beachcroft Wansbroughs**; Georges Vandersanden at **CMS DeBacker**; Frank Fine at **EC Competition Law Advocates**; Konstantinos Adamantopoulos at **Hammonds**; and Izzet Sinan at **Morgan Lewis**.

CUSTOMS, TRADE, WTO AND ANTI-DUMPING

Sidley Austin Brown & Wood LLP's presence in Washington, DC, Geneva and Brussels underscores its status as a world leader in trade law matters. In the ten years since the WTO was created the firm has been involved in over 200 of the 300-plus complaints brought: advising Brazilian sugar producers' association UNICA in Brazil's complaint

CUSTOMS, TRADE, WTO AND ANTI-DUMPING

SIDLEY AUSTIN BROWN & WOOD LLP ✪
WILMER CUTLER PICKERING HALE AND DORR LLP ✪

GIDE LOYRETTE NOUEL ✪
HAMMONDS
HOGAN & HARTSON L.L.P. ✪
McDERMOTT WILL & EMERY/ STANBROOK LLP ✪
VAN BAEL & BELLIS ✪
VERMULST VERHAEGHE & GRAAFSMA
WHITE & CASE LLP AVOCATS ADVOCATEN

Covington & Burling ✪
Crosby & Co Law Firm ✪
Freshfields Bruckhaus Deringer
Herbert Smith LLP ✪

Cleary, Gottlieb, Steen & Hamilton LLP ✪
Crowell & Moring ✪
Eversheds
Mayer, Brown, Rowe & Maw LLP ✪
Steptoe & Johnson LLP ✪

Clifford Chance
Heuking Kühn Lüer Wojtek ✪
Kemmler Rapp Böhlke
Latham & Watkins LLP
O'Melveny & Myers LLP ✪
Squire, Sanders & Dempsey L.L.P. ✪
Taylor Wessing ✪

Firms are listed A-Z in tiers which are ranked in order of priority
✪ Indicates firm displays contact details at the end of this chapter.

against the European Communities concerning export subsidies for sugar being a recent example. Representing Honeywell before the Directorate-General for Trade in the high-tenacity yarn investigation showcased the firm's anti-dumping capabilities, and in respect of customs Umicore, 3M and Cargill are all clients. Richard Weiner leads a 'proactive and constructive' team that 'spends time trying to understand the economics'.

Marco Bronckers anchors the trade group at **Wilmer Cutler Pickering Hale and Dorr LLP**, which has a transatlantic link to one of the strongest practices in Washington, DC. WTO litigation is a strong point, with Boeing requiring representation in connection with all aspects of its dispute with Airbus over subsidies to large civil aircraft. The firm also represents a major WTO member government in its negotiations on access to medicines within the context of patent protection envisaged in the TRIPS agreement, and aids several Asian governments on their negotiating positions in bilateral and multilateral frameworks. Claus-Dieter Ehlermann is a former chairman of the WTO Appellate Body.

The experienced Olivier Prost is highly regarded both within **Gide Loyrette Nouel** and beyond. The firm assisted the African Caribbean and Pacific countries in their intervention before the WTO Arbitrators in the Banana arbitration, and assists Arcelor in the first anti-dumping proceedings initiated by Russia against certain steel products originating in the EU.

Konstantinos Adamantopoulos leads a team at **Hammonds** which is regularly involved in EU investigations, WTO law and dispute settlement proceedings, bilateral and multilateral relations of third countries with the EU, customs and indirect taxation and the free movement of goods. EU-Russia relations expert Edward Borovikov, and Jonathan Branton, are also recommended.

'She is very good with clients, incredibly hardworking, and knows her stuff back to front', says one client of **Hogan & Hartson L.L.P.**'s Lourdes Catrain, who is praised in other quarters for having 'a deep knowledge of trade law whilst being practical and business oriented'. Acting for a Chinese company on the anti-dumping investigation on plastic sacks and bags from China is one of a number of matters that the firm is currently instructed on.

The 'authoritative' and 'well-connected' Clive Stanbrook is a leading figure at **McDermott Will & Emery/Stanbrook LLP**, who along with Philip Bentley was one of the original pioneers in developing a Brussels international trade practice. The resurgence of countervailing cases in the EU since the Uruguay Round means that the firm has seen significant growth in this area, where it has represented Indian exporters in proceedings involving PET film, PET chips, micro-diskettes and recordable CDs. Successes in the seminal anti-dumping cases of *Eurocoton v Council* and *Philips v Council* were significant recent highlights.

At **Van Bael & Bellis**, WTO panel member Jean-François Bellis has advised international clients in countless anti-dumping cases as well as in many of the less frequently used EC countervailing, safeguard and 'trade barriers' proceedings. The firm has recently acted for the Brazilian Government in a WTO dispute concerning the EU's imposition of anti-dumping duties on imports of tube and pipe fittings from Brazil.

Paul Waer's departure means that *Vermulst Waer & Verhaeghe* is now known as **Vermulst Verhaeghe & Graafsma**. Recommended partners include Edwin Vermulst and Folkert Graafsma, who represents clients in trade litigation proceedings concerning anti-dumping, anti-subsidy, safeguards, origin and customs law.

White & Case LLP Avocats Advocaten is a good choice for anti-dumping matters, working as it does both for European manufacturers seeking the imposition of measures as well as exporters wishing to avoid them. The firm recently represented four European producers of hand pallet trucks in a complaint against dumped imports of Chinese trucks. Ian Forrester and up and coming associate James Killick are recommended in a team which has impressive 'depth of understanding' and 'very good contacts at the Commission'.

Covington & Burling's alliance with strategic consulting firm Kissinger McLarty Associates provides clients with access to diplomats, business leaders, negotiators and intelligence analysts. The firm regularly represents the Council of Ministers in anti-dumping and anti-subsidy cases before the European courts, and acts both for private clients and the Commission in WTO disputes. David Harfst and Georg Berrisch are the key figures.

Crosby & Co Law Firm's Ursula O'Dwyer is currently representing Eurofonte in an anti-dumping complaint and EU investigation on behalf of the European castings industry against certain castings originating in China, as well as one exporter and two importers producing lever-arch mechanisms in China in an ongoing investigation.

Dr Michael Schütte is the key contact at **Freshfields Bruckhaus Deringer**, which is currently representing Infineon Technologies in the WTO dispute settlement procedure initiated against the EU and US concerning countervailing duties on the imports of DRAMS into the EU and US. The firm is also active in the anti-dumping arena.

Herbert Smith LLP's Craig Pouncey represented the Government of Antigua and Barbuda in its successful WTO action against the US ban on cross-border gambling and betting services, which was the first-ever WTO dispute on an e-commerce issue and one of the first disputes under GATS. The firm also acted for Chiquita Brands on its high-profile litigation against the Commission concerning the EU's failure to comply with the outcome of a WTO dispute settlement procedure.

Mittal Steel is a big-name client of **Cleary, Gottlieb, Steen & Hamilton LLP**, whom the firm is currently advising in anti-dumping proceedings and proceedings relating to subsidies paid in Central and Eastern European countries. George Bustin and Till Müller-Ibold are the main partners.

Dr Robert MacLean is the key contact at **Crowell & Moring**, whose presence in Washington, DC allows the firm to service clients in the US and EU. All aspects of trade law are advised upon, with MacLean regularly involved in litigation before the CFI.

Eversheds predominantly advises on trade regulatory and defence work, with a particular focus on export controls and sanctions. The team has expertise in the interaction of US and EU export controls relating to defence, industrial products and design, and encryption software. Market access and customs disputes are also undertaken.

Mayer, Brown, Rowe & Maw LLP has recently been appointed by the Commission to undertake an evaluation of EU trade defence instruments, and has advised the Thai Government on EU trade law and WTO issues. Anti-dumping-wise the firm represented Chinese exporters of plastic bags and sacks on an EU investigation.

At **Steptoe & Johnson LLP** James Searles advises on EU external trade measures, customs, intra-EU trade obstacles and international market access issues. In the anti-dumping arena he represents the interests of both exporters and importers. The 'indispensable' Iain MacVay is an expert in the use of EU market access mechanisms such as the Trade Barriers Regulation.

We also recommend: Tony Reeves at **Clifford Chance**; Gabrielle Williamson at **Heuking Kühn Lüer Wojtek**; Rainer Bierwagen at **Kemmler Rapp Böhlke**; Jean Paul Poitras at **Latham & Watkins LLP**; Susan Ols at **O'Melveny & Myers LLP**; Dan Horovitz at **Squire, Sanders & Dempsey L.L.P.**; and Franziska Wagner at **Taylor Wessing**.

EU REGULATORY

Many of the firms listed in the **EU Regulatory** table have wide-ranging practices cutting across numerous different industries. Consequently, there follows a non-exhaustive list of recommended advisers in each sector.

EU regulatory – Agriculture: McDermott Will & Emery/Stanbrook LLP advises on food and agriculture approvals, particularly the registration and marketing of genetically modified organisms, traceability, health requirements, labelling and packaging; and **Gide Loyrette Nouel** is recommended for agrifood matters.

EU regulatory – Energy: Freshfields Bruckhaus Deringer advises various clients on the Commission's energy sector inquiry; **Norton Rose** has extensive knowledge of the electricity and gas markets in Europe and has acted for leading electricity companies, oil and gas majors, governments and governmental bodies. **O'Melveny & Myers LLP** recently advised a client in relation to the compatibility with the EU Gas Directives and national implementing legislation of its pricing mechanism for supply of gas to third parties.

EU regulatory – Environment: Environmental specialist Michael Renouf recently joined **Berwin Leighton Paisner LLP** from **Crosby & Co Law Firm**. **DLA Piper Rudnick Gray Cary** Professor Geert Van Calster's team caters for all the environmental and energy practices of the DLA Group network; **Hogan & Hartson L.L.P.** advises companies on EU chemicals legislation, as well as the impact of the Regulation on Hazardous Substances (ROHS) and the Waste Electrical and Electronic Equipment Directive (WEEE); **Hunton & Williams LLP**'s Professor Lucas Bergkamp counsels on EU health and safety regulation issues for chemical, electronics, consumer goods and other companies; and **Lovells** is representing US Steel in CFI proceedings challenging the Commission's decision to limit C02 emissions in Slovakia. **McDermott Will & Emery/Stanbrook LLP** recently established a programme for compliance with WEEE and ROHS for a major supplier of components for electrical and electronic products; **Sidley Austin Brown & Wood LLP** counsels Honeywell in a number of high-profile environmental, health and safety and consumer protection issues; Reshad Forbes is the key contact at **Van Bael & Bellis**, which is praised by clients for being 'professional, fast, very flexible and always ready to meet the customer's schedule and requirements'; **White & Case LLP Avocats Advocaten** advises Toyota on EU environmental legislation, including measures regulating fuel quality and the current regulatory framework on motor vehicle emissions; and **Wilmer Cutler Pickering Hale and Dorr LLP** has advised IT and telecoms equipment companies on compliance with WEEE and ROHS.

EU regulatory – Food and drugs: Gide Loyrette Nouel is assisting Tate & Lyle in the reform of the EC sugar organisation with a view to securing its access to raw materials and ensuring fair competition within the new regime between refineries and beet producers; **Hogan & Hartson L.L.P.**'s Jacqueline Mailly 'has the right contacts and a good feel for the way things are going'; **Hunton & Williams LLP** advises SMEs and multinationals on compliance, enforcement, legislative and policy issues; **Lovells** represents a number of food and feed manufacturers on issues such as the use of innovative ingredients, health and nutritional claims and traceability; **McDermott Will & Emery/Stanbrook LLP** counsels clients on their obligations concerning a wide range of regulations including compliance with registration, notification, inspection, advertising, packaging, labelling and marketing requirements; **McKenna Long & Aldridge LLP** recently conducted a risk assessment for generic drugs for product liability purposes in four jurisdictions; **Norton Rose** advises the Metro Group in connection with regulatory issues; **Sidley Austin Brown & Wood LLP**'s Maurits Lugard counsels Herbalife on, amongst other matters, EU rules on irradiated foods; and **Wilmer Cutler Pickering Hale and Dorr LLP** has recently recruited former EU Commissioner for Health and Consumer Protection David Byrne.

EU regulatory – Information technology: Catherine Erkelens is recommended at **Bird & Bird**; **Covington & Burling** advises on compliance issues arising in connection with electronic contracts and signatures, network and information security, cybercrime, e-advertising and e-promotion, content control, jurisdiction in internet transactions, digital copyright and data protection; at **DLA Piper Rudnick Gray Cary** privacy expert Dr Rosa Barcelo recently joined the firm from the Commission; Kees Kuilwijk is respected both within **Steptoe & Johnson LLP** and beyond; and **McDermott Will & Emery/Stanbrook LLP** advises clients on their

EU REGULATORY

Akin Gump Strauss Hauer & Feld
Allen & Overy LLP ✪
Arnold & Porter LLP ✪
Cleary, Gottlieb, Steen & Hamilton LLP ✪
Clifford Chance
Covington & Burling ✪
Freshfields Bruckhaus Deringer
Hengeler Mueller ✪
Hogan & Hartson L.L.P. ✪
Jones Day ✪
Keller & Heckman
Linklaters ✪
Lovells ✪
McDermott Will & Emery/Stanbrook LLP ✪
McKenna Long & Aldridge LLP ✪
NautaDutilh
Norton Rose
SJ Berwin LLP ✪
Sidley Austin Brown & Wood LLP ✪
Slaughter and May ✪
Squire, Sanders & Dempsey L.L.P. ✪
Stibbe ✪
Van Bael & Bellis ✪
Weil, Gotshal & Manges LLP
White & Case LLP Avocats Advocaten
Willkie Farr & Gallagher LLP ✪
Wilmer Cutler Pickering Hale and Dorr LLP ✪

Ashurst ✪
Baker & McKenzie ✪
Beachcroft Wansbroughs ✪
Berwin Leighton Paisner LLP
Bird & Bird ✪
CMS DeBacker ✪
Crosby & Co Law Firm ✪
Crowell & Moring ✪
DLA Piper Rudnick Gray Cary ✪
Dechert LLP ✪
Gibson, Dunn & Crutcher LLP
Gide Loyrette Nouel ✪
Gleiss Lutz ✪
Haarmann Hügel ✪
Hammonds
Herbert Smith LLP ✪
Heuking Kühn Lüer Wojtek ✪
Howrey LLP ✪
Hunton & Williams LLP ✪
Kemmler Rapp Böhlke
Latham & Watkins LLP
Lontings & Partners ✪
Mayer, Brown, Rowe & Maw LLP ✪
Morrison & Foerster LLP ✪
O'Connor and Company
O'Melveny & Myers LLP ✪
Olswang
Simmons & Simmons ✪
Skadden, Arps, Slate, Meagher & Flom LLP
Steptoe & Johnson LLP ✪
Taylor Wessing ✪
Vermulst Verhaeghe & Graafsma

Firms are listed A-Z in tiers which are ranked in order of priority
✪ *Indicates firm displays contact details at the end of this chapter.*

obligations concerning data on their European employees and customers, data collection and use and transfer of this data outside the EU.

EU regulatory – Pharmaceuticals and biotechnology:
Lontings & Partners' non-profit and trade associations department deals with EU regulatory issues relating to medical products and devices; **Lovells**' Christopher Thomas assists manufacturers on the grant of marketing authorisations, compliance with promotional and advertising requirements and other issues such as innovative gene therapy; **McDermott Will & Emery/Stanbrook LLP** advises clients on pan-European pharmaceutical product approval programmes and importation and movement within the EU; **Norton Rose** represents Pfizer in relation to distribution and regulatory issues connected with the placing on the market of pharmaceutical products; **Hogan & Hartson L.L.P.** is, according to one client, 'the most thorough and responsive firm I have worked with', with Linda Horton commended for bringing a 'global perspective'; and **Sidley Austin Brown & Wood LLP** advises a leading biotechnology company on EU rules and policies regarding biotech products, including the moratorium on new approvals.

EU regulatory – Telecoms: Cleary, Gottlieb, Steen & Hamilton LLP's John Temple Lang was formerly the director responsible for telecommunications and media in the Competition Directorate-General of the Commission; Gerald Oberst and George Metaxas are recommended at **Hogan & Hartson L.L.P.**, which advises SES Global on satellite regulatory issues in Europe and beyond; **Dechert LLP**'s Isabelle Rahman is an expert in the area; **Gibson, Dunn & Crutcher LLP**'s Peter Alexiadis has a world-class reputation; and **Wilmer Cutler Pickering Hale and Dorr LLP** is one of Brussels' leading telecoms firms.

EU regulatory – Transport: Ashurst advises P&O, National Express and various rail franchisees; **Norton Rose** represents shipowners, ports, airlines, tour operators, travel agents, financiers, governments and regulators on all aspects of aviation, shipping and rail competition, regulation and political matters; **Lovells** has maritime capabilities as well as an air practice that has advised airlines on negotiations between the EU and third countries on Open Skies; **McDermott Will & Emery/Stanbrook LLP** advises on the licensing of carriers and rights and obligations of carriers under EU rules, particularly in the air transport sector; **O'Melveny & Myers LLP** advised Eurocontrol in relation to the implementation of its air safety rules into the EU legal order; and **Wilmer Cutler Pickering Hale and Dorr LLP** represents a number of international airlines and steers the Star Alliance through all of its major regulatory proceedings in Europe.

ALLEN & OVERY LLP

UITBREIDINGSTRAAT 80
2600 ANTWERPEN

Telephone: +32 3 287 72 22
Fax: +32 3 287 72 44
E-mail: info.belgium@allenovery.com
Website: www.allenovery.com

Languages
Dutch, English, French, German, Italian, Spanish

Other offices
Amsterdam, Bangkok, Beijing, Brussels, Bratislava, Budapest, Dubai, Frankfurt, Hamburg, Hong Kong, London, Luxembourg, Madrid, Milan, Moscow, New York, Paris, Prague, Rome, Shanghai, Singapore, Tokyo, Turin, Warsaw

Number of lawyers 2,304
at this office 24

Contact
Wim Dejonghe

CATEGORIES OF WORK

Corporate and M&A
Wim Dejonghe,
Woutere Van de Voorde

Employment, pensions and incentives
Pieter De Koster

Public and administrative
Fabienne Martens

Banking, finance and capital markets
Sylvia Kierszenbaum, Filip Tanghe

Litigation and ADR
Luc Demeyere

Environment and planning
Axel Craeybeckx

Media and entertainment
Filip Van Elsen

Insolvency and restructuring
Luc Demeyere, Filip Tanghe

IT, internet and telecoms
Filip Van Elsen

BAKER & McKENZIE

MEIR 24
2000 ANTWERP

Telephone: +32 3 213 40 40
Fax: +32 3 213 40 45
E-mail: baker.br@bakernet.com
Website: www.bakernet.com

Languages
Dutch, English, French, German

Other offices
The member firms of Baker & McKenzie International, a Swiss Verein, have 70 offices in 38 countries around the world. For a complete list, please visit www.bakernet.com.

Number of lawyers 3,300+
at this office 15

Contacts
Koen Vanhaerents, François Gabriel

CATEGORIES OF WORK

Banking and finance
J Cerfontaine

Corporate finance
J Cerfontaine

Dispute resolution
K De Winter, J Cerfontaine

Intellectual property
K De Winter

International/commercial
K De Winter

IT/communications
K De Winter

Real estate, construction, environment and tourism
P Mallien

CMS DEBACKER

AMERIKALEI 92
2000 ANTWERP

Telephone: +32 3 206 01 40
Fax: +32 3 206 01 50
E-mail: info@cms-db.com
Website: www.cms-db.com

Languages
Dutch, English, French, German, Italian, Spanish

Number of lawyers 50
at this office 6

Contact
Trudo Motmans

Other CMS alliance member firms
CMS Adonnino Ascoli & Cavasola Scamoni, Italy; CMS Albiñana & Suárez de Lezo, Spain; CMS Bureau Francis Lefebvre, France; CMS Cameron McKenna, UK; CMS Derks Star Busmann, Netherlands; CMS von Erlach Henrici, Switzerland; CMS Hasche Sigle, Germany; CMS Reich-Rohrwig Hainz, Austria

CATEGORIES OF WORK

Corporate law, mergers and acquisitions

Banking, securities and finance

Bankruptcy and insolvency

Commercial law, distribution, IP and IT

Litigation and dispute resolution

Employment and pensions

Real estate, construction and town planning

Tax

European law, competition, state aids

Environment

Public and administrative law, public procurements, public utilities, public/private partnerships, energy, telecoms, health and hospitals

ELEGIS – BUYLE DIERYCK MAINGAIN

BRUSSELSTRAAT 59
2018 ANTWERPEN

Telephone: +32 3 238 78 50
Fax: +32 3 237 98 99
E-mail: bdm@elegis.be
Website: www.elegis.be

Languages
Dutch, English, French, German

Other offices
Brussels, Eupen, Liege, Namur

Number of lawyers 107
at this office 10

Member
AIJA; AEDB; Euro Franchise Lawyers; IBA; ICC; UIA

CATEGORIES OF WORK

Commercial litigation
Werner van der Veeken, Hugo Callens

Corporate
Hugo Callens

Banking and finance
Christian Dieryck

Labour law
Marina Van der Auweraert

Competition, antitrust
Christian Dieryck, Werner van der Veeken

Maritime and marine insurance
Paul Verguts, Christian Dieryck

Transportation
Paul Verguts, Christian Dieryck

Construction and project development
Hugo Callens

Arbitration
Christian Dieryck, Paul Verguts

Distribution
Christian Dieryck

Environment
Werner van der Veeken

Real estate
Hugo Callens

ELEGIS – HUYBRECHTS ENGELS CRAEN & PARTNERS

BRUSSELSTRAAT 59
2018 ANTWERPEN

Telephone: +32 3 244 15 60
Fax: +32 3 238 41 40
E-mail: hec@elegis.be
Website: www.elegis.be

Languages
Dutch, English, French, German

Other offices
Brussels, Eupen, Liege, Namur

Number of lawyers 107
at this office 26

Member
TerraLex; European Criminal Bar Association; Belgium Maritime Law Association

CATEGORIES OF WORK

Corporate and commercial litigation
Peter Engels, Annemie Coox

Banking and finance
Marc A Huybrechts, Edmond J Brondel

Shipping and transport
Marc A Huybrechts, Wouter Den Haerynck

Employment
MC Craen, Dominique Neirynck

Criminal law
Peter Engels, Edmond Brondel

Insurance
Wouter Den Haerynck, Dominique Neirynck

Construction and project development
Luc Janssens, Peter Engels

Arbitration
Marc A Huybrechts

Distribution
Peter Engels, Edmond J Brondel

Real estate and environment
Peter Engels, Wim Slosse

Administrative law
Wim Slosse, Peter Engels

EU and competition
Annemie Coox, Wouter Den Haerynck

KEGELS & CO
ADVOCATEN

MECHELSESTEENWEG 196
2018 ANTWERPEN

Telephone: +32 3 257 17 71
Fax: +32 3 257 14 74
E-mail: info@kegels-co.be
Website: www.kegels-co.be

Languages
Dutch, English, French, German, Spanish

Number of lawyers 10

CATEGORIES OF WORK

Maritime
Tony Kegels, André Kegels

Inland waters
Tony Kegels

Road and air carriage
Dirk Noels, Valerie Diercken

Transport intermediaries
Dirk Noels, Koen Kerstens

EU and competition
André Kegels

Agency/distribution
Dirk Noels, Valerie Diercken

Arbitration
Tony Kegels, Mathieu Verly

Banking and finance
Kristin Verhaegen

Litigation
André Kegels, Dirk Noels

General contracts
Tony Kegels, Dirk Noels

Insurance
Tony Kegels, Tom Valckx

Customs
André Kegels, Patricio Diaz Gavier

Employment and labour
Dirk Noels, Koen Kerstens

Liability
Kristin Verhaegen, Sarah Stas

Insolvency
Kristin Verhaegen, Koen Kerstens

TILLEMAN VAN HOOGENBEMT

MEIR 24, BUS 6
2000 ANTWERP

Telephone: +32 3 220 64 00
Fax: +32 3 220 64 19
E-mail: filip.tilleman@tvh-law.be

Languages
Dutch, English, French, German

Other offices
Brussels, Paris*

Number of Lawyers 12
at this office 9

Contact
Filip Tilleman

CATEGORIES OF WORK

Labour law
Filip Tilleman,
Herman van Hoogenbemt

Restructuring and transfer of undertakings
Filip Tilleman,
Herman van Hoogenbemt

National and international social security law
Herman van Hoogenbemt,
Yves Jorens

Discrimination and harassment
Filip Tilleman

European labour law
Yves Jorens

Pension plans
Herman van Hoogenbemt

Criminal law
Michael Verhaeghe

Commercial law
Ann De Wael

THE FIRM

Tilleman van Hoogenbemt (TVH) is a niche firm specialising in all legal matters related to national and international employment. Its founders, Filip Tilleman and Herman van Hoogenbemt, were partners in the labour department of the former Benelux firm Loeff Claeys Verbeke. Both have published numerous books and articles on all aspects of labour law and are frequent speakers at conferences.

Yves Jorens is professor of national and international social security law in the faculty of law at the universities of Gent and Antwerp. He is an expert in, and has written many books and articles, on European social law and international employment. He is also project director of an European Observatory for the Social Security of Migrant Workers, commissioned by the European Commission, which gives him wide access to social security authorities throughout the EU.

AREAS OF PRACTICE

The firm mainly focuses its interest on all topics of labour law, both individual (dismissals, working time, remuneration, harassment, etc) and collective (collective redundancies, negotiations with unions, transfer of undertakings, strikes, etc), social security law, international employment, and any other employment-related branch of the law (tax law, criminal law, privacy, unfair competition of former employees, intellectual property, etc).

In order to support its activities in its major field of interest, the firm also conducts a general business law practice, as well as a criminal law practice, focused on social criminal law.

Although the firm has a strong academic background, its main purpose is to provide its clients with concrete solutions, based on a thorough knowledge of a client's business and needs and a no-nonsense approach. TVH lawyers are strongly committed to providing clients with workable and clear solutions without entering into legal details if these are not relevant for business people. If necessary, clients' interests are strongly defended before all possible courts.

The firm as a whole is strongly committed to a cost-effective approach, thus aiming at giving more value for money. As a result, the firm has succeeded in keeping its fees substantially below market average.

TVH serves all kinds of business clients, including both global and local companies. In order to serve its internationally orientated clients, the firm has established an informal network of correspondents in a number of European countries, thus avoiding the additional costs of setting up a formal organisation, while having recourse to specialised services abroad. However, due to its frequent involvement in cases related to cross-border employment between Belgium and its neighbouring countries, the firm has set up formal links with like-minded firms in France (Pierre-Phillippe Franc in Paris) and the Netherlands (Houben Advocaten in Breda).

AFSCHRIFT

AVENUE LOUISE 208
1050 BRUSSELS

Telephone: +32 2 646 46 36
Fax: +32 2 644 38 00
E-mail: avocats@afschrift.com
Website: www.afschrift.com

Languages
Croatian, Dutch, English, French, German, Hebrew, Italian, Slovenian, Spanish

Other offices
Geneva, Madrid

Number of lawyers 20

Member
TELFA (Trans European Law Firms Alliance)

CATEGORIES OF WORK

Income tax
Muriel Igalson, Filip Goddevriendt

Corporate tax
Pascale Hautfenne, Natacha Auvertin

Tax restructuring
Martin Van Beirs, Sophie Vanhaelst

International taxation
Thierry Afschrift, Pascale Hautfenne

Gifts and estate
Sylvie Leyder,
Valérie-Anne de Brauwere

Real estate taxation
Sophie Vanhaelst, Muriel Igalson

VAT
Anne Rayet, Inès Wouters

Tax litigation
Anne Rayet, Sylvie Leyder

White-collar crime
Thierry Afschrift, Sabrina Scarna

ALLEN & OVERY LLP

AVENUE DE TERVUEREN 268 A
1150 BRUSSELS

Telephone: +32 2 780 22 22
Fax: +32 2 780 22 44
E-mail: info.belgium@allenovery.com
Website: www.allenovery.com

Languages
Dutch, English, French, German, Italian, Spanish, Russian

Other offices
Amsterdam, Antwerp, Bangkok, Beijing, Bratislava, Brussels, Budapest, Dubai, Frankfurt, Hamburg, Hong Kong, London, Luxembourg, Madrid, Milan, Moscow, New York, Paris, Prague, Rome, Shanghai, Singapore, Tirana, Tokyo, Turin, Warsaw

Number of lawyers 2,304
at this office 97

Contact
Wim Dejonghe

CATEGORIES OF WORK

Aviation
Werner Eyskens

Banking and finance
Peter Bienenstock

Capital markets
Dirk Meeus, Peter Bienenstock

Corporate and M&A
Dirk Meeus, Pierre-Olivier Mahieu

Employment, pensions and incentives
Pieter De Koster

Environment and planning
Gauthier van Thuyne

EU and competition law
Michael J Reynolds, Direk Arts

Insolvency and restructuring
Koen Van den Broeck, Werner Eyskens

Intellectual property
Geert Glas

IT, internet and telecoms
Geert Glas

Litigation and ADR
Joost Everaert, Koen Van den Broeck

Media and entertainment
Geert Glas

Real estate
Bruno de Duve, Daniel Gillet

Public and administrative
Véronique Vanden Acker

State aids
Michel Struys

Taxation
Bruno de Duve, Patrick Smet

Trade law and antidumping
Jacques Steenbergen

Energy
Joost Everaert

ALTIUS (IN COOPERATION WITH TIBERGHIEN)

AVENUE DU PORT, 86C B414
1000 BRUSSELS

Telephone: +32 2 426 14 14
Fax: +32 2 426 20 30
Website: www.altius.com

Languages
Dutch, English, French

Number of lawyers 50

Contact
Johan De Bruycker
(johan.debruycker@altius.com)

CATEGORIES OF WORK

Commercial contracts and IT
Herman De Bauw

Banking and finance
Johan De Bruycker

Intellectual property
Paul Maeyaert

Employment law
Sylvie Dubois

Mergers and acquisitions
Philippe Jadoul,
Carine Van Regenmortel,
Alexis Goeminne

Commercial litigation
Christophe Ronse

Competition law
Carmen Verdonck

Property
Carine Van Regenmortel,
William Timmermans

ARNOLD & PORTER LLP

11 RUE DES COLONIES
KOLONIËNSTRAAT 11
1000 BRUSSELS

Telephone: +32 2 517 66 00
Fax: +32 2 517 66 03
Website: www.arnoldporter.com

Languages
Arabic, Bengali, Chinese, Ebrou, Estonian, Farsi, Filipino, French, German, Greek, Hebrew, Hindustani/Punjabi/Urdu, Hungarian, Italian, Japanese, Konkani (Indian), Latin, Marathi, Portuguese, Russian, Sesotho, Spanish, Turkish, Vietnamese

Other offices
Denver, London, Los Angeles, McLean (Virginia), New York, San Francisco, Washington DC

Number of lawyers 633
at this office 6

International groupings
The World Law Group

CATEGORIES OF WORK

Antitrust, competition and trade regulation
Marleen Van Kerckhove (Brussels), Bill Baer (DC), Tim Frazer (London)

Bankruptcy
Brian Leitch (Denver)

Corporate and commercial
Jeremy Willcocks (London), Steve Kaplan (DC)

Environmental
Thomas Milch (DC)

EU regulatory
Ian Dodds-Smith (London)

Financial institutions
Patrick Doyle (DC)

Food, drug and medical devices
Daniel Kracov (DC), Dara Corrigan (DC)
Ian Dodds-Smith (London)

Intellectual property and technology
Joel Freed (DC), David Apatoff (DC)

International arbitration
Jean Kalicki (DC)

International trade
Larry Schneider (DC)

Life sciences, biotech
Richard Johnson (DC),
Lincoln Tsang (London)

Litigation
Robert Weiner (DC)

Product liability
Ian Dodds-Smith (London)

Tax
Dick Hubbard (DC)

Telecoms/media and Internet
Michael Ryan (London),
Patrick J Grant (DC)

Real estate
Gary Humes (DC),
Lee Narrow (London)

ASHURST

AVENUE LOUISE 489
1050 BRUXELLES

Telephone: +32 2 626 19 00
Fax: +32 2 626 19 01
Website: www.ashurst.com

Languages
Dutch, English, Flemish, French, Greek, Italian, Spanish

Other offices
Dubai, Frankfurt, London, Madrid, Milan, Munich, New Delhi*, New York, Paris, Singapore, Tokyo

Number of lawyers 748
at this office 31

Contacts
Julian Ellison, Carl Meyntjens

CATEGORIES OF WORK

- EU law
- Competition, information technology, telecommunications, energy, transport, insurance and financial services
- International trade law, dumping, subsidies and origin rules
- Litigation and representation before the European Courts in Luxembourg
- Public procurement
- State aid
- Belgian law
- Cross-border M&A/MBO/LBO
- Banking/capital markets/ EASDAQ listings
- Company/commercial
- Employment

BIRD & BIRD

AVENUE D'AUDERGHEM 22-28
1040 BRUSSELS

Telephone: +32 2 282 60 00
Fax: +32 2 282 60 11
E-mail: brussels@twobirds.com
Website: www.twobirds.com

Languages
English, Dutch, French, German, Italian, Spanish

Other offices
Beijing, Düsseldorf, Frankfurt, Hong Kong, London, Madrid, Milan, Munich, Paris, Rome, Stockholm, The Hague

Number of lawyers 472
at this office 20

Contact
Paul Hermant

CATEGORIES OF WORK

- Aviation and aerospace
- Banking and financial services
- Commercial
- Communications
- Competition and EU
- Corporate
- Dispute resolution
- Employment
- Internet and e-commerce
- Information technology
- Intellectual property
- Life sciences
- Media and sport
- Mergers and acquisitions
- Public and administrative
- Real estate

BAKER & McKENZIE

AVENUE LOUISE 149
EIGHTH FLOOR
1050 BRUSSELS

Telephone: +32 2 639 36 11
Fax: +32 2 639 36 99
E-mail: baker.br@bakernet.com
Website: www.bakernet.com

Languages
Dutch, English, French, German, Greek, Italian

Other offices
The member firms of Baker & McKenzie International, a Swiss Verein, have 70 offices in 38 countries around the world. For a complete list, please visit www.bakernet.com.

Number of lawyers 3,300+
at this office 55

Contacts
Koen Vanhaerents, François Gabriel

CATEGORIES OF WORK

Banking and finance
I Maes, A De Raeve

Corporate finance
K Vanhaerents, P Leys

Dispute resolution
P Sculier

Employment
J Slootmans, F Gabriel

Intellectual property
P Sculier

International/commercial
A Gutermann

IT/communications
D Fesler, A Gutermann

Real estate, construction, environment and tourism
D Lechien

Tax
A Huyghe, P Lion

THE FIRM

Baker & McKenzie is a leading global law firm with 70 offices in 38 countries. A multinational network of over 3,300 legal professionals offers clients resources and knowledge in every area of business law in virtually every important financial and commercial centre in the world.

Baker & McKenzie has been established in Europe for over 40 years, having opened its first European offices in 1957. Since then, the European and Middle Eastern network has grown to 29 offices, giving it unparalleled geographical coverage.

The Brussels office opened in 1957. In 1998, Baker & McKenzie set up a dedicated European Law Centre in Brussels, which serves as the firm's centre of expertise on all issues of European Union law.

In March 2002, Baker & McKenzie merged with the Antwerp-based law practice of Jan Cerfontaine, Pascal Mallien and Koen De Winter.

Baker & McKenzie aims to provide clients with practical solutions by combining technical excellence with a creative and results-oriented approach.

AREAS OF PRACTICE

Baker & McKenzie co-ordinates its core practice areas on local, regional and global levels, giving most of its lawyers experience in more than one jurisdiction, as well as providing multinational teams of specialists.

Utilising a global practice group structure and ground-breaking technology coupled with a personal, detailed understanding of a client's specific business, Baker & McKenzie is able to organise its extensive resources to provide focused and strategic counsel to clients.

Baker & McKenzie in Brussels has advised on the structuring of transactions and the conduct of business in conformity with both local and European Community law, in a broad range of practice areas, including corporate and commercial; banking and finance; securities and capital markets transactions; international taxation; pensions and executive compensation; commercial litigation and arbitration; mergers and acquisitions; real estate; environmental law; intellectual property and information technology; and employment law.

Baker & McKenzie International is a Swiss Verein with member law firms around the world.

BAKER & McKENZIE
EUROPEAN LAW CENTRE

AVENUE LOUISE 149
EIGHTH FLOOR
1050 BRUSSELS

Telephone: +32 2 639 36 11
Fax: +32 2 639 36 99
Website: www.bakernet.com

Languages
Dutch, English, French, German, Italian

Other offices
The member firms of Baker & McKenzie International, a Swiss Verein, have 70 offices in 38 countries around the world. For a complete list, please visit www.bakernet.com.

Number of lawyers 3,300+
at this office 7

Contacts
Fiona Carlin, Thomas Lampert

CATEGORIES OF WORK

European cartels and transatlantic investigations
F Carlin, Th Lampert, K Haegeman

European merger control and co-ordination of multinational merger control
Th Lampert, N Niejahr, F Carlin

General European competition law (distribution systems, licensing, other corporation agreements and competition law compliance)
F Carlin, Th Lampert, J Haans, K Haegeman

Internal market
N Niejahr, F Carlin

Public procurement
N Niejahr

State aids
N Niejahr, K Haegeman

Telecommunications, energy and regulated industries
F Carlin, Th Lampert

THE FIRM

Baker & McKenzie is a leading global law firm with 70 offices in 38 countries. A multinational network of over 3,300 legal professionals offers clients resources and knowledge in every area of business law in virtually every important financial and commercial centre in the world.

Baker & McKenzie has been established in Europe for over 40 years, having opened its first European offices in 1957. Since then, the European and Middle Eastern network has grown to 29 offices, giving it unparalleled geographical coverage.

The Brussels office opened in 1957. In 1998, Baker & McKenzie set up a dedicated European Law Centre (ELC) in Brussels, which serves as the firm's centre of expertise on all issues of European Union law.

In March 2002, Baker & McKenzie merged with the Antwerp-based law practice of Jan Cerfontaine, Pascal Malien and Koen De Winter.

The firm aims to provide clients with practical solutions by combining technical excellence with a creative and results-oriented approach.

The European Law Centre brings together lawyers from different legal and linguistic backgrounds (EU) who specialise in EU law and policy, whilst being fully integrated within Baker & McKenzie's global and European network. Among its leading lawyers, the ELC counts: Fiona Carlin (managing partner of the European Law Centre with over 15 years' experience in Brussels, chair of the Competition Law Committee and vice-president of the Board of Amcham EU); and Dr Thomas Lampert (partner and specialist in EU and German competition law).

Baker & McKenzie International is a Swiss Verein with member law firms around the world.

AREAS OF PRACTICE

Baker & McKenzie co-ordinates its core practice areas on local, regional and global levels, enabling it to provide clients with a multinational team of specialists where appropriate. The European Law Centre (ELC) is the focal point of Baker & McKenzie's European Competition Law Practice Group, comprising 130 lawyers.

As such, the European Law Centre regularly provides advice on the competition law implications of mergers, joint ventures and other complex transactions. When transactions are required to be notified to national regulators, the office co-ordinates such notifications, in unison with members of the firm's global antitrust group, which is present in every major antitrust centre around the world.

The European Law Centre is also regularly engaged in cartel work dealing with both the European Commission and national competition authorities. It regularly prepares tailored competition compliance programmes for its clients and offers targeted competition audits. It is also active in the European Commission's sectoral investigations into the energy and insurance sectors.

The European Law Centre has extensive experience in advising clients, including governments, on EU state aid matters, such as the implications of being recipients of state subsidies, preferential tax treatment and other forms of state aid, and also helps clients who are at a competitive disadvantage in comparison to their competitors who have received state aid.

The European Law Centre frequently monitors and advises on other areas of EU legislation, such as internal market issues, telecommunications and e-commerce law, environmental and energy law, the public procurement rules, and constitutional matters and legislative procedures.

BEACHCROFT WANSBROUGHS

CHAUSSÉE DE WATERLOO 412F
1050 BRUSSELS

Telephone: +32 2 541 85 80
Fax: +32 2 541 85 85
E-mail: info@bwlaw.co.uk
Website: www.bwlaw.co.uk

Languages
Dutch, English, French, German, Italian, Spanish

Other offices
Birmingham, Bristol, Leeds, London, Manchester, Winchester

Number of lawyers 816

Contact
Julie Nazerali (resident partner)

CATEGORIES OF WORK

Commercial
Simon Hodson

Litigation
Trevor Chamberlain,

Beachroft Wansbroughs Consulting
Richard Hobbs

Construction
John Vasey

Commercial property
Michael Bothamley

Corporate services
Laurence Markham

Employment
Elizabeth Adams

Financial services
Nigel Frudd

Health
Nigel Montgomery

Injury risk
Tania Sless

Mutual law
Peter Lindsay

Professional risk
Richard Beaty

Projects/PFI
Malcolm Austwick

Public law
Julian Gizzi

Risk counsel
Tony Cherry

Technology, media and telecommunications
Nick Holland

THE FIRM

Beachcroft Wansbroughs is a leading commercial UK law firm with 1,374 employees led by 144 partners, many of whom are recognised as leading experts in their field. Operating across seven offices in the UK and one in Brussels, the firm's lawyers deliver national and international expertise at a local level.

The firm was nominated for Law Firm of the Year at the 2005 *Legal Business* Awards, where it was described as 'fast becoming a major force in commercial, health, projects and insurance sectors'.

Its lawyers take considerable care to understand their clients, their strategic objectives and the environment in which they operate. As a result they have a solid reputation as trusted business advisers who deliver pragmatic and timely legal advice.

Teams work in a proactive way aimed at anticipating and preventing problems before they become major issues, and work with clients to find solutions through mediation rather than litigation; or to minimise impact where litigation is unavoidable.

AREAS OF PRACTICE

The firm is increasingly receiving instructions from global and overseas organisations to deal with their UK, EU and cross-border legal requirements. International organisations utilise Beachcroft Wansbroughs for the full breadth of their services, and in particular:

Competition, EU and regulatory: the Brussels office advises public and private clients in a variety of industry sectors. It has specialist expertise in delivering a range of competition advice from obtaining cross-jurisdictional competition clearance, to advising on behavioural aspects of competition, dominance, pricing, cartel leniency, distribution agreements, technology transfer, proceedings before the European Commission and the Courts, devising and tailoring competition compliance programmes and training throughout EMEA and public procurement. Combining their experience with specialists throughout the firm's UK offices, the team provides a full EU legal service in areas as diverse as free movement, data protection, intellectual property, financial services, telecommunications, lobbying the EU institutions and employment.

Corporate: the corporate team is experienced in dealing with complex cross-border transactions which involve multiple and diverse jurisdictions. It advises on acquisitions and disposals; AIM flotations; banking and finance; capital restructuring; equity and debt funding; insolvency; joint ventures; mergers; management buy-outs; VAT planning; tax and trusts and is supported by UK and Brussels based European law and competition experts.

Financial services: the financial services division is a unique alliance of lawyers, regulatory consultants and international experts with experience covering UK and international financial services. Clients include businesses and individuals regulated by the FSA, international businesses requiring FSA approval and foreign government agencies requiring enforcement support programmes. The firm also advises on change of control, design and regulation of new collective investment schemes and passporting between EU regulatory authorities, approved persons and the prevention of financial crime and terrorist financing.

Technology, media and telecoms: much of the TMT team's work is of an international nature acting for large US and European multinationals in various transactions around EMEA, and advising on issues such as outsourcing transactions, global data protection and cross-border commercial contracts and corporate governance issues. Most of the team are ex in-house lawyers and/or dual qualified in many EU countries.

Counselex: through Beachcroft Wansbroughs, clients have access to Counselex, a global network of law firms who have cross-border experience across a broad spectrum of legal services of special significance in the global business arena. A number of the firms are award winning in their jurisdiction and internationally.

BREDIN PRAT

118 AVENUE DE CORTENBERGH
1000 BRUXELLES

Telephone: +32 2 639 27 10
Fax: +32 2 646 03 11

Languages
Dutch, English, French

Other offices
Paris

Number of lawyers 80
at this office 4

CATEGORIES OF WORK	
General EU law	**European litigation**
EC competition	**State aid**
Merger control	

THE FIRM

Bredin Prat is a Paris-based law firm specialised in business law and in particular high-level mergers and acquisitions (including major French privatisations) and litigation. The Paris office has acquired a widely recognised expertise in the field of domestic and EU competition law with its highly respected partners Robert Saint-Esteben and Hugues Calvet.

The Brussels Office was founded in 1999. In 2003, Marc Pittie became the Brussels-based partner in charge of the office, heading a team of four EU specialised lawyers, members of the Paris or the Brussels Bar.

Through previous experience in private practice and as a clerk at the Court of First Instance in Luxembourg, Marc Pittie has wide experience of international transactions as well as behavioural cases before the European Commission and the European courts. The Brussels office has also developed an in-depth understanding of the internal politics of the Commission and good working relationships with its officials, as well as a strong insight of litigation in front of the European Community courts.

The Brussels practice is fully integrated within the Paris office's competition law practice group with a total number of 11 lawyers dedicated to EU and national competition.

AREAS OF PRACTICE

The firm advises on all aspects of competition law including merger control, abuse of a dominant position, cartels, state aids, regulatory matters and commercial transactions, both at a counselling and litigation stage. Its Brussels-based lawyers are able to give advice and opinions on EU, French and/or Belgian law in French, English and Dutch, and appear in front of European as well as national jurisdictions.

Having been involved in many major cases involving both French and multinational companies, the firm has gained special expertise in complex and highly sensitive transactions and litigation cases.

The Brussels office has acquired specific experience in the fields of telecoms, the entertainment industry, banking facilities and also various industrial sectors.

Through the Paris office, the firm is able to offer a full range of services, advising on M&A and corporate as well as tax aspects. Relying on its 'Best-Friends' network, Bredin Prat also offers assistance on an international basis, especially as regards international antitrust filings and clearances in the context of multi-jurisdictional transactions and multi-jurisdictional cartel investigations.

CMS DEBACKER

CHAUSSÉE DE LA HULPE 178
1170 BRUSSELS

Telephone: +32 2 743 69 00
Fax: +32 2 743 69 01
E-mail: info@cms-db.com
Website: www.cms-db.com

Languages
Dutch, English, French, German, Italian, Spanish

Number of lawyers 50
at this office 44

Contact
Stanislas van Wassenhove

Other CMS alliance member firms
CMS Adonnino Ascoli & Cavasola Scamoni, Italy; CMS Albiñana & Suárez de Lezo, Spain; CMS Bureau Francis Lefebvre, France; CMS Cameron McKenna, UK; CMS Derks Star Busmann, Netherlands; CMS von Erlach Henrici, Switzerland; CMS Hasche Sigle, Germany; CMS Reich-Rohrwig Hainz, Austria

CATEGORIES OF WORK

Corporate law, mergers and acquisitions

Banking, securities and finance

Bankruptcy and insolvency

Commercial law, distribution, IP and IT

Litigation and dispute resolution

Employment and pensions

Real estate, construction and town planning

Tax

European law, competition, state aids

Environment

Public and administrative law, public procurements, public utilities, public/private partnerships, energy, telecoms, health and hospitals

CMS EU LAW OFFICE

AVENUE LOUISE 200
1050 BRUXELLES

Telephone: +32 2 650 04 20
Fax: +32 2 650 04 22
E-mail: eulawoffice@cmslegal.com
Website: www.cmslegal.com

Languages
English, French, German, Dutch, Italian

Other CMS alliance offices advising on EU law
Aberdeen, Düsseldorf, Frankfurt, Hamburg, London, Lyon, Madrid, Milan, Munich, Paris, Rome, Stuttgart, Vienna, Utrecht, Zurich

Number of lawyers 2,000+
at this office 8

Other CMS alliance members
CMS Adonnino Ascoli & Cavasola Scamoni (Italy); CMS Albiñana & Suárez de Lezo (Spain); CMS Bureau Francis Lefebvre (France); CMS Cameron McKenna (UK); CMS DeBacker (Belgium); CMS Derks Star Busmann (Netherlands); CMS von Erlach Henrici (Switzerland); CMS Hasche Sigle (Germany); CMS Reich-Rohrwig Hainz (Austria).

Contacts Michael Bauer, Robert Bosman

CATEGORIES OF WORK

Competition and antitrust

Merger control

State aid

Anti-dumping and subsidies

WTO regulation

EU customs law

Free movement of goods and services

Distribution and franchising

EU litigation

Lobbying of EU institutions

CLAEYS & ENGELS, member of ius laboris

BOULEVARD DU SOUVERAIN 280
1160 BRUSSELS

Telephone: +32 2 761 46 00
Fax: +32 2 761 47 00
E-mail: info@claeysengels.be
Website: www.claeysengels.be

Languages
Dutch, English, French, German

Other offices
Antwerp, Ghent, Kortrijk, Liège

Number of lawyers 60
at this office 35

Contacts
Thierry Claeys, Chris Engels, Pieter Smedts, Eric Carlier, Olivier Debray, Lutgarde Sommerijns, Luc Bihain, Jean-Paul Lacomble, Henri-François Lenaerts, Bart Adriaens, Ann Witters, An Van Damme, Bart Vanschoebeke, Jan Van Gysegem, Patrick Maerten, Inge Lamberts

Member
ius laboris, International Employment Law, Pensions and Employee Benefits Alliance

CATEGORIES OF WORK

Labour law (including traditional labour law, collective labour relations, European labour law, criminal aspects of labour law, restructuring and transfer of undertakings)

Social security

Supplementary pensions

Human resources fiscal matters

Compensation and benefits

Company law

THE FIRM

Claeys & Engels is a specialist law firm offering a full range of legal services in all areas concerning human resources and personnel policy. Each subject is dealt with by a specialist team of lawyers experienced both in providing advice and litigation. In addition the firm's lawyers draft and implement with the client, internal policies and codes of conduct that dovetail with the human resources policy of the client. The firm is the first specialist office with a full service to both national and international clients on all aspects of human capital.

In view of the growing internationalisation of the economy, Claeys & Engels is actively participating in a specialist international network known as ius laboris, International Employment Law, Pensions and Employee Benefits Alliance. This co-operative resource association was formed in January 2001, with its registered office in Brussels and counts over 1,200 lawyers in more than 70 cities.

AREAS OF PRACTICE

The office deals with all aspects of labour law: individual dismissals, company work rules, organisation of working hours, safety at work, temporary work, cross-border employment and international secondment, wages and related aspects. It also helps clients in matters of collective labour law. It advises on the rules governing the operation of the employee representative bodies within the undertaking, trade union delegations and the European Works Council. It also offers advice and assistance in negotiating and drafting company-level collective bargaining agreements, and similarly protects clients' interests in legal proceedings arising from employee representative elections.

Claeys & Engels is active in criminal aspects of labour law and in labour enforcement law (this particularly concerns administrative fines that may be imposed for labour law offences).

The firm offers advice on and assistance with collective or individual negotiations in connection with restructuring, transfers of undertakings as a result of mergers, demergers or acquisitions, and outsourcing.

A number of lawyers specialise in the various branches of social security (especially social security legislation, health and disability insurance, etc). These issues are also handled in an international context. The pensions team has in-depth knowledge of all legal aspects of supplementary pensions and years of experience guarantee a multidisciplinary and thorough approach.

Claeys & Engels also includes a team of lawyers specialised in all tax matters related to human resources. The approach takes into account both the individual aspects and those related to the undertaking as a whole, while fully integrating all the incidences concerning employment law, social security and complementary pensions.

The firm has first-hand experience in offering legal advice integrated with human resources through helping set up or reorganise undertakings. The firm expertly intervenes in the setting up of new labour force membership, the integration of pension schemes, healthcare and other cafeteria schemes and in the establishment of new remuneration policies or cost reimbursements.

Claeys & Engels equally possesses specific experience in the setting up of procedures and management systems for executives and expatriated directors or recipients of salary splits or other forms of remuneration within an international context.

Company law is an essential instrument in the organisation and functioning of a business. The firm has broad skills to offer its clients in this field, especially on the following points: the functioning of the board of directors, corporate governance, management buy-ins, option plans for shares and warrants – the status of directors, the process of company management, shareholder agreements, the holding of general assemblies. It assists its clients in more specialised topics, such as conflicts between shareholders or questions of public or criminal liability.

CLEARY GOTTLIEB STEEN & HAMILTON LLP

RUE DE LA LOI 57
1040 BRUSSELS

Telephone: +32 2 287 20 00
Fax: +32 2 231 16 61
Website: www.clearygottlieb.com

Languages
Bulgarian, Danish, Dutch, English, Finnish, French, Gaelic, German, Italian, Norwegian, Portuguese, Russian, Spanish, Swedish

Other offices
Cologne, Frankfurt, Hong Kong, London, Milan, Moscow, New York, Paris, Rome, Tokyo, Washington DC

Number of lawyers 847
at this office 64

CATEGORIES OF WORK

Banking, finance and capital markets

Commercial/corporate

EU and competition law

EU litigation and arbitration

EU regulatory

Information technology

Intellectual property

Media and entertainment

Merger control

Mergers and acquisitions

State aid

Trade

CROSBY & CO
LAW FIRM

188A AVENUE DE TERVUREN
1150 BRUSSELS

Telephone: +32 2 233 37 47
Fax: +32 2 233 37 40
E-mail: mail@crosbyandco.be
Website: www.crosbyandco.be

Languages
Dutch, English, French, German, Italian, Portuguese, Spanish

Number of lawyers 6

Contacts
Scott Crosby (head of firm),
Richard Lang (associate),
Andreas Schoepgens (associate),
Silvia Santoro (associate),
Jane Golding (of counsel),
Conor Maguire (of counsel)

CATEGORIES OF WORK

All aspects of European law, including contentious matters before the Courts of the European Communities in Luxembourg, the Court of Human Rights in Strasbourg and the Belgian courts

COVINGTON & BURLING

KUNSTLAAN 44, AVENUE DES ARTS
1040 BRUSSELS

Telephone: +32 2 549 52 30
Fax: +32 2 502 15 98
Website: www.cov.com

Languages
Dutch, English, French, German, Hungarian, Italian, Polish, Portuguese, Russian, Spanish

Other offices
London, New York, San Francisco, Washington DC

Number of lawyers 550+
at this office 20

International groupings
Please see www.cov.com for firm affiliations

CATEGORIES OF WORK

Anti-dumping and anti-subsidy
Georg Berrisch

Belgian litigation
Alain Strowel, Genevieve Micheaux

Competition
David Hull, Georg Berrisch

Corporate and commercial
Henriette Tielemans, Genevieve Micheaux

Data protection
Henriette Tielemans

Distribution and franchising
Henriette Tielemans, David Hull

E-commerce and internet
David Harfst

Export controls and sanctions
Georg Berrisch

Life sciences
Peter Bogaert

Intellectual property
Alain Strowel

Legislative
David Harfst, Georg Berrisch

EU litigation
Georg Berrisch

Merger control
David Hull

Public procurement
Georg Berrisch

State aid
Georg Berrisch

Telecommunication and broadcasting
David Harfst, Alain Strowel

WTO trade policy and customs
David Harfst, Georg Berrisch

WTO dispute settlement
Georg Berrisch, David Harfst

THE FIRM

Covington & Burling, founded in 1919, is an international firm of over 550 lawyers with offices in Washington DC, New York, San Francisco, London and Brussels. The Brussels office, founded in 1989, is active in a wide area of EU and domestic law and policy issues.

AREAS OF PRACTICES

The firm advises on all aspects of competition law including merger control, abuse of a dominant position, cartels, and commercial transactions. Lawyers also have particular expertise in dealing with issues at the intersection of competition law and IP law, joint ventures (including B2B ventures), trade association matters, and the structuring of pan-European distribution and licensing agreements. The firm has in-depth experience in a range of industries, including pharmaceuticals, biotechnology, software, telecommunications, motor vehicles, and construction equipment. It routinely handles transatlantic competition matters with antitrust lawyers in its US offices.

Covington & Burling has a diverse international trade practice encompassing trade policy, WTO dispute resolution, import/export controls, customs, anti-dumping, trade facilitation, and subsidy matters, among other areas. The firm advises both private industry and governments, and regularly represents the Council of Ministers in anti-dumping cases before the European Courts. Its particular strength and expertise lies in advising clients on transatlantic trade disputes, and its Brussels trade practice is fully integrated with the Washington and London offices. The trade practice is led by Stuart Eizenstat, former US ambassador to the EU.

The life sciences practice covers pharmaceuticals and biotechnology, cell and tissue products, devices, novel and functional foods, animal feeds, chemicals, biocides, and electronic goods, amongst others. It includes regulatory strategies, advice under community and national rules, regulatory exclusivity, borderline issues, safety and environmental reviews, approvals, clinical trials, promotion, internet activities, data privacy, and policy and legislative work. The European life sciences practice is fully integrated between the Brussels and London offices and together with the firm's leading US practice, provides a leading service to life sciences clients.

The Brussels office has deep expertise in IP, acting for major clients in copyright and trade mark litigation. It handles litigation directly in Belgium and co-ordinates it in other European countries. The practice has extensive legislative experience in IP policy matters, including with the European Commission and EU Member States. The firm also has a sophisticated licensing practice, notably in the field of technology. The IP team works closely with lawyers from the London office, and clients include companies from the software, media, biotechnology and pharmaceutical sectors.

The IT team assists leading companies and trade associations on a broad range of issues, including electronic contracts, security and encryption, illegal internet content, internet advertising and promotion, digital copyright, jurisdiction over internet transactions, codes of conduct, data protection in relation to e-commerce, cyber crime, and the regulation of 'cookies' and 'spam'. Working closely with offices in London, Washington, New York and San Fransisco, and where appropriate with local counsel, the firm provides integrated multi-regional advice to companies doing business worldwide via the internet and on-line services.

The firm has extensive experience handling issues related to the EU Data Protection Directive and the EU Electronic Communications Data Protection Directive. It has assisted clients with privacy audits and provided pan-European advice on compliance with national requirements, including rules governing notification, on-line privacy, direct marketing, human resources, and health privacy. The firm has assisted clients with transborder data flow issues, including drafting global codes of conduct and intra-company agreements, and advising on the 'Safe Harbour' regime for data transferred to the US. Clients include technology and pharmaceutical companies, trade associations, companies with significant internet website issues, and telecommunications providers.

CROWELL & MORING

RUE ROYALE 71
1000 BRUSSELS

Telephone: +32 2 282 40 82
Fax: +32 2 230 63 99
E-mail: egybels@crowell.com
rmaclean@crowell.com
Website: www crowell.com

Languages
Dutch, English, French, German, Mandarin, Serbian, Spanish, Swedish

Other offices
Irvine (California), London, Washington DC

Number of lawyers 306
at this office 17

Contacts
Emmanuel Gybels, Robert MacLean

CATEGORIES OF WORK

EU competition law
Werner Berg, Thomas De Meese

Litigation
Emmanuel Gybels

Commercial law
Emmanuel Gybels

Intellectual property
Kristof Roox

WTO law
Robert MacLean

EU anti-dumping and customs
Robert MacLean

EU litigation
Werner Berg, Robert MacLean

Telecommunications law
Thomas De Meese

International arbitration
Emmanuel Gybels

EU regulatory law
Thomas De Meese, Werner Berg

CRUYPLANTS ELOY WAGEMANS & PARTNERS

RUE DEFACQZ 78
1060 BRUSSELS

Telephone: +32 2 534 20 20
Fax: +32 2 534 30 18
E-mail: info@cew-law.be
Website: www.cew-law.be

Languages
Dutch, English, French, German, Italian

Number of lawyers 26

Member
Interlex; Jurismundi

CATEGORIES OF WORK

Arbitration

Banking and finance

Commercial law and litigation

Competition law and European law

Contracts

Copyright and media

Corporate law

Disciplinary law

Distribution law

Health law

Insolvency

Insurance and liability

Intellectual property rights

Labour law

Mediation

Mergers and acquisitions

Non-profit organisations and foundations

Real estate

Sports law

Tax law and litigation

Trade practices

White-collar crime

DLA PIPER RUDNICK GRAY CARY

106 AVENUE LOUISE
1050 BRUSSELS

Telephone: +32 2 500 15 00
Fax: +32 2 500 16 00
E-mail: yves.tavernier@dlapiper.com
Website: www.dlapiper.be

Languages
Italian, Dutch, English, French, German, Greek, Spanish, Swedish

Other offices
Austria, Belgium, Bosnia-Herzegovina, China, Croatia, Czech Republic, Denmark*, Egypt*, France, Georgia, Germany, Hong Kong, Hungary, Italy, Japan, Netherlands, Norway*, Poland*, Russia, Singapore*, Slovakia, South Africa*, Spain, Sweden*, Thailand, UK, Ukraine, United Arab Emirates, US

Number of lawyers 3,100
at this office 100

Contacts
Steven De Keyser (Managing Director – Continental Europe), Yves Tavernier (Managing Partner Belgium)

CATEGORIES OF WORK

Banking and finance
Yves Brosens

Business support and restructuring
Christian Van Buggenhout

Commercial and projects
Koen De Maeyer, Francis Goffin, Herman Lemaire

Corporate, mergers and acquisitions, private equity
Dirk Caestecker, Jean-Michel Detry

Environmental and administrative
Bob Martens

EU and competition
David Cox, Bertold Bär-Bouyssière, Jean Naslin

Labour law
Eddy Lievens

Litigation and arbitration
Andre Faurès

Public-private partnership
Bob Martens, Koen De Maeyer

Real estate
Els Empereur, Dirk Caestecker

Supreme Court litigation
Pierre Van Ommeslaghe

Tax law
Marc De Munter

Technology, media and communications (IT/IP and outsourcing)
Louis Puts, Patrick Van Eecke, Kristof De Vulder

Trade, anti-dumping and WTO
Prof Geert Van Calster

Transport and logistics
Koen De Maeyer

THE FIRM

DLA Piper Rudnick Gray Cary is a leading global legal services provider with approximately 3,100 lawyers in 58 offices across 22 countries. The organisation is committed to building long-term relationships with its clients and supports their strategic and operational needs both locally and internationally.

DLA Piper is a founding member of an exclusive alliance of full-service legal organisations with a shared vision. DLA Piper Group, established in 1999, has members across Europe, Africa, the Middle East, Asia, and the US, which deliver expert local know-how and integrated international solutions.

AREAS OF PRACTICE

DLA Piper Rudnick Gray Cary invests in its clients to understand what their needs really are and how value can be added to their business. Lawyers of DLA Piper Rudnick Gray Cary differentiate themselves by their speed of response and their desire to put the client first. A team typically consists of lawyers able to really understand and empathise with clients' commercial needs, both locally and on a broader international level.

DLA Piper Rudnick Gray Cary's lawyers specialise in all aspects of business law and regularly transact on a cross-border basis. The firm is organised to provide a range of essential business advice aimed at meeting clients' day-to-day legal requirements, not just on international mergers and acquisitions and banking, but also on people and employment, commercial dealings, litigation, insurance, marine, aviation and plans for restructuring and expansion, as well as administrative and environmental matters, real estate, competition, outsourcing, public-private partnerships, tax, information technology and intellectual property.

DE WOLF & PARTNERS

ELITE HOUSE
SQUARE DU BASTION 1A
PORTE DE NAMUR
1050 BRUSSELS

Telephone: +32 2 289 64 64
Fax: +32 2 503 48 58
E-mail: avocats@dewolf-law.be
Website: www.dewolf-law.be
www.businessandlaw.be

Languages
Dutch, English, French, German, Italian, Swedish Spanish

Number of lawyers 34

Contact
Patrick De Wolf

Member
Osborne Clarke Alliance

CATEGORIES OF WORK

Commercial
Luc Stalars, Stefan Deswert

Company
Patrick De Wolf, Frank Weinand

Tax
Olivier Bertin

Labour
Francois Lagasse, Thierry Vierin

Property and construction
Gilles Carnoy

Information technology
Jean-Paul Triaille

Arbitration
Patrick De Wolf

Intellectual property
Jean-Paul Triaille, Gaëtane Schmitz

DECHERT LLP

480 AVENUE LOUISE
1050 BRUSSELS

Telephone: +32 2 535 54 11
Fax: +32 2 535 54 00
E-mail: richard.temko@dechert.com
Website: www.dechert.com

Languages
Dutch, English, French, German, Italian

Other offices
Austin, Boston, Charlotte, Frankfurt, Harrisburg, Hartford, London, Luxembourg, Munich, Newport Beach, New York, Palo Alto, Paris, Philadelphia, Princeton, San Francisco, Washington DC

Number of lawyers 900+
at this office 17

Contacts
Richard Temko (managing partner),
Isabelle Rahman (EU law) (isabelle.rahman@dechert.com),
René H Gonne (corporate and securities, corporate finance, M&A, energy law) (rene.gonne@dechert.com),
Eric Deltour (corporate, M&A, joint ventures, private equity) (eric.deltour@dechert.com)

CATEGORIES OF WORK

Aviation

Mergers and acquisitions

Company law

Private equity

Banking and finance

Real estate

Bankruptcy

Structured finance

Commercial law

Taxation

Employment law

Venture capital

Energy law

EC competition law

Intellectual property

Telecommunications

Joint ventures

Financial services

Leasing

State aids

Litigation and arbitration

ELEGIS – BUYLE DIERYCK MAINGAIN

RUE AUGUSTE DE BOECK 54
1140 BRUXELLES

Telephone: +32 2 240 15 20
Fax: +32 2 240 15 30
E-mail: bdm@elegis.be
Website: www.elegis.be

Languages
Dutch, English, French, German

Other offices
Antwerp, Eupen, Liege, Namur

Number of lawyers 107
at this office 36

Member
AIJA; AEDBF; Euro Franchise Lawyers; IBA; ICC; UIA

CATEGORIES OF WORK

Commercial litigation
André Lombart, Daniel De Jaeger

Corporate
Jean Pierre Renard

Banking and finance
Jean-Pierre Buyle, Christophe Steyaert

Labour law
Bernard Maingain

Competition, antitrust
Christophe Steyaert

Intellectual property
Daniel De Jaeger

Contracts
Philippe Colle

Real estate and construction
Françoise Balon

Distribution and franchising
André Lombart, Daniel De Jaeger

Computer law
Christophe Steyaert

Tax
Marc Marlière

Mergers and acquisitions
Jean Pierre Renard, Bernard Maingain

Bankruptcy and insolvency
Jean Pierre Renard, Philippe Colle

Financial criminal law
Jean-Pierre Buyle, Jean Pierre Renard

Insurance law
Philippe Colle

Patrimony rights
Françoise Balon

EUBELIUS

GOEDHEIDSSTRAAT 5-7
RUE DE LA BONTÉ
1000 BRUSSELS

Telephone: +32 2 543 31 00
Fax: +32 2 543 31 01
E-mail: brussels@eubelius.com
Website: www.eubelius.com

Languages
Dutch, English, French, German

Other offices
Antwerp, Kortrijk

Number of lawyers 92
at this office 73

Contact
Koen Geens (partner)

CATEGORIES OF WORK

Corporate and securities law; mergers and acquisitions; capital markets

Taxation

Litigation, liability and insurance

Insolvency and creditors' rights

Regulated sectors and privatisation (telecommunications, postal services, broadcasting and public transport)

IT and e-commerce

Business and finance

Competition and EU law

Succession planning and family businesses

Real estate

Environmental and administrative law

White-collar crime and human rights

GIDE LOYRETTE NOUEL

VIEW BUILDING
RUE DE L'INDUSTRIE, 26-38
1040 BRUSSELS

Telephone: +32 2 231 11 40
Fax: +32 2 231 11 77
E-mail: gln.brussels@gide.com
Website: www.gide.com

Other offices
Algiers, Beijing, Belgrade, Bucharest, Budapest, Casablanca, Hanoi, Istanbul, London, Moscow, New York, Paris, Prague, Riyadh, Shanghai, Tunis, Warsaw

Number of lawyers 586
at this office 15

Contacts
Antoine Gosset-Grainville (gossetgrainville@gide.com),
Olivier Prost (prost@gide.com)

CATEGORIES OF WORK

EU and competition

International trade

Anti-dumping and countervailing duty proceedings

GATT/WTO regulations

Agriculture and food processing industry law

Customs law

Free movement of individuals, capital, goods and services

Distribution and franchising

Litigation

Information technology

Telecommunications

E-commerce and the Internet

Public procurement

GLEISS LUTZ
RECHTSANWÄLTE

RUE GUIMARD 7
1040 BRUSSELS

Telephone: +32 2 551 10 20
Fax: +32 2 512 15 68
E-mail: info@gleisslutz.com
Website: www.gleisslutz.com

Languages
Dutch, German, English, French, Italian, Mandarin, Cantonese, Polish, Portuguese, Spanish, Russian, Czech, Slovak

Other offices
Berlin, Frankfurt, Munich, Stuttgart, Prague, Warsaw

Number of lawyers 225
at this office 6

Contact
Dr Ulrich Soltesz

CATEGORIES OF WORK

German and international law

General EU law

Competition, antitrust

Mergers control

Anti-dumping and subsidies law

State aid

EU litigation

International trade law

German antitrust and commercial law

HAARMANN HÜGEL

9, ROND POINT SCHUMAN
PO BOX 14
1040 BRUSSELS

Telephone: +32 2 286 81 10
Fax: +32 2 286 81 18
Website: www.haarmannhuegel.com
www.hugelaw.com

Languages
English, French, German

Other offices
Vienna

Number of lawyers 32

CATEGORIES OF WORK

Antitrust law (including co-ordination of multi-jurisdiction antitrust proceedings)
Dr Rainer Roniger, Dr Astrid Ablasser, Martine Maier

Merger control law (including co-ordination of multi-jurisdiction filings)
Dr Rainer Roniger, Martina Maier, Dr Astrid Ablasser

State aid law
Martina Maier, Dr Rainer Roniger

Public procurement law
Dr Rainer Roniger, DDr Christian Schneider

Distribution
Dr Rainer Roniger, Dr Astrid Ablasser

Energy
DDr Christian Schneider, Dr Rainer Roniger

Transport
Martina Maier, DDr Christian Schneider

EC litigation
Martina Maier, Dr Rainer Roniger

General EU law
Martina Maier, Dr Rainer Roniger, Dr Meinhard Novak

HANOTIAU & VAN DEN BERG

AVENUE LOUISE 480/9
1050 BRUSSELS

Telephone: +32 2 290 39 00
Fax: +32 2 290 39 39
E-mail: info@hvdb.com
Website: www.hvdb.com

Languages
Dutch, English, French, German, Portuguese

Other offices
Paris

Number of lawyers 17

CATEGORIES OF WORK

International arbitration and litigation, including:

Competition

Construction and engineering

Corporate

Distribution and franchising

Energy and natural resources

Banking and finance

Information and communication technology

Intellectual property

Joint ventures, consortia and co-operation

Sales and purchasing

Transport and air law

Post M&A litigation

Supreme Court work

HENGELER MUELLER

AVENUE DE CORTENBERGH 118
BOITE 2
1000 BRUXELLES

Telephone: +32 2 788 55 00
Fax: +32 2 788 55 99
E-mail: hmbrx@hengeler.com
Website: www.hengeler.com

Other offices
Düsseldorf, Frankfurt, Berlin, Munich, London

Number of lawyers 192
at this office 5

Contact
Dr Bernhard Maassen

CATEGORIES OF WORK

EU and German competition law

State aid

Merger control

Healthcare and life sciences

European regulatory affairs

HERBERT SMITH

15 RUE GUIMARD
1040 BRUXELLES

Telephone: +32 2 511 74 50
Fax: +32 2 511 77 72
E-mail: contact@herbertsmith.com
Website: www.herbertsmith.com

Languages
Dutch, English, Finnish, French, German, Italian, Spanish, Swedish

Other offices
Bangkok, Beijing, Hong Kong, London, Moscow, Paris, Shanghai, Singapore, Tokyo

Number of lawyers 1,089
at this office 9

CATEGORIES OF WORK

Competition
Craig Pouncey, Veronica Roberts

Media and telecoms
Craig Pouncey, Veronica Roberts

Customs, trade and WTO
Craig Pouncey, Lode van den Hende

Public procurement
Craig Pouncey, Adrian Brown

Intellectual property
Hanna Anttilainen

State aids
Craig Pouncey, Lode Van Den Hende

Mergers
Veronica Roberts

Regulatory
Adrian Brown

HEUKING KÜHN LÜER WOJTEK

AVENUE LOUISE 140
1050 BRUSSELS

Telephone: +32 2 646 20 00
Fax: +32 2 646 20 40
E-mail: brussels@heuking.de
Website: www.heuking.de

Languages
German, English, French, Dutch, Italian

Other offices
Berlin, Chemnitz, Cologne, Düsseldorf, Frankfurt, Hamburg, Munich

Number of lawyers 6

Contact
Gabrielle H Williamson, JD

CATEGORIES OF WORK

General EC law

Competition law and merger control

State aids

EC and WTO trade and customs law

Environmental, health and safety regulation

Energy regulation

Product regulation and liability

Telecoms, media and IT law

Transportation and postal services law

Aviation law

Intellectual property rights

Labour law and social policy

German and European M&A transactions

THE FIRM

Heuking Kühn Lüer Wojtek was founded in Düsseldorf, Germany, in 1971. Since then, the firm has spread geographically, and Heuking Kühn now has seven significant offices in Germany, as well as an office in Brussels.

The firm has an extensive international network of law firms, enabling it to provide its clients with seamless 'one-stop shopping', on international transactions and regulatory matters. Since its formation, Heuking Kühn Lüer Wojtek has specifically chosen to remain an independent law firm. It is Heuking Kühn Lüer Wojtek's philosophy that, to provide the best possible service to its clients, the firm must be able to co-operate with various other law firms which are at the top of the profession in their respective countries. This gives the firm the ability to make alternative counsel suggestions to its clients, giving the clients a choice of the best suitable law firm or lawyer in each country and for each matter. Over the last 30+ years, Heuking Kühn Lüer Wojtek has developed excellent relationships with the key firms in all of the major jurisdictions worldwide.

Heuking Kühn Lüer Wojtek is a name which is synonymous with legal competence. The firm is one of the largest commercial law firms in Germany, with more than 170 specialised lawyers and tax advisers, representing the interests of national and international clients. Included in the client list are large and medium-sized German and international companies in all areas of the manufacturing industry, as well as trade and service industries, associations, governmental and public sector organisations and private clients and trusts.

The firm prides itself on substantive legal competence and on the excellent education and continuing legal education of its lawyers. Moreover, virtually all of the lawyers are German-English bilingual.

Extensive specialisation and comprehensive knowledge of specific industry sectors provide the basis of all of Heuking Kühn Lüer Wojtek's legal counselling. Experienced partners and carefully selected associate lawyers develop innovative solutions to complex legal problems. The lawyers regularly work in their specific practice area groups and also in multi-group and multi-disciplinary teams with clients and outside consultants or advisers. Entrepreneurial thinking on behalf of firm clients, as well as efficient, quality, cost-effective and timely work and the highest personal dedication are key components of Heuking Kühn Lüer Wojtek's culture.

AREAS OF PRACTICE

Heuking Kühn Lüer Wojtek is a full-service commercial law firm. Cross-border and cross-sector knowledge in combination with a deep understanding of business reasoning enables service to clients with the broadest possible support in all their negotiations and business decisions. This applies equally to M&A transactions, to legal advice on company structure, business risk management, negotiations and negotiation tactics, training, crisis and insolvency counselling, corporate financial matters, and complex litigation and arbitration. Thanks to a variety of strong business clients, the firm has built long-term relationships with its clients and can assist them, beginning with the establishment of a business, followed by implementing business goals, including day-to-day legal work, reorganisations, acquisitions and divestitures.

Heuking Kühn Lüer Wojtek is actively involved with its clients in providing regulatory counselling in all areas of commercial law, as well as assisting them in organising and implementing their M&A transactions in Germany, throughout Europe, and internationally. Heuking Kühn Lüer Wojtek has particular expertise in German and EU company law; competition law, merger control, state aids and regulated industries (including energy; telecommunications; and transport, postal services and shipping law); taxation; employment law; finance and banking; international trade and customs; insurance; litigation, arbitration and mediation; bankruptcy and insolvency; environment, health and safety law; product liability; product-specific regulation; real estate and construction law; IP, IT and media law; and private clients and family law.

HOGAN & HARTSON LLP

VIEW BUILDING
RUE DE L'INDUSTRIE 26
1040 BRUSSELS

Telephone: +32 2 505 09 11
Fax: +32 2 505 09 96
E-mail: chatton@hhlaw.com
Website: www.hhlaw.com

Languages
English, Dutch, French, German, Italian, Russian, Spanish, Greek, Hungarian

Other offices
Baltimore, Beijing, Berlin, Boulder, Budapest, Caracas, Colorado Springs, Denver, Geneva, Hong Kong, London, Los Angeles, Miami, Moscow, Munich, New York, Northern Virginia, Paris, Shanghai, Tokyo, Warsaw, Washington DC

Number of lawyers 1,101
at this office 15

Contact
Catriona Hatton

CATEGORIES OF WORK

- **European and international competition law**
- **EU regulatory and policy issues**
- **International trade**
- **Food and agriculture**
- **Life sciences**
- **Communications**
- **Energy liberalisation**
- **Environment**
- **Data protection**
- **State aids**

HOUTHOFF BURUMA

BOULEVARD DE L'EMPEREUR 5
1000 BRUSSELS

Telephone: +32 2 507 98 00
Fax: +32 2 507 98 98
Website: www.houthoff.com

Languages
Dutch, English, French, German

Other offices
Amsterdam, London, Luxembourg*, Rotterdam, The Hague

Number of lawyers 305
at this office 11

Contact
Gerard van der Wal

CATEGORIES OF WORK

- **Competition law**
- **International trade and customs law**
- **Trade with non-member countries**
- **Intellectual property law**
- **EU law**
- **Agricultural law**
- **European litigation**
- **Pharmaceutical law**

HOWREY LLP

AVENUE DES NERVIENS 9-31
1040 BRUSSELS

Telephone: +32 2 741 10 11
Fax: +32 2 741 10 12
Website: www.howrey.com

Languages
Dutch, English, French, German, Greek, Italian, Portuguese, Spanish, Swedish

Other offices
Amsterdam, Chicago, East Palo Alto, Houston, Irvine, London, Los Angeles, Northern Virginia, Paris, Salt Lake City, San Francisco, Taipei, Washington DC

Number of lawyers 565
at this office 26

Contacts
Trevor Soames (head of antitrust)
Carl De Meyer (head of IP)

CATEGORIES OF WORK

All aspects of European and US competition and antitrust law and policy

European and national merger control: clearance of M&A and joint ventures

European and international cartel investigations, private antitrust litigation and arbitration (including damages actions)

Abuse of dominant position/ monopolisation issues

Competition litigation and advocacy

Antitrust corporate governance and risk management issues

State aid

Transport and energy

Telecoms, media and broadcasting

Intellectual property, including national and international patent litigation and all aspects of trade marks and copyrights, as well as unfair competition and competition law

Global litigation and dispute resolution

Global counselling

HUNTON & WILLIAMS

AVENUE LOUISE 326, BOX 6
1050 BRUXELLES

Telephone: +32 2 643 58 00
Fax: +32 2 643 58 22
E-mail: info@hunton.com
Website: www.hunton.com

Languages
Dutch, English, French, German, Italian, Spanish

Other offices
Atlanta, Bangkok, Charlotte, Dallas, Hong Kong, Houston, Knoxville, London, McLean, Miami, New York, Norfolk, Raleigh, Richmond, Singapore, Washington DC

Number of lawyers 850+
at this office 7+

Contacts
Prof Lucas Bergkamp, Hervé Cogels, Christopher Kuner, R Hewitt Pate, Michael Rosenthal

CATEGORIES OF WORK

Biotechnology/FDA/healthcare
Lucas Bergkamp

Chemical
Lucas Bergkamp

Competition
R Hewitt Pate, Michael Rosenthal

Consumer protection
Lucas Bergkamp

Corporate and commercial
Hervé Cogels, Charles Ashton

Corporate finance
Hervé Cogels, Peter Kavanagh

E-commerce
Christopher Kuner

Environmental
Lucas Bergkamp

Internet
Christopher Kuner

Labour law
Hervé Cogels, Lucas Bergkamp

Liability
Lucas Bergkamp

Privacy/data protection
Christopher Kuner

Product and trade regulation
Lucas Bergkamp

Project finance
Swati Patel, Peter Maxfield

JANSON BAUGNIET

187 CHAUSSÉE DE LA HULPE
1170 BRUSSELS

Telephone: +32 2 675 30 30
Fax: +32 2 675 30 31
E-mail: email@janson.be
Website: www.janson.be

Languages
Dutch, English, French, German

Number of lawyers 60

Contacts
Henri-Paul Lemaitre, Flip Petillion

CATEGORIES OF WORK

Administrative and environmental law

Banking and finance

Bankruptcy and reorganisation

Civil and commercial contracts

Company law, M&A, securities regulation

Construction, public procurement contracts

Criminal law, human rights

Distribution

Employment and labour law

Healthcare and pharmaceuticals

Intellectual property and information technology

Liabilities and insurance

Litigation, arbitration, ADR

Media and telecommunications law

Real estate, lease contracts

Tax

Trade and competition law

JONES DAY

AVENUE BRAND WHITLOCK 165
1200 BRUXELLES

Telephone: +32 2 645 14 11
Fax: +32 2 645 14 45
Website: www.jonesday.com

Languages
Dutch, English, French, German, Italian, Spanish

Other offices
Atlanta, Beijing, Chicago, Cleveland, Columbus, Dallas, Frankfurt, Hong Kong, Houston, Irvine, London, Los Angeles, Madrid, Menlo Park, Milan, Moscow, Mumbai*, Munich, New Delhi*, New York, Paris, Pittsburgh, San Diego, San Francisco, Shanghai, Singapore, Sydney, Taipei, Tokyo, Washington DC

Number of lawyers 2,200
at this office 30

*In association with Pathak & Associates

CATEGORIES OF WORK

Lending/structured finance and derivatives
Thierry Buytaert

Commercial contracts
Luc Houben

Mergers and acquisitions
Luc Houben, Howard Liebman

Corporate law
Luc Houben, Thierry Buytaert

Antitrust and competition law
Bernard Amory, Alexandre Verheyden, Eric Morgan de Rivery, Thomas Jestaedt, Vincent Brophy

Labour and employment
Chantal Biernaux

International litigation and arbitration
Geoffroy de Foestraets, Sébastien Champagne

Media law
Geoffroy de Foestraets

Real estate
Luc Houben, Thierry Buytaert

Tax law
Howard Liebman

Telecommunications law
Bernard Amory, Alexandre Verheyden

Intellectual property and technology
Mireille Buydens

LAWELL

BASTION TOWER
PLACE DU CHAMP DE MARS 5/B11
1050 BRUSSELS

Telephone: +32 2 736 40 90
Fax: +32 2 735 87 14
E-mail: mail@lawell-lawyers.com
Website: www.lawell-lawyers.com

Languages
Dutch, English, French, German, Spanish

Other offices
Paris

Number of lawyers 10

Contacts
Alain A Henderickx, Jean-Louis Lodomez, Luc Godin

Member
Brussels Bar; Paris Bar

CATEGORIES OF WORK

Corporate, M&A, private equity

Commercial and distribution

EU and international mobility/ expatriates

EU regulatory

Intellectual property

Labour

Litigation and arbitration

National and international tax

Pensions and benefits, social security

Restructuring and bankruptcy

Technology, media and communications

Trade, competition, anti-dumping and WTO

White-collar crime

LAWFORT

WOLUWEDAL 20
SINT-STEVENS-WOLUWE
1932 BRUSSELS

Telephone: +32 2 710 78 11
Fax: +32 2 710 78 53
E-mail: firstname.name@lawfort.be
Website: www.lawfort.be

Languages
All European languages

Other offices
Antwerp, Ghent, Prague

Number of lawyers 120

Contact
Marc Vandemeulebroeke (managing partner)

International groupings
Alliance with Pekin & Bayar, Turkey

CATEGORIES OF WORK

Administrative and energy law
Guy Block

Arbitration and mediation
Herman Verbist

Commercial, distribution, IP law
Wilfried Van Looveren, Annick Mottet, Bruno De Vuyst, Eric Laevens

Corporate structuring, M&A, business recovery
Marie Evrard, Stéphane Bertouille, Phillippe Van den Broecke, Katrin De Saedeleir

Employment and human resources
Véronique Pertry, Frank Ruelens, Stefan Nerinckx, Rudi Desmet

Financial services
Marc Vandemeulebroeke, Koen Vanderheyden

Real estate, environment
François de Montpellier, Ciska Servais

Tax law
Ignaas Behaeghe

ICT and e-business
Jos Dumortier

Transport and logistics, aviation and tourism
Marc Van Looveren

Pharmaceutical
Bruno De Vuyst

LEBOEUF, LAMB, GREENE & MACRAE LLP

ARTS/LUX BUILDING
RUE DU LUXEMBURGSTRAAT 14A
1000 BRUSSELS

Telephone: +32 2 227 09 00
Fax: +32 2 227 09 09
E-mail: eclaes@llgm.com
Website: www.llgm.com

Languages
Afrikaans, Dutch, English, French, German, Greek, Italian, Kyrgyz, Russian, Spanish

Other offices
Albany, Almaty, Beijing, Boston, Chicago, Hartford, Houston, Jacksonville, Johannesburg, London, Los Angeles, Moscow, New York, Paris, Pittsburg, Riyadh, San Francisco, Washington DC

Number of lawyers 650+
at this office 10

Contact
Etienne Claes

CATEGORIES OF WORK

Corporate
Etienne Claes, Eric Bodson

Antitrust
Peter Crowther, Teresa Zueco

Energy
Etienne Claes

Litigation
Bertold F Theeuwes, Frederick Peels

Intellectual property
Eric Bodson

Employment
Etienne Claes, Bertold F Theeuwes

Technology
Eric Bodson

Environmental
Etienne Claes

Insurance/reinsurance
Alexandros Iatrou

White-collar crime
Etienne Claes

LINKLATERS DE BANDT

RUE BREDERODE 13
1000 BRUSSELS

Telephone: +32 2 501 94 11
Fax: +32 2 501 94 94
Website: www.linklaters.com

Languages
All commercial and local languages in the countries where Linklaters operates

Other offices
Amsterdam, Antwerp, Bangkok, Beijing, Berlin, Bratislava, Bucharest, Budapest, Cologne, Dubai, Frankfurt am Main, Hong Kong, Lisbon, London, Luxembourg, Madrid, Milan, Moscow, Munich, New York, Paris, Prague, Rome, São Paulo, Shanghai, Singapore, Stockholm, Tokyo, Warsaw

Number of lawyers 2,000 worldwide

Contact
Jean-Pierre Blumberg

CATEGORIES OF WORK

Mergers and acquisitions
Jean-Pierre Blumberg, Jean-Marie Nelissen Grade

Technology, media and telecommunications
Tanguy Van Overstraeten

Capital markets
François De Bauw

EU and competition
Gerwin Van Gerven, Alec Burnside

Banking
Jacques Richelle

Employment, pensions and benefits
Luc Vanaverbeke

Tax
Ivo Onkelinx

Public, administrative
Lieve Swartenbroux

Real estate
Jacques Périlleux

Litigation, arbitration
Johan Verbist

Intellectual property
Jean-Christophe Troussel

Projects
Jean-Pierre Blumberg, Frédéric Falla

LIEDEKERKE WOLTERS WAELBROECK KIRKPATRICK

3 BOULEVARD DE L'EMPEREUR
1000 BRUXELLES

Telephone: +32 2 551 15 15
Fax: +32 2 551 14 14
E-mail: info@liedekerke-law.be
Website: www.liedekerke-law.be

Languages
Dutch, French, English, German, Danish, Italian, Spanish

Number of lawyers 120

CATEGORIES OF WORK

Banking
Jan Vincent Lindemans

Finance – capital markets
Thierry Tilquin, Piet van Overbeke

Corporate – M&A
Philippe Malherbe, Thierry Tilquin

Intellectual property
Martine Demeur

Taxation
Daniel Garabedian, Jacques Malherbe

Competition
Jules Stuyck

International law – WTO law
Nicolas Angelet

Insolvency
Paul Vandepitte

Employment law
Paul Geerebaert, Vincent Busschaert

Real estate
Yves Delacroix, Valérie Simonart

Environment
Bernard Deltour, Dirk Lindemans

Administrative law
Dirk Lindemans, Bernard Deltour

Aviation and transport
Marc Godfroid

Commercial litigation
Aimery de Schoutheete, Joe Sepulchre

Arbitration
Joe Sepulchre

Insurance
Pol Glineur

THE FIRM

Established in 1965, Liedekerke Wolters Waelbroeck Kirkpatrick is one of the oldest law firms in Belgium. It is also one of the largest Belgian independent law firms with 120 lawyers. A number of them teach or have taught in renowned law faculties in Belgium or abroad, and are well-known figures in the legal world. The firm offers a broad range of services in the principal areas of expertise in business law and possesses a great deal of competence and a high reputation in general commercial law, including contract drafting and litigation, both nationally and internationally.

In each area, Liedekerke's aim is to offer high-quality, personalised services in which legal rigour is allied to solid practical experience and consideration of the economic need of its clients. Its approach is very much client-focused, always looking for the balance between good knowledge of the environment in which the client operates, and effective and creative legal advice. The firm works in Dutch, French and English, and several of its partners and associates are fluent in other languages as well. Relations with clients are built on a long-term perspective and the development of personal relationships.

The firm advises and represents domestic, foreign and multinational companies in the financial, property, industrial and service sectors, public authorities and international organisations, charitable organisations and private individuals. Liedekerke has long been developing relations with top-grade world corporations and foreign law firms of the first order.

AREAS OF PRACTICE

As a full-service law firm, Liedekerke Wolters Waelbroeck Kirkpatrick advises on practically all areas in business law including the various branches of civil and commercial law; tax, accountancy and estate planning; finance and corporate; social security and labour law; public and administrative law; real estate; transport and insurance; intellectual and industrial property; white-collar crime; European law and competition; international law including international economic law, human rights law and international criminal law. The firm has advised in numerous M&A and financial transactions in Belgium. It provides a full range of corporate and M&A services, including: advice on creation of undertakings, operations of companies, transfer of shares and assets, co-operation between undertakings; choice of the most appropriate form of reorganisation, negotiating and drafting documents, domestic and European Union merger control units.

The firm's activity covers all aspects of legal practice: consultations, negotiation and drafting of agreements; advice and assistance in the operations conducted by its clients or with which they are confronted, mediation; dispute resolution; participation in the drafting of legislative texts. The firm conducts proceedings before the national, European and international jurisdictions, both judicial and arbitral, the Court of Cassation, the Council of State and the Belgian Constitutional Court. Liedekerke Wolters Waelbroeck Kirkpatrick has always regarded the experience and handling of disputes as an essential complement to its advising activity.

LONTINGS & PARTNERS

TOUR & TAXIS
HAVENLAAN
AVENUE DU PORT 86C B113
1000 BRUSSELS

Telephone: +32 2 787 90 00
Fax: +32 2 787 90 99
E-mail: lontings.partners@lontings.be
Website: www.lontingsandpartners.be

Languages
English, French, Dutch, German

Number of lawyers 42

CATEGORIES OF WORK

Corporate and finance
Dirk Lontings, Vincent Dirckx

Commercial and insurance
Hugo Keulers

Non-profit and trade associations
Dirk Lontings

ICT and IP
Hugo Keulers

Regulatory, environment and real estate
Wouter Neven

Employment, pensions and benefits
Alexander Vandenbergen, Jan Hofkens

Tax litigation
Alain Claes

THE FIRM

Lontings & Partners maintains, with some pride, that it is a law firm with a distinct vision, believing not only in legal professionalism, but also in enthusiasm, commitment and involvement.

All specialists in their own fields, the firm's lawyers offer high-quality services to organisations in all necessary areas of the law. Lontings & Partners maintains the expertise, structure and commitment necessary to collaborate closely with clients, assisting them in achieving their business objectives, both in Belgium and abroad.

Lontings & Partners operates on an interpersonal level with key figures in clients' organisations, making time for the managing director, general manager, sales director, human resources director, finance and administration director, or any professional who appreciates clear and comprehensive legal advice. The firm strives to establish long-term professional relationships with clients and contacts. Throughout the changes that affect organisations, the firm endeavours to maintain steadfast counsel so that loyalty and mutual trust can grow.

Meticulous recruiting is a priority. Lawyers at Lontings & Partners, a number of whom hold university posts, have excellent academic credentials and a wealth of experience.

AREAS OF PRACTICE

Lontings & Partners is an independent full-service Belgian law firm that is active in all areas of the law relevant to companies, business and non-profit organisations.

The firm is structured around the following seven departments: corporate and finance; commercial and insurance; employment, pensions and benefits; ICT and IP; non-profit and trade associations; regulatory, environment and real estate; and tax litigation.

More information can also be obtained on the firm's website: www.lontingsandpartners.be.

LOVELLS

AVENUE LOUISE 523
BOÎTE 24
1050 BRUXELLES

Telephone: +32 2 647 06 60
Fax: +32 2 647 11 24
E-mail: information@lovells.com
Website: www.lovells.com

Languages
Dutch, English, French, German, Italian, Spanish

Other offices
Alicante, Amsterdam, Beijing, Berlin, Budapest*, Chicago, Düsseldorf, Frankfurt, Hamburg, Ho Chi Minh City, Hong Kong, London, Madrid, Milan, Moscow, Munich, New York, Paris, Prague, Rome, Shanghai, Singapore, Tokyo, Warsaw, Zagreb*

Number of lawyers 1,600
at this office 17

Contact
Tom McQuail

CATEGORIES OF WORK

Competition, antitrust and merger control

Trade law and regulation

Dumping, customs and tariffs

Internal market legislation, regulatory issues and public policy

Telecommunications and energy

Company and commercial law

Mergers and acquisitions

Banking, finance and securities law

Real estate and intellectual property

Employment law

LOYENS

WOLUWE ATRIUM
NEERVELDSTRAAT 101-3
1200 BRUSSELS

Telephone: +32 2 743 43 43
Fax: +32 2 743 43 10
E-mail: information@loyens.com
Website: www.loyens.com

Languages
Chinese, Dutch, English, French, German, Italian, Spanish

Other offices
Amsterdam, Antwerp (Loyens), Arnhem, Aruba, Curaçao, Eindhoven, Frankfurt, Geneva, London, Luxembourg (Loyens Winandy), New York, Paris, Rotterdam, Singapore, Tokyo, Zurich

Number of lawyers 710
at this office 104

CATEGORIES OF WORK

General tax
Christian Chéruy

Private client
Saskia Lust

Tax litigation
Jan van Besien

Indirect tax
Thierry Charon

Employment law, compensation, benefits and pensions
Carl Bevernage, Christian Willems, Jean-Louis Davain

IP, ICT and media
Benoit Van Asbroeck

Banking and finance
Wilfred Goris, Grégoire Jakhian, Marc Vermylen

Corporate law and M&A
Roel Nieuwdorp, Grégoire Jakhian

EU, competition and regulatory
Koen Platteau

Real estate
Wilfred Goris, Christophe Laurent

Commercial law
Geert Bogaert, Yves Van Couter

Litigation, arbitration and ADR
Martine De Roeck

MANNHEIMER SWARTLING

AVENUE DE TERVUEREN 13
1040 BRUXELLES

Telephone: +32 2 732 22 22
Fax: +32 2 736 96 52
Website: www.mannheimerswartling.se

Languages
Dutch, English, Finnish, French, German, Swedish

Other offices
Berlin, Frankfurt, Gothenburg, Helsingborg, Malmö, New York, St Petersburg, Stockholm

Number of lawyers 330
at this office 4

Contact
Johan Coyet

CATEGORIES OF WORK

Competition law, merger control

EC law

Free movement of goods, services, persons and capital

Public procurement

State aid

Trade law

Telecommunications and media

Energy

MARX, VAN RANST, VERMEERSCH & PARTNERS

TERVURENLAAN 270
270 AVENUE DE TERVUEREN
1150 BRUXELLES

Telephone: +32 2 285 01 00
Fax: +32 2 230 33 39
E-mail: info@mvvp.be
Website: www.mvvp.be

Languages
English, Dutch, French, German, Italian

Number of lawyers 25

CATEGORIES OF WORK

Corporate law
Kristoffel Vermeersch, Nicole Van Ranst

Mergers and acquisitions
Nicole Van Ranst, Kristoffel Vermeersch

Commercial law
Anne Jonlet, Jan Ravelingien, Bernard Caris

Intellectual property
Peter Marx, Herman Croux

Media and entertainment law
Peter Marx, Herman Croux

Trade practices and competition
Anne Jonlet, Jan Ravelingien, Bernard Caris

Labour and employment law
Rafaël Claes, Bruno Blanpain

Business immigration
Bernard Caris, Rafaël Claes

Real estate
Stefaan Verbouwe

Regulatory affairs and public law
Stefaan Verbouwe

Tax and finance
Kristoffel Vermeersch

Litigation and arbitration
Anne Jonlet, Herman Croux, Jan Ravelingien

MAYER BROWN ROWE & MAW LLP

AVENUE DES ARTS, 52
1000 BRUSSELS

Telephone: +32 2 502 55 17
Fax: +32 2 502 54 21
E-mail: kdesai@mayerbrownrowe.com
Website: www.mayerbrownrowe.com

Languages
Dutch, English, French, German, Italian, Russian, Spanish

Other offices
Berlin, Charlotte, Chicago, Cologne, Frankfurt, Houston, London, Los Angeles, Mexico City (correspondence office), New York, Palo Alto, Paris, Beijing and Shanghai (partner offices), Washington DC

Number of lawyers 1,300
at this office 9

CATEGORIES OF WORK

Competition
Kiran Desai,
Dr Jens Peter Schmidt

Customs, trade, WTO and anti-dumping
Paulette Vander Schueren

EU regulatory
Kiran Desai

Government affairs
Dr Günter Burghardt

McDERMOTT WILL & EMERY/STANBROOK LLP

RUE PÈRE EUDORE DEVROYE 245
1150 BRUSSELS

Telephone: +32 2 230 50 59
Fax: +32 2 230 57 13
Website: www.mwe.com

Languages
All main business languages

Other offices
Boston, Chicago, Düsseldorf, London, Los Angeles, Miami, Munich, New York, Orange County, Rome, San Diego, Silicon Valley, Washington DC

Number of lawyers 1,000
at this office 12

Contacts
Clive Stanbrook QC, Scott S Megregian, Philip Bentley QC

CATEGORIES OF WORK

EU and competition
Clive Stanbrook QC, Scott S Megregian

State aid and public procurement
Philip Bentley QC, Ian Rose

EU and regulatory
Ian Rose, Frank Schoneveld

International trade and customs
Philip Bentley QC, Clive Stanbrook QC

Anti-dumping and countervailing proceedings
Philip Bentley QC, Clive Stanbrook QC

European environmental, health, safety and consumer goods regulations
Frank Schoneveld

McGUIREWOODS LLP

250 AVENUE LOUISE
BTE 64
1050 BRUSSELS

Telephone: + 32 2 629 42 11
Fax: + 32 2 629 42 22
Website: www.mcguirewoods.com

Languages
Dutch, English, French, German, Spanish

Other offices
Almaty (Kazakhstan), Atlanta, Baltimore, Charlotte, Charlottesville, Chicago, Jacksonville, Los Angeles, New York, Norfolk, Pittsburgh, Richmond, Tysons Corner, Washington DC

Number of lawyers 725
at this office 17

CATEGORIES OF WORK

Administrative law, product liability
Emmanuel de Cannart d'Hamale

Advertising
Xavier Van der Mersch

Agency, distribution and franchising
Emmanuel de Cannart d'Hamale, Xavier Van der Mersch

Aviation, competition and antitrust, eastern Europe
John Barnum

Banking and finance
Hubert André-Dumont, Christiane Zuniga

Corporate and commercial, corporate finance, M&A and joint ventures
Hubert André-Dumont, Xavier Van der Mersch

Project finance
Hubert André-Dumont, Christiane Zuniga

E-commerce and internet, computer and information technology
Emmanuel de Cannart d'Hamale

Employment and benefits, transnational tax matters
Xavier Van der Mersch

Inward investment
Hubert André-Dumont, Xavier Van der Mersch

Litigation and arbitration
Emmanuel de Cannart d'Hamale, John Barnum

Mining and Africa
Hubert André-Dumont, Emmanuel de Cannart d'Hamale

Real estate and construction
Hubert André-Dumont

McKENNA LONG & ALDRIDGE LLP

2 AVENUE DE TERVUEREN
1040 BRUSSELS

Telephone: +32 2 278 12 11
Fax: +32 2 278 12 00
E-mail: brussels@mckennalong.com
Website: www.mckennalong.com

Languages
Dutch, English, French, German, Italian, Romanian, Spanish

Other offices
Atlanta, Denver, Los Angeles, Philadelphia, San Diego, San Francisco, Washington DC

Number of lawyers 385
at this office 9

Contact
Claudio Mereu

CATEGORIES OF WORK

Environmental
Ursula Schliessner, Robert A Matthews

Food and drug
Ursula Schliessner, Claudio Mereu

European litigation
Claudio Mereu, Robert A Matthews

Coporate and commercial
Richard WIllis

Product safety/product liability
Ursula Schliessner

European business and regulatory
Koen Van Maldegem, Claudio Mereu

European competition law
Claudio Mereu, Koen Van Maldegem

International arbitration and litigation
Koen Van Maldegem, Claudio Mereu

Public procurement and international dispute resolution
Claudio Mereu, Peter Sellar

MORGAN LEWIS

7 RUE GUIMARD
1040 BRUSSELS

Telephone: +32 2 507 75 00
Fax: +32 2 507 75 55
E-mail: info@morganlewis.com
Website: www.morganlewis.com

Languages
English, Dutch, French, German, Spanish, Swedish, Turkish

Other offices
Boston, Chicago, Dallas, Frankfurt, Harrisburg, Irvine, London, Los Angeles, Miami, New York, Palo Alto, Paris, Philadelphia, Pittsburgh, Princeton, San Francisco, Tokyo, Washington DC

Number of lawyers 1,200+
at this office 2

CATEGORIES OF WORK

EC and national merger control, joint ventures, distribution and IP licensing
Izzet M Sinan, Jonathan Uphoff

Telecommunications and technology
Izzet M Sinan

THE FIRM

Morgan Lewis, with more than 1,200 lawyers in 19 offices in the US, Europe and Asia is one of the largest law firms in the world.

Morgan Lewis represents clients across the globe, from mergers and acquisitions and joint ventures to technology and outsourcing; from fraud and money laundering to employment and property. With its international reach Morgan Lewis can resolve differing and conflicting laws in a number of jurisdictions to produce optimum results for its clients. The firm's lawyers understand the problems and complexities of transactional litigation and cross-border negotiation and can advise on US and EU regulatory matters.

The firm's clients are diverse and include Fortune 250 companies, leading financial services and investment banking organisations, as well as pioneers in the e-commerce and internet sector. The firm also represents high-net-worth individuals. All clients receive the same high level of care and benefit from the firm's local presence in a global market.

The firm handles a vast diversity of legal work including antitrust, business and commercial litigation, business and finance, corporate transactions, employment, labour and benefits, energy and utilities, insurance, intellectual property, international arbitration, investment management, life sciences, mergers and acquisitions, real estate, outsourcing, securities, sport, tax and technology.

AREAS OF PRACTICE

Morgan Lewis, Brussels is fully integrated with the firm's 18 other offices and offers a strong pan-European service in combination with its London, Frankfurt and Paris lawyers. The Brussels office opened 17 years ago and is an important element of one of the world's largest and most sophisticated antitrust practices. The firm provides clients with the full spectrum of antitrust services, from preventive counselling and merger control to advice on cutting-edge antitrust issues to defence of 'bet the company' antitrust litigation including, in particular, international cartel cases. The firm focuses on effective strategies, careful structuring and skilled implementation to provide clients with tailored, cost-effective and innovative solutions, to enable them to meet their business objectives. Morgan Lewis antitrust lawyers work as one worldwide, integrated team, irrespective of office location, and the team is particularly experienced in addressing complex multi-jurisdictional issues.

The Brussels office is routinely involved in cross-border mergers and acquisitions, international joint ventures and the structuring and restructuring of multinational groups. In this context, the firm's expertise in global tax strategy and European company law and formation has enabled Morgan Lewis to provide material assistance to colleagues and clients in timely conception and execution of such complex transactions.

MORRISON & FOERSTER LLP

AVENUE MOLIÈRE 262
1180 BRUSSELS

Telephone: +32 2 347 04 00
Fax: +32 2 347 18 24
Website: www.mofo.com

Languages
Dutch, French, German, Italian, Swedish

Other offices
Beijing, Century City, Denver, Hong Kong, London, Los Angeles, New York, Northern Virginia, Orange County, Palo Alto, Sacramento, San Diego, San Francisco, Shanghai, Singapore, Tokyo, Walnut Creek, Washington DC

Number of lawyers 975
at this office 5

Contact
Christopher Norall (cnorall@mofo.com)

CATEGORIES OF WORK

Competition
Christopher Norall, Rony Gerrits

Privacy/data protection
Karin Retzer

Intellectual property
Karin Retzer

Licensing
Karin Retzer

Internet/e-commerce
Karin Retzer

Trade
Christopher Norall

THE FIRM

With more than one thousand lawyers in nineteen offices around the world, Morrison & Foerster offers clients comprehensive, global legal services in business and litigation. The firm is distinguished by its unsurpassed expertise in technology and life sciences. The firm has one compelling mission: to deliver success for its clients.

Morrison and Foerster's Brussels office was established in 1991. The Brussels office plays a key role in the firm's highly-integrated antitrust and global technology practices. The office has lawyers qualified to practice under national laws in Belgium, Germany, Sweden and the United States.

AREAS OF PRACTICE

Morrison & Foerster offer a cutting-edge European competition law practice, far-reaching expertise on compliance with EU and member state privacy laws and internet regulation, and broad multi-jurisdictional transactional experience, in particular technology licensing, joint ventures, outsourcing, distribution and ISP contracts.

Competition and merger regulation: extensive experience particularly in the technology sector, including representing companies in investigations and litigation before the European Commission and National competition authorities, representing companies in merger notifications, both at EU and member state level, and general antitrust counselling. Recent transactions include representing Thomson on an EU merger control proceeding relating to Thomson's acquisition of a 33% share in Contentguard; representing Panasonic in its complaint to the European Commission against Qualcomm's alleged abusive licensing terms; representing Matsushita in connection with the European Commission's investigation of patent pool licensing terms of DVD technology and representing Hitachi in obtaining EU merger regulation clearance of its acquisition of the hard disc business of IBM.

Privacy: the firm provides strategic advice on EU and member state privacy laws, and assists with worldwide data protection compliance projects and privacy of communications in the workplace. Lawyers have experience in consulting and negotiating with the European Commission, the European Parliament and with national data protection authorities throughout Europe.

E-commerce: the office's lawyers have substantial expertise in e-commerce issues, ranging from the enforceability of online contracts, the legal aspects of internet auctions, liability imposed on internet service providers, digital signatures and taxation of internet transactions. The Brussels office covers matters including content licensing and collaboration agreements and the adoption of policies relating to the provision of e-commerce products and services.

Intellectual property: services include advising on technology licensing, distribution and joint venture agreements, international dispute resolution, and EU developments affecting IP rights, including initiatives on copyright, trade marks, patents, design rights and databases.

Trade: the Brussels office has experience in anti-dumping, anti-subsidy, customs and WTO-related issues. The firm's attorneys have advised governments on GATT/WTO dispute resolution proceedings.

Intellectual agility is the hallmark of Morrison & Foerster. The firm applies it to every matter – from the complex to the routine – to ensure the best outcome for clients.

MONARD–D'HULST

TERVURENLAAN 270
1150 BRUSSELS

Telephone: +32 2 234 67 10
Fax: +32 2 280 47 79
Email: info@monard-dhulst.be
Website: www.monard-dhulst.be

Languages
Dutch, English, French, German, Italian

Other offices
Hasselt*, Kortrijk*

Number of lawyers 66

Contacts
See website

CATEGORIES OF WORK	
Banking/finance	Labour/employment
Commercial	Liability/insurance
Corporate	M&A/private equity
Dispute resolution/arbitration	Media/entertainment
Environment/administrative	Private estates
Fraud/white-collar crime	Real estate/construction
Insolvency/restructuring	Securities/capital markets
Intellectual property/TMT	Tax/tax litigation

O'MELVENY & MYERS LLP

BLUE TOWER
AVENUE LOUISE 326
1050 BRUSSELS

Telephone: +32 2 642 41 00
Fax: +32 2 642 41 90
E-mail: brussels@omm.com
Website: www.omm.com

Languages
English, French, Danish, Dutch, German, Italian, Mandarin, Norwegian, Portuguese, Spanish

Other offices
Beijing, Century City, Hong Kong, London, Los Angeles, Newport Beach, New York, San Francisco, Shanghai, Silicon Valley, Tokyo, Washington DC

Number of lawyers 1,049
at this office 10

Contact
Riccardo Celli

CATEGORIES OF WORK	
EU and national merger control	State aid
European and international cartel investigations	Antitrust litigation
Leniency applications	Public procurement
Compliance programmes	General EU law
Global antitrust counselling	Regulatory law in transport, energy and financial services sectors
Trade, customs, WTO and anti-dumping	Abuse of dominant market position

PESTALOZZI LACHENAL PATRY

165 AVENUE LOUISE
1050 BRUXELLES

Telephone: +32 2 646 60 10
Fax: +32 646 75 34
E-mail: bru@plplaw.ch
Website: www.plplaw.ch

Languages
English, French, German

Other offices
Geneva, Zurich

Number of lawyers 103
at this office 3

Member
Lex Mundi

CATEGORIES OF WORK

Swiss and EC competition law
Christophe Rapin

EC and WTO trade law and regulations
Christophe Rapin

EC corporate and commercial law
Christophe Rapin

PHILIPPE & PARTNERS

LOUISE AVENUE 240 1ST FLOOR
1050 BRUXELLES

Telephone: +32 2 600 52 00
Fax: +32 2 600 52 01
Website: www.philippe-law.com

Languages
English, Dutch, French, German, Italian, Luxembourgish, Portuguese, Spanish, Slovak, Russian

Other offices
Charleroi, Liege, Luxembourg

Number of lawyers 47
at this office 20

CATEGORIES OF WORK

Intellectual property and trade practices
Isabelle Goes, Marc De Witte

Distribution
Isabelle Goes, Marc De Witte

Contracts (public and private, national and international)
Denis Philippe, Marjorie Allo

Public law
Christophe Dubois

Employment and social security law
Geoffroy Lemaire, Frédéric Robert

Tax Law
Odile Deladrière, Geert De Neef

Real estate
Philippe Bossard, Murielle Mc Sorley

Energy law
Denis Philippe, Marc Gouden

European law (notably competition)
Denis Philippe, Francesco Apruzzi

Corporate law, mergers and acquisitions
Willy Platteeuw, Geert De Neef

Energy law
Denis Philippe, Marc Gouden

Banking and financial law
Murielle Mc Sorley, Denis Philippe

Debt recovery
Isabelle Goes, Phillippe Bossard

Insolvency and reorganisation
Charles Bullman, Edgar Kempeners

Torts, liabilities and insurance
Marc Gouden, Isabelle Goes

SJ BERWIN LLP

SQUARE DE MEEÛS 19
BOÎTE 3
1050 BRUXELLES

Telephone: +32 2 511 53 40
Fax: +32 2 511 59 17
E-mail: brussels@sjberwin.com
Website: www.sjberwin.com

Languages
English, French, German, Italian, Portuguese, Spanish

Other offices
Berlin, Frankfurt, London, Madrid, Milan, Munich, Paris, Turin

Number of lawyers 550
at this office 19

Contact
Ramon Gallardo

CATEGORIES OF WORK

- Competition
- Consumer and sanitary
- Energy and national resources
- Environment
- International litigation/dispute resolution and arbitration
- Corporate law
- Mediation/bilateral
- Private clients
- Funding
- Mergers and acquisitions
- Shipping and transport
- Trade laws
- Major Article 85 notifications (restrictive practices)
- EC merger regulation notifications
- State aid
- Agriculture and fisheries law
- EU trade law
- EU and national aspects of biotech regulation
- Agrochemicals
- EU litigation
- EU customs law
- Consulting and lobbying (EU public affairs)

SIDLEY AUSTIN LLP

SQUARE DE MEEUS 35
1000 BRUSSELS

Telephone: +32 2 504 64 00
Fax: +32 2 504 64 01
Email: rweiner@sidley.com
Website: www.sidley.com

Languages
Dutch, English, French, Greek, Italian, Norwegian, Spanish, Swedish

Other offices
Beijing, Chicago, Dallas, Frankfurt, Geneva, Hong Kong, London, Los Angeles, New York, San Francisco, Shanghai, Singapore, Tokyo, Washington DC

Number of lawyers 1,600+
at this office 15

Contacts
Richard LA Weiner, Laurent A Ruessmann, Maurits Lugard, Stephen Spinks

CATEGORIES OF WORK

- Global and EU trade policy
- WTO law and negotiations
- Dispute resolution
- EU trade remedies
- Customs
- Competition/antitrust
- State aid
- EU regulatory
- Financial services
- Food and agriculture
- Healthcare, pharmaceuticals, medical services
- Telecommunications
- Energy liberalisation
- Privacy/data protection
- Environmental

SIMMONS & SIMMONS

AVENUE LOUISE 149 B 16
1050 BRUXELLES

Telephone: +32 2 542 09 60
Fax: +32 2 542 09 61
E-mail: enquiries@simmons-simmons.com
Website: www.simmons-simmons.com

Languages
Dutch, English, French, German

Other offices
London, Rotterdam, Paris, Lisbon, Milan, Rome, Düsseldorf, Frankfurt, Madrid, Padua, Oporto, Madeira, Abu Dhabi, Qatar, Hong Kong, Shanghai, Tokyo, New York, Dubai

Number of lawyers 764
at this office 14

Contact
Anthony Orr

CATEGORIES OF WORK

Corporate

Banking

Capital markets

Projects, PFI

EU, competition

Dispute resolution

Intellectual property

Employment

Financial markets

Pharmaceutical and biotechnology

Energy and utilities

Transport

Consumer goods

SIMONT BRAUN

AVENUE LOUISE 149
PO BOX 20
1050 BRUSSELS

Telephone: +32 2 543 70 80
Fax: +32 2 543 70 90
E-mail: info@simontbraun.be
Website: www.simontbraun.be

Languages
Danish, Dutch, English, French, German, Greek, Hebrew, Italian, Polish, Portuguese

Number of lawyers 50

CATEGORIES OF WORK

Arbitration and litigation
John Bigwood, Paul Alain Foriers

Commercial law
Béatrice Thieffry,
Alain Vandemeulebroeke

Company law
Paul Alain Foriers, Sandrine Hirsch

Criminal financial law
Jean-François Terlinden

Finance and banking
Michèle Grégoire, Vanessa Marquette

Intellectual property and competition law
Fernand de Visscher, Eric De Gryse

Labour law
Baudouin Paquot, Sylvie Lacombe

Mergers and acquisitions
Sandrine Hirsch, Vanessa Marquette

Real estate and construction
Thomas Braun, Michèle Borgers

Administrative law
Katelijne Ronse

Supreme Court
Lucien Simont

Tax law
Baudouin Paquot

Trade practices, e-commerce and distribution
Laurent de Brouwer, Emmanuel Cornu

Entertainment, media and information technology
Benoit Michaux

SLAUGHTER AND MAY

AVENUE DE CORTENBERG 118
1000 BRUSSELS

Telephone: +32 2 737 94 00
Fax: +32 2 737 94 01
E-mail: brussels@slaughterandmay.com
Website: www.slaughterandmay.com

Other offices
London, Paris, Hong Kong

Number of lawyers 566
at this office 10

Contacts
John Boyce, Michael Rowe

CATEGORIES OF WORK

Competition law including merger control, antitrust, cartel investigations
John Boyce, Michael Rowe

Litigation and representation before national courts and the European Courts in Luxembourg
John Boyce, Michael Rowe

State aid
John Boyce, Michael Rowe

Public procurement
John Boyce, Michael Rowe

Internal market issues
John Boyce, Michael Rowe

International trade law, dumping, subsidies
John Boyce, Michael Rowe

THE FIRM

Slaughter and May has an extensive international practice covering a wide range of corporate, commercial and financial work, with offices in London, Brussels, Paris and Hong Kong. It provides a comprehensive and integrated service covering all the areas in which corporate and other clients look for advice in order to implement their business decisions.

The firm's approach to international work places quality of advice and a long-standing in-depth knowledge of the jurisdiction at the heart of its strategy. It has close working relationships with leading independent law firms in all the major jurisdictions. These relationships allow the firm to provide the best legal advice worldwide in a seamless and integrated manner.

Established in 1989, the Brussels office focuses on EU and competition law matters. The Brussels team is led by two resident partners, John Boyce and Michael Rowe, and comprises in total about ten lawyers operating as an integral part of the firm's Competition Group.

The Slaughter and May Competition Group has close working relationships with leading competition specialists in independent law firms across the EU, as well as outside Europe. It is able to draw on these relationships to assemble tailor-made integrated teams of lawyers who have the best expertise and contacts in each jurisdiction for particular cases (from multi-jurisdictional merger cases to international cartel proceedings). A number of the European firms with whom the firm works also have offices in Brussels. This further facilitates the close working relationships and contacts between the firm's competition practices and extends to joint training, secondments, and know-how and technology exchanges.

AREAS OF PRACTICE

The Brussels office advises on all aspects of competition law. In particular, it advises on merger control notifications to the European Commission and to national competition authorities. It also represents clients on complaints and investigations under Articles 81 and 82 of the EC Treaty (and equivalent national laws) and the rules of state aid. The office also monitors other EU developments (such as internal market issues and trade issues) and maintains regular contact with Commission officials.

The relationships the firm has with other leading EU competition practices mean that it is particularly well-placed to deal with issues under the new regime of increased co-operation within the European Competition Network (the network established between the European Commission and the 25 EU Member States' national competition authorities as from 1 May 2004).

Further details on other areas of practice within the firm are provided in the London office entry of this publication.

SQUIRE, SANDERS & DEMPSEY L.L.P.

165, AVENUE LOUISE, BOX 13-14
1050 BRUSSELS

Telephone: +32 2 627 11 11
Fax: +32 2 627 11 00
E-mail: bhartnett@ssd.com
Website: www.ssd.com

Languages
Dutch, English, Finnish, French, German, Hebrew, Hungarian, Italian, Spanish, Swedish

Other offices
Beijing, Bratislava, Budapest, Caracas, Cincinnati, Cleveland, Columbus, Hong Kong, Houston, London, Los Angeles, Miami, Moscow, New York, Palo Alto, Phoenix, Prague, Rio de Janeiro, San Francisco, Santa Domingo, Shanghai, Tallahassee, Tampa, Tokyo, Tysons Corner, Warsaw, Washington DC, West Palm Beach, Bucharest*, Buenos Aires*, Dublin*, Kyiv*, Milan*, Santiago*

Number of lawyers 800+
at this office 14

Contact Brian Hartnett

Member
American Chamber of Commerce

CATEGORIES OF WORK

Belgian commercial
Anthony Van der Hauwaert

Computer technology, multimedia services
Anthony Van der Hauwaert, Oliver Geiss

Environmental
Cristiana Spontoni

EU competition law
Brian Hartnett, Rebecca O'Donnell

EU state aid
Brian Hartnett, Oliver Geiss

Food and drugs, pharmaceuticals
Cristiana Spontoni

Hospitality and leisure
Kenneth Hatton

Intellectual property
Rebecca O'Donnell, Oliver Geiss

International trade, WTO
Dan Horovitz, Seppo Puustinen

International transactions
Kenneth Hatton, Anthony Van der Hauwaert

Mergers and acquisitions/ joint ventures
Brian Harnett, Rebecca O'Donnell

Power generation, energy
Rebecca O'Donnell

Telecoms
Thomas Ramsey, Ann LaFrance, Rebecca O'Donnell

THE FIRM

Founded in 1890, Squire, Sanders & Dempsey is a multi-jurisdictional law firm with approximately 800 lawyers practising in offices in Europe, the Americas and Asia. The firm's practice covers most substantive areas of the law, with an emphasis on business and finance matters.

The firm operates as a single global partnership, which ensures client accountability and the seamless delivery of uniformly high-quality legal services throughout the world. The firm's lawyers come from many countries and cultures, are licensed to practise in both common law and civil law jurisdictions, and communicate with clients in their native languages. Today, the firm remains committed to the fundamental principles ordained by its founders: to serve clients effectively and to maintain the professional standards that distinguish both the firm and its people.

AREAS OF PRACTICE

The firm is organised around four major practice areas: advocacy, business, capital markets and regulated industries. Within these practice areas, the firm's work can be divided into numerous areas of specialisation, including banking, bankruptcy and restructuring, biotechnology and pharmaceuticals, communications, competition law, trade law, converging technologies, corporate, energy, environmental, health care, intellectual property, international dispute resolution, labour and employment, litigation, mergers and acquisitions, privatisations, project finance, real estate, securities and taxation.

Since its opening in 1975, the Brussels office has been engaged primarily in the practice of European Community (EC) law, representing a wide range of multinational companies.

The Brussels office regularly represents clients before the European Commission on matters of competition law, trade and customs law, energy and environmental regulation, intellectual property law, telecoms regulations, pharmaceutical regulations and other areas of EC law. The office also regularly represents clients before the Court of Justice challenging the decisions of the European Commission.

Ongoing contact with the EC institutions keeps lawyers apprised of new and emerging regulatory policies and practices relating to sectoral or topical issues affecting clients. In addition, the Brussels lawyers have spearheaded a number of key regulatory projects for the European Commission and other national regulatory bodies relating to the implementation of EU regulation.

The Brussels office functions bilingually in English and French, and many of the lawyers are European nationals qualified to advise on their respective national laws. Clients receive advice not only on their rights and obligations at the EC level, but also on the laws of the major member states (France, Czech Republic, Hungary, Slovakia, Germany, Italy, Spain, Belgium, Ireland, Finland and the UK) and the implementation of the Community Law into those national legal systems. In addition, European and other clients are represented in all legal aspects of investments in the United States as well as cross-border mergers and acquisitions, privatisation matters, and other international business transactions. Similarly, American clients are advised on their legal matters throughout the European Community and Central and Eastern Europe.

Many of the Brussels office lawyers are acknowledged leaders in their fields of expertise.

STEPTOE & JOHNSON LLP

AVENUE LOUISE 240
BOX 5
1050 BRUSSELS

Telephone: +32 2 626 05 00
Fax: +32 2 626 05 10
Website: www steptoe.com

Languages
Dutch, English, French, German, Italian

Other offices
London, Los Angeles, New York, Phoenix, Washington DC

Number of lawyers 439
at this office 9

Contacts
Jean Russotto, Philip Woolfson, Kees Kuilwijk, James Searles

Member
Lex Mundi

CATEGORIES OF WORK

Financial services
Jean Russotto, Philip Woolfson

Competition
Kees Kuilwijk, Craig Simpson

Environment
James Searles, Darren Abrahams

International trade
James Searles

Insurance and reinsurance
Philip Woolfson, Simon Arnot

Biotechnology and pharmaceuticals
Jean Russotto, Craig Simpson

International tax
Eric Osterweil

Information technology
Kees Kuilwijk

Belgian domestic corporate, commercial and financial services law
Michael Olislaegers

THE FIRM

Steptoe & Johnson LLP is a multinational partnership with offices in Brussels, London, Washington DC, New York, Phoenix and Los Angeles. With more than 400 lawyers worldwide, Steptoe & Johnson provides counsel and representation in virtually every area of law. In over 50 years of practice, the firm has gained an international reputation for vigorous representation of clients before government agencies, successful advocacy in litigation and arbitrations and creative and practical advice in guiding business transactions.

The Brussels office provides legal services in three principal areas: European Union and international; Belgian corporate and commercial and international tax.

The firm's Brussels lawyers draw on a broad range of knowledge and experience. British, Belgian, Dutch, French, Swiss, Canadian and US lawyers advise on matters involving their national legal systems and on issues raised in the context of the European Union (EU), the World Trade Organisation and other international fora.

AREAS OF PRACTICE

The Brussels legal team has a long and distinguished history of working with EU institutions. Its regulatory competence is diverse, including EU/international trade, biotechnology and chemicals regulation, financial services and insurance, environment, technology and communications, competition and litigation. Supplementing the EU regulatory practice, the Brussels office also offers counsel on Belgian corporate, financial and commercial issues, and on international tax and structuring.

Brussels office clients come from all across the globe. The firm represents national and multinational companies, European and international trade associations.

With over 30 years' experience in Brussels, its services include: assessment of new regulatory proposals; legal support and lobbying strategy to influence regulatory proposals; advice on implementation and application of EU law in the member states; advice on validity of EU laws; challenges to member state laws through EU administrative procedures or judicial proceedings; challenges to EU decisions before the EU courts; and advice and advocacy on compliance with international laws of measures adopted by the EU or its member states.

The firm regularly advises clients in the following substantive areas of law: banking and other financial services; competition/antitrust; consumer protection; environment; life sciences; insurance; market access (within and outside the EU); and technology, e-commerce and telecommunications.

It currently advises clients in the following industrial and service sectors: agricultural products; banking; biotechnology; chemicals; consumer products; direct selling; food and drink; insurance; information and communications technologies; medical devices; motor vehicles; pharmaceuticals; and plant protection products and biocides.

Steptoe & Johnson LLP has concluded a cooperation agreement with Olislaegers & De Creus, an independent Belgian law firm (located in its office) that also serves as the Belgian law practice for the clients of Steptoe & Johnson. The firms work closely together to provide seamless expertise on Belgian national law, particularly corporate, commercial and finacial services aspects. The Olislaegers & De Creus co-operation with Steptoe & Johnson, in turn, gives the firms Belgian corporate clients access to distinguished counsel in the major business centres of both Europe and the United States.

The international tax practice offers tax planning for, and implementation of, structures for corporate entities doing business in a wide variety of jurisdictions, as well as representation of clients before tax administrations and the courts.

STIBBE

RUE H WAFELAERTSSTRAAT 47-51
1060 BRUSSELS

Telephone: +32 2 533 52 11
Fax: +32 2 533 52 12
E-mail: info@stibbe.be
Website: www.stibbe.com

Languages
Dutch, English, French, German, Italian, Spanish

Other offices
Amsterdam, London, New York

Number of lawyers 276
at this office 108

Contact
Oliver Clevenbergh

CATEGORIES OF WORK

Administrative law
David D'Hooghe

Banking, finance and capital markets
Jan Peeters

Competition/EU regulatory
Peter Wytinck

Construction
Vera Van Houtte

Corporate and commercial
Olivier Clevenbergh

Dispute resolution
Jean-Pierre Fierens

Environment and permits
Jan Bouckaert

Fraud and white-collar crime
Hans Van Bavel

Information technology
Erik Valgaeren

Intellectual property
Brigitte Dauwe

Labour and employment
Jean-Philippe Cordier

Mergers and acquisitions
Marc Fyon

Real estate
Rudy Nauwelaerts

Tax
Werner Heyvaert

TAYLOR WESSING

TRÔNE HOUSE
4 RUE DU TRÔNE
1000 BRUSSELS

Telephone: +32 2 289 60 60
Fax: +32 2 289 60 70
E-mail: brussels@taylorwessing.com
Website: www.taylorwessing.com

Languages
Dutch, English, French, German

Other offices
Alicante*, Berlin, Brussels, Cambridge, Dubai*, Düsseldorf, Frankfurt, Hamburg, Munich, London, Paris, Shanghai*

Number of lawyers 598
at this office 13

Contacts
Marc Picat, Christine Flion, Jean Van Steenwinckel

Member
Interlex; Unilaw

CATEGORIES OF WORK

Corporate, M&A

Employment and pensions

Environment and town planning

Tax law

Estate planning

Commercial and contracts law

IP

Dispute resolution

EU law and internal market

EU and national competition law

EU and national merger control

EU state aid

EU public procurement

EU regulatory affairs

Trade and WTO

Life sciences and healthcare

TIBERGHIEN (IN COOPERATION WITH ALTIUS)

AVENUE DU PORT, 86C/419
1000 BRUSSELS

Telephone: +32 2 773 40 00
Fax: +32 2 773 40 55
Email: info@tiberghien.com
Website: www.tiberghien.com

Languages
Dutch, English, French, German

Other offices
Antwerp

Number of lawyers 43

Contact
Bernard Peeters
(bernard.peeters@tiberghien.com)

CATEGORIES OF WORK

Tax (including individual and corporate income tax; VAT; customs and excise law; European/international tax law; inheritance tax; stamp duties and equivalent taxes; real estate taxes-registration and mortgage taxes; local and environmental taxes)

Tax litigation

Estate planning

Family property law

UGGC & ASSOCIÉS

AVENUE ALBERT ELISABETH 46
BOÎTE 1
1200 BRUSSELS

Telephone: +32 2 736 66 14
Fax: +32 2 736 68 18
E-mail: avocats@uggc-law.be
Website: www.uggc-law.be

Languages
Arabic, Dutch, English, French, German, Italian, Spanish

Other offices
Casablanca, Paris

Number of lawyers 95
at this office 8

CATEGORIES OF WORK

Tax and corporate law
Jean-Nicolas Goossens

Commercial law
Philip Van Doorn,
Willem-Henri van Rijckevorsel

Competition and EC law
Philip Van Doorn

Real estate and construction
Willem-Henri van Rijckevorsel

Arbitration and mediation
Philip Van Doorn

VAN BAEL & BELLIS

AVENUE LOUISE 165
1050 BRUSSELS

Telephone: +32 2 647 73 50
Fax: +32 2 640 64 99
Email: info@vanbaelbellis.com
Website: www.vanbaelbellis.com

Languages
Arabic, Bulgarian, Dutch, English, Finnish, French, German, Greek, Italian, Japanese, Polish, Russian, Spanish, Swedish, Ukrainian

Other offices
Geneva

Number of lawyers 60

CATEGORIES OF WORK

EC and national competition law

EC and international trade law (anti-dumping and other trade protection measures; customs law; WTO)

Regulatory law (pharmaceuticals, aviation, telecommunications, energy)

Belgian business law

Arbitration and litigation

Mergers and acquisitions and corporate law

Intellectual property and IT

Employment

Pharmaceutical law

Tax

EU regulatory (environment, consumer protection, product safety)

VERHAEGEN WALRAVENS

6 CHAUSSÉE DE BOONDAEL
1050 BRUSSELS

Telephone: +32 2 640 96 97
Fax: +32 2 648 08 09
E-mail: info@verwal.net
Website: www.verwal.net

Languages
Dutch, English, French, German, Portuguese, Spanish

Number of lawyers 25

International groupings
European Legal Alliance

CATEGORIES OF WORK

Corporate and commercial
Jacques Verhaegen, Philip Walravens

Dispute resolution
Eric Cusas, Philip Walravens

Banking and finance
Pierre Frühling

Aviation
Pierre Frühling

Fraud and white-collar crime
Emmanuel Roger France, Eric Cusas

IT
Emmanuel Roger France

Employment
Anne Kamp

M&A
Jacques Verhaegen, Philip Walravens

Real estate
Jacques Verhaegen, Eric Cusas

ADVOKATFIRMAN VINGE

RUE DU LUXEMBOURG 3
1000 BRUSSELS

Telephone: +32 2 501 07 00
Fax: +32 2 501 07 07
Website: www.vinge.se

Languages
English, French, Swedish

Other Offices
Gothenburg, Helsingborg, Hong Kong, London, Malmö, Paris, Shanghai, Stockholm

Number of lawyers 300
at this office 4

Contact
Olle Rislund

Member
Scandinavian Law Alliance with Kromann Reumert (Denmark) and Thommessen (Norway); Lex Mundi

CATEGORIES OF WORK	
Banking and finance	Litigation and arbitration
Bankruptcy and liquidation	M&A
China practice	Marketing
Corporate finance, capital markets	Media
Employment and benefits	Private equity funds
EU and antitrust	Public procurement
Financial services and regulations	Real estate and environmental
General corporate	Tax
Insurance	Telecommunications
Intellectual property	Transport
IT	

THE FIRM

With some 300 fee-earners, Vinge is one of the largest law firms in Scandinavia. The firm is a member of the Scandinavian Law Alliance together with Kromann Reumert in Denmark and Thommessen in Norway.

Vinge has offices in Stockholm, Gothenburg, Malmö and Helsingborg as well as in London, Paris, Brussels, Hong Kong and Shanghai. The firm's clients include domestic and international commercial enterprises, financial institutions and state and regulatory bodies. Vinge is committed to providing the highest-quality legal advice and experience for all matters in which the firm becomes involved, to the highest professional standards.

Innovation, creativeness and a business-orientated, problem-solving approach are at the core of the practice. The firm's size means that there are resources available to handle large and complex domestic and cross-border transactions within tight time frames. At the same time, there is a strong focus on responsiveness and personal commitments to clients. Vinge's motto is: A good commercial lawyer sees beyond the law.

AREAS OF PRACTICE

Vinge specialises in all aspects of commercial law and is consistently ranked amongst the leading law firms in Scandinavia in a number of key practice areas. Vinge's extensive network of contacts comprises independent law firms, consultants and investment banks with whom the firm works regularly on domestic and cross-border deals and projects.

The firm takes an overall approach as well as providing in-depth knowledge by working together with major foreign law firms. Vinge has developed a wide international network which is available to its clients. The firm's broad experience and expertise means that it is called upon to handle all kinds of commercial law issues. It has learned from experience what resources and services are required in order to find the right solutions to clients' problems.

Vinge does everything it can to help clients to achieve success in their business. The firm sees beyond the problems and seeks the solutions.

WILLKIE FARR & GALLAGHER LLP

AVENUE LOUISE 480/3B
1050 BRUSSELS

Telephone: +32 2 290 18 20
Fax: +32 2 290 18 21
Website: www.willkie.com

Languages
French, English, Dutch, German, Norwegian

Other offices
Frankfurt, London, Milan, New York, Paris, Rome, Washington DC

Number of lawyers 590
at this office 11

Contacts
Xavier Dieux, Marc van der Woude

CATEGORIES OF WORK

Mergers and acquisitions

Litigation and arbitration

Corporate finance

Aviation

Banking law

Competition

Business reorganisation/ restructuring

Energy law

WILMER CUTLER PICKERING HALE AND DORR LLP

BASTION TOWER
PLACE DU CHAMP DE MARS 5
1050 BRUXELLES

Telephone: +32 2 285 49 00
Fax: +32 2 285 49 49
Email: law@wilmerhale.com
Website: www.wilmerhale.com

Languages
Czech, Dutch, English, French, German, Greek, Italian, Russian, Spanish

Other offices
Baltimore, Beijing, Berlin, Boston, London, Munich, New York, Northern Virginia, Oxford, Palo Alto, Waltham, Washington DC

Number of lawyers 1,100
at this office 26

CATEGORIES OF WORK

Aviation	**International trade**
Belgian commercial law	**Litigation**
Cartel investigations	**Media and sports law**
Competition	**Merger control**
Environment	**Public procurement**
EU regulatory	**State aids**
Financial services	**Telecommunications and regulated industries**
Information technology and intellectual property	**Transactions, corporate**

THE FIRM

WilmerHale offers unparalleled legal representation across a comprehensive range of practice areas that are critical to the success of its clients. The firm has over 1000 lawyers operating in five countries and practices at the very top of the legal profession. The depth and scope of the practice give it the ability to anticipate obstacles, seize opportunities and get the case resolved or the deal done – and the experience and know-how to prevent it from being undone.

WilmerHale was formed in May 2004 through the merger of two leading law firms, Hale and Dorr LLP and Wilmer Cutler Pickering LLP. The formation of the new firm fused two historic traditions of pro bono and public services. This commitment continues to be an integral part of the cultural fabric of the firm.

WilmerHale's Brussels office, established in 1990, concentrates on complex, challenging issues at the intersection of business, law and policy. The success of the Brussels office can be attributed to the continued work in these areas, as well as to the careful combination of an exceptional group of lawyers from across Europe and North America.

AREAS OF PRACTICE

WilmerHale is internationally recognised for its premier practices in antitrust and competition; aviation; bankruptcy; civil and criminal trial and appellate litigation; communications; corporate; defence and national security; financial institutions; intellectual property counseling and litigation; international arbitration; life sciences; securities regulation, enforcement and litigation; tax; and trade. In each practice area, WilmerHale lawyers bring the same insight, dedication to excellence, and commitment to client service needed for its clients to achieve their business objectives. Major areas of activity in the Brussels office include:

EU antitrust/competition: the firm is well versed in all aspects of the law, including merger control, cartel investigations, behavioral issues and state aid. The firm also has extensive experience in obtaining regulatory clearance of multi-jurisdictional mergers and joint ventures from national competition authorities and advises on national competition law.

Customs, trade, WTO and anti-dumping: the firm's lawyers counsel and represent clients in all areas of international trade regulation, with a special focus on anti-dumping and disputes before the WTO.

IT, communications and e-commerce: the firm has many years of practice in all aspects of these industries and advises extensively on pan-European and global issues, including regulation, transactions and privacy and data protection.

EU regulatory: the firm handles complex regulatory and legislative issues across industry sectors including aviation, financial services, energy, life sciences and environment.

Court litigation: the firm's Brussels lawyers have extensive experience in litigating contentious EU law issues before the European courts in Luxembourg, as well as before national courts.

Corporate: the firm's regulatory practices benefit from the support of experienced commercial lawyers.

LAGA

BERKENLAAN 8A
1831 DIEGEM

Telephone: +32 2 800 70 00
Fax: +32 2 800 70 01
E-mail: info@laga.be
Website: www.laga.be

Languages
Dutch, English, French, German, Russian, Spanish

Other offices
Antwerp, Brussels, Kortrijk, Namur

Number of lawyers 100+

International groupings
American Chamber of Commerce, Belgian Venturing Association, Belgian Franchising Association, Union Professionelle du Secteur Immobilier, Genootschap Advocaten Publiekrecht, Forum Milieuadvocaten, IFA, IBA, IAPIP, The Belgian Chapter of the International Chamber of Commerce

CATEGORIES OF WORK

Corporate law
Hilde Laga, Philippe Ernst

Mergers and acquisitions
Thomas Denys

Capital markets
Thomas Denys

Asset and structured finance
Werner Van Lembergen

Banking and financial law
Werner Van Lembergen, Philippe Ernst

Private equity
Thomas Denys

Commercial law
Christiane Cunningham, Bart De Moor

Real estate law
Collette De Ridder, Dirk Van Heuven

Insolvency and reorganisation
Bart De Moor

European and competition law
Guillemette Smadja,
Beatrice Vanden Abeele

Employment social security and immigration law
Erwin Vandervelde, Ilse Govaert

Public law
Dirk Van Heuven

Tax and real estate tax law
Benoit Nibelle, Johan Speecke

Private client advisory and estate planning
Mark Delboo

Dispute resolution
Hilda Laga, Bart De Moor

THE FIRM

With over 100 lawyers and an extensive specialisation, Laga is one of the most prominent law firms in Belgium. Partners and senior lawyers at the firm include lawyers with over 20 years' experience at the bar, as well as lawyers from a wide range of professional backgrounds including academia, tax and legal consultancy, industry and the banking world.

Laga also has offices in Antwerp, Brussels, Kortrijk and Namur; and works with top firms throughout Europe with which it has built up privileged relationships.

Laga is a full-service law firm comprised of lawyers who specialise in a wide range of disciplines. The firm works for multinational groups, financial institutions and government bodies. National and medium-sized businesses, start-ups, non-profit organisations and individuals are also part of the firm's client portfolio. This diversity is a direct consequence of Laga's unique blend of talents and profiles as well as its structure, which enables the firm to both efficiently address frequently asked questions and resolve complex and international legal issues.

AREAS OF PRACTICE

The corporate law/mergers and acquisitions/private equity/capital markets department specialises in group restructuring, corporate governance, acquisitions, divestitures, management buy-outs and joint ventures, IPO's, delistings and mergers and due diligences.

The banking and finance team provide advice on financial services, hybrid financing, assets, securities, cross-border leasing, venture capital, project financing, investment funds, advice for institutional investors and regulatory advice.

Commercial law work includes commercial distribution (agency, distributorships and franchise), sale of goods, bills of exchange, commercial leases, sureties and transport.

The firm's experts provide advice and assistance in many areas of employment and social security law, from drawing up and terminating contracts and drafting collective agreements to creating work regulations and pension schemes. They have also acquired extensive experience in dealing with mass redundancies and restructuring measures.

The firm's private client advisory and estate planning practice has extensive knowledge and experience in domestic and international estate planning; this encompasses family, property and security, income tax, hybrid financing structures, offshore planning and wealth tax.

The European law department provides a wide range of high-quality services on competition, state aids, public procurement and EU funding. The department has an extensive track record of working with the European Commission.

The insolvency and reorganisation department is made up of commercial law practitioners with extensive experience in advising distressed companies, and the creditors of distressed companies, and devising and implementing corporate recovery plans.

Active in public law, the firm also deals with construction, environment and public procurement.

The real estate team has extensive experience in civil property law and contract law relating to property; as well as town planning and finance structuring.

The tax practice offers clients creative, multi-jurisdictional tax planning and high-quality personalised advisory services in a broad range of tax matters; including M&A, international and local corporate restructuring.

In the area of dispute resolution, the firm has been involved in several civil and criminal law suits, particularly in the fields of corporate and employment law litigation. Also in responsibility cases involving industrial risk. Some of the firm's experienced lawyers are also appointed as arbitrators, mediators or legal experts on a regular basis.

DE WOLF LAW FIRM

ETIKHOVESTRAAT 6
9680 MAARKEDAL

Telephone: +32 5 523 52 00
Fax: +32 5 530 06 51
E-mail: dewolf@lawfirmdewolf.com
Website: www.lawfirmdewolf.com

Languages
English, French, German

Number of lawyers 6

CATEGORIES OF WORK

Public procurement (including EU law)
Carlos De Wolf, Jozef Timmermans

Construction law
Carlos De Wolf, Leen De Smet

Project finance
Carlos De Wolf

Environmental law
Carlos De Wolf, Karolien Beké

Insurance law
Hilde Van Parys

Real estate law
Carlos De Wolf, Leen De Smet

Company law (including public law companies)
Jozef Timmermans

Planning and zoning
Carlos De Wolf, Karolien Beké

BOSNIA-HERZEGOVINA

Population	**4.2 million**
Number of lawyers (Federation of Bosnia and Herzegovina)	**680**
(Republika Srpska)	**412**
Professional title	**Advokat**
Currency	**Mark**
Index	
Corporate and M&A	130
Intellectual property	131
Country index	5

Following its declaration of independence from the Socialist Federation of Yugoslavia, in March 1992, Bosnia-Herzegovina (BiH) suffered serious conflict. The struggle to recover from three years of bloody inter-ethnic war, during which 250,000 citizens died in the battle between Bosnian Muslims, Croats and Serbs, lingers. The 'Dayton Agreement', signed in December 1995, struck a balance resulting in the development of three ethnically based spheres of influence dominated by party organisations, not necessarily corresponding with the formal structures of a government. These informal units in many ways determined the rule of law and role of politics in the legal process. Reforms have since been introduced in order to strengthen central government.

Today, although an EU-led peacekeeping force remains in place, the peace has outlasted the war and BiH is a single state within internationally recognised borders with a State-level government and separate, fully elected governments in two entities, 'Federation of BiH' and 'Republica Srpska'. International administration has helped the country maintain fragile peace and work to repair the damage wreaked by war continues to make progress.

The country is ideally located, enjoys a rich tradition of successful participation in international projects and has a highly qualified and motivated labour force, proficient in foreign languages. Its development has progressed over the last six years but rather discouragingly for a country considering itself a potential candidate for EU membership, remains well below the average level in the EU.

BILLING

Billing is complicated in BiH and depends on many variables. Generally, tariffs are set by the Bar Association and domestic firms charge €50-€100 per hour for a consultation. Alternatively, lawyers may agree a fee with clients and can do this by way of a written contract.

At the beginning of 2005, Parliament initiated a change in the law by setting a limit on the amount lawyers can charge. However, this change was imprecise and has not yet been fully implemented.

MARKETING

Suppression of advertising law firms' services has a longstanding tradition and was established to prevent unfair competition and to ensure the protection of clients. According to the Statute on the Bar Association, lawyers are permitted to publish limited details on a board outside the office, a letterhead, a professional listing of lawyers and a website.

ECONOMY

BiH is the poorest political order in the former Yugoslav Republic and has been plagued by prolonged economic dysfunction. The pre-war economy was diversified with a large industrial base and well-educated workforce. The war had a devastating effect on the economy, virtually paralysing trade and ceasing almost all exports. The economy was further disadvantaged by the framework within which it has been forced to develop. Two serious problems remain: a sizeable current account deficit; and high unemployment rates, estimated at around 44%.

Thankfully, BiH is entering a phase of positive economic development and stability. In 2000 the rate of economic growth increased by 10%. GDP has seen a steady rise in recent years and in 2004 it grew to around 5%. Foreign direct investment remains low, hindered by excessive layers of bureaucracy, political interference and corruption. However, there is an increasing presence of large, international corporations. The country receives a substantial amount of reconstruction and humanitarian aid from the international community but needs to prepare for an era of declining assistance.

The economy is heavily dependent on imports and in most sectors the market is dominated by goods or services from Croatia, Serbia and Montenegro, Slovenia, Austria, Italy and Germany. Agriculture is predominantly privatised but farms are mostly small and inefficient. Domestic production is extremely limited and industry greatly overstaffed, a hangover of the socialist economic structure of Yugoslavia.

An extensive transition of the market economy has begun in BiH and government at all levels is working towards fulfilling conditions set by the European Commission before negotiations can begin on the Stabilisation and Accession Agreement.

LEGAL MARKET

It is difficult to find reputable lawyers in BiH. Those with the best education and language skills often

The largest firms

1	Maniega & Soler Abogados	9
2	Branko & Vladimir Maric	7
	Branko Maric, Law Office	7
	Wolf Theiss	7
5	Ruzica Topic, Attorney at Law	6
6	Amila Ferizovic Kunosic, Attorney at Law	3
	Bojana Tkalcic-Dulic & Olodar Prebanic, Lawyers Office	3
	Emir Kovacevic, Attorney at Law	3
	IKRP Roka & Partners Ltd	3
	Karabdic Kerim, Advokat	3
	Lansky, Ganzger & Partner d.o.o.	3
12	DLA Weiss-Tessbach in cooperation with local attorneys	2
13	Zlatko Sehovic, Attorney at Law	1

These figures represent the total number of lawyers in this country only, and have been supplied by the firms themselves. The figures should be accurate as at 1 January 2006.

take on highly paid posts with government bodies, though it has been suggested that this will change as the legal market evolves.

The legal market in BiH is undeveloped and mainly consists of independent lawyers' offices with one or two lawyers and one administrative employee. The current law stipulates that a lawyer must have practised for five years before he is allowed to hire an associate. This rule is criticised for being discriminatory and the Office of the High Representative is looking into this discrepancy.

There is no real presence of foreign firms in BiH, with the exception of a few Austrian firms: **DLA Weiss-Tessbach in cooperation with local attorneys**, **Wolf Theiss** and **Lansky, Ganzger & Partner d.o.o.**. However, there is room in the market for more foreign firms and as the legal market develops, further arrivals are possible. Progress in the legal market is hindered by the existence of the two separate entities but foreign lawyers believe the market will follow those of Croatia and Slovenia and more multi-lawyer firms will begin to appear.

LEGISLATIVE DEVELOPMENTS

The complex legal and regulatory framework in BiH is a serious impediment to the country's progression. There are, nevertheless, ongoing attempts to reform the territory. In 2004 BiH passed State-level framework laws on land registration and accounting and auditing.

The American Bar Association Central European and Eurasian Law Initiative (CEELI) has had a big influence on legal reform in BiH. CEELI targets legal and professional reform and is particularly focused on capacity building for lawyers and strengthening the organised Bar. CEELI has also been working with the bar associations in BiH to form a unified structure and in past years succeeded in encouraging the various bar associations in the Federation to unify into one joint association. CEELI's criminal law reform programme recently focused on Criminal Procedure Code and Criminal Code reform.

CORPORATE AND M&A

CORPORATE AND M&A

Bojana Tkalcic-Dulic & Olodar Prebanic, Lawyers Office
Branko Maric, Law Office ✪
DLA Weiss-Tessbach in cooperation with local attorneys ✪

Amila Ferizovic Kunosic, Attorney at Law
IKRP Roka & Partners Ltd
Karabdic Kerim, Advokat ✪
Lansky, Ganzger & Partner d.o.o.
Pasalic & Pasalic, Lawyers Office
Ruzica Topic, Attorney at Law
Wolf Theiss ✪

Emir Kovacevic, Attorney at Law
Irena Mojovic, Advokatska Kancelarija
Zlatko Sehovic, Attorney at Law

Firms are listed A-Z in tiers which are ranked in order of priority
✪ Indicates firm displays contact details at the end of this chapter.

The three attorneys at **Lawyers Office Bojana Tkalcic-Dulic & Olodar Prebanic** are accomplished in corporate and commercial law. Clients include embassies, international banks, multinational companies and global organisations. In 2005 the firm advised international investors in privatisation projects and prime acquisitions of companies and banks in BiH. The firm's clients are very satisfied with the quality of work and praise the firm's 'in-depth analysis of problems, straightforward problem-solving skills, proactive thinking and advising on alternative solutions'.

The commercial department at **Law Office Branko Maric** comprises a team of experienced lawyers specialised in commercial transactions. The firm offers a wide range of legal services for companies of all sizes, within all business sectors and is particularly dominant in the banking and finance sector – in the last year the firm has acted in numerous acquisitions of banks and insurance companies in BiH. The firm represented the EBRD in banking matters and Coca-Cola, Benetton and Volkswagen in privatisation procedures. Clients declare Maric and his associate to be 'professional, pleasant, co-operative and efficient'. **Law Office Branko Maric** moves up a place to the top tier this year due to its professional reputation and ability to propose optimum solutions.

DLA Weiss-Tessbach in cooperation with local attorneys co-operates with a local office in BiH. The office consists of three lawyers specialising in corporate, finance and real estate law. The firm represents subsidiaries of some of the world's leading banks and assists foreign clients with the establishment of local presences. In 2005 the firm handled the acquisition of Mittal Steel by the Kuwaiti Investment Office.

The three-lawyer team at **Amila Ferizovic Kunosic, Attorney at Law** boasts long-term, legal experience with a reputation for being accessible without a formalistic, complicated approach. Head of the office, Amila Kunosic-Ferizovic, previously worked at the Ministry of Justice and as a Vice-Public Prosecutor. Highlights over the year include advocating a change in court practice in BiH. Clients praise Ferizovic's high level of professional knowledge and quality of legal expertise.

Advokat Karabdic Kerim currently comprises two attorneys but expansion and relocation are imminent. The firm prides itself on high-speed, high-quality, solution-oriented legal services with particular expertise in privatisation law. The firm has just undertaken the representation of Sony and Hyundai and assisted a leading, international law firm with the review of an EU directive.

Austrian firm, **Lansky, Ganzger & Partner d.o.o.** has a subsidiary office in BiH, which assists foreign investors in joint ventures and M&A. The firm has completed significant work involving legal due diligence and advised on the establishment in BiH of international banks and other financial institutions.

Lawyers Office Pasalic & Pasalic diligently practises civil rights and compensation law. This father-daughter partnership has a long history in BiH and offers services in several languages. The firm advises several big-name clients including Hyundai, Xerox and Mercedes-Benz. Last year the firm represented a dominant car manufacturer in a €50m damages compensation claim. Respect is gained for the firm's responsiveness, commitment to deadlines and specific advice.

Ruzica Topic, Attorney at Law specialises in company establishment in BiH and is supported by a team of six attorneys. The firm has represented the World Bank, Deloitte & Touche and the EBRD and was responsible for the legal services provided in the biggest privatisation project in the Republic of Srpska, involving a government institution. The firm is experienced in advising foreign entities such as multinational manufacturers, industrial companies and trading companies in establishing and developing a business presence in BiH. Topic's clients claim the direction and representation they receive is 'honest, thorough and always in the client's best interests'.

Wolf Theiss has a branch in BiH comprising two attorneys, Renuka Kukanesen and Sandra Mueller. Last year the firm carried out due diligence work for large corporations and prepared a labour by-law for the Bosnian subsidiary of a leading software company. Clients are happy with the quality of work carried out by the firm.

Advokatska Kancelarija Irena Mojovic is highly experienced in corporate and commercial practice, particularly in matters involving the incorporation and registration of companies. The firm has advised several large Bosnian companies on privatisation matters. One client believes Mojovic, who possesses 30 years of experience as a lawyer and judge, to be 'the best lawyer in Bosnia'.

Sole practitioner **Zlatko Sehovic, Attorney at Law** has been active in BiH since 1988. He represents clients in many European countries and speaks German and English fluently. Sehovic primarily advises on indemnity cases against Bosnian companies and major clients include Lufthansa and Bank of Austria.

INTELLECTUAL PROPERTY

BiH experiences problems with the adequate protection of IPRs. The country's porous borders make it a distribution point for pirated goods. There are few attorneys specialising in this area of law, but after receiving criticism from the IP Alliance in 2004, an effort to make improvements is expected.

INTELLECTUAL PROPERTY

Branko Maric, Law Office ✪
Pasalic & Pasalic, Lawyers Office

Emir Kovacevic, Attorney at Law
Wolf Theiss ✪

Firms are listed A-Z in tiers which are ranked in order of priority
✪ Indicates firm displays contact details at the end of this chapter.

Law Office Branko Maric is one of the few offices registered as a trade mark agency in BiH. Advice on all issues regarding IP is available. Maric is lauded by clients as 'an absolute leader and authority in his office' and is very well connected in legal circles in BiH.

Specialist IP firm **Lawyers Office Pasalic & Pasalic** represents a number of prestigious, global companies including Kraft Foods, Levi Strauss and Nestlé. Clients comment that the firm is very responsive and has an eye for detail. Partners Inja and Rizah Pasalic, are capable patent agents. In 2005 the firm represented the world's biggest food and beverage company in a trade mark infringement case. One very satisfied client reports 'Inja Pasalic is smart, skilled, straightforward, in short a dream lawyer'.

Wolf Theiss's subsidiary office handles IP and IT work through Georg Kresbach, a Vienna-based partner. Last year the firm represented international clients in cross-border, counterfeit claims.

LAW OFFICE BRANKO MARIC

MEHMEDA SPAHE 24
71000 SARAJEVO

Telephone: +387 33 716 030
Fax: +387 33 716 036/210 316
E-mail: maric.b@bih.net.ba

Languages
Bosnian, Croatian, English, French, German, Italian, Serbian

Number of lawyers 7

International groupings
The South East Europe Legal Group (SEE Legal)

CATEGORIES OF WORK

Arbitration and mediation
Visnja Dizdarevic

Banking
Branko Maric, Visnja Dizdarevic

Corporate
Branko Maric, Dijana Ivanovic

Energy/utilities
Visnja Dizdarevic

Indemnity claims
Predrag Radovanovic, Ezmana Hadziavdic

Consumer protection and product liability
Emina Pasagic

Intellectual property
Emina Pasagic

Privatisation
Branko Maric, Dijana Ivanovic

Real estate/construction law and project development
Emina Pasagic, Ezmana Hadziavdic

Taxation
Branko Maric

Telecoms/ IT
Branko Maric

Trade and other civil litigation
Predrag Radovanovic, Dzana Smailagic-Hromic

THE FIRM

The Law Office Maric was established in 1959 when its founder Dr Vladimir Maric left the position of president of the Commercial Court in Sarajevo and started a private practice as an attorney at law. Dr Maric's speciality at that time determined the present profile of the Office. The firm developed strongly after Bosnia and Herzegovina opened to foreign investments and foreign capital. The firm's specialisation, high professional level of service and communication with clients in the major world languages, as well as its ability to deal with all situations arising on the Bosnian and Herzegovina market, definitely placed it among the leading law offices in the country.

The Law Office Maric undertakes a wide range of contentious and non-contentious legal activities for diverse clients, these include: companies, partnerships, individuals, governments and governmental departments. Most of the firms' work is on an international level, and many of its clients are based abroad. The Office's aim is to always provide a high quality service in a friendly manner, applying the highest professional standards.

AREAS OF PRACTICE

Banking: Almost all banks in Bosnia and Herzegovina with a share of foreign capital have been clients of the Office, either regarding due diligence reports by acquisitions, consulting upon investments, solutions for organisational restructuring, or problems with their ongoing business activities. The firm has prepared studies for the World Bank, as well as the Bank Privatisation Unit of the Ministry of Finance of the Federation of Bosnia and Herzegovina. On the basis of the Office's suggestions, the concept of privatisation has been defined for a great number of banks currently operating in the Federation of Bosnia and Herzegovina.

Corporate: Law Office Branco Maric has extensive experience in incorporation and registration of companies, as well as in organisation, acquisition, sales, mergers, restructurings and corporate governance. The commercial department, comprised of a team of skilled lawyers, specialises in commercial transactions, the sale and distribution of merchandise, commercial agreements, secured transactions and commercial litigation.

Privatisation: Since the beginning of the privatisation process in Bosnia and Herzegovina and the firm's first privatisation agreement representing the Coca-Cola Company, it has taken part in the most important privatisation procedures performed, both in the capacity of sole legal advisers and in cooperation with large international law firms.

Real estate: The Office deals with real estate investments as a whole, and advises clients at all stages of the project, from planning to completion and leasing; letters of intent to acquisition and continuous counselling.

Energy: Since the transformation of the energy and utility sector in Bosnia and Herzegovina has been in process, the Office in partnership with an international consulting firm has been chosen to provide legal advice during the entire reorganisation process in the areas of the transfer and distribution of electrical energy and water management; financed by the European Union and USAID.

Telecoms: The firm has considerable experience regarding the acquisition of licenses in the mobile telephone sector, as well as regarding all activities of internet service providers, since it participated in providing solutions to problems relating to the distribution of domains in Bosnia and Herzegovina.

Indemnity claims: The Office has been engaged in indemnity claims in insurance matters, and is experienced in the execution of indemnification requests and court proceedings related to these requests. The Law Office participated as a local consultant in the creation of all insurance laws, including both applicable laws as well as laws in the process of adoption.

Intellectual property: The Office is one of the few offices that is registered as a trade mark agent in Bosnia and Herzegovina. Besides official trademark protection it provides counselling on all issues regarding intellectual property, including authors rights, trade marks and brands.

DLA WEISS-TESSBACH

IN COOPERATION WITH LOCAL ATTORNEYS

FRA ANDJELA ZVIZDOVICA 1/10
71000 SARAJEVO

Telephone: +387 33 295 236
Fax: +387 33 295 242
E-mail: sarajevo@dlapiper.com
Website: www.dlapiper.com

Languages
Bosnian, Croatian, English, Serbian

Other offices
Austria, Belgium, China, Croatia, Czech Republic, Denmark*, Egypt*, France, Georgia, Germany, Hong Kong, Hungary, Italy, Japan, Netherlands, Norway*, Poland*, Russia, Singapore*, Slovakia, South Africa*, Spain, Sweden*, Thailand, UK, Ukraine, United Arab Emirates, US

Number of lawyers 3,100
at this office 3

Contact
Barbara Novosel (Vienna)

Member
DLA Piper Group

CATEGORIES OF WORK

General commercial	**Corporate**
Banking and finance	**Mergers and acquisitions**
Real estate	**Litigation**
Privatisation	

THE FIRM

DLA Weiss-Tessbach was established in 1878 in Austria and is one of the longest-established law firms in the country. Since 1989, the firm has undergone a dynamic expansion across Central and Eastern Europe, growing from 15 to over 100 lawyers and from one to seven offices, including Sarajevo, where it operates in co-operation with local attorneys. DLA Weiss-Tessbach will continue to expand in the Central and Eastern European region as countries adjust to EU membership.

DLA Weiss-Tessbach is part of DLA Piper Rudnick Gray Cary, one of the leading global legal service organisations, with approximately 3,100 lawyers in 58 offices across 22 countries. The organisation is committed to building long-term relationships with its clients and supports their strategic and operational needs both locally and internationally.

AREAS OF PRACTICE

The firm has strengthened its core areas of expertise (commercial and corporate, M&A, banking and finance, general commercial law, real estate), and advises its clients as a full-service firm in all relevant areas of business law, including administrative law, employment law, IT and telecoms, technology, intellectual property, venture capital and capital markets.

DLA Weiss-Tessbach has well-established relations with clients of various backgrounds. The firm advises medium-sized enterprises as well as leading (often publicly listed) international and domestic industrial groups, service providers, banks and other financial institutions and individuals.

DLA Weiss-Tessbach has established a particular reputation for its ability to handle cases in international cross-border contexts. The firm is renowned for its expertise in the structuring and implementation of projects and transactions in Bosnia, as well as in other countries in Central and Eastern Europe. It carefully views the ongoing developments in the Central and Eastern European region with the aim of combining the needs of the constantly changing international legal market and industry, whilst also upholding the high standard of service that the firm has always been able to offer to its clients.

ADVOKAT KARABDIC KERIM

BRAVADZILUK 8
71000 SARAJEVO

Telephone: +387 61 177 527
Fax: +387 33 531 500
E-mail: karabdic@bih.net.ba

Languages
English, German

Number of lawyers 3

Contact
Kerim Karabdic

Member
Juritax

CATEGORIES OF WORK

General commercial practice	Family law
Business law	Corporate and commercial
Property law	Banking and finance
Privatisation	Environment
Investments	Intellectual property
Charitable organisations	Foreign direct investment
International arbitration	Energy and natural resources

WOLF THEISS

FRA. ANDJELA ZVIZDOVICA 1
UNITIC TOWER
71000 SARAJEVO

Telephone: +387 33 296 444
Fax: +387 33 296 425
Website: www.wolftheiss.com

Languages
German, English, Bosnian

Other offices
Belgrade, Bratislava, Bucharest, Ljubljana, Prague, Tirana, Vienna, Zagreb

Number of lawyers 161
at this office 5

Contacts
Dieter Spranz, Renuka Kukanesen

CATEGORIES OF WORK

Arbitration, litigation

Banking and finance

Construction, real estate and leasing

Corporate counsel

Intellectual property

Labour

M&A

Reorganisation and restructuring

THE FIRM

Wolf Theiss was founded in 1957 in Vienna and today is one of the leading law firms in the CEE/SEE region. Over the past few years the firm has experienced extraordinarily dynamic growth, both domestically and internationally.

Wolf Theiss has established a network of nine offices* in Albania, Austria, Bosnia and Herzegovina, Croatia, the Czech Republic, Romania, Serbia and Montenegro, Slovakia and Slovenia. In 2005 alone, Wolf Theiss opened two new offices, in Bucharest and Sarajevo. The firm also regularly assists its clients with projects in Bulgaria, Hungary, Macedonia, Moldova, Poland, Turkey and Ukraine, in co-operation with local attorneys.

The firm's dynamic growth is also reflected in its increase in personnel. At present, Wolf Theiss employs over 350 individuals at nine locations – compare this to 30 employees in one office, Vienna, ten years ago and the growth is apparent.

*The firm's operations in the various locations are set up in compliance with local law and the Bar rules requirements which include the form of co-operation with independent local attorneys.

BULGARIA

Population	7.5 million
Number of lawyers	10,500
Professional title	Attorney
Currency	Lev (BGL)

Index

Bulgaria is now on track to becoming a fully functioning political democracy and market economy after its period under the communist sphere of influence between 1946 and 1990. It held its first multi-party election in 1990, joined Nato in 2004, and aims to join the EU in 2007 alongside Romania.

A general election in 2005 brought to power a coalition led by the Bulgarian Socialist Party (BSP), with BSP leader Sergei Stanishev elected Prime Minister. He replaced Simeon Saxe-Coburg-Gotha, who was both Prime Minister (2001-2005), and Tsar of Bulgaria (1943-1946).

BILLING

Fees at Bulgarian firms are generally lower than at international firms. Billing is generally by the hour, with rates ranging from €50 to €120 for an associate, €150 to €180 for a senior associate, and €150 to €300 an hour for a partner. Flat fees are common for certain procedures such as standard intellectual property matters.

MARKETING

As part of an effort to harmonise Bulgarian legal practice with EU standards, a new code of practice published in 2005 prohibits the disclosure of clients in marketing material. However, the new code has been criticised as poorly drafted and a source of a degree of confusion, as it neglects to mention whether it is acceptable to name clients that have consented to disclosure. Firms seem to apply different interpretations to the new code, and a majority of Bulgarian firms have well-produced and informative websites, many of which still reveal a good deal of client-related information.

IN-HOUSE LAWYERS

In-house teams at large companies will generally comprise no more than one or two lawyers, although the major Bulgarian banks tend to have larger legal departments.

In-house lawyers are not required to be members of the Bar, but must pass the Ministry of Justice's legal examination to provide legal opinion. In-house lawyers may however, represent employers in court.

ECONOMY

Under communism Bulgaria had a strong agricultural sector but its main industries such as steel, heavy chemicals, electronics and armaments were ill-suited to competition in a post-communist environment. The loss of protected markets led to a steep decline in output in the early and mid-1990s when Bulgaria became the poorest of the former Soviet satellite states in Central and Eastern Europe.

A minor recovery emerged in 1994. Unfortunately, this was derailed during 1996 due to short-sighted economic reforms and an unstable and de-capitalised banking system. 1997 saw ambitious reforms, including the introduction of a currency board regime. Inflationary pressures were curtailed, and growth and stability returned.

The country has since made significant progress. The privatisation process is well underway, with the banking sector now almost entirely privatised. 70% of Bulgaria's employees now work in the private sector. In 2004 the government finally managed to offload the state telecommunications company after nearly two years of legal wrangling. The only large privatisation still to be completed, other than granting concessions in the energy and resources sectors, is that of Bulgartabac, the giant state tobacco company. Recent attempts to privatise it have ended in failure. It now looks as if it will be broken up and sold bit by bit.

EU accession, planned for 2007, is a major incentive for foreign investment, which is vital to the country's much-needed economic growth. The IMF projects growth will be 5.7% in 2005 and 5.5% in 2006. Presently Germany and Austria are the most significant investors in Bulgaria, although Greece, Turkey and other proximate jurisdictions also play a part.

LEGAL MARKET

Although the market does feature international firms, so far the only one of a truly global scale to have opened is **CMS Cameron McKenna LLP;** fellow CMS Group member **CMS Reich-Rohrwig Hainz** operates a separate four-lawyer practice in Sofia. **CMS Cameron McKenna LLP** entered Bulgaria to service Advent, a major global client now significantly involved in Bulgarian telecommunications. The firm has now merged with *Hayhurst Robinson*. Others, such as Italy's **Studio Legale Sutti**, Austria's **Schönherr** and

The largest firms

1	Georgiev, Todorov & Co	48
2	Djingov, Gouginski, Kyutchukov & Velichkov	42
3	LIC-Penkov, Markov & Partners	38
4	Batkov, Stoev, Botev & Associates	35
5	Borislav Boyanov & Co	29
6	Seplex Law Offices	27
7	Novel Consult	23
8	Kambourov & Partners	22
9	LEGACOM Antov & Partners Law Firm	18
	Landwell Bulgaria	18
11	Eurolex Bulgaria Limited	17
12	Varadinov & Co Attorneys-at-Law	15
13	Dimitrov, Petrov & Co	14
14	Arsov, Natchev, Ganeva	13
	CMS Cameron McKenna LLP	13
	TelecomLex Consult - Cheresheva, Nachev & Partners	13
17	Dobrev, Kinkin & Lyutskanov Law Firm	12
	Simeonov & Dermendjiev	12
19	Borissov Law Office	11
	Interius	11
21	Braykov's Legal Office	10
	Deloitte Bulgaria EOOD	10
	KPMG Bulgaria OOD	10
	PI Partners	10
25	Atanassov & Ivanov Law Firm	9
	Sabev & Partners Law Firm	9
	Sutti, Studio Legale	9

These figures represent the total number of lawyers in this country only, and have been supplied by the firms themselves. The figures should be accurate as at 1 January 2006.

Greece's **IKRP Rokas & Partners OOD** have focused Central and Eastern European strategies and are present to facilitate the significant investments from neighbouring countries.

While it is likely that more firms will enter the market post EU-accession, expect no gold rush. Bulgaria is probably too small to warrant the entry of big international firms for purely strategic reasons. Like **CMS Cameron McKenna LLP**, the large internationals that do enter in future are likely to do so by following a big client on the back of a major acquisition or project. Many firms will remain content to conduct Bulgarian business out of other regional centres such as Vienna, Bratislava and Bucharest.

Legal practice in Bulgaria to some extent mirrors the difficult reforms of its judicial and regulatory bodies necessary for EU entry. Harmonisation with EU laws has now reached over 90%. Unfortunately, the country still has some way to go as aspects of the legal profession still suffer from vested interests that hinder progress towards transparent international practice standards. This is particularly the case with regards to the court system. It is often said that successful litigation is more about having the right contacts than the right argument. There were reports in October 2005 of a plan to sack 900 (relatively junior) investigating magistrates as part of an effort to clean up before EU accession. But some observers claim that this action is merely for show, and unlikely to root out the core of the problem, which may be much higher up the ladder.

Among domestic firms significantly involved in cross-border work, **Borislav Boyanov & Co** and **Djingov, Gouginski, Kyutchukov & Velichkov** are particularly credited for the way they have built practices embracing Western standards. Other commendable firms include **Georgiev, Todorov & Co**, **LIC-Penkov, Markov & Partners**, **Kambourov & Partners**, and **Novel Consult**.

BANKING AND FINANCE

BORISLAV BOYANOV & CO ✪
DJINGOV, GOUGINSKI, KYUTCHUKOV & VELICHKOV ✪
GEORGIEV, TODOROV & CO ✪
LIC-PENKOV, MARKOV & PARTNERS ✪

CMS Cameron McKenna LLP ✪
DIA Consult - Law Office
Dobrev, Kinkin, Lyutskanov & Partners ✪
Eastlaw
Eurolex Bulgaria Limited
Kambourov & Partners ✪
Landwell Bulgaria ✪
Novel Consult
Spasov & Bratanov ✪

Andonov & Radinska
Arsov, Natchev, Ganeva ✪
Boteva & Kantutis
Dospevsky & Partners, Law Office
Interius
KPMG Bulgaria OOD
LEGACOM Antov & Partners Law Firm ✪
PI Partners ✪
Seplex Law Offices
Simeonov & Dermendjiev

Atanassov & Ivanov Law Firm ✪
IKRP Rokas & Partners OOD
LGK & Co Law Office
Modus Consult
Sutti, Studio Legale ✪
Vladimirov Law Office

Firms are listed A-Z in tiers which are ranked in order of priority
✪ Indicates firm displays contact details at the end of this chapter.

BANKING AND FINANCE

In recent years **Borislav Boyanov & Co** has been significantly involved in the privatisation of Bulgaria's banking sector, and has advised several foreign banks starting operations in the country. Recently it acted for 16 banks on a €285m syndicated loan, and was active in significant real estate finance transactions, including advising the EBRD on the financing of a large hotel on the Balkan Peninsula, and a €35m deal to finance the acquisition of Bulgaria's largest department store. The firm counts Citibank and CSFB among its clients.

Djingov, Gouginski, Kyutchukov & Velichkov appears to work at the forefront of innovation in Bulgarian banking transactions. It worked on a securitisation of a major power plant in 2005, advised a number of international investment banks on derivatives transactions, represented a major international investment bank on a limited recourse acquisition financing, and advised a range of foreign banks on regulatory issues. Partners Stephan Kyutchukov, Vessela Stancheva and Nikolai Gouginski are recommended.

Although **Georgiev, Todorov & Co**'s workload is becoming increasingly concerned with concessions, projects, ITC and litigation, one should not discount its banking credentials. Clients have included ABN Amro, Bulgarian National Bank and Commerzbank, and it acted for the EBRD in establishing First Investment Bank. It has since advised the EBRD on secured lending projects. Other notable work includes handling the sale as a going concern of one of Bulgaria's largest-ever insolvent banks, and advising Mitsui on a €1bn project financing of a power plant.

LIC-Penkov, Markov & Partners has extensive experience, advising both banks and Bulgarian companies with regards to cross-border lending/borrowing. The firm also acted on the privatisations of Post Bank and the United Bulgarian Bank, two of Bulgaria's largest banks.

Regional player *Hayhurst Robinson* has brought a good deal of banking expertise to **CMS Cameron McKenna LLP**. Renata Petkova is reported to be a rising star among Bulgarian banking lawyers. The firm is notable for its involvement in project financings, notably advising two multinational investment banks on the US$58m financing of the Galata gasfield.

DIA Consult - Law Office has experience of advising banks on obtaining licences and maintaining contacts with state supervisory bodies, although the firm's strongest suit is insurance. In 2005 the firm advised the Bulgarian subsidiary of a major European insurance company on the establishment of an insurance brokerage in the Russian Federation. Antoaneta Dimolarova is recommended.

Vladimir Kinkin, Theodor Bojinov and Roumen Lyutskanov headline **Dobrev, Kinkin, Lyutskanov & Partners**' banking practice, which advises European banks, notably ING and Depfa Bank. The firm is particularly active in the financing of projects.

The National Bank of Bulgaria uses **Eastlaw** for advice on bank licensing and privatisation matters. Partner Angel Kalaidjiev is recommended from a firm that has also acted for foreign banks and insurance companies on licensing and starting operations in the country, notably ING and American Credit Bank.

Project finance is a great strength at **Eurolex Bulgaria Limited**. Various international financial institutions, including the EBRD, use the firm for funding Bulgarian projects. The firm also acts for Bulgarian banks in non project-related matters, such as loans and securitisations.

In 2005 Yavor Kambourov and Vladimir Rangeloff at **Kambourov & Partners** were involved in arranging capital increases and refinancings for Bulgarian banks. Of particular note was its work for a major international investment bank on the legal and financial structuring of the privatisation of a significant state-owned company, and providing legal representation to a bank on an €80m securitisation of an LBO transaction.

Landwell Bulgaria's Nikolay Bebov is a specialist in the regulatory aspects of Bulgaria's financial services laws. Various banking work includes conducting due diligence prior to banking mergers and acquisitions, advising a major Scandinavian bank on marine mortgages, and representing an international insurance group on the registration of a life business.

Novel Consult has become particularly involved in sorting out bad debts in recent years, devising legal tools for quick litigation in debt collecting, and working on debt restructuring programmes for Elit Bank, First Private Bank and Popular Co-operative Bank. The firm also advises international banks on direct lending, and reports growth in project finance-related transactions.

Spasov & Bratanov's Georgi Spasov has fifteen years of experience as a finance lawyer under his belt. A recognised expert in his field in Bulgaria, he is particularly recommended for cross-border lending. In recent years he advised foreign syndicates containing some of the world's best-known banks on a number of €100m + loans to Bulgarian entities.

After advising the Mall of Sofia on its €34m syndicated loan, **Andonov & Radinska** continued its work as legal advisor to Bulgaria's largest-ever real estate development, even when GE and Quinlan Partnership became major shareholders in the venture in 2005. The firm has since advised on €14m of new loans to the project, and the hedging of all loans via interest rate swaps.

Arsov, Natchev, Ganeva rises up the rankings this year by demonstrating its capability to handle large, cross-border lending, acting on a US$124m syndicated loan to Lukoil's Bulgarian subsidiary.

Nina Boteva of **Boteva & Kantutis** has a rare speciality in anti-money laundering. The firm counts Bank Austria, Nordvestbank and Eteva Bank among its clients, and conducted due diligence for a large Italian Bank on a possible acquisition in 2005.

Seplex Law Offices has a track record advising foreign and domestic banks. In 2005 it advised the EBRD on projects within the country, and continued to be active advising its foreign clients on their borrowings from local banks.

Atanassov & Ivanov Law Firm is carving out a niche in debt recovery and is involved in pioneering factoring in Bulgaria, notably advising a German collection company through 2005.

CAPITAL MARKETS

BORISLAV BOYANOV & CO ✪
DIMITROV, TCHOMPALOV & TODOROVA LTD
DJINGOV, GOUGINSKI, KYUTCHUKOV & VELICHKOV ✪
LANDWELL BULGARIA ✪
SPASOV & BRATANOV ✪

Arsov, Natchev, Ganeva ✪
Batkov, Stoev, Botev & Associates ✪
DIA Consult - Law Office.
Eastlaw
Georgiev, Todorov & Co ✪
Kambourov & Partners ✪
Novel Consult

Firms are listed A-Z in tiers which are ranked in order of priority
✪ Indicates firm displays contact details at the end of this chapter.

CAPITAL MARKETS

Borislav Boyanov & Co has been at the forefront of Bulgarian securities over the years. It advised on the country's first-ever sovereign eurobond issue, and more recently acted for the Bulgarian Ministry of Finance on the execution of a master ISDA agreement with the International Bank of Reconstruction and Development. In 2005 the firm advised a major international investment bank on a REPO transaction of the shares of a major telecommunications company.

While most firms in this grouping tend to focus on international investment, boutique outfit **Dimitrov, Tchompalov & Todorova Ltd** is unique in specialising in Bulgarian securities matters. It is possibly Bulgaria's leading firm for debt and equity traded on the Bulgarian Stock Exchange, although it is also now beginning to advise foreign clients. In 2005 the firm advised on the listing in Sofia of Bulgaria's first REIT. Iordan Tchompalov is commended for his 'accurate and well-expressed knowledge'.

Djingov, Gouginski, Kyutchukov & Velichkov works with foreign investment banks on capital markets matters, including JP Morgan, Citibank and UBS. In 2005 the firm advised a London-based stockbroker on the Alternative Investment Market (London) IPO of a major company's Bulgarian real estate assets. The firm also advises a host of investment banks, and a famous US-based hedge fund, on Bulgaria-related derivatives transactions.

Landwell Bulgaria advised First Investment Bank on a ground-breaking eurobond issue in 2005. It was Bulgaria's first bond issue under Basel II, and the country's first subordinated issue. The firm previously advised First Investment Bank on a number of other innovative issues, including a hybrid debt/equity instrument. It is now also carving out a successful niche in mutual funds, advising both foreign funds that invest in Bulgaria, and domestic funds investing outside the country.

In addition to bank lending, **Spasov & Bratanov** has experience of debt capital markets work. In recent years it advised foreign banks and banking syndicates on eurobond offerings by Bulgarian companies.

Arsov, Natchev, Ganeva is advising Bloomberg in connection with the expansion of electronic trading platforms for securities and other financial instruments in Bulgaria.

Batkov, Stoev, Botev & Associates has advised the major shareholder of Mobiltel with regards to an option contract, and the issuer with regards to Mobitel's €200m senior notes listing in Luxembourg.

DIA Consult - Law Office advises companies on share issuance, acquisitions and disposals. It is also adept at fixed-income work, including mortgage bonds and convertible bonds. In 2004 it advised Industrial Holdings of Bulgaria on a convertible issue.

Eastlaw has experience of tapping the capital markets as part of the privatisation process. It has advised companies on capital increases via public offers of shares, and has helped to float specialist funds on the stock market that invest in privatisations.

Georgiev, Todorov & Co advises the Bulgarian Financial Supervision Commission on the legal aspects of various capital markets issues.

Kambourov & Partners acts for a major Bulgarian stockbroker and advised it in 2005 on the Bulgarian Stock Exchange IPO of a major state-owned company.

Novel Consult has been an active participant in the development of Bulgarian securities markets. The firm participated in the preparation of the rules of trade of the Stock Exchange, and worked on a legal framework for the Ministry of Industry on the public offering of shares as a means of privatisation.

CORPORATE AND M&A

According to a foreign lawyer working in Bulgaria, 'the service provided by **Borislav Boyanov & Co** clearly stands out'. It advises a number of well-known international companies such as Allied Domecq and adidas-Salomon AG, and is the first from Bulgaria to place a representative in Brussels. The firm features leading corporate practitioners in Borislav Boyanov and Yordan Naydenov, and should appeal to clients with operations spanning the region due to its co-founding of *Central and Eastern Europe Law Offices (CELO)*, an association of eight leading firms across the region. The firm was involved in some high-profile transactions in 2005, notably advising a Greek Mobile operator on its €400m acquisition of the country's second-biggest GSM operator.

Big-name clients such as Nokia, Carlsberg A/S and Accor use **Djingov, Gouginski, Kyutchukov & Velichkov** for ongoing advice with regards to their Bulgarian operations. The firm offers a full service from EU competition advice through to employment, e-commerce and IP. But it is in M&A where the firm really shines. With quality lawyers such as telecoms expert Violetta Kunze (who is based in the firm's affiliated office in Frankfurt), Kalina Tchakarova and Zdravka Ugrinova, who is described as 'an excellent commercial lawyer' by one client, the firm has excellent resources. Advising Bank Austria on its acquisition of Hebros Bank and GE Commercial Finance on its acquisition of the Mall of Sofia stand out among several recent, big-ticket transactions.

With 39 fee-earners, including recommended commercial lawyers Vladimir Penkov and Ivan Markov, **LIC-Penkov, Markov & Partners** is one of the largest firms in Bulgaria, with sufficient resources to cover the commercial legal needs of most clients. The firm is adept at all forms of commercial contracts and employment matters, and has advised foreign companies such as Heineken Group and Siemens Information and Communications. The firm is also active in domestic M&A, having advised brewer Ariana AD in its merger with Zagorka AD, and the Coca-Cola Hellenic Bottling Company in its acquisition of eight domestic bottling and distribution companies.

Hayhurst Robinson's (now **CMS Cameron McKenna LLP**'s) Sofia-based partner David Butts specialises in acquisitions, notably for private equity investors. The firm's Central and Eastern European footprint appeals to diversified investors throughout the region, so a number of leading venture capital houses and private equity firms, such as Baring Private Equity Partners, are clients. But the firm also acts for trade investors, and recently advised OTP Bank on its €311m acquisition of DSK Bank, the former Bulgarian national savings bank.

Other than offering general corporate advice and corporate transactional services, **DIA Consult - Law Office** is notable for its work with insurance companies, particularly Allianz, whose Bulgarian subsidiaries are regular clients. The firm is advising the Bulgarian Financial Supervision Commission on the draft insurance code to transpose EU directives.

Eurolex Bulgaria Limited is less transactional than many firms of its calibre, focusing instead on providing legal counsel to its clients, many of whom are public sector commercial entities, such as the Bulgarian Energy Efficiency Fund. Foreign clients do feature however, and include a leading European Pharmaceutical company. It also has a good track record in insolvency and liquidation.

World-leading companies Mitsui and Microsoft turn to **Georgiev, Todorov & Co** for general legal consulting. Whilst not quite matching the transactional resources of its rivals, the firm sets itself apart by having very strong litigation credentials, both in the general corporate context, and more specifically in IP and competition. The firm was notably successful in a competition case for Microsoft in 2005.

Kambourov & Partners' ongoing clients include a global German energy company, which it advised on the privatisation of Bulgaria's energy distribution network in 2005. The firm is described as 'solid and capable' and has a good record in dispute resolution due to the experience of name partner Yavor Kambourov.

Landwell Bulgaria recruited four new senior staff in 2005, including Laura Kapelovska, a specialist in competition matters, and Hristo Gradinarski, an experienced litigator. The firm has notable strengths in conducting due diligence of Bulgarian companies on behalf of potential foreign investors.

LEGACOM Antov & Partners Law Firm's clients include Colgate-Palmolive, Bank Austria and Pfizer. Notable corporate practitioners include Christo Andov and Georgi Vassilev.

One client lauds 'the outstanding level of service' provided by the 'proactive and helpful' **Seplex Law Offices** team. Led founder by Sergei Penev, the firm notably advises AT&T on general corporate matters, and has acted as Bulgarian counsel on several international mergers. Its client list is notably weighted towards IT and telecommunications companies.

In recent years **Andonov & Radinska** was involved in some big projects that generated a good deal of quality corporate work. For example, in 2005 it advised Mall of Sofia on its disposal of a

CORPORATE AND M&A

BORISLAV BOYANOV & CO ✪
DJINGOV, GOUGINSKI, KYUTCHUKOV & VELICHKOV ✪
LIC-PENKOV, MARKOV & PARTNERS ✪

CMS Cameron McKenna LLP ✪
DIA Consult - Law Office
Eurolex Bulgaria Limited
Georgiev, Todorov & Co ✪
Kambourov & Partners ✪
Landwell Bulgaria ✪
LEGACOM Antov & Partners Law Firm ✪
Seplex Law Offices

Andonov & Radinska
Arsov, Natchev, Ganeva ✪
Atanassov & Ivanov Law Firm ✪
Borissov Law Office ✪
Boteva & Kantutis
Braykov's Legal Office
Deloitte Bulgaria EOOD ✪
Eastlaw
KPMG Bulgaria OOD
PI Partners ✪
Sabev & Partners Law Firm ✪
Simeonov & Dermendjiev
Sutti, Studio Legale ✪

Batkov, Stoev, Botev & Associates ✪
Dobrev, Kinkin, Lyutskanov & Partners ✪
Goleminov & Goleminov
IKRP Rokas & Partners OOD
Interius
Modus Consult
Niesar & Diamond LLP and Todorova Law Offices Business Banking Corporate Environmental Legal Consultancy
Novel Consult
Spasov & Bratanov ✪

A & M Partners
Bazlyankov Stanoev & Tashev
Chernev, Komitova & Partners
Coeler Legal Consulting EOOD
Dardov, Assenov & Partners
Dimitrov, Petrov & Co ✪
Dimitrov, Tchompalov & Todorova Ltd
Interjures Bulgaria Ltd
InterLex Consult
Kazakov & Kazakov & Co
LGK & Co Law Office
Schönherr ✪
Stoyanov Mittov Tanev
Stoeva, Kuyumdjieva & Vitliemov
TelecomLex Consult - Cheresheva, Nachev & Partners ✪
Teralex Consult
Varadinov & Co Attorneys-at-Law ✪
Vladimirov Law Office
Yalnazov & Dzhikov

Firms are listed A-Z in tiers which are ranked in order of priority
✪ Indicates firm displays contact details at the end of this chapter.

50% stake to GE and Quinlan Partnership. Meanwhile, its involvement in the Stara Zagora Gas PPP led to restructuring work, with the firm converting the PPP into a complex joint stock company involving a variety of classes of shareholding. Ongoing clients include Familia Supermarkets and Scania. The firm is 'recommended as lawyers of first choice to any foreign investor', by one client.

Arsov, Natchev, Ganeva partners Svetlana Ganeva and Vladimir Natchev are fluent French speakers, which accounts for the firm's relationship with a number of high-profile French clients, such as Vivendi and Danone, and its fruitful working relationship with French firm **Gide Loyrette Nouel**. It also features German-speaking lawyers. The firm recently capitalised on Bulgaria's Nato membership by scooping the cream of Bulgaria's first orders from Western defence contractors, advising Eurocopter (EADS) on the sale of 18 military helicopters to Bulgaria via an offset agreement, and Armaris on a US$1bn sale of four vessels for the Bulgarian Navy.

International companies that retain the services of **Atanassov & Ivanov Law Firm** include a leading Greek mobile phone retailer, a world famous Japanese vehicle manufacturer, and an iconic global sportswear brand. The firm's practice is evenly spilt between ongoing counsel and transactional work.

New firm **Borissov Law Office** has three partners, each with experience of working with foreign clients. Its track record includes advising the EBRD on investments in several Bulgarian companies, and acting for the government in the potential sale of the Bulgarian Telecommunications Company (BTC) to Koc Holding and Turk Telecom. Founding partner Plamen Borrisov led the work on the attempted Bulgartabac privatisation whilst a senior counsel at **Kambourov & Partners**. He is described as 'a very capable lawyer', and his firm is picking up some excellent mandates.

Boteva & Kantutis has considerable experience with employee share and option schemes, and with liquidation and bankruptcy matters.

Braykov's Legal Office focuses on international companies and has advised BAT, Diageo, IBM, Kodak and Xerox, notably in matters concerning IP and employment. The firm, led by Valentin Braykov, has a network of associate offices spread around the country to best serve its clients, and is noted for its litigation credentials.

Accounting firm **Deloitte Bulgaria EOOD**'s Borislav Stratev was formerly head of legal at the Bulgarian National Bank. He is recommended for legal and tax due diligence of companies undergoing privatisation or acquisition.

The Sofia office of **PI Partners**, a regional firm with additional offices in Athens and Bucharest, and a member of Ernst & Young's legal network, doubled its numbers in 2005, with four new hires joining at associate level. The firm gained a major banking client in 2005, and continued to advise British Telecom's Bulgarian subsidiary on corporate matters. The firm is particularly recommended for employment contract advice to companies that intend to use complicated staff remuneration structures in their Bulgarian operations.

Sabev & Partners Law Firm advises the Bulgarian subsidiaries of foreign corporations, including a major generic pharmaceuticals manufacturer that commends the 'very good service' provided by the firm with regards to their restructuring in 2005. It was also involved in UNCITRAL arbitrations arising out of the country's privatisation programme, for which it has been credited for its 'legal excellence, with commercial and practical judgement'.

Simeonov & Dermendjiev services Bulgarian state institutions and foreign companies from around the globe. The firm is particularly noteworthy for its international litigation and arbitration experience. Iyalo Dermendjiev is a specialist arbitrator, whilst Julian Varbanov specialises in the IP field.

In 2005 **Studio Legale Sutti** added M&A specialist Kloyan Georgiev Uzunov to its steadily growing corporate team led by Tzvetelina Dimitrova. The firm has a strong Italian client base, although the Sofia office mostly advises Bulgarian enterprises.

Aside from providing commercial advice to long-term clients, notably, Mobiltel, **Batkov, Stoev, Botev & Associates** is recognised as a leading firm for commercial litigation. The firm represented a competitor in the investigation of alleged state-aid worth €80m granted to BTC in 2004.

Dobrev, Kinkin, Lyutskanov & Partners' corporate clients include Cilag, Abbott Laboratories and International Aero Engines. The firm expanded its offices in 2005, recruited four new corporate lawyers, and promoted EU law specialist Theodor Bojinov to partner. The firm advised on the acquisition of a cement factory in 2005.

With its affiliation to San Francisco firm **Niesar Curls Bartling LLP, Niesar & Diamond LLP and Todorova Law Offices Business Banking Corporate Environmental Legal Consultancy** advises a good stock of US clients, although the firm has also advised a number of European companies, notably UK names such as Rolls-Royce and Prudential. The firm has a strong specialism in environmental law through Liliana Maslarova.

Novel Consult's strengths are in commercial contracts and litigation arising out of commercial contracts. Many of the firm's key clients are in the IT and telecoms fields. The firm worked on all contracts and licences for an international software and hardware company in Bulgaria, and is becomingly increasingly involved in advising Bulgaria's privatised telecoms companies.

Spasov & Bratanov has advised on post-privatisation sales and leveraged buy-outs within Bulgaria, often for foreign private equity funds. Bokyo Bratanov and Georgi Spasov are recommended.

Capital markets specialist **Dimitrov, Tchompalov & Todorova Ltd** shares commercial work with **Stoeva, Kuyumdjieva & Vitliemov**, which advises the local subsidiary of a major international drinks company on general corporate matters.

IT, TELECOMS AND MEDIA

Borislav Boyanov & Co has been a heavyweight telecoms player since it was involved in Bulgaria's first attempted telecoms privatisation back in 1997. Vodafone's use of the firm on applying for a Bulgarian licence in 2000, and its work on the €400m acquisition of Bulgaria's second GSM operator for a leading Greek network in 2005 demonstrate the firm's continued standing over the years. The firm also has a solid media practice under Damien Simeonov, which in 2005 closed a US$26m acquisition of Bulgaria's largest cable TV operator. A solid group of patent and trade mark attorneys under Natasha Andreeva completes the offering.

Dimitrov, Petrov & Co is a full-service firm with particular strengths in the IT and telecoms fields. It has served clients of the calibre of Nokia, Siemens and Orbitel in recent years. In 2004 the firm advised Cable & Wireless on its acquisition of a majority stake in Mobikom Radiotelecommunication, one of three mobile network operators in Bulgaria. It also acts for the Bulgarian telecoms regulator, advising it in 2004 with respect to the issuance of both a TV broadcasting licence, and a national GSM licence. Recommended lawyers include George Dimitrov, who specialises in e-commerce, and Katya Glushkova, a media law expert.

Djingov, Gouginski, Kyutchukov & Velichkov covers the full TMT spectrum. It has represented well-known global companies in IP matters, notably Reuters and Carlsberg, and has represented media companies, including a couple of major film studios, on an assortment of corporate and IP matters. The firm also has a strong track record with telecoms companies through Frankfurt-based Violetta Kunze. Nokia is a client.

Georgiev, Todorov & Co's experience with IT companies is demonstrated by the fact that Microsoft uses the firm as its legal counsel in Bulgaria. The firm is also advising Elbit Systems on a €50m modernisation of Bulgarian military helicopters, and now advises BTC on day-to-day matters after successfully representing it in a major competition case in 2005.

Kambourov & Partners went before the Supreme Administrative Court in 2005 to challenge the issuance of a GSM licence on behalf of a major Bulgarian GSM network. The firm also counts Nokia's Bulgarian subsidiary as a

IT, TELECOMS AND MEDIA

BORISLAV BOYANOV & CO ✪
DIMITROV, PETROV & CO ✪
DJINGOV, GOUGINSKI, KYUTCHUKOV & VELICHKOV ✪
GEORGIEV, TODOROV & CO ✪
KAMBOUROV & PARTNERS ✪
LIC-PENKOV, MARKOV & PARTNERS ✪
SEPLEX LAW OFFICES

CMS Cameron McKenna LLP ✪
Deloitte Bulgaria EOOD ✪
Eurolex Bulgaria Limited
Landwell Bulgaria ✪
TelecomLex Consult - Cheresheva, Nachev & Partners ✪

Arsov, Natchev, Ganeva ✪
Batkov, Stoev, Botev & Associates ✪
Borissov Law Office ✪
Braykov's Legal Office
Dobrev, Kinkin, Lyutskanov & Partners ✪
Interius
Novel Consult
Patent Universe
Teralex Consult
Varadinov & Co Attorneys-at-Law ✪

Andonov & Radinska
Eastlaw
Sabev & Partners Law Firm ✪
Simeonov & Dermendjiev
Sutti, Studio Legale ✪

Firms are listed A-Z in tiers which are ranked in order of priority
✪ *Indicates firm displays contact details at the end of this chapter.*

client. Away from telecoms, the firm advised on a large public software procurement and acted for a major regional advertising agency on a joint venture with a local entertainment company.

LIC-Penkov, Markov & Partners has wide-ranging TMT ability. Its telecommunications clout is demonstrated by its selection by Avdent, the international private equity fund, to act as its local legal counsel on its purchase of 65% of the shares of state telecoms company BTC as part of its privatisation. Other telcos that have used the firm include Vodafone, Telefonica and Cable & Wireless. In the IT field, the firm has advised the likes of Sony Ericsson and ProSoft, whilst the firm also provides comprehensive legal services to radio and TV operators, notably Radio City EOOD.

Over the years **Seplex Law Offices** has built up considerable experience in the telecoms sector having been active in the privatisation of BTC, and advising AT&T on an ongoing basis. The firm's client portfolio also includes global leaders in the IT field, notably Cisco Systems.

After advising private equity group Advent through their acquisition of BTC, **CMS Cameron McKenna LLP** was retained by Advent and BTC as ongoing legal advisor. The Sofia team is led by 'thorough and proactive' Peter Valert, who has a strong track record in the TMT field. The firm's recent merger with *Hayhurst Robinson* brings significant additional capability in this area.

Eurolex Bulgaria Limited has a track record of working with broadcasters and publishers. In 2005 it acted for a British broadcaster on its acquisition of a Bulgarian TV station and successfully represented an association of Bulgarian broadcasters in a competition case against a collection of foreign and Bulgarian music publishers. The firm was also involved in establishing a body to regulate Bulgaria's journalists.

Between Galina Bunkova, who heads the IP practice, and Lilia Andonova, the firm's telecoms expert, **Landwell Bulgaria** is well positioned to advise on a range of IP, IT and telecoms matters. In 2004, it was active in trade mark disputes and registration for international clients and advised on data protection issues relating to the establishment of the country's first credit reference agency.

TelecomLex Consult - Cheresheva, Nachev & Partners is particularly specialised in the regulatory aspects of telecoms law and is advising the Bulgarian government in relation to the harmonisation of Bulgarian telecommunications regulations with those of the EU.

Arsov, Natchev, Ganeva advised the Communications Regulation Commission on the issuance of third national GSM licence. The firm is also advising Bloomberg on electronic trading platforms for securities.

Teralex Consult has uniquely carved out a niche as a specialist media firm. Partners Katya Glushakova and Alexander Ivanov spend more than half their time advising clients in the television and radio fields. Highlights in recent years include successfully representing a TV station before the Competition Commission, and advising on the reconstruction and modernisation of a state radio broadcaster.

Varadinov & Co Attorneys-at-Law advised US investors on their acquisition of Bulgaria's largest cable operator, and continued to advise the acquired company on general corporate matters, as well as further acquisitions in the cable TV market worth around €25m.

Studio Legale Sutti is the co-ordinator of the *Global Alliance for e-Commerce Law*. Its Sofia practice boasts IT specialist Irena Mihaleva.

MARITIME

Vladimirov Law Office

Eurolex Bulgaria Limited
LGK & Co Law Office
LIC-Penkov, Markov & Partners ✪

Firms are listed A-Z in tiers which are ranked in order of priority
✪ *Indicates firm displays contact details at the end of this chapter.*

MARITIME

Vladimirov Law Office runs a full-service shipping practice out of its Sofia and Varna offices. The four-partner practice headed by the recommended Vladimir Vladimirov regularly works with a number of international firms, including **Holman Fenwick & Willan** and **Ince & Co**, on shipping-related matters. In addition to acting for shipowners from Bulgaria, Greece and Cyprus, the firm represents several insurance companies, notably Allianz, and British P&I clubs, including West of England and Steamship Mutual. The firm was involved in several maritime disputes in 2005.

Eurolex Bulgaria Limited continues to be engaged in due diligence for the privatisation of various Bulgarian ports, and advised a large Italian defence contractor on the procurement procedure for the construction of four naval vessels for the Bulgarian fleet in 2005.

LGK & Co Law Office has a commendable shipping practice that covers most contentious and non-contentious maritime work. Clients include Coeclerici Group, Navigation Maritime Bulgaria and Unitainer.

LIC-Penkov, Markov & Partners operates a maritime practice out of its Varna and Burgas offices. The firm is advising Cammell Laird Holdings, a UK-based shipbuilder, with regards to the rehabilitation of the Varna Shipyard. The firm also advised the Privatisation Agency on the sale of the Bulgarian Commercial Sea Fleet and the Bulgarian River Navigation Fleet.

PRIVATISATION AND FOREIGN INVESTMENT

Borislav Boyanov & Co has been involved in transferring key parts of the Bulgarian State apparatus to the private sector since the privatisation process began in 1992. In recent years the firm has advised on the successful privatisation of Bulgaria's largest bank, Bulbank. That was the country's most valuable completed privatisation project until 2005, when three international power companies paid €693m for 67% of the electricity network from seven state-owned companies, which were also advised by **Borislav Boyanov & Co**, whilst **Djingov, Gouginski, Kyutchukov & Velichkov** advised the acquirer, CEZ in the deal.

The combination of *Hayhurst Robinson* and **CMS Cameron McKenna LLP** brings together considerable privatisation and foreign investment experience. *Hayhurst Robinson* has been involved in banking privatisation and **CMS Cameron McKenna LLP** advised client Advent on the privatisation of BTC.

PRIVATISATION AND FOREIGN INVESTMENT

BORISLAV BOYANOV & CO ⭘
CMS CAMERON McKENNA LLP ⭘
DJINGOV, GOUGINSKI, KYUTCHUKOV & VELICHKOV ⭘
GEORGIEV, TODOROV & CO ⭘
KAMBOUROV & PARTNERS ⭘
LIC-PENKOV, MARKOV & PARTNERS ⭘
SEPLEX LAW OFFICES

Borissov Law Office ⭘
Eastlaw
Eurolex Bulgaria Limited
KPMG Bulgaria OOD
LEGACOM Antov & Partners Law Firm ⭘
Schönherr ⭘

Arsov, Natchev, Ganeva ⭘
Atanassov & Ivanov Law Firm ⭘
Batkov, Stoev, Botev & Associates ⭘
Deloitte Bulgaria EOOD ⭘
PI Partners ⭘
Spasov & Bratanov ⭘
Tascheva & Partner

Firms are listed A-Z in tiers which are ranked in order of priority
⭘ Indicates firm displays contact details at the end of this chapter.

Djingov, Gouginski, Kyutchukov & Velichkov has been involved in most of Bulgaria's privatisations. It continued to advise the government and CSFB on the privatisation of major thermal power plants in Bulgaria, and a Danish company in its successful bid for the concessions to run the Varna and Burgas airports in 2005.

After providing local legal advice with respect to the privatisation of BTC, 2005 saw **Georgiev, Todorov & Co** active advising both foreign investors and granting bodies with regards to concessions for the running of airports, highways and ports. The patient and good-humoured Ivan Todorov is recommended.

The well-regarded Vladimir Rangeloff of **Kambourov & Partners** advised a German multinational power company with regards to the privatisation of Bulgaria's electricity distribution network, and advised one of the few remaining state-owned companies through its privatisation process in 2005.

An 18-strong team at **LIC-Penkov, Markov & Partners** has spent much of the last two years working for Advent International on its privatisation of BTC, the state-owned telecoms company. Prior to that, the firm advised on a wide range of privatisations in the banking, commercial navigation, glass, food, tobacco and chemical industries.

Seplex Law Offices has enjoyed broad involvement in the Bulgarian privatisation process. Recent work involved advising foreign investors on their involvement in the privatisation of businesses as diverse as film studios, thermo power plants and airports. Previous work involved advising significant foreign multinationals and consortiums on their bids to participate in the privatisation of the county's telecommunications and electricity infrastructure.

Eastlaw works on mid-sized privatisations, usually involving the domestic capital markets.

Eurolex Bulgaria Limited has particular experience in the utilities and infrastructure sectors. Its popularity with public sector bodies and municipalities has brought the firm a good deal of privatisation work over the years. More recent clients have included foreign private investors, and the firm is branching out into non-core areas, for example providing due diligence to a Welsh studio in 2005 on the privatisation of Bulgaria's national film studio.

LEGACOM Antov & Partners Law Firm advised CA-IB Corporate Finance with regards to the privatisation of aspects of the Bulgartabac state tobacco monopoly.

Austrian firm **Schönherr** opened a Sofia office in 2004 to further its strategy of engaging in cross-border investments within the Central and Southern European region. Its Bulgaria team expanded to seven lawyers in 2005, and advised EVN on a large investment in the country's electricity distribution sector.

Batkov, Stoev, Botev & Associates is representing Russia's leading energy producer in its involvement in the privatisation of thermo-electric power stations at Varna, Bobovdol and Russe.

Spasov & Bratanov has advised on several large post-privatisation sales, including leveraged buy-outs.

PROJECTS, ENERGY AND NATURAL RESOURCES

Borislav Boyanov & Co covers almost all aspects of the projects spectrum, from advising banks on finance through to acting for sponsors in the resources, energy and infrastructure fields. In addition to advising the government on the recent electricity network privatisation, the firm completed some major projects work in 2005. It advised a major international investment bank with respect to regulatory and constitutional aspects of the financing of Bulgaria's first large-scale PPP project - the €700m Trakia highway. Previously the firm advised ENEL on a €580m financing to modernise power generation units as part of the Maritsa East III Project.

Through its merger with *Hayhurst Robinson*, **CMS Cameron McKenna LLP** has acquired has considerable expertise and experience in the energy sector across the region, most notably on the finance side. The firm advised two international financial institutions on the financing of the development of the Galata gas field in recent years and is very active in the energy and resources sector in neighbouring Romania.

Djingov, Gouginski, Kyutchukov & Velichkov's capability is demonstrated by the range of work it has done in recent years. The firm is notably advising CSFB on both a green field hydro-electric project, and (in conjunction with the Bulgarian Government) on the privatisation of thermal plants at Varna and Bobiv. On the finance side the firm advised Merrill Lynch on limited recourse acquisition financing to a major regional steel company, and the ERBD on the securitisation of one of the Maritza East plants. The firm also acted for a regional investment fund on the financing for an offshore gas extraction project. Georgi Gouginski is particularly recommended for energy-related matters.

With Japanese heavy industry player Mitsui as a client, **Georgiev, Todorov & Co** gets its fill of projects work in the energy and infrastructure sectors. It advised a consortium including Mitsui, Toshiba and the Japanese Bank of International Cooperation with respect to the €260m rehabilitation of the Maritza East 2 thermal power plant. The firm is also active in the process of granting major concessions to foreign investors concerning the running of infrastructure assets.

In addition to its work on the Mall of Sofia project, **Andonov & Radinska** is gaining

PROJECTS, ENERGY AND NATURAL RESOURCES

BORISLAV BOYANOV & CO ⭘
CMS CAMERON McKENNA LLP ⭘
DJINGOV, GOUGINSKI, KYUTCHUKOV & VELICHKOV ⭘
GEORGIEV, TODOROV & CO ⭘

Andonov & Radinska
Arsov, Natchev, Ganeva⭘
Atanassov & Ivanov Law Firm ⭘
Dobrev, Kinkin, Lyutskanov & Partners ⭘
Eastlaw
Eurolex Bulgaria Limited
Kambourov & Partners ⭘
Landwell Bulgaria ⭘
LIC-Penkov, Markov & Partners ⭘
Novel Consult
Spasov & Bratanov ⭘
Varadinov & Co Attorneys-at-Law ⭘

Borissov Law Office ⭘
Batkov, Stoev, Botev & Associates ⭘
Boteva & Kantutis
Delchev, Simeonov & Partners ⭘
Sabev & Partners Law Firm ⭘
Schönherr ⭘
Sutti, Studio Legale ⭘
Stoeva, Kuyumdjieva & Vitliemov

Firms are listed A-Z in tiers which are ranked in order of priority
⭘ Indicates firm displays contact details at the end of this chapter.

experience of PPP projects through its advice to the Municipality of Stara Zagora on the construction, development and operation of its first gas network. The firm advised the municipality on financing the project through loans and preference shares, and on the restructuring of the PPP company.

Arsov, Natchev, Ganeva is one of Bulgaria's leading law firms with respect to hydro-electric plants and projects. It was involved in the privatisation of several hydro-electric plants, and has acted as legal counsel on the construction of new plants in the Iskar and Struma river valleys.

Through 2005 **Atanassov & Ivanov Law Firm** advised the project company with regards to an engineering and procurement contract for the Maritza East lignite power plant, having previously advised US-based Entergy on its €600m investment in the project. The firm's projects and resources credentials are verified by one client who states: 'We work in several Eastern European countries. This firm is by far the best we have found.'

Dobrev, Kinkin, Lyutskanov & Partners advises on the restructuring, rehabilitation and financing of energy projects, notably in gas supply, district heating, power supply and transportation. It has a good relationship with German Bank Depfa, who the firm has acted for in project financings, such as €30m for the reconstruction of Toplofikazia-Rousse power plant, and €226m for Bulgaria's largest coal-fired power station.

Eastlaw's list of ongoing clients includes the Bulgarian subsidiaries of Rexoil and Shell. The latter was advised by the firm on its of purchase of Amoco Bulgaria, and on the setting up and incorporation of its Shell Gas Bulgaria subsidiary, which included the construction and start-up of a gas-filling plant.

In 2005 **Eurolex Bulgaria Limited** advised a Czech client on its proposed acquisition of three thermal power plants in 2005, and is advising a Russian group in connection with a licence for regional gas distribution and the construction of network facilities. The firm's real strength, however, is advising the public sector on privatisations. The firm counts numerous municipalities as clients. Managing partner Andrey Delchev is president of the Bulgarian Petrol and Gas Association, whilst Stoyan Barzakov is currently managing the development of regulatory legislation in the water and energy sectors.

In addition to providing ongoing advice to a multinational energy company on its Bulgarian operations during and after its involvement in the €695m privatisation of the electricity sector, **Kambourov & Partners** has been active in litigation concerning gas distribution licences and due diligence for overseas investors in the mining sector.

Landwell Bulgaria advises the Bulgarian subsidiary of Turkish petrol distributor Opet Aygas, which is investing US$100m to build 60 gas stations in Bulgaria by 2007.

LIC-Penkov, Markov & Partners has acted for Salini Costruttori on Bulgarian infrastructure projects for the construction and operation of motorways, gas distribution networks and waste management plants.

Novel Consult's banking practice is becoming increasingly involved in project financings, which now comprise about 35% of the firm's workload. Particularly notable is its 2003 work for the EBRD alongside **Linklaters** on the €650m financing of the Maritza East III power plant. Managing Partner Petya Kolcheva is a specialist in concessions, energy and infrastructure at the municipal level.

Spasov & Bratanov has a broad range of energy experience. It mainly advises lenders, but also has experience of working with project sponsors. The firm worked on the country's largest water financing to date, advising the EBRD as lender. Other notable recent work includes advising a Japanese bank on financing for a major power project, and acting for a UK-listed oil and gas producer on its exploration and development of Bulgarian offshore reserves.

In 2004/2005 **Varadinov & Co Attorneys-at-Law** represented companies involved in a large highway PPP project, and provided legal advice and contracts for a US$140m natural gas drilling project. Yavor Varadinov and Galina Gergova both specialise in the law related to concessions.

Delchev, Simeonov & Partners provides commercial services to a major global engineering company participating in the construction of one of Bulgaria's largest power plants.

REAL ESTATE AND CONSTRUCTION

The Bulgarian Real estate market appears to be reaching fever pitch as the country approaches EU accession, with foreign investors speculating that the country's traditionally low market prices will harmonise with EU levels in time. Much investment is from companies and funds investing in commercial developments, but a notable appetite among private investors (particularly from Britons), for direct residential real estate, notably along the Black Sea coast and at the country's ski resorts, is driving a construction boom.

Foreign companies and individuals may invest directly in property, but if they want to buy land, they must set up a company in Bulgaria to hold it. Setting up such companies, handling real estate and land acquisitions for foreigners, and advising on real estate construction projects is arguably the biggest growth area for Bulgarian law firms at present. The gold rush is unlikely to last long and already there are some rumours of a bubble, but for now few commercial firms are willing to eschew the sector.

Many of **Andonov & Radinska**'s clients are quite real estate-heavy, such as Familia supermarkets, which the firm advised on leases in 2005. The firm is notable for its various work on the Mall of Sofia mega-project, ranging from project finance, through drafting and finalising lease terms for its retail premises, and the settlement of construction claims in relation to the project.

Borislav Boyanov & Co has worked on many of Bulgaria's high-profile real estate deals, often on the financing side. Property finance work in 2005 includes advising Bulbank on a €35m financing of Bulgaria's largest department store, and representing the EBRD in a finance transaction for Grand Hotel Hermitage. Volume transactional work is evidenced by the fact that McDonald's uses the firm for site purchases and leases, whilst the firm has advised on construction projects ranging from buildings through to oil pipelines, gas distribution and water. Nikolay Nikolov is recommended.

Hayhurst Robinson has translated its sound project finance experience into a growing real estate finance practice across its Central and Eastern European jurisdictions. The firm advised two banks on their financing of two hotel complexes on the Black Sea coast, and advised Baring Private Equity Partners (equity) and a multinational financial institution (debt), on the financing of a US$60m winery in Bulgaria. Its merger with **CMS Cameron McKenna LLP** in 2006, arguably the market leader for Central and Eastern European real estate, has boosted the overall offering, making this practice extremely attractive to companies and portfolio investors with pan-regional interests.

Although **Djingov, Gouginski, Kyutchukov & Velichkov** handles standalone real estate transactions through Stephan Kyutchukov, the firm's experience of big-ticket real estate derives largely from its commercial transactions. For

REAL ESTATE AND CONSTRUCTION

Andonov & Radinska
Borislav Boyanov & Co ✪
CMS Cameron McKenna LLP ✪
Djingov, Gouginski, Kyutchukov & Velichkov ✪
Dobrev, Kinkin, Lyutskanov & Partners ✪
Eurolex Bulgaria Limited
Kambourov & Partners ✪
LIC-Penkov, Markov & Partners ✪
Seplex Law Offices

Georgiev, Todorov & Co ✪
PI Partners ✪
Schönherr ✪
Sutti, Studio Legale ✪
Tascheva & Partner
Varadinov & Co Attorneys-at-Law ✪

Firms are listed A-Z in tiers which are ranked in order of priority
✪ *Indicates firm displays contact details at the end of this chapter.*

example, in 2005 the firm advised on the real estate aspects of the acquisition of the Mall of Sofia and conducted due diligence on the real estate assets of an offshore company's Bulgarian subsidiary, prior to its listing on the Irish Stock Exchange.

Dobrev, Kinkin, Lyutskanov & Partners has extended its projects expertise into a growing residential real estate practice, led by Sophia Bayrakova. The firm's practice is mostly residential and has developed close working relationships with agencies in Ireland, the UK and Spain.

Eurolex Bulgaria Limited's experience of managing big investment projects on behalf of its public sector clients has yielded an accomplished construction practice. The firm continues to represent the Municipality of Sofia, advising it on an underground construction project beneath Sofia Central Train Station in 2005. The firm's experience is now recognised by foreign investors, notably Israeli companies which instructed it in relation to land acquisition and the construction of large residential complexes in Sofia.

'Very efficient' **Kambourov & Partners** has built relationships with foreign agencies offering residential Bulgarian real estate to investors. In response to demand from British investors, the firm has moved its extremely personable senior associate Radoslav Alexandrov to represent the firm in London. Through 2005 the firm advised on numerous small real estate and land transactions with a combined value of around €27m.

Major clients that **LIC-Penkov, Markov & Partners** advises with regards to building projects include Strabag, a major German construction company, and the Coca-Cola Hellenic Bottling Company.

In 2005 **Seplex Law Offices** advised Bulgaria-based US institutions and foreign property funds on the legal aspects of property transactions and construction activity in the country.

With its emphasis on dispute resolution, **Georgiev, Todorov & Co** is worth considering should a need arise for construction-related litigation, or European arbitration services.

Oil and gas distribution group OMV is a major client of **Schönherr**. The firm is advising it on the acquisition and development of sites for its downstream businesses in Bulgaria, and is working with a major European real estate developer in connection with a shopping mall project in Sofia.

Senior partner Nelly Tascheva's firm, **Tascheva & Partner** is recommended to German and Austrian clients for property-related deals. In recent years it has been active in a number of multi-million euro retail and industrial real estate acquisitions and construction projects. Recent transactions include advising German clients on the construction of a large cherry processing facility and a refrigerator factory.

Varadinov & Co Attorneys-at-Law has advised a telecommunications client on the construction aspects of building its cable network, and has a record of advising hotel groups on real estate transactions.

ARSOV, NATCHEV, GANEVA

36 SHIPKA STREET
3RD FLOOR
1504 SOFIA

Telephone: +359 2 946 3349
Fax: +359 2 946 3348
E-mail: info@anglaw.com
Website: www.anglaw.com

Languages
English, French, German, Russian

Number of lawyers 14

International groupings
International Bar Association;
Bulgarian Dutch Business Club

CATEGORIES OF WORK

Corporate and commercial
Marin Arsov, Jivko Rokov

Capital markets and securities
Marin Arsov, Stoil Hristov

Real estate and construction
Marin Arsov, Stoil Hristov

Public procurement
Svetlana Ganeva, Marin Arsov

Insolvency and debt collection
Vladimir Natchev, Marin Arsov

Environmental law
Jivko Rokov, Milena Georgieva

Litigation and arbitration
Marin Arsov, Vladimir Natchev

Employment and human resources
Jivko Rokov, Dessislava Lukarova

Aviation law
Svetlana Ganeva, Vladimir Natchev

Telecommunications and media
Marin Arsov, Milena Georgieva

Energy law
Marin Arsov, Stoil Hristov

Foreign investments
Svetlana Ganeva, Dessislava Lukarova

Joint ventures
Marin Arsov, Jivko Rokov

Banking and finance
Vladimir Natchev, Stoil Hristov

Administrative law
Svetlana Ganeva, Marin Arsov

ATANASSOV & IVANOV LAW FIRM

9 HRISTO BELCHEV STREET
1000 SOFIA

Telephone: +359 2 981 4331
Fax: +359 2 980 7660
E-mail: office@atanassovivanov.com
Website: www.atanassovivanov.com

Number of lawyers 9

CATEGORIES OF WORK

Project finance
Ilian Ivanov, Stoyan Atanassov

Corporate and commercial
Stoyan Atanassov, Ilian Ivanov

Banking and finance
Ilian Ivanov, Stoyan Atanassov

Tax and planning
Ilian Ivanov, Maria Dimitrova

Employment
Ilian Ivanov, Maria Dimitrova

Securities regulations
Stoyan Atanassov, Denitza Stoyanova

Real estate
Stoyan Atanassov, Mihaela Staynova

Mergers and acquisitions
Stoyan Atanassov, Ilian Ivanov

Foreign investments
Ilian Ivanov, Stoyan Atanassov

Litigation
Ilian Ivanov, Stoyan Atanassov

BATKOV, STOEV, BOTEV & ASSOCIATES

48 ALABIN STREET
1000 SOFIA

Telephone: +359 2 933 5611
Fax: +359 2 933 5614
E-mail: office@batkov.com
Website: www.batkov.com

Languages
English, French, German, Russian

Number of lawyers 37

Member
Interlegal

CATEGORIES OF WORK

Administrative
Todor Batkov, Martin Yordanov

Banking
Todor Batkov, Ventsislav Stoev

Civil law
Boyko Botev, Alexander Angelov

Corporate and commercial
Georgi Georgiev,
Boris Liakov

Labour and social security
Anna Avramova, Rossen Stoyanov

Litigation and arbitration
Boyko Botev, Stoyan Yakimov

Privatisation and foreign investments
Ventsislav Stoev,
Nikola Rachev

Tax
Ventsislav Stoev, Georgi Georgiev

Telecommunications
Todor Batkov, Martin Yordanov

THE FIRM

Batkov, Stoev, Botev & Associates was founded in 1991. Since then it continues growing steadily – today it is one of the major law companies in Bulgaria. Nowadays it numbers 37 lawyers working in various practice areas, nine trainees and office staff.

The new and the larger office of the company is situated in the centre of the city of Sofia – opposite the building of the Courts of Justice.

The firm's main task is to provide creative, practical advice at the highest quality level based not only on the knowledge of the matters, but also on understanding the clients' businesses and needs, and the industries in which they operate. The result: creative, prompt, cost-effective, satisfactory and value-added solutions to its clients.

Lawyers work both individually and in teams created for the single purpose of delivering solutions for the firm's clients.

In order to render quality services, the firm is constantly involved in its members' enhancing their knowledge in specific areas of practice.

The nature of the firm's clients varies from multinational companies through the entire range of privately owned companies, and commercial entities to individuals.

AREAS OF PRACTICE

Batkov, Stoev, Botev & Associates understand that it is impossible for a lawyer to specialise in all legal matters. But the breadth of its experience and the diversity of its knowledge enables the firm to handle multiple matters demanding large numbers of lawyers on tight deadlines – while producing the highest quality legal work. The firm works extensively with a broad range of industries, including: telecommunications; software; banking; financial services; pharmaceutical; healthcare; media; intellectual property; manufacturing; real estate; retail; energy, oil, and gas; technology; transportation.

Batkov, Stoev, Botev & Associates represents clients in proceedings before national agencies and governmental bodies. Several attorneys have also represented state agencies in specialised matters. Batkov, Stoev, Botev & Associates is ready to assist clients in various types of government and regulatory matters.

Batkov, Stoev, Botev & Associates helps forward its clients in: loan and finance agreements; estate and trust administration; counselling investors in obtaining and closing financial agreements; increase or reduction of capital; advice on the setting up and running of business in Bulgaria; mergers and acquisitions counselling; negotiation, drafting and enforcement of various commercial contracts.

The telecommunications sector is unique and dynamic in nature. Batkov, Stoev, Botev & Associates is a leading adviser on the financing, regulatory and commercial aspects of national telecoms financings and projects. Whether a bank, a telecom operator, an investor, a state agency or a government, the firm can assist on the full spectrum of transactions and activities in the telecommunications sector.

During the last few years the firm's lawyers have been actively involved in the privatisation and foreign investment processes in Bulgaria. The law firm has represented investors for more than ten years.

Litigation is one of the firm's significant practice areas. Batkov Stoev, Botev & Associates represent clients at both trial, appellate and supreme court levels throughout the country. Experience includes almost every type of general civil, administrative, and commercial litigation.

With colleagues in other countries, the firm can give co-ordinated cross-border advice on various tax issues.

Batkov, Stoev, Botev & Associates is the first Bulgarian law company to have been elected a member of Interlegal – the international network of law firms.

BORISLAV BOYANOV & CO

**24 PATRIARCH
EVTIMII BOULEVARD
1000 SOFIA**

Telephone: +359 2 981 3103
Fax: +359 2 981 7733
E-mail: mail@boyanov.com
Website: www.boyanov.com

Languages
Bulgarian, English, German, Russian, Spanish

Other offices
Bourgas, Brussells, Sevlievo, Varna

Number of lawyers 34

Contact
Borislav T Boyanov

Member
SEE Legal; CELO; Terralex; World Services Group

CATEGORIES OF WORK

Corporate, M&A
Yordan Naydenov

IT, telecommunications and media
Damian Simeonov

Finance
Damian Simeonov

Banking
Svetlina Kortenska

Energy and natural resources
Alexander Chatalbashev

Capital markets
Alexander Chatalbashev

Commercial
Raina Dimitrova

Litigation and arbitration
Kina Chuturkova

Competition
Peter Petrov

Employment
Violeta Hristova

Property and construction
Nikolay Nikolov

Lobbying and public affairs
Borislav T Boyanov

Intellectual property
Natasha Andreeva

BORISSOV LAW OFFICE

**NDK ADMINISTRATIVE BUILDING
1 BULGARIA SQUARE
PO BOX 246
1463 SOFIA**

Telephone: +359 2 811 7751
Fax: +359 2 811 7752
E-mail: office@borissov-law.com
Website: www.borissov-law.com

Languages
English, German, Russian

Number of lawyers 11

Contact
Plamen M Borissov

CATEGORIES OF WORK

Administrative and public law

Environment

Banking and finance

Insurance

Business advisory

Intellectual property and technology

Capital markets

Litigation

Construction

Mergers and acquisitions

Consumer law

Private clients

Competition

Privatisation

Corporate and commercial

Property

Corporate recovery and insolvency

Taxation

Employment

Telecommunications

Energy and natural resources

CMS CAMERON McKENNA EOOD LAW OFFICE

14 TSAR OSVOBODITEL BLVD
FLOOR 2, 1000 SOFIA

Telephone: +35 92 921 9910
Fax: +35 92 921 9919
E-mail: info@cms-cmck.com
Website: www.law-now.com

Languages
Bulgarian, English, German, Russian

Other offices
Aberdeen, Bristol, Bucharest, Budapest, Edinburgh, Hong Kong, London, Moscow, Prague, Warsaw

Number of lawyers 587

Contact
Peter Valert

International groupings
CMS Cameron McKenna is a member of CMS, the alliance of major European law firms providing clients with a full range of legal and tax services. CMS's activities are co-ordinated through EEIG, registered in Brussels.

CATEGORIES OF WORK

Privatisation
Peter Valert, Kalina Milanova, Reneta Petkova

Banking and international finance
Katerina Kraeva, Reneta Petkova, David Butts

Corporate and commercial
Peter Valert, Katerina Kraeva, Anna Rizova-Clegg, Teodora Ivanova, Lyubomir Dabov, Zlatina Ruseva, Boris Smolyanov

Projects, utilities, infrastructure
Kalina Milanova, Anna Rizova-Clegg, Reneta Petkova, David Butts, Lyubomir Dabov

Real estate
Kalina Milanova, Lyubomir Dabov, David Butts, Elisa Ivanova, Teodora Ivanova

Telecommunications
Peter Valert, Anna Rizova-Clegg

Competition
Anna Rizova-Clegg, Teodora Ivanova, Zlatina Ruseva

CMS REICH-ROHRWIG HAINZ

TZAR OSVOBODITEL BLVD 14
1000 SOFIA

Telephone: +359 2 921 9921
Fax: +359 2 921 9929
E-mail: sofia@cms-rrh.com
Website: www.cms-rrh.com

Languages
Bulgarian, English, German

Other offices
Belgrade, Bratislava, Brussels, Prague, Vienna, Zagreb

Number of lawyers 71
at this office 4

Contacts
Peter Huber, Gentscho Pavlov

Member
CMS Alliance of major European law firms; World Law Group

CATEGORIES OF WORK

Corporate and commercial

Mergers and acquisitions

Telecommunications

Intellectual property

Privatisation and foreign investment

Project finance, construction and real estate

Employment

Public procurement

DELCHEV, SIMEONOV & PARTNERS

8 KALOYAN STREET
2ND FLOOR
1000 SOFIA

Telephone: +359 2 888 40 8216
Fax: +359 2 988 0018
E-mail: office@dsp-lawfirm.com
Website: www.dsp-lawfirm.com

Languages
English, French, Russian, Spanish

Number of lawyers 9

CATEGORIES OF WORK

Antitrust, competition and trade
Emil Delchev, Emil Simeonov

Bankruptcy
Emil Delchev

Corporate, commercial
Emil Delchev, Emil Simeonov

Dispute resolution
Emil Delchev, Emil Simeonov

Employment
Snezhana Stoyanova, Emil Simeonov

Intellectual property
Emil Delchev, Emil Simeonov

Mergers and acquisitions
Emil Delchev

Real estate
Emil Simeonov, Snezhana Stoyanova

Tax
Emil Delchev

DELOITTE BULGARIA EOOD

55 ALEXANDER STAMBOLIJSKI BOULEVARD
1000 SOFIA

Telephone: +359 2 980 8500
Fax: +359 2 980 0436
Website: www.deloitte.bg

Languages
English, French, Russian

Other offices
Varna

Number of lawyers 10

CATEGORIES OF WORK

Banking and finance
Borislav Stratev

Commercial contracts
Petko Iliev

Concessions
Elena Kalapova

Media and entertainment
Elena Kalapova

Corporate and commercial
Borislav Stratev, Petko Iliev

Energy
Elena Kalapova

EU and competition
Petko Iliev

Real estate
Borislav Stratev, Rosen Aleksandrov

Government contracts
Borislav Stratev

Insurance law
Ekaterina Souleva

Intellectual property, IT and media
Rosen Aleksandrov

Labour law
Rosen Aleksandrov

Mergers and acquisitions
Borislav Stratev, Ekaterina Souleva

Privatisation
Borislav Stratev

Procurement
Ekaterina Souleva

Tax law
Borislav Stratev, Dinko Yordanov

DIMITROV, PETROV & CO

36 PATRIARH EVTIMII BLVD
ENTR. B, FL. 4
1000 SOFIA

Telephone: +359 2 988 7361
Fax: +359 2 987 7096
E-mail: info@dpc.bg
Website: www.dpc.bg

Languages
Bulgarian, English, French, German, Italian, Russian, Spanish,

Other offices
Varna

Number of lawyers 14
at this office 12

Member
IBA; Meritas

CATEGORIES OF WORK

Corporate and commercial
Bogdan Petrov

Computers and technology
George Dimitrov

Real estate
Alexander Todorov

Telecommunications
Miroslav Ognyanov

Mergers and acquisitions
Bogdan Petrov

Lobbying
George Dimitrov

Antitrust
Miroslav Ognyanov

Banking and finance institutions
Angel Kalaidjiev

Administrative
Alexander Todorov

Business litigation
Margarita Kalaidjieva

Intellectual property
Plamena Nikolaeva

International business
Angel Kalaidjiev

Taxation
Margarita Kalaidjieva

Construction
Bogdan Petrov

Insurance
Angel Kalaidjiev

Advertising and media
George Dimitrov

DJINGOV, GOUGINSKI, KYUTCHUKOV & VELICHKOV

10 TSAR OSVOBODITEL BOULEVARD
1000 SOFIA

Telephone: +359 2 932 1100
Fax: +359 2 980 3586
E-mail: dgkv@dgkv.com
Website: www.dgkv.com

Languages
English, French, German, Russian

Other offices
Frankfurt am Main

Number of lawyers 46

Contacts
Assen Djingov, Marius Velichkov

CATEGORIES OF WORK

Privatisation
Zdravka Ugrinova

General corporate
Assen Djingov

Banking
Stephan Kyutchukov

Securities
Vessela Stancheva

Project finance
Stephan Kyutchukov

Mergers and acquisitions
Zdravka Ugrinova

Tax
Viara Todorova

Construction
Stephan Kyutchukov

Litigation
Stephan Kyutchukov

Telecommunications
Violetta Kunze

Secured transactions
Stephan Kyutchukov

Energy
Georgi Gouginski

Competition
Nikolai Gouginski

Environmental law
Stephan Kyutchukov

Commercial property
Stephan Kyutchukov

Commercial contracts
Georgi Gouginski

IP, IT and media
Kalina Tchakarova

Labour law
Kalina Tchakarova

THE FIRM

Founded in 1994, Djingov, Gouginski, Kyutchukov & Velichkov is now one of Bulgaria's largest and most prominent law firms.

AREAS OF PRACTICE

The firm acts as legal adviser to global commercial banks, such as HVB, BNP Paribas, Citibank, Société Générale and TC Ziraat Bank for their Bulgarian operations. It acted as counsel to IFC, AIG, Bank Austria and MKB for the acquisition of shares in major Bulgarian banks; EBRD, IFC, Commerzbank and two major German funds for the establishment of a Bulgarian micro finance bank, and Paribas for the first Euro Bond issue for Sofia. It has advised UBS, Rabobank, JP Morgan and Barclays Bank on various regulatory matters, and US and European investment banks and securities firms on their operations on the Bulgarian market of stocks, bonds and T-bills. The firm has been involved in Bulgaria's largest privatisation deals: Bulgarian Telecommunications Company and State Savings Bank, as counsel to the government. The firm also represented OMV for acquisition of the state-owned gasoline retail company; Deutsche Bank for the acquisition of the three main domestic pharmaceutical companies; Nomura, Société Générale and KBC Bank in their acquisitions of Bulgaria's three largest banks; SKF in the privatisation of a bearings plant; ČEZ in the privatisation of Bulgarian electricity distribution companies and Copenhagen Airports for the concession of two major Bulgarian airports. The firm also acts in consortium with CSFB as counsel to the government for the sale of three major thermal power stations.

The firm's leading position in the field of project finance and corporate finance is founded upon high expertise in lending, debt finance and securitisation. The firm is counsel to WB, EBRD, IFC, JBIC, BSTDB, CSFB, KfW and Deutcshe Bank on the financing of various infrastructure, construction and financial projects. Recently, the firm advised OTP and DSK Bank on financing of the Sofia Mall and Merill Lynch on the financing of Global Steel Holdings Ltd for the acquisition of a major regional steel company.

In the field of telecoms and media, the firm has represented a consortium of investors for MobilTel acquisition – the largest M&A deal in CEE for 2004; Magyar Telekom Rt for the acquisition of Bulgaria's largest alternative wireline telecom and internet provider; Sanoma Magazines and Handelsblatt for the acquisition of a Bulgarian publishing business; Playboy for the publishing of its magazine in Bulgaria; Warner Bros for the hiring of Bulgarian extras; Reuters and Bloomberg for their Bulgarian activity; Gazprombank for the acquisition of shares in a media holding structure; Intel and Bulgaria's second-largest GSM operator on regulatory matters; Telecom Italia in a tender for a GSM licence, and so on.

The firm's trade mark practice group, representing, among others, Deutsche Telekom, Hugo Boss, ENI and Gallaher, enlarged its trade mark portfolio by adding Carlsberg Bulgaria, Servier Laboratories and Tabacalera.

In the real estate sector, the firm advised on Bulgaria's largest real estate acquisition of TzM, Sofia's largest trade and office centre, and it recently acted as counsel to GE Commercial Finance on the acquisition of a 50% stake in the Sofia Mall.

In the energy and infrastructure sector, the firm has advised AES, Entergy, Enel, EnergoPro, Rolls-Royce Power Ventures and RWE Power AG on their investment projects; OMV for the construction of a nationwide network of petrol stations; Anglian Water and Thames Water for three major water concessions.

The firm advises on all aspects of labour and social security law. Major clients include SKF, Carlsberg, OMV, Accor, Aventise Pharma, among others.

Further clients include, among others: Abbot, Alcatel, AndersenLegal IP, BP, Bristol Myers Squibb, Cable & Wireless, Cereol, Chase Manhattan, Chevron Texaco, Coca-Cola, DMG, Eli Lilly, Enron, Ford, Estée Lauder, GE International, Hörmann KG, Hilton, ING Barings, Interoute, Japan Tobacco, Kempinski Hotels, Lukoil, Morgan Stanley, Nokia, OTE, Shell, Standard Bank London, Swisscom, Volvo, VP Market Group, Whirlpool, and Western Union.

DOBREV, KINKIN & LYUTSKANOV LAW FIRM

8 TSAR IVAN SHISHMAN STREET
1000 SOFIA

Telephone: +359 2 980 3475
Fax: +359 2 980 4261
E-mail: lawfirm-office@lawfirm-bg.org
Website: www.lawfirm-bg.com

Languages
English, German, Russian

Number of lawyers 12

Contacts
Roumen Lyutskanov, Theodore Bojinov

Member
European Law Firm (ELF)

CATEGORIES OF WORK

Privatisation and foreign investment
Vladimir Kinkin, Theodore Bojinov

Corporate and commercial
Vladimir Kinkin, Theodore Bojinov

Banking and finance
Roumen Lyutskanov, Theodore Bojinov

Real estate and construction
Roumen Lyutskanov, Sophia Bayrakova

Property
Adriana Nacheva, Maria Boiadjieva

Insurance, transportation and maritime
Roumen Lyutskanov, Sophia Bayrakova

Concessions and public procurement
Grozdan Dobrev, Elisaveta Sokolova

Tax and tax planning
Vladimir Kinkin, Daniela Petkova

Civil litigation and arbitration
Alexander Georgiev, Silvia Spassova

Copyright and patent law
Daniela Petkova, Elisaveta Sokolova

Telecommunications and IT
Elisaveta Sokolova, Iassen Hristev

Trade regulations, consumers' rights protection, competition
Grozdan Dobrev, Iassen Hristev

Energy
Roumen Lyutskanov, Sophia Bayrakova

Family and inheritance
Adriana Nacheva, Maria Boiadjieva

Labour and social securities
Grozdan Dobrev, Adriana Nacheva

THE FIRM

Dobrev, Kinkin & Lyutskanov Law Firm was founded in 1989. It was among the first law firms to be established after the changes in Bulgaria in the 1990s. The firm is a company, constituted and operating in accordance with the Bar Act. The firm works in partnership with leading worldwide law firms on several international projects. The firm serves the commercial and investment activities of its clients. The firm's experience and expertise allow it to assist its clients to accomplish their objectives.

Dobrev, Kinkin & Lyutskanov Law Firm provides legal services mainly in the fields of commercial and civil law. The firm has earned a good reputation and authority among numerous local and foreign investors through providing services in their investment, privatisation and post-privatisation projects. The firm provides legal services in the privatisation of enterprises in various economic sectors, such as the chemical industry, machine-building, electronics, banking, transport, tourism, food industries, media and cinema, trade and services.

AREAS OF PRACTICE

Property law and construction law are a focus of the firm's practice. The firm offers advice to clients on the acquisition, design, construction, supervision, development and management of real estate.

Financial law, taxation and banking law are priorities of the firm. The firm offers legal services to local and foreign banks, preparing due diligence reports and reviews in the case of financing and implementation of various projects and related collateral.

The firm provides advice to banks and financial institutions in extending inter-bank and syndicated loans and in establishing inter-bank consortia.

The team's professionalism in providing legal services in connection with infrastructure projects, transportation and insurance is well known to the companies in these sectors.

The firm has long experience in the registration, licensing and acquisition of banks. Tax planning and tax consultations constitute an important part of the firm's work.

The firm provides legal services in the field of company law: registration, custodian services, restructuring, acquisition and liquidation of companies. The firm offers legal services to companies in bankruptcy proceedings. The firm's attorneys-at-law have been registered on the list of trustees approved by the Minister of Justice of the Republic of Bulgaria. The firm provides legal services in the acquisition of enterprises, ie due diligence reports, conduct of negotiations and drafting of contracts.

The firm's services also cover the field of competition law, including representation of its clients before the Competition Protection Commission.

Maritime law is an important aspect of the firm's activities. The practice includes consultations on the conclusion and implementation of maritime transportation contracts, claims, litigation, and arrest of vessels.

The firm provides legal assistance in the registration of trade marks, industrial designs and patents. The firm offers legal defence to its clients in the sphere of intellectual property rights.

The firm assists with consultancy, participation in negotiations and drawing up of contracts in all spheres of economic life. The firm participates in negotiating insurance contracts and defends its clients against insurance companies, including in international insurance cases.

The firm provides legal defences to its clients before all Bulgarian courts and before domestic and international arbitration tribunals. Lawyers of the firm specialise in mediation and alternative dispute resolution. The firm's practice areas include recognition and enforcement of foreign court judgments and arbitration awards.

Dobrev, Kinkin & Lyutskanov Law Firm provides high-quality, focused, responsive and cost-effective services to its selected clientele, which includes renowned names among the banks, as well as among the investment, manufacturing and trading companies.

GEORGIEV, TODOROV & CO

27 PARCHEVICH STREET
1000 SOFIA

Telephone: +359 2 937 6527
Fax: +359 2 937 6525
E-mail: office@georg-tod.com
Website: www georg-tod.com

Languages
Armenian, English, French, German, Greek, Italian, Russian, Spanish

Other offices
Bourgas, Plovdiv, Rousse, Stara Zagora, Varna, Veliko Tarnovo

Number of lawyers 48
at this office 32

Contact
Ms Gergana Popova

Member
Lawyers Associated Worldwide (LAW)

CATEGORIES OF WORK

Corporate and commercial
Alexander Katzarsky, Arno Mamassian

Mergers and acquisitions
Alexander Katzarsky, Arno Mamassian

Privatisation
Ivan Todorov, Christina Koycheva

Project finance
Rossitsa Baltajieva, Christina Koycheva

Banking
Rossitsa Baltajieva, Ivan Todorov

Telecommunications, IT, media
Alexander Pachamanov,
Rossitsa Baltajieva

Energy
Ivan Todorov, Dimitar Danailov

Securities
Alexander Katzarsky, Arno Mamassian

EU law
Bogdan Drensky, Marina Marinova

Unfair competition
Valery Tarandov,
Alexander Pachamanov

Taxation
Dimitar Danailov, Rossitsa Baltajieva

Real estate
Valery Tarandov, Liubomir Alexandrov

Insolvency
Valentin Georgiev, Valery Tarandov

Licences and concessions
Ivan Todorov, Rossitsa Baltajieva

Administrative appeals
Ivan Todorov, Dimitar Danailov

Litigation and arbitration
Teodor Chipev, Ivan Todorov

THE FIRM

GTC provides business law services, with particular emphasis on the financial, telecom, IT and energy sectors for a large domestic client base and a range of foreign investors, such as Microsoft Corporation (USA), Mitsui & Co (Japan), Advent International (USA), UPS Europe (Belgium), ABN AMRO Bank (the Netherlands), Montgomery Watson Harza (Belgium), the Bulgarian National Bank, the Bulgarian Finance Supervision Commission, Rompetrol (Romania), Piraeusbank (Greece), Raiffeisenbank (Austria), Intelcan (Canada), Imperial Tobacco (UK), Europa Capital Management (UK), etc.

Since its establishment in 1991, GTC has gained extensive international experience and has often been a pioneer. For instance, GTC provided advice regarding: the first projects for the reconstruction of airforce facilities in compliance with NATO standards (2003); the sale of the biggest insolvent bank as a going concern (2002); the first issuing of Eurobonds by a Bulgarian entity (1999); the first merger of private banks (1998), etc.

One of the important reasons for the speedy development of the firm is that GTC combines successful consultancy work with an outstanding litigation practice. Thus the firm is able to use its specific knowledge of court precedents to avoid possible problems for the clients. Lawyers from GTC have represented clients in some of the largest arbitration and litigation cases in Bulgaria.

AREAS OF PRACTICE

Examples of the most recent (2004) consultancy and litigation work include:

Support to Advent International as buyer of the Bulgarian telecommunications company (the state owned ex-monopolist in the provision of fixed telephony). The overall financial effect from the transaction exceeds €1bn, which makes it the biggest privatisation in Bulgaria. Apart from complex advice and assistance in negotiations, the firm defended the buyer in more than 12 cases of appeal with the Supreme Administrative Court. All cases were closed with a final court decision in favour of the client. As recognition for GTC's role in the process the firm was retained as long-term outside counsel to support BTC in its day-to-day activities as well as in the obtaining of GSM3 license.

Support to Mitsui & Co, Toshiba Corp and the Japanese Bank of International Cooperation with repect to the rehabilitation of four units of Maritza Iztok 2 Thermal Power Plant. Maritza Iztok 2 accounts for approximately 17% of the total electricity produced in Bulgaria. GTC successfully advised on Bulgarian law as well as EU competition issues, and defended the client before the Supreme Adminsitrative Court with respect to state aid issues. The firm also managed to ensure the issuing of a state guarantee in favour of JBIC.

A brochure providing more details is available upon request.

KAMBOUROV & PARTNERS

55 NEOFIT RILSKI STREET
1000 SOFIA

Telephone: +359 2 986 9999
Fax: +359 2 986 9995
E-mail: office@kambourov.biz
Website: www.kambourov.biz

Languages
English, French, German, Italian, Russian, Spanish

Number of lawyers 23

Contacts
Yavor Kambourov, Vladimir Rangeloff

CATEGORIES OF WORK

Foreign investments
Yavor Kambourov, Vladimir Rangeloff

Privatisation
Yavor Kambourov, Vladimir Rangeloff

Litigation and arbitration
Yavor Kambourov, Vladimir Rangeloff

Banking law and bank insolvency
Yavor Kambourov, Stefan Gugushev

Insolvency proceedings
Yavor Kambourov, Hristina Kirilova

Intellectual property and copyright
Yavor Kambourov, Mitko Karushkov

Taxation and customs issues
Emil Emanuilov, Vladimir Rangeloff

Employment and social security issues
Emil Emanuilov, Nikolay Bandakov

Commercial law (including mergers and acquisitions)
Vladimir Rangeloff, Stefan Gugushev

Corporate law
Mitko Karushkov, Stefan Gugushev

Telecommunications, TV, movie industry
Mitko Karushkov, Yavor Kambourov

Energy sector, mining
Vladimir Rangeloff, Stefan Tzakov

Concessions
Stefan Tzakov, Stefan Gugushev

Competition and consumer protection
Mitko Karushkov, Atanas Shopov

THE FIRM

Since its establishment in 1988, Kambourov & Partners has proven to be one of the leading and fastest-growing law firms in Bulgaria. Over the last two years, the firm has more than doubled its number of lawyers and significantly increased the number of its projects and partners. Today, the office comprises two partners, six senior associates, 12 associates, and three legal trainees.

Kambourov & Partners is a law firm of unique values, identity and 'personality', with a passion for client service. The firm's trademark is flexibility, offering extensive experience, professionalism, integrity and a highly personal approach. Kambourov & Partners has a reputation for providing quality legal services within the shortest possible time limits. The firm advises mostly foreign multinational companies and institutions. Due to the growing amount of trans-border projects, the firm has appointed a permanent representative in London.

AREAS OF PRACTICE

Banking and finance: The firm provides financial advice and services to investors, lenders, borrowers, issuers, underwriters, sponsors and venture capital firms. Clients include large Bulgarian banks and major international financial institutions. The firm provides assistance in day-to-day banking operations as well as consultancy on investment projects, project finance, application of thin cap rules and avoidance of double taxation.

Capital markets and public offering: Kambourov & Partners acts for several Bulgarian investment intermediaries, advising on the sale of shares through public offering and other transactions taking place on the regulated capital market. The firm's lawyers have gained substantial expertise in privatisation deals involving public offering.

Energy and natural resources: Kambourov & Partners acted for one of Europe's energy giants in the privatisation of the Bulgarian energy distribution companies, and continues to provide consultancy in the post-privatisation integration process. The firm also offers advisory services to a number of energy enterprises operating in Bulgaria.

Foreign investments, M&A and privatisation: Kambourov & Partners offers its clients a full range of legal services including legal due diligence, drafting transaction documentation, assistance in negotiating the terms of the deal, participation in tenders for assignment of public procurements and concessions, assistance in obtaining all necessary permits and government authorisations.

Intellectual property: The IP team provides due diligence, TM research and monitoring, registration of trade marks, appellations of origin and industrial design, copyright protection, drafting of licensing agreements and contracts for assignment of exclusive and and non- exclusive rights over IPs and IP infringement litigation.

Liquidation, insolvency and restructuring: These are areas where the firm has specific expertise and specialisation. Kambourov & Partners' senior partner has been active as an assignee-in-bankruptcy in major Bulgarian enterprises, among which are some of the former leading Bulgarian banks.

Real estate and construction: Kambourov & Partners provide legal advice on all aspects of property investments under Bulgarian law. The firm's lawyers are experienced in the elaboration of financing schemes involving the support of credit institutions. Relevant experience includes negotiation of construction contracts pursuant to FIDIC rules.

Telecoms and media: The firm has been heavily involved in the legal work on a number of telecom projects, including the privatisation of the Bulgarian national telecom The firm consulted a couple of large international movie companies on the possible schemes for financing movies in Bulgaria.

Tax: The firm provides tax advice to Bulgarian and foreign employees, managers and members of the managing corporate bodies. It also offers company tax planning, M&A and international tax planning and interpretation and application of Avoidance of Double Taxation Treaties.

LIC-PENKOV, MARKOV & PARTNERS

BL 22, ENTR A
IZTOK DISTRICT
1113 SOFIA

Telephone: +359 2 971 3935
Fax: +359 2 971 1191
E-mail: lega@bg400.bg
Website: www.licpenkov-markov.com

Languages
Bulgarian, English, French, German, Russian

Other offices
Bourgas, Dobrich, Lovech (2), Pleven (and Troyan), Rousse, Sofia (2), Stara Zagora, Targovishte, Varna, Vratsa

Number of lawyers 57
at this office 23

International groupings
Lex Mundi; Eurojuris (Germany); Bulgarian International Business Association; Business Club of German Economy; German-Bulgarian Industrial Chamber

CATEGORIES OF WORK

Commercial and business
Vladimir Penkov, Ivan Markov

Privatisation
Vladimir Penkov

Foreign investment
Vladimir Penkov

Joint venture
Vladimir Penkov

Banking and financial
Ivan Markov, Laghezar Raichev

Mergers and acquisitions
Vladimir Penkov, Svetlin Adrianov

Antitrust and competition
Svetlin Adrianov

Consumer protection
Svetlin Adrianov

Telecoms
Svetoslav Dimitrov

Labour
Dimitar Chorbadjiev

Tax
Dimitar Slavchev

Real estate
Todorin Pakerov

Commercial (international)
Vladimir Penkov, Milena Gaydarska

Licensing
Vladimir Penkov

Litigation
Todorin Pakerov

Arbitration (international)
Vladimir Penkov

Customs
Roman Stoyanov

Maritime
Krastio Georgiev

THE FIRM

Established in 1990, LIC-Penkov, Markov & Partners is now one of the largest law firms in Bulgaria, with offices in Sofia and nine other major Bulgarian cities. The firm employs 57 lawyers and a comprehensive team of support staff. The firm has strong co-operative links with Lansky, Ganzger & Partners (Vienna), Niebaum, Kohler, Punge, Söder (Dortmund). Lega InterConsult was the first domestic firm to be admitted to the Bulgarian International Business Association (BIBA), an association of foreign investors in the country. Since 2003 it has been a member of the Business Club of German Economy in Bulgaria. In 2005 the firm was certified under the ISO 9001:2000 management system standard for comprehensive legal services and consultations, thus becoming the first law firm in Bulgaria to be granted such certification.

The firm is noted for its commitment to research. It has published articles on: the harmonisation of Bulgarian and EU corporate and commercial law for the Bulgarian Centre for the Study of Democracy; *The EU: Towards an Institutional Infrastructure*; tax and development; Customs Acts and regulation. The firm contributes to specialised publications such as the *International Privatisation Law Review*. LIC-Penkov, Markov & Partners also publishes its own newsletter, the first of its kind in Bulgaria and with a circulation of 2,200, that provides up-to-date legal information to governmental and non-governmental institutions, embassies, businesses and individual experts in the legal and economic sectors. The firm is active in the preparation of bills and legal regulations concerning issues including concessions, privatisations and electronic signature.

Lawyers at the firm regularly take part in international legal and business forums, including in recent years: the 1999 UN forum on new trends in competition law in Brno; the 2000 international conference of the Centre for Energy Efficiency in Sofia; the Fourth Session of the Bulgarian-German Committee Conference for Economic Co-operation in Hanover.

AREAS OF PRACTICE

The firm's main areas of practice are commercial and business law with particular emphasis on corporate law, privatisation, foreign investment, joint ventures, banking and financial law, mergers and acquisitions, antitrust and competition, consumer protection, telecoms, labour law, tax law, real estate, international commercial law, licensing, litigation and international arbitration. LIC-Penkov, Markov & Partners are specialists in the provision of legal advice on the international aspects of commercial, company and civil law. Lawyers at the firm are recognised experts in many of the fields mentioned.

One of the firm's main activities is advising overseas clients on investment opportunities in Bulgaria. LIC-Penkov, Markov & Partners advises on the legal regulations relating to taxation, customs procedures, export and import, currency, employment and social security and their relation to the contemporary investment climate.

The recognised strength of LIC-Penkov, Markov & Partners' legal presence in the investment sector has led to its involvement in some of the largest investment projects in the region. The firm's major international clients include The Coca-Cola Company, directly and through Leventis Group and Clarina; Heineken, in Brewinvest and Brewmasters' investment in Bulgarian breweries; Hewlett-Packard; the European Bank for Reconstruction and Development (EBRD); DaimlerChrysler AG; Siemens AG; Willi Betz Group in its distribution of Mercedes-Benz and Chrysler; Bayer AG; Sumitomo Corporation; National Bank of Greece; Cargill; Salini; Advent International; Titan Cement; Galagher Int; Telefónica; Enichem; Karelia Tobacco; Laufen; Knauf; Chimco (Bulgaria); Lafarge, Autotechnica (authorised importer of Audi and Seat); Frech; Alu Koenig Stahl; BASF AG; Velux A/S; Alcoa; Carrefour Marinopoulos SA; Carrier Hellas Air-conditioning; Casa Group Plc; TBIH Group. The firm also advises the government of Bulgaria and the Swiss Federation with regard to financing projects in Bulgaria.

LANDWELL BULGARIA

7TH FLOOR
9-11 MARIA LOUISA BLVD
1000 SOFIA

Telephone: +359 2 935 5100
Fax: +359 2 935 5166
E-mail:
irina.tsvetkova@bg.landwellglobal.com
Website: www.landwellglobal.com/bg

Languages
Arabic, English, French, German, Italian, Spanish, Russian

Number of lawyers 21

Contacts
Irina Tsvetkova (partner),
Nikolay Bebov (senior managing associate)

International groupings
Landwell, correspondent law firms of PricewaterhouseCoopers

CATEGORIES OF WORK

Banking and finance law
Irina Tsvetkova, Galina Bunkova

Capital markets law
Nikolay Bebov, Maria Urmanova

Commercial contracts law, secured transactions
Galina Bunkova, Georgy Georgiev

Company law
Maria Urmanova

Construction law, concessions, real estate law, property investments
Peter Takov, Hristo Gradinarski

Dispute resolution
Hristo Gradinarski

Employment law
Polina Ganeva

Energy law
Polina Ganeva, Nikolay Bebov

Intellectual property and data protection
Galina Bunkova

M&A, privatistion
Irina Tsvetkova, Georgy Georgiev

Project finance
Nikolay Bebov, Hristo Gradinarski

Technology, internet, pharmaceuticals law
Galina Bunkova

THE FIRM

Landwell Bulgaria has had a notable presence on the Bulgarian legal market since 2002, with the core team in the firm working together since 1998. Landwell Bulgaria has completed a series of projects of significance for Bulgaria, such as Eurobond issues (Bulgarian aspects), implementation of a Class One investment in co-operation with the BulgariaInvest Agency, structuring of debt/equity hybrid instruments for banks, registration for public offer of foreign UCITS, creation of the first private credit bureau in Bulgaria and approval of personal data processing procedures applied by it, real estate acquisition advice, gas distribution company acquisition, and gas and electricity deregulation services. Landwell Bulgaria is a dynamic, innovative and multi-expertise business law practice.

The firm is a member of the international legal network "Landwell" and a correspondent law firm of PricewaterhouseCoopers in Bulgaria. Landwell Bulgaria also co-operates on an ad hoc basis with a number of international firms of lawyers across the globe.

The firm's client base consists of both leading international investors in Bulgaria and high-growth Bulgarian companies. Among the many notable names are entities within the UniCredit/HVB Group, Société Générale Group, Raiffeisen Zentralbank Group, Deutsche Bahn Group (Railion – LS Danubuis), EFG Eurobank Ergasias Group, Alliance and Leicester Group, Opet Aygaz (Koç Group), Montupet, AMGA, M Real, and many others.

AREAS OF PRACTICE

Financial services law: regulatory: banking laws and regulations, including prudential regulations and Basle II advice; securities firms regulatory work; financial conglomerates; equities and bonds issues, including Eurobonds, floatation of companies; collective investment schemes; insurance; pension schemes; real estate investment trusts; other forms of securitisation; deal structuring: bank loans and syndicated loans; distribution of financial products, including collective investment schemes; acquisitions; tender offers; title finance: leasing and auto-leasing; factoring; M&A and privatisation; project finance; securities litigation.

Real estate and construction: acquisitions: pre-acquisition due diligence, acquisition and conveyancing; structuring of payments; collateralisation; regulatory advice: zoning rules, construction and use permits; concessions: procedures and project finance in concession-related projects; construction law: construction administrative law and construction contracts, application of FIDIC-based contracts; investments related to real estate: financing of projects; investment vehicles; regulatory activities for hotels: obtaining and maintenance of categorisation.

Energy and utilities law: electricity deregulation: new rules and trends for electricity; renewable energy; trading rules and exchanges; project finance aspects; nuclear energy: decommissioning; construction of new capacities; international treaties in the nuclear sector; gasification: licensing procedures; transit; distribution; the water sector: water concessions; public service obligations; oil and gas: retail and wholesale trade in oil and gas; public obligations (compulsory stocks, quality requirements).

Intellectual property and personal data protection: trademarks: registration and maintenance; studies; copyright: copyright-related clauses in construction contracts; the music business; TV; personal data protection: regulatory advice and representation before the regulator; IP litigation.

General company and commercial law: company law: registration and maintenance of companies; increase and reduction of share capital; company secretarial services: commercial contracts: sale and purchase; distribution; loans; leases; franchise; agency; shipping and forwarding agreements; internet contracts; consumer protection and fair trade practices; secured transactions: mortgages; bank guarantees; negotiable instruments as collateral; registered pledges.

Other areas of practices: competition and EU law; dispute resolution; employment law; international private law; technology, internet, pharmaceuticals law; transport law (in particular, rail, aviation, marine).

LEGACOM ANTOV & PARTNERS LAW FIRM

1ST FLOOR
3 YANKO ZABUNOV STREET
1408 SOFIA

Telephone: +359 2 950 1030
Fax: +359 2 950 1070
E-mail: legacom@legacom.com
Website: www.legacom.com

Languages
Bulgarian, English, French, Greek, Russian

Number of lawyers 18

CATEGORIES OF WORK

Banking and finance

Commercial property/real estate

Corporate and commercial

Dispute resolution – litigation and arbitration

Employment

Energy and natural resources

Environment

Foreign direct investment

Infrastructure and project finance

Insurance

Media and entertainment

Mergers and acquisitions

Privatisation

Shipping and transport

PI PARTNERS

BUSINESS PARK
BUILDING 10, FLOOR 2
MLADOST 4
1715 SOFIA

Telephone: +359 2 817 7100
Fax: +359 2 817 7111
E-mail: pi.partners@bg.eylaw.com
Website: www.eylaw.com/bg

Languages
Bulgarian, English, French, German, Russian, Slovak, Spanish

Other offices
Athens, Bucharest, Istanbul, Thessaloniki

Number of lawyers 60
at this office 7

Contact
Anelia Dinova (anelia.dinova@bg.eylaw.com)

International groupings
Ernst & Young

CATEGORIES OF WORK

Banking, finance and securities
Diana Valkova

M&A and privatisations
Anelia Dinova

Commercial and corporate
Milen Rusev

Human capital services and labour
Boyan Kirtchev

Litigation and arbitration
Milen Rusev

Real estate
Konstantin Ilin

SABEV & PARTNERS LAW FIRM

59 SOLUNSKA STREET
1000 SOFIA

Telephone: +359 2 953 1273
Fax: +359 2 953 1767
E-mail: office@sabevandpartners.com
Website: www.sabevandpartners.com

Languages
English, French, German, Russian

Number of lawyers 9

Contact
Mrs Boryana Boteva

CATEGORIES OF WORK

Corporate and commercial
George Sabev, K Kavaldjieva

Capital markets and securities
George Sabev, Stefan Stefanov

Taxation
B Boteva, Nevena Stoeva

Competition
Assen Alexiev

Intellectual property
Assen Alexiev

Property and construction law
Violeta Dikova, K Kavaldjieva

Employment and social security
B Boteva, Kostya Karaivanov

Environment
Katilin Popov

Litigation and dispute resolution
A Alexiev, Stefan Stefanov

Public procurement
Stefan Stefanov, Nevena Stoeva

Privatisation and concessions
Boryana Boteva, Nevena Stoeva

Telecommunications and IT
Assen Alexiev

Administrative
George Sabev, Stefan Stefanov

EU law
Violeta Dikova, Katilin Popov

International arbitration
B Boteva, Assen Alexiev

Bankruptcy
George Sabev, Stefan Stefanov

Foreign investments
Boryana Boteva, Violeta Dikova

Mergers and acquisitions
George Sabev, Stefan Stefanov

SCHÖNHERR
BULGARIA EOOD

SOLUNSKA 27
1000 SOFIA

Telephone: +359 2 933 1070
Fax: +359 2 986 1105
E-mail: office@schoenherr.bg
Website: www.schoenherr.at

Languages
Bulgarian, German, English

Other offices
Belgrade, Brussels, Bucharest, Kyiv, Ljubljana, Vienna, Zagreb (co-operation office)

Number of lawyers 130
at this office 8

Contacts
Christoph Lindinger (ch.lindinger@schoenherr.at),
Markus Piuk (m.piuk@schoenherr.at),
Alexandra Doytchinova (a.doytchinova@schoenherr.bg)

CATEGORIES OF WORK

International and Bulgarian practice

International contracts and foreign investments

Banking securities and finance

Project finance

M&A

Privatisations

Public private partnership

Real estate and commercial property

EU law

Competition

SPASOV & BRATANOV

35 SLAVYANSKA STREET
1000 SOFIA

Telephone: +359 2 980 1808
Fax: +359 2 980 2510
E-mail: office@sbn-law.com
Website: www.sbn-law.com

Languages
Bulgarian, English, French, German, Russian

Number of lawyers 7

Contact
Georgi Spasov, LLM

Member
BBCC; BIBA

CATEGORIES OF WORK

Banking and finance
Georgi Spasov, Vassil Hadjov

Commercial and company law
Jana Djambazova, Boyko Bratanov

Mergers and acquisitions
Jana Djambazova, Georgi Spasov

Corporate finance
Vassil Hadjov, Georgi Spasov

Capital markets
Georgi Spasov, Vassil Hadjov

Litigation
Boyko Bratanov, Georgi Spasov

Arbitration
Boyko Bratanov, Georgi Spasov

Energy and infrastructure projects
Vassil Hadjov, Jana Djambazova

Concessions
Georgi Spasov, Jana Djambazova

Real estate
Jana Djambazova

Tax law
Boyko Bratanov

STUDIO LEGALE SUTTI

UL MOSKOVSKA 27A
1000 SOFIA

Telephone: +359 2 980 3275
Fax: +359 2 988 5015
E-mail: maildesk@sutti.com
Website: www.sutti.com

Languages
Bulgarian, Croatian, English, French, German, Italian, Japanese, Romanian, Russian, Serbian, Spanish

Other offices
Belgrade, Bucharest, Genoa, London, Milan, Rome, Tokyo, Zagreb

Contact
Tzvetelina Dimitrova

CATEGORIES OF WORK

Company, commercial law

Banking and finance

Mergers and acquisitions

Distribution, agency and franchising

Debt collection and insolvency

Commercial property law

Intellectual property

Patent and trade mark agency service

White-collar crime

EC, competition and antitrust law

IT and TLC law

Litigation and arbitration

Employment, labour law

Administrative law

Environmental law

TELECOMLEX CONSULT – CHERESHEVA, NACHEV & PARTNERS

2ND FLOOR
24 PRAGUE BLVD
1606 SOFIA

Telephone: +359 2 952 2745
Fax: +359 2 951 6478
E-mail: cheresheva@tlc.bg
nachev@tlc.bg
Website: www.tlc.bg

Languages
Bulgarian, English, French, Russian

Number of lawyers 13
at this office 9

CATEGORIES OF WORK

Corporate governance
Vesselina Tsankova, Margarita Mileva

Mergers and acquisitions
Ilonka Raichinova, Yasna Stavreva

Commercial and tax law
Vesselina Tsankova, Ilonka Raichinova

Securities and capital markets
Sylvia Cheresheva, Ilonka Raichinova

Competition and EU law
Dragia Dragiev, Yasna Stavreva

Regulatory
Sylvia Cheresheva, Damyan Ganchev

IT and e-communications
Sylvia Cheresheva, Damyan Ganchev

Intellectual property and e-commerce
Damyan Ganchev, Vesselina Tsankova

Media and entertainment
Damyan Ganchev, Ivailo Bourkov

Infrastructure and project finance
Sylvia Cheresheva, Iliya Nachev

Family business and investment funds
Iliya Nachev, Nadezhda Boncheva

Real estate
Iliya Nachev, Nadezhda Boncheva

Construction
Iliya Nachev, Sylvia Cheresheva

Employment and social security
Yasna Stavreva, Mila Velcheva

Administrative law and process
Mila Velcheva, Margarita Rangelova

Litigation and arbitration
Yasna Stavreva, Georgi Gatev

VARADINOV & CO ATTORNEYS-AT-LAW

**38 VASSIL LEVSKI BLVD.
1000 SOFIA**

Telephone: +359 2 963 2776
Fax: +359 2 963 3291
E-mail: maildesk@varadinovlaw.com
Website: www.varadinovlaw.com

Languages
Bulgarian, English, French, German, Italian, Russian

Number of lawyers 15

Contact
Iva Ivanova Zgurova

CATEGORIES OF WORK

Company and commercial law
Yavor Grigorov Varadinov

Banking and finance
Silviya Krasteva Krasteva-Kochkova

Mergers and acquisitions
Yavor Grigorov Varadinov

Distribution, agency and franchising
Lyubomir Nikolaev Talev

Debt collection and insolvency
Anna Asenova Penakova

Commercial property law
Galina Ivanova Gergova

Intellectual property
Julia Kamenova Georgieva,
Yavor Grigorov Varadinov

Patent and trade mark agency service
Julia Kamenova Georgieva,
Yavor Grigorov Varadinov

IT and TLC law
Anna Asenova Penakova

Litigation and arbitration
Yanislava Ivanova Chankova

Employment and labour law
Yanislava Ivanova Chankova

Administrative law
Milen Atanasov Shopov

Environmental law
Julia Kamenova Georgieva

Project finance
Silviya Krasteva Krasteva-Kochkova,
Yavor Grigorov Varadinov

Dispute resolution
Yavor Grigorov Varadinov

Privatisation
Galina Ivanova Gergova,
Yavor Grigorov Varadinov

THE FIRM

Varadinov & Co Attorneys-at-Law was established in 1990 by the managing partner, Yavor Grigorov Varadinov. The firm's office is situated in the centre of Sofia and initially comprised of three attorneys-at-law, which has now grown to its current size of 15 attorneys-at-law. Many of the firm's attorneys have attained recognition as specialists in their areas of practice.

Varadinov & Co is a competitive law firm that always aims to efficiently resolve clients cases. The firm has a solid domestic position and strong European and US connections.

AREAS OF PRACTICE

Varadinov & Co Attorneys-at-law is focused on providing legal services for corporate clients, and commercial law is the firm's core area of practice. The firm has a large amount of corporate and multinational clients, the interests of which have contributed to the firm's development in various areas of law and business. Varadinov & Co's main areas of practice include corporate law, project finance, company and commercial law, mergers and acquisitions, foreign investments, concessions, banking law, tax law, corporate finances, real estate law, telecommunications, intellectual property, administrative law, litigation, arbitration and privatisation. The firm also deals with a lot of international construction work. It is noted for its cross-border work in the Gulf region where some of the firm's clients are general contractors.

The firm's intellectual property expertise includes trade marks, designs, patents and copyright law.

For further information, please visit: www.varadinovlaw.com.

CROATIA

Population	**4.5 million**
Number of lawyers	**2,828**
Professional title	**Odvjetnik**
Currency	**Croatian Kuna (HVK)**

Index

Croatia obtained independence from Yugoslavia in 1991 and is rapidly emerging as a future member of the EU. It is located in what is widely termed as southeastern Europe. It nestles between Bosnia-Herzegovina and Slovenia, and its southern coastline runs along the Adriatic Sea. Its attractive coastline, which boasts a temperate climate, has attracted a dramatic increase in tourism in recent years. Croatia now boasts one of the fastest-growing economies in the region.

BILLING

The Croatia Bar Association has strict guidelines on fees and lawyers pay close attention to these rules. Croatia has a three-level legal profession, which includes partners, registered attorneys and trainees. As it takes some four years to train in a law firm, before qualifying as a registered attorney, the junior level of law firms can be a significant portion of the practice and is often an integral segment of the business. Croatia's most prominent partners bill in the range of €300 per hour, experienced registered attorneys charge some €190 to €240, with junior associates (trainees) requesting an hourly rate of between €100 and €180.

MARKETING

The Croatia Bar Association is showing signs of softening its traditionally conservative approach to marketing, though firms are still prohibited from advertising.

IN-HOUSE LAWYERS

In-house lawyers are not members of the Croatia Bar Association. As with other jurisdictions, in-house legal teams are becoming increasingly prominent and will often work alongside private practice to efficiently complete a transaction or other legal mandate.

POLITICAL AND ECONOMIC CLIMATE

Croatia applied to join the EU in 2003, and could gain membership as early as 2007. The Croatian region was always one of Yugoslavia's most prosperous areas, though perhaps not as wealthy as what is now Slovenia. The economy has developed strongly in recent years despite a dip in 2000. Though unemployment is high at 14%, the nation's blossoming tourism industry has become a pivotal driver of growth. A swathe of real estate and infrastructure developments has become integral to this dynamic economy and much of this is tourism related. The EU accession process has also accelerated fiscal and structural reform. GDP growth has hovered around 4% over the last few years.

With much of Croatia's industry now privatised, the economy has become increasingly dynamic and international. Some 90% of the banking sector is now foreign owned. The industrial and manufacturing sectors, chemicals and food remain important businesses. In recent years Germany, Austria, Italy and the US have proved to be the major sources of investment into Croatia, but the UK has provided increasing amounts of capital, notably in the real estate and tourism sectors. Very much part of the global economy, Croatia is now home to major multinationals like Deutsche Telekom and Heineken.

LEGAL MARKET

Croatia's rapid emergence has seen the legal profession playing an important role in foreign investment and the construction and financing of real estate and commercial property. Most prominent lawyers and law firms do not specialise further than this broad demand.

The Croatian legal market's rapid development has seen the emergence of a range of dominant firms in recent years. **Hanzekovic, Radakovic and Partners** and **Zuric i Partneri** were the ascendant firms following Croatia's independence in 1991, but in the following period, firms like **Bogdanovic, Dolicki & Partners (in assoc with Lovells)**, **Markovic & Pliso** and **Porobija & Porobija** have emerged with the increasing prominence and experience of their partners and the exploitation of affiliations and connections with foreign law firms. In the last three years **Savoric & Partners** has surfaced as a leading name and through the efforts of name partner Boris Savoric, the firm has gained a series of cross-border and high-profile instructions. Other up-and-coming firms include **Juric Law Offices** and **Law Office Babic**, where once again the esteemed presence of their founding partners has won the attention of foreign and domestic clients.

Foreign law firms are not allowed to practise law in Croatia, but local firms are allowed to create affiliations 'in order to carry out activities of

The largest firms

1	PricewaterhouseCoopers	84
2	Bogdanovic & Dolicki (in association with Lovells)	20
	Vukic, Jelusic, Sulina Stankovic, Jurcan & Jabuka	20
4	Zuric i Partneri	19
5	Markovic & Pliso	14
	Porobija & Porobija	14
	Vukmir & Associates	14
8	Hanzekovic, Radakovic and Partners	13
9	Divjak, Topic & Bahtijarevic	11
10	Savoric & Partners	10
11	KPMG Croatia d.o.o.	9
	Miroljub Macesic, Law Offices	9
13	Babic, Law Office	8
	Crnalic in co-operation with CMS Reich-Rohrwig Hainz	8
15	Boric, Law Office	7
	Sutti, Studio Legale	7
17	Dragicevic, Law Office	6
	Nikolina Golubic in co-operation with Schönherr Rechtsanwälte GmbH	6
	Travas & Partners	6
20	Cipcic-Bragadin, Law Firm	5
	Vedris & Partners	5
	Wolf Theiss Vienna in cooperation with Croatian lawyers	5
23	Cirkveni, Law Office	4
	DLA Weiss-Tessbach/Branch for International Legal Consulting/in cooperation with local attorneys	4
	Juric Law Offices	4
	Ljubenko, Law Office	4
	Pliso Rajic Milicic	4

These figures represent the total number of lawyers in this country only, and have been supplied by the firms themselves. The figures should be accurate as at 1 January 2006.

common interest and to provide mutual service' according the Croation Bar Association. This has allowed new law firms to emerge with a formal affiliation to an international firm. **DLA Weiss-Tessbach/Branch for International Legal Consulting/in cooperation with local attorneys**; **Nikolina Golubic in co-operation with Schönherr Rechtsanwälte GmbH** and **Wolf Theiss Vienna in cooperation with Croatian lawyers** are examples of Croatian practices which are essentially an arm of an international firm. Yet with the Croatian Bar's demand that all those practising domestic law should be Croatian citizens and registered local attorneys, it limits the direct influence of foreign players on these practices.

Other firms employ looser arrangements. **Bogdanovic, Dolicki & Partners (in assoc with Lovells)** is allied to international law firm **Lovells**, but not in name. **Porobija & Porobija** is known to work with UK-based international firm **Linklaters** on a frequent basis, but this is far from an exclusive arrangement.

Even if the Croatian legal market is further liberalised to allow the presence of foreign lawyers and international law firms, it is unlikely that anything will develop beyond the current 'affiliation' arrangement. Croatia is a small jurisdiction and globally minded law firms have become more focused on core markets and large economies. Connections will remain important to international law firms, but offices in smaller jurisdictions (where the ability to make substantial profits is limited) is unlikely.

LEGISLATIVE DEVELOPMENTS

Legal reform is by its nature an ongoing process, but Croatia's coalition government has paid close attention to transforming a structure that was formerly founded on Communist principles. The issues of consumer protection, competition and state aid, and intellectual property rights are foremost elements of legal reform. The judiciary has undergone significant change and with the EU accession process in full swing, the jurisdiction is obliged to harmonise its legal structure in line with the EU.

BANKING, FINANCE AND CAPITAL MARKETS

Bogdanovic, Dolicki & Partners (in assoc with Lovells) has developed a strong internationally oriented brand thanks in part to its association with UK-based international firm **Lovells**. Banking, finance and capital markets instructions now represent an important pillar of the practice. The firm is known to have represented such global names as Deutsche Bank and Commerzbank, while also having a strong background in equity and debt securities. In 2003, partner Tin Dolicki worked alongside **Lovells** on the project financing of the Central Waste Water Treatment Plant in Zagreb.

Hanzekovic, Radakovic and Partners is one of Croatia's oldest and most established law firms. It continues to operate a niche but substantial business in debt recovery. It has impressive connections to Croatia's leading banks, with partner Irine Jelcic Husien having an excellent reputation.

Markovic & Pliso has a fine banking and finance practice that should be acknowledged for its record in project finance. In this regard it has represented the EBRD and a succession of other foreign financial institutions. Zoran Markovic has an excellent reputation, but the departure of Kristijan Galic to **Law Office Boric** in October 2004 was a loss.

Porobija & Porobija's esteemed record in banking and finance has brought it to the attention of foreign banks including strong regional player, Erste Bank. The EBRD has also proved to be a fruitful client over the years and thus the firm's record has developed strongly in project financing. Boris Porobija has an outstanding reputation.

Zuric i Partneri enjoys an established presence in Croatia, being one of the nation's oldest law firms. As also one of the largest firms in the jurisdiction, it has attracted a broad array of

BANKING, FINANCE AND CAPITAL MARKETS

BOGDANOVIC, DOLICKI & PARTNERS (IN ASSOC WITH LOVELLS) ✪
HANZEKOVIC, RADAKOVIC AND PARTNERS ✪
MARKOVIC & PLISO
POROBIJA & POROBIJA ✪
ZURIC I PARTNERI ✪

Babic, Law Office ✪
Boric, Law Office
Divjak, Topic & Bahtijarevic
Juric Law Offices ✪
Savoric & Partners ✪
Travas & Partners

Crnalic in co-operation with CMS Reich-Rohrwig Hainz ✪
DLA Weiss-Tessbach/Branch for International Legal Consulting/in cooperation with local attorneys ✪
Matic-IKRP ✪
Miroljub Macesic, Law Offices ✪
Nikolina Golubic in co-operation with Schönherr Rechtsanwälte GmbH
PricewaterhouseCoopers
Vukmir & Associates
Wolf Theiss Vienna in cooperation with Croatian lawyers ✪

Firms are listed A-Z in tiers which are ranked in order of priority
✪ Indicates firm displays contact details at the end of this chapter.

local and international finance sector clients. The firm's record in projects, privatisation and latterly PPP-style developments has evidently given it a sound understanding of financial structures and instruments. In this regard Bojan Fras has an eminent standing.

Boris Babic of **Law Office Babic** has an impressive record in banking and finance, having advised on several acquisitions of local banks by foreign investors over the years. The firm continues to provide standard loan advice, but has of late worked on a major restructuring of a loan portfolio. Its international standing was demonstrated by its advice to a major international bank providing the acquisition financing for the purchase of a local company. The firm has also worked alongside international firms such as **Pillsbury Winthrop Shaw Pittman LLP**, **Paul, Weiss, Rifkind, Wharton & Garrison LLP** and **Baker & McKenzie LLP** on financing arrangements.

The arrival of Kristijan Galic from **Markovic & Pliso** in October 2004, significantly enhanced **Law Office Boric**'s banking and finance credentials. Galic has a strong background in syndicated lending having represented a series of international banks. In 2005, he provided Croatian law advice relating to the re-admission of a UK company to the London Stock Exchange, which included the financing of its Croatian subsidiaries.

Divjak, Topic & Bahtijarevic has an impressive record in banking and finance. In 2005 it represented the acquirer of a mid-sized Croatian bank. It also advised an Austrian investment fund in connection with the first listing of foreign securities on the Croatian Stock Exchange. Barclays Bank and JP Morgan Chase have mandated the firm in recent years.

Juric Law Offices should be identified for its finance background. The firm frequently provides advice to foreign lenders and also several venture capital funds, while often working alongside international law firms. In 2005 the firm advised a Croatian ministry in relation to two major World Bank loan agreements. Sanja Juric is the sole partner.

Savoric & Partners has handled a series of mandates for the EBRD, including advising on the financing of Croatia's Getro d.d. to expand its supermarket chain and the financing of Croatia's largest cement company, Nasicecement. As ever, name partner Boris Savoric is pivotal to winning these instructions, but the arrival of Marin Vice Vujicic to the firm in 2004 significantly enhanced its banking and finance capability.

Travas & Partners has a prominent finance practice under Aleksej Miskovic, Robert Travas and Marko Frkovic. The firm frequently represents foreign banks and works alongside international law firms. In 2005 it advised on a substantial loan facility to one of Croatia's largest food and retail companies. The firm represented the lenders in the €27m financing of the development of a commercial complex in the Adriatic city of Rijeka. The firm has represented international banks such as Deutsche Bank and in 2005 advised Bank Austria for the first time. The firm regularly advises banks in respect of bankruptcy proceedings.

Crnalic in co-operation with CMS Reich-Rohrwig Hainz seconded a senior associate to the **CMS Reich-Rohrwig Hainz** Vienna office in 2005 with a view to developing the Croatian firm's banking capability. The firm now has six resident lawyers with Austrian partner Gregor Famira spending in excess of 50% of his time in the Zagreb office.

DLA Weiss-Tessbach/Branch for International Legal Consulting/in cooperation with local attorneys boasts a healthy list of international banking clients, many hailing from its Central and Eastern European headquarters in Vienna. The Zagreb office is best known for real estate and project finance, as well as municipal finance matters. Vienna-based Barbara Novosel oversees the practice.

Matic-IKRP has represented a variety of international and domestic banks over the years. It has fine global connections.

Law Offices Miroljub Macesic regularly advises foreign banks on the financing of new buildings in shipyards. The firm also advises the buyers of new buildings on a less frequent basis.

Nikolina Golubic in co-operation with Schönherr Rechtsanwälte GmbH is recommended for real estate finance. Six lawyers are resident in the Zagreb office with Vienna partners Michael Lagler and Martin Ebner overseeing operations. Ebner and his team advised on one of the largest finance transactions in Croatia during 2005.

PricewaterhouseCoopers is recognised for project finance work, including wastewater plants. Croatian citizen Don Markusic heads the department and holds Australian and UK legal qualifications, but is yet to be admitted in Croatia.

Vukmir & Associates is also experienced in finance matters, including straight lending and more structured instruments.

Wolf Theiss Vienna in cooperation with Croatian lawyers has handled several transactions on behalf of key client Bank Austria. The firm's Vienna headquarters has a strong finance background.

CORPORATE AND M&A

Bogdanovic, Dolicki & Partners (in assoc with Lovells) is an established brand in Croatia and a clear leader in corporate and commercial law. Founding partner Tin Dolicki is widely regarded as an absolute authority on corporate law and one of the most respected lawyers in Croatia. The firm is regarded by clients as 'very good from a legal point of view' and its record in high-value and cross-border transactions is pre-eminent. The firm is renowned for its international connections and has a solid relationship with UK-based international firm **Lovells**. Mladen Markoc is also highly regarded.

Markovic & Pliso is known for its representation of blue-chip domestic corporates such as state-owned Croatian television company, HRT. The firm is prominent in a range of industries, notably in real estate-related transactions and privatisations. Zoran Markovic is widely acknowledged as one of the leading corporate advisers in Croatia, while fellow name partner Miroslav Pliso is known for his broad legal ability.

Porobija & Porobija has a tremendous reputation in Croatia. It frequently advises VIPnet, the first private GSM provider in Croatia and affiliate of Telekom Austria. Boris Porobija remains the firm's key partner and is responsible for much of the business. The firm often works alongside international law firm **Linklaters**, a measure of its transactional credibility and has an esteemed record in major Croatian projects and privatisations.

Savoric & Partners has a burgeoning reputation and is widely regarded as the most dynamic and forward-thinking firm in Croatia. In recent years it has risen to prominence by acting for financial institutions in multi-million euro transactions. In 2004 it recruited two new partners and is now considered one of the most capable law firms in Croatia, despite not having the experience levels of some of its competitors.

Zuric i Partneri has an outstanding record and is known for being the longstanding leader in corporate and M&A work. Ratko Zuric and Bojan Fras remain celebrated names in corporate and commercial law. The firm retains an esteemed presence in Croatia and has an impressive client base that includes IBM, Cisco and T-Mobile. In recent years it has advised on a series of high-profile, cross-border transactions. Its senior partners remain some of the most sought-after advisers on high-value deals, while in the next generation, Lucija Reicher-Zuric is gaining a formidable reputation.

Law Office Babic has a strong corporate practice dominated by instructions from foreign clients. The firm has also developed close ties with a series of international law firms, bolstering its referral base and high-value transactional record. The firm, led by Boris Babic is also known for competition law advice, having advised on the Croatian element of a major international merger. The firm is also known for its work in the transport, hotel and tourism sectors. Senior figures Marija Gregoric and Luka Tadic-Colic have also proved themselves worthy of recommendation. 'What impressed me the most was their ability to come up with creative legal solutions for various problems,' one client said. 'They are not afraid to voice disagreement with the client, a quality which I find often lacking in law firms.'

DLA Weiss-Tessbach/Branch for International Legal Consulting/in cooperation with local attorneys has a firmly established presence in Croatia, having been located there

CORPORATE AND M&A

BOGDANÓVIC, DOLICKI & PARTNERS (IN ASSOC WITH LOVELLS) ✪
MARKOVIC & PLISO
POROBIJA & POROBIJA ✪
SAVORIC & PARTNERS ✪
ZURIC I PARTNERI ✪

BABIC, LAW OFFICE ✪
DLA WEISS-TESSBACH/BRANCH FOR INTERNATIONAL LEGAL CONSULTING/IN COOPERATION WITH LOCAL ATTORNEYS ✪
HANZEKOVIC, RADAKOVIC AND PARTNERS ✪

Divjak, Topic & Bahtijarevic
Juric Law Offices ✪
Matic-IKRP ✪
PricewaterhouseCoopers
Travas & Partners
Vukmir & Associates

Boric, Law Office
Cipcic-Bragadin, Law Firm
Cirkveni, Law Office ✪
Crnalic in co-operation with CMS Reich-Rohrwig Hainz ✪
Dragicevic, Law Office
KPMG Croatia d.o.o.
Miroljub Macesic, Law Offices ✪
Nikolina Golubic in co-operation with Schönherr Rechtsanwälte GmbH
Petrak Law Offices
Simunovic & Batur, Law Firm
Vukic, Jelusic, Sulina Stankovic, Jurcan & Jabuka
Wolf Theiss Vienna in cooperation with Croatian lawyers ✪

Firms are listed A-Z in tiers which are ranked in order of priority
✪ Indicates firm displays contact details at the end of this chapter.

since 1997. As part of one of the fastest-growing international law firms and one with an exceptionally strong brand in Central and Eastern Europe, the Croatian branch has built a prestigious record in cross-border transactions. Vienna-based Barbara Novosel oversees the Croatian office's operations. As a consequence, the Croatian practice frequently advises Austrian banks and industrial corporates on real estate developments and other projects.

Hanzekovic, Radakovic and Partners is one of the most recognised brands in Croatia having been established for well over a decade. These days it has a solid banking client base and has a profitable debt recovery business. Milan Radakovic remains a highly regarded individual, while Snjezana Posavec Mitrov is commended for corporate law advice. The firm is the Croatian member of the *Lex Mundi* international network of independent law firms.

Divjak, Topic & Bahtijarevic has a healthy list of foreign clients, demonstrating its eminence in Croatia and ability to deliver 'high-quality legal support' according to clients. In 2005 it advised the Austrian company OMV in corporate matters relating to the construction and development of a chain of petroleum stations. AstraZeneca, Lockheed Martin and McCann Ericksson have also been recent clients of the firm. Ten lawyers comprise the firm led by Saàa Divjak, Emir Bahtijaveric and Damir Topic. 'The firm's high quality is based on its capacity to respond to all our needs in diverse legal areas and at the same time they respond promptly and competently,' one client said.

Juric Law Offices represents a significant number of foreign investors, often working alongside international law firms such as **Clifford Chance** and **Allen & Overy LLP**. In recent years the firm has built an eminent reputation for work in the pharmaceuticals sector. In 2005 it assisted a Slovenian company in connection with the restructuring of its Croatian subsidiary. It also represented a US company seeking to purchase assets from a bankrupt Croatian entity. Sanja Juric leads the firm that includes three other lawyers.

Matic-IKRP has a strong foreign investment focus and is part of the global network headed by Greek firm **I.K. Rokas & Partners in association with Nika Eleftheria and Karypidou Illiana**.

PricewaterhouseCoopers represents numerous international investors in Croatia and recently advised Tele2 on the establishment of its operations in the country. The firm is not authorised to provide local law advice, but currently works alongside domestic firm **Law Office Modric** on Croatian matters. Don Markusic, an Australian of Croatian heritage, leads the practice. Motorola is another high-profile client.

Travas & Partners is a longstanding adviser of the largest private Croatian company Agrokor, which has given it both domestic and international prominence. It has worked with **Clifford Chance**, **Shearman & Sterling LLP** and **Allen & Overy LLP** on cross-border mandates. The firm provided Croatian counsel (working alongside international adviser **Allen & Overy LLP**) on the restructuring of Metropolis Advertising Group. Aleksej Miskovic is recommended.

Vukmir & Associates is led by the highly regarded Mladen Vukmir and the firm has risen to prominence on the back of his prestigious intellectual property business. Consequently, the firm boasts a fine range of technology-oriented clients, most notably from the telecoms, IT and software industries and this has provided it with some challenging corporate instructions. Clients also include several leading multinational brands.

Law Office Boric should be acknowledged for its work in the property sector. Mirjana Boric has represented foreign and domestic investors for many years, with significant activity in the tourism sector in recent times. The firm retains a strong client base of Austrian investors in particular and also advised one of the parties involved in the merger of a Croatian IT manufacturer and retailer. The firm has also provided advice to several local telecoms-related companies on regulatory matters.

Law Firm Cipcic-Bragadin has represented a series of private equity funds in recent years and Silvije Cipcic-Bragadin is an elected vice-president of the Croatian Private Equity and Venture Capital Association.

Law Office Cirkveni's esteemed presence in Croatia is demonstrated by its role as advisers to Croatian Telecom, which it advised on the arrangement of the dividend and advance dividend pay-out during 2005. Though a small firm of six lawyers, it has built a much-coveted client portfolio. Neven Cirkveni is the firm's key rainmaker.

Crnalic in co-operation with CMS Reich-Rohrwig Hainz grew from two lawyers to six during 2005. It is headed by Gregor Famira who spends more than 50% of his time in Zagreb, while also returning to **CMS Reich-Rohrwig Hainz**'s headquarters in Vienna on a frequent basis. The firm's active property business has developed rapidly with it now having represented a series of UK investors looking to acquire Croatian assets. UK property developers now drive some 40% of the business. The firm is also close to the regional auditors.

Law Office Dragicevic is another strong name in intellectual property law thanks to the high profile of Mladen Dragicevic. The firm is particularly noted for its trade mark protection work and has represented esteemed clients such as Bennetton and Pfizer over the years. Debt recovery is also a key area of the business.

Paul Suchar leads **KPMG Croatia d.o.o.**'s Croatian practice with a sizeable team of lawyers. Unsurprisingly it has significant experience of representing foreign corporates in relation to their Croatian interests. As the firm is prevented from offering Croatian law advice at this time it works closely with **Law Firm Simunovic & Batur**.

Law Offices Miroljub Macesic is best known for real estate developments beyond its particularly high profile in shipping. The firm recently advised on a significant development in Istria. The firm often works alongside other Croatian firms on major instructions and is particularly prolific in litigation.

Nikolina Golubic in co-operation with Schönherr Rechtsanwälte GmbH has built a practice in the insurance and pharmaceutical sectors. It frequently represents Austrian and German investors, but has advised clients from as far afield as Sweden in connection with their Croatian interests. The firm is also noted for its real estate practice.

Petrak Law Offices has three lawyers and offers general commercial expertise.

Law Firm Simunovic & Batur has a close connection to **KPMG Croatia d.o.o.**. As a consequence the firm has developed a healthy record acting for foreign investors, particularly in the manufacturing, tourism, insurance and financial sectors.

Vukic, Jelusic, Sulina Stankovic, Jurcan & Jabuka is the leading firm in Rijeka and has firmly established itself as a leading shipping practice. The firm has also managed to develop a name in corporate law and has become increasingly involved in property and infrastructure developments. Gordan Stankovic and Zoran Vukic are both highly regarded.

Wolf Theiss Vienna in cooperation with Croatian lawyers provides advice in relation to Croatian matters from its Belgrade office. It is part of the leading Austrian firm and Central and Eastern Europe-focused **Wolf Theiss**. It has consequently represented a series of Austrian entities, particularly banks, in relation to their Croatian interests. Property and IT matters have been especially prominent.

FOREIGN INVESTMENT, PROJECTS AND PRIVATISATION

The era of privatisation has virtually ended, though firms with extensive experience of such transactions are well placed with increasing amounts of foreign capital coming into Croatia's economy. Real estate developments and transactions have proved increasingly active and fruitful for Croatia's top law firms.

Bogdanovic, Dolicki & Partners (in assoc with Lovells) has a prestigious record in privatisations, infrastructure developments and real estate transactions. The firm benefits from its close association with **Lovells**, which gives it access to investors from Germany and the UK in particular. German real estate developers have provided a significant portion of the business in recent years.

Hanzekovic, Radakovic and Partners is another long-established firm in the fields of privatisation and infrastructure development. The firm represents both banks and sponsors in relation to Croatian projects.

Markovic & Pliso has a rich history of roles in property developments, especially hotel projects. The firm has a strong regional profile gaining the attention of foreign investors from Central and Eastern Europe as well as Western Europe. It is one of several Croatian firms to gain mandates from the EBRD. The firm is also prominent in infrastructure developments.

Porobija & Porobija has a notable record of sponsor and bank representations in respect of property and infrastructure developments. In recent years the firm has represented the banks (including the EBRD) on the construction of a major wastewater treatment plant in Zagreb. It advised on the first-ever multiplex cinema in Croatia and the second-phase financing of the Istrian toll motorway. Boris Porobija is the key individual and often works alongside international law firms such as **Linklaters**. Sanja Porobija is recommended for real estate developments.

FOREIGN INVESTMENT, PROJECTS AND PRIVATISATION

BOGDANÓVIC, DOLICKI & PARTNERS (IN ASSOC WITH LOVELLS) ✪
HANZEKOVIC, RADAKOVIC AND PARTNERS ✪
MARKOVIC & PLISO
POROBIJA & POROBIJA ✪
SAVORIC & PARTNERS ✪
ZURIC I PARTNERI ✪

BABIC, LAW OFFICE ✪
DLA WEISS-TESSBACH/BRANCH FOR INTERNATIONAL LEGAL CONSULTING/IN COOPERATION WITH LOCAL ATTORNEYS ✪
JURIC LAW OFFICES ✪

Boric, Law Office
Cipcic-Bragadin, Law Firm
Cirkveni, Law Office ✪
Crnalic in co-operation with CMS Reich-Rohrwig Hainz ✪
Divjak, Topic & Bahtijarevic
Dragicevic, Law Office
Matic-IKRP ✪
PricewaterhouseCoopers
Simunovic & Batur, Law Firm
Travas & Partners
Vukmir & Associates
Wolf Theiss Vienna in cooperation with Croatian lawyers ✪

Firms are listed A-Z in tiers which are ranked in order of priority
✪ Indicates firm displays contact details at the end of this chapter.

Savoric & Partners has developed an impressive record in foreign entity representation. Recently it advised a consortium of Croatian companies alongside Swedish telecoms operator Tele2 in the public tender for a Croatian GSM and UMTS mobile operator.

Zuric i Partneri is firmly established in the infrastructure development and projects segment thanks to its presence in the market during the early stages of the privatisation phase right through to modern-day foreign investment. The firm has represented German and Austrian investors in recent years including German construction company Walter Bau on Croatian motorway developments.

Law Office Babic has worked on some ten privatisation mandates over the years. The firm frequently represents the foreign investor in such issues and regularly works alongside an international law firm. Its credentials were augmented by its advisory role on a recent major infrastructure BOT project in Croatia valued in excess of €150m.

DLA Weiss-Tessbach/Branch for International Legal Consulting/in cooperation with local attorneys has an eminent reputation for Croatian projects making use of its impressive client portfolio of Austrian investors and financiers, as well as its broad international business. Real estate developments have provided a significant source of business in recent years. It also has the experience of working on one of Croatia's largest privatisations to date, having represented Deutsche Telekom in the privatisation of Hrvatski Telekom.

Juric Law Offices has received mandates from several foreign banks in connection with Croatian projects and developments. In 2003 it represented the bidder in relation to a major Croatian privatisation. The firm has worked with several international law firms on significant projects over the years.

Law Office Boric represents a significant number of foreign investors, particularly from Austria and Germany. Much of the work is property related thanks to the efforts of Mirjana Boric. It has advised on several hotel industry privatisations over the years.

Law Firm Cipcic-Bragadin's emergence as a small but fervent force in Croatia was demonstrated by its role as counsel to Constructa-grad (the Croatian subsidiary of a French construction company) on a series of projects in Croatia.

Law Office Cirkveni has handled a series of significant privatisations in recent years. It advised Kerum on its €50m acquisition by way of privatisation in the tourist industry.

Crnalic in co-operation with CMS Reich-Rohrwig Hainz frequently represents Austrian and German investors looking to acquire assets in Croatia. Of late however, it has secured a significantly greater number of instructions from UK property developers.

Divjak, Topic & Bahtijarevic has an established record in foreign investment and infrastructure development. In 2005 it represented Czech company Papirius in the acquisition of the largest Croatian office supply company. It also advised GTC International in the construction of the largest shopping and business centre in Croatia.

Law Office Dragicevic has a prestigious intellectual property business, which has given it access to numerous foreign technology companies looking to make investments in Croatia.

Matic-IKRP is a prominent name in the projects arena. The firm is particularly strong in the maritime and shipping sector, but has developed an impressive record in infrastructure developments.

PricewaterhouseCoopers is experienced in projects having represented numerous wastewater plants and municipalities. In recent years it has advised on the construction of several wastewater plants, acting for concessionaires and municipalities.

Law Firm Simunovic & Batur provides representation to a range of foreign real estate investors. Property acquisitions and investments in Zagorje and Dalmatia have been particularly active for the firm. It frequently works alongside **KPMG Croatia d.o.o.**.

Travas & Partners has significant experience of property development projects across Croatia, though many of its roles have been for the financiers.

Vukmir & Associates' excellent IP practice has brought it onto the radar screen of numerous international investors. Partner Sanja Tkalec Kovac should be identified in this respect.

Wolf Theiss Vienna in cooperation with Croatian lawyers boasts a prominent list of Austrian and international investors. From its Belgrade office it has worked on a series of projects including a marina development on the Croatian coast.

SHIPPING

MIROLJUB MACESIC, LAW OFFICES ⭘
VUKIC, JELUSIC, SULINA STANKOVIC, JURCAN & JABUKA

Juric Law Offices ⭘

Firms are listed A-Z in tiers which are ranked in order of priority
⭘ *Indicates firm displays contact details at the end of this chapter.*

SHIPPING

Two firms dominate the shipping sector and are based in the key European port of Rijeka. In 2003, the World Bank approved a US$156.5m loan to the Croatia Rijeka Gateway project, which has further augmented the city's position in the shipping sector. Rijeka-based **Law Offices Miroljub Macesic** is widely regarded as the most adept and experienced firm when it comes to shipping matters. The firm frequently defends parties against cargo claims, and is also involved in ship finance and construction. The firm also advises foreign banks on the financing of new buildings in shipyards. Miroljub Macesic leads a firm of eight lawyers, two of which are based in Zagreb.

The sizeable **Vukic, Jelusic, Sulina Stankovic, Jurcan & Jabuka** operates a blossoming legal practice, a main pillar of the business being shipping. The firm is known for admiralty, ship finance and ship-building legal advice, with Gordon Stankovic very much to the fore.

Juric Law Offices is recognised for its finance background in the shipping sector. During 2005, the firm continued its role as adviser to the secured lenders to a significant shipyard in bankruptcy.

LAW OFFICES MIROLJUB MAĆEŠIĆ

POD KASTELOM NO 4
PO BOX 366
51000 RIJEKA

Telephone: +385 51 215 010
Fax: +385 51 215 030
E-mail: macesic@macesic.hr

Languages
English, French, Italian

Other offices
Zagreb

Number of lawyers 9
at this office 6

CATEGORIES OF WORK

Banking and finance

Commercial property, real estate

Corporate and commercial

Dispute resolution – litigation and arbitration

Foreign direct investment

Infrastructure and project finance

Insolvency/corporate restructuring

Insurance

Intellectual property

Mergers and acquisitions

Private client

Privatisation

Shipping and transport

LAW OFFICE BABIĆ

NOVA CESTA 60
10000 ZAGREB

Telephone: + 385 1 382 1124
Fax: + 385 1 382 0451
E-mail: boris.babic@babiclawoffice-zg.hr

Languages
Croatian, English

Number of lawyers 8

CATEGORIES OF WORK

M&A
Boris Babić, Luka Tadić-Čolić

Competition
Boris Babić, Marija Gregorić

Labour and employment
Boris Babić, Marija Gregorić

Real estate and property
Marija Gregorić, Katarina Škvorc

Corporate and commercial
Marija Gregorić, Katarina Škvorc

Dispute resolution
Luka Tadić-Čolić, Katarina Škvorc

Banking and finance
Boris Babić

Life sciences
Boris Babić, Marija Gregorić

BOGDANOVIĆ & DOLIČKI
IN ASSOCIATION WITH LOVELLS

UL ALEXANDERA VON HUMBOLDTA 4B/III
10000 ZAGREB

Telephone: +385 1 615 9595
Fax: +385 1 615 7733
E-mail: information@lovells.com
Website: www.lovells.com

Languages
English, German

Other offices
Alicante, Amsterdam, Beijing, Berlin, Brussels, Budapest*, Chicago, Düsseldorf, Frankfurt, Hamburg, Ho Chi Minh City, Hong Kong, London, Madrid, Milan, Moscow, Munich, New York, Paris, Prague, Rome, Shanghai, Singapore, Tokyo, Warsaw

Number of lawyers 1,600
at this office 19

Contact
Tin Dolicki

CATEGORIES OF WORK

Mergers and acquisitions	Contract
Banking, securities and finance	Construction, building
Commercial law (general)	EU law
Competition, antitrust	Trade marks, intellectual property
Companies, corporations	Arbitration and litigation

LAW OFFICE CIRKVENI

RADIĆEVA 27
10000 ZAGREB

Telephone: + 385 1 485 1252
Fax: + 385 1 485 1245
E-mail: mail@cirkveni.hr
Website: www.cirkveni.hr

Languages
English, French, German, Italian

Number of lawyers 6

CATEGORIES OF WORK

Foreign investments	Banking and finance
Privatisations	Taxation
Mergers and acquisitions	Property and real estate
Corporate and securities	Administrative
Antitrust	Bankruptcy
Commercial	Arbitration and litigation
Product liability	

CRNALIC

IN CO-OPERATION WITH CMS REICH-ROHRWIG HAINZ

JURIŠIĆEVA 24
10000 ZAGREB

Telephone: +385 1 482 5600
Fax: +385 1 482 5601
E-mail: zagreb@cms-rrh.com

Languages
Croatian, English, German

Other offices
Belgrade, Bratislava, Brussels, Prague, Sofia, Vienna

Number of lawyers 71
at this office 8

Contacts
Gregor Famira, Jasmina Crnalić

Member
CMS Alliance of major European law firms; World Law Group

CATEGORIES OF WORK

Banking and finance

Capital markets

Commercial property, real estate and construction

Competition

Corporate and commercial

Dispute resolution

Intellectual property

Labour and employment

Mergers and acquisitions

Privatisation

Regulatory/public procurement

HANŽEKOVIĆ, RADAKOVIĆ & PARTNERS

RADNIČKA CESTA 22
10000 ZAGREB

Telephone: +385 1 618 4611
Fax: +385 1 618 4816
E-mail: hanrad@zg.t-com.hr

Languages
Croatian, English, French, German, Serbian, Macedonian, Slovenian, some Italian

Other offices
Dubrovnik*, Osijek*, Požega*, Rijeka*, Sisak*, Split*, Varaždin*, Zadar*

Number of lawyers 13

Contact
Marijan Hanžeković

Member
Lex Mundi

CATEGORIES OF WORK

Banking and finance
Damir Metelko, Irina Jelčić

Litigation
Milan Radaković, Domagoj Truhar

Joint ventures, construction law, PPP projects, concessions
Jasminka Čorda Truhar

Corporate law and labour law
Snježana Posavec Mitrov, Ana Crnković

Real estate, commercial law
Kruno Knežević, Zvonimir Buterin

Telecommunications, energy
Domagoj Truhar, Zvonimir Buterin

Mergers and acquisitions
Irina Jelčić

Securities, capital markets
Damir Metelko, Kruno Knežević

Arbitration
Marijan Hanžeković, Jasminka Čorda Truhar

Intellectual property law, environmental law
Andrea Domac, Valentina Kučić

Execution law
Zvonimir Buterin, Iva Markotić

DLA WEISS-TESSBACH/BRANCH FOR INTERNATIONAL LEGAL CONSULTING/IN COOPERATION WITH LOCAL ATTORNEYS

FRANE PETRICA 4
10000 ZAGREB

Telephone: +385 1 485 4200
Fax: +385 1 485 4241
E-mail: zagreb@dlapiper.com
Website: www.dlapiper.com

Languages
Bosnian, Croatian, English, German, Polish, Italian, Serbian

Other offices
Austria, Belgium, Bosnia-Herzegovina, China, Czech Republic, Denmark*, Egypt*, France, Georgia, Germany, Hong Kong, Hungary, Italy, Japan, Netherlands, Norway,* Poland*, Russia, Singapore*, Slovakia, South Africa*, Spain, Sweden*, Thailand, UK, Ukraine, United Arab Emirates, US

Number of lawyers 3,100
At this office 4

Contact
Barbara Novosel (Vienna)

Member
DLA Piper Group

CATEGORIES OF WORK

General commercial	**Corporate**
Banking and finance	**Mergers and acquisitions**
Insolvency	**Litigation**
Real estate	

THE FIRM

DLA Weiss-Tessbach was established in 1878 in Austria and is one of the longest-established law firms in the country. Since 1989, the firm has undergone a dynamic expansion across Central and Eastern Europe, growing from 15 to 100 lawyers and from one to seven offices, including Zagreb, where it operates in co-operation with local attorneys. DLA Weiss-Tessbach will continue to expand in the Central and Eastern European region as countries adjust to EU membership.

DLA Weiss-Tessbach is part of DLA Piper Rudnick Gray Cary, one of the leading global legal services organisations, with approximately 3,100 lawyers in 58 offices in 22 countries across Europe, Africa, the MIddle East, Asia and the US.

The organisation is committed to building long-term relationships with its clients and supports their strategic and operational needs, both locally and internationally.

AREAS OF PRACTICE

The firm has strengthened its core areas of expertise (commercial and corporate, M&A, banking and finance, general commercial law, real estate), and advises its clients as a full-service firm in all relevant areas of business law, including administrative law, employment law, IT and telecoms, technology, intellectual property, venture capital and capital markets.

DLA Weiss-Tessbach has well-established relations with clients of various backgrounds. The firm advises medium-sized enterprises as well as leading (often publicly listed) international and domestic industrial groups, service providers, banks and other financial institutions and individuals.

DLA Weiss-Tessbach has established a particular reputation for its ability to handle cases in international cross-border contexts. The firm is renowned for its expertise in the structuring and implementation of projects and transactions in Croatia, as well as in other countries in Central and Eastern Europe. It carefully monitors the ongoing developments in the Central and Eastern European region with the aim of combining the needs of the constantly changing international legal market and industry, whilst also upholding the high standard of service that the firm has always been able to offer to its clients.

JURIC LAW OFFICES

BUDMANIJEVA 5
10000 ZAGREB

Telephone: +385 1 618 3789
Fax: +385 1 618 3803
E-mail: info@juriclaw.hr

Languages
Croatian, English, French, German, Italian, Spanish

Number of lawyers 4

Contact
Sanja Jurić

International groupings
IBA; ABA

CATEGORIES OF WORK

Banking, finance and capital markets
S Jurić

Corporate and commercial
S Jurić

Dispute resolution and arbitration
S Jurić

Foreign direct investment
S Jurić

Foreign investment, projects and privatisations
S Jurić

Infrastructure and project finance
S Jurić

Insolvency and corporate restructuring
S Jurić

Mergers and acquisitions
S Jurić

Telecommunications
S Jurić

Public procurement
S Jurić

Public-private partnership
S Jurić

MATIĆ-IKRP

BEDNJANSKA 14
10000 ZAGREB

Telephone: +385 1 617 0791
Fax: +385 1 617 0792
Email: tin.matic@zg.htnet.hr
Website: www.rokas.com

Languages
English, German, Italian, Spanish

Other offices
Athens, Belgrade, Bucharest, Piraeus, Skopje, Sofia, Ljubljana, Sarajevo

Number of lawyers 53
at this office 3

Member
IBA; Croatian Bar Association; Croatian American Bar Association; Croatian Arbitration Association; American Chamber of Commerce in Croatia

CATEGORIES OF WORK

Arbitration
Tin Matić

Banking and finance
Tin Matić

Bankruptcy
Tin Matić

Civil litigation
Iskra Bubas

Commercial
Iskra Bubas

Company
Iskra Bubas

Franchising
Tin Matić

E-commerce
Tin Matić

Investment
Tin Matić

Transport
Iskra Bubas

Real estate
Igor Mucalo

Export/import
Tin Matić

Mediation
Tin Matić

Competition
Tin Matić

Family
Igor Mucalo

LAW OFFICES MIROLJUB MAĆEŠIĆ

MIHANOVIĆEVA 16
10000 ZAGREB

Telephone: +385 1 457 7248
Fax: +385 1 457 6795
E-mail: macesic@macesic.hr

Languages
English, French, Italian

Other offices
Rijeka

Number of lawyers 9
at this office 3

CATEGORIES OF WORK

- Banking and finance
- Commercial property, real estate
- Corporate and commercial
- Dispute resolution – litigation and arbitration
- Foreign direct investment
- Infrastructure and project finance
- Insolvency/corporate restructuring
- Insurance
- Intellectual property
- Mergers and acquisitions
- Private client
- Privatisation
- Shipping and transport

POROBIJA & POROBIJA

GALLERY IMPORTANNE
IBLEROV TRG 10/VII
PO BOX 92
10000 ZAGREB

Telephone: +385 1 469 3999
Fax: +385 1 469 3900
E-mail: porobija@porobija.hr
Website: www.porobija.hr

Languages
English, French, German, Hungarian

Number of lawyers 14

CATEGORIES OF WORK

- Administrative and regulatory law
- Banking and finance
- Bankruptcy
- Capital markets
- Commercial law
- Company law
- Competition law
- Concessions
- Construction law
- Energy and infrastructure
- Litigation and arbitration
- Mergers and acquisitons
- Privatisation
- Project financing
- Public utilities
- Real estate
- Tax law
- Telecommunications

ŠAVORIĆ & PARTNERS

ANDRIJE HEBRANGA 27
10000 ZAGREB

Telephone: +385 1 485 5900
Fax: +385 1 485 6232
E-mail: boris.savoric@savoric.com

Languages
English, German

Number of lawyers 10

Member
American Chamber of Commerce, Croatia

CATEGORIES OF WORK

Banking and finance
Boris Šavorić, Marin Vice Vujicic

Mergers and acquisitions
Boris Šavorić, Ivan Simac

Corporate and commercial, insurance
Boris Šavorić, Marin Vice Vujicic

Telecommunications
Boris Šavorić, Ivan Simac

Litigation and arbitration
Boris Šavorić, Helena Sjaus

Competition
Boris Šavorić, Marin Vice Vujicic

Securities, project finance
Boris Šavorić, Marin Vice Vujicic

Corporate finance
Boris Šavorić, Marin Vice Vujicic

Real estate
Helena Sjaus, Gordon Kunstek

Employment
Helena Sjaus

Cross-border transactions
Boris Šavorić, Marin Vice Vujicic

Information technology
Ivan Simac

Insolvency, corporate restructuring
Marin Vice Vujicic

Intellectual property
Ivan Simac

Media, entertainment, privatisation
Boris Šavorić

Private client
Helena Sjaus

THE FIRM

Šavorić & Partners is recognised as having young and dynamic, yet experienced lawyers, offering a full range of quality legal services. The firm has been constantly growing from the day it was established. The office operates as a team of ten lawyers offering a complete solution to problems arising while doing business in Croatia. Šavorić & Partners has established good relations and often operates with a number of reputable international law firms such as Baker & McKenzie; Squire, Sanders & Dempsey; Simmons & Simmons; Weil, Gotshal & Manges; LeBoeuf, Lamb, Greene & MacRae; Ropes & Gray; Clyde & Co; and Freshfields.

All partners have a long history of professional experience and comprehensive knowledge in their areas of practice. The firm advises international clients on major corporate and financial transactions, and assists foreign investors in joint ventures and mergers and acquisitions in Croatia.

AREAS OF PRACTICE

The firm's client base consists of some of the largest Croatian companies and clients from the US and Europe: European Bank for Reconstruction and Development, Deutsche Bank, RTL Group, Henkel, AIG, UBS, Nestlé, McDonald's, L'Oreal France, Hachette Distribution Services, Schering-Plough, SAS Rezidor hotels, Generali, Enron Corp,Croatia Osiguranje, Iskon Internet, IntesaBCI, PBZ, Quaestus, Baupost, Lorenz & Bahlsen, GE Group, Croatian Bank for Reconstruction and Development, and more.

Significant projects and transactions for the firm include advising the European Bank for Reconstruction and Development in the city of Karlovac project and Getro project. The firm advised the selling shareholder over the sale of equity interest in leading Croatian company, Oktal-Pharma, to German strategic partner Anzag. The firm acted for a consortium of leading Croatian companies: Nexe; PBZ; Jamnica; Lura; Dalekovod; IGH; and Konstruktor, with Swedish operator Tele2, in winning international tender for the third Croatian GSM and UMTS mobile operator. The firm acted as legal adviser to Privredna Banka Zagreb (as sponsor) and Croatia Insurance d.d. (as issuer) in listing of all ordinary and preference shares of Croatia Insurance d.d. into the Quotation I of Zagreb Stock Exchange. The firm acted for IntesaBCI in bidding for Nova Bank and in the preparation of a securitisation project for certain public debts.

The firm advises German/Luxembourg television and media group RTL and a consortium of leading Croatian companies Agrokor, Podravka, Atlantic group and HVB (Splitska) bank in winning the tender for the first privatised Croatian television channel and the starting-up of a TV station in Croatia. The firm also advised the European Bank for Reconstruction and Development in financing (with Zagrebacka Bank), one of the largest Croatian cement industries, Nasicecement in a syndicated loan. The firm advised European Bank for Reconstruction and Development in a financing of the City of Zagreb solid waste programme. The firm acted as legal adviser to the sellers (capital venture funds) of Overseas, the largest parcel delivery company in Croatia, in the sale of shares to the strategic purchaser Austrian Post. Partner Boris Savoric was appointed by Enron Corp and Weil, Gotshal & Manges as legal advisers for the restructuring and liquidation of Enron business operations in Croatia. The firm recently acted in the acquisition of two hotels on the Adriatic coast.

The firm represents AIG (American Insurance Group which has been insuring all UN vehicles and operations in Croatia). The firm is also very active in a number of MBO and LBO projects as well as in real estate development projects.

STUDIO LEGALE SUTTI

PRILAZ GJURE DEZELICA 12
10000 ZAGREB

Telephone: +385 1 481 8972
Fax: +385 1 481 8979
E-mail: maildesk@sutti.com
Website: www.sutti.com

Languages
Bulgarian, Croatian, English, French, German, Italian, Japanese, Portuguese, Romanian, Russian, Serbian, Spanish

Other offices
Belgrade, Bucharest, Genoa, London, Milan, Rome, Sofia, Tokyo

Contact
Brian Dinter

CATEGORIES OF WORK

- Company, commercial law
- Banking and finance
- Mergers and acquisitions
- Distribution, agency and franchising
- Debt collection and insolvency
- Commercial property law
- Intellectual property
- Patent and trade mark agency service
- White-collar crime
- EC, competition and antitrust law
- IT and TLC law
- Litigation and arbitration
- Employment, labour law
- Administrative law
- Environmental law

ŽURIĆ I PARTNERI

GUNDULIĆEVA 63
10000 ZAGREB

Telephone: +385 1 488 1333
Fax: +385 1 485 6704
E-mail: info@zuric-i-partneri.hr

Languages
English, French, German, Italian, Slovenian

Number of lawyers 19

Contacts
Bojan Fras, Tomislav Tus, Branimir Škurla, Duško Žurić

CATEGORIES OF WORK

- Banking
- Commercial
- Competition
- Concessions
- Construction
- Corporate
- Energy
- Arbitration
- Finance and securities
- Intellectual property
- Labour
- Litigation
- Privatisation
- Property
- Telecoms and information technology

WOLF THEISS VIENNA IN CO-OPERATION WITH CROATIAN LAWYERS

PRAŠKA 10
10000 ZAGREB

Telephone: +385 1 492 5400
Fax: +385 1 492 5450
E-mail: zagreb@wolftheiss.com
Website: www.wolftheiss.com

Languages
Croatian, English, German, Italian

Other offices
Belgrade, Bratislava, Bucharest, Ljubljana, Prague, Sarajevo, Tirana, Vienna

Number of lawyers 161
at this office 5

Contact
Ralf Peschek (contact for Croatian matters)
Please refer to Vienna entry for contact details

CATEGORIES OF WORK

Arbitration, litigation, mediation	**IT and IP**
Banking, capital markets, securities, projects finance, investment funds	**Real estate, construction and leasing**
Corporate and M&A	**Retail law**
Employment and labour	

THE FIRM

Wolf Theiss was founded in 1957 in Vienna, and today is one of the leading law firms in the CEE/SEE region. Over the past few years the firm has experienced extraordinarily dynamic growth, both domestically and internationally.

Wolf Theiss has established a network of nine offices* in Albania, Austria, Bosnia and Herzegovina, Croatia, the Czech Republic, Romania, Serbia and Montenegro, Slovakia and Slovenia. In 2005 alone, Wolf Theiss opened two new offices, in Bucharest and Sarajevo. The firm also regularly assists its clients with projects in Bulgaria, Hungary, Macedonia, Moldova, Poland, Turkey and Ukraine, in co-operation with local attorneys.

The firm's dynamic growth is also refelcted in its increase in personnal. At present, Wolf Theiss employs over 350 individuals at nine locations – compare this to 30 employees in one office, Vienna, ten years ago and the growth is apparent.

*The firm's operations in the various locations are set up in compliance with local law and the Bar rules requirements which include the form of co-operation with independent local attorneys.

CYPRUS

Population	800,000
Number of lawyers	1,600
Professional title	Dikigoros
Currency	Cyprus Pound (CY£)

Index

The island of Cyprus is located in the east Mediterranean Sea, south of Turkey, east of Lebanon and north of Egypt. Britain administered Cyprus from 1878 although Turkey retained formal sovereignty until 1923. The Republic of Cyprus gained independence in 1960, at which point tensions between the Greek and Turkish communities on the island increased. In 1974 a coup by extremists, backed by the then Greek military junta, was followed by the invasion of the northern part of the island by Turkish troops. Since 1974 the island has been partitioned. The 'Turkish Republic of Northern Cyprus' remains unrecognised internationally except by Turkey. Diplomatic efforts to reunite the island continue, although these received a setback in April 2004 when a referendum to approve the Annan settlement was rejected by Greek Cypriots. There are signs that, at a practical level, the two communities are choosing to work together but that there is no political will to resolve the partition. In December 2005 the North/South division gained a high-profile, political and populist dimension when Cherie Blair QC, wife of British Prime Minister, Tony Blair, agreed to act, in what may well be a precedent-setting case, for a British couple ordered to demolish their North Cyprus home and pay compensaton to the original Greek Cypriot landowner

In 2004, Cyprus entered the EU as a divided nation and the *acquis*, the EU body of law, remains suspended in the north. This article covers the southern part of the island, the truncated, democratic, Republic of Cyprus.

Cyprus has a population of about 800,000 which divides roughly 3:1 between Greek and Turkish communities. Most of the Greek Cypriot population lives in the larger urban centres and in particular the two largest, the capital, Nicosia (Lefkosia in Greek, Lefkosa in Turkish) and the largest port and industrial city, Limassol. Greek and Turkish are the official languages of Cyprus although English is widely spoken and used in business.

BILLING

Although contingency fees are not permitted in Cyprus, fixed-fee arrangements and retainers are negotiated. Cypriots enjoy a long tradition of vigorous bargaining; overseas clients should not be intimidated. Hourly rates vary quite widely. Senior partners' charges range from €325 to €525 per hour, associates and junior partners, €170 to €325.

MARKETING

The increasing pressure on Cypriot lawyers to look for off-island business has seen a sharp increase in the number of effective and useful websites, many offering access to informative articles and briefing booklets covering aspects of Cypriot law. We also note an increase in the number of overseas branches and associations, mainly in Eastern Europe and the CIS.

IN-HOUSE LAWYERS

The amount of legal work in Cyprus does not justify in-house counsel except in the larger banks and insurers. Law firms are prepared to strike preferred terms with clients at reduced rates.

ECONOMY

Cyprus' economy is biased towards the services sector (75%) with tourism (30- 40%) and financial services (20%) dominating. Industry and construction contribute about 20% of GDP and agriculture 5%. The Cypriot government is attempting to promote industrial production by attracting new hi-tech manufacturing and encourage a restructuring of the traditional food, beverages and plastics industries. GDP has grown steadily over the last five years and the Greek Cypriot part of Cyprus ranks as one of the more prosperous Mediterranean areas. Efforts to bring the economy into line for Eurozone membership in 2007, combined with a slack fiscal policy, have produced inflationary pressures and an increasing PSBR. At the end of 2005 there were signs that the fiscal deficit was falling slightly, partly as a result of a successful tax amnesty, but further restraint of public-sector expenditure seems essential if the deficit is to reduce further.

Cyprus' geographical position, backed by a sound infrastructure of telecoms, excellent transport links, well-educated workforce and stable legal system, has created a perfect International Business Centre for servicing Eastern Europe, the Middle East and North Africa. Cyprus also has reciprocal investment-protection agreements with several countries in the region. Recent regulatory changes in response to EU membership demands and international standardisation offer greater protection to investors and bank customers. However, a standardisation of the tax treatment of local companies and IBCs, which now suffer a uniform

The largest firms

1	Andreas Neocleous & Co	48
2	Chrysses Demetriades & Co Law Office	38
3	L Papaphilippou & Co	20
4	Patrikios Pavlou & Co	19
	Tassos Papadopoulos & Co	19
6	Christodoulos G. Vassiliades & Co	18
7	George L Savvides & Co	17
	K Chrysostomides (Dr) & Co	17
9	Papacharalambous & Angelides	15
	Scordis, Papapetrou & Co	15
11	Georgiades & Pelides	12
12	Antis Triantafyllides & Sons	11
	Michael Kyprianou & Co	11
14	George Y Yiangou & Co	10
15	Lellos P Demetriades Law Office	9
	Polakis Sarris & Co Lawyers	9
17	Christos M Triantafyllides Law Firm	8
	Eliades, Paschalides, Hadjianastasiou & Co	8
	Kinanis - Pyrgou & Co	8
	Kyriacos Th Michaelides & Co Law Office	8
21	Cacoyannis & Demetriou	6
	Chryssafinis & Polyviou	6
23	Andrew Demetriou & Co, Law Office of	5
	Michaelides & Michaelides	5
25	Antonis Andreou & Co	4
	Karides, Karides & Georghiades	4
	Yiannos G Georgiades and Co. Law Firm	4

These figures represent the total number of lawyers in this country only, and have been supplied by the firms themselves. The figures should be accurate as at 1 January 2006.

10% corporation tax rate, may limit future development of the sector.

Cyprus remains an important shipping centre and currently claims sixth position globally for registered tonnage. All major international maritime conventions have been adopted since EU membership.

LEGAL SYSTEM

Cyprus has a common law system based on English Law with some civil law adaptations. Most statutes are officially translated into English.

LEGAL MARKET

Cyprus law firms originally addressed the limited local market but the development of the island as an OFC/IBC has, over the past ten years, seen the rather inward-looking profession revitalised by second-generation partners. Most of the firms mentioned have adopted a policy of expansion by recruitment, selecting well-educated young lawyers, many of whom are not only educated in overseas universities but have also qualified as lawyers both in Cyprus and in other jurisdictions. It seems likely that, as this intake gains experience, the pace of modernisation will be increased. In the meantime, overseas clients can be assured that the quality of Cypriot lawyers is generally high, and up to international expectations, although some firms do present in a slightly old-fashioned way.

Bench-mark firm for the new order is Limassol-headquartered **Andreas Neocleous & Co** which also offers offices in Nicosia and Paphos. The firm consistently attracts client accolades and now fields 56 lawyers in Cyprus and 22 overseas. **Andreas Neocleous & Co** has deservedly established a reputation for consistent high quality and performance. Also excellent firms, each with a different personality and niche skills are, **Chryssafinis & Polyviou** and **Chrysses Demetriades & Co Law Office**. Ambitious **Patrikios Pavlou & Co** moved into purpose-built offices in 2005 and now offers full, international-standard, facilities.

FOREIGN OFFICES

Andreas Neocleous & Co has added a Brussels branch to a regional network which includes expanding offices in Moscow, Budapest, Kiev and Prague. **L Papaphilippou & Co** offers offices in Warsaw and Athens in addition to three island branches. **Kyriacos Th Michaelides & Co Law Office** also has an Athens branch. **Patrikios Pavlou & Co** is currently in discussions with law firms in Russia and Eastern Europe which are expected to crystallise into an international association early in 2006.

International players do take a proportion of the high-value work. **Pinsent Masons**' PFI group advised the Cyprus government on the first PPP project to close on the island – the Cyprus Airports PPP: Hermes Consortium, an SPV with international and Cypriot backers acquired a 25-year concession to operate Larnaca and Paphos airports. Mark Coker is leading the **Freshfields Bruckhaus Deringer** team which is advising the mandated lead arrangers on the financing of the transaction.

BANKING AND FINANCE

Law firms reported a buoyant year for banking and finance instructions in 2005, borne along on the wave of investment into Eastern Europe and the CIS. There was also a good deal of high-value claims work and some interesting litigation on banking confidentiality.

Andreas Neocleous & Co's top-tier team continues to act for many of the major global banks, including Barclays, Goldman Sachs and UBS, while maintaining a strong hold on the local market. The eighteen-strong team, headed by name partner Andreas Neocleous, has built on traditional strengths in lending and private equity to develop expertise in structured finance, securitisation and product innovation.

Chryssafinis & Polyviou acts for Cyprus Development Bank, Bank of Cyprus and other major regional players; Polis Polyviou is recognised as a top-class banking lawyer.

Chrysses Demetriades & Co Law Office has acted for several global banks, including CSFB, but is best known for expertise and competence in maritime finance. Eliana Constantinidou heads the shipping finance department; Marion Coukidou-Madella is also recommended.

Lex Mundi member **Dr K Chrysostomides & Co** represents major banks such as Barclays and SocGen. The firm offers the full range of banking and finance support including ship mortgage expertise.

BANKING AND FINANCE

ANDREAS NEOCLEOUS & CO ✪
CHRYSSAFINIS & POLYVIOU
CHRYSSES DEMETRIADES & CO LAW OFFICE

K CHRYSOSTOMIDES (DR) & CO
L PAPAPHILIPPOU & CO
MICHAEL KYPRIANOU & CO ✪
TASSOS PAPADOPOULOS & CO

Antis Triantafyllides & Sons
Georgiades & Pelides
Montanios & Montanios
Patrikios Pavlou & Co ✪

Papacharalambous & Angelides ✪
Yiannos G Georgiades and Co. Law Firm

Firms are listed A-Z in tiers which are ranked in order of priority
✪ Indicates firm displays contact details at the end of this chapter.

L Papaphilippou & Co acts as general counsel for several banks and handles the full range of commercial finance law. The firm offers particular expertise in all aspects of shipping finance.

The Limassol office of **Michael Kyprianou & Co**, which provides a first-class service to banking clients including ING, ABN and ANZ Banking Group, boasts niche expertise in aircraft leasing. Pavlos Aristodemou heads the three-lawyer team which was instructed by **Herbert Smith LLP** and ABN Amro to deal with the Cyprus aspects of a US$1bn syndicated loan to Russian oil giant TNK.

Tassos Papadopoulos & Co advises the progressive and expanding Laiki Group (Cyprus Popular Bank Group). Marios Eliades is recommended.

Antis Triantafyllides & Sons celebrated fifty years in practice in 2005 and continues to provide competent support in banking and finance law.

Georgiades & Pelides handles bank and institutional financing within an internationally biased, business-orientated practice.

Montanios & Montanios is recommended for shipping finance.

Patrikios Pavlou & Co's banking and finance team attracts high-value instructions from global players and the firm's strength in litigation ensures some interesting work. During 2005 **Patrikios Pavlou & Co** represented Ukranian Privatbank in the successful defence of a Court application for disclosure of client details where the funds at issue amounted to US$800m.

Papacharalambous & Angelides, a competent, eight-lawyer firm, is active in the banking and finance market.

Yiannos G Georgiades and Co. Law Firm represents the Cyprus Popular Bank in contentious matters.

CORPORATE AND M&A

Between January and November 2005, 12,500 new companies were registered in Cyprus compared to 11,500 for the whole of 2004. It follows that corporate and commercial lawyers report a busy period. International work is particularly brisk and EU-related advice is also in demand. Lawyers have emphasised that much of the new work is high quality, such as 'open' investment vehicles undertaking projects in Eastern Europe, and that the anonymous ownership of the 'tax haven days' is firmly in retreat.

Andreas Neocleous & Co's corporate group is commended for 'accuracy and speed' and continues to attract a diverse range of complex, high-value work, from M&A, to cross-border reorganisations for clients including Commerzbank AG, Dell and Vodafone. Widely commended Elias Neocleous, called to both the English and Cypriot bars, is probably the island's most prolific legal author. **Andreas Neocleous & Co**'s corporate group also boasts experienced and highly recommended Kyriakos Georgiades.

Former minister Christos Mavrellis heads the heavyweight corporate group at **Chrysses Demetriades & Co Law Office**. The firm, *inter alia*, acts for F&C Emerging Markets' Russian Investment Company SICAV.

Tassos Papadopoulos & Co holds its place in the top tier with an impressive range of blue-chip clients including Cyprus Trading Corporation. During the past year the firm has handled a wide range of corporate instructions including joint ventures and syndication agreements. Marios Eliades is active in international corporate matters.

Antis Triantafyllides & Sons continues to attract quality instructions. The Nicosia-based firm has a branch office in Paris. Rather more traditional than some firms, **Antis Triantafyllides & Sons** offers a very solid core of experienced partners noted for sound advice in cross-border investment. Clients include Hoffman-la Roche and Cyprus Grain Commission.

Chryssafinis & Polyviou is very well respected and punches above its weight in corporate, as in banking. Polis Polyviou is commended as a first-class, practical lawyer. The firm acts for Cyprus Airways Group.

Nicosia-based **Dr K Chrysostomides & Co**'s corporate team recruited two lawyers in the autumn of 2005. The well-respected firm offers a full-service corporate team although high-profile Dr Kypros Chrysostomides remains absent from the practice as a member of the Cyprus government. **Dr K Chrysostomides & Co** has advised on the setting up of captive insurance companies in Cyprus.

Patrikios Pavlou & Co's Stavros Pavlou and a team of four service a wide range of corporate clients from inward investors to Cyprus Stock Exchange-quoted companies. The firm is active in the regional market and noted for sound drafting in high-value transactions. **Patrikios Pavlou & Co** is one of the first law firms to be involved in the new Dubai Stock Exchange; as we went to press the firm is working on a holding company flotation likely to go to market at between US$40m and US$70m. **Patrikios Pavlou & Co** also advised in connection with the flotation of a Bulgarian property fund on London's AIM.

Law Office of Andrew Demetriou & Co offers an effective corporate team; the four-partner firm favours a practical, client-centred, approach which has attracted a loyal following. The firm has acted for, *inter alia*, Cyprus Forest Industries, and the Electricity Authority of Cyprus.

Georgiades & Pelides effectively addresses the international client and has excellent contacts with UK Magic Circle firms. Recent clients include Centaur Financial Services.

L Papaphilippou & Co offers a substantial corporate department, highly active in international work and known for insurance matters.

CORPORATE AND M&A

ANDREAS NEOCLEOUS & CO ✪
CHRYSSES DEMETRIADES & CO LAW OFFICE
TASSOS PAPADOPOULOS & CO

ANTIS TRIANTAFYLLIDES & SONS
CHRYSSAFINIS & POLYVIOU
K CHRYSOSTOMIDES (DR) & CO
PATRIKIOS PAVLOU & CO ✪

Andrew Demetriou & Co, Law Office of ✪
Georgiades & Pelides
L Papaphilippou & Co
Michael Kyprianou & Co ✪

Christos M Triantafyllides Law Firm
Kyriacos Th Michaelides & Co Law Office ✪
Papacharalambous & Angelides ✪

Christodoulos G. Vassiliades & Co
Kinanis – Pyrgou & Co
Markides, Markides & Co
Nicos Papacleovoulou, Law Chambers
Yiannos G Georgiades and Co. Law Firm

Firms are listed A-Z in tiers which are ranked in order of priority
✪ Indicates firm displays contact details at the end of this chapter.

Michael Kyprianou & Co attracts a steady flow of blue-chip international instructions and referrals. Past clients have included Thomson Multimedia and the Herald Tribune.

Christos M Triantafyllides Law Firm offers a full-service practice; the firm acts of Hull Blyth Arazouzos, the travel and shipping group.

Three-partner, Nicosia-based **Kyriacos Th Michaelides & Co Law Office** provides a sound service.

Papacharalambous & Angelides is an energetic, competent firm with a young partner profile which should move up the tiers as the newcomers gain experience.

Christodoulos G. Vassiliades & Co is a good-quality, eleven-partner firm which provides a full-service corporate practice, headed by Koula Demetriou. **Christodoulos G. Vassiliades & Co** attracts a steady flow of overseas instructions.

A first listing for **Kinanis – Pyrgou & Co**, whose recruitment policies over the last few years have created a young, outward-looking firm which addresses the mid-range corporate market effectively.

Markides, Markides & Co, one of Cyprus' longest-established law firms, offers a full corporate service from its Nicosia office.

Paphos-based **Law Chambers Nicos Papacleovoulou** offers a north London branch. The firm offers a competent, full-service corporate practice which is a real mid-market alternative to the dominant Nicosia firms.

Yiannos G Georgiades and Co. Law Firm has been working with accountancy firm Baker Tilley International for a number of mutual clients and also acts for Alitalia.

DISPUTE RESOLUTION

ANDREAS NEOCLEOUS & CO ✪
KYRIACOS TH MICHAELIDES & CO LAW OFFICE ✪
PATRIKIOS PAVLOU & CO ✪
TASSOS PAPADOPOULOS & CO

ANTIS TRIANTAFYLLIDES & SONS
CHRYSSES DEMETRIADES & CO LAW OFFICE
L PAPAPHILIPPOU & CO
MARKIDES, MARKIDES & CO
MICHAEL KYPRIANOU & CO ✪

Andrew Demetriou & Co, Law Office of ✪
K Chrysostomides (Dr) & Co
Montanios & Montanios
Polakis Sarris & Co Lawyers

Christodoulos G. Vassiliades & Co
Papacharalambous & Angelides ✪
Scordis, Papapetrou & Co
Yiannos G Georgiades and Co. Law Firm

Firms are listed A-Z in tiers which are ranked in order of priority
✪ *Indicates firm displays contact details at the end of this chapter.*

DISPUTE RESOLUTION

The high-value investment flows now passing through Cyprus have inevitably generated disputes and the demand for resolution advice is growing. Law firms are now promoting Cyprus as an arbitration jurisdiction with some success. In many instances where capital projects are involved, arbitration clauses bring in international aspects and Cypriot lawyers are increasingly familiar with running actions alongside foreign law firms. In this section we have singled out those firms which have the capacity to handle complex, high-value international matters as well as litigation in the Cypriot courts.

Takis Christofourou heads **Andreas Neocleous & Co**'s 22-fee-earner litigation group, which divides into four practice teams. During 2005 the firm handled several multi-million dollar commercial actions, involving enterprises as diverse as oilfields and football teams. As well as obtaining a number of Mareva injunctions, **Andreas Neocleous & Co** claimed the first Cypriot Norwich Pharmacal Order, and acted in several high-value employment, probate and divorce cases.

Kyriacos Th Michaelides & Co Law Office offers a solid team of litigators, with particular strength in IP. Name partner Kyriacos Michaelides has a long-track record on high-profile cases.

Patrikios Pavlou & Co enters the dispute resolution top tier, having worked hard to establish an impressive share of the high-value litigation and arbitration market. The 21-lawyer firm is set to strengthen its corporate litigation team in 2006 by signing a senior associate from a second-tier rival. During 2005 **Patrikios Pavlou & Co** handled a US$5m arbitration before the Vienna Arbitration Court, and is currently working, jointly with a Swedish firm, on a Stockholm-based arbitration between an Austrian client and the Ukranian Energy Authority. Stavros Pavlou, **Patrikios Pavlou & Co**'s key litigator, is acting for ex-heavyweight boxing champion Lennox Lewis in a £10m claim against his former manager.

Pambos Ioannides, **Tassos Papadopoulos & Co**'s senior partner, acted as lead counsel for N K Shacolas in the successful defence of an US$18m bank guarantee action brought by the Federal Bank of Lebanon which became the longest-ever commercial court hearing in Cyprus, nearly 200 days.

Antis Triantafyllides & Sons boasts a strong litigation practice with several lawyers called to the Bar both in Cyprus and England.

Chrysses Demetriades & Co Law Office fields three litigation partners specialising in commercial and partnership matters.

L Papaphilippou & Co's nine litigators are particularly experienced in banking, insurance and maritime matters.

Former Attorney General Alecos Markides of **Markides, Markides & Co** receives peer acclaim as 'one of the leading local litigators'.

Michael Kyprianou & Co name partner Michael Kyprianou is a noted advocate, as is Menelaos Kyprianou. The firm handles some complex international work.

Law Office of Andrew Demetriou & Co is highly recommended for disputes in construction and development projects.

Dr K Chrysostomides & Co's litigation group is led by experienced Alexandros Taliadoros.

Montanios & Montanios' Eric Montanios is rated for shipping and aviation disputes.

Polakis Sarris & Co Lawyers has a solid reputation for litigation, particularly commercial credit disputes.

Christodoulos G. Vassiliades & Co offers a reliable litigation department boasting good contacts with banks including Cyprus Popular Bank and Hellenic Bank. Irene Anastasiou is recommended.

Papacharalambous & Angelides' Pavlos Angelides is an experienced commercial litigator and vice-president of the Nicosia Bar Association. The firm has recently recruited several promising young lawyers and should build quickly.

Patrikios Pavlou & Co's seven-strong litigation team led by Soteris Pittas and Chrysostomos Nicolaou, is familiar with the full range of corporate litigation and continues to attract quality instructions.

Former Cyprus government spokesman Michalis Papapetrou of **Scordis, Papapetrou & Co** is a well-connected and effective litigator.

Yiannos G Georgiades and Co. Law Firm name partner Yiannos Georgiades is well known as a litigator and has represented such global players as Coca-Cola and Kelloggs in brand protection matters.

EU AND COMPETITION

ANDREAS NEOCLEOUS & CO ✪
LELLOS P DEMETRIADES LAW OFFICE

Firms are listed alphabetically
✪ *Indicates firm displays contact details at the end of this chapter.*

EU AND COMPETITION

Most firms mentioned in the corporate and M&A section have developed competence in EU and competition law: the firms listed here offer specialists in the field.

Andreas Neocleous & Co, now with the advantage of a Brussels office, advises BT, Mitsubishi and Volvo. Elias Neocleous heads the team.

Lellos P Demetriades Law Office's Joanna Loizidou, formerly vice-president of the Cyprus Competition Commission, is recommended for competition advice.

INTELLECTUAL PROPERTY

Firms have been busy with IP work as Cyprus' buoyant economy draws in international consumer electronics, telecoms and pharmaceuticals players. Brand protection actions in fashion, music, film and perfumes are on the increase.

Andreas Neocleous & Co handles all aspects of IP work and is experienced in dealing with major international players in the pharmaceutical, software and telecoms sectors.

Chrysses Demetriades & Co Law Office's Thomas Keane is a noted authority on international IP issues, particularly copyright and licensing.

Lellos P Demetriades Law Office has established a strong reputation in anti-piracy and anti-counterfeit work in music, fashion, and film.

Dr K Chrysostomides & Co boasts considerable expertise in and experience of IP across the board but is particularly strong on patent protection and anti-counterfeiting issues where a 'hands-on' approach is required.

L Papaphilippou & Co has developed a strong following in the television sector since the state monopoly was substantially divested. **L Papaphilippou & Co** acts for Antenna TV and its international associate company Antenna Satellite, as well as Fred TV.

Michael Kyprianou & Co punches above its weight in IP and has edged close to the top tier with a series of large brand trade mark and design rights instructions.

Christodoulos G. Vassiliades & Co, hitherto noted for trade mark work, now fields a youthful IP group which is gaining in strength and depth.

Markides, Markides & Co name partners, Alecos Markides and Hermione Markides are the Cypriot contributors to *Enforcement of Intellectual Property Rights through Border Measures in the EU.*

INTELLECTUAL PROPERTY

ANDREAS NEOCLEOUS & CO ✪
CHRYSSES DEMETRIADES & CO LAW OFFICE
LELLOS P DEMETRIADES LAW OFFICE

K Chrysostomides (Dr) & Co
L Papaphilippou & Co
Michael Kyprianou & Co ✪

Christodoulos G. Vassiliades & Co
Markides, Markides & Co
Papacharalambous & Angelides ✪
Polakis Sarris & Co Lawyers
Yiannos G Georgiades and Co. Law Firm

Firms are listed A-Z in tiers which are ranked in order of priority
✪ Indicates firm displays contact details at the end of this chapter.

Eleni Papacharalambous of **Papacharalambous & Angelides** has developed useful niche expertise in internet brand and goodwill protection.

Polakis Sarris & Co Lawyers offers IP advice within a competent commercial office.

In addition to brand-protection work mentioned in the **Dispute resolution** section, **Yiannos G Georgiades and Co. Law Firm** advises Saba Kypris, the Cyprus office of major international patent and trade mark company Saba on IP matters and is assisting CAA Travel Media to launch a TV channel in the UK.

MARITIME AND ADMIRALTY

The number of Admiralty cases has been declining for many years and we have now combined the maritime and admiralty law sections. Cyprus maintains a strong position in world shipping by virtue of generous fiscal and flagging policies, which are now fully aligned with international standards. The long tradition of shipping has developed considerable legal expertise in 'dry' work.

Andreas Neocleous & Co's maritime department, headed by experienced Panayiotis Neocleous, has been busy with high-value construction contracts and purchase deals. The firm's able banking team lends support where financing and refinancing is involved.

Highly rated **Chrysses Demetriades & Co Law Office** fields three shipping partners and handles all admiralty and dry shipping matters including arbitration.

L Papaphilippou & Co's George Pamborides, the author of *International Shipping Law*, is superbly qualified to handle maritime matters of the greatest complexity. Senior partner Andreas Haviaras worked as a shipping operations manager before being called to the Bar and augments his recognised legal expertise with 'hands-on' experience.

MARTIME AND ADMIRALTY

ANDREAS NEOCLEOUS & CO ✪
CHRYSSES DEMETRIADES & CO LAW OFFICE
L PAPAPHILIPPOU & CO
MONTANIOS & MONTANIOS

GEORGE L SAVVIDES & CO
TASSOS PAPADOPOULOS & CO

K Chrysostomides (Dr) & Co
Michael Kyprianou & Co ✪
Polakis Sarris & Co Lawyers

Christodoulos G. Vassiliades & Co
Emilios Lemonaris
Patrikios Pavlou & Co ✪
Yiannos G Georgiades and Co. Law Firm

Firms are listed A-Z in tiers which are ranked in order of priority
✪ Indicates firm displays contact details at the end of this chapter.

Montanios & Montanios ranks as *primus inter pares* in admiralty and maritime work. Well known Acis Montanios heads a five-strong team.

George L Savvides & Co handles admiralty and maritime work and has been instructed by Stelmar.

Tassos Papadopoulos & Co is recommended for marine insurance advice.

Dr K Chrysostomides & Co deals with registration and transfers and frequently acts for mortgagees where injunctions are required to prevent alienation of vessels.

Michael Kyprianou & Co handles ship sales and purchases.

Polakis Sarris & Co Lawyers offers a full service to shipowners, from registration to sales, purchase and management.

Christodoulos G. Vassiliades & Co is expert in the shipping registration field; the firm has been appointed Deputy Registrar for Athens-based Belize International Merchant Marine Registry.

Emilios Lemonaris offers a comprehensive service to shipowners.

Patrikios Pavlou & Co acted in one of the few admiralty cases of 2005 and successfully stayed the action on a US$40m collision claim. The firm's Soteris Pittas is an experienced admiralty litigator.

Yiannos G Georgiades and Co. Law Firm name partner Yiannos Georgiades boasts wide experience in shipping matters and a track record of publications in the field.

REAL ESTATE AND CONSTRUCTION

The Cyprus construction sector is busy, with residential and hotel developers particularly active. Several major infrastructure projects have also required expert legal input. Most firms listed in the corporate and commercial section handle property deals and property finance. The firms listed here offer wider expertise.

REAL ESTATE AND CONSTRUCTION

ANDREW DEMETRIOU & CO, LAW OFFICE OF ✪

ANDREAS NEOCLEOUS & CO ✪
TASSOS PAPADOPOULOS & CO

Nicos Papacleovoulou, Law Chambers
Papacharalambous & Angelides ✪
Patrikios Pavlou & Co ✪
Yiannos G Georgiades and Co. Law Firm

Firms are listed A-Z in tiers which are ranked in order of priority
✪ Indicates firm displays contact details at the end of this chapter.

Law Office of Andrew Demetriou & Co name partner Andrew Demetriou is internationally active in high-value projects. Demetriou is international and general counsel, as well as a main board director of, D G Jones and Partners, the global construction consultants and project managers.

Andreas Neocleous & Co boasts wide experience in construction from commercial development, including golf courses and marinas, to major civil engineering projects such as the Paphos – Polis Chrisochou road scheme.

Tassos Papadopoulos & Co acted for the Hermes Consortium, the successful bidder in the major airport concession contract throughout the complex, three-year negotiations.

Law Chambers Nicos Papacleovoulou's property and construction expertise has developed along with the Paphos building boom. The firm is recommended both to developers and private clients for transactional matters, disputes and property finance.

Papacharalambous & Angelides is a full-service, Nicosia-based firm with four branch offices in Cyprus, ideally positioned to handle property matters across the island. The firm, which has expanded rapidly through the recruitment of well-qualified young lawyers, has a strong network of international associates.

Patrikios Pavlou & Co assisted GM subsidiary General Ionics to submit a bid for the purchase of the Dhekalia desalination plant.

Four-partner **Yiannos G Georgiades and Co. Law Firm** is active in the construction sector.

TAX

Most commercial lawyers in Cyprus are highly competent in tax law and know their way around Cyprus' double tax conventions. Some lawyers note that the major accountancy firms are more frequently met on tax issues than other law firms.

Andreas Neocleous & Co offers 'highly professional and effective representation' according to one long-term client. The tax group continues its long-term assistance to Itera SA as the gas giant moves through a complex

TAX

ANDREAS NEOCLEOUS & CO ✪
CHRYSSES DEMETRIADES & CO LAW OFFICE
MICHAEL KYPRIANOU & CO ✪
PATRIKIOS PAVLOU & CO ✪
TASSOS PAPADOPOULOS & CO

Christodoulos G. Vassiliades & Co
Georgiades & Pelides
K Chrysostomides (Dr) & Co
Kinanis – Pyrgou & Co
Lellos P Demetriades Law Office
Papacharalambous & Angelides ✪

Firms are listed A-Z in tiers which are ranked in order of priority
✪ *Indicates firm displays contact details at the end of this chapter.*

restructuring and during 2005 **Andreas Neocleous & Co** advised Merrill Lynch over taxation issues on portfolio acquisitions and disposals in the CIS and Ukraine. Elias Neocleous is well known for his international tax expertise.

Chrysses Demetriades & Co Law Office offers a comprehensive tax planning and compliance service. The legal team is backed by chartered accountants.

Michael Kyprianou & Co continues to receive a high number of corporate tax referrals from leading firms in Europe and the US.

Patrikios Pavlou & Co specialises in international tax planning and can offer full corporate and trust services.

Tassos Papadopoulos & Co's Nicholas Papadopoulos is a rising star in tax law.

Christodoulos G. Vassiliades & Co offers comprehensive international tax services and, through associated companies, trust services and asset management.

Dr K Chrysostomides & Co offers sound taxation competence within a holistic business planning approach.

Kinanis – Pyrgou & Co name partners Christos Kinanis and Melina Pyrgou, supported by promising associates, offer international tax planning which is particularly well targeted at the CIS and other former 'eastern bloc' countries.

ANDREAS NEOCLEOUS & CO

NEOCLEOUS HOUSE
199 ARCH MAKARIOS III AVENUE
3608 LIMASSOL

Telephone: +357 25 36 28 18
Fax: +357 25 35 92 62
E-mail: info@neocleous.com
Website: www.neocleous.com

Languages
Czech, English, French, German, Greek, Hungarian, Italian, Russian, Spanish, Turkish, Ukrainian

Other offices
Brussels, Budapest, Kiev, Moscow, Nicosia, Paphos, Prague

Number of lawyers 75
at this office 38

Member
International Attorneys' Club; International Bar Association; International Business Law Consortium; International Tax Planning Association

CATEGORIES OF WORK

Companies, corporate management, trustee and fiduciary services
Andreas Neocleous, Elias Neocleous

Tax law and international tax planning
Andreas Neocleous, Elias Neocleous

Admiralty and international trade law
Panayiotis Neocleous, Maria Ioannou

Banking law, finance, insolvency
Anna Panayiotidou, Christina Hadjigiorki

Administrative law
Christos Melides, Christina Christou

Real estate, wills, land law and administration of estates
Lefkios Tsikkinis, George Christoforou

Internet, e-commerce and information technology law
Elias Neocleous, Nicolas Ktenas

Shipping companies, ship registration, ship finance and aviation
Panayiotis Neocleous, Costas Stamatiou

Corporate finance, capital markets, securities
Elias Neocleous, Kyriakos Georgiades

Matrimonial and family law
Christos Melides, Anna Panayiotidou

European law
Andreas Neocleous, Elias Neocleous

General litigation
Takis Christoforou, Antonis Glykis

Arbitration (local and international)
Andreas Neocleous, Christos Melides

Intellectual property and trade marks
Nicholas Ktenas, Elena Papachristoforou

THE FIRM

Andreas Neocleous & Co is one of the leading firms in the Eastern Mediterranean, with 75 lawyers and six tax consultants. Internationally focused, with a broad practice offering a full range of services, its expanding client base ranges from private individuals to multinational organisations.

The firm has offices in six countries and has recently expanded its activities in Moscow and opened an office in Brussels. The firm has a particular expertise in Eastern Europe and CIS cross-border corporate finance transactions and joint venture projects, with clients including international banks and financial institutions, insurance, energy, telecommunications and broadcasting companies, and US and UK 'Magic Circle' firms.

AREAS OF PRACTICE

Admiralty and maritime: handles collisions, charterparty disputes and executions of judgments against shipping companies worldwide. It also deals with all aspects of ship finance and registration under the Cypriot and other flags.

Banking and finance: advises major financial institutions on all aspects of financial services and banking. The firm has strong links with commercial and investment banks, trust companies and underwriters.

Corporate and commercial/mergers and acquisitions: advises on corporate management and governance, formation, merger and acquisition of companies in Cyprus and abroad, corporate reconstruction and reorganisation, capital raising and private equity work.

Competition and European Union law: advises multinational enterprises investing or considering an investment in Cyprus on competition and merger control issues.

Intellectual property: advises on the acquisition, registration and protection of all types of intellectual property. The firm specialises in high-level advice to international clients on the protection and exploitation of intellectual property using Cyprus-based structures.

Litigation and arbitration: as well as handling all types of litigation, this department conducts domestic and international arbitration, mediation and other forms of ADR.

Infrastructure and project finance: the firm assists clients on landmark developments, global PFI and PPP projects. Advice is specifically tailored to dovetail with the corresponding commercial, banking and finance and tax aspects.

Tax law and international tax planning: the department advises on tax law and treaties, plans structures for multinational companies and handles tax disputes. The Cyprus tax regime provides attractive tax planning opportunities for cross-border investment and company reorganisations.

PATRIKIOS PAVLOU & CO

PATRICIAN CHAMBERS
332 AGIOU ANDREOU STREET
PO BOX 54543
3725 LIMASSOL

Telephone: +357 25 87 15 99
Fax: +357 25 34 45 48
E-mail: info@pavlaw.com
Website: www.pavlaw.com

Languages
English, French, German, Greek, Italian, Russian, Ukrainian

Other offices
Nicosia*

Number of lawyers 21
at this office 17

Member
International Tax Planning Association (ITPA); International Bar Association (IBA); European Association of Lawyers (AEA); International Association of Young Lawyers (AIJA)

CATEGORIES OF WORK

Corporate and commercial law
Stavros Pavlou, Soteris Pittas, Lia Iordanou Theodoulou

International tax planning
Stavros Pavlou, Andria Andreou

Banking and finance
Stavros Pavlou, Stella Louka Pavlou

Litigation and arbitration
Soteris Pittas, Chrysostomos Nicolaou

European law
Stavros Pavlou, Chrysostomos Nicolaou

Shipping
Patrikios Pavlou, Soteris Pittas

Intellectual property
Patrikios Pavlou, Andria Andreou

Real estate, wills and probate
Patrikios Pavlou, Andria Andreou

Information technology
Stavros Pavlou, Andria Andreou

Internet and e-commerce
Stavros Pavlou, Andria Andreou

LAW OFFICE OF ANDREW DEMETRIOU & CO

31 EVAGORAS AVENUE
1ST FLOOR, EVAGORAS COMPLEX
1066 NICOSIA

Telephone: +357 22 67 50 90
Fax: +357 22 67 58 65
E-mail: reception@ademetriou.com
Website: www.ademetriou.com

Languages
English, French, German, Greek, Italian

Number of lawyers 5

Contact
Andrew Demetriou (managing partner)

Member
Cyprus Bar Association; International Bar Association; Chartered Institute of Arbitrators; World e-Business Law Report (panel members); Roster of UN Center on Transnational Corporations (panel members)

CATEGORIES OF WORK

Construction
Andrew Demetriou

Arbitration
Andrew Demetriou, Christos Frakalas

Litigation
Andrew Demetriou, Stella J Stephani

Telecommunications
Andrew Demetriou, Elena Michail-Pikis

EU and competition
Elena Michail-Pikis, Christos Frakalas

Commercial
Andrew Demetriou, Elena Michail-Pikis

Family law
Stella J Stephani

Consumer law
Christos Frakalas

Energy and natural resources
Andrew Demetriou, Elena Michail-Pikis

Quality manager
Nadja Phasoulli

COSTAS INDIANOS & CO

ADVOCATES AND LEGAL CONSULTANTS

4 DIAGORAS STREET
KERMIA HOUSE FLATS 601-602
1097 NICOSIA

Telephone: +357 22 67 52 31
Fax: +357 22 66 96 78
E-mail: indianos@indianos.com.cy
Website: www.indianos.com.cy

Languages
English, French, Greek, Italian, Spanish

Other offices
Larnaca

Number of lawyers 5
at this office 3

CATEGORIES OF WORK

Shipping/maritime
Anthony Indianos, Rena David

Corporate and commercial
Anthony Indianos, Rena David

Tax planning
Anthony Indianos, Rena David

Real estate
Anthony Indianos, Andreas Papasiantis

Family
Anthony Indianos, Andreas Papasiantis

EU
Anthony Indianos, Andreas Papasiantis

Intellectual property
Anthony Indianos, Andreas Papasiantis

Civil litigation
Anthony Indianos, Andreas Papasiantis

Debt collection
Anthony Indianos, Andreas Papasiantis

Criminal litigation
Anthony Indianos, Andreas Papasiantis

Administrative litigation
Anthony Indianos, Andreas Papasiantis

Immigration
Anthony Indianos, Andreas Papasiantis

KYRIACOS TH MICHAELIDES & CO

66 IPPOKRATOUS STREET
1015 NICOSIA
PO BOX 21548
1510 NICOSIA

Telephone: +357 22 45 24 00
Fax: +357 22 76 18 78
E-mail: online@ktmlaw.com
Website: www.ktmlaw.com

Languages
English, German, Greek

Other offices
Athens

Number of lawyers 9
at this office 8

CATEGORIES OF WORK

General litigation/civil litigation
Kyriacos Th Michaelides

Company law (incorporating management, trustee services)
Christiana K Michaelides,
Renos K Michaelides

Commercial law
Christiana K Michaelides

Arbitration
Kyriacos Th Michaelides

Intellectual property
Renos K Michaelides

Banking, finance and capital markets
Christiana K Michaelides

Construction
Kyriacos Th Michaelides

Property and administration of estates
Christiana K Michaelides,
Renos K Michaelides

Administrative
Kyriacos Th Michaelides

MICHAEL KYPRIANOU & CO

6TH FLOOR
2 AGIAS ELENIS STREET
PO BOX 28765
1060 NICOSIA

Telephone: +357 22 44 77 77
Fax: +357 22 76 78 80
E-mail: info@kyprianou.com.cy
Website: www.kyprianou.com.cy

Languages
English, French, German, Greek, Russian

Other offices
Limassol, Paphos

Number of lawyers 10
at this office 6

Contact
Menelaos Kyprianou

Member
Multilaw; Eurolink for Lawyers;
The Middle Temple; ITPA; IBA; INTA; AIJA

CATEGORIES OF WORK

Company law (incorporation of companies, trustee and fiduciary services)
Anna Grigorieva

Tax law and international tax planning
Menelaos Kyprianou

Ship registration and finance
Tonia Antoniou, Menelaos Kyprianou

Admiralty and international trade law
Menelaos Kyprianou

Franchising, mergers and acquisitions
Menelaos Kyprianou, Pavlos Kyprianou

Litigation and arbitration
Michael Kyprianou, Menelaos Kyprianou

Banking law, finance and insolvency
Demos Christodoulou, Elli Florentzou

Law of e-commerce
Tonia Antoniou, Elli Florentzou

Real estate, wills and administration of estates
Michael Kyprianou, Michael Hasikos, Savvas Savvides, Nicolas Nicolaou

European law
Pavlos Kyprianou

Intellectual property
Tonia Antoniou

PAPACHARALAMBOUS & ANGELIDES

**10 THEMISTOKLI DERVI STREET
1ST FLOOR
PO BOX 24901
NICOSIA 1305**

Telephone: +357 22 67 01 89
Fax: +357 22 67 69 76
Email: office@palaw.com.cy
Website: www.palaw.com.cy

Languages
English, French, Greek, Romanian

Other offices
Athens*, Bahrain, Brussels*, Bucharest*, Dubai, Kuwait, Larnaca*, Limassol*, London*, Moscow*, New York*, Paphos*, Paralimni*, Sofia*, Riyadh

Number of lawyers 15
at this office 12

Contact
Stavroulla Ioannou Kyrou
(stavroulla@palaw.com.cy)

CATEGORIES OF WORK

Litigation

Company law (registering local companies' trade marks, patents, trade names and counterfeits)

Offshore company registration and administration

Banking

Public and administrative law

Intellectual property

Trusts

Family

Registration of companies into the Cyprus Stock Exchange

Commercial law

Civil and criminal proceedings

Labour law

Consultancy

Investment issues

Financial companies

THE FIRM

Papacharalambous & Angelides was founded by Andreas Papacharalambous and Pavlos Angelides in 1983 and is based in the centre of Nicosia, the capital of Cyprus. However, prior to this, Andreas Papacharalambous and Pavlos Angelides maintained their own offices, begun in 1976 and 1977 respectively.

AREAS OF PRACTICE

Papacharalambous & Angelides began as a small office with two partners and has now expanded and evolved into a large firm consisting of 12 in-house qualified lawyers and has association with lawyers in all the main towns in Cyprus including Larnaca, Limassol, Paphos and Paralimni. It covers a wide range of areas of practice and the members of the firm are very experienced in all these areas, being able to offer advice with particular emphasis on general litigation, company law, family law, public and administrative law, and civil and criminal proceedings.

Moreover, the firm covers all areas concerning athletic and sports law together with any rights and regulations within this area. In addition, the law firm offers consultation to many semi-governmental organisations. Papacharalambous & Angelides also specialises in stock exchange activities both within Cyprus and Greece. The firm also has an extensive international client base and has associate offices including permanent representation in Greece, Romania, Bulgaria, Belgium, Saudi Arabia, Nigeria and the UK. The firm has recently expanded to Israel and France, and has strong links with many other European countries.

The firm tries to keep up with all current developments in the law so as to be more effectively and efficiently able to serve its clients. It has recently set up a website, providing information and updates on the firm.

A brochure providing more details is available on request.

CZECH REPUBLIC

Population	**10.2 million**
Number of lawyers	**6,000**
Professional title	**Advokat**
Currency	**Koruna (Kc)**

Index

The Czech Republic has been through a dramatic transformation in the last 20 years, and it cannot be under-estimated how nascent the country's economic environment remains. Much praise was heaped on Czechoslovakia's people when they pulled off the peaceful Velvet Revolution in 1989, and communism was rejected in the most civilised way possible. The first free elections were held in June 1990, and then came the so-called Velvet Divorce, of the Czech Republic and Slovakia, and so a new country was born in 1993.

The country's capital, Prague, could hold its own against any European capital city, and tourists flood in by the coach load. The country achieved EU accession in 2004, and has not suffered the kind of mass population flows that were feared, and were indeed realised in neighbouring Poland.

The business environment is thus still very much developing and evolving to find its place in the new-world order. Corruption is still an issue, and an unstable political environment continues to hamper some foreign direct investment (FDI). The general election in 2002 produced a coalition government led by Vladimir Spidla, but that collapsed in June 2004. His former deputy Stanislav Gross moved to form a new government with the same coalition, only to see it collapse less than a year later. In April 2004 Jiri Paroubek took over as prime minister, and the ruling Czech Social Democratic Party has since recovered some popularity. It looks likely that the party will now remain in power, alongside its two junior coalition members, until the general election scheduled for 2006, which is currently wide open.

ECONOMY

Until 2004, the government's main task was preparation for EU accession in May 2004. With that achieved, membership is now demanding more legislative and administrative reform, as well as improvements in industrial productivity levels to stimulate growth.

After accession the government set about tackling the current-account deficit, by raising taxes and cutting expenditure. With the strong performance of exports, that has been successful: in 2004 exports amounted to US$66.7bn and imports ran at US$67.5bn, with a trade deficit much lower than it had been in 2003.

Now, the Czech National Bank has indicated it is worried about the potential impact of rising oil prices on consumer prices, so interest rate rises appear imminent. What's more, the government will have to be vigilant to restrain the economy's tendency to overheat and absorb imports. Further fiscal and pensions system reforms will be needed if the country is to adopt the Euro, though politically that remains some way off.

Most of the Czech Republic's trade is with the EU, which purchases some 86% of its exports and provides 72% of its imports. Germany is its closest trading partner, responsible for one-third of all imports and exports, with Slovakia next up.

Since revolution, the decline in the industrial sector's contribution to GDP has been marked, and has led to rising unemployment. Total employment was 38% in 1990 but is now nearer the 30% typical of Central Europe, though at levels well below those seen in Poland and Slovakia.

The private sector accounted for a mere 4% of GDP at the start of the transition, but it has expanded rapidly after a wave of privatisations through the 1990s, and its share of the economy passed 80% in 2002. Most of the privatisations have now finished, but the structural change has been immense. There are now more than 2.1 million registered businesses, compared to just 18,000 back in 1990.

The country has proved one of the most successful of the transition economies in attracting FDI. Incentives were brought in in 1998 that have stimulated both greenfield and brownfield projects, and since 1993 nearly €40bn in FDI has been recorded. The country benefits from its position at the heart of Europe, with good access to both established Western economies like that of Germany, and the emerging Eastern markets. The highway network is in need of investment, but there are plans to double it by 2007 and it is already the densest in the region.

There is a skilled and productive workforce that has attracted much investment from the automotive industry, and is feeding a large research and development sector at comparatively low cost. Multinationals like Panasonic, Honeywell, Motorola and Mercedez-Benz run research and design centres in the republic. The attractiveness of Prague itself, plus strong IT and language skills, are further making the country a haven for offshoring units.

Hopes were raised of an uptick on the Prague Stock Exchange in 2004, when the IPO of pharmaceutical company Zentiva was five-times oversubscribed in both Prague and London. It was

The largest firms

1	Procházka Randl Kubr	50
2	Linklaters	49
3	Kocián Solc Balastík	47
4	Nörr Stiefenhofer Lutz	40
5	White & Case	39
6	Salans	38
7	Brzobohaty Broz & Honsa, v.o.s.	33
	Kríz and Belina	33
9	Balcar, Polansky & spol.	31
10	Allen & Overy, Praha Advokátní kancelár	30
	Pokorny, Wagner a Spol.	30
12	Havel & Holásek	29
	Peterka & Partners v.o.s.	29
14	Baker & McKenzie V.O.S.	28
	Weil, Gotshal & Manges	28
16	Clifford Chance	27
17	Glatzová & Co	26
18	Squire, Sanders & Dempsey, v.o.s., advokátní kancelár	23
	Vejmelka & Wünsch, v.o.s.	23
	Vyskocil, Kroslak a Spol.	23
21	CMS Cameron McKenna v.o.s.	22
	Konecná & Safár	22
23	Felix a spol.	21
24	Cermak Horejs Myslil a spol	20
	Rödl & Partner	20
	Sodomka Soucek Jindra Mokry & Partners	20

These figures represent the total number of lawyers in this country only, and have been supplied by the firms themselves. The figures should be accurate as at 1 January 2006.

the first float since 1937, and given that it followed a €680m secondary offering of Cesky Telecom shares in December 2003 by KPN and Swisscom, there were hopes it might be the start of a trend. Alas, local companies have not so far emerged to follow in Zentiva's footsteps.

BILLING

With the emergence of a band of strong local law firms, all lawyers operating in the country have experienced increased fee pressure in the last few years. It is not necessarily the domestic players pushing rates down, either, but rather the international firms apparently buying up work as the dip in privatisations left associates under-employed.

The Czech law firms are doing evermore complex work, but their fee levels remain lower generally than those of international players. For equity partners, the domestic firms are charging between €140 and €320 per hour, while rates at continental European law firms range from €200 to €550, and the US and UK firms bill €350 to €450. The dollar exchange rate has hit the latter numbers, and has served to push the average down for international firms.

Most billing is still done on an hourly rate, though clients are increasingly sophisticated and are demanding both more flexible arrangements, and root-and-branch rate reviews.

MARKETING

The law severely restricting marketing was changed in September 2003, but the change has had a limited impact. In theory, firms can now advertise their services far more freely but in practice, few firms have done so.

As the number of new firms in the Prague market increases – often young partners emerging from hard-hit international firms to set up on their own – profile-raising is becoming more of a necessity, and competition is pushing it onto the agenda of many more players.

IN-HOUSE LAWYERS

The status of in-house lawyers remains high in comparison to other countries in the region, and there are more frequent instances of partners leaving law firms to take in-house positions with multinational corporations or banks. Top lawyers continue to aspire to work in private practice, though, and the increasing number of small law firms is providing a platform for a new generation of highly trained young lawyers.

LEGAL MARKET

A wave of privatisations in the Czech Republic in the 1990s attracted a similar inflow of international law firms, particularly US firms staffed by partners with Czech descendants, and UK Magic Circle players looking to roll out across Central and Eastern Europe.

That period was one of boom for those that were on the ground, but with the wave of privatisations coming to an end, Prague offices have started to look more vulnerable. The year 2005 saw the exit from the market of both **Hogan & Hartson** and **Dewey Ballantine**. The three English firms with sizeable presences: **Allen & Overy, Praha Advokátní kancelár**, **Clifford Chance**, and **Linklaters**, have done some serious navel-gazing and have all, in their own way, restructured for the new environment. Some partners have returned to the London offices of their firms.

Today, it is FDI and its requisite real estate demands that is driving legal activity in Prague. With much of that investment coming from neighbouring countries, German and Austrian firms like **Gleiss Lutz**, **Haarmann Hemmelrath**, **Nörr Stiefenhofer Lutz** and **Wolf Theiss** have picked up important instructions and are following their clients into the country with some success.

Most significant, though, is surely the emergence of a band of strong local law firms. Often these practices have been started by partners leaving the international practices to set up alone, and they are now attracting young local talent. With these firms benefiting from an inflow of referrals from overseas law firms that do not have a presence in the region, they are quickly gaining experience in evermore complex transactions.

What's more, with the Czech private sector gaining traction, and with FDI now reasonably mature, there is a growing volume of mid-sized transactions that do not interest the international firms in Prague, on which local firms like **Brzobohatý Broz & Honsa, v.o.s.**, **Glatzová & Co**, **Havel & Holásek** and **Procházka Randl Kubr** are well-placed to advise.

Boutique specialist players are also emerging, like **Kines** for TMT, **Cermak Horejs Myslil a spol** and **Vyskocil, Kroslak a Spol.** for patents and trade marks, and **Peterka & Partners v.o.s.**, which is a Czech firm specialising in work for French investors.

Finally, it is of note that the large, former state-owned businesses are now investing outside of the Czech Republic, and are looking for legal advisers that can help them region-wide. While playing to the strengths of the international firms, this is also driving local firms into collaborations beyond their home borders.

BANKING, FINANCE AND CAPITAL MARKETS

Despite the flotation in 2004 of Czech pharmaceutical company Zentiva, activity on the Prague Stock Exchange remains uninspiring. Those firms offering capital markets expertise generally do so as part of a broader finance

BANKING, FINANCE AND CAPITAL MARKETS

ALLEN & OVERY, PRAHA ADVOKÁTNÍ KANCELÁR ✪
CLIFFORD CHANCE
WHITE & CASE

LINKLATERS ✪
WEIL, GOTSHAL & MANGES ✪

BAKER & McKENZIE V.O.S. ✪
BALCAR POLANSKÝ NORTON ROSE
CMS CAMERON McKENNA V.O.S. ✪
PROCHÁZKA RANDL KUBR ✪

Brzobohatý Broz & Honsa, v.o.s. ✪
Glatzová & Co ✪
Havel & Holásek ✪
Salans
Squire, Sanders & Dempsey, v.o.s., advokátní kancelár ✪
Wolf Theiss ✪

EY Law / Weinhold Legal
Felix a spol. ✪
Gide Loyrette Nouel ✪
Gleiss Lutz ✪
Giese & Partner
Haarmann Hemmelrath ✪
Haslinger/Nagele & Partner, v.o.s.
Nörr Stiefenhofer Lutz ✪
Pokorný, Wagner a Spol. ✪
Sodomka Soucek Jindra Mokry & Partners
Vejmelka & Wünsch, v.o.s. ✪
Vyskocil, Kroslak a Spol.

Firms are listed A-Z in tiers which are ranked in order of priority
✪ Indicates firm displays contact details at the end of this chapter.

offering, and any capital markets experts that were resident in Prague have returned to the London offices of their law firms as privatisations have come to an end. As a result, the *Legal 500* has combined last year's capital markets commentary with a broader banking and finance section for 2006.

Banking and finance work in the Czech Republic is dominated by the local practices of large international law firms, particularly **Allen & Overy, Praha Advokátní Kancelár**, **Clifford Chance** and **White & Case**.

Allen & Overy, Praha Advokátní Kancelár partners Mikuláš Touška and Václav Valvoda are two of the best-known finance lawyers in the country, and work on the biggest deals around. In 2005, they advised Calyon as mandated lead arrangers in connection with the CZK1.975bn financing of Karneval Media. On the capital markets side, the firm worked for JP Morgan on the financing of Oskar Mobile, the third-largest mobile operator in the Czech Republic, in relation to €325m of high-yield bonds and a multi-currency syndicated loan of €40m.

Clifford Chance's team, led by Vlad Petrus, is described as 'extremely thorough and professional' for complex transactions, on which it is able to draft in considerable resource from across the region. The team worked for HVB Bank and Erste Bank on a restructuring of secured loan facilities to the largest leveraged buy-out in Central Europe to date, the US$380m acquisition of coal mining company OKD.

The **White & Case** team, led by the impressive Jan Matejcek, acts for a list of banks that includes ABN Amro, Bawag Bank, Erste Bank, CSOB, Czech Export Bank, Dresdner, Deutsche Bank and the EBRD. The firm worked for listed Czech pharma group Zentiva funding its CZK3bn acquisition of a 51% stake in Sicomed in Romania, one of the largest unsecured acquisition financings ever executed in the Czech Republic, and the second-largest foreign acquisition by a Czech company ever.

In the second tier, **Linklaters**'s team is led by managing associate Ondřej Žváček after partner Francis Kucera returned to London. The team has a base in real estate finance, but is expanding into acquisition finance for both borrowers and lenders. Žváček acted for Czech bank CSOB on a syndicated loan for Mostecká uhelná of up to €125m.

Weil, Gotshal & Manges has a team of four partners who, though members of a US law firm, have incredible penetration of the local market. With a borrower-led banking team, the highlight was advising Czech Airlines on the financing of its new fleet of 12 aircraft for US$500m. On the capital markets side, the firm represented the Czech Ministry of Labour and Social Affairs in a share exchange deal involving two Czech power companies for a value of about CZK2.4bn.

In the third tier, **Baker & McKenzie V.O.S.** acted for HVB Bank on a major refinancing, and also works for Czech bank CSOB. Clients praise the team's good knowledge of the local market, and commercial sense.

Balcar Polanský Norton Rose has a bank-led practice run by the firm's former managing partner in Moscow Simon Renton and the highly rated Jaroslav Polanský. The team is well versed in work on distressed loans, and works with banks including Kormerčni banka, ABC International, HSBC Bank and ABN Amro. Polanský led the team advising on the sale of receivables in connection with the liquidation of Union Banka, in liquidation.

CMS Cameron McKenna V.O.S. has a five-lawyer team led by the popular Paul Stallebrass, one of the few experts on leveraged acquisition financings in the region. He splits his time between Prague and Bucharest, and works with clients including Advent International, AIG, Deutsche Bank, Erste Bank and JP Morgan Partners. As well as acquisition finance, the office is well versed in property and project finance.

Procházka Randl Kubr partner Martin Aschenbrenner is highly rated for debt capital markets work, particularly domestic structured bond issues. The firm works for financial institutions, including ABN Amro, CSOB, ING, HVB Bank, Morgan Stanley and Citibank. Partner Robert Nemec advised ABN Amro on a CZK2.1bn loan to Alliachem in 2005.

In the fourth tier, **Brzobohatý Broz & Honsa, v.o.s.** is one of the highly rated Czech firms, though it has felt the loss of Tomas Brzobohatý, who took a senior management role with a client. The firm still acts for several leading banks and insurance companies.

Glatzová & Co's team is praised by clients as 'one of the best local firms in the Czech market'. The firm acted for Commerzbank on a €3m structured loan to a car manufacturer, and on a €85m lease and loan financing for Corinthia Group.

Havel & Holásek, led by name partner Jaroslav Havel, is a new addition to our tables for banking and finance, having expanded its client base in the last year. The group now regularly acts for Erste Bank, ABN Amro Asset Management, and ING Group. The firm acts for ABN Amro and Julius Baer Investment Funds on all aspects of the operation and distribution of their foreign-based investment funds in the Czech Republic, including registration with the Czech Securities Commission.

Salans acted for the Czech government-owned debt administration and consolidation agencies in the sale of a CZK15bn package of non-performing loans, and represented Raiffeisenbank in the financing of a large residential project in Prague. Partner Olga Humlová is recommended.

Squire, Sanders & Dempsey, v.o.s., advokátní kancelár retains a small but active presence in the Czech Republic, and is popular with banking clients.

Wolf Theiss acts for a number of Austrian and German banks doing deals in the Czech Republic. In 2005, the firm advised Erste Bank on the refinancing of a €100m loan to IDAG, the purchaser of three project companies. The Prague office also advised Equita Management, the private equity firm, on the financing of its acquisition of VAG Armaturen for an undisclosed amount, and worked on the securitisation of the new syndicated financing.

CORPORATE AND M&A

Three firms dominate the market for major corporate deals in the Czech Republic: **Linklaters**, **Weil, Gotshal & Manges** and **White & Case**. With the deals market increasingly busy, the growing number of mid-market acquisitions is playing to the strengths of the local firms, who are now gaining a greater share of M&A volume.

The **Linklaters** corporate practice in Prague is run by the experienced Lukas Sevcik, and includes a total of 25 fee-earners. The firm last year acted for bidders in the two largest privatisations, those

CORPORATE AND M&A

LINKLATERS ✪
WEIL, GOTSHAL & MANGES ✪
WHITE & CASE

Allen & Overy, Praha Advokátní kancelář ✪
Baker & McKenzie V.O.S. ✪
Brzobohatý Broz & Honsa, v.o.s. ✪
CMS Cameron McKenna v.o.s. ✪
Clifford Chance
Glatzová & Co ✪
Havel & Holásek ✪
Kocián Solc Balastík
Procházka Randl Kubr ✪

Balcar Polanský Norton Rose
EY Law / Weinhold Legal
Gide Loyrette Nouel ✪
Haarmann Hemmelrath ✪
Lovells ✪
Nörr Stiefenhofer Lutz ✪
Peterka & Partners v.o.s. ✪
Salans
Squire, Sanders & Dempsey, v.o.s., advokátní kancelár ✪
Vejmelka & Wünsch, v.o.s. ✪
Wolf Theiss ✪

Cermak Horejs Myslil a spol ✪
Giese & Partner
Gleiss Lutz ✪
Pokorný, Wagner a Spol. ✪
Rowan Legal
Vyskocil, Kroslak a Spol.

Firms are listed A-Z in tiers which are ranked in order of priority
✪ Indicates firm displays contact details at the end of this chapter.

of Cesky Telecom and Vitkovice Steel, and worked for Vodafone on its acquisition of the mobile operator Oskar for US$4.4bn. The team worked for JP Morgan Partners and Bancroft on the country's largest private equity transaction, when they bought Nowaco for more than €100m, and advised power company CEZ on its purchase of Electrica Oltenia in Romania, for an undisclosed amount.

Weil, Gotshal & Manges managing partner Karel Muzikár is one the best-connected lawyers in the Prague market, and his team of three other partners is advising all the major state-owned and formerly state-owned companies. The firm represented Cesky Telecom in the sale of the government's majority stake to Telefónica for US$3.3bn, and worked for OSINEK, the government holding company, on the sale of Vitkovice Steel, one of the largest Czech steel mills, to EVRAZ for CZK7.05bn.

At **White & Case**, partners Jan Matejcek and Ivo Barta are described as 'excellent' and 'outstanding' by clients. They advised the National Property Fund and CKA on the privatisation of Unipetrol, the major Czech petrochemical group, for US$600m, and are increasingly acting for major Czech companies expanding overseas. The largest of these was the €281.5m acquisition by CEZ of three Bulgarian electricity companies, while Barta also worked on Zentiva's US$102m purchase of Sicomed in Romania.

In our second tier, **Allen & Overy, Praha Advokátní Kancelár**'s corporate team is led by regional managing partner Jane Townsend. She advised Ceská Rafinérská and its shareholders on the conversion of its refinery from a profit centre to a cost centre, while in M&A the firm worked for the Ministry of Finance in the acquisition of a shareholding in CEPS, a transmission grid company.

Baker & McKenzie V.O.S. has made significant headway in its local M&A practice in the last year, and is one of the international firms that challenges the top three. In 2005, the firm won two of the most significant mandates, though clients were unsuccessful in their bids. The firm did its first work for Shell, in its ultimately unsuccessful bid for BP's gas stations in the Czech Republic, and worked for the Blackstone Group in its bid to acquire a controlling stake in Cesky Telecom.

Brzobohatý Broz & Honsa, v.o.s. is one of the leading Czech firms for corporate work. Name partner Josef Broz heads the group, which is praised by clients.

CMS Cameron McKenna v.o.s.'s corporate group is run by Ian Parker, who works with seven others. His focus is on private equity deals, where he acts for funds including DBG Eastern Europe, Advent International and JP Morgan. The firm advised Belgacom in an ultimately fruitless bid for Cesky Telecom, and worked for Advent on the acquisition of CCS, a provider of petrol loyalty cards, from JP Morgan Asset Management.

Clifford Chance's corporate clients in the country include the EBRD and International Power. The firm hired Alex Cook as a partner from **Allen & Overy, Praha Advokátní Kancelár**, and promoted Emil Holub to the partnership, with both given a brief to focus on corporate work. The pair is advising a number of Russian companies on their interests in the Czech Republic.

Glatzová & Co is praised by one client for its 'in-depth knowledge of the market and service that is just as good as at the international firms'. The firm advised a group of shareholders including RWE and EON on the sale of Alliatel, and worked for Cinergy Global Resources on the sale of Cinergetika, a power plant, to Slávia Capital Asset Management.

Havel & Holásek has a 13-lawyer corporate and M&A team, and advised České dráhy, the operator of Czech railways, on the transformation of its business into two independent entities. Partner Jaroslav Havel advised UK project company Davis Langdon & Everest on its acquisition of Czech group KLMG Building Management.

Kocián Solc Balastík moves up in our tables this year, having established a solid reputation in the market for corporate work and receiving high praise from competitors. The firm scooped the work to advise Telefónica, the successful bidder for Cesky Telecom.

Procházka Randl Kubr is a strong local player, and has a steady flow of mid-market transactions. The firm advised Russia's Sistema on the corporate restructuring of its Czech operations, and provides public procurement and commercial advice to Morgan Stanley locally. On the M&A side, partner Robert Nemec worked for GTS Czech in its buyout of Alliatel.

In our fourth tier, **Balcar Polanský Norton Rose** partner Simon Renton runs a bank-led practice that also provides strong commercial advice to clients, and EU law advice.

At **EY Law / Weinhold Legal**, the partners are praised by one client for being 'very customer-orientated', while the team at **Gide Loyrette Nouel** works for major French clients including L'Oréal Group, BIC, Arcelor and BNP Group in their Czech operations.

Haarmann Hemmelrath is a German firm with a significant tax practice. It advised Mediatel, a Czech issuer of Yellow Pages directories, on due diligence and antitrust issues.

Lovells has a two-partner office, which is real estate led. It acts for clients including Doughty Hanson.

Nörr Stiefenhofer Lutz is another German firm, and works for major clients like Skoda, Volkswagen and Wintershall Gas.

PETERKA & PARTNERS v.o.s. is a Czech firm that acts for clients like engineering company Lutos, and restoration and conservation company Gema Art Group.

Salans partner Alena Bányaiová advised foreign investor Ispat International on the Czech, Polish, Romanian and Kazakh aspects of its US$17.bn merger with LNM to form Mittal Steel.

Squire, Sanders & Dempsey, v.o.s., advokátní kancelár partner Vladimira Papirnik works for the Czech government's Revitalisation Agency on the restructuring of companies in difficulties.

Vejmelka & Wünsch, v.o.s. is a two-partner local firm with strong connections to leading international law firms not present in Prague. Through referrals, it advised on the restructuring of Swarovski in the Czech Republic, and worked on the Myllykoski foreign investment, which saw €450m invested in the largest European paper mill project.

Wolf Theiss advised US private equity fund Cerberus Partners on the Czech aspects of its €130m acquisition of automotive business GenCorp.

DISPUTE RESOLUTION

Contentious work is an expanding practice area for most law firms in the Czech Republic, and only

DISPUTE RESOLUTION

BAKER & McKENZIE V.O.S. ✪
SALANS
WEIL, GOTSHAL & MANGES ✪
WHITE & CASE

Brzobohatý Broz & Honsa, v.o.s. ✪
Cermak Horejs Myslil a spol ✪
Kocián Solc Balastík
Peterka & Partners v.o.s. ✪
Procházka Randl Kubr ✪
Squire, Sanders & Dempsey, v.o.s., advokátní kancelár ✪

Allen & Overy, Praha Advokátní kancelár ✪
Balcar Polanský Norton Rose
CMS Cameron McKenna v.o.s. ✪
Clifford Chance
Gide Loyrette Nouel ✪
Glatzová & Co ✪
Linklaters ✪
Nörr Stiefenhofer Lutz ✪
Vejmelka & Wünsch, v.o.s. ✪
Vyskocil, Kroslak a Spol.

Firms are listed A-Z in tiers which are ranked in order of priority
✪ *Indicates firm displays contact details at the end of this chapter.*

a small number of them hold themselves out as specialists in the area. Whilst the majority of firms present in Prague will be capable of conducting dispute resolution work for their corporate clients when matters arise, the four firms in our top tier have dedicated teams.

At **Baker & McKenzie V.O.S.**, the contentious practice is run by partner Martin Hrodek. His work last year included advising insurance company CSOB Pojistovna in its successful defence of a CZK1bn arbitration claim initiated by an insurance broker. The practice also acts for Cesky Telecom.

Salans partners Marek Nosek and Alena Bányaiová provide dispute resolution advice. Nosek advised Biocel in proceedings before the Supreme Court of the Czech Republic and the Constitutional Court of the Czech Republic, while Bányaiová represented ON Semiconductor in litigation arising from a transfer of all assets and liabilities to the majority shareholders.

Weil, Gotshal & Manges represents Nomura in various arbitrations and litigation arising out of its failed investment in Investicni a postovni banka, and works for Czech gas pipeline operator CEPRO. The team also advised OSINEK in competition proceedings and investigations before the Czech office for the Protection of Economic Competition, and the European Commission.

At **White & Case**, practice head Monika Rutland represented Czech bank CSOB in a record-setting arbitration, where they won €640m. The eight-year case involved a dispute between the bank and the Slovak Republic regarding the breach by the Republic of an agreement signed in 1993 to restructure the bank in anticipation of its privatisation.

In our second tier, **Brzobohatý Broz & Honsa, v.o.s.**'s disputes team is headed by partner Frantisek Honsa. He works on commercial disputes in the Czech courts, arbitrations, and some criminal law.

Cermak Horejs Myslil a spol is a Czech firm with an unrivalled reputation for contentious intellectual property work.

At **Kocián Solc Balastík**, name partner Alexandr Kocián is highly regarded for litigation, arbitration and criminal law, and is a new entrant to our table.

PETERKA & PARTNERS v.o.s. acted for Czech bank PPF in a case relating to the takeover of IPB by CSOB, with state aid of between €3-€6bn. It also works for Czech manufacturer Lutos in litigation before the French courts over product liability. Name partner Ondrej Peterka is the best-known personality, specialising in French disputes.

Procházka Randl Kubr acts for its financial institution clients in litigation matters, and works for local operations of European insurers in insurance and reinsurance settlements.

The local office of US law firm **Squire, Sanders & Dempsey, v.o.s., advokátní kancelár** is home to partner Lubos Tichy, an international dispute resolution specialist.

In our third tier, **Allen & Overy, Praha Advokátní Kancelár** worked last year for a government agency suing for an unpaid bill of CZK99m under a commercial contract before the Czech Court of Arbitration, and advised the Czech subsidiary of an international media company in a dispute related to unfair competition acts by former employees.

Balcar Polanský Norton Rose has represented the administrators of both the major banks that have been forced into administration, Agrobanka and IPB, and last year advised on the liquidation of Union banka, and the related disputes.

CMS Cameron McKenna v.o.s.'s team specialises in media-related disputes, and advises the government and financial institutions in various contentious issues. The firm advised two individuals in arbitration with a large Swiss energy company, and the firm worked for Warner Bros on IP disputes following infringements in the Czech market.

Clifford Chance partner Vlad Petrus heads the firm's local litigation team, and has acted in intellectual property and unfair competition disputes in the last year.

Gide Loyrette Nouel advises companies including Candia, Beauté Prestige International and L'Oréal in litigation related to trade mark protection and infringement matters in the Czech Republic.

Glatzová & Co is a strong local Czech player which advises its core corporate clients when they are involved in contentious matters.

Linklaters in Prague works on commercial disputes and trade mark protection cases, arbitration, IP, banking and real estate litigation. The firm was hired by CKA to defend it in an arbitration initiated by what is now Vitkovice Holding, which was seeking the return of alleged unjustified enrichment. The defence was successful. The team, led by Luděk Vrána, also won two tenders to work for the Czech Republic in arbitration over alleged breaches of regulations on the protection of foreign investment.

Nörr Stiefenhofer Lutz won arbitration proceedings for four German distributors of Budweiser Budvar beer against the state-owned brewery regarding the invalidity of their termination of the distributors' agreements. The firm also works for Lekarny Lloyds in court proceedings against its former managing director.

Vejmelka & Wünsch, v.o.s. is a strong local firm working for international businesses in arbitration cases.

Vyskocil, Kroslak a Spol. is a leader in intellectual property work, and in Czech court litigation and libel work. The firm represents a number of high-profile individuals in libel matters against the Czech media.

REAL ESTATE AND CONSTRUCTION

The real estate market in the Czech Republic remains incredibly active, with both development programmes and FDI driving demand. **CMS Cameron McKenna V.O.S.**'s Prague managing partner, Hilary McDowell, is one of the biggest personalities in the country for such work, and advised a fund managed by TMW Pramerica Immobilien on the acquisition of two office buildings in Prague, one of which was home to the Prague Stock Exchange. The firm also worked for Orco on the construction aspects of two large residential projects in Prague.

Linklaters moves up into the first tier of our rankings for real estate this year, with partner Klára Štěpánková receiving plaudits in the market. She acts for major real estate clients including CGI, Invesco, iii fund, Immoeast, Ballymore and HVB Bank, and has also worked for large institutions like Czeck Railways and Komerčni banka on real estate projects.

Salans is now home to perhaps the biggest name in commercial property work in the Czech Republic, partner Evan Lazar, who used to practise at **Weil, Gotshal & Manges**. He works for AIG/Lincoln on development, construction, financing and leasing of The Park in Prague, and for GE Commercial Finance Real Estate, Heitman International and TK Development in the sale of the Euro Mall Brno Shopping Centre.

At **White & Case**, partner Monika Rutland is responsible for the real estate practice, and is advising the first Czech real estate investment funds, CEE Property Development Portfolio and Czech & Slovak Property Fund, on various

REAL ESTATE AND CONSTRUCTION

CMS CAMERON McKENNA V.O.S. ✪
LINKLATERS ✪
SALANS
WHITE & CASE

Allen & Overy, Praha Advokátní kancelár ✪
Baker & McKenzie V.O.S. ✪
Balcar Polanský Norton Rose
Brzobohatý Broz & Honsa, v.o.s. ✪
Clifford Chance
Glatzová & Co ✪
Havel & Holásek ✪
Peterka & Partners v.o.s. ✪

Lovells ✪
Procházka Randl Kubr ✪
Squire, Sanders & Dempsey, v.o.s., advokátní kancelár ✪
Weil, Gotshal & Manges ✪
Wolf Theiss ✪

Ambruz & Dark ✪
EY Law / Weinhold Legal
Gide Loyrette Nouel ✪
Giese & Partner
Gleiss Lutz ✪
Haarmann Hemmelrath ✪
Nörr Stiefenhofer Lutz ✪
Sodomka Soucek Jindra Mokry & Partners
Vejmelka & Wünsch, v.o.s. ✪

Firms are listed A-Z in tiers which are ranked in order of priority
✪ Indicates firm displays contact details at the end of this chapter.

transactions. The firm is also working for Doughty Hanson, the UK real estate developer, on a new office building development in Prague.

In our second tier, **Allen & Overy, Praha Advokátní kancelár** works for Skanska in relation to an acquisition of land in Prague, and also on real estate litigation. The team is advising several Japanese investors on greenfield investments in the Czech Republic, and is working for Norbrook Laboratories in its acquisition of a pharmaceutical production facility from Aliachem.

Baker & McKenzie V.O.S. is growing its real estate profile in the Czech Republic, and is increasingly representing developer clients. Last year the firm advised Cesky Telecom on its plan to divest €250m-worth of real estate, the biggest-ever such divestiture in the country. The team won new client Parkridge CE Developments, advising it on a distribution centre outside Prague.

Balcar Polanský Norton Rose represents clients on all sorts of real estate issues, ranging from due diligence to project financing and the drafting of construction agreements.

Brzobohatý Broz & Honsa, v.o.s. is a local Czech firm with a good reputation for real estate work.

Clifford Chance has a long-standing relationship with shopping centre developer Carrefour, but has in the last year diversified its client base into other areas, including winning work for CSOB on the sale and partial lease-back of eight office buildings in Prague. Other clients include ING Real Estate, IKEA, and Europe Capital Partners. The team is led by partner Emil Holub.

Glatzová & Co is a strong Czech firm, and advised Tesco on the real estate aspects of its acquisition of Carrefour hypermarkets last year.

Havel & Holásek has a six-lawyer real estate team, led by partner Jan Holásek. Clients include the Czech Airport Authority, the Czech Road Authority, British shopping centre developer Freeport, and Swedish construction company Skanska.

PETERKA & PARTNERS v.o.s. is a local firm that is advising a number of significant foreign investors in connection with real estate projects in the Czech Republic.

In our third tier, **Lovells** is a new addition to our table. Clients include Tesco, ING Real Estate Fund and Doughty Hanson.

Procházka Randl Kubr partner Daniel Rosicky leads his firm's property practice, which accounts for around 10% of its work. The firm is advising an international opportunity fund on the development of two logistics parks.

Squire, Sanders & Dempsey, v.o.s., advokátní kancelár's real estate practice is led by partner Radek Janecek, who works for owners, developers, and investors.

Weil, Gotshal & Manges retains a strong real estate practice, despite the departure of Evan Lazar to **Salans**. The firm worked for Goldman Sachs in its tender to buy the €300m property portfolio of Cesky Telecom.

Wolf Theiss advises major Austrian and German investors in real estate, including work for Immoeast Immobilien, which is listed on the Vienna Stock Exchange, on the acquisition of a real estate portfolio in Prague. The firm is also working for Irish real estate developer Parker Green on its first investment in the Czech Republic.

TMT

The telecommunications industry is one of the most active in the Czech Republic, and 2005 was a particularly busy year given the privatisation of Cesky Telecom and the sale of the country's mobile operator Oskar.

Law firms active in TMT in Prague cover three principal areas: regulatory work, including intellectual property work; transactions; and disputes. The team at **Baker & McKenzie V.O.S.** is led by partner Gabriela Vendlova, and is particularly active in the information technology arena. In 2005, Vendlova advised Czech bank CSOB on the acquisition of banking and software equipment from local manufacturer PVT, and worked for securities trading system UNIVYC on IT legislation aspects.

TMT

BAKER & McKENZIE V.O.S. ✪
CMS CAMERON McKENNA V.O.S. ✪
CERMAK HOREJS MYSLIL A SPOL ✪
KINES
WEIL, GOTSHAL & MANGES ✪

Allen & Overy, Praha Advokátní kancelár ✪
Balcar Polanský Norton Rose
Glatzová & Co ✪
Linklaters ✪
Procházka Randl Kubr ✪
Vyskocil, Kroslak a Spol.
White & Case

Brzobohatý Broz & Honsa, v.o.s. ✪
Havel & Holásek ✪
Squire, Sanders & Dempsey, v.o.s., advokátní kancelár ✪
Traplová Hakr Kubát Law and Patent Offices
Vejmelka & Wünsch, v.o.s. ✪

Firms are listed A-Z in tiers which are ranked in order of priority
✪ Indicates firm displays contact details at the end of this chapter.

CMS Cameron McKenna V.O.S.'s practice in Central and Eastern Europe is led by Peter Valert. The firm works for media companies entering the Czech Republic, like Motion Picture Association, Warner Brothers, and Universal Pictures. On the telecoms side, the firm advised Belgacom on its failed bid for Cesky Telecom, and for GMT Communications Partners, a private equity fund, on its attempted purchase of Aliatel.

Cermak Horejs Myslil a spol is a local Czech firm that is the leading one in the country for advising on patent and trade mark protection.

Kines was set up in 2004 by Stephen Kines as a specialist TMT firm, and covers the entire region from its Prague headquarters. The only such firm in the country, its focus saw it advise Microsoft on multiple projects across Central and Eastern Europe, and it worked for Vodafone on the bidding for its 3G licence.

Weil, Gotshal & Manges, through partner Karel Muzikár, has one of the best regulatory practices in the Czech Republic. The firm worked for Cesky Telecom in its privatisation and all of its other commercial activities, and worked for Karneval Media, one of the two largest Czech cable TV networks, on retail price legislation issues.

In our second tier, **Allen & Overy, Praha Advokátní kancelár** advised European Computer Systems on setting up a Czech subsidiary, worked for Virgin Enterprises in a domain name dispute, and acted for Lycos Europe, News International and Swisscom in the Czech Republic.

Balcar Polanský Norton Rose works for adidas, AIG and MCI WorldCom on TMT matters in the Czech Republic.

Glatzová & Co is a local firm that advised Aliatel shareholders on its sale, and is active in the deals and regulatory arena for telecoms companies.

Linklaters' TMT practice is incorporated into its corporate and M&A team, and partner-level expertise is offered from London. The firm works for Vodafone in the Czech Republic, and advised it on its acquisition of Czech mobile operator Oskar Mobil. It also advised ClearChannel buying InterKoncert's promotions business, and worked for BT, TeliaSonera and Microsoft on various regulatory, IT and corporate matters.

Procházka Randl Kubr has identified IT, IP and e-commerce as a growth area, and the firm is advising a leading mobile operator and a fixed-line operator in licensing and regulatory compliance.

Vyskocil, Kroslak a Spol. is a specialist in fields such as advertising, where it acts for Ogilvy & Mather, film rights, where it advises Universal Pictures, and music publishing rights, where clients include Sony BMG Entertainment, Universal Music and Warner Music.

White & Case's Czech TMT group is headed by Václav Jerman, and last year advised JP Morgan Securities leading a group of underwriters on the dual listing of Central European Media Enterprises on the Prague Stock Exchange, raising US$709m.

TAX

In tax, **White & Case** has the largest team of any law firm in the Czech Republic, with 11 fee-earners, many of whom joined from the local arm of Arthur Andersen. They are described by one client as 'definitely the best people in the Czech tax advisory market', and are led by partner Ales Cechel. The team is the only one at a law firm that competes with the Big Four accountants, and clients include CEZ, on acquisition-related tax advice, and Zentiva.

Linklaters partner Ton Kemp handles complex tax structuring on M&A, finance and real estate transactions, and also works on international tax planning issues for clients across the region. Last year the firm worked for Merrill Lynch and Global Steel Holdings on the tax aspects of Global Steel's €150m acquisition of Bulgarian steel company Kremikovtzi, requiring tax planning in Bulgaria, Luxembourg and the Netherlands.

At **Allen & Overy, Praha Advokátní Kancelár**, the team advised Deutsche Telekom on the implementation of an employee incentive scheme, and worked for JP Morgan arranging a €250m facility for Oskar Mobil, and a €325m high-yield bond issue by them. Other clients on the tax side include Credit Lyonnais and ICN Czech Republic.

Baker & McKenzie V.O.S.'s tax practice in Prague is run by Pavel Fekar, and the team has advised on the VAT consequences of payment cards, an analysis of the social security position of expatriates, and on the Czech tax aspects of emission trading and receivables trading.

Procházka Randl Kubr is a new addition to our table this year, having added a tax consulting practice with the hire of two new partners from Deloitte. Richard Svejda and Marek Moudry have arrived with their teams, having been responsible for Deloitte's FSI clients in the Czech Republic, and been technical advisers to the deputy finance minister of the Czech Republic in their previous positions. The firm can now offer all tax services, including corporate, personal and value-added tax expertise. Clients of the team include Barclays Capital, CAIB Corporate Finance, CP Leasing, Prague Airport, and Wood & Co.

TAX

WHITE & CASE

LINKLATERS ✪

ALLEN & OVERY, PRAHA ADVOKÁTNÍ KANCELÁR ✪
BAKER & McKENZIE V.O.S. ✪
PROCHÁZKA RANDL KUBR ✪

Haarmann Hemmelrath ✪
Nörr Stiefenhofer Lutz ✪
Salans

Firms are listed A-Z in tiers which are ranked in order of priority
✪ *Indicates firm displays contact details at the end of this chapter.*

ALFERY & PARTNER

VÁCLAVSKÉ NÁMĚSTÍ 40
110 00 PRAGUE 1

Telephone: +420 221 111 777
Fax: +420 221 111 788
E-mail: info@alferypartner.com
Website: www.alferypartner.com

Languages
Czech, English, German

Number of lawyers 10

CATEGORIES OF WORK

Corporate and commercial
Dr Cihláfi, Dr Brejcha

Intellectual property
Dr Hodková, Dr Cihláfi

Mergers and acquisitions
Dr Hrdina, Dr Brejcha

Litigation
Dr Hrdina, Dr Brejcha

Employment
Dr Hodková, Dr Krayzlová

Tax
Ing Alfery, Ing Mašek

Real estate, construction
Dr Hrdina, Dr Cihlář

E-commerce
Dr Hodková, Dr Krajzlová

Competition and EU
Dr Hrdina, Dr Brejcha

ALLEN & OVERY, PRAHA ADVOKÁTNI KANCELÁŘ

V CELNICI 4
5TH FLOOR
110 00 PRAGUE 1

Telephone: +420 222 107 111
Fax: +420 222 107 107
E-mail: information@allenovery.com
Website: www.allenovery.com

Languages
Czech, English, French, German, Japanese

Other offices
Amsterdam, Antwerp, Bangkok, Beijing, Bratislava, Brussels, Budapest, Dubai, Frankfurt, Hamburg, Hong Kong, London, Luxembourg, Madrid, Milan, Moscow, New York, Paris, Rome, Shanghai, Singapore, Tokyo, Turin, Warsaw

Number of lawyers 2,304
at this office 28

Contacts
Jane Townsend, Mikuláš Touška, Václav Valvoda, Jan Myška

CATEGORIES OF WORK

Arbitration/litigation
Jane Townsend, Mikuláš Touška

Insolvency/restructuring
Mikuláš Touška

Banking/finance
Mikuláš Touška, Václav Valvoda

Mergers and acquisitions
Jane Townsend, Jan Myška

International capital markets
Václav Valvoda, Mikuláš Touška

Private equity and venture capital
Jane Townsend

Corporate/commercial
Jane Townsend, Jan Myška

Privatisation
Jan Myška, Mikuláš Touška

Derivatives
Mikuláš Touška, Václav Valvoda

Project finance
Jane Townsend, Mikuláš Touška

Energy
Jane Townsend, Jan Myška

Real estate
Václav Valvoda, Ivan Telecký

EU and competition
Václav Valvoda, Jan Halama

Trade finance
Mikuláš Touška

AMBRUZ & DARK

ADVOKATI VOS

BUSINESS COMMUNITY CENTER
KATERINSKA 40/466
120 00 PRAGUE 2

Telephone: +420 251 152 911
Fax: +420 251 157 911
E-mail:
firstname.lastname@ambruzdark.com
Website: www.ambruzdark.com

Languages
English, German, French, Russian, Spanish

Other offices
Brno

Number of lawyers 19

Contacts
Vladimir Ambruz, Jan Spacil

Member
Landwell, correspondent law firms of PricewaterhouseCoopers

CATEGORIES OF WORK

Commercial and competition
Vladimir Ambruz, Jan Spacil

Financial services
Jan Spacil, Jiri Markvart

Corporate restructuring
Vladimir Ambruz, Jan Spacil

Intellectual property
Marketa Penazova, Klara Valentova

Dispute resolution
Ludvik Juricka, Jiri Markvart

Mergers and acquisitions
Vladimir Ambruz, Jan Spacil

Employment and human resources
Klara Novakova, Klara Valentova

Public law
Vladimir Ambruz, Jiri Markvart

EU law
Tomáš Babáček, Lukaš Poddaný

Real estate
Ludvik Juricka, Katerina Vyslouzilova

THE FIRM

Ambruz & Dark is a correspondent law firm of Landwell.

Landwell is one of the largest international law practices with 2,800 business and tax lawyers worldwide. Landwell provides a full range of legal services through specialists organised in global networks. Landwell's main focus is on cross-border M&A transactions and corporate transformation projects. Working closely with PricewaterhouseCoopers, Landwell is a market leader in the design and delivery of complex corporate change. This is achieved through a focus on strong local capabilities with a global outlook and by ensuring that its implementation skills match its legal ones.

AREAS OF PRACTICE

Landwell provides a full range of business law services, through specialist lawyers organised in global networks. In this way, consistent high standards of advice and service are guaranteed for both international and local clients. Landwell's international strengths include: legal consulting on mergers and acquisitions; corporate structuring; financial services; real estate; technology, media and communications; and employment law.

BAKER & McKENZIE v.o.s.

PRAHA CITY CENTRE
KLIMENTSKÁ 46
110 02 PRAGUE 1

Telephone: +420 236 045 001
Fax: +420 236 045 055
E-mail: office.prague@bakernet.com
Website: www.bakernet.com

Languages
English, French, German, Russian, Slovak, Spanish, Ukrainian

Other offices
The member firms of Baker & McKenzie International, a Swiss Verein, have 70 offices in 38 countries around the world. For a complete list, please visit www.bakernet.com.

Number of lawyers 3,300+
at this office 28

Contacts
Borys Dackiw, Alexandr César

CATEGORIES OF WORK

Arbitration and dispute resolution

Banking and finance

Bankruptcy and corporate restructuring

Capital markets

Competition law

Employment and labour law

General corporate and commercial

Information technology/ e-commerce

Intellectual property

Mergers and acquisitions

Private equity

Real estate and construction

Tax

Telecommunications

BRZOBOHATÝ BROŽ & HONSA

KLIMENTSKÁ 1207/10
110 00 PRAGUE 1

Telephone: +420 234 091 355
Fax: +420 234 091 366
E-mail: legal@bbh.cz
Website: www.bbh.cz

Languages
Czech, English, French, German, Russian, Slovak, Spanish

Number of lawyers 33

CATEGORIES OF WORK

Banking and finance
Tomáš Otruba

Capital markets
Tomáš Otruba

Mergers and acquisitions
Josef Brož

Dispute resolution
František Honsa, Vladimír Uhde

Commercial property and real estate
Jan Petřík

Insurance
Petr Mlejnek

Corporate and commercial
Jiří Němec

Insolvency and corporate restructuring
Josef Brož

Information technology
Jan Petřík

Competition
Jiří Němec

Fraud and white-collar crime
František Honsa, Vladimír Uhde

Media and entertainment
Vladimír Uhde

Energy and natural resources
Jiří Němec

ČERMÁK HOŘEJŠ MYSLIL A SPOL.

LAWYERS AND PATENT ATTORNEYS

NÁRODNÍ 32
110 00 PRAHA 1

Telephone: +420 296 167 111
Fax: +420 224 946 724
E-mail: intelprop@apk.cz
Website: www.cermakhorejsmyslil.cz

Languages
English, French, German, Russian, Slovak,

Number of lawyers 20

Contact
Dr Karel Čermák

Member
Interleges; AIPPI; LIDC; INTA; LES; TAGLaw

International groupings
In association with Bušová Ursínyová Bušö
Bratislava, Slovak Republic

CATEGORIES OF WORK

Intellectual property
Dr Karel Čermák, Dr Jan Matějka

Pharmaceuticals
Dr Karel Čermák Jr, Mgr Ondrej Cerych

Trade marks
Dr Jan Matějka, Kateřina Floriánová

Unfair competition
Dr Karel Čermák, Dr Lukáš Lorenc

Commercial/corporate
Dr Ing Richard Myslil, Dr Stanislav Myslil

Construction and tax
Dr Karel Čermák Jr

Mergers and acquisitions
Dr Karel Čermák Jr, Dr Ing Richard Myslil

Competition
Dr Ing Richard Myslil

Commercial litigation
Mgr Michal Hanko, Dr Stanislav Myslil

Dispute resolution – litigation and arbitration
Dr Karel Čermák Jr, Dr Stanislav Myslil

E-commerce and government business/regulatory
Dr Karel Čermák Jr

Antipiracy
Dr Antonín Křížek

Foreign direct investment and privatisation
Dr Stanislav Myslil

Information technology
Dr Karel Čermák

Insolvency, corporate restructuring
Dr Ing Richard Myslil

Labour law
Dr Ing Richard Myslil, Mgr Michal Hanko

Private client
Dr Jan Matějka

THE FIRM

The legal firmČermák Hořejš Myslil a spol. was established in 1990 but for over 40 years some partners of the firm have specialised in the fields of industrial and intellectual property law and international commercial law. The firm comprises approximately 20 in-house lawyers, four patent attorneys and approximately 40 specialised and administrative employees, including legal and technical translators and a number of experienced and specially educated (through the Institute of Industrial-Legal Education and Industrial Property Office) trade mark and patent officers.

Through its Slovak associates Bušová Ursínyová Bušo it provides all kinds of legal services in Slovakia.

AREAS OF PRACTICE

The firm has a long tradition and extensive experience in providing legal services in the fields of arbitration, industrial and other intellectual property law, commercial law, company law and foreign investment. In the patent area, it has experts in all technical fields, ranging from mechanical engineering to biotechnology. It also has experience in some specialised fields related to intellectual property, such as pharmaceuticals, foods tariffs, domain name disputes, and technical standards, including litigation. It is this tradition and experience that have made Čermák Hořejš Myslil a spol. one of the most highly demanded firms for representation within these legal fields by Czech and Slovak, as well as foreign and supranational, clientele.

CMS CAMERON McKENNA V.O.S.

KAROLINY SVETLE 25
110 00 PRAGUE 1

Telephone: +420 221 098 888
Fax: +420 221 098 000
E-mail: info@cms-cmck.com
Website: www.law-now.com

Languages
Czech, English, German

Other offices
Aberdeen, Bristol, Bucharest, Budapest, Edinburgh, Hong Kong, London, Moscow, Sofia, Warsaw

Number of lawyers 587
at this office 35

Contact
Hilary McDowell

International grouping
CMS Cameron McKenna is a member of CMS. CMS is the alliance of major European law firms providing clients with a full range of legal and tax services. CMS's activities are co-ordinated through EEIG, registered in Brussels.

CATEGORIES OF WORK

Real estate
Hilary McDowell, Iveta Placha

Telecoms
Ian Parker

Banking and finance
Paul Stallebrass

Litigation and arbitration
Peter Valert

Corporate
Ian Parker, Helen Rodwell

Technology
Peter Valert

Energy, projects and construction
Helen Rodwell

IP, media and entertainment
Peter Valert

e|n|w|c ATTORNEYS AT LAW

EISELSBERG NATLACEN WALDERDORFF CANCOLA V.O.S.

U PRAŠNÉ BRÁNY 1
110 00 PRAHA 1

Telephone: +420 224 819 216
Fax: +420 224 819 217
E-mail: prag@enwc.com
Website: www.enwc.com

Languages
English, French, German, Hungarian, Italian, Polish, Slovak

Other offices
Bratislava, Brno, Budapest, Vienna, Warsaw

Number of lawyers 47
at this office 11

Contacts
Dr Georg Walderdorff, Dr Erwin Hanslik

CATEGORIES OF WORK

Company and commercial

Banking and finance

Intellectual property

Labour and employment

Mergers and acquisitions

Real estate

International arbitration and litigation

Construction and building

EU and competition

DLA WEISS-TESSBACH

MÁNESOVA 5
120 00 PRAHA

Telephone: +420 224 234 413
Fax: +420 222 246 065
E-mail: prague@dlapiper.com
Website: www.dlapiper.com

Languages
Czech, English, French, German, Slovak

Other offices
Austria, Belgium, Bosnia-Herzegovina, China, Croatia, Denmark*, Egypt*, France, Georgia, Germany, Hong Kong, Hungary, Italy, Japan, Netherlands, Norway*, Poland*, Russia, Singapore*, Slovakia, South Africa*, Spain, Sweden*, Thailand, UK, Ukraine, United Arab Emirates, US

Number of lawyers 3,100
at this office 11

Contact
Jörg Nürnberger

Member
DLA Piper Group

CATEGORIES OF WORK

Corporate	Financing
Mergers and acquisitions	Real estate
Intellectual property	General commercial

THE FIRM

DLA Weiss-Tessbach was established in 1878 in Austria and is one of the longest-established law firms in the country. Since 1989, the firm has undergone a dynamic expansion across Central and Eastern Europe, growing from 15 to 100 lawyers and from one to seven offices, including Prague. DLA Weiss-Tessbach will continue to expand in the Central and Eastern European region as countries adjust to EU membership.

DLA Weiss-Tessbach is part of DLA Piper Rudnick Gray Cary, one of the leading global legal services organisations, with approximately 3,100 lawyers in 58 offices across 22 countries. The organisation is committed to building long-term relationships with its clients and supports their strategic and operational needs both locally and internationally.

AREAS OF PRACTICE

The firm has strengthened its core areas of expertise (commercial and corporate, M&A, banking and finance, general commercial law, real estate), and advises its clients as a full-service firm in all relevant areas of business law, including administrative law, employment law, IT and telecoms, technology, intellectual property, venture capital and capital markets.

DLA Weiss-Tessbach has well-established relations with clients of various backgrounds. The firm advises medium-sized enterprises as well as leading (often publicly listed) international and domestic industrial groups, service providers, banks and other financial institutions and individuals.

DLA Weiss-Tessbach has established a particular reputation for its ability to handle cases in international cross-border contexts. The firm is renowned for its expertise in the structuring and implementation of projects and transactions in the Czech Republic, as well as in other countries in Central and Eastern Europe. It carefully monitors the ongoing developments in the Central and Eastern European region with the aim of combining the needs of the constantly changing international legal market and industry, whilst also upholding the high standard of service that the firm has always been able to offer to its clients.

FELIX A SPOL.

U NIKOLAJKY 5
150 00 PRAGUE

Telephone: +420 251 081 111
Fax: +420 251 081 122
E-mail: akfelix@akfelix.cz
Website: www.akfelix.cz

Languages
Czech, English, German, Polish, Russian

Number of lawyers 22

International Groupings
Nomos Group

CATEGORIES OF WORK

Banking, finance, securities	Fraud and white-collar crime
Commercial property, real estate	Insolvency, restructuring
Competition and trade	Intellectual property and IT
Corporate and commercial	Mergers and acquisitions
Construction and building	Private client
Dispute resolution	Shipping and transport
Employment, pensions, benefits	Tax
Foreign direct investment	

GIDE LOYRETTE NOUEL

KRAKOVSKÁ 9
110 00 PRAGUE 1

Telephone: +420 222 871 111
Fax: +420 222 871 112
Website: www.gide.com
Email: gln.prague@gide.com

Other offices
Algiers, Beijing, Belgrade, Brussels, Bucharest, Budapest, Casablanca, Hanoi, Istanbul, London, Moscow, New York, Paris, Riyadh, Shanghai, Tunis, Warsaw

Number of lawyers 586
at this office 12

Contact
François Veit (veit@gide.com)

CATEGORIES OF WORK

Foreign investment	Real estate transactions and financing
Company law	Tax – customs law
Mergers and acquisitions	International trade
Restructuring	Intellectual property
Banking and finance	Labour
Joint ventures	Litigation and arbitration
Privatisation	Public law

GLATZOVÁ & CO

BETLÉMSKÝ PALÁC
HUSOVA 5
110 00 PRAGUE 1

Telephone: +420 224 401 440
Fax: +420 224 248 701
E-mail: office@glatzova.com
Website: www.glatzova.com

Languages
Czech, English, French, German, Russian, Slovak

Number of lawyers 26

CATEGORIES OF WORK

Utility law
Vít Horáček, Renáta Zbranková

Anti-monopoly
Vladimíra Glatzová, Vít Horáček

M&A
Vladimíra Glatzová, Dana Schweigelová

Labour
Renáta Zbranková, Marie Janšová

Banking and financial markets
Vladimíra Glatzová, Dana Schweigelová

General commercial
Vladimíra Glatzová, Renáta Zbranková

Telecoms and IT
Vít Horáček, Jindřich Jelínek

Insurance
Vladimíra Glatzová, Dana Schweigelová

Real estate
Vít Horáček, Gabriel Achour

Arbitration and litigation
Vít Horáček, Renáta Zbranková

Intellectual property
Vít Horáček

Construction
Renáta Zbranková, Gabriel Achour

THE FIRM

Glatzová & Co was founded in 1994 by Vladimíra Glatzová as a sole practice. The firm has since expanded to a team of 26 attorneys and has come to be regarded as one of the leading commercial law firms in the Czech Republic.

Described as a 'natural choice for domestic advice' in *Chambers Global* 2005, Glatzová & Co has won repeated praise for its work. In the on-line *Legal 500 – Europe, Middle East & Africa* and *IFLR Guide to the World's Leading International Business Law Firms*, as well as *Global Counsel 3000*, it is ranked as a recommended Czech firm in the areas of M&A, privatisation, real estate, joint ventures, banking and finance and capital markets. Its partners and senior associates are listed in other specialist publications among the world's leading lawyers in the areas of M&A, privatisation, real estate and corporate finance. The principal clients of the firm are major Western investors or their Czech subsidiaries across a diverse range of commercial sectors. The following entities are representative: ABB, Africa Israel Group, AIG, AstenJohnson, Buderus, Cinergy, Citibank, CTP Project Invest, E.ON, FCE Credit, First Reserve Corporation, Ford, Immorent ČR, Komerčni banka, Mondi, Hunter Douglas, Imperial Tobacco, Kolbenschmidt, Messer Group, Mittal Steel, Ondeo Services (formerly Lyonnaise des Eaux), Orco, Rockwool, Tesco, Volvo.

Glatzová & Co enjoys a reputation for the technical excellence of its lawyers, who are known for their sensitivity to clients' commercial objectives, their multi-jurisdictional experience and training and their strong links with major Western European and North American law firms. The firm boasts a number of high-profile specialists in the areas of Czech utilities law, banking and finance, IP law and litigation, real estate, privatisation and competition.

AREAS OF PRACTICE

The firm offers advice on cross-border and domestic transactions and operations to businesses, financiers, governmental bodies, international organisations and private individuals.

Glatzová & Co has an almost perfect track record in the handling of anti-monopoly/competition matters. It co-ordinated the Czech approval of a host of multinational mergers and also participated in the filing and defence of numerous complaints against competitors. In recent years, it has secured the domestic authorisation of mergers including Tesco/Carrefour; Hoechst AG/Rhone-Poulenc SA; Bayer AG/Hoechst AG/BASF AG; RWE AG/VEW AG; Brenntag AG/Stinnes AG; LNM Steel Group (now Mittal Steel)/Nová Hut' a.s.; Léčiva a.s./Slovakfarma a.s.; E.ON AG/Ruhrgas AS; and Claas KGaA mbH/Renault Agriculture SA. Glatzová & Co is active in regulatory issues in the telecom and energy sectors, including representation of alternative telecoms against the legacy provider and the issue of public subsidies across many commercial areas. It also counsels Ford and Volvo on the regulatory requirements for their distribution arrangements in the Czech Republic, including EU law compliance.

Glatzová & Co's attorneys are adept at managing all stages of M&A transactions. They have participated in the majority of significant privatisations in the Czech Republic, and are regularly retained to advise on the Czech law aspects of high-profile international transactions including deals across the steel, pharmaceutical, utilities and terrestrial, cable and satellite broadcasting sectors. The firm also provides advice on employment issues, business formation, licensing and IP protection, arbitration, litigation and compliance with filing and reporting obligations

The firm's construction and real estate practices represent international investors, architects, resort owners, construction companies, property developers and others in real estate acquisitions and sales, architectural and construction work, retail and leisure schemes, joint ventures, greenfield projects, leasing and related litigation. In the last year alone, Glatzová & Co has co-ordinated a number of key commercial, corporate, industrial and residential projects, including large-scale residential and shopping centre construction projects in Prague. The firm was also the first to introduce a legal framework for time-sharing schemes in the Czech Republic.

GLEISS LUTZ
RECHTSANWÄLTE

JUGOSLÁVSKÁ 29
120 00 PRAGUE 2

Telephone: +420 224 007 500
Fax: +420 224 007 555
E-mail: info@gleisslutz.com
Website: www.gleisslutz.com

Languages
Dutch, English, French, German, Italian, Polish, Portuguese, Russian, Spanish, Slovak

Other offices
Berlin, Brussels, Frankfurt, Munich, Stuttgart, Warsaw

Number of lawyers 225
at this office 19

Contact
Dr Martin Kubánek

CATEGORIES OF WORK

Czech, Slovak and international practice

Banking, securities and finance

Commercial law (general)

Companies, corporations

Competition, antitrust

Employment, labour

Environment and pollution control

Mergers and acquisitions

Tax

Trade marks, intellectual property

HAARMANN HEMMELRATH

PALÁC MYSLBEK
OVOCNÝ TRH 8
110 00 PRAGUE 1

Telephone: +420 224 490 000
Fax: +420 224 490 033
E-mail:
prague@haarmannhemmelrath.com
Website:
www.haarmannhemmelrath.com

Languages
English, French, German, Italian, Russian, Slovak, Vietnamese

Other offices
Bielefeld, Bucharest, Budapest, Düsseldorf, Frankfurt, Hamburg, Leipzig, Moscow, Munich, Paris, Shanghai, Warsaw

Number of lawyers 226

CATEGORIES OF WORK

Corporate and business law
Pavel Vincík, Arthur Braun

Mergers and acquisitions, reorganisations
Arthur Braun, Dr Thu Nga Haškovcova

IP, antitrust, EU, media
Arthur Braun, Tomas Cihula

Real estate transactions
Dr Thu Nga Haškovcova, Arthur Braun

Environmental and energy law
Pavel Vincík, David Vosol

Labour law
Dr Stepanka Wiesnerova

International tax law
Ian Rowbotham

Czech tax law
Jitka Kolarova, Ondřej Homolka

Corporate finance, banking, leasing
Dr Thu Nga Haškovcova, David Vosol

Computer/internet law
Hedvika Hartmanova

Litigation/arbitration
Hedvika Hartmanova

HAVEL & HOLÁSEK

TYN 1049/3
110 00 PRAGUE 1

Telephone: +420 224 895 950
Fax: +420 224 895 980
E-mail: office@havelholasek.cz
Website: www.havelholasek.cz

Languages
English, Czech, French, German, Italian, Russian, Slovak, Spanish

Number of lawyers 29

CATEGORIES OF WORK

Banking and finance
Jaroslav Havel, Robert Nešpůrek

Bankruptcy
Jaroslav Havel, Marek Vojáček

Corporate
Jaroslav Havel, Marek Vojáček

Commercial transactions
Jaroslav Havel, Robert Nešpůrek

Due diligence
Jaroslav Havel, Michael Mullen

EC law
Robert Nešpůrek

Economic competition
Robert Nešpůrek

Employment
Jaroslav Havel, Daniel Zejda

Engineering and construction
Jan Holásek, Josef Hlavička

Greenfield projects
Jan Holásek, Michael Mullen

Intellectual property
Robert Nešpůrek, Michael Mullen

Joint ventures and foreign investment
Jan Holásek, Michael Mullen

Mergers and acquisitions
Jaroslav Havel, Michael Mullen

Public private partnerships
Jaroslav Havel, Robert Nešpůrek

Public tenders and procurement
Jan Holásek, Daniel Zejda

Real estate
Jan Holásek, Michael Mullen

Securities
Robert Nešpůrek, Marek Vojáček

Telecommunications and media
Robert Nešpůrek

KONEČNÁ & ŠAFÁŘ

ŠIROKÁ 36/5
110 00 PRAGUE 1

Telephone: +420 221 990 455
Fax: +420 221 990 450
E-mail: praha@konecna-safar.com
Website: www.konecna-safar.com

Languages
English, French, German, Hungarian, Italian, Russian, Slovak, Spanish

Other offices
Bratislava

Number of lawyers 28

Contacts
Pavel Šafář, Radka Konečná

Member
American Law Firm Association; Association of European Lawyers; Czech Transportation Law Society; Geneva Group International; Association for Real Estate Market Development

CATEGORIES OF WORK

Corporate and commercial law
Klára Zemanová, Tomáš Zacha

Competition law
Tomáš Zacha

Mergers and acquisitions
Radka Konečná, Pavel Šafář

Project finance
Radka Konečná

Securities
Pavel Šafář

Restructuring and bankruptcy
Pavel Šafář

Real estate development
Radka Konečná

Commercial litigation
Ales Chamrád, Václav Beneš

Arbitration
Pavel Šafář, Tomáš Zacha

Shipping
Pavel Šafář

Debt collecting
Tomáš Zacha

Labour and employment
Klára Zemanová, Hana Ševelová

Intellectual property law
Hana Ševelová, Václav Beneš

Telecommunication
Hana Ševelová

Oil, gas and mining
Pavel Šafář

Tax advisory services
David Staněk, Milan Tomček

KOTRLÍK BOURGEAULT ANDRUŠKO

ADRIA PALACE - 5TH FLOOR
JUNGMANNOVA 31
110 00 PRAHA 1

Telephone: +420 224 990 000
Fax: +420 224 990 001
E-mail: pkotrlik@kotrlik.com
Website: www.kotrlik.com

Languages
Czech, English, French, German, Slovak

Number of lawyers 10

Contact
Petr Kotrlík

CATEGORIES OF WORK

- **Mergers and acquisitions**
- **Competition**
- **Litigation**
- **General corporate law**
- **Arbitration**
- **Joint ventures**
- **Privatisations**
- **Intellectual property**
- **Banking and capital markets**
- **International trade**
- **Project finance**
- **Telecommunications**
- **Energy and natural resources**
- **Real estate**
- **Environmental law**

KŘÍŽ & BĚLINA

DLOUHÁ 13
110 00 PRAHA 1

Telephone: +420 221 890 936
Fax: +420 224 819 343
E-mail: recepce@akkb.cz
Website: www.akkb.cz

Languages
Czech, English, German, French, Russian, Armenian

Number of lawyers 33

International groupings
Eurojuris

CATEGORIES OF WORK

Contracts
Miroslav Bělina, Petr Poledne

Company law
Miroslav Bělina, Žofie Chromcová

Copyright law, trade marks law, patent law and other intellectual and industrial property rights
Veronika Křesťanová, Tomáš Dobřichovský

Right of privacy and publicity, press law and media law
Jan Kříž, Josef Fiřt

Protection against unfair competition and the abuse of participation in competition
Jan Kořán, Tomáš Hejduk

Litigation
Petr Poledne, Tomáš Hejduk

Labour law (including collective bargaining), social security law
Miroslav Bělina, Bára Sadílková

Civil law, family law
Petr Poledne, Věra Zemanová

Administrative law
Jan Sviták, Zuzana Špírková

Tax law, finance law (including banking), law on foreign exchange and the application of customs regulation
Martin Bělina, Jan Sviták

Criminal law
Martin Rotta

LINKLATERS

PALÁC MYSLBEK
NA PŘÍKOPĚ 19
117 19 PRAGUE 1

Telephone: +420 221 622 111
Fax: +420 221 622 199
Website: www.linklaters.com

Languages
Czech, Dutch, English, French, German

Other offices
Amsterdam, Antwerp, Bangkok, Beijing, Berlin, Bratislava, Brussels, Bucharest, Budapest, Cologne, Dubai, Frankfurt am Main, Hong Kong, Lisbon, London, Luxembourg, Madrid, Milan, Moscow, Munich, New York, Paris, Rome, São Paulo, Shanghai, Singapore, Stockholm, Tokyo, Warsaw

Number of lawyers 2,000 worldwide

Contact
Jason Mogg

CATEGORIES OF WORK

Arbitration
Luděk Vrána

Banking and capital markets
Ondřej Žváček, Robert David

Commercial
Luděk Vrána

Competition/antitrust
Luděk Vrána, Daniel Čekal

Corporate reorganisations/ privatisations and foreign investment
Lukas Sevcik, Luděk Vrána,

Employment
Luděk Vrána

Energy
Kamil Blažek

Infrastructure/PPP
Kamil Blažek

Insolvency
Luděk Vrána

Insurance
Lukas Sevcik

Intellectual property
Karin Pomaizlová

Mergers and acquisitions/corporate
Lukas Sevcik, Luděk Vrána

Private equity/venture capital
Lukas Sevcik

Project finance
Jason Mogg

Real estate/construction
Klára Štěpánková, Bryan Wilson

Tax
Ton Kemp, Bohdana Pražská

Telecoms, media and entertainment
Hana Gawlasová

LOVELLS

SLOVANSKÝ DŮM
NA PŘÍKOPĚ 22
110 00 PRAHA 1

Telephone: +420 221 411 700
Fax: +420 224 210 004
E-mail: information@lovells.com
Website: www.lovells.com

Languages
English, French, German, Russian, Spanish

Other offices
Alicante, Amsterdam, Beijing, Berlin, Brussels, Budapest*, Chicago, Düsseldorf, Frankfurt, Hamburg, Ho Chi Minh City, Hong Kong, London, Madrid, Milan, Moscow, Munich, New York, Paris, Rome, Shanghai, Singapore, Tokyo, Warsaw, Zagreb*

Number of lawyers 1,600
at this office 25

Contact
Tomas Bettelheim

CATEGORIES OF WORK

Banking and capital markets

Dispute resolution

Intellectual property and competition issues

Mergers and acquisitions

Project finance

Technology transfers and franchising

Commercial and other real estate-related services

Environmental law and regulations

Joint ventures

Privatisation

Public tenders

NÖRR STIEFENHOFER LUTZ

NA PŘÍKOPĚ 15
110 00 PRAGUE 1

Telephone: +420 233 112 111
Fax: +420 233 112 112
E-mail: info@noerr.com
Website: www.noerr.com

Languages
Czech, English, German, French, Russian, Slovak, Spanish

Other offices
Berlin, Bratislava, Bucharest, Budapest, Dresden, Düsseldorf, Frankfurt, Moscow, Munich, New York, Warsaw

Number of lawyers 256
(+ 66 tax advisers, public accountants and tax assistants)
at this office 40
(36 locally, comprising 20 lawyers, 16 professionals in the tax and audit department and 4 attorneys in Munich and Berlin)

Contacts
Jaroslav Melzer, Libor Prokeš, Barbara Kusak, Roman Ženatý

CATEGORIES OF WORK

Arbitration and dispute resolution

Banking, project finance and capital markets

Energy

EU, antitrust and competition

General commercial practice

General corporate practice

Insurance

IP and unfair competition

Labour and employment

M&A, joint ventures, corporate reorganisations (MBO, MBI)

Media and entertainment

Pharmaceuticals

Private equity and venture capital

Privatisation, greenfield investment

Real estate, commercial property, construction

Tax

Telecoms and IT

PETERKA & PARTNERS v.o.s

NA PŘÍKOPĚ 15
110 00 PRAGUE 1

Telephone: +420 246 085 300
Fax: +420 246 085 370
E-mail: office@cabinet.cz
Website: www.cabinet.cz

Languages
Czech, English, French, German, Slovak, Spanish, Russian

Other offices
Bratislava

Number of lawyers 39
at this office 29

Contact
Ondřej Peterka

Member
TerraLex®; International Lawyers Network (ILN)

CATEGORIES OF WORK

Company and commercial
Ondřej Peterka

Mergers and acquisitions
Ondřej Peterka

Competition law
Ondřej Peterka

Real estate development and construction
Pavla Přikrylová

Litigation and arbitration
Jiří Černý

Intellectual property
Hynek Peroutka

Labour law
Hynek Peroutka

Securities and finance
Jan Liška

Tax law
Magdaléna Vyškovská

Bankruptcy law
Hynek Peroutka

IT, finance
Jan Liška

International law
Ondřej Peterka

European law
Hynek Peroutka

POKORNÝ, WAGNER & PARTNER

KAROLÍNY SVĚTLÉ 301/8
110 00 PRAGUE 1

Telephone: +420 224 229 287-9
Fax: +420 224 229 290
E-mail: office@p-w.cz
Website: www.p-w.cz

Languages
Czech, English, French, German, Slovak

Number of lawyers 30

Contacts
Radek Pokorný, Richard Wagner

CATEGORIES OF WORK

Banking and finance	Energy and natural resources
Capital markets	Intellectual property
Competition	Media and entertainment
EU law	Mergers and acquisitions
Corporate and commercial	Telecommunications
Litigation and arbitration	Due diligence

PROCHÁZKA RANDL KUBR

JÁCHYMOVA 2
110 00 PRAHA 1

Telephone: +420 221 430 111
Fax: +420 224 235 450
E-mail: office@prk.cz
Website: www.prk.cz

Languages
English, French, German, Russian, Slovak

Number of lawyers 50+

Contacts
Daniel Rosicky, Pavel Randl

Member
Lex Mundi; ius laboris, International Employment Law Pensions and Employee Benefits Alliance

CATEGORIES OF WORK

Banking	Bankruptcy and restructurings
Finance and capital markets	Telecommunications and media
Mergers and acquisitions	Litigation and arbitration
General corporate	Insurance and reinsurance
Real estate	Comprehensive tax practice
Labour and employment	Intellectual property

SQUIRE, SANDERS & DEMPSEY, v.o.s.,
ADVOKÁTNÍ KANCELÁŘ

VÁCLAVSKÉ NÁMĚSTÍ 57/813
110 00 PRAGUE 1

Telephone: +420 221 662 111
Fax: +420 221 662 222
E-mail: vpapirnik@ssd.com
Website: www.ssd.com

Languages
English, French, German, Polish, Russian, Slovak, Spanish, Swedish

Other offices
Beijing, Bratislava, Brussels, Budapest, Caracas, Cincinnati, Cleveland, Columbus, Hong Kong, Houston, London, Los Angeles, Miami, Moscow, New York, Palo Alto, Phoenix, Rio de Janeiro, San Francisco, Santa Domingo, Shanghai, Tallahassee, Tampa, Tokyo, Tysons Corner, Warsaw, Washington DC, West Palm Beach, Bucharest*, Buenos Aires*, Dublin*, Kyiv*, Milan*, Santiago*

Number of lawyers 800+
at this office 23

Contact Vladimira Papirnik

Member
American Chamber of Commerce;
Association for Foreign Investment;
Czech-French Chamber of Commerce

CATEGORIES OF WORK

Arbitration and litigation	**Joint ventures**
Banking and finance	**International transactions**
Bankruptcy and restructuring	**Labour and employment**
Competition law	**Mergers and acquisitions**
Corporate and commercial	**Project finance**
EU law	**Real estate**
Energy	**Telecoms**
Greenfield investments	**Venture capital**
Intellectual property	

THE FIRM

Founded in 1890, Squire, Sanders & Dempsey is a multi-jurisdictional law firm with approximately 800 lawyers practising in offices in Europe, the Americas and Asia. The firm's practice covers most substantive areas of the law, with an emphasis on business and finance matters.

The firm operates as a single global partnership, which ensures client accountability and the seamless delivery of uniformly high-quality legal services throughout the world. The firm's lawyers come from many countries and cultures, are licensed to practise in both common law and civil law jurisdictions, and communicate with clients in their native languages. Today, the firm remains committed to the fundamental principles ordained by its founders: to serve clients effectively and to maintain the professional standards that distinguish both the firm and its people.

Established in 1991, the Prague office provides a full range of legal services to Czech, foreign and multinational commercial clients. It maintains an extensive practice that utilises comprehensive international experience with essential local knowledge in a broad and varied transactional and financing practice. The office advises clients on complex transactions and restructurings in the Czech Republic and throughout Central and Eastern Europe, and works closely with the firm's Brussels and other Western European offices on matters involving EU law and the integration of the Czech Republic into the EU.

AREAS OF PRACTICE

The firm is organised around four major practice areas: advocacy, business, capital markets and regulated industries. Within these practice areas, the firm's work can be divided into numerous areas of specialisation, including banking, bankruptcy and restructuring, biotechnology and pharmaceuticals, communications, competition law, converging technologies, corporate, energy, environmental, healthcare, intellectual property, international dispute resolution, labour and employment, litigation, mergers and acquisitions, privatisations, project finance, real estate and securities.

The Prague office has extensive experience with foreign investment in the Czech Republic. It is one of the founding members of the Association for Foreign Investments, an organisation whose primary goal is to promote the Czech Republic abroad and to support CzechInvest, the Czech agency for foreign direct investment, in attracting foreign ventures. The office handles a variety of corporate matters and has extensive experience in the areas of privatisation transactions, mergers and acquisitions and greenfield investments, handling some of the most prominent transactions in the Czech Republic. In addition, the office's expansive real estate practice includes counselling foreign and domestic investors on a range of matters including acquisitions, financings and foreclosures.

In the financing field, the Prague office places a strong emphasis on lending and capital markets and represents clients including international lenders, borrowers, trustees, underwriters, credit enhancers, and national and multinational development organisations in transactions ranging from commercial loans to project financing and asset-backed financing.

The Prague office specialises in international litigation and arbitration, representing clients in bilateral investment treaty arbitrations as well as in commercial disputes under all leading institutional rules including the ICC, UNCITRAL, LCIA, Stockholm and Vienna Rules.

The firm's Prague lawyers are an integral part of the Czech legal community and are active in civic and business organisations including the American Chamber of Commerce in the Czech Republic.

VEJMELKA & WÜNSCH V.O.S.

ITALSKÁ 27
120 00 PRAHA 2

Telephone: +420 222 253 050
Fax: +420 222 253 090
E-mail: prague@vejwun.cz
Website: www.vejmelkawuensch.cz

Languages
Czech, English, German, Russian, Slovak, Swedish

Number of lawyers 23

Contacts
Josef Vejmelka, Petr Wünsch

CATEGORIES OF WORK

Corporate and M&A

Finance, banking and securities

Competition and trade

Intellectual property and IT

Tax

Real estate

Environmental planning and regulatory

Employment, pensions and benefits

Dispute resolution and arbitration

WEIL, GOTSHAL & MANGES

CHARLES BRIDGE CENTER
KRIZOVNICKÉ NÁM. 1
110 00 PRAGUE 1

Telephone: +420 221 407 300
Fax: +420 221 407 310
Website: www.weil.com

Other offices
Austin, Boston, Budapest, Brussels, Dallas, Frankfurt, Houston, London, Miami, Munich, New York, Paris, Providence, Shanghai, Silicon Valley, Singapore, Warsaw, Washington DC, Wilmington

Number of lawyers 1,200
at this office 29

Contact
Karel Muzikar (managing partner)

CATEGORIES OF WORK

Aviation	**Litigation, dispute resolution**
Banking and finance	**Mergers and acquisitions**
Bankruptcy and restructuring	**Private equity and venture capital**
Capital markets	**Privatisation**
Competition and regulatory	**Real estate**
Employment	**Telecoms**
IP and technology	

THE FIRM
Weil, Gotshal & Manges is a leader in the marketplace for sophisticated, international legal services. With more than 1,200 lawyers across the US, Europe and Asia, the firm serves many of the most successful companies in the world in their high-stakes matters and transactions. Weil Gotshal has built a world-class team of lawyers by pursuing a strategy of steady, purposeful growth. It continues to build upon a balanced platform of practices and locations without acquiring any debt. The firm's three primary departments – corporate, litigation/regulatory and restructuring – provide healthy diversification in all economic cycles, while its international expansion over the past decade has resulted in a quarter of the firm's lawyers now being in Europe.

AREAS OF PRACTICE
The firm's antitrust/competition practice advises on international M&A regulatory notifications, antitrust distribution counselling, cartels, litigation and government and state competition policy.

The corporate department is the firm's largest, with lawyers in the US and across Europe. The department advises international financial institutions and corporate clients in complex public and private mergers and acquisitions, private equity deals, strategic alliances and other commercial transactions.

The firm's corporate governance practice is recognised as the pre-eminent counsellor of corporate boards, management and institutional investors on the full range of governance issues, including board composition, structure and processes; executive and director compensation; director responsibilities, including in connection with mergers, spin-offs and other extraordinary transactions; internal and governmental investigations of alleged accounting or other corporate misconduct; and shareholder initiatives.

The firm is recognised as a market leader in the handling of complex and innovative finance transactions internationally. The firm advises on a wide range of financing activities and has particular expertise in acquisition finance, asset-based finance, debt re-structuring and insolvency, debt and equity capital markets, derivatives, high yield debt, securitisation, structured finance and telecom and multimedia financing.

The firm has a leading intellectual property and technology practice and advises a number of the world's major technology, media and telecommunications companies. It also acts for investors in technology, media and communications entities. The practice handles patent infringement, outsourcing transactions, strategic alliances, cross-border mergers and acquisitions, investments and IPOs. The firm advises on the protection and exploitation of IP and on a wide range of e-commerce matters including data protection. It has expertise in regulatory telecoms matters.

The firm's litigation practice advises international clients on all major areas of the law and has extensive experience in all aspects of dispute resolution. It advises clients in jury trials and appeals, as well as arbitration and alternative dispute forums.

The firm's real estate practice handles complex real estate transactions (including finance, securitisations, development, leasing, sales, acquisitions and debt restructurings) across the US and Europe. It also advises clients on real estate M&A transactions and transactions involving real estate investment trusts.

The firm has one of the largest, most broadly based bankruptcy and business reorganisation practices in the world. The department has been involved in virtually all major chapter 11 reorganisation cases in the US and in major national and international out of court debt restructurings.

The tax department provides advice to a broad range of international clients, covering many economic sectors. The department works closely with the firm's other departments to find innovative solutions to problems that present various and competing multidisciplinary considerations.

WOLF THEISS
ATTORNEYS AT LAW

KLIMENTSKÁ 10
110 00 PRAHA 1

Telephone: +420 251 018 611
Fax: +420 251 018 625
E-mail: praha@wolftheiss.com
Website: www.wolftheiss.com

Languages
Czech, German, English, French

Other offices
Belgrade, Bratislava, Bucharest, Ljubljana, Sarajevo, Tirana, Vienna, Zagreb

Number of lawyers 161
at this office 15

Contacts
Paul Sestak, Erik Steger, Lenka Smoliková, Pavel Marc, Rainer Frank, Jan Horký

CATEGORIES OF WORK

Arbitration, litigation, mediation	**Eastern Europe**
Banking, capital markets, securities, project finance, investment funds	**IT and IP**
Contracts	**Labour and industrial relations**
Corporate and M&A	**Real estate, construction and leasing**

THE FIRM

Wolf Theiss was founded in 1957 in Vienna, and today is one of the leading law firms in the CEE/SEE region. Over the past few years the firm has experienced extraordinarily dynamic growth, both domestically and internationally.

Wolf Theiss has established a network of nine offices* in Albania, Austria, Bosnia and Herzegovina, Croatia, the Czech Republic, Romania, Serbia and Montenegro, Slovakia and Slovenia. In 2005 alone, Wolf Theiss opened two new offices, in Bucharest and Sarajevo. The firm also regularly assists its clients with projects in Bulgaria, Hungary, Macedonia, Moldova, Poland, Turkey and Ukraine, in co-operation with local attorneys.

The firm's dynamic growth is also refelcted in its increase in personnel. At present, Wolf Theiss employs over 350 individuals at nine locations – compare this to 30 employees in one office, Vienna, ten years ago and the growth is apparent.

*The firm's operations in the various locations are set up in compliance with local law and the Bar rules requirements which include the form of co-operation with independent local attorneys.

DENMARK

Population	5.40 million
Number of lawyers	4,800
Professional title	Advokat
Currency	Danish Krone (DKr)

Index

Denmark is by far the smallest of the Nordic countries by land mass. It is also the most disparate, attached to Western Europe by the slenderest of peninsulas and spreading out over 400 islands, most of which lie in the straits between Sweden and Germany.

Funen and Zealand are the two largest islands, with the latter lying just off the coast of Sweden's southern tip. Copenhagen, Denmark's capital city is on Zealand. Odense, Denmark's third city is in Funen, whilst Aarhus, the second city is on the Jutland pennisula.

Culturally and economically, Denmark has strong ties to both Sweden and Norway. It also has a friendly but more competitive relationship with its former colonies Iceland and Greenland. Danes are a conscientious people enjoying one of highest rates of GDP per head in the world as well as being among the most energy-efficient.

BILLING

Billing rates remain relatively reasonable, with hourly rates ranging from about €375 to €400 for a senior partner and approximately €150 to €200 for a fully qualified assistant. Clients generally agree that Denmark's largest law firms, collectively known as the Big Four, are more expensive than their smaller rivals.

MARKETING

The Danish Bar Association forbids direct marketing to clients, although firms are otherwise allowed to advertise however they wish. Although the Danish market remains fairly conservative, in recent years more aggressive marketing efforts have come into focus, with some firms now beginning to advertise in newspapers, and hire external consultants. Nevertheless, the Danish business community is very close-knit and the need for marketing remains limited.

IN-HOUSE LAWYERS

Denmark has over 450 in-house lawyers and its largest companies generally maintain sizeable in-house teams. It is not uncommon for in-house lawyers to move into private practice and vice versa. Increasingly, firms are seconding lawyers to favoured clients and offering in-house counsel the opportunity to experience private practice.

ECONOMIC AND POLITICAL CLIMATE

Denmark is the world's 26th largest economy with GDP growing at around 3% in 2005 and predicted to grow at over 2.5% in 2006. Services account for 70% of the workforce and unemployment has been below the European average for a number of years. A stable 25% of the economy is devoted to the manufacturing sector. Overall, the economy has performed well for over a decade and the Danish current account has been in surplus since 1998.

The Danish Central Bank closely shadows moves by the European Central Bank, although the country remains solidly outside the Eurozone. Germany is Denmark's chief trading partner, followed by the UK and Sweden. Manufactured goods comprise the bulk of visible exports (75%).

As with other Nordic countries, government spending is relatively high, partly because of a large public sector, which employs almost one-third of the total workforce. The private sector is dominated by small and medium-sized enterprises (SMEs), with less than 12% of the work force employed by companies of more than 500 employees.

Denmark's right-of-centre government returned to power for a second term in 2005 following a general election early in the year. Prime Minister Anders Fogh Rasmussen continues to lead a minority coalition that comprises the Liberal Party and the Conservative Party but requires the support of the populist Danish People's Party to legislate.

LEGAL SYSTEM

Denmark's legal system is based on statute. Law school graduates must go through a three-year apprenticeship at a firm, followed by a Bar exam before they are granted admission by the Minister of Justice. There is no distinction between barristers and solicitors in Denmark, though to gain rights of audience before the High Court, lawyers must have experience in the District Courts. To appear before the Supreme Court requires at least five years of successful experience in the High Court, and the completion of an additional exam.

LEGAL MARKET

2005 was an excellent year for firms in Denmark as a reinvigorated M&A market fuelled confidence, profits and expectations across the board. The biggest debates of recent years, particularly those relating to conflicts of interest and the optimum size of firms in a small country, continued apace.

The largest firms

1	Bech-Bruun	250
2	Kromann Reumert	220
3	Plesner	150
4	Gorrissen Federspiel Kierkegaard	120
5	Dahl, Koch & Boll, Advokatfirmaet	95
6	Vingardshus, Advokaterne	90
7	DLA Nordic	75
	Lett Law Firm	75
9	Poul Schmith Law Firm	71
10	Delacour	52
11	Accura Advokataktieselskab	45
12	Jonas Bruun	41
13	Lind Cadovius	40
14	Hjejle Gersted Mogensen	38
	Rønne & Lundgren	38
16	Plougmann & Vingtoft	36
17	Mazanti-Andersen, Korsø Jensen & Partnere	35
18	Focus Advokater LLP	34
	MAQS Advokatbyrå	34
20	Tommy V Christiansen, Advokatfirmaet	31
21	Philip & Partners	28
22	Lund Elmer Sandager	27
23	Norsker & Co. Law Firm	25
	Osborne Clarke	25
25	Bang + Regnarsen	24

These figures represent the total number of lawyers in this country only, and have been supplied by the firms themselves. The figures should be accurate as at 1 January 2006.

If there was ever pressure on the Big Four firms – **Bech-Bruun**, **Kromann Reumert**, **Plesner** and **Gorrissen Federspiel Kierkegaard** – to downsize then this was only slightly in evidence. Instead, smaller firms such as **DLA Nordic**, **Accura Advokataktieselskab** and **Lett Law Firm** were clearly intent on growing as fast as possible. How to recruit quality lawyers in a small market is perhaps the biggest issue facing every firm.

The Big Four continue to dominate all aspects of the market, employing approximately as many lawyers between them as the next fifteen commercial firms combined.

Bech-Bruun and **Kromann Reumert** are by far the biggest firms, with the former having over 240 lawyers in Denmark. It is noticeable that these two firms have not grown much in recent years and many suspect that **Plesner** and **Gorrissen Federspiel Kierkegaard** are at a more sensible size.

Bech-Bruun, in particular, witnessed the departure of some leading partners in 2005, with brothers Jacob and Michael Vinther, and Jon Dyhre Hansen all leaving for **Accura Advokataktieselskab**; a massive coup for the 50-lawyer firm. A fourth senior partner Poul Hvilsted departed for **DELACOUR**, an Aarhus firm beginning to make a name in Copenhagen

Rumours and worries about conflicts of interest at the Big Four have been a popular topic in the mainstream Danish press for the last two years. In general, **Bech-Bruun** is regarded as being most at risk having grown more quickly, through more mergers than its rivals (approximately seven in the last fifteen years alone) and consequently having inherited a wider client base. But in reality, conflicts are a daily problem for any large firm in a country as small as Denmark and all the largest firms admit to being hampered by the situation.

In the eyes of many, **Kromann Reumert** is said to have the best brand of any firm in Denmark. However, this has not stopped it saying goodbye to highly prized names, including over six partners and senior associates to **Rønne & Lundgren** in recent years.

When faced with the need to refer large matters elsewhere, it is not uncommon that a big firm might have to ask four, five or even six other firms before finding one that is not conflicted. In extreme cases, such as the recent sale of Chr Hansen, which attracted upwards of 15 bidders, companies have been forced to go without local legal advice being unable to find any capable firm that is not already engaged. To many of the leading firms this state of affairs is to Denmark's shame.

That the Big Four are often conflicted is of direct benefit to a second tier of smaller but highly capable home-grown firms, including **Jonas Bruun**, **Lett Law Firm**, **Lind Cadovius**, **Accura Advokataktieselskab** and **Nielsen & Nørager**.

Among this second tier there are significant differences in strategy. **Accura Advokataktieselskab** has grown from 30 to 50 lawyers in less than one year, and is perhaps the most talked-about firm in Denmark at the moment with its punchy, transaction-heavy approach. **Lett Law Firm** also attracts attention, following a series of mergers, which has seen it push the 100-fee-earner barrier. **Lett Law Firm** has ambitions to form a Big Five although it has not yet achieved the international capability or corporate base to merit that status.

At the other end of the scale, **Jonas Bruun** and **Hjejle Gersted Mogensen** are highly traditional practices with fewer than 40 lawyers but widely respected for their quality. **Jonas Bruun**, in particular, which has never made a lateral hire nor lost a partner, remains the first choice for the Big Four when conflicted on a transaction.

In the eyes of clients the only difference between the Big Four and the second tier is that the larger firms are able to offer a faster and more efficient service around the clock, as and when the client needs it.

Finally, other firms worthy of special mention in 2005 include **Bender von Haller Dragsted**, which was the result of a merger between niche IT-practices *Advokatfirmaet Bender.dk* and *von Haller Law Firm.*

Finally, 100-lawyer **Poul Schmith Law Firm** is the Kammeradvokaten (primary adviser to the Danish State) and is commended by peers for its skills in all practice areas.

REGIONAL FIRMS

With the exception of **Plesner**, all the Big Four firms have sizeable offices in Aarhus, Denmark's second city. However, the opportunities for growth outside of Copenhagen are limited and in recent years it is notable that Aarhus' two largest home-grown firms, **Abel & Skovgård Larsen Advokatfirma** and **DELACOUR**, have both established a presence in the capital.

Elsewhere, **Lett Law Firm** deliberately shunned Aarhus and acquired the Kolding office of **Dahl, Koch & Boll Advokatfirmaet** in 2004, which is in a highly industrial region of Jutland known locally as 'The Triangle'. No other firm has followed its lead, although the **Dahl, Koch & Boll Advokatfirmaet** network maintains four offices across Jutland. **Focus Advokater LLP** is based in Odense.

ACCOUNTANCY-LINKED FIRMS

There are no accountancy-linked firms in Denmark, although **Rønne & Lundgren**, formerly part of the *Andersen Legal* network, maintains a close but informal relationship with Deloitte & Touche.

FOREIGN FIRMS

As a whole, Denmark has largely been overlooked by foreign firms. The country has few of the attractions of Sweden such as large multinational companies and plentiful natural resources. A DKK1bn (€134m) deal is very large by Danish standards but much less interesting to firms used to deals of £1bn (€1.45bn) in London. **Eversheds Advokataktieselskab** and **Osborne Clarke** are the only two foreign firms to venture into Denmark and they maintain only small offices in the country.

FOREIGN OFFICES AND LINKS

Few Danish firms have rigid ties with firms abroad, because there is generally not enough work flowing into Denmark from one source to warrant such an alliance. The Big Four do not choose to work exclusively with London's Magic Circle but will court the top twenty or so London practices. As a member of the *DLA Group*, **DLA Nordic** (formerly *Lindh Stabell Horten* in Denmark) is the only firm able to claim exclusive ties. It markets itself as a pan-Scandinavian law firm, with integrated offices in Norway, Denmark and Sweden.

MAQS Advokatbyrå also has offices in Sweden, Poland and Estonia and an exclusive alliance with Finnish firm **Krogerus Attorneys Ltd**.

Philip & Partners has a long history of co-operation with **Baker & McKenzie**, though the relationship is not exclusive.

As part of the *Scandinavian Law Alliance*, **Kromann Reumert** has strong links with fellow members **Thommessen Krefting Greve Lund** and **Vinge**, two of the top firms in Norway and Sweden respectively. This is by no means an exclusive relationship, and if a client requires it they will work with other Scandinavian firms. The Alliance also benefits from shared offices in Brussels and London. **Kromann Reumert** is also a member of *Lex Mundi*.

Bech-Bruun has had a small office in Moscow since 1996, when it opened it at a client's behest.

Several mid-sized firms have offices in Germany. **Bang + Regnarsen** boasts a five-lawyer office in Hamburg, as well as a strategic alliance with German firm **Schlawein Naab Partnerschaft** and a co-operativie agreement with Sweden's **Danowsky & Partners Advokatbyrå**. Odense-based **Focus Advokater LLP** also has a Hamburg practice called **Dänische Advokaten** as well as an exclusive relationship with France's **Cabinet Shefet**.

BANKING AND FINANCE

There is a limited market for banking and finance in Denmark, with the Big Four dominating whatever work is available. However the banks themselves tend to have large in-house teams that will undertake the most specialised work themselves. The banks also stipulate that most of the work in this sector be governed by English law and therefore the most lucrative and complex deals are often passed to London firms. With this in mind some of the Big Four have been active in recruiting UK and US lawyers.

BANKING AND FINANCE

BECH-BRUUN ✪
GORRISSEN FEDERSPIEL KIERKEGAARD
KROMANN REUMERT ✪
PLESNER ✪

Accura Advokataktieselskab ✪
DLA Nordic ✪
Eversheds Advokataktieselskab
Jonas Bruun ✪

Lett Law Firm ✪
Lind Cadovius ✪
Nielsen & Nørager ✪

Firms are listed A-Z in tiers which are ranked in order of priority
✪ *Indicates firm displays contact details at the end of this chapter.*

Seven partners comprise **Bech-Bruun**'s banking and finance team, which is a subset of the capital markets group, headed by Steen Halmind. More than any other firm, **Bech-Bruun** is able to claim serious international credibility owing to the 2004 arrival of UK solicitor Ian Tokley from **Herbert Smith LLP**, where he had been a senior finance partner. Tokley was made up to partner at his new firm in 2005 and in tandem with Halmind was active for Barclays Capital in a number of leading transactions including acting for Barclays Capital in €1.5bn syndicated financing of DONG (Danish Oil and Natural Gas), for lenders Citigroup and Goldman Sachs in the €4bn acquisition of ISS, and for JP MorganChase in a US$31bn financing of Danske Bank. A number of private equity houses also use the firm, as do **Clifford Chance**, **Linklaters** and **Cravath, Swaine & Moore LLP**.

Approximately one-tenth of **Gorrissen Federspiel Kierkegaard**'s fee-earners are employed by a finance department that has long been viewed by many as the leader. In the eyes of peers it 'continues to make very good running'; an opinion that is well-substantiated by a deal list that includes advice to CVC Capital partners, purchasers of a DKK1.27bn (€170m) stake in Post Danmark, and advice provided to lender HSH Nordbank on two deals worth close to DKK1.5bn (€201m) in total. It also advised buyers EQT and Goldman Sachs on their financing of the DKK22bn (€2.9bn) purchase of ISS, the biggest transaction of 2005. 'Razor-sharp' Herman Federspiel and Henrik Lind are senior figures in the industry, with Michael Steen Jensen also recommended.

Kromann Reumert's banking group is regarded as 'excellent' by peers and clients alike with Kim Rasmussen attracting the highest praise. A strong blue-chip client base means that the firm is often seen on the borrower side, acting for ISS in 2005 as well as TDC, the recipient of a €650m syndicated facility. On the lender side, it is noticeably strong among Scandinavian banks, counting Carnegie, Sydbank, Nordea, HSH Nordbank and FIH Erhvervsbank as regular clients. 2005 also found the firm working with **Allen & Overy LLP** advising a trio of international lenders on a DKK2bn (€268m) multi-currency revolving facility for Tryg Vesta; and acting alone for two Scandinavian banks as lead arrangers in a €455m refinancing of Denmark's Nycomed.

International clients declare themselves to be very pleased with **Plesner**'s 'sophisticated' banking group which 'possesses a better commercial sense than most other firms we know'. Caspar Münter, Thomas Maaberg Hansen and Jørgen Permin are the most frequently cited names, awarded 'high marks' by clients and peers. Permin has a good reputation in acquisition finance, having acted for EQT Partners and Altor Equity partners as purchasers in two deals worth DKK2.3bn (€308m) and for Danish-listed Contex Holding, in its purchase of a Massachusetts printer for US$77m. Asset-based and project finance are other areas in which the firm excels, being particularly active in the shipping and aviation sectors.

In line with its burgeoning reputation for M&A, **Accura Advokataktieselskab** is increasingly recognised for its finance capabilities, particularly acquisition finance. Claus Bennetsen is the leading figure and he is supported by new partner Kim Toftgaard. Both were employed by the likes of Svenska Handelsbanken, RBS, and Blackstone in 2005. When advising the latter **Accura Advokataktieselskab** worked closely with **Ashurst**.

DLA Nordic is hailed for its 'quality and international standards', especially in regard to leveraged buyouts where Søren Thyssen Valerius impresses. 'Straightforward' Valerius was hired from **Kromann Reumert** in 2004 and has rapidly built a team to rival the top tier, as was demonstrated in early 2005 when the firm was appointed to HSH Nordbank's panel alongside **Kromann Reumert** and **Gorrissen Federspiel Kierkegaard**. HSH wasted no time in instructing the firm to advise on its role as lead counsel to the agent and arranger of a €600m financing facility in connection with Nordic Capital's acquisition of Falck. Similar transactions could be quoted for Danske, Nordea and FIH Erhvervsbank.

Transaction finance is a leading strength of **Eversheds Advokataktieselskab** where Vibeke Krag and Troels Askerud garner respect for their skills. A small team on the ground in Copenhagen is supported by a wider network international transaction team, which can be called upon to assist, as it did in 2004 when the firm advised buyer Svenska Enskilda Banken on the DKK2.7bn sale of Codan Life and Pension. Clients declare themselves to be 'very satisfied' with this set-up. ABN Amro and Ikano are also clients.

Both of Scandinavia's two largest banks, Nordea and Danske, employ the services of **Jonas Bruun**, which has a greater history of acting in specialised and complex finance transactions than any other second-tier firm. It advised financial institution Danish Ship Finance on its conversion from a foundation to a limited liability company and offer of DKK1.1bn (€147m) worth of shares to investors. Per Magid and Henrik Dahl are the leading names.

Lett Law Firm has a range of domestic litigation, outsourcing and finance work for financial institutions, some of which are drawn from the firm's leading insurance practice. Chairman Soren Jenstrup is active for Nykredit, Denmark's largest mortgage provider in disputes with shareholders, whilst Eurohypo is an important client of the Kolding office, which provides advice on real estate finance.

Hans Madsen of **Lind Cadovius** offers specialist securitisation and SPV products to clients such as Nordea. His colleague Frantz Palludan is more finance orientated, although this is not a huge source of work for the firm.

Nielsen & Nørager has niche expertise in the foundation and financing of private equity funds and some experience of advising larger lenders such as Nordea and JP Morgan. Morten Eldrup-Jørgensen is by far the best-known name. Arne Gerlyng-Hansen has departed the firm to become CEO of a Danish company, leaving his work in the hands of associates Thomas Weisbjerg and Jan Presfeldt.

Also recommended for advice to smaller Danish banks and financiers are Henning Hansen at **Philip & Partners**; **Hjejle Gersted Mogensen**; and **Mazanti-Andersen, Korsø Jensen & Partnere**, where J Korsø Jensen is highly recommended for his work in Jutland.

CAPITAL MARKETS

There is considerable expectation about the prospects for capital markets work in 2006, with a number of new listings being mooted. Flickers of the anticipated activity were apparent in 2005, which saw two IPOs and a healthy increase in secondary offerings. That said, the work remains concentrated in the hands of a specialist few.

With the market still not back to full fitness it was always going to be difficult for **Bech-Bruun** to reach the same heights in 2005 as it did in the summer of 2004 when it was active in four transactions valued at at least €10bn in total. Most prominent in 2005 were two rights issues in the domestic market by Pharmexa and Bavarian Nordic in which Jørgen Reimer Jensen advised ING Bank and Nordea Corporate Finance respectively. However, in anticipation of good times, Steen Halmind has increased the size of his team to nine partners by introducing corporate partner Peter M Andersen as back-up to N E Nielsen who heads a listed company practice. International securitisation expert Ian Tokley remains the firm's wildcard on the global scene.

Klaus Søgaard of **Gorrissen Federspiel Kierkegaard** is highly regarded for his securities law expertise and draws on the firm's strength in the banking arena to consistently attract some of the biggest deals. Highlights of 2005 included advice provided to the managers on a US$3bn EMTN issue by Jyske Bank; advice provided to KomunneKredit on its issue of CHF200m (€130m) fixed-rate notes; and to the managers of a €1.8bn bonds issue by the Danish Government.

CAPITAL MARKETS

BECH-BRUUN ✪
GORRISSEN FEDERSPIEL KIERKEGAARD
KROMANN REUMERT ✪
PLESNER ✪

Accura Advokataktieselskab ✪
DLA Nordic ✪
Jonas Bruun ✪
Nielsen & Nørager ✪

Firms are listed A-Z in tiers which are ranked in order of priority
✪ *Indicates firm displays contact details at the end of this chapter.*

Kromann Reumert had a sterling 2005 and some rivals now concede its position as 'number one'. Following the firm's work at the Copenhagen Stock Exchange for Group 4 Falck in 2004, spring 2005 found partner Marianne Philip in the same place delivering advice to Pharmexa and Bavarian Nordic on their rights issues. In the summer Philip had to be accompanied by half-a-dozen other partners, including Jørgen Kjegaard Madsen and Carsten Fode, in order to provide advice on various matters relating to a public tender, a de-listing, a secondary offering and the sale of shares in Post Danmark. Finally, autumn brought the biggest transactions of all as Caroline Pontoppidian worked with **Weil, Gotshal & Manges**, London, advising TrygVesta on its IPO, the biggest in Denmark for ten years; and Madsen was appointed to act for Copenhagen Airports, the subject of a prominent public offer.

Working closely with **Davis Polk & Wardwell**, **Plesner** advised the underwriters in the TrygVesta IPO. It also won two important instructions from DONG, advising first on its receipt of a €1.5bn syndicated loan facility and second in connection with its issue of Luxembourg-listed Eurobonds and hybrid securities nominally worth a total of €1.6bn. Jørgen Permin remains the lead name, although Thomas Maaberg Hansen, adviser to HSH Nordbank as arranger of two Danish bond listings, is also recommended. Catherine Kendal Tholstrup and senior associate Anna Iversen run a derivatives practice.

As capital markets activity has increased so too has **Accura Advokataktieselskab**'s work in this area and it now enters the table for the first time. It was counsel to Enskilda Securities for the public offering by SparNord Bank. It is especially active in listings of structured bond products.

DLA Nordic is another new entrant, having significantly increased its capital markets activity, not least owing to historic ties to the municipalities involved in the sale of major energy companies. A strong lender-orientated finance practice adds weight here, as does Dan Moalem's venture capital practice.

Jonas Bruun is counsel to the Danish Ministry of Finance in the ongoing privatisation of state energy company DONG, which is set to result in the biggest IPO in Danish history. The firm is also the preferred choice of some banking clients for verification of prospectuses.

Unusually for a Danish firm, capital markets work is a substantial portion of **Nielsen & Nørager**'s business, which is heavily involved in an active biotech sector that often requires fund-raising advice. Private equity houses investing in this sector are also important clients. As the smallest firm in the table **Nielsen & Nørager** is inevitably not leading in the biggest transactions but Morten Eldrup-Jørgensen's 'technical and thorough approach' wins plaudits. Verification of prospectuses is another a source of work.

CORPORATE AND COMMERCIAL

Bech-Bruun is the biggest firm by headcount in both Copenhagen and Aarhus and it is the principal adviser to AP Møller Mærsk, Denmark's largest listed company. Size is beneficial to its international standing with **Bech-Bruun** the best-known of all Danish firms beyond Scandinavia. Size was also a necessity for any firm handling the massive global requirements of the Chr Hansen sale in 2005 and the AP Møller Mærsk merger in 2003, both of which it did. Significantly, it is the most cosmopolitan firm in Denmark, employing Swedish-, German-, US-, UK- and Canadian-qualified lawyers and English is the official language of the firm.

Like **Bech-Bruun**, **Gorrissen Federspiel Kierkegaard** is also well known for the quality of its international links, which it has built up over many years. It is a frequent recipient of work from some of the leading firms around the world, including **Slaughter and May**, **Herbert Smith LLP** and **Davis Polk & Wardwell**. Perhaps because of this **Gorrissen Federspiel Kierkegaard** has traditionally been home to a more international client base than its peers, with German supermarket Lidl being a relatively new addition. Although it is the smallest of the Big Four, its expertise in cross-border transactions, finance and shipping is universally respected.

Kromann Reumert, Denmark's second-largest firm, is known for the unrivalled quality of its corporate client base, which reads like a roll-call of Denmark's leading brands: ISS, Novo, TDC, Carlsberg, Danisco, DONG, Vestas and Copenhagen Airports. Clients are impressed by the 'corporate-like' way in which the firm operates although, in common with the rest of the Big Four, this has not stopped a trickle of senior staff leaving for smaller firms, most visibly to

CORPORATE AND COMMERCIAL

BECH-BRUUN ✪
GORRISSEN FEDERSPIEL KIERKEGAARD
KROMANN REUMERT ✪
PLESNER ✪

Accura Advokataktieselskab ✪
DLA Nordic ✪
Hjejle Gersted Mogensen
Jonas Bruun ✪
Lett Law Firm ✪
Lind Cadovius ✪
Nielsen & Nørager ✪
Philip & Partners ✪

Mazanti-Andersen, Korsø Jensen & Partnere ✪
Rønne & Lundgren ✪

Delacour ✪
Eversheds Advokataktieselskab
Focus Advokater LLP ✪
MAQS Advokatbyrå
Osborne Clarke

Lassen Ricard ✪
Lund Elmer Sandager
Norsker & Co. Law Firm

Firms are listed A-Z in tiers which are ranked in order of priority
✪ *Indicates firm displays contact details at the end of this chapter.*

Rønne & Lundgren. Overall in 2005 **Kromann Reumert** increased its stature and strength in the market.

Plesner operates from a single Danish office and with 130-lawyers is often considered by observers of the market to have achieved a better size than the rest of the Big Four. International clients are unanimous in praising the firm for the 'high quality' of its work, and it is noticeable that many clients also cite the speed at which the firm responds to requests. Transactional work remains an important driver of growth overall, although the firm offers a full service to clients, including Siemens, GE group companies, Telenor and Le Meridien Hotels. Steen E Christensen is chairman of the board of directors of Nykredit Group.

Managing partner Kåre Stolt has engineered impressive growth at **Accura Advokataktieselskab**, which has grown from 30 to 50 lawyers in one year. Nor has this growth been mere ballast, with the arrival of partners Michael Vinther, Jacob Vinther and Jon Dyhre Hansen (all from **Bech-Bruun**) bearing testament to excellent quality and ambition at the firm. **Accura Advokataktieselskab** continues to be best known for M&A, real estate and tax but it also maintains a wider corporate following that includes domestic clients Carlsberg, Coloplast, Logstor and Vestas; and multinationals Coca-Cola, ChevronTexaco, Arriva, Unilver and Vivendi.

Copenhagen Energy is an important and active client of **DLA Nordic**'s 15-fee-earner corporate team, which was instructed to advise it on corporate restructuring worth more than €2.7bn. Public-sector and energy companies are an important source of work, as is the biotech sector, private equity funds and Rolls-Royce. Nicolai Horten is noted as head and Dan Moalem for 'drive and energy'.

Hjejle Gersted Mogensen is a commercial firm that is highly respected for a strong tradition. Following the promotion of two associates and a merger with a small professional indemnity firm, there are now 16 partners at the firm. Søren Lehmann Nielsen is the contact.

Jonas Bruun is a traditional 40-lawyer firm that in the eyes of peers has 'really got its strategy right'. A mix of foreign and domestic clients, including longstanding relationships with leading Danish banks, government institutions and energy-sector corporates, coupled with a universally acknowledged reputation for 'quality and professionalism' means that the firm is never short of work. Although all the lawyers at the firm work in various disciplines, Mogens Ebeling and Henning Aasmul-Olsen are most readily identifiable here.

If the top tier of firms is traditionally collectively known as the 'Big Four' the swelling of **Lett Law Firm** to nearly 100 lawyers has made it increasingly difficult to identify the leaders by size alone. Though it has not yet the international reach or longstanding reputation of these firms, it is its avowed ambition in the long-term to be seen as a member of a 'Big Five'. Litigation, insurance, and administrative law are leading disciplines and Volvo, Danish State Railways and NyKredit are leading clients.

Lind Cadovius mixes regular commercial work with a shot of larger transactions. It is firmly embedded in the second tier of firms behind the so-called Big Four, being the perfect size to win referrals from them as well as to attract long-term loyalty from mid-sized Danish companies.

Danish medium-sized businesses are a fountain of work for 17-lawyer **Nielsen & Nørager**, though larger clients such as Michelin also provide regular instruction. In academic terms, the firm stands apart from competitors in that two of its practising partners are doctors of law and one is a professor of law. Partners Eigil Lego Andersson and Olaf Andersen are recommended. Morten Eldrup-Jørgensen is chair of *Uni Law*, an alliance that also includes the UK's **Taylor Wessing**.

Corporate and commercial remains the mainstay of **Mazanti-Andersen, Korsø Jensen & Partnere**'s business, which also includes white-collar crime. Clients are typically in the construction and banking sectors.

Thirty-eight lawyer **Rønne & Lundgren** made significant strides forward in 2005 in establishing itself as a real estate- and M&A- focused firm of 'genuine good quality' and it now rises one tier. It has hired an impressive clutch of senior associates and partners from **Kromann Reumert** in recent years as it seeks to bolster its credentials across the board. It maintains a close but informal relationship with Deloitte & Touche. WPP is a client for corporate matters.

New entrant **DELACOUR** traditionally derived most of its work from SMEs in Jutland, prior to opening an office in Copenhagen in 2003 with the intention of growing a practice of similar proportions in Zealand. Although determinedly a full-service firm, it has identified IP, M&A, transport and public procurement as leading strengths.

Eversheds Advokataktieselskab has niche corporate finance capability that belies its size, as well as tax, employment and banking practices. Troels Askerud is responsible for corporate matters.

Full-service **Focus Advokater LLP**, Funen's most famous firm, has followed the lead of other regional practices in opening an office in Copenhagen. This is the firm's third office with one partner also based permanently in Hamburg. A close alliance with France's **Cabinet Shefet** in Paris and Nice is also of note. In addition to a growing real estate business, Funen's world-class greenhouse industry is a source of work.

Thirty-five lawyer **MAQS Advokatbyrå** has big ambitions to raise the profile of its office in Denmark, and achieved a measure of success in this regard in 2005. EU and competition, shipping, insurance and IP are particular focus areas, though a full service is offered.

Peers state that it is 'impossible to discount' **Osborne Clarke**'s position in the market although with only three partners on the ground in Copenhagen it is limited in the services it can offer. Managing partner Anders Hansen is the most readily identifiable figure.

Steen Lassen of **Lassen Ricard** has been appointed to represented Danish Prime Minister Anders Fogh Rasmussen in connection with investigations being made by the Danish Minister of Justice and parliament.

DISPUTE RESOLUTION

The Danish court system roughly breaks down into three tiers: district courts, high courts, including the Eastern High Court (Østre Landsret) and the Western High Court (Vestre Landsret), and at the top, the Supreme Court (Højesteret). Added to these there are specialised courts such as the Labour Court and the Maritime and Commercial Court. It should be noted that 100-lawyer **Poul Schmith Law Firm** which works almost exclusively as prosecutor for the State, and is hence not included here, is widely regarded as among the best litigation firms in Denmark.

Litigation is a growing business at **Gorrissen Federspiel Kierkegaard**, which dedicates 12 partners to the area, although only four of these are Copenhagen based. It was the first of the Big Four firms to create a specialised disputes group with Arne Bierfreund, Axel Kierkegaard and Henrik Christup comprising a trio of senior stars.

DISPUTE RESOLUTION

GORRISSEN FEDERSPIEL KIERKEGAARD
HJEJLE GERSTED MOGENSEN
LETT LAW FIRM ✪
PLESNER ✪

BECH-BRUUN ✪
JONAS BRUUN ✪
KROMANN REUMERT ✪
LIND CADOVIUS ✪
MAZANTI-ANDERSEN, KORSØ JENSEN & PARTNERE ✪
PHILIP & PARTNERS ✪

DLA Nordic ✪
Dahl, Koch & Boll, Advokatfirmaet
Johan Schlüter Law Firm ✪
Nielsen & Nørager ✪
Norrbom & Vinding Law Firm, member of ius laboris ✪
Norsker & Co. Law Firm
Osborne Clarke
Tommy V Christiansen, Advokatfirmaet
Viltoft & Høberg-Petersen ✪

Firms are listed A-Z in tiers which are ranked in order of priority
✪ *Indicates firm displays contact details at the end of this chapter.*

Oluf Engell of **Hjejle Gersted Mogensen** is one of the most highly-rated litigators of his generation. The firm's disputes group is widely billed as its premier department and it can only have been strengthened by a merger with legacy *Fisch-Thomsen & Partners*, a four-partner firm best known for professional indemnity.

Lett Law Firm has long possessed a specialised litigation department that, in addition to the tax and insurance litigation in which the firm excels, has acted in some of Denmark's most prominent cases. Most of note is Rene Offersen's ongoing role as defence counsel to politician Peter Brixtofte in a highly publicised case concerning allegations of abuse of power. Offersen also recently acted with Jesper Lett in a Supreme Court case for TDC, whilst Georg Lett acted in two asset stripping claim cases; the first for seller Nordea and the second in the Supreme Court against LGT Bank Liechtenstein.

Clients cite **Plesner**'s 'excellent strategies' as a selling point of its eight-partner litigation group, which has expertise in insurance, construction, IP, tax and competition. Torben Bondrop, Michael Rosenmejer and Michael Rekling are three of the best-known names, whilst Peter Fogh and Peter Wengler- Jørgensen are recognised international arbitrators. There are also five qualified mediators at the firm.

Bech-Bruun has specialist litigators in employment, insurance, maritime, taxation and IT, and is experienced in arbitration. There is no single partner in charge of litigation overall but Morten Ulrich, Jes Anker Mikkelsen and Carsten Pedersen are most prominent. Ulrich recently successfully represented the personnel of Squadron 722 of the Danish Air Force in a Supreme Court case against the Ministry of Defence.

Per Magid, **Jonas Bruun**'s 'excellent' senior litigator, represented the Russian Federation in the Danish High Court in relation to registration of title to immovable properties formerly held by the Soviet Union. A clutch of other partners offers litigation and arbitration expertise.

Following the lead of its competitors, **Kromann Reumert** has moved towards the formation of a distinct disputes group. Mogens Skipper-Pedersen is the partner charged with the task of forming the team. He can call on good resources across the firm, with clients especially citing Erling Borcher for his 'success' as an IP litigator and employment litigator Claus Juel Hansen as 'an excellent lawyer and one of Denmark's finest'.

Lind Cadovius is justifiably proud of a strong litigation tradition, which continues to see the department play a leading role in life at the firm, even as other firms have downscaled their capabilities. Håkon Djurhuus is recommended for real estate disputes and as an arbitrator; Mats Berendt for white-collar crime; Jess Thierson for tax litigation; and Nicolai Westergaard for employment.

J Kørso Jensen of **Mazanti-Andersen, Korsø Jensen & Partnere** maintains a leading name for litigation and arbitration, particularly construction and white-collar crime.

It is a requirement of being a partner at **Philip & Partners** that a lawyer is also admitted to the Supreme Court and it is expected that all partners appear before this court at least five times during their career. Mogens Gaarden, a leading representative of the State in Surpeme Court cases is one of the best-known. The arrival of Steen Rode from **Poul Schmith Law Firm** adds significant strength in employment disputes.

Lars Carsten heads a litigation group at **DLA Nordic** comprising 15 fee-earners, spread across all of the firm's departments. Lawyers at the firm make regular Supreme Court appearances.

Partners Jacob Norager-Nielsen, Eigil Lego Anderson and Michael Wiisbye are all Supreme Court Advocates at **Nielsen & Nørager**. It recently defended a leading Danish business magazine from libel charges.

Advokatfirmaet Tommy V Christiansen is included because of the pre-eminence of name partner Tommy V Christiansen in tax litigation, whilst **Viltoft & Høberg-Petersen** is unrivalled in construction litigation.

EU AND COMPETITION

Though the Big Four are dominant it is difficult for them to maintain full-time practices in this area because of a limited market.

EU AND COMPETITION

KROMANN REUMERT ✪

BECH-BRUUN ✪
GORRISSEN FEDERSPIEL KIERKEGAARD
PLESNER ✪

Hjejle Gersted Mogensen
Jonas Bruun ✪
Lett Law Firm ✪
Lind Cadovius ✪
MAQS Advokatbyrå
Nielsen & Nørager ✪

Accura Advokataktieselskab ✪
DLA Nordic ✪
Mazanti-Andersen, Korsø Jensen & Partnere ✪
Viltoft & Høberg-Petersen ✪

Firms are listed A-Z in tiers which are ranked in order of priority
✪ *Indicates firm displays contact details at the end of this chapter.*

When the work is available **Kromann Reumert** is able to provide by far the largest dedicated EU and competition practice in Denmark, calling on the services of a mammoth 15-lawyer team. A number of competitors note that the firm is 'without doubt number one' and clients speak positively of its abilities, of which less than half are directed towards transactional support. Jens Munk Plum heads a department that also includes Morten Kofman and Erik Mohr Mersing, a specialist in UK- and US-related competition matters. The firm shares a Brussels office with its colleagues in the *Scandanavian Law Alliance*.

Bech-Bruun boasts involvement in every dawn raid issued by the Danish Competition Board in 2005, and advised leading heating and sanitation company Bravida in relation to an investigation into cartel activity in the industry. Peter Stig Jakobsen and Simon Evers Hjelmborg comprise a two-partner team, which also represents Viasat, Telia Sonera, and DSB, the latter in public procurement.

'Leading individual' Jan-Erik Svensson continues to head **Gorrissen Federspiel Kierkegaard**'s EU and competition team, which was fully active in support of the firm's impressive activities on the transactional side. Associate Martin Dittmer is recommended as 'up and coming'.

Karen Dyekjær of **Plesner** is cited by peers as 'a leader in her field' and she is well supported by Katja Høegh who receives the 'highest recommendation' from clients impressed by her 'deep knowledge, analytical skills and easy-to-understand conclusions'. Høegh filed a complaint for Gråhundbus to the Danish Competition Commission against DSB.

Hjejle Gersted Mogensen boasts long experience of competition law and merger notifications. It has represented foreign clients before the ECJ.

According to the market **Jonas Bruun** offers the most direct challenge to the four leaders in this field. The bulk of its work is transactional support though it also attracts large cases on a standalone basis. Not least of these is Jeppe Skadhauge and Olaf Koktvedgaard's work as counsel to TV2 in proceedings before the European Commission.

EU and competition at **Lett Law Firm** is divided into four areas: public procurement; competition; food and medicines regulation; and free movement of goods. It is perhaps best known for public procurement where it has a strong client base of Danish municipalities. In competition, Georg Lett has been counsel to Feta cheese in a long-running series of cases before the European Court of First Instance and European Court of Justice. Susie Ekstrand heads the niche food and medicine practice.

Competition was originally a small support function for **Lind Cadovius**' M&A group but in the past two years it has seen significant growth. Work for Post Danmark is largely responsible, with the newly privatised company employing its advice on public procurement matters. Lotte Hummelshøj and Søren Zinck are the names to note.

The arrival of partner Thomas Ryhl from **Plesner** has seriously strengthened **MAQS Advokatbyrå**'s EU and competition practice, earmarked as an area ripe for rapid growth. Ryhl joins an internationally focused team that acted for Scandinavian ferry company Scandlines on an investigation by the Danish competition authorities, and for various publishing houses in a case before the European Commission.

Henrik Peytz, cuts a well-known figure at **Nielsen & Nørager**, which as Danish counsel to Michelin is frequently engaged by the French company to advise on competition matters. Peytz also has a leading media following.

Jesper Fabricius, who joined **Accura Advokataktieselskab** from **Lett Law Firm** in early 2005 has one of the best reputations of any competition lawyer in Denmark, especially for public procurement. Although his practice at **Accura Advokataktieselskab** remains young he has established a solid client following that includes the municipalities of Copenhagen and Frederiksberg, Arriva and Logstor.

Lise Groesmeyer builds on **DLA Nordic**'s traditional strength in the public sector to provide public procurement advice. Groesmeyer supports competition specialist Andreas Christensen, formerly of **Bech-Bruun**, who demonstrates 'commitment and dedication'.

Kirsten Frijs is the primary contact for competition law matters at **Mazanti-Andersen, Korsø Jensen & Partnere** which represents Danish clients in relations with the Danish competition authorities and litigates in competition-related disputes.

EMPLOYMENT

NORRBOM & VINDING LAW FIRM, MEMBER OF IUS LABORIS ✪

BECH-BRUUN ✪

DLA Nordic ✪
Elmer & Partnere, Advokatfirmaet
Kromann Reumert ✪
Lind Cadovius ✪
Plesner ✪
Schebye & Jacobsen, Advokatfirmaet

Accura Advokataktieselskab ✪
Eversheds Advokataktieselskab
Gorrissen Federspiel Kierkegaard
Jonas Bruun ✪
Lett Law Firm ✪
Mazanti-Andersen, Korsø Jensen & Partnere ✪
Philip & Partners ✪
Poul Schmith Law Firm
Rønne & Lundgren ✪

Firms are listed A-Z in tiers which are ranked in order of priority
✪ *Indicates firm displays contact details at the end of this chapter.*

EMPLOYMENT

Employment law is a growing concern for firms in Denmark although international clients express concern that the country lags some way behind other Western jurisdictions.

Few firms attract as many superlatives as employment boutique **Norrbom & Vinding Law Firm, member of ius laboris**, 'variously described as 'the out-and-out leader' and 'five years ahead of everyone else'. Established in 1998, the six-partner firm acts exclusively for management in both the public and private sectors and successfully represented Dansk Supermarket before the Supreme Court in a case concerning the right to wear headscarves at work. Some of Denmark's leading corporates, who would ordinarily use only the biggest firms, retain this firm on all employment law matters. Mariann Norrbom is internationally renowned and, in 2006, assumes the chair of the IBA's employment committee, a rare honour for a Danish lawyer. Jørgen Vinding is also recommended.

Martin Ulrich heads a quartet of partners at employer-focused **Bech-Bruun**, which 'has good people in the hardcore areas of employment law', including managing partner Lars Svenning Andersen and Bjarke Vejby. Both Vejby and Ulrich attract the highest praise for their work which includes advice to TDC, Maersk, IBM, and Novo Nordisk, among others. The firm is particularly well known for its public-sector work and advises the City of Copenhagen.

Finn Schwarz heads a specialised and broad-skilled employment group at **DLA Nordic**, which works closely with colleagues in Sweden and Norway to provide clients (generally employers) with a pan-Scandinavian service. Clients include Scientific Atlanta, Motorola, Danish employment law group SITA, Chubb and Mattel; the latter being attracted to the firm by the employment group alone.

Niche employment practice **Advokatfirmaet Elmer & Partnere** acts solely for employees and trade unions.

Clients of Claus Juel Hansen, co-head of **Kromann Reumert**'s employment practice praise his 'exceptional service and responsiveness' and 'would not hesitate to recommend him'. Stock options, benefits and major disputes are areas in which he excels. Hansen is 'ably supported' by Helene Amsinck who has been active for key client DONG in relation to all of its consolidation activity.

Nicolai Westergaard at **Lind Cadovius**, a permanent judge in Denmark's Labour Court, is also a noted talent for advice to trade unions and employees. Demonstrating impressive ability to cater for all parties in the labour market, Westergaard's colleague Birgette Horn is active for employers.

Plesner is 'doing a good job and going in the right direction' under the headship opf Tina Reissmann who presides over a 'fresh and energetic team'. The firm does not yet have the long-established reputation of some of its peers but increasingly wins challenging mandates for the likes of LEGO, Bonnier Group and Coca-Cola.

Advokatfirmaet Schebye & Jacobsen is another niche employee and trade union firm that is based in Aarhus and Copenhagen. Ulla Jacobsen in Aarhus and Karen-Margrethe Schebye in Copenhagen are contacts.

Accura Advokataktieselskab continues to build its practice, which initially existed to provide support on the transactional side but is now beginning to win work on a stand-alone basis. Anne Katherine Schøn heads a three-lawyer team that acts for Air France, Canon and KLM.

Hans Juhler continues to develop a practice at **Eversheds Advokataktieselskab**, recently assisting a much larger firm on HR due diligence for a large transaction.

Five lawyers comprise an employment team at **Gorrissen Federspiel Kierkegaard**, which is primarily engaged on transactional support work. Anne Birgett Gammeljord is the head.

The arrival of recommended employment specialist and litigator Steen Rode from **Poul Schmith Law Firm** has bolstered **Philip & Partners**' employment credentials. Rode is active for public and private-sector clients.

New entrants **Jonas Bruun** and **Lett Law Firm** also have small employment teams, as does **Rønne & Lundgren** where compliance programmes are an important source of work.

ENERGY
JONAS BRUUN ✪
KROMANN REUMERT ✪
BECH-BRUUN ✪
DLA NORDIC ✪
GORRISSEN FEDERSPIEL KIERKEGAARD
LETT LAW FIRM ✪
LIND CADOVIUS ✪
PLESNER ✪
Philip & Partners ✪

Firms are listed A-Z in tiers which are ranked in order of priority
✪ *Indicates firm displays contact details at the end of this chapter.*

ENERGY

The energy sector has long proved a lucrative source of work in Denmark and 2005 was no exception. In particular, the largest energy company, state-owned Danish Oil and Natural Gas (DONG), grew larger still when it acquired much of the recently privatised electricity industry (though still subject to EU competition authority approval at the time of writing). Renewable energy sources are also popular in Denmark, which boasts approximately one windmill per 1000 head of population.

Peers regard Claus Høeg Madsen and **Jonas Bruun** as 'standing out in regards to insight into gas and electricity regulatory issues'. Besides **Kromann Reumert**, **Jonas Bruun** is the firm most frequently identified by peers and clients as identifiable with quality energy-sector advice. Madsen advised the Ministry of Finance, owner of DONG, in relation to the latter's acquisitions and has assisted electricity company NESA on pricing disputes. Other clients include Energi E2, Naturgas Fyn and the Danish Competition Council.

Clients regard **Kromann Reumert** as 'some way ahead of the pack,' not least because it has long been the primary adviser to DONG on corporate matters. This year, it is elevated one tier not only on the strength of its unmatched transactional achievements in the gas, electricity and wind sectors but also owing to recommendations for its regulatory expertise. Anders Stubbe Arndal is consistently singled out by energy-sector clients for the 'brilliance of his M&A and energy expertise'.

Per Hemmer heads **Bech-Bruun**'s energy team, which spans both the Copenhagen and Aarhus offices. Gas and electricity are the leading areas of expertise.

Clients express 'happiness' with **DLA Nordic**'s services, which cater for electricity, heating, water, and gas industry bodies in both transactional and regulatory matters. Klavs Gravesen is the commanding presence in a team that has built up plenty of expertise as the primary adviser to Copenhagen Energy for many years, although its recent purchase by DONG may require that the firm further branch out. New partner Søren Hornbæk Svendsen, who arrived from an in-house position at DONG in late 2005, may be the answer here, already winning the firm a first instruction from his former employer. Other clients include NESA, E.ON and Dansk Energi.

Gorrissen Federspiel Kierkegaard continues as lead counsel to Elsam in relation to the proposed merger with DONG, now pending before European competition authorities. Jan-Erik Svensson is on the board of the Danish Association of Energy Lawyers.

Legacy *Lett, Vilstrup & Partnere* was the traditional counsel for Royal Dutch Shell in Denmark and this work has now passed to **Lett Law Firm**, adding an international aspect to a strong domestic practice. Heating and electricity are areas of specialisation with the firm receiving increasing instructions from Energi E2 as well as continuing to act for distribution companies Energi Fyn, TRE-FOR and RAVDEX.

When not using **Kromann Reumert**, **Lind Cadovius** is the first port of call for DONG, which has employed the firm for over two decades. 'One of Denmark's top three energy lawyers,' Hans Madsen is renowned for his gas purchase abilities.

Gas and electricity distribution companies are the primary source of work for **Plesner**, which is also a recipient of instructions from DONG. No single partner is employed full time in this sector, with the firm drawing on different departments to provide corporate, competition, litigation and, increasingly, regulatory advice. For example, IT partner Michael Rekling acted for gas transmission company Gastra in connection with its merger with electricity transmission companies; and corporate partners Poul Flemming Hansen and Caspar Munter assisted electricity distribution company SEAS-NVE on the divestiture of a 25% shareholding in Energi E2 to DONG.

Philip & Partners enters the table on the back of Jesper Rothe's work for Vattenfall, which has a high-profile contract with DONG to acquire electricity production capacity. Russian wholesalers DFN Oil and Staroil are also clients.

ENVIRONMENT

Despite the departure of leading public law advocate Poul Hvilsted, **Bech-Bruun** continues to retain a leading individual in the shape of Henriette Soja. Soja is assisted by two other partners in a projects-orientated team that acts for Copenhagen Harbour and the constructor of the underground train to the new Ørestad development.

Mogens Moe, who joined **DLA Nordic** from **Plesner** in 2002, remains one of the foremost environmental law lawyers in Denmark. Moes is one of eight partners in a public law group that draws on **DLA Nordic**'s historic ties to Danish municipalities, including the City of Copenhagen.

ENVIRONMENT
BECH-BRUUN ✪
DLA NORDIC ✪
LETT LAW FIRM ✪
LIND CADOVIUS ✪
MAZANTI-ANDERSEN, KORSØ JENSEN & PARTNERE ✪
PLESNER ✪
Delacour ✪
Kromann Reumert ✪

Firms are listed A-Z in tiers which are ranked in order of priority
✪ *Indicates firm displays contact details at the end of this chapter.*

Clients cite Moe's 'long experience of Danish environmental law' as a key selling point.

Legacy *Lett, Vilstrup & Partnere* had a leading reputation for environmental law owing to the expertise of 'highly specialised' Vivi Bruhn Knudsen, and this has now been assumed whole into **Lett Law Firm**. It has an enviable client base acting for insurance companies and energy companies and, most impressively, Royal Dutch Shell, which uses the firm exclusively.

Litigator and environmental law specialist Håkon Djuurhus of **Lind Cadovius** enjoys a 'very high standing' in the market. He also teaches environmental law on behalf of the Danish Bar Association.

Mazanti-Andersen, Korsø Jensen & Partnere's former chairman of the Danish Association of Environmental Law Birgitte Refn Wenzel has concentrated on environmental law for over a decade and is thus one of the most experienced practitioners in what remains a relatively new field.

Plesner rises one tier on the strength of the work of Søren Stenderup Jensen and a team of eight lawyers that is particularly active in environmental matters relating to the life sciences and pharmaceuticals industries. Much of the practice is litigation based.

Poul Hvilsted, formerly of **Bech-Bruun** and now of **DELACOUR**, is also recommended for his environmental expertise, particularly on zoning disputes. He won a landmark decision over a department store in Jutland.

Aarhus associate partner Kim Trenskov has a good reputation and is the primary name to note at **Kromann Reumert**. Partner Jørgen B Jepsen also attracts praise, although he is only engaged in this area for a small part of his time.

IT AND E-COMMERCE

Denmark has few world-beating companies of which to boast and has therefore identified knowledge and services, particularly IT-related, as a potential selling point.

No other lawyer in Scandinavia wins as much praise for their outsourcing skills as Ole Horsfeldt

IT AND E-COMMERCE

BECH-BRUUN ✪
BENDER VON HALLER DRAGSTED ✪
KROMANN REUMERT ✪

ELVANG & PARTNERE, ADVOKATFIRMAET

DLA Nordic ✪
Nielsen & Nørager ✪
Plesner ✪

Accura Advokataktieselskab ✪
Dahl, Koch & Boll Advokatfirmaet
Gorrissen Federspiel Kierkegaard
Johan Schlüter Law Firm ✪
Lett Law Firm ✪
MAQS Advokatbyrå
Philip & Partners ✪
Poul Schmith Law Firm
Rønne & Lundgren ✪

Firms are listed A-Z in tiers which are ranked in order of priority
✪ *Indicates firm displays contact details at the end of this chapter.*

at **Bech-Bruun**, who is regularly name-checked by firms across the Nordic region. Horsfeldt is co-head of a team that also includes Janne Glæsel and Niels M Andersen. It was active on two projects for AP Møller-Mærsk in 2005; the first an outsourcing of requirements to IBM globally and, the second, on an ERP project.

The amalgamation of three of Denmark's finest IT teams – namely legacy *Advokatfirmaet Bender.dk*, legacy *von Haller Law Firm*, and Nicolai Dragsted of **MAQS Advokatbyrå** – to form **Bender von Haller Dragsted** has created the largest and most specialised IT group under one Danish roof. Branding itself as offering IT networking, IT expertise, and IT experience, and active for both vendors and customers on all commercial matters, the only question that remains is whether there will be enough work to feed 16 lawyers, though early indications were positive, with the firm reporting that domain name issues and public procurement were busy areas. Nicolai Dragsted, Martin von Haller Grønbæk and Hanne Bender are leading lights.

'Understanding the client's language and acronyms', **Kromann Reumert** wins high praise from clients. Lau Normann Jørgensen is the partner attracting most praise, heading a team that acted for insurer Tryg in a DKK600m (€80m) outsourcing and technology programme and for Cisco in its acquisition of KISS Technology. The firm identifies systems procurement and outsourcing as strengths.

Seven-partner **Advokatfirmaet Elvang & Partnere**, one of the first boutique firms to be established in Denmark, offers specialist IT advice and other services to IT-sector clients. Name partner Kristian Elvang-Gøransson is a leading brand in his own right and most impressively represents SAP in Denmark. Kim Hansen is also regarded as 'really very good' by the market.

Micheal Goeskjær's IT team at **DLA Nordic**, a sub-set of a wider technology-media-communications group, benefits substantially from the wider *DLA Group* network. In particular, the firm often works with the London office on IT-outsourcing transactions and with the Belgian office advising the European Commission on commercial practices in the region. Motorola is a client.

Nielsen & Nørager's senior partner Jacob Nørager-Nielsen, author of a famous IT contract law book, is billed as 'the father of IT law' in Denmark. Nørager-Nielsen acts for JH Schultz, one of the world's oldest printers and printer for the government. Litigation and IT contracts are the bulk of the firm's work with Nørager-Nielsen said 'to do, and to do well, anything that is asked of him'.

Eight lawyers have specialist IT skills at **Plesner** where Per Håkon Schmidt is the leading name. In line with the firm's wider business, the IT group is strong on the transactional side, advising Siemens on a number of important outsourcings, as well as witnessing growth in disputes, particularly in relation to e-commerce.

Dahl, Koch & Boll Advokatfirmaet is included on the back of strong recommendations for a young and upcoming IT-practice in Jutland.

Peer Petersen is the leading IT authority at **Philip & Partners** and acts for Apple and Sony as part of his wider entertainment practice. Established links to **Baker & McKenzie** are of use here.

Outsourcing is an area of growth for **Rønne & Lundgren** which draws on ties to Deloitte & Touche to generate work here. IT has traditionally been a focus for the firm.

INSOLVENCY

There are eighteen lawyers appointed to the Maritime and Commercial Court in Copenhagen and these are invariably the recipients of the biggest cases, though there was little new work in 2005.

Troels Tuxen presides over a seven-partner insolvency group at **Bech-Bruun**, which is unrivalled on sheer size. Tuxen is most active in restructuring work and often acts with the firm's capital markets and corporate groups. Ole Borch has the leading reputation of the moment, not least owing to his position as Chair of the IBA's insolvency sub-committee. Three **Bech-Bruun** partners are assigned to the Maritime and Commercial Court compared to two or less at each of its rivals.

Michael Zeigler, head of a three-partner team at **Plesner**, has the foremost reputation of any insolvency practitioner in Denmark. Pernille Bigaard, a colleague of Zeigler at the Maritime and Commercial Court, follows close behind in reputation and is a certified mediator. Peter Bang provides insolvency litigation expertise.

INSOLVENCY

BECH-BRUUN ✪
PLESNER ✪

GORRISSEN FEDERSPIEL KIERKEGAARD
KROMANN REUMERT ✪

Accura Advokataktieselskab ✪
Bang + Regnarsen
DLA Nordic ✪
Jonas Bruun ✪
Lett Law Firm ✪
Lind Cadovius ✪
Lund Elmer Sandager
Mazanti-Andersen, Korsø Jensen & Partnere ✪
Philip & Partners ✪
Poul Schmith Law Firm

Firms are listed A-Z in tiers which are ranked in order of priority
✪ *Indicates firm displays contact details at the end of this chapter.*

Aarhus-based Aage Tang Andersen has a leading reputation at **Gorrissen Federspiel Kierkegaard**. In Copenhagen, Axel Kierkegaard and Anne Birgitte Gammeljord are recommended.

Søren Aamann Jensen is the day-to-day head of **Kromann Reumert**'s insolvency team following the retirement of Kurt Skovlund in 2005. Work continues for Credit Finance Denmark, the subsidiary of a Norwegian company, Imerco, an ironmongery company, and for Teleglobe Danmark, a telecoms business. Two partners are appointed to the Maritime and Commercial Court.

Though not the firm's biggest business, Jesper Trommer Volf's insolvency practice at **Accura Advokataktieselskab** continues to attract a steady stream of work. Volf was counsel to the German trustees regarding the Danish aspects of the prominent Phoenix Kapitaldienst bankruptcy and is one of two trustees appointed to the estate of bankrupt contractor J&B Entreprise, the biggest and highest-profile insolvency of 2005. A close relationship with the banks via the firm's M&A department is a plus.

Bang + Regnarsen has two assigned to the Maritime and Commercial Court.

Caspar Moltke at **DLA Nordic** has been a permanent trustee of the Maritime and Commercial Court for 12 years. Among other matters, including reconstruction, the firm represents creditors and undertakes debt collection. It was administrator to the bankruptcy estates of shipping companies GT-Linien and Østersøens Færgedrift.

Claus Høeg Madsen and Per Magid of **Jonas Bruun** continue to act as trustees for listed Danish Steelworks and Bluetel respectively.

Insolvency is a leading discipline at **Lett Law Firm**'s Kolding office in Jutland.

Lars Skanvig and Henrik Andersen are well-respected insolvency practitioners at **Lind Cadovius**, although a dearth of large bankruptcies in 2005 has mostly seen them employed in other areas.

J Kørso Jensen and Henrik Sanders of **Mazanti-Andersen, Korsø Jensen & Partnere** are court-appointed trustees. The restructuring of Farum Municipality, in which the firm is involved, continues.

Philip & Partners' Erik Mahlberg is frequently appointed by the courts in bankruptcy cases. Mahlberg is handling the bankruptcy of Aarhus Flydedok, a floating dock, which went bankrupt in 1999 and which is particularly complex owing to its role as a base for the Danish Navy.

Poul Schmith Law Firm, chief adviser to the government, also advises a number of private-sector clients in insolvency matters.

INSURANCE

The Danish insurance market is a limited market and the bulk of the work is litigation.

The merger between *Lett, Vilstrup & Partnere* and *Lett & Co* to form **Lett Law Firm** has created an insurance litigation powerhouse that in terms of breadth of services and client base brooks no rivals. Denmark's leading non-life insurers are all clients including Tryg, Codan, TopDanmark and Alm Brand; as are life-side pension providers, Nordea, Danica and PFA. Links to some of the world's most renowned insurance firms including **Barlow Lyde & Gilbert**, **Clyde & Co** and **Lovells** mean that international clients are not lacking and AIG, Axa, Gerling, Hiscox, CNA and General Cologne are frequent users of the firm. In 2005, the latter two successfully employed Michael Grønbach in a DKK40m (€5.4m) reinsurance dispute, due to go to appeal before the Supreme Court in 2006. Georg Lett has a 'unique standing' in general, whilst Susie Stærk Ekstarnd is recommended for product liability, as is Pernille Sølling, who also has a strong pensions practice.

Bech-Bruun's shipping and transport group is also responsible for insurance work, particularly litigation. Henrik Valdorf-Hansen successfully represented Tryg in a liability case against SAS.

A 20-lawyer team at **Kromann Reumert** sits in both Aarhus and Copenhagen and offers expertise across the board, including reinsurance, whilst making its strongest imprint in liability and coverage disputes. Litigator Morten Samuelssson heads the group and has a strong professional negligence and D&O practice. Christina Neugebauer is recommended for personal injury cases.

Mikael Rosenmejer of **Plesner** continues to act as counsel to Scandinavian Tobacco Company in proceedings against the company by smokers claiming damages. Litigator Torben Bondrop has three cases pending before the Supreme Court, two for an insurer and one concerning product liability. A ten-lawyer team is respected by the markets for its ability to attract international work.

INSURANCE

LETT LAW FIRM ✪

Bech-Bruun ✪
Kromann Reumert ✪
Plesner ✪

DLA Nordic ✪
Gorrissen Federspiel Kierkegaard
Jonas Bruun ✪
Nielsen & Nørager ✪
Rønne & Lundgren ✪

Firms are listed A-Z in tiers which are ranked in order of priority
✪ *Indicates firm displays contact details at the end of this chapter.*

DLA Nordic predominantly represents insurers in personal injury and other liability cases.

Corporate partner Henning Aasmul-Olsen of **Jonas Bruun** is a regular adviser to Tryg on corporate and regulatory matters.

Michael Wiisbye heads up insurance work at **Nielsen & Nørager**, which acts for a number of insurers in both regulatory and claims work, including IF, one of Scandinavia's largest insurers, and a client for over two decades.

New entrant **Rønne & Lundgren** boasts a strong foundation of foreign insurance-sector clients including Genworth, Ace and Aon, as well as corporates from other sectors faced with insurance-related problems. The work is mainly non-contentious and the firm enjoys referrals from leading international firms such as **Lovells**.

INTELLECTUAL PROPERTY

Kromann Reumert has one of the largest, if not the largest, dedicated IP group in Denmark with a partner working almost full-time in each of three sub-groups: patents, trade marks, and marketing. Patent litigation in the pharmaceutical sector, trade mark litigation for leading brand owners and product imitation cases continue to comprise a bulk of the group's work. Nicolai Lindgreen attracts the highest praise for his work as a patent litigator, with Erling Borcher and Frank Bøggild also recommended.

Plesner's leading IP and life sciences group is 'service minded and competent' with clients appreciative of the 'commerciality of its advice'. Twenty-two lawyers comprise the group, which has long been a flagship department at the firm. It has an especially high reputation for patent, copyright and trade mark litigation, acting for Nike and LEGO among others, and in Peter Ulrik-Plesner boasts the most frequently recommended lawyer. Karen Dyekjær is recommended for her life sciences work whilst clients also praise junior members of the team including Mikkel Vittrup, Tanja Meedum and Britt-Mari Fog.

Bech-Bruun's 20-lawyer IP team continues to work closely with the firm's leading media and IT practices, although head Janne Glæsel now focuses more exclusively on IPR work. Glæsel impressed in two cases in 2005, successfully representing business paper Børsen in a trade mark dispute before the Supreme Court and acting for Metro newspapers in a similar case before the Maritime and Commercial Court. Klaus Ewald Madsen is recommended by peers for his patent litigation skills.

INTELLECTUAL PROPERTY

KROMANN REUMERT ✪
PLESNER ✪

BECH-BRUUN ✪
DLA NORDIC ✪
JOHAN SCHLÜTER LAW FIRM ✪

Accura Advokataktieselskab ✪
Bender von Haller Dragsted ✪
Delacour ✪
Elvang & Partnere, Advokatfirmaet
Gorrissen Federspiel Kierkegaard
Lett Law Firm ✪
Philip & Partners ✪

Jonas Bruun ✪
Lassen Ricard ✪
MAQS Advokatbyrå
Nielsen & Nørager ✪
Norsker & Co. Law Firm
Osborne Clarke
Rønne & Lundgren ✪
Viltoft & Høberg-Petersen ✪

Firms are listed A-Z in tiers which are ranked in order of priority
✪ *Indicates firm displays contact details at the end of this chapter.*

DLA Nordic's IP team is going from strength-to-strength following the impressive hire of partners Ole Damsbo and Anders Valentin from **Johan Schlüter Law Firm**. Damsbo is among the best-known patent litigators in Denmark and joins a team that is already well established in the market for trade mark and copyright disputes, not least owing to the reputation of managing partner Jens Jakob Bugge. Clients are also pleased to commend the firm for the ease in which 'it is always possible to get hold of a partner or qualified associate. One to watch.

For copyright matters Johan Schlüter of **Johan Schlüter Law Firm** reigns supreme although the departure of Ole Damsbo to **DLA Nordic** is undoubtedly a setback for its patent litigation work. The firm is active solely in IP, IT, e-commerce, media and entertainment and related EU and Competition law.

Medical and life sciences companies form a significant bulk of the client base of Karsten Kielland's IP team at **Accura Advokataktieselskab**. Merck, Wyeth, Genzyme and Specsavers are clients.

Niche firms **Bender von Haller Dragsted** and **Advokatfirmaet Elvang & Partnere** are included on the strength of their niche IT talents, which also require related IP skills.

DELACOUR has a three-partner IP department headed by Johnny Petersen, that is increasing its visibility domestically and also internationally, following an informal relationship with **Bird & Bird**. Patents are a leading competence, although it is also active in trade mark and copyright matters. Asger Heine Jensen and Aarhus-based Carsten Lorentzen are recommended, the latter being active for eyewear manufacturer Lindberg.

Gorrissen Federspiel Kierkegaard has yet to make much of an impression on the market in regard to IP, traditionally operating a small practice under the guise of an in-house agency, GFK Designs and Trademarks. However, at the close of 2005, the firm announced that it was entering into partnership with **Plougmann & Vingtoft**, a patent and trade mark agency formerly in partnership with **Johan Schlüter Law Firm**. How this new relationship will fare remains to be seen.

Registration matters, protection issues, licensing, franchising and disputes are features of **Lett Law Firm**'s work. The firm benefits from niche links to the food sector.

IP is an important source of work for Peer Petersen and **Philip & Partners**. As counsel to the Karen Blixen Foundation, Petersen had a busy year in 2005 following a new film about the author's life, which attracted intense media coverage. Petersen also advised on the creation of a new foundation for education grants to be funded by proceeds from the works of Selinko, another Danish author etched on the national psyche.

Media-leader **Lassen Ricard** is admitted to the table on the strength of recommendations for its IP work, which generally sees it protecting the interests of its media-sector clients.

IP is the fastest-growing department at **MAQS Advokatbyrå** where Jeppe Brogaard Clusen is in charge of a team that was very active in customs and civil seizures work in 2005. The firm acts only for trade mark owners, counting some of the world's biggest companies among its clients.

Disney Corporation is a regular client of **Nielsen & Nørager** on IP matters as are the firm's biotech clients, which use it when entering into licensing and franchise agreements.

MEDIA AND ENTERTAINMENT

In the eyes of the market **Bech-Bruun** is 'without doubt the leader' now said to be 'taking work back from its competitors'. Partner Strange Beck has a 'formidable' reputation, acting for British-based broadcaster Viasat and Metro Newspapers in various prominent cases in 2005. For film matters Per Neumann is first choice for many, acting for Wallander Film & TV and new movie channel Scandinavia, among others. Senior associate Nina Henningson continues to attract considerable praise.

Johan Schlüter Law Firm enjoys an 'enviable position' insofar as, more than others, its name is synonymous with top media and IP advice. Name partner Johan Schlüter remains the driving force in respect of entertainment work, whilst Lars Hallgreen is singled out for the excellence of his sports practice. The firm is active in the television, radio, phonogram, videogram, author, publishing and distribution markets. Torben Steffensen is recommended for his litigation skills.

MEDIA AND ENTERTAINMENT

BECH-BRUUN ✪
JOHAN SCHLÜTER LAW FIRM ✪
LASSEN RICARD ✪

Nielsen & Nørager ✪
Plesner ✪

DLA Nordic ✪
Kromann Reumert ✪
Philip & Partners ✪

Jonas Bruun ✪
MAQS Advokatbyrå
Rønne & Lundgren ✪
Viltoft & Høberg-Petersen ✪

Firms are listed A-Z in tiers which are ranked in order of priority
✪ *Indicates firm displays contact details at the end of this chapter.*

Although active in a number of areas, it is for media work, and broadcasting in particular, that six-partner **Lassen Ricard** attracts the greatest superlatives. Peter Lambert and Steen Lassen are the star names in a team that acts for Sony Music, Danish broadcasters DR and TV2 and the BBC.

The name of Ole Finn Nielsen and **Nielsen & Nørager** is regarded as being synonymous with the film industry. Nielsen's clients include Danish and foreign film companies, leading individuals such as director Bille August, the Disney Corporation; and TV company SBS.

Per Håkon Schmidt and Michael Vilhelm Nielsen are both recommended at **Plesner**, which remains best known for its sports-sector work, particularly football. The firm acts for leading Danish team, Aarhus Elite AGF and Nielsen sits on the board of the Super League Division Association. Music, film and radio are other areas of expertise.

Warner Brothers and merchandise agency Kidz Entrtainment are leading clients of 'swift and professional' **DLA Nordic**, where Bastian Rankløve heads a media and entertainment team. Distribution, licence, wireless and television agreements are areas of expertise.

Book and newspaper publishing is an area of strength for **Kromann Reumert** with the firm having historically advised the Danish Newspaper Publishers Association and the Danish Publishers Association. Martin Dahl Pedersen and Erik Mohr Mersing are the leading names at a firm, which also represents football body, the Danish Players Association.

Philip & Partners rises one tier on the strength of the work of Peer Petersen, who acts for Sony BMG, the Karen Blixen Foundation and EMI. Petersen enjoys widespread industry contacts but generally only acts for companies in the music and film industries, as opposed to artists.

Jonas Bruun advises Danish TV station TV2 and has occasionally acted for DR, the second station. Henrik Dahl also acts for various newspapers including Berlingske Group.

Kåre Wancsher, drummer with the group *Michael Learns to Rock*, is also an associate at **MAQS Advokatbyrå** where he advises musicians on contracts.

Rønne & Lundgren enters the table on the back of work for advertising agency WPP and various film production companies.

Bjørn Høberg-Petersen has developed a niche, part-time practice at **Viltoft & Høberg-Petersen**, acting for actors. He also represents the Danish Actor's Association (DAA).

Although not specialising in the area and therefore not in the table, **Lind Cadovius** is also recommended for notable past successes, not least those of partner Frantz Palluden who was counsel to one time Danish pop sensation Aqua, which had a major hit with 'Barbie Girl'.

MERGERS AND ACQUISITIONS

The top-tier firms attract the largest M&A deals every time. However owing to conflict of interest rules that forbid any firm from acting for more than one bidder in controlled auctions, a second tier of firms is also guaranteed a role in an increasing number of transactions. At the close of 2005 a public tender for telecoms operator TDC was made by a consortium of private equity funds, which at €10.2bn was set to be the largest LBO in Europe ever.

Internationally, **Bech-Bruun** enjoys one of the most recognisable names of any Danish firm. Top-ten US firms speak highly of it as does a national UK firm, impressed with its ability to 'tailor a transaction to us with a degree of expertise that we haven't witnessed in Germany or elsewhere'. Global reach was especially important in 2005 when the firm was instructed by global food ingredients business Chr Hansen to advise it on its DKK8bn (€1.1bn) sale to PAI partners – a deal which required **Bech-Bruun** to instruct 28 other law firms across the globe and to employ a new IT system to manage over 40,000 requests from numerous bidders. The above transaction would have swamped a smaller firm but **Bech-Bruun** was also able to find time to advise target Maersk Data, the shareholders of Falck; buyers Altor, Swedish BNS Industrier and Siemens; and the sellers of Cyber City. In total it advised purchasers, sellers or targets on deals worth over DKK23.5bn (€3.1bn) and was chosen by the consortium of private equity funds to advise on their DKK76bn (€10.2bn) tender for TDC (with **Simpson Thacher & Bartlett LLP**). Group head Søren Meisling is a

MERGERS AND ACQUISITIONS

BECH-BRUUN ✪
GORRISSEN FEDERSPIEL KIERKEGAARD
KROMANN REUMERT ✪
PLESNER ✪

Accura Advokataktieselskab ✪
Jonas Bruun ✪

DLA Nordic ✪
Hjejle Gersted Mogensen
Lett Law Firm ✪
Lind Cadovius ✪

Eversheds Advokataktieselskab
Nielsen & Nørager ✪
Philip & Partners ✪
Rønne & Lundgren ✪

Delacour ✪
Focus Advokater LLP ✪
Lassen Ricard ✪
MAQS Advokatbyrå
Mazanti-Andersen, Korsø Jensen & Partnere ✪

Firms are listed A-Z in tiers which are ranked in order of priority
✪ Indicates firm displays contact details at the end of this chapter.

'powerful rainmaker' and is well supported by Mikkel Baaring Lerche and Jacob Hjortshøj.

Despite being approximately half the size of its two biggest rivals **Gorrissen Federspiel Kierkegaard**'s deal value in the first half of 2005 was larger than that of any other independent Nordic firm. The biggest of these deals was advice provided to buyers EQT and Goldman Sachs on the DKK 22bn (€3bn) purchase of ISS, the largest M&A of the year. Nordic Capital also proved to be a valuable client, calling on the firm to advise it on its DKK13.4bn (€1.8bn) and DKK5.3bn (€710m) purchases of Nycomed and Falck, respectively. Demonstrating that it is also adept on the other side, it acted for Brandtex, which sold its entire share capital to EQT. Managing partner Niels Heering, Klaus Søgaard and corporate finance partner Tomas Haagen Jensen are some of those recommended.

Having a strong blue-chip client base means that 'solution-orientated' **Kromann Reumert** is never far from the biggest deals, acting for targets ISS in the biggest completed transaction of 2005 and TDC in what will likely be the biggest transaction ever. Acting for the target was, in fact, a recurring theme of 2005 with the firm also active for the board of Falck, TDC Forlag and Aarhus United in other sales totalling over DKK12bn (€1.6bn). On the buyer's side **Kromann Reumert** remains the primary adviser to DONG, for a long time one of the most enviable mandates. Clients commend a 'solid team that is always available' whilst singling out Anders Stubbe Arndal for his 'expert negotiation skills'. Henrik Møgelmose and Mogens Skipper-Pedersen are other leading names. Møgelmose in particular impressed with his advice to the government in conjunction with **Poul Schmith Law Firm** on the privatisation of Post Danmark.

'A 24/7 firm that is really keyed in to what big internationals want', **Plesner** has enjoyed great success in rebranding itself as an aggressive M&A-hungry powerhouse in recent years. In 2004 this culminated in the firm achieving the psychologically important feat of advising on more deals and a higher total value of deals than any other Danish firm. In a narrow market it would be hard to achieve the same year-on-year but early signs looked to show that the firm would again emerge as the leader by deals completed in 2005. Advice to buyers was a prominent feature with the firm acting for Goldman Sachs, which purchased ISS together with EQT; for IBM on its DKK4.5bn (€630m) purchase of Maersk Data; EQT, which purchased Brandtex; and Norway's Telenor, purchaser of CyberCity for €185m. It also acted for Nycomed, which was sold to Nordic Capital for DKK13.4bn (€1.8bn), the second biggest M&A of the year; and for Legoland (in conjunction with **Clifford Chance**) in its sale to Blackstone. Jacob Bier is the most frequently cited name although Christian Th Kjolbye and Finn Lerno are also commended for being 'figures of experience'.

Two very different firms are vying for the position of being the leading firm for M&A after the Big Four. **Accura Advokataktieselskab** is the newest entrant, drawing praise from clients who are 'thoroughly satisfied' and impressed by 'commitment and solid commercial acumen'. More than half the firm's income is derived from M&A and it was active in over DKK40bn (€5.4bn) worth of transactions in the first three-quarters of 2005 including advice to lender EQT in two deals totalling over DKK13bn (€1.7bn), and to buyers Actavis, Blackstone in deals worth DKK8bn (€1.1bn). Thomas Weincke and Kåre Stolt are leading names in a 'thoroughly hands-on' team that stands best placed to steal work from the leaders following the arrival of brothers Jacob and Michael Vinther from **Bech-Bruun**.

Jonas Bruun has long enjoyed a monopoly as the only firm able to compete on equal terms with the Big Four. The quality of its work is perhaps unrivalled and it is far and away the leading choice for the Big Four when conflicted. On some measures Henning Aasmul-Olsen was the leading M&A lawyer in Denmark in 2005, advising on a higher total value of deals than any other. Having 40 lawyers only, **Jonas Bruun** is but a third of the size of **Gorrissen Federspiel Kierkegaard**, the smallest of the Big Four, nevertheless relative to its size it regularly advises on a far higher value of deals than any other firm. The firm is particularly strong in the energy sector where it acted for the Ministry of Finance, owner of DONG, in relation to DONG's merger with Elsam. Mogens Ebeling and Claus Høeg Madsen are also leading names.

Clients of **DLA Nordic** pronounce themselves as 'very happy' with the services of an M&A team that was most prominent in 2005 as adviser to Copenhagen energy on its €2.7bn restructuring, which included various transactions. Jim Øksenebjerg's negotiation skills are identified as a source of particular satisfaction for clients.

Hjejle Gersted Mogensen is recommended for smaller transactional work, particularly up to approximately DKK500m (€67m). On larger matters, Chrsitian Schow Madsen advised the former owners of CyberCity on its €185m sale to Telenor and Oluf Engell was retained by the bondholders in ISS during the sale of its share capital, as well as advising a bidder in the sale of ChrHansen.

Lett Law Firm remains focused on SME sector and its Kolding office continues to generate praise in this regard. It acted for a bidder in the Chr Hansen auction and for Energi E2 in the sale of power stations to Vattenfall. With over 100 lawyers now at the firm it is looking to broaden its footprint in this market.

Although M&A is not the dominant focus for **Lind Cadovius** that it is for some other firms, nevertheless it has experience of employing almost its whole staff on transactions when the need arises. In common with others, 2005 was a successful year and it acted for the buyers of TDC Forlag in conjunction with **Clifford Chance**, as well as being employed by the buyer of Chr Hansen (with **Weil, Gotshal & Manges**).

Jens Arnesen of **Eversheds Advokataktieselskab** was busiest in 2005, particularly in regard to private equity funds and transaction finance. The firm regularly draws on the resources of its international and growing Scandinavian alliance.

Morten Eldrup-Jørgensen and **Nielsen & Nørager** remain a favoured choice for referrals from larger firms on small- and medium-sized transactions. Private equity funds, including Atrium and Partners also provide significant business, although the firm was most often seen acting for unsuccessful bidders in 2005.

Philip & Partners represented bidders in the NetTestand TDC Forlag auctions, a bank in the sale of ISS, and the sellers of Aarhus United, which was sold for DKK2.3bn (€300m) in autumn 2005. Jesper Rothe is the contact at a firm known for its links to US clients.

Between 12 and 15 of **Rønne & Lundgren**'s 38 lawyers are active in M&A, a core feature of the firm's business and reputation. The largest firms happily recommend this firm, which was active in numerous deals in 2005, especially on the real estate side. Most notable was Henrik Juul Hansen's work for Kerr-Mcgee on the DKK18bn (€2.4bn) sale of its oil interests and for Meinl European Land in its €1bn acquisition of FORAS Holding.

Frans Rossen, formerly a senior associate at **Bech-Bruun**, is the name to note at **DELACOUR** , which has a fledgling M&A practice in

Copenhagen. Rossen is also a German-qualified lawyer and the firm's most impressive transaction to date was acting for Deutsche Post in its bid for 25% of the shares of Post Danmark in 2004.

Lassen Ricard is recommended for M&A expertise in the media sector, where it acts for TV 2, among others.

Lars Lokdam is responsible for M&A at **MAQS Advokatbyrå** in Copenhagen, which is not an overriding practice area although it has seen considerable growth of late. Most notable is advice provided to a multinational on the Danish aspects of its multi-billion dollar sale and other work in connection with property deals in which the firm's Swedish offices excel.

J Korsø Jensen at **Mazanti-Andersen, Korsø Jensen & Partnere** is regarded as 'excellent' for smaller domestic deals.

REAL ESTATE AND CONSTRUCTION

REAL ESTATE AND CONSTRUCTION

BECH-BRUUN ✪
KROMANN REUMERT ✪
PLESNER ✪

ACCURA ADVOKATAKTIESELSKAB ✪
VILTOFT & HØBERG-PETERSEN ✪

DLA Nordic ✪
Gorrissen Federspiel Kierkegaard
Jonas Bruun ✪
Lind Cadovius ✪
Lund Elmer Sandager
Rønne & Lundgren ✪

Hjejle Gersted Mogensen
Lett Law Firm ✪
Mazanti-Andersen, Korsø Jensen & Partnere ✪
Westergaard & Alstrøm

MAQS Advokatbyrå
Nielsen & Nørager ✪
Philip & Partners ✪

Firms are listed A-Z in tiers which are ranked in order of priority
✪ Indicates firm displays contact details at the end of this chapter.

Torben Schøn is a prominent figure at **Bech-Bruun**, although the departure of cohort Jon Dyhre Hansen to **Accura Advokataktieselskab** means that he alone possesses a market-leading reputation for real estate at the firm. Nevertheless with upwards of 35 lawyers devoted to real estate there is plenty of room for new talent to emerge. German banks are a significant source of work and the firm recently won the right to represent co-owner Steen & Strøm in the sale of half of Fields shopping centre in Ørestad, in one of the largest property transactions ever.

In Niles Balselv and Flemming Horn Andersen, **Kromann Reumert** possesses two of Denmark's two top-five real estate lawyers. A 30-fee-earner property and construction team is commended by clients for 'effectiveness, professionalism and timeliness' with Andersen particularly praised for 'the humanity he injects into the client relationship'. Balslev and Andersen were active in five major Danish transactions in 2005, worth almost DKK8bn (€1.1bn) in total.

'Leading real estate mind' Leif Djurhuus co-heads a 12-lawyer group at **Plesner** in tandem with Peer Meisner. It regularly acts for Keops, Steen & Strøm, Sjælso Gruppen, Schauamnn and the Nordea group, with clients explaining that they are 'definitely very satisfied' with ' consistently high levels of service'. In 2005, Meisner advised TK Development on its sale of its 50% ownership of Field's shopping centre in Copenhagen. The firm also boasts a leading, 12-lawyer construction group, in which Peter Fogh is prominent.

The arrival at **Accura Advokataktieselskab** of leading real estate partner Jon Dyhre Hansen from **Bech-Bruun**, perhaps the biggest move of 2005, alters the balance of power within the market. Though **Accura Advokataktieselskab** was not traditionally best known for its real estate work, the addition of Dyhre to Henik Groos' nine-lawyer team suddenly makes the firm every inch a contender at the top. Highlights of 2005 included advice to Keops on real estate purchases in Sweden totalling over DKK8bn (€1.1bn).

Although it is also active in other practice areas, the dominance of **Viltoft & Høberg-Petersen**'s construction team means that the market often refers to this firm as a niche construction firm, such is the strength of its reputation. It is for this that the firm enjoys a high ranking in the table. Partners Michael Gjedde-Nielsen and Hans Lykke Hansen are both construction experts acting for public and private-sector clients, including the metro system in the prominent Ørestad development.

Clients who have used **DLA Nordic** for real estate matters are particularly complementary about the way it follows up its work with 'a call by the partner to ensure that services rendered have fully met expectations'. These services predominantly comprise lease agreements for domestic and foreign clients of the firm, as well as some construction and project development expertise. Michael Neumann is the contact.

Thomas Stampe of **Gorrissen Federspiel Kierkegaard** continues to represent CGI, Commerzbank's Equity fund, with regard to its acquisition of 50% of shares in Field's shopping centre. Overall the firm devotes fewer resources to real estate than its larger rivals with Aarhus-based Peter Sjøgreen heading a small team best-known for its work for Lidl supermarkets.

Christian Sinding is recommended by peers for his transactional prowess in real estate matters at **Jonas Bruun**. Poul Heidmann advises on planning, environmental and regulatory aspects of real estate.

Frantz Palluden of **Lind Cadovius** won an impressive mandate to advise the City of Copenhagen on the Ørestad development, the creation of a whole new district, which, when completed, will be equivalent to Denmark's fifth-largest city by size.

Lund Elmer Sandager is strong in both real estate and construction with Steen Raagaard Andersen acting as a point of contact for both. Sjælsø Gruppen is a client.

Real estate is **Rønne & Lundgren**'s flagship practice in the eyes of the market and a strong reputation attracts recruits with Klaus Höxbro from **Eversheds Advokataktieselskab**, Niels Kjaergaard of **Viltoft & Høberg-Petersen** and Niels Gram-Hanssen of **Kromann Reumert** all joining as partners in the past two years. The firm ascends the table on the back of strength in property development, real estate finance, sale of large portfolios and non-contentious construction expertise.

Sixteen lawyers, predominantly real estate focused, departed **Norsker & Co. Law Firm** in 2006 for **Lett Law Firm**.

Ninety per cent of **Westergaard & Alstrøm**'s work is commercial property-related. In addition to private clients, the firm advises over 30 local municipalties.

Philip & Partners is a new entrant owing to the construction expertise of Claus Kaare Pedersen who has a significant client following among major construction companies. The firm is advising one of the first constructors on the ground in Ørestad.

SHIPPING AND TRANSPORT

The shipping and transport market is a narrow market with perhaps only between thirty and forty lawyers specialising in the area. The top tier of three firms account for about 60% of the total market.

A four-partner shipping and transport team at **Bech-Bruun** advises shipowners, managers, P&I clubs, cargo owners, insurers and carriers on shipping and multi-modal transport matters. Head Jes Anker Mikkelsen is the most highly respected member of a team that advised the Chinese *Fu Shan Hai* following its collision with the *Gdynia* in 2003, the largest collision of recent times. Shipping giant Maersk, Denmark's largest and most prestigious company, is a core client of the firm. Other clients include P&I clubs, UK Club, West of England and GARD.

Gorrissen Federspiel Kierkegaard is a recognised leader in shipping on the owner-side, where it acts for major Danish shipowners Norden and Sandlines, and several P&I clubs. Head Alex Laudrup wins plaudits for his wet work, whilst Peter Appel is acknowledged as 'pre-eminent within the industry'. Finally, the firm has a close association with UK shipping firms such as **Watson, Farley & Williams LLP** and **Richards**

SHIPPING AND TRANSPORT

BECH-BRUUN ✪
GORRISSEN FEDERSPIEL KIERKEGAARD
KROMANN REUMERT ✪

Bang + Regnarsen
Delacour ✪
Focus Advokater LLP ✪

DLA Nordic ✪
Lett Law Firm ✪
Mazanti-Andersen, Korsø Jensen & Partnere ✪
Philip & Partners ✪
Plesner ✪
Viltoft & Høberg-Petersen ✪

Firms are listed A-Z in tiers which are ranked in order of priority
✪ *Indicates firm displays contact details at the end of this chapter.*

Butler and has also acted for airlines, including Maersk Air.

Along with **Gorrissen Federspiel Kierkegaard**, **Kromann Reumert** is a traditional leader in shipping, particularly on the finance side where it wins most respect. Henrik Thal Jantzen is commended for his work on the wet side and Christian Hennings on the dry side. Litigation continues to be a substantial part of its practice.

Ulla Fabricius heads **Bang + Regnarsen**'s well-reputed shipping practice which sits in offices in Copenhagen and Hamburg. Contracts and liability issues are the bulk of the work.

DELACOUR has a six-lawyer transportation group to rival the first tier in size and reach if not yet in tradition. The practice has grown substantially with the arrival of Anders Hedetoft from **Kromann Reumert**, who is particularly well versed in customs law. Hedetoft now heads the team in tandem with Henrik Kleis, who has a strong client following at the Port of Aarhus. Airlines are also a source of business.

Peter Ringsted of **Focus Advokater LLP** is one of the most highly-regarded shipping lawyers in Denmark, recognisable by all in the market. Ringsted is active for both financiers and ship owners nationally and, in 2005, was also busy at the firm's Hamburg office advising owners and banks in respect of Antiguan registrations.

Mediterranean Shipping Company is a client of **DLA Nordic**. Telecoms and commercial partner Hans Abildstrøm is the contact point.

Lett Law Firm is the principal adviser to Danish State Railways (DSB).

Jens Hjortskov is in charge of shipping matters at **Philip & Partners**, which acts for a number of Far Eastern shipping companies, including Jan Ming Line. Hjortskov, who is dual Swedish- and Norwegian-qualified, also advises on the sale and purchase of aircraft.

Peter Fogh is the chief shipping and transport partner at **Plesner**. Fogh is particularly active on the contentious side. Clients who have used the firm for ship finance, another strength, express their 'full satisfaction' with its 'timely service'. Aviation finance is a third strength.

Viltoft & Høberg-Petersen has a specialist knowledge of maritime penal law and maritime pollution and has acted for crews in salvage disputes.

TAX

Bech-Bruun has severely boosted its standing with the hire of a team from **Gorrissen Federspiel Kierkegaard** headed by Anders Oreby Hansen, who has 15-years' experience as a tax specialist, and Michael Serup who joins from **Advokatfirmaet Tommy V Christiansen** in Aarhus. Hansen joins Nikolaj Bjørnholm in Copenhagen who is singled out for considerable praise by peers and clients alike. With 18-lawyers, the firm's practice is the biggest and it ascends to the top tier this year as the chief competitor to **Plesner**. Like that firm it is seeking to win work back from the dominant accountancy practices and offers planning, transfer pricing, litigation and transactional support.

Plesner is in possession of a ten-lawyer tax group 'every bit as good as a superb reputation suggests'. Much of that reputation is owing to Hans Severin Hansen, 'by far the most experienced tax lawyer in Denmark', and a permanent adviser to the Ministry of Taxation. The firm wins greatest praise for its litigation capability though some major international clients are beginning to instruct it in other areas that would typically be the remit of Big Four accountancy practices. These clients state that the firm is 'able to provide a better level of opinion on most issues' and that its expertise 'is growing all the time'. Partner Lasse Esjberg Christensen and senior associate Anders Endicott Pedersen are noted as 'business-like and efficient'.

Tax continues to be an area in which 'young and innovative' **Accura Advokataktieselskab** is said to excel, although this is perhaps not surprising given its former relationship with PwC, where Kåre Stolt and the 'very capable' Lars Fogh were partners. Fogh undertakes most of the tax work these days, which is primarily transactional tax advice and, unusually for a Danish law firm, complex structuring advice. Kaspar Bostian joined the firm from **Poul Schmith Law Firm**, adviser to the Ministry of Taxation.

Aarhus-based **Advokatfirmaet Tommy V Christiansen** is a tax boutique that is known throughout Denmark for its tax litigation work. Name partner Tommy V Christiansen enjoys an enduring reputation.

Hjejle Gersted Mogensen has traditionally been recognised as a leader in the Danish tax market, particularly in contentious work. Søren Lehmann Nielsen is perceived by the market to be 'doing very well' here.

TAX

BECH-BRUUN ✪
PLESNER ✪

ACCURA ADVOKATAKTIESELSKAB ✪
TOMMY V CHRISTIANSEN, ADVOKATFIRMAET

Hjejle Gersted Mogensen
Kromann Reumert ✪
Lett Law Firm ✪
Lind Cadovius ✪
Nielsen & Nørager ✪

DLA Nordic ✪
Dahl, Koch & Boll Advokatfirmaet
Dania Advokater A/S (Dania Law Firm Ltd)
Gorrissen Federspiel Kierkegaard
Mazanti-Andersen, Korsø Jensen & Partnere ✪
Rønne & Lundgren ✪

Firms are listed A-Z in tiers which are ranked in order of priority
✪ *Indicates firm displays contact details at the end of this chapter.*

Arne Ottosen and Jan Børjesson are the partners in a cross-office tax team at **Kromann Reumert**. Ottosen is based in Copenhagen and wins plaudits for his litigation skills.

Lett Law Firm remains best known for its tax litigation capabilities. It is the firm of choice for the Ministry of Taxation when **Poul Schmith Law Firm** is conflicted. Claus Holberg and Jesper Lett are contact points.

Name partner Jørgen Cadovius of **Lind Cadovius** undertakes tax planning whilst Jess Theirson does a 'good job' as a tax litigatior.

Henrik Peytz of 'highly regarded' **Nielsen & Nørager** is commended by peers. Peytz has acted in several principal court cases and is known for his EU tax law expertise. 'Up-coming' Jacob Larson supports him. The firm also provides a limited range of tax planning advice.

Dahl, Koch & Boll Advokatfirmaet enters the table following the hire of Michael Amstrup and his team from **Norsker & Co. Law Firm**.

Gorrissen Federspiel Kierkegaard's small tax team was severely depleted by the departure of recommended partner Anders Oreby Hansen and his team to **Bech-Bruun**.

Rønne & Lundgren began developing an all-round tax focus following its departure from the *Andersen Legal* network in 2002. Prior to that it had only offered tax litigation capability. Since then, despite continuing links to Deloitte & Touche, it has added a wider non-contentious service, with Jørn Qviste being prominent.

TELECOMS

The telecoms market has been relatively stable in Denmark in recent years owing to the dominance of a limited number of players, each with its own preferred counsel. The exit of Orange from the

TELECOMS

BECH-BRUUN ✪
JONAS BRUUN ✪
KROMANN REUMERT ✪
LETT LAW FIRM ✪
PLESNER ✪

Accura Advokataktieselskab ✪
DLA Nordic ✪
MAQS Advokatbyrå

Firms are listed A-Z in tiers which are ranked in order of priority
✪ *Indicates firm displays contact details at the end of this chapter.*

market in 2004 was seen as evidence that there was little room for new business. However the growth of mobile telephony services in 2005 and the expected sale of TDC, far and away the dominant provider in the market, has renewed interest in this sector.

Telia is the stand-out client of **Bech-Bruun**'s two partner telecoms group, recommended by peers for its leading regulatory expertise. The firm impresses most for its transactional prowess in this sector, not least in the sale of CyberCity to Telenor for €190m.

'Excellent' **Jonas Bruun** has been in the vanguard of telecoms regulatory advisers since the market first took off in the early 1990s. Traditionally the firm was primary counsel to SONOFON, Denmark's second-largest telecoms provider after TDC, although the purchase of this company by Telenor in 2004 has now seen this work pass to **Plesner**. To compensate for this, the firm is turning its attention to assisting its energy-sector clients in their rapid diversification into broadband provision.

Kromann Reumert is a primary adviser to TDC, especially on corporate matters, and not least on its anticipated sale. Torben Waage is recommended for his 'thorough knowledge of all things telecoms'. Also of note in 2005 was advice provided to Broadcast Service Denmark, a joint venture in connection with the establishment of digital terrestial TV (DVB-T), which blends telecoms, media and IT expertise.

TDC is also an important client of **Lett Law Firm**, which undertakes regulatory and technology-related work, as well as procurement and litigation. How this relationship will stand in the face of TDC's expected purchase remains to be seen. The National IT and Telecom Agency is another client.

Plesner is the firm most in the ascendant in regard to telecoms, having entered the table for the first time last year and continuing through to the top tier this time. The activities of its client Telenor are largely responsible for its rise, with the Norwegian company purchasing Denmark's SONOFON in 2004 and generating new mandates for the firm. Finally, the 'level-headed' abilities of Christian Th. Kjølbye also contribute to the firm's success. Younger partner Niels Christian Ellegaard lends support.

Accura Advokataktieselskab, which won a first instruction from secondary mobile operator Debitel in 2005, is a new entrant this year. Other telecoms-sector clients include Cable & Wireless, Swisscom and Alcatel, although the bulk of its work for these is corporate and commercial-related.

Telecoms is an area of strength for **DLA Nordic**, which represents service providers such as Motorola, Global Crossing, Tele2, and Colt. A slow 2005 in terms of instruction on regulatory matters was met by an increasing volume of litigation.

Dankse Telecom is a client of new entrant **MAQS Advokatbyrå**, which identifies the telecoms sector as an area in which it can grow in Denmark.

BECH-BRUUN

FRUE KIRKEPLADS 4
8100 AARHUS C

Telephone: +45 72 27 00 00
Fax: +45 72 27 00 27
E-mail: info@bechbruun.com
Website: www.bechbruun.com

Languages
English, French, German, Russian, the Scandinavian languages

Other offices
Copenhagen, Moscow

Number of lawyers 254
at this office 60

CATEGORIES OF WORK

Capital markets	IT law and telecommunications
Company law	Litigation
Construction law and real estate	Media and entertainment
Corporate consulting	Mergers and acquisitions
Employment and labour law	Private law
Energy supply	Public law
Environmental law	Russian law
EU and competition law	Taxation
Insolvency and restructuring	Tort and insurance
Intellectual property rights	Transport law
International law	

DELACOUR

LILLE TORV 6
PO BOX 505
8100 AARHUS C

Telephone: + 45 70 11 11 22
Fax: + 45 70 11 11 33
E-mail: delacour@delacour.dk
Website: www.delacour.dk

Languages
English, French, German, the Scandinavian languages

Other offices
Copenhagen

Number of lawyers 52
at this office 41

Member
Advoc, an international network of independent law firms

CATEGORIES OF WORK

Arbitration and litigation	Insolvency
Banking and finance	Insurance
Business set-up in China and eastern Europe	Intellectual property and IT
Corporate and commercial	Mergers and acquisitions
Directorship	Real estate and construction
Employment	Tax
Environment	Transport and maritime law
EU and competition	

LETT LAW FIRM

VAERKMESTERGADE 25, 8TH
8100 AARHUS C

Telephone: +45 86 12 86 00
Fax: +45 86 12 86 56
E-mail: lett@lett.dk
Website: www.lett.dk

Languages
English, German, the Scandinavian languages

Other offices
Copenhagen, Kolding

Number of lawyers 75
at this office 11

CATEGORIES OF WORK

- Mergers and acquisitions
- Corporate and commercial
- Competition/antitrust
- Insolvency
- Insurance and liability
- International trade
- Litigation and arbitration

BECH-BRUUN

LANGELINIE ALLÉ 35
2100 COPENHAGEN

Telephone: +45 72 27 00 00
Fax: +45 72 27 00 27
E-mail: info@bechbruun.com
Website: www.bechbruun.com

Languages
English, French, German, Italian,
the Scandinavian languages

Other offices
Aarhus, Moscow

Number of lawyers 254
at this office 190

CATEGORIES OF WORK

- Capital markets
- Company law
- Construction law and real estate
- Corporate consulting
- Employment and labour law
- Energy supply
- Environmental law
- EU and competition law
- Insolvency and restructuring
- Intellectual property rights
- International law
- IT law and telecommunications
- Litigation
- Media and entertainment
- Mergers and acquisitions
- Private law
- Public law
- Russian law
- Taxation
- Tort and insurance
- Transport law

ACCURA

ACCURA ADVOKATAKTIESELSKAB

STRANDVEJEN 60
2900 HELLERUP
COPENHAGEN

Telephone: +45 39 45 39 50
Fax: +45 39 45 39 60
E-mail: info@accura.dk
Website: www.accura.dk

Languages
English, French, German, the Scandinavian languages

Number of lawyers 46

Contact
Claus Bennetsen

CATEGORIES OF WORK

Commercial and competition
Annemette Thorgaard, Jesper Fabricius

Company law
Michael Vinther, Karsten Kielland

Corporate structuring
Kåre Stolt, Lars Fogh

Dispute resolution
Lars Bruun, Henrik Groos

Technology, media and communications
Martin Kasten

Employment and human resources
Nicole Offendal, Anne Kathrine Schøn

Financial services
Kim Toftgaard, Claus Bennetsen

Insolvency law/ financial restructuring
Jesper Trommer Volf

Intellectual property
Jesper Fabricius, Karsten Kielland

Mergers and acquisitions
Kåre Stolt, Thomas Weincke, Michael Vinther, Jacob Vinter

Real estate
Jon Dyhre Hansen, Henrik Groos

Tax
Henriette la Cour, Lars Fogh

Life sciences
Thomas Weincke, René Thornfeldt Perdersen

Venture capital
Claus Bennetsen, Jesper Trommer Volf

THE FIRM

Accura law firm is one of the fastest-growing major law firms in Denmark. Since its formation, the firm's goal has been to meet the professional legal counselling needs of any Danish or international company. Accura collaborates with a highly developed network of well-reputed international law firms from around the world.

The firm aims to provide an attractive working environment, and the ever-increasing number of qualified candidates applying for new jobs at the firm suggests it is on the right track. Supplementary training for employees is an indispensable part of the firm's business development, and many employees have supplemented their Danish legal education with additional studies or work experience overseas. Many have considerable business experience from outside the sphere of legal business.

AREAS OF PRACTICE

Accura Advokataktieselskab strives to make a difference in the Danish business community. The firm meets the requirements of modern businesses who need expert competencies, and is always able to set up teams of advisers possessing in-depth legal insight and a broad range of business knowledge.

A combination of international and domestic expertise, of specialists and generalists, and of legal and business affairs has enabled the firm to work together with numerous major, well-known and well-respected Danish and international companies. Accura Advokataktieselskab has a flat and modern organisational structure with short chains of command and operates in teams to best meet its clients' needs from every angle. The firm values efficiency, determination, creativity, independent analysis and superior legal expertise, believing that it is important to demonstrate its commitment and to be readily available to its clients, maintaining an open and ongoing dialogue with them, ensuring that they are kept well informed of proceedings.

The firm considers relationships quintessential: if its working relationship with clients is not based on mutual respect and inspiration, the firm cannot add value to its clients' businesses. Clients benefit from cross-border and cross-discipline inspiration and expertise, something that the firm considers of the utmost importance. By utilising and developing its international legal network at all levels, the firm experiences mutual inspiration.

In brief, what the firm aims to do is to generate inspiring relationships.

BENDER VON HALLER DRAGSTED

PAKHUS 4
KALKBRÆNDERILØBSKAJ 4
2100 COPENHAGEN

Telephone: +45 72 24 12 12
Fax: +45 72 24 12 13
E-mail: mail@bvhd.dk
Website: www.bvhd.dk

Languages
English, French, German, the Scandinavian languages

Number of lawyers 16

Contact
Nicolai Dragsted

CATEGORIES OF WORK

IT law and contracts
All lawyers

Arbitration
Peter Lind Nielsen, Jesper Langemark

Company law
Benjamin Lundström, Martin von Haller Grønbæk

Construction law
Peter Dann Jørgensen

Data protection
Birgitte Toxværd, Nis Peter Dall

Domain names
Kasper Heine

Intellectual property
Kasper Heine, Hanne Bender

Internet law
Martin von Haller Grønbæk, Jesper Langemark

IT project contracts
Hanne Bender, Nicolai Dragsted

M&A regarding IT companies
Jesper Langemark

Mediation
Benjamin Lundström, Kasper Heine

Open source
Martin von Haller Grønbæk

Outsourcing
Nicolai Dragsted, Henne Bender

Public procurement
Peter Dann Jørgensen, Peter Lind Nielsen

Telecommunication
Peter Lind Nielsen, Nicolai Dragsted

DELACOUR

HAMMERENSGADE 1
1267 KØBENHAVN K

Telephone: +45 70 11 11 22
Fax: + 45 70 11 11 33
E-mail: delacour@delacour.dk
Website: www.delacour.dk

Languages
English, German, French, the Scandinavian languages

Other offices
Aarhus

Number of lawyers 52
at this office 11

Member
Advoc, an international network of independent law firms

CATEGORIES OF WORK

Arbitration and litigation

Banking and finance

Corporate and commercial

Employment

Environment

EU and competition

Insurance

Intellectual property and IT

Life science

Mergers and acquisitions

Public sector

Real estate and construction

DLA NORDIC

VED STRANDEN 18, PO BOX 2034
1012 COPENHAGEN

Telephone: +45 77 30 40 50
Fax: +45 77 30 40 77
E-mail: info@dlanordic.dk
Website: www.dlanordic.com

Languages
English, French, German, Hebrew, the Scandinavian languages

Other offices
Bergen, Oslo, Stockholm

Number of lawyers 220
at this office 75

Contacts
Jens Jakob Bugge (managing partner), Kjeld Rask (COO)

Member
DLA Piper Group

CATEGORIES OF WORK

Banking and finance
Søren Thyssen Valerius

Capital markets
Torsten Hoffmeyer, Dan Moalem

Corporate and commercial
Jim Øksnebjerg, Dan Moalem

Dispute resolution – litigation and arbitration
Lars Carstens, Andreas Christensen

EU and competition
Lise Goesmeyer, Andreas Christensen

Employment
Finn Schwarz, Nicolai Mallet, Erik Wendelboe Christiansen

Energy
Klavs Gravesen, Søren Hornbæk Svendsen

IT and e-commerce
Michael Goeskjær, Mads Nygaard Madsen

Insolvency
Casper Moltke, Steen Klein

Insurance
Nicolai Horten

Intellectual property
Jens Jakob Bugge, Bastian Rankløve

Media and entertainment
Bastian Rankløve, Jens Jakob Bugge

Mergers and acquisitions
Jacob Kornerup, Torsten Hoffmeyer

Real estate and construction
Michael Neumann, Thomas Krucov Jensen

Shipping and transport
Hans Abildstrøm

Tax
Jim Øksnebjerg, Bjarne Becher Jensen

Telecommunications
Michael Goeskjær, Hans Abildstrøm

THE FIRM

DLA Nordic is the only Nordic law firm with offices in Copenhagen, Oslo, Bergen and Stockholm. The firm ranks among the leading law firms in its respective home markets in Denmark, Norway and Sweden. Each office provides a complete range of integrated legal services across borders, both in the local market and on a global basis.

DLA Nordic is part of DLA Piper Rudnick Gray Cary Group, an exclusive alliance of international full-service legal organisations with a shared vision. Established in 1999, the group now has members across Europe, Africa, the Middle East, Asia and the US, which deliver expert local know-how and integrated international solutions.

DLA Nordic's vision is to be the leading Nordic law firm, and is based on the observation that many clients have operations in all three countries. It is a modern, growing practice with a distinct client service focus; legal advice is based on a proactive approach and an understanding of the client's business. The firm offers a thorough and cost-effective mode of work, knowledge and insight in the local business environment, seamless Scandinavian and international legal services, and commercially based solutions.

AREAS OF PRACTICE

Banking and finance: advises on a wide range of Scandinavian and international financial institutions in various acquisition and asset finance transactions, plus regulatory work and derivatives.

Capital markets: developed practice significantly in 2004 by boosting its top-tier private equity and venture capital capabilities, as well as public equity.

Corporate and commercial: advises on corporate acquisitions, finance and securities law, venture capital and all areas of corporate law.

Employment: handles all types of employment issues, including staff policy, individual contracts, corporate reorganisations and collective agreements.

Energy: advises primarily national energy companies, municipalities and financial institutions on regulatory matters, mergers, acquisitions, sales, company establishments and restructures on construction and strategic issues.

IT and e-commerce: significant expertise in IT law, including internet-related issues (eg domain name disputes, illegal copying and downloading of copyrighted material).

Intellectual property: a growing IP department dealing with every aspect of intellectual property rights and with significant experience regarding trade mark infringement actions, patent litigation, cases about parallel import and counterfeited goods.

Media and entertainment: advises advertising agencies, record companies, radio and television companies, media companies, musicians and actors.

Mergers and acquisitions: offers advisory services to purchasers, sellers, intermediaries, financial partners and consultants, ranging from the initial strategic considerations to subsequent quality management of acquired company.

Real estate and construction: advises public and private sector clients on all issues in relation to real estate, environmental and construction law.

Telecommunications: advises clients across all sectors on the fast-changing telecoms industry, primarily around intellectual property rights.

The firm also gives other advice on areas including dispute resolution, insurance, tax, insolvency, shipping and transport, EU and competition.

LAW FIRM J.P. GALMOND & CO

HC ANDERSENS BOULEVARD 51
4 TV
1553 COPENHAGEN V

Telephone: +45 33 13 45 30
Fax: +45 33 93 55 30
E-mail: galmond@galmond.dk

Languages
Danish, English, German, Russian

Other offices
Hamburg, Moscow, St Petersburg

Number of lawyers 12
at this office 5

CATEGORIES OF WORK

- Agency and sales agreements
- Bankruptcy
- Company law
- Construction
- Employment
- Finance
- Intellectual property and competition
- IT and telecoms
- Law of tort
- Leasing, purchase and sale of real estate
- Litigation and arbitration
- Mergers and acquisitions, issues and transfer of business ownership
- Establishment of subsidiaries
- International finance
- Legal service on a regular basis
- M&A and contract law
- Project support

THE FIRM

The firm was established in 1983 when Mr JP Galmond took over a law firm whose core business areas included acting as legal advisers to the German Embassy in Copenhagen. A large number of the firm's clients were German companies operating in the Danish market. German and European companies still form part of the firm's client base which, however, primarily comprises a large number of Danish and Russian companies.

J.P. Galmond & Co has had a representation office in Hamburg since 1985. The firm started doing business in Russia in 1989, and a representation office was set up in 1992 in St Petersburg. At present the firm includes 12 lawyers.

AREAS OF PRACTICE

J.P. Galmond & Co provides all-round legal advice on international and national business operations. The firm has built up large and broad experience within company and commercial law, which it draws on when rendering legal services to small, medium-sized and large businesses including companies listed on the stock exchange in Denmark and abroad.

The firm's top priority is to ensure prompt, efficient and results-oriented legal advice and its aim is to provide concrete and practical solutions of a high professional standard to clients.

The establishment of offices in Russia and Germany means that it is uniquely positioned to render legal services to both national and international clients in Western and Eastern Europe.

In the firm's offices in St Petersburg and Moscow it has specialised in cross-border M&A and advice on telecoms, finance and company law.

The office has regular co-operation partners in most European countries and the USA.

JOHAN SCHLÜTER ADVOKATFIRMA

SUNDKROGSGADE 9
2100 COPENHAGEN

Telephone: +45 33 63 96 50
Fax: +45 33 6396 60
E-mail: info@jslaw.dk
Website: www.jslaw.dk

Languages
English, German, French, the Scandinavian languages

Other offices
Aarhus

Number of lawyers 18

Contact
Johan Schlüter

CATEGORIES OF WORK

Commercial and company law
J Schlüter, P Mollerup, L Halgreen

Litigation
T Steffensen

Arbitration
J Schlüter, T Steffensen

Copyright
J Schlüter, NB Jørgensen

Trade marks
A Ellermann

Patent
J Plesner Mathiasen

Sports
L Halgreen

Media and entertainment
J Schlüter, KS Schierbeck

IT – internet
NB Jørgensen

EU and competition
J Schlüter, L Halgreen, P Mollerup

JONAS BRUUN ADVOKATFIRMA

BREDGADE 38
1260 COPENHAGEN K

Telephone: +45 33 47 88 00
Fax: +45 33 47 88 88
E-mail: jb@jblaw.dk
Website: www.jonasbruun.dk

Languages
English, French, German, Russian

Number of lawyers 40

CATEGORIES OF WORK

Arbitration and litigation

Banking and finance

Capital markets

Commercial property

Company and commercial

Construction

EU and competition

Energy

Environment

Intellectual property

Mergers and acquisitions

Telecommunications, media and entertainment

KROMANN REUMERT

5 SUNDKROGSGADE
2100 COPENHAGEN

Telephone: +45 70 12 12 11
Fax: +45 70 12 13 11
E-mail: cph@kromannreumert.com
Website: www.kromannreumert.com

Languages
English, Dutch, French, German, the Scandinavian languages

Other offices
Aarhus, Brussels, London

Number of lawyers 222
at this office 172

Member
Lex Mundi; Scandinavian Law Alliance

CATEGORIES OF WORK

Banking and finance	IT and telecommunications
Commercial and company	Litigation and arbitration
Competition	Maritime and transportation
Employment and labour	Mergers and acquisitions
Energy	Real property, environmental and construction law
Insolvency	Shipping
Insurance and tort law	Stock exchange regulation
Intellectual property, media and marketing law	Tax law

LETT LAW FIRM

RÅDHUSPLADSEN 4
1550 COPENHAGEN V

Telephone: +45 33 77 00 00
Fax: +45 33 77 00 01
E-mail: lett@lett.dk
Website: www.lett.dk

Languages
English, French, German, the Scandinavian languages

Other offices
Aarhus, Kolding

Number of lawyers 75
at this office 48

CATEGORIES OF WORK

Public/administrative law	Food law
Environmental law	Public procurement
Mergers and acquisitions	Intellectual property
Corporate and commercial	IT and e-commerce
Tax	Telecoms
Dispute resolution	Employment and labour
Insurance and liability	Media and entertainment
Energy	Banking and finance
Shipping and transport	Real estate and construction
EU and competition	

LASSEN RICARD

LAW FIRM

31 AMALIEGADE
1256 COPENHAGEN

Telephone: +45 33 32 20 12
Fax: +45 33 32 24 74
E-mail: lrlaw@lrlaw.dk
Website: www.lassenricard.dk

Languages
English, French, German, Norwegian, Swedish

Number of lawyers 14

CATEGORIES OF WORK	
Banking and finance	**IT**
Company and commercial	**Litigation and arbitration**
Construction	**Media and entertainment**
EU and competition	**Mergers and acquisitions**
Intellectual property	**Telecommunications**

THE FIRM

Lassen Ricard is an international law firm advising mainly on commercial law issues, and in particular, on cases relating to international matters.

Lassen Ricard attach importance to the personal contact between the client and the attorneys, or team of attorneys, who advise the client, to ensure an essential relationship of trust.

It is crucial for the firm to offer legal service of the highest professional standard. Lassen Ricard has a close, non-exclusive co-operation with distinguished law firms abroad.

In addition to their legal degrees from Danish universities, several of the firm's attorneys hold degrees from foreign universities, such as Harvard Law School, University of Delaware, Duke Law School, University of Chicago Law School, City of London College and George Washington University.

The attorneys of Lassen Ricard are authorised to appear before all Danish courts, including the Danish Supreme Court. They have extensive experience pleading before arbitral tribunals and also act as judges in arbitration tribunals. In addition, the firm has experience in pleading before the European Court of Justice.

AREAS OF PRACTICE

Lassen Ricard provides a full range of services within corporate and commercial law, media, entertainment and intellectual property law, mergers and acquisitions, EU and competition law, IT, telecoms and litigation. Among Lassen Ricard's clients within said areas are a large number of international companies, as well as large and mid-size Danish companies. The firm also assists some of their clients by being appointed board members.

Lassen Ricard has extensive knowledge within intellectual property and is the leading Danish law firm within media and entertainment representing a large number of broadcasters and broadcasting organisations, as well as record companies, theatres, artists etc.

Representative clients include: Agfa; Banctec; Bayer; British Broadcasting Corporation; Biomet; Discovery Communications Europe; Danish Radio and Television; Danish TV2; Eurosport; Matsushita; Nord-Deutscher Rundfunk; Norwegian Radio and Television; TV2 Norway; Rai; Seiko; Sony Music Entertainment; Zweites Deutsches Fernsehen; Maxxium (Remy Martin, Jim Beam, Highland Distillers); RTL Plus; Sakata; Sat-1; Swedish Radio and Television; The Union of Broadcasting Organisations regarding Denmark, Norway, Sweden and Iceland; The Presidium of the Danish Parliament; The EU Environment Agency; and Kaukomarkkinat.

LIND CADOVIUS

38 ØSTERGADE
PO BOX 2256
1019 KØBENHAVN K

Telephone: +45 33 33 81 00
Fax: +45 33 33 81 01
E-mail: law.office@lindcad.dk
Website: www.lindcad.dk

Languages
English, German, French, the Scandinavian languages

Number of lawyers 40

CATEGORIES OF WORK

Company and commercial
Jørgen Cadovius, Frantz Palludan

Mergers and acquisitions
Frantz Palludan, Hans Madsen, Søren Jørgensen

Banking and finance
Frantz Palludan

IT
Hans Madsen, Marlene W Plas

Intellectual property
Mads Berendt

Insolvency law
Henrik Andersen, Lars Skanvig

Construction and real estate
Mads Berendt

Media and entertainent
Jens Krogh Petersen

Insurance
Nicolai Westergaard

Arbitration and litigation
Mads Berendt, Håkun Djurhuus, Nicolai Westergaard

Employment, labour law
Nicolai Westergaard, Birgitte Horn

Tax
Jess Thiersen

Energy
Hans Madsen, Marlene W Plas

Competition and EU law
Lotte Hummelshøj, Søren Zinck

Environment
Håkun Djurhuus

White-collar crime
Mads Berendt

NIELSEN & NØRAGER

METROPOL
FREDERIKSBERGGADE 16
1459 COPENHAGEN K

Telephone: +45 33 11 45 45
Fax: +45 33 11 80 81
E-mail: info@nnlaw.dk
Website: www.nnlaw.dk

Languages
English, French, German, the Scandinavian languages

Number of lawyers 17

Member
Unilaw

CATEGORIES OF WORK

Arbitration and litigation
Jacob Nørager-Nielsen, Eigil Lego Andersen

Banking and finance
Morten Eldrup-Jørgensen, Thomas Weisbjerg

Company and commercial
Ole Finn Nielsen, Morten Eldrup-Jørgensen

Construction
Halfdan Krag Jespersen, Jacob Nørager-Nielsen

Corporate finance, M&A
Morten Eldrup-Jørgensen, Eigil Lego Andersen

EC and competition
Henrik Peytz

Insurance
Michael S Wiisbye

Information technology
Jacob Nørager-Nielsen

Media and entertainment
Ole Finn Nielsen

Real estate
Marianne Kjær Stolt, Halfdan Krag Jespersen

Taxation
Henrik Peytz, Jan Presfeldt

Employment
Marianne Kjær Stolt

Telecoms
Henrik Peytz

Biotech
Morten Eldrup-Jørgensen, Jan Presfeldt

MAZANTI-ANDERSEN, KORSØ JENSEN & PARTNERE

69 ST KONGENSGADE
1264 KØBENHAVN K

Telephone: +45 33 14 35 36
Fax: +45 33 19 37 37
E-mail: info@mazanti.dk
Website: www.mazanti.dk

Languages
English, French, German, Italian, Russian, the Scandinavian languages

Number of lawyers 35

CATEGORIES OF WORK

Mergers and acquisitions	Finance and banking
Litigation and arbitration	International contract
Insolvency	Intellectual property
Company and commercial	Tax
Franchising law	EU and competition
Employment and labour law	Family, matrimonial
Marketing law	Environment
Public law	Construction law and real estate

THE FIRM

The firm was initially established in 1853 and is today one of the oldest law firms in Denmark. The firm was formed by CCV Liebe, a prominent Danish lawyer and politician, whose lead was followed by his son, Otto Liebe, who was both the first chairman of the Danish Bar Association and, in 1920, Prime Minister of Denmark. From 1932, the firm was headed by Leif Gamborg and, since 1958, by J Mazanti-Andersen, Jørgen and Hans Henrik Gamborg. The partners have continued the firm's tradition in relation to corporate and procedural law and established and developed its international basis and practice.

The firm has grown considerably over the years. Mazanti-Andersen, Korsø Jensen & Partnere's practice areas cover corporate and commercial law, the M&A department is strong, and the firm represents both substantial international and national clients in litigation and national and international arbitration.

It is the opinion of the firm that legal services in relation to clients' activities outside Denmark are best provided for by the use of local counsel in the country in question. Consequently, the firm, instead of setting up branch offices outside Denmark, participates in comprehensive, formalised international co-operation and has legal connections in every continent. Due to these relationships, the firm's clients are assured that legal problems in individual foreign countries are solved by local lawyers with a high degree of personal involvement and competence.

Today, the firm is among the largest and well-esteemed law firms in Denmark, and is renowned for its professional competence, dynamism and integrity.

AREAS OF PRACTICE

Mazanti-Andersen, Korsø Jensen & Partnere has extensive experience in corporate and commercial law, M&A and litigation and arbitration. The firm also has a department dealing with environmental issues. It is the stated objective of the firm to provide professional services, reflecting a creative and progressive attitude in all respects, responding to national and international clients' demands for innovative and commercial solutions of complex problems.

The firm is constantly seeking to maintain its up-to-the-minute legal expertise and all the lawyers participate on a regular basis in extensive legal training programmes within specific areas of law. Many of the firm's lawyers also lecture on corporate and commercial law at universities in Denmark and abroad.

It has been the experience of the firm that most clients prefer a consistent, personal service. Consequently, it is a fundamental objective of the firm's operation to charge one lawyer with sole responsibility for monitoring and co-ordinating the affairs of each client, to ensure that they have a clear line of contact with the firm. Mazanti-Andersen, Korsø Jensen & Partnere has the following structure: one client – one contact person – one team. If complicated projects demand the expertise from different parts of the firm, the necessary resources are made available to any client at short notice.

The active promotion of specialisations within the firm ensures that the firm is able to adapt its practice to meet developments in the business community together with the future needs and requirements of its clients. The firm has at its disposal all the necessary technical facilities, including an extensive computer-based legal library connected to external databases.

NORRBOM & VINDING, member of ius laboris

LAW FIRM

DAMPFÆRGEVEJ 26
2100 COPENHAGEN

Telephone: +45 35 25 39 40
Fax: +45 35 25 39 50
E-mail: nv@nv-law.dk
Website: www.nv-law.dk

Languages
English, French, Italian, Spanish, the Scandinavian languages

Number of lawyers 23

Contacts
Mariann Norrbom, Jørgen Vinding, Morten Langer, Yvonne Frederiksen

Member
ius laboris, International Employment Law, Pensions and Employee Benefits Alliance

CATEGORIES OF WORK

- **All aspects of labour law**
- **All aspects of employment law**
- **Company staff policies**
- **Compensation and benefits**
- **European labour law**
- **Criminal aspects of labour law**
- **Restructuring and transfer of undertakings**
- **Social security**
- **Employee participation**
- **Pension schemes**
- **Tax issues relating to employment law**

THE FIRM

Norrbom & Vinding is a niche law firm dealing with all aspects of labour and employment law, exclusively for the management side. Although the firm is relatively new, it has 25 years of experience within its area of expertise, and a core of the firm's attorneys have worked together for more than 15 years. The firm is one of the first specialist offices in Denmark with a full service to both national and international clients on all aspects of law related to human resources.

Norrbom & Vinding is a member of ius laboris, International Employment Law Pensions and Employee Benefits Alliance. The alliance was formed in January 2001 and today numbers more than 1,200 lawyers in Europe, North and South America.

AREAS OF PRACTICE

Labour law: the firm advises managements in both public and private companies on the negotiation, interpretation and termination of collective agreements, and it frequently participates in industrial disputes procedures. The firm also advises companies on the establishment of European works councils.

Norrbom & Vinding offers advice on, and assistance with, both collective and individual aspects in connection with transfer of undertakings, restructuring, redundancies and outsourcing.

Pensions: pensions are an element of human resources attracting increasing interest. The firm assists on the drafting and implementation of company-based pension plans, pension issues relating to termination of employment and expatriation. The firm also offers advice on taxation aspects in relation to pensions.

Individual employment law: even within the very traditional area of employment law – the individual employment relationship – various developments in recent years have led to more complex legal problems. The firm's advice and sparring with HR departments within this area includes: recruitment procedures, employment contracts, material changes in existing employment conditions, severance agreements, discrimination, equal treatment, maternity/paternity leave, freedom of association and data protection.

Company policies: HR departments base their work on company policies to quite a large extent. Such policies may deal with issues ranging from alcohol policies, anti-harassment measures, the use of e-mail, and distribution of anniversary bonuses, to rules on absence due to sickness. The firm's advice on such aspects includes assessment of policies in relation to collective agreements and legislation, possible legal action in relation to non-compliance with company policies and review of policies with regard to sustainable development issues.

Benefits: today, pay is often a combination of many different elements, leading to an increase in the need for advice in relation to both the pay concept as such and to tax issues. In this area, Norrbom & Vinding assists on the composition of individual payroll packages and the development, implementation and subsequent administration of bonus, incentive and employee share programmes.

PHILIP & PARTNERS

VOGNMAGERGADE 7
1120 KØBENHAVN K

Telephone: +45 33 13 11 12
Fax: +45 33 32 80 45
E-mail: lawoffice@philip.dk
Website: www.philip.dk

Languages
English, German, Italian, Norwegian, Swedish

Number of lawyers 35

CATEGORIES OF WORK

Banking and finance
Erik Malberg, Henning Hansen

Capital markets
Erik Korre Horten, Henning Hansen

Contracts
Claus Kaare Pedersen

Corporate and commercial
Peer B Petersen, Jesper Rothe

Dispute resolution
Mogens Gaarden, Steen Rode

Employment
Steen Rode

Energy
Jesper Rothe

Environment
Mogens Gaarden

EU and competition law
Erik Malberg, Jesper Rothe

Insolvency
Erik Malberg, Henning Hansen

Insurance
Mogens Gaarden, Steen Rode

IT and e-commerce
Jesper Rothe, Peer B Petersen

Media and entertainment
Peer B Petersen

Mergers and acquisitions
Henning Hansen, Jesper Rothe

Real estate and construction
Claus Kaare Pedersen, Jens Hjortskov

Shipping and transport
Jens Hjortskov, Steen Rode

Tax
Martin Simonsen, Thomas Frøbert

Telecoms
Henning Hansen, Jens Hjortskov

PLESNER

37 AMERIKA PLADS
2100 COPENHAGEN

Telephone: +45 33 12 11 33
Fax: +45 33 12 00 14
E-mail: plesner@plesner.com
Website: www.plesner.com

Languages
English, French, German, Italian, Norwegian, Polish, Swedish

Number of lawyers 150

CATEGORIES OF WORK

Commercial law and companies

Intellectual property

Telecommunications and media

Information technology

Commercial property

Tax

EU law

Banking, securities and finance

Construction law, environmental and building law

Energy and mining law

Corporate finance

Insurance

Mergers and acquisitions

Litigation and arbitration

Bankruptcy, insolvency

Competition law and unfair marketing

Product liability and consumer law

Labour law

RØNNE & LUNDGREN

TUBORG HAVNEVEJ 18
POSTBOX 90
2900 COPENHAGEN HELLERUP

Telephone: +45 35 25 25 35
Fax: +45 35 25 25 36
E-mail: info@rl.dk
Website: www.ronnelundgren.com

Languages
English, German, Italian, the Scandinavian languages, Cantonese

Number of lawyers 38

Contacts
Finn Rønne, Benny Schwartz

CATEGORIES OF WORK

Corporate and commercial	**Litigation and arbitration**
Administrative	**Media and entertainment**
Employment	**Mergers and acquisitions**
EU and competition	**Real property and construction**
Insolvency and reorganisation	**Financing and securities regulation**
Insurance and tort	**Succession**
IP and marketing	**Tax (including international tax)**
IT	**Finance and banking**

VILTOFT & HØBERG-PETERSEN
ADVOKATAKTIESELSKAB

GOTHERSGADE 109
1123 KØBENHAVN K

Telephone: +45 33 14 93 00
Fax: +45 33 14 32 56
E-mail: viltoft@viltoft.dk
Website: www.viltoft.dk

Languages
English, French, German, Icelandic, the Scandinavian languages

Number of lawyers 11

CATEGORIES OF WORK

Construction law Michael Gjedde-Nielsen, Hans Lykke Hansen	**Arbitration** Hans Lykke Hansen, Michael Gjedde-Nielsen
Labour and employment law Bjørn Høberg-Petersen, Jakob Juul	**Energy law** Jakob Juul
Copyright/entertainment law Bjørn Høberg-Petersen	**Computer law** Claus Berg, Jakob Juul
Contract law Claus Berg, Michael Gjedde-Nielsen	**Environmental law** Michael Gjedde-Nielsen, Claus Berg
Public procurement law Hans Lykke Hansen, Michael Gjedde-Nielsen	**Criminal law** Bjørn Høberg-Petersen

LETT LAW FIRM

JERNBANEGADE 31
6000 KOLDING

Telephone: +45 75 50 40 00
Fax: +45 75 54 10 50
E-mail: lett@lett.dk
Website: www.lett.dk

Languages
English, French, German, the Scandinavian languages

Other offices
Aarhus, Copenhagen

Number of lawyers 75
at this office 16

CATEGORIES OF WORK

Mergers and acquisitions	**Intellectual property**
Corporate and commercial	**IT and e-commerce**
Competition/antitrust	**Telecommunications**
Tax	**Employment and labour**
Litigation and arbitration	**EU and competition**
Insurance and liability	**Banking and finance**
Insolvency	**Energy**
Real estate and construction	**Capital markets**
Public procurement	

FOCUS ADVOKATER LLP

ENGLANDSGADE 25
POSTBOX 906
5100 ODENSE C

Telephone: +45 63 14 20 20
Fax: +45 63 14 20 30
E-mail:mail@focus-advokater.dk
Website: www.focus-advokater.dk

Languages
English, French, German, Spanish

Other offices
Copenhagen, Hamburg, Paris*, Nice*

Number of lawyers 43
at this office 33

Contacts
Peter Ringsted, Michael Clemmensen

CATEGORIES OF WORK

Arbitration and litigation	**Insolvency**
Banking, securities and finance	**Intellectual property**
Companies, commercial law (general)	**Mergers and acquisitions**
Construction	**Ship and aircraft finance**
EU and competition	**Tax**
Environmental law	**Transport**

EGYPT

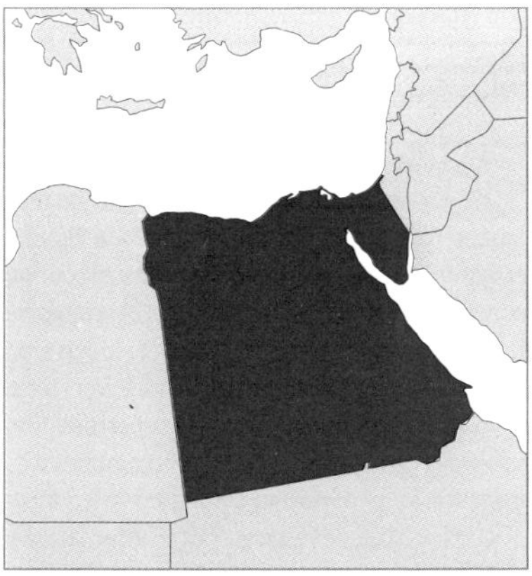

Population	**74 million**
Number of lawyers	**n/a**
Professional title	**Attorney at law**
Currency	**Egyptian pound (E£)**

Index

In September 2005 the President of the past 24 years, Hosny Mubarak, won Egypt's first-ever presidential election by a landslide, amidst opposition calls of electoral irregularities. Politicians are divided as to whether the election represents the first steps towards the democratisation of Egypt, or was manipulated by Mubarak to reinforce the legitimacy of his authoritarian regime (the main opposition party The Muslim Brotherhood was banned from standing.)

Prior to the election, Egypt was subject to a great deal of diplomatic pressure from the United States to initiate democratic reform and it is clear that Egypt will continue to enhance its political and economic ties with the world's only superpower.

Unfortunately Egypt continues to be a target for extremists and in July 2005 terrorist bomb attacks killed 88 people in the resort of Sharm el-Sheikh. Such acts of violence will hopefully not impact upon the mood of optimism in Egypt, that after 50 years of authoritarian rule, the nation has taken significant steps towards democracy.

ECONOMY

The Egyptian economy is continuing to experience dramatic growth of around 6% per annum, particularly with exports and public quoted companies, though for the majority of the workforce based in the suburbs, these areas remain overcrowded, poor and lacking in investment.

President Mubarak was re-elected partly on the promise to continue with economic reforms to help facilitate investment, as well as increasing levels of state salaries and maintaining subsidies. These reforms will also be crucial in reducing high unemployment (a conservative estimate puts it at 10%).

Egypt's dependence on substantial government debt, continues to limit the ability of financial institutions to invest domestically (approximately one third of banking assets are tied up in the same), which in turn detracts companies from expanding and generating more jobs.

Another pressing long-term concern that must be addressed before economic development can be sustained, is that of the skills deficit of the Egyptian workforce. The Egyptian education system has been criticised for failing to sufficiently equip school leavers with transferable skills and continuing professional development of the workforce is largely ignored by companies.

Oil remains a foundation of the Egyptian economy, (40% of exports) together with tourism which represents a US$6.6bn industry. In September 2005 the Egyptian government announced plans for a US$5bn oil refinery, which hopefully will counter any fall in tourism as a consequence of the July bomb attacks.

With a population of over 74 million, it is essential that the Egyptian economy not only grows, but also diversifies, so that the benefits of economic reform and greater investment will impact upon many rather than the few.

BILLING

Associates working in leading Cairo practices expect to charge from US$100 to US$250 per hour for international work, while partners charge from US$200 to US$350 per hour. Fees for domestic clients are generally lower.

IN-HOUSE LAWYERS

There has been a gradual movement within large financial institutions to establish in-house legal departments, with fee-earners being recruited from respected domestic practices.

MARKETING

There are no restrictions on Egyptian law firms marketing their services. Domestic firms' websites mirror those of Western practices, detailing the legal services provided, significant clients represented and resumés of the leading partners.

LEGAL MARKET

The Egyptian legal market is mainly comprised of home-grown practices, though in the past 20 years there has been a gradual influx of international firms joining forces with domestic partnerships. Foreign lawyers are only permitted to practise within the jurisdiction if they have an association with a local firm, which in turn must have practitioners registered at the Egyptian Bar Association. Accordingly, **Baker & McKenzie** is allied with **Helmy, Hamza & Partners**, **Denton Wilde Sapte** has its association with **El Oteifi Law Office**, **Trowers & Hamlins** is twinned with **Nour Law Office** and German firm **Amereller**

The largest firms

1	Zaki Hashem & Partners, Attorneys at Law	42
2	Al Kamel Law Office	33
3	Sarwat A. Shahid Law Firm	29
4	Ibrachy & Dermarkar	25
5	Kosheri, Rashed & Riad	22
6	Baker & McKenzie	21
7	Denton Wilde Sapte	19
8	Sherif Saad Law Offices	16
9	Abu-Ghazaleh Legal	13
	Karim Adel Kamel Law Office	13
11	Hassouna & Abou Ali	12
	Hilmy Law Firm	12
13	Nabil Farag Law Firm	11
	Nadoury & Nahas Law Offices	11
15	Mena Associates in association with Amereller Rechtsanwälte	8
16	ELOMC Lawyers	7
	Sharkawy Law Office	7
18	Trowers & Hamlins	6

These figures represent the total number of lawyers in this country only, and have been supplied by the firms themselves. The figures should be accurate as at 1 January 2006.

Rechtsanwälte has **Mena Associates** as its Egyptian partner. In October 2005 **DLA Matouk Bassiouny** was formed. It is the first Middle Eastern office of global firm **DLA Piper Rudnick Gray Cary UK LLP**. John Matouk and Omar Bassiouny have extensive corporate, commercial and capital markets expertise in Egypt.

White & Case has 50 years of experience advising in the region, as well as having an office in Riyadh, Saudi Arabia. Recently the firm represented EBIC on the creation and maintenance of a US$450m ammonia plant in the Egyptian Gulf of Suez.

Leading local firms have enhanced their international presence by joining strategic alliances of law firms. **Ibrachy & Dermarkar** is a member of *TAGLaw*, **Nadoury & Nahas Law Offices** is party to *Lex Africa*, whereas **Shalakany Law Office** is affiliated to *Lex Mundi*.

The main commercial centre in Egypt for legal work is Cairo. All major facets of corporate and commercial practice are offered in the capital, together with a great deal of project finance-based work, which reflects the high level of investment activity currently driving the Egyptian economy. On a lesser scale, in Alexandria there is some shipping work.

BANKING AND FINANCE

Baker & McKenzie has an expanding office (six new associates were hired in 2005), which mirrors its expanding banking and finance workload. For Morgan Stanley it acted as arranger for a US$1.5bn oil forward sale and securitisation, with Mohamed Ghannam leading the team, as well as advising on an ongoing US$500m remittance securitisation for a major Egyptian bank. Mohamed Ghannam together with other international partner Mohamed Talatt represented Telecom Egypt in an E£2bn (US$347m) corporate bond issue.

The finance team spearheaded by Bridget McKinney at **Denton Wilde Sapte** continues to attract high-profile work, acting as local counsel for Italian bank Banca IMI in a €1.2bn equity financing for the Sawiris family, as part of a bidding consortium for Wind Telecom. The firm advised BNP Paribas on the financing, delivery and leaseback of seven A300-600 Airbus aircraft worth US$750m.

With six partners and 15 associates **Kosheri, Rashed & Riad** has finance expertise, together with high-profile banking clients. It acted on the US$700m acquisition of Misr America International Bank, and is currently working on the sale of Egyptian Commercial Bank.

Shalakany Law Office has an experienced group of lawyers advising on all aspects of banking and finance, as well as being the first in Egypt to apply new financial products, such as GDRs (Global Depository Receipts) and leveraged buy-outs.

BANKING AND FINANCE

BAKER & McKENZIE ✪
DENTON WILDE SAPTE ✪
KOSHERI, RASHED & RIAD ✪
SHALAKANY LAW OFFICE
TROWERS & HAMLINS

Hassouna & Abou Ali
Ibrachy & Dermarkar
Zaki Hashem & Partners, Attorneys at Law

Firms are listed A-Z in tiers which are ranked in order of priority
✪ *Indicates firm displays contact details at the end of this chapter.*

2005 was a productive year for the finance team at **Trowers & Hamlins** led by Sara Hinton. For Exim-Bank the group is acting as local counsel on a proposed US$300m financing of an ammonia plant, and was also the first firm to advise on establishing a factoring company in the free-zone.

Hassouna & Abou Ali, a two-partner firm supported by eight associates, has maintained its reputation for undertaking cutting-edge work. For a USAID (US Agency for International Development) funded project, it developed a unique legal framework for the introduction of real estate financing and securitisation. 'Their work is thorough and most professional; they are focused, responsible and practical,' reported one client.

Advising on five key transactions in the past 12 months, **Ibrachy & Dermarkar** has a group led by 'very professional' finance specialist Ashraf Elibrachy, that has been instructed by international investment banks Calyon, West LB and MCC as local counsel. The team also negotiated the assignment of a financing agreement for the Islamic Corporation for the Development of the Private Sector, and reported on regulatory issues on behalf of the Day Berry & Howard Foundation.

As one of the largest practices in Egypt with 48 attorneys, **Zaki Hashem & Partners, Attorneys at Law** is a full-service law firm with an impressive blue-chip client list: Heineken, Nissan and Vodafone Egypt, amongst others. For the Overseas Private Investment Corporation it acted on a major oil and gas deal, and for IT company Raya Holding SAE, advised on a capital increase and secondary private placement worth E£300m (US$52m).

CORPORATE AND M&A

Baker & McKenzie's corporate team had a very busy year, acting on a plethora of takeovers, mergers and joint ventures for leading global players. It advised Barclays Bank on its potential bid for local bank Misr International; American Express was represented in the merger of its Egyptian branches with the Egyptian American Bank; and Mars UK appointed the team for the

CORPORATE AND M&A

BAKER & McKENZIE ✪
DENTON WILDE SAPTE ✪
SHALAKANY LAW OFFICE
ZAKI HASHEM & PARTNERS, ATTORNEYS AT LAW

Hassouna & Abou Ali
Ibrachy & Dermarkar
Mena Associates in association with Amereller Rechtsanwälte
Trowers & Hamlins

Al Kamel Law Office
Kosheri, Rashed & Riad ✪
Nadoury & Nahas Law Offices
Sarwat A. Shahid Law Firm

Karim Adel Kamel Law Office
The Egyptian Law Firm

Firms are listed A-Z in tiers which are ranked in order of priority
✪ *Indicates firm displays contact details at the end of this chapter.*

purposes of establishing a local manufacturing company. Other deals included a US$550m construction materials takeover and US$130m telecommunications joint venture.

The 21-attorney 'knowledgeable, thorough and responsive' team at **Denton Wilde Sapte** has acted on a 'first' in Egypt, on behalf of BNP Paribas documenting, negotiating and registering five A320-200 Airbus finance leases for Egypt Air. This was the first registration of a foreign finance lessor in the Finance Lease Department of the Ministry of Investment under the new Finance Lease Law. Other high-profile work undertaken consists of a US$900m petrochemical joint venture and advising Islamic and African venture capital funds on share purchases of domestic concerns.

With 57 attorneys, **Shalakany Law Office** is fully equipped to offer a wide range of corporate and commercial services encompassing joint ventures, international corporate structures and company administration.

Zaki Hashem & Partners, Attorneys at Law has historically been at the forefront of corporate practice in Egypt. 2005 cemented this reputation, with the firm acting for Vodafone Egypt in the restructuring and licensing of its entire mobile phone operations in Egypt. Other significant deals were a US$300m purchase by global beverage company Heineken of domestic rival Al Ahram Beverages Company; acting on behalf of Nissan for a US$25m acquisition of a manufacturing asset; and for Raya Holding, advising on a E£300m (US$52m) private placement.

Hassouna & Abou Ali specialises in high-profile corporate and commercial work. On behalf of the American University in Cairo the firm advised on a US$100m new university campus project, and for Egyptian Telephone Equipment Company negotiated a licence agreement with Qualcomm. One client commented: 'Their work performed was outstanding and in a timely manner.'

Ibrachy & Dermarkar with 22 attorneys continues to act for leading aviation companies in corporate and commercial matters, British Airways, Air France-KLM and Lufthansa are amongst its clients. Two substantial deals advised on, with both teams being led by partner Ashraf Elibrachy, were the acquisition of Egyptian Fertilzers Company by TATA Chemicals Limited; and Piraeus Bank's acquisition of the Egyptian Commercial Bank.

The 13-attorney team at **Mena Associates in association with Amereller Rechtsanwälte** has had a diverse range of corporate instructions in 2005, ranging from representing a *Fortune 500* company in the bankruptcy of its local distributor, to a US$100m joint venture in the aviation industry. The firm was also instructed on one of the two largest LNG projects in Egypt, and is valued for being 'quick, responsive, taking into account the practical needs.'

Sara Hinton's team at **Trowers & Hamlins** had a brisk year, notably acting for Vodafone on a share swap relating to a 50:50 joint venture with Telecom Egypt, and for cable manufacturers Leoni, negotiating all relevant agreements in relation to their Egyptian expansion. Other advice given varies from dealing with a major Gulf investment company's corporate restructuring of its investments, to representing a large overseas investor in its share purchase of a domestic concern. One oil and gas industry client commented it is 'a law firm we trust and rely on.'

Thirty-three-attorney firm, **Al Kamel Law Office** has the capacity to undertake a broad spectrum of corporate and commercial work.

Kosheri, Rashed & Riad counts Caterpillar Egypt, Philip Morris and Colgate-Palmolive amongst its clients, as well as acting on the acquisition of the Eastern Tobacco Company in 2005.

Three-partner firm (split between two offices in Cairo and Alexandria) **Nadoury & Nahas Law Offices** acts for UPS Egypt regarding its operations within the jurisdiction, including the acquisition of a freight company, and reviewing agreements between UPS and Loutfy Mansour International Distribution Company.

Acting on behalf of banks, construction companies, embassies and insurance companies, **Sarwat A. Shahid Law Firm** has a team of 21 attorneys and regularly provides advice on investments, joint ventures and acquisitions.

With 13 attorneys, **Karim Adel Kamel Law Office**, led by name partner Karim Adel Kamel, acted on two significant deals in 2005; the share sale of a local concern to the French company Santesurf and establishing a new joint stock company Amadeus Egypt as a subsidiary of Amadeus Global Travel Distribution.

Two-partner and eight-attorney **The Egyptian Law Firm** counts embassies, international corporations and local companies as clients, with attorney Yaser Gamaluddin Hamam being noted as 'very helpful' by clients.

DISPUTE RESOLUTION

BAKER & McKENZIE ✪
KOSHERI, RASHED & RIAD ✪

Denton Wilde Sapte ✪
Hassouna & Abou Ali
Hazem Gomaa (Dr), Law Office of
Ibrachy & Dermarkar
Karim Adel Kamel Law Office
Mena Associates in association with Amereller Rechtsanwälte
Nadoury & Nahas Law Offices
Shalakany Law Office
Trowers & Hamlins
Zaki Hashem & Partners, Attorneys at Law

Ashraf Law Firm

Firms are listed A-Z in tiers which are ranked in order of priority
✪ *Indicates firm displays contact details at the end of this chapter.*

DISPUTE RESOLUTION

The 18-strong Cairo office of **Baker & McKenzie** continues to be instructed on high-profile litigation, over the past year representing football federation FIFA, hotel group Radisson SAS, and global conglomerate ICI Uniquema. 'They are a good respectful firm with a good name and reputation,' praised one client.

Kosheri, Rashed & Riad is led by two litigation heavyweights; 'top-notch' managing partner Dr Riad and senior partner Professor Kosheri (vice- president of the International Chamber of Commerce in Paris). The firm acted on two of the largest disputes in 2005; an E£600m (US$104m) telecommunications claim and a US$250m media dispute. One client that instructed the firm on a three-year arbitration commented that the service is 'first class in every respect'.

Arbitration comprises the majority of the contentious caseload at **Denton Wilde Sapte**, with the firm acting as lead counsel for an international insurance company, a multinational mining company and for construction companies, providing 'excellent support both from a quality and from response time standpoint.'

Hassouna & Abou Ali represented an international French contractor in its dispute with a major Egyptian contractor, concerning the call of performance bonds in a US$7m contract. This case was heard before the Cairo Regional Center for International Commercial Arbitration.

The two-partner dispute resolution group at **Ibrachy & Dermarkar** is headed by Dr Bahieldin Elibrachy and Dr Mahmoud Mokhtar Berairy. They are currently handling a complex multi-jurisdictional commercial mediation between a Gulf-based company and a *Fortune 500* company. Smaller arbitrations have been handled on behalf of construction and utility companies.

Achieving a favourable outcome on behalf of CNA Insurance in a US$20m case in the Court of First Instance, has dominated the litigation caseload for **Karim Adel Kamel Law Office** in 2005, with Ossama Badawy heading the litigation and arbitration department.

Mena Associates in association with Amereller Rechtsanwälte specialises in seven-figure litigation and arbitration, the highlight of which in 2005 was representing a major European contractor in a €100m arbitration.

In 2005 **Nadoury & Nahas Law Offices** acted on two arbitrations in Alexandria and Cairo. The former was between two domestic companies, the latter saw the firm represent international corporation ALU Glass against Korean company, Doosan Construction & Engineering.

Being one of the first Egyptian practices to exploit the opening in the market for commercial arbitration expertise, **Shalakany Law Office** boasts a dedicated team which undertakes around ten new arbitrations on an annual basis. Name partner Dr Khaled El Shalakany is a fellow of the Chartered Institute of Arbitrators, and acts as an arbitrator himself in various disputes.

Advising on big-value disputes is the foundation of the dispute resolution practice at **Trowers & Hamlins**. The team is acting on behalf of a major technology equipment company on a US$20m technology transfer agreement dispute, and for a principal investor in a dairy plant project regarding its multi-million dollar dispute with an equipment supplier.

The renowned dispute resolution department at **Zaki Hashem & Partners, Attorneys at Law** has expertise to represent international and domestic clients at all courts in Egypt. Currently inactive partner Dr Nabil Elaraby is a judge at the International Court of Justice in The Hague.

'Characterised by competence and integrity' six-attorney practice **Ashraf Law Firm** specialises in criminal defence litigation, winning four significant cases before the Egyptian Supreme Court in 2005. The firm represents high-profile individuals, as well as banks and engineering companies.

INTELLECTUAL PROPERTY

With a global reputation for IP expertise, **Baker & McKenzie** does not disappoint, with the team focusing on patent and trade mark infringement claims. For hotel group Sheraton the firm was retained to advise on trade name and trade mark infringement. The firm has also recently advised GlaxoSmithKline on patent issues, and the use of generics within the pharmaceutical industry.

The world's largest research-based pharmaceutical company Pfizer instructs **Denton Wilde Sapte** as local counsel, to protect the intellectual property of key products such as Viagra. The team also has advised on counterfeiting and copyright law.

Shalakany Law Office offers a broad range of IP advice, encompassing patent, copyright and trade mark law. The firm has strong links with the relevant government IP agencies, and is experienced in IP litigation.

With IP professor Ms Nermien Al-Ali leading the team, **Ibrachy & Dermarkar** acts as IP counsel for global corporations Siemens and Bayer, as well as advising on franchising, licensing and creative technology issues for other international clients.

Representing pharmaceutical, IT and music companies, **Zaki Hashem & Partners, Attorneys at Law** has an experienced IP team, with particular expertise in IP audit for the purpose of acquiring and licensing intellectual property rights.

INTELLECTUAL PROPERTY

BAKER & McKENZIE ✪
DENTON WILDE SAPTE ✪
SHALAKANY LAW OFFICE

Hazem Gomaa (Dr), Law Office of
Ibrachy & Dermarkar
Kosheri, Rashed & Riad ✪
Zaki Hashem & Partners, Attorneys at Law

Firms are listed A-Z in tiers which are ranked in order of priority
✪ Indicates firm displays contact details at the end of this chapter.

OIL AND GAS

Baker & McKenzie has been instructed as local counsel for Egypt LNG and its sponsors in relation to an Egyptian LNG liquefaction project, as well as setting up concession assignments in Alamein and the West Mediterranean Block 1.

Continuing to undertake high-profile work, **Ibrachy & Dermarkar** represents mostly financial institutions on their investments in the Egyptian oil and gas market. For Standard Bank London, the firm acted as local counsel on a US$65m senior common terms agreement.

Acting on one of the biggest oil and gas projects for Spanish-based utility company Union Fenosa, **Zaki Hashem & Partners, Attorneys at Law** established the legal structure of the first liquefied natural gas (LNG) project in Egypt worth US$1.7bn. The practice has handled such major instructions since the origination of oil concessions in the 1960s.

Kosheri, Rashed & Riad represents Marathon Oil Corporation, BP Amoco, Elf Oil Germany and the Ministry of Oil regarding its operations in Egypt.

OIL AND GAS

BAKER & McKENZIE ✪
IBRACHY & DERMARKAR
ZAKI HASHEM & PARTNERS, ATTORNEYS AT LAW

Denton Wilde Sapte ✪
Kosheri, Rashed & Riad ✪
Trowers & Hamlins

Firms are listed A-Z in tiers which are ranked in order of priority
✪ Indicates firm displays contact details at the end of this chapter.

PRIVATISATION

BAKER & McKENZIE ✪
DENTON WILDE SAPTE ✪
IBRACHY & DERMARKAR

Kosheri, Rashed & Riad ✪
Sarwat A. Shahid Law Firm

Firms are listed A-Z in tiers which are ranked in order of priority
✪ Indicates firm displays contact details at the end of this chapter.

PRIVATISATION

Egypt is continuing with a steady stream of privatisations. One of the few remaining state-owned industries, the insurance sector in September 2005 was given the green light by the Egyptian government to be sold into private hands.

Advising on a number of investments in newly privatised companies, **Baker & McKenzie** has been active in the banking, manufacturing and chemicals industries. The firm was instructed by Barclays regarding its 40% acquisition of Cairo Barclays Bank, as well as being seller's counsel for the sale of the Bank of Alexandria.

A US$900m PPP project dominated **Denton Wilde Sapte**'s privatisation caseload in 2005. On behalf of Canadian multinational petrochemical company Methanex, the team was instructed to draft all documentation and set up the joint venture agreement between the client and EChem, an Egyptian public sector petrochemical holding company.

Ibrachy & Dermarkar is currently acting on the high-profile privatisation of Telecom Egypt, as well as for DIB Egypt LLC in its purchase of a privatised cotton and textiles company. Ashraf Elibrachy is leading both teams.

PROJECTS AND INFRASTRUCTURE

Advising frequently on the largest projects in Egypt, **Baker & McKenzie** has considerable strength and depth. It represented an international and local consortium on a E£3bn (US$520m) light rail project. The firm has also acted for sponsors of a US$600m ammonia plant and for the joint

PROJECTS AND INFRASTRUCTURE

BAKER & McKENZIE ✪
TROWERS & HAMLINS

Al Kamel Law Office
Denton Wilde Sapte ✪
Ibrachy & Dermarkar
Kosheri, Rashed & Riad ✪
Shalakany Law Office
Zaki Hashem & Partners, Attorneys at Law

Firms are listed A-Z in tiers which are ranked in order of priority
✪ Indicates firm displays contact details at the end of this chapter.

sponsor of a US$700m petrochemical plant. On behalf of the National Bank of Egypt the team acted as lender's counsel regarding the US$130m finance of a linear alkyl benzene project.

Trowers & Hamlins has been retained to advise a major client on the construction of a magnesium smelter plant, and for an international resource company, a private free-zone company is being established by the team for the development of a US$80.5m mining project. Exim-Bank has also been advised regarding the financing of a major fertiliser project.

Ibrachy & Dermarkar has recently advised Hutchison Port Holding on the innovative structuring of a new company for the purposes of converting, constructing and operating new container terminals at Alexandria and El Dekheila ports.

The two main instructions for **Zaki Hashem & Partners, Attorneys at Law** in 2005, were representing the Egyptian Fertilizer Company in a US$250m loan transaction, and also restarting the largest BOT road project in Egypt that was initiated in 2001.

SHIPPING

With the key shipping route of the Suez Canal, there are a large number of small maritime and shipping law practices in the ports of Alexandria and Port Said.

'The lawyers are responsive, quick and proactive' at nine-attorney practice **ELOMC Lawyers**, which is based in Alexandria. Specialising in shipping and maritime litigation, the firm is instructed by shipping lines and P&I clubs. Senior partner Mohamed Faramawy 'is very friendly and responds without delay.'

SHIPPING

ELOMC LAWYERS
KOSHERI, RASHED & RIAD ✪
SHALAKANY LAW OFFICE

Abou Ali
Eldib Advocates
Nadoury & Nahas Law Offices

Firms are listed A-Z in tiers which are ranked in order of priority
✪ Indicates firm displays contact details at the end of this chapter.

Though not core to **Kosheri, Rashed & Riad**, or to **Shalakany Law Office**, these firms are relied upon by their international clients to deal with shipping-related questions when they arise.

A two-partner, six-associate firm based in Port Said, **Abou Ali** represents several P&I clubs; Britannia Steam Ship Insurance Association Limited, Steamship Mutual Underwriting Association Limited and London Steamship Owners' Mutual Insurance Association Limited. The practice is associated with **Hassouna & Abou Ali** in Cairo.

Nadoury & Nahas Law Offices, with offices in Cairo and Alexandria, recently handled a substantial shipping litigation case between a multinational pipeline company and a P&I club.

TELECOMS

Baker & McKenzie has been instructed by Telecom Egypt in a number of its significant projects in 2005, including an E£2bn (US$347m) corporate bond issue, a US$130m share purchase in Vodafone Egypt, and acting as local counsel for their Algeria Project with Orascom Technologies.

TELECOMS

BAKER & McKENZIE ✪
IBRACHY & DERMARKAR
TROWERS & HAMLINS
ZAKI HASHEM & PARTNERS, ATTORNEYS AT LAW

Denton Wilde Sapte ✪
Kosheri, Rashed & Riad ✪

Firms are listed A-Z in tiers which are ranked in order of priority
✪ Indicates firm displays contact details at the end of this chapter.

'Very efficient, responsive and fast' **Ibrachy & Dermarkar** has acted as legal counsel for Siemens and Huawei Tech Investment Company, on two supplier credit agreements involving international borrowers, guarantors and lenders. The value of the deals amounted to €30m and US$25m respectively.

Trowers & Hamlins represents global leaders in telecoms, most notably Vodafone, where the 50:50 joint venture between Vodafone Egypt and Telecom Egypt was advised upon. Other clients represented include a leading French player regarding its Egyptian investments, and reporting on regulatory issues for the sale and distribution of pre-paid international calling cards for a large telecommunications company.

Vodafone Egypt is a client of **Zaki Hashem & Partners, Attorneys at Law**, which was advised on the restructuring of its business and also on the E£4bn (US$694m) merger with Telecom Egypt. The firm has a strong historical grounding in telecommunications, previously advising on the introduction of pay phones and mobile phones in Egypt.

BAKER & McKENZIE

WORLD TRADE CENTER
1191 CORNICH EL NIL, 18TH FLOOR
CAIRO

Telephone: +20 2 579 1801-6
Fax: +20 2 579 1808
Website: www.bakernet.com

Languages English, French, German

Other offices
Almaty, Amsterdam, Antwerp, Baku, Bangkok, Barcelona, Beijing, Berlin, Bogotá, Bologna, Brasilia, Brussels, Budapest, Buenos Aires, Calgary, Cancun, Caracas, Chihuahua, Chicago, Dallas, Düsseldorf, Frankfurt, Geneva, Guadalajara, Hanoi, Ho Chi Minh City, Hong Kong, Houston, Jakarta, Juarez, Kuala Lumpur, Kyiv, London, Madrid, Manama, Manila, Melbourne, Mexico City, Miami, Milan, Monterrey, Moscow, Munich, New York, Palo Alto, Porto Alegré, Paris, Prague, Rio de Janeiro, Riyadh, Rome, St Petersburg, San Diego, San Francisco, Santiago, São Paulo, Shanghai, Singapore, Stockholm, Sydney, Taipei, Tijuana, Tokyo, Toronto, Valencia, Vienna, Warsaw, Washington DC, Zurich

Number of lawyers 3,300+
at this office 21

Contact
Taher Helmy

CATEGORIES OF WORK

Administrative law
Kamal Aboulmagd, Hazim Rizkana

Arbitration
Samir M Hamza, Hazim Rizkana

Banking and finance
Taher Helmy, Hazim Rizkana

BOOT projects
Samir M Hamza, Mohammad Talaat

Commercial law, general
Samir M Hamza, Mohammad Talaat

Environmental law
Samir M Hamza, Hatem Soliman

Intellectual property law
Hazim Rizkana, Mohammad Talaat

Labour law
Mohammad Talaat,
Mohamed Abdallah

Litigation
Hazim Rizkana, Saber Soliman

Mergers and acquisitions
Taher Helmy, Mohammed Ghannam

Privatisation
Taher Helmy, Hazim Rizkana

Securities
Taher Helmy, Hazim Rizkana

Tax
Samir M Hamza, Suzan Farid

Telecommunications law
Samir M Hamza,
Mohammed Ghannam

THE FIRM

Founded in Chicago in 1949, Baker & McKenzie is a leading law firm with 70 offices in 38 countries. A multinational network of over 3,300 legal professionals offers clients resources and knowledge in every area of business law, in virtually every important financial and commercial centre in the world.

Baker & McKenzie has been established in Europe for over 40 years, having opened its first European offices in 1957. Since then, the European and Middle Eastern network has grown to 29 offices, giving it unparalleled geographical coverage.

The Cairo office of Baker & McKenzie (Helmy, Hamza & Partners) was established in 1985. It is the only law firm in Egypt that combines a detailed knowledge of local law and the ability to offer the experience of an international law firm with access to a vast global network of resources and legal expertise.

The clients of the Cairo office include large multinational corporations and local businesses. Baker & McKenzie's worldwide network of offices enables the Cairo office to refer Egyptian clients wishing to do business abroad to its own offices located in that particular jurisdiction.

As part of the Baker & McKenzie international network, the Cairo office is deeply committed to furthering its clients' business both within the Middle East region and globally.

Baker & McKenzie International is a Swiss Verein with member law firms around the world.

AREAS OF PRACTICE

Baker & McKenzie co-ordinates its core practice areas on local, regional and global levels, giving most of its lawyers experience in more than one jurisdiction, as well as providing multinational teams of specialists.

Utilising a global practice group structure and ground-breaking technology coupled with a personal, detailed understanding of a client's specific business, Baker & McKenzie is able to organise its extensive resources to provide focused and strategic counsel to clients.

The Cairo office can advise clients on all legal issues, from purely domestic issues to the most complex cross-border or multi-jurisdictional transactions, tax planning or disputes. More specifically, it provides legal services to both domestic and international companies in a diverse range of specialisation including corporate, banking and finance, commercial, taxation, privatisation, transfer of technology, intellectual property, telecommunications, capital markets, joint ventures, restructuring, mergers and acquisitions, debt-equity swaps, oil and gas. The firm also conducts a strong commercial litigation and international arbitration practice.

The Cairo office is heavily involved in the issuance of Global Depository Receipts (GDRs) of shares of Egyptian companies, including participating in the preparation of offering circulars. The scope of activities carried out in the corporate practice is widespread; from advising and assisting in the bidding for Egypt's first private power plant project on a 'BOOT' (build, own, operate, and transfer) basis, to advising on the legal issues of transporting Egyptian antiquities from Egypt for exhibition in various American cities.

The government called upon the firm's expertise in the recent amendments to the Copyright Law, as well as drafting the Telecommunications and Environmental Laws.

DLA MATOUK BASSIOUNY

13 EL BIRGASS STREET
GARDEN CITY
CAIRO

Telephone: +20 2 792 0075
Fax: +20 2 795 4221
Website: www.dlapiper.com/egypt

Languages
Arabic, English, French

Number of lawyers 17

Contacts
John Matouk, managing partner (john.matouk@dlamatoukbassiouny.com), Omar Bassiouny, executive partner (omar.bassiouny@dlamatoukbassiouny.com)

Member
DLA Piper Group

CATEGORIES OF WORK

Aviation	**Intellectual property**
Banking and finance	**Energy and infrastructure**
Corporate, privatisation and commercial	**Real estate**
Dispute resolution	**Tourism**
Employment	

THE FIRM

DLA Matouk Bassiouny advises on a wide range of corporate, commercial and banking matters across several practice areas and sectors. The firm's lawyers are trained and qualified both locally and internationally, and are fully conversant in English, Arabic and French and with the cultural and business practices in both local and international jurisdictions. Based in Cairo, the firm is especially well placed to assist clients in neighbouring North African countries, based on similarities of legal systems, language and culture, as well as geographical proximity.

The firm is experienced in representing clients with all the main regulatory and financial authorities in Egypt, including the main commercial tribunals, the Central Bank of Egypt, the Capital Markets Authority and the Cairo and Alexandria Stock Exchanges.

The firm is also a member of DLA Piper Group, an exclusive alliance of international full-service legal organisations with a shared vision. Established in 1999, the group now has members across Europe, Africa, the Middle East, Asia and the US, which deliver expert local know-how and integrated international solutions.

AREAS OF PRACTICE

Aviation: assists international clients in all aspects of the sector. It maintains strong working relationships with the national airline and the Civil Aviation Authority.

Banking and finance: provides advice on asset-based finance, infrastructure and project finance, trade and real estate finance. It has a strong sector knowledge and maintains close relationships with Egyptian financial institutions.

Corporate, privatisation and commercial: experienced in acquisitions, start-ups, company formations and administration. Advises on corporate, contractual and partnership structures, on the ongoing relationships between venture partners, on exit strategies and on due diligence issues. It advises foreign investors on all aspects of privatisation public/private participation projects, including due diligence, negotiations, document drafting, target company management and labour restructuring and regulatory compliance. It also provides a wide range of services on the formation of legal entities and their continued corporate compliance. These services are individually tailored to each client's specific needs.

Dispute resolution: headed by Walid Salem and Ahmed Amin, former general counsel of Bank Misr, one of Egypt's four largest banks. The practice is highly experienced in commercial arbitration and is registered with the Cario Regional Centre for Commercial Arbitration.

Employment: advises by combining the clients' strategy with the practicalities of local implementation. It covers acquisitions, restructurings, recruitment and terminations and provides local support to international clients.

Intellectual property: offers a comprehensive service covering patents, trade marks, copyright, design rights, unfair competition and the protection of goodwill and trade secrets. Sectors covered include IT, pharmaceuticals, healthcare, biotechnology and other science-based industries, media, entertainment and leisure industries and retail and distribution.

Energy and infrastructure: advises international oil and gas industry on a broad range of transactional and regulatory issues. It works with international clients, from independents focusing on upstream activities to fully integrated oil and gas companies, distribution companies and consortia, as well as commercial banks and other financers. It also covers electricity sector restructurings, regulation and independent power stations. The practice has advised private companies on major electricity industry privatisations, restructurings and acquisitions.

Real estate: advises on all aspects of commercial real estate transactions.

DENTON WILDE SAPTE

9 SHAGARET EL DOR STREET
ZAMALEK
CAIRO

Telephone: +20 2 736 5128
Fax: +20 2 736 7717
E-mail: cairo@dentonwildesapte.com
Website: www.dentonwildesapte.com

Languages
Arabic, Dutch, English, French, German

Other offices
Abu Dhabi, Almaty, Dubai, Istanbul, London, Milton Keynes, Moscow, Muscat, Paris, Tashkent

Number of lawyers 683
at this office 23

Contact
Bridget McKinney

CATEGORIES OF WORK

- Arbitration
- Aviation
- Banking and finance
- Capital markets
- Company establishment
- Constitutional and administrative law
- Construction
- Intellectual property
- Joint ventures
- Labour law
- Litigation
- Mergers and acquisitions
- Oil and gas
- Privatisation
- Projects
- Telecommunications

KOSHERI, RASHED & RIAD

16 MAAMAL EL SOKKAR STREET
GARDEN CITY
CAIRO 11451

Telephone: +20 2 795 4795
Fax: +20 2 795 8521
E-mail: samiakr@link.net
Website: www.krr-law.com

Languages
English, French, Arabic

Other offices
Paris*

Number of lawyers 22

Contacts
Dr Tarek Riad, Dr Hatem Gabr, Hala Riad, Dr Ahmed El-Kosheri

CATEGORIES OF WORK

- Arbitration and business litigation
- Corporate and commercial
- Mergers and acquisitions
- Privatisation and capital markets
- Construction
- Labour law
- Energy and natural resources
- Government business/ regulatory and environment
- Asset finance and securitisation
- Insurance
- Aviation and maritime affairs
- BOT projects
- Oil concessions
- Maritime matters
- Foreign direct investment and competition
- Telecommunications and media and entertainment
- Banking and finance
- Infrastructure and project finance
- Tax
- Commercial property, real estate
- Intellectual property
- Information technology and e-commerce
- World Trade Organisation agreements and dispute resolution
- Up/downstream gas agreements

ESTONIA

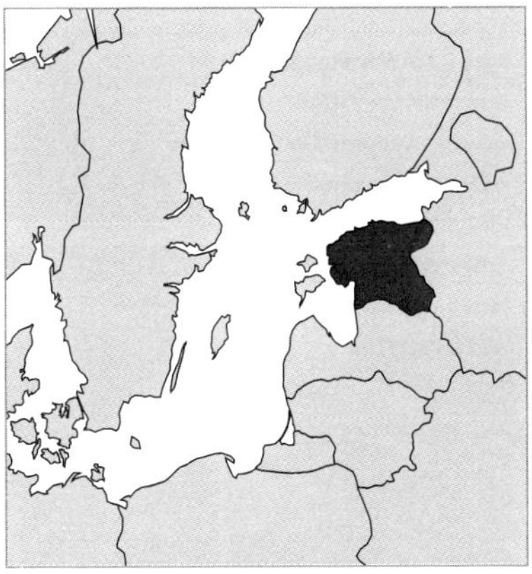

Population	1.4 million
Number of lawyers	450
Professional title	Advokaat
Currency	Estonian kroon (EEK))

Index

Estonia shares borders with Russia and Latvia and is the smallest, most northerly of the three former Soviet Baltic States. The country entered the EU and Nato in 2004 just a decade after the final departure of Russian troops, developments hard to imagine in such a short period of time.

Estonia offers a welcoming climate to foreign investors and its proximity to Russia facilitates trade with the West.

BILLING

Average hourly rates vary between €100 to €200 depending on the type of case and level of expertise of the attorney. Rates for international clients may differ.

MARKETING

The Estonian Bar is very strict on marketing and it is illegal for lawyers to directly advertise their firms. However, many Bar members get around these stringent rules with various forms of indirect marketing such as writing articles for publications and sponsoring events. Most firms have websites in English and Estonian.

IN-HOUSE LAWYERS

Large Estonian banks and companies house their own legal departments but will often outsource to law firms on complicated corporate matters.

ECONOMY

Estonia is among the fastest-growing economies in the region attributable to its steady increase in foreign investment, liberal taxation system and favourable location. The World Bank recently ranked the country as number 16 in the world for its agreeable business climate.

GDP was 7.8% in 2004 influenced by the balanced state budget, stable convertible currency and liberal trade and investment laws. GDP is forecast at a healthy 6.5% for 2005 due to a significant increase in export volumes.

Limited natural resources emphasise the service sector as a primary economic engine. A skilled and adaptable workforce creates a good basis for a knowledge-oriented economy. The economy benefits from strong electronics and telecommunications sectors and tourism is a rapidly developing market.

Fiscal practices and performances have been solid and impressive with the country generating a budget surplus in 2001. The unemployment rate is still above average for Europe but is decreasing after growth in the job market in 2001. Expeditious privatisation further aided Estonia's reform programme.

Foreign investors are attracted by the multitude of benefits explaining the surge of investment witnessed, particularly in the banking sector where almost 100% is foreign owned. The country has the most liberal trade and investment laws in the world taken advantage of by countries such as Sweden and Finland.

In spite of these advantages, Estonia's economy is not entirely unflawed. There is a current risk of the economy overheating by growing too fast. The increase in inflation is notable and with plans to join the single currency in 2007 Estonia needs to fight further increases, preventing a similar situation to that of Latvia, where inflation rates have rocketed, seriously effecting industry.

LEGAL MARKET

The Estonian legal market is relatively small but its development has echoed economic growth. Estonian legislation, originally based on the codified German legal system, is rapidly changing with new and amended laws regularly appearing. In 2005 a new Commercial and Civil Procedure Code had a drastic impact on the legal system.

The presence of foreign firms is slowly increasing with a notable escalation of international firms referring work through larger, local firms since the country's accession to the EU. It has been suggested that there may be an influx of international firms opening offices in Estonia as the legal market develops.

The gap between firms at each end of the spectrum is forecast to grow with those at the lower end remaining more domestically focused. The legal market is in a phase of maturation and with a high proportion of young, newly qualified lawyers there is healthy competition between firms and a very modern service with lawyers demonstrating excellent language skills.

The Estonian legal market is dominated by a few key firms: **Lepik & Luhaäär LAWIN**, **Raidla & Partners** and **Tark & Co.** The merger *of Luiga, Mugu & Borenius* and *Mody, Haal Glimstedt Law Firm* resulted in the emergence of **Luiga Mody Hääl**

The largest firms

1	Raidla & Partners	30
2	Tark & Co	27
3	Sorainen Law Offices	25
4	Luiga Mody Hääl Borenius	24
5	Lepik & Luhaäär LAWIN	23
6	Paul Varul, Advokaadibüroo	19
	Teder, Glikman & Partnerid, Law Firm	19
8	Aivar Pilv, Law Office	16
9	Concordia Attorneys at Law	14
	Lextal Law Firm	14
11	Hedman Osborne Clarke Alliance	9
12	Lasvet Patent and Trademark Agency	8
	Ots & Co, Law Office	8
	Pohla & Hallmägi	8
15	Aavik, Arvisto & Partners, Law Office	7
	Tamme & Otsmann, Law Firm	7
17	HETA, Advokaadibüroo	6
	Laus & Partners, Law Office	6
	Leppik & Partners	6
	Lillo & Lóhmus, Law Office	6
	MAQS Advokatbyrå	6
22	AAA Baltic Service Company	5
	Hough, Hübner, Hütt & Partners	5
24	Keevallik & Partners, Law Office	3
	Malsco Law Office	3
	V Kaasik & Co, Law Office	3

These figures represent the total number of lawyers in this country only, and have been supplied by the firms themselves. The figures should be accurate as at 1 January 2006.

Borenius causing a new battle in the ranks. The Estonian branch of **Sorainen Law Offices** continues to make progress and further strengthened its reputation in 2005 with the addition of several key attorneys including tax specialist Lucs Nijs.

An interesting development in 2005 was the appearance of Estonia's first Scandinavian firm, **MAQS Advokatbyrå**, which opened a five-partner office. It is early days but the firm is already instructed by several international blue-chip corporates and financial institutions and has the potential to be very successful in the market. Partner Karolina Ullman is Estonian, allowing the office the advantage of a good local market knowledge.

As in Latvia and Lithuania, Baltic partnering became very popular in Estonia in the last two years with larger firms forming alliances in order to provide pan-Baltic coverage. First to set the trend in 2004 was **Lepik & Luhaäär LAWIN** who formed an alliance with **Lideika, Petrauskas, Valiunas ir partneriai LAWIN** in Lithuania and **Klavins & Slaidins LAWIN** in Latvia. With more than 80 lawyers, the grouping combines the legal services of three top-tier firms.

Quickly following suit was **Raidla & Partners** with the formation of structured partnership *RoschierRaidla*. The grouping includes **Roschier Holmberg**, Finland, **Norcous & Partners**, Lithuania and **Lejins, Torgans & Partners**, Latvia. With over 170 lawyers and a recently opened office in Sweden, the alliance is the largest of its kind providing full Nordic-Baltic coverage.

Luiga Mody Hääl Borenius recently formed a link with **Foigt & Partners/Regija Borenius** in Lithuania and **Liepa, Skopina / BORENIUS** in Latvia, employing over 100 lawyers in total.

Referred to as 'one of the most noteworthy developments in the legal field' pan-Baltic network *Baltic Legal Solutions* comprises **Law Firm Teder, Glikman & Partnerid** in Estonia, **Kronbergs & Cukste** in Latvia and **Jurevicius, Balciunas & Bartkus** in Lithuania. The firms were formerly linked with Ernst & Young but severed ties in the summer of 2005.

Sorainen Law Offices offers full Baltic coverage with branches in Riga, Tallinn, Vilnius and Helsinki.

Law Office Ots & Co Estonia, **Law Firm Saladzius & Partners** Lithuania and **Baltmane & Bitans Law Office** Latvia, co-operate in a pan-Baltic grouping.

Hedman Osborne Clarke Alliance works alongside offices in Helsinki and St Petersburg.

BANKING AND FINANCE

BANKING AND FINANCE

LEPIK & LUHAÄÄR LAWIN ⭘
LUIGA MODY HÄÄL BORENIUS ⭘
RAIDLA & PARTNERS ⭘
SORAINEN LAW OFFICES ⭘
TARK & CO ⭘

MAQS Advokatbyrå
Teder, Glikman & Partnerid, Law Firm ⭘

Aare Raigi Advokaadibüroo
Aivar Pilv, Law Office ⭘
Hedman Osborne Clarke Alliance
HETA, Advokaadibüroo ⭘
Hough, Hübner, Hütt & Partners
Keevallik & Partners, Law Office
Laus and Partners, Law Office ⭘
Lextal Law Firm
Paul Varul, Advokaadibüroo ⭘
Pohla & Hallmägi
Straus & Partners, Law Firm
Tehver & Partners, Law Office

Firms are listed A-Z in tiers which are ranked in order of priority
⭘ Indicates firm displays contact details at the end of this chapter.

Lepik & Luhaäär LAWIN is well-known in Estonia as the first private law office founded in the post-war period, comprising 25 highly skilled attorneys. Founding member and banking and finance expert Peeter Lepik has been recognised as one of the world's leading finance lawyers. Last year the firm advised several large international banks on requirements enacted in the Securities Market Act and other finance-related issues.

Full-service **Luiga Mody Hääl Borenius** offers a comprehensive finance practice. After a merger between *Luiga, Mugu & Borenius* and *Mody, Haal Glimstedt Law Firm* in August 2005, the firm now boasts a diverse range of 25 individually specialised lawyers. In the past year the firm has advised international finance groups, banks and government institutions on various complex transactions, some valued in excess of one billion Euro.

Leading attorney Raino Paron heads the banking and finance team at Estonia's largest firm **Raidla & Partners**. Paron's expertise may be linked with his time spent working at the World Bank and the IMF. Also deserving mention is partner Jüri Raidla, chairman of the Estonian Banking Association, who is recommended for his 'breadth of knowledge and experience both on a technical and practical level'. A significant case for the firm in 2005 was representing Estonia's largest shipping company during refinancing for the construction of a new passenger vessel.

Pan-Baltic **Sorainen Law Offices**' banking and finance department has been very active in the last 12 months. The firm advised a major European financier on insider dealing of third-party takeover bids for publicly traded shares and also counselled a significant global industrial group on Baltic security matters related to global refinancing. The firm recently organised the very first conference in Estonia concerning the possibilities and experience of PPP, further raising its profile in this sector. 'Keeping promises and constant availability' are strengths appreciated by clients.

Specialist banking and finance partner Hannes Vallikivi at **Tark & Co**, receives praise from contemporaries and clients alike for his aptitude. In 2005 the firm handled the largest-ever share acquisition in the history of the Baltic countries for Hansabanka, valued at €1.7bn. The firm also acted as local counsel for a bank syndicate on a financing issue for the global restructuring of the Hagemayer Group worth €615m. Clients state 'attorneys are incredibly confident in an international setting whilst being well connected locally'.

MAQS Advokatbyrå recently emerged as the only international firm in the Estonian market and has since continued to grow both in terms of quality of work and reputation. Banking and finance is a cornerstone of the firm's practice with attorneys demonstrating particular expertise in the areas of property, asset, acquisition and export finance. In 2005 the firm represented Hansapank in a dispute with a bankrupt company.

Eighteen-lawyer **Law Firm Teder, Glikman & Partnerid** was established in 2004, combining two of Estonia's oldest firms, *Teder & Partnerid* and *Glikman & Glikman*. The firm's banking and finance lawyers focus on project finance, electronic banking and securities. Predominantly working with financial institutions, the firm counts Sampo Bank and a dominant Baltic bank amongst its clients.

Aare Raigi Advokaadibüroo specialises in banking and finance and has acted as general counsel for Estonia's second-largest bank for ten years. In 2005 the firm successfully represented Hansapank in a dispute with a claimant seeking the revocation of a €7.3m share-purchase agreement. Clients claim attorneys at the firm are 'thorough, detail oriented and do not lose their head in severe conflict situations'.

The banking and finance department at **Law Office Aivar Pilv** comprises a stable team with long-term experience and profound analytical skills. The firm provides legal assistance in transactions involving various financial matters including the organisation of bond issues and the issuing of derivatives instruments. The firm has practical experience in representing clients before the Stock Exchange Arbitration Court to protect the rights and interests of companies. Clients include one of the largest banks in the Baltic States.

Hedman Osborne Clarke Alliance advises financial institutions and individuals on all aspects of banking and finance. Lawyers at the firm are renowned in this field and offer a first-class service combining technical excellence and a commercial approach. The firm is engaged by one of the three largest banks in Estonia for financial matters. In 2005 the firm advised clients in Iceland and Norway on international banking and insurance issues.

Attorneys at **Law Office Keevallik & Partners** have vast experience of advising foreign banks and financial institutions in connection with their investments in Estonia. The firm's widespread international contacts and range of working languages enable it to render high-quality legal assistance to both domestic and foreign clients who praise the firm for its 'excellent timekeeping, accuracy and ability to offer appropriate solutions'.

Law Office Laus and Partners is comprised of eight lawyers headed by partners Raivo Laus and Madis Kiisa. Last year the firm handled banking and finance transactions for many large international banks valued at up to €20m.

Lextal Law Firm is respected for its strong banking and finance capabilities. The firm recently handled the bankruptcy proceedings of a leading Estonian alcoholic beverage manufacturer. A significant addition to the firm last year was Alar Urm who spent 13 years as head of the legal department of the Ministry of Finance. The firm deserves acclaim for its 'excellent communication and language skills'.

The eight lawyers at **Pohla & Hallmägi** are experienced in banking and finance. The firm represents major financial institutions in the Baltic countries and partner Jüri Ploom is a qualified bankruptcy trustee. Clients are enthused by the firm's 'professionalism, knowledge and great experience in international law'.

Law Office Tehver & Partners may be a young firm but it already boasts renowned banking and finance clients. Partners Jaanus Tehver and Toomas Laanemaa are experts in financial law and receive acclaim for their 'dedication, commitment, smooth and efficient communication and knowledge'. One satisfied client comments: 'They are the quickest lawyers I have ever seen.'

CORPORATE AND M&A

The reputation of the corporate and M&A team at **Lepik & Luhaäär LAWIN** is reflected in its enviable client list which includes Statoil and Procter & Gamble. The firm offers high-quality, cross-border advice. Name partners Peeter Lepik and Toomas Luhaäär are key players at the firm, ensuring it retains a top position in this year's table. In 2005 the firm advised many esteemed clients on corporate issues including setting up subsidiaries in Estonia.

The widely acclaimed M&A team at **Raidla & Partners** is headed by Sven Papp, formerly of **White & Case LLP**. Last year the firm handled a transaction valued at €500m on behalf of an Estonian telephone operating company. Some of the world's leading companies entrust this firm with their M&A work and satisfied clients claim that without the lawyers of **Raidla & Partners** their businesses would not be a success.

2005 was a busy year for **Sorainen Law Offices**' commercial and M&A department. A significant deal included advising eBay on the acquisition of Skype Tecnologies SA for a consideration of €2.1bn. Head of the pan-Baltic corporate practice group Karin Madisson recently became a partner and is considered a veritable expert on Estonian company law. Clients 'appreciate the quick response to requests and the fact the firm constantly keeps you informed on how the case is developing'.

Tark & Co advises a host of the world's largest companies on corporate matters. In 2005 the firm handled several of Estonia's most significant M&A transactions and is currently working on establishing the first European financial company in the Baltic States by merging Estonian, Latvian and Lithuanian regulated financial institutions. 'The firm is miles ahead of competitors,' claims one satisfied client.

Luiga Mody Hääl Borenius is widely experienced in domestic and multi-jurisdictional M&A. The firm has advised, organised transactions and conducted due diligence for several major international corporations. Clients praise the firm's 'perfect timing, professional advice and excellent communication skills'.

MAQS Advokatbyrå has a rapidly growing client base and, with five partners in the Estonian office, offers high-quality services. Foreign investment is a key practice area and in 2005 the firm advised an international supermarket retailer on its establishment in Estonia and continually advises one of the world's largest multinational companies on corporate issues.

CORPORATE AND M&A

LEPIK & LUHAÄÄR LAWIN ✪
RAIDLA & PARTNERS ✪
SORAINEN LAW OFFICES ✪
TARK & CO ✪

Luiga Mody Hääl Borenius ✪
MAQS Advokatbyrå
Paul Varul, Advokaadibüroo ✪
Teder, Glikman & Partnerid, Law Firm ✪

A Jakobson & A Jaroslavski, Advokaadibüroo
Aare Raigi Advokaadibüroo
Aavik, Arvisto & Partners, Law Office
Aivar Pilv, Law Office ✪
Edith Sassian & Co, Law Office
Hedman Osborne Clarke Alliance
HETA, Advokaadibüroo ✪
Hough, Hübner, Hütt & Partners
Keevallik & Partners, Law Office
Laus and Partners, Law Office ✪
Lextal Law Firm
Ots & Co, Law Office ✪
Pohla & Hallmägi
Straus & Partners, Law Firm
Tehver & Partners, Law Office
V Kaasik & Co, Law Office

Firms are listed A-Z in tiers which are ranked in order of priority
✪ Indicates firm displays contact details at the end of this chapter.

Attorneys at **Advokaadibüroo Paul Varul** are experienced in M&A and the firm handled several important deals in 2005. The firm also welcomed three new associate lawyers and continues to expand. Clients praise the firm's 'excellent accessibility' and claim 'lawyers are available even outside office hours'.

Law Firm Teder, Glikman & Partnerid offers high-quality business advice to domestic and international clients.

Sworn advocates Alla Jackobson and Anatoly Jaroslavsky of **Advokaadibüroo A Jakobson & A Jaroslavski** have many years of experience in corporate and M&A. Amongst the firm's clients are Russian and Ukrainian Embassies.

Aare Raigi Advokaadibüroo specialises in all areas of business law with corporate and M&A work spilling over into other practice areas. 'I appreciate the firm's individual approach and the considerable extent of care placed upon solving problems,' professes one satisfied client.

Marko Aavik of **Law Office Aavik, Arvisto & Partners** specialises in corporate and M&A. Last year the six-lawyer team handled work related to the increase and decrease of share capital for various domestic and international companies. The firm specialises in pharmaceuticals and medical regulatory work. Clients highly recommend the services of the firm and compliment the lawyers' 'profound depth of knowledge'.

Law Office Aivar Pilv aims to render high-quality legal assistance on an internationally recognised level. The firm has a competent 21-lawyer team that advises global and domestic clients on founding companies and subsidiaries in Estonia and abroad and on all M&A matters.

Former judge Edith Sassian heads small but efficient **Law Office Edith Sassian & Co**. Clients from a multitude of countries respect Sassian's reputation as 'an experienced lawyer with the ability to handle complex cases'.

The 11 lawyers at **Hedman Osborne Clarke Alliance** provide a full range of legal services in all areas of corporate and business law. Last year the firm represented Estonia's second-largest oil company in corporate matters and also advised an international tobacco company on extending its scope to Estonia. The firm recently benefited from the arrival of respected corporate attorney Kenno Vilippus from **Law Firm Teder, Glikman & Partnerid**.

Advokaadibüroo HETA is well connected in Europe and advises international and domestic clients on foreign investment and corporate matters.

Law Office Keevallik & Partners specialises in commercial law. The firm's membership of international legal associations enables it to develop close professional co-operation with foreign colleagues and clients. The firm provides legal advice to foreign and local companies and a significant client is a leading Finnish agricultural group. Name partner Toomas Keevallik is a highly recommended lawyer who clients believe is available '24/7'.

The eight lawyers at **Law Office Laus and Partners** are competent in corporate and M&A. The firm has handled legal issues for various government institutions and large Estonian companies.

The specialist eight-lawyer corporate and M&A team at **Lextal Law Firm** is experienced in IPOs, takeovers, restructuring and establishment of foreign companies. Key attorneys include 'intelligent, calm and steady' partners Üllar Talviste and Ants Karu. Satisfied clients commend the firm's 'mutual understanding and business knowledge'.

Leading partner Maivi Ots of **Law Office Ots & Co** specialises in corporate and M&A. The firm represents leading national banks and property companies and advises in relation to takeovers and company establishment. Clients profess the lawyers at this firm to be 'dedicated, educated and orientated to understand customers' needs'.

Pohla & Hallmägi offers a comprehensive corporate and M&A practice. The firm is consulted by a number of international companies and recently advised on the merger of Estonia's main airports.

Partner Ilmar Straus, formerly of *Law Firm Glikman & Glikman*, heads the corporate and M&A team at **Law Firm Straus & Partners**. The ten-lawyer firm was established in 2004 and already boasts an enviable client base and attention-grabbing courtroom successes. Esteemed clients include an international pharmaceutical giant and one of the world's largest automaker corporations. The firm is commended for its 'thorough understanding of client's business needs'.

'Experienced and knowledgeable' partners Janus Tehver and Toomas Laaneaa of **Law Office Tehver & Partners** handled several large insurance and takeover transactions in 2005. Satisfied clients state that 'although the firm is relatively new there is no quality difference from some of the bigger firms and attorneys are good at suggesting solutions rather than just pointing out problems'.

EU AND COMPETITION

Since Estonia's accession to the EU in 2005 the EU and competition department at **Raidla & Partners** has continued to flourish. The firm's work mainly involves advising clients on how their companies are affected by EU rules and regulations. Clients state that lawyers at the firm are 'practical problem solvers who work with clients to resolve and avoid problems'.

Carri Ginter, **Sorainen Law Offices**, is a reputable EU expert who holds an LLM in European law and lectures at the Institute of Law of the University of Tallinn. In 2005 the firm assisted a leading UK firm with filing issues and the submission of appropriate documentation to the Estonian Competition Board.

Tark & Co advises numerous leading national and international companies on a full range of EU and competition matters including dominant position and competition law compliance. Partner Kaja Leiger specialises in competition practice and is acknowledged as one of the best in the field.

EU AND COMPETITION

RAIDLA & PARTNERS ✪
SORAINEN LAW OFFICES ✪
TARK & CO ✪

Aivar Pilv, Law Office ✪
Keevallik & Partners, Law Office
Lextal Law Firm
Ots & Co, Law Office ✪

Firms are listed A-Z in tiers which are ranked in order of priority
✪ *Indicates firm displays contact details at the end of this chapter.*

2005 was an active year for **Law Office Aivar Pilv** particularly with providing legal opinions on the interpretation and implementation of competition law on issues concerning mergers and unfair competition that have set precedents in the courts. Recently the firm represented the Competition Board in a dispute involving the cancellation of unreasonably high call tariffs. The firm's leading lawyers in this field are Aivar Pilv, Ilmar-Erik Aavakivi and Piret Blankin.

Law Office Keevallik & Partners is actively involved in EU and competition law. The firm has assisted clients in obtaining approvals from the Estonian Competition Board and advised on several international merger proceedings connected to EC legislation in 2005. Clients proclaim the firm 'keeps promises and is excellent at negotiating'.

Lextal Law Firm was involved in high-profile EU cases in 2005 including representing a client in the first-ever complaint involving Estonia to go before the European Court of Justice. The firm also advised the European Commission on a legal study of the transposition of 25 environmental directives.

Law Office Ots & Co has been active in EU and competition practice since Estonia's accession into the EU in 2005. Key work has included the drafting and revision of agreements on behalf of various national and global corporations. Partner Toomas Pikamäe specialises in this area. Clients claim that 'lawyers at the firm show great expertise in their field and the friendly and informal atmosphere allows them to reach the core of the problem'.

IP, IT AND TELECOMS

In 2005 **Lepik & Luhaäär LAWIN** welcomed the return of telecommunications expert Pirkko-Liis Harkmaaa, who had been working for the European Commission. The firm provides a full range of high-quality services with star clients including Coca-Cola and Toyota. Last year the firm advised many well-known brands on trade mark

IP, IT AND TELECOMS

LEPIK & LUHAÄÄR LAWIN ✪
LUIGA MODY HÄÄL BORENIUS ✪
RAIDLA & PARTNERS ✪
TEDER, GLIKMAN & PARTNERID, LAW FIRM ✪

AAA Baltic Service Company
MAQS Advokatbyrå
Sorainen Law Offices ✪
Straus & Partners, Law Firm
Tark & Co ✪

Aare Raigi Advokaadibüroo
Aivar Pilv, Law Office ✪
Edith Sassian & Co, Law Office
Hedman Osborne Clarke Alliance
Keevallik & Partners, Law Office
Lextal Law Firm
Paul Varul, Advokaadibüroo ✪
Pohla & Hallmägi
Tehver & Partners, Law Office

Firms are listed A-Z in tiers which are ranked in order of priority
✪ *Indicates firm displays contact details at the end of this chapter.*

infringement and patent protection issues. The firm was also involved in the drafting of the new Estonian telecommunications law.

Viive Kaur of **Luiga Mody Hääl Borenius** is hailed as a 'leading mind in IP' in Estonia. Last year the firm advised one of the world's foremost financial services groups regarding electronic trading systems and on-line contracts.

The creative and innovative lawyers at **Raidla & Partners** are competent in IP, IT and telecoms practice and the firm is renowned in this area for its profound knowledge of telecoms law. The firm advises AS Elion, Estonia's largest telecommunications provider, on various regulatory issues. Partner Sven Papp is hailed 'a very good IP lawyer'.

The IP, IT and telecoms specialists at **Law Firm Teder, Glikman & Partnerid** are highly regarded for their advice on complex and sophisticated matters. Last year the firm carried out IP audits concerning regulatory and compliance issues and participated in nearly all major telecoms and IT transactions.

AAA Baltic Service Company specialises in IP. Head of office and experienced patent attorney Urmas Kernu previously worked at the Institute of Cybernetics of the Academy of Sciences as the Head of Patent and Scientific Information Department. During his time in this job Kernu prepared Estonian copyright law regarding software and has since published articles on Estonian IP law. Last year the firm represented one of the world's leading consumer goods companies in a copyright dispute. Clients praise the firm for its 'efficient, excellent and professional work'.

MAQS Advokatbyrå has a broad knowledge of all aspects of IP. Several attorneys are patent and trade mark agents or have experience working in various industries. The firm recently acquired the IP portfolio of one of the world's leading fashion designers and has been advising the company on IP infringement issues.

Sorainen Law Offices has experienced considerable growth in its IP, IT and telecoms work in the last 12 months. The firm advises a major IT service provider in Europe on the use of trade marks and related risks in Estonia. The firm also advises a dominant global IT products and services provider on various legal matters including advising on the conclusion of internet agreements.

Law Firm Straus & Partners provides a broad spectrum of high-quality legal services and has a particularly strong IP department led by Anu Uritam, previously of *Law Firm Glikman & Glikman*, who is reputed to be one of Estonia's top IP lawyers. Adding further strength to the department is prominent copyright specialist Heike Pisuke. In 2005 the firm attained success in two major Supreme Court decisions, in one the Supreme Court formulated its first decision on the limits of free quotations and free use of reproductions of artistic works. Clients profess the firm to be 'the best for Copyright law'.

Tark & Co advises the world's leading drinks company on trade mark dispute issues and a prominent international mobile phones supplier on localisation of service terms.

Aare Raigi Advokaadibüroo is engaged by numerous companies for IP and IT-related issues and the firm recently advised a large Estonian bank on a trade mark protection matter. Clients highlight the firm's key strengths as being flexibility and client orientation.

Law Office Aivar Pilv has extensive experience in IP-related matters particularly in the area of copyright protection for works of literature, art and research. The firm represents clients in disputes arising as a result of using and registering objects of IP and in the IP Appellate Committee and in court. The firm has also represented state institutions in telecommunications disputes. Key individuals are Andres Aavik, Piret Blankin and Ilmar-Erik Aavakivi.

Former judge and sole practitioner Edith Sassian (**Law Office Edith Sassian & Co**), has been a member of the Estonian Board of Appeals of Industrial Property since 1995 and has great experience of IP litigation and arbitration.

All-round **Law Office Keevallik & Partners** is well known for its work in IP. In the last 12 months the firm has successfully represented several corporate clients in litigation involving internationally known trade marks. The firm also represents some of Estonia's biggest telephone and information mediation companies. Accuracy is a key strength highlighted by clients.

Last year **Lextal Law Firm** increased its team of reputable lawyers with the arrival of Eneken Tikk, renowned for her competence in matters relating to the 'information society'. The firm handles a full range of IP work and in the last two years has been actively involved in the contentious area of internet development. Clients state the firm is 'easy to access, even at weekends and in the evenings, responds quickly and has excellent negotiation skills'.

Full-service **Advokaadibüroo Paul Varul** offers a competent IP, IT and telecoms practice. Last year the firm was responsible for drafting a new telecommunication services act. Clients claim 'the firm's success is down to the lawyers' flexibility and broad range of expertise'. Ants Mailend deserves mention for his expertise and 'frank and honest nature'.

Andres Hallmägi of **Pohla & Hallmägi** is a renowned IT and IP expert who recently represented an Estonian company in revolutionary litigation on the use of digital signatures in civil procedure. The firm's 'expeditious responses in the shortest possible time' receive praise from clients.

Law Office Tehver & Partners is experienced in IP Law and has handled patent and industrial property protection matters for government institutions.

MARITIME AND TRANSPORT

Lepik & Luhaäär LAWIN is highly regarded for its maritime practice. The firm advises one of the largest shipping companies in the Baltic region and also Estonian Shipping Company. Maritime specialist Professor Heiki Lindpere has been acknowledged as an expert in this field.

Malsco Law Office specialises in maritime law. Highlights include representing Estonia's biggest shipping importer during a dispute concerning the import of sugar brought about by recent EU accession. The firm retains the majority of Estonia's shipowners and operators as clients. Partner Indrek Nuut was formerly legal adviser to the Estonian Shipowners Association.

Sorainen Law Offices recently co-operated with an international firm during the representation of a defendant against a claim for compensation for the profit lost as a result of environmental pollution. The firm also advised an Icelandic refinancier regarding security aspects of the refinancing of shrimp ship operators.

In 2005 **Aare Raigi Advokaadibüroo** represented the Estonian Railway Inspectorate in a dispute involving railway undertakings and also advised a leading bank on ship financing arrangements.

Maritime law specialist Piret Lappert advises clients on maritime property and transport law at **Hedman Osborne Clarke Alliance**.

The six lawyers at **Law Office Keevallik & Partners** have a great deal of experience in transportation matters. The firm has been consulted by clients in connection with providing services in Estonian ports.

MARITIME AND TRANSPORT

LEPIK & LUHAÄÄR LAWIN ✪
MALSCO LAW OFFICE
SORAINEN LAW OFFICES ✪

Aavik, Arvisto & Partners, Law Office
Hedman Osborne Clarke Alliance
HETA, Advokaadibüroo ✪
Keevallik & Partners, Law Office
Lextal Law Firm
Luiga Mody Hääl Borenius
MAQS Advokatbyrå
Pohla & Hallmägi
Raidla & Partners ✪
Tark & Co ✪
Teder, Glikman & Partnerid, Law Firm ✪

Firms are listed A-Z in tiers which are ranked in order of priority
✪ Indicates firm displays contact details at the end of this chapter.

Lextal Law Firm is competent in legal matters related to the transfer and encumbering of ships, chartering and maritime insurance.

Luiga Mody Hääl Borenius advises Estonian Air on aviation matters and also advised one of the largest Nordic banking groups regarding the financing of a large shipping company.

MAQS Advokatbyrå recently represented the Ministry of Finance in a case involving the public procurement of radar systems. The firm also advises one of Tallinn's ports on business matters.

Attorneys at **Pohla & Hallmägi** deal with a vast amount of maritime and transport transactions. Name partner and maritime law expert Asko Pohla has represented a number of oil transportation companies, major ports and a railroad operator as well as Norwegian, Swedish, Russian and Estonian shipyards. Clients state the approach of the firm is 'creative, frank and ethical'.

Last year **Tark & Co** advised shipping companies on the establishment of subsidiaries and the transfer of operations. The firm also represented a client in court in relation to Estonia's biggest oil pollution case.

Law Firm Teder, Glikman & Partnerid has seen an increase of work in this sector since EU accession. Clients range from local public companies to significant global players and include a major rail network.

REAL ESTATE AND CONSTRUCTION

Prodigious **Lepik & Luhaäär LAWIN** has handled a large volume of construction transactions in the last year and many lawyers at the firm have expertise in the field. Last year the firm advised the most important casino group in the Baltic States on the construction of the largest casino-hotel. Other notable clients include several of the largest construction and real estate companies in the Baltic region and various state authorities.

After the merger of two top-tier law firms in August 2005 **Luiga Mody Hääl Borenius** now has a crack team of real estate and construction attorneys including expert partners Jaanus Mody and Marti Hääl, lauded 'excellent lawyers'. The firm represents several of the Baltic States' largest real estate companies in their day-to-day legal matters and handled the acquisition and future development of the largest wind-park in Estonia in 2005.

Last year **Raidla & Partners** represented a major Norwegian real estate group in its acquisition of a large office building in Tallinn owned by an Estonian company. Jüri Raidla leads the department and one peer from a major London firm deems him 'the most impressive lawyer I have ever met'. Clients praise the firm's ability to 'accommodate even the most impossible deadlines'.

In 2005 **Sorainen Law Offices** handled one of Estonia's benchmark property transactions when advising a Finnish property investment company on the acquisition of a shopping centre worth €62.1m. The firm also advised a major sports equipment manufacturer in the sale of a large office and industrial estate using an innovative transaction structure and advising on environmental matters.

Tark & Co is constantly raising its profile in this field and is engaged by various domestic and international companies for advice on Estonian real estate issues. In 2005 the firm provided assistance to the country's leading commercial enterprise in connection with the development and opening of one of Estonia's largest shopping malls. The firm's 'very high level of professional flexibility' receives praise from clients.

MAQS Advokatbyrå advises foreign and domestic companies on real estate matters. The firm is retained by Port of Miiduranna to advise on its real estate transactions. The firm has particular expertise in the area of sales and lease-backs of large real estate portfolios.

Law Firm Teder, Glikman & Partnerid houses one of the most active teams of real estate specialists in the country. The firm represents a number of both domestic and international real estate companies and investment funds.

Aare Raigi Advokaadibüroo is retained by one of Estonia's key players in the real estate market and also by the Department of Housing Economy of Tallinn City Government. The firm advised a major transit terminal for oil products on construction matters last year. 'A confidential atmosphere, professionalism and full co-operation,' left one client very satisfied with the firm's services.

Ülle Kullör of **Hedman Osborne Clarke Alliance** advised on several construction and property development projects in 2005 and counselled an array of international clients in connection with property acquisitions including advising a number of foreign capital companies on real estate development projects.

Name partner Toomas Keevallik, **Law Office Keevallik & Partners,** offers expertise in matters concerning construction and real estate. Clients include several major real estate developers and building companies. The firm provides construction-related advice in connection with infrastructure and residential and industrial development.

REAL ESTATE AND CONSTRUCTION

LEPIK & LUHAÄÄR LAWIN ✪
LUIGA MODY HÄÄL BORENIUS ✪
RAIDLA & PARTNERS ✪
SORAINEN LAW OFFICES ✪
TARK & CO ✪

MAQS Advokatbyrå
Teder, Glikman & Partnerid, Law Firm ✪

Aare Raigi Advokaadibüroo
Aavik, Arvisto & Partners, Law Office
Aivar Pilv, Law Office ✪
Hedman Osborne Clarke Alliance
Keevallik & Partners, Law Office
Lextal Law Firm
Paul Varul, Advokaadibüroo ✪
Pohla & Hallmägi
Straus & Partners, Law Firm
Tehver & Partners, Law Office
V Kaasik & Co, Law Office

Firms are listed A-Z in tiers which are ranked in order of priority
✪ Indicates firm displays contact details at the end of this chapter.

Lextal Law Firm has a team of three lawyers handling real estate and construction matters for several of Estonia's dominant construction companies. The firm has represented major customers in EU funded projects.

In 2005 **Advokaadibüroo Paul Varul** handled numerous noteworthy real estate and construction cases. Satisfied clients highlight the 'customer-oriented corporate culture and pleasant communication'.

Partners Asko Pohla, Jüri Ploom and Toivo Viilup of **Pohla & Hallmägi** are experienced in this field and currently assist foreign and domestic investors in the development of new living and commercial areas and the purchase of shopping centres in Estonia.

Partner Paavo Paas handles the real estate work at **Law Firm Straus & Partners.** Daily transactions include leasing, purchasing, environmental and financing issues. The firm's most noteworthy client in this department is the biggest real estate developer in the Baltic States. 'Responsiveness and a solution-oriented manner' are appreciated by clients.

Law Office Tehver & Partners has advised and represented several large corporations and institutions on big-value construction matters. Clients praise the firm's 'sharpness and ability to work in both the Estonian and English languages'.

TAX

AIVAR PILV, LAW OFFICE ✪
LEPIK & LUHAÄÄR LAWIN ✪
LUIGA MODY HÄÄL BORENIUS ✪
SORAINEN LAW OFFICES ✪

Aare Raigi Advokaadibüroo
Aavik, Arvisto & Partners, Law Office
Hedman Osborne Clarke Alliance
HETA, Advokaadibüroo ✪
Hough, Hübner, Hütt & Partners
Keevallik & Partners, Law Office
Straus & Partners, Law Firm
Lextal Law Firm
Paul Varul, Advokaadibüroo ✪
Raidla & Partners ✪
Rödl & Partner
Tark & Co ✪
Teder, Glikman & Partnerid, Law Firm ✪

Firms are listed A-Z in tiers which are ranked in order of priority
✪ *Indicates firm displays contact details at the end of this chapter.*

TAX

Law Office Aivar Pilv is among the leading Estonian firms for tax issues; the Customs and Tax Board receives regular advice from this firm on interpretation of tax law. The firm has thorough expertise in this area and has contributed to the development of judicial practice on several principal issues. Recognised lawyers include sworn advocates Aivar Pilv, Erki Kergandberg and Margus Lentsius.

Lepik & Luhaäär LAWIN offers extensive experience, having handled a number of complex international issues. Tax specialist Rolan Jankelevitsh offers comprehensive expertise. The tax department at the firm recently advised the Estonian government in a dispute with the European Commission regarding surplus sugar stocks. Esteemed clients include Hoffman-La Roche and Electrolux.

Marti Hääl of **Luiga Mody Hääl Borenius** is one of Estonia's top tax law experts. Tax litigation is a key practice area at the firm, gaining it remarkable recognition. Several significant cases have been secured in court against the Estonian Tax Board. Last year the firm acted on behalf of a leading Estonian investment bank in carrying out complex analysis of alternative investment structures covering the local and international taxation structure and recommending the optimal fund structure.

The addition of tax expert Luc Nijs in 2005 significantly upped the profile of **Sorainen Law Offices**' tax department. Last year the firm provided pan-Baltic advice to a capital markets provider on tax issues related to stock borrowing and equity derivatives. The firm also advised a real estate investment company on tax planning for the acquisition of hotels.

Lawyers at **Aare Raigi Advokaadibüroo** have developed in-depth expertise in Estonian tax laws and partner Aare-Heino Raig is renowned in this arena. A significant transaction last year involved representing a large Estonian bank in a dispute with Estonian tax authorities. Clients believe the firm 'understands the big picture and the social implications and developments of business'.

Hedman Osborne Clarke Alliance offers experienced, multi-lingual tax services to domestic and foreign clients. Mari-Liis Liinat is an adept tax lawyer.

Law Office Keevallik & Partners endeavours to provide sophisticated legal services and has increased its tax-related work in the past year advising both corporate and private clients. The firm is constantly growing with new areas of expertise appearing every year and a rapidly increasing client base.

Lextal Law Firm showcased its tax capabilities last year when representing a client against the tax authorities in a highly significant transaction. The firm impresses clients with its 'rapid turnaround skills and extremely good accessibility'.

Advokaadibüroo Paul Varul offers a specialised tax service. The busy department is headed by partner Helmut Pikmets who has more than 14 years of experience. The firm is able to work in an advisory capacity as well as having excellent litigation skills. Clients assert the firm 'has a good reputation and public image and shows outstanding competence'.

Asko Pohla and Taimar Ehrlich represent clients in tax disputes and planning at **Pohla & Hallmägi**.

Law Firm Straus & Partners is adept in tax practice. Last year partner Priit Lätt represented a large foods company in a high-profile case involving the Estonian Customs and Tax Board. Lätt has also been actively involved in disputes over the post-clearance recovery of import duties. Clients praise the firm's punctuality and thoroughness.

Tark & Co boasts outstanding tax expertise. The firm counsels clients on all Estonian tax-related issues including tax planning and due diligence. The firm co-operates with **Baker & McKenzie LLP**, the Tax and Customs Board and the Ministry of Financial Affairs.

Law Firm Teder, Glikman & Partnerid advises clients on complex tax cases, working closely with national tax and customs authorities, aiming to provide the most current information on customs and tax policies.

LAW OFFICE AIVAR PILV

VABADUSE VÄLJAK 10
10146 TALLINN

Telephone: +372 6 404 650
Fax: +372 6 404 653
E-mail: info@apilv.ee
Website: www.apilv.ee

Languages
English, Estonian, Finnish, German, Russian

Other offices
Tartu

Number of lawyers 16
at this office 13

Member
TAGLaw

CATEGORIES OF WORK

Bankruptcy law
Aivar Pilv, Margo Lemetti

Corporate law
Ilmar-Erik Aavakivi, Margo Lemetti

Contracts
Ilmar-Erik Aavakivi, Kristina Uuetoa-Tepper

Banking and finance law
Erki Kergandberg, Margus Lentsius

Property law
Kristina Uuetoa-Tepper, Margus Lentsius

Intellectual property law
Andres Aavik, Ilmar-Erik Aavakivi

Labour law
Kristina Uuetoa-Tepper, Piret Blankin

Valuation of business projects
Ilmar-Erik Aavakivi, Siiri Traat

Land and ownership reform
Tarmo Pilv, Raul Talts

Administrative law
Aivar Pilv, Kristina Uuetoa-Tepper

Customs law
Kristina Uuetoa-Tepper, Erki Kergandberg

Taxation (tax law)
Aivar Pilv, Erki Kergandberg

Telecommunications
Piret Blankin, Ilmar-Erik Aavakivi

Competition law
Aivar Pilv, Ilmar-Erik Aavakivi

Copyright
Andres Aavik, Raul Talts

White-collar crime
Aivar Pilv, Tarmo Pilv

Arbitration and litigation
Aivar Pilv, Erki Kergandberg

CONCORDIA ATTORNEYS AT LAW

LENNUKI 22
10145 TALLINN

Telephone: +372 6 262 062
Fax: +372 6 262 061
E-mail: law@concordia.ee
Website: www.concordia.ee

Languages
English, Estonian, Finnish, German, Russian

Number of lawyers 12

International groupings
European Law Firm; Estonian Bar Assocation

CATEGORIES OF WORK

Corporate and commercial
Andres Vutt

Banking and finance
Ott Saame

Real estate
Jaanus Mägi

Litigation
Andres Past

Intellectual property
Anto Variku

Mergers and acquisitions
Andres Vutt

Construction law
Ott Saame

Contracts
Ott Saame

Insolvency
Kaidar Sultson

Criminal law
Helen Haal, Monika Mägi

Labour law
Anto Variku

Competition
Andres Vutt

Constitutional law
Mihkel Tasa

Administrative law
Mihkel Tasa

ADVOKAADIBÜROO HETA

RÜÜTLI 4
10130 TALLINN

Telephone: +372 6 996 611
Fax: +372 6 442 889
E-mail: heta@heta.ee
Website: www.heta.ee

Languages
English, Estonian, Finnish, German, Russian

Number of lawyers 5

CATEGORIES OF WORK

Banking and finance
Taavi Pihlakas, Mati Maksing

Corporate and commercial
Taavi Pihlakas, Kaido Pihlakas

Litigation and arbitration
Triinu Vernik, Mati Maksing

Contracts
Kaido Pihlakas, Mati Maksing

Tax law
Mati Maksing, Taavi Pihlakas

Real estate
Taavi Pihlakas, Kaido Pihlakas

Construction and planning
Taavi Pihlakas, Kaido Pihlakas

Competition
Mati Maksing, Taavi Pihlakas

Mergers and acquisitions
Taavi Pihlakas, Mati Maksing

Privatisation
Kaido Pihlakas, Taavi Pihlakas

Bankruptcy law
Taavi Pihlakas, Mati Maksing

Administrative law
Triinu Vernik, Kaido Pihlakas

Labour law
Mati Maksing, Triinu Vernik

Insurance
Kaido Pihlakas, Triinu Vernik

LAW OFFICE LAUS & PARTNERS

NAFTA 1
10152 TALLINN

Telephone: +372 6 622 640
Fax: +372 6 622 641
E-mail: lawoffice@lauspartners.ee
Website: www.lauspartners.ee

Languages
English, Estonian, Finnish, Russian

Number of lawyers 6

CATEGORIES OF WORK

Banking and finance
Raivo Laus, Madis Kiisa

Corporate and commercial
Raivo Laus, Alo Pormeister

Administrative
Kalev Aavik, Janek Väli

Commercial property/real estate
Madis Kiisa, Viktor Särgava

Competition and EU
Kalev Aavik, Janek Väli

Construction
Janek Väli, Viktor Särgava

Litigation and arbitration
Raivo Laus, Madis Kiisa

Mergers and acquisitions
Raivo Laus, Alo Pormeister

Tax and customs
Raivo Laus, Madis Kiisa

Shipping and transport
Raivo Laus, Viktor Särgava

Telecommunications
Madis Kiisa, Viktor Särgava

Criminal law
Alo Pormeister, Janek Väli

Intellectual property
Janek Väli, Kalev Aavik

Family and succession law
Alo Pormeister, Viktor Särgava

Citizenship and migration
Kalev Aavik, Alo Pormeister

Media and entertainment
Janek Väli, Kalev Aavik

Environment
Kalev Aavik, Alo Pormeister

LEPIK & LUHAÄÄR LAWIN

DUNKRI 7
10123 TALLINN

Telephone: +372 6 306 460
Fax: +372 6 306 463
E-mail: tallinn@lawin.ee
Website: www.lawin.ee

Languages
English, Finnish, German, Russian, Swedish

Number of lawyers 23

Contacts
Peeter Lepik, Toomas Luhaäär

Member
Estonian Bar Association;
International Bar Association

International groupings
LAWIN; Lex Mundi; LAW

CATEGORIES OF WORK

Corporate and commercial
Peeter Lepik, Martin Simovart

Trade and investments
Toomas Luhaäär, Rolan Jankelevitsh

Mergers and acquisitions
Martin Simovart

Construction
Liina Linsi

Real estate
Liina Linsi, Marika Jaanson

Banking and finance, capital markets
Peeter Lepik, Martin Simovart

Competition
Martin Simovart

Contracts
Peeter Lepik, Martin Simovart

Dispute resolution, litigation and arbitration
Liina Linsi, Vesse Võhma

Intellectual property
Pirkko-Liis Harkmaa

Tax
Toomas Luhaäär, Rolan Jankelevitsh

Employment
Liina Linsi, Triinu Hiob

Insolvency
Toomas Luhaäär, Vesse Võhma

Shipping and transport
Heiki Lindpere, Liina Linsi

Telecoms
Pirkko-Liis Harkmaa

Insurance
Vesse Võhma, Kaidi Reiljan-Sihvart

THE FIRM

Lepik & Luhaäär LAWIN, founded in 1990, is now one of the leading and largest law firms in Estonia and the Baltic States. The firm advises in all major fields of business law and is distinguished by the excellence of its services, its extensive experience and employing of leading specialists in Estonia.

The firm is a member of LAWIN, a group of leading Baltic law firms also including Klavins & Slaidins from Latvia and Lideika, Petrauskas, Valiunas ir partneriai LAWIN from Lithuania. LAWIN currently has over 80 lawyers, making it the largest legal presence working in the Baltics.

Lepik & Luhaäär LAWIN represents international clients in most legal issues and areas, including corporate and commercial law, corporate finance, banking and securities, construction and real estate, competition, investments, intellectual property, employment, taxation, insolvency law and litigation. The firm is experienced in assisting clients establish businesses and invest in the Republic of Estonia. The firm's specialists work in five practice groups: corporate and M&A, finance and tax, property and environment, trade and technology, and dispute resolution and transport.

AREAS OF PRACTICE

The lawyers of the firm regularly deal with a broad range of international corporate and business transactions, including the establishment of branch offices in Estonia and subsidiaries in Estonia and abroad. Lawyers of the firm deal with the preparation of supply and other export contracts, commercial contracts, agency, distributorship as well as franchising arrangements. The firm has been advising several major US and European financial institutions while structuring the finance to local entities. The lawyers of the firm handle the acquisition of companies and advise clients on subscription and share purchase agreements, corporate charters, shareholders' agreements and other agreements among shareholders; several of them also have a profound experience in banking, finance and securities sectors.

The firm also assists and represents clients in securities transactions and has substantial experience in advising on the implementation of legislation and regulation regarding investment into a wide range of areas in the Estonian economy. With the development of private equity market over recent years, strong emphasis has been placed on different private equity issues. Lepik & Luhaäär LAWIN has substantial expertise in handling matters related to competition law, including merger control, special and exclusive rights, unfair competition and restriction of competition. The lawyers of the firm have assisted clients in applying for exemptions and state aid and represented clients in competition matters both before the Competition Board and in courts.

The firm represents clients in a wide variety of aspects related to taxation, including tax planning and development of specific tax structures and project evaluation on legal and financial aspects, in order to diminish, within the law, tax exposures on investments, mergers and acquisitions.

LUIGA MODY HÄÄL BORENIUS

PARNU MNT 15
10141 TALLINN

Telephone: +372 6 651 888
Fax: +372 6 651 899
E-mail: lmh@lmh.ee
Website: www.lmh.ee

Languages
English, Estonian, Finnish, German, Russian

Number of lawyers 26

Other Borenius group member firms
Borenius & Kemppinen (Helsinki);
Liepa, Skopina/Borenius (Riga);
Foigt & Partners/Regija Borenius (Vilnius)

CATEGORIES OF WORK

Banking and finance
Sten Luiga, Priit Pahapill

Contracts
Peeter Kutman, Margus Mugu

Corporate and commercial
Sten Luiga

Competition
Sten Luiga, Peeter Kutman

IP, IT and telecoms
Peeter Kutman, Viive Kaur

Litigation, arbitration
Jaanus Mody, Marti Hääl

Maritime and transport
Margus Mugu

Mergers and acquisitions
Sten Luiga, Priit Pahapill

Real estate and construction
Jaanus Mody, Margus Mugu

Insolvency
Jaanus Mody, Margus Mugu

Infrastructure
Peeter Kutman, Sten Luiga

Capital markets
Priit Pahapill, Sten Luiga

Labour law
Marti Hääl

Tax
Marti Hääl

LAW OFFICE OTS & CO

PÃRNU MNT 15
4TH FLOOR
10141 TALLINN

Telephone: +372 6 141 990
Fax: +372 6 141 999
E-mail: info@otsco.ee
Website: www.otsco.ee

Languages
English, Estonian, Finnish, French, German, Russian

Number of lawyers 8

CATEGORIES OF WORK

Company law
Maivi Ots, Randu Riiberg

M&A
Maivi Ots, Randu Riiberg

Property law
Maivi Ots, Maris Kuurberg

Intellectual property law
Maivi Ots

Constitutional and administrative law
Toomas Pikamäe

Tax law
Toomas Pikamäe

Competition law
Toomas Pikamäe

Law of obligations
Maris Kuurberg, Raiko Lipstok

Planning and construction
Maris Kuurberg

Bankruptcy law
Randu Riiberg

Labour law
Randu Riiberg, Annika Raidmaa

Public procurement law
Raiko Lipstock

Customs law
Rando Maisvee

European Union law
Rando Maisvee, Tambet Toomela

Immigration law
Annika Raidmaa

ADVOKAADIBÜROO PAUL VARUL ATTORNEYS-AT-LAW

AHTRI 6A
10151 TALLINN

Telephone: +372 6 264 300
Fax: +372 6 264 306
E-mail: tallinn@varul.ee
Website: www.varul.ee

Languages
English, Estonian, Finnish, German, Russian

Other offices
Tartu

Number of lawyers 19
at this office 17

International groupings
International Business Law Consortium (IBLC); Euro-American Lawyers Group (EALG)

CATEGORIES OF WORK

Administrative
Paul Varul

Banking and finance
Helmut Pikmets

Commercial property, real estate
Mikk Löhmus, Leonid Tolstov

Competition
Ants Mailend, Vaido Pöldoja

Construction and planning
Mikk Löhmus, Vadim Pilimonov

Corporate and commercial
Paul Varul, Leonid Tolstov

Litigation and arbitration
Aldo Kaljurand, Mikk Löhmus

Employment
Anu Sander, Kersti Kull

Energy and natural resources
Ants Mailend, Mikk Löhmus

Infrastructure and project finance
Aldo Kaljurand, Kristina Vind

Insolvency, corporate restructuring
Paul Varul, Tarmo Peterson

Insurance
Karl Haavasalu, Ingeri Luik

Intellectual property
Ants Mailend

Media and entertainment
Matti Laarmaa

RAIDLA & PARTNERS

ROOSIKRANTSI 2
10119 TALLINN

Telephone: +372 6 407 170
Fax: +372 6 407 171
E-mail: email@raidla.ee
Website: www.raidla.ee

Languages
English, Finnish, German, Russian, Swedish

Other offices
Helsinki*, Riga*, Stockholm*, Vilnius*

Number of lawyers 33

International groupings
Roschier Raidla; ius laboris, International Employment Law, Pensions and Employee Benefits Alliance

CATEGORIES OF WORK

Banking and finance, capital markets
Raino Paron

Corporate and commercial
Sven Papp

Dispute resolution, litigation and arbitration
Toomas Vaher

Energy and natural resources
Sven Papp, Jaanus Ikla

Insolvency/corporate restructuring
Toomas Vaher, Raino Paron, Sven Papp

Insurance
Raino Paron

Intellectual property
Ants Nomper

Infrastructure
Jüri Raidla, Raino Paron, Sven Papp

Mergers and acquisitions
Sven Papp, Raino Paron

Privatisation
Jüri Raidla

Shipping and transport
Toomas Vaher

Tax
Monika Sehver

Telecommunications
Sven Papp, Kristi Reinson

Real estate development
Jüri Raidla, Jaanus Ikla

E-commerce
Raino Paron

Competition
Raino Paron, Tanel Kalaus

SORAINEN LAW OFFICES

PARNU ROAD 15
10141 TALLINN

Telephone: +372 6 400 900
Fax: +372 6 400 901
E-mail: sorainen@sorainen.ee
Website: www.sorainen.com

Languages
English, Estonian, Finnish, French, German, Latvian, Lithuanian, Polish, Russian, Swedish

Other offices
Riga, Vilnius

Number of lawyers 65
at this office 25

CATEGORIES OF WORK

Mergers and acquisitions
Toomas Prangli, Aku Sorainen

Property and construction law
Kaido Loor, Triin Toomemets

Financial and securitites law
Kaido Loor, Pekka Puolakka

Company law
Karin Madisson, Risto Agur

Trade, distribution and services
Evelin Parn-Lee, Pekka Puolakka

Insurance
Kaido Loor

Competition and public procurement law
Pekka Puolakka, Evelin Parn-Lee

Employment law
Toomas Prangli, Katrin Sarap

Taxation law
Kaido Loor, Konstantin Kotivnenko

Litigation and arbitration
Carri Ginter, Carry Plaks

Intellectual property and IT law
Kaido Loor, Evelin Parn-Lee

Energy and environmental law
Toomas Prangli

THE FIRM

Sorainen Law Offices was established in 1995 in Tallinn, Estonia. The firm was expanded to Latvia and Lithuania in 1997 and 1999 respectively. The firm has grown steadily and is today one of the leading Baltic law firms, with 65 lawyers, including 10 partners, in its three offices. Many lawyers of the firm are widely recognised 'experts' in their areas of practice.

The firm's offices in Estonia, Latvia and Lithuania are part of a fully integrated, pan-Baltic legal practice with a strong international element dedicated to providing high-quality legal services to foreign investors and to local businesses in the region.

AREAS OF PRACTICE

The firm's strategic focus is on M&A, with a strong commitment also to property and construction law and financial and securities law. Consequently, the firm is constantly involved in most major M&A transactions in the Baltic countries.

Sorainen Law Offices has built its practice through organic growth and outstanding service. Being a full service business law firm, Sorainen Law Offices assists domestic and international clients in all corporate areas, competition, banking and finance, insurance, corporate and commercial, shipping and transport, property, IT and telecoms, IPR, employment, tax, insolvency and restructuring, litigation and arbitration.

As a truly integrated pan-Baltic law firm, Sorainen Law Offices offers a focused, proactive, business-minded and co-ordinated approach to client service in relation to cross-border transactions.

More detailed information is provided upon request.

LAW FIRM TAMME & OTSMANN

ROOSIKRANTSI 11
10119 TALLINN

Telephone: +372 6 976 090
Fax: +372 6 976 091
E-mail: abtamme@abtamme.ee
Website: www.abtamme.ee

Languages
English, Estonian, Finnish, German, Russian

Number of lawyers 7

Contact
Lea Nõmme

CATEGORIES OF WORK

Mergers and acquisitions
Tõnis Tamme, Ergo Blumfeldt

Company and commercial law
Ergo Blumfeldt, Risto Käbi

Real estate and construction
Tõnis Tamme, Urmas Kiik

Banking and project finance
Ergo Blumfeldt, Tõnis Tamme

Mediation and litigation
Villu Otsmann, Urmas Kiik

Competition law
Villu Otsmann, Risto Käbi

Intellectual property
Risto Käbi

IT and telecommunications
Risto Käbi

Employment law
Merlin Salvik, Kai Priks

Tax law
Villu Otsmann

Shipping and transport
Tõnis Tamme

ADVOKAADIBÜROO TARK & CO

ROOSIKRANTSI 2
10119 TALLINN

Telephone: +372 6 110 900
Fax: +372 6 110 911
E-mail: tarkco@tarkco.ee
Website: www.tarkco.com

Languages
English, Finnish, French, German, Russian, Swedish

Number of lawyers 27

Member
Estonian Bar Association;
International Bar Association

CATEGORIES OF WORK

Banking and finance
Hannes Vallikivi, Meelis Hint

Mergers and acquisitions
Risto Vahimets, Marit Savi

Securities
Hannes Vallikivi, Meelis Hint

Commercial and company law
Aare Tark, Toomas Taube

EU and competition law
Kaja Leiger, Margit Lahevee

Energy law and infrastructure projects
Kaja Leiger, Imbi Jürgen

Intellectual property
Toomas Taube, Piret Luiga

Employment
Toomas Taube, Sille Allikmets

Tax
Risto Vahimets, Piret Jesse

Insolvency
Maidu Kaasik, Allar Aru

Telecommunications
Kaja Leiger, Aet Bergmann

Litigation and arbitration
Jaan Lindmäe, Andres Suik

Environment
Kaja Leiger, Imbi Jürgen

Shipping and transport
Toomas Taube, Piret Luiga

Commercial property and real estate
Risto Vahimets, Minni-Triin Park

TEDER, GLIKMAN & PARTNERID

TORNIMÄE 2, 18TH FLOOR
10145 TALLINN

Telephone: +372 665 7070
Fax: +372 665 7071
E-mail: info@tgplegal.ee
Website: www.tgplegal.ee

Languages
English, Estonian, Finnish, German, Russian, Swedish

Number of lawyers 60
at this office 19

Contact
Tarmo Laanetu

Member
Baltic Legal Solutions;
American Chamber of Commerce Estonia;
The British-Estonian Chamber of Commerce;
Estonian Bar Association;
Swedish Chamber of Commerce in Estonia

CATEGORIES OF WORK

Corporate and commercial
Mariana Hagström, Daisy Tauk

Dispute resolution, litigation and arbitration
Indrek Teder, Leon Glikman

Mergers and acquisitions
Daisy Tauk, Mariana Hagström

IT, IP and telecommunications
Mariana Hagström, Daisy Tauk

EU and competition
Mariana Hagström

Construction and planning
Leon Glikman, Indrek Teder

Finance and banking
Indrek Teder, Mariana Hagström

Infrastructure and transportation
Mariana Hagström, Indrek Teder

Insurance
Leon Glikman, Indrek Teder

Energy, chemicals and utilities
Indrek Teder

Real estate
Leon Glikman, Indrek Teder

Employment
Daisy Tauk

Health services and medical
Mariana Hagström

Tax
Tuuve Tiivel

Population	5.22 million
Number of lawyers	1.7 million
Professional title	Asianajaja
Currency	Euro (€)

Index

Finland has long had a close association with neighbours Russia and Sweden, and this can still be seen today in the Finnish business world, where trade with Russia remains important. During the 18th century, the land known as 'Finland' was twice occupied by Russian forces, and seemed to be a bone of contention between Sweden and Russia. In 1808 Finland was conquered outright by the Russian Emperor Alexander I, and became an autonomous Grand Duchy in union with the Russian Empire until 1917, when the nation finally declared independence for the first time. Since gaining independence, and apart from a brief civil war in 1918, Finland has remained a stable nation. In the Second World War Finland had to defend itself against both Germany, and the Soviet Union. The Soviet Union continued to have some influence in Finnish politics after the war, but Finland managed to maintain a democratic government and free market, in a period which saw rapid economic growth and increased wealth and stability. From a battle-scarred agrarian nation, the Finland of today is developed, technologically advanced, independent, and unlike the other Baltic States, a keen and early supporter of the European Union, becoming a member state in 1995.

Finland is one of the world's only countries still to be growing. Made up of many thousands of lakes and islands, Finland continues to grow at a rate of 7sq km a year. This heavily forested nation's northern end is within the Arctic Circle and experiences the midnight sun. However the surreal image of this expanding, water-based land, with 24-hour light through winter is not mirrored by the political situation, which is considerably more conventional. Finland has a semi-presidential system, with the president formally responsible for foreign policy, but with most executive power lying with the cabinet and prime minister, who is chosen by the parliament. The parliament, or Eduskunta, consists of 200 members, and has supreme legislative authority, with the ability to alter the Constitution of Finland, and override presidential vetoes. The current prime minister is Matti Vanhanen, who took over in June 2003, and he heads a government of 18 ministers made up of the Centre Party, the Social Democratic party, and the Swedish People's party. The next election will be in 2007.

BILLING

Partners at the larger firms in Finland are charging an average of approximately €350 to €400 per hour. Some of the leading partners may even charge up to €400 per hour. Associates bill from €200 to €300 per hour, with rates decreasing considerably outside Helsinki. Increasingly lawyers have not been charging hourly fees, but agreeing fixed fees and contingency fees with clients.

MARKETING

There is nothing to prevent Finnish firms from advertising, and most firms have their own websites. There are now several professional legal publications in Helsinki, and the increased media coverage has created a more aggressive marketing approach in the market. However, many firms will not divulge information about their clients.

IN-HOUSE LAWYERS

The larger Finnish companies have in-house legal teams, with telecoms giant Nokia housing a team as large as any law firm in Finland. Senior lawyers in these departments are almost considered as highly as their counterparts in the top law firms. The in-house lawyers at these companies will advise on the majority of issues faced by their employers, with outside firms brought in to provide specialist advice, and to work on the larger, more complex deals, particularly on mergers, and in litigation. In-house lawyers are not permitted to be members of the Bar in Finland.

ECONOMY

Finland has a high standard of living, with a largely industrialised, free-market economy. Finland has been rated as the most competitive country in the world by the World Economic Forum, and is considered to be one of the least corrupt nations on the planet. The key economic sectors are manufacturing, engineering, telecommunications and the electronics industries. Trade is very important to the economy, with exports equalling one third of GDP.

Agriculture is not a strong contributor to the Finnish economy, and rural areas have seen a rise in unemployment, despite the importance of the forestry industry. Finland benefited from the technology boom in the '90s, and considerable foreign investment in the TMT sector. Despite the downturn in recent years in this sector, the Finnish economy has remained stable, with a steady, if unspectacular rise being currently observed. Growth over the last two years has been greater

The largest firms

1	Hannes Snellman Attorneys at Law Ltd	104
2	Roschier Holmberg	103
3	Castrén & Snellman Attorneys Ltd	76
4	Borenius & Kemppinen	54
5	Krogerus Attorneys Ltd	44
6	Fennica Attorneys Ltd	29
7	Dittmar & Indrenius	26
8	Peltonen, Ruokonen & Itäinen Attorneys At Law	25
9	Merilampi Marttila Laitasalo	22
	Veikko Palotie & Co	22
11	Hammarström Puhakka Partners, Attorneys Ltd	21
12	Bützow Nordia	19
	Waselius & Wist	19
14	Luostarinen Mettälä Räikkönen	18
	Mäkitalo Rämö Juutilainen Oy, Attorneys-at-Law	18
	Procopé & Hornborg	18
17	Ernst & Young	17
	Juridia Attorneys-At-Law, Ltd	17
	White & Case Oy, Asianajotoimisto	17
20	Ace Law Ltd	15
	Susiluoto Attorneys-at-Law Ltd	15
22	Laakso, Lukander & Ruohola	14
	Sivenius, Suvanto & Co Oy	14
24	Heikkilä & Co Attorneys at Law Ltd.	13

These figures represent the total number of lawyers in this country only, and have been supplied by the firms themselves. The figures should be accurate as at 1 January 2006.

than expected, with a total production increase of around 3.7%. Investment in real estate increased by 4%, and there has been a slight decrease in unemployment. More of the same is predicted for the near future.

LEGAL MARKET

Again, there has been little dramatic change in the legal market of Finland. The firms report an increase in activity, unsurprisingly mirroring the general health of the economy. In particular, 2005 seems to have been a good year for M&A and has seen foreign investment in real estate. The technology sector is providing a healthy amount of work, though not as much as during the boom a few years ago.

Hannes Snellman Attorneys at Law Ltd and **Roschier Holmberg** continue to lead the market, and provide the benchmark for competitors. These firms are considerably larger than all the other firms in Finland, are recognised for the quality of their advice, and have a plethora of big-name clients. **Roschier Holmberg** reports an increase in the pharmaceutical and biotechnology sectors, and has opened up four offices in technology parks around the country.

Several firms are chasing the two Finnish frontrunners, and **Castrén & Snellman Attorneys Ltd** leads the pack. With an excellent M&A record and top-rated practices in our ratings in several areas, this is a top-quality firm, and has been described as the most recognised in the country. Other contenders include **Borenius & Kemppinen**, which has seen a lot of growth in recent years following systematic investment. **Krogerus Attorneys Ltd** is another growing firm, with several offices around the country, and a strong national presence. **Fennica Attorneys Ltd** and **Merilampi Marttila Laitasalo** are two other firms making significant strides.

Asianajotoimisto White & Case Oy remains the leading foreign firm in the market and provides a viable alternative to the large domestic firms, particularly to international clients seeking advice in banking and finance or capital markets, where the firm's presence across Europe and the US is extremely valuable.

FOREIGN OFFICES AND ASSOCIATIONS

Interaction with Russia and the Baltic States is important to the Finnish, and several firms have offices in their neighbours' cities. At the end of 2005, **Roschier Holmberg** opened an office in Stockholm. **Borenius & Kemppinen** works in alliance across the Baltic region through associated *Borenius Group* law firms in Estonia, Latvia and Lithuania. **Castrén & Snellman Attorneys Ltd** has an office in St Petersburg, and **Hedman Osborne Clarke Alliance**, a member of UK firm **Osborne Clarke**'s European alliance, has offices in Helsinki, Tallinn, St Petersburg and Frankfurt.

BANKING AND FINANCE

Hannes Snellman Attorneys at Law Ltd's finance team is led by Kari Lautjarvi, who is also president of the Finnish Bar Association. The firm acts for Nordea Bank Finland, Deutsche Bank and Citigroup. The team worked on the arrangement of Sampo Plc's €550m credit facility, and advised on the financing of the E18 Lohja-Muurla expressway construction. Matti Engelberg is an experienced practitioner.

Luostarinen Mettälä Räikkönen has a focus on banking and finance. Kimmo Mettälä leads the nine-strong team, reputed for the quality of its work. In 2005 the firm represented HVB Banque Luxembourg SA on a €260m senior facilities agreement, and HVB Capital Markets on a US$252m note purchase agreement. The firm acted for Wavin Holding in connection with its €860m facility. Other clients included StyroChem Finland Oy, the Bank of Scotland, and HSH-Nordbank AG.

Roschier Holmberg remains one of the benchmark firms, led by the prolific Gunnar Westerlund. 2005 saw the team act for Handelsbanken Capital Markets in its acquisition by Forestia Holding Oy for €172m, a complicated finance transaction. The firm acted for Hypo Real Estate Bank in the €350m financing of the acquisition of Finnish shopping centres from Ilmarinen, the largest-ever cross-border real estate transaction in Finland. The firm also acted on one

BANKING AND FINANCE

HANNES SNELLMAN ATTORNEYS AT LAW LTD ✪
LUOSTARINEN METTÄLÄ RÄIKKÖNEN ✪
ROSCHIER HOLMBERG ✪
WHITE & CASE OY, ASIANAJOTOIMISTO

Borenius & Kemppinen ✪
Castrén & Snellman Attorneys Ltd ✪
Waselius & Wist ✪

Dittmar & Indrenius ✪
Fennica Attorneys Ltd ✪
HH Partners, Attorneys-at-Law, Ltd ✪
Krogerus Attorneys Ltd ✪
Merilampi Marttila Laitasalo ✪

Bützow Nordia
Hammarström Puhakka Partners, Attorneys Ltd ✪
Peltonen, Ruokonen & Itäinen Attorneys At Law ✪

Procopé & Hornborg
Veikko Palotie & Co ✪

Firms are listed A-Z in tiers which are ranked in order of priority
✪ Indicates firm displays contact details at the end of this chapter.

of the first public securitisations, representing Citigroup, Nordea Securities and NorScan Properties in a deal valued at €775m.

Asianajotoimisto White & Case Oy has a very strong banking practice, led by one of the leading lawyers in the country, executive lawyer Petri Haussila. Partners Timo Airisto and Risto Ojantakanen are also highly rated. The firm had a busy 2005, representing Altor Equity Partners in the acquisition of GE Healthcare's dental imaging equipment business. The team also acted for Hypo Real Estate Bank International in the financing of an acquisition and lease-back of three Nokia offices in Finland. Other major clients included Deutsche Bank and Nordic Capital.

Borenius & Kemppinen has been involved in some complex transactions, mainly advising on the financing of acquisitions, and real estate fund management. Acting for some large international clients; Jari Vikiö leads the team.

Castrén & Snellman Attorneys Ltd reports a busy 2005 for the banking and finance team, led by partners Pekka Lehtinen and Merja Kivela. Work included a loan arrangement from Nordea Bank, Eurohypo and SEB to Citycon Oyj, restructuring arrangements for Metsäliitto Cooperative and M-real Corporation, and a securitisation for Fitch Ratings Ltd.

Waselius & Wist expanded in 2005, and continues to recruit into its thriving banking and finance practice. Founding partner Jan Waselius acts for blue-chip clients such as Credit Suisse and Sampo Bank.

Dittmar & Indrenius is very active cross-border. The banking and finance team is smaller than many of its rivals, but does not lack in quality, with partners such as Markus Troberg and Jan Ollila. The client list includes Bank of America.

Fennica Attorneys Ltd's Jori Taipale runs the banking and finance practice. In 2005 he acted for Finndomo Holding Ltd on a facilities agreement relating to the acquisition of the company's share capital, a deal worth tens of millions of euro. He also represented, with partner Pekka Takki, the European Directories Consortium led by Macquarie Capital Alliance Group on the financing of the purchase of Yellow Brick Road Group for €1.8bn.

Taina Tuohino and managing partner Arto Kukkonen of **HH Partners, Attorneys-at-Law, Ltd** are active in banking and finance. Ms Tuohino recently acted for a group of private investors, while Arto Kukkonen has been assisting a long-term client on the issues relating to the leasing of large projects.

Krogerus Attorneys Ltd moves up a tier this year, on the basis of its strong showing in banking and finance. The firm acts for domestic and international banks and financial institutions. Partner Juha Wessman heads the department and specialises in project and structured finance, PPP transactions and real estate financing. Partner Mikko Mali also advises on acquisition financing, and PPP transactions.

Merilampi Marttila Laitasalo's banking and finance practice is led by partner Ari Keinänen, an experienced practitioner who has been actively involved in developing Finnish corporate law. Jukka Laitasalo, one of the firm's founding partners, has an excellent reputation in banking, with particular experience in insolvency.

CAPITAL MARKETS

Roschier Holmberg had another active year, with partner Dimitrios Himonas leading on most of the major deals. He led on the €5bn Sampo Housing Loan Bank issue, the first jumbo covered bond from the Nordic countries. He also, with Thomas Lindholm, represented the Republic of Finland in the €770m offering of shares in Fortum Oyj. Other clients in 2005 included ABN Amro Rothschild, Société Générale, JP Morgan and Merrill Lynch.

Waselius & Wist has one of the top capital markets practices, with partner Tarija Wist possessing an excellent reputation. The major highlight of 2005 was acting for Merrill Lynch, Morgan Stanley and ABN Amro Rothschild on the public offering of Neste Oil Oyj.

Asianajotoimisto White & Case Oy's team, again led by the impressive Petri Haussila, is a market leader in capital markets. An already strong group, including parters Timo Airisto and Risto Ojantakanen was further empowered in 2005 by the return of senior associate Mikko Hulkko from the firm's London office. Recent deals include representing JP Morgan in the €725m rights offering of OKO Bank, the proceeds of which form part of the financing for the acquisition of Pohjola Group. The firm acted for Fortum Corporation and its subsidiary Neste Oil Corporation in a spin-off and simultaneous listing of Neste Oil on the Helsinki Stock Exchange. This was the largest IPO in Finland for seven years.

Borenius & Kemppinen advised a large Finnish company in the listing of the company's shares on the Helsinki Stock Exchange. The team, led by partner Ari-Pekka Saanio also advised another major client in its directed share issue.

Castrén & Snellman Attorneys Ltd partners Merja Kivelä, Pekka Lehtinen and Jari Sonninen form a powerful team, acting on Kone Oyj's demerger, working on IPOs for Inion Oy, and on the acquisition of shares in Turun Arvokiinteistöt Oyj for Nordea Bank.

Hannes Snellman Attorneys at Law Ltd was particularly active in equity capital markets transaction in 2005. Led by Kari Lautijärvi, the team acted for OKO Bank on the €2bn public tender offer for all shares in Pohjola-Yhtymä Oyj. The firm also represented Deutsche Bank on the Finnish €5bn bond issue.

HH Partners, Attorneys-at-Law, Ltd partners Jari Nikupaavola and Arto Kukkonen lead this practice at the firm.

Krogerus Attorneys Ltd's Mikko Mali heads the team in conjunction with Mika Ståhlberg. The client list includes a number of major venture capital investors, as well as listed companies. The focus in 2005 was on public tenders, with an international aspect, and mergers of listed companies.

Luostarinen Mettälä Räikkönen's capital markets team is anchored by well-regarded finance expert Kimmo Mettälä. The firm represented Nordea Bank on the update of the €1bn EMTN programme for Elisa Communications Corporation, and advised a Finnish client on ISDA master agreements.

Merilampi Marttila Laitasalo's team is headed by Pekka Merilampi and Ari Keinänen. Each has an excellent reputation, Merilampi particularly for his corporate knowledge, and Keinänen has expertise in securities transactions, such as public tender offers and IPOs. The firm advised Fortum and Neste Oil Corporation in the spin-off and IPO of Neste Oil on the Helsinki Stock Exchange.

CAPITAL MARKETS

ROSCHIER HOLMBERG ✪
WASELIUS & WIST ✪
WHITE & CASE OY, ASIANAJOTOIMISTO

Borenius & Kemppinen ✪
Castrén & Snellman Attorneys Ltd ✪
Hannes Snellman Attorneys at Law Ltd ✪

HH Partners, Attorneys-at-Law, Ltd ✪
Krogerus Attorneys Ltd ✪
Luostarinen Mettälä Räikkönen ✪
Merilampi Marttila Laitasalo ✪

Fennica Attorneys Ltd ✪
Peltonen, Ruokonen & Itäinen Attorneys At Law ✪

Firms are listed A-Z in tiers which are ranked in order of priority
✪ Indicates firm displays contact details at the end of this chapter.

CORPORATE AND M&A

Hannes Snellman Attorneys at Law Ltd has 49 fee-earners in this area, and it is by far the largest practice in the firm. Accordingly, the firm is a market leader. The combined experience of partners Juhani Mäkinen, Carl-Henrik Wallin, Tuomo Vähäpassi and managing partner Johan Aalto drives this impressive team, which includes 17 partners in total. In 2005 the team advised on the acquisition of Holiday Club Finland Oy for €120m, and the tender offer of €436m for Cloetta Fazer AB by Oy Karl Fazer Ab. The firm also advised Wärtsilä Oyj Abp on the €533m acquisition of Ruukki, Skf and Wärtsilä.

Roschier Holmberg has a reputation as the market leader in corporate transactions. Partner Ulf-Henrik Kull led on many of the larger transactions in 2005, and Mika Alanko and Kaj Swanjlung also carry impressive reputations.

CORPORATE AND M&A

HANNES SNELLMAN ATTORNEYS AT LAW LTD ✪
ROSCHIER HOLMBERG ✪

Borenius & Kemppinen ✪
Castrén & Snellman Attorneys Ltd ✪
Dittmar & Indrenius ✪
Fennica Attorneys Ltd ✪
Krogerus Attorneys Ltd ✪
Luostarinen Mettälä Räikkönen ✪
Merilampi Marttila Laitasalo ✪
Waselius & Wist ✪
White & Case Oy, Asianajotoimisto

HH Partners, Attorneys-at-Law, Ltd ✪
Hammarström Puhakka Partners, Attorneys Ltd ✪
Laakso, Lukander & Ruohola ✪
Peltonen, Ruokonen & Itäinen Attorneys At Law ✪
Procopé & Hornborg
Veikko Palotie & Co ✪

Bützow Nordia
Gahmberg, Hästö & Co ✪
Hedman Osborne Clarke Alliance
Heinonen & Co ✪
Juridia, Attorneys-At-Law, Ltd ✪
Kallioinen, Tolppanen, Salminen & Co, Attorneys at Law, Ltd ✪
Mäkitalo Rämö Juutilainen Oy, Attorneys-at-Law ✪
Sivenius, Suvanto & Co Oy ✪
Susiluoto Attorneys-at-Law Ltd

Firms are listed A-Z in tiers which are ranked in order of priority
✪ *Indicates firm displays contact details at the end of this chapter.*

Managing partner Lennart Simonsen and senior partner Thomas Lindholm are also active in the area. Highlights in 2005 include the merger of Cooperative Tradeka Corporation and Wihuri Oy, acting for Outokumpu Oyj in the €598m sale of its copper business, and representing Eriken Luxembourg in its €345m sale to Kemira Oyj.

Borenius & Kemppinen has been particularly active on the M&A front, advising on some of the most significant acquisitions in 2005. In addition the firm has provided general corporate advice to a mix of international and large domestic companies, including the reorganisation of distribution networks in Europe and Japan for one client. Partner Nina Wilkman heads the practice.

Castrén & Snellman Attorneys Ltd is hot on the heels of the leading two firms when it comes to M&A work. Petta Lehtinen and Johan Åkermarck are highly recommended, and these two partners form part of a 34-strong team. 2005 saw the practice really blossom, with 58% growth in activity. The team represented CapMan Capital Management Oyj on the acquisition of Notex Yhtiöt and Okman Group, and acted for OMHEX AB on the acquisition of the National Stock Exchange of Lithuania and the Central Securities Depository of Lithuania.

Dittmar & Indrenius has a strong focus on M&A. As a small firm the emphasis is on quality, creating a compact team which performs to the highest standard for multinational clients. Markus Troberg, the managing partner, is an experienced corporate practitioner, and advised on the first-ever cross-border bank merger in Finland. In 2005 the firm advised on the Nordic Broadcasting acquisition of Alma Finnish Broadcasting, worth €460m.

Fennica Attorneys Ltd's corporate team had a busy year. Partner Matti Ylä-Mononen joined in March 2005 from **Merilampi Marttila Laitasalo** and with Jori Tapale and Jaako Hietala forms a formidable team. Clients include Elisa Corporation, Finndomo Holding, Nanso Ltd and Sponsor Capital Oyj.

Krogerus Attorneys Ltd's corporate practice was strengthened in 2005 with the arrival of two associates. Partners Hannu Krogerus, Mikko Mali, and Mika Ståhlberg are the department's leading lights. With five offices across the country the firm is well placed to serve clients outside Helsinki.

Luostarinen Mettälä Räikkönen, with industrious name partner Kimmo Mettälä again leading the way, had a busy year. The firm represented Suomen Osuuskappojen Keskuskunta in its acquisition of €52m of shares of Sumoen Spar Oyj. The firm also acted on the sales of Boyfood Oy, Nöjesguiden Oy, and JHC Arena Holding Oy. Keijo Raikonen is a leading name.

Pekka Merilampi and Ari Keinänen lead the **Merilampi Marttila Laitasalo** corporate practice. Senior partner Pekka Merilampi is one of the leading corporate experts in Finland, has sat on the board of several legislative committees, and was conferred by the President of Finland the honorary title of Lagman in 1998. The corporate practice is the central pillar of the firm. M&A specialist Jani Ylä-Autio joined the firm from **Roschier Holmberg** as a partner.

Waselius & Wist provides top-quality corporate advice, comparable to the larger firms. Founding partners Tarija Wist and Jan Waselius are excellent practitioners, acting on some large transactions. The firm acted for JC Decaux on the acquisition of Viacom Outdoor Oy, and represented Aviation Capital Group on the acquisition of Boullioun Aviation Services. Almonova Oyj is also a client.

Asianajotoimisto White & Case Oy represented Kemira Plc in its acquisition of Finnish Chemicals, for a value of €345m. The firm also advised Nordic Capital in the acquisition of Outokumpu Copper for €599m. The firm's global reach was of value in these deals. The practice has an M&A focus, with partner Risto Ojantakanen in particular specialising in the field.

HH Partners, Attorneys-at-Law, Ltd's impressive corporate practice mainly worked on M&A transactions in 2005. The firm's clients included several major Finnish companies, a US-based software company, and an Australian investment bank, all advised on acquisitions. Taina Tuohino and Arto Kukkonen are recommended for their expertise.

Hammarström Puhakka Partners, Attorneys Ltd has a good corporate practice with partners Jörgen Hammarström, Juho Lenni-Taattola and Pekka Puhakka experienced M&A advisers.

Ari Savela and Leif Itäinen in **Peltonen, Ruokonen & Itäinen Attorneys At Law**'s corporate practice are recommended. The firm acts for a number of major domestic companies, and several international clients.

Procopé & Hornborg's corporate practice is at the core of its business. Managing partner Ismo Hentula is recommended. The client base is primarily made up of companies in the energy and telecoms sectors.

Though particularly known for its insolvency work, **Veikko Palotie & Co** managing partner Tauno Palotie is recommended for his M&A expertise and heads a strong corporate practice, augmented by the merger last year with *Ahola & Sokka*.

DISPUTE RESOLUTION

Castrén & Snellman Attorneys Ltd remains a market leader in dispute resolution, thanks in large part to the expertise of highly rated partners Juoko Huhtala and Marko Hentunen. This is an important part of the firm's business, reflected by this very strong team consisting of five partners, four specialist counsels and nine associates. The practice is based on commercial disputes, but also works on some high-profile white-collar crime cases. Partner Niklas Langenskiöld specialises in maritime, transport, aviation and insurance law.

Hannes Snellman Attorneys at Law Ltd has the largest dispute resolution team in the country, with a considerable share of the market. Partner Patrik Lindfors heads the team, which has a focus on transaction-based work, and conflict management, now with an increasingly international aspect.

Merilampi Marttila Laitasalo's Ari Kantor specialises in commercial litigation. Founding partner Jukka Laitasalo is acknowledged for his versatile experience in arbitration and litigation. In the firm's Tampere office, Lassi Kettula runs a strong litigation practice specialising in liability issues.

Roschier Holmberg's litigation team is led by partners Eva Nordman and Rainer Hilli. They are active in patent litigation, representing Anheuser-Busch in the 'Budweiser' trade mark case, before the Supreme Court and European Court of Justice. The team has ongoing cases concerning supplementary patent protection, invalidation and infringement for pharmaceuticals, genomics and biochemistry, with clients such as Pfizer and Gillette. Petri Taivalkoski is leading a team representing the majority of Finnish power

DISPUTE RESOLUTION

CASTRÉN & SNELLMAN ATTORNEYS LTD ⊙
HANNES SNELLMAN ATTORNEYS AT LAW LTD ⊙
MERILAMPI MARTTILA LAITASALO ⊙
ROSCHIER HOLMBERG ⊙

Borenius & Kemppinen ⊙
Dittmar & Indrenius ⊙

Aminoff & Weissenberg, Attorneys Ltd ⊙
Fennica Attorneys Ltd ⊙
HH Partners, Attorneys-at-Law, Ltd ⊙
Krogerus Attorneys Ltd ⊙
Luostarinen Mettälä Räikkönen ⊙
Peltonen, Ruokonen & Itäinen Attorneys At Law ⊙
Veikko Palotie & Co ⊙
Waselius & Wist ⊙

Bützow Nordia
Hammarström Puhakka Partners, Attorneys Ltd ⊙
Laakso, Lukander & Ruohola ⊙
Pirilä & Pöyhönen
Procopé & Hornborg
Susiluoto Attorneys-at-Law Ltd

Firms are listed A-Z in tiers which are ranked in order of priority
⊙ Indicates firm displays contact details at the end of this chapter.

transmission companies in an appeal against the Energy Market Authority's decision regarding electricity pricing.

In 2005 **Borenius & Kemppinen** was particularly active in patent and trade mark litigation. The team of Seppo Kemppinen, Pekka Tarkela, Ben Rapinoja, and Kristiina Harenko is one of the best in this field.

Dittmar & Indrenius provides commercial litigation and arbitration advice both in Finland and abroad. Clients include banking groups, insurance companies, and a large automotive manufacturer. The firm's partners frequently act as arbitrators in commercial arbitration proceedings.

Aminoff & Weissenberg, Attorneys Ltd is primarily a shipping and transport firm, but due to these specialisations has a thriving litigation practice. Founding partners Jan Aminoff and Ulla von Weissenberg lead the team.

Fennica Attorneys Ltd has a renowned dispute resolution practice in large part due to Marko Wainio. He was involved in several highly significant, groundbreaking cases in 2005. Tom Vapaavuori is also highly recommended.

HH Partners, Attorneys-at-Law, Ltd's Jari Nikupaavola is a specialist litigator and arbitrator. In 2005 his clients included large Finnish software, metal, and technology companies, in a wide range of disputes.

Krogerus Attorneys Ltd's dispute resolution practice advises small-to-medium-sized companies. The team has expertise in tort, labour law, tax, environment, insurance and property issues. Marja Ramm-Schmidt and Jari Pekka Alho enjoy impressive reputations.

Luostarinen Mettälä Räikkönen's Raimo Seppälä leads the dispute resolution team, and name partner Keijo Raikkonen is also active in the area. The team represented Sampo Bank in its litigation against Sponda Plc, and acted in an international arbitration in London.

Peltonen, Ruokonen & Itäinen Attorneys At Law has seen a fairly busy year in litigation. Jukka Peltonen has a wealth of experience in both criminal and civil cases, and has been involved in over 100 arbitration proceedings.

Veikko Palotie & Co's Mika Pakarinen is an experienced litigator and arbitrator.

Waselius & Wist's Jan Waselius saw a rise in litigious work in 2005. He has been involved in some high-profile arbitration cases, and some insider trading, and market abuse cases.

EU AND COMPETITION

Castrén & Snellman Attorneys Ltd has one of the strongest competition practices in Finland, led by highly regarded partner Hannu Pokela. In 2005 the team noted a change in competition work, as merger control legislation changed, and self-assessment became more prevalent. Partner Johan Åkermarck, and associate Sari Hiltunen are also leaders in the field. The team advised Fortum Oyj on the establishment of a joint venture, and Suomi Mutual Life Assurance Company on a number of transactions.

Hannes Snellman Attorneys at Law Ltd's team is headed by partner Mika Savola, an experienced litigator. He is particularly active in cartel cases, and has been advising one of the defendants in the ongoing asphalt cartel case, one of the largest of its kind. Partner Tapani Manninen is an experienced competition lawyer, and Mika Pohjonen is widely considered to be the leading expert in public procurement matters.

Krogerus Attorneys Ltd has gained a number of clients in the media, food, and electricity sectors, adding to its strength in telecoms. The firm has a large team of experts, including Katri Joenpolvi, Mikko Pirttilä, and Petteri Metsä-Tokila, who were joined by Molla Mäkilaine from **Asianajotoimisto White & Case Oy**. The team is rated for the level of complexity of the issues it provides quality advice on.

Luostarinen Mettälä Räikkönen has one of the liveliest competition practices in Finland. The team is representing UPM Kymmene Corporation in one of the largest and most significant antitrust investigations to involve a Finnish company. The firm is currently involved in several cartel investigations, and is launching a complaint with the EC over discriminatory treatment of pharmaceutical products. Jukka Luostarinen is one of the most experienced lawyers in the area.

EU AND COMPETITION

CASTRÉN & SNELLMAN ATTORNEYS LTD ⊙
HANNES SNELLMAN ATTORNEYS AT LAW LTD ⊙
KROGERUS ATTORNEYS LTD ⊙
LUOSTARINEN METTÄLÄ RÄIKKÖNEN ⊙
ROSCHIER HOLMBERG ⊙

Borenius & Kemppinen ⊙
Fennica Attorneys Ltd ⊙
Merilampi Marttila Laitasalo ⊙
Procopé & Hornborg
Waselius & Wist ⊙
White & Case Oy, Asianajotoimisto

HH Partners, Attorneys-at-Law, Ltd ⊙
Morini & Kiikeri International Law Firm
Peltonen, Ruokonen & Itäinen Attorneys At Law ⊙
Reims & Co
Veikko Palotie & Co ⊙

Firms are listed A-Z in tiers which are ranked in order of priority
⊙ Indicates firm displays contact details at the end of this chapter.

Roschier Holmberg has advised its clients in several cartel investigations, and Commission investigations on an EU level, and in the US. Clients in 2005 included Carlsberg, IBM, and Industri Kapital AB. Christian Wik has an excellent reputation in the field, and Nikko Hukkinen is also very active.

Borenius & Kemppinen recruited partner Ilkka Aalto-Setälä from **Asianajotoimisto White & Case Oy** as the new head of department. He is a highly rated EU and competition lawyer. The team also includes partner Janne Kairo. The practice was active advising members of the automotive industry in 2005, with partner Riku Paanila also advising.

Fennica Attorneys Ltd's Jori Taipale has given EU and competition advice in a number of distribution agreements, M&A transactions, joint ventures and public procurement-related matters. He advised Elisa Corporation on a public tender offer.

Merilampi Marttila Laitasalo's EU and competition team is headed by Arttu Mentula. He has extensive experience in merger control clearances before the Finnish Competition Authority and the European Commission, and recently represented Rautaruukki Corporation and Wärtsilä Corporation in the merger control filings before the European Commission regarding the creation of a new joint venture with Aktiebolaget SKF. Erkko Ruohoniemi is a specialist counsel, concentrating on competition matters.

Lotta Uusitalo at **Procopé & Hornborg**, one of the firm's five partners, has a strong reputation for her competition work for Finnish and international clients.

Waselius & Wist advises on all aspects of competition law, particularly for corporate clients. Partner Mikka Eerola heads the practice.

Asianajotoimisto White & Case Oy's competition practice centres around Petri Haussila and senior associate Tanja Törnkvist. The firm assisted Kemira Oyj in the acquisition of Finnish Chemicals Oyj for €345m, with notification submitted to the relevant authorities in Finland, Sweden and Norway.

MARITIME AND TRANSPORT

Aminoff & Weissenberg, Attorneys Ltd is a niche firm with an excellent reputation. It specialises in maritime and transport law, with matters relating to insurance, carriage of goods and passengers, charterparty and bill of lading disputes, collision, salvage, sale and purchase of vessels, CMR matters and pollution. Jan Amoinoff and Ullavon Weisenberg are leaders in this field, and founded the firm. Clients tend to be international vessel owners and their underwriters.

Castrén & Snellman Attorneys Ltd's Niklas Langenskiöld is one of the handful of leading maritime and transport lawyers in the country. Unlike the other two top firms in this sector, **Castrén & Snellman Attorneys Ltd** is a full-service firm, but its maritime and transport practice is an important focus. The firm advises in all issues and is very strong on the disputes side.

Gahmberg, Hästö & Co has two areas of focus, corporate and commercial, and maritime and transport. Name partner Henrik Gahmberg heads the maritime and transport practice, and can call on his 30 years of experience in the area. He is often instructed to litigate in complex and extensive matters before national courts as well as before international panels of arbitrators. The firm's clients include marine and P&I underwriters, shipowners, some of the world's largest shipping companies, and the Finnish Maritime Administration.

HH Partners, Attorneys-at-Law, Ltd's Johan Bardy has 20 years' experience in maritime and transport law, and has acted in some of Finland's highest-profile cases. He represents both domestic and foreign corporations, shipowners, trucking companies and P&I clubs.

MARITIME AND TRANSPORT

AMINOFF & WEISSENBERG, ATTORNEYS LTD ⊙
CASTRÉN & SNELLMAN ATTORNEYS LTD ⊙
GAHMBERG, HÄSTÖ & CO ⊙

HH Partners, Attorneys-at-Law, Ltd ⊙
Hannes Snellman Attorneys at Law Ltd ⊙
Luostarinen Mettälä Räikkönen ⊙
Veikko Palotie & Co ⊙

Borenius & Kemppinen ⊙
Bützow Nordia
Procopé & Hornborg
Roschier Holmberg ⊙

Firms are listed A-Z in tiers which are ranked in order of priority
⊙ *Indicates firm displays contact details at the end of this chapter.*

Hannes Snellman Attorneys at Law Ltd's Mariehamn office, where the shipping practice is based, is headed by Kenneth Neoveus. Neoveus specialises in shipping finance.

Luostarinen Mettälä Räikkönen partners Kimmo Mettälä and Janne Tuulos advised on the tender process organised by the Finnish Road Administration to design, build, finance and operate the Lohja-Muurla E18 motorway project.

Veikko Palotie & Co's transport practice is strongly influenced by business with neighbouring Russia. The firm provides shipping and road transport advice to large internationally operating companies.

REAL ESTATE AND CONSTRUCTION

The team at **Castrén & Snellman Attorneys Ltd** enjoyed a very interesting year, acting on some large projects, such as the construction of a shopping centre, several hotel deals, and the financing of the E18 motorway construction. Partners Mika Ilveskero and Uwe Uusitalo head the practice. The team worked on the sale and lease-back of property for Oy Agfa-Gevaert Ab, and on the acquisition of Kesko real estate properties by Nordisk Renting Oy.

Veikko Palotie & Co has a strong practice, with partners Asta Siponen, Teemu Kauttu, Veli Leinonen and Lauri Tolvanen all specialising in a variety of property issues.

Fennica Attorneys Ltd has a thriving real estate practice thanks to the efforts of Pekka Raatikainen and Jaako Hietala. The firm is involved in all aspects of real estate work, both contentious and non-contentious. Marko Wainio continues to advise major institutional clients on various aspects of commercial property and construction law, while regularly lecturing at the University of Helsinki.

HH Partners, Attorneys-at-Law, Ltd has a very good reputation particularly for its construction advice, acting frequently on litigious matters and in arbitration proceedings. Eero Kajander and Jari Nikupaavola are recommended.

REAL ESTATE AND CONSTRUCTION

CASTRÉN & SNELLMAN ATTORNEYS LTD ⊙
VEIKKO PALOTIE & CO ⊙

Fennica Attorneys Ltd ⊙
HH Partners, Attorneys-at-Law, Ltd ⊙
Hammarström Puhakka Partners, Attorneys Ltd ⊙
Merilampi Marttila Laitasalo ⊙
Roschier Holmberg ⊙

Borenius & Kemppinen ⊙
Bützow Nordia
Juridia, Attorneys-At-Law, Ltd ⊙
Laakso, Lukander & Ruohola ⊙

Firms are listed A-Z in tiers which are ranked in order of priority
⊙ *Indicates firm displays contact details at the end of this chapter.*

Hammarström Puhakka Partners, Attorneys Ltd partner Kari Marttinen specialises in real estate and construction law, with expertise in planning and zoning, pollution and the environment.

Merilampi Marttila Laitasalo's real estate and construction team has benefited from foreign investment. The experienced team has advised on some complex real estate transactions, often involving the provision of advice on the financing structures required. Ari Keinänen leads the team.

Roschier Holmberg's real estate practice acted for Eurohypo AG in the purchase and lease-back of Pohjola Ltd's headquarters in Helsinki. The team also acted on the acquisition by Merrill Lynch, O'Connor Capital Partners and Genesta Property of six commercial properties. Gunnar Westerlund and Kaj Swanljung lead the department.

TMT AND IP

The TMT practice at **Borenius & Kemppinen** has an impressive client list, particularly in the IT sector. The team advises several multinational corporations. The IP practice provides a considerable amount of litigious advice, including acting in a landmark case before the ECJ. Kristina Harenka is recommended for IP work and is an expert on new media and licensing. Pekka Tarkela and Seppo Kemppinen advise on IP and IT-related disputes. Ben Rapinoja specialises in life sciences.

Castrén & Snellman Attorneys Ltd's team has seen an active year, though the market is not as strong as five years ago. Nokia and Pfizer are important clients for the firm. IT and outsourcing were important areas of work in 2005. IT expert Kimmo Rekola is a client favourite, and Johan Akermarck and Paulina Tenhunen are specialists in the pharmaceutical sector.

Fennica Attorneys Ltd has a genuine focus on TMT, and as a result has forged an impressive reputation in the field. Partners Pekka Raatikainen and Kari-Matti Lehti lead the way, particularly with regards to outsourcing and telecoms. The firm acted for SAP Finland on several major software and consulting projects, advised Elisa Plc on outsourcing, and represented Teleca AB on worldwide frame agreement negotiations. The firm was also active in three different patent disputes in 2005, a large proportion of the total number in Finland.

Hannes Snellman Attorneys at Law Ltd's technology group advises on intellectual property issues, IPR strategies, IT, media and marketing. Kaisa Fahlund heads the group, and specialises in IPR and IT with a special emphasis on complex IT system deliveries and outsourcing arrangements. The firm's key clients include Microsoft, and Accenture. The 12-lawyer team is one of Finland's strongest, and includes partner Mikko Heinonen who advises several technology start-ups.

Krogerus Attorneys Ltd represents major Finnish clients, from both the private and public

TMT AND IP

BORENIUS & KEMPPINEN ✪
CASTRÉN & SNELLMAN ATTORNEYS LTD ✪
FENNICA ATTORNEYS LTD ✪
HANNES SNELLMAN ATTORNEYS AT LAW LTD ✪
KROGERUS ATTORNEYS LTD ✪
ROSCHIER HOLMBERG ✪

HH Partners, Attorneys-at-Law, Ltd ✪
Susiluoto Attorneys-at-Law Ltd

Backström & Co ✪
Dittmar & Indrenius ✪
Heinonen & Co ✪
Luostarinen Mettälä Räikkönen ✪
Merilampi Marttila Laitasalo ✪
Pirilä & Pöyhönen
Veikko Palotie & Co ✪
Waselius & Wist ✪

Ace Law Ltd
Juridia, Attorneys-At-Law, Ltd ✪
Laakso, Lukander & Ruohola ✪
Peltonen, Ruokonen & Itäinen Attorneys At Law ✪
Procopé & Hornborg

Firms are listed A-Z in tiers which are ranked in order of priority
✪ *Indicates firm displays contact details at the end of this chapter.*

sectors, on their IT procurement and outsourcing needs. Juah Pekka Katainen leads the team, with Katri Joenpolvi noted for her expertise in telecoms. The IP practice has continued to grow, with the arrival of Arto Hakkarainen to take the reins from the departed Jan Vidjeskog. The firm continues to build on its strength in this area, following last year's promotion to the top tier.

Roschier Holmberg advised clients through a tumultuous period during 2004 and 2005. The firm advised a number of Finnish IT companies on licensing and launching new products. Rainer Hilli leads the team, which acted for a number of mobile technology companies, notably Flexotronics on its acquisition of Finnish ODM Microcell Oy. The team has been active in outsourcing and disputes in the communications sector, advised SBS Broadcasting on the acquisition of Finnish digital television channel TV5, and acted for Nokia in its divestment of its PMR business. On the IP front the firm has been involved in several patent disputes, acting for Anheuser-Busch, Pfizer, Gillette, and GlaxoSmithKline. Janne Kairo, formerly a partner at **Borenius & Kemppinen** joined the team in 2005.

HH Partners, Attorneys-at-Law, Ltd has a strong IT practice, representing some household names. Alf-Ole Wanamo has over 30 years of experience in this sector. The IP practice, led by Esa Korkeamaki, has been handling plenty of litigation of late. Partner Taino Tuohino is very active in e-commerce, aiding international clients with the localisation of a webpage, advising on online betting, and assisting in launching a website.

Susiluoto Attorneys-at-Law Ltd is well regarded for its IP work, particularly by clients from the telecoms and IT sectors. Name partner Tapio Susiliuoto leads the team, Petri Järvensivu has expertise in IT supply, and Mari Lampenius specialises in copyright and trade mark issues, product liability, and advertising and marketing for the pharmaceutical market.

Backström & Co is a firm built around its IP practice, with founding partner Peter Backström known as a leading individual in the field.

Dittmar & Indrenius has a strong TMT practice, with long-term clients such as GlaxoSmithKline, Pfizer and Hewlett-Packard. In 2005 United Technologies Group and Microsoft were added to the list. The firm also advised on the Nordic Broadcasting acquisition of Alma Broadcasting.

Heinonen & Co is a full-service firm with a particular emphasis on IP. Six of the firm's eight lawyers have IP expertise, with partner Hann-Maija Elo at the cutting edge of anti-counterfeiting matters.

Luostarinen Mettälä Räikkönen's Kimmo Mettälä acts for clients in the chemical and pharmaceutical sectors, and Raimo Seppälä is active for technology clients.

Merilampi Marttila Laitasalo's practice is gaining a reputation for its contentious work, particularly in patent litigation. Ari Kantor is well regarded for his work in the telecoms and energy markets. Tapio Väätäinen specialises in IP matters, while founding partner Tuomo Marttila, based in the Tampere office, is an expert in patent litigation.

Pirilä & Pöyhönen provides good IP advice, with name partner Kalle Pirilä boasting considerable experience.

One of **Veikko Palotie & Co**'s strongest areas is providing advice to the telecoms and IT sectors. IP is also of increasing significance to the firm. Mika Pakarinen specialises in IP, media and entertainment law, and Teemu Kauttu advises on IT issues.

Waselius & Wist acts for both domestic and international clients, particularly advising on IP matters. Mikko Eerola and Jan Waselius are recommended.

TAX

HH Partners, Attorneys-at-Law, Ltd managing partner Arto Kukkinen is one of the leading international tax specialists in Europe, and hence the firm's tax practice is a market leader and a regular in our top tier. The firm provides advice to clients on cross-border structuring, project finance, acquisitions, personal taxation and excise duty. Many clients are software, IT and telecoms companies listed in Finland or the US.

Hannes Snellman Attorneys at Law Ltd's tax team is now led by Ossi Haapaniemi, who was made up to partner in 2005. He was formerly a tax manager at Arthur Andersen, and is at the cutting edge of tax issues. The practice is focused on transaction-based issues.

Roschier Holmberg has improved an already strong corporate tax practice with the addition of Vesa Rasinaho. He was appointed as a specialist counsel for tax and structuring. He joins Gunnar Westerlund, one of the country's leading experts, and head of the corporate tax team. The firm's tax practice is cross-border, and benefits from the strong transactional nature of the corporate practice. The practice has won awards for its innovative work across Europe.

Borenius & Kemppinen has been joined by Dr Janne Juusela, one of the leading tax experts in Finland, and a writer and lecturer on the subject. The firm rises in the rankings to reflect Dr Juusela's status and the quality of the firm's work.

Specilist counsel Sari Laaksinen leads **Castrén & Snellman Attorneys Ltd**'s tax group, supported by three associates. The firm acts for a mix of international and domestic clients on all tax issues.

Hammarström Puhakka Partners, Attorneys Ltd provides good tax advice, Matti Nenonen being the foremost specialist within the firm.

Peltonen, Ruokonen & Itäinen Attorneys At Law's tax practice acts for an impressive client list and is led by Taija Kaijalainen.

Waselius & Wist's Niklas Thibblin is a respected tax specialist.

TAX

HH PARTNERS, ATTORNEYS-AT-LAW, LTD ✪
HANNES SNELLMAN ATTORNEYS AT LAW LTD ✪
ROSCHIER HOLMBERG ✪

Borenius & Kemppinen ✪
Castrén & Snellman Attorneys Ltd ✪

Hammarström Puhakka Partners, Attorneys Ltd ✪
Peltonen, Ruokonen & Itäinen Attorneys At Law ✪
Waselius & Wist ✪

Firms are listed A-Z in tiers which are ranked in order of priority
✪ *Indicates firm displays contact details at the end of this chapter.*

AMINOFF & WEISSENBERG, ATTORNEYS LTD

KORKEAVUORENKATU 34
00130 HELSINKI

Telephone: +358 9 6840 477
Fax: +358 9 6840 4740
E-mail: jan.aminoff@jaflaw.fi
Website: www.jaflaw.fi

Languages
English, Swedish

Number of lawyers 4

CATEGORIES OF WORK

Maritime law	General corporate and business law
Transport law	Contract law
Aviation law	Tort law
Insurance law	Insolvency
Sale and purchase of vessels	Litigation, arbitration and arrest proceedings

BACKSTRÖM & CO
ATTORNEYS AT LAW

ET MAKASIINIKATU 4
00130 HELSINKI

Telephone: +358 9 6689 940
Fax: +358 9 6689 9410
E-mail: info@backstrom.fi
Website: www.backstrom.fi

Languages
English, German, Swedish

Number of lawyers 4

Contacts
Peter Backström, Petri Eskola

Member
Eurojuris International EEIG

CATEGORIES OF WORK

Intellectual property	Corporate and commercial
Patents, trade marks	Commercial litigation, arbitration
Competition law	Contract law
Agency law, distribution	Damages and product liability

BORENIUS & KEMPPINEN

YRJÖNKATU 13A
00120 HELSINKI

Telephone: +358 9 615 333
Fax: +358 9 6153 3499
E-mail: info@borenius.com
Website: www.borenius.com

Languages
English, Estonian, Finnish, French, German, Latvian, Lithuanian, Russian, Spanish, Swedish

Number of lawyers 54

Other Borenius group member firms
Liepa, Skopina/Borenius (Riga);
Luiga Mody Hääl Borenius (Tallinn);
Foigt & partners/Regija Borenius (Vilnius)

CATEGORIES OF WORK

Banking and finance	Labour
Capital markets	Dispute resolution
Commercial contracts	Mediation
Company law	Private clients
Corporate governance	Antitrust and marketing law
Energy	Public procurement
Mergers and acquisitions	Brands and designs
Private equity	Data protection and trade secrets
Real estate and construction	IP litigation
Ship finance	IT and telecommunications
Arbitration	Life sciences
Associations and foundations	Media and entertainment
Insolvency	Tax

THE FIRM

Borenius and Kemppinen (B&K) was established in 1911, it has experienced rapid growth in recent years and is today one of the leading law firms in Finland. The firm provides comprehensive business law services in Finland and the Baltic region through its associated offices in Riga, Latvia; Tallinn, Estonia and Vilnius, Lithuania. In addition, B&K has branch offices at Innopoli 2, a technology centre in Espoo, and in Tampere.

B&K's commitment to the success of its' clients is firmly founded on strong expertise, long-term commitment, genuine involvement, experience and innovation. The firm's teams of renowned experts combine local and international expertise with a co-ordinated and dedicated approach in order to ensure the highest quality of service.

AREAS OF PRACTICE

B&K provides its domestic and international clients with expert advice on matters relating to business and corporate law, including cross-border M&A, venture capital/private equity and capital markets transactions. B&K's lawyers also specialise in complex legal issues regarding intellectual property law, marketing and antitrust law and merger control rules. The firm provides advice in the highly specialised fields of IP/IT such as biotechnology, digital content production, data networks and telecommunications.

B&Ks' approach to business challenges is team-orientated, combining strong and diverse expertise with a thorough business understanding.

For further information, please contact Ari-Pekka Saanio (partner), Tel: +358 9 6153 3417 or E-mail: ari-pekka.saanio@borenius.com

CASTRÉN & SNELLMAN

EROTTAJANKATU 5A
00130 HELSINKI

Telephone: +358 9 228 581
Fax: +358 9 601 961
E-mail: firstname.surname@castren.fi
Website: www.castren.fi

Languages
English, Finnish, French, German, Italian, Russian, Swedish

Other offices
St Petersburg

Number of lawyers 79
at this office 76

Contact
Pekka Jaatinen (managing partner)

CATEGORIES OF WORK

Mergers and acquisitions
Jan Kuhlefelt, Jari Sonninen

Capital markets
Merja Kivelä

Private equity and venture capital
Kimmo Rekola, Mårten Janson

Banking and finance
Pekka Lehtinen

General corporate
Mika Ilveskero

Tax
Sari Laaksonen

IP and technology
Kimmo Rekola, Petri Rinkinen

Life sciences
Johan Åkermarck

EU and competition
Hannu Pokela

Insolvency
Pauliina Tenhunen

Dispute resolution
Marko Hentunen

Employment
Jan Örndahl

Environment and real estate
Elina Lampi-Fagerholm

Maritime, transport and aviation
Niklas Langenskiöld

Commercial agreements
Uwe Uusitalo

Energy
Juha Väyrynen

Insurance
Pekka Jaatinen, Mika Ilveskero

DITTMAR & INDRENIUS

POHJOISESPLANADI 25A
00100 HELSINKI

Telephone: +358 9 681 700
Fax: +358 9 652 406
E-mail: firstname.surname@dittmar.fi
Website: www.dittmar.fi

Languages
English, French, German, Swedish

Number of lawyers 26

Contacts
Markus Troberg, Antti Kuusimäki,
Jan Ollila, Petteri Uoti, Juha-Pekka Mutanen

CATEGORIES OF WORK

Mergers and acquisitions	**Dispute resolution**
Finance and capital markets	**Corporate and commercial**

THE FIRM

Dittmar & Indrenius is one of Finland's leading international law firms focused on mergers and acquisitions, finance and capital markets, dispute resolution and corporate and commercial.

Dittmar & Indrenius is frequently involved in large transactions, often with a cross-border dimension.

The firm provides its clients with a professional service of the highest calibre, combining technical excellence with commercial awareness and a practical, constructive approach to legal issues.

The firm maintains close contacts with leading law firms in the world, but is not tied to any formal network or association of firms.

The firm serves its clients in English, Finnish, French, German and Swedish.

AREAS OF PRACTICE

International work is an essential part of the firm's practice. Dittmar & Indrenius has a broad experience in cross-border mergers and acquisitions, and commercial and financial matters.

Dittmar & Indrenius represents leading international companies and institutions with various sectors, such as banking, finance, private equity, venture capital, insurance, information technology, telecommunications, manufacturers, automobiles, pharmaceuticals, consumer goods and services, aviation, consultancy, construction, energy, entertainment and media. Dittmar & Indrenius also acts for a number of governments and international organisations.

FENNICA ATTORNEYS LTD

MANNERHEIMINTIE 8
00100 HELSINKI

Telephone: +358 9 6226 670
Fax: +358 9 6226 677
E-mail: contact@fennica.fi
Website: www.fennica.fi

Languages
English, French, German, Swedish

Number of lawyers 29

Contacts
Jori Taipale, Pekka Takki

CATEGORIES OF WORK

Banking and finance
Jori Taipale, Jaakko Hietala

Capital markets
Harri Hynninen, Matti Ylä-Mononen

Competition
Jori Taipale, Jaakko Hietala

Intellectual property
Pekka Raatikainen, Tom Vapaavuori

IT and telecommunications
Pekka Takki, Kari-Matti Lehti

General corporate and commercial
Jaakko Hietala, Harri Hynninen

Mergers and acquisitions
Matti Ylä-Mononen, Jori Taipale

Litigation and arbitration
Tom Vapaavuori, Marko Wainio

Real estate and construction
Marko Wainio, Jaakko Hietala

FORUM PARTNERS ATTORNEYS LTD

MANNERHEIMINTIE 20 B
00100 HELSINKI

Telephone: +358 9 3515 055
Fax: +358 9 3515 011
Website: www fp.fi

Languages
English, Finnish, French, German, Swedish

Number of lawyers 9

CATEGORIES OF WORK

Company law and international restructuring
Martti Lavonsalo

Legal due diligence
Martti Lavonsalo

National and international contract law
Martti Lavonsalo, Harri Metso

Banking, insurance and finance operations
Martti Lavonsalo, Harri Metso

Intellectual property rights and IT law
Harri Metso

Competition law and public procurement
Toni Huopalainen, Harri Metso

Labour law
Pekka Suominen

Energy law
Toni Huopalainen

Insolvency law
Pekka Suominen

Dispute resolution
Pekka Suominen

Transportation
Harri Metso

GAHMBERG, HÄSTÖ & CO

POHJOINEN MAKASIINIKATU 7 A 6
00130 HELSINKI

Telephone: +358 9 6869 880
Fax: +358 9 6869 8850
E-mail: ghetco@ghetco.com

Languages
English, French, German, the Scandinavian languages

Number of lawyers 9

Contact
Henrik Hästö

International groupings
Mackrell International

CATEGORIES OF WORK

Corporate and commercial
Henrik Hästö, Niclas Salingre

Mergers and acquisitions
Henrik Hästö

Maritime and transport
Henrik Gahmberg, Herman Ljungberg

Insurance
Henrik Gahmberg, Herman Ljungberg

Competition and EU
Mirko Pennanen

Real estate and environment
Niclas Salingre

Finance, securities
Henrik Gahmberg, Henrik Hästö

Dispute resolution
Henrik Hästö, Henrik Gahmberg, Herman Ljungberg, Niclas Salingre

Tax
Henrik Hästö

Employment
Niclas Salingre

HH PARTNERS, ATTORNEYS-AT-LAW, LTD

MANNERHEIMINTIE 14 A
00100 HELSINKI

Telephone: +358 9 177 613
Fax: +358 9 653 873
E-mail: hhpartners@hhpartners.fi
Website: www.hhpartners.fi

Languages
English, Swedish

Number of lawyers 12

Contact
Mr Arto Kukkonen (managing partner)

CATEGORIES OF WORK

Capital market

Commercial

Construction

Contracts and competition

Corporate and corporate finance

Dispute resolution

Environment

Insolvency

Insurance

Information technology and communications

Intellectual property

Maritime and transport

Media and marketing

Mergers and acquisitions

Real estate

Taxation and employment

HAMMARSTRÖM PUHAKKA PARTNERS

BULEVARDI 1A
00100 HELSINKI

Telephone: +358 9 474 21
Fax: +358 9 474 2222
E-mail: firstname.surname@hpplaw.fi
Website: www.hpplaw.fi

Languages
English, Finnish, French, German, Swedish

Number of lawyers 21

Contacts
Jörgen Hammarström, Pekka Puhakka

International groupings
Legalink

CATEGORIES OF WORK

Corporate and contracts
Jörgen Hammarström, Jaana Klinga

Dispute resolution
Pekka Puhakka, Antti Palmujoki

Competition law
Tuomas Saraste, Jouni Alanen, Vesa Silaskivi

Mergers and acquisitions
Jörgen Hammarström, Pekka Puhakka

Insolvency law
Juho Lenni-Taattola, Matti Nenonen

Environmental law, property and real estate
Kari Marttinen, Jouni Alanen

Employment law
Pekka Puhakka, Klaus Nyblin

IT and telecoms
Tuomas Saraste, Pekka Puhakka, Vesa Silaskivi

Public procurement
Jouni Alanen, Tuomas Saraste

THE FIRM

Hammarström Puhakka Partners, Attorneys Ltd specialises in business law. The firm is dedicated to first-class, responsive and personal service, and its purpose is to help its clients to achieve their personal business goals.

The central operational principles of Hammarström Puhakka Partners are a high level of legal expertise and reliability, and a line of action which is cost efficient and concentrated on the essential issues in the interest of the client. The firm promises individually customised solutions to its clients' needs.

AREAS OF PRACTICE

The firm provides services to its domestic and foreign clients in all central areas of law, and on any issues related to contracts, companies and compensations. The firm has exceptionally strong experience and expertise in antitrust, competition and marketing law, EU law, intellectual property, insolvency (liquidations and corporate restructuring), environmental law and employment law.

A significant part of Hammarström Puhakka Partners' assignments are international and the firm's lawyers provide services in Finnish, Swedish, English, German and French. The services provided by the firm's international networks are at the disposal of its clients.

Hammarström Puhakka Partners' policy is to support the resolution of disputes through negotiations. Should proceedings not be reasonably unavoidable, the firm has particularly good facilities and experience to litigate or arbitrate any issue. Several of the firm's lawyers act as arbitrators.

HANNES SNELLMAN

ETELÄRANTA 8
00130 HELSINKI

Telephone: +358 9 228 841
Fax: +358 9 177 393
E-mail:
hannes.snellman@hannessnellman.fi
Website: www.hannessnellman.fi

Languages
English, French, German, Swedish

Other offices
Turku, Mariehamn

Number of lawyers 104

Contact
Johan Aalto (managing partner)

Member
Loan Market Association; Finnish Bar Association; International Bar Association; International Chamber of Commerce

CATEGORIES OF WORK

M&A
Carl-Henrik Wallin, Tuomo Vähäpassi, Mikko Heinonen

Technology and litigation
Kaisa Fahllund

Competition and litigation
Mika Savola

Finance and capital markets
Kari Lautjärvi

Dispute resolution
Patrik Lindfors

THE FIRM

Founded in 1909 by Hannes Snellman, the firm is one of the two largest in Finland. The firm focuses on transactions and conflict management.

Hannes Snellman has developed a broad network of international industrial and financial contacts. The firm regularly advises on international matters and maintains close ties with foreign law firms worldwide.

Hannes Snellman advises international clients on a regular basis, including leading financial institutions, major international corporations, industrial groups, leading investment banks and service companies. Geographically, the clients come mostly from the US, UK and continental Europe as well as Scandinavia.

AREAS OF PRACTICE

The M&A group's activities encompass both domestic and international transactions, such as MBO, LBO and joint venture arrangements as well as other M&A assignments. The group advises clients in cross-border transactions and acts as lead counsel in international projects. It also provides special knowledge in capital investments and expertise in tax, labour and company law. Competition, EU legislation, and IP matters are particularly strong complementary areas supporting the M&A practice.

The finance and capital markets group is one of the leaders in the field in Finland. The group represents domestic and foreign credit institutions and investment firms, issuers, mezzanine lenders and borrowers in domestic and international financing transactions. A major focus has been on demanding multilateral cross-border transactions, but the market knowledge gained through them is useful also in bilateral negotiations between lenders and corporate customers. The firm's tax group works alongside the finance and capital markets group, specialising in all tax aspects of transactions and M&A as well as tax work in relation to financial instruments. Several lawyers from the finance and capital markets group have gained considerable recognition in their field of expertise.

The technology and litigation group advises clients especially on information and communications technology (ICT) and intellectual property rights (IPR) issues, such as ICT system deliveries and procurement, software development and outsourcing arrangements, R&D projects, IPR strategies, technology licensing, life science, telecoms, e-commerce, data protection, media and marketing. Another focus of the group is IPR and ICT related litigation. Apart from traditional IPR litigation, typical cases include illegal copying of software and databases, industrial espionage, misappropriation of trade secrets as well as unfair trade practices.

The dispute resolution group deals with litigation, arbitration, mediation and matters concerning bankruptcies and insolvency both in Finland and abroad. The group is also effective in pre-empting disputes. The arbitration practitioners of the group and of the firm have extensive experience as counsels, chairpersons and arbitrators in domestic and international proceedings. This experience has been gained from both ad hoc and institutional proceedings, eg under the Finnish Arbitration Act, the Arbitration Rules of the Arbitration Institute of the Central Chamber of Commerce of Finland and under the ICC Arbitration Rules. Many international arbitration proceedings have provided the arbitration practitioners of the firm with invaluable and wide-ranging experience.

The competition and litigation group specialises in assignments related to substantive and procedural aspects of competition law. The team has broad experience in handling cases related to eg merger control, cartels and other competition restrictions before national competition authorities and the European Commission. In addition, its work involves litigation and other assignments related to public procurement and claims for damages based on competition law infringements. The group's knowledge covers the entire field of competition law, including the assessment of competition problems, their prevention through compliance programmes, and litigation before courts and tribunals.

HEINONEN & CO

FREDRIKINKATU 51-53 B
PO BOX 671
00100 HELSINKI

Telephone: +358 9 2530 0600
Fax: +358 9 6944 352
E-mail: mail@heinonen.com
Website: www.heinonen.com

Languages
English, Finnish, French, German, Swedish

Number of lawyers 9

Other offices
Alicante

Member
Eurofranchise Lawyers (an association of independent European franchise lawyers); Finnish Bar Association; AIPPI; INTA; ECTA; FICPI; IBA; representatives before OHIM; ELF European law Firm

CATEGORIES OF WORK

Advertising and marketing

Competition and EU

Corporate and commercial

Dispute resolution – litigation and arbitration

Franchising

Information technology, e-commerce

Insolvency, corporate restructuring

Intellectual property

Labour

Media and entertainment

Telecommunications

JURIDIA LTD ATTORNEYS-AT-LAW

MUNKKISAARENKATU 2
00150 HELSINKI

Telephone: +358 9 6841 230
Fax: +358 9 6225 400
E-mail: firstname.lastname@juridia.com
Website: www.juridia.com

Languages
Danish, English, Finnish, French, German, Swedish

Number of lawyers 17

Contact
Hannu Rintala

Member
EuroLaw; EEIG

CATEGORIES OF WORK

Mergers and acquisitions
Olli Iirola, Hannu Rintala

Company
Olli Iirola, Mika Taberman

Venture capital and private equity
Kimmo Oila, Olli Iirola

Intellectual property
Kimmo Oila, Iikka Sainio

IT and telecoms
Kimmo Oila, Hannu Rintala

Litigation
Tero Routamo, Antti Merilainen

Arbitration
Olli Iirola, Kimmo Oila

Capital markets
Olli Iirola, Mika Taberman

Corporate tax
Henri Steiner

Employment
Pekka Jäntti, Kari Parkkinen

Insolvency
Harri Lindfors, Tero Routamo

Commercial contracts
Peter Salovaara, Henri Steiner

Construction
Ilkka Koivisto

EU and competition
Marko Mononen, Hannu Rintala

KALLIOINEN, TOLPPANEN, SALMINEN & CO
ATTORNEYS AT LAW, LTD

YRJÖNKATU 8 A 2
00120 HELSINKI

Telephone: +358 9 6126 090
Fax: +358 9 607 344
E-mail: helsinki@ktslaw.net
Website: www.ktslaw.net

Languages
English, German, Swedish

Other offices
Hämeenlinna, Tampere

Number of lawyers 10
at this office 3

Contact
Jari Salminen

CATEGORIES OF WORK

Banking and finance operations
Jukka Reilin

Company law
Jari Salminen

Contract law
Mika Backman, Tuomo Kareila

Family law
Ruut Kallioinen

Insolvency and bankruptcy
Juha Kallioinen

Insurance law
Juha Kallioinen

Labour law
Timo Jarmas, Mika Backman

Litigation and arbitration
Jari Salminen, Jarkko Hankaa

Mergers and acquisitions
Harri Tolppanen

Real estate and construction
Harri Tolppanen

KROGERUS ATTORNEYS LTD

POHJOINEN MAKASIINIKATU 6A
PO BOX 143
00130 HELSINKI

Telephone: +358 9 6226 520
Fax: +358 9 631 811
E-mail: helsinki@krogerus.com
Website: www.krogerus.com

Languages
English, French, German, Swedish

Other offices
Jyväskylä, Kuopio, Oulu, Vantaa

Number of lawyers 44

Contact
Juna Pekka Katainen

Member
IGAL (Intercontinental Grouping of Accountants & Lawyers); ICC (International Chamber of Commerce); TAGLaw; IBA (International Bar Association)

CATEGORIES OF WORK

Corporate and commercial law
Juha Pekka Katainen, Hannu Krogerus

Mergers and acquisitions
Mikko Mali, Mika Ståhlberg

EU and competition
Katri Joenpolvi

Telecommunications and IT law
Katri Joenpolvi, Juha Pekka Katainen

Banking and finance (including project finance)
Juha Wessman, Mikko Mali

Capital markets
Mika Ståhlberg, Mikko Mali

Intellectual property
Juha Pekka Katainen, Juha Taipale

Real estate
Pasi Kapanen, Juha Wessman

Litigation
Jari-Pekka Alho, Kimmo Penttilä

Arbitration
Jari-Pekka Alho, Marja Ramm-Schmidt

Corporate restructuring and insolvency
Jarmo Makkonen, Jari-Pekka Alho

Labour law
Jari-Pekka Alho

Tax
Pekka T Talari

Technology and media law
Juha Pekka Katainen, Juha Taipale

Venture capital and private equity
Mika Ståhlberg, Mikko Mali

THE FIRM

Founded in 1992, Krogerus Attorneys Ltd specialises in Finnish and international business law. The firm has offices in Helsinki, Jyväskylä, Kuopio, Oulu and Vantaa.

Krogerus operates its business first and foremost on understanding the clients' businesses and their objectives. The firm's founders have long experience working as counsel for major Finnish industrial firms, banks and public administration, and they use this experience to its fullest extent when advising their clients.

The legal services offered to clients are tailored in co-operation with the clients themselves to suit their current needs. The firm's clients are large and medium-sized domestic and foreign corporations and financial institutions. Krogerus also serves smaller companies, especially internationally orientated ones, in central, eastern and northern Finland. The firm also advises different sectors of public administration in Finland and abroad.

In order to offer the best possible services to its clients, the firm has established contacts with a number of investment and commercial banks, authorities and law firms, as well as auditing firms both in Finland and abroad.

AREAS OF PRACTICE

The firm's areas of practice are mergers and acquisitions, capital markets, venture capital and private equity, project finance, EU and competition law, technology and media, telecommunications, corporate restructuring, insolvency and litigation and arbitration.

M&A: the firm has advised various industrial buyers and sellers, private equity and venture capital funds, MBO and MBI teams and investors in numerous M&A transactions and investments in a broad variety of businesses ranging from IT, technology and telecoms sector to cosmetics. The firm has also advised the Finnish government in a number of privatisation transactions.

Capital markets and finance: the firm and its partners have advised in various IPOs and public offerings, as well as mergers and demergers of listed companies. The firm has frequently acted as legal adviser in the field of project finance, as well as public-private-partnership (PPP) and real estate financing transactions.

Competition law: the firm has advised clients in dealing with the Finnish Competition Authority and the Commission of the European Union in issues concerning all fields of competition law, such as compliance work, negotiations with authorities (particularly M&A cases) and litigation.

EU law: Krogerus has assisted clients in numerous assignments concerning European law. The assignments vary from litigation and negotiations with the Commission of the European Union to monitoring of the regulatory developments in certain fields of EC law. The firm has been selected as the legal adviser for EU in Finland (Eurojus).

Technology and media: the firm has advised various major companies in their IT and technology procurement cases (including outsourcing agreements) and regularly advises leading Finnish IT, technology and media vendors on a full range of their commercial contractual issues. The firm constantly represents clients providing services and products to Nokia in their major framework and other contract negotiations with Nokia Corporation. The firm has worked especially on IT and technology projects in the field of banking and financing, telecommunications, e-business and contract manufacturing.

Corporate restructuring and insolvency: the firm's lawyers have wide experience in operating as official receivers in bankrupts' estates, voluntary and legal liquidation proceedings, acting as administrators in corporate restructurings and representing creditors in all such proceedings.

Dispute resolution: the firm serves major business clients in litigation and arbitration processes. Some of the firm's lawyers also act as mediators.

LUOSTARINEN METTÄLÄ RÄIKKÖNEN

ATTORNEYS AT LAW

MANNERHEIMINTIE 14 B
9TH FLOOR
00100 HELSINKI

Telephone: +358 9 5860 100
Fax: +358 9 5860 1060
E-mail: mail@lmrlaw.fi
Website: www.lmrlaw.fi

Languages
English, Finnish, French, German, Spanish, Swedish

Number of lawyers 18

CATEGORIES OF WORK

Banking and finance	**Mergers and acquisitions**
Capital markets	**Company and commercial**
Private equity and venture capital	**EU and competition**
Arbitration and litigation	**Energy**
Privatisation	**Telecommunications and IT**
Intellectual property	**Employment and labour law**
Insurance	**Agency, distributorship and licensing**

THE FIRM

Luostarinen Mettälä Räikkönen (LMR) is a business law firm focusing on corporate and commercial law, competition, mergers and acquisitions, banking and finance, and general business law including dispute resolution. The firm's aim is to provide legal services of the highest quality in a practical and cost-efficient manner. The lawyers of LMR have gained extensive experience both internationally and in Finland from a number of financial institutions and manufacturing sectors as well as retail businesses. The international and in-house experience of the firm's partners and other lawyers provides a very good basis for LMR to effectively and successfully provide legal services to domestic and international clients. LMR currently consists of 18 full-time lawyers, five of whom are partners, assisted by well-qualified support staff. The professional competence of the firm is highlighted by the fact that over 70% of LMR's lawyers have a postgraduate university degree either in law or economics, and almost 40% of its lawyers have postgraduate law degrees from universities outside Finland.

AREAS OF PRACTICE

LMR routinely advises clients in cross-border commercial transactions, comprising mergers and acquisitions, joint ventures, licensing, distribution and franchising arrangements, large-scale construction and other investment projects, and other cross-border matters. The firm's international clients include, among others, US, European and Finnish listed and unlisted companies, banks, insurance companies and investment banks, private equity firms, and governmental entities.

In the areas of banking, finance and securities markets, LMR is frequently recognised as one of the leading law firms in Finland and the firm advises clients in a broad range of matters, including public and private borrowing transactions such as EMTN programmes and syndicated loans, acquisition finance transactions, securitisation and other structured finance arrangements, project and trade finance, debt and equity capital markets operations, private placements, governmental and multilateral financial institutions, derivatives transactions, portfolio transfers, investments, listings, and counselling on securities market regulations. LMR has experience with the documentation and consummation of deals for international banks, investment banks and corporate clients. The experience covers both planning financing deals and their implementation.

In the corporate area, LMR regularly represents corporate clients, private equity firms and other parties in cross-border M&A transactions, and the firm's services cover the transaction from the due diligence and bidding stage to the drafting and negotiation of the legal documentation and the completion of the transaction. The firm has extensive experience of advising clients in a number of diverse sectors, including various manufacturing industries, mining, pulp and paper, telecommunications, banking, insurance, retail businesses and service industries.

The firm is also recognised as one of the leading Finnish law firms in the area of competition law, where the firm's services range from advice to clients in relation to compliance programs, notifications to the competition authorities in connection with M&A transactions, and different types of litigious matters and proceedings, including representation of clients in cartel investigations before Finnish and EU authorities. The firm also advises both private companies and state and local authorities on public procurement law and handles litigation relating to procurement processes.

In the area of general business law advice, the firm provides advice and legal representation to clients in a broad range of matters extending from the establishment of a company to advice on various contractual matters, employment and labour law issues, and dispute resolution where the firm has an active practice in representing clients both in court as well as domestic and international arbitration proceedings. The firm is well known for its specialised litigation capabilities in the areas of banking and insurance disputes.

MÄKITALO RÄMÖ JUUTILAINEN OY

ATTORNEYS AT LAW

ETELÄESPLANADI 18
00130 HELSINKI

Telephone: +358 9 6844 410
Fax: +358 9 6844 4141
E-mail: attorneys@mrjlaw.fi
Website: www.mrjlaw.fi

Languages
English, Finnish, French, German, Malay, Polish, Spanish, Swedish

Number of lawyers 14

CATEGORIES OF WORK

Banking and finance
Risto Rämö, Juha Mäkitalo

Mergers and acquisitions
Juha Mäkitalo, Risto Rämö, Jaana Juutilainen

Corporate and commercial law
Juha Mäkitalo, Jaana Juutilainen

Intellectual property
Risto Rämö

IT and telecoms
Jani Rantanen, Juho Lönnblad

Competition, EU
Risto Rämö

Distribution, agency and franchise
Jaana Juutilainen

Environment
Jaana Juutilainen, Mikko Pimiä

Real estate and construction
Mikko Pimiä, Mika Alanen

Life sciences
Risto Rämö, Heidi Ilvessalo

Litigation, arbitration
Mikko Pimiä, Jaana Juutilainen

Insolvency
Mikko Pimiä, Mika Alanen

Taxation
Mika Alanen, Mikko Pimiä

Labour
Marcus Blomfelt

MERILAMPI MARTTILA LAITASALO

ETELÄESPLANADI 22 A
00130 HELSINKI

Telephone: +358 9 686 481
Fax: +358 9 6864 8484
E-mail: law.offices@mmllaw.fi
Website: www.mmllaw.fi

Languages
English, French, German, Swedish

Other offices
Tampere

Number of lawyers 22
at this office 18

Contacts
Ari Keinänen, Arttu Mentula

CATEGORIES OF WORK

Mergers and acquisitions
Ari Keinänen, Jani Ylä-Autio

Corporate law
Pekka Merilampi, Tuomo Marttila

Banking and finance
Jukka Laitasalo, Merja Blankenstein

Labour
Jani Ylä-Autio

Real estate
Ari Keinänen, Jani Ylä-Autio

Capital markets
Ari Keinänen, Pekka Merilampi

Competition and EU
Arttu Mentula, Erkko Ruohoniemi

Public procurement
Arttu Mentula, Erkko Ruohoniemi

Intellectual property
Tuomo Marttila, Tapio Väätäinen

Insolvency
Jukka Laitasalo, Tapio Väätäinen

Torts and product liability
Ari Kantor, Lassi Kettula

Dispute resolution
Jukka Laitasalo, Ari Kantor

THE FIRM

Merilampi Marttila Laitasalo Attorneys at Law Ltd (MML) was established in 1992, following the split of the biggest Finnish law firm at the time, and has grown steadily since then. The clientele consists of international and domestic companies.

MML is especially recognised in the fields of mergers and acquisitions, company law and corporate governance, competition and EU, capital markets, litigation and arbitration, as well as banking and finance.

AREAS OF PRACTICE

The firm is constantly involved in a number of major M&A, corporate restructuring and capital markets transactions. Senior partner Pekka Merilampi, and partners Ari Keinänen and Jani Ylä-Autio, are well known in this area. The firm is continuously advising a wide range of listed and other major companies, including many top 20 listed companies.

MML advised Fortum Corporation and Neste Oil Corporation in the spin-off and IPO of Neste Oil on the Helsinki Stock Exchange, the value of which was €577m. In addition, the firm advised the Swedish public company Axfood AB on its sale of majority shareholdings in the Finnish listed company Spar Finland Plc to SOK. Other notable clients include Sanoma WSOY companies and Lassila & Tikanoja Plc. The firm is also continuously advising and representing both international and domestic clients in large real estate portfolio transactions.

MML has an established history of advising clents in various matters related to banking and finance. Partners Ari Keinänen and Jukka Laitasalo are well known in this area. Specialist counsel Merja Blankenstein is also actively involved in a number of matters related to this area, with a strong focus on financing matters. The firm represented a number of domestic and international banks in a €575m syndicated multicurrency facility arrangement to a Finnish listed company.

MML is continuously involved in various competition law matters. The firm advised and represented Rautaruukki Corporation and Wärtsilä Corporation before the EU Commission, regarding the creation of a new joint venture, Oy Ovako Ab (turnover €1.3bn), with Swedish-listed company Aktiebolaget SKF. Partner Arttu Mentula was in charge of the merger control filings, assisted by specialist counsel Erkko Ruohoniemi. Furthermore, MML represented the Swedish-listed company Axfood AB and Spar FInland Plc before the Finnish Competition Authority in the highly debated transaction in which SOK acquired control over Spar FInland, also active in the daily consumer goods market. In addition, the firm and its competition lawyers are involved in major cartel proceedings, such as the Asphalt cartel case, self-assessment, abuse of a dominant position, private enforcement and public procurement cases.

The firm frequently represents various parties in international and national arbitration, both as arbitrators and counsels. Furthermore, MML and its experts, especially partners Jukka Laitasalo, Ari Kantor and Lassi Kettula, are continuously appearing before courts in various disputes, including mergers and acquisitions and securities market disputes.

PELTONEN, RUOKONEN & ITÄINEN

ATTORNEYS AT LAW LTD

FREDRIKINKATU 48A
00100 HELSINKI

Telephone: +358 9 4176 030
Fax: +358 9 4176 0417
E-mail: office@peltonenlaw.fi
Website: www.peltonenlaw.fi

Languages
English, French, German, Swedish

Number of lawyers 25

CATEGORIES OF WORK

Banking and financing, energy
Hans Sundblad, Mikko Ojala

Capital markets
Mikko Ojala, Ari Savela

Corporate law
Ari Savela, Leif Itäinen

Mergers and acquisitions
Leif Itäinen, Hans Sundblad

Trade and industry
Jukka Peltonen, Kalevi Tervanen

Intellectual property, technology, telecoms, media and entertainment
Jussi Savonen, Kalevi Tervanen

Litigation and arbitration
Jukka Peltonen, Esa Salonen

Insurance, transportation and liability
Esa Salonen, John-Henrik Spåre

Reinsurance, insurance regulatory issues, transportation/liability
Kalevi Tervanen

EU and international law
Ari Savela, Anne Petäjäniemi-Björklund

Competition law
Anne Petäjäniemi-Björklund, Juri-Pekka Kainulainen

Employment law
Pekka Ruokonen, Katriina Vierula

Tax law
Leif Itäinen, Tuija Kaijalainen, Jere Törmänen

Environment, real estate, construction
Jukka Peltonen, Mikko Kärkkäinen

Insolvency and asset recovery
Leif Itäinen, Jussi Savonen

Private client
Harriet Lagus

THE FIRM

Finnish Business Law Firm Peltonen, Ruokonen & Itäinen (Peltonen) was founded in 1970 by Jukka Peltonen, an eminent and hard-working old-school lawyer. The firm established a reputation as one of the leading Finnish law firms in the 1970s and has since possessed the strength in depth to handle complex transactions and disputes. In its practice, the firm focuses on the professional skills and expertise of its attorneys, and is known to operate with an emphasis on highest-quality client service.

The firm's work covers such industries and businesses as energy, shipbuilding, food processing, retail, materials processing, telecommunications, technology, media, transportation, construction, banking, finance, insurance and reinsurance and the securities markets.

Peltonen's clientele consists of major Finnish and international corporations, banks and other financial institutions, insurance companies, SMEs and growth business enterprises, and family businesses, as well as private customers. Governmental agencies and municipalities use the firm's services on a regular basis. The firm also continues the tradition of attending to the legal affairs of private individuals.

The firm represents foreign clients in their operations in Finland and also offers access to the Nordic and Baltic markets through its well-established cross-border co-operation with premier law firms in Sweden, Denmark, Estonia, Latvia and Lithuania. Peltonen advises Finnish clients on their export, financing and investment activities abroad using its network of law firms in Europe, the Americas and Asia.

AREAS OF PRACTICE

Peltonen, Ruokonen & Itäinen offers its services in all areas of business and commercial law.

The firm is involved in company and commercial law, including takeovers, mergers and acquisitions, joint ventures, strategic alliances and corporate restructurings. Peltonen's attorneys advise in corporate financing arrangements, credit and equity issues, venture capital financing arrangements, share and bond issues and corporate listings, as well as project financing. The firm's legal work in energy infrastructure, for instance in project financing for building a new nuclear power plant in Finland, is one of the landmarks of this practice in Finland. Peltonen, Ruokonen & Itäinen is a member of ISDA.

Peltonen's work in the insurance industry makes it among the leading practices in Finland. The firm provides services in insurance regulatory issues and insurance-related corporate transactions and captive insurance. The firm's insurance and reinsurance law specialists advise on contentious and non-contentious matters, including contract drafting, facultative insurance and reinsurance coverage issues, policy interpretation, property damage, business interruption and liability insurance, errors and omissions and professional negligence.

The firm's litigation practice team provides a comprehensive service to its clients. The firm's attorneys have extensive experience in domestic and international arbitrations and large-scale litigations in the general courts, administrative and special courts and governmental agency proceedings, including the Finnish Competition Authority and Market Court. The firm also has long-standing experience in handling multi-jurisdictional litigations. The firm has one of the leading defence lawyer practices in lawyers' liability cases in the country.

Peltonen has a well-established practice in EU law, competition law and public procurement proceedings. The firm has a significant and fast-growing client portfolio of technology, software and content companies using the firm's services in IPR and patent law and venture capital issues.

The firm regularly advises both Finnish and foreign companies on Finnish employment law and practice. The firm is a member of the European Employment Lawyers Association.

Peltonen, Ruokonen & Itäinen has wide-ranging expertise in bankruptcy, corporate restructuring and distraint affairs.

ROSCHIER HOLMBERG

KESKUSKATU 7A
00100 HELSINKI

Telephone: +358 20 5066 000
Fax: +358 20 5066 100
E-mail: roschier@roschier.com
Website: www.roschier.com

Languages
English, French, German, Swedish

Other offices
Stockholm, Oulu, Tampere, Turku, Vaasa

Number of lawyers 111
at this office 89

Contacts
Tomas Lindholm (senior partner),
Lennart Simonsen (managing partner)

Member
ius laboris, International Employment Law, Pensions and Employee Benefits Alliance; Lex Mundi; Roschier Raidla

CATEGORIES OF WORK

Corporate advisory and disputes (Corporate advisory and general commercial; EU and competition advisory; arbitration and ADR; litigation)

Technology, media and communications (intellectual property; IT and communications; IP and technology transactions)

Transactions and finance (M&A; private equity; public company transactions; banking and finance; venture capital)

THE FIRM

Roschier Holmberg, as a leading law firm in the Nordic region with its main office in Finland, operates in the international marketplace. The firm's clients include leading domestic and global corporations, financial service and insurance institutions, investors, growth and other private companies with international operations, governments and municipalities.

As a member of RoschierRaidla, an integrated cross-border operation of some 185 lawyers in five jurisdictions, including Roschier Holmberg in Finland and in Sweden, Raidla & Partners in Estonia, Lejins, Torgans & Partners in Latvia and Norcous & Partners in Lithuania, the firm offers direct access to the Baltic rim market and cross-border solutions based on uniform quality and best practices of international standard by premier law firms in each jurisdiction.

AREAS OF PRACTICE

Roschier Holmberg has a leading M&A practice both in large-scale transactions involving public companies and in private equity deals. The firm concentrates its dispute and compliance advisory on the corporate advisory and disputes practice group that is responsible for all aspects of corporate senior advice. The transactions and finance practice group provides M&A services relating to public and private companies, including private equity and venture capital work. The practice group also advises on financing as well as equity and debt capital markets functions. While the competition law service is integrated into the corporate advisory group, the technology service, provided by the technology, media and communications practice group, incorporates intellectual property and technology transactions in its portfolio.

SIVENIUS, SUVANTO & CO OY

PACIUKSENKATU 21
00270 HELSINKI

Telephone: +358 9 5306 760
Fax: +358 9 5306 7699
E-mail: info@sisulaw.com
Website: www.sisulaw.com

Languages
English, Finnish, Swedish

Number of lawyers 14

CATEGORIES OF WORK

Commercial (general)
Juha Sivenius, Jukka Suvanto

Corporate
Juha Sivenius, Peter Bützow

Mergers and acquisitions
Juha Sivenius, Jukka Suvanto

Litigation
Juha Sivenius, Olli Hoppu

Arbitration
Juha Sivenius, Peter Bützow

Insolvency
Peter Bützow, Kari Huttunen

Transport
Olli Hoppu

Compensation claims
Jukka Suvanto, Olli Hoppu

Environmental
Olli Hoppu

Labour
Peter Bützow, Jarmo Henriksson

Banking, securities and finance
Peter Bützow, Mika Jauhiainen

Intellectual property
Jarmo Henriksson

Competition
Olli Hoppu, Mika Jauhiainen

Insurance
Jukka Suvanto, Olli Hoppu

Construction
Juha Sivenius, Peter Bützow

VEIKKO PALOTIE & CO

ALEKSANTERINKATU 44 A
00100 HELSINKI

Telephone: +358 9 228 831
Fax: +358 9 2288 3300
E-mail: palotie@veikkopalotie.fi
Website: www.veikkopalotie.fi

Languages
English, French, German, Swedish

Number of lawyers 23

CATEGORIES OF WORK

Arbitration

Banking and finance

Commercial litigation

Competition and EU law

Real estate and construction

Corporate and commercial

Damages and product liabilty

Distribution, agency and franchise

Employment, labour

Environment

Insolvency/corporate restructuring

Insurance

IPR and information technology

Media and entertainment

Mergers and acquisitions

Telecommunications

WASELIUS & WIST

ETELÄESPLANADI 24A
00130 HELSINKI

Telephone: +358 9 6689 520
Fax: +358 9 6689 5222
E-mail: ww@ww.fi
Website: www.ww.fi

Languages
English, Finnish, French, German, Swedish

Number of lawyers 19

Contacts
Jan Waselius, Tarja Wist, Lauri Peltola, Mikko Eerola, Nina Rosenlew

CATEGORIES OF WORK

- Finance law
- Capital markets
- Banking law
- Mergers and acquisitions
- Industrial property
- Taxation
- Antitrust and competition
- Labour law
- Litigation and arbitration
- General corporate and business law
- Real property

LAAKSO, LUKANDER & RUOHOLA

YLIOPISTONKATU 15 B
20100 TURKU

Telephone: +358 2 2733 777
Fax: +358 2 2337 777
E-mail: turku@llr.fi
Website: www.llr.fi

Languages
English, French, German, Spanish, Swedish

Other offices
Helsinki, Pori, Salo

Number of lawyers 14
at this office 11

Contacts
Harri Lukander, Jarkko Ruohola

CATEGORIES OF WORK

- Agency and distribution
- Arbitration and litigation
- Company and commercial
- Construction
- Contract
- EC and competition
- Environment
- Extractable land resources
- Family
- Insolvency and bankruptcy
- Intellectual property and e-commerce
- Labour
- Licensing
- Mergers and acquisitions
- Tax
- IT and telecommunications
- Real estate

FORMER YUGOSLAV REPUBLIC OF MACEDONIA

Population	**2.1 million**
Number of lawyers	**2,118**
Professional title	**Advokat**
Currency	**Macedonian denar (MKD)**
Index	
Corporate and M&A	298
Country index	**5**

The Former Yugoslav Republic of Macedonia (FYROM) narrowly escaped the violence suffered in the Balkan states following the break-up of Yugoslavia in 1991. In spite of this the country was struck by great civil unrest in 2001 causing an uprising of rebels and an ethnic shooting war due to resentment on the part of the Albanian minority demanding greater rights.

Eventually a peace deal was struck under the Orhid agreement resulting in Albanian fighters laying down their arms and amendments to the Constitution being made at the end of 2001 formally acknowledging the rights of ethnic Albanians who make up about a quarter of the population. In August 2004 the Macedonian Parliament approved controversial legislation redrafting local boundaries and allowing ethnic Albanians more independence.

The violent events of 2001 seriously damaged both the economy and the nation's social fabric. The country is now in desperate need of a government that will include ethnic Albanians in national decision-making and economic life. Since independence, elected governments have proved to be self-seeking and corrupt and two 2002 Crisis Group reports concluded that corruption threatened the state's very existence. Current President and former Prime Minister Branko Crvenkovski came into office in 2004, after predecessor Boris Trajovski tragically died in a plane crash, claiming to have learnt from mistakes made whilst running the government in the mid-1990s.

On a more positive note the impact of the Ohrid agreement, relative stability of government, heavy investment of EU economic and political capital, democratic presidential elections in 2004 and the possibility of entry into Nato in 2007 indicates that FYROM is on the path to rehabilitation.

FYROM has applied to join the EU but, while progress is being made, there is still a lot of ground to be covered before required standards are achieved.

BILLING

The Macedonian Bar Association suggests guidelines for billing tariffs, however fees are usually negotiated between lawyers and clients on an individual basis. Hourly rates vary between €100 and €200.

MARKETING

The Macedonian Bar Association does not have strict marketing rules and most firms now have websites.

ECONOMY

FYROM has had an unfortunate economic history. After gaining independence in 1991, Macedonia was the least-developed of the Yugoslav republics. A Greek trade embargo until 1996, absence of infrastructure and a reputation of political instability and corruption are among a host of hindrances impeding development. The crisis in 2001 further disrupted matters, pushing back prospects of economic growth and revival and resulting in GDP shrinkage of 4.5%. GDP is gradually making a recovery and was estimated at 1.3% in 2004. Unemployment is another grave problem with more than 30% of the population out of work.

The economy remains small, having barely crossed the threshold from developing to transitional. The industrial sector, mostly established before independence, is large, providing jobs to approximately a third of those in formal employment and comprising about 18% of GDP. The sector is inefficient, unprofitable and badly organised.

A large proportion of industry is now privatised but the shielded and opaque way in which the privatisations were carried out has reinforced accusations of government corruption.

The country's banking sector is rapidly advancing due to the implementation of regulatory improvements and increased supervision, and agriculture and tourism offer potential.

Prime Minister Vlado Buckovski pledged his economic team would come up with a programme to strengthen the economy and attract foreign direct investment. At present the biggest deterrent for foreign investors is confidence about the security of their assets, but there is hope that the programme will improve this.

LEGAL MARKET

Macedonian law prevents foreign firms from opening offices in the country. However, some international firms achieve Macedonian coverage by a system of referrals to local offices and with the gradual increase of foreign investment, local lawyers believe this type of co-operation will grow.

The legal market is in a period of expansion and development with several of the larger firms, for example **Lawyers Antevski** and **Law Office Polenak**, joining alliances.

A notable change in 2005 was the establishment of **MENS LEGIS CAKMAKOVA Advocates** following the departure of Biljana Cakmakova from **MENS LEGIS Law Firm** in September 2005.

The largest firms

1	Polenak, Law Office	12
2	Antevski, Lawyers	9
3	Debarliev, Dameski & Kelesoska Attorneys at Law	8
	Mens Legis Law Firm	8
5	IKRP Rokas and Partners DOOEL	6
6	Peluso & Associates L.T.D.	5
7	Joanidis, Law & Patent Office	4
	Kolevski, Law Office	4
9	Knezovic & Associates, Law Office	3
	Sofronievski, Law & Patent Office	3

These figures represent the total number of lawyers in this country only, and have been supplied by the firms themselves. The figures should be accurate as at 1 January 2006.

LEGISLATIVE DEVELOPMENTS

The government is taking steps to improve the current low level of foreign investment with legislation to ensure foreign investors receive equal treatment. Major incentives were implemented, including the Law on Customs and the Law on Profit Taxes, to provide tax exemptions to outside investors. The Trade Companies Law that regulates business activity was replaced in May 2004 by more progressive legislation.

A transparent regulatory system ensures that nothing impedes foreign investments. However, excessive bureaucratic red tape poses difficulties in government administration and provides further opportunities for corruption. In 2002 the government established an Anti-Corruption Commission and two major anti-corruption laws: the Law on Money Laundering Prevention and the Law on Corruption Prevention were introduced in an ongoing battle to combat bribery and corruption in public administration.

CORPORATE AND M&A

Lawyers Antevski is the largest firm in the country with nine lawyers in total. The firm advises various foreign diplomatic and consular missions in Macedonia, including several international embassies. The firm was actively involved in foreign direct investment projects in 2005 and recently advised AVON Cosmetics in connection with the establishment of an affiliate company in Macedonia. Other big-name clients include World Bank Group and Ernst & Young who the firm counsels on tax, real estate and commercial issues in relation to FYROM.

The three-lawyer team at **Law Office Knezovic & Associates** offers excellent multi-jurisdictional advice on corporate and M&A matters. Leading partner, Dejan Knezovic, plans to expand the office in the next 12 months. In 2005 the firm was involved in one of the most significant transactions of the year when it acted for Macedonia's power company in a privatisation matter. Esteemed clients include British American Tobacco and Mittal Steel, the world's largest steel company.

Established in 1946, **Law Office Polenak** is the most experienced law firm in the country. The firm is active in the rapidly developing banking sector and has handled transactions involving the enforcement of loans and debt and financing matters for government institutions. The firm also advises foreign investors on the establishment and creation of companies and M&A issues.

The eight 'remarkable' lawyers at **MENS LEGIS CAKMAKOVA Advocates** offer a full range of legal services to local and international clients and co-operate with large international firms. The firm advised the EBRD on a copyright protection issue and the US Agency for International Development on a corporate governance and company law project. A whole host of global corporations instruct this firm including Procter & Gamble, Forever Living Products and McDonald's. Clients praise the firm's speed and accessibility and particularly recommend the high level of professionalism that managing partner Biljana Cakmakova demonstrates.

CORPORATE AND M&A

Antevski, Lawyers
Knezovic & Associates, Law Office
Polenak, Law Office

Mens Legis Cakmakova Advocates
Mens Legis Law Firm
Peluso & Associates L.T.D.

Aleksander T. Pulejkov, Law Office
Dukoski Law Office
IKRP Rokas and Partners DOOEL
Joanidis, Law & Patent Office
Kolevski, Law Office
Monevski Law Firm
Panova, Law Office & Patent Bureau
Sofronievski, Law & Patent Office

Firms are listed A-Z in tiers which are ranked in order of priority

Founding member of **MENS LEGIS Law Firm**, Ljubica Ruben, has over 20 years of experience and is engaged as an EU expert through a European agency. The firm's seven lawyers and 15 outsourcing consultants have advised on several key deals in the last 12 months including on the privatisation of Macedonia's telecommunications company. Other noteworthy clients include IBM, the Macedonian Ministry of Economy and Western Union. Clients class 'excellent communication, efficiency and professionalism' as particular strengths.

With offices in Rome, Milan and New York **Peluso & Associates L.T.D.** is well connected and offers specialist business knowledge in a range of languages. Virtually all clients are international and the firm handles numerous referrals from US firms. The firm demonstrated its capabilities in 2005 when representing Akitech, a subsidiary of Alitalia, in a dispute with a Macedonian airline valued at US$2m. The firm has recently been requested to act as general counsel for two *Fortune 500* companies.

IKRP Rokas and Partners DOOEL has an office in Skopje. The firm advises Stepanska Bank and a distributor of Nokia phones on banking, corporate and telecoms matters.

Monevski Law Firm counts the World Bank and the Ministry of Economy amongst its clients. In 2005 the firm handled corporate matters related to a hydropower plant and has advised on an Energy Efficiency Development project.

Law Office & Patent Bureau Panova specialises in corporate and international matters. The firm recently advised the Embassy of the US on a land purchase transaction and assisted Mitchel Group Inc with the evaluation of the Macedonia Court Modernisation Project.

Sole practitioner Ana Sofronievski, **Law & Patent Office Sofronievski**, is assisted by two trainee la wyers. The firm handles corporate matters for various domestic and foreign companies.

DEBARLIEV, DAMESKI & KELESOSKA ATTORNEYS AT LAW

11 OKTOMVRI 115 A 2/2-4
1000 SKOPJE

Telephone: +389 2 3136 530
Fax: +389 2 3215 470
E-mail: ddk@ddklaw.com.mk
Website: www ddklaw.com.mk

Languages
Croatian, English, French, German, Serb

Number of lawyers 8

Contact
Dragan Dameski

CATEGORIES OF WORK

Business, foreign investments, privatisations, property, international trade, tax, telecommunications, mergers and acquisitions, banking
Ivan Debarliev

Antitrust, administrative, corporate, commercial, banking and securities, bankruptcy
Dragan Dameski

Corporate, insurance, employment, leases, contracts, debt collection, litigation, intellectual property
Emilija Kelesoska Soljakovska

Population	61.3 million
Number of lawyers	40,000
Professional title	Avocat
Currency	Euro (€)

Index

France is divided into 96 metropolitan departments, which are grouped into 22 regions. The heart of this centralised structure is Paris, the capital and epicentre of the country's business and legal community. As a result, Paris is home to both the country's leading indigenous law firms and a host of foreign law firms principally from the US and the UK.

Outside of Paris, Lyon, the capital of the Rhône-Alpes region, is France's second economic centre. The country's two other major centres of business are Lille and Marseille. Like Lyon, Lille is largely industrial while Marseille, the Mediterranean hub port, is the economic and maritime capital of the South. Other important cities include Nantes, Rennes, Bordeaux, Toulouse, Montpellier and Strasbourg. Law firms in the regions are dealt with at the end of the chapter.

BILLING

Fees are generally negotiated with the client in advance. The majority of firms work on an hourly rate basis. Hourly billing is quite a recent development for French firms, very much a result of the Anglo-Saxon firms' influence. Some firms prefer a flat fee. Contingency fees, which were officially prohibited, are now increasingly used.

Hourly billing rates range from €155 for junior lawyers to €520 for senior partners, though in some cases more may be charged on particularly complex issues. Generally, rates outside Paris are around one-third lower than in Paris.

MARKETING

The French legal profession is governed by a strict code of professional ethics (especially with regard to publicity). However, law firms are increasingly opening up to marketing, particularly in the Paris market where more than 60 foreign firms are represented.

IN-HOUSE LAWYERS

In-house lawyers are to be found in all larger companies. Most legal departments handle the majority of work themselves, seeking outside help only with regard to specific questions and, of course, litigation. In the case of certain small and medium-sized companies, a law firm might serve as an external legal department.

THE LEGAL MARKET

The profession was modified in 1992 by merging the *avocats* with the *conseils juridiques*. The resulting change was an important one: law firms were thus given an opportunity to provide a complete service adapted to the needs of business clients.

While the two professions are generally harmoniously intertwined in Paris, the picture is slightly different in the provinces where there is often still a distinction between firms engaged in court work and those supplying out-of-court legal services.

There are about 40,000 avocats in France, of which approximately 45% are registered at the Paris Bar. In the regions, few firms boast more than ten avocats, although there are some exceptions, notably in Lyon. The number of firms active on a national scale is small. The largest is **Fidal**, with 20 regional directorates and 100 offices. The other law firms previously linked to the Big Four accountancy firms maintain offices in several cities outside Paris: **Landwell & Associés** in Bordeaux, Grenoble, Lille, Lyon, Marseille, Montpellier, Nantes, Rennes, Strasbourg; **Taj** in Marseille, Lyon, Bordeaux, Tours, Lille; and **Ernst & Young Société d'Avocats** in Bordeaux, Grenoble, Lille, Lyon, Marseille, Monaco, Montpellier, Nantes, Nice, Saint-Etienne, Strasbourg, Toulouse.

The other firm with a national spread is the labour law specialist **Barthélémy & Associés, member of ius laboris** with offices in 14 cities (Paris, Lille, Rennes, Strasbourg, Clermont-Ferrand, Lyon, Bordeaux, Toulouse, Nîmes, Montpellier, Marseille, Nice, Nantes, Saint-Etienne).

Compared to Anglo-Saxon firms, the size of French practices may appear modest. Where French firms have chosen expansion, this has often been done in order to acquire an international dimension (**Gide Loyrette Nouel** for example).

At the same time, there are also a number of medium-sized firms in Paris which do not compete in size but are regarded as centres of excellence (for example, **Bredin Prat** and **Darrois Villey Maillot Brochier**, to name two). Fifty or so Anglo-Saxon firms are represented in Paris. Their contribution to the development of the legal market is undisputed and a number of these firms are well represented in our tables.

There are comparatively few other countries represented in the French legal market. German firms, for example, have tended to turn their expansion plans more towards Eastern Europe.

The largest firms

1	Fidal	1,285
2	Landwell & Associés	660
3	Ernst & Young Société d'Avocats	413
4	CMS Bureau Francis Lefebvre	356
5	Gide Loyrette Nouel	309
6	Taj	250
7	Freshfields Bruckhaus Deringer	243
8	Barthélémy & Associés, member of ius laboris	220
9	Clifford Chance	191
10	Salans	160
11	Linklaters	150
12	Lefèvre Pelletier & associés	140
13	Lovells	122
14	Latham & Watkins	120
15	Allen & Overy LLP	115
16	Baker & McKenzie SCP	105
17	Ginestié Magellan Paley-Vincent	102
18	August & Debouzy	90
	Orrick, Herrington & Sutcliffe	90
20	Cleary, Gottlieb, Steen & Hamilton LLP	87
21	Jones Day	85
22	Shearman & Sterling LLP	84
23	UGGC & Associés	83
	White & Case LLP	83
25	Bignon Lebray & Associés	80
	DS Avocats	80
	De Pardieu Brocas Maffei	80
28	Bredin Prat	76
29	Alain Bensoussan	75
	Lamy Lexel Avocats Associés	75
	Norton Rose	75
32	Fromont, Briens & Associés	72
	Herbert Smith LLP	72

These figures represent the total number of lawyers in this country only, and have been supplied by the firms themselves. The figures should be accurate as at 1 January 2006.

Nonetheless, four main German firms have offices in Paris: **Brandi Dröge Piltz Heuer & Gronemeyer**; **Haarmann Hemmelrath**; **Grützmacher Gravert Viegener**; and **BSR Rödl & Partners**. Dutch firm **Loyens & Loeff** is also present.

Scandinavia is represented in France by Swedish firm **Vinge**, and southern Europe by Italian firm **Carnelutti Studio Legale Associato**, and Spanish firms **J A Cremades et Associés** and **Cuatrecasas**.

LINKS ABROAD

Twenty-five French firms based in Paris maintain a presence abroad, varying from a small office staffed by one or two *avocats* to a larger, structured office, often the result of a merger with a local firm.

Five firms have a strong foreign presence. At the end of the 1980s, **Gide Loyrette Nouel** took on an important strategic route to expansion in the international markets. Hence the setting up of offices in Riyadh, New York, and Brussels, followed by Warsaw, Moscow, Bucharest, Budapest, Prague, Istanbul, Hanoi, Beijing, Shanghai and, more recently, Tunis, Casablanca, Algiers and Belgrade. **Gide Loyrette Nouel** also opened in London in 2003 with a 30-lawyer banking and finance team from **Sidley Austin**. Today one-third of the firm's lawyers is located abroad, in offices generally headed by a French partner.

Salans has a presence in London and the US, in Moscow and Warsaw as well as St Petersburg, Kyiv, Almaty, Baku and Atyrau. The firm is also present in Prague, Bratislava, Bucharest, Istanbul and Shanghai.

CMS Bureau Francis Lefebvre is represented all over Europe, being part of the *CMS* alliance. But **CMS Bureau Francis Lefebvre** already had offices abroad, which have, in some cases, merged with the *CMS* offices in the same cities. To date, the firm is present in Brussels, Bucharest, Buenos Aires, Casablanca, Düsseldorf, Montevideo, Moscow, New-York, Sao Paulo, Shanghai. The firm also hosts a five-lawyer team specialising in African law.

Vovan & Associés has offices in Italy, China, Vietnam and Thailand, while **DS Avocats** is well represented in China, Singapore, Vietnam, South Korea, the UK, Belgium and Spain.

A number of other firms have successfully developed internationally in niche areas, often by accompanying particular clients. There are also firms that have developed special competence in EU law, such as **Bredin Prat**, **Coutrelis & Associés**, **UGGC & Associés** and **Vogel & Vogel**, as well as specialists in environmental law, **Huglo Lepage & Associés Conseil**. **Vogel & Vogel** is present in Frankfurt, while **JP Karsenty & Associés** is in London, Brussels and Milan, and **Ngo Miguérès & Associés** in Milan too. **Ginestié Magellan Paley-Vincent** is in London. As for the US, **JeantetAssociés**, **Sokolow, Carreras & Associés** and **Thieffry & Associés** have an office in New York. **Ngo Miguérès & Associés** is in Mexico. **KGA Avocats** can be found in Singapore, **Lefèvre Pelletier & Associés** in Hong Kong and Canton, **Thieffry & Associés** in Shanghai, **Adamas** in Beijing, Shanghai, Guangzhou, Taipei and Seoul, **Ngo Miguérès & Associés** and **Flécheux & Associés** (in partnership) in Hanoi and Ho Chi Minh City. Finally, a few firms are represented in Africa: **Ernst & Young Société d'Avocats** has offices in the Ivory Coast, Gabon, Senegal, Guinea, Cameroon, Congo, Morocco and Tunisia; **KGA Avocats** is also established in the Ivory Coast; and **UGGC & Associés** is in Morocco.

THE BIG FOUR

What we call here the Big Four are the former legal arms of the Big Four accountancy firms which are now working independently. The legal arms of the Big Four accountants had displayed grand ambitions in the 1990s. These have been overshadowed by the fall-out from the Sarbanes-Oxley law and the Loi de Sécurité Financière in France. Their growth has been particularly visible in the regions, though, where a few top local firms have been taken over. In Paris, they have not reached the top, except in the tax area; the restrictions imposed on their activities and the subsequent moves of lawyers towards traditional law firms have somewhat slowed their growth. Even if the Big Four firms now carry unquestionable weight, sustained by name as well as international connections, they are not real competitors to traditional firms, working in different fields, or for different types of clients.

Fidal has the most extensive representation nationwide and is also largest in terms of number of lawyers. **Landwell & Associés** is the combination of *Price Waterhouse Juridique et Fiscal* and *Coopers & Lybrand CLC Juridique et Fiscal* in 1999.

More recently, in September 2002, Brussels approved the merger between *HSD Ernst & Young* and *Archibald*, the legal arms of *Ernst & Young* and *Andersen Legal* in France, to create *Ernst & Young Société d'Avocats*, now known as **Ernst & Young Société d'Avocats**. The merger wasn't processed without loss, various teams having left the firm to other Big Four or to traditional firms.

The other Big Four is **Taj**, the new name for *Deloitte & Touche Juridique et Fiscal*. The firm is now independent from the audit and accountancy activities.

MOVES, MERGERS AND SPLITS

After the rush of UK firms at the end of the 1990s, it is now US firms that are very active in the Paris market place. The trend started off with the arrival in 2002-03 of **Orrick, Herrington & Sutcliffe**, **Mayer, Brown, Rowe & Maw LLP**, **Weil, Gotshal & Manges** and **Latham & Watkins** by taking over local *cabinets*. These firms have kept growing with significant lateral acquisitions for the latter two in the private equity field for instance. More recently, *Moquet Borde & Associés* joined **Paul, Hastings,**

Janofsky & Walker (Europe) LLP, at the beginning of 2004. At the same time, **Morgan Lewis** set up in Paris with a group split from **De Pardieu Brocas Maffei**. Finally, at the end of 2005, **Orrick, Herrington & Sutcliffe** merged with Paris heavyweight *Rambaud Martel*, combining its banking and finance strength with the strong corporate and litigation practice of the French firm. Other US firms have grown in 2005 too. **Proskauer Rose LLP** cashed in on defections from *Rambaud Martel* before the merger by taking on a team notably strong in real estate and construction law. At the same time, as *Rambaud Martel* announced its merger with **Orrick, Herrington & Sutcliffe**, some partners decided to go their own way: **Reed Smith Rambaud Charot LLP** is one result of this, allowing the US-based firm to set foot in France, after Germany and the UK. At the beginning of 2006, **Salans** also welcomed a team from *Rambaud Martel*, comprising five partners and ten associates with capability in corporate and restructuring.

As for **Dechert**, it has welcomed six of the eight partners (and their teams) from *Coudert Frères* when its office closed down. Also, IP boutique firm *Cousté & Cousté* has become the Paris office of US firm **Howrey LLP**. **Hogan & Hartson MNP** ended its correspondence link with **Cariddi, Mee, Rué** to set up its own Paris office, while developing its whole European network. **DLA Piper Rudnick Gray Cary UK LLP** is now linked with **Cariddi, Mee, Rué** and operates as **DLA Piper Rudnick Gray Cary US LLP, correspondents of CARIDDI, MEE, RUE, association d'avocats au barreau de Paris**.

On the French side, **Bredin Prat** and **Slaughter and May** have reinforced their 'best-friends' relationship as the Magic Circle firm decided to close down its Paris office (although maintaining a representative office to work on the English law aspects of work in France). M&A and finance teams consequently joined **Bredin Prat** but some partners remain **Slaughter and May** partners, while being integrated in the French firm. *Caubet Chouchana Meyer* split and a group of four partners has set up **BMS', Association d'Avocats**, a 12-lawyer firm strong in the real estate field, *Magellan* and *Ginestié Paley-Vincent & Associés* merged to form **Ginestié Magellan Paley-Vincent** in Paris and Lyon. In the same towns, 15 lawyers from **Ernst & Young Société d'Avocats** joined **Adamas** and *Croizat & Huguenin* merged with Paris firm **Carbonnier Lamaze Rasle & Associés**.

At the same time, a bundle of small firms were created, proof that the French market is not the sole preserve of global firms: **Sarrau Thomas Couderc**, a private equity specialist with partners joining from **Denton Wilde Sapte** and **Landwell & Associés**; **Senave, Noreils, Ang**; **La Boétie**, to mention a few.

ADMINISTRATIVE AND PUBLIC LAW

Allen & Overy LLP has succeeded in establishing a strong reputation with partners Noël Chahid-Nouraï and Frédéric Mion. The team offers a full range of advice on various matters, including public procurement contracts and PPP, regulatory and environmental issues, privatisation, litigation, public aspects of M&A, financings, tax and stock-exchange transactions. The public law practice has been involved recently in the fields of infrastructure, telecommunications, energy and increasingly in the media industry. Significant deals include advising the French Ministry of Justice on the €900m PPP programme for 18 prisons; the city of Le Havre on a PPP project; Sanef (motorways) for its partial privatisation and several entities on initiatives by toll road companies; and BDPME and the Ministry of Finance on its transformation of ANVAR into a commercial company and the creation of a new public entity (Oseo); M6 on regulatory issues.

David Préat is the partner in charge at **Clifford Chance**. The team is completed by Patrick Hubert and Rémi Sermier (of-counsels), and complements strong projects, EU/competition and corporate practices. **Clifford Chance** advised Eurely Consortium in the tender process of the European satellite positionning system, Galileo; the French Government and Imprimerie Nationale on the restructuring of this undertaking; Lyon-Turin Ferroviaire on the finalising of the high-speed rail link between France and Italy; and the State in connection with the award of motorway concessions. At the same time, the team is in a good position in the emerging PPP market with notable experience in the hospital field (Centre Hospitalier Sud Francilien).

At **Freshfields Bruckhaus Deringer**, Thierry Laloum, along with six associates handles public law-related cases. The firm is particularly strong in financial public law and PPP but also handles general administrative and environmental law. The team advised the Centre Hospitalier Universitaire de Caen in relation to its enlargement by way of a PPP and two consortiums in relation to their bid for new hospitals; a consortium in relation to its bid for the award of the concession of the French A 65 motorway; ABN Amro in relation to the arrangement of the first joint bond offering (*emprunt obligataire groupé*) involving 11 French local governments (*communautés urbaines*); the Neuf Cegetel group in relation to several negotiations and disputes related to rights of way fees; and Gaz de France in a dispute related to the construction of a gas transportation infrastructure in France.

Two partners handle administrative law at **Gide Loyrette Nouel**: Laurent Deruy and Michel Guénaire. Their practice covers the major areas, primarily public contracts, public enterprises, public finances and local authorities. They assist the State, local authorities, public enterprises and numerous private companies and groups, both as advisers and on litigation. They have significant involvement in the issues relating to the

ADMINISTRATIVE AND PUBLIC LAW

ALLEN & OVERY LLP ✪
CLIFFORD CHANCE
FRESHFIELDS BRUCKHAUS DERINGER
GIDE LOYRETTE NOUEL ✪

BOIVIN & ASSOCIÉS
DS AVOCATS
GRANGE & ASSOCIÉS
HUGLO LEPAGE & ASSOCIÉS CONSEIL ✪
LINKLATERS ✪
SUR – MAUVENU ET ASSOCIÉS
UGGC & ASSOCIÉS ✪

Adamas ✪
Ashurst ✪
August & Debouzy
Baker & McKenzie SCP ✪
Bird & Bird ✪
Bruno Kern Avocats
De Castelnau
JeantetAssociés ✪
Jones Day ✪

Bignon Lebray & Associés
Darrois Villey Maillot Brochier ✪
Flécheux & Associés
Franklin ✪
GAIA
Gibson, Dunn & Crutcher LLP
KGA Avocats
Latournerie Wolfrom & Associés ✪
Lovells ✪
Norton Rose
Orrick, Herrington & Sutcliffe ✪
Salans
Veil Jourde ✪

AdDen
Ader Amigues & Jolibois
Berlioz & Co
Carbonnier Lamaze Rasle & Associés
Cazin
CMS Bureau Francis Lefebvre ✪
De Pardieu Brocas Maffei ✪
Debevoise & Plimpton LLP ✪
Denton Wilde Sapte ✪
Ernst & Young Société d'Avocats
Fidal ✪
Ginestié Magellan Paley-Vincent ✪
Goutal & Alibert
Granrut Avocats
Lefèvre Pelletier & associés ✪
Lussan Brouillaud
Matharan Pintat Avocats
Molas et Associés
Neveu Sudaka & Associés
Pichavant & Chétrit
Sartorio & Associés
Stasi et Associés
Watson, Farley & Williams LLP ✪
White & Case LLP

Firms are listed A-Z in tiers which are ranked in order of priority
✪ Indicates firm displays contact details at the end of this chapter.

enforcement of the new PPP contractual scheme, the reinforcement of the country's administrative decentralisation policy and continued endeavors to implement the provisions of the EU gas directives and foster the opening of the electricity market. **Gide Loyrette Nouel** recently advised a French public undertaking in the construction and operation of a major Northern Europe waterway; ENEL in the framework of the set-up of a partnership with EDF on the joint financing of the EPR nuclear reactor programme; financial institutions and construction companies on the French Government's new prisons programme; and a major US construction equipment company in securing public subsidies for its French operations.

Boivin & Associés has been active in administrative law for a long time, and Jean-Pierre Boivin's doctrinal contribution to the matter is unrivalled. He is director of the IDPA (*Institut de Droit Public des Affaires du Barreau de Paris*). The firm has developed particular strength in administrative contracts, public markets, and delegation of public services, alongside a top environmental practice. The firm has advised Eurotunnel since 1985 in relation to its concession and urban planning matters; Veolia in adminstrative contracts, public markets, concession matters and PPP projects; an international telecoms operator in the drafting of contracts with local authorities; and an international bank in monitoring and financing an important development project in Paris.

DS Avocats has a team of eight lawyers active in public business law. The partners involved in this area are Daniel Chausse, Jean-François Bizet and Frédéric Lévy in Paris, and Romain Granjon in Lyon, who joined from **Adamas**. They advise local communities, communes, public companies and construction companies regarding town-planning, environmental or public markets issues and provision of public services.

At **Grange & Associés**, Claude Grange is undisputedly the best known specialist in public law related to construction matters in France. The seven-lawyer firm specialises in construction project management, public market and delegation of public services management, town-planning and environment. It advises a wide panel of French towns, regions, ministries and various public entities, as well as ports, airports, hospitals, motorway companies and the building industry.

Even though the firm is now more visible in environment law, for which it is a leader in France, **Huglo Lepage & Associés Conseil** has its origins in administrative litigation, and half of the work is still dedicated to the matter. Christian Huglo, Corinne Lepage and their teams advise and defend various local and regional authorities and departments. Their activities encompass administrative law, town-planning, business public law, contracts, markets, delegation and public/private partnerships

Paul Lignières is in charge of public law at **Linklaters**. He is a PPP specialist, deals with delegation of public services, liberalisation of utilities and handles public aspects of corporate and financial transactions, in conjunction with other departments. He and his team have sound knowledge of various sectors where public aspects are vital: infrastructure (rail transport for instance), energy, telecoms, defence, health, education.

Four-partner, eight-associate **Sur - Mauvenu et Associés** focuses on public company and commercial law (at a French and European level), particularly with regard to the provision of public services, such as transport and town-planning, and with a good knowledge of administrative contracts (including PPP, concessions, delegation of public services, etc). Marie-Thérèse Sur-Le Liboux is considered an inventive practitioner.

UGGC & Associés' Jean-Nicolas Clément handles environmental issues; Bernard Lamorlette is developing a town-planning practice; and Thierry dal Farra is a specialist in public contracts, public markets and PPP, as well as public litigation, and often works for the French State.

Adamas is based in Lyon and Paris and has developed expertise in public law over the last 40 years. The team now numbers five partners (including Alain-Serge Mescheriakoff and Claude Ferradou) and ten associates, and offers services spanning environmental law, public markets, town-planning and provision of public services.

Ashurst is involved in public law through its projects/PPP activity, notably on infrastructure (Michel Lequien). The team acts on many projects including the Perpignan-Bettembourg rail-road project and hospitals, among others.

At **August & Debouzy**, Olivier Debouzy leads the 15-lawyer team specialising in public, regulatory and competition law, with partners Christian Pierret and Dominique de Combles de Nayves. Areas covered include procurement contracts (including PPP), public liability (with major public transport litigations), privatisation, regulation of regulated sectors, such as defence, telecoms, space and tobacco.

Baker & McKenzie SCP is active in public law through Arnaud Cabanes, who is also an environmental law specialist, and Emmanuel Guillaume, on the telecoms side. The firm advises EDF, SAGEP, Conseil Général des Hauts-de-Seine and ADP.

At **Bird & Bird**, the team is led by Jean-Dominique Bloch and also comprises two of-counsels (Christophe Barthélémy joined in 2005 from Electricité de France where he was Company Secretary). The department covers the whole range of public law with a focus on the contractual aspects (public markets, delegations and the like), regulation and public-private issues, in all the areas where the firm specialises: telecoms, IT, health and life sciences, defence and aviation.

Bruno Kern Avocats opened his firm specialising in public law in 2001, after being in charge of the department at *Archibald Andersen*. The 12-lawyer firm is mainly active in the field of public contracts, notably working for public entities, like the Ville de Paris, the Syndicat des Transports d'Ile de France and some French *régions*.

Law firm **de Castelnau** specialises in local public law or decentralisation law and works for public or semi-public entities.

JeantetAssociés has two partners active in public law: Pascal Martin and, a former conseiller d'Etat arrived in 2004, Marc Fornacciari. Historically present in four major areas, public markets, town-planning, environment and liability, the firm is now developing an interest in the deregulated sectors (telecoms, electricity), and PPP. **Jeantet-Associés** advised Air France in the case of the terminal 2E collapse at Roissy airport.

Philippe Delelis is **Jones Day**'s public law expert. He specialises in the field of public contracts, procurement, public service concessions, occupation of public land, PPPs, deregulation, public finance and restructurings. He also has experience in issues related to privatisations, deregulation of public services and utilities networks, such as energy and telecoms. He represents the Institut National de la Santé et de la Recherche Médicale (INSERM) in connection with the implementation of a PPP relating to Toulouse's Canceropôle; and Airbus in connection with the occupation of public land required by the A380 construction.

The commercial public law team at **Bignon Lebray & Associés** is led by Lionel Roche (in Lyon) who joined from **Adamas**.

Darrois Villey Maillot Brochier practises public law, owing to François Sureau, a former member of the Conseil d'Etat. He handles public aspects of M&A and is equally involved in privatisation (ASF, GDF).

Michel Bazex deals with administrative law at **Flécheux & Associés** and handles, for example, competition law with public aspects.

At **Franklin**, Jérôme Michel and a four-lawyer team are active for local authorities in the context of public contracts. At the same time, they have knowledge of corporate and regulatory issues related to the energy market (electricity) in France and Eastern countries. Town-planning and environment are also covered.

GAIA handles all types of public contracts, such as concession contracts and PPP. The team, comprising two partners (Jean-Louis Péru and Patrice Cohen-Seat) and five associates combines expertise in public and environmental law.

Gibson, Dunn & Crutcher LLP recruited Nicolas Baverez from **Brandford-Griffith & Associés** in 2004. He deals with economic public law and is an expert in privatisations and private/public issues. Among his clients are SNCF and GDF.

At **KGA Avocats**, the partner in charge is Laurent-Xavier Simonel.

Jean Latournerie is well-known. **Latournerie Wolfrom & Associés** is involved in public contracts, urban planning and civil engineering law, deregulation and privatisations.

Lovells has a dedicated PPP and economic public law practice headed by Jacques Bertran de Balanda. The firm is involved in major bidding exercises (prisons, hospitals, roads, rail), advising the Galileo Joint Undertaking for the concession of the satellite radio navigation system.

Norton Rose has a PPP expert, Philippe Mallea. He has experience in real estate projects involving the public and private sectors (hospitals).

Orrick, Herrington & Sutcliffe is active in public law through two partners coming from *Rambaud Martel*: Frédéric Torron and Bruno Richard have an advisory and contentious practice. Covered areas include public markets, regulation, administrative responsibility, and capital-opening of semi-public entities.

Salans has an economic public law practice with François Froment-Meurice and Paul Falcone, two former *conseillers d'Etat*. They handle public contracts, financings and litigation with a good knowledge of French overseas territories.

Pierre-Alain Jeanneney is in charge of public law at **Veil Jourde**. A former member of the Conseil d'Etat, he acts in all sectors affected by deregulation for clients such as Air France, France Télécom and RATP.

AVIATION

Beaumont Garnault is undoubtedly the leading French aviation firm, now that it is the Paris office of reputed London aviation specialist **Beaumont & Son - Aviation at Clyde & Co.** Acting for the national carrier and its insurers, the firm and its partners do, however, also work for other carriers and handle some matters for manufacturers. Services provided span finance, product and accident liability, insurance and regulatory issues. Fernand Garnault heads the six-lawyer boutique firm.

Gide Loyrette Nouel's aviation practice covers all air transport litigation, mortgages and insurance or reinsurance problems relating to such disputes. Philippe Rames is the main partner involved, whereas Neil McGilchrist, ex-president of **Beaumont & Son - Aviation at Clyde & Co** joined as a consultant in 2005. The team advises on a permanent basis major aircraft manufacturers, such as Aérospatiale, EADS, Eurocopter, ATR, and Socata, in relation to product liability, accidents, and major aviation insurers such as La Réunion Aérienne, Axa and Allianz. Additionally, the team regularly advises foreign manufacturers such as Saab, Commander and Volvo Aero and has a good practice regarding aircraft and engine maintenance business with industrial operators such as Seca, Sogerma and Air France.

AVIATION

BEAUMONT GARNAULT

Gide Loyrette Nouel ✪

Norton Rose

Bird & Bird ✪
Bouckaert Ormen Passemard Sportes ✪
Clyde & Co ✪
Decker & Associés
Rembauville-Nicolle & Bureau - Rbm2l
Soulez Larivière et Associés ✪

Denton Wilde Sapte ✪
Holman Fenwick & Willan ✪
Penlaw Selarl ✪
Rappaport Hocquet
Simmons & Simmons ✪

Firms are listed A-Z in tiers which are ranked in order of priority
✪ Indicates firm displays contact details at the end of this chapter.

Norton Rose works mainly in aviation finance but is also involved in insolvency, work-outs and restructurings, insurance, repossessions and other contentious matters (George Paterson, Owen Mulholland).

At **Bird & Bird**, product liability expert Vonnick Le Guillou joined from **Clyde & Co**. She belongs to the international aviation and aerospace group with lawyers in Belgium, Germany, Sweden and the UK. Contractual and regulatory advice is also provided.

Insurance specialist **Bouckaert Ormen Passemard Sportes** is regularly involved in aviation cases, usually representing US and UK clients in their disputes with French manufacturers.

Clyde & Co handles aviation issues arising from of its work for insurers. Gérard Honig is Airbus' lawyer and advised on the Airbus A320 crash in the UAE. He also advised Aérospatiale in the Concorde case.

Although there is some aviation activity in Paris, we would also recommend **Decker & Associés** in Toulouse, where the industry is well represented.

Rembauville-Nicolle & Bureau - Rbm2l's Patrice Rembauville-Nicolle maintains a strong reputation. He is Boeing's lawyer in France for all matters relating to accidents and, more generally, aviation litigation. He represented Dunlop in the Concorde crash.

Soulez Larivière et Associés is well known for its aviation expertise. Clients include the Direction Générale de l'Aviation Civile and Snecma.

At **Denton Wilde Sapte**, Brett Hailey is an aircraft finance specialist.

Holman Fenwick & Willan acts on a regular basis for Safair, Delta Airlines, American Airlines, RyanAir and Air Canada.

Penlaw SELARL has built a strong aviation practice in Paris. The firm regularly handles litigation and advisory work for Middle-East Airline, Sabena Technics and various US leasing corporations.

Rappaport Hocquet handles crash cases, generally advising the victims. The firm also works for pilots and air crew unions.

Simmons & Simmons' Jeremy Arscott handles aircraft finance.

BANKING AND FINANCE

Allen & Overy LLP's team consists of seven partners: three French - Luc Rentmeesters, Christophe Jacquemin, Jonathan Nabarro; and four English - Rod Cork, Adrian Mellor, Tim Scales and Vikki Greatorex. The client base features a number of large, international banks. The finance practice is international, covering acquisition finance, syndicated loans, structured finance, telecoms, real estate, projects, asset finance and corporate restructurings. **Allen & Overy LLP** advised Citigroup on a US$500m commercial and export credit-backed financing for Wataniya Telecom; Mizuho Corporate Bank on the financing of the tertiary LBO of Actaris from Montagu Private Equity backed by LBO France (€605m); the lead arranger on the €1bn financing of the acquisition of Framatome Connectors International by Bain Capital from Areva; the banks in relation to refinancing the indebtedness of Rhodia; the French Ministry of Justice regarding the construction of 18 penitentiaries (€900m); Autoroutes du Sud de la France on a €1bn credit facility; and Inco Ltd and Goro Nickel SA on a US$500m French tax lease.

The **Clifford Chance** finance team works on complex structured finance transactions and securitisations on an international level, including real estate deals. (Richard Parolai and Jonathan Lewis). The firm is involved in acquisition and LBO finance (Diane de Moüy), and is also well known for employee share plans as well as debt restructuring, general banking and regulatory advice (Olivier Bertin-Mourot). Thierry Arachtingi, who arrived from **White & Case LLP**, is an acquisition and property finance expert. **Clifford Chance** advised Calyon on a €500m credit facility arranged for Neuf Télécom; Duke Street Capital in relation to the financing of the acquisition of the Proclif Group (clinics); Colony Capital in relation to the financing of the acquisition of Buffalo Grill together with Colyzeo (€340m); Rexel on a securitisation transaction; ABN Amro on a €225m pan-European securitisation for a producer of chocolate; and Risanamento on the financing of the acquisition of two real estate portfolios from SFL in Paris (€180m).

De Pardieu Brocas Maffei is regarded by many as the number one French banking firm and works closely with a few US firms. The practice covers regulatory, advisory and contentious

BANKING AND FINANCE

ALLEN & OVERY LLP ✪
CLIFFORD CHANCE
DE PARDIEU BROCAS MAFFEI ✪
FRESHFIELDS BRUCKHAUS DERINGER
GIDE LOYRETTE NOUEL ✪
LINKLATERS ✪

ASHURST ✪
LATHAM & WATKINS
ORRICK, HERRINGTON & SUTCLIFFE ✪
SHEARMAN & STERLING LLP
WHITE & CASE LLP

Cleary, Gottlieb, Steen & Hamilton LLP ✪
Debevoise & Plimpton LLP ✪
Herbert Smith LLP ✪
JeantetAssociés ✪
Jones Day ✪
Lovells ✪
Norton Rose

August & Debouzy
Ayache Salama & Associés ✪
Bignon Lebray & Associés
Bredin Prat ✪
Chaintrier & Associés
Dechert ✪
Denton Wilde Sapte ✪
Dubarry Le Douarin Veil ✪
Ernst & Young Société d'Avocats
Eversheds-Frere Cholmeley
Ince & Co ✪
Kramer Levin Naftalis & Frankel LLP ✪
Lefèvre Pelletier & associés ✪
Lussan Brouillaud
Mayer, Brown, Rowe & Maw LLP ✪
Morgan Lewis ✪
NomoS ✪
Paul, Hastings, Janofsky & Walker (Europe) LLP ✪
SJ Berwin ✪
Salans
Simmons & Simmons ✪
Sullivan & Cromwell LLP
UGGC & Associés ✪
Willkie Farr & Gallagher LLP ✪

Firms are listed A-Z in tiers which are ranked in order of priority
✪ Indicates firm displays contact details at the end of this chapter.

matters (the latter being a traditional strength), with solid activity in derivatives and structured finance. The firm undertakes a wide range of finance work for clients such as banks and large insurance companies, as well as some investment companies. Antoine Maffei, Pierre Minor and Olivier Hubert are well-known specialists. In 2005, the firm was active in acquisition and LBO finance, on the borrowers' or banks' sides, advising the borrower in the financing of the takover bid of Foncière des Régions (€900m); the banks in the financing of the takeover bid of Quiksilver for Rossignol (€500m); and Wendel Investissement in the stapled financing related to the LBO sale of Wheelabrator Allevard (€310m). **De Pardieu Brocas Maffei** is also involved in project and asset finance, in fields such as satellites, ship, and mobile phone networks. At the same time, the firm handled a multitude of syndicated loans and was instructed by the banks (BNP Paribas) in the €335m corporate loan issued for Pinguely-Haulotte. The firm has acquired PPP capacity under Yves-René Guillou.

Freshfields Bruckhaus Deringer's finance group boasts no less than 11 partners, including Michel Quéré, Jean-Luc Michaud, Hervé Kensicher, Glenn Matheson and Véronique Collin. Although the firm's activities are diverse, certain practice areas merit special mention: structured finance and complex financing arrangements, property finance, and transactions with an elaborate tax dimension. The firm is also involved in aviation and acquisition/LBO finance. Among major work, we would mention acting as counsel to Eurotunnel in connection with the restructuring of its debt; Euro Disney on all aspects of the legal and financial restructuring of the group; France Antilles on a syndicated loan of €150m for refinancing of acquisition Pathé SA on the second refinancing of Europalaces; Bayerische Landesbank on the financing of the acquisition of a property located at avenue Montaigne in Paris (€157.5m); and BNP Paribas as arranger in relation to the financing of a portion of a nickel-cobalt industrial production complex in New Caledonia under a French tax lease structure for Goro Nickel (US$451m).

Gide Loyrette Nouel's 80-lawyer team is active in all areas of banking and finance. In addition to project finance, capital markets and securitisation, the firm is also involved in structured finance (Eric Cartier-Millon, Kamel Ben Salah), and in financial institutions and services (Jean-Guillaume d'Hérouville, Stéphane Puel). The team works closely with the London (seven partners) and New York (two new partners in 2005) offices. The firm advised Société Générale in the €60.2m LMBO financing of the acquisition of Financière Mory by Mory S.A.S; Natexis Banques Populaires and Calyon in the €126.8m LBO financing of the acquisition of Financière Courtepaille; the mandated lead arrangers in the €3.1bn LBO financing of the acquisition of Rexel by CDR, Eurazeo and Merrill Lynch Private Equity; Axa Reim in relation to the structuring of a *Société Civile de Placement Immobilier (SCPI)*; Veolia Environnement in the €4bn multicurrency revolving facility; the arrangers in the €2bn revolving multi-currency facility granted to Vinci SA; and the mandated lead arrangers in the €1.6bn refinancing of existing indebtedness of Vivarte.

Three types of activity are especially well developed at **Linklaters**: acquisition and leveraged finance, structured finance and mainstream banking (including syndicated loans). PPP and property financings are aslo dealt with. Partners involved are Bertrand Andriani, Olivier Jauffret, Nathalie Hobbs, Arnaud Fromion and Jean-Jacques Essombè (a regulatory specialist). The firm represented ING Finance France SA and ING Bank NV in relation to a secondary LBO of the Terreal Group; Suez on a public tender offer for Electrabel shares for an amount of €11.2bn and share capital increase by Suez for an amount of €2.5bn; Metrovacesa in relation to its cash public offer for 100% of Gecina (enterprise value €8.57bn); and the mandated lead arrangers on the EDF €6bn multi-currency revolving credit facility.

Ashurst is certainly one of the premier firms in the acquisition finance field – with Laurent Mabilat, Diane Sénéchal and James Collis (who arrives from London) – although it also carries out project/PPP, structured, property and restructuring work. The acquisition finance work principally involves LBO financing for French banks, as well as acting for foreign banks with operations in France and investment funds. A number of CDOs/CLOs, securitisations and property financings have also been completed in recent months. In 2005, the firm advised Calyon and Intermediate Capital Group plc on the acquisition financing of Picard Surgelés by BC Partners (€1.3bn); BNP Paribas on the financing of the acquisition of Saur by PAI Partners from Bouygues (€1bn); Goldman Sachs and Natexis Banques Populaires on the leveraged recapitalisation of Frans Bonhomme; EHI Fund, established by Property Fund Management plc and Jones Lang LaSalle, on the structuring of the fund (€700m); and Natexis Banques Populaires in respect of Valoris CLO Plc (€300m).

Latham & Watkins has a good name in banking, finance and capital markets, with a balanced clientele of banks and borrowers. The firm handles acquisition and LBO finance, structured finance, real estate finance, project and asset finance. Three partners are mainly active: Etienne Gentil, Dominique Basdevant and Xavier Farde. Last year, the firm was instructed by Citigroup and Euro Hypo in the €2.6bn financing of the acquisition by Starwood of Taittinger; CIC in the €430m financing of the acquisition of retirement home group Medidep; Société Générale, BNP Paribas and BECM in the financing of the public offering launched by Foncière des Régions for Bail Investissement (€900m); the arrangers of the €300m PIK loan for the recapitalisation of Eutelsat; and Eurofima in the €220m French tax leasing of Alstom-Bombardier locomotives leased to SNCB.

Orrick, Herrington & Sutcliffe's reputation derives from its asset finance practice, which covers all industrial sectors and accounts for one-third of the finance activity. The remainder is made up of general banking and traditional credit agreements (very often for borrowers), project finance, and financial disputes. The firm is one of few with wide knowledge of cross-border tax lease financings. The finance practice additionally covers property, shipping and trade finance. Partners, including David Syed, Raphaële Courtier and Stuart McAlpine (Alain Gautron left for **Norton Rose**), represented a syndicate of European banks, in a US$840m financing for the purchase of two cruise vessels, the largest container ships to be built in the world; BNP Paribas as lessor in a series of export credit-backed aircraft lease transactions involving 12 Airbus aircraft (US$650m); Cegetel in connection with a €1bn revolving credit facility transaction; and Vivendi Universal group in connection with a six billion Moroccan Dirham financing to finance the acquisition of a 16% stake in Maroc Telecom.

Shearman & Sterling LLP is very active in acquisition and LBO finance (Martin Lebeuf works for French and US banks) but also handles property finance, syndicated loans and high-yield issues (Christophe Dugué, Manuel Orillac). The firm has expertise in derivatives instruments, is very active in cross-border financings, handling structured and specialised finance work. Recent deals include advising Eurazeo, Texas Pacific Group and GSCP in connection with the leveraged recapitalisation of Eutelsat (€2.4bn); Morgan Stanley, JPMorganChase, Merrill Lynch, RBS and CCF as arrangers for the senior facilities supporting the leveraged buyout of Rexel (€2.4bn); and Neuf Telecom in connection with the €500m syndicated facilities supporting the merger between Neuf Telecom and Cegetel.

White & Case LLP is known for project finance, LBO and acquisition finance, structured and asset finance, very often on the banks' side but increasingly for the borrowers, and is developing real estate, high-yield and securitisation activities. Gilles Peigney is well known for his acquisition and LBO practice. Thomas McDonald is in charge of asset finance (aviation and shipping). (Thierry Arachtingi left for **Clifford Chance**.) The firm is active in the energy and commodities finance markets. **White & Case LLP** represented Starwood Capital Group in connection with the acquisition of a controlling stake in Groupe Taittinger and Société du Louvre, and in connection with a public tender offer for the remaining shares; the underwriters in connection with the senior and second lien secured financing of the recapitalisation of Eutelsat (€1.775bn of senior debt, €475m of second lien debt and an additional €300m of PIK debt); BNP Paribas and Société Générale in connection with the €2.22bn financing of the recapitalisation of TDF; Calyon and Aareal Bank in the €170.5m acquisition facility granted to a group of investors represented by UBS for the acquisition of the Rive Défense office building located in Nanterre; and Société Générale in the French tax lease financing of a container for CMA CGM (US$297m).

Cleary, Gottlieb, Steen & Hamilton LLP represents borrowers and lenders in a wide range of financings, such as acquisition finance, syndicated bank financings and structured and derivative financing transactions. Recent experience includes being counsel to Vestar Capital Partners Europe in connection with its €287m senior refinancing of the acquisition of OGF; a consortium of banks in the debt restructuring of Penauille Polyservices; Unibail in connection with its €500m and €600m syndicated credit facilities; BNP Paribas in connection with the financing of the acquisition of Galeries Lafayette, including €750m secured senior facility, €470m bridge financing and €838m subordinated bond offering; and Havas in its €150m syndicated credit facility.

Debevoise & Plimpton LLP's practice is a French/UK/US one with partner in charge Pierre Clermontel and of-counsel Eryl Besse. Clients are equally balanced between banks and blue-chips, and activities are focused on acquisition/LBO finance and corporate credit facilities. Recent deals include advising Eutelsat in its €1.3bn credit facility; Pernod Ricard on the €9.3bn credit facility in connection with the financing of its acquisition of Allied Domecq; and the acquiring consortium and Rexel on the financing of the €3.7bn leveraged acquisition of Rexel.

Herbert Smith LLP had a team of two partners – Georges Dirani and Clotilde Dirnat – and seven associates; at the time of writing, it emerged that Dirnat is leaving the firm. Main areas of expertise include international debt finance, acquisition finance, structured finance, securitisations and derivatives. The client base is evenly split between banks and national and international borrowers. **Herbert Smith LLP** works with Société Générale, BNP Paribas, Calyon, ING, Natexis and, more recently,CIC Crédit Mutuel and HSBC. Recent experience includes advising HSBC and Calyon on a €1bn syndicated credit facility to Autoroutes du Sud de la France SA; CIC Crédit Mutuel and HSBC as co-arrangers in a €400m receivables financing structured around a securities structure for Autalis; Barilla Holdings SPA/Harry's in connection with a substantial restructuring of the existing debt of the group; and Société Générale and Calyon as co-arrangers of a €250m secured acquisition financing to Smoby.

The **JeantetAssociés** team is growing and is led by Jean-Maurice Gaillard, with partners Jean-François Adelle, Philippe Portier and Thierry Brun. The firm has developed particular expertise in financial aspects of M&A, complex structured financings, notably in the property area and tax-related cases, acting for borrowers and increasingly for financial institutions, including Calyon and Merrill Lynch, for buyers and sellers. Last year's highlights include advising Hypo Real Estate Capital France in the financing of the acquisition by the Qatar Islamic Bank of the Colgate Towers and of a real estate portfolio located in Courbevoie; Compagnie des Alpes in a €260m syndicated credit; and the Royal Bank of Scotland in the €100m financing of the Hotel Plaza Athénée.

Jones Day handles acquisition finance, asset and structured finance transactions, especially in the real estate field, and tax-driven financings. Moreover, the private equity sector is developing and the firm has recently been representing investment funds in LBOs. The partners in charge are Philippe Billot and Pierre-Nicolas Ferrand. The firm represented Bouwfonds Property Finance BV in the financing of the construction of a 70,000 sq m commercial center in the Paris region (€155m); RBS in connection with the financing of two bridge secured multi-option, multi-currency revolving facilities granted to two funds of funds; RTE on financial issues related to the debt restructuring (€7bn) in connection with the creation of RTE EDF Transport; and Atos Origin SA in connection with a €1.2bn syndicated multicurrency revolving facility agreement.

Lovells is very active in banking and finance and has now established relationships with major players such as Groupe Caisses d'Epargne, Société Générale, BNP Paribas, Natexis Banques Populaires, Barclays Bank Plc, Alstom, EDF and Suez. Its activities include acquisition finance (mainly for banks and investment funds), asset finance (on behalf of banks and aviation companies), international trade and commodities in emerging countries, project finance and PPP, property and regulatory work, debt restructurings, syndicated loans and e-banking. Jacques Bertran de Balanda and Richard Jadot are the partners in charge. **Lovells** advised Société Générale with respect to the recapitalisation of the LBO of Novacap (Rhodia spin-off) for Bain Capital; Crédit Agricole on the €200m long-term credit facilities for the financing of the sale and leaseback of 14 Carrefour hypermarkets in Spain, Italy and Greece; and EDF in a €6bn multi-currency syndicated credit facility.

Norton Rose's practice revolves around three types of work – asset finance, acquisition finance and project finance. The firm boasts a first-class reputation in shipping (Nigel Ward and Alain Gautron who arrived from **Orrick, Herrington & Sutcliffe**), aviation finance (George Paterson) and is developing trade finance, renewable energy finance and PPP activities (Philippe Mallea). In less than two years, the team has broadened, with three lateral hires and two internal promotions. The work centres on structured finance for banks of all nationalities (**Norton Rose** has been appointed to the Société Générale and BNP Paribas panels), and large French companies. General banking and finance (Martin Gdanski) is also covered. The firm has advised CCF and Société Générale on lease financings of rolling stock for the Swiss and Belgian railways; the banks on the acquisition financing of several international cable networks; the banks on several French and international wind farm financings;

Société Générale on its tax lease structures for two container ships for Evergreen; and various consortiums and public clients in the PPP financings of several hospital projects.

CAPITAL MARKETS

Allen & Overy LLP has a leading practice in both France and Europe. The firm's partners devoted to capital markets work in Paris are principally Dan Lauder and François Poudelet, while Pierre Gissinger is well known for his derivatives expertise. The firm is primarily active in the fields of debt, regulatory, warrants and derivatives, under French, English and US law, acting principally for French and international banks, although the firm is developing the equity side with US securities law capacity. For instance, the firm advised Société Générale regarding the issue by Wendel Investissement of €300,000,000 4.375% bonds due 2017. **Allen & Overy LLP** has been active in an increasing number of Tier 1, own-fund transactions recently, advising Thomson in relation to the issue of €500m deeply subordinated notes, and in activities related to the Prospectus Directive. The firm remains a leader in EMTN programmes, advising many French banks and corporates. On the equity side, the team has been involved in the €885m capital increase of Sanef and listing on Eurolist by Euronext, and the structuring of a €850m securitisation for RCI Banque, advising the arrangers.

Cleary, Gottlieb, Steen & Hamilton LLP enjoys an excellent reputation for its equities practice worldwide. In Paris, the firm's expertise manifests itself in French and US securities law with a complete range of international equity offerings, equity derivatives and other derivatives transactions, structured financings, capital securities offerings and convertible, exchangeable and straight debt offerings. The French/US team includes Pierre-Yves Chabert, Robert Bordeaux-Groult, Andrew Bernstein, John Brinitzer and Russell Pollack. Recent Experience includes advising the underwriters in connection with the initial public share offering of Mercialys, the real estate affiliate of Casino; Gaz de France in its €4.5bn IPO; Euro Disney SCA and The Walt Disney Company in the €253m underwritten rights offering of Euro Disney shares; BNP Paribas, JP Morgan and Société Générale, as initial purchasers, in a €450m convertible bonds offering by Air France, convertible and/or exchangeable into new or existing shares of Air France-KLM; and Natexis Banques Populaires in its €300m offering of deeply subordinated Tier 1 notes.

Primarily involved in debt-related matters (Jonathan Lewis, Richard Parolai and Cedric Burford), **Clifford Chance**'s practice has extended to securitisations and equity offerings (Edward Kamman). The firm is active in both non-contentious (including employee share plans with Olivier Bertin-Mourot) and contentious equity work. On the equity side, **Clifford Chance** advised Erap on the French Government's €3.3bn sale of 6 to 8% of its stake in France Télécom; Maroc Télécom on its double listing in Casablanca and Paris (€812m); and EDF on the sale through an accelerated book-building process of its interest in Total (€2.565bn). On the debt side, major deals include advising Société Générale in relation to a debut €600m bond issue by SFR; the City of Paris on the establishment of a €2bn EMTN programme; and Deutsche Bank in relation to the issue of €300m deeply subordinated floating rate Tier 1 notes by Natexis Banques Populaires, listed on the Luxembourg Stock Exchange.

CAPITAL MARKETS

ALLEN & OVERY LLP ✪
CLEARY, GOTTLIEB, STEEN & HAMILTON LLP ✪
CLIFFORD CHANCE
FRESHFIELDS BRUCKHAUS DERINGER
GIDE LOYRETTE NOUEL ✪
LINKLATERS ✪
SHEARMAN & STERLING LLP

DE PARDIEU BROCAS MAFFEI ✪
DEBEVOISE & PLIMPTON LLP ✪
LATHAM & WATKINS
LOVELLS ✪
SKADDEN, ARPS, SLATE, MEAGHER & FLOM LLP
SULLIVAN & CROMWELL LLP
WILLKIE FARR & GALLAGHER LLP ✪

Brandford-Griffith & Associés ✪
Bredin Prat ✪
Darrois Villey Maillot Brochier ✪
Davis Polk & Wardwell
Hogan & Hartson MNP ✪
Jones Day ✪
Orrick, Herrington & Sutcliffe ✪
Paul, Hastings, Janofsky & Walker (Europe) LLP ✪
Simmons & Simmons ✪
White & Case LLP

Ashurst ✪
Baker & McKenzie SCP ✪
DLA Piper Rudnick Gray Cary US LLP, correspondents of Cariddi, Mee, Rue, association d'avocats au barreau de Paris ✪
Fried, Frank, Harris, Shriver & Jacobson LLP
Gibson, Dunn & Crutcher LLP
Herbert Smith LLP ✪
JeantetAssociés ✪
Kramer Levin Naftalis & Frankel LLP ✪
LeBoeuf, Lamb, Greene & Macrae LLP ✪
Norton Rose
Reinhart Marville Torre
Salans
Veil Jourde ✪

Firms are listed A-Z in tiers which are ranked in order of priority
✪ Indicates firm displays contact details at the end of this chapter.

Freshfields Bruckhaus Deringer retains its position as one of the leaders in both international (offshore) and domestic securitisations. For example, Société Générale, BNP Paribas and Calyon were advised in relation to a €4.5bn synthetic residential mortgage-backed securitisation originated by Crédit Logement and BNP Paribas was advised as arranger of a trade receivables securitisation programme involving some French, Italian and US affiliates of the Hachette Filipacchi Presse group, and replacing a purely European programme. Within the capital markets sector, the firm handles the placement of complex credit derivatives. Its client base is largely made up of banks. The partners involved are Hervé Touraine, Véronique Collin, Ian Falconer, Antonin Besse and Dougall Molson. On the debt side, the firm assisted Crédit Foncier de France on a number of issues of *obligations foncières* (covered bonds), and ABN Amro as arranger on the first multi-issuer bond issue involving French local governments. On the equity side, Patrick Bonvarlet and Linda Hesse (US securities) are active, advising France Télécom on the partial financing for the acquisition of Spanish mobile operator Amena by way of a €3bn capital increase including public offers in France, Belgium, Germany, the Netherlands, Spain and the UK; Calyon and Morgan Stanley in a €7.9bn debt facility for Suez, to part-fund its offer for the 49.9% minority stake in Belgian utility Electrabel, and as global coordinators and bookrunners of the related €2.3bn rights issue by Suez.

Gide Loyrette Nouel has a leading practice in debt and equity issues (Arnaud Duhamel and Jean-Marc Desaché), derivatives and structured products (Alban Caillemer du Ferrage). One of the firm's main strength rests in its expertise in securitisation (both domestic and offshore) with Xavier de Kergommeaux, Gilles Saint Marc and Patrice Doat. The firm is also active in stock exchange introductions and dual listings. Work accomplished last year includes a €1.75bn securitisation transaction arranged by Natexis Banques Populaires and listed on the Paris Stock Exchange, the first issuance of bonds by a French FCC under the new legal and regulatory framework. Since 2004, the derivatives group has been advising ISDA on banking and financial regulatory issues in France. At the same time, the Investment Management team is counsel to French and international asset management companies carrying out business in France, advising the Fonds de Réserve des Retraites (the French State pension fund, (FRR)) on the structuring of its private equity investments (€1.5bn). Also, **Gide Loyrette Nouel** represented the lead managers in the €2.4bn senior credit facilities and €600m high-yield subordinated notes issued for Rexel; Rue du Commerce in its IPO; and Lehman Brothers and BNP Paribas in the issuance of ADS in the US and new shares on the Nouveau Marché for Infovista. Furthermore, the firm assists issuers, arrangers and dealers on the setting up, updates and/or issue of numerous tranches under EMTN Programmes of Morgan Stanley Dean Witter, Merrill Lynch, Calyon, Société Générale, La Poste, Ville de Paris, Région Ile de France, Alcatel, Lafarge, etc. It currently advises the French State in the privatisation of Gaz de France and Electricité de France.

Linklaters' six-partner specialised practice offers debt, equity, derivatives and growing securitisation expertise. The firm advises both lenders and borrowers and is developing both high-yield and US practices (Tom O'Neill). In the equity securities sector, the firm is primarily active with regard to pure stocks and shares and also handles the development of debt products convertible into and/or exchangeable for stocks and shares. Gilles Endréo is very well regarded. Other partners include Cenzi Gargaro and Philippe Herbelin. The team also has a good knowledge of credit derivatives, warrants, OTC products under French or English law for banks and companies, and EMTN programmes (having dealt with 40 programmes in 2004/2005). Highlights over the year include assisting Suez on its share capital increase for an amount of €2.4bn to partly refinance a public tender offer for Electrabel; the arrangers on the French State privatisation and IPO of Gaz de France, the largest in the world for three years (€4.5bn); and Calyon, as Arranger, in connection with the restructuring of a multi-jurisdictional securitisation of trade receivables originated by twelve entities, members of the CEGELEC group. The team was also involved in the issue of the *obligations assimilables du Trésor* (OAT) due April 2055 by The Republic of France (€6bn).

Shearman & Sterling LLP is one of the top firms on the equity side, especially with regard to offerings with an international dimension, equity-linked and high-yield offerings. The firm has been involved in almost every privatisation since 1986, acting for issuers (EDF, Air France, among others), the Treasury or underwriters for listings in Paris and New York and other international offerings. The Paris-based capital markets group is also a leader in the field of employee offerings. Active partners are Robert Treuhold, Hervé Letréguilly, Sami Toutounji, Manuel Orillac and Bertrand Sénéchal. Recent highlights include assisting ABN Amro Rothschild and Société Générale in connection with a Rule 144A/Regulation S secondary offering of ordinary shares of Air France-KLM by the Republic of France (€700m); France Télécom in the sale of 8% of the capital of Pages Jaunes to institutional investors through an accelerated book building (€440m); Rhodia in its offering of 8% senior notes due 2010 to refinance its debt (€500m); and the underwriters in connection with the €3bn rights offering of ordinary shares by France Télécom.

Alongside a traditional practice in securities issues and complex derivatives (the firm is strongly involved in the structuring of warranted products intended to investment funds and leveraged financial products), **De Pardieu Brocas Maffei** is distinguished by its expertise in payment systems, compensation and delivery rules (particularly the new European regulation on multi-product compensation instruments). Antoine Maffei, Olivier Hubert and Pierre Minor have also been active in the implementation of worldwide offerings of shares (GDF, ASF, Air France, Crédit Agricole, Suez, among others) assisting banks or issuers, and increased their presence in securitisation transactions, notably European securitisations of receivables and real estate debts (CMBS), advising the note trustee and security trustee in the pan-European securitisation of receivables via a FCC for Smurfit. At the same time, a great deal of equity and debt transactions are handled, such as a €400m programme of super-subordinated notes for AGF, and a capital increase for Crédit Agricole in 15 countries.

Debevoise & Plimpton LLP is active in equity and equity linked transactions although some debt issues are also dealt with through the establishment of EMTN programmes (for PPR). The most visible partner in this practice is Pierre Clermontel, with Marc Castagnède and Raman Bet-Mansour also active within a 20-lawyer team. Clients are equally broken down between banks and corporates. Recently, the firm was instructed by Alstom in its bond issue that raised €600m and in its €1bn global offering of bonds; Rexel in the issuance and sale of €600m of high-yield notes through a global offering with Rule 144A in the US; the underwriters in the €233m capital increase by Scor; and Aar and Calyon on the IPO of Nexity.

At **Latham & Watkins**, several partners are active alongside the M&A practice, while Roberto Cristofolini and Basil Zotiades, as well as Patrick Singer and John Watson, are entirely dedicated to capital markets. The team covers French and foreign securities and stock exchange issues and is active in domestic and international IPOs, share offerings and equity linked matters. The recent arrivals have reinforced the equity, equity linked, subordinated debt and high-yield offerings aspects and established US expertise in Paris. **Latham & Watkins** advised Société Générale in the IPO of Meetic; Axa Investment Managers in the establishment of a multi-issuer, multi-currency synthetic CDO programme and the issuance of a series of notes linked to a portfolio of investment grade reference entities, in excess of €640m; and CSFB, BNP Paribas and Calyon in the high-yield issue of €500m 8% senior notes due 2010 by Rhodia.

Lovells is involved in major debt transactions with Philip Boys and Sharon Lewis, who is also an international securitisation expert and now head of the worldwide practice. Jean-Norbert Pontier, a securitisations and derivatives expert, joined from **Sidley Austin** London in 2005. The team (13 fee-earners) also handles equity issues, repackagings, derivatives, IPOs, financial services and funds work. **Lovells** advised Alstom on the refinancing of €4.9bn bonding guarantee programme of up to €8bn and over €2bn of disposals; BNP Paribas as lead manager on French law aspects of 18 CDOs with an aggregate issue amount of €1.2bn; the Suez Group and its subsidiary Genfina on a public offer, worth in excess of €1.4bn, which enabled the Suez Group to divest their interest in Fortis; and EDF on several major financings (€7.8bn and ¥12bn).

The Paris office of **Skadden, Arps, Slate, Meagher & Flom LLP** handles privatisations with international placement aspects (Air France, ASF, APRR, France Télécom, EADS) and stock exchange introductions in Paris and New York. The firm also handles equity-linked work and securitisations. Traditionally on the underwriters' side, **Skadden, Arps, Slate, Meagher & Flom LLP** increasingly acts for issuers. Partners involved are Pierre Servan-Schreiber, Armand Grumberg and David Revcolevschi. Major deals include advising the underwriters in the privatisation of France Télécom (€5.5bn) and the offering by France Télécom of convertible bonds (€1.1bn); the underwriters in the €1.3bn IPO of Société des Autoroutes Paris Rhin Rhône; Scor in its €232m capital increase; and Air France-KLM in the sale by the French Republic of its stake (US$905m) as well as in the forthcoming employee offering by the company.

Sullivan & Cromwell LLP plays an important part in placing European operators on international markets, particularly in the US. The practice covers the whole range of products from IPOs and privatisations to private placements, including 144A. Partners include Richard Vilanova, Nikolaos Andronikos, Dominique Bompoint and Richard Asthalter. In 2005, the firm was involved in various privatisations (France Télécom, Areva, EDF, SANEF), advising the French Treasury, the underwriters or the issuers. It was also instructed by Axa in a €68m multi-year securitisation; the underwriters in a French and international offering of shares in Eutelsat (€3bn); the underwriters in the US$1.1bn capital increase of Metrovacesa; and Thomson in a US$500m private placement to Silverlake Partners of exchangeable/ convertible bonds.

Willkie Farr & Gallagher LLP is very active on the equity side (Laurent Faugérolas, Daniel Hurstel). It is involved in stock market introductions (with expertise in transactions combining public offerings in Europe with private placement in the US), global equity offerings, private placements of securities and debt offerings, usually acting for the issuer. In 2004/2005, the team was instructed on the equity offerings of French highway company SAPRR, BioMérieux and Nexity and advised Schneider Electric on two issuances of notes under a €2.95bn EMTN programme.

Brandford-Griffith & Associés is regularly involved in capital markets, advising issuers, banks and financial institutions on stock market listings (working in partnership with several highly-ranked firms in the US), or in the context of privatisations (Snecma in 2005). The team (Henri Brandford-Griffith, Laurent Sablé) also handles financial instruments issuings and participates in the creation of new financial products and new issuing structures. Recent deals include advising the banks in the capital increase of Euro Disney, and the banks in the IPO of Rue du Commerce and the banks in the IPO of NextRadioTV (BFM-RMC).

Besides major privatisations (France Télécom, Snecma, Sernam), **Bredin Prat** has expertise in various complex financial instruments, mainly on the equity side for issuers, and works on a regular basis with **Davis Polk & Wardwell** in the US for M&A-related issues. The firm was involved in the IPO of Lazard.

Darrois Villey Maillot Brochier is also involved in capital markets issues. A privatisation specialist (François Sureau) and an expert in stock exchange-related transactions (Marie-Noëlle Dompé) are also part of the firm. The firm advised Groupe Caisse d'Epargne in the context of the IPO of Lazard and Autoroutes du Sud de la France and GDF in their privatisations.

In the past five years, the Paris office of **Davis Polk & Wardwell** has represented the issuers or underwriters in numerous international securities offerings by French issuers, including Alstom, Axa, Dassault Systemes and Rhodia. Recent deals include advising the French Finance Ministry on its secondary offering of 152 million shares of France Télécom, and IXIS Corporate & Investment Bank, Lazard Frères Banque, BNP Paribas and Calyon as lead managers in the €253m Rule 144A/Regulation S rights offering of common stock by Euro Disney.

At **Hogan & Hartson MNP**, Jean-Marc Franceschi joined from **Jones Day**. He is mainly active on the equity side and is involved in IPOs, capital increases, issues of shares, convertible bonds and secondary offers. He advised UBS, financial adviser to AS Watson in the €350m takeover of Marionnaud and Penauille Polyservices in connection with a €157m capital increase and friendly takeover launched by CCF recycling.

After Jean-Marc Franceschi left for **Hogan & Hartson MNP** in 2005, **Jones Day** recruited Frank Martin Laprade from **Clifford Chance** to join forces with Renaud Bonnet and Philippe Billot. Debt, equity and securitisation transactions are dealt with, mainly on the issuer's side. Highlights of the practice include several high-profile transactions, such as France Télécom's most important acquisition since Orange in 2000 (Amena), one of the largest French PIPE deals (Completel), and several IPOs (eg Satimo and most recently Staff and Line on the Alternext market of Euronext Paris).

Orrick, Herrington & Sutcliffe has an increasingly important practice covering all aspects of capital markets, bond issues with the original firm's partners (Raphaële Courtier, Véronique Roualet) and equity issues with ex-*Rambaud Martel* corporate partners who are experts in privatisations and stock-exchange transactions. The firm advised Renault SA in the update of its €7bn EMTN programme, and Vivendi Universal in two fixed-rate note issuances for the amounts of €600m and €630m. Securitisations are also handled.

Paul, Hastings, Janofsky & Walker (Europe) LLP's capital markets team, with Aline Poncelet, was reinforced by the arrival of two of-counsels dealing with equity offerings and debt financings (Scott Saks and Erwan Barre). The firm is also recognised as an expert in the area of corporate governance.

Simmons & Simmons' capital markets team is led by Arnauld Achard and focuses on structured securities, securitisation, CDOs (cash and synthetic), derivatives, funds and regulatory work. Clients include Barclays, Lehman Brothers, Citigroup and IXIS Asset Management.

White & Case LLP's practice concentrates on complex structured transactions. Last year, the team that includes Vincent Morin, Gilles Peigney and other coprorate partners, advised Echostar in its negotiations with Archos and its subscription of newly issued Archos preferred shares; the bondholders (Oceane) in the public exchange offer launched by Infogrammes; and Wendel Investissement in the acquisition of Bureau Veritas which included an offer of Wendel Investissement listed shares to Bureau Veritas shareholders in France and abroad.

CONSTRUCTION

CONSTRUCTION

BOUSQUET

PROSKAUER ROSE LLP ✪

GRANGE & ASSOCIÉS
KARILA & ASSOCIÉS
LEFÈVRE PELLETIER & ASSOCIÉS ✪

- Bignon Lebray & Associés
- Cabouche Gabrielli Marquet
- Caston
- Charles Sirat - Jean-Paul Gilli
- Clyde & Co ✪
- Flécheux & Associés
- Foucaud Tchekhoff Pochet & Associés
- Gide Loyrette Nouel ✪
- Le Mazou Associés
- Michel Tirard
- Naba et Associés
- Neveu Sudaka & Associés
- Orrick, Herrington & Sutcliffe ✪
- Raffin & Associés
- Vatier & Associés ✪
- White & Case LLP

Firms are listed A-Z in tiers which are ranked in order of priority
✪ Indicates firm displays contact details at the end of this chapter.

Bousquet's long-standing and close relationship with leading French construction company Bouygues has allowed this *généraliste* firm to develop a leading specialist construction practice, with seven dedicated lawyers. The firm also advises on property transactions.

The other leading firm is **Proskauer Rose LLP**, after a specialised team from *Rambaud Martel* joined at the end of 2005 with Christophe Lapp, Jean-Philippe Sorba and Emmanuelle Payrau-Sorba. It lists major public contractors among its clientele (Roissy CDG airport, Ministry of Finance, Pompidou Centre, among others). The construction department has attained a position of strength in recent years, being especially highly regarded for contract work and major construction projects, where the firm deals with the financing, building, maintenance and exploitation of the project. The firm also handles partnership contracts, insurance and disputes.

Claude Grange (**Grange & Associés**) is a leading expert in French public construction law. With partners Florence Alonso-Martin and Rajess Ramdenie, the firm has an impressive track record in town-planning, infrastructure management and delegation of public services, mainly on the public actors' side, but also working alongside major French building companies.

In construction insurance, **Karila & Associés** is a first-choice firm. Jean-Pierre Karila advised on the Crédit Lyonnais fire case and is expert on the liability of builders, property developers, architects, and research consultancies.

Real estate accounts for a significant part of **Lefèvre Pelletier & Associés**' practice. Construction and town-planning are frequent matters for the firm, including on the litigation and arbitration side. The firm is often instructed on the developer's side.

The activity of **Cabouche Gabrielli Marquet**, **Caston**, **Clyde & Co**, **Neveu Sudaka & Associés**, **Raffin & Associés** and **Naba et Associés**, is very much linked to insurance, and **Charles Sirat - Jean-Paul Gilli** more to town-planning. **Gide Loyrette Nouel** is well known for high-level construction litigation cases. Jean-Jacques Raquin and Eric Martin-Impératori are experts in the negotiation of acquisition contracts and in the processes required to obtain all related administrative authorisation. **Le Mazou Associés** has particular expertise in property development (project management, sales and acquisitions). **Michel Tirard** is well known for advising property developers on planning matters.

The team at **Orrick, Herrington & Sutcliffe** (formerly *Rambaud Martel*) comprises Frédéric Torron and Bruno Richard.

Foucaud Tchekhoff Pochet & Associés and **Bignon Lebray & Associés** are also recommended.

At **White & Case LLP**, the team comprises partners Christopher Seppala on the construction arbitration side, and Jacques Bouillon on the corporate side.

CORPORATE AND COMMERCIAL

As in previous years, it is important to point out that we have omitted firms like **Bredin Prat**, **Darrois Villey Maillot Brochier** and **Brandford-Griffith & Associés** from this section on the basis that their activity, high-level though it is, is largely transactional M&A and does not cover the full range of corporate and commercial work. See the separate Mergers and acquisitions section, below.

Gide Loyrette Nouel remains the benchmark French firm and has the highest number of renowned teams in Paris: M&A, banking and finance, capital markets, commercial property, public law, IP, litigation, arbitration, labour, tax, transport and insurance, to mention some of them. With 17 offices abroad and some 200 lawyers outside France, **Gide Loyrette Nouel** is also one of the few French firms with an international presence. This year again, the firm has carried on its development with double-digit turnover growth.

International firm **Cleary, Gottlieb, Steen & Hamilton LLP** continues to enjoy the enviable position of being a US firm regarded locally as a fully-fledged French firm equipped with polyvalent lawyers working on non-standard issues. Traditionally known for its banking clientele, the firm has expanded its commercial practice, as evidenced by its evermore-frequent incursions into high-level takeover bids. Equally, the firm has taken its place among the best firms in other practice areas, such as capital markets and privatisation, tax, European law and is becoming increasingly visible in litigation and arbitration.

Clifford Chance's origins in Paris are in finance and property. The practice is now vast: the main areas of activity remain financing (of acquisitions, projects and property), but other strengths include M&A and private equity, capital markets, EU and competition, environmental law, tax, public law, litigation and arbitration. 2004-05 was a year of consolidation, with 3% growth in turnover.

After several years of impressive growth, **Freshfields Bruckhaus Deringer**'s turnover is now stable. Although the firm continues to be recognised for its banking, finance and capital markets work (with a new US equities capability), its activities in cross-border M&A also rank highly. The firm's arbitration practice is recognised worldwide. Additional strengths include employment, property, tax, litigation, IP, energy and public law, and competition and EU law.

CORPORATE AND COMMERCIAL

GIDE LOYRETTE NOUEL ✪

CLEARY, GOTTLIEB, STEEN & HAMILTON LLP ✪
CLIFFORD CHANCE
FRESHFIELDS BRUCKHAUS DERINGER
LATHAM & WATKINS
LINKLATERS ✪
ORRICK, HERRINGTON & SUTCLIFFE ✪

ALLEN & OVERY LLP ✪
CMS BUREAU FRANCIS LEFEBVRE ✪
DE PARDIEU BROCAS MAFFEI ✪
JEANTETASSOCIÉS ✪
JONES DAY ✪
LOVELLS ✪
PAUL, HASTINGS, JANOFSKY & WALKER (EUROPE) LLP ✪
SALANS
SHEARMAN & STERLING LLP
WHITE & CASE LLP
WILLKIE FARR & GALLAGHER LLP ✪

Ashurst ✪
August & Debouzy
Baker & McKenzie SCP ✪
Bird & Bird ✪
Herbert Smith LLP ✪
Lefèvre Pelletier & associés ✪
Norton Rose
Sullivan & Cromwell LLP
UGGC & Associés ✪
Veil Jourde ✪

Bignon Lebray & Associés
DS Avocats
Debevoise & Plimpton LLP ✪
Dechert ✪
Denton Wilde Sapte ✪
Ernst & Young Société d'Avocats
Fidal ✪
Flécheux & Associés
Franklin ✪
Ginestié Magellan Paley-Vincent ✪
Granrut Avocats
Hughes Hubbard & Reed LLP ✪
Kahn & Associés
Morgan Lewis ✪
SJ Berwin ✪
Simmons & Simmons ✪
Sokolow, Carreras & Associés
Skadden, Arps, Slate, Meagher & Flom LLP
Weil, Gotshal & Manges ✪

Continued

Latham & Watkins, after an impressive year in 2004 with six significant lateral hires that brought the number of partners in the Paris office to 34, had a busy 2005 integrating the new teams which have generated a lot of work. These changes have strenghtened the practices in private equity, capital markets and litigation. **Latham & Watkins** is now more visible in the Paris market and a true full-service firm with strong teams in corporate, finance, IP/IT and media, EU and competition, employment, tax and litigation. Securitisation and arbitration are also developing.

Initially well known in Paris for corporate and finance law, **Linklaters** has increased its scope and has become a full-service firm. This expansion is especially pronounced in the areas of tax, EU law, property, IP, public law and M&A, including stock-exchange issues and private equity. The historically well-developed capital markets practice is now complemented by impressive banking and finance expertise, including project finance.

Orrick, Herrington & Sutcliffe is now a major full-service firm after merging with *Rambaud Martel*. Although it was only half of the French firm that joined the US structure at the end of 2005, the profile of the new firm brings together one of the best possible combinations of high-level litigation and top advisory practices. *Rambaud Martel* brought strong M&A, corporate, commercial and dispute resolution teams, while **Orrick, Herrington & Sutcliffe** was already a top player on the finance scene. Other areas of law where the two firms can combine strengths are tax, competition, labour, IP/IT, insolvency, public, real estate, construction and insurance law.

Allen & Overy LLP hosts 115 lawyers in Paris and has been expanding quickly over the past few years, with double-digit turnover growth in 2004/2005. The M&A, banking and finance and capital markets teams remain the pillars of the practice, but with growing tax, competition (with a lateral hire in 2005), administrative, labour law and dispute resolution expertise. **Allen & Overy LLP** also has a top-tier intellectual property department. The firm boasts a highly international client base, acting in particular for a large number of major banks.

CMS Bureau Francis Lefebvre's activity is solid, supported by a wide client base. Belonging to the *CMS* alliance has strengthened the firm's international presence and its transactional practice. The firm remains the reference for tax in France. That said, **CMS Bureau Francis Lefebvre** now achieves half of its turnover from its other advisory activities with a strong employment law team and abilities in real estate, EU and competition, and corporate/M&A. The firm is also present in Lyon and Strasbourg.

Still considered one of the jewels in the banking and finance sector, **De Pardieu Brocas Maffei** is a multi-service firm, complementing its traditional activities in banking and finance with M&A, capital markets, commercial property, insolvency, litigation, insurance and tax. In 2005, **De Pardieu Brocas Maffei** continued growing, especially in property, M&A, public and EU law.

JeantetAssociés has decided to concentrate on practice areas with high added value and, after reducing its size considerably a few years ago and increasing its profitability at the same time, the firm is now growing. **JeantetAssociés** practises in areas related to M&A and litigation and is also visible in finance, EU and competition, tax, employment, real estate, insolvency and public law. The firm is determined to carry on as an independent player.

Still strong in coporate/M&A, finance, EU and competition, real estate, litigation and arbitration, **Jones Day** is increasingly visible in public law/PPP, environment, tax and capital markets, with lateral hires in these areas. Other fields covered include IP and labour law.

Lovells is a full-service firm, with a stable turnover despite the reduced size of its coporate department after a few departures in 2005. Development is now again centred on corporate activities, whilst **Lovells** remains strong in banking, finance (including PPP) and capital markets. The firm is also strong in IP/IT, competition, and restructuring. The growing litigation dimension of the firm is worth mentioning.

Moquet Borde & Associés is now **Paul, Hastings, Janofsky & Walker (Europe) LLP**'s Paris office. The firm's core business remains corporate/M&A and litigation but other assets include tax, EU and competition, commercial property, white-collar crime, corporate governance and stock exchange law. It has strengthened its international corporate and capital markets capacity with the addition of US attorneys.

A French/US firm with a presence in Eastern Europe from its origins, international firm **Salans** is now well balanced between Europe, North America and the East. The firm totals 450 lawyers with about 130 partners worldwide, one-third of them in Paris. A full-service firm, **Salans** is particularly prominent in pharmaceuticals, luxury goods, aerospace, sport and venture capital. The firm's more visible areas of expertise are M&A, IP/IT, tax, arbitration and litigation and it has strenghtened its property, IP, corporate, labour, public and banking practices in 2005/2006, notably by welcoming a 15-lawyer team from *Rambaud Martel*. Other developments are expected in antitrust.

Shearman & Sterling LLP has built its practice in Paris around international arbitration and equity capital markets expertise. The arbitration practice has expanded considerably into litigation, often with an international dimension, and the firm's knowledge of the stock markets complements a good practice in the financial markets and in M&A, where the firm is willing to develop (private equity and stock market transactions). The firm is also active in EU and competition law, in tax and environment. The client base is mainly industrial and includes large international organisations.

At **White & Case LLP**, the finance practice is large, covering acquisitions and all types of structured finance, projects and property. The M&A activity, an all-round practice with a strong involvement in LBOs, is also recommended, as are the arbitration, litigation, EU and competition, employment, tax, real estate and construction teams.

CORPORATE AND COMMERCIAL
Continued

Adamas ✪
Ayache Salama & Associés ✪
BMH Avocats - Breitenstein Meillassoux Hauser ✪
Bersay & Associés ✪
Cotty Vivant Marchisio & Lauzeral
Courtois Lebel
De Gaulle Fleurance & Associés ✪
Deprez Dian Guignot ✪
Dubarry Le Douarin Veil ✪
Eversheds-Frere Cholmeley
Fried, Frank, Harris, Shriver & Jacobson LLP
Gibson, Dunn & Crutcher LLP
Hammonds Hausmann
Hogan & Hartson MNP ✪
KGA Avocats
Kramer Levin Naftalis & Frankel LLP ✪
Landwell & Associés
LeBoeuf, Lamb, Greene & Macrae LLP ✪
Ngo Miguérès & Associés
NomoS ✪
Proskauer Rose LLP ✪
Reed Smith Rambaud Charot LLP ✪
Stehlin & Associés
Taj ✪
Vivien & Juvigny

Continued

US-based **Willkie Farr & Gallagher LLP** is renowned for M&A, being a leader in LBOs in Paris. The firm also enjoys a good reputation in tax, capital markets and finance. Lately, it lost an insolvency team.

Ashurst is known particularly for its M&A, LBO and acquisition finance expertise. The client base is mainly made up of banks and investment funds from around the globe. The firm is also developing tax, property, EU law and litigation/arbitration practices, in order to offer an integrated practice across Europe.

August & Debouzy is a young, full-service firm founded in 1995 and comprising 85 lawyers. The firm's main practices include M&A, privatisation, administrative and economic law, employment, IT, IP and real estate, not to mention its contentious expertise. Clients include France Télécom, Vivendi Universal, Philip Morris, Air France and Microsoft. The firm has an international network of best friends with firms such as **Covington & Burling** (US) and **Nabarro Nathanson** (UK).

Baker & McKenzie's Paris office focuses on company law and M&A, particularly in the industrial fields, but the firm also has strong practices in tax, IP, telecoms and IT, EU and competition, real estate, public and environmental law, labour and litigation. It intends to develop in the banking and finance field.

Bird & Bird offers a service with a specialisation in the media, communications and information technology sectors, as well as expertise in all aspects of business law: EU and competition law, IP (with the arrival of a new team in 2005), life sciences, tax, labour law, litigation, public law, corporate, aviation and private equity. The team comprises 65 lawyers, including 16 partners.

Herbert Smith LLP is well established in Paris, and is consolidating in its core business – corporate work, finance, projects/energy, litigation/arbitration, the latter two being areas where the firm is particularly strong. Other practices include IP, EU law, tax and employment. In 2005, the firm recruited a strong real estate team. **Herbert Smith LLP** also enjoys an international alliance with **Stibbe** and **Gleiss Lutz**.

Lefèvre Pelletier & Associés stands out for its expertise in commercial property (38% of its turnover), but has diversified into other areas of commercial practice. Notably, the firm is active in M&A/LBO, labour, tax, finance, insurance and litigation. The firm's turnover has doubled in four years. It now numbers 140 lawyers including 30 partners and has offices in Hong Kong and Canton, opened in 2005.

Norton Rose's practice in Paris is well balanced between corporate and commercial on the one hand and banking and finance on the other. Thus, the firm is active in asset finance (with a major lateral hire in this practice in 2005), structured, acquisition, project/PPP and energy finance and its corporate capability encompasses M&A, private equity, IP/IT, competition, tax, employment and dispute resolution. Further expansion is expected in the real estate field.

Sullivan & Cromwell LLP's practice centres on international securities offerings by French issuers, privatisation and M&A. The firm is also recognised for its project finance and tax expertise. Some 30 lawyers, including seven partners, work in the Paris office.

UGGC & Associés, with around 90 lawyers, is a commercial all-rounder, as active in M&A as it is in public law, insolvency and dispute resolution. Tax, labour law, corporate and public law are the areas where growth is particularly significant. The firm has further offices in Brussels and Casablanca.

Veil Jourde has two main areas of activity. In M&A, the firm is involved in public offerings, privatisations, LBOs and restructurings. Its reputation is equally well established in litigation, including criminal and commercial proceedings. At the same time, the firm is involved in other areas such as tax, IP and contracts, public law and insolvency.

Bignon Lebray & Associés is a general commercial firm, offering both advisory and contentious capability. **Bignon Lebray & Associés** is a founder member of *Meritas* and has offices in Lyon, Lille and Aix-en-Provence, thus covering France from north to south. The firm's range of services includes company law, M&A, banking and finance, tax, labour, international mobility, property and construction, public and IP/media law.

With about 90 lawyers, **DS Avocats** is a full-service firm known particularly for its EU and competition practice as well as business administrative law. Moreover, the firm is one of the few French firms with offices in Asia (China, Singapore, South Korea and Vietnam), as well as in Lyon, Brussels, London and Barcelona.

The activities of **Debevoise & Plimpton LLP** in Paris revolve around six core practices: M&A, private equity, capital markets, finance, EU/competition and arbitration. The firm offers some 40 lawyers, and has experienced steady growth since 2002 with the arrival of several high-calibre practitioners.

When *Coudert Frères* closed down in the summer 2005, six out of the eight partners and 30 associates joined forces with the Paris office of **Dechert**. The new firm comprises 11 partners active in corporate, M&A, private equity and financings, litigation and arbitration, life sciences, tax and labour law. The firm retains an international clientele, mainly industrial, and is working on reinforcing its French corporate activities.

Denton Wilde Sapte's activity revolves around four areas: technology, media and telecoms; energy, transport and infrastructure; real estate and retail; and financial institutions. The firm is active in M&A and joint ventures, litigation, IP/IT, tax and employment and is strengthening in finance and public law.

Ernst & Young Société d'Avocats is the new entity formed after the two legal arms of the international MDPs merged in Paris at the end of 2002. Despite losses affecting the tax and corporate practices, the new firm boasts 600 fee-earners in 13 offices across France. The core business revolves around corporate tax, labour law, human capital and M&A, but the firm is also present in indirect tax, IP/IT and litigation/ arbitration.

National firm **Fidal** is best known for its tax expertise and for being the largest firm in the country. However, the Paris office is also extensively involved in labour law, company and commercial issues and competition, for a clientele of small and medium-sized companies and blue-chips. Additionally, the firm offers niche practices such as health, tourism and sports law.

Flécheux & Associés is made up of eight partners active in public and environmental law, construction, insurance, M&A, IP, distribution and commercial law. The contentious dimension of the firm is important, including white-collar crime. Abroad, **Flécheux & Associés** has an office in Vietnam, is close to a firm in Belgium and has links with Lebanon and North Africa.

Franklin has expertise in M&A, projects, administrative law, litigation and IT. The 40-strong firm has also set up tax, employment and private equity teams. The firm regularly acts for blue-chips like France Télécom and SNCF.

Ginestié, Paley-Vincent & Associés merged with *Magellan* in 2005 to form **Ginestié Magellan Paley-Vincent**, a firm with offices in Paris and Lyon and with a foothold in London and Milan (opened in 2005). The firm's main focus is M&A, with specialisms in LBOs and risk capital. Other services offered include international tax, IP/IT, litigation, health and labour law.

Granrut Avocats is comprised of 40 lawyers and specialises in corporate, insolvency, IP and media, banking, public and environmental law, real estate and insurance, labour law, mainly with a contentious angle (including arbitration and white-collar crime). In the past two years, the firm has doubled in size and four partners have joined the firm. Alliances have been established with UK firm **Pinsent Masons** and Scandinavian firm **MAQS Advokatbyrå**.

Hughes Hubbard & Reed LLP's most visible practice is international arbitration. However, the firm remains active in corporate and corporate finance, IT, commercial property and labour law. The firm has recently increased its capacity in arbitration, corporate and tax.

Kahn & Associés' practice is entirely dedicated to new technology and e-commerce. Clients include international IT companies with interests in France, investment funds and traditional French blue-chips embarking on e-commerce and start-up projects.

Morgan Lewis was born in 2004 when the firm from Philadelphia took over an 18-lawyer team from **De Pardieu Brocas Maffei**. In 2005, a finance team joined from **Orrick, Herrington & Sutcliffe**. The practice is full service with a strong corporate department and expertise in finance, labour, competition, new technologies, tax and public law.

The Paris office of **SJ Berwin** opened in 2001 and has grown to a practice of some 40 lawyers. A leading private equity firm in Paris, **SJ Berwin** has expertise in fund formation, LBOs and M&A, tax and EU and competition, and developed the financing aspect of acquisitions and the real estate capacity in 2005 with the arrival of two partners.

Simmons & Simmons' activity is equally split between three main practices: corporate and projects, litigation and arbitration, finance and capital markets. Employment and tax are also dealt with. The firm is now focusing on specific areas like energy, finance and pharmaceuticals. It

CORPORATE AND COMMERCIAL
Continued

ASA Avocats Associés
Ader Amigues & Jolibois
Alerion ✪
Alexen Avocats
Avens Lehman & Associés
BMS', Association d'Avocats
Barbé Carpentier Thibault Groener & Associés
Barsi Doumith & Associés
Berlioz & Co
Bernard Hertz Béjot
Bernet Castagnet Wantz & Associés
Bertagna
Bousquet
Carbonnier Lamaze Rasle & Associés
Cayol, Cahen & Associés
Chaintrier & Associés
Cornet Vincent Ségurel
Cournot Association d'Avocats ✪
Curtis, Mallet-Prevost, Colt & Mosle LLP ✪
DLA Piper Rudnick Gray Cary US LLP, correspondents of Cariddi, Mee, Rue, association d'avocats au barreau de Paris ✪
Delsol & Associés ✪
Falque & Associés
Farthouat Asselineau & Associés
Foucaud Tchekhoff Pochet & Associés
Gaillot, Bouchony & Associés
LMT Avocats
LSK & Associés
La Boétie
Lacourte Balas & Associés
Lamy & Associés ✪
Lamy Lexel Avocats Associés
Lartigue Tournois & Associés
Latournerie Wolfrom & Associés ✪
Lipworth, Cabinet ✪
Lussan Brouillaud
Mayer, Brown, Rowe & Maw LLP ✪
Moisand Boutin & Associés
Neveu Sudaka & Associés
P.D.G.B.
Pascal Wilhelm & Associés
Racine
Ratheaux ✪
Reinhart Marville Torre
Senave, Noreils, Ang
Soulier
Taylor Wessing ✪
Thieffry & Associés
Vaïsse, Brémond, Rambert & Associés
Vatier & Associés ✪
Vendôme
Vovan & Associés
Wilinski Scotto & Associés
Winston & Strawn LLP ✪

Firms are listed A-Z in tiers which are ranked in order of priority
✪ Indicates firm displays contact details at the end of this chapter.

suffered the loss of three partners in 2005, affecting mainly the private equity and finance activities.

Sokolow, Carreras & Associés is the new name for *Sokolow Dunaud Mercadier Carreras* after a few lawyers left in 2004 for **Latham & Watkins** and **Norton Rose**. Its contentious practice is noted, as well as its company law and M&A work, including private equity. Media and IP also account for a significant part of the firm's business and it benefits from offices in Brussels and New York.

With 30 lawyers in Paris, **Skadden, Arps, Slate, Meagher & Flom LLP** is known for its M&A (especially in public transactions) and capital markets work. The firm particularly stands out in cross-border deals and investments abroad and acts for major companies in the banking, telecoms, air and space, entertainment and luxury goods sectors. Areas of development are M&A-related litigation, tax and international arbitration.

Weil, Gotshal & Manges merged with *Serra, Leavy & Cazals* in January 2003. The firm, with about 35 lawyers, is active in corporate, M&A, LBOs (with one of the best teams in Paris), tax, litigation, media and IT law, insolvency and European law. It is growing quickly and the insolvency capacity was increased by the arrival of a high-level team.

Adamas is in Lyon (40 lawyers) and in Paris (15). Abroad, the firm has five offices in Asia (China, Taiwan, Korea) and one in Brussels. An all-round corporate law firm (M&A, IP, contracts, distribution, labour, among other areas), **Adamas** is visible in litigation/arbitration, public and environmental law, with a focus on international matters.

Ayache Salama & Associés now comprises 35 lawyers, half of them being active in corporate finance. Tax and public law have always been core practice areas, with the addition of private equity expertise following the merger with *Tordjman & Associés* in 2004 adding welcome expertise. The firm is also active in litigation (post-merger and white-collar crime), distribution and competition.

BMH Avocats - Breitenstein Meillassoux Hauser is a mid-size firm active in corporate and commercial law, intellectual property and new technologies. Its practice is also directed towards Germany with several bi-cultural practitioners within the 25-lawyer team.

Twenty-five lawyers, including three partners and two of-counsels, work for **Bersay & Associés**. Activity is mostly international, at 60%, with clients including some of the biggest industrial companies in France, as well as some multinationals. The firm handles M&A, capital investment, restructurings, dispute resolution, competition and distribution, IP and telecoms, contracts, labour and tax. An office in Toulouse was opened in 2005.

Created in 2004, **Cotty Vivant Marchisio & Lauzeral** is a promising young firm with 18 lawyers. Its core activities are M&A, restructurings and acquisition finance, commercial and securities litigation and employment law.

Courtois Lebel was created in 1969 and is now made up of eleven partners. The firm has eight departments: IP, IT, health law, projects and industrial risk, competition and distribution, banking law, M&A and stock exchange law and labour law.

De Gaulle Fleurance & Associés houses 38 lawyers, including seven partners, and was formed from a split from **August & Debouzy** in 2001. Work rests on two main activities: corporate (including financings, restructurings, tax) and IP/IT, media, with expertise in the health sector.

Initially active in a media/IP/advertising niche, **Deprez Dian Guignot** has now widely increased its scope of interventions. With some 40 lawyers, the firm specialises in banking and finance, corporate law and M&A, insolvency, labour law, competition, and IP/IT.

Dubarry Le Douarin Veil was created 20 years ago as a commercial litigation firm. It has since developed advisory and contentious practices in the following fields: banking and finance, corporate/M&A (with a lateral hire in 2005), insolvency, labour and competition, and finally IP/IT, an area where the firm is particularly visible. The firm now counts 45 lawyers and is a founding member of *The European Legal Alliance*.

Eversheds-Frere Cholmeley has developed consistently in the past three years in Paris and is now structured around four core activities: corporate/M&A, litigation/arbitration (with the arrival of a new partner this year) and, more recently set up, employment, banking and finance and real estate.

Fried, Frank, Harris, Shriver & Jacobson LLP is getting more visible in Paris with the recruitment of two teams in 2005: one in M&A/private equity, and the other in insolvency (signing at the same time an alliance with insolvency and commercial litigation firm, **Lantourne Duret & Associés**). Main areas of practice remain M&A, corporate finance and capital markets.

Gibson, Dunn & Crutcher LLP in Paris (17 fee-earners) concentrates on corporate, mainly private and public acquisitions, very often for French clients in connection with a US/France transaction. The firm recently acquired a public law capacity and also handles capital markets work and tax law.

Thirty-two-lawyer **Hammonds Hausmann** is the result of the merger in 2001 of *Hausmann & Associés* with UK firm **Hammonds** and is dedicated to M&A and private equity, commercial law and IT, dispute resolution, tax and employment law. Clients have an industrial (space, defence) or contractual (distribution, joint ventures) profile.

Hogan & Hartson MNP has an office in Paris since the end of 2004 when it ended its correspondence link with **Cariddi, Mee, Rué**. The firm is building up a new team with strengths in telecoms, capital markets, EU and competition, labour law, and with further developments expected in tax, projects, M&A and arbitration.

Fifty-lawyer **KGA Avocats** in Paris, Lyon, Bordeaux and Marseille, is the result of a merger with the Paris office of *Theodore Goddard* and *Klein & Associés* in 1993. The firm's practice is a general corporate and international one with a focus on dispute resolution, M&A, IP, property, labour and public law and specific areas covered such as space, sport, defence, media and Francophone Africa law.

When **Clifford Chance** merged with *Rogers & Wells*, lawyers of the Paris office of the US firm joined **Kramer Levin Naftalis & Frankel LLP**. The firm has now 20 lawyers in Paris mainly specialising in corporate law with a financial angle, and also dealing with litigation, insolvency and tax. Recent developments include the arrival of an insurance specialist and a labour law team. The firm corresponds with **Berwin Leighton Paisner LLP** in the UK.

Landwell & Associés numbers some 415 lawyers across France (ten offices). Like the other former Big Four firms, a good proportion of its work lies in corporate tax, but labour law, private tax and all other types of advisory work are also handled.

LeBoeuf, Lamb, Greene & Macrae LLP is made up of 22 lawyers and work is equally divided between dispute resolution, corporate and private equity (venture capital) with the arrival of a new partner, insurance and reinsurance. The firm also has capability in contracts, tax, employment and capital markets.

Ngo Miguérès & Associés has always been an international firm, has two offices in Vietnam (in partnership with **Flécheux & Associés**) and is also in Italy and Mexico. The firm's 40 lawyers handle corporate and commercial matters for international investors and can also deal with contracts, banking law, IP/IT, labour and tax law, litigation.

NomoS has more than 35 lawyers and is developing a complete range of services, with a focus on media/communications and IT/IP, private equity, consumer goods, distribution, and the food and health industries.

Proskauer Rose LLP's Paris office is its only one outside the US. It recently doubled in size by welcoming a team from *Rambaud Martel* made of six partners with a strong reputation in construction and related areas (public law, insurance, property etc). More generally, the firm's core practices are: corporate, commercial, labour, tax and commercial litigation. **Proskauer Rose LLP** represents a wide variety of US and other multinational groups with business activities in France and Europe, as well as some of the largest French companies in the financial, oil, chemical, pharmaceutical, telecoms, consumer products and leisure sectors.

Reed Smith Rambaud Charot LLP is a split from *Rambaud Martel* at the time of the merger with **Orrick, Herrington & Sutcliffe**. Four partners set up the Paris office of the US firm. Their activity is both advisory (corporate/M&A/LBO) and contentious, serving the traditional areas covered by the firm: pharmaceuticals and health, financial services, distribution and industry.

Stehlin & Associés is a mid-size firm (30 lawyers) mainly active in corporate and tax but that also covers IT and public law. It is part of *Osborne Clark Alliance* and *Interlaw* and works for several US companies such as Nike and Pizza Hut.

Taj is the new name of *Deloitte & Touche Juridique et Fiscal*. With offices in seven cities in France and some 250 lawyers and tax specialists, the firm is most active in tax but covers other areas of law. Some industries where it is active include; health, property, defence, food, luxury, distribution, textile, and sport.

Vivien & Juvigny was born when two teams got together in 2004. The first one originated from various international firms and set up the firm in 2000 around an international corporate, M&A, tax and labour practice. The second one, coming from *Rambaud Martel*, brought two EU and competition partners and a pharmaceutical law partner. The firm now numbers 21 lawyers.

ASA Avocats Associés is a major firm in Strasbourg with an office in Paris. More information is available in the final section, **The Regions**.

Ader Amigues & Jolibois was founded by ex-head of the Paris Bar Henri Ader. Its practice is predominantly contentious with eight partners dealing with general business litigation, arbitration, white-collar crime, bankruptcy and press law.

Alerion was founded by seven partners, most of them formerly a *Bignon Lebray & Associés*. More than 25 lawyers are active with a focus on property, construction and insurance. They also handle corporate law, M&A, documentary credit, tax, employment, competition, distribution, and health law.

Alexen Avocats is an EIG of several firms in the process of merging with offices in Paris, Lyon and Marseille. They are mainly active in corporate/M&A, tax, labour law, IT, international trade and customs. Clients are mostly found among mid-cap companies.

Avens Lehman & Associés was set up in 1990. With 15 lawyers, the firm belongs to the *BGI* network and is visible in EU and competition law but also active in labour law, IP/IT/media, corporate and commercial. 60% of the activity is contentious.

BMS', Association d'Avocats was created when *Caubet Chouchana Meyer* split up in 2005. Four partners set up the firm with a focus on the real estate business, although tax, private equity and distribution are also dealt with.

Barbé Carpentier Thibault Groener & Associés' core activity is corporate law with eight out of eleven partners specialising in M&A, private equity and joint ventures. Clients are foreign groups at 80% (US, UK and Asia mainly). Other areas of law covered are competition, labour law, IP, projects, contracts and distribution, insolvency and litigation.

Bernard Hertz Béjot has always had an international vocation with 75% of its clients foreign and seven partners bilingual English or trilingual German. Its business law activity is equally balanced between litigation and counsel: M&A, corporate and commercial, competition, IP/IT, insurance and stock market law.

Bernet Castagnet Wantz & Associés was created in 2003 by an ex-**Shearman & Sterling LLP** partner and two litigators, later joined by a tax expert. The firm advises mid-cap companies in international transactions and has a general contentious practice for clients like clinics.

Bertagna has eight lawyers who are active in company and commercial law, labour and insurance, litigation. From its origins back in 1991 the firm has had close links with Italy, Greece, United States, and Great Britain (in alliance with **Berrymans Lace Mawer**).

Carbonnier Lamaze Rasle & Associés' practice is still based on the name partners' specialities: public law, M&A, media law, banking law. More recently, the firm has developed expertise in tax, international corporate, press law, competition and distribution in the luxury goods industry. In 2005, it merged with *Croizat & Huguenin* in Lyon.

Chaintrier & Associés has some 30 lawyers including nine partners. Founded in 1982, the firm assists his clients in M&A and corporate finance. Other practice areas are tax, contracts and distribution, insolvency, labour law and litigation.

Cornet Vincent Ségurel is a major firm in Nantes with an office in Paris. More information are available in the **The Regions** section.

Cournot Association d'Avocats is a medium-sized firm with 25 lawyers. Its core business is corporate and M&A but it also works in employment law, litigation and arbitration and IT. Clients are industrials and financial institutions.

Curtis, Mallet-Prevost, Colt & Mosle LLP is a New York firm with ten offices around the world. The Paris office work is the reflection of the firm's global strengths: corporate and international arbitration. Three partners are active in France.

Delsol & Associés is a major firm in Lyon with an office in Paris. More information is available in the **The Regions** section.

Falque & Associés is a full-service firm with 30 lawyers. Areas of law handled include IP, litigation and arbitration, commercial property, corporate, tax, employment.

Founded in 1968 **Farthouat Asselineau & Associés** is above all a litigation firm. It is also very active in white-collar crime and arbitration. Some 20 lawyers (ten partners) also assist their clients in company, insurance and labour law.

Foucaud Tchekhoff Pochet & Associés has been practising for more than 30 years. Its 11 partners are active in corporate law, M&A, banking and finance, IP/IT, labour law, competition and distribution, litigation and arbitration. Sport law, tax and real property are also handled.

Gaillot, Bouchony & Associés has four partners and specialises in international business law, helping French and foreign companies in their investments and activities in and outside France. Main areas of law covered are M&A, litigation, international trade, labour law, IP, press law, telecoms and media,

LMT Avocats is a firm with strong Franco-German activity although international business law is handled in a broader sense. Twenty-five lawyers offer capability in M&A, tax, labour law, industrial risks, pharmeceuticals law, IP, litigation and arbitration.

LSK & Associés has seven partners and is mainly active in M&A/LBO and general corporate work including financings and restructurings.

La Boétie is the result of the merger of several teams from various firms (**Clifford Chance**, **NomoS**, *BDFT*) in 2004. Five of the eight partners have a general corporate practice (including private equity). The rest is made of international contracts, tax, insolvency, litigation, IP/IT and media law.

Lacourte Balas & Associés was founded in 1973 and has eight partners. Half of its activity is related to the real estate industry, an area where the firm is increasingly visible with recent hires. The firm is also involved in general corporate and finance work, including their contentious aspects. It has a link with a US firm.

LAMY & ASSOCIES and **Lamy Lexel Avocats Associés** are major firms in Lyon with offices in Paris. More information is available in the **The Regions** section.

Lartigue Tournois & Associés specialises in media law, corporate and commercial law, and in labour law. It also has abilities in transport and insurance and has strong links with the Arabic world.

Latournerie Wolfrom & Associés was set up in 1995 by lawyers from *Moquet Borde & Associés* and has now more than 20 lawyers. The firm is particularly visible in new technologies, public law, financings, insolvency, commercial law and distribution.

Cabinet Lipworth was created by Frank Lipworth in 1997 after years spent at **Nabarro Nathanson** and **Bredin Prat**. Five lawyers handle M&A, joint ventures, corporate finance, commercial law and litigation. The firm is close to firms in the UK and in Switzerland.

Lussan Brouillaud is an 18-lawyer law firm founded in 1932 and with strong activity in banking law (litigation, regulatory etc). A second important activity is press law and human rights, within a broader contentious practice that includes white-collar crime. Finally, a corporate and M&A practice is developing, while public law is handled by an individual firm on the same premises (**Cazin**). The firm has a good knowledge of Bulgaria and Azerbaijan.

In Paris, **Mayer, Brown, Rowe & Maw LLP** has more than 30 lawyers with a general corporate and corporate finance practice. The firm has been very active on the private equity scene recently, while being less successful in the setting up of a property team. It also deals with structured finance, capital markets, tax and environment.

Nine-partner **Moisand Boutin & Associés** originates from *PriceWaterhouse Juridique et Fiscal*. It has a strong tax practice but the arrival of a corporate partner in 2005 has increased its involvement in other areas of law. M&A, IP, banking and finance, dispute resolution, employment and real estate are all on offer.

Neveu Sudaka & Associés now has ten partners. The firm offers a full service (corporate and commercial, banking and finance, insolvency) but is especially known in the property and construction fields where it covers all aspects, including leases, town-planning, public law and insurance.

Founded in 1985, **P.D.G.B.** dedicates about half of its activity to tax work (seven partners out of 19). Other important practice areas are labour law and M&A (three new partners arrived in 2005, including two specialists of Franco-German relationships), with a renowned team in venture capital.

Pascal Wilhelm & Associés is active in some specific areas: advertising, media, supermarkets and distribution. The four partners handle litigation, competition and distribution law, public law, IP and media law.

Racine has offices in Paris, Lyon, Marseille and Bordeaux. With some 40 lawyers, it is a full-service firm, without a tax capacity though. Half of the activity is contentious and the firm is part of the *TAGlaw* network.

Ratheaux is a major firm in Lyon with an office in Paris. More information can be found in **The Regions** section.

Reinhart Marville Torre is correspondant to Canadian firm **Davies Ward Phillips & Vineberg LLP**. Business is equally spread between counsel and litigation. Contentious work is mainly financial and corporate litigation as well as IP, labour and competition. Corporate work, including capital markets, is handled for clients in the capital investment, pharmaceuticals and supermarkets sectors.

Senave, Noreils, Ang is a split from **Duclos Thorne Mollet-Viéville & Associés**. Three partners have a general corporate practice with a focus on IP, labour law, M&A, media law, contract, commercial litigation and white-collar crime.

Soulier is a major firm in Lyon with an office in Paris. See **The Regions** for further information.

Taylor Wessing is a European firm with main offices in the UK, Germany and France and a presence in Brussels, Alicante, Dubai and Shanghai. A full-service firm with an industry focus (IT and telecommunications, life sciences and healthcare, media and entertainment, leisure, fashion etc), **Taylor Wessing** was set up in Paris in 2003 with teams from the Big Four and is growing quickly with more than 60 lawyers, including 15 partners.

Thieffry & Associés has always had an interest in international business with offices in New York and Shanghai. The contentious dimension of the firm is strong (including arbitration and white-collar crime) but general corporate and commercial work is widely carried out: M&A, contracts and distribution, EU and competition, environment, construction, tax, transport law.

With a litigation background, **Vatier & Associés** is active in arbitration, labour law, public and health law, and white-collar crime. The firm is growing in property and corporate.

Founded in 2004 by lawyers from **Jones Day** and *Coopers & Lybrand Juridique et Fiscal*, **Vendôme** has some ten lawyers. They work for small- and mid-cap French and international clients in the pharmaceuticals, biotechnology and computer science industries, assisting on corporate, M&A, private equity, dispute resolution, labour, tax, insurance and property issues.

Half of **Vovan & Associés**' 40 lawyers are in foreign offices: Brussels, Rome, Milan, Beijing, Hanoi, Ho Chi Minh City and Bangkok. In France, the firm is in Paris, Marseille and Lyon. A great amount of work is related to foreign investment in France and French investment abroad. Clients are assisted on all aspects of general business law.

Wilinski Scotto & Associés was set up in 1997 by partners from Anglo-Saxon firms. Twenty lawyers among which five partners assist a French and international clientele in corporate issues, including private equity as the firm often advises the management in LBO deals, commercial law and projects, labour law, construction and real estate, and dispute resolution.

Winston & Strawn LLP has ten partners in France and the firm has enjoyed steady growth since 1995. Its activity is mainly corporate and commercial but litigation and arbitration are also handled. Finally, the firm has a special knowledge of environmental and energy issues.

DISPUTE RESOLUTION: COMMERCIAL LITIGATION

In addition to its acknowledged expertise in stock exchange and European disputes, **Bredin Prat** also handles general commercial litigation. Issues covered include investment agreements, business, company and asset transfer agreements, construction and distribution agreements in a wide range of markets including telecoms, pharmaceuticals, the motor industry and energy. The firm's clientele is based in Europe, the Middle East and the US, and the disputes are subject to a wide range of different laws. Partners include Jean-François Prat, Didier Martin, Louis-Christophe Delanoy, Claude Bendel and Sylvie Morabia.

Gide Loyrette Nouel's contentious capability is vast and each department undertakes litigation. In addition, eight partners are specifically in charge of litigation and are specialists in all kinds of disputes organised into three main areas of activity: commercial law, corporate crime and company/financial institution law. Litigation partners include Jean-Marie Burguburu, *Bâtonnier* (head of the Paris Bar) between 1 January 2004

DISPUTE RESOLUTION: COMMERCIAL LITIGATION

BREDIN PRAT ✪
GIDE LOYRETTE NOUEL ✪
ORRICK, HERRINGTON & SUTCLIFFE ✪

DARROIS VILLEY MAILLOT BROCHIER ✪
DE PARDIEU BROCAS MAFFEI ✪
FRESHFIELDS BRUCKHAUS DERINGER
JEANTETASSOCIÉS ✪

Cleary, Gottlieb, Steen & Hamilton LLP ✪
Clifford Chance
Granrut Avocats
Herbert Smith LLP ✪
Latham & Watkins
Linklaters ✪
Lovells ✪
Paul, Hastings, Janofsky & Walker (Europe) LLP ✪
Salans
Simmons & Simmons ✪
Veil Jourde ✪
White & Case LLP

Ashurst ✪
Baker & McKenzie SCP ✪
Bouckaert Ormen Passemard Sportes ✪
Dechert ✪
Flécheux & Associés
Jones Day ✪
Lussan Brouillaud
Shearman & Sterling LLP
Soulez Larivière et Associés ✪
UGGC & Associés ✪
Vatier & Associés ✪
Willkie Farr & Gallagher LLP ✪

August & Debouzy
Bird & Bird ✪
Brandford-Griffith & Associés ✪
CMS Bureau Francis Lefebvre ✪
Dubarry Le Douarin Veil ✪
Franklin ✪
Hauteclocque Larroumet
LeBoeuf, Lamb, Greene & Macrae LLP ✪
Lefèvre Pelletier & associés ✪
Norton Rose

Continued

DISPUTE RESOLUTION: COMMERCIAL LITIGATION Continued

- Ader Amigues & Jolibois
- Allen & Overy LLP ✪
- Ayache Salama & Associés ✪
- Barbé Carpentier Thibault Groener & Associés
- Barsi Doumith & Associés
- Berlioz & Co
- Bernet Castagnet Wantz & Associés
- Bersay & Associés ✪
- Bignon Lebray & Associés
- Cotty Vivant Marchisio & Lauzeral
- Denton Wilde Sapte ✪
- Ernst & Young Société d'Avocats
- Eversheds-Frere Cholmeley
- Fidal ✪
- Ginestié Magellan Paley-Vincent ✪
- Hammonds Hausmann
- Hughes Hubbard & Reed LLP ✪
- KGA Avocats
- Kramer Levin Naftalis & Frankel LLP ✪
- Latournerie Wolfrom & Associés ✪
- Montravers & Partners
- Ngo Miguérès & Associés
- NomoS ✪
- Racine
- Reinhart Marville Torre
- Sarrau Thomas Couderc
- Savin Martinet Associés ✪
- Sokolow, Carreras & Associés
- Taylor Wessing ✪
- Thieffry & Associés
- Vaïsse, Brémond, Rambert & Associés
- Viguié Schmidt
- Weil, Gotshal & Manges ✪
- Winston & Strawn LLP ✪

Firms are listed A-Z in tiers which are ranked in order of priority
✪ *Indicates firm displays contact details at the end of this chapter.*

and 2006, Gilles Duquet, Michel Pitron and Didier Laigo.

At **Orrick, Herrington & Sutcliffe**, every *avocat* previously at *Rambaud Martel* (the two firms merged as of 1 January 2006) has a litigation background and very often litigation feeds the other practices within the firm. The contentious practice is broad, covering public, social and commercial law as well as construction, or insolvency issues. White-collar crime, stock-exchange litigation and arbitration are also handled.

Darrois Villey Maillot Brochier handles sophisticated cases, often linked with M&A deals, shareholders and white-collar crime. The firm's contentious practice is highly regarded.

De Pardieu Brocas Maffei's contentious practice is traditionally focused on commercial, banking, finance and insurance law, although it also handles property disputes, insolvency, and white-collar crime. Jacques Henrot, Dominique Lefort, Constance de la Hosseraye and Paul Talbourdet's clients are mainly banks and financial institutions.

Freshfields Bruckhaus Deringer's main activities in litigation are corporate, commercial and banking law, securities and shareholder conflicts, business crime law, mediation, restructuring, collective procedures and bankruptcy, insurance and product liability. Elie Kleiman, Philippe Hameau and Stéphane Bénouville are the litigation partners.

Around 50% of **JeantetAssociés**' turnover springs from contentious work. Most of the partners handle litigation as it arises within their own area of expertise. **JeantetAssociés** is traditionally a strong litigation French firm.

Cleary, Gottlieb, Steen & Hamilton LLP's Jean-Yves Garaud handles litigation relating to product liability or post-M&A and restructuring cases, very often in an international context.

Clifford Chance is active in both cross-border and French litigation. Jean-Pierre Grandjean and Thomas Baudesson are the partners entirely dedicated to general corporate and commercial litigation, although various partners handle contentious matters. Clients include Volvo, Airbus, Carrefour, Cegetel/SFR, Moulinex, LVMH and Swissport.

Granrut Avocats' litigation practice is broad. In addition to criminal matters (Bernard du Granrut, Stéphane Micheli), the firm is also active in press law and media (Jean Castelain), public law (Marc Bellanger), property (Pierre-Yves Rossignol), labour law (Laurent Ribadeau-Dumas, René Fremy) and insolvency.

Herbert Smith LLP undertakes a wide range of commercial litigation, a traditional strength of the firm's practice globally. Industrial and product liability (in the aviation sector significantly), banking and finance (working for major banks), and white-collar crime are the three areas where Denis Chemla, Charles Kaplan and their team are active.

At **Latham & Watkins**, four partners (Patrick Dunaud, Valérie Bouaziz Torron, Emmanuel Drai and Laure Marcilhacy) and one of-counsel are fully dedicated to litigation, teaming with ten partners in the other departments involved in litigation/arbitration matters (antitrust, IP, media, telecoms, insolvency, distribution and employment). The firm is particularly involved in disputes involving corporate, securities law, acquisition litigation and professional liability.

Linklaters is stong in M&A litigation and handles complex, cross-border commercial disputes and criminal/regulatory investigations (often involving more than one jurisdiction). Arnaud de la Cotardière leads the team. Numerous lawyers also handle their own disputes (M&A, IP, EU and competition, etc).

At **Lovells**, Marc Henry deals mainly with corporate, insolvency and finance litigation and arbitration, while Thomas Rouhette is involved in commercial litigation with an emphasis on distribution, product liability and insurance. The litigation team is 13 fee-earners strong.

Paul, Hastings, Janofsky & Walker (Europe) LLP is very active in general litigation, with a strong white-collar crime team. Its contentious practice encompasses commercial litigation, banking and financial matters, stock market litigation, responsibility, and insolvency.

Salans' litigation team numbers nine partners and covers the whole spectrum of disputes with an emphasis on international and cross-border matters.

Simmons & Simmons' team comprises 16 lawyers and has particular expertise in product liability and distribution litigation (pharmaceuticals), stock exchange, banking and finance litigation, contentious and regulatory work for the food industry, IP, and commercial distribution litigation.

Veil Jourde's reputation rests on three fields: criminal financial matters and arbitration; insolvency; and financial, stock market and commercial litigation, with partners Jean Veil, Georges Jourde and Barbara Lévy.

While **White & Case LLP**'s litigation team is able to advise on all aspects of commercial litigation, the firm has a number of areas of particular expertise that include financial litigation, insolvency, white-collar crime and administrative litigation. Partners Emmanuel Rosenfeld, Jean-Luc Boussard, Reinhard Dammann and Philippe Métais are involved in high-profile cases such as Elf Aquitaine/Le Floch Prigent and CDR/Executive Life.

Ashurst's litigation team is increasingly visible. Led by Jean-Pierre Farges, the seven-lawyer team boasts a diverse practice that encompasses commercial litigation, white-collar-crime, public law litigation, insolvency and restructuring.

At **Baker & McKenzie SCP**, 11 lawyers handle dispute resolution, including partner Jean-Dominique Touraille. Areas of expertise include distribution, commercial litigation, transport, contracts, industrial risk, insolvency and banking.

Bouckaert Ormen Passemard Sportes was formed through a split from **Norton Rose**. The firm handles commercial and financial litigation and half of the work is related to the insurance and reinsurance sector.

Dechert, with a team led by Xavier Nyssen (previously **Coudert Frères**), is active in post-acquisition litigation, bank guarantees litigation, criminal and civil liability of company auditors and managers, trade regulation, advertising law, unfair competition, distribution agreements, pharmaceuticals and oil production-sharing contracts.

Three quarters of **Fléchuex & Associés**' activity is contentious with interventions in a broad range of matters such as competition, construction, public law, insurance and professional liability, IP and commercial law. Some white-collar crime is also handled, as is arbitration.

At **Jones Day**, Laurent Martinet's eight-lawyer team handles product liability, competition and distribution litigation, restructuring.

Lussan Brouillaud is renowned in litigation with partners Jean-Yves Dupeux and François Martineau well known. Their reputation is in banking and press litigation, in white-collar crime, but they are also active in general commercial litigation.

Shearman & Sterling LLP's team is involved in post arbitral matters. Some of the activity emanates from the M&A and corporate finance departments but this diverse international practice also handles other sorts of disputes.

At **Soulez Larivière et Associés**, Daniel Soulez Larivière is well known, while **UGGC & Associés**' litigation team numbers 14 lawyers. Areas of activity include transport and medical liability.

Vatier & Associés is the other half of the former *Granrut Vatier Baudelot & Associés*. Particularly noteworthy is work relating to public law, insolvency and white-collar crime.

Five lawyers are dedicated to litigation at **Willkie Farr & Gallagher LLP** and Dominique Mondoloni deserves a mention. The firm handles cases relating to administrative law, town-planning and property, but also undertakes litigation in IP, banking and telecoms.

DISPUTE RESOLUTION: INTERNATIONAL ARBITRATION

The four-partner team at **Freshfields Bruckhaus Deringer** enjoys an enviable reputation, and Jan Paulsson deserves special mention as a leading arbitrator and a public international law expert. Of the other three partners, Eric Schwartz has solid experience in the construction sector, Peter Turner and Nigel Blackaby's specialities are in investor/State cases, in South America for the latter. Elie Kleiman and Constantine Partasides are also active. The practice is wide and well established, covering many ICC and CIRDI cases in various sectors, including telecoms, energy, construction, investment, financial services and joint ventures, among others.

Shearman & Sterling LLP's Paris team, led by Emmanuel Gaillard who also leads the 80-lawyer worldwide group, comprises some 30 associates and four other partners (Christophe Dugué, Philippe Pinsolle, Todd Wetmore and Fernando Mantilla-Serrano; David Reed was transferred to London). The six core areas of the practice are: investment (where **Shearman & Sterling LLP** represents *Yukos v Russian Federation*), energy, business combinations, construction, financial and insurance, and general commercial arbitration. These arbitrations (75 pending cases whose total value was over US$52bn) had their venues in 18 different locations throughout the world and were subject to over 25 governing laws. Partners also regularly act as arbitrator.

At **Gide Loyrette Nouel**, Pierre Raoul-Duval heads up the seven-partner arbitration practice. Philippe Nouel's status on the international arbitration scene in Paris also merits special mention, as well as Christian Camboulive, Carole Malinvaud and Rupert Reece's work. The arbitration cases handled by the team during 2005 concerned areas such as investments, banking, joint venture contracts, construction projects, oil and gas, defence, M&A, telecommunications, distribution and IP matters, acting for governments, state-owned entities or private companies and investors. In more general terms, the arbitration cases handled by the team during 2005 (around 40) were conducted in either French or English and pursuant to the ICC or ICSID rules in Paris, London and elsewhere. Several *ad hoc* (generally UNCITRAL) cases were also handled.

White & Case LLP also possesses an excellent reputation. Stephen Bond, Christopher Seppala and Michael Polkinghorne are frequently mentioned and all act as arbitrators. Andrew McDougall, Philippe Sarrailhé, Reinhard Dammann and consultant Christophe Seraglini are also active, with a team of 12 associates. The worldwide global team has more than 80 practioners. The areas in which the firm practises are construction, international joint ventures and investment, oil and gas, telecoms, banking, as well as litigation on behalf of, or against, governments.

At **Darrois Villey Maillot Brochier**, Matthieu de Boisseson has a first-class reputation in arbitration. He often acts as arbitrator for various international institutions and also advises multinational companies. Two young partners are also active, including rising star Pierre Duprey, as counsels in matters relating to M&A.

At **Dechert**, the international arbitration practice (previously *Coudert Frères*'), is led by Philip Dunham and Eduardo Silva Romero. The firm's main activities centre on a specialisation in construction, investments and corporate, distribution and energy.

Delvolvé Rouche handles a range of issues including finance, investment, joint ventures and construction. A large number of ICC arbitrations are undertaken by the firm, as are ad hoc proceedings. Jean-Louis Delvolvé acts mainly as an arbitrator.

Derains & Associés also has a good reputation; Yves Derains frequently appears before various international arbitration courts. The firm also has wide experience as counsel in arbitrations, either institutional or ad hoc, and is known for its construction, energy, natural resources, international commerce and international finance expertise. It houses four partners, including Jean Georges Betto. Alain Bourdeaux, legal head at Vinci Construction Grands Projets, joined the firm in 2005.

DISPUTE RESOLUTION: INTERNATIONAL ARBITRATION

FRESHFIELDS BRUCKHAUS DERINGER
SHEARMAN & STERLING LLP

GIDE LOYRETTE NOUEL ✪
WHITE & CASE LLP

DARROIS VILLEY MAILLOT BROCHIER ✪
DECHERT ✪
DELVOLVÉ ROUCHE *
DERAINS & ASSOCIÉS
JONES DAY ✪
LAZAREFF, SERGE *
SALANS

B Moreau - Lawyers
Bredin Prat ✪
Cleary, Gottlieb, Steen & Hamilton LLP ✪
Clifford Chance
Eversheds-Frere Cholmeley
Herbert Smith LLP ✪
Hughes Hubbard & Reed LLP ✪
Latham & Watkins

Curtis, Mallet-Prevost, Colt & Mosle LLP ✪
Debevoise & Plimpton LLP ✪
Denton Wilde Sapte ✪
JeantetAssociés ✪
KGA Avocats
Linklaters ✪
Lovells ✪
Michael Lee
Norton Rose
Orrick, Herrington & Sutcliffe ✪
Paul-A. Gélinas *
Philippe Leboulanger
Shadbolt & Co LLP
Simmons & Simmons ✪
Winston & Strawn LLP ✪

Ader Amigues & Jolibois
Ashurst ✪
Augendre
August & Debouzy
Baker & McKenzie SCP ✪
Berlioz & Co
Bernard Hertz Béjot
Bernards
Bertagna
Bouckaert Ormen Passemard Sportes ✪
Bouloy Grellet & Godin
Brandford-Griffith & Associés ✪
Castaldi Mourre Sprague
Gravel Leclerc & Associés
Hammonds Hausmann
Holman Fenwick & Willan ✪
Lamy & Associés ✪
Lefèvre Pelletier & associés ✪
Ngo Miguérès & Associés
Paul, Hastings, Janofsky & Walker (Europe) LLP ✪
Teynier, Pic & Associés
Thieffry & Associés
UGGC & Associés ✪
Veil Jourde ✪

** Firms mainly active as an arbitrator*
Firms are listed A-Z in tiers which are ranked in order of priority
✪ Indicates firm displays contact details at the end of this chapter.

PUBLIC INTERNATIONAL LAW

Cleary, Gottlieb, Steen & Hamilton LLP ✪ *Robert Greig*
Eversheds-Frere Cholmeley *Rodman Bundy*
Freshfields Bruckhaus Deringer *Jan Paulsson*

Firms are listed alphabetically
✪ *Indicates firm displays contact details at the end of this chapter.*

At **Jones Day**, Michael Bühler is the head of the firm's European dispute resolution practice and is the full German member of the International Court of Arbitration of the ICC; John Crawford and Sigvard Jarvin complete the team. Work includes cases in the fields of engineering, construction, oil and gas, trade, know-how transfer, joint ventures and shareholder agreements.

Serge Lazareff is considered one of the best arbitrators in France. He arbitrates in conflicts in various sectors, among them construction, international project finance and distribution contracts.

Six partners, two of-counsels and six associates advise on arbitration matters at **Salans** and handle on average 65 cases a year (one-third as arbitrator). Lawyers involved include expert in Russian law Jeffrey Hertzfeld, former UNCC Commissioner, Carl Salans, current vice-president of the ICC Court, and Sarah François-Poncet. Bruno Leurent left for **Winston & Strawn LLP**. Arbitrations are equally divided between East-West, Middle East and Africa, the US and Europe. Areas covered are energy, joint ventures, hotels, construction, investment and post-acquisitions.

B Moreau - Lawyers' solid reputation is based largely on the expertise of Bertrand Moreau. He is president of the Comité Français de l'Arbitrage (CFA). He and his team advise on both domestic and international arbitrations.

Bredin Prat handles financial and commercial arbitrations, and those relating to investment. Louis Christophe Delanoy and Tim Portwood merit mention. Areas covered include telecoms, pharmaceuticals, the motor industry, agriculture and energy for a clientele based in Europe, the US and the Middle East.

At **Cleary, Gottlieb, Steen & Hamilton LLP**, Jean-Yves Garaud, Robert Greig and Claudia Hannacker (counsel) handle general commercial arbitration as well as sovereign arbitration and international public law.

At **Clifford Chance**, Jason Fry and Jean-Pierre Grandjean are the most active partners in this area, with some ten lawyers working with them. Renowned Professor Pierre Mayer acts as a consultant.

Eversheds-Frere Cholmeley's team is made of three partners: Rodman Bundy, David Sellers and Louis Degos. The latter, Secretary-General of the Comité Français de l'Arbitrage, arrived from **B Moreau - Lawyers** to develop internal and international commercial arbitration. Rodman Bundy is a very renowned international public law specialist with a sound knowledge of the energy sector. David Sellers' activity is in projects, investments, energy and construction.

Herbert Smith LLP's arbitration practice in Paris is headed up by Charles Kaplan. The group acts in international commercial matters covering a wide range of industries, including energy and natural resources, international investment and large-scale construction and engineering projects.

Hughes Hubbard & Reed LLP's eight-lawyer arbitration team operates under the leadership of José Rosell and Axel Baum (counsel). Some 20 cases are handled at the same time, mainly in the US$100m area. The firm undertakes arbitration work relating to multinational deals on behalf of manufacturers or governments in cases of investment, joint ventures, competition, environment, licences and, more recently, energy and construction. Central and Eastern Europe and Latin America are the two main areas of focus.

The international arbitration team at **Latham & Watkins** is headed by Laurent Jaeger and Mark Beckett, the latter having relocated from the New York office. The firm's expertise is in disputes between states and investors, construction, energy, environment and trade.

DISPUTE RESOLUTION: STOCK MARKET LITIGATION

Respected names at **Bredin Prat** include Paris legend Jean-François Prat who heads the team, Didier Martin and Sylvie Morabia.

Meanwhile, **Darrois Villey Maillot Brochier** boasts the considerable skills of Jean-Michel Darrois who is supported by Philippe Villey, Emmanuel Brochier, Hervé Pisani and Marie-Noëlle Dompé.

At **Linklaters**, Thierry Vassogne is famous and, along with Marc Loy, is very active in stock market litigation.

Orrick, Herrington & Sutcliffe, Jean-Pierre Martel (previously *Rambaud Martel*), is highly recommended.

Other recommended firms and individuals include: **Brandford-Griffith & Associés** (Henri-Brandford Griffith and Diane Pasturel); **Cleary, Gottlieb, Steen & Hamilton LLP** (Pierre-Yves Chabert, Jean-Yves Garaud, Catherine Peulvé); **Clifford Chance** (Frédéric Peltier); **Cotty Vivant Marchisio & Lauzeral** (Thierry Cotty); **Freshfields Bruckhaus Deringer** (Patrick Bonvarlet and Elie Kleiman); **Gide Loyrette Nouel** (Youssef Djehane); **JeantetAssociés** (Georges Terrier); **Latham & Watkins** (Patrick Dunaud); **Paul, Hastings, Janofsky & Walker (Europe) LLP** (Dominique Borde); **Reed Smith Rambaud Charot LLP** (Mathieu Rambaud); **Simmons & Simmons** (Thierry Gontard); **Sullivan & Cromwell LLP** (Dominique Bompoint); **Veil Jourde** (Jean Veil); and **Viguié Schmidt** (Nicolas Viguié and Yves Schmidt).

DISPUTE RESOLUTION: STOCK MARKET LITIGATION

BREDIN PRAT ✪
DARROIS VILLEY MAILLOT BROCHIER ✪
LINKLATERS ✪
ORRICK, HERRINGTON & SUTCLIFFE ✪

Brandford-Griffith & Associés ✪
Cleary, Gottlieb, Steen & Hamilton LLP ✪
Freshfields Bruckhaus Deringer
Gide Loyrette Nouel ✪
JeantetAssociés ✪
Veil Jourde ✪

Clifford Chance
Cotty Vivant Marchisio & Lauzeral
Latham & Watkins
Paul, Hastings, Janofsky & Walker (Europe) LLP ✪
Reed Smith Rambaud Charot LLP ✪
Simmons & Simmons ✪
Sullivan & Cromwell LLP
Viguié Schmidt

Firms are listed A-Z in tiers which are ranked in order of priority
✪ *Indicates firm displays contact details at the end of this chapter.*

DISPUTE RESOLUTION: WHITE-COLLAR CRIME

The following lawyers are recommended for white-collar crime: Jean-François Prat and Eric Dezeuze (**Bredin Prat**); Jean-Michel Darrois, Marie-Noëlle Dompé, and Emmanuel Brochier (**Darrois Villey Maillot Brochier**); Jean-René Farthouat (**Farthouat Asselineau & Associés**); **Francis Szpiner**; Jean-Marie Burguburu and Kiril Bougartchev (**Gide Loyrette Nouel**); **Hervé Témime**; **Jean-Yves Leborgne**; Jean-Yves Liénard (**Liénard Ardaillion-liénard Landon** in Versailles); Olivier Metzner (**Metzner Associés**); **Philippe Lemaire**; **Thierry Herzog**; Thierry Lévy (**Thierry Lévy, Orly Rezlan et Associés**); Jean Veil and Georges Jourde (**Veil Jourde**);

Our list also includes: Roger Doumith (**Barsi Doumith & Associés**); **Christine Courrégé**; Bernard Dartevelle (**Dartevelle Benazeraf Merlet Dubest**); Pierre Cornut-Gentille (**French Cornut-Gentille**); Bernard du Granrut (**Granrut Avocats**); **Jean-Paul Lévy**; Georges Terrier, Bernard Gorny, Henri Hajdenberg and Philippe Blaquier-Cirelli (**JeantetAssociés**); Georges Kiejman (**Kiejman & Marembert**); Paul Lombard and Olivier Baratelli (**Lombard & Associés**); Yves Baudelot (**Lysias**); **Michel Zaoui**; **Olivier Schnerb**; Jean-Pierre Martel (**Orrick, Herrington & Sutcliffe**, ex-*Rambaud Martel*); Michel Jéol and Sylvie-Claire d'Arvisenet (**Paul, Hastings, Janofsky & Walker (Europe) LLP**); Daniel Soulez Larivière (**Soulez Larivière et Associés**); Bernard Vatier (**Vatier & Associés**); Emmanuel Rosenfeld (**White & Case LLP**); Xavier Flécheux (**Flécheux & Associés**).

DISPUTE RESOLUTION: WHITE-COLLAR CRIME

BREDIN PRAT ✪
DARROIS VILLEY MAILLOT BROCHIER ✪
FARTHOUAT ASSELINEAU & ASSOCIÉS
FRANCIS SZPINER
GIDE LOYRETTE NOUEL ✪
HERVÉ TÉMIME
JEAN-YVES LEBORGNE
LIÉNARD ARDAILLION-LIÉNARD LANDON
METZNER ASSOCIÉS
PHILIPPE LEMAIRE
THIERRY HERZOG
THIERRY LÉVY, ORLY REZLAN ET ASSOCIÉS
VEIL JOURDE ✪

Barsi Doumith & Associés
Christine Courrégé
Dartevelle Benazeraf Merlet Dubest
French Cornut-Gentille
Granrut Avocats
Jean-Paul Lévy
JeantetAssociés ✪
Kiejman & Marembert
Lombard & Associés
Lussan Brouillaud
Lysias
Michel Zaoui
Olivier Schnerb
Orrick, Herrington & Sutcliffe ✪
Paul, Hastings, Janofsky & Walker (Europe) LLP ✪
Soulez Larivière et Associés ✪
Vatier & Associés ✪
White & Case LLP

Ayache Salama & Associés ✪
August & Debouzy
Bourguet Kneusé Vallette
Brandford-Griffith & Associés ✪
Cayol, Cahen & Associés
Clifford Chance
Dubarry Le Douarin Veil ✪
Eric Hemmerdinger
Fischer Tandeau de Marsac Sur & Associés
Flécheux & Associés
Franklin ✪
Freshfields Bruckhaus Deringer
Lafarge Associés
Montbrial et Associés
Pierre Haik
Proskauer Rose LLP ✪
Roland Poynard
Thieffry & Associés

Firms are listed A-Z in tiers which are ranked in order of priority
✪ *Indicates firm displays contact details at the end of this chapter.*

EU, COMPETITION AND DISTRIBUTION

Robert Saint-Esteben of **Bredin Prat** is a leading practitioner, and Hugues Calvet is also very well known, while in Brussels, Marc Pittie is the partner in charge. Recent highlights include cases such as Financière Galaxies/B&B Hotel Group (counsel to Eurazeo); Liberty Surf/Telecom Italia (counsel to Telecom Italia); and Invensys Building Systems/Schneider Electric (counsel to Schneider Electric).

While **Cleary, Gottlieb, Steen & Hamilton LLP** is characterised by a long-established practice in Brussels, the Paris team has a wide practice and is involved in major merger control work, cartel and abuse of dominance investigations, state aid proceedings and litigation. It now numbers five lawyers, including two partners: Antoine Winckler and François Brunet. Recent deals include advising Neuf Telecom in its acquisition of Cegetel; EADS and Nokia in the context of the acquisition by EADS of Nokia's Professional Mobile Radio business; Sanofi Aventis, Merck and Lilly France in connection with the rejection by the French Competition Council of a request for interim measures filed by Phoenix-Pharma; and the French Government in the context of the appeal against the European Commission's decision regarding alleged state aid granted to France Télécom.

Clifford Chance is a major player in EU and competition law with Claude Lazarus. Michel Debroux left for **Hogan & Hartson MNP**, while Stanislas Martin arrived as of-counsel; he used to be the deputy financial advisor of the French representation at the European Union in Brussels. The team advises on all aspects of EU and French merger control, anti-competitive practices, state aid, and competition matters, in close link with the 38 antitrust partners worldwide. **Clifford Chance** advised SFR in the deal with Neuf Telecom who acquired SFR's fixed telephone subsidiary Cegetel; EDF on the competition law aspects of the possible acquisition of Edison and on the notification of joint control over Edison together with AEM; and the LFP (Ligue de Football Professionnel) on the allotment of the television broadcasting rights of the French Premier League.

Vogel & Vogel is a specialist EU and competition boutique. Founded in 1990, the firm currently numbers 35 lawyers with further offices in Brussels and Frankfurt. Its practice is particularly well developed in the automobile, audiovisual and telecoms sectors. The firm advised Renault in antitrust proccedings before the French Competition Council against the SPEA; TPS in a case against Neuf Telecom before the Paris Court of Appeal; Yamaha in a case before the Paris Court of Appeal against the CNPA; GE in the GE/Honeywell versus European Commission merger control case; and Eurazeo in the acquisition of Fraikin.

At **Freshfields Bruckhaus Deringer**, the team, consisting of partners Jacques-Philippe Gunther and Jérôme Philippe, plus some 14 associates, is active in merger regulation. It also handles French and European competition aspects as well as monopoly issues in the media and telecoms sectors. The French office works in close co-operation with the other offices in Europe. Recent highlights include representing Solvay on the merger control issues linked with the acquisition of Fournier, a French pharmaceutical company; Gaz de France in relation to

EU, COMPETITION AND DISTRIBUTION

BREDIN PRAT ✪
CLEARY, GOTTLIEB, STEEN & HAMILTON LLP ✪
CLIFFORD CHANCE
VOGEL & VOGEL ✪

FRESHFIELDS BRUCKHAUS DERINGER
GIDE LOYRETTE NOUEL ✪
JONES DAY ✪
LATHAM & WATKINS
LINKLATERS ✪
VIVIEN & JUVIGNY
WHITE & CASE LLP

Allen & Overy LLP ✪
Ashurst ✪
CMS Bureau Francis Lefebvre ✪
Coutrelis & Associés
DS Avocats
Darrois Villey Maillot Brochier ✪
Fourgoux & Associés
JeantetAssociés ✪
Lovells ✪
Meffre & Grall ✪
Shearman & Sterling LLP

Avens Lehman & Associés
Baker & McKenzie SCP ✪
De Pardieu Brocas Maffei ✪
Hogan & Hartson MNP ✪
Morgan Lewis ✪
Norton Rose
Orrick, Herrington & Sutcliffe ✪
Paul, Hastings, Janofsky & Walker (Europe) LLP ✪
Salans
Weil, Gotshal & Manges ✪

August & Debouzy
Bersay & Associés ✪
Bird & Bird ✪
Brandford-Griffith & Associés ✪
Debevoise & Plimpton LLP ✪
Denton Wilde Sapte ✪
Deprez Dian Guignot ✪
Dubarry Le Douarin Veil ✪
Ernst & Young Société d'Avocats
Eversheds-Frere Cholmeley
Fidal ✪
Flécheux & Associés
Funck-Brentano Gewelbe Brousseau
Granrut Avocats
Herbert Smith LLP ✪
LSK & Associés
NomoS ✪
SJ Berwin ✪
Sokolow, Carreras & Associés
Thieffry & Associés
UGGC & Associés ✪

Firms are listed A-Z in tiers which are ranked in order of priority
✪ *Indicates firm displays contact details at the end of this chapter.*

the acquisition and privatisation of the Belgium operator SPE; France Télévision on the creation of a new international news TV channel; and Buena Vista Home Entertainment in responding to a statement of objections and to the final report established by the French Competition Council, related to its sale practices of Disney videotapes to distributors.

The EU and competition department of **Gide Loyrette Nouel** in Paris comprises seven partners including Xavier de Roux and distribution specialists Antoine Choffel and Joëlle Salzmann. All work with a European dimension is handled in conjunction with the Brussels office (Antoine Gosset-Grainville); altogether the team numbers 50 lawyers. The firm advises on all aspects of competition law including merger control, cartels, abuse of dominant position, state aid, vertical restraints and also specialises in distribution law, consumer protection, tobacco law, product liability, advertising, and unfair competition disputes. **Gide Loyrette Nouel** was involved in a large number of merger filings and was counsel to Pernod Ricard in the acquisition of Allied Domecq; Sofiproteol/Diester Industrie in the creation of a jointly contractual subsidiary with the group Bunge; and to Caisse d'Epargne for the notification to the European Commission of the joint venture with Crédit Agricole. In antitrust matters, the firm represented SNCF before the French Competition Council, where British Airways was challenging the pricing policy of SNCF; Natexis Banques Populaires in the procedure launched by the European Commission against various French banks active in the French CB organisation (credit card network); and to Intermarché in judicial proceedings against Carrefour for unfair competition behaviour due to the capture of numerous supermarkets.

At **Jones Day**, Eric Morgan de Rivery is a well-known specialist in deregulation, with a focus on telecoms, electricity, transport and media matters. The practice now numbers eight lawyers, with teams in Brussels and all over Europe; the concentration of expertise in Washington, DC is another asset. **Jones Day** represented France Télécom in its US$10.7bn acquisition of a controlling interest in Auna; BP in its successful appeal of the French Competition Council decision to impose competition law fines on BP and other oil companies; Apple before the French Competition Council in an alleged case of abuse of dominance where the rejection of VirginMega's complaint was obtained; and Elf Aquitaine/Total SA with general assistance before the European Commission and the Tribunal of First Instance of the European Communities in several cartel cases involving chemicals.

The Paris office of **Latham & Watkins** boasts three partners and six other lawyers devoted to competition law. The firm opened an office in Brussels in February 2002, while in the US, it fields a further 15 antitrust lawyers. Alain Georges has a good knowledge of financial matters, the hotel and hi-tech industries. In 2005, he advised Groupement des Cartes Bancaires and the ten banks in a cartel case in the payment-card sector and NMPP in a series of proceedings for alleged abuses of dominance. Christophe Clarenc is a deregulation expert (telecoms, gas, electricity, post) and represents France Télécom in most of its competition disputes, for example in the proceeding against T-Online, Free, LDCom and Bouygues Télécom; Hugues Vallette-Viallard has national and international expertise in structuring distribution networks and litigation between industrials and distributors.

Linklaters' French competition group, led by Olivier d'Ormesson and Anne Wachsmann, comprises ten lawyers and is very active in EU and French merger control, state aid and high-profile antitrust cases before the French Competition Council and the European Commission. The year's highlights include advising Kronenbourg in the context of an investigation closed by a favourable decision regarding their acquisitions of distributors in France; Automobiles Peugeot SA and Peugeot Nederland NV on various Article 81 vertical restraint issues following dawn raids carried out by the European Commission; Metrovacesa on its bid for Gecina; and Alcatel with the notification to the European Commission of the creation of two joint ventures (Alenia Space and Telespazio). The team was also active in state aid with cases such as advising SNCM before the CFI, and British Telecom in respect of electronic communications network assets. The Paris office further benefits from the combined EU practice in Brussels, which now numbers some 130 lawyers including 30 partners.

Olivier de Juvigny is a raising star in French competition and EU law. He is a partner at **Vivien & Juvigny**, joining in 2004 from *Rambaud Martel* with a team including Iñaki Saint-Esteben. The practice includes merger control, antitrust litigation, state aid and distribution matters. Several deals involving CAC 40 companies and investment funds were notified lately and the firm has developed an agreements and abuse of dominant position litigation practice in fields as varied as the media, financial services, sport, supermarkets and industrial goods for professionals. The firm advised BNP Paribas in responding to a statement of objections sent by the European Commission to the main French banks in the credit card sector, and BNP Paribas in the notification of the Cetelem-Cofinoga deal following the takeover of Galeries Lafayette. **Vivien & Juvigny** is also counsel to two pharmaceutical companies, including Johnson and Johnson, on a regular basis.

At **White & Case LLP**, Jean-Patrice de la Laurencie has a strong reputation in EU and competition law and works with a team of six in Paris. The work carried out involves a lot of merger control but also includes antitrust matters – on the advisory and contentious sides – state aid and distribution. **White & Case LLP** was instructed by Starwood Capital Group in its acquisition of Taittinger and of Société du Louvre; Wendel Investissement on antitrust matters relating to the purchase of Bureau Veritas; and BNP Paribas on a major acquisition (the matter involved a stake in Galeries Lafayette and acquisition of Cofinoga). Other clients include Canal + and L'Oréal.

Olivier Fréget joined **Allen & Overy LLP** from **Bird & Bird**. He is mainly active in deregulation-related litigation. Areas of expertise include telecoms, transport, media, life sciences and pharmaceuticals.

Chantal Momège at **Ashurst** is active in state aid, antitrust, notifications, deregulation and distribution law. Her team was involved in the notification of the restructuring of the French rail freight (Fret SNCF). She advised the Ministry of Transport on the launching of the 'motorway of the sea' project between France and Spain and assisted Electrabel during the acquisition of a stake in SHEM.

Bernard Geneste, Jean-Paul Tran Thiet and Melchior Wathelet at **CMS Bureau Francis Lefebvre** handle EU and competition law in regulated sectors, in the transport, telecoms and energy industries.

Coutrelis & Associés is well known for its expertise in European Community Law in counselling, lobbying and litigation. The team numbers ten lawyers between Paris and Brussels offices. Its most developed practices are French and EU antitrust law, food and drug law, GMO issues and customs law. The firm handles cases for or against the European Commission and has thus far appeared in more than 65 cases before the European Court of Justice or the Court of First Instance in Luxembourg.

Claude Lucas de Leyssac and his team at **DS Avocats** handle all aspects of competition, distribution and European law. The firm has an office in Brussels.

Top M&A firm **Darrois Villey Maillot Brochier** launched its competition practice in 2002 with Didier Théophile. He handles concentrations and abuses of dominant position for clients such as La Poste and TPF.

Fourgoux & Associés is active in competition law (cartels, dominant position, unfair competition) and distribution with a focus on the food industry. It has an office in Brussels.

At **JeantetAssociés**, Loraine Donnedieu de Vabres heads the practice, while senior of-counsel Henry Lesguillons, Paul Cocchiello and young partner Thomas Picot are also active. The practice is wide and covers merger control and M&A-related matters, litigation, state aid, compliance programmes, antitrust, distribution and WTO issues in areas such as construction, public works, port infrastructure, cable, insurance, energy, supermarkets, industrial waste, space industry, drinks and the environment.

Pierre de Montalembert at **Lovells** handles competition work for clients such as Alstom,

Barclays, ExxonMobil, PepsiCo, SAS Carte Bleue, PMU, 3i and other private equity houses. The team works closely with the Brussels office.

Jean-Marie Meffre and Jean-Christophe Grall, **Meffre & Grall**, have good experience of French restrictive practices law and antitrust law. The firm numbers 12 lawyers.

Jean-Mathieu Cot is a young and well-regarded EU and competition specialist at **Shearman & Sterling LLP**.

Hervé Lehman, at **Avens Lehman & Associés**, is active in cartels and abuse of dominant position, state aid and merger control.

Alex Dowding, Mireille Dany and Régis Fabre at **Baker & McKenzie SCP** are recommended. They are active in antitrust cases and merger control and have expertise in distribution matters, advising Connex on European State aids issued in relation to the privatisation of SNCM and Platinum/Diac on merger control notifications.

De Pardieu Brocas Maffei's Philippe Guibert heads the four-lawyer practice. The team has developed a strong antitrust litigation practice and works on merger control issues, notably in the insurance, banking, private equity, property and industrial fields.

Hogan & Hartson MNP recently recruited Michel Debroux, a partner at **Clifford Chance**. He is a deregulation specialist with a sound knowledge of the energy and telecom sectors.

At **Morgan Lewis**, Jean Leygonie is an EU and competition specialist who also handles corporate work.

Laure Givry at **Norton Rose** is in charge of merger control and antitrust, state aid and distribution law.

At **Orrick, Herrington & Sutcliffe**, Marianne Mousseron, ex-*Rambaud Martel*, handles concentrations law, antitrust issues and has good knowledge of distribution cases. The other partner is Philippe Rincazaux, who was at *Coudert Frères* before joining **Orrick, Herrington & Sutcliffe**.

Paul, Hastings, Janofsky & Walker (Europe) LLP's competition practice is managed principally by Pierre Kirch who divides his time between the Paris and Brussels offices. Together with Béatrice Honorat, he provides services in the area of competition law relating both to advice and litigation.

At **Salans**, Mélanie Thill-Tayara is recommended, while Cyrille Couadou is the EU and competition specialist at **Weil, Gotshal & Manges**.

EMPLOYMENT

With 180 lawyers spread across 14 offices, **Barthélémy & Associés, member of ius laboris** is the only large firm specialising in employment law. Jacques Barthélémy (founder of the firm), Alain Sauret (chairman), and Pascal Lagoutte (director of the Paris office), are well-known, as are Michel Morand (acting for health and social trade associations) and Bruno Serizay (a social security expert). The firm covers all aspects of labour law and is particularly well known for its work in collective negotiations, acting for 70 employer federations, among them the largest employers.

EMPLOYMENT

BARTHÉLÉMY & ASSOCIÉS, MEMBER OF IUS LABORIS ✪

AUGUST & DEBOUZY
CMS BUREAU FRANCIS LEFEBVRE ✪
FLICHY & ASSOCIÉS ✪
FRESHFIELDS BRUCKHAUS DERINGER
FROMONT, BRIENS & ASSOCIÉS ✪
GIDE LOYRETTE NOUEL ✪

Baker & McKenzie SCP ✪
Coblence & Associés
Fidal ✪
Ginestié Magellan Paley-Vincent ✪
JeantetAssociés ✪
Latham & Watkins
Lefèvre Pelletier & associés ✪
Proskauer Rose LLP ✪
Salans

Clifford Chance
Cotty Vivant Marchisio & Lauzeral
Ernst & Young Société d'Avocats
Hughes Hubbard & Reed LLP ✪
Landwell & Associés
Lovells ✪
Morgan Lewis ✪
Norton Rose
Orrick, Herrington & Sutcliffe ✪
Simmons & Simmons ✪
UGGC & Associés ✪
White & Case LLP

Continued

August & Debouzy has a team of 25 lawyers dedicated to employment law, with Emmanuelle Barbara, Philippe Durand, Marie-Hélène Bensadoun, Fabienne Haas and Virginie Devos the partners in charge. In a few years, the team has become one of the few main players in Paris. The firm mostly handles general work, collective procedures, M&A and restructuring, financial issues, social security, pensions and benefits and corporate managers law. Contentious work is also carried out and the firm is increasingly involved in research and training, while handling labour law for other firms.

CMS Bureau Francis Lefebvre's employment law team is made up of eight partners and 35 lawyers. Nicolas de Sevin, Laurent Marquet de Vasselot, Pierre-Jean Sinibaldi, Jacques Nicolas, Nicolas Callies and Jean-Claude Anisten are well-known partners. The areas covered are M&A, national and international reorganisations, collective redundancy and site closings, collective negotiations and organisation of working time, deffered benefits and international mobility. Contentious work is developing.

Flichy & Associés was founded by Hubert Flichy who has an excellent reputation. Very much a niche practice, the firm comprises some 28 lawyers including eight partners – with the arrival of Anne le Bault de la Morinière from *Rambaud Martel* – and acts only on high-level issues for industrial companies, banks, and numerous pension funds. Restructurings, social plans and collective contentious matters constitute the bulk of its work.

In 2004, employment law boutique *Bélier et Associés* joined forces with the labour team led by Pascale Lagesse at **Freshfields Bruckhaus Deringer**. The whole team now numbers more than 20 lawyers (Emmanuel Bénard being the third partner) and is very active in collective and contentious issues, Gilles Bélier being a leading player in major employment cases. The firm also handles industrial restructurings with international aspects, employee share schemes, benefit and pension plans, social security, working time implementation and dispute resolution.

Originally from Lyon, **Fromont, Briens & Associés**, a partner firm of **LAMY & ASSOCIES**, has developed a comprehensive practice in Paris with Gilles Briens since 1995. The firm is particularly renowned in social security matters but also handles employment law and has a strong litigation practice, including white-collar crime.

At **Gide Loyrette Nouel**, Joël Grangé heads the employment department, backed up by Professor Gérard Couturier. The team is particularly involved in restructurings and M&A, collective redundancy plans, transfer of undertakings and collective disputes, with a strong litigation practice (Gilles Duquet, Aurélien Boulanger and Baudoin de Moucheron). The firm's labour and employment practice traditionally has an international outlook and, with 35 lawyers, offers significant resources. Employee savings and pension schemes, health and safety regulations, social security issues and employment-related crime, are also dealt with.

Baker & McKenzie SCP's team comprises 16 employment lawyers, with partners Denise Broussal, who is French-American, and Gilles Jolivet. Clients are both US-based and French. Two lawyers are dedicated entirely to litigation and work encompasses a lot of M&A-related cases and outsourcings.

Chantal Giraud Van Gaver at **Coblence & Associés** is also recommended. The team comprises five partners specialising in employment law and covering the whole spectrum of labour issues.

At **Fidal**, Sylvain Niel is well known and other partners handle employment law in Paris, including Philippe d'Harcourt, Jean-Paul Fels and Jacques Brunel. The department handles French and international work contracts, collective agreements, salaries and wages, pensions, flexible time management and staff representation institutions. **Fidal** also undertakes contentious proceedings.

EMPLOYMENT Continued

- Alexen Avocats
- Allen & Overy LLP ✪
- Bardavid Tourneur & Halphen
- Bersay & Associés ✪
- Bignon Lebray & Associés
- Bird & Bird ✪
- Cleary, Gottlieb, Steen & Hamilton LLP ✪
- Dechert ✪
- Courtois Lebel
- Denton Wilde Sapte ✪
- Dubarry Le Douarin Veil ✪
- Eversheds-Frere Cholmeley
- Falque & Associés
- Franklin ✪
- Granrut Avocats
- Hammonds Hausmann
- Herbert Smith LLP ✪
- Hogan & Hartson MNP ✪
- Jones Day ✪
- Kahn & Associés
- Lafarge Associés
- Lamy Lexel Avocats Associés
- Latournerie Wolfrom & Associés ✪
- NomoS ✪
- Paul, Hastings, Janofsky & Walker (Europe) LLP ✪
- Racine
- Sokolow, Carreras & Associés
- Sutra et Associés
- Taj ✪
- Taylor Wessing ✪
- Touati Avocats A La Cour, Cabinet ✪
- Tuffal Nerson
- VoxLaw

Firms are listed A-Z in tiers which are ranked in order of priority

✪ Indicates firm displays contact details at the end of this chapter.

The names of Dominique de la Garanderie, a former head of the Paris Bar, as well as Marie-Alice Jourde at **Ginestié Magellan Paley-Vincent** deserve a mention for their expertise in labour law.

At **JeantetAssociés**, Jean Néret is well known and the other partner is Anne-Elisabeth Combes. The firm is active in contentious matters, accidents at work, major industrial incidents, working time or litigation against the URSSAF, and major industrial restructurings.

At **Latham & Watkins**, Agnès Cloarec, Deborah Sankowicz and a team of eight lawyers devote a large part of their time to labour aspects of company restructurings and outsourcings, with a particular focus on the banking, food, advertising, hotel and catering sectors. Half of the work is contentious.

Lefèvre Pelletier & Associés is active in labour law with a team of ten lawyers, headed by Françoise Pelletier and Marie-Daphné Fishelson. Industries covered include banking, telecoms, luxury, hotel, press and pharmaceuticals.

Yasmine Tarasewicz and five associates make up the labour team at US firm **Proskauer Rose LLP**. Tarasewicz is notable for her expertise in labour law for US companies with operations in France.

Salans has an important labour and employment department, comprising 14 lawyers and this was reinforced with the arrival of a small team from *Rambaud Martel* early in 2006. Department head, Jean-Louis Magnier focuses on advice in restructuring, collective negotiations and remuneration policies, contentious work, and retirement and pension plans. Amongst the clients are several large US companies, a major French bank, foreign banks present in France, hotel chains, pharmaceutical laboratories and several aviation and maritime companies.

At **Clifford Chance**, Viviane Stulz (counsel) is in charge.

Antoine Vivant, of **Cotty Vivant Marchisio & Lauzeral**, handles a great deal of restructurings for national and international corporates and also has a contentious activity.

Ernst & Young Société d'Avocats has a 90-lawyer team and covers the whole range of labour law, with Roselyne Sands specialising in international issues.

The two partners in charge at **Hughes Hubbard & Reed LLP** are Nadine Voisin and Thierry Brezillon. They handle both collective and individual work, on the advisory and contentious sides, with a focus currently on de-localisation and merger-related audits.

With a team of some 50 lawyers, **Landwell & Associés** covers all aspects of labour law. Partners include William Phillips. The firm is mostly involved in restructurings, social plans, relocation and stock option plans.

At **Lovells**, Philippe Thomas focuses on labour law, mainly in the context of M&A transactions and reorganisations, assisting clients in the setting up of remuneration schemes, or acting for private equity funds on the replacement of top managers.

At **Morgan Lewis**, François Vergne heads the three-lawyer employment team that arrived from **De Pardieu Brocas Maffei**.

Norton Rose's employment team is led by Claire Fougea and mainly works for French subsidiaries of foreign groups.

At **Orrick, Herrington & Sutcliffe**, the team is made up of partners Christine Guillot-Bouhours and Françoise Mertz-Lhuillier from *Rambaud Martel* (Anne le Bault de la Morinière is now at **Flichy & Associés**).

Simmons & Simmons' team is led by Laure Joncour. She advises major US and international financial institutions and other international corporate clients on employment, restructuring, collective issues, mass redundancies, employee profit-sharing schemes, international projects, among other issues.

UGGC & Associés' labour practice comprises three partners: Roseline Sauser, Pascal Bathmanabane, Sophie Uettwiller.

EMPLOYMENT (EMPLOYEES)

- Bouaziz Benamara
- Florence Lyon-Caen
- Grumbach & Associés
- Henry Albouy Dudeffant
- Lachaud Lepany Associés
- Legrand & Associés
- Ravisy & Associés ✪
- Wizenberg Cohen-Seat Grinsnir Peru

Firms are listed alphabetically

✪ Indicates firm displays contact details at the end of this chapter.

At **White & Case LLP**, the seven-lawyer team, led by François Farmine and counsel Christiane Lefebvre has an all-round employment practice and handles contentious work and restructurings in conjunction with the corporate department.

EMPLOYMENT (EMPLOYEES)

The eight firms listed are active on behalf of employees. They act for trade unions and works councils, from giving legal advice, including crisis management, to litigation. The firms frequently work together in cases of collective redundancies. Some of the lawyers act for several unions.

ENVIRONMENT

Environmental law makes up 50% of the work for **Boivin & Associés**' Jean-Pierre Boivin and his team of ten lawyers. The other partner is Manuel Pennaforte. The firm is increasingly active in projects in the oil, chemicals, water, waste, nuclear power, and iron and steel sectors, and also advises companies in the pharmaceuticals industry. Recent cases include advising TotalFinaElf regarding the wreck of the *Erika*; AZF on the explosion of its chemical plant in Toulouse; Kodak in relation to pollution at former site of Vincennes; BP France in important soil pollution matters; and sizeable international firms specialising in waste regarding dioxin pollution cases.

Huglo Lepage & Associés Conseil's roots are in administrative litigation and the firm has now developed into a pre-eminent name in environmental law. Many large cases over the years have contributed to the firm's reputation: *Amoco Cadiz*, the Alsace potash mines, Creys Malville and the pollution of the Rhine and, more recently, the *Erika* and the *Prestige*. Moreover, Corinne Lepage was Minister for the Environment from 1995 to 1997. The practice is split equally between advisory and contentious work and the firm handles all matters relating to the environment, including EU-related issues and M&A. Activities linked with the health and biotechnologies sectors are developing.

Adamas' practice in environmental law matters is mainly focused on five areas: handling

ENVIRONMENT

BOIVIN & ASSOCIÉS
HUGLO LEPAGE & ASSOCIÉS CONSEIL ✪

Adamas ✪
Clifford Chance
Gide Loyrette Nouel ✪
Pichavant & Chétrit
Savin Martinet Associés ✪
UGGC & Associés ✪
Winston & Strawn LLP ✪

Allen & Overy LLP ✪
Baker & McKenzie SCP ✪
Bignon Lebray & Associés
De Pardieu Brocas Maffei ✪
GAIA
Granrut Avocats
Jones Day ✪
Laurence Lanoy
Otto Associés
Salans
Soulez Larivière et Associés ✪
Thieffry & Associés

Firms are listed A-Z in tiers which are ranked in order of priority
✪ *Indicates firm displays contact details at the end of this chapter.*

of contaminated sites-related issues; outsourcing of environmental industrial management; environmental audits in relation to M&A; water; waste and energy related public procurement; and servicing and risk management of closed minefields. Environmental law is now handled by a dedicated team of four full-time lawyers in Paris and two in Lyon, under the leadership of Yvan Razafindratandra. **Adamas** has offices in China, Korea and in Taiwan, and increasingly handles issues related to environmental law for foreign companies investing in China. Clients include the Communauté Urbaine de Lyon, an international luxury group and a tyre manufacturer.

Four associates and one partner (Pierre Bechman), work full-time within **Clifford Chance**'s environmental practice which covers a broad range of matters relating to the environment. The work is mainly contentious. For instance, the firm has been advising Volvo since 1999 in a series of multi-jurisdictional claims arising out of the Mont Blanc Tunnel disaster.

At **Gide Loyrette Nouel**, environmental cases are dealt with by David Desforges and Laurent Deruy. The four-lawyer team is involved in major industrial acquisitions and site restructuring operations. The firm has expertise in four segments of environmental law: advice, litigation, contractual work and audit. Areas covered range from regulated industrial activities to emissions, wastewater, waste treatment, noise nuisance, mining and nuclear law, and polluted sites. A strong emphasis was recently put on the new regulation of emissions allocation and trading. Banks, financial institutions and various types of industrials are advised. David Desforges advised Nova Chemicals in the set-up of the BP-Nova Chemicals joint venture in the polymers market.

Pichavant & Chétrit was formed by a split from **GAIA** in 2003. Jean-Daniel Chétrit is an environmental specialist, whose work involves the redevelopment of urban and polluted sites, obtaining authorisations, planning permission for registered industrial plants and expropriation cases.

Savin Martinet Associés deals with every type of environmental law issue. Its services include regulatory audits, purchase and sale audits, environmental risk analysis, the negotiation of environmental clauses in contracts (liability guarantees, etc), help with classified facilities, and case-monitoring in conjunction with French authorities. Patricia Savin covers all aspects of pollution and nuisance law, including facilities classified for environmental protection, water, air, waste, all types of spills or releases, hazardous materials transport and storage, among others. The problems associated with asbestos, termites, lead and VOCs, in particular in the real property field, are a speciality. Mining and quarries law is also a speciality.

Jean-Nicolas Clément is the public/environment law specialist at **UGGC & Associés**. Aside from some town-planning activities, he devotes 90% of his time to environmental work (with a balanced advisory/contentious practice). Clément has built his reputation in the nuclear, quarry, waste and hydrocarbon sectors.

Vincent Sol and Joëlle Herschtel head the environment practice at **Winston & Strawn LLP**, supported by six associates. Vincent Sol is a member of the Conseil Supérieur des Installations Classées and an expert in polluted ground. The firm offers a global service encompassing civil, criminal and administrative litigation, and acquisition audits. Among the firm's clients are large manufacturers in the chemicals, pharmaceuticals, automotive, steel, energy and waste sectors. The team advised Rhodia in connection with the closure of an industrial site in Lille. Forty lawyers are dedicated to the matter across offices in Paris, Chicago and Washington, DC.

Environmental law at **Allen & Overy LLP** is handled by Noël Chahid-Nouraï and Frédéric Mion on M&A-related matters, regulatory issues (for instance in relation with the implementation of the European Directive on WEEE and RoHS), and litigation.

Baker & McKenzie SCP is active in environmental law through Arnaud Cabanes. Clients include international and French companies facing environmental issues in connection with their industrial activities (United Technologies, Quaker Chemical, Alcan, BASF, BP). Moreover, the firm has specific expertise in climate change.

Lionel Roche, **Bignon Lebray & Associés**, advises industrial companies on their environmental issues/obligatons.

At **De Pardieu Brocas Maffei**, Jacques Henrot deals with environmental issues for insurance companies, banks and industrials, while Yves-René Guillou is the public law specialist.

At **GAIA**. Jean-Louis Péru deals with environment issues related to town-planning or waste treatment.

Granrut Avocats merits a mention for the work of Christophe Bourdel in environmental law (industrial risk, soil pollution and oil-related issues).

At **Jones Day**, Françoise Labrousse (who arrived from **Shearman & Sterling LLP**) has made a name for herself in environmental work, both on the transactional and litigation/arbitration sides, particularly in health and safety-related matters.

Laurence Lanoy is also an environmental lawyer who works independently.

Caroline London at **Otto Associés** carries out environmental work, largely from a local community perspective. She is also active in a national context, advising increasingly on environmental audits.

Salans' Jean-Christophe Honlet is active in the field, particularly regarding industrial site remediation issues on the contentious and non-contentious sides. He is also involved in arbitrations and works closely with the energy group.

Daniel Soulez-Larivière at **Soulez Larivière et Associés** was appointed by TotalFinaElf to represent the company in two major environmental accidents – the sinking of *Erika* and the explosion of the AZF chemical plant in Toulouse. The firm is also involved in asbestos litigation.

Patrick Thieffry, at **Thieffry & Associés**, specialises in European environmental law.

HEALTH AND LIFE SCIENCES

At **Bird & Bird**, a life sciences practice has developed under Paule Drouault-Gardrat. She is mainly active in the pharmaceutical, biotechnology and medical equipment industries and handles both advice and litigation on regulatory, IP, commercial aspects as well as product liability. At the same time, Marc Lipskier in active in pharmaceutical liability.

De Gaulle Fleurance & Associés is active in pharmaceutical regulation, contracts, IP, data protection and litigation, through Louis de Gaulle, Frank Valentin and Jean-Marie Job.

At **Dechert**, Alain Decombe (previously *Coudert Frères*) has developed life sciences expertise, with three associates, on the corporate and regulatory sides.

At **Simmons & Simmons**, Jacques-Antoine Robert is well regarded for his product liability practice in the pharmaceutical industry, having for instance successfully represented GlaxoSmithKline before the French Supreme Court in a case involving the alleged side effects of the Hepatitis B vaccine.

HEALTH AND LIFE SCIENCES

BIRD & BIRD ✪
DE GAULLE FLEURANCE & ASSOCIÉS ✪
DECHERT ✪
SIMMONS & SIMMONS ✪

Alain Bensoussan
Augendre
Baker & McKenzie SCP ✪
Bernet Castagnet Wantz & Associés
Courtois Lebel
Ginestié Magellan Paley-Vincent ✪
Intuity
Jones Day ✪
LeBoeuf, Lamb, Greene & Macrae LLP ✪
Taylor Wessing ✪
Vivien & Juvigny

Firms are listed A-Z in tiers which are ranked in order of priority
✪ *Indicates firm displays contact details at the end of this chapter.*

At **Augendre**, Geneviève Augendre is active on the contractual and contentious aspects relating to clinics, hospitals, doctors and has knowledge of the biotechnology sector. She sits at the *Conseil National de l'Ordre des Médecins*.

Baker & McKenzie SCP has a worldwide healthcare and pharmaceuticals practice group represented in France by Laurent Epstein and Henry de Suremain, mainly on the corporate and regulatory sides.

Bernet Castagnet Wantz & Associés has clients among clinics in health contractual law and restructurings.

Alain Gorny is a specialist at **Courtois Lebel**, active in unfair competition, comparative advertising and product liability issues, while Catherine Paley-Vincent is a health specialist at **Ginestié Magellan Paley-Vincent**, mainly on the contentious side.

Christophe Hénin is a pharmaceutical litigation specialist at **Intuity** (he used to work at **Proskauer Rose LLP**).

Jones Day's Laurent Martinet is active in product liability in the health industry.

LeBoeuf, Lamb, Greene & Macrae LLP's involvement in the life sciences area is on the corporate and litigation aspects.

At **Taylor Wessing**, Alain de Foucault arrived from **LeBoeuf, Lamb, Greene & Macrae LLP** and is active on the company (BioMérieux) and venture capital sides.

At **Vivien & Juvigny**, Etienne Gouesse is a pharmaceutical liability specialist.

IT, TELECOMS AND THE INTERNET

Alain Bensoussan is one of the leading IT specialist firms, Alain Bensoussan having been one of the first lawyers to specialise in the field about 20 years ago. Renowned lawyers include Pascal Arrigo, Benoît de Roquefeuille, Isabelle Tellier. The firm's practice centres on computing (which accounts for almost half of its activity), telecoms, communications and multimedia - traditionally the firm's three main areas of activity, to which the internet, biotechnology and health, as well as space law are natural additions. About 90 lawyers work in the Paris, Lyon and Grenoble offices.

Bird & Bird is a sector-focused, full-service international firm specialising in the communications and IT industries and covering all aspects of business law. Frédérique Dupuis-Toubol is one of the most renowned experts in telecommunications in France, while Olivier Fréget adds competition ability and Jean-Dominique Bloch public law expertise in this area. Stéphane Lemarchand's IT activity is directed towards computer science, e-business and litigation, acting for both providers and users. Ariane Mole is a data protection specialist. For **Bird & Bird**, contract negotiations and regulation form the core of the firm's practice, but litigation, outsourcing and PPP issues are increasingly important. The client base comprises large users of computer technology and computer services companies. The firm also handles internet issues (including IP work, contracts and corporate issues), and in the field of telecoms, the firm exclusively represents new entrants into the French market.

Ten partners and some 30 associates are active at **Kahn & Associés**. The firm traditionally acts for multinationals (mainly US, but also European and Israeli) and their French operations, but also for start-ups and venture capital funds. Among its clients are hardware manufacturers, software producers and distributors, makers of equipment and peripherals, computer goods and services providers, all sorts of hi-tech and telecoms companies and more traditional companies. The firm's activity is structured round computer science (hardware and software), internet, multimedia and telecoms. **Kahn & Associés** offers a wide range of expertise including corporate, M&A, IP, labour law and litigation. The firm has an office in Nice Sophia Antipolis, France's Silicon Valley.

Salans' IT team, consisting of four partners and 12 associates, is one of the leaders in the new technologies sector and is respected in the fields of computing, multimedia, internet and telecommunications. Christiane Féral-Schuhl is particularly well known. Along with Bruno Grégoire Sainte-Marie, the team has been active both in transactional work and litigation in the IT field since the '80s. Michael Hancock and Jeroen Luchtenberg both have telecoms backgrounds and now deal with a broad range of international and domestic telecoms, internet, cable television and media transactions, reorganisations and disputes. In the last few years, the Paris group has become particularly active in French and international outsourcing contracts. The group represents a broad range of French and international clients including industry leaders, start-ups, software developers, service providers, media and telecommunications conglomerates, computer consultants, multimedia companies and inventors.

Baker & McKenzie SCP's IT department is co-headed by Emmanuel Guillaume, former head of

IT, TELECOMS AND THE INTERNET

ALAIN BENSOUSSAN
BIRD & BIRD ✪
KAHN & ASSOCIÉS
SALANS

Baker & McKenzie SCP ✪
Clifford Chance
Derriennic & Associés
Franklin ✪
Gide Loyrette Nouel ✪
Iteanu & Associés
Latham & Watkins

August & Debouzy
BMH Avocats - Breitenstein Meillassoux Hauser ✪
Bersay & Associés ✪
Courtois Lebel
De Gaulle Fleurance & Associés ✪
Dubarry Le Douarin Veil ✪
Latournerie Wolfrom & Associés ✪
Orrick, Herrington & Sutcliffe ✪

Alterman Benezra, SCP
Bernard Hertz Béjot
Bignon Lebray & Associés
Cabinet de La Taille
Cayol, Cahen & Associés
DS Avocats
Denton Wilde Sapte ✪
Deprez Dian Guignot ✪
Ernst & Young Société d'Avocats
Ginestié Magellan Paley-Vincent ✪
Herbert Smith LLP ✪
Hogan & Hartson MNP ✪
Hughes Hubbard & Reed LLP ✪
LeBoeuf, Lamb, Greene & Macrae LLP ✪
Lovells ✪
Morgan Lewis ✪
NomoS ✪
Norton Rose
Racine
Taylor Wessing ✪
Watson, Farley & Williams LLP ✪
Weil, Gotshal & Manges ✪

Firms are listed A-Z in tiers which are ranked in order of priority
✪ *Indicates firm displays contact details at the end of this chapter.*

the legal department at France Télécom, and Rémy Bricard (IT/internet); Christian Blomet and Denise Lebeau-Marianna are the other partners. While telecoms is a very important area for the firm, both nationally and internationally, **Baker & McKenzie SCP** is also strong in computing and the internet. The team has been particularly active recently in litigation, data protection and outsourcing. Among clients, we can mention Oracle, Valeo, France Télécom and Canal +.

Marc d'Haultfoeuille heads the seven-lawyer CMT team at **Clifford Chance**, which covers computer law, multimedia and video games, hi-tech aspects of IP, and telecoms for French and foreign operators investing in France, advising Saint-Gobain, Airbus and Sagem on the review of their worldwide telecoms infrastructure. The firm is also involved in e-commerce and the internet, data protection and cryptology, and also handles arbitration and litigation. It advised ABN Amro and Saint-Gobain on outsourcing projects, as well as Carrefour on various worldwide IT agreements.

Comprising ten lawyers, six of them partners, **Derriennic & Associés** is a leading firm in the new technologies sector. With 30 years' experience in the computing field, Jean-Noël Derriennic is particularly highly regarded, although the firm is now expanding into telecoms and internet issues. The firm's client base spans software suppliers, as well as companies and administrative bodies using computer services.

At **Franklin**, Bradley Joslove leads the new technology department. The firm is very active in the cable industry and in the internet (eBay), and handles outsourcing projects for big institutional French clients. Recently, a Japanese clientele has been developed.

On the telecoms side, **Gide Loyrette Nouel** is very active in international bids, handling both regulatory and transactional issues. It handled the merger of TD and Cegetel creating the second fixed telecoms operator in France; the French Army on the outsourcing of its telecoms networks; and several telecoms new entrants in all regulatory matters before the French regulator, ART. The firm is also active in the IT and internet fields, drafting for instance agreements for several US-based, worldwide groups for the transfer and use outside the EU of personal data initially processed by subsidiaries established within the EU territory, and handles litigation on the user side. The partners in charge are Grégoire Goussu, Rémy Fekete and Olivier Cousi.

Iteanu & Associés has ten lawyers specialising in IT and e-commerce. The firm comprises three departments: corporate, contracts and litigation. Its activities include computing (service companies, publishers), telecoms (new service providers, equipment manufacturers) and a communication/ audiovisual/internet focus.

At **Latham & Watkins**, seven lawyers devote themselves to IT full time. One of the main facets of the firm's work is linked to its expertise in EU law – licences, relations with the regulatory authorities (ART) – although litigation (and arbitration) are also handled; Christophe Clarenc provides general representation to France Télécom in antitrust and telecommunications law. As for Laurent Szuskin, he is active in telecoms (counsel and contracts), computing and new technologies, working for providers and users with an emphasis on outsourcing renegotiation contracts, and computer public markets litigation. For instance, he provides general assistance to La Poste in the drafting and negotiation of various IT contracts.

August & Debouzy's IP/IT specialist, Isabelle Renard, is an engineer. The team has developed expertise in all IT, internet and computer science matters, dealing for instance with outsourcing and security audits of information systems.

At **BMH Avocats - Breitenstein Meillassoux Hauser**, André Meillassoux is a specialist in computer law and contracts.

Bersay & Associés' Martine Georges is a very respected name in the telecoms industry. She is involved in the negotiation and drafting of information technology contracts, regulatory aspects of the matter, and related dispute resolution.

At **Courtois Lebel**, Hervé Gabadou and a three-lawyer team are entirely dedicated to IT and communications issues, working for hi-tech operators and banks, insurance, publishing and pharmaceutical companies.

Louis de Gaulle, Julien Horn and Franck Valentin, all partners of **De Gaulle Fleurance & Associés**, advise clients on e-commerce, computer-hacking and data-processing issues. Clients include Microsoft and MSN.

At **Dubarry Le Douarin Veil**, four partners, including Bruno Ducoulombier, are active, mainly in the computer science area in which the firm has been advising a major player for many years. It also handles systems organisation, externalisation and litigation for both editors and users.

Latournerie Wolfrom & Associés is active in computer science, data protection, multimedia, e-business, and telecoms. Marie-Hélène Tonnellier is the partner in charge and works for clients such as SNCF (voyages-sncf.com), Tiscali, Fnac and Predica.

At **Orrick, Herrington & Sutcliffe**, François Bloch has experience in French and cross-border transactions, with an emphasis on telecommunications, media, IT/internet, entertainment and IP law. He advised Nec and Bloomberg on all IT agreements. Other clients in the telecoms area include Neuf Telecom and Qualcomm. David Masson joined from *Rambaud Martel* and is the other partner.

We also mention: **SCP Alterman Benezra** (Henri Alterman); **Cabinet de la Taille**; **Bernard Hertz Béjot** (Michel Béjot); **Bignon Lebray & Associés** (Anne-Marie Pecoraro); **Cayol, Cahen & Associés** (Bernard Cahen); **DS Avocats**; **Denton Wilde Sapte** (Gilles Vercken); **Deprez Dian Guignot** (Vincent Fauchoux); **Ernst & Young Société d'Avocats** (Jean-Pascal Amoros); **Ginestié Magellan Paley-Vincent** (Isabelle Gavanon); **Herbert Smith LLP** (Alexandra Neri); **Hogan & Hartson MNP** (Winston Maxwell); **Hughes Hubbard & Reed LLP** (Christopher Mesnooh); **LeBoeuf, Lamb, Greene & Macrae LLP** (Olivier Laude); **Lovells** (Milan Chromecek and Marie-Aimée de Dampierre); **Morgan Lewis** (Florence Guthfreund-Roland); **NomoS** (Eric Lauvaux); **Norton Rose** (Hervé Castelnau); **Taylor Wessing** (Marc Schuler); **Watson, Farley & Williams LLP** (Lucien Rapp); and **Weil, Gotshal & Manges** (Claude Serra).

INSOLVENCY

Sonier Poulain & Associés is the market leader and is the result of the merger between *Sonier & Associés* and *Poulain & Associés* in 2005. Gabriel Sonier and Jean-Paul Poulain are very well considered within the profession and they were joined by expert Philippe Dubois from **JeantetAssociés**. A system of correspondents enables Gabriel Sonier's firm to maintain special relationships with banks (OBC, Crédit Foncier de France, Merrill Lynch, JP Morgan and Deutsche Bank) and other law firms that lack a specialist within their own organisation. The firm acted in the main bankruptcies in France in the past few years: Moulinex/Brandt, UBS (Valfond Group), Léon de Bruxelles, Complétel, Alcatel Réseaux d'Entreprises - Marine Communication, and Immobilière Hôtelière.

Highly praised Jean-Dominique Daudier de Cassini joined **Weil, Gotshal & Manges** at the end of 2005 with three associates. He used to work at **Willkie Farr & Gallagher LLP**. The team also includes Philippe Druon. They work notably with the New York office where the practice is very strong. They advise companies on recovery procedures, restructurings and risk management, and also deal with strategies to safeguard against insolvency and management liability. The team is also active in difficult LBOs, private equity being another strength of the firm.

At **De Pardieu Brocas Maffei**, Jacques Henrot, Paul Talbourdet, Antoine Maffei and Emmanuel Fatôme handle insolvency matters. They work for lenders and increasingly for borrowers in an international context, and have been involved in many defective LBO financings and debt renegotiations recently acting for KBC Bank, Société Générale, and a major lender to Eurotunnel. Other cases include Federal Mogul, Prologue Software, Valiance, Metaleurop and Valfond. The firm works on a regular basis with specialists **Bingham McCutchen LLP**, **Cadwalader, Wickersham & Taft LLP**, **Sidley Austin LLP** and **Kirkland & Ellis LLP**.

INSOLVENCY

SONIER POULAIN & ASSOCIÉS ✪

WEIL, GOTSHAL & MANGES ✪

DE PARDIEU BROCAS MAFFEI ✪
GIDE LOYRETTE NOUEL ✪
SANTONI-PACCIONI
VEIL JOURDE ✪

Fauvet, La Giraudière & Associés
Freshfields Bruckhaus Deringer
JeantetAssociés ✪
Saigne Sigrist
Salans

Ashurst ✪
Ernst & Young Société d'Avocats
Fried, Frank, Harris, Shriver & Jacobson LLP
Lantourne Duret & Associés
UGGC & Associés ✪
Vatier & Associés ✪
White & Case LLP
Willkie Farr & Gallagher LLP ✪

Allen & Overy LLP ✪
Bernard Lagarde
Bignon Lebray & Associés
Cleary, Gottlieb, Steen & Hamilton LLP ✪
Clifford Chance
Denton Wilde Sapte ✪
Dubarry Le Douarin Veil ✪
Franklin ✪
Jones Day ✪
Kuntz & Associés ✪
Latham & Watkins
Lefèvre Pelletier & associés ✪
Lovells ✪
Lussan Brouillaud
Norton Rose
Orrick, Herrington & Sutcliffe ✪
Pardo Boulanger & Associés ✪
Paul, Hastings, Janofsky & Walker (Europe) LLP ✪
Simmons & Simmons ✪

Firms are listed A-Z in tiers which are ranked in order of priority
✪ Indicates firm displays contact details at the end of this chapter.

At **Gide Loyrette Nouel**, Olivier Puech has a very good reputation and Jean-Michel Lucheux also merits a mention. They specialise in amicable restructurings (*ad hoc mandates* and *conciliations*) and the management of bankruptcy proceedings and have capability in all related litigation. The firm was involved in the restructuring of Metaleurop SA.

Marc Santoni and Bruno Paccioni at **Santoni-Paccioni** are leading insolvency lawyers. They have been active in the takeover of bankrupt companies Thermatech, FI System and Locatel and have worked on the Alstom and Rhodia debt restructurings. They also assist funds when they have difficulties with their investments.

At **Veil Jourde**, Guilhem Brémond is the insolvency expert, working mainly for rescuers (Balmain/Mugler, LVMH/Cryo, etc), while Georges Jourde – a highly regarded litigator – is often on the banks and financial institutions' side.

François Fauvet at **Fauvet, La Giraudière & Associés**, is also renowned. He was for example advsising MAAF in the AOM/Air Liberté case.

Philippe Hameau and Stéphane Bénouville at **Freshfields Bruckhaus Deringer** work for shareholders, banks and debtors. They advised a Belgian credit institution in relation to the restructuring of a real estate company; a European aerospace company, claimant in a liability claim against an official liquidator (*liquidateur judiciaire*); Euro Disney in connection with the restructuring of its debt; and Morgan Stanley in relation to insolvency proceedings commenced against certain clients.

At **JeantetAssociés**, Georges Terrier, Yvon Dréano and Philippe Portier are active in insolvency matters while a young partner, Didier Malka is entirely dedicated to the matter (Philippe Dubois is now at **Sonier Poulain & Associés**). They act on all sides - for the companies, for the creditors, and for the rescuers. They have advised CADIF and Deutsche Bank in the Penauille company debt restructuring, Gaudriot in its bankruptcy, and Crédit Lyonnais in claims against the Moulinex and Brandt banking pool.

Philippe Saigne, **Saigne Sigrist**, has a well-recognised practice, advising financial institutions, brokerage firms and credit houses in their insolvency proceedings.

At **Salans**, Michel Jockey and Pierre-Gilles Wogue arrived from Rambaud Martel in early 2006 and bring good reputations in insolvency and restructuring matters.

Jean-Pierre Farges (**Ashurst**); Jean-Yves Marquet and Hanker Sorensen (**Ernst & Young Société d'Avocats**); David Chijner (**Fried, Frank, Harris, Shriver & Jacobson LLP**) and Maurice Lantourne (**Lantourne Duret & Associés**), who are linked by an exclusive partnership; Bernard Grelon and Thierry Montéran (**UGGC & Associés**); Bernard Vatier (**Vatier & Associés**); Jean-Luc Boussard, Reinhard Dammann and Philippe Métais (**White & Case LLP**); and Alexandra Bigot (**Willkie Farr & Gallagher LLP**), are also recommended.

INSOLVENCY (RECEIVERS)

BIGOT LYONNET
JEAN-PAUL PETRESCHI
OLTRAMARE FOURCAULT
POUDENX BAYLE

Firms are listed alphabetically

INSOLVENCY (RECEIVERS)

Four firms are set apart due to their very well-defined activities. **Bigot Lyonnet**, **Poudenx Bayle**, **Oltramare Fourcault** and **Jean-Paul Petreschi** advise receivers and their representatives.

INSURANCE

Clyde & Co is undoubtedly the best insurance firm in France. The firm is well placed on international insurance matters, with a particular focus on reinsurance. At the same time, it is involved in sectors such as aviation, shipping and transport, energy and natural resources, construction (industrial risks business), and acted in the main insolvency and corporate restructurings in the insurance industry over the last few years. The firm advises almost all the insurance and reinsurance companies (AXA, AGF, MMA, Royal & SunAlliance, and Scor to name a few) and also works for industrial companies (product liability) such as Alcatel and Airbus. Recently, the firm has been involved in major tunnel fires in France, an important plane crash in Egypt and product liability cases in the pharmaceutical industry. Well-known insurance specialists include Gérard Honig, Jean-Marie Preel (an industrial risks specialists), and Bernard Mettetal (reinsurance and insurance insolvency).

New firm **Bouckaert Ormen Passemard Sportes**' Christian Bouckaert has a strong reputation through acting for many leading European and US insurers, as well as commercial and industrial clients on a variety of contentious and non-contentious matters. He is also a well-known reinsurance specialist (arbitration). Pascal Ormen, Rémi Passemard and Carole Sportes are the other partners involved and deal with a variety of cases - industrial risk, civil liability, pharmaceutical liability, corporate executives' liability, life insurance, insolvency, aviation, and the whole range of insurance and reinsurance litigation and arbitration. In recent years, the firm represented the reinsurers involved in the Toulouse AZF explosion; a group of insurers in the context of collapsing mines in the Lorraine area; a group of insurers in the collapse of the Roissy terminal; and on a reinsurance case related to the World Trade Center in New York.

At **Gide Loyrette Nouel**, Emmanuel Fontaine and Philippe Rames handle insurance issues linked to the firm's activities in shipping, aviation, construction, industrial risks and product liability. The team has been advising on insurance products contracts, due diligence, insurance contract distribution, insurance company regulation (authorisation, merger) and various insurance and reinsurance disputes. For instance, the firm acted on behalf of EDF on the organisation of the distribution scheme for associated automobile insurance products; BNP Paribas Assurances on pre-litigation filing

INSURANCE

CLYDE & CO ✪

BOUCKAERT ORMEN PASSEMARD SPORTES ✪

GIDE LOYRETTE NOUEL ✪
LEBOEUF, LAMB, GREENE & MACRAE LLP ✪

Beaumont Garnault
Bouloy Grellet & Godin
Cabouche Gabrielli Marquet
Caston
De Pardieu Brocas Maffei ✪
Hascoët Trillat
Herbert Smith LLP ✪
Holman Fenwick & Willan ✪
Ince & Co ✪
Karila & Associés
Lefèvre Pelletier & associés ✪
Naba et Associés
Neveu Sudaka & Associés
Périnne, Ribierre & Redding
Proskauer Rose LLP ✪
Raffin & Associés
Rembauville-Nicolle & Bureau - Rbm2l
Tétaud Lambard Jami & Associés

Bertagna
CMS Bureau Francis Lefebvre ✪
Clifford Chance
Delormeau & Associés
Denton Wilde Sapte ✪
Elkaim Pagani Monteret-Amar
Flécheux & Associés
Granrut Avocats
Kramer Levin Naftalis & Frankel LLP ✪
Linklaters ✪
Lovells ✪
Orrick, Herrington & Sutcliffe ✪
Paul, Hastings, Janofsky & Walker (Europe) LLP ✪
Reed Smith Rambaud Charot LLP ✪

Firms are listed A-Z in tiers which are ranked in order of priority
✪ *Indicates firm displays contact details at the end of this chapter.*

involving a major French life Insurer; and AXA on a securitisation deal regarding a motor insurance portfolio.

LeBoeuf, Lamb, Greene & Macrae LLP is internationally renowned for its insurance practice, on the regulatory, corporate and contentious sides, including reinsurance litigation. Jean Alisse handles the work in Paris with US partner William Marcoux. Xavier Périnne, who had joined from **Clyde & Co** in 2004, set up his own firm a year later, **Périnne, Ribierre & Redding**.

Other firms are worth a mention: construction experts **Karila & Associés**, **Cabouche Gabrielli Marquet**, **Caston**, **Neveu Sudaka & Associés**, and **Naba et Associés**; shipping specialists **Bouloy Grellet & Godin**, **Ince & Co**, **Holman Fenwick & Willan** and **Rembauville-Nicolle & Bureau - Rbm2l**; aviation specialist **Beaumont Garnault**; insurance firms **Hascoët Trillat**, **Périnne, Ribierre & Redding**, **Tétaud Lambard Jami & Associés** and **Raffin & Associés**; and full-service firms **De Pardieu Brocas Maffei**, **Herbert Smith LLP** (Charles Kaplan and Denis Chemla), **Proskauer Rose LLP** (Christophe Lapp and Emmanuelle Payrau-Sorba), and **Lefèvre Pelletier & associés**.

INTELLECTUAL PROPERTY: FULL-SERVICE FIRMS

At **Allen & Overy LLP**, Pierre Lenoir leads a team of nine lawyers. He works primarily in patents and trade marks. Within the patents area, the firm advises a number of important international pharmaceutical clients, while in trade marks, the client base is focused on retailers. Work is both contentious and non-contentious and benefits from the international network.

Isabelle Leroux and Yves Bizollon (arrived from **LAMY & ASSOCIES** with a team of four associates) are the partners in charge of **Bird & Bird**'s IP department. Leroux handles trade marks while Bizollon's expertise is more in the patents field. Areas of expertise include food, pharmaceuticals, telecoms, media, computers, mechanicals, fashion, sport, design and toys.

Grégoire Triet and Arnaud Michel head the IP department at **Gide Loyrette Nouel**, which also comprises nine associates. Patent litigation, trade mark and copyright are the focus of the practice. Longstanding clients include Levi-Strauss and Philip Morris. Grégoire Triet is President of the AAPI (Association des Avocats de Propriété Industrielle).

Linklaters' IP specialist is Denis Monégier du Sorbier who is particularly known for his patent expertise. The team is developing international oriented advisory work, especially in M&A-derived IP work (including LBOs and IPOs), with a client portfolio including hi-tech and pharmaceutical companies. **Linklaters** has a strong European IP team, notably in Cologne and London.

At **Lovells**, the IP department is three-partners (Milan Chromecek, Dominique Ménard and Marie-Aimée de Dampierre) and 13-lawyers strong and some 100 lawyers deal with IP in Europe. The practice can be divided into four areas: dispute resolution; asset management; media and entertainment; and information technology. About 80% of the clients come from the Paris IP practice and include Ford, Diageo, Canon, Estée Lauder, GlaxoSmithKline, Deutsche Telekom and Total.

Two partners head **August & Debouzy**'s 15-lawyer IP department: Isabelle Renard and Mahasti Razavi. They handle trade marks, patents, copyright and commercial contracts. Areas in which the firm is active include the defence industry, banking and finance, telecoms and IT, media, health and pharmaceuticals. Contentious work is growing with an increased number of patents cases.

At **Deprez Dian Guignot**, Pierre Deprez, Philippe Dian and Vincent Fauchoux deal with trade marks and copyright in the media, entertainment and luxury goods fields. The firm has also set up an autonomous department specialising in trade mark advice, including registration.

The IP/IT group at **Freshfields Bruckhaus Deringer** is composed of seven lawyers, including

INTELLECTUAL PROPERTY: FULL-SERVICE FIRMS

ALLEN & OVERY LLP ✪
BIRD & BIRD ✪
GIDE LOYRETTE NOUEL ✪
LINKLATERS ✪
LOVELLS ✪

August & Debouzy
Deprez Dian Guignot ✪
Freshfields Bruckhaus Deringer
Latham & Watkins
Salans

Baker & McKenzie SCP ✪
Clifford Chance
De Gaulle Fleurance & Associés ✪
Denton Wilde Sapte ✪
Flécheux & Associés
Herbert Smith LLP ✪
NomoS ✪

Bersay & Associés ✪
Bignon Lebray & Associés
BMH Avocats - Breitenstein Meillassoux Hauser ✪
CMS Bureau Francis Lefebvre ✪
Coblence & Associés
DS Avocats
Dubarry Le Douarin Veil ✪
Ernst & Young Société d'Avocats
Ginestié Magellan Paley-Vincent ✪
Granrut Avocats
Jones Day ✪
Lamy & Associés ✪
Paul, Hastings, Janofsky & Walker (Europe) LLP ✪
Simmons & Simmons ✪
Sokolow, Carreras & Associés
Taylor Wessing ✪
Thieffry & Associés
UGGC & Associés ✪
Veil Jourde ✪

Firms are listed A-Z in tiers which are ranked in order of priority
✪ *Indicates firm displays contact details at the end of this chapter.*

partner Xavier Buffet Delmas, who is increasingly visible. The practice covers all areas of IP/IT and specialises in litigation concerning patents, trade marks, design and model trade marks, mergers and acquisitions, technology licences, personal data protection, e-commerce and dispute resolution. Clients include L'Oréal, Colgate, Renault, Gaz de France, Weight Watchers International and Nintendo.

The team, at **Latham & Watkins** numbers 13 lawyers, including partners Emmanuel Baud, Patrick Dunaud and Jean-Christophe Tristant. Among fields covered are media, sport, agribusiness and life sciences.

Gérard Delile heads the **Salans** IP practice which covers all classical IP matters and teams up with the strong IT group when necessary. Pierre Lubet and David Masson arrived from *Rambaud Martel* in early 2006. The firm serves as counsel to international leaders in such fields as IT and software, videogames, pharmaceuticals and chemicals, transport, foods and beverages, toys and games, haute-couture, fragrance and cosmetics, furniture design, luxury goods and tobacco.

Baker & McKenzie SCP's six-lawyer team is headed by Jean-François Bretonnière. It mainly deals with trade marks and trade mark litigation (with a large Asian clientele). Areas of expertise include pharmaceuticals, franchise and distribution, telecoms and publishing.

Clifford Chance's Christian Lachèze handles both trade mark and patent litigation. Jean-Frédéric Gaultier is the other partner to mention.

At **De Gaulle Fleurance & Associés**, the IP/IT team is made up of 13 lawyers and encompasses trade marks, patents, technology transfer and domain names in areas such as health, computers and industry, and artistic copyright in the media industry. Clients include 20th Century Fox, Dreamworks, MSN, Microsoft, Grévin & Cie and AFP.

Two partners (Stefan Naumann and Gilles Vercken) and one of-counsel (Michel Vivant) handle IP at **Denton Wilde Sapte** within the TMT department.

At **Flécheux & Associés**, Marie-Anne Gallot le Lorier is the IP specialist. She handles a great deal of copyright issues, working for publishing houses and in the IT sector.

Herbert Smith LLP's IP team is led by Alexandra Néri and numbers six lawyers. They work for French and international clients on contentious and non-contentious issues: an internet search engine, supermarkets groups, an international music producer, fashion and luxury companies, the leading French civil nuclear company, and a French research organisation, among others.

NomoS' Eric Lauvaux and Héléna Delabarre are in charge of IP and handle litigation as well as advice and audits in areas such as hi-tech, film and music.

INTELLECTUAL PROPERTY: BOUTIQUES

ARMENGAUD GUERLAIN
COURTOIS LEBEL
COUSIN & MOATTY
DUCLOS THORNE MOLLET-VIÉVILLE & ASSOCIÉS
ESCANDE
GAULTIER LAKITS - JOSSE SZLEPER
GILBEY DE HAAS
GREFFE
PHILIPPE COMBEAU
VÉRON & ASSOCIÉS

Cléry de La Myre Mory
Corinne Champagner Katz
Hirsch & Associés
Hoffman
Hollier-Larousse
Howrey LLP ✪
Jean-Louis Lagarde
Michel Huet
Nataf & Fajgenbaum & Associés

Firms are listed A-Z in tiers which are ranked in order of priority
✪ Indicates firm displays contact details at the end of this chapter.

INTELLECTUAL PROPERTY: BOUTIQUES

Patents (electronics, pharmaceuticals) and trade marks (fashion) account for the majority of the work at **Armengaud Guerlain**. Jacques Armengaud is vice-president of the Association of Intellectual Property Lawyers and Stéphane Guerlain of the Association des Praticiens du Droit des Marques et des Modèles (APRAM).

At **Courtois Lebel**, three partners, among them Arnaud Casalonga, cover patents trade marks and author rights. IT litigation and advice.

Pierre Cousin, at **Cousin & Moatty**, sources a significant proportion of turnover from patents work, particularly in the fields of pharmaceuticals, chemicals, mechanics and optics.

Intellectual property represents 50% of **Duclos Thorne Mollet-Viéville & Associés**' activity. Five dedicated lawyers handle about 100 cases per year covering patent litigation, trade marks and copyright issues.

Escande is particularly known for its work in unfair competition, trade marks and is increasingly active in patent litigation. Michel-Paul Escande's clients include some big names in the automotive, luxury goods and food sectors.

Geoffroy Gaultier heads **Gaultier Lakits - Josse Szleper** (formerly *Cabinet Mathély*), which comprises five lawyers. The firm handles substantial amounts of patent litigation.

Richard John Gilbey and Charles de Haas at **Gilbey de Haas** are recommended.

At **Greffe**, IP is the largest practice area and caters to a diverse client base boasting a number of names in the fashion (haute-couture and ready-to-wear) and industrial sectors.

Philippe Combeau and his two associates deal with around 30 patent litigation cases per year. The firm's client base is diverse and includes large pharmaceutical companies.

Pierre Véron of **Véron & Associés** is highly praised for his work in patent litigation. Ten lawyers (also including Isabelle Romet, Thomas Bouvet and Sabine Agé) focus on patents, trade marks, designs and models, with cases such as Rhodia/Asec, Daiichi Kigenso, Winthrop/Astra-Zeneca, Sandoz/Glaxo, Depagne/Sogexi. The firm is in Paris and Lyon.

Other recommended specialists include: Olivier de La Myre Mory and Alain Cléry (**Cléry de La Myre Mory**); **Corinne Champagner Katz**; Marc-Roger Hirsch (**Hirsch & Associés**); Serge Hoffman (**Hoffman**); Christian Hollier-Larousse (**Hollier-Larousse**); Marina Cousté (**Howrey LLP**); **Jean-Louis Lagarde**; **Michel Huet**; and Fabienne Fajgenbaum (**Nataf & Fajgenbaum & Associés**).

INTELLECTUAL PROPERTY: PATENT AND TRADE MARK ATTORNEYS

This chapter introduces the best patent and trade mark attorneys in France (CPI - *conseils en propriété industrielle*). Still part of a separate profession (although the debate regarding merger with lawyers is ongoing), the CPI firms handle IP portfolio management. Some 550 experts have the title of CPI. Those that specialise in patents have a science background and are engineers (*ingénieurs*), those in charge of trade marks studied law and are legal consultants (*juristes*). Some of them have both qualifications.

Cabinet Beau de Loménie is one of the top industrial property firms. With some 50 *conseils* (35 engineers, and 15 law specialists), among them six partners, it is the biggest firm in France. The firm has offices in Lille, Lyons, Marseille (with four consultants in each of them) and in Munich (with a German consultant) for European patents. As far as patents are concerned, three departments can be identified chemistry/biochemistry/biotechnology; electronics/computer science; and mechanics/physics. Of note, the firm has two UK specialists in its chemistry department, a UK and a US consultant in the electronics department, and someone of Japanese nationality. 45% of the clients come from abroad. Among the firm's clients are Messier-Bugatti, Poclain Hydraulics, Habitat and Spontex.

Germain & Moreau is a growing firm and has doubled size in ten years. With now some 15 engineers and 12 trade mark specialists, it is a young firm the headquarters of which is in Lyons but with offices in Paris (four *juristes* and two engineers), Saint-Etienne and in Neuchâtel (Switzerland). **Germain & Moreau**'s reputation lies in offering a well-balanced practice covering

INTELLECTUAL PROPERTY: PATENT AND TRADE MARK ATTORNEYS

BEAU DE LOMÉNIE, CABINET
GERMAIN & MOREAU
LAVOIX
PLASSERAUD
REGIMBEAU
SANTARELLI

Breese Derambure Majerowicz
Casalonga Josse
EGYP - Gutmann Plasseraud
Harlé et Phélip, Cabinet
Hirsch Pochart
Loyer Peuscet Brema
Novagraaf
Orès

Armengaud Jeune Lepeudry
Boettcher
Brevalex
Inlex Conseil
Lhermet La Bigne & Rémy
Markplus International
Netter
Vidon
Weinstein

Firms are listed A-Z in tiers which are ranked in order of priority

patents and trade marks, the latter making up 50% of turnover. Fields covered are vast with for instance a patents department specialising in biotechnology, chemistry, pharmacology and a strong clientele in the wine industry. Litigation is also handled.

Lavoix is renowned. The firm has more than 30 *conseils en propriété industrielle*. Its Lyons office is important (seven *conseils*) and the firm is also present in Toulouse and Clermont-Ferrand. Three-quarters of the activity is dedicated to patents and broken down between general mechanics and physics (slightly prevailing), chemistry/pharmacology and biotechnologies, electronics and computer science. **Lavoix** is one of the firms with the most sizeable proportion of national clients (75%), and works very closely with small and medium-sized French companies, as well as multinationals with French origins.

With some 56 industrial property consultants, **Plasseraud** is another strong player in Paris that has doubled its workforce in five years. It also has an office in Lyons where two engineers and a legal adviser are active. The patent activities are split between chemistry/pharmaceuticals/biotechnologies (25% of the turnover) and mechanics/electricity/computer science (50%). The rest is dedicated to trade marks. **Plasseraud** also has a Japanese ambassador who represents the firm in Japan.

Regimbeau has 45 *ingénieurs* and *juristes* and a total of 145 people spread between offices in Paris, Rennes and Lyons. The patents department is divided into two areas: biotechnology and pharmacology; telecoms, electronics, computers and mechanics, notably for clients in the semi-conductor and silicium industries. The trade mark activity is particularly visible in the banking and food industries. **Regimbeau** is also renowned for its contentious activity.

Santarelli was born in March 2003, following the merger of *Rinuy, Santarelli* and *Bonnet-Thirion*. It is especially renowned for its litigation practice: among the 30 consultants that form the firm, 20 patent and ten trade mark specialists, half have contentious abilities and three *conseils* are fully dedicated to litigation. As far as patents are concerned, the firm covers the whole technological spectrum but is especially renowned in biotechnology, electronics and telecoms. Another speciality is the cooperation between engineers and legal experts who team up for licensing activities for example. An American partner and a British engineer work for the firm. **Santarelli** also has further offices in Toulouse and Marseille.

Breese Derambure Majerowicz is the result of last year's merger between *BDSA – Bouju Derambure Bugnion* and *Breese Majerowicz*. The staff of approximately 100 includes 30 trade mark and patent attorneys. Patent activity constitutes 60% of the business. Its areas of expertise include: life sciences, biotechnology, pharmacology and cosmetics, chemistry, engineering sciences, telecommunications, computer science, packaging, food, real estate, automotive, aeronautics, textiles and luxury goods. The firm is active in patent and IP rights litigation as well as in services such as financial valuation and strategy. Its domestic client base is 75% and the current 25% international base in US and Japan is expanding.

Founded in 1867, **Casalonga Josse** has a team specialising in European patent law in Munich, a team specialising in EC trade mark law in Alicante, and an office in Grenoble. In Paris, the patents activity is broken down between two departments: mechanics/electricity/electronics and chemistry/pharmacology/biotechnologies. Some 20 engineers work there. The legal department comprises five IP consultants, a New York Bar lawyer, and an Alicante Bar lawyer. At the same time, the firm deals with its clients' contentious matters.

EGYP - Gutmann Plasseraud was originally formed from a split from **Plasseraud** 15 years ago, and its founding partners have now made way for the five women partners heading the firm. Apart from Paris, the firm has offices in Lyons and Alicante. 70% of the work is dedicated to patents, with specific expertise in biotechnology. The firm is also well known in mechanics, electronics and physics. In trade marks, areas of excellence include the food industry, luxury goods, marks of origin (wines and champagnes) and collective trade marks (franchises). 10% of the clients are international.

Cabinet Harlé et Phélip is a very old firm, the origins of which date back to the 19th century. Today, the firm has eight consultants (eight engineers and four legal advisors) and a secondary office in Nantes. In the patents department, the activity is wide and covers chemistry, biotechnology, mechanics, construction, physics, electronics and software. Of note, **Cabinet Harlé et Phélip** has a doctor of engineering on its team. Litigation is important and makes up 10% of the turnover. Clients are both international and national technology companies. The firm is also active in trade marks and works for small and medium-sized companies.

Hirsch Pochart is a firm of *conseil en propriété industrielle* working very closely to law firm, **Hirsch & Associés**. The latter numbers 15 lawyers among which six have a double training engineer/lawyer, whereas **Hirsch Pochart** has eight consultants. The lawyers do not deal with administrative work and 85% of the activity of **Hirsch Pochart** comes from the law firm. Clients are international (45%) and the work breaks down as follows: 45% patents; 30% trade marks; 25% litigation.

Loyer Peuscet Brema comrpises three firms that firms share premises and have some 15 consultants altogether. Two associates work in the Nantes office. All areas of intellectual property are tackled, including contentious issues, and the firm is especially active in the following areas for patents: mechanics, aeronautics, hydraulics, chemistry, biology, electronics and information systems.

Novagraaf in France has 31 patent and trade mark attorneys. Trade marks and patents are dealt with in distinct structures: Novagraaf France for trade marks and Novagraaf Technologies for patents. The firm was born from the merger between *Novamark* that existed in France, Belgium and Switzerland, with *Markgraaf*, present in the Netherlands and the UK. In 2002, the firm *Ballot*, a patent specialist, joined Novagraaf Technologies, bringing at the same time offices in Metz, Lorient, Besançon and Toulon. The European network is non-exclusive. In France, trade marks (Johan Van Den Bossche) make up 55% of the business and all areas are included with specific expertise in the wine industry. As far as patents (Jean-Louis Sommier) are concerned, 12 engineers are active in electronics/software, mechanics/ metallurgy and chemistry/biotechnology.

Orès was founded in 1972 and its activity is mainly dedicated to patents. Fourteen engineers are active in the following areas: biotechnology, chemistry, pharmacology, textiles/paper/rubber/plastic, food, mechanics, electronics and physics. Four *juristes* handle trade marks.

MEDIA AND ENTERTAINMENT FULL-SERVICE FIRMS

BIGNON LEBRAY & ASSOCIÉS
BIRD & BIRD ✪
DE GAULLE FLEURANCE & ASSOCIÉS ✪
DENTON WILDE SAPTE ✪
DEPREZ DIAN GUIGNOT ✪
GIDE LOYRETTE NOUEL ✪
GRANRUT AVOCATS
LATHAM & WATKINS
NOMOS ✪
SALANS
SOKOLOW, CARRERAS & ASSOCIÉS
WAN AVOCATS

Allen & Overy LLP ✪
August & Debouzy
Carbonnier Lamaze Rasle & Associés
Clifford Chance
Hogan & Hartson MNP ✪
La Boétie
Pascal Wilhelm & Associés
Taylor Wessing ✪
Vatier & Associés ✪
Weil, Gotshal & Manges ✪

Firms are listed A-Z in tiers which are ranked in order of priority
✪ Indicates firm displays contact details at the end of this chapter.

MEDIA AND ENTERTAINMENT: FULL-SERVICE FIRMS

Bignon Lebray & Associés' media team is led by Anne-Marie Pecoraro. Well-known within the music industry (she advises artists and editors), the activities of her team also encompass TV, cinema, press and publishing.

At **Bird & Bird**, Alexandre Vuchot is a specialist in media and sports law and has considerable experience in broadcasting rights acquisition. He represents domestic and international media companies on regulatory issues and transactional matters.

De Gaulle Fleurance & Associés handles intellectual property, contracts and litigation in the media and entertainment industries.

At **Denton Wilde Sapte**, Gilles Vercken has a strong competence in media and entertainment. A former head of legal of Sacem-Sdrm and Saces and legal director of Ellipse Canal+ Cable, he is very active in media, technology and IP, especially in television, radio, music, publishing and video games.

Deprez Dian Guignot (Pierre Deprez, Philippe Dian, Vincent Fauchoux) represents advertising agencies, publishers and press agencies, French and European TV cable or satellite channels, among them a French national TV channel, content providers and other media. The firm also has expertise in entertainment law - movie, TV/radio, music and video games.

Gide Loyrette Nouel's practice in the media field focuses on film and television, especially financing production and distribution. Olivier Cousi and Rémy Fekete provide a wide range of services including assistance to independent producers and to financing institutions, negotiation of all forms of national, international distribution and co-production agreements and litigation.

Jean Castelain is the media expert at **Granrut Avocats**. He heads a four-lawyer team and works for major companies in the music business (EMI, Warner) and the French union of music publishers CSDEM, TV networks (France Télévision), the collecting society SCAM and film producers.

At **Latham & Watkins**, partners Patrick Dunaud, Emmanuel Drai and their teams have expertise in the fields of film and television, working for major corporations such as TF1, Europsort, TPS, CNN, Time Warner, HBO, Endemol and Fox. Work is carried out on the corporate, litigation and regulatory sides.

NomoS has a media team with Eric Lauvaux, a specialist in the music industry. Héléna Delabarre is the other partner. The firm is developing a name in the audiovisual sector.

The media and audiovisual team in **Salans**' Paris office is greatly involved in the world of entertainment, music, television and audiovisual production activities. Bruno Grégoire Sainte Marie and his team assist music and film producers, singers, musicians, conductors, national theatres, agents, etc.

At **Sokolow, Carreras & Associés**, three litigation partners have media expertise: Alain Barsikian, Jean-Michel Iscovici and Pierre-Olivier Chartier.

At **WAN Avocats**, Isabelle Wekstein and Jean Aittouares handle publishing (for publishers, authors and retailers), audiovisual (motion picture, television and music companies) and all other types of entertainment matters, as well as media concentration cases before the European Commission and trade mark rights.

Allen & Overy LLP is active on the corporate, IP and regulatory sides, working for M6, Paris Première, Ouest-France and the Cannes Film Festival.

August & Debouzy is counsel to various publishers of daily newspapers, magazines and trade organisations for contentious and IP-related matters.

At **Carbonnier Lamaze Rasle & Associés**, Michel Rasle is very active in television (Arte and other national channels), radio (Radio France, RFI) and has some activities in press and publishing. Eric Morain handles press white-collar crime.

Clifford Chance is involved in TV rights matters and is active in sports law issues (Marc d'Haultfoeuille and Yves Wehrli act for the French football league). The team advised NRJ Group and MTV Networks on various legal issues and Turner Broadcasting on distribution issues.

At **Hogan & Hartson MNP**, Winston Maxwell handles media and communications issues, both transactional and regulatory, notably in the TV and cable industries.

La Boétie is present in the fields of music and audiovisual with an activity related to contracts, co-productions, financings (cinema, television radio).

Pascal Wilhelm & Associés has a five-lawyer team with clients in various media: television (Canal+), press (Marianne, 20 minutes), radio (MFM) and also carries out a lot of work for advertising agencies.

Taylor Wessing advises in the media area with Arnaud de Senilhes and Christian Valsamidis. They are especially strong in the cinema industry and are involved in many productions, but clients also include press and music groups.

At **Vatier & Associés**, Ann Creelman and Olivier Saumon are active.

Claude Serra, at **Weil, Gotshal & Manges**, is an expert on corporate and financial television-related issues, with clients in the cable industry for instance. He also advises producers and financial institutions.

MEDIA AND ENTERTAINMENT: NEWSPAPERS AND MAGAZINES

Yves Baudelot (**Lysias**), Jean-Yves Dupeux (**Lussan Brouillaud**), Christophe Bigot (**Bauer & Bigot**), and Bruno Landry (**Dartevelle Benazeraf Merlet Dubest**) are acknowledged as excellent *avocats* who represent their publishing clients in court, as well as advising them on more traditional areas of press law, such as violations of privacy, defamation and image rights.

Christophe Bigot advises Hachette Filipacchi, Le Nouvel Observateur, Le Point, Télérama, le Groupe Liaisons. Since January 2000, he has been a name partner of **Bauer & Bigot**, which specialises in communications law.

Bruno Landry (**Dartevelle Benazeraf Merlet Dubest**) also concentrates on the written word, working mainly for the Groupe Express (*L'Express, Lire*) and Hachette Filipacchi (*France Dimanche, Télé 7 Jours*), with Laurent Merlet. Political and business personalities are also defended.

Lussan Brouillaud has two lawyers handling communications and media: Jean-Yves Dupeux and Thierry Massis. They regularly represent the interests of various French magazines, including those published by Prisma Presse.

Yves Baudelot, a partner at **Lysias**, is active in media law, specialising in journalism and editorial matters. Clients include *Le Monde* and specialist financial and business papers.

MEDIA AND ENTERTAINMENT NEWSPAPERS AND MAGAZINES

BAUER & BIGOT
DARTEVELLE BENAZERAF MERLET DUBEST
LUSSAN BROUILLAUD
LYSIAS

Firms are listed alphabetically

MEDIA AND ENTERTAINMENT BOOK PUBLISHING

BAUER & BIGOT
DARTEVELLE BENAZERAF MERLET DUBEST
DOMINIQUE DE LEUSSE DE SYON
ZYLBERSTEIN & HALPERN

Firms are listed alphabetically

MEDIA AND ENTERTAINMENT: BOOK PUBLISHING

Christophe Bigot, **Bauer & Bigot**, boasts publishing houses Albin Michel and Flammarion among his clients.

The name partners of **Dartevelle Benazeraf Merlet Dubest** are exclusive legal advisers to the Gallimard Group, but also work for Flammarion and the National Publishers Association (Syndicat National de l'Edition).

Dominique de Leusse de Syon represents Le Seuil as well as a number of smaller publishing houses.

At **Zylberstein & Halpern**, Jean-Claude Zylberstein is renowned for his practice in copyright in the publishing sector. He works for Plon, Robert Laffont, Libella and Editis, mainly on libel and plagiarism cases. In the same firm, Anne Boissard is also well known.

MEDIA AND ENTERTAINMENT: TELEVISION/RADIO

Louis Bousquet, at **Bousquet**, has for many years acted as legal counsel to the Bouygues Group. The firm became active in media law during the privatisation of TF1. Its practice covers issues ranging from corporate transactions to regulatory matters. Partners Olivier Sprung and Philippe Moncorps also handle TV and radio work.

At **Carbonnier Lamaze Rasle & Associés**, around half of Michel Rasle's time is spent on TV-related work (Arte). Teamed with three associates, Rasle regularly undertakes both advisory and litigation work for other TV channels and radio stations (Radio France, RFI).

MEDIA AND ENTERTAINMENT TELEVISION/RADIO

BOUSQUET
CARBONNIER LAMAZE RASLE & ASSOCIÉS
CHEMOULI DAUZIER ET ASSOCIÉS
DEPREZ DIAN GUIGNOT ✪
LATHAM & WATKINS
MARTINE COISNE
WEIL, GOTSHAL & MANGES ✪

Firms are listed alphabetically
✪ Indicates firm displays contact details at the end of this chapter.

Pierre-Louis Dauzier, at **Chemouli Dauzier et associés**, works for Canal+ and also for radio stations.

Televisual matters are also to the fore at **Deprez Dian Guignot**, where partner Philippe Dian is exclusive adviser to a national TV station. The firm handles all areas of law for this client, from commercial to press law.

At **Latham & Watkins**, Patrick Dunaud works for distributors (Eurosport, TPS, TF1). The firm handles negotiations linked with sports law and is very active in the cable and satellite sectors (CNN, Time Warner).

Martine Coisne advises a private broadcaster and several medium-sized film and TV production companies.

Claude Serra at **Weil, Gotshal & Manges** is another acknowledged expert in broadcast media law. His clientele includes a number of cable companies, which he advises on infrastructure matters, as well as production companies and institutional investors.

MEDIA AND ENTERTAINMENT: FILM

The six lawyers at **Bitoun & Associés** enjoy close and longstanding links with the film industry, advising directors, scriptwriters, actors, producers and TV production companies.

At **Gide Loyrette Nouel**, Olivier Cousi and Rémy Fekete provide a wide range of services including assistance to independent producers and to financing institutions.

Michel Libermann is based in Paris and New York, where he advises major players in the European film industry on the US market and vice-versa. Areas covered in the US are contracts, co-production, multi-source financing and the acquisition and marketing of licensing rights.

Christian Valsimidis at **Taylor Wessing** heads an eight-lawyer team. He advises mainly producers and film directors and is involved in great deal of productions.

Walker, Borowsky & Haidar offers a wide range of services covering all TV and film-related legal issues: project finance, loan guarantees, capital markets transactions, negotiations with actors and their agents, contracts, co-production agreements, distribution and dealing with public regulators and censors. The client base consists of TV stations, capital investors, banks, and French, US, British, German and Scandinavian actors' agents.

MEDIA AND ENTERTAINMENT FILM

BITOUN & ASSOCIÉS
GIDE LOYRETTE NOUEL ✪
MICHEL LIBERMANN
TAYLOR WESSING ✪
WALKER, BOROWSKY & HAIDAR

Firms are listed alphabetically
✪ Indicates firm displays contact details at the end of this chapter.

MEDIA AND ENTERTAINMENT MUSIC

BIGNON LEBRAY & ASSOCIÉS
GRANRUT AVOCATS
JEAN ENNOCHI
NICOLAS BOESPFLUG
NOMOS ✪

Firms are listed alphabetically
✪ Indicates firm displays contact details at the end of this chapter.

MEDIA AND ENTERTAINMENT: MUSIC

A handful of French lawyers work regularly for the major companies and have become experts in this highly specialised area of law. Amongst them, Anne-Marie Pecoraro (**Bignon Lebray & Associés**), **Jean Ennochi**, Jean Castelain at **Granrut Avocats**, Eric Lauvaux at **NomoS** and **Nicolas Boespflug** are all highly regarded.

MERGERS AND ACQUISITIONS

Bredin Prat is involved in most of the major transactions. Its outstanding reputation is due to the names of Jean-François Prat (public offerings and stock market battles) and Didier Martin (privatisations) but the corporate team (including Elena Baxter, Sébastien Prat, Philippe Beurier, Olivier Assant, Emmanuel Masset, and Patrick Dziewolski, to mention a few), is one of the biggest teams in France. The firm also distinguishes itself by having US and English partners and has developed strong working relationships abroad with **Cravath, Swaine & Moore LLP** and **Davis Polk & Wardwell** in the US and, in Europe, with celebrated best friends **Slaughter and May** (UK), **Hengeler Mueller** (Germany), **Bonelli Erede Pappalardo** (Italy), and **Uría Menéndez** (Spain). The link with **Slaughter and May** was strengthened at the beginning of 2006 by the integration of the M&A team of the Magic Circle firm when it decided to withdraw from the French market. Among major recent transactions, we can mention counsel to the Taittinger family in the acquisition of Groupe Taittinger by Starwood Capital; Gécina in its acquisition by Metrovacesa; Snecma in its merger with Sagem; the funds in the acquisition of Rexel; Equant in its acquisition by France Télécom; and Accor in the PIPE investment by Colony Capital. The firm was also active in the privatisations of Snecma, Sernam and France Télécom.

Cleary, Gottlieb, Steen & Hamilton LLP is involved in public bids (Pierre-Yves Chabert), as well as in transnational transactions, and is well positioned for privatisations. Other partners involved include Jean-Michel Tron, François Jonemann, Marie-Laurence Tibi, John Brinitzer, Valérie Lemaitre and Jean-Marie Ambrosi (private equity). The firm represented Euronext in its potential offer for the London Stock Exchange;

MERGERS AND ACQUISITIONS

BREDIN PRAT ✪

CLEARY, GOTTLIEB, STEEN & HAMILTON LLP ✪
DARROIS VILLEY MAILLOT BROCHIER ✪
LINKLATERS ✪

CLIFFORD CHANCE
FRESHFIELDS BRUCKHAUS DERINGER
GIDE LOYRETTE NOUEL ✪
LATHAM & WATKINS
ORRICK, HERRINGTON & SUTCLIFFE ✪
SULLIVAN & CROMWELL LLP

Ashurst ✪
Brandford-Griffith & Associés ✪
De Pardieu Brocas Maffei ✪
JeantetAssociés ✪
Jones Day ✪
Paul, Hastings, Janofsky & Walker (Europe) LLP ✪
Shearman & Sterling LLP
Skadden, Arps, Slate, Meagher & Flom LLP
Veil Jourde ✪
Willkie Farr & Gallagher LLP ✪

Allen & Overy LLP ✪
Baker & McKenzie SCP ✪
Debevoise & Plimpton LLP ✪
Herbert Smith LLP ✪
Lovells ✪
Norton Rose
SJ Berwin ✪
Salans
Weil, Gotshal & Manges ✪
White & Case LLP

August & Debouzy
CMS Bureau Francis Lefebvre ✪
Cotty Vivant Marchisio & Lauzeral
Davis Polk & Wardwell
Dechert ✪
Denton Wilde Sapte ✪
Eversheds-Frere Cholmeley
Franklin ✪
Gibson, Dunn & Crutcher LLP
Ginestié Magellan Paley-Vincent ✪
Hughes Hubbard & Reed LLP ✪
LeBoeuf, Lamb, Greene & Macrae LLP ✪
Lefèvre Pelletier & associés ✪
Morgan Lewis ✪
Simmons & Simmons ✪
UGGC & Associés ✪

Continued

BNP Paribas in the €2.2bn buyout of Groupe Galeries Lafayette and the related tender offer; Equant NV, a subsidiary of France Télécom, in the acquisition by France Télécom of the 45.8% interest in Equant that it did not previously own; Areva in the €1bn sale of FCI to Bain Capital; Neuf Télécom in connection with its acquisition of Cegetel; Bouygues in the €1bn sale of SAUR to PAI Partners; and BC Partners in its €1.3bn acquisition of Picard Surgelés from Candover.

The four name partners at **Darrois Villey Maillot Brochier** are highly active in M&A and Jean-Michel Darrois is particularly well known. Olivier Diaz also deserves a mention. The firm frequently handles public bids, (friendly or hostile with contentious aspects), as well as a number of more classic M&A transactions. In 2004/2005, it advised Bouygues in the disposal of shares of SAUR; Marionnaud in connection with the takeover bid by AS Watson; Pernod Ricard in the acquisition of Allied Domecq; AGF in the acquisition of Gécina; and the Moulin family in the takeover bid on Galeries Lafayette. **Darrois Villey Maillot Brochier** works closely with New York M&A powerhouse **Wachtell, Lipton, Rosen & Katz**.

Three main areas merit mention at **Linklaters**: takeover bids (Thierry Vassogne, Marc Loy, Thierry Riguet, Bertrand Cardi); private acquisitions and joint ventures (Alain Garnier, Patrick Rignell); and LBOs (Fabrice de la Morandière, Michel Frieh). Patrick Laporte left for **Debevoise & Plimpton LLP**. The team, that includes in total 50 lawyers (including 11 partners), was involved in the public tender offer by Suez on Electrabel for an amount of €11.2bn and the share capital increase by Suez for an amount of €2.5bn; the Meyer family in the framework for the cash offer for Galeries Lafayette; the cash public offer by Metrovacesa for Gecina (enterprise value € 8.57bn); the sale of UGC Cinemas Holdings Limited to a subsidiary of Cineworld UK Limited owned by Blackstone; the recommended public offer by Pernod Ricard to acquire Allied Domecq plc; the acquisition of a 50.5% stake by Adecco in Altedia; and the Saur LBO (€1bn).

Clifford Chance handles both classic M&A work and more complex transactions, such as public bids or LBOs. The firm has a broad client base, which includes numerous French and foreign investment funds, and is on good terms with a number of investment banks. **Clifford Chance**'s nine-partner team includes Marcus Billam, Frédéric Peltier, Christophe Salamon, Thierry Schoen, Yves Wehrli and Catherine Astor-Veyres. The firm recently acted for Colony on the acquisition of Buffalo Grill (€158m); Air France in the disposal to BC Partners and Cinven of its 23% holding in Amadeus; France Télécom on its disposal of its remaining 36% stake in TDF to Charterhouse Capital Partners, CDC Equity Capital and Caisse des Dépôts et Consignations; Pathé on the sale of four of its TV channels; EADS on the sale by EADS Telecom of various worldwide activities to Aastra and Lagassé; Kohlberg Kravis Roberts on the French aspects of the acquisition of Toys R Us (€6.7bn); and Clayton Dubilier & Rice, Eurazeo and Merrill Lynch Global Private Equity on the acquisition from PPR of Rexel (€4.1bn).

At **Freshfields Bruckhaus Deringer**, nine partners handle M&A, including Yves de Mahenge,

MERGERS AND ACQUISITIONS
Continued

Adamas ✪
Ayache Salama & Associés ✪
BMH Avocats - Breitenstein Meillassoux Hauser ✪
Barbé Carpentier Thibault Groener & Associés
Bernard Hertz Béjot
Bernet Castagnet Wantz & Associés
Bersay & Associés ✪
Bignon Lebray & Associés
Bird & Bird ✪
Courtois Lebel
De Gaulle Fleurance & Associés ✪
Dubarry Le Douarin Veil ✪
Ernst & Young Société d'Avocats
Fidal ✪
Fried, Frank, Harris, Shriver & Jacobson LLP
Haarmann Hemmelrath ✪
Hammonds Hausmann
Hogan & Hartson MNP ✪
Kahn & Associés
Kramer Levin Naftalis & Frankel LLP ✪
Landwell & Associés
Mayer, Brown, Rowe & Maw LLP ✪
NomoS ✪
Orrick, Herrington & Sutcliffe ✪
Ratheaux ✪
Sokolow, Carreras & Associés
Taylor Wessing ✪
Taj ✪
Vatier & Associés ✪
Viguié Schmidt
Vivien & Juvigny

Firms are listed A-Z in tiers which are ranked in order of priority
✪ *Indicates firm displays contact details at the end of this chapter.*

Patrick Bonvarlet, Jean-Claude Cotoni, Isabelle MacElhone, Antoine Vignial, Bertrand Pellet and Fabrice Cohen. Arnaud Pérès left for **Davis Polk & Wardwell**. The firm handles both French M&A issues and those with an international dimension, private equity transactions, public offers for listed companies, IPOs, secondary rights issues and capital restructurings. Major recent transactions include advising Solvay in relation to its acquisition of Fournier Pharma (€1.3bn); Goldman Sachs Capital Partners on its acquisition of the cable business of Pirelli (€1.3bn); AS Watson (Hutchison Whampoa), on its recommended public offer to acquire Marionnaud (€535m); Cinven on the acquisition of Amadeus for a consideration of €4bn; Cinven on the leveraged recapitalisation of Eutelsat (€2.5bn); and Lehman Brothers on its joint acquisition, with Starwood Capital Group, of Le Meridien's hotel portfolio through a 50/50 joint venture (£1bn).

The 17-partner M&A team at **Gide Loyrette Nouel** (the biggest in France) remains one of the most prominent, with a special mention to Youssef

Djehane, Antoine Bonnasse and Olivier Puech. Christophe Eck, Didier G Martin, Jean-Emmanuel Skovron and Serge Tatar are also well known. Recent highlights include advising France Télécom and Canal+ on the joint sale of their cable network operations; the French Treasury on the opening of GDF's capital; SNCF Participations on the sale of its stake in the share capital of Cegetel in the scope of the merger Cegetel/9Telecom; Tiscali for the sale of its French listed subsidiary, Liberty Surf, to Telecom Italia; and Johnson Controls Inc on the sale of its French subsidiary, Johnson Controls Engine Electronics, to Valeo.

Latham & Watkins is active in classic M&A as well as in private equity, an area where the firm is now a leader with the arrival of Thomas Forschbach and a team from **Ashurst** in autumn 2004. Some nine partners, with a special mention to Dominique Basdevant, Patrick Beauvisage, Nicolas Bombrun, Pierre Descheemaeker and Olivier du Mottay, regularly handle M&A work. Recent highlights include acting for Sagard in the acquisition of Kiloutou (€175m); Bain Capital in its acquisition of FCI from Areva (€1bn); Electra Partners in the joint MBO acquisition with CVC Capital Partners of part of the CPI Group (€450m); Spectrum Equity Investors in the €2.4bn leveraged finance recapitalisation by shareholders of their ownership interests in Eutelsat; and MediMedia in the sale of its professional and medical publishing businesses to Reed Elsevier (€230m).

The M&A team at **Orrick, Herrington & Sutcliffe** comes mainly from *Rambaud Martel* and has established its reputation on the basis of its practice in major transactions involving listed companies. Jean-Pierre Martel is among the leading lawyers called in the country's most important stock market battles. Other partners include Jean-Michel Leprêtre, Luc Saucier, Fabrice Patrizio, Arnaud Larrousse, Bertrand Delafaye and three **Orrick, Herrington & Sutcliffe** partners: George Yates, François Bloch and Nathalie le Bris. For example, the firm advised Gecina in the takeover bid launched by Metrovacesa; BNP Paribas in the sale of 19.2% of Eiffage shares and of 20.8% of Carbone Lorraine shares; Vinci in the procedure organised by the French Government to sell its controlling stake in Autoroutes du Sud de la France; Galeries Lafayette in the takeover bid launched by SEMAD; and the French Ministry of Finance, along with Calyon and Morgan Stanley, on the privatisation of Electricité de France.

Sullivan & Cromwell LLP has recognised capabilities to provide both French and US legal advice on domestic and cross-border transactions. Richard Asthalter, Gérard Mazet, William Torchiana and Dominique Bompoint handle significant deals. The firm's highlights for 2005 include assisting CCF Recycling in the US$766m bid to acquire Penauille Polyservices; advising the financial advisors to France Télécom on the US$735m bid to buy the remaining shares in Equant; and advising the financial advisors to Metrovacesa on the US$7.3bn acquisition of Gecina. **Sullivan & Cromwell LLP** was also involved in the privatisations of Areva, EDF, France Télécom and Sanef.

LEVERAGED BUY-OUTS

ASHURST ✪
LATHAM & WATKINS
LINKLATERS ✪
WEIL, GOTSHAL & MANGES ✪
WILLKIE FARR & GALLAGHER LLP ✪

Clifford Chance
Freshfields Bruckhaus Deringer
Gide Loyrette Nouel ✪
Mayer, Brown, Rowe & Maw LLP ✪
SJ Berwin ✪
White & Case LLP

Ayache Salama & Associés ✪
Bredin Prat ✪
Cleary, Gottlieb, Steen & Hamilton LLP ✪
Darrois Villey Maillot Brochier ✪
Jones Day ✪
Lefèvre Pelletier & associés ✪
Lovells ✪
Orrick, Herrington & Sutcliffe ✪
P.D.G.B.
Salans
Sarrau Thomas Couderc
Shearman & Sterling LLP
Veil Jourde ✪
Wilinski Scotto & Associés

Allen & Overy LLP ✪
August & Debouzy
Baker & McKenzie SCP ✪
Bird & Bird ✪
Brandford-Griffith & Associés ✪
CMS Bureau Francis Lefebvre ✪
De Pardieu Brocas Maffei ✪
Debevoise & Plimpton LLP ✪
Dechert ✪
Ernst & Young Société d'Avocats
Franklin ✪
Fried, Frank, Harris, Shriver & Jacobson LLP
Ginestié Magellan Paley-Vincent ✪
HPML
JeantetAssociés ✪
La Boétie
LeBoeuf, Lamb, Greene & Macrae LLP ✪
NomoS ✪
Norton Rose
Paul, Hastings, Janofsky & Walker (Europe) LLP ✪
Simmons & Simmons ✪
Sokolow, Carreras & Associés
Taj ✪
Taylor Wessing ✪
UGGC & Associés ✪

Firms are listed A-Z in tiers which are ranked in order of priority
✪ Indicates firm displays contact details at the end of this chapter.

Ashurst's practice focuses on LBOs, on both the equity and the debt sides. The firm is also involved in straight acquisitions. The team numbers 20 lawyers, with partners Frédéric Pinet, Guy Benda and Bertrand Delaunay. In 2005, the team assisted Charterhouse Capital Partners LLP, CDC Entreprises Equity Capital and Caisse des Dépôts et Consignations on the acquisition of a 36% interest in Télédiffusion de France (TDF); Stirling Square Capital Partners on the acquisition of Permaswage and the DMC division of the Deutsch Company; and Fox International Channels Group on the acquisition by Fox of one of the leading French cable and satellite travel and leisure channels from Pathé SAS.

Brandford-Griffith & Associés is widely dedicated to M&A work, with a strong focus on public transactions – Henri Brandford-Griffith has notably been active in mergers involving stock exchange battles such as BNP/Paribas and TotalFina/Elf Aquitaine. Cross-border transactions, stock exchange litigation and LBOs are also handled. Recently, the partners (also including Nigel Hartridge, Vanina Paolaggi, Jérôme Brosset and Guillaume Kessler) advised Wendel Investissements in connection with its offer for Groupe Taittinger; Ripplewood Holding in connection with the acquisition of Power Systems' activities from Alcatel; Crédit Agricole SA in Lazard's project of going public; LBO France Gestion and EDM in their acquisition of Groupe Rocamat; Banque Palatine in the takeover bid for Eurosic; and SNPE on the acquisition of Tessenderlo.

At **De Pardieu Brocas Maffei**, Thierry Brocas and his teams have a top clientele in the banking, insurance and real estate areas, although the number of industrial clients is growing. The team also includes Guillaume Touttée, Frédéric Bucher, Stéphane Illouz and Pascale Gros, who arrived from *Coudert Frères*. They all handle increasing volumes of international and private equity deals. The firm advised Wendel Investissement in its bid for the acquisition of Taittinger and in connection with the sale of Wheelabrator Allevard to LBO France; Suren on the public tender offer for Medidep; Pernod Ricard in connection with the acquisition of the French subsidiaries of Allied Domecq; Foncière des Régions in the context of the takeover bid for Bail Investissement Foncière; and the shareholders (Apax Partners and Galileo Partners), in the IPO of Rue du Commerce on Euronext.

M&A continues to be one of the areas in which **JeantetAssociés** excels, especially cross-border, advising banks as well as industrials and, more recently, Anglo-Saxon funds. Eleven partners are active in M&A, among which Georges Terrier, Philippe Blaquier-Cirelli, Yvon Dréano, Christophe Perchet and Philippe Portier stand out. Recently, the firm advised the Meyer family in the sale of its stake in Galeries Lafayette to BNP Paribas; Bain Capital LLC in the acquisition of Toys R Us;

FUND FORMATION

SJ BERWIN ✪

Debevoise & Plimpton LLP ✪
Dechert ✪
Sarrau Thomas Couderc

Firms are listed A-Z in tiers which are ranked in order of priority
✪ Indicates firm displays contact details at the end of this chapter.

Vallourec Group in the acquisition of V&M Tubes; Areva in the acquisition of Alstom's T&D business; **JeantetAssociés** also acted in the privatisation of Compagnie des Alpes (C3D Group). The firm traditionally represents Suez, LVMH and Areva.

At **Jones Day**, Wesley Johnson handles major cross-border negotiated transactions, while other partners involved include Sophie Hagège, Gaël Saint Olive and My Linh Vu-Grégoire. The firm is traditionally on the seller side and regularly advises clients like Rhône-Poulenc, Rhodia, La Poste and Renault. At the same time, Olivier Edwards and Renaud Bonnet are private equity and venture capital specialists, involved in technology/biotech transactions. Recent deals include advising Harsco Corporation in its acquisition of Hünnebeck Group GmbH (€140m); Sanofi-Aventis in its sale of the assets of the worldwide oral healthcare division (including Fluocaril) to Procter & Gamble; France Télécom in its €6.4bn acquisition, via its subsidiary Orange S.A., of 80% of the shares of Auna, Spain's third-biggest mobile telecom operator; and EMME Multimedia SA in the acquisition of Hachette Multimedia's distribution business.

At **Paul, Hastings, Janofsky & Walker (Europe) LLP**, some eight partners are involved in M&A. Transactions often have a stock exchange dimension (Dominique Borde, Aline Poncelet) and the firm is involved in privatisations, property deals for funds (Andrew Armfelt) and private equity (Olivier Deren). The team is getting more international with the arrival of three American lawyers, including partner Joel Simon (corporate finance). Major recent transactions include representing KPMG in the acquisition of Salustro Reydel; a group of investors in Eutelsat in the sale of certain indirect shareholdings of Eutelsat to Texas Pacific Group and Spectrum; Shiseido in connection with a sale of one of its subsidiaries; Hachette Livre in relation to the sale of Dalloz Edition to Francis Lefebvre; and the French government in connection with the privatisation of Dagris.

Three partners handle M&A at **Shearman & Sterling LLP** – Cyrille Niedzielski, Hubertus Sulkowski and Jacques Naquet-Radiguet (Jacques Epstein left for **Lefèvre Pelletier & associés** – mainly in deals with a cross-border element and increasingly in private equity. **Shearman & Sterling LLP** has been very active in privatisations in recent years, on the issuer side (EDF, Air France). The firm advised Apax Partners in the LBO of Outremer Telecom; Société Générale in its acquisition of Hanseatic Bank (€190m); Merrill Lynch Global Private Equity as part of a consortium of investors in their acquisition of Rexel SA from PPR (€3.7bn); the Permal Group in its restructuring and sale to Legg Mason, Inc (US$1.4bn); and France Télécom in its acquisition of 80% interest in Amena (€6.4bn).

Skadden, Arps, Slate, Meagher & Flom LLP is active in both public and private M&A, with a few LBOs. The practice is diverse and complements strong corporate finance expertise. Partners involved are Pierre Servan-Schreiber, Christopher Baker, Laurent Cohen-Tanugi, Armand Grumberg and Blaine Fogg (of-counsel who arrived from New York). In 2005, the firm advised Institut Français du Pétrole in the sale of its 34% stake in Geoservices to a subsidiary of Astorg; Fournier Pharma in connection with its €1.2bn acquisition by Solvay; Quiksilver, Inc in its US$318m acquisition of Rossignol; and The Stanley Works in its €416m acquisition of Facom from Fimalac.

Jean Veil of **Veil Jourde** has an M&A practice dealing with listed companies, public takeover bids and privatisations. Private acquisitions, LBOs and restructurings are dealt with by Guillaume Kuperfils, Ariel Harroch and Daniel Katz. Patrick Jaïs and a team left for **Fried, Frank, Harris, Shriver & Jacobson LLP**. The firm advises Vivendi Universal on a general basis and funds like Atria, Apax, ABN Amro Capital and Eurazeo, among others. Recently **Veil Jourde** acted for Generali in the acquisition of Zurich; Atria in the €96m acquisition of FPEE; L'Oréal, controlling shareholder of Sanofi, in the takeover bid for Aventis; Eurazeo in the merger with Rue Impériale (€2.6bn); and Vivendi Universal in the sale of Monaco Telecom to Cable & Wireless.

Willkie Farr & Gallagher LLP handles both LBOs (where it is among the top Paris firms, with Daniel Payan and three young partners), and M&A, including domestic and cross-border tender offers, both negotiated and unsolicited (Daniel Hurstel and Laurent Faugérolas). The team was involved in the €1bn acquisition by PAI Partners of Sydsvenska Kemi AB, a holding company of the Swedish group Perstorp, from Industri Kapital; the €337bn acquisition by Ebro Puleva of all of the issued capital of Panzani from Financière Panzani and its management; the €430m acquisition by funds advised or managed by Goldman Sachs Capital Partners of a 15.8% interest in Eutelsat; the €300m acquisition by CGG of 60% of the share capital of Exploration Resources ASA; and in the €1bn cash tender offer of Foncière des Régions for each ordinary share of Bail Investissement.

The M&A team at **Allen & Overy LLP** handles both French and cross-border transactions. The team, led by partners Edouard Didier, Jean-Claude Rivalland, Nicolas Bichot, Armelle Walters-Renaud and Frédéric Moreau, has been active in the following areas: media and telecoms, advising UBM on the acquisition of the French Medical Press from Santemedia Holding; pharmaceuticals, advising Biomet France in relation to the acquisition of Biobank; and financial services, advising Société Générale in relation to the acquisition of Euro Bank in Poland.

Baker & McKenzie SCP's M&A practice consists of corporate group restructurings, transactional work, and stock exchange-related deals. The firm is also becoming more involved in private equity, working for funds like One Equity Partners and Platinum Equity. The team includes Eric Lasry, Laurent Epstein, Laurent Barbara, Marc Mariani (real estate) and Raphaële François-Poncet (listed companies). They advised One Equity Partners in the acquisition of LBC sold by Fimalac (€243m); Platinum Equity in the acquisition of the trading operations and certain assets of the Logistics Division of Hays Logistics (€114m); and WP Carey in the acquisition of a portfolio of five real estate companies sold by Lone Star and Deutsche Bank.

Debevoise & Plimpton LLP's M&A and private equity practice is still oriented towards US clients but international transactions are increasingly handled for French companies. Partners involved are Antoine Kirry, Marc Castagnède and Raman Bet-Mansour, whereas Patrick Laporte joined from **Linklaters**. The firm is also widely involved in private equity, representing ABN Amro and Merrill Lynch Investment Managers in the formation of funds dedicated to the French market. M&A lawyers represented Pernod Ricard in its US$14bn acquisition of Allied Domecq; Axa and Finaxa in their €5bn merger; a private equity fund in the €3.7 LBO of Rexel; Equant in its going-private and de-listing transaction involving France Télécom; and AGF Private Equity and a European family in their LBO of Médi-Partenaires.

Herbert Smith LLP is developing an M&A practice, with four partners (Philippe Trosset, Jacques Buhart, Bruno Basuyaux and Frédéric Grillier) and one of-counsel involved on a permanent basis (Anne Maréchal left). The firm advised LogicaCMG plc on its proposed 'one-for-two' rights issue and €930.3m acquisition of Unilog SA; Fortune Brands on its acquisition of a number of major spirits and wines brands from Allied Domecq; Eurotunnel SA on its successive equity and debt restructurings and on its relationship with shareholders; and the French Government with regards to Snecma and Sagem's decision to examine the merger of the two groups.

Lovells' M&A team is made of three partners (Robert Follie, Arnaud Latscha and Gilles de Poix) whilst the private equity arm also includes three partners (Jon Harry, Monique Sentilles-Dupont and Alexis Terray). They work for large international clients, developing at the same time a quality French clientele. Recent deal highlights include advising Barclays Bank plc in the acquistion by Barclays of ING's personal and private banking businesses in France; BBA Group plc in the acquisition by Signature Flight Support Paris of the French company Privatair; the management and the company on the acquisition of Camaieu SA by Axa Private Equity; and 3i on the buyout of Fermetures Le Nouy.

The **Norton Rose** M&A department is headed by Jean-François Mercadier, and numbers four other partners among which are Hervé Castelnau (a media and telecoms specialist), Alain Malek (a Middle East and Africa expert), and Pascale Gallien (a private equity and venture capital lawyer). Areas of expertise include energy, transport, financial institutions, media, telecoms and biotechnology. The firm is on the panel of clients such as Société Générale, BNP Paribas and HSBC and is the exclusive advisor to Nestlé. Deal highlights include advising HSBC CCF in the disposal of NetValor to Médiatis; Nestlé in the acquisition of Proteika; Nexo in the setting up of an agreement with Yamaha Corporation; and ONA (Morocco) in its bid for the third Moroccan fixed telecoms licence and its acquisition of four state-owned companies.

SJ Berwin's Paris office was created in 2001 and its M&A practice is developing with a strong focus on LBOs. The private equity specialist has four partners dedicated to the matter: Christophe Digoy, Maxence Bloch, Pierre-Louis Périn and Colin Millar, who arrived from **Simmons & Simmons**. Laurence Pinot-Lacan joined **August & Debouzy**. George Pinkham has been a specialist in funds establishment for years (working with four other specialised partners), and the firm can cash in on his knowledge of funds to build up transactional activity. Recently, **SJ Berwin** advised Barclays Private Equity in connection with the acquisition of Laho Equipment (€110m); ING Parcom Private Equity in the acquisition of Courtepaille (€200m); and Medica France on its recapitalisation (€296.6m).

Salans has an extensive M&A practice, with 12 partners of French, US or German nationality (including Paul Morel, John Flanigan, Pascal Chadenet, John Speers, François Vignaud and Johannes Jonas) covering cross-border and French M&A, stock market operations, joint ventures and private equity. The capacity was increased at the beginning of 2006 with the arrival of a team from *Rambaud Martel* comprising ten lawyers, including three partners. The firm recently advised a Northern European group of investors on the acquisition of a French pharmaceutical company; Fonds Partenaires-Gestion (Lazard) on the acquisition of Mondial Tissus and Heytens from Apax (€170m); Alcan in the sale of its laminated tubs business; CarlsonWagonLit on the acquisition of Frantour from Accor; and Süddeutscher Verlag on the sale of CB News to a management team and institutional investors.

At **Weil, Gotshal & Manges**, Claude Serra handles classic and public M&A, while the private equity team is very well considered; David Aknin is renowned and other partners are Emmanuelle Henry and Frédéric Cazals. 2004/2005 deals include advising Faiveley Transport in the acquisition of Sab Wabco from Vestar Capital Partners (€310m); PAI partners in the LBO acquisition of Saur from Bouygues (€1.037bn); the vendors in the sale of Amena to Orange through a capital increase of France Télécom (€10.6bn); and Suez on the acquisition of Electrabel (€11.2bn).

White & Case LLP has a good M&A practice, especially on the private equity side (partners involved are François Leloup and Vincent Morin). Other partners are Philippe Sarrailhé, Bernard Tézé and Eric Laplante. Cashing in on its leading reputation in LBOs, where it has the ability to advise on both equity and financing, the firm has succeded in expanding to industrial M&A, using its US, UK and domestic law capability. **White & Case LLP** advised Starwood Capital Group in its acquisition of Taittinger and of Société du Louvre (€2.6bn); Eurazeo and Carlyle Group, in their sale of Terreal SA to LBO France (€860m); Danisco Venture in its investment in the French food safety and protectant company TMI Europe SA; and Industri Kapital in its acquisition of Bonna Sabla from AXA Private Equity and other shareholders (€235m).

Other leading private equity specialists not mentioned before include Xavier Jaspar at **Mayer, Brown, Rowe & Maw LLP**; Françoise Monod at **P.D.G.B.**; Bernard Ayache, David Ayache, Alain Levy, Olivier Tordjman (**Ayache Salama & Associés**); and Lionel Scotto, Henri Pieyre de Mandiargues (**Wilinski Scotto & Associés**). Also, created in 2005, is **Sarrau Thomas Couderc**, a 45-lawyer firm (half of them being tax specialists) specialising in private capital, advising private equity actors, private and family groups, managers of big companies; on the LBO side they advise funds and managers. Jean-Bernard Thomas and David de Pariente are recommended.

PROJECT FINANCE AND ENERGY: PROJECT FINANCE

PROJECT FINANCE AND ENERGY: PROJECT FINANCE

ALLEN & OVERY LLP ✪
CLIFFORD CHANCE
GIDE LOYRETTE NOUEL ✪
HERBERT SMITH LLP ✪
LINKLATERS ✪

Ashurst ✪
Bredin Prat ✪
De Pardieu Brocas Maffei ✪
Freshfields Bruckhaus Deringer
Norton Rose
Simmons & Simmons ✪
Sullivan & Cromwell LLP
White & Case LLP

Cleary, Gottlieb, Steen & Hamilton LLP ✪
Curtis, Mallet-Prevost, Colt & Mosle LLP ✪
JeantetAssociés ✪
Latham & Watkins
Lovells ✪
Orrick, Herrington & Sutcliffe ✪

Firms are listed A-Z in tiers which are ranked in order of priority
✪ Indicates firm displays contact details at the end of this chapter.

Allen & Overy LLP's projects practice is led by Tim Scales and Rod Cork, assisted by the public law practice. They advise banks, sponsors and other institutions on various projects, including those involving multi-lateral institutions and export credit agencies. The firm is active in various sectors, particularly energy and natural resources, infrastructure and telecoms, with a growing focus on North Africa and across the Central and Eastern European region, and very visible on the PPP market. **Allen & Overy LLP** is involved in major deals such as the financing of the Obajana Cement project (US$798m) in Nigeria; the financing of the AES-Sonel capital investment programme (€400m) in Cameroon; the financing of four wind farm projects for EDF in Portugal (€220m); the financing of a cereal terminal in the Port of Djibouti; and advising the French Ministry of Justice on the PPP for the construction of 18 prisons (€900m).

Clifford Chance retains an outstanding Paris office, where Michael Elland-Goldsmith, Anthony Giustini and two counsels head up a projects practice principally advising banks and sponsors. The PPP practice is strong in the infrastructure and hospital areas. Other sectors where the firm has solid experience include power and leisure facilities. The firm is counsel to the Centre Hospitalier Sud Francilien on the €200m PPP financing of the Corbeil-Essonnes hospital; Lyon Turin Ferroviaire on the structuring of the project of a rail link between Lyon and Turin; Etablissement Public pour le Palais de Justice de Paris with regard to the PPP of the new Paris Court House; Royal Bank of Scotland on the €100m financing of the extension of the Toulouse underground; and the lender in connection with the financing of a reverse osmosis water desalination plant in Algeria.

Gide Loyrette Nouel's lawyers (Emmanuel Fontaine, John Crothers, Bruno de Cazalet, Rupert Reece and François Krotoff) are mainly present in countries with a strong French influence – Maghreb, Africa, Vietnam and China, and in Eastern European countries where the firm has offices. The firm increased its North African capacity with the opening of offices in Algiers and Casablanca in 2003/2004 in addition to the Tunis office. Areas of focus include infrastructure, water, electricity and telecommunications. Recently, the firm has advised a bidding consortium on the financing and construction and operation of the A65 toll motorway concession; the IFC and the Civil Aviation Authority on PSP in the BOT expansion of the Hajj Terminal for the International Airport at Jeddah; the Government of Bulgaria on the drafting and negotiation of the concession contract for the Bourgas and Varna airports; and the Ministry of Post Telegraph and Telephone of Iran, together with BNP Paribas, on the award of the first GSM licence (approximately €3.5bn) to a private sector telecommunications operator.

Herbert Smith LLP is active on the sponsors' side in a wide range of sectors, including oil, gas, mining, water, electricity, telecoms and infrastructure (pipelines, refineries, power plants), but increasingly represents banking clients and state entities. Geographically, the firm acts mainly in Africa (60% of the work, this year in new countries like Mauritania, Tunisia, Angola, Equatorial Guinea and Libya), but also in Europe and the Middle East, for clients increasingly coming from new countries (China, Japan, Russia, India). The group consists of 13 lawyers, including five partners, notably Neil Brimson, Stéphane Brabant, Bertrand Montembault and Laurent Vandomme. In 2004/2005, the firm advised British Gas Tunisia Limited on the development of the Barca Project in Tunisia; CNPC, the major Chinese oil company, on the acquisition from Kufpec of oil and gas interests in Tunisia; Eurotunnel in relation to its debt structure and issues of a corporate nature; EDF in relation to the negotiation of long-term service agreements with Alstom Power for the maintenance of the Azito Power Plant in Côte d'Ivoire; and ABSA/NedBank on a US$40m financing for High River Gold of its interests in the Taparko gold mine project in Burkina Faso.

Maybe less pre-eminent in volume but not in technical ability, **Linklaters** has been active in project finance for many years, advising for example the Eurotunnel banking syndicate on both French and English law. Bertrand Andriani is highly praised and the firm is increasingly active in France and well positioned in the emerging PPP market with a new public law team (Paul Lignières). Simon Ratledge is the other partner. **Linklaters** represented ABN Amro and Depfa on the financing of a logistical support platform at the Douai hospital; CDC and CNCE on the research and anciliary facilities at the 15/20 eye hospital; ACS/Urbaser on the Marseille incinerator, the biggest environmental project in France and a premiere in waste treatment PPP in France; and Falconbridge on the Koniambo integrated mine, power and port project in New Caledonia.

Ashurst is active in the growing PPP market in France, having worked in the past in Central and Eastern Europe, in the Middle East and in West Africa. Mainly working for sponsors, the firm also represents international institutions, lenders and governments. Michel Lequien deals with the whole projects (BOT, concessions, public law, regulation, etc, Laurent Mabilat and Diane Sénéchal being in charge of the financing aspects). The team advised TP Ferro SA, Eiffage, ACS on the high-speed rail link Perpignan-Figueras HSL project; the French Ministry of Equipment and Transport on the 'motorway of the sea' project, a regular international maritime transport service between France and Spain; and various consortiums on their tender offers for PPP hospital and motorways projects.

Slaughter and May's team joined **Bredin Prat** at the beginning of 2006. It advises sponsors, companies and lenders on the structuring and financing of major projects (with a focus on gas and electricity) around the world. Examples of work include advising Wataniya Telecom in relation to a US$490m financing for the third GSM network in Algeria; Cora in relation to various EBRD financings of hypermarkets in Romania and Hungary; and BNP Paribas and Calyon as syndicate agents of the Euro Disney credits.

De Pardieu Brocas Maffei mainly advises banks, and has advised on credits guaranteed by Coface. The firm has experience in Asia, having assisted a syndicate on the establishment of the TGV in Korea, and on Laibin B in China. **De Pardieu Brocas Maffei** advised Calyon, WestLB and Citibank in the financing and restructuring of a cellular phone project in Algeria (Orascom); the borrower in the €480m financing of a telecoms project in Algeria (Wataniya); and Société Française d'Eolienne in the financings of wind farm projects in France.

Freshfields Bruckhaus Deringer offers project management from the bid to the setting up of the project and the financing (Jean L'Homme, Thomas Hechl, with Thierry Laloum for the public aspects, Yves de Mahenge and Joseph Huse for the corporate side). The major areas covered are water, power, oil and gas, mines, transport and telecommunications. Traditionally, **Freshfields Bruckhaus Deringer** advises sponsors and multilateral organisations, but also acts for banks and governments. The team advised Gaz de France on various projects, including the gas compression station of Cuvilly; a leading company in connection with its participation in the project company for a power project in Algeria; Eurotunnel on various aspects of its business; Tangier Mediterranean Special Agency (TMSA) in connection with the new seaport in Morocco; and ABB Utilities in connection with a sub-contract for the construction of a hospital in Malta.

Norton Rose mainly advises banks, but also sponsors, with Martin Gdanski and Nigel Ward well-known partners. Phillipe Mallea is a PPP expert who worked for Bouygues in hospital projects in the UK. Recent work concerned the advice to consortiums (Cari, Eiffage, Bouygues) and public clients (Saint-Nazaire, Pontoise, Roanne hospitals) in PPP transactions in the health sector. **Norton Rose** also acted for BNP Paribas on the financing for Boralex of wind power projects in France. The firm is involved in renewable energies and active in the oil and gas sectors, particularly offshore, advising leading French oil companies and banks on oil and gas projects and on trade/commodities transactions in Africa, the Middle East and Kazakhstan.

At **Simmons & Simmons**, Australia-born Christophe Asselineau is the partner in charge. The five-lawyer team mainly works for sponsors, with a strong focus on energy and mining, and is also active in the French energy market (cogeneration). Recent deals include representing the Office National d'Assainissement and Algérienne des Eaux in its negotiation with Suez on the 18-year PPP of the drinking and waste water management of the city of Algiers; and Black & Veatch in relation to the first IWPP in Algeria.

Sullivan & Cromwell LLP's project finance activity is headed by Richard Vilanova and Nikolaos Andronikos. The firm has advised European principals for many years on project finance matters, particularly in South America, Africa, and the Middle East, and is currently advising on several pending projects in the oil, mining and natural gas/petrochemicals sectors.

At **White & Case LLP**, Paule Biensan and Jacques Bouillon are in charge. The firm advises sponsors, governments and financial institutions on projects all over the world, notably in Africa in a variety of sectors, including power, infrastructure, mining and telecoms. For example, the projects team advised the banks on the financing of the high-speed railway portion to be built between France and Spain (€1.1bn); Alcan/Pechiney on the financing of the de-bottlenecking of Bauxite mining facilities owned by CVG Bauxilum CA in Venezuela (US$228m); and Royal Bank of Scotland as lender and investor in a PPP hospital project in the southwest France.

PROJECT FINANCE AND ENERGY: ENERGY

We also mention firms involved in the contractual, corporate and regulatory aspects of energy and infrastructure projects. In addition to specialists already mentioned above, the following firms are recommended.

At **CMS Bureau Francis Lefebvre**, Jean-Pierre Andrieux, a partner in the tax team active in Algeria for many years, was joined in 2004 by five lawyers specialising in African law from **Ernst & Young Société d'Avocats**. The firm has an office in Morocco and other countries covered are Algeria, Tunisia, Cameroon, Gabon, Ghana, Guinea and Senegal.

Thierry Lauriol and his team (three associates and African consultants) specialise in projects, energy and natural resources at **JeantetAssociés**. They are mainly active on the African continent

PROJECT FINANCE AND ENERGY: ENERGY

CMS BUREAU FRANCIS LEFEBVRE ✪
CLIFFORD CHANCE
GIDE LOYRETTE NOUEL ✪
HERBERT SMITH LLP ✪
JEANTETASSOCIÉS ✪
LEBOEUF, LAMB, GREENE & MACRAE LLP ✪
SALANS

Ashurst ✪
Cleary, Gottlieb, Steen & Hamilton LLP ✪
Eversheds-Frere Cholmeley
Franklin ✪
Freshfields Bruckhaus Deringer
Haarmann Hemmelrath ✪
Lovells ✪
Norton Rose
Orrick, Herrington & Sutcliffe ✪
Simmons & Simmons ✪
Sokolow, Carreras & Associés

Firms are listed A-Z in tiers which are ranked in order of priority
✪ Indicates firm displays contact details at the end of this chapter.

(and also North America, Arab countries and overseas French territories) where they handle regulatory, contractual and contentious aspects of projects, and give consultations on OHADA law to banks. Areas of expertise include mining, but also oil and gas. Jean-François Adelle deals with financing aspects.

Jean-Claude Petilon was *Coudert Frères'* projects and Africa expert within a seven-fee-earner team comprising French and African lawyers. They now work for **LeBoeuf, Lamb, Greene & Macrae LLP**. Their recent involvement in privatisations (Madagascar, Gabon) completes wider expertise in projects with, for instance in 2004, legal assistance to a major LNG project in Equatorial Guinea and to an international mining group holding interests in Burkina Faso, Senegal, Zimbawe and Ivory Coast.

Salans assists dozens of oil companies in their operations in Eastern Europe, the CIS and Asia, where the firm has offices, in a wide scope of corporate, banking and finance, administrative, international arbitration and local litigation matters. Partners involved (other than arbitration ones) are James Hogan and Theodore Matheny.

Jean-Pierre Vignaud at **Cleary, Gottlieb, Steen & Hamilton LLP** advises developing countries (Africa) and international groups in transactions in the fields of energy, water, infrastructure and telecommunications, and in the context of privatisations.

At **Eversheds-Frere Cholmeley**, Rodman Bundy is a public international law litigator. He is involved in oil and gas matters for OPEP governments and multinationals. The team is also active in francophone Africa on a regular basis.

Jérôme Michel, at **Franklin**, is involved in energy projects in France and abroad and advised the Ukrainian and Mauritanian governments on reforms of respectively the energy market and the land and planning legislation.

At **Haarmann Hemmelrath**, Héctor Farina's areas of expertise are corporate law, foreign investments, particularly in the energy sector, and international contracts. He previously worked at **Denton Wilde Sapte**. He acts as counsel for various utilities companies in their investments in Africa and Latin America. Outside France, the firm is involved in the energy sector on a wider scale.

Lovells is active in the oil and gas market with companies such as BHP Billiton, ExxonMobil and Statoil, mainly in Africa. It also handles financings and PPP, with a dedicated team of experts (Jacques Bertran de Balanda) that has worked on toll motorway concessions and hospital projects.

At **Orrick, Herrington & Sutcliffe**, Pascal Agboyibor regularly represents both corporations and multinational banks, lenders and participants in power generation, telecommunications, hotels and resort facilities, manufacturing equipment, railway equipment, and aircraft equipment financings and transactions.

Sokolow, Carreras & Associés (Nicolas Sokolow) takes part in infrastructure, industrial and extraction projects. All the stages of the project are dealt with: contracts, setting up of entities, financings, relationships with international financial institutions and States.

REAL ESTATE

Clifford Chance's real estate team now numbers two partners (François Bonteil and Ronald Austin), a counsel, three senior associates and 12 associates. The team is active both on the financing and transaction sides, with a clientele including Anglo-Saxon funds. The tax side is also dealt with. **Clifford Chance** advised Patron Capital Partners on the acquisition of a real estate portfolio including Tour Anjou in La Défense and two Center Parcs (Pierre & Vacances) for a value of €450m; GE Commercial Finance Real Estate France on the acquisition of Foncière Ariane (85 buildings, €350m); and Standard Life on the sale of a real estate portfolio to Teachers (five buildings, €493m). Other clients include Risanamento, Lasalle, Axa Reim, Carlyle Real Estate etc.

De Pardieu Brocas Maffei is very active in corporate and financing aspects of commercial property, working for French and foreign investors, banks (acting as lenders/finance leasers), investment banks providing advisory services in the property field, users and property developers like Cogedim. The firm is also widely involved in litigation related to insurance, buying and selling issues. Jacques Henrot heads the department; Paul Talbourdet, Emmanuel Fatôme and Stéphane Illouz are also recommended and five other partners are regularly involved. They acted for Foncière des Régions on its tender offer for shares in Bail Investissement; a fund managed by AXA Reim France on the acquisition of a portfolio of office buildings in France built and sold by the developer Lazard; Foncière des Murs on the acquisition from Accor of 128 hotels; Bank of Scotland as arranger of a credit facility to finance several property asset deals, or share deals, in France; BNP Paribas on the financing of the purchase and development by Colony of an office building located in Vélizy; and La Poste Direction Immobilière for the sale and leaseback of part of its property assets portfolio.

Working in very close collaboration with a firm of notaries, **Freshfields Bruckhaus Deringer** offers a broad spectrum of property services. The clientele comprises UK, French and European investors, investment funds (US and German), major developers, banks, financial institutions and insurance companies. Recently, the firm has been active advising on property securitisations (national and offshore) and on the setting up of real estate funds. Sixteen associates and two partners handle property work: Benoît Marcilhacy, Pascal Schmitz, with Hervé Kensicher for financings, and real estate tax capacity on top. The firm advised Deutsche Bank on the acquisition and leaseback of AutoDistribution's property portfolio; Apollo in the disposal (through a share sale) to Morgan Stanley Eurozone Office Fund of the Pascal Towers, in La Défense (Paris); Blackstone in the acquisition of a portfolio of commercial buildings located in France and in Poland; and Hines in the sale to AXA REIM of the company holding six buildings in Meudon.

Gide Loyrette Nouel has a strong international practice and has been active in property law since the 1970s, when it started advising UK investors in Paris. The team comprises eight partners among which Gérard Tavernier, Frédéric Nouel, Jean-Jacques Raquin, Eric Martin-Impératori and Renaud Baguenault de Puchesse stand out. The scope of the practice is wide and includes advising on the restructuring of loan portfolios, the externalisation of the State's real estate assets, and property financing. Clients are mostly of German, US and Middle Eastern origin. Last year, **Gide Loyrette Nouel** advised KanAm Grund Kapitalanlagegesell-schaft mbH and Whitehall on the acquisition of Le Stadium in Saint-Denis (15,000 sq m); Unibail in relation to the acquisition of a real estate complex located in Levallois, for the development of 85,000 sq m of office and retail space (€386m); Vivendi Universal on the sale of its shares in the Romanian company that owns the Athénée Palace Hotel in Bucharest, operated by the Hilton Group; and Unibail on the sale to Risanamento SpA of 50, avenue Montaigne, Paris (€233m).

The other top French firm is **Lefèvre Pelletier & Associés**, where real estate continues to

REAL ESTATE

CLIFFORD CHANCE
DE PARDIEU BROCAS MAFFEI ✪
FRESHFIELDS BRUCKHAUS DERINGER
GIDE LOYRETTE NOUEL ✪
LEFÈVRE PELLETIER & ASSOCIÉS ✪

JONES DAY ✪
LINKLATERS ✪

Ashurst ✪
Baker & McKenzie SCP ✪
Salans
White & Case LLP

BMS', Association d'Avocats
CMS Bureau Francis Lefebvre ✪
Herbert Smith LLP ✪
Lacourte Balas & Associés
Latham & Watkins
Orrick, Herrington & Sutcliffe ✪
Paul, Hastings, Janofsky & Walker (Europe) LLP ✪
UGGC & Associés ✪
Zurfluh Lebatteux & Associés

August & Debouzy
Bignon Lebray & Associés
DS Avocats
Denton Wilde Sapte ✪
Dubarry Le Douarin Veil ✪
Ernst & Young Société d'Avocats
Eversheds-Frere Cholmeley
Fidal ✪
Hughes Hubbard & Reed LLP ✪
JeantetAssociés ✪
Lovells ✪
Mayer, Brown, Rowe & Maw LLP ✪
Neveu Sudaka & Associés
Norton Rose
Racine
SJ Berwin ✪
Vatier & Associés ✪

Firms are listed A-Z in tiers which are ranked in order of priority
✪ Indicates firm displays contact details at the end of this chapter.

account for 38% of the overall turnover. Philippe Lefèvre is an expert in property investment and fellow name partner Philippe Pelletier is expert in rent and co-ownership issues. Pierre Popesco left for **Herbert Smith LLP** with a team. Clients include property investors, banks, promoters, builders and insurance companies, among others. With ten partners and some 35 associates, this is the largest team in Paris. Last year it assisted Accor in the disposal of 128 hotels for which the company becomes leaseholder, the leases being indexed to the activity (more than €1bn); Aerium in the acquisition of several shopping centres and supermarkets in Poland, Czech Republic, Slovakia and Turkey (€376m); and ING Reim on the acquisition of the Vache Noire shopping centre from AM Development France (€200m).

Jones Day's real estate team is headed by Jean-Louis Martin, while Vincent Agulhon handles tax and Philippe Billot financings. The ten-lawyer team (including the tax specialists) is mainly dedicated to investment for major Anglo-Saxon, German and French funds. It advised Morgan Stanley Eurozone Office Fund in connection with its acquisition of a real estate company owning the Tours Pascal at La Défense; UBS Real Estate on the acquisition of an office building of 15,000 sq m located at Suresnes (Paris region); Lasalle Investment Management in the setting-up of two joint ventures (€300m); and Apollo Real Estate Advisors in the setting-up of two joint ventures with local French partners.

Linklaters' commercial property team, led by Françoise Maigrot, acts on complex deals, town-planning as well as environment, construction and property financing/securitisation. They work closely with strong corporate, finance, tax and public/PPP teams. The firm was active in deals such as the cash public offer by Metrovacesa for 100% of Gecina; the acquisition by Teachers Insurance and Annuity Association of America of a real estate portfolio from Standard Life Investments (€493m); the IPO for Casino of its property company; the Douai Logipôle PPP project (Hôpital de Douai); and the financing of various property portfolios for a Middle Eastern fund.

The real estate team at **Ashurst** comprises partners Dorothée Bontoux and Philippe None, with Diane Sénéchal for the financing aspects, and works closely with a notary firm. They advise funds and investors in acquisitions, financing and tax issues related to property deals, town-planning and commercial leases. The firm advised Marriott International on most of its French projects and Deka Immobilien GmbH on all French leases; the joint venture La Ferme (French and Swiss investors) in relation to the development of 600 residential dwellings close to the Franco-Swiss border; the joint venture between Bank of Scotland and Fairmont Hotels in relation to the acquisition of the Monte Carlo Grand Hotel in Monaco; and EHI Fund, a high-income fund investing in industrial real estate, on its structuring (€700m).

Baker & McKenzie SCP increased its presence in commercial property in 2004 and is increasingly visible on the market. In addition to the expertise of Eric Pomonti, that of Olivier Mesmin – a property tax expert – and Marc Mariani – a corporate lawyer – has to be mentioned. Clients include foreign investors and French corporates on property transactions and commercial leases. They are for example Qatar Islamic Bank, Morgan Stanley Real Estate Fund, Société Foncière Lyonnaise and Foncière des Régions.

Salans recruited Henry Lazarski in late 2004. He worked for a long time at **Clifford Chance** and had joined **Mayer, Brown, Rowe & Maw LLP** in 2003 when he had to retire from the UK-based international firm. He is one of the most renowned property experts in Paris and works for numerous international funds and investors, which will complement **Salans**' traditional activity on the users' side.

Although young, the real estate team at **White & Case LLP** has developed alongside the more established construction and arbitration practices. Emmanuel Rosenfeld is well respected. He is a specialist in litigation and real estate, and works for funds, very often US-based. Franck Peter is the other partner. The group covers transactional work and the whole range of real estate issues. They advised Klépierre in the acquisition of shopping centres in Poland and in the Czech Republic (€420m); Tertial, a subsidiary of Caisse des Dépôts & Consignations, in the development and sale of a major and widely-publicised shopping centre in Montpellier (€200m); and the City of Boulogne-Billancourt on the redevelopment of the former industrial land of Renault (€600m).

BMS', Association d'Avocats is also recommended. It is a split from the former *Caubet Chouchana Meyer*. The new firm advises investment and pensions funds as well as Anglo-Saxon businesses investing in France, and is mainly involved in the office property business but also works in commercial real estate. Michel Meyer and Robert Meilichzon are widely involved in property issues.

CMS Bureau Francis Lefebvre (Jean-Luc Tixier) is active in real estate transactions, acting for Deutsche Bank and Inovalis. The firm is also involved in commercial leases (Philippe Riglet) and corporate aspects of property (Philippe Rosenpick).

Herbert Smith LLP recruited well-regarded real estate expert Pierre Popesco and a team (five associates) at the end of 2005. They used to work for **Lefèvre Pelletier & associés**. Popesco's work will be focused on international transactional real estate matters, working for French and German companies such as insurers and developers, REITs and French and foreign investment funds.

Half of the activity of **Lacourte Balas & Associés** is dedicated to real estate transactions, covering all sorts of investments and disivenstments, financings, promotion, construction, town-planning, tax and leases. Thierry Lacourte, Jean-Claude Balas are well-known and were joined in 2005 by Jean-Pierre Daniel from **Mayer, Brown, Rowe & Maw LLP**.

The real estate team at **Latham & Watkins** (Dominique Basdevant and Pierre Descheemaeker) handles real estate projects with an emphasis on financings and property transactions, having particular experience with office buildings, retail premises, hotels, casinos and industrial real estates.

Orrick, Herrington & Sutcliffe's practice focuses on commercial leases and property in general, both on the advisory and contentious sides. Catherine Saint-Geniest (ex-*Rambaud Martel*) works closely with public law and construction departments, while Alfred Fink has considerable experience in advising foreign investors on commercial property matters. Financings are handled by Sylvie Perrin.

At **Paul, Hastings, Janofsky & Walker (Europe) LLP**, Andrew Armfelt works for funds and operators on corporate and equity aspects of transactions. He also handles arbitration and is particularly visible in the hotel and tourism industries.

UGGC & Associés handles financial and commercial aspects of property projects, with a special focus on town-planning (Bernard Lamorlette). Clients include major property developers and publics entities.

Zurfluh Lebatteux & Associés specialises in co-ownership.

Real estate: leases: We recommend **Bruno Boccara & Associés**, where Bruno Boccara and Danièle Lipman-Boccara are renowned specialists. Other lawyers include Marie-Odile Vaissié and Philippe Pelletier (**Lefèvre Pelletier & associés**); Jean-Pierre Blatter (**Blatter, Raclet & Associés**); **Bousquet**; André Guillemain and Marie-Laurence Sainturat (**Guillemain Banide & Sainturat**); André Jacquin (**Jacquin Maruani**); **Jehan Barbier**; Catherine Saint-Geniest (**Orrick, Herrington & Sutcliffe**); **Philippe-Hubert Brault**; Dorothée Bontoux (**Ashurst**); Philippe Riglet (**CMS Bureau Francis Lefebvre**); **Freshfields Bruckhaus Deringer**; and Eric Martin-Impératori (**Gide Loyrette Nouel**).

SHIPPING

Bouloy Grellet & Godin's Luc Grellet handles trade, industrial risk, charterparty, international credit documentation, international sales and arbitration. He advised the shipowner in the *Erika* case. Philippe Godin is a specialist in transport and advises forwarding agents and insurance companies on the freight side.

UK-based **Holman Fenwick & Willan** currently comprises some 20 lawyers, with further offices in Rouen and Nantes. Best-known partners are Jean-Jacques Ollu and Guillaume Brajeux, Olivier Purcell and Timothy Clemens-Jones. They have recognised experience in French and international litigation (contentious matters account for 90% of the firm's activity). Within its broad practice, the firm focuses on charterparty, admiralty, insurance, international trade and customs law, industrial risks, ship finance, and international debt recovery. Recently, the firm was involved in many large shipping casualties (*Estonia*, *Ievoli Sun*, among others).

Ince & Co has twelve lawyers in Paris and Le Havre involved in maritime law. Gilles Gautier handles shipping and marine insurance litigation. The other partners are Fred Vroom (for the finance aspects) and Andrew Charlier (general non-

SHIPPING

BOULOY GRELLET & GODIN
HOLMAN FENWICK & WILLAN ✪
INCE & CO ✪
RICHARDS BUTLER
RICHEMONT NICOLAS & ASSOCIÉS
VILLENEAU ROHART SIMON & ASSOCIÉS

Clyde & Co ✪
Gide Loyrette Nouel ✪
Le Berre Engelsen Witvoet
Rembauville-Nicolle & Bureau - Rbm2l

Courtois & Finkelstein
Dagorne - Huchet
Laroque & Associés
Lassez & Associés ✪
Penlaw Selarl ✪
Schmill Lombrez
Tinayre Cleach et Associés

Firms are listed A-Z in tiers which are ranked in order of priority
✪ *Indicates firm displays contact details at the end of this chapter.*

contentious matters). Jérôme de Sentenac is in charge of the Le Havre office, with Mathieu Croix specialising in shipping litigation. Jacques Le Vaillant handles contentious work. Clients include maritime transport companies and insurers.

Fellow UK firm **Richards Butler** fields ten lawyers in Paris, four of them partners, specialising in shipping matters. The practice is broad, covering transport litigation, incidents at sea, international sales, insurance, reinsurance and protective measures. The two partners in charge, Peter Iglikowski and Lars Lewis, are of British origin and possess the dual qualification of French *avocat* and British solicitor. The firm is involved in the *Erika* case, acting for the shipowners.

Richemont Nicolas & Associés' Henri de Richemont is well regarded. Known as a P&I clubs and shipowners' lawyer, he and his five-lawyer team also act for charters and other road and maritime transport operators. The firm was involved in maritime cases such as the *Tanio* and the *Erika* wrecks.

Villeneau Rohart Simon & Associés' eight-lawyer practice focuses on maritime law. Patrick Simon and Jean-Serge Rohart are particularly well known, the latter being President of the Association Française de Droit Maritime. The firm has forged a reputation for dealing with major accidents, such as *Amoco Cadiz* and *Estonia*. The majority of the work is international and clients include P&I clubs and shipowners.

UK firm **Clyde & Co** has a strong maritime practice, headed by Gildas Rostain whose activity is mainly contentious, for international shipowners, shippers, shipyards, P&I clubs and insurers. The team comprises nine lawyers in total, Rozenn Lopin being the other partner. The firm is assisting Bureau Veritas in the *Erika* wreck; the

SHIPPING FINANCE

Ince & Co ✪
Norton Rose
Orrick, Herrington & Sutcliffe ✪
Watson, Farley & Williams LLP ✪

Firms are listed alphabetically
✪ *Indicates firm displays contact details at the end of this chapter.*

insurer of the shipowner of the *Sherbro*; and the shipyard where the *Estonia* was built

At **Gide Loyrette Nouel**, Emmanuel Fontaine is recognised as a specialist in financing and shipbuilding transactions, as well as in maritime pollution. He has been involved in all the major cases since the *Amoco Cadiz* and *Torrey Canyon* cases (*Erika*, *Prestige* being the most recent), as well as other large shipping losses such as the mv *Monarch of the Seas*. Philippe Rames is specialised in insurance and industrial risks. The team also advises shipowners, insurers and shipbuilders, such as Chantiers de l'Atlantique, in shipping and transport litigation, as well as in financing and shipbuilding transactions and has developed a practice in large leisure boats transactions and disputes.

Four-partner, three-associate **Le Berre Engelsen Witvoet** focuses on shipping, general transport law, insurance, international arbitration, product liability and commercial litigation. In maritime law, the firm is particularly active on the litigation side.

Rembauville-Nicolle & Bureau - Rbm2l has offices in Paris and Le Havre. Patrice Rembauville-Nicolle and Xavier Bureau act for shipowners, P&I clubs and shippers.

We also recommend the following niche firms: **Courtois & Finkelstein**; **Dagorne - Huchet**; **Laroque & Associés**; **Lassez & Associés**; **Penlaw SELARL**; **Schmill Lombrez**; and **Tinayre Cleach et Associés**.

We also mention here four leaders in shipping finance in France: **Ince & Co** (Fred Vroom); **Norton Rose** (Nigel Ward and Alain Gautron who arrived from **Orrick, Herrington & Sutcliffe**); **Orrick, Herrington & Sutcliffe** (Stuart McAlpine); and **Watson, Farley & Williams LLP** (Nigel Moss, Laurence Martinez-Bellet and Jean Thibaud).

TAX

CMS Bureau Francis Lefebvre is without doubt the pre-eminent tax practice in Paris and benefits from various expert teams (no less than 30 lawyers specialising in VAT for example). The firm and its 74 partners enjoy an excellent reputation, particularly Jean-Claude Bouchard, Jean Guilmoto and Laurent Chatel on the domestic side. Pierre Sébastien Thill, Bruno Gouthière, Bruno Gibert, Stéphane Gelin, Edouard Milhac and Pierre-Jean

Douvier are frequently mentioned for their international expertise. The latter group was reinforced with the arrival of a three-partner team specialising in transactional and international tax from **Ernst & Young Société d'Avocats**, and a chief economist advising on transfer pricing policy. The practice covers company tax law, restructurings and M&A, transfer pricing as well as assistance in fiscal control, in sectors such as real estate, banking and insurance, energy, telecoms, pharmaceuticals, life sciences and the hotel industry. Its international reach has obviously been broadened through the alliance sealed with *CMS*, and the French firm is heavily involved in developing the tax practice of other members.

The tax practice at **Bredin Prat** is headed by Renaud Streichenberger who is a leading international corporate tax expert. The seven-lawyer team also boasts two other partners, Edouard Sicot and Yves Rutschmann and is being joined by a team from **Slaughter and May** at the time of writing. A significant part of the activity is related to major cross-border transactions handled by the M&A team, like the acquisitions of Gécina, Groupe Taittinger, Accor and the creation of CACEIS (Crédit Agricole – Caisse d'Epargne Investor Services). The firm also has an expertise in innovative financial products and real estate (specifically regarding the new tax regime for French listed real estate investment companies SIIC).

Cleary, Gottlieb, Steen & Hamilton LLP is a leader in innovative tax transactions pertaining to prominent public M&A and capital markets deals as well as to private equity deals. Gilles Entraygues is widely praised. Three other partners also focus on tax matters within the firm's broad practice: Arnaud de Brosses, Pascal Coudin and Jean-Michel Tron, who also handles M&A.

The **Linklaters** team comprises seven lawyers, including two partners: Philippe Derouin, a well-known tax specialist, and Annick Lainé-Audouard. The tax work handled is very much linked to its corporate and finance practices, often with an international dimension. Major transactions include public and private M&A deals, corporate reorganisations and, on the finance side, CDO-CLO issues and structured financings, in the real estate field for instance. Some contentious work is also carried out. Recent deals include the public offer by Suez on Electrabel; the cash offer for Galeries Lafayette launched by SEMAD; the cash public offer by Metrovacesa for 100% of Gecina; the sale of Montagu Private Equity's stake in Actaris to LBO France; the cross-border mezzanine financing for a secondary LBO of the Terreal Group; and the IPO of Gaz de France.

Clifford Chance's tax department comprises some 16 lawyers, including four partners – Eric Davoudet, Eric Zeller, Alexandre Lagarrigue and Julien Ruderman. The tax practice is strongly linked to the real estate (Lasalle, Risanamento), structured finance (Société Générale, Deutsche Banke, CDC Ixis) and corporate practices, notably in the private equity sector (Carlyle, Duke Street Capital). The group has developed particular expertise in structuring investment funds (Butler Capital Partners, Barclays Private Equity) and employee share plans (Suez, Steria). The practice is mainly advisory.

Freshfields Bruckhaus Deringer's team comprises four partners and eleven associates. Antoine Colonna d'Istria, Eric Thomas, James Vaudoyer and Cyril Valentin deal with international M&A, financial tax and real estate matters. They represented Whitehall, Ixis and GE in connection with the refinancing of a multi-billion-euro real estate portfolio related to France Télécom; Lehman Brothers in connection with the restructuring of the Meridien Hotels group; and Calyon as arranger of a pan-European trades receivables securitisation programme for Rhodia.

Willkie Farr & Gallagher LLP's tax practice numbers three partners (Allard de Waal, Marie-Hélène Raffin, Bernard Le Pezron), plus five associates. Their activity is close to the general activity of the firm and therefore concerns M&A and LBOs in an international context. Financial tax, tax consolidation, patrimonial tax and stock options are also handled, while clients include banks, private equity funds, and companies in the entertainment, pharmaceuticals, automotive, steel, telecoms and audiovisual areas.

Allen & Overy LLP's team comprises six lawyers, and the activity is split between financial products (Siamak Mostafavi) and corporate (Patrice Couturier). Cross-border, tax-enhanced financings and French/US tax-driven deals, structuring of the acquisition of real estate portfolios, tax aspects of securitisations, asset finance and employee stock option plans are areas of growth.

Arsene is a young and rapidly growing tax firm founded by ex-Big Four partners in 2004, Frédéric Donnedieu de Vabres (previously managing partner of *Archibald Andersen*), Oilivier Vergniolle and Roland Schneider. With 22 lawyers, including six partners, **Arsene** covers the whole range of company tax, with a focus on international corporate matters, and widened its scope of interventions in 2005 by recruiting two specialists and their teams: Alain Recoules, VAT and finance (**Landwell & Associés**), and François Lugand, real estate (**Taj**).

Baker & McKenzie SCP's tax practice now comprises more than 25 tax advisers, including three partners, among them Pierre-Yves Bourtourault, Véronique Millischer and Olivier Mesmin, a property tax specialist. They specialise in international tax optimisation, restructurings, VAT, contentious matters, and personal patrimonies and are particularly visible in the industrial and property fields.

At **Gide Loyrette Nouel**, Richard Beauvais, Olivier Dauchez, Gilbert Ladreyt and Guillaume

TAX

CMS BUREAU FRANCIS LEFEBVRE ✪

BREDIN PRAT ✪
CLEARY, GOTTLIEB, STEEN & HAMILTON LLP ✪
LINKLATERS ✪

Clifford Chance
Freshfields Bruckhaus Deringer
Willkie Farr & Gallagher LLP ✪

Allen & Overy LLP ✪
Arsene
Baker & McKenzie SCP ✪
Gide Loyrette Nouel ✪
Latham & Watkins
Shearman & Sterling LLP
Sullivan & Cromwell LLP
White & Case LLP

Ashurst ✪
August & Debouzy
Brandford-Griffith & Associés ✪
De Pardieu Brocas Maffei ✪
Dechert ✪
JeantetAssociés ✪
Jones Day ✪
Lefèvre Pelletier & associés ✪
Morgan Lewis ✪
Paul, Hastings, Janofsky & Walker (Europe) LLP ✪
Orrick, Herrington & Sutcliffe ✪
Salans
Veil Jourde ✪

Alexen Avocats
Barsi Doumith & Associés
Bignon Lebray & Associés
Bird & Bird ✪
Denton Wilde Sapte ✪
Eversheds-Frere Cholmeley
Franklin ✪
Ginestié Magellan Paley-Vincent ✪
Haarmann Hemmelrath ✪
Herbert Smith LLP ✪
Kléber
LeBoeuf, Lamb, Greene & Macrae LLP ✪
Lovells ✪
Mayer, Brown, Rowe & Maw LLP ✪
Moisand Boutin & Associés
NomoS ✪
Norton Rose
P.D.G.B.
SJ Berwin ✪
Sarrau Thomas Couderc
Simmons & Simmons ✪
Sokolow, Carreras & Associés
Stehlin & Associés
Taylor Wessing ✪
Thieffry & Associés
UGGC & Associés ✪
Watson, Farley & Williams LLP ✪
Weil, Gotshal & Manges ✪

Firms are listed A-Z in tiers which are ranked in order of priority
✪ Indicates firm displays contact details at the end of this chapter.

Goulard are the tax partners. Their activity has a strong international dimension and is highly transaction orientated They work in conjunction with specialists from other departments in the firm: M&A, finance and real estate. The tax department also plays an active role in corporate, finance, employee benefits, tax ruling and litigation.

Latham & Watkins' tax specialists are Olivier Delattre, Christian Nouel and Xavier Renard. The firm's tax team comprises nine lawyers and encompasses international tax, M&A and private equity, financings and financial products, real estate issues, as well as employee-related and transfer pricing issues. In particular, the team is very active in restructurings and acquisitions and also handles contentious work. About one third of the business is auto-generated.

Niels Dejean and Isabelle Chauvet are the tax specialists at **Shearman & Sterling LLP**. The six-lawyer team advises on all aspects of business taxation, including tax planning, LBOs and LMBOs, design and set up of new financial products, and assistance in the resolution of tax controversies. The tax lawyers also frequently advise in M&A, financing and capital markets transactions, domestic or cross-border with expertise in the fields of structured finance, tax restructuring, transfer-pricing and acquisitions.

Sullivan & Cromwell LLP, with Jean-Pierre Le Gall (of-counsel) and Gauthier Blanluet, provides both US and French advice on the broad array of transactional capital markets and M&A matters.

Alexandre Ippolito and Norbert Majerholc are the two partners in charge at **White & Case LLP**). The activity is related to the M&A practice, such as the acquisition of Taittinger by Starwood Capital Group, and the financial expertise of the firm with regular work on a range of complex structured financial products transactions.

We also strongly recommend: Catherine Charpentier (**Ashurst**); Xavier Rohmer and Philippe Lorentz (**August & Debouzy**); Pierre Ullmann (**Brandford-Griffith & Associés**); Emmanuel Chauve (**De Pardieu Brocas Maffei**); Yann de Kergos (**Dechert**); Dominique Godet (**JeantetAssociés**); Vincent Agulhon and Christopher Potter, previously at **Ashurst** (**Jones Day**); Eric Ginter, Thierry Pons, Pierre Appremont (**Lefèvre Pelletier & associés**); Patrice Lefèvre-Péaron (**Morgan Lewis**) ; Roland Poirier and Stéphane Salou (**Orrick, Herrington & Sutcliffe**); Henri de Feydeau and Alain Jouan (**Paul, Hastings, Janofsky & Walker (Europe) LLP**); Bernard Chesnais, François Froment-Meurice, Benoît Giraux, Sandra Hazan (**Salans**); and Ariel Harroch (**Veil Jourde**).

TAX: THE BIG FOUR

What we call here the Big Four are the former legal arms of the Big Four accountancy firms, which are now completely separated. These firms handle a great deal of tax work and have been isolated as their profile is different from firms mentioned in the previous section.

TAX: THE BIG FOUR
ERNST & YOUNG SOCIÉTÉ D'AVOCATS
FIDAL ✪
Landwell & Associés
Taj ✪

Firms are listed A-Z in tiers which are ranked in order of priority
✪ Indicates firm displays contact details at the end of this chapter.

The merger between *HSD Ernst & Young* and *Archibald* gave birth to a new heavyweight on the Paris tax scene. The scope of tax issues covered by **Ernst & Young Société d'Avocats** is impressive, ranging from international taxation to tax aspects of acquisitions and restructurings, indirect taxation (VAT/customs duties), arbitration and tax litigation, as well as company taxation, supply chain, transfer pricing and tax management for wealthy individuals. Well-known tax specialists include Patrick Dibout (European tax law), Robert Tarika and Antoine Morterol (international tax), Hervé Lehérissel and Antoine Glaize. In addition the merged firm did suffer a number of other defections.

Fidal's unsurpassed national reach underlines its strength, working primarily for a client base made up of small and medium-sized businesses. The Paris office undertakes larger advisory roles, but also day-to-day tax declarations and executive tax matters. The tax practice is built on well-known names such as Pierre-Yves Demazière (asset tax), Eric Lecocq (litigation), Jean-Luc Menu (corporate), François Bon and Guillaume de Brondeau (international), Jean-Dominique Delannoy (asset, insurance, real estate), Marc Ctetté (real estate) and finally Jean-Louis Dieudonné (VAT).

Apart from a focus on individual taxation (comprising executives and expatriates) led by Michael Jaffe and Georges Morisson-Couderc, **Landwell & Associés** also boasts a well-established company tax department with a focus on international tax, M&A, transfer-pricing, VAT and customs and real estate. Robert Magnan (banking and finance) has a good reputation. Hervé-Antoine Couderc and David Pariente (private equity) left for **Sarrau Thomas Couderc**, and Alain Recoules (indirect taxes) for **Arsene**.

At **Taj**, tax work represents 90% of the total turnover (70% for company tax and 20% for individual tax). Bernard Boutemy (litigation), and Gianmarco Monsellato (transfer-pricing) are well known.

THE REGIONS

We mention here the leading law firms in the regions. This list includes the Big Four. Some of these firms are also represented in Paris and, for that reason, can sometimes be direct competitors to Parisian firms.

Adamas has offices in Lyon, Paris, Brussels and in Asia (Beijing, Shanghai, Taipei, Canton, Seoul). The firm's activities revolve around four departments: public and environmental law, Asia and foreign investments in China, international business law (M&A, arbitration, IP), and general litigation.

Strasbourg-based **Alexandre Lévy Kahn** is renowned throughout the region for its superb company and commercial work and the firm's four partners and nine associates also handle tax, labour, real estate, insurance, banking, EU and IP cases. The firm has a largely court-based practice.

Also in Strasbourg, **ASA Avocats Associés** is very highly regarded. A variety of areas are covered: company and commercial, banking and finance, commercial property, distribution and competition. The firm has an office in Paris.

Bignon Lebray & Associés is in Paris, Lyon, Lille and Aix-en-Provence. The firm is active in general corporate and commercial law, M&A, banking law, collective procedures, labour law, tax, public and environment law, IP and media, real estate, distribution and competition, international mobility, for French and international clients. It is part of the *Meritas* network (previously *CLA*).

CJA Beucher is considered a quality, full-service practice in the Pays de Loire region (Angers) and enjoys a good reputation. Its practice is advisory as well as contentious and its core activity is corporate, tax and labour law. Patrick Beucher is particularly acknowledged for his expertise within the food industry.

CMS Bureau Francis Lefebvre Lyon is the new name of *Boyer Clément Pégand* after the Paris tax and business law heavyweight increased its stake in the firm to 51% in 2003. With a clientele of mid-size businesses and subsidiaries of large manufacturing, retail and service corporations based in the Rhône-Alpes region, the firm is active in corporate, labour, public, health and tax laws and litigation. Forty-six lawyers work in Lyon.

Camille & Associés is one of the oldest firms in Toulouse and also has an office in Barcelona. With 15 lawyers, the firm is well regarded for its work in commercial, banking, labour and property law and has a varied clientele encompassing the industrial, retail and service industry sectors.

Carbonnier Lamaze Rasle & Associés is present in Lyon after merging with *Croizat & Huguenin* in 2005. The latter was initially the office of *Moquet Borde & Associés* in Lyon after the Paris office joined **Paul, Hastings, Janofsky & Walker (Europe) LLP**. The firm is an all-rounder with a focus on M&A/LBO, finance and company law, very often related to foreign investments.

Cornet Vincent Ségurel is indisputably one of the major players in general company and commercial law in the western region of the country. Comprising some 40 lawyers in Nantes and Paris, it is the product of a successful merger between a firm of *avocats* and a firm of *conseils juridiques*. The firm is notably active in insolvency,

THE REGIONS

Adamas *Lyon*
Alexandre Lévy Kahn *Strasbourg*
ASA Avocats Associés *Strasbourg*
Bignon Lebray & Associés *Aix-en-Provence, Lille, Lyon*
CJA Beucher *Angers*
CMS Bureau Francis Lefebvre Lyon ✪ *Lyon*
Camille & Associés *Toulouse*
Carbonnier Lamaze Rasle & Associés *Lyon*
Cornet Vincent Ségurel *Nantes*
Decker & Associés *Toulouse*
Delsol & Associés ✪ *Lyon*
Duel *Lille*
Dutat Lefebvre & Associés *Lille*
Duteil Avocat ✪ *Lyon*
Ernst & Young Société d'Avocats *12 offices*
Fidal ✪ *100 offices*
Lamy & Associés ✪ *Lyon*
Lamy Lexel Avocats Associés *Lyon, Alps*
Landwell & Associés *nine offices*
Lebas & Associés *Lille*
Legalis *Lille*
Morvilliers Sentenac *Toulouse*
Racine *Bordeaux, Lyons, Paris*
Ratheaux ✪ *Lyon, Nice*
Requet Chabanel *Lyon*
Soulier *Lyon*
Taj ✪ *six offices*

Firms are listed alphabetically
✪ *Indicates firm displays contact details at the end of this chapter.*

distribution, employment, transport, property, tax and public law.

Decker & Associés of Toulouse has six partners and is renowned for its commercial practice which is particularly strong in banking and aviation law. A large proportion of the client base consists of commercial banks and the firm has developed close and successful relationships within this sector, often being called upon to advise on the financing of M&A transactions. The firm also has a number of clients in the food sector.

Delsol & Associés is the result of the split at *Bignon, Lebray, Delsol & Associés* in 2003. It numbers eleven partners (nine in Lyon and two in Paris). The firm acts for a national and international clientele in business law – M&A, company law, tax, labour, litigation, public law, construction – with some niche expertise in the tourism sector, for associations and the professions.

In Lille, **Duel** has 11 partners and 19 associates who handle company and employment law, commercial law, construction and insolvency. The firm has further offices throughout the region (Douai, Tourcoing, Béthune), as well as in Paris. Clients include local companies, banks and insurance companies.

Dutat Lefebvre & Associés has offices in Lille, Valenciennes and Cambrai and its 22 partners are active in all areas of law, including tax, labour, insurance, construction, M&A and white-collar crime. They advise regional companies and handle litigation.

Duteil Avocat is a boutique firm in Lyon that handles M&A and stock exchange issues, often in an international context.

Ernst & Young Société d'Avocats, the new ensemble formed by the merger between *HSD Ernst & Young* and *Archibald* has offices in 12 cities (Bordeaux, Grenoble, Lille, Lyon, Marseille, Monaco, Montpellier, Nantes, Nice, Saint-Etienne, Strasbourg, Toulouse). The merger only affected Lyon and Strasbourg, the only cities where the previous member of the *Andersen Legal* network had offices. The Lyon office is especially strong. The firm's three main areas of activity are tax, labour law and corporate/M&A, but depending on the office, skills have been developed in various areas of law, like banking and finance in Lyon for instance.

With a network of 100 offices in 20 regional centres, **Fidal** has offices all over France. The strength of the firm is in general corporate and commercial work, tax and labour law but it is increasingly handling contentious work.

LAMY & ASSOCIES is considered one of the major general commercial practices in Lyon. Its staff of about 120 avocats (including **Fromont, Briens & Associés**) in Lyon and Paris is organised into specialist teams. Though the firm has built up its reputation in a broad range of areas on the basis of its litigation expertise, it does not handle labour law, this being undertaken instead by **Fromont, Briens & Associés**, with which **LAMY & ASSOCIES** has a partnership. The firm is the French member of *Terralex*.

Lamy Lexel Avocats Associés has a staff of 75 lawyers divided between Paris, Lyon, Annecy, Chambéry and Albertville. In Lyon, 40 lawyers act for medium and large companies. Apart from traditional activity in company and commercial law, the firm's expertise also encompasses distribution, tax and public law, sports law (with a dedicated ten-lawyer team), as well as litigation/arbitration and labour law, which has always been one of its strengths, especially in the Paris office.

Landwell & Associés has nine offices outside Paris (Bordeaux, Grenoble, Lille, Lyon, Marseille, Montpellier, Nantes, Rennes, Strasbourg). The biggest one is Lyon with some 40 lawyers specialising in tax law, but also in company law, contracts, restructurings and M&A. The firm also handles labour law and contentious work in fields such as banking and collective proceedings.

Based in Lille and with 20 lawyers, **Lebas & Associés** is particularly well regarded for the quality of its trial work, but has been developing an advisory practice which now comprises half of the firm's activity. The firm has a good reputation in company and commercial law. The client base includes national and regional institutions and mail order companies.

One of the important firms in the Northeast region (based in Roubaix, near Lille) is **Legalis**, although this is more due to its good reputation and substantial client base than its size. The practice covers company and commercial law, competition and insolvency. The firm is particularly well regarded for the quality of its trial work. Clients are mainly small and medium-sized companies, although there are also several larger banking and industrial clients.

Toulouse-based **Morvilliers Sentenac** enjoys a superb reputation locally and keeps growing with three lateral hires over the year. Sixteen lawyers represent a regional and national client base mainly in the medical and pharmaceutical sectors, including some major laboratories. Other strings to the firm's bow include IP, a solid reputation for tax, company law, insolvency and M&A, and banking and IT, as well as particular experience in international relations.

Racine is in Paris, Bordeaux, Lyon and Marseille. In addition to a general activity in corporate, M&A and private equity, the firm is also active in IT, employment, public law, construction and property, competition, with a particular profile in contentious issues. **Racine** is part of *TAGlaw*.

Ratheaux comprises 30 lawyers, 11 of them partners, with a solid reputation in business law (company law, tax, contracts), while developing know-how in other fields such as labour law, securities and regulation, and economic law. The firm handles a lot of work for international companies wishing to establish themselves in France. Two further offices are located in Paris and Nice.

Requet Chabanel, in Lyon, is active in company law, tax, economic law and labour law. The firm has a partnership with two other firms to handle litigation and intellectual property. Eight partners and ten associates compose the team.

With offices in Paris, Brussels and Lyon, **Soulier** has established a good name in national and international law and belongs to the *World Law Group*. The firm acts on all aspects of corporate, business and commercial law, with abilities in M&A, international contracts and competition, commercial litigation and white-collar crime. Other areas of expertise include IP, media, employment and sports law.

Taj has offices in Marseille, Lyon, Bordeaux, Tours and Lille and 35 partners. The firm offers a full service, with a special focus on national and international M&A, commercial law, tax, labour law and insolvency.

DELSOL & ASSOCIÉS

12 QUAI ANDRÉ LASSAGNE
69001 LYON

Telephone: +33 4 72 10 20 30
Fax: +33 4 72 10 20 31
Website: www.delsolavocats.com

Languages
English, German, Italian, Spanish

Other offices
Paris

Number of lawyers 37
at this office 29

Contacts
Jean-Philippe Delsol, Amaury Nardone

CATEGORIES OF WORK

Corporate, mergers and acquisitions, private equity
Jean-Philippe Delsol, Philippe Dumez, Amaury Nardone

Associations, foundations and third sector
Alexis Becquart, Laurent Butstraën, Xavier Delsol

Tax law
Paulette Trillat

Labour and employment law
Etienne Joulie

Construction and real estate
Nathalie Peyron

Administrative and public law
Aldo Sevino

Litigation
Pierre-Marie Durade-Replat

Restructurings
Jean-Philippe Delsol

Stock exchange regulations
Amaury Nardone

Bankruptcy proceedings
Philippe Dumez, Pierre-Marie Durade-Replat

The professions
Michel Duquaire

DUTEIL AVOCAT

7 PLACE ANTONIN PONCET
69002 LYON

Telephone: +33 4 78 37 24 24
Fax: +33 4 78 37 24 34
E-mail: online@duteil-avocat.com
Website: www.duteil-avocat.com

Languages
English, French

Number of lawyers 5

Contacts
François Duteil, Delphine Descamps, Olivia Boyron

CATEGORIES OF WORK

Mergers and acquisitions

Stock exchange engineering

Financial engineering

Banking, finance and securities

Capital investment

Venture capital

Equity investment

Corporate law

LAMY & ASSOCIÉS

40 RUE DE BONNEL
69484 LYON CEDEX 03

Telephone: +33 4 78 62 14 00
Fax: +33 4 78 62 14 99
E-mail: info@lamy-associes.com
Website: www.lamy-associes.com

Languages
English, German, Italian, Spanish

Other offices
Paris

Number of lawyers 37
at this office 34

Member
TERRALEX

CATEGORIES OF WORK

International arbitration
Christoph Martin Radtke,
Anne Covillard

International law and European law
François Balsan,
Christoph Martin Radtke

Commercial and corporate disputes
Philippe Genin,
Anne Bolland-Blanchard

Competition, distribution and consumption
Anne Covillard, Rémi Llinas,
Carole Girerd

Insolvency and reorganisation
Gérard Legrand, Philippe Genin

Finance and banking law
Gérard Legrand

Tax law and dispute resolution
Gérard Legrand, Hugues Martin

Property disputes, technical and technological litigation
Yves Bizollon, Jean-Guillaume Monin

Criminal law for business
Philippe Genin

Industrial and intellectual property
Yves Bizollon, Jean-Guillaume Monin

Corporate
Dominique Grivet, Pierre-Jean Ferry

Mergers and acquisitions
François Balsan, Eric Baroin

Health
Bruno Lamy, Anne Bolland-Blanchard

RATHEAUX

40 RUE DE BONNEL
69484 LYON CÉDEX 03

Telephone: +33 4 72 61 75 75
Fax: +33 4 78 60 00 09
E-mail: ratheaux@ratheaux.fr
Website: www.ratheaux.fr

Languages
English, German, Italian, Spanish

Other offices
Nice, Paris

Number of lawyers 35

Member
EEIG Consulegis

CATEGORIES OF WORK

Corporate and company
Pierre Cote, André Monet

Tax law and litigation
Serge Berrettoni, Christian Muller

Mergers and acquisitions
Michel Bottazzi,
Gaëtan de la Bourdonnaye

Private equity, venture capital
Pierre Cote, Michel Belin

Labour, employment law
Marie-Claude Chautard

Commercial litigation
Sylvain Roussat, Bernard Ughetto

IP copyright, patents and trade marks
Bernard Ughetto

Contracts, competition, distribution
Henri Saint-Père

Bankruptcy, debt collection
Michel Bottazzi, Sylvain Roussat

LMBO, joint ventures
Henri Saint-Père, Michel Belin

International arbitration
Bernard Ughetto

Pensions, social security
Marie-Claude Chautard

EU, international and foreign investment
Henri Saint-Père

VAT, excise and customs
Serge Berrettoni, Christian Muller

Corporate restructuring, asset deals
Michel Bottazzi, André Monet

Product liability, industrial risks
Sylvain Roussat, Bernard Ughetto

CMS BUREAU FRANCIS LEFEBVRE

1-3 VILLA ÉMILE BERGERAT
92522 NEUILLY-SUR-SEINE CEDEX

Telephone: +33 1 47 38 55 00
Fax: +33 1 47 38 55 55
E-mail: info@cms-bfl.com
Website: www.cms-bfl.com

Languages
English, German, Italian, Mandarin, Portuguese, Russian, Spanish

Other offices
Brussels, Bucharest, Buenos Aires, Casablanca, Düsseldorf, Lyon, Montevideo, Moscow, New York, São Paulo, Shanghai, Strasbourg

Number of lawyers 435
at this office 303

Contact
Pierre-Sébastien Thill

Member
CMS, the alliance of major independent European law firms

CATEGORIES OF WORK

Direct taxation

VAT

Registration fees – wealth tax

Local taxes

International taxation

Customs & Excise duties

Employment law

International law

Corporate law, M&A

Insolvency law

Patrimonial law

Dispute and arbitration

Contracts and regulations

Banking and finance, insurance

Real estate and public law

Intellectual property and information technology law

Competition, distribution and customer law

EU law and dispute

Local authorities, semi-public companies and local public sector

Africa: business law and taxation

FIDAL

14 BVD DU GÉNÉRAL LECLERC
92527 NEUILLY-SUR-SEINE CEDEX

Telephone: +33 1 47 38 54 00
Fax: +33 1 47 38 54 99
E-mail: valerie.climent@fidal.fr
Website: www.fidal.fr

Languages
English, Spanish, German, Italian, Polish, Russian, Chinese, Portuguese

Other offices
Brussels; 100 offices throughout France

Number of lawyers 1,285

CATEGORIES OF WORK

Tax law
Yann de Givré

International corporate tax
Nathalie Cordier-Deltour, Hervé Bidaud

Company law, M&A
André Guengant

Private equity
Guy Roulin

Labour and employment law
Gérard Kesztenbaum

Estate planning – wealth preservation and transmission
Pierre Berger

Competition and distribution law
Dominique Ferré

IP/IT
Dominique Ferré

Litigation and dispute resolution
Bruno Berger-Perrin

Public sector
Eric Gintrand

European law
Frédéric Puel

Banking law and taxation
Yves Robert

Insurance law and taxation
Michel Braun

Real property law and taxation
Marc Cretté

Environment law
Bruno Wertenschlag

Financial markets and regulations
Philippe D'Hoir

Health
Michel Guérin

Sports
Denis Provost

THE FIRM

Fidal was created in 1922.

The firm has developed since and now numbers 100 offices all over France and in Brussels.

AREAS OF PRACTICE

With about 1,300 lawyers in France and correspondents in 150 other countries, Fidal is the 'leading business law firm in France in terms of income and size' (source: *'Juristes Associés' – 'radiographie des cabinets d'avocats d'affaries en France'*).

The law firm offers its clients a three-tier service: national, with a strong presence in Paris (nearly 400 lawyers) and in regions throughout France; European, with the support of its Brussels office, specialising in EU issues; and international, with 200 lawyers dedicated to international matters.

Fidal's lawyers advise several tens of thousands of businesses of all sizes, from multinationals to small and mid-sized businesses, all of which benefit from the same high standards of quality and knowledge of the client's market. The firm's organisation is based on specialised departments which cover the traditional areas of business law (tax law, employment law, company law, mergers and acquisitions, distribution law, antitrust law, intellectual property law, estate planning, and litigation). To meet the distinct needs of certain market segments, the firm has developed practice groups with specialised expertise in these markets (public sector, listed companies, capital investment, retirement and contingency funds, safety-prevention, associations and social economy, health, sports law, food and agricultural industries, etc).

Fidal's organisation is also supported by a single legal and tax research and development department, which is a valuable source of forward thinking and pro-active solutions, and, through a rigorous training policy, dedicated to reinforcing the firm's specialised practice areas and to managing the quality of the firm's client relations.

For more information, visit the website at www.fidal.fr.

TAJ

181 AVENUE CHARLES DE GAULLE
92524 NEUILLY-SUR-SEINE

Telephone: +33 1 40 88 22 50
Fax: +33 1 40 88 22 17
Website: www.taj.fr

Languages
Arabic, Dutch, English, German, Italian, Japanese, Portuguese, Russian, Spanish

Other offices
Bordeaux, Lille, Lyon, Marseille, Tours

Number of lawyers 250

Contact
Pascale Ponroy (pponroy@taj.fr) – communication manager

CATEGORIES OF WORK

Corporate tax
Sophie Blégent-Delapille

Indirect tax, VAT and customs
Odile Courjon

Individual tax and international mobility
Anne Vaucher, Patrick Tyrrell

International tax restructuring
Sophie Blégent-Delapille

Real estate tax
Rachid Arras, Benoît Dambre

Transfer pricing
Gianmarco Monsellato

Banking and financial tax
Marie-France Vernay

Joint venture, corporate reorganisation, takeovers
Jean-Victor Prévost

Contracts, distribution and competition law
Jean-Victor Prévost

Insolvency law, bankruptcy
Stéphanie Chatelon

Public law
Frédéric Gosme

Labour law
Véronique Béal-Child

THE FIRM

Taj is one of the leading French law firms and advises groups on their international tax and legal strategies. It employs more than 350 professionals, including 34 partners.

These professionals offer an extensive range of services covering most aspects of tax and legal matters to French and foreign multinationals, small- and medium-sized companies, public and private institutions, and government organisations.

The firm's clients are guaranteed continuous and tailored support in all stages of their growth and development. Its experts combine the ability to solve complex tax and legal problems with financial and economic understanding, to provide a response adapted to corporate strategic issues.

Certain teams are entirely dedicated to specific sectors of activity for a better understanding of clients' concerns and to provide the best response adapted to their needs and expectations.

Taj develops its expertise in highly diversified sectors such as health, real estate, aeronautics, defence, food industry, luxury goods, distribution, textiles and sport.

Taj serves its clients in co-ordination with the 20,000 Deloitte tax professionals located in 150 countries across the globe. Taj has access to the tools and methodologies of the global tax practice of Deloitte and is committed to maintain the same high standards of client service and quality.

AREAS OF PRACTICE

Taj is specialised in a wide range of both domestic and international tax and legal work to multinational corporations, international financial institutions, and sovereign governments.

The office provides clients with legal and tax assistance and advice on mergers and acquisitions, joint venture, reorganisation and structuring in France. Its lawyers also have cohesive experience of cross-border and multi-jurisdictional transactions.

The firm's bankruptcy and insolvency department represents institutional investors. It also acts regularly for unsecured creditors, and business debtors.

The firm is actively involved in corporate international tax planning, VAT and custom duty planning. The practice serves all the international tax planning and dispute-related needs of national and multinational clients, including co-ordination of multi-country planning, transfer pricing, profit reparation, planning strategic tax consulting, value-added tax issues, and custom duty planning.

Clients are advised on social law matters including employment contracts, landing redundancies, relations with trade union, international transfers and so on.

ADAMAS

5 RUE DE CASTIGLIONE
75001 PARIS

Telephone: +33 1 53 45 92 22
Fax: +33 1 53 45 92 20
E-mail: paris@adamas-lawfirm.com
Website: www.adamas-lawfirm.com
www.adamas-asia.com

Languages
English, German, Mandarin, Spanish

Other offices
Lyon, Beijing, Shanghai, Guangzhou, Taipei, Seoul

Number of lawyers 50

CATEGORIES OF WORK

Mergers and acquisitions, investments (Lyon office)
Hervé Le Blanc, Robert Guillaumond

Mergers and acquisitions, investments (Paris office)
Jérôme Gertler, Dominique Gerry

International arbitration
Robert Guillaumond

Administrative law, public law
Alain Serge Mescheriakoff, Claude Ferradou

Environmental law
Yvan Razafindratandra

Corporate law and contracts
Jean-Marie Tochio, Denis Santy

Industrial property rights
Barbara Bertholet

Social law, labour law
Jean-Michel Ghinsberg, Sylvain Letemplier

Banking law
Hervé Le Blanc

Taxation
Jean-Claude Chocque

Urban planning and development
Georges Xynopoulos

China law, investments in China
Franck Desevedavy, Olivier Dubuis

China law: corporate law and contracts
Arnaud Depierrefeu, Olivier Lefebure

Investments in India
Olivier Dubuis, Delphine Gieux

ALERION

5 RUE JEAN MERMOZ
75008 PARIS

Telephone: +33 1 58 56 97 00
Fax: +33 1 58 56 97 01
E-mail: paris@alerionavocats.com
Website: www.alerionavocats.com

Languages
French, English, Spanish, German, Korean, Chinese

Number of lawyers 40

CATEGORIES OF WORK

Banking and finance
Dominique Doise, Philippe Mathurin

Bankruptcy
Philippe Mathurin

Corporate and business law
Pierre-Olivier Brouard, Christophe Gerschel

M&A
Pierre-Olivier Brouard, Jacques Bouyssou

Private equity, capital markets
Jacques Bouyssou, Pierre-Olivier Brouard

Competition, distributorship, EC
Catherine Robin

Labour law
Jacques Perotto

International investment
Joong-Ho Kim

Tax law
Christophe Gerschel

Commercial property and real estate
Philippe Mathurin

Product liability and insurance
Philippe Mathurin, Patrick Lescop De Moÿ

Litigation, arbitration
Dominique Doise, Jacques Bouyssou

Public law
Philippe Mathurin

Sports and entertainment
Christophe Gerschel

Korean business law
Joong-Ho Kim

Health and medical law
Remi Pellet

ALLEN & OVERY LLP

EDOUARD VII
26 BOULEVARD DES CAPUCINES
75009 PARIS

Telephone: +33 1 40 06 54 00
Fax: +33 1 40 06 54 54
E-mail: information@allenovery.com
Website: www.allenovery.com

Languages
Arabic, English, French, German, Italian, Spanish

Other offices
Amsterdam, Antwerp, Bangkok, Beijing, Bratislava, Brussels, Budapest, Dubai, Frankfurt, Hamburg, Hong Kong, London, Luxembourg, Madrid, Milan, Moscow, New York, Paris, Prague, Rome, Shanghai, Singapore, Tokyo, Turin, Warsaw

Number of lawyers 2,304
at this office 117

Contacts
Edouard Didier (senior partner), Isabelle Epp (marketing contact)

CATEGORIES OF WORK

Banking/syndications

Acquisition finance/private equity

Securitisation/asset finance

Projects/telecoms finance

Corporate/commercial

Mergers and acquisitions

Restructuring

Intellectual property/ information technology

Real estate

EU and competition

Employment, pensions and incentives

Public, administrative and environmental

Debt and equity capital markets

Derivatives

Tax

Structured financings

Financial services

ASHURST

18 SQUARE EDOUARD VII
75009 PARIS

Telephone: +33 1 53 53 53 53
Fax: +33 1 53 53 53 54
Website: www.ashurst.com

Languages
English, French, German, Portuguese, Spanish

Other offices
Brussels, Dubai, Frankfurt, London, Madrid, Milan, Munich, New Delhi*, New York, Singapore, Tokyo

Number of lawyers 748
at this office 65

Contact
Frédéric Pinet

CATEGORIES OF WORK

Corporate
Frédéric Pinet, Guy Benda, Bertrand Delaunay

International finance
Laurent Mabilat, Diane Sénéchal, James Collis

Private equity
Frédéric Pinet, Guy Benda, Bertrand Delaunay (corporate), Laurent Mabilat, Diane Sénéchal, James Collis (international finance), Catherine Charpentier (tax)

Restructuring and insolvency
Jean-Pierre Farges, Bertrand Delaunay, Sophie Nicolas

Energy, transport and infrastructure
Michel Lequien

Tax
Catherine Charpentier

Competition
Chantal Momège

Real estate
Dorothée Bontoux, Philippe None

Litigation and arbitration
Jean-Pierre Farges

Employment
Alexandre Jaurett

AYACHE SALAMA & ASSOCIÉS

47 AVENUE HOCHE
75008 PARIS

Telephone: + 33 1 58 05 38 05
Fax: +33 1 58 05 38 00
E-mail: b.ayache@ayache-salama.com

Languages
English, German, Spanish

Number of lawyers 35

Contacts
Denis Salama, Bernard Ayache

Member
Law Exchange International (LEI)

CATEGORIES OF WORK	
Mergers and acquisitions	**Competition law**
Private equity	**Distribution law**
Banking and finance	**Public economic law**
Corporate law	**Tax law**
Arbitration	**Intellectual property**
Litigation	**Real estate**

THE FIRM
The specialist commercial law firm Ayache Salama & Associés advises and represents French and foreign companies in a wide range of legal areas.

The firm's client base comprises mainly large companies, predominantly in the industrial sector, and also a large number of investment banks, financial institutions and investment funds.

AREAS OF PRACTICE
Although Ayache Salama & Associés' commercial law practice encompasses both non-contentious advice and litigation, today the firm mainly acts in an advisory capacity.

Ayache Salama & Associés advises on mergers and acquisitions transactions – an area that has seen considerable growth within the firm, in traditional industries, as well as in the new economy. The firm also handles financial markets work and regularly advises large industrial concerns and investment funds on their acquisition deals. It is also involved in LBO financing, eurobonds and derivative products. In addition, Ayache Salama & Associés has considerable expertise relating to legal disputes in the banking, stock market and financial sectors.

The firm provides contentious and non-contentious advice in the area of competition and distribution law. These practice areas constitute a significant part of the firm's overall practice, due to the large number of large distribution chains, both French and overseas, in its client base. This area of expertise is complemented by an excellent knowledge of the legal matters affecting the commercial property business, and, in particular, shopping centres.

Ayache Salama & Associés' intellectual property practice has expertise in brands, designs and models and patents.

Tax lawyers at the firm have solid experience in both domestic and international company and private tax law.

The firm is also involved in economic public law and local authority law, acting mainly on behalf of banks, local authorities, and public enterprises. The public law department is led by an attorney who is a professor of law (professeur agrégé des facultés de droit).

BMH AVOCATS
BREITENSTEIN MEILLASSOUX HAUSER

29 RUE DU FAUBOURG SAINT-HONORÉ 75008 PARIS

Telephone: +33 1 42 66 63 19
Fax: +33 1 42 66 64 81
E-mail: bmh@bmhavocats.com
Website: www.bmhavocats.com

Languages
English, German, Russian, Spanish

Number of lawyers 20

Contact
Dr Martin Hauser (Paris)

CATEGORIES OF WORK

E-commerce and information technology
André Meillassoux

Intellectual property
Martin Hauser

Mergers and acquisitions
Olivier Hoebanx, Thomas Jahn

Company law
Olivier Hoebanx

Health and pharmaceutical law
Catherine Nelken

Energy
Martin Hauser, Anouk Darcet-Felgen

Commercial litigation
Olivier Hoebanx, Anouk Darcet-Felgen

EC law (antitrust)
Catherine Nelken

International arbitration
Martin Hauser, Olivier Hoebanx

Labour and social law
Anne-Marie Senechal-L'Homme

BAKER & McKENZIE

32 AVENUE KLÉBER BP 2112 75771 PARIS CEDEX 16

Telephone: +33 1 44 17 53 00
Fax: +33 1 44 17 45 75
E-mail: paris.info@bakernet.com
Website: www.bakernet.com

Languages
English, German, Italian, Japanese, Spanish

Other offices
The member firms of Baker & McKenzie International, a Swiss Verein, have 70 offices in 38 countries around the world. For a complete list, please visit www.bakernet.com.

Number of lawyers 3,300+
at this office 105

Contacts
Laurent Epstein, Denise Broussal

CATEGORIES OF WORK

Corporate law
Marie-Francoise Bréchignac, Pierre Ray

Competition, distribution
Mireille Dany, Alex Dowding, Régis Fabre

Employment and immigration law
Denise Broussal, Gilles Jolivet

Information technology
Rémy Bricard

Intellectual property
Jean-François Bretonnière

Litigation and arbitration
Jean-Dominique Touraille

Mergers and acquisitions
Laurent Barbara, Eric Lasry, Laurent Epstein, Alyssa Gallot

Pharmaceutical and healthcare industries
Laurent Epstein, Henry de Suremain

Public and environmental law
Arnaud Cabanes

Real estate
Eric Pomonti, Marc Mariani, Olivier Mesmin

Securities law
Raphaële François-Poncet

Telecommunications
Emmanuel Guillaume

Tax
Pierre-Yves Bourtourault, Véronique Millischer, Olivier Mesmin

BARTHÉLÉMY & ASSOCIÉS, member of ius laboris

5-7 RUE D'ATHÈNES
75009 PARIS

Telephone: +33 1 44 95 48 00
Fax: +33 1 45 63 99 62
E-mail: bysauret@barthelemy-associes.fr
Website: www.barthelemy-associes.fr

Languages
English, Spanish

Other offices
Bordeaux, Clermont Ferrand, Lille, Lyon, Marseille, Montpellier, Nantes, Sophia Antipolis, Nîmes, Rennes, Saint Etienne, Strasbourg, Toulouse

Number of lawyers 220
at this office 90

Contacts
Alain Sauret, Pascal Lagoutte

Member
ius laboris, International Employment Law Pensions and Employee Benefits Alliance

CATEGORIES OF WORK

Labour and employment law	**Working time**
Compensation and benefits	**Social security**
Pensions	**Sports law**
Restructuring plans	**Executive employment contracts**
Collective labour law	**Litigation and dispute resolution**
Works council	**Health and safety at work**

THE FIRM

Established in 1964 by Jacques Barthélémy, the law partnership of Barthélémy and Associates is one of France's leading employment law practices with 220 lawyers.

The firm is located in Paris, but the partnership has 14 well-staffed branch offices in France's most important cities.

The firm is ISO 9001 certified.

AREAS OF PRACTICE

Barthélémy and Associates was one of the first firms in the country to specialise in labour law, social security, and pension law. The firm is able to provide assistance in all areas relating to the application of labour and employment law for companies with a view to preventing or resolving individual or collective employment disputes.

Barthélémy works closely with leading universities and academic centres in the field of professional training, research, and the development of legislative reform. Several of the partners collaborate actively with a variety of specialist legal publications.

BERSAY & ASSOCIÉS

31 AVENUE HOCHE
75008 PARIS

Telephone: +33 1 56 88 30 00
Fax: +33 1 56 88 30 01
E-mail: contact@bersay-associes.com
Website: www.bersay-associes.com

Languages
English, German, Hebrew, Italian, Portuguese, Spanish

Contacts
Jérôme Bersay, Yves Ardaillou, Emmanuel Shulte

CATEGORIES OF WORK

Mergers and acquisitions	Insolvency/corporate restructuring
Corporate and commercial	Labour and employment
Capital markets	Intellectual property
Business law	Information tecchnology
Banking and finance	E-commerce
Tax	Telecommunications
Competition law	Media and entertainment
Commercial property/real estate	Fraud and white-collar crime
Dispute resolution – litigation and arbitration	Shipping and transport

THE FIRM

Bersay & Associés is an international law firm known for its high-quality legal services.

Founded by Jérôme Bersay, the firm has experienced fast-paced growth, going from two lawyers in 1998 to 27. Most of the lawyers within the firm have previously worked for a leading Anglo-Saxon and/or French firm.

Bersay & Associés was the first Paris law firm to be certified ISO 9001 in 1998. Bersay & Associés stands apart from other firms because of its strategic approach and total availability. The firm's lawyers are recognised for their creativity and for their responsiveness.

Bersay & Associés has a strong international focus. All its lawyers work in French and in English and most of them work in at least a third language (ie German, Spanish, Italian, Portuguese, Hebrew). To facilitate its international activities, the firm has established working relationships with high-quality firms throughout the world. Bersay & Associés has chosen to remain independent from network organisations which would require the firm to work with designated foreign firms as it prefers to choose highly qualified foreign correspondents with the right expertise for the specific assignment.

AREAS OF PRACTICE

Bersay & Associés offers a wide range of expertise covering the main facets of the company's operations: corporate and capital markets (ie mergers and acquisitions, long-term financing transactions, joint ventures, shareholders' agreements, shareholders' disputes, IPOs); commercial, competition and EU law (ie merger control, antitrust, distribution); business law; banking and finance; insolvency/corporate restructuring; commercial property/real estate; tax (ie corporate tax, international transactions, long-term financing transactions, litigation); labour and employment (compensation and benefits, collective and individual claims, restructuring and layoff plans etc); intellectual property/information technology (patent, trade mark, copyright, domain name, software, internet, e-commerce, media and entertainment, and telecommunications matters).

The firm's practice is equally balanced between transactional work and litigation/arbitration.

BIRD & BIRD

CENTRE D'AFFAIRES EDOUARD VII
3 SQUARE EDOUARD VII
75009 PARIS

Telephone: +33 1 42 68 60 00
Fax: +33 1 42 68 60 11
E-mail: paris@twobirds.com
Website: www.twobirds.com

Languages
English, French, German

Other offices
Beijing, Brussels, Düsseldorf, Frankfurt, Hong Kong, London, Madrid, Milan, Munich, Rome, Stockholm, The Hague

Number of lawyers 472
at this office 66

Contact
Frédérique Dupuis-Toubol

CATEGORIES OF WORK

Advertising

Aviation and aerospace

Broadcasting (national and EU)

Communications

Competition and EU law

Corporate finance

Data protection

Employment law

Energy

Information technology

Internet and e-commerce

Intellectual property

Life sciences

Litigation and dispute resolution

Media, film and entertainment

Product liability

Public law

Sport

Tax

BOUCKAERT ORMEN PASSEMARD SPORTES (BOPS)

SOCIÉTÉ D'AVOCATS

47 RUE DUMONT D'URVILLE
75116 PARIS

Telephone: +33 1 70 37 39 00
Fax: +33 1 70 37 39 01
E-mail: cabinet.bops@bopslaw.com
Website: www.bopslaw.com

Languages
English, German, Italian, Spanish

Number of lawyers 20

Contacts
Christian Bouckaert, Pascal Ormen, Rémi Passemard, Carole Sportes

CATEGORIES OF WORK

Arbitration
Christian Bouckaert, Pascal Ormen

Aviation
Christian Bouckaert, Carole Sportes

Bankers liability
Rémi Passemard

Construction contracts
Pascal Ormen, Rémi Passemard

D&O liability
Rémi Passemard

Environmental risks
Pascal Ormen, Carole Sportes

Industrial risks
Pascal Ormen, Rémi Passemard

Insolvency law
Rémi Passemard

Insurance litigation
All partners

Life insurance
Pascal Ormen, Rémi Passemard

Pharmaceutical/medical liability
Carole Sportes, Christian Bouckaert

Product liability
Christian Bouckaert, Carole Sportes

Regulatory and policy wording
Pascal Ormen

Reinsurance
Christian Bouckaert, Pascal Ormen

BRANDFORD-GRIFFITH & ASSOCIÉS

9 RUE DES PYRAMIDES
75001 PARIS

Telephone: +33 1 44 55 44 55
Fax: +33 1 44 55 44 00
E-mail: office@brandfordgriffith.com

Languages
English, French

Number of lawyers 25

Contacts
Henri Brandford-Griffith, Nigel Hartridge

CATEGORIES OF WORK

Stock exchange
Henri Brandford-Griffith, Vanina Paolaggi, Jérôme Brosset, Guillaume Kessler

Mergers and acquisitions
Henri Brandford-Griffith, Nigel Hartridge, Vanina Paolaggi, Guillaume Kessler

Litigation and arbitration
Yves Repiquet, Diane Pasturel, Henri Brandford-Griffith

Capital markets
Laurent Sablé

Private equity/LBO
Jérôme Brosset, Vanina Paolaggi, Guillaume Kessler, Eytan Hanouna

Competition
Florent Prunet

Tax
Pierre Ullmann

CPLC PARTNERS

7 RUE DE PHALSBOURG
75017 PARIS

Telephone: +33 1 40 53 40 30
Fax: +33 1 40 53 40 31
E-mail: avocats@cplc-partners.com

Languages
Dutch, English, French, Italian

Other offices
Le Mans

Number of lawyers 9
at this office 7

CATEGORIES OF WORK

Commercial law
Thierry Pariente, Véronique Lemeur-Baudry

Litigation
Thierry Pariente, Cécile Cabana-Draut

EU law and competition
Véronique Lemeur-Baudry

Corporate law
Georges Civalleri

Distribution law
Véronique Lemeur-Baudry, Thierry Pariente

New technology law
Thierry Pariente

Tax
Georges Civalleri

Business restructuring
Georges Civalleri

BREDIN PRAT

130 RUE DU FAUBOURG SAINT-HONORÉ
75008 PARIS

Telephone: +33 1 44 35 35 35
Fax: +33 1 42 89 10 73
E-mail: bredinprat@bredinprat.com

Languages
English, German, Italian, Polish, Russian, Spanish

Other offices
Brussels

Number of lawyers 80
at this office 76

CATEGORIES OF WORK

Mergers and acquisitions	**EC and French competition law**
Securities law	**Banking and finance**
Litigation and arbitration	**Company and commercial**
Tax	**Capital markets**
Public law	**Financing**

THE FIRM

Founded in the 1960s, Bredin Prat specialises in business law, in particular high-level mergers and acquisitions (including major French privatisations). It also undertakes work in finance and capital markets, competition law, tax law, commercial litigation and arbitration, and white-collar criminal law.

Approximately three-quarters of the firm's lawyers are French. Four American partners, one British partner and British and American associates make up the balance of the firm. Practice is conducted in both French and English.

Bredin Prat has chosen to remain independent from network organisations which would require the firm to work with designated firms or offices outside of France. The firm has instead chosen the route of developing strong working relationships with several firms in all the European capitals and in the United States (and to a more limited extent in Asia) which can be called upon to form the appropriate international team for specific transborder or multi-jurisdictional transactions. More specifically in Europe, Bredin Prat is part of an active network of leading independent firms, including Slaughter and May in the UK, Hengeler Mueller in Germany, Bonelli Erede Pappalardo in Italy, and Uría Menéndez in Spain. Individuals of Bredin Prat and these other firms regularly work together as one integrated team to provide clients with first-class and seamless legal advice worldwide.

In early 1999, a group of Brussels-based lawyers specialising in European Community law joined the firm to open Bredin Prat's Brussels office.

The Brussels office represents an integrated expansion of the European competition law group in Paris.

In November 2002, a high-level tax team of lawyers joined the firm.

AREAS OF PRACTICE

Following the firm's tradition of specialisation in chosen practice areas or in specific types of transactions – as opposed to a broad-based corporate, commercial practice – the firm's transactional work today is concentrated on securities and public takeover law, significant (and often cross-border or multi-jurisdictional) mergers, acquisitions, divestitures, joint ventures, reorganisations, privatisation, tax, financing and corporate finance.

Similarly, a significant part of Bredin Prat's litigation practice – representing French and foreign clients before the French courts, French and European Community regulatory bodies and French and international arbitral tribunals – is today concentrated in the areas of finance, securities law, corporate law, tax law, competition and antitrust law, and white-collar criminal matters related to the foregoing. The firm's traditional civil and private international law practice in particularly significant matters continues to represent an important part of its litigation and arbitration practice.

The firm's Brussels office practises European Community law with a particular focus on competition law, mergers and state aids.

CLEARY GOTTLIEB STEEN & HAMILTON LLP

12 RUE DE TILSITT
75008 PARIS

Telephone: +33 1 40 74 68 00
Fax: +33 1 45 63 66 37
Website: www.clearygottlieb.com

Languages
Arabic, Dutch, English, French, German, Greek, Italian, Japanese, Polish, Romanian, Russian, Spanish, Swedish

Other offices
Brussels, Cologne, Frankfurt, Hong Kong, London, Milan, Moscow, New York, Rome, Tokyo, Washington DC

Number of lawyers 847
at this office 90

CATEGORIES OF WORK

Arbitration and litigation

Banking and finance

Capital markets/securities

Competition law

Debt restructuring

Energy and project finance

Joint ventures

Mergers and acquisitions

Privatisations

Structured finance

Securitisation

Tax

CLYDE & CO
SOCIÉTÉ D'AVOCATS

12 RUE MAGELLAN
75378 PARIS CEDEX 08

Telephone: +33 1 44 43 88 88
Fax: +33 1 44 43 88 77
Video conference: +33 1 44 43 88 99
E-mail: paris.office@clydeco.fr
Website: www.clydeco.com

Languages
English, German, Italian, Spanish

Other offices
Abu Dhabi, Belgrade, Caracas, Cardiff, Dubai, Guildford, Hong Kong, London, Moscow, Nantes, Piraeus, Rio de Janeiro, St Petersburg, Shanghai, Singapore

Number of lawyers 409
at this office 38

Contacts
Gildas Rostain, Gérard Honig, Bernard Mettetal

CATEGORIES OF WORK

Arbitration
Gérard Honig, Bernard Mettetal

Aviation
Gérard Honig, Simon Ndiaye

Construction contracts
Jean-Marie Preel, Clarisse Billot

Environmental
Bernard Mettetal

Professional indemnity and directors' and officers' liability
Gérard Honig, Bernard Mettetal

Shipping
Gildas Rostain, Rozenn Lopin

Insolvency law
Bernard Mettetal

Insurance and reinsurance
Gérard Honig, Bernard Mettetal

Product liability – industrial risks
Jean-Marie Preel, Gérard Honig

Life insurance and regulatory
Bernard Mettetal, Gérard Honig

COURNOT ASSOCIATION D'AVOCATS

**89-91 RUE DU FAUBOURG SAINT HONORÉ
75008 PARIS**

Telephone: +33 1 40 06 19 19
Fax: +33 1 40 06 19 20
E-mail: sjcournot@cournotavocats.com

Languages
English, French, German, Italian

Number of lawyers 20

Contact
Stéphane Cournot

Member
Washington DC Bar; Paris Bar

CATEGORIES OF WORK

Arbitration (national/international)
Laurent Paris

Capital markets
Richard Dehé

Employment
Laurence Pinchou

Insolvency
Stéphane J Cournot

Mergers and acquisitions
Stéphane J Cournot, Richard Dehé, Arnaud de Corbière

Tax
Richard Dehé

Corporate and commercial
Stéphane J Cournot, Arnaud de Corbière

Commercial litigation
Laurent Paris, Laurence Pinchou

IT, telecoms and internet
Yann Breban

Intellectual property, trade marks
Laurence Pinchou

Project finance
Richard Dehé

White-collar crime
Laurent Paris

CURTIS, MALLET-PREVOST, COLT & MOSLE LLP

**15 RUE D'ASTORG
75008 PARIS**

Telephone: +33 1 42 66 39 10
Fax: +33 1 42 66 39 62
E-mail: info@cm-p.com
Website: www.cm-p.com

Languages
English, French

Other offices
Frankfurt, Houston, London, Mexico City, Milan, Muscat, New York, Stamford, Washington DC

Number of lawyers 187
at this office 7

Contacts
Yves E Lepage, Geoffroy Lyonnet, Peter M Wolrich

Member
American Society of International Law; French Arbitration Committee; International Chamber of Commerce; Institute of International Business Law and Practice; London Court of International Arbitration

CATEGORIES OF WORK

International transactions
Peter M Wolrich, Geoffroy Lyonnet

Mergers and acquisitions
Geoffroy Lyonnet, Yves E Lepage

EU law

Contracts
Peter M Wolrich, Geoffroy Lyonnet

Litigation and arbitration
Peter M Wolrich, Geoffroy Lyonnet

Structured finance
Yves E Lepage

Antitrust

Infrastructure and project finance
Yves E Lepage

Privatisation
Yves E Lepage

Transnational joint ventures
Yves E Lepage

Power generation
Yves E Lepage

Petroleum and petrochemical contracts
Yves E Lepage, Peter M Wolrich

Construction contracts
Yves E Lepage, Peter M Wolrich

Equipment sale and leaseback
Yves E Lepage

Investment management
Geoffroy Lyonnet

DLA PIPER RUDNICK GRAY CARY US LLP,

CORRESPONDENTS OF CARIDDI, MEE, RUE, ASSOCIATION D'AVOCATS AU BARREAU DE PARIS

12 RUE DE LA PAIX
75002 PARIS

Telephone: +33 1 40 15 24 00
Fax: +33 1 40 15 24 03
E-mail: info@dlapiper.com
Website: www.dlapiper.com

Languages
English, French, German, Dutch, Spanish, Portuguese, Italian, Albanian, Vietnamese

Other offices
Austria, Belgium, Bosnia-Herzegovina, China, Croatia, Czech Republic, Denmark*, Egypt*, Georgia, Germany, Hong Kong, Hungary, Italy, Japan, Netherlands, Norway*, Poland*, Russia, Singapore*, Slovakia, South Africa*, Spain, Sweden*, Thailand, UK, Ukraine, United Arab Emirates, US

Number of lawyers 3,100
at this office 30

Contact
Alan F Cariddi

CATEGORIES OF WORK

Corporate, mergers and acquisitions
Alan F Cariddi, Christine Bougis-Stentz

Banking and finance
Carol AF Umhoefer, Anne-Noëlle Charvillat-Carrez

Commercial and bankruptcy
Christine Bougis-Stentz, Bruce C Mee

HR and employment
Bijan E Eghbal

Litigation and arbitration
Bruce C Mee

Securities and capital markets
Anne Maréchal

Intellectual property and information technologies
Carol AF Umhoefer, Bruce C Mee, Patrick Boiron

Insurance
Bruce C Mee

Real estate
Philippe X Ledoux

Tax
Fabrice Rué

Structured and project finance/public-private partnerships
Fabrice Rué

Media and communication
Patrick Boiron

THE FIRM

DLA Piper Rudnick Gray Cary is a leading global legal services provider with approximately 3,100 lawyers in 58 offices across 22 countries. The organisation is committed to building long-term relationships with its clients and supports their strategic and operational needs both locally and internationally. The firm's practice in Paris is particularly international; its experience reaches beyond France, the US and the UK to include the laws, practices and business customs of other jurisdictions in Europe, South America and Asia.

The affiliated Paris office of DLA Piper Rudnick Gray Cary US LLP is composed of experienced French and US attorneys, practising as avocats (attorneys-at-law), admitted without restriction to the Paris Bar. The firm engages in a substantial and diversified practice in France and represents clients active not only in the EU but also in many other countries throughout the world.

The firm's key strengths are its relationship-driven approach, its business-like attitude, and its broad service capability, as well as its local knowledge and long-standing experience.

AREAS OF PRACTICE

The firm's Paris office focuses in particular on corporate law, including mergers and acquisitions, joint ventures, and strategic investments; securities law and capital markets; tax; banking and finance; real estate; French and European commercial law (including bankruptcy); intellectual property, media and information technologies; labour and employment; and arbitration and litigation.

The firm's clients are mid-sized and large French, European, Japanese and US companies, commercial banks, multinational corporations, private equity and other investment funds, and leading investment banks. The firm is familiar with a wide variety of business sectors, including advertising, telecommunications, media, e-commerce, computer software, medical devices, professional and consumer electronics, textiles, retail apparel, video games, toys and games, food and beverages, banking, insurance, real estate, hotels, energy, chemicals, cosmetics and pharmaceuticals.

The firm's objective is to bring to its clients a clear understanding of the French legal system and of the cultural context in which it operates. The firm's lawyers work closely together in order to ensure that the client's economic objectives can be achieved within the constraints imposed by French law.

DARROIS VILLEY MAILLOT BROCHIER

69 AVENUE VICTOR HUGO
75116 PARIS

Telephone: + 33 1 45 02 19 19
Fax: + 33 1 45 01 91 68
E-mail:
firstinitialsurname@darroisvilley.com

Languages
Dutch, English, German, Italian, Spanish

Number of lawyers 35

Contacts
Jean-Michel Darrois, Matthieu de Boisséson

CATEGORIES OF WORK

Mergers and acquisitions
Alain Maillot, Olivier Diaz

Complex corporate transactions
Philippe Villey

Stock exchange law
Marie-Noëlle Dompé

Governmental and privatisation matters
François Sureau

EU, regulatory matters
Didier Théophile

International arbitration
Matthieu de Boisséson, Pierre Duprey

Criminal business law
Jean-Michel Darrois

Litigation
Emmanuel Brochier

International matters
Andrew Plump, David Scemla

Private equity
Alain Maillot, Oliver Diaz

THE FIRM

Darrois Villey Maillot Brochier is a highly specialised firm of 35 lawyers concentrating on, and limiting its practice to, two distinct but often related activities. The firm provides advisory services concerning complex corporate and financial operations including: mergers and acquisitions; tender offers and tender offer defences; company reorganisations; stock exchange and company law issues; and privatisations and related transactions with governmental bodies and administrations, including European Union regulatory advice and compliance services. The firm also renders services concerning litigation and arbitration matters, including particularly, international arbitration matters arising out of such corporate and financial operations, specialising in complex corporate and securities regulation issues. The firm's expertise in regard to these activities has evolved since its creation in 1982 as a result of its consistent involvement in major acquisitions and tender offers in France and in the resolution of highly visible business disputes.

The firm is frequently involved in friendly combinations and reorganisations of major multinational enterprises, and has handled many unusually complex combinations in regulated industries. The evolution of the firm's activities in cross-border and international matters enables the partners of the firm to act as advisers to multinational clients with respect to their investment strategies and to co-operate with leading independent firms in other jurisdictions, such as Wachtell, Lipton, Rosen & Katz in New York.

Over the years, the firm has maintained close client relationships with many major multinational enterprises, for which it has acted both as strategic adviser and transaction counsel, either alone or in co-operation with selected firms in other jurisdictions. The firm also maintains close and ongoing relationships with the major investment banks active in the key financial market places.

AREAS OF PRACTICE

Mergers and acquisitions: since the time of its formation, the firm has been involved in major acquisitions, securities regulation matters and corporate financial transactions. From its early landmark tender offer matters, the firm has consistently been involved in the major corporate events in its marketplace. The complex corporate and financial operations handled by the firm include privatisation and related transactions involving enterprises controlled by the state and governmental entities. The firm currently advises the French State and state entities on several significant matters.

Litigation and arbitration: throughout its history, the firm has been involved in high-profile litigation and arbitration matters. A significant number of such matters arise out of corporate and financial operations, particularly complex securities regulation issues. However, the range of the firm's litigation activity extends to both civil and criminal matters. The firm's partners include a recognised authority on international arbitration and the firm is generally involved in several such matters, both as counsel to parties in arbitration and through the appointment of partners as arbitrators.

Finance and capital markets: the firm often advises on the financial aspects and structures involved in the corporate transactions which it handles, including advice concerning the conception, documentation and implementation of securities issues in the capital markets in France as well as elsewhere in Europe and North America. The firm both advises its clients directly and acts in co-operation with other firms and investment banks in structuring and co-ordinating such securities issues.

Corporate and tax: in the course of its involvement with combinations and reorganisations of enterprises, the firm is often called upon to advise on French and international investment and tax structures and to co-ordinate the creation and implementation of such structures. The firm's clients for such advice also include investment funds from various countries and selected individual and family group investors.

DE GAULLE FLEURANCE & ASSOCIÉS

11 RUE PORTALIS
75008 PARIS

Telephone: +33 1 56 64 00 00
Fax: +33 1 56 64 00 01
E-mail: ecourville@dgfla.com
Website: www.dgfla.com

Languages
English, French, Spanish

Number of lawyers 37

Contacts
Emilie Courville, Sandrine Nuissier

CATEGORIES OF WORK

Intellectual property and information technology
Louis de Gaulle, Julien Horn

Commercial and competition law
Louis de Gaulle, Frank Valentin

Corporate
Gilles Gaillard, Didier Bruère-Dawson

Capital investment and financing
Henri-Nicolas Fleurance, Bénédicte Colin

Taxation and estate planning
Henri-Nicolas Fleurance, Vincent Schmitt

Real estate
Henri-Nicolas Fleurance, Bénédicte Colin

Labour and employment law
Bénédicte Colin, Etienne Pujol, Claire Lavergne

Health
Jean-Marie Job, Frank Valentin

Administrative law and regulatory matters
Louis de Gaulle

Litigation and arbitration
Arnaud de Barthès de Montfort, Julien Horn

THE FIRM

De Gaulle Fleurance & Associés is a business law firm. It aims to offer its clients a high-value-added, prompt, customised and pragmatic service with an international approach. Through its flexible and effective organisation, the firm supports its clients both in the transactional and litigation areas.

The firm has centred its development on the complementary nature of its practice groups to co-ordinate any case by using transverse skills.

AREAS OF PRACTICE

The firm counts many US and UK companies among its clients, whom it advises both on French and Community law matters and on their activities in Europe (including Eastern Europe) and in Africa. The firm also accompanies its French-based clients in their domestic and international transactions.

The firm assists clients in devising and implementing their commercial, sourcing, protection and defence policy in connection with all aspects of commercial and competition law in the context of the specific regulatory frameworks applicable. In this respect, the firm drafts, negotiates and conducts due diligences of contracts, and places the defence of the commercial interests of its clients at the core of its practice.

For maximum effectiveness the firm has developed expert know-how focusing on transverse competences. In particular, the firm supports its clients in connection with acquisitions, disposals, restructuring, project financing or refinancing and the launch of international operations. It has developed significant skills in the area of real estate portfolios covering properties for office, commercial, mixed and residential use and state-owned real estate. Throughout such transactions, the firm provides services in relation to contract drafting, negotiation and analysis, legal and tax due diligence, preparation of research papers and opinions. During each engagement, the firm ensures that its counsels fully comply with its clients' financial and operational constraints.

While hiring, training and firing is part and parcel of the normal life of a business, there can be significant implications lurking behind such apparently straightforward matters. The firm assists and represents its clients in striking a balance between their legitimate business interests and those of employees, while complying with the complex, fast-changing rules of French labour and employment law.

De Gaulle Fleurance & Associés provides advisory and litigation assistance and support to its clients in the development of their policy for the protection, exploitation and defence of their intellectual property assets. It is active in all areas pertaining to intellectual property, new technologies, telecoms and related matters. The firm provides services to all types of industries such as information technology, telecoms, e-commerce, cinema, television, entertainment, music, press, advertising and promotional events (including sports).

The firm also provides support to its clients in all areas related to health law and biotech industry in the context of national and EU regulations. The firm's client base comprises pharmaceutical companies, biotech companies and research entities, enterprises manufacturing or distributing proprietary medicines, manufacturers of medical equipment and companies from the health services sector. The international outreach in this area was confirmed with a co-operation agreement with the American firm Patton Boggs which is one of the leading Washington firms and has been ranked the top lobbying practice.

The French economy is characterised by strong interventionism by the state, local government and state bodies and corporations. The firm therefore accompanies its clients, as advisers and litigators, in all issues they face involving administrative law, in their relations with the authorities and in interpreting specific rules.

DE PARDIEU BROCAS MAFFEI

64-66 AVENUE D'IÉNA
BP 2004
75761 PARIS CEDEX 16

Telephone: +33 1 53 57 71 71
Fax: +33 1 53 57 71 70
Website: www.de-pardieu.com

Languages
Arabic, Dutch, English, German, Italian, Russian, Spanish

Number of lawyers 80

Contact
Charles-Henri de Pardieu (senior partner)

CATEGORIES OF WORK

Banking and finance
CH de Pardieu, A Maffei, P Minor, O Hubert

Capital markets, securitisation
A Maffei, P Minor, O Hubert

Competition, EU law
Ph Guibert

Corporate finance
T Brocas, P Minor, G Touttée

Corporate law
T Brocas, G Touttée, S Illouz, P Gros

Employment and labour law

Environmental law
J Henrot, P Talbourdet

Information technology and intellectual property

Insurance, reinsurance
P Talbourdet, G Touttée

Litigation and arbitration
J Henrot, D Lefort, P Talbourdet

M&A, stock exchange regulations
T Brocas, G Touttée, F Bucher, S Illouz, P Gros

Private equity
T Brocas, G Touttée, F Bucher

Public law
Ph Guibert, YR Guillou

Real estate and real estate finance
J Henrot, P Talbourdet, E Fatôme, P Gebarowski

Restructuring and insolvency
J Henrot, A Maffei, P Talbourdet, E Fatôme

Tax
E Chauve

White-collar crime
D Lefort

THE FIRM

The firm initially earned its reputation, both in France and internationally, in banking and finance. It is now a full-service firm with a wide range of practice areas.

Partners of De Pardieu maintain regular contact with overseas law firms, among them some of the most renowned firms in the major international business and financial centres. Its relationships with these firms enables De Pardieu to bring together multi-disciplinary teams to work on cross-border transactions at any time and to ensure the successful completion of these transactions in the relevant jurisdictions.

The firm's international activities extend to Europe, the US and Asia.

The firm represents banks, financial institutions, insurance companies, service companies and industry.

AREAS OF PRACTICE

De Pardieu Brocas Maffei operates in teams specialising in the key areas of business law. Its lawyers have extensive international expertise.

The firm has expertise in banking and finance, capital markets, corporate law, M&A, stock exchange regulation, real estate and real estate finance, insolvency and restructuring, EU and competition, tax, insurance and litigation.

DEBEVOISE & PLIMPTON LLP

21 AVENUE GEORGE V
7008 PARIS

Telephone: +33 1 40 73 12 12
Fax: +33 1 47 20 50 82
E-mail: akirry@debevoise.com
Website: www.debevoise.com

Languages
Czech, Danish, English, Farsi, French, Spanish

Other offices
Hong Kong, Frankfurt, London, Moscow, New York, Shanghai, Washington DC

Number of lasers 660+
at this office 40

CATEGORIES OF WORK

Mergers and acquisitions
Antoine Kirry, Patrick Laporte

International dispute resolution
Barton Legum, Michael M Ostrove

Financing
Pierre Clermontel, Eryl Besse

Capital markets
Pierre Clermontel, Raman Bet-Mansour

Private equity buyouts
Antoine Kirry, Marc Castagnéde

Tax
Pierre-Pascal Bruneau

DENTON WILDE SAPTE

5 AVENUE PERCIER
75008 PARIS

Telephone: +33 1 53 05 16 00
Fax: +33 1 53 05 97 27
E-mail: paris@dentonwildesapte.com
Website: www.dentonwildesapte.com

Languages
English, French, German, Italian, Spanish

Other offices
Abu Dhabi, Almaty, Cairo, Dubai, Istanbul, London, Milton Keynes, Moscow, Muscat, Tashkent

Number of lawyers 683
at this office 40

Contact
Sena Agbayissah

CATEGORIES OF WORK

Asset finance

IT and e-business

Banking and finance

Media and advertising

Competition and distribution

Mergers and acquisitions

Corporate law

Private equity

Dispute resolution

Project finance

Employment law

Property law

Insolvency

Structured finance

Insurance law

Tax

Intellectual property

DECHERT

7 PLACE D'IÉNA
75116 PARIS

Telephone: +33 1 53 65 05 00
Fax: +33 1 53 65 05 05
E-mail: jonathan.schur@dechert.com
alain.decombe@dechert.com
Website: www.dechert.com

Languages
English, French, German, Italian, Russian, Spanish

Other offices
Austin, Boston, Brussels, Charlotte, Frankfurt, Harrisburg, Hartford, London, Luxembourg, Munich, Newport Beach, New York, Palo Alto, Philadelphia, Princeton, San Francisco, Washington DC

Number of lawyers 900+
at this office 40

Contacts
Alain Decombe (managing partner), Jonathan A Schur (managing partner)

CATEGORIES OF WORK

Labour law
Kathie Claret, Monique Béguiachvili

Litigation
Xavier Nyssen

IP/IT
Kathie Claret

Construction/infrastructures
Philip Dunham, Gillian Lemaire

Corporate/M&A
Jay Aragonés, Bertrand Caradet, Alain Decombe, Jonathan Schur

Banking and finance
Bertrand Caradet, Joseph Smallhoover

Arbitration
Philip Dunham, Gillian Lemaire, Xavier Nyssen, Eduardo Silva Romero

Pharmaceuticals/medical devices
Alaine Decombe, Jonathan Schur

Tax
Yann de Kergos

THE FIRM

The attorneys of Dechert's Paris office are highly experienced in the full scope of international business law and represent multinational clients in France and throughout the key economies of the world. Established in 1995, Dechert's Paris office team of five partners and ten associates provides clients with exceptional legal services for a variety of industries, notably pharmaceutical products and medical devices, finance, manufacturing, technology and e-commerce, utilities, construction and engineering. Well versed in all aspects of French and European law, the firm's lawyers publish regularly on product liability, intellectual property and trade secrets, media liability and financial law.

AREAS OF PRACTICE

The firm's legal services expertise spans a broad range of transactional services – from mergers and acquisitions to general corporate and commercial advice, corporate finance, restructurings and the creation of companies in France and other jurisdictions, including US, UK, Belgium, Germany and Luxembourg. For financial institutions and related businesses, the firm advises on the creation of various types of French mutual and investment funds and on banking and securities regulations. Dechert also represents clients in the areas of bank lending, notably asset-based lending and project finance, as well as in secured lending and structured finance. The Paris office handles a significant number of litigation and arbitration matters involving all aspects of business law.

DEPREZ DIAN GUIGNOT

21 RUE CLÉMENT MAROT
75008 PARIS

Telephone: +33 1 53 23 80 00
Fax: +33 1 53 23 80 01
Website: www.ddg.fr

Languages
English, German, Portuguese, Spanish

Number of lawyers 35

Member
INTA; International Fiscal Association

CATEGORIES OF WORK

Intellectual property, litigation
Pierre Deprez, Vincent Fauchoux

Information technology
Vincent Fauchoux

Trade marks
Jacques Beaumont

Media
Philippe Dian

EU and competition law
Pierre Deprez, Jean-Christophe André

Food and drugs
Jean-Christophe André

Arbitration and litigation
Emmanuel Bouttier, Frederic Fournier

Mergers and acquisitions
Michel Guignot, Ana-Paula Reis Lopes, Hervé de Kervasdoué

Labour law
Laurent Carrié

Public law
Laurent Gravier

FRANKLIN

26 AVENUE KLÉBER
75116 PARIS

Telephone: +33 1 45 02 79 00
Fax: +33 1 45 02 79 01
E-mail: info@franklin-paris.com
Website: www.franklin-paris.com

Languages
English, German, Italian, Russian, Spanish

Number of lawyers 41

CATEGORIES OF WORK

Mergers and acquisitions
Yam Atallah, Alexandre Marque, Mark Richardson

Administrative law, environment
Jérôme Michel

Project finance
Jérôme Michel

Company, commercial
Yam Atallah, Alexandre Marque, Mark Richardson

Information technology, telecommunications
Bradley Joslove

Private equity (MBO/LBO, fund structuring, ventures)
Yam Atallah, Alexandre Marque, Mark Richardson

Tax
Jean-Christophe Bouchard

Intellectual property
Yann Colin

Arbitration and litigation
Yann Colin

Advertising, competition and distribution
Jérôme Michel

EU law
Jérôme Michel

Media and entertainment
Yann Colin

Labour
Patrick Thiébart

DUBARRY LE DOUARIN VEIL

6 PLACE DE NARVIK
75008 PARIS

Telephone: +33 1 44 30 25 00
Fax: +33 1 44 30 25 01
E-mail: dlv@dlvlaw.com
Website: www.dlvlaw.com

Languages
English, German, Hebrew, Italian, Spanish

Number of lawyers 45

Contacts
Pierre-François Veil, Yann Le Douarin, Pierre de Girard

Member
Founding member of the European Legal Alliance (Belgium, England, France, Germany, Ireland, Italy, Scotland, Spain)

CATEGORIES OF WORK

- **Litigation and arbitration**
- **Corporate, M&A, private equity**
- **Commercial contracts**
- **Information technology**
- **Intellectual and industrial property, media**
- **Distribution and product liability**
- **Competition, antitrust law**
- **Criminal business law**
- **Financial market law**
- **Banking, securities and finance**
- **Insolvency, restructuring**
- **Tax**
- **Employment and labour law**
- **Real estate**
- **Health care**

THE FIRM

Dubarry Le Douarin Veil is a long-standing and well-established law firm based in Paris. Founded in 1984, the firm specialises in business law, offering commercial clients a wide range of legal services.

The firm's activities cover both non-contentious advice and litigation for a domestic and international client base. The firm works closely with its clients to provide a quality service in all matters of their business activities.

The majority of the firm's lawyers have considerable experience of the full range of commercial legal practice and are able to offer specialist services against this general commercial background. Clients benefit from the firm's lawyers being able to offer legal solutions in a business environment.

Dubarry Le Douarin Veil has a total staff of more than 70, including 15 partners. The firm operates with flexible and responsive teams of lawyers, drawn from different disciplines, to provide the optimum service to its clients.

In addition, as a founding member of the European Legal Alliance, Dubarry Le Douarin Veil offers pan-European expert advice on a wide range of practice areas. The European Legal Alliance brings together seven commercial law firms under a single brand and is based in Belgium, England, France, Germany, Ireland, Italy, Scotland and Spain.

AREAS OF PRACTICE

Dubarry Le Douarin Veil has wide experience in assisting both French and foreign clients from all over the world, from different business and industry sectors, in commercial and corporate matters.

The firm has particular expertise in the field of corporate law, mergers and acquisitions, private equity, commercial and banking litigation, intellectual property and information technology law, tax, real estate, and employment law.

The firm offers clients complete assistance and advice from start-up and formation, throughout its operations, offering the client the full range of advice where necessary.

The firm's lawyers are experienced in acquisitions, sales, IPOs, mergers and takeovers. The firm has considerable expertise in advising foreign clients on establishing business operations in France.

The firm is able to offer contentious and court practice in all of the practice areas listed above.

FLICHY & ASSOCIÉS

7 RUE KEPLER
75116 PARIS

Telephone: +33 1 56 62 30 00
Fax: +33 1 56 62 30 01
E-mail: flichy@flichy-associes.com
Website: www.flichy-associes.com

Number of lawyers 32

Contacts
Hubert Flichy, Claire Toumieux

Member
EELA; IBA; AVOSIAL

CATEGORIES OF WORK

Labour law

THE FIRM

Flichy & Associés is among France's leading employment law firms.

Founded in February 1999 by Hubert Flichy, in partnership with Isabelle Ayache-Revah and Philippe Montanier, the firm has since experienced continuous growth. Claire Toumieux, Philippe Langlois and Arnaud Chaulet joined the partnership in May 2000, April 2001, and January 2003. Anne le Bault de la Morinière (from Rambaud Martel) and Florence Aubonnet also joined the partnership in January 2006.

The sole practice area of the eight partners and 25 associates of Flichy & Associés is employment law and social security law; it has become well known for its handling of redundancy schemes, issues relating to working hours and the labour aspects of restructuring operations. The firm's clientele is essentially made up of French, British and American companies, in industry, banking and telecommunications.

AREAS OF PRACTICE

Flichy & Associés' practice is dedicated to employment law and social security law. It has concentrated on negotiations, labour disputes and issues arising from restructuring operations and from mergers and acquisitions. Another area of expertise involves the labour aspects of transnational operations, as well as mobility and expatriation.

Flichy & Associés also advises on all aspects of social security law (basic and complementary benefits), high-risk individual disputes and company savings plans and on labour issues arising in publicly owned companies.

FROMONT, BRIENS & ASSOCIÉS

5 RUE BOUDREAU
PARIS 75009

Telephone: +33 1 44 51 63 80
Fax: +33 1 44 51 63 89
E-mail: info@fromont-briens.com
Website: www.fromont-briens.com

Languages
English, German, Italian, Spanish

Other offices
Lyon

Number of lawyers 72
at this office 37

International groupings
Terralex

CATEGORIES OF WORK

Pensions and social protection
Gilles Briens, Catherine Millet-Ursin

Social security
David Rigaud, Jean-Jacques Fournier

Restructuring plans – audit
Philippe Clément, Cédric Guillon

Working time
Marilyn Favier, Béatrice Mounier-Bertail

Labour litigation
Yves Fromont, Hugues Pélissier

Collective labour law
Frédéric Leclercq, Marie-Laurence Boulanger

Works council
David Calvayrac, Jean-Sébastien Capisano

Compensation and benefits
Frank Wismer, Emilie Zieleskiewicz

Executive employment contracts
Hélène Saïd, Nicolas Chavrier

GINESTIÉ MAGELLAN PALEY-VINCENT

10 PLACE DES ETATS-UNIS
75116 PARIS

Telephone: +33 1 57 57 50 00
Fax: +33 1 57 57 52 00
E-mail: paris@ginestie.com
Website: www.ginestie.com

Languages
English, French, German, Italian, Spanish

Other offices
London, Lyon, Milan

Number of lawyers 47
at this office 31

Contact
Francoise Ciaudo-Ginestié

CATEGORIES OF WORK

Mergers and acquisitions/ private equity
Philippe Ginestié, Bernard Laurent-Bellue, Anne Dabezies

Corporate
Florence Cotillon, Franck Bourgeois

Stock exchange
Jean-Christophe Vidal

Information technology
Isabelle Gavanon

IP, copyright and trade marks
Francoise Ciaudo-Ginestié

Tax
Brigitte Berdugo, Martial Buono, Christophe Billet

Medical law/family law
Catherine Paley-Vincent

Commercial/banking
Emmanuelle Bouretz

Public affairs
Catherine Jeancolas

Competition/biotechnology
Francois Xavier Testu

GIDE LOYRETTE NOUEL

26 COURS ALBERT 1ER
75008 PARIS

Telephone: +33 1 40 75 60 00
Fax: +33 1 43 59 37 79
E-mail: info@gide.com
Website: www.gide.com

Languages
Arabic, Bulgarian, Chinese, Czech, English, German, Hungarian, Italian, Polish, Romanian, Russian, Spanish, Turkish, Vietnamese

Other offices
Algiers, Beijing, Belgrade, Brussels, Bucharest, Budapest, Casablanca, Hanoi, Istanbul, London, Moscow, New York, Prague, Riyadh, Shanghai, Tunis, Warsaw

Number of lawyers 586

Contacts
Gérard Tavernier (tavernier@gide.com), Xavier de Kergommeaux (kergommeaux@gide.com)

CATEGORIES OF WORK

Arbitration
Pierre Raoul-Duval, Christian Camboulive

Bankruptcy, insolvency
Jean-Michel Lucheux, Olivier Puech

Economic law, EU
Joëlle Salzmann, Antoine Choffel

Finance, project finance
Emmanuel Fontaine, Kamel Ben Salah

Intellectual property
Arnaud Michel, Grégoire Triet

IT, internet, e-commerce
Grégoire Goussu, Rémy Fekete

Labour law
Joël Grangé, Baudouin de Moucheron

Litigation
Gilles Duquet, Aurélien Boulanger

Media and entertainment
Olivier Cousi, Rémy Fekete

M&A, corporate law
Youssef Djehane, Hugues Mathez

Public law, environmental law
Laurent Deruy, Michel Guénaire

Real estate, property law
Renaud Baguenault, Stanislas Dwernicki

Tax
Richard Beauvais, Olivier Dauchez

Telecommunications
Rémy Fekete, Olivier Cousi

Transport, maritime and insurance
Emmanuel Fontaine, Philippe Rames

White-collar crime
Jean-Marie Burguburu, Kiril Bougartchev

THE FIRM

Building from a premier position in France into a powerful independent international law firm, Gide Loyrette Nouel operates out of 18 offices around the world. With more than 580 lawyers and legal consultants, including 96 partners, drawn from over 30 nationalities, the firm offers some of the most respected specialists in each of the various sectors of national and international finance and business law.

For more than 80 years, Gide Loyrette Nouel has been offering legal advice and assistance to companies, public and private institutions, and governments. Constantly demanding the highest quality from its lawyers, the firm is able to assist clients in resolving all manner of legal issues, no matter how complex or diverse.

The firm has offices in Europe (Belgrade, Brussels, Bucharest, Budapest, Istanbul, London, Moscow, Paris, Prague and Warsaw), in the US (New York), in the Middle East (Riyadh), in North Africa (Algiers, Casablanca, and Tunis) and in Asia (Hanoi, Beijing and Shanghai).

AREAS OF PRACTICE

Lawyers at Gide Loyrette Nouel advise and represent clients in all aspects of commercial law. Over 80 lawyers at the firm work on mergers and acquisitions, takeover bids, public offers of exchange, stocks and bond issues, stock exchange flotations, and privatisations, both in Paris and abroad.

Gide Loyrette Nouel's banking and finance team is one of the most prominent in the market, offering French, English and US banking and finance law capability: more than 120 lawyers, located mainly in Paris, London and New York, deal with all aspects of banking and finance law, in particular all types of financing (including classic bank financing, structured finance, acquisition finance, project finance and securitisation), international debt and capital securities issues, accounting, and derivative and structured products.

The firm is also renowned for its real estate law practice. It acts on behalf of investors, property developers, or tenants at all stages of real estate transactions, in France and abroad. In addition, Gide Loyrette Nouel's lawyers have a well-established reputation in arbitration, litigation, tax law, labour law and public law. They have developed a high level of expertise in matters relating to patents, brands, information technology law, the internet, e-commerce, media and telecommunications. Finally, by virtue of its presence in Brussels for more than 35 years, the firm has a proven track record in economic and EU law. In particular, it is regarded as a leader in the fields of competition, WTO and anti-dumping law.

In order to provide its clients with the best possible service in Paris and abroad, the firm operates through multinational and multi-disciplinary teams.

GRÜTZMACHER GRAVERT VIEGENER

12 RUE D'ASTORG
75008 PARIS

Telephone: +33 1 44 51 05 70
Fax: +33 1 42 66 33 68
E-mail: paris@gg-v.net
Website: www gg-v.de

Languages
English, French, German

Other offices
Frankfurt am Main, Hamburg

Number of lawyers 28
at this office 9

International groupings
TAG Law; TIAG

CATEGORIES OF WORK

Corporate tax law
Johannes Viegener, Pascal Schultze

Commercial and company law
Bénédicte Querenet-Hahn

Mergers and acquisitions
Thomas Führlbeck, Pascal Schultze

Corporate finance
Thomas Führlbeck, Pascal Schultze

Real estate
Thomas Führlbeck

HAARMANN HEMMELRATH

23, RUE BALZAC
75008 PARIS

Telephone: +33 1 53 53 02 80
Fax: +33 1 53 53 02 81
E-mail:
paris@haarmannhemmelrath.com
Website:
www.haarmannhemmelrath.com

Languages
Dutch, English, German, Italian, Japanese, Mandarin, Spanish

Other offices
Bielefeld, Bucharest, Budapest, Düsseldorf, Frankfurt, Hamburg, Leipzig, Moscow, Munich, Prague, Shanghai, Warsaw

Number of lawyers 226
at this office 27

CATEGORIES OF WORK

General corporate
Anja Droege, Bruno Lefébure

Mergers and acquisitions
Yann François, Anja Droege

Banking finance
Dr Bernd Sagasser

Private equity, venture capital
Dr Bernd Sagasser, Marc-Alexis Fauvet

International tax law
Jacques Prats, Dr Bernd Sagasser, Jacques-Henry de Bourmont

National tax law
Jacques Prats, Jacques-Henry de Bourmont

Real estate transactions
Yann François, Silke Nadolni, Jacques-Henry de Bourmont

Litigation and arbitration
Marc-Alexis Fauvet, Nathalie Sinavong

Competition and EU law
Martina Maier, Nathalie Sinavong

State aids
Martina Maier, Dr Antje Luke

IPO
Marc-Alexis Fauvet

German law
Dr Bernd Sagasser, Dr Antje Luke

Insolvency law
Marc-Alexis Fauvet

Energy and natural resources
Hector Farina

China desk
Bruno Lefébure

HERBERT SMITH

20 RUE QUENTIN BAUCHART
75008 PARIS

Telephone: +33 1 53 57 70 70
Fax: +33 1 53 57 70 80
E-mail: contactparis@herbertsmith.com
Website: www.herbertsmith.com

Languages
Arabic, Dutch, English, French, German, Greek, Hebrew, Italian, Russian, Spanish

Other offices
Bangkok, Beijing, Brussels, Hong Kong, London, Moscow, Shanghai, Singapore, Tokyo

Number of lawyers 1,089
at this office 73

CATEGORIES OF WORK

Corporate finance, M&A
Jacques Buhart, Bruno Basuyaux

Project finance
Stéphane Brabant, Neil Brimson

International finance and banking
Georges Dirani

Employment
Sophie Brézin

IP/IT
Alexandra Neri

Tax
Jean-Luc Calisti

Real estate
Pierre Popesco

Litigation and arbitration
Denis Chemla, Charles Kaplan

Competition, EU and distribution law
Jacques Buhart, Dominique Brault

HOGAN & HARTSON MNP

69 AVENUE FRANKLIN ROOSEVELT
75008 PARIS

Telephone: +33 1 55 73 23 00
Fax: +33 1 55 73 23 10
E-mail: wjcurtin@hhlaw.com
Website: www.hhlaw.com

Languages
Dutch, English, French, German, Spanish

Other offices
Baltimore, Beijing, Berlin, Boulder, Brussels, Budapest, Caracas,Colorado Springs, Denver, Geneva, Hong Kong, London, Los Angeles, Miami, Moscow, Munich, New York, Northern Virginia, Shanghai, Tokyo, Warsaw, Washington DC

Number of lawyers 1,101
at this office 20

Contact
William J Curtin

CATEGORIES OF WORK

Capital markets

Intellectual property

Competition

Litigation and arbitration

Corporate

Mergers and acquisitions

Data privacy

Regulatory of investment in France

Environment and energy

Telecommunications and media law

HOLMAN FENWICK & WILLAN

65 RUE D'ANJOU
75008 PARIS

Telephone: +33 1 44 94 40 50
Fax: +33 1 42 65 46 25
E-mail: holmans@hfw-france.com
Website: www.hfw.com

Languages
English, Italian, Polish, Spanish

Other offices
Dubai, Hong Kong, London, Melbourne, Piraeus, Rouen, Shanghai, Singapore

Number of lawyers 209
at this office 18

CATEGORIES OF WORK

Admiralty
Jean-Jacques Ollu, Oliver Purcell

Shipping litigation and arbitration
Timothy Clemens-Jones, Guillaume Brajeux

International trade
Timothy Clemens-Jones, Jean-Jacques Ollu

Commercial litigation
Guillaume Brajeux, Stéphane Sélégny

Insurance and reinsurance
Oliver Purcell, Jean-Jaques Ollu

Finance, company and commercial
Sybille Elleboode-Merlier, Janet Butterworth

Industrial risk
Guillaume Brajeux, Jean-Jacques Ollu

European law
Timothy Clemens-Jones, Edouard Tay Pamart

Customs and excise
Guillaume Brajeux, Edouard Tay Pamart

Ship finance
Timothy Clemens-Jones, Janet Butterworth

Labour law
Stéphane Sélégny

THE FIRM

Holman Fenwick & Willan is an international law firm specialising in shipping and transport, trade and energy, insurance and reinsurance and commercial law. The firm has a reputation worldwide for excellence and innovation. It has one of the largest international arbitration and dispute resolution practices of its kind, with offices in Europe, the Middle East and Asia Pacific.

The firm's international practice is founded upon its principal offices in London, Paris, Piraeus, Hong Kong, Shanghai, Singapore and Melbourne and over 120 years' experience of working with other law firms in jurisdictions throughout the world.

The Paris office was opened in 1977 and together with an office in Rouen (opened 1994), the firm has 24 lawyers in France. Shipping and maritime litigation and arbitration, including Admiralty work, represents about 50% of the firm's activities in France. The firm has a growing insurance, reinsurance, customs and industrial risk practice, which together with general commercial and international litigation and arbitration represents another 30%.

The commercial practice also continues to grow. The firm's offices in France are involved in most aspects of corporate and commercial law, including labour law, project, asset and structured finance, and mergers and acquisitions.

AREAS OF PRACTICE

All aspects of shipping including Admiralty, international trade, insurance and reinsurance, customs law, commercial litigation and arbitration, financial, company, commercial and labour law, all relevant aspects of European law, aviation, project, asset and structured finance, and mergers and acquisitions.

HOWREY LLP

29 BOULEVARD RASPAIL
75007 PARIS

Telephone: +33 1 42 22 46 11
Fax: +33 1 45 44 97 04
E-mail: coustem@howrey.com
Website: www.howrey.com

Languages
English, German, Spanish

Other offices
Amsterdam, Chicago, East Palo Alto, Houston, Irvine, London, Los Angeles, Northern Virginia, Salt Lake City, San Francisco, Taipei, Washington DC

Number of lawyers 565
at this office 5

Contact
Marina Cousté

Member
INTA; LES France; AIPPI; APRAM; EPLA

CATEGORIES OF WORK

Industrial and intellectual property: patents
Marina Cousté, François Jonquères, Florent Guilbot

Trade marks, copyright, designs
Marina Cousté, Amaury de Saint-Amand, Charlotte Portmann

Computer law and technology information
Marina Cousté, Charlotte Portmann

Advertising and competition
Marina Cousté, François Jonquères

Biotechnologies
Marina Cousté, François Jonquères

HUGHES HUBBARD & REED LLP

47 AVENUE GEORGES MANDEL
75116 PARIS

Telephone: +33 1 44 05 80 00
Fax: +33 1 45 53 15 04
E-mail: rosell@hugheshubbard.com
Website: www.hugheshubbard.com

Languages
Arabic, English, German, Italian, Portuguese, Spanish

Other offices
Jersey City, Los Angeles, Miami, New York, Tokyo, Washington DC

Number of lawyers 27

Contacts
Merrikay Hall, José Rosell

CATEGORIES OF WORK

Arbitration, litigation
Axel Baum, José Rosell

Bankruptcy, insolvency
Thierry Brezillon

Labour, employment
Nadine Voisin, Thierry Brezillon

Real estate and construction
Claire Ayer

Corporate M&A and commercial
Merrikay Hall, Christian Belloin

IP, technology, media and telecoms
Christopher Mesnooh

HUGLO LEPAGE & ASSOCIÉS CONSEIL

40 RUE DE MONCEAU
75008 PARIS

Telephone: +33 1 56 59 29 59
Fax: +33 1 56 59 29 39
E-mail: paris@huglo-lepage.com
Website: www.huglo-lepage.com

Languages
Dutch, English, German, Italian, Spanish

Other offices
Brussels

Number of lawyers 42

Member
GESICA

CATEGORIES OF WORK

Environmental law
C Huglo, C Lepage, M Wemaëre

Environmental audit
C Huglo, C Lepage, A Moustardier

European law
C Lepage, M Wemaëre

Classified installations law
C Huglo, A Moustardier

Healthcare
C Huglo, RP Drai

Medical law
RP Drai

Biotechnology
C Lepage, I Cassin, Ph Feitussi

Consumer protection
C Lepage, I Cassin

Zoning and planning
I Cassin, E Bineteau

Urban planning
I Cassin, E Bineteau

Building law
RP Drai, E Bineteau

Public law
C Lepage, C Huglo

Local government law
E Bineteau, O Schmitt

Economic public law
MY Benjamin, O Schmitt

Public procurement
MY Benjamin, O Schmitt

Corporate finance, M&A
Ph Feitussi

JONES DAY

120 RUE DU FAUBOURG
SAINT-HONORÉ
75008 PARIS

Telephone: +33 1 56 59 39 39
Fax: +33 1 56 59 39 38
Website: www.jonesday.com

Languages
Chinese, English, German, Italian, Russian, Spanish, Swedish, Turkish, Vietnamese

Other offices
Atlanta, Beijing, Brussels, Chicago, Cleveland, Columbus, Dallas, Frankfurt, Hong Kong, Houston, Irvine, London, Los Angeles, Madrid, Menlo Park, Milan, Moscow, Munich, New Delhi, New York, Pittsburgh, San Diego, San Francisco, Shanghai, Singapore, Sydney, Taipei, Tokyo, Washington DC

Number of lawyers 2,200
at this office 87

CATEGORIES OF WORK

Administrative and public law
Philippe Delelis

Arbitration
Michael W Bühler

Banking and structured finance
Philippe Billot, Pierre-Nicolas Ferrand

Corporate finance, capital markets
Philippe Billot, Frank Martin Laprade

Corporate and commercial litigation
Laurent Martinet

Environmental, health and safety
Françoise Labrousse

EU and competition
Eric Morgan de Rivery

Insolvency
Pierre-Nicolas Ferrand

Intellectual property
Catherine Muyl

Labour law
Anne Boileau

Mergers and acquisitions
Wesley R Johnson Jr

Real estate
Jean-Louis Martin

Tax
Vincent Agulhon, Christopher Potter

Private equity (venture capital, LBO)
Olivier Edwards, Renaud Bonnet

INCE & CO

45 AVENUE KLÉBER
75116 PARIS

Telephone: +33 1 53 76 91 00
Fax: +33 1 53 76 91 26
E-mail: firstname.lastname@incelaw.com
Website: www.incelaw.com

Languages
Dutch, English, French, Spanish

Other offices
Hamburg, Hong Kong, Le Havre, London, Piraeus, Shanghai, Singapore

Number of lawyers 228
at this office 12

Contacts
Gilles Gautier, Fred Vroom

Ince & Co in France is a transnational grouping between Ince & Co and SCP Gautier Vroom & Associés

CATEGORIES OF WORK

Aviation
Fred Vroom

Business and finance
Fred Vroom, Andrew Charlier

Commercial disputes
Gilles Gautier

Energy
Gilles Gautier, Fred Vroom

Insurance and reinsurance
Gilles Gautier

Shipping and trade
Gilles Gautier, Fred Vroom, Andrew Charlier

THE FIRM

Ince & Co is an international law firm, with offices in Hamburg, Hong Kong, Le Havre, London, Paris, Piraeus, Shanghai and Singapore. The firm practises English, French, German and Hong Kong law, in six main business strands. With a clear grasp of clients' commercial needs, Ince & Co provides non-contentious business and finance advice for clients in a wide range of industries, and also deploys all methods of dispute resolution.

AREAS OF PRACTICE

Aviation: with a team that 'really understands the aviation business' (*The Legal 500*, 2005) and with in-depth market knowledge, Ince & Co has the flexibility to handle any kind of aviation matter anywhere in the world – from aircraft purchase to major incidents and lesser accidents worldwide. The firm often deploys legal tools to solve problems that appear to be mainly commercial in nature. For crises or disasters, the Ince Worldwide Emergency Response Service is only a phone call away.

Business and finance: the firm's team of specialist commercial lawyers works with clients to find the answers that help drive their businesses forward. With the combination of high levels of commercial nous and a capacity for hard work, the firm can help clients achieve their goals – whether acquisition, disposal, joint venture or conclusion of a complex commercial contract. Ince & Co's experience ranges from management buy-outs, through the resolution of shareholder disputes to difficult employment issues.

Commercial disputes: once described in the press as 'brutal litigators', the firm also has a lighter touch. Ince & Co's expertise covers all forms of dispute resolution, ranging from dialogue, through ADR to arbitration and court proceedings. Where litigation is judged to be in a client's interests, or is unavoidable, the firm draws on immense experience in the commercial courts of the countries where it has offices, and a worldwide network of correspondent lawyers. The firm's cases come from many sectors, including sport, entertainment and financial services.

Energy: the firm has been in the oil and gas business for as long as many of its clients. Since the early days of North Sea development, the firm's energy practice has spread all around the world, both onshore and off, from exploration and drilling to FPSOs and refineries. It now extends to renewable sources such as wind.

Insurance and reinsurance: Ince & Co's team serves clients who provide coverage, those who broke it and those who purchase it. Whether the case is contentious or non-contentious and however straightforward or complex the subject matter insured, the firm offers all the legal services required in these industries. The firm's direct insurance practice covers all manner of insurance claims, including marine and energy insurance, political contingent and credit risk, and coverage disputes. Reinsurance is also a strong area of focus for the firm. The team advises on, among other things, every aspect of run-off business.

Shipping and trade: the firm provides all the legal services required by the shipping and commodities industries. The firm counts among its clients many of the world's leading shipowners, charterers, shipbuilders, traders, banks and insurers. *The Legal 500* refers to the firm's 'unrivalled knowledge of the market' and its 'strength in depth'.

Emergency Response: Ince & Co operates a 24-hour emergency response service, 365 days a year. It has vast experience of the practical and legal problems following a major emergency, disaster or crisis. Its teams can respond immediately to a wide range of incidents, from accidents in the aviation, shipping, energy, hotel and rail sectors, through natural disasters and disease, to terrorist acts. Tel: +44 20 7283 6999.

The contact details for the Le Havre office are: 136 Rue Victor Hugo, 76600 Le Havre. Telephone: +332 3522 1888. Fax: +332 3522 1880. E-mail: firstname.lastname@incelaw.com. For all Le Havre matters please contact Jérôme de Sentenac or Mathieu Croix.

JEANTETASSOCIÉS

87 AVENUE KLÉBER
75116 PARIS

Telephone: +33 1 45 05 80 08
Fax: +33 1 47 04 20 41
E-mail: info@jeantet.fr
Website: www.jeantet.fr

Languages
English, German, Italian, Spanish

Other offices
New York

Number of lawyers 70

Contacts
Georges Terrier, Yvon Dréano, Philippe Portier

CATEGORIES OF WORK

Mergers and acquisitions	**Business criminal law**
Banking and finance	**Administrative law**
Antitrust, competition and distribution	**Bankruptcy, insolvency and restructuring**
International contracts and trade	**Real estate**
Tax	**Energy and natural resources**
Labour law	**Litigation and alternative dispute resolution**

THE FIRM

JeantetAssociés is one of France's premier independent law firms.

Founded in Paris in 1924, JeantetAssociés is a full-service firm with significant activity in long-term financing operations and litigation. The firm has 70 lawyers, of which 23 are partners (all members of the Paris Bar), and it is structured so as to be able to act as a single, multi-disciplinary legal and tax team.

The firm has had an international focus since it was founded and, more particularly, since the 1950s, when a large proportion of its foreign clients were from the US. During the last two decades, it has diversified its client base so that, while a third are still North American, a third are now large French industrial and financial groups and the remaining third are mostly European.

To further reinforce existing close relationships with its US-based clientele, the firm established an office in New York in 1991. This office has since grown its practice by attracting new US companies doing business in France, including American law firms, which need assistance with their clients' transatlantic matters. Moreover, the New York office provides support to French clients investing in the US by liaising, advising and co-ordinating on any pertinent legal matter with local American law firms.

On the other continents, JeantetAssociés maintains excellent connections with foreign independent law firms, particularly in Europe and the US.

AREAS OF PRACTICE

JeantetAssociés offers a wide but selected range of legal services to companies (banking, financial and industrial groups) and institutions – public or private, national or international – and government bodies.

JeantetAssociés' practice is focused on areas of law requiring high added value, particularly mergers and acquistions, corporate restructurings, banking and finance, tax, competition, labour law and administrative law.

KRAMER LEVIN NAFTALIS & FRANKEL LLP

47 AVENUE HOCHE
75008 PARIS

Telephone: +33 1 44 09 46 00
Fax: +33 1 44 09 46 01
Website: www.kramerlevin.com

Languages
English, French, German, Italian, Arabic

Other offices
New York

Number of lawyers 317
at this office 20

CATEGORIES OF WORK

Mergers and acquisitions	**Real estate**
Corporate securities and finance	**Employment and labour law**
Banking law and capital markets	**Foreign investment**
Structured financings and securitisations	**Insurance law**
Reorganisations and bankruptcy	**Litigation and arbitration**

THE FIRM

Kramer Levin Naftalis & Frankel LLP is a premier, full-service law firm with offices in New York and Paris and an alliance with UK-based Berwin Leighton Paisner LLP (London and Brussels). Kramer Levin's strong focus on client service and its single-minded commitment to excellence have enabled it to build long-term relationships with major domestic and international corporations, institutions and individuals that look to it for innovative and practical solutions for both everyday and complex matters. As leading practitioners in their respective fields, Kramer Levin attorneys guide Global 1000 companies and emerging growth entities, across a broad range of industries, to help them fully realise their business goals.

AREAS OF PRACTICE

The Paris office of Kramer Levin Naftalis & Frankel LLP represents a wide range of French, European and overseas clients. The office offers its clients a full-service legal practice, ranging from complex transactions and sophisticated financial products to cutting-edge business litigation. All of the lawyers working in the Paris office are admitted to the Paris Bar; many of them are also admitted in New York or other US jurisdictions and/or hold law degrees from other countries including Italy, Germany and Austria. Thanks to a network including the New York headquarters, the firm's alliance in London and Brussels and its privileged relations with top law firms in other jurisdictions, the clients of Kramer Levin's Paris office benefit from worldwide coverage, providing them with local solutions to their legal needs.

KUNTZ & ASSOCIÉS

9 RUE SCRIBE
75009 PARIS

Telephone: +33 1 44 94 95 00
Fax: +33 1 44 94 95 09
E-mail: info@kuntz-avocats.com
Website: www.kuntz-avocats.com

Languages
French, English, German

Number of lawyers 8

CATEGORIES OF WORK

Bankruptcy
Jean-Emmanuel Kuntz, Sabine Rotkopf

Business restructuring
Jean-Emmanuel Kuntz,
Vincent Pierre Merat

Insolvency
Jean-Emmanuel Kuntz, Sabine Rotkopf

Litigation
Jean-Emmanuel Kuntz,
Marie-Agnès Descrozaille

Commercial law
Jean-Emmanuel Kuntz, Sabine Rotkopf

Social law
Sabine Rotkopf, Hélène Lefevre

Mergers and acquisitions
Jean-Emmanuel Kuntz

Banking law
Vincent Pierre Merat

Civil law
Sabine Rotkopf

Business law
Jean-Emmanuel Kuntz,
Vincent Pierre Merat

Competition law
Marie-Agnès Descrozaille,
Sabine Rotkopf

LASSEZ ET ASSOCIÉS

51 AVENUE MONTAIGNE
75008 PARIS

Telephone: +33 1 42 56 44 81
Fax: +33 1 45 61 91 12
E-mail: lassezavocats@mac.com

Languages
English, Italian

Number of lawyers 6

CATEGORIES OF WORK

Shipping and transportation

International trade

Arbitration

Litigation

Insurance

LATOURNERIE WOLFROM & ASSOCIÉS

**164 RUE DU FAUBOURG SAINT HONORÉ
75008 PARIS**

Telephone: +33 1 56 59 74 74
Fax: +33 1 56 59 74 75
E-mail: contact@latournerie-wolfrom.com
Website: www.latournerie-wolfrom.com

Languages
English, German, Italian, Spanish

Number of lawyers 27

CATEGORIES OF WORK

Mergers and acquisitions
Christian Wolfrom, Pierre Lafarge

Corporate and company
Christian Wolfrom, Pierre Lafarge

Banking and finance
Christian Wolfrom, Pierre Lafarge

Capital markets and business start-ups
Christian Wolfrom, Pierre Lafarge

Copyright and intellectual property
Marie-Hélène Tonnellier

IT, internet and e-commerce
Marie-Hélène Tonnellier

Commercial law and commercial litigation
Nathalie Karpik, Marie-Hélène Tonnellier

Distribution and competition
Nathalie Karpik, Marie-Hélène Tonnellier

Libel
Jean Latournerie, Nathalie Karpik

Telecoms
Terence Cabot, Marie-Hélène Tonnellier

Administrative and public law
Jean Latournerie, Terence Cabot

Environment
Jean Latournerie, Terence Cabot

Unfair competition
Nathalie Karpik

Litigation and arbitration
Nathalie Karpik, Jean Latournerie

Media, broadcasting, entertainment
Marie-Hélène Tonnellier

Employment and labour law
Joëlle Hannelais

Town planning
Terence Cabot

LEBOEUF, LAMB, GREENE & MACRAE LLP

**130 RUE DU FAUBOURG SAINT-HONORÉ
75008 PARIS**

Telephone: +33 1 53 93 77 00
Fax: +33 1 42 56 08 06
E-mail: olaude@llgm.com
Website: www.llgm.com

Languages
English, French, German, Italian, Spanish

Other offices
Albany, Almaty, Beijing, Boston, Brussels, Chicago, Hartford, Houston, Jacksonville, Johannesburg, London, Los Angeles, Moscow, New York, Pittsburg, Riyadh, San Francisco, Washington DC

Number of lawyers 650+
at this office 22

Contact
Olivier Laude

CATEGORIES OF WORK

Dispute resolution
Olivier Laude

Insurance law
Jean Alisse

Corporate M&A
René de Monseignat, Stephen Walters

Capital markets
Stephen Walters, René de Monseignat

Private equity
Stephen Walters

Energy
René de Monseignat, Olivier Laude

Media and intellectual property
Olivier Laude

Trust and estates
René de Monseignat

Real estate
René de Monseignat, Olivier Laude

White-collar crime
Olivier Laude

LEFÈVRE PELLETIER & ASSOCIÉS

136 AVENUE DES CHAMPS-ELYSÉES
75008 PARIS

Telephone: +33 1 53 93 30 00
Fax: +33 1 53 93 30 30
E-mail: info@lpalaw.com
Website: www.lpalaw.com

Languages
Chinese, Dutch, English, French, German, Russian, Spanish

Other offices
Guangzhou, Hong Kong

Number of lawyers 145
at this office 140

CATEGORIES OF WORK

Real estate
Simon Lowe

Litigation and arbitration
Pierre Lévêque

M&A and corporate law
Jean-Luc Bédos

Business law
Vincent Lunel

Banking and finance
Christophe Jacomin

Tax law
Eric Ginter, Thierry Pons

Insurance law
Philippe Lefèvre

Labour law
Mary-Daphné Fishelson

LINKLATERS

25 RUE DE MARIGNAN
75008 PARIS

Telephone: +33 1 56 43 56 43
Fax: +33 1 43 59 41 96
Website: www.linklaters.com

Languages
All commercial and local languages in the countries where Linklaters operates

Other offices
Amsterdam, Antwerp, Bangkok, Beijing, Berlin, Bratislava, Brussels, Bucharest, Budapest, Cologne, Dubai, Frankfurt am Main, Hong Kong, Lisbon, London, Luxembourg, Madrid, Milan, Moscow, Munich, New York, Prague, Rome, São Paulo, Shanghai, Singapore, Stockholm, Tokyo, Warsaw

Number of lawyers 2,000 worldwide

Contacts
Nathalie Hobbs, Alain Garnier, Arnaud de La Cotardière

CATEGORIES OF WORK

Banking

Capital markets

Commercial

Corporate/M&A

EU and competition

Employment

Intellectual property

Litigation and arbitration

LBOs/private equity

Projects

Public law/public-private partnerships

Real estate

Financial services

Tax

Technology, media and telecommunications

CABINET LIPWORTH

**18 AV FRANKLIN D ROOSEVELT
75008 PARIS**

Telephone: +33 1 53 75 41 41
Fax: +33 1 53 75 14 12
E-mail: office@cabinet-lipworth.com
Website: www.cabinet-lipworth.com

Languages
Cantonese, English, Mandarin

Number of lawyers 6

CATEGORIES OF WORK

Mergers and acquisitions
Frank Lipworth, Myriam Smith

Banking (financing, syndications)
Frank Lipworth, Iris Bellanger

Private equity
Frank Lipworth, Myriam Smith

Financial markets
Iris Bellanger, Olivier Arwacher

Commercial leases
Myriam Smith

IT agreements
Iris Bellanger, Garance Grandchamp

Associations
Olivier Arwacher, Myriam Smith

Commercial litigation
Frank Lipworth, Myriam Smith

Music contracts
Frank Lipworth, Garance Grandchamp

Regulatory matters (financial services)
Frank Lipworth, Myriam Smith

Acquisitions of receivable portfolios
Frank Lipworth, Iris Bellanger

International joint ventures
Frank Lipworth, Iris Bellanger

LOVELLS

**6 AVENUE KLÉBER
75116 PARIS**

Telephone: +33 1 53 67 47 47
Fax: +33 1 53 67 47 48
E-mail: information@lovells.com
Website: www.lovells.com

Languages
English, German, Italian, Spanish

Other offices
Alicante, Amsterdam, Beijing, Berlin, Brussels, Budapest*, Chicago, Düsseldorf, Frankfurt, Hamburg, Ho Chi Minh City, Hong Kong, London, Madrid, Milan, Moscow, Munich, New York, Prague, Rome, Shanghai, Singapore, Tokyo, Warsaw, Zagreb*

Number of lawyers 1,600
at this office 107

Contact
Robert Follie

CATEGORIES OF WORK

Aviation

Banking, project finance

Bankruptcy

Business restructuring

Capital markets, structured finance

Consumer and advertising law

Competition and EU law

Corporate law

Distribution law

Employment law

E-commerce

Insurance law

IP, technology and media

Litigation and arbitration

Oil and gas

Outsourcing

Pharmaceutical and biosciences

Private equity

Real estate

Public law

Public/private partnerships and economic public law

Tax, including cross-border

Telecommunications

Venture capital and management buy-outs

MAYER BROWN ROWE & MAW LLP

41 AVENUE HOCHE
75008 PARIS

Telephone: +33 1 53 53 43 43
Fax: +33 1 53 96 03 83
Website: www.mayerbrownrowe.com

Languages
English, French, German, Italian, Korean, Russian, Spanish

Other offices
Berlin, Brussels, Charlotte, Chicago, Cologne, Frankfurt, Houston, London, Los Angeles, Mexico City (correspondence office), New York, Palo Alto, Beijing and Shanghai (partner offices), Washington DC

Number of lawyers 1,300
at this office 36

CATEGORIES OF WORK

Corporate/M&A/private equity
Xavier Jaspar, Alexis Dargent

Banking and finance/capital markets
Jean-Philippe Lambert, Jean-Pierre Lee

Real estate
Jean-Philippe Lambert

Tax
Laurent Borey, Benjamin Homo

Litigation and arbitration
Jean-Philippe Lambert

Employment and labour
Laurence Dumure Lambert

MEFFRE & GRALL

80 AVENUE MARCEAU
75008 PARIS

Telephone: +33 1 53 57 31 70
Fax: +33 1 47 20 90 40
E-mail: meffregrall@mgavocats.fr
Website: www.mgavocats.fr

Languages
English, French, German, Italian, Spanish

Number of lawyers 11

International groupings
LEXLINK

CATEGORIES OF WORK

French and EU competition law
JC Grall, JM Meffre, C Guet, N Kouchnir-Cargill, C Grass, T Lamy

Distribution law
JC Grall, T Lamy, C Guet, N Kouchnir-Cargill, C Grass

Media, entertainment and intellectual property
JC Grall, E Laur

Marketing law
JC Grall, N Kouchnir-Cargill, T Lamy

Litigation
E Bordenave, N Kouchnir-Cargill, E Le Morhedec

Information technology
T Lamy

Employment
E Bordenave

MORGAN LEWIS

68 RUE DU FAUBOURG SAINT-HONORÉ 75008 PARIS

Telephone: +33 1 53 30 43 00
Fax: +33 1 53 30 43 01
E-mail: info@morganlewis.com
Website: www.morganlewis.fr
www.morganlewis.com

Languages
Arabic, Croatian, English, French, German, Italian, Serbian, Spanish

Other offices
Boston, Brussels, Chicago, Dallas, Frankfurt, Harrisburg, Irvine, London, Los Angeles, Miami, New York, Palo Alto, Philadelphia, Pittsburgh, Princeton, San Francisco, Tokyo, Washington DC

Number of lawyers 1,200+
at this office 26

CATEGORIES OF WORK

M&A, competition, administrative and environmental law, joint ventures
Jean Leygonie

M&A, private equity, privatisations, securities
Anne Tolila

Acquisition finance, structured finance, project finance
Stéphan Alamowitch

Antitrust
Jean Leygonie

Outsourcing, IT and IP, e-commerce, new technology, telecoms
Florence Guthfreund-Roland

Labour and employment
François Vergne

Taxation
Patrice Lefèvre-Péaron

Litigation
Thierry Dalmasso

THE FIRM

Morgan Lewis, with more than 1,200 lawyers in 19 offices in the US, Europe and Asia, is one of the largest law firms in the world.

Morgan Lewis represents clients across the globe, from mergers and acquisitions and joint ventures to technology and outsourcing; from fraud and money laundering to employment and property. With its international reach, Morgan Lewis can resolve differing and conflicting laws in a number of jurisdictions to produce optimum results for its clients. The firm's lawyers understand the problems and complexities of transactional litigation and cross-border negotiation and can advise on US and EU regulatory matters. The firm's clients are diverse and include Fortune 250 companies, leading financial services and investment banking organisations, as well as pioneers in the e-commerce and internet sector. The firm also represents high-net-worth individuals. All clients receive the same high level of care and benefit from the firm's local presence in a global market. The firm handles a vast diversity of legal work including antitrust, business and commercial litigation, business and finance, corporate transactions, employment, labour and benefits, energy and utilities, insurance, intellectual property, international arbitration, investment management, life sciences, mergers and acquisitions, real estate, outsourcing, securities, sport, tax and technology.

AREAS OF PRACTICE

Morgan Lewis Paris is fully integrated with the firm's 18 other offices and offers a strong pan-European service in combination with its Brussels, Frankfurt and London lawyers. The Paris office opened 18 months ago and has brought top-tier clients and broad experience across industries to the firm. Morgan Lewis Paris works closely with US and European colleagues and offers particular strength in the areas of corporate law, labour and employment, antitrust and technology.

The Paris office assists clients in a wide variety of complex financial transactions, including secured lending, leasing, securitisations, trade finance and project finance deals as well as restructuring and debt trading. The firm's Paris lawyers have participated in many pioneering transactions from business securitisations to double-dip corporate financing. They also focus on complex capital markets work including issuance of deeply subordinated debts, warrants or high-yield bonds. The recent addition of Stéphan Alamowitch to the Paris team has increased the acquisition, project and structured finance capability. All the lawyers in the Paris office are members of the Morgan Lewis business and finance practice, of which the main focus is M&A, private equity, privatisation, tax and securities law. The Paris team also provides advice to the telecommunications industry. Clients include large multinational telecommunications and IT companies. The office also offers a unique pan-European outsourcing practice with the other Morgan Lewis offices in London and Frankfurt.

Morgan Lewis, Paris has a strong labour and employment law practice. Its lawyers help clients negotiate the ever-changing landscape of laws that govern the workplace in France and, together with the London and US offices, they offer decades of experience in French, European Union and international labour laws.

The Paris office also offers a team of lawyers who focus on antitrust and competition issues. The team provides a full range of services, from preventive counselling to defence of 'bet the company' litigation.

The Paris tax department focuses on French and international tax law and represents clients before courts and administrative bodies that have jurisdiction over tax matters. In addition, it assists clients on VAT and EU tax law, project finance, especially for government authorities, electronic payment systems and privatisation or relative matters, such as joint ventures between state-owned companies and the private sector. The Paris team also advises individuals and estates of substantial wealth in connection with management or restructuring of personal financial interests.

NOMOS

13 RUE ALPHONSE DE NEUVILLE
75017 PARIS

Telephone: +33 1 43 18 55 00
Fax: +33 1 43 18 55 55
E-mail: nomos@nomosparis.com
Website: www.nomosparis.com

Languages
English, German, Italian, Spanish

Number of lawyers 35

Contacts
Eric Lauvaux, Christophe Pecnard

Member
IBA; IAEL; AEC; AFDIT; ACEECA

CATEGORIES OF WORK

Media and entertainment
Héléna Delabarre, Eric Lauvaux

Intellectual property, IT
Héléna Delabarre, Eric Lauvaux

EC and French competition law, distribution law
Christophe Pecnard, Emmanuelle Voisset

Advertising and consumer law
Christophe Pecnard, Emmanuelle Voisset

International arbitration
James Lightburn

Tax law
Jean-Claude Bignon, Anne-Marie Hatchondo

Mergers and acquisitions
Matthieu Bringer, James Lightburn, Jean-François Pourdieu

Private equity
Jean-François Pourdieu

Labour law
Anne Ciret

THE FIRM

Founded in 1998, NomoS is a young, modern practice which is highly specialised in developing industry sectors and nurtures a close working relationship with its clients. The firm's name did not belong to a founding partner but actually means 'custom having the force of law' in ancient Greek.

Today, the firm employs 35 lawyers, 10 of whom are partners.

AREAS OF PRACTICE

NomoS is active both in an advisory capacity and in contentious matters. The firm acts as the legal partner of its French and international clients, which include large groups and dynamic small to medium-sized companies, assisting them in their day-to-day operations as well as in their more unusual transactions.

The firm is involved in the following areas of commercial law: mergers and acquisitions, company law, labour law, intellectual property and IT law, tax law, competition law, distribution law and consumer law.

The firm is particularly active within developing industry sectors, such as private equity, media/communications/entertainment, new technologies, distribution, food processing and advertising. NomoS advises its clients over the long term, enabling the firm's lawyers to build long-standing relationships with its clients.

Within the firm, legal work is undertaken by teams who combine an in-depth understanding of each client's marketplace with specialist legal knowledge.

The firm does not belong to a network or alliance, but has developed a 'web' of trusted correspondents within each of its main areas of activity.

NOVE7 AVOCATS

113 RUE DE L'UNIVERSITÉ
75007 PARIS

Telephone: +33 1 56 89 36 36
Fax: +33 1 56 89 36 37
Website: www.nove7.com

Languages
English, French, German, Italian, Spanish

Other offices
Bordeaux

Number of lawyers 28
at this office 24

Contacts
François Illouz (francois.illouz@nove7.com), Alexis Gramblat (alexis.gramblat@nove7.com)

CATEGORIES OF WORK

Commercial law
François Illouz, Alexis Gramblat

Corporate, M&A, bankruptcy
Michele Jaudel, Eric Lapchin

IP, media and communications law
François Illouz, Danielle Elkrief

Information technology and industrial property
Joël Heslaut, Danielle Elkrief

Tax Law
Eric Lapchin, Didier Brezillon

Real estate law
Michel Simonet, Anne Tartary

Labour law
Michele Jaudel, François Illouz

Sports law
Alexis Gramblat, François Illouz

PAUL, HASTINGS, JANOFSKY & WALKER (EUROPE) LLP

30 AVENUE DE MESSINE
75008 PARIS

Telephone: +33 1 42 99 04 50
Fax: +33 1 45 63 91 49
E-mail: info@paulhastings.com
Website: www.paulhastings.com

Languages
English, German, Italian, Spanish, Bulgarian, Russian

Other offices
Atlanta, Beijing, Brussels, Hong Kong, London, Los Angeles, Milan, New York, Orange County, Palo Alto, San Diego, San Francisco, Shanghai, Stamford, Tokyo, Washington DC

Number of lawyers 50

Contact
Dominique Borde

CATEGORIES OF WORK

Mergers, acquisitions, dispositions and joint ventures

Capital markets, securities and privatisations

Private equity

Project finance

Banking and finance

Dispute resolution and arbitration

White-collar crime

Intellectual property

Real estate

EU/competition law

Employment

Tax

Regulatory and public administrative law

Insurance

ORRICK, HERRINGTON & SUTCLIFFE

25 BOULEVARD DE L'AMIRAL BRUIX
75782 PARIS CEDEX 16

Telephone: +33 1 53 53 75 00
Fax: +33 1 53 53 75 01
Website: www.orrick.com

Other offices
Hong Kong, London, Los Angeles, Milan, Moscow, New York, Orange County, Pacific Northwest (Portland, Seattle), Rome, Sacramento, San Francisco, Silicon Valley, Taipei, Tokyo, Washington DC

Number of lawyers 850
at this office 90

Contacts
David Syed, Stéphane Salou, Jean-Pierre Martel

CATEGORIES OF WORK

Corporate, mergers and acquisitions, restructurings, joint ventures, strategic alliances

Capital markets

Securities and stock exchange regulation

Private equity

Corporate finance

Project finance

Asset finance

Insolvency

Contract law

Banking and structured finance

Litigation, dispute resolution, arbitration and mediation

Tax (corporate, structuring, real estate, income and litigation)

Antitrust and competition law

Administrative and regulatory law

Employment law

White-collar crime

IP, technology, media, telecoms and IT

Real estate and construction

Maritime and transport

Insurance law

THE FIRM

Orrick is an international law firm with more than 850 lawyers located in Asia, Europe and North America. In Europe, Orrick has approximately 200 lawyers across five offices, located in London, Milan, Paris, Rome and Moscow. With the firm's European expansion, Orrick now has 16 offices across three continents. Much of Orrick's client work in Europe involves cross-border transactions and financings that span Europe, the Middle East, Africa, Asia and the Americas. To support the demands of its clients, Orrick has made seamless client service its number one goal across the firm. As a result, the firm's European lawyers can call on the substantial resources of Orrick's other offices around the world to provide clients with the expertise required to support their transactions. Above all, Orrick's name stands for excellence in legal services; integrated, responsive client teams throughout the world; innovative leadership and management; and a commitment to the firm's core values, which govern these business standards. Effective 1 January 2006, Orrick merged with Rambaud Martel, one of the largest pre-eminent French, full-service law firms renowned for its corporate practice, including a respected practice in mergers and acquisitions and stock exchange regulation. This merger created an unparalleled source of corporate legal counsel in France and around the world.

AREAS OF PRACTICE

Orrick's Paris office is highly respected for its work on major cross-border and domestic transactions involving transactional work, litigation and other forms of dispute resolution. Orrick's Paris finance practice covers a range of disciplines, from litigation, international arbitration, commercial and structured finance to asset and project finances. The firm's finance lawyers advise on transactions ranging from traditional credit agreements and public debt issues to complex cross-border lease financings, including secured and unsecured lending, asset-backed financing, letters of credit, asset-backed commercial paper financings, lease finance and aircraft finance in structured finance. Orrick's lawyers also represent issuers, arrangers, trustees and investors in structured finance and capital markets transactions. The energy and project finance group in Paris serves clients in the energy, communications and other key infrastructure sectors. The Paris maritime practice handles domestic and international ship finance transactions, acting for financial institutions, banks, ship owners and operators on all aspects of their business.

Orrick's Paris corporate practice, strengthened by the merger with Rambaud Martel, advises public and private companies (listed and non-listed), banks, financial institutions, investment and venture capital funds on all aspects of corporate law at every stage of their growth and development, and includes a range of industries, such as luxury goods, automotive, food and retail industries, as well as telecoms, construction, commodities (water, electricity and gas), and many service industries. The firm's expertise also includes mergers and acquisitions, joint ventures and strategic alliances, strategic technology transactions, corporate formations, financings at all stages of development, restructurings, securities, information technology and intellectual property, as well as general corporate counselling. Orrick's corporate lawyers draw upon the experience of other practice groups to provide assistance with antitrust, tax, executive compensation and employee benefits, intellectual property, employment, real estate and litigation issues. The real estate group represents clients in all phases of real estate investment, financing, development, and operations, with work ranging from traditional purchases, sales, leases, and financings to highly complex portfolio acquisitions and multi-jurisdictional transactions.

PARDO BOULANGER & ASSOCIÉS

74 AVENUE DE WAGRAM
75017 PARIS

Telephone: +33 1 46 22 56 56
Fax: +33 1 46 22 56 66
E-mail: avocats@pba-avocats.com

Number of lawyers 10

CATEGORIES OF WORK

Bankruptcy litigation
Olivier Pardo, Catherine Boulanger, Ludovic Landivaux, Xavier Cazottes

Banking
Olivier Gedin

Real estate
Laurence Dauxin-Nedelec, Catherine Boulanger

Insolvency and business reconstruction
Ludovic Landivaux, Xavier Cazottes

White-collar crime and corporate internal investigations
Olivier Pardo, Ludovic Landivaux
Jean-Charles Teissedre, Michaël Cahn

THE FIRM

Pardo Boulanger and Associés is one of the top bankruptcy law firms in Paris, and is also known for its corporate law expertise. The firm was founded by Olivier Pardo. Before opening his own practice, Olivier was a criminal court judge and then special consultant to the Minister of Justice, at which time he helped to develop the bankruptcy law of 1994. Olivier has partnered with Catherine Boulanger, who is another well-known lawyer in Paris, and Ludovic Landivaux, who has been praised for his solid legal work. All three partners went through the Institute of Political Studies in Paris, otherwise known as l'Institut d'Etudes Politiques de Paris or Sciences Po Paris.

Working alongside the three partners are three junior partners and four associates, all of whom have years of experience that have helped establish Pardo Boulanger as the leading firm that it is today.

AREAS OF PRACTICE

Pardo Boulanger offers a variety of legal services in order to satisfy the diverse needs of its clients. However, the firm is well known in the areas of bankruptcy litigation, private and commercial real estate, banking law, white-collar crime and corporate internal investigations, corporate law, insolvency and business reconstruction, European business law and European corporate law. Other areas of practice include arbitration and alternative dispute resolution, commercial law, conflict resolution between shareholders, contracts, drafting charters and by-laws, drafting contracts between associates and shareholders, drafting transfers of company shares and stocks, dispute resolution between shareholders, employer responsibility, corporate tax, employee responsibility, insurance, matters of dispute, media law (television, radio), mergers and acquisitions, penal law, private law (contractual liability and civil liability), public law (public markets and delegation of public services), calls for tender, and social welfare law.

PENLAW SELARL

23 RUE D'ANJOU
75008 PARIS

Telephone: +33 1 44 51 59 70
Fax: +33 1 44 51 59 71
E-mail: h.page@penlaw.fr

Languages
English, French

Other offices
London*

Number of lawyers 6

Contacts
Henry Page, Sophie Denassieu

CATEGORIES OF WORK

- Aviation
- Maritime
- Insurance
- Transport of goods
- Banking
- International arbitration
- Commercial disputes
- Letter of credit disputes
- Disputes relating to states – commercial and other
- Sale of goods
- Real property (commercial and other)
- Employment law
- Mergers and acquisitions
- Tax planning
- Corporate structures
- Shareholder agreements/disputes

THE FIRM

Penlaw (previously the Paris office of Penningtons) was founded in the early 1990s and is staffed by lawyers qualified both under English and French law. Penningtons Solicitors LLP in England consists of over 60 partners, over 150 lawyers and a total staff of over 380. Its head office is situated in the City and it carries out a wide variety of work.

The Paris office originally advised on corporate matters, particularly cross border. Since 1994, with the arrival of a new team of lawyers, the office has changed emphasis and now provides a one-stop service for, on the one hand, purely French problems (mainly commercial), both contentious and non-contentious and, on the other hand, international problems relating to aviation, shipping, international trade, letters of credit and other commercial disputes. Since 1997 it has developed a further area of specialisation in aviation to become one of the recognised aviation firms in France. In 2005, Penlaw SELARL became a separate legal entity from Penningtons after Penningtons changed to LLP status.

The lawyers in Penlaw consist of dual (English and French) qualified lawyers and pure French avocats. As a consequence, the firm is well equipped to deal with both international and domestic legal issues. It is the policy of the office to be concise and clear in its advice, to negotiate special fee arrangements where appropriate and to find the most cost-effective and efficient solution for clients whether in disputes or in non-contentious matters. Penlaw can deal efficiently with a broad range of international and domestic problems in a no-nonsense and competitive manner using its London office where necessary for procedural support and back up.

AREAS OF PRACTICE

The firm specialises in a variety of matters. The firm is recognised as an aviation specialist and regularly handles matters relating to aircraft purchase, finance, lease, registration and maintenance contracts. The firm has also been successful in litigation arising out of aviation-related matters. In the area of maritime law, the firm acts regularly for English P&I clubs, for owners, charterers and others of many nationalities. The firm regularly represents maritime clients before all the usual jurisdictions in France and England (courts and arbitration). The lower charge-out rates in Paris compared to most London firms are found by many clients to give rise to a significant saving in cost without sacrificing quality. The firm also acts for a number of insurers and steel and other traders in connection with transport-related problems, quality disputes and documentary credit matters.

The firm deals with international arbitrations before the ICC, LCIA and Stockholm Chamber of Commerce. One particular area of expertise is the enforcement of judgments/awards (or securing claims) against debtors whose assets are difficult to locate or seize, including foreign states. All problems relating to the seizure of assets both in France and in many other jurisdictions are included within the firm's specialist areas of knowledge.

As well as commercial disputes of all natures, the firm deals with non-contentious commercial matters such as agency and distribution contracts, real property transactions (both commercial and other), mergers and acquisitions, tax planning and advice on international corporate structures. The firm also has expertise in private client work including employment law, personal injury and matters relating to tax planning and inheritance.

PROSKAUER ROSE LLP

68 RUE DU FAUBOURG SAINT-HONORÉ 75008 PARIS

Telephone: +33 1 53 05 60 00
Fax: +33 1 53 05 60 05
E-mail: jlcuadrado@proskauer.com
Website: www.proskauer.com

Languages
English, French, Spanish, German

Other offices
Boca Raton, Boston, Los Angeles, Newark, New Orleans, New York, Washington DC

Number of lawyers 701
at this office 32

Contact
Jean-Luc Cuadrado

CATEGORIES OF WORK

Corporate, commercial, mergers and acquisitions
Guillaume Kellner

International transactions and private equity
William Krisel, Delia Spitzer

Securities law
Guillaume Kellner

Labour, employment
Yasmine Tarasewicz, Béatrice Pola

Tax
Jean-Luc Cuadrado

Civil, product and professional liability
Valérie Lafarge-Sarkozy, Emmanuelle Payrau-Sorba

Bankruptcy
Valérie Lafarge-Sarkozy

Major projects/construction
Christophe Lapp, Jean-Philippe Sorba

Administrative law
Christophe Lapp, Jean-Philippe Sorba

Antitrust
Christophe Lapp

White-collar defence
Philippe Goossens

Insurance law
Emmanuelle Payrau-Sorba

RAVISY & ASSOCIÉS

4 BOULEVARD ST MICHEL 75006 PARIS

Telephone: +33 1 53 10 99 99
Fax: +33 1 53 10 99 98
E-mail: avocats@prudhommes.com
Website: www.prudhommes.com

Languages
English, French, Portuguese

Number of lawyers 6

Contact
Philippe Ravisy

CATEGORIES OF WORK

Employment law
Philippe Ravisy, Susana Lopes dos Santos

Social security law
Didier Médecin, Susana Lopes dos Santos

Negotiation coaching
Philippe Ravisy, Didier Médecin

Litigation (individual disputes)
Susana Lopes dos Santos, Didier Médecin

Work contracts
Philippe Ravisy, Géraldine Tchemenian

Health, safety and working conditions
Philippe Ravisy, Didier Médecin

Labour disputes
Géraldine Tchemenian, Philippe Ravisy

REED SMITH RAMBAUD CHAROT LLP

42 AVENUE RAYMOND POINCARÉ
75016 PARIS

Telephone: +33 1 76 70 40 00
Fax: +33 1 76 70 41 19
E-mail:
firstinitialsurname@reedsmith.com
Website: www.reedsmith.com

Languages
English, French, Spanish

Other offices
Century City, Coventry, London, Los Angeles, Munich, New York, Newark, Northern VA, Oakland, Philadelphia, Pittsburgh, Princeton, San Francisco, Washington DC, Wilmington

Number of lawyers 1,078
at this office 14

CATEGORIES OF WORK

Commercial litigation
Marie Albertini, Beniot Charot

Corporate
Mathieu Rambaud, Philippe Lecler

Employment
Séverine Martel

Arbitration
Benoit Charot, Marie Albertini

Healthcare
Mathieu Rambaud, Phillippe Lecler

M&A
Mathieu Rambaud, Phillippe Lecler

Outsourcing
Mathieu Rambaud, Phillippe Lecler

Product liability
Benoit Charot

Insurance/reinsurance litigation
Benoit Charot

Professional negligence
Benoit Charot, Marie Albertini

Pharmaceuticals/biotechnology
Mathieu Rambaud, Benoit Charot

THE FIRM

Reed Smith is a leading international law firm. The firm has grown rapidly over the past few years through a series of strategic mergers and lateral additions and it now has over 1,000 lawyers across 14 US and four European cities. A strong presence on both coasts of the US makes the firm ideally positioned to offer clients a transatlantic capability. It continues to invest in key markets to meet clients' needs and, in 2005, opened its first offices in mainland Europe, in Munich and Paris.

Reed Smith represents clients, large and small, across a great number of legal disciplines and many industry sectors. In Europe, its key industries are financial services and life sciences. Its firmwide clients include financial institutions, pharmaceutical companies, manufacturers, healthcare providers and insurers, communications and media companies and real estate developers and government bodies.

AREAS OF PRACTICE

Reed Smith's core services in Europe are corporate, life sciences, financial services, litigation, employment, real estate and TMT.

Corporate: the firm's largest department handles a wide variety of corporate and commercial transactions for, in particular, US and European clients. The department's expertise includes mergers and acquisitions, corporate finance, competition and corporate tax. It enjoys a strong track record in alternative investment market–related work.

Life sciences: the department supports leading-edge companies in pharmaceuticals, biotechnology, diagnostics, medical devices and healthcare. The firm advises life sciences companies on debt and equity financing and partners with clients through all phases of development, production, marketing and distribution of products. It is also widely acknowledged for its work defending clients in high-profile, multi-jurisdictional product liability claims.

Financial services: the financial services group advises on capital market products, consumer financial services, regulatory advice (Financial Services and Market Act 2000) and transactions (acquisitions, divestitures, restructurings). It also has a transatlantic project finance team.

Commercial litigation: the firm handles substantial commercial disputes and is particularly well known for its work in international asset recovery, financial regulation and multi-jurisdictional claims. Specific areas of expertise include product liability claims, insolvency and corporate restructuring, intellectual property and domestic and international arbitration. It has a dedicated team of French-speaking advocates.

Employment: the team provides a full service to employers and HR professionals encompassing service agreements and employment contracts, employee benefits, business transfers, dismissals, redundancies, discrimination and trade union law. It also advises on all EU aspects of employment law and offers transactional and non-transactional pensions advice. In addition, the UK business immigration team is recognised as one of the leading practices in the country and provides corporate clients and individual foreign investors with advice in connection with residence and working in the UK.

Real estate: the real estate group advises on high-value acquisitions and disposals for corporate clients in the retail, financial, services, media and manufacturing industries. High-level property litigation, contentious and non-contentious planning and infrastructure expertise is an additional strength of the team.

TMT and IP/IT: the firm represents a variety of media and entertainment, technology and telecommunications companies on all contractual, commercial, intellectual property and regulatory aspects. The firm works closely with broadcast clients and cable companies on all issues relating to broadcasting and the convergence of communication technologies. It advises on outsourcing, licensing, and other technology transactions.

SJ BERWIN

64 AVENUE KLÉBER
75116 PARIS

Telephone: +33 1 44 34 63 46
Fax: +33 1 44 34 63 47
E-mail: info-paris@sjberwin.com
Website: www.sjberwin.com

Languages
English, French, Portuguese, Spanish

Other offices
Berlin, Brussels, Frankfurt, London, Madrid, Milan, Munich, Turin

Number of lawyers 550
at this office 35

Contact
George Pinkham

CATEGORIES OF WORK

Private equity, fund structuring
George Pinkham, Sylvie Vansteenkiste

Private equity, corporate, MBO/LBO
Christophe Digoy, Maxence Bloch

EU and competition
Marc Lévy

Tax law
Sylvie Vansteenkiste

Corporate finance, M&A
Pierre-Louis Périn

Venture capital
Pierre-Louis Périn

SAVIN MARTINET ASSOCIÉS

66 RUE DU FAUBOURG
SAINT-HONORÉ
75008 PARIS

Telephone: +33 1 53 43 22 20
Fax: +33 1 53 43 22 21
E-mail: contact@smaparis.com
Website: www.smaparis.com

Languages
Dutch, English, German, Spanish, Italian

Number of lawyers 14

CATEGORIES OF WORK

Criminal, civil and administrative litigation, arbitration and mediation
Yvon Martinet, Arnaud Constant

Regulatory audits, risk audits, environmental and social reporting
Patricia Savin, Yvon Martinet

Corporate business law, retail and competition, customs
Yvon Martinet, Arnaud Constant

Health and safety law
Patricia Savin, Yvon Martinet

Food and consumer law
Yvon Martinet

Environmental law
Patricia Savin

Polluted sites, land law
Patricia Savin

Natural resources law
Patricia Savin, Yvon Martinet

SIMMONS & SIMMONS

SOLICITORS, AVOCATS À LA COUR, RECHTSANWALT

5 BOULEVARD DE LA MADELEINE
75001 PARIS

Telephone: +33 1 53 29 16 29
Fax: +33 1 53 29 16 30
E-mail: enquiries@simmons-simmons.com
Website: www.simmons-simmons.com

Languages
English, French, German

Other offices
London, Rotterdam, Lisbon, Milan, Rome, Düsseldorf, Frankfurt, Brussels, Madrid, Padua, Oporto, Madeira, Abu Dhabi, Qatar, Hong Kong, Shanghai, Tokyo, New York, Dubai

Number of lawyers 764
at this office 52

Contact
Thierry Gontard

CATEGORIES OF WORK

Corporate	Employment
Banking	Financial markets
Capital markets	Pharmaceutical and biotechnology
Taxation	Energy and utilities
Projects, PFI	TMT
EU, competition	Aerospace and defence
Litigation/arbitration	Transport
Intellectual property	Consumer goods
Real estate	

SONIER POULAIN ET ASSOCIÉS

46 AVENUE D'IENA
75116 PARIS

Telephone: +33 1 53 23 43 00
Fax: +33 1 53 23 43 09
E-mail:
sonier-poulain@sonier-poulain.com

Languages
English, German, Spanish

Number of lawyers 17

Member
INSOL International; INSOL Europe; Association des Praticiens des Procedures Collectives; Association Nationale des Juristes de Banque

CATEGORIES OF WORK

Insolvency, bankruptcy and restructuring	Intellectual property
Commercial law	Tax law, stock exchange law and banking
Corporate law	Labour and employment
Mergers and acquisitions	Competition law
International real estate	Litigation, arbitration

SLAUGHTER AND MAY

ENGLISH SOLICITORS

112 AVENUE KLÉBER
75784 PARIS CEDEX 16

Telephone: +33 1 44 05 60 00
Fax: +33 1 44 05 60 60
E-mail: paris@slaughterandmay.com
Website: www.slaughterandmay.com

Other offices
London, Brussels, Hong Kong

CATEGORIES OF WORK

General corporate and commercial
Peter Deckers. Andrew McClean

Capital markets
Peter Deckers, Andrew McClean

Banking
Peter Deckers, Andrew McClean

Project finance
Peter Deckers

THE FIRM

Slaughter and May, a leading international law firm with a worldwide corporate, commercial and financing practice, established its office in Paris in 1974. Slaughter and May in Paris practises English law.

Slaughter and May aims to provide a professional service of the highest calibre, combining technical excellence with commercial awareness and a practical, constructive approach. This is reinforced by its hands-on approach and the flexibility of its working method which enables it to provide the highest quality of advice and service across the world. Through the firm's other offices and close working relationships with lawyers from leading independent law firms around the world, Slaughter and May is able to provide its clients with a fully integrated and seamless international service of the highest quality.

AREAS OF PRACTICE

Slaughter and May advises clients on the legal aspects of an extensive range of commercial, financial and banking transactions. The core practice area is financing, including complex asset finance and project finance. Rather than develop single specialisms, lawyers in the core practice areas are encouraged to adopt a multidisciplinary approach and the firm is well known for its innovative work.

SOULEZ LARIVIÈRE ET ASSOCIÉS

22 AVENUE DE LA GRANDE-ARMÉE
75017 PARIS

Telephone: +33 1 47 63 37 22
Fax: +33 1 42 67 83 05
E-mail: avocats@soulezlariviere.com
Website: www.soulezlariviere.com

Languages
English, French

Number of lawyers 9

CATEGORIES OF WORK

Commercial litigation and arbitration

Aviation

Environment

Industrial risk

Torts, insurance, liability

Product liability

Construction

Criminal litigation

Corporate crime, including involuntary manslaughter

International criminal law

Human and civil rights

TAYLOR WESSING

42 AVENUE MONTAIGNE
75008 PARIS

Telephone: +33 1 72 74 03 33
Fax: +33 1 72 74 03 34
E-mail: paris@taylorwessing.com
Website: www.taylorwessing.com

Languages
English, French, German Spanish

Other offices
Alicante, Berlin, Brussels, Cambridge, Dubai*, Düsseldorf, Frankfurt, Hamburg, London, Munich, Shanghai

Number of lawyers 598
at this office 65

Member
Interlex

CATEGORIES OF WORK

Banking and finance
Arnaud de Senilhes

Media and entertainment
Christian Valsamidis, Arnaud de Senilhes

Corporate and commercial
Gilles Amsallem, Pascal Roux, Frédéric Guy

M&A
Gilles Amsallem, Pascal Roux, Noro-Lanto Ravisy

Capital markets
Noro-Lanto Ravisy, Pascal Roux

Tax
Claire Deleris, Christophe Flaicher

Employment
Claudia Jonath

Competition and EU, regulatory, administrative, lobbying
Olivier de Chazeaux

IP, IT
Marc Schuler

Dispute resolution
Paul-Albert Iweins, Benjamin Sarfati

Insurance
Arnaud Bertrand

Real estate
François Verdot

CABINET TOUATI

15 RUE D'ASTORG
75008 PARIS

Telephone: +33 1 42 94 00 08
Fax: +33 1 42 94 08 84
E-mail: jjtouati@cabinet-touati.com
Website: www.cabinet-touati.com

Languages
English, Spanish

Number of lawyers 4

Member
Franco-British Chamber of Commerce; EELA; ABA; IBA

CATEGORIES OF WORK	
Employment and labour law	**Criminal law**
Employee benefits	**Social security law**

THE FIRM

The law firm was founded in 1998 by Jean-Jacques Touati. Focusing on employment law, with an increasing emphasis on international practice and tailored services, the firm places its extensive litigation experience at the service of its advisory role. Jean-Jacques Touati was formerly a lecturer at the University of Law in Paris, and was a lawyer in labour law at several international law firms and is renowned for his articles and books on transfer of undertakings, as well as on reasons for dismissals. He is the author of the two studies in dismissal for gross negligence and in serious cause, of the prestigious collection 'Juris-classeur Employment Law Encyclopedia', and also has an extensive practice in litigation.

AREAS OF PRACTICE

The team, accustomed to working for companies and international groups with a global view, provides advisory and litigation services in all areas of labour law, including restructuring and redundancy, employee representations, benefits and retirement, termination, social security and labour litigation, international mobility, executive packages.

UGGC & ASSOCIÉS

47 RUE DE MONCEAU
75008 PARIS

Telephone: +33 1 56 69 70 00
Fax: +33 1 56 69 70 71
E-mail: uggc@uggcavocats.com
Website: www.uggcavocats.com

Languages
Arabic, Dutch, English, German, Italian, Spanish

Other offices
Brussels, Casablanca

Number of lawyers 95
at this office 83

CATEGORIES OF WORK

Corporate law, mergers and acquisitions
Jean-Jacques Uettwiller, Bernard Grelon, Pascal Squercioni

Tax law
Michel Turon, Antoine Gabizon, Laurent Chambaz

Transport law
Michel Gout

Litigation and arbitration
Bernard Grelon, Michel Gout, Jean-François Canat

ADR/mediation
Jean-François Canat, Thierry Montéran

Real estate and urban planning
Bernard Lamorlette

Public law
Thierry Dal Farra, Bernard Lamorlette, Jean-Nicolas Clément

Environment
Jean-Nicolas Clément

Bankruptcy/insolvency
Thierry Montéran, Bernard Grelon

Labour law
Roseline Sauser, Pascal Bathmanabane, Sophie Uettwiller

EU competition law and intellectual property law
Elisabeth Logeais, Corinne Khayat, Michel Ponsard

Art law
Jean-François Canat

Trust law
Laurent Chambaz

VATIER & ASSOCIÉS

12 RUE D'ASTORG
75008 PARIS

Telephone: +33 1 53 43 15 55
Fax: +33 1 53 43 15 78
E-mail: acr@vatier-associes.com
Website: www.vatier-associes.com

Languages
English, French

Number of lawyers 26

CATEGORIES OF WORK

Arbitration
Bernard Vatier

Litigation (general commercial, enforcement)
Bernard Vatier, Daniel Paquet

Litigation (criminal, white-collar)
Bernard Vatier, Olivier Saumon

Competition, distribution, direct selling law
Arnaud Moquin

Corporate (including all aspects of company law, joint ventures)
Arnaud Moquin, Frederic Gourdon, Ann Creelman

Bankruptcy, insolvency
Bernard Vatier, Olivier Saumon

M&A, corporate restructuring
Ann V Creelman, Frederic Gourdon, François Hugonin

Tax
François Hugonin

Property (construction, promotion, financing, urban development, zoning)
Daniel Paquet

Labour and employment law
Marie-Sylvie Vatier, Arnaud Moquin

Health (pharmaceutical – malpractice for public and private institutions, distribution of regulated products and services)
Olivier Saumon, Céline Roquelle-Meyer

Intellectual property
Oliver Saumon

VEIL JOURDE

38 RUE DE LISBONNE
75008 PARIS

Telephone: +33 1 56 69 56 69
Fax: +33 1 53 53 94 94
E-mail: contact@veilpartners.com
Website: www.veilpartners.com

Languages
English

Number of lawyers 32

CATEGORIES OF WORK

Mergers and acquisitions
Jean Veil, Guillame Kuperfils, Ariel Harroch, Marie-Charlotte Trebuchet

Stock exchange regulations (public transactions)
Jean Veil, Ariel Harroch

Restructuring
Georges Jourde, Guilhem Bremond

Tax
Ariel Harroch

Litigation and arbitration
Jean Veil, Georges Jourde, Eric Deubel

Public law
Pierre-Alain Jeanneney

ADVOKATFIRMAN VINGE

21 RUE JEAN GOUJON
75008 PARIS

Telephone: +33 1 53 53 42 30
Fax: +33 1 53 53 42 31
Website: www.vinge.se

Languages
Swedish, English, French, German

Other Offices
Brussels, Gothenburg, Helsingborg, Hong Kong, London, Malmö, Shanghai, Stockholm

Number of lawyers 300
at this office 4

Contact
Anders B Åberg

Member
Scandinavian Law Alliance with Kromann Reumert (Denmark) and Thommessen (Norway); Lex Mundi

CATEGORIES OF WORK

Banking and finance	**Litigation and arbitration**
Bankruptcy and liquidation	**M&A**
China practice	**Marketing**
Corporate finance, capital markets	**Media**
Employment and benefits	**Private equity funds**
EU and antitrust	**Public procurement**
Financial services and regulations	**Real estate and environmental**
General corporate	**Tax**
Insurance	**Telecommunications**
Intellectual property	**Transport**
IT	

THE FIRM

With some 300 fee-earners, Vinge is one of the largest law firms in Scandinavia. The firm is a member of the Scandinavian Law Alliance together with Kromann Reumert in Denmark and Thommessen in Norway.

Vinge has offices in Stockholm, Gothenburg, Malmö and Helsingborg as well as in London, Paris, Brussels, Hong Kong and Shanghai. The firm's clients include domestic and international commercial enterprises, financial institutions and state and regulatory bodies. Vinge is committed to providing the highest quality legal advice and experience for all matters in which the firm becomes involved, to the highest professional standards.

Innovation, creativeness and a business-orientated, problem-solving approach are at the core of the practice. The firm's size means that there are resources available to handle large and complex domestic and cross-border transactions within tight time frames. At the same time, there is a strong focus on responsiveness and personal commitments to clients. Vinge's motto is: A good commercial lawyer sees beyond the law.

AREAS OF PRACTICE

Vinge specialises in all aspects of commercial law and is consistently ranked amongst the leading law firms in Scandinavia in a number of key practice areas. Vinge's extensive network of contacts comprises independent law firms, consultants and investment banks with whom the firm works regularly on domestic and cross-border deals and projects.

The firm takes an overall approach as well as providing in-depth knowledge by working together with major foreign law firms. Vinge has developed a wide international network which is available to its clients. The firm's broad experience and expertise means that it is called upon to handle all kinds of commercial law issues. It has learned from experience what resources and services are required in order to find the right solutions to clients' problems.

Vinge does everything it can to help clients to achieve success in their business. The firm sees beyond the problems and seeks the solutions.

VOGEL & VOGEL

30 AVENUE D'IÉNA
75116 PARIS

Telephone: +33 1 53 67 76 20
Fax: +33 1 53 67 76 25
E-mail: info@vogel-vogel.com
Website: www.vogel-vogel.com

Languages
English, German, Spanish

Other offices
Brussels, Frankfurt

Number of lawyers 35

Contact
Joseph Vogel

CATEGORIES OF WORK

European competition law
Louis Vogel, Joseph Vogel

French competition law
Louis Vogel, Joseph Vogel

Merger control
Louis Vogel, Joseph Vogel

State aid
Louis Vogel, Joseph Vogel

Unfair competition law
Charles S Fahrner, Xavier Henry

Media and telecoms
Louis Vogel, Joseph Vogel

Product liability, defence to consumer actions
Charles S Fahrner

Distribution law (franchising, agency, selective distribution, termination of dealerships)
Joseph Vogel, Xavier Henry

Advertising
Charles S Fahrner

Litigation/arbitration
Louis Vogel, Joseph Vogel

Relations between France and Germany
Louis Vogel, Charles S Fahrner

Relations between France and the USA
Louis Vogel, Joseph Vogel

Automobile distribution
Joseph Vogel, Xavier Henry

THE FIRM

Louis and Joseph Vogel founded the firm of Vogel & Vogel in 1990. Since its creation the firm has grown steadily and now employs 25 attorneys (two partners and 23 associates) and 10 consultant lawyers. Vogel & Vogel, in recognition of the growing international nature of business, has always placed great importance on being able to offer its clients an international service. Accordingly, the firm has established offices in Paris, Frankfurt and Brussels. The firm has also established legal relations with other law firms around the world so as to ensure its clients a comprehensive service.

The success of Vogel & Vogel can be traced to its commitment to excellence and its promise to provide the highest quality service to its clients. Vogel & Vogel listens to its clients and seeks to become an effective tool in fulfilling their business objectives. The firm places great importance on developing long-standing relationships with its clients so as to allow the development of a true culture of understanding.

AREAS OF PRACTICE

The firm is particularly recognised for its expertise in the areas of EU and French competition law, distribution law matters, automobile law, product liability and generally all areas of international and French commercial law practice. The firm also specialises in the field of Franco-German and Franco-American legal relations. To this end both Louis and Joseph Vogel are qualified lawyers with the New York Bar.

When working with clients the firm seeks not only to advise them comprehensively as to the legal issues before them, but also endeavours to use the law as an instrument of their commercial policy. Consequently, the firm does not merely offer legal solutions, but rather seeks to apply the law in tandem with its client's business strategy. The firm is dedicated to offering a constructive, efficient and friendly service. Client contact is welcomed and partner participation is guaranteed.

WATSON, FARLEY & WILLIAMS

WATSON, FARLEY & WILLIAMS LLP

150 AVENUE DES CHAMPS-ELYSÉES
75008 PARIS

Telephone: +33 1 56 88 21 21
Fax: +33 1 56 88 21 20
Website: www.wfw.com

Languages
Afrikaans, Arabic, Cantonese, Danish, Dutch, English, French, German, Greek, Gujarati, Hebrew, Hindi, Italian, Malay, Mandarin, Marathi, Norwegian, Polish, Russian, Spanish, Swahili, Swedish, Thai

Other offices
Bangkok, Hamburg, London, New York, Piraeus, Rome, Singapore

Number of lawyers 198
at this office 17

CATEGORIES OF WORK

Banking and finance
Laurence Martinez-Bellet, Nigel Moss

Shipping and ship finance
Nigel Moss, Laurence Martinez-Bellet

Corporate
Bertrand Dumon

Trade finance and commodities
Nigel Moss, Laurence Martinez-Bellet

Private equity
Gilles Cervoni, Bertrand Dumon

Tax
Gilles Cervoni

Structured finance
Laurence Martinez-Bellet, Gilles Cervoni

Public and administrative law, PPP
Lucien Rapp

Project finance
Laurence Martinez-Bellet, Nigel Moss

Competition and antitrust
Lucien Rapp

Arbitration
Lucien Rapp, David Kavanagh

THE FIRM

Established in 1982, Watson, Farley & Williams is an international corporate and commercial law firm recognised for its excellence in banking, structured and asset financing and particularly in the transport and energy sectors. The firm also advises in a number of specialist areas in corporate law, litigation and tax law. The Paris office was opened in 1989.

The firm specialises in finance law, capital markets, corporate law, contract law, public law and private equity. The clientele of the Paris office comprises mainly French and foreign banks, investment funds and major industrial groups, both French and international.

The Paris office shares the firm's reputation for excellence in shipping finance and is also involved in aircraft finance transactions. It specialises in leasing and was the first law firm in France to implement the GIE tax regime. It is also involved in structured and commodity finance and derivatives.

The Paris office has an established practice in corporate law, including mergers and acquisitions, with or without leverage, and private equity, reinforced by the recent arrival of Bertrand Dumon.

The Paris office also has a major expertise in public and administrative law, competition and antitrust and EU law, especially in the fields of telecommunications, information technology, energy and transport, where it has been prominent in operations in the public sector (PPPs).

The Paris tax team deals with all the tax implications arising from the above transactions, both in France and internationally and now benefits from a well-established reputation for providing tax advice for mergers and acquisitions and finance transactions, as well as in estate planning.

The Paris arbitration team, led by Prof. Lucien Rapp and David Kavanagh and comprising dual-qualified French and English lawyers, has extensive experience in large-scale international arbitrations, including investment treaty and sovereign disputes, under all major institutional rules.

AREAS OF PRACTICE

A key feature is the firm's division into four international practice areas. These groups are not divided by location, but work together internationally for the firm's international clients.

International finance group: the firm's lawyers advise all project participants, covering areas such as general banking finance, structured finance, securities and capital markets, derivatives, trade finance, asset finance, project finance, cross-border tax leverage lending and leasing and work outs and insolvencies. The group has particular expertise and experience in a number of industry sectors heavily dependent on the financing of large capital assets.

International corporate group: clients have access to a wide range of domestic and international expertise covering all aspects of international corporate law, including M&A and disposals, public offerings of securities, management buy-outs and buy-ins, business and asset sales, debt structuring, equity financings, corporate restructurings, international privatisations and commercial agreements, such as distributorship, outsourcing purchase and agency agreements and joint ventures and partnerships. The group offers specialist advice on real property, intellectual property, employment/pensions, service agreements, share option and incentive schemes, executive immigration and EU competition.

International litigation group: large-scale litigation, arbitration and dispute resolution matters are handled on a worldwide basis. The firm's lawyers have represented clients involved in international disputes in banking, construction, offshore oil and gas, power and energy, international trade, shipping and aviation. The group also advises on the enforcement of security over vessels, marine pollution and insurance, shipbuilding, charterparties, and offshore oil and gas contracting.

International tax group: the firm advises on domestic/cross-border tax leasing, non-asset-based structured finance, tax planning, investigations, litigation and indirect tax. They also give advice on all types of transactions.

WEIL, GOTSHAL & MANGES

2 RUE DE LA BAUME
75008 PARIS

Telephone: +33 1 44 21 97 97
Fax: +33 1 42 89 57 90
Website: www.weil.com

Other offices
Austin, Boston, Brussels, Budapest, Dallas, Frankfurt, Houston, London, Miami, Munich, New York, Prague, Providence, Shanghai, Silicon Valley, Singapore, Warsaw, Washington DC, Wilmington

Number of lawyers 1,200
at this office 35

Contacts
Claude Serra, David Aknin

CATEGORIES OF WORK

Competition	**Private equity**
Corporate finance	**Regulation**
Intellectual property	**Reorganisation and restructuring**
Litigation, arbitration and dispute resolution	**Taxation**
Mergers and acquisitions	

THE FIRM

Weil, Gotshal & Manges is a leader in the marketplace for sophisticated, international legal services. With more than 1,200 lawyers across the US, Europe and Asia, the firm serves many of the most successful companies in the world in their high-stakes matters and transactions. Weil Gotshal has built a world-class team of lawyers by pursuing a strategy of steady, purposeful growth. It continues to build upon a balanced platform of practices and locations without acquiring any debt. The firm's three primary departments – corporate, litigation/regulatory and restructuring – provide healthy diversification in all economic cycles, while its international expansion over the past decade has resulted in a quarter of the firm's lawyers now being in Europe.

AREAS OF PRACTICE

The firm's antitrust/competition practice advises on international M&A regulatory notifications, antitrust distribution counselling, cartels, litigation and government and state competition policy.

The corporate department is the firm's largest, with lawyers in the US and across Europe. The department advises international financial institutions and corporate clients in complex public and private mergers and acquisitions, private equity deals, strategic alliances and other commercial transactions.

The firm's corporate governance practice is recognised as the pre-eminent counsellor of corporate boards, management and institutional investors on the full range of governance issues, including board composition, structure and processes; executive and director compensation; director responsibilities, including in connection with mergers, spin-offs and other extraordinary transactions; internal and governmental investigations of alleged accounting or other corporate misconduct; and shareholder initiatives.

The firm is recognised as a market leader in the handling of complex and innovative finance transactions internationally. The firm advises on a wide range of financing activities and has particular expertise in acquisition finance, asset-based finance, debt restructuring and insolvency, debt and equity capital markets, derivatives, high yield debt, securitisation, structured finance and telecom and multimedia financing.

The firm has a leading intellectual property and technology practice and advises a number of the world's major technology, media and telecommunications companies. It also acts for investors in technology, media and communications entities. The practice handles patent infringement, outsourcing transactions, strategic alliances, cross-border mergers and acquisitions, investments and IPOs. The firm advises on the protection and exploitation of IP and on a wide range of e-commerce matters including data protection. It has expertise in regulatory telecoms matters.

The firm's litigation practice advises international clients on all major areas of the law and has extensive experience in all aspects of dispute resolution. It advises clients in jury trials and appeals, as well as arbitration and alternative dispute forums.

The firm's real estate practice handles complex real estate transactions (including finance, securitisations, development, leasing, sales, acquisitions and debt restructurings) across the US and Europe. It also advises clients on real estate M&A transactions and transactions involving real estate investment trusts.

The firm has one of the largest, most broadly based bankruptcy and business reorganisation practices in the world. The department has been involved in virtually all major chapter 11 reorganisation cases in the US and in major national and international out of court debt restructurings.

The tax department provides advice to a broad range of international clients, covering many economic sectors. The department works closely with the firm's other departments to find innovative solutions to problems that present various and competing multidisciplinary considerations.

WILLKIE FARR & GALLAGHER LLP

21-23 RUE DE LA VILLE L'EVÊQUE
75008 PARIS

Telephone: +33 1 53 43 45 00
Fax: +33 1 40 06 96 06
Website: www.willkie.com

Languages
English, French, German

Other offices
Brussels, Frankfurt, London, Milan, New York, Rome, Washington DC

Number of lawyers 590
at this office 54

Contacts
Daniel Payan, Daniel Hurstel

CATEGORIES OF WORK

Mergers and acquisitions
Daniel Payan, Laurent Faugérolas, Daniel Hurstel, Annette Péron, Jeffrey Fouts, Eduardo Fernandez, Christophe Garaud, Cédric Hajage, Emmanuel Scialom

Securities and capital markets
Laurent Faugérolas, Daniel Hurstel, Daniel Payan

Business reorganisation and restructuring
Alexandra Bigot, Patricia Le Marchand

Tax
Allard de Waal, Bernard Le-Pezron, Marie-Hélène Raffin, Philippe Grudé

Litigation
Dominique Mondoloni

WINSTON & STRAWN LLP

21 AVENUE VICTOR HUGO
75116 PARIS

Telephone: +33 1 53 64 82 82
Fax: +33 1 53 64 82 20
E-mail: info@winston.com
Website: www.winston.com

Languages
Creole, Chinese, English, French, German, Hebrew, Italian, Spanish

Other offices
Chicago, Geneva, London, Los Angeles, Moscow, New York, San Francisco, Washington DC

Number of lawyers 850
at this office 34

Contact
Vincent Sol

CATEGORIES OF WORK

Corporate
Patrick Murray, W Paul Bishop, Alexandre Brue, Robert Flanigan, Jérôme Herbet, Antoine Martin, Vincent Trevisani

Energy
Vincent Trevisani

Environmental
Vincent Sol, Joelle Herschtel

Labour and employment relations
Sébastien Ducamp

Dispute resolution – litigation – arbitration
Joel Alquezar, Bruno Leurent, Gilles Bigot, Alexandre Bailly

Public & business law
Frédéric Scanvic

GERMANY

Population	**82.5 million**
Number of lawyers	**116,000**
Professional title	**Rechtsanwalt Rechtsanwältin**
Currency	**Euro (€)**

Index

Germany is a federal state that covers a substantial geographical area between Western and Central and Eastern Europe. It stretches from the border with Denmark and the North Sea, to the South, where it meets the Alps mountain range of Austria and Switzerland. Germany has 16 states, each with its own parliament, judiciary and administration. In 2002 it adopted the euro (€).

The head of government changed in 2005, with Chancellor Gerhard Schröder's term of office ending in November, Schröder having been in power since 27 October 1998. His successor Angela Merkel is the first female German chancellor and she heads a 'grand coalition' between the Christian Democratic Union Party and the Social Democratic Party. Both have dominated German politics over the years and commentators have speculated that the two traditionally rival factions will find consensus hard to reach in government. There is much conjecture as to when the 'grand coalition' may break down.

Beyond central government, Germany's federal structure indulges significant power to the regional states. Closely allied to this is an economy that is strikingly decentralised. Though Frankfurt is the financial centre and the home of Germany's Stock Exchange, it is a relatively small city and many banks are based outside, notably in Hamburg. Berlin is of course the administrative hub and an important media centre, while one of the most active industrial and manufacturing regions is the Rhine-Ruhr and many of Germany's leading law firms have offices nearby in Cologne and Düsseldorf. Furthermore with the Federal Cartel Office in Bonn, firms also have an incentive to be based in the region, particularly as EU modernisation has confirmed greater powers on national antitrust regulators.

Hamburg, in the north, is the country's second-largest city and is home to Europe's second-biggest port. Most of Germany's shipping law specialists are based here. It is also a media centre, having traditionally hosted a number of major publishing houses. Family-owned businesses and trading companies are an important part of the regional economy.

Stuttgart, and the Swabian district, is another important contributor to the economy. Medium-sized and family owned businesses (Mittelstand) are plentiful, while blue-chip corporates such as DaimlerChrysler and Porsche are also present. Southwest of Stuttgart is the Bavarian capital, Munich. Munich is a prosperous city and the surrounding region has become home to the tech boom. Siemens is based here, while a host of biotech and pharmaceutical companies have also chosen the area as their home. Following this development, many of the world's most acquisitive private equity funds have set up operations in Munich.

BILLING

Undoubtedly German lawyers' fees are lower than in London and New York. Nevertheless as German firms have traditionally operated a different model to UK outfits the difference in rates won't be immediately apparent. German firms tend to operate a low gearing structure with fewer associates to every partner. To some extent this means partners are obliged to deal with the demanding aspects of a mandate as well as the more straightforward issues. This has a direct effect on fees, with partners having to accommodate the two-levelled nature of their practice and hence premium rates have to follow. Nevertheless, Germany's improving economy and the fact that firms are becoming more Anglo-Saxon in nature means fees are rising steadily. According to the German Lawyers' Fee Regulations (BRAGO), the fee charged by a lawyer should be based on the value of the case in question. These fees were supposed to be adjusted in 2002 but the proposed reform failed.

Hourly rates for partners at international law firms are now often above €300. Local firms will however charge significantly less. Anecdotal evidence from clients suggests that the billing procedure should be negotiated before a firm is instructed. With the advent of competitive pitches and legal panels, law firms will normally set out a fee structure before taking on work.

MARKETING

Germany has become a truly international legal market and subsequently the attitudes towards marketing are no longer conservative. Competition amongst law firms and lawyers has encouraged firms to promote their services as best they can. In previous years, individual partners relied on their own reputations to win business. This situation remains to a degree, with a handful of leading partners being integral to client relationships. **Shearman & Sterling LLP**'s Georg

The largest firms

1	**Freshfields Bruckhaus Deringer**	**563**
2	**Clifford Chance**	**434**
3	**CMS Hasche Sigle**	**420**
4	**Linklaters Oppenhoff & Rädler**	**330**
5	**Lovells**	**310**
6	**Taylor Wessing**	**237**
7	**Luther Rechtsanwaltsgesellschaft mbH**	**230**
	White & Case LLP	**230**
9	**Hengeler Mueller**	**203**
10	**Beiten Burkhardt**	**191**
	Nörr Stiefenhofer Lutz	**191**
12	**Gleiss Lutz**	**186**
13	**Baker & McKenzie**	**159**
14	**Heuking Kühn Lüer Wojtek**	**158**
15	**Allen & Overy LLP**	**127**
16	**Graf von Westphalen Bappert & Modest**	**123**
17	**Buse Heberer Fromm**	**113**
18	**Latham & Watkins LLP**	**111**
19	**Flick Gocke Schaumburg**	**110**
20	**GSK Gassner Stockmann & Kollegen**	**107**
21	**Haarmann Hemmelrath**	**105**
22	**Rödl & Partner GbR**	**101**
23	**Shearman & Sterling LLP**	**100**
24	**GÖRG Partnerschaft von Rechtsanwälten**	**95**
25	**FPS Fritze Paul Seelig**	**90**

These figures represent the total number of lawyers in this country only, and have been supplied by the firms themselves. The figures should be accurate as at 1 January 2006.

Thoma for instance is known to have outstanding connections to German corporates such as Allianz and DaimlerChrysler. But with the onset of professional marketing and business development departments amongst the international players, designed to promote the firm and to win pitches, the rest are to some extent obliged to play ball. Websites are virtually ubiquitous for all the major law firms in Germany. Most will also reveal further details about their track records in the various practice areas. Following the revision of the official Code of Conduct for Lawyers (Berufsordnung) in 1997, most firms will employ marketing strategies to promote their services. Prior to this, marketing activities were strictly forbidden.

Most firms now publish their recent instructions or at least reveal something of their recent workload to the press. Many will also list the firms that acted for the other parties in a transaction or mandate and hence the press is able to build an accurate picture of the leading advisers in the various legal disciplines.

IN-HOUSE LAWYERS

In-house legal departments (Rechtsabteilungen) are much more prominent in Germany than in many other jurisdictions. This has a profound effect on the legal market, where for instance BMW has an immense in-house department that virtually never seeks outside counsel. Other blue-chip corporates like Siemens have sizeable in-house teams that rarely instruct private practice. With the onset of specialisation this is changing and private practice law firms have worked hard to develop their specific industry knowledge. Yet with so many in-house departments moving in the same direction, employing their resources to the various legal areas, law firms have to be realistic about which clients will provide them with consistent levels of business.

ECONOMY

Germany's economy recovered in 2005 and anecdotal evidence suggests that the legal market is busier than it has been for some five years. Germany's economy has performed poorly since 2000 and unemployment has reached concerning levels, particularly in Eastern Germany or the former German Democratic Republic. Invariably re-integration of West and East Germany has been a long and arduous process. It is fair to say that Eastern Germany has struggled to embrace a new capitalist and free-trade culture and this despite significant funds being provided by central government.

Berlin's re-emergence as the administrative capital was expected to enable it to become a key business centre again. It has struggled to achieve this and **Clifford Chance**'s closure of its office there suggested that many law firms no longer saw it as an essential place to exist. That said the growth of the media sector there has enthused many others.

Germany's unemployed grew to 10.6% of the population in 2004. GDP growth was a meagre 1.7%. It has one of the slowest-growing economies in the EU. Insolvencies, including that of KirchMedia, have been prevalent.

LEGAL MARKET

2005 was a relatively uneventful year compared to the previous year. In 2004, severe restructuring particularly among the Anglo-German international firms saw groups of partners exit and look for alternative places to pursue their legal careers. **Clifford Chance**, **Linklaters Oppenhoff & Rädler** and **Lovells** were the most obvious, but **Freshfields Bruckhaus Deringer** has not escaped the need to review the performance of its partnership and make some serious changes.

While many partners have sought new homes to extend their careers, numerous others have moved firms for bureaucratic and remuneration reasons. The lockstep compensation structure operated mainly by firms of a UK origin has become somewhat unpopular amongst Germans. Furthermore the levels of management in UK firms tends to be greater, conflicting with the widespread consensus amongst German partners that they prefer to concentrate on the day-to-day business or as many of them refer to as being intrinsically entrepreneurial.

In 2004, many new firms spun-off from large international outfits, but in 2005 the market regained some semblance of stability.

Lovells' former Germany managing partner Oliver Felsenstein chose to join **Clifford Chance** and further enhance the Magic Circle firm's prestigious privat e equity practice. **Lovells** also lost Oliver Kessler and Jens Rinze who elected to launch **Sidley Austin**'s new Frankfurt office.

Over at **Haarmann Hemmelrath**, the shock resignation of founding partner Wilhelm Haarmann precipitated a throng of departures, mainly amongst the most senior individuals. Andreas Oldenbourg who left to launch **Oldenbourg Plus**, Heinrich Rodewig and Thomas Krempl moved to **Taylor Wessing** and Christoph von Einem switched over to **White & Case LLP**. The Berlin office was taken over by international law firm **Salans** at the start of 2006, while at the same time former founding partner Wilhelm Haarmann launched a spin-off firm. Other partners have also sought new homes and inevitably the future of the firm has been thrown into question.

Aside from this, the profitability pressures on many international firms appear to have hindered them from electing large numbers of new partners. The direct result is that many senior associates have departed from the large international firms to either launch new practices or take partnership at another firm. **GREENFORT Partnerschaft von Rechtsanwälten** was launched in April 2005, comprising former senior associates from **Freshfields Bruckhaus Deringer** and **Hengeler Mueller**.

ANTITRUST

Freshfields Bruckhaus Deringer's leading European practice is augmented by a formidable team in Germany. With the respected Martin Klusmann leading the German department alongside the immensely experienced Gerhard Wiedemann, the firm has a department capable of dealing with the full range of antitrust issues including merger control, cartel issues and abuse of dominance cases. **Freshfields Bruckhaus Deringer** also has an established German team in Brussels.

Gleiss Lutz features Germany's leading antitrust lawyer, Rainer Bechtold (Stuttgart) and the department is now headed by Ingo Brinker (Munich). Established clients include DaimlerChrysler, Volkswagen, Munich Re and Infineon, demonstrating the firm's eminence in this segment. Matthias Karl is a truly up-and-coming name, while the firm is well represented in Brussels through Ulrich Soltécz and Simon Hirsbrunner.

Hengeler Mueller has an established track record in merger control, but also a burgeoning business in cartel issues and abuse of dominance. Jochen Burrichter is another prominent name in the German antitrust sector and with an impressive three partners in Brussels and a fruitful relationship with **Slaughter and May** in London, **Hengeler Mueller** offers essential European coverage. Thus it was chosen to represent Deutsche Börse on its bid to acquire the London Stock Exchange, one of the most complex and long-running merger hearings of recent years.

CMS Hasche Sigle boasts a sizeable department featuring 12 partners who have extensive experience of antitrust matters. The firm is particularly strong in the utilities sector, with recent involvement in a gas cartel investigation. Harald Kahlenberg remains the firm's key name, with an outstanding reputation.

With Dirk Schröder in the driving seat, **Cleary, Gottlieb, Steen & Hamilton LLP**'s Cologne-based antitrust practice boasts a range of prestigious regular clients, including Citigroup, Deutsche Telekom, Deutsche Post, Bayer and E.ON. The team handles some 40% merger control work as well as a significant amount of cartel cases. Lead partner Dirk Schröder has an outstanding reputation and should also be commended for antitrust litigation. The younger Romina Polley is also emerging as a leading name, while excellent German antitrust partner Stephan Barthelmess in Brussels should also be noted. Wolfgang Deselaers has transferred to Cologne.

Though **Linklaters Oppenhoff & Rädler** has a strong operation in Cologne under Wolfgang Deselaers, its Brussels branch, where it houses several German partners, gains numerous recommendations from clients. Anne Federle is picked out in particular for being extremely dedicated and hard working, but clients also applaud the firm's strong industry knowledge. 'They know the company, our products and our industry,' one said. Cologne partner Daniela Seeliger is also applauded by clients who also support the election of Carsten Grave to the partnership. Both are recommended for abuse of dominance cases.

Shearman & Sterling LLP's fine antitrust practice is headed by the excellent Hans-Jurgen Meyer Lindemann. It has a formidable portfolio of blue-chip clients thanks in part to the fabulous connections of the corporate department, but this has brought the team into a series of challenging instructions, allowing it to further build its business on a standalone basis. The firm represented LuK before the German Federal Cartel Office and the Tribunal de Grande Instance in Paris, in relation to an alleged abuse of a dominant position in the dual-weighted flywheels market.

ANTITRUST

FRESHFIELDS BRUCKHAUS DERINGER
GLEISS LUTZ ✪

HENGELER MUELLER ✪

CMS Hasche Sigle ✪
Cleary, Gottlieb, Steen & Hamilton LLP ✪
Linklaters Oppenhoff & Rädler ✪
Shearman & Sterling LLP
Wilmer Cutler Pickering Hale and Dorr LLP ✪

Baker & McKenzie ✪
Clifford Chance
Latham & Watkins LLP
Lovells ✪
Oppenländer Rechtsanwälte
Schulte Rechtsanwaltsgesellschaft mbH

Allen & Overy LLP ✪
Bird & Bird ✪
Gibson, Dunn & Crutcher LLP
Graf von Westphalen Bappert & Modest ✪
Haver & Mailänder
Heuking Kühn Lüer Wojtek ✪
Hogan & Hartson Raue L.L.P. ✪
Jones Day
Mayer, Brown, Rowe & Maw LLP ✪
McDermott Will & Emery Rechtsanwälte Steuerberater LLP ✪
Nörr Stiefenhofer Lutz ✪
Norton Rose Vieregge
SJ Berwin LLP ✪
Taylor Wessing ✪
White & Case LLP

Firms are listed A-Z in tiers which are ranked in order of priority
✪ *Indicates firm displays contact details at the end of this chapter.*

Wilmer Cutler Pickering Hale and Dorr LLP has a world-leading antitrust practice and its Berlin branch is playing an evermore important role in supporting this esteemed brand. Ulrich Quack remains a prominent name in the market, as is the seasoned Karlheinz Quack. Despite the firm's reputation in Germany for representing the public sector, it has provided counsel to a series of significant blue-chip corporates in the national and European courts. It is also known for merger control issues and boasts blue-chip clients such as Bayer Healthcare and Deutsche Telekom.

Baker & McKenzie's senior level features Jörg-Martin Schultze in Frankfurt and Thomas Lampert in Brussels. The team completed a successful leniency application to the European Commission during 2005. Compliance audits have been an integral part of the practice in recent months.

Clifford Chance's antitrust presence is largely based in Dusseldorf under the auspices of the respected Joachim Schütze. The firm's blossoming M&A business brings the practice a sizeable number of merger control mandates. It is also well regarded for state aid cases with Holger Wissel to the fore. The practice is known in particular for its work in the telecoms, healthcare and energy sectors. Martin Bechtold leads the German-facing practice from Brussels.

State aid is very much the core of **Latham & Watkins LLP**'s esteemed practice, led by Marco Núñez Müller. The team has handled several important cases in the aviation sector of late. The department also provided merger control advice to Clerical Medical and was instructed on a significant cartel case in the paper recycling industry. With Andreas Weitbrecht in Brussels, the firm has a well-rounded practice.

Lovells' depleted ranks following the loss of Thomas Jestaedt to **Jones Day** in Brussels, leaves Düsseldorf-based partner Martin Sura shouldering much of the firm's heavy antitrust burden. With Walter Klosterfelde's imminent retirement, it was essential that the firm's senior ranks were augmented and with Christian Bahr's election to the partnership, the firm went some way to achieving this. The firm's private equity clients have brought a significant portion of merger control work to the practice and it continues to be heavily involved in cartel investigations.

Albrecht Bach at **Oppenländer Rechtsanwälte** is highly reputed and the firm is known for its role in many cartel infringement cases. It should also be recognised for antitrust litigation.

Schulte Rechtsanwaltsgesellschaft mbH is particularly strong in the financial services segment and a significant portion of the firm's business is antitrust thanks to the efforts of Josef Schulte and Michael Ewen and a sizeable team. The firm's prestigious client base has included names such as Deutsche Bank.

Allen & Overy LLP's growing presence in antitrust law brought it into two major cartel investigations during 2005. The team, headed by Ellen Braun, includes of-counsel Hermann-Josef Bunte and offers a strong presence, mainly in Hamburg.

Bird & Bird's practice is headed by Klaus-Jürgen Michaeli and is supported by several senior individuals in the firm's highly regarded intellectual property department, who have years of antitrust experience. The firm represented DRK, alleging abuse of dominant position by Chiron in connection with parent loyalties, this outlining the firm's strong IP influenced practice.

Gibson, Dunn & Crutcher LLP's antitrust practice is led by Michael Walther, which balances some 70% national filings against 30% EU filings. Walther comes from an IP background.

Graf von Westphalen Bappert & Modest's notable antitrust practice is linked in part to the firm's strengths in the pharmaceuticals, chemicals and foodstuffs sectors. Though much of its workload is merger control, leading partners Carsten Bittner and Lothar Harings are also known for cartel case capabilities.

Stuttgart-based **Haver & Mailänder** has another established practice backed by a Brussels office. The firm is best known for media and telecoms-related work as well as state aid issues.

Heuking Kühn Lüer Wojtek has added further credibility to its antitrust practice with the hire of **Wilmer Cutler Pickering Hale and Dorr LLP** senior associate Rainer Velte as a partner in Berlin in 2005. Gabrielle Williamson, based in Brussels, has an excellent reputation for state aid, cartels and broader antitrust matters.

Hogan & Hartson Raue L.L.P. has a stellar practice, most notably in the media sector. Christoph Wagner and Eckhard Bremer should be identified in this respect. The firm frequently represents ProSiebenSat.1 in antitrust matters.

Jones Day's Frankfurt-based antitrust practice is led by Carsten Gromotke, but was significantly enhanced by the arrival of former **Lovells** partner Thomas Jestaedt in Brussels. The German operation has a prestigious record in high-value merger control.

Christofer Eggers leads the department at **Mayer, Brown, Rowe & Maw LLP** which features the respected Hans-Georg Kamann. The firm has broad expertise and represented BASF AG in a major vitamin cartel case.

McDermott Will & Emery Rechtsanwälte Steuerberater LLP should be noted for its antitrust work in the technology sector. Thomas Hauss leads the practice which has recently acquired a major mobile telecoms company as a new client. The team often represents major international corporations in connection with their German antitrust demands.

Nörr Stiefenhofer Lutz has a solid media-related practice with Berlin partner Karsten Metzlaff leading the cartel practice. Consolidation in the broadcasting sector has been an important source of business in recent years.

Norton Rose Vieregge's competition practice is headed by Michael Jürgen Werner and represents prestigious clients such as easyJet, Imperial Logistics and Carlsberg.

SJ Berwin LLP has a leading European antitrust practice now augmented by the increasing prominence of the firm's German operation, particularly in Munich. Alexander Rinne heads the practice which is active on a domestic and international level.

Taylor Wessing's technology and IP practice provides the basis for its EU and competition business. Its burgeoning corporate transactional business is also an important source of merger control work.

Hamburg-based Jörg Schmeding and Antje Mattfeld lead **White & Case LLP**'s antitrust efforts. Its transaction-related expertise was demonstrated by its advice to EDEKA Zentrale on the merger control filings regarding its takeover of SPAR AG.

BANKING AND FINANCE

Allen & Overy LLP remains a key player in the market, best known for its quality acquisition finance practice. Of late it has made inroads into the active real estate finance and NPL sectors, as well as the project finance arena, with Peter Stenz advising the banks on helicopter, wind-park and power station mandates. Practice head Peter Hoegen is leading the firm's initiative in the real estate and NPL markets, for clients such as ABN Amro, Eurohypo and Barclays Capital. German senior partner Neil Weiand remains a prominent name in bank lending and clients appreciate his insight and his 'sense of ease when explaining things to a client'. Hoegen and Matthew Howard are working hard to develop the firm's brand in structured finance and securitisation. Wolfgang Melzer leads the asset finance practice.

Clifford Chance's strong banking and finance brand is significantly augmented by a large, evidently capable and broadly skilled team in Frankfurt. With notable strength in obvious areas such as acquisition, leveraged and asset finance, the firm also boasts a strong reputation in project finance for both domestic and broader international work under Nick Wong, Riko Vanezis (particularly airports) and Beda Wortmann. The firm has handled several transactions in Turkey on behalf of HypoVereinsbank and in Central and Eastern Europe. Riko Vanezis remains an important figure in the area of aircraft finance for a variety of banks. Beda Wortmann is the firm's key real estate finance practitioner, again for a prestigious list of banks and borrowers. On acquisition finance, Bettina Steinhauer and Barbara Mayer-Trautmann lead in Frankfurt and Munich respectively, the latter also being known for leveraged buy-outs.

Linklaters Oppenhoff & Rädler continues to offer a prominent and respected acquisition finance practice led by Carl-Peter Feick. 'From my perspective they have a depth of talent that not many of the other Frankfurt-based law firms can rival,' one client enthused. Of late, the practice has engaged more actively in the real estate finance market as well as further involvement in the NPL sector. For acquisition and real estate finance, clients commend the up-and-coming Sabine Felix in particular. 'She is an extremely well organised lawyer and very clear in her recommendations,' one said. The team also includes experienced partner Eva Reudelhuber who clients praise for her quick response times and effective management. Clients also value the 'strong performance' of Frankfurt-based English partner John Stansfield and newly elected partner Marc Trinkaus, a syndicated lending and acquisition finance specialist. In addition, Andreas Steck provides solid bank supervisory and regulatory expertise. 'They take a more collaborative approach as a culture and are prepared to give more colour on legal interpretation,' one client added.

BANKING AND FINANCE

ALLEN & OVERY LLP ✪
CLIFFORD CHANCE
LINKLATERS OPPENHOFF & RÄDLER ✪

FRESHFIELDS BRUCKHAUS DERINGER
HENGELER MUELLER ✪
WHITE & CASE LLP

GLEISS LUTZ ✪
MILBANK, TWEED, HADLEY & McCLOY LLP ✪

Ashurst ✪
Baker & McKenzie ✪
CMS Hasche Sigle ✪
Cleary, Gottlieb, Steen & Hamilton LLP ✪
Latham & Watkins LLP
Lovells ✪
Mayer, Brown, Rowe & Maw LLP ✪
Norton Rose Vieregge

Debevoise & Plimpton LLP ✪
Dewey Ballantine LLP ✪
GSK Gassner Stockmann & Kollegen ✪
Görg Partnerschaft von Rechtsanwälten ✪
Haarmann Hemmelrath ✪
Nörr Stiefenhofer Lutz ✪
Shearman & Sterling LLP
Simmons & Simmons ✪
Taylor Wessing ✪
Weil, Gotshal & Manges ✪

Bette – Brink, Rechtsanwälte ✪
Graf von Westphalen Bappert & Modest ✪
Luther Rechtsanwaltsgesellschaft mbH ✪
SJ Berwin LLP ✪

Firms are listed A-Z in tiers which are ranked in order of priority
✪ Indicates firm displays contact details at the end of this chapter.

Freshfields Bruckhaus Deringer covers all areas of financing, with particular potency in the active real estate segment. Aircraft, ship and rolling stock financing remain core to the business and the firm traditionally dominates this sector with the experienced Dirk Schmalenbach and Konrad Schott to the fore. In acquisition finance the firm tends to be borrower led, but with an increased focus on finance as a whole it is gradually being rewarded by more instructions from banks such as Citibank and Deutsche Bank. Yorck Jetter and Ralph Kästner are leading this initiative, while Christian Bunsen and Daniel Reichert-Facilides head up project finance.

Hengeler Mueller continues to be a first port of call for clients with particularly complex demands and in bank regulatory issues, and structured finance, the firm is hard to match. A fine mix of mandates from leading investment banks as well as corporates continues with the excellent Hendrig Haag advising adidas-Salomon on a revolving credit facility, and the firm has also played a significant role in the NPL sector having advised Citigroup on its acquisition of an NPL portfolio from Hypo Real Estate, through a joint venture with Eurohypo. On the acquisition finance front the firm represented Deutsche Bank and CSFB on Axel Springer's purchase of a majority stake in ProSiebenSat.1. Thomas Cron, Johannes Tieves and Martin Geiger should be noted in this respect, while on structured finance there is no lawyer with a greater reputation than Stefan Krauss.

White & Case LLP now warrants a more prestigious standing in the banking and finance arena and this is reflected in a promotion in the rankings. The firm is now a trusted adviser of several leading banks in Germany and much credit should be given to Annica Lindegren who is applauded by one client for being 'always supportive and very good with the client and other parties'. Others see real value in her experience and constant availability. **White & Case LLP** is also trusted with high-value transactions thanks to what banks regard as a sizeable team with quality across the department. Clients also highlight Stephen Hodgson as a 'top lawyer' for project finance, though he is commended for his all-round experience, technical acumen and 'putting things in perspective'. Commerzbank remains a key client, but a broader portfolio of banking clients that trust the firm with high-value and complex transactions suggests that its promotion in the rankings this year is well deserved. Eberhard Meincke leads the team in Hamburg, known in particular for regulatory work and being the relationship partner for HSH Nordbank.

Gleiss Lutz is commended for dramatic steps forward in acquisition finance, much to the credit of department head Burkhard Jäkel. The traditionally borrower-led practice is gaining recognition from the banks thanks in part to the efforts of Andreas Wölfle on secondment to **Herbert Smith LLP** in London. Furthermore, the firm's efforts to augment its Frankfurt office have not gone unnoticed by banks. Helge Kortz and Olaf Otting (regulatory issues) should also be mentioned.

Milbank, Tweed, Hadley & McCloy LLP boasts a small but excellent finance team led by Rainer Magold, regarded by clients as the 'guru of acquisition finance in Germany'. Magold and his team are thought to be 'experienced and pleasant to deal with' and effective on mid-cap to high-value transactions. He is also known in particular for private equity sector financing for both borrowers and banks. Associate Thomas Ingenhoven is also highlighted by clients as an extremely capable young lawyer.

Ashurst's banking and finance standing should be augmented by the arrival of 'dynamic and experienced' Tom Beckerhoff from **Norton Rose Vieregge** in January 2006. Beckerhoff provides greater expertise across the finance arena, but gives the firm vital project finance capabilities. Clients have expressed a need for the firm to develop greater levels of expertise and experience across the team and Beckerhoff's arrival should go some way to achieving this. It remains a strong player in acquisition and leveraged finance, particularly in relation to private equity transactions, where the firm has represented borrowers such as key client Bain Capital. Furthermore, lead partner Stephan Kock is becoming increasingly active in the active real estate finance sector. Andreas Zahn provides the structured finance acumen.

Following the departure of Rainer Magold and Christina Ungeheuer to **Milbank, Tweed, Hadley & McCloy LLP**, **Baker & McKenzie**'s practice is no longer dominated by acquisition finance instructions. Though in Munich partner Michael Foundethakis and department head Olaf Gebler this discipline is ably covered, with the former being identified by one client as having 'flexibility and creativity in finding solutions and reaching consent in difficult situations'. The firm remains strong in aircraft finance for clients such as Lufthansa and Eurowings, while it is increasingly eminent in project finance for banks including Dresdner.

CMS Hasche Sigle's acquisition finance practice is driven to a major extent by its private equity business with Christoph Schücking, Herbert Wiehe (formerly **Norton Rose Vieregge**) and Mark Riede to the fore. The Hamburg office provides much of the asset finance strength, in the ship and rolling stock sectors in particular.

Cleary, Gottlieb, Steen & Hamilton LLP's excellent reputation in Germany extends to banking and finance where it represented Citigroup Financial Products in the formation of a consortium to acquire a €394m real estate loan portfolio from Hypo Real Estate Bank. John Palenberg led on the transaction, but Christof von Dryander should be mentioned for strong banking connections and regulatory knowledge. The firm's esteemed record also includes advising Citigroup on the acquisition of a €2.4bn NPL portfolio from Eurohypo, outlining its reputation in the banking sector.

Latham & Watkins LLP's Uwe Eyles is one of the foremost banking regulatory lawyers in Germany. The firm is also strong in leveraged finance, with international clients such as CSFB and Goldman Sachs now delivering instructions on a regular basis. Unusually, the firm handles much of the business from Hamburg, through Nikolaus Lorenz in particular, but its efforts to grow in Frankfurt have proved crucial in winning the attentions of domestic and international banks.

Lovells' regulatory and asset finance reputation dominates and again unusually Berlin-based Thomas Lindemann and Andreas Schwennicke are the firm's most recognised practitioners. Its excellent media standing has provided a solid basis for a flourishing film finance practice, but the aviation sector has also been fruitful. Acquisition and leveraged finance for the firm's bustling private equity business should not go unnoticed.

Mayer, Brown, Rowe & Maw LLP remains strong in the structured finance sector with considerable run-off from its active role in Germany's active NPL sector on behalf of key clients Lone Star and Eurohypo. Manfred Heeman retains an esteemed reputation with Jörg Wulfken also a key name.

Norton Rose Vieregge is carving out a position as the alternative to the dominant and large firms in Germany. Clients expressed an appreciation of its efficient role on multi-jurisdictional transactions, though recognised that the size of the team and its relative lack of experience limits its exposure to higher-value deals. Ralf Springer is commended by clients for 'putting the problems of the client on centre stage and trying to provide solutions rather than answers'. His acquisition finance expertise is 'undoubted' according to one, though his background is in asset finance, particularly in the aviation sector. Senior associate Tomas Gärdfors is also widely praised for understanding the 'commercial fundamentals' and 'economics' of transactions. 'He's very responsive, down to earth, direct and never loses his sense of humour and that makes working with him so enjoyable,' one client said. He led the team advising Commerzbank on the closing of €140m senior credit facilities to support the refinancing of OEM automotive supplier Carcoustics International GmbH. Dirk Trautmann is becoming increasingly active in project finance, though the departure of Tom Beckerhoff to **Ashurst** is a loss.

Debevoise & Plimpton LLP's strength is in asset finance, through the vastly experienced Hans Bertram-Nothnagel. Much of the work is in the aviation sector with clients such Swiss International Airlines.

Dewey Ballantine LLP's Philipp von Ilberg is an eminent acquisition finance and syndicated lending lawyer and with the firm's expanding resources in Frankfurt it is making a further impact. Bernd Fahrholz was chairman of the board of management at Dresdner Bank, before joining the firm in 2003, giving it further banking credibility. Von Ilberg is greatly admired by local and international banks.

GSK Gassner Stockmann & Kollegen's strong real estate practice has enabled the firm to develop an impressive property finance business, with the firm now representing a significant portion of the most active real estate investment funds in Germany. Markus Escher provides notable bank regulatory expertise. Bertold Frisch in Frankfurt should also be mentioned.

GÖRG Partnerschaft von Rechtsanwälten is gaining prominence in the project finance sector thanks in part to the efforts of Frankfurt partner Mark Kersting. However in 2005, the firm's Cologne office advised on the largest project-financed power plant project ever in Germany, a 800 Megawatt gas/steam project in Hamm-Uentrop in which the firm advised the sponsors led by Trianel, on matters which included a debt financing of around €350m. It is also becoming increasingly active in the NPL sector thanks to its roots as a top-tier restructuring firm.

Haarmann Hemmelrath's London office is providing the firm with greater credentials in the banking and finance sector. In real estate refinancing it is increasingly prominent as well as in the lucrative NPL sector. During 2005, the firm advised JP MorganChase on the acquisition of a non-performing and sub-performing loan portfolio from DZ Bank in Frankfurt. David von Saucken, Gordon Stewart (London) and Andreas Lehmann led the team. Andreas Lehmann also advised Lone Star on the acquisition of a NPL portfolio from Aareal Bank.

Nörr Stiefenhofer Lutz's borrower-oriented practice is led by the experienced Hans-Günther Nordhues. Leveraged work in the private equity sector is growing, but the firm is also making inroads with the key investment banks.

Shearman & Sterling LLP's small banking and finance practice is known especially for refinancing restructuring and a growing element of acquisition finance work. At present its corporate profile completely overshadows what it has on the finance side, but the efforts of Johannes Kremer and Andreas Diem are going some way to achieving parity. Diem recently advised HVB and Mizuho as co-arrangers on financing the acquisition of ATU Auto Teile-Unger group by KKR.

Continual investment into the finance sector has brought rewards to **Simmons & Simmons**. Thanks in no small part to the efforts of the widely admired Ingrid Kalisch, the firm has begun to represent banks such as ING, Barclays and ABN Amro in Germany. It also provided acquisition finance advice to a borrower in the tourism sector. With the arrival of Frank Thomas, having disbanded his old firm, **Simmons & Simmons** now has substantial aircraft and rolling stock finance business. Stephen Moller leads the structured finance segment.

Following the hire of Claus Goedecke, **Taylor Wessing**'s banking and finance department has been further enhanced by the arrival of real estate finance specialist Reinhard Bartholomäi and structured finance expert Thomas Kulzer, both from **Freshfields Bruckhaus Deringer**. Property finance is especially active for both international investors and banks. Peter Seeman should be noted for acquisition finance issues.

Weil, Gotshal & Manges should be identified for borrower work in particular. The practice appears largely driven by its burgeoning private equity business and in turn, its acquisitive clients in the NPL market. Tom Schorling is the key individual in this respect.

Other practices with solid traditions in banking and finance include **Bette – Brink, Rechtsanwälte** where Klaus Bette and Ulrich Brink are known to represent both domestic and international clients.

Not the classic name in banking, **Graf von Westphalen Bappert & Modest** has concentrated hard on developing this area, alongside UK alliance partner **Wragge & Co LLP**. Like many other firms, it is also active in the NPL sector. Michael Nicolaus and Frank Büchler are the key partners, with Clemens Jobe on the NPL side.

Luther Rechtsanwaltsgesellschaft mbH retains a banking presence despite the loss of respected practice head Ingrid Kalisch to **Simmons & Simmons** in 2003.

SJ Berwin LLP's Thomas Schrell is becoming increasingly recognised by the banking sector and is known for having a 'sharp mind' and being a good 'technician' particularly in relation to structuring the debt. He appears to be actively building his business at the firm following his defection from **Lovells** in 2004.

CAPITAL MARKETS

In terms of pure expertise, **Cleary, Gottlieb, Steen & Hamilton LLP** boasts one of the foremost capital markets practices in Germany with an impressive market share of the nation's most prestigious and demanding transactions. The firm has represented clients such as HypoVereinsbank for many years and in 2004 it acted for Deutsche Post and Deutsche Postbank in Postbank's €1.5bn IPO. Overall the firm tends to gain more issuer representation, but many of these mandates come as a result of recommendations from underwriters. Its New York origins provide a healthy flow of general SEC work for DAX 30 companies listed in the US. The firm has also handled several capital increases for clients such as HypoVereinsbank and TUI. Individuals such as Gabriele Apfelbacher and Christof von Dryander have outstanding reputations and uphold the firm's immense standing in Germany.

Freshfields Bruckhaus Deringer's stellar equity capital markets practice has its roots in the firm's esteemed corporate client base. In recent years capital increases have driven the practice, but with IPO activity on the way back, the firm will inevitably gain a considerable market share. Ernst Thomas Emde is an experienced securities lawyer and is ably supported by senior figures such as corporate head Andreas Fabritius. Andreas König is commended for his work on the debt side, where the firm is developing its business particularly in equity-linked products and some high-yield bond work.

Hengeler Mueller has a powerful equity and debt practice. Its stellar securitisation practice has of late shown a little more activity, but a series of prestigious convertible and exchangeable bond mandates outlines its continuing leading position in the market. Torsten Busch and Wolfgang Groß are often applauded. Inevitably, when the equity markets return, the firm's impressive corporate and banking client base will ensure a prominent position. The firm frequently works alongside New

CAPITAL MARKETS

CLEARY, GOTTLIEB, STEEN & HAMILTON LLP ✪
FRESHFIELDS BRUCKHAUS DERINGER
HENGELER MUELLER ✪

Allen & Overy LLP ✪
Clifford Chance
Linklaters Oppenhoff & Rädler ✪
Shearman & Sterling LLP
Sullivan & Cromwell LLP

Baker & McKenzie ✪
CMS Hasche Sigle ✪
Gleiss Lutz ✪
Lovells ✪

Davis Polk & Wardwell
Fried, Frank, Harris, Shriver & Jacobson LLP
Haarmann Hemmelrath ✪
Heisse Kursawe Rechtsanwälte Partnerschaft ✪
Hölters & Elsing
Latham & Watkins LLP
Mayer, Brown, Rowe & Maw LLP ✪
Milbank, Tweed, Hadley & McCloy LLP ✪
Norton Rose Vieregge
Sidley Austin LLP
Skadden, Arps, Slate, Meagher & Flom LLP
Taylor Wessing ✪
White & Case LLP

Firms are listed A-Z in tiers which are ranked in order of priority
✪ Indicates firm displays contact details at the end of this chapter.

York firm **Davis Polk & Wardwell** on securities issues.

One of **Allen & Overy LLP**'s real successes of the last few years must be its rise to prominence in equity capital markets, thanks largely to the efforts of the excellent and amiable Michael Schlitt. Clients have applauded Schlitt's industrious efforts to win and retain business. Some 85% of instructions come from banks including Morgan Stanley and Deutsche Bank. Of late the firm has been involved in several block trade transactions and equity-linked deals, including advising sole book-runner Nomura International on a €1.1bn exchangeable bond by KfW into ordinary registered shares of Deutsche Post. However, clients believe the firm needs to acquire greater experience and expertise on the straight debt side.

A significant influx of bond mandates keeps **Clifford Chance** very much in the minds of the leading banks and issuers and this including an increasingly prominent record in high yield. Markus Pfüller and Sebastian Maerker are the lead partners for prestigious clients such as JP Morgan Securities, Commerzbank AG, Deutsche Bank AG and Dresdner Bank AG. On the straight equity side, the firm advised the banks on a €700m IPO including a 144A tranche.

Linklaters Oppenhoff & Rädler's reputation in the equity-linked field continues to grow at pace with its involvement in eight out of 11 such transactions in the German market in 2004. Clients applaud Berthold Kusserow and his team for their work on bond deals. The group advised HSH Nordbank on a €15bn debt issuance programme, comprising notes and derivative notes and was the first debt issuance programme for issuer HSH Nordbank, the first to be approved by BaFin, the German regulator, following the new Prospectus Directive. Raymond Fisher leads the US securities team in Germany, which has enabled the firm to penetrate the growing high-yield market, mainly for issuers. Herbert Harrer should also be recommended for equity transactions. On straight equity deals the firm has a solid position, but not in the same league as **Hengeler Mueller** and **Freshfields Bruckhaus Deringer**.

Despite its eminent US/German combination, **Shearman & Sterling LLP**'s capital markets record is not as formidable as its corporate/M&A practice. Yet with its tremendous German client base it is often fed with securities instructions and similarly its burgeoning client base is an important source of business. Stephan Hutter is the firm's most recognised securities partner and advised the underwriters, led by Deutsche Bank and Merrill Lynch as joint global coordinators and joint bookrunners, on OMV Aktiengesellschaft's combined €657m capital increase and €550m convertible bond offering in December 2004.

Sullivan & Cromwell LLP is now a force in the German capital markets sector, particularly following the arrival of Wolfgang Feuring from **Freshfields Bruckhaus Deringer** in 2001. In June 2005, it provided German and US counsel to the underwriters of the Federal Republic of Germany's US$5bn global bond offering including a 144A tranche. It also represented the issuer Premiere AG on its €1.2bn IPO including 144A offering in March 2005.

Baker & McKenzie's capital markets practice is now led by Manuel Lorenz following the departure of senior names such as Peter Veranneman and Hans-Peter Leube. Nevertheless Andreas Lohner was elected to the partnership in 2005 and will go some way to re-invigorating the senior ranks.

CMS Hasche Sigle should be noted for equity expertise, for both issuers and underwriters for mid-sized transactions. Christoph Schücking and Andreas Zanner are recommended.

Gleiss Lutz recently advised Standard Life in connection with its demutualisation and potential flotation on the London Stock Exchange. Hoimar von Ditfurth confirmed his excellent credentials on this mandate, while Kilian Bälz provided further support. The firm is gaining a greater share in IPOs with several instructions now coming from prominent underwriters in the German market. The firm is also historically strong on the bonds side.

Lovells' capital markets practice received a heavy blow when key partners Oliver Kessler and Jens Rinze left to launch **Sidley Austin**'s Frankfurt office in 2006. The two partners are better known for structured products and securitisation and thus the firm will be confident of retaining a solid equity business of a series of capital increases in recent years.

Davis Polk & Wardwell works closely with **Hengeler Mueller** and has a small operation in Frankfurt driven largely by debt transactions. With **Hengeler Mueller** it advised the Federal Republic of Germany on its first foreign currency bond issue, a US$5bn bond due 1 June, 2010. The vastly experienced Patrick Kenadjian leads the office.

Former **Hölters & Elsing** partners Sven Schulte-Hillen and Juergen van Kann launched **Fried, Frank, Harris, Shriver & Jacobson LLP**'s practice in 2004. Prior to joining they worked on Deutsche Postbank's €1.5bn IPO in June 2004.

Haarmann Hemmelrath is recommended for Central and Eastern European issuers notably on Eurobond mandates. Convertible bonds and secondary issuances are also an important area of practice. Andreas Lehmann is widely respected, but the departure of Mirko Sickinger to **Heuking Kühn Lüer Wojtek** was another loss.

Heisse Kursawe Rechtsanwälte Partnerschaft's Alexander Honrath is one of the few capital markets specialists to be based in Munich. Bayerische Landesbank and UBS Deutschland are key clients.

Hölters & Elsing represented Deutsche Post AG on its IPO in June 2004 alongside **Cleary, Gottlieb, Steen & Hamilton LLP** as co-counsel. Wolfgang Holters led the team.

Like its international profile in the capital markets environment, **Latham & Watkins LLP**'s German operation has built a position of pre-eminence in high-yield bonds. At one stage the firm had advised on seven out of the first 11 issuances that comprised a German component. The firm was also IPO counsel for the dual-track listing of Viterra. In 2005, the firm handled two MTN programmes under the new German Prospectus Directive. Underwriters are the key sources of business. Rudolf Haas and Philipp von Randow have excellent reputations and are leading the high-yield initiative.

Mayer, Brown, Rowe & Maw LLP's sustained period of investment into its Frankfurt office has given it a greater profile in the capital markets sector particularly following the arrival of Peter Nägele from **Clifford Chance** and Ulrike Binder from **CMS Hasche Sigle** in 2005. The firm subsequently received several IPO mandates in 2005.

Milbank, Tweed, Hadley & McCloy LLP frequently advises on US institutional private placements and recapitalisations. Christian Droop is recommended and holds dual qualification in Germany and the US.

Norton Rose Vieregge has a notable debt-oriented practice headed by Rüdiger Litten. Credit-linked notes instructions have been a valuable source of business. Clients include DZ Bank.

Former **Lovells** partners Oliver Kessler and Jens Rinze left to launch **Sidley Austin**'s Frankfurt office in 2006. The two partners are known for structured products and securitisation, and are suitably equipped to cater to the firm's global strength in this sector.

Skadden, Arps, Slate, Meagher & Flom LLP's Peter Veranneman, who joined from **Baker & McKenzie** in 2005 has an excellent reputation in both IPOs and capital increases.

Taylor Wessing's Claus Goedecke is another well-known corporate finance lawyer and is also known more recently for capital increases.

White & Case LLP is strong on the debt side with Jochen Artzinger-Bolten to the fore, but its increased presence on IPOs should be noted thanks to the efforts of partners such as Volker Land in Hamburg and Markus Hauptmann in Frankfurt. During 2005, the firm boasted market share of IPOs beyond any other firm. It is also one of few firms to concentrate on IPOs from its Hamburg branch.

CORPORATE AND M&A

Freshfields Bruckhaus Deringer's advisory role to Unicredito on its €15.4bn acquisition of HypoVereinsbank endorses the firm's longstanding position at the head of the market. The mandate was won by global corporate head Andreas Fabritius (an Italian speaker) and in so doing demonstrated the exceptional talent that

CORPORATE AND M&A

FRESHFIELDS BRUCKHAUS DERINGER
HENGELER MUELLER ✪

CLEARY, GOTTLIEB, STEEN & HAMILTON LLP ✪
CLIFFORD CHANCE
GLEISS LUTZ ✪
LINKLATERS OPPENHOFF & RÄDLER ✪
SHEARMAN & STERLING LLP

Allen & Overy LLP ✪
CMS Hasche Sigle ✪
Latham & Watkins LLP
Lovells ✪
Nörr Stiefenhofer Lutz ✪
Taylor Wessing ✪
Weil, Gotshal & Manges ✪
White & Case LLP

Baker & McKenzie ✪
Beiten Burkhardt ✪
Bird & Bird ✪
Buse Heberer Fromm ✪
GSK Gassner Stockmann & Kollegen ✪
Görg Partnerschaft von Rechtsanwälten ✪
Graf von Westphalen Bappert & Modest ✪
Haarmann Hemmelrath ✪
Heuking Kühn Lüer Wojtek ✪
Hölters & Elsing
Jones Day
Mayer, Brown, Rowe & Maw LLP ✪
McDermott Will & Emery Rechtsanwälte Steuerberater LLP ✪
Norton Rose Vieregge
P+P Pöllath + Partners ✪
Skadden, Arps, Slate, Meagher & Flom LLP

Gibson, Dunn & Crutcher LLP
Hogan & Hartson Raue L.L.P. ✪
Luther Rechtsanwaltsgesellschaft mbH ✪
Morgan Lewis ✪
Rittstieg Rechtsanwälte

Continued

the firm has to offer. Fabritius leads a significant group of leading corporate and transactional lawyers of which there are too many to name. Ralph Wollburg and Axel Eppe are worthy of particular note. The firm's immense size and reputation for representing blue-chip corporates means that it is rarely out of the picture on high-value transactions. It advised E.ON on its sale of Viterra, a show of the firm's public M&A abilities. The firm's broad resources mean that it is also frequently involved in mid-cap deals.

Hengeler Mueller's esteemed position in corporate and commercial law is undeniable as it continues to be a key trusted adviser of DAX 30 corporates and supervisory boards across Germany. In Michael Hoffmann-Becking it boasts Germany's leading corporate lawyer, though he is edging towards retirement. Yet with names such as Maximilian Schiessl, Andreas Austmann and Oleg de Lousanoff the firm has an assured longstanding legacy and remains strong internationally thanks to formal relationships with firms such as New York's **Davis Polk & Wardwell** and London's **Slaughter and May**. In 2005 it advised HypoVereinsbank's supervisory board on its €15.4bn acquisition by Unicredito. Its corporate law strength was demonstrated by its representation of HSBC Trinkaus & Burkhardt in its conversion to a stock corporation. Michael Hoffmann-Becking and Andreas Austmann led the corporate team.

Cleary, Gottlieb, Steen & Hamilton LLP has become an integral thread in the fabric of German corporate transactions and no longer trades merely on its impressive record in securities. 2005 saw it advise HypoVereinsbank on its €15.4bn acquisition by Unicredito as well as Deutsche Post on its €3.7bn acquisition of Exel and Deutsche Postbank AG on its €1.8bn takeover of BHW Holding. The firm's increasing prominence in corporate transactions is thanks in no small part to the connections of the heralded Christof von Dryander, but also the presence of Gabriele Apfelbacher and Klaus Riehmer who worked on the Unicredito deal. US partner Ward Greenberg played a prominent role on the Deutsche Post transaction. In light of its involvement in a series of bulge-bracket transactions it must now surely be regarded as one of the leading M&A practices in Germany.

Clifford Chance must now be considered as a serious competitor to the current established leaders – **Freshfields Bruckhaus Deringer** and **Hengeler Mueller**. When it comes to the financial services, energy and healthcare sectors, the firm is nearly always involved in the major corporate transactions. Beyond these sectors, the firm is known to provide corporate law advice to 15 of the DAX 30 companies on a regular basis, following an initiative to increase the firm's connections to publicly listed companies. In this respect the firm's sectoral approach to various industries appears to have also paid off with it now consistently ranking in the top three in M&A league tables. Wolfgang Richter is one of the firm's senior names when it comes to stock corporation law, with the experienced Thomas Gasteyer and Andreas Dietzel providing further credibility to the firm. Arndt Stengel (head of the listed companies group), Kersten Von Schenck and Diana Weber-Rey are also frequently commended.

Gleiss Lutz continues its hot streak of headline-grabbing mandates with it representing Swiss Re on its US$6.8bn acquisition of GE Insurance Solutions from General Electric Company in 2005. The deal was led by Gerhard Wegen (one of the best-connected lawyers in Germany) and Hansjörg Scheel, with the firm working alongside its alliance partners – London's **Herbert Smith LLP** and Benelux firm **Stibbe** and close-friends in the US, **Simpson Thacher & Bartlett LLP**. It yet again demonstrated the firm's international standing, which in many ways outstrips its domestic position. 'I couldn't talk too highly of them. The quality of the work is off the scale sometimes,' one foreign client said, having been disappointed with the standard of advice from other advisers in previous years. Gerhard Wirth provides vital domestic stock corporation law expertise. Stefan Mutter and Bodo Riegger should also be commended, while clients also praise Hoimar von Ditfurth.

Linklaters Oppenhoff & Rädler has a sizeable corporate and commercial practice led by Wolfgang Sturm which is gaining prominence, but still has some way to go to be the firm of choice for blue-chip domestic corporates. When it comes to M&A, deals tables would suggest **Linklaters Oppenhoff & Rädler** lags behind **Freshfields Bruckhaus Deringer**, **Hengeler Mueller** and even **Clifford Chance**. Nevertheless, in senior names such as Georg Maier-Reimer, the firm does boast solid credentials, which have resulted in some prestigious corporate mandates such as advising Intermarché on the squeeze-out of the minority shareholders of SPAR Handels-AG. The 'excellent' Hans-Ulrich Wilsing led the team, which is commended by clients for squeeze-out instructions. In M&A, Stephan König, Wolfgang Sturm, Michael Lappe and Peter Erbacher are a few of the firm's most respected partners. On the private equity front, the firm's representation of Fortress on its €3.5bn acquisition of real estate company Gagfah in 2004 established the firm's credentials in this arena.

Shearman & Sterling LLP has an immense standing in the German market with a multitude of domestic and international blue-chip clients. Georg Thoma (Germany's best-connected lawyer) is responsible for much of this with his links to corporates such as Allianz Group and DaimlerChrysler. Of late the firm has handled several large transactions for Axel Springer including its acquisition of ProSiebenSat.1. In September 2005, it advised on a landmark transaction, representing Allianz on its cross-border €5.7bn merger with subsidiary Riunione Adriatica di Sicurtà (RAS) including the conversion of Allianz AG into a European Company (Societas Europaea). Georg Thoma, Hans Diekmann (Düsseldorf) and Roger Kiem (Frankfurt) led the corporate team.

Allen & Overy LLP is steadily developing its corporate profile, now representing DAX 30 clients like TUI, SAP and Bilfinger Berger on a regular basis. It has a long way to go to reach parity with **Freshfields Bruckhaus Deringer** and **Hengeler Mueller** but several high-profile and high-value M&A mandates are helping its emergence. Arguably its more prolific partners are in Hamburg with Helge Schaefer and Cornelius Fisher-Zernin playing a significant role. Hans Schoneweg and Mark Hoenike should be acknowledged in Frankfurt. The firm is strongest in the telecoms, energy and financial services sectors.

CMS Hasche Sigle is now the second-largest law firm in Germany having absorbed **Norton Rose Vieregge**'s Cologne office in January 2005. Some 40% of its business is based around corporate and M&A with 190 lawyers and 75 partners, and following the launch of its Cologne office it is now representing Deutsche Bank in the many bidding processes in Germany to acquire NPLs. Klaus Jäger is the lead partner. The firm remains strong in the energy and insurance sectors, but continues to be ensconced in its traditional client portfolio of Mittelstand companies. Thomas Meyding, Axel Sigle, Florian Bauer and Thomas Meyer are often regarded as the firm's leading corporate lawyers.

Latham & Watkins LLP's Joachim von Falkenhausen leads the corporate department that includes the excellent Christoph von Teichman, both in Hamburg. Private equity has become an increasingly important element of the practice and with a greater corporate finance capability in Frankfurt, after much investment, the department has become significantly stronger over the last two years. The firm has also become a significant name in privatisations, having recently advised the District of Munich on the sale of two hospitals and the City of Hamburg on a major transaction involving nursing homes. The firm won the latter mandate after a competitive bid involving 12 other law firms. Henning Schneider is a member of the corporate department, but specialises on the public sector side.

Lovells boasts a leaner practice following several partner defections over the last two years. Yet it retains a strong presence in the energy sector thanks in part to the efforts of Hamburg partner Andreas Meyer, while Volker Triebel remains the firm's most recognised corporate lawyer. The firm has also developed an impressive Nordic business in Germany. Michael Witzel and Tim Brandi are also important members of the team, while the private equity practice remains strong despite the departure of Oliver Felsenstein to **Clifford Chance**.

Nörr Stiefenhofer Lutz's recruitment efforts over the last two years has enabled it to make a greater impact on a corporate level, particularly in Berlin where it hired Thorsten Reinhard from **Freshfields Bruckhaus Deringer** in November 2005. He follows respected individuals such as Alexander Ritvay who returned to the firm in 2005. The firm's fine media reputation makes it hard to ignore when it comes to corporate transactions in this sector. It teamed up with **Shearman & Sterling LLP** on Axel Springer's acquisition of ProSiebenSat.1, demonstrating its media aptitude. On the private equity side the firm has represented Allianz Capital Partners alongside **O'Melveny & Myers LLP** in New York as well as Montagu. The firm is also known for its Central and Eastern European workload as well as the automotive sector with Tobias Bürgers to the fore. Thomas Schulz heads the practice alongside Alexander Ritvay.

Taylor Wessing's sizeable corporate/M&A practice features some 73 corporate lawyers and has been augmented by a series of excellent lateral hires in recent months. Well-known corporate partners Heinrich Rodewig and Thomas Krempl joined the firm in Munich on 1 October, from **Haarmann Hemmelrath**. The firm has also recruited a series of senior associates from **Freshfields Bruckhaus Deringer**. Hamburg partner Bernhard Kloft leads a practice that remains a key player in mid-cap M&A and acting for traditional Mittelstand companies, as well as remaining a technology-focused firm. In this regard **Taylor Wessing** has also carved out a niche acting for US West Coast investors with interests in the German economy. Clients regard it as one of the 'top-five firms in mid-sized transactions' and note its 'cultural fit to the German market' as well as its 'commercial sense'. The seasoned Munich partner Klaus Zimmermann is commended for his 'commercial approach' and 'international experience'. Clients also identify his younger colleague Stephan Heinemann as a leading individual.

One of Germany's most dynamic firms at present, **Weil, Gotshal & Manges** has positioned itself with overwhelming success as the choice firm for buyers and investors. Private equity and distressed funds are the key sources of mandates. Over the last two years it has advised distressed fund Lone Star on its acquisition of several NPL portfolios. Private equity clients including Cerberus, Texas Pacific Group and Saban Capital have brought it into some of the highest-value deals of 2005. Germany managing partner Gerhard Schmidt remains the firm's key rainmaker, but partners such as Uwe Hartmann have proved vital in handling the numerous mandates from Lone Star. The firm's Munich office, opened in February 2004 is now responsible for up to 40% of revenues in Germany, advising private equity funds such as Apax.

White & Case LLP continues to mix a healthy business of challenging corporate mandates with sizeable M&A transactions. It advised EDEKA Zentrale, Germany's leading retail group, on the acquisition of SPAR Handels-AG, led by Frankfurt partner Markus Hauptmann. The experienced Jörg Schmeding is commended by clients for being 'practical, effective and communicating well'. Frank Evers heads the M&A practice in Hamburg, where the firm boasts a range of Nordic clients on its books. 'We value the long-term relationship we have with them and their understanding of how we work and of our businesses,' one client said. Frankfurt based Andreas Stilken and Christoph Papenheim are also commended by clients. The firm is also highly regarded for privatisation work.

Despite the recent departure of a senior team of corporate lawyers including Matthias Jaletzke and Bernd Mayer to **Skadden, Arps, Slate, Meagher & Flom LLP**, **Baker & McKenzie** retains an impressive list of corporate clients, including DaimlerChrysler, Degussa and Siemens, which appear confident of instructing the firm on an ongoing basis. In June 2005, the team closed on behalf DaimlerChrysler the sale of debis AirFinance BV to Cerberus Capital Management. The immensely respected Dirk Oberbracht led on the transaction, while the equally prominent Wilhelm Hebing heads the M&A group.

Another stellar year for **Beiten Burkhardt** peaked in August 2005 when it teamed up with **Simpson Thacher & Bartlett LLP** to advise adidas-Salomon on the €3.1bn acquisition of Reebok International. **Beiten Burkhardt** handled

CORPORATE AND M&A Continued

- **Aderhold v. Dalwigk Knüppel Rechtsanwaltsgesellschaft GmbH ✪**
- **Ashurst ✪**
- **Büsing, Müffelmann & Theye**
- **DLA Piper Rudnick Gray Cary ✪**
- **Dechert LLP ✪**
- **Dewey Ballantine LLP ✪**
- **Esche Schümann Commichau**
- **Fried, Frank, Harris, Shriver & Jacobson LLP**
- **Glauber Steinberg Stenger Hannemann Uhlmannsiek**
- **Göhmann Wrede Haas Kappus & Hartmann**
- **Greenfort Partnerschaft von Rechtsanwälten**
- **Happ Luther & Partner**
- **Haver & Mailänder**
- **Heisse Kursawe Rechtsanwälte Partnerschaft ✪**
- **Hoffmann Liebs Fritsch & Partner (HLFP)**
- **Honert Funke Maute Neumayer**
- **Huth Dietrich Hahn ✪**
- **Kaye Scholer (Germany) LLP ✪**
- **Kuhn Carl & Norden**
- **Milbank, Tweed, Hadley & McCloy LLP ✪**
- **PPR & Partner ✪**
- **Rödl & Partner**
- **SJ Berwin LLP ✪**
- **Salger Rechtsanwälte**
- **Scheidermair Rechtsanwälte**
- **Sibeth Partnerschaft Rechtsanwälte Steuerberater Wirtschaftsprüfer ✪**
- **Simmons & Simmons ✪**
- **Thümmel, Schütze & Partner ✪**
- **Waldeck Rechtsanwälte Partnerschaftsgesellschaft**
- **Willkie Farr & Gallagher LLP ✪**
- **Wilmer Cutler Pickering Hale and Dorr LLP ✪**

Firms are listed A-Z in tiers which are ranked in order of priority
✪ Indicates firm displays contact details at the end of this chapter.

the German law aspects of the deal and was led by Thomas Sacher in Nuremberg. It continues to be active in mid-cap transactions and advised varetis AG on the €20.8m sale of its core business, enquiry and database solutions to the Volt Group. The firm is also a leader in public procurement.

Bird & Bird's entry into the German market has been swift and effective, and it has shrewdly built on a strong corporate brand established by the excellent Alexander Schröder-Frerkes. Lufthansa and Kerr McKee are key clients thanks to his prominence. Corporate finance specialist Erich Michel joined from **Norton Rose Vieregge** in 2004, having an esteemed record in privatisations on behalf of government bodies and also a frequent adviser of 3i over the years. The firm's sectoral focus on technology and life sciences has attracted the attention of several national and international private equity investors. The arrival of Jiri Jaeger from **Haarmann Hemmelrath** on 1 November is another boon to the firm's corporate practice.

Buse Heberer Fromm's M&A practice is headed by Christian Quack, with the Hamburg office being the most active of its network in 2005. The firm is part of the *European Legal Alliance*, which includes UK firm **Field Fisher Waterhouse** and the two recently worked on a wind energy sector transaction, involving setting up the project company and revising the purchase agreements. **Buse Heberer Fromm**'s Berlin office represented the buyer of a significant real estate portfolio while the traditional Mittelstand business of the entire firm remains important. The Essen and Berlin offices are known for their strength in the energy sector, with the Hamburg office having a solid profile in the medical devices industry. Life science, hotels, food and pulp and paper are also important business areas.

Further recruitment and investment has brought **GSK Gassner Stockmann & Kollegen** onto a greater national standing. In 2005 it recruited Eckart Petzold and a team from **Lovells** to its Düsseldorf office. Petzold should be noted for his Italian/German workload. Andreas Bauer is boosting the firm's profile in the private equity sector, while Gregor Seikel is noted for property-related transactional work.

GÖRG Partnerschaft von Rechtsanwälten is a leader in restructuring and insolvency with its Cologne office particularly renowned. Stock corporation law advice and squeeze-outs are important areas of the business. Klaus Hubert Görg boasts an outstanding reputation, while the progress of its Frankfurt office has been important to its corporate profile.

Graf von Westphalen Bappert & Modest concentrates on the mid-cap market, but with its strong international outlook it handles a significant portion of inbound and outbound investments. The firm represented one client in a €250m acquisition of a European consortium. Its M&A stronghold is in Freiburg with Gerhard Manz, Barbara Mayer and Albert Schröder the most recognised names. The firm's association with **Wragge & Co LLP** in the UK is of obvious benefit.

Haarmann Hemmelrath is now without many of its senior partners after a sustained exodus. Well-known names such as Andreas Oldenbourg who departed in October 2005 to set up his own firm, and founding partner Wilhelm Haarmann who left along with four other partners to set up his own practice on 1 January 2006. It results in the firm having a more junior range of partners. The firm will hope to retain a healthy client base of Mittelstand companies as well as advising DAX 30 corporates such as Siemens and DaimlerChrysler. Several transactions in Cental and Eastern Europe are indicative of the firm's international nature. It is also well known for its record in telecoms transactions, both in Germany as well as in Central and Eastern Europe. In June 2005, it advised Bulgaria's Mobiltel and its Austrian majority shareholder M-Tel Holding on its takeover by Telekom Austria.

Heuking Kühn Lüer Wojtek's corporate business is driven largely by German and foreign medium-sized businesses with a €50m-€500m turnover. Düsseldorf partner Hironaga Kaneko has also developed the firm's Japanese clientele, many of which have a presence in the city. The firm has an emphasis on energy, IT and media sectors and has also developed its client base through its excellent employment law practice. However, the firm is arguably most recognised for its work in the energy sector. The arrival of five partners, including Mirko Sickinger from the Cologne office of **Haarmann Hemmelrath** was a significant coup. Name partners Ralf Wojtek and Wolfgang Kühn are key individuals.

Hölters & Elsing remains a strong player in corporate and M&A much to the credit of names partners Wolfgang Hölters and Siegfried Elsing. The firm is also close to the public sector with it advising the Federal Republic of Germany on the privatisation of Deutsche Bahn. It is known for its advice to Mittelstand companies, but has also listed corporates such as Deutsche Postbank AG as clients, as well as representing a large number of foreign investors, mainly from the US. Younger partners Stefan Weinheimer and Wilhelm Nolting-Hauf are also recommended.

Another prominent player in the NPL sector, **Jones Day** continues to develop its transactional business. Ansgar Rempp and Volker Kammel have been important members of the team in this market. Clients including Bayer AG, BT, and Abbott Laboratories are examples of the firm's prestigious client portfolio when it comes to M&A.

Mayer, Brown, Rowe & Maw LLP remains a key player in Germany's active NPL sector and in real estate-related transactions. The firm is becoming increasingly recognised for its representation of hedge funds and distressed debt acquirors such as Lone Star. The arrival of Markus Strelow from **Ashurst** in 2004 was a boon in this respect. Clients praise Cologne partner Joachim Modlich for his 'pragmatism' and 'speed', while Frankfurt partners Rüdiger Herrmann and Mark Walker should also be recommended.

From its two bases in Düsseldorf and Munich, **McDermott Will & Emery Rechtsanwälte Steuerberater LLP** has shown commitment to the German market and been rewarded with significant business in the mid-cap sector. It is notably strong in the technology and media arenas and is becoming more involved in the NPL market. Konsantin Günther and Christian von Sydow lead a growing department that covers smaller transactions in the venture capital area right up to multi-million euro deals.

Norton Rose Vieregge has impressed a range of clients, particularly in relation to regional or Central and Eastern European work. 'We have never come across a law firm that has been as responsive as this. We appreciate the effort they put into serving us as a client. They have a willingness to change their delivery process to the extent that we've developed products together,' one said. Campbell Steedman is commended for his work in Central and Eastern Europe and clients have expressed admiration for his co-ordination of multi-jurisdictional mandates. Steedman has handled several major instructions from Romania and Bulgaria, while also remaining the firm's relationship partner for Nestlé. He returned to the London office in April 2006. Andreas Börner is also commended by clients. Nevertheless, several clients have expressed concern at the firm's limited resources, being 'too thin' in Germany following its Cologne office joining **CMS Hasche Sigle** in January 2005. Dirk Otto is considered an 'innovative dealmaker'.

P+P Pöllath + Partners is noted for its advice to managers and supervisory boards, often in connection with a significant transaction. Reinhard Pöllath and Matthias Bruse are frequently commended in this respect and are known for being excellent M&A lawyers. Though relatively small with some 65 lawyers the firm has an excellent reputation in private equity transactions, fund structuring and tax advice.

Skadden, Arps, Slate, Meagher & Flom LLP advised Louis Dreyfus Energy Holdings on its sale of the Wilhelmshaven refinery in Germany and the UK-based Louis Dreyfus Refining and Marketing to ConocoPhillips in 2005. The deal demonstrated the firm's European transactional record but also its growing presence in Germany. Matthias Jaletzke and Bernd Mayer are recommended.

Gibson, Dunn & Crutcher LLP's small Munich office boasts several immensely respected partners, this despite the tragic death of the excellent Christoph Hoebbel in May 2005. Philip Martinius was elected to the partnership in January 2005 and he links up with fine corporate partners Benno Schwarz (known for Russian and Central and Eastern European work) and Christoph Kuhmann. Private equity business has driven much of the practice including the representation of Investcorp, a global client. The team also represents Infineon and several German venture capital investors. The firm also advised Süd Chemie in a major transaction.

Hogan & Hartson Raue L.L.P. further enhanced its corporate standing with the hire of Jochen Schäfer from **Rödl & Partner** in November 2005. This comes after significant investment into its Munich office with Henning Mennenoeh (life science specialist) joining from **Allen & Overy LLP** in 2004. The firm's corporate media practice is one of the strongest in Germany and this was outlined by it providing lead counsel to the Saban consortium on the €2.5bn sale of its controlling stake in ProSiebenSat.1.

Luther Rechtsanwaltsgesellschaft mbH remains a pivotal firm in the energy and utilities sectors, particularly privatisations. The Düsseldorf and Cologne region is its stronghold, though it has a broader national presence. Wilhelm Niggemann is recommended.

The small yet powerful **Morgan Lewis** is a making rapid progress. With additional strength now in the tax arena, the firm is making further headway in the private equity and hedge fund sector. It also has a remarkably impressive list of corporate clients thanks in no small part to the efforts of managing partner Christian Zschocke. The firm tends to work on small- to mid-cap transactions.

Hamburg boutique **Rittstieg Rechtsanwälte** has an outstanding reputation for mid-cap to high-value M&A and is trusted corporate adviser to an impressive client base. Andreas Rittstieg and Rüdiger Zeller are respected partners.

Aderhold v. Dalwigk Knüppel Rechtsanwaltsgesellschaft GmbH is recommended for restructuring and corporate turnaround. Reinhard von Dalwigk has a prestigious record in this area. Public and private sector clients provide frequent instructions, including North Rhine Westphalia and Mobilcom. It is allied to MDP RölfsPartner, which is an obvious boost to this area of business. Thorsten Prigge and Jörg Swoboda also hold excellent reputations.

Private equity continues to be the bedrock of **Ashurst**'s corporate and M&A practice, though the departure of Jörg Kirchner to **Latham & Watkins LLP** is a loss. Simon Beddow has transferred from London to head the firm's German operation but also to further integrate the strong private equity capability in Germany with the excellent practice in the UK. The firm is also known for its work in the sports sector thanks to Frankfurt managing partner Hermann Schlindwein.

Bremen-based **Büsing, Müffelmann & Theye** is recommended for media-related work with the experienced Herbert Müffelmann and Constantin Frick to the fore. Offices in Frankfurt and Berlin give it further national credibility.

DLA Piper Rudnick Gray Cary continued its rapid development in 2005 having been established by former **GÖRG Partnerschaft von Rechtsanwälten** managing partner Ulrich Juengst in 2004. It has hired prolifically and in 2005 opened a crucial Frankfurt office to add to its global credentials. Its Hamburg office advised Weener Plastik Packaging Group on its acquisition of Euro-Matic in the UK. Klaus von Gierke led the corporate team.

Dewey Ballantine LLP's expanding resources in corporate should be noted. In Rudolf Coelle, Markus Federle and Benedikt von Schorlemer the firm has created a team with real credibility in just a short space of time.

Hamburg-based **Esche Schümann Commichau** is another favourite of Mittelstand companies and runs an MDP model. Klaus Kamlah is respected for stock corporation law.

Glauber Steinberg Stenger Hannemann Uhlmannsiek is another strong Hamburg-based boutique. Jan Volker Glauber is known for his work in the insurance sector.

Well-connected to several German blue-chip companies, **Göhmann Wrede Haas Kappus & Hartmann** handles the full range of corporate matters. Klaus-Dieter Hartmann is one of several respected partners.

Frankfurt firm **GREENFORT Partnerschaft von Rechtsanwälten** was launched in April 2005, comprising of former senior associates from **Freshfields Bruckhaus Deringer** and **Hengeler Mueller**. The new firm has already acquired some prestigious business including advising Technitrol on the acquisition of the ignition coil, coil and transformer businesses of era Group. Daniel Röder led the team.

Happ Luther & Partner remains a strong Hamburg player noted for its eminence in stock corporation law and local M&A. Wilhelm Happ is a frequent adviser to supervisory boards and is an acknowledged stock corporation law expert. Jörgen Tielmann is also noted for stock corporation issues, but has become increasingly active in international M&A, advising on a substantial transaction in the software navigation sector. Hubertus Freiherr von Der Recke is a lawyer, tax adviser and auditor.

Heisse Kursawe Rechtsanwälte Partnerschaft established a formal alliance with UK firm **Eversheds LLP** giving it access to a prominent global legal network. Since splitting from the defunct *ARCON Rechtsanwälte Schmidt-Sibeth Heisse Weisskopf Kursawe* it has won roles on a series of cross-border transactions. Matthias Heisse is recommended in this respect.

Hoffmann Liebs Fritsch & Partner (HLFP) is based in Düsseldorf and Berlin. It boasts a list of foreign and mid-sized German clients and is also allied to the UK's **Pinsent Masons**.

Honert Funke Maute Neumayer is a strong Munich-based boutique and one which has provided advice to a series of prestigious clients. Much of the work is also tax driven. Jürgen Honert and Jochen Neumayer should be acknowledged.

Huth Dietrich Hahn has an able M&A practice, with a strong presence in Hamburg and northern Germany. Karl Freiherr von Hahn and Ralf Stucken are widely commended.

Kaye Scholer (Germany) LLP has become a growing presence in the German market. Much of the work comes from foreign investors, but domestic mandates should also be noted including Harald Rieger representing the Honsel family in the sale of their stakes in Honsel AG during a secondary buy-out by Ripplewood.

Kuhn Carl & Norden is a prestigious small firm in Stuttgart. It has obtained some rather impressive roles in significant transactions over the years.

Milbank, Tweed, Hadley & McCloy LLP's excellent private equity practice may overshadow what else it has achieved in the mainstream corporate transactional field, but Peter Nussbaum and Norbert Rieger's efforts should not go unnoticed having gained several advisory roles for publicly listed companies. The election of Munich-based Ulrike Dormann to the partnership, demonstrates the ongoing development of the business.

PPR & Partner remains a strong player with foreign companies particularly those in the software sector. Fifty per cent of the firm's business is M&A oriented thanks to the efforts of Theo Rauh and Hans-Peter Palenberg. Rauh, in particular, is applauded by clients. 'He is very pragmatic, hard working, always easy to reach and contributes excellent ideas on how best to negotiate,' one said. The firm has also been appointed as co-coordinating lawyers for a multi-jurisdictional transaction in Europe. It has represented US publicly listed company RPM in a series of transactions. The firm should also be noted for venture capital expertise, led by Jochen Herbst.

Rödl & Partner mixes a traditionally strong and geographically broad client base of Mittelstand companies with a clear international outlook. The firm has extended across the globe offering a multi-disciplinary service to mainly German clients in connection with their foreign interests. Christian Rödl and Michael Wiehl should be picked out for corporate M&A advice.

SJ Berwin LLP is particularly strong on the funds structuring side and private equity transactions. Thomas Pauls and Christoph Brenner are two notable names on the transactional side, where the firm frequently advises Deutsche Beteiligungs.

Salger Rechtsanwälte's rapid development was halted in 2005 when a sector of the firm quit to join **Scheidermair Rechtsanwälte**

Scheidermair Rechtsanwälte is a sizeable Frankfurt-based practice boasting vastly experienced individuals such as Manfred Scheidermair. In recent years the firm has expanded the partnership rapidly with a five-partner team joining from **Salger Rechtsanwälte** in 2005.

SIBETH Partnerschaft Rechtsanwälte Steuerberater Wirtschaftsprüfer has generated an impressive business since launching on 1 January 2005. The corporate work is very much influenced by the firm's excellent real estate practice. The team led by Andreas Kloyer is particularly active with real estate investment funds, though straight corporate work from technology, biotech and life sciences clients is a healthy component.

Simmons & Simmons' corporate and private equity practice is headed by Franz-Josef Schöne. The firm has yet to break into the sort of high-value transactions that it would advise on in London, but in mid-cap and smaller private equity deals it deserves recognition.

Thümmel, Schütze & Partner is another strong Mittelstand adviser. The firm is best known in Stuttgart and the south German region where it has its headquarters. Rolf Schütze and Roderich Thümmel are well known.

Waldeck Rechtsanwälte Partnerschaftsgesellschaft is known for privatisation work. Over the years, the partners have represented a series of public authorities, as well as banks and corporates. Werner Waldeck leads the firm.

Willkie Farr & Gallagher LLP lost key partner Thomas Heymann, when he launched **Heymann & Partner** in 2005. Deutsche Bank and Swiss Re are key clients of his. Respected partner Markus Wenserski remains at **Willkie Farr & Gallagher LLP** and he was joined by Jochen Winter from **Linklaters Oppenhoff & Rädler** in 2006. They provide a solid basis for it to go forward.

Wilmer Cutler Pickering Hale and Dorr LLP's office in Munich and a sizeable operation in Berlin see it mixing technology and media business, with a strong regulatory and antitrust practice. Roland Steinmeyer has an established corporate reputation.

DISPUTE RESOLUTION

DISPUTE RESOLUTION

CLIFFORD CHANCE
FRESHFIELDS BRUCKHAUS DERINGER
HENGELER MUELLER ✪
LINKLATERS OPPENHOFF & RÄDLER ✪

Allen & Overy LLP ✪
Baker & McKenzie ✪
CMS Hasche Sigle ✪
Gleiss Lutz ✪
Lovells ✪
Nörr Stiefenhofer Lutz ✪
Shearman & Sterling LLP

Haver & Mailänder
Heuking Kühn Lüer Wojtek ✪
Hölters & Elsing
Latham & Watkins LLP
Lörcher & Lörcher

Aderhold v. Dalwigk Knüppel Rechtsanwaltsgesellschaft GmbH ✪
Ashurst ✪
Beiten Burkhardt ✪
Brödermann & Jahn ✪
Broglie, Schade & Partner GbR
Buse Heberer Fromm ✪
Danckelmann & Kerst
Esche Schümann Commichau
FPS Fritze Paul Seelig ✪
Graf von Westphalen Bappert & Modest ✪
Gurland
Haarmann Hemmelrath ✪
Jones Day
Luther Rechtsanwaltsgesellschaft mbH ✪
Mayer, Brown, Rowe & Maw LLP ✪
Schwarz Kelwing Wicke Westpfahl ✪
Simmons & Simmons ✪
Taylor Wessing ✪
White & Case LLP
Wilkinson, Barker, Knauer, Leitermann
Wilmer Cutler Pickering Hale and Dorr LLP ✪

Firms are listed A-Z in tiers which are ranked in order of priority
✪ *Indicates firm displays contact details at the end of this chapter.*

Clifford Chance has one of the largest and broadest practices in Germany, with an impressive array of partners handling both litigation and arbitration. Banking, securities, corporate and insurance sector disputes provide a significant portion of its business. White-collar crime, product liability and construction cases are also important segments. Fabian von Schlabrendorff is identified for banking disputes, with Uwe Hornung for white-collar crime issues.

Freshfields Bruckhaus Deringer has concentrated more resources into its dispute resolution team in recent years. With three partners having transferred from the corporate department to the disputes team, it has enabled the practice to offer an even more commercial and pragmatic service. US-related disputes and insurance cases have been areas of increased activity. Rolf Trittmann is often identified as a leading exponent of dispute resolution, both in litigation and arbitration proceedings, including ICC arbitrations. Senior name Reinhart Densch retired in 2005.

Hengeler Mueller's Peter Heckel is one of Germany's leading practitioners and is known for both litigation and arbitration. Corporate, banking and securities disputes remain the mainstay of the practice, with Markus Meier another prominent individual. The group represented Deutsche Telekom in the prominent *Federal Republic of Germany v Toll Collect* case which Heckel led alongside Henning Bälz.

Linklaters Oppenhoff & Rädler had a truly stellar 2005 with involvement in several of Germany's highest-profile and landmark cases. The firm was mandated by the Federal Republic of Germany on the *Toll Collect* case. Senior figure and arbitration guru Klaus Günther led the **Linklaters Oppenhoff & Rädler** team. Klaus Saffenreuther is another important individual and Peter Klappich leads the practice that richly deserves its first-tier status.

Allen & Overy LLP's strength is in finance-related disputes and the firm's core clientele remains German and international banks, such as Commerzbank and Deutsche Bank. Carsten Salger leads the department, which includes the respected Cornelius Fischer-Zernin.

Baker & McKenzie has a large and respected practice featuring individuals such as Günther Pickrahn, a leading name in dispute resolution who is becoming increasingly known for mediation matters. In this respect the firm is carving out several niche areas in which it is becoming increasingly dominant. This includes insolvency litigation and an increasing focus on arbitration. Jürgen Mark, Stephan Spehl and Jörg Risse should also be identified as leading practitioners.

CMS Hasche Sigle boasts extensive resources for litigation and arbitration, with greater profile in the latter thanks to the efforts and expertise of the pre-eminent Klaus Sachs, with Dorothee Ruckteschler (Stuttgart) and Helmut Borngräber (Düsseldorf) also of immense calibre. Clients endorse the firm for its faultless preparation and performance in court.

Gleiss Lutz is recommended for both domestic and international disputes, with the excellent Stefan Rützel and Stephan Wilske often noted for their expertise in this segment. Following its stellar role acting for the State of Baden-Württemberg in a massive €1.1bn state liability case, the firm continues to advise a range of German and foreign clients including DaimlerChrysler and GE Capital on various issues. Frequent appearances in ICC arbitration proceedings demonstrate the high regard in which this blossoming practice is held.

Lovells' centres of excellence in dispute resolution are in Munich and Frankfurt. The team is known for energy disputes including arbitrations as well as product liability cases in which the German team played a key role in a major international mandate. Insolvency and white-collar crime are also prominent areas for the practice, where Detlef Haas should be recognised. Five partners are dedicated to dispute resolution. Volker Triebel (one of Germany's leading practitioners), Alexander Loos and Thilo von Bodungen are recommended.

Insurance and product liability remains a key segment of **Nörr Stiefenhofer Lutz**'s dispute resolution practice. Munich-based partner Michael Molitoris has an outstanding reputation while Patricia Nacimiento is rapidly becoming one of the leading names in arbitration.

Shearman & Sterling LLP's esteemed reputation brought it into the *Toll Collect* arbitration and *Bombardier v DaimlerChrysler* case. In this respect, its dispute resolution practice has compiled an impressive track record to build on. Richard Kreindler in particular has become increasingly recognised for high-profile arbitrations as well as litigation. Senior figure Jochem Reichert is also frequently commended.

Haver & Mailänder is noted for arbitration expertise in particular with an emphasis towards corporate and transactional-related disputes. Rolf Winkler and Klaus Gerstenmaier are highly regarded.

Heuking Kühn Lüer Wojtek's record in arbitration proceedings is becoming increasingly impressive thanks in part to the work of name partner Wolfgang Kühn, who also sits as an arbitrator. The firm is also known for its role in shareholder disputes in the newspaper industry.

Hölters & Elsing partner Siegfried Elsing is a respected arbitration counsel who successfully represented **Haarmann Hemmelrath** in a major dispute. Of-counsel Otto Sandrock is known for both appearing as an arbitrator and counsel.

Latham & Watkins LLP should now be regarded as one of the leading firms in securities litigation thanks to the efforts of former **Clifford Chance** partner Bernd-Wilhelm Schmitz, who joined with a team in 2004. He recently represented Deutsche Telekom in one of the largest securities disputes to take place in Germany. Schmitz is also handling several other securities cases, acting for banks and financial institutions. Sebastian Seelmann-Eggebert should be noted for his recent arbitration work.

Lörcher & Lörcher's Gino Lörcher is a senior figure in arbitration proceedings and is often appointed as an arbitrator.

Aderhold v. Dalwigk Knüppel Rechtsanwaltsgesellschaft GmbH has a solid reputation for contentious work and has handled complex disputes on behalf of a series of blue-chip names in both a domestic and international context.

Ashurst's practice includes two partners and ten associates, with greater involvement in antitrust litigation where the firm benefits from having employed an economist in Germany for several years.

Beiten Burkhardt's strong media and sports background has provided it with ongoing and impressive contentious business. It also boasts a forensic practice under Hans-Jürgen Schroth.

Brödermann & Jahn's Eckart Brödermann is another high-profile litigator, while **Broglie, Schade & Partner GbR** concentrates on professional indemnity in the medical sector.

Buse Heberer Fromm is known for white-collar crime cases thanks to the presence of key partner Ulrich Bent in Berlin.

Danckelmann & Kerst's Hans Beeg is an experienced arbitration specialist including in cases before the ICC in Paris.

Hamburg-based **Esche Schümann Commichau** and national firm **FPS Fritze Paul Seelig** have solid litigation expertise, the latter particularly in IP.

Graf von Westphalen Bappert & Modest's Friedrich Graf von Westphalen (Cologne) and Klaus Landry (Hamburg) frequently sit as arbitrators and often hear cases involving international trade disputes. Henrich Heggemann (Cologne) is recognised for his expertise in building and construction arbitration proceedings and recently represented an Eastern European government in a case against a Turkish contractor.

Jens Bredow at **Gurland** is also known for being a prominent arbitrator.

In Rainer Bommert **Haarmann Hemmelrath** boasts a litigator of exceptional calibre and with the arrival of Francis Bellen from **Clifford Chance** in February 2005, the firm's dispute resolution capability has been somewhat augmented.

Jones Day's Thomas Mahlich is one of the leading litigators in Germany and is backed by an esteemed global firm with excellent contentious credentials. He is also known especially for white-collar crime cases.

Luther Rechtsanwaltsgesellschaft mbH is another firm with a strong forensic practice and boasts the services of the excellent Ulrich Theune.

Mayer, Brown, Rowe & Maw LLP's Ulf Grundmann and his team are better known for IP-related disputes but boast a range of blue-chip clients that instruct the firm on mainstream corporate cases.

Schwarz Kelwing Wicke Westpfahl's Walter Eberl is an arbitration and mediation specialist and regularly appears before the ICC.

Simmons & Simmons' Hans-Hermann Aldenhoff is applauded by clients. 'The team presented the case well in court and the research and backup was excellent,' one client remarked. The team is particularly strong in the financial services sector, as well as in employment disputes.

Taylor Wessing is recommended for IP-related disputes with Dietrich Max to the fore. The firm should also be commended for product liability.

White & Case LLP is known for insolvency and banking disputes and has a stellar international arbitration practice. Experienced names such as Hans-Jürgen Hüesker lend the firm further credibility.

Wilmer Cutler Pickering Hale and Dorr LLP's public sector capability and contentious experience is also worthy of note.

EMPLOYMENT

Following the amalgamation of the former **Norton Rose Vieregge** Cologne office in 2005, **CMS Hasche Sigle** possesses the critical mass, the depth of expertise, the nationwide spread and the client base to stand it out as one of the leading firms in Germany. Major clients include DaimlerChrysler, Deutsche Telekom and Cisco Systems, and transactional, restructuring and day-to-day advice are all strengths. Matthis Kappus is a top practitioner in the field.

EMPLOYMENT

CMS HASCHE SIGLE ✪
FRESHFIELDS BRUCKHAUS DERINGER
GLEISS LUTZ ✪

Baker & McKenzie ✪
CBH Cornelius Bartenbach Haesemann & Partners, member of ius laboris ✪
Küttner Rechtsanwälte
Linklaters Oppenhoff & Rädler ✪
Schmitt-Rolfes, Faltermeier, Staudacher ✪

Allen & Overy LLP ✪
Ashurst ✪
avocado rechtsanwälte
Beiten Burkhardt ✪
Clifford Chance
Fäber Rechtsanwälte
Graf von Westphalen Bappert & Modest ✪
Hengeler Mueller ✪
Heuking Kühn Lüer Wojtek ✪
Hogan & Hartson Raue L.L.P. ✪
Kasper, Knacke, Wintterlin & Partner
Kliemt & Vollstädt
Latham & Watkins LLP
Loh Von Hülsen Michael Rechtsanwälte
Lovells ✪
Luther Rechtsanwaltsgesellschaft mbH ✪
Neef & Schrader
Nörr Stiefenhofer Lutz ✪
Simmons & Simmons ✪
Taylor Wessing ✪
Tschöpe, Schipp, Clemenz
White & Case LLP

B.B.O.R.S Rechtsanwälte
Bird & Bird ✪
Buse Heberer Fromm ✪
DLA Piper Rudnick Gray Cary ✪
Dechert LLP ✪
Eckert Dörsam Klette
Haarmann Hemmelrath ✪
Hoffmann Liebs Fritsch & Partner (HLFP)
Jones Day
KSB Intax
Mayer, Brown, Rowe & Maw LLP ✪
McDermott Will & Emery Rechtsanwälte Steuerberater LLP ✪
Melchers
Norton Rose Vieregge
PPR & Partner ✪
Salans
Wilmer Cutler Pickering Hale and Dorr LLP ✪

Firms are listed A-Z in tiers which are ranked in order of priority
✪ Indicates firm displays contact details at the end of this chapter.

Freshfields Bruckhaus Deringer continues to be a force in the market despite the departure of Walter Ahrens to set up his own practice and the retirement of Hans Christian Netzel. The Employment Pensions Benefits practice shines in an improving M&A market, while technical expertise is there in abundance, particularly in Düsseldorf through Hans Josef Willemson. Georg Annuß is driving the Munich team forward in its second year of existence, and Berlin remains strong in public sector work.

Ten dedicated partners at **Gleiss Lutz** indicate a large team across four offices, but the firm's position at the top of the market also reflects tremendous expertise. T-Online was advised on its merger with Deutsche Telekom AG, one of many acquisition-related mandates, Infineon instructed the firm on the staff reduction of 800 employees, and it also handled a four-way spin-off of Air Liquide. The managing director of RTL 2 was also reinstated to his position after being removed by a majority shareholder without notice, an unusual mandate which displayed the level of technical knowledge and ability to think outside the box of lawyers at the firm.

Although **Baker & McKenzie** is active in M&A and outsourcing support work, the bulk of the workload is restructuring mandates with major global clients being advised on some extremely large and complex procedures. Gregor Dornbusch heads a team which is also proficient in pensions and benefits matters.

CBH Cornelius Bartenbach Haesemann & Partners, member of ius laboris advises an impressive collection of clients including Allianz, SAS, Toyota and Saturn on day-to-day matters, and the unusual expertise in employee invention rights stands the firm out.

'Well organised' **Küttner Rechtsanwälte** is a niche employment firm of longstanding excellence, with particular expertise in negotiating with workers' committees and unions on restructurings from offices in Berlin and Cologne. German and international manufacturing and industrial companies comprise the majority of the client base, while it also advises several media and publishing companies.

Linklaters Oppenhoff & Rädler is frequently involved in the biggest restructurings for some major clients, including Bankgesellscheft Berlin, Bayerische Landesbank and others. The team provides sterling support to its M&A team, particularly in the Frankfurt office under new team head Michael Tepass, and a major mandate was the relocation of a credit card business from Frankfurt to Dusseldorf for RBS. Elsewhere the teams are more business restructuring oriented, particularly in Cologne where former department head Karl-Dietmar Cohnen and redundancy programme expert Gilbert Wurth operate. Munich houses pensions expertise. Day-to-day mandates include advice on codes of conduct, while Texas-based ACS is advised on 'insourcing' human resource activities.

Versatile Munich niche firm **Schmitt-Rolfes, Faltermeier, Staudacher** combines advice to an enviable corporate client list, which includes Siemens, Hypovereinsbank and MAN, with acting for senior employees in high-value disputes. Name partner Peter Staudacher is a notable figure.

Allen & Overy LLP advises an international client base on operations in Germany from offices in Frankfurt and Hamburg, leveraging off the firm's global Employment, Pensions and Incentives Group. With a potent M&A group, the firm is also exposed to clients on supporting corporate transactions which gives it a largely banking and corporate-oriented client base. In pure employment matters, Anja Breitfeld's team advises on collective bargaining agreements, the structuring of individual employment contracts and executive dismissals, while restructuring remains a huge area of work.

Ashurst is getting on some varied and interesting high-profile mandates, including the closure of the German holding company of Servisair/Globeground, which involved some litigation, negotiation with works council, and the plant relocation of IMG. The majority of the team's instructions come from M&A transactions. Tobias Neufeld returned from **Cleary, Gottlieb, Steen & Hamilton LLP** in 2005.

avocado rechtsanwälte built on a strong foundation of mandates concerning works councils and trade union disputes for a client base of banking, publishing and industrial companies to increasingly support its corporate group in M&A-related matters. The three-partner team displays good technical know-how.

Beiten Burkhardt has notable employment expertise in its Munich office, where it acts for Munich Airport, and also advised manufacturer Garuhe on a mass dismissal in a production plant.

Clifford Chance houses eight employment lawyers in both the Frankfurt and Düsseldorf offices, with a pick-up in the transactional market providing substantial work in the Frankfurt office in particular; Siemens' divestiture to BenQ was a notable example. The team also works increasingly closely with the private equity team. Restructuring clients included major publishers, while more frequent instructions come from the Mittelstand. Outsourcing provides more international activity for the venerable Berndt Gach and his team.

Düsseldorf-based **Fäber Rechtsanwälte** has an unusually strong media and entertainment sector focus, with clients hailing from the IT, film and sports industries, as well as banking and biotech circles. The firm is recognised for litigation expertise.

Graf von Westphalen Bappert & Modest has always been active in restructuring, mass dismissals and the like, and has recently turned its hand more to advising public authorities, including the Hanseatic City of Hamburg, on employment aspects of PPP projects. Andrea Benkendorff, based in Dresden, has specific expertise in this area and also counts church-related organisations among clients.

Hengeler Mueller leverages off a powerful coporate practice to advise on some large-scale transaction-related mandates including the sale of ThyssenKrupp's real estate group to MSREF. It also advised Bombardier on a restructuring and compliance system implementation. Hans-Joachim Liebers is very active.

Heuking Kühn Lüer Wojtek's employment expertise is strong in Cologne and Munich, although the recruitment of Stefan Fischer and Joachim Littig into the Berlin office increases the firm's national reach. Restructuring continues to drive the practice alongside mandates in transaction support.

Hogan & Hartson Raue L.L.P. advises some high-profile and varied clients on employment matters, including Berlin Airports Corporation, Gucci's German subsidiaries and the German Heart Institute in Berlin on various ongoing matters. Gernod Meinel is a highly respected figure, and despite a concentration in the Berlin office the Munich office is also impressively active.

Stuttgart-based **Kasper, Knacke, Wintterlin & Partner** enjoys international contacts through the Integrated Advisory Group, a multi-disciplinary professional advisory group. It remains a solid niche employment firm, handling all aspects of collective bargaining agreements, share options and pension plans. Wolfgang Hesse is recommended.

Kliemt & Vollstädt has established itself in the market over its three-year existence as a very credible firm. Clients in the metals and chemicals industries are advised alongside professional sportspeople, government ministries and public authorties, as well as company directors. Restructuring and turnaround scenarios are also handled. Name partners Michael Kliemt and Oliver Vollstädt have impeccable pedigrees, and locations in Frankfurt, Berlin and Düsseldorf give it good national coverage.

Latham & Watkins LLP boasts a genuinely international outlook and client base, with around 50% of its clients English speaking, including foreign shareholders. Around half the work done is in transaction support, although retrenchment and restructuring of mid-sized companies still accounts for a large proportion of its activity; a recent mandate was the politically sensitive closure of the Hamburg aluminium plant, employing 550 people. The firm matches depth of resources with superb technical ability.

Loh Von Hülsen Michael Rechtsanwälte is nominated by peers as a sound firm in empoyment matters. The firm offers consulting services and a strong line in dispute resolution. With clients in federal and governmental bodies, as well as major manufacturers, the firm's continued excellence in this sector during its five-year lifespan under Ernesto Loh justifies a move up the rankings this year.

Lovells' large and growing employment team continues to be engaged on some large restructuring mandates, but has also performed well on some prestigious corporate mandates, including for Motorola. British American Tobacco was advised on the reorganisation of its Bayreuth operation. BMW instructs the firm on pensions issues, while GlaxosmithKline and Allianz are other notable clients. Frankfurt-based Thomas Ubber is practice group head, the excellent Eckhard Schwarz leads the Hamburg department, and Jonas Müller in Berlin is active in employee representation.

Luther Rechtsanwaltsgesellschaft mbH continues to show well in the employment market, with project reorganisations an area of expertise.

Hanover-based **Neef & Schrader** is a three-partner niche practice of high expertise.

Strongest in Berlin, **Nörr Stiefenhofer Lutz** nevertheless offers good emplyment advice and expertise across the network. The reorganisation of Philip Morris GmbH in Munich and Berlin showed the benefits of this nationwide coverage and depth of resources in the 23-lawyer team, with 94 complaints against the dismissal notice filed, and 40 proceedings in Berlin being handled largely successfully. Stefan Tomcic, Heidi Mahr and Hans-Christoph Schimmelpfennig handle varied mandates, from outsourcing to transactional support, for the likes of Siemens, Credit Suisse First Boston and Allianz.

Employment continues to be the success story at **Simmons & Simmons**, which couples a superb German operation, serving investment banks and DAX 30 clients, with an awesome international network, which keeps major clients such as General Electric at the firm. A recent major mandate has been to oversee the gradual winding down of a major manufacturer's operations in Germany. Hans-Hermann Aldenhoff's expertise also spills over into white-collar crime, where he acts for corporates on directors' liability matters and pension fraud.

Headed out of Hamburg by Axel Filges but located around the country, **Taylor Wessing**'s ten-partner employment team is versatile. It handles day-to-day matters for the likes of Panasonic Electric Works (Europe) AG, Google Germany GmbH and various other DAX 30 clients, and advised Repower AG on a large restructuring and Finisair Corp on a restructuring mandate supporting its acquisition of an Infineon subsidiary.

Guterslöh-based **Tschöpe, Schipp, Clemenz** is a niche practice with a national outlook, advising the Mittelstand and larger companies on restructuring, pension schemes and all aspects of employment law. Management boards are also advised.

White & Case LLP is increasingly versatile in its activities, no longer existing as the corporate support function it once was. Restructuring, employee share programmes and spin-offs were all handled by Ingrid Deuchler's impressive outfit, and clients such as Mobilcom, Motorola GmbH and Kraft Foods Deutschland all contribute to the firm's rise up the rankings for 2006.

Markus Sondermann at new firm **B.B.O.R.S Rechtsanwälte** has mainly advised US and Italian-owned German companies on negotiations with works councils and reconciliation plans.

Bird & Bird derives its employment practice from its corporate team, as a result offering advice on employment aspects of corporate deals. It also shows well in standalone matters, advising O2 on legal aspects of its works constitution and an international manufacturer on a proposed outsourcing mandate, following on from a similar mandate for British Telecom where its international presence was a key strength. Martin Nebling heads the team.

Strong in Essen and active in Düsseldorf, **Buse Heberer Fromm** is active in day-to-day consultation work with clients, as well as restructuring and reorganisations. New clients such as Cap Gemini underline the firm's progress in the market.

DLA Piper Rudnick Gray Cary's annex of *Coudert Brothers LLP*'s former Frankfurt operation brings outsourcing and restructuring expert Michael Magotsch to the firm.

Dechert LLP's employment practice is very much a corporate transaction-focused entity, although Olaf Fasshauer has expertise in wrongful dismissal and employment-related litigation.

Eckert Dörsam Klette represents a major IT company on complex employment disputes.

Haarmann Hemmelrath advises predominantly on restructuring mandates as part of corporate deals. Friederike Göbbels in Munich is the key contact.

Hoffmann Liebs Fritsch & Partner (HLFP) advises companies on restructuring mandates and pension schemes, and has increased its share of the corporate support market.

Jones Day enjoys good relations with international pharmaceutical, telecoms and technology clients in Germany, and has branched out relationships to include employment advice. Transactional support is at the core, although collective agreement law and works council matters also feature.

KSB INTAX, based in northern Germany, tends to handle employment mandates as part of a full service to clients, who include manufacturing and automobile companies.

Mayer, Brown, Rowe & Maw LLP is making inroads into the market, advising some of the more reputed names among the firm's clients including Gillette and Google on outsourcing, minor restructuring and corporate support matters. Guido Zeppenfeld is establishing himself.

McDermott Will & Emery Rechtsanwälte Steuerberater LLP leverages off an increasingly impressive corporate practice to attach itself to some large-scale, post-merger integration mandates.

Melchers advises clients, including from the aerospace and industrial sectors, on restructurings incorporating negotiations with works councils and trade unions.

Norton Rose Vieregge enjoys good relations with Nestlé, having advised it on the employment issues of an acquisition, and also performed on several restructurings. INVESCO was advised on the split-off and reorganisation of elements of its German business. Cornelia Marquardt heads the team.

PPR & Partner offers a largely M&A support function or restructuring, but also engages in negotiations with works councils.

Salans has good restructuring expertise in Berlin through Thomas Wahlig and the former **Haarmann Hemmelrath** team.

Wilmer Cutler Pickering Hale and Dorr LLP runs an employment team from within its corporate group which is primarily focused on transactional work. Its litigation capability was bolstered in 2005 by the recruitment of Anja Mengel from **Linklaters Oppenhoff & Rädler**.

IP: COPYRIGHT

CMS Hasche Sigle is proficient in all areas of IP, with Hamburg and Cologne headquarters of expertise, particularly in press and television broadcasting matters. Ulrich Külper heads the team from Hamburg, while Albrecht Pilz and Gordian Hasselblatt lend litigation skills in Cologne.

Stuttgart-based IP niche specialist **Löffler Wenzel Sedelmeier** has an historically outstanding reputation in IP matters, and remains a leading firm according to rivals.

Lovells' all-round excellence in IP is reflected in a copyright practice which is geared towards media and IT. Royalties and licensing agreements are handled, including mobile content licensing, as are personality rights disputes on behalf of publishers and software companies.

Baker & McKenzie enjoys a prominent position in the market and is at the cutting edge of new developments having advised on the first registered community designs dispute in the country. Around 60% of the firm's activities in the sector are contentious, with design rights a particular feature for the year. Biotechnology licensing is also an increasing area. Michael Fammler's team advises The Body Shop, among other big-name clients. Bettina Goldman left the firm in 2004 to take up an in-house position.

Beiten Burkhardt maintains a strong presence across all IP fields with large dedicated teams in each sector. Copyright issues are handled for the firm's big publishing client base and music collecting society GEMA is another client.

Despite being a niche industrial property-focused firm, **Boehmert & Boehmert** reaches across Germany, Spain, France and China. In copyright matters, an artist-heavy client base including musicians, actors, film directors and authors are guided in all aspects of copyright

IP: COPYRIGHT

CMS HASCHE SIGLE ✪
LÖFFLER WENZEL SEDELMEIER
LOVELLS ✪

Baker & McKenzie ✪
Beiten Burkhardt ✪
Boehmert & Boehmert
Freshfields Bruckhaus Deringer
Harmsen Utescher ✪
Hertin Anwaltssozietät
McDermott Will & Emery Rechtsanwälte Steuerberater LLP ✪
Schwarz Kelwing Wicke Westpfahl
Taylor Wessing ✪
Unverzagt – von Have

Bird & Bird ✪
Gleiss Lutz ✪
Graf von Westphalen Bappert & Modest ✪
Heuking Kühn Lüer Wojtek ✪
Latham & Watkins LLP
Lausen Rechtsanwälte
Linklaters Oppenhoff & Rädler ✪
Rospatt Osten Pross ✪
Sasse & Partner
Schweizer (Prof), Kanzlei
Wilmer Cutler Pickering Hale and Dorr LLP ✪

Allen & Overy LLP ✪
Ashurst ✪
avocado rechtsanwälte
Becker Büttner Held, Rechtsanwälte Wirtschaftsprüfer Steuerberater
Buse Heberer Fromm ✪
Hogan & Hartson Raue L.L.P. ✪
Kropp-Olbertz Schulte-Franzheim Seibert
Lichte Rechtsanwälte
Norton Rose Vieregge
PPR & Partner ✪
Shearman & Sterling LLP
White & Case LLP

Firms are listed A-Z in tiers which are ranked in order of priority
✪ Indicates firm displays contact details at the end of this chapter.

protection. Wilhelm Nordemann in Potsdam is well regarded.

Boasting a terrific reputation across Europe, **Freshfields Bruckhaus Deringer** offers both contentious and non-contentious advice from all its offices in Germany, with the concentration of expertise in Frankfurt. Recent increases in activity have been in data protection, in connection with offshore outsourcing mandates, and technology transfer block exemption matters. Transactional support remains strong. It is a large and well-versed operation, helmed by Peter Chrocziel.

Hamburg niche outfit **Harmsen Utescher** advises on contentious and non-contentious work, with a healthy music client base and increasing activity in digital exploitation issues. The firm also has a forte in design rights.

Hertin Anwaltssozietät celebrated its 60th anniversary in 2005, continuing in its traditions of delivering top-notch niche IP services. Christlieb Klages advises an artist-heavy client base on copyright protection, while new instructions from Sony BMG on anti-piracy matters are a valid indication of how far the firm punches above its weight.

McDermott Will & Emery Rechtsanwälte Steuerberater LLP displayed its growing expertise in a variety of contentious cases incorporating image rights infringements and musical copyright, as well as advising on general issues such as software licensing and research project issues.

Schwarz Kelwing Wicke Westpfahl has a very credible all-round media practice which crosses over into IP matters, while it is also known for advertising work including unfair competition.

Taylor Wessing has a strong client base in software and technology in Berlin under Andreas Meissner, advising Fujitsu Siemens on copyright fees. Publishing is very strong in the Munich office, where the arrival of Reinhard Gaertner is a massive asset in the press field. Fellow new arrival in Munich, Sylbie Gierschmann brings data protection know-how. Hamburg offers excellent broadcasting and funding services under Marin v. Albrecht, and Carl A Claussen has a strong sports practice and is active in marketing and image rights advice.

Unverzagt – von Have advises ten Bundesliga footballers on sponsorship and image rights and also advises advertising agency Saatchi & Saatchi. The fact that it has retained Microsoft in respect of copyright advice on its new operating system speaks volumes for the growing reputation of the firm.

Bird & Bird has increasing involvement in design copyright, with matters handled from within the firm's lauded IP practice.

Gleiss Lutz is currently advising Hewlett-Packard on a litigious issue, and also advises US media clients on licensing matters including distribution, merchandising and advertising.

Graf von Westphalen Bappert & Modest made significant gains in the market with the recruitment of Walter Scheuerl from **Lovells** who brings expertise in unfair competition, an adjunct to a specialisation in advising agencies on the development of advertising campaigns.

Heuking Kühn Lüer Wojtek's focus on non-contentious works leads it into media and publishing matters including licensing agreements. IT copyright matters are also handled by a national team which includes experts Michael Schmittmann in Düsseldorf, Søren Pietzcker in Hamburg and Rudolf du Mesnil in Frankfurt.

Latham & Watkins LLP has a good publishing client base, advising *Der Speigel* on general IP rights, while Amazon Deutschland also uses the firm for similar matters. An excellent relationship with Stage Entertainment GmbH also provides licensing mandates, and design right protection instructions from furniture manufacturers have been a feature of the year. Andrea Jager-Lenz and Ulrich Börger are valued experts.

Lausen Rechtsanwälte's copyright activity is mainly oriented around the media sector, where film and entertainment companies and publishing houses are advised on licensing and distribution, as well as some litigation issues. Privacy rights are also handled.

Linklaters Oppenhoff & Rädler is strong in the entertainment sector, with film and television an area of note. Copyright and antitrust go increasingly hand in hand.

Rospatt Osten Pross has a terrific reputation in the market and has had since its inception in 1946. The modern firm has strength in 3D design rights and general all-round IP litigation drives the firm.

Music specialist **Sasse & Partner** has a booming rights clearance and licensing practice, advising on new forms of exploitation including online and mobile phone platforms.

Kanzlei Prof Schweizer, and particulary name partner Robert Schweizer, has a highly reputed name in press matters with clients across the printed and electronic media world. Rivals attribute the firm with a keen focus on its target market.

Wilmer Cutler Pickering Hale and Dorr LLP uses its IP capability in tandem with an increasing presence in corporate circles. Licensing issues are also handled by Christian Breuer and his team. Lastminute.com GmbH was advised on unfair competition matters.

The celebrated Henning Harte-Bavendamm continues to drive the IP practice at **Allen & Overy LLP**, with a standing in the market that is attracting the highest-calibre clients. The firm is an increasingly important advisor to Sony, expanding its role with the music giant on litigation matters, while design rights also provided a good deal of contentious work. The firm is more prominent on the corporate support side, advising on the use of the WestLB name in an acquisition.

Ashurst's IP offering supports its M&A practice well, although litigation matters have included advising a UK publishing house against a German collecting society. The firm is also active in software and hardware development.

avocado rechtsanwälte is active in the publishing sector, advising in print and especially electronic media circles on advertising and information exploitation, as well as supporting outsourcing projects.

Becker Büttner Held, Rechtsanwälte Wirtschaftsprüfer Steuerberater handles online music copyright issues.

Buse Heberer Fromm is active in advising on design rights, particularly in the fashion industry, while advertising agencies, IT clients and publishing houses round off the client base. The firm enjoys a fruitful relationship with **Field Fisher Waterhouse** in the UK.

Hogan & Hartson Raue L.L.P. has a burgeoning reputation in German media circles, boosted by clients such as Axel Springer and lawyers such as Christoph Wagner, while Cologne-based **Kropp-Olbertz Schulte-Franzheim Seibert** represents publishers, authors and artists.

Despite the loss of Carsten Bartholl to **Taylor Wessing**, **Lichte Rechtsanwälte** remains a firm of longstanding high repute in the music industry, with many agencies, producers and record companies all instructing the firm. Walter Lichte is a top-ranked figure.

PPR & Partner has leveraged off a food industry client base to advise on labelling and advertising matters. The firm also advises clients on the use of photography in advertising.

Shearman & Sterling LLP is mostly engaged in IP issues related to corporate transactions. Thomas Nägele is the key figure.

White & Case LLP is active in trade secret litigation.

IP: PATENTS AND REGISTERED DESIGNS (DISPUTE RESOLUTION)

Bird & Bird boasts one of the country's leading patent lawyers in co-head of the international IP department and chairman of the firm's Germany offices, Wolfgang von Meibom. He is backed by a market-leading team across its German offices. A truly international patent litigation practice advises predominantly overseas clients, making good use of the firm's improving specialist European network, but also maintains many Mittelstand clients. A heavy biotech workload has recently been supplemented with a raft of instructions from the electronics industry, including from Nokia and Electrolux, and new clients Thomson and Creative. Research and development agreements are also handled.

Munich-based **KLAKA Rechtsanwälte** is a market-leading boutique, with a reputation in pharmaceutical-related litigation that is unsurpassed due to the excellent Michael Nieder and Olaf Giebe. New technology issues were a major feature of the year, particularly in telecoms where it represented longstanding clients in infringment proceedings against some of the world's biggest telecoms companies.

Lovells' celebrated patent practice continues to excel, with one high-profile telecoms-related dispute highlighting the firm's technical expertise and resources, both in Germany and London; the Düsseldorf office alone houses 20 patent lawyers. Also worthy of note is a run of 'patent ambush' cases, and an increasing presence in pharmaceutical litigation matters came with new clients. Andreas von Falck deservedly earns the praise of many of his fellow practitioners.

Rospatt Osten Pross has been a renowned patents practice for nearly sixty years, and the continuing presence of Peter von Rospatt and Horst von der Osten gives the firm a certain grandeur. An array of excellent junior lawyers also has a reputation for good technical knowledge.

IP, PATENTS AND REGISTERED DEISGNS (DISPUTE RESOLUTION)

BIRD & BIRD ✪
KLAKA RECHTSANWÄLTE ✪
LOVELLS ✪
ROSPATT OSTEN PROSS ✪

Bardehle Pagenberg Dost Altenburg Geissler ✪
Krieger, Mes & Graf von der Groeben
Lichtenstein, Körner & Partner
Preu, Bohlig & Partner
Reimann Osterrieth Köhler Haft Rechtsanwälte ✪
Wildanger Kehrwald Graf v. Schwerin & Partners

Boehmert & Boehmert
Gleiss Lutz ✪
Harmsen Utescher ✪
Lorenz Seidler Gossel
Taylor Wessing ✪

CBH Cornelius Bartenbach Haesemann & Partners, member of ius laboris ✪
CMS Hasche Sigle ✪
Freshfields Bruckhaus Deringer
Grünecker, Kinkeldey, Stockmair & Schwanhäusser
Hoffmann.Eitle
Mayer, Brown, Rowe & Maw LLP ✪
Patzina Rechtsanwälte
Simmons & Simmons ✪
White & Case LLP

Allen & Overy LLP ✪
Baker & McKenzie ✪
Beiten Burkhardt ✪
Buse Heberer Fromm ✪
Hengeler Mueller ✪
Hertin Anwaltssozietät
Hogan & Hartson Raue L.L.P. ✪
Jones Day
Latham & Watkins LLP
Linklaters Oppenhoff & Rädler ✪
Löhde Leo Schmidt-Hollburg & Witte
McDermott Will & Emery Rechtsanwälte Steuerberater LLP ✪
Wilmer Cutler Pickering Hale and Dorr LLP ✪

Firms are listed A-Z in tiers which are ranked in order of priority
✪ *Indicates firm displays contact details at the end of this chapter.*

Although it handles patent prosecutions, **Bardehle Pagenberg Dost Altenburg Geissler**'s main area of focus is in litigation, where clients include technology and biotechnology companies from the US. Offices in Paris and Alicante, in addition to its German presences in Düsseldorf and Munich, give it a broad European spread, allied to a liaison office in Shanghai.

Düsseldorf-based industrial property specialists **Krieger, Mes & Graf von der Groeben** has a traditional focus on patent and utility model law. In the patents field the firm is exclusively active in litigation with a heavy focus on forensic work. There is a high level of technical knowledge among its lawyers, epitomised by former Bayer AG patent in-house counsel and IP veteran Ulrich Krieger, while Peter Mes also impresses. Günther Gretz has retired.

Lichtenstein, Körner & Partner, with offices in Dresden, Stuttgart and Alicante, has a history of advising US clients on German and European patent issues. The expertise of Eberhard Körner is a big pull for clients.

Preu, Bohlig & Partner is a longstanding specialist firm of high repute in the market, with offices in Dusseldorf, Hamburg, Munich and Berlin.

Reimann Osterrieth Köhler Haft Rechtsanwälte is an excellent IP boutique formed by ex-**Clifford Chance** partners Thomas Reimann and Christian Osterrieth, and former **Taylor Wessing** partner Martin Köhler. Prestigious clients from the telecoms, electronics and other industries are testament to the high regard in which the individuals are held in the market, and the arrival of Thomas Schmitz further strengthens the team.

Dusseldorf-based IP boutique **Wildanger Kehrwald Graf v. Schwerin & Partners** continues to be a big presence in litigation circles after around 40 years in the market. Roland Kehrwald and Wolf Graf Schwerin advise German and international companies predominantly on patent infringement litigation, with technology and biotechnology particular areas of activity.

Although **Boehmert & Boehmert**'s key patents office is Munich, the firm has patent expertise present throughout the firm's significant German network of offices. In addition to standard expertise in life sciences and biotechnology, this justifiably renowned firm has expertise in semi-conductor and software technology, displaying a wide spread of experience and specific sector knowledge.

Gleiss Lutz's patent litigation practice is the most dynamic of the firm's respected IP practices. The firm enjoys close links with clients in the automotive industry, where it is involved in a patent arbitration case, and also is prominent in the healthcare and pharmaceutical sectors.

IP specialist **Harmsen Utescher** has a long history in the patents market where clients hail from the chemicals, biotech, IT and mechanical engineering sectors. Michael Schaeffer is very well known.

Munich-based **Lorenz Seidler Gossel** has advised on contentious and non-contentious patent issues for over 40 years, and retains a good standing in the market.

Taylor Wessing places a strong focus on IP/IT, and the development of its patent litigation practice, including several lateral hires, is a reflection of the dedication shown. Active in the medical and pharmaceutical fields, the firm's international network is a valuable asset.

CBH Cornelius Bartenbach Haesemann & Partners, member of ius laboris boasts the expertise of the venerable Kurt Bartenbach, whose technical knowledge, experience and specialist expertise in employee inventions mark him out in the field.

Patents and utility patents are notable areas of work at **CMS Hasche Sigle**, including a focus on matters in the food industry.

Freshfields Bruckhaus Deringer is developing well in patent litigation, advising clients such as Motorola, Intel and Microsoft and making use of a potent European network, working closely in particular with its Amsterdam office. German strength is mainly focused in Düsseldorf. The practice also incorporates a pharmaceuticals and life sciences sector group and links up with the antitrust team.

Grünecker, Kinkeldey, Stockmair & Schwanhäusser is a specialist IP firm with a superb reputation in patents work, primarily in registrations and prosecution, but also houses a very capable litigation practice. Specific areas of expertise include material science and nanotechnology.

Hoffmann.Eitle is a respected name in the market and a London office gives it an unusual dimension. A large and talented team means it can handle the biggest mandates.

Increasingly impressive across the board in IP, **Mayer, Brown, Rowe & Maw LLP**'s patent practice is following this pattern, advising the likes of Dior and Nokia on design-related matters. The firm is also attempting to increase its exposure in the pharmaceutical world by tapping into its existing client base previously only served in corporate matters.

Small Frankfurt operation **Patzina Rechtsanwälte** advises clients on infringement matters as well as negotiating and drafting licence agreements.

Under Peter Meyer, **Simmons & Simmons** is developing a reputation that exceeds its diminutive size. Close connections with the firm's sister offices in Rotterdam and Tokyo mean that the office works very much as part of an international structure on litigation matters. New instructions from US pharmaceutical clients boost the firm's profile.

Allen & Overy LLP is increasingly active in the pharmaceuticals and biotech markets, an area led by Wolfgang Witz in Frankfurt. Global licence agreements and litigation are handled, with several cases in the misappropriation of confidential information showcasing good skills in that area.

Baker & McKenzie's patent litigation work is handled from within the general litigation group.

Beiten Burkhardt advises a strong industrial and manufacturing client base on litigation and advisory matters.

Buse Heberer Fromm advises on patent litigation and licensing agreements.

Hengeler Mueller has increased its patent litigation presence in Düsseldorf having represented a number of IT clients, supplementing an existing licensing capability.

Hertin Anwaltssozietät's strength lies in the pharmaceutical and biotech sectors, working closely alongside its trade mark department on disputes.

Henning Mennenöh is a key figure in the biotech sphere at **Hogan & Hartson Raue L.L.P.** but his focus is more corporate.

Jones Day combines patent litigation and, unusually for an international firm, patent prosecution in Munich. Chemistry and pharmaceutical industries are well served, thanks to a sector focus on life sciences, and Friedrich Klinkert also has expertise in automotive safety engineering. The three-partner team shows good knowledge and depth.

Latham & Watkins LLP's comparatively small team exists primarily as a support function to the corporate team, but is increasingly active in patent litigation and risk management issues.

At **Linklaters Oppenhoff & Rädler** a small team advises the firm's multinational client base on litigation matters and technology-driven transactional matters, as well as research and development and licensing issues. Coca-Cola is a client.

Löhde Leo Schmidt-Hollburg & Witte leverages off a good media client base to offer patent litigation advice in that sector in particular.

McDermott Will & Emery Rechtsanwälte Steuerberater LLP is increasingly strong in patents work, advising on software and hardware patents. The firm is also looking at moving into the biotech sector.

Wilmer Cutler Pickering Hale and Dorr LLP is active in the pharmaceutical and life science sectors, with Procter & Gamble and Pfizer instructing the firm on European patents.

IP: PATENTS AND REGISTERED DESIGNS (REGISTRATIONS)

The comments below refer to firms that house significant registration and prosecution capability in the form of patent attorneys.

Boehmert & Boehmert is an old hand in the market, with an array of talented patent attorneys in all of its many offices. Patent prosecution is the firm's main focus.

Eisenführ, Speiser & Partner boasts exceptional capability in the chemistry field, while the arrival of senior patent attorney Joachim Glaeser from his own former firm brings vast experience to the Bremen office. Clients include Philips, Nokia, Nike and Kellogg's. The firm has expanded from its Bremen base to Munich, Berlin and Hamburg.

Grünecker, Kinkeldey, Stockmair & Schwanhäusser and **Hoffmann.Eitle** are outstanding patents practices, with expertise in science and technology.

Based in Munich and Düsseldorf, **König . Szynka . Tilmann . Von Renesse** specialises in biotech work, although its expertise is broad and includes optical sciences and engineering.

IP, PATENTS AND REGISTERED DEISGNS (REGISTRATIONS)

Boehmert & Boehmert
Eisenführ, Speiser & Partner
Grünecker, Kinkeldey, Stockmair & Schwanhäusser
Hoffmann.Eitle
König . Szynka . Tilmann . Von Renesse
Uexküll & Stolberg ✪

Bardehle Pagenberg Dost Altenburg Geissler
Harmsen Utescher ✪
Hertin Anwaltssozietät
Viering, Jentschura & Partner
Vossius & Partner

Firms are listed A-Z in tiers which are ranked in order of priority
✪ *Indicates firm displays contact details at the end of this chapter.*

Uexküll & Stolberg's reputation in the biotech fields is elevated by the well-known Ingeborg Völker. The client base is mostly US, and includes ExxonMobil, Colgate, Johnson & Johnson and Black & Decker. The firm has offices in Munich and Hamburg, and the team houses both patent attorneys and attorneys at law.

Bardehle Pagenberg Dost Altenburg Geissler continues to advise on patent prosecution and registration matters from a European network.

Hertin Anwaltssozietät houses two patent attorneys in a growing team which focuses on the biotech and pharmaceutical sectors, advising research institutes.

IP: TRADE MARKS

Bird & Bird's superb IP offering extends to trade mark work where portfolio management for multinational clients is the focus of the team. The fact that the team remains at the cutting edge of the market was exemplified in protecting Deutsche Telekom's registered colour trade mark against revocation proceedings. The firm continues to advise the client in a triumvirate with **Lovells** and **Mayer, Brown, Rowe & Maw LLP**, and also increased its prosecution offering during 2005. New clients Audi AG and the Discovery Channel point to a growing reputation, not least due to the expertise of Wolfgang von Meibom, Klaus-Jürgen Michaeli and their formidable team.

Linklaters Oppenhoff & Rädler offers global clients protection advice worldwideh and also offers portfolio valuation for calculations of royalties for licensing. Unfair competition is a particular strength, with the firm advising on all aspects from market entry to litigation. Deutsche Post remains a major client, with its entire trade mark portfolio managed out of the Cologne office as well as its sponsorship of the FIFA World Cup 2006, while others come from the pharmaceuticals, media and food industries.

Lovells has significant expertise in Hamburg, from where it advises the likes of AB and Volvo, although increasing demand from existing clients has led to more activity out of Munich and Frankfurt.

Baker & McKenzie excels in M&A support, where it handled the trade mark issues surrounding a French takeover of a German company in the electronics field, and in standalone matters, where a global client base of telecoms, IT, clothing and automotive companies engage the firm. These include The Body Shop, which was advised on a franchise dispute, and advertising agency Leo Burnett Worldwide, Inc. More unusually, the firm advised on complex questions of transfer-pricing within the scope of a company audit. Globally, the firm rolled out its Global IP Manager system, administering over 200,000 trade marks worldwide, while domestically Michael Fammler heads a large and multi-skilled team.

One of the finest all-round IP niche firms in Germany, **Boehmert & Boehmert** runs thoroughly impressive trade mark practices from Munich and Bremen, encompassing all portfolio management issues from applications, searches and infringements. Michaela Huth-Dierig heads the department.

Of the all-round boost given to **CMS Hasche Sigle**'s IP capability by the takeover of the former **Norton Rose Vieregge** Cologne office, the firm's trade mark team was particularly enhanced.

Freshfields Bruckhaus Deringer's experience in the market means it is well placed to offer strategic litigation, with the resources to handle less straightforward matters. The usual core areas of sponsorship, advertising, unfair competition and portfolio management are handled with aplomb.

Gleiss Lutz's trade mark expertise is mainly housed in its Stuttgart office where the excellent Stefan Völker is based, with an emphasis on prosecution work. Clients advised on general matters include several automotive clients such as DaimlerChrysler, a reflection of the firm's long-standing connections in the automotive industry. Other matters incorporate licensing and unfair compeition, where it has acted for Volkswagen and T-Mobile. Munich is also a busy office.

Hamburg-based **Harmsen Utescher** holds a longstanding presence in the market, as well as the near-unanimous respect of its peers.

Lichtenstein, Körner & Partner's Carmen Lichtenstein and Thomas Sambuc are known for swift and client-focused service in trade mark matters. The IP practice advises numerous US clients.

IP specialist **Lorenz Seidler Gossel** has respectable trade mark capability, and is popular with technology clients.

Mayer, Brown, Rowe & Maw LLP continues to make strides, handling worldwide trade mark filing strategies and portfolio management for Deutsche Telekom as part of a triumverate with **Lovells** and **Bird & Bird**. In contentious matters Ulrich Brückmann successfully advised on the lifting of a trade mark injunction, which came alongside other mandates for Nike and Gillette. The firm has also developed products on parallel imports and anti-counterfeiting measures; terrific progress for a little over a year in the market.

Nörr Stiefenhofer Lutz handles some global trade mark portfolios, and also represented Henkel KgaA, as well as its Czech and Polish subsidiaries, on unfair competition issues in those territories.

Taylor Wessing is increasing its share of the trade mark market, advising major fashion and sports apparel retailers in very high-profile disputes, and showing particularly strongly in unfair competition matters for clients including Dyson. The firm's strength lies primarily in Munich and Düsseldorf, and it operates closely with excellent teams in Paris and London on pan-European portfolio management.

Unverzagt – von Have retains a top-notch trade mark practice despite its diversification into a more expansive media field. It handles trade mark, sponsorship and advertising issues for the City of Hamburg related to the upcoming FIFA World Cup.

Trade marks are the overriding focus of the IP offering at **White & Case LLP**, with the excellent Christian Rohnke at the forefront. Litigation is the main driver, with clients such as Microsoft engaging the firm in unfair competition mandates. FIFA is also instructing the firm on licensing deals.

Allen & Overy LLP continues to make progress, advising Knoll on its pan-European trade mark strategy, and Levi Strauss & Co on protection and litigation.

Friederike Bahr handles trade marks at the Munich office of **Beiten Burkhardt**, especially for various sporting clients including FIFA, FC Bayern Munich and the German Golf Association.

Eisenführ, Speiser & Partner has successfully branched out from its origins as a patent prosecution firm to establish itself in the trade mark field, leveraging off a stellar client list including Philips to advise on anti-counterfeiting and registered design rights.

Hengeler Mueller splits trade mark expertise equally between Frankfurt and Düsseldorf, with six lawyers in each office. Litigation matters are handled predominantly out of Düsseldorf. Domestic clients include high street brand names while overseas instructions tend to come from technology and pharmaceutical companies. A move up the rankings this year reflects a growing presence in the market.

On top of **KLAKA Rechtsanwälte**'s top-notch patents practice, the firm has significant expertise in trade mark and unfair competition work through Andreas Schulz.

Andrea Jaeger-Lenz at **Latham & Watkins LLP** is a top-notch trade mark lawyer, advising clients that require and receive a broadly skilled practice with international connections. Nestlé is a long-term client, while the firm's increasing focus on litigation has led to such prestigious instructions as challenging infringments of the Red Cross trade mark.

IP: TRADE MARKS

BIRD & BIRD ⊙
LINKLATERS OPPENHOFF & RÄDLER ⊙
LOVELLS ⊙

Baker & McKenzie ⊙
Boehmert & Boehmert
CMS Hasche Sigle ⊙
Freshfields Bruckhaus Deringer
Gleiss Lutz ⊙
Harmsen Utescher ⊙
Lichtenstein, Körner & Partner
Lorenz Seidler Gossel
Mayer, Brown, Rowe & Maw LLP ⊙
Nörr Stiefenhofer Lutz ⊙
Taylor Wessing ⊙
Unverzagt – von Have
White & Case LLP

Allen & Overy LLP ⊙
Beiten Burkhardt ⊙
Eisenführ, Speiser & Partner
Hengeler Mueller ⊙
Klaka Rechtsanwälte ⊙
Latham & Watkins LLP

Bardehle Pagenberg Dost Altenburg Geissler
FPS Fritze Paul Seelig ⊙
Graf von Westphalen Bappert & Modest ⊙
Grünecker, Kinkeldey, Stockmair & Schwanhäusser
Hertin Anwaltssozietät
Heuking Kühn Lüer Wojtek ⊙
Hoffmann.Eitle
Kleiner Rechtsanwälte
McDermott Will & Emery Rechtsanwälte Steuerberater LLP ⊙
Meissner, Bolte & Partner
Patzina Rechtsanwälte
Schwarz Kelwing Wicke Westpfahl ⊙

Buse Heberer Fromm ⊙
CBH Cornelius Bartenbach Haesemann & Partners, member of ius laboris ⊙
Clifford Chance
Happ Luther & Partner
Heussen Rechtsanwaltsgesellschaft mbH
Jones Day
Klinger & Kollegen
Luther Rechtsanwaltsgesellschaft mbH ⊙
PPR & Partner ⊙
Rospatt Osten Pross ⊙
Siebeke Lange Wilbert
Simmons & Simmons ⊙
Spitz · Gaul · Golda
Uexküll & Stolberg ⊙
Wilmer Cutler Pickering Hale and Dorr LLP ⊙

Firms are listed A-Z in tiers which are ranked in order of priority
⊙ Indicates firm displays contact details at the end of this chapter.

Bardehle Pagenberg Dost Altenburg Geissler handles a portfolio of world-famous brands based in Germany and beyond from its offices in Düsseldorf, Munich, Paris, Alicante and Shanghai.

FPS Fritze Paul Seelig has a strong reputation in piracy cases, although registration matters are also handled.

On top of unfair competition expertise, engaged by clients including Wilkinson Sword, **Graf von Westphalen Bappert & Modest** enjoys good contacts in the food industry, advising one big name confectionary and beverage group.

Grünecker, Kinkeldey, Stockmair & Schwanhäusser houses a 20-strong department comprised of trade mark attorneys and lawyers, handling prosecution, litigation and licensing in fields such as computer science and technology.

Hertin Anwaltssozietät's expertise in IP spills over into the trade mark field where Hermann-Josef Omsells advises major insurer HUK COBERG on all litigious trade mark matters and unfair competition. Bild Zeitung is advised on its internet portal.

Heuking Kühn Lüer Wojtek gears its trade mark work towards advertising, and unfair competition in particular, with Japanese and US clients furnishing the firm with a lot of its work.

Although patent attorneys by trade, **Hoffmann.Eitle** retains a credible trade mark practice.

Kleiner Rechtsanwälte advises chemical, IT and food companies. The firm has offices in Düsseldorf, Stuttgart and Mannheim.

McDermott Will & Emery Rechtsanwälte Steuerberater LLP handles trade mark issues as part of a general approach to IP. Work includes unfair competition and the adaptation of a trade mark portfolio across Europe.

Meissner, Bolte & Partner includes trade mark expertise in its array of IP capabilities.

Patzina Rechtsanwälte handles trade marks and passing-off issues for designer labels Ferrari, Swatch and others. Andreas Bock heads the team.

Schwarz Kelwing Wicke Westpfahl's highly respected practice advises IKEA, among others, on trade mark registration and infringement.

Buse Heberer Fromm houses its trade mark expertise mainly in the Hamburg office where it advises US clients on licence agreements and Jette Joop.

CBH Cornelius Bartenbach Haesemann & Partners, member of ius laboris offers consultancy services and litigation advice to such luminary clients as DaimlerChrysler AG, Haribo and Deutsche Lotto und Totoblock.

Clifford Chance's IP department offers strong support in transactional matters.

Happ Luther & Partner has very specialised expertise in the form of former tobacco industry in-house counsel Geert Johan Seelig. His work for Imperial Tobacco includes advising on innovative trade mark strategies which incorporate 3D design registrations in light of the increasing clampdowns on tobacco advertising. Pharmaceutical clients are also advised on litigious issues including unfair competition.

Jones Day covers all aspects of trade mark work, from piracy and border confiscation, to unfair competition, protection of secrets, and German and European design law. Christian Meister enjoys good penetration of the textile, cosmetics and technology industries, while a sector focus on life sciences provides specialised support.

Klinger & Kollegen has expanded its trade mark advice to cover aspects of Internet domain law.

PPR & Partner has built on a trade mark administration practice to advise a manufacturing company on the protection of its trade marks against former sister companies.

Rospatt Osten Pross's superb reputation in IP matters extends to trade mark matters, where the firm most notably managed to have the colour blue registered as a trade mark for its petrol station client.

Simmons & Simmons, in addition to patents work, is also active in trade marks, establishing new relationships with Japanese pharmaceutical clients.

Spitz · Gaul · Golda has a media and fashion client base that includes adidas, Marco Polo and Konami. Name partner Volker Spitz is an anti-counterfeit and piracy specialist.

Frank Dettmann is the trade mark specialist at **Uexküll & Stolberg**, where his clients include Colgate and Tiffany.

Wilmer Cutler Pickering Hale and Dorr LLP's Christian Breuer handles trade mark rights and disputes for clients in the IT, media and automotive sectors.

INFORMATION TECHNOLOGY

Freshfields Bruckhaus Deringer is tremendously impressive, with a large and talented team in Germany supported by an enviable international network, an atttraction for its multinational client base which includes Hewlett-Packard, Mars Group, Microsoft, Nintendo, SEAT and Sony. Good examples of this capability include advising Adobe on the localisation of a services agreement and technical consulting agreement in seven jurisdictions around the world. IT outsourcing for banks and other private companies has increased, bringing with it more data-protection issues. Peter Chrocziel heads the multi-disciplinary IP/IT team jointly with Avril Martindale in London.

SSW Schneider Schiffer Weihermüller remains a force in the German market, with the venerable Jochen Schneider still pulling the strings at this niche firm. Outsourcing remains a key strength, with public procurement an increasingly impressive area driven by hospital clients. Software licensing and development and data protection are other areas particularly recommended.

INFORMATION TECHNOLOGY

FRESHFIELDS BRUCKHAUS DERINGER
SSW SCHNEIDER SCHIFFER WEIHERMÜLLER ✪

Baker & McKenzie ✪
Bartsch und Partner GbR
CMS Hasche Sigle ✪
Clifford Chance
Lovells ✪
Nörr Stiefenhofer Lutz ✪

Beiten Burkhardt ✪
Buse Heberer Fromm ✪
Gleiss Lutz ✪
Latham & Watkins LLP
Linklaters Oppenhoff & Rädler ✪
McDermott Will & Emery Rechtsanwälte Steuerberater LLP ✪
SHS Schreiber Hahn Schmidt
Taylor Wessing ✪
White & Case LLP
Willkie Farr & Gallagher LLP ✪
Witte

Allen & Overy LLP ✪
avocado rechtsanwälte
Bird & Bird ✪
Brehm & v. Moers
Godefroid & Pielorz
Graf von Westphalen Bappert & Modest ✪
Haarmann Hemmelrath ✪
Harmsen Utescher ✪
Haver & Mailänder
Hengeler Mueller ✪
Heuking Kühn Lüer Wojtek ✪
Heussen Rechtsanwaltsgesellschaft mbH
Jones Day
Löhde Leo Schmidt-Hollburg & Witte
Mayer, Brown, Rowe & Maw LLP ✪
Norton Rose Vieregge
Oppenländer Rechtsanwälte
PPR & Partner ✪
Reed Smith LLP ✪
Rödl & Partner GbR
Schwarz Kelwing Wicke Westpfahl ✪
Schweizer (Prof), Kanzlei
Velten Franz Jakoby
Wilmer Cutler Pickering Hale and Dorr LLP ✪

Firms are listed A-Z in tiers which are ranked in order of priority
✪ Indicates firm displays contact details at the end of this chapter.

Outsourcing continues to be a focal point of **Baker & McKenzie**'s terrific IT practice, with recent mandates including IT infrastructure and call centre outsourcings for the likes of global clothing retailers, manufacturers and finance companies, deals which were invariably cross border. IT service providers are also advised on bidding for projects, and e-commerce is a strength. The launch of a global music download platform showcased the firm's international breadth.

Karlsruhe-based **Bartsch und Partner GbR** is a commercial firm with a technology focus. Michael Bartsch leads a team high on online technology expertise.

CMS Hasche Sigle shows expertise in transactional matters, with experience in structuring agreements for outsourcing projects. New media is an area of activity, in both transactional and litigation circles. The multi-disciplinary approach serves clients well.

An expert team in **Clifford Chance**'s Frankfurt office is geared towards large-scale outsourcing and systems integration deals, particularly for banking clients, where the firm's huge resources can be deployed efficiently. Smaller teams operate out of the Munich and Düsseldorf offices.

Lovells shows well in outsourcing, particularly in the telecoms sector where T-Online is a major client. Wolfgang Büchner heads a multi-skilled team out of Munich. Stefan Schuppert heads a vibrant e-commerce team based in Munich, handling internet issues including legal issues surrounding hyperlinks and online advertising, and Hamburg, which is geared towards direct marketing. Amazon GmbH, Axel Springer and the German Direct Marketing Association are all clients.

Nörr Stiefenhofer Lutz is strong in all areas of the media, and the two Munich-based partners Peter Bräutigam and Andreas Leupold certainly uphold that tradition in an excellent IT and e-commerce department. Outsourcing continues to be a key area, with connections to Central and Eastern Europe a big asset, while the Stuttgart office advised CCP Systems GmbH on an embedded technology roll-out in co-operation with IBM. E-commerce issues are handled for the likes of eBay.

Beiten Burkhardt's relationship with the Ministry of Defence extends to instructions on several large outsourcing projects, and the firm also has experience in the establishment of internet platforms.

Buse Heberer Fromm's IT practice is centred in Frankfurt, with smaller teams in Essen and Hamburg. An inter-disciplinary outfit specialises in outsourcing mandates with the two biggest of the year both valued at around the €250m mark. More upmarket clients are coming to the firm, unusually more often from the supplier side. The firm also transfers its IT expertise to PPP matters where necessary.

Gleiss Lutz handles a varied workload, from outsourcing, including tenders and contracts, to e-commerce, and software development and licensing. Disputes arising from domain names and outsourcing issues are also frequent activities for the firm. Stefan Weidert heads the practice from Berlin.

Latham & Watkins LLP has good expertise in Frankfurt, where Ulrich Wuermeling is known for work in IT and telecoms. The firm shows strongest in the corporate arena, where it can combine strength in M&A and industry specialisation. Silicon Valley clients are key to the firm, as are investment banks increasingly. Outsourcing is also handled.

Following the departures of Margot Gräfin von Westerholt to **P+P Pöllath + Partners** and Kornelius Kleinlein to **Hogan & Hartson Raue L.L.P.**, **Linklaters Oppenhoff & Rädler** now focuses on contractual and outsourcing work, in which the Berlin office advises satellite operator SES Astra SA. The firm also enjoys close contact with major finance clients in similar transactions. Christian Hey is based in Cologne and Munich, and oversees the Frankfurt operation.

McDermott Will & Emery Rechtsanwälte Steuerberater LLP is generally strong in media matters, and information technology is no exception. Key client T-Online is advised on e-commerce matters, the firm was instructed by a leading European smart card manufacturer on its participation in the German health card project, and IPTV streaming solutions were also handled for a German ISP. A combination of good technical knowledge and a commercial approach to the sector are outstanding aspects.

Klaus Sommerlad at Frankfurt-based **SHS Schreiber Hahn Schmidt** drives a reputable outsourcing practice.

With a strong technology focus across the firm, including in corporate, it is no surprise to see **Taylor Wessing** making progress in IT. Kai Westerwelle brought Microsoft to the firm when he joined from **Clifford Chance** in 2003, and the relationship continues to thrive. E-government investment is another growing area. Eleven partners comprise one of the largest specialist IT teams in Germany. New arrival Detlef Klett from **Luther Rechtsanwaltsgesellschaft mbH** brings sector-specific disputes expertise, a good asset to a previously transaction-focused practice which was also boosted by the arrival of Reinhardt Gaertner from **Bird & Bird**.

White & Case LLP continues to show strongly in its focal area of outsourcing, advising the Dräger Group, Sparkasse and Fiduci, as well as several municipally owned entities on outsourcing mandates. The return of Jost Kotthoff from **Shearman & Sterling LLP** in June 2005, along with Detlev Gabel, brought further banking client connections with Deutsche Bank in particular. A major airline was also advised on the purchase of core software. Tobias von Tucker arrived into the fledgling Munich office from **Haarmann Hemmelrath**.

Willkie Farr & Gallagher LLP has always focused on technology as a key area since it opened in Germany, and remains a top-notch practice in outsourcing and IT project agreements with clients mainly hailing from the banking and finance sector, including Deutsche Bank and Accenture. Sven-Erik Heun brings additional regulatory and antitrust nous.

Munich-based IT boutique **Witte** has a good reputation at the smaller end of the market, offering advice on a range of issues in the technology field, mostly to clients in the industry.

Allen & Overy LLP continues to impress in outsourcing, advising INFO AG and Glidepath on various IT and data processing mandates, while several banks are also advised on various matters. Software development and licence agreements are also coming to the fore in Mark Hoenike's Hamburg-based practice.

avocado rechtsanwälte offers a full service in IT, advising start-ups to global corporations, with particular activity in outsourcing-related disputes incorporating data-protection matters.

The departure of Reinhardt Gaertner to **Taylor Wessing** not long after he arrived put the brakes on **Bird & Bird**'s progress in the market. However, the efforts of Alexander Duisberg means the firm maintains a relationship with major electronics, telecoms and technology clients on general commercial and public procurement matters. E-commerce is a growth area, and the firm has experience in voice-over-IP matters. Another was boost was the arrival of Susanne Koch from **Willkie Farr & Gallagher LLP** and further recruits have been targeted.

Media boutique **Brehm & v. Moers** houses an active, three-partner multimedia practice helmed by Benedikt Wemmer in Berlin. Concept development is a key area for the firm.

Dusseldorf-based commercial firm **Godefroid & Pielorz** gears its e-commerce expertise towards a client core of banks and small companies.

Klaus Brisch in the Cologne office of **Graf von Westphalen Bappert & Modest** is part of an increasingly specialised and focused IT operation at the firm which is particularly active with telecoms clients including Deutsche Telekom AG and T-Systems International GmbH. More cutting-edge work involves electronic billing and signatures, and e-government continues to be a notable area.

Hamburg IP boutique **Harmsen Utescher** advises on domain name disputes, as well as delivery and maintenance contracts.

Haver & Mailänder in Stuttgart is well versed in e-commerce matters, while **Hengeler Mueller** provides advice on media and internet-related matters.

Heuking Kühn Lüer Wojtek's Michael Schmittman has a strong presence in cable and satellite licensing, with SES Astar a longstanding client. Recent work includes advising local federal broadcaster NRV on various politically interesting matters, and forays have been made into broadband licences and online gambling.

At **Jones Day**, Hans-Werner Moritz is particularly active in the hardware and software industries, with manufacturers the key clients. Distributors, e-commerce providers and ISPs also engage the firm, particularly US and Swiss companies. Expertise stretches from outsourcing-related matters to piracy, data protection and licensing, incorporating top-notch technical know-how.

Löhde Leo Schmidt-Hollburg & Witte advises on software licensing, distribution and consulting projects, as well as global alliances and patent litigation.

Mayer, Brown, Rowe & Maw LLP has expanded from an outsourcing base to incorporate software licensing and data protection issues. The team dovetails with employment and antitrust lawyers at the firm.

Stuttgart-based commerical firm **Oppenländer Rechtsanwälte** advises companies on software projects and data-processing systems implementation. Markus Köhler is the internet and e-commerce contact.

PPR & Partner advises an array of software producers, something of a specialism for the firm.

Reed Smith LLP enters the table for 2006 having taken former **Freshfields Bruckhaus Deringer** IT expert Stefan Rippert from **Haarmann Hemmelrath**. His previous activities have included outsourcing, software projects and IT roll-outs for the likes of T-systems International and Bank of Tokyo Mitsubishi.

Rödl & Partner GbR advises several e-commerce, internet and multimedia companies.

Schwarz Kelwing Wicke Westpfahl notes an increase in e-commerce work, supplementing several domain name disputes.

Kanzlei Prof Schweizer advises e-commerce, software and market research institute clients.

Düsseldorf-based commercial firm **Velten Franz Jakoby** has a focus on multimedia, including internet law and telecommunications generally. It shows an understanding of the 'nuts and bolts' of the industry.

Wilmer Cutler Pickering Hale and Dorr LLP runs its IT practice out of a good corporate department, where Klaus Schubert advises clients from the IT and semiconductor industries. Combined skills were displayed in the transfer of technology for a micro-processor plant in Germany.

INSOLVENCY AND RESTRUCTURING

INSOLVENCY AND RESTRUCTURING

BRINKMANN & PARTNER
HWW WIENBERG WILHELM
HESS RECHTSANWÄLTE
KÜBLER
SCHULTZE & BRAUN ✪
WELLENSIEK RECHTSANWÄLTE – PARTNERSCHAFTSGESELLSCHAFT

Clifford Chance
Görg Partnerschaft von Rechtsanwälten ✪
Hermann
Jaffé Rechtsanwälte Insolvenzverwalter
Leonhardt & Partner
Tiefenbacher ✪
White & Case LLP

Allen & Overy LLP ✪
Gleiss Lutz ✪
Heuking Kühn Lüer Wojtek ✪
Jones Day
Linklaters Oppenhoff & Rädler ✪
Metzeler, van Betteray, Buchalik
Nörr Stiefenhofer Lutz ✪
Piepenburg – Gerling Rechtsanwälte
Weil, Gotshal & Manges ✪
Weiland (Dr) & Partner

Amend & Collegen
Andres (Dr) & Schneider
Ashurst ✪
CMS Hasche Sigle ✪
Dithmar Westhelle Assenmacher Zwingmann & Partner
Feser & Spliedt
Freshfields Bruckhaus Deringer
Graf von Westphalen Bappert & Modest ✪
Haarmann Hemmelrath ✪
Hengeler Mueller ✪
Johlke, Niethammer & Partner
Kaye Scholer (Germany) LLP ✪
Kebekus & Zimmermann
Kirkland & Ellis International LLP
Latham & Watkins LLP
Lieser, Rombach & Kollegen
Lovells ✪
McDermott Will & Emery Rechtsanwälte Steuerberater LLP ✪
Rödl & Partner
Salans
Shearman & Sterling LLP
Simmons & Simmons ✪
Taylor Wessing ✪

Firms are listed A-Z in tiers which are ranked in order of priority
✪ Indicates firm displays contact details at the end of this chapter.

In Germany, most insolvency instructions are handled by niche firms, where individuals are appointed as administrators. The larger firms' activities come, with limited exceptions, under general restructuring advice.

In terms of sheer volume of insolvency mandates, **Brinkmann & Partner** matches any firm in the market due to a good reputation and a spread of 12 offices across the country. Multi-site companies and conglomerates are key clients, and include property company Graubner KG and several media businesses.

Insolvency specialists **HWW Wienberg Wilhelm** has extended its network recently with new offices in various locations bringing its coverage up to 18 locations. The firm contains some vastly experienced figures.

HESS Rechtsanwälte is now based in Erfurt and Mainz, and is an insolvency boutique.

Although a full-service firm, **Kübler** is best known for market-leading insolvency expertise, which incorporates administration and restructuring. The firm is based across Germany, and also has an office in Poland. Name partner Bruno Kübler has over 25 years of experience in the market.

Schultze & Braun combines insolvency and restructuring with tax advice as part of a multi-disciplinary concept which offers a commercial approach to the sector. Corporate reorganisation and labour issues are also handled across its 25 German offices. Edgar Grönda and Eberhard Braun are notable figures.

Insolvency specialists **Wellensiek Rechtsanwälte – Partnerschaftsgesellschaft** houses some of the most experienced administrators in the market, including name partner Jobst Wellensiek, a father figure in the sector in which he has practised for over 30 years. Alfred Hagebusch adds distressed debt trading expertise, while Christopher Seagon advises both debtors and creditors.

Clifford Chance enjoys long standing in the market, with a reputation for representing banks that surpasses many rivals. Kolja von Bismark and his team have advised on the largest mandates, with Bankgesellschaft Berlin a client. The firm continues to advise Sony/Columbia Pictures on the fall-out of the Kirch collapse, and has also advised on the restructuring of a major retailer. A particular source of work has been the collapse of US companies affecting their German subsidiaries.

GÖRG Partnerschaft von Rechtsanwälten has its roots in restructuring and insolvency, and remains a top-quality corporate restructuring outfit. Although it took a major role in the Kirch restructuring and worked with the administrators of Babcock Borsig on its restructuring, its main focus is advising clients from the Mittelstand on pre-insolvency turnaround advice and overseas banks as creditors. Klaus Hubert Görg remains a pivotal figure in the market, while Jobst-Freidrich v Unger and Roland Hoffman-Theinert are key lawyers on the corporate side.

Hermann is another multi-disciplinary outfit, fielding tax auditors and accountants to provide an all-round insolvency service to its clients. The firm is known for advising creditors or advising stricken companies on rehabilitation matters, including founding rescue and continuation companies.

Jaffé Rechtsanwälte Insolvenzverwalter advises on a huge volume of cases from its five offices across the country. The firm made its name on the Kirch insolvency and related litigation, and has taken this reputation for multi-regional insolvencies forward. Acting exclusively for banks and concentrating on insolvency rather than restructuring means that the firm has established itself as a leading firm for these specific issues.

Leonhardt & Partner, based in Berlin, advises on major insolvency proceedings and receivership work. Peter Leonhardt heads the practice.

Tiefenbacher combines insolvency advice with tax expertise from specialists within the six-office firm. Thomas Kohl is the head of the insolvency practice which has advised on a huge number of insolvencies across the country, and also acts increasingly internationally.

Based in Hamburg but with practitioners across the network, **White & Case LLP** fields a large, multi-skilled and versatile team. Klaus Pannen remains one of the few lawyers at an international firm to still be appointed as an administrator by the courts, and he works alongside Frank Evers on restructuring mandates, incorporating debt and equity swaps. Good relationships with banks mean lots of NPL deals, while the firm has also been active in advising investors in purchasing insolvent companies.

Allen & Overy LLP's expertise in finance spills over into insolvency and restructuring work. The Frankfurt office is also a key element of the firm's continental NPL transactions practice. Peter Hoegen's practice has been heavily involved in distressed debt trading in recent times, while the refinancing of syndicated credit facilities for Schefenacker AG is a good example of the team's performance at the top of the market. Banks, particularly investment banks, fill out most of the client base.

Gleiss Lutz's key instruction for 2005 was advising JP MorganChase as a creditor of Primacom, a cross-border matter which followed a failed acquisition. Elsewhere, the firm's superb employment team lends weight and value working alongside Andreas Spahlinger's insolvency outfit, with pre-insolvency turnarounds a feature as much as restructurings and insolvencies.

Heuking Kühn Lüer Wojtek is strongest in Düsseldorf, Cologne and Berlin, although it houses insolvency and restructuring capability in Hamburg and Cheminitz. The firm is establishing a reputation for crisis management thanks to Hans-Jochem Lüer, Peter Fissenewert and Achim Freiherr von Griessenbeck.

Jones Day was heavily involved in the NPL trading market throughout 2005, advising US and German banks as purchasers predominantly, while restructuring was also a feature. Mayflower and its English administrator were advised on the sale of its German subsidiaries. Volker Kammel continues to impress as the dedicated partner.

Four of **Linklaters Oppenhoff & Rädler**'s eight insolvency and restructuring partners are based in Frankfurt, although Wolfgang Sturm heads the highly credible corporate-focused group out of Cologne. The group has advised joint administrators of Automold GmbH and ISA Deutschland GmbH, creditors of Schulte GmbH and has handled a debt-equity swap for a major multinational. With an international client base, a lot of work has been centred around the insolvencies of US subsidiaries in Germany.

Metzeler, van Betteray, Buchalik's Wolfgang van Betteray heads a practice out of Düsseldorf which is well known for its expertise in heavyweight insolvencies and restructurings, particularly in the media sector following its involvement in the Kirch insolvency. Trust solutions are another strength.

Nörr Stiefenhofer Lutz is strongest for insolvency matters in Berlin, where Thomas Hoffman resides, while partners also sit in Munich and Düsseldorf. The firm has advised creditors on restructuring, both pre- and post-insolvency, and distressed debt trading. The firm also advised **Jaffé Rechtsanwälte Insolvenzverwalter** as insolvency trustee on the Kirch collapse, a high-profile mandate which reflects the firm's increasing presence in the market.

Although a small firm, seven-lawyer **Piepenburg – Gerling Rechtsanwälte** has a good name in the Düsseldorf market, with further offices in Cologne and Potsdam.

With the corporate expertise of Gerhardt Schmidt also being put to frequent use in the restructuring world, **Weil, Gotshal & Manges** is carving an excellent reputation in debt-for-equity swaps, having advised Augusta Technologie AG on its recapitalisation. Uwe Hartmann is another key figure, and Deutsche Bank increasingly instructs the firm on restructuring matters.

Insolvency-geared **Dr Weiland & Partner**, and in particular name partner Gerd Weiland, is experienced in administrative receivership matters. The firm also has an office in Paris in addition to Hamburg and Berlin.

Enormously experienced name partner Angelika Amend at **Amend & Collegen** has advised on a high volume of insolvencies in recent years, with clients hailing from the media, construction and fashion industries.

Dr Andres & Schneider is a niche firm based in Düsseldorf. Name partner Winfred Andres is recommended.

Ashurst ramped up insolvency capability for 2006 with the hire of Ingo Scholz and his eight-strong team from **Haarmann Hemmelrath**. This came alongside partner hires in the London office, indicating the firm's strong intentions in the market.

CMS Hasche Sigle fields a small practice with a good track record advising companies from the Mittelstand. The firm is often appointed as administrator, and is increasingly active in the NPL field.

Dithmar Westhelle Assenmacher Zwingmann & Partner combines insolvency expertise with tax and business advice from its offices in Kassel and Erfurt.

Feser & Spliedt is a ten-lawyer, Berlin-based insolvency specialist with particular experience in the building, construction and social services sectors. Dr Jürgen Spliedt and Udo Feser are recommended.

Freshfields Bruckhaus Deringer successfully geared its NPL expertise to a growing market sector, utilising its strength in various areas such as tax and real estate. Restructuring continued to be a fertile area, with Apollo AG instructing the firm on the financial restructuring of takeover target PrimaCom AG. A bank consortium also engaged the firm on the debt rescheduling of the KarstadtQuelle group. Lars Westpfahl heads the group from Hamburg.

Graf von Westphalen Bappert & Modest has good insolvency and restructuring expertise, in Freiburg through Frank Büchler, and Munich with Ernst Lindl and Clemens Jobe. The firm represents companies in trouble and creditors securing claims, and is ramping up its reputation in the NPL trading sector, where Jobe has advised financial institutions and a real estate asset management company.

Haarmann Hemmelrath continues to be busy in the NPL and restructuring markets, having advised JP Morgan on the recent acquisition of an NPL portfolio. It is frequently active in advising banks as creditors. Stefan Denkhaus in Hamburg is noted for insolvency administration. The departure of Ingo Scholz to **Ashurst** so soon after he joined from **Skadden, Arps, Slate, Meagher & Flom LLP** was a surprising development.

Hengeler Mueller's powerful corporate and finance teams lend significant weight in the insolvency arena, the firm having advised on several takeovers of insolvent companies and banks, as well as advising Deutsche Telekom on the restructuring of subsidiaries. Reinhold Ernst in Düsseldorf has a growing reputation.

Hamburg boutique **Johlke, Niethammer & Partner** has a good reputation for receivership work, an area in which Horst Johlke, a veteran of 40 years in the market, remains active.

Kaye Scholer (Germany) LLP advises banks as creditors on insolvencies, while **Kebekus & Zimmermann** is a Düsseldorf-based specialist practice.

Although **Kirkland & Ellis International LLP** is a private equity boutique, it has advised on various administrations and Chapter 11 restructurings throughout Europe, on deals led out of the US. The firm is also active in the trading of distressed asset portfolios.

Latham & Watkins LLP combined insolvency and real estate skills to advise the insolvent AGIV Real Estate AG in the sale of Deutsche Real Estate AG to Whitehall, a €300m transaction. Elsewhere, major US, UK and German banks were advised as creditors and debt providers, and the firm ramped up its distressed debt trading activity. Christoph von Teichmann and Nikolaus Lorenz are highly regarded.

Lieser, Rombach & Kollegen's name partner Jens Lieser heads a practice that has been active in the market for nearly four decades. The firm is housed in Koblenz and Erfurt.

Lovells is active in the media sector, leveraging off a superb practice and heavyweight client list.

NPL deals and restructuring work is a major part of **McDermott Will & Emery Rechtsanwälte Steuerberater LLP**'s output. Christian von Sydow advised Morgan Stanley on an equity swap in the

NPL field, while the firm has also advised several US clients on restructuring of joint ventures.

Rödl & Partner advises insolvent company clients in the main, utilising expertise in real estate and tax to maximise asset value returns, and a huge German and international network for multi-site clients.

Salans' takeover of the Berlin office of **Haarmann Hemmelrath** brought the trusteeship expertise of Andreas Ziegenhagen to the firm.

Shearman & Sterling LLP entered the NPL arena in 2005, advising Dresdner Bank on the sale of a non-core business portfolio.

Simmons & Simmons' insolvency work is inextricably linked to its impressive employment practice, while the firm has advised on the acquisition of insolvent assets.

Taylor Wessing beefed up its restructuring capability with the recruitment of corporate partners Thomas Krempl and Heinrich Rodewig from **Haarmann Hemmelrath**.

INVESTMENT FUNDS

Hengeler Mueller has the leading investment funds practice, particularly with regards to hedge funds and in the open-ended regulated field. The practice is further strengthened by the firm's eminent regulatory expertise and the excellence of key partner Thomas Paul. **Hengeler Mueller** is also known for funds restructuring and in Edgar Wallach and Michael Thoma it has two further partners with excellent credentials.

Clifford Chance is strong on both closed-end and open-ended funds. The firm has a world-renowned investment funds practice and with its Frankfurt office's rapid development in Germany, the department is going to greater heights. Sven Zeller leads the department alongside tax specialist Hans Stamm.

Freshfields Bruckhaus Deringer is better known for open-ended funds instructions and for its work in the restructuring segment. Domestic and foreign funds are advised by the team which includes Ernst Emde and Gunnar Schuster. Both partners have close connections to BaFin, the financial services regulator.

Linklaters Oppenhoff & Rädler's Alexander Vogt is a respected name in the investment funds environment in Germany. The team which includes Andreas Streck is becoming better known for fund restructuring and working with closed-end funds for retail investors. The practice should also be regarded as one of the best equipped to handle the structuring of both open-ended and closed-end funds. The firm's strength in London and beyond is a major asset as well as having a formidable tax practice in Germany.

Norton Rose Vieregge's Frank Herring is a prominent name in open-ended funds and regulatory issues. He is particularly active in the hedge fund and real estate fund sectors.

INVESTMENT FUNDS

HENGELER MUELLER ✪

CLIFFORD CHANCE
FRESHFIELDS BRUCKHAUS DERINGER
LINKLATERS OPPENHOFF & RÄDLER ✪
NORTON ROSE VIEREGGE

Allen & Overy LLP ✪
CMS Hasche Sigle ✪
Fassbender Schmitt-Walter Nissen
GSK Gassner Stockmann & Kollegen ✪
Gleiss Lutz ✪
Heimann
Lovells ✪
P+P Pöllath + Partners ✪
SJ Berwin LLP ✪

Firms are listed A-Z in tiers which are ranked in order of priority
✪ *Indicates firm displays contact details at the end of this chapter.*

Other firms with investment funds expertise include **Allen & Overy LLP** based on its eminent financial services connections; **CMS Hasche Sigle**, for regulatory advice to banking clients; Munich-based **Fassbender Schmitt-Walter Nissen** for structuring closed-end real estate funds; **Gleiss Lutz** for shari'ah law-compliant funds where Kilian Bälz should be noted for his fluent Arabic and for advising Parsoli Global Islamic Equity Fund on the launch of its distribution system in Germany; Hamburg-based **Heimann** where Carl Graf Hardenberg is widely praised; **Lovells**, with a strong hedge fund structuring business; **P+P Pöllath + Partners**, which boasts private equity fund structuring guru Andreas Rodin; and **SJ Berwin LLP**, which has a similarly outstanding practice in private equity fund structuring, though Uwe Steininger's departure is a loss.

MARITIME AND SHIPPING

CMS Hasche Sigle's maritime economy group is geared towards the financial side of the market, while wet and dry matters in general are handled for shipyards, shipping companies, insurers, logistics companies and others. The majority of this large and skilled team is based in Hamburg where practice head Volker Looks and Dieter Rabe enjoy prestigious reputations.

Celebrating 75 years in the market in 2005, **Dabelstein & Passehl** can lay a claim to longevity in the market as a mark of its continued success. Based in Leer and Hamburg, the two biggest mandates for the year reflected its increasing penetration of the insurance market, advising insurers on the *Pride of America* and *ENA II* casualties. For shipowners, the firm advised the P&I club and owners of the *Michelle* following a collision. While vastly experienced in disputes, including arbitrations, the firm is also very active in new shipbuilding matters, predominantly advising owners including Blohm & Voss.

MARITIME AND SHIPPING

CMS HASCHE SIGLE ✪
DABELSTEIN & PASSEHL ✪
INCE & CO ✪
LEBUHN & PUCHTA
SCHACKOW & PARTNER (DR)

Ahlers & Vogel
Blaum Dettmers Rabstein
Remé Rechtsanwälte
Segelken & Suchopar
Taylor Wessing ✪

BBL Bracker Böhlhoff & Lübbert Rechtsanwälte
Cyrus Makowski
Dirksen & Schwadtke
Ehlermann (Dr) & Jeschonnek
Esche Schümann Commichau
Freshfields Bruckhaus Deringer
Heuking Kühn Lüer Wojtek ✪
Kretschmar von Teuffel Leverkus

Bollmann & Partner GbR ✪
Johansson Rechtsanwälte – Notare
Lauprecht Rechtsanwälte Notare

Firms are listed A-Z in tiers which are ranked in order of priority
✪ *Indicates firm displays contact details at the end of this chapter.*

A blend of UK and German qualified lawyers gives **Ince & Co** a more rounded and versatile offering than other shipping firms. For example, it enables the firm to advise German banks on loan agreements under local law, but can also advise on assignments under UK law. Shipbuilding, ship finance, and sale and purchase agreements comprise the bulk of the firm's workload, with a US$1bn fleet financing a highlight for the first-rate Jan Hungar. The firm also took a role on the *ENA II* accident fallout, displaying its capability in casualty work, advising the salvors.

Hamburg firm **Lebuhn & Puchta** is a highly commercial operation boasting the talents of Johannes Trost, Ulrich Stall, Heinrich-Werner Goltz and the excellent Christian Breitzke. Wet and dry claims of all kinds are handled with genuine expertise by a specialist insurance department whose clients include shipowners, underwriters and P&I clubs. Ship financing, and charter and purchase agreements are also handled by this market-leading outfit.

Dr Schackow & Partner is ostensibly a full-service firm, which means its shipping practice is rooted in commercial expertise, contributing to its commercial approach to clients. Julius Drumm has a fine reputation which attracts P&I clubs, shipyards and ship financiers to the firm.

Ahlers & Vogel is widely spread in Germany with offices in Rostock, Hamburg and Bremen, and it also benefits from membership of the *North Sea*

Group, an international network. A full-service firm, it is nevertheless best known for shipping matters as part of all-round expertise in transport, both contentious and non-contentious. Rolf Herber is singled out by peers as a top-notch lawyer, while his Hamburg colleague Ronald Wöhrn and Bremen-based Wolfgang Dierks are also worthy of mention.

Full-service firm **Blaum Dettmers Rabstein** handles shipping matters from Hamburg and Bremen, home of the recommended Joachim Bartels, Claus Holzhüter and the bulk of the team. Cargo-owners and insurance companies favour the firm.

Hamburg-based **Remé Rechtsanwälte** is heavily involved in shipbuilding contractual matters, as well as labour and tax issues related to the industry, while in disputes the firm handles wet and dry matters, with particular expertise in collisions and oil pollution. Pilotage law is another specialism. Name partner Thomas Remé and Hartmut von Brevern are recommended.

Segelken & Suchopar focuses on insurance matters in relation to all forms of transportation, advising insurers, logistics companies and freight carriers from offices in Berlin and Hamburg. In maritime issues, transportation insurers are the key clients.

Taylor Wessing's strong arbitration practice is very visible in the shipping market, with Christophe Hasche standing out. The firm acts for shipyards and regulatory authorities on wet and dry matters, and also has significant expertise in aviation casulty disputes. On the financing side, the firm advised Blohm & Voss GmbH on the contracts for several luxury yachts, as well as other shipbuilders on container vessel construction. Klaus Kostka is another key figure.

BBL Bracker Böhlhoff & Lübbert Rechtsanwälte more than doubled in size in 2005 with the arrival as partners of Bernd Koch, Heiko Giermann and Alexander Mittman. The firm traditionally advises shipowners, operators, importers and exporters, and insurers. Finance, logistics contracts and cargo claims litigation are cornerstones of the practice.

Cyrus Makowski is a member of the *Cyrus Ross Group*, with alliance partners across Europe including **Philip Ross & Co** in London. The commercial firm handles shipbuilding and financing. Joachim Cyrus is well known.

Shipping boutiques **Dirksen & Schwadtke**, home of experts Klaus Dirksen and Hans-Joachim Schwadtke, and ship finance specialists **Dr Ehlermann & Jeschonnek** carry good reputations in Hamburg.

Although not a shipping practice per se, Hamburg-based **Esche Schümann Commichau** advises shipping clients on commercial insurance matters through Joachim Umlauf.

Freshfields Bruckhaus Deringer has capable shipping expertise, in both contentious and non-contentious matters, as part of a wider transport practice in Berlin.

Heuking Kühn Lüer Wojtek advises on wet and dry matters from its Hamburg office, where Ulrich Wittkopp heads the team.

Kretschmar von Teuffel Leverkus advises on registration and shipbuilding contracts for international shipping companies, ship builders and dockyards. Name partner Nikolai von Teuffel is an experienced practitioner.

Hamburg-based **Bollmann & Partner GbR** also has an office in St Petersburg. The firm advises German, European and Chinese clients.

Johansson Rechtsanwälte – Notare, located in Kiel, advises clients from Germany, Scandinavia and the Baltic States on shipping issues.

MEDIA, ENTERTAINMENT AND PRESS

MEDIA, ENTERTAINMENT AND PRESS

BREHM & V. MOERS
NÖRR STIEFENHOFER LUTZ ✪
SCHWARZ KELWING WICKE WESTPFAHL ✪

CMS Hasche Sigle ✪
Clifford Chance
Hogan & Hartson Raue L.L.P. ✪
Kornmeier Kollegen Rechtsanwälte
Lichte Rechtsanwälte
Lovells ✪
McDermott Will & Emery Rechtsanwälte Steuerberater LLP ✪
Poll & Ventroni
Unverzagt – von Have

Bird & Bird ✪
Freshfields Bruckhaus Deringer
Hengeler Mueller ✪
Hertin Anwaltssozietät
Latham & Watkins LLP
Linklaters Oppenhoff & Rädler ✪
Prinz, Neidhardt, Engelschall
Sasse & Partner
Schertz Bergmann Rechtsanwälte
Taylor Wessing ✪

Allen & Overy LLP ✪
Ashurst ✪
avocado rechtsanwälte
Bartsch und Partner GbR
Beiten Burkhardt ✪
Buse Heberer Fromm ✪
CBH Cornelius Bartenbach Haesemann & Partners, member of ius laboris ✪
Damm & Mann
Fromm · Maurer
Frömming & Partner
Gleiss Lutz ✪
Görg Partnerschaft von Rechtsanwälten ✪
Graf von Westphalen Bappert & Modest ✪
Heuking Kühn Lüer Wojtek ✪
Heussen Rechtsanwaltsgesellschaft mbH
Jones Day
Kamin & Wilke
Kuhn Carl & Norden
Lausen Rechtsanwälte
Ouart & Kollegen (Dr)
Rittershaus ✪
Scheuermann Westerhoff Strittmatter
Schweizer (Prof), Kanzlei
Senfft Kersten Nabert & Maier
Thümmel, Schütze & Partner ✪
White & Case LLP
Wilmer Cutler Pickering Hale and Dorr LLP ✪

Firms are listed A-Z in tiers which are ranked in order of priority
✪ Indicates firm displays contact details at the end of this chapter.

Across its four offices, **Brehm & v. Moers** offers expertise in film funding, production, broadcasting and publishing in the top bracket. In Munich, Stefan v Moers enjoys a prominent position in the film market, holding a role as head of the supervisory board of Babelsberg Studios, while activities in 2005 included, alongside the regular production work, insolvency matters and conversion of companies from GmbH to AG. The firm is also advising increasing numbers of investors in the market. Wolfgang Brehm in the Berlin office handles international productions for the likes of Paramount and Warner, while Frankfurt houses good publishing expertise, which includes a new line in libel checking of autobiographies. The Hamburg office advises state-owned radio stations. Internet piracy is another new area.

With a long and distiguished history in the market, **Nörr Stiefenhofer Lutz** is synonymous with media matters in Germany. Following the demise of key client Kirch, new clients such as AETN of New York, which instructed the firm on the licensing of the History Channel and establishing a German subsidiary, and publisher Passauer Verlagsgruppe are proof that it just keeps moving forward. Activities in 2005 included music contract disputes, testament to a growing presence in the field, and film financing. Alexander Liegl and Alexander Ritvay have good penetration of the sports market, while Johannes Kreile cuts an experienced figure as head of the department.

Schwarz Kelwing Wicke Westpfahl continues to hold a strong position in the film financing market, increasing its client share of private equity funds investing in media and production companies. The corporate firm also sees its fair share of M&A work in the sector, advising the Thomson Group on acquisitions of publishing companies. Transactional work makes up the bulk of the firm's activities.

CMS Hasche Sigle thrives in press and publishing, with clients including AOL and publishing house NDR. The firm advises Bundesliga clubs on marketing and counterfeit merchandising specifically, and sports marketing issues are an area of expertise generally. Copyright issues are handled for clients in the entertainment industries.

Although known for heavyweight corporate activity in the entertainment sphere, **Clifford Chance** is also proficient in technical media matters, incuding licensing agreements in film and television.

Hogan & Hartson Raue L.L.P. gets better and better, mirroring its global status as a serious media player. The firm took a role on Axel Springer's takeover of ProSiebenSat, and also advised ProSiebenSat on various other matters, as well as MTV Europe. Jan Hegemann and Peter Raue are very astute practitioners.

Kornmeier Kollegen Rechtsanwälte is based in Cologne and Frankfurt. The firm has particular strength in new media issues, both contentious and non-contentious, which was further boosted by the arrival of former sole practioner Petra Marwitz in 2005.

Lichte Rechtsanwälte is a small but potent operation acting predominantly in music on the contractual side. The departure of Carsten Bartholl to **Taylor Wessing** is a blow, however.

Lovells is carving a reputation for itself in advising on personality rights, having advised Electronic Arts and Bauer Publishing on such issues in 2005. Privacy was also a feature, with the firm advising Axel Springer, a client which continues to furnish the firm with quality litigation instructions. Publishing houses and broadcasters, including ProSiebenSat.1, make up the majority of the client base. Volker Meinberg is an admired figure, and Albert Kitzler gives the firm a presence in the film production industry.

McDermott Will & Emery Rechtsanwälte Steuerberater LLP takes a commercial approach to the sector, where Ralf Weisser is extremely active in broadcasting matters, advising on regulatory, cable allocation and distribution rights, and licensing litigation. NBC/Universal instructs the firm on a host of matters, including corporate, while RTL is one of several major broadcasting clients. T-Online is advised in connection with video-on-demand issues. Hans-Joachim Schreiber is active in advising a mix of venture capitalists and corporates in investments in the sector.

Poll & Ventroni has a high profile in media circles, with clients in music, software, press and technology engaging the firm's renowned expertise in new media copyright protection. Trade mark work is touched upon, but it is cutting-edge copyright work in the sector that the firm is rightly lauded for.

Impressive media boutique **Unverzagt – von Have** counts copyright, film and television, trade mark, and press and publishing as its core areas. On the publishing side, the firm enjoys close relations with Bertelsmann among others. Internet piracy and film funding are growing areas. Advertising mandates include co-ordinating a European advertising campaign for Toyota, while Saatchi & Saatchi is another notable client. The departure of Alexander von Kalckreuth from the Berlin office means the firm is now focused on advising publishers in press matters.

Bird & Bird enjoys good penetration of the sports sponsorship market, with programmes in German football, including the FIFA World Cup 2006, cycling and Formula 1, driving releationships with major clients Deutsche Telekom and T-Mobile. Individual footballers, including Lukas Podolski, are also advised on image rights. Dr Joseph Fesenmair heads the team from the Munich office, although both Munich and Düsseldorf house two partners each.

Freshfields Bruckhaus Deringer is a major player in corporate media circles, advising EM.TV Beteilgungs GmbH & Co. KG on the sale of a share in Tele Munich Group, and Gruner + Jahr on the acquisition of an Axel Springer business, and a subsequent joint venture including the two. The firm is also high up on the television broadcasting ladder, being very involved in the breakthrough of Viacom and NBC into the German market. Michael Haidinger oversees the German operation from Hamburg, jointly heading the firmwide group with London-based Simon Marchant.

Hengeler Mueller is active from the Berlin office, where over half of a team of 12 lawyers focuses exclusively on TMT. Clients such as Kabel Deutschland and Freenet Mobilcom were advised on major corporate deals in 2005, although the firm specialises in regulatory work, particularly in telecoms. Both contentious and non-contentious matters are handled by Wolfgang Spoerr and his team.

IP boutique **Hertin Anwaltssozietät** continues to be an impressive outfit, with 60 years in the market. It advises the German Association of Independent Film Makers on contractual matters, in addition to a number of film companies including Ziegler Film GmbH. Celebrity clients also instruct the firm on defamation and personality rights issues, a legacy of its history in press matters.

Although **Latham & Watkins LLP** is active in media regulatory matters, the majority of its press work is contentious, where its top clients are Axel Springer and Spiegel Verlag. This practice is based exclusively in Hamburg. In entertainment, Stageholding is advised on theatre production, and a new client Ticketonline has brought the firm into the burgeoning ticketing arena, where it has advised on corporate matters, including sales of agencies and subsidiaries, and the creation of joint ventures in Switzerland and Austria.

Linklaters Oppenhoff & Rädler's media expertise is mainly based in Berlin, where Stefan Lütje covers publishing and internet-based content, and in particular film and television, with the likes of Viacom, MTV, CBS, Paramount and Nickelodeon comprising the client base. Michaela Sopp concentrates on media finance matters in Munich.

Matthias Prinz at **Prinz, Neidhardt, Engelschall** focuses on press litigation, being perhaps the best-connected lawyer in the print media. He is invariably involved in the highest-profile cases, with a celebrity client base seeking representation on defamation and privacy matters.

Sasse & Partner is a niche media practice with an excellent reputation in music matters among independent labels, advising on corporate issues as well as contractual matters. The International Federation of Phonographic Industries is another client, while high-net-worth individuals from the industry are given access to tax advice thanks to a joint venture with tax consultants Wirtschaftsprüfungsgesellschaft ZWP Rotonda in Cologne. The firm also offers advice in print media, predominantly to the press and authors. Helge Sasse is the key figure, based in Cologne.

Schertz Bergmann Rechtsanwälte is a Berlin-based spin-off from **Hertin Anwaltssozietät**, comprising of partners Christian Schertz, a libel expert acting for private individuals, and Simon Bergmann, who specialises in media labour law and sports. Clients hail from the entertainment industry and politics. Publishing houses are also advised.

Taylor Wessing built on a solid publishing and marketing core in Munich and a television practice in Berlin with the recruitment of Carsten Bartholl from Hamburg music boutique **Lichte Rechtsanwälte**. He brings a corporate focus to that area for the international firm with a history of advising on music licensing for films, which tallies with the film production and funding expertise in the Berlin office. The arrival of Reinhard Gaertner from **Bird & Bird** into Munich brings more publishing connections to a firm which already advises clients such as Condé Nast.

Allen & Overy LLP's burgeoning relationship with Sony BMG, particularly on the licensing, broadcasting and distribution side, gives the firm an entry in the table this year.

Ashurst has good knowledge of the publishing and technology sectors, and enjoys a fruitful relationship with sports client IMG.

avocado rechtsanwälte is most active in privacy and defamation actions, advising publishing houses in particular, while the representation of a client in an international research enterprise over the unauthorised use of film footage showed good technical application of the law. Sports sponsorship is also handled.

Bartsch und Partner GbR is particularly active in new media, advising software companies, internet providers and publishers on data protection and copyright.

Beiten Burkhardt has enjoyed good standing in the market for years thanks in the main to a huge publishing client base, production houses Walt Disney, Universal and Paramount, and various smaller broadcasting houses and private radio stations all instructing the firm.

Buse Heberer Fromm is very active in defamation matters through Hamburg-based Michael Nesselhauf, former in-house counsel at *Der Spiegel*, whose client list is an array of celebrities and sportspeople, as well as several publishing houses.

CBH Cornelius Bartenbach Haeseman & Partners, member of ius laboris offers general copyright protection advice to film and theatre production companies.

Berlin IP boutique **Damm & Mann** specialises in libel matters, advising a number of publishing and broadcasting houses including Bertelsmann AG, RTL and *Frankfurter Allgemeine Zeitung*, as well as several politicians. Name partners Roger Mann and Renate Damm are at the forefront of the well-respected practice.

Gleiss Lutz specialises in advice to publishing houses, while **Graf von Westphalen Bappert & Modest** handles film and entertainment matters, mainly production, from its Cologne, Berlin and Hamburg offices. RTL is a client, while publishing houses, music production companies and advertising houses fill out the client base.

Heuking Kühn Lüer Wojtek is active in film and television funding, as well as print advertising and publishing. Name media clients are advised on straightforward corporate matters as well as sector specific issues including distribution and copyright. The Discovery Channel, one of many broadcasting clients, is advised on new digital broadcasting projects by Michael Schmittman in Düsseldorf, who also specialises in new media issues.

Always strong in IP generally, the arrival of a former in-house counsel at Sony Music Entertainment gives **Jones Day** a presence in entertainment law.

Hamburg-based **Kamin & Wilke** is known and respected for music work.

Kuhn Carl & Norden advises private radio stations and publishing houses on commercial matters including the formation of broadcasting companies, from its Stuttgart base.

Media companies are the focus at **Lausen Rechtsanwälte**, where standard licensing and copyright advice is supplemented by sector-specific expertise in employment. Merchandising and advertising is a speciality, while new media in general is a strength at this dynamic and commercially geared firm.

Dr Ouart & Kollegen enters the table this year following the arrival of senior associates from **Allen & Overy LLP** and **Schwarz Kelwing Wicke Westpfahl**, and an impressive track record in advising a professional football club in some high-profile litigation.

Broadcasting is the focus at **White & Case LLP**, which is advising the Federal Republic of Germany on the establishment of a national digital radio network, and Premiere Fernsehen on the restructuring of its business as a platform for Pay TV services.

Wilmer Cutler Pickering Hale and Dorr LLP is strong in Munich as a result of legacy firm *Hale & Dorr*'s presence in the market. Clients include publishing houses and Frieda Springer, major shareholder in Axel Springer AG.

PRIVATE EQUITY

Clifford Chance's world-leading private equity practice is supported by a tremendous group in Germany. It is best known for representing UK and European buy-out funds, but its ability to attract instructions from US players such as KKR demonstrates the German practice's leading credentials. With the arrival of **Lovells**' esteemed rainmaker Oliver Felsenstein, the department was even further enhanced, though it still lacks a really significant presence in Munich, where many other law firms and funds house much of their German resources. Christopher Kellett and Mario Schmidt remain formidable individuals, while clients continually highlight the team's experience, commercial approach and all-round ability.

Though no longer the force it was in Munich following the loss of Peter Nussbaum and Norbert Rieger, **Freshfields Bruckhaus Deringer** remains a prominent firm on the German private equity scene. Hamburg's Nils Matthias Koffka and Frankfurt partner Andreas von Werder are key individuals and the firm still retains clients such as BC Partners, 3i and Permira.

Hengeler Mueller's transactional eminence is not lost on buy-out funds and sellers in the private equity arena. A blossoming relationship with KKR, which it often advises alongside regular US counsel **Simpson Thacher & Bartlett LLP** shows that it is serious about fund representation. It is also a frequent adviser to Blackstone and in Maximilian Schiessl it boasts one of the nation's most respected private equity specialists. Jochen Vetter should also be commended.

Following a fabulous 2004, when **Linklaters Oppenhoff & Rädler** represented Fortress Group on its €3.5bn acquisition of Gemeinnutzige Aktien-Gesellschaft für Angestellten-Heimstaetten (Gagfah), the firm continues to advise the financial investor on its German bids. It advised Fortress on the €1.5bn acquisition of NILEG Immobilien from Norddeutsche Landesbank. Jochen Winter, once again led the team on this high-value transaction but then left in January 2006 to join **Willkie Farr & Gallagher LLP**; a significant loss to the practice. The firm has also advised Terra Firma Capital Partners on several bids as well as PAI Partners, Candover Partners and HgCapital.

Milbank, Tweed, Hadley & McCloy LLP had an outstanding year following the launch of its Munich practice in 2004. Eminent partners Peter Nussbaum and Norbert Rieger have handled several instructions from Apax and Carlyle respectively, while the firm has leveraged off its network to attain mandates from Cerberus and Goldman Sachs PAI in Germany. Tax partner Rolf

PRIVATE EQUITY

CLIFFORD CHANCE

FRESHFIELDS BRUCKHAUS DERINGER
HENGELER MUELLER ✪
LINKLATERS OPPENHOFF & RÄDLER ✪
MILBANK, TWEED, HADLEY & MCCLOY LLP ✪
WEIL, GOTSHAL & MANGES ✪

Gleiss Lutz ✪
Latham & Watkins LLP
Lovells ✪
P+P Pöllath + Partners ✪
Skadden, Arps, Slate, Meagher & Flom LLP

Allen & Overy LLP ✪
Ashurst ✪
Baker & McKenzie ✪
CMS Hasche Sigle ✪
Debevoise & Plimpton LLP ✪
Dechert LLP ✪
Haarmann Hemmelrath ✪
Kirkland & Ellis International LLP
McDermott Will & Emery Rechtsanwälte Steuerberater LLP ✪
Nörr Stiefenhofer Lutz ✪
SJ Berwin LLP ✪
Shearman & Sterling LLP
Taylor Wessing ✪
White & Case LLP
Willkie Farr & Gallagher LLP ✪

Firms are listed A-Z in tiers which are ranked in order of priority
✪ *Indicates firm displays contact details at the end of this chapter.*

Füger has also proved to be a pivotal member of the team. The election of Munich-based Ulrike Dormann to the partnership, indicates the progress of the firm in Germany. In December 2005, the firm advised Apax Partners and Goldman Sachs Capital Partners on the sale of their shareholdings in Kabel Deutschland to Providence Equity Partners.

Weil, Gotshal & Manges' stellar record in private equity allowed it to advise on one of the largest media transactions in history when it represented P7S1 Holding on the sale of its controlling interest in ProSiebenSat.1 Media AG, Germany's largest commercial television group, to Axel Springer AG. P7S1 Holding is a private equity consortium led by Saban Capital. The firm is also an active adviser of funds such as Cerberus and Texas Pacific Group. Tobias Geerling, Stephan Grauke and Jürgen Börst should be commended without forgetting chief rainmaker Gerhard Schmidt. The firm also advised Texas Pacific and TPG-Axon on the acquisition of shareholdings in mobilcom AG from France Télécom, outlining its strength in high-value and complex transactions.

Gleiss Lutz's emergence in the corporate transactional field extends to private equity with several roles for blue-chip funds such as Blackstone, Ripplewood and General Atlantic

Partners. The firm mainly acts for US-based funds thanks to its close connections to US firms such as **Simpson Thacher & Bartlett LLP**. Rainer Loges leads the private equity practice which includes key partners Gerhard Wegen (the firm's chief rainmaker), Jan Bauer, Christian Cascante and Fred Wendt in Berlin.

Latham & Watkins LLP has developed a significantly greater profile in private equity thanks to its international connections and the efforts of German partners including Hans-Jürgen Lütt in Frankfurt. The German portion of the firm has become closer to international client Carlyle and also BC Partners on a purely domestic basis. Apollo Real Estate and CSFB Private Equity have also become important clients. The recent hire of Jörg Kirchner from **Ashurst** gives the firm a significant boost particularly with his connections to Bain Capital, Carlyle, EQT and Cinven.

Lovells' private equity practice was dealt a significant blow with the departure of Oliver Felsenstein to **Clifford Chance** in 2005. In new department head Joachim Habetha and his team, the firm retains the requisite talent and expertise to continue its impressive run of form in major transactions. HgCapital, Terra Firma, Doughty Hanson, EQT and Permira are previous clients of the practice and are expected to continue instructing the firm in the future.

Just eight years old, **P+P Pöllath + Partners** has a strong all-round private equity practice, noted for funds structuring, funds formation and transactions. In this regard, the firm's strong tax capability is of great value. On the buy-out front, Apax, EQT and Carlyle have all been fruitful clients over the years. Matthias Bruse is a fine transactional lawyer with Andreas Rodin one of the leading names in fund formation.

Skadden, Arps, Slate, Meagher & Flom LLP's German operation is benefiting from the success of the London office, which has now brought funds such as Doughty Hanson into the business. Matthias Jaletzke is now representing the fund in Germany. It continues to represent Apax on a frequent basis. The firm also has a strong position in the mid-market through Barclays and EQT. Walter Henle is the practice's most senior name.

Allen & Overy LLP has yet to really establish itself as a true private equity player, though its international profile and the efforts of Hamburg corporate partner Helge Schäfer deserve recognition.

Ashurst's fine private equity practice remains a key player thanks in no small part to the efforts of former partner Jörg Kirchner in Munich and Hermann Schlindwein in Frankfurt. (Kirchner has now joined **Latham & Watkins LLP** and frequently represents Bain Capital, Carlyle, EQT and Cinven). Schlindwein acts for Advent International and Electra. Schlindwein represented Advent International on its investment in Casa Reha Betriebs-und Beteiligungsgesellschaft in October 2005. Private equity continues to be a core business to the firm in Germany, but Kirchner's departure leaves a significant gap to fill.

Baker & McKenzie's Dirk Oberbracht remains a key name and the firm retains some distinction in the private equity market despite the loss of Walter Henle and Matthias Jaletzke to **Skadden, Arps, Slate, Meagher & Flom LLP** in 2004. In June 2005, the firm represented Madison Dearborn Partners on its acquisition of Sirona Dental from EQT. This was the first-ever tertiary buy-out in Germany. One Equity Partners and Apax Partners also continue to instruct the firm, suggesting that departures have not affected the practice to the same extent as many would have expected. Wilhelm Hebing and Florian Kästle are also recommended.

CMS Hasche Sigle's immense size and multitude of offices around Germany has enabled it to gain a foothold in the private equity sector. It is regularly instructed by BC Partners, with Udo Simmat and Martin Bell often as lead partners. Platinum Equity is also a key client.

Debevoise & Plimpton LLP has a solid global relationship with Clayton, Dubilier & Rice, for which it has provided advice in Germany on a series of transactions. Providence Equity Partners is also a regular client. Thomas Schürrle is highly recommended.

Dechert LLP's three-partner private equity and venture capital practice in Munich following the promotion of Volkmar Bruckner (recent recruit from **Baker & McKenzie**) to the partnership and hire of Berthold Hummel from long-term client 3i gives the firm even greater credibility in the sector. Federico Pappalardo and his team continue to work for 3i as well as CVC Equity Partners.

Haarmann Hemmelrath's loss of Christoph von Einem to **White & Case LLP** is a blow, but it remains strong on the fund structuring side and in mid-cap transactions.

Kirkland & Ellis International LLP launched its German practice at the end of 2004, following the arrival of Volker Kullman from **Clifford Chance**. Several other partners have transferred from London and New York and the Munich office has become an immediate force in private equity. Dearborn Partners and Permira are expected to be lucrative clients and the firm operates from the same building as key international client Bain Capital.

McDermott Will & Emery Rechtsanwälte Steuerberater LLP should be identified for its venture capital business under Hans-Joachim Schreiber, though private equity business is also growing.

Thomas Schulz and Georg Schneider lead **Nörr Stiefenhofer Lutz**'s private equity group. The firm has represented Allianz Capital Partners alongside **O'Melveny & Myers LLP** in New York as well as Montagu Private Equity.

SJ Berwin LLP is recommended for tax structuring, but it is gaining a further presence in transactional matters for clients such as Electra, 3i and Alpha Capital. Thomas Pauls is highlighted in this respect.

Thomas König and Harald Selzner are **Shearman & Sterling LLP**'s most recognised partners within the private equity sector. The firm often represents the seller in such transactions but of late has represented Goldman Sachs Capital Partners Allianz Capital Partners and CVC.

Peter Hellich (Düsseldorf) and head of corporate Bernhard Kloft (Hamburg) lead **Taylor Wessing**'s increasingly esteemed private equity practice acting for funds such as Granville Baird Capital Partners and Equity Partners. Clients favour the firm for mid-cap transactions.

White & Case LLP is the process of building its private equity business having represented funds such as EQT in recent years. Its recruitment of **Haarmann Hemmelrath**'s Christoph von Einem, to launch a Munich office in early 2006 was a significant development. Frankfurt partners Markus Hauptmann and Andreas Stilcken are also highly regarded.

Willkie Farr & Gallagher LLP has a strong global brand in private equity and Germany has gone some way to matching the excellent reputation of the firm's Paris office. Despite the loss of Thomas Heymann to launch **Heymann & Partner**, it retains a host of talented individuals including Markus Wenserski and the arrival of Jochen Winter from **Linklaters Oppenhoff & Rädler** in January 2006 provides a significant boost to the practice.

PUBLIC SECTOR

Clifford Chance fields a versatile and all-round impressive environmental practice, offering advice on contaminated land in brownfield developments, emissions-trading and waste management, often on transaction-related mandates. The German energy group remains active, ably supporting the real estate team on wind farm acquisitions. Industrial private companies and state entities to a lesser extent comprise the client base.

Klaus-Peter Dolde and Rainard Menke are the driving forces behind the excellent **Dolde & Partner** in Stuttgart. The firm has a recognised track record in all aspects of public law, with environmental expertise incorporating pollution and recycling. Public procurement and energy are other strengths.

Freshfields Bruckhaus Deringer is carving a niche for itself in schools PPP projects, having taken the Offenbach project to the implementation phase and taking new instructions on another schools PPP project from the City of Schwarzenbek. The team lends weight to a good project finance team which has been involved on a waste incineration plant, and it remains active on infrastructure projects in Eastern Europe.

Although the public sector offering at **Gleiss Lutz** is aligned strongly with its real estate practice, it still impresses for advising on a wide variety of matters, from hospital financing to emissions-trading and regulatory litigation matters. In the latter, the firm excelled in defending the State of Baden Württemberg against an alleged breach of official duty. In the private sector, major clients instruct Ralf Thaeter's lauded energy team, while various mobile phone operators fill out the client base.

Redeker Sellner Dahs & Widmaier has expertise across the board in public law matters, but it is environmental law where the firm really stands out. Pollution, waste and conservation matters are all areas of strength, backing up very good planning and construction work for a largely institutional client base. Offices in London and Brussels give the firm good European penetration.

Baker & McKenzie brings its public sector expertise to the fore in real estate and telecoms matters. In telecoms, the firm has expertise in advising regulators on outsourcing issues and government authorities on legal reforms, but also takes instructions from private companies in real estate, particularly on planning and environmental issues arising from new developments. The firm advised the City of Hamburg on the privatisation of all hospitals in the city.

Nuclear safety is a forte of all-round environment specialists **Gaßner, Groth, Siederer & Coll**. Other mandates typically involve wastewater and pollution issues related to urban developments, where the firm has good regulatory expertise.

Regulatory matters are a strength at **Hengeler Mueller**, both for investors and enterprises on site clean-ups and new plant developments, while the expert team also provides good support in corporate transactions with environmental and compliance issues. RWE is a key client on energy matters, and state aid is another relevant area where the firm boasts expertise of the highest calibre.

Hogan & Hartson Raue L.L.P. made further strides in the market with the recruitment of Kornelius Kleinlein from **Linklaters Oppenhoff & Rädler** into the Munich office. He brings expertise in infrastruture, having advised the government on the Toll Collect project. The firm's Berlin office continues to impress in advising on potential de-regulation matters, and is also working alongside the London office providing institutional support to the Russian Federation regarding the implementation of the Kyoto Protocol.

With a history in the privatisation market, **Linklaters Oppenhoff & Rädler** is also prominent in PPP work, epitomised by its advice to the Bilfinger Berger and Laing consortium on the privately financed extension of highways. Public sector bodies are also advised, the most notable being the Federal Transport Ministry in the ongoing dispute over the delayed introduction of the lorry toll system, an arbitration and restructuring mandate. Ian Andrews' relocation to London deprives the Frankfurt office of his top-notch finance expertise, although he remains active on projects in both Germany and Austria. The public procurement practice is headed out of Berlin by new partner Jan Endler, alongside the successful energy practice which advises investors in newly privatised utilities. Recent deals include the acquisition of two wind farms, and the firm's versatile environment practice supplements various practice areas across the firm, in corporate, civil, criminal and public law.

With strength in finance, **Lovells** enjoys good market penetration in construction, projects and public procurement.

Nörr Stiefenhofer Lutz is strong in energy, with department head Wolfgang Kässer's standing bringing in mandates from Germany and Eastern Europe. Gas supply contracts and joint ventures between oil supply companies were handled, as were disputes in fuel and energy management regulation, including a cross-border dispute with a Hungarian element.

White & Case LLP is carving a very creditable reputation for itself in the public sector, offering environmental, privatisation and deregulation advice. In environmental matters, it is active mainly in the Hamburg and Berlin offices, the latter particularly noted for work in the healthcare sector on wastewater and facilities management. Both public entities and private parties are advised, and the firm is ramping up its financing activities in the sector. Environmentally friendly energy is another focus, with energy in particular a busy area; the firm is advising on several pipeline projects in association with offices in Russia. Berlin and Düsseldorf are the key centres here.

Wilmer Cutler Pickering Hale and Dorr LLP combines rare expertise in regulatory matters and aviation to field a specialised team of high calibre from Berlin, in particular Natalie Lübben. The firm advises major international air carriers, and has taken a role advising Frankfurt Airport on an environmental matter concerned with the nearby presence of a chemical plant, and Zurich Airport on an overflight dispute. Elsewhere, the presence of Matthias Wissman, former Federal Minister of Transport is a huge asset to its lobbying presence, while telecoms, IT and energy are other areas of activity for this very impressive firm.

Zenk Rechtsanwälte is a public law-oriented commercial firm with offices in Berlin, Hamburg, Cologne and Brussels. Environmental issues are a strength in this sector, especially soil contamination on proposed building sites, while the firm shows strongly in all other facets of public law, specifically public procurement, local government and hospital financing.

Drawing on significant expertise in environmental matters, the traditional core of the practice, **Allen & Overy LLP** is increasingly active in advising clients on banned substances. The firm

PUBLIC SECTOR

CLIFFORD CHANCE
DOLDE & PARTNER
FRESHFIELDS BRUCKHAUS DERINGER
GLEISS LUTZ ✪
REDEKER SELLNER DAHS & WIDMAIER

Baker & McKenzie ✪
Gaßner, Groth, Siederer & Coll
Hengeler Mueller ✪
Hogan & Hartson Raue L.L.P. ✪
Linklaters Oppenhoff & Rädler ✪
Lovells ✪
Nörr Stiefenhofer Lutz ✪
White & Case LLP
Wilmer Cutler Pickering Hale and Dorr LLP ✪
Zenk Rechtsanwälte

Allen & Overy LLP ✪
Baumeister, Rechtsanwälte
Beiten Burkhardt ✪
Buse Heberer Fromm ✪
CMS Hasche Sigle ✪
Eisenmann Wahle Birk
Graf von Westphalen Bappert & Modest ✪
Heuking Kühn Lüer Wojtek ✪
Lenz and Johlen
Quaas und Partner, Anwaltskanzlei

---

avocado rechtsanwälte
Ashurst ✪
Baumann Rechtsanwälte
Becker Büttner Held, Rechtsanwälte Wirtschaftsprüfer Steuerberater
Bird & Bird ✪
Böckmann (Dr) & Partner GbR
Bogsch, Jäger, Schwarzer
CBH Cornelius Bartenbach Haesemann & Partners, member of ius laboris ✪
Caemmerer – Bender – Lenz
GSK Gassner Stockmann & Kollegen ✪
Görg Partnerschaft von Rechtsanwälten ✪
Günther, Heidel, Wollenteit, Hack
Haarmann Hemmelrath ✪
Jones Day
Köhler & Klett, Rechtsanwälte
Latham & Watkins LLP
Leinemann & Partner
Loh Von Hülsen Michael Rechtsanwälte
Luther Rechtsanwaltsgesellschaft mbH ✪
Mannheimer Swartling ✪
Niedersberg (Dr) Rechtsanwalt
Norton Rose Vieregge
Schulte-Wissermann (Dr), Kunz Müller und Kollegen
Seufert Rechtsanwälte
Sibeth Partnerschaft Rechtsanwälte Steuerberater Wirtschaftsprüfer ✪
Simmons & Simmons ✪
Thümmel, Schütze & Partner ✪
Taylor Wessing ✪

Firms are listed A-Z in tiers which are ranked in order of priority
✪ *Indicates firm displays contact details at the end of this chapter.*

PUBLIC SECTOR: ENERGY

BECKER BÜTTNER HELD, RECHTSANWÄLTE WIRTSCHAFTSPRÜFER STEUERBERATER
CLIFFORD CHANCE
FRESHFIELDS BRUCKHAUS DERINGER
GLEISS LUTZ ✪

Allen & Overy LLP ✪
Buse Heberer Fromm ✪
CMS Hasche Sigle ✪
Dolde & Partner
Hogan & Hartson Raue L.L.P. ✪
Linklaters Oppenhoff & Rädler ✪
Nörr Stiefenhofer Lutz ✪
White & Case LLP

Baker & McKenzie ✪
Baumann Rechtsanwälte
Böckmann (Dr) & Partner GbR
Eisenmann Wahle Birk
Günther, Heidel, Wollenteit, Hack
Haarmann Hemmelrath ✪
Hengeler Mueller ✪
Heuking Kühn Lüer Wojtek ✪
KSB Intax
Latham & Watkins LLP
Mannheimer Swartling ✪
Niedersberg (Dr) Rechtsanwalt

Firms are listed A-Z in tiers which are ranked in order of priority
✪ Indicates firm displays contact details at the end of this chapter.

is also noted for emissions-trading and pollution disputes, in which it has recently advised paper-production companies, while waste management is a longstanding strength. Frankfurt is the home of the team, led by the excellent Thomas Pschera, but the Hamburg office also houses some telecoms-related expertise. In PPP matters, the firm has advised Deutsche Bank on toll systems. Cornelius Fischer-Zernin heads up energy issues.

Baumeister, Rechtsanwälte is recommended for environmental, waste, water and pollution expertise. The 18-lawyer head office in Münster receives additional support from a smaller Leipzig office.

Beiten Burkhardt is generally acknowledged as a major player in the sector, with enviable contacts in public authorities. A showcase for the firm's standing, resources and aptitude was the privatisation of the German army's IT system. The firm also enjoys a longstanding relationship with Munich Airport, handling employment matters predominantly for the client.

Buse Heberer Fromm is expanding its interests in the energy sector, with a recent history in geothermal power plant investment now supplemented by risk analysis of wind farm investment. The growing Düsseldorf office has advised a governmental authority on price-fixing allegations in the pharmaceutical market.

CMS Hasche Sigle has particular strength and expertise in the wind energy sector, while project development financing is another core area of this impressive team.

Eisenmann Wahle Birk has most of its lawyers based in its home city of Stuttgart, where Hans-Jörg Birk is recommended in the firm's flagship areas of construction, planning and environmental law. Dresden is a smaller outpost for the firm.

Graf von Westphalen Bappert & Modest continues to be strong in public planning and construction law, having displayed this expertise on airport developments in the past which also incorporated emission controls and aviation law. Furthermore, the firm also has a good track record in privatisation, having advised on the complete privatisation of several hospitals. A further string to the practice's bow came with the arrival of Ingrid Reichling from **Beiten Burkhardt**, bringing public procurement expertise in construction, health and IT.

Heuking Kühn Lüer Wojtek continues to advance in the public sector, with the recruitment of Thomas Nickel from **Lovells** into the firms' Frankfurt office. The move is designed to strengthen the network's capability in the PPP and public procurement markets outside of the flagship Düsseldorf office, where Ute Jaspar and Peter Kamphausen are privatisation experts. Water, waste, transport and hospitals are the areas of focus, with local authorities and utilities companies comprising the bulk of the firm's clients; recent work includes the sale of the Hanseatic Trade Centre in Hamburg under Carsten Wagner.

Planning and construction are areas of particular competence at Cologne firm **Lenz and Johlen**, combining these strengths with environmental expertise on PPP projects. Heribert Johlen heads a growing team of 15.

Stuttgart firm **Anwaltskanzlei Quaas und Partner** focuses on all aspects of public sector work with particular expertise in planning and construction, incorporating environmental law. It is frequently engaged in the health sector where Michael Quaas and Jens-Michael Kuhlmann are renowned figures. Public sector aspects of aviation projects are also handled well.

avocado rechtsanwälte covers the full spectrum of public law from its Cologne office, with public procurement an increasing area of focus. Energy and environmental expertise comes into play advising clients in the chemicals and paper industries, especially on soil contamination issues and waste incineration. Emissions-trading is another key area, with the firm advising private companies on applications for licences.

Becker Büttner Held, Rechtsanwälte Wirtschaftsprüfer Steuerberater is superb in energy and renewable energy mandates, advising dozens of energy-supply companies on restructuring, formation of grid companies and project finance structuring, with tax, corporate and regulatory issues all capable of being handled. Emissions-trading is also a strength, while waste management, including wastewater management and privatisation, and transport are also areas of recommendation.

PUBLIC SECTOR: ENVIRONMENT

DOLDE & PARTNER
FRESHFIELDS BRUCKHAUS DERINGER
GAßNER, GROTH, SIEDERER & COLL
GLEISS LUTZ ✪
REDEKER SELLNER DAHS & WIDMAIER

Allen & Overy LLP ✪
Baker & McKenzie ✪
Baumeister, Rechtsanwälte
Clifford Chance
Köhler & Klett, Rechtsanwälte
Lenz and Johlen
Linklaters Oppenhoff & Rädler ✪
Zenk Rechtsanwälte

---

avocado rechtsanwälte
Bogsch, Jäger, Schwarzer
CMS Hasche Sigle ✪
Eisenmann Wahle Birk
Graf von Westphalen Bappert & Modest ✪
Günther, Heidel, Wollenteit, Hack
Hengeler Mueller ✪
Heuking Kühn Lüer Wojtek ✪
Hoffmann Liebs Fritsch & Partner (HLFP)
Mayer, Brown, Rowe & Maw LLP ✪
Norton Rose Vieregge
Simmons & Simmons ✪
Taylor Wessing ✪
White & Case LLP

Firms are listed A-Z in tiers which are ranked in order of priority
✪ Indicates firm displays contact details at the end of this chapter.

Internationally focused **Bird & Bird** advanced in public law with the recruitment of René Voigtländer as senior consultant from **Mayer, Brown, Rowe & Maw LLP** bringing expertise in regulatory issues in biotech and energy to complement department head Jan Byok's public procurement and cartel strength. The firm also handles ensuing litigation matters.

GSK Gassner Stockmann & Kollegen excels in high-profile PPP work, with past mandates including the construction of the holocaust monument in Berlin, and various schools and prison projects. Deutschebahn is advised on rail projects. The firm has expanded from a base of construction mandates to IT, with a client base of local and state authorities.

GÖRG Partnerschaft von Rechtsanwälten's public sector expertise is based exclusively in Berlin, although its presence stretches across Germany; for example the firm is advising on all public law aspects of the construction of a power plant on North Westphalia. In environmental matters, it advises a mix of private industrial companies, and city and local authorities.

Energy matters are handled well at **Haarmann Hemmelrath**, not least owing to a potent European network, with offices in Prague,

Paris and London showing particular expertise. E.ON is a major client, while private equity investment into projects remains a focus.

Jones Day's public sector work incorporates planning regulation advice, but is generally more public procurement oriented, especially in the healthcare sector, advising private bidders, and privatised transportation, advising local authorities on tenders. The firm's superb antitrust network comes into play frequently in this area.

KSB INTAX made inroads into the energy sector with the recruitment of former in-house counsel Henning Recknagel, who brings expertise in regulatory, business and antitrust issues.

Latham & Watkins LLP is most active in environmental matters, particularly pollution control, as well as public water supplies. It advises public and private entities.

Leinemann & Partner has leveraged off a strong public utility construction practice to emerge in public sector law. Recent mandates include advising on two unlawful administrative regulation mandates concerning the public tendering procedures for motorway construction.

Loh Von Hülsen Michael Rechtsanwälte is small but distinguished, with Gerhard Michaels a foremost expert who is frequently engaged by government authorities on building regulatory matters and associated disputes. The firm advised the Federal Republic of Germany in its lawsuit against former Chancellor Kohl concerning the release of documents of the State Security Service of the former GDR, a mandate which speaks volumes about the esteem in which the firm is held.

Luther Rechtsanwaltsgesellschaft mbH is known for privatisation work, with a history in hospitals and public utilities projects.

Mayer, Brown, Rowe & Maw LLP shows well in environmental matters, especially in advising Deutsche Post AG and DHL Aviation NV on the expansion of Frankfurt Airport incorporating a dispute over a proposed night-flight ban, and associated infrastructure requirements. Markus Geisler's team is strong in aviation matters, and also leverages off a strong pharmaceutical client base to advise on the transport of hazardous chemicals around the world.

Norton Rose Vieregge approaches public procurement and PPP work from a competition and antitrust perspective, with a particular focus on transport, having advised the German Ministry of Transport, Construction and Housing on a motorway widening programme, one of the largest PPP projects in Germany. State aid issues are an area of particular expertise for Michael Jürgen Werne.

SIBETH Partnerschaft Rechtsanwälte Steuerberater Wirtschaftsprüfer continues to operate on several long-term mandates inherited form legacy firm *ARCON*, including several water-related litigation and contractual matters.

Already known for environmental regulatory work, **Simmons & Simmons** advised a UK energy company on a joint venture in Germany.

Taylor Wessing has a good record in water PPP matters on the financing side. The practice overlaps with a very credible construction and development offering, where it makes use of a good environmental practice, but most of the firm's activities are on the transactional front in public procurement and privatisation mandates. Transport projects are an area in which the firm is increasingly active.

Hoffmann Liebs Fritsch & Partner (HLFP) houses niche expertise in product liability in environment and technology, while emerging energies is another focus.

Thümmel, Schütze & Partner has public procurement strength in its Stuttgart office, while its Dresden office handles restructuring of state and municipally owned companies in view of the revised Municipal Code in Saxony.

REAL ESTATE AND CONSTRUCTION

Clifford Chance was given a fine start in the German real estate market, merging as it did with sector leaders *Punder, Volhard, Weber & Axster*, and the firm continues to be a very impressive outfit. Residential and retail portfolio transactions dominated the year, as well as government-owned sale and leasebacks, large and complicated deals which showcased the firm's depth of resources, client connections with the likes of Whitehall, Apollo and Tishman Speyer, and all-round capability including top-notch tax expertise. The firm has also been active in wind farm acquisitions. A setback came in the failure of the firm to hang on to its respected Berlin team following the closure of that office, but lawyers such as Klaus Minuth in the core Frankfurt team embody a top-ranked practice.

Freshfields Bruckhaus Deringer makes good use of its international network, garnering an enviable private equity client base including Fortress, MSREF and Blackstone. Increasing investment into the German market, especially in retail and leisure schemes, has accounted for much of the firm's activities in the last year. As well as these high-profile investors, the firm is visible more on the seller side, with the cities of Hamburg and Dresden being advised on some high-profile sales of state properties. German clients have also been advised in investments, particularly in Asia, while the high-level banking expertise at the firm lends weight to a very good financing practice. Johannes Conradi is a tremendously impressive figure.

Known especially for hotel work, **CMS Hasche Sigle** enjoys a good working relationship with alliance partners **CMS Cameron McKenna LLP** across several jurisdictions in Europe.

Latham & Watkins LLP's practice is mainly based in Hamburg, where Jürgen Hübner is an especially respected figure in the market, although an effort is being made to bring up the numbers in the Munich office. Following market trends, the firm has been heavily involved in advising German clients on large-scale disposals, while new international investors, private equity funds and venture capitalists are instructing it on

REAL ESTATE AND CONSTRUCTION: REAL ESTATE

CLIFFORD CHANCE
FRESHFIELDS BRUCKHAUS DERINGER

CMS Hasche Sigle ✪
Latham & Watkins LLP
Lovells ✪
White & Case LLP

Allen & Overy LLP ✪
Baker & McKenzie ✪
GSK Gassner Stockmann & Kollegen ✪
Gleiss Lutz ✪
Görg Partnerschaft von Rechtsanwälten ✪
Graf von Westphalen Bappert & Modest ✪
Linklaters Oppenhoff & Rädler ✪
Taylor Wessing ✪

---

avocado rechtsanwälte
Hengeler Mueller ✪
Hölters & Elsing
Luther Rechtsanwaltsgesellschaft mbH ✪
Mayer, Brown, Rowe & Maw LLP ✪
Nörr Stiefenhofer Lutz ✪
O & P Oberthür & Partner ✪
Schäfer, Riedl, Viechtl, Weichler, Segbers
Sibeth Partnerschaft Rechtsanwälte Steuerberater Wirtschaftsprüfer ✪
Wagensonner Luhmann Breitfeld Helm

Ashurst ✪
Bartsch und Partner GbR
Buse Heberer Fromm ✪
CBH Cornelius Bartenbach Haesemann & Partners, member of ius laboris ✪
Dechert LLP ✪
German Greek Law Group - Ziouvas
Gibson, Dunn & Crutcher LLP
Haarmann Hemmelrath ✪
Happ Luther & Partner
Heisse Kursawe Rechtsanwälte Partnerschaft ✪
Heuking Kühn Lüer Wojtek ✪
Heussen Rechtsanwaltsgesellschaft mbH
Hogan & Hartson Raue L.L.P. ✪
KSB Intax
Leinemann & Partner
McDermott Will & Emery Rechtsanwälte Steuerberater LLP ✪
Melchers
Norton Rose Vieregge
P+P Pöllath + Partners ✪
PPR & Partner ✪
Salans
Zirngibl Langwieser

Firms are listed A-Z in tiers which are ranked in order of priority
✪ Indicates firm displays contact details at the end of this chapter.

REAL ESTATE AND CONSTRUCTION: CONSTRUCTION

HEIERMANN FRANKE KNIPP
KAPELLMANN UND PARTNER
LOVELLS ✪
SCHILLING DR MARBACH PROF NIEMÖLLER DR GRIEM & PARTNER

CMS Hasche Sigle ✪
GSK Gassner Stockmann & Kollegen ✪
Gleiss Lutz ✪
Leinemann & Partner

---

avocado rechtsanwälte new
Bornheim, v. Rosenthal & Kollegen
Clifford Chance
Graf von Westphalen Bappert & Modest ✪
Haarmann Hemmelrath ✪
Hecker, Werner, Himmelreich & Nacken
Heuking Kühn Lüer Wojtek ✪
Hölters & Elsing
Koeble, Donus, Fuhrmann, Locher & Partner
Kupferschmid, Englert, Pichl, Grauvogl & Kollegen
Mock Rechtsanwälte
Nörr Stiefenhofer Lutz ✪
O & P Oberthür & Partner ✪
Sibeth Partnerschaft Rechtsanwälte Steuerberater Wirtschaftsprüfer ✪
Taylor Wessing ✪
White & Case LLP

Allen & Overy LLP ✪
Bartsch und Partner GbR
Happ Luther & Partner
Hengeler Mueller ✪
Heussen Rechtsanwaltsgesellschaft mbH
KSB Intax
Kaye Scholer (Germany) LLP ✪
Latham & Watkins LLP
PPR & Partner ✪
Wagensonner Luhmann Breitfeld Helm

Firms are listed A-Z in tiers which are ranked in order of priority
✪ Indicates firm displays contact details at the end of this chapter.

the purchasing side. An international practice is also advising German investors in investments across Europe, including CEE.

Lovells carries a global reputation for excellence in real estate, as well as an international client base, into a recovering German investment arena. Clients such as Bank of Scotland and ING Real Estate, instructing the firm as financiers and joint venture investors, keep the firm at the top end of the market. Roland Bomhard in Düsseldorf and Ingo Winterstein in Frankfurt enjoy good reputations, while efforts to increase the firm's presence on the financial side in Munich and Hamburg bode well for the future. The firm remains a force in construction projects, all of which justify promotions in both categories this year.

White & Case LLP continues to access the real estate market successfully through it finance activities, taking various roles advising on the acquisition finance then securitising the portfolio. HSH Nordbank continues to be a key client on the real estate side, and RBS was advised on the Viterra transaction, while the arrival of Thomas Flatten from **Allen & Overy LLP** brings further expertise in this area. Hamburg-based partner Jan-Peter Kecker and Berlin-based partner Endrik Lettau head the department.

Real estate finance is the focus at **Allen & Overy LLP**, where the firm's superb banking team turns its capabilities to structured financing, portfolio deals and securitisation take-outs. Recent deals for Peter Hoegen and his Frankfurt-based team include advising a bank on the €265m securitisation of a residential portfolio, a subsidiary of Viterra AG, and other banks on the acquisition of office and retail portfolios. International banks such as Hypo Real Estate Bank International, Credit Suisse First Boston and ABN Amro are typical clients. The firm also handles litigation issues arising from real estate financings.

Baker & McKenzie integrates real estate mandates with public law issues, running the two practices in tandem, an approach which has paid off with a number of major instructions including the privatisation of all hospital premises for the City of Hamburg. In the private sector, two major new institutional investors from abroad engaged the firm for the first time on large acquisitions, and portfolio and asset management for the likes of Siemens and Sony round off a thoroughly impressive year for the firm.

GSK Gassner Stockmann & Kollegen is building an increasingly laudable track record in real estate and PPP work, with particular strength in the Berlin and Düsseldorf offices. A new three-way alliance with **Nabarro Nathanson** and Paris firm **August & Debouzy** is built around the real estate market, and has led to the firm increasing its share of international clients investing in Germany, including Aviva. The firm advised Deutsche Telekom on the sale of Residenzpost, and advises Fairacre on the investment side. Former **Clifford Chance** partner Michael Eggersberger is a key figure, while new capability on the finance side was epitomised by Dirk Brückner and Otto Gassner's work advising Allianz Arena GmbH on the financing of the new Allianz Arena in Munich. UBS, Credit Suisse and Eurohypo are other clients.

Detlef Schmidt's real estate team at **Gleiss Lutz** continues to show well in the project development sphere, while portfolio transfers, in line with the progress of the market, provided significant mandates and showcased the firm's ability to handle large due diligence requirements. On the financing side, the firm advised Hypo Real Estate London as lender on the acquisition of Lloyds of London, working closely with alliance partner **Herbert Smith LLP**.

GÖRG Partnerschaft von Rechtsanwälten was given a huge lift in 2005 with the arrival of many of the excellent former **Clifford Chance** team in Berlin, led by Jan Lindner-Figura. A focus on classic real estate work yields instructions on transactional and project development mandates, including one from an Anglo-Indian investor comprising the acquisition, development and lettings issues illustrating the all-round capablity of the team. The team has also advised local authority vendors on major portfolio transactions.

Graf von Westphalen Bappert & Modest made considerable efforts to reshape its real estate practice in the past year following the departure of several members to **SIBETH Partnerschaft Rechtsanwälte Steuerberater Wirtschaftsprüfer**. Ulrich Stuhlfelner brings construction expertise from former firm **Rupprecht Bestelmeyer Stuhlfelner**, while the firm also took three lawyers from the now defunct Berlin office of **Clifford Chance**. New developments and construction are the strengths of the firm, with transactional work an increasing feature. The firm's association with UK firm **Wragge & Co LLP** is a potentially good asset.

Restructured nearly two years ago, **Linklaters Oppenhoff & Rädler** combines excellence in tax and fund structuring to excel on the high-end financing side of the market. Private equity clients such as Fortress favour the firm, specifically department head Michael Steinbrecher, in transactions such as the NILEG Immobilien acquisition.

Taylor Wessing grows more and more visible in the transaction market, with Daniel Ajzensztejn increasingly active in Hamburg. Typically, international investors instruct the firm on deals worth between €20m and €100m, including new developments, with Israeli clients a growing feature; the firm advised Israeli investor Summit Real Estate Holdings Ltd on the €142.6m acquisition and financing of an investment fund subsidiary, comprising a ten-building office portfolio.

avocado rechtsanwälte's real estate strength is centred in Berlin and Düsseldorf, where transactional expertise is matched by private and public planning, and construction experience. Project management of commercial and leisure developments is a forte. The firm also advised a project development company on the planning and construction of an embassy of the Federal Republic of Germany in an Eastern state. Three new lawyers in Munich show the firm's ambition in that city too.

As well as getting on some huge corporate real estate mandates, for example the sale of ThyssenKrupp's residential real estate group to MSREF, straightforward portfolio transactions are also a feature of **Hengeler Mueller**'s activities, with recent deals being conducted in the residential, commercial and retail sectors.

Hölters & Elsing is building a decent real estate team which is increasingly winning some notable mandates in transactions and developments.

Luther Rechtsanwaltsgesellschaft mbH has broad coverage of Europe, bringing increasing involvement in Central and Eastern European markets, particularly in infrastructure.

Mayer, Brown, Rowe & Maw LLP, with its strength and focus on finance, is advising an array of private equity clients on investments in residential portfolios. The firm also advised Eurohypo AG on the sale of a portfolio under a joint venture with Citigroup, a €2.4bn deal.

Nörr Stiefenhofer Lutz enjoys a good relationship with McDonald's, advising on the full range of landlord/tenant and construction matters.

Hamburg firm **O & P Oberthür & Partner** has geared its considerable expertise towards some major projects in northern Germany in recent years, with construction and infrastructure projects including PPPs to the fore. The firm also handles architectural law.

A growing full-service real estate team at **SIBETH Partnerschaft Rechtsanwälte Steuerberater Wirtschaftsprüfer** is particularly noted for advising contractors on projects, as well as investment banks and vehicles from abroad on new developments across the country. The firm has also secured various NPL portfolios on real estate interests. Thomas Richter is the figurehead.

Ashurst is building a real estate investment practice from within its finance team, advising predominantly financiers and banks.

Bartsch und Partner GbR is active in development work, where it advises an array of commercial builders, architects, banking houses and hotel groups on industrial facility, health and leisure projects.

Buse Heberer Fromm has advised English clients in investments in German real estate; international clients of the firm tend to be private equity groups. An area of note has been advising potential investors on risk analysis of investment in wind farms. The firm is also active in negotiating the re-leasing of retail portfolios, mostly on the tenant side, and also houses a commendable construction team.

CBH Cornelius Bartenbach Haesemann & Partners, member of ius laboris combines real estate and public law expertise to show well on construction mandates, with 22 lawyers operating from bases in Cologne and Cottbus.

Dechert LLP shows in the real estate market on the back of financing mandates for the likes of Bank of America and various private equity firms.

Gibson, Dunn & Crutcher LLP is emerging in the real estate market thanks to the efforts of tax expert Jeffery Trinklein's fund-structuring expertise, which has been geared towards foreign investment banks active in the German market. Clients also include a Russian group.

Haarmann Hemmelrath continued to progress in the same areas of housing facility portfolio transactions as it did in 2004, when it leveraged off strength in corporate and tax to advise on the GAGFAH transaction. New mandates included advising Bauwert Property Group on the €200m sale of the German Growth Portfolio, and Cerberus Investment LLC on investments in Wohnungsbaugesellschaft. The arrival of Frank Oprée into the Munich office from **Graf von Westphalen Bappert & Modest** is a boost.

Happ Luther & Partner makes an entrance into the table for 2006 following the annex of *Gemoll Rechtsanwälte,* headed by Guido Gemoll who specialises in real estate receiverships.

Formerly the *ARCON* office in Munich, **Heisse Kursawe Rechtsanwälte Partnerschaft** took the Munich-based real estate team of **Kapellmann und Partner**, following the decision of the former *ARCON* real estate team in the city to join **Graf von Westphalen Bappert & Modest**.

Heuking Kühn Lüer Wojtek leverages off a strong PPP presence to field a good construction output rooted in public sector or PPP work. Clients are invariably public entities, and projects have included the Hanseatic Trade Centre in Hamburg, the Treptowers in Berlin, and the Congress Centres in Frankfurt and Chemnitz.

Hogan & Hartson Raue L.L.P. is breaking into the real estate market, advising WP Carey International LLC on a €100m acquisition and leaseback, as well as other due diligence matters on divestments.

KSB INTAX combined good contacts in the sports world with an improving construction and projects presence to advise the franchise company for the reconstruction of the football stadium in Lower Saxony.

Kaye Scholer (Germany) LLP has carved a niche in plant construction work under Ulrich Trost, undertaking both contentious and non-contentious matters for engineering and construction clients.

Leinemann & Partner is a foremost firm in Germany for construction in the public sector, bringing together expertise in both areas to advise on projects including the international PPP of the Hungarian Cultural Institute, and litigation issues surrounding the Lehrter Bahnhof in Berlin.

McDermott Will & Emery Rechtsanwälte Steuerberater LLP's new partner Norbert Schulte is establishing a presence for the firm in the real estate market, with Blackstone instructing the firm on transactions.

Melchers advised overseas investors in a €120m acquisition in Germany in 2005.

Norton Rose Vieregge combines a solid finance practice with excellent network clients in RBS and HBOS to retain a presence in the real estate finance market. German property bank AHBR is another key client, alongside Carlsberg.

Private equity boutique **P+P Pöllath + Partners** is emerging in real estate following its recruitment of a former **Clifford Chance** team in Berlin, which boasted a serious pedigree in the market, and thanks to an upsurge of private equity investment in German real estate.

PPR & Partner specialises in commercial tenancy agreements, where it advises mainly its commercial and corporate clients.

Former **Haarmann Hemmelrath** partner Barbara Busch brings portfolio transaction expertise of high calibre to **Salans**.

Greek firm **German Greek Law Group - Ziouvas** is increasingly active in the real estate market from a Munich base, having diverted resources to this area in recent times.

Zirngibl Langwieser advised several real estate funds on investments in Germany.

STRUCTURED FINANCE AND SECURITISATION

Clifford Chance's top-tier practice continues to set the bar high in terms of ability across the various disciplines, experience, leading expertise and impressive resources. Peter Scherer is undoubtedly a leading name in credit derivatives and synthetic structures, backed by the excellent Marc Benzler. The firm's esteemed securitisation record was demonstrated by it representing Goldman Sachs and Deutsche Bank as lead managers on the Federal Republic of Germany's synthetic securitisation of the Russian Federation's debt to Germany under the Paris Club debt obligations agreement. The firm remains dominant in synthetic and True Sale securitisations. Michael Weller should be commended in this respect.

In Stefan Krauss, **Hengeler Mueller** has the leading name in securitisation. Clients recognise his immense experience and grasp of the 'core issues'. The firm continues to lead on True Sale transactions and recently advised Ocean Star 2004 on the global shipping loan securisation of

STRUCTURED FINANCE AND SECURITISATION

CLIFFORD CHANCE
HENGELER MUELLER ⭘

LINKLATERS OPPENHOFF & RÄDLER ⭘

Allen & Overy LLP ⭘
Cleary, Gottlieb, Steen & Hamilton LLP ⭘
Freshfields Bruckhaus Deringer
Lovells ⭘
Sidley Austin

Ashurst ⭘
Baker & McKenzie ⭘
Haarmann Hemmelrath ⭘
Mayer, Brown, Rowe & Maw LLP ⭘
Simmons & Simmons ⭘
White & Case LLP

Firms are listed A-Z in tiers which are ranked in order of priority
⭘ Indicates firm displays contact details at the end of this chapter.

HSH Nordbank. Martin Geiger is also recommended.

Linklaters Oppenhoff & Rädler's brand in structured finance and derivatives is firmly established, with a blossoming reputation in synthetic securitisations. It represented Merrill Lynch as arranger and lead manager, KfW (intermediary) and Bank of New York (Trustee) on the synthetic securisation of residential mortgage loans originated by Northern Rock under the KfW PROVIDE scheme. 'The teams are always flexible and give all-round advice to a transaction for all relevant aspects. You can use Linklaters for complex structures,' one client said. Peter Waltz is known for structured equity products and Kurt Dittrich for True Sale structures. Of late the firm represented JP Morgan Securities as the arranger of a €2bn secured MTN programme. This was the first time in the German retail market that structured notes with a particular repackaging structure had been employed. Berthold Kusserow leads the practice.

Allen & Overy LLP's finance record is augmented by Matthew Howard in this sector and Peter Stenz who is now concentrating much of his time on securitisation matters. The firm's emergence in this area is demonstrated by its advisory role for Hypo Real Estate Bank International as sole arranger of a €246.55m commercial mortgage backed securitisation by Valesco Funding plc.

Cleary, Gottlieb, Steen & Hamilton LLP remains a key adviser to Standard & Poor's in relation to RMBS, CMBS and other synthetic and True Sale securitisation structures. The firm also advised Goodyear on a pan-European securitisation programme providing up to €275m of financing. Thomas Buhl, Christof von Dryander and Werner Meier should be identified as the leading advisers at the firm.

Freshfields Bruckhaus Deringer's Bernhard Kaiser and Andreas Bartsch are key to the firm's securitisation business and includes English partner Stuart Axford. In 2004 the firm represented the Federal Republic of Germany on the synthetic securitisation of the Russian Federation's debt to Germany under the Paris Club debt restructuring agreement.

Lovells' loss of Oliver Kessler to join **Sidley Austin** is a significant blow to its structured finance and securitisation aspirations. The firm retains a track record to build on having represented Fitch, Soc Gen and Nomura over the years.

Ashurst's Andreas Zahn remains a solid name in the structured finance sector, particularly in mortgage-backed securitisations, structured note mandates and derivatives. He has won mandates from Deutsche Bank, WestLB and other German banks.

Baker & McKenzie's Dietmar Helms has experience of securitisation issues and has represented clients such as Dresdner Bank over the years.

Haarmann Hemmelrath has increased its presence in ABS programmes with Cologne partner Andreas Lehmann featuring prominently.

Mayer, Brown, Rowe & Maw LLP's supremely active securitisation practice took on another series of headline-grabbing mandates. This follows its advice to a syndicate of banks led by ABN Amro on the securitisation of €1.25bn German auto loan receivables originated by Volkswagen Bank through the German-based securitisation SPV Driver One GmbH in 2004. IN 2005 it advised a consortium led by WestLB and BNP Paribas on another securisation of German auto loans by Volkswagen Bank. Ralf Hesdahl leads the practice.

Simmons & Simmons' profile in structured finance is growing thanks to the efforts of banking and finance head Ingrid Kalisch and English partner Stephen Moller. The firm has a strong link to London where German partner Bodo Schaar is located. In April 2005 the firm advised the arrangers of the asset-backed notes issued by Lavoro Finance in respect of loan receivables originated by Banca Nazionale del Lavoro.

White & Case LLP's hire of the excellent Ulf Kreppel has significantly bolstered its presence in securitisation, with the firm representing both originators and banks. Kreppel had spent some years in London while with **Allen & Overy LLP**, learning these new structured approaches to raising finance. He now concentrates almost entirely on securitsation matters, including True Sale Initiative models.

TAX

Flick Gocke Schaumburg has a traditionally fervent practice backed by a sizeable team of partners and associates which continues to expand. The firm's broad expertise is well known, and it has been brought in to advise on the tax aspects of a series of high-value M&A deals in recent years. Furthermore, its client base reflects the calibre of the practice with a range of DAX-listed companies frequently instructing the firm. Clients and competitors frequently commend Thomas Rödder for top quality and commercially oriented advice. Detlev Piltz and Harald Schaumburg are also recommended.

Freshfields Bruckhaus Deringer is arguably the only firm to offer expertise across the entire discipline, with a strong record in areas ranging from private equity to real estate. A stellar record on M&A transactions coming from its esteemed corporate practice should not overshadow the allure of the tax department itself that has proved particularly effective in winning its own business. Despite the loss of Rolf Füger to **Milbank, Tweed, Hadley & McCloy LLP** in 2004 and the departure of Hans-Gerd Wienands to an in-house position at Messer Griesheim, the practice remains immensely respected. Michael Randerath continues to attract accolades for solutions-driven advice, while department head Stephan Eilers adds to the department's integrity.

TAX

FLICK GOCKE SCHAUMBURG ✪
FRESHFIELDS BRUCKHAUS DERINGER

LINKLATERS OPPENHOFF & RÄDLER ✪

Allen & Overy LLP ✪
Clifford Chance
Gleiss Lutz ✪
Haarmann Hemmelrath ✪
Hengeler Mueller ✪
Lovells ✪
Peters, Schönberger & Partner ✪
Shearman & Sterling LLP

CMS Hasche Sigle ✪
Dewey Ballantine LLP ✪
McDermott Will & Emery Rechtsanwälte Steuerberater LLP ✪
Nörr Stiefenhofer Lutz ✪
P+P Pöllath + Partners ✪
Rödl & Partner GbR

Ashurst ✪
Baker & McKenzie ✪
Cleary, Gottlieb, Steen & Hamilton LLP ✪
Debevoise & Plimpton LLP ✪
Gibson, Dunn & Crutcher LLP
Graf von Westphalen Bappert & Modest ✪
RP Richter & Partner
SJ Berwin LLP ✪
Streck Mack Schwedhelm
White & Case LLP

Alpers & Stenger
Beiten Burkhardt ✪
BTU Simon Schneider Göckel
Buse Heberer Fromm ✪
Caemmerer – Bender – Lenz
Böckmann (Dr) & Partner GbR
Esche Schümann Commichau
Fassbender Schmitt-Walter Nissen
Heuking Kühn Lüer Wojtek ✪
Honert Funke Maute Neumayer
Jones Day
KSB Intax
Kapp, Ebeling & Partner
Latham & Watkins LLP
Luther Rechtsanwaltsgesellschaft mbH ✪
Morgan Lewis ✪
Müller-Horn, Püschel & Luther
PNHR Pelka Niemann Hollerbaum Rohde
PPR & Partner ✪
Raupach & Wollert-Elmendorff Rechtsanwaltsgesellschaft mbH
Simmons & Simmons ✪
Taylor Wessing ✪
Zacher & Partner

Firms are listed A-Z in tiers which are ranked in order of priority
✪ Indicates firm displays contact details at the end of this chapter.

Linklaters Oppenhoff & Rädler is a strong competitor with a broad practice noted for real estate, private equity and structured finance-related tax advice. Its burgeoning business evidently enabled it to elect two new partners in 2005: Florian Lechner and Oliver Rosenberg. In terms of experienced partners, the firm has a lot to offer and that coupled with exceptionally broad expertise makes it an increasingly powerful player. Jens Blumenberg (Frankfurt) and Karl Schäfer (Munich) are two of the most prominent partners, while Munich managing associate Thomas Elser and Frankfurt partner Martin Krause are identified by clients as very capable.

Eugen Bogenschütz is the key figure at **Allen & Overy LLP** and has delivered the firm essential tax credibility. Bogenschütz has advised multinational clients for some years including ITT Industries and Pfizer, and is one of Germany's leading corporate tax advisers. Asmus Mihm provides further tax-structuring credentials – having had an esteemed career at **Hengeler Mueller** and Goldman Sachs, he is a pivotal figure for the firm's financial services business. The team is particularly strong in structured finance and capital markets-related work.

Clifford Chance's Frankfurt office houses the core of its tax practice with Munich and Düsseldorf also playing an important role. The firm handles tax issues across the full range of financing, real estate, investment vehicles and corporate transactional matters, and leading investment banks remain core to the business. Manfred Benkert and Heinz-Günter Gondert are frequently touted as the firm's leading names in corporate transactional related tax matters.

Gleiss Lutz's tax practice has become increasingly prominent in transactions in recent years, in both M&A and private equity, but also acquisition financing and of late real estate finance projects. The firm should also be noted for its frequent advice to municipalities involved in privatisations. Stefanie Beinert, Achim Dannecker, Sven-Christian Witt and Michael Marquardt are the key partners, while the arrival of the immensely well-regarded Harald Plewka from **Haarmann Hemmelrath** is a significant boost.

Haarmann Hemmelrath's MDP approach is an obvious asset in this area, with wealth tax specialists and advisers. It is a frequent adviser of financial services entities. Stefan Busch represented Bankgesellschaft Berlin in relation to the transfer of its property business to the Federal State of Berlin. Busch is a key name and is based in Berlin, with Alexander Hemmelrath and Claus Schild in Munich, Obviously the departure of Wilhelm Haarmann will leave a significant gap to fill.

Hengeler Mueller's prestigious corporate and finance business ensures a healthy and demanding flow of business for its esteemed tax practice. The four-partner practice includes the excellent Friedhelm Jacob, Martin Klein, Hermann-Josef Tries and Ernst-Thomas Kraft and boasts blue-chip clients such as Bayer, Deutsche Telekom and RWE. The department is also increasingly active in relation to the firm's burgeoning private equity business.

Despite the departure of Joerg Siegels to **Morgan Lewis**, **Lovells** remains a key player in tax with particular strength in private equity transactions, real estate, and insurance and re-insurance. Following Siegels' departure, the core of the team is based in Düsseldorf under Christoph Kueppers and in Munich under Stephan Geibel. Kueppers has specialised in insurance and reinsurance for many years, but the firm's blossoming private equity and real estate practices remain key drivers of this quality tax practice. Private equity funds Terra Firma and HgCapital have instructed the team on several transactions.

Munich-based **Peters, Schönberger & Partner**'s name partners Jürgen Peters and Christopher Schönberger have outstanding reputations for transactionally oriented tax advice. Klaus Höfner should also be identified as a leading practitioner, while the MDP handles the full range of tax instructions for DAX-listed companies to wealthy individuals.

Shearman & Sterling LLP's small yet powerful practice boasts the services of Reinhard Stockum and Gottfried Breuninger, both of whom have good reputations. A series of departures at partner level has reduced its capacity (Hanno Berger joining **Dewey Ballantine LLP** in 2004 for instance), but as usual with **Shearman & Sterling LLP**, size never appears to be a hindrance. Contented clients over the years have included Allianz and DaimlerChrysler.

CMS Hasche Sigle's expansive mode has not excluded tax with Angelika Thies joining the Munich office from Ernst & Young in 2004. Corporate transactions, finance and international tax matters remain the driving force behind the business and the firm launched a separate tax consultancy function in Munich and Stuttgart in 2002, to operate alongside the lawyers. Wolf-Georg von Rechenberg and Kurt Gratz have excellent reputations.

Dewey Ballantine LLP has become a key player on the tax scene following the hire of Hanno Berger from **Shearman & Sterling LLP** in 2004. Berger and his team have an impressive client portfolio of financial institutions, including Deutsche Bank, Commerzbank and Dresdner Bank. Clients also highlight Berger's creativity and commercial approach. Following the firm's growth on the corporate law side, the tax team has managed to develop its business beyond the financial institution stronghold.

McDermott Will & Emery Rechtsanwälte Steuerberater LLP now has a sizeable tax practice in line with its esteemed department in the US. Arndt Raupach is still heavily involved in day-to-day issues despite being nearly 70. Dirk Pohl is a leading name, particularly in tax litigation for multinationals. The firm brought in an additional team including four partners from KPMG in April 2005.

In February 2006 **Nörr Stiefenhofer Lutz** hired World Tax Service WTS board member Stefan Hölzemann as a partner giving the firm further international credibility in tax aspects including cross-border restructurings. The firm retains its deeply entrenched connections to the Mittelstand as well as several DAX 30 companies. It should also be identified for its tax advice relating to film finance. Georg Edelmann and Silvia Sparfeld are highly regarded.

P+P Pöllath + Partners was launched as a tax boutique and flourished into a formidable corporate and private equity boutique. Unsurprisingly, tax still plays a key role with Thomas Töben, Michael Best and Wolfgang Tischbirek (a recent recruit from **Shearman & Sterling LLP**) as the lead partners. The firm is often applauded for its tax structuring in private equity transactions.

Rödl & Partner GbR's multi-disciplinary approach is very much driven by its tax advisory practice which has acquired a prestigious business, ranging from clients in its traditional Mittelstand heartland, right through to multinational clients which it serves through its extensive global network. Christian Rödl is known for both tax and corporate advice and is backed by a large team across Germany.

Ashurst has tax teams based in Munich and Frankfurt, mainly allied to the firm's corporate finance business, but also a stellar showing in funds structuring for clients such as WestLB. Leveraged financing and continued involvement in real estate financing has kept the department particularly active. Clients in Munich include HypoVereinsbank, HSBC and Allianz, while in Frankfurt the team represents Lehman Brothers and WestLB.

Baker & McKenzie has continued its period of consolidation with Stephan Schnorberger joining from PwC in August 2005 to launch a new transfer-pricing group at the firm. This follows the arrival of former head of VAT at KPMG Germany, Nicole Looks in 2004. **Baker & McKenzie**'s global reputation remains a key attraction to multinational clients. Christian Brodersen leads the practice.

Cleary, Gottlieb, Steen & Hamilton LLP's Daniel Weyde is the firm's key tax partner. With the firm's wide-ranging activity in finance, M&A and capital markets, Weyde has been exposed to some particularly challenging instructions, including providing tax counsel to Citigroup on its €2.4bn joint venture with Eurohypo to trade non-performing loans.

Debevoise & Plimpton LLP has an eminent tax reputation particularly in the private equity sector thanks to the efforts of Friedrich Hey. He advised on the tax aspects of Kabel Deutschland's acquisitions of three other German regional cable network operators in 2005, which comprised several private equity investors.

Gibson, Dunn & Crutcher LLP's Hans Martin Schmid (formerly **Shearman & Sterling LLP**) has an impressive tax record.

Graf von Westphalen Bappert & Modest operates a multi-disciplinary practice featuring lawyers, accountants and tax advisers. The firm is best known for its tax planning advice to medium-sized and Mittelstand companies. In this regard, the automotive, food, medical equipment and real estate sectors are most active, but also with a further emphasis on PPP projects and privatisation. Günter Maier and Matthias von Rönn are the most recognised partners.

Munich-based **RP Richter & Partner** spun off from Ernst & Young's tax department in 2001 and since then has built an impressive business based around private clients, mid-sized companies and now several DAX companies. High-profile clients in the car rental, utilities and manufacturing sectors suggest the firm has come some way since its launch. Of the 55 professionals at the firm, 19 are lawyers with six of these also being tax advisers. Wolfgang Richter is the firm's chief rainmaker.

SJ Berwin LLP derives from a tax-driven business which has become a leader in private equity funds formation and structuring. In this regard Rüdiger Knopf is one of the foremost tax specialists in the private equity area.

Cologne-based **Streck Mack Schwedhelm** is known for tax disputes and name partner Michael Streck has an excellent reputation. The firm also has offices in Berlin and Munich.

White & Case LLP boasts eminence in corporate transactions, privatisations and finance-driven tax. Gerhard Laule, Günther Kahlert and Andreas Knebel have excellent reputations.

In the final tier we recommend Hamburg's **Alpers & Stenger** which should be identified for a noted regional presence, while **Beiten Burkhardt**'s Munich-based partner Hans Volckens is recognised by clients for his impressive ability in relation to demanding tax mandates.

Also in Munich, **BTU Simon Schneider Göckel** has an established tax brand; as does **Buse Heberer Fromm** following the arrival of further resources; and **Caemmerer - Bender - Lenz** in Erfut, Freiburg and Karlsruhe. **Dr Böckmann & Partner GbR** is a prominent name in Berlin.

Esche Schümann Commichau is allied to a firm of accountants and has a profile that extends well beyond its Hamburg base. Klaus Stolberg is highly reputed.

Fassbender Schmitt-Walter Nissen is commended by clients for investment funds structuring and thus its tax practice plays a valuable role.

Heuking Kühn Lüer Wojtek has expanded its tax practice with Dieter Bohnert (also known for white-collar crime), Wolfram Meven, and Gerd Kostrzewa very much to the fore. Jörg Schewe in Hamburg should also be mentioned. The firm works with KPMG and Ernst & Young on a frequent basis.

Bavarian firm **Honert Funke Maute Neumayer**; **Jones Day** where Joachim Borggräfe is popular with the Mittelstand; **Kapp, Ebeling & Partner**; Hanover-based **KSB INTAX**, which boasts the presence of the excellent Christian Knoke; **Latham & Watkins LLP** which is experienced in the private equity sector handling the tax matters related to leveraged buy-outs and other transactions (Götz Wiese is the lead partner) are also recommended.

Luther Rechtsanwaltsgesellschaft mbH; **Morgan Lewis** which is now well and truly on the map following the arrival of Jörg Siegels from **Lovells** in 2005; **Müller-Horn, Püschel & Luther**; the historically strong **Raupach & Wollert-Elmendorff Rechtsanwaltsgesellschaft mbH** ; **PNHR Pelka Niemann Hollerbaum Rohde**; **PPR & Partner**; **Simmons & Simmons** led by Hans-Jörg Wittmann; **Taylor Wessing**; and **Zacher & Partner** all merit mention.

TELECOMS

The size of the team, the variety of work and the complexity and size of the deals all contribute to **Baker & McKenzie**'s continuing presence at the top of the market. Joachim Scherer and Ulrich Ellinghaus combine public law and telecoms to provide market-leading regulatory advice, with the Regulatory Authority for Telecommunications and Post and the Federal Ministry of Economics and Labour seeking out the team for high-profile instructions. Feasibility studies are another notable strength.

Freshfields Bruckhaus Deringer is highly reputed in the corporate arena, where private equity houses, particularly Apollo Management, have been flooding the firm with acquisition mandates. Kabel Deutschland was also advised on the flotation of a corporate bond, and O2 was counselled on antitrust and licensing issues pending its merger with Telefónica.

Piepenbrock & Schuster is rooted in new media and telecommunications, advising on business, regulatory and litigation matters. A team of techincally knowledgeable former in-house counsel is epitomised by Hermann-Josef Piepenbrock, a deregulation expert, and Martin Geppert. A business consulting arm, Piepenbrock & Schuster Consulting AG, was established in 2004.

Regulatory expert firm **Redeker Sellner Dahs & Widmaier** is very active in telecoms, advising clients including Deutsche Telekom AG on matters before the the Regulatory Authority for Telecommunications and Post, incorporating antitrust issues.

Mark Hoenike heads a corporate-oriented telecoms practice within **Allen & Overy LLP**'s communications, media and technology group. Versatel and Swisscom are key clients, having been advised on various acquisitions, while Morgan Stanley, Goldman Sachs, Deutsche Bank AG and Citibank instructed the firm on the acquisition of Kabel Deutschland. Deutsche Bahn AG was advised on commercial agreements relating to the rollout of WLAN networks in railway stations. Helge Schäfer is another leading light in a team which also handles regulatory issues for its clients.

Clifford Chance offers telecoms advice from the perspective of antitrust and regulatory experts Martin Wissman and Joachim Schütze in Düsseldorf, while Bernd Meyer-Witting in the Frankfurt office brings corporate expertise to all forms of media. The firm leverages successfully off its financial and institutional client base.

Wolfgang Spoerr heads a lively telecoms practice in **Hengeler Mueller**'s Berlin office, which handles high-profile corporate mandates as well as regulatory issues which recently included issues relating to the digitalisation of cable networks and the allocation of free-to-air channels.

Already strong in regulatory matters, **Hogan & Hartson Raue L.L.P.**'s recruitment of Kornelius Kleinlein from **Linklaters Oppenhoff & Rädler** further advanced the firm's client base

TELECOMS

BAKER & McKENZIE ✪
FRESHFIELDS BRUCKHAUS DERINGER
PIEPENBROCK & SCHUSTER
REDEKER SELLNER DAHS & WIDMAIER

Allen & Overy LLP ✪
Clifford Chance
Hengeler Mueller ✪
Hogan & Hartson Raue L.L.P. ✪
McDermott Will & Emery Rechtsanwälte Steuerberater LLP ✪
Wilmer Cutler Pickering Hale and Dorr LLP ✪

---

avocado rechtsanwälte
B.B.O.R.S Rechtsanwälte
Bird & Bird ✪
CMS Hasche Sigle ✪
DLA Piper Rudnick Gray Cary ✪
Gleiss Lutz ✪
Haarmann Hemmelrath ✪
Haver & Mailänder
Heuking Kühn Lüer Wojtek ✪
Hölters & Elsing
Kraatz & Kraatz
Latham & Watkins LLP
Linklaters Oppenhoff & Rädler ✪
Lovells ✪
Nörr Stiefenhofer Lutz ✪
Norton Rose Vieregge
Taylor Wessing ✪
Velten Franz Jakoby
White & Case LLP
Wilkinson, Barker, Knauer, Leitermann
Willkie Farr & Gallagher LLP ✪

Firms are listed A-Z in tiers which are ranked in order of priority
✪ Indicates firm displays contact details at the end of this chapter.

and know-how. Aside from regulatory matters, recent mandates have included acquisitions for Texas Pacific Group and Apax Partners. Christoph Wagner and Christian von Hammerstein are the department's incumbent experts.

McDermott Will & Emery Rechtsanwälte Steuerberater LLP advises T-Online on its IT requirements, and is also garnering an excellent reputation for antitrust advice to telecoms and internet clients. Telecoms clients also engage the firm on regulatory and contractual matters.

Wilmer Cutler Pickering Hale and Dorr LLP advises such luminary clients as AOL Inc, on online content liability issues, and has a particular strength in regulatory matters from its Berlin office where Natalie Lübben is instructed by Deutsche Telekom AG and Time Warner.

avocado rechtsanwälte's telecoms expertise is geared towards antitrust mandates. Telco Services GmbH is a client.

B.B.O.R.S Rechtsanwälte has established itself during its short existence as a very capable operation in the regulatory field, with Peter Radler's fusion of public sector and telecoms expertise coming to the fore. The firm advised Telefónica Deutschland before the Regulator on line-sharing rates, and Tele2 Deutschland on several mandates including a DSL product matter before the Regulator.

Although **Bird & Bird** boasts clients such as Deutsche Telekom and T-Mobile, the firm's advice has traditionally been on the trade mark and sponsorship side. However, the arrival of Christian Kessel from **Baker & McKenzie** brings valuable expertise on the commercial and contractual side, while activities in outsourcing and Voice-over-IP services have broadened the firm's appeal.

CMS Hasche Sigle is especially skilled on the regulatory side, with Christian Scherer-Leydecker a prominent figure. Network operators are the client focus, with Mobil.com a key contact.

DLA Piper Rudnick Gray Cary took *Coudert Brothers LLP*'s telecoms expertise in 2005.

Haarmann Hemmelrath combines expertise in Paris and Germany successfully, advising communications providers on telecoms set-ups across Europe. Bernd Sagasser and Stephan Rippert are the key figures.

Heuking Kühn Lüer Wojtek's presence in telecoms is mainly on the regulatory side, where satellite providers and network operators comprise the majority of the Hamburg-based team's clients.

Kraatz & Kraatz is a niche telecoms and IT firm located at Kronberg im Taunus, showing significant technical expertise in advising many overseas clients on regulatory and contractual matters. Franz Kraatz helms the practice.

Latham & Watkins LLP' telecoms expertise is mainly geared to advising Deutsche Telekom on ongoing security litigation mandates, although it is expanding to smaller US clients based in Germany.

The departure of Kornelius Kleinlein to **Hogan & Hartson Raue L.L.P.** has left **Linklaters Oppenhoff & Rädler** short on telecoms regulatory expertise at partner level, although the firm boasts some talented associates. In outsourcing and commercial telecoms work, spilling over into cartel matters, the firm remains more than competent, with a lot of activity in the cable and broadband markets.

Lovells' telecoms expertise is mainly housed in Munich under Wolfgang Büchner. It serves stellar clients such as T-Online International AG and Deutsche Telekom on a mix of contractual, regulatory and IP-related issues, including email surveillance. Start-ups and and licensing issues are also handled.

Although **Nörr Stiefenhofer Lutz** houses telecoms expertise across its offices, the focal point is Berlin where Alexander Ritvay and Karsten Metzlaff possess immense experience in transactional and regulatory matters, respectively. Major mandates involved due diligence on the transmission of programmes related to the ongoing takeover of ProSiebenSat.1 by Axel Springer, a mandate which was handled with great proficiency. The firm also advised European service providers on pan-European infrastructrure agreements and represented RTL in successful cartel proceedings.

Taylor Wessing has refocused on regional telecoms operators, bringing its commendable IT expertise to the fore.

White & Case LLP, already known for corporate and outsourcing deals in the sector, is increasing its share of the regulatory market. O2 remains a key client, with Martin Hoffman advising it on complex regulatory matters, while Martin Munz and Norbert Wimmer are good practitioners. The return of Jost Kotthoff from **Shearman & Sterling LLP** brings closer connections with major banks.

Wilkinson, Barker, Knauer, Leitermann has all-round expertise in media, telecoms and IT, on the business and regulatory sides.

SCHULTZE & BRAUN

EISENBAHNSTR 19-23
77855 ACHERN

Telephone: +49 78 41 70 80
Fax: +49 78 41 70 83 01
E-mail: mail@schubra.de
Website: www.schubra.de

Languages
English, French, Italian, Japanese, Basic Mandarin

Other offices
Berlin, Bremen, Chemnitz, Dessau, Dresden, Erfurt, Frankfurt, Freiburg, Halle, Hamburg, Hanover, Karlsruhe, Kassel, Konstanz, Leipzig, Magdeburg, Mannheim, Munich, Nürnberg, Offenburg, Oldenburg, Osnabrück, Rostock, Rottweil, Saarbrücken, Stuttgart

Number of lawyers 71
at this office 26

International groupings
AEPPC/EIPA; IBA Committee J; International Insolvency Institute

CATEGORIES OF WORK

Insolvency
Dr Eberhard Braun, Dr Ferdinand Kießner

Banks and banking
Dr Peter de Bra

Litigation and arbitration
Christian Forcher

Forensic services
Otto Lakies

Company law
Harald Kroth

Construction law
Judith Franz

Corporate law
Achim Frank

Criminal law
Alexander Schork

Economic law
Martina Dietrich, Dr Andreas Beck

Family law
Barbara Meider

International law
Anneroso Tashiro, Ellen Delzant

Labour and employment
Bertram Wolf, Joachim Zobel

Corporate restructuring
Jens Weber, Volker Beissenhirtz

Security
Dr Rainer Riggert, Roland Fendel

Tax
Arno Abenheimer

THE FIRM

Schultze & Braun is an association of five companies with lawyers, auditors, tax consultants and sworn accountants. The services it offers cover the whole range of legal and tax counselling requirements for individuals, craftsmen, trade and industry. Schultze & Braun currently has a staff of about 450.

Fritz Beck's independent tax counselling practice was founded in 1949. 1969 saw the arrival of Wolfgang Schultze as tax consultant, thereby establishing the firm. The composite company of Schultze & Braun was formed in 1975, as tax consultants and lawyers. The insolvency department was reorganised in 1980, thereby extending the firm's activities. In 1987, Schultze & Braun included auditing as part of its service.

AREAS OF PRACTICE

Schultze & Braun offers in its partnership comprehensive counselling in all legal and tax matters – it is both a specialist and a generalist. A host of highly qualified specialists all within one organisation deal with each case according to its specific problems.

As one of the first composites, Schultze & Braun surmounted the division of the professions of the legal adviser and the tax consultant in 1975.

The advantages of this are still obvious today – countless legal points are bound up with tax matters, and almost every tax problem has a legal question in the background.

Even within the field of legal advice, no one person can master the full range of court work, civil and public law.

What is more, business matters are becoming increasingly important. This means that it is now part of the role of the auditor to determine the most opportune legal and commercial organisational arrangements. Thus, for example, it would be unthinkable to run a company without an operational report system.

Liquidity planning and profits planning by comparing desired and actual figures are important prerequisites for successful company management. Schultze & Braun also pays particular attention to these points.

Securities management and realisation through pools of trusts are features of the work of the business law department; the department works with this conceptually and operationally for banks and suppliers on problems where furnishing collateral, securities management and realisation are all involved, with or without liquidation proceedings.

Schultze & Braun deals with business problems, cost accounting, budget planning and supervision, advice on establishment, and investment and financial analysis, as well as drawing up annual reports and index and comparative accounts. Presentation of accounts and balance sheets for French and English as well as German companies is a further area of the firm's activity.

Schultze & Braun is also prepared to act in companies' boards of directors and as executors of wills.

BAKER & McKENZIE LLP

FRIEDRICHSTRASSE 79-80
10117 BERLIN

Telephone: +49 30 20 38 76 00
Fax: +49 30 20 38 76 99
Website: www.bakernet.com

Languages Dutch, English, French, Italian, Russian, Spanish

Other offices Almaty, Amsterdam, Antwerp, Baku, Bangkok, Barcelona, Beijing, Bogotá, Bologna, Brasilia, Brussels, Budapest, Buenos Aires, Cairo, Calgary, Cancun, Caracas, Chicago, Chihuahua, Dallas, Düsseldorf, Frankfurt, Geneva, Guadalajara, Hanoi, Ho Chi Minh City, Hong Kong, Houston, Jakarta, Juarez, Kuala Lumpur, Kyiv, London, Madrid, Manama, Manila, Melbourne, Mexico City, Miami, Milan, Monterrey, Moscow, Munich, New York, Palo Alto, Paris, Porto Alegré, Prague, Rio de Janeiro, Riyadh, Rome, St Petersburg, San Diego, San Francisco, Santiago, São Paulo, Shanghai, Singapore, Stockholm, Sydney, Taipei, Tijuana, Tokyo, Toronto, Valencia, Vienna, Warsaw, Washington DC, Zürich

Number of lawyers 3,300+
at this office 16+

CATEGORIES OF WORK

Administrative law
Frank-Rainer Töpfer

Banking and finance
Wilhelm Hebing

Company and commercial law
Ulrich Hennings, Peter Wessels

Environmental law
Frank-Rainer Töpfer

IP, media and dispute resolution
Stefan Dittmer

Labour law
Alexander Wolff

Law of the former German Democratic Republic
Frank-Rainer Töpfer

Litigation and arbitration
Stefan Dittmer, Frank-Rainer Töpfer

Mergers and acquisitions
Wilhelm Hebing, Ulrich Hennings, Peter Wessels, Thorsten Seidel

Privatisation
Wilhelm Hebing, Frank-Rainer Töpfer, Thorsten Seidel, Christian Birkholz

Real estate
Frank-Rainer Töpfer, Peter Wessels

Tax
Christian Birkholz, Wilhelm Hebing

THE FIRM

Baker & McKenzie has provided sophisticated legal advice and services to many of the world's most dynamic and global organisations for more than 50 years. With a network of more than 3,300 locally qualified, internationally experienced lawyers in 38 countries, the firm has the knowledge and resources to deliver the broad scope of quality legal services required to respond effectively to both international and local needs – consistently, confidently and with a sensitivity for cultural, social and legal practice differences.

Baker & McKenzie has been established in Europe for over 40 years, having opened its first European offices in 1957. Since then, the European and Middle Eastern network has grown to 29 offices, giving it unparalleled geographical coverage.

The Frankfurt am Main office was formed in 1962; the office in Berlin was opened on 1 March 1990; the Munich office on 1 April 1997; and the Düsseldorf office on 1 April 1999.

Since their formation, the German offices have advised their clients on all questions of German, European and international industrial and commercial law with particular emphasis on cross-border and multinational transactions. At present, more than 170 attorneys-at-law (Rechtsanwälte), tax advisers, and varying numbers of foreign admitted lawyers work in the German offices.

All attorneys are at least bilingual; most of them have completed additional graduate legal studies at foreign law schools. Several attorneys are simultaneously admitted as CPAs, tax advisers, tax attorneys, attorneys for administrative law or attorneys for labour law.

AREAS OF PRACTICE

Baker & McKenzie co-ordinates its core practice areas on local, regional and global levels, giving most of its lawyers experience in more than one jurisdiction, as well as providing multinational teams of specialists.

Utilising a global practice group structure and ground-breaking technology coupled with a personal, detailed understanding of a client's specific business, Baker & McKenzie is able to organise its extensive resources to provide focused and strategic counsel to clients.

Baker & McKenzie advises multinational enterprises, large German companies, medium-sized enterprises, banks and insurance companies, as well as institutions and entities under public law in all questions of German, European, and international industrial and commercial law including company law, competition and cartel law, intellectual property, banking and finance, labour law, administrative law, and tax law. Furthermore, the firm handles litigation and arbitration matters. Several partners have expertise in specialised areas of law, such as European Community law, the law of cosmetics, food and drug law, trade marks, franchising, corporate finance, new financial products, government procurement, real estate transactions, and media telecommunications law.

Baker & McKenzie International is a Swiss Verein with member law firms around the world.

BEITEN BURKHARDT

KURFÜRSTENSTRASSE 72-74
10787 BERLIN

Telephone: +49 30 26 47 10
Fax: +49 30 26 47 11 23
E-mail: bblaw-berlin@bblaw.com
Website: www.bblaw.com

Languages
Cantonese, Czech, English, French, Hungarian, Italian, Mandarin, Polish, Russian, Slovak, Spanish, Ukrainian

Other offices
Beijing, Brussels, Cologne, Düsseldorf, Frankfurt am Main, Hong Kong, Kiev, Leipzig, Moscow, Munich, Nuremberg, St Petersburg, Shanghai, Warsaw

Number of lawyers 249
at this office 28

CATEGORIES OF WORK

- Company law
- Banking and finance
- Tax law
- European law and cartel law
- Foundation, association, societies and sports law
- Industrial property rights
- Labour law
- Procurement law
- Public law
- Information technology
- Estate planning and succession rules
- Copyright law
- Litigation and arbitration
- Telecommunication law
- Real estate law
- Advertising law
- Media law

BUSE HEBERER FROMM

KURFÜRSTENDAMM 217
10719 BERLIN

Telephone: +49 30 32 79 42 0
Fax: +49 30 32 79 42 22
E-mail: berlin@buse.de
Website: www.buse.de

Languages
English, French, Italian, Russian, Spanish, Turkish

Other offices
Düsseldorf, Essen, Frankfurt am Main, Hamburg, Munich, New York, Palma de Mallorca, Sydney, Zurich

Number of lawyers 120
at this office 24

Member
The European Legal Alliance: Beauchamps (Ireland); Dubarry Le Douarin Veil (France); Field Fisher Waterhouse (England); Harper Macleod (Scotland); Jimenez de Parga (Spain); La Scala & Associati (Italy)

CATEGORIES OF WORK

- Banking and finance
- Antitrust and merger control
- Commerce, transport, insurance
- Commercial delinquency
- Corporate/M&A
- Industrial property and copyrights
- Information technology and telecommunications
- Labour and employment
- Litigation and arbitration, national and international
- Press and media
- Property and construction
- Public law
- Tax

CMS HASCHE SIGLE

MARKGRAFENSTRASSE 36
CARREE AM GENDARMENMARKT
10117 BERLIN

Telephone: +49 30 20 36 00
Fax: +49 30 20 36 02 90
E-mail: berlin@cms-hs.com
Website: www.cms-hs.com

Languages
Dutch, English, French, Italian, Spanish

Other offices
Belgrade, Brussels, Chemnitz, Cologne, Dresden, Düsseldorf, Frankfurt, Hamburg, Leipzig, Moscow, Munich, Prague, Stuttgart

Number of lawyers 420
at this office 28

Other CMS alliance member firms
CMS Adonnino Ascoli & Cavasola Scamoni, Italy; CMS Albiñana & Suárez de Lezo, Spain; CMS Bureau Francis Lefebvre, France; CMS Cameron McKenna, UK; CMS DeBacker, Belgium; CMS Derks Star Busmann, Netherlands; CMS von Erlach Henrici, Switzerland; CMS Reich-Rohrwig Hainz, Austria

CATEGORIES OF WORK

Corporate

Mergers and acquisitions

Private equity and venture capital

Banking

Stock trading and capital markets

Competition and merger control

State aid and EU law

Intellectual property, copyright, media and press

Individual and collective labour law

Real estate and construction

IT and telecommunications

Tax

Estate planning

Insolvency

Utilities

Public commercial and environment, procurement

Distribution and franchise law

Insurance

Maritime, shipping and transport

Litigation and arbitration

GSK GASSNER STOCKMANN & KOLLEGEN

MOHRENSTRASSE 42
10117 BERLIN

Telephone: +49 30 20 39 07 0
Fax: +49 30 20 39 07 44
E-mail: berlin@gsk.de
Website: www.gsk.de

Languages
English, French, German, Italian, Russian

Other offices
Düsseldorf, Frankfurt, Hamburg, Heidelberg, Munich, Stuttgart

Number of lawyers 107
at this office 16

Contacts
Dr Christian R Schmidt (Berlin), Dr Andreas Bauer (Munich), Dr Andreas May (Frankfurt), Dr Philipp Jebens (Hamburg), Dr Peter Ladwig (Stuttgart), Dr Eckart Petzold (Düsseldorf), Wolfgang Böhm (Heidelberg)

CATEGORIES OF WORK

Corporate
Dr Christian R Schmidt, Dr Michael Stobbe

Mergers and acquisitions
Dr Rainer Stockmann, Dr Michael Stobbe

Venture capital and private equity
Dr Rainer Stockmann

Real estate, project finance, construction
Dr Lorenz Claussen, Dr Oda Wedemeyer

Commercial lease
Dr Christian R Schmidt, Dr Lorenz Claussen

Infrastructure, public sector, public procurement
Dr Lorenz Claussen, Dr Oda Wedemeyer

Notarial services
Dr Lorenz Claussen, Stefan Aldag

Banking and finance, capital markets
Dr Rainer Stockmann, Dr Michael Stobbe

Intellectual property and unfair competition
Dr Christian R Schmidt, Dr Jörg Kahler

Information technology
Dr Christian R Schmidt, Dr Jörg Kahler

Antitrust and merger control
Dr Christian R Schmidt, Dr Michael Stobbe

Labour/employment law
Dr Christian R Schmidt

Litigation and arbitration
Dr Christian R Schmidt, Dr Oda Wedemeyer

Taxation
Dr Rainer Stockmann, Dr Michael Stobbe

GLEISS LUTZ
RECHTSANWÄLTE

FRIEDRICHSTADT-PASSAGEN
QUARTIER 206
FRIEDRICHSTRASSE 71
10117 BERLIN

Telephone: +49 30 80 09 79 0
Fax: +49 30 80 09 79 97 9
E-mail: info@gleisslutz.com
Website: www.gleisslutz.com

Languages
Dutch, English, French, Italian, Mandarin, Cantonese, Polish, Portuguese, Spanish, Russian, Czech, Slovak

Other offices
Frankfurt, Munich, Stuttgart, Brussels, Prague, Warsaw

Number of lawyers 225
at this office 45

Contact
Dr Ralf Thaeter LLM

CATEGORIES OF WORK

- German, EC and international law
- Banking, securities and finance
- Commercial law (general)
- Companies, corporations
- Competition, antitrust
- Electronic commerce, internet law
- Employment, labour
- Environment and pollution control
- Insurance
- Litigation and arbitration
- Mergers and acquisitions
- Real estate
- Tax
- Telecommunications, media and broadcasting
- Trade marks, intellectual property

GÖRG
PARTNERSCHAFT VON RECHTSANWÄLTEN

TIERGARTEN DREIECK
KLINGELHÖFERSTRASSE 5
10785 BERLIN

Telephone: +49 30 88 45 03 0
Fax: +49 30 88 27 15 0
E-mail: berlin@goerg.de
Website: www.goerg.de

Languages
English, French, Italian, Portuguese, Russian, Spanish

Other Offices
Cologne, Essen, Frankfurt

Number of lawyers 97
at this office 36

CATEGORIES OF WORK

- Restructuring/insolvency law
- Employment law
- Real estate/construction law/projects
- IP/IT/media law/general commercial
- Corporate/M&A/banking and finance/tax law
- Regulatory/public law
- Litigation and arbitration
- International transactions

GRAF VON WESTPHALEN BAPPERT & MODEST

RAUCHSTRASSE 26
10787 BERLIN

Telephone: +49 30 72 61 11 0
Fax: +49 30 72 61 11 12 3
E-mail: berlin@westphalen-law.com
Website: www.westphalen-law.com

Languages
English, French, Greek, Italian, Russian, Spanish, Turkish

Other offices
Cologne, Dresden, Frankfurt, Freiburg, Hamburg, Munich, Alicante, Brussels, Vienna

Number of lawyers 123
at this office 12

Contact
Dr Lorenz Czajka

In exclusive co-operation with
Wragge & Co, UK

CATEGORIES OF WORK

- Corporate, private equity
- Mergers and acquisitions, privatisation
- Commercial and international trade
- Real estate, construction and project development
- Corporate real estate
- Distribution
- Arbitration and litigation
- EC law
- Antitrust law
- Customs regulation
- Public private partnership
- Intellectual property, product piracy and unfair trading
- Administrative, planning and environmental
- Labour and employment
- Information technology, media and entertainment
- Tax, accounting
- Banking, insolvency
- Product liability and insurance
- Life sciences

HENGELER MUELLER

CHARLOTTENSTRASSE 35/36
10117 BERLIN

Telephone: +49 30 20 37 40
Fax: +49 30 20 37 43 33
E-mail: hmbln@hengeler.com
Website: www.hengeler.com

Other offices
Düsseldorf, Frankfurt, Munich, Brussels, London

Number of lawyers 192
at this office 26

Contact
Dr Julius Budde

CATEGORIES OF WORK

- M&A/corporate
- Private equity
- Equity capital markets
- Banking and finance
- Insolvency and reorganisation
- Litigation and arbitration
- Central and Eastern Europe
- Regulatory and environment
- Privatisation and PPP
- Public sector restructuring
- Public procurement
- Healthcare and life sciences
- Telecommunications and media
- Real estate

HEUKING KÜHN LÜER WOJTEK

FRIEDRICHSTRASSE 149
10117 BERLIN

Telephone: +49 30 88 00 97 0
Fax: +49 30 88 00 97 99
E-mail: berlin@heuking.de
Website: www.heuking.de

Languages
German, English, French

Other offices
Brussels, Chemnitz, Cologne, Düsseldorf, Frankfurt, Hamburg, Munich

Number of lawyers 17

Contact
Prof Dr Peter Fissenewert

CATEGORIES OF WORK

Corporate law	**Environmental law**
Mergers and acquisitions	**Arbitration**
Merger control and competition law	**Administrative law**
Litigation	**Labour law**
Privatisations	**Real estate and construction law**
Public tenders and bids	**Insolvency and crisis management**
Banking law	**Tax law**
Financial services	**Public procurement law**
Energy law	

THE FIRM

Heuking Kühn Lüer Wojtek was founded in Düsseldorf, Germany, in 1971. Since then, the firm has spread geographically, and Heuking Kühn now has seven significant offices in Germany, as well as an office in Brussels.

The firm has an extensive international network of law firms, enabling it to provide its clients with seamless 'one-stop shopping', on international transactions and regulatory matters. Since its formation, Heuking Kühn Lüer Wojtek has specifically chosen to remain an independent law firm. It is Heuking Kühn Lüer Wojtek's philosophy that, to provide the best possible service to its clients, the firm must be able to co-operate with various other law firms which are at the top of the profession in their respective countries. This gives the firm the ability to make alternative counsel suggestions to its clients, giving the clients a choice of the best suitable law firm or lawyer in each country and for each matter. Over the last 30+ years, Heuking Kühn Lüer Wojtek has developed excellent relationships with the key firms in all of the major jurisdictions worldwide.

Heuking Kühn Lüer Wojtek is a name which is synonymous with legal competence. The firm is one of the largest commercial law firms in Germany, with more than 170 specialised lawyers and tax advisers, representing the interests of national and international clients. Included in the client list are large and medium-sized German and international companies in all areas of the manufacturing industry, as well as trade and service industries, associations, governmental and public sector organisations and private clients and trusts.

The firm prides itself on substantive legal competence and on the excellent education and continuing legal education of its lawyers. Moreover, virtually all of the lawyers are German-English bilingual.

Extensive specialisation and comprehensive knowledge of specific industry sectors provide the basis of all of Heuking Kühn Lüer Wojtek's legal counselling. Experienced partners and carefully selected associate lawyers develop innovative solutions to complex legal problems. The lawyers regularly work in their specific practice area groups and also in multi-group and multidisciplinary teams with clients and outside consultants or advisers. Entrepreneurial thinking on behalf of firm clients, as well as efficient, quality, cost-effective and timely work and the highest personal dedication are key components of Heuking Kühn Lüer Wojtek's culture.

AREAS OF PRACTICE

Heuking Kühn Lüer Wojtek is a full-service commercial law firm. Cross-border and cross-sector knowledge in combination with a deep understanding of business reasoning enables service to clients with the broadest possible support in all their negotiations and business decisions. This applies equally to M&A transactions, to legal advice on company structure, business risk management, negotiations and negotiation tactics, training, crisis and insolvency counselling, corporate financial matters, and complex litigation and arbitration. Thanks to a variety of strong business clients, the firm has built long-term relationships with its clients and can assist them, beginning with the establishment of a business, followed by implementing business goals, including day-to-day legal work, reorganisations, acquisitions and divestitures.

Heuking Kühn Lüer Wojtek is actively involved with its clients in providing regulatory counselling in all areas of commercial law, as well as assisting them in organising and implementing their M&A transactions in Germany, throughout Europe, and internationally. Heuking Kühn Lüer Wojtek has particular expertise in German and EU company law; competition law, merger control, state aids and regulated industries (including energy; telecommunications; and transport, postal services and shipping law); taxation; employment law; finance and banking; international trade and customs; insurance; litigation, arbitration and mediation; bankruptcy and insolvency; environment, health and safety law; product liability; product-specific regulation; real estate and construction law; IP, IT and media law; and private clients and family law.

HOGAN & HARTSON RAUE LLP

POTSDAMER PLATZ 1
10785 BERLIN

Telephone: +49 30 72 61 15 0
Fax: +49 30 72 61 15 10 0
E-mail: gmeinel@hhlaw.com
Website: www.hhlaw.com

Languages
English, French, Hebrew, Italian, Spanish

Other offices
Baltimore, Beijing, Boulder, Brussels, Budapest, Caracas, Colorado Springs, Denver, Geneva, Hong Kong, London, Los Angeles, Miami, Moscow, Munich, New York, Northern Virginia, Paris, Shanghai, Tokyo, Warsaw, Washington DC

Number of lawyers 1,101
at this office 39

Contact
Gernod Meinel

CATEGORIES OF WORK

Mergers and acquisitions	Infrastructure projects
Corporate law	Internet and e-commerce
Tax and customs	Antitrust law
Banking and capital markets	Public procurement law
Project finance	Intellectual property
Privatisation	Media and telecommunications
Labour law	Real estate
Litigation and arbitration	Construction
Insolvency law	Utilities
Copyright, publishing and press law	Healthcare and biotechnology
Patents and trade marks	Sports and entertainment
Environmental law	Life sciences

LOVELLS

SCHLÜTERSTRASSE 37
10629 BERLIN

Telephone: +49 30 88 91 90
Fax: +49 30 88 91 91 00
E-mail: reception.berlin@lovells.com
Website: www.lovells.de

Languages
English, French

Other offices
Alicante, Amsterdam, Beijing, Brussels, Budapest*, Chicago, Düsseldorf, Frankfurt, Hamburg, Ho Chi Minh City, Hong Kong, London, Madrid, Milan, Moscow, Munich, New York, Paris, Prague, Rome, Shanghai, Singapore, Tokyo, Warsaw, Zagreb*

Number of lawyers 1,600
at this office 31

Contact
Johannes Meinel

CATEGORIES OF WORK

Corporate/M&A, private equity	Intellectual property
Restructuring and insolvency	Real estate
Banking	Projects
Antitrust and unfair competition	Technology, media, telecommunications
Capital markets	Litigation, product liability
Project finance, public private partnerships	International arbitration
Tax	Food and drug regulations
Employment	Law of Eastern Europe

MANNHEIMER SWARTLING

RECHTSANWÄLTE UND SCHWEDISCHE ADVOKATEN

MAUERSTRASSE 83-84
10117 BERLIN

Telephone: +49 30 22 66 99 0
Fax: +49 30 22 66 99 10
Website: www.mannheimerswartling.se

Languages
English, French, Swedish

Other offices
Brussels, Frankfurt, Gothenburg, Helsingborg, Malmö, New York, St Petersburg, Stockholm

Number of lawyers 330
at this office 10

Contact
Jürgen Busch

CATEGORIES OF WORK

- Banking and securities
- Corporate
- Employment
- Energy
- Environment
- EU and competition
- Intellectual property
- Litigation and arbitration
- Mergers and acquisitions
- Real estate and construction

NÖRR STIEFENHOFER LUTZ

CHARLOTTENSTRASSE 57
10117 BERLIN

Telephone: +49 30 20 94 20 00
Fax: +49 30 20 94 20 94
E-mail: info@noerr.com
Website: www.noerr.com

Languages
English, French, German, Italian, Polish, Spanish

Other offices
Bratislava, Bucharest, Budapest, Dresden, Düsseldorf, Frankfurt, Munich, Moscow, New York, Prague, Warsaw

Number of lawyers 256
(+ 66 tax advisers, public accountants and tax assistants)
at this office 42
(+6 tax advisers, public accountants and tax assistants)

Contact
Mr Hans Christian Kirchner

CATEGORIES OF WORK

- Administrative law
- Antitrust law
- Audit and accounting services
- Banking law
- Company and tax law
- International and commercial law
- Litigation
- Media and entertainment law
- Mergers and acquisitions
- Planning and zoning
- Real estate
- Reorganisation
- Restitution claims and restoration of property in eastern Germany
- Trade, industry and labour law

P+P PÖLLATH + PARTNERS

POTSDAMER PLATZ
LINKSTRASSE 2
10785 BERLIN

Telephone: +49 30 25 35 30
Fax: +49 30 25 35 39 99
E-mail: ber@pplaw.com
Website: www.pplaw.com

Languages
English, French

Other offices
Frankfurt, Munich

Number of lawyers 66
at this office 30

Contacts
Andreas Rodin, Thomas Toeben

CATEGORIES OF WORK

Private equity

Real estate

M&A

Restitution

Corporate finance

Family (high-net-worth, succession)

Tax

Trusts, foundations, charities

SJ BERWIN LLP

RECHTSANWÄLTE – STEUERBERATER – WIRTSCHAFTSPRÜFER

KURFÜRSTENDAMM 63
10707 BERLIN

Telephone: +49 30 88 71 71 50
Fax: +49 30 88 71 71 66
E-mail: berlin@sjberwin.com
Website: www.sjberwin.com

Languages
English, French, Spanish

Other offices
Brussels, Frankfurt, London, Madrid, Milan, Munich, Paris, Turin

Number of lawyers 550
at this office 12

Contact
Dr Frank Vogel

CATEGORIES OF WORK

Corporate law
Dr Frank Vogel, Dr Andreas Wuesthoff

Private equity
Dr Frank Vogel, Dr Frank Ludwig

Venture capital
Dr Frank Vogel, Dr Andreas Wuesthoff

Fund structuring
Dr Jan Dirk Heerma, Dr Daria Salus

M&A, joint ventures
Dr Frank Vogel, Dr Frank Ludwig

Tax
Dr Till Fock

Intellectual property
Dr Jan Dirk Heerma

Banking and financial services
Dr Till Fock

Alternative investments
Dr Till Fock

SCHWARZ KELWING WICKE WESTPFAHL

KURFÜRSTENDAMM 220
10719 BERLIN

Telephone: +49 30 88 59 27 0
Fax: +49 30 88 22 26 0
E-mail: berlin@skwlaw.de
Website: www.skwlaw.de

Languages
English, French, German, Spanish

Other offices
Dresden, Frankfurt am Main, Munich

Number of lawyers 58
at this office 17

Member
Terralex; PLG

CATEGORIES OF WORK

Administrative
Matthias Druba, Dr Klaus Jankowski

Banking and finance
Hellmut Sieglerschmidt, Christoph von Arnim

Commercial property, real estate
Helge Eimers, Ralph Nielebock, Christian Rahns, Christoph von Arnim, Dietrich Wicke, Matthias Druba, Helmut Sieglerschmidt

Construction
Dr Olaf Kreißl, Dr Klaus Jankowski

Corporate and commercial
Hellmut Sieglerschmidt, Christian Rahns, Christoph von Arnim

Employment
Monika Birnbaum, Dr Alexandra Henkel

Media and entertainment
Prof Dr Alexander Freys, Dr Frank Brauner

Public procurement, public services
Ermbrecht Rindtorff

Environment
Ermbrecht Rindtorff, Dr Klaus Jankowski

Film and television/trade marks, intellectual property, copyright
Prof Dr Alexander Freys, Dr Frank Brauner

Insolvency law
Dr Olaf Kreißl

Unfair competition
Prof Dr Alexander Freys, Monika Birnbaum

Privatisation and restitution (East Germany)
Matthias Druba

Dispute resolution – litigation and arbitration
Monika Birnbaum, Helge Eimers, Dr Alexandra Henkel

TAYLOR WESSING

HAUS MENDELSSOHN
JÄGERSTR 51
10117 BERLIN

Telephone: +49 30 88 56 36 0
Fax: +49 30 88 56 36 46
E-mail: berlin@taylorwessing.com
Website: www.taylorwessing.com

Languages
English, Dutch, French, Italian, Mandarin, Spanish

Other offices
Alicante*, Brussels, Cambridge, Dubai*, Düsseldorf/Neuss, Frankfurt, Hamburg, London, Munich, Paris, Shanghai*

Number of lawyers 598
at this office 33

Member
World Law Group; Tech Law Group

CATEGORIES OF WORK

Banking and finance
Claus Goedecke, Peter Seemann

China desk
Florian Ranft

Commercial
Dr Christoph Hasche

Corporate/M&A
Bernhard Kloft

Employment and pensions
Axel C Filges

EU law/antitrust
Dr Marco Hartmann-Rüppel, Markus Wirtz

Intellectual property
Dr Sabine Rojahn

Life science
Dr Ulrich Steffen

Media and entertainment
Martin von Albrecht

Private client
Romana Traichel

Projects and finance
Dr Rüdiger von Hülst

Public commercial law
Dr Walter Potthast

Real estate and construction
Jan Wunschel

Regulatory affairs
Andreas Haak

Tax
Bernd Michel

Technology/IT/telecoms
Jörg Wimmers

WILMER CUTLER PICKERING HALE AND DORR LLP

FRIEDRICHSTR. 95
10117 BERLIN

Telephone: +49 30 20 22 64 00
Fax: +49 30 20 22 65 00
Website: www.wilmerhale.com

Languages
English, French, German, Italian, Russian, Spanish

Other offices
Baltimore, Beijing, Boston, Brussels, London, Munich, New York, Northern Virginia, Oxford, Palo Alto, Waltham, Washington

Number of lawyers 1,100
at this office 46

CATEGORIES OF WORK

Antitrust and competition/ merger control, EU law
Ulrich Quack, Stefan Ohlhoff

Aviation
Dieter Lange, Matthias Wissmann

Corporate
Roland Steinmeyer, Alexander Kollmorgen

Energy/environment
Martin Seyfarth

International arbitration and litigation
Gary Born, Wolfgang Rosener

IP/IT and litigation
Klaus Schubert

Labour and employment
Anja Mengel

M&A and financial services
Roland Steinmeyer, Christian Crones

Public procurement
Natalie Lübben

Public policy
Matthias Wissmann, Martin Seyfarth

Real estate, notary
Frank Roitzsch, G Graf zu Castell-Castell

Tax
Oliver Bugge

Telecommunications and media
Natalie Lübben

THE FIRM

WilmerHale offers unparalleled legal representation across a comprehensive range of practice areas that are critical to the success of its clients. The firm has over 1,000 lawyers operating in five countries and practices at the very top of the legal profession. The depth and scope of the practice give it the ability to anticipate obstacles, seize opportunities and get the case resolved or the deal done – and the experience and know-how to prevent it from being undone.

In Germany, the firm offers legal services with approximately 55 lawyers from offices in Berlin and Munich. The Berlin office has a special focus on complex competition and regulatory matters, often involving sensitive political issues and has established a strong corporate transactions practice group. Clients come primarily from the technology (including biotechnology), media, aviation, energy, telecommunication and travel industries, as well as from the banking and financial services sector. The Munich office focuses on providing specialised legal services for media and technology companies, venture capitalists and investment banks.

AREAS OF PRACTICE

Antitrust/competition: The Berlin office has one of the leading antitrust and competition groups in Germany, which works closely together with members of the firm's practice group in Brussels, London, Boston and Washington.

The team has extensive experience in obtaining regulatory clearance of mergers, acquisitions and joint ventures in Germany and before the European Commission; in advising and representing clients before German and European authorities and courts with regard to dominance and market access issues, competition law aspects of horizontal and vertical agreements, cartel investigations and compliance programs.

Aviation: the firm's German aviation practice is fully integrated in the firm's aviation practice group, consisting of more than 30 lawyers. The German team has extensive expertise in all aspects of international, EU and national aviation matters, such as air traffic rights, market access, airspace allocation, airport regulations, landing charges, the European Single Sky initiative, slot allocation and ground handling.

Corporate/M&A: the German corporate group, with over 30 lawyers in Berlin and Munich, provides the full range of corporate and commercial legal services to domestic and international clients. It has long-standing experience in complex domestic and international mergers and acquisitions, privatisations, reorganisations and liquidations, as well as in real estate transactions, property development matters and financing transactions.

Energy/environment: the firm's energy lawyers advise clients on all aspects of energy regulation, from third-party access and supply and transportation agreements to emissions trading, unbundling, the German Renewable Energy Sources Act and the German Combined Heat and Power Act. In the environmental sector, the team has a crucial market position for advice in collective industry initiatives.

IP/IT: the firm's IP team is based in Berlin and Munich and comprises about ten lawyers. The team advises and represents clients regarding all IP issues, both contentious and non-contentious. The team's work includes trade marks, patent and utility model issues, IT/ e-commerce/outsourcing, copyright, unfair trade practices law and IP litigation. The group has a strong focus on the IT sector.

Legal strategy and public policy: the Berlin team has successfully taken on the Washington DC office's tradition of working at the crossroads of law, business and politics. The team has a substantial track record in handling politically sensitive matters, especially in regulated industries.

Telecommunications and media: the German team works with clients in the fixed, mobile and broadband sectors. It assists clients in structuring specialised commercial solutions and in developing regulatory strategies.

HAARMANN HEMMELRATH

WELLE 15
33602 BIELEFELD

Telephone: + 49 521 16 45 0
Fax: + 49 521 16 45 13 3
E-mail:
bielefeld@haarmannhemmelrath.com
Website:
www.haarmannhemmelrath.com

Languages
English, French, German

Other offices
Bucharest, Budapest, Düsseldorf, Frankfurt, Hamburg, Leipzig, Moscow, Munich, Paris, Prague, Shanghai, Warsaw

Number of lawyers 226

CATEGORIES OF WORK

Company and commercial law
Henning Rolf, Katrin Kaßmann, Claudia Leipelt

Company succession
Henning Rolf, Katrin Kaßmann

Contract law
Henning Rolf, Claudia Leipelt

Labour law
Claudia Leipelt

Mergers and acquisitions
Henning Rolf

Tax law
Katrin Kaßmann, Henning Rolf

FLICK GOCKE SCHAUMBURG

JOHANNA-KINKEL-STRASSE 2-4
53175 BONN

Telephone: +49 228 95 940
Fax: +49 228 95 94 100
E-mail: bonn@fgs.de
Website: www.fgs.de

Languages
English, French, Italian, Spanish

Other offices
Berlin, Frankfurt

Number of lawyers 120
at this office 90

Contacts
Prof Dr Harald Schaumburg,
Prof Dr Thomas Rödder,
Dr Andreas Schumacher, Dr Stephan Göckeler

CATEGORIES OF WORK

German and international tax law	Transfer pricing
Corporate and business law	Estate planning
Mergers and acquisitions	Real estate transactions
Reorganisation of group structures	Tax litigation
IPOs	Customs law
Inbound and outbound investment	Due diligence and special audits

THE FIRM

Flick Gocke Schaumburg is an independent law firm with a clear focus on international tax, corporate and M&A work. The firm has established itself as Germany's leading tax law practice, combining the experience of lawyers and economists to develop tailor-made and tax efficient legal structures and solutions. European Tax Law Firm of the Year 2003 (*Chambers* Award); German Tax Firm of the Year 2005 (*International Tax Review* European Award).

The firm's international work primarily involves international tax law, corporate law with M&A, cross-border conversions, transfer pricing structures and the implementation of holdings and joint ventures. The firm has developed strong personal relations with many premier consultants abroad through intense co-operation on transnational projects.

The firm's clients include multinational enterprises, affiliated corporations, family-owned businesses and high-net-worth individuals. The firm regularly acts, inter alia, for banks, investment funds and insurance companies, the telecommunications sector, chemicals companies, the energy industry, car manufacturers, mechanical engineering companies and airlines.

AREAS OF WORK

International taxation: the firm's activities include international tax planning and application of double taxation treaties; negotiations of advance agreements with tax authorities; representation in tax audits and closing talks; tax, administrative and constitutional litigation; legal and financial analysis of investment funds; development and support of transfer pricing systems; legal representation before customs authorities and in foreign trade matters.

Corporate and business law: FGS deals with joint ventures and other forms of co-operation; drafting and amending of shareholders' agreements; articles of incorporation and partnership agreements; resolution of disputes among owners of a business enterprise; evaluation and negotiation of takeover bids and of compensation for dissenting shareholders.

Inbound and outbound investment: the firm is active in tax efficient structuring of direct sales, permanent establishments and subsidiaries; establishing, maintaining and winding up operations in Germany and abroad; transfer of tangible and intangible property; cross-border M&A.

M&A: the firm handles tax efficient acquisitions or sales of companies and ownership interests, management buyouts and leveraged buyouts, the formation and reorganisation of corporations and partnerships; the incorporation and optimisation of business entities; the structuring of affiliated groups and intra-group transactions; tax efficient capital increases, contributions or property in exchange for ownership interests, divisions and other group reorganisations.

Estate planning: advice is provided on the transfer of family-owned businesses, lifetime gratuitous transfers to prospective heirs, international estate planning, and the execution of wills.

Due diligence and special audits: the firm offers legal, tax and financial due diligence; statutory and voluntary audits; national and international group financial statements; verification of transfer prices and other special examinations; evaluation of business enterprises and appraisal of controlling systems.

CMS HASCHE SIGLE

HARTMANNSTRASSE 7
09111 CHEMNITZ

Telephone: +49 371 3 69 74 0
Fax: +49 371 3 69 74 21
E-mail: chemnitz@cms-hs.com
Website: www.cms-hs.com

Languages
English

Other offices
Belgrade, Berlin, Brussels, Cologne, Dresden, Düsseldorf, Frankfurt, Hamburg, Leipzig, Moscow, Munich, Prague, Stuttgart

Number of lawyers 420
at this office 7

Other CMS alliance member firms
CMS Adonnino Ascoli & Cavasola Scamoni, Italy; CMS Albiñana & Suárez de Lezo, Spain; CMS Bureau Francis Lefebvre, France; CMS Cameron McKenna, UK; CMS DeBacker, Belgium; CMS Derks Star Busmann, Netherlands; CMS von Erlach Henrici, Switzerland; CMS Reich-Rohrwig Hainz, Austria

CATEGORIES OF WORK

Corporate

Mergers and acquisitions

Private equity and venture capital

Banking

Stock trading and capital markets

Competition and merger control

State aid and EU law

Intellectual property, copyright, media and press

Individual and collective labour law

Real estate and construction

IT and telecommunications

Tax

Estate planning

Insolvency

Utilities

Public commercial and environment, procurement

Distribution and franchise law

Insurance

Maritime, shipping and transport

Litigation and arbitration

HEUKING KÜHN LÜER WOJTEK

WESTSTRASSE 16
09112 CHEMNITZ

Telephone: +49 371 38 20 30
Fax: +49 371 38 20 31 00
E-mail: chemnitz@heuking.de
Website: www.heuking.de

Languages
German, English, French, Russian

Other offices
Berlin, Brussels,Cologne, Düsseldorf, Frankfurt, Hamburg, Munich

Number of lawyers 8

Contact
Annemarie Rott

CATEGORIES OF WORK	
International corporate law	**Commercial law**
Mergers and acquisitions	**Tax law**
Joint ventures	**Labour law**
Customs and trade law	**Financial and banking law**
Property transactions	**Litigation and arbitration**
Construction law	**Energy law**

THE FIRM

Heuking Kühn Lüer Wojtek was founded in Düsseldorf, Germany, in 1971. Since then, the firm has spread geographically, and Heuking Kühn now has seven significant offices in Germany, as well as an office in Brussels.

The firm has an extensive international network of law firms, enabling it to provide its clients with seamless 'one-stop shopping', on international transactions and regulatory matters. Since its formation, Heuking Kühn Lüer Wojtek has specifically chosen to remain an independent law firm. It is Heuking Kühn Lüer Wojtek's philosophy that, to provide the best possible service to its clients, the firm must be able to co-operate with various other law firms which are at the top of the profession in their respective countries. This gives the firm the ability to make alternative counsel suggestions to its clients, giving the clients a choice of the best suitable law firm or lawyer in each country and for each matter. Over the last 30+ years, Heuking Kühn Lüer Wojtek has developed excellent relationships with the key firms in all of the major jurisdictions worldwide.

Heuking Kühn Lüer Wojtek is a name which is synonymous with legal competence. The firm is one of the largest commercial law firms in Germany, with more than 170 specialised lawyers and tax advisers, representing the interests of national and international clients. Included in the client list are large and medium-sized German and international companies in all areas of the manufacturing industry, as well as trade and service industries, associations, governmental and public sector organisations and private clients and trusts.

The firm prides itself on substantive legal competence and on the excellent education and continuing legal education of its lawyers. Moreover, virtually all of the lawyers are German-English bilingual.

Extensive specialisation and comprehensive knowledge of specific industry sectors provide the basis of all of Heuking Kühn Lüer Wojtek's legal counselling. Experienced partners and carefully selected associate lawyers develop innovative solutions to complex legal problems. The lawyers regularly work in their specific practice area groups and also in multi-group and multidisciplinary teams with clients and outside consultants or advisers. Entrepreneurial thinking on behalf of firm clients, as well as efficient, quality, cost-effective and timely work and the highest personal dedication are key components of Heuking Kühn Lüer Wojtek's culture.

AREAS OF PRACTICE

Heuking Kühn Lüer Wojtek is a full-service commercial law firm. Cross-border and cross-sector knowledge in combination with a deep understanding of business reasoning enables service to clients with the broadest possible support in all their negotiations and business decisions. This applies equally to M&A transactions, to legal advice on company structure, business risk management, negotiations and negotiation tactics, training, crisis and insolvency counselling, corporate financial matters, and complex litigation and arbitration. Thanks to a variety of strong business clients, the firm has built long-term relationships with its clients and can assist them, beginning with the establishment of a business, followed by implementing business goals, including day-to-day legal work, reorganisations, acquisitions and divestitures.

Heuking Kühn Lüer Wojtek is actively involved with its clients in providing regulatory counselling in all areas of commercial law, as well as assisting them in organising and implementing their M&A transactions in Germany, throughout Europe, and internationally. Heuking Kühn Lüer Wojtek has particular expertise in German and EU company law; competition law, merger control, state aids and regulated industries (including energy; telecommunications; and transport, postal services and shipping law); taxation; employment law; finance and banking; international trade and customs; insurance; litigation, arbitration and mediation; bankruptcy and insolvency; environment, health and safety law; product liability; product-specific regulation; real estate and construction law; IP, IT and media law; and private clients and family law.

ADERHOLD V. DALWIGK KNÜPPEL
RECHTSANWALTSGESELLSCHAFT GMBH

COLONIUS CARRE
SUBBELRATHER STRASSE 15A
50823 COLOGNE

Telephone: +49 221 93 70 45 21
Fax: +49 221 93 70 45 90
E-mail: info@roelfspartner.de
Website: www.roelfspartner.de

Languages
German, English, French, Spanish

Other offices
Berlin, Dortmund, Düsseldorf, Frankfurt, Leipzig

Number of lawyers 40
at this office 5

Contacts
Dr Norbert Knittlmayer, Dr Norbert Knüppel

International groupings
In co-operation with RölfsPartner, an independent member of Baker Tilly International

CATEGORIES OF WORK

Corporate	Litigation and arbitration
Corporate restructuring	Mergers and acquisitions
Information technology	Private equity

CMS HASCHE SIGLE

THEODOR-HEUSS-RING 19-21
50668 COLOGNE

Telephone: +49 221 77 16 0
Fax: +49 221 77 16 11 0
E-mail: cologne@cms-hs.com
Website: www.cms-hs.com

Languages
Dutch, English, French, Italian

Other offices
Belgrade, Berlin, Brussels, Chemnitz, Dresden, Düsseldorf, Frankfurt, Hamburg, Leipzig, Moscow, Munich, Prague, Stuttgart

Number of lawyers 420
at this office 60

Other CMS alliance member firms
CMS Adonnino Ascoli & Cavasola Scamoni, Italy; CMS Albiñana & Suárez de Lezo, Spain; CMS Bureau Francis Lefebvre, France; CMS Cameron McKenna, UK; CMS DeBacker, Belgium; CMS Derks Star Busmann, Netherlands; CMS von Erlach Henrici, Switzerland; CMS Reich-Rohrwig Hainz, Austria

CATEGORIES OF WORK

Corporate	IT and telecommunications
Mergers and acquisitions	Tax
Private equity and venture capital	Estate planning
Banking	Insolvency
Stock trading and capital markets	Utilities
Competition and merger control	Public commercial and environment, procurement
State aid and EU law	Distribution and franchise law
Intellectual property, copyright, media and press	Insurance
Individual and collective labour law	Maritime, shipping and transport
Real estate and construction	Litigation and arbitration

CBH CORNELIUS BARTENBACH HAESEMANN & PARTNERS, member of ius laboris

BISMARCKSTRASSE 11-13
50672 COLOGNE

Telephone: +49 221 95 19 00
Fax: +49 221 95 19 09 0
E-mail: cbh@cbh.de
Website: www.cbh.de

Languages
Dutch, English, French, Hungarian, Italian, Russian, Spanish

Other offices
Berlin, Cottbus

Number of lawyers 60
at this office 55

Contacts
Werner M Mues, Ernst Eisenbeis, Manfred Hecker

Member
ius laboris, International Employment Law, Pensions and Employee Benefits Alliance

CATEGORIES OF WORK

Employment
Werner M Mues, Ernst Eisenbeis

Intellectual property
Jens Kunzmann

Construction, real estate
Manfred Haesemann, Joachim Strieder

Public private partnership
Manfred Haesemann

Corporate
Manfred Hecker

M&A, company and commercial
Dieter Korten

Banking
Paul Assies

Public administration
Stefan Hertwig

Litigation/arbitration
Johannes Ristelhuber

THE FIRM

CBH offers highly specialised legal services, from solving individual legal issues to ongoing comprehensive support of companies and groups of companies in key areas of practice, including continuous consulting services in the preliminary stages of legal problems. CBH develops strategies and represents clients in dealings with government agencies and authorities, in litigation and in arbitration.

AREAS OF PRACTICE

In employment law, CBH focuses on continuous legal services for HR departments of companies, develops and implements restructuring programs and corporate changes, and handles disputes with individual employees. Services comprise negotiations with unions, staff, committees and work councils and litigation in labour courts throughout Germany. As the German member of ius laboris, the firm is able to provide international services in all sectors of employment law.

In intellectual property CBH works on employee inventions, patents, licences, unfair competition, trade marks and trade names.

Corporate and M&A work includes establishing and restructuring of companies, transactions and IPOs.

The property and construction team provides consulting services to investors, the construction industry and government institutions, in planning, acquisition and construction, financing and marketing of property.

A team of specialists for public administration law works on property-related issues and in the field of environmental care.

CLEARY GOTTLIEB STEEN & HAMILTON LLP

THEODOR-HEUSS-RING 9
50668 COLOGNE

Telephone: +49 221 80 04 00
Fax: +49 221 80 04 01 99
Website: www.clearygottlieb.com

Languages
English, French, German, Spanish

Other offices
Brussels, Frankfurt, Hong Kong, London, Milan, Moscow, New York, Paris, Rome, Tokyo, Washington DC

Number of lawyers 847
at this office 14

CATEGORIES OF WORK

- Commercial
- Competition law
- Corporate
- Joint ventures
- Mergers and acquisitions

GÖRG
PARTNERSCHAFT VON RECHTSANWÄLTEN

SACHSENRING 81
50677 KÖLN

Telephone: +49 221 33 66 00
Fax: +49 221 33 66 08 0
E-mail: cologne@goerg.de
Website: www.goerg.de

Languages
Dutch, English, French, Italian, Spanish

Other Offices
Berlin, Essen, Frankfurt

Number of lawyers 97
at this office 44

CATEGORIES OF WORK

- Restructuring/insolvency law
- Employment law
- Real estate/construction law/projects
- IP/IT/media law/general commercial
- Corporate/M&A/banking and finance/tax law
- Regulatory/public law
- Litigation and arbitration
- International transactions

DLA PIPER RUDNICK GRAY CARY

HOHENZOLLERNRING 72
50672 COLOGNE

Telephone: +49 221 277 277 0
Fax: +49 221 277 277 10
E-mail: ulrich.juengst@dlapiper.com
Website: www.dlapiper.com/germany

Languages
Arabic, Dutch, English, French, German, Russian, Spanish

Other offices
Austria, Belgium, Bosnia-Herzegovina, China, Croatia, Czech Republic, Denmark*, Egypt*, France, Georgia, Germany, Hong Kong, Hungary, Italy, Japan, Netherlands, Norway*, Poland*, Russia, Singapore*, Slovakia, South Africa*, Spain, Sweden*, Thailand, UK, Ukraine, United Arab Emirates, US

Number of lawyers 3,100
at this office 22

Contact
Dr Ulrich Jüngst

Member
DLA Piper Group

CATEGORIES OF WORK

Banking and finance
Abdul Aziz A Al-Yaqout

Corporate, anti-trust
Dr Martin Schulte

Corporate, mergers and acquisitions
Dr Ulrich Jüngst

Commercial
Dr Thomas Jansen

HR and employment
Dr Bernd Borgmann

Corporate, insolvency
Abdul Aziz A Al-Yaqout

Insurance and reinsurance
Dr Herbert Palmberger

Litigation
Dr Markus Beaumart

Project finance – PPP
Dr Frank Roth

Real estate
Dr Markus Beaumart

Technology, media and communications
Dr Thomas Jansen

THE FIRM

DLA Piper Rudnick Gray Cary is a leading global legal services provider with approximately 3,100 lawyers in 58 offices across 22 countries. The organisation is committed to building long-term relationships with its clients and supports their strategic and operational needs both locally and internationally.

In Germany, DLA Piper Rudnick Gray Cary is a 50-lawyer-strong team with offices in Cologne, Frankfurt and Hamburg. The firm comprises highly experienced, well-established German lawyers. It specialises in all aspects of business law, from corporate and project finance to real estate, employment and IT/media. The firm plans to open offices in other major cities in Germany in the next year as part of its strategy to build a national practice across the country.

DLA Piper is a founding member of an exclusive alliance of full-service legal organisations with a shared vision. DLA Piper Group, established in 1999, has members across Europe, Africa, the Middle East, Asia and the US, which deliver expert local know-how and integrated international solutions.

AREAS OF PRACTICE

Banking and finance: acting for financial institutions on such topics as leveraged and acquisition finance, asset-based finance, infrastructure and project finance, real estate finance and securitisation and capital markets. The firm offers expertise in all financing techniques and products.

Competition: advice and litigation services in all areas of anti-trust and competition law. With the Brussels EU and competition law team and the US antitrust and trade regulations group, the firm advises globally on a wide range of domains.

Corporate, mergers and acquisitions: advises mid-sized and large organisations on all types of transactional and advisory matters and has a growing international reputation within the corporate market.

Commercial: structuring transactions, drafting a whole range of civil and commercial law contracts and participation in business negotiations.

HR and employment: practical experience of helping clients mould their people strategies and work practices, including preparation of employment contracts, assistance in labour disputes and redundancy, in outsourcing, post-merger integration and restructuring.

Insolvency: working alongside senior management, the boards of private and public companies and shareholders to identify trading difficulties and financial pressures with their businesses. The firm's services include identifying risks, rescue operations, solvent reconstructions, asset and debt recovery and creative use of formal insolvency proceedings.

Insurance and reinsurance: advises clients on a wide range of matters, including product, contract and regulatory advice to German and international insurers and reinsurers; D&O insurance; alternative risk transfer; and investments by insurers under German insurance regulation.

Litigation: experience in all aspects of commercial dispute management, working in partnership with clients to manage the litigation process so as to minimise risk and maximise certainty.

Project finance – PPP: as the demand for project finance and PPPs expands, the firm acts for service providers, banks and contracting authorities advising on the local commercial environment, as well as the requirements of international project finance.

Real estate: services to corporate occupiers, developers, financial institutions and the public sector covering all aspects of commercial real estate transactions, including development and financing work. Advises on turnkey plant and infrastructure projects.

Technology, media and communications: contentious and non-contentious advice on all kinds of technology and IP/media-related matters and transactions, with special experience in IT, outsourcing, data protection, telecommunications and in media/TV, sports, sponsorship, unfair competition, and all kinds of intellectual property rights.

HEUKING KÜHN LÜER WOJTEK

MAGNUSSTRASSE 13
50672 COLOGNE

Telephone: +49 221 20 52 0
Fax: +49 221 20 52 1
E-mail: koeln@heuking.de
Website: www.heuking.de

Languages
German, English, French, Spanish, Swedish

Other offices
Berlin, Brussels, Chemnitz, Düsseldorf, Frankfurt, Hamburg, Munich

Number of lawyers 32

Contact
Dr Hans-Jochem Lüer

CATEGORIES OF WORK

Corporate and partnership law, mergers and acquisitions

General commercial law

Competition, merger control

Insurance, reinsurance

Banking and finance

Insolvency and restructuring

Telecommunications law

Media, publishing, copyright

Industrial property

Food and drug law

Employment and labour law

THE FIRM

Heuking Kühn Lüer Wojtek was founded in Düsseldorf, Germany, in 1971. Since then, the firm has spread geographically, and Heuking Kühn now has seven significant offices in Germany, as well as an office in Brussels.

The firm has an extensive international network of law firms, enabling it to provide its clients with seamless 'one-stop shopping', on international transactions and regulatory matters. Since its formation, Heuking Kühn Lüer Wojtek has specifically chosen to remain an independent law firm. It is Heuking Kühn Lüer Wojtek's philosophy that, to provide the best possible service to its clients, the firm must be able to co-operate with various other law firms which are at the top of the profession in their respective countries. This gives the firm the ability to make alternative counsel suggestions to its clients, giving the clients a choice of the best suitable law firm or lawyer in each country and for each matter. Over the last 30+ years, Heuking Kühn Lüer Wojtek has developed excellent relationships with the key firms in all of the major jurisdictions worldwide.

Heuking Kühn Lüer Wojtek is a name which is synonymous with legal competence. The firm is one of the largest commercial law firms in Germany, with more than 170 specialised lawyers and tax advisers, representing the interests of national and international clients. Included in the client list are large and medium-sized German and international companies in all areas of the manufacturing industry, as well as trade and service industries, financial institutions, associations, governmental and public sector organisations and private clients and trusts.

The firm prides itself on substantive legal competence and on the excellent education and continuing legal education of its lawyers. Moreover, virtually all of the lawyers are German-English bilingual.

Extensive specialisation and comprehensive knowledge of specific industry sectors provide the basis of all of Heuking Kühn Lüer Wojtek's legal counselling. Experienced partners and carefully selected associate lawyers develop innovative solutions to complex legal problems. The lawyers regularly work in their specific practice area groups and also in multi-group and multidisciplinary teams with clients and outside consultants or advisers. Entrepreneurial thinking on behalf of firm clients, as well as efficient, quality, cost-effective and timely work and the highest personal dedication are key components of Heuking Kühn Lüer Wojtek's culture.

AREAS OF PRACTICE

Heuking Kühn Lüer Wojtek is a full-service commercial law firm. Cross-border and cross-sector knowledge in combination with a deep understanding of business reasoning enables service to clients with the broadest possible support in all their negotiations and business decisions. This applies equally to M&A transactions, to legal advice on company structure, business risk management, negotiations and negotiation tactics, training, crisis and insolvency counselling, corporate financial matters, and complex litigation and arbitration. Thanks to a variety of strong business clients, the firm has built long-term relationships with its clients and can assist them, beginning with the establishment of a business, followed by implementing business goals, including day-to-day legal work, reorganisations, acquisitions and divestitures.

Heuking Kühn Lüer Wojtek is actively involved with its clients in providing regulatory counselling in all areas of commercial law, as well as assisting them in organising and implementing their M&A transactions in Germany, throughout Europe, and internationally. Heuking Kühn Lüer Wojtek has particular expertise in German and EU company law; competition law, merger control, state aids and regulated industries (including energy; telecommunications; and transport, postal services and shipping law); taxation; employment law; finance and banking; international trade and customs; insurance; litigation, arbitration and mediation; bankruptcy and insolvency; environment, health and safety law; product liability; product-specific regulation; real estate and construction law; IP, IT and media law; and private clients and family law.

LUTHER RECHTSANWALTSGESELLSCHAFT MBH

LUDWIGSTRASSE 8
50667 COLOGNE

Telephone: +49 221 2779 500
Fax: +49 221 2779 510
E-mail: contact@luther-lawfirm.com
Website: www.luther-lawfirm.com

Languages
Chinese, Dutch, English, French, Italian, Japanese, Polish, Portuguese, Russian, Spanish, Swedish

Other offices
Berlin, Brussels*, Budapest*, Dresden, Düsseldorf, Essen, Eschborn/Frankfurt am Main, Hamburg, Hanover, Leipzig, Mannheim, Munich, New York*, Nuremberg, Singapore*, Stuttgart

Number of lawyers 230
at this office 39

CATEGORIES OF WORK

Antitrust and EU law
Dr Thomas Kapp (Stuttgart)

Banks, capital markets, insurance companies
Dr Wolfgang Richter (Berlin)

Commercial and distribution law
Volker Steimle (Cologne)

Company organisation and management
Dr Jörg Rodewald (Munich)

Transaction advice
Dr Axel Zitzmann (Düsseldorf)

Corporate law
Dr Jörg Rodewald (Munich)

Environmental and energy law
Dr Arndt Begemann (Essen)

Financing consulting
Dr Wolfgang Richter (Berlin)

Industrial property and copyright law
Dr Markus Sengpiel (Cologne)

Labour law
Axel Braun (Cologne)

Litigation and dispute resolution
Dr Ulrich Theune (Hamburg)

Media, IT, electronic commerce, and telecoms
Dr Fritjof Börner (Cologne)

Medical law
Thomas Henßler (Hamburg)

Public sector consulting services
Dr Christian Ziche (Dresden)

Real estate and construction law
Stefan Sihler (Berlin)

Restructuring and insolvency consulting
Reinhard Willemsen (Cologne)

ADERHOLD V. DALWIGK KNÜPPEL
RECHTSANWALTSGESELLSCHAFT GMBH

SAARLANDSTRASSE 23
44139 DORTMUND

Telephone: +49 231 77 66 62 0
Fax: +49 231 77 66 64 11
E-mail: info@roelfspartner.de
Website: www.roelfspartner.de

Languages
German, English

Other offices
Berlin, Cologne, Düsseldorf, Frankfurt, Leipzig

Number of lawyers 40
at this office 8

Contacts
Dr Christian Hoppe, Dr Wolfgang Nockelmann

International groupings
In co-operation with RölfsPartner, an independent member of Baker Tilly International

CATEGORIES OF WORK

Agency and distribution

Banking and finance

Corporate

Corporate restructuring

Intellectual property and licensing

Litigation and arbitration

Mergers and acquisitions

Notarial services

Real estate

Product liability

CMS HASCHE SIGLE

AN DER DREIKÖNIGSKIRCHE 10
01097 DRESDEN

Telephone: +49 351 82 64 40
Fax: +49 351 8 26 47 16
E-mail: dresden@cms-hs.com
Website: www.cms-hs.com

Languages
English

Other offices
Belgrade, Berlin, Brussels, Chemnitz, Cologne, Düsseldorf, Frankfurt, Hamburg, Leipzig, Moscow, Munich, Prague, Stuttgart

Number of lawyers 420
at this office 3

Other CMS alliance member firms
CMS Adonnino Ascoli & Cavasola Scamoni, Italy; CMS Albiñana & Suárez de Lezo, Spain; CMS Bureau Francis Lefebvre, France; CMS Cameron McKenna, UK; CMS DeBacker, Belgium; CMS Derks Star Busmann, Netherlands; CMS von Erlach Henrici, Switzerland; CMS Reich-Rohrwig Hainz, Austria

CATEGORIES OF WORK

- Corporate
- Mergers and acquisitions
- Private equity and venture capital
- Banking
- Stock trading and capital markets
- Competition and merger control
- State aid and EU law
- Intellectual property, copyright, media and press
- Individual and collective labour law
- Real estate and construction
- IT and telecommunications
- Tax
- Estate planning
- Insolvency
- Utilities
- Public commercial and environment, procurement
- Distribution and franchise law
- Insurance
- Maritime, shipping and transport
- Litigation and arbitration

NÖRR STIEFENHOFER LUTZ

LOUIS-BRAILLE-STRASSE 5
01099 DRESDEN

Telephone: +49 351 81 66 00
Fax: +49 351 816 60 81
E-mail: info@noerr.com
Website: www.noerr.com

Languages
English, French, German, Italian, Russian

Other offices
Berlin, Bratislava, Bucharest, Budapest, Düsseldorf, Frankfurt, Moscow, Munich, New York, Prague, Warsaw

Number of lawyers 256
(+ 66 tax advisers, public accountants and tax assistants)
at this office 16
(+1 tax adviser, public accountants and tax assistants)

Contact
Otto Stolberg-Stolberg

CATEGORIES OF WORK

- Administrative/environmental law
- Banking law
- Company and commercial law
- Construction law
- East German (formerly DDR) law, especially commercial law
- Greenfield investments
- International private and contract law
- Labour law and industrial relations
- Law relating to commercial leases
- Mergers and acquisitions
- Planning and construction law
- Property and real estate law
- Restitution claims/investment law
- Tax law

ADERHOLD V. DALWIGK KNÜPPEL

RECHTSANWALTSGESELLSCHAFT GMBH

GRAFENBERGER ALLEE 159
40237 DÜSSELDORF

Telephone: +49 211 69 01 03
Fax: +49 211 69 01 355
E-mail: info@roelfspartner.de
Website: www.roelfspartner.de

Languages
German, English

Other offices
Berlin, Cologne, Dortmund, Frankfurt, Leipzig

Number of lawyers 40
at this office 13

Contacts
Dirk Lange, Thorsten Prigge

International groupings
In co-operation with RölfsPartner, an independent member of Baker Tilly International

CATEGORIES OF WORK

Banking and finance	Litigation and arbitration
Corporate law	Mergers and acquisitions
Corporate restructuring	Private equity
Environmental law	Real estate
Insolvency law	Tax
Labour law	

BIRD & BIRD

KARL-THEODOR-STRASSE 6
40213 DÜSSELDORF

Telephone: +49 211 20 05 60 00
Fax: +49 211 20 05 60 11
E-mail: duesseldorf@twobirds.com
Website: www.twobirds.com

Languages
English, French, German, Mandarin

Other offices
Beijing, Brussels, Frankfurt, Hong Kong, London, Madrid, Milan, Munich, Paris, Rome, Stockholm, The Hague

Number of lawyers 472
at this office 45

Contacts
Wolfgang von Meibom (chairman),
Dr Alexander Schröder-Frerkes (vice-chairman)

CATEGORIES OF WORK

Arbitration	Litigation
Aviation and aerospace	Life sciences
Commercial	Media
Communications	Outsourcing
Corporate/M&A/private equity	Private client
Employment	Public procurement
EU and competition/antitrust	Real estate
Intellectual property	Regulatory
IT and e-commerce	Sport and sponsorship

BAKER & McKENZIE LLP

NEUER ZOLLHOF 2
40221 DÜSSELDORF

Telephone: +49 211 31 11 60
Fax: +49 211 31 11 61 99
Website: www.bakernet.com

Languages
Dutch, English, French, Hungarian, Italian

Other offices Almaty, Amsterdam, Antwerp, Bahrain, Baku, Bangkok, Barcelona, Beijing, Berlin, Bogotá, Bologna, Brasilia, Brussels, Budapest, Buenos Aires, Cairo, Calgary, Cancun, Caracas, Chicago, Chihuahua, Dallas, Frankfurt, Geneva, Guadalajara, Hanoi, Ho Chi Minh City, Hong Kong, Houston, Jakarta, Juarez, Kuala Lumpur, Kyiv, London, Madrid, Manila, Melbourne, Mexico City, Miami, Milan, Monterrey, Moscow, Munich, New York, Palo Alto, Paris, Porto Alegré, Prague, Rio de Janeiro, Riyadh, Rome, St Petersburg, San Diego, San Francisco, Santiago, São Paulo, Shanghai, Singapore, Stockholm, Sydney, Taipei, Tijuana, Tokyo, Toronto, Valencia, Vienna, Warsaw, Washington DC, Zürich

Number of lawyers 3,300+
at this office 16+

CATEGORIES OF WORK

Commercial law
Jürgen Mark, Heiko Plassmeier

Company law
Barbara Deilmann, Stephan Semrau

Information technology, media and computer law
Heiko Plassmeier

Labour law
Markus Kappenhagen

Capital markets
Barbara Deilmann, Stephan Semrau

Mergers and acquisitions
Joachim Drude, Thomas Menke

Litigation and arbitration
Jürgen Mark, Heiko Plassmeier

Product liability
Jürgen Mark

Private equity and venture capital
Joachim Drude, Thomas Menke

Tax
Stephan Schnorberger

THE FIRM

Baker & McKenzie has provided sophisticated legal advice and services to many of the world's most dynamic and global organisations for more than 50 years. With a network of more than 3,300 locally qualified, internationally experienced lawyers in 38 countries, the firm has the knowledge and resources to deliver the broad scope of quality legal services required to respond effectively to both international and local needs – consistently, confidently and with a sensitivity for cultural, social and legal practice differences.

Baker & McKenzie has been established in Europe for over 40 years, having opened its first European offices in 1957. Since then, the European and Middle Eastern network has grown to 29 offices, giving it unparalleled geographical coverage.

The Frankfurt am Main office was formed in 1962; the office in Berlin was opened on 1 March 1990; the Munich office on 1 April 1997; and the Düsseldorf office on 1 April 1999.

Since their formation, the German offices have advised their clients on all questions of German, European and international industrial and commercial law with particular emphasis on cross-border and multinational transactions. At present, more than 170 attorneys-at-law (Rechtsanwälte), tax advisers, and varying numbers of foreign admitted lawyers work in the German offices.

All attorneys are at least bilingual; most of them have completed additional graduate legal studies at foreign law schools. Several attorneys are simultaneously admitted as CPAs, tax advisers, tax attorneys, attorneys for administrative law or attorneys for labour law.

AREAS OF PRACTICE

Baker & McKenzie co-ordinates its core practice areas on local, regional and global levels, giving most of its lawyers experience in more than one jurisdiction, as well as providing multinational teams of specialists.

Utilising a global practice group structure and ground-breaking technology coupled with a personal, detailed understanding of a client's specific business, Baker & McKenzie is able to organise its extensive resources to provide focused and strategic counsel to clients.

Baker & McKenzie advises multinational enterprises, large German companies, medium-sized enterprises, banks and insurance companies, as well as institutions and entities under public law in all questions of German, European, and international industrial and commercial law including company law, competition and cartel law, intellectual property, banking and finance, labour law, administrative law, and tax law. Furthermore, the firm handles litigation and arbitration matters. Several partners have expertise in specialised areas of law, such as European Community law, the law of cosmetics, food and drug law, trade marks, franchising, corporate finance, new financial products, government procurement, real estate transactions, and media telecommunications law.

Baker & McKenzie International is a Swiss Verein with member law firms around the world.

BUSE HEBERER FROMM

KÖNIGSALLE 100
40215 DÜSSELDORF

Telephone: +49 211 38 80 00
Fax: +49 211 37 36 78
E-mail: duesseldorf@buse.de
Website: www.buse.de

Languages
English, French, Italian, Spanish

Other offices
Berlin, Essen, Frankfurt am Main, Hamburg, Munich, New York, Palma de Mallorca, Sydney, Zurich

Number of lawyers 120
at this office 16

Member
The European Legal Alliance: Beauchamps (Ireland); Dubarry Le Douarin Veil (France); Field Fisher Waterhouse (England); Harper Macleod (Scotland); Jimenez de Parga (Spain); La Scala & Associati (Italy)

CATEGORIES OF WORK

- Banking and finance
- Antitrust and merger control
- Commerce, transport, insurance
- Commercial delinquency
- Corporate/M&A
- Industrial property and copyrights
- Information technology and telecommunications
- Labour and employment
- Litigation and arbitration, national and international
- Press and media
- Property and construction
- Public law
- Tax

CMS HASCHE SIGLE

BANKSTRASSE 1
40476 DÜSSELDORF

Telephone: +49 211 49 34 0
Fax: +49 211 49 20 09 7
E-mail: duesseldorf@cms-hs.com
Website: www.cms-hs.com

Languages
English, French, Spanish

Other offices
Belgrade, Berlin, Brussels, Chemnitz, Cologne, Dresden, Frankfurt, Hamburg, Leipzig, Moscow, Munich, Prague, Stuttgart

Number of lawyers 420
at this office 28

Other CMS alliance member firms
CMS Adonnino Ascoli & Cavasola Scamoni, Italy; CMS Albiñana & Suárez de Lezo, Spain; CMS Bureau Francis Lefebvre, France; CMS Cameron McKenna, UK; CMS DeBacker, Belgium; CMS Derks Star Busmann, Netherlands; CMS von Erlach Henrici, Switzerland; CMS Reich-Rohrwig Hainz, Austria

CATEGORIES OF WORK

- Corporate
- Mergers and acquisitions
- Private equity and venture capital
- Banking
- Stock trading and capital markets
- Competition and merger control
- State aid and EU law
- Intellectual property, copyright, media and press
- Individual and collective labour law
- Real estate and construction
- IT and telecommunications
- Tax
- Estate planning
- Insolvency
- Utilities
- Public commercial and environment, procurement
- Distribution and franchise law
- Insurance
- Maritime, shipping and transport
- Litigation and arbitration

HAARMANN HEMMELRATH

MARTIN-LUTHER-PLATZ 26
40212 DÜSSELDORF

Telephone: +49 211 83 99 0
Fax: +49 211 83 99 13 3
E-mail:
dusseldorf@haarmannhemmelrath.com
Website:
www.haarmannhemmelrath.com

Languages
Bulgarian, Croatian, Czech, Dutch, English, French, Hungarian, Italian, Japanese, Mandarin, Norwegian, Polish, Portuguese, Romanian, Russian, Slovak, Spanish, Vietnamese

Other offices
Bielefeld, Bucharest, Budapest, Frankfurt, Hamburg, Leipzig, Moscow, Munich, Paris, Prague, Shanghai, Warsaw

Number of lawyers 226

CATEGORIES OF WORK

Mergers and acquisitions
Thomas Bula

Corporate finance

Venture capital, private equity

Fund structuring
Torsten Grob

Banking, leasing
Dr Bernd Sagasser

Corporate and business law
Kai Schöneberger

IP, IT, antitrust, EU law

Inheritance law

Public law and regulatory matters, environment and energy law, privatisation

Litigation, mediation, arbitration
Dr Günter Fußbahn

Corporate recovery, insolvency
Hans-Jörg Hegerl

International tax law
Dr Bernd Sagasser, Thomas Bula

National tax law and compliance
Ralf Lohmann, Thomas Bula

Corporate taxation

Accounting
Joerg Schoberth, Susann Ihlau

HENGELER MUELLER

BENRATHER STRASSE 18-20
40213 DÜSSELDORF

Telephone: +49 211 83 04 0
Fax: +49 211 83 04 17 0
E-mail: hmdus@hengeler.com
Website: www.hengeler.com

Other offices
Frankfurt, Berlin, Munich, Brussels, London

Number of lawyers 192
at this office 69

Contact
Dr Matthias Blaum

CATEGORIES OF WORK

M&A

Private equity and venture capital

General corporate and corporate restructuring

Equity capital markets

Banking and finance

Litigation and arbitration

Competition

IP/IT

Regulatory and environment

Telecommunications and media

Insolvency and reorganisation

Real estate

Energy

HEUKING KÜHN LÜER WOJTEK

CECILIENALLEE 5
40474 DÜSSELDORF

Telephone: +49 211 60 05 50 0
Fax: +49 211 60 05 50 50
E-mail: duesseldorf@heuking.de
Website: www.heuking.de

Languages
German, English, French, Japanese

Other offices
Berlin, Brussels, Chemnitz, Cologne, Frankfurt, Hamburg, Munich

Number of lawyers 50

Contacts
Dr Wolfgang Kühn, Dirk Kolvenbach

CATEGORIES OF WORK

Corporate, partnerships, international mergers and acquisitions, general commercial law

German and international tax law

Private clients and family office

Competition, merger control, antitrust

Banking and finance

Insurance

Leasing and finance

Litigation, arbitration and mediation

Administrative law

Entertainment, media, publishing, copyright

Industrial property

Employment and labour law

Real estate transactions and construction law

Environmental law

Family law

Telecommunications and IT law

Procurement and public/private partnerships

THE FIRM

Heuking Kühn Lüer Wojtek was founded in Düsseldorf, Germany, in 1971. Since then, the firm has spread geographically, and Heuking Kühn now has seven significant offices in Germany, as well as an office in Brussels.

The firm has an extensive international network of law firms, enabling it to provide its clients with seamless 'one-stop shopping', on international transactions and regulatory matters. Since its formation, Heuking Kühn Lüer Wojtek has specifically chosen to remain an independent law firm. It is Heuking Kühn Lüer Wojtek's philosophy that, to provide the best possible service to its clients, the firm must be able to co-operate with various other law firms which are at the top of the profession in their respective countries. This gives the firm the ability to make alternative counsel suggestions to its clients, giving the clients a choice of the best suitable law firm or lawyer in each country and for each matter. Over the last 30+ years, Heuking Kühn Lüer Wojtek has developed excellent relationships with the key firms in all of the major jurisdictions worldwide.

Heuking Kühn Lüer Wojtek is a name which is synonymous with legal competence. The firm is one of the largest commercial law firms in Germany, with more than 170 specialised lawyers and tax advisers, representing the interests of national and international clients. Included in the client list are large and medium-sized German and international companies in all areas of the manufacturing industry, as well as trade and service industries, associations, governmental and public sector organisations and private clients and trusts.

The firm prides itself on substantive legal competence and on the excellent education and continuing legal education of its lawyers. Moreover, virtually all of the lawyers are German-English bilingual.

Extensive specialisation and comprehensive knowledge of specific industry sectors provide the basis of all of Heuking Kühn Lüer Wojtek's legal counselling. Experienced partners and carefully selected associate lawyers develop innovative solutions to complex legal problems. The lawyers regularly work in their specific practice area groups and also in multi-group and multidisciplinary teams with clients and outside consultants or advisers. Entrepreneurial thinking on behalf of firm clients, as well as efficient, quality, cost-effective and timely work and the highest personal dedication are key components of Heuking Kühn Lüer Wojtek's culture.

AREAS OF PRACTICE

Heuking Kühn Lüer Wojtek is a full-service commercial law firm. Cross-border and cross-sector knowledge in combination with a deep understanding of business reasoning enables service to clients with the broadest possible support in all their negotiations and business decisions. This applies equally to M&A transactions, to legal advice on company structure, business risk management, negotiations and negotiation tactics, training, crisis and insolvency counselling, corporate financial matters, and complex litigation and arbitration. Thanks to a variety of strong business clients, the firm has built long-term relationships with its clients and can assist them, beginning with the establishment of a business, followed by implementing business goals, including day-to-day legal work, reorganisations, acquisitions and divestitures.

Heuking Kühn Lüer Wojtek is actively involved with its clients in providing regulatory counselling in all areas of commercial law, as well as assisting them in organising and implementing their M&A transactions in Germany, throughout Europe, and internationally. Heuking Kühn Lüer Wojtek has particular expertise in German and EU company law; competition law, merger control, state aids and regulated industries (including energy; telecommunications; and transport, postal services and shipping law); taxation; employment law; finance and banking; international trade and customs; insurance; litigation, arbitration and mediation; bankruptcy and insolvency; environment, health and safety law; product liability; product-specific regulation; real estate and construction law; IP, IT and media law; and private clients and family law.

LOVELLS

KENNEDYDAMM 17
40476 DÜSSELDORF

Telephone: +49 211 13 68 0
Fax: +49 211 13 68 10 0
E-mail: receptiondus@lovells.com
Website: www.lovells.de

Languages
Dutch, English, French, Italian, Portuguese, Russian, Spanish

Other offices
Alicante, Amsterdam, Beijing, Berlin, Brussels, Budapest*, Chicago, Frankfurt, Hamburg, Ho Chi Minh City, Hong Kong, London, Madrid, Milan, Moscow, Munich, New York, Paris, Prague, Rome, Shanghai, Singapore, Tokyo, Warsaw, Zagreb*

Number of lawyers 1,600
at this office 56

Contact
Erhard Keller

CATEGORIES OF WORK

Corporate/M&A, private equity

Restructuring and insolvency

Banking

Antitrust and unfair competition

Capital markets

Project finance, public private partnerships

Tax

Employment

Intellectual property

Real estate

Projects

Technology, media, telecommunications

Litigation, product liability

International arbitration

Food and drug regulations

Law of Eastern Europe

McDERMOTT WILL & EMERY
RECHTSANWÄLTE STEUERBERATER LLP

STADTTOR 1
40219 DÜSSELDORF

Telephone: +49 211 30 21 10
Fax: +49 211 30 21 15 55
Website: www.mwe.com

Languages
All main business languages

Other offices
Boston, Brussels, Chicago, London, Los Angeles, Miami, Munich, New York, Orange County, Rome, San Diego, Silicon Valley, Washington DC

Number of lawyers 1,000
at this office 11

CATEGORIES OF WORK

Antitrust and regulatory
Dr Thomas Hauss

Capital markets
Konstantin Günther

Corporate
Konstantin Günther

Intellectual property
Dr Thomas Hauss

Labour and employment
Volker Teigelkötter

Mergers and acquisitions
Konstantin Günther

Private equity
Konstantin Günther, Dr Norbert Schulte

Real estate
Konstantin Günther, Dr Norbert Schulte

NÖRR STIEFENHOFER LUTZ

VICTORIAPLATZ 2
40477 DÜSSELDORF

Telephone: +49 211 49 98 60
Fax: +49 211 49 98 61 00
E-mail: info@noerr.com
Website: www.noerr.com

Languages
English, French, German, Italian, Russian, Spanish

Other offices
Berlin, Bratislava, Bucharest, Budapest, Dresden, Frankfurt, Moscow, Munich, New York, Prague, Warsaw

Number of lawyers 256
(+ 66 tax advisers, public accountants and tax assistants)
at this office 18

Contact
Dr Stefan Tomicic

CATEGORIES OF WORK

Administrative and regulatory law

Company and tax law

Construction law

Insolvency, reorganisation

Insurance law

International and commercial law

Labour law

Litigation, civil law

Mergers and acquisitions

Professional liability

Real estate

PPR & PARTNER

ATTORNEYS CERTIFIED PUBLIC ACCOUNTANT TAX ADVISORS

KÖNIGSALLEE 70
40212 DÜSSELDORF

Telephone: +49 211 82 89 29 0
Fax: +49 211 82 89 29 29
E-mail: kontakt@ppr-partner.de
Website: www.ppr-partner.de

Languages
English, French, Italian, Spanish

Number of lawyers 14

Contacts
Dieter G Pape, Dr Theo Rauh

Member
Lexwork International

CATEGORIES OF WORK

Capital markets
Dr Jochen Herbst

Competition and antitrust
Jörg Meyer, Thomas Brosig

Construction and real estate
Markus Melcher

Economic administration
Dr Jochen Herbst, Thomas Brosig

Employment
Dieter G Pape, Dr Andreas Zens

Environment
Dr Jochen Herbst

Foodstuffs
Jörg Meyer

French law
Sophie Renault, Dr Andreas Zens

Information technology
Dr Stephan Wolff, Thomas Brosig

International commercial
Dr Theo Rauh, Dr Stefan Wolff

Inheritance and inheritance tax
Hans-Peter Palenberg, Frank Dittschar

Mergers and acquisitions
Dr Theo Rauh, Klaus T Stalpers

National and international tax
Hans-Peter Palenberg, Klaus T Stalpers

Sale and distribution
Dr Andreas Zens, Dr Stephan Wolff

Trade marks, intellectual property
Jörg Meyer, Florian Geyer

REIMANN OSTERRIETH KÖHLER HAFT

DÜSSELDORFER STRAßE 189
40545 DÜSSELDORF

Telephone: +49 211 55 02 20
Fax: +49 211 550 22 55 0
E-mail: contact@rokh-ip.com
Website: www.rokh-ip.com

Languages
German, English, French, Italian, Danish

Number of lawyers 10

CATEGORIES OF WORK

National and multi-jurisdictional patent litigation
Dr Thomas Reimann,
Dr Christian Osterrieth, and all other lawyers at the firm

Trade marks
Dr Christian Osterrieth,
Thomas Schmitz

Design law
Klaus Haft, Kay N Kasper

Unfair competition law
Dr Martin Köhler, Thomas Schmitz

Copyright law
Kay N Kasper, Thomas Schmitz

Employee invention law
Dr Michael Trimborn, Kay N Kasper

Product liability law
Dr Christine Kanz

Licensing
Dr Christian Osterrieth,
Dr Christine Kanz

Research and development agreements
Dr Christian Osterrieth, Dr Christine Kanz

IP due diligence within transactions
Dr Martin Köhler, Dr Michael Trimborn

IP opinions
Dr Thomas Reimann,
Dr Christian Osterrieth

Arbitration and mediation
Dr Thomas Reimann,
Dr Christian Osterrieth

ROSPATT OSTEN PROSS
RECHTSANWÄLTE

PO BOX 11 09 35
KAISER-FRIEDRICH-RING 56
40509 DÜSSELDORF

Telephone: +49 211 57 72 45 0
Fax: +49 211 57 72 45 55
E-mail: mail@rospatt.de
Website: www.rospatt.de

Languages
English, French

Other offices
Mannheim

Number of lawyers 11
at this office 10

CATEGORIES OF WORK

Patents, utility models

Trade marks

Design patents

Copyrights

Unfair competition

Product liability

Litigation, arbitration, licensing

SIMMONS & SIMMONS

KÖNIGSALLEE 98A
40215 DÜSSELDORF

Telephone: +49 211 47 05 30
Fax: +49 211 47 05 35 3
E-mail: enquiries@simmons-simmons.com
Website: www.simmons-simmons.com

Languages
Dutch, English, French, German, Spanish

Other offices
London, Rotterdam, Paris, Lisbon, Milan, Rome, Frankfurt, Brussels, Madrid, Padua, Oporto, Madeira, Abu Dhabi, Qatar, Hong Kong, Shanghai, Tokyo, New York, Dubai

Number of lawyers 764
at this office 25

Contact
Jane Newman

CATEGORIES OF WORK

Corporate	**Intellectual property**
Banking	**Employment**
Capital markets	**Financial markets**
Taxation	**Pharmaceutical and biotechnology**
Projects, PFI	**Energy and utilities**
EU, competition	**TMT**
Dispute resolution	**Transport**

TAYLOR WESSING

KÖNIGSALLEE 92A
40212 DÜSSELDORF

Telephone: +49 211 83 87 0
Fax: +49 211 83 87 10 0
E-mail: duesseldorf@taylorwessing.com
Website: www.taylorwessing.com

Languages
Dutch, English, French, Italian, Mandarin, Spanish

Other offices
Alicante*, Berlin, Brussels, Cambridge, Dubai*, Frankfurt, Hamburg, London, Munich, Paris, Shanghai*

Number of lawyers 598
at this office 55

Member
World Law Group; Tech Law Group

CATEGORIES OF WORK

Banking and finance
Claus Goedecke, Peter Seemann

China desk
Florian Ranft

Commercial
Dr Christoph Hasche

Corporate/M&A
Bernhard Kloft

Employment and pensions
Axel C Filges

EU law/antitrust
Dr Marco Hartmann-Rüppel, Markus Wirtz

Intellectual property
Dr Sabine Rojahn

Life science
Dr Ulrich Steffen

Media and entertainment
Martin von Albrecht

Private client
Romana Traichel

Projects and finance
Dr Rüdiger von Hülst

Public commercial law
Dr Walter Potthast

Real estate and construction
Jan Wunschel

Regulatory affairs
Andreas Haak

Tax
Bernd Michel

Technology/IT/telecoms
Jörg Wimmers

BETTE – BRINK

SEMMELWEISSTRASSE 12
99096 ERFURT

Telephone: +49 361 34 74 00
Fax: +49 361 34 74 09 9
E-mail: bette-brink@erfurt.juropartner.de
Website: www.bette-brink.de

Languages
English, French, Russian, Spanish

Other offices
Berlin, Mainz

Number of lawyers 12
at this office 4

Member
Juropartner (European Society for Economic Interests)

CATEGORIES OF WORK

Construction law
Birgit Anuschek, Christian Stückrad

Industrial relations law
Birgit Anuschek, Dr Susanne Salzmann

Commercial law
Birgit Anuschek

Company law
Christian Ceranski

Law for the promotion of the fuel and electricity industries
Christian Ceranski

Leasing law
Christian Ceranski

Liability law
Christian Stückrad

Law of the new Federal States
Birgit Anuschek

Computer law
Christian Ceranski

Banking law
Christian Ceranski

BUSE HEBERER FROMM

HUYSSENALLEE 86-88
45128 ESSEN

Telephone: +49 201 175 80
Fax: +49 201 175 84 00
E-mail: essen@buse.de
Website: www.buse.de

Languages
English, French, Italian, Spanish

Other offices
Berlin, Dusseldorf, Frankfurt am Main, Hamburg, Munich, New York, Palma de Mallorca, Sydney, Zurich

Number of lawyers 120
at this office 13

Member
The European Legal Alliance:
Beauchamps (Ireland); Dubarry Le Douarin Veil (France); Field Fisher Waterhouse (England); Harper Macleod (Scotland); Jimenez de Parga (Spain); La Scala & Associati (Italy)

CATEGORIES OF WORK

Banking and finance

Antitrust and merger control

Commerce, transport, insurance

Commercial delinquency

Corporate/M&A

Industrial property and copyrights

Information technology and telecommunications

Labour and employment

Litigation and arbitration, national and international

Press and media

Property and construction

Public law

Tax

GÖRG
PARTNERSCHAFT VON RECHTSANWÄLTEN

BREDENEYER TOR
ALFREDSTRASSE 279
45133 ESSEN

Telephone: +49 201 43 77 60
Fax: +49 201 43 77 620
E-mail: essen@goerg.de
Website: www.goerg.de

Languages
English, French, Russian

Other Offices
Berlin, Cologne, Frankfurt

Number of lawyers 97
at this office 8

CATEGORIES OF WORK

- **Restructuring/insolvency law**
- **Employment law**
- **Corporate/M&A**
- **Litigation and arbitration**
- **Real estate/construction law/ projects**
- **International transactions**
- **General commercial**

ADERHOLD V. DALWIGK KNÜPPEL
RECHTSANWALTSGESELLSCHAFT GMBH

FRIEDRICH-EBERT-ANLAGE 54
60325 FRANKFURT AM MAIN

Telephone: +49 69 63 14 68 10
Fax: +49 69 63 14 68 43
E-mail: info@roelfspartner.de
Website: www.roelfspartner.de

Languages
German, English, French

Other offices
Berlin, Cologne, Dortmund, Düsseldorf, Leipzig

Number of lawyers 40
at this office 5

Contacts
Dr Detlef Koch, Jörg Swoboda

International groupings
In co-operation with RölfsPartner, an independent member of Baker Tilly International

CATEGORIES OF WORK

- **Corporate**
- **Mergers and acquisitions**
- **Fund structuring**
- **Private equity**
- **Labour law**
- **Real estate**

ALLEN & OVERY LLP

TAUNUSTOR 2
60311 FRANKFURT AM MAIN

Telephone: +49 69 26 48 50 00
Fax: +49 69 26 48 58 00
E-mail: information.germany@allenovery.com
Website: www.allenovery.com

Languages
Dutch, English, French, German, Italian, Japanese, Polish, Spanish

Other offices
Amsterdam, Antwerp, Bangkok, Beijing, Bratislava, Brussels, Budapest, Dubai, Hamburg, Hong Kong, London, Luxembourg, Madrid, Milan, Moscow, New York, Paris, Prague, Rome, Shanghai, Singapore, Tokyo, Turin, Warsaw

Number of lawyers 2,304

Contacts
Dr Cornelius Fischer-Zernin,
Dr Neil George Weiand

CATEGORIES OF WORK

- **Asset financing/leasing**
- **Antitrust/competition law**
- **Arbitration**
- **Regulatory**
- **Bond issues**
- **Restructuring**
- **Company law**
- **Derivatives**
- **Employment law**
- **Energy law, energy trading**
- **Environmental law**
- **Equity capital markets**
- **Global loans**
- **IP/IT**
- **Joint ventures and takeovers**
- **Leveraged finance**
- **Litigation**
- **Mergers and acquisitions**
- **Pharmaceutical and bioscience**
- **Private equity, MBO and LBOs**
- **Project finance**
- **Public and administrative law**
- **Real estate and finance**
- **Securitisation**
- **Tax**
- **Telecommunications law**

ASHURST

OBERLINDAU 54-56
60323 FRANKFURT AM MAIN

Telephone: +49 69 97 11 26
Fax: +49 69 97 20 52 20
Website: www.ashurst.com

Languages
English, French, German

Other offices
Brussels, Dubai, London, Madrid, Milan, Munich, New Delhi*, New York, Paris, Singapore, Tokyo

Number of lawyers 748
at this office 43

Contact
Simon Beddow

CATEGORIES OF WORK

Banking and securities finance
Andreas Zahn

Competition and EU
Gaby Eickstädt

Corporate and commercial
Reinhard Eyring, Hermann Schlindwein

Tax
Klaus Herkenroth

Private equity
Hermann Schlindwein

Real estate
Stephan Kock

Public law
Jutta Geiger

Public procurement law
Jutta Geiger

Employment
Andreas Vogel

Intellectual property/ information technology
Manja Epping

Mergers and acquisitions
Reinhard Eyring, Hermann Schlindwein

Sport
Hermann Schlindwein

Venture capital
Reinhard Eyring

BAKER & McKENZIE LLP

BETHMANNSTRASSE 50-54
60311 FRANKFURT AM MAIN
Telephone: +49 69 29 90 80
Fax: +49 69 29 90 81 08
Website: www.bakernet.com

Languages
English, French, Italian, Portuguese, Russian, Spanish

Other offices
Almaty, Amsterdam, Antwerp, Baku, Bangkok, Barcelona, Beijing, Berlin, Bogotá, Bologna, Brasilia, Brussels, Budapest, Buenos Aires, Cairo, Calgary, Cancun, Caracas, Chicago, Chihuahua, Dallas, Düsseldorf, Geneva, Guadalajara, Hanoi, Ho Chi Minh City, Hong Kong, Houston, Jakarta, Juarez, Kuala Lumpur, Kyiv, London, Madrid, Manama, Manila, Melbourne, Mexico City, Miami, Milan, Monterrey, Moscow, Munich, New York, Palo Alto, Paris, Porto Alegré, Prague, Rio de Janeiro, Riyadh, Rome, St Petersburg, San Diego, San Francisco, Santiago, São Paulo, Shanghai, Singapore, Stockholm, Sydney, Taipei, Tijuana, Tokyo, Toronto, Valencia, Vienna, Warsaw, Washington DC, Zürich

Number of lawyers 3,300+
at this office 100+

CATEGORIES OF WORK

Administrative and environmental law
Joachim Scherer, Ulrich Ellinghaus

Antitrust and competition law
Jörg-Martin Schultze

Banking and finance
Dietmar Heims, Olaf Gebler

Capital markets
Manuel Lorenz

Company and commercial
Ulf Wauschkuhn

Food and drugs
Thilo Räpple

Information technology, media and computer law
Matthias Scholz

Intellectual property, trade marks
Michael Fammler

Labour law
Günther Heckelmann, Gregor Dornbusch

Litigation and arbitration
Günter Pickrahn

Mergers and acquisitions
Florian Kästle, Dirk Oberbracht

Product liability
Axel Hamm

Real estate and construction
Georg von Franckenstein

Tax
Christian Brodersen, Ulrich Ränsch

Telecommunications
Joachim Scherer, Ulrich Ellinghaus

Venture capital
Florian Kästle, Dirk Oberbracht

THE FIRM

Baker & McKenzie has provided sophisticated legal advice and services to many of the world's most dynamic and global organisations for more than 50 years. With a network of more than 3,300 locally qualified, internationally experienced lawyers in 38 countries, the firm has the knowledge and resources to deliver the broad scope of quality legal services required to respond effectively to both international and local needs – consistently, confidently and with a sensitivity for cultural, social and legal practice differences.

Baker & McKenzie has been established in Europe for over 40 years, having opened its first European offices in 1957. Since then, the European and Middle Eastern network has grown to 29 offices, giving it unparalleled geographical coverage.

The Frankfurt am Main office was formed in 1962; the office in Berlin was opened on 1 March 1990; the Munich office on 1 April 1997; and the Düsseldorf office on 1 April 1999.

Since their formation, the German offices have advised their clients on all questions of German, European and international industrial and commercial law with particular emphasis on cross-border and multinational transactions. At present, more than 170 attorneys-at-law (Rechtsanwälte), tax advisers, and varying numbers of foreign admitted lawyers work in the German offices.

All attorneys are at least bilingual.

AREAS OF PRACTICE

Baker & McKenzie co-ordinates its core practice areas on local, regional and global levels, giving most of its lawyers experience in more than one jurisdiction, as well as providing multinational teams of specialists.

Utilising a global practice group structure and ground-breaking technology coupled with a personal, detailed understanding of a client's specific business, Baker & McKenzie is able to organise its extensive resources to provide focused and strategic counsel to clients.

Baker & McKenzie advises multinational enterprises, large German companies, medium-sized enterprises, banks and insurance companies, as well as institutions and entities under public law in all questions of German, European, and international industrial and commercial law including company law, competition and cartel law, intellectual property, banking and finance, labour law, administrative law, and tax law. Furthermore, the firm handles litigation and arbitration matters. Several partners have expertise in specialised areas of law, such as European Community law, the law of cosmetics, food and drug law, trade marks, franchising, corporate finance, new financial products, government procurement, real estate transactions, and media telecommunications law.

Baker & McKenzie International is a Swiss Verein with member law firms around the world.

BEITEN BURKHARDT

BOCKENHEIMER ANLAGE 15
MOZARTPLATZ
60322 FRANKFURT

Telephone: +49 69 75 60 95 0
Fax: +49 69 75 60 95 512
E-mail: bblaw-frankfurt@bblaw.com
Website: www.bblaw.com

Languages
Cantonese, Czech, English, French, Hungarian, Italian, Mandarin, Polish, Russian, Slovak, Spanish, Ukrainian

Other offices
Beijing, Berlin, Brussels, Cologne, Düsseldorf, Hong Kong, Kiev, Leipzig, Moscow, Munich, Nuremberg, St Petersburg, Shanghai, Warsaw

Number of lawyers 249
at this office 40

CATEGORIES OF WORK

- Company law
- Banking and finance
- Tax law
- European law and cartel law
- Foundation, association, societies and sports law
- Industrial property rights
- Labour law
- Procurement law
- Public law
- Information technology
- Estate planning and succession rules
- Copyright law
- Litigation and arbitration
- Telecommunication law
- Real estate law
- Advertising law
- Media law

BIRD & BIRD

TAUNUSANLAGE 1
60329 FRANKFURT AM MAIN

Telephone: +49 69 74 22 26 00 0
Fax: +49 69 74 22 26 01 1
E-mail: frankfurt@twobirds.com
Website: www.twobirds.com

Languages
English, French, German, Spanish

Other offices
Beijing, Brussels, Düsseldorf, Frankfurt, Hong Kong, London, Madrid, Milan, Munich, Paris, Rome, Stockholm, The Hague

Number of lawyers 472
at this office 10

Contacts
Erich Michel, Christian Kessel

CATEGORIES OF WORK

- Arbitration
- Aviation and aerospace
- Commercial
- Communications
- Corporate/M&A/private equity
- Employment
- EU and competition/antitrust
- Intellectual property
- IT and e-commerce
- Litigation
- Life sciences
- Media
- Outsourcing
- Private client
- Public procurement
- Real estate
- Regulatory
- Sport and sponsorship

BUSE HEBERER FROMM

GROSSE GALLUSSTRASSE 1-7
60311 FRANKFURT AM MAIN

Telephone: +49 69 97 10 97 0
Fax: +49 69 97 10 97 10
E-mail: frankfurt@buse.de
Website: www.buse.de

Languages
English, French, Italian, Portuguese, Spanish

Other offices
Berlin, Düsseldorf, Essen, Hamburg, Munich, New York, Palma de Mallorca, Sydney, Zurich

Number of lawyers 120
at this office 22

Member
The European Legal Alliance:
Beauchamps (Ireland); Dubarry Le Douarin Veil (France); Field Fisher Waterhouse (England); Harper Macleod (Scotland); Jimenez de Parga (Spain); La Scala & Associati (Italy)

CATEGORIES OF WORK

- Banking and finance
- Antitrust and merger control
- Commerce, transport, insurance
- Commercial delinquency
- Corporate/M&A
- Industrial property and copyrights
- Information technology and telecommunications
- Labour and employment
- Litigation and arbitration, national and international
- Press and media
- Property and construction
- Public law
- Tax

CMS HASCHE SIGLE

BARCKHAUSSTRASSE 12-16
60325 FRANKFURT/MAIN

Telephone: +49 69 71 70 10
Fax: +49 69 71 70 14 04 10
E-mail: frankfurt@cms-hs.com
Website: www.cms-hs.com

Languages
English, French, Spanish

Other offices
Belgrade, Berlin, Brussels, Chemnitz, Cologne, Dresden, Düsseldorf, Hamburg, Leipzig, Moscow, Munich, Prague, Stuttgart

Number of lawyers 420
at this office 40

Other CMS alliance member firms
CMS Adonnino Ascoli & Cavasola Scamoni, Italy; CMS Albiñana & Suárez de Lezo, Spain; CMS Bureau Francis Lefebvre, France; CMS Cameron McKenna, UK; CMS DeBacker, Belgium; CMS Derks Star Busmann, Netherlands; CMS von Erlach Henrici, Switzerland; CMS Reich-Rohrwig Hainz, Austria

CATEGORIES OF WORK

- Corporate
- Mergers and acquisitions
- Private equity and venture capital
- Banking
- Stock trading and capital markets
- Competition and merger control
- State aid and EU law
- Intellectual property, copyright, media and press
- Individual and collective labour law
- Real estate and construction
- IT and telecommunications
- Tax
- Estate planning
- Insolvency
- Utilities
- Public commercial and environment, procurement
- Distribution and franchise law
- Insurance
- Maritime, shipping and transport
- Litigation and arbitration

CLEARY GOTTLIEB STEEN & HAMILTON LLP

MAIN TOWER
NEUE MAINZER STRASSE 52
60311 FRANKFURT AM MAIN

Telephone: +49 69 97 10 30
Fax: +49 69 97 10 31 99
Website: www.clearygottlieb.com

Languages
English, French, German, Italian, Polish, Portuguese, Spanish, Swedish

Other offices
Brussels, Cologne, Hong Kong, London, Milan, Moscow, New York, Paris, Rome, Tokyo, Washington DC

Number of lawyers 847
at this office 41

CATEGORIES OF WORK

- Banking and finance
- Capital markets/securities
- Commercial
- Competition law
- Corporate
- Joint ventures
- Litigation and arbitration
- Mergers and acquisitions
- Tax

CURTIS, MALLET-PREVOST, COLT & MOSLE LLP

STAUFENSTRASSE 42
60323 FRANKFURT AM MAIN

Telephone: +49 69 97 14 42 0
Fax: +49 69 97 14 42 33
E-mail: info@cm-p.com
Website: www.cm-p.com

Languages
Arabic, English, French, German

Other offices
Houston, London, Mexico City, Milan, Muscat, New York, Paris, Stamford, Washington DC

Number of lawyers 187
at this office 3

Contacts
Carl A Ruggiero, Dr Holger Jung, Marc V Kramer

Member
International Bar Association;
American Chamber of Commerce in Germany;
Frankfurt Bar Association

CATEGORIES OF WORK

- Mergers and acquisitions
- International corporate/commercial
- Investment management
- Banking
- Financial markets
- Arab laws
- International litigation/arbitration

DLA PIPER RUDNICK GRAY CARY

WESTHAFEN TOWER
WESTHAFENPLATZ 1
60327 FRANKFURT AM MAIN

Telephone: +49 69 27 13 30
Fax: +49 69 27 13 31 00
E-mail: michael.magotsch@dlapiper.com
Website: www.dlapiper.com/germany

Languages
Chinese, English, French, Italian, Korean, Spanish

Other offices
Austria, Belgium, Bosnia-Herzegovina, China, Croatia, Czech Republic, Denmark*, Egypt*, France, Germany, Georgia, Hong Kong, Hungary, Italy, Japan, Netherlands, Norway*, Poland*, Russia, Singapore*, Slovakia, South Africa*, Spain, Sweden*, Thailand, UK, Ukraine, United Arab Emirates, US

Number of lawyers 3,100
at this office 14

Contact
Michael Magotsch

Member
DLA Piper Group

CATEGORIES OF WORK

Corporate, mergers and acquisitions
Rainer Jacob, Dr Kirsten Girnth, Michael Ghaffar

HR and employment
Michael Magotsch

Technology, media and communications
Dr Kirsten Girnth

Capital markets/IPO/venture capital
Martin Heinsius

Real estate
Rainer Jacob

Asia desk
Michael Ghaffar

Tax
Martin Heinsius

THE FIRM

DLA Piper Rudnick Gray Cary is a leading global legal services provider with approximately 3,100 lawyers in 58 offices across 22 countries. The organisation is committed to building long-term relationships with its clients and supports their strategic and operational needs both locally and internationally.

In Germany, DLA Piper Rudnick Gray Cary is a 50-lawyer-strong team with offices in Cologne, Frankfurt and Hamburg. The office comprises well-established German lawyers who are highly experienced in both national and international legal work. It specialises in all aspects of business law, from corporate and project finance to real estate, employment and IT/media. There are plans to open offices in other major cities in Germany within the next year as part of its strategy to build a national practice across the country.

DLA Piper is a founding member of an exclusive alliance of full-service legal organisations with a shared vision. DLA Piper Group, established in 1999, has members across Europe, Africa, the Middle East, Asia and the US, which deliver expert local know-how and integrated international solutions.

AREAS OF PRACTICE

Corporate, mergers and acquisitions: advises mid-sized and large organisations on all types of transactional and advisory matters and has a growing international reputation within the corporate market.

HR and employment: practical experience of helping clients mould their people strategies and work practices, including preparation of employment contracts, assistance in labour disputes and redundancy, in outsourcing, post-merger integration and restructuring.

Technology, media and communications: contentious and non-contentious advice in all kinds of technology and IP/media-related matters and transactions, with special experience in IT, outsourcing, data protection, telecommunications and in media/TV productions, sports, sponsorship, and unfair competition, as well as the exploitation, protection and enforcement of all kinds of intellectual property rights.

Capital Markets/IPO/venture capital: advises on IPOs, secondary offerings, dual listings, delistings, tax-driven derivatives, public takeover matters, and compliance, as well as regulatory matters.

Real estate: services to corporate occupiers, developers, financial institutions, and the public sector, covering all aspects of commercial real estate transactions, including development and financing work. Advice on turnkey plant and infrastructure projects.

Asia desk: outbound advice of businesses active in Asia and inbound advice to Asian clients in Germany on all types of transactional and advisory matters, with the ability to work in Mandarin and in Korean.

Tax: advice on tax-efficient investment structures for real estate and shipping investments, M&A transactions, tax planning for post-merger integration, and tax efficient investment structures for regulated industries such as investment funds, banks and other financial institutions.

DEBEVOISE & PLIMPTON LLP

TAUBENSTRASSE 7-9
60313 FRANKFURT AM MAIN

Telephone: +49 69 20 97 50 00
Fax: +49 6 20 97 55 55
E-mail: dfhickok@debevoise.com
Website: www.debevoise.com

Languages
English, German

Other offices
Hong Kong, London, Moscow, New York, Paris, Shanghai, Washington DC

Number of lawyers 660+
at this office 13

CATEGORIES OF WORK

Mergers and acquisitions
Dr Thomas Schürrle, David F Hickok

Restructuring
Dr Thomas Schürrle

Private equity funds
Marcia MacHarg, Dr Friedrich EF Hey

Corporate tax
Dr Friedrich EF Hey

Capital markets
David F Hickok, Philipp von Holst

Financing
Hans Bertram-Nothnagel, Philipp von Holst

Dispute resolution
Dr Thomas Schürrle

Aviation
Hans Bertram-Nothnagel, Philipp von Holst

Competition
Dr Thomas Schürrle, Philipp von Holst

DECHERT LLP

TRIANON
MAINZER LANDSTRASSE 16
60325 FRANKFURT AM MAIN

Telephone: +49 69 97 16 82 45
Fax: +49 69 97 16 83 71
E-mail: joseph.smallhoover@dechert.com
Website: www.dechert.com

Languages
English, French, German

Other offices
Austin, Boston, Brussels, Charlotte, Harrisburg, Hartford, London, Luxembourg, Munich, Newport Beach, New York, Palo Alto, Paris, Philadelphia, Princeton, San Francisco, Washington DC

Number of lawyers 900+

Contact
Joseph Smallhoover (managing partner)

CATEGORIES OF WORK

Bank financing and securitisation
Joseph J Smallhoover

Financial services
Joseph J Smallhoover

Mergers and acquisitions
Joseph J Smallhoover

Private equity
Joseph J Smallhoover

Corporate finance and securities
Joseph J Smallhoover

Alternative investment funds
Joseph J Smallhoover

Bankruptcy/corporate recovery and insolvency
Joseph J Smallhoover

Domestic and international tax
Joseph J Smallhoover

Finance and real estate
Joseph J Smallhoover

DEWEY BALLANTINE LLP

TAUNUS ANLAGE 1
60329 FRANKFURT

Telephone: +49 69 36 39 30
Fax: +49 69 36 39 33 33
E-mail: frankfurt@deweyballantine.com
Website: www.deweyballantine.com

Languages
English, French, German

Other offices
Austin, Beijing, East Palo Alto, Houston, London, Los Angeles, Milan, New York, Rome, Warsaw, Washington DC

Number of lawyers 550+
at this office 34

Contacts
Dr Hanno Berger (hberger@deweyballantine.com), Philipp von Ilberg (pilberg@deweyballantine.com)

CATEGORIES OF WORK

Mergers and acquisitions
Markus Federle, Rudolf Coelle, Benedikt von Schorlemer

Private equity
Markus Federle, Rudolf Coelle, Benedikt von Schorlemer, Philipp von Ilberg

Capital markets
Bernd Fahrholz, Philipp von Ilberg

Tax
Hanno Berger, Bernulph von Crailsheim, Peter Happe, Dieter Lübbehüsen

Banking and finance
Bernd Fahrholz, Philipp von Ilberg

Asset management and banking regulatory
Kai-Uwe Steck

FPS FRITZE PAUL SEELIG

ESCHERSHEIMER LANDSTRASSE 25-27
60322 FRANKFURT AM MAIN

Telephone: +49 69 95 95 70
Fax: +49 69 95 95 71 66
E-mail: frankfurt@fps-law.de
Website: www.fps-law.de

Languages
English, French, Italian, Russian, Spanish

Other offices
Berlin, Düsseldorf, Hamburg, Munich

Number of lawyers 90
at this office 53

Contact
Dr Robin L Fritz

Member
Meritas

CATEGORIES OF WORK

Company, mergers and acquisition

Commercial property and real estate

Corporate

Capital markets

Trade and distributor contracts

Tax

Construction, leasing

Real estate

Public private partnership (PPP)

Public procurement

Competition and EU

Mergers and acquisitions

Energy and environmental

Banking and insolvency

Product liability, insurers' liability

EC law

Employment

New media, e-commerce, computer

IT, media and entertainment

Insurance

Antitrust

Arbitration and litigation

IP, product piracy, unfair trading

Sponsoring

GSK GASSNER STOCKMANN & KOLLEGEN

TAUNUSANLAGE 21
60325 FRANKFURT AM MAIN

Telephone: +49 69 71 00 03 0
Fax: +49 69 71 00 03 44
E-mail: frankfurt@gsk.de
Website: www.gsk.de

Languages
English, French, German

Other offices
Berlin, Düsseldorf, Hamburg, Heidelberg, Munich, Stuttgart

Number of lawyers 107
at this office 16

Contacts
Dr Christian R Schmidt (Berlin), Dr Andreas Bauer (Munich), Dr Andreas May (Frankfurt), Dr Philipp Jebens (Hamburg), Dr Peter Ladwig (Stuttgart), Dr Eckart Petzold (Düsseldorf), Wolfgang Böhm (Heidelberg)

CATEGORIES OF WORK

Corporate
Dr Gregor Seikel, Dr Volker Holl

Mergers and acquisitions
Dr Gregor Seikel, Dr Volker Holl

Venture capital and private equity
Dr Gregor Seikel

Real estate, project finance, construction
Dr Andreas May, Holger Lampe

Infrastructure,public sector, public procurement
Dr Andreas May, Philipp Klingen

Taxation
Dr Gregor Seikel

Commercial lease
Dr Rainer Werum, Dr Josef Maria Wodicka

Banking and finance, capital markets
Dr Rainer Werum

Information technology
Philipp Klingen, Dr Gregor Seikel

Litigation and arbitration
Dr Oliver N Moufang, Holger Lampe

GLEISS LUTZ
RECHTSANWÄLTE

MENDELSSOHNSTAßE 87
60325 FRANKFURT

Telephone: +49 69 95 51 4 0
Fax: +49 69 95 51 41 98
E-mail: info@gleisslutz.com
Website: www.gleisslutz.com

Languages
Dutch, English, French, Italian, Mandarin, Cantonese, Polish, Portuguese, Spanish, Russian, Czech, Slovak

Other offices
Berlin, Munich, Stuttgart, Brussels, Prague, Warsaw

Number of lawyers 225
at this office 50

Contact
Dr Hoimar von Ditfurth

CATEGORIES OF WORK

German, EC and international law

Banking, securities and finance

Commercial law (general)

Companies, corporations

Competition, antitrust

Electronic commerce, internet law

Employment, labour

Environment and pollution control

Insurance

Litigation and arbitration

Mergers and acquisitions

Real estate

Tax

Telecommunications, media and broadcasting

Trade marks, intellectual property

GÖRG
PARTNERSCHAFT VON RECHTSANWÄLTEN

PLATZ DER EINHEIT 2
60327 FRANKFURT

Telephone: +49 69 17 00 00 17
Fax: +49 69 17 00 00 27
E-mail: frankfurt@goerg.de
Website: www.goerg.de

Languages
English, French

Other offices
Berlin, Cologne, Essen

Number of lawyers 97
at this office 9

CATEGORIES OF WORK

Restructuring/insolvency law

Employment law

Real estate/ construction law/projects

IP/IT/media law/ general commercial

Corporate/M&A/banking and finance/tax law

Regulatory/public law

Litigation and arbitration

International transactions

GRÜTZMACHER GRAVERT VIEGENER

BROSSSTRASSE 6
60487 FANKFURT AM MAIN

Telephone: +49 69 97 96 10
Fax: +49 69 97 96 11 00
E-mail: frankfurt@gg-v.de
Website: www gg-v.de

Languages
English, French, German, Italian, Spanish

Other offices
Hamburg, Paris

Number of lawyers 28
at this office 10

International groupings
TAG Law; TIAG

CATEGORIES OF WORK

Corporate, tax, auditing
Dr Rolf Grützmacher, Katrin Gäbler

Commercial and company law
Dr K Gravert, Matthias Krämer

Mergers and acquisitions
Dr Kay Jess, Amselm Gehling

Corporate finance
Dr Kay Jess, Amselm Gehling

Information technology/ intellectual property
Dr Andreas Bittner, Amselm Gehling

Insolvency law
Axel Raap, Dr Olaf Büchler

Construction and real estate
Dr Kay Jess, Dr Andreas Bittner

Non-profit organisations
Dr Siegbert Schneider, Katrin Gäbler

Employment and labour
Dr Arno Maier-Bridou

HAARMANN HEMMELRATH

NEUE MAINZER STRASSE 75
60311 FRANKFURT AM MAIN

Telephone: +49 69 92 05 90
Fax: +49 69 92 05 91 33
E-mail: frankfurt@haarmannhemmelrath.com
Website: www.haarmannhemmelrath.com

Languages
Croatian, English, French

Other offices
Bielefeld, Bucharest, Budapest, Düsseldorf, Hamburg, Leipzig, Moscow, Munich, Paris, Prague, Shanghai, Warsaw

Number of lawyers 226

CATEGORIES OF WORK

Mergers and acquisitions
Dr Rainer Bommert

Corporate law
Dr Siddharta Schwenzer, Dr Rainer Bommert

IPO, capital markets
Dr Andreas Fillmann

Private equity/venture capital

Banking
Dr Andreas Fillmann

Telecommunications, media, technology

Litigation, forensic services, arbitration
Dr Rainer Bommert

Real estate
Barbara Busch

International tax

National tax
Barbara Busch

Transfer pricing

Insolvency, restructuring, distressed debt

Structured finance
Barbara Busch

HENGELER MUELLER

BOCKENHEIMER LANDSTRASSE 51
60325 FRANKFURT

Telephone: +49 69 17 09 50
Fax: +49 69 72 57 73
E-mail: hmffm@hengeler.com
Website: www.hengeler.com

Other offices
Düsseldorf, Berlin, Munich, Brussels, London

Number of lawyers 192
at this office 88

Contact
Dr Christof Jäckle

CATEGORIES OF WORK

Banking, finance and capital markets

Bank regulatory law

Asset management

Syndicated lending

Acquisition finance

Project finance

Derivatives

Equity capital markets

Debt capital markets

Asset-backed securities

M&A/corporate

Private equity

Tax

Competition

Labour and employment

IP/IT

Insolvency and reorganisation

Real estate

Litigation and arbitration

HEUKING KÜHN LÜER WOJTEK

GRÜNEBURGWEG 102
60323 FRANKFURT

Telephone: +49 69 97 56 10
Fax: +49 69 97 56 12 00
E-mail: frankfurt@heuking.de
Website: www.heuking.de

Languages
German, English, French

Other offices
Berlin, Brussels, Chemnitz, Cologne, Düsseldorf, Hamburg, Munich

Number of lawyers 11

Contact
Rudolf du Mesnil de Rochemont

CATEGORIES OF WORK

Mergers and acquisitions, business start-ups

Competition law and merger control

Banking and finance, capital markets

IP, IT, copyright, entertainment, media, publishing, data protection

Regulatory compliance

Property development, real estate, public administration

Commercial, distribution, advertising, franchising law

Employment law

Litigation and arbitration

THE FIRM

Heuking Kühn Lüer Wojtek was founded in Düsseldorf, Germany, in 1971. Since then, the firm has spread geographically, and Heuking Kühn now has seven significant offices in Germany, as well as an office in Brussels.

The firm has an extensive international network of law firms, enabling it to provide its clients with seamless 'one-stop shopping', on international transactions and regulatory matters. Since its formation, Heuking Kühn Lüer Wojtek has specifically chosen to remain an independent law firm. It is Heuking Kühn Lüer Wojtek's philosophy that, to provide the best possible service to its clients, the firm must be able to co-operate with various other law firms which are at the top of the profession in their respective countries. This gives the firm the ability to make alternative counsel suggestions to its clients, giving the clients a choice of the best suitable law firm or lawyer in each country and for each matter. Over the last 30+ years, Heuking Kühn Lüer Wojtek has developed excellent relationships with the key firms in all of the major jurisdictions worldwide.

Heuking Kühn Lüer Wojtek is a name which is synonymous with legal competence. The firm is one of the largest commercial law firms in Germany, with more than 170 specialised lawyers and tax advisers, representing the interests of national and international clients. Included in the client list are large and medium-sized German and international companies in all areas of the manufacturing industry, as well as trade and service industries, associations, governmental and public sector organisations and private clients and trusts.

The firm prides itself on substantive legal competence and on the excellent education and continuing legal education of its lawyers. Moreover, virtually all of the lawyers are German-English bilingual.

Extensive specialisation and comprehensive knowledge of specific industry sectors provide the basis of all of Heuking Kühn Lüer Wojtek's legal counselling. Experienced partners and carefully selected associate lawyers develop innovative solutions to complex legal problems. The lawyers regularly work in their specific practice area groups and also in multi-group and multidisciplinary teams with clients and outside consultants or advisers. Entrepreneurial thinking on behalf of firm clients, as well as efficient, quality, cost-effective and timely work and the highest personal dedication are key components of Heuking Kühn Lüer Wojtek's culture.

AREAS OF PRACTICE

Heuking Kühn Lüer Wojtek is a full-service commercial law firm. Cross-border and cross-sector knowledge in combination with a deep understanding of business reasoning enables service to clients with the broadest possible support in all their negotiations and business decisions. This applies equally to M&A transactions, to legal advice on company structure, business risk management, negotiations and negotiation tactics, training, crisis and insolvency counselling, corporate financial matters, and complex litigation and arbitration. Thanks to a variety of strong business clients, the firm has built long-term relationships with its clients and can assist them, beginning with the establishment of a business, followed by implementing business goals, including day-to-day legal work, reorganisations, acquisitions and divestitures.

Heuking Kühn Lüer Wojtek is actively involved with its clients in providing regulatory counselling in all areas of commercial law, as well as assisting them in organising and implementing their M&A transactions in Germany, throughout Europe, and internationally. Heuking Kühn Lüer Wojtek has particular expertise in German and EU company law; competition law, merger control, state aids and regulated industries (including energy; telecommunications; and transport, postal services and shipping law); taxation; employment law; finance and banking; international trade and customs; insurance; litigation, arbitration and mediation; bankruptcy and insolvency; environment, health and safety law; product liability; product-specific regulation; real estate and construction law; IP, IT and media law; and private clients and family law.

KAYE SCHOLER (GERMANY) LLP

SCHILLERSTRASSE 19
60313 FRANKFURT

Telephone: +49 69 25 49 40
Fax: +49 69 25 49 44 44
E-mail: frankfurt@kayescholer.com
Website: www.kayescholer.com

Languages
English

Other offices
Chicago, London, Los Angeles, New York, Shanghai, Washington DC, West Palm Beach

Number of lawyers 500
at this office 14

Contact
Dr Harald Rieger

Member
AmCham (American Chamber of Commerce)

CATEGORIES OF WORK

Corporate
Dr Harald Rieger, Michael Mölling

M&A and private equity
Matthias Götz, Dr Klaus Eyber

Corporate finance and capital markets
Matthias Götz, Till Hafner

Antitrust
Dr Harald Rieger,
Dr Sebastian Jungermann

Litigation and dispute resolution
Dr Klaus Eyber, Britta Jungermann

National and international tax law
Dr Joachim Borggräfe,
Dr Martin Weger

Pharmaceutical and biotech
Dr Gottfried Freier

Contracts and national and international engineering and construction law
Dr Ulrich Trost, Dr Heinz-Bodo Führ

Real estate
Thomas Krall

LINKLATERS OPPENHOFF & RÄDLER

MAINZER LANDSTRASSE 16
60325 FRANKFURT AM MAIN

Telephone: +49 69 71 00 30
Fax: +49 69 71 00 33 33
Website: www.linklaters.com

Languages
All commercial and local languages in the countries where Linklaters operates

Other offices
Germany: Berlin, Cologne, Munich; worldwide: Amsterdam, Antwerp, Bangkok, Beijing, Bratislava, Brussels, Bucharest, Budapest, Dubai, Hong Kong, Lisbon, London, Luxembourg, Madrid, Milan, Moscow, New York, Paris, Prague, Rome, São Paulo, Shanghai, Singapore, Stockholm, Tokyo, Warsaw

Number of lawyers 2,000 (worldwide)
330 (Germany)

Contacts
Michael Lappe (German senior partner),
Markus Hartung (German managing partner)

CATEGORIES OF WORK

M&A/corporate
Wolfgang Sturm (*Cologne*)

Banking and finance
Carl-Peter Feick (*Frankfurt*)

Tax
Karl Schäfer (*Munich*)

Real estate
Michael Steinbrecher (*Frankfurt*)

IP, trade marks and copyrights
Stefan Lütje (*Berlin*)

EU and cartel law
Wolfgang Deselaers (*Cologne/Brussels*)

Litigation and arbitration
Peter Klappich (*Cologne*)

Employment
Michael Tepass (*Frankfurt*)

Public law, environmental law
Jan Endler (*Berlin*)

TMT
Christian Hey (*Cologne*)

Regulated markets
Kai Pritzsche (*Berlin*)

Private equity
Ulrich Wolff (*Frankfurt*)

Insolvency and restructuring
Wolfgang Sturm (*Cologne*)

Media
Stefan Lütje (*Berlin*)

Healthcare
Peter Klappich (*Cologne*)

LOVELLS

UNTERMAINANLAGE 1
60329 FRANKFURT AM MAIN

Telephone: +49 69 96 23 60
Fax: +49 69 96 23 61 00
E-mail: reception.frankfurt@lovells.com
Website: www.lovells.de

Languages
English, French, Italian, Polish, Russian, Spanish

Other offices
Alicante, Amsterdam, Beijing, Berlin, Brussels, Budapest*, Chicago, Düsseldorf, Hamburg, Ho Chi Minh City, Hong Kong, London, Madrid, Milan, Moscow, Munich, New York, Paris, Prague, Rome, Shanghai, Singapore, Tokyo, Warsaw, Zagreb*

Number of lawyers 1,600
at this office 91

Contact
Hans-Peter Loew

CATEGORIES OF WORK

Corporate/M&A, private equity	Intellectual property
Restructuring and insolvency	Real estate
Banking	Projects
Antitrust and unfair competition	Technology, media, telecommunications
Capital markets	Litigation, product liability
Project finance, public private partnerships	International arbitration
Tax	Food and drug regulations
Employment	Law of Eastern Europe

MANNHEIMER SWARTLING
RECHTSANWÄLTE UND SCHWEDISCHE ADVOKATEN

WILDUNGER STRASSE 9
60487 FRANKFURT AM MAIN

Telephone: +49 69 97 40 12 0
Fax: +49 69 74 10 14 3
Website: www.mannheimerswartling.se

Languages
English, French, Swedish

Other offices
Berlin, Brussels, Gothenburg, Helsingborg, Malmö, New York, St Petersburg, Stockholm

Number of lawyers 330
at this office 10

Contact
Christian Bloth

CATEGORIES OF WORK

Banking and securities	Intellectual property
Corporate	Litigation and arbitration
Employment	Mergers and acquisitions
Environment	Real estate and construction
EU and competition	Sports

MAYER BROWN ROWE & MAW LLP

BOCKENHEIMER LANDSTRASSE 98-100 60323 FRANKFURT/MAIN

Telephone: +49 69 79 41 0
Fax: +49 69 79 41 10 0
E-mail: frankfurt@mayerbrownrowe.com
Website: www.mayerbrownrowe.com

Languages
English, French, Italian, Spanish

Other offices
Berlin, Brussels, Charlotte, Chicago, Cologne, Houston, London, Los Angeles, Mexico City, Beijing, Shanghai (correspondence offices); New York, Palo Alto (partner offices); Paris, Washington DC

Number of lawyers 1,300
at this office 75

Contact
Reinhart Lange (managing partner)

CATEGORIES OF WORK	
Corporate	**Biotech**
M&A	**Pharma**
Private equity	**Life science**
Banking and finance	**Information technology**
Securitisation	**Telecommunications**
Intellectual property	**Internet and media**
Antitrust and competition	**Litigation**
Real estate	**Dispute resolution**
Environment	**Equity capital markets**
Employment pensions/benefits	**Outsourcing**
Tax	**Aviation and airports**
Insolvency	

THE FIRM

Mayer, Brown, Rowe & Maw LLP is a leading international law practice with over 400 partners and 1,300 lawyers worldwide. It serves its international clients from 13 offices: Berlin, Brussels, Charlotte, Chicago, Cologne, Frankfurt, Houston, London, Los Angeles, New York, Palo Alto, Paris and Washington DC. In addition to these offices, Mayer, Brown, Rowe & Maw LLP has a network of well established contacts throughout Europe to assist in regional matters as well as representative offices in Beijing and Shanghai.

AREAS OF PRACTICE

30 partners and a total of 90 lawyers in the offices in Frankfurt am Main, Cologne and Berlin advise German and international clients on the full range of legal issues. In doing so, the firm's lawyers draw upon their in-depth local knowledge of the Germany market and practices as well as the resources of a major international law firm.

Firmwide, Mayer, Brown, Rowe & Maw represents major multinational corporations, financial institutions and insurance companies, public utilities, trade associations, governments, companies of every size and industry, start-up ventures, and many non-profit organisations as well.

In Germany, the firm's core areas of practice are as follows: corporate, M&A, private equity, banking and finance, securitisation, intellectual property, antitrust and competition, real estate, environment, employment and labour, tax, insolvency, biotech, pharmaceutical and life science, information technology, telecommunications, litigation and dispute resolution.

Furthermore, through the firm's belief that thorough knowledge of the firm's client's operations is indispensable, to fully meet the individual needs of different jurisdictions, the firm has built up branch-specific intelligence in numerous business fields over many years. These include: biotech, pharmaceutical and life science, chemicals, automotive, steel, metal processing, machine tool engineering, building construction, property development and management, planning, food and beverages, consumer goods, retail textiles, financial service and insurance, information technology, telecommunications, internet and media, and sports marketing.

MILBANK, TWEED, HADLEY & McCLOY LLP

FRANKFURTER WELLE
AN DER WELLE 4
60422 FRANKFURT AM MAIN

Telephone: +49 69 75 93 71 70
Fax: +49 69 75 93 83 03
E-mail: info@milbank.com
Website: www.milbankeurope.com

Other offices
Hong Kong, London, Los Angeles, Munich, New York, Singapore, Tokyo, Washington DC

Number of lawyers 520
at this office 10

Contact
Dr Rainer Magold

CATEGORIES OF WORK

Banking and acquisition finance
Dr Rainer Magold,
Dr Christina Ungeheuer

Debt and equity capital markets
Christian Droop

THE FIRM

Milbank is committed to providing high-quality legal services wherever the firm practices. The firm recruits from among the most promising lawyers and is committed to their training as well as providing opportunities for promotion. Milbank draws on its strengths globally to ensure that it can address the needs of its clients wherever they are.

Milbank's Frankfurt team focuses on complex domestic and cross-border financing transactions, ranging from acquisitions to corporate, structured, asset and project financings. Working as an integral team, the firm's Frankfurt lawyers provide comprehensive advice on the German, US and English law aspects of financings in the public and private markets to banking, private equity, underwriter/arranger and corporate issuer clients.

AREAS OF PRACTICE

The acquisition and corporate finance practice of partners Dr Rainer Magold and Dr Christina Ungeheuer has enjoyed long-standing recognition as a leading practice in the market. It is complemented by the firm's international debt and equity capital markets practice, led by partner Christian Droop.

From the firm's Frankfurt and Munich offices the firm provides fully integrated legal advice on corporate, tax and finance matters to clients doing business or investing in Germany. The firm's Frankfurt and Munich lawyers also work closely with the firm's London and New York offices and leverage the complementary strengths of Milbank's global finance and banking expertise in the conception and execution of some of the most intricate and innovative transactions in Europe.

MORGAN LEWIS

GUIOLLETTSTRASSE 54
60325 FRANKFURT AM MAIN

Telephone: +49 69 71 40 07 11
Fax: +49 69 71 40 07 10
E-mail:
frankfurtoffice@morganlewis.com
Website: www.morganlewis.de
www.morganlewis.com

Languages
English, French, German, Italian, Spanish

Other offices
Boston, Brussels, Chicago, Dallas, Harrisburg, Irvine, London, Los Angeles, Miami, New York, Palo Alto, Paris, Philadelphia, Pittsburgh, Princeton, San Francisco, Tokyo, Washington DC

Number of lawyers 1,200+
at this office 25

CATEGORIES OF WORK

Projects and transactions
Dr Christian Zschocke, Nils Rahlf

Antitrust
Dr Jürgen Beninca

Financial services
Dr Uwe Jahn

Taxation
Dr Jörg Siegels

Labour
Dr Walter Ahrens

THE FIRM

Morgan Lewis, with more than 1,200 lawyers in 19 offices in the US, Europe and Asia, is one of the largest law firms in the world.

Morgan Lewis represents clients across the globe, from mergers and acquisitions and joint ventures to technology and outsourcing; from fraud and money laundering to employment and property. With its international reach, Morgan Lewis can resolve differing and conflicting laws in a number of jurisdictions to produce optimum results for its clients. The firm's lawyers understand the problems and complexities of transactional litigation and cross-border negotiation and can advise on US and EU regulatory matters.

The firm's clients are diverse and include Fortune 250 companies, leading financial services and investment banking organisations, as well as pioneers in the e-commerce and internet sector. The firm also represents high-net-worth individuals. All clients receive the same high level of care and benefit from the firm's local presence in a global market.

The firm handles a vast diversity of legal work including antitrust, business and commercial litigation, business and finance, corporate transactions, employment, labour and benefits, energy and utilities, insurance, intellectual property, international arbitration, investment management, life sciences, mergers and acquisitions, real estate, outsourcing, securities, sport, tax and technology.

AREAS OF PRACTICE

The Frankfurt office opened 17 years ago and is a successful, highly specialised office concentrating on projects and transactions mainly in mergers and acquisitions, public and private equity. The team also focuses on financial services especially securities, capital markets and derivatives. Other areas of activity include emerging business, IP projects, antitrust, tax and labour. The lawyers in the Frankfurt office are qualified in German law as well as some other international jurisdictions and are experienced in handling complex, cross-border assignments. Morgan Lewis, Frankfurt is fully integrated with the firm's 18 other offices and offers a strong pan-European service in combination with its Brussels, London and Paris lawyers.

The Frankfurt team provides advice internationally, regardless of whether it is for activities in Germany or other countries. Morgan Lewis, Frankfurt uses the firm's e-technology to interact with clients across the globe and ensure smooth working practices despite differing time zones, thus ensuring the German market is accessible for international clients.

The Frankfurt office expanded its tax capability in 2005 by the addition of Dr Jörg Siegels and increased its capabilities to include labour and employment law in 2006 (with Dr Walter Ahrens).

NÖRR STIEFENHOFER LUTZ

FRIEDRICHSTRASSE 2-6
60323 FRANKFURT AM MAIN

Telephone: +49 69 97 14 77 0
Fax: +49 69 97 14 77 100
E-mail: info@noerr.com
Website: www.noerr.com

Languages
Arabic, English, French, German, Italian, Russian, Spanish

Other offices
Berlin, Bratislava, Bucharest, Budapest, Dresden, Düsseldorf, Moscow, Munich, New York, Prague, Warsaw

Number of lawyers 256
(+ 66 tax advisers, public accountants and tax assistants)
at this office 32

Contact
Dr Thomas Bergmann

CATEGORIES OF WORK

Banking and finance	Mergers and acquisitions
Capital markets	Private clients
Commercial law	Public and administrative law
Company	Real estate and development
German and EC antitrust and cartel law	Tax law
Labour law	Unfair competition law
Litigation and arbitration	

P+P PÖLLATH + PARTNERS

HAUPTWACHE
ZEIL 127
60313 FRANKFURT AM MAIN

Telephone: +49 69 24 70 47 0
Fax: +49 69 24 70 47 30
E-mail: fra@pplaw.com
Website: www.pplaw.com

Languages
English, French

Other offices
Berlin, Munich

Number of lawyers 66
at this office 6

Contacts
Ralph Wagner, Wolfgang Hohensee

CATEGORIES OF WORK

Private equity	Real estate
M&A	Restitution
Corporate finance	Family (high-net-worth, succession)
Tax	Trusts, foundations, charities

RITTERSHAUS
LAW OFFICES

MAINZER LANDSTRASSE 61
60329 FRANKFURT AM MAIN

Telephone: +49 69 27 40 40 0
Fax: +49 69 27 40 40 25
E-mail: info@rittershaus.net
Website: www.rittershaus.net

Languages
English, French, Italian, Russian, Spanish

Other offices
Mannheim

Number of lawyers 32
at this office 8

Contacts
Wendelin Frhr von Ketelhodt,
Dr Wolf-Henrik Friedrich

CATEGORIES OF WORK

Companies, corporations
Wendelin Frhr von Ketelhodt,
Dr Wolf-Henrik Friedrich

Mergers and acquisitions
Dr Wolf-Henrik Friedrich,

Competition, antitrust
Dr Wolf-Henrik Friedrich,

Inheritance law
Dr Wolf-Henrik Friedrich,
Wendelin Frhr von Ketelhodt

Banking, securities and finance
Wendelin Frhr von Ketelhodt,

Contract
Jörg Döhrer, Mark Oliver Kühn

Real property and construction law
Wendelin Frhr von Ketelhodt,
Dr Wolf-Henrik Friedrich

Sports and entertainment
Dr Wolf-Henrik Friedrich

IT law, e-business
Mark Oliver Kühn

Employment, labour
Jörg Döhrer

Notary office
Wendelin Frhr von Ketelhodt

SJ BERWIN LLP
RECHTSANWÄLTE – STEUERBERATER – WIRTSCHAFTSPRÜFER

POSEIDON-HAUS
HAMBURGER ALLEE 1
60486 FRANKFURT AM MAIN

Telephone: +49 69 50 50 32 50 0
Fax: +49 69 50 50 32 49 9
E-mail: frankfurt@sjberwin.de
Website: www.sjberwin.com

Languages
Danish, English, French, Greek

Other offices
Berlin, Brussels, London, Madrid, Milan, Munich, Paris, Turin

Number of lawyers 550
at this office 32

Contacts
Rüdiger Knopf, Anthony Tulloch

CATEGORIES OF WORK

Private equity MBOs, M&A
Rüdiger Knopf

Venture capital funds
Anthony Tulloch

Estate planning
Dr Andreas Söffing

Corporate taxation
Gerald Thomas, Markus Hill

Financial due diligence
Dr Gunter Franzke

Commercial law
Stephan Schmidt,
Dr William Panagiotides

Corporate law/VC transactions/IPOs
Dr Michael Roos, Dr Tobias Lenz

Corporate finance, M&A
Sebastian Gronstedt

Employment law
Dr Holger Thomas

SCHWARZ KELWING WICKE WESTPFAHL

MÖRFELDER LANDSTR 117
60598 FRANKFURT

Telephone: +49 69 63 00 01 0
Fax: +49 69 63 55 22
E-mail: frankfurt@skwlaw.de
Website: www.skwlaw.de

Languages
Arabic, English, French, German

Other offices
Berlin, Dresden, Munich

Number of lawyers 58
at this office 12

Contacts
Stefan Kridlo, Michael Wahl, Dr Tatjana Schroeder

Member
Terralex; PLG

CATEGORIES OF WORK

Corporate and commercial law
Dr Manfred Westpfahl, Stefan Kridlo, Dr Tatjana Schroeder

Real estate law, conveyancing
Stefan Kridlo, Dr Manfred Westpfahl

Banking and finance
Wilfried Maas, Dr Jan Marwede

Arbitration and litigation
Martin Stück, Wilfried Maas

Unfair competition
Dr Kerstin Degenhardt

Labour and employment law
Michael Wahl

Succession law
Dr Manfred Westpfahl

Copyright, trade marks, intellectual property
Martin Stück

Mergers and acquisitions
Stefan Kridlo, Dr Tatjana Schroeder

Information technology
Dr Oliver M Bühr

Construction law
Julian Westpfahl

SIMMONS & SIMMONS

MESSETURM
FRIEDRICH-EBERT-ANLAGE 49
60308 FRANKFURT AM MAIN

Telephone: +49 69 90 74 54 0
Fax: +49 69 90 74 54 54
E-mail: enquiries@simmons-simmons.com
Website: www.simmons-simmons.com

Languages
Dutch, English, French, German, Spanish

Other offices
London, Rotterdam, Paris, Lisbon, Milan, Rome, Düsseldorf, Brussels, Madrid, Padua, Oporto, Madeira, Abu Dhabi, Qatar, Hong Kong, Shanghai, Tokyo, New York, Dubai

Number of lawyers 764
at this office 15

Contact
Ingrid Kalisch

CATEGORIES OF WORK

Corporate

Banking

Capital markets

Taxation

Projects, PFI

EU, competition

Dispute resolution

Intellectual property

Employment

Financial markets

Pharmaceutical and biotechnology

Energy and utilities

TMT

Transport

THÜMMEL, SCHÜTZE & PARTNER

GRUENEBURGWEG 102
60323 FRANKFURT

Telephone: +49 69 95 91 35 0
Fax: +49 69 95 91 35 30
E-mail: frankfurt@tsp-law.com
Website: www.tsp-law.com

Languages
German, English, French

Other offices
Berlin, Brussels, Dresden, Singapore, Stuttgart

Number of lawyers 58
at this office 14

Contact
Dr Hans-Jochen Otto

CATEGORIES OF WORK

Banking and finance
Dr Jochen Mittag, Dr Gabriele Fontane

Corporate and commercial
Marcus Rauschenberger

Mergers and acquisitions
Dr Hans-Jochen Otto,
Dr Gabriele Fontane,
Marcus Rauschenberger

Private equity
Dr Hans-Jochen Otto,
Dr Gabriele Fontane,
Marcus Rauschenberger

Tax
Dr Hans-Jochen Otto

THE FIRM

Thümmel, Schütze & Partner (TSP) was founded in 1973 in Stuttgart, where it still maintains its head office. Since its foundation it has established three further German offices at Frankfurt am Main, Dresden and Berlin. In addition to its German offices, TSP has been operating for more than 20 years in Singapore, the only German law firm with such a long-term presence in the Southeast Asian region.

The client structure of the firm corresponds to its services and international work: numerous well-known German and international banks as well as internationally orientated large and medium-sized enterprises regularly call on TSP's legal expertise. TSP is not affiliated with any other law firm, but it does maintain long-standing relationships with an assortment of leading foreign law firms.

Since the rise of the German private equity market about 15 years ago, TSP has advised private equity funds in their investments in Germany. The services include tax and legal transaction structuring, due diligence, acquisition finance and post-acquisition restructurings. In addition to private equity funds, TSP advises individuals and privately held companies of the German Mittelstand in divestment situations.

AREAS OF PRACTICE

TSP frequently advises mid-size and large companies in transaction work, often in cross-border transactions. As in the area of private equity, TSP offers transaction-related tax advice and provides legal services relating to all transaction stages.

TSP's services in the area of banking/capital markets range from general banking law, payment transactions, cash management, bank supervision, secured lending ad the documentation of financial products and structured financing. TSP has long-term experience in the issuing of securities, in particular the issuing of warrants, certificates, bonds and other derivatives. In addition, TSP regularly advises banks in finance-related litigation.

TAYLOR WESSING

SENCKENBERGANLAGE 20-22
60325 FRANKFURT AM MAIN

Telephone: +49 69 9 71 30 0
Fax: +49 69 9 71 30 10 0
E-mail: frankfurt@taylorwessing.com
Website: www.taylorwessing.com

Languages
English, Dutch, French, Italian, Mandarin, Spanish

Other offices
Alicante*, Berlin, Brussels, Cambridge, Dubai*, Düsseldorf/Neuss, Hamburg, London, Munich, Paris, Shanghai*

Number of lawyers 598
at this office 38

Member
World Law Group; Tech Law Group

CATEGORIES OF WORK

Banking and finance
Claus Goedecke, Peter Seemann

China desk
Florian Ranft

Commercial
Dr Christoph Hasche

Corporate/M&A
Bernhard Kloft

Employment and pensions
Axel C Filges

EU law/antitrust
Dr Marco Hartmann-Rüppel, Markus Wirtz

Intellectual property
Dr Sabine Rojahn

Life science
Dr Ulrich Steffen

Media and entertainment
Martin von Albrecht

Private client
Romana Traichel

Projects and finance
Dr Rüdiger von Hülst

Public commercial law
Dr Walter Potthast

Real estate and construction
Jan Wunschel

Regulatory affairs
Andreas Haak

Tax
Bernd Michel

Technology/IT/telecoms
Jörg Wimmers

WILLKIE FARR & GALLAGHER LLP

SENCKENBERGANLAGE 16
60325 FRANKFURT AM MAIN

Telephone: +49 69 79 30 20
Fax: +49 69 79 30 22 22
Website: www.willkie.com

Languages
English, French, Italian

Other offices
Brussels, London, Milan, New York, Paris, Rome, Washington DC

Number of lawyers 590
at this office 16

Contact
Sven-Erik Heun

CATEGORIES OF WORK

Telecoms, internet, media, and entertainment (TIME)

Intellectual property

Corporate and financial services

Information technology

Litigation

Mergers and acquisitions

Private equity

Restructuring

Tax

Real estate

Capital markets

WEIL, GOTSHAL & MANGES

TAUNUSANLAGE 1 (SKYPER)
60329 FRANKFURT AM MAIN

Telephone: +49 69 21 65 96 00
Fax: +49 69 21 65 96 99
Website: www.weil.com

Other offices
Austin, Boston, Brussels, Budapest, Dallas, Houston, London, Miami, Munich, New York, Paris, Prague, Providence, Shanghai, Silicon Valley, Singapore, Warsaw, Washington DC, Wilmington

Number of lawyers 1,200
at this office 41

Contact
Gerhard Schmidt (managing partner)

CATEGORIES OF WORK

Banking and finance	**Private equity**
Litigation	**Restructuring**
Mergers and acquisitions	**Taxation**

THE FIRM

Weil, Gotshal & Manges is a leader in the marketplace for sophisticated, international legal services. With more than 1,200 lawyers across the US, Europe and Asia, the firm serves many of the most successful companies in the world in their high-stakes matters and transactions. Weil Gotshal has built a world-class team of lawyers by pursuing a strategy of steady, purposeful growth. It continues to build upon a balanced platform of practices and locations without acquiring any debt. The firm's three primary departments – corporate, litigation/regulatory and restructuring – provide healthy diversification in all economic cycles, while its international expansion over the past decade has resulted in a quarter of the firm's lawyers now being in Europe.

AREAS OF PRACTICE

The firm's antitrust/competition practice advises on international M&A regulatory notifications, antitrust distribution counselling, cartels, litigation and government and state competition policy.

The corporate department is the firm's largest, with lawyers in the US and across Europe. The department advises international financial institutions and corporate clients in complex public and private mergers and acquisitions, private equity deals, strategic alliances and other commercial transactions.

The firm's corporate governance practice is recognised as the pre-eminent counsellor of corporate boards, management and institutional investors on the full range of governance issues, including board composition, structure and processes; executive and director compensation; director responsibilities, including in connection with mergers, spin-offs and other extraordinary transactions; internal and governmental investigations of alleged accounting or other corporate misconduct; and shareholder initiatives.

The firm is recognised as a market leader in the handling of complex and innovative finance transactions internationally. The firm advises on a wide range of financing activities and has particular expertise in acquisition finance, asset-based finance, debt restructuring and insolvency, debt and equity capital markets, derivatives, high-yield debt, securitisation, structured finance and telecom and multimedia financing.

The firm has a leading intellectual property and technology practice and advises a number of the world's major technology, media and telecommunications companies. It also acts for investors in technology, media and communications entities. The practice handles patent infringement, outsourcing transactions, strategic alliances, cross-border mergers and acquisitions, investments and IPOs. The firm advises on the protection and exploitation of IP and on a wide range of e-commerce matters including data protection. It has expertise in regulatory telecoms matters.

The firm's litigation practice advises international clients on all major areas of the law and has extensive experience in all aspects of dispute resolution. It advises clients in jury trials and appeals, as well as arbitration and alternative dispute forums.

The firm's real estate practice handles complex real estate transactions (including finance, securitisations, development, leasing, sales, acquisitions and debt restructurings) across the US and Europe. It also advises clients on real estate M&A transactions and transactions involving real estate investment trusts.

The firm has one of the largest, most broadly based bankruptcy and business reorganisation practices in the world. The department has been involved in virtually all major chapter 11 reorganisation cases in the US and in major national and international out of court debt restructurings.

The tax department provides advice to a broad range of international clients, covering many economic sectors. The department works closely with the firm's other departments to find innovative solutions to problems that present various and competing multidisciplinary considerations.

ALLEN & OVERY LLP

KEHRWIEDER 12
20457 HAMBURG

Telephone: +49 40 82 22 12 0
Fax: +49 40 82 22 12 20 0
E-mail: information@allenovery.com
Website: www.allenovery.com

Languages
Dutch, English, French, German, Hungarian, Italian, Japanese, Polish, Spanish

Other offices
Amsterdam, Antwerp, Bangkok, Beijing, Bratislava, Brussels, Budapest, Dubai, Frankfurt, Hong Kong, London, Luxembourg, Madrid, Milan, Moscow, New York, Paris, Prague, Rome, Shanghai, Singapore, Tokyo, Turin, Warsaw

Number of lawyers 2,304

Contacts
Dr Cornelius Fischer-Zernin,
Dr Neil George Weiand

CATEGORIES OF WORK

Asset financing/leasing	**IP/IT**
Antitrust/competition law	**Joint ventures and takeovers**
Arbitration	**Leveraged finance**
Banking regulatory	**Litigation**
Bond issues	**MBO and LBOs**
Business restructurings	**Mergers and acquisitions**
Company law	**Private equity**
Derivatives	**Project finance**
Employment law	**Public and administrative law**
Energy law	**Real estate and finance**
Environmental law	**Securitisation**
Equity capital markets	**Tax**
Global loans	**Telecommunications law**

BOLLMANN & PARTNER GbR

STADTHAUSBRUECKE 12
20355 HAMBURG

Telephone: +49 40 37 86 87 0
Fax: +49 40 37 86 87 20

Languages
English, French

Other offices
Copenhagen, St Petersburg

Number of lawyers 5

Contacts
Dr Michael Boemke
(dr.boemke@bollmann-hh.de),
Dr Knut Suhr
(dr.suhr@bollmann-hh.de),
Alexander Schmidt
(a.schmidt@bollmann-hh.de),
Verena Zahn
(verena.zahn@web.de)

CATEGORIES OF WORK

Company law
Dr Michael Boemke, Dr Knut Suhr

International sales law
Dr Knut Suhr, Dr Michael Boemke

Agency
Dr Knut Suhr, Dr Michael Boemke

Arbitration
Dr Knut Suhr, Dr Michael Boemke

Litigation
Verena Zahn, Alexander Schmidt

Employment law
Verena Zahn

Labour law
Verena Zahn

Transport and maritime law
Dr Knut Suhr, Alexander Schmidt

Administrative law
Alexander Schmidt

Tax
Jobst-Günther Maeder

Family law
Verena Zahn

BRÖDERMANN & JAHN

NEUER WALL 71
HAMBURG 20354

Telephone: +49 40 37 09 05 0
Fax: +49 40 37 09 05 55
E-mail: broedermann@german-law.com
Website: www.german-law.com

Languages
English, French, German, Portuguese, Spanish, Swedish

Number of lawyers 9

Contacts
Dr Eckart Brödermann, Dr Phillip von Dietze

Member
Consulegis

CATEGORIES OF WORK

Mergers and acquisitions
Dr Eckart Brödermann,
Dr Phillip von Dietze

Corporate law
Dr Phillip von Dietze

Arbitration and international litigation
Dr Eckart Brödermann,
Dr Andrea Tiedemann

Commercial law, distribution, franchise
Dr Phillip von Dietze, Tina Denso

IT law
Dr Eckard von Bodenhausen

Customs
Tina Denso

Insurance
Dr Eckard von Bodenhausen

European law
Dr Eckart Brödermann,
Dr Phillip von Dietze

Antitrust law (including merger control)
Dr Phillip von Dietze

Conflict of laws
Dr Eckart Brödermann,
Dr Andrea Tiedemann

Labour law
Dr Andrea Tiedemann

Inheritance law
Dr Andrea Tiedemann

Real estate
Dr Eckard von Bodenhausen

Trade marks
Dr Phillip von Dietze

BUSE HEBERER FROMM

HARVESTEHUDER WEG 23
20149 HAMBURG

Telephone: +49 40 41 99 90
Fax: +49 40 41 99 91 69
E-mail: hamburg@buse.de
Website: www.buse.de

Languages
Chinese, English, French, Italian, Portuguese, Spanish, Swedish

Other offices
Berlin, Düsseldorf, Essen, Frankfurt am Main, Munich, New York, Palma de Mallorca, Sydney, Zurich

Number of lawyers 120
at this office 25

Member
The European Legal Alliance:
Beauchamps (Ireland); Dubarry Le Douarin Veil (France); Field Fisher Waterhouse (England); Harper Macleod (Scotland); Jimenez de Parga (Spain); La Scala & Associati (Italy)

CATEGORIES OF WORK

Banking and finance

Antitrust and merger control

Commerce, transport, insurance

Commercial delinquency

Corporate/M&A

Industrial property and copyrights

Information technology and telecommunications

Labour and employment

Litigation and arbitration, national and international

Press and media

Property and construction

Public law

Tax

CMS HASCHE SIGLE

STADTHAUSBRÜCKE 1-3
20355 HAMBURG

Telephone: +49 40 37 63 00
Fax: +49 40 37 63 04 06 00
E-mail: hamburg@cms-hs.com
Website: www.cms-hs.com

Languages
English, French, Italian, Spanish

Other offices
Belgrade, Berlin, Brussels, Chemnitz, Cologne, Dresden, Düsseldorf, Frankfurt, Leipzig, Moscow, Munich, Prague, Stuttgart

Number of lawyers 420
at this office 69

Other CMS alliance member firms
CMS Adonnino Ascoli & Cavasola Scamoni, Italy; CMS Albiñana & Suárez de Lezo, Spain; CMS Bureau Francis Lefebvre, France; CMS Cameron McKenna, UK; CMS DeBacker, Belgium; CMS Derks Star Busmann, Netherlands; CMS von Erlach Henrici, Switzerland; CMS Reich-Rohrwig Hainz, Austria

CATEGORIES OF WORK

Corporate	**IT and telecommunications**
Mergers and acquisitions	**Tax**
Private equity and venture capital	**Estate planning**
Banking	**Insolvency**
Stock trading and capital markets	**Utilities**
Competition and merger control	**Public commercial and environment, procurement**
State aid and EU law	**Distribution and franchise law**
Intellectual property, copyright, media and press	**Insurance**
Individual and collective labour law	**Maritime, shipping and transport**
Real estate and construction	**Litigation and arbitration**

DLA PIPER RUDNICK GRAY CARY

JUNGFERSTIEG 7
20354 HAMBURG

Telephone: +49 40 1 88 88 0
Fax: +49 40 1 88 88 11
E-mail: klaus.vongierke@dlapiper.com
Website: www.dlapiper.com/germany

Languages
English, French, German, Italian, Russian, Swedish

Other offices
Austria, Belgium, Bosnia-Herzegovina, China, Croatia, Czech Republic, Denmark*, Egypt*, France, Germany, Georgia, Hong Kong, Hungary, Italy, Japan, Netherlands, Norway*, Poland*, Russia, Singapore*, Slovakia, South Africa*, Spain, Sweden*, Thailand, UK, Ukraine, United Arab Emirates, US

Number of lawyers 3,100
at this office 14

Contact
Dr Klaus von Gierke

Member
DLA Piper Group

CATEGORIES OF WORK

Commercial
Dr Klaus von Gierke

Litigation and arbitration
Dr Johannes Matz

Corporate, mergers and acquisitions
Dr Klaus von Gierke

Marine
Carsten Grau

HR and employment
Volker von Alvensleben

Technology, media and communications
Kristina Maier

THE FIRM

DLA Piper Rudnick Gray Cary is a leading global legal services provider with approximately 3,100 lawyers in 58 offices across 22 countries. The organisation is committed to building long-term relationships with its clients and supports their strategic and operational needs both locally and internationally.

In Germany, DLA Piper Rudnick Gray Cary is a 50-lawyer-strong team with offices in Cologne, Frankfurt and Hamburg. The office has well-established German lawyers who are highly experienced in both national and international legal work. It specialises in all aspects of business law, from corporate and project finance to real estate, employment and IT/media. There are plans to open offices in other major cities in Germany within the next year as part of its strategy to build a national practice across the country.

DLA Piper is a founding member of an exclusive alliance of full-service legal organisations with a shared vision. DLA Piper Group, established in 1999, has members across Europe, Africa, the Middle East, Asia and the US, which deliver expert local know-how and integrated international solutions.

AREAS OF PRACTICE

Corporate, mergers and acquisitions: advises mid-sized and large organisations on all types of transactional and advisory matters and has a growing international reputation within the corporate market.

Commercial: structuring transactions, drafting a whole range of civil and commercial law contracts and participation in business negotiations.

HR and employment: practical experience of helping clients mould their people strategies and work practices, including preparation of employment contracts, assistance in labour disputes and redundancy, in outsourcing, post-merger integration and restructuring.

Marine: offers specialised legal advice in all fields of transport and maritime law, ranging from traditional maritime law over European land transport law, based on the CMR Convention, to the complex and still developing laws on combined and multimodal transports.

Technology, media and communications: provides contentious and non-contentious advice in areas of IT/outsourcing, sports, e-commerce, data protection and privacy.

Litigation: experience in all aspects of commercial dispute management, working in partnership with clients to manage the litigation process so as to minimise risk and maximise certainty.

DABELSTEIN & PASSEHL

GROSSE ELBSTRASSE 36
22767 HAMBURG

Telephone: +49 40 31 77 97 0
Fax: +49 40 31 77 97 77
E-mail: hamburg@da-pa.com
Website: www.da-pa.com

Languages
English, French, Spanish

Other offices
Leer

Number of lawyers 12

CATEGORIES OF WORK

Carriage of goods/bill of lading
Dieter Schwampe, Rüdiger Warnke

Yacht building and insurance
Jan Dreyer, Stefan Schrandt

Ship finance
Thomas Brüggemann, Stefan Schrandt

Ship arrest
Thomas Brüggemann

Ship and plant construction
Jan Dreyer, Stefan Schrandt

German-English legal proceedings
Rüdiger Warnke, Esther Mallach

Land and air transport
Esther Mallach, Rüdiger Warnke

Charterparty disputes
Thomas Brüggemann,
Dieter Schwampe

Insurance
Dieter Schwampe, Jan Dreyer

DÄNISCHE ADVOKATEN

FOCUS ADVOKATER LLP

AN DER ALSTER 71
20099 HAMBURG

Telephone: +49 40 24 91 92
Fax: +49 40 24 04 09
E-mail:mail@daenische-advokaten.de
Website: www.focus-advokater.dk

Languages
English, French, Spanish, the Scandinavian languages

Other offices
Copenhagen, Odense, Paris*, Nice*

Number of lawyers 43
at this office 1

Contacts
Knud K Damsgaard, Uwe Teichert

The categories listed apply only to Focus Advokater, the firm's office in Denmark

CATEGORIES OF WORK

Arbitration and litigation

Banking, securities and finance

Companies, commercial law (general)

Construction

EU and competition

Environmental law

Insolvency

Intellectual property

Mergers and acquisitions

Ship and aircraft finance

Tax

Transport

HAARMANN HEMMELRATH

JUNGFERNSTIEG 30
20354 HAMBURG

Telephone: +49 40 35 00 60
Fax: +49 40 35 00 61 33
E-mail: hamburg@haarmannhemmelrath.com
Website: www.haarmannhemmelrath.com

Languages
English, French, Japanese, Mandarin

Other offices
Bielefeld, Bucharest, Budapest, Düsseldorf, Frankfurt, Leipzig, Moscow, Munich, Paris, Prague, Shanghai, Warsaw

Number of lawyers 226

CATEGORIES OF WORK

Corporate and business
Dr Oliver Tomat

Mergers and acquisitions
Thilo Rohde

Privatisation

Legal and tax reorganisation
Dr Thomas Lübbehüsen

Capital markets
Dr Oliver Tomat

Real estate development
Dr Marc Biebelheimer

Banking law, leasing

International tax
Dr Thomas Lübbehüsen

National tax
Marco Berndt, Jan Rickauer

Audit and accounting services
Holger Böge

Due diligence services
Uwe Wolf

Corporate restructuring, insolvency
Stefan Ulrich Denkhaus, Friedrich von Kaltenborn-Stachau

Labour law
Dr Daniela Heise

HARMSEN UTESCHER

ALTER WALL 55
20457 HAMBURG

Telephone: +49 40 37 69 09 0
Fax: +49 40 37 69 09 99
E-mail: contact@harmsen.utescher.com
Website: www.harmsen.utescher.com

Languages
English, French, Italian

Number of lawyers 19

CATEGORIES OF WORK

German and international trade mark law

Patent and utility-model law

Unfair competition law

IT and new media law

Copyright law, registered design law

Pharmaceutical law, medical products law

Food and cosmetics law

German and European antitrust law

Media law

Sports law

HEUKING KÜHN LÜER WOJTEK

BLEICHENBRÜCKE 9
20354 HAMBURG

Telephone: +49 40 35 52 80 0
Fax: +49 40 35 52 80 80
E-mail: hamburg@heuking.de
Website: www.heuking.de

Languages
German, English, French, Italian, Spanish

Other offices
Berlin, Brussels, Chemnitz, Cologne, Düsseldorf, Frankfurt, Munich

Number of lawyers 31

Contact
Dr Stefan Duhnkrack

CATEGORIES OF WORK

- Corporate, partnerships, international mergers and acquisitions, general commercial law
- Competition, merger control and state aids
- Project finance
- Insurance
- Litigation and arbitration
- Environmental and public law
- Energy law
- Entertainment, media, publishing, copyright
- Intellectual property law
- Property and real estate law
- Employment and labour law
- Maritime law
- Transport law, postal services and logistics
- IT, e-commerce and telecommunications

THE FIRM

Heuking Kühn Lüer Wojtek was founded in Düsseldorf, Germany, in 1971. Since then, the firm has spread geographically, and Heuking Kühn now has seven significant offices in Germany, as well as an office in Brussels.

The firm has an extensive international network of law firms, enabling it to provide its clients with seamless 'one-stop shopping', on international transactions and regulatory matters. Since its formation, Heuking Kühn Lüer Wojtek has specifically chosen to remain an independent law firm. It is Heuking Kühn Lüer Wojtek's philosophy that, to provide the best possible service to its clients, the firm must be able to co-operate with various other law firms which are at the top of the profession in their respective countries. This gives the firm the ability to make alternative counsel suggestions to its clients, giving the clients a choice of the best suitable law firm or lawyer in each country and for each matter. Over the last 30+ years, Heuking Kühn Lüer Wojtek has developed excellent relationships with the key firms in all of the major jurisdictions worldwide.

Heuking Kühn Lüer Wojtek is a name which is synonymous with legal competence. The firm is one of the largest commercial law firms in Germany, with more than 170 specialised lawyers and tax advisers, representing the interests of national and international clients. Included in the client list are large and medium-sized German and international companies in all areas of the manufacturing industry, as well as trade and service industries, associations, governmental and public sector organisations and private clients and trusts.

The firm prides itself on substantive legal competence and on the excellent education and continuing legal education of its lawyers. Moreover, virtually all of the lawyers are German-English bilingual.

Extensive specialisation and comprehensive knowledge of specific industry sectors provide the basis of all of Heuking Kühn Lüer Wojtek's legal counselling. Experienced partners and carefully selected associate lawyers develop innovative solutions to complex legal problems. The lawyers regularly work in their specific practice area groups and also in multi-group and multidisciplinary teams with clients and outside consultants or advisers. Entrepreneurial thinking on behalf of firm clients, as well as efficient, quality, cost-effective and timely work and the highest personal dedication are key components of Heuking Kühn Lüer Wojtek's culture.

AREAS OF PRACTICE

Heuking Kühn Lüer Wojtek is a full-service commercial law firm. Cross-border and cross-sector knowledge in combination with a deep understanding of business reasoning enables service to clients with the broadest possible support in all their negotiations and business decisions. This applies equally to M&A transactions, to legal advice on company structure, business risk management, negotiations and negotiation tactics, training, crisis and insolvency counselling, corporate financial matters, and complex litigation and arbitration. Thanks to a variety of strong business clients, the firm has built long-term relationships with its clients and can assist them, beginning with the establishment of a business, followed by implementing business goals, including day-to-day legal work, reorganisations, acquisitions and divestitures.

Heuking Kühn Lüer Wojtek is actively involved with its clients in providing regulatory counselling in all areas of commercial law, as well as assisting them in organising and implementing their M&A transactions in Germany, throughout Europe, and internationally. Heuking Kühn Lüer Wojtek has particular expertise in German and EU company law; competition law, merger control, state aids and regulated industries (including energy; telecommunications; and transport, postal services and shipping law); taxation; employment law; finance and banking; international trade and customs; insurance; litigation, arbitration and mediation; bankruptcy and insolvency; environment, health and safety law; product liability; product-specific regulation; real estate and construction law; IP, IT and media law; and private clients and family law.

HUTH DIETRICH HAHN

WARBURGSTRASSE 50
20354 HAMBURG

Telephone: +49 40 41 52 50
Fax: +49 40 41 52 51 11
E-mail: info@hdh.net
Website: www.hdh.net

Languages
English, French, Spanish

Number of lawyers 20

CATEGORIES OF WORK

Mergers and acquisitions, corporate finance
All partners

IPO
All partners

Corporate law
All partners

Private equity
All partners

Tax law
All partners

Venture capital
Dr Röttger

Real property law
Dr Stucken, Herr Strasburger

Antitrust law
Dr Aries

Public law
Herr Strasburger

Media law
Dr Aries

Succession planning, heritage law
Dr Wittuhn

THE FIRM

Huth Dietrich Hahn was established in 1990 and currently has 20 lawyers. The firm has the advantage of being big enough to take on and deal effectively with considerably large matters, for example in the field of mergers and acquisitions, whilst also retaining a reputation for advising individual clients on smaller matters.

All of the partners of the firm have had considerable working experience in the legal profession in different jurisdictions, with some of the firm's partners having graduated with Masters Degrees in the United States.

As a result of such extensive international experience and expertise, the firm has been able to associate with and establish a network with other firms of foreign lawyers. Such firms were selected by Huth Dietrich Hahn on the strength of the high-quality services which they provide to their clients and accordingly, the firm is able to offer its clients services not only within Germany and the rest of Europe, but in almost all countries worldwide.

AREAS OF PRACTICE

The firm specialises in the field of acquisitions and mergers, and is able to provide a broad range of advice on acquisitions, restructuring and corporate finance. The firm will advise the client throughout the transaction, from the letter of intent, during the due diligence process, and throughout negotiation, whilst also advising on the tax implications of the transaction, restructuring and financing. The firm is also able to provide related services in the areas of antitrust and labour law.

Huth Dietrich Hahn's practice also covers matters of IPOs of companies, and further areas of the firm's expertise include real property, the laws of succession (in particular with respect to companies), tax law for both corporate bodies and individuals, antitrust law, European Community law and public law (especially in the areas of East German law).

INCE & CO

GROSSE ELBSTRASSE 47
22767 HAMBURG

Telephone: +49 40 38 08 60
Fax: +49 40 38 08 61 00
E-mail: firstname.lastname@incelaw.com
Website: www.incelaw.com

Languages
English, French, German, Italian, Polish, Russian, Sinhalese, Spanish

Other offices
Hong Kong, Le Havre, London, Paris, Piraeus, Shanghai, Singapore

Number of lawyers 228
at this office 11

Contact
Detlef Zschoche

CATEGORIES OF WORK

Aviation
Axel Salander, Jan Hungar

Business and finance
Detlef Zschoche, Jan Hungar

Commercial disputes
Axel Salander, Detlef Zschoche, David McInnes

Energy
Axel Salander

Insurance and reinsurance
Detlef Zschoche, Jan Hungar, David McInnes

Shipping and trade
Detlef Zschoche, Axel Salander, David McInnes, Jan Hungar

THE FIRM

Ince & Co is an international law firm, with offices in Hamburg, Hong Kong, Le Havre, London, Paris, Piraeus, Shanghai and Singapore. The firm practises English, French, German and Hong Kong law, in six main business strands. Underpinning the firm's expertise is a clear grasp of clients' commercial needs. Ince & Co provides non-contentious business and finance advice for clients in a wide range of industries, and also deploys all methods of dispute resolution.

AREAS OF PRACTICE

Aviation: with a team that 'really understands the aviation business' (*The Legal 500*, 2005) and with in-depth market knowledge, Ince & Co has the flexibility to handle any kind of aviation matter anywhere in the world – from aircraft purchase to major incidents and lesser accidents worldwide. The firm often deploys legal tools to solve problems that appear to be mainly commercial in nature. For crises or disasters, the Ince Worldwide Emergency Response Service is only a phone call away.

Business and finance: the firm's team of specialist commercial lawyers works with clients to find the answers that help drive their businesses forward. With the combination of high levels of commercial nous and a capacity for hard work, the firm can help clients achieve their goals – whether acquisition, disposal, joint venture or conclusion of a complex commercial contract. Ince & Co's experience ranges from management buy-outs, through the resolution of shareholder disputes to difficult employment issues.

Commercial disputes: once described in the press as 'brutal litigators', the firm also has a lighter touch. Ince & Co's expertise covers all forms of dispute resolution, ranging from dialogue, through ADR to arbitration and court proceedings. Where litigation is judged to be in a client's interests, or is unavoidable, the firm draws on immense experience in the commercial courts of the countries where it has offices, and a worldwide network of correspondent lawyers. The firm's cases come from many sectors, including sport, entertainment and financial services.

Energy: the firm has been in the oil and gas business for as long as many of its clients. Since the early days of North Sea development, the firm's energy practice has spread all around the world, both onshore and off, from exploration and drilling to FPSOs and refineries. It now extends to renewable sources such as wind.

Insurance and reinsurance: Ince & Co's team serves clients who provide coverage, those who broke it and those who purchase it. Whether the case is contentious or non-contentious and however straightforward or complex the subject matter insured, the firm offers all the legal services required in these industries. The firm's direct insurance practice covers all manner of insurance claims, including marine and energy insurance, political contingent and credit risk, and coverage disputes. Reinsurance is also a strong area of focus for the firm. The team advises on, among other things, every aspect of run-off business.

Shipping and trade: from shipyard to scrapyard, from factory to receiver, from finance to flotation, the firm provides all the legal services required by the shipping and commodities industries. The firm counts among its clients many of the world's leading shipowners, charterers, shipbuilders, traders, banks and insurers. *The Legal 500* refers to the firm's 'unrivalled knowledge of the market' and its 'strength in depth'.

Emergency Response: Ince & Co operates a 24-hour emergency response service, 365 days a year. It has vast experience of the practical and legal problems following a major emergency, disaster or crisis. Its teams can respond immediately to a wide range of incidents, from accidents in the aviation, shipping, energy, hotel and rail sectors, including pollution and contamination, through natural disasters and outbreaks of disease, to terrorist acts. Tel: +44 20 7283 6999.

LOVELLS

WARBURGSTRASSE 50
20354 HAMBURG

Telephone: +49 40 41 99 30
Fax: +49 40 41 99 32 00
E-mail: reception.hamburg@lovells.com
Website: www.lovells.de

Languages
English, French, Italian, Russian, Spanish

Other offices
Alicante, Amsterdam, Beijing, Berlin, Brussels, Budapest*, Chicago, Düsseldorf, Frankfurt, Ho Chi Minh City, Hong Kong, London, Madrid, Milan, Moscow, Munich, New York, Paris, Prague, Rome, Shanghai, Singapore, Tokyo, Warsaw, Zagreb*

Number of lawyers 1,600
at this office 52

Contact
Volker Meinberg

CATEGORIES OF WORK

- **Corporate/M&A, private equity**
- **Restructuring and insolvency**
- **Banking**
- **Antitrust and unfair competition**
- **Capital markets**
- **Project finance, public private partnerships**
- **Tax**
- **Employment**
- **Intellectual property**
- **Real estate**
- **Projects**
- **Technology, media, telecommunications**
- **Litigation, product liability**
- **International arbitration**
- **Food and drug regulations**
- **Law of Eastern Europe**

O & P OBERTHÜR & PARTNER

ARNOLD-HEISE-STRASSE 10
20249 HAMBURG

Telephone: +49 40 35 50 57 0
Fax: +49 40 35 50 57 13
E-mail: info@oberthuer.de
Website: www.oberthuer.de

Languages
English, French, Spanish

Number of lawyers 7

Contact
Ms Andrea Bohl

CATEGORIES OF WORK

- **Public real estate law**
- **Private real estate law (including consultancy, preparation of project management and other contracts)**
- **Construction law**
- **Architectural law**
- **Legal consultancy (purchase and sale, valuation and commercialisation of properties, realisation of major building schemes during the course of approval procedure, etc)**
- **Commercial and environmental law**
- **Public duty and fee**
- **Public contracts**
- **Placing of public orders**
- **Federal air pollution**
- **Neighbourhood problems**
- **Expropriation and eminent domain**
- **Development costs**
- **Development schemes**

TAYLOR WESSING

NEUER WALL 44
20354 HAMBURG

Telephone: +49 40 3 68 03-0
Fax: +49 40 3 68 03 28 0
E-mail: hamburg@taylorwessing.com
Website: www.taylorwessing.com

Languages
Dutch, English, French, Italian, Mandarin, Spanish

Other offices
Alicante*, Berlin, Brussels, Cambridge, Dubai*, Düsseldorf/Neuss, Frankfurt, London, Munich, Paris, Shanghai*

Number of lawyers 598
at this office 54

Member
World Law Group; Tech Law Group

CATEGORIES OF WORK

Banking and finance
Claus Goedecke, Peter Seemann

China desk
Florian Ranft

Commercial
Dr Christoph Hasche

Corporate/M&A
Bernhard Kloft

Employment and pensions
Axel C Filges

EU law/antitrust
Dr Marco Hartmann-Rüppel, Markus Wirtz

Intellectual property
Dr Sabine Rojahn

Life science
Dr Ulrich Steffen

Media and entertainment
Martin von Albrecht

Private client
Romana Traichel

Projects and finance
Dr Rüdiger von Hülst

Public commercial law
Dr Walter Potthast

Real estate and construction
Jan Wunschel

Regulatory affairs
Andreas Haak

Tax
Bernd Michel

Technology/IT/telecoms
Jörg Wimmers

UEXKÜLL & STOLBERG

BESELERSTR 4
22607 HAMBURG

Telephone: +49 40 89 96 54 0
Fax: +49 40 89 96 54 88
E-mail: postmaster@uex.de
Website: www.uex.de

Languages
English, German

Other offices
Munich

Number of lawyers 23
at this office 21

CATEGORIES OF WORK

Patents and licensing – chemistry
Dr Allard von Kameke, Dr Peter Franck

Patents and licensing – biotechnology
Ingeborg Voelker, Dr Albrecht von Menges

Patents and licensing – medical and electrical engineering
Jürgen Suchantke, Arnulf Huber

Trade marks
Dr Frank Dettmann, Dr Allard von Kameke

Design registration
Jürgen Suchantke, Dr Frank Dettmann

Unfair competition
Dr Frank Dettmann

WATSON, FARLEY & WILLIAMS

WATSON, FARLEY & WILLIAMS LLP

VAN-DER-SMISSEN-STRAßE 9
HAMBURG 22767

Telephone: +49 40 80 80 34 40
Fax: +49 40 80 80 34 41 0
Website: www.wfw.com

Languages
Afrikaans, Arabic, Cantonese, Danish, Dutch, English, French, German, Greek, Gujarati, Hebrew, Hindi, Italian, Malay, Mandarin, Marathi, Nowegian, Polish, Russian, Spanish, Swahili, Swedish, Thai

Other offices
Bangkok, London, New York, Paris, Piraeus, Rome, Singapore

Number of lawyers 198
at this office 13

Contacts
Lothar Wegener, Thomas Hollenhorst, Maren Brandes

CATEGORIES OF WORK

- **Asset/ship finance**
- **Project finance**
- **Trade finance**
- **Leasing**
- **Workouts and restructuring**
- **Financial services**
- **M&A**
- **Private equity**
- **Corporate finance**
- **Energy projects**
- **Real estate**
- **Marine and other insurance**
- **Shipbuilding, ship repair**
- **Commercial and finance litigation**
- **International and domestic arbitration**
- **Marine litigation**
- **Tax**

TIEFENBACHER

IM BREITSPIEL 9
69126 HEIDELBERG

Telephone: +49 62 21 31 13 10
Fax: +49 62 21 31 13 11
Website: www.tiefenbacher.de
E-mail: ID@tiefenbacher.de

Languages
English, French, Italian, Spanish

Other offices
Chemnitz, Dresden, Erfurt, Hamburg, Jena, Stuttgart

Number of lawyers 43
at this office 18

Contact
Thomas Kohl MBA

Member
Association of European Lawyers (AEL); ALFA International; International Business Law Consortium (IBLC); Transatlantic Law International (TALI)

CATEGORIES OF WORK

Banking and finance
Peter Pfennigs

Leasing
Peter Pfennigs, Ingo Schellpeper

Commercial and corporate
Jürgen Dernbach, Tobias Bieber

Insolvency
Jürgen Dernbach, Karsten Wagner

Tax
Jürgen Dernbach, Dr Harald Riedel

IP, IT, competition
Thomas Kohl MBA, Thorsten Ehrhard

Labour law
Peter Pfennigs, Annemarie Böttcher

Construction and architecture
Dr Johannes Bickel, Christof Werkle

Family law
Ingrid Möllinger

Commercial agents law
Judith Hasel, Christiane Seidel

Succession
Christof Werkle

Energy
Dr Birgit Chorianopoulos

EU and international
Thomas Kohl MBA, Marcello Di Stefano

M&A
Thomas Kohl MBA

CMS HASCHE SIGLE

AUGUSTUSPLATZ 9
04109 LEIPZIG

Telephone: +49 341 2 16 72 0
Fax: +49 341 2 16 72 33
E-mail: leipzig@cms-hs.com
Website: www.cms-hs.com

Languages
English, French, Italian

Other offices
Belgrade, Berlin, Brussels, Chemnitz, Cologne, Dresden, Düsseldorf, Frankfurt, Hamburg, Moscow, Munich, Prague, Stuttgart

Number of lawyers 420
at this office 22

Other CMS alliance member firms
CMS Adonnino Ascoli & Cavasola Scamoni, Italy; CMS Albiñana & Suárez de Lezo, Spain; CMS Bureau Francis Lefebvre, France; CMS Cameron McKenna, UK; CMS DeBacker, Belgium; CMS Derks Star Busmann, Netherlands; CMS von Erlach Henrici, Switzerland; CMS Reich-Rohrwig Hainz, Austria

CATEGORIES OF WORK

Corporate

Mergers and acquisitions

Private equity and venture capital

Banking

Stock trading and capital markets

Competition and merger control

State aid and EU law

Intellectual property, copyright, media and press

Individual and collective labour law

Real estate and construction

IT and telecommunications

Tax

Estate planning

Insolvency

Utilities

Public commercial and environment, procurement

Distribution and franchise law

Insurance

Maritime, shipping and transport

Litigation and arbitration

HAARMANN HEMMELRATH

NEUMARKT 9A
04109 LEIPZIG

Telephone: +49 341 12 63 0
Fax: +49 341 12 63 13 3
E-mail:
leipzig@haarmannhemmelrath.com
Website:
www.haarmannhemmelrath.com

Languages
English, French, Russian

Other offices
Bielefeld, Bucharest, Budapest, Düsseldorf, Frankfurt, Hamburg, Moscow, Munich, Paris, Prague, Shanghai, Warsaw

Number of lawyers 226

CATEGORIES OF WORK

Corporate and business law
Bernd Brinkmann

Mergers and acquisitions
Bernd Brinkmann

Intellectual property, antitrust, EU law, media law, telecommunications
Bernd Brinkmann

Corporate recovery, insolvency
Niels Bahr

Public law
Dr Gabriel Glos

National tax law and compliance
Niels Bahr

Audit and accounting services
Niels Bahr

Construction law
Axel Heuchert

Labour law
Dr Dagmar Unger

Litigation, mediation, arbitration
Bernd Brinkmann

BETTE – BRINK

GROSSE BLEICHE 60-62
55116 MAINZ

Telephone: +49 61 31 28 77 00
Fax: +49 61 31 28 77 09 9
E-mail: bette-brink@mainz.juropartner.de
Website: www.bette-brink.de

Languages
Czech, English, French, Polish, Spanish

Other offices
Berlin, Erfurt

Number of lawyers 12
at this office 7

Member
Juropartner (European Society for Economic Interests)

CATEGORIES OF WORK

Banking law
Dr Ulrich Brink, Tomasz Stockhaus

Company law
Dr Ulrich Brink, Almut Diederichsen

Fiscal law
Dr Ulrich Brink

Leasing law
Dr Ulrich Brink, Peter Schultz

Industrial relations law
Christian v der Lühe, Bengt Scheiner

Company environment law
Christian v der Lühe

European law
Almut Diederichsen, Christian v der Lühe

International private law
Almut Diederichsen

Law governing factoring and financing
Barbara Samuelsen, Dr Ulrich Brink

RITTERSHAUS
LAW OFFICES

HARRLACHWEG 4
68163 MANNHEIM

Telephone: +49 621 42 56 0
Fax: +49 621 42 56 25 0
E-mail: info@rittershaus.net
Website: www.rittershaus.net

Languages
English, French, Italian, Russian, Spanish

Other offices
Frankfurt

Number of lawyers 32
at this office 24

Contacts
Prof Dr Christof Hettich, Rainer Dietmann

CATEGORIES OF WORK

Companies, corporations
Prof Dr Christof Hettich, Dr Martin Bürmann

Mergers and acquisitions
Rainer Dietmann, Verena Eisenlohr LLM

Competition, antitrust
Dr Daniel Weisert, Dr Bernd M Zinow

Real property and construction law
Andreas Pauli, Britta Martensen

Administrative and public law
Andreas Schmidt LLM

Arbitration
Prof Dr Gerald Rittershaus, Prof Dr Christof Hettich

Private clients, inheritance law
Dr Martin Bürmann, Dr Patrick Certa

Employment, labour
Dr Andreas Notz, Dr Annette Sättele

Sports and entertainment
Rainer Dietmann, Nico Rittershaus

Tax
Prof Dr Christoph Hettich, Rainer Dietmann

Insolvency law, restructuring
Andreas Schmidt LLM

Private equity
Verena Eisenlohr LLM, Dr Barbara von Horstig

ROSPATT OSTEN PROSS
RECHTSANWÄLTE

JANDERSTRASSE 8
68199 MANNHEIM

Telephone: +49 621 84 55 37 5
Fax: +49 621 84 55 37 6
E-mail: mail@rospatt.de
Website: www.rospatt.de

Languages
English, French

Other offices
Düsseldorf

Number of lawyers 11
at this office 1

CATEGORIES OF WORK

Patents, utility models

Trade marks

Design patents

Copyrights

Unfair competition

Product liability

Litigation, arbitration, licensing

ASHURST

PRINZREGENTENSTRASSE 18
80538 MÜNCHEN

Telephone: +49 89 24 44 21 100
Fax: +49 89 24 44 21 101
Website: www.ashurst.com

Languages
English, French, German

Other offices
Brussels, Dubai, Frankfurt, London, Madrid, Milan, New Delhi*, New York, Paris, Singapore, Tokyo

Number of lawyers 748
at this office 20

Contact
Simon Beddow

CATEGORIES OF WORK

Arbitration
Karl Wach

Corporate and commercial
Reinhard Eyring, Hermann Schlindwein

Employment
Andreas Vogel

Intellectual property/ information technology
Manja Epping

Insolvency
Karl Wach

Litigation
Karl Wach

White-collar crime
Karl Wach

Mergers and acquisitions
Reinhard Eyring, Hermann Schlindwein

Private equity
Hermann Schlindwein

Venture capital
Reinhard Eyring

Tax
Klaus Herkenroth

BAKER & McKENZIE LLP

THEATINERSTRASSE 23
80333 MÜNCHEN

Telephone: +49 89 55 23 80
Fax: +49 89 55 23 81 99
Website: www.bakernet.com

Languages
English, French, Italian, Polish, Spanish

Other offices Almaty, Amsterdam, Antwerp, Baku, Bangkok, Barcelona, Beijing, Berlin, Bogotá, Bologna, Brasilia, Brussels, Budapest, Buenos Aires, Cairo, Calgary, Cancun, Caracas, Chicago, Chihuahua, Dallas, Düsseldorf, Frankfurt, Geneva, Guadalajara, Hanoi, Ho Chi Minh City, Hong Kong, Houston, Jakarta, Juarez, Kuala Lumpur, Kyiv, London, Madrid, Manama, Manila, Melbourne, Mexico City, Miami, Milan, Monterrey, Moscow, New York, Palo Alto, Paris, Porto Alegré, Prague, Rio de Janeiro, Riyadh, Rome, St Petersburg, San Diego, San Francisco, Santiago, São Paulo, Shanghai, Singapore, Stockholm, Sydney, Taipei, Tijuana, Tokyo, Toronto, Valencia, Vienna, Warsaw, Washington DC, Zürich

Number of lawyers 3,300+
at this office 25+

CATEGORIES OF WORK

Banking and finance
Michael Foundethakis

Capital markets
Andreas Lohner

Company and commercial law
Ulf Wauschkuhn

Information technology, media and computer law
Wolfgang Fritzemeyer, Christoph Rittweger

Intellectual property
Constanze Ulmer-Eilfort, Wolfgang Fritzemeyer

Labour law
Bernhard Trappehl, Mark Zimmer

Litigation and arbitration
Stephan Spehl, Truiken Heydn

Mergers and acquisitions
Florian Kästle, Jörg Wössner, Udo Henkel

Private equity and venture capital
Florian Kästle, Udo Henkel

Tax
Udo Henkel

THE FIRM

Baker & McKenzie has provided sophisticated legal advice and services to many of the world's most dynamic and global organisations for more than 50 years. With a network of more than 3,300 locally qualified, internationally experienced lawyers in 38 countries, the firm has the knowledge and resources to deliver the broad scope of quality legal services required to respond effectively to both international and local needs – consistently, confidently and with a sensitivity for cultural, social and legal practice differences.

Baker & McKenzie has been established in Europe for over 40 years, having opened its first European offices in 1957. Since then, the European and Middle Eastern network has grown to 29 offices, giving it unparalleled geographical coverage.

The Frankfurt am Main office was formed in 1962; the office in Berlin was opened on 1 March 1990; the Munich office on 1 April 1997; and the Düsseldorf office on 1 April 1999.

Since their formation, the German offices have advised their clients on all questions of German, European and international industrial and commercial law with particular emphasis on cross-border and multinational transactions. At present, more than 170 attorneys-at-law (Rechtsanwälte), tax advisers, and varying numbers of foreign admitted lawyers work in the German offices.

All attorneys are at least bilingual.

AREAS OF PRACTICE

Baker & McKenzie co-ordinates its core practice areas on local, regional and global levels, giving most of its lawyers experience in more than one jurisdiction, as well as providing multinational teams of specialists.

Utilising a global practice group structure and ground-breaking technology coupled with a personal, detailed understanding of a client's specific business, Baker & McKenzie is able to organise its extensive resources to provide focused and strategic counsel to clients.

Baker & McKenzie advises multinational enterprises, large German companies, medium-sized enterprises, banks and insurance companies, as well as institutions and entities under public law in all questions of German, European, and international industrial and commercial law including company law, competition and cartel law, intellectual property, banking and finance, labour law, administrative law, and tax law. Furthermore, the firm handles litigation and arbitration matters. Several partners have expertise in specialised areas of law, such as European Community law, the law of cosmetics, food and drug law, trade marks, franchising, corporate finance, new financial products, government procurement, real estate transactions, and media telecommunications law.

Baker & McKenzie International is a Swiss Verein with member law firms around the world.

BARDEHLE PAGENBERG DOST ALTENBURG GEISSLER

INTELLECTUAL PROPERTY FIRM OF ATTORNEYS-AT-LAW AND PATENT ATTORNEYS

GALILEIPLATZ 1
81679 MÜNCHEN

Telephone: +49 89 92 80 50
Fax: +49 89 92 80 54 44
E-mail: info@bardehle.de
Website: www.bardehle.com

Languages
Chinese (Mandarin), Dutch, English, French, Hungarian, Italian, Polish, Portuguese, Romanian, Russian, Spanish

Other offices
Alicante, Düsseldorf, Paris

Number of lawyers 50
at this office 37

Member
Information Technology Law Group Europe; AIPPI; FICPI; LES; INTA; AIPLA; GALA; ECTA; USTA; ALAI; CLA; German Association for the Protection of Industrial Property and Copyright Law (GRUR); VPP

CATEGORIES OF WORK

- Industrial and intellectual property (prosecution, litigation, counselling)
- Patents
- Trade marks
- Copyrights
- Design protection
- Antitrust EU law
- Software protection
- Unfair competition
- Licensing of all types of rights
- Intellectual property searches
- Portfolio valuations
- Computers, information technology
- Biotechnology
- Pharmaceuticals
- Chemistry
- Medical devices

BEITEN BURKHARDT

GANGHOFERSTRASSE 33
80339 MUNICH

Telephone: +49 89 35 06 50 0
Fax: +49 89 35 06 51 23
E-mail: bblaw-muenchen@bblaw.com
Website: www.bblaw.com

Languages
Cantonese, Czech, English, French, Hungarian, Italian, Mandarin, Polish, Russian, Slovak, Spanish, Ukrainian

Other offices
Beijing, Berlin, Cologne, Düsseldorf, Frankfurt am Main, Hong Kong, Kiev, Leipzig, Moscow, Nuremberg, St Petersburg, Shanghai, Warsaw

Number of lawyers 249
at this office 61

CATEGORIES OF WORK

- Company law
- Banking and finance
- Tax law
- European law and cartel law
- Foundation, association, societies and sports law
- Industrial property rights
- Labour law
- Procurement law
- Public law
- Information technology
- Estate planning and succession rules
- Copyright law
- Litigation and arbitration
- Telecommunication law
- Real estate law
- Advertising law
- Media law

BIRD & BIRD

PACELLISTRASSE 14
80333 MUNICH

Telephone: +49 89 35 81 60 00
Fax: +49 89 35 81 60 11
E-mail: muenchen@twobirds.com
Website: www.twobirds.com

Languages
English, French, German, Mandarin

Other offices
Beijing, Brussels, Düsseldorf, Frankfurt, Hong Kong, London, Madrid, Milan, Paris, Rome, Stockholm, The Hague

Number of lawyers 472
at this office 21

Contacts
Dr Joseph Fesenmair, Dr Ulrich Goebel

CATEGORIES OF WORK

- Arbitration
- Aviation and aerospace
- Commercial
- Communications
- Corporate/M&A/private equity
- Employment
- EU and competition/antitrust
- Intellectual property
- IT and e-commerce
- Life sciences
- Litigation
- Media
- Outsourcing
- Private client
- Public procurement
- Real estate
- Regulatory
- Sport and sponsorship

BUSE HEBERER FROMM

MAXIMILIANSPLATZ 18
80333 MUNICH

Telephone: +49 89 24 22 33 0
Fax: +49 89 24 22 33 10
E-mail: muenchen@buse.de
Website: www.buse.de

Languages
English, French, Italian, Spanish

Other offices
Berlin, Düsseldorf, Essen, Frankfurt am Main, Hamburg, New York, Palma de Mallorca, Sydney, Zurich

Number of lawyers 120
at this office 12

Member
The European Legal Alliance: Beauchamps (Ireland); Dubarry Le Douarin Veil (France); Field Fisher Waterhouse (England); Harper Macleod (Scotland); Jimenez de Parga (Spain); La Scala & Associati (Italy)

CATEGORIES OF WORK

- Banking and finance
- Antitrust and merger control
- Commerce, transport, insurance
- Commercial delinquency
- Corporate/M&A
- Industrial property and copyrights
- Information technology and telecommunications
- Labour and employment
- Litigation and arbitration, national and international
- Press and media
- Property and construction
- Public law
- Tax

CMS HASCHE SIGLE

BRIENNER STRASSE 11/V
80333 MÜNCHEN

Telephone: +49 89 23 80 70
Fax: +49 89 23 80 71 10
E-mail: muenchen@cms-hs.com
Website: www.cms-hs.com

Languages
Dutch, English, French, Italian, Russian, Spanish

Other offices
Belgrade, Berlin, Brussels, Chemnitz, Cologne, Dresden, Düsseldorf, Frankfurt, Hamburg, Leipzig, Moscow, Prague, Stuttgart

Number of lawyers 420
at this office 57

Other CMS alliance member firms
CMS Adonnino Ascoli & Cavasola Scamoni, Italy; CMS Albiñana & Suárez de Lezo, Spain; CMS Bureau Francis Lefebvre, France; CMS Cameron McKenna, UK; CMS DeBacker, Belgium; CMS Derks Star Busmann, Netherlands; CMS von Erlach Henrici, Switzerland; CMS Reich-Rohrwig Hainz, Austria

CATEGORIES OF WORK

Corporate

Mergers and acquisitions

Private equity and venture capital

Banking

Stock trading and capital markets

Competition and merger control

State aid and EU law

Intellectual property, copyright, media and press

Individual and collective labour law

Real estate and construction

IT and telecommunications

Tax

Estate planning

Insolvency

Utilities

Public commercial and environment, procurement

Distribution and franchise law

Insurance

Maritime, shipping and transport

Litigation and arbitration

DECHERT LLP

THERESIENSTRASSE 6
80333 MÜNCHEN

Telephone: +49 89 21 21 63 0
Fax: +49 89 21 21 63 33
E-mail: federico.pappalardo@dechert.com
Website: www.dechert.com

Languages
English, French, German, Italian

Other offices
Austin, Boston, Brussels, Charlotte, Frankfurt, Harrisburg, Hartford, London, Luxembourg, Newport Beach, New York, Palo Alto, Paris, Philadelphia, Princeton, San Francisco, Washington DC

Number of lawyers 900+
at this office 10

Contact
Federico Pappalardo (managing partner)

CATEGORIES OF WORK

Mergers and acquisitions
Federico G Pappalardo, Dr Volkmar Bruckner

Private equity
Federico G Pappalardo, Berthold Hummel, Dr Volkmar Bruckner

Venture capital
Federico G Pappalardo, Berthold Hummel, Dr Volkmar Bruckner

Corporate finance and securities
Dr Olaf Faßhauer, Thomas Gierath

Employee benefits and executive compensation
Dr Olaf Faßhauer

Labour and employment
Dr Olaf Faßhauer, Giovanni Russo

Bank financing and securitisation
Federico G Pappalardo, Dr Olaf Faßhauer

Capital markets
Federico G Pappalardo, Dr Volkmar Bruckner

Tax
Thomas Gierath

FROHWITTER

POSSARTSTRASSE 20
81679 MÜNCHEN

Telephone: +49 89 99 80 90
Fax: +49 89 99 80 95 55
E-mail: info@frohwitter.com
Website: www.frohwitter.com

Languages
English, French, German, Italian, Romanian, Russian

Number of lawyers 12

CATEGORIES OF WORK

Patent and trade mark prosecution
Dr Thomas Leske

Biotechnology, biochemical, pharmacy
Dr Christian Helbig, Dr Norman Klix

Mechanical engineering
Dr Thomas Leske

Electronics
Dr Edward Tomlinson

Computer and IT
Jan Gigerich, Dr Roman Sedlmaier

Medical devices
Dr Bettina Hermann, Dr Norman Klix

Telecommunications
Jan Gigerich, Roland Brachmann

Patent litigation
Bernhard Frohwitter, Dr Ludwig Vohland

Unfair competition, design and trade mark
Dr Tatjana Kowal-Wolk, Dr Ludwig Vohland

IP commercialisation
Jan Gigerich, Dr Roman Sedlmaier

International patent strategy, intellectual property counselling, licensing hi-tech patent practice
Bernhard Frohwitter

GSK GASSNER STOCKMANN & KOLLEGEN

LUDWIGSTRASSE 10
80539 MÜNCHEN

Telephone: +49 89 28 81 74 0
Fax: +49 89 28 81 74 44
E-mail: muenchen@gsk.de
Website: www.gsk.de

Languages
English, French, German, Italian, Russian

Other offices
Berlin, Düsseldorf, Frankfurt, Hamburg, Heidelberg, Stuttgart

Number of lawyers 107
at this office 30

Contacts
Dr Andreas Bauer (Munich), Dr Christian R Schmidt (Berlin), Dr Andreas May (Frankfurt), Dr Philipp Jebens (Hamburg), Dr Peter Ladwig (Stuttgart), Dr Eckart Petzold (Düsseldorf), Wolfgang Böhm (Heidelberg)

CATEGORIES OF WORK

Corporate
Dr Andreas F Bauer, Dr Madeleine Detzner-Molnia

Mergers and acquisitions
Dr Andreas F Bauer, Dr Madeleine Detzner-Molnia

Venture capital and private equity
Dr Andreas F Bauer, Dr Madeleine Detzner-Molnia

Real estate, project finance, construction
Dr Otto Gaßner, Dr Dirk Brückner, Dr Michael Eggersberger

Commercial lease
Dr Thomas Haller, Dr Maximilian Schilling

Infrastructure, public sector, public procurement
Dr Otto Gaßner, Dr Andreas Geiger, Dr Wolfgang Würfel

Banking and finance, capital markets
Dr Otto Gaßner, Dr Theo Waigel, Dr Markus Escher, Dr Christian Waigel

Intellectual property and unfair competition
Dr Madeleine Detzner-Molnia

Information technology
Dr Andreas F Bauer

Antitrust and merger control
Dr Christian Waigel

Labour/employment law
Dr Andreas F Bauer

Litigation and arbitration
Dr Thomas Haller, Dr Maximilian Schilling

Taxation
Dr Andreas F Bauer, Dr Madeleine Detzner-Molnia

GLEISS LUTZ
RECHTSANWÄLTE

PRINZREGENTENSTRASSE 50
80538 MUNICH

Telephone: +49 89 21 66 70
Fax: +49 89 21 66 71 11
E-mail: info@gleisslutz.com
Website: www.gleisslutz.com

Languages
Dutch, English, French, Italian, Mandarin, Cantonese, Polish, Portuguese, Spanish, Russian, Czech, Slovak

Other offices
Berlin, Frankfurt, Stuttgart, Brussels, Prague, Warsaw

Number of lawyers 225
at this office 17

Contact
Dr Ingo Brinker

CATEGORIES OF WORK

German, EC and international law

Banking, securities and finance

Commercial law (general)

Companies, corporations

Competition, antitrust

Electronic commerce, internet law

Employment, labour

Insurance

Litigation and arbitration

Mergers and acquisitions

Tax

Trade marks, intellectual property

HAARMANN HEMMELRATH

MAXIMILIANSTRASSE 35
80539 MUNICH

Telephone: +49 89 21 63 60
Fax: +49 89 21 63 61 33
E-mail:
munich@haarmannhemmelrath.com
Website:
www.haarmannhemmelrath.com

Languages
Czech, Danish, English, French, Italian, Polish, Russian

Other offices
Bielefeld, Bucharest, Budapest, Düsseldorf, Frankfurt, Hamburg, Leipzig, Moscow, Paris, Prague, Shanghai, Warsaw

Number of lawyers 226

CATEGORIES OF WORK

Corporate and business law
Ivo Ziganke

Mergers and acquisitions

Due diligence
Ivo Ziganke, Dr Christian Wiggers

Reorganisation, corporate recovery
Hansjörg Zelger

Audit and accounting services
Hubertus Eichler, Hansjörg Zelger

Real estate, environmental law
Dr Alexander Venus

Fund structuring, leasing
Prof Dr Alexander Hemmelrath, Jürgen Fahrenberg

IP, antitrust, EU law, media law

Corporate finance, venture capital, private equity
Dr Sven Beyer

Labour law

International tax law
Prof Dr Alexander Hemmelrath, Prof Dr Claus Schild

National tax law and compliance
Doris Pflieger-Steininger, Stefan Heinrichshofen

Healthcare
Prof Dr Georg Nagler

HEISSE KURSAWE
RECHTSANWÄLTE PARTNERSCHAFT, MEMBER OF EVERSHEDS INTERNATIONAL

MAXIMILIANSPLATZ 5
80333 MÜNCHEN

Telephone: +49 89 54 56 50
Fax: +49 89 54 56 52 01
E-mail: munich@heisse-kursawe.com
Website: www.heisse-kursawe.com

Languages
English, French, German, Italian, Spanish

Number of lawyers 42

Contacts
Dr Matthias Heisse, Dr Alexander Honrath

CATEGORIES OF WORK

- Corporate law, reorganisations
- Corporate finance, capital markets
- Mergers and acquisitions
- Construction and engineering
- Real estate
- Labour law, employment
- EU law
- Commercial law (general)
- Banking
- Trade marks, intellectual property, media law
- Competition, antitrust
- Litigation and arbitration
- Tax
- Administrative and environment
- Probate and family law
- Estate planning
- Internet, IT and computer law

HENGELER MUELLER

LEOPOLDSTRASSE 8-10
80802 MUNICH

Telephone: +49 89 38 33 80
Fax: +49 89 38 33 83 33
E-mail: hmmuc@hengeler.com
Website: www.hengeler.com

Other offices
Düsseldorf, Frankfurt, Berlin, Brussels, London

Number of lawyers 192
at this office 10

Contact
Dr Gerhard Lang

CATEGORIES OF WORK

- M&A/corporate
- Private equity
- Capital markets
- Banking and finance
- Telecommunications and media
- Health care and life sciences
- Real estate
- Central and Eastern Europe

HEUKING KÜHN LÜER WOJTEK

PRINZREGENTENSTRASSE 48
80538 MUNICH

Telephone: +49 89 54 03 10
Fax: +49 89 54 03 15 40
E-mail: muenchen@heuking.de
Website: www.heuking.de

Languages
German, English, French

Other offices
Berlin, Brussels, Chemnitz, Cologne, Düsseldorf, Frankfurt, Hamburg

Number of lawyers 14

Contact
Dr Mathias Schroeder

CATEGORIES OF WORK

Corporate law	**Construction**
Mergers and acquisitions	**Real estate**
Commercial law	**Labour law**
Litigation	**Information technology**
Restructuring	**Intellectual property rights**
Property transactions	

THE FIRM

Heuking Kühn Lüer Wojtek was founded in Düsseldorf, Germany, in 1971. Since then, the firm has spread geographically, and Heuking Kühn now has seven significant offices in Germany, as well as an office in Brussels.

The firm has an extensive international network of law firms, enabling it to provide its clients with seamless 'one-stop shopping', on international transactions and regulatory matters. Since its formation, Heuking Kühn Lüer Wojtek has specifically chosen to remain an independent law firm. It is Heuking Kühn Lüer Wojtek's philosophy that, to provide the best possible service to its clients, the firm must be able to co-operate with various other law firms which are at the top of the profession in their respective countries. This gives the firm the ability to make alternative counsel suggestions to its clients, giving the clients a choice of the best suitable law firm or lawyer in each country and for each matter. Over the last 30+ years, Heuking Kühn Lüer Wojtek has developed excellent relationships with the key firms in all of the major jurisdictions worldwide.

Heuking Kühn Lüer Wojtek is a name which is synonymous with legal competence. The firm is one of the largest commercial law firms in Germany, with more than 170 specialised lawyers and tax advisers, representing the interests of national and international clients. Included in the client list are large and medium-sized German and international companies in all areas of the manufacturing industry, as well as trade and service industries, associations, governmental and public sector organisations and private clients and trusts.

The firm prides itself on substantive legal competence and on the excellent education and continuing legal education of its lawyers. Moreover, virtually all of the lawyers are German-English bilingual.

Extensive specialisation and comprehensive knowledge of specific industry sectors provide the basis of all of Heuking Kühn Lüer Wojtek's legal counselling. Experienced partners and carefully selected associate lawyers develop innovative solutions to complex legal problems. The lawyers regularly work in their specific practice area groups and also in multi-group and multidisciplinary teams with clients and outside consultants or advisers. Entrepreneurial thinking on behalf of firm clients, as well as efficient, quality, cost-effective and timely work and the highest personal dedication are key components of Heuking Kühn Lüer Wojtek's culture.

AREAS OF PRACTICE

Heuking Kühn Lüer Wojtek is a full-service commercial law firm. Cross-border and cross-sector knowledge in combination with a deep understanding of business reasoning enables service to clients with the broadest possible support in all their negotiations and business decisions. This applies equally to M&A transactions, to legal advice on company structure, business risk management, negotiations and negotiation tactics, training, crisis and insolvency counselling, corporate financial matters, and complex litigation and arbitration. Thanks to a variety of strong business clients, the firm has built long-term relationships with its clients and can assist them, beginning with the establishment of a business, followed by implementing business goals, including day-to-day legal work, reorganisations, acquisitions and divestitures.

Heuking Kühn Lüer Wojtek is actively involved with its clients in providing regulatory counselling in all areas of commercial law, as well as assisting them in organising and implementing their M&A transactions in Germany, throughout Europe, and internationally. Heuking Kühn Lüer Wojtek has particular expertise in German and EU company law; competition law, merger control, state aids and regulated industries (including energy; telecommunications; and transport, postal services and shipping law); taxation; employment law; finance and banking; international trade and customs; insurance; litigation, arbitration and mediation; bankruptcy and insolvency; environment, health and safety law; product liability; product-specific regulation; real estate and construction law; IP, IT and media law; and private clients and family law.

HOGAN & HARTSON RAUE LLP

SCHACKSTRAßE 1
80539 MUNICH

Telephone: +49 89 20 50 88 80
Fax: +49 89 20 50 88 81 0
E-mail: jhegemann@hhlaw.com
Website: www.hhlaw.com

Languages
English, French

Other offices
Baltimore, Beijing, Berlin, Boulder, Brussels, Budapest, Caracas, Colorado Springs, Denver, Geneva, Hong Kong, London, Los Angeles, Miami, Moscow, New York, Northern Virginia, Paris, Shanghai, Tokyo, Warsaw, Washington DC

Number of lawyers 1,101
at this office 8

Contacts
Jan Hegemann, Steven Ballew

CATEGORIES OF WORK

Entertainment

Media

Life science

Corporate law

Project finance

Copyright

Publishing and press law

Internet and e-commerce

Life sciences/biotechnology

Intellectual property

Mergers and acquisitions

Banking and capital markets

Litigation and arbitration

Public procurement law

Telecommunications

Private equity

Venture capital

KLAKA RECHTSANWÄLTE

DELPSTRASSE 4
81679 MÜNCHEN
(BOGENHAUSEN)

Telephone: +49 89 99 89 19 0
Fax: +49 89 98 00 36
E-mail: info@klaka.com
Website: www.klaka.com

Languages
English, Spanish

Number of lawyers 10

CATEGORIES OF WORK

Patent law, utility models, employee inventions
Michael Nieder, Olaf Giebe

Trade mark law, firm name
Andreas Schulz, Ralf Hackbarth

Copyright law, design patents
Wolfgang Götz,
Ralf-Michael Burkhardt

Unfair competition law
Michael Brass, Stefan Eck

Antitrust law, public procurement
Wolfgang Straub, Michael Nieder

Trade mark prosecution
Oliver Rauscher

Food and drug law
Andreas Schulz, Michael Nieder

IT and internet law
Ralf Hackbarth, Michael Brass

Press and media law
Ralf-Michael Burkhardt,
Andreas Schulz

General commercial, banking law
Wolfgang Straub,
Ralf-Michael Burkhardt

Energy law
Wolfgang Straub

LOVELLS

KARL-SCHARNAGL-RING 5
80539 MÜNCHEN

Telephone: +49 89 29 01 20
Fax: +49 89 29 01 22 22
E-mail: reception.munich@lovells.com
Website: www.lovells.de

Languages
English, French, Italian, Polish, Russian

Other offices
Alicante, Amsterdam, Beijing, Berlin, Brussels, Budapest*, Chicago, Düsseldorf, Frankfurt, Hamburg, Ho Chi Minh City, Hong Kong, London, Madrid, Milan, Moscow, New York, Paris, Prague, Rome, Shanghai, Singapore, Tokyo, Warsaw, Zagreb*

Number of lawyers 1,600
at this office 81

Contact
Christoph Hiltl

CATEGORIES OF WORK

Corporate/M&A, private equity

Restructuring and insolvency

Banking

Antitrust and unfair competition

Capital markets

Project finance, public private partnerships

Tax

Employment

Intellectual property

Real estate

Projects

Technology, media, telecommunications

Litigation, product liability

International arbitration

Food and drug regulations

Law of Eastern Europe

McDERMOTT WILL & EMERY
RECHTSANWÄLTE STEUERBERATER LLP

NYMPHENBURGER STRASSE 3
80355 MUNICH

Telephone: +49 89 12 71 20
Fax: +49 89 12 71 11 1
Website: www.mwe.com

Languages
All main business languages

Other offices
Boston, Brussels, Chicago, Düsseldorf, London, Los Angeles, Miami, New York, Orange County, Rome, San Diego, Silicon Valley, Washington DC

Number of lawyers 1,000
at this office 31

CATEGORIES OF WORK

Antitrust and regulatory
Dr Oliver Steffens

Capital markets
Christian von Sydow

Corporate
Dr Martin Kock, Dr Jörg Kretschmer

Intellectual property
Dr Boris Uphoff

Media, entertainment and press
Dr Ralf Weisser, Dr Wolfgang von Frentz, Oliver Kächele, Claudia Sendlbeck Schickor

Information technology
Dr Oliver Steffens, Dr Wolfgang von Frentz

Mergers and acquisitions
Dr Jorg Kretschmer, Christian von Sydow

Private equity
Dr Martin Kock, Hans-Joachim Schreiber

Taxation
Dr Dirk Pohl, Dr Joachim Giehl, Markus Roth

Telecoms
Dr Ralf Weisser, Dr Wolfgang von Frentz

MILBANK, TWEED, HADLEY & McCLOY LLP

**MAXIMILIANSTRASSE 15
(MAXIMILIANHÖFE)
80539 MÜNCHEN**

Telephone: +49 89 25 55 93 60 0
Fax: +49 89 25 55 93 70 0
E-mail: info@milbank.com
Website: www.milbankeurope.com

Other offices
Frankfurt, Hong Kong, London, Los Angeles, New York, Singapore, Tokyo, Washington DC

Number of lawyers 520
at this office 14

Contact
Dr Rolf Füger

CATEGORIES OF WORK

Corporate advisory (Aktien- und Konzernrecht)
Dr Norbert Rieger

Equity capital markets
Dr Peter Nussbaum

M&A and private equity
Dr Peter Nussbaum, Dr Norbert Rieger

Tax
Dr Rolf Füger

THE FIRM

Milbank is committed to providing high-quality legal services wherever the firm practises. The firm recruits from among the most promising lawyers and is committed to their training as well as providing opportunities for promotion. Milbank draws on its strengths globally to ensure that it can address the needs of its clients wherever they are.

AREAS OF PRACTICE

The lawyers in the firm's Munich office concentrate on practice areas in which they have received recognition in the German market; specifically, mergers and acquisitions, including public core corporate transactions (particularly for those involving public stock corporations), tax and financial structuring, and equity capital markets. The Munich office focuses on servicing listed companies in complex transactions and on advising the private equity industry. This approach leverages the firm's complementary global corporate finance practice, including in Milbank's Frankfurt office. From the firm's Munich and Frankfurt offices the firm provides fully integrated legal advice on corporate, tax and finance matters to clients doing business or investing in Germany.

NÖRR STIEFENHOFER LUTZ

BRIENNER STRASSE 28
80333 MÜNCHEN

Telephone: +49 89 28 62 80
Fax: +49 89 28 01 10
E-mail: info@noerr.com
Website: www.noerr.com

Languages
Afrikaans, Czech, Dutch, English, French, German, Hungarian, Italian, Persian, Portuguese, Romanian, Russian, Spanish, Swedish, Slovakian

Other offices
Berlin, Bratislava, Bucharest, Budapest, Dresden, Düsseldorf, Frankfurt, Moscow, New York, Prague, Warsaw

Number of lawyers 256
(+ 66 tax advisers, public accountants and tax assistants)
at this office 93
(+19 tax advisers, public accountants and tax assistants)

Contact
Dr Dieter Schenk

CATEGORIES OF WORK

Audit and accounting services	**Law relating to tax offences**
Aviation law	**Litigation and arbitration**
Banking, capital investment, project financing	**Media law, IT law and new media**
Corporate law (including corporate finance, venture capital, IPO)	**Mergers and acquisitions, antitrust law**
Distribution law (including franchising, leasing, agency)	**Privatisation**
Environmental law and product liability	**Reorganisation and insolvency**
Intellectual property and copyright	**Tax law (national and international)**
Labour law and restructuring	**Zoning, construction and real estate**

THE FIRM

Nörr Stiefenhofer Lutz is among the highest profile law firms on the European legal market, at the same time one of the few independent German law firms dealing with major national and international transactions and projects. With a current strength of more than 300 professionals, the firm serves a stable base of international groups, medium-sized companies and wealthy private individuals.

Nörr Stiefenhofer Lutz stands for unrestricted full service. In contrast to many other large offices, which have withdrawn from areas not immediately connected with acquisitions and mergers, Nörr Stiefenhofer Lutz continues to offer its services over the entire spectrum of commercial law, specifically drawing attention to its commitment to labour law, intellectual property law, litigation and arbitration.

The firm's multidisciplinary approach follows logically from its full-service philosophy. In major transactions and reconstructions in particular, financial and tax parameters play at least as important a part as the legal details. For this reason, approximately 20% of the firm's professionals are tax advisors and auditors, many of them with long experience in leading positions in industry and business.

AREAS OF PRACTICE

Nörr Stiefenhofer Lutz is strongly present internationally, as well as nationally. Its five German offices are situated in the most important commercial centres. By concentrating expertise in particular offices – media law in Munich and Berlin, corporate finance in Frankfurt, antitrust law in Berlin and IT business in Munich – the firm can respond to the particular requirements of its clients.

The chosen focus of the international offices is central and eastern Europe. Nörr Stiefenhofer Lutz identified the potential of this region at an early stage, and has guided investors on the ground in this market since the end of the 1980s, in the planning and implementation of their projects. In the western European and Anglo-American legal world, as well as in other parts of the world, the firm can rely on a closely connected and long-established network of 'best friends'. Furthermore, Nörr Stiefenhofer Lutz is a member of Lex Mundi, the world's leading association of independent law firms. A representative office in New York serves to support contacts with US clients.

Offices in Germany: Berlin, Düsseldorf, Dresden, Frankfurt am Main, Munich.

Offices abroad: Bratislava, Bucharest, Budapest, Moscow, Prague, Warsaw.

P+P PÖLLATH + PARTNERS

FÜNF HÖFE
KARDINAL-FAULHABER-STRASSE 10
80333 MUNICH

Telephone: +49 89 24 24 00
Fax: +49 89 24 24 09 99
E-mail: muc@pplaw.com
Website: www.pplaw.com

Languages
English, French

Other offices
Berlin, Frankfurt

Number of lawyers 66
at this office 30

Contacts
Andrea von Drygalski, Matthias Bruse

CATEGORIES OF WORK

Private equity	**Real estate**
M&A	**Restitution**
Corporate finance	**Family (high-net-worth, succession)**
Tax	**Trusts, foundations, charities**

PETERS, SCHÖNBERGER & PARTNER

SCHACKSTRASSE 2
80539 MÜNCHEN

Telephone: +49 89 38 17 20
Fax: +49 89 38 17 22 04
E-mail: psp@pspmuc.de
Website: www.pspmuc.de

Languages
English, French, Italian, Russian, Spanish

Number of lawyers 14
(+22 tax advisers and CPAs)

Member
DFK International; Eurolegal

CATEGORIES OF WORK

Company law/capital market Dr K Höfner, Dr C Wallner	**Reorganisation tax** Dr K Höfner, H Dörfler
Family office, global custody Ch Schönberger, S Gross	**Shareholder moderation/mediation** B Winterstetter
Film production/taxation of artists H Dörfler, Dr C Wallner	**Corporate and commercial** Dr K Höfner, Dr K Maierhofer
International tax Dr J Peters, R W Graf	**IT** S Gross, Dr A-M Wagner
Real estate and building Ch Schönberger, R Fürholzer	**Due diligence** B Winterstetter, Dr K Höfner
Mergers and acquisitions B Winterstetter, Dr K Höfner	**Law regarding fiscal offences** U Derlien, M Schencking
Management buy-out Dr K Maierhofer, S Nowack	**Tax conversion law** Dr K Höfner, H Dörfler
Determination of succession Ch Schönberger, Dr K Höfner	**Insolvency law** Dr K Maierhofer, Dr C Wallner
Foundations/public charity J Doppstadt, Dr K Maierhofer	**Labour law** Dr K Maierhofer, Dr C Wallner

REED SMITH LLP

FÜNF HÖFE
THEATINERSTRASSE 8
80333 MUNICH

Telephone: +49 89 20 30 41 0
Fax: +49 89 20 30 41 99
E-mail:
firstinitialsurname@reedsmith.com
Website: www.reedsmith.com

Languages
English, French, German

Other offices
Century City, Coventry, London, Los Angeles, New York, Newark, Northern VA, Oakland, Paris, Philadelphia, Pittsburgh, Princeton, San Francisco, Washington DC, Wilmington

Number of lawyers 1,078
at this office 9

CATEGORIES OF WORK

Corporate
Michael Fischer

Financial services
Stefan Kugler

Litigation
Etienne Righthammer

Mergers and acquisitions
Michael Fischer

Employment
Oliver Heeder

Funds
Stefan Kugler

TMT
Stephan Rippert

IP/IT
Stephan Rippert

Life sciences
Stephan Rippert

THE FIRM

Reed Smith is a leading international law firm. The firm has grown rapidly over the past few years through a series of strategic mergers and lateral additions and it now has over 1,000 lawyers across 14 US and four European cities. A strong presence on both coasts of the US makes the firm ideally positioned to offer clients a transatlantic capability. It continues to invest in key markets to meet clients' needs and, in 2005, opened its first offices in mainland Europe, in Munich and Paris.

Reed Smith represents clients, large and small, across a great number of legal disciplines and many industry sectors. In Europe, its key industries are financial services and life sciences. Its firmwide clients include financial institutions, pharmaceutical companies, manufacturers, healthcare providers and insurers, communications and media companies and real estate developers and government bodies.

AREAS OF PRACTICE

Reed Smith's core services in Europe are corporate, life sciences, financial services, litigation, employment, real estate and TMT.

Corporate: the firm's largest department handles a wide variety of corporate and commercial transactions for, in particular, US and European clients. The department's expertise includes mergers and acquisitions, corporate finance, competition and corporate tax. It enjoys a strong track record in alternative investment market-related work.

Life sciences: the department supports leading-edge companies in pharmaceuticals, biotechnology, diagnostics, medical devices and healthcare. The firm advises life sciences companies on debt and equity financing and partners with clients through all phases of development, production, marketing and distribution of products. It is also widely acknowledged for its work defending clients in high-profile, multi-jurisdictional product liability claims.

Financial services: the financial services group advises on capital market products, consumer financial services, regulatory advice (Financial Services and Market Act 2000) and transactions (acquisitions, divestitures, restructurings). It also has a transatlantic project finance team.

Commercial litigation: the firm handles substantial commercial disputes and is particularly well known for its work in international asset recovery, financial regulation and multi-jurisdictional claims. Specific areas of expertise include product liability claims, insolvency and corporate restructuring, intellectual property and domestic and international arbitration. It has a dedicated team of French-speaking advocates.

Employment: the team provides a full service to employers and HR professionals encompassing service agreements and employment contracts, employee benefits, business transfers, dismissals, redundancies, discrimination and trade union law. It also advises on all EU aspects of employment law and offers transactional and non-transactional pensions advice. In addition, the UK business immigration team is recognised as one of the leading practices in the country and provides corporate clients and individual foreign investors with advice in connection with residence and working in the UK.

Real estate: the real estate group advises on high-value acquisitions and disposals for corporate clients in the retail, financial, services, media and manufacturing industries. High-level property litigation, contentious and non-contentious planning and infrastructure expertise is an additional strength of the team.

TMT and IP/IT: the firm represents a variety of media and entertainment, technology and telecommunications companies on all contractual, commercial, intellectual property and regulatory aspects. The firm works closely with broadcast clients and cable companies on all issues relating to broadcasting and the convergence of communication technologies. It advises on outsourcing, licensing as well as other technology transactions.

SJ BERWIN LLP

RECHTSANWÄLTE – STEUERBERATER – WIRTSCHAFTSPRÜFER

MARIA-THERESIA-STRASSE 5
81675 MUNICH

Telephone: +49 89 89 08 10
Fax: +49 89 89 081 10 0
E-mail: munich@sjberwin.com
Website: www.sjberwin.com

Languages
English, French

Other offices
Berlin, Brussels, Frankfurt, London, Madrid, Milan, Paris, Turin

Number of lawyers 550
at this office 22

Contact
Dr Alexander Rinne

CATEGORIES OF WORK

Corporate law
Thomas Pauls, Dr Justus F Binder

Venture capital
Dr Justus F Binder

Fund structuring
Dr André Gloede

Alternative investments
Achim Pütz

Banking and financial services
Achim Pütz

Tax law
Dr Michael Kreft, Dr André Gloede

Private equity
Thomas P Pauls

EU and competition
Dr Alexander Rinne

M&A, joint ventures
Thomas Pauls, Dr Michael Kreft

SSW SCHNEIDER SCHIFFER WEIHERMÜLLER

BAVARIARING 27
80336 MUNICH

Telephone: +49 89 54 34 91 00
Fax: +49 89 54 34 92 00
E-mail: info@ssw-muc.de
Website: www.ssw-muc.de

Languages
German, English, French

Number of lawyers 15

CATEGORIES OF WORK

Software contracts and projects for users
Prof Dr Jochen Schneider, Michaela Witzel

Software contracts and projects for providers
Elke Bischof, Kerstin Scheefeld

E-commerce
Frieder Backu, Isabell Conrad

Unfair competition
Frieder Backu, Ludwig Antoine

Labour and employment law
Ludwig Antoine, Isabell Conrad

IP
Prof Dr Jochen Schneider, Michaela Witzel

Data protection, privacy law
Prof Dr Jochen Schneider, Isabell Conrad

Tax law
Dr Bernd Schiffer, Frieder Backu

Outsourcing
Prof Dr Jochen Schneider, Michaela Witzel

Public procurement
Elke Bischof, Kerstin Scheefeld

Corporate law
Dr Bernd Schiffer, Frieder Backu

Software distribution and antitrust law
Prof Dr Jochen Schneider, Michaela Witzel

SCHMITT-ROLFES FALTERMEIER STAUDACHER

ANWALTSSOZIETÄT

DESTOUCHESSTRASSE 4
80803 MUNICH

Telephone: +49 89 38 38 40 0
Fax: +49 89 38 38 40 20
E-mail: info@sfs-law.de

Languages
English, French, Russian

Number of lawyers 8

CATEGORIES OF WORK

Employment and labour law

Collective labour relations

Collective dismissals

European employment law

Compensation and benefits

Pensions

Expatriates

SCHWARZ KELWING WICKE WESTPFAHL

WITTELSBACHERPLATZ 1
80333 MÜNCHEN

Telephone: +49 89 28 64 00
Fax: +49 89 28 09 43 2
E-mail: muenchen@skwlaw.de
Website: www.skwlaw.de

Languages
Czech, English, French, Italian, Spanish

Other offices
Berlin, Dresden, Frankfurt am Main

Number of lawyers 58
at this office 28

Contacts
Prof Dr Mathias Schwarz,
Dr Michael Brauch

Member
Terralex; PLG

CATEGORIES OF WORK

Corporate and commercial law
Dr Armin Schwerdtfeger

Real estate law, conveyancing, construction
Dr Josef Zeller, Dr Andreas Mylaeus

Media and entertainment
Dr Christoph Haesner, Dr Ulrich Fuchs

Internet and e-commerce
Dr Andreas Peschel-Mehner

Trade marks, intellectual property
Dr Dorothee Altenburg

Arbitration and litigation
Dr Josef Zeller, Dr Daniel Kaboth

Mediation
Prof Dr Mathias Schwarz

Mergers and acquisitions
Dr Sebastian v Wallwitz,
Dr Michael Brauch,
Dr Matthias Nordmann

Banking and finance
Dr Ulrich Muth

Unfair competition
Dr Ulrich Muth,
Dr Andreas Peschel-Mehner

Labour and employment law
Dr Bernd Joch

Probate, succession law
Dr Josef Zeller, Sigrid Koppenhöfer

Copyright
Prof Dr Mathias Schwarz,
Dr Konstantin Wegner

SIBETH PARTNERSCHAFT RECHTSANWÄLTE STEUERBERATER WIRTSCHAFTSPRÜFER

OBERANGER 34-36
80331 MÜNCHEN

Telephone: +49 89 38 80 80
Fax: +49 89 38 80 81 01
E-mail: munich@sibeth.com
Website: www.sibeth.com

Languages
Catalan, English, French, Italian, Russian, Spanish

Other offices
Erfurt

Number of lawyers 44
at this office 36

Contacts
Dr Andreas Kloyer, Thomas Richter

CATEGORIES OF WORK

Corporate law, reorganisation
Dr Georg Anders

Corporate finance, capital markets
Dr Andreas Kloyer

Mergers and acquisitions, restructuring
Cornelia Weber

Private equity, venture capital
Dr Andreas Kloyer

Tax
Rupert Klar

Accounting, funds
Rupert Klar

Construction and engineering
Thomas Richter

Real estate
Dr Michael Grünwald

Property finance
Dr Michael Grünwald

Public sector
Dr Wolfgang Weisskopf

Labour law, employment
Axel Metzner

Commercial law (general)
Axel Metzner

Probate and estate planning
Dr Hans Schmidt-Sibeth

Commercial property
Ralf Josef Dörner

TAYLOR WESSING

ISARTORPLATZ 8
80331 MUNICH

Telephone: +49 89 2 10 38-0
Fax: +49 89 2 10 38 30 0
E-mail: muenchen@taylorwessing.com
Website: www.taylorwessing.com

Languages
English, Dutch, French, Italian, Mandarin, Spanish

Other offices
Alicante*, Berlin, Brussels, Cambridge, Dubai*, Düsseldorf/Neuss, Frankfurt, Hamburg, London, Paris, Shanghai*

Number of lawyers 598
at this office 57

Member
World Law Group; Tech Law Group

CATEGORIES OF WORK

Banking and finance
Claus Goedecke, Peter Seemann

China desk
Florian Ranft

Commercial
Dr Christoph Hasche

Corporate/M&A
Bernhard Kloft

Employment and pensions
Axel C Filges

EU law/antitrust
Dr Marco Hartmann-Rüppel, Markus Wirtz

Intellectual property
Dr Sabine Rojahn

Life sciences
Dr Ulrich Steffen

Media and entertainment
Martin von Albrecht

Private client
Romana Traichel

Projects and finance
Dr Rüdiger von Hülst

Public commercial law
Dr Walter Potthast

Real estate and construction
Jan Wunschel

Regulatory affairs
Andreas Haak

Tax
Bernd Michel

Technology/IT/telecoms
Jörg Wimmers

WEIL, GOTSHAL & MANGES

MAXIMILIANHÖFE
MAXIMILIANSTRASSE 13
80539 MUNICH

Telephone: +49 89 24 24 30
Fax: +49 89 24 24 33 99
Website: www.weil.com

Other offices
Austin, Boston, Budapest, Brussels, Dallas, Frankfurt, Houston, London, Miami, New York, Paris, Prague, Providence, Shanghai, Silicon Valley, Singapore, Warsaw, Washington DC, Wilmington

Number of lawyers 1,200
at this office 23

Contact
Gerhard Schmidt (managing partner)

CATEGORIES OF WORK

Banking and finance	**Private equity**
Litigation	**Restructuring**
Mergers and acquisitions	**Taxation**

THE FIRM

Weil, Gotshal & Manges is a leader in the marketplace for sophisticated, international legal services. With more than 1,200 lawyers across the US, Europe and Asia, the firm serves many of the most successful companies in the world in their high-stakes matters and transactions. Weil Gotshal has built a world-class team of lawyers by pursuing a strategy of steady, purposeful growth. It continues to build upon a balanced platform of practices and locations without acquiring any debt. The firm's three primary departments – corporate, litigation/regulatory and restructuring – provide healthy diversification in all economic cycles, while its international expansion over the past decade has resulted in a quarter of the firm's lawyers now being in Europe.

AREAS OF PRACTICE

The firm's antitrust/competition practice advises on international M&A regulatory notifications, antitrust distribution counselling, cartels, litigation and government and state competition policy.

The corporate department is the firm's largest, with lawyers in the US and across Europe. The department advises international financial institutions and corporate clients in complex public and private mergers and acquisitions, private equity deals, strategic alliances and other commercial transactions.

The firm's corporate governance practice is recognised as the pre-eminent counsellor of corporate boards, management and institutional investors on the full range of governance issues, including board composition, structure and processes; executive and director compensation; director responsibilities, including in connection with mergers, spin-offs and other extraordinary transactions; internal and governmental investigations of alleged accounting or other corporate misconduct; and shareholder initiatives.

The firm is recognised as a market leader in the handling of complex and innovative finance transactions internationally. The firm advises on a wide range of financing activities and has particular expertise in acquisition finance, asset-based finance, debt restructuring and insolvency, debt and equity capital markets, derivatives, high-yield debt, securitisation, structured finance and telecom and multimedia financing.

The firm has a leading intellectual property and technology practice and advises a number of the world's major technology, media and telecommunications companies. It also acts for investors in technology, media and communications entities. The practice handles patent infringement, outsourcing transactions, strategic alliances, cross-border mergers and acquisitions, investments and IPOs. The firm advises on the protection and exploitation of IP and on a wide range of e-commerce matters including data protection. It has expertise in regulatory telecoms matters.

The firm's litigation practice advises international clients on all major areas of the law and has extensive experience in all aspects of dispute resolution. It advises clients in jury trials and appeals, as well as arbitration and alternative dispute forums.

The firm's real estate practice handles complex real estate transactions (including finance, securitisations, development, leasing, sales, acquisitions and debt restructurings) across the US and Europe. It also advises clients on real estate M&A transactions and transactions involving real estate investment trusts.

The firm has one of the largest, most broadly based bankruptcy and business reorganisation practices in the world. The department has been involved in virtually all major chapter 11 reorganisation cases in the US and in major national and international out of court debt restructurings.

The tax department provides advice to a broad range of international clients, covering many economic sectors. The department works closely with the firm's other departments to find innovative solutions to problems that present various and competing multidisciplinary considerations.

WILMER CUTLER PICKERING HALE AND DORR LLP

MAXIMILIANSTR. 31
80539 MÜNCHEN

Telephone: +49 89 24 21 30
Fax: +49 89 24 21 32 13
Website: www.wilmerhale.com

Languages
English, French, German

Other offices
Baltimore, Beijing, Berlin, Boston, Brussels, London, New York, Northern Virginia, Oxford, Palo Alto, Waltham, Washington

Number of lawyers 1,100
at this office 9

CATEGORIES OF WORK

Corporate
Hubert Besner, Rainer Kreifels

Life sciences
Hubert Besner

IP/IT and litigation
Florian von Baum

M&A
Hubert Besner, Rainer Kreifels

Labour and employment
Manfred Schmid

Telecommunications and media
Florian von Baum

THE FIRM

WilmerHale offers unparalleled legal representation across a comprehensive range of practice areas that are critical to the success of its clients. The firm has over 1,000 lawyers operating in five countries and practices at the very top of the legal profession. The depth and scope of the practice give it the ability to anticipate obstacles, seize opportunities and get the case resolved or the deal done – and the experience and know-how to prevent it from being undone.

In Germany, the firm offers legal services with approximately 55 lawyers from offices in Berlin and Munich. The Berlin office has a special focus on complex competition and regulatory matters, often involving sensitive political issues and has established a strong corporate transactions practice group. Clients come primarily from the technology (including biotechnology), media, aviation, energy, telecommunication and travel industries, as well as from the banking and financial services sector. The Munich office focuses on providing specialised legal services for media and technology companies, venture capitalists and investment banks.

AREAS OF PRACTICE

The principal practice areas of the Munich office are:

Corporate/M&A: the German corporate group, with over 30 lawyers in Berlin and Munich, provides the full range of corporate and commercial legal services to domestic and international clients. It has long-standing experience in domestic and international mergers and acquisitions, privatisations, reorganisations and liquidations, as well as in real estate transactions, property development matters and financing transactions.

A main focus of the Munich corporate practice is legal advice for technology and life sciences companies in a wide range of corporate, securities and employment matters.

IP/IT: the firm's intellectual property team is based in Berlin and Munich and comprises about 10 lawyers. The team advises and represents clients regarding all IP issues, both contentious and non-contentious. The spectrum of the team's work includes trademarks, patent and utility model issues, IT/e-commerce/outsourcing, copyright (mainly software), unfair trade practices law and all aspects of IP litigation, including preliminary injunctive relief (mostly in the field of trademark and unfair trade practices) and patent infringement litigation. The group has a strong focus on the IT sector (e-commerce companies, software companies and the semi-conductor industry), followed by the life sciences sector, including licensing and medical trial agreements and other regulatory aspects of medical law.

Telecommunications and media: the firm's German communications team works with clients in the fixed, mobile and broadband sectors. The firm assists clients in structuring specialised commercial solutions and in developing regulatory strategies.

CMS HASCHE SIGLE

SCHÖTTLESTRASSE 8
70597 STUTTGART

Telephone: +49 711 976 40
Fax: +49 711 976 49 00
E-mail: stuttgart@cms-hs.com
Website: www.cms-hs.com

Languages
Dutch, English, French, Italian, Spanish

Other offices
Belgrade, Berlin, Brussels, Chemnitz, Cologne, Dresden, Düsseldorf, Frankfurt, Hamburg, Leipzig, Moscow, Munich, Prague

Number of lawyers 420
at this office 88

Other CMS alliance member firms
CMS Adonnino Ascoli & Cavasola Scamoni, Italy; CMS Albiñana & Suárez de Lezo, Spain; CMS Bureau Francis Lefebvre, France; CMS Cameron McKenna, UK; CMS DeBacker, Belgium; CMS Derks Star Busmann, Netherlands; CMS von Erlach Henrici, Switzerland; CMS Reich-Rohrwig Hainz, Austria

CATEGORIES OF WORK

Corporate

Mergers and acquisitions

Private equity and venture capital

Banking

Stock trading and capital markets

Competition and merger control

State aid and EU law

Intellectual property, copyright, media and press

Individual and collective labour law

Real estate and construction

IT and telecommunications

Tax

Estate planning

Insolvency

Utilities

Public commercial and environment, procurement

Distribution and franchise law

Insurance

Maritime, shipping and transport

Litigation and arbitration

GSK GASSNER STOCKMANN & KOLLEGEN

KRONENSTRASSE 30
70174 STUTTGART

Telephone: +49 711 220 45 79 0
Fax: +49 711 220 45 79 44
E-mail: stuttgart@gsk.de
Website: www.gsk.de

Languages
English, French, German

Other offices
Berlin, Düsseldorf, Frankfurt, Hamburg, Heidelberg, Munich

Number of lawyers 107
at this office 9

Contacts
Dr Christian R Schmidt (Berlin), Dr Andreas Bauer (Munich), Dr Andreas May (Frankfurt), Dr Philipp Jebens (Hamburg), Dr Peter Ladwig (Stuttgart), Dr Eckart Petzold (Düsseldorf), Wolfgang Böhm (Heidelberg)

CATEGORIES OF WORK

Corporate
Dr Peter Ladwig, Dr Peter Bauschatz

Mergers and acquisitions
Dr Peter Ladwig

Venture capital and private equity
Dr Peter Ladwig

Taxation
Dr Peter Bauschatz

Real estate, project finance, construction
Dr Thomas Lang

Commercial lease
Dr Thomas Lang

Infrastructure, public sector
Dr Wolfram Sandner

Public procurement
Dr Wolfram Sandner

Capital markets
Dr Peter Ladwig

GLEISS LUTZ
RECHTSANWÄLTE

MAYBACHSTRASSE 6
70469 STUTTGART

Telephone: +49 711 89 97 0
Fax: +49 711 85 50 96
E-mail: info@gleisslutz.com
Website: www.gleisslutz.com

Languages
Dutch, English, French, Italian, Mandarin, Cantonese, Polish, Portuguese, Spanish, Russian, Czech, Slovak

Other offices
Berlin, Frankfurt, Munich, Brussels, Prague, Warsaw

Number of lawyers 225
at this office 73

Contact
Prof Dr Gerhard Wegen LLM

Stuttgart is the head office of this firm

CATEGORIES OF WORK

German, EC and international law

Banking, securities and finance

Commercial law (general)

Companies, corporations

Competition, antitrust

Electronic commerce, Internet law

Employment, labour

Environment and pollution control

Insurance

Litigation and arbitration

Mergers and acquisitions

Real estate

Tax

Telecommunications, media and broadcasting

Trade marks, intellectual property

HENNERKES, KIRCHDÖRFER & LORZ

JAHNSTRASSE 43
70597 STUTTGART

Telephone: +49 711 725 79 0
Fax: +49 711 725 79 20
E-mail: info@hennerkes.de
Website: www.hennerkes.de

Languages
English, French

Number of lawyers 10

CATEGORIES OF WORK

Mergers and acquisitions
Prof Rainer Kirchdörfer, Dr Rainer Lorz

Tax
Prof Rainer Kirchdörfer

Initial public offerings
Prof Dr Hennerkes,
Prof Rainer Kirchdörfer

Estate planning
Prof Dr Hennerkes, Dr Rainer Lorz

Corporate finance, capital markets
Prof Rainer Kirchdörfer, Dr Rainer Lorz

Reorganisations
Prof Rainer Kirchdörfer,
Dr Andreas Wiedemann

Company
Prof Dr Brun-Hagen Hennerkes,
Prof Rainer Kirchdörfer

Insolvency
Dr Andreas Wiedemann

Trusts and foundations
Dr Rainer Lorz, Dr Rainer Kögel

Commercial
Dr Andreas Wiedemann,
Dr Rainer Kögel

International law
Dr Rainer Lorz

Competition and antitrust
Dr Rainer Kögel

Employee stock ownership plans
Dr Andreas Wiedemann

Financing
Dr Rainer Lorz,
Dr Andreas Wiedemann

THÜMMEL, SCHÜTZE & PARTNER

URBANSTRASSE 7
70182 STUTTGART

Telephone: +49 711 166 70
Fax: +49 711 166 72 90
E-mail: stuttgart@tsp-law.com
Website: www.tsp-law.com

Languages
German, English, French, Italian, Spanish

Other offices
Berlin, Brussels, Dresden, Frankfurt am Main, Singapore

Number of lawyers 58
at this office 32

Contact
Dr René-Alexander Hirth

CATEGORIES OF WORK

Antitrust, competition and trade regulation
Dr Harro Wilde

Arbitration
Prof Dr Rolf A Schütze,
Prof Dr Roderich C Thümmel

Banking and finance
Dr Hervé Edelmann,
Dr Susanne Kratzsch

Corporate and commercial
Dr Werner Oldenburg,
Dr René-Alexander Hirth

D&O liability
Prof Dr Roderich C Thümmel

Employment
Ralf Fuhrmann, Dr Andreas Chmel

IP and technology
Dr Tilo Bodendorf,
Dr Thomas R Klötzel

Litigation
Prof Dr Rolf A Schütze,
Dr Hervé Edelmann

Media and press
Dr Tilo Bodendorf, Dr Harro Wilde

M&A, private equity
Prof Dr Roderich C Thümmel,
Dr René-Alexander Hirth

Patent litigation
Dr Thomas R Klötzel

Private clients
Dr Günther H Raiser

Product liability
Dr Susanne Kratzsch

Project management
Dr Martin Asal

Public procurement
Severin Birkmann

Real estate
Severin Birkmann, Dr Martin Asal

THE FIRM

Thümmel, Schütze & Partner (TSP) was founded in 1973 in Stuttgart. Since then the firm has grown steadily and today comprises almost 60 lawyers, including a notary in Stuttgart and a notary in Berlin. In addition to its German offices, TSP has been operating for more than 20 years in Singapore, the only German law firm with such a long-term presence in the Southeast Asian region. Over the years, TSP has advised on and participated in numerous prominent commercial transactions with a focus on cross-border investment, mergers and acquisitions, corporate internationalisation and restructuring, as well as German and international litigation and arbitration.

The client structure of the firm corresponds to its services and international work: numerous well-known German and international banks as well as internationally orientated large and medium-sized enterprises regularly call on TSP's legal expertise.

TSP is not affiliated with any other law firm, but it does maintain long-standing bilateral ties with renowned foreign law firms across the globe. TSP's lawyers appreciate the opportunity to work in teams with international clients' management, their legal departments and local external counsel alike. TSP's ultimate objective is to provide prime legal services while finding efficient and creative solutions for the individual client's needs whether for specific issues or comprehensive interdisciplinary projects. In pursuance of its philosophy, TSP always tries to combine the advantages of a continuous personal working relationship of the client with the specific partner of the firm and the vast resources of TSP as a firm in terms of specialist expertise.

GHANA

Population	**21 million**
Number of lawyers	**3,000 (approx)**
Professional title	**Barrister; solicitor**
Currency	**Cedi (GHC))**

Index

In 1957, Ghana became the first sub-Saharan African colony to gain independence. As implied by the territory's British imperial name of the Gold Coast, Ghana benefits from a rich endowment of natural resources, including not only gold, but timber, bauxite, diamonds and manganese, which generates double the per capita income of its neighbours Côte d'Ivoire, Burkina Faso and Togo. However, the average per capita GDP estimate of US$2,300 (2004) conceals the huge inequalities of an economy in which 60% of the labour force is engaged in subsistence agriculture. Aids/HIV continues to have a significant impact on economic output and life expectancy. UNAIDS estimates that 4.9% of the population of 21 million are Aids/HIV positive; significantly less than the sub-Saharan average of 7.5%, but nonetheless a major problem for the government.

Ghana has suffered one-party government and two periods of military rule since independence but the 'Third Republic' constitutional democracy established in 1992 now seems secure. With an independent judiciary and a free press, Ghana is something of a model for the development of a functioning democracy in the region.

President John Kufuor was re-elected in December 2004 for a four-year term and his NPP (New Patriotic Party) clinched a narrow overall majority in the 230-seat Parliament. The political stability which has prevailed in Ghana since 1992 has encouraged the development of close ties with its West African neighbours, principally through the 15 nation strong Economic Community of West African States (ECOWAS). Ghana also is a leading member of the African Union and the fifth largest contributor to UN operations in the region.

The benefits of stability also show in international support for Ghana, which, despite much socio-political progress, remains heavily reliant on aid. Since 2003 about a third of development assistance to Ghana has been delivered by the MDBS (Multi Donor Budgetary Support) pooled funding initiative supported by the World Bank, the EU and nation states including the UK and France. The MDBS framework provides not only cash but support for good practice in governance and macro-economic management. Corruption in Ghana is regarded as moderate for the region.

BILLING

International clients should treat fees in Ghana as negotiable. The high inflation rate has rendered the cedi a fairly volatile currency and local rates for routine work are understandably not available to inward investors. Most firms are happy to discuss fees in advance and agree fixed or contingency rates for defined instructions. For guidance, 'international' hourly charge out rates for partners in Ghana generally fall in the range €125 to €175, with assistants being billed from €80 upwards according to experience.

POLITICAL CLIMATE

President John Kufuor, an Oxford-educated English barrister with long political experience, has tried to break down the tribal bonds which tend to dominate African politics and develop an inclusive democracy while promoting outward-looking regional and global policies. The National Reconciliation Commission set up by Kufuor in 2002 to examine the human rights abuses of the 1980s, submitted its report to the Ghanaian government in April 2005 but its findings have not yet been made public. Ghana's human rights record is now generally considered good. The Ghana Poverty Reduction Strategy, monitored by the IMF, continues to make progress alongside policies promoted to improve health, education and development of the rural economy.

Regionally, Ghana has established a reputation for constructive diplomacy. President Kufuor's two-year terms as chairman of ECOWAS came to an end in 2005. During his term, Kufuor was one of the principal brokers in the deal which ended Liberia's 14-year civil war. ECOWAS's wider economic aspirations towards a common regional currency, a common agricultural policy and a West African 'power pool' are proving difficult to achieve.

ECONOMY

Ghana's economy is founded largely on agriculture and mineral extraction; cocoa and gold are the major export commodities. Tourism also contributes to foreign earnings. Remittances from expatriate Ghanaians now comprise a significant flow; the Bank of Ghana reported inward remittances from private individuals of US$305m in the first quarter of 2005. This largesse reflects one of Ghana's main impediments to development: according to World Bank research,

45% of graduate and skilled Ghanaians work in the EU or North America.

Most industrial production supplies domestic and regional markets. Ghana has a well-developed downstream oil industry with a large refinery at Port Tema, 30km east of Accra; crude oil is supplied from Nigeria. The construction of the long-planned, US$620m, West African Gas Pipeline, which will link the Nigerian gas-fields with Ghana, Togo and Benin, began in September 2005; the project is backed by Shell, Chevron and the World Bank.

The IMF is broadly content with Ghana's macroeconomic performance and business confidence is firm. Growth for 2005 is put at 5.8%, inflation is falling and budget deficits have declined. The now independent Bank of Ghana's provisional headline inflation rate for the first three months of 2005 was about 15%, a significant improvement on the 24% rate in 2003.

Despite progress, and a clear commitment from government to move Ghana forward, the challenges facing the economy are huge. Infrastructure improvements to telecoms, roads and energy distribution are proceeding slowly although initiatives are in place to accelerate these. Bureaucratic impediments to private sector expansion remain. Privatisation has featured in the Ghanaian economy since 1988 and several hundred state-owned enterprises have been divested in whole or in part; Ghana Telecom for instance was privatised in 1996. In January 2005 Ghana began the partial privatisation of its under-performing water company supported by a loan of US$103m from the World Bank

LEGAL SYSTEM AND LEGAL MARKET

The Ghanaian legal system is founded on English common law with customary law adaptation where appropriate. The fairly high level of public confidence in the legal system derives as much from the comparatively low level of judicial corruption as from the 1992 constitution which guarantees the independence of the judiciary.

Despite the improving rate of economic growth and inward investment, it seems unlikely that the market for legal services will reach a size in the medium term sufficient to tempt an international firm to open an Accra office. Practices with regional networks in Africa and the Middle East do undertake work in Ghana, for instance, **Norton Rose** was recently instructed by Gold Fields Limited, the South African mining company, to advise on the Ghanaian aspects of a US$2.1bn merger deal with IAMGold, a Canadian company. **Denton Wilde Sapte**'s London and Cairo offices work closely with local firm **Bentsi-Enchill & Letsa** on high-value deals. **Denton Wilde Sapte** has advised on trade financing for the Ghana Cocoa Board, major power projects and, on behalf of Standard Chartered Bank, a US$20m syndicated facility for Ghana Telecoms. **Æ LEX**, with three branches in Nigeria, has a full-service Accra office; the firm boasts particular strengths in the oil, gas and petroleum sectors.

Ghanaian law firms are increasingly addressing the international markets. The internet has facilitated marketing and some firms' websites are both sophisticated and informative. Several firms have established international links. **Bentsi-Enchill & Letsa** is sole Ghanaian member of *Lex Mundi*, **Fugar & Co** belongs to regional network *Lex Africa* and **Laryea, Laryea & Company P.C.** boasts *TerraLex* membership.

CORPORATE AND M&A

Five-partner **Bentsi-Enchill & Letsa** boasts an excellent reputation as a professional firm, and is hugely popular with commercial clients for corporate finance, securitisation and M&A due diligence. In September 2005 **Bentsi-Enchill & Letsa** worked with **Gide Loyrette Nouel MNP** in London on behalf of Iroko Securities Limited to create a ground-breaking repackaging of Ghanaian promissory notes utilising a Mauritian SPV. Founding partner and 'class-act' Kojo Bentsi-Enchill is an accomplished corporate lawyer who gained early experience at **Shearman & Sterling LLP** in New York, while Ace Anan Ankomah is expert in international matters, including taxation.

Fugar & Co now fields 14 lawyers. Founder William Fugar has a reputation for resolute commerciality, and Iris Richter-Addo offers a niche specialisation in IP, particularly 'traditional knowledge' with reference to genetic patenting. **Fugar & Co**'s expertise in capital markets received recognition when the firm was asked to assist the Ghana Stock Exchange and the government in drafting regulations for Collective Investment Schemes. The firm attracts numerous referrals from the region through membership of *Lex Africa* as well as working with leading global law firms such as **Mayer, Brown, Rowe & Maw LLP**; **Baker & McKenzie LLP**; and **Slaughter and May**. **Fugar & Co**'s high-calibre corporate finance and securities practice features prominently in mining sector transactions. The firm has also recently been instructed by First Boston Bank, and the Caterpillar Corporation.

Hesse & Hesse's David Hesse, a recognised authority on banking and intellectual property matters, recently worked with **Howrey LLP** to register Intel Corporation trade marks in Ghana. Partner Larsey Mensah is Ghana's environmental law guru. The growing firm now fields 11 fee-earners, attracts a blue-chip following and works with overseas law firms such as **Cleary, Gottlieb, Steen & Hamilton LLP**. A notable litigation victory was claimed by **Hesse & Hesse** in 2005 when a US$1.5m negligence claim against Merchant Bank (Ghana) Limited was successfully defended, and amongst a sheaf of interesting transactional instructions, the firm were lead advisors to AfriCap Microfinance on its acquisition of a 19% stake in Mozambique's Socremo Banco de Microfinancas.

CORPORATE AND M&A

BENTSI-ENCHILL & LETSA ✪

Fugar & Co
Hesse & Hesse
JLD Legal Consultancy Services ✪
Tetteh & Co

Awoonor Law Consultancy
Kudjawu & Co
Laryea, Laryea & Company P.C.
Reindorf Chambers
Sam Okudzeto & Associates

Firms are listed A-Z in tiers which are ranked in order of priority
✪ Indicates firm displays contact details at the end of this chapter.

JLD Legal Consultancy Services is frequently involved in Ghana's high-profile corporate transactions. Commercially minded senior partner, LSE alumna Joyce Darko, called to both the English and Ghanaian bars, 'is excellent; one of the best people in Ghana' according to one client. During 2005 **JLD Legal Consultancy Services** acted in the Total Oil Ghana Limited merger with Mobil Oil Ghana Limited, and for Ghana Commercial Bank in connection with the issue and flotation of new shares on the Ghana Stock Exchange. **JLD Legal Consultancy Services** also acted successfully for Sarah Lee DE International BV over trade mark infringement in Ghana.

Current president of the Ghanaian Bar Association, Kwami Tetteh, name partner at **Tetteh & Co**, has a long list of blue-chip clients including AngloGold Ashanti and Barclays Bank Ghana Limited. **Tetteh & Co** fields seven experienced lawyers offering a full-service corporate and commercial practice, including litigation. The firm boasts particular expertise in the telecoms sector having set up and dealt with the syndicated financing of Millicom Ghana Limited, the country's first mobile telephone operator, and a recent credit line to Ghana Telecom to facilitate network expansion. **Tetteh & Co**, is currently advising IT player Webintec Group on WAN exploitation.

Three-lawyer **Awoonor Law Consultancy** brings a pragmatic, commercial approach to dispute resolution. Name partner Ekow Awoonor is an experienced operator who has recently advised on the complex acquisition of a majority interest in Phyto-Riker Pharmaceuticals Ghana Limited. **Awoonor Law Consultancy** acts as local counsel for Fortis Bank (Nederland) NV and in 2005 advised Louis Dreyfus Corporation in connection with a rolling commodity finance deal.

Kudjawu & Co is recommended as a 'very good' general commercial practice. Name partner Norbert Kujdawu has served on the founding board of the Ghana Stock Exchange and as a director of the Bank of Ghana. Stanley Amarteifio, commended as a strong practitioner, boasts wide experience in insurance matters. **Kudjawu & Co** also offers the services of patent attorneys.

Laryea, Laryea & Company P.C. fields six fee-earners from two offices in Accra; name partner Kenneth Laryea is recommended for his 'commitment, thoroughness and decorum'. As well as a full-service commercial practice, **Laryea, Laryea & Company P.C.** is perhaps Ghana's premier firm for shipping. It advised Teledesic in obtaining a high-speed broadband frequency telecoms licence and has represented a number of leading airlines including KLM and Singapore Airlines.

'Professional, dedicated and thorough' **Reindorf Chambers**, 'well-respected by the judiciary and the legal community', is particularly noted for expertise in mining and energy matters. Fui Tsikata, head of **Reindorf Chambers**, until recently, taught the Natural Resources Law course at Accra University; but has succumbed to client demands and is now in full time practice. Tsikata has acted for numerous major mining and power players including Gold Fields Ghana and St Jude Resources. During 2005 **Reindorf Chambers** advised CAL Bank on its conversion from private to public company and subsequent listing. **Reindorf Chambers** made a useful hire in 2005 with ex-Ernst & Young Ghana tax consultant Kizzita Mensah joining.

Sam Okudzeto of **Sam Okudzeto & Associates** is, perhaps, Ghana's most venerable practising lawyer, a former member of the Ghana parliament and former president of the Ghana Bar Association. Okudzeto chaired a presidential commission into a football stadium disaster in Accra and is currently Chairman of the Commonwealth Human Rights International Advisory Commission. **Sam Okudzeto & Associates** acts for a range of corporate and commercial clients including mining companies, foreign investment companies and embassies. In December 2005 Sam Okudzeto successfully represented Ghana Guinness Breweries Limited in a fast-track interlocutory hearing brought by a minority shareholder to prevent the AGM proceeding.

PROJECTS AND PRIVATISATION

With over 300 state-owned enterprises privatised since 1988, the scope for further divestment is limited; only the controversial privatisation of Ghana's urban water system seems imminent. Major projects, however are in train. With aid investment more strictly monitored by donors and increased stability in the region encouraging inward investment, demand for legal services in major capital projects seems set to grow over the short and medium terms.

Many of the firms mentioned for commercial and corporate expertise will enter the market but at present, we mention those firms which have demonstrated the capacity and expertise to handle major long-term project work.

Bentsi-Enchill & Letsa has been involved throughout the divestment programme, and acted in connection with the State Insurance Corporation, Ghana Aluminium and Ghana Sugar Estates privatisations. The firm is very active in the energy and mining sector: Kojo Bentsi-Enchill serves on the technical committee of the Ghana Energy Commission. **Bentsi-Enchill & Letsa** has solid experience in the petroleum sector and advised Korean SK Engineering & Construction on the financing of its US$250m contract for the construction of a residual fluid catalytic cracker at Tema oil refinery which is due to be commissioned in September 2006.

Fugar & Co has represented the foreign purchaser of the government interest in Ghana Film Corporation; and more recently advised on the privatisation of the water sector and on the funding of new gold mining projects.

Laryea, Laryea & Company P.C.'s blue-chip clientele includes ALCOA, which the firm is advising in negotiations with the Ghana Government to create an integrated aluminium industry; and CMS Generation, which is being represented in connection with a major power plant expansion.

During 2005 **Reindorf Chambers** advised Barclays Bank on the financing of the Trafigura Beheer BV £36m mooring facility at Tema Port. **Reindorf Chambers**' Fui Tsikata was involved in the country's first and largest privatisation ten years ago, the sale of shares in Ashanti Goldfields.

PROJECTS AND PRIVATISATION

Bentsi-Enchill & Letsa ✪
Fugar & Co
Laryea, Laryea & Company P.C.
Reindorf Chambers

Firms are listed alphabetically.
✪ *Indicates firm displays contact details at the end of this chapter.*

BENTSI-ENCHILL & LETSA

1ST FLOOR
TEACHERS' HALL COMPLEX
EDUCATION LOOP
(OFF BARNES ROAD)
ADABRAKA
ACCRA

Telephone: +233 21 221 171
Fax: +233 21 226 129
Website: www.belonline.org

Languages
English, French

Number of lawyers 21

International groupings
Ghana Member of Lex Mundi;
Denton Wilde Sapte Africa Association

CATEGORIES OF WORK

Corporate finance
Kojo Bentsi-Enchill

Capital restructuring
Kojo Bentsi-Enchill

Banking
Kojo Bentsi-Enchill

Trade and project finance
Kojo Bentsi-Enchill

Privatisation
Kojo Bentsi-Enchill

Intellectual property
Kojo Bentsi-Enchill

Energy
Kojo Bentsi-Enchill

Environment
Kojo Bentsi-Enchill

Mining and natural resources
Kojo Bentsi-Enchill

Foreign investment
Kojo Bentsi-Enchill

Property and conveyancy
Divine Kwaku Duwose Letsa

Trusts and estate matters
Divine Kwaku Duwose Letsa

Insurance
Divine Kwaku Duwose Letsa

Aviation and shipping
Divine Kwaku Duwose Letsa

Labour and employment
Kojo Bentsi-Enchill

Family and adoption
Divine Kwaku Duwose Letsa

Litigation
Ace Anan Ankomah

Dispute resolution
Ace Anan Ankomah

JLD LEGAL CONSULTANCY SERVICES

NO 6 SENCHI STREET
AIRPORT RESIDENTIAL AREA
ACCRA

Telephone: +233 21 782 711
Fax: +233 21 784 477
E-mail: jld@jldlaw.net
Website: www.jldlaw.net

Languages
English, French

Number of lawyers 7

Contact
Ms Joyce Darko

Member
Ghana Bar Association; Ghana National Committee of OHADA; Ghana Arbitration Centre; Ghana Association of Chartered Mediators and Arbitrators

CATEGORIES OF WORK

Corporate and commercial law
Joyce Darko, Pala Kwawukume

Mergers and acquisitions
Joyce Darko, Victor Anku-Tsede

Building and engineering contracts
Joyce Darko

Minerals and mining law
Joyce Darko

Alternative dispute resolution
Joyce Darko, Kwasi Prempeh-Eck

Laws of immovable property
Kwasi Prempeh-Eck, Victor Anku-Tsede

Nationality and immigration
Joyce Darko, Kwasi Prempeh-Eck

Contracts
Joyce Darko, Pala Kwawukume

Securities industry law
Joyce Darko, Pala Kwawukume

Law of natural resources
Joyce Darko

Law of taxation
Victor Anku-Tsede, Pala Kwawukume

Insurance claims
Abla Masoperh, Pala Kwawukume

Labour issues and industrial relations
Kwasi Prempeh-Eck, Victor Anku-Tsede

Intellectual property
Pala Kwawukume, Victor Anku-Tsede

Litigation
Victor Anku-Tsede, Pala Kwawukume

Human rights law
Abla Masoperh

Electronic (internet) law
Pala Kwawukume

Telecommunications law
Pala Kwawukume

GIBRALTAR

Population	**27,884**
Number of lawyers	**144**
Professional title	**Solicitor; barrister**
Currency	**Gibraltar pound/pound sterling)**

Index

Gibraltar is located on the southern coast of Spain, more specifically on the Strait of Gibraltar, which links the Atlantic Ocean with the Mediterranean Sea, in between Europe and Africa. Also known as 'Gib' or 'the Rock', Gibraltar is a self-governing British overseas territory and one of the most densely populated territories in the world.

Historically, the issue of sovereignty over Gibraltar has been the source of great controversy between Spain and the United Kingdom, presenting itself as one of the thorns in international relations between both countries. In 2002, both the Spanish and British governments agreed on joint sovereignty over Gibraltar, but a referendum was carried out by the Gibraltarian government and a majority of 98.97% of voters in Gibraltar voted against the shared sovereignty plan. The constitution states that there can be no transfer of sovereignty against the wishes of the people, and whilst this is the case the situation is unlikely to change. In October 2004, however, foreign ministers from both countries agreed to enter into further dialogue about Gibraltar's future status. The dispute, which has lasted for almost three centuries, seems to have settled down under the rule of Spanish acting Prime Minister, José Luís Rodriguez Zapatero.

As a British overseas territory, Gibraltar's chief of state is Queen Elizabeth II, represented by Governor and Commander-in-Chief, Sir Francis Richards, since May 2003. The head of government is currently Chief Minister Peter Caruana (elected to office in 1996) and his cabinet is comprised of a Council of Ministers appointed by the governor, in consultation with the Chief Minister, from among the 15 elected members of the House of Assembly.

Defence and foreign affairs remain the responsibility of the UK. Gibraltar's enviable position within the EU but outside the EU VAT area means it can offer tax-exempt company status.

BILLING

Hourly billing is the general custom in Gibraltar and lawyers' rates may vary from around €120 for a junior associate to €570 for a senior partner.

MARKETING

Marketing rules in Gibraltar are relaxed compared with more conservative neighbour Spain. However whilst some firms actively promote themselves, some of the more established ones are reluctant to do so, relying instead on word-of-mouth recommendation to generate business.

IN-HOUSE LAWYERS

Gibraltar's major businesses do not have the tradition of employing in-house lawyers. Even where they do exist, law firms are still called upon to advise on certain matters.

ECONOMY

Tourism, offshore finance and shipping make the greatest contributions to the economy, with telecoms and e-business emerging as a fourth pillar. The telecoms sector is consolidating itself through the establishment of specialised businesses such as satellite control centres and web-hosting. The Rock's thriving and increasingly sophisticated financial services sector has evolved thanks to Gibraltar's unique status as an offshore finance centre within Europe exempt from levying VAT. Banks, insurance companies and investment services can also benefit from special 'passporting rights' granted to Gibraltar, through which they are able to access the EU financial markets.

LEGAL SYSTEM

Gibraltar's legal system is based on English common law and statutes. The legal profession is fused, meaning lawyers – whether solicitors or barristers – carry out similar work; no distinction is made between the two in respect of rights of audience. The profession's governing body is the General Council of the Bar, but disciplinary powers are vested in the Chief Justice. The civil courts in Gibraltar are, in ascending order: the Court of First Instance; the Supreme Court; the Court of Appeal; and the Privy Council in London. The laws of Gibraltar were launched on-line in 2004, and can be found on the government's website at www.gibraltarlaw.gov.gi

LEGAL MARKET

Traditionally, the Gibraltar legal market was comprised of small family firms and sole practitioners and, unsurprisingly, few people specialised. Family practices are still a major feature of the market, but are increasingly shaping themselves into full-service firms with separate

The largest firms

1	Hassans	52
2	Marrache & Co	28
3	Isola & Isola	20
4	Triay and Triay	15
5	Triay Stagnetto Neish	11
6	Attias & Levy	9
7	Cruz & Co	3
	Stephen Bullock & Company	3
9	Budhrani & Co	2
	Massias & Partners	2
	Nuñez & Co	2
12	Glaisyers	1
	R A Triay & Co	1

These figures represent the total number of lawyers in this country only, and have been supplied by the firms themselves. The figures should be accurate as at 1 January 2006.

departments. **Hassans**, established in the 1930s, is the largest firm on the Rock and was the first to model itself in this way. The firm's growth in size seems unstoppable and it is now close to being three times larger than the second largest. The oldest firm is **Isola & Isola**, which was set up in 1892, followed closely by **Triay and Triay**, which celebrated its centenary in 2005.

Triay Stagnetto Neish was formed in 2001 following the merger between *Louis W Triay & Partners* and *Stagnetto & Co*, which had both been active since the 1950s. **Denton Wilde Sapte** closed its Gibraltar office in February 2006; it was the only international with a presence in Gibraltar. **Marrache & Co** was the first law firm to open its own office in London in addition to representative offices in Lisbon and Marbella. There is a noticeable gap between these firms and the smaller practices recommended both in terms of size and the type of transactions handled. The latter still attract a wide range of clients and remain first choice for some because of the personal service they offer.

BANKING AND FINANCE

Gibraltar continues to consolidate its position as a buoyant and reputable finance centre. Financial institutions are supervised by the independent Financial Services Commission, which applies strict regulatory standards equivalent to those in the UK. Such is the credibility of its financial regulation that the Rock has been heralded a benchmark jurisdiction in Europe.

It is an attractive choice for financial institutions as it is the only finance centre within the EU exempt from levying VAT. It also offers banks and insurance companies the opportunity to access, or 'passport' their services into the European market.

The finance sector is also becoming increasingly diversified and sophisticated. The insurance sector has experienced major growth; nearly 50 companies are now licensed on the Rock compared to just 11 three years ago. Apart from the obvious tax privileges, an added attraction for investors is the accessibility and efficiency of the regulators. Gibraltar has also become a European centre for derivatives trading, and has been approved by Liffe and Eurex (Eurex opened a new access point for member firms there in 2004). Other specialist areas include securitisation and repackaging.

Hassans boasts a large number of the leading banking and finance specialists. The firm's practice spans corporate structures (special purpose vehicles), licensing and establishment of financial institutions, regulatory and compliance advice, repackaging of debt, restructuring of credit institutions, securitisation of assets and setting up of credit institutions. **Hassans** originally set up most of the major banks and insurance companies in Gibraltar. Valerie Holliday and Nigel Feetham are the key partners in the banking and finance department.

BANKING AND FINANCE

HASSANS ✪
TRIAY AND TRIAY ✪

Isola & Isola

Marrache & Co ✪
Massias & Partners
Triay Stagnetto Neish

Attias & Levy
Charles A Gomez, Barrister-at-Law
Nuñez & Co
Stephen Bullock & Company

Firms are listed A-Z in tiers which are ranked in order of priority
✪ *Indicates firm displays contact details at the end of this chapter.*

Another highly reputed practice in Gibraltar is **Triay and Triay** whose offering spans banking (having advised several foreign banks importing their own domestic background into their Gibraltar operations), insurance (advising both on the formation of insurance companies, and the onward requirements of conducting insurance business) and financial services (assisting with all other activities requiring licensing under the Financial Services Ordinance). The firm is regularly involved in large transactions. Robert Vasquez and Javier Triay are highly regarded for their expertise in this field.

Isola & Isola boasts well-established expertise in the banking sector. Clients include a number of major international investment banks. Partner Christian Hernandez is recommended.

Marrache & Co boasts in-depth experience in banking and investment matters. While providing sound advice in the setting up of banking or investment schemes, the firm is also capable of offering a wide range of wealth-structuring services. Managing partner Benjamin Marrache has acted on a number of high-profile deals in the jurisdiction.

Massias & Partners is regularly involved in high-profile operations for a number of international banks. The firm also boasts strong expertise in securitisations. Partner Isaac Massias is a well-known practitioner in Gibraltar.

Triay Stagnetto Neish's solid banking and finance practice also boasts insurance capabilities. The firm has acted and continues to act for numerous insurers and captive insurers in Gibraltar. Partner Charles Lavarello is frequently involved in property financing transactions.

One of the main fortes at **Attias & Levy** is financial services issues, having most notably acted in the insurance sector for the underwriters in a misselling case. Name partners Abraham Levy (banking), Levi Attias (financial services) and partner Keith Azopardi (financial services) are the firm's key individuals in this field.

Also enjoying a solid reputation in Gibraltar, **Charles A Gomez, Barrister-at-Law** has advised on various debt recovery issues.

Nuñez & Co's clients include investment management firms and banks. Paul and Joseph Nuñez are recommended practitioners.

Stephen Bullock & Company has advised a number of international clients in several banking and finance matters.

CORPORATE AND M&A

Gibraltar is a magnet for offshore company formations owing to its status as a major finance centre within the EU.

Corporate and commercial is **Hassans**' most important practice area. The firm has three major focus points: acting for major US, Canadian and European-listed groups (a large number of them *Fortune 100* companies) in corporate restructurings – one of the firm's major growth areas spearheaded by partner Michael Castiel; internet betting operations, especially acting for London Stock Exchange-listed companies PartyGaming Plc and 888.com, namely advising on the setting up of internet betting companies, applying for licences and securing the Gibraltar side for the listing of the companies – another of the major growth areas in the firm, led by Peter Montegriffo; and the private client and trusts area, where senior partner James Levy QC leads the firm's advice on general structuring work (personal trusts and corporate structures). Highlights include advising General Electric in connection with its US$500m sale of 60% of GE Capital International Services to General Atlantic Partners and Oakhill Capital Partners.

Isola & Isola's corporate practice spans corporate and trust matters, particularly the formation of offshore companies and trusts within the jurisdiction and abroad, and is regularly involved in multi-jurisdictional transactions with a Gibraltar element. Managing partner Peter A Isola is considered one of the best corporate practitioners in Gibraltar. The firm's company management business, Fiduciary Management Ltd, is the largest in Gibraltar.

Triay and Triay is regarded as a leading practice in the corporate and commercial field. Its expertise includes having the largest practice in intellectual property in Gibraltar. The firm's corporate and commercial work spans a wide range of matters, from company incorporations to shareholder and joint venture agreements, and M&A.

With solid cross-border expertise **Marrache & Co** has a well-established corporate team handling numerous international restructurings on behalf of well-known listed companies. Senior partner Isaac Marrache spearheads the practice and has acted for a number of high-profile domestic and international clients.

CORPORATE AND M&A

HASSANS ✪

ISOLA & ISOLA

TRIAY AND TRIAY ✪

Marrache & Co ✪

Triay Stagnetto Neish

Attias & Levy

Charles A Gomez, Barrister-at-Law

Eric C Ellul & Co

Cruz & Co

Glaisyers

Massias & Partners

R A Triay & Co

Stephen Bullock & Company

Firms are listed A-Z in tiers which are ranked in order of priority

✪ *Indicates firm displays contact details at the end of this chapter.*

Triay Stagnetto Neish provides a wide range of commercial, financial and corporate advice. The firm has a large client base, which includes both local and international clients and has established a solid practice covering a variety of areas, including corporate finance, commercial and construction contracts, joint venture and partnerships, M&A and management buy-outs and take-overs.

With 12 lawyers (including two partners) **Attias & Levy** is one of the five largest firms in Gibraltar. Abraham Levy is frequently involved on the Gibraltar end of multi-jurisdictional deals. The firm offers advisory and managerial services to numerous private and corporate clients.

Charles A Gomez, Barrister-at-Law's main area of expertise is company incorporation and management.

Incorporation of companies and offshore structuring and tax planning are a few of the strengths at **Eric C Ellul & Co**.

Cruz & Co's head of practice is Paul Borge. Clients include large City firms, small companies and private individuals. The firm is able to provide advice on all aspects of corporate and commercial, including company formations, asset management, and drafting shareholding and loan agreements.

Massias & Partners' well-respected expertise in this field spans advice on purchase of assets and setting up structures in the UK and elsewhere.

R A Triay & Co can also provide sound corporate and commercial advice on a wide range of matters.

Stephen Bullock & Company's corporate practice spans advice on company incorporations and on setting up tax-efficient structures for international and domestic clients.

CORPORATE TAX

HASSANS ✪

ISOLA & ISOLA

TRIAY AND TRIAY ✪

TRIAY STAGNETTO NEISH

Marrache & Co ✪

Attias & Levy

Charles A Gomez, Barrister-at-Law

Glaisyers

Firms are listed A-Z in tiers which are ranked in order of priority

✪ *Indicates firm displays contact details at the end of this chapter.*

CORPORATE TAX

Gibraltar is awaiting a decision from the European Court of Justice relating to its overdue corporate tax reforms, which were due to come into place in July 2003. Although approved by EU finance ministers, the draft laws were subsequently found to be in breach of EU rules on state aid by the Competition Commissioner. The government has challenged this decision.

Hassans senior partner James Levy QC is head of tax at the firm. He offers broad experience in corporate and international tax work, and has earned a reputation in Gibraltar for innovation in these areas. He was involved in setting up one of the first substantial unit trusts in Gibraltar and recently advised on the drafting and piloting of a bill through the Gibraltar House of Assembly relating to a bank's conversion from a subsidiary to a branch. Michael Castiel led the firm's advice to General Electric in the multi-jusrisdictional tax and corporate structure put in place to facilitate the US$500m sale of 60% of GE Capital International Services to two leading private equity firms.

With full-service capability in corporate tax advisory, **Isola & Isola** is another of the well-established practices. The firm advises private clients on tax and offshore trust matters.

Triay and Triay boast solid tax expertise spanning financial and tax planning and business taxation.

Triay Stagnetto Neish has in partners Louis W Triay QC and Lewis B Triay two of the most respected practitioners in Gibraltar.

Marrache & Co has in Benjamin and Isaac Marrache its best-known tax experts, offering multi-jurisdictional tax planning expertise. Clients of the firm include high-net-worth individuals and increasingly sports personalities.

Charles A Gomez, Barrister-at-Law has acted on behalf of the authorities in numerous tax cases in Gibraltar.

Name partner Abraham Levy, at **Attias & Levy**, is regularly involved private client tax issues.

DISPUTE RESOLUTION

HASSANS ✪

ISOLA & ISOLA
TRIAY AND TRIAY ✪
TRIAY STAGNETTO NEISH

Attias & Levy
Budhrani & Co
Charles A Gomez, Barrister-at-Law
Cruz & Co
Eric C Ellul & Co
Marrache & Co ✪
R A Triay & Co
Stephen Bullock & Company

Firms are listed A-Z in tiers which are ranked in order of priority
✪ Indicates firm displays contact details at the end of this chapter.

DISPUTE RESOLUTION

Hassans' disputes practice is going from strength to strength. Louis Baglietto spearheads the litigation team, the largest and one of the finest in Gibraltar, recently strengthened with the arrival of expert partner Daniel Feetham from **Isola & Isola**. James Levy QC and Louis Baglietto led the firm's successful advice to the Transport and General Workers Union in a matter of breach of contract by the British MoD, which culminated in a groundbreaking ruling by the Gibraltarian court establishing that it had jurisdiction over the British government. John Restano is also recommended in commercial litigation and shipping.

Isola & Isola saw one of its star partners leave for **Hassans** last year, but still offers a quality practice. Peter J Isola and Rebecca Mahon are two of the firm's best-known personalities.

Triay and Triay has established a solid reputation for the efficient and imaginative representation of clients' interests in litigation matters. Senior partner Joseph E Triay QC and JE Triay junior (who specialises in asset tracing in liquidations and bankruptcies) are highly respected litigators.

Triay Stagnetto Neish's outstanding litigation practice advises on almost all aspects of litigation and also has considerable experience in arbitration and Alternative Dispute Resolution.

Attias & Levy's litigation practice spans commercial, financial, property and public administrative disputes. Keith Azopardi is the firm's head of practice and has, most notably, represented one of the two main unions in Gibraltar in a case against the Ministry of Defence.

Charles A Gomez, Barrister-at-Law's quality litigation team has advised a number of foreign clients on a wide variety of contentious matters including banking litigation and insolvency, tax litigation, construction arbitration, employment disputes, as well as professional and medical negligence, and personal injury.

IT AND TELECOMS

HASSANS ✪
ISOLA & ISOLA
MARRACHE & CO ✪
TRIAY AND TRIAY ✪

Attias & Levy

Firms are listed A-Z in tiers which are ranked in order of priority
✪ Indicates firm displays contact details at the end of this chapter.

Kerrin Drago brings her strong personal injury expertise to **Cruz & Co**'s busy litigation department.

Eric C Ellul & Co has in Eric C Ellul MBE and Mark Ellul its best-known personalities in this field.

Marrache & Co's litigation expert is Tony Christodoulides, who has experience in anti-money laundering cases.

Personal injury work is also a major strength at **R A Triay & Co**.

Stephen Bullock & Company mainly deals with civil and criminal litigation issues involving maritime law.

IT AND TELECOMS

The telecoms market remains very small despite liberalisation, so there is little in the way of legal activity. Gibraltar is, however, developing its profile as an e-commerce centre, and lawyers have mainly been occupied with work generated through the growth of the on-line betting and gaming sector.

Hassans advises several governments, which are deregulating their industries on the framing of suitable legislation, including the government of Gibraltar on the implementation of legislation on telecoms. Other clients include global and local operators seeking advice on regulatory environments, namely Gibraltar's main telecoms network Gibtelecom. Partner Peter Montegriffo is the firm's expert in this field.

Isola & Isola's clients include a number of businesses in the on-line gaming sector, while **Marrache & Co** is also recommended in the telecoms sector; Benjamin Marrache is experienced.

Triay and Triay has advised on-line betting businesses in relation to IT issues. Robert Vasquez is the firm's best-known personality.

Attias & Levy has experience in the field, namely dealing with applications for telecoms licences.

PRIVATE CLIENT

HASSANS ✪
ISOLA & ISOLA
MARRACHE & CO ✪
TRIAY AND TRIAY ✪

Glaisyers
Triay Stagnetto Neish

Attias & Levy
Charles A Gomez, Barrister-at-Law
Massias & Partners

Firms are listed A-Z in tiers which are ranked in order of priority
✪ Indicates firm displays contact details at the end of this chapter.

PRIVATE CLIENT

Hassans offers quality advice to a wide range of private clients, spanning acquisition of residential status, advice and structure for wealth protection and enhancement, for both residents and non-residents, establishment of trusts, including discretionary trusts and asset-protection trusts and a full range of tax advice. The firm has advised in excess of £3bn-worth in property investment structuring transactions and has a number of high-net Israeli private clients with investments in the UK.

Isola & Isola's Peter A Isola brings solid expertise in various matters involving trust and tax planning advice.

Marrache & Co has a strong focus in private client matters, with Benjamin Marrache developing the firm's trusts capability.

Triay and Triay advises private clients on financial and tax planning, personal and business taxation, creation, management and reorganisation of trusts, probate and winding up of estates upon death, property and family and asset management. F Javier Triay, James Ramagge and Charles Simpson are the expert partners in this field.

Triay Stagnetto Neish's renowned private client practice collects high praise from clients and rivals alike. Managing partner Louis B Triay is one of the best-known individuals in the field.

Trusts work, structuring and asset holding are some of the issues **Attias & Levy** advises on within the general private client area. The firm's head of department is name partner Levi Attias.

Charles A Gomez, Barrister-at-Law boasts solid trusts experience.

Massias & Partners' private client work covers trusts, tax planning, and asset structuring.

REAL ESTATE AND CONSTRUCTION

Gibraltar has experienced a boom in property development over the last 15 years, largely owing to the reclamation of harbour land, which has led to an increase in real estate. Residential construction has been the fastest growth area, but many believe this has now reached its peak. Firms are increasingly advising developers and individuals with interests in Spain and Portugal, and some have created Spanish departments to meet demand.

REAL ESTATE AND CONSTRUCTION

HASSANS ✪
ISOLA & ISOLA
MARRACHE & CO ✪
TRIAY AND TRIAY ✪
TRIAY STAGNETTO NEISH

Attias & Levy
Charles A Gomez, Barrister-at-Law
Eric C Ellul & Co
Massias & Partners

Firms are listed A-Z in tiers which are ranked in order of priority
✪ *Indicates firm displays contact details at the end of this chapter.*

Hassans' real estate team is led by Dick Azopardi who has been developing Spanish law capacity to satisfy the needs of ex-pats requiring property and tax advice in Spain. Spanish-qualified lawyer Raoul Guittierez who is advising clients in this area enhances the team's international capability.

Isola & Isola has a leading practice in real estate and construction matters, having acted for one of the largest residential developers in Gibraltar. One of the firm's best-known personalities is Albert J Isola.

Marrache & Co covers all aspects of Gibraltarian, English and Spanish property laws as well as offering capability in setting up financial structures in property transactions.

Spanning conveyancing and commercial and residential property development projects, **Triay and Triay**'s well-respected real estate practice has advised a number of international banks in Gibraltar. Abraham B Serfaty QC and Julian R Triay are the partners in charge.

Triay Stagnetto Neish spans property development issues, conveyancing and is particularly experienced in dealing with Spanish and Portuguese property issues. Partner Charles Lavarello is the firm's best-known personality and has advised a number local and foreign developers and investors.

Another of the main fortes at **Attias & Levy** is property work. The firm regularly acts for banks, property developers and landlords. Stephen Catania is in charge of the firm's property practice, while Abraham Levy also takes part in some important property instructions.

A number of **Charles A Gomez, Barrister-at-Law**'s clients are individuals purchasing properties in Gibraltar.

Eric C Ellul & Co's real estate capabilities include conveyancing, regularly assisting clients with property transactions in Spain and Portugal.

Conveyancing work is also a mainstay at **Massias & Partners**, whose clients are often involved in some of the biggest property transactions in Gibraltar.

SHIPPING

Even though the shipping market has been very quiet recently, as a major shipping destination and the second biggest bunkering port in Europe, Gibraltar has some excellent shipping lawyers.

Triay and Triay enjoys a leading reputation within the shipping industry, advising a number of international clients in ship finance and registration, shipping litigation and advocacy in the Admiralty Jurisdiction of the Supreme Court of Gibraltar. The firm is also involved in drafting of security documentation. The firm's best-known personalities in the field are senior partner Joseph Emanuel Triay QC and James Ramagge.

Lewis Baglietto heads **Hassans**' litigation and shipping team, with John Restano being the firm's expert. The firm boasts strong expertise in ship arrest work and has, over the years, established close links with major English shipping law firms and been involved in a number of important admiralty cases, most of which have a strong international aspect.

Isola & Isola has in Christian Hernandez its most prominent shipping expert. He boasts particular expertise in ship arrest and is invariably involved in the majority of shipping cases in Gibraltar. Clients include the International Transport Worker's Federation, P&I clubs, banks and shipowners.

SHIPPING

TRIAY AND TRIAY ✪

HASSANS ✪
ISOLA & ISOLA

R A TRIAY & CO
TRIAY STAGNETTO NEISH

Attias & Levy
Charles A Gomez, Barrister-at-Law
Cruz & Co
Eric C Ellul & Co
Marrache & Co ✪

Firms are listed A-Z in tiers which are ranked in order of priority
✪ *Indicates firm displays contact details at the end of this chapter.*

R A Triay & Co's well-known Raymond Triay is the firm's head of practice. His experience as a maritime lawyer is widely acclaimed in the market, especially in ship finance and registration and arrests.

Joint senior partner AV Stagnetto QC and Guy Stagnetto provide solid expertise within **Triay Stagnetto Neish**'s shipping practice. The firm acts for major international shipping entities as well as international P&I clubs and is regularly involved in ship arrests.

Attias & Levy has been quite active in the litigation side of shipping issues. Keith Azopardi spearheads litigation advice, while Levi Attias also has experience in shipping registration issues.

Both **Charles A Gomez, Barrister-at-Law** and **Cruz & Co** boast solid expertise in ship and yacht registrations, ship arrests and litigation matters.

Eric C Ellul & Co's shipping expertise covers ship arrests, registration of vessels and representing both crew members and shipowners in disputes.

Marrache & Co represents a variety of international owners, cargo interests and banking institutions with vessel-oriented businesses and claims and is active in the registration of vessels in Gibraltar. The firm also boasts expertise in yacht registration.

HASSANS
INTERNATIONAL LAW FIRM

57-63 LINE WALL ROAD
PO BOX 199
GIBRALTAR

Telephone: +350 79000
Fax: +350 71966
E-mail: info@hassans.gi
Website: www.gibraltarlaw.com

Languages
Chinese (Cantonese, Mandarin), English, French, Hebrew, Italian, Portuguese, Spanish

Number of lawyers 55

Contacts
James Levy QC (senior partner), Michael Castiel

Member
TerraLex

CATEGORIES OF WORK

Corporate and commercial
James Levy QC, Michael Castiel

Banking
Tony Provasoli, Valerie Holliday

Litigation
David Dumas QC, Gilbert Licudi

Tax
James Levy QC, Chris White

Private client
James Levy QC, Javier Chincotta

Telecommunications
Tony Provasoli

Employment
Gilbert Licudi

Pensions, trusts
Peter C Montegriffo, Gilbert Licudi

Company management
James Levy QC, Desmond Reoch

Admiralty, maritime
Lewis Baglietto, John Restano

Insurance
Nigel Feetham

Bankruptcy, insolvency
David Dumas QC

Property, real estate
Dick Azopardi

Corporate redomiciliations
Michael Castiel, Nigel Feetham

Securitisation
Nigel Feetham

Dispute resolution
David Dumas QC, Lewis Baglietto

Internet gaming
Peter C Montegriffo, Javier Chincotta

Funds
Daniel Feetham

THE FIRM

Hassans was founded in 1939, and is the largest law firm in Gibraltar. It was the first in Gibraltar to structure itself as a modern international law firm, with separate departments for different fields of specialisation. Its aim is to give a high-quality, personal and effective service to its clients of whatever size or nature. The firm has an international clientele, which it continues to develop. It has links with major London, continental and US law firms.

Three quarters of the firm's work is related to international clients. Many of them use Gibraltar companies and trusts to structure their fiscal, fiduciary or investment requirements and, over the years, strong links have been forged with major multinationals, financial institutions, banks, law and accountancy firms worldwide. Gibraltar's status as part of the EU is a significant factor in attracting such institutions and businesses. The firm's international clients come, above all, from the US, the UK, Israel and Europe (in particular Luxembourg, the Netherlands, Spain and Portugal). They include major multinationals, banks and building societies.

AREAS OF PRACTICE

Corporate and commercial: The firm provides a full range of legal services for clients ranging from small businesses to major multinationals. It advises corporate clients working in or through Gibraltar on a wide variety of cross-border transactions and financing structures. Other matters handled include international corporate restructures, joint ventures, M&A, corporate franchising, tax and e-commerce.

Litigation: The department handles most aspects of litigation, with a niche focus on international commercial and trust litigation. The firm's litigators practise as both barristers and solicitors, and provide a full range of litigation services at all levels for both local and international clients.

International finance and banking: The firm has particular experience in banking and financial markets. Its lawyers also advise in banking regulation and licensing work, including the establishment of offshore operations and regulatory advice, as well as the implementation of various legal and tax structures including repackaging and securitisation. It is the only firm in Gibraltar to combine specialist expertise in derivatives regulation with a substantial banking, tax and securitisation practice.

Telecoms: The firm has advised on the privatisation of the government of Gibraltar's telephone services and advises one of the main carriers. The firm advises on all aspects of telecoms, including broadcasting and wireless telegraphy, and was instructed by the International Telecommunications Union to report on telecoms legislation in the Caribbean region.

Private client: The firm has specialist lawyers who regularly advise on all aspects of private client matters, including asset protection trusts, domiciliation and taxation.

Drafting: The firm advised the government on the transposition of EU Directives into Gibraltar law. This work has concerned legislation relating to financial services and telecoms. Contacts have also been established with a number of other governments requiring assistance in this area.

Trust and company administration: Through an associated company (Line Management Services Ltd), the firm provides administration services for companies and trusts. Among the users of these services are international clients, advised on Gibraltar trusts and offshore companies.

Maritime: The firm has strong links with major English shipping firms and has been involved in a number of significant international admiralty cases. It also handles ship registration and finance.

Property: The firm acts for most of the major local and international developers and builders. It advises in matters of secured lending, mortgages and charges for most banks and building societies in Gibraltar.

Internet gaming: The firm has advised some of the major on-line betting operators on setting up their operations in Gibraltar and on their IPOs on the London Stock Exchange. The firm has also been heavily involved in assisting the Gibraltar government and industry in drafting the new Gambling Ordinance, which has modernised gaming legislation.

MARRACHE & CO

5 CANNON LANE
PO BOX 85
GIBRALTAR

Telephone: +350 79918
Fax: +350 73315
E-mail: marrache@marrache.com
Website: www.marrache.com

Languages
English, French, Italian, Portuguese, Spanish

Other offices
Lisbon, London, Marbella, Milan, Prague

Number of lawyers 43
at this office 29

International groupings
Lex Mundi; WSG; STEP; ITPA; IBA

CATEGORIES OF WORK

Company/commercial
Isaac Marrache, Carol Haw

Property and construction
Leanne Turnbull

Private client
Benjamin Marrache, Neil Lopez

Spanish department
Gabriel Garcia Benavides

Litigation
Anthony Christodoulides

Restructurings and financial services
Jeevan Daswani

Admiralty and shipping
Penny Garcia

Sports management
D Suissi

THE FIRM

The Marrache family arrived in Gibraltar 300 years ago and, over the years, the firm of Marrache & Co has grown to its current size of over 29 lawyers and fee-earners making it one of the largest firms on the Rock of Gibraltar.

Marrache & Co has an established reputation as an international law firm in Gibraltar. With over 80% of its current workload being of an international nature this cross-border expertise is what differentiates the firm from other firms on the Rock. The fact that Marrache & Co is the only Gibraltarian law firm with offices in London, Lisbon and Marbella results in the firm being able to act as a one-stop point for clients requesting cross-border advice in the Iberian Peninsula.

The firm is divided into eight departments and the firm's corporate arm, Gibland Secretarial Services Ltd, manages over 3,500 companies.

Marrache & Co is reviser of the Martindale Hubbell directory and is the Gibraltar member of the World Service Group Association and member of the Bars of England and Wales, Portugal and Spain. The firm is also a member of the International Tax Planning Association, the International Bar Association, the American Bar Association, the Society of Trust and Estate Practitioners and the Pension Lawyers Association.

AREAS OF PRACTICE

Marrache & Co provides commercially focused legal services for a global client base comprising multinational business and private clients who are seeking advice on Gibraltar law.

The firm has always been at the forefront of innovation, and has accumulated a wealth of experience in client care due to its direct, hands-on approach. Consistently ranked in the top tier of directories in banking and finance, private client, litigation, insolvency and restructuring, the firm's in-depth knowledge of the use of offshore structures in tax planning has earned it a reputation as being consistent, professional and first class.

The firm is unique in the provision of sports management advice in Gibraltar, it has acted on behalf of many celebrities in the field of sport, including the renowned footballer David Beckham and many international golf players, who have either taken up residence in the Iberian Penninsular or sought advice on their tax status.

The Spanish department, comprising six qualified bilingual Spanish lawyers, has acted in most of the developments in the Spanish Costa del Sol and acts on behalf of The Royal Bank of Scotland (Gibraltar) Ltd in most of its lending for Spanish properties.

The private client department advises international clients on the use of Gibraltar trusts and is at the forefront of the industry in attracting high-net-worth individuals to Gibraltar to become residents within the meaning of the tax-advantageous residency programme.

The commercial and restructuring departments have been involved in several major corporate restructurings on behalf of well-renowned listed companies, including the largest commercial transaction in Gibraltar's history involving the merger of three multinational pharmaceutical companies which is now in its third year of reorganisation.

The firm also advises in respect of listings in the London Stock Exchange and the Alternative Investment Market.

Finally, members of the litigation department have been involved in high-profile complex cases during the last year which have served to enhance their reputation as very effective litigators and highly regarded insolvency practitioners.

TRIAY AND TRIAY

28 IRISH TOWN
PO BOX 15
GIBRALTAR

Telephone: +350 72020
Fax: +350 72270
E-mail: lawyers@triay.com
Website: www.triay.com

Languages
English, French, Hebrew, Spanish

Number of lawyers 14

Contact
JE Triay Jnr

International groupings
Association of European Lawyers; International Lawyers Group; LEXLINK; ITPA

CATEGORIES OF WORK

Banking
FJ Triay

Company and commercial
AB Serfaty QC, FJ Triay

Employment
MW Isola, JR Triay

Family
C Simpson

Insurance
FJ Triay

Investment schemes and financial services
RM Vasquez

Litigation
AA Vasquez QC, JE Triay

Insolvency
AB Serfaty QC

Personal injuries
MW Isola, SP Triay

Property
AB Serfarty QC, JR Triay

Shipping and Admiralty
JE Triay, J Ramagge

Taxation
RM Vasquez

Telecommunications and e-commerce
RM Vasquez

Trusts
JE Triay, FJ Triay

Wills and probate
SP Triay, JR Triay

GREECE

Population	**11 million**
Number of lawyers	**25,000**
Professional title	**Dikigoros**
Currency	**Euro (€)**

Index

Greece is officially known as the Hellenic Republic and occupies the most south-easterly position in Europe. Situated in the Balkans, it also has access to the emerging markets of the Black Sea, Eastern Europe and the eastern Mediterranean. Bordering Albania, the Former Yugoslav Republic of Macedonia, Bulgaria and Turkey, it combines an impressive landscape of towering mountains with in excess of 1400 islands, the largest of which is Crete.

Prime Minister Costas Karamanlis leads the country's centre-right New Democracy party following its landslide victory in the March 2004 elections. Characterised by a mixed economy, the State continues to play a pervasive role in the economy despite an ongoing privatisation programme which to date has included; the Hellenic Telecommunications Organisation (OTE); Public Power Corporation; Public Gas Corporation (DEPA); Ionian Bank; and Pireaus Port Authority. Less of a priority in the years immediately preceding the Athens Olympics in 2004, it was expected that on its completion the privatisation process would continue with renewed vigour. However, for all Prime Minister Karamanlis' bold claims of raising €1.5bn through the sale of key assets, 2005 was a relatively damp squib, with only a secondary offering in OPAP and the ongoing Olympic Airlines privatisation worthy of note.

BILLING

The standard method of billing is on an hourly rate. However in a competitive market it is increasingly common for firms to offer fee caps and fee estimates. Depending on the seniority of the lawyer, rates vary from approximately €70 to €450.

MARKETING

A strict Greek Lawyers Code prohibits the advertising of legal services. Nevertheless, the code is being amended to reflect a more liberalised attitude to marketing. Websites are permitted however, and many firms also publish on various aspects of the Greek legal landscape.

IN-HOUSE LAWYERS

Most large companies and banks have their own in-house lawyers. In-house lawyers are legally permitted to work in outside practices as well, although some firms do not allow this.

ECONOMY

For a long time the Greek economy has been one of the under-performers of the EU countries. High unemployment, high inflation and a large public deficit have all contributed to this dubious honour. Whilst recovery is far from complete there are signs that an improvement is underway.

In many respects the recent staging of the Olympics in Athens provided the boost that the economy required. As well as heralding a huge upsurge in investment (GDP growth was almost 4% above the average across the EU as a whole in the years preceding the Games), it also led to an improvement in the transport and infrastructure system. Particularly impressive is the 680km Egnatia motorway which runs across nothern Greece and the Athens Metro which carries in the region of 400,000 passengers daily. The unmitigated success of the Olympics and a vigorous advertising campaign has also had a knock-on effect on the tourist industry, which in 2005 reported an increase of around 6%.

Foreign Direct Investment (FDI) is still relatively low however, and prior to the EU's enlargement, the country reported the lowest foreign investment levels of all the member states. This is the result of a myriad of factors: militant trade unions; high corporate tax rates; a heavily regulated labour market; and high levels of bureaucracy. It also faces the increasing challenge of neighbouring countries, such as Romania and Bulgaria, which offer lower labour costs and corporate taxes, and the prospect of high GDP growth rates. The incumbent government has reacted to these challenges with the introduction of a new investment incentives law and a tax law that calls for a progressive reduction of corporation taxes from the current 35% down to an eventual 25%.

LEGAL MARKET

Whilst the Greek market is still dominated by family run law firms, this is changing, albeit at a very slow rate. Medium-to-large firms are ushering in a change in respect to both working methods and business structuring. Whilst the Greek legal system is not sufficiently evolved to allow specialisation in areas to the exclusion of others, law firms are developing departments based along practice areas.

Whilst it is true that many of the law firms in Greece are organised in such a way as to represent

The largest firms

1	Kyriakides - Georgopoulos Law Firm	54
2	I.K. Rokas and Partners	45
	Kallimopoulos, Loukopoulos, Chiotellis Law Firm	45
4	Zepos & Yannopoulos	43
5	Sarantitis Law Firm	40
6	Vgenopoulos & Partners	39
7	M & P Bernitsas	35
	PI Partners	35
9	Tsibanoulis & Partners Law Firm	33
10	Norton Rose	32
11	Karatzas & Partners Law Firm	30
12	Avramopoulos & Partners Law Firm	25
13	TJ Koutalidis, Law Office	24
14	Theo V Sioufas, Law Offices	23
15	Daniolos, Issaias and Partners Law Offices	22
	Lykourezos Law Offices	22
17	Calavros and Partners	21
18	C. Papacostopoulos & Associates	20
	Elias Paraskevas Attorneys at Law	20
	Fotis Kremmydas - Philippos Doris & Associates	20
	S. A. Felios & Associates	20
	Voutyras Zannas & Associates	20
23	Gr J Timagenis	19
24	Bahas, Gramatidis & Partners	18
	Ballas, Pelecanos & Associates	18
	Lambadarios Law Offices	18

These figures represent the total number of lawyers in this country only, and have been supplied by the firms themselves. The figures should be accurate as at 1 January 2006.

little more than loose co-habitation arrangements, a recent Bill has been introduced with the aim of encouraging the formal incorporation of law firms. As well as introducing tax incentives, and reducing from five to two the number of partners necessary to incorporate, the Bill has also done away with the rule that previously bestowed partnership on a lawyer who had worked at a firm for three years after qualification.

Cross-border network alliances continue to be a major driver for generating international work. **PI Partners** is aligned to **EY Law**, which in turn is associated to Ernst & Young. **Kremalis – Law Firm, member of ius laboris** underscores its employment focus through its membership of *ius laboris*, the international employment law, pensions and employee benefits alliance. **Zepos & Yannopoulos** is a member of *Lex Mundi*, while **Sarantitis Law Firm** is the exclusive Greek member of *World Services Group*. **Moussas & Tsibris Attorneys at Law** is a member of *Transatlantic Law International*. IP specialist, **Metaxopoulos. Law Firm** is a member of the *ALAI* and also belongs to Brussels-based *TELFA*. **Avramopoulos & Partners Law Firm** is a member of the *State Capital Global Law Firm Group* and is regularly instructed by US and northern European corporates.

Other less formal collaborations also exist and in common with the majority of the firms, **Dr Helen Papaconstantinou, John Filias & Associates** consults a number of specialist consultants for certain areas of work. The firm collaborates with 45 technical counsellors who provide invaluable consultancy services based on their technical expertise in patent matters.

Karatzas & Partners Law Firm, **Kyriakides – Georgopoulos Law Firm**, **M & P Bernitsas** and **Law Office TJ Koutalidis** are all leading firms across a range of practice areas. Other high performers are **Zepos & Yannopoulos**, which benefits from leading tax and real estate departments; leading insurance law firm **I.K. Rokas and Partners**; and **Vgenopoulos & Partners**, which combines a first-rate corporate client base with strong banking prowess.

FOREIGN OFFICES

The wider Balkan region is opening up increasingly fertile opportunities for Greek law firms. **PI Partners** has affiliated offices in Romania and Bulgaria which operate under the PI trade name. **German Greek Law Firm – Ziouvas** has a German office in Berlin.

FOREIGN FIRMS

Norton Rose is in the unique position of being the only international firm in the country with full-service capability. With offices in Athens and Piraeus, the firm has truly established itself as a major name in the region, and often competes toe-to-toe with some of the country's most important law firms. The firm's strong ship financing practice has begun to leverage more instructions in relation to straight banking work. In the corporate sphere, whilst international clients make up the bulk of the practice, it is also making in-roads into the domestic market.

The vast majority of foreign firms have a presence in the port of Piraeus. Situated close to Athens, it is home to the Greek shipping industry and a financial centre in its own right. Firms represented are **Clyde & Co**; **Constant & Constant**; **Hill Taylor Dickinson**; **Holman Fenwick & Willan International**; **Stephenson Harwood Consultants O.E.**; **Law Office Reece & Tomazos in association with Richards Butler**; **Watson, Farley & Williams**; and **Ince & Co**.

BANKING, FINANCE AND CAPITAL MARKETS

Karatzas & Partners Law Firm has a strong track record for both banking and capital markets work. In the capital markets, it was instructed by UBS in relation to the Agricultural Bank of Greece's major pre-emptive rights issue. It also advised OPAP in its recent secondary offering. The firm is the clear market leader in securitisation transactions and recently advised Citigroup Global Markets and UBS in the €750m RMBS transaction originated by the Bank of Piraeus. Alexander Metallinos is highly regarded by peers.

Headed by Konstantinos Vouterakos, **Kyriakides – Georgopoulos Law Firm**'s impressive banking practice continues to flourish and reports an increase in instructions from both Barclays and RBS. Alpha Bank remains a key client and the recent recruitment of the bank's in-house counsel, Despina Doxaki, has bolstered an already strong team.

M & P Bernitsas acts for a plethora of domestic and international banks on a range of domestic and cross-border financings. The firm acted as local counsel (**Allen & Overy LLP** was UK counsel) for a syndicate of international and domestic banks in a €850m loan facility to OTE. In the capital markets, the firm represented Bank of America Securities (in collaboration with US firm **Milbank, Tweed, Hadley & McCloy LLP**) in the US private placement of US$176m of notes issued by Delta Holdings. This transaction was the first private placement of notes of a Greek listed company in the US. Athanasia Tsene heads the department and is recommended by both clients and peers alike.

Law Office TJ Koutalidis advised JP Morgan and Deutsche Bank on the €1.6bn financing of the LBO of TIM Hellas Telecommunications. On the capital markets side, it advised Lambrikis Press on the block trade of 50% of its share capital. The firm advised AthEx in relation to potential changes to the legal framework governing the Greek capital markets. Dr Nikos Pimblis has an excellent reputation for securities issues.

Zepos & Yannopoulos advises many of the country's largest banking and capital markets

BANKING, FINANCE AND CAPITAL MARKETS

KARATZAS & PARTNERS LAW FIRM ✪
KYRIAKIDES – GEORGOPOULOS LAW FIRM
M & P BERNITSAS ✪
TJ KOUTALIDIS, LAW OFFICE ✪
ZEPOS & YANNOPOULOS ✪

Elias Paraskevas Attorneys at Law ✪
Moratis – Passas
Moussas & Tsibris Attorneys at Law ✪
Norton Rose
PI Partners ✪
Tsibanoulis & Partners Law Firm ✪
Vgenopoulos & Partners ✪

Calavros and Partners ✪
Dracopoulos & Vassalakis ✪
E Stratigis, Law Office
Gr J Timagenis
I.K. Rokas and Partners
Sarantitis Law Firm ✪
Theo V Sioufas, Law Offices

Avramopoulos & Partners Law Firm ✪
Bahas, Gramatidis & Partners
Ballas, Pelecanos & Associates ✪
C Papacostopoulos & Associates ✪
Chrysses Demetriades & Co Law Office
Daniolos, Issaias and Partners Law Offices
Dryllerakis & Associates ✪
George Lazarimos & Sons
Markatos – Lamnides Athens Law Firm
Politis & Partners ✪
Roussos & Hatzidimitriou Law Offices ✪
S & A Papadimitriou & Co ✪
Stavropoulos & Partners ✪

Anagnostopoulos Bazinas Fifis ✪
Apostolos Georgiades & Associates
Kallimopoulos, Loukopoulos, Chiotellis Law Firm ✪
Lambadarios Law Offices ✪
Reece & Tomazos in association with Richards Butler, Law Office

---

Firms are listed A-Z in tiers which are ranked in order of priority
✪ Indicates firm displays contact details at the end of this chapter.

players on a range of financing and regulatory matters. The firm advises a number of major international players including Merrill Lynch, American Express and JP Morgan in the regulatory requirements of the Greek Capital Market Commission. Other highlights include advising Eurohypo on the financing of a major shopping centre development in Thessalonika.

Elias Paraskevas Attorneys at Law provides high-calibre banking expertise to an impressive portfolio of largely international financial institutions such as UBS, Fortis and Credit Suisse. The firm recently advised Finova Capital in restructuring the financing arrangements of an aircraft leased to a Greek operator. In the capital markets, the firm advised the Greek government in relation to the intended securitisation of overdue tax claims. It was also instructed in relation to the offering of 5% of the issued share capital in TIM Hellas. The firm receives frequent referrals from well-known international law firms.

Moratis – Passas has a fine reputation for banking work. Name partner George Moratis receives excellent feedback.

Moussas & Tsibris Attorneys at Law offers expertise across a wide range of disciplines including corporate, asset and acquisition financing. Michael Tsibris has a pre-eminent reputation in the market and is known by his peers as 'one of the finest capital markets lawyers around'. The firm advised the Mytilineos Group in its purchase of a majority shareholding in Aluminium of Greece. Nicholas Moussas acts as legal counsel to the Hellenic Deposit Guarantee Fund.

Benefiting from both Greek and UK-qualified lawyers, **Norton Rose** acts for an impressive portfolio of domestic and international banks including Morgan Stanley, Alpha Bank, CSFB and Calyon. The firm was instructed by Alpha Bank both in the restructuring of a US$20m syndicated loan facility to the Ashluk Group of Romania and in the arrangement of a US$75m syndicated facility to a leading Greek metals company. In the capital markets, it advised Diana Shipping in its US$230m NYSE IPO. Dimitri Sofianopoulos heads a team that is recommended by clients for its 'high degree of professionalism and expertise'.

PI Partners' first-rate capital markets team advised the underwriters in the €1.3bn part-privatisation of OPAP. The firm also advised Delta Holdings in the placement of €200m corporate notes to US institutional investors. Stathis Potamitis is a member of the Athens Exchange Legal Council.

Tsibanoulis & Partners Law Firm acts for an impressive roster of securities and investment services firms, including Pegasus Securities, Eurocorp Securities, Energon Capital Finance and Eurocorp Finance. Dr Dimitris Tsibanoulis is a member of the Hellenic Capital Markets Commission and has an excellent reputation for investment and capital markets regulatory advice. The firm recently advised Pancreta Bank on the first bond loan to be issued in Greece by a co-operative bank.

Vgenopoulos & Partners acts for several international and domestic banks including Aegean Baltic, Marfin and BNP Paribas. The firm offers excellent ship financing capabilities.

Calavros and Partners is involved in the restructuring project of the Agricultural Bank of Greece.

Gr J Timagenis has been involved in an impressive number of IPOs for Greek shipping companies in the US markets, including the listing and follow-on equity offering of Diana Shipping onthe NYSE.

Sarantitis Law Firm advised First Business Bank on a number of issues including a syndicated loan agreement to a major Russian industrial unit and the implementation of its electronic banking services. The firm continues to receive regular instructions in its role as the National Westminster Bank's exclusive Greek counsel.

Avramopoulos & Partners Law Firm advised the Bank of Attica in the issuance of a €100m bond loan. Other highlights include advising Attica Ventures (one of the Bank of Attica's affiliate companies), in several share participations in domestic corporates.

Daniolos, Issaias and Partners Law Offices, **G. C. Economou & Associates** and **Roussos & Hatzidimitriou Law Offices** all have excellent ship financing capabilities.

Headed by managing partner Evangelos Politis, **POLITIS & PARTNERS**' banking department advises local and international banks on a range of asset, project and leveraged financings. The firm is advising in the project financing of a major technological park in Athens. In the capital markets, the firm is advising Sanyo in the private placement of securities in its subsidiaries Arcadia Digital and Arcadia Master. Clients include Hellenic Bank Limited Group and Eurocorp.

S & A Papadimitriou & Co advises corporates and financial institutions in a range of financing activities. It advised a major domestic industrial group in relation to several multi-million Euro loan and project funds agreements.

Anagnostopoulos Bazinas Fifis is an excellent litigation practice that has a growing focus on securities and banking litigation.

Kallimopoulos, Loukopoulos, Chiotellis Law Firm advises lenders and borrowers in a full range of financing matters. The firm has a burgeoning reputation for securitisation work.

Lambadarios Law Offices represented Aventurine in its issuance of a €20m convertible bond loan with Marfin Bank. The firm also provides regulatory advice to a number of AthEx-listed corporates.

CORPORATE AND M&A

Karatzas & Partners Law Firm's 'thorough and efficient' M&A department advised leading Greek mobile operator, Cosmote, in its acquisition of mobile telecommunications companies in Bulgaria and FYROM. Active in the private equity market, the firm advised APAX Partners and Texas Pacific Group in the €1.11bn acquisition of 80.87% of TIM Hellas' shares from Telecom Italia and the €350m acquisition of Q Phone. Managing partner Catherine Karatzas is recommended.

Kyriakides – Georgopoulos Law Firm offers a full service to clients across a range of industries including transport, manufacturing and pharmaceuticals. In the M&A market, the firm has advised clients on the acquisition of a steel mill, a shipyard and a pharmaceutical company. The firm

CORPORATE AND M&A

KARATZAS & PARTNERS LAW FIRM ✪
KYRIAKIDES – GEORGOPOULOS LAW FIRM
M & P BERNITSAS ✪
SARANTITIS LAW FIRM ✪
TJ KOUTALIDIS, LAW OFFICE ✪
VGENOPOULOS & PARTNERS ✪
ZEPOS & YANNOPOULOS ✪

Bahas, Gramatidis & Partners
Ballas, Pelecanos & Associates ✪
Calavros and Partners ✪
Dryllerakis & Associates ✪
Elias Paraskevas Attorneys at Law ✪
I.K. Rokas and Partners
Norton Rose
PI Partners ✪

Gr J Timagenis
Papaconstantinou, Law Offices ✪
Theo V Sioufas, Law Offices

Avramopoulos & Partners Law Firm ✪
Basil T Patkos, Law Offices
C Papacostopoulos & Associates ✪
Daniolos, Issaias and Partners Law Offices
Dontas Law Offices
Kallimopoulos, Loukopoulos, Chiotellis Law Firm ✪
Markatos – Lamnides Athens Law Firm
Massouridis Stavropoulos & Associates
Metaxopoulos. Law Firm ✪
Moratis – Passas
Moussas & Tsibris Attorneys at Law ✪
Reece & Tomazos in association with Richards Butler, Law Office
Roussos & Hatzidimitriou Law Offices ✪
S & A Papadimitriou & Co ✪
S. A. Felios & Associates ✪
Souriadakis, Frangakis, Skaltsas & Associates ✪
Tsibanoulis & Partners Law Firm ✪

A Voutsas Law Office
Anagnostopoulos Bazinas Fifis ✪
Chrysses Demetriades & Co Law Office
Cocalis & Psarras Law Firm ✪
Dracopoulos & Vassalakis ✪
Fotis Kremmydas – Philippos Doris & Associates ✪
German Greek Law Group – Ziouvas
Lambadarios Law Offices J
Mourgelas & Scandamis
Nikitaides & Associates
Nomos Thessaloniki Law Firm
P Sotiropoulos (Dr) Law Office
Politis & Partners ✪
Stavropoulos & Partners ✪
Thanos Masoulas & Partners, Law Firm
Theologidis Lascaratos Mitrakos Myrillos
Voutyras Zannas & Associates

Firms are listed A-Z in tiers which are ranked in order of priority
✪ Indicates firm displays contact details at the end of this chapter.

is often instructed by corporates wishing to establish subsidiaries in Balkan countries.

Headed by Angeliki Vasaka, **M & P Bernitsas**' 'technically sound and responsive' corporate department offers expertise across a range of corporate activity. The firm advised Telecom Italia on the sale of its 80% stake in TIM Hellas. Other highlights include advising Alcan Inc on the sale of its majority shareholding in Aluminium de Greece. The 'top-notch' Nikos Papachristopoulos has an excellent reputation for M&A.

Sarantitis Law Firm advised International Radio Network Holdings in the acquisition of a 90% stake in Italian radio station, Rock FM. Jointly headed by Yiannis Sarantitis and Dorotheos Samoladas, the department advises an impressive range of public and private sector clients, including Telenor, Agricultural Bank of Greece, Gamesa and Deloitte. The firm continues to play an active role in the establishment of offshore and Greek limited liability companies.

Under the expert leadership of Dr Tryfon Koutalidis, **Law Office TJ Koutalidis**' corporate department advises an impressive stable of national and international corporates including Vodafone-Panafon, Intracom and Diageo Hellas. It advised Aramco on the sale of its €400m shareholding in Motor Oil Hellas and Intracom in its acquisition of a minority shareholding in Forthnet, the domestic internet access provider.

Vgenopoulos & Partners recently advised International Shipping Enterprises on its US$607m acquisition of Navios Maritime Holdings. Other clients include Dell, Samsonite and Sony Ericsson.

Zepos & Yannopoulos advised a number of multinational companies on establishing subsidiaries in Greece including Footlocker, La Redoute and Sfera Joven. On the transactional side, the firm has been involved in high-profile acquisitions for Iberdrola (acquisition of Rokas) and Lenovo (acquisitions of IBM's PC business in Greece).

Ballas, Pelecanos & Associates made a number of impressive client acquisitions in 2005, including Chiquita International, Avaya and IMS Health. The firm is exclusive corporate counsel to both Ford Motor Hellas and Microsoft Hellas.

Calavros and Partners' broad-based corporate practice acts for an impressive array of multinational clients including Glaxosmithkline Group, Merck & Co, Panasonic and Johnson & Johnson. The firm was recently instructed by Greek Duty Free Shops in its acquisition of a stake in the national duty free company of an Asiatic country.

Dryllerakis & Associates has been instructed in relation to the acquisition of a number of fish farms. The firm continues to advise the textiles group, Klonatex, in its restructuring. Emmanuel Dryllerakis receives plaudits from his peers, specifically in relation to the tax and accounting aspects of corporate transactions.

Elias Paraskevas Attorneys at Law has excellent links with a number of UK and US-based law firms and is frequently involved in transactions with a strong international flavour. The firm is regularly instructed by international companies establishing a local subsidiary in Greece. In the M&A market, the firm acted as local counsel in the sale of Boots Healthcare International (**Slaughter and May** led the transaction) and advised a Greek insurance company in the divestment of its share in a major local mobile telecommunications company. Managing partner Dimitris Pareskevas 'is astute and commercial' and has an excellent reputation as an M&A lawyer.

Aided by its international network of offices, **I.K. Rokas and Partners** provides all-embracing corporate and commercial advice to international and national corporates. The firm has an excellent pedigree in the insurance sector.

Headed by Elena Tsohou, **Norton Rose** offers Greek and UK law expertise to a client base that includes a mix of local and international clients including OPAP, Morgan Stanley and Credit Agricole. The firm advised the venture capital arm of Fortis Bank in the sale of its 25% shareholding in a joint venture shipping company.

PI Partners offers a good all-round service to a range of domestic and international corporates. The firm advised Alpha Bank in the €152m acquisition of Serbian bank, Jubanka A.D Beograd. The firm is increasingly involved in corporate restructuring and was recently court-appointed commissioner of troubled listed domestic construction company, Embedos.

Theo V Sioufas, Law Offices offers corporate and commercial assistance to a number of prominent players in the shipping industry.

Avramopoulos & Partners Law Firm advised Bank of Attica in the sale of one of its subsidiary's to Eurobank. It also advised Mitsis Hotels on its acquisition of a substantial hotel complex on the island of Corfu.

Predominantly known as a media and IP firm, **Metaxopoulos. Law Firm** is increasing its focus on the corporate arena. Clients speak highly of this 'high-quality and reactive team' and single out Kriton Metaxopoulos and Valérie Monso for praise.

Moussas & Tsibris Attorneys at Law offers day-to-day corporate and commercial assistance to both national and international corporates.

Law Office Reece & Tomazos in association with Richards Butler advised Nike in the establishment of a subsidiary in Greece.

S & A Papadimitriou & Co advised Global Finance in the acquisition of a controlling shareholding in AthEx-listed company, Eurodrip A.V.E.G.E. The firm is also active in the private equity market and is instructed by leading domestic venture capital firm, Global Finance.

Tsibanoulis & Partners Law Firm has been active in the M&A market and was involved in the merger between Bayer Hellas and Bayer CropScience. It has also been involved in a number of sizeable acquisitions in the transport and raw materials sectors.

Lambadarios Law Offices offers corporate and commercial advice to an impressive array of multinationals including Procter & Gamble Hellas, Goodyear Dunlop, SonyBMG Hellas and Mercedez Benz Hellas.

Mourgelas & Scandamis offers full-service corporate and commercial advice to a range of national and multinational corporates. The firm is involved in the contractual framework for the security for the forthcoming Asian games in Qatar. Name partner Gregory Mourgelas is recommended.

POLITIS & PARTNERS' clients include Lavipharm, Sanyo Hellas, Libra Holidays Group and Bosch Rexroth Group. Clients appreciate the firm's 'direct, efficient and responsive advice' and single out Evangelos Politis for praise.

Nomos Thessaloniki Law Firm has a strong German client base through its strong links with the Greek/German Chamber of Commerce, as does **German Greek Law Firm – Ziouvas**, which also has an office in Berlin.

DISPUTE RESOLUTION

Anagnostopoulos Bazinas Fifis offers civil and criminal litigation expertise to a range of national and international clients. It successfully represented three US airline operators and the Worldspan Group in its €40m dispute with the Greek State. The firm is a leader in medical negligence litigation and is instructed by Iaso Clinics. Ilias Anagnostopoulos heads a team that includes insolvency expert George Bazinas.

Ballas, Pelecanos & Associates advises clients across all sectors in relation to disputes relating to contracts for sale and product liability. The team recently successfully defended a number of automotive manufacturers/distributors in a range of dealer claims.

Kyriakides – Georgopoulos Law Firm offers expertise across a range of civil, white-collar and public law disputes. Recent highlights include successfully representing Pioneer Europe in a major ICC arbitration regarding the termination of a distribution agreement. Clients include McDonald's Hellas, DHL and Coca-Cola HBC.

Metaxopoulos. Law Firm's market-leading disputes practice offers overarching expertise to an impressive range of national and international clients. Led by Kriton Metaxopoulos and Vivian Vassilopoulou, the firm is defending a leading European livestock breeder in a €5.2m claim brought against it by Greek stock breeders for losses suffered as a result of the sale of defective cattle. Well-known for its IP expertise, the firm recently successfully represented the Greek distributors of the Oliver Stone movie, *Alexander*, in relation to attempts to prohibit its distribution on the grounds of its alleged depiction of Alexander as a homosexual.

PI Partners has an excellent track record for arbitration, both under ICC and Greek law. Recent highlights include successfully defending Tetrapak Hellas against a €2m claim for the termination of a commercial lease agreement. The firm continues to advise ELPET in ICC arbitration proceedings against FYROM.

DISPUTE RESOLUTION

Anagnostopoulos Bazinas Fifis ✪
Bahas, Gramatidis & Partners
Ballas, Pelecanos & Associates ✪
Gr J Timagenis
I.K. Rokas and Partners
Kyriakides – Georgopoulos Law Firm
Metaxopoulos. Law Firm ✪
PI Partners ✪
Sarantitis Law Firm ✪
TJ Koutalidis, Law Office ✪
Theo V Sioufas, Law Offices
Vgenopoulos & Partners ✪
Zepos & Yannopoulos ✪

A Voutsas Law Office
Apostolos Georgiades & Associates
Avramopoulos & Partners Law Firm ✪
Calavros and Partners ✪
Daniolos, Issaias and Partners Law Offices
Dryllerakis & Associates ✪
Economou & Economou Law Office
Elias Paraskevas Attorneys at Law ✪
Flogaitis, Pamboukis, Siuoutis Tzavaras & Associates
G E Bairactaris & Partners
Holman Fenwick & Willan International ✪
Kremalis – Law Firm, member of ius laboris ✪
Karatzas & Partners Law Firm ✪
Kyriakides – Georgopoulos Law Firm
M & P Bernitsas ✪
Moussas & Tsibris Attorneys at Law ✪
Norton Rose
Papaconstantinou, Law Offices ✪
Politis & Partners ✪
Reece & Tomazos in association with Richards Butler, Law Office
S & A Papadimitriou & Co ✪
Souriadakis, Frangakis, Skaltsas & Associates ✪
Tsibanoulis & Partners Law Firm ✪

Firms are listed A-Z in tiers which are ranked in order of priority
✪ Indicates firm displays contact details at the end of this chapter.

Instructed in both a stand-alone capacity and off the back of its corporate client base, **Sarantitis Law Firm** offers first-rate litigation capability. Recent highlights include advising First Business Bank in a dispute with ASEPT. The firm also continues to advise Greek magazine publisher, Attica Publications, in a dispute regarding ownership of the rights of the Greek edition of *PC Magazine*.

At **Law Office TJ Koutalidis**, Dr Anna Mantakou heads an excellent arbitration practice that recently achieved a notable success on behalf of Intracom in a €168m contractual dispute with OTE International and others. The firm has also represented Hochtief A G Consortia in numerous tendering disputes regarding Greek motorway concession projects. Gregory Lipothetis heads the litigation practice.

Vgenopoulos & Partners offers litigation expertise across a range of commercial and corporate matters. The firm recently achieved a favourable result for a retail client in arbitration proceedings resulting from the project management of a large hypermarket in the north of Greece.

Zepos & Yannopoulos recently acted for Stanleybet before the Administrative Supreme Court in relation to OPAP's gaming monopoly. Other highlights include representing Louis Vuitton in numerous anti-counterfeiting disputes.

Apostolos Georgiades & Associates represents Attikos Helios in proceedings against Hellenic Tourist Property. In collaboration with **White & Case LLP**'s Paris office the firm is representing Hochtief in a significant claim against the Athens International Airport and French Thales in a dispute regarding the air navigation system of the new Athens airport.

Calavros and Partners has a leading reputation for construction and engineering arbitration. Name partner Professor Constantin Calavros is well known and is a member of the board of the Hellenic Institute of Arbitration.

Dryllerakis & Associates is involved in a number of domestic and international arbitrations for corporates. John Dryllerakis recently acted as an ICC arbitrator in relation to a public works dispute. Professor Spyropoulos is involved in a number of cases before the Administrative Supreme Court.

Kremalis – Law Firm, member of ius laboris is a niche employment practice offering non-contentious and contentious advice to a range of national and multinational clients including Sony, IBM and Toyota. Professor Konstantinos Kremalis is a member of the Greek Board of Mediators and Arbitrators.

Karatzas & Partners Law Firm regularly represents its banking and insurance clients in disputes relating to the non-payment of loans and insurance claims.

M & P Bernitsas represented Hallmark Cards in a major commercial dispute. Panayotis Bernitsas heads the practice.

Moussas & Tsibris Attorneys at Law advises corporates, individuals and insurance companies in insurance disputes. It also has a growing reputation in securities disputes and advises clients in relation to insider dealing and breach of securities regulations. Nicholas Moussas is recommended.

Headed by UK-qualified lawyer Chris Hobbs, **Norton Rose**'s disputes practice offers expertise in both Greek and English law to clients such as Delta Airlines, Banca Intesa and Tatersalls. The UK law capacity is most useful in shipping disputes (where contracts are usually governed by UK law) but is also beneficial in cross-border disputes.

POLITIS & PARTNERS advises corporate clients in a range of insurance, antitrust, tort and commercial disputes. The firm successfully represented a corporate client in a multi-million Euro construction project dispute. Dr Panayotis Glavinis has an excellent reputation for international commercial arbitrations and was recently appointed Greek member to the Commission of Arbitration of ICC (Paris).

S & A Papadimitriou & Co represented a leading private company in a contractual dispute against the Greek State, while **Tsibanoulis & Partners Law Firm** offers expertise in both civil matters and white-collar crime.

EU AND COMPETITION

M & P Bernitsas has an excellent pedigree for EU law matters and advises national and international companies in relation to advisory and contentious work – where it frequently appears before the European Commission. The firm represents the Greek subsidiary of a German automotive manufacturer in competition compliance issues following the recent regulations affecting the industry. Panayotis Bernitsas is a practitioner of impeccable credentials and has a focus on the transport, steel and coal industries.

Ballas, Pelecanos & Associates offers 'comprehensive and complete' knowledge of EU and competition law. The firm regularly appears before the Greek Competition Authority in relation to merger filings and hearings. The department is very active within the automotive industry and advises a significant proportion of Greek importers and sales companies on compliance issues relating to EU regulations on motor vehicle distribution.

Calavros and Partners offers broad-ranging EU and competition law expertise to both national and international clients. The firm's reputation was bolstered by its representation of GlaxoSmithKline regarding its alleged anti-competitive behaviour. The decision is pending in what the European Commission itself described as one of the three major current competition cases.

Dryllerakis & Associates' competition practice offers expertise across a broad range of disciplines, from merger filings to antitrust litigation. Previously a member of the Greek Competition Committee, senior partner John Dryllerakis has vast expertise at the very heart of national competition issues. The firm recently concluded a case on behalf of a major Greek supermarket in relation to allegations of concerted practices.

At **Kyriakides – Georgopoulos Law Firm**, Anastasia Dritsa heads a team that has been involved in a number of significant antitrust cases. Clients include Coca-Cola HBC, BAT and Alsthom.

Mourgelas & Scandamis Law Firm specialises in EU and competition law and is the result of a merger between *Scandamis cum suis* and *G Mourgelas and Partners Law Firm*. One of the country's pre-eminent figures in EU and competition law, Nicos Scandamis receives rave reviews from his peers. The firm has recently acted for the Hellenic Petroleum Marketing Companies Association in a major dispute with the Greek State regarding its refusal to refund VAT in alleged contravention of an EU directive.

EU AND COMPETITION

M & P BERNITSAS ✪

BALLAS, PELECANOS & ASSOCIATES ✪
CALAVROS AND PARTNERS ✪
DRYLLERAKIS & ASSOCIATES ✪

Avramopoulos & Partners Law Firm ✪
Bahas, Gramatidis & Partners
Kyriakides – Georgopoulos Law Firm
Mourgelas & Scandamis Law Firm
Papaconstantinou, Law Offices ✪
PI Partners ✪
TJ Koutalidis, Law Office ✪
Zepos & Yannopoulos ✪

A Voutsas Law Office
Cocalis & Psarras Law Firm ✪
Elias Paraskevas Attorneys at Law ✪
I.K. Rokas and Partners
Sarantitis Law Firm ✪
Souriadakis, Frangakis, Skaltsas & Associates ✪
Vgenopoulos & Partners ✪

Firms are listed A-Z in tiers which are ranked in order of priority
✪ *Indicates firm displays contact details at the end of this chapter.*

PI Partners successfully represented Procter & Gamble regarding an exclusive supply agreement with Rolco Vianil. Group leader, Xenephon Paparrigopoulos, heads the EU studies department of the Scientific Service of the Hellenic Parliament.

Led by Professor Mastromanolis, **Zepos & Yannopoulos**' EU and competition team advised Banco Comercial Portugues in its merger notification before the Greek Competition Commission. Carrefour is a major client.

Elias Paraskevas Attorneys at Law advised on the merger control issues relating to Boots' divestment of its international healthcare business. It also recently advised a venture capital company on the State Aid provisions in its proposed financing of a foreign consortium's bid to acquire Olympic Airlines.

ENERGY

Karatzas & Partners Law Firm has expertise in the financing of energy projects particularly in relation to wind parks.

Kyriakides – Georgopoulos Law Firm has a long and established reputation in the energy sector having previously played a central role for the Greek State in the liberalisation of the gas and electricity markets. The firm acts for an impressive portfolio of clients from a range of sectors, including the likes of the Public Gas Corporation, Deutsche Bank and Regal Petroleum. On the financing side, the firm has been instructed by a number of banks in relation to wind projects.

ENERGY

Karatzas & Partners Law Firm ✪
Kyriakides – Georgopoulos Law Firm
M & P Bernitsas ✪
PI Partners ✪
Sarantitis Law Firm ✪
Zepos & Yannopoulos ✪

Apostolos Georgiades & Associates
Elias Paraskevas Attorneys at Law ✪
I.K. Rokas and Partners
Kallimopoulos, Loukopoulos, Chiotellis Law Firm ✪
Tsibanoulis & Partners Law Firm ✪
Vgenopoulos & Partners ✪

Firms are listed A-Z in tiers which are ranked in order of priority
✪ *Indicates firm displays contact details at the end of this chapter.*

A leading player in the energy field, **M & P Bernitsas** advises private and public sector clients in relation to energy and environmental compliance issues. The team offers expertise in regulatory matters, as well as advising major energy and utilities companies in M&A and capital markets-related activity.

PI Partners advises Hellenic Petroleum on various issues relating to the regulation of the energy markets. On the contentious side, the firm is representing a subsidiary of ORMAT in a dispute with the Development Company of the Municipality of Milos.

Sarantitis Law Firm's clients include Statoil, Gamesa, Diekat Energy and Energy Developments (UK).

Zepos & Yannopoulos has been particularly active in the renewable energy market, where there has been a lot of investment activity. The firm advised Spanish energy company, Iberdrola, in its acquisition of domestic energy company, Rokas. The firm advised the Hellenic Regulatory Authority on the drafting of the new electricity trading and operating code. Clients include ChevronTexaco, Edison Trading and Eurus Energy.

Elias Paraskevas Attorneys at Law offers expertise in energy regulatory matters.

Tsibanoulis & Partners Law Firm acted for a bank in the financing of a wind farm project.

IT AND TELECOMS

Avramopoulos & Partners Law Firm advises an impressive roster of leading telecoms companies including EDS, AT Kearney, Nortel Networks and LCC International.

M & P Bernitsas is instructed by a number of major IT and telecoms players in relation to

IT AND TELECOMS

AVRAMOPOULOS & PARTNERS LAW FIRM ✪
M & P BERNITSAS ✪
SARANTITIS LAW FIRM ✪
TJ KOUTALIDIS, LAW OFFICE ✪

Bahas, Gramatidis & Partners
Ballas, Pelecanos & Associates ✪
Calavros and Partners ✪
Chrysses Demetriades & Co Law Office
Cocalis & Psarras Law Firm ✪
Dryllerakis & Associates ✪
I.K. Rokas and Partners
Karatzas & Partners Law Firm ✪
Kyriakides – Georgopoulos Law Firm
Reece & Tomazos in association with Richards Butler, Law Office
Themistos Law Offices
Vgenopoulos & Partners ✪
Zepos & Yannopoulos ✪

Drakopoulos Law Firm ✪
PI Partners ✪
Politis & Partners ✪

Firms are listed A-Z in tiers which are ranked in order of priority
✪ *Indicates firm displays contact details at the end of this chapter.*

licensing and regulatory issues. Panayotis Bernitsas is recommended.

Sarantitis Law Firm's clients include Deutsche Telekom, Albania Mobile Communications, Craig Wireless Group and Uunet Hellas LCC.

Law Office TJ Koutalidis' Nikitas Fortsakis heads a telecoms department that provides a range of contentious and non-contentious advice to clients such as Vodafone-Panafon, Bloomberg and Intracom.

Ballas, Pelecanos & Associates' clients include Microsoft, Matav, Kenwood and Equant.

Calavros and Partners advises Greek telecommunications provider, Hellenic Telecommunications Organisation (OTE).

Cocalis & Psarras Law Firm advised the Public Gas Corporation (DEPA) in telecoms-related investments.

Dryllerakis & Associates has represented alternative local telecoms carrier, Lannet, in a number of matters before the telecoms regulator, the NRA.

Karatzas & Partners Law Firm advised leading Greek mobile operator, Cosmote, in several acquisitions.

Zepos & Yannopoulos' clients include Nokia, Cisco, Hewlett-Packard, Bull and Ericsson.

Drakopoulos Law Firm acts for Vivodi Telecom, a major domestic alternative fixed-line telecommunications provider.

PI Partners advises BT on the legal and regulatory issues relating to the establishment of a branch in Greece.

INSURANCE

I.K. ROKAS AND PARTNERS

Gr J Timagenis
Kremalis – Law Firm, member of ius laboris ✪
Sarantitis Law Firm ✪
Theo V Sioufas, Law Offices

Bahas, Gramatidis & Partners
C Papacostopoulos & Associates ✪
Daniolos, Issaias and Partners Law Offices
German Greek Law Group – Ziouvas
Karatzas & Partners Law Firm ✪
Souriadakis, Frangakis, Skaltsas & Associates ✪
Vgenopoulos & Partners ✪
Zepos & Yannopoulos ✪

Firms are listed A-Z in tiers which are ranked in order of priority
✪ *Indicates firm displays contact details at the end of this chapter.*

INSURANCE

I.K. Rokas and Partners' market-leading insurance group receives glowing reviews from its competitors. The firm acts for an impressive portfolio of insurance companies, individual policyholders and corporates, and offers the full range of expertise from claims and policy-related litigation, to regulatory advice.

Kremalis – Law Firm, member of ius laboris provides private insurance advice across a range of areas including occupational pension funds, social security, compensation and employee benefits.

Gr J Timagenis; **Sarantitis Law Firm** and **Theo V Sioufas, Law Offices** are all strong shipping firms and have excellent insurance capabilities.

Karatzas & Partners Law Firm acts for Greek automotive insurer, Omega Insurance, in relation to insurance issues and day-to-day corporate and commercial matters.

INTELLECTUAL PROPERTY

DONTAS LAW OFFICES
HELEN PAPACONSTANTINOU (DR), JOHN FILIAS & ASSOCIATES ✪
METAXOPOULOS. LAW FIRM ✪

A Voutsas Law Office
Ballas, Pelecanos & Associates ✪
Kallimopoulos, Loukopoulos, Chiotellis Law Firm ✪
Patrinos & Kilimiris
Sarantitis Law Firm ✪

Bahas, Gramatidis & Partners
Cocalis & Psarras Law Firm ✪
D. S. Oekonomidis (Dr) and Partners Law Offices
Daniolos, Issaias and Partners Law Offices
Dryllerakis & Associates ✪
German Greek Law Group – Ziouvas
I.K. Rokas and Partners
Karatzas & Partners Law Firm ✪
Kyriakides – Georgopoulos Law Firm
Ladas & Ladas
Lambadarios Law Offices ✪
M & P Bernitsas ✪
Moussas & Tsibris Attorneys at Law ✪
Souriadakis, Frangakis, Skaltsas & Associates ✪
Tavlaridis Tsimikalis & Kalonarou
Thanos Masoulas & Partners, Law Firm
Themistos Law Offices
Vgenopoulos & Partners ✪
Zepos & Yannopoulos ✪

Firms are listed A-Z in tiers which are ranked in order of priority
✪ *Indicates firm displays contact details at the end of this chapter.*

INTELLECTUAL PROPERTY

One of the country's premier IP law practices, **Dontas Law Offices**, boasts an impressive client base including multinationals such as Gant, Nokia, Sara Lee and Volvo. The firm was involved in a number of high-profile cases in 2005 including successfully representing adidas in its 'four stripes' litigation. It has a prominent anti-piracy team and is frequently involved in counterfeit seizures.

IP boutique **Dr Helen Papaconstantinou, John Filias & Associates** offers contentious and non-contentious expertise across a range of IP issues relating to patents, trade marks and designs. Senior partner Dr Helen Papaconstantinou is a revered practitioner who is also currently serving as the vice-president of the AIPPI Group of Greece.

Metaxopoulos. Law Firm offers contentious and non-contentious IP advice to an impressive raft of media and entertainment clients that is the envy of its competitors. The firm was recently instructed by a domestic DVD production company, Victory Music, in relation to obtaining the licence of DVD rights for the Athens 2004 Olympic Games. On the contentious side, the firm is involved in a continuous stream of copyright infringement actions on behalf of the Greek collective anti-piracy organisation (EPOE). The firm is also active in patent and trade mark protection and infringement matters.

Ballas, Pelecanos & Associates represents Microsoft, Levi Strauss, Philip Morris and Imperial Tobacco in anti-counterfeiting, and anti-piracy matters. The firm is Greek representative of the ICC's Counterforce network.

Sarantitis Law Firm's four-lawyer team offers a broad spread of both soft and hard IP advice. The team advises Greek mobile telecommunications provider, Cosmote, in the protection of its IP rights both domestically and throughout Europe.

Karatzas & Partners Law Firm manages the trade mark portfolios of several AthEx-listed companies including Biossol, Imaco and Nikas.

Headed by Irene Kyriakides, **Kyriakides – Georgopoulos Law Firm**'s IP department has reported a considerable increase in workload and has picked up new clients from the food and beverages industry. Starbucks remains a key client and the firm has represented it in numerous trade mark disputes with local retailers.

Lambadarios Law Offices advised Sony BMG on copyright issues relating to a number of its artists. The firm was also involved in trade mark infringement disputes on behalf of both Telecom Italia Mobile and Aspis Real Estate.

Moussas & Tsibris Attorneys at Law successfully acted for printing manufacturer, OKI Electric, in relation to a major IP and anti-counterfeit dispute.

Vgenopoulos & Partners was instructed by a major international mobile phone company in relation to anti-counterfeit matters.

PROJECTS AND PRIVATISATION

Elias Paraskevas Attorneys at Law is instructed by a consortium in the bidding process for a major motorway project. On the privatisation side, the firm advised a venture capital company that provided the funding to the Olympic Investors Consortium in the privatisation of Olympic Airlines. Dimitris Paraskevas has an excellent pedigree for privatisation work having previously served as Secretary for Privatisation of the Ministry of Development.

Aided by its first-rate banking client base, **Karatzas & Partners Law Firm** is often instructed in relation to the financing of some of the country's largest projects. Highlights include advising German bank, HVB, as the intermediary in the €30m financing of the Loutra Kylinis hotel complex.

M & P Bernitsas advised the Greek State in its 16.4% offering of its stake in OPAP. The team has strong political involvement, and is frequently instructed by the State in relation to drafting of privatisation-related legislation. Dimitris Roussis and Dimitris Bernitsas are recommended.

Avramopoulos & Partners Law Firm advised the Greek and US consortium of York Capital Management and Olympic Investors, in their bid for Olympic Airlines.

Calavros and Partners advised NBG International, as financial adviser to Greek Duty Free Shops, in relation to the sale of 79.7% of the latter's share capital.

PI Partners advised the underwriters in the OPAP offering. On the projects side, the firm is advising one of the bidders in the tender for the construction of the Ionian Motorway.

Law Office TJ Koutalidis, in collaboration with **Dryllerakis & Associates**, advised Aegean Airways in its failed bid in the ongoing privatisation saga of Olympic Airways. On the projects side, the firm is advising a consortium led by Hochtief AG as preferred bidder for the new toll road Maliakos – Kleidi Project.

Ballas, Pelecanos & Associates continues to advise Science Applications International Corporations on the post-2004 Olympic Games implementation of the US$300m security contract (**Lambadarios Law Offices** is co-counsel)

Cocalis & Psarras Law Firm advised a multinational consortium of investors in the tender for the Thessaloniki Metro. The firm is currently advising the Public Power Corporation in its participation in the privatisation of three power generation companies in Bulgaria.

Lambadarios Law Offices advised on a venture capital group's bid for the State-owned Olympic Airlines.

PROJECTS AND PRIVATISATION

ELIAS PARASKEVAS ATTORNEYS AT LAW ✪
KARATZAS & PARTNERS LAW FIRM ✪
M & P BERNITSAS ✪

Avramopoulos & Partners Law Firm ✪
Calavros and Partners ✪
Dryllerakis & Associates ✪
Kyriakides – Georgopoulos Law Firm
PI Partners ✪
Sarantitis Law Firm ✪
TJ Koutalidis, Law Office

Apostolos Georgiades & Associates
Bahas, Gramatidis & Partners
Ballas, Pelecanos & Associates ✪
Cocalis & Psarras Law Firm ✪
Dracopoulos & Vassalakis ✪
I.K. Rokas and Partners
Lambadarios Law Offices ✪
Norton Rose
S & A Papadimitriou & Co ✪
Vgenopoulos & Partners ✪
Zepos & Yannopoulos ✪

Firms are listed A-Z in tiers which are ranked in order of priority
✪ Indicates firm displays contact details at the end of this chapter.

REAL ESTATE AND CONSTRUCTION

Vgenopoulos & Partners advises Carrefour Marinopoulos in relation to several real estate matters. The firm is also instructed by the developers of one of the largest commercial and entertainment centres in Greece.

Zepos & Yannopoulos offers market-leading advice to a range of developers, financial institutions and investors. The firm advised EuroHypo Bank on the €70m financing of a major shopping mall development in Thessalonika. It also advised a major international fund on the regulatory issues pursuant to the development of a major real estate plot into a hotel and golf course.

Drakopoulos Law Firm has an impressive hotels practice and recently acted for First Choice in relation to the construction, management and lease of a €12.5m hotel in Cephalonia. The firm is also instructed by international developer, Plaza Centers, on the development of a €20m shopping centre in Athens.

REAL ESTATE AND CONSTRUCTION

VGENOPOULOS & PARTNERS ✪
ZEPOS & YANNOPOULOS ✪

Apostolos Georgiades & Associates
Bahas, Gramatidis & Partners
C Papacostopoulos & Associates ✪
Daniolos, Issaias and Partners Law Offices
Drakopoulos Law Firm ✪
Elias Paraskevas Attorneys at Law ✪
Fotis Kremmydas – Philippos Doris & Associates ✪
German Greek Law Group – Ziouvas
Kallimopoulos, Loukopoulos, Chiotellis Law Firm ✪
Karatzas & Partners Law Firm ✪
Kyriakides – Georgopoulos Law Firm
M & P Bernitsas ✪
Metaxopoulos. Law Firm ✪
Moussas & Tsibris Attonerys at Law ✪
Themistos Law Offices

Firms are listed A-Z in tiers which are ranked in order of priority
✪ Indicates firm displays contact details at the end of this chapter.

Elias Paraskevas Attorneys at Law has an international flavour to its real estate practice. The firm advised clients in relation to property transactions in the Balkans and Switzerland.

With an office in Cologne, **German Greek Law Firm – Ziouvas** has a strong German flavour to its client base. The firm continues to benefit from its involvement in the German-Hellenic Association for the Protection of Real Estate Abroad and represents the interests of over 800 of its German-speaking members.

Karatzas & Partners Law Firm advised a subsidiary of Lamda Development in the development of the largest shopping centre in Greece.

Moussas & Tsibris Attorneys at Law specialises in the transfer of real estate assets to and from offshore companies in various jurisdictions.

SHIPPING AND MARITIME

Gr J Timagenis is widely admired for its shipping expertise and serves a varied portfolio of clients including shipowners, P&I clubs and international banks across a broad range of shipping matters.

Norton Rose offers one of the most comprehensive and complete shipping practices around, and deservedly moves up a notch in our rankings. Benefiting from its impressive international reach, the firm is one of the leaders in ship financing matters and is regularly instructed by all the major local and international banks. Led by the highly regarded Dimitri Sofianopoulos, the team advised HSH Nordbank in the US$500m loan facility to facilitate the Restis Group's acquisition of a fleet of bulkers. The 'robust

SHIPPING AND MARITIME

GR J TIMAGENIS
NORTON ROSE
SARANTITIS LAW FIRM ✪
THEO V SIOUFAS, LAW OFFICES

VGENOPOULOS & PARTNERS ✪

Clyde & Co
Constant & Constant
Daniolos, Issaias and Partners Law Offices
G E Bairactaris & Partners
Hill Taylor Dickinson
Holman Fenwick & Willan International ✪
Ince & Co ✪
PI Partners ✪
Panos D Mavroyannis & Partners
Paul C Avrameas & Partners Law Office
Reece & Tomazos in association with Richards Butler, Law Office
Roussos & Hatzidimitriou Law Offices ✪
Scorinis Law Offices
Watson, Farley & Williams ✪

Basil T Patkos, Law Offices
Deucalion Rediadis & Sons
German Greek Law Group – Ziouvas
I.K. Rokas and Partners
Karatzas & Partners Law Firm ✪
S & A Papadimitriou & Co ✪
Stephenson Harwood Consultants O.E.
TJ Koutalidis, Law Office ✪
Theologidis Lascaratos Mitrakos Myrillos

Antony Antapassis – George Albouras Law Office
Calavros and Partners ✪
Chrysses Demetriades & Co Law Office
Constantin Mattheos Law Offices
I. Savramis & Partners Law Offices
Lallis Voutsinos & Anagnostopoulos
P Sotiropoulos (Dr) Law Office
Souriadakis, Frangakis, Skaltsas & Associates ✪
Tsibanoulis & Partners Law Firm ✪

Firms are listed A-Z in tiers which are ranked in order of priority
✪ *Indicates firm displays contact details at the end of this chapter.*

and commercial' Chris Hobbs heads a litigation team that is particularly strong on dry matters. The firm is acting for the owners in a major dispute (US$9m+) with a Chinese yard relating to pre- and post-delivery defects of the purchased vessels.

Sarantitis Law Firm offers a broad range of contentious and non-contentious expertise to banks, shipyards, shipowners and P&I clubs. On the financing side, the firm advised First Business Bank on in excess of 25 loan agreements to facilitate the financing of new-builds and second-hand vessels. The firm has niche expertise in the luxury yacht market and recently advised Alfa Yachting on the €50m sale of one of its yachts. On the contentious side, the firm advised Israel Shipyards in a dispute with the Greek State over the late payment of several vessels. Vassilis Sarantitis is a well-known individual in the field.

Theo V Sioufas, Law Offices has a stellar reputation in the Greek shipping market. Specialising in ship financing, the firm acts for an impressive portfolio of Greek banks.

Vgenopoulos & Partners has a first-rate reputation in relation to ship financing, and is frequently instructed by banks such as HSH Nordbank and Aegean Baltic Bank. Recent highlights include advising HSH Nordbank on the US$520m acquisition financing of Navios Maritime Holdings.

Perhaps best-known as a cargo practice par-excellence, **Clyde & Co** is experienced in the full gamut of both wet and dry work including charter-party disputes, general average and collisions. Martin Hall heads a team that offers both Greek and UK law expertise and includes master mariner Russell Rawlings. Clients include Transmed Shipping and Golden Union Shipping.

Backed by its impressive network of world-wide offices, **Holman Fenwick & Willan International** has an excellent track record for both wet and dry expertise. On the wet side, Charles Lowe is frequently involved in major collisions and has an excellent reputation for his salvor work. Whilst on the dry side, the firm benefits from the expertise of David Pitlarge. Dan Tindall is building up the firm's shipping finance practice.

Headed by Jonathan Elvey, **Ince & Co** acts for owners and P&I clubs in relation to a myriad of wet and dry matters. The firm's excellent admiralty practice offers a 24-hour emergency response service for marine casualties.

Headed by dual-qualified partner John Reece, **Law Office Reece & Tomazos in association with Richards Butler**'s shipping department offers expertise in a full range of wet and dry shipping matters including charter-party and shipbuilding disputes, casualties and cargo claims. The firm recently advised Eukor Car Carriers and their P&I club following a fire on board their vessel, the *Aniara*.

One of the pre-eminent and most highly-respected shipping finance firms in the region, **Watson, Farley & Williams** boasts an impressive client base that includes the majority of major domestic and international banks, and major corporate borrowers. George Paleokrassas heads a team that was recently instructed by a syndicate of international banks in relation to a ten-year, US$250m revolving credit facility to Tsakos Energy Navigation. Jeremy Watson is well-known.

S & A Papadimitriou & Co is involved in a number of dry shipping disputes on behalf of ship-owners. Highlights include advising a leading Greek shipowner in a contract of affreightment dispute.

Chrysses Demetriades & Co Law Office, which operates locally as **G. C. Economou & Associates**, has an excellent shipping practice that is frequently involved in major ship purchases for clients.

TAX

ZEPOS & YANNOPOULOS ✪

Dryllerakis & Associates ✪
Stavropoulos & Partners ✪

Avramopoulos & Partners Law Firm ✪
Bahas, Gramatidis & Partners
Ballas, Pelecanos & Associates ✪
C Papacostopoulos & Associates ✪
Chrysses Demetriades & Co Law Office
Dracopoulos & Vassalakis ✪
I.K. Rokas and Partners
Kaldis Law Offices
Karatzas & Partners Law Firm ✪
Kyriakides – Georgopoulos Law Firm
M & P Bernitsas ✪
Massouridis Stavropoulos & Associates
Metaxopoulos. Law Firm ✪
Moratis – Passas
Papaconstantinou, Law Offices ✪
Sarantitis Law Firm ✪
Souriadakis, Frangakis, Skaltsas & Associates ✪
TJ Koutalidis, Law Office ✪
Theo V Sioufas, Law Offices
Vgenopoulos & Partners ✪

Firms are listed A-Z in tiers which are ranked in order of priority
✪ *Indicates firm displays contact details at the end of this chapter.*

TAX

With no fewer than 17 lawyers at its disposal, **Zepos & Yannopoulos**' tax team offers strength and depth that far outstrips its competitors. Recent highlights include advising Deutsche Bank on the regulatory and tax issues on the restructuring of its real estate investments in Greece. The firm's highly regarded tax litigation team recently represented a Japanese car manufacturer in a major dispute before the ECJ, relating to the assessment of Greek customs duty.

Dryllerakis & Associates is frequently involved in major tax litigation on behalf of corporate clients. On the advisory-side, the firm offers expertise in compliance issues in relation to Greece's notoriously complex tax regime.

Stavropoulos & Partners' Ioannis Stavropolous is a revered practitioner who is frequently instructed in relation to the country's most complex and important tax issues.

Ballas, Pelecanos & Associates has a focus on transfer pricing and permanent establishment issues.

M & P Bernitsas offers contentious and non-contentious tax advice to its strong corporate client base.

Vgenopoulos & Partners successfully represented a major Italian construction company before the Supreme Administrative Court, regarding the application of Italian-Greek double tax relief.

AFENDRAS & PARTNERS LAW OFFICES

38 SINA & SKOUFA STREET
106 72 ATHENS

Telephone: +30 210 364 6105
Fax: +30 210 364 3191
E-mail: afendras@afendras.gr
Website: www.afendras.gr

Languages
English, French, German, Italian

Number of lawyers 17

Contacts
Stavros Afendras, Yota Psarogiorgou

CATEGORIES OF WORK

Mergers and acquisitions
S Afendras, E Kastrinaki

Capital markets
S Afendras, Y Psarogiorgou

Banking and finance
S Afendras, S Panagiotopoulos

Energy
Y Psarogiorgou, K Altourk

Investment
S Afendras, V Vilaras

Corporate
A Konstas, Y Psarogiorgou

Telecommunications
Ch Doukas, E Karamalli

Commercial and civil
Ch Doukas, E Kastrinaki

Civil law
A Konstas, D Kabourmalis

Taxation
S Afendras, N Zorbala

Corporate criminal
M Spanoudaki, O Kapachtsi

European law
E Kastrinaki, A Evaggeliou

Sports
S Panagiotopoulos, Y Psarogiogou

Intellectual property
Ch Doukas, D Kabourmalis

THE FIRM

The firm was formed initially by Stavros D Afendras in 1986. At the beginning, the firm provided services mainly in the fields of European and corporate law. Progressively, the firm grew, and in order to cover the needs of its clientele, expanded its services into other areas of law.

The firm's offices are located at the heart of the Athens city centre and staffed with lawyers that are specialised and qualified to deal with the areas of law listed above.

AREAS OF PRACTICE

Afendras & Partners Law Offices provide a full range of corporate and commercial law services, from company establishment to advising on mergers and acquisitions. Other principal practice areas include banking and finance, capital markets, investment and securities, as well as tax and insolvency procedures. In the field of industry and enterprises, the firm has extensive experience in energy, telecommunications and investment projects.

Afendras & Partners' clientele consists of major local and international companies, as well as financial institutions and important investors in the field of industry.

Legal advice is also offered in relation to Greek civil law matters and sports law. Anticipating the demand for legal expertise in several practice law areas, the office established certain groups of specialised lawyers, in order to meet client requirements.

ANAGNOSTOPOULOS BAZINAS FIFIS

ODOS ALOPEKIS 11
106 75 ATHENS

Telephone: +30 210 725 4800
Fax: +30 210 725 4835
E-mail: info@abf.gr
Website: www.abf.gr

Languages
English, French, German

Number of lawyers 17

Contacts
IG Anagnostopoulos, GB Bazinas

Member
Fraudnet; ICC

CATEGORIES OF WORK

Litigation	Securities regulation
Arbitration and ADR	Product liability
Corporate and commercial	Fraud and white-collar crime
Insolvency and corporate restructuring	Tax and customs offences
Banking and finance	Environment
Mergers and acquisitions	Extradition and mutual assistance
Media and entertainment	Money laundering
Information technology	Corruption practices
Construction	Competition and antitrust

THE FIRM

The firm was established in 1990 and assumed its present form in 1996 with the union of Anagnostopoulos & Fifis, Counsellors & Attorneys at Law with Law Offices GB Bazinas, with the aim of utilising the synergies of comprehensive representation in business matters of a contentious nature.

It pioneered the integration of top-level commercial law counsel with expert representation in relation to economic and corporate crime, and ranks among the country's premier providers of litigation and dispute management services. The firm today is recognised as a dynamic, niche legal service provider with a distinctive character and market position.

AREAS OF PRACTICE

The firm is active in a variety of work areas. Although litigation has traditionally formed the core of its work, today the firm offers a wide range of consultative services in matters of Greek, European and international law to a number of major international and domestic corporations from the energy, defence, banking and financial services, aviation, telecommunications, automobiles, pharmaceuticals, raw materials, information technology and media sectors, as well as domestic and foreign public and governmental organisations.

The firm ranks among the country's premier providers of dispute management services and among the clear leaders in the domain of economic and corporate crime. With one of the country's strongest litigation teams, the firm is able to offer across-the-board tactical options to a wide international and domestic corporate client base.

The firm has an extensive corporate and commercial law practice and is regularly instructed in relation to both mainstream international business transactions and highly innovative projects, such as combined IT and credit transactions, transfer of technology projects and spin-off companies. It regularly acts on such matters as corporate acquisitions, shareholder minority disputes, group structuring and implementation, EU-funded projects and directors' liability.

Noted for its experience with complex international litigation, cross-border insolvency and related proceedings, as well as voluntary and enforced corporate restructuring, the firm is regularly instructed to advise and represent creditors, debtors, turnaround professionals and foreign liquidators in matters of Greek and European insolvency law.

The firm performs a significant volume of mainstream banking and financial services law work, including secured and unsecured credit, documentary credit, revolving facilities and post-petition funding in the course of domestic or cross-border restructuring. It is regularly involved in the drafting and enforcement of security over a variety of assets, including vessels, aircraft, securities and real estate, either in conjunction with the drafting of lender or other documentation, or tracking master agreements governed by the laws of the major credit and paper markets.

After acquiring, in 2002, a specialist media law practice, the firm is able to offer top-notch consulting and representation in all aspects of media and IT, including print media, free-to-air and subscriber television and radio, production, advertising and Internet law.

Regularly acting for several prime international and domestic financial institutions in contentious and non-contentious securities regulation matters, the firm enjoys a growing international reputation for both its consultative and its litigious work in this domain.

The firm also advises and represents some of the largest international and domestic corporations in relation to securities regulation, corporate criminal liability, tax and customs offences, money laundering, corruption practices, extradition and mutual assistance, product liability and environmental liability matters. Name partner Professor Ilias G Anagnostopoulos has served as lead counsel in most of the major economic and corporate crime cases over the past 15 years.

AVRAMOPOULOS & PARTNERS LAW FIRM

70 PANORMOU STREET
115 23 ATHENS

Telephone: +30 210 691 2200
Fax: +30 210 691 1211
E-mail: info@avralaw.gr
Website: www.avramopoulos.com

Languages
English, French, German, Greek, Italian

Other offices
Nicosia*

Number of lawyers 25

Contact
Vassilis D Avramopoulos

Member
The State Capital Law Firm Group

CATEGORIES OF WORK

Corporate, commercial and tax	**Labour and social insurance**
Mergers and acquisitions	**Commercial property, real estate**
Privatisation and investments	**Media and entertainment**
IT and telecommunications	**Hotel and resort development**
EU and competition law	**Gaming and licensing**
Banking, finance and securities	**Aviation**
Construction and public procurement	**Intellectual property**
Infrastructure and project finance	**Government business, regulatory**
Litigation and arbitration	**Sports law**

THE FIRM

Avramopoulos & Partners provides a comprehensive business law service for its clients, both domestic and international. The key areas of its service are set out below.

AREAS OF PRACTICE

Commercial and corporate services: the commercial department acts for corporate business and banking clients, both Greek and international in a number of areas including joint ventures, mergers and acquisitions, management buy-outs, corporate reorganisations, franchising, distribution and agency agreements, asset financing and commercial lending.

The firm also regularly advises domestic and international clients regarding investments in Greece and is also active in the area of private finance initiatives both from the state and business client point of view.

IT and telecommunications: the firm is very well regarded and advises and represents in Greece some of the world's leading companies in the area of information technology and telecommunications.

Having played a major role in structuring, negotiating and documenting major corporate and commercial ventures and in advising on significant regulatory issues, we have gained an in-depth knowledge of the Greek telecommunications regulatory framework.

Labour and social insurance: the firm has extensive experience across the entire labour, employment and social insurance law, including litigation and labour dispute resolution, employment contract negotiation, drafting and termination, as well as transfer of business and outsourcing.

Banking finance and securities: the firm is substantially involved in the sectors of banking, finance and capital markets, including legal services regarding the underwriting procedure for the listing of companies in the Athens stock market, consulting regarding the regulatory aspects for the listing/initial public offerings (IPO) of new stocks in the Athens stock market, agreements for the provision of investment services and especially discretionary portfolio management agreements, consulting regarding the sector of private banking, tax issues raised for the best management of clients' assets, term loan agreements, credit facilities, revolving credit facilities, loan note instruments, syndicated loans, and tax law consulting regarding the above matters.

Hotel and resort development: they have developed an exceptionally strong expertise in this area, having handled the development, acquisition, financing and operation of various large and well-known hotels and resorts in Greece.

Detailed information is available upon request.

BALLAS, PELECANOS & ASSOCIATES

10 SOLONOS STREET
KOLONAKI
106 73 ATHENS

Telephone: +30 210 362 5943
Fax: +30 210 364 7925
E-mail: balpel@otenet.gr

Languages
English, French, German, Italian

Number of lawyers 18

Contact
George A Ballas

Member
Counterforce Network; International Bar Association; European Patent Institute

Formerly Simitis Law Offices, established in 1930

CATEGORIES OF WORK

- Company and commercial
- Corporate law
- Foreign investments
- Privatisation and projects
- Mergers and acquisitions
- Corporate finance
- EU and competition (unfair and antitrust)
- Industrial and intellectual property
- Patents, trade marks, designs (including litigation)
- Copyright and allied rights (including litigation)
- Licences, franchising
- Contract
- Litigation and arbitration

C. PAPACOSTOPOULOS & ASSOCIATES

3 STRATIGOU TOMBRA STREET
AGHIA PARASKEVI
153 42 ATHENS

Telephone: +30 210 606 2325
Fax: +30 210 606 2111
E-mail: info@cpalaw.gr
Website: www.cpalaw.gr

Languages
English, French, German, Italian

Number of lawyers 20

Contacts
Mr Constantine Papacostopoulos,
Ms Angela Iliadis

Member
IFA International;
Greek Association For Commercial Law

CATEGORIES OF WORK

- Tax advice and planning
- Mergers and acquisitions
- Securities
- Corporate finance
- Property finance
- Capital markets
- Banking and finance
- Litigation
- Arbitration
- Commercial and company law
- Legal audits
- EU and competition law
- Corporate recovery
- Media and entertainment
- Energy and infrastructure projects
- Construction – real estate
- Intellectual property
- Telecommunications and ICT
- E-business
- Labour law and social security
- Public sector
- Shipping and transportation

CALAVROS AND PARTNERS

19 VRANA STREET
(SIDESTREET TO KATEHAKI AVE)
11525 ATHENS

Telephone: +30 210 369 8700
Fax: +30 210 369 8750
E-mail: calavros@calavros.com
Website: www.calavros.com

Languages
English, French, German

Number of lawyers 14

Member
International Association for Civil Procedure & International Arbitration; International Association for Comparative Law; International Federation for European Law; Comparative Law Society

International groupings
In association with Habscheid–Thyssen (Dresden-Munich-Lausanne)

CATEGORIES OF WORK	
Commercial and corporate law	Immigration
EU and competition	Capital markets, banking, investment
Mergers and acquisitions	Litigation and arbitration
Spin-offs and privatisations	Administrative law
Pharmaceutical law	Tax law
Telecommunications	Labour and social security law
Intellectual and industrial property	Private international law
Contract law	Environmental law
Civil law	Criminal law

THE FIRM

Calavros and Partners law firm was established in 1980 and is already acclaimed as one of the leading and most esteemed Greek law firms. Managed by a forward-thinking team of partners under the leadership of Professor Constantin Calavros, Calavros and Partners enjoys a well-established reputation for its commitment to providing top-quality, comprehensive and business-orientated legal services.

Calavros and Partners enjoys a well established reputation due to its commitment to always providing top-quality legal services. The firm's overall approach is to combine excellence in results with taking extra care to keep close, personal contact with clients throughout the handling of every case. It is for this reason that the firm has chosen to associate with lawyers from diverse legal backgrounds with sophisticated expertise, who are capable of attending clients' needs in the most efficient manner. It is this mentality that has always led the firm to co-operate with the most reputable law firms in Europe and internationally. The firm's goal remains to provide practical solutions that meet clients' requirements cost effectively.

Equipped with the latest technology, with continuous back-up by an in-house computer expert, the firm not only ensures secured and speedy inter-networking but also guarantees a prompt and timely response to all its clients, meeting the changing conditions of today's demanding business world.

AREAS OF PRACTICE

Calavros and Partners has a broad commercial practice and is distinguished for servicing multinational private and public sector companies, as well as Greek companies seeking to expand their business abroad. The firm offers a comprehensive range of legal services spanning the entire spectrum of corporate and commercial activities, with outstanding expertise in mergers and acquisitions, join ventures, privatisations, international transactions and commercial contracts, foreign investments, antitrust law and unfair competition, agency and distribution, industrial and intellectual property, software and computer law, banking and finance, EU law, real estate matters, civil law, human rights protection law, administrative law, tax law, and civil and commercial litigation and arbitration. In particular, having had the opportunity to undertake a full range of corporate and commercial assignments with regard to numerous mergers and acquisitions, the firm has gained distinctive experience in handling all corporate affairs which are affected by a merger or acquisition.

Calavros & Partners is proud to consider itself an expert in all fields of pharmaceutical law, including anticompetitive behaviour, patent protection, biotechnologies, marketing practices, pricing and reimbursement, consumer law, product liability, licensing, clinical trials, and parallel trade. Advising Greek and multinational pharmaceutical companies during the last years has given the firm the opportunity to deepen its knowledge and experience of the whole Greek and EU complex legal framework regarding medicinal products, and their development, protection and circulation, as well as their pricing and reimbursement by the national health insurance systems.

The firm has been appointed as special legal adviser to the Association of Pharmaceutical Companies doing Business in Greece (SFEE) – the firm's managing partner, Professor Constantin Calavros, has been representing SFEE in law-making committees operating either under the Ministry of Health and/or the National Drug Organisation (EOF), being greatly involved in the legal drafting of both ministerial decisions and interpretative circulars which concern fundamental regulatory issues of the pharmaceutical industry, such as allowable marketing practices, marketing expenses etc.

The firm is also renowned for its pioneering work in the developing area of telecoms. It has assumed the responsibility to handle transactions of immense significance that exceed the boundaries of Greece. Such expertise remains constantly updated by the firm's uninterrupted consulting of public and private undertakings that remain active in the telecoms market.

COCALIS & PSARRAS

14 SOLONOS STREET
106 73 ATHENS

Telephone: +30 210 361 3661
Fax: +30 210 364 1258
E-mail: info@tclaw.gr
Website: www.tclaw.gr

Languages
English, French, German, Italian

Number of lawyers 11

Contact
Dimitri Cocalis

CATEGORIES OF WORK

Mergers and acquisitions
DN Cocalis, S Papadopoulou

Investment
DN Cocalis, L Ioannidou

Banking and finance
DN Cocalis, L Ioannidou

Competition
AC Psarras, DN Cocalis

Telecoms
AC Psarras, S Papadopoulou

IT
AC Psarras, DN Cocalis

Intellectual property
AC Psarras, J Georgountzou

Media
AC Psarras, S Papadopoulou

Energy
DN Cocalis, S Papadopoulou

Aviation
AC Psarras, L Ioannidou

Selective distribution network
AC Psarras, P Gavrilis

Commercial
S Papadopoulou, L Ioannidou

Contract
DN Cocalis, S Papadopoulou

Corporate
N Raxi, L Ioannidou

Litigation
N Raxi, S Papadopoulou

Tax
DN Cocalis, P Gavrilis

Arbitration
DN Cocalis, AC Psarras

Advertising
AC Psarras, J Georgountzou

THE FIRM

Cocalis & Psarras was originally established in 1913 and has concentrated since its early days on corporate clients and a 'boutique' policy, which has allowed it to offer specialised and personalised services of a high standard to Greek and foreign clients, for almost a century. The firm's client base is mainly European, North American, Japanese and South Korean, with establishments or interests in Greece, the Balkans and the Mediterranean area; it includes private sector entities, banks, states, state organisations, independent administrative authorities, public sector enterprises, utilities, lawyers, auditors, consulting firms and other business-orientated professionals. Cocalis & Psarras is an incorporated partnership of lawyers, under PD 518/1989.

AREAS OF PRACTICE

The firm efficiently covers all the areas of practice listed above, with particular emphasis and expertise in M&A, investment, banking and financing, competition, telecommunications, IT, intellectual property, media, energy, aviation, and selective distribution networks. The firm has long experience in providing comprehensive legal services on an outsourcing basis to several national and international clients.

DRACOPOULOS & VASSALAKIS

6 OMIROU STREET
105 64 ATHENS

Telephone: + 30 210 322 7000
Fax: + 30 210 322 7111
E-mail: info@dvlaw.gr

Languages
English, French, German, Greek

Number of lawyers 12

CATEGORIES OF WORK

Capital markets	**Project finance**
M&A	**Corporate taxation**
Banking	**Corporate finance**
Energy	**Privatisations**

DRAKOPOULOS LAW FIRM

7 HASIOTI STREET
N FILOTHEI
151 23 ATHENS

Telephone: +30 210 683 6561
Fax: +30 210 683 6538
E-mail: info@drakopoulos-law.com
Website: www.drakopoulos-law.com

Languages
English, French, German, Italian, Spanish

Number of lawyers 10

Member
IBA; CLA

CATEGORIES OF WORK

Commercial and corporate law P Drakopoulos, I Scandalis	**Intellectual/industrial property law** Dr V Papakonstantinou, D Markopoulou
International trade law P Drakopoulos, I Scandalis	**Computer law** Dr V Papakonstantinou, M Katsoula
Mergers and acquisitions P Drakopoulos, I Scandalis	**Labour law** A Economou, I Kolias
Administrative law A Economou, V Tsoukala	**Litigation** A Economou, V Tsoukala
Antitrust and unfair competition law P Drakopoulos, D Markopoulou	**Consumer products** A Economou, D Markopoulou
Civil law A Economou, I Kolias	**Stock Exchange** A Economou, I Scandalis
Media and advertising Dr V Papakonstantinou, D Markopoulou	**Construction and real estate** Dr V Papakonstantinou, M Katsoula
Tourism Dr V Papakonstantinou, M Katsoula	**Securities** A Economou, I Scandalis
Telecommunications Dr V Papakonstantinou, D Markopoulou	**Taxation** A Economou, I Scandalis

DRYLLERAKIS & ASSOCIATES

25 VOUKOURESTIOU STREET
106 71 ATHENS

Telephone: +30 210 362 8159
Fax: +30 210 364 4218
E-mail: lawoffice@dryllerakis.gr
Website: www.dryllerakis.gr

Languages
English, French, German, Italian, Russian, Spanish

Number of lawyers 17

Contact
JC Dryllerakis

Member
International Business Law Consortium (IBLC)

CATEGORIES OF WORK	
Company and commercial	Securities and stock exchange
Competition	Gaming law
Tax	Privatisation and projects
Mergers and acquisitions	Finance
Foreign investment	Real estate
Trade marks	Arbitration and litigation
Information technology	

THE FIRM

The formation of Dryllerakis & Associates as a firm of lawyers has been considered necessary in order to secure the best organisation and a better quality of service in the substantial and serious matters that the firm handles.

The firm has operated in Athens since 1970, and in its present form since 1978. In 1994, the firm's name changed from Theofanopoulos-Dryllerakis to its current name. The firm has five partners. It offers a full range of professional legal and administrative services. The senior partner and special adviser have experience that stems from positions as general counsel and general tax counsel in major multinationals, and also from participation in management teams and boards of directors of Greek and international companies.

AREAS OF PRACTICE

Dryllerakis & Associates is oriented towards providing consultation to international clients and businesses in general. The firm also has a long tradition in mergers and acquisitions work and has handled more than 40 cases so far, it also has special experience in tax law, environmental law and business contracts. The firm has also successfully handled important privatisation cases.

All the lawyers have extensive experience in court practice and arbitration. Senior lawyers frequently handle matters in the Supreme Courts and especially in the Conseil D'Etat and the Supreme Administrative Court.

All the lawyers are fluent in English and most of them have a working knowledge of French, while others speak a variety of languages including German, Spanish, Italian and Russian.

Allocation of cases is based on several criteria such as expertise and seniority, specialisation and availability.

The company operates from its head office (as above) as well as in a neighbouring building at 30 Voulourestiou Street. Both buildings are served by modern communication systems that allow inter-office communication, telephone conferencing, etc; as well as being fully equipped with a modern computer network system.

The senior partners participate in the board of directors and the management of several major companies including clients of the firm (such as Barilla's affiliate, Belersdorf, Hyatt, Shell, etc) and offers them significant experience in current managerial and business issues which develop the firm's legal knowledge and facilitate the provision of advice and solutions to clients' specific legal needs.

Owing to the participation of the senior partner, Mr JC Dryllerakis in the public administrative process, the firm has substantial experience in this field and concerning the way subjects are treated by the administration. Mr Dryllerakis was a regular member of the Independent Competition Committee for six years and a member of the board of directors of the Capital Markets Committee for two years, assisting in the regulation of the capital market. He has participated in the drafting committees of several pieces of legislation, the office having been assigned to the drafting of the law for liquidation of the Restructuring Organisation.

Representative clients include: Aegean Airlines, AEPI SA, Allatini SA, Barilla, Beiersdorf AG, Blue Palace Hotel, Danone Group, Delta Dairy Products SA, Grande Bretagne, IBM Hellas SA, ICC Inc, EFG Eurobank Ergasias SA, EFG Eurobank Properties, Eurocorp AEPEY, Exelixi Portfolio Investments SA, Exxon Corporation, Forthnet SA, Hyatt Regency Hotels & Tourism (Hellas) A.E., Klonatex Group, Leo Burnett, Lectra SA, LoyalWard Ltd, SCA Packaging A.E., Minoan Lines, Natalys SA, Nintendo, Paneuropean Oil & Ind. Hold.SA, Petrola Hellas AEBE, Pechiney (Aluminium de Grece), Raytheon Co, Shell SA, Sonae-Charagionis SA, Tate & Lylle/Amylum Group, Tesa SA, TVX Gold Inc.

ELIAS PARASKEVAS ATTORNEYS AT LAW

7 ASKLEPIOU STREET
106 79 ATHENS

Telephone: +30 210 361 0333
Fax: +30 210 364 5329
E-mail: info@paraskevaslaw.com
Website: www.paraskevaslaw.com

Languages
English, French, German, Italian

Number of lawyers 20

Contact
Dimitris Paraskevas, managing partner (dparaskevas@paraskevaslaw.com),
Beth Tate Hondros, deputy managing partner (bhondros@paraskevaslaw.com)

CATEGORIES OF WORK

Mergers and acquisitions
Dimitris Paraskevas

Privatisation and projects
Dimitris Paraskevas

Banking, finance and capital markets
Dimitris Paraskevas

Company and corporate governance
Olga Galazoula

Employment law
Irini Charisiadou

Real estate
Dimitris Paraskevas

EU and competition
Irene Grammatopoulou

IT and telecoms
Constantinos Ploubis

Litigation and dispute resolution
Irini Charisiadou, Beth Tate Hondros

Cross-border transactions
Dimitris Paraskevas, Beth Tate Hondros

FOTIS KREMMYDAS-PHILIPPOS DORIS AND ASSOCIATES

37 ACADEMIAS AVE, 5TH FLOOR
106 72 ATHENS

Telephone: +30 210 363 6084
Fax: +30 210 361 8841
E-mail: info@kremlaw.gr

Languages
English, French, German

Other offices
London

Number of lawyers 21
at this office 18

CATEGORIES OF WORK

Company law
Fotis Kremmydas, Efi Kyriazi

Business transactions
Fotis Kremmydas, Dimitris Boukis

Tax
Costis Mallios, Fanny Karayianni

Litigation
Roula Liossi, Fanny Karayianni

Arbitration
Fotis Kremmydas, Roula Liossi

Family and inheritance
Patricia Adamopoulou,
Fanny Karayianni

Property law
Efi Kyriazi, Froso Dimakou Kiaou

Labour law
Nicholaos Dounavis, Costis Mallios

Intellectual property
Dimitris Boukis, Patricia Adamopoulou

Banking and finance
Dimitris Boukis, Costis Mallios

G. C. ECONOMOU & ASSOCIATES

11 KANARI STREET
KOLONAKI
106 71 ATHENS

Telephone: +30 210 364 0030
Fax: +30 210 364 0082
E-mail: economou@gce-associates.gr

Languages
English, French, Greek, Italian

Other offices
Piraeus, Cyprus

Number of lawyers 45
at this office 7

Contacts
G C Economou, Yiannis Lymperopoulos

CATEGORIES OF WORK

Shipping and ship finance

Commercial and company law

Banking, finance and capital matters

Mergers and acquisitions

Project finance

International tax planning, corporate structuring and trusts

EU internal market, competition, e-trade

International trade

Real estate

Litigation and arbitration

Insurance and professional negligence

Gaming law

Intellectual property

Telecommunications

GEORGE K STEFANAKIS & ASSOCIATES

18 AKADIMIAS STREET
106 71 ATHENS

Telephone: +30 210 361 8722
Fax: +30 210 363 9409
E-mail: info@stefanakislawfirm.gr

Languages
English, French, German, Italian

Number of lawyers 14

CATEGORIES OF WORK

Corporate and commercial
KP Papadiamantis, IG Stefanaki

Tax
A Chatjitjani

Labour
S Fanourgakis, IK Konstantinou

Civil law and litigation
GK Stefanakis, NG Deskas

Arbitration
GK Stefanakis, KP Papadiamantis

Insolvency
GK Stefanakis, NG Deskas

Insurance
NG Deskas

Economic criminal law
NG Deskas, IK Konstantinou

Intellectual and industrial property
GK Stefanakis, KP Papadiamantis

EU law, competition and agency
KP Papadiamantis, AA Kortesis

Foreign investments and project finance
KP Papadiamantis, IG Stefanaki

Mergers and acquisitions
KP Papadiamantis, IK Konstantinou

Real estate
NG Deskas, S Sideraki

Wills and estate planning
A Chatjitjani, S Sideraki

Administrative
GK Stefanakis, KP Papadiamantis

Public works and procurement
GK Stefanakis, KP Papadiamantis

Information technology
IG Stefanaki, AA Kortesis

LAW OFFICES HAROULA CONSTANDINIDOU

62A SKOUFA STREET
106 80 ATHENS

Telephone: +30 210 363 6567
Fax: +30 210 363 6088
E-mail: constandinidou@ath.forthnet.gr
Website: www.constandinidou.gr

Languages
English, French, German

Other offices
Paris*

Number of lawyers 11
at this office 7

Member
Athens Bar Association; International Bar Association; International Academy of Matrimonial Lawyers; International Society of Family Law; National Council for Abducted Children (reunite); Association of Private International Law

CATEGORIES OF WORK

International family law
Haroula Constandinidou, Konstantinos Stavropoulos

Family law
Haroula Constandinidou, Joanna-Natalie Stavropoulou

International private law
Haroula Constandinidou, Konstantinos Stavropoulos

General practice
Maria Dilana, Joanna-Natalie Stavropoulou

Inheritance law
Konstantinos Stavropoulos, Panagiotis Panteloukas

Corporate law
Haroula Constandinidou, Maria Dilana

Real estate
Joanna-Natalie Stavropoulou, Panagiotis Panteloukas

International child abduction
Haroula Constandinidou, Konstantinos Stavropoulos

Commercial law
Karl-Andreas Psichas, Konstantinos Stavropoulos

Trade marks
Maria Dilana, Panagiotis Panteloukas

Civil litigation
Maria Dilana, Karl-Andreas Psichas

Civil law
Maria Dilana, Panagiotis Panteloukas

European law
Panagiotis Panteloukas, Ioannis Somarakis

IKONOMOPOULOS & PARTNERS

4 KOUMBARI STREET
106 74 ATHENS

Telephone: +30 210 361 3615
Fax: +30 210 364 1806
E-mail:
ikonomopoulos@ikonomopoulos.gr
Website: www.ikonomopoulos.gr

Languages
English, French, German, Italian

Number of lawyers 12

Contact
Harris Ikonomopoulos

CATEGORIES OF WORK

Corporate and commercial

Tax

Administrative

Banking and finance

Energy and natural resources

Foreign and direct investment

Government business, regulatory

Civil law and litigation

Privatisation

PPPs

EU and competition

Intellectual property

IT and telecoms

Dispute resolution/arbitration

Criminal law

Construction

Public works and procurement

DR HELEN PAPACONSTANTINOU, JOHN FILIAS & ASSOCIATES

LAW OFFICES

2 COUMBARI STREET
KOLONAKI
106 74 ATHENS

Telephone: +30 210 362 5757
Fax: +30 210 362 6742
E-mail: mail@hplaw.biz
Website: www.hplaw.biz

Languages
Dutch, English, French, German, Italian, Spanish

Number of lawyers 15

Contact
John Filias (general manager)

CATEGORIES OF WORK

Trade mark law
E Yazitzoglou, M Theodoridou

Patent law,
M Athanassiadou, H Voelkel

Litigation in patents
Dr H Papaconstatinou, T Goussios

Litigation in trade marks
E Lappa, A Chandanou

Competition law – copyright
Dr H Papaconstantinou, T Goussios

Community trade marks
K Delouka, A Roussou

International trade marks
E Yazitzoglou, M Theodoridou

Licensing
K Delouka, D Katsouli

Maintenance of trade marks
D Karatza

Searching – watching
D Karatza, I Louvis

European patents, SPCs
C Dimou, A Roussou

Customs monitoring procedures
F Kardiopoulis

Domain names
F Kardiopoulis, E Lappa

Designs
M Athanassiadou

THE FIRM

The firm Dr P D Theodorides & Dr H G Papaconstantinou, which started as a solo practice, was founded by Panagiotis Theodorides in 1920 and is one of the oldest trade mark and patent firms in Greece. In order to better serve its clients and maintain a competitive practice which covers the broad spectrum of intellectual property law, the firm evolved into two distinct branches in 1996, one under the old firm name (Law Office Dr P D Theodorides – Dr H G Papaconstantinou) covering trade marks, domain names, copyright and related litigation, and the other under the name Dr Helen Papaconstantinou, John Filias & Associates, covering patents, designs, utility models and related litigation. Dr Helen Papaconstantinou, who graduated from the University of Athens with a law degree and holds a Dr Juris degree from the Free University of Berlin, has headed the firm since 1986. In addition to being active in numerous other international organisations (INTA, ITMA, CIPA ao), Dr Helen Papaconstantinou is vice president of the AIPPI Group of Greece, member of the executive committee of FICPI, member of the board and former secretary general of the European Patent Institute and a council member of ECTA.

Over the past 85 years, the firm has grown steadily to become the largest firm of its kind in Greece. The firm's staff consists of 41 people, including 15 attorneys, most of whom possess postgraduate degrees from Greece and abroad, with considerable experience in intellectual property matters over many years of practice, five paralegals and four foreign secretaries. Three of the firm's attorneys are European patent attorneys, one is a UK barrister and one has extensive experience in international arbitration practice in the USA. Most of the firm's attorneys are members of various professional bodies.

The firm is able to serve foreign clients in English, French, German, Spanish, Italian and Dutch. The firm collaborates closely with 42 technical counsellors who have accredited degrees in sciences. The majority of them are or have been involved in academic research, are competent translators for English, French and German, and provide consulting services based on their technical expertise in patent matters.

AREAS OF PRACTICE

The firm specialises in intellectual property law, including patents, trade marks, copyright, designs, domain names, supplementary protection certificates for plant protection and medicinal products, unfair competition, customs monitoring procedures and all related litigation. It also offers expert consulting and quality advice in all areas of industrial and intellectual property law as well as on franchising distribution and license agreements and on advertising, marketing and consumer law.

The firm's client base covers a very broad spectrum. Its clients range from trade mark and patent departments of large and small international companies directly represented by the firm, through to multinational and small companies represented by the firm indirectly through trade mark and patent agents from all over the world.

In addition to its intellectual property activities in Greece, the firm maintains a close collaboration with law offices in Cyprus and all the Arabic countries, and has acquired experience in the handling of trade mark and patent matters in these countries for many years.

The firm of Dr Helen Papaconstantinou, John Filias & Associates is both flexible and adaptable in its ability to serve multifarious needs of clients. As a result, it has expanded its scope of representation to include intellectual property matters from all Balkan countries.

KALLIMOPOULOS, LOUKOPOULOS, CHIOTELLIS LAW FIRM

2 YPSILANTOU STR
106 75 ATHENS

Telephone: +30 210 726 4500
Fax: +30 210 726 4510
E-mail: legal@klclawfirm.com
Website: www.klclawfirm.com

Languages
English, French, German, Greek, Italian, Russian

Other offices
Sofia, Bucharest, Brussels

Number of lawyers 50
at this office 44

CATEGORIES OF WORK

Corporate, competition, joint ventures

Mergers and acquisitions

Commercial contracts/agency/ distribution

Franchising

Media, sports and entertainment

Intellectual and industrial property

Aviation and transport

IT, telecoms and e-commerce

Banking

Securities and stock exchange

Project finance and venture capital

EU court representation

European Commission

State aid

Dispute resolution, litigation, arbitration

Privatisations

Environmental law

Public procurement and concessions

Administrative law

Tax planning, structure and disputes

Employment law

KARATZAS & PARTNERS LAW FIRM

8 OMIROU STREET
105 64 ATHENS

Telephone: +30 210 371 3600
Fax: +30 210 323 4363
E-mail: mail@karatza-partners.gr

Languages
English, French, German, Greek

Number of lawyers 30

International groupings
International Swaps and Derivatives Association, Inc

CATEGORIES OF WORK

Banking and finance
Catherine Karatzas, Christina Papanikolopoulou

Mergers and acquisitions
Alexander Metallinos, Anna Manda

Capital markets
Catherine Karatzas, Alexander Metallinos

Securities
Alexander Metallinos, Christina Papanikolopoulou

Corporate and commercial
Catherine Karatzas, George Minoudis

Litigation
Christina Faitakis, Vassiliki Salaka

Real estate
Christina Faitakis, Vassiliki Salaka

Intellectual property
George Minoudis

Media and entertainment
Vassiliki Salaka, George Minoudis

Insurance
Vassiliki Salaka

Energy and natural resources
Christina Faitakis

KIORTSIS & ASSOCIATES LAW OFFICES
ESTABLISHED 1951

7 MAVROKORDATOU STREET
106 78 ATHENS

Telephone: +30 210 380 2914
Fax: +30 210 380 2401
E-mail: info@kiortsis.gr
Website: www.kiortsis.gr

Languages
English, French, German, Greek

International groupings
International Association for the Protection of Intellectual Property (AIPPI); Institute of Professional Representatives before the European Patent Office (EPI); European Communities Trade Mark Association (ECTA); International Trademark Association (INTA); International Federation of Industrial Property Attorneys (FICPI)

CATEGORIES OF WORK

Unfair competition

Copyrights

Intellectual property

Industrial property

Greek trade marks

Community trade marks

International trade marks

Greek patents

European patents

International patent applications

Utility models

Greek designs

Community designs

International design applications

Domain names

KREMALIS – LAW FIRM, member of ius laboris

35, KYRILLOU LOUKAREOS STR
114 75 ATHENS

Telephone: +30 210 643 1387
Fax: +30 210 646 0313
E-mail: secr.athens@kremalis.gr
Website: www.kremalis.gr

Languages
English, French, German, Italian, Spanish

Number of lawyers 12

Contacts
Konstantinos Kremalis (kkremalis@kremalis.gr), Vasiliki Sofogianni (secr.athens@kremalis-gr)

Member
ius laboris, International Employment Law, Pensions and Employee Benefits Alliance

CATEGORIES OF WORK

Labour and employment law (including mediation and arbitration, consulting, litigation, compensation and benefits, expatriation, drafting and negotiations for individual and collective agreements, restructuring, transfer and merger of undertakings)

International and European employment and social law

Media and internet law

Social security law (including retirement protection, pension funds, health and medical law, social policy research projects)

Administrative law

Constitutional law

Tax law

Private insurance law (including life and group insurance, occupational schemes)

International private law

LAMBADARIOS LAW OFFICES

3 STADIOU STREET
105 62 ATHENS

Telephone: +30 2 10 322 4047
Fax: +30 2 10 322 6368
E-mail: lambalaw@lambalaw.gr
Website: www.lambadarioslaw.gr

Languages
English, French, German, Japanese, Spanish

Number of lawyers 18

CATEGORIES OF WORK

Corporate, company law
Nondas Lambadarios,
Dimitrios Lambadarios

Banking, finance
Nondas Lambadarios

Structured finance
Nondas Lambadarios

Arbitration, mediation
Constantinos Lambadarios

Foreign investments
Dimitrios Lambadarios

Telecommunication
Nondas Lambadarios

Litigation
John Filiotis

Environmental
Stefanos Lambadarios

Securities, capital markets
Dimitrios Lambadarios

Mergers and acquisitions
Nondas Lambadarios

Intellectual property
Katerina Malanou

Taxation
Maria Fronista

Competition law
Constantinos Lambadarios

European community law
Nikos Trataros

Labour law
Maria Fronista

Civil law
John Filiotis

Urban planning
Dimitrios Lambadarios

THE FIRM

Lambadarios Law Offices was founded in 1863 by Konstantinos E Lambadarios Sr in Athens and has been operating continuously since then with a well respected Greek and international clientele. The firm today numbers 20 lawyers and five partners, all located at its offices in the centre of Athens. Many of the firm's partners and associates are well respected individuals in their fields of expertise both nationally and internationally. Specifically, two of the partners are alumni of Cleary, Gottlieb, Steen & Hamilton, giving the firm a unique advantage in working with international clients.

Mr Constantinos Lambadarios Sr (1915-2002), after completing his studies at Harvard Law School, returned to Greece with unique expertise in foreign investments. Through his hard work and considerable experience the firm established itself as a leader in the field of foreign direct investments during the 1960s and 1970s. Since then it continues to advise a number of international corporations that came to invest in Greece during that era, such as Goodyear and Procter and Gamble. With a solid base of clients, the firm has grown under the leadership of Mr Epaminondas Lambadarios and Mr Dimitrios Lambadarios, who, after completing their studies at Harvard Law School and the University of London and joining the firm in 1970, have successfully and considerably diversified the categories of work that the firm offers to its clients.

It is the firm's policy to strive to provide a high level of legal advice without disregarding personal contact with clients. Proof of this approach is that the firm has clients who have been with it for 30 years.

AREAS OF PRACTICE

The firm specialises in a wide variety of both domestic and international commercial work offering a high level of legal services to its clients worldwide. The firm's client base includes banks, financial institutions, insurance corporations, large industrial and commercial sector corporations and private individuals.

Since the early 1960s the firm has advised foreign clients who wish to establish businesses in Greece. The firm has an extensive foreign clientele, mainly based in North America and the European Union, that has either established business in Greece or requires legal advice on a wide range of legal subjects relating to doing business with a Greek partner. The firm's domestic clientele is equally strong, with representative clients from the banking sector, insurance, commercial and private individuals. The main work done by the firm relates to corporate law, mergers and acquisitions, banking, structured finance and securities, having advised clients entering the Athens Stock Exchange. Moreover, the firm has represented foreign and domestic clients in numerous litigations and arbitrations in the ICC. The firm's intellectual property expertise includes trade mark, patent and copyright law and advises clients such as Sony Music SA. Recently the firm, recognising the impact of environmental legislation on the way business is conducted, decided to create an environmental law department that advises clients on issues relating to their business.

Please contact the firm for more details or visit the website.

LYKOUREZOS LAW OFFICES

19 DIMOKRITOU STREET
106 73 ATHENS

Telephone: +30 210 360 7913/4
Fax: +30 210 360 7983
Website: www.lykourezoslawoffices.gr

Languages
English, French, German, Italian, Spanish

Number of lawyers 22

Contact
Alexandros Lykourezos

CATEGORIES OF WORK

Administrative law and litigation
Z Saloustros, K Lidorikis

Banking law, securities regulation
A Nestorides, I Papakonstantinou

International business law
A Nestorides, I Papakonstantinou

Civil, commercial litigation, arbitration
A Nestorides, I Papakonstantinou

Competition law
F Karra, D Georgiopoulou

Criminal law, white-collar crime, extradition
A Lykourezos, P Machas

Energy and utilities law
N Davrados, V Strantzia

Family law
I Papakonstantinou, Y Nousia

Intellectual property law
A Nestorides, I Papakonstantinou

Mergers and acquisitions
A Lykourezos, I Papakonstantinou

Privatisations, public sector projects
N Davrados, E Mamalakis

Concession agreements
N Davrados, E Mamalakis

Real estate development and construction law
K Lidorikis, Z Saloustros

Sports law
N Davrados, E Mamalakis

Tax law
V Strantzia

Telecommunications and media law
A Nestorides, D Georgiopoulou

Trade, corporate and contract law
A Nestorides, K Lidorikis

M & P BERNITSAS

5 LYKAVITTOU STREET
106 72 ATHENS

Telephone: +30 210 361 5395
Fax: +30 210 364 0805
E-mail: bernitsas@bernitsaslawoffices.gr
Website: www.bernitsaslawoffices.gr

Languages
English, French, German, Italian, Spanish

Number of lawyers 35

CATEGORIES OF WORK

Aviation
K Papantonopoulou

Banking and finance
A Tsene

Capital markets
N Papachristopoulos

Company and commercial
L Vasaka

Energy, natural resources and environmental
A Almyroudi

EU and competition
A Almyroudi

Food and beverages, medicinal products/medical devices
Y Chryssospathis

Human rights
D Mirasyesi

Intellectual property and IT
Y Chryssospathis

Labour
K Papantonopoulou

Land and property
L Vasaka

Litigation, arbitration and dispute resolution
P Bernitsas

Mergers and acquisitions
L Vasaka, N Papachristopoulos

Privatisations
D Roussis

Project finance
D Georgacopoulos

Public procurement (works, supplies, services)
D Roussis

Tax
N Papachristopoulos

Telecommunications and media
P Bernitsas

METAXOPOULOS. LAW FIRM

54 VASILISSIS SOPHIAS AVENUE
115 28 ATHINAI

Telephone: +30 210 725 7614
Fax: +30 210 729 7610
E-mail:
metaxopoulos@metaxopouloslaw.gr
Website: www.metaxopouloslaw.gr

Languages
English, French, German, Italian, Spanish

Other offices
Brussels, Salonika*

Number of lawyers 15

Member
Trans-European Law Firms Association (TELFA); Global Advertising Lawyers Alliance (GALA); Association Litteraire et Artistique Internationale (ALAI)

CATEGORIES OF WORK

Intellectual property
I Daroussou, K Metaxopoulos

Company law
A Metaxopoulos, K Metaxopoulos

Commercial law
V Vassilopoulou, F Stathopoulou

Privatisation and projects
K Metaxopoulos, V Monso

Litigation and arbitration
F Stathopoulou, K Metaxopoulos

EU and competition law
V Monso, A Elianou

Labour law
Y Kapelaris, A Kappou

Civil law
E Tsakoumi, M Nikolaraki

Industrial property
K Vossos, A Kappou

Mergers and acquisitions
V Monso, A Elianou

Real estate
M Nikolaraki, F Stathopoulou

Adminsitrative law
F Stathopoulou, L Papa

Tax, banking, finance
V Vassilopoulou, K Metaxopoulos

Media, entertainment, telecoms
K Metaxopoulos, K Vossos

Stock exchange law
F Stathopoulou, E Tsakoumi, V Vassilopoulou

Public procurement
E Tsakoumi, V Monso

IT broadcast law
K Vossos, L Papa

MOUSSAS & TSIBRIS

34 ASKLIPIOU ST
106 80 ATHENS

Telephone: +30 210 339 2070 3
Fax: +30 210 339 0591
E-mail: info@moussastsibris.gr
Website: www.moussastsibris.gr

Languages
English, French, German, Italian

Number of lawyers 10

CATEGORIES OF WORK

Corporate
M Tsibris, N Moussas

Commercial
E Voulgarides, L Tsapara

Banking
N Moussas, M Tsibris

Insurance
N Moussas, V Moussas

Financial markets regulation
M Tsibris, G Plagou

Distributorships
V Moussas, K Tzamalouka

Franchising
N Moussas, K Tzamalouka

International trade
N Moussas, G Plagou

Commercial and civil litigation
V Moussas, E Arvanitopoulos

Tax
L Papahatzi

Real estate
V Moussas, D Dragonea

Telecommunications, media
N Moussas, G Plagou

Sports law
N Moussas, V Moussas

PI PARTNERS

**11TH KM, NATIONAL RD
THENS-LAMIA, METAMORPHOSI
144 51 ATHENS**

Telephone: +30 210 288 6550
Fax: +30 210 288 6910
E-mail: pi.partners@gr.eylaw.com
Website: www.eylaw.com/gr

Languages
English, French, German, Greek, Italian, Spanish, Turkish

Other offices
Bucharest, Istanbul, Sofia, Thessaloniki

Number of lawyers 60
at this office 34

Contacts
Stathis Potamitis (stathis.potamitis@gr.eylaw.com), George Bersis (giorgos.bersis@gr.eylaw.com)

International groupings
Ernst & Young

CATEGORIES OF WORK

Banking, finance and securities
Stathis Potamitis, George Bersis

M&A and privatisations
Johnny Vekris, Stathis Potamitis

Commercial and corporate
Johnny Vekris, Tati Iliadou

Human capital services and labour
Tati Iliadou

EU law and markets under regulation
Xenophon Paparrigopoulos

Intellectual property, patents and trade marks
Xenophon Paparrigopoulos

Litigation and arbitration
Xenophon Paparrigopoulos

Real estate
Johnny Vekris

Shipping
Johnny Vekris

LAW OFFICES PAPACONSTANTINOU

**4 QUEEN SOPHIA AVENUE
106 74 ATHINAI**

Telephone: +30 210 729 5750
Fax: +30 210 729 5756
E-mail: hpaplaw@ath.forthnet.gr

Languages
English, French, German

Number of lawyers 8

Contact
Dr Helen Papaconstantinou

CATEGORIES OF WORK

Company and commercial

EU law

Mergers and acquisitions

Securities and stock exchange

Banking and finance

Labour law

Tax

Competition law

Insurance

Intellectual property

Real estate

Litigation and arbitration

Public works and procurement

Franchising and agency

POLITIS & PARTNERS

24 PATR IOAKIM STREET
106 75 ATHENS

Telephone: +30 210 729 7252
Fax: +30 210 725 1144
E-mail: asaratsi@egplaw.gr
Website: www.egplaw.gr

Languages
English, French, German, Italian

Number of lawyers 7

Contact
Angeliki Saratsi

CATEGORIES OF WORK

Banking and finance
Evangelos Politis, Nicholas Anastopoulos

Corporate and commercial
Evangelos Politis, Angeliki Saratsi

Securities – capital markets
Evangelos Politis, Nicholas Anastopoulos

Dispute resolution
Angeliki Saratsi, Prof Dr Panayotis Glavinis

Litigation
Evangelos Politis, Nicholas Anastopoulos

International arbitration
Prof Dr Panayotis Glavinis

Internet and e-commerce law
Angeliki Saratsi, Katerina Somou

IT and telecommunication law
Angeliki Saratsi, Vassilis Demponos

Project finance
Prof Dr Panayotis Glavinis, Evangelos Politis

Intellectual property
Angeliki Saratsi, Vassilis Demponos

Labour and employment law
Evangelos Politis, Nicholas Anastopoulos

Real estate
Katerina Somou, Vassilis Demponos

S & A PAPADIMITRIOU & CO

241 SYNGROU AVE
& 2 ALIKARNASSOU STR
NEA SMIRNI
171 22 ATHENS

Telephone: +30 2 10 940 9960
Fax: +30 2 10 940 9043
E-mail: office@saplegal.gr

Languages
English, French

Number of lawyers 6

Member
ICC; European Lawyers Union; Greek Association for Civil Law; Greek Association for Commercial Law; Greek Association for Maritime Law; International Bar Association

CATEGORIES OF WORK

Investments

Law of contracts

Civil law

Estate planning, wills and inheritance

Establishment of foundations in Greece and abroad

Corporate law

Mergers and acquisitions

Banking and finance law

International trade law and law of transport

Shipping and maritime law, ship finance

Litigation and arbitration

S. A. FELIOS & ASSOCIATES

10 NEOFYTOU VAMVA STREET
KOLONAKI
106 74 ATHENS

Telephone: +30 210 729 9630
Fax: +30 210 729 9651
Video conferences: +30 210 729 9155
E-mail: contact@felioslawfirm.gr
Website: www.felioslawfirm.gr

Languages
Dutch, English, French, German, Italian, Spanish

Number of lawyers 20

Member
Libralex European Economic Interest Group

CATEGORIES OF WORK

Corporate and commercial
Evangelia Vouza, Maria Skagou

International investments
Sotiris Felios, Maria Skagou

Competition law
Sotiris Felios, Maria Skagou

Telecoms, IT and the internet
Maria Skagou

New technologies
Maria Skagou

Broadcasting and advertising law
Maria Skagou, Evangelia Vouza

Sports law
Nikos Markopoulos

Art law
Sotiris Felios, Maria Skagou

Intellectual property
Mari Damaskopoulou

Banking and financial
Manolis Fellios, Nikos Markopoulos

Stock exchange law
Evangelia Vouza, Manolis Felios

Taxation
Voula Marousaki

Real estate
Maria Nelly Pavlous, Lary Hanou

Aviation law
Dionysia Papastamos

Energy
Sotiris Felios, Evangelia Vouza

EU law
Evangelia Vouza, Valerie Baller

Administrative law
Evangelia Vouza, Ioanna Christopoulou

Labour law
Mari Damaskopoulou, Maria Skagou

THE FIRM

Established as a law office in 1975 by Sotiris Felios and now operating as a law firm, S. A. Felios & Associates is recognised as one of the most prominent law firms in Greece. Four years ago, the firm moved to its new offices in Neofytou Vamva Street, Kolonaki. The firm has the latest technology and employs 20 attorneys and six paralegals, with secretarial support. The firm also operates offices in Brussels since January 2004.

AREAS OF PRACTICE

Corporate law and related matters: finance; commercial contracts (exclusive or non-exclusive agency, distribution, supply, franchising); industrial property; advising major companies on establishment, operation, M&A, privatisations and investments; commercial arbitration and international transaction agreements; acquisition of shares; joint ventures; participation in public procurement procedures; establishment and operation of companies and branch offices; management agreements and related subjects; and consumer protection policy issues.

Competition law: supporting companies before the Greek Competition Committee and the European authorities; matters of transfer of control over businesses; antitrust; consummation of transactions exceeding the thresholds of Law 703/77, as well as the degree of implementation of the Greek legislation with EU antitrust specifications.

Telecoms, IT, new technologies and broadcasting: acquisition of telecoms licences and company shareholding; provision of services, supply of equipment and network operation (including mobile telephone networks); call-centre operations and services (including licensing, privacy, data protection, and the legal aspects of conducting market surveys); the creation and operation of websites, e-commerce and other Internet services (including issues related to the security of e-commerce transactions, encrypted signatures, identification of data, and so on); protection of personal data.

Sports law: club ownership; transfer of players; employment contracts; financing and construction of sports stadiums; commercial agreements for the exploitation of sports rights, including TV rights, sponsorship and marketing agreements and representation, as well as organisation of the Olympic Games in 2004 (including the Cultural Olympiad).

Art law: artist-dealer relations; private sales; IP and copyright (including their application to works produced or distributed through new means and technologies); trade marks.

Banking and finance, stock exchange law and taxation: corporate and inter-bank lending; debt restructuring; financial counsellor services and agreements; due diligence; financing of activities (including major construction works); investments; restructuring or participation in projects financed by European funds and programmes; bank mergers and acquisitions; advice and representation before authorities with reference to stock exchange law (including listing, transfer of shares and compliance); advising clients on their present and potential tax liability.

Real estate: acquisition, sale and lease of real estate with a view to developing activities; expropriations; town planning; real estate investment funds.

Aviation law: activities ranging from tax- and finance-related issues to disputes between airlines and their customers.

Energy: analysing regulatory frameworks; advising on the operational aspects of restructuring; production of electricity from environmentally friendly sources; due diligence.

EU law: advice and representation before the European authorities, including the directorates of the European Commission, as well as the courts of the EU; advice on the implementation of EU directives in Greece.

Labour law: all aspects of employment relations, representing clients before the courts and public authorities or in negotiations with labour unions. The firm also practises administrative law and public procurement.

SARANTITIS LAW FIRM

9 ANAGNOSTOPOULOU STREET
106 73 ATHENS

Telephone: +30 210 367 0400
Fax: +30 210 362 1595
E-mail: athens@sarantitis.com
Website: www.sarantitis.com

Languages
English, French, German, Italian, Spanish

Other offices
Piraeus, Thessaloniki

Number of lawyers 40
at this office 22

Contacts
Mr Yiannis Sarantitis, Mr Dorotheos Samoladas

CATEGORIES OF WORK

Corporate and commercial	**EU law**
Banking and finance	**Taxation**
Foreign investments	**Telecommunications, IT and media**
Privatisations	**Maritime law**
Labour law	**Arbitration and litigation**

THE FIRM

Sarantitis Law Firm serves its clients internationally from offices in all three major financial centres of Greece: Athens, Piraeus and Thessaloniki. Sarantitis is regarded as one of the leading law firms in Greece, being, at the same time, one of the largest in size. Established by its senior partner in 1965, today the firm represents an impressive list of companies, banks and enterprises within Greece and abroad. Sarantitis handles substantial transactions, while continuing to provide the personal services its clients value.

In order to provide broader and more effective legal services, Sarantitis co-operates closely with other firms around the world in such cities as New York, London, Paris, Rome, Moscow, Oslo, Hong Kong, Brussels and Tokyo. The firm's local network of correspondents covers Greece, Cyprus and the Balkans, with the main emphasis on business centres and commercial ports.

AREAS OF PRACTICE

From its head office in Athens, Sarantitis offers a diverse corporate and commercial practice ranging from general corporate representation to important M&A activity, including privatisation projects in the Greek public sector as well as in other Balkan countries. The team specialising in stock exchange and security law has extensive experience on high-profile IPOs, as well as private equity transactions. The firm has, for the last 30 years, provided legal consultancy services to banks and other financial institutions dealing with a variety of financial products and other services. The firm's banking practice has been involved in various aspects of banking law, beginning with the establishment of foreign banks in Greece, their operation and expansion, takeovers/mergers, transfers of shares, purchase and sale of retail and commercial operations.

The team of lawyers specialising in IT, media and telecoms law has gained the trust and the responsibility to represent leading firms in the Balkans and across Europe. Sarantitis holds a leading position in providing expertise in drafting and successfully negotiating the full spectrum of IT and telecoms projects, having engaged in some of the major IT projects, internet law cases and telecoms contracts that have marked the development of these markets in Greece.

The Piraeus office has an influential presence in one of Europe's largest shipping and trading centres, having significantly participated in the legal affairs of the Greek shipping sector for over 35 years. Due to its longstanding presence and active involvement in this particular field of law, the firm is not only known as the oldest, but also as one of the foremost national firms specialising in maritime law in the region.

Thessaloniki, which is an autonomous economic centre and major port in the north of Greece, serves as a gateway to the greater Balkan area, which enables Sarantitis to serve their clients in their business activities in Northern Greece and the Balkan region. Members of the Thessaloniki office practice corporate and commercial law and have been engaged in substantial legal cases in the areas of taxation, property development and real estate, major franchising as well as maritime law.

SOURIADAKIS, FRANGAKIS, SKALTSAS & ASSOCIATES

6 KRIETZOTOU STREET
ATHENS 106 71

Telephone: +30 210 362 6888
Fax: +30 210 363 1631
E-mail: info@sofralaw.gr
Website: www.sofralaw.gr

Languages
English, French, German, Italian,

Number of lawyers 15

Contact
M Souriadakis

CATEGORIES OF WORK

Company and commercial
N Frangakis, M Souriadakis

EU and competition
N Frangakis, D Papacharalampous, E Kanataki

Privatisation and projects
M Souriadakis, D Skaltsas

Litigation and arbitration
N Frangakis, D Skaltsas, M Souriadakis

Intellectual property
M Souriadakis, Dr G Ladoyannis

Banking and finance
M Souriadakis, C Vassilopoulou

Mergers and acquisitions
N Frangakis, M Souriadakis

Insurance
N Kazantzi, M Ioannidou

Civil law and property
M Pachygianni, Dr G Ladoyannis

ECHR
N Frangakis, E Kanataki

IT and telecommunications
N Frangakis, C Vassilopoulou

Media and entertainment
M Souriadakis, D Papacharalampous

Energy and infrastructure projects
N Frangakis, Dr G Ladoyannis

Real estate
N Kazantzi, M Pachygianni, C Vassilopoulou

Employment
M Ioannidou,C Vassilopoulou

STAVROPOULOS & PARTNERS

18 VALAORITOU STREET
106 71 ATHENS

Telephone: +30 210 363 4262
Fax: +30 210 363 3204
E-mail: info@stplaw.com
Website: www.stplaw.com

Languages
English, French, German, Spanish

Number of lawyers 16

Contact
Ioannis Stavropoulos (managing partner)

CATEGORIES OF WORK

Corporate and commercial

Taxation

Mergers and acquisitions

Competition

EU law

Finance and banking

Securities

Real estate and construction

Trade marks and patents

Administrative law

Litigation and arbitration

LAW OFFICE TJ KOUTALIDIS

4 VALAORITOU STREET
106 71 ATHENS

Telephone: +30 210 360 7811
Fax: +30 210 360 0069
E-mail: info@koutalidis.gr
Website: www.koutalidis.gr

Languages
English, French, German, Italian, Spanish

Number of lawyers 24

CATEGORIES OF WORK

Shipping and aviation
TJ Koutalidis, KJ Protopapa

Banking and finance
NC Koritsas, NV Salakas

Construction
DC Hadjigrigoriadis, PE Koutalidis

Corporate
TJ Koutalidis, NC Koritsas

European law
NP Fortsakis, E Pilati

Infrastructure
GP Logothetis, EN Courakis

Investment law
NE Pimblis, IE Deloucas

Litigation and arbitration
A Mandakou, GP Logothetis

Mergers and acquisitions
KJ Protopapa, KN Kyriakakis

Taxation
NC Koritsas, GD Naskaris

TSIBANOULIS & PARTNERS LAW FIRM

18 & 24 OMIROU STREET
106 72 ATHENS

Telephone: +30 210 367 5100
Fax: +30 210 367 5115
E-mail: info@tsibanoulis.gr

Languages
English, French, German, Spanish

Other office
Piraeus

Number of lawyers 33

Contacts
Dr D Tsibanoulis, Caroline Friedrich, Elena Bailas, Vasso Vouga

Member
European Financial Market Lawyers Group (EFMLG); German Greek Law Association; International Federation for European Law (FIDE); Greek Competition Law Society; Greek Commercial Law Society; International Bar Association (IBA); EU Clearing and Settlement Legal Certainty Group; European Banking and Finance Law Society

CATEGORIES OF WORK

Banking and finance
Dr D Tsibanoulis, E Bailas

Capital markets
Dr D Tsibanoulis, M Komis

European financial markets
Dr D Tsibanoulis, Dr E Avgouleas

Private equity, venture capital
C Friedrich, C Trihas

Structured finance and derivatives
Dr E Avgouleas, Dr T Katsas

Project finance
E Bailas, A Leoutsea

E-commerce and internet banking
Dr D Tsibanoulis, M Komis

Corporate and commercial
C Friedrich, S Garavela

Mergers and acquisitions
C Friedrich, A Apostolaki

Real estate and commercial leasing
A Apostolaki, C Frentzos

Antitrust
M Perraki, N Tryfonidou

Intellectual property
M Perraki, A Goulandris

Privatisation
Dr D Tsibanoulis, E Bailas

Litigation
Dr D Karamagiolis, M Stenou

Corporate taxation
E Bailas, A Apostolaki

Shipping law and shipping finance
V Vouga, M Liouta

THE FIRM

Tsibanoulis & Partners has established a reputation as one of Greece's leading law firms in the fields of banking law and financial services, capital market regulation and securities law, offering quality legal services to major Greek and international banking and financial institutions, blue-chip corporations and high-net-worth individuals. The firm has seven partners and 26 associates. Most are multi-lingual and hold qualifications from leading European and American universities. Many of the firm's lawyers are qualified in other European jurisdictions allowing the firm to offer clients both multi-jurisdictional experience and legal expertise in order to meet their changing needs in the international market effectively. Work is conducted in Greek, English, French, German and Spanish.

AREAS OF PRACTICE

The firm's reputation for transactional work, including international bond issues, syndicated loan facilities, structured finance, derivatives and securitisations, and general corporate work, is among the best in the field. Partners from the firm have acted in several cross-border acquisitions of banks and other financial institutions, major corporate mergers and acquisitions, banking and corporate restructurings, securities and project finance transactions. Since November 2000, managing partner Dr Dimitris Tsibanoulis has been lead adviser to the government of the Republic of Cyprus for the reform of its capital markets law. The firm's Piraeus office represents both domestic and international banks, financial institutions and ship owners in all aspects of finance and litigation.

Standing out for its extensive experience in the areas of banking, finance and corporate law and the commercial awareness of its lawyers, the firm regularly acts for foreign governments, international and domestic financial institutions, large investment services firms, multinational corporations and companies listed in the Athens Stock Exchange together with major European and US law firms. The firm offers legal advice on a variety of corporate, finance and banking law matters including stock exchange and securities regulations, and on the structuring of finance facilities and highly complex and innovative products, and acts for them in the context of a large number of complex credit, finance and corporate transactions, including mergers and acquisitions, joint ventures and partnership agreements.

Responding to its clients' needs, Tsibanoulis & Partners also runs a sizeable general corporate and commercial practice, offering comprehensive advice and conducting commercial and labour law litigation and contentious work. The firm is frequently asked to act for its clients in a variety of commercial law agreements including franchise, licensing, agency and distribution, industrial and intellectual property contracts, and provides expert advice on corporate taxation, tax-driven structures and various aspects of EU law.

VGENOPOULOS & PARTNERS

LAW FIRM

15 FILIKIS ETERIAS SQUARE
106 73 ATHINAI

Telephone: +30 210 720 6900
Fax: +30 210 723 1462
E-mail: mail@vplaw.gr
Website: www.vplaw.gr

Languages
English, French, German, Italian, Russian

Other offices
Piraeus, Salonika*

Number of lawyers 51
at this office 32

Contacts
Loukas Roufos, Eliana Paschalides, John Papapetros

CATEGORIES OF WORK

Aviation
Dr Alexandros Kalantzis, Calliope Metaxotou

Banking and finance, securitisation
John Papapetros, Calliope Metaxotou

Capital markets
Loukas Roufos, Stephanos Karaiskakis

Real estate and construction
Eliana Paschalides, Nikos Damigos

EU law and competition
Dr Alexandros Kalantzis, Dr Ioanna Anastassopoulou

Corporate and commercial
Loukas Roufos, Angelos Georgoussis

Dispute resolution
Eliana Paschalides, Milto Papangelis

Litigation
Aris Anghelakos, George Iatridis

Energy and natural resources
Dr Alexandros Kalantzis, Dr Ioanna Anastassopoulou

Government business, regulatory
Stephanos Karaiskakis, Aris Anghelakos

Insurance
Dr Alexandros Kalantzis

Intellectual property
Laoura Liberopoulou

Mergers and acquisitions
Loukas Roufos, Stephanos Karaiskakis

Shipping and transport
John Papapetros, Milto Papangelis

Tax
Angelos Georgoussis

Telecommunications
Dr Alexandros Kalantzis

THE FIRM

Vgenopoulos & Partners is a Greek law firm that was established in 1983 in Piraeus by its current senior partners.

In the beginning, the firm's main area of practice was shipping law, covering all aspects of the law as it relates to shipping and shipping finance. Within a short period of time the firm expanded into other areas of practice, summarised in the list of categories of work above. Given the number of lawyers working for the Athens and Piraeus offices of the firm (39 lawyers in total), Vgenopoulos & Partners is one of the largest firms in Greece.

The firm's policy is to combine a personal approach with the highest professional standards and to provide clients with clear, comprehensive and business-orientated legal services and with rapid responses in changing business situations. The firm is highly sensitive to the importance of preserving the confidentiality of client information as well as to the need for effective cost management. Although the firm is continually expanding, it remains a young and enterprising practice.

Most of the firm's attorneys have studied at postgraduate level in foreign universities and have had experience and training in law offices in western Europe. Many of the firm's attorneys regularly participate in seminars, conferences and other continuing legal education programmes. All of the firm's offices are equipped with the latest technology, tailored to meet the needs of modern commercial clients.

AREAS OF PRACTICE

The firm is organised into several practice groups, each headed by a highly experienced partner and staffed by specialised and experienced lawyers.

Vgenopoulos & Partners' clients consist of local and international banks and financial institutions, multinational companies and joint ventures, local and foreign-based manufacturers, insurers and service companies, foreign law firms and shipping companies.

ZEPOS & YANNOPOULOS

75 KATEHAKI & KIFISSIAS AVE
115 25 ATHENS

Telephone: +30 210 696 7000
Fax: +30 210 699 4640
E-mail: info@zeya.com
Website: www.zeya.com

Languages
English, French, German, Italian, Spanish

Other offices
Athens, Salonika

Number of lawyers 43
at this office 41

Contacts
Dimitrios Zepos, Yerassimos Yannopoulos

Member
Lex Mundi

CATEGORIES OF WORK

Banking and finance
V Digenopoulos, T Mitsidis

Capital markets
V Lazarakou, S Papastavrou

Commercial and tax litigation
V Digenopoulos, G Katrinakis

Corporate and commercial law
D Zepos, C Sarantis

Energy
C Sarantis, M Kolia

EU and competition
E Mastromanolis, I Koimtzoglou

International taxation
Y Yannopoulos, M Stavrinou

IT and e-commerce
P Kakouris, D Cozonis

Labour law
C Kabilafkas, R Papakonstantinou

Mergers and acquisitions
V Lazarakou, M Allamani

Privatisations and projects
T Mitsidis, M Kolia

Real estate
C Kallideris, M Allamani

Taxation
Y Yannopoulos, V Moraitis

Telecommunications
S Papastavrou, A Skolarikou

VAT
A Karopoulos

Intellectual property
S Melegou, N Christoforidis

GERONYMAKIS AND PARTNERS LAW OFFICE

89 KOLOKOTRONI STREET
18535 PIRAEUS

Telephone: +30 210 422 4407
Fax: +30 210 412 5608
E-mail: geronymakis@geronymakis.com
Website: www.geronymakis.com

Languages
English, French, German, Italian, Spanish

Number of lawyers 12

Member
Euréseau

CATEGORIES OF WORK

Maritime law
George Geronymakis, Efrossini Velli

Yachting law: S&P agreements; yacht building agreements, disputes; offshore/onshore corporate services; VAT issues, registrations, claims
George Geronymakis, Xanthippos Korovinis, Anna Psatha, Efrossini Velli, Elianna Halida

Yacht financing (loan agreements)
Efrossini Velli, Anna Psatha

Yacht financing (leasing agreements)
George Geronymakis, Xanthippos Korovinis

International tax planning
George Geronymakis, Tasos Avrantinis, Xanthippos Korovinis

Commercial law
Tasos Avrantinis, Lena Fragi, Aggeliki Chatzistavrou

Company law
Tasos Avrantinis, Aggeliki Chatzistavrou

Real estate law
Zetta Pierratou, Lena Fragi

Taxation law
Tasos Avrantinis, Maria Papafotiou

Aviation law
Zetta Pierratou, Lena Fragi

Banking law
Zetta Pierratou, Aggeliki Chatzistavrou

Litigation
Zetta Pierratou, Tasos Avrantinis, Maria Papafotiou

HOLMAN FENWICK & WILLAN

INTERNATIONAL

6TH FLOOR
86 FILONOS STREET
185 36 PIRAEUS

Telephone: +30 210 429 3978
Fax: +30 210 429 3118
E-mail: holmans@hfw.com.gr
Website: www.hfw.com

Languages
English, French, German, Greek, Spanish

Other offices
Dubai, Hong Kong, London, Melbourne, Paris, Rouen, Shanghai, Singapore

Number of lawyers 209
at this office 10

CATEGORIES OF WORK

Admiralty and marine insurance
Dimitri Vassos

Marine litigation/arbitration
David Pitlarge, Gareth Williams

Commercial litigation/arbitration, international trade
Gareth Williams, Dimitri Vassos

Commodities
Gareth Williams

Insurance/reinsurance
Dimitri Vassos

Shipping and project finance
Dan Tindall

THE FIRM

Holman Fenwick & Willan is an international law firm specialising in shipping and transport, trade and energy, insurance and reinsurance and commercial law. The firm has a reputation worldwide for excellence and innovation. It has one of the largest international arbitration and dispute resolution practices of its kind, with offices in Europe, the Middle East and Asia Pacific.

The firm's international practice is founded upon its principal offices in London, Paris, Piraeus, Hong Kong, Shanghai, Singapore and Melbourne and over 120 years' experience of working with other law firms in jurisdictions throughout the world.

The Piraeus office was opened in 1993 to provide enhanced services to one of the shipping industry's most important strategic centres. The office provides services in relation to English law matters with the emphasis on commercial and shipping-related litigation and casualties. The office has particular expertise in marine and insurance matters, including hull and cargo claims, charterparty disputes, casualty investigation and collisions, salvage, oil pollution, wreck removal, constructive and actual total losses, sale and purchase and commodity-related and other commercial issues.

AREAS OF PRACTICE

Shipping litigation/Admiralty, commercial litigation, marine insurance and project finance.

INCE & CO

7TH FLOOR
137 FILONOS STREET
185 36 PIRAEUS

Telephone: +30 210 429 2543
Fax: +30 210 429 3318
E-mail: firstname.lastname@incelaw.com
Website: www.incelaw.com

Languages
English, French, Greek

Other offices
Hamburg, Hong Kong, Le Havre, London, Paris, Shanghai, Singapore

Number of lawyers 228
at this office 8

Contacts
Jonathan Elvey, Antonis Lagadianos

CATEGORIES OF WORK

Aviation
Jonathan Elvey

Business and finance
Antonis Lagadianos

Commercial disputes
Jonathan Elvey, Antonis Lagadianos

Energy
Jonathan Elvey, Antonis Lagadianos

Insurance and reinsurance
Jonathan Elvey, Antonis Lagadianos

Shipping and trade
Jonathan Elvey, Antonis Lagadianos

THE FIRM

Ince & Co is an international law firm, with offices in Hamburg, Hong Kong, Le Havre, London, Paris, Piraeus, Shanghai and Singapore. The firm practises English, French, German and Hong Kong law, in six main business strands. Underpinning the firm's expertise is a clear grasp of clients' commercial needs. Ince & Co provides non-contentious business and finance advice for clients in a wide range of industries, and also deploys all methods of dispute resolution.

AREAS OF PRACTICE

Aviation: with a team that 'really understands the aviation business' (*The Legal 500*, 2005) and with in-depth market knowledge, Ince & Co has the flexibility to handle any kind of aviation matter anywhere in the world – from aircraft purchase to major incidents and lesser accidents worldwide. The firm often deploys legal tools to solve problems that appear to be mainly commercial in nature. For crises or disasters, the Ince Worldwide Emergency Response Service is only a phone call away.

Business and finance: the firm's team of specialist commercial lawyers works with clients to find the answers that help drive their businesses forward. With the combination of high levels of commercial nous and a capacity for hard work, the firm can help clients achieve their goals – whether acquisition, disposal, joint venture or conclusion of a complex commercial contract. Ince & Co's experience ranges from management buy-outs, through the resolution of shareholder disputes to difficult employment issues.

Commercial disputes: once described in the press as 'brutal litigators', the firm also has a lighter touch. Ince & Co's expertise covers all forms of dispute resolution, ranging from dialogue, through ADR to arbitration and court proceedings. Where litigation is judged to be in a client's interests, or is unavoidable, the firm draws on immense experience in the commercial courts of the countries where it has offices, and a worldwide network of correspondent lawyers. The firm's cases come from many sectors, including sport, entertainment and financial services.

Energy: the firm has been in the oil and gas business for as long as many of its clients. Since the early days of North Sea development, the firm's energy practice has spread all around the world, both onshore and off, from exploration and drilling to FPSOs and refineries. It now extends to renewable sources such as wind.

Insurance and reinsurance: Ince & Co's team serves clients who provide coverage, those who broke it and those who purchase it. Whether the case is contentious or non-contentious and however straightforward or complex the subject matter insured, the firm offers all the legal services required in these industries. The firm's direct insurance practice covers all manner of insurance claims, including marine and energy insurance, political contingent and credit risk, and coverage disputes. Reinsurance is also a strong area of focus for the firm. The team advises on, among other things, every aspect of run-off business.

Shipping and trade: from shipyard to scrapyard, from factory to receiver, from finance to flotation, the firm provides all the legal services required by the shipping and commodities industries. The firm counts among its clients many of the world's leading shipowners, charterers, shipbuilders, traders, banks and insurers. *The Legal 500* refers to the firm's 'unrivalled knowledge of the market' and its 'strength in depth'.

Emergency Response: Ince & Co operates a 24-hour emergency response service, 365 days a year. It has vast experience of the practical and legal problems following a major emergency, disaster or crisis. Its teams can respond immediately to a wide range of incidents, from accidents in the aviation, shipping, energy, hotel and rail sectors, including pollution and contamination, through natural disasters and outbreaks of disease, to terrorist acts. Tel: +44 20 7283 6999.

ROUSSOS & HATZIDIMITRIOU LAW OFFICES

5-7 FILELLINON STREET
185 36 PIRAEUS

Telephone: +30 2 10 429 4200
Fax: +30 2 10 429 4625
E-mail: office@roussoshatzidimitriou.com

Languages
English, French, German, Spanish

Number of lawyers 11

Member
Eurolegal

CATEGORIES OF WORK

Litigation
Costas Roussos, Costas Cotsiyannis

Commercial
Zafiris Hatzidimitriou,
Ioanna Dimopoulou

Corporate
Io Grekoussi, Costas Cotsiyannis

Admiralty and maritime
Costas Roussos, Zafiris Hatzidimitriou

Maritime insurance
Costas Roussos, Areti Arvaniti

Banking and investment
Zafiris Hatzidimitriou,
John Christoforidis

Contracts
Costas Cotsiyannis, Areti Arvaniti

Real estate
Costas Roussos, Costas Cotsiyannis

Mergers and acquisitions
Zafiris Hatzidimitriou,
John Christoforidis

Ship finance
Costas Roussos, Io Grekoussi

Privatisation
Costas Roussos, Zafiris Hatzidimitriou

Civil law
Costas Roussos, Costas Cotsiyannis

Industrial and intellectual property
Costas Cotsiyannis,
Angeliki Antonopoulou

Employment
Costas Cotsiyannis, Maria Giakoumi

Telecommunications
Zafiris Hatzidimitriou,
Angeliki Antonopoulou

WATSON, FARLEY & WILLIAMS

WATSON, FARLEY & WILLIAMS GREEK BRANCH

8TH FLOOR, IONIAN BUILDING
DEFTERAS MERARCHIAS 2
185 36 PIRAEUS

Telephone: +30 210 459 4000
Fax: +30 210 459 4004
Website: www.wfw.com

Languages
Afrikaans, Arabic, Cantonese, Danish, Dutch, English, French, German, Greek, Gujarati, Hebrew, Hindi, Italian, Malay, Mandarin, Marathi, Norwegian, Polish, Russian, Spanish, Swahili, Swedish, Thai

Other offices
Bangkok, Hamburg, London, New York, Paris, Rome, Singapore

Number of lawyers 198
at this office 9

Contacts
George Paleokrassas, Jeremy Watson

CATEGORIES OF WORK

Ship finance

Commercial shipping and corporate shipping

Tax and tax-based leasing

Property

EU law

Banking, international finance, trade finance, project finance

Capital markets – public and private equity and debt issues

Sale and purchase, new building contract sales and resales

GUERNSEY

Population	60,000
Number of lawyers	80
Professional title	Advocate
Currency	Pound sterling (£))

Index

Guernsey and Jersey are both crown dependencies, part of the British Isles, but not part of the United Kingdom. Guernsey is the smaller of the two islands, although the Bailiwick of Guernsey also includes the islands of Alderney, Sark and Herm.

Matters relating to foreign relations and defence are looked after for the Channel Islands by the Crown through the UK government. The Channel Islands are neither full nor associate members of the EU (although they fall within the common customs area and therefore levy the common external tariff). Their relationship with the EU is determined by Protocol 3 to the UK's Treaty of Accession.

BILLING

Typically fees are charged on the basis of an hourly rate decided in advance by the parties. Scale fees exist for conevyancing work. However, fees may vary depending on the lawyer instructed and the job in hand. Clients can expect costs not dissimilar to those charged by City of London firms: around £160 for a newly qualified lawyer, rising to around £350 at partner level.

MARKETING

Law firms are free to advertise within the framework of the Rules of Professional Conduct.

THE LEGAL 500

Readers should note that the following is taken from the **Offshore Britain** section of the 2005 edition of *The Legal 500* (UK edition), available at www.legal500.com.

LEGAL MARKET

Guernsey has one of Europe's premier captive insurance markets, with over 750 insurance entities, from captive managers to international life insurers. The dominance of the financial services industry on the island means that clients expect to receive a high level of legal know-how and expertise. Unusually for a jurisdiction which handles a large volume of trust litigation, there is no well-established system of law reports, unlike its Channel Islands counterpart, Jersey.

With around 100 advocates registered with the Guernsey Bar, the legal community is close-knit and competitive. Interestingly, this has led to the emergence of niche practices, which are well positioned to benefit from the conflicts endemic in such a small market.

2004 saw two new legal practices established: the high-street focused **Trinity Chambers** and **AO HALL Advocates**, set up by former **Carey Olsen** high-flyers Alison Ozanne and Louise Hall.

Five firms lead the market, **Babbe Le Pelley Tostevin**, **Carey Olsen**, **Collas Day**, **Ozannes** and **Ogier**. Prestigious **Ozannes** has shown commitment to its Guernsey base, a focus which has paid dividends. The firm has impressive strength in-depth in every practice area, and fields an array of high-calibre partners. This, combined with an enviable client base of blue-chip institutions, makes the firm a formidable player. Its strategy of gentle expansion contrasts with **Carey Olsen**, which has made huge strides across the region in recent years. Following its 2003 merger it is the largest pan-Channel Islands firm, with 12 partners in Guernsey, a ten-partner team in Jersey, and a presence in Alderney. It also has the advantage of a London office. The firm has considerable expertise across the board and good connections for referral work.

The chasing pack consists of **Collas Day** and **Babbe Le Pelley Tostevin**, both quality firms which are regularly instructed on high-level work, but lack the consistency of the main players across the full breadth of practice areas. The experienced property practitioner Chris Bound heads the seven-partner team at **Collas Day**, while the dynamic Andrew Laws spearheads the practice at **Babbe Le Pelley Tostevin**, following the retirement of Richard Babbe.

Ogier has a smaller presence on Guernsey compared to its dominance in Jersey, with just three partners. One of these is former **Carey Olsen** associate Simon Davies, who has joined to add litigation expertise to the financial services-focused practice. The bijou but skilled practice benefits from referrals from Jersey, and the firm's new Cayman practice.

Wedlake Bell Guernsey and **Turcan Connell** are the only two mainland firms with a presence on the island. **Wedlake Bell Guernsey** focuses on UK property work, while **Turcan Connell** has a private client focus.

The largest firms

1	Carey Olsen	50
2	Ozannes	32
3	Collas Day	21
4	Ogier	20
5	Babbe Le Pelley Tostevin	16
6	AO HALL Advocates	7
7	SG Law	4
8	Ashton Allen Barnes	3
	Randell & Loveridge	3
	Wedlake Bell Guernsey	3
11	Mourant du Feu & Jeune	2

These figures represent the total number of lawyers in this country only, and have been supplied by the firms themselves. The figures should be accurate as at 1 January 2006.

COMMERCIAL AND BANKING

CAREY OLSEN
OZANNES

Babbe Le Pelley Tostevin
Collas Day
Ogier ✪

Firms are listed A-Z in tiers which are ranked in order of priority
✪ Indicates firm displays contact details at the end of this chapter.

COMMERCIAL LITIGATION

OZANNES

CAREY OLSEN

BABBE LE PELLEY TOSTEVIN
COLLAS DAY

AO Hall Advocates
Ogier ✪

Firms are listed A-Z in tiers which are ranked in order of priority
✪ Indicates firm displays contact details at the end of this chapter.

COMMERCIAL AND BANKING

Carey Olsen is frequently instructed by Channel Islands banks and, like the other leading Guernsey firms, benefits from City referrals. Highlights for 2004 include acting for Carlyle Group in the acquisition of an interest in QinetiQ, a company privatised by the British government, and acting for GMAC on a £292m loan for a UK property acquisition. Team leaders Nigel Carey and Graham Hall are assisted by Ben Morgan and newly made-up partner Darren Bacon, who are both commended by clients for their 'practical, timely advice'.

Ozannes has established commercial and banking expertise, advising the full range of financial institutions and blue-chip companies, as well as handling referrals. The esteemed Peter Harwood heads the three-partner practice. Major transactions in 2004 include acting as Guernsey legal adviser to Barclays Bank on a £1.3bn senior mezzanine and junior financing of the acquisition of AA Corporation Ltd and its subsidiaries. The 'methodical' Gavin Farrell and 'capable' David Moore are recommended, while Jessica Roland is building a reputation for employee downsizing work.

Babbe Le Pelley Tostevin's best-known personalities for financial services are Mark Helyar and Simon Howitt. Highlight instructions include acting in the Channel Island's largest deal of 2004; Royal Bank of Scotland's £240m purchase of the Condor Ferries Group from ABN Amro.

The skilled Ian Kirk heads the three-partner team at **Collas Day**, who is praised by clients for his broad commercial repertoire. The team acted on all the major M&A deals on the island in 2004; including acting for Affiliated Managers Group, a US investment management group, on the acquisition of four Guernsey fund management companies within the Genesis group, and four Guernsey registered funds as part of a multi-jurisdictional transaction. Chris Bound also provides commercial expertise.

Ogier's William Simpson has a superb reputation for corporate and commercial work. Roger Le Tissier acts for Investec CI, Close Brothers and SG Hambro.

COMMERCIAL LITIGATION

Ozannes has a formidable commercial litigation practice. The firm has acted on all of the landmark litigation cases in the past year; including advising the Jersey Fishermen's Association on challenging Guernsey legislation imposing a local fishing licensing regime. A well-staffed team which includes high-calibre individuals such as 'fighter' Peter Ferbrache, 'technically competent' insolvency and asset-tracing expert Jeremy Wessels, 'skilled' Robert Shepherd, and 'experienced' Gordon Dawes means that the firm is capable of running more than one major case at a time. An enviable client base spans financial services companies, blue-chip companies, local businesses and City firms.

The 'technically outstanding' John Greenfield heads the six-partner practice at **Carey Olsen**. The team has now integrated the trusts litigation team into the litigation group, bringing partners Russell Clark and Michael Eades, and senior associate Paul Buckle, into the fold. Highly rated advocate Alison Ozanne has left to set up her own practice with employment expert Louise Hall, while Gill Dinnings retired. In 2005 the firm successfully advised on a landmark application to place a Protected Cell Company (PCC) into administration.

Babbe Le Pelley Tostevin's litigation team was bolstered by the arrival of Ian Swan from **Crown Office Chambers**. The 'highly professional' Andrew Laws, who specialises in asset tracing and fraud matters, heads the team which gains instruction on prominent financial services disputes. A growing client list includes a significant number of insurers and trade unions. Geoff Allez has significant expertise in mediation.

Collas Day's Mark Ferbrache is well known in the market for his work as a litigator and acts on complex commercial litigation, including asset tracing. Paul Richardson, the other partner in the firm's busy commercial litigation practice, is also highly regarded. The firm successfully represented Lady Bathurst in a complex trust action against Carey Olsen Trust Company, a leading trusts case.

AO HALL Advocates is one to watch for the future. Alison Ozanne attracts considerable client loyalty and high regard, described as 'highly responsive and quick to understand client priorities' and 'a pleasure to work with'. Spearheading the practice together with Louise Hall, the pair are focusing on litigation, trusts and employment.

Ogier has added litigation capacity to its practice in Guernsey, with the recruitment of Simon Davies from **Carey Olsen**. At the time of writing the nascent practice has yet to demonstrate its capacity, but has the advantage of being able to draw on considerable strength in Jersey.

INSURANCE

High-level insurance advice is bread and butter work to Guernsey lawyers, due to the predominance of the captive insurance market on the island. Expertise in protected cell companies is in demand, and advice on insurance-based products used in private client wealth management is on the rise.

Captives expert Michael Eades spearheads **Carey Olsen**'s insurance practice, capitalising on the firm's longstanding experience in captive insurance. Graham Hall is recommended for his experience in captives formation, while London-based Fiona Fleming also acts on insurance matters.

At **Ozannes**, trio Peter Harwood, David Moore, and Chris Anderson have significant expertise in advising local captive insurers and the international insurance industry. The team continues to garner instructions from London blue-chip insurers and friendly societies. Key clients include AON Insurance Managers, Royal Bank of Scotland and White Rock Insurance PCC Ltd. In 2004 the firm acted as Guernsey adviser on the insurance aspects of the acquisition of Abbey National by Banco Santander.

Babbe Le Pelley Tostevin has particular strength in the insurance market, acting for many of the island's captive insurance companies, and providing corporate governance advice. The firm works closely with the regulator and has significant expertise in developments in modern protected cell company (PCC) legislation, working both for and against the regulator.

Collas Day has two new recruits to its insurance practice, Sally Ross-Basinger and Gareth Bell, both from City firms, who join the knowledgeable Ian Kirk. Key clients include the Guernsey Financial Services Commission, Catholic National Mutual and Lombard Insurance Group.

INSURANCE

CAREY OLSEN
OZANNES

Babbe Le Pelley Tostevin

Collas Day
Ogier ✪

Firms are listed A-Z in tiers which are ranked in order of priority
✪ *Indicates firm displays contact details at the end of this chapter.*

INVESTMENT FUNDS

CAREY OLSEN
OZANNES

OGIER ✪

Babbe Le Pelley Tostevin
Collas Day

Firms are listed A-Z in tiers which are ranked in order of priority
✪ *Indicates firm displays contact details at the end of this chapter.*

INVESTMENT FUNDS

Carey Olsen's five-partner practice consists of Nigel Carey, Ben Morgan, Graham Hall, Darren Bacon and Fiona Fleming in the London office. The team continues to secure new clients on the full gamut of funds work; open-ended and closed-ended funds, private equity, hedge funds, alternative strategy funds, property financing structures and limited partnership structures. Graham Hall in particular is recommended for his innovative approach to SPV work, including protected cell companies.

Ozannes fields highly experienced practitioners Peter Harwood, David Moore and Gavin Farrell, who advise across the range of structured products, derivatives and share issues; including in 2004 acting as Guernsey legal adviser to Hermes Investment Management Ltd on the establishment of a fund of hedge funds listed on the Irish Stock Exchange. An impressive client list includes Merrill Lynch and Morgan Stanley.

Ogier's Roger Le Tissier is active in advising on investment funds, handling the full spectrum of high-value fund work. William Simpson is highly rated by clients.

Energetic duo Mark Helyar and Simon Howitt are the core investment funds specialists at **Babbe Le Pelley Tostevin**. Major clients include Royal Bank of Scotland and Heritage Fund.

Collas Day's Sean Cheong is experienced in establishing complex and innovative finance structures. Highlight transactions include advising Kintyre LLP and clients of Scottish Widows Investment Partnership in the sale of the McKenzie property portfolio to clients of Insight Investments for £150m, by way of transfers to several Guernsey partnerships.

PERSONAL TAX, TRUSTS AND PENSIONS

Carey Olsen has the largest trusts team in Guernsey, which also has considerable contentious capacity. Active practitioners include the 'highly commercial' Russell Clark, who has developed a specialist compliance, trusts and fiduciary regulation practice, the highly regarded Michael Eades, currently chairman of the Guernsey Bar Council, who has particular expertise in charitable trusts, and pensions expert Paul Buckle. Clients are local fiduciary companies such as Kleinwort Benson (Guernsey) Trustees Ltd, Baring Trustees (Guernsey) Ltd and Fairfax Insurance Ltd.

PERSONAL TAX, TRUSTS AND PENSIONS

CAREY OLSEN
OZANNES

Babbe Le Pelley Tostevin
Collas Day
Ogier ✪

Ashton Allen Barnes

Turcan Connell
Wedlake Bell Guernsey

Firms are listed A-Z in tiers which are ranked in order of priority
✪ *Indicates firm displays contact details at the end of this chapter.*

Ozannes' highly experienced St John Robilliard heads the dedicated trusts department which consists of six partners and a total of eight fee-earners. The firm is frequently instructed to appear in contentious trust appeals before the Guernsey Court of Appeal and has handled several landmark cases. A diverse range of clients includes accountants, trust companies, private individuals and banks, both on and off the island. David Moore is recommended for regulatory appeals and negotiations with the Guernsey Financial Services Commission.

Babbe Le Pelley Tostevin's two-partner private client group is headed by senior partner Nick Tostevin, while the other half of the duo is family expert Michael Riddiford. Geoff Allez acts for many of the major Guernsey Trusts service providers.

The 'sensible and pragmatic' Paul Richardson is recommended for private client and corporate trust issues at **Collas Day**, while John Lewis and Peter Atkinson both provide pensions expertise.

Ogier associate Alison MacKrill handles trusts and private client matters.

Ashton Allen Barnes' Raymond Ashton is a knowledgeable tax and trusts expert, who has expertise in advising high-net-worth individuals as well as maintaining a sharp reputation as an academic.

REAL ESTATE

Babbe Le Pelley Tostevin's Piers Dereham (formerly at **Linklaters**) heads the team, which represents clients in significant commercial property developments such as the Royal Hotel development site and the refinancing of the Admiral Park site. The firm boasts the largest domestic conveyancing practice on the island.

The 'superb' Ian Beattie heads the commercial property practice at **Carey Olsen**, while Jason Morgan deals with residential transactions, as well as disputes. The team had a successful year, acting

REAL ESTATE

BABBE LE PELLEY TOSTEVIN
CAREY OLSEN
COLLAS DAY
OZANNES

Wedlake Bell Guernsey

Firms are listed A-Z in tiers which are ranked in order of priority

in over £75m worth of commercial property deals for both developers and investors. Highlights include acting in the sale of the Bristol & West loan portfolio, and acting for the purchaser of the largest and most expensive office block in Guernsey.

Collas Day's property specialists Richard Ogier and Chris Bound head a solid property practice, which counts heavyweights such as Royal Bank of Scotland International Ltd and Bank of Butterfield International (Guernsey) among its clients. Chris Bound has considerable expertise in security instructions.

Ozannes is a major player in the commercial property market. Colourful personality Roger Perrot oversees a busy, three-partner practice, which also has contentious capacity, in particular in advising on development appeals. A broad client base includes the government and local authorities, developers and landowners, as well as high-net-worth individuals and financial institutions.

'First-class' senior partner Quentin Spicer at **Wedlake Bell Guernsey** advises UK clients on property matters.

MOURANT DU FEU & JEUNE

PO BOX 543, EASTWING
TRAFALGAR COURT
ADMIRAL PARK
ST PETER PORT GY1 6HJ

Telephone: +44 1481 715601
Fax: +44 1481 715602
E-mail: mdfj@mourant.com
Website: www.mourant.com

Languages
English, French, German, Italian, Portuguese, Spanish

Other offices
London, Cayman Islands, Jersey

Number of lawyers 80

Member
Lex Mundi

CATEGORIES OF WORK

Capital markets
Robert Hickling

Banking
James Ruane

Corporate structures
James Ruane

Dispute resolution and litigation
Jonathan Speck

Corporate and commercial
Wendy Malorey

Employment
Wendy Malorey

Trusts
Giles Corbin

Funds
Jaqueline Richomme

Property
Elizabeth Breen

Financial services
Simon Gould

Fund administration
Robert Short

Corporate structures administration
Robert Short

Property fund administration
Paul Le Marquand

Private wealth management
Alan Binnington

OGIER

COUTTS HOUSE
LE TRUCHOT
ST PETER PORT GY1 1WD

Telephone: +44 1481 721672
Fax: +44 1481 721575
E-mail: info@ogier.com
Website: www.ogier.com

Languages
English, French

Other offices
Cayman Islands, Jersey, London

Number of lawyers 120
at this office 20

Member
Association of European Lawyers (AEL); STEP; Guernsey International Lawyers Association; EVCA; BVCA

CATEGORIES OF WORK

Banking
William Simpson, Roger Le Tissier

Securitisation and structured finance
William Simpson, Roger Le Tissier

Mergers and acquisitions
William Simpson, Roger Le Tissier

Investment funds
Roger Le Tissier, William Simpson

Corporate and commercial
William Simpson, Roger Le Tissier

Litigation
William Simpson, Simon Davies

Corporate finance
William Simpson, Roger Le Tissier

Trust and estate planning
William Simpson, Marcus Leese

Private client
William Simpson, Marcus Leese

Employment law
William Simpson, Marcus Leese

Regulatory
Roger Le Tissier

THE FIRM

Ogier is one of the leading offshore providers of legal and administration services with approximately 500 employees across offices in Jersey, Guernsey, London and the Cayman Islands.

Ogier has developed an extensive portfolio of international clients and continues to provide legal and administration services for these clients through its dedicated teams.

A large proportion of the firm's qualified lawyers have worked in some of the world's leading financial centres and bring exceptional experience and expertise sought by today's clients.

AREAS OF PRACTICE

Banking: Ogier is widely regarded as a premier firm for banking and international finance. It specialises in advising on all areas of banking, security, structured finance, banking regulation and the establishment of banks.

Corporate and commercial: Ogier's highly experienced and extensive team covers mergers and acquisitions, employment and privacy laws, IT/IP and e-commerce.

Securitisation: Ogier has one of the leading and largest securitisation and capital markets teams, with particular expertise in asset-backed securities, CBOs, ABCP and structured notes.

Structured finance: the structured finance team covers structured equity, asset finance and tax neutral transactions.

Investment funds: Ogier's fund practice comprises one of the largest funds teams in Guernsey, Jersey and the Cayman Islands, and advises on the establishment and structuring of funds as well as on regulatory and compliance issues.

Trusts: the trust and estate planning group has one of the largest trusts teams exclusively dedicated to advising trust companies, intermediaries and individuals in matters of trust law.

Private client: Ogier continues to develop and grow its private client practice. The private client team can provide a full range of administration services to trusts, companies and limited partnerships established in the Channel Islands, as well as to entities established elsewhere.

Fiduciary services: Ogier Fiduciary Services provides professional administration and accounting services to trusts, companies and limited partnerships.

HUNGARY

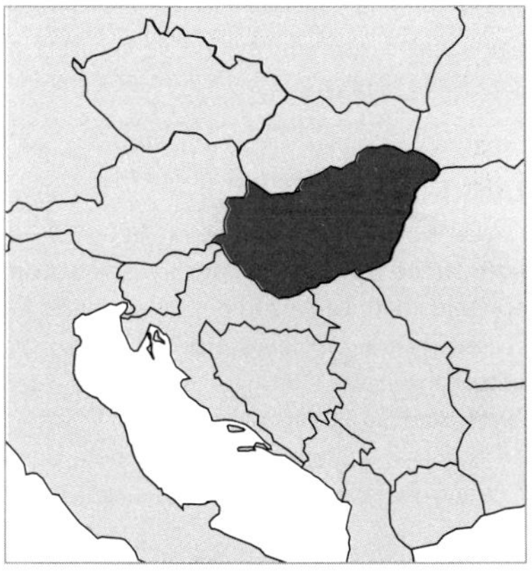

Population	**10.2 million**
Number of lawyers	**8,000**
Professional title	**Attorney**
Currency	**Hungarian Forint (Ft)**

Index

Landlocked Hungary links old and new Europe, lying between established EU member Austria, new EU members Slovakia and Slovenia and future members Romania (expected to join in 2007), and Croatia, currently in negotiations about a joining date. Its other neighbours are Serbia and Montenegro, and Ukraine. Hungary itself joined the EU in May 2004 and has been a Nato member since 1999. President László Sólyom took office in August 2005 for a five-year term. Prime Minister Ferenc Gyurcsány, of the Hungarian Socialist Party, has been in office since October 2004 and the next parliamentary elections are due to be held in 2006.

BILLING

A relatively high number of lawyers for the size of the country means that competition is fierce, keeping fees relatively stable at all of the firms. Clients can expect to pay from between €100 an hour to €400 an hour for partners' work, exceptionally rising as high as €500 an hour for specialist advice from a senior partner at an international firm. Work carried out by assistants is likely to be charged at between €80 and, where they are working in an international law firm, €100 an hour. Some clients specify a fixed fee, others pay by the hour but often firms will give an estimate based on hourly rates.

MARKETING

Regulations set by the Hungarian Bar mean that firms cannot advertise. One avenue of promotion they can use is their own website. However, law firms are limited to including general descriptions of their experience on a site, and cannot, for example, use online examples of work done for clients.

IN-HOUSE LAWYERS

In-house lawyers at Hungary's larger companies handle most day-to-day issues, through to representing them in court. However, they will go out of house for specialist advice or when dealing with complex issues.

ECONOMY

Hungary, once a centrally planned economy, is now a successful market economy.

Growth in GDP was put at 3.9% in 2004 and has seen a continued uplift as a result of accession to the EU on 1 May 2004. The confidence of foreign investors appears to have strengthened following accession, with real estate funds eager to invest in a buoyant market. In recent years the economy has grown on average faster than the original 15 EU member states, but has lagged behind the average growth of the ten states that joined on 1 May 2004.

The services sector accounts for almost two-thirds of GDP, with strengths in financial advice, real estate, and business advice, while a manufacturing-led industrial sector is responsible for about a quarter. Flourishing industries include road-building and construction, reflecting a buoyant property market. Hungary is losing low-skill manufacturing as the cost of labour exceeds that of Eastern European countries but is at the same time building knowledge-based industries such as IT and pharmaceuticals.

Inflation has fallen from 14% in 1998 to 7% in 2004, boosting consumer spending, while unemployment remains at about 6%. In capital markets, equity deals have continued be static, as has been the case since the Russian financial crisis of 1998, but a market for fixed-income bonds is gathering strength. M&A activity, however, has been buoyant, fuelled by low valuations and increasing foreign confidence. Germany is Hungary's largest foreign economic partner, with Austria not far behind.

Shifting the terms of analysis, 80% of GDP comes from the private sector and the rest from the public sector. Sweeping privatisation has reached Budapest Airport which is being bought by UK group BAA, and means the only significant areas still to pass from public to private, and often foreign, ownership are the health service and state-owned airline Malév. A referendum was held on the future of the health service in 2004, but a low turnout invalidated the result, and no further date has yet been set. It is now unlikely to take place before the 2006 elections, which are expected to be held in May. Attempts to sell Malév have as yet come to nothing.

The privatisation process is approaching maturity with an increase in the number of PPPs and the financing of projects to expand the motorway network, which when completed will also have a significant effect on the economy.

The largest firms

1	Martonyi és Kajtár Baker & McKenzie	40
2	Oppenheim és Társai Freshfields Bruckhaus Deringer	38
3	CMS Cameron McKenna LLP	34
4	Köves Clifford Chance	32
5	Réti, Antall & Madl LANDWELL	30
6	Berecz & Andrékó Linklaters	28
	Horváth & Partners DLA Weiss-Tessbach	28
8	Réczicza White & Case LLP	25
9	Nagy és Trócsányi	24
10	SBG & K Patent and Law Offices	23
	Szecskay - Attorneys at Law	23
12	Siegler Law Office/Weil, Gotshal & Manges	20
13	Gide Loyrette Nouel - Molnár & Ferenczy	18
	Szabó, Kővári, Tercsák és Társai Ügyvédi Iroda (in cooperation with Salans)	18
	Éva Hegedûs (Dr.) in association with Allen & Overy LLP	18
16	Kovács Réti Szegheö Attorneys at Law	15
	Nógrádi Law Office	15
	Nörr Stiefenhofer Lutz	15
	Sándor Szegedi Szent-Ivány & Komáromi	15
20	Bogsch & Partners	14
	Burai - Kovács & Partners	14
	Bán S Szabó & Partners	14
	CHSH Szécsényi Ugyvédi Iroda Cerha Hempel Spiegelfeld Hlawati	14
24	Erös Üqyvédi Iroda Squire, Sanders & Dempsey LLP	13
25	Bihary, Balassa & Partners Attorneys at Law	12
	Squarra & Partos (in association with Lovells)	12

These figures represent the total number of lawyers in this country only, and have been supplied by the firms themselves. The figures should be accurate as at 1 January 2006.

LEGAL MARKET

Budapest is home to almost two million people, or a fifth of Hungary's population, and its legal community is similarly concentrated in the capital. International clients have been investing in the country since the privatisations of the 1990s and interest continues today, with property now a prime market. With the foreign money came foreign law firms, setting up office in Budapest in partnership with Hungarian firms in accordance with local Bar Association rules.

Regionalisation means more transactions involving several Central European countries and Hungarian law firms are consulted on the local aspects of multinational deals, benefiting firms in international networks. Overall, the amount of legal work has increased, but has not yet prompted many new entrants into the market.

The top Hungarian firms are now taking their regional expertise into the newly emerging markets of Central and Eastern Europe, among them **Köves Clifford Chance**, which provides an all-round service to clients in Hungary, as well as in Romania, Bulgaria, Serbia and Croatia.

During 2005, well-respected **Réczicza White & Case LLP** increased its focus on business outside as well as inside Hungary's borders and partner Rob Irving spent much of 2005 working in Romania's fast-growing economy. **Martonyi és Kajtár Baker & McKenzie**, whose co-founder János Martonyi is a former Hungarian foreign minister, rates highly for the experience and expertise from years working for an impressive roster of multinational clients.

CMS Cameron McKenna LLP and *Hayhurst Robinson* have merged to create a firm known under the 'CMS Cameron McKenna' name and the move will strengthen its position in the region. Former *Hayhurst Robinson* Budapest managing partner Balázs Máthé, who was previously head of corporate at **Berecz & Andrékó Linklaters** and a leading M&A specialist, opted not to go with the merger, preferring to set up alone.

Siegler Law Office/Weil, Gotshal & Manges continues to strengthen, and is particularly known for M&A, with expertise in sectors including energy, broadcasting and real estate.

Many domestic law firms are well regarded, some boasting extensive links within the country's political establishment. Established law firm **Nagy és Trócsányi** is one such firm; counsel Professor László Sólyom is currently on leave of absence to serve as Hungarian President, and partner László Trocsanyi is a former Hungarian ambassador to Brussels. **Forgó, Varga and Partners** was founded in 2000 to focus on M&A. Since then it has strengthened its position in TMT, dispute resolution and PPP. **Danubia** and **SBG & K Patent and Law Offices** are both known for an in-depth approach to patent and trade mark law.

Other notable Hungarian firms include **Sándor Szegedi Szent-Ivány & Komáromi**, which grew by 50% in 2005 and is a member of Eversheds International. **Szecskay – Attorneys at Law**, **Burai – Kovács & Partners**, and **Bogsch & Partners** are others.

German and Austrian companies have led investment into Hungary, and those linked to German firms and serving a large German-speaking clientele include **Luther, Fest & Kajli Attorneys**, **Haarmann Hemmelrath** and **Nörr Stiefenhofer Lutz**.

French firm **Gide Loyrette Nouel – Molnár & Ferenczy** is often the first port of call for French clients, but it also employs native speakers of English and German.

BANKING AND FINANCE

Berecz & Andrékó Linklaters' 'experienced' seven-strong banking and capital markets team represents both banks and borrowers. In 2005 it advised banks providing HUF52.9bn to the Hungarian State Railway Company, and represented the Student Loan Centre in financing the country's student loan system, both deals involving the government. Work is said to be 'flawless'.

During the last year, the team at **CMS Cameron McKenna LLP** worked on high-profile deals including the first public procurement financing of a heating plant, for banking client Kereskedelmi és Hitelbank Rt. Refinancings for banking clients included the Dorottya Udvar office building.

BANKING AND FINANCE

BERECZ & ANDRÉKÓ LINKLATERS ✪
CMS CAMERON McKENNA LLP ✪
ÉVA HEGEDÛS (DR.) IN ASSOCIATION WITH ALLEN & OVERY LLP ✪
KÖVES CLIFFORD CHANCE

Gárdos, Füredi, Mosonyi, Tomori, Law Office of
Horváth & Partners DLA Weiss-Tessbach ✪
Martonyi és Kajtár Baker & McKenzie ✪
Oppenheim és Társai Freshfields Bruckhaus Deringer
Réczicza White & Case LLP
Siegler Law Office/Weil, Gotshal & Manges ✪
Squarra & Partos (in association with Lovells) ✪

Bihary, Balassa & Partners Attorneys at Law ✪
Burai – Kovács & Partners
Erös Üqyvédi Iroda Squire, Sanders & Dempsey LLP ✪
Gide Loyrette Nouel – Molnár & Ferenczy ✪
Nagy & Pintér Hogan & Hartson ✪
Nagy és Trócsányi ✪
Nörr Stiefenhofer Lutz ✪
Réti, Antall & Madl LANDWELL
Sándor Szegedi Szent-Ivány & Komáromi
Szecskay – Attorneys at Law ✪

Firms are listed A-Z in tiers which are ranked in order of priority
✪ *Indicates firm displays contact details at the end of this chapter.*

Dr. Éva Hegedûs in association with Allen & Overy LLP advises both international banks and borrowers, including Raiffeisen Bank on a £30m credit facility given to a Hungarian company, MKB bank on a student accommodation PFI project, and Hungarian energy company MOL on a €700m credit facility arranged by a banking consortium, one of the biggest loans provided to a company in Central Europe. Banking clients say the firm 'assists greatly' their operations.

Managing partner Péter Köves leads the team at **Köves Clifford Chance**, which worked in 2005 on refinancings, syndicated loan agreements and for major German and US banks. Its experience includes major motorway financings and it is recommended for 'excellent service'.

Banking is one of the core specialist areas covered by **Law Office of Gárdos, Füredi, Mosonyi, Tomori**, and it can advise on setting-up and licensing banks and other institutions giving credit.

Horváth & Partners DLA Weiss-Tessbach works for banks including Barclays Bank and project and construction companies in financing and refinancing deals, many involving commercial property. During 2005, the firm hired two new banking and finance associates from the Hungarian Financial Supervisory Authority.

The team at **Martonyi és Kajtár Baker & McKenzie** is led by Zoltán Martonyi, recommended for his 'professional preparedness, style of negotiation and willingness of cooperation', and advises banks including Hungarian OTP Bank. In 2005 it worked for Raffeisen International Fund Advisory on the sale of investment units in Hungary.

Oppenheim és Társai Freshfields Bruckhaus Deringer advises banks on regulatory issues, and both banks and borrowers on financing. The team also works in Slovakia, the Czech Republic, and Romania and advised Credit Suisse and Deutsche Bank on financing the acquisition of the Carl Zeiss Group. Clients praise a 'business-minded and goal-oriented attitude, innovative thinking and high level of commitment'.

Réczicza White & Case LLP represented foreign and domestic lending banks including Anglo-Irish Bank and Commerzbank and continued to work for international banks financing the M5 motorway concession, advising on the third, €150m phase. It is recommended for its handling of complex transactions.

Clients recommend the team at **Siegler Law Office/Weil, Gotshal & Manges** for banking expertise. It has received some 30 mandates from clients, including both banks and borrowers, over the last year. The firm focuses on regulatory work and financing deals for clients including Citigroup subsidiary CitiInsurance and Hungarian steel company Dunaferr, this last on a €65m export credit facility.

Squarra & Partos (in association with Lovells) has advised both banks and investors, and has an emphasis on commercial property. It worked for ING Real Estate Finance, investing in Budapest shopping centre the Pólus Centre, and OTP Bank when it financed two acquisitions by Swiss-owned developer SCD Hungary.

Hungarian and foreign banks and financial institutions form a significant part of the client list at **Bihary, Balassa & Partners Attorneys at Law**.

Burai - Kovács & Partners advises banks and venture capital investors providing finance for acquisitions.

Erös Üqyvédi Iroda Squire, Sanders & Dempsey LLP represents international and domestic banks on a variety of financial issues.

Dr Balázs Ferenczy, former chief legal counsel of Credit Lyonnais Hungária Rt, heads the banking team at **Gide Loyrette Nouel - Molnár & Ferenczy**. It concentrates on banking law and investments, advising borrowers in Hungary, Romania, Russia and Ukraine on real estate and energy deals.

Nagy & Pintér Hogan & Hartson specialises in media and pharmaceuticals and in 2005 represented a major international film company in financing a film shot in Hungary and cinema operator and film distributor InterCom Rt on the Hungarian tax implications of a major loan from a Canadian bank.

The team at **Nagy és Trócsányi** represents a number of regionally important banks including CIB Bank and Raiffeisen Bank.

Nörr Stiefenhofer Lutz gained experience in the banking field during the foundation of the Hypobank, now HVB Bank, in the early 1990s and has continued to represent the bank as its main counsel. Structured and municipal finance are among the issues it handles for clients such as Bayerische Landesbank.

Réti, Antall & Madl LANDWELL advises a number of international lending banks and investment funds, as well borrowers, on finance deals, regulation and other matters.

In 2004 and 2005 **Sándor Szegedi Szent-Ivány & Komáromi** acted for the lenders of a syndicated loan to a Hungarian state-owned bank, and advised a US borrower and its Hungarian guarantor on a credit agreement and related security agreements.

The team at **Szecskay - Attorneys at Law** is particularly active in financing real estate deals, representing both banks and property developers building office buildings and shopping centres.

CAPITAL MARKETS

The fundraising markets were dominated by government eurobond issues in 2005, although a market is now expected to open up for project bonds. No significant IPOs completed in what is widely seen as a dormant market perhaps because of the expense of flotations, leaving investment funds available to potential borrowers. The Hungarian Capital Markets Act was amended on 1 July 2005 to include the EU Prospectus Directive.

Berecz & Andrékó Linklaters' team is led by managing partner Csaba Berecz and managing associate Dr Andrea Miskolczi, previously of the Frankfurt Stock Exchange. They advised on a major bond issue by the Hungarian Privatisation Authority, and on two IPOs, including that of low-cost airline SkyEurope Airlines on exchanges in Warsaw and Vienna. Deutsche Bank, Citigroup and Nomura are among international clients.

Dr Zoltán Lengyel, capital markets partner at **Dr. Éva Hegedûs in association with Allen & Overy LLP**, leads a team of four advising international investment banks and companies on debt, equity and bond issues, derivatives and structured finance. It acted for Morgan Stanley on a US$1.5bn fixed-rate bond issue by the Republic of Hungary and for Hungarian energy firm MOL on its first eurobond issue.

Köves Clifford Chance has been active in the bond market, advising banks including HSBC, UBS, Dresdner Kleinwort Wasserstein and BNP Paribas on issues of eurobonds and sovereign debt. Significant deals of 2004/2005 included advising Citigroup Global Markets and BNP Paribas on a €1bn sovereign debt issue by the Republic of Hungary.

Réczicza White & Case LLP advised on the first private placing from HVB Mortgage Bank Hungary, a euro mortgage bond valued at €15m, as well as handling a Yankee bond offering for the Hungarian Government Debt Management Agency.

Capital markets and finance partner Konrád Siegler at **Siegler Law Office/Weil, Gotshal & Manges**, 'probably the best security lawyer', has wide expertise in stockmarket transactions as well as bond issues. Work in 2005 included advising

CAPITAL MARKETS

BERECZ & ANDRÉKÓ LINKLATERS ✪
ÉVA HEGEDÛS (DR.) IN ASSOCIATION WITH ALLEN & OVERY LLP ✪
KÖVES CLIFFORD CHANCE
RÉCZICZA WHITE & CASE LLP
SIEGLER LAW OFFICE/WEIL, GOTSHAL & MANGES ✪

CMS Cameron McKenna LLP ✪
Erös Üqyvédi Iroda Squire, Sanders & Dempsey LLP ✪
Gárdos, Füredi, Mosonyi, Tomori, Law Office of
Gide Loyrette Nouel - Molnár & Ferenczy ✪
Horváth & Partners DLA Weiss-Tessbach ✪
Martonyi és Kajtár Baker & McKenzie ✪
Oppenheim és Társai Freshfields Bruckhaus Deringer
Squarra & Partos (in association with Lovells) ✪
Szecskay - Attorneys at Law ✪

Firms are listed A-Z in tiers which are ranked in order of priority
✪ *Indicates firm displays contact details at the end of this chapter.*

German utilities group E.ON on disputes connected to the squeeze-out of minority shareholders in three Hungarian electricity companies, and Investor Holding Rt on its takeover offer for grain trader Agrimill.

CMS Cameron McKenna LLP can advise on public offerings and takeovers as well as bond issues. In 2005 it advised Invitel Rt, a subsidiary of Magyar Telecom BV, on a €165m refinancing of its senior debt facilities, linked to a €142m high-yield bond issue.

Erös Üqyvédi Iroda Squire, Sanders & Dempsey LLP advises on loan facilities, eurobonds, syndicated financings and bond issues. In 2005 it advised clients from a start-up Hungarian business going through fundraising, and a leading US tyre and rubber company on the use of its Hungarian shareholdings in a loan refinancing.

Law Office of Gárdos, Füredi, Mosonyi, Tomori has particular expertise in advising securities firms, advising clients in both public and private placements.

Gide Loyrette Nouel – Molnár & Ferenczy is building a securitisation practice under the aegis of banking and finance partner Dr Balázs Ferenczy and regularly advises on European ABS securitisations involving Hungarian asset classes.

Horváth & Partners DLA Weiss-Tessbach has the expertise to advise on stock market listings and bond issues, including, in 2005, a €1.5bn eurobond issue. It advised an Austrian company on the delisting from five different stock exchanges, including Budapest, of its newly acquired Hungarian ceramics company and was instructed on the secondary offering of shares in leading Hungarian chemicals business BorsodChem in one of the largest non-governmental share sales to date. Clients cite its 'well-deserved' reputation as a capital markets legal adviser, saying it gives a 'quality' and 'professional' service.

Martonyi és Kajtár Baker & McKenzie acts on stock market listings, bond issues and securitisation. It advised OTP Bank Rt on a €1bn EMTN and a €25m eurobond issue, and represented MOL on the flotation of its shares on the Warsaw Stock Exchange.

Oppenheim és Társai Freshfields Bruckhaus Deringer has experience advising clients including First Hungary Fund, ABN Amro and Euroclear on Hungarian capital markets regulations, and is also briefing a number of multinational investment banks on the market.

Partner László Partos is the capital markets expert at **Squarra & Partos (in association with Lovells)**, and advises Hungarian banks on listing funds on the stock market. In 2005, he continued to work with minority shareholders in Brau Union Group, following its takeover by Heineken.

Szecskay – Attorneys at Law has experience in both the IPO and bond markets, advising in 2005 on a potential listing on the Budapest Stock Exchange and on an Austrian/German bond issue. In 2004 it acted for the country's largest drugs manufacturer during its privatisation, a process that involved issuing bonds that were exchangeable for shares in the company.

COMPETITION

In the wake of the country's accession to the EU, competition has proved a fast-growing and fast-changing area of law, since lawyers now have to consider the implications of European as well as Hungarian law.

The seven-member team led by partner Zoltán Barakonyi at **Martonyi és Kajtár Baker & McKenzie** handles issues from mergers, cartel and market dominance, to compliance, antitrust, EU law and consumer protection for multinationals and their Hungarian subsidiaries and is rated as 'one of the best – or even the best – competition practices in Hungary'. In 2005 it successfully represented a Hungarian telecommunications company against price-fixing allegations, and several construction companies in ongoing road-building cartel cases that include a high-profile motorway cartel case.

The five members of **Réczicza White & Case LLP**'s team excel in advising on the competition aspects of mergers. In addition, its unfair competition practice, led by senior associate Szabolcs Posta, has continued to grow and represents multinationals in disputes with competitors or in market investigations. Clients include Electricité de France (EdF) and pharmaceuticals group Colgate-Palmolive.

Berecz & Andrékó Linklaters' developing practice advises international and national clients on the competition aspects of mergers, state aid, unfair competition, and abuse of market position and cartels. In 2005 it represented South Korean company Hankook Tire Co on the state aid aspects of opening a new €500m factory in the country, and an international financial organisation facing a cartel enquiry.

During 2005 **Köves Clifford Chance** advised the Hungarian State on the antitrust aspects of contracts with construction companies on the M5 and M6 motorways, Hyundai on the restructuring of its Hungarian distribution and repair network and names including the General Electric Company, IMS Health and Pfizer on competition law as it relates to mergers.

Oppenheim és Társai Freshfields Bruckhaus Deringer has seen growing demand for its seven-strong team's knowledge of EU law since accession. The practice advises energy companies and blue-chip multinationals including Eli Lilly and Volvo, and has been working with IT clients ahead of government cartel investigations into the industry.

Lawyers from **Bán S Szabó & Partners** regularly appear before Hungarian competition and appeal courts, representing multinational and domestic clients. They act on the competition aspects of acquisitions, cross-border work and distribution and licensing agreements.

COMPETITION

MARTONYI ÉS KAJTÁR BAKER & McKENZIE ✪
RÉCZICZA WHITE & CASE LLP

Berecz & Andrékó Linklaters ✪
Köves Clifford Chance
Oppenheim és Társai Freshfields Bruckhaus Deringer

Bán S Szabó & Partners
Erös Üqyvédi Iroda Squire, Sanders & Dempsey LLP ✪
Éva Hegedûs (Dr.) in association with Allen & Overy LLP ✪
Gide Loyrette Nouel – Molnár & Ferenczy ✪
Kovács Réti Szegheö Attorneys at Law ✪
Nagy & Pintér Hogan & Hartson ✪
Nagy és Trócsányi ✪
Réti, Antall & Madl LANDWELL
SBG & K Patent and Law Offices
Sándor Szegedi Szent-Ivány & Komáromi ✪
Siegler Law Office/Weil, Gotshal & Manges ✪
Szecskay – Attorneys at Law ✪

Firms are listed A-Z in tiers which are ranked in order of priority
✪ Indicates firm displays contact details at the end of this chapter.

In 2005, lawyers from **Erös Üqyvédi Iroda Squire, Sanders & Dempsey LLP** advised a Central and Eastern European food manufacturer and a US energy company on merger control issues and also represented a Hungarian mortgage loan company on an intellectual property infringement case before the Hungarian Competition Council.

Dr. Éva Hegedûs in association with Allen & Overy LLP represents national and international clients on issues arising from transactions, regulation and anti-competitive behaviour. The firm has advised telecoms and media clients including Hungarian mobile phone company Pannon GSM.

Dr István Molnár heads the expanding competition team at **Gide Loyrette Nouel – Molnár & Ferenczy** which advises clients including pharmaceutical and automotive companies, on the effect of EU competition law on the Hungarian market.

Partner Dr Tamás Matarits is the specialist in competition, trade and EU law at independent law firm **Kovács Réti Szegheö Attorneys at Law**. The firm represents both Hungarian and foreign businesses, in the wholesale, pharmaceutical and food sectors, on issues from cartels to merger control.

Nagy & Pintér Hogan & Hartson's expertise in competition lies in advising pharmaceutical and food companies. It represented Schering-Plough in an unfair drug promotion case against a competitor before the consumer protection authorities, the first case of its kind in Hungary.

At **Nagy és Trócsányi**, Péter Nagy, working with **Allen & Overy LLP**, represented Hungarian mobile phone operator Pannon GSM against cartel allegations involving the country's three major operators. Other clients include US tobacco company Philip Morris.

Réti, Antall & Madl LANDWELL handles work from exclusivity agreements, antitrust and unfair market practices to merger control, compliance and state aid. Notably, it represented Swiss publishing house the Ringier Group on its acquisition of Hungarian political newspaper Népszabadság Rt.

Patent and trade mark specialist **SBG & K Patent and Law Offices** represents foreign and domestic companies on Hungarian law as it relates to mergers, antitrust and unfair competition cases.

Sándor Szegedi Szent-Ivány & Komáromi has worked on cases of unfair market practices in the nutritional and food-production market and regularly handles merger-related notifications to the Competition Office.

Competition lawyers at **Siegler Law Office/Weil, Gotshal & Manges** work closely with its M&A team and in 2005 they advised the consortium of Fraport AG and Deutsche Bank AG on the competition aspects of their bid for Budapest Airport and Macquarie Communications Infrastructure Group on its plans to buy a majority stake in broadcast tower company Antenna Hungária.

Szecskay – Attorneys at Law advises on the competition aspects of mergers and takes cases before the Hungarian Competition Authority. Among its clients are a spirits company and a leading pharmaceutical business.

CORPORATE AND COMMERCIAL

Berecz & Andrékó Linklaters handles complex as well as general issues for international and Hungarian companies including mobile phone company Pannon GSM, BorsodChem Rt, RWE subsidiary Mátrai Power Plant Rt and leading courier company DHL. Managing partner Csaba Berecz is in charge following the departure of former head of corporate Balázs Máthé, although a successor is likely to be appointed during 2006. Clients cite high service levels and 'comprehensive support'.

The team of specialists at **Köves Clifford Chance** prides itself on giving an all-round service, and is described as 'one of the most reliable firms'. During 2005 it worked for clients including CSFB in its role representing the Hungarian State on the €1.8bn sale of Budapest Airport.

Martonyi és Kajtár Baker & McKenzie counts multinationals including Pepsi Cola, Ford, adidas and Reebok International among the clients of this wide-ranging practice, led by name partner Géza Kajtár. In the last year work included advising an IT multinational on its Hungarian distribution model.

'Excellent' **Réczicza White & Case LLP** continues to work with high-profile clients including the EBRD, Nestlé and Colgate-Palmolive.

CORPORATE AND COMMERCIAL

BERECZ & ANDRÉKÓ LINKLATERS ✪
KÖVES CLIFFORD CHANCE
MARTONYI ÉS KAJTÁR BAKER & McKENZIE ✪
RÉCZICZA WHITE & CASE LLP
SIEGLER LAW OFFICE/WEIL, GOTSHAL & MANGES ✪

CMS Cameron McKenna LLP ✪
Erös Üqyvédi Iroda Squire, Sanders & Dempsey LLP ✪
Éva Hegedûs (Dr.) in association with Allen & Overy LLP ✪
Forgó, Varga and Partners ✪
Horváth & Partners DLA Weiss-Tessbach ✪
Luther, Fest & Kajli Attorneys ✪
Nagy & Pintér Hogan & Hartson ✪
Nagy és Trócsányi ✪
Oppenheim és Társai Freshfields Bruckhaus Deringer

Bihary, Balassa & Partners Attorneys at Law ✪
Burai – Kovács & Partners
Dezsö & Partners
Gárdos, Füredi, Mosonyi, Tomori, Law Office of
Gide Loyrette Nouel – Molnár & Ferenczy ✪
Haarmann Hemmelrath ✪
Kovács Réti Szegheö Attorneys at Law ✪
Nógrádi Law Office
Nörr Stiefenhofer Lutz ✪
Réti, Antall & Madl LANDWELL
SBG & K Patent and Law Offices
Sándor Szegedi Szent-Iványi & Komáromi ✪
Squarra & Partos (in association with Lovells) ✪
Szecskay – Attorneys at Law ✪

Bálintfy & Partners Law Office
Bán S Szabó & Partners
Bárd, Cseri & Partners ✪
Bogsch & Partners
CHSH Szécsényi Ugyvédi Iroda Cerha Hempel Spiegelfeld Hlawati ✪
de Capoa e Associati, Studio Legale
Déri & Lovrecz
Füsthy & Mányai Law Office
Heinzelmann & Partners, Attorneys at Law
Kovacs Barborjak Kende Kendvai & Katona
Marai & Associates
Radványi & Partners
Simon & Petz Attorneys-at-law
Szabó, Kővári, Tercsák és Társai Ügyvédi Iroda (in cooperation with Salans)
Szalma, Ferenczi & Partners
Udvarhelyi & Partners

Firms are listed A-Z in tiers which are ranked in order of priority
✪ *Indicates firm displays contact details at the end of this chapter.*

One client described it as the 'one of the top law firms we've worked with, worldwide'.

Siegler Law Office/Weil, Gotshal & Manges counts Philip Morris, Reuters, affiliates of RWE and UCB Hungary and energy companies BP, CEZ (Czech Power Company), and El Paso Oil & Gas among the companies it advises on corporate and commercial issues. The firm comes recommended for its 'focus on relevant issues, clear advice and timely responses'.

Time has yet to tell what **CMS Cameron McKenna LLP**'s merger with *Hayhurst Robinson* will mean for this 'excellent' law firm, which specialises in advising pharmaceutical, technology and media companies, as well as handling more general corporate work. It worked on the regional aspects of IBM's sale of its PCD business to Singapore-based Lenovo in 2005.

Erös Üqyvédi Iroda Squire, Sanders & Dempsey LLP acts for companies looking to invest in or expand in the country and beyond. US lawyer Kevin Connor is the managing partner of both the Budapest and Bratislava offices, and advises Central European and multinational enterprises on international business law.

Dr Éva Hegedûs leads the corporate practice at **Dr. Éva Hegedûs in association with Allen & Overy LLP**, advising a number of multinationals on an ongoing basis. They include drinks company SAB Miller, BT Hungary, Viasat Broadcasting (UK) Ltd and Versatel Telecom International.

Forgó, Varga and Partners works largely for international companies on the regulatory, commercial, employment, and public procurement aspects of their business. Recommended for 'high-quality advice, the ability to handle complex transactions and commercial sense', it specialises in working with TMT and pharmaceutical businesses. Clients include the Hungarian franchisee of hair salon group Essensuals and chocolate maker Stollwerck Hungary.

'Reliable' and 'professional' **Horváth & Partners DLA Weiss-Tessbach** works for Hungarian and international retailers, especially in the fields of food and furniture and, recently, biotechnology. It advised venture capital firm VCP Energy AG on a planned €35m investment in a Hungarian power plant and Budapest Stock Exchange-listed plastic manufacturer Pannonplast Rt on a restructuring.

Luther, Fest & Kajli Attorneys, led by managing partner Arne Gobert, advises large international businesses on their Hungarian investments. 'Extremely responsive, fast and thorough,' the firm works for a multinational oil and gas company and advises Deutsche Lufthansa and German telecoms manufacturing company Balda Solutions in their Hungarian operations. Employment law is a key area.

Nagy & Pintér Hogan & Hartson gives 'highest-quality, quick and sensitive' service to clients ranging from employment matters to insolvency and restructuring. It is particularly known for its work with pharmaceutical companies, including leading independent Hungarian pharmaceutical company Richter Gedeon Rt, Herbalife International of the US and

Schering-Plough, but also works for media and entertainment companies.

Coca-Cola's Hungarian production company, Samsung Electronics, Philip Morris, German discount supermarket chain Lidl and a UK insurer call on **Nagy és Trócsányi**, a firm that is 'reliable' and 'open to last-minute requests' for corporate and commercial work.

Masterfoods Hungary was among clients calling on corporate law advice from **Oppenheim és Társai Freshfields Bruckhaus Deringer** during the last year, on issues including restructuring. The firm, which has a 'high level of commitment, flexibility and a business-minded attitude' also represented DB Systems in negotiations with MÁV Hungarian State Railways and is still active on its big deal of late 2004, advising E.ON Ruhrgas International on its takeover of MOL's gas businesses.

Bihary, Balassa & Partners Attorneys at Law's team works with both multinationals and SMEs investing in Hungary, advising on corporate issues from insolvency, mergers and employment law, to media and energy law.

Burai – Kovács & Partners, led by managing partner János Burai-Kovács, advises large international companies on corporate and commercial issues, with a focus on M&A.

Dezsö & Partners advises international clients including Alcatel Hungary on issues from company formation and administration to restructuring.

Law Office of Gárdos, Füredi, Mosonyi, Tomori has experience from the privatistions of the gas and edible oils and detergent industries, from where a number of its current clients hail.

Gide Loyrette Nouel – Molnár & Ferenczy focuses on general work and corporate restructurings, sometimes following M&A, for a range of clients, many of which are French.

Haarmann Hemmelrath's Budapest office counts Parmalat, Merloni Indesit and DaimlerChrysler among its clients, handling issues from distribution and employment agreements to insolvency and restructuring. It also advised an Irish investor putting money into a new regional airport in Hungary.

Kovács Réti Szegheö Attorneys at Law represents clients including a Japanese automotive glass maker, tyre manufacturer Bridgestone, and multinationals Agfa and Fuji. It works with international clients from the wine, meat, and milk industries as well as a pharmaceuticals company.

Nógrádi Law Office is known for working with medium-sized companies on corporate and real estate issues.

Nörr Stiefenhofer Lutz represents a number of international household names in sectors from pharmaceuticals and electronics to drinks.

Réti, Antall & Madl LANDWELL specialises in working with US and Canadian businesses with offshore businesses in Hungary. Accession to the EU means this offshore regime is being replaced, but the firm is still advising its client base of some 25 companies under the new rules, which continue to offer low-tax benefits. It also advises its other clients on general corporate and commercial work.

SBG & K Patent and Law Offices advises foreign and domestic companies on general corporate law, including commercial agreements and employment law. It has a particular focus on working with small and medium-sized companies doing business internationally, and those for whom intellectual property issues are important.

Sándor Szegedi Szent-Ivány & Komáromi's specialisations include employment law. The firm also works on issues such as commercial and work contracts, tenders and public procurement, for clients including the Hungarian subsidiary of a leading multinational IT, telecoms and electronics business. Managing partner Tamás Sándor was involved in drafting both the new and the previous Companies Act.

General corporate work forms a major part of the practice at **Squarra & Partos (in association with Lovells)** which has advised, among others, a number of pharmaceutical and biotechnology businesses.

Szecskay – Attorneys at Law, a 'dependable and trusted adviser' offering 'personalised and devoted attention' is retained by the Hungarian subsidiaries of leading US and German multinationals, as well as large domestic companies. It has worked on corporate restructurings for international and Hungarian companies and has expertise in employment issues.

Bálintfy & Partners Law Office is a long-established Budapest law firm, set up in 1988 by lawyers who previously worked in-house at various companies, and has a reputation in the field of employment law.

Bán S Szabó & Partners advises clients, including multinational companies and their Hungarian subsidiaries, on corporate law issues ranging from foreign investment in Hungary, to corporate governance, company law and reporting.

Bárd, Cseri & Partners has 20 fee-earners, led by partners Dr Zsuzanna Cseri and Dr Károly Bárd. It works for multinational insurance companies, logistics firms and real estate investors from as far afield as Ireland, Israel, Britain, Belgium and the US.

Bogsch & Partners advises longstanding multinational clients including McDonald's and IBM on the local aspects of running their business.

CHSH Szécsényi Ugyvédi Iroda Cerha Hempel Spiegelfeld Hlawati has a strong client base in Austria and Germany. In 2005, the firm advised E.ON on restructuring its Hungarian subsidiaries and a leading Austrian construction company on a PPP tender to build and operate a prison.

The Budapest office of Italian law firm **Studio Legale de Capoa e Associati** is staffed by seven lawyers from both Italy and Hungary, advising companies from both countries.

Déri & Lovrecz gives an all-round corporate and commercial service to multinationals investing in Hungary.

Marai & Associates was founded in 1992 by former **Martonyi és Kajtár Baker & McKenzie** lawyer Maria Márai and now has two partners, an associate and five counsel. It advises Hungarian and foreign investors on business opportunities in the country and across general corporate law.

Radványi & Partners can advise its international corporate clients in Dutch and Flemish, as well as English and Hungarian, in areas such as banking, international trade, telecoms, tax and dispute resolution and general commercial law.

Corporate and commercial work accounts for 50% of the workload at **Simon & Petz Attorneys-at-law** where longstanding clients include banknote technology company Jura Group, and the Hungarian operation of an international electronics blue-chip company.

Szabó, Kővári, Tercsák és Társai Ügyvédi Iroda (in cooperation with Salans) handles routine corporate and commercial work for British, German, Dutch and Israeli clients investing in Hungary. Recent work includes advising a UK company on a joint venture to build a sports centre worth up to €800m in north Budapest, and a German construction company closing a Hungarian subsidiary.

Szalma, Ferenczi & Partners advises medium-sized companies from Hungary, Germany, Austria, Holland and Israel and has expanded with the arrival of banking and finance specialist and name partner Katalin Ferenczi. Its electronic information management systems allow the firm to sign and file documents electronically and clients to monitor progress online.

Udvarhelyi & Partners advises predominantly German, Austrian and British clients on corporate and commercial issues including cross-border issues and litigation.

DISPUTE RESOLUTION

'Exceptional' energy expert Zoltán Faludi of **Köves Clifford Chance** won HUF3bn for a client in an arbitration case during 2005, while colleague Péter Lakatos advised electronics and telecoms clients on product recall and litigation.

At **Nagy és Trócsányi**, Péter Nagy, described by peers as Budapest's leading litigator and by clients as 'terrific' and 'aggressive', represented international and domestic clients including the Hungarian government before arbitration courts as far afield as Paris, Washington, and Vienna, as well as taking some half dozen cases before the arbitration courts attached to the Hungarian Chamber of Commerce.

Erös Üqyvédi Iroda Squire, Sanders & Dempsey LLP has represented Hungarian banks

DISPUTE RESOLUTION

KÖVES CLIFFORD CHANCE
NAGY ÉS TRÓCSÁNYI ✪

Erös Ügyvédi Iroda Squire, Sanders & Dempsey LLP ✪
Réczicza White & Case LLP
Szecskay – Attorneys at Law ✪

Berecz & Andrékó Linklaters ✪
Bogsch & Partners
Burai – Kovács & Partners
Danubia
Forgó, Varga and Partners ✪
Martonyi és Kajtár Baker & McKenzie ✪
Nógrádi Law Office
Oppenheim és Társai Freshfields Bruckhaus Deringer
Siegler Law Office/Weil, Gotshal & Manges ✪

Bálintfy & Partners Law Office
Dezsö & Partners
Gárdos, Füredi, Mosonyi, Tomori, Law Office of
Kovács Réti Szegheö Attorneys at Law ✪
Réti, Antall & Madl LANDWELL
SBG & K Patent and Law Offices
Sándor Szegedi Szent-Iványi & Komáromi ✪

Firms are listed A-Z in tiers which are ranked in order of priority
✪ Indicates firm displays contact details at the end of this chapter.

and investsment funds in litigation, as well as advising major players in the Hungarian electricity market on compliance issues related to long-term supply agreements.

In the past four years the Budapest office of **Réczicza White & Case LLP** has represented clients with claims worth more than €500m in Hungarian arbitration and other disputes. It is representing a pharmaceutical company in a price agreement dispute with the Republic of Hungary that is expected to form a precedent when it has been heard before the Court of Appeal.

Dr András Szecskay of **Szecskay – Attorneys at Law**, who 'ranks among the elite lawyers in Hungary' has a strong reputation among peers for his handling of litigation. He has been instructed on cases relating to intellectual property, the pharmaceutical industry, mergers and privatisation issues by major Hungarian businesses, as well as a public authority on a major international pollution case.

Berecz & Andrékó Linklaters' dispute resolution practice focuses on trade mark litigation and other intellectual property issues. During 2005 managing associate András Lendvai represented perfume company the Lancaster Group in anti-counterfeiting disputes including a pioneering community trade mark infringement case.

Bogsch & Partners advises on dispute resolution in relation to its intellectual property clients as well as working on damage claims and employment issues.

Burai – Kovács & Partners represents its international clientele on litigation and arbitration, including tax litigation.

Danubia specialises in litigation and enforcement actions to protect both patents and trade marks.

Forgó, Varga and Partners acts before a number of different courts, primarily in the fields of pharmaceuticals and telecoms. It has represented the Hungarian State Privatisation and Holding Company on a multi-million dollar international arbitration in Austria and Slovakia.

The maturing dispute resolution team at **Martonyi és Kajtár Baker & McKenzie** has represented the Hungarian subsidiary of a multinational agricultural company in a defamation case brought by a competitor, and is advising a major Hungarian construction company as it challenges a US$6.6m fine imposed by the Hungarian Competition Authority following allegations of a cartel in motorway construction tenders.

Oppenheim és Társai Freshfields Bruckhaus Deringer represents clients such as leading Hungarian construction company Strabag, food company HJ Heinz UK, and German energy company RWE's local distribution companies, on contract and general commercial disputes before the courts and in arbitration hearings. In 2005 it represented Canadian railway company Bombardier, disputing a tender run by the Hungarian State Railways.

Siegler Law Office/Weil, Gotshal & Manges has become an important port of call for US companies and their subsidiaries looking to pursue disputes and arbitration in Hungary, for blue-chip names including HJ Heinz, Donna Karan New York (DKNY), and the Hungarian-American Enterprise Fund.

Bálintfy & Partners Law Office works for Hungarian, English and German-speaking clients, companies and individuals.

Tax litigation is the primary focus of the dispute resolution practice at **Dezsö & Partners**. It also advised Swiss railway company Stadler in a dispute involving Bombardier and Hungarian State Railways.

The litigation practice at **Law Office of Gárdos, Füredi, Mosonyi, Tomori** concentrates on the firm's specialist areas of capital markets and securities work.

Kovács Réti Szegheö Attorneys at Law has two chartered arbitrators and mediators, Dr Kálmán Gyárfás and Dr Attila Kovács.

Réti, Antall & Madl LANDWELL handles dispute resolution work where relevant to its existing clients. In particular, it has handled a large number of disputes related to employment law.

SBG & K Patent and Law Offices works for its clients in tax disputes in addition to protecting intellectual property rights.

Sándor Szegedi Szent-Iványi & Komáromi regularly represents clients involved in employment and construction disputes.

ENERGY

The rising price of oil has made the management and regulation of energy resources important in Hungary as elsewhere. Companies are now looking beyond the country's borders to other Eastern European countries for supplies, and interest in renewable sources is growing.

Berecz & Andrékó Linklaters represents energy companies on sector-specific regulation and public procurement and general corporate issues. RWE subsidiary the Mátrai Power Plant, E.ON, Lukoil and a wind farm company are among its clients.

Zoltan Faludi of **Köves Clifford Chance** comes highly recommended as an energy expert. During the past year his clients included German energy company E.ON, the Association of Gas Distribution companies and US company EETEK.

Strengths in both the renewable and traditional energy markets keep **Réczicza White & Case LLP** at the forefront of this sector. It has advised Electricité de France (EdF) on state aid and unfair competition issues and worked with BIL Investment Hungary and Spanish wind-power company Preneal SA on a proposed pioneering wind farm development, to be built in conjunction with Hungarian wind energy companies.

Burai – Kovács & Partners has wide-ranging experience on exploration and pipeline issues. It advised Hungarian energy company MOL on issues including cross-border pipeline work and worked with multinational oil and gas companies on mining licences and concessions.

CMS Cameron McKenna LLP has experience of acting for large clients, including Budapest Power Plant, on regulatory and cost matters.

Erös Ügyvédi Iroda Squire, Sanders & Dempsey LLP works for major companies in the Hungarian electricity market and in 2005 also advised El Paso on the power plant it runs with its joint venture partner.

Dr. Éva Hegedûs in association with Allen & Overy LLP has taken a strong position on energy-related project finance, advising banks including OTP Bank Rt and Kereskedelmi és Hitelbank Rt, and borrowers on energy projects. It has also advised trading and generation companies on electricity-trading agreements.

Luther, Fest & Kajli Attorneys represents both a multinational oil and gas exploration company and advises on the development of wind farms. It has experience of advising a petrol station network.

Martonyi és Kajtár Baker & McKenzie brings its competition expertise to bear in the energy markets, advising clients such as E.ON Hungária and the Hungarian subsidiary of RWE, on the potential effects of liberalisation of the energy

ENERGY

BERECZ & ANDRÉKÓ LINKLATERS ✪
KÖVES CLIFFORD CHANCE
RÉCZICZA WHITE & CASE LLP

Burai – Kovács & Partners
CMS Cameron McKenna LLP ✪
Erös Üqyvédi Iroda Squire, Sanders & Dempsey LLP ✪
Éva Hegedûs (Dr.) in association with Allen & Overy LLP ✪
Luther, Fest & Kajli Attorneys ✪
Martonyi és Kajtár Baker & McKenzie ✪
Oppenheim és Társai Freshfields Bruckhaus Deringer
Siegler Law Office/Weil, Gotshal & Manges ✪
Szecskay – Attorneys at Law ✪

Gide Loyrette Nouel – Molnár & Ferenczy ✪
Réti, Antall & Madl LANDWELL
Sándor Szegedi Szent-Ivány & Komáromi ✪

Firms are listed A-Z in tiers which are ranked in order of priority
✪ *Indicates firm displays contact details at the end of this chapter.*

market, as well as on regulatory, market dominance and merger control issues.

Oppenheim és Társai Freshfields Bruckhaus Deringer advises on the liberalisation of energy markets. In 2005 it represented Swiss electricity company Atel AG, on its purchase of a major Hungarian power plant and related start-up of a regional trading company.

Siegler Law Office/Weil, Gotshal & Manges represents a broad range of power generation companies, gas, electricity distribution and renewables companies including BP, E.ON and the shareholders of United Bio Fuels Holding Hungary AG on regulatory, corporate and commercial issues.

Szecskay – Attorneys at Law has wide experience in advising 'satisfied' energy companies, acting recently on heat-supply agreements, electricity price-setting, and acquisitions in the sector.

Gide Loyrette Nouel – Molnár & Ferenczy has a history of working on energy privatisations and today advises urban heating and water companies on issues including project finance.

Réti, Antall & Madl LANDWELL played an active part in the privatisation of the domestic energy industry, and its more recent experience includes long-term energy contracts. Clients include a Hungarian metal producer which works with the energy sector.

Sándor Szegedi Szent-Ivány & Komáromi has advised energy companies on M&A.

INTELLECTUAL PROPERTY

Berecz & Andrékó Linklaters is recommended for the 'exceptional commitment and success' of its IP team on issues from regulation and border measures to patent and trade mark enforcement and disputes. During 2005 it successfully challenged counterfeiters by bringing the first community trade mark dispute on behalf of international perfume company the Lancaster Group, a case which went to the Hungarian Court of Appeal.

Patent attorneys and general attorneys work closely together at highly specialist IP firm **Danubia**, to protect inventions, ideas and branding through filing and enforcing patents, trade marks and related law.

SBG & K Patent and Law Offices files and protects patents and other IP protection for domestic and international clients at home and abroad. The firm advises in particular on patenting software, semi-conductors and business methods and is well regarded by peers.

Oppenheim és Társai Freshfields Bruckhaus Deringer handles copyright, trade mark and domain name registrations and disputes, as well as data protection matters. It also has links to patent filing experts. Clients of its five-strong team include technology companies, notably Microsoft, as well as Caterpillar and Hungarian pharmaceutical industry body AIPM.

Szecskay – Attorneys at Law handles trade mark filings but its strength is in handling patent and trade mark-related disputes. It is instructed by large Hungarian and international companies including a major pharmaceutical company.

Bogsch & Partners has expertise across the range of intellectual property issues, from filing trade marks and patents to dealing with licences, brand-renewal issues and acting when rights are infringed for pharmaceutical companies, fast food restaurants, tobacco and IT companies.

Kovács Réti Szegheö Attorneys at Law helps luxury goods companies protect brands, advising a leading Hungarian cosmetics company and LVMH, owner and distributor of Kenzo, Christian Dior, and Givenchy perfumes.

Köves Clifford Chance advises existing clients on IP. It recently carried out due diligence for Bridgepoint Capital on its acquisition of music and book licensing company Mediasat Group.

IP registrations, enforcement and piracy issues are where the expertise of **Martonyi és Kajtár Baker & McKenzie** lies and it has worked for food and drink companies and a major Japanese electronics business.

At **Nagy és Trócsányi** intellectual property is handled where issues emerge from other transactions.

Réczicza White & Case LLP's two specialist areas lie in trade mark disputes and investigations and in software licences, with clients in the banking, sports and media sectors.

Réti, Antall & Madl LANDWELL registers trade marks and some patents, and litigates to protect them and other IP issues. It advises Swiss publishing group Ringier on IP issues.

Sándor Szegedi Szent-Ivány & Komáromi is active in registering trade marks, dealing with licence contracts and litigation on copyright and trade mark infringement.

Siegler Law Office/Weil, Gotshal & Manges has represented Danubius Hotels on trade mark and intellectual property issues, DMX Music on copyright and in a dispute involving payment of royalties, Donna Karan in lawsuits concerning copied DKNY goods and Híd Rádio Rt, publisher of Hungarian tabloid *Színes Bulvár*, on trade mark infringement and disputes.

INTELLECTUAL PROPERTY

BERECZ & ANDRÉKÓ LINKLATERS ✪
DANUBIA
SBG & K PATENT AND LAW OFFICES

Oppenheim és Társai Freshfields Bruckhaus Deringer
Szecskay – Attorneys at Law ✪

Bogsch & Partners
Kovács Réti Szegheö Attorneys at Law
Köves Clifford Chance
Martonyi és Kajtár Baker & McKenzie ✪
Nagy és Trócsányi ✪
Nógrádi Law Office
Réti, Antall & Madl LANDWELL
Sándor Szegedi Szent-Ivány & Komáromi ✪
Siegler Law Office/Weil, Gotshal & Manges ✪

Firms are listed A-Z in tiers which are ranked in order of priority
✪ *Indicates firm displays contact details at the end of this chapter.*

MERGERS AND ACQUISITIONS

Investor confidence in Hungary has continued to grow, boosted to some extent by EU accession, leading to a higher number of acquisitions. At the same time local companies are looking to build a presence across the region.

Berecz & Andrékó Linklaters represented a bidder for Budapest Airport, the largest privatisation project yet in Hungary, and a major Hungarian bank as it made acquisitions around the region. Private equity is a specialism and JP Morgan and Bancroft Private Equity are among recent clients.

Dr. Éva Hegedûs in association with Allen & Overy LLP represented telecoms and pharmaceuticals companies on acquisitions, and also worked with Swisscom on its successful bid for a majority stake in Antenna Hungária. It advised a consortium bidding for Budapest Airport.

Köves Clifford Chance sees itself as an all-rounder, but M&A is a particular focus. Clients see it as 'capable of handling the most difficult deals without involving London-based colleagues'. In

MERGERS AND ACQUISITIONS

BERECZ & ANDRÉKÓ LINKLATERS ✪
ÉVA HEGEDÛS (DR.) IN ASSOCIATION WITH ALLEN & OVERY LLP ✪
KÖVES CLIFFORD CHANCE
MARTONYI ÉS KAJTÁR BAKER & McKENZIE ✪
RÉCZICZA WHITE & CASE LLP
SIEGLER LAW OFFICE/WEIL, GOTSHAL & MANGES ✪

CMS Cameron McKenna LLP ✪
Erös Üqyvédi Iroda Squire, Sanders & Dempsey LLP ✪
Forgó, Varga and Partners ✪
Nagy és Trócsányi ✪
Oppenheim és Társai Freshfields Bruckhaus Deringer

Dezsö & Partners
Gide Loyrette Nouel – Molnár & Ferenczy ✪
Horváth & Partners DLA Weiss-Tessbach ✪
Kovács Réti Szegheö Attorneys at Law ✪
Luther, Fest & Kajli Attorneys ✪
Nagy & Pintér Hogan & Hartson ✪
Nógrádi Law Office
Nörr Stiefenhofer Lutz ✪
Réti, Antall & Madl LANDWELL
Sándor Szegedi Szent-Ivány & Komáromi ✪
Squarra & Partos (in association with Lovells) ✪
Szecskay – Attorneys at Law ✪

Burai – Kovács & Partners
Gárdos, Füredi, Mosonyi, Tomori, Law Office of
SBG & K Patent and Law Offices
Szabó, Kővári, Tercsák és Társai Ügyvédi Iroda (in cooperation with Salans)

Firms are listed A-Z in tiers which are ranked in order of priority
✪ Indicates firm displays contact details at the end of this chapter.

2005 it advised private equity investor Warburg Pincus in its acquisition of Euromedic International, one of the highest-value private equity deals seen in the region during the year, and CSFB, representing the Hungarian State, on the sale of Budapest Airport.

The nine-strong dedicated M&A team at **Martonyi és Kajtár Baker & McKenzie** is recommended for 'strategic thinking, flexibility and creativity'. It is working with businesses as they look to expand in the region, among them Magyar Telecom on buying stakes in Telekom Crne Gore, of Montenegro, and T-Systems Hungary Kft. It also advised Hungarian energy company Mol on the sale of its natural gas businesses in late 2004, a deal that media reports put at nearly €2bn.

Name partner István Réczicza of **Réczicza White & Case LLP** advised BAA, the winning bidder in the privatisation of Budapest Airport during 2005, while partner Rob Irving led a team advising management of Euromedic International on its sale to Warburg Pincus in one of the biggest deals of the year and represented AIG-CET Capital Management (Poland) Ltd on its acquisition of a stake in Romanian engineering-to-facilities management conglomerate UTI Group, one of the largest private equity deals so far seen in Romania.

Siegler Law Office/Weil, Gotshal & Manges has particular expertise in private equity and venture capital. A team led by managing partner David Dederick represented the shareholders of Euromedic International in the US$100m sale of the company to Warburg Pincus in one of the largest private equity deals of 2005. In addition it advised Fraport AG and Deutsche Bank AG on their bid for Budapest Airport. It is praised for 'constructive solutions' in 'tight timeframes'.

CMS Cameron McKenna LLP works with international and domestic companies, and is recommended for its work with media and pharmaceutical companies. During 2005 it advised shareholders of Elekthermax Ltd on its sale to Candy Elettrodomestici Srl, and IBM on the Hungarian aspects of the transfer of its PCD business to Lenovo.

Erös Üqyvédi Iroda Squire, Sanders & Dempsey LLP's staff represented bidders for Antenna Hungária and for national airline Malév during 2005, as well as working on a number of corporate acquisitions.

Forgó, Varga and Partners is recommended for 'quality and speed'. The firm is working on the refinancing of the motorways and on the privatisation of Budapest Airport. Clients also include aerospace group EADS Group, which it advised on the Hungarian aspects of its acquisition of Nokia's Professional Mobile Radio business and Austrian Post, represented on its acquisition of a Hungarian postal company.

Nagy és Trócsányi advised on the acquisition of a company by NKT Group.

Oppenheim és Társai Freshfields Bruckhaus Deringer represents both domestic and international companies on M&A within Hungary and advises on the Hungarian aspects of international deals handled by the firm's network. It worked for UniCredit on its proposed merger with HVB, and Pearson on the restructuring of its Hungarian investments, and has a 'good knowledge of the Hungarian regulatory system'.

Dezsö & Partners advised a bidder tendering for Budapest Airport and a leading US sportswear manufacturer and retailer on buying a chain of shops in Hungary.

The team at **Gide Loyrette Nouel – Molnár & Ferenczy**, led by managing partner Jacques de Servigny, largely advises French companies in sectors including supermarkets and food production, and also worked on the privatisation of Budapest's exhibition park.

Horváth & Partners DLA Weiss-Tessbach has advised bidders on privatisation projects, among them a consortium of investors bidding for Budapest Airport, and a bidder in the Antenna Hungária privatisation.

Partner Dr András Réti is the M&A specialist at **Kovács Réti Szegheö Attorneys at Law**, which recently represented the Carnex Group in acquisitions within the food industry and worked on the takeover of a Hungarian car windscreen maker by a US investor.

Luther, Fest & Kajli Attorneys has acted on a number of complex transactions, including for a major listed French company on the acquisition of 20 Hungarian subsidiaries and their subsequent restructuring.

Nagy & Pintér Hogan & Hartson advised Hungarian pharmaceutical company Richter Gedeon in acquiring land and then building a joint venture factory in India. It also represented an investor buying a stake in a secondary Hungarian airport.

Nógrádi Law Office advises mid-sized businesses on corporate growth.

Lawyers at **Nörr Stiefenhofer Lutz** have handled acquisitions and restructurings for Italian, British and German companies in sectors from white goods to software and energy.

Réti, Antall & Madl LANDWELL's experience is in advising on privatisations. It represented the state privatisation agency on the sale of Dunaferr and exhibition hall Hungexpo, and bidders for broadcasting tower business Antenna Hungária and Budapest Airport during 2005.

Sándor Szegedi Szent-Ivány & Komáromi has handled mergers, acquisitions and related restructurings in a wide range of industries. In 2005 it represented the Austrian purchaser of a printing house and worked on the restructurings of a multinational media group and a major Hungarian car dealer group.

Squarra & Partos (in association with Lovells) represents international companies, including Icelandic pharmaceuticals firm Actavis when it bought Kéri Pharma.

Szecskay – Attorneys at Law advised bankers financing acquisitions and buyers and sellers in a number of major privatisations carried out in 2004 and 2005.

Burai – Kovács & Partners handles company acquisitions by Hungarian companies outside the country and foreign companies inside Hungary. It recently represented a paper production company buying businesses in Bulgaria, and UK and French investors buying a Hungarian broadcasting group.

Law Office of Gárdos, Füredi, Mosonyi, Tomori handles regular M&A work including in the area of finance and capital markets.

Szabó, Kővári, Tercsák és Társai Ügyvédi Iroda (in cooperation with Salans) represents clients beyond the Hungarian border, where recent work includes advising a US stock market-listed company on the sale of its IT and internet subsidiary based in Slovakia to an investor there.

PROJECT FINANCE

BERECZ & ANDRÉKÓ LINKLATERS ✪
CMS CAMERON McKENNA LLP ✪
KÖVES CLIFFORD CHANCE
OPPENHEIM ÉS TÁRSAI FRESHFIELDS BRUCKHAUS DERINGER

Éva Hegedûs (Dr.) in association with Allen & Overy LLP ✪
Horváth & Partners DLA Weiss-Tessbach ✪
Martonyi és Kajtár Baker & McKenzie ✪
Nagy és Trócsányi ✪
Réczicza White & Case LLP

Bihary, Balassa & Partners Attorneys at Law ✪
Nörr Stiefenhofer Lutz ✪
Siegler Law Office/Weil, Gotshal & Manges ✪
Squarra & Partos (in association with Lovells) ✪
Szecskay – Attorneys at Law ✪

Firms are listed A-Z in tiers which are ranked in order of priority
✪ Indicates firm displays contact details at the end of this chapter.

PROJECT FINANCE

The continuing move towards privatisation and towards funding infrastructure expansion through PPP has fuelled the market over the last year. The financing of planned expansion of the motorway network is particularly significant.

Berecz & Andrékó Linklaters has built its reputation for project finance on major public deals such as the development of the motorway network, on which it acted for the Hungarian government during 2004 and is instructed for its 'experience and regional presence'. It also represented banks on the privatisation of exhibition space Hungexpo and the development of a shopping centre in Romania.

CMS Cameron McKenna LLP has experience of both privatisation and public procurement financings, advising a construction consortium on its bid for the first phase of the M6 motorway concession.

Köves Clifford Chance worked for the Ministry of Economy and Transport in 2004 and early 2005 on a complex PPP to finance the €750m restructuring of the M5 motorway, billed as the first genuine road PPP transaction in the country. The firm's Péter Köves and Gergely Horváth also advised a number of banks providing project financing on the construction of the €470m M6.

The **Oppenheim és Társai Freshfields Bruckhaus Deringer** team, led by Ottó Daróczi, has experience of some of Hungary's highest-profile project finance deals, including acting for the M6 motorway concession consortium on a potential refinancing. It advised several parties in the privatisation of Budapest Airport, including a bidder and a lender.

Partner Marcell Németh leads the six-strong banking and finance team at **Dr. Éva Hegedûs in association with Allen & Overy LLP** on projects, including advising Budapest Airport on the rebuilding of Terminal 1, the Municipality of Budapest on a major property development project and MVB bank on a student accommodation PFI in Eastern Hungary.

Horváth & Partners DLA Weiss-Tessbach has a standalone team dealing with PPP. In 2005 it worked for Erste Bank Hungary, funding a number of office, apartment and hotel buildings, and advised a consortium including construction company Strabag Rt and Erste Bank on PPP projects to build schools, university buildings and a penitentiary.

Property and education are core areas for the project finance team at **Martonyi és Kajtár Baker & McKenzie** that is working on deals in Hungary and neighbouring Ukraine.

Nagy és Trócsányi has strong experience in advising both banks and borrowers. Name partner Péter Nagy advises the National Motorway Corporation on fundraising to expand the motorway network, while partner Péter Berethalmi has advised Inteligo on financing for low-cost airline WizzAir.

Réczicza White & Case LLP advised Thales SA and T-Systems in their successful negotiations of a long-term PPP contract with the Budapest Transportation Authority. The team, recommended for its handling of 'complex' transactions, advised four international banks on funding the motorway system during 2004 and continues to work on the final €150m phase of the M5 project.

Bihary, Balassa & Partners Attorneys at Law advises Hungarian and foreign investors entering the market on legal issues relating to projects.

Nörr Stiefenhofer Lutz represents a number of international banks involved in project finance deals.

The team at **Siegler Law Office/Weil, Gotshal & Manges** works on commercial property financings and refinancings for clients including GTC Global Trade Centers in both Croatia and Romania. It is also advising Hungarian bank OTP Bank on issues including the €100m development of a new digital communications system, to be financed through PPP.

Squarra & Partos (in association with Lovells)' experience is in PPP projects and the firm has also worked on motorway financing.

Szecskay – Attorneys at Law acts for both banks and property companies on financing high-value real estate developments. It has advised international investors looking into future PPP financing of schools, hospitals, prisons and other infrastructure.

REAL ESTATE

CMS CAMERON MCKENNA LLP ✪
RÉCZICZA WHITE & CASE LLP

Berecz & Andrékó Linklaters ✪
Dezsö & Partners
Erös Üqyvédi Iroda Squire, Sanders & Dempsey LLP ✪
Horváth & Partners DLA Weiss-Tessbach ✪
Köves Clifford Chance
Luther, Fest & Kajli Attorneys ✪
Martonyi és Kajtár Baker & McKenzie ✪
Nagy és Trócsányi ✪
Nógrádi Law Office
Oppenheim és Társai Freshfields Bruckhaus Deringer
Réti, Antall & Madl LANDWELL
Siegler Law Office/Weil, Gotshal & Manges ✪
Szabó, Kővári, Tercsák és Társai Ügyvédi Iroda (in cooperation with Salans)

CHSH Szécsényi Ugyvédi Iroda Cerha Hempel Spiegelfeld Hlawati ✪
Dessewffy Bellák & Partners Law Office
Éva Hegedûs (Dr.) in association with Allen & Overy LLP ✪
Gide Loyrette Nouel – Molnár & Ferenczy ✪
Haarmann Hemmelrath ✪
Kovács Réti Szegheö Attorneys at Law ✪
Nagy & Pintér Hogan & Hartson ✪
Nörr Stiefenhofer Lutz ✪
Sándor Szegedi Szent-Ivány & Komáromi ✪
Squarra & Partos (in association with Lovells) ✪
Szecskay – Attorneys at Law ✪

Firms are listed A-Z in tiers which are ranked in order of priority
✪ Indicates firm displays contact details at the end of this chapter.

REAL ESTATE

Hungary is seeing keen interest in real estate, which has intensified since its accession to the EU further boosted market confidence. Real estate deals usually include M&A work, with transactions structured, for tax reasons, around the sale of companies holding a single asset – the property.

CMS Cameron McKenna LLP has a strong reputation for its advice to developers, real estate funds and financing banks. Its seven-strong team, led by partner Dr Gábor Czike, continued in 2005 to advise Bouygues, the developer of a major entertainment, shopping and hotel complex the Kerepesi Project, while working on a number of multi-million euro acquisitions of office buildings and shopping centres.

Réczicza White & Case LLP has seen its real estate practice grow rapidly, working for UK, US and German real estate funds and shopping centre developer Plaza Centers (Europe) in Hungary, Poland and the Czech Republic. Clients recommend Greg Medley and István Réczicza at 'one of the top law firms we've used worldwide,' for 'creativity and commercialism'.

Berecz & Andrékó Linklaters has strengthened its practice with the recruitment of a new, five-strong team. Department head Dr Katalin Dévald has been with the firm since

August 2005 and her experience on major projects including the Four Seasons Hotel Gresham Palace and the Bank Center office building are likely to boost the practice's standing in future. The firm acts for real estate funds, banks and German construction company Hochtief on its first development projects in Hungary.

Dezsö & Partners works for real estate funds including Deutsche Bank Real Estate and IVG, part of the Deutsche Telekom Group, as well as other UK, Irish and Dutch investors. Partner Katalin Veszely is well known in the field.

Audi and financial advisers Guardian Managers Ltd were among the real estate clients of **Erös Üqyvédi Iroda Squire, Sanders & Dempsey LLP,** which also represented a number of US manufacturers establishing new plants in Hungary and a group of European real estate investors.

In 2005 **Horváth & Partners DLA Weiss-Tessbach** recruited two new associates to a practice which represents international real estate investors and developers including Talentis Programiroda Kht, developer of the Talentis golf and leisure centre.

Köves Clifford Chance's approach to real estate has previously been in terms of financing, but its clients now include real estate funds, investment banks and German industrial company INA Shaffler Group, buying land for a factory.

Luther, Fest & Kajli Attorneys advises leading real estate funds and developers from the UK, the US, and Germany on the buying, selling and leasing of commercial property and is recommended for its 'very high-quality, extremely thorough' approach, backed up by 'a lot of experience and a strong understanding of Hungarian law'.

Tesco Global is one of the major clients at **Martonyi és Kajtár Baker & McKenzie**'s commercial property practice, which deals with services from sales and acquisitions to leases and specialises in providing related tax advice. The five-member team, led by name partner Géza Kajtár, also advised clients including Europolis Invest and the Hungarian subsidiary of AIG/Lincoln Properties.

Nagy és Trócsányi advises international development companies from Hungary, Germany, Poland and beyond.

Oppenheim és Társai Freshfields Bruckhaus Deringer advises on building, buying and selling logistics centres, office buildings, shops and hotels. Notably it has worked with Spanish developer Fadesa to buy land for the Budapest Central Passage development, a €45m, 80-hectare mixed-use development.

Réti, Antall & Madl LANDWELL buys property including office buildings and industrial plants on behalf of real estate funds. The capacity of its real estate practice, however, has been somewhat limited by the departure of partners including real estate specialist Katalin Veszely to form rival practice **Dezsö & Partners**.

The focus at **Siegler Law Office/Weil, Gotshal & Manges** is primarily on real estate transactions, both inside and outside Hungary, although it has construction law expertise as well. Clients include the DeBenedetti Group in the financing of a residential and retail development in Bulgaria and Rockspring Property Management in acquisitions, developments and leasings within the region.

Szabó, Kővári, Tercsák és Társai Ügyvédi Iroda (in cooperation with Salans) worked with international property investors before joining the real estate-focused **Salans** network, but the year and a half since then has seen its practice strengthen. The firm represents developers from Holland, Sweden and the UK, advising on the buying, selling and leasing of offices and industrial buildings, and is strongly recommended by clients.

CHSH Szécsényi Ugyvédi Iroda Cerha Hempel Spiegelfeld Hlawati advises Austrian, German and Hungarian property investors on acquisitions and sales. They include, notably, Vienna-listed developer Immoeast on deals including the €210m acquisition of a chain of shopping centres.

The highest-profile job at **Dessewffy Bellák & Partners Law Office** in 2005 was advising Real 4 You Group on building its Duna Tower skyscraper in Budapest. The firm works for predominantly Austrian, German and Hungarian investors and acted for the local franchise of a well-known US fast food chain on buying sites.

Dr. Éva Hegedûs in association with Allen & Overy LLP specialises in providing finance for real estate deals. In 2005 they included advising the Municipality of Budapest on a major property development project.

British solicitor Charles Cruden now heads the real estate department at **Gide Loyrette Nouel – Molnár & Ferenczy** following the move in-house of partner Dr Judit Gaál. Deals across the region have included acting for global logistics company ProLogis on its €70m acquisition of Hungary's largest logistics park, Harbor Park.

Haarmann Hemmelrath is instructed by foreign and domestic investors and banks on residential and commercial property acquisitions and advised on the construction of a water theme park.

Kovács Réti Szegheö Attorneys at Law advises developers and construction companies from Germany, Austria, Israel and Spain, including Skanska. The firm is also advising Japanese tyre manufacturer Bridgestone on a greenfield development.

Nagy & Pintér Hogan & Hartson deals primarily with commercial and educational property, working for both the American International School of Budapest and the International Christian School of Budapest.

Real estate is a primary focus for the team at **Nörr Stiefenhofer Lutz** where recent work includes advising on the sale of the MOM-Park MFC retail and office building on behalf of Bayerische Landesbank and Bayerische Hausbau International. Other clients include Spanish real estate developer Habitat.

Sándor Szegedi Szent-Ivány & Komáromi works with investors building hotels and related developments both inside and outside Hungary. In 2005 it also advised on the sale of an office building.

Squarra & Partos (in association with Lovells) advises on buying and selling office buildings, industrial and retail property, representing the Dawnay Day group, when it bought four Hungarian shopping centres from the Plaza Group.

Szecskay – Attorneys at Law specialises in advising greenfield investors and developers, on retail and industrial parks. It has worked with a major French supermarket chain and has represented a number of Hungarian wine cellars buying or leasing rural premises.

TMT

Technology, media and telecoms are growing industries in Hungary, and a new Media Act is scheduled for publication in 2006.

British telecoms company BT is among the blue-chip names that come to **Berecz & Andrékó Linklaters** for legal advice on regulatory issues from a team led by associate Dr András Lendvai. The firm also advised Belgian media sales business RMB on the management buyout of its Hungarian subsidiary.

TMT

BERECZ & ANDRÉKÓ LINKLATERS ✪
ÉVA HEGEDÛS (DR.) IN ASSOCIATION WITH ALLEN & OVERY LLP ✪
KÖVES CLIFFORD CHANCE
RÉCZICZA WHITE & CASE LLP

CMS Cameron McKenna LLP ✪
Forgó, Varga and Partners ✪
Martonyi és Kajtár Baker & McKenzie ✪
Nagy és Trócsányi ✪
Oppenheim és Társai Freshfields Bruckhaus Deringer
Réti, Antall & Madl LANDWELL
SBG & K Patent and Law Offices
Siegler Law Office/Weil, Gotshal & Manges ✪

Bogsch & Partners
Danubia
Gide Loyrette Nouel – Molnár & Ferenczy ✪
Haarmann Hemmelrath ✪
Horváth & Partners DLA Weiss-Tessbach ✪
Kovács Réti Szegheö Attorneys at Law ✪
Squarra & Partos (in association with Lovells) ✪
Szecskay – Attorneys at Law ✪

Firms are listed A-Z in tiers which are ranked in order of priority
✪ Indicates firm displays contact details at the end of this chapter.

Dr. Éva Hegedûs in association with Allen & Overy LLP advises national and international telecoms clients including BT and KPN Telecom on regulatory and related issues. In 2005 it acted for Swisscom on its successful bid for Antenna Hungária.

The team at **Köves Clifford Chance** has been concentrating on identifying regulatory opportunities in the region and has worked with its Washington, DC office to advise on the setting up of a telecoms regulatory body.

Réczicza White & Case LLP's expertise in telecoms regulation was called upon by Hungary's National Telecommunications Authority (NHH) for matters including advice on the third generation of mobile operator licences. It also worked with EADS Secure Networks which took over Nokia's professional mobile radio business in Hungary.

CMS Cameron McKenna LLP works for 'satisfied' IT clients including Siemens Hungary and has drafted contracts for the Bulgarian Telecom Company as the Eastern European state looks to put in place its next generation mobile phone network.

Forgó, Varga and Partners also acted for EADS on the Hungarian aspects of its acquisition of Nokia's professional radio business. In 2005 the firm, known for 'high service levels' strengthened its list of technology clients, which includes Logica CMG, EDS, Bloomberg, Blaupunkt and T-Com.

Martonyi és Kajtár Baker & McKenzie represents names including Deutsche Telekom subsidiaries Magyar Telecom and T-Com, which are expanding in the region. The firm's competition expertise is also brought to bear here.

Nagy és Trócsányi advised ORTT, the Hungarian National Board of Radio and Television, and Hungary's second-largest mobile phone company Pannon GSM on a number of matters, while partner Tibor Bogodan chaired the board of lawyers drafting the State's forthcoming Media Act.

Oppenheim és Társai Freshfields Bruckhaus Deringer is strong in media and broadcasting, and advised Sanoma on the launch of a new television channel and MTV on integrating its Viva TV Hungarian subsidiary into its business. Technology clients include, most notably, Microsoft.

Réti, Antall & Madl LANDWELL advises printing and media companies, including Swiss publishing group Ringier, which owns the leading Hungarian tabloid newspaper and bought, during 2005, the country's leading political paper. It also handles corporate work for IT companies.

SBG & K Patent and Law Offices advises businesses in this sector on the intellectual property-related issues.

Siegler Law Office/Weil, Gotshal & Manges works with broadcasters, particularly on M&A. Deals have included Emmis Communications Corporation's acquisitions of radio businesses in Hungary, Poland, Slovakia and Bulgaria.

Technology, media and telecoms companies are regular clients of **Bogsch & Partners** thanks to expertise in intellectual property. It also advises on issues related to software, domain names and internet and digital operations and represents the BBC in its Hungarian operations.

Danubia works with scientific and technology businesses on protecting their intellectual property rights, and takes enforcement action when they are infringed.

Gide Loyrette Nouel – Molnár & Ferenczy's focus is on media issues. Name partner István Molnár advised Hungarian media company Multi Reklám between 1993 and 2004.

Haarmann Hemmelrath has acted as counsel to Deutsche Telekom on employment-related issues.

Horváth & Partners DLA Weiss-Tessbach is taking on more TMT work, and advised a production company when it made a film in Hungary.

Kovács Réti Szegheö Attorneys at Law handles regulatory and licence issues for a Hungarian satellite system operator.

Squarra & Partos (in association with Lovells) has experience in telecoms, and represents a number of clients in the sector including a major broadband provider.

Szecskay – Attorneys at Law has represented technology companies, but perhaps more significantly has advised Hungarian ministries and regulatory bodies on e-commerce lawmaking.

TAX

Many law firms are agreed that tax advisers at the Big Four accountancy firms are the primary source of advice in this market. However law firms also have their own qualified tax advisers and lawyers in order to provide advice on the tax aspects of issues they are dealing with.

Berecz & Andrékó Linklaters has a dedicated tax team of three associates, who advise on the tax aspects of the firm's M&A and private equity deals.

Senior tax adviser István Keményfy at **Köves Clifford Chance** specialises in transactional tax issues, allowing the firm to give an all-round service to its clients.

Oppenheim és Társai Freshfields Bruckhaus Deringer has a three-member dedicated tax team, advising both high-net-worth individuals and local and foreign companies on income tax, corporate tax, VAT and other related areas.

The tax ligitation work of **Réti, Antall & Madl LANDWELL** complements the work of its partner, Big Four accountancy partner PricewaterhouseCoopers and the two work closely together, referring work to each other.

TAX

BERECZ & ANDRÉKÓ LINKLATERS ✪
KÖVES CLIFFORD CHANCE
OPPENHEIM ÉS TÁRSAI FRESHFIELDS BRUCKHAUS DERINGER
RÉTI, ANTALL & MADL LANDWELL

Burai – Kovács & Partners
Éva Hegedûs (Dr.) in association with Allen & Overy LLP ✪
Gide Loyrette Nouel – Molnár & Ferenczy ✪
Martonyi és Kajtár Baker & McKenzie ✪
Réczicza White & Case LLP

CMS Cameron McKenna LLP ✪
Haarmann Hemmelrath ✪
Nógrádi Law Office
Nörr Stiefenhofer Lutz ✪

Firms are listed A-Z in tiers which are ranked in order of priority
✪ Indicates firm displays contact details at the end of this chapter.

Burai – Kovács & Partners handles tax litigation for its international clients.

Dr. Éva Hegedûs in association with Allen & Overy LLP advises offshore US and Canadian companies on tax benefits, and in 2005 also worked with Goldman Sachs International and Deutsche Telekom on tax issues.

Gide Loyrette Nouel – Molnár & Ferenczy's dedicated tax team provides general tax consultancy as well as working on the tax aspects of mergers, acquisitions, corporate restructurings and real estate deals carried out elsewhere in the group.

A main focus of the tax team at **Martonyi és Kajtár Baker & McKenzie** is on the tax aspects of the real estate deals it services, although it also leads tax restructurings for blue-chip clients.

Tax litigation is a specialism at **Réczicza White & Case LLP**'s Budapest office.

The tax practice at **CMS Cameron McKenna LLP** specialises in advising private equity investors on tax issues in the region and also has strengths in VAT and tax breaks related to film financing.

Haarmann Hemmelrath has particular expertise in VAT, putting VAT systems in place for the Hungarian operation of an international car manufacturer as well as advising on corporate tax law.

Nörr Stiefenhofer Lutz employs both tax advisors and auditors in its tax department, who advise Bombardier Transportation, Lindner and Max Aicher Group among others.

ANDREAS NEOCLEOUS & CO – TULLER & KLESICS

BALASSI BU 25
1055 BUDAPEST

Telephone: +36 1 311 3135
Fax: +36 1 354 0677
E-mail: info.budapest@neocleous.com
Website: www.neocleous.com

Languages
English, German, Russian and local languages where Andreas Neocleous & Co operates

Other offices
Brussels, Limassol, Paphos, Nicosia, Moscow, Kiev, Prague

Number of lawyers 75
at this office 7

CATEGORIES OF WORK

Company and commercial law

Tax law and international tax planning

Intellectual property

IBC services

Litigation and arbitration

Property and construction

Leasing

Internet, e-commerce and IT law

Banking and finance

Project finance

Real estate

EC law

BÁRD, CSERI & PARTNERS

KRISZTINA KRT 39/B
1013 BUDAPEST

Telephone: +36 1 489 2020
Fax: +36 1 489 2022
E-mail: office@parallellaw.hu
Website: www parallellaw.hu

Languages
English, French, German, Italian

Number of lawyers 10

Member
Central East Europe Integration Group (CIG)

CATEGORIES OF WORK

Real estate
Dr Zsuzsanna Cseri, Dr Petra Lencs

Competition and antitrust
Dr Zsuzsanna Cseri, Dr Karoly Bárd

Mergers and acquisitions
Dr Karoly Bárd, Dr Zsuzsanna Cseri

Insurance
Dr Karoly Bárd

Arbitration
Dr Karoly Bárd

Employment
Dr Gabriella Nagy, Dr Erika Berdi

Media, publishing, newspapers
Dr Mariann Koranyi

EC laws
Dr Zsuzsanna Cseri

Insolvency and business recovery
Dr Mariann Koranyi

Corporate and commercial law
Dr Zsuzsanna Cseri, Dr Petra Lencs

Banking and finance
Dr Zsuzsanna Cseri, Dr Tibor Keves

BERECZ & ANDRÉKÓ LINKLATERS

AKADÉMIA BANK CENTER
SZÉCHENYI RAKPART 3
1054 BUDAPEST

Telephone: +36 1 428 4400
Fax: +36 1 428 4444
Website: www.linklaters.com

Languages
All commercial and local languages in the countries where Linklaters operates

Other offices
Amsterdam, Antwerp, Bangkok, Beijing, Berlin, Bratislava, Brussels, Bucharest, Cologne, Dubai, Frankfurt am Main, Hong Kong, Lisbon, London, Luxembourg, Madrid, Milan, Moscow, Munich, New York, Paris, Prague, Rome, São Paulo, Shanghai, Singapore, Stockholm, Tokyo, Warsaw

Number of lawyers 2,000 worldwide

Contact
Dr Csaba Berecz

CATEGORIES OF WORK

Corporate and commercial
Dr Csaba Berecz, David Davies

Mergers and acquisitions
David Davies

Banking
Dr Csilla Andrékó, Dr Csaba Berecz

Capital markets
Dr Csaba Berecz, Dr Andrea Miskolczi

Project finance
Dr Csilla Andrékó, Dr Gábor Pázsitka

Intellectual property
Dr András Lendvai

Energy regulatory
Dr Andrea Miskolczi

Tax
Dr Gábor Antal

EU/competition
Dr Dániel Kaszás

Technology, media and telecommunications
Dr András Lendvai

Real estate
Dr Katalin Dévald

Environmental
Dr Péter Peremiczki

Dispute resolution
Dr András Lendvai

BIHARY, BALASSA & PARTNERS ATTORNEYS AT LAW

HARANGVIRÁG U.5
1026 BUDAPEST

Telephone: +36 1 391 4491
Fax: +36 1 200 8047
E-mail: office@biharybalassa.hu
Website: www.biharybalassa.hu

Languages
English, French, German

Number of lawyers 12

CATEGORIES OF WORK

Banking and financial services

Company law

Competition law, unfair competition, antitrust law

Construction law

Dispute resolution and arbitration

Foreign investment in Hungary

Internet law

Joint ventures

Labour law

Media law

Mergers and acquisitions

Privatisation

Project finance

Public procurement

Real property law

Technology transfer

Telecommunications

CHSH SZÉCSÉNYI UGYVÉDI IRODA CERHA HEMPEL SPIEGELFELD HLAWATI

BUDAY LÁSZLO U 12
1024 BUDAPEST

Telephone: +36 1 345 4535
Fax: +36 1 345 4543
E-mail: office.chsh@szecsenyi.com
Website: www.chsh.at

Languages
English, German, Hungarian, Russian

Other offices
Brussels, Bucharest, Vienna

Number of lawyers 76
at this office 14

Contacts
Lászió Szécsényi, Alfred Nemetschke, Walter Anderi, Johannes Aehrenthal

CATEGORIES OF WORK

Banking, securities and finance
Kinga Hetényi, Gábor Érdi

Companies and corporations
Judit Vadász, Lászió Nanyista

Mergers and acquisitions
Kinga Hetényi, Judit Vadász

Arbitration and litigation
Margit Balogh

Commercial law and contracts
Kinga Hetényi

Franchising and distribution
Kinga Hetényi

Real estate, construction and buildings
Lászió Szécsényi

Privatisation and telecommunications
Lászió Szécsényi, Margit Balogh

Regulation, administrative and consitutional law
Margit Balogh

International and comparitive law
Lászió Szécsényi, Margit Balogh

CMS CAMERON McKENNA LLP

YBL PALACE, 3RD FLOOR
KAROLYI MIHALY UTCA 12
1053 BUDAPEST

Telephone: +36 1 483 4800
Fax: +36 1 483 4801
E-mail: info@cms-cmck.com
Website: www.law-now.com

Languages
English, French, German, Hungarian

Other offices
Aberdeen, Bristol, Bucharest, Edinburgh, Hong Kong, London, Moscow, Prague, Sofia, Warsaw

Number of lawyers 587
at this office 53

Contact
Gabriella Ormai

International grouping
CMS Cameron McKenna is a member of CMS. CMS is the alliance of major European law firms providing clients with a full range of legal and tax services. CMS's activities are co-ordinated through EEIG, registered in Brussels.

CATEGORIES OF WORK

Company and commercial
Dr Gabriella Ormai, Dr Balazs Kokeny

Corporate finance, M&A, capital markets
Dr Gabriella Ormai, Robert Hayhurst, Dr Ferenc Matrai, Dr Aniko Kircsi

Dispute resolution, litigation, ADR
Dr Milan Kohlrusz, Dr Nikoletta Szederjessy

E-commerce, IT, telecoms
Dr Gabriella Ormai, Dr Balazs Kokeny

Intellectual property and media
Dr Gabriella Ormai

International finance, banking and restructuring
Alex Doughty, Dr Erika Papp

Property and construction
Dr Gabor Czike

Tax
Dr Gabriella Ormai

Energy and projects
Dr Ferenc Matrai, Dr Peter Simon

Pharmaceuticals
Dr Gabriella Ormai

ERÖS ÜGYVÉDI IRODA
SQUIRE, SANDERS & DEMPSEY L.L.P.

ANDRÁSSY ÚT 64
1062 BUDAPEST

Telephone: +36 1 428 7111
Fax: +36 1 428 7100
E-mail: aeros@ssd.com
Website: www.ssd.com

Languages
English, French, German, Hungarian, Italian, Romanian, Russian, Slovak, Spanish

Other offices
Beijing, Bratislava, Brussels, Caracas, Cincinnati, Cleveland, Columbus, Hong Kong, Houston, London, Los Angeles, Miami, Moscow, New York, Palo Alto, Phoenix, Prague, Rio de Janeiro, San Francisco, Santo Domingo, Shanghai, Tallahassee, Tampa, Tokyo, Tysons Corner, Warsaw, Washington DC, West Palm Beach, Bucharest*, Buenos Aires*, Dublin*, Kyiv*, Milan*, Santiago*

Number of lawyers 800+
at this office 13

Contact Ákos Eros

Member
American Chamber of Commerce; Joint Venture Association, Hungary; Hungary-Japan Economic Club; Hungarian Chamber of Commerce

CATEGORIES OF WORK

Capital markets
Kevin Connor, Dr Ákos Mester

Corporate finance, banking
Dr Ákos Erös, Kevin Connor

EU competition law
Dr Ákos Mester

Infrastructure, project asset finance
Kevin Connor, Dr Ákos Erös

Intellectual property
Dr Ákos Mester

International arbitration
Dr Iván Szász, Dr Judit Kelemen

International transactions
Dr Ákos Erös, Kevin Connor

Labour law
Dr Judit Nádor, Csaba Vari

Litigation
Dr Judit Kelemen, Artúr Tamási

Mergers and acquisitions
Dr Ákos Erös

Power generation, energy
Dr Ákos Erös, Artúr Tamási

Privatisations
Dr Iván Szász, Dr Ákos Erös

Real estate
Kevin Connor, Dr Ákos Mester

Securities
Dr Ákos Erös, Dr Ákos Mester

THE FIRM

Founded in 1890, Squire, Sanders & Dempsey is a multi-jurisdictional law firm with approximately 800 lawyers practising in offices in Europe, the Americas and Asia. The firm's practice covers most substantive areas of the law, with an emphasis on business and finance matters.

The firm operates as a single global partnership, which ensures client accountability and the seamless delivery of uniformly high-quality legal services throughout the world. The firm's lawyers come from many countries and cultures, are licensed to practise in both common law and civil law jurisdictions, and communicate with clients in their native languages. Today, the firm remains committed to the fundamental principles ordained by its founders: to serve clients effectively and to maintain the professional standards that distinguish both the firm and its people.

AREAS OF PRACTICE

The firm is organised around four major practice areas: advocacy, business, capital markets and regulated industries. Within these practice areas, the firm's work can be divided into numerous areas of specialisation, including banking, bankruptcy and restructuring, biotechnology and pharmaceuticals, communications, competition law, converging technologies, corporate, energy, environmental, healthcare, intellectual property, international dispute resolution, labour and employment, litigation, mergers and acquisitions, privatisations, project finance, real estate, securities and taxation.

Since its opening in 1991, the Squire Sanders Budapest office has served as an adviser to clients on key privatisation and investment opportunities, financing and securitisations, mergers and acquisitions, joint ventures, intellectual property, regulatory, communications, energy, real estate, labour and environmental issues. A multilingual staff of lawyers includes Western-trained foreign lawyers.

Considered one of the leading law firms in Hungary, the Budapest office provides counsel to Hungarian firms and foreign entities doing business in the region as well as to governmental institutions.

Intellectual property rights, joint ventures and licensing arrangements are among the matters lawyers handle for clients. In addition, the Budapest office has represented a number of businesses in connection with cross-border litigation, arbitration and commercial transactions.

e|n|w|c ATTORNEYS AT LAW

EISELSBERG NATLACEN WALDERDORFF CANCOLA

DOROTTYA U 1
1051 BUDAPEST

Telephone: +36 1 327 0407
Fax: +36 1 327 0410
E-mail: budapest@enwc.com
Website: www.enwc.com

Languages
Czech, English, French, German, Italian, Polish, Slovak

Other offices
Bratislava, Brno, Prague, Vienna, Warsaw

Number of lawyers 47
at this office 7

Contacts
Dr Raimund Cancola, Dr Roland Kölcsey-Rieden

CATEGORIES OF WORK

Company and commercial

Intellectual property

Mergers and acquisitions

International arbitration and litigation

Banking and finance

Insurance

Labour and employment

Real estate

Construction and building

EU law

DR ÉVA HEGEDÛS IN ASSOCIATION WITH ALLEN & OVERY LLP

MADÁCH TRADE CENTER
MADÁCH IMRE UTCA 13-14
1075 BUDAPEST

Telephone: +36 1 483 2200
Fax: +36 1 268 1515
E-mail: information@allenovery.com
Website: www.allenovery.com

Languages
English, French, German, Hungarian

Other offices
Amsterdam, Antwerp, Bangkok, Beijing, Bratislava, Brussels, Dubai, Frankfurt, Hamburg, Hong Kong, London, Luxembourg, Madrid, Milan, Moscow, New York, Paris, Prague, Rome, Shanghai, Singapore, Tokyo, Turin, Warsaw

Number of lawyers 2,304
at this office 19

Contacts
Éva Hegedûs, Zoltàn Lengyel, Marcell Németh

CATEGORIES OF WORK

Banking/finance
Marcell Németh

International capital markets
Zoltán Lengyel

Corporate/commercial
Eva Hegedûs

Derivatives
Zoltán Lengyel

Energy
Marcell Németh

Environment
Éva Hegedûs

EU law
Tamás Riesz, Éva Hegedûs

Competition
Tamás Riesz

Intellectual property

PPP
Marcell Németh

Mergers and acquisitions
Éva Hegedûs

Privatisation
Éva Hegedûs, Zoltán Lengyel

Project finance and trade finance
Marcell Németh

Real estate
Éva Hegedûs, Tamás Riesz

Telecommunications/media
Tamás Riesz

Offshore
Ágnes Bejó

Tax
Levente Torma

Private equity
Éva Hegedûs, Marcell Németh

FORGÓ, VARGA & PARTNERS

LAW FIRM

ALKOTÁS U 17-19 (DÉLI POINT)
III FLOOR
1123 BUDAPEST

Telephone: +36 1 214 0080
Fax: +36 1 214 0078
E-mail: office@forgovarga.com

Languages
English

Number of lawyers 10

Contacts
Zoltán Forgó, János Tamás Varga

CATEGORIES OF WORK

- Company law
- Mergers and acquisitions
- Venture capital
- Privatisation
- Internet
- E-commerce
- Information technology
- Intellectual property rights
- PPP, infrastructure
- Telecommunications
- Media
- Commercial law
- Competition law
- Labour law
- Litigation
- Arbitration
- Pharmaceuticals

GIDE LOYRETTE NOUEL

EMKE BUILDING
RÁKÓCZI ÚT 42, BP 409
1072 BUDAPEST

Telephone: +36 1 411 7400
Fax: +36 1 411 7440
E-mail: gln.budapest@gide.com
Website: www.gide.com

Other offices
Algiers, Beijing, Belgrade, Brussels, Bucharest, Casablanca, Hanoi, Istanbul, London, Moscow, New York, Paris, Prague, Riyadh, Shanghai, Tunis, Warsaw

Number of lawyers 586
at this office 18

Contacts
Jacques de Servigny (servigny@gide.com),
István Molnár (molnar@gide.com),
Balázs József Ferenczy (ferenczy@gide.com)

CATEGORIES OF WORK

- Mergers and acquisitions
- Privatisation
- Company law
- Real estate transactions and financing
- Project finance
- Banking and finance
- Capital markets and business leasing
- Telecommunications
- Communications and media – new technologies
- Competition and distribution
- Intellectual property
- Employment law and social benefits
- Tax
- Arbitration and litigation
- Energy, environment and transport

HORVÁTH & PARTNERS DLA WEISS-TESSBACH

ALKOTÁS U. 50
1123 BUDAPEST

Telephone: +36 1 325 3020
Fax: +36 1 325 3021
E-mail: budapest@dlapiper.com
Website: www.dlapiper.com

Languages
English, German, Hungarian

Other offices
Austria, Belgium, Bosnia-Herzegovina, China, Croatia, Czech Republic, Denmark*, Egypt*, France, Georgia, Germany, Hong Kong, Italy, Japan, Netherlands, Norway*, Poland*, Russia, Singapore*, Slovakia, South Africa*, Spain, Sweden*, Thailand, UK, Ukraine, United Arab Emirates, US

Number of lawyers 3,100
at this office 27

Contact
Dr Mónika Horváth

Member
DLA Piper Group

CATEGORIES OF WORK

Corporate/M&A
Dr Mónika Horváth, Dr András Posztl

Banking/projects/real estate
Dr Péter Györfi-Tóth,
Dr Rita Hoffmann

General commercial/ labour law/litigation
Dr Helga Fehér

Intellectual property
Dr Rita Hoffmann

THE FIRM

Horváth & Partners, the Budapest office of DLA Weiss-Tessbach has 27 lawyers. Established in 1878, DLA Weiss-Tessbach is one of Austria's oldest law firms. It was one of the first international firms to open an office in Hungary (1989). Across Central and Eastern Europe, DLA Weiss-Tessbach has seven offices. It will continue to expand in the region as countries adjust to EU membership.

The firm is part of DLA Piper Rudnick Gray Cary, a leading global legal services provider with approximately 3,100 lawyers in 58 offices across 22 countries. The organisation is committed to building long-term relationships with its clients and supports their strategic and operational needs both locally and internationally.

AREAS OF PRACTICE

The firm has strengthened its core areas of expertise (commercial and corporate, M&A, banking and finance, general commercial law, real estate), and advises its clients as a full-service law firm in all relevant areas of business law, including administrative law, employment law, IT and telecoms, technology, intellectual property, venture capital and capital markets.

It has well-established relations with clients of various backgrounds. The firm advises small and medium-sized enterprises as well as leading (often publicly listed) international and domestic industrial groups, service providers, banks and other financial institutions and individuals.

The firm has established a particular reputation for its ability to handle cases in international cross-border contexts. It is renowned for its expertise in the structuring and implementation of projects and transactions in Hungary, as well as in other countries in Central and Eastern Europe. It carefully views the ongoing developments in the Central and Eastern European region with the aim of combining the needs of the constantly changing international legal market and industry, whilst also upholding the high standard of service that the firm has always been able to offer to its clients.

HAARMANN HEMMELRATH

DEÁK FERENC U. 15
1052 BUDAPEST

Telephone: +36 1 484 0484
Fax: +36 1 484 0433
E-mail: budapest@haarmannhemmelrath.com
Website: www.haarmannhemmelrath.com

Languages
Bulgarian, Croatian, Czech, Dutch, English, Finnish, French, Italian, Japanese, Mandarin, Norwegian, Polish, Portuguese, Romanian, Russian, Slovak, Spanish, Vietnamese

Other offices
Bielefeld, Bucharest, Düsseldorf, Frankfurt, Hamburg, Leipzig, Moscow, Munich, Paris, Prague, Shanghai, Warsaw

Number of lawyers 226

CATEGORIES OF WORK

Mergers and acquisitions
Dr Andrea Jádi Németh, John Wager

Corporate
Dr Andrea Jádi Németh

Labour
Dr Eszter Berta

International tax
Dr Eszter Berta

Arbitration and litigation
Dr Andrea Jádi Németh, John Wager

Greenfield investments
Martin Wodraschke

Commercial real estate
Dr Andrea Jádi Németh, Dr Eszter Berta

Banking and project finance (construction)
Dr Eszter Berta, John Wager

Joint ventures and investments in central and eastern Europe
Dr Martin Wodraschke

KOVÁCS RÉTI SZEGHEÖ ATTORNEYS AT LAW

ZUGLIGETI ÚT 41
1121 BUDAPEST

Telephone: +36 1 275 2785
Fax: +36 1 275 2784
E-mail: krs@krs.hu
Website: www.krs.hu

Languages
English, French, German, Hungarian, Italian

Number of lawyers 15

Contact
Dr Tamas Matarits

Member
Central and Eastern European Law Offices (CELO); Balms Group International (BGI); Geneva Group International (GGI); Lawyers Associated Worldwide (LAW)

CATEGORIES OF WORK

Corporate and commercial
Dr Attila Kovács

Mergers and acquisitions
Dr András Réti

Commercial property
Dr Attila Kovács

Greenfield investment
Dr Olga Réti

Competition, trade, EU law
Dr Tamás Matarits

Intellectual property
Dr Zita Tamás

Labour and employment law
Dr Zita Orbán

Insolvency law
Dr Tamás Matarits

Arbitration, litigation, ADR
Dr Kálmán Gyárfás

LUTHER, FEST & KAJLI ATTORNEYS-AT-LAW

VÁCI ÚT 20
1132 BUDAPEST

Telephone: +36 1 451 8640
Fax: +36 1 451 8669
E-mail: arne.gobert@hu.ey.com

Languages
English, French, German, Hungarian

Other offices
Athens, Berlin, Bratislava, Brusssels, Bucharest, Chisinau, Cologne, Courbevoie, Dresden, Düsseldorf, Eindhoven, Ekaterinburg, Eschborn, Essen, Frankfurt, Grenoble, Hamburg, Hanover, Istanbul, Kiev, Leipzig, Lyon, Madrid, Mannheim, Marseille, Milan, Montpellier, Moscow, Munich, Nantes, Naples, Nice, Paris, Poznan, Prague, Riga, Rome, Rotterdam, Salonica, Sofia, St Petersburg, Strasbourg, Stuttgart, Tallin, Tbilisi, Toulouse, Turin, Vienna, Vilnius, Warsaw, Wroclaw, Yuhno-Sakhalins, Zurich

Number of lawyers 1,500

Contact Dr Arne Gobert (managing partner)

International groupings
Luther

CATEGORIES OF WORK

Corporate law and M&A
Dr Arne Gobert, Dr Attila Fest

Energy, oil and gas
Dr Arne Gobert

Real estate
Dr Arne Gobert, Dr Linda Kajli

IP/IT
Dr Attila Fest

Labour law
Dr Imre Krisch, Dr Arne Gobert

Corporate insolvency and bankruptcy
Dr Linda Kajli

Litigation and arbitration
Dr Imre Krisch, Dr Attila Fest

Competition law
Dr Imre Krisch

Commercial law
Dr Linda Kajli, Dr Attila Fest

EU law
Dr Arne Gobert, Dr Linda Kajli

Banking and finance
Dr Attila Egri, Dr Linda Kajli

Media and entertainment
Dr Arne Gobert, Dr Attila Fest

THE FIRM

Luther, Fest & Kajli Attorneys-at-Law, registered in the capital of Hungary, Budapest, is an international business consultant law firm. The company, founded in 2002, as a spin-off from a leading Hungarian law firm and international network (Andersen Legal), is one of the leading counsels in Hungary, connected to an international network of attorneys-at-law. The firm offers its clients legal services of the highest standard. The firm's clients are registered companies from the USA, the EU, and the Middle East, as well as local companies and institutions, private companies and entities.

The firm offers legal services in all areas of commercial business activities. Additionally, the quality of its legal counselling is ensured by professional qualifications of its staff. The firm sets the highest personnel requirements for its staff and strongly supports the continuing education and specialisation of its attorneys-at-law.

The extensive international dimensions of Luther, Fest & Kajli Attorneys-at-Law are based both on its team of multilingual attorneys, with dual language qualifications, and the firm's access to the global network of Ernst & Young.

The firm undertakes legal counselling services not only in Hungarian, but also in English, German and French.

AREAS OF PRACTICE

The firm co-operates, both on domestic and international matters, with one of the largest counselling firms in the world, Ernst & Young. Ernst & Young has more than 110,000 employees in 670 locations in over 140 countries.

To provide the best service for its clients the firm often works with business and tax advisers, and with various other professionals. In exercising this co-operation, the firm regularly combines its legal, tax and other services, and for international matters it can involve business advisers or foreign experts.

The firm's German co-operation partner, Luther Rechtsanwaltsgesellschaft is one of the largest German law firms with approximately 250 attorneys in 14 seats in Germany and abroad, such as German Desks in New York and Singapore. Luther, Fest & Kajli Attorneys-at-Law provides legal advice in several fields of law in close co-operation with Ernst & Young.

There is a demand for domestic and foreign professionals with special knowledge within the expanding complexity of international business. The firm is capable of providing its clients with comprehensive international and country-specific professional advice beyond its pure legal services, and to include related multidisciplinary activities.

As a law firm dealing primarily with business matters the firm has accumulated in-depth experience in the domains of energy, real estate and construction law, corporate, commercial and M&A, tax, customs law, general private law, project development, banking and finance, intellectual property and copyright, public commercial law (including competition, cartel and public procurement legislation).

MARTONYI ÉS KAJTÁR BAKER & McKENZIE

ANDRÁSSY ÚT 102
1062 BUDAPEST

Telephone: +36 1 302 3330
Fax: +36 1 302 3331
E-mail: janos.martonyi@bakernet.com
Website: www.bakernet.com

Languages
Croatian, English, French, German, Spanish

Other offices
The member firms of Baker & McKenzie International, a Swiss Verein, have 70 offices in 38 countries around the world. For a complete list, please visit www.bakernet.com.

Number of lawyers 3,300+
at this office 40

Contact
János Martonyi (managing partner)

CATEGORIES OF WORK

Banking and finance
Zoltán Martonyi

Capital markets
Zoltán Martonyi

Commercial property, real estate
Géza Kajtár, Tivadar Fütty

Competition and EU law
Zoltán H Barakonyi, Péter Vörös

Corporate/mergers and acquisitions
Pál P Takács, Ines K Radmilovic

Dispute resolution
János Martonyi, József Antal

General commercial
Géza Kajtár

Information technology
Andrea Soós, Emese Szitási

Intellectual property
Zoltán H Barakonyi, Krisztián Tivadar

Labour law
Pál P Takács, Ákos Fehérváry

Pharmaceuticals/healthcare
Zoltán H Barakonyi, Helga Biró

Privatisations
János Martonyi, Pál P Takács

Tax
Géza Kajtár, Gergely Riszter

Telecommunications
Péter Vörös, Emese Szitási

Venture capital/private equity
Pál P Takács

NAGY & PINTÉR HOGAN & HARTSON
LAW OFFICE

BANK CENTER, GRANITE TOWER
BUDAPEST V, SZABADSÁG TÉR 7-9
1054 BUDAPEST

Telephone: +36 1 302 9050
Fax: +36 1 302 9060
E-mail: knagykoppany@hhlaw.com
Website: www.hhlaw.com

Languages
English, French, German, Russian, Spanish

Other offices
Baltimore, Beijing, Berlin, Boulder, Brussels, Caracas, Colorado Springs, Denver, Geneva, Hong Kong, London, Los Angeles, Miami, Moscow, Munich, New York, Northern Virginia, Paris, Shanghai, Tokyo, Warsaw, Washington DC

Number of lawyers 1,101
at this office 8

Contact
Kornelia Nagy-Koppany

CATEGORIES OF WORK

Mergers, acquisitions and divestitures

Company formation and corporate counselling

Pharmaceutical and healthcare

Entertainment and gambling

Venture capital and private equity

Corporate finance

Bankruptcy, insolvency and corporate restructurings

Competition law

Labour and employment

Intellectual property

Technology transfer

Real estate

Telecommunications and e-commerce

NAGY ÉS TRÓCSÁNYI

UGOCSA U 4/B
1126 BUDAPEST

Telephone: +36 1 487 8700
Fax: +36 1 487 8701
E-mail: budapest_office@nt.hu
Website: www.nt.hu

Languages
English, French, German

Other offices
New York

Number of lawyers 25
at this office 24

Member
Lex Mundi

CATEGORIES OF WORK

- Antitrust and competition law
- Arbitration and litigation
- Aviation law
- Banking and corporate finance
- Capital markets and securities
- Commercial law
- Commercial real property
- Company and trade law
- Construction
- Energy law
- Greenfield investments
- Intellectual property
- Joint ventures
- Media
- Mergers and acquisitions
- Taxes
- Telecommunications
- Trade marks

NÖRR STIEFENHOFER LUTZ

FÖ UTCA 14-18
1011 BUDAPEST

Telephone: +36 1 224 0900
Fax: +36 1 224 0495
E-mail: info@noerr.com
Website: www.noerr.com

Languages
English, French, German, Hungarian, Italian, Russian

Other offices
Berlin, Bratislava, Bucharest, Dresden, Düsseldorf, Frankfurt, Moscow, Munich, New York, Prague, Warsaw

Number of lawyers 256
(+ 66 tax advisers, public accountants and tax assistants)
at this office 15
(+ 4 tax advisers, public accountants and tax assistants)

Contacts
Zsolt K Radnóczy, László Mészáros

CATEGORIES OF WORK

- Auditing
- Banking and finance law
- Commercial law
- Competition and antitrust law
- Construction law
- Corporate law
- Energy law
- Environment law
- Insurance law
- Intellectual property and trade mark law
- Labour law
- Real estate law
- Tax law

SIEGLER LAW OFFICE/WEIL, GOTSHAL & MANGES

BANK CENTER
GRANITE TOWER
SZABADSÁG TÉR 7
1054 BUDAPEST

Telephone: +36 1 301 8900
Fax: +36 1 301 8901
Website: www.weil.com

Other offices
Austin, Boston, Brussels, Dallas, Frankfurt, Houston, London, Miami, Munich, New York, Paris, Prague, Providence, Shanghai, Silicon Valley, Singapore, Warsaw, Washington DC, Wilmington

Number of lawyers 1,200
at this office 20

Contact
David Dederick

CATEGORIES OF WORK

Banking and finance	**Labour and employment**
Capital markets	**Mergers and acquisitions**
Competition	**Private equity and venture capital**
Dispute resolution	**Privatisation**
Energy	**Project finance**
General corporate and commercial	**Real estate**
IP, technology and communications	**Telecoms and media**

THE FIRM

Weil, Gotshal & Manges is a leader in the marketplace for sophisticated, international legal services. With more than 1,200 lawyers across the US, Europe and Asia, the firm serves many of the most successful companies in the world in their high-stakes matters and transactions. Weil Gotshal has built a world-class team of lawyers by pursuing a strategy of steady, purposeful growth. It continues to build upon a balanced platform of practices and locations without acquiring any debt. The firm's three primary departments – corporate, litigation/regulatory and restructuring – provide healthy diversification in all economic cycles, while its international expansion over the past decade has resulted in a quarter of the firm's lawyers now being in Europe.

AREAS OF PRACTICE

The firm's antitrust/competition practice advises on international M&A regulatory notifications, antitrust distribution counselling, cartels, litigation and government and state competition policy.

The corporate department is the firm's largest, with lawyers in the US and across Europe. The department advises international financial institutions and corporate clients in complex public and private mergers and acquisitions, private equity deals, strategic alliances and other commercial transactions.

The firm's corporate governance practice is recognised as the pre-eminent counsellor of corporate boards, management and institutional investors on the full range of governance issues, including board composition, structure and processes; executive and director compensation; director responsibilities, including in connection with mergers, spin-offs and other extraordinary transactions; internal and governmental investigations of alleged accounting or other corporate misconduct; and shareholder initiatives.

The firm is recognised as a market leader in the handling of complex and innovative finance transactions internationally. The firm advises on a wide range of financing activities and has particular expertise in acquisition finance, asset-based finance, debt restructuring and insolvency, debt and equity capital markets, derivatives, high yield debt, securitisation, structured finance and telecom and multimedia financing.

The firm has a leading intellectual property and technology practice and advises a number of the world's major technology, media and telecommunications companies. It also acts for investors in technology, media and communications entities. The practice handles patent infringement, outsourcing transactions, strategic alliances, cross-border mergers and acquisitions, investments and IPOs. The firm advises on the protection and exploitation of IP and on a wide range of e-commerce matters including data protection. It has expertise in regulatory telecoms matters.

The firm's litigation practice advises international clients on all major areas of the law and has extensive experience in all aspects of dispute resolution. It advises clients in jury trials and appeals, as well as arbitration and alternative dispute forums.

The firm's real estate practice handles complex real estate transactions (including finance, securitisations, development, leasing, sales, acquisitions and debt restructurings) across the US and Europe. It also advises clients on real estate M&A transactions and transactions involving real estate investment trusts.

The firm has one of the largest, most broadly based bankruptcy and business reorganisation practices in the world. The department has been involved in virtually all major chapter 11 re-organisation cases in the US and in major national and international out of court debt restructurings.

The tax department provides advice to a broad range of international clients, covering many economic sectors. The department works closely with the firm's other departments to find innovative solutions to problems that present various and competing multidisciplinary considerations.

SÁNDOR SZEGEDI SZENT-IVÁNY & KOMÁROMI

A MEMBER OF EVERSHEDS INTERNATIONAL

PASARETI ÚT 59
1026 BUDAPEST

Telephone: +36 1 394 3121
Fax: +36 1 392 4949
E-mail: office@sandor-advocat.hu
Website: www.sandor-advocat.hu

Languages
English, German, Russian

Number of lawyers 15

Contact
Dr Tamás Sándor

CATEGORIES OF WORK

Corporate law

Commercial law

Project finance

Real estate, construction law

Energy and utilities

Telecommunications

Banking and financial services

Competition law

Mergers and acquisitions, privatisation

Antitrust and cartel law

Media law

Labour law

Public procurement

Administrative, environmental law

Litigation and arbitration

SQUARRA & PARTOS

IN ASSOCIATION WITH LOVELLS

ANDRÁSSY UT 2
1061 BUDAPEST

Telephone: +36 1 474 2080
Fax: +36 1 474 2081
E-mail: information@lovells.com
Website: www.lovells.com

Other offices
Alicante, Amsterdam, Beijing, Berlin, Brussels, Chicago, Düsseldorf, Frankfurt, Hamburg, Ho Chi Minh City, Hong Kong, London, Madrid, Milan, Moscow, Munich, New York, Paris, Prague, Rome, Shanghai, Singapore, Tokyo, Warsaw, Zagreb*

Number of lawyers 1,600
at this office 13

Contact
Dr Thomas Squarra

CATEGORIES OF WORK

Banking

Corporate/commercial including M&A

Venture capital, private equity

Capital markets

Telecommunications

Dispute resolution

E-commerce

Real estate

Intellectual property

Employment law

Litigation/arbitration

SZECSKAY – ATTORNEYS AT LAW

KOSSUTH TÉR 16-17
1055 BUDAPEST

Telephone: +36 1 472 3000
Fax: +36 1 472 3001
E-mail: info@szecskay.com
Website: www.szecskay.com

Number of lawyers 23

Languages
English, French, German

Contacts
Dr András Szecskay, Dr Judit Budai, Laurent A Niddam

CATEGORIES OF WORK

Corporate/M&A
András Szecskay, Orsolya Görgényi

Banking and finance
Judit Budai, Szabolcs Gáll

Project finance/PPP
András Szecskay, Patrick Tausz

Competition law
Judit Budai, Katalin Grósz

Litigation/arbitration
András Szecskay, Laurent Niddam

Intellectual property
Gábor Faludi, Gusztáv Bacher

Real estate
Patrick Tausz, Hédi Bozsonyik

Commercial and civil law
Gábor Faludi, Judit Gulás

Employment law
Hédi Bozsonik, Katalin Grósz

E-commerce/IT/telecommunications
Gábor Faludi, Judit Budai

Media and entertainment
Szabolçs Gáll, Stefan Moldovan

Energy law
Katalin Grósz, Judit Gulás

Environmental law
Katalin Grósz, Anikó Keller

Administrative law
András Szecskay, Attila Jásdi

Constitutional law
Katalin Grósz, Judit Gulás

EU law
Judit Budai, Andrea Bayer

Insolvency
Hédi Bozsonyik, Anikó Keller

Public procurement
András Szecskay, Hédi Bozsonyik

ICELAND

Population	295,000
Number of lawyers	1,000
Professional title	Lawyer; Advocate
Currency	Icelandic Krona (ISK)

Iceland, Europe's most westerly country, lies in the North Atlantic, just south of the Arctic Circle but warmed by the Gulf Stream. The rocky and partially glaciated interior is uninhabitable and Reykjavík, the capital, with its hinterland, is home to nearly two thirds of Iceland's 300,000 inhabitants.

Iceland became an independent republic in 1944 after centuries as a dependency of Norway and, latterly, Denmark. The last general election for the 63-member Althing was held in 2003 when a centre-right coalition retained control; the next general election is due in 2007. Halldór Ásgrímsson, leader of the liberal Progressive Party, took over as Prime Minister in September 2004 under a deal struck with the conservative Independence Party.

Although a member of Nato, Iceland has no armed forces and relies for defence on the US, which maintains a controversial military base in Keflavík. Iceland is a member of the European Economic Area (EEA). The government remains opposed to membership of the EU, mainly because of the potential threat to Iceland's valuable fisheries.

With a per capita GDP of over US$33,000, Iceland now ranks in the top ten most affluent countries in the world. Fishing has traditionally been the mainstay of the country, which possesses few natural resources other than the substantially under-exploited geothermal and hydro-power which have stimulated the ongoing development of power-intensive aluminium and ferrosilicon processing. In recent years the government has encouraged diversification. Tourism has grown in importance and industry has expanded into new, hi-tech areas such as biotechnology and software.

BILLING

Icelandic law firms generally bill by the hour although preferred client terms may be negotiated. Work for international clients is charged at higher rates than for domestic market. Typical hourly rates for international instructions would be €175 – €275 for partners and €125 – €175 for associates.

MARKETING

Advertising by law firms must be conducted in accordance with the Iceland Bar Association's Code of Conduct which prohibits exaggeration of expertise. Although most of the larger firms now have websites, the paucity of inward investment has left most Icelandic lawyers to concentrate on local business promotion by networking.

IN-HOUSE LAWYERS

Iceland's financial sector now employs some 10% of working lawyers, who are represented by Félag lögfræðinga fjármálafyrirtækja, the Association of In-House Lawyers in Financial Institutions. This practice follows the precedent set when banks were state-controlled. For instance, Kaupthing Bank, the investment and corporate bank which was one of the main movers in Skipti ehf, the winning bidder for Iceland Telecom, houses a legal services division which supports the revenue-generating activities as well as advising on regulatory matters. The loss of transactional work now that the financial sector is booming, is causing some concern among independent lawyers.

ECONOMY

From the late 1980s, Iceland has followed policies of market liberalisation, fiscal consolidation, privatisation and structural reform which one commentator has described as creating 'the Nordic Tiger'. From 1998 to 2002, there were some problems as the economy overheated when consumption took over from a period of rising exports; inflation rose as high as 9% and the króna depreciated rapidly before the economy turned round, the current account deficit disappeared and inflation fell. Since 2003 the Icelandic economy has again been on the move; in 2004 GDP growth rose to 6.2% and during 2005, ICEX, the Iceland Stock Exchange, posted a rise of 64%. As we go to press, net foreign debt, aggravated by the capital inflows required to fund aluminium-related investments, has increased to 89% of GDP and there are again signs that consumer expenditure, fed by a surge in mortgage lending, is causing some inflationary pressure.

However, the Iceland Central Bank is resolved to bring inflation back to the target of 2.5% and in October 2005 raised its policy interest rate to 10.25%, with the stated intention of 'maintaining a tight monetary policy for longer than has previously been expected'.

Falling tax rates have followed economic liberalisation and efforts have been made to

The largest firms

1	LOGOS - Legal Services	28
2	Lex Law Offices	20
3	Reykjavik Law Firm	11
4	Jonsson & Hall	10
5	AM Praxis	8
	Juris Law Office	8
	Lagastod - Sigurmar K Albertsson	8
8	Landslog Law Offices	7
	Landwell	7
10	Attorneys at Hofdabakki	6
11	Lögmenn Klapparstig	5
12	Fjeldsted, Blöndal & Fjeldsted	4
	LM Attorneys	4
	Lögfrædipjónustan ehf	4
15	Adalsteinsson & Partners	3
	Lögborg	3
	Löggardur ehf	3
	Páll Arnór Pálsson hrl & Ragnar Baldursson hdl	3
	Soleyjargotu 17, Law Office Solicitors	3
	Solnes Law Office	3
21	Backman & Björgvinsson	2
	JP Lögmenn	2
	Sigurjonsson & Thor	2
24	Faktor Patentbureau ehf	1
	Kjartan Ragnars Law Offices	1

These figures represent the total number of lawyers in this country only, and have been supplied by the firms themselves. The figures should be accurate as at 1 January 2006.

simplify the tax system. The current corporate tax rate is 18%, which is expected to fall as monetary policy brings the economy back into balance.

One of the main features of the Icelandic economy in recent years has been the expansion of Icelandic companies into foreign markets, largely by acquisition. In effect, ambitious Icelandic operations, particularly in food processing, pharmaceuticals and financial services have acquired subsidiaries to expand both productive capacity and potential markets. Scandinavian and UK business have been the main targets; in the six months to June 2005, approximately €2bn of Icelandic money was invested in the UK alone. Icelandic banks are particularly aggressive and have been described as 'world players'. Certainly the top three Icelandic banks are very well placed in the Nordic market; it was reported in December 2005 that the three largest, KB Bank, Íslandsbanki and Landsbanki had a total 2,100 employees working overseas, mostly in Scandinavia, as against 3,000 in Iceland.

Foreign investment in Iceland is restricted by law. Inward investment in fisheries, fish processing, energy and aviation is either prohibited or limited, although EEA resident investors are more lightly sanctioned than others. Large-scale investments in aluminium and power projects were started in 2003 and are scheduled for completion in 2008, at which time Iceland's aluminium production should rise to approximately 35% of visible exports.

In September 2005 Iceland Telecom was sold to Skipti ehf, an investment vehicle backed by a number of investment banks, pension funds and other investors, for ISK66.1bn.

Iceland's business reputation took a knock in July 2005 when Jón Ásgeir Jóhannesson, CEO of the expansionary Baugur Group, and associates, were faced with multiple charges of fraud, many of them extremely trivial, which led to the withdrawal of a bid for UK supermarket chain Somerfield. Jóhannesson, who is represented by Gestur Jonsson of **Jonsson & Hall**, vigorously denied any wrongdoing and the District Court subsequently dropped all counts. The Supreme Court subsequently returned eight charges to the District Court, which has since refused an application to drop proceedings. A second appeal has been made to the Supreme Court and a decision is awaited as we go to press.

LEGAL SYSTEM AND LEGAL MARKET

Iceland's civil law system is based on Danish law and the 1944 constitution. Eight district courts (Héraðsdòmur) have jurisdiction over civil and criminal cases. Appeal is to the Supreme Court (Hæstiréttur) in which cases may be heard by up to seven justices according to importance and complexity.

Membership of the Iceland Bar Association (Lögmannafélag Íslands) is mandatory for practising attorneys (lögmaður). The current membership is approximately 600 of whom about 200 have rights of audience in the Supreme Court. The Association is responsible for setting professional standards and representing its members. Disciplinary matters are handled by an independent Disciplinary Board, to which the Bar Association can appoint two out of five members.

The modest legal market in Iceland is incapable of supporting many full-service firms and the majority of attorneys are sole practitioners. The larger firms sometimes experience conflict of interest issues, not only because of the market size but because senior practitioners take executive jobs in quangos and larger companies. There is, therefore, potential for mergers amongst smaller players to create client choice.

LOGOS – Legal Services, with 25 lawyers, is the largest firm on island and co-owner of IP consultancy and patent attorney firm **A&P Arnason Intellectual Property Group**. **Lex Law Offices**, with 14 partners and six associates, is second in size terms and operated as *Lex-Nestor* throughout 2005 following the merger with Nestor Lögmenn. Ten-lawyer **Jonsson & Hall** is ambitious and offers keen competition in business law. A number of smaller firms are extremely competent in the mid-range or offer niche expertise which matches that of the big players.

INTERNATIONAL ASSOCIATIONS

LOGOS – Legal Services is the Icelandic member of both *Lex Mundi* and *Terralex* and in January 2006 will open a London office in conjunction with three other Nordic law firms, Denmark's **Kromann Reumert**, Norway's **Thommessen Krefting Greve Lund**, and Sweden's **Vinge**.

Jonsson & Hall is a member of *State Capital Global Law Firm Group*. **Landwell** is part of the PricewaterhouseCoopers network and **Reykjavik Law Firm** is a member firm of *The Association of European Lawyers*.

BANKING AND FINANCE

Most Icelandic banks handle a good deal of transactional and regulatory work in-house and although some instructions do reach law firms, the full benefit of Icelandic banking expansion is likely to be enjoyed by firms in Scandinavia and the UK. Foreign banks are frequently represented and there was some substantial syndicated financing work in 2005.

Ólafur Haraldsson of **Lex Law Offices** is recommended for banking and finance matters, particularly where real estate is involved. Thorunn Gudmundsdóttir acts for the Icelandic National Bank, and Birgir Már Ragnarsson handles external work for Straumur Investment Bank. The firm continues to act for the major banks on a variety of work.

BANKING AND FINANCE

LEX LAW OFFICES ✪
LOGOS – LEGAL SERVICES ✪

Jonsson & Hall ✪
Landwell ✪

AM Praxis
Attorneys at Hofdabakki ✪
LM Attorneys
Landslog Law Offices
Reykjavik Law Firm

Firms are listed A-Z in tiers which are ranked in order of priority
✪ Indicates firm displays contact details at the end of this chapter.

LOGOS – Legal Services was legal advisor to Actavis Group in the June 2005 subscription offer to raise funds for the acquisition of US-listed pharmaceutical company Alpharma. Partners Jakob Möller and Ottar Palsson conducted the legal due diligence in connection with a share issue by KB Bank on behalf of Deutsche Bank. The firm handles collection work through the Kollekta ehf joint venture with **Lögborg**. Belgian qualified Sophie Romaniello brings wide experience of mainland European practice to a strong office.

Jonsson & Hall has established a solid reputation as a good all-round commercial firm which acts for the major Icelandic banks and foreign banks with Icelandic interests.

Landwell has expanded to eight lawyers and continues to attract blue-chip instructions. During 2005, the firm advised regular client Kaupthing Bank over €94m of senior and mezzanine finance when Icelandic investors purchased Spanish pharmaceutical companies Lesvi and Inke from Procter & Gamble. **Landwell** also advised a syndicate led by Barclays in relation to £500m senior debt and an ICEX-listed £100m bond issue when Bakkavör Group acquired LSE-listed Geest Plc.

Supreme Court attorney Hróbjartur Jónatansson of **AM Praxis** is widely experienced in financial matters and is licensed to operate investment companies. **AM Praxis** operates recoveries unit, AM Kredit plc.

Björn Líndal, partner in **Attorneys at Hofdabakki** and former MP, has experience of director-level involvement in major financial institutions including a period as MD of Landsbanki Islands' retail operations.

LM Attorneys' Kristján Thorbergsson acts for several banks, including Reykjavík Savings Bank, on a regular basis.

Landslog Law Offices now fields five partners and three associate lawyers. The well-respected and well-connected firm has acted for the Savings Bank of Keflavík, the third-largest savings bank in Iceland, and Invest in Iceland Agency, a Ministry of Industry & Commerce initiative.

Reykjavik Law Firm's clients include investment house Atorka and the Federation of Icelandic Banks and Securities dealers.

CORPORATE AND M&A

Several ICEX flotations and an active M&A market both on island and offshore kept law firms busy throughout 2005, and several firms have been recruiting.

Jonsson & Hall continues to act for blue-chip players including Kogun, Alcoa, Iceland Express and Shell Iceland. Name partner Gestur Jonsson is a respected all-rounder. Hordur Felix Hardarson is rising rapidly in stature from his 2001 admission as a Supreme Court attorney; he assisted with the international shipping merger between Geest Line and Samskip.

Prestigious **Lex Law Offices** handles a string of blue-chip clients including Icelandic Alloys, Air Atlanta and European Investment Bank. Jónas Aðalsteinsson, who serves on several corporate boards, ranks as one of Iceland's commercial law gurus. The firm's corporate clients include Shell Iceland, investment bank Straumur and retailer Hagar.

LOGOS – Legal Services' Gunnar Sturlusson and Ottar Palsson advised Flugleidir Icelandair Group on the purchase the Icelandic Bluebird Cargo Company for ISK3.8bn and the assumption of debt obligations for aircraft of another ISK1.4bn. The firm also worked with Morgan Stanley on the report to the State Privatisation Committee on the divestment of Iceland Telecom.

Five-partner, three-associate **AM Praxis** is known for building strong client relations and acts for Apple Computers and Nike. The practice offers strong core corporate and commercial expertise. Sveinn Jónatansson is a solid all-rounder with tax expertise.

Hreinn Loftsson, the founder of **Attorneys at Hofdabakki** is chairman of retail group Baugur.

CORPORATE AND M&A

JONSSON & HALL ✪
LEX LAW OFFICES ✪
LOGOS – LEGAL SERVICES ✪

AM Praxis
Attorneys at Hofdabakki ✪
Landslog Law Offices
Landwell ✪
Reykjavik Law Firm
Taxis Attorneys

Fulltingi Legal Services
JP Lögmenn
Juris Law Office
LM Attorneys

Firms are listed A-Z in tiers which are ranked in order of priority
✪ Indicates firm displays contact details at the end of this chapter.

The six-lawyer firm has a sound reputation for commercial work.

Landslog Law Offices represents expansionary Ossur, the leading international inventor and manufacturer of prosthetics, orthotics and synthetic bones, and Samkaup Ltd, Iceland´s third-largest retail chain. **Landslog Law Offices** has a reputation for establishing long-term client relationships and total commitment. Garöar Garöarsson is widely experienced and respected, with particular knowledge of international business law. Jón Sveinsson is Chairman of the Foreign Investment into Iceland Commission and the Privatisation Commission.

Landwell's market position edges closer to the top tier. The firm has strong international capabilities and fields highly experienced Baldvin Bjorn Haraldsson, who is also called to the French Bar, and Asgeir A Ragnarsson, also called to the New York Bar. Again the firm managed to take more than its share of the recent quality instructions, undertaking the legal review for Landsbanki as underwriter of a listing on ICEX, and acting for a syndicate led by Bank of Scotland in relation to the Mosaic Fashions hf IPO in June 2005.

Reykjavik Law Firm offers comprehensive coverage of the corporate and commercial field. Guðrun H Brynleifsdóttir, former deputy director of the Internal Revenue, is recommended for international tax issues and managing partner Steinar Thór Guðgeirsson brings a wealth of experience to corporate and insolvency work. **Reykjavik Law Firm**'s clients included car importer Brimborg and brewery Egill Skallgrimsson.

Seven-lawyer **Taxis Attorneys** remains Iceland's premier tax law practice and is also noted for strength in inward investment advice, M&A and high-net-worth private client work. Jon Elvar Gudmondsson returned to the firm as a partner in September 2005 after a period of study in the Netherlands to rejoin well-known former Internal Revenue Directorate chief, Gardar Valdimarsson. During 2005 **Taxis Attorneys**' impressive range of work included a major corporate reorganisation in the financial sector, several international acquisitions, and the provision of tax advice to some of the largest Icelandic multinationals and major foreign clients.

Fulltingi Legal Services has consolidated well since the 2001 merger and now fields 12 lawyers. The firm is particularly strong in corporate work and handled the sale of a 55% stake in Iceland Seafood Group by parent SIF to Feldir Investment Ltd.

Five-lawyer **JP Lögmenn** is best known for insolvency work but also offers a general commercial and corporate practice.

In January 2006, full-service firm *Legalis Law Office* merged with **Juris Law Office**.

LM Attorneys' clients include Skýrr the IT supplier, and genomics player deCode Genetics.

DISPUTE RESOLUTION

JONSSON & HALL ✪
LEX LAW OFFICES ✪
LOGOS – LEGAL SERVICES ✪

Adalsteinsson & Partners
Attorneys at Hofdabakki ✪
Landslog Law Offices

AM Praxis
JP Lögmenn
Juris Law Office
Reykjavik Law Firm
Taxis Attorneys

Firms are listed A-Z in tiers which are ranked in order of priority
✪ *Indicates firm displays contact details at the end of this chapter.*

DISPUTE RESOLUTION

The name partners at **Jonsson & Hall** are experienced and respected litigators, noted for a robust approach. Ragnar Hall has vast experience as both defender and prosecutor. Gestur Jonsson's main interests are in commercial litigation and arbitration.

Lex Law Offices boasts a strong litigation group from which Supreme Court attorneys Karl Axelsson, and Ólafur Haraldsson (who has maritime law expertise) are particularly recommended. The firm acts for one of Iceland's leading insurers, Sjóvá-Almennar.

At **LOGOS – Legal Services** Hakon Arnason and Jakob R Möller lead a strong litigation team. Möller has experience at a European level; he appeared before the EFTA court in a precedent-setting competition matter on behalf of Fagtún ehf. The firm is recommended for all commercial dispute resolution, particularly insurance matters.

Adalsteinsson & Partners' name partner Ragnar Adalsteinsson is arguably Iceland's most able litigator and certainly its best-known human rights advocate. Adalsteinsson won in the precedent-setting *Ragnhildur Guðmundsdóttir v State of Iceland* medical privacy case and also assisted the Falun Gong movement to file a writ under the UN Convention Against Torture against Chinese security boss Luo Gan during his brief visit to Iceland. Sigríður Rut Júlíusdóttir, the second partner in this small and effective firm, has also won a reputation for effective advocacy and represented the former prime minister in defamation litigation.

Hreinn Loftsson, senior partner at well-connected **Attorneys at Hofdabakki** successfully represented Landsvirkjun, the Icelandic national power company, in Supreme Court litigation over environmental impact procedures on a power station construction project. Thordur Bogason, who has considerable experience in European and constitutional law, represented Landsvirkjun in the District Court.

All five partners at **Landslog Law Offices** are Supreme Court attorneys. The firm has strong connections with the University of Iceland. Vilhjálmur Vilhjálmsson is Iceland's foremost authority on wet shipping law and an effective insurance litigator.

AM Praxis fields two Supreme Court attorneys. Hróbjartur Jónatansson is seen as a strong litigator and is recommended generally for commercial and corporate work, as well as his IT specialisation.

JP Lögmenn's main reputation lies in insolvency litigation.

Legalis Law Office's merger into **Juris Law Office** brings three Supreme Court attorneys.

Jóhannes Albert Sævarsson, a **Reykjavik Law Firm** partner, is a strong all-round litigator, recommended for contractual disputes and administrative law matters. Colleague Tómas Jónsson is also effective across the field and has particular interests in IT and IP.

Taxis Attorneys is recommended for tax dispute instructions. During 2005 the firm represented a major Italian construction company and its Icelandic branch before the State Tax Board and through the courts.

EU AND COMPETITION

Although Iceland is not an EU member, EEA law is important, particularly competition law, and several of the leading law firms have partners or associates who have worked in Brussels.

Lex Law Offices built up a wealth of experience in competition matters while advising the Icelandic Competition Authority during the three-year investigation into oil price fixing that resulted in record fines for the cartel members. Supreme Court advocate and former president of the Icelandic Bar Association, Thorunn Guðmundsdóttir is a solid corporate litigator with impressive experience in insurance matters.

LOGOS – Legal Services has wide experience of competition work and has, among other things, acted for shipping company Eimskip, airline Icelandair and insurer VÍS.

Jonsson & Hall's Hordur Felix Hardarson, a Supreme Court attorney, is the firm's EU specialist. The firm has recently represented clients involved in the oil cartel inquiry.

Juris Law Office's Andri Árnason, associate professor at Reykjavík University, and chairman of the Court of Arbitration of the Iceland Chamber of Commerce Board since 2005, specialises in competition law.

Landwell added to its EU and competition credentials by hiring Rannveig Sigurðardóttir from **Allen & Overy Luxembourg** during 2005.

Stefán Geir Thórisson at **Lögmenn Klapparstig** brings three years' experience as an EFTA surveillance officer to good use in his competition practice. Another former EFTA hand, Eggert B Ólafsson specialises in EEA law, competition and state aid law at **Reykjavik Law Firm**. **AM Praxis** includes competition law within a small but sound commercial and corporate office. **Attorneys at Hofdabakki**'s Thordur Bogason has experience of both EFTA and Althing secretariats. Jón Sveinsson **Landslog Law Offices** has considerable experience in competition law.

EU AND COMPETITION

LEX LAW OFFICES ✪
LOGOS – LEGAL SERVICES ✪

Jonsson & Hall ✪
Juris Law Office
Landwell ✪
Lögmenn Klapparstig
Reykjavik Law Firm

AM Praxis
Attorneys at Hofdabakki ✪
Landslog Law Offices

Firms are listed A-Z in tiers which are ranked in order of priority
✪ *Indicates firm displays contact details at the end of this chapter.*

EMPLOYMENT

Iceland is a signatory to the EEA agreement and therefore incorporates all EU employment and social directives into its national laws. The labour force is highly unionised and strict procedures apply to redundancy. There is, therefore, a growing market for law firms in employment-related matters although much of this is routine and handled by sole practitioners.

Jonsson & Hall represents parties from each part of the employment spectrum; employers, employees and trades unions. Clients include Alcoa. Gestur Jonsson specialises in labour law and Ragnar Halldor Hall served as a Labour Court judge before joining the firm.

Experienced Jakob R Möller heads the employment team at **LOGOS – Legal Services**

AM Praxis' Thórarinn V Thórarinsson was President of the Confederation of Icelandic Employers for nearly 15 years before joining the firm. He maintains his interest in employment law and represented Italian construction company Impreglio in connection with labour issues on a hydroelectric construction project.

EMPLOYMENT

JONSSON & HALL ✪
LOGOS – LEGAL SERVICES ✪

AM Praxis

Firms are listed A-Z in tiers which are ranked in order of priority
✪ *Indicates firm displays contact details at the end of this chapter.*

INTELLECTUAL PROPERTY, IT AND TELECOMS

LOGOS – LEGAL SERVICES ✪

AM Praxis
Adalsteinsson & Partners
Faktor Patentbureau ehf
Jonsson & Hall ✪
Juris Law Office
Lex Law Offices ✪
Reykjavik Law Firm

Fjeldsted, Blöndal & Fjeldsted
GH Sigurgeirsson
Kjartan Ragnars Law Offices
LM Attorneys

Firms are listed A-Z in tiers which are ranked in order of priority
✪ Indicates firm displays contact details at the end of this chapter.

INTELLECTUAL PROPERTY, IT AND TELECOMS

Iceland's move into new technologies, which has stimulated several domestic companies to become global players in biotechnology and pharmaceuticals, has also spurred Iceland's lawyers, particularly younger ones, to develop considerable expertise in IP and IT.

LOGOS – Legal Services worked with **Linklaters** and other prestigious European law firms on a report on data protection in the enlarged EU. The firm is affiliated to patent attorneys **A&P Arnason Intellectual Property Group**. **LOGOS – Legal Services** has acted for Actavis, the pharmaceutical company, both on corporate and IP matters. Hjördis Halldorsdottir has a specialist interest in e-business.

AM Praxis' Hróbjartur Jónatansson has considerable expertise in IP matters with particular strengths in computer law. Jonatsson is an expert in software licences and Thórarinn V Thórarinsson, who served as Chairman of Iceland Telecom before joining the firm in 2002, is known as a hands-on lawyer who brings a pragmatic approach to problems.

Adalsteinsson & Partners' Sigríður Rut Júlíusdóttir is expert in copyright and legal advisor to the Icelandic Writers Association. Ragnar Adalsteinsson was lead advisor to mobile operator TAL when it was party to the merger which created Og Vodafone in 2003.

Faktor Patentbureau Ehf, is still headed by founder Jón L Arnalds, Supreme Court sttorney, and Iceland's venerable IP supremo. The firm handles patent, trade mark, design, and copyright law, domain names, licensing and franchising as well as providing post-registration services such as annuity administration.

Jonsson & Hall handles IP, IT and telecoms work and has a specialist niche in musical copyright.

Juris Law Office's Andri Árnason advised Iceland Telecom for many years prior to its privatisation in 2005.

Lex Law Offices' Erla S Árnadóttir has wide experience in data protection, trade mark and patent law; she has been a reserve member of Copyright Committee since 1995. The firm acts for Icelandic Savings Bank on computer contracts. Partner Ragnheiður M Ólafsdóttir worked as a lawyer at the Icelandic Patent Office before joining **Lex Law Offices**.

Reykjavik Law Firm's Tómas Jónsson's main practice areas lie in information technology, telecoms and IP law. The firm acts for IT service provider Nýherja.

Skúli Fjeldsted of **Fjeldsted, Blöndal & Fjeldsted** is recommended for trade mark matters. **GH Sigurgeirsson**, headed by the experienced attorney of the same name, has specialised in IP work for over 30 years and offers a full-service trade mark practice as well as handling patent applications.

Kjartan Ragnars Law Offices is a similar specialist non-contentious IP practice headed by Kjartan Ragnars. Five-lawyer **LM Attorneys** offers niche strengths in IP work and telecoms. Kristján Thórbergsson is regarded as a heavyweight practitioner in a practice whose clients include Skyrr, Ten Systems and IMC Iceland.

MARITIME AND TRANSPORT

Three lawyers at **LOGOS – Legal Services** specialise in the transport sector. Einar Baldvin Axelsson is a recognised leader in maritime matters and qualified as a ship broker to extend his expertise. Erlendur Gislason specialises in aviation law, as does Othar Örn Petersen. The firm's clients include shipping major Eimskip.

AM Praxis' Astridur S Thorsteinsson has considerable experience and expertise in maritime and aviation law and was previously employed as general counsel for the Icelandic Civil Aviation Administration. **AM Praxis** also acts for Icelandair.

Jonsson & Hall's Hörður Felix Harðarson represented budget airline Iceland Express in a competition dispute with national carrier Icelandair. The firm also acts for Samskip.

LM Attorneys' Jóhannes Björnsson is a noted authority on fishing matters who acts for both the National Association of Fishing and the Federation of Icelandic Fishing Vessels. In 2000, Björnsson took the case of a trawler owner in dispute with the Icelandic government before the European Court of Human Rights and negotiated a satisfactory settlement between hearing and verdict.

Vilhjálmur Viljhálmsson of **Landslog Law Offices** is an expert on wet shipping matters and author of a Norwegian published paper on marine salvage. Garðar Garðarsson handles shipping and fisheries matters. The firm acts for shipping company Samskip and insurer Sjóvá-Almennar.

Lex Law Offices' managing-partner Helgi Jóhannesson and colleague Lilja Jónasdóttir are active shipping lawyers. The firm acts for Samskip and is well versed in dry shipping matters.

Law Office Solicitors Soleyjargotu 17 specialises in marine insurance and cargo claims. Partner Gardar Briem is Iceland correspondent for the global Charterers' P&I Club and other shipowners' mutuals.

MARITIME AND TRANSPORT

LOGOS – LEGAL SERVICES ✪

AM Praxis
Jonsson & Hall ✪
LM Attorneys
Landslog Law Offices
Lex Law Offices ✪
Soleyjargotu 17, Law Office Solicitors

Firms are listed A-Z in tiers which are ranked in order of priority
✪ Indicates firm displays contact details at the end of this chapter.

PROJECTS AND PFI

Although privatisation in Iceland has substantially run its course, PFI initiatives are now reaching the market. Major capital projects are ongoing and seem set to increase.

Landwell is providing ongoing advice to Austurhöfn ehf, a joint venture company established by the Icelandic government and the city of Reykjavík in connection with the East Harbour Project, which will provide concert, conference and hotel facilities. The 40-year contract, which **Landwell** is drafting and negotiating, is worth in the region of US$350m. **Landwell** also advised the prevailing consortium bidder in the Iceland Telecom privatisation.

Lex Law Offices was instructed by Bechtel International in connection with a major aluminium smelter construction contract. **LOGOS – Legal Services**' Othar Örn Petersen is also recommended for project finance matters.

PROJECTS AND PFI

Landwell ✪
Lex Law Offices ✪
LOGOS – Legal Services ✪

Firms are listed alphabetically
✪ Indicates firm displays contact details at the end of this chapter.

ATTORNEYS AT HOFDABAKKI

HOFDABAKKI 9
6TH FLOOR
110 REYKJAVÍK

Telephone: +354 587 1286
Fax: +354 587 1247
E-mail: logmenn@justice.is
Website: www.justice.is

Languages
Danish, English

Number of lawyers 6

Contacts
Hreinn Loftsson (hreinn.loftsson@justice.is),
Thordur Bogason (thordur.bogason@justice.is)

CATEGORIES OF WORK

Commercial and company law
Hreinn Loftsson, Thordur Bogason

Competition law
Hreinn Loftsson, Thordur Bogason

EU law and administrative law
Thordur Bogason, Björn Lindal

Mergers and acquisitions
Thordur Bogason, Hreinn Loftsson

Banking and finance
Björn Lindal

Litigation
Thordur Bogason, Hreinn Loftsson

Energy, infrastructure, environment
Thordur Bogason

Insurance
Hreinn Loftsson

JONSSON & HALL

SUDURLANDSBRAUT 4
108 REYKJAVÍK

Telephone: +354 414 4100
Fax: +354 414 4101
E-mail: law@law.is
Website: www.law.is

Languages
English, the Scandinavian languages

Number of lawyers 10

Member
State Capital Global Law Firm Group

CATEGORIES OF WORK

Arbitration

Banking and finance

Company and commercial

Commercial litigation

Competition

Insolvency

Insurance

IP law

Labour and employment

Media and entertainment

Mergers and acquisitions

International investments

Securities law

LANDWELL

SKOGARHLID 12
105 REYKJAVÍK

Telephone: +354 550 0500
Fax: +354 550 0505
E-mail: landwell@is.landwellglobal.com
Website: www.landwellglobal.com/is

Languages
Danish, English, French, German

Number of lawyers 8

Contacts
Asgeir A Ragnarsson, Baldvin B Haraldsson

International groupings
Part of Landwell International Network of Law Firms

CATEGORIES OF WORK

Commercial and company law
Baldvin B Haraldsson,
Katrin H Hallgrimsdottir

Mergers and acquisitions
Asgeir A Ragnarsson,
Einar B Arnason

Banking and finance
Baldvin B Haraldsson,
Asgeir A Ragnarsson, Einar B Arnason

Corporate restructuring
Kari Kjartansson

Securities
Asgeir A Ragnarsson,
Einar B Arnason

Competition law
Katrin H Hallgrimsdottir,
Einar B Arnason

Intellectual property
Gudrun Bergsteinsdottir

EU law
Rannveig B Sigurdardottir,
Gudrun Bergsteinsdottir

Employment law
Katrin H Hallgrimsdottir

Public law
Kari Kjartansson

Technology, media and communications
Asgeir A Ragnarsson,
Einar B Arnason

Arbitration
Baldvin B Haraldsson

Litigation
Baldvin B Haraldsson,
Gudrun Bergsteinsdottir

THE FIRM

Landwell was formed in 1998 by its current senior partners, Mr Asgeir A Ragnarsson and Mr Baldvin B Haraldsson. Landwell Iceland has grown considerably during the past few years in response to the needs of previous and new clients. The firm has a strong local team of attorneys, representing one of the leading law practices in Iceland in the field of corporate and commercial law. The attorneys at Landwell Iceland have an extensive education and experience in their field; and are members of the bars in Iceland, Paris and New York.

The firm enjoys the healthy growth of its corporate clients, some of which are leading banks and financial institutions. Landwell's main focus has always been on the corporate and business sector with a strong speciality in cross-border M&A transactions and finance.

AREAS OF PRACTICE

Landwell Iceland is working on many of the largest and most complex international M&A and banking and finance deals in the country. The firm advises many of the largest Icelandic banks on a case by case basis in relation to their local and international high profile transactions. The firm specialises in corporate and commercial law and is one of the leading firms in banking and finance and M&A. Landwell Iceland feel they are the most international law firm in Iceland as the vast majority of their work is cross-border; the firm regularly works with many of the world's leading law firms, including several magic circle firms.

The firm is focused on delivering complete solutions to their clients whether in Iceland or abroad. It has well-established relationships with leading law practices all over the world, which allows them to assist clients effectively in cross-border transactions. Many of Landwell's clients view the firm's cross-border practice and expertise as one of its strongest aspects.

LEX LAW OFFICES

SUNDAGÖRDUM 2
PO BOX 8975
128 REYKJAVÍK

Telephone: +354 590 2600
Fax: +354 590 2606
E-mail: lex@lex.is
Website: www.lex.is

Languages
English, German, the Scandinavian languages

Number of lawyers 20

Contact
Helgi Jóhannesson (managing director)

CATEGORIES OF WORK

Banking, securities and finance
Ólafur Haraldsson, Ragneiður M Òlafsdóttir

Corporate and commercial law
Helgi Jóhannesson, Jónas A Aðalsteinsson

Mergers and acquisitions
Jónas A Aðalsteinsson, Helgi Jóhannesson

Foreign investments, international contracts
Thorunn Guðmundsdóttir, Ólafur Haraldsson

EU
Ólafur Haraldsson, Thorunn Guðmundsdóttir

Administrative law
Halldór Jónsson, Karl Axelsson

Bankruptcy, insolvency
Helgi Jóhannesson, Heimir Örn Herbertsson

Public procurement
Erla S Árnadóttir, Eirikur Thorlaksson

Maritime and transport law
Ólafur Haraldsson, Lilja Jonasdóttir

Trade marks
Ragneiður M Òlafsdóttir, Lilja Jonasdóttir

Copyright, licensing, intellectual property
Erla S Árnadóttir, Ragneiður M Òlafsdóttir

Tax
Halldór Jónsson, Gardar Gislason

Labour law
Heidrún Jónsdóttir, Eirikur Thorlaksson

Energy and environmental law
Halldór Jónsson, Jónas A Aðalsteinsson

Insurance, accident, injury claims
Lilja Jónasdóttir, Ólafur Haraldsson

Competition law
Heimir Örn Herbertsson, Thórunn Guðmundsdóttir

LOGOS

LEGAL SERVICES – SINCE 1907

EFSTALEITI 5
103 REYKJAVÍK

Telephone: +354 540 0300
Fax: +354 540 0301
E-mail: logos@logos.is
Website: www.logos.is

Languages
English, French, German, Spanish, the Scandinavian languages

Other offices
London

Number of lawyers 26

Contact
Gunnar Sturluson (managing partner)

CATEGORIES OF WORK

Aviation
Othar Örn Petersen, Erlendur Gíslason

Banking, securities and finance
Pétur Gudmundarson, Jakob R Möller

Insurance, injury claims, labour
Hákon Árnason, Jakob R Möller

Construction, building
Othar Örn Petersen, Erlendur Gíslason

Insurance
Hákon Árnason

Litigation
Hákon Árnason, Jakob R Möller

Tax
Bjarnfredur Ólafsson

Intellectual property
Árni Vilhjálmsson, Ragnar T Árnason

Companies, corporations
Pétur Gudmundarson, Gunnar Sturluson

Commercial law (general)
Pétur Gudmundarson, Gudmundur J Oddsson

Admiralty, maritime
Einar Baldvin Axelsson, Pétur Gudmundarson

Competition law and EU/EEA law
Árni Vilhjálmsson, Helga Melkorka Óttarsdóttir

Mergers and acquisitions
Gunnar Sturluson, Helga Melkorka Óttarsdóttir

Licensing and IT law
Hjördis Halldórsdóttir, Árni Vilhjálmsson

IRAN

Population	**69.5 million**
Number of lawyers	**15,000**
Professional title	**Attorney**
Currency	**Rial (IR)**
Index	
Corporate and commercial	630
Country index	**5**

As a consequence of the 1979 revolution led by the supporters of Ayatollah Khomeini, the theocratic regime of the Islamic Republic of Iran was established. Since then, this oil-rich nation which borders internationally significant states including Iraq, Afghanistan and Pakistan, has had a tumultuous social, economic and political 25 years.

The present Supreme Leader of Iran and its effective ruler, Ayatollah Ali Khamenei, is responsible for preserving the policies of the Islamic Republic of Iran, as well as being the commander-in-chief of the armed forces and security operations.

His second-in-command and highest official in the country is the President of Iran, the current incumbent Mahmoud Ahmadinejad was elected in June 2005. There is a 290-member parliament (or Majlis) and an 86-strong Assembly of Experts whose main role as clerics is to elect the Supreme Leader. The Council of Guardians (twelve jurists) ensures parliamentary laws conform with Islamic shari'ah law, while the Expediency Council mediates disputes between the Majlis and The Council of Guardians.

Middle East analysts have blamed this plethora of clerical and non-religious ruling bodies for inhibiting internal reform and effective decision-making in Iran, due to the various representatives' interests often being diametrically opposed.

Iran's oscillation between pragmatic and ideological concerns has also marred bilateral and international relations. Other Middle Eastern states have difficulty trusting it, because of Iran's historical propagation of Islamic revolution in neighbouring states, such as Bahrain in 1981 (plot to overthrow the government) and Saudi Arabia in 1987 (rioting Iranian pilgrims during the Hajj), as well as its support for extremist groups including Hezballah in Lebanon and Hamas in Israel.

Most detrimental to its standing on the international stage, has been the cessation of diplomatic relations with the US as a consequence of the Iranian students' siege of the US Embassy in 1979. In 1988 the *USS Vincennes* shot down an Iranian Airbus A300B2 killing 290 civilians and since 1995 the superpower has imposed crippling sanctions on Iran, forbidding US companies from trading with it. The US cites Iran's alleged support of international terrorism, its opposition to the Middle East peace process, subversive behaviour towards its neighbours, poor human rights and its efforts to develop nuclear weapons as the five blocks to lifting sanctions.

The nuclear issue continued to be prominent in 2005. In August 2005 Iran restarted its uranium enrichment programme, the need to develop nuclear fuel was cited by President Ahmadinejad in his reasoning to the UN. The EU3 (England, Germany and France) have threatened to report it to the UN Security Council, as the programme will also enable development of nuclear weapons, and relations have been strained further still, due to Iran's reluctance to allow random UN inspections of its facilities.

BILLING

Typical fees for Iranian lawyers start at around US$150 per hour for junior attorneys, and range between US$200 and US$300 for leading practitioners. Fees are generally reduced for domestic clients, who often do not require knowledge of international law or foreign language skills.

MARKETING

Neither the Iranian government nor regional authorities restrict practitioners from marketing their practices via websites, direct mailing or brochures. The Iranian Bar Association forbids firms referring to themselves as 'International Law Firms', though this prohibition is often ignored.

ECONOMIC CLIMATE

The heart of the Iranian economy has oil pumping through its veins, holding 10% of the world's proven resources, and it is the second-largest OPEC producer. Some 80–90% of total export earnings and 40–50% of the government's budget derive from oil. Following Russia, Iran possesses the second-largest natural gas reserves in the world.

Despite this abundance of valuable natural resources, since the 1979 revolution the Iranian economy has failed to sustain growth and successfully develop. Key industries in Iran are in state hands, including petroleum, banking, utilities and mining. State control has been criticised for inhibiting the proper exploitation of these industries, due to competing ideological and pragmatic objectives within the government. Economists argue that privatisation of key industries such as oil, will facilitate improvements

The largest firms

1	Adib Law Firm	11
2	Parviz Savrai (Dr) & Associates, International Law Office	10
	Shamsaei (Dr) & Associates	10
4	Behrooz Akhlagi (Dr) and Associates, International Law Office	9
5	Foreign Legal Affairs Group	8
	Tavakoli & Shahabi	8
7	J Bokharai & Associates, Law Offices of	7
8	Ali Laghaee (Dr) & Associates Inc International, Law Offices	6
	Hami Legal Services	6
	Jamal Seifi (Dr) & Associates	6
	Raysan Patent & Trademark Agents	6
12	A.A.Atai & Associates, Law Offices	5
	M Ebadi Tabrizi & Associates, Law Offices	5
14	Atieh Associates	4
	Torossian, Avanessian & Associates	4
16	Abbas Mohajerian & Partners	3
	Albert Bernardi & Associates, Law Offices	3
18	Alavi & Associates	2
	Z A Afshari Law Firm	2
	de Capoa e Associati, Studio Legale	2

These figures represent the total number of lawyers in this country only, and have been supplied by the firms themselves. The figures should be accurate as at 1 January 2006.

in management and efficiency, resulting in greater profitability, especially as Iran already has one of the most highly educated workforces in the Middle East. Frustratingly, traditionalists consistently oppose reform, knowing that the loss of state control may result in reduced state power and influence over the electorate. The election in June 2005 of the conservative Ahmadinejad government will not remove this hurdle to progress.

The inability of the Iranian economy to effectively grow is also inhibited by a its high budget deficit. US$7.25bn per year is spent by the Iranian government on subsidies for foodstuffs and gasoline, resulting in budget funds being diverted to pay for them, rather than being earmarked for investment in new technologies. There has been some investment to help diversify away from reliance on oil into petrochemicals and agricultural products (dates, flowers and pistachios). Agriculture is one of the largest employers, with 22% of the country's workforce.

The facilitation of foreign investment has also been recognised as key to Iran's future economic success. In May 2002 the Expediency Council approved the Law on Attraction and Protection of Foreign Investment, but implementation had been delayed due to disagreements between reformers and conservatives. One significant foreign oil-based investment entered into with a Japanese consortium in February 2004, was a US$2.5bn buy-back project guaranteeing Iran annual revenues of US$17.4bn once fully operational. Similar joint projects will be limited without further legislation to create an improved climate for foreign investment.

Foreign investment has also been restricted due to Iran's poor bilateral and international relations. The eight-year war with Iraq (1980–1988) and allegations of the Islamic Republic's propagation of Islamic revolution and disruptive behaviour towards its Middle Eastern neighbours has detracted investment. In August 2005, the Iranian government recommencing its nuclear uranium enrichment programme, may lead to further economic sanctions if it is referred to the UN Security Council.

LEGAL MARKET

All of the leading domestic firms in Iran are based in the capital Tehran, which is also the home of the Iranian parliament, stock exchange and Central Bank of Iran. Approximately 8,000 attorneys are members of the Central Bar Association in Tehran, with the other 7,000 practising attorneys members of the 11 provincial bar associations. In contrast to other Middle Eastern states with highly developed legal markets, the typical Iranian law firm has fewer than ten attorneys and currently no international firm has offices in the country, save for **Studio Legale de Capoa e Associati** an Italy-based practice, which has an associate office in Tehran. International firms which have offices elsewhere in the region (including **Allen & Overy LLP**, **Denton Wilde Sapte**, **Norton Rose** and **Towers & Hamlins**) have resources to undertake work within the jurisdiction independently, or in tandem with local practitioners. The likelihood of international firms entering into associations with local firms will depend on the expansiveness of the Iranian government's privatisation programme and legislative reform to facilitate foreign investment, which in turn may lead to a dramatic increase in demand for multi-jurisdictional legal services.

Attorneys may work as consultants, or have public bodies and private companies as clients, but are not permitted to be on the payroll as employees of either.

CORPORATE AND COMMERCIAL

The **Law Offices A.A.Atai & Associates** is comprised of two name partners supported by five associates. The firm has an established track record advising international companies operating in Iran, with particular strength in regulation and commercial contracting. For Millicom International Cellular SA of Luxembourg, advice was provided on the setting up of a joint venture company, and Swiss company Glencore International's purchase of an Iranian food company involved substantial commercial contracting expertise. One client who has used the firm for 20 years in litigation matters singled out senior partner Mr Ali Akbar Atai as being 'particularly skilled, competent and effective'.

Adib Law Firm, a ten-attorney practice headed by the eponymous Dr Mohammad Adib, has an impressive global client base, including international airline Gulf Air, Japanese trading company Mitsui, and Canadian bank CIBC. The firm has been in existence for over 25 years and Dr Adib has great experience in international arbitration.

Respected by peers and clients alike, four-attorney practice **Atieh Associates** continues to punch above its weight, with a wide range of legal advice being given in the telecommunications, banking, oil and gas and transport sectors. Prominent international clients include banking giants ABN Amro, BNP Paribas and Commerzbank, and global food company Heinz. Managing partner Mr Babak Namazi has been recognised as giving 'excellent, responsive and commercial' advice. Significant work undertaken in the past year ranges from negotiating oil exploration contracts/buy-back arrangements, giving legal advice to the second successful recipient of a GSM mobile phone licence in Iran, and advising on a proposed trans-national railway.

With two partners and three assistants, the **Law Offices of M Ebadi Tabrizi & Associates** is an up-and-coming general commercial and litigation practice representing mainly German and Nordic clients on inward investment. One major German industrial company commented

CORPORATE AND COMMERCIAL

A.A.ATAI & ASSOCIATES, LAW OFFICES ✪
ADIB LAW FIRM
ATIEH ASSOCIATES
M EBADI TABRIZI & ASSOCIATES, LAW OFFICES
PARVIZ SAVRAI (DR) & ASSOCIATES, INTERNATIONAL LAW OFFICE
TAVAKOLI & SHAHABI

Alavi & Associates
Albert Bernardi & Associates, Law Offices
Ali Laghaee (Dr) & Associates Inc International, Law Offices
Hami Legal Services
J Bokharai & Associates, Law Offices of
J Nouraei & M Mostafavi Law Office
Jamal Seifi (Dr) & Associates
Shamsaei (Dr) & Associates ✪
Torossian, Avanessian & Associates

Firms are listed A-Z in tiers which are ranked in order of priority
✪ *Indicates firm displays contact details at the end of this chapter.*

that the firm's services were of 'high professional quality, effective and successful', and a Norwegian shipping concern commended principal Mahmoud Ebadi, who 'knows his job very well' when arranging joint ventures with Iranian companies. Mr H Malak, the other partner in the firm, is recommended for his handling of complex long-term litigation work, while assistant Mr K Afshar has been noted for his ability to apply both Iranian penal law and commercial law in resolving disputes.

Twelve-attorney practice, **International Law Office Dr Parviz Savrai & Associates** is a full-service law firm with Dr Parvaz Savrai himself and Dr Goldoust Jouybari the leading lights. Significant international clients represented are Japanese trading company Kanematsu, where a broad spectrum of corporate advice has been given, GKN plc (both in England and in Germany) and Buhler Holding AG in Germany.

Recognised as being one of the leading practices in Iran, eight-attorney corporate firm **Tavakoli & Shahabi** has been recommended for its 'commitment, competence, superior quality and promptness'. With a client list mostly comprised of *Fortune 500* names, the practice has recently advised on a number of joint ventures in the automotive and pharmaceutical industries, as well as being retained by a leading oil company in relation to a multi-million dollar LNG project. Name partner Mostafa Shahabi has been noted for his integrity, and one high-profile client who has retained the firm for ten years, praised him and the firm as being 'crucial in ensuring that the litigation process was conducted transparently at all times' in the difficult Iranian litigation environment.

Oil and gas specialist **Alavi & Associates**, with recommended name partner Mansour Alavi leading a four-attorney team, has a number of high-profile international drilling and oil industry clients. One oil construction company which employs the firm to undertake all its legal services within the jurisdiction, rates the work as 'A-plus', and another client specialising in oilfield tubular products, commented that the firm is comprised of 'professionals who know what they are speaking about, with a high ethical standard.'

One of the longest-established Iranian law firms, with 50 years of practice (and which continues to be run by its founding partner) is **Law Offices of Albert Bernardi & Associates**. The firm focuses on litigation, shipping, corporate and intellectual property work and currently advises three embassies in Iran.

Law Offices Dr Ali Laghaee & Associates Inc International has 12 attorneys and intellectual property (contentious and non-contentious) is the primary speciality of the firm. The recent hire of Mr Ashoory has boosted the IP infringements department already headed by Dr Ali Laghaee and Mr Alireza Laghaee. Both are noted by clients for their professional work and knowledge of local IP laws and regulations.

Hami Legal Services specialises in IP work, with a team of four attorneys supported by two patent and trade mark agents. The firm also has expertise in the fields of immigration, shipping and corporate law, in which founding partner Hassan Badamchi has been practising for 30 years.

With two partners and three attorneys, **Law Offices of J Bokharai & Associates** possesses a wide range of knowledge in all aspects of commercial and corporate law and similar to other smaller Iranian practices, has strength and depth in advising foreign companies on the registration and protection of their intellectual property in Iran.

J Nouraei & M Mostafavi Law Office is a three-partner corporate and commercial practice with a mainly German client base.

Dr Jamal Seifi & Associates is run by leading international arbitration expert, Dr Jamal Seifi with five attorneys assisting him including a sitting judge (Mr Lashakari) and oil and gas expert (Mr Shafe). In 2005 the 'clear and very articulate' Dr Seifi acted on an important arbitration concerning a major petrochemical complex in Iran, as well as acting on a Zurich-based arbitration between Iranian and Korean companies. The firm has also been instructed as local counsel for a major Chinese company's US$1bn aluminium smelter construction project in Iran.

Dr Shamsaei & Associates is an 11-strong practice supported by two independent associate attorneys. The firm has capabilities across the commercial board, areas of practice such as oil and gas, banking and finance, commercial litigation and foreign investment are catered for. With the latter the firm has expertise to deal with buy-back arrangements and BOT arrangements.

Torossian, Avanessian & Associates is a relatively young practice, but is also respected for its expertise in banking and finance. The firm has some blue-chip clients, with name partner Ida Avanessian specialising in foreign investment and international projects.

LAW OFFICES A.A.ATAI & ASSOCIATES, ATTORNEYS AT LAW

NO 8, 3RD FLOOR, 14TH STREET
KHALED ISLAMBOLI AVENUE
(VOZARA)
15117 TEHRAN

Telephone: +98 21 8871 3850
Fax: +98 21 8871 5252
E-mail: atai@ataiassociates.com
Website: www.ataiassociates.com

Languages
English, Farsi

Number of lawyers 5

Contact
Mr Ali Akbar Atai

CATEGORIES OF WORK

Company and commercial	**Joint venture**
International business law	**Labour law**
Investment law	**Shipping and transportation**
Energy and natural resources	**Dispute resolution**
Banking and financial law	**Corporate and contract law**
Agency law	**Marine law**
International trade law	**Litigation**

THE FIRM

The law firm of A.A.Atai & Associates has offered a full range of legal services since 1975, and has developed an enviable reputation as one of Iran's leading international law firms, largely due to its ability to combine an understanding of international markets with dependable interpretation of relevant developments in Iran's legal system.

AREAS OF PRACTICE

Located in Tehran, the firm regularly advises European and Asian companies operating in Iran's oil, gas, transportation, telecoms and banking industries on a wide range of business matters, including setting up representative offices, investing in free trade and special economic zones, establishing joint ventures and participating in major government sponsored economic projects.

The firm is available to advise, draft, interpret and negotiate documents in English as well as Farsi.

DR SHAMSAEI & ASSOCIATES

12TH APT NO 22
5TH ST GANDI AVENUE
TEHRAN

Telephone: +98 21 879 3043
Fax: +98 21 877 3371
E-mail:
drshamsaei@iranbusinesslawyers.com
Website: www.iranbusinesslawyers.com

Languages
Arabic, English, French, Japanese

Number of lawyers 11

Contact
Dr M Shamsaei (Mobile: +98 912 1176 351)

Member
Juritax; International Bar Association (IBA)

In association with
Middle East Association

CATEGORIES OF WORK

- Foreign investment
- Buy-back arrangements
- International business contracts
- BOT schemes
- Patents and trade marks
- Banking and finance
- Commercial litigation
- Insurance
- Arbitration
- Shipping and marine law
- Oil and gas
- Telecommunication law
- Agency law

IRELAND

Population	**3.9 million**
Number of lawyers	**6,500 solicitors**
	1,400 barristers
Professional title	**Solicitor; barrister**
Currency	**Euro (€)**

Index

Twenty six counties in Ireland have been independent since 1921, forming the Republic in 1949. Years of poverty, emigration and high taxation have been reversed through Ireland's membership of the EU. Ireland has been closely engaged with the European Union project since joining the EEC in 1973, and adopting the euro in 2002. Now it is the country all the accession states wish to emulate. Hitting its stride in the 1990s, the economy quickly earned the 'Celtic Tiger' tag. The government had a key role in Ireland's success, creating the landmark International Financial Services Centre as a base for the wave of global financial institutions which poured into the country, attracted by a 10% tax rate. US manufacturers also arrived in droves to set up European operations in Ireland. Ten years on, the economy has steadied. The tax rate has changed to (a still competitive) 12.5%, and new entrants are more likely to be high-end pharma or biotech companies than manufacturers.

BILLING

The Irish legal market is highly competitive, putting pressure on fees. Capped fees and agreed fees are the norm, particularly when dealing with the public sector. Partners' hourly rates range between €300 and €450.

MARKETING

The marketing regime for law firms is governed by The Solicitors (Amendment) Act 2002, which specifies the information which may be included in an advertisement, and introduced a ban on advertisements in 'an inappropriate location.' Damages claims for personal injury cannot be mentioned in an advertisement. Websites and electronic communications are also covered by the Act, which states that advertisements should not be false, misleading or reflect badly on other solicitors.

IN-HOUSE LAWYERS

In-house lawyers make up a substantial percentage of the legal market, with over 600 of the Republic's 6,500 solicitors working in-house. There is a steady transition of in-house lawyers to private practice, and vice versa.

ECONOMY

Although the 'Celtic Tiger' era has well and truly passed, the economy is thriving.

GDP is forecast to grow by 4.7% in 2006 and 4.5% in 2007: a positive outlook. New industry is at the forefront, as the focus has shifted from large-scale manufacturing to high-end biotech and pharma operations. A score of US multinationals have their European headquarters in Ireland, enticed by the competitive 12.5% tax rate and a well-educated, English-speaking workforce. The ambition of the new breed of super-rich Irish entrepreneurs created by the boom has outgrown the country's borders, as they snap up high-profile property acquisitions in the UK, Eastern Europe and China. New roads projects are in full swing; part of the National Development Plan 2000-2006 which is investing over €52bn in health, education, roads, water, waste services and transport.

LEGAL SYSTEM

Ireland's legal system is derived from that in the UK, although unlike the UK it has a US-style written constitution. It is a common law jurisdiction, modified by national legislation, although as an EU member the rulings of the European Court of Justice take precedence over national law.

LEGAL MARKET

The dominant players in the legal market are the Big Five: **A&L Goodbody**, **Arthur Cox**, **McCann FitzGerald**, **Matheson Ormsby Prentice** and **William Fry**. The Big Five field considerably more fee-earners than any other firm and cover the full range of industry specialisms.

In a surprise move, *Binchys* merged with **Maples and Calder** in January 2006, providing Irish law experience for the Cayman Islands-based law firm.

Several mid-tier firms also have notable expertise in certain areas, for example; **BCM Hanby Wallace** excels in employment, **Dillon Eustace** has a niche in investment funds, while **LK Shields** has a formidable reputation for IP. The mid-tier firms have provided the most exciting developments of the year. Ambitious **O'Donnell Sweeney** linked up with **Eversheds LLP** in the first such arrangement between an Irish and a UK firm. **Mason Hayes+Curran** has not rested on its laurels, but has boosted its full-service capability with key

The largest firms

1	McCann FitzGerald	265
2	A&L Goodbody	242
3	Matheson Ormsby Prentice	226
4	Arthur Cox	210
5	William Fry	194
6	O'Donnell Sweeney	87
7	BCM Hanby Wallace	80
8	Dillon Eustace	70
	Mason Hayes+Curran	70
10	Beauchamps	56
11	Eugene F. Collins	45
12	LK Shields	41
13	Ronan Daly Jermyn	40
14	WhitneyMoore	34
15	Landwell Solicitors	27
16	O'Flynn Exhams	24
17	Holmes O'Malley Sexton	23
18	Maples and Calder	21
19	Ivor Fitzpatrick & Company	20
20	PJ O'Driscoll & Sons	19
21	Orpen Franks	17
22	Noel Smyth & Partners	15
23	Conway Kelleher Tobin	14
24	Nolan Farrell & Goff	13
25	GJ Moloney & Co Solicitors	12
	Kennedy McGonagle Ballagh incorporating Bell Branigan O'Donnell & O'Brien	12
	Kilroys	12
	Lennon Heather & Company	12
	McEvoy Partners	12
	Reddy Charlton McKnight	12

These figures represent the total number of lawyers in this country only, and have been supplied by the firms themselves. The figures should be accurate as at 1 January 2006.

hires. In 2005 Suzanne Carter, the former Head of Taxation at Vodafone, joined the firm to lead the tax practice, while Justin McKenna joined the corporate and securities law team from **LK Shields**. The firm also opened has an office in London.

Elsewhere, changes of personnel include Nicola Palmer's departure from **LK Shields** to bolster **Matheson Ormsby Prentice**'s commercial property practice, and was replaced by Jim Gollogley. Also at **LK Shields**, Hugh Garvey has taken over the mantle of managing partner from Larry Shields. Food and life sciences specialist Raymond O'Rourke left **Mason Hayes+Curran**, while the other expert in the field, Maree Gallagher, left **Arthur Cox** to form her own consultancy practice.

LINKS ABROAD

Of the Big Five, **William Fry** is the only one not to have a London office, although the firm opened in New York in June 2005. **Mason Hayes+Curran** has joined the London scene, opening its doors in February 2005.

In the US **Arthur Cox**, **McCann FitzGerald**, **Mason Hayes+Curran**, **Matheson Ormsby Prentice** and **A&L Goodbody** all have offices in New York, while the latter also has a presence in Boston, as does **Dillon Eustace**. **Matheson Ormsby Prentice** also has a second US office in Palo Alto. **A&L Goodbody** and **McCann FitzGerald** are the only firms represented in continental Europe, with offices in Brussels, although **Dillon Eustace** has an alliance with **Arendt & Medernach** in Luxembourg and, uniquely, an office in Tokyo.

Nearer to home, a number of the top and mid-tier have link-ups with Northern Irish firms. **Arthur Cox** is the only firm to span both North and South through **Arthur Cox Northern Ireland**. **McCann FitzGerald** is allied to **L'Estrange & Brett**, forming the *North South Legal Alliance*; **William Fry** has formed links with **Tughans**; while **Matheson Ormsby Prentice** has the *All Island Legal Alliance* with **Cleaver Fulton Rankin**. Among the mid-tier firms, **Mason Hayes+Curran** has an *i-law alliance* with **Carson McDowell**; and **Eugene F. Collins** is 'best friends' with **C & H Jefferson**.

BANKING AND fiNANCE

Aviation finance aficionado Catherine Duffy heads **A&L Goodbody**'s banking practice, while Stephen Haughey and Séamus Ó'Cróinín are able banking and finance practitioners. Examples of high-quality instructions include acting for Anglo Irish Bank in syndicated facilities to fund the €291m development of Phase 1 of Spencer Dock in Dublin, the second-largest development financing completed in Ireland. Major clients include corporate heavyweights such as Air France, Quinlan Private and ING Bank.

BANKING AND FINANCE

A&L GOODBODY ✪
ARTHUR COX ✪
DILLON EUSTACE ✪
MATHESON ORMSBY PRENTICE ✪
McCANN FITZGERALD ✪
WILLIAM FRY ✪

Eugene F. Collins ✪
LK Shields ✪
Mason Hayes+Curran ✪

BCM Hanby Wallace ✪
Beauchamps ✪
Ivor Fitzpatrick & Company ✪
Kilroys
O'Donnell Sweeney ✪
Robert Ryan & Associates
Ronan Daly Jermyn ✪

Dockrell Farrell
E P Fanning & Co, Solicitors
Landwell Solicitors ✪
Maples and Calder ✪
PJ O'Driscoll & Sons ✪
Reddy Charlton McKnight ✪
WhitneyMoore

Firms are listed A-Z in tiers which are ranked in order of priority
✪ *Indicates firm displays contact details at the end of this chapter.*

Arthur Cox recruited Fiona O'Neill from **CMS Cameron McKenna LLP**, to boost its already strong banking and finance team. Clients love Gráinne Hennessy, whom they praise for her 'spot-on commercial advice'. The team acted for Legg Mason in the US$3.7bn acquisition of the asset management business of Citigroup. A top-drawer client list includes Anglo Irish Bank, First Active, and Merrill Lynch.

Property partners Paul Eustace and Michael Barker have expertise in secured lending at **Dillon Eustace**. A steady workload includes advising on the creation of complex tax-driven property structures for the acquisition of property in Ireland and across Europe. Quality clients include Irish Life & Permanent and Bank of Scotland.

'The exceptionally well-informed' William Prentice heads the banking and finance department at **Matheson Ormsby Prentice**, which now includes Joe Beashel, former MD of Invesco's Irish operations. A wide-ranging client base includes both domestic and international banks such as Bank of Ireland and Citigroup. A key instruction in 2004 was advising IIB Bank and KBC Bank on the €350m refinancing of the existing facilities of the Kingspan Group.

Renowned banking and finance specialist **McCann FitzGerald** has a breadth of practice that ranges from aircraft finance to derivatives and covered bonds. The team is peopled with strong players such as John Cronin, the 'distinguished' Roy Parker, Eamon de Valera and Niall Powderly.

Catherine Deane and Hilary Marren are asset finance experts. Highlights include advising ABN Amro on a €300m loan to Oracle Technology Company.

The six-partner team at **William Fry** regularly acts for lenders, sponsors and investors in property-based transactions both in Ireland and in Europe. Prestigious instructions include acting for the Serpentine consortium that purchased the site of the proposed new AIB premises at Ballsbridge, Dublin for over €367m. Neville O'Byrne and Elaine Hanly both have excellent reputations.

Gerard Coll heads **Eugene F. Collins**' banking and finance practice, while Laura McDermott and Leonora Malone both boast considerable banking expertise. A major highlight in 2005 was advising the *Leinster Leader* on the sale of 100% of the shares in the company to Johnston Press for €138.6m.

LK Shields' banking and financial services unit had a busy 2005, dealing with a raft of work including the launch of Arlington UK Balanced Property Fund and the launch of Protego Real Estate Funds. The team specialises in advising top financial institutions and corporates on debt financing structures, including intricate fund structures that use derivatives. Clients include Grupo Banco Santander, Citibank and Bank of Ireland. David Williams and Joseph Galvin head the team.

Mason Hayes+Curran's 'commercially adept' Kevin Hoy advises lenders and borrowers on a broad mix of finance, such as secured and unsecured loans and the arrangement of syndicated facilities. The three-partner team counts Bank of Ireland, Bank of Scotland (Ireland), AIB, ACC Bank and Ulster Bank amongst its key clients. In 2005 the firm advised Warren Acquisitions on Irish law aspects of the €2.3bn purchase of Warner Chilcott, a pharmaceutical company.

Highlights for **BCM Hanby Wallace** include acting for the Avoca Capital Group in their latest €400m capital fund raising. Paul McGennis and Ciara Gunning provide considerable banking expertise.

Ivor Fitzpatrick & Company continues to be retained by Ireland's major financial institutions, including Bank of Ireland, Bank of Scotland and Irish Nationwide Building Society, for which the firm has completed a high volume of transactions. The firm has a strong reputation for asset-secured commercial lending. Anne McHale is an accomplished banking and finance practitioner.

Kilroys is a niche corporate firm that has investment funds expertise; but which also offers financial services advice to its clients. Eamon Jones provides banking and finance capability.

Stephen Rodgers, formerly of **A&L Goodbody**, is a key banking partner at **O'Donnell Sweeney**, as is Patricia Heffernan, who has significant skill in secured lending, particularly for commercial property transactions. The team advised IFG Group on the €13.3m sale of 50% of IFG Insurance and Mortgage Services and LFG Mortgage and Assurance Services to GE Capital Woodchester.

Two-partner **Robert Ryan & Associates** has a concentrated banking focus which advises both international and domestic clients.

Cork-based **Ronan Daly Jermyn** continues to be a key adviser to a number of the well-known banks, including Bank of Ireland, Bank of Scotland, Ulster Bank, ACC Bank and IIB Bank. Frank Daly and Tom Fox are highly sought after for their banking prowess.

CAPITAL MARKETS

In the Irish context this section principally refers to the debt markets, as there is scant activity in the Irish equity markets. An upward trend is the flotation of Irish companies on AIM.

A&L Goodbody has a star-studded team that includes John Olden, Eithne Fitzgerald, Ciaran Rogers and Paul White. Extensive expertise covers the gamut of debt and equity issuances for private and public companies in Ireland, Europe and the US. An example of the quality of instructions is advising the Irish subsidiaries of GE Capital on an EMTN programme, and also advising British Energy on Irish law securities and company law.

Arthur Cox has one of Ireland's top capital markets practices, which is integrated with structured finance. A strong Irish client base generates a substantial flow of domestic debt capital markets work. City pedigree practitioners Cormac Kissane and Glenn Butt lead the field and are popular with clients. The team acted for EBS Building Society on an issue of €125m hybrid Tier 1 securities, and advised Grafton Group on its US$350m private placement into the US.

The 'respected' Tim Scanlon heads an impressive capital markets practice at **Matheson Ormsby Prentice**, while Turlough Galvin, who straddles tax and capital markets, is highly rated by clients and practitioners alike. Highlights of the past 12 months include acting for AgCert International on its IPO on the London and Dublin stock exchanges, and advising on two rights issues by Waterford Wedgwood to raise approximately €100m each. **McCann FitzGerald** advised Davy Stockbrokers on this transaction.

A sample capital markets transaction at **McCann FitzGerald** is advising FireOne Group on its IPO and admission to AIM. The corporate finance group, which includes luminaries such as Barry Devereux, regularly advises Irish and international clients on IPOs, bond issues, rights issues and open offers. There has been a steady flow of bond issues and instructions on the establishment of MTN and CP programmes for debt capital markets. The team also boasts unique expertise on Irish covered bonds, courtesy of banking supremo Roy Parker.

William Fry has a diverse practice, advising Irish corporations and global financial entities on bond issues, the establishment of commercial paper and MTN programmes. The team is also active in venture capital financing, acting for both investors and companies in the private equity market. The firm advised Ardagh Glass Group in its public bond offering for over €126m. According to clients, Elaine Hanly is 'superlative'.

Dillon Eustace has an established reputation for its investment funds practice, which it augments with the capacity to undertake corporate finance work, through its corporate and commercial practice headed by Lorcan Tiernan.

Highlights for **Eugene F. Collins** include advising Anglo Irish Bank on the issue of £300m preference shares, the largest-ever equity issue by an Irish bank. The team also advised the same banking institution on the update and increase of its MTN programme to €10bn. Eileen Grace has a first-class reputation for her capital markets expertise.

LK Shields is experienced in advising on public offerings and the private placing of equity and debt securities, as well as on compliance issues with the Irish Stock Exchange. Joseph Gavin is recommended.

The 'brilliant' Paul Egan at **Mason Hayes+Curran** was joined by Justin McKenna from **LK Shields**, strengthening the capital markets team. The firm continues to advise on a number of public-to-private transactions involving companies quoted the Irish Stock Exchange, as well as advising Calyx Group on the placing of shares and listings on AIM in a deal worth €13m.

CAPITAL MARKETS

A&L GOODBODY ✪
ARTHUR COX ✪
MATHESON ORMSBY PRENTICE ✪
McCANN FITZGERALD ✪
WILLIAM FRY ✪

Dillon Eustace ✪
Eugene F. Collins ✪
LK Shields ✪
Mason Hayes+Curran ✪

BCM Hanby Wallace ✪
Beauchamps ✪
Kilroys
O'Donnell Sweeney ✪

Firms are listed A-Z in tiers which are ranked in order of priority
✪ Indicates firm displays contact details at the end of this chapter.

CONSTRUCTION

Projects expert Kevin Feeney leads the four-partner projects and construction group at **A&L Goodbody**, which includes former **Pinsent Masons** partners Dudley Solan and Eamonn Conlon in its ranks. In 2005 the team advised a syndicate of Irish banks (led by Anglo Irish Bank)

CONSTRUCTION
A&L GOODBODY ✪ McCANN FITZGERALD ✪
ARTHUR COX ✪ HUSSEY FRASER ✪ WILLIAM FRY ✪
Matheson Ormsby Prentice ✪
BCM Hanby Wallace ✪ Beauchamps ✪ Eugene F. Collins ✪ LK Shields ✪ Mason Hayes+Curran ✪ Noel Smyth & Partners O'Donnell Sweeney ✪ Ronan Daly Jermyn ✪ WhitneyMoore
Dillon Eustace ✪

Firms are listed A-Z in tiers which are ranked in order of priority
✪ Indicates firm displays contact details at the end of this chapter.

on the construction funding of the Spencer Dock Development, and acted for Shell Oil and Gas Exploration on the development of the Corrib Gas Terminal Building, a new onshore gas terminal building. The practice also has substantial expertise in the construction of windfarms and power stations in Ireland.

McCann FitzGerald has an excellent name for construction and PPP. Clients rate Tim Bouchier Hayes for 'his intelligent, thoughtful approach'. Highlights include advising John Sisk & Sons, the contractor, on contracts for the development of the Dundrum Shopping Centre, the largest shopping centre development in Ireland.

Arthur Cox won a score of lead roles in Ireland's major construction projects in 2004 and 2005. The 13-fee-earner construction team advised the Railway Procurement Agency on four major track extensions to the LUAS Light Rail Network, as well as rolling-stock upgrades, and advised Mowlem on the high-profile Dublin Port Tunnel project. Ted Williams leads the team.

Construction specialist **Hussey Fraser** reaps a host of high-quality instructions, and has considerable strength in construction arbitration. In 2005 the firm acted in a major arbitration in a hearing on liability, in which the arbitrator found in the client's favour. This was one of largest claims ever made in an Irish arbitration. Anthony Hussey is a talented practitioner.

William Fry's construction practice has extensive experience of advising the employer, project sponsor and the financier. The six-fee-earner team has a dual advisory and contentious approach. Highlights include advising Private Investors on the €45m extension and renovation of the Shelbourne Hotel Dublin, and acting for Aughinish Alumina on the development of its 150MW combined heat and power plant. Liam McCabe heads the able team.

Matheson Ormsby Prentice' s construction capacity has settled since the departure of Mark Varian to **O'Donnell Sweeney** in 2004. Damien Keogh handles disputes, while Richard Stowe deals with the advisory work, for a core contractor client base. The team regularly advises consortia on contracts relating to schools, harbour development and waste recycling. Disputes work includes advising one of Ireland's largest building contractors in High Court proceedings against an employer in respect of non-payment and wrongful termination of a contract.

BCM Hanby Wallace has strong links with developers, which results in a raft of first-class instructions. Tim Kinney heads the department, which is acting for the developer on the Dundrum Shopping Centre. The team has a wide remit of construction and engineering contracts, sub-contracts and consultancy agreements, as well as advising on project agreements and related sub-contracts on PFI/PPP projects.

Eugene F. Collins' strong commercial property practice reaps quality construction work for industry clients such as PJ Walls and Pierse Contracting. Mark Walsh is 'knowledgeable and reliable.'

New arrival Jim Gollogley heads the construction unit at **LK Shields**. The team counts public and semi-state authorities, private contractors, developers, occupiers and tenants on its client list. Key instructions include acting on the €100m development of a harbour company's property.

Formerly of **Pinsent Masons**, Rory Kirrane is team leader of **Mason Hayes+Curran**'s construction practice, which acts for indigenous contractors and developers on significant residential and retail projects, as well as multinationals such as Ericsson and Masonite on disputes arising in relation to building or engineering contracts. The team is acting for Eco Wind Power on turbine supply and construction contracts related to the Geevagh wind farm.

Ex-**Matheson Ormsby Prentice** Mark Varian and his team have considerably boosted **O'Donnell Sweeney**'s construction capability. The firm acts for a broad mix of clients from the construction sector: employers, developers, contractors and banks. Major clients include industry heavyweights such as such as John Sisk & Sons, PJ Walls, Treasury Holdings, Manor Park and Ulster Bank.

Cork-based **Ronan Daly Jermyn** acts for a number of the major construction companies in Ireland, leveraging off its strong commercial property expertise.

Dillon Eustace acts for a number of financial institutions and developers on the construction side.

CORPORATE AND M&A

M&A and corporate finance are healthy, with activity in the media and healthcare sectors at a mid-market level. A notable trend in 2005 was the surge in private equity, as investments mature, creating significant profits for private equity houses.

CORPORATE AND M&A
A&L GOODBODY ✪ ARTHUR COX ✪ MATHESON ORMSBY PRENTICE ✪ McCANN FITZGERALD ✪ WILLIAM FRY ✪
MASON HAYES+CURRAN ✪
BCM HANBY WALLACE ✪ DILLON EUSTACE ✪ EUGENE F. COLLINS ✪ LK SHIELDS ✪ O'DONNELL SWEENEY ✪
Beauchamps ✪ Ivor Fitzpatrick & Company ✪ Landwell Solicitors ✪ Maples and Calder ✪ McEvoy Partners ✪ WhitneyMoore
Dockrell Farrell Gore & Grimes ✪ KLW Kilroys PJ O'Driscoll & Sons ✪ Reddy Charlton McKnight ✪ Ronan Daly Jermyn ✪
Brian O'Donnell & Partners Conway Kelleher Tobin Holmes O'Malley Sexton Maurice Power O'Flynn Exhams Orpen Franks Robert Ryan & Associates Sweeney McGann Vincent & Beatty

Firms are listed A-Z in tiers which are ranked in order of priority
✪ Indicates firm displays contact details at the end of this chapter.

A&L Goodbody boasts several experienced practitioners: Paul White, who heads the department, Eithne Fitzgerald and the 'versatile' John Given. The firm has strength across the spectrum of corporate finance, M&A and private equity. In 2005, the firm advised eircom on the €420m recommended acquisition of Meteor Mobile Communications and acted for SR Technics on its acquisition of FLS Aerospace, the Danish technical aircraft, component and engine services provider. A sterling client list includes AIB, Heiton Group and the Department of Finance.

Clients are full of praise for the core partners in the corporate and commercial practice at **Arthur Cox**. Ciarán Bolger is a 'leader in the field', James O'Dwyer 'an intelligent and experienced lawyer', while Brian O'Gorman is 'commercially astute'. The team pulls in impressive M&A work; in 2005 acting for the sellers in the €450m disposal of Superquinn to Select Retail Holdings and advising UGC in the €325m acquisition of ntl Ireland via a Morgan Stanley conduit. An impressive client list includes heavyweights such as CRH, Fyffes and Paddy Power.

Matheson Ormsby Prentice scooped a coveted role advising NAB on its €1.4bn disposal of National Irish Bank and Northern Bank to Danske Bank; the largest M&A transaction in 2004. The team also garners substantial private equity and venture capital instructions, including the establishment of International Securities Trading Corporation, an Irish company formed to acquire assets in the financial services sector. Andrew Doyle is 'an excellent corporate lawyer', while Tim Scanlon and Patrick Spicer are also recommended.

Head of corporate and public M&A at **McCann FitzGerald**, Barry Devereux and his team advise a broad mix of clients from indigenous entrepreneurs to state bodies and global multinationals. Paul Heffernan heads a separate private M&A and commercial team. Major highlights of 2005 include advising PacketExchange on relocation of the holding company of the group to Ireland, and also on a raft of private equity investments. Clients include GlaxoSmithKline, Kingspan Group and Diageo. Owen O'Connell is recommended.

William Fry has a well-earned reputation as an excellent M&A firm. A raft of impressive instructions include advising the largest shareholder block, the Doyle family, on the Jury's Doyle Hotel Group takeover, estimated at €1bn-plus. On the corporate finance side the team advised Waterford Wedgwood on two rights issues, each raising approximately €100m. A strong portfolio of plcs includes DCC, Tullow Oil and McInerney. Bryan Bourke and Myra Garrett are both 'highly capable' operators.

Mason Hayes+Curran has a broad-based practice that handles a wide range of commercial and corporate, venture capital, corporate finance and inward investment work, as well as advising on significant public-to-private transactions. Highlights include advising AIG Global Sports and Entertainment Fund LLP on its investment in Setanta Sports Holdings and handling Ely Group's admission to AIM. Paul Egan's team was boosted by the addition of able practitioner Justin McKenna from **LK Shields**.

Colin Sainsbury and Sean Wallace are the key partners in **BCM Hanby Wallace**'s corporate and commercial practice. In 2005 the team advised on a raft of M&A transactions, including handling the acquisition of AGB Scientific by VWR International, and Prime Carrier's acquisition of Am-Beo. Venture capital investments and fundraisings also account for a considerable chunk of the workload; in 2005 the firm acted for Avoca Capital Group on its latest €400m capital fundraising.

Dillon Eustace has significant corporate and commercial capability. Major clients include Chatt Holdings, a US venture capital administrator. The firm also has a compliance and regulatory unit that advises on corporate governance, auditing and accounting issues. Lorcan Tiernan is a recommended practitioner.

Eugene F. Collins has solid corporate and commercial expertise, with clients describing the firm as 'efficient, competent and providing an excellent service.' Key instructions include advising on the Irish aspects of the €730m sale of Stanley Leisure to William Hill, and acting for Western Wireless in the acquisition of minority shares in Meteor Mobile Holdings. Eileen Grace, Anthony Collins and Gerard Coll are rated practitioners in the corporate and commercial team.

The seven-partner practice at **LK Shields** covers the full breadth of corporate and commercial law, handling M&A, flotations, private equity, inward investment and commercial contracts. Highlights include advising William Hill on the acquisition of the Irish operations of Stanley Racing, and handling Ormonde Mining's admission to AIM and the Irish Stock Exchange. Gerard Halpenny and Marco Hickey are admired for their 'efficiency and responsiveness'. Justin McKenna has left join **Mason Hayes+Curran**.

David O'Beirne heads the corporate and commercial team at **O'Donnell Sweeney**, while Francis Hackett, managing partner of the firm, regularly advises on major transactions. The firm has a particular focus on advising privately owned companies in traditional industries. A major recent instruction was advising Century Homes on its €98m sale to Kingspan. Also notable was advising on the disposal by the founding shareholders of Caulfield Group to an MBO team.

An example of a major transaction for **Beauchamps** in the past year is acting as the lead advisor on the €50m development of the Radisson Hotel and Resort in Co Cavan. Shaun O'Shea heads a busy five-partner team, which includes Gary Rice, who has carved a niche in regulatory and sports law.

Ivor Fitzpatrick & Company acted as lead lawyers to the vendor shareholders in the tradesale of the Retail Petroleum System group of companies to Torex Retail, an AIM-listed international retail systems business. Andy McConnell and John King are recommended.

Edward Evans heads **Landwell Solicitors**' corporate and commercial team. Highlights include advising Cross Atlantic Capital Partners and 4th Level Ventures on private equity investments made in Irish technology and biotech companies. Other notable instructions include advising Irish newspapers on the outsourcing of back office functions as part of restructuring projects.

Corporate finance is a key focus at **Maples and Calder** (formerly *Binchys*). In 2005, the team acted for International Marketing and Sales Group in a number of fundraisings from private investors with a total value of US$4.2m. Jennifer Caldwell heads the practice.

The four-partner practice at **McEvoy Partners**, headed by Bernard McEvoy, has dealt with a raft of AIM flotations over the past year, including that of Adwalker, Ovoca Resources, Persian Gold and Vimio. On the M&A side, the team acted on the sale of Fitzpatrick's Hotel in Bunratty, estimated at €11m.

WhitneyMoore advises on the full breadth of corporate and commercial matters, including venture capital, M&A and corporate governance.

Dockrell Farrell's key commercial partners are John Dockrell and Brendan O'Donovan. The firm deals with a broad scope of corporate and commercial matters.

Gore & Grimes has expertise in the disposal of private and public companies.

Dynamic corporate boutique **KLW** is recommended. John Kehoe garners considerable praise from clients for being 'very trustworthy; he practises law in a 'City' way.'

Niche practice **Kilroys** has a high reputation for corporate and commercial expertise.

PJ O'Driscoll & Sons, which is located in Dublin and Cork, regularly advises a broad mix of companies and financial institutions, both Irish and international, on a wide remit of corporate transactions, while Dublin firm **Reddy Charlton McKnight** has a good reputation in the market.

Cork-based **Ronan Daly Jermyn** has an impressive corporate and commercial practice: one of the best outside Dublin. A quality client list that includes Musgrave Group, GSK and Eli Lilly, was expanded by client gains Dairygold and Dynea, the international adhesives group. The team has expertise in venture capital, acting for venture capital houses on technology fundraisings. John Dwyer and Garvan Corkery have good reputations.

DISPUTE RESOLUTION

The new Commercial Court, set up in 2004, has successfully speeded up the progress of cases, but the tight deadlines it imposes has stretched firms with limited resources.

Peter Law heads **A&L Goodbody**'s 12-partner team, which includes the 'highly competent' Caroline Preston. The practice is developing an excellent reputation in mediation. A steady flow of high-value work includes acting for BUPA Ireland in a significant dispute, challenging legislation that may allow for the imposition of an annual €34m levy, payable in favour of a dominant state-owned insurer.

Arthur Cox's strong team contains the experienced David O'Donohoe and Conor McDonnell. The team acted in the landmark case of 2005: advising Fyffes Group in proceedings against DCC for alleged insider dealing, a case which pivots around the sale of DCC's stake in Fyffes in February 2000. This is the first civil insider trading case ever brought in Ireland. The team is also advising a large group of Irish bookmakers in proceedings against the British Horse Racing

DISPUTE RESOLUTION

A&L GOODBODY ✪
ARTHUR COX ✪
MATHESON ORMSBY PRENTICE ✪
McCANN FITZGERALD ✪
WILLIAM FRY ✪

EUGENE F. COLLINS ✪
LK SHIELDS ✪
MASON HAYES+CURRAN ✪

BCM HANBY WALLACE ✪
BEAUCHAMPS ✪
DILLON EUSTACE ✪
IVOR FITZPATRICK & COMPANY ✪
O'DONNELL SWEENEY ✪
RONAN DALY JERMYN ✪

Conway Kelleher Tobin
Dockrell Farrell
Duncan Grehan & Partners
Kilroys
Landwell Solicitors ✪
Maples and Calder ✪
Reddy Charlton McKnight ✪
Simon McAleese Solicitors
WhitneyMoore

Firms are listed A-Z in tiers which are ranked in order of priority
✪ Indicates firm displays contact details at the end of this chapter.

Board (BHRB) in a dispute over the BHB's alleged database rights.

Matheson Ormsby Prentice's dispute resolution practice is jointly headed by the 'experienced' Michael Tyrell and Stuart Margetson, who is considered 'a leader in the field.' Consistent with the firm's focus on specialisms, the team has strengths across the dispute resolution spectrum, from IP, retail and leisure, employment, professional negligence and product liability. Key cases in 2005 include advising National Irish Bank on regulatory issues in the largest ever High Court inquiry into an Irish bank.

McCann FitzGerald has a wide ranging practice, from administrative law to employment and IP. The team continues to advise the state development company that procured the National Aquatic Centre in a series of high-profile disputes over contractual arrangements for the operation of the Centre. Roddy Bourke has a superlative reputation.

William Fry fields some talented partners in its dispute resolution practice: Owen O'Sullivan for commercial litigation, Carol Plunkett for IP and Michael Kealey for defamation. The team was instructed on the biggest case of 2005, *Fyffes v DCC*, in which the sum of around €100m is being claimed in damages. An impressive roll call of clients includes Red Bull, Flogas Ireland, Arnotts and Boots.

Terry Leggett at **Eugene F. Collins** has an excellent reputation. Also recommended is Ronan O'Neill, who specialises in medical and IP litigation. Highlight cases include advising Shell Ireland in the ongoing dispute with landowners and objectors to its €900m gas pipeline and onshore terminal facilities in Mayo, and advising an international accountancy firm in a €50m professional negligence claim in the Commercial Court.

LK Shields' busy four-partner practice is headed by Edmund Butler and Hugh Garvey. A steady flow of instructions includes advising Frank Dunlop, a key witness in the Mahon Tribunal, which is investigating allegations of political bribery and planning corruption. The team has also acted in a number of significant and complex shareholder disputes.

Litigation is a core strength at **Mason Hayes+Curran**, where the team is headed by the 'skilful' Declan Black. The firm has advised on a raft of high-value disputes before the Commercial Court, acting for Xilinx Ireland in a €26m claim by parties alleging to be commercial agents.

BCM Hanby Wallace's Gerald Butler heads the dispute resolution practice. The firm specialises in advising insurance heavyweights on insurance claims, health and safety legislation and professional negligence and malpractice. The firm is expanding its general commercial litigation capacity.

Gabriel Daly heads **Beauchamps**' dispute resolution practice. A busy workload includes handling the 16 plaintiff actions against the tobacco companies and the State, for damages arising out of the alleged failure of the State to properly regulate the manufacture and sale of tobacco products. Mark Heslin and Claire Callanan are recommended for employment expertise.

Dillon Eustace handles a broad mix of personal injury, maritime, aviation, insurance and commercial litigation. Key instructions include acting for a leading international bank in defence of a claim by an international investment fund for losses arising out of an investment contract. Paul Gill has particular expertise in defamation.

Ivor Fitzpatrick & Company moves up a tier this year in recognition of the firm's commitment to dispute resolution. Deirdre Courtney heads the team, while Susan Stapleton handles the civil litigation. The firm has a thriving judicial review practice, in 2005 resisting a challenge to a decision of the Broadcasting Commission of Ireland to award an alternative Rock Radio licence to a radio station trading as 'Phantom FM'. The team is also active in the major tribunals and has honed expertise in this field.

In late 2004 **O'Donnell Sweeney** recruited the former managing partner of **Landwell Solicitors**, Jim Trueick, so gaining a formidable litigator and employment law expert. The team also includes quality practitioners Dermot McEvoy and Norman Fitzgerald. Major highlights include advising a company in a significant claim against the Department of Agriculture and a major corporate, which successfully settled in favour of **O'Donnell Sweeney**'s client.

Ronan Daly Jermyn has substantial dispute resolution expertise, acting in the high-profile tribunals including the Flood and Moriarty tribunals. Judicial review is also a niche within the practice. In 2005 the firm advised in the significant case of *O'Callaghan v Judge Alan Mahon & ors*, which challenged the working of a tribunal which focuses on planning matters and payment.

EU AND COMPETITION

Dr Vincent Power is an acknowledged EU and competition expert at **A&L Goodbody**. The five-fee-earner team includes Grainne Pyne, a senior economist. In 2005 the team advised on a raft of merger notifications, and also handled the competition aspects of eircom's €420m acquisition of Meteor Mobile Communications. Other key instructions include advising Johnston Press on its €138.6m acquisition of the *Leinster Leader* and the €95m acquisition of Local Press.

Arthur Cox has a first-class competition group led by two experienced partners, John Meade and Patrick O'Brien. The team has a concentrated focus on competition law and merger control, and recently advised Bank of America on the Irish competition and regulatory aspects of its merger with MBNA. Major clients include An Post, Dairygold, Eagle Star, Viridian and Ulster Bank.

The 'pragmatic' Helen Kelly at **Matheson Ormsby Prentice** is praised by clients for providing 'business-friendly advice, to which other firms do not come close' as well as scoring points for being 'fun to work with'. The five-fee-earner group has strength in merger control and also in cartel work. High-profile instructions include advising Hewlett-Packard Ireland on the multiple acquisition of companies including Synstar and Schlumberger Ireland.

Gerard FitzGerald and Damian Collins are well-known EU and competition practitioners at **McCann FitzGerald**. A varied workload is demonstrated by examples: the firm has advised O2 on a range of competition matters, including advising on ComReg's decision to designate O2 an operator with significant market power, and has acted for the Voluntary Health Insurance Board in state aid proceedings initiated before the EC Court of First Instance by BUPA.

William Fry has an extensive competition law practice, with expertise in public procurement. The team acts for an array of state bodies: FAS, the Office of Public Works, Dublin City Council and the Rail Procurement Agency. Regulatory advice is also provided to clients in the telecoms, media, financial services and industrial sectors, which include Sky Jefferson Smurfit Group, Waterford Wedgwood and Red Bull. John Handoll heads the practice.

EU AND COMPETITION

A&L GOODBODY ✪
ARTHUR COX ✪
MATHESON ORMSBY PRENTICE ✪
McCANN FITZGERALD ✪
WILLIAM FRY ✪

Beauchamps ✪
Eugene F. Collins ✪
LK Shields ✪
Landwell Solicitors ✪
Mason Hayes+Curran ✪

Conway Kelleher Tobin
Dillon Eustace ✪
Dockrell Farrell
Kilroys
O'Donnell Sweeney ✪
Robert Ryan & Associates
Ronan Daly Jermyn ✪
WhitneyMoore

Firms are listed A-Z in tiers which are ranked in order of priority
✪ *Indicates firm displays contact details at the end of this chapter.*

EMPLOYMENT

ARTHUR COX ✪
BCM HANBY WALLACE ✪

A&L GOODBODY ✪
MASON HAYES+CURRAN ✪
MATHESON ORMSBY PRENTICE ✪
McCANN FITZGERALD ✪
WILLIAM FRY ✪

LK Shields ✪
Landwell Solicitors ✪
O'Donnell Sweeney ✪
Ronan Daly Jermyn ✪

Beauchamps ✪
Conway Kelleher Tobin
Dillon Eustace ✪
Eugene F. Collins ✪
Ivor Fitzpatrick & Company ✪
Simon McAleese Solicitors
WhitneyMoore

Firms are listed A-Z in tiers which are ranked in order of priority
✪ *Indicates firm displays contact details at the end of this chapter.*

Beauchamps has recruited associate Tim Jordan, formerly of *Coudert Brothers* in Brussels, to boost its EU and competition practice. The firm advises both Irish and international companies as well as state bodies on the full spectrum of EU and competition law issues, from merger control and public procurement to cartel and dominance matters. One to watch.

Also Brussels-trained is David Dillon at **Eugene F. Collins**, who is building up a solid EU and competition practice. Major highlights include advising one of Ireland's largest petroleum suppliers on an investigation by the Competition Authority. On the transactional side, the firm advised Select Retail Holdings on its acquisition of Superquinn.

LK Shields' remit covers both EU and Irish competition law, including advice on restrictive practices, abuse of a dominant position and merger control. Examples of work undertaken include advising ISS Group on various competition law matters and IAWS Group, a major food and agri-business group, on the competition law aspects of transactions. Clients' favourite Marco Hickey heads the EU and competition unit.

Garrett Breen at **Landwell Solicitors** is a specialist in regulatory law, advising both companies and individuals, as well as regulatory authorities. The firm acts for the Office of Utility Regulation in Guernsey, advising on electricity, postal and telecommunications matters. The Commission for Aviation Regulation is another key client.

Mason Hayes+Curran regularly advises on merger notifications, including obtaining merger clearances in several European jurisdictions for Barlo Group in its acquisition of the Quinn Group. Anthony Burke heads the practice.

EMPLOYMENT

Arthur Cox has a demonstrated commitment to employment expertise, with three partners dedicated to the practice area and leading employment expert Dr Mary Redmond as a consultant to the group. The team acts for the full spectrum of employers; including both Irish and global corporations, listed, private, not-for-profit and public sector clients. Seamus Given is recommended.

Gary Byrne is one of Ireland's leading employment practitioners at **BCM Hanby Wallace**. This busy practice thoroughly deserves its reputation for excellence in the field. The team regularly handles complex and high-profile employment cases, and is currently acting for Ryanair in a challenge in the Supreme Court to the High Court and Labour Court decisions under the controversial Industrial Relations (Miscellaneous Provisions) Act 2004. Michelle Ní Longáin and Michael Kennedy are experienced practitioners.

A&L Goodbody's employment law group advises on complex Irish and EU employment law. Ian Moore heads the six-partner practice, while Alison Fanagan is active on the health and safety side, regularly defending companies and directors against prosecution by the Health and Safety Authority. A key instruction was advising the International Rugby Board in a dispute with Geoffrey Evans over replacing him as head of rugby development. Ian Moore heads the practice.

Mason Hayes+Curran has a varied client base that spans both the public and private sectors. AIB, Kellogg's and Merrill Lynch are major clients. Highlights include advising a Japanese multinational on the closure of two facilities in Dublin and also acting for a UK supermarket withdrawing from the Republic. On the contentious side the team regularly deals with equal pay disputes before the Equality Tribunal. Peter McInnes and Emer Gilvarry are both 'on the ball,' according to clients.

Paul Glenfield heads the newly merged employment, pensions and benefits law group at **Matheson Ormsby Prentice**. The firm has a strong health and safety practice. Clients are drawn from diverse industry sectors, and include prestigious Irish and multinational companies such as Hewlett-Packard, Microsoft, Citigroup and National Irish Bank.

Terence McCrann has a great reputation for his employment expertise at **McCann FitzGerald**. The team of eight lawyers handles both contentious and advisory work for household names such as Argos, Bank of Ireland, Diageo and University College Cork.

William Fry has a solid employment practice that regularly advises Ireland's most successful companies, both domestic and international, such as Jefferson Smurfit Group, Hibernian Group and Tesco. The combined employment and pensions group has contentious and non-contentious capacity, advising on outsourcings, TUPE and the full range of employment issues. Boyce Shubotham is a 'wise head'.

Michael Kavanagh heads the employment unit at **LK Shields**, which advises both Irish and multinational employers on all aspects of employment law. The team advised on a raft of disputes involving directors, shareholder employees and former employees. Major clients include IAWS Group, a major food and agri-business group, and Boylesports.

Landwell Solicitors scoops considerable employment work from its PwC connections, and takes a proactive approach to advice. Colleen Cleary is the resident employment law specialist, advising corporate clients and HR professionals on the full spectrum of employment issues, including corporate restructuring.

Jim Trueick, former managing partner of **Landwell Solicitors**, has joined David Fagan at **O'Donnell Sweeney**, boosting the team's expertise. Highlights of 2005 include advising a sizeable multinational telecommunications company in the acquisition of a specialist IT provider.

Jennifer Cashman has expertise at Cork-based **Ronan Daly Jermyn**. The experienced

Fergus Long also heads the team. In 2005 the team successfully represented University College Cork (UCC) in the High Court and Supreme Court over an equality claim taken against UCC by a number of security operatives.

ENERGY AND NATURAL RESOURCES

Arthur Cox has one of the largest dedicated energy teams and an outstanding client list, including energy heavyweight Viridian Group. The team reaps the lion's share of key energy and resources projects in Ireland, including acting for Viridian Group on the development of the €250m development of the Huntstown Phase 2 Power Project. Another major instruction was advising Northern Ireland Energy Holdings on the £185m acquisition of Premier Transmission, the owner of the Scotland-to-Northern Ireland gas pipeline. Alex McLean and John Glackin have weighty expertise.

'Dynamo' Michael O'Connor heads **Matheson Ormsby Prentice**'s energy and natural resources group, which has maintained its reputation for quality instructions. The team advised Arcon International Resources on the mining aspects of its recommended €93.4m offer by Lundin Mining, and advised Tynagh Energy on the development and financing of a 400MW independent power plant.

Projects guru Kevin Feeney is a central player in the four-partner energy team at **A&L Goodbody**. Project financing is a focus; recent deals include acting on a dual mandate basis for SWS Natural Resources and Barclays Bank on the project financing of the Gneeves and Kilgarvan windfarms. The team is also advising the private equity investor, HgCapital, on its equity investment in the 32MW project financed Sorne windfarm in Donegal.

Mason Hayes+Curran counts both regulatory bodies and energy companies on its client list. Key instructions are providing advice on the oil exploration industry for Dragon Oil, and advising the CER and Northern Ireland Energy Regulator on the development of an all-Ireland market. Wind farm projects are also a particular focus. Practitioners who are active in the field are John Kettle, Kevin Hoy and Tony Burke.

McCann FitzGerald's client list includes significant players in the energy sector, such as Bord Gáis Eireann, which the team advises on corporate and regulatory matters, commercial arrangements and project financing, as well as on the establishment and distribution of its gas distribution and supply business in Northern Ireland. Patricia Lawless has a good reputation.

Aislinn O'Farrell heads a busy two-partner team at **William Fry**, which moves up a tier this year in recognition of the quality of its workload. Major instructions include acting for RWE Energy (Ireland) on gas supply, operation and maintenance and electricity revenue issues relating to the Tynagh Energy Ireland plant at Tynagh, Co Galway. The team also provides advice on the full spectrum of emissions and emissions-trading matters to clients such as Edenderry Power, Aughinish and Smurfit.

Eileen Prendergast at **BCM Hanby Wallace** has project finance expertise, while at **Beauchamps**, Ainsley Heffernan is the chief partner in the energy and natural resources unit which advises on power projects.

Dillon Eustace advises a mixture of financiers, exploration companies and state bodies. The firm acts for the leading Irish gas operator on licensing and other issues relating to the supply of gas within Ireland. Paul Eustace is active in energy matters.

Banking and finance partner Leonora Malone is the key energy contact at **Eugene F. Collins**.

LK Shields is a new entrant to our table this year, in recognition of growing expertise in this area. Philip Daly heads the practice, which acts for the largest renewable energy provider in Ireland in the development of wind farms in Ireland.

O'Donnell Sweeney has considerable experience of advising on wind farm project development and financing, advising on projects worth €190m in the past 12 months.

Ronan Daly Jermyn has Enterprise Oil as a significant client, which is developing a gas field off the West Coast. In 2005 the firm also added Bord Gáis Eireann to the client list.

WhitneyMoore has some energy capability.

ENERGY AND NATURAL RESOURCES

ARTHUR COX ✪
MATHESON ORMSBY PRENTICE ✪

A&L GOODBODY ✪
MASON HAYES+CURRAN ✪
McCANN FITZGERALD ✪
WILLIAM FRY ✪

BCM Hanby Wallace ✪
Beauchamps ✪
Dillon Eustace ✪
Eugene F. Collins ✪
LK Shields ✪
O'Donnell Sweeney ✪
O'Flynn Exhams
Ronan Daly Jermyn ✪
WhitneyMoore

Firms are listed A-Z in tiers which are ranked in order of priority
✪ Indicates firm displays contact details at the end of this chapter.

IT, TELECOMS AND E-COMMERCE

Arthur Cox's technology group has been expanded by a internal merger with the Life Sciences and Pharmaceuticals group and is now overseen by three partners: John Menton, Declan Hayes and Raymond Hurley. Professor Robert Clark acts as a consultant. The team regularly acts for US multinational technology and pharmaceutical companies as well as emerging and domestic technology companies. An impressive client list includes PayPal, Athlone Institute of Technology, Cisco Systems and eBay.

The team at **Matheson Ormsby Prentice** has a first-class reputation and a client base to match. Don McAleese and Anne-Marie Bohan are standing counsel for the Irish-based operations of Microsoft, Google, Hewlett-Packard and Xerox, as well as being retained by the Department of Communications, Marine and Natural Resources to advise on the Electronic Communications legislation. Technology clients find both partners 'exceptionally talented lawyers' and comment that the firm offers a 'superlative level of service'; the firm also gains full marks for 'showing enthusiasm for the client's business.'

William Earley, Paul Lavery and Susan O'Halloran are highly capable practitioners at **McCann FitzGerald**. The team is adviser to O2 Communications (Ireland) and British Telecom (Esat BT) as well as providing e-commerce advice to Diageo, the National Gallery of Ireland and Motorola.

William Fry's IT and e-commerce practice has strength on outsourcing, new media and data protection. In 2005 the firm added Yahoo! to a burgeoning client list, which already includes household names such as Siemens, IONA Technologies and IBM. The team also acted for Royal & SunAlliance in the first major IT infrastructure outsourcing since 2000 – to IBM. Carol Plunkett is recommended on the disputes side.

IT, TELECOMS AND E-COMMERCE

ARTHUR COX ✪
MATHESON ORMSBY PRENTICE ✪
McCANN FITZGERALD ✪
WILLIAM FRY ✪

A&L GOODBODY ✪
MASON HAYES+CURRAN ✪

Eugene F. Collins ✪
LK Shields ✪
Landwell Solicitors ✪
O'Donnell Sweeney ✪

BCM Hanby Wallace ✪
Beauchamps ✪
Dockrell Farrell
Kilroys

Conway Kelleher Tobin
Dillon Eustace ✪
Maples and Calder ✪
Ronan Daly Jermyn ✪
Simon McAleese Solicitors

Firms are listed A-Z in tiers which are ranked in order of priority
✪ Indicates firm displays contact details at the end of this chapter.

John Whelan heads the three-partner practice at **A&L Goodbody**, which has a steady flow of instructions, regularly advising on e-commerce and outsourcing. Highlights for 2005 include advising eircom on the outsourcing of its IT and call centre functions to Capita, and acting for IBEC on the outsourcing of its IT functions to Fujitsu. The team also advised Apple on the Irish rollout of its iTunes packages.

Tony Burke and John Kettle at **Mason Hayes+Curran** advise a host of public purchasers on their IT procurements including the national broadcaster, RTE, the Office for the Director of Public Prosecutions and the National Food Safety Board. The pair have a formidable reputation for 'responsiveness' and for 'handling whatever is thrown at them.'

Eugene F. Collins has a solid client base of technology and e-commerce clients, including Columbia Ventures Corporation, which the firm regularly advises on e-commerce issues, telecommunications, deregulation and licensing. David Hackett, former in-house counsel at GSM Association, heads the team of three fee-earners.

LK Shields' IT and e-commerce practice falls within the ambit of the IP unit. The team has experience of advising on an array of IT contracts, from software licensing to service level agreements. A varied client base includes start-up, incubator and early stage companies as well as entrepreneurs. On the contentious side the team regularly handles e-commerce disputes over domain names and other internet-related disputes.

Following Carol Plunkett's departure from **Landwell Solicitors** to **William Fry**, Garrett Breen heads the technology, media and communications group, which regularly advises internet-based retailers. Recent work includes conducting data protection audits for a large multinational internet seller.

Tony McGovern at **O'Donnell Sweeney** has substantial IT and e-commerce expertise. Highlights of 2005 include acting for Similarity Systems on its €5.5m fundraising led by Trinity Venture Capital. A growing client list includes several large software companies, which the team advises on licensing in Ireland and abroad.

Darren Daly and Sean Wallace cover the full IT and e-commerce remit at **BCM Hanby Wallace**.

Beauchamps has recruited Maureen Daly to head the IP practice, which includes IT and e-commerce work. Mark Pery-Knox Gore also has expertise in the technology field.

The eponymous John Dockrell at **Dockrell Farrell** is the main contact for IT and e-commerce at the firm.

Patrick Ryan head the IT and e-commerce team at **Kilroys**, which has a number of technology companies on the client list, including Telenor, Norway's biggest telecoms company.

INSOLVENCY AND CORPORATE RESTRUCTURING

ARTHUR COX ✪
EUGENE F. COLLINS ✪
MATHESON ORMSBY PRENTICE ✪
McCANN FITZGERALD ✪
WILLIAM FRY ✪

A&L GOODBODY ✪
MASON HAYES+CURRAN ✪
WHITNEYMOORE

LK Shields ✪
O'Donnell Sweeney ✪
Ronan Daly Jermyn ✪

Beauchamps ✪
Ivor Fitzpatrick & Company ✪
Landwell Solicitors ✪
Reddy Charlton McKnight ✪

Firms are listed A-Z in tiers which are ranked in order of priority
✪ Indicates firm displays contact details at the end of this chapter.

INSOLVENCY AND CORPORATE RESTRUCTURING

A consequence of Ireland's economic success is a downturn in insolvency. Most work in this sector is focused on restructuring, corporate compliance and advising clients on managing the growing corporate regulatory burden.

Arthur Cox reaps a raft of instructions from its close links with the Big Four accountancy practices, as well as the key Irish banks, such as Ulster Bank, Bank of Ireland and AIB. Highlight instructions include advising the joint administrator of Rover Ireland. Eugene McCague and William Day are experienced practitioners in the field.

Barry O'Neill and Doug Smith lead a busy practice at **Eugene F. Collins**, which has a wealth of experience in bankruptcy, company restructurings and schemes of arrangement, receiverships and voluntary liquidations. Clients consider both practitioners to be 'first port of call' for corporate restructuring.

Matheson Ormsby Prentice's insolvency and corporate restructuring team regularly advises financial institutions, public and private companies, and insolvency professionals on the full spectrum of corporate restructuring and insolvency. The team scooped a high-profile instruction in 2004 acting for the official liquidator of Eurofood, the Irish subsidiary of Parmalat. The 'capable' Rod Ensor heads the department, while Tony O'Grady provides contentious capability.

Jane Marshall and Emma Crowley are key insolvency practitioners at **McCann FitzGerald**. Highlight instructions include advising on the Irish aspects of the international restructuring of Flightlease (Ireland) (in liquidation). The team is also acting on the receivership of the Keytech Plastics.

William Fry's two-partner insolvency and corporate recovery team is led by Michael Quinn. Mark Traynor is the other half of the duo. The team has been involved in a raft of Ireland's high-profile insolvencies acting for liquidators, examiners and receivers, covering a breadth of industry from manufacturing to financial services.

Paul Dobbyn and David Baxter are joint team leaders at **A&L Goodbody**'s experienced, four-partner insolvency unit. The team is currently advising the majority bondholders in the high-profile liquidation of Parmalat's Irish subsidiary, Eurofood.

Litigator Declan Black heads the **Mason Hayes+Curran** insolvency team, while newly made up partner Maurice Phelan is also active in the area. Core instructions emanate from domestic insolvency practitioners, although the firm also advises parties in cross-border insolvencies with an Irish element.

WhitneyMoore regularly advises companies and individuals as well as insolvency professionals. Paul Hayes heads the practice.

LK Shields' seven-strong team has an established track record in advising on the substantial restructurings of major corporates based in Ireland. Hugh Garvey and Edmund Butler are recommended.

Norman Fitzgerald at **O'Donnell Sweeney**, like all the firms in our table, benefits from referral work from the mid-size and large accountancy firms. A varied client base includes liquidators, creditors and companies or directors.

Cork firm **Ronan Daly Jermyn** provides insolvency expertise to diverse sectors of industry. Nicholas Comyn is recommended.

INSURANCE

Our insurance section encompasses firms that advise insurance companies on industry regulation and those that focus on insurance disputes, such as personal injury claims.

A&L Goodbody has strength on the contentious and advisory aspects of insurance. Major instructions include advising Standard Life on its demutualisation project, and acting for Partner Re, a significant Bermuda insurer, on the establishment of its European headquarters. The practice encompasses regulation and M&A for a diverse client base of domestic and international insurers, including Hibernian, Irish Life, Prudential and Zurich. James Grennan is an accomplished practitioner.

Matheson Ormsby Prentice's 'capable' Liam Flynn spearheads the corporate and regulatory arm of the insurance practice, while Sharon Daly is active on the contentious side. A sterling client base includes Ark Life, AXA Ireland, Carphone Warehouse Insurance and Medical Protection Society. Highlights of 2005 include advising Banco

INSURANCE
A&L GOODBODY ✪ MATHESON ORMSBY PRENTICE ✪ WILLIAM FRY ✪
Arthur Cox ✪ Dillon Eustace ✪ McCann FitzGerald ✪
Mason Hayes+Curran ✪
Beauchamps ✪ Dockrell Farrell Ivor Fitzpatrick & Company ✪ Kilroys LK Shields ✪ Landwell Solicitors ✪ O'Donnell Sweeney ✪ Ronan Daly Jermyn ✪ WhitneyMoore
BCM Hanby Wallace ✪ Duncan Grehan & Partners Eugene F. Collins ✪ Good & Murray Smith & Company Gore & Grimes ✪ Maples and Calder ✪
Firms are listed A-Z in tiers which are ranked in order of priority ✪ *Indicates firm displays contact details at the end of this chapter.*

Santander on the Irish regulatory aspects of its £30bn acquisition of Abbey National.

William Fry fields four fee-earners who advise all sectors of the insurance industry: insurance, life assurance, reinsurance as well as insurance intermediaries. Key instructions include advising AXA Cessions on an innovative 'catbond' structure, which involved establishing an Irish special purpose reinsurance company that provided coverage against losses arising from windstorms, collaterised with a bond issue. Regulatory work is also a specialism. The 'responsive and practical' John Larkin leads the team.

At **Arthur Cox** a first-class client list includes a raft of prestigious insurance companies such as Royal & SunAlliance, Eagle Star and Allianz. The firm acts for insurance companies on every facet of business, as well as advising on insurance regulation. Carl O'Sullivan heads the busy practice.

The insurance unit at **Dillon Eustace** has a strong regulatory focus, handled by Andrew Bates. Major clients include life and non-life insurers, reinsurance captives and insurance captives. The team also has a substantial personal injury defence practice, which defends both domestic and international insurers. Kieran Cowhey has expertise in defence litigation.

McCann FitzGerald fields several highly able practitioners in the insurance field, including litigators Roddy Bourke and Helen Collins. An impressive client list includes Allianz, Barclays Insurance, Chubb and Royal & SunAlliance. The team advises the Medical Defence Union on medical negligence cases, professional indemnity claims and Medical Council disciplinary proceedings.

Lorcan Buckley leads the team at **Mason Hayes+Curran**, which acts for all the major insurance companies active in Ireland. The firm has a strong defence insurance practice, handling claims for a number of large retailers and construction companies. Eagle Star Insurance and Hibernian are on the client list.

Beauchamps' Claire Callanan and Gabriel Daly regularly handle insurance disputes, while Berchmans Gannon advises a raft of healthcare insurance providers in Ireland, providing a depth of experience in clinical indemnity litigation.

Dockrell Farrell is active in insurance defence litigation for both domestic and international insurers, while at **Ivor Fitzpatrick & Company** civil litigator Susan Stapleton also has experience on the insurance defence side, in particular of mass torts.

Kilroys specialises in advising clients in the non-life insurance sector on insurance arbitration, insurance regulation and compliance and insurance policy drafting and review. The team also specialises in credit insurance and re-insurance. Anthony Laying and Eamon Jones are key contacts at the firm.

LK Shields focuses on insurance litigation; handled by three partners, Edmund Butler, Michael Kavanagh and Laurence Shields. The team has carved a strong niche in professional negligence, acting in defence of claims against solicitors, accountants, engineers and architects.

Landwell Solicitors focuses on regulatory compliance, while at **O'Donnell Sweeney** Norman Fitzgerald has expertise in professional negligence claims and is advising a professional services firm in a key case.

Ronan Daly Jermyn has the biggest defence litigation practice outside Dublin, which regularly handles work for all the major insurance companies. The team also advises public bodies such as the State Claims Agency and the Clinical Indemnity Board, which deals with all the medical negligence cases in Ireland.

John Lynch heads a busy insurance defence litigation practice at **WhitneyMoore**, advising insurers and self-insured clients.

INTELLECTUAL PROPERTY

The three-partner practice at **LK Shields** handles both advisory and contentious work on the gamut of IP, including trade marks, patents, copyright and franchising. In 2005 the team advised Ranbaxy Laboratories in its dispute against Warner-Lambert over the drug Atorvastatin. A major client is News International Newspapers, which the firm advises on all its contentious and advisory IP issues in Ireland and abroad. The departure of 'first-class' Patricia McGovern, who left in early 2006 to set up her own practice, is a loss to the firm.

INTELLECTUAL PROPERTY
LK SHIELDS ✪ MATHESON ORMSBY PRENTICE ✪ McCANN FITZGERALD ✪ WILLIAM FRY ✪
A&L GOODBODY ✪ ARTHUR COX ✪
Beauchamps ✪ Eugene F. Collins ✪ Mason Hayes+Curran ✪ WhitneyMoore
BCM Hanby Wallace ✪ Dillon Eustace ✪ Dockrell Farrell Gleeson McGrath Baldwin Landwell Solicitors ✪ O'Donnell Sweeney ✪ Reddy Charlton McKnight ✪ Ronan Daly Jermyn ✪ Simon McAleese Solicitors
Firms are listed A-Z in tiers which are ranked in order of priority ✪ *Indicates firm displays contact details at the end of this chapter.*

In 2005 **Matheson Ormsby Prentice** launched an associated trade mark filing firm, MOP Trademark Advisers, which adds another dimension to a thriving IP practice. Team head Alistair Payne provides commercial IP advice, while Michael Tyrell handles the contentious arm. The team regularly advises on the IP element of corporate transactions and on the commercialisation of IP assets and trade mark protection programmes. Major clients include the National Lottery, Nokia and Next.

Clients find Grace Smith and Yvonne McNamara at **McCann FitzGerald** 'efficient, proactive and commercial, while at the same time cost conscious'. The team deals with the full spectrum of advisory and contentious matters concerning trade marks, patents and copyright. Key instructions include advising adidas in disputes over the three striped band, and James Joyce estate on copyright.

William Fry acts for a litany of household names ranging from Associated Newspapers to Pfizer, Tesco, Starbucks and Waterford Crystal. On the contentious side, Carol Plunkett is renowned as a leading IP expert who 'handles the concerns of clients with attention and aplomb.' Highlights for the firm in 2005 include acting for Pfizer in two patent disputes and advising Hutchison 3G Ireland on its entry into the Irish market. David Cullen, who leads the advisory side of the practice, is an experienced practitioner.

John Whelan heads the four-partner department at **A&L Goodbody**, which has a sturdy advisory and contentious IP practice. The team regularly advises on patents, copyright, trade marks, passing off, designs and trade secrets. Highlights include acting for Abbott Laboratories in defending a patent revocation, and continuing to advise Danone on trade mark and patent matters.

Arthur Cox benefits from the expertise of Professor Robert Clark, a consultant to the technology and IP Group. The team advises blue-chip corporates, as well as academic institutions such as University College Dublin and Dublin City University. Key instructions in 2005 include advising Vodafone on a trade mark infringement and domain name conflict case, and acting for Waterford Crystal in an action for trade mark infringement against Cavan Crystal. John Menton heads the team.

Beauchamps has considerably boosted its practice with the hire of Maureen Daly from **A&L Goodbody**. The firm advises high-calibre clients such as Levi Strauss, Timberland and the Craft Council of Ireland, and is certainly one to watch.

David Hackett and Ronan O'Neill have IP expertise at **Eugene F. Collins**. The team recently advised Western Wireless International on all the IP implications of the €420m sale of its subsidiary Meteor Mobile Communications to eircom. On the contentious side, the team has advised on a raft of trade mark and copyright infringement actions.

Mason Hayes+Curran has a wide remit which covers branding, corporate and technology transfer IP. Major highlights include advising Dublin City University on the creation of Centres of Excellence, and advising cornflake specialists Kellogg's in High Court trade mark proceedings. Richard Woulfe has expertise on IP disputes.

Ken Parkinson at **WhitneyMoore** is 'the grandfather of patent litigation', providing 'matchless' expertise on intellectual property disputes.

INVESTMENT FUNDS

A&L Goodbody fields a dynamic and experienced team, which provides the full spectrum of legal advice to a blue-chip client base. Investment funds expertise is supplemented by regulatory listing and taxation capability. Brian McDermott leads the three-partner team, which advised Bramdean Asset Management in establishing a suite of Dublin-based UCITS funds and its Irish management company, and acted for Perpetual Trustees Australia on the establishment of a front office investment management operation in Ireland: PI Investment Management.

Arthur Cox's listings service is now in its second year, under the watchful eye of Helen Berrill. On the pure investment funds front, the five-fee-earner team has advanced expertise, having advised on the largest number of UCITS III conversions. Highlights for 2005 include advising Legg Mason on the takeover of the Citibank funds in Ireland. Kevin Murphy is recommended.

INVESTMENT FUNDS

A&L GOODBODY ✪
ARTHUR COX ✪
DILLON EUSTACE ✪
MATHESON ORMSBY PRENTICE ✪

McCANN FITZGERALD ✪
WILLIAM FRY ✪

Kilroys
LK Shields ✪
Mason Hayes+Curran ✪

Firms are listed A-Z in tiers which are ranked in order of priority
✪ Indicates firm displays contact details at the end of this chapter.

Dillon Eustace's name is synonymous with cutting-edge investment funds work. According to clients, the firm provides 'first-class' advice on a breadth of funds, from private equity and property funds to hedge funds. The firm has international reach through its alliance with **Arendt & Medernach** in Luxembourg and its presence in Boston and Tokyo; in Japan the firm is a market leader in the establishment of retail funds for sale. An impressive client base includes Barings, Fidelity, AIG and PIMCO. Andrew Bates is recommended.

Matheson Ormsby Prentice acts for some of the largest promoters of investment funds in Dublin including Goldman Sachs, Citigroup, Lehman Brothers and INVESCO. The firm also has a growing client list of hedge fund managers. Clients benefit from a parallel regulatory risk management and compliance practice, headed by the experienced Joe Beashel. Michael Jackson and James Scanlon head the practice, which offers funds expertise from its London office.

A leading light of the funds practice at **McCann FitzGerald** is Maire O'Connor, formerly of Ernst & Young. Clients admire O'Connor for 'her ability to make decisions, which is key' and find the team 'efficient and professional'. The funds practice handles Abbey National Treasury Services' Irish funds work. Other clients include AIB Fund Management and IBM UK, which the team has advised on a diversified global fund. Ambrose Loughlin is recommended.

William Fry's Patricia Taylor has significant technical capability. The seven-partner team regularly handles the establishment of funds and provides ongoing advice to those funds, as well as advising on the establishment of UCITS III conversions. Clients number several of the largest global fund promoters, such as Barclays Global Investors.

The former head of investment funds at the Irish Stock Exchange, Hilary Griffey, heads the investment funds practice at **Kilroys**. The firm provides advice to fund promoters and service providers on establishing and operating investment funds in Ireland.

LK Shields' funds practice has a broad focus, advising companies and third-party managers on mutual funds, hedge funds, treasury issues, structured finance and derivatives transactions. Highlight instructions include advising three international investment managers on setting up Irish regulated fund structures for investment in commercial property in the UK and Europe. Joseph Galvin and David Williams head the practice.

Fionán Breathnach heads **Mason Hayes+Curran**'s growing investment funds practice which covers investment funds regulation, alternative investments and hedge funds.

LIFE SCIENCES

Life sciences is a burgeoning area of practice for firms, as Ireland is a growing hub for the pharmaceutical and biotech industries.

At **A&L Goodbody** Cliona Hickey heads the contentious arm, while the 'through and sensible' David Widger acts on the advisory side. The team advises major players in life sciences and healthcare on inward investment projects, regulatory updates, corporate finance and waste management. An impressive client base includes Pfizer, Bayer, Baxter and Amgen.

Declan Hayes leads the practice at **Arthur Cox** to which Maree Gallagher is a consultant. The firm is advising on the establishment of a €2.2bn biopharma campus, the largest facility of its type in the world, and also handled the acquisition, estimated at over €100m, of Mednova by Abbott Laboratories.

Following the departure of Tom Maher to an in-house position, Karen Holmes and Robert O'Shea jointly head the life sciences practice at **Matheson Ormsby Prentice**, which contains a number of industry recruits. The team advises a wide spectrum of clients in the pharmaceutical, biotechnology, medical technology and healthcare sectors. Recent instructions include advising Opsona Therapeutics on its spin-out from Trinity College, Dublin, and also advising on the same company's US$8m financing from Seroba, IVC, Genentech and Enterprise Ireland.

McCann FitzGerald fields a cross-disciplinary team with IP experts Yvonne McNamara and Susan O'Halloran advising on regulatory matters.

LIFE SCIENCES

A&L GOODBODY ✪
ARTHUR COX ✪
MATHESON ORMSBY PRENTICE ✪
McCANN FITZGERALD ✪
WILLIAM FRY ✪

BCM Hanby Wallace ✪
Maree Gallagher Associates
Mason Hayes+Curran ✪

Ronan Daly Jermyn ✪

Firms are listed A-Z in tiers which are ranked in order of priority
✪ Indicates firm displays contact details at the end of this chapter.

Highlights of the past year include advising West Pharmaceutical Services on the Irish legal aspects of its acquisition of Tech Group, as well as acting for Azur Pharma on its equity fundraising.

William Fry draws strength from its sterling corporate practice, which regularly advises life sciences heavyweights such as DCC Healthcare and Sterile Technologies. The firm also acts for a raft of domestic and international venture capital firms investing in the life sciences sector. Clients are well serviced in the event of a dispute, through litigator Carol Plunkett. The team acted for the University of Pittsburgh Medical Centre on its joint venture with Eurocare Healthcare to operate a private oncology clinic in Waterford.

Former Elan lawyer Colin Sainsbury at **BCM Hanby Wallace**, has a loyal client following. The growing practice acts for diverse range of pharmaceutical, biotech and medical devices companies, governmental bodies and research institutions; both Irish and international. Stand-out transactions include advising Newport Pharmaceuticals on its strategic alliance with Bioaccelerate for the co-development of a chronic fatigue drug, and acting for Bank of Scotland (Ireland) on the financing of an acquisition by Alltracel Pharmaceuticals.

Maree Gallagher Associates is the leading agriculture and food specialist in Ireland. Maree left **Arthur Cox** in 2005 to form her own consultancy practice, which provides high-level regulatory expertise in the food and pharmaceutical sector.

Mason Hayes+Curran has established a dedicated life sciences unit, which advises the industry on venture capital funding, licensing collaborations and strategic alliances. The team, headed by ex-Elan lawyer Martin Kelleher, recently advised a domestic diagnostic device manufacturing company on material transfer agreements, manufacturing outsourcing agreements and technology transfers.

MARITIME AND SHIPPING

'Safe pair of hands' Catherine Duffy at **A&L Goodbody** is very knowledgeable in shipping finance. The firm advises on the full scope of maritime and shipping matters, such as ship financing, claims work and maritime litigation. Recent instructions include advising a major Irish bank in the financing of a large fishing vessel, and acting for Irish Ferries on the deregistration of vessels.

Dillon Eustace has a strong reputation for wet shipping, and is also active in shipping finance. Major clients include a high proportion of P&I clubs and all the major ferry companies, such as Stena.

McCann FitzGerald advises on a range of maritime and transport matters, including ship arrest; collision, salvage and pollution claims and salvage claims, as well as having a strong presence in shipping finance and registration. A solid shipping client base includes P&I clubs Bilbroughs, Britannia, Steamship and Sunderland Marine. Petria McDonnell has considerable expertise.

MARITIME AND SHIPPING

A&L GOODBODY ✪
DILLON EUSTACE ✪
McCANN FITZGERALD ✪

ARTHUR COX ✪
MATHESON ORMSBY PRENTICE ✪

Conway Kelleher Tobin
Kennedy McGonagle Ballagh incorporating Bell Branigan O'Donnell & O'Brien
Ronan Daly Jermyn ✪
Vincent & Beatty

Firms are listed A-Z in tiers which are ranked in order of priority
✪ Indicates firm displays contact details at the end of this chapter.

Arthur Cox's Kathleen Garrett is recommended. The team covers all aspects of wet and dry shipping to a high standard.

Helen Kelly and Michael O'Connor both provide shipping and transport expertise at **Matheson Ormsby Prentice**. Highlight instructions include advising Stena AB on its acquisition of assets and vessels from P&O, and acting for P&O Maritime Services, the preferred bidder, on the procurement of ship management services by the public sector.

Mason Hayes+Curran is active on ship finance and regularly acts in both wet and dry shipping disputes. Key clients include the Marine Institute, which the firm is advising on the collection of scientific data in the fishing industry and European quotas.

MEDIA AND ENTERTAINMENT

A&L Goodbody fields several practitioners with media and entertainment expertise, notably London-based Geraldine East and Paul White. The firm regularly acts as production lawyers on feature films, as well as advising on high-profile television productions. A niche focus is sports law, which is handled by Eoin MacNeill, who advises on major sporting events. On the client list is the Football Association of Ireland and Nissan Ireland, which the firm advises on sponsorship of the Nissan Irish Open.

James Hickey is the key practitioner at **Matheson Ormsby Prentice**, with extensive experience of film and television financing and production. The two-partner practice has advised on a raft of well-known films and TV series. Major clients include Irish copyright collection societies IMRO and MCPS Ireland.

Simon McAleese Solicitors has carved an impressive niche in defamation, with specialist practitioners Simon McAleese and Paula Mullooly providing considerable expertise. The firm is retained to advise on pre-publication and post-publication complaints and litigation by Independent Newspapers. Other key clients include Mirror Group newspapers, Penguin and Random House.

MEDIA AND ENTERTAINMENT

A&L GOODBODY ✪
MATHESON ORMSBY PRENTICE ✪
SIMON MCALEESE SOLICITORS

McCANN FITZGERALD ✪
RONAN DALY JERMYN ✪
WILLIAM FRY ✪

Arthur Cox ✪
BCM Hanby Wallace ✪
Beauchamps ✪
Dillon Eustace ✪
Eugene F. Collins ✪
Gleeson McGrath Baldwin

Dockrell Farrell
E P Fanning & Co, Solicitors
Ivor Fitzpatrick & Company ✪
LK Shields ✪
Landwell Solicitors ✪
Lennon Heather & Company
Maples and Calder ✪
Mason Hayes+Curran ✪
WhitneyMoore

Firms are listed A-Z in tiers which are ranked in order of priority
✪ Indicates firm displays contact details at the end of this chapter.

A cross-departmental team at **McCann FitzGerald** regularly advises clients such as the Mirror Group, The Sunday Times, the National Gallery of Ireland and the James Joyce estate. The firm's media and entertainment practice is also strong in film financing.

Richard Martin at **Ronan Daly Jermyn** has built up a strong media and entertainment practice, advising all the papers in the wide-ranging Irish Examiner Group on pre-publication and defamation issues. Other key clients include local radio stations, including the leading provincial station 96FM. On the contentious side the firm was instructed in the high-profile case of *Irish Times v Judge Murphy and ors* in the Supreme Court, which concerned the fundamental rights of the media to report court cases.

William Fry has strength across the media and entertainment sector, operating as a multi-disciplinary six-partner team. A notable client gain in 2005 was internet search engine Yahoo!. Other major instructions include acting for RTE in the establishment of TG4, the Irish language channel. The 'effective and charming' Michael Kealey is an experienced defamation expert.

Colin Kavanagh is a recommended practitioner in **Arthur Cox**'s media and entertainment unit. The firm advises a diverse media client base on transactional, IP, regulatory and disputes issues. An impressive client list includes media heavyweights such as RTE, Warner Bros and Turner Broadcasting as well as individual writers, musicians and actors.

BCM Hanby Wallace acts as Irish solicitors to Sky News. Pamela Cassidy is an accomplished practitioner.

Gary Rice heads a niche sports law practice at **Beauchamps**, which advises a raft of well-known sports organisations.

Dillon Eustace's Paul Gill has a superb reputation in defamation. The firm also advises a number of newspapers, including *The Star*.

Litigator Terry Leggett is the media and entertainment contact at **Eugene F. Collins**, while **Gleeson McGrath Baldwin** has an established client base of well-known national and international artists, composers, orchestras, publishers, promoters and record companies.

MERGERS AND ACQUISITIONS

A&L Goodbody has an impressive M&A practice which headlines on a raft of large-scale transactions. In 2005, an impressive deal sheet included advising eircom on its €420m takeover of Meteor Mobile Communications, Royal Dutch Shell Ireland on the €200m disposal of its Irish retail and commercial business to Topaz Distribution and Logistics, and Quinlan Private on its €330m disposal of the Savoy Hotel to Fairmont Hotel Group. The 'practical and sensible' John Given heads the M&A practice, while Eithne Fitzgerald, head of corporate finance, is an adept practitioner.

Arthur Cox has a first-class reputation for M&A work and a team stocked with exceptional lawyers: Brian O'Gorman, Ciaran Bolger, Colm Duggan and James O'Dwyer all have a loyal client following. The team advised Gillette on the Irish aspects of its US$57bn acquisition by P&G, and through the use of Chinese walls, acted on both sides of UGC's €319m acquisition of ntl Ireland via a Morgan Stanley conduit.

M&A is core to **William Fry**'s corporate and commercial practice and a cornerstone of the firm's high reputation. The 13-partner team acted on a score of transactions in 2004 and 2005, such as advising Select Retail Holdings on the €450m acquisition of the Superquinn supermarket group. The team also scooped a landmark instruction in 2005, advising the Jefferson Smurfit Group on its merger negotiations with Kappa Packaging, which, if successful, will be the largest merger in Irish corporate history. Owen O'Connell has a superb reputation. Other stand out practitioners are Myra Garrett, Bryan Bourke and Ken Casey.

The M&A team at **Matheson Ormsby Prentice** fields quality practitioners such as Andrew Doyle, Robert Heron, Tim Scanlon and Patrick Spicer. The team has the size and expertise

MERGERS AND ACQUISITIONS

A&L GOODBODY ✪
ARTHUR COX ✪
WILLIAM FRY ✪

MATHESON ORMSBY PRENTICE ✪
McCANN FITZGERALD ✪

LK Shields ✪
Mason Hayes+Curran ✪

BCM Hanby Wallace ✪
Dillon Eustace ✪
Eugene F. Collins ✪
KLW
Landwell Solicitors ✪
McEvoy Partners ✪
O'Donnell Sweeney ✪
Ronan Daly Jermyn ✪
WhitneyMoore

Beauchamps ✪
Dockrell Farrell
Gore & Grimes ✪
Ivor Fitzpatrick & Company ✪
Kilroys
Maples and Calder ✪
PJ O'Driscoll & Sons ✪
Reddy Charlton McKnight ✪
Robert Ryan & Associates

Firms are listed A-Z in tiers which are ranked in order of priority
✪ Indicates firm displays contact details at the end of this chapter.

to advise on the biggest deals in the market; advising on the largest M&A transaction in 2004; acting for NAB on its €1.4bn disposal of National Irish Bank and Northern Bank to Danske Bank.

McCann FitzGerald also had a meaty role in the biggest deal of 2004; advising Danske Bank on its €1.4bn acquisition of Northern Bank and NIB. On the domestic front, the team advised Kingspan on its €91m purchase of Century Homes, a specialist in timber-frame technology. Clients report that Barry Devereux is 'extremely bright and focused.'

Clients at **LK Shields** rate Gerard Halpenny for his 'practical and commercial attitude to doing business'. Marco Hickey is also a favourite. The corporate and commercial practice, which has a bias towards M&A and corporate finance, acted on several key deals in 2004 and 2005; advising William Hill on its acquisition of the Irish operations of Stanley Bookmakers, and acted for Santander Asset Management on the restructuring of the Irish Asset Management Group.

Mason Hayes+Curran has a busy M&A practice, advising ntl as Irish legal adviser in the sale of its broadcasting business to a consortium led by Macquarie Communications Infrastructure Group, and also acting for the sellers of Lake Communications on its US$45m acquisition by Inter-Tel Lake. David O'Donnell and Liam Brazil are recommended.

Ex-Elan lawyer Colin Sainsbury at **BCM Hanby Wallace** is highly rated by clients (particularly those in the pharmaceutical and biotech sectors) for his expertise. The growing team is regularly instructed on both domestic and international transactions, including advising on the acquisition of AGB Scientific by VWR International, and on Prime Carrier's acquisition of Am-Beo.

The team at **Dillon Eustace** advised Johnston Press in the UK on the acquisition of the *Leinster Leader*; one of the largest transactions in 2005. Lorcan Tiernan heads the corporate and commercial department, while ex-**Arthur Cox** Abigail Kennedy spearheads the M&A work.

Eugene F. Collins regularly advises on mid-market deals. The firm also scooped instruction on the *Leinster Leader* deal, acting for the *Leinster Leader*, the target of the €138.6m acquisition by Johnston Press. Other highlight instructions include advising BNP Paribas on the sale of BNP Paribas Finance to Fexco. Team head Gerald Coll is 'highly competent'.

KLW is building up a strong reputation for complex M&A. John Kehoe, formerly of **Mason Hayes+Curran**, is praised by clients for his 'business-orientated, City approach'.

Corporate and financial services specialist Edward Evans at **Landwell Solicitors** is a solid dealmaker, while Gerry Bohan has M&A expertise.

Niche outfit **McEvoy Partners** continues to build up its practice, acting for Stafford Holdings in its €40m purchase of Lifestyle Sports. Bernard McEvoy has a good reputation.

O'Donnell Sweeney scooped a major domestic instruction advising Century Homes on its €98m sale to Kingspan, and also acted for Merrion Stockbrokers, part of the Merrion Capital Group, on the sale of 49.9% of Jordan Grand Prix to Midland Group. David Beattie is recommended.

Ronan Daly Jermyn advised on a raft of significant deals in 2004 and 2005, including the €25m sale of Farran Technologies to Smiths Group, the UK-based hi-tech engineering business, and acting for Premier Recruitment on its acquisition of Nigel Lynn Associates, a major independent finance and accountancy recruiter in the UK. Adrian Wall and Garvan Corkery are experienced practitioners.

WhitneyMoore has considerable M&A experience. Therese Rochford is recommended.

PENSIONS AND EMPLOYEE BENEFITS

Sheena Doggett heads the employment benefits group at **A&L Goodbody**, which advises on every facet of employee incentive schemes. A solid client base includes Irish quoted and private companies, encompassing sectors such as financial services, technology, pharmaceutical and manufacturing. Robert Buckley spearheads the pensions team, which regularly advises international insurance companies on pensions and life assurance products.

PENSIONS AND EMPLOYEE BENEFITS

A&L GOODBODY ✪
ARTHUR COX ✪
BCM HANBY WALLACE ✪
LK SHIELDS ✪
MATHESON ORMSBY PRENTICE ✪
McCANN FITZGERALD ✪
O'DONNELL SWEENEY ✪
WILLIAM FRY ✪

Beauchamps ✪
Landwell Solicitors ✪
Mason Hayes+Curran ✪
WhitneyMoore

Firms are listed A-Z in tiers which are ranked in order of priority
✪ Indicates firm displays contact details at the end of this chapter.

Arthur Cox's Declan Drislane and Philip Smith both provide considerable expertise on pension schemes, as well as advising on the pension element of large-scale corporate transactions. An impressive client list includes IBM Ireland, Masterfoods, RTE and Gallaher Tobacco.

BCM Hanby Wallace's superlative employment expertise is a springboard to advising on pensions and employee benefits. Managing partner Gary Byrne heads the team.

Fiona Thornton heads the highly rated pensions and employee benefits group at **LK Shields**, which also has pensions litigation capacity. Key instructions in 2004 and 2005 include advising the Construction Industry Federation on the reorganisation of its industry wide pension scheme, and advising AIB on the introduction of its new employee share plan.

Brian Buggy leads **Matheson Ormsby Prentice**'s pensions practice, which is part of the employment, pensions and benefits group. The team provides legal advice to corporate clients and trustees on the full range of pension schemes and employee benefits, with a particular focus on employee benefit structures and pensions reorganisation.

The pensions and employee benefits group at **McCann FitzGerald** boasts an impressive client list that includes both international and domestic corporates such as Air France, Pfizer Ireland Pharmaceuticals and Sherry Fitzgerald. The experienced Maureen Dolan oversees the practice, which advises statutory bodies, trustees and employees on pension arrangements and employee benefit and incentive plans.

O'Donnell Sweeney's fast-expanding pensions and regulatory practice is headed by Peter Fahy, who regularly advises on employee share schemes. Highlights of 2004 and 2005 include advising the Department of Transport on pension funds, and the eircom ESOP on the eircom IPO.

Michael Wolfe heads **William Fry**'s pensions team, while Maura Roe spearheads the employee benefits share schemes unit, which works closely with the tax department. On the pensions side, a wide remit covers the pension element of corporate deals, wind ups and scheme mergers.

PLANNING AND ENVIRONMENT

Alison Fanagan heads the four fee-earner team at **A&L Goodbody**, which has substantial experience on both advisory and disputed planning and environment matters. An established client list covers the pharmaceutical, manufacturing, energy, aviation and waste industries. Major highlights of 2004 and 2005 include advising ING Bank in the defence of planning judicial review proceedings in opposition to a €40m factory outlet development in Co Louth.

Arthur Cox has one of the largest dedicated planning and environment groups in Ireland. Deborah Spence spearheads the practice, which is geared towards providing expertise to the firm's enviable client base in the industrial and manufacturing sectors. The team benefits from the expertise of Dr Yvonne Scannell, a leading specialist in the field. Key instructions include advising the largest private waste infrastructure provider in Ireland, Greenstar, in defending a third-party legal challenge to approval for an engineered residual waste facility in Co Kildare.

Matheson Ormsby Prentice's property partner Patrick Sweetman heads the planning and environment group, while Stuart Margetson regularly advises on disputes. The team provides expertise on high-profile infrastructure projects, and in 2005 advised lenders Barclays Bank on the environmental aspects of a 343MW CCGT plant (IPP).

PLANNING AND ENVIRONMENT

A&L GOODBODY ✪
ARTHUR COX ✪
MATHESON ORMSBY PRENTICE ✪
McCANN FITZGERALD ✪

BCM Hanby Wallace ✪
Beauchamps ✪
William Fry ✪

Dillon Eustace ✪
O'Donnell Sweeney ✪
Ronan Daly Jermyn ✪

Eugene F. Collins ✪
LK Shields ✪
Landwell Solicitors ✪
Mason Hayes+Curran ✪
WhitneyMoore

Firms are listed A-Z in tiers which are ranked in order of priority
✪ Indicates firm displays contact details at the end of this chapter.

Stand-out practitioners at **McCann FitzGerald** for planning and the environment are Michael O'Reilly and Michelle Doyle. The team advised the National Roads Authority on a number of planning and environment concerns arising from road development, such as a challenge to the proposed M3 near the historically significant Hill of Tara in County Meath. Other clients include Ballymun Regeneration, Shell E&P Ireland and Dublin Airport Authority.

In line with its strong reputation in property, **BCM Hanby Wallace** also handles the attendant planning, development and environmental issues. Brian Wallace is experienced.

Newly made up partner Ainsley Heffernan heads the planning and environmental unit at **Beauchamps**, which regularly advises property developers, manufacturers, pharmaceutical companies and energy suppliers. Commercial property partner Niall Coleman also has planning and environmental expertise.

William Fry's cross-departmental planning and environmental team has strengths in waste management, IPPC licensing, contaminated land and protected area controls as well as advising on the new EU Carbon Emissions Trading Scheme. Barrister Conor Linehan heads the unit.

Commercial property partner Paul Eustace at **Dillon Eustace** has planning and environmental experience, while at **O'Donnell Sweeney** Rory O'Donnell and Sean Greene are active.

In 2005 regional firm **Ronan Daly Jermyn** advised in the high-profile case of *O'Callaghan v Mahon & ors* in the Supreme Court, which challenged the working of the Planning Tribunal into certain planning matters and payment.

PROJECT FINANCE AND PPP

A&L Goodbody has a strong team, which fields sector experts Kevin Feeney and former **Pinsent Masons** partners Eamonn Conlon and Dudley Solan. An impressive client list includes both the public and private sectors in Ireland, Northern Ireland and abroad. Highlight instructions include advising the Department of Environment and Science on the Cork School of Music project, which closed in September 2005, and advising the Railway Procurement Agency on its partnership arrangements with developers of the B1 extension to the Luas light railway.

In 2004 and 2005 **Arthur Cox** won two prime public sector legal mandates, acting for the National Development Finance Agency (NDFA) and Rail Procurement Agency (RPA). The team also advised the sole arranger, Barclays Bank, on the Cork School of Music PPP. The experienced Ted Williams leads the team, ably supported by 'the top banking lawyer in town' Grainne Hennessy, as well as Angus Creed in Belfast.

Matheson Ormsby Prentice fields a three-partner practice, headed by the 'dedicated' Michael O'Connor, which regularly advises banks,

PROJECT FINANCE AND PPP

A&L GOODBODY ✪
ARTHUR COX ✪
MATHESON ORMSBY PRENTICE ✪
McCANN FITZGERALD ✪
WILLIAM FRY ✪

Mason Hayes+Curran ✪
O'Donnell Sweeney ✪

BCM Hanby Wallace ✪
Beauchamps ✪
Dillon Eustace ✪
Eugene F. Collins ✪
Kilroys
LK Shields ✪
Ronan Daly Jermyn ✪
WhitneyMoore

Firms are listed A-Z in tiers which are ranked in order of priority
✪ *Indicates firm displays contact details at the end of this chapter.*

developers and state bodies. A major instruction for the firm was advising the borrower, Tynagh Energy, on the largest project financing to reach financial close in Ireland during 2004 to 2005, the €330m Tynagh IPP. The firm also advised the lead contractor in the Cork School of Music PPP.

McCann FitzGerald has a superb track record for projects work, advising on all the Irish PPPs to reach financial close to date, across a diverse range of market sectors. Clients are impressed by Tim Bouchier-Hayes, and 'admire him very highly'. The firm has advised the National Roads Authority on all the roads projects. Claire Lenny is also a skilled practitioner.

William Fry's cross-departmental projects team has a strong public sector focus, advising Dublin City Council on the O'Devaney Gardens Regeneration Project, the second urban regeneration PPP deal in Ireland, and acting for the Rail Procurement Agency on the procurement of an integrated ticketing system for transport in the Greater Dublin area. Sonja Price, construction specialist Liam McCabe and environment and planning expert Conor Linehan are all active on PPP deals.

Mason Hayes+Curran has PPP expertise on the energy side, advising on producers with small-scale wind farms or hydro plants. The firm is also involved in bids for roads projects, as well as advising on potential PPP projects in sectors such as housing.

Patrick Ryan at **Kilroys** is the chief contact for public procurement work, while at **LK Shields** Philip Daly and Fiona Thornton are both provide advice on PPPs. Highlights for the firm include acting for one of the largest semi-state harbour authorities on the infrastructure and commercial development of port facilities.

Ronan Daly Jermyn has PPP expertise, continuing to advise on the €100m treatment plant for Cork City.

REAL ESTATE

A&L Goodbody's Mairead Sherlock is a leading light in the commercial property practice, while Stephen O'Riordan and consultant Tom O'Connor are highly rated. A raft of prestigious instructions includes advising AIB on the €350m sale and leaseback of the AIB headquarters in Ballsbridge. The team also acted for Quinlan Private on the €785m acquisition of the BP portfolio in Knightsbridge.

John Walsh at **Arthur Cox** is much admired by clients, who proclaim him to be 'a legend.' The able commercial property practice includes over 25 lawyers, including seven partners. The team acted for Sean Dunne in the much-publicised acquisition of Jury's Hotel & The Towers in Ballsbridge, for a reported €260m, and also acted for the seller in the disposal of Superquinn, a national supermarket chain, which included the sale of nine large shopping centres and property chain. Mark Barr is also recommended.

Lonan McDowell and Jim Murphy have solid reputations at **McCann FitzGerald**. The firm excels in property finance, and scooped a sizeable instruction acting for both the consortium of investors which purchased the site of AIB's headquarters in Ballsbridge for €367.5m and for AIB, the funding bank; the largest-ever property acquisition in Ireland.

William Fry fields several big hitters; joint team heads the 'highly competent and skilful' Nora White and Edward Spain, and Andrew Muckian, formerly of **Matheson Ormsby Prentice**. The 28-fee-earner team acts for institutions, developers, investors and an expanding number of international retailers. The firm boasts long-established expertise in tax-driven property transactions: in 2005 acting for Select Retail Holdings on the €400m acquisition of the Superquinn supermarket chain. The team also acted for TopShop/TopMan in the letting of its new flagship store in St Stephen's Green.

BCM Hanby Wallace has scooped several of the largest redevelopment projects in Ireland, acting for the developer. A landmark instruction was advising on the €500m construction, development, financing and letting of Dundrum Shopping Centre, the biggest shopping centre in Ireland. Another example is Athlone Town Centre; a €150m mixed-use development and one of Ireland's largest private development projects. Paul McGennis and Paul Walsh are recommended.

Beauchamps has established property expertise and boasts an impressive client base of investors and developers. Aidan Marsh heads the seven-partner team, which advised Redquartz on the property aspects on its €33.5m acquisition of the Holiday Inn at Dublin Airport from the Intercontinental Hotel Group, and acted for Dulcedo on the €110m Manor Mills development in Maynooth, Co Kildare, a mixed retail, office and residential development.

REAL ESTATE

A&L GOODBODY ✪
ARTHUR COX ✪
McCANN FITZGERALD ✪
WILLIAM FRY ✪

BCM HANBY WALLACE ✪
BEAUCHAMPS ✪
MATHESON ORMSBY PRENTICE ✪
O'DONNELL SWEENEY ✪

Dillon Eustace ✪
Eugene F. Collins ✪
LK Shields ✪
Mason Hayes+Curran ✪
Ronan Daly Jermyn ✪
WhitneyMoore

Dockrell Farrell
Ivor Fitzpatrick & Company ✪
Maples and Calder ✪
Noel Smyth & Partners
Reddy Charlton McKnight ✪

Conway Kelleher Tobin
Kilroys

Firms are listed A-Z in tiers which are ranked in order of priority
✪ *Indicates firm displays contact details at the end of this chapter.*

Nicola Palmer has joined **Matheson Ormsby Prentice** from **LK Shields**. The firm acted for the joint venture of Park Developments and John Sisk & Sons contractors in a major residential development project at Hanover Quay, Dublin and again for the duo in a major residential marina development at Greystones, Co Wicklow. Patrick Sweetman heads the department.

Joseph Stanley and Alan Murphy are industrious practitioners at **O'Donnell Sweeney**. The team advised a major indigenous retail group on its retail expansion and development, and also acted on a number of sizeable retail developments in Dundalk, Tralee, Arklow and Meekstown. Highlights include advising Spencer Dock Development Company on the residential element of Spencer Dock, the largest urban regeneration project in Dublin.

Paul Eustace and Michael Barker head the practice at **Dillon Eustace**, which acts for a raft of banks and financial institutions on property financing. A healthy client list also includes numerous retail multiples, such as Carphone Warehouse, Reid Furniture and the Irish sandwich retailer Munchies.

David Ensor heads a busy practice at **Eugene F. Collins**, which has a mixed client base of investors, developers, retailers and financial institutions. In 2005 the firm added a raft of UK retail clients, including New Look and Harvey Norman, to its client list. Notable recent instructions include advising Pierse Contracting on the acquisition of a 332-unit site in Carrickmines, Co Dublin.

It is all change at **LK Shields**, as Nicola Palmer has left to join **Matheson Ormsby Prentice**, being replaced by Jim Gollogley. The team advises on high-value property transactions in Ireland and abroad for a varied client base of state and semi-state bodies, developers and major financial institutions.

Declan Curran heads the property team at **Mason Hayes+Curran**. A key instruction for the firm was advising Rhatigan Group on its €80m purchase of the Westgate site, an important central Dublin development. The team also has a healthy client list of retail clients, such as Subway, Specsavers, Fat Face and Toni & Guy.

Ronan Daly Jermyn has one of the strongest commercial property teams in Ireland outside Dublin. John O'Dwyer leads the team, which has been instructed on a raft of matters both regionally and nationally. Highlights include advising on a number of new hotels, including the new Radisson SAS in Cork.

Michael Carney heads the commercial property practice at **WhitneyMoore**. The team regularly acts for investors in tax-driven hotel and nursing home schemes and has also advised developers in a number of residential schemes. Major clients include Green Property, British Land and Irish Life.

Dockrell Farrell's remit includes all aspects of commercial conveyancing, including office, retail, industrial and housing developments. Ernest Farrell heads the practice, while **Maples and Calder Solicitors** (formerly *Binchys*) acts for a diverse mix of owners, developers, investors and financial institutions as well as landlord and tenant.

Alfred Thornton leads the commercial property team at **Ivor Fitzpatrick & Company**, which acted for Lalco Holdings in the €50m acquisition of the Chocolate Factory, a mixed-use residential and commercial site.

Thomas Marren heads the three-partner practice at **Reddy Charlton McKnight**, which advises on all aspects of commercial property.

STRUCTURED FINANCE AND SECURITISATION

Ciarán Rogers heads a strong team of 19 fee-earners at **A&L Goodbody**, which has acted on over 100 securitisations and structured products transactions in the past 12 months. The raft of deals included advising the Irish issuing vehicle, German Postal Pensions Securitisation, on the high-profile €7.5bn securitisation of German pension receivables, and acting for DEPFA Bank in its synthetic securitisation of a portfolio of its PPP/PEI loan book, the first securitisation of this asset class in Europe.

Arthur Cox advises originators, lead managers, rating agencies and issuers on the full spectrum of structured finance and securitisation transactions. The 'highly competent' Cormac Kissane heads the team. An impressive client base includes top investment banks such as Citibank, Barclays Capital, Merrill Lynch, ABN Amro and Bank of America. A highlight transaction was advising Barclays Capital on the establishment of Bank of Ireland's €10bn mortgage-covered securities programme.

STRUCTURED FINANCE AND SECURITISATION

A&L GOODBODY ✪
ARTHUR COX ✪
MATHESON ORMSBY PRENTICE ✪
McCANN FITZGERALD ✪

DILLON EUSTACE ✪
WILLIAM FRY ✪

LK Shields ✪

Firms are listed A-Z in tiers which are ranked in order of priority
✪ Indicates firm displays contact details at the end of this chapter.

Matheson Ormsby Prentice has substantial expertise in advising on complex structured finance: from CDOs and CLOs to warehousing, tax and regulatory arbitrage. In 2004 and 2005, the team advised lead managers BNP Paribas and Barclays Capital on the issue of £300m of Tier 1 Capital preference shares by Anglo Irish Bank, and also advised AIB on a hybrid Tier 1 €1bn capital issue. Clients praise team head Turlough Galvin for being 'technically very good and commercial' and admire his 'honest and frank manner.'

McCann FitzGerald's Roy Parker 'utterly blows away the competition', according to clients, who also recommend Fergus Gillen for securitisation. A raft of quality work includes advising on the establishment of the Bank of Ireland Mortgage Bank, the first Irish covered bond bank in the mortgage sector, and also acting for the bank's inaugural €2bn mortgage covered security issue.

Dillon Eustace is active on structured finance transactions. The establishment of a tax team, led by ex-PwC David Lawless, augments this expertise. Key instructions include advising Gazprombank on a raft of structured finance transactions, and acting for a major insurance group on assurance-backed securitisation and repackaging transactions. Mark Thorne is recommended.

William Fry's structured finance and securitisation team includes Elaine Hanly, considered by clients to be 'one of the best on banking', and experienced practitioners Orla Brennan, John Larkin and Martin Phelan. Standout transactions over the past year include advising AXA Cessions on an innovative 'catbond' structure, which involved establishing an Irish special purpose reinsurance company that provided coverage against losses arising from windstorms, collaterised with a bond issue. Another major instruction was advising Brenntag GmbH on an €300m trade receivables securisation.

LK Shields has been busy handling a steady flow of pre-securitisation funding transactions, in addition to advising on a high volume of repackaging transactions for one of Europe's well-known investment banks. David Williams and Joseph Galvin head the practice.

TAX

Matheson Ormsby Prentice's formidable tax team maintains pole position in the Republic. Clients consider managing partner Liam Quirke to be 'one of the finest tax lawyers in Dublin' and also shower praise on the 'versatile' Turlough Galvin. Standout transactions in 2005 include advising on the €3.5bn Overture CDO, which was Europe's largest CDO involving a syndicate of over 40 banking institutions. The 23-fee-earner team also provides Irish tax advice in the US.

The experienced Peter Maher heads **A&L Goodbody**'s 12-fee-earner tax team, which clients find 'very user-friendly with good, prompt service'. Highlights for 2004 and 2005 include advising on the Irish tax aspects of the Standard Life demutualisation, and acting for Real Estate Opportunities on the share purchase of target companies from Treasury Holdings. John Hickson, David Glynn, James Somerville and Andrew Quinn are also active in tax.

Arthur Cox has a fast-expanding tax team headed by the impressive Conor Hurley, and which also includes the highly rated Caroline Devlin. The firm is at the forefront of structured finance and capital markets transactions, and provides the tax expertise to match. In 2005, the team advised on the tax aspects of the €326m sale of ntl Ireland to UGC via a Morgan Stanley conduit.

Tax experts at **McCann FitzGerald** include Julie Quin, Colm Fanning and consultant Michael Ryan. The firm has a wealth of expertise in structured finance, augmenting the tax team, which has a focus on tax-based finance. An example of the quality of

TAX

MATHESON ORMSBY PRENTICE ✪

A&L GOODBODY ✪
ARTHUR COX ✪
McCANN FITZGERALD ✪
WILLIAM FRY ✪

BCM Hanby Wallace ✪
Dillon Eustace ✪
Mason Hayes+Curran ✪
Ronan Daly Jermyn ✪

Firms are listed A-Z in tiers which are ranked in order of priority
✪ Indicates firm displays contact details at the end of this chapter.

work undertaken is advising CIBC World Markets on the tax aspects of a CDO transaction; one of the first to be facilitated in Ireland following the introduction of a conditional VAT exemption for collective portfolio management services.

Martin Phelan heads the tax practice at **William Fry**, which has sound referral links to the major accountancy firms. The team advises on both transactional tax planning and tax litigation. Highlights in 2005 include advising Jefferson Smurfit Group on its trade receivables securitisation.

BCM Hanby Wallace and **Dillon Eustace** are building up serviceable tax practices: experienced PwC tax partner David Lawless heads a growing team at **Dillon Eustace**.

Mason Hayes+Curran has recruited Suzanne Carter, former Director of Taxation at Vodafone Ireland, to spearhead its emerging tax practice. One to watch.

Outside Dublin **Ronan Daly Jermyn** has recruited John Cuddigan from Ernst & Young to boost its tax expertise.

BARRISTERS

Of the senior counsel there are a number of names that stand out: Dermot Gleeson, Paul Gallagher, Donal O'Donnell, Michael Collins, Richard Nesbitt, John Gordon and Paul Gardiner. Eoin McGonigal and Michael Cush are also worthy of mention.

Other recommendations are Dan O'Keeffe, Ian Finlay, Eoin McCullough and Bill Shipsey. Popular choices of junior counsel for instructing solicitors are Oisín Quinn, David Barniville and Eileen Barrington.

For specific sector expertise we recommend the following:

For IP, John Gordon and Richard Nesbitt, Brian O'Moore and Denis McDonald. Clued-up juniors are Michael Howard and John Breslin.

For construction, senior counsel Dermot Gleeson and Paul Gallagher have considerable expertise, while up-and-coming juniors are Reg Jackson and Peter Shanley, both of whom are commercially focused.

In the agriculture sector, we recommend senior counsel Gerard Hogan and juniors Anthony O'Connor, James O'Reilly and Richard Nesbitt.

Senior counsel Gerard Durcan is instruction of choice for EU and competition work, together with Michael Collins, Paul Sreenan and Gerard Hogan.

For tax work, Thomas McCann shines, while John Farrell is a coveted choice for property.

A number of barristers have an employment focus, including Tom Mallon, Frank Callanan, Gerard Durcan, Ercus Stewart, Ian Finlay, John Rogers, Roderick Horan and Mark Connaughton.

In insurance, the list of luminaries includes the adaptable Paul Sreenan, together with Michael Collins, Dennis McDonald, Colm Allen, Murray McGrath and David Barniville.

Brian McGovern and Denis McDonald are both popular choices for shipping matters.

PJ O'DRISCOLL & SONS

73 SOUTH MALL
CORK

Telephone: +353 21 230 0800
Fax: +353 21 427 4709
E-mail: enquiries@pjodriscoll.ie
Website: www.pjodriscoll.ie

Languages
English, French

Number of lawyers 19

CATEGORIES OF WORK

Commercial
Edward O'Leary, Liosa O'Sullivan

Banking
Justin Fennell, Brendan Hogan

Construction
Joan Kiely, Patricia O'Brien

Agriculture
Barry O'Driscoll, Henry O'Sullivan

Commercial property
Patricia O'Brien, Elaine O'Driscoll

Dispute resolution
Michael O'Driscoll, PJ O'Leary

Employment
Kieran Doran, Michelle Creed

Insolvency
Edward O'Leary, PJ O'Leary

Intellectual property
Liosa O'Sullivan

Media and entertainment
Elaine O'Driscoll

Mergers and acquisitions
Edward O'Leary, Justin Fennell

Planning and environment
Elaine O'Driscoll, Joan Kiely

Private clients
Barry O'Driscoll

RONAN DALY JERMYN

12 SOUTH MALL
CORK

Telephone: +353 21 480 2700
Fax: +353 21 480 2790
E-mail: info@rdj.ie
Website: www.rdj.ie

Languages
English, French, German

Number of lawyers 40

Contact
John Dwyer (managing partner)

CATEGORIES OF WORK

Corporate, M&A
Frank Daly, Garvan Corkery

Inward investment
John Dwyer, Garvan Corkery

IT and e-commerce
Garvan Corkery, Adrian Wall

Tax
John Cuddigan

Employment
Fergus Long, Jennifer Cashman

Insolvency and debt recovery
Nicholas Comyn, Fergal Dennehy

Banking and finance
Frank Daly, Thomas Fox

Media and defamation
Richard Martin, John Buckley

PPP/construction
Finola McCarthy, Margaret Ring

Commercial property
John Dwyer, Pat Ahern

Litigation/dispute resolution
Fergus Long, Richard Martin

Maritime
Richard Martin, James O'Sullivan

Private client
John Jermyn, Rosemary Horgan

Matrimonial and family law
Rosemary Horgan

A&L GOODBODY

INTERNATIONAL FINANCIAL SERVICES CENTRE
NORTH WALL QUAY
DUBLIN 1

Telephone: +353 1 649 2000
Fax: +353 1 649 2649
E-mail: law@algoodbody.ie
Website: www.algoodbody.ie

Languages
Dutch, French, German

Other offices
Boston, London, New York

Number of lawyers 215

Contact
Paul Carroll (managing partner)

CATEGORIES OF WORK

Banking and financial services
Catherine Duffy (department head)

Corporate
Paul White (department head)

Litigation and dispute resolution
Peter Law (department head)

Pensions
Roddy Buckley (department head)

Private client
Michael O'Gorman (department head)

Property
Mairead Sherlock (department head)

Tax
Peter Maher (department head)

Mergers and acquistions
John Given

Corporate finance
Eithne FitzGerald

Venture capital
John Olden

Capital markets
John Olden, Ciaran Rogers

Inward investment
John Coman

Partnerships
John Olden

Projects and construction
Kevin Feeney, Eamonn Gill

Asset finance
Catherine Duffy

Securitisation
Ciaran Rogers

Outsourcing
John Whelan

Insurance
James Grennan

EU, regulatory and competition
Vincent Power

Compliance and corporate financial governance
Kevin Allen

Insolvency and corporate recovery
David Baxter

IP, telecoms and technology
John Whelan

Investment funds
Brian McDermott

ADR and mediation
Joe Kelly

Sports law
Eoin MacNeill

Leisure and licensing
Joe Kelly

Life sciences and healthcare
David Widger, Cliona Hickey

Media and entertainment
Geraldine East

Environmental and planning
Alison Fanagan

Food and agriculture
John Coman

Employment
Ian Moore

Pensions and employee incentives
Eamon Brady, Sheena Doggett

Debt recovery
Eileen Roberts

Product liability
Caroline Preston

A&L Goodbody Consulting
Peter Brennan

Corporate offences
Joe Kelly

ARTHUR COX

EARLSFORT CENTRE
EARLSFORT TERRACE
DUBLIN 2

Telephone: +353 1 618 0000
Fax: +353 1 618 0618
E-mail: mail@arthurcox.com
Website: www.arthurcox.com

Languages
English, French, German, Italian, Spanish

Other offices
Belfast, London, New York

Number of lawyers 223
at this office 195

CATEGORIES OF WORK

Mergers and acquisitions, corporate finance
Ciarán Bolger, Colm Duggan

Capital markets
Glenn Butt, Cormac Kissane

Corporate and commercial
Michael Meghen, Brian O'Gorman

Tax-based financing, corporate and capital taxation
Conor Hurley, Caroline Devlin

Banking
William Johnston, Kathleen Garrett

Project and asset finance
Grainne Hennessy, Liam Carney

Inward investment
Declan Hayes, Declan Drislane

International financial services and funds
Carl O'Sullivan, Sarah Cunniff

Corporate restructuring and insolvency
Eugene McCague, William Day

Securitisation
Cormac Kissane, Grainne Hennessy

EU and competition law
John Meade, Patrick O'Brien

Technology
John Menton, Rob Corbet

Pensions
Declan Drislane, Philip Smith

Employee share schemes
Stephen Hegarty, Anne Corrigan

Commercial property
John Walsh, Mark Barr

Commercial litigation
Conor McDonnell, Andrew Lenny

Professional negligence
Donogh Crowley, Margaret Muldowney

Defamation
Donogh Crowley

Insurance litigation
David O'Donohoe, Greg Glynn

Employment and industrial relations
John V O'Dwyer, Séamus Given

Energy and natural resources
Alex McLean

Environment and planning
Deborah Spence, Yvonne Scannell

Telecommunications
Patrick McGovern, Ann Marie Kearney

Intellectual property
David O'Donohoe, Louise Carey

Food law
Declan Hayes

Construction/ public private partnerships
Ted Williams, Niav O'Higgins

Product liability
Isabel Foley, David O'Donohoe

Projects
Patrick McGovern, Alex McLean

BCM HANBY WALLACE

88 HARCOURT STREET
DUBLIN 2

Telephone: +353 1 418 6900
Fax: +353 1 418 6901
E-mail: info@bcmhw.com
Website: www.bcmhw.com

Languages
French, German, Spanish

Number of lawyers 80

Contact
Gary Byrne (managing partner)

CATEGORIES OF WORK

Arbitration and dispute resolution
Gerard W Butler, Helen Wilkinson, Kieran Johnston

Administrative law
Duncan Inverarity

Capital markets
Sean Wallace, Barry MacCarthy

Commercial property and development
Michael Walsh, Catherine Guy

Commercial property finance
Paul McGennis, Ciara Gunning, Mark Kavanagh, Deirdre McBennett

Construction
Tim Kinney, Fiona O'Neill

Corporate/commercial
Feargal Brennan, Colin Sainsbury, Enda Newton

Corporate banking
Paul McGennis, Eileen Prendergast

Corporate finance, M&A
Feargal Brennan, Sean Wallace

Employment
Gary Byrne, Michael Kennedy

Equality and discrimination
Michelle Ni Longain

Family law
Orlaith McCarthy

Health services
Sinéad Kearney, Olive Doyle

ICT
Sean Wallace

Leisure and licensing
Daniel Murphy, Alan Adams

Life sciences and intellectual property
Colin Sainsbury, Alex Nesbitt

Litigation
Gerard W Butler, Louise Holmes, Kieran Johnston

Pensions and employee benefits
Gary Byrne, Margaret Pilkington

Planning and environmental
Brian Wallace

Private client and estate planning
Jane Mathews, Carolyn Wallace

Project finance and PPP
Tim Kinney

Residential property
James Moran, Daniel Murphy, Alan Adams, Aileen Cosgrove

Tax
Nicola Walsh

BEAUCHAMPS

DOLLARD HOUSE
WELLINGTON QUAY
DUBLIN 2

Telephone: +353 1 418 0600
Fax: +353 1 418 0699
E-mail: securemail@beauchamps.ie
Website: www.beauchamps.ie

Languages
English, French, German, Italian

Number of lawyers 56

Contacts
Imelda Reynolds (managing partner),
Órlagh McKeon (marketing manager)

CATEGORIES OF WORK

Banking and finance
Daniel Cashman, Aisling Foley

Commercial property
Aidan Marsh, Imelda Reynolds

Competition and regulated markets
Timothy Jordan

Construction law
Maitiu O'Donaill, Richard Liddy

Corporate and commercial
Shaun O'Shea, John White

Employment
Claire Callanan, Mark J Heslin

Franchising
Imelda Reynolds, Daniel Cashman

Healthcare
Aisling Gannon, Berchmans Gannon

Public private partnerships
Niall Coleman

IP/IT
Maureen Daly, Gary Rice

Litigation
Gabriel Daly, Philip Smith

Planning and environmental
Ainsley Heffernan, Niall Coleman

Private client
John Cunningham, Joseph Bowe

Public and professional law
Gary Rice, Dermot Casserly

Residential property development
Kate O'Connor

Sport
Gary Rice

Corporate finance, mergers and acquisitions
Maire Cunningham,
Mark Pery-Knox-Gore

DILLON EUSTACE

GRAND CANAL HOUSE
1 UPPER GRAND CANAL STREET
DUBLIN 4

Telephone: +353 1 667 0022
Fax: +353 1 667 0042
E-mail: info@dilloneustace.ie
Website: www.dilloneustace.ie

Languages
French, German, Italian

Other offices
Boston, Tokyo

Number of lawyers 90

Contacts
David Dillon (senior partner),
Mark Thorne (managing partner)

CATEGORIES OF WORK

Banking and finance
David Dillon, Mark Thorne

Admiralty and maritime
Paul Gill, Paul Breen

Commercial litigation
Kieran Cowhey

Employment
John Doyle, Niamh Loughran

Listings
Tara O'Callaghan, Ian McLaughlin

Insurance (life/non-life)
Andrew Bates, Brian Dillon

Corporate and commercial
Lorcan Tiernan, Catherine McKnight

Defamation
Paul Gill

Aviation
Kieran Cowhey

Insolvency/corporate recovery
David Dillon, Lorcan Tiernan

Energy and natural resources
Paula Kelleher, Paul Eustace

Holiday and travel law
John Doyle

IFSC/ financial services
David Dillon, Andrew Bates

Investment funds
Andrew Bates, Brian Kelliher

Insurance litigation
Lorna Kennedy, Paul Breen

Regulatory compliance
Paul Kelleher, Paul Ryan

Litigation and arbitration
Kieran Cowhey, Paul Gill

Tax
David Lawless

Mergers and acquisitions
Lorcan Tiernan, Abigail Kennedy

Inward investment
Mark Thorne, Paul Eustace

Commercial property/construction
Paul Eustace, Michael Barker

Arbitration/ADR
John Doyle

Securitisation
Mark Thorne, David Lawless

Healthcare
Andrew Bates, John Doyle

EUGENE F COLLINS

TEMPLE CHAMBERS
3 BURLINGTON ROAD
DUBLIN 4

Telephone: +353 1 202 6400
Fax: +353 1 667 5200
E-mail: lawyer@efc.ie
Website: www.efc.ie

Languages
French, German

Number of lawyers 45

Contact
David Cantrell (managing partner)

CATEGORIES OF WORK

Mergers and acquisitions
Anthony Collins, Gerard Coll

Banking, securities and finance
Laura MacDermott, Eileen Grace

Companies, corporations
Anthony Collins, Leonora Malone

Capital markets
Eileen Grace, Leonora Malone

Competition, regulation
David Geary

Commercial litigation
Terry Leggett, Ronan O'Neill

Property, real estate
David Ensor, John Territt

Bankruptcy, insolvency
Barry O'Neill, Terry Leggett

Intellectual property
David Hackett

Information technology
David Hackett

Labour
Maura Connolly

Defamation
Terry Leggett

Directors advice
Eileen Grace

Arbitration
Michael Carrigan

Immigration
David Cantrell

Private client
John Costello

Energy
Leonora Malone

GORE & GRIMES

CAVENDISH HOUSE
SMITHFIELD
DUBLIN 7

Telephone: +353 1 872 9299
Fax: +353 1 872 9877
E-mail: solrs@goregrimes.ie
Website: www.goregrimes.ie

Languages
English, French

Number of lawyers 11

Contact
Brian O'Neill

CATEGORIES OF WORK

Company and commercial
Anthony Gore-Grimes, Brian O'Neill

Mergers and acquisitions
Brian O'Neill, Anthony Gore-Grimes

Commercial property
John Gore-Grimes, Karl Hayes, Caroline Gore-Grimes

Private client litigation
David Martin, Liam Collins

Intellectual property
Brian O'Neill, Helen Gore-Grimes

Arbitration
John Gore-Grimes

Commercial litigation
David Martin

Planning and environmental law
John Gore-Grimes

Family law
Mary Hayes, Alan Finnerty

Property and development
John Gore-Grimes, Collette Hunt
Caroline Gore-Grimes

Probate and trusts
Karl Hayes

EU and competition
Anthony Gore-Grimes

Employment
Helen Gore-Grimes, Brian O'Neill

HUSSEY FRASER

17 NORTHUMBERLAND ROAD
DUBLIN 4

Telephone: +353 1 668 1966
Fax: +353 1 668 2621
E-mail: husseyfraser@securemail.ie
Website: www.husseyfraser.ie

Languages
English

Number of lawyers 6

CATEGORIES OF WORK

Construction law
Anthony Hussey, Siobhan Kenny

Construction dispute resolution
Malcolm Fraser, Andrew Rush

Health and safety
Malcolm Fraser

Environmental law
Malcolm Fraser

Employment law
Anne Barrett

Commercial and corporate law
Siobhan Kenny

Commercial litigation
Malcolm Fraser

Commercial conveyancing
Siobhan Kenny

Matrimonial and family law
John Browne

General litigation
Anne Barrett

IVOR FITZPATRICK & COMPANY
SOLICITORS

44-45 ST STEPHENS GREEN
DUBLIN 2

Telephone: +353 1 678 7000
Fax: +353 1 678 7004
E-mail: info@ivorfitzpatrick.ie
Website: www.ivorfitzpatrick.ie

Languages
French, German, Spanish

Number of lawyers 20

Contact
Ivor Fitzpatrick

CATEGORIES OF WORK

Corporate and commercial banking, corporate finance
Anne McHale, Alfred Thornton, Andreas McConnell

Commercial property, construction
Jennifer Blunden, Alfred Thornton

Mergers and acquisitions, project finance and capital markets
John King, Anne McHale, Andreas McConnell

Civil litigation
Susan R Stapleton

Dispute resolution and commercial litigation
Deirdre Courtney, Mary Claire Markey

Product liability, medical negligence
Susan R Stapleton

Employment and HR support
Mary Claire Markey

Administration of estates, matrimonial law
Susan R Stapleton

Administrative and broadcasting law
Dympna Murphy

Insolvency and insurance
Deirdre Courtney, Margaret Scully

Debt management
Margaret Scully

Intellectual property, IT, telecoms and commerce
John King

Media and entertainment
Deirdre Courtney, John King

Asset finance, maritime and shipping
Ivor Fitzpatrick

Corporate tax, EU and competition
Cormac Gordon, John King

LK SHIELDS
SOLICITORS

39-40 UPPER MOUNT STREET
DUBLIN 2

Telephone: +353 1 661 0866
Fax: +353 1 661 0883
E-mail: email@lkshields.ie
Website: www.lkshields.ie

Languages
English, French, German, Italian

Number of lawyers 50

Contacts
Hugh Garvey (managing partner), Laurence K Shields (chairman)

International groupings
ius laboris International Employment Law, Pensions and Employee Benefits Alliance

CATEGORIES OF WORK

Corporate and commercial
Laurence K Shields, Emmet Scully

Banking and finance
Joseph Gavin, David Williams

Corporate finance
Gerard Halpenny, Emmet Scully

Employment and employee benefits
Michael Kavanagh, Fiona Thornton

Public/private partnerships and public procurement
Philip Daly, Richard Curran

Intellectual property and technology
Eoin Cunneen, Deirdre Kilroy

Commercial property
Jim Gollogley, Gerry O'Hanlon

EU competition law
Marco Hickey, Derval O'Halloran

Commercial litigation and dispute resolution
Edmund Butler, Michael Kavanagh

Insolvency and bankruptcy
Hugh Garvey, Edmund Butler

Pensions
Fiona Thornton

THE FIRM

A premier and dynamic firm providing client-focused practical, timely, cost-effective and innovative legal solutions. Founded in 1988, the firm was, and remains, ranked among the leading law firms in Ireland. The firm has acted in some of the most complex and high-profile legal transactions and proceedings. It is noted for successfully adding specialist services to its core activities such as employment, pensions, financial services and competition, in all of which it competes successfully at the top level.

LK Shields Solicitors' dynamic business environment, and client-focused approach, enables consistent delivery of quality legal advice across multiple practice areas. The firm is constantly looking forward, anticipating change and striving to improve its standards and client services. The firm's solicitors are young, ambitious and forward facing. They work to attain an in-depth knowledge of clients' business environments, enabling them to facilitate the provision of first-class legal solutions. The firm's growing client base is made up of a multitude of successful and enterprising businesses, both in Ireland and internationally.

AREAS OF PRACTICE

The firm is structured around three integrated departments: business law, litigation and dispute resolution and property. Each department is comprised of industry-focused units that combine the knowledge of the firm's solicitors.

The business law department is the largest of the three departments and comprises a number of successful specialist units with an outstanding reputation, particularly in mergers and acquisitions, banking and financial services, commercial, employment and intellectual property. Other practice areas of major strength within the firm are EU law and competition law, corporate finance and restructuring.

The litigation and dispute resolution department houses one of the top teams of litigators in the City. It acts in numerous high-profile cases, including representing clients before the recently introduced Commercial Court requiring intensive activity and fast turnaround. This department continues to expand its litigation, arbitration and mediation services for commercial clients in the Irish courts and in international disputes.

The property department is enjoying rapid growth, acting and advising on all aspects of commercial property transactions in Ireland. The firm's lawyers have strong technical and commercial capability, whilst also liaising with appropriate experts and professionals in other disciplines in the property field. The firm regularly advises on premium-value property transactions in Ireland, including for semi-State bodies.

The firm's legal expertise is augmented by the excellent support provided by its secretarial and accounting staff, IT department and its library and information centre.

LK Shields Solicitors' main areas of practice are: corporate and business law, intellectual property, mergers and acquisitions, banking and financial services, asset finance, capital markets, investment funds, insolvency, securitisation, litigation and dispute resolution including mediation and arbitration, insurance litigation, shareholder disputes, professional negligence defence, insolvency, EU law, competition law, employment, employment benefits, pensions, healthcare, property, construction, energy and natural resources, planning and environment, project finance, corporate tax, insurance, private client services, public procurement, public private partnerships, media and entertainment, and company secretarial.

LANDWELL
SOLICITORS

GARDNER HOUSE
WILTON PLACE
DUBLIN 2

Telephone: +353 1 662 6655
Fax: +353 1 662 6788
E-mail: info@ie.landwellglobal.com
Website: www.landwellglobal.com/ie

Languages
English, French, German

Number of lawyers 25

Contacts
Edward Evans, Gerry Bohan, Garrett Breen, Ursula McMahon, Pauline Louth, Colleen Cleary

International groupings
Landwell, worldwide network of law firms

CATEGORIES OF WORK

Commercial and competition
Edward Evans, Gerry Bohan, Pauline Louth

Corporate structuring
Ursula McMahon

Dispute resolution
Garrett Breen, Ita Guilfoyle

Technology, media and communications
Garrett Breen

Employment and human resources
Colleen Cleary

Financial services
Edward Evans

Intellectual property
Garrett Breen

Mergers and acquisitions
Gerry Bohan, Edward Evans, Pauline Louth

Public law
Garrett Breen

Real estate
Gerry Bohan

MAPLES AND CALDER

40 LOWER BAGGOT STREET
DUBLIN 2

Telephone: +353 1 667 9800
Fax: +353 1 661 6239
E-mail: dublininfo@maplesandcalder.com
Website: www.maplesandcalder.com

Languages
English, Irish

Other offices
BVI, Cayman Islands, Dubai, Hong Kong, Jersey, London

Number of lawyers 140
at this office 19

Contacts
Jennifer Caldwell, Julian Reddyhough

CATEGORIES OF WORK

Capital markets

Corporate

Entertainment and media law

Employment and pensions law

EU law

Insurance

Investment funds

Insolvency and corporate restructuring

Information technology and e-commerce

Irish tax law

Finance

Litigation

Local practice

Regulatory and financial services

Trusts/selected private client services

MASON HAYES+CURRAN

6 FITZWILLIAM SQUARE
DUBLIN 2

Telephone: +353 1 614 5000
Fax: +353 1 614 5001
E-mail: mail@mhc.ie
Website: www.mhc.ie

Languages
English, French, German, Spanish

Other offices
London, New York

Number of fee-earners 130

Contact
Declan Moylan (managing partner)

CATEGORIES OF WORK

Administrative/public bodies
Niall Michel, Brian Hunt

Banking, securities and finance
Kevin Hoy, Christine O'Donovan

Biotechnology
Martin Kelleher, Philip Nolan

Capital markets
Paul Egan, Niamh Callaghan

Commercial recoveries
Colman Curran

Company secretarial and corporate compliance
Paula Phelan, Elaine Keating

Construction law
Rory Kirrane, Vanessa Byrne

Corporate and business law, including M&A
Paul Egan, David O'Donnell

Dispute resolution
Declan Black, Emer Gilvarry

EU and competition law
Tony Burke, John Kettle

Employment law
Emer Gilvarry, Richard Woulfe

Energy and natural resources
Kevin Hoy, William Carmody

Environmental and planning law
Ailbhe Gilvarry, Declan Curran

IT and telecoms
Tony Burke, Philip Nolan

Insolvency and corporate recovery
Declan Black, Maurice Phelan

Insurance litigation
Lorcan Buckley

Intellectual property
Tony Burke, Richard Woulfe

Investment funds and insurance
Fionán Breathnach

Inward investment
Declan Moylan, Liam Brazil

Inward investment from US
Declan Moylan, Daniel Walsh (resident in New York)

Life sciences
Martin Kelleher, John Kettle

Litigation and arbitration
Emer Gilvarry, Declan Black

Maritime law
Helen Noble

Media and entertainment
John Kettle, Philip Nolan

Pensions
John Kettle

Private client
Nora Larkin

Public law and government investigations
Niall Michel, Brian Hunt

Public private partnerships
Kevin Hoy

Real estate
Declan Curran, Vanessa Byrne

Regulated industries
Tony Burke, John Kettle

Securities law
Paul Egan, Niamh Callaghan, Justin McKenna

Taxation
Suzanne Carter

MATHESON ORMSBY PRENTICE

30 HERBERT STREET
DUBLIN 2

Telephone: +353 1 619 9000
Fax: +353 1 619 9010
E-mail: mop@mop.ie
Website: www.mop.ie

Languages
Dutch, French, German, Italian, Spanish

Other offices
London, New York, Palo Alto (CA)

Number of lawyers 230

CATEGORIES OF WORK

Asset finance
Chris Quinn, Anthony Walsh

Asset management
Michael Jackson, James Scanlon

Banking
Patrick Molloy, William Prentice

Capital markets
Michael Jackson, Tim Scanlon

Commercial litigation and dispute resolution
Stuart Margetson, Michael Tyrrell

Commercial property – development
Owen O'Sullivan, Patrick Sweetman

Commercial property – investment
Cara O'Hagan, Nicola Palmer

Commercial property – retail
Deirdre Morris, Cara O'Hagan

Corporate and commercial
Andrew Doyle, Patrick Spicer

Corporate restructuring and insolvency
Rod Ensor, Tony O'Grady

EC, competition and regulatory
Helen Kelly

Employment, pensions and benefits
Brian Buggy, John Dunne, Paul Glenfield

Energy and natural resources
Peter O'Brien, Michael O'Connor

Information technology
Anne-Marie Bohan, Don McAleese

Insurance
Sharon Daly, Liam Flynn

Intellectual property
Alistair Payne, Michael Tyrrell

Inward investment
Robert O'Shea, John Ryan

Life sciences
Karen Holmes, Stuart Margetson

Media and entertainment
Ruth Hunter, James Hickey

Mergers and acquisitions
Robert Heron, George Brady

Outsourcing
Anne-Marie Bohan, Patrick Spicer

Planning and environmental
Stuart Margetson, Patrick Sweetman

Private client
Paraic Madigan, Graham Richards

Private equity
Edward Miller, Stanley Watson

Privatisations
Robert Heron, Michael O'Connor

Projects and construction
Damien Keogh, Michael O'Connor

Regulatory risk and financial services compliance
Joe Beashel

Retail and leisure
Lorraine Compton, Nicola Palmer

Structured finance, securitisation and repackaging
Tara Doyle, Turlough Galvin

Tax
Liam Quirke, John Ryan

Transport and shipping
Bríd Munnelly

Venture capital
Edward Miller, Tim Scanlon

McCANN FITZGERALD

2 HARBOURMASTER PLACE
INTERNATIONAL FINANCIAL SERVICES CENTRE
DUBLIN 1

Telephone: +353 1 829 0000
Fax: +353 1 829 0010
E-mail: postmaster@mccannfitzgerald.ie
Website: www.mccannfitzgerald.ie

Languages
Dutch, French, German, Italian, Japanese, Spanish

Other offices
Brussels, London, Belfast* (North South Legal Alliance with L'Estrange & Brett)

Number of lawyers 267+

CATEGORIES OF WORK

Banking and financial services
Ronan Molony, Niall Powderly

Capital markets
Roy Parker, Richard Rice

Commercial property
Colin Keane, Lonan McDowell

Commercial disputes
David Clarke, Helen Collins

Corporate and commercial
William Earley, Paul Heffernan

Corporate finance, M&A
Barry Devereux, David Byers

Employment and pensions
Terence McCrann, Maureen Dolan

Energy
Patricia Lawless, Gerald FitzGerald

Insolvency and restructuring
Jane Marshall, Emma Crowley

Construction
Timothy Bouchier-Hayes, Max Abrahamson

Competition and EU
Damian Collins (Brussels), Gerald FitzGerald

Intellectual property
Grace Smith, Yvonne McNamara

Investment funds
Ambrose Loughlin, Máire O' Connor

Maritime and transport
Petria McDonnell, Mark Pearson

Private client
Susan O'Connell, Muriel Walls

Product liability
Roderick Bourke, Helen Collins

Public private partnership/PFI
Timothy Bouchier-Hayes, Eamonn O'Hanrahan

McEVOY PARTNERS

CANADA HOUSE
65-68 ST STEPHEN'S GREEN
DUBLIN 2

Telephone: +353 1 415 5900
Fax: +353 1 476 0551
E-mail: info@mcevoypartners.ie
Website: www.mcevoypartners.ie

Languages
English, French, German

Number of lawyers 12

Contact
Bernard McEvoy

CATEGORIES OF WORK

Mergers and acquisitions

Management buy-outs/buy-ins

IPOs/flotations

Commercial property

Intellectual property

Competition

Equity/debt fundraising

Franchising/distribution

Corporate restructuring

Entertainment

Information technology

Employment

O'DONNELL SWEENEY
SOLICITORS

ONE EARLSFORT CENTRE
EARLSFORT TERRACE
DUBLIN 2

Telephone: +353 1 664 4200
Fax: +353 1 664 4300
E-mail: info@odonnellsweeney.ie
Website: www.odonnellsweeney.ie

Languages
French, German, Italian, Spanish

Number of lawyers 87

Member
Eversheds International Association

CATEGORIES OF WORK

Banking and finance
Patricia Heffernan, Steven Rodgers

Capital markets
David Beattie, Chelita Healy

Commercial property
Joseph Stanley, Rory O'Donnell

Company and commercial
David Beattie, David O'Beirne

Construction
Mark Varian, Dermot McEvoy

Dispute resolution
Dermot McEvoy, Norman Fitzgerald

Employee benefits, pensions
David Beattie, Peter Fahy

Employment law
David Fagan, Jim Trueick

Energy and natural resources
David Beattie, Mark Varian

EU, competition
Seán Ryan

Information technology
Tony McGovern, Peppe Santoro

Insolvency
Norman Fitzgerald, Mark Woodcock

Insurance, regulatory
Peter Fahy, Francis Hackett

Intellectual property
Tony McGovern, Feilim O'Caoimh

Landlord and tenant
Sean Greene, Alan Murphy

Mergers and acquisitions
Joseph R Sweeney, Francis Hackett, David O'Beirne

Planning and environment
Sean Greene, Rory O'Donnell

Projects and PPP
Mark Varian, Kerri Crossen

Telecoms
Francis Hackett

REDDY CHARLTON MCKNIGHT

12 FITZWILLIAM PLACE
DUBLIN 2

Telephone: +353 1 66 19 500
Fax: +353 1 67 89 192
E-mail: rcmck@rcmck.com
Website: www.rcmck.com

Languages
English, French, Irish, Italian, Polish

Number of lawyers 12

Contact
Paul Keane (managing partner)

International groupings
Interleges

CATEGORIES OF WORK

Corporate and commercial
Paul Keane, Barbara Galvin, Richard Hammond

Commercial and residential property
Tom Marren, Christina McGowan

Litigation and dispute resolution
Lorna McAuliffe, Gerard Charlton, Laurence Fenelon, Lorraine Rowland

Private client
Gerard Charlton, Richard Hammond

Company secretarial
Maeve Walsh

Construction law
Paul Keane, Deirdre Ni Fhloinn

Insolvency and corporate recovery
Paul Keane, Richard Hammond

Employment and industrial relations
Lorna McAuliffe, Barbara Galvin

Sports law
Lorna McAuliffe, Laurence Fenelon

WILLIAM FRY

FITZWILTON HOUSE
WILTON PLACE
DUBLIN 2

Telephone: +353 1 639 5000
Fax: +353 1 639 5333
E-mail: info@williamfry.ie
Website: www.williamfry.ie

Languages
English, French, German, Italian, Spanish

Number of lawyers 194

Other offices
Belfast* (Tughans Solicitors), New York

CATEGORIES OF WORK

Arbitration and dispute resolution
Owen O'Sullivan, Michael Kealey

Asset management
Dan Morrissey, Tara O'Reilly

Banking and financial services
Neville O'Byrne, Elaine Hanly

Capital markets
Ken Casey, Brendan Heneghan

Construction
Liam McCabe, Andrew Muckian

Corporate and commercial
Alvin Price, Myra Garrett

E-commerce
Victor Timon, David Cullen

Employment
Boyce Shubotham, Maura Roe

Energy and waste management
Aislinn O'Farrell, Bryan Bourke

EU/competition
John Handoll, Cormac Little

Insolvency and corporate recovery
Michael Quinn, Barry Cahir

Insurance
John Larkin, Paul Murray

Intellectual property
Carol Plunkett, David Cullen

Investment funds
Daniel Morrissey, Declan O'Sullivan

Inward investment
Brendan Cahill, David Carthy

Life sciences and healthcare
Alvin Price, David Cullen

Litigation
Owen O'Sullivan, Carol Plunkett

Media and broadcasting
Michael Kealey, Ken Casey

Mergers and acquisitions
Owen O'Connell, Brendan Cahill

Pensions/employee share schemes
Michael Wolfe, Maura Roe

Planning and environmental
Conor Linehan, Liam McCabe

Project finance (PPP)
Liam McCabe, Elaine Hanly

Property
Nora White, Edward Spain

Public procurement
John Handoll, Cormac Little

Securitisation
Elaine Hanly, Daragh Bohan

Taxation
Martin Phelan, Michael O'Connor

Technology
Myra Garrett, Victor Timon

Telecommunications
John Handoll, Victor Timon

Trusts and estates
Edmund Fry, Nora Lillis

ISLE OF MAN

Population	**60,000**
Number of lawyers	**192 (110 Manx advocates and 82 registered practitioners)**
Professional title	**Advocate**
Currency	**Pound sterling (£))**

Index

The Isle of Man continues to build on its reputation as a well-regulated financial services centre. The insurance sector in particular goes from strength to strength.

While maintaining strong links with the UK mainland, the commercial success of the jurisdiction means that, like Jersey and Guernsey, dependence on the UK is waning as more institutional clients come from overseas – increasingly from the US, the Middle East (UAE) and South Africa.

The Manx Bar is a fused profession and Manx advocates enjoy rights of audience and also undertake the role played by solicitors on the mainland. In addition, it is straightforward for advocates to register as solicitors on the mainland. However, UK solicitors do not enjoy reciprocal rights. Foreign lawyers have, since 1986, only been able to practise as Registered Legal Practitioners – restricted from undertaking conveyancing, litigation or being probate practitioners. In May 1997, the Isle of Man Law Society reluctantly voted to relax the rules forbidding non-Manx lawyers from becoming members of the Bar. However, multinational partnerships between lawyers are still prohibited. The rules continue to restrict the areas of practice foreign lawyers may undertake.

BILLING

The Advocates' Scale Fees Act (1963) lays down four scale fees covering every aspect of legal services. However, fees may vary depending on the lawyer instructed and the job in hand. Clients can expect costs not dissimilar to those charged by City of London firms: around £160 for a newly qualified lawyer, rising to around £350 at partner level.

MARKETING

Advocates may advertise their services reasonably freely although there are regulations which demand that any publicity be accurate and in good taste.

THE LEGAL 500

Readers should note that the following is taken from the **Offshore Britain** section of the 2005 edition of *The Legal 500* (UK edition), available at www.legal500.com.

LEGAL MARKET

The Isle of Man is well known as a hub for captive insurance, shipping and, more recently, internet gaming. Although the island lacks a cohesive marketing body for the island (such as Jersey Finance, or the IDA in Ireland) to publicise its competitive advantages, significant measures have been introduced to make the island a destination for investors and financial institutions.

From April 2006, the government plans to roll out a non-discriminatory corporate tax regime, with income tax being abolished altogether. The Isle of Man is a regulated jurisdiction which caters for a wide variety of funds, including the Experienced Investor Fund, which has been in place since 1999. Protected Cell Company (PCC) legislation was introduced in 2004 and the new Companies Act, due to come into force in 2006, is anticipated to make the island an even more favourable place for financial institutions to do business.

Cains Advocates Limited and **Dickinson Cruickshank** are the island's two largest firms. The two firms were jointly instructed by the Treasury Department of the Isle of Man Government to advise and draft the new Isle of Man Companies Bill, due to come into force in 2006. Internationally focused **Cains Advocates Limited** has five directors, and recruited four fee-earners in 2004, bringing the total number of lawyers to 25. The firm benefits from frequent referrals from Magic Circle firms and has a permanently staffed London office to facilitate this process.

Forty-one fee-earner **Dickinson Cruickshank** reaps a steady flow of instructions from blue-chip institutions based both in the Isle of Man and in the UK. The firm has across-the-board expertise and is looking to ramp up its funds capability.

Simcocks deals with the full range of commercial work and has a focus on UK tax mitigation planning. It was the first Isle of Man firm to open a London office.

Compact **Quinn Kneale** has a solid corporate and commercial practice, dealing with a steady flow of UK and international instructions. The firm fields some experienced and adept practitioners.

Two-advocate firm **MannBenham Limited** is a highly capable outfit, which concentrates on corporate and commercial work, as well as providing niche specialisms in timeshare trusts and gaming licences, counting a raft of online casinos and bookmakers among its clients.

The largest firms

1	Dickinson Cruickshank	37
2	Cains Advocates Limited	30
3	Simcocks	17
4	Quinn Kneale	8
5	Mann & Partners	6
6	Gough & Co.	5
	MannBenham Limited	5
	Stuart Smalley & Co LLC	5
9	Carter Jones McDonald	4
	Carters	4
	Kelly Luft Stanley Ashton	4
	Laurence Keenan, Advocates & Solicitors	4
	Maitland	4
14	Corlett Bolton	3
	Dougherty & Associates	3
	Gelling Johnson Farrant	3
	Mark Moroney Advocates	3
18	PhilipConwayThomas	2
19	Andrew Bridson - Advocate & Commissioner of Oaths	1
	Conti Advocates	1
	Hyde & Hanson	1
	Richard Penn	1

These figures represent the total number of lawyers in this country only, and have been supplied by the firms themselves. The figures should be accurate as at 1 January 2006.

The acclaimed **Mann & Partners** receives very positive feedback from clients for its commercial approach and speedy turnaround time. The firm has a strong reputation in commercial litigation, regulatory matters and employment: in 2004, the firm set up a distinct employment unit headed by John Aycock in anticipation of the introduction of new employment legislation.

Stuart Smalley & Co LLC is primarily a tax-focused practice, advising an entrepreneurial client base on fiscal mitigation. The lawyers benefit from the support of tax accountants.

Part of the international South African practice of **Webber Wentzel Bowens**, **Maitland** has a thriving practice in the Isle of Man, advising both South Africans and wealthy Europeans on their financial affairs.

Shirley McDonald at **Carter Jones McDonald** has carved out a superb reputation for the firm's criminal practice.

Niche litigation practice **Gough & Co.** is headed by Alan Gough, who is acknowledged to be an outstanding advocate.

BANKING AND FINANCE

Many blue-chip financial institutions have a presence on the Isle of Man, including Royal Bank of Scotland International, Coutts, Merrill Lynch, National Australia Group (Northern Bank) and Barclays International. The firms recommended here are capable of handling high-value banking and structured finance transactions with an international element. Niche specialisms in aircraft, ship finance and film are also core to most practices.

Cains Advocates Limited has the capacity to act on large-scale, high-value transactions. Mike Pinson is recommended, while Andrew Fingret provides expertise in film financing, acting on eight such deals in 2004. Funds specialist Simon Harding left to join **Dickinson Cruickshank**.

Dickinson Cruickshank is regularly instructed on major international transactions, including in 2004 acting on securitisations for Aston Partners Ltd and Cambridge Place Partners. The team also advised Northern Bank Ltd on the reorganisation of its Isle of Man subsidiary bank and disposal to Danske Bank. Nick Verardi is recommended, as is Joanne Kelly for aircraft leasing. Recent recruits include Simon Harding and Faye Moffett.

BANKING AND FINANCE

CAINS ADVOCATES LIMITED
DICKINSON CRUICKSHANK

Mann & Partners
Simcocks

Firms are listed A-Z in tiers alphabetically

COLLECTIVE INVESTMENT FUNDS

CAINS ADVOCATES LIMITED

Dickinson Cruickshank
Mann & Partners
MannBenham Limited
Simcocks

Firms are listed A-Z in tiers alphabetically

The 'impressive' Paul Branford handles banking and finance matters at **Mann & Partners**, advises on international financing and refinancing transactions, acting for both lenders and borrowers.

Simcocks advises banking clients including Barclays on regulatory and supervisory issues. The team has a particular focus on the formation and management of collective investment schemes.

COLLECTIVE INVESTMENT FUNDS

Funds work is a growing area for Manx law firms, as the government is trying to encourage fund managers and large third-party administrators to move over from popular funds destination Dublin.

Ahead of the pack is **Cains Advocates Limited**, which reaps the lion's share of fund work on the island. Although other firms are now beefing up their fund practices, **Cains Advocates Limited** maintains its position comfortably ahead of its competitors. The firm fields several experienced practitioners, including Richard Vanderplank, who heads the regulatory and mutual funds group, Andrew Baker and Mike Edwards. The team handles a broad range of collective and closed-end investment vehicle formations. The team was joined by Jim Hughes, formerly of Bank of Bermuda Group.

Dickinson Cruickshank advises its blue-chip client base on the establishment of both institutional and retail funds. Highlight instructions in 2004 include establishing an Isle of Man experienced investor fund for Charlotte Square. The team has been boosted by the arrival of Simon Harding from **Cains Advocates Limited**.

The 'responsive' Paul Branford of **Mann & Partners** has an excellent reputation for meticulous compliance work. The firm is building up its collective funds practice and also handles EIF instructions.

Bijou practice **MannBenham Limited** is forging a reputation in the EIF market, while at **Simcocks**, Phil Games and David Spencer are active practitioners in the funds arena.

COMMERCIAL

As well as having the capacity to act as Isle of Man counsel in international financial transactions, law firms also service the technology and electronic payment processing companies lured to the

COMMERCIAL

CAINS ADVOCATES LIMITED	
DICKINSON CRUICKSHANK	
Gough & Co.	
Maitland	
Mann & Partners	
MannBenham Limited	
Simcocks	
Quinn Kneale	
Stuart Smalley & Co LL	
Andrew Bridson - Advocate & Commissioner of Oaths	

Firms are listed A-Z in tiers alphabetically

island by the government's fiscal incentives. Lucrative niche sectors include the space industry, ship registration and, due to the flexible regulatory framework, gambling licences. An aircraft register, similar to the highly successful shipping register, is due to be rolled out in 2006.

Cains Advocates Limited fields an array of experienced advocates in its well-respected corporate and commercial team. Head of department Andrew Corlett sits on the IOM Treasury Strategy Group, Mike Pinson and Andrew Baker are acknowledged M&A specialists, while Mike Edwards has a strong reputation in ship finance. In 2004, former **Allen & Overy LLP** lawyer Chris Ewan joined the film and media law unit of the team.

Dickinson Cruickshank's expanding corporate and commercial department continues to flourish. In 2004, the team handled a steady flow of AIM listings, such as acting as Isle of Man counsel for the £10m listing of Renewable Energy Holdings Plc. Other highlight instructions include advising Northern Trust Ltd on the acquisition of the Barings group of companies, dealing with the Isle of Man banking subsidiaries. Simon Cain is an 'astute, canny' practitioner while Joanne Kelly and Nick Verardi both have strong reputations for high-value M&A and MBOs. The firm also has a considerable bank of expertise in shipping matters.

Paul Kerruish heads the commercial team at **Gough & Co.**, which handles an assortment of commercial contracts and corporate instructions for mid-market clients.

Clients find **Maitland** 'exceptional'. The firm provides high-level international tax planning to a mixed clientele of South African émigrés and European high-net-worth individuals. Colin Bird is recommended.

Clients praise 'proactive' and 'impressive' Chris Murphy at **Mann & Partners**, who 'produces quality work and always keeps them in the loop'. The firm has a strong reputation for specialised regulatory work, as well as expertise in gaming law and e-commerce.

MannBenham Limited has a dedicated commercial and corporate focus. The team, headed by Tim Mann, is capable of handling a broad range of commercial instructions for its clientele, the majority of which are corporate service providers. In 2004, the firm acted in a number of M&A transactions in the corporate service industry. The other half of the duo, Miles Benham, is also recommended.

Ita McArdle heads a capable commercial team at **Simcocks**, which fields eight corporate and commercial specialists. The firm acts for a mixed client base of large international companies and small businesses.

Quinn Kneale has a solid commercial practice which deals with a range of corporate and commercial instructions. President of the Isle of Man Law Society Jeremy Callin is recommended for his expertise

Jonathan Smalley of **Stuart Smalley & Co LLC** has a good reputation for his 'hands-on method of tackling international tax planning conundrums'.

Andrew Bridson of **Andrew Bridson - Advocate & Commissioner of Oaths** advises Isle of Man companies on corporate and commercial matters, as well as providing opinions to leading banks on Manx companies.

COMMERCIAL LITIGATION

The Isle of Man has a fused profession, with a Bar of around 100 advocates, but can import QCs from the UK to act on particularly complex cases, or if an unreasonable demand is brought to bear on the practice.

The 'impressive' Seth Caine heads the litigation team at **Cains Advocates Limited** which boasts a wealth of expertise in international fraud, asset-tracing and insolvency work. Peter Clucas is experienced in anti-money-laundering, while experienced Giles Hill handles insolvency matters.

First-class advocate Paul Morris heads **Dickinson Cruickshank**'s commercial dispute resolution team and is also senior partner of the firm. Chris Cope is recommended for international fraud and asset-recovery work. The firm scooped a high-profile instruction in 2004, acting for Roys Poyiadjis in a high-profile case brought by the US government for the recovery of the alleged proceeds of a corporate fraud. The case is significant as it is unusual for substantial proceedings to be issued in the Isle of Man.

COMMERCIAL LITIGATION

CAINS ADVOCATES LIMITED	
DICKINSON CRUICKSHANK	
MANN & PARTNERS	
Gough & Co.	
MannBenham Limited	
Simcocks	
Quinn Kneale	
Andrew Bridson - Advocate & Commissioner of Oaths	

Firms are listed A-Z in tiers alphabetically

The excellent John Aycock heads the litigation practice at **Mann & Partners**, which regularly receives chunky referral work from UK and US firms, as well as its peers on the island. Highlight instructions in 2004 include acting for the spouse of deposed Pakistani Prime Minister Benazir Bhutto in defending an action brought by a liquidator. The team has strength in both private and governmental work, and has set up an employment law unit to deal with the increase in claims. Associate Chris Brooks has joined from **Cains Advocates Limited**.

Gough & Co. has a determined litigation focus, with Alan Gough viewed by his peers as one of the best litigators on the island. Alan Gough is supported by associates Christopher Webb and Charles Coleman. The team handles a breadth of contentious matters, providing particular expertise in asset-tracing and insolvency work.

Although predominantly focused on its commercial and corporate practice, the litigation team at **MannBenham Limited** attracts some significant trust litigation. The firm is increasingly instructed on cross-border litigation actions which involve Isle of Man companies. Miles Benham, who heads the department, has a solid reputation for his negotiation skills and is considered to have a commercial approach.

The litigation department at **Simcocks** is headed by Chris Arrowsmith and handles substantial commercial and insolvency work. Kevin O'Riordan has expertise in divorce cases for high-net-worth individuals.

At three-partner team **Quinn Kneale**, Jonathan Wild has a growing reputation for his skills as an advocate in the firm's commercial litigation practice.

Andrew Bridson - Advocate & Commissioner of Oaths is primarily a niche litigation practice. Former **Mann & Partners** advocate Andrew Bridson acts for both beneficiaries and trustees in trust disputes; defending and obtaining injunctions, freezing and disclosure orders. The practice also handles property litigation and banking disputes.

INSURANCE

There is a demand for insurance work on the Isle of Man due to the preponderance of financial institutions linked to the 'captive' institutional market or the retail life sector. The Insurance and Pensions Authority regulates a growing pensions market, which encompasses a variety of pension products, from major international schemes to bespoke expatriate schemes.

INSURANCE
CAINS ADVOCATES LIMITED
SIMCOCKS
Dickinson Cruickshank
Mann & Partners
Firms are listed A-Z in tiers alphabetically

David Bermingham handles a steady flow of captive insurance work at **Cains Advocates Limited**, while former **Denton Wilde Sapte** lawyer Ben Hughes specialises in pensions and employee benefits.

David Spencer at **Simcocks** has an excellent reputation for insurance advice. The firm has a strong insurance practice, acting for many of the captive insurance companies on the island.

Dickinson Cruickshank's Nick Verardi was involved in numerous insurance instructions in 2004, including setting up a number of new companies on the island. The team also has considerable experience in setting up captive insurance companies. Major clients include Canada Life International.

Mann & Partners' client list includes several major insurance and life assurance companies, including Royal Skandia and Direct Line.

PERSONAL TAX, TRUSTS AND PROBATE

As an offshore jurisdiction, the Isle of Man has a well-established bank of legal expertise specialising in private client and trusts work. As well as trust management and formation, trust litigation is on the rise as trusts set up in the 1960s reach maturity and spark disputes between beneficiaries.

Jeremy Walton heads the practice at **Cains Advocates Limited**, which can call on the contentious expertise of Seth Caine, who is an active player in trust litigation. The team acts for high-net-worth individuals and major trust companies.

PERSONAL TAX, TRUSTS AND PROBATE
CAINS ADVOCATES LIMITED
DICKINSON CRUICKSHANK
Mann & Partners
MannBenham Limited
Simcocks
Stuart Smalley & Co LLC
Firms are listed A-Z in tiers alphabetically

At **Dickinson Cruickshank**, Sharon Roberts heads the four-partner department, ably supported by two assistants. John Rimmer has an outstanding reputation for his succession planning and asset protection, as well as trust litigation. A snapshot of work in 2004 includes advising a trustee on trust and lending documentation in connection with the acquisition of a £100m property, and advising protectors over multi-millon-pound trust disputes with trustees. A sterling client list includes government departments, local authorities, a raft of high-net-worth individuals and leading trust companies.

Mann & Partners provides advice on all aspects of private client and trust law. At **MannBenham Limited**, Timothy Mann handles both contentious and non-contentious private client and trust work. Philip Games at **Simcocks**' private client practice works alongside the commercial group to provide trust and tax advice to an entrepreneurial clientele. English solicitor Martine Fleming at **Stuart Smalley & Co LLC** is recommended for her timely advice to high-net-worth individuals, while Jonathan Smalley has built up a reputation for trust-related crisis management. Clients also benefit from the firm's firm taxation focus.

REAL ESTATE
CAINS ADVOCATES LIMITED
DICKINSON CRUICKSHANK
SIMCOCKS
Gough & Co.
Kelly Luft Stanley Ashton
Mann & Partners
Firms are listed A-Z in tiers alphabetically

REAL ESTATE

Advocates report that the commercial property market was relatively flat in 2004, so at this stage of its cycle this practice area has not been a core generator of profits.

Head of department Jeremy Walton and former **Lovells** solicitor Mike Polson are the major personalities in the commercial property team at **Cains Advocates Limited.** A blue-chip client list includes well-known entities Manx Electricity Board and Royal Skandia Life.

Mark Humphrey at **Dickinson Cruickshank** is recommended for substantial commercial property instructions, including property financing, while consultant Geoffrey Karran has expertise in advising on complex planning issues.

Simcocks has a strong client base of developers, to which the team provides an in-depth advisory and transactional service. Irini Newby is a leading light of the practice.

Gough & Co. and **Kelly Luft Stanley Ashton** both have solid commercial property capability.

Mann & Partners' Chris Murphy acts for institutional and private investors in the acquisition, disposal and leasing of commercial and private property. The client list includes local property development and construction companies.

ISRAEL

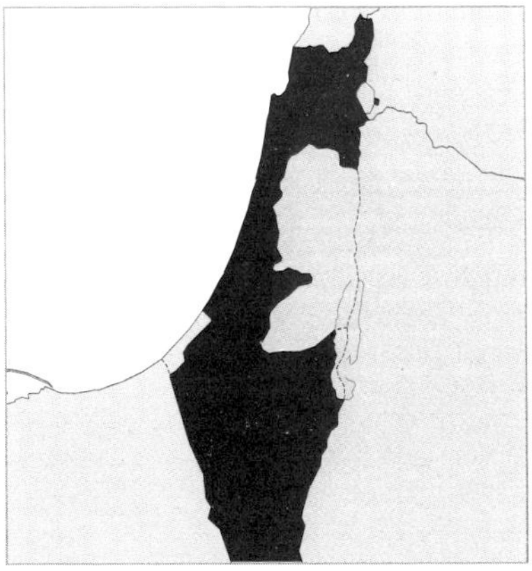

Population	**6.6 million**
Number of lawyers	**27,000**
Professional title	**Advocate**
Currency	**New Israeli Shekel (NIS))**

Index

Israel, located at the point where Europe, Asia and Africa meet, shares borders with Lebanon, Syria, Jordan and Egypt, as well as with the disputed Palestinian territories.

It is a small and diverse country, with Tel Aviv, Haifa and Jerusalem typical of the dense urban centres that contrast with the 5% of the community that live in rural co-operative communities called kibbutzim and moshavim.

The vast majority (some 80%) of the population is Jewish, though there is also a large Arab presence.

Israel has long been at the heart of global politics, and remains so. Since its creation in the wake of World War II, Israel has had a series of disputes with neighbouring Arab states and the Palestinian community over land, borders and recognition, which continue today.

There is a sense in the country that recent progress towards peace will continue. The security situation and the economy are both seen to be improving, stimulated in part by the relative political stability that has prevailed in recent years.

Prime Minister Ariel Sharon left the right-wing Likud party in late 2004 to set up his own Kadima party to fight the forthcoming election, in order to further his changes of negotiating peace with the Palestinians, after hardliners objected to his decision to withdraw from the Gaza Strip. Senior figures, including former labour leader Shimon Peres, have followed him. The peace process remains central to political and business life in Israel.

BILLING

An hourly rate is widely used for most work, though pre-agreed or percentage fees may apply to certain transactions in areas such as project finance and real estate. Rates for associates can start at around US$150 per hour, rising to over US$400 per hour for partners. At many firms, hourly rates are set to increase modestly next year, though they have remained stable for the last few years.

MARKETING

Minor shifts in the marketing activities permitted for law firms in Israel suggest that liberalisation is favourable, the practice of direct advertising having once been strictly prohibited. Only smaller firms had taken up the limited promotional activity that is permitted, but now larger firms are starting to sponsor conferences and events, as well as developing more sophisticated internet sites.

IN-HOUSE LAWYERS

The number of lawyers in Israel grows rapidly, and a typical estimate is that it has doubled in size in the last seven years. A plentiful supply of legal talent, at least at junior level, has lowered the cost of employment and has led to many more firms, including smaller enterprises, hiring in-house counsel. However, most significant matters are still referred to external law firms.

ECONOMY

The progress that has been made so far, towards peace and through the economic reform programme of Finance Minister Benjamin Netanyahu, has helped to lift Israel's economy, with greater interest in the maturing hi-tech sector noticeable in 2005. Also, the rebound in the tourism industry shows perceptions are shifting about the security situation.

With its strengths in research and development, IT, agro-technology and biotechnology, Israel's economic fortunes are less closely tied to the to local or political factors than to the global economy, the relative buoyancy of which has attracted a growing level of foreign investment in Israel. Legislative changes including the introduction of tax exemptions for foreign companies active in certain sectors of the Israeli market have also encouraged foreign investment.

LEGAL MARKET

There has been a strong trend toward consolidation at the top end of the Israeli legal market and some notable mergers have taken place. The latest of these is the joining of *Goldfarb, Levy, Eran & Co* with the practice of *Dankner, Lusky & Co* to form **Goldfarb, Levy, Eran, Meiri & Co.**, which is now among the largest law firms in the country and cements its place with firms like **Yigal Arnon & Co**, **S. Horowitz & Co** and **Herzog, Fox & Neeman** in Israel's 'Magic Circle'.

Gilead Sher's firm joined forces to become part of **Aaronsohn Sher Aboulafia Amoday & Co Law Offices**, and other significant mergers are expected early in 2006, with the aim of allowing larger firms to offer full-service capability, while

The largest firms

1	Herzog, Fox & Neeman	104
2	Goldfarb, Levy, Eran, Meiri & Co.	95
3	Balter, Guth, Aloni & Co	80
4	Yigal Arnon & Co	78
5	Meitar Liquornik Geva & Leshem Brandwein	71
6	S. Horowitz & Co	70
7	Naschitz, Brandes & Co.	64
8	Fischer Behar Chen Well Orion & Co	60
9	M. Firon & Co Advocates and Notaries	59
10	Gross, Kleinhendler, Hodak, Halevy, Greenberg & Co	57
11	Gornitzky & Co	56
12	Shiboleth, Yisraeli, Roberts, Zisman and Moshe H. Ne'eman, Ben-Artzi & Co.	55
13	Yehuda Raveh & Co.	46
14	M Seligman & Co	45
	S Friedman & Co, Advocates	45
	Zellermayer, Pelossof & Co., Advocates	45
17	Gilat, Bareket & Co, Attorneys at Law	40
	Reinhold Cohn & Partners, Patent Attorneys	40
19	Pearl Cohen Zedek Latzer	36
20	Caspi & Co	35
21	Danziger, Klagsbald & Co	33
22	Zysman, Aharoni, Gayer & Co	32
23	Berkman Wechsler Sahar Bloom & Co	31
24	Aaronsohn Sher Aboulafia Amoday & Co Law Offices	30
	Erdinast, Ben Nathan & Co., Advocates	30
	Weksler, Bregman & Co., Advocates	30

These figures represent the total number of lawyers in this country only, and have been supplied by the firms themselves. The figures should be accurate as at 1 January 2006.

developing strength in depth in specialist areas of law.

Key splits were also a feature of the market, most notably with the break-up of *Eitan, Pearl, Latzer & Cohen-Zedek* into **Eitan Law Group** and **Pearl Cohen Zedek Latzer**.

Key departures include Ori Rosen's from what is now **Danziger, Klagsbald & Co** to set up his own firm, and Joshua Rosensweig's split from **Gornitzky & Co** to form **Rosenram Business Development Ltd**.

FOREIGN FIRMS

To practise local law, which is conducted in Hebrew, lawyers must be locally qualified, and though their numbers are growing there are still relatively few qualified in both UK and Israeli law, though more are US and Israel-qualified. Also, restrictions on partnerships with foreign firms have left the major domestic firms in a position to handle high-value, international transactions, often working closely with foreign law firms.

INTERNATIONAL NETWORKS

Given the restrictions on affiliations with international law firms, many Israeli firms are members of international networks, such as *TagLaw*, *InterLaw* or *World Law Group*. International Chambers of Commerce are also an important source of foreign business for Israeli firms.

BANKING AND FINANCE

Herzog, Fox & Neeman includes the highly respected Alan Sacks, Ehud Sol and Gil White in a team that acts for major domestic banks, including Bank Hapoalim, as well as many of the large investment banks with a presence in Israel. It remains highly active on the borrower side and receives strong recommendations. Eliot Sacks adds capability in regulatory and derivatives matters.

The representation of domestic banks in major financings secures **Kantor Elhanani Tal & Co**'s place in the rankings. Founding partner Dalia Tal heads the banking and capital markets practice group, which handles M&A in the financial sector as well as banking law.

S. Horowitz & Co can claim a large banking department, including Ruth Oren, Anthony Bloch, Michelle Lieberman, Hugh Kowarsky and Clifford Davis, along with the banking litigation skills of Alex Hertzman and Ehud Arzi. Present on the majority of major financings on behalf of banks, the firm continues to build on its position as a leading firm in this sector. A highlight was the financing of the Alagem/Phoenix bid for a controlling interest in Bezeq.

Banking and finance is the strongest practice area for **Weksler, Bregman & Co., Advocates**, which receives praise from both clients and peers. It focuses largely on work for domestic banks, with clients such as Investec (Israel) and United Mizrahi Bank.

Caspi & Co recently represented Bank Hapoalim and Bank Leumi in the sale of their asset management business. The firm has a presence in structured finance and has developed a growing practice acting for a large proportion of domestic hedge funds, which are relatively new to Israel. Menachem Feder is also a leading expert on derivatives trading.

Efrati, Galili, Lahat & Co has been busy on behalf of buyers for mutual funds that have been sold off by banks under the requirements of new legislation, acting for banks such as United Mizrahi Bank on the sale of provident funds.

BANKING AND FINANCE

HERZOG, FOX & NEEMAN ✪
KANTOR ELHANANI TAL & CO
S. HOROWITZ & CO ✪
WEKSLER, BREGMAN & CO., ADVOCATES ✪

CASPI & CO ✪
EFRATI, GALILI, LAHAT & CO ✪
GOLDFARB, LEVY, ERAN, MEIRI & CO. ✪
GORNITZKY & CO ✪
MEITAR LIQUORNIK GEVA & LESHEM BRANDWEIN ✪
YEHUDA RAVEH & CO. ✪
YIGAL ARNON & CO ✪

Amit, Pollak, Matalon & Co
Danziger, Klagsbald & Co ✪
Fischer Behar Chen Well Orion & Co ✪
Gross, Kleinhendler, Hodak, Halevy, Greenberg & Co ✪
Heskia-Hacmun Law Firm ✪
S Friedman & Co, Advocates ✪
Shiboleth, Yisraeli, Roberts, Zisman and Moshe H. Ne'eman, Ben-Artzi & Co. ✪
Yaacov Salomon, Lipschutz & Co ✪
Yuval Levy & Co ✪
Zellermayer, Pelossof & Co., Advocates ✪

Avniel, Salomon & Co
Balter, Guth, Aloni & Co
Baratz, Horn & Co
Barnea & Co ✪
ES Shimron, I Molho, Persky & Co ✪
Ephraim Abramson & Co
Erdinast, Ben Nathan & Co., Advocates ✪
Haim Zadok & Co ✪
Hamburger Evron & Co. Law Offices & Notaries
J Weinroth (Dr) & Co ✪
Levy, Meidan & Co ✪
M Porath & Co
M Seligman & Co
Naschitz, Brandes & Co. ✪
Shavit Bar-On Gal-On Tzin Nov Yagur, Law Offices ✪

Firms are listed A-Z in tiers which are ranked in order of priority
✪ Indicates firm displays contact details at the end of this chapter.

The merger between *Goldfarb, Levy, Eran & Co* and *Dankner Lusky & Co* to create **Goldfarb, Levy, Eran, Meiri & Co.** was accompanied by the promotion to partner of associates, including Ariel Rosenberg, who specialises in banking and finance and has growing experience on complex, international transactions. Innovative deals, such as the partnership between an Israeli insurance company and a US investment bank, indicate the quality of its work.

Gornitzky & Co is a large firm that handles a significant amount of work for domestic banks and insurance companies, as well as advising corporate clients on financing. The departure of Joshua Rosensweig still leaves Zvi Ephrat and Moriel Matalon in a practice that offers a wide range of expertise.

Meitar Liquornik Geva & Leshem Brandwein is well regarded, particularly on institutional lending, asset-backed loans and syndicated financing. The firm also advises on derivatives transactions and related ISDA documentation. Dror Brandwein and Clifford Felig are prominent partners.

Lisa Tross heads the banking and finance department at **Yehuda Raveh & Co.**, representing construction companies, banks, universities and statutory authorities. The firm acts for foreign and domestic banks, with key deals including a US$250m loan provision from an Israeli bank, and a US$1.3bn credit facility.

Yigal Arnon & Co is a highly respected firm and is a strong player in the corporate finance sector. Amnon Lorch and Shiri Shaham include banking law in their diverse range of skills.

Amit, Pollak, Matalon & Co, formerly *Amit, Pollak, Matalon & Ben-Naftali, Erez & Co*, continues to represent some of Israel's leading corporates, banks and insurance companies in finance-related matters.

Danziger, Klagsbald & Co, previously *Danziger, Klagsbald, Rosen & Co*, recently represented a consortium of US banks in a US$100m loan to an Israeli corporation. Ronen Matry is supported by four associates in a busy team that acts for clients including Bank Leumi, Israel Discount Bank and Bank Hapoalim.

Fischer Behar Chen Well Orion & Co is widely respected, particularly for its asset finance and securitisation expertise. As well as representing major Israeli banks and insurance companies, it has also acted in the financing of major privatisations.

Though part of its commercial transactions team, the banking and finance expertise at **Gross, Kleinhendler, Hodak, Halevy, Greenberg & Co** is strong in its own right.

Heskia-Hacmun Law Firm's Amos Hacmun has represented a consortium of banks in regard to a large credit facility, and can count foreign banks among its clients. As well as helping financial institutions set up operations in Israel, the firm also advises on regulatory and financing matters.

S Friedman & Co, Advocates sees a large amount of finance work stemming from the firm's aviation and shipping practice, though it is also developing a larger entertainment finance practice.

Shiboleth, Yisraeli, Roberts, Zisman and Moshe H. Ne'eman, Ben-Artzi & Co. seems set to grow its standing in the banking and finance sector.

Yaacov Salomon, Lipschutz & Co counts Israel's second-largest bank among its clients and has a large team dedicated to its activities, including Alexander Samuel, Jaacov Riwanowitch, Dror Timor and David Goldenblatt.

Yuval Levy & Co couples financing expertise with its corporate and commercial practice. It has advised banks and insurance companies, as well as being involved in many corporate finance transactions.

Zellermayer, Pelossof & Co., Advocates has acted for international investment banks as well as domestic and foreign borrowers, with Avi Pelossof seen as a leading light.

Avniel, Salomon & Co's Yoav Salomon has a good reputation, as does the team at **Balter, Guth, Aloni & Co** for many aspects of commercial lending.

Baratz, Horn & Co, formerly *Baratz, Bar-Nathan, Horn & Co*, has the respected Yuval Horn's expertise in corporate and structured finance deals.

Barnea & Co's Micky Barnea advises foreign lenders in all aspects of financing, and recently represented Investec and Romania's Piraeus Bank.

Ephraim Abramson & Co partners Ephraim Abramson and Harry Grynberg represented a foreign participant in the bidding process during the privatisation of a major domestic bank.

Haim Zadok & Co's Nitza Posner, formerly legal advisor to the Special Credits Division of Bank Hapoalim, often represents creditors and debtors in major corporate crises, and recently acted for several unsecured creditors in the collapse of Clubmarket, a major chain of supermarkets.

Levy, Meidan & Co, previously *Joseph Levy & Co*, maintains a presence in banking and finance.

M Seligman & Co's Gabriel Hake and **Shavit Bar-On Gal-On Tzin Nov Yagur, Law Offices**' Hanit Nov and Liad Ziv are also worthy of note.

CAPITAL MARKETS AND SECURITIES

Caspi & Co has a long-standing reputation for representing financial institutions and capital consumers, with banks, insurers, underwriters and issuers of securities regularly seeking the firm's advice. Its capital markets practice has market-leading expertise in securities, spanning many asset classes, and it is often called upon to handle equity funding for new and mature clients.

Goldfarb, Levy, Eran, Meiri & Co. has strengthened its presence as a result of the merger between *Goldfarb, Levy, Eran & Co* with *Dankner Lusky & Co*, from which Ido Zemach is among the five partners added. Neil Nachum Stowe often represents Israeli companies in public offerings on foreign stock exchanges such as Nasdaq and AIM. The firm recently acted for underwriters in the public offering on the Tel Aviv Stock Exchange of Sapiens and for Retalix on its Nasdaq public offering.

The team at **Gross, Kleinhendler, Hodak, Halevy, Greenberg & Co** often advises issuers. Partners Joseph Gross, Gene Kleinhendler and Amir Halevy have been frequent authors on securities law. The firm has also become an important advisor on debt financing, through its focus on securitisation.

Herzog, Fox & Neeman is recommended for advising on public offerings and private placements in Israel and Europe. Ehud Sol and newly promoted partners Chaim Freidland and Efrat Ram act for domestic and foreign investors and issuers, as well as for underwriters of

CAPITAL MARKETS AND SECURITIES

CASPI & CO ✪
GOLDFARB, LEVY, ERAN, MEIRI & CO. ✪
GROSS, KLEINHENDLER, HODAK, HALEVY, GREENBERG & CO ✪
HERZOG, FOX & NEEMAN ✪
MEITAR LIQUORNIK GEVA & LESHEM BRANDWEIN ✪
S. HOROWITZ & CO ✪
YIGAL ARNON & CO ✪

Barnea & Co ✪
Efrati, Galili, Lahat & Co ✪
Fischer Behar Chen Well Orion & Co ✪
Gornitzky & Co ✪
M. Firon & Co Advocates and Notaries ✪
Naschitz, Brandes & Co. ✪
S Friedman & Co, Advocates ✪
Shiboleth, Yisraeli, Roberts, Zisman and Moshe H. Ne'eman, Ben-Artzi & Co. ✪
Yaacov Salomon, Lipschutz & Co ✪
Zellermayer, Pelossof & Co., Advocates ✪

Balter, Guth, Aloni & Co
Cohen, Cohen, Yaron-Eldar & Co., Law Offices
Ephraim Abramson & Co
Haim Samet, Steinmetz, Haring & Co
Kantor Elhanani Tal & Co
M Seligman & Co
Tulchinsky Stern & Co ✪
Weksler, Bregman & Co., Advocates ✪

Amit, Pollak, Matalon & Co
Baratz, Horn & Co
Cohen Legal Partners ✪
Danziger, Klagsbald & Co ✪
Erdinast, Ben Nathan & Co., Advocates ✪
Haim Zadok & Co ✪
J Weinroth (Dr) & Co ✪
Levy, Meidan & Co ✪
M Porath & Co
Melcer & Co Law Offices
Volovelsky, Dinstein & Co
Zysman, Aharoni, Gayer & Co

Firms are listed A-Z in tiers which are ranked in order of priority
✪ Indicates firm displays contact details at the end of this chapter.

placements on the Tel Aviv Stock Exchange (TASE), the New York Stock Exchange (NYSE) and Nasdaq. Expanding this department is a key goal and significant hires are imminent.

Meitar Liquornik Geva & Leshem Brandwein saw a lot of work in 2005, much of it relating the US securities market. Its securitisation and derivatives expertise are also sought after. It has handled many IPOs including Saifun Semiconductors on Nasdaq for US$136m, in which it represented the underwriters, and Adamind Ltd on AIM. It is also strong in domestic capital markets work

S. Horowitz & Co has an impressive list of clients, including Credit Suisse First Boston, Goldman Sachs, JP Morgan and Morgan Stanley, for which it acts on matters arising from securities offerings in Israel. The securitisation of parking lot receipts for a municipality in Tel Aviv, and the issue of its debt securities on TASE, were recent highlights. Hugh Kowarsky, Clifford Davis, Asgad Stern and Avigail Kastiel are the main players.

Yigal Arnon & Co has acted for issuers and underwriters in numerous listings and public offerings on TASE and in many public offerings in the US and Europe over the years. Its experience is recognised in the market, and Shiri Shaham is among those with securities and banking law expertise.

Micky Barnea, senior partner at **Barnea & Co** has seen his firm continue its successful growth. Its ties with the UK market have seen it acting on London Stock Exchange (LSE) listings of Israeli companies. Its AIM team, including Simon Jaffa, has also been busy with listings for Poly Information and Amiad.

Efrati, Galili, Lahat & Co has also acted on AIM flotations, as well as listings on TASE. It recently acted for Alony-Hetz in capital-raising activities, as well as other major domestic corporates.

Fischer Behar Chen Well Orion & Co is notable for securitisation and structured finance capability. It acted on the securitisation of property tax receipts for the city of Ramla, which is now a model for other municipalities to adopt. It is also involved in debt restructuring for a major telecoms client in a cross-border matter. It also acted for Azrieli Group in the acquisition of debt issued by commercial real estate companies to Bank Leumi pension funds.

Gornitzky & Co has experience in complex equity and debt securities, having advised investment banks, brokers and corporates on international IPOs and secondary offerings, dual listings, asset securitisations and post-M&A restructuring. The firm retains expertise in US and UK securities law.

Partners Rivi Firon-Irani and Alon Alpert, along with senior associate Nimrod Bashan, handle capital market deals at **M. Firon & Co Advocates and Notaries**, which is praised by clients for its diligence and high standards of professionalism. Clients include one of Israel's main institutional investors.

Naschitz, Brandes & Co. maintains its reputation for US securities work.

Asher Rabinowitz at **S Friedman & Co, Advocates** is known for his securitisation skills, and he recently represented Metal Tech in its flotation on AIM.

Shiboleth, Yisraeli, Roberts, Zisman and Moshe H. Ne'eman, Ben-Artzi & Co. acts for issuers, underwriters, equity funds and institutional investors in a broad-ranging practice.

Yaacov Salomon, Lipschutz & Co has a strong team with in David Goldenblatt, Merav Arad-Salomon, Oren Harpaz and Raanan Rawitz, who was recently promoted to partner. The firm is active in share offerings and debentures on the stock exchange, private issues and the raising of capital in foreign markets.

Zellermayer, Pelossof & Co., Advocates also has experience of TASE listings, as well as foreign offerings, in both the debt and equity markets.

Balter, Guth, Aloni & Co maintains a good reputation, while **Cohen, Cohen, Yaron-Eldar & Co., Law Offices** continues to build on successes in the IPO market with the addition of Tali Yaron-Eldar to expand its commercial and securities expertise.

Ephraim Abramson & Co has the capable Ephraim Abramson, Harry Grynberg and Jeffrey Rashba handling securities work.

Founding partner Dalia Tal heads the banking and capital markets practice group at **Kantor Elhanani Tal & Co**, which is seen as a strong player in the securities market.

Gabriel Hake and Tamar Luz at **M Seligman & Co** are notable practitioners, while the teams at **Tulchinsky Stern & Co** and **Weksler, Bregman & Co., Advocates** are also well regarded.

Amit, Pollak, Matalon & Co has securities expertise to accompany its strengths in corporate and commercial law, while **Baratz, Horn & Co**, formerly *Baratz, Bar-Nathan, Horn & Co*, also remains active.

Young firm **Cohen Legal Partners**, set up by David Cohen in 2002, has experience in Israeli and UK securities law as part of a general practice firm with a niche in corporate funding, particularly on AIM. The firm acts for a number of technology companies.

Haim Zadok & Co's senior partner Tzachi Feldman recently represented Israel Petrochemical Enterprises and Mashav Initiating and Development Ltd in a capital fundraising from institutional investors of NIS805m (US$180m) for Mashav and NIS150m (US$34m) for Petrochemical.

COMPETITION

CASPI & CO ✪
DANZIGER, KLAGSBALD & CO ✪
RON GAZIT, ROTENBERG & CO ✪
ZVI AGMON LAW OFFICES

FISCHER BEHAR CHEN WELL ORION & CO ✪
HERZOG, FOX & NEEMAN ✪
LEVY, MEIDAN & CO ✪
S. HOROWITZ & CO ✪
SHAVIT BAR-ON GAL-ON TZIN NOV YAGUR, LAW OFFICES ✪

Erdinast, Ben Nathan & Co., Advocates ✪
Gornitzky & Co ✪
Gross, Kleinhendler, Hodak, Halevy, Greenberg & Co ✪
Kantor Elhanani Tal & Co
S Friedman & Co, Advocates ✪
Weinstock-Zecler & Co ✪
Yigal Arnon & Co ✪
Yuval Levy & Co ✪

Amit, Pollak, Matalon & Co
Efrati, Galili, Lahat & Co ✪
Haim Zadok & Co ✪
Zell, Goldberg & Co

Firms are listed A-Z in tiers which are ranked in order of priority
✪ *Indicates firm displays contact details at the end of this chapter.*

COMPETITION

Caspi & Co's team remains strong despite the loss of David Tadmore from the antitrust department. The remaining talent handles a large volume of important matters before the Antitrust Commission in regard to mergers, price-fixing and monopoly operation. A full service, from notification to complex litigation, is the firm's strategy.

Sharon Klainman-Sofer is a partner in **Danziger, Klagsbald & Co**'s litigation practice group who has specialist knowledge of antitrust law. She advises on competition aspects of M&A, partnerships, strategic alliances and distribution agreements and also handles complex litigation. Avigdor Klagsbald is also experienced in antitrust matters.

Ron Gazit, Rotenberg & Co emphasises competition law within its broad practice. In 2005, it cleared a beverage-sector recycling joint venture in a restrictive practices tribunal, represented supermarket chain SuperSol, defended Central Bottling Co in an antitrust claim and acted in cases relating to credit-card interchange fee arrangements.

Zvi Agmon Law Offices has expanded its department at associate level to accommodate more work. The firm remains one of the most highly recommended in this practice area, in part because of its tight focus on competition law and class actions.

Fischer Behar Chen Well Orion & Co has a relatively large team of four lawyers devoted to antitrust matters. It has been active in litigation regarding cartel claims for clients like Telrad Networks. Clients come from many sectors, including gas, financial services and automotive. Recent highlights include representing Visa Cal in its ongoing request before the Israeli Antitrust Commissioner.

Herzog, Fox & Neeman's team is led by the respected corporate lawyer Ehud Sol, supported by associate Gal Rozent. It remains active in major competition matters, largely derived from its significant commercial clients.

Levy, Meidan & Co, formerly *Joseph Levy & Co*, is well regarded for competition work, which is among its key strengths. It acts for Visa International in groundbreaking work in regard to credit card interchange fees and counts two statutory monopolies (the Israel Postal Authority and Israel Airport Authority) as important clients. Dairy foods company Tnuva is also a client. Regulatory advice, civil and criminal matters all feature in the firm's competition work.

S. Horowitz & Co is the preferred competition firm for many leading Israeli companies, including major players in the pharmaceutical, energy and media sectors. Hagai Doron is the leading light in Asgad Stern's team, which sees numerous antitrust matters arising from its corporate clients.

Shavit Bar-On Gal-On Tzin Nov Yagur, Law Offices is often consulted as a lawyer's lawyer by firms seeking competition expertise. Tzahi Yagur is a prominent author on competition law and highly regarded as a leader in his field.

Erdinast, Ben Nathan & Co., Advocates has represented corporate clients in their antitrust proceedings. It has particular experience in the broadcast media and telecommunications sectors.

Alex Kesary and Lily Doron act in major antitrust cases for significant clients like Aviation Services Ltd and other fuel companies in Israel, giving **S Friedman & Co, Advocates** a place in the rankings. The well-regarded David Malkoff has expertise in EU competition law for the shipping and transport sectors.

Weinstock-Zecler & Co's Niv Zecler has acted for key clients such as telecoms company Bezeq before the Antitrust Tribunal and the Supreme Court. It recently acted in an indictment against numerous gas companies concerning a supply cartel.

Yuval Levy & Co often appears before the Commissioner of Restrictive Trade Practices for approvals of mergers. Opher Levy is seen as a growing authority on antitrust matters. The firm acted for Leumi Card in the antitrust tribunal over credit card interchange fees between issuing and acquiring banks.

Amit, Pollak, Matalon & Co advises banks, insurance companies, real estate developers, software developers and VC funds on competition law. The antitrust department was involved in the research into competition legislation for the Knesset Economics Committee.

As part of its M&A and litigation practices **Efrati, Galili, Lahat & Co** advises many corporate clients on antitrust matters. Highlights include representing the Dead Sea Bromine Group, together with US counsel, in proceedings instituted in the US by the Federal Trade Commission. It is currently acting in a number of civil class actions pending in the US regarding the same matter.

Haim Zadok & Co's senior partner Gideon Toledano represents importers of vehicles and the Israel Motor Vehicle Importers Association, recently acting for all 21 importers in Israel in negotiations with the Antitrust Authority.

Zell, Goldberg & Co recently advised a *Fortune 500* company in the aerospace sector on competition law issues. Marc Zell and Chaim Crown are the key players.

CORPORATE AND M&A

The merger of *Goldfarb, Levy, Eran & Co* with *Dankner Lusky & Co* to form **Goldfarb, Levy, Eran, Meiri & Co.** makes the firm a big-hitter in terms of size, breadth and expertise. Its client base is bigger following the merger, and it has promoted Dubi Zoltak and Neil Nachum Stowe to partner level, recognising their capabilities in large commercial transactions and international M&A deals. Ashok Chandrasekhar is also active, while the firm can count Intel Corp, Discount Investment Corporation and Scitex Digital Printing as clients for M&A and tenders.

Gross, Kleinhendler, Hodak, Halevy, Greenberg & Co is still highly recommended for the strength of its corporate law unit and its commercial transactions team, in which Eytan Greenberg and David Hodak are active in regard to M&A deals.

Herzog, Fox & Neeman has enviable expertise in Alan Sacks, Ehud Sol, Janet Pahima and others on the corporate side, while Amir Seraya, Anthony Leibler, Yael Bar-Shai and Tal Dror deal with commercial work. Standout deals indicating the quality of the firm's practice include Israel Equity Ltd's acquisition of Israeli bottle manufacturer Phoenicia, and Koor Industries US$146m sale of holdings in Tadiran Communications.

Meitar Liquornik Geva & Leshem Brandwein has notable expertise, not least in Clifford Felig, for a broad range of corporate and commercial work on a domestic and international basis. Recent M&A work includes acting for Shopping.com in its sale to eBay for US$626m, and Tecnomatix in its sale to UGS for US$230m.

S. Horowitz & Co added Keith Shaw, previously of **Zell, Goldberg & Co** in 2005 and still prominent in corporate deals are Ruth Oren, Anthony Bloch, Hugh Kowarsky and Avigail Kastiel. The firm recently acted for Bell South and also represented Supersol, the country's largest food retailer, on its acquisition of Clubmarket. Among the many highlights were a defence sector joint venture and representation of Bank Hapoalim in its acquisition of a controlling stake in C Kredi ve Kalkinma Bankasi.

Yigal Arnon & Co may be witnessing the retirement of Paul Baris and Yigal Arnon, but a

CORPORATE AND M&A

GOLDFARB, LEVY, ERAN, MEIRI & CO. ✪
GROSS, KLEINHENDLER, HODAK, HALEVY, GREENBERG & CO ✪
HERZOG, FOX & NEEMAN ✪
MEITAR LIQUORNIK GEVA & LESHEM BRANDWEIN ✪
S. HOROWITZ & CO ✪
YIGAL ARNON & CO ✪

BARNEA & CO ✪
CASPI & CO ✪
EFRATI, GALILI, LAHAT & CO ✪
FISCHER BEHAR CHEN WELL ORION & CO ✪
GORNITZKY & CO ✪
M. FIRON & CO ADVOCATES AND NOTARIES ✪

Danziger, Klagsbald & Co ✪
Kantor Elhanani Tal & Co
Naschitz, Brandes & Co. ✪
Shavit Bar-On Gal-On Tzin Nov Yagur, Law Offices ✪
Shiboleth, Yisraeli, Roberts, Zisman and Moshe H. Ne'eman, Ben-Artzi & Co. ✪
Tulchinsky Stern & Co ✪
Yehuda Raveh & Co. ✪
Zellermayer, Pelossof & Co., Advocates ✪

Aaronsohn Sher Aboulafia Amoday & Co Law Offices
Amit, Pollak, Matalon & Co
Balter, Guth, Aloni & Co
Baratz, Horn & Co
ES Shimron, I Molho, Persky & Co ✪
Ephraim Abramson & Co
Erdinast, Ben Nathan & Co., Advocates ✪
Haim Zadok & Co ✪
M Porath & Co
M Seligman & Co
Pearl Cohen Zedek Latzer ✪
Ron Gazit, Rotenberg & Co ✪
S Friedman & Co, Advocates ✪
Y. Ben-Dror & Co Law Offices
Yaacov Salomon, Lipschutz & Co ✪
Yuval Levy & Co ✪
Zell, Goldberg & Co

Avital, Dromi & Co ✪
Avniel, Salomon & Co
Berkman Wechsler Sahar Bloom & Co
Cohen Legal Partners ✪
Epstein, Chomsky, Osnat & Co.
Haim Samet, Steinmetz, Haring & Co
Hamburger Evron & Co. Law Offices & Notaries
Heskia-Hacmun Law Firm ✪
J Weinroth (Dr) & Co ✪
Levy, Meidan & Co ✪
Melcer & Co Law Offices
Miron, Bension & Prywes
Primes, Shiloh, Givon, Meir, Law Firm
Raved, Magriso, Benkel & Co.
Weinstock-Zecler & Co ✪
Weksler, Bregman & Co., Advocates ✪

Firms are listed A-Z in tiers which are ranked in order of priority
✪ Indicates firm displays contact details at the end of this chapter.

strong team remains in the form of David Schapiro, Barry Levenfeld and David Osbourne. The firm is still called upon for top-level commercial transactions and corporate matters.

Though a relatively young firm, **Barnea & Co** is fast developing a reputation, particularly on the strengths of its ties with firms and markets in the UK. Simon Jaffa is prominent among those working for large Israeli companies as well as multinationals. Recent highlights include representing Cellcom during the sale of controlling stakes in the company by Bell South and Safra. Other clients include Emerson Electric, Johnson & Johnson, SAP, Piraeus Bank, Nomura Bank and ICC Chemicals.

Caspi & Co is widely recommended in the market, having represented IDB, the largest holding company in Israel, on its purchase of a 90% stake of Cellcom in two separate tranches from Bell South and Safra. The firm's M&A team was kept busy, and won plaudits for its representation of food company Tnuva in an arrangement with Yoplait in France in regard to their operations in Eastern Europe.

Efrati, Galili, Lahat & Co has developed from its platform in hi-tech to offer broader corporate and commercial services. It was Israeli counsel to Ivax Inc in its acquisition by leading pharmaceutical company Teva for around US$7.5bn, and advises Alony-Hetz Assets and Investments on acquisitions.

Fischer Behar Chen Well Orion & Co is among the largest and most prestigious firms in Israel and this is reflected in its corporate work, which includes work on the privatisation of Bank Leumi in 2005. The firm began in 1998 with ten lawyers and now has around 60, and this growth is derived from work on major deals including Perrigo's acquisition of the Agis pharmaceutical company for over US$800m; and Sheer Networks in its acquisition by Cisco. The firm also represented the State of Israel in the privatisations of IDB and Bank Leumi.

Gornitzky & Co has a prominent individual in Pinkhas Rubin, and the firm was involved in M&A deals for leading Israeli corporates in 2005.

M. Firon & Co Advocates and Notaries is highly recommended by its clients, who pick out managing partner Zvi Firon, along with Rivi Irani, and Niv Sever, for their high-quality professionalism and timely services. The firm is active in complex M&A deals, with clients from the hotel, defence and wholesale sectors. It also advises telecoms, hi-tech and insurance companies on corporate matters. It handles work relating to Eastern Europe, as it has an office in Romania, as well a representative offices in Ukraine, Serbia and Montenegro, and Bulgaria.

Danziger, Klagsbald & Co's practice is headed up by Yoram Danziger, working with partner Oren Shenkar and six associates. Though former name partner Ori Rosen left in 2005 to set up his own firm, the firm is still active for major clients in the technology sector, for which it acts in M&A work. It handles both foreign and domestic clients.

Kantor Elhanani Tal & Co's corporate and commercial practice group acts for numerous Israeli corporations, and increasingly represents members of international consortia. M&A, asset and stock sales and purchases, spin-offs and hi-tech investments are among its many strengths.

Naschitz, Brandes & Co. has the notable Gil Brandes in a respected practice.

Shavit Bar-On Gal-On Tzin Nov Yagur, Law Offices has represented large companies including Israel Chemicals, Gadot, Bank Hapoalim, Bank Leumi, Bank Discount, Oracle and Sunrider, and joins this year's rankings on the basis of its broad expertise and growing reputation.

Tapping into new markets has been a recent feature of **Shiboleth, Yisraeli, Roberts, Zisman and Moshe H. Ne'eman, Ben-Artzi & Co.**'s work, the firm having established a presence in Shanghai to capitalise on the growing volume of business between Israel and China. As Japanese investors once again look to Israel, the firm has acted for two corporations headquartered in Japan. This accompanies its existing domestic activity.

Tulchinsky Stern & Co was on the side of Teva Pharmaceutical Industries in its US$7.5bn acquisition of IVAX Corporation, which typifies the scale and complexity of work the firm is used to handling.

A leading firm in Jerusalem, **Yehuda Raveh & Co.** is noted for the expertise of Lisa Tross, as well as the M&A capabilities of Yehuda Raveh and Yehuda Glatt, whose activity is often for clients in the hi-tech sector. Carmit Bar-On has developed a client base in the hotel and tourism sectors, with Isrotel among the key clients.

Zellermayer, Pelossof & Co., Advocates has a large corporate and commercial department, which a client describes as 'second to none' for quality and client-oriented service. Michael Zellermayer is a prominent business lawyer in Israel, while partner Avi Ortal has an emerging profile.

Aaronsohn Sher Aboulafia Amoday & Co Law Offices expanded with the arrival of Gilead Sher's practice, significantly increasing its capabilities in this area.

Amit, Pollak, Matalon & Co, previously *Amit, Pollak, Matalon & Ben-Naftali, Erez & Co*, represents domestic corporates, banks, insurance companies, real estate developers, contractors, public entities, cooperatives and hi-tech enterprises. The commercial practice works closely with the securities team.

Baratz, Horn & Co's Benjamin Baratz is known for his commercial law expertise, while Yael Baratz specialises in large international transactions including cross-border M&A. Yuval Horn is also active in commercial and corporate deals.

ES Shimron, I Molho, Persky & Co comes highly recommended in the market, and **Haim Zadok & Co** can call on the experience of Ilan Shavit in corporate reorganisation and liquidations. He represents clients such as the Israeli Vehicle Importers Association as well as many independent vehicle importers and dealerships.

Ephraim Abramson & Co is another strong Jerusalem firm, and recently worked for a contender in the sale of a large stake in Bank Leumi and in other privatisations. Ephraim Abramson, Avraham Aberman, Harry Grynberg and Jeffrey Rashba are the key individuals, whose work includes the sale of a local soccer team and acquisitions for a German software company.

Erdinast, Ben Nathan & Co., Advocates benefits from the promotion to partner of Roy Caner, who specialises in M&A, international transactions and investment funds. Yoav Dankner was also promoted to partner in recognition of skills in M&A and general commercial and corporate advice.

M Porath & Co counts important players in the telecoms sector among its corporate clients, and has also advised Israeli subsidiaries of major international companies in the technology sector on commercial issues.

M Seligman & Co's Eli Zohar, Gabriel Hake and Zvi Bar-Natan are sought after, the latter having joined from what is now **Baratz, Horn & Co.**

Pearl Cohen Zedek Latzer's capabilities extend beyond its hi-tech specialism and clients speak very highly of the quality of its broader corporate services. Doron Latzer is seen as a highly capable corporate lawyer. Though it advises many hi-tech companies on commercial matters, its scope is expanding.

Ron Gazit, Rotenberg & Co acts for Israeli and foreign clients, including public and private companies in the manufacturing, commercial technology, telecoms and services industries. It recently helped in securing a franchise agreement on Stella Artois beer for an affiliate of the Central Bottling Company, and an Orangina franchise for another CBC affiliate in Romania. The firm has added corporate lawyer Dina Frankenthal for her experience in representing US and Israeli VC investors, financial institutions and corporations.

S Friedman & Co, Advocates' Charles Gottlieb represented Kagoor Networks Inc in its sale to Juniper Networks Inc, and acts for large Israeli corporations.

Y. Ben-Dror & Co Law Offices recently represented the Israeli subsidiary of Boston Communication Group Inc in an acquisition of assets from PureSight Ltd, and handles commercial work for several hi-tech clients.

Haifa firm **Yaacov Salomon, Lipschutz & Co**'s Moshe Lipschutz, Joseph Gillor, David Goldenblatt, Raanan Rawitz, Merav Arad-Salomon and Oren Harpaz are in demand, while **Yuval Levy & Co** represents an expanding base of foreign and domestic companies, including new clients Global Factoring Ltd and internet payment service company Paycard Ltd. Existing clients include Lockheed-Martin, Iskoor Metals & Steel and DaimlerChrysler Financial Services Ltd.

Zell, Goldberg & Co's Marc Zell and Sonia Shnyder represented a Russian joint venture in technology acquisition matters in a busy year.

Clients are full of praise for David Cohen and his team at **Cohen Legal Partners**, while **Epstein, Chomsky, Osnat & Co.**'s practice is growing after the arrival of Ami Osnat's team.

Heskia-Hacmun Law Firm has targeted corporate work from Germany by hiring two German-qualified associates Simone Faran and Tom Franz. Clients in agriculture, hi-tech and retail have generated significant work.

Levy, Meidan & co formerly *Joseph Levy & Co*, is often involved in large M&A deals, complementing corporate advice with its expertise in competition law.

Weinstock-Zecler & Co recently acted for a major Israeli drugstore chain in penetrating the Chinese market through M&A.

DISPUTE RESOLUTION

Always a strong discipline for the firm, litigation remains key to **Caspi & Co**, which had another banner year. The firm, which was retained by Philip Morris USA for its tobacco litigation, had a significant victory in recent international arbitration in the electronics sector, dealt with by Menachem Feder. Managing partner Ram Caspi is seen as one of the country's most senior litigators, and his practice now boasts two newly promoted partners in Geva Haniv and Yoram Barr.

Goldfarb, Levy, Eran, Meiri & Co. now has five litigation partners, including Omri Kaufman, who specialises in commercial and administrative matters, constitutional and public law. He often acts in regard to tenders, antitrust issues, telecoms and civil disputes.

Gornitzky & Co also appointed new partners in Erez Harel and Lior Porat in a practice that continues to excel in this field.

Alex Hertzman handles international litigation at **S. Horowitz & Co**, while Yehoshua Horesh is the main force for domestic work. Clients like oil company Paz and Israel Electric Corp regularly engage his services. Asgad Stern and Ehud Arzi are also prominent in one of the country's leading teams. Major clients from the pharmaceutical, energy, leisure, retail and transport markets also feature, as does the defence of a product liability claim for pharma giant Teva.

Danziger, Klagsbald & Co's practice is recommended. Avigdor Klagsbald heads a dispute resolution group with three other partners – Erez Tikolsker, Sharon Klainman-Sofer and Amir Shraga. It represented Prime Minister Ariel Sharon in investigations relating to election funding, Bank Hapoalim in a recent investigation, and leading telecoms company Bezeq.

Fischer Behar Chen Well Orion & Co continues to grow rapidly in both size and standing. Reuven Behar and Gil Orion are highly regarded litigation partners in a practice that counts Israel's three leading insurance companies, the national water company, and the Bank of Israel among its clients The defence of numerous class actions and appearing in arbitrations feature strongly in its work.

Tuvia Erlich, David Zailer and Joseph Ashkenazi are prominent in a large litigation and arbitration team at **Herzog, Fox & Neeman**, which acts in a broad range of matters from contractual claims, fraud, securities disputes and class actions to antitrust litigation. Yaacov Sharvit and Baruch Katzman are also highly regarded.

Dr J Weinroth & Co's Jacob Weinroth is well known is Israel as a leading litigator, particularly in commercial matters. Fellow partner Avraham Weinroth also specialises in litigation in a practice that also handles white-collar crime and class action claims.

M. Firon & Co Advocates and Notaries' involvement in complex, high-profile cases, along with high praise from clients, see it enter this year's rankings. The department has been active in commercial disputes, class actions, judicial reviews, antitrust, securities and insolvency matters. Zvi Firon and Efrat Rand are the most significant partners.

M Seligman & Co's Eli Zohar is widely respected as a quick-thinking litigator at the head of a good team. The practice grew in 2005 with the arrival of Zvi Bar-Nathan's dispute resolution practice from the firm now known as **Baratz, Horn & Co**, which brought three new partners to the firm. The firm thus maintains its prominence despite the departure of Chaim Zelichov and others to form **Chaim Zelichov & Co,. Advocates and Notaries**.

The longstanding reputation of **Yigal Arnon & Co** endures, characterised by its aggressive strategies. This sees the firm remain active in the broadest range of litigation matters, form white-collar criminal defence to class actions.

Yuval Levy & Co still has a strong reputation built on partners like Yuval Levy and Yechiel Kasher. The firm has acted for Israel's largest credit card company, the Israeli Airport Authority, a domestic oil and gas company, a mobile phone operator, and many others in sectors such as finance, manufacturing, shipping and retail.

Amit, Pollak, Matalon & Co comes well recommended to clients seeking specialist litigation expertise. Class actions feature strongly among recent matters, though the firm has also been active for banks, insurance companies, real estate developers and contractors, investment banks, venture capital funds, software houses and hi-tech enterprises. It also advises governmental companies, public entities, cooperatives, industrial concerns and political organisations.

Barnea & Co has been involved in significant environmental litigation, including matters concerning the pollution of Haifa Bay, and insolvency cases. The arrival of Zohar Lande as head of litigation from **Gornitzky & Co** brings more heavyweight expertise on board. One high-profile case saw the firm represent Fremantle Media in an action against Channel 2.

DISPUTE RESOLUTION

CASPI & CO ✪
GOLDFARB, LEVY, ERAN, MEIRI & CO. ✪
GORNITZKY & CO ✪
S. HOROWITZ & CO ✪

DANZIGER, KLAGSBALD & CO ✪
FISCHER BEHAR CHEN WELL ORION & CO ✪
HERZOG, FOX & NEEMAN ✪
J WEINROTH (DR) & CO ✪
M. FIRON & CO ADVOCATES AND NOTARIES ✪
M SELIGMAN & CO
YIGAL ARNON & CO ✪
YUVAL LEVY & CO ✪

Amit, Pollak, Matalon & Co
Barnea & Co ✪
Efrati, Galili, Lahat & Co ✪
Gross, Orad, Schlimoff & Co.
Haim Zadok & Co ✪
Naschitz, Brandes & Co. ✪
Yehuda Raveh & Co. ✪

Aaronsohn Sher Aboulafia Amoday & Co Law Offices
Gross, Kleinhendler, Hodak, Halevy, Greenberg & Co ✪
Heskia-Hacmun Law Firm ✪
Kantor Elhanani Tal & Co
Meitar Liquornik Geva & Leshem Brandwein ✪
S Friedman & Co, Advocates ✪
Shiboleth, Yisraeli, Roberts, Zisman and Moshe H. Ne'eman, Ben-Artzi & Co. ✪
Tulchinsky Stern & Co ✪
Weksler, Bregman & Co., Advocates ✪
Zell, Goldberg & Co

Avniel, Salomon & Co
Baratz, Horn & Co
Berkman Wechsler Sahar Bloom & Co
Chaim Zelichov & Co,. Advocates and Notaries
Ephraim Abramson & Co
Erdinast, Ben Nathan & Co., Advocates ✪
Hermann, Makov & Co
J Segev (Dr) Law Offices
Levy, Meidan & Co ✪
M Porath & Co
Miron, Bension & Prywes
Raved, Magriso, Benkel & Co.
Ron Gazit, Rotenberg & Co ✪
Seligsohn Gabrieli Levit & Co
Shavit Bar-On Gal-On Tzin Nov Yagur, Law Offices ✪
Tik, Gilad & Co – Law Offices
Yaacov Salomon, Lipschutz & Co ✪

Firms are listed A-Z in tiers which are ranked in order of priority
✪ *Indicates firm displays contact details at the end of this chapter.*

Class actions have provided more work for **Efrati, Galili, Lahat & Co**. They included the representation of Bezeq in a claim arising from its public offering prospectus, and many matters for a major Israeli bank. The firm acts in disputes for longstanding clients such as Dead Sea Bromine Group.

Gross, Orad, Schlimoff & Co. was created by the recent merger of *Baruch Gross & Co* with Sigal Schlimoff and Harry Orad, formerly of *R Levitan & Co*. While commercial law is its focus, the litigation department is a major strand of the firm's capabilities, and insurance litigation is now a strong feature. A recent case includes a notable medical malpractice claim involving alleged misuse of eggs for IVF treatment.

Eyal Rosovsky is a noted commercial litigator at **Haim Zadok & Co**, where he is currently acting for clients such as Carmel Olefins in a large pollution litigation.

Naschitz, Brandes & Co. has a respected litigation practice covering commercial matters, product liability, banking, securities and insurance litigation.

Dispute resolution is a key practice area for **Yehuda Raveh & Co.** where Yuval Grayevksy has defended class actions on behalf of clients in the financial sector, claims against leisure sector operators and a major project consortium. Other highlights include US$5bn real estate litigation in regard to numerous agricultural settlements and international arbitrations in civil and commercial matters.

Aaronsohn Sher Aboulafia Amoday & Co Law Offices is where Gilead Sher's practice now operates, bringing the newly merged firm into the rankings.

Gross, Kleinhendler, Hodak, Halevy, Greenberg & Co has a respected practice, while **Heskia-Hacmun Law Firm**'s Dor Heskia is notable for involvement in internet-related actions and the representation of fashion and retail companies, leading entrepreneurs and projects companies.

Kantor Elhanani Tal & Co's litigation practice group is headed by founding partners Israel Kantor and Yaron Elhanani. It is recommended in the market and acts for financial services clients that also benefit from the firm's strong banking and securities expertise.

Meitar Liquornik Geva & Leshem Brandwein continues to be seen as one of the major firms in Israel and its dedicated litigation group often acts for international and large domestic concerns, including Merck in Israel in a Vioxx-related class action. It is also representing the US government in matters concerning its new consulate in Jerusalem.

S Friedman & Co, Advocates' Alex Kesary handles labour and commercial litigation, while Itamar Anaby's expertise is also in demand. Lily Doron acts in antitrust litigation. The firm defended large Israeli corporations against class actions in 2005 and has made an impression in significant labour disputes.

Zell, Goldberg & Co maintains its standing having acted for a major independent oil exploration company in a challenge over the closure of the Israeli Marine Economic Zone, and for an Israeli food producer in a case before the US State Court. Jeffrey Michels and Oded Revivi are the notable partners.

Though a relatively small firm, **Avniel, Salomon & Co** has Yoav Salomon, who is considered a leading litigator. Recent highlights include acting for a multinational company based in Germany in a claim against an Israeli government-owned company and the State of Israel.

Chaim Zelichov & Co,. Advocates and Notaries' name partner comes highly recommended. Having left **M Seligman & Co** in early 2005, he now acts with Yaron Ben-Dan for many private claimants. The firm recently represented a foreign company suing the Israel aviation industry for a large sum regarding an allegation of a breach of contract.

Ephraim Abramson & Co's Yair Assael and Avraham Aberman are sought after, as is Moshe Lador, the former District Attorney for Jerusalem, who joined the firm in 2005. The firm specialises in commercial litigation and white-collar criminal matters.

Erdinast, Ben Nathan & Co., Advocates maintains a strong practice, as does **Levy, Meidan & Co**, formerly *Joseph Levy & Co*, which handles significant antitrust litigation.

M Porath & Co has handled major cases in sectors such as construction and cosmetics.

Raved, Magriso, Benkel & Co.'s litigation department, headed by Joseph Benkel, has made a name for itself in commercial litigation, class actions and derivatives claims.

Shavit Bar-On Gal-On Tzin Nov Yagur, Law Offices' Yuval Gal-On and Amir Witkon are worthy of note.

ENERGY AND NATURAL RESOURCES

Gornitzky & Co maintains its reputation for infrastructure work, which it built upon gas, oil, electricity, power and water desalination projects, such as the long-running development at Ashkelon. Its experience in large BOT developments is second to none.

Herzog, Fox & Neeman has long been involved in water, gas and power projects. The firm is highly recommended for the projects expertise of Michael Fox, Yaakov Brandt and Mark Phillips, as well as the experience of Adam Eytan. Though the development of some major energy and infrastructure schemes slowed in Israel in 2005, the firm remains well placed on key deals.

M. Firon & Co Advocates and Notaries is currently involved in an international deal with a foreign gas company in regard to long-term gas supplies to Israel, worth in the region of US$2.5bn. The department, led by Eldad Firon, acts for major domestic and international corporations and comes highly recommended by clients.

The Israel Electric Corporation is a major client for **S. Horowitz & Co**. The firm is currently representing it in regard to a large natural gas supply deal. Paz Fuel Company is a client, as is Shafir, for which the firm acted in regard to the construction of a regional purification system. Yehoshua Horesh, Amir Caspari and Hugh Kowarsky are among the notable practitioners in a practice that can also call on extensive project finance expertise.

Balter, Guth, Aloni & Co has acted for cooperative organisations, including kibbutzim and moshavim, in regard to agriculture and water use law, in which the firm has developed specialised expertise. Water purification, sewage and waste disposal projects are part of its portfolio.

Caspi & Co represents clients in the oil, gas and power sectors, assisting with joint ventures, project financing and concessions. Its energy team adds industry-specific expertise to the firm's wider capabilities in corporate governance, transactions, finance and litigation.

Corporate work for investors in the energy sector is part of **Efrati, Galili, Lahat & Co**'s practice, which recently represented a bidder in the tender for the Israel Natural Gas project. It also has clients active in the water sector.

Goldfarb, Levy, Eran, Meiri & Co. joins the rankings as it now incorporates the expertise formerly at *Dankner, Lusky & Co*.

ENERGY AND NATURAL RESOURCES

GORNITZKY & CO ✪
HERZOG, FOX & NEEMAN ✪
M. FIRON & CO ADVOCATES AND NOTARIES ✪
S. HOROWITZ & CO ✪

Balter, Guth, Aloni & Co
Caspi & Co ✪
Efrati, Galili, Lahat & Co ✪
Goldfarb, Levy, Eran, Meiri & Co. ✪
Meitar Liquornik Geva & Leshem Brandwein ✪
S Friedman & Co, Advocates ✪
Shiboleth, Yisraeli, Roberts, Zisman and Moshe H. Ne'eman, Ben-Artzi & Co. ✪
Yaacov Salomon, Lipschutz & Co ✪

ES Shimron, I Molho, Persky & Co ✪
Ephraim Abramson & Co
Haim Zadok & Co ✪
Yigal Arnon & Co ✪
Zell, Goldberg & Co
Zellermayer, Pelossof & Co., Advocates ✪

Firms are listed A-Z in tiers which are ranked in order of priority
✪ *Indicates firm displays contact details at the end of this chapter.*

Meitar Liquornik Geva & Leshem Brandwein is seen as having strengths in project development, while **S Friedman & Co, Advocates** counts leading fuel companies, including Israel's principal air fuel supplier Aviation Services Ltd, among its clients.

Shiboleth, Yisraeli, Roberts, Zisman and Moshe H. Ne'eman, Ben-Artzi & Co. has gained experience on the many BOT, BOO and PFI projects that have been initiated in recent years, having represented local and foreign contractors.

Yaacov Salomon, Lipschutz & Co has acted for Israel's national electricity company, among other energy clients. David Goldenblatt and Raanan Rawitz are the key players.

Ephraim Abramson & Co, **ES Shimron, I Molho, Persky & Co**, **Haim Zadok & Co** and **Yigal Arnon & Co** also retain significant capability in this sector, while **Zell, Goldberg & Co** recently acted in the formation of a consortium purchasing crude oil from a producer in the Persian Gulf.

Zellermayer, Pelossof & Co., Advocates has been active in the development of gas sector projects.

HI-TECH

Danziger, Klagsbald & Co remains a force in the hi-tech sector, though the departure of prominent partner Ori Rosen to set up his own firm is significant. Ayal Shenhav still acts for clients such as Apax, BRM, Cedar, Evergreen, Gemini, Genesis, Reed Elsevier Ventures and Veritas. Recent transactions include investment by funds in Celletra Ltd, Chiaro Networks, Dune Medical Devices and Viola Networks Inc.

Goldfarb, Levy, Eran, Meiri & Co. is stronger after the merger of *Goldfarb, Levy, Eran & Co* with *Dankner, Lusky & Co*, and has added to its list of partners with the promotion of Ido Zemach and Dubi Zoltak, who have experience advising venture capital funds and hi-tech companies. Recent work includes the representation of Intel in its acquisition of OPlus Technologies.

Meitar Liquornik Geva & Leshem Brandwein is a strong practice for hi-tech work and comes highly recommended in the market. Its expertise in technology development, licensing, procurement and distribution is sought after. It also acts for a growing number of e-commerce companies.

Yigal Arnon & Co has a separate life sciences practice, within which it advises biotechnology, pharmaceutical, medical devices and healthcare service companies. It also acts for academic research centres and their investors.

Efrati, Galili, Lahat & Co has expertise in e-commerce within its technology group, acting for software and hardware manufacturers, internet and information-processing firms, as well as clients in the pharmaceutical, medical devices and biotechnology sectors. Recent clients include Teva, West Pharmaceuticals and VC fund Genesis Partners. The firm also represented Brainspark Plc, the controlling shareholder in Geosim Systems, and is general counsel to the Meytav Technologics Enterprises incubation centre.

HI-TECH

DANZIGER, KLAGSBALD & CO ✪
GOLDFARB, LEVY, ERAN, MEIRI & CO. ✪
MEITAR LIQUORNIK GEVA & LESHEM BRANDWEIN ✪
YIGAL ARNON & CO ✪

Efrati, Galili, Lahat & Co ✪
Fischer Behar Chen Well Orion & Co ✪
Gornitzky & Co ✪
Herzog, Fox & Neeman ✪
M. Firon & Co Advocates and Notaries ✪
Pearl Cohen Zedek Latzer ✪
S Friedman & Co, Advocates ✪
S. Horowitz & Co ✪
Shiboleth, Yisraeli, Roberts, Zisman and Moshe H. Ne'eman, Ben-Artzi & Co. ✪
Yehuda Raveh & Co. ✪
Zellermayer, Pelossof & Co., Advocates ✪

Aaronsohn Sher Aboulafia Amoday & Co Law Offices
Amit, Pollak, Matalon & Co
Avital, Dromi & Co ✪
Baratz, Horn & Co
Barnea & Co ✪
Berkman Wechsler Sahar Bloom & Co
Cohen, Cohen, Yaron-Eldar & Co., Law Offices
Eitan Law Group
Erdinast, Ben Nathan & Co., Advocates ✪
Eyal Khayat, Zolty, Neiger & Co
Kantor Elhanani Tal & Co
Naschitz, Brandes & Co. ✪
Ron Gazit, Rotenberg & Co ✪
Schuman, Livnat & Mayer
Weinstock-Zecler & Co ✪
Yossifoff, Cohen & Co Law Offices

Balter, Guth, Aloni & Co
Caspi & Co ✪
Heskia-Hacmun Law Firm ✪
M Porath & Co
Ori Rosen & Co., Law Offices
Raved, Magriso, Benkel & Co.
Tulchinsky Stern & Co ✪
Volovelsky, Dinstein & Co
Y. Ben-Dror & Co Law Offices
Yuval Levy & Co ✪
Zell, Goldberg & Co
Zysman, Aharoni, Gayer & Co

Firms are listed A-Z in tiers which are ranked in order of priority
✪ Indicates firm displays contact details at the end of this chapter.

The technology department of **Fischer Behar Chen Well Orion & Co** has seen clients progress from formation, through financing to IPOs and M&A activity. The industry-specific knowledge of partners Avi Fischer, Avraham Well, Eran Yaniv and Atir Hardof-Jaffe is often called upon in major matters.

The team at **Gornitzky & Co** resides in the broader hi-tech and communications practice. The firm draws clients from the broadcasting, IT, e-commerce, biotechnology and pharmaceuticals sectors, for many of which it acts as general corporate counsel as well as providing specific advice on technology law and venture capital funding.

Herzog, Fox & Neeman has prioritised the hi-tech sector as a source of work, with Janet Pahima, Hanan Haviv and Ran Chai notable in a practice that straddles hi-tech and intellectual property. Eldar Ben Ruby and Jan Wimpfheimer specialise in venture fund formation. The department picked up lawyers from the former *Eitan, Pearl, Latzer & Cohen-Zedek* in 2005, and further expansion is anticipated.

M. Firon & Co Advocates and Notaries represents a large and growing number of significant Israeli hi-tech clients, who speak in the highest terms of quality of work and the constructive approach of its lawyers.

Pearl Cohen Zedek Latzer took a large proportion of partners and associates from the break-up of *Eitan, Pearl, Latzer & Cohen-Zedek* in 2005, with Zeev Pearl, Dekel Shiloh and Guy Yonay amongst those active in the group. As well as M&A in the sector, the firm offers accompanying services in licensing, litigation and, above all, intellectual property. It has clients active in wireless communication, image processing, consumer electronics, endoscopy, medical and industrial lasers, enterprise software and Internet application development.

S Friedman & Co, Advocates has a good track record of acting for technology companies and financial institutions investing in the sector. It has notable depth in technology finance and leasing.

Anthony Bloch, Clifford Davis, Mordechay Malca and Avigail Kastiel were all involved in hi-tech transactions for **S. Horowitz & Co** in 2005. Clients include Tel Aviv University, in regard to the formation of a venture capital fund, Yeda Research and Development for spin-offs and financing, and online news portal YNet.

Shiboleth, Yisraeli, Roberts, Zisman and Moshe H. Ne'eman, Ben-Artzi & Co., which has a notable affiliate office in New York, has hi-tech and biotechnology expertise, representing mature companies in the sector as well as start-ups, venture capital funds and various kinds of investor.

Yehuda Raveh and Yehuda Glatt offer general corporate advice to hi-tech clients, as well as handling industry-specific matters at **Yehuda Raveh & Co.**. The firm has a reputation for establishing technology incubators in Israel and includes large R&D companies, software developers and semiconductor businesses among its clients

Zellermayer, Pelossof & Co., Advocates' hi-tech expertise centres on its representation of numerous venture capital funds in providing seed money or advanced-stage funding. It also represents hi-tech companies in general corporate matters, having taken some through early stages of formation.

Aaronsohn Sher Aboulafia Amoday & Co Law Offices was previously *Aaronsohn, Aboulafia, Gal-On, Tzin, Amoday & Co*. Its reorganisation through changes at partner level leaves its technology market expertise intact.

Amit, Pollak, Matalon & Co acts for hi-tech companies and their foreign and domestic venture capital investors. Banks, insurance companies, real estate developers and contractors, venture capital funds and software houses are among its clients with interests in this sector.

Avital, Dromi & Co's Esther Sternbach, Arie Lamay and Ori Rahat often act for hi-tech companies, though the firm's telecoms practice is better known. Media technology developers and broadcasters are among its important clients.

Baratz, Horn & Co's Yael Baratz excels in biotechnology licensing, while Eli Belkind specialises in computer law, as well as corporate and commercial law as it relates to hi-tech companies. Major industrial plants and entrepreneurs feature as clients.

Micky Barnea's experience of technology matters and securities has underpinned the success of **Barnea & Co**'s practice, which was involved in AIM listings last year. The firm acts for foreign and domestic venture capital funds in financing hi-tech companies, and in 2005 helped Surf Communication Solutions in its third round of fundraising from investors such as Texas Instruments, Giza and Pitango.

Berkman Wechsler Sahar Bloom & Co's focus is advising on the protection and exploitation of hi-tech companies' proprietary assets, and it has built up expertise in negotiating clinical trial agreements, OEM, VAR and other manufacturing, distribution and technology transfer transactions.

Cohen, Cohen, Yaron-Eldar & Co., Law Offices saw more key funding and M&A transactions for clients in medical imaging, measurement, device development and software markets in 2005.

Eitan Law Group is a result of the break-up of *Eitan, Pearl, Latzer & Cohen-Zedek* in February 2005. The strength of its technology practice is an important part of its expanding scope as a commercial law firm.

Erdinast, Ben Nathan & Co., Advocates made Yoav Dankner a partner in 2005. His general corporate practice includes work for hi-tech companies and venture capital funds, often advising on cross-border transactions.

Eyal Khayat, Zolty, Neiger & Co's name partners Eyal Khayat and Amir Zolty have been involved in major matters, including working with Singapore-based law firms in the first IPO of an Israeli technology company (Sarin Technologies Ltd) on Singapore's stock exchange.

Kantor Elhanani Tal & Co's provided comprehensive legal services to the sector through its hi-tech and telecommunications practice group, which represents companies and investors in all stages of corporate development and which has advised numerous foreign investors both in hi-tech investments, as well as the total acquisition of Israeli hi-tech companies.

Gil Brandes of **Naschitz, Brandes & Co.** is noted for his expertise in hi-tech matters.

Ron Gazit, Rotenberg & Co has several clients in the broadcast media, mobile telecommunications and internet-related sectors. The firm is assisting commercial broadcaster Keshet Broadcasting in regard to new agreements with royalty agencies.

Schuman, Livnat & Mayer's Russell D Mayer, Barry Schuman and Chen Livnat come highly recommended, as does Gideon Weinstock at **Weinstock-Zecler & Co**.

Ori Rosen & Co., Law Offices joins the table this year, having been formed by partner Ori Rosen following his departure from what is now **Danziger, Klagsbald & Co**. His expertise makes him a leading practitioner in hi-tech and biotechnology matters.

INSURANCE

Levitan, Sharon & Co has senior partner Rachel Levitan, who has the most prestigious reputation for insurance matters in Israel. Her firm was formerly *R Levitan & Co*, from which Sigal Schlimoff and Harry Orad departed to join **Gross, Orad, Schlimoff & Co.**. She now works with fellow senior partner Peggy Sharon, and notable partners Tammy Greenberg, Sharon Shefer, Dror Zamir and Moshe Abady in a specialist insurance and reinsurance practice that commands the highest respect.

Balter, Guth, Aloni & Co has acted for Israel's largest insurance groups, handling claims processing, personal injury and property damage. It also deals with liability matters, including professional malpractice and product liability. It acts for Israeli governmental body Avner, which supervises claims from traffic accidents.

Clal Insurance was a client of **Efrati, Galili, Lahat & Co** in a merger of three Israeli insurance companies. The firm also represents international insurers involved in projects work in Israel. It is currently involved in a high-value, multi-jurisdictional matter arising from damages claimed for alleged exposure to pesticides.

Gross, Orad, Schlimoff & Co.'s Harry Orad is an expert in financial lines insurance, while Jonathan Gross's expertise puts him on the insurance committee of the Israeli Bar Association. A commercial firm with a strong litigation practice, it is best known for its insurance and reinsurance work. It recently acted for insurers in the largest-ever bank safe deposit box loss in Israel's history, as well as in many aviation claims.

INSURANCE

LEVITAN, SHARON & CO ✪

Balter, Guth, Aloni & Co
Efrati, Galili, Lahat & Co ✪
Gross, Orad, Schlimoff & Co.
M. Firon & Co Advocates and Notaries ✪
M Seligman & Co
Naschitz, Brandes & Co. ✪
S. Horowitz & Co ✪

Aaronsohn Sher Aboulafia Amoday & Co Law Offices
Baratz, Horn & Co
Chaim Zelichov & Co,. Advocates and Notaries
Goldfarb, Levy, Eran, Meiri & Co. ✪
Gornitzky & Co ✪
Hermann, Makov & Co
Meitar Liquornik Geva & Leshem Brandwein ✪
S Friedman & Co, Advocates ✪
Sahar, Stobiecki & Co
Shavit Bar-On Gal-On Tzin Nov Yagur, Law Offices ✪
Yaacov Salomon, Lipschutz & Co ✪
Yehuda Raveh & Co. ✪

Firms are listed A-Z in tiers which are ranked in order of priority
✪ Indicates firm displays contact details at the end of this chapter.

M. Firon & Co Advocates and Notaries' work for three of Israel's largest insurance companies merits it a high ranking this year.

M Seligman & Co's Daphna Zadicario-Ely and Shone Helin-Grinbom sustain a capable practice despite the loss of Chaim Zelichov, while insurance capabilities are a key part of the identity of **Naschitz, Brandes & Co.**.

S. Horowitz & Co acts for Phoenix, Israel's largest insurer, and Gerling, which is active in Europe, particularly Germany. Clal Insurance is a key client for matters relating to D&O policy. The firm has also handled fund investments for AIG. Alex Hertzman and Ehud Arzi are the key partners.

Chaim Zelichov & Co,. Advocates and Notaries has the established practice built up by the name partner during his time at **M Seligman & Co**. He acts for many private claimants but also represents Migdal Insurance and its reinsurers in recent claims for bodily and property damages following the collapse of Versailles Hall in Jerusalem. It also acted for an Italian insurance company and a number of foreign reinsurers in 2005.

Goldfarb, Levy, Eran, Meiri & Co. has consolidated as a leading, full-service firm in Israel following its merger activities in late 2005, and insurance is still a major part of its broad services.

Meitar Liquornik Geva & Leshem Brandwein offers insurance expertise to accompany its top-level corporate practice, while **S Friedman & Co, Advocates** often represents insurers in regard to P&I clubs.

Shavit Bar-On Gal-On Tzin Nov Yagur, Law Offices' Ofer Bar-On and Amir Witkon are also notable specialists.

INTELLECTUAL PROPERTY

Gilat, Bareket & Co, Attorneys at Law works as litigation arm of top patent attorneys **Reinhold Cohn & Partners, Patent Attorneys**. Together they make up the Reinhold Cohn Group, for which the firm handles litigation, licensing and commercial law matters. David Gilat and Eran Bareket are seen as credible players, their recent highlights including complex biotech litigation *Israel Bio Engineering Project v Sereno*, a major patent infringement case representing Israel's three largest long-distance telephone service providers.

Boutique intellectual property firm **Luthi & Co** acts in many of the important IP cases in Israel. It acts for leading generic pharmaceutical companies and has been heavily involved in the debate on domestic patent extension legislation, which could significantly impact that market. Its reputation as a leading practice is upheld throughout the legal market.

S. Horowitz & Co has the widely respected Tal Band, whose practice has a formidable patent prosecution department. Recent work includes acting for Pfizer in litigation relating to Viagra, and handing trade marks for Anheuser Busch. Generic pharma producer Teva, Israel's largest company, is an important IP client, while the firm has also represented Nokia and Alcatel in patent litigation. Hugh Kowarsky handles the licensing of inventions of the Weizman Institute of Sciences and Technology. Avi Ordo acted in a matter arising from infringement of the Botox trade mark, while Ran Vogel acts for Teva and Bristol Myers Squibb.

Seligsohn Gabrieli Levit & Co is widely seen as one of the leading firms, with an established reputation in all aspects of IP work, from complex litigation to registration.

Dr Shlomo Cohen & Co Law Office has perhaps the best-known name in Israel in the IP field. Another boutique IP practice, it has a broad client base in the pharmaceutical, chemical, biotechnology, aerospace, entertainment, aviation, electronics, defence, computer hardware, software, fashion, cosmetics, food and publishing sectors. Shlomo Cohen teaches IP courses at law schools in the Hebrew University and Tel Aviv University.

Eitan Law Group emerges from last year's break-up of *Eitan, Pearl, Latzer & Cohen-Zedek* with the considerable expertise of Tally Eitan, who has a prominent reputation in IP. Though it is pursuing a broader commercial focus, rendering IP services to a wide range of industries is still core to the practice.

Clients praise the prompt and efficient services of **Ellen B. Shankman & Associates**, which has acted for major international brands thanks to its tight focus on high-level IP work.

INTELLECTUAL PROPERTY

GILAT, BAREKET & CO, ATTORNEYS AT LAW ✪
LUTHI & CO ✪
S. HOROWITZ & CO J
SELIGSOHN GABRIELI LEVIT & CO
SHLOMO COHEN (DR) & CO LAW OFFICE

Eitan Law Group
Ellen B. Shankman & Associates ✪
Luzzatto & Luzzatto Patent Attorneys ✪
Pearl Cohen Zedek Latzer ✪
Yigal Arnon & Co ✪
Zysman, Aharoni, Gayer & Co

Efrati, Galili, Lahat & Co ✪
Goldfarb, Levy, Eran, Meiri & Co. ✪
Gross, Kleinhendler, Hodak, Halevy, Greenberg & Co ✪
Herzog, Fox & Neeman ✪

Amit, Pollak, Matalon & Co
Avital, Dromi & Co ✪
Balter, Guth, Aloni & Co
Berkman Wechsler Sahar Bloom & Co
ES Shimron, I Molho, Persky & Co ✪
Ehrlich & Partners
Haim Samet, Steinmetz, Haring & Co
Heskia-Hacmun Law Firm ✪
Jeremy M. Ben-David & Co. Ltd
Raved, Magriso, Benkel & Co.
S Friedman & Co, Advocates ✪
Shiboleth, Yisraeli, Roberts, Zisman and Moshe H. Ne'eman, Ben-Artzi & Co. ✪
Volovelsky, Dinstein & Co

Firms are listed A-Z in tiers which are ranked in order of priority
✪ Indicates firm displays contact details at the end of this chapter.

Principally acting as patent attorneys **Luzzatto & Luzzatto Patent Attorneys** also acts in high-value litigation, including copyright infringement. Dr Kfir Luzzato, Michael Hackmey and Miriam Hackmey are the leading partners at the firm.

Pearl Cohen Zedek Latzer, formerly part of *Eitan, Pearl, Latzer & Cohen-Zedek*, has notable individuals in Zeev Pearl, Mark Cohen, Nachman Cohen-Zedek, Dekel Shiloh and Guy Yonay. Head of the trade mark department, Dor Cohen-Zedek, and Yosi Barkai, who leads the prosecution department in Israel, were among new partners appointed recently. The Tel Aviv office works closely with a flourishing office in New York. Clients include many multinational corporations dealing in Israel.

Grouping IP with corporate partnering work, **Yigal Arnon & Co** helps foreign and domestic companies with the development, protection and exploitation of intellectual property rights. It has clients from diverse sectors including software development, telecommunications, semiconductors, biotechnology and electro-optics.

Zysman, Aharoni, Gayer & Co is the Israeli arm of international venture law firm **ZAG-S&W**, which offers integrated services for companies active in the US and Israel. Within this unique structure, IP services feature strongly.

Efrati, Galili, Lahat & Co has an established hi-tech practice, so IP issues are important to many of its clients. The firm advises them on issues such as licensing, though not patents, and has been involved in trade mark disputes.

Goldfarb, Levy, Eran, Meiri & Co. has developed IP capability to support the needs of its corporate clients, in a similar way to **Gross, Kleinhendler, Hodak, Halevy, Greenberg & Co** and **Herzog, Fox & Neeman**, where Neil Wilkoff, Meir Linzen and Karen Elburg are among the well-known figures.

Avital, Dromi & Co's Arie Lamay and David Blum are worthy of note.

Heskia-Hacmun Law Firm joins the table after significant IP matters for an Israeli internet file-sharing company.

S Friedman & Co, Advocates is also added for its advice to technology, logistics and transport clients on the exploitation of intellectual property rights. Charles Gottlieb and Doron Herman have experience of IP-backed financing and lending.

PROJECTS AND INFRASTRUCTURE

Representing the Vid desalination company in the final phase of construction of the world's largest reverse osmosis plant in Ashkelon was a highlight for **Gornitzky & Co**, which still merits its high position in our rankings.

Herzog, Fox & Neeman has the highly regarded Mark Phillips, who specialises in project finance, alongside the respected Adam Eytan. It has been closely involved in many of the largest, longstanding infrastructure projects. Michael Fox and Yaakov Brandt are also prominent.

M. Firon & Co Advocates and Notaries acts for some of the largest construction companies in Israel, and increasingly has a part in international projects, with recent deals in Portugal, Bulgaria, Jamaica, the US and Africa. Tamar Firon-Smorodinsky represents major consortia in BOT project tenders.

S. Horowitz & Co continues its involvement for banks in the late stages of the light railway projects in Jerusalem and Tel Aviv. Ruth Oren, Anthony Bloch, Michelle Lieberman and Clifford Davis handle projects and finance, while Yehuda Horesh and Amir Caspari often work on infrastructure development. Road, bridge and water projects feature in recent work

Yehuda Raveh & Co. is respected for its capabilities in BOT and PFI work, particularly Yehuda Raveh and Yehuda Glatt. Yuval Grayevsky, who often acts in large construction projects, is also notable. The firm can claim some involvement in longstanding matters such as the light railway developments and the Ashkelon water desalination plant. It also has ongoing projects in the energy, education and healthcare sectors.

PROJECTS AND INFRASTRUCTURE

GORNITZKY & CO ✪
HERZOG, FOX & NEEMAN ✪
M. FIRON & CO ADVOCATES AND NOTARIES ✪
S. HOROWITZ & CO ✪
YEHUDA RAVEH & CO. ✪
YIGAL ARNON & CO ✪
ZELLERMAYER, PELOSSOF & CO., ADVOCATES ✪

CASPI & CO ✪
FISCHER BEHAR CHEN WELL ORION & CO ✪
GOLDFARB, LEVY, ERAN, MEIRI & CO. ✪
LEVY, MEIDAN & CO ✪
MELCER & CO LAW OFFICES

Aaronsohn Sher Aboulafia Amoday & Co Law Offices
Baratz, Horn & Co
Barnea & Co ✪
Efrati, Galili, Lahat & Co ✪
Erdinast, Ben Nathan & Co., Advocates ✪
Gross, Kleinhendler, Hodak, Halevy, Greenberg & Co ✪
S Friedman & Co, Advocates ✪
Yaacov Salomon, Lipschutz & Co ✪

Firms are listed A-Z in tiers which are ranked in order of priority
✪ Indicates firm displays contact details at the end of this chapter.

With a long-standing reputation in this area **Yigal Arnon & Co** remains a presence in the market, with developments in energy, road, railway and water projects among its recent work. The practice benefits from the firm's other strengths in tax, real estate, litigation and commercial law.

Zellermayer, Pelossof & Co., Advocates has a good standing in the market for business law, which extends to projects work, including major BOT and BOO transactions. Gas exploration, development and distribution work has been important for one key client, while water desalination projects have also featured.

The renowned Ram Caspi has experience in project finance, giving **Caspi & Co** its standing in the market. The firm often acts for sponsors, suppliers, insurers and ratings agencies in project-related matters,

Fischer Behar Chen Well Orion & Co's notable work includes the deal for the electrification of Israel's railways, representing construction company Danya Cebus, and a project for the use of liquid natural gas (LNG) for power production, in which it acted for the pipeline company.

Dankner, Lusky & Co and *Golfarb, Levy, Eran & Co* were both listed in our rankings for project finance. Their merger to create one of Israel's largest firms: **Goldfarb, Levy, Eran, Meiri & Co.** pools the expertise in both teams and consolidates the firm's strength in this area.

Levy, Meidan & Co, formerly known as *Joseph Levy & Co*, maintains its reputation in project finance, also a key area to **Melcer & Co Law Offices**, which has had another active year despite the slowdown in Israel's development of major infrastructure projects.

Aaronsohn Sher Aboulafia Amoday & Co Law Offices now houses the projects expertise of Gilead Sher, making it a capable player in the sector.

Baratz, Horn & Co's Yael Baratz is kept busy with large engineering and construction projects.

Barnea & Co joins the rankings having had some part in Israel's largest BOT projects, the long-standing light railway developments. Simon Jaffa spent much of his time on those deals in 2005, with the Jerusalem Light Railway due for imminent financial close. The firm was also party to the railway electrification project and its team of five lawyers is quickly establishing its presence.

Water projects feature strongly for **Efrati, Galili, Lahat & Co**, whose partner Karin Mayer is a university lecturer on project finance. The firm's experience covers sewage, desalination, energy and transportation work.

Erdinast, Ben Nathan & Co., Advocates has a prominent practice in energy and infrastructure matters, often acting for equity investors and developers. Partner Uri Noy's experience of such projects and his litigation skills make him a notable practitioner.

The team at **Gross, Kleinhendler, Hodak, Halevy, Greenberg & Co** is well versed in BOT, BOO and PFI projects work, bringing together the firm's strengths in commercial, finance, securities and tax law. Yaron Herman and David Hodak are the leading partners.

S Friedman & Co, Advocates' Ami Safran and David Malkoff have project finance experience. Recent work includes a number of multi-jurisdictional matters in the shipbuilding sector.

David Goldenblatt and Raanan Rawitz are the prominent practitioners at **Yaacov Salomon, Lipschutz & Co**.

REAL ESTATE

Goldfarb, Levy, Eran, Meiri & Co. now incorporates the strong real estate practice of *Dankner, Lusky & Co*, which joined with *Goldfarb, Levy, Eran & Co*'s existing team to boost its capabilities and provide a broader context of services to support major property transactions.

Shraga F Biran & Co is particularly known for its real estate work, backed up by a sound commercial practice. Its work on securing the approval for a planning scheme that will relocate the agricultural market in Tel Aviv and construct a commercial and residential neighbourhood on its former site in the city centre, guarantees its leading presence in this practice area. International real estate deals also feature strongly.

Weksler, Bregman & Co., Advocates is still amongst the leading firms for commercial, residential and real estate development, having been involved in the construction of large shopping malls and hotels. The firm acts for Africa Israel Investments, which is active in land development, construction and the hotel sector.

Tamar Hausner-Raveh and Uri Yamin are the key partners at **Yehuda Raveh & Co.**, which often represents developers and statutory authorities in industrial, residential and commercial real estate deals. It acts for owners of large shopping malls and for the Company for the Development of Central Jerusalem, which is responsible for rebuilding commercial enterprises in the centre of the city. It also advises non-profit organisations such as the Abraham Foundation.

Caspi & Co's Yoram Barr was recently made a partner in the litigation and real estate practices, where the firm has traditionally been strong. It acts for both purchasers and sellers in commercial and residential transactions, where the workload continues to grow.

Danziger, Klagsbald & Co represented operations of Dankner Investments in Eastern Europe, including the purchase of property in Prague for the construction of 170 residential units, and a site in Budapest for 700 residential units. It acted in the sale of units in the Lev Hasavyonim project in Modi'in and represents commercial centres like Haifa Mall and Weizmann Science Campus.

The rapid growth of **Fischer Behar Chen Well Orion & Co** in recent years continues, generating more commercial and residential real estate work. It has been busy with the acquisition of interests in major mall and office tower projects, and worked on planning and zoning matters for a major oil refinery development.

Erez Harel is a new litigation partner at **Gornitzky & Co** who also has experience of real estate transactions. Yaron Elhawi is another newly promoted partner in the practice.

Herzog, Fox & Neeman's well-established reputation as a commercial law firm includes strengths in property transactions, often as part of a broader portfolio of commercial and finance services. Yaakov Brandt, Yael Bar-Shai, Adam Eytan and Moshe Hardi are the key players.

Kantor Elhanani Tal & Co's real estate and property development group is led by founding partner Yaron Elhanani. It often acts for construction companies, local and foreign investors in land acquisition, planning, zoning and contractual matters.

M. Firon & Co Advocates and Notaries acts for a leading Israeli construction company, which has been central to many large real estate transactions. Itzhak Narkiss heads the real estate department, which also acts for housing developers. Raphael Melman leads on construction matters, including hospital and hotel projects.

REAL ESTATE

GOLDFARB, LEVY, ERAN, MEIRI & CO. ✪
SHRAGA F BIRAN & CO
WEKSLER, BREGMAN & CO., ADVOCATES ✪
YEHUDA RAVEH & CO. ✪

Caspi & Co ✪
Danziger, Klagsbald & Co ✪
Fischer Behar Chen Well Orion & Co ✪
Gornitzky & Co ✪
Hamburger Evron & Co. Law Offices & Notaries
Herzog, Fox & Neeman ✪
Kantor Elhanani Tal & Co
M. Firon & Co Advocates and Notaries ✪
Meitar Liquornik Geva & Leshem Brandwein ✪
Miron, Bension & Prywes
Naschitz, Brandes & Co. ✪
S Friedman & Co, Advocates ✪
S. Horowitz & Co ✪
Yaacov Salomon, Lipschutz & Co ✪
Yigal Arnon & Co ✪
Yossifoff, Cohen & Co Law Offices
Yuval Levy & Co ✪

Aaronsohn Sher Aboulafia Amoday & Co Law Offices
Amit, Pollak, Matalon & Co
Balter, Guth, Aloni & Co
Baratz, Horn & Co
Barnea & Co ✪
Berkman Wechsler Sahar Bloom & Co
Cohen, Cohen, Yaron-Eldar & Co., Law Offices
Cohen Wilchek & Co
Efrati, Galili, Lahat & Co ✪
Gross, Kleinhendler, Hodak, Halevy, Greenberg & Co ✪
Haim Zadok & Co ✪
Hermann, Makov & Co
J Weinroth (Dr) & Co ✪
Levy, Meidan & Co ✪
M Porath & Co
Raved, Magriso, Benkel & Co.
Ron Gazit, Rotenberg & Co ✪
Shavit Bar-On Gal-On Tzin Nov Yagur, Law Offices ✪
Tik, Gilad & Co – Law Offices
Volovelsky, Dinstein & Co
Zysman, Aharoni, Gayer & Co

Firms are listed A-Z in tiers which are ranked in order of priority
✪ *Indicates firm displays contact details at the end of this chapter.*

S Friedman & Co, Advocates acted for construction companies Gav-Yam and A Dori, and also acts for hi-tech centre MATAM, the City of Haifa and other municipal bodies in real estate transactions. David Malkoff, Doron Schweppe and Keren Betser are the key people.

S. Horowitz & Co has large clients whose corporate work generates some major real estate transactions. Recent highlights include involvement in the sale of Gaza Strip commercial greenhouses. Amir Caspari and Yehoshua Horesh are among the notable practitioners.

Yaacov Salomon, Lipschutz & Co's Joseph Gillor, Ofer Schweizer and Hanoch Morgenstern have built reputations in real estate work.

Yigal Arnon & Co's team includes Nira Kuritzky, known for specialised real estate and commercial work.

Yuval Levy & Co has been active in regard to the construction and development of shopping centres, hotels, residential and commercial property.

Amit, Pollak, Matalon & Co represents local and international developers, construction companies and investors.

Barnea & Co's reputation continues to grow on numerous property deals for UK and European investors.

Cohen, Cohen, Yaron-Eldar & Co., Law Offices has extended its capabilities with the addition of Tali Yaron-Eldar to the practice.

Efrati, Galili, Lahat & Co has large real estate and investment companies as clients, for which it has acted in the acquisition of development sites. It has also handled the acquisition of interests in REITs.

Ron Tzin and Yuval Gal-On are the principal partners in real estate at **Shavit Bar-On Gal-On Tzin Nov Yagur, Law Offices**.

SHIPPING AND TRANSPORT

David Malkoff, Alex Kesary and Amir Cohen Dor are leaders in maritime law who give **S Friedman & Co, Advocates** its dominant standing in this sector. As well as its leading shipping practice, the firm is also seeing greatly increased aviation finance activity. Charles Gottlieb and Ami Safran handle high-value deals, including a large financing of the acquisition of commercial jets from Boeing and Airbus.

Hermann, Makov & Co handles some shipping-related claims, but its real strength is in the aviation sector. With a major domestic airline as a client its aviation finance work is of the highest quality.

John Harris of Haifa firm **Zaslansky & Harris** is highly praised for his 'professional, knowledgeable and prompt' service. An expert in maritime law, he leads a practice that also handles clients in the aviation sector. Matters for vessel owners and dry cargo purchasers feature.

Caspi & Co had a steady year, acting for longstanding clients in new transport-related matters.

Herzog, Fox & Neeman also maintains a solid presence for shipping and transport work, with Alan Sacks and Mark Phillips seeing considerable activity in the aircraft sector.

Ilan Orly & Co has five lawyers, all focused on shipping, marine insurance and transport matters, mainly for Israeli clients. It is seeing more work in vessel registration and construction, particularly of large yachts, and in charter-party claims.

Cargo claims make up a significant amount of the shipping work for **Leshem-Kipperman, Law Offices & Notary**, as they do for **Naschitz, Brandes & Co.**.

Primes, Shiloh, Givon, Meir, Law Firm acts for clubs, many from London, in P&I representations in Israel. It also advises funding agents, port authorities and a leading maritime insurance company, mostly in cargo claims.

S. Horowitz & Co does no shipping work, but is active for major commercial clients in the airline sector, where industry-specific knowledge is highly valued. International airlines and logistics companies seek out its services.

Jacov Rubin handles cargo matters and insurance claims in both the marine and aviation sectors. It is currently acting for foreign clients in claims against carriers, though it mostly represents Israeli companies.

M Seligman & Co's Roy Blecher has gained experience in transport matters, as has **Yaacov Salomon, Lipschutz & Co**'s Joseph Gillor.

SHIPPING AND TRANSPORT

S FRIEDMAN & CO, ADVOCATES ✪

Hermann, Makov & Co
Zaslansky & Harris

Caspi & Co ✪
Herzog, Fox & Neeman ✪
Ilan Orly & Co
Leshem-Kipperman, Law Offices & Notary ✪
Naschitz, Brandes & Co. ✪
Primes, Shiloh, Givon, Meir, Law Firm
S. Horowitz & Co ✪

Elkes, Ascher & Co.
Jacov Rubin
M Seligman & Co
Yaacov Salomon, Lipschutz & Co ✪

Firms are listed A-Z in tiers which are ranked in order of priority
✪ *Indicates firm displays contact details at the end of this chapter.*

TAX

Dr Avi Alter & Co Law Offices' name partner is widely considered to be one of the most able tax lawyers in the country, often consulted on changes to tax legislation. Ziv Sharon is also highly regarded. The firm, which focuses purely on tax, handles most aspects of international and domestic taxation, including litigation. Its key clients include banks, insurance companies, hi-tech ventures, government ministries and large individual investors.

Shekel & Co. specialises in advising large clients on tax matters. Partners Moshe Shekel, Yaniv Shekel, Ofer Elboim and Itamar Katz are the leading lights. The firm's focus on corporation tax

TAX

AVI ALTER & CO (DR) LAW OFFICES ⊙
SHEKEL & CO.

D Potchebutzky Law Offices
Danziger, Klagsbald & Co ⊙
Gornitzky & Co ⊙
Gross, Kleinhendler, Hodak, Halevy, Greenberg & Co ⊙
Herzog, Fox & Neeman ⊙
S Friedman & Co, Advocates ⊙
S. Horowitz & Co ⊙
Yigal Arnon & Co ⊙
Zellermayer, Pelossof & Co., Advocates ⊙

A Rafael & Co
Amit, Pollak, Matalon & Co
Balter, Guth, Aloni & Co
Berkman Wechsler Sahar Bloom & Co
Cohen, Cohen, Yaron-Eldar & Co., Law Offices
Goldfarb, Levy, Eran, Meiri & Co. ⊙
M. Firon & Co Advocates and Notaries ⊙
M Seligman & Co
Naschitz, Brandes & Co. ⊙
Pearl Cohen Zedek Latzer ⊙
Shiboleth, Yisraeli, Roberts, Zisman and Moshe H. Ne'eman, Ben-Artzi & Co. ⊙
Tulchinsky Stern & Co ⊙
Weksler, Bregman & Co., Advocates ⊙
Yaacov Salomon, Lipschutz & Co ⊙
Yehuda Raveh & Co. ⊙
Yossifoff, Cohen & Co Law Offices

Firms are listed A-Z in tiers which are ranked in order of priority
⊙ Indicates firm displays contact details at the end of this chapter.

law, working closely with clients' financial departments and their CPAs, is appreciated in major matters, such as a petition to the Supreme Court demanding the annulment of an amendment to the stamp duty tax law, and the tax planning of a new dental network with over 40 branches. Clients include major domestic holding companies, public and private businesses and high-net-worth foreign individuals.

D Potchebutzky Law Offices' Gideon Klugman is well regarded as a leading tax lawyer in a firm that has a long tradition of excellence in this area.

Danziger, Klagsbald & Co's Ayal Shenhav is firmly established after joining the firm two years ago. He acts for many of Israel's leading entrepreneurs and venture capital funds. He advises on the tax implications of large M&A deals and assists domestic and foreign companies with employee stock options plans. Providing a tax opinion to AudioCodes Ltd for its convertible debt offering on Nasdaq was a recent highlight.

One of **Gornitzky & Co**'s leading tax experts Joshua Rosensweig left in 2005 to form a new firm with Revital Aviram. However, the renowned expertise of Pinhas Rubin and managing partner Moriel Matalon is still brought to bear on tax-related matters including litigation.

Samuel Borenstein heads **Gross, Kleinhendler, Hodak, Halevy, Greenberg & Co**'s tax department, which has been continuing to grow over the last two years. Ester Koren Dalal is also prominent in an active practice.

Herzog, Fox & Neeman is highly recommended as a capable tax firm, with Meir Linzen picked out as a leading light. Yaakov Neeman, Eldar Ben-Ruby, Eliot Sacks and Anat Shavit make up a busy team.

S Friedman & Co, Advocates' Doron Schweppe is an authority on corporate and real estate tax matters, while Doron Herman advises multinational companies on cross-border tax structures. The tax department is closely aligned with the firm's corporate, securities and technology teams.

Leor Nouman at **S. Horowitz & Co** advises major clients like Nokia Corporation's Israeli subsidiary on tax issues, and assisted with the tax implications of a Bristol-Myers Squibb subsidiary's cessation of activities in Israel. The work derives largely from its strong corporate and banking practices, but the tax department has been a focus of development within the firm over the last two years.

Harry Kirsh is important to **Yigal Arnon & Co**'s tax practice with his long experience of international tax matters for corporates and individuals. His previous experience as legal counsel within the Income Tax Commission saw him work on the interpretation of tax treaties, and he remains active in Israel's high-value tax matters.

Zellermayer, Pelossof & Co., Advocates has a broad practice, active in domestic and international corporate tax matters, and in real estate tax issues. Strengths in commercial, M&A, securities and finance law provide a context for its tax work.

Amit, Pollak, Matalon & Co advises on tax structures, government and local authority permits and incentive-based exemptions.

Goldfarb, Levy, Eran, Meiri & Co. houses strong tax expertise in its greatly expanded full-service practice.

M Seligman & Co's Aaron Michaeli is a notable tax practitioner.

Alexander Samuel, Moshe Lipschutz and Eran Seraya at **Yaacov Salomon, Lipschutz & Co** are capable in complex tax matters.

Yehuda Raveh & Co. has strong tax expertise that accompanies the firm's commercial and corporate finance activities. Professor Isaac Hadari is well known and currently serves as chairman of the Tax Commission for the Israel Bar Association.

TELECOMS

AVITAL, DROMI & CO ⊙
HERZOG, FOX & NEEMAN ⊙
RON GAZIT, ROTENBERG & CO ⊙
S. HOROWITZ & CO ⊙

CASPI & CO ⊙
ERDINAST, BEN NATHAN & CO., ADVOCATES ⊙
ES SHIMRON, I MOLHO, PERSKY & CO ⊙
FISCHER BEHAR CHEN WELL ORION & CO ⊙
GOLDFARB, LEVY, ERAN, MEIRI & CO. ⊙
GORNITZKY & CO ⊙
YIGAL ARNON & CO ⊙
ZELLERMAYER, PELOSSOF & CO., ADVOCATES ⊙

Eitan Law Group
Ephraim Abramson & Co
Epstein, Chomsky, Osnat & Co.
Gross, Kleinhendler, Hodak, Halevy, Greenberg & Co ⊙
J Weinroth (Dr) & Co ⊙
Levy, Meidan & Co ⊙
M Seligman & Co
Meitar Liquornik Geva & Leshem Brandwein ⊙
Pearl Cohen Zedek Latzer ⊙
Schuman, Livnat & Mayer
Shiboleth, Yisraeli, Roberts, Zisman and Moshe H. Ne'eman, Ben-Artzi & Co. ⊙
Yaacov Salomon, Lipschutz & Co ⊙
Yehuda Raveh & Co. ⊙
Zysman, Aharoni, Gayer & Co

Firms are listed A-Z in tiers which are ranked in order of priority
⊙ Indicates firm displays contact details at the end of this chapter.

Avital, Dromi & Co is seen as the number one firm for regulatory matters. Esther Sternbach and Ori Rahat lead the telecoms practice, which counts leading Israeli hi-tech and telecoms companies among its clients, often in their ventures abroad. It also acts for foreign entities entering the Israeli market. Work in telecommunications, broadcast media, infrastructure and content provision all feature strongly.

Herzog, Fox & Neeman is regarded as a leader in this field, Yaacov Sharvit, Ran Tal and Amir Seraya among the notable individuals. It is active in transactional work and regulatory matters for telecommunications, satellite, cable and mobile phone companies. It also has a hand in telecoms infrastructure projects.

Ron Gazit, Rotenberg & Co advises clients in the broadcast media, mobile telecommunications and internet sectors. The firm is assisting commercial broadcaster Keshet Broadcasting in regard to new agreements with royalty agencies, and also represents the firm in licensing and the acquisition of programming. Long-time client Partner Communications launched its 3G phone network in 2005 and the firm assisted with securing interactive and video content. It is involved in regulatory matters concerning the ongoing legislative reform in Israel's telecoms sector.

S. Horowitz & Co represented the successful bidder for Israel's Channel 2. Asgad Stern and Hagai Doron, who acts for MTV, are prominent. The firm acted for Cellcom's controlling shareholder Bell South, in matters concerning cellular to landline interconnections and represents international media companies like Warner Brothers. The financing of telecoms infrastructure projects is a major focus.

Caspi & Co recently acted for large domestic holding company IDB on a major acquisition in the telecommunications sector. The firm remains a contender for large transactions.

Erdinast, Ben Nathan & Co., Advocates has been prominent in this sector, representing a cellular network operator, a leading landline operator and numerous broadcasting companies. Regulatory advice and litigation are within the team's scope.

ES Shimron, I Molho, Persky & Co has a reputation for groundbreaking regulatory and licensing work, having been an early entrant to telecommunications law in Israel. These remain the firm's strengths and clients from media, broadcasting and telecoms sectors seek its advice.

Fischer Behar Chen Well Orion & Co includes Channel 10 and an independent television station among the broadcast clients for which it firm acts on all fronts, from regulatory advice to litigation. It also represents cable operators, and mobile network company Cellcom.

Now among the largest firms in Israel, **Goldfarb, Levy, Eran, Meiri & Co.** is familiar with the telecoms field mostly through major acquisitions such as the recent purchase of a stake in Cellcom worth US$1.3bn.

Gornitzky & Co's hi-tech and communications team is drawn from its skilled corporate, finance and projects lawyers. Its work for telecommunications start-ups continues, as do matters in the broadcasting and e-commerce sectors.

Gil Oren at **Yigal Arnon & Co** is highly regarded. His diverse corporate practice includes specific telecommunications capability. His expertise encompasses regulatory and licensing advice as well as complex transactional work.

Zellermayer, Pelossof & Co., Advocates acts for large telecoms and data communications providers, with regulatory work, financing and acquisitions all featuring. The highly regarded Michael Zellermayer has experience in such matters.

Ephraim Abramson & Co, which is centred in Jerusalem but has a branch in Tel Aviv, has Jeffrey Rashba and Harry Grynberg active in this area.

The telecommunications law credentials of **Epstein, Chomsky, Osnat & Co.** have been improved with the arrival of the former head of telecoms and media in Israel's antitrust authority.

Pearl Cohen Zedek Latzer's significant presence in the hi-tech sector provides the backdrop for its telecommunications work, which is still a feature for the firm following the recent split of *Eitan, Pearl, Latzer & Cohen-Zedek*.

Schuman, Livnat & Mayer's Barry Schuman is a notable individual, as is Joseph Gillor at **Yaacov Salomon, Lipschutz & Co**.

AVITAL, DROMI & CO

53 HASHALOM ROAD
(VERED TOWER)
GIV'ATAYIM 53454

Telephone: +972 3 573 3000
Fax: +972 3 573 4000
E-mail: adlaw@adlaw.co.il

Languages
English, Hebrew

Other offices
Granot

Number of lawyers 15
at this office 13

CATEGORIES OF WORK

Telecommunications
Esther Sternbach, Ori Rahat

International commercial transactions
Arie Lamay

Information technology and hi-tech
Esther Sternbach, Arie Lamay, Ori Rahat

Intellectual property
David Blum, Arie Lamay

Litigation
Itzhak Fink

Communications licensing
Ori Rahat, Esther Sternbach

Competition
Liad Sider, Esther Sternbach, Ori Rahat

Corporate and commercial
Esther Sternbach, Arie Lamay, Liad Sider, Ori Rahat, Ram Tsiddon

Energy and natural resources
Liad Sider

Infrastructure projects
Liad Sider, Jacob Dromi

Agricultural sector and real estate
Liad Sider, Ram Tsiddon

Chapter 11 proceedings
Arie Lamay, Ram Tsiddon

Capital markets and securities
Arie Lamay, Liad Sider

Project finance and infrastructure
Liad Sider, Ram Tsiddon

THE FIRM

Avital, Dromi & Co was established in 1986 by Gideon Avital and Jacob Dromi. Since then, the firm has grown and become a specialist in various fields of law, including telecommunications and entertainment, international and commercial.

The firm is one of the leading law firms in Israel in the field of telecommunications and entertainment law as well as various related fields.

The telecommunications and entertainment team at Avital, Dromi & Co consists of seasoned lawyers with vast experience and expertise in this field. Esther Sternbach, formerly chief legal adviser to Bezeq, the Israeli Telecommunications Corporation, was for the last four years a lecturer on telecommunications law in the law faculty of the Hebrew University in Jerusalem.

The activities of the firm involve frequent and close contact with all relevant regulatory authorities and governmental bodies in Israel. In order to remain informed of regulatory and technological developments worldwide, Avital, Dromi & Co maintains intensive, ongoing, working relationships with several US and European law firms that specialise in similar fields of practice.

AREAS OF PRACTICE

Avital, Dromi & Co represents Israel's leading telecommunications and hi-tech companies. The firm also represents foreign companies that have activities, interests and operations in Israel's growing telecommunications sector and local companies engaged in telecommunications ventures worldwide (Europe, US, South America and Asia).

The firm regularly advises telecommunications companies, inter alia, the Israeli cable TV and telecoms operators, content providers, cellular operators, ISPs and international calls operators, on the legal, commercial and regulatory aspects of their activities. These include participation in negotiations, preparation of various agreements for the purchase of content from foreign and local publishers, programmers and producers, dealing with competitive issues, regulatory matters concerning the content of television programming and advice concerning the cable operators' entry into telecommunications service provision.

The firm also specialises in a broad range of transactions relating to transmission, infrastructure and content. The firm accompanies its clients through all stages of their transactions: representation in the commercial negotiation; solving problems that arise during negotiation; examining legal aspects; drafting contracts; and, whenever required, obtaining permits from the authorities.

Avital, Dromi & Co also provides legal services to foreign companies, cellular operators, internet service providers, satellite telecommunication companies and added-value services licensees that operate on local telephony, cable and cellular infrastructure. The firm provides its clients with licensing, commercial, contractual advice and general legal support.

Among the firm's other prominent clients are private and public companies that are involved in worldwide activities, mainly in the hi-tech and telecommunications infrastructure sectors. The firm also specialises in licensing agreements for software and technology and provides its clients with legal and commercial services worldwide.

In recent years, the firm has become intensively involved in the privatisation of Israel's agricultural sector whilst representing many 'kibbutzim' (co-operative associations). Avital, Dromi & Co has also provided these kibbutzim with legal services in the process of entry of investors to their industries. The firm's northern branch in Granot was established mainly to provide these services.

Avital, Dromi & Co has also accompanied large projects related to the opening of Israel's electricity market to competition and other infrastructure projects.

YAACOV SALOMON, LIPSCHUTZ & CO

64 HAMEGINIM AVENUE
HAIFA 33264

Telephone: +972 4 814 0500
Fax: +972 4 855 7038
E-mail: office-haifa@ysl-law.com

Languages
Arabic, English, French

Other offices
Tel Aviv

Number of lawyers 28
at this office 23

Contact
David Goldenblatt
(david-goldenblatt@ysl-law.com)

CATEGORIES OF WORK

General law practice

Corporate and commercial

Taxation

Securities and investments

Banks and banking

Labour

International joint ventures

Insurance

Franchises and franchising

Licensing

Litigation

Real estate and construction

Town planning

Capital markets

Energy

Patents and trade marks

Shipping and Admiralty

BARNEA & CO

AMZUR HOUSE
8 HASADNAOT STREET
HERZLIYA PITUACH 46728

Telephone: +972 9 960 0700
Fax: +972 9 951 6002
E-mail: mbarnea@barlaw.co.il
Website: www.barlaw.co.il

Languages
English, Hebrew, Italian, French, Spanish, German

Number of lawyers 17

Contacts
Michael Barnea, Simon Jaffa

CATEGORIES OF WORK

Securities and capital markets
Michael Barnea

Mergers and acquisitions
Michael Barnea, Simon Jaffa

International transactions
Simon Jaffa

Private equity
Michael Barnea

Litigation and arbitration
Zohar Lande

Project finance
Simon Jaffa

Corporate and commercial
Michael Barnea, Simon Jaffa

Technology law
Michael Barnea

Real estate
Aya Lavi-Bezalel

Private client, trusts
Simon Jaffa, Aya Lavi-Bezalel

Banking
Simon Jaffa

COHEN LEGAL PARTNERS

50 BASEL STREET
HERZLIYA PITUACH 46646

Telephone: +972 9 957 5011
Fax: +972 9 957 7826
E-mail: admin@clplegal.com
Website: www.clplegal.com

Languages
English, French, Hebrew, Italian, Portuguese, Russian, Spanish

Number of lawyers 4
at this office 3

Contact
David Cohen

Member
Israel- British Law Association; STEP; IBA; International Association of Jewish Lawyers and Jurists; Law Society of England and Wales; Israel Bar

CATEGORIES OF WORK

Corporate law
David Cohen

Securities law
David Cohen

International securities law
David Cohen

Commercial law
Martyn Felix

International business law
David Cohen

Technology law
David Cohen

Property law
Martyn Felix

PEARL COHEN ZEDEK LATZER

5 SHENKAR ST
PO BOX 12704
HERZLIYA PITUACH 46733

Telephone: +972 9 972 8000
Fax: +972 9 972 8001
E-mail: main@pczlaw.com
Website: www.pczlaw.com

Languages
English, German, French, Hebrew

Other offices
New York

Number of lawyers 28
at this office 20

Member
AIPPI; MARQUES; INTA; FICBI; ECTA; AIPLA

CATEGORIES OF WORK

Corporate and commercial
Doron Latzer, Jody Stein

Copyright and cyber law
Daniel Bustanai, Dor Cohen-Zedek

Litigation
Zeev Pearl, Nachman Cohen-Zedek, Daniel Bustanai

Patent prosecution
Mark Cohen, Dekel Shiloh

Patent counselling and opinions
Mark Cohen, Guy Yonay

Employment, labour, benefits and options
Kalia Klein

Tech transactions and licensing, tech transfer
Zeev Pearl, Hili Blum

Trade marks and designs
Nachman Cohen-Zedek, Dor Cohen-Zedek

Biotech/pharma
Mark Cohen, Rachel Teitelbaum

Defence industries
Nachman Cohen-Zedek, Yosi Barkai

Electronics and semi-conductors
Dekel Shiloh, Guy Yonay

Information and communication technologies
Zeev Pearl, Dekel Shiloh

Manufacturing and industrial products
Nachman Cohen-Zedek, Yosi Barkai

Medical devices
Zeev Pearl, Mark Cohen

Pharma regulatory
Zeev Pearl, Irit Gordon

Video and display technologies
Zeev Pearl, Guy Yonay

YEHUDA RAVEH & CO

26 USISHKIN STREET
PO BOX 7722
JERUSALEM 91077

Telephone: +972 2 563 5232
Fax: +972 2 561 7101
E-mail: lawfirm@yraveh.co.il
Website: www.yraveh.co.il

Languages
English, French, Hebrew, Hungarian

Other offices
Haifa, Tel Aviv

Number of lawyers 48

CATEGORIES OF WORK

Infrastructure projects
Yehuda Raveh, Yehuda Glatt

Intellectual property
Gabi Robenbach

Building and development
Lisa Tross, Yuval Grayevsky

Taxation
Professor Itzhac Hadari

Mergers and acquisitions
Yehuda Raveh, Yehuda Glatt

Litigation
Yuval Grayevsky, Haim Stern

Antitrust
Carmit Bar-On

Environmental matters
Sara Shalom

Hi-tech
Yehuda Glatt

Banking
Lisa Tross, Yehuda Raveh

International law and transactions
Yehuda Raveh, Yehuda Glatt

Privatisation of government
Yehuda Raveh

Corporate
Yehuda Raveh, Lisa Tross

Hotels
Carmit Bar-On

THE FIRM

The firm was established in the 1940s by Gideon Hausner, and has grown to be one of Israel's largest law firms. Mr Hausner served as the Attorney General of Israel and as a cabinet minister in the country's government.

Today the firm is led by Mr Yehuda Raveh, and has a staff of 71 lawyers, associates and administrative personnel. The firm has grown from two lawyers in 1979 to 48. The firm has offices throughout the country in Jerusalem, Tel Aviv, and Haifa.

AREAS OF PRACTICE

All aspects of commercial and corporate law, including, among others, real estate development and infrastructure projects (BOT), hotels, banking and insurance, mergers and acquisitions, corporate and project finance, national and international capital markets, privatisation, international transactions, litigation, environmental projects, intellectual property, bankruptcy cases, licensing, distributorship, trust of all kinds and estate planning.

The firm possesses special expertise in rendering services to foreign residents and foreign investors, be they large conglomerates, medium or small-size corporations, or individuals. The firm has developed a unique knowledge of Israel's Free Trade Agreements with the EU and with the US and Canada, and the potential benefits of the use of such FTAs to manufacturers and exporters aiming at the EU and the US market.

The firm's main fields of specialisation are BOT and infrastructure projects, public and private income generating projects such as the Cross-Israel Highway, railways and light trains, sewage and water projects, student dormitories and tourist accommodation, shopping centres, office buildings and parking facilities. Mr Raveh was chosen to serve as a member of the BOT expert group of The United Nations.

The firm has been involved in the establishment and legal representation of technological incubators in Israel. The firm represents one of the largest R&D companies in the country and advises several other hi-tech companies. Mr Raveh serves as the president of one of the largest hi-tech groups of investors in start-up companies. The group has invested seed money in many hi-tech companies and continues to do so successfully.

The firm represents major developers and constructors of both residential and commercial projects and industrial parks all over the country. The firm has expertise in hotel development and hotel management throughout Israel and represents numerous owners, developers and major national and international hotel companies.

The firm advises banking clients on a case-by-case basis, on different matters ranging from legal options on various banking matters, to negotiations of complicated project finance, conducting due diligence process for banks and other lending institutions and serving as receivers and liquidators in bankruptcy cases.

The firm has developed unique expertise in the telecommunications field, including television, cable TV and the internet.

The firm handles extensive distributorship agreements, mergers and acquisitions (mainly for foreign investors), telecommunications transactions, bankruptcy and liquidation proceedings and intellectual property matters.

The firm's tax department accompanies all transactions handled by the firm, covering local and international corporate and individual tax aspects.

LUZZATTO & LUZZATTO PATENT ATTORNEYS

OMER INDUSTRIAL PARK
OMER 84965

Telephone: +972 8 646 7070
Fax: +972 8 646 7080
E-mail: mail@luzzatto.co.il
Website: www.luzzatto.co.il

Languages
Czech, English, French, Hebrew, Hindi, Italian, Russian

Other offices
Jerusalem, Ramat Gan

Number of lawyers 18

Member
AIPPI; INTA; FICPI

CATEGORIES OF WORK

General intellectual property practice
Dr Esther Luzzatto, Michal Hackmey (patent attorney)

Patents prosecution
Prof Emanuel Manzurola, Michal Hackmey (patent attorney)

Trade mark and service marks prosecution
Adv Miriam Hackmey, Adv Ronen Sasson

Designs prosecution
Zadok Fuerst (patent attorney), Adv Avi Lavon

Patent and trade mark prosecution
Dr Kfir Luzzatto, Zadok Fuerst (patent attorney)

IP international practice
Haim Chechik (patent attorney), Adv Gilad S Hadary

Trade mark searches
Adv Oren Weiner, Adv Ronen Sasson

Patent searches
Dr Bruce Alpert, Zadok Fuerst (patent attorney)

IP due diligence for mergers and acquisitions
Dr Kfir Luzzatto, Adv Avi Lavon

THE FIRM

The firm was established in Italy by Riccardo Luzzatto in 1869, and since then has concentrated on intellectual property. The family firm was moved to Israel in 1976 by Edgar Luzzatto, the grandson of Riccardo Luzzatto. The firm has grown significantly in recent years and currently has three separate offices in Jerusalem, Ramat-Gan and Omer. The firm has acquired substantial experience in patent litigation, such as oppositions, cancellation proceedings, infringement actions and the like, in Israel and abroad. Moreover, the firm provides in-depth analysis of international intellectual property issues during the due diligence process of mergers and acquisitions.

AREAS OF PRACTICE

The firm offers a full range of services in connection with intellectual property. It specialises in patent drafting and prosecution, with experts in all fields of science and technology, trade and service marks prosecution and design. The firm also handles litigation in proceedings before the Registrar of Patents, Trademarks and Design and is of-counsel in legal proceedings before the Israeli courts. It also provides consulting services, searches and opinions in the IP field.

DANZIGER, KLAGSBALD & CO

**7 MENACHEM BEGIN ST
(28 BEZALEL STREET)
GIBOR SPORT BUILDING
RAMAT GAN 52521**

Telephone: +972 3 611 0700
Fax: +972 3 611 0707
E-mail: office@danklaw.co.il
Website: www.danklaw.co.il

Languages
Dutch, English, French, Hebrew

Number of lawyers 34

Contact
Dr Yoram Danziger

CATEGORIES OF WORK

Corporate law
Yoram Danziger

Hi-tech
Ayal Shenhav

Litigation
Avigdor Klagsbald

Real estate, banking and bankruptcy
Ronen Matry

Taxation
Ayal Shenhav

THE FIRM

Danziger, Klagsbald & Co is one of Israel's leading law firms, serving prominent Israeli and international companies, financial institutions and individuals. The firm brings a multi-disciplinary, expert approach to corporate, civil, criminal and administrative law matters, from planning and developing strategy to conducting transactions to litigation disputes. Danziger, Klagsbald & Co represents a diversity of clients, from hi-tech start-up companies to international conglomerates, from the owners of family businesses to politicians and heads of state. The firm assists Israeli clients in their local and international activities and international companies conducting business in Israel. The practice is focused around six major groups: litigation, corporate, hi-tech, real estate, banking and bankruptcy, and tax.

AREAS OF PRACTICE

The corporate practice group has an active international practice, representing both Israeli companies operating internationally and international corporations doing business in Israel. The group serves as legal counsel to numerous private and publicly traded companies. Its clients include issuers, underwriters, placement agents and investors.

The litigation practice group represents domestic and international individuals and business enterprises of all sizes before courts and arbitration panels. The firm's litigators have argued and won numerous cases before the Israeli Supreme Court, district and magistrates courts, and other judicial and administrative tribunals. They have set several notable precedents in the areas of company law, constitutional law, bids and tenders, antitrust, and white-collar and economic crime.

The hi-tech practice group is recognised as a national leader in the representation of venture capital funds and hi-tech companies. The group advises companies on a range of day-to-day, corporate and commercial business issues, including private placements, technology agreements, option plans, international operations, employment law, protecting intellectual property and more, and has been involved in numerous mergers and acquisitions, representing both purchasers and sellers. The group counsels many of Israel's top venture capital and investment banking firms, as well as numerous companies in the fields of software, hardware, semiconductors, communications, internet, e-commerce, and the life-sciences markets. Additionally, the group represents individual entrepreneurs, venture capitalists, financial service organisations, noted research institutions and high-growth private and public companies, all in major technology fields.

The real estate practice group has extensive experience in real estate development, having managed countless properties and construction projects in Israel and abroad. In addition, the group is actively involved in the formation of real estate funds that intend to invest in both Israeli and non-Israeli projects.

The banking and bankruptcy practice group assists financially troubled companies in structuring main receiverships and other creditor arrangements. Members of the group have personally served as receivers of several Israeli conglomerates and as the liquidators of many others.

The tax practice group provides general tax advice to multinational companies, venture capital funds, private technology companies, high-net-worth individuals and others. The group has obtained many advance tax rulings from the Israeli tax authorities.

M. FIRON & CO ADVOCATES AND NOTARIES

16 ABBA HILLEL SILVER STREET
52506 RAMAT GAN
POB 3381, 52136 RAMAT GAN

Telephone: +972 3 754 0050
Fax: +972 3 754 0055
E-mail: firon@firon.co.il

Languages
Bulgarian, English, French, Hebrew, Italian, Spanish

Other offices
Be'er Sheva, Jerusalem

Number of lawyers 66
at this office 59

Contact
Zvi Firon

Member
Interlaw

CATEGORIES OF WORK

Dispute resolution, litigation and arbitration
Zvi Firon, Renato Jarach

Private client
Zvi Firon, Michael Firon

Energy, infrastructure and natural resources
Eldad Firon, Tamar Smorodinsky

Construction
Itzhak Narkiss, Eran Rosenberg

Government, labour and administration litigation
Renato Jarach, Efrat Rand

Capital markets and corporate and commercial
Rivi Irani, Alon Alpert

Corporate and commercial and tax
Raphael Melman, Shay Huberman

Development of international real estate and infrastructure projects
Itzhak Narkiss, Haim Sarov

Intellectual property and hi-tech projects
Eldad Firon, Jacob Sarov

Commercial property, real estate
Raphael Melman, Gili Riesel

THE FIRM

Over 50 years of legal service have earned M. Firon & Co a leading position among Israel's law firms. M. Firon & Co was founded by Adv Michael Firon and the late Yaacov S Shapiro, former Minister of Justice.

Today, headed by the accomplished lawyer Adv Zvi Firon, the firm is classed by *The Legal 500 – EMEA* as one of the leading law firms in Israel and is listed by *Dun & Bradstreet* among the ten largest law firms in the country, with 59 attorneys, including 18 partners.

AREAS OF PRACTICE

Corporate and business: under the management of Adv Zvi Firon, the firm attends to the legal planning and execution of complex mergers, acquisitions and restructuring of entities for its clients operating in the hotel industry, private defence industry, trade and wholesale, including all tax implementations. Likewise, it represents and advises clients with regard to the formation of joint ventures, the acquisition of property and shares, as well as providing legal services to insurance firms, telecommunications companies and hi-tech clients.

Real estate: headed by Adv Itzhak Narkiss, this department handles real estate transactions on a large scale and provides ongoing services to some of Israel's leading housing and construction companies.

Energy and natural resources: ranked by *The Legal 500 – EMEA* among the three leaders in this category, the department, led by Adv Eldad Firon, is involved in the country's most significant energy transactions, representing domestic and international major corporations.

Construction: this department, headed by Adv Raphael Melman, has been involved in some of the most extensive construction projects in Israel, including hospitals, hotels, commercial and residential developments.

Stock exchange and commercial: under the supervision of Adv Rivi-Irani, this department provides a full range of legal services to corporations, foreign banks, members of the Tel Aviv Stock Exchange, insurance companies and other organisations operating in the financial sector.

Litigation: the sizeable litigation department, managed by Advs Zvi Firon and Efrat Rand, handles all kinds of civil and commercial litigation, and is best known for its involvement in complex business disputes.

Infrastructure: this department, headed by Adv Tamar Firon-Smorodinsky, represents major consortiums in crucial BOT project tenders, including the light railway system in Jerusalem and Tel Aviv, energy, water and waste disposal projects, roads and tunnels, ports and marinas, as well as gas and oil installation projects.

Public and administrative: under the direction of Adv Renato Jarach, former director of the High Court of Justice Department of the State Attorney General's Office, this department handles many significant cases before the Supreme Court.

International activity: led by Adv Itzhak Narkiss, M. Firon & Co works closely with both Israeli and foreign investors active in Israel and abroad, especially in Eastern Europe, finding legal solutions to further their business objectives. Together with Adv Ron Bar-Nir, the firm operates law offices in Romania, Serbia and Montenegro, Ukraine and Bulgaria. The firm also represents clients with businesses in various African states, the Caribbean and South America.

Individual law: M. Firon & Co specialises in the provision of general legal advice and solutions to both private clients and privately held entities, including advice in the fields of tax, inheritance law, wills and legal settlements, etc.

M. Firon & Co has many high-profile clients, including Israel's largest hotel chain, two of the country's largest construction corporations, the largest HMOs, the largest private defence industry, investment and development companies both in Israel and abroad, Israel's largest telecommunications corporations, industrial and hi-tech corporations, retail and wholesale trade in all sectors, local authorities, and various public and government institutions.

MEITAR LIQUORNIK GEVA & LESHEM BRANDWEIN

16 ABBA HILLEL SILVER ROAD
RAMAT GAN 52506

Telephone: +972 3 610 3100
Fax: +972 3 610 3111
E-mail: meitar@meitar.com
Website: www.meitar.com

Languages
English, Hebrew

Number of lawyers 71

CATEGORIES OF WORK

Corporate
Dan Geva, Dror Brandwein

Litigation
Israel Leshem, Israel Pfeffer

Securities
Cliff Felig, Dan Shamgar

Venture capital and start-ups
Maya Liquornik, David Chertok

Mergers and acquisitions
Dan Geva, Dan Shamgar

Technology
Maya Liquornik, Bill Galkin

Labour and employment
Moti Arad

Antitrust and administrative
Moti Arad

White-collar crime
Israel Leshem, Nadav Weisman

Commercial transactions
Yoram Movshovitz, Edo Likhovski

Telecoms
Daphna Nechmad, Ronen Bezalel

Life sciences
David Chertok, Raanan Lerner

Insurance
Dror Brandwein

Banking and derivatives
Cliff Felig, David Glatt

Real estate
Amos Goren

Taxation
Meir Akunis

THE FIRM

Meitar Liquornik Geva & Leshem Brandwein is a leading Israeli law firm with a reputation for excellence on domestic and international matters. MLG&LB provides clients with comprehensive expert counsel and representation in a variety of business contexts, from sophisticated transactions to complex litigation and beyond. The approach has always been to ensure that each client's matters are handled by the best professionals in the relevant area of expertise, with a view towards meeting their business objectives. Clients are represented from both the international and domestic Israeli business communities and professionals offer clients in-depth knowledge of, and expertise in, a number of disciplines and industries, hands-on international legal experience and innovative thinking.

Working closely with clients and with their non-Israeli counsel, the firm facilitates cross-border transactions, bridge international boundaries and assists clients by opening doors both in Israel and overseas. Through all stages of clients' growth, from seed financing, through private and public offerings, mergers and acquisitions and beyond, the firm brings distinct added value and among the finest international and domestic representation to clients to help them achieve their strategic goals. The firm regularly assists non-Israeli clients in understanding the local business culture and landscape, including its local players, as well as regulatory processes and the Israeli judiciary.

MLG&LB's clients include leading multinational and domestic corporations, private and publicly traded companies in areas such as technology, communications, pharmaceutical and medical, media and publishing, energy, construction, banking, financial services and advertising, venture capital funds and investment companies, investment banks, holding companies and high-net-worth individuals.

MLG&LB was created by the merger of two leading Israeli law firms, Meitar, Liquornik, Geva & Co and Leshem, Brandwein & Co., each leaders in their respective fields.

AREAS OF PRACTICE

Corporate and securities: a major part of the firm's work consists of venture capital investments; public offerings; M&A; private placements; equity and debt offerings in Israel and abroad; banking and derivatives; and securitisations. The firm also specialises in corporate restructuring, including splits, spin-offs, share buy-backs, joint ventures and management buy-outs. The firm acts regularly in corporate, partnership and joint venture formation, establishment and implementation of stock option and compensation plans, and financing transactions.

Litigation: this department handles a wide range of commercial litigation, including contests for corporate control and class actions, labour law and insurance matters. Its attorneys appear in all Israeli courts, arbitration proceedings, and specialised courts and regulatory bodies.

Technology: the firm is intensively involved in structuring and negotiating the international transactions of its clients: OEM; licensing; distribution; VAR; joint development; outsourcing and similar agreements with expertise in complex software transactions. The firm handles all aspects of deals including: participation in negotiations on the commercial terms; drafting of agreements; setting up local entities; creating financial arrangements; ensuring protection of intellectual property rights; and co-operating with local counsel worldwide.

Telecoms: the firm acts for one of Israel's largest conglomerates involved in telecoms provision, represents one of Israel's three international operators, and has represented clients in tenders for cellular operations, as well as in many regulatory, telecoms and antitrust issues.

Taxation: the firm provides tax advice and planning in a range of areas: international taxation; corporate tax planning; employee compensation plans; real estate; trusts and estates; and personal tax planning.

General legal services: the firm also provides services in areas such as: real estate, banking and commercial papers; regulatory matters; labour-related issues; antitrust and other matters.

TULCHINSKY STERN & CO

14 ABBA HILLEL ROAD
RAMAT GAN 52506

Telephone: +972 3 751 9181
Fax: +972 3 751 1127
E-mail: tel@tslaw.co.il

Languages
Hebrew, English, French, Romanian, Bulgarian

Other offices
Jerusalem

Number of lawyers 23

CATEGORIES OF WORK

Corporate and securities
Menachem Tulchinsky, Yaacov Michlin

Corporate finance and M&A
Doron Stern, Baruch Peri

Taxation
Menachem Tulchinsky, Isaac Marciano

Commercial Litigation
Menachem Tulchinsky, Doron Stern

Mediation and arbitration
Isaac Marciano

Intellectual property and commercial information
Yaacov Michlin, Alon Tabak

Venture capital finance
Doron Stern, Ariel Fuss, Alon Tabak

Real estate and hotel management
Yossi Ratnovsky, Doron Stern

Employment and labour
Chagit Pedael, Yossi Ratnovsky

Environmental law
Chagit Pedael

THE FIRM

Tulchinsky Stern & Co was founded in 1995 by Adv Menachem Tulchinsky and Adv Doron Stern. Since its establishment, two features have characterised the firm's practice: its knowledge and expertise of commercial transactions and its relationships with leaders of the Israeli and international business community. In the years following its founding, the firm's capabilities, reputation and client base have grown significantly. For this reason, the firm today represents commercial interests from Israel, North America and Europe. Similarly, the firm enjoys close working relationships with leading North American and European law firms, enabling it to provide a seamless, international legal service.

AREAS OF PRACTICE

The firm specialises in providing advice and assistance to a wide variety of Israeli and international clients in a range of practice areas. It advises multinational corporations as well as small business entities and private individuals. The corporate practice assists clients in the planning and implementation of complex and innovative finance transactions, including private placement transactions, in local and foreign markets. Specifically, the firm was involved in the Issuance by Teva Pharmaceutical Industries Ltd, one of the firm's larger clients, of convertible debentures in the US in an aggregate amount of US$900m, and was also invovled in Israel's largest private placement, the US$100m investment in Chiaro Networks Ltd. The M&A practice has been involved in deals of virtually every possible size and structure, ranging from private company acquisitions, stock-swap transactions and asset sales. Tulchinsky Stern & Co was recently involved in the US$7.4bn acquisition of Ivax Corporation by Teva, and handled the largest merger in Israeli history, as well as the US$3.4bn merger of Teva with Sicor Inc, and facilitating the US$5bn merger of Chromatis Neworks with Lucent Technologies. The firm's venture capital team provides a full range of services in both venture fund formation and portfolio investment, developing experience in a variety of fields, with a particular emphasis in the bio-tech and hi-tech sector. Tulchinsky Stern & Co also successfully represent start-up companies from before incorporation to their public offering or acquisition, and often beyond, through venture capital financings, public offerings, mergers and acquisitions, executive compensation and employee benefits, commercial aggreements and IP and corporate partnering.

In addition to the firm's corporate and commercial practice, it has long been recognised as a leading tax advisor, in both Israeli and international tax matters, assisting all types of business entities. The firm's knowledge and experience enables it to develop tax-efficient structures for corporate and project finance transactions and new capital market instruments and products, and provide strategic tax advice and constructive and innovative solutions to all tax problems. The firm also has a strong IP practice, and IP attorneys represent many clients from the technological and pharmaceutical sectors. Broad experience has developed expertise in the areas of intellectual property licensing, with a specific proficiency in the licensing of hi-tech and pharmaceutical intellectual property, including *inter alia*, distribution and marketing agreements, research and development agreements.

The litigation team has diverse and extensive experience, representing both Israeli and non-Israeli clients in litigation matters. In respect of alternative dispute resolution, senior partners are well known as experienced mediators and arbitrators in a wide variety of areas.

In addition, the practice includes real estate, environmental and employment law. The firm's client list speaks for itself, and includes some of Israel's and the international community's leading corporations.

ELLEN B. SHANKMAN & ASSOCIATES

13 WEIZMAN STREET
REHOVOT 76280

Telephone: +972 8 946 5310
Fax: +972 8 946 8779
E-mail: ellen@ellenshankman.com
Website: www.ellenshankman.com

Other offices
Park Tamar Rehovot

Contact
Ellen Shankman

CATEGORIES OF WORK

Intellectual property

Branding strategies

Trade marks

Copyright

Licensing

Domain names

Internet law

Notary

DR AVI ALTER & CO

LAW OFFICES

8 SHAUL HAMELECH BLVD
TEL AVIV 64733

Telephone: +972 3 696 6633
Fax: +972 3 696 6663
E-mail: info@altertax.co.il
Website: www.altertax.co.il

Languages
English, German, Hebrew, Russian

Number of lawyers 16

CATEGORIES OF WORK

International/national taxation
Anat Tenne, Udi Shostak

International/national tax planning
Dr Avi Alter, Ziv Sharon

Direct and indirect taxation
Udi Shostak, Nir Horenstein

Tax rulings in Israel and abroad
Amichai Pery, Anat Tenne

Taxation of mergers and acquisitions
Nir Horenstein, Helena Ben-Baruch

Taxation of public offerings, ESOPs and ESPPs
Amichai Pery, Shlomi Regev

VAT taxation
Arie Levovitsh, Ziv Sharon

Estate and trust law
Arie Levovitsh, Ziv Sharon

Taxation of hi-tech companies and employees
Shlomi Regev, Ori Kalif

Tax litigation
Ziv Sharon, Nir Horenstein

Arbitration
Helena Ben-Baruch, Nadav Sagi, Michal Raveh

Hybrid instruments taxation
Kobi Tsarfaty, Avi Fridman, Guy Reshtick

Tax settlement/tax treaties
Itai Hochberg, Ori Kalif

Israeli tax legislation – advisers and initiators
Dr Avi Alter, Ziv Sharon

Corporate taxation
Dr Avi Alter, Udi Shostak

CASPI & CO

33 YAVETZ STREET
TEL AVIV 65258

Telephone: +972 3 796 1000
Fax: +972 3 796 1001
E-mail: office@caspilaw.com
Website: www.caspilaw.com

Number of lawyers 35

Contact
Norman Menachem Feder

CATEGORIES OF WORK

Administrative and constitutional
Ram Caspi, Gad Ticho

Civil
Ram Caspi

Commercial and corporate (domestic)
Ram Caspi

Commercial and corporate (international)
Norman Menachem Feder

Competition
Norman Menachem Feder

Communications
Yossi Abadi

Construction and housing
Assaph Caspi

Criminal
Navot Tel-Tzur

Energy
Ram Caspi

Finance (derivatives/structured)
Norman Menachem Feder

Finance (project)
Norman Menachem Feder

Litigation and arbitration
Gad Ticho, Navot Tel Zur

Real estate and conveyancing
Yzik Naimi, Guy Caspi

Securities
Ami Gilad

Transportation
Orna Kedar

ES SHIMRON, I MOLHO, PERSKY & CO

PLATINUM TOWER
21 HA'ARBA'AH STREET
TEL AVIV 64739

Telephone: +972 3 685 3685
Fax: +972 3 685 3853
E-mail: officeta1@smplaw.co.il
Website: www.smplaw.co.il

Languages
English, French, German, Hebrew, Italian

Other offices
Jerusalem

Number of lawyers 23
at this office 10

Contact
Orrin Persky

CATEGORIES OF WORK

Corporate and commercial
Isaac Molho, David N Shimron

Mergers and acquisitions
Isaac Molho, Orrin Persky

Competition and antitrust law
Jakob Melcer, Dov Abramowitz

Telecoms and entertainment law
Isaac Molho, Dov Abramowitz

Charitable organisations
Isaac Molho, David N Shimron

Energy
David N Shimron, Dov Abramowitz

Labour
Michal Arlosoroff, Tal Ranel-Cohen

Liquidation, insolvency and bankruptcy
Isaac Molho, Jakob Melcer

Real estate development
Orrin Persky, David N Shimron

Intellectual property
Isaac Molho, Michal Shur-Ofry

Hi-tech
Isaac Molho, Shai Ganor

Banking and securities
David N Shimron, Michal Arlosoroff

Government authorities
David N Shimron, Shai Ganor

Civil and commercial litigation
Orrin Persky, Michael Rabello

Wills and trusts
Orrin Persky, Michal Arlosoroff

Venture capital
Isaac Molho, Shai Ganor

EFRATI GALILI LAHAT & CO

6 WISSOTSKY STREET
TEL AVIV 62338

Telephone: +972 3 545 2020
Fax: +972 3 604 0111
E-mail: office@egl.co.il
Website: www.egl.co.il

Languages
Chinese, English, French, Hebrew, Spanish

Number of lawyers 20

Contact
Karin Mayer Rubinstein (adv, partner)

CATEGORIES OF WORK

- General corporate and commercial
- Mergers and acquisitions
- Capital markets and securities
- Venture capital, private equity
- Technology
- Life sciences and pharmaceuticals
- Privatisation
- Infrastructure and project finance
- Government and municipalities
- Joint ventures
- International transactions
- Competition and antitrust
- Litigation, dispute resolution
- Class actions
- Environment and energy
- Wills, trusts and estates
- Insurance
- Labour law
- Real estate and tourism
- Intellectual property
- Media, advertising and entertainment
- Banking and finance
- Venture capital and investment funds
- Foreign direct investments

GILAT, BAREKET & CO, ATTORNEYS AT LAW

ASSOCIATED WITH REINHOLD COHN & PARTNERS

5 HAR SINAI STREET
PO BOX 4480
TEL AVIV 61044

Telephone: +972 3 566 7999
Fax: +972 3 566 9030
E-mail: info@gilatadv.co.il
Website: www.rcip.co.il

Languages
Arabic, English, French, German, Hebrew, Portuguese

Number of lawyers 40
at this office 15

Contact
Daphna Gilat (Adv)

CATEGORIES OF WORK

- Intellectual property
- Information technology
- Hi-tech, computers and software
- Antitrust and trade regulations
- Pharmaceuticals, biotechnology
- Commercial and corporate
- Technology transfer
- Franchises
- Litigation
- Advertising and marketing

ERDINAST, BEN NATHAN & CO

25 NACHMANI STREET
TEL AVIV 65794

Telephone: +972 3 621 2500
Fax: +972 3 525 0896
E-mail: ebnlaw@ebnlaw.co.il
Website: www.ebnlaw.co.il

Languages
English, French, Hebrew

Number of lawyers 30

CATEGORIES OF WORK

Corporate and commercial law	**International transactions**
Commercial litigation	**Mergers and acquisitions**
Telecoms and media	**Energy and infrastructure**
Venture capital	**Project finance**
Technology	**Banking and finance**
Intellectual property	**Class actions**
Antitrust	**Constitutional law**
Securities	**Administrative law**

THE FIRM

Erdinast, Ben Nathan & Co was established in 1988 by Giora Erdinast and Rami Ben-Nathan. The firm is located in the heart of Tel Aviv's business district and consists of 30 advocates (seven partners and 23 associates) and several trainee advocates. Having played a major role in some of the most complex transactions and legal proceedings conducted in Israel in recent years, the firm is recognised as one of the leading commercial law firms in the country.

The firm represents some of the most prominent corporations and institutions in the Israeli economy, and has developed a wide-ranging international network. The firm's client roster includes publicly traded corporations, multinational corporations, entrepreneurial companies, venture capital funds, insurance companies, banks, and financial institutions.

Most of the firm's attorneys graduated with honours, some are admitted to the New York State Bar, and others have served as assistant teachers and lecturers in various fields of law or on the editorial boards of their universities' legal publications.

The firm's multilingual legal team provides a profound knowledge and deep understanding of the markets, both local and overseas, in which the firm is involved. Work is undertaken with a commercial approach and in a highly professional manner.

AREAS OF PRACTICE

The firm specialises in civil and commercial law, with particular emphasis on corporate law, mergers and acquisitions, media and communications, antitrust law, capital markets, banking, project finance, class actions, and commercial litigation.

The firm acts as general counsel to businesses of all types, including some of the leading corporations in Israel, and serves as special counsel in a variety of matters. The firm routinely represents its clients in complex transactions, including multinational transactions, investment agreements, financing agreements, mergers and acquisitions, takeovers, public and private offerings, entrepreneurial agreements, BOT and PFI agreements, and various other commercial agreements. The firm also represents various corporate clients in a wide variety of commercial litigation with a special focus on mergers and acquisitions, class actions, antitrust law, banking law, communications and media law, and petitions to the High Court of Justice on fundamental issues of administrative law.

In order to maintain and enhance its position at the forefront of the Israeli legal community, the firm constantly expands and diversifies its legal competencies in response to changes in the economy and in the corporate world. The firm's growing reputation in the areas of communications and hi-tech in recent years and its focus on project finance and banking law are examples of this approach.

The firm is morally and professionally committed to the exercise of its professional capacity for the good of the public at large and is always prepared to consider pro-bono representation.

FISCHER BEHAR CHEN WELL ORION & CO

3 DANIEL FRISCH ST
TEL AVIV 64731

Telephone: +972 3 694 4111
Fax: + 972 3 609 1116
E-mail: fbc@fbclawyers.com
Website: www.fbclawyers.com

Languages
Arabic, English, French, German, Hebrew, Hungarian, Serbo-Croatian, Spanish, Yiddish

Number of lawyers 60

CATEGORIES OF WORK

Litigation	**Intellectual property**
Corporate	**Regulatory**
Technology and life sciences	**Telecommunications**
Antitrust and competition	**Infrastructure and project finance**
Real estate	

THE FIRM

Founded in 1958, Fischer Behar Chen Well Orion & Co is one of Israel's foremost law firms, dedicated to providing full legal service to a broad spectrum of clients. FBC offers its clients sophisticated and high calibre counselling together with a dynamic and pragmatic approach to the practice of law. Recognised for its ability to address challenging legal issues creatively and successfully, FBC prides itself on professional excellence and dedication to its clients.

Over the last decade, FBC has grown significantly, expanding the scope of its resources and fields of practice. The breadth of the firm's expertise affords clients access to legal knowledge and experience in a wide range of disciplines. Attorneys within each practice area provide precise and in-depth counsel in their individual fields, while the firm's culture fosters co-operation among attorneys in different practice areas.

Many of the firm's lawyers hold degrees in business, economics and accounting, consistent with FBC's belief that successful attorneys should bring a broad perspective to their legal practice. The firm also includes native English-speaking attorneys as well as attorneys who have practiced extensively in leading law firms in the United States. In addition, the firm's network includes relationships with accounting, legal and other professionals, both in Israel and abroad, and these alliances enrich the firm's expertise in its global practice of law.

FBC represents prominent domestic and international clients in various industries and business sectors, including banking, investment, insurance, manufacturing, aviation, real estate, infrastructure, telecoms, hi-tech, and venture capital. The firm is regularly involved in a range of transactions and litigations, including some of the largest and highest profile in Israel.

AREAS OF PRACTICE

FBC's corporate attorneys regularly counsel privately held and public companies in all major aspects of corporate law. FBC has one of the leading banking and financial institution practices in Israel, where it has represented the State of Israel in the privatisation of two of Israel's principal banks, as well as one of the most highly regarded corporate restructuring practices in the country.

The litigation practice area is a cornerstone of FBC. Attorneys in this practice area represent a broad range of clients, ranging from the apex of Israel's economy, including its leading banks, financial institutions, and insurance companies, to major foreign businesses and multinational companies, to other public and private entities and individuals.

FBC has one of the fastest growing and dynamic high-quality real estate practices in Israel. The firm handles major real estate transactions in Israel and abroad and has extensive experience in representing entrepreneurs, developers, property owners and potential purchasers.

FBC's antitrust department has been recognised as Israel's leader in this field. Attorneys counsel clients in many of the country's principal economic sectors and provide ongoing advice in all major aspects of competition law.

FBC's technology and life sciences group is well recognised for representing a variety of clients, including domestic and international companies, underwriters, and investors, in high-profile transactions in the technology and venture capital markets.

FBC's intellectual property practice counsels clients on a wide variety of issues covering all types and aspects of IP. In addition to having substantial experience in transactions and litigation involving IP in both traditional and emerging media, the firm also advises clients on matters of copyright registration, licensing and transfer of ownership.

As in many jurisdictions, companies wishing to do business in Israel have to contend with a complex network of regulations and agencies at a variety of governmental levels. FBC specialises in helping clients navigate through the regulatory labyrinth in a wide variety of fields of business.

FBC represents major clients in all the principal telecoms business sectors in Israel and has extensive experience in all aspect of infrastructure projects.

GOLDFARB, LEVY, ERAN, MEIRI & CO

2 WEIZMANN STREET
TEL AVIV 64239

Telephone: +972 3 608 9999
Fax: +972 3 608 9909
E-mail: gle@glelaw.com
Website: www.glelaw.com

Languages
English, French, German, Hebrew, Spanish

Other offices
Tel Aviv

Number of lawyers 100
at this office 75

Contact
Yehuda M Levy (managing partner)

CATEGORIES OF WORK

Banking and finance
Yehuda M Levy, Oded Eran

Securities
Oded Eran, Amir Tzafrir, Adam Klein, Ashok J Chandrasekhar

Corporate and commercial
Rami Sofer, Levy Amitay, Nechama Brin

Corporate finance and capital markets
Yehuda M Levy, Oded Eran, Amir Tzafrir, Ashok J Chandrasekhar

Intellectual property
Marc Rabin

Telecommunications
Zvi Hauser

Mergers and acquisitions
Yehuda M Levy, Oded Eran, Ashok J Chandrasekhar

Infrastructure
Amir Tzafrir

Civil and commercial litigation
Reuven Reif, Aran Meiri, Hagit Blaiberg

Taxation
Tal Atsmon

Zoning, planning and construction
Tamar Migdal

Insurance
Rami Sofer

Transportation projects
Aran Meiri, Rami Sofer

Labour and employment
Ofer Ravid

Real estate, construction and development
Levy Amitay, Avi Arad

THE FIRM

Goldfarb, Levy, Eran, Meiri & Co is one of the largest and most highly regarded full-service law firms in Israel. The firm is the result of the merger of Goldfarb, Levy, Eran & Co, which was established in 1972, and Dankner-Lusky & Co, which was established in 1984. The firm carries on a general full-service business practice and serves a wide range of Israeli and foreign clients, with special emphasis on international transactions, financing, securities, mergers and acquisitions, real estate, taxation and related actvitites.

The clients of the firm include leading Israeli companies in their operations in Israel and abroad, major foreign firms in connection with their activities in and with Israel and local governmental entities. The firm has particularly extensive experience in counselling and representing the hi-tech sector, including both industrial firms and their venture capital backers and representing major Israeli construction companies in real estate transactions and projects in Israel and abroad.

The firm combines expertise in the Israeli legal system and business context with an extensive international background. In addition to professional training and experience in Israel, a number of partners and associates have had United States practice and legal education (many being member of various US bar jurisdictions), and others have had substantial exposure to the legal and commercial scene in the United States, Western Europe and other countries.

AREAS OF PRACTICE

As a policy, Goldfarb, Levy, Eran, Meiri & Co does not disclose clients or transactions in which it has been involved. In general, however, the firm has broad experience with public offerings and private placements in Israel, the US, Europe and elsewhere, and with other aspects of business financing. The firm also has a thorough understanding and deep involvement in the legal aspects of the Israeli real estate market and accompanied major real estate projects in Israel and abroad. A major part of the firm's work consists of counselling, negotiating and providing other legal services in connection with purchases, sales, merger and acquisitions of businesses and business assets; incorporation of companies, partnerships and venture funds; public and private equity and debt offerings, loans and other forms of financing; banking matters; licensing of patents, technology and trade marks; purchase contracts and marketing agreements of various types, including distributorships, agencies and franchising, supply agreements; product development programmes; employment agreements including stock options and other forms of employee and executive compensation; and a variety of other commercial transactions and activities.

The firm regularly deals with governmental bodies and regulatory authorities, including those responsible for Israel's investment and incentive programs. Merger and acquisition transactions are an important part of the firm's practice and expertise, including mergers among Israeli corporations, mergers of foreign corporations with Israeli corporations and mergers of Israeli corporations with foreign corporations. The firm has also guided the restructuring of very large Israeli conglomerates. The firm has experience in handling infrastructure development projects. The legal services that are provided include assistance in obtaining permits, concessions and approvals, representation in the tenders, and representation in negotiation and in related matters.

GORNITZKY & CO

45 ROTHSCHILD AVENUE
TEL AVIV 65784

Telephone: +972 3 710 9191
Fax: +972 3 560 6555

Languages
English, French, German, Spanish

Other offices
Herzliya Pituach

Number of lawyers 61

Contacts
Pinhas Rubin, Moriel Matalon, Ariel Zelichov, Zvi Ephrat

CATEGORIES OF WORK

Commercial

Corporate

Mergers and acquisitions

Antitrust

International business transactions

Agency, distribution and franchise agreements

Securities and public offerings

Taxation and international taxation

Trusts and estates

Financing

Banks and banking

Insurance

Real estate

Infrastructure projects and project finance

Litigation

Arbitration and mediation

White-collar crimes

Class actions

Liquidation, insolvency and bankruptcy

Hi-tech and venture capital

Telecommunications

Energy projects

THE FIRM

As one of Israel's first law firm's dating back to 1938, Gornitzky & Co has the distinction of being a leading provider of legal services. In the past several years, Gornitzky & Co has been classified as a leading firm in different legal fields by the editorial departments of the main international guides. Additionally, many of the firm's partners have attained positions of recognition as experts in their fields of practice and serve on the boards of directors of some of Israel's largest institutions.

Gornitzky & Co boasts one of the largest and very well regarded legal teams in Israel, which is headed by Advocate Pinhas Rubin. The firm takes pride in its legal staff members, who, in most cases, started their legal careers in the firm after being chosen from the best academic institutions in Israel and abroad and continue to prove their high professional qualities and abilities daily.

Gornitzky & Co is committed to providing professional one-stop shop service of the highest quality, combining legal knowledge and expertise with commercial and business understanding. The firm's market presence is confirmed through its ability to service the government, leading local and international corporate institutions and their consistently high ranking in the major international legal guides.

AREAS OF PRACTICE

Gornitzky & Co's clientele includes the State of Israel, domestic and international commercial and corporate clients, from multinational corporations to public and private companies, to private investors and individuals. Gornitzky & Co represents its clientele primarily in the following fields of practice:

Corporate, commercial, M&A, antitrust (consultation regarding antitrust issues, including obtaining approvals from government agencies such as the controller of restrictive trade practices), international transactions and agency, distribution and franchise agreements (representing both local and foreign clients), securities and public offerings (on the Tel-Aviv stock exchange and on foreign stock exchanges).

Taxation and international taxation, (advise major investors including individuals and companies on the structuring of large transnational projects), trust and estates, financing and investments, insurance (commercial and corporate advice to many major insurance companies in Israel) banks and banking (representing many of the major Israeli banks). Some of the firm's senior partners have also served, or continue to serve as, members of the board of directors of domestic as well as international banks.

Real estate (act as external general counsel to many public and private real estate companies in domestic and international property transactions and in corporate and commercial fields), hotels and tourism (constant consultation to several international hotel chains in commercial, corporate, real estate and labour law issues), infrastructure projects and project finance (tenders, bids and consultation regarding desalination, power stations, toll highway and light rail projects).

Litigation (representing individuals and entities in all Israeli courts in different varying issues of corporate, commercial and tax law), white-collar crimes (representing influential individuals and officers of public corporations in hearings before the state attorney and the district attorney and in the Israeli courts), class actions arbitration and mediation (serving as arbitrators and mediators, chosen by the relevant parties and by the Israeli courts and representation of parties in arbitration and mediation), liquidation, bankruptcy and insolvency (representing companies, liquidators and creditors. In addition Gornitzky & Co and its attorneys have been nominated by the court and by the creditors as liquidators of large Israeli companies).

Hi-tech, and start-ups, venture capital funds, communications and telecommunications companies, including representation of Israel's sole satellite licensee (advice regarding corporate, legislative and taxation issues); acts as external general counsel of oil and gas companies, industrial and pharmaceutical companies and their shareholders.

GROSS, KLEINHENDLER, HODAK, HALEVY, GREENBERG & CO

AZRIELI CENTER ONE
CIRCULAR BUILDING
TEL AVIV 67021

Telephone: +972 3 607 4444
Fax: +972 3 607 4422
E-mail: amir@gkh-law.com
Website: www.gkh-law.com

Languages
English, Arabic, French, German, Spanish, Hebrew

Number of lawyers 57

Contacts
Prof Joseph Gross (chairman),
Amir Halevy (managing partner)

CATEGORIES OF WORK

Commercial and corporate	**Taxation**
Securities and underwriting	**Commercial property**
Technology and venture capital	**Real estate**
Mergers and acquisitions	**Litigation**
Investments	**Antitrust and competition**
Intellectual property	**Labour and employment**
Cross-border transactions	

THE FIRM

Gross, Kleinhendler, Hodak, Halevy, Greenberg & Co, (GKH) (est 1979) is Israel's leading corporate and securities law firm, providing superior and innovative legal services.

GKH is engaged in all aspects of corporate and commercial legal practice, representing a large number of publicly held corporations traded on US, Israeli and European stock exchanges. The firm also represents international investment banks, privately held corporations of all sizes, newly formed businesses, partnerships and joint ventures. Clients served comprise a broad range of industrial, commercial, energy, retail, transportation, financial, and service enterprises. The firm's expertise includes representation before government ministries, regulatory agencies and the Bank of Israel.

Several firm members are licensed to practise in the US and Europe, and much of the firm's work is conducted in English.

AREAS OF PRACTICE

GKH's attorneys advise on a wide range of corporate matters including corporate governance, dividend distributions, compensation, indemnification and insurance of officers and directors, and shareholder agreements.

Commercial transactions: GKH's work in this area encompasses all forms of domestic and international commercial transactions, including the perfection of security interests in tangible and intangible property, and franchising. The firm's attorneys draft commercial contracts including licensing, lease, distribution and manufacturer representation agreements, as well as agency and non-competition agreements.

GKH's restrictive trade department conducts ongoing reviews of issues relating to various transactions, handles local and international merger filings and exemption requests related to restrictive arrangements.

Public financing, securities and corporate finance: specialising in both US and Israeli securities law, GKH has represented hundreds of issuers in connection with domestic and international, equity and debt securities offerings. The firm also counsels major international underwriters and investment banks in connection with securities offerings of Israeli companies and other aspects of their activities in Israel. GKH's attorneys represent clients in private placements, bridge financing, mezzanine financing, credit agreements, project finance, securitisation and repurchase agreements.

GKH have long been advising clients on formation of start-ups through to public and private offerings, in Israel, the US and Europe. GKH also counsels venture capital funds on their structure, and handles financing rounds from seed through mezzanine financing. The firm's IP department provides services with regard to trade marks, licensing arrangements and real-time consultation with international patent attorneys working in affiliation with GKH.

Renowned for its involvement in complex reorganisations, and in M&A activities of large Israeli and multinational organisations, GKH provides comprehensive coverage from structuring transactions, tax planning, negotiation, court submissions, and representation before regulatory bodies. The firm represents offerors and offerees in tender offers and takeovers, and acts as counsel in proxy contests.

Tax: GKH provides strategic tax planning to corporations on a variety of transactions and to individuals on complex tax issues. The department also prepares opinions relating to interpretation of tax laws.

GKH's rapidly expanding litigation department deals with all aspects of commercial litigation, including claims filed in Israel by or against multinational organisations and government agencies.

GKH provides advice on all aspects of employment law ranging from representation at tribunals to retirement benefits counselling senior officers.

Telecommunications: specialising in company restructuring, cross-ownership and preparation of tender offers, the firm also provides advice and opinions to local regulatory authorities concerning the establishment and implementation of new laws and practices. GKH's ongoing observation of global developments in this field provide its internationally active clients with a full range of current advice.

HAIM ZADOK & CO

RUBINSTEIN BUILDING
18TH FLOOR
20 LINCOLN STREET
TEL AVIV 67134

Telephone: +972 3 625 4000
Fax:+972 3 625 4040
E-mail: general@zadokco.co.il
Website: www.zadokco.co.il

Languages
Hebrew, English, French, Arabic, German

Number of lawyers 29

Contact
Adv Ilan Shavit (Stricks)

CATEGORIES OF WORK

Banking and finance
Ilan Shavit, Nitza R Posner

Bankruptcy and reorganisation
Ilan Shavit, Nitza R Posner

Investment
Tzachi Feldman,
Gideon (Doni) Toledano

International business
Dan Meridor, Gideon (Doni) Toledano

Arbitration and mediation
Dan Meridor, Eyal Rosovsky

Real estate
Avi Drexler, Tzachi Feldman

Litigation and dispute resolution
Eyal Rosovsky, Ilan Shavit

Criminal (white-collar)
Eyal Rosovsky

Constitutional and administrative
Dan Meridor

Capital market and hi-tech
Tzachi Feldman

Liquidation and receivership
Ilan Shavit, Nitza R Posner

Environmental
Ehood Schneider

Competition
Gideon (Doni) Toledano

Infrastructure
Ehood Schneider

Government business/regulatory
Dan Meridor

Corporate and commercial
Tzachi Feldman,
Gideon (Doni) Toledano

HESKIA-HACMUN LAW FIRM

AZRIELI CENTER
THE TRIANGULAR TOWER
TEL AVIV 67023

Telephone: +972 3 608 1122
Fax: +972 3 608 1123
E-mail: main@hh-law.co.il
Website: www.hh-law.co.il

Languages
English, German, Hebrew

Number of lawyers 5

Contacts
Dor Heskia, Amos Hacmun

Member
German-Israeli Lawyers Association;
Israeli-German Chamber of Commerce;
American-Israeli Chamber of Commerce and Industry; British-Israeli Chamber of Commerce;
Japan-Israeli Chamber of Commerce;
Swiss-Israeli Chamber of Commerce

CATEGORIES OF WORK

Corporate and commercial

Dispute resolution, litigation and arbitration

Telecommunications and technology

Banking and finance

Mergers and acquisitions

HERZOG, FOX & NEEMAN

ASIA HOUSE
4 WEIZMANN STREET
TEL AVIV 64239

Telephone: +972 3 692 2020
Fax: +972 3 696 6464
E-mail: hfn@hfn.co.il
Website: www.hfn.co.il

Languages
Hebrew, English, French

Number of lawyers 104

Contacts
Meir Linzen, Alan Sacks, Ehud Sol

Member
World Law Group; International Bar Association

CATEGORIES OF WORK

Corporate
Alan Sacks, Ehud Sol

Mergers and acquisitions
Alan Sacks, Ehud Sol, Janet-Levy Pahima, Anthony Leibler

Capital markets and securities
Ehud Sol, Chaim Friedland, Efrat Ram, Ilanit Landsman Yogev

Banking and finance
Alan Sacks, Gil White

Telecoms and media
Yaacov Sharvit, Ran Tal

Venture capital and investment funds
Janet Levy Pahima, Eldar Ben-Ruby

Infrastructure development and project finance
Michael Fox, Mark Phillips, Adam Eytan

Commercial litigation and arbitration
Tuvia Erlich, David Zailer, Yossi Ashkenazi

Tax
Yaakov Neeman, Meir Linzen, Eldar Ben-Ruby

Real estate and construction
Yaakov Brandt, Moshe Hardy

Labour and employment
Orly Gerbi

Energy and natural resources
Michael Fox, Adam Eytan

Commercial law
Amir Seraya

Intellectual property and IT
Neil Wilkof

Antitrust and competition
Ehud Sol, Gal Rozent

Internet and e-commerce
Meir Linzen, Gil White, Ran Tal

Administrative and public law
Yaakov Neeman, Yaacov Sharvit

THE FIRM

Herzog, Fox & Neeman (HFN) is one of Israel's foremost corporate and commercial law offices representing leading companies worldwide. HFN was founded in 1972 by the late Chaim Herzog, later to become the sixth president of the State of Israel; Michael Fox, formerly a partner in a London law firm; and Dr Yaakov Neeman, author of numerous books and articles on tax law and one of Israel's foremost authorities on income tax. HFN has grown into one of Israel's best-known international corporate law firms. Its legal staff comprises a significant number of native English speakers with experience in leading international firms in the US, the UK and Australia.

AREAS OF PRACTICE

The firm's principal practice areas are corporate; M&A; tax; banking and finance; infrastructure development and project finance; capital markets and securities; commercial litigation; IP/IT; telecoms; property and construction; energy and natural resources; the internet and e-commerce; venture capital; employment; and antitrust and competition.

The corporate department at HFN is among the largest and most experienced in Israel, with much of its work internationally sourced. The lawyers in this department have a wealth of experience in a range of corporate work, including: share purchases/sales; joint ventures; mergers; corporate reorganisations; and asset purchases/sales. The firm continues to feature prominently in significant international transactions.

HFN's tax department is the largest and most broadly experienced of any Israeli law firm and covers all aspects of taxation relating to commercial activities in Israel. It's main focus is the provision of tax advice to Israeli and cross-border transactions.

HFN advises leading American and European international banks and has a strong following from local and investment banks. The banking department has been involved in virtually all the major PFI projects in Israel.

HFN is known internationally for its substantial experience in project finance and infrastructure, representing banks and concessionaires in high-profile Israeli projects, involving telecoms, tunnels, natural gas extraction and pipelines, power projects, desalination, toll roads and transport.

HFN's securities and capital markets practice enjoys a leading reputation for its cross-border work and is well known for its work involving local and international underwriters and public offering of securities listed on the Tel Aviv Stock Exchange, the New York Stock Exchange, Nasdaq, as well as European markets.

The IT/IP department works with the corporate group on technology transactions and also covers a variety of IT/IP activities, including licensing and technology transfer, trade mark prosecution, litigation, computer and cyberspace law and copyright matters.

The telecoms and media department has become a leader in its field representing a number of international telecoms corporations as well as bidders in all major telecoms in Israel.

The real estate, construction and property development department provides a complete service to foreign and domestic developers.

HFN's litigation department is one of the largest and best-resourced in Israel, able to deploy many lawyers for complex commercial actions both domestic and cross-border, and representing many multinationals conducting litigation in Israel.

HFN represents a large and ever-growing number of domestic and international venture capital funds and private investors, as well as the portfolio companies in which they invest, through the whole development process of incubation, start-up, emergence and maturity.

The energy and natural resources department has been at the forefront of recent growth in this sector including the exploitation of Israel's natural gas resources.

Further information can be found on the HFN website: www.hfn.co.il.

DR J WEINROTH & CO

14 WEIZMAN STREET
WEIZMAN CENTER
TEL AVIV 64239

Telephone: +972 3 718 1111
Fax: +972 3 718 1112
E-mail: office@weinrothlaw.com

Languages
English, French, German

Number of lawyers 21

Contact
Oded Nesher

CATEGORIES OF WORK

Civil litigation
Dr Jacob Weinroth

Securities regulation
Dr Avraham Weinroth

Dispute resolution and arbitration
Dr Avraham Weinroth

Government business/regulatory
Dr Avraham Weinroth

Fraud and white-collar crime
Dr Jacob Weinroth

Insolvency/corporate restructuring
Dr Jacob Weinroth

Banking and finance
Dr Avraham Weinroth

Commercial property
Dr Avraham Weinroth

Corporate and commercial
Dr Avraham Weinroth

Insurance
Dr Jacob Weinroth

Commercial litigation
Dr Jacob Weinroth,
Dr Avraham Weinroth

Private client
Dr Jacob Weinroth,
Dr Avraham Weinroth

THE FIRM

Dr J Weinroth & Co is considered to be among Israel's leading litigation practices. The firm also offers clients the full range of first-rate legal services; from commercial law, banking, securities, insurance and real estate transactions; through to family law, including wills and estates.

Market surveys in the Israeli press, as well as surveys among the country's lawyers themselves, have consistently placed Dr J Weinroth & Co as the firm most people would want to represent them in any litigation. Indeed, the 2001 edition of *The European Legal 500* stated: 'For issues of Israeli white-collar crime and civil and commercial litigation, the reputation of Dr J Weinroth & Co is unchallenged'. The firm represents clients before all the country's courts, tribunals and arbitration committees, including the Supreme Court, and handles all types of litigation, from criminal, to civil and commercial, including class action suits.

Since 1974, Dr J Weinroth & Co has been engaged in the practice of Israeli and international law. The firm's members are all Israeli lawyers, and a number also have international qualifications. The firm comprises two partners and 19 associate lawyers, and this enables it to provide a professional and personal service to all its clients. The size of the firm, the close ratio of partners to associates, and the efficient and professional support staff, ensure that each case receives the rigorous attention that it requires.

Jacob Weinroth, the firm's founder and senior partner, is an enormously respected figure within the legal community. He is one of the country's best-known lawyers, having represented Israel's Presidents and Prime Ministers in high-profile cases. He is also an expert in commercial law. The other partner is Dr Avraham Weinroth, a specialist in banking, public law, property law, commercial law, securities and administrative law and litigation.

AREAS OF PRACTICE

In addition to litigation, the firm has a reputation for providing high-quality legal services in many different areas, especially in the corporate, commercial and real estate fields. The firm has been involved in facilitating major domestic and international transactions, including the taxation aspects of such work. In addition, the firm has established a reputation in the expanding fields of antitrust and competition law, and also offers expertise in liquidations, torts, banking and securities.

The firm is best known for its representation of high-profile national and international personalities, such as the late President Ezer Weizman, Prime Minister Ariel Sharon, former Prime Minister and current Finance Minister Benjamin Netanyahu, Transport Minister Meir Sheetrit, Agriculture Minister Israel Katz, Minister without Portfolio and former Justice Minister Tzachi Hanegbi, former Police Minister Shlomo Ben-Ami, former Infrastructure Minister Yosef Paritski, former Minister Salah Tarif, former MK Nehama Ronen, and Israel's Counsel-General in the Hague, Urel Yhzhaki. Dr J Weinroth & Co represents Russian magnate billionaire Michael Cherney, as well as diamond magnate Dan Gertler and the family of the late business tycoon Shaul Eisenberg.

The client list of the firm speaks for itself, and includes the most prominent Israeli and international companies and businesses, such as the Histadrut Trade Union Movement, major insurance companies and pension funds, including Menorah and the Phoenix, many diamond manufacturing companies, Bezeq International (a leading international communications company), Ofer Brothers (the owners of the Israel Corp, and United Mizrahi Bank), PricewaterhouseCoopers, the Taic family (owners of luxury hotels in Israel), Dubek Ltd (the leading Israeli tobacco company), Magen David Adom Ambulance Service, The Cross-Israel Highway Co, Palace America (high-quality sheltered housing), Avrech (a gasoline station chain) and Migdalei Be'eri (a prestigious Tel Aviv residential complex).

LESHEM-KIPPERMAN, LAW OFFICES & NOTARY

13 BALFOUR STREET
TEL AVIV 65211

Telephone: +972 3 629 0780
Fax: +972 3 629 0789
E-mail: lk@leshem-kipperman.co.il
Website: www.leshem-kipperman.com

Languages
English

Number of lawyers 3

Contacts
Moshe Leshem, Irit Leshem-Kipperman

CATEGORIES OF WORK

Air transportation

Aviation, commercial and regulatory matters

Transportation cargo recoveries

Aircraft purchase, lease and finance

Admiralty, marine and shipping

Litigation and arbitration

Tort law, product liability

Insurance

LEVITAN, SHARON & CO

57 YIGAL ALON STREET
TEL AVIV 67891

Telephone: +972 3 688 6768
Fax: +972 3 688 6769
E-mail: office@levitansharon.co.il

Languages
English, German, Hebrew

Number of lawyers 27

Contacts
Rachel Levitan, Peggy Sharon

Member
International Bar Association (IBA); Professional Liability Underwriting Society (PLUS); Federation of Defense and Corporate Counsel (FDCC); International Association of Insurance Law (AIDA); Aviation Insurance (AIA)

CATEGORIES OF WORK

Insurance and reinsurance
Rachel Levitan

Aviation/products
Peggy Sharon

Claims handling/TPA
Sharon Shefer

Jewellers block
Sharon Shefer

Dispute resolution/ litigation and arbitration
Tammy Greenberg

D&O litigation
Rachel Levitan

Financial lines insurance/ fraud litigation
Moshe Abady

Real estate
Dror Zamir

Insurance corporate/regulatory work
Irit Shapira-Weber

International litigation including deposition services
Peggy Sharon

Product liability
Rachel Levitan

LEVY, MEIDAN & CO

4 KOIFMAN STREET
TEL AVIV 68012

Telephone: +972 3 510 2491
Fax: +972 3 510 2493
E-mail: main@ljlaw.co.il

Languages
Hebrew, English, Spanish

Number of lawyers 23

CATEGORIES OF WORK

Antitrust/competition law
Joseph Levy, Michal Schwartz

Securities
Amir Nachlieli, Asher Bichoonski

Banking
Noa Meidan, Ziv Neuman

Trade
Joseph Levy, Tal Dagan

Communications
Amir Nachlieli, Oded Kahana

Commercial
Joseph Levy, Noa Meidan

Government contracts and tenders
Joseph Levy, Noa Meidan

Project finance
Joseph Levy, Noa Meidan

Corporate
Amir Nachlieli, Oded Kahana

Litigation
Eyal Blizovsky

Administrative law
Eyal Blizovsky,
Tamar Heimowitz-Richter

Property law
Tal Dagan, Avital Dagan

THE FIRM

Levy, Meidan & Co (formerly known as Joseph Levy & Co) was established in 1992, and employs 23 lawyers. Based in Tel Aviv, the firm has an active domestic and international practice and serves as a regular outside counsel or as a project specialist to a number of major corporations, banks, investment groups, and trade associations. The firm's advice is also sought by national and municipal government entities such as the Ministry of Finance, Ministry of Transportation, the Ministry of National Infrastructures and the Ministry of the Environment.

AREAS OF PRACTICE

The firm has extensive experience in tenders law. The firm's lawyers were actively involved in the process by which legislation of the Mandatory Tenders Law and its regulations were enacted in the Knesset – Israel's Parliament. The firm has been engaged in the preparation of tenders; is accompanying tender processes on behalf of various government ministries; and is representing local and overseas clients in various legal proceedings, in tenders established by the state, municipalities, government companies, public bodies, etc.

The firm has drawn up the tender and the concession agreement for the Carmel Tunnels Project and provides legal counsel to the Ministries of Finance and Transportation on this project. The Carmel Tunnels is a build, operate and transfer (BOT) project for the privatisation of Haifa Metropolitan's major transportation infrastructure, granting a concession for collecting tolls. The firm represents a major highway developer for the Tel Aviv Metropolitan, and also acts as an adviser for the tender committee which selected the concessionaire for a Private Finance Initiative (PFI) toll highway between the cities of Modi'in and Tel Aviv.

The firm has drawn up the tender documents and the concession agreement for the setting up of a seawater desalination project for 100 million cubic meters of water annually in south Israel. This is also a BOT project and the firm acts as legal counsel to the Ministries of Finance, National Infrastructures and the Environment and the Water Commission on this project. In addition, the firm has drawn up the tender documents and the concession agreement for seawater desalination facilities on a BOO basis. For this project, the firm also acts as legal counsel for the Ministries of Finance, National Infrastructures and the Environment and the Water Commission. Currently, the firm acts as legal counsel to the Ministry of Finance, National Infrastructures and the Environment and the Water Commission in a third desalination project in Israel for 100 million cubic metres a year. The firm was an adviser to two of the largest banks in Israel in the bridge financing of a large-scale natural gas project and represented Credit Suisse First Boston in the issuance of secured notes for the project.

The firm participated in preparing the tender for the selection of the country's second cellular phone operator. The firm is currently an adviser to one of the largest international telecommunications and internet services provider companies in Israel.

The firm has developed extensive practical experience in the area of antitrust. The firm provides ongoing legal advice to various entities on such topics as the application of programs for the internal enforcement of the Israeli Antitrust Law, and represents clients before the Antitrust Authority and the Antitrust Tribunal. In this respect, the firm represents a major food manufacturer and distributor, a leading international credit card company, a major metropolitan public transportation company and a satellite broadcasting company.

The firm assisted one of Israel's largest mortgage banks in establishing, formulating and structuring a secondary market for mortgages. The firm also formulated the protocol agreements to regulate the secondary mortgage market. In addition it has represented a leading worldwide software provider in the acquisition of several Israeli hi-tech companies.

LUTHI & CO

AMERICA HOUSE
35 SHAUL HAMELECH BLVD
PO BOX 33113
TEL AVIV 64927

Telephone: +972 3 695 2268
Fax: +972 3 695 1120
E-mail: mail@luthi.co.il
Website: www.luthi.co.il

Languages
English

Number of lawyers 11

Contacts
Richard Luthi, Christopher Brice

CATEGORIES OF WORK

Patents

Confidential information

Data protection

Trade marks, service marks and brand protection

Copyright, designs; author's and moral rights

Pharmaceuticals and biotechnology

Food technology

Agricultural and industrial chemicals

Information and communications technology

Materials science

Aviation and space technology

Imaging and photography

Toys, games and sports equipment

NASCHITZ, BRANDES & CO.

5 TUVAL STREET
TEL AVIV 67897

Telephone: +972 3 623 5000
Fax: +972 3 623 5005
E-mail: info@nblaw.com
Website: www.nblaw.com

Languages
English, French, German, Hebrew, Hungarian, Russian, Spanish

Other offices
Haifa

Number of lawyers 64
at this office 52

Member
International Attorneys Club; Mackrell International; International Bar Association; AIDA International Insurance Law Association; Israel Maritime Law Association

CATEGORIES OF WORK

Litigation
Peter Gad Naschitz, Gil Atar, Tamar Arad Kareth, Ofer Motola, Ethan A Naschitz, Azriel Rothman

Emerging growth companies
Sharon A Amir, Eran Ballan, Gil Brandes, Jonathan Feuchtwanger, Noga Devecseri Spira

Mergers and acquisitions, joint ventures
Hanina Brandes, Sharon A Amir, Aaron M Lampert

Mediation
Ofer Motola, Yoav Razin, Yaron Horovitz

Banking
Pnina Broder Manor, Ethan A Naschitz

Intellectual property
Shimon Chertow, Jonathan Feuchtwanger, Yaron Horovitz

Competition law
Hanina Brandes, Yoav Razin

Capital markets
Aaron M Lampert

Real estate
Zacharia Feit, Shmuel Lechner

Shipping and transport
Peter Gad Naschitz, Ethan A Naschitz

THE FIRM

Naschitz, Brandes & Co. is one of Israel's largest and most prominent law firms. The firm's 19 partners and more than 60 associates and articled clerks provide sophisticated advice to clients on the full gamut of civil matters.

Naschitz Brandes attorneys possess specialised knowledge in a broad variety of areas of legal practice, allowing the firm to advise on the most complex domestic and multinational commercial transactions, and to handle a broad variety of civil disputes. With a head office in Tel-Aviv and a branch office in Haifa, Naschitz Brandes serves Israeli and international clients. The firm works closely with leading law firms in other countries to provide clients with comprehensive services around the world.

The firm's attorneys are committed to the development of the legal profession, continuing legal education and community service. Its attorneys are active in the Israeli Bar, and in various initiatives related to the legal profession. Naschitz Brandes has been an instrumental force in legislative and regulatory reform, in areas ranging from agriculture law, antitrust law, securities law to tax law. The firm also prepares position papers and drafts legislation on issues of public interest. Its attorneys regularly lecture at seminars and conferences on areas related to the firm's expertise.

AREAS OF PRACTICE

The firm's corporate practice ranges from the representation of start-up companies in the hi-tech and biotechnology arenas, to the representation of the largest public and governmental companies, investors in these companies, venture capital funds and financial services professionals who advise these companies. The firm has played a leading role in many major and innovative commercial transactions, corporate mergers and acquisitions, and joint ventures. The firm's clients include Fortune 500 corporations and leading information technology companies, ranging from software houses to telecommunications hardware manufacturers to fabless chip manufacturers. Naschitz Brandes' team serves these clients by combining the sophistication that comes from the firm's traditional representation of the largest multinational corporations with the creativity, flexibility and openness that are an essential element of the firm's philosophy. The firm has far-ranging experience in related commercial fields such as the representation of banks and financial services institutions.

Naschitz Brandes' highly respected litigation practice covers a wide spectrum of areas, including general commercial, product liability, banking, insurance, maritime, securities and intellectual property. The firm's attorneys appear regularly before all courts countrywide, and have been instrumental in many landmark decisions. Naschitz Brandes has been involved in precedent-setting corporate law cases, including cases relating to shareholders' rights and disputes, class actions, shareholder derivative suits, compensation claims upon termination of distribution and similar relationships, and securities law cases.

Naschitz Brandes regularly represents the leading Israeli and international insurance and reinsurance companies – advising on commercial and regulatory issues, and representing these companies in litigation and subrogation matters. The firm is involved in the largest fire, casualty and property cases, including all significant Israeli tobacco and environmental claims.

Additionally, for the last 40 years Naschitz Brandes has been one of the leading maritime law firms in Israel. With a network of professional correspondents worldwide, the firm serves as the primary Israeli correspondent and representative firms for leading foreign law firms, insurers and ship owners. Beside a broad recovery and subrogation practice, the firm has been involved in the most significant Israel-related cases and arbitrations involving total loss, general average or salvage.

In addition, the firm is prominent in the areas of bankruptcy law, intellectual property law and labour law.

REINHOLD COHN & PARTNERS, PATENT ATTORNEYS

21 AHAD HA'AM STREET
PO BOX 4060
TEL AVIV 61040

Telephone: +972 3 710 9333
Fax: +972 3 560 6405
E-mail: info@rcip.co.il
Website: www.rcip.co.il

Languages
Arabic, English, French, German, Hebrew, Portuguese, Russian, Spanish

Other offices
Jerusalem

Number of lawyers 40
at this office 26

Contact
Dr Bossmat Gonen

CATEGORIES OF WORK

Life sciences and chemistry
Ilan Cohn, Bossmat Gonen

Trade marks
David Gilat, Ronit Barzik-Soffer

Hi-tech
Ehud Hausman, Jonathan Topper

Litigation and commercial law
David Gilat, Eran Bareket

Technology, law technology
David de Vries, Ena Pugatsch

RON GAZIT ROTENBERG & CO

46 ROTHSCHILD BLVD
ALROV TOWER, 12TH FLOOR
TEL AVIV 66883

Telephone: +972 3 711 1711
Fax: +972 3 711 1700
E-mail: mail@rgr.co.il
Website: www. rgr.co.il

Languages
Dutch, English, French, Hebrew

Number of lawyers 28

Contact
Mr Ron Gazit

CATEGORIES OF WORK

Corporate
Ron Gazit

Information technology
Ron Gazit

Complex litigation
Yaron Reiter

Competition/antitrust
Eyal Roy Sage

Dispute resolution
Ron Gazit, Yaron Reiter

Intellectual property
Eyal Roy Sage

Mergers and acquisitions
Benjamin Rotenberg

Telecommunications/new media
Eyal Roy Sage

Commercial property
Amir Amar

Media
Benjamin Rotenberg

Procurement
Benjamin Rotenberg

Venture capital
Ron Gazit

S FRIEDMAN & CO

ADVOCATES

**THE TRADE TOWER
25 HAMERED ST
PO BOX 50222
TEL AVIV 61500**

Telephone: +972 3 796 1500
Fax: +972 3 796 1501
E-mail: tel-aviv@friedman.co.il
Website: www.friedman.co.il

Languages
Arabic, English, French, Hebrew, Italian

Other offices
Haifa, Herzliya Pituach

Number of lawyers 45

Contacts (partners)
Amiram Safran, Asher Rabinowitz, David Malkoff, Alexander Kesary, Sarit Molcho, Itamar Anaby, Doron Schweppe, Charles B Gottlieb, Lily Doron, Amir Cohen-Dor, Michael Safran, Keren Betser

CATEGORIES OF WORK

- **Banking, finance and international transactions**
- **Mergers and acquisitions and securities**
- **Corporate (including labour and restrictive trade practices)**
- **Real estate and infrastructure development**
- **Litigation and dispute resolution and insurance**
- **Taxation (domestic and international)**
- **Maritime, aviation and transportation**
- **Technology and venture capital**

THE FIRM

Since the firm's establishment in 1939, S Friedman & Co has been one of Israel's most distinguished law firms; it has been at the forefront of the development of Israel's legal community and jurisprudence. The firm has a long-established international practice and provides efficient, value-added 'one-stop' legal services as 'outside in-house' counsel to some of Israel's largest multinational enterprises with global operations. The firm also acts for multinational enterprises and financial institutions, marketing connections with their Israeli operations. S Friedman & Co embraces a multidisciplinary team approach towards counselling clients, maximising their ability to provide clients with integrated, seamless and cost-efficient advice and services.

AREAS OF PRACTICE

Banking and finance: S Friedman & Co has extensive cross-border experience in the fields of corporate, project and cross-border finance in each of the firm's practice areas. It has an international banking practice representing domestic and international banks and financial institutions.

Shipping and transportation: S Friedman & Co is pre-eminent in maritime and transportation law in Israel, it has a long and distinguished history. The firm advises major international shipping concerns in all aspects of their businesses, with particular expertise in fleet acquisition and asset-backed finance along with taxation, regulatory and insurance liability issues. The firm also advises the State of Israel in various shipping matters.

Aviation: the firm has an active aircraft finance practice including advising clients on security and registration issues in the State of Israel.

Corporate, labour and employee benefits: S Friedman & Co advises multinational enterprises on corporate matters pertaining to their holdings, acquisitions and divestitures in Israel. The firm also represents and advises shareholders, officers and directors on corporate governance and shareholder relations. It's labour lawyers are well versed in all aspects of labour law and executive compensation.

Anti-trust competition: the firm has an active competition law practice, advising multinational and domestic corporations on competition issues.

Litigation and ADR: S Friedman & Co's litigation department represents both domestic and foreign institutions and individuals in an array of complex commercial, civil, regulatory and insurance-related litigation at all levels of the judiciary; in arbitrations and before all forms of regulatory bodies in the state of Israel in a cost-effective manner.

Securities and M&A: the firm advises its clients on private placements, initial public and secondary offerings. It is a pioneer in securitisation both on the public and private markets in Israel. Its M&A expertise encompasses the array of the firm's practice groups and includes contested and friendly acquisitions and takeovers, tender offers, proxy contests, divestitures and leveraged buy-outs.

Real estate and infrastructure: S Friedman & Co represent some of the country's largest developers, contractors, investors, financial institutions and landowners in all aspects of the development process and infrastructure development.

Tax: the firm has a full-service tax department handling domestic and international tax issues and planning. It also has expertise in tax-related litigation.

Venture law and IP: the firm is experienced in advising venture capitalists and international financial institutions in private equity preferred share and convertible note financings, most typically of a cross-border nature. It is closely partnered with its technological clients to help them develop efficient strategies for the best exploitation of their intellectual property.

S. HOROWITZ & CO

31 AHAD HA'AM STREET
TEL AVIV 65202

Telephone: +972 3 567 0700
Fax: +972 3 566 0974
E-mail: info@s-horowitz.co.il
Website: www.shorowitz.com

Languages
English, German, Hebrew

Number of lawyers 71

Contacts
Tal Band, Clifford Davis

Member
Lex Mundi

CATEGORIES OF WORK

Dispute resolution
Yehoshua Horesh, Alex Hertman, Asgad Stern, Ehud Artzi

Corporate and commercial
Ruth Oren, Anthony Bloch, Clifford Davis, Michelle Liberman

Mergers and acquisitions
Anthony Bloch, Clifford Davis, Avigail Kastiel

Banking and finance
Ruth Oren, Anthony Bloch, Clifford Davis, Hugh Kowarsky

Competition
Asgad Stern, Hagai Doron

Capital markets and securities
Asgad Stern, Avigail Kastiel

Energy and natural resources
Yehoshua Horesh, Alex Hertman, Eliya Zunz

Life sciences and pharmaceuticals
Tal Band, Avi Ordo

Project finance and infrastructure
Anthony Bloch, Clifford Davis, Michelle Liberman

Intellectual property
Tal Band, Hugh Kowarsky, Avi Ordo

Employment and employee benefits
Shoshana Gavish

Tax
Leor Nouman

Telecoms and media
Asgad Stern, Hagai Doron, Clifford Davis

Commercial property
Yehoshua Horesh, Amir Caspari

Insurance
Alex Hertman, Ehud Arzi

Criminal (white-collar)
Ilan Sofer

SHAVIT BAR-ON GAL-ON TZIN NOV YAGUR, LAW OFFICES

SONOL TOWER
52 MENACHEM BEGIN
TEL AVIV 67137

Telephone: +972 3 791 2800
Fax: +972 3 791 2801
Email: contact@sbilaw.com
Website: www.sbilaw.com

Languages
English, Hebrew

Number of lawyers 27

Contact
Ilan Shavit

Member
ELG - European Law Group

CATEGORIES OF WORK

Company and commercial
Ilan Shavit, Ofer Bar-On

Mergers and acquisitions
Ilan Shavit, Tzahi Yagur

Hi-tech start-ups and venture capital
Ilan Shavit, Amir Witkon

Commercial and residential property
Yuval Gal-On, Ron Tzin

Litigation and arbitration
Ofer Bar-On, Yuval Gal-On

Zoning and planning law
Yuval Gal-On, Ron Tzin

Municipal law and taxation
Ofer Bar-On, Ravit Baram-Mazor

International business development
Josef Lederman

Liquidation and insolvency
Ofer Bar-On, Hanit Nov

Banking law
Hanit Nov, Liat Naggar-Snir

Antitrust and competition law
Tzahi Yagur, Hilit Arel

Labour law
Hanit Nov, Liad Ziv

Mining law
Ilan Shavit, Ravit Baram-Mazor

Environmental law
Ron Tzin, Tal Tsafrir

BOT projects
Tzahi Yagur, Mirit Topf Katzurin

Taxation law
Hanan Nitzan (CPA), Doron Budovitz (attorney and CPA)

International network (ELG – European Law Group)
Ilan Shavit, Ofer Bar-On

SHIBOLETH, YISRAELI, ROBERTS, ZISMAN AND MOSHE H. NE'EMAN, BEN-ARTZI & CO.

46 MONTEFIORE STREET
TEL AVIV 65201

Telephone: +972 3 710 3311
Fax: +972 3 710 3322
Website: www.shibolet.com

Languages
English, French, Hebrew

Other offices
New York

Number of lawyers 70
at this office 55

Contacts
Yaacov Yisraeli (manager@shibolet.com),
Moshe H Ne'eman (office@nsblaw.com)

Member
Terralex, Worldwide Network of Independent Law Firms

CATEGORIES OF WORK

Corporate

Commercial

Mergers and acquisitions

Securities

Capital markets

Banking and finance

Corporate governance

High-tech and bio-tech

Intellectual property

Project finance and infrastructure

Litigation

Telecommunications

Media and entertainment

Real estate

Employment law

Tax

Regulatory practice

Insurance

WEINSTOCK-ZECLER & CO

1 AZRIELI CENTER
132 PETACH TIKVA ROAD
TEL AVIV 67021

Telephone: +972 3 696 8333
Fax: +972 3 696 4222
E-mail: law@w-z.co.il

Languages
English, French

Number of lawyers 9

CATEGORIES OF WORK

Competition and antitrust
Niv Zecler

Corporate law and financing
Gidon Weinstock, Ofer Argov

Dispute resolution/litigation and arbitration
Niv Zecler, Gidon Weinstock

Banking
Gidon Weinstock, Ofer Argov

WEKSLER, BREGMAN & CO., ADVOCATES

SHALOM TOWER
9 ACHAD HA'AM STREET
TEL AVIV 65251

Telephone: +972 3 511 9393
Fax: +972 3 511 9394
E-mail: office@wblaw.co.il
Website: www.wblaw.co.il

Languages
English, French, Hebrew, Japanese

Number of lawyers 30

CATEGORIES OF WORK

Corporate
Adv Uri Bregman, Adv Ora Dvir

Company
Adv Ofer Yankovich, Adv Dror Toren

Real estate and BOT projects
Adv Uri Bregman, Adv Avi Ben-Yaakov

Banking and finance
Adv Ora Dvir, Adv Ofer Yankovich

Commercial
Adv Uri Bregman, Adv Dror Toren

Commercial Property
Adv Guy Kasher

Securities and capital markets
Adv Ora Dvir, Adv Ofer Yankovich

Public offering
Adv Ofer Yankovich, Adv Ora Dvir

Planning and zoning
Adv Taly Salton-Yeshua

International commercial transactions
Adv Uri Bregman, Adv Dror Toren

Hi-tech investments
Adv Dror Toren, Adv Ron Salpeter

Litigation and arbitration
Adv Doron Dan, Adv Amit Pines

Liquidation and receivership
Adv Amit Pines, Adv Yael Moshkovich

Employment and labour
Adv Dror Toren, Adv Yaron Rossman

Mergers and acquisitions
Adv Uri Bregman, Adv Dror Toren

Antitrust; tender law
Adv Amit Pines, Adv Ofer Yankovich

THE FIRM

Established in 1936, the firm of Weksler, Bregman & Co is one of the most prominent corporate and commercial law firms in Israel. The firm, with 30 attorneys, has a general, full-service business practice, with specialisation in real estate, securities, banking and commercial transactions. Weksler, Bregman & Co's clientele encompasses corporations and public bodies in these sectors.

AREAS OF PRACTICE

The firm services its corporate clients through the organisation of business structures. These include: the establishment and ongoing representation of corporations, partnerships, branches of foreign corporations in Israel and joint venture entities; negotiation, counselling and other services relating to asset purchase transactions, and mergers and acquisitions; the drafting of R&D and technology and licensing agreements, franchise, marketing, agency and distributorship agreements, stock option schemes, and a variety of other types of commercial agreements and documents.

The firm has vast experience in commercial, residential and industrial real estate development and infrastructure projects, ranging from the construction of commercial centres, large residential areas, shopping malls and hotels, and is intensively involved in all aspects of the Cross-Israel Highway project. The firm represents a leading Israeli investment company, engaged in land development, construction, insurance, trade, hotels and tourism, including the regional franchise for a major international hotel chain.

The firm offers broad expertise in the securities field and has extensive experience in public offerings and private placements, representing both issuers and underwriters. It serves as legal counsel to the Tel Aviv Stock Exchange and has handled the public offerings of leading Israeli banks and investment and holding companies. The firm also provides corporate planning in the selection and design of business structures, and in the financing of corporate reorganisations and other transactions. The firm's work also includes the preparation of documentation, the conducting of due diligence reviews, and complex negotiations with regulatory and securities and exchange authorities.

The firm provides services for a number of Israeli and international entrepreneurs, companies and venture funds in hi-tech, providing counselling in the areas of company, securities, intellectual property and employment law.

The firm renders legal services to banking institutions in Israel. Work performed includes counselling, negotiations, legal opinions, issuance of various types of governmental licences and other related services.

The firm deals with governmental bodies and agencies and advises its clients on the establishment of incentive-based investments in industry and tourism. In serving its clientele in cross-border transactions, the firm also offers the services of an Israeli lawyer with extensive legal experience in Japan and South Korea.

Weksler, Bregman & Co represents clients in commercial litigation, arbitration and labour disputes. The firm supervises foreign litigation on behalf of its Israeli clientele and represents foreign clients in Israeli courts.

The firm offers broad expertise in matters relating to liquidation and receivership procedures of corporations, and the firm's lawyers act as liquidators or receivers of companies, especially on behalf of banks.

YEHUDA RAVEH & CO

RUBINSTEIN HOUSE
20 LINCOLN STREET
TEL AVIV 67134

Telephone: +972 3 562 0303
Fax: +972 3 561 8558
E-mail: ravehtlv@ravehtlv.co.il
Website: www.yraveh.co.il

Languages
English, French, Hebrew, Hungarian

Other offices
Haifa, Jerusalem

Number of lawyers 48

CATEGORIES OF WORK

Infrastructure projects
Yehuda Raveh, Yehuda Glatt

Building and development
Lisa Tross, Yuval Grayevsky

Mergers and acquisitions
Yehuda Raveh, Yehuda Glatt

Antitrust
Carmit Bar-On

Hi-tech
Yehuda Glatt

International law and transactions
Yehuda Raveh, Yehuda Glatt

Corporate
Yehuda Raveh, Lisa Tross

Intellectual property
Gabi Robenbach

Taxation
Professor Itzhac Hadari

Litigation
Yuval Grayevsky, Haim Stern

Environmental matters
Sara Shalom

Banking
Lisa Tross, Yehuda Raveh

Privatisation of government
Yehuda Raveh

Hotels
Carmit Bar-On

DR ZEEV HOLENDER LAW OFFICES

40 MONTEFIORE STREET
TEL AVIV 65201

Telephone: +972 3 566 5005
Fax: +972 3 566 5015
E-mail: holender@holender.co.il

Languages
Dutch, English, French, Hebrew, Spanish

Other offices
Amsterdam, Budapest

Number of lawyers 6

CATEGORIES OF WORK

Corporate and commercial

National and international taxation

National and international tax planning

Capital markets and securities

Public offerings

Private placements

Technology and venture capital

International commercial transactions

Real estate

Oil and gas

Communication and film production

Arbitration and mediation

Mergers and acquisitions

Litigation

YIGAL ARNON & CO

ADVOCATES AND NOTARY

1 AZRIELI CENTER
PO BOX 33777
TEL AVIV 67021

Telephone: +972 3 608 7777
Fax: +972 3 608 7724
E-mail: info@arnon.co.il
Website: www.arnon.co.il

Languages
English, French, Hebrew

Other offices
Jerusalem

Number of lawyers 79
at this office 54

CATEGORIES OF WORK

Antitrust and competition
Ronit Amir Yaniv

Banking and financial services
Amnon Lorch, Shiri Shaham

Bankruptcy and creditors' rights
Dror Vigdor, Doron Tamir

Corporate finance
David Schapiro, Orly Tsioni

Emerging growth companies
Barak Platt, Gil Oren, Orly Tsioni

IP and corporate partnering
Barry Levenfeld

Labour law, executive compensation and employment benefits
Hagai Shmueli, Ben Sandler

Life sciences
Barry Levenfeld, Barak Platt

Litigation
Yigal Arnon, Dror Vigdor, Barak Tal

Mergers and acquisitions
Barry Levenfeld, David Schapiro

Project finance
David Schapiro, Doron Tamir

Public tenders
Amnon Lorch, Doron Tamir

Real estate and development
Rami Kook, Amalia Meshi

Securities
David Schapiro, Shiri Shaham

Tax
Harry Kirsh

Telecommunications
Gil Oren, David Osborne

Venture capital
Barry Levenfeld, Barak Platt

THE FIRM

Yigal Arnon & Co is one of Israel's largest and most dynamic law firms. It provides a full spectrum of legal services to a wide-ranging client base. Clients seek out Yigal Arnon & Co when looking for professionalism, service and integrity to resolve complex and challenging problems.

Clients choose the firm for its good business judgment, a multi-disciplinary legal approach and a thorough understanding of the clients' objectives. A reputation for achieving timely and positive results has attracted high-profile clients, demanding cases and exceptional lawyers.

AREAS OF PRACTICE

Antitrust and competition: provides antitrust counselling and litigation services encompassing monopolies, strategic alliances, exclusive commercial relationships and M&A.

Banking and finance: represents Israeli and overseas commercial banks, investment banks and stock exchanges in: obtaining licences for local operations; banking and money laundering regulations; complex derivatives, securitisation; stock lending and hedging.

Bankruptcy and creditors' rights: represents troubled companies and creditors, receivers and liquidators of major enterprises in connection with creation and enforcement of security interests, debt restructuring, loan syndications, reorganisations and liquidation proceedings.

Corporate finance: one of the largest corporate finance practices in Israel negotiates private placement, venture capital and debt financing; domestic and international strategic alliances, joint ventures and other corporate partnering arrangements; public offerings and M&A.

Emerging growth companies: specialises in representation from before creation through and beyond their public offering or acquisition.

IP and corporate partnering: extensive experience in proprietary asset exploitation, strategic partnerships, technology transfer, manufacturing, distribution and marketing, with particular expertise in software, e-commerce, telecommunications, semiconductors and biotechnology.

Labour law: provides tax and regulatory advice regarding private and public company employee option and stock purchase plans; also handles labour and employment matters, including executive employment.

Life sciences: works with international and domestic companies including biotechnology, pharmaceutical, bioinformatics, medical devices and healthcare service companies; universities and academic centres.

Litigation: one of the foremost litigation practices in Israel, represents clients in complex and high-profile litigation: commercial litigation, white-collar crime, class action defence; unfair competition, environmental matters, employment issues; real estate, banking and insurance cases.

M&A: has assisted domestic and overseas companies in many of the country's largest, most significant and most complex transactions.

Project finance and public tenders: represents Israeli and overseas companies and financial institutions in infrastructure, electricity generation, semiconductor manufacture, roads, railways, waterworks and waste management projects on BOT and more traditional bases.

Real estate and development: assists major Israeli and international construction companies, financial institutions, real estate developers and individual entrepreneurs active in various projects: commercial, industrial, office, shopping centre, hotel, resort, residential and mixed-use real estate.

Securities: assists clients in listings and in over 100 public offerings in the US and Europe for the issuer, underwriter or key selling shareholders.

Tax: covers the Israeli tax aspects of financial instruments, transfer pricing for international groups, technology transfer, M&A, venture funds, employee stock options, and tax planning for high-net-worth individuals.

Telecoms: clients includes cable television companies, internet providers, global fibre infrastructure companies, telecom equipment manufacturers and internet (voiceover IP) telephony companies; also assists in securing broadcast licences, establishing program distribution, determining rate regulations and preparing fixed-line and wireless access permits.

Venture capital: represents many prominent Israeli and overseas venture capital funds; deals in fund formation and has assisted funds in hundreds of portfolio investments.

YUVAL LEVY & CO

YUVAL LEVY HOUSE
8 NESS ZIONA ST
TEL AVIV 63904

Telephone: +972 3 517 2303
Fax: +972 3 516 4185
E-mail: office@yuvalaw.co.il
Website: www.yuvalaw.co.il

Languages
English, Hebrew

Number of lawyers 18

Member
Legal Network International
(an association of independent law firms);
Counselex Global Ltd

CATEGORIES OF WORK

Corporate
Prof Yuval Levy, Opher Levy

Commercial litigation
Prof Yuval Levy, Yechiel Kasher

Commercial
Tamar Krongrad, Ohad Maymon

Intellectual property
Prof Yuval Levy, Nir Kehat

International transactions
Tamar Krongrad, Ohad Maymon

Antitrust and unfair competition
Opher Levy, Yechiel Kasher

Mergers and acquisitions
Opher Levy, Tamar Krongrad

Environmental law
Idit Reiter, Yigal Borochovsky

Criminal litigation
Prof Yuval Levy, Livnat Kalina

Banking
Prof Yuval Levy, Ohad Maymon

Securities
Opher Levy, Tamar Krongrad

Arbitration
Yechiel Kasher, Nir Kehat

Reorganisation and insolvency
Yechiel Kasher, Yigal Borochovsky

Financing
Opher Levy, Tamar Krongrad

Real property
Opher Levy, Yuval Bracha

THE FIRM

Prof Yuval Levy founded the firm of Yuval Levy & Co in 1973, having been a partner in one of Israel's top law firms specialising in commercial, maritime and international law. Since its establishment, the firm has expanded in size and fields of practice, and now comprises 18 attorneys (seven partners and 11 associates). The professional staff hold degrees from top-ranking Israeli and American universities, and many of the attorneys graduated with honours, hold graduate degrees, have served as teaching assistants, or have otherwise excelled, and are recognised, in their fields.

The firm represents a myriad of domestic and international clients, and enjoys a strong reputation in antitrust and intellectual property litigation, commercial litigation, the credit card industry, environmental law, securities law, hi-tech, mergers and acquisitions, corporate and transactional law, and financing. As the sole Israeli member of the Legal Network International (an association of 40 independent law firms strategically located in more than 25 countries worldwide) Yuval Levy & Co provides worldwide representation to its clients in key geographic markets where and when needed, utilising lawyers uniquely qualified and positioned to assist in all aspects of international and foreign law.

The firm's partners have been recognised consistently in the last few years by Dun & Bradstreet, and are regularly cited in Israeli media and professional publications regarding their fields of expertise.

AREAS OF PRACTICE

Commercial litigation: the firm's litigation spans a wide variety of areas of law, particularly antitrust, environmental law, intellectual property, and commercial disputes. The firm's members appear in all court and administrative forums in Israel, as well as arbitrational forums, and have represented inter alia, major Israeli financial institutions and worldwide corporate entities. Members of the firm have appeared before the Supreme Court of Israel in numerous claims. Particularly noteworthy is this firm's extensive representation of clients before the Commissioner.

Corporate law and financing: Yuval Levy & Co provides legal counsel to leading banking and financial institutions in Israel, and serves as general counsel to Leumi Card Ltd, the credit card subsidiary of Bank Leumi le-Israel. The firm specialises in the reorganisation of existing corporate entities, and in negotiations for mergers, purchases and sales of companies, partnerships and joint ventures of various types, and has advised both lenders and lendees on international financing projects from overseas.

Technology: as part of its ongoing representation of corporate entities, Yuval Levy & Co focuses on IP protection, licensing arrangements, and research and development projects. The firm's members have extensive experience in negotiating and drafting computer hardware and software agreements, as well as technology transfer agreements. Yuval Levy & Co provides ongoing services regarding marketing agreements of various types (distributorships, agencies and OEM agreements).

Real estate: the firm has a thriving property practice, with its reputation steadily growing in 'start-to-finish' representation of property entrepreneurs in large projects throughout the country – the building of malls, hotels, and residential and commercial properties. The litigation aspect of the firm's property practice touches on contractual aspects (disputes between purchasers and sellers, as well as those between entrepreneurs and tenants) and criminal ones (regarding violations of urban planning laws). The firm has had significant 'wins' in the field of urban planning.

Environmental law: the firm provides legal counselling in a wide range of environmental aspects including regulatory and compliance services.

Bankruptcy and liquidation: members of the firm have served, and continue to serve, as liquidators/receivers of private and public companies. The firm has waged legal battles on behalf of clients in connection with liquidation and bankruptcy proceedings and have handled numerous and extensive litigation dealings with companies in liquidation.

Additional information can be obtained from www.yuvalaw.co.il.

ZELLERMAYER, PELOSSOF & CO., ADVOCATES

THE RUBINSTEIN HOUSE
20 LINCOLN STREET
TEL AVIV 67134

Telephone: +972 3 625 5555
Fax: +972 3 625 5500
E-mail: general@zelpel.com
Website: www.zelpel.com

Languages
English, French, German, Hebrew, Spanish

Number of lawyers 45

Contacts
Michael Zellermayer, Avi D Pelossof, Eli Mei-Tal, Guy Tsafrir, Guy Even-Ezra, Helit Ben-Israel, Dr Avraham Ortal, Mimi Zemah, Ofer Shapira

CATEGORIES OF WORK

Corporate and commercial law

Mergers and acquisitions, joint ventures

Banking and corporate financing

Securities and capital markets

Tax law

Telecommunications

Energy and infrastructure

Licensing and technology transfer

Labour law

Litigation

Real estate and zoning

Environmental law

Bankruptcy and liquidation

THE FIRM

Zellermayer, Pelossof & Co. was founded in 1984 by Michael Zellermayer (chairman). Until 1988, he was a leading partner at a New York firm. He handled more than 100 leveraged buy-outs in the 1980s, has extensive experience in M&As, and specialises in all forms of corporate finance. He has been deeply involved in the telecoms market, including representing the successful bidder for the second cellular licence, handling the country's two largest telecoms acquisitions, and representing several multinationals in their Israeli operations. Managing partner Avi D Pelossof joined the firm in 1986. He has extensive industry experience, having served as the CEO of Israel's largest food manufacturer (Elite), chairman of Haifa Chemicals and the Tel Aviv Stock Exchange, a director of Israel Aircraft Industries, and has advised the Industrialists Association. Most of the firm's lawyers have international experience, and most of the firm's clients and activities are international.

AREAS OF PRACTICE

The firm specialises in all spheres of business law, in particular corporate and securities, administrative, licensing, tax, real estate, labour, telecoms, and environmental laws; as well as in commercial litigation. Its broad expertise allows the firm's lawyers to provide full legal support in an array of advanced business activities, in Israel and worldwide. The firm's clients, being a multitude of nationalities, cover a broad range of industrial, finance, technology and energy businesses, governmental and private.

M&As: a full range of transactional experience covers all deal aspects from negotiations and tax planning, to handling antitrust and other regulatory matters, performing due diligence, covering securities issues, as well as IP, labour relations, and real estate. This enables the firm to be regularly involved in some of the largest transactions in the country, such as representation of: the winning consortium in the government bid for the privatisation of Bezeq – The Israel Telecommunication Corp Ltd, one of the country's largest privatisations ever.

Telecoms: in addition to its presence in the M&A field, the firm advises and represents major telecoms/datacom service and equipment companies in their ongoing affairs, such as regulatory and government matters, infrastructure, real estate, financing, labour, and participates in legislative advisory committees.

Technology: represents several US VC funds in the establishment of their Israeli companies and represents numerous fast-growing hi-tech companies, thus forming a meeting point for entrepreneurs and institutional investors. The firm has advised on major technology privatisation projects, including the Ministry of Defence's Armament Development Authority (Rafael), Israel Aircraft Industries and the Government Biological Institute.

Banking and capital markets: advises major investment banks and financial institutions, from underwriting and project financing to speciality products and retail. The firm has advised on numerous public offerings of Israeli companies in the US and European equity markets.

Project financing and government bids: experience includes representing consortia in bidding for government franchises in communications, for BOT infrastructure projects and others, such as the representation of a consortium of banks and financial sponsors in the leveraged acquisition of one of the world's largest BOPP manufacturers. The firm represented the winning bidder in the government's bid for the sale of Bezeq and in the negotiations for the financing of such bid.

Gas and energy: experience includes representing several gas exploration, development and distribution ventures, including the owners of the current largest natural gas reserves in Israel, as well as the country's cement monopoly, and IPP projects.

Environmental: representation of Israeli and multinational companies in transactions related to environmental solutions, and the adjustment of the activities of senior Israeli organisations to the new environmental laws.

ITALY

Population	**58.1 million**
Number of lawyers	**148,000**
Professional title	**Avvocato**
Currency	**Euro (€)**

Index

The Kingdom of Italy, declared in 1861, was replaced in 1946 by a Democratic Republic. Italy's young-nation status is often felt in the strength of regional over national ties yet the country has been at the forefront of Europe: a charter member of the EEC and signatory to the 1999 Economic and Monetary Union.

Italy is the world's seventh-largest economy and possesses diversified industry, sharing approximately the same total and per capita output as France and the UK. Small and medium-sized family businesses excel in the processing and manufacturing of high-quality design goods while the major industries are precision machinery, motor vehicles, chemicals, pharmaceuticals, textiles and clothing. Manufacturing accounts for about 25% of GDP and approximately 90% of merchandise exports, yet most raw materials, and more than 75% of energy requirements, are imported. This market economy remains split between a developed industrial north, dominated by private companies, and a less advanced, welfare-dependent agricultural south with 20% unemployment.

For the past decade, Italy has pursued tight fiscal policies in order to meet EU requirements and has benefited from lower interest and inflation rates. The current government has enacted reforms to fuel competitiveness and long-term growth but because of the general economic slowdown and union opposition, Italy has moved sluggishly to implement structural reforms of its tax burden, rigid labour market and generous pension system. It has breached the 3% EU deficit ceiling and public debt stands at 108% of GDP.

In addition, the Republic is not without socio-economic problems: high unemployment, euro dissatisfaction, illegal immigration, fear of terrorism and organised crime.

Times remain politically turbulent. Domenico Siniscalco, the Italian Finance Minister, resigned over a scandal involving the Bank of Italy and the Prime Minister, Silvio Berlusconi, is regularly judicially investigated for corruption. His House of Freedoms coalition comprises the Forza Italia party, the conservative National Alliance, the moderate Union of Christian Democrats and the populist Northern League. Issues dividing them are electoral system changes, the budget and Mr Berlusconi's leadership. National elections loom in April 2006. Meanwhile, the government has passed a bill redefining the constitution, strengthening the prime minister's authority, reducing the head of state's powers and conferring more autonomy on the nation's 20 regions over education, healthcare and law and order. Southern politicians fear that their access to state financial resources will be restricted but a referendum to uphold the bill's passage into law is expected to take place after the 2006 election.

The northeast of Italy is a particularly vibrant region. Padua, in the Veneto region, is an important commercial centre with a strong hi-tech sector specialising in electronics, fibre optics, pharmaceuticals and chemicals. Vicenza, Verona and Treviso are also crucial to the region's economy and have prospered from its development.

To the west, Milan is Italy's primary business centre. Most leading commercial law firms have a presence here. Still further west, Turin is thriving, its rapidly expanding textiles and telecoms industries reducing the city's historic dependence on Fiat. Turin's hosting of the 2006 Winter Olympics has improved local infrastructure and communications.

Nearby in Liguria, Genoa, a major commercial port, leads the country in shipping and insurance and is developing booming electronics and communications sectors. Bologna and Florence, the central-north's other major commercial centres, are also flourishing business cities.

Rome is the country's second commercial and legal centre. It houses the government, the Supreme Court and the competition authorities, and is fundamental to administrative, antitrust and litigation lawyers. Most leading law firms maintain an office in Rome.

South of the capital, the disparity between the richer industrial north and the rural south is apparent. Agriculture and tourism remain the main sources of income, although the EU has poured money into southern Italy to bring its technology and telecoms industries in line with the north. Naples is an important shipping hub yet trails behind Genoa as Italy's maritime centre and remains a target for organised crime. Along with reducing the budget deficit and reforming Italy's pension system (state pensions account for 15% of GDP), boosting commercial activity in the south remains a priority for the government.

BILLING

The method for calculating charge-out rates depends on the practice area. For commercial legal advice in private equity, finance and real estate, a fee of between 0.5% and 3.0% of the transaction

The largest firms

1	Gianni, Origoni, Grippo & Partners	312
2	EY Law	275
3	Bonelli Erede Pappalardo	243
4	Chiomenti Studio Legale	193
5	Tonucci, Studio Legale	183
6	Allen & Overy - Studio Legale Associato	163
7	Clifford Chance	149
8	NCTM - Studio Legale Associato	140
9	Freshfields Bruckhaus Deringer	124
10	Professionale Associato a Baker & McKenzie, Studio	112
11	Sutti, Studio Legale	105
12	LexJus	100
13	Macchi di Cellere Gangemi	95
	Pavia e Ansaldo	95
15	Lawfed - Rubino-Sammartano e Associati	89
16	Simmons & Simmons	78
17	Pirola Pennuto Zei & Associati	75
	Ughi e Nunziante	75
19	Agnoli Bernardi e Associati	73
20	Hammonds Rossotto	71
21	d'Urso Munari Gatti, Studio Legale Associato	66
22	Carnelutti Studio Legale Associato	65
23	Lovells	62
24	CMS Adonnino Ascoli & Cavasola Scamoni	60
	Pedersoli e Associati	60
26	Nunziante Magrone	56
27	De Berti Jacchia Franchini Forlani	55

These figures represent the total number of lawyers in this country only, and have been supplied by the firms themselves. The figures should be accurate as at 1 January 2006.

value is usually charged. This figure varies according to the firm instructed and the nature and complexity of the work. Competition for work is fierce and firms are often willing to be flexible on fees. Clients are increasingly sophisticated, sometimes opting for capped bills, caring less about how the work is done or how much time is incurred and more about results at competitive prices.

Hourly rates are allowed for contentious work. Senior partners may bill between €500 and €600 per hour while junior partners levy rates of between €200 and €350 per hour and mid-level associates are charged out at between €100 and €200 per hour. International firms charge substantially more than mid-sized corporate firms and, as with transactional work, costs increase for more complex matters.

MARKETING

Marketing is a relatively recent concept to the Italian legal system, the professional advertising code only amended in 1999. Lawyers may provide information regarding their firms, including areas of specialisation and conference participation, via legal directories, brochures and the internet but the Bar Council's ethical code prevents direct advertising and public comment. Recently, Italy's national Bar agreed to review its blanket ban on advertising and client disclosure after sustained pressure from ASLA, set up in 2004 to represent the country's commercial law firms. Nonetheless, traditional sole practitioners prefer to rely on personal contact and word-of-mouth referrals. Most firms, reluctant to invest in public relations, remain without marketing strategies. However, owing to the same economic factors that led to more competitive fees, the business development plans of Anglo-Saxon counterparts are being studied by large Italian firms.

IN-HOUSE LAWYERS

Senior Italian lawyers often wear several hats. Noted commercial practicioners sometimes work as professors, politicians or directors of companies belonging to corporate clients. However, following the Parmalat and Cirio scandals, corporate governance has been scrutinised and regulatory reforms introduced along the transparent lines of Sarbanes-Oxley in the US.

LEGAL PROFESSION

The majority of firms remain in the hands of sole practitioners or small family-run practices, where lawyers are generalists without specific areas of expertise. Conversely, numerous boutiques, led by university professors, offer academic yet commercialised advice, often in tax, intellectual property and dispute resolution.

In response to client demand and the presence of international firms, larger commercial law practices, predominantly in Milan or Rome, are taking note of Anglo-Saxon models and expanding. Clients are benefiting from specialised partners and their back-up teams, resulting in a faster, more efficient service, while younger lawyers are enticed by the more equitable remuneration of the international partnerships.

LEGAL MARKET

It has been a turbulent year of lateral hires, team defections and splits. The international firms are here to stay but not necessarily in happy fusion with Italian practices. US and UK partnerships are keen to tap into the domestic clients to which Italian lawyers have access, increasingly appointing Italians as managing partners, and Italian firms are lured by international networks and cross-border transactions. Expectations on both sides are sometimes disappointed. Senior associates and junior partners may welcome international lockstep systems and the chance to be 'managed' within a structure whose ethos and career path suits them, but others opt to found new Italian practices when their previously independent firms merge.

The up-shot is constant movement that, in turn, fuels change. Italian lawyers are also shifting allegiances between UK and US firms. Fear of mass defections by local lawyers is making even staunchly traditional firms consider new management systems. Founding Italian partners are resistant to change yet feel compelled to tackle the issue of succession to ensure that their firms last beyond their retirement.

US firms continue to make their presence felt. 'Global but local' **Cleary, Gottlieb, Steen & Hamilton LLP** is reaping the rewards of hiring rainmaker Roberto Casati from **Allen & Overy – Studio Legale Associato** and has recently opened in Turin. **Orrick, Herrington & Sutcliffe** boosted its administrative and construction law departments by recruiting Guido Bardelli and Maria Alessandra Bazzani from **Studio Legale Tributario in Association with Ernst & Young** and project finance experts Claudio Guccione and Domenico Galli from the same source. **Jones Day** appointed Marco Lombardi as its first Italian partner-in-charge.

English firm **Bird & Bird** opened its second Italian office in Rome, assisted by antitrust and communications lawyer Eutimio Monaco and litigator Osvaldo Lombardi, recruited from **Ughi e Nunziante**. **Freshfields Bruckhaus Deringer**'s Philip Richards returned to London and Bruno Castellini now heads Milan. Luigi Chessa, former co-managing partner at **Clifford Chance** rejoined after a two-year absence. **Lovells** strengthened its corporate practice in Rome by welcoming Antonio di Pasquale and a three-strong team from **Pavia e Ansaldo**, while **Ashurst** hired respected **Allen & Overy – Studio Legale Associato** project finance partner Franco Vigliano and three associates for its Milan office.

Some Italian firms are also benefiting from market volatility. **NCTM – Studio Legale Associato** hired Giuliano Berruti from **Pavia e Ansaldo** to its administrative law department and Corrado Verna joined the banking team from **Studio Legale Tributario in Association with Ernst & Young. DLA Piper Rudnick Gray Cary** recruited banking partner Francesco Squerzoni from **Freshfields Bruckhaus Deringer**, labour partner Ciaudio Morpurgo from **Vita Samory, Fabbrini e Associati** and Giulio Azzanretto from **Macchi Di Cellere Gangemi**. Gian Luca Rabitti defected from **Clifford Chance** to **Chiomenti Studio Legale**, while corporate partner Marco Frazzica switched from **CMS Adonnino Ascoli & Cavasola Scamoni** to **De Berti Jacchia Franchini Forlani. Pedersoli e Associati** was busy recruiting at all levels. Litigation partner Andrea Magliani and six professionals joined from *Magliani e Associati*, M&A and private equity specialist Enrico Zattoni arrived from former *Morano e Associati* and Alfredo Malguzzi and Giovanni Bandera were hired to found a new tax department.

The market was shocked by another series of high-profile splits. In October, *McDermott Will & Emery/Carnelutti* de-merged and **Carnelutti Studio Legale Associato**'s fifty-strong Milan team returned to independence. Banking and corporate lawyers Massimo Trentino and Filippo Mazza stayed in Rome with **McDermott Will & Emery Studio Legale Associato** alongside eight other lawyers.

Late in 2005, half of **Pavia e Ansaldo** left to create seventy-fee-earner **Agnoli Bernardi e Associati**, led by Maurizio Bernardi and Marcello Agnoli at the same Milan address with branches in Rome, Turin and Padua. **Studio Legale Associato a White & Case** endured a difficult year. A six-lawyer team left the firm for **Varrenti, Bassan, Lenzi e Associati Studio Legale e Tributario**. Executive partner Alberto Morano also departed, being replaced by New York partner Sean Geary less than a year after *Morano & Associati* was acquired. In addition, the nine-lawyer Rome branch was closed to concentrate on the banking and commercial work stemming from Milan, and the Turin office split off to form a standalone, eight-lawyer practice, headed by Gianpiero Basso.

Studio Santa Maria ended its exclusive alliance with UK partner **Berwin Leighton Paisner LLP** but the pair remain non-exclusive allies for referral purposes. **Norton Rose** suffered a blow when managing partner, Roberto Cornetta, left to set up the Milan office of international firm **Paul, Hastings, Janofsky & Walker (Europe) LLP**.

The year did not pass without new merger announcements or office openings. **PGL – Puopolo Geffers Luise & Associati** hooked up with *Studio Legale lacobelli* to form **PGRB – Puopolo Geffers Rosen & Bosin** with offices in Milan, Rome and Naples. **Bonelli Erede Pappalardo** acquired Milanese practice *Studio Sica*, taking on 20 administrative lawyers, and international firm **SJ Berwin** opened in Milan and Turin, hiring the above-mentioned Alberto Morano to focus on the buy-out and acquisition finance sectors.

BANKING, FINANCE AND CAPITAL MARKETS

The market has been relatively slow, reflecting global economic trends and exacerbated by Italy's specific economic and political problems. Inward investment has been deterred by corruption and protectionism fears as evidenced by the BNL and Banca Antonveneta cases. However, the PPP and project finance sectors have been active, especially in healthcare.

Allen & Overy – Studio Legale Associato's strength in banking, finance and capital markets remains unchallenged. The ICM department had an exceptional year, advising BNP Paribas and Mediobanca as joint global co-ordinators on the IPO of Aeroporto di Venezia Marco Polo SpA-SAVE and represented Barclays Capital, Merrill Lynch and UBS on the Republic of Argentina's US$81bn debt exchange offer. Notwithstanding Andrea Arosio's 2005 departure, the banking team has been busy, acting for ABN Amro Bank NV, Deutsche Bank AG London and Banca Intesa as mandated lead arrangers of €9bn senior liens and credit facilities in support of Weather Investments SA's high-profile bid for Wind Telcommunicazioni SpA. Merrill Lynch, Banca Popolare di Lodi Scarl and Unicredit Banca Mobiliare SpA are securitisation clients. The firm has offices in Milan, Rome, Padua and Turin.

Fifty-three-partner **Bonelli Erede Pappalardo** has offices in Milan, Rome, Genoa, Brussels and London. Amongst a plethora of impressive deals the banking, finance and capital markets team advised Autogrill SpA on a €500m financing, and the EBRD on the issue and listing of €150m callable bonds that are linked to CMS rates. The firm operates ' non-exclusive, best-friends' links with **Bredin Prat** in France, **Slaughter and May** in the UK, **Uría Menéndez** in Spain and **Hengeler Mueller** in Germany.

Outstanding Giorgio Cappelli leads the eight-partner banking and finance team at 38-partner **Chiomenti Studio Legale**, while Enrico Giordano and Manfredi Vianini Tolomei advise on capital markets and securitisation. The strategic alliance with **Skadden, Arps, Slate, Meagher & Flom LLP**, aimed at combining respective strengths in US, Italian and English law, remains in place. In 2005, the firm was involved in the Alitalia restructuring and assisted numerous foreign banks in connection with Parmalat affairs.

Clifford Chance's finance and capital markets team comprises 15 partners. The banking and projects group, led by the widely respected trio of Charles Adams, Giuseppe De Palma and Massimo Novo, is known for its leveraged acquisition and project finance work. This team acted for Banca Intesa as lead arranger on a €400m Sicily power project and for Société Générale on the acquisition financing for Necta Vending Group as well as representing Banca IMI in connection with the €1.2bn financing to Weather for the Wind Telecommunicazioni acquisition. In debt and equity capital markets Filippo Emanuele was involved in the Marr and Italease IPOs, while the securitisation department worked on top-end deals such as the €4.37bn SCIP II restructuring. Silvio Riolo and Michele Crisostomo have been active in structured finance, particularly in derivatives, assisting JP Morgan as underwriter of a disposal of a €2.1bn interest in Mediaset. Capital markets partner Franco Grilli is praised for 'combining very good local advice and knowledge with an international feel' and the firm is commended generally for its 'securitisation

BANKING, FINANCE AND CAPITAL MARKETS

ALLEN & OVERY – STUDIO LEGALE ASSOCIATO ✪
BONELLI EREDE PAPPALARDO
CHIOMENTI STUDIO LEGALE ✪
CLIFFORD CHANCE
GIANNI, ORIGONI, GRIPPO & PARTNERS ✪

ASHURST ✪
CLEARY, GOTTLIEB, STEEN & HAMILTON LLP ✪
FRESHFIELDS BRUCKHAUS DERINGER
LINKLATERS ✪
NCTM – STUDIO LEGALE ASSOCIATO ✪
SIMMONS & SIMMONS ✪

Dewey Ballantine Studio Legale ✪
Giliberti Pappalettera Triscornia e Associati ✪
Grimaldi e Associati
Loiacono e Associati ✪
Lovells ✪
Macchi di Cellere Gangemi ✪
Norton Rose
Orrick, Herrington & Sutcliffe ✪
Pedersoli e Associati ✪
Tonucci, Studio Legale ✪
Vita Samory, Fabbrini e Associati ✪

Beltramo, Studio Legale
Bird & Bird ✪
CMS Adonnino Ascoli & Cavasola Scamoni ✪
DLA Piper Rudnick Gray Cary ✪
Delfino e Associati, Willkie Farr & Gallagher LLP, Studio Legale ✪
Galgano ✪
Jones Day ✪
McDermott Will & Emery Studio Legale Associato ✪
PGRB – Puopolo Geffers Rosen & Bosin ✪
Pavia e Ansaldo
Ughi e Nunziante ✪

Firms are listed A-Z in tiers which are ranked in order of priority
✪ *Indicates firm displays contact details at the end of this chapter.*

know-how, prompt and comprehensive assistance' as well as having the 'crtitical mass to conduct large and complex transactions'.

Gianni, Origoni, Grippo & Partners' Alberto Giampieri leads 34 banking and finance lawyers who are spread between Rome, Milan and London, while Antonio Segni is in charge of a 31-strong capital markets team. The firm assisted Credit Suisse, BNP Paribas, Deutsche Bank, Nomura and Hypo-und Vereinsbank on a €4.9bn financing and represented Merrill Lynch and Fortress in connection with NPLs. In debt capital markets the firm acted for Telecom Italia Capital SA and Capitalia on Luxemburg Stock Exchange placements, while in equity capital markets the department advised Banca Caboto and MCC Capitalia on the offering of units in a €750m real estate fund. Massimo Desiderio recently joined the banking team.

Ashurst managing partner Riccardo Agostinelli specialises in structured finance, banking and debt restructuring. The firm advised insurance company Fondiaria-SAI SpA on the issue of performance bonds relating to the €2.5bn Santa Giulia development project and Mediobanca–Banca di Credito Finanziario SpA on the €3.3bn financing payable for Transalpina di Energia Srl's acquisition of Edison.

Six partners make up the Milan and Rome offices of **Cleary, Gottlieb, Steen & Hamilton LLP** whose banking team acts on global offerings for Italian issuers and advises multinational companies offering securities to Italian Investors. Michael Volkovitsch focuses on corporate finance and securities, and Giuseppe Scasselati-Sforzolini on capital markets. The firm was international counsel to Enel SpA in connection with the Italian Ministry of Economy and Finance's sale of 28% of Enel's share capital and is ongoing counsel to DeRigo SpA who want to be the first Italian issuer to de-list from the New York Stock Exchange and to the Republic of Argentina in relation to its external debt restructuring. One client commends the firm for its expertise in interpreting US law and corporate governance to the benefit of Italian corporations.

Freshfields Bruckhaus Deringer's Enrico Castellani looks after banking and finance, while Bruno Castellini and Carlo Kostka run the securities side to the equity capital markets team. The firm acted for a pool of lenders in connection with the €4.9bn secured financing for the acquisition of shares in Banca Antonveneta and advised Deustche Bank in relation to Alitalia's restructuring. In debt capital markets, this group represented Unicredit Banca Mobiliare, ABN Amro and Euro Capital Structures as arrangers on a €1bn securitisation of car loans. Sixteen lawyers, led by Franco Campomori, look after project finance, assisting infrastructure sponsors and financiers. In 2005, the projects team represented Siemens AG in connection with the Rome metro Line C extension and Interbanca on its financing of a waste-to-energy power plant in southern Italy.

Despite its small size **Linklaters** continues to attract high-level instructions. Milan-based partner Sarosh Mewawalla advised the mandated lead arrangers on the €5bn financing of BNL, and DEPFA Bank on the innovative financing of a PPP relating to the A3 motorway extension from Salerno to Reggio Calabria. In capital markets, Luigi Sensi represented Deutsche Bank and Unicredit Banca Mobiliare SpA in Fastweb SpA's €800m global offering, as well as Merrill Lynch International and Banca IMI SpA on the IPO of food service distributor Marr SpA.

Alberto Toffoletto and Stefano Padovani of **NCTM – Studio Legale Associato** are known for their bank-related regulatory advice in relation to Consob and Banca d'Italia. The banking and finance team of the 33-partner firm focuses on bank lending, leveraged acquisition and recapitalisation financing, its core activities comprising single bank and syndicated loans, project finance and securitisation, guarantees and credit facility letters. In 2005, this department assisted De Agostini SpA and Toro Assicurazioni SpA on the €700m global offering of Toro Assicurazioni shares and Royal Bank of Scotland, Unicredit Banca D'Impresa, Cassa di Risparmio di Lucca and Unicredit Banca Mobiliare on a €245m land loan.

Marco Franzini and Nino Lombardo look after banking matters at 15-partner **Simmons & Simmons**. Regular client Unicredit Banca d'Impresa was assisted on a €50m staple financing for the Bluvacanze acquisition. In debt capital markets and securitisation the firm has been exceptionally active. Rome-based Filippo Pingue acted on a €640m healthcare receivables transaction in the region of Lazio for Banca Intesa SpA and advised Nomura on the issue of the first public asset-backed zero coupon note in Italy. Managing partner Richard Slater and Andrea Cristaudi, the latter recruited to the Milan office from **Allen & Overy – Studio Legale Associato**, look after financial services and have expanded their client base to first-tier domestic institutions like Banca Fideuram and Scottish Widows.

Dewey Ballantine Studio Legale has made huge inroads into the banking and finance scene. The firm acted for Weather on the acquisition financing of Wind, Italy's third-largest telecommunications operator and the €10bn debt refinancing linked to the M&A deal. The department has a dynamic three-pronged approach to transactions, making use of Bruno Gattai in Milan, Stefano Speroni in Rome and Ugo Giordano in London. The team also assisted Efibanca SpA on a €160m debt restructuring issue.

Giliberti Pappalettera Triscornia e Associati has expertise in complex corporate and structured finance transactions. The firm advised Seat Pagine Gialle SpA on a €2.6bn refinancing with Royal Bank of Scotland and Impregilo in the restructuring of €800m of debt. Enrico Giliberti, Carlo Pappalettera and Alessandro Triscornia are highly recommended for their professionalism, preparation, and ability to meet deadlines. One client confirms that he is 'fully satisfied with their performance' and that 'I found them very competent and supporting'. Other clients include Investitori Associati, Permira, Ferretti SpA and the CIR Group.

Grimaldi e Associati's banking and finance group is led by partners Vittorio Grimaldi and Francesco Novelli, both highly respected for their privatisation and capital markets work. Of interest, the department advised the ordinary members of Cirio in relation to the company structure divestment procedure. Giovanni Ragnoni Bosco Lucarelli was recently hired from **Freshfields Bruckhaus Deringer** with a view to expanding the firm's structured finance capabilities.

In response to client demand, three-partner **Loiacono e Associati** recently opened a London office. Managing Partner and ex-investment banker Dario Loiacono, together with Marina Jaudenes, advise numerous Italian banking and industrial clients on the development of technically challenging financial products as well as disgruntled investors like BPI when seeking indemnity for CDO losses. The firm is counsel to the Italian Stock Exchange. Merrill Lynch, Bear Stearns and Calyon rank as clients.

Andrew Welbourn heads banking and finance at **Lovells**. The practice had a strong year in projects, having advised Astaldi SpA's sponsor consortium on the landmark €250m Mestre Hospital financing which is expected to pave the way for further deals in the PPP sector. In acquisition finance the department acted for Dresdner Kleinwort Wasserstein, Barclays Capital and Bayerische Hypo-und Vereinsbank on a €700m syndicated financing, and for Société Général on a €300m export credit financing. In capital markets the team represented ABN Amro Bank NV in setting up a €650m securitisation programme. One client describes the firm as being 'serious, committed and pragmatic'. Francesco Curreli recently joined as partner from **Bonelli Erede Pappalardo**.

Macchi Di Cellere Gangemi has its main offices in Rome, Milan and Bologna, with smaller branches in Verona, Treviso, Vicenza and Paris. Claudio Visco and Giuseppe Schiavello are in charge of banking, finance and capital markets. The firm advises on asset-based and structured finance, particularly in the field of real estate portfolio financing and the structuring of securitisation transactions linked to performing and non-performing mortgage loans. Several banks and financial companies wishing to open branches and subsidiaries in Italy are clients, as well as corporate entities wanting to issue shares, bonds, structured notes and warrants in Italy and abroad.

Despite **Norton Rose** losing its managing partner Roberto Cornetta to **Paul, Hastings,**

Janofsky & Walker (Europe) LLP the firm was involved in significant project finance and debt capital deals as well as syndicated financings for IPPs and airport privatisations. The firm advised ABN Amro, Banca Intesa, Banca Antonveneta and Interbanca on the €133m financing of the Mestre Hospital project, unique in being the first UK-style hospital PPP project in Italy. One client commends the lawyers' 'high degree of knowledge in the export credit field' and for being 'very quick in their responses, competitive in their cost structure and available even at short notice'. Michael Taylor receives particularly glowing reviews. Other clients listed are Fortis Bank SA/NV-Succursale in Italia, Banca Caboto SpA and IVECO SpA, a global truck manufacturing subsidiary of Fiat.

Ten-partner **Orrick, Herrington & Sutcliffe** is active in debt restructuring, bankruptcy, project and structured financings and healthcare receivables. Milan-based partner Daniela Andreatta has assisted Lehman Brothers in purchasing Parmalat debt, while Patrizio Messina in Rome is known for his securitisation, structured finance and leveraged finance work, focusing mainly on advice in cross-border and domestic asset-backed financing. The firm advised IXIS Corporate & Investment Bank and ICCREA Banca SpA as co-arrangers of mortgage loan receivables valued at €450m, and Benetton Group SpA on a €500m syndicated revolving credit facility.

The number of fee-earners at Milan firm **Pedersoli e Associati** has shot up to sixty. Its remarkable lateral hire of Andrea Arosio and his ten-strong banking team, including securitisation and derivative products expert Dario Longo, from **Allen & Overy – Studio Legale Associato** paid dividends in 2005. The firm acted for Euro Capital Structures Limited in connection with a €3bn mortgage transaction and IXIS CIB on €400m loan securitisations, while Unipol Assicurazioni SpA was assisted in its €4.96bn acquisition financing of Banca Nazionale del Lavoro SpA. Other impressive clients include Banca Intesa, BNP Paribas and Mediobanca.

Studio Legale Tonucci has offices in Rome, Milan, Florence and Padua. Livio Esposizione runs the banking and finance group while Mauro Baldisonni looks after structured finance and privatisation. The firm advised Fabbrica Immobiliare SGR in setting up a €800m property fund and Deutsche Bank AG in relation to €320m of health sector credits in Lazio.

Forty-five-lawyer **Vita Samory, Fabbrini e Associati** is based in Milan but has a smaller office in Rome. In 2005, Francesco Scassaro assisted on the listing of Caleffi as well as on the IPO of Marr, a market leader in food distribution and textiles manufacturing. Interbanca is also a client.

At Rome-based **Studio Legale Beltramo** Susanna Beltramo and eight fee-earners specialise in EMTN programmes and asset-backed floating rate notes relating to healthcare receivables. Clients comprise Banca Agrileasing SpA and Finnmeccanica SpA.

Bird & Bird has made significant investments into its banking and finance department, headed by Raimondo Maggiore. BNL Fondi Immobiliari SGRpA was recently advised in connection with real estate funds Fondo Dinamico and Fondo Umbria. Aureo Gestioni, Pioneer Investments and Stefanel SpA are further clients.

Paolo Bonolis' arrival made a difference to **CMS Adonnino Ascoli & Cavasola Scamoni**. In 2005, the firm advised one international bank on the implementation of a multi-jurisdictional cash-pooling system and assisted another client on the creation of a revolving facility security package for a ski resort development.

Federico Sutti is **DLA Piper Rudnick Gray Cary**'s regional managing partner, Elisabetta Poltronieri runs the asset finance team and new arrival Francesco Squerzoni is leading the banking and finance group. The firm acted on a mortgage loan grant for the purchase and development of a €68m commercial centre and represented CommerzBank Ag Milan Branch on the syndication of a €450m acquisition loan.

Studio Legale Delfino e Associati, Willkie Farr & Gallagher LLP has 30 attorneys working from Milan and Rome. The practice focuses on acquisition finance, capital markets and securities law. Deustche Bank, Merck and Italenergia are clients.

Francesco Galgano and Davide Contini are key banking and finance partners at boutique firm **Galgano**. Forty lawyers are spread between offices in Milan and Bologna. The firm acts on a range of asset finance projects, securitisations, debt and equity transactions, banking contracts and financial restructurings. Clients tend to be industrial corporations, banks, institutional investors and technology businesses.

Ettore Scandale is in control of asset finance, banking and capital markets at **Jones Day**. In 2005, the department represented Consult & Partners SpA in relation to the €179m funding of a stake in Autostrada Brescia-Verona-Vicenza-Padova SpA. The firm also acts for WestLB AG.

The two practices making up *McDermott Will & Emery/Carnelutti* have gone their separate ways. Highly respected banking and finance lawyers Massimo Trentino and Marco Pressi have remained in Rome at **McDermott Will & Emery Studio Legale Associato**.

Gianfranco Puopolo runs the banking and finance team at **PGRB – Puopolo Geffers Rosen & Bosin**, recently joined by Arrigo Montella, a *commercialista* and project finance specialist. The firm represented US hedge funds, Stark Investment and Cargill, on the assignment of receivables for Parmalat creditors.

Pavia e Ansaldo has had a troubled time. Half the firm left to set up **Agnoli Bernardi e Associati** but the practice retained the respected Roberto Zanchi who continues to advise on banking and corporate finance matters.

Marcello Gioscia heads the banking department at 11-partner **Ughi e Nunziante**. The firm recently acted for Banco de Bilbao Argentaria in connection with its high-profile bid for Banca Nazionale del Lavoro.

CORPORATE AND M&A
Milan and Rome

The economy has not fully recovered but the volume of M&A and private equity transactions has increased, particularly the number of IPO mandates received.

Competitors and clients alike recognise the strength of **Bonelli Erede Pappalardo**'s corporate group. Sergio Erede, Franco Bonelli, Roberto Cera and Alberto Saravalle are noted as exceptional lawyers. In 2005, the firm advised Banca Nazionale del Lavoro SpA on the €6.6bn takeover bid by Banca Bilbao Vizcaya Argentaria and Autogrill SpA on its €768m bid for Aldeasa SA, the Spanish airport operator. Further, the corporate team acted for Banca Antonveneta SpA in connection with the incredible ABN Amro takeover and worked on Morgan Stanley's behalf in the creation of a joint venture between MSREF Funds and Pirelli Real Estate & C SpA.

Chiomenti Studio Legale retains a sterling reputation in the market. The 14-partner corporate and M&A department is headed by Carlo Croff and further complemented by 58 fee-earners. In 2005, the firm advised TIM SpA in relation to Telecom SpA's €90m bid and ENEL SpA in connection with the high-profile €12.1bn acquisition of Wind Telecomunicazioni SpA, while Vittorio Tadei led Fintecna SpA in its €900m bid for Alitalia Servizi SpA. According to one client Michele Carpinelli is the 'best lawyer in Italy on certain aspects of transactional law'. Francesco Tedeschini and Franco Agopyan also receive glowing reports.

Gianni, Origoni, Grippo & Partners' department is backed by 29 partners and 100 assistants. The practice is a key player at Italian, international and cross-border level. Francesco Gianni and Filippo Troisi are known for their work on public and private M&A, joint ventures and privatisation. Alessandro Giuliani represents domestic and foreign corporations, financial institutions and private equity and venture capital funds in relation to investments, divestments and financing. Amongst a plethora of transactions, the firm assisted Cassa Depositi e Prestiti in the acquisition of a 30% stake in Terna, Credit Suisse First Boston on Unipol Assicurazioni SpA's tender offer for the ordinary shares of Banca Nazionale del Lavoro SpA and MTS SpA, the largest bond stock exchange in Europe, on the acquisition of its control by Euronext and Borsa Italiana. On the private equity side, Goldman Sachs was advised on the acquisition of Pirelli Cavi, and Efibanca SpA and Meliorbanca SpA on the acquisition by Clessidra SGR of Sisal SpA's share capital.

M&A star Roberto Casati led global practice **Cleary, Gottlieb, Steen & Hamilton LLP** in advising ABN Amro on the much-profiled €6.3bn takeover of Italian-listed banking group Banca Antonveneta. The firm has multi-jurisdictional expertise in corporate and merger transactions and works closely with its antitrust and tax departments. The firm also represented Euronext in its €245m acquisition of a controlling stake in MTS and advised AEM SpA on its €12.8bn joint acquisition of Edison SpA, Italy's second-largest energy company, and Hypo Vereinsbank AG on its €19.2bn merger with Unicredito. One client describes Giuseppe Scasselati-Sforzolini as 'outstanding' and a 'very diligent and organised lawyer, good on detail and creative'. William B McGurn also receives glowing praise.

Eleven partners direct **Clifford Chance**'s corporate group from Milan, Rome and Padua. The department had a bumper year in M&A deals and listings, acting on the Electricité de France SA takeover of Edison, and on the IPOs of IGD, Itallease and Marr. The Marzotto and Donà families were assisted on the tender and launch offer for listed Zignago ordinary shares, valued at €240m. The firm enhanced its Rome presence with corporate partner Tiziana Del Prete's arrival from **Gianni, Origoni, Grippo & Partners**.

Mario Ortu and Fabrizio Arossa are the contact partners for **Freshfields Bruckhaus Deringer**'s M&A group. Recent highlights included advising Unicredito Italiano on its takeover of Hypo Vereinsbank and Goldman Sachs Principal Investment Area on the acquisition of Pirelli Cavi e Sistemi. The corporate restructuring team has also been active, having represented a number of lenders, borrowers and financial advisers on insolvency restructurings.

Seven-partner Milan firm **Giliberti Pappalettera Triscornia e Associati** continues to expand its core business of commercial and corporate law. Highly recommended partner Alessandro Triscornia represented Finanziaria Coin Srl in the sale of a €181m stake in Gruppo Coin SpA. M&A lawyer Carlo Pappalettera is also widely respected.

NCTM – Studio Legale Associato recently advised Bridgepoint Capital on the €250m sale of its SEA Società Europea Autocaravan SpA holding. This cross-border deal was innovative in its tax structuring, being the first management leveraged buyout under the new tax rules. One client believes Paolo Montironi to be 'one of the best M&A lawyers in Italy, with fantastic technical ability', while another describes Giuliano Lanzavecchia as 'young, yet brilliant'.

Pedersoli e Associati strengthened its corporate and commercial department by hiring M&A and private equity specialist Enrico Zattoni who is developing the firm's pharmaceutical and biotechnology practice. One client expounds: 'He is very succinct and gives clear and consistent advice. He is dedicated to achieving a positive outcome for us and takes extra effort to complete projects.' Another client confirms his 'outstanding legal competence, as well as unusual ability to understand, and interact with proficiency in the commercial side of our deals'. Carlo Pedersoli advised Unipol Assicurazioni SpA on its €4.96bn acquisition of BNL SpA, while Antonio Pedersoli assisted Telecom Italia Spa on its €950m purchase of internet businesses Virgilio and Tin.it. Other established clients are Banca Intesa and BPU. Enzo Pulitanò, a corporate governance expert, is of-counsel to the firm.

Allen & Overy – Studio Legale Associato is making a stealthy recovery after losing star lawyer Roberto Casati. Paolo Cerina is head of the nine-partner corporate department that advised UBS (Italia) SpA on its acquisition of Etra SIM SpA, the Italian financial intermediary firm, and represented Morgan Stanley on the exchange offer for Hypo-Vereinsbank by Unicredit Italiano. Meanwhile, Finnmeccanica SpA was assisted on a complex multi-jurisdictional defence sector deal with BAE Systems.

Nine partners advise on M&A and corporate and commercial transactions at **Studio Professionale Associato a Baker & McKenzie**. In 2005, the firm represented LVMH on its €470m corporate restructuring and Gruppo CISA on its high-profile corporate capital sale and trade mark transfer. One client expounds: 'Its worldwide presence is unsurpassed. It has extremely good attorneys and is very efficient and responsive. It is able to handle anything we need and resolve it in a timely, competent and economical fashion. **Studio Professionale Associato a Baker & McKenzie** is unmatched in my experience in working as a team; its various departments interact extremely effectively.'

Studio Legale Delfino e Associati, Willkie Farr & Gallagher LLP has a strong reputation in M&A and private equity. Maurizio Delfino assisted Electricité de France in the €12bn joint acquisition of Edison, Italy's second-largest power group, marking the end of a four-year dispute. In addition, the firm advised Russian steel producer OAO Severstal in its purchase of a €430m stake in Lucchini SpA, a deal that is expected to mark Severstal as one of the world's top-ten steel revenue producers.

Dewey Ballantine Studio Legale has gone from strength to strength. The firm recently advised Weather Investments SA in the largest-ever leveraged buyout in Europe and private equity fund 3i on its biggest deal to date in Italy, the €115m acquisition of a stake in Giochi Preziosi, the fourth-largest toy manufacturer in the world. The practice also represents Italcementi SpA, ABN Amro and Finnmeccanica SpA. One client commends Bruno Gattai for having 'a lot of commercial sense' and for 'being very reliable and transparent on fees'.

Milan-based **Studio Legale Associato d'Urso Munari Gatti** also has offices in Rome and

CORPORATE AND M&A
Milan and Rome

BONELLI EREDE PAPPALARDO
CHIOMENTI STUDIO LEGALE ✪
GIANNI, ORIGONI, GRIPPO & PARTNERS ✪

CLEARY, GOTTLIEB, STEEN & HAMILTON LLP ✪
CLIFFORD CHANCE
FRESHFIELDS BRUCKHAUS DERINGER
GILIBERTI PAPPALETTERA TRISCORNIA E ASSOCIATI ✪
NCTM – STUDIO LEGALE ASSOCIATO ✪
PEDERSOLI E ASSOCIATI ✪

Allen & Overy – Studio Legale Associato ✪
Studio Professionale Associato a Baker & McKenzie ✪
Delfino e Associati, Willkie Farr & Gallagher LLP, Studio Legale ✪
Dewey Ballantine Studio Legale ✪
d'Urso Munari Gatti, Studio Legale Associato
Galgano ✪
Grimaldi e Associati
Lovells ✪
Macchi di Cellere Gangemi ✪
Simmons & Simmons ✪
Vita Samory, Fabbrini e Associati ✪

Ashurst ✪
CMS Adonnino Ascoli & Cavasola Scamoni ✪
Carnelutti Studio Legale Associato ✪
Curtis, Mallet-Prevost, Colt & Mosle LLP in associazione con Gilioli, Alemani, Bocchiola, Tamburini e Par ✪
DLA Piper Rudnick Gray Cary ✪
De Berti Jacchia Franchini Forlani ✪
Grande Stevens: Studio Legale Associazione Professionale
Jones Day ✪
McDermott Will & Emery Studio Legale Associato ✪
Orrick, Herrington & Sutcliffe ✪
PGRB – Puopolo Geffers Rosen & Bosin ✪
Piergrossi Bianchini Eversheds
Sutti, Studio Legale ✪
Tonucci, Studio Legale ✪
Ughi e Nunziante ✪
White & Case, Studio Legale Associato

Abbatescianni e Associati
Haarmann Hemmelrath
Lombardi Molinari e Associati ✪
Mazzoni E Associati – Verusio E Cosmelli Studi Legali Associati
Tributario, Studio Legale, in Association with Ernst & Young
Varrenti, Bassan, Lenzi e Associati Studio Legale e Tributario

---

Firms are listed A-Z in tiers which are ranked in order of priority
✪ Indicates firm displays contact details at the end of this chapter.

Bologna. The firm had an active year in M&A, closing on 11 transactions during the third quarter alone and assisting De Agostini Partecipazioni SpA in relation to the IPO of Toro Assicurazioni SpA. Other clients include Mediobanca and Lehman Brothers.

Galgano's Milan office has been involved in numerous commercial transactions such as Wabtec Corporation's acquisition of Rutger SpA and GE Equity's disinvestment from Vimercati SpA. Other clients of note are UBS, Yahoo!, Calyon and Julius Baer.

Rome-based **Grimaldi e Associati** recently advised Lucchini in connection with a sale of 62% of Lucchini SpA and acted for Taylor's HPM when the latter acquired the Sandretto Group. Partners Vittorio Grimaldi and Roberto Cappelli are well known for their advice to public and private companies.

Leah Dunlop's corporate and commercial department at **Lovells** has benefited significantly from the recent IPO revival and has been active in insolvency and corporate restructuring transactions. Advent International is a frequent private equity client for whom the firm acted in relation to the secondary buyout of Gruppo Argenta, a leading domestic vending machine operator and SABMiller, the international brewer, was assisted on its acquisition of a €162.5m stake in Birra Peroni. Major new clients include Patriarch Partners LLC and Brown Foreman, the Jack Daniels producer. Key recommended lawyers are recently hired Antonio di Pasquale and Andrea Accomero.

Macchi di Cellere Gangemi is known for corporate restructuring and commercial litigation, offering specific advice on agency and franchise contracts, outsourcing and lease agreements, transportation, joint ventures and corporate governance. Name partner Luigi Macchi di Cellere is a highly respected corporate lawyer and litigator.

Marco Franzini looks after **Simmons & Simmons**' corporate matters in Milan and commercial partner Nino Lombardo is based in Rome. The firm advised Marazzi Gruppo Ceramiche SpA on its US$103m acquisition of Welor Kerama, Russia's leading manufacturer of tiles and ceramics and GKN on its 50% shareholding sale in AgustaWestland to its JV partner, Finmeccanica, Italy's leading aerospace and defence company. Also of interest the practice worked with 3i on a range of investment transactions.

Eleven-partner **Vita Samory, Fabbrini e Associati**'s Guido Testa and Luca Fabbrini are both known for their M&A and private equity work. The firm represents corporate institutions, Sirti SpA being a typical client. Name partner Luigi Vita Samory is highly regarded for corporate dispute resolution work.

Daniele Raynaud leads **Ashurst**'s department in Milan, focusing strongly on M&A and private equity. The firm acted for Banca Intesa SpA on its €70m shareholding sale in Epiclink SpA, an ISP, to Telecom Italia SpA and advised Fondo Interbancario di Investimento Azionario SpA on its €20m shareholding acquisition in Synergia 2000 SpA. Recently, the practice has received an increased number of IPO mandates.

Pietro Cavatola at eighteen-partner **CMS Adonnino Ascoli & Cavasola Scamoni** is known for his work in the energy sector. The firm represented a major international company in its acquisition of a leading supplier of microbiological products to the food and defence sectors.

Alberto Rittatore advises on commercial and corporate matters from the Milan office of the newly formed **Carnelutti Studio Legale Associato** together with ex-**Studio Legale Tonucci** lawyer Goffredo Guerra.

Eight-partner **Curtis, Mallet-Prevost, Colt & Mosle LLP in associazione con Gilioli, Alemani, Bocchiola, Tamburini e Par** is led by Michele Tamburini. The firm has been involved in infrastructure and restructuring work on behalf of Parmalat SpA and the Kosovo Trust Agency.

DLA Piper Rudnick Gray Cary has offices in Milan and Rome. Federico Sutti is the firm's best-known lawyer. In 2005, the department acted for Progetto Elettronica 92 Srl in liquidazione on the €6m sale of two subsidiaries and assisted a foreign bank on its sale of two Italian entities.

De Berti Jacchia Franchini Forlani has 67 lawyers working from Milan, Rome, Brussels and Moscow. Marco Frazzica recently joined the firm, bringing with him an established Scandinavian clientele, including multinationals active in the automotive and steel sectors. Dai Nippon Printing Co Ltd, the world's largest printing company, is a client.

Turin-based **Grande Stevens: Studio Legale Associazione Professionale** has branch offices in Milan and Rome. Name partner Franzo Grande Stevens remains closely linked to the Fiat Group.

The corporate and commercial department of **Jones Day**, run by Giovanni Marini and Ettore Scandale, offers legal advice in relation to M&A, joint ventures and corporate governance. The firm assisted private equity fund JZ International in its acquisition of Previnet SpA, a market-leader in outsourcing administration services, and Algol SpA on its sale of a networking, storage and Ip telephony dealer.

Rome-based lawyers Massimo Trentino, Filippo Mazza, former managing partner of **Studio Legale Delfino e Associati, Willkie Farr & Gallagher LLP** and Carsten Steinhauer advise on commercial and corporate matters at **McDermott Will & Emery Studio Legale Associato**.

Alessandro De Nicola and Luigi Colombo of ten-partner **Orrick, Herrington & Sutcliffe** are known for their corporate legal work. Of note, the practice assisted Gentium, an Italian pharmaceutical company during its listing process on the New York Stock Exchange and advised Ampliter NN on share placements by Citigroup. Other clients include Finlombardia SpA, Regione Lombardia and Eurus Energy BV, a subsidiary of the largest wind power developer in Japan. The department boosted its M&A capability with the arrival of Anna Spanò from **Studio Legale Tributario in Association with Ernst & Young**

PGRB – Puopolo Geffers Rosen & Bosin acted on ten M&A transactions ranging from €30m to €150m in the first six months of the year and recently assisted System Management Capital in its acquisition of a large Czech steel manufacturer. One client describes Gianfranco Puopolo as 'a lawyer and a business man who understands the big picture and addresses all issues, while keeping the business in perspective. He is a deal maker because he drives and follows the deal through'.

Thirteen-partner **Piergrossi Bianchini Eversheds** is based in Milan with a smaller office in Rome. The firm's commercial and corporate law department has continued to benefit from its alliance with UK-based **Eversheds LLP**. The practice acts for a number of multinational groups and mid-sized entities, recently advising on a share capital acquisition matter and on a pharmaceutical company equity sale.

In addition to numerous Italian offices **Studio Legale Sutti** now has branches in the UK, Eastern Europe and Japan. M&A name partner Stefano Sutti leads the corporate and public business law department. Of interest, the firm advised electronics service company Elcoteq Network Corporation on its €150m acquisition of an Italian competitor and acted for document storage business, Recall, on its takeover of Italian company Shuttle. One client says: 'While SLS is a full-service business firm, what it does best in our view is crisis management and dealing with multinational issues.'

At **Studio Legale Tonucci**, Andrea Rosi Piermartini and Daniele Santosuosso advise on general corporate matters while Marco Nicolini and ex-*McDermott Will & Emery/Carnelutti* Oreste Marchini look after M&A. In 2005, this department acted for LBO France in its €548m leveraged buy-out of multinational Actaris SA, as well as representing San Paolo IMI on its acquisition of Albanian bank BIA. Of further note the practice advised Volkswagen Group in the €90m sale of Europcar Lease Srl. Giovanni Mangialardi and Gaetano Guerreri offer energy and environmental law expertise. The firm has been in merger talks for some time with IP boutique **Franzosi Dal Negro Pensato Setti** and recently commenced discussions regarding a formal alliance with US giant **Mayer, Brown, Rowe & Maw LLP**

Ughi e Nunziante has offices in Milan and Rome. M&A partner Gianni Nunziante recently acted on the fourth tranche public placement of ENEL shares as advisor to the offeror Ministry of Economy and assisted Veolia on its purchase of Enel Hydro in addition to representing Tiscali on its sale of search engine company Excite to Ask Jeeves.

Notwithstanding domestic troubles, six-partner **Studio Legale Associato a White & Case** notched up some important transactions over the last year. The firm assisted Banche Popolari Unite and Centrobanca SpA in the US$53m sale of their interests in Italian and private equity funds and advised Sanpaolo IMI Private Equity SpA and Quadrivio SGR SpA on the sale of US$87m share capital in Carpine SpA, a vending machine company. Umberto Piatelli is known for his private equity expertise while Andrea De Santis is recommended for M&A work.

Abbatescianni e Associati's managing partner Riccardo Roversi carries out M&A work, often with a competition slant, while Edoardo Tedeschi specialises in energy law. Recently, the firm advised a French company on its acquisition of a public transport company.

The Milan office to international law firm **Haarmann Hemmelrath** is managed by Barnaba Ricci. This commercial practice focuses strongly on company law and real estate transactions.

Lombardi Molinari e Associati recently acted for Efibanca SpA in its €117m bid for Bormioli Rocco SpA.

Rome-based **Mazzoni E Associati – Verusio E Cosmelli Studi Legali Associati** also has offices in Milan, Pisa and Lucca. Giovanni Verusio is recommended for compliance advice.

Studio Legale Tributario in Association with Ernst & Young has 130 lawyers working from full-service offices all over Italy.

Seventeen-partner **Varrenti, Bassan, Lenzi e Associati Studio Legale e Tributario** opened in Milan in June 2004 and is made up of ex-**Studio Legale Associato a White & Case** and **Ughi e Nunziante** lawyers. The firm assisted Proton Group, a cleaning company for hospitality venues, in its recent acquisition of the Cagiva Group. A branch office is in Moscow.

DISPUTE RESOLUTION

BONELLI EREDE PAPPALARDO
LOMBARDI MOLINARI E ASSOCIATI ✪

Allen & Overy – Studio Legale Associato ✪
Studio Professionale Associato a Baker & McKenzie ✪
Chiomenti Studio Legale ✪
Cleary, Gottlieb, Steen & Hamilton LLP ✪
Freshfields Bruckhaus Deringer
Lovells ✪
Norton Rose
Pedersoli e Associati ✪
Schlesinger – Anelli, Studio Legale

Abbatescianni e Associati
Clifford Chance
Galgano ✪
Orrick, Herrington & Sutcliffe ✪
Piergrossi Bianchini Eversheds
Sutti, Studio Legale ✪

Firms are listed A-Z in tiers which are ranked in order of priority
✪ Indicates firm displays contact details at the end of this chapter.

DISPUTE RESOLUTION

No longer the exclusive domain of the professors, this sector is now considered a growth market and accordingly larger firms are investing in litigation departments. The processing of a case in Italy is notorious for cost and delay and firms are increasingly offering dispute resolution advice. Arbitration is also becoming a preferred mechanism for settling major commercial disputes.

Five partners at **Bonelli Erede Pappalardo** work on commercial litigation, representing high-profile clients in civil law proceedings. The firm is especially interested in the contentious aspects of banking, finance and corporate transactions, advising on breach of contract matters, enforcement injunctions of performance bonds and applications to overturn shareholders' meeting resolutions. The firm's litigation practice further extends to personal injury, defamation, privacy and data protection. In 2005, the group acted for Enel SpA in an arbitration against a Venezuelan petroleum company and represented a number of Belgian investors in a dispute with the Republic of Egypt regarding Suez Canal dredging work.

Ten-partner **Lombardi Molinari e Associati** acts on complex litigation and arbitration matters, often in the corporate, banking and insolvency sectors. The firm assisted Parmalat SpA and others in claims for damages and claw-back actions. Giuseppe Lombardi and Ugo Molinari are highly esteemed litigators.

Massimo Greco and Alberto Nanni are co-heads of litigation at **Allen & Overy – Studio Legale Associato**. The firm assisted CSFB on a €275m claw-back action deriving from the Parmalat insolvency and Rabobank in a €30m Cirio debt-recovery action.

Claudio Camilli is head of the dispute resolution practice at **Studio Professionale Associato a Baker & McKenzie** that represented Banca Popolare di Bari SpA on a €15m stock purchase agreement arbitration. Gianfranco Di Garbo's employment team acted for Dai Telecom Italia SpA on collective dismissal and discrimination matters.

Powerhouse **Chiomenti Studio Legale** has strong litigation capabilities, particularly in relation to commercial and financial disputes on behalf of multinational corporations, banks, telecommunications companies, software writers and real estate companies. The department boasts a number of key lawyers who regularly find themselves on arbitration matters before the International Centre of Settlement of International Disputes. The firm has been active in Parmalat matters on behalf of foreign banks.

Litigation and international arbitration are major components of **Cleary, Gottlieb, Steen & Hamilton LLP**'s practice. William B McGurn's team represents corporations and financial institutions in complex financial and commercial disputes and was counsel to ABN Amro before the domestic and European courts in relation to its high-profile and ultimately successful bid for Banca Antonveneta that involved a criminal investigation, share-freezing and Consob's suspension of the original Banca Popolare Italiana tender and mandatory offers. Ferdinando Emanuele assisted the Republic of Argentina on its successful defence against claims relating to its external indebtedness and also won a €180m settlement for Bancomext, the Mexican export credit agency.

At **Freshfields Bruckhaus Deringer** six fee-earners specialise in insolvency litigation. In relation to the Parmalat affair, the firm acted for Deutsche Bank, HSBC and Merrill Lynch on claw-back actions totalling €180m and tortious claims valued at €2bn. Amedeo Rampolla and five associates in Milan look after employment-related litigation.

Lovells' 14-lawyer dispute resolution group is directed by product liability expert Francesca Rolla. The firm has assisted British American Tobacco Italia SpA in hundreds of claims brought against the company in Italy and advised the official liquidator of Eurofood in its appeal against a court decision to declare the company insolvent in relation to Parmalat's extraordinary administration. The firm also works on contentious insolvency matters and multi-jurisdictional litigation in the pharmaceutical and automotive fields. One client commends the practice's 'professionalism, and determination' to win a case on its behalf.

Cristina Pagni leads the 16-strong dispute resolution team at **Norton Rose**, advising on a broad range of cross-border and domestic litigation in commercial, insurance and public law, in addition to IP, bankruptcy and employment matters.

Pedersoli e Associati's litigation department was strengthened by the arrival of Andrea Magliani and his entire group from *Magliani e Associati*. The department, now numbering 20 fee-earners, specialises in international commercial arbitration and cross-border disputes, particularly in the insurance sector.

Milan-based corporate boutique **Studio Legale Schlesinger – Anelli**, led by the indefitagable Professor Piero Schlesinger, was once part of *Studio Schlesinger Lombardi*. The firm is applauded by competitors for its dispute resolution work and has a close working relationship with IP boutique **Trevisan & Cuonzo Avvocati**.

At Milan-based **Abbatescianni e Associati** Girolamo Abbatescianni is known for his commercial arbitration and litigation work, particularly in relation to post-acquisition disputes, while Luca Failla provides contentious labour law advice.

Fabio Guastadisegni heads **Clifford Chance**'s dispute resolution team from Milan, while of-counsel Carmelo Alessio is in Rome. The firm has acted in connection with the default of one of Italy's largest airline companies.

Galgano's name in litigation is inextricably linked to that of founding partner Professor Francesco Galgano whose practice offers dispute resolution advice pertaining to civil, commercial and banking law, as well as IP and employment matters.

Luigi Colombo and Diego Rigatti at **Orrick, Herrington & Sutcliffe** act on litigation and arbitration matters. The firm assisted Ansaldo SpA before the Court of Milan on a turn-key contract relating to the construction of the largest desalination plant in the world.

Riccardo Buizza of **Piergrossi Bianchini Eversheds** is recommended for his expertise in product liability disputes.

Studio Legale Sutti acted for Dorel Netherlands on a pre-contractual liability case against an Italian competitor and advised manufacturing company Fata Automaton SpA in litigation relating to €35m bank guarantees issued by Società Italian Cauzioni SpA. Federal Express is regularly assisted on employment matters.

EU REGULATORY AND COMPETITION

Six partners and 18 associates handle antitrust matters at **Bonelli Erede Pappalardo**. Ex-EC Director-General for Competition, Aurelio Pappalardo, and Professor Luca Radicati are noted specialists. The firm recently advised AITEC, the European association of cement producers on gas emission-trading rights, and ENEL on alleged abuse of position proceedings. Also of interest, this department acted for TIM on cartel issues.

Cleary, Gottlieb, Steen & Hamilton LLP is a recognised leader in antitrust and regulatory work at domestic and European level. Outstanding lawyer Mario Siragusa and his team represented ABN Amro before the European Commission in connection with the hotly contested €6.3bn bid for Banca Antonveneta. The firm also advised Alitalia on recapitalisation and state aid issues and was counsel to Merck & Co before the Italian Antitrust Authority. The practice benefits from close ties to its Brussels and Frankfurt offices.

At **Clifford Chance**, Cristoforo Osti and four other lawyers advise on a range of competition topics, comprising abuse of dominance, restrictive practices, cartel enquiries, merger control and state aid. Clients include ExxonMobil Meditteranea Srl, Pfizer Italia Srl and GS SpA.

Freshfields Bruckhaus Deringer's antitrust, competition and trade group is run by Tommaso Salonico in Rome where advice is offered on merger control, state aid regulations and unilateral abuse of market power. Gas Natural was represented on its bid for Endesa, one of the four major Italian electricity generators. In utilities, the firm regularly assists Edison and AEM Milano and in pharmaceuticals the client base welcomed new clients Boehringer Inghelheim and Altana Pharma. Marcello Clarich and Fabrizio Arossa are highly recommended.

Alberto Pera, ex-Secretary General of the Italian Antitrust Authority heads **Gianni, Origoni, Grippo & Partners**' three-partner competition department. The firm is extremely active in merger control issues, restrictive practices, state aid and regulatory matters in the energy and telecoms sector. Clients include Telecom Italia, Trenitalia and Finmeccanica.

At **Allen & Overy – Studio Legale Associato** Silvia D'Alberti runs the antitrust department. Advice has been given to Wolters Kluwer on the antitrust aspects of the De Agostini Profesionale and UTET Professionale acquisitions. Finnmeccanica SpA is another notable client.

Studio Professionale Associato a Baker & McKenzie's six-lawyer competition and EU regulatory team advises on antitrust and cartel matters. New client Syrio Pharma SpA was successfully defended against alleged price-fixing in the artificial baby food market and IMX Poste Italy, the only private group in the European postal sector, was advised in an alleged abuse of dominant position case.

Rome-based Francesco Tedeschini manages the competition and EU department at **Chiomenti Studio Legale**, highly esteemed for its antitrust clearance and state aid work and benefiting from strong links to a Brussels office. The firm was recently involved in the notorious Wind deal. Key personalities are Andrea Giardina, Gianluca Belotti and Stefania Bariatti.

De Berti Jacchia Franchini Forlani also has an office in Brussels. Roberto Jacchia is known for representing large multinationals in the pharmaceutical, food, beverage and gaming industries. Clients describe the service as 'seamless and focused' and Giovanni Indirli, who has extensive ECJ experience, has joined the practice as counsel.

Giorgio Mondini and Giacomo Monelli at six-partner **Studio Legale Mondini-Rusconi** are known for their competition and antitrust advice. The firm assisted a worldwide media and entertainment company in an unfair competition matter and a leading Italian pharmaceutical company in an exclusive rights dispute.

NCTM – Studio Legale Associato's regulatory team is an offshoot of the banking department, advising financial institutions on legislative changes and providing representation before the regulatory authorities. The antitrust and competition group is an extension of the commercial practice, assisting on pre-merger filings, compliance programmes and attendances before the Italian Antitrust Authority and European Commission. Clients include Microsoft, Telecom Italia, Bridgepoint Capital and Ferrari.

Studio Rossi is known for its antitrust expertise. Ex-Consob President Guido Rossi advised ABN Amro in connection with the Banca Antonveneta affair.

Studio Santa Maria has offices in Rome and Milan and hosts an Italian desk from US firm **Greenberg Traurig LLP**. The firm advises the Italian government and numerous blue-chip clients on antitrust law, international trade and dumping, and recently assisted several Italian banks in a €3bn state aid proceeding. Other clients are the Italian Football League and the Municipality of Milan.

Filippo Fioretti heads the commercial and competition group at **Simmons & Simmons**, advising in particular on EU and Italian competition authorities' investigations. Piergiorgio Pepe has expertise in the transport, energy and consumer goods sectors, one client describing his aviation sector knowledge as 'outstanding'. The firm advised Endesa Europa SL on merger control issues arising from its Eurosviluppo Elettrica acquisition and Dolomiti Energia SpA on state aid issues. According to one client the practice 'manages to be a step ahead and very prompt and proactive' and 'has a well-trained and experienced system of internal co-ordination, information-sharing and brainstorming'.

Rino Caiazzo heads antitrust and regulation matters at **Ughi e Nunziante**. This department advised BT Albacom and Colt Telecom against Telecom Italia in an abuse of dominant position case that culminated in the largest-ever fine in

EU REGULATORY AND COMPETITION

BONELLI EREDE PAPPALARDO
CLEARY, GOTTLIEB, STEEN & HAMILTON LLP ✪

CLIFFORD CHANCE
FRESHFIELDS BRUCKHAUS DERINGER
GIANNI, ORIGONI, GRIPPO & PARTNERS ✪

Allen & Overy – Studio Legale Associato ✪
Studio Professionale Associato a Baker & McKenzie ✪
Chiomenti Studio Legale ✪
De Berti Jacchia Franchini Forlani ✪
Mondini-Rusconi, Studio Legale ✪
NCTM – Studio Legale Associato ✪
Rossi, Studio
Santa Maria, Studio
Simmons & Simmons ✪
Ughi e Nunziante ✪

DLA Piper Rudnick Gray Cary ✪
Guarino, Studio Legale
Rucellai & Raffaelli
Sutti, Studio Legale ✪

Firms are listed A-Z in tiers which are ranked in order of priority
✪ Indicates firm displays contact details at the end of this chapter.

Italy of €152m being handed down to a single company. In addition, the firm represented Bristol Myers Squibb on a successful defence of a cartel case in the artificial baby milk sector.

New to the table is **DLA Piper Rudnick Gray Cary** in Milan. It offers competition advice at domestic and European level. Francesca Sutti represented Weather Investments II Sarl in relation to the notorious Wind telecommunications deal, filing a concentration with the Italian Competition Authority. Other clients include Thüga Italia Srl and the AXA Group.

Rome-based **Studio Legale Guarino** is recommended for antitrust law. Founding partner Giuseppe Guarino is an ex-minister of finance and trade.

Rucellai & Raffaelli hosts offices in Milan, Rome and Bologna. Enrico Raffaelli is respected by peers for excellent advice on European, antitrust and competition law.

Studio Legale Sutti recently acted for IPLOM SpA, an Italian oil company, on antitrust matters and assisted Seleco Multimedia on a €100m state aid case.

INTELLECTUAL PROPERTY

Intellectual property is a niche practice area that demands lawyers of exceptional technical ability. In addition to providing sound non-contentious IP advice, often linked to M&A due diligence duties, international firms are boosting their IP litigation capabilities to compete with the boutiques that traditionally dominate this field. The top professors: Sena, Vanzetti, Floridia and Franzosi receive glowing references from professional colleagues. And while patent agents like Jacobacci are building small legal teams ancillary to their main practices, some larger firms are offering patent agency services, often complemented by significant investments into their IT systems.

A new IP code was introduced in 2005, repealing over 40 current laws and establishing a new procedure, expected to be faster than the judicial proceedings provided by the Italian Civil Procedure Code.

Independent firm **Trevisan & Cuonzo Avvocati** has offices in Milan, Rome and Parma. IP is the firm's core business and it is particularly known for its industry-patent litigation in pharmaceuticals and biotechnology. Trade mark prosecution and enforcement work has been carried out for Unilever, Porsche and Philips Electronics and anti-counterfeiting assistance given to Caterpillar, while Halliburton was represented in the practice's largest IP dispute of the year. Mainstream IP contract, licensing and domanin name advice is also provided. Clients contacted confirm complete satisfaction.

Massimiliano Mostardini and Giovanni Galimberti co-manage the IP department at 37-lawyer firm **Bird & Bird**. The firm is young, having opened in 2003, but the department has

INTELLECTUAL PROPERTY

TREVISAN & CUONZO AVVOCATI ✪

BIRD & BIRD ✪
FRANZOSI DAL NEGRO PENSATO SETTI

Studio Professionale Associato a Baker & McKenzie ✪
Hammonds Rossotto
Lovells ✪
Mondini-Rusconi, Studio Legale ✪
Pellegrino & Dragotti, Studio Legale
Rapisardi, Studio Legale ✪

Allen & Overy – Studio Legale Associato ✪
Bonelli Erede Pappalardo
Cleary, Gottlieb, Steen & Hamilton LLP ✪
De Berti Jacchia Franchini Forlani ✪
Freshfields Bruckhaus Deringer
Gianni, Origoni, Grippo & Partners ✪
Pavia e Ansaldo
Simmons & Simmons ✪
Sutti, Studio Legale ✪
Tonucci, Studio Legale ✪

Firms are listed A-Z in tiers which are ranked in order of priority
✪ *Indicates firm displays contact details at the end of this chapter.*

considerable experience in contentious and non-contentious matters, particularly in patent, trade mark and design litigation, internet domain name disputes and copyright. One client appreciates Giovanni Galimberti's 'straight-to-the-point' attitude. Clients include Puma Italia Srl, Smith International Inc, Electrolux AB and Edwards Lifesciences Inc.

Milan firm **Franzosi Dal Negro Pensato Setti** is known for exceptional IP patent enforcement advice at domestic and international levels. Offices are also run from Rome and Bologna.

Studio Professionale Associato a Baker & McKenzie's IP department, headed by Lorenzo de Martinis, advises on trade marks, copyright and licensing and Roberto Ramponi leads the IP prosecution practice. Significant investments have been made in a state-of-the-art IT platform from which clients can access their trade mark portfolios. Clients include Hewlett-Packard, Calvin Klein and Zippo Manufacturing Company, the latter having been assisted on a complex international patent issue. The firm is recommended for its 'know-how, competence and reliability'.

Hammonds Rossotto's Milan and Rome offices have extensive experience of intellectual property matters, including trade marks, copyright, domain name disputes, global brand creations and the protection of online rights. The firm represents several music industry clients.

Luigi Mansani runs IP matters at **Lovells**. The department has advised Brandt Italia SpA, Nissan Motor Co and Deutsche Telekom AG in trade mark litigation. The practice offers expertise in patent, copyright and design issues and clients tend to be major national and foreign companies.

Giorgio Mondini, Anna Carabelli and Alessandro Fano of **Studio Legale Mondini-Rusconi** specialise in contentious and non-contentious intellectual property issues, comprising general copyright, anti-counterfeiting merchandising and internet domain issues. The firm boasts a wealth of global media clients and recently assisted an entertainment multinational on a trade mark infringement of a US television series.

Studio Legale Pellegrino & Dragotti deals almost exclusively with IP matters. Gualtiero Dragotti is the firm's managing partner, while Giovanni Pellegrino is senior counsel on international arbitrations. The practice benefits from alliances with patent and trade mark attorneys and in 2005 the firm underwent a major expansion programme in terms of size and range of services offered. Domestic clients include Gruppo Coin and Chemi, while internationally this boutique acts for US enterprise Wilson Tool and Dutch company Kickers International. One client commends the firm for its responsiveness and the 'perfect functioning of its internal teams'.

IT-focused **Studio Legale Rapisardi** is known for patent, trade mark and domain name work in the domestic and international arena. In addition to its niche team of lawyers, the firm provides and co-ordinates teams of engineers, technicians and agents, and offers a computer-based patent management system for clients to access.

Roberto Donnini and Massimiliano Molinari of **Allen & Overy – Studio Legale Associato** assist Twentieth Century Fox on an ongoing basis in relation to IP issues.

Bonelli Erede Pappalardo has a niche intellectual property practice that advises on contentious and non-contentious matters, focusing particularly on patents, trade marks, software copyright, data protection, franchising contracts and merchandising arrangements for the fashion industry. Clients include Armani, De Agostini and Luxottica.

Mario Siragusa is the IP partner at **Cleary, Gottlieb, Steen & Hamilton LLP**. Recently, the firm defended Gucci SpA against lawsuits relating to the non-renewal of worldwide licences for brand perfumes and cosmetics products and assisted Merck & Co Inc in relation to a court refusal to license intellectual property rights.

Maria Cristina Franchini at **De Berti Jacchia Franchini Forlani** is known for her patent litigation in the pharmaceutical and durable consumables sectors. According to one client the firm possesses 'outstanding capacity in getting to the point'.

Matteo Orsingher leads **Freshfields Bruckhaus Deringer**'s IP team. This department has considerable experience in the licensing and litigating of patent and trade mark matters and has worked for Wella on a major trade mark dispute and Rodale International in negotiating domestic and international licences for the publication of the company's numerous magazines. Other impressive clients comprise Fox International Channels and The Walt Disney Company Italia.

Nino Di Bella heads **Gianni, Origoni, Grippo & Partners**'s ten-strong team dedicated to patent, trade mark and copyright matters. The firm regularly acts on anti-counterfeiting litigation for adidas, Hasbro and Nokia.

Gian Paolo di Santo of **Pavia e Ansaldo** advises on intellectual property rights and related litigation.

Rome-based Filippo Fioretti is head of IP at **Simmons & Simmons**. The firm provides contentious and non-contentious IP advice, particularly in the TMT, pharmaceutical and biotechnology sectors. Media company Dreamworks SKG was assisted on its Italian dubbing agreements and Organon SpA was represented on trade mark licence agreements.

Studio Legale Sutti specialises in 'soft' and contentious IP, recently advising plastic products company Okbaby Srl on a reassignment matter before the Naming Authority. According to one client, the firm has 'an outstanding IP practice', regarding Simona Cazzaniga as a 'rising star in respect of patent enforcement'. The firm has its own in-house patent agents.

Alessandro Del Ninno runs **Studio Legale Tonucci**'s IP department, recently acting for Renato Balestra Haute Couture, an Italian fashion house, on the licensing and €20m sale of IP assets.

REAL ESTATE

Real estate is still regarded as a growth area worthy of domestic and international investment. Interestingly, whereas interest has previously tended to be focused in the north, the central and southern regions are now attracting investment. In addition to portfolio acquisitions, foreign investors are targeting the Italian retail sector, particularly shopping centres, offices and warehouses.

Roberto Cera and Alberto Saravalle lead the field at **Bonelli Erede Pappalardo**. In 2005, the firm advised Pirelli & Co Real Estate SGR SpA on the transfer of a €877m property portfolio, Enel SpA on the €1.4bn sale of New Real SpA, Beni Stabili SpA on a joint venture with Fiat Partecipazioni SpA and GEFIM SpA that concerned the acquisition of numerous property assets, and CSFB Real Estate Capital Funds in relation to Immobiliare Fondo di Previdenza Lavoratori Giornali's purchase of a Rome and Genoa-based portfolio.

At **Chiomenti Studio Legale**, Michele Carpinelli, Francesco Tedeschini and Filippo Modulo recently led Pirelli & Co Real Estate SpA, Deutsche Bank Real Estate Opportunities IB and Investitori Associati – Borletti Family on an €888m acquisition of La Rinascente SpA.

REAL ESTATE

BONELLI EREDE PAPPALARDO
CHIOMENTI STUDIO LEGALE ✪
CLIFFORD CHANCE
FRESHFIELDS BRUCKHAUS DERINGER
GIANNI, ORIGONI, GRIPPO & PARTNERS ✪

Allen & Overy – Studio Legale Associato ✪
Ashurst ✪
DLA Piper Rudnick Gray Cary ✪
Jones Day ✪
Mondini-Rusconi, Studio Legale ✪
Norton Rose
Pedersoli e Associati ✪
Portalupi & Partners ✪

Carnelutti Studio Legale Associato ✪
Delli Santi & Partners
Lombardi Molinari e Associati ✪
Lovells ✪

Firms are listed A-Z in tiers which are ranked in order of priority
✪ *Indicates firm displays contact details at the end of this chapter.*

Partners Paolo Rulli and Massimo La Torre guide the real estate group at **Clifford Chance**. The firm assisted Carlyle Group on its €255m acquisition of properties in central Rome, Milan and Turin. Other clients include Società Sviluppo Commerciale Srl, Nexity International and the Di Veroli Group.

Marzio Longo leads a 14-strong property team at **Freshfields Bruckhaus Deringer** that offers expertise in real estate funds, development projects and the finance, regulatory and tax sides to projects. The firm assisted Morgan Stanley Real Estate Funds/Pirelli & Co Real Estate on the acquisition of 250 properties and Mills Corporation on the award by the Municipality of Rome of the concession for the re-development of the Rome-based ex-Mercati Generali complex. According to one client the 'performance of Marzio Longo is exceptional as it combines legal expertise, market knowledge and commercial mindset'.

Mario Amoroso's real estate department at **Gianni, Origoni, Grippo & Partners** was boosted in 2005 by the arrival of Francesco Marzari and Eugenio Falcone, specialists in zoning and land use. The department provides advice on portfolio disposals and acquisitions and works closely with the banking team in relation to real estate securitisations. Clients include Antonveneta GE, AIG Lincoln, Hines and Pirelli & Co Real Estate.

Allen & Overy – Studio Legale Associato derives substantial real estate work from its banking and finance group. The property team advised Hines European Development Fund in relation to the acquisition and development of the Garibaldi-Repubblica development project and APN/UKA, an Australian investment fund, in connection with shopping mall acquisitions.

Eva Maschietto heads property matters at **Ashurst**. The firm advised Spazio Industriale 3 Srl, a joint venture between Soros Real Estate Investors and Pirelli & Co Real Estate SpA, on a portfolio purchase from Prada SpA and represented insurance company Milano Assicurazioni on a JV linked to Milan's €600m City of Fashion project.

DLA Piper Rudnick Gray Cary's Olaf Schmidt is noted for his real estate acumen. The firm assisted DEGI, a management company that runs real estate funds, on the acquisition of the Ministero della Salute project in Rome E.U.R. – Europarco. One client says that the firm 'has the most experienced in-depth knowledge of the Italian real estate market that we have found so far'. Another client says that managing partner Federico Sutti 'has always provided an excellent point of trust' and that 'good seamless services have been provided by more junior staff'.

Marco Lombardi and Giovanni Marini advise on real estate at **Jones Day**. The department acts for real estate funds, investment banks and developers, representing ING Real Estate Development International BV on its joint venture acquisition of development land in Parma, and Electronic Data Systems on the multi-jurisdictional sale and leaseback of buildings in Pomezia. Other notable clients are Wal-Mart and Hugo Boss.

Giorgio Mondini and Luca Tiberi offer real estate assistance at **Studio Legale Mondini-Rusconi**. In 2005, the firm advised a major sportswear and equipment manufacturer in connection with its commercial property leases.

Fourteen lawyers at **Norton Rose** offer advice on real estate, interacting closely with their tax, finance and dispute resolution teams. Dutch company Corio has been assisted on a number of commercial property investments in Italy. Key figures in this department are Nicolò Juvara and new managing partner Paolo Daviddi.

Antonio Pedersoli runs **Pedersoli e Associati**'s real estate team. The firm acts for Pirelli & Co Real Estate on a number of development and commercial portfolios and advised Banca Popolari Unite Scpa on a €150m property company sale. Mario Botte, former corporate legal manager of Arcon Italia Srl, was recruited to the real estate and property finance practice. Enrico Zattoni is commended by one client for advice that is 'well beyond expectations'.

Real estate is the core business of boutique practice **Portalupi & Partners**, focusing on portfolio acquisitions and disposals, developments and the setting up of real estate funds. The firm's exceptionally specialised team also provides advice on zoning, building and environmental issues.

After the *McDermott Will & Emery/Carnelutti* split, partner Guido Inzaghi remained in Milan at **Carnelutti Studio Legale Associato** where he continues to advise on commercial developments and urban planning matters.

Seven-partner Rome firm **Delli Santi & Partners**, led by Riccardo Delli Santi, specialises in due diligence, town planning and feasibility studies associated with portfolio acquisitions. Clients include DEKA Immobilien Investment GMBH and Citylife Consortium.

Lombardi Molinari e Associati recently advised Lehman Brothers Real Estate Funds and Pirelli Real Estate SpA on a €150m property transaction.

Lovells' real estate department is led by Marco Rota Candiani. The firm assisted AMB in relation to a development of a multi-phase logistics site near Milan. One client comments: 'They have a very good understanding of the corporate, tax and real estate issues that large international investors need to evaluate and address as part of making a large cross-border investment. Overall, we were impressed by the level of co-ordination and responsiveness from their entire team.'

TMT

The decline in the telecoms market has slightly receded. The incumbents and mobile operators still dominate, yet traditional telecoms models are threatened by broadband take-ups and VoIP, a broadband medium connection utilised to make free voice calls over the internet. The government has supported the development of an IT economy by introducing a number of incentives and financial contributions for companies operating in this sector.

Bonelli Erede Pappalardo remains closely linked to Telecom Italia. The firm represented the incumbent operator on the restructuring of its communications activities in the Mediterranean region and before competition authorities in relation to the acquisition of a French ISP. Also of note, the TMT department advised Telefónica before the European Commission with regards to the acquisition of Cesky Teleco, the Czech telecoms entity.

Studio Professionale Associato a Baker & McKenzie's Lorenzo de Martinis runs the firm's IT and communications department, offering expertise in the financial cards and payment systems markets. Clients include SIA and First Data Corporation who are leading providers of technology services to financial markets as well as H3G SpA and Giorgio Armani SpA. One client reports that the firm 'is an international network of competent, professional and pragmatic lawyers, who definitely understand the requirements of the company and are able to merge their technical competence with the pragmatic requirement of the decision maker in the client'.

Luca Fossati heads TMT matters at **Chiomenti Studio Legale**. The department is closely tied to the firm's M&A, capital markets and project finance teams. Advice is given to the telecommunications industry on licence assignments, network set ups, bond offerings and regulatory issues. Instructions also derive from clients working in the third-generation mobile and fixed-line telephony sectors.

TMT

BONELLI EREDE PAPPALARDO

STUDIO PROFESSIONALE ASSOCIATO A BAKER & McKENZIE ✪
CHIOMENTI STUDIO LEGALE ✪
CLEARY, GOTTLIEB, STEEN & HAMILTON LLP ✪
CLIFFORD CHANCE
FRESHFIELDS BRUCKHAUS DERINGER
GALGANO ✪
GIANNI, ORIGONI, GRIPPO & PARTNERS ✪

Allen & Overy – Studio Legale Associato ✪
Bird & Bird ✪
Carnelutti Studio Legale Associato ✪
NCTM – Studio Legale Associato ✪
Portolano Colella Cavallo Studio Legale ✪
Simmons & Simmons ✪
Sutti, Studio Legale ✪
Ughi e Nunziante ✪

Abbatescianni e Associati
Dalla Vedova
Dewey Ballantine Studio Legale ✪
Guarino, Studio Legale
Hammonds Rossotto
Lovells ✪
PGRB – Puopolo Geffers Rosen & Bosin ✪

Firms are listed A-Z in tiers which are ranked in order of priority
✪ *Indicates firm displays contact details at the end of this chapter.*

Cleary, Gottlieb, Steen & Hamilton LLP is a recognised authority in pay television, voice and data communications, internet services and software products, specifically advising on pricing issues, x-DSL technology, TV licence agreements and film distribution. The firm represented SKY Italia Srl against anti-competition claims filed in court.

Clifford Chance provides corporate, regulatory and finance assistance to a plethora of multinational TMT clients. Nicholas Wrigley advised broadband operator FASTWEB SpA on its €798m global offering, while Michele Crisostomo represented JPMorganChase in connection with the €14.5bn takeover of TIM.

Freshfields Bruckhaus Deringer advises on the regulatory aspects of telecommunications transactions, also focusing on technology outsourcing, new media and e-commerce contracts. This Rome-based department worked with directory company Il Numero Italia on advertising and data protection issues and assisted Fox International Channels on the TMT aspects to its broadcasting channels. Further clients of note are Bentley Systems, Hewlett-Packard and H3G.

Marco Consonni at **Galgano** advises on internet strategy, e-commerce, data protection, TV broadcasting agreements and advertising. The roster of clients includes Yahoo!, eBay, Expedia, Vodafone, MTV and Saatchi & Saatchi.

Gianni, Origoni, Grippo & Partners' TMT department is headed by Andrea Mazziotti di Celso. The firm assisted Blackstone Wind in its bid for Wind SpA and La7 on the acquisition of Elefante TV, a national broadcasting licensee. Other clients are Sky TV and KPN.

Allen & Overy – Studio Legale Associato represents Twentieth Century Fox on an ongoing basis in relation to entertainment law issues.

Joining the table this year is four-partner **Bird & Bird**. Recruited from **Ughi e Nunziante**, rising star Eutimio Monaco helped set up the new Rome office. The firm was involved in several abuse of dominant position proceedings filed on behalf of telecommunications operators. Heavyweight clients include TELE2 Italia SpA, Italy's second fixed-line operator and Eutelia, the fourth-largest telecoms operator in Italy. Assistance was also provided to Infonxx when it entered the directory market.

Nicolò Bastianini of Milan practice **Carnelutti Studio Legale Associato** is described by one client as 'outstanding' and as having 'achieved great results in a complicated regulatory environment'. Partner Giangiacomo Olivi is also highly recommended.

NCTM – Studio Legale Associato offers expertise in relation to new technologies contracts and regulatory issues. Vittorio Noseda advised British Telecom on its €411m acquisition of Albacom SpA. Other notable clients are Dell Computer, Siemens and I Net SpA.

Niche Rome practice **Portolano Colella Cavallo Studio Legale** focuses on the transactional, regulatory and litigation sides of TMT, notably terrestrial and satellite content and agreements, sports contracts, website issues and e-commerce. One client commends the firm for its 'fresh, modern approach and strong commercial focus'. The firm's client base boasts a plethora of international media clients as well as fashion houses and software companies.

Filippo Fioretti and Nino Lombardo direct **Simmons & Simmons**' TMT department from Rome. The firm recently advised CONSIP SpA, a state-owned company authorised to carry out e-procurement activities and IT product acquisitions for the Italian government on internet public tender issues, and assisted Elitel SpA on the launch of the new VoIP service. This department also works with Telecom Italia SpA as well as Datamat SpA and IDT Global Ltd.

Studio Legale Sutti provides full-service assistance to the hi-tech sector, recently advising Bticino on the regulatory issues involved in the establishment of an independent television broadcasting company and representing Scandinavian telecoms company Ascade on the licensing of routing-pricing software to an Italian incumbent. The firm also assisted Immogest and Galileo with personal data processing compliance issues.

Ughi e Nunziante advised BT Albacom and Colt Telecom in connection with a crucial collective dominance case against Telecom Italia. Rino Caizzo has an excellent reputation for his regulatory-based work in the telecoms sector.

At ten-partner **Abbatescianni e Associati** Federico Ferrara specialises in music and entertainment law.

Fourteen-lawyer **Dalla Vedova** is based in Rome. Marco Dalla Vedova is known for his telecoms advice. The firm acts for a number of *Fortune 500* companies as well as foreign governments.

Stefano Speroni led **Dewey Ballantine Studio Legale** in advising Weather Investments SA on its acquisition of Wind Telecomunicazioni SpA from Enel SpA. The €12.2bn transaction represented the second-largest leveraged buy-out worldwide, ever.

Studio Legale Guarino's Giuseppe Guarino is regarded by peers as an expert in telecommunications.

Hammonds Rossotto provides tailored advice on software development and licensing, source code escrow agreements, website hosting and data protection.

Luigi Mansani leads an IT team of six fee-earners at **Lovells**. The firm assisted eBay in the legal management of its website and PayPal Inc on the establishment of its website, its legal and privacy policies, user agreements and electronic money issuance.

PGRB – Puopolo Geffers Rosen & Bosin's Frank Geffers and Angela Rinaldi have advised Amadeus GTD, a leading global distribution system and technology provider to the travel industry, on its software agreements. The Italian Ministry of Defence is represented on privacy, video surveillance and anti-spamming matters.

TAX

Boutiques offering contentious and non-contentious tax advice retain positions of prominence in this sector. However, in response to client demand and in the interests of increased revenues, some larger commercial practices are investing in stand-alone tax departments, hiring both tax lawyers and *dottori commercialisti*.

Professor Tomasso Di Tanno heads the exceptional tax practice **Di Tanno e Associati**. Clients include Microsoft, Lehman Brothers International and Vodafone Omnitel NV.

Maisto e Associati is recognised as a top tax boutique. Led by Gugliemo Maisto the firm has offices in Milan, Rome and London and is formally allied to **Clifford Chance**.

Enrico Vitali heads seven-partner **Vitali Romagnoli Piccardi E Associati**. The firm handles all aspects of tax law connected to cross-border transactions and is known for its outstanding tax advice in M&A, banking and finance, and litigation. Clients are investment banks, multinationals and private equity bodies and the firm shares an alliance with Italian giant **Gianni, Origoni, Grippo & Partners**. Name-partner Giulio Tremonti recently returned to government as Finance Minister.

Luigi Biscozzi and Raffaele Nobili at Milan firm **Biscozzi Nobili** are highly esteemed for their legal tax expertise.

Andrea Silvestri runs a 13-strong tax group at **Bonelli Erede Pappalardo** that works closely with the firm's M&A team yet is also instructed on its own merits at domestic and international levels. Ex-**Maisto e Associati** lawyer Andrea Manzitti recently joined the department.

Full-service firm **Camozzi & Bonissoni** has 20 partners and 130 professionals in Milan and Rome, advising on international tax planning, transfer-pricing and tax litigation. The practice has working relationships with **Slaughter and May** in the UK and **Hengeler Mueller** in Germany.

Corrado Grande and Giuseppe Andrea Giannantonio head **Chiomenti Studio Legale**'s 18-strong tax group. Specialist advice is offered in relation to M&A, company restructurings, tax planning and litigation. Partner Michele Carpinelli is highly esteemed for his tax law capabilities.

TAX

DI TANNO E ASSOCIATI ✪
MAISTO E ASSOCIATI
VITALI ROMAGNOLI PICCARDI E ASSOCIATI

Biscozzi Nobili
Bonelli Erede Pappalardo
Camozzi & Bonissoni
Chiomenti Studio Legale ✪
Fantozzi e Associati
Franco Gallo, Studio Associato Legale Tributario fondato da
Freshfields Bruckhaus Deringer
Macchi di Cellere Gangemi ✪
NCTM – Studio Legale Associato ✪
Uckmar, Studio

Abbatescianni e Associati
Allen & Overy – Studio Legale Associato ✪
Ashurst ✪
Studio Professionale Associato a Baker & McKenzie ✪
CMS Adonnino Ascoli & Cavasola Scamoni ✪
Gianni, Origoni, Grippo & Partners ✪
Tonucci, Studio Legale ✪

Carnelutti Studio Legale Associato ✪
Dewey Ballantine Studio Legale ✪
Fiorentini, Studio Legale Tributario
Lovells ✪
Norton Rose
Santa Maria, Studio
Simmons & Simmons ✪

Firms are listed A-Z in tiers which are ranked in order of priority
✪ Indicates firm displays contact details at the end of this chapter.

Fantozzi e Associati's 40 tax lawyers and advisors are spread between Rome, Milan, Bologna and Lugano, the latter office building up a Swiss client base. The firm's name is inextricably linked to the outstanding reputation of founding partner Augusto Fantozzi who used to be Minister of Finance and Foreign Trade. The practice is a member of the *Tax and Global Alliance* network.

Three-partner boutique **Studio Associato Legale Tributario fondato da Franco Gallo** has offices in Rome and Milan. The practice's advisers are recognised experts in VAT, tax assessments, international fiscal matters and corporate income tax. The firm has a collaborative agreement with **Ripa Di Meana Avv. Vittorio Studio Legale** in Rome.

Freshfields Bruckhaus Deringer provides stand-alone tax advice and transaction-related structuring yet liaises closely with the firm's M&A, real estate and finance teams. The six-lawyer team, led by Renato Paternollo, represented Goldman Sachs Capital Partners Funds on tax issues. Other clients are Edison and Lehman brothers.

Four partners advise on tax at **Macchi di Cellere Gangemi**. Bruno Gangemi is nationally esteemed, his practice covering business taxation, domestic and international VAT, taxation of employees, M&A fiscal structuring and litigation.

Piermauro Carabellese leads the tax team at **NCTM – Studio Legale Associato**, targeting areas such as domestic and international litigation, capital markets and financial transactions as well as providing specific tax structuring advice to M&A transactions. Clients include Clessidra Capital Partners, British Telecom and British Aerospace.

Studio Uckmar's 15-lawyer firm has offices in Milan, Rome, Genoa and Buenos Aires. Victor Uckmar is a highly considered tax specialist. The firm is a founding member of *Acbgroup*, a network of over 50 associated law firms.

Abbatescianni e Associati has offices in Milan, Rome and Brescia. Angelo C Colombo and his *dottori commercialisti* act for corporate clients, offering tax planning, structuring advice and due diligence services within the domestic and international arena. The firm is a member of an alliance with UK-based **Osborne Clarke**.

Allen & Overy – Studio Legale Associato has benefited from the recruitment of 15 tax professionals from **Haarmann Hemmelrath**. In 2005, this department, led by Andrea Manganelli, assisted Global Garden Products Italy SpA on its group restructuring and advised ECO SpA in relation to divestment plans.

Ashurst's Stefano Serbini offers specialist tax advice in relation to M&A, tax-driven financial products and contentious fiscal matters.

Studio Professionale Associato a Baker & McKenzie's three-partner team, led by Gerardo Boniello, specialises in corporate tax restructuring. Clients comprise Dai Telecom-Telit, LVMH and Estée Lauder. Of-counsel Carlo Gnetti and tax associate Silvia Brandoni recently joined the firm.

One-third of **CMS Adonnino Ascoli & Cavasola Scamoni**'s partners provide tax advice. Pietro Adonnino, ex-member of the Superior Finance Council of the Italian Ministry of Finance, advises on national and international tax issues.

Partner Massimo Agostini and seven associates handle tax matters at **Gianni, Origoni, Grippo & Partners**, usually linked to M&A, banking and corporate finance transactions. Recently, the firm assisted Cassa Depositi e Prestiti in its acquisition of a stake in Terna. A crucial alliance is in place with tax boutique **Vitali Romagnoli Piccardi E Associati**.

At **Studio Legale Tonucci** two partners and eight fee-earners practise tax planning and auditing. The firm acquired *Studio Grimaldi & Associati* in 2004.

Gilberto Comi heads a four-partner tax department at **Carnelutti Studio Legale Associato**, offering direct and indirect taxation advice, and tax planning services.

Luca Dezzani runs **Dewey Ballantine Studio Legale**'s tax department. In 2005 the firm assisted Weather Investments SA in its tax structuring of the Wind Telecommunicazioni SpA acquisition and worked on the reorganisation of Moby SpA, a leader in ferryboat transportation in Italian waters,

Seven-partner **Studio Legale Tributario Fiorentini** advises on contentious and non-contentious tax matters and acts as defending counsel at Supreme Court level. A number of banks and foreign companies are listed as clients.

Lovells' three-partner tax practice, led by Fulvia Astolfi and Andrea Accornero, has built on its earlier hiring of Domenico Borzumato and Serena Pietrosanti from *Andersen Legal* and bolstered its Italian client base. The firm provided tax structuring advice to Luxottica Grup SpA in connection with its acquisition of retail businesses in China.

Antonello Lupo runs **Norton Rose**'s tax team, offering tax efficiency and structuring advice to multinational and Italian companies, often relating to global tax rules and treaties.

Ex-**Maisto e Associati** lawyer Stefano Simontacchi heads **Studio Santa Maria**'s tax department, advising in domestic and international taxation and corporate restructuring.

At **Simmons & Simmons** *dottori commercialisti* Michele Citarella and Ernesto Caso have developed a tax practice that focuses on the financial, corporate and employment sectors. Key clients are Banca Intesa SpA, Barclays Capital and Finanziaria Internazionale Srl.

OTHER LEADING FIRMS

Coccia DeAngelis & Associati Studio Legale E Tributario ✪
Nunziante Magrone ✪
Padovan, Studio Legale
Rosauer, Studio Legale
Toffoletto e Soci, member of ius laboris ✪

Albertazzi & Associati Studio Legale
Barzano & Zanardo
Bernascone & Soci, Studio Legale ✪
Biolato Longo Ridola & Mori
CBM & Partners
Cajola & Associati ✪
Cannata Pierallini in associazione con Coudert Brothers, Studio Legale
Capaccioli s.r.l., Studio
Coggiatti, Studio Legale
Corno, Studio – Avvocati
de Meo & Associati, Studio Legale
Dore & Associati
Floridia, Studio Legale
Forlati – Minelli – Rizzi, Studio Legale
Franceschelli, Studio Legale
Frau & Partners SLA
Fusillo & Associati, Studio Legale
Grieco e Associati
JMU – Law Firm
Jenny & Partners ✪
LGV Avvocati ✪
Lawfed – Rubino-Sammartano e Associati ✪
Lega Colucci Morri e Associati Studio Legale e Tributario
Marena, Bonvicini, Aghina e Ludergnani
Mastellone, Studio Legale
McNabb Associates, P.C
Montanari & Associati
Nodari & Associati, Studio Legale
Olivieri Ciapetti & Partners, Studio Legale
Pinci & Associates, PLLC
Pojaghi, Studio Legale
Sardo, Studio Legale
Sena & Tarchini
Tosi & Partners
Watson, Farley & Williams Studio Legale Associato ✪
Zambelli Luzzati Meregalli e Associati

Firms are listed A-Z in tiers which are ranked in order of priority
✪ Indicates firm displays contact details at the end of this chapter.

OTHER LEADING FIRMS

The following firms, generally siuated in Milan or Rome, are recommended either as specialist boutiques or smaller, full-service commercial practices.

Rome-based **Coccia DeAngelis & Associati Studio Legale E Tributario** is led by Massimo Coccia. Noted for its sports law expertise the firm advised the Italian Olympic Committee (CONI) on the implementation of new sports legislation. The practice also has a prominent energy law department and represented Gas Intensive in an abuse of dominant position matter.

Nunziante Magrone is based in Rome with additional offices in Milan, Turin and Bologna. The firm advises on commercial, financial, regulatory and tax matters and recently assisted COS SpA on its acquisition of Finsiel SpA, a market leader in IT. One client says of Marco Mazzeschi: 'We have been very satisfied with his work. He understands the Italian legal system and local political climate, and is very adept at working matters through to resolution'.

Marco Padovan heads **Studio Legale Padovan** in Milan, where 23 fee-earners advise on asset and project finance, securitisation, general commercial and corporate matters, international trade law and dispute resolution. The practice has extensive links abroad and has handled litigation in Israel, Finland and the US, as well as representing Italian contractors on highway and dam projects. Branch offices exist in Rome and Treviso.

Four lawyers operate from **Studio Legale Rosauer**'s Rome base. The firm focuses on commercial and corporate law, general litigation and international arbitration. It is a member of *Mackrell International*, a global referral network comprising independent law firms.

Toffoletto e Soci, member of ius laboris is primarily known for its employment law practice. Advice is provided on collective agreements, trade union negotiations and employment due diligence during M&A. The firm's membership of *ius laboris*, an alliance of leading employment law firms, gives the firm a significant international presence.

Milan firm **Albertazzi & Associati Studio Legale** is a general commercial practice that also specialises in energy law.

Barzano & Zanardo has offices in Rome, Milan, Turin, Vicenza and Biella. The firm specialises in patent and trade mark registration, often in the Republic of San Marino. Clients include ENI SpA and Cadbury Schweppes.

Corporate finance lawyer Gabriele Bernascone leads Milan-based **Studio Legale Bernascone & Soci.**. The firm recently acted for an international consumer products company in its procurement of an Italian coatings enterprise and advised a Japan-based insurance company on medical malpractice cases. The practice is a founding member of *ADINCOM*, an Italian organisation that focuses on the interaction between science and legislation.

Biolato Longo Ridola & Mori is a Rome-based commercial practice that is known for its pharmaceutical advertising expertise. Shipping and property law services are also provided.

Six-partner **CBM & Partners** offers legal guidance in general corporate matters, M&A, real estate, arbitration, employment and administrative law.

Milan firm **Cajola & Associati** has represented Lexmark International Inc and Brother Industries Ltd on trade mark enforcement rights in Italy and Lindeteves Jacoberg Ltd, a listed Singapore electric motor manufacturer company, in connection with cross-border disputes. The practice is a member of the *INTERLEGAL* network of international law firms.

Rome-based **Studio Legale Cannata Pierallini in associazione con Coudert Brothers** has a significant aviation practice that represents European air transport companies and manufacturers in employment law, insurance and commercial aircraft acquisitions. The firm also advises on banking, finance, insolvency, joint ventures and antitrust law.

Studio Capaccioli s.r.l. is based in Florence with Rome, Milan and Ferrara branches. The practice advises on banking and finance, M&A, shipping law and tax planning. The firm recently worked on an equity JV in Hong Kong and on the business and legal restructuring of an Italian air transport company.

Studio Legale Coggiatti was founded in Rome in 1996 and advises on company and commercial matters, telecommunications, labour, banking and sports law. The firm is allied to **Studio Legale Mastellone** in Florence and **Studio Legale Sardo** in Milan and is a member of *InterAct EEIG*.

Studio Corno – Avvocati is based in Lissone, 15kms from Milan. Partner Giorgio Corno, also a UK-qualified solicitor, and six fee-earners offer commercial legal advice with particular emphasis on e-commerce, insolvency and corporate restructuring. The firm gains international referrals from *LaWorld*, a global network of independent law firms.

Michele de Meo leads **Studio Legale de Meo & Associati**, a Rome-based firm with offices in Naples, Milan and Civitavecchia. The practice advises on commercial and corporate law, shipping, general litigation and ADR.

Dore & Associati is in Cagliari, the capital of Sardinia. Carlo Dore and 13 fee-earners advise on banking, real estate, competition, labour and tax law. The firm is allied to Florence practice **Studio Legale Vannini** and recently opened a branch in Brussels to focus on EU matters.

Boutique **Studio Legale Floridia** is recommended for trade mark, patent and anti-counterfeiting litigation.

Venice-based **Studio Legale Forlati – Minelli – Rizzi** is known as a litigation firm that also carries out commercial and corporate work. The practice is a member of the *Eurojuris International* network.

Studio Legale Franceschelli is a niche Milan firm that advises on company and contracts law in addition to competition and IP matters.

Frau & Partners SLA has offices in Milan, Rome and Verona. Managing Partner Maurizio Codurri is recommended for international business, financing and tax law.

Studio Legale Fusillo & Associati is a full-service practice in Rome focusing strongly on international arbitration, corporate law and IP.

General commercial and banking practice **Grieco e Associati** also offers corporate litigation advice. Based in Rome and Milan, the firm acts for Autostrade, General Motors and Enel.

Florence-based **JMU – Law Firm** is run by Jacopo Monaci Naldini, whose performance one client describes as 'exemplary'. The practice boasts English mother-tongue capabilities and advises on general commerce, project finance, real estate and trust law.

Jenny & Partners' core business is corporate and commercial law with a strong emphasis on banking, finance and energy law. The firm recently recruited M&A partner Gianmarco Mileni Munari and litigator Barbara Micelli from **Ashurst**.

LGV Avvocati's core business is IP. The practice offers expertise in copyright, trade mark and patent disputes. Clients include phonogram producers and the Business Software Alliance. Partner Roberto Vallenti is secretary to the Intellectual Property Rights Committee at the American Chamber of Commerce.

Milan-based **Lawfed – Rubino-Sammartano e Associati** has branches in Rome, Genoa and Turin and is a member of *Lawfed*, a network of independent law and accountancy firms. Mauro Rubino-Sammartano is reputed for his excellence in arbitration and is the current President of the European Court of Arbitration.

Lega Colucci Morri e Associati Studio Legale e Tributario is a new legal and tax advisory firm in Milan comprising 16 partners, many of whom are ex-Magic Circle. A second office recently opened in China.

Nine-partner **Marena, Bonvicini, Aghina e Ludergnani** has offices in Milan and Bologna that specialise in corporate, finance and commercial matters. Clients include pharmaceutical and fashion multinationals, merchant banks and several private equity players.

Florence-based **Studio Legale Mastellone** provides assistance in relation to civil, company and commercial law, litigation, transportation, real estate and employment. The firm is allied to **Studio Legale Coggiatti** in Rome and **Studio Legale Sardo** in Milan.

McNabb Associates, P.C is a boutique criminal defence firm operating from Milan, London, Washington, DC and Houston. Expertise is offered in international extradition cases, mainly connected to money laundering and mail and bank fraud allegations originating from the US.

Alberto Montanari heads commercial boutique **Montanari & Associati** that advises on M&A, corporate law and arbitration. Clients range from small businesses to large corporate entities like Siemens.

Studio Legale Nodari & Associati is recommended for its advice in corporate and commercial matters as well as litigation.

Fourteen-lawyer **Studio Legale Olivieri Ciapetti & Partners** has offices in Modena, Florence and Reggio Emilia that advise on a range of commercial practice areas.

Pinci & Associates, PLLC is an international practice with offices in Milan, Rome, Florence, Naples, New York and Athens. Several clients are multinational corporations with commercial, IP or TMT interests in Europe and the US.

Founding partner Alberto Pojaghi of **Studio Legale Pojaghi** in Milan is a specialist in competition and antitrust matters, intellectual property, arbitration and international law.

Milan-based **Studio Legale Sardo** is part of an alliance with **Studio Legale Coggiatti** in Rome and **Studio Legale Mastellone** in Florence.

Sena & Tarchini is known for outstanding patent and trade mark litigation work. The client base comprises pharmaceutical companies and fashion houses.

Tosi & Partners is based in Milan but has an office in Piacenza. This boutique is well known in the fields of data protection, data security and hi-tech law. Professor Emilio Tosi serves as arbitrator on numerous Italian and international associations.

Carlo Galdo of **Watson, Farley & Williams Studio Legale Associato**'s Rome office is highly regarded for his shipping finance expertise. Eugenio Tranchino specialises in corporate and projects work for major corporations and lenders.

Milan-based **Zambelli Luzzati Meregalli e Associati** is a full-service commercial firm allied to **Studio Legale Beltramo** and **ACLAW – Ceccon & Associati**.

BOLOGNA

Bologna, situated in north-central Italy, is the capital of the Emilia-Romagna region. The presence of international corporations is slight, with small to medium-sized companies providing most of the commercial activity. Key industries include food production, car manufacturing, clothing, footwear and engineering.

BOLOGNA Leading firms

Studio Professionale Associato a Baker & McKenzie opened its third Italian office in Bologna in 2002 when it merged with *Studio Bernini* to form **Studio Bernini associato a Baker & McKenzie**. This office is headed by the ex-Minister of Foreign Trade Giorgio Bernini, a leading expert in international arbitration, competition and antitrust law.

Corporate and arbitration lawyers Pietro Buccarelli and Federico Dettori are in charge of **Galgano**'s 40 lawyers working between Bologna and Milan. In 2005, Professor Fancesco Galgano was appointed by the Court of Padua to represent

BOLOGNA Leading firms

Bernini associato a Baker & McKenzie, Studio
Galgano
Gianni, Origoni, Grippo & Partners

---

de Capoa e Associati, Studio Legale
Derra, Meyer & Partner
Macchi di Cellere Gangemi
Morresi, Studio Legale

Firms are listed A-Z in tiers which are ranked in order of priority

Banca Antonveneta's interests while its two major shareholders battled out the takeover. In addition, the firm advised Unipol on a proposed acquisition of Banca Nazionale del Lavoro.

Gianni, Origoni, Grippo & Partners' Bologna office recently worked on the Cassina SpA acquisition and acted for Parmalat on the sale of Parma Calcio AC.

Full-service practice **Studio Legale de Capoa e Associati** has branches in Milan and Treviso in addition to associated offices in Budapest, Bucharest, Tehran, Los Angeles and Warsaw.

Derra, Meyer & Partner is based both in Germany and Italy and is the legal adviser to the German consulates in Rome, Bologna and Rimini. The practice is active in M&A, dispute resolution, employment, tax and energy law.

Macchi di Cellere Gangemi has been in Bologna since 2003 and offers general commercial and corporate legal services.

Studio Legale Morresi has offices in Bologna, Treviso and Brussels. This full-service commercial firm provides advice on corporate law, IP, antitrust issues and international arbitration.

GENOA

Genoa, the provincial capital of the Liguria Region, is near Turin in north-western Italy and has a population of approximately 650,000. The city boasts a major port that remains dominated by the shipping and insurance sectors, and in recent years has a seen a revival of its commercial and industrial activities. Historically, the city has been known for its ship-building and steelworks but the finance, electronics and computer sectors have emerged on a national and international level. Recently, a number of structural works and urban programmes were implemented as a result of Genoa being the 2004 European City of Culture.

GENOA Leading firms

Bonelli Erede Pappalardo has 37 professionals in Genoa, offering advice mainly in corporate and finance law, and litigation. Founding partner Professor Franco Bonelli is nationally and locally esteemed.

GENOA Leading firms

Bonelli Erede Pappalardo
Uckmar, Studio

Afferni Crispo & C., Studio Legale
Piccinini & Associati
Pinci & Associates, PLLC
Sutti, Studio Legale

Acquarone, Studio
Kielland Bressler, Studio Legale
Riccomagno, Studio Legale

Firms are listed A-Z in tiers which are ranked in order of priority

Victor Uckmar of five-partner **Studio Uckmar** is highly regarded for his tax expertise.

Commercial firm **Studio Legale Afferni Crispo & C.** has a secondary office in Milan. Advice is provided on M&A, bankpruptcy, litigation and IP law. Vittorio Afferni and Giorgio Schiano di Pepe are professors at the University of Genoa.

Piccinini & Associati is recommended for commercial, shipping, transport and litigation matters. Several Italian and international insurance companies are clients.

Pinci & Associates, PLLC is a full-service law firm with offices in Milan, Rome, Florence, Naples, New York and Athens. Several clients are multinational corporations with interests in Europe and the US.

Studio Legale Sutti's original Genoa office, run by Giuliano Pennini, advises on shipping and maritime issues, employment law and local litigation. In 2005, this office represented windsurf manufacturers Royal Ten Gate on a €2.3m dispute.

Professor Lorenzo Acquarone leads recommended commercial practice **Studio Acquarone**.

Studio Legale Kielland Bressler is recommended for shipping finance.

Studio Legale Riccomagno specialises in maritime and transportation law, international contracts and arbitration. The firm is a member of *IBLC*, an association of law and accountancy firms, and *Unilex*, a network of Italian law firms.

NAPLES

The Naples peninsula, extending into the central Mediterranean, is in the Campania region and the major industrial centre of southern Italy. Over the past decade, efforts have been made to tackle political corruption and improve the city's infrastructure, yet economic development remains considerably slower than in the north. Consequently, few international law firms are present.

Naples' commercial port is a significant shipping and maritime centre with close export links to China and home to southern Italy's major airport. The automotive and aeronautical industries are important features of the economy and a large Fiat plant is located here. Food production and tourism are also crucial to the region.

NAPLES Leading firms

Studio Legale de Meo & Associati is a medium-sized firm with offices in Naples, Rome, Milan and Civitavecchia. Michele de Meo, former founding partner of **Ughi e Nunziante** is reputed for his shipping law and litigation expertise.

Four-partner **Studio Legale Avv Prof Michele Sandulli & Associati** also has offices in Rome and Avellino. The firm acts on corporate, insolvency, and competition law, as well as litigation. Clients include Ariete SpA, the electrical household appliances company, and Banca di Napoli SpA.

NAPLES Leading firms

de Meo & Associati, Studio Legale
Michele Sandulli (Avv Prof) & Associati, Studio Legale

Carnelutti, Studio Legale
Gianni, Origoni, Grippo & Partners
PGRB – Puopolo Geffers Rosen & Bosin ✪
Scognamiglio, Studio Legale

A.L. Advisory
Lauro, Studio Legale
Militerni Nardone Ceceri & Associati
Morace & Co.

Firms are listed A-Z in tiers which are ranked in order of priority

Studio Legale Carnelutti's office in Naples (not be confused with the reincarnated **Carnelutti Studio Legale Associato** that recently split from **McDermott Will & Emery Studio Legale Associato**) is known for its shipping law and litigation advice.

Gianni, Origoni, Grippo & Partners opened in Naples in 2003. The practice works closely with the Milan, Rome, Bologna and Padua offices.

Rome-based **PGRB – Puopolo Geffers Rosen & Bosin** has three fee-earners working from Naples. Claudio Pepe worked on the tax aspects of a project for Skytanking concerning jet fuel facilities at the city's airport.

Studio Legale Scognamiglio is a ten-lawyer firm specialising in real estate, M&A, dispute resolution and maritime law. Clients include Bank of China and Toro Assicurazioni. Further offices are in Rome and Torre del Greco, and the firm is looking to open in Shanghai to service European clients active in the Asian market.

Paolo Di Martino and Claudio Porzo head up niche practice **A.L. Advisory**. The firm's core business is banking and finance but international arbitration and ADR work are also carried out.

Studio Legale Lauro advises on international shipping and maritime law as well as general commercial matters.

Four-partner **Militerni Nardone Ceceri & Associati** also has offices in Milan, Rome and Bergamo. This practice advises on M&A, arbitration, banking and administrative law.

Morace & Co. provides legal expertise on maritime issues, ship finance and dispute resolution. The firm has offices in Rome and Cagliari.

PADUA

Padua, in the Veneto region, is one of the most prosperous areas of north-eastern Italy and a popular place for large domestic and international firms to establish a presence. It is less affected by external economic change as it is less reliant on

PADUA Leading firms
Clifford Chance
Gianni, Origoni, Grippo & Partners
Simmons & Simmons ✪
Agnoli Bernardi e Associati
LCA Avvocati e Commercialisti D'Impresa
Tonucci, Studio Legale
ACLAW – Ceccon & Associati ✪
Cantaluppi & Partners
Pirola Pennuto Zei & Associati

Firms are listed A-Z in tiers which are ranked in order of priority
✪ Indicates firm displays contact details at the end of this chapter.

finance as Milan or the big-ticket deals. The region has strong services, mechanical, electronics, optical, pharmaceutical and textiles sectors. Nearby Vicenza is known for its base chemical companies in relation to the tanning industry and Treviso for furniture manufacturing.

PADUA Leading firms

Clifford Chance's Padua office is a full-service branch that works closely with the Milan and Rome teams, while also generating instructions locally.Gianandrea Rizzi has extensive experience in corporate and commercial matters, litigation and international arbitration.

Gianni, Origoni, Grippo & Partners has 14 fee-earners working on M&A, real estate, labour and litigation. Five professionals were added in 2005 and corporate lawyer Stefano Beghi was made partner. The office assisted Pirelli & Co Real Estate in connection with a huge development project of Portogruaro/Fossalta. Other clients include Diesel SpA for corporate issues and Cassa di Risparmio di Padova e Rovigo for labour matters.

Simmons & Simmons corporate lawyer Paolo Brugnera directs the Padua office, recently representing the Law Debenture Trust Corporation on the €1.2bn Cirio Group insolvency claim and SET Distribuzione on a €180m electricity distribution network acquisition.

Pavia e Ansaldo no longer has a presence in Padua. Its entire team left to form **Agnoli Bernardi e Associati** at the same address where contracts partner Giorgio Spanio leads a nine-strong legal team. The firm advises on corporate and private equity work, banking and finance, and litigation. Niche advice is also offered in sports and privacy law, and additional offices are in Milan, Rome and Turin.

Twelve-partner **LCA Avvocati e Commercialisti D'Impresa** is a multidisciplinary firm specialising in banking, corporate, antitrust and tax law. Additional offices are in Milan, Venice, London and Munich. The practice is a member of the *Euro Pacific Legal Group* and recently established an Australian desk for Italian clients looking to do business in Australia.

Studio Legale Tonucci's Padua office is run by Carlo Scarpa. The firm's head office is in Rome with branches in Milan, Florence, Bucharest and Tirana.

ACLAW – Ceccon & Associati is a full-service firm that has associated offices in Rome, Milan, Pordenone and Budapest.

Cantaluppi & Partners' core business is IP, namely patent, design, trade mark, copyright and domain names issues.

Pirola Pennuto Zei & Associati is recommended for legal tax advice.

TURIN

Turin, capital of the Piedmont region, is situated below the Alps in north-western Italy. The city, with a population of around 900,000, is a key site for manufacturers and hi-tech companies as well as being home to Fiat, the largest private sector employer in Italy. Despite being affected by the general economic slump, foreign investment is active. The area surrounding Turin features an important aerospace district that generates an annual turnover of around €1.3bn; Motorola has a research centre here and Italian coffee producers Ferrero and Lavazza are present.

Law firms in Turin represent multinational corporations and small to medium-sized companies and manufacturers. In early 2006, Turin hosted the Winter Olympic Games, providing an economic boost to the city. Improved infrastructure and communications, through the construction of a high-speed rail link between Lyon and Milan and a city subway, are expected to bring in investment.

TURIN Leading firms
Allen & Overy – Brosio e Associati – Studio Legale Associato ✪
Grande Stevens: Studio Legale Associazione Professionale
Agnoli Bernardi e Associati
Bin Avvocati Associati
Buffa, Bortolotti & Mathis
Frignani e Associati Studio Legale
Hammonds Rossotto
Jacobacci & Associati, Studio Legale
Tosetto Weigmann e Associati
Gamna, Studio Legale
Pirola Pennuto Zei & Associati

Firms are listed A-Z in tiers which are ranked in order of priority
✪ Indicates firm displays contact details at the end of this chapter.

TURIN Leading firms

Carlo Pavesio runs **Allen & Overy – Brosio e Associati – Studio Legale Associato**'s Turin branch, focusing on commercial law, M&A, antitrust and competition, technology licensing and litigation.

Grande Stevens: Studio Legale Associazione Professionale is a full-service law firm with additional offices in Milan and Rome. Franzo Grande Stevens is a highly respected commercial lawyer and a member of the National and Turin Bar Council. The practice is historically linked to its client Fiat.

Pavia e Ansaldo no longer has a presence in Turin. Its entire team left to form **Agnoli Bernardi e Associati** at the same address, a full-service law firm, with 70 professionals offering legal advice from Turin, Padua, Milan and Rome. For tax matters, the practice enjoys a working relationship with boutique **Di Tanno e Associati**.

Twenty-five-lawyer **Bin Avvocati Associati** is led by Marino Bin. In 2005, Melinda Geary, a common law expert and Daniele Pisanello, and IP and food lawyer, were recruited. Clients include ITW, global designers and producers of engineered fasteners, and Agenzia Torino, who are responsible for building the infrastructure for Turin's Winter Olympic Games.

Buffa, Bortolotti & Mathis specialises in trade law, antitrust matters and international litigation. The firm has a working relationship with Milan firm **Studio Legale Squassi & Gullo** and is a member of the *European Law Group*. Clients include Italian exporters and foreign companies setting up in Italy.

Frignani e Associati Studio Legale is recommended for franchising and competition law. The firm also advises on antitrust, litigation, IP and international trade.

Ten partners work from **Hammonds Rossotto**'s Turin office, assisting Italian and foreign clients in corporate and commercial matters, litigation and credit recovery.

Studio Legale Jacobacci & Associati also has offices in Milan and Rome. The firm is a former patent office that is admired for its 'soft' and contentious IP work that also advises on corporate and merger issues. Clients range from start-up ventures to huge multinational corporations in the fashion, biotechnology, electronics and Formula 1 businesses.

Tosetto Weigmann e Associati has a 'best-friends' agreement with Milan-based **Vita Samory, Fabbrini e Associati**. The firm advises on commercial and M&A transactions but is particularly known for its IP and litigation practice. Branch offices operate from Milan and Rome.

Studio Legale Gamna is recommended for corporate and bankruptcy advice.

Multi-disciplinary firm **Pirola Pennuto Zei & Associati** specialises in tax law. Additional offices are in Milan and Rome.

Gianni, Origoni, Grippo & Partners recently opened in Turin, led by Moreno Martini.

AGNOLI BERNARDI E ASSOCIATI

VIA DELLA MOSCOVA 3
20121 MILANO

Telephone: +39 02 63 28 51
Fax: +39 02 63 28 58 10
E-mail: info.milano@agnoli-bernardi.it
Website: www.agnoli-bernardi.it

Languages
Dutch, English, French, German, Hebrew, Italian, Mandarin, Romanian, Russian, Spanish

Other offices
Padua, Rome, Turin

Number of lawyers 73

International groupings
International Bar Association (IBA); AIFI (Italian Private Equity and Venture Capital Association); NED Community (Non-Executive Directors Community); EVCA (European Venture Capital Association)

CATEGORIES OF WORK

Corporate, M&A and private equity
Marcello Agnoli, Maurizio Bernardi

Banking and finance
Maurizio Bernardi, Francesca de Fraja

Communications
Francesca Lodigiani, Fabrizio De Luca

Litigation and arbitration
Paolo Berruti, Giorgio Spanio, Paolo Bianco

Labour litigation
Alberto Musy, Guido Zingoni

Privacy law
Gerolamo Pellicanò

Sport law
Giorgio Spanio, Gerolamo Pellicanò

Competition and EU
Marcello Agnoli, Nicolas Lievens

Intellectual property
Francesca Lodigiani, Caterina Quaranta

Administrative law
Paolo Berruti, Ermanno Vaglio

ALLEN & OVERY – STUDIO LEGALE ASSOCIATO

VIA MANZONI, 41/43
20121 MILAN

Telephone: +39 02 29 04 91
Fax: +39 02 29 04 93 33
E-mail: information@allenovery.com
Website: www.allenovery.com

Languages
English, French, German, Italian, Spanish

Other offices
Amsterdam, Antwerp, Bangkok, Beijing, Bratislava, Brussels, Budapest, Dubai, Frankfurt, Hamburg, Hong Kong, London, Luxembourg, Madrid, Moscow, New York, Paris, Prague, Rome, Shanghai, Singapore, Tokyo, Turin, Warsaw

Number of lawyers 2,304
at this office 100

Contacts
Roberto Casati (senior partner),
G. Massimilano Danusso (managing partner),
Emanuele Borganti (head of operations in Italy)

CATEGORIES OF WORK

Corporate
Paolo Cerina

Banking
Giancarlo Castorino

Tax
Andrea Manganelli

ICM
G. Massimilliano Danusso

Litigation
Massimo Greco

ASHURST

VIA SANT'ORSOLA 3
20123 MILAN

Telephone: +39 02 85 42 31
Fax: +39 02 85 42 34 44
Website: www. ashurst.com

Languages
English, French, Italian, Spanish

Other offices
Brussels, Dubai, Frankfurt, London, Madrid, Munich, New Delhi*, New York, Paris, Singapore, Tokyo

Number of lawyers 748
at this office 27

Contacts
Daniele Raynaud, Riccardo Agostinelli

CATEGORIES OF WORK

Corporate and commercial
Daniele Raynaud

Real estate
Daniele Raynaud

Private equity
Daniele Raynaud

Mergers and acquisitions
Daniele Raynaud

International finance
Riccardo Agostinelli, Maura Magioncalda

Banking
Riccardo Agostinelli, Maura Magioncalda

Capital markets
Leonardo Proni

Tax
Stefano Serbini

Employment
Francesco Simoneschi

Litigation
Francesco Simoneschi

Competition and EU

Regulatory

Intellectual property/ information technology

ASTOLFO DI AMATO E ASSOCIATI

LARGO AUGUSTO 1
20122 MILAN

Telephone: +39 02 76 01 74 97
Fax: +39 02 76 00 44 12
E-mail: diamatoeassociati@diamato.net
Website: www.diamato.net

Languages
English, French, Italian

Other offices
Naples, Rome

Number of lawyers 20

Contact
Alessio Di Amato

Member
Multilaw

CATEGORIES OF WORK

General practice

Corporate law

Banking law

Securities regulation

Business crime

White-collar crime

Tax crime

Bankruptcy

Litigation and arbitration

Contract law

Intellectual property, rights advertising and marks law

Information technology law

Telecommunications, media and entertainment law

Antitrust and trade regulation

European Union law

Foreign investments

International business transactions

STUDIO PROFESSIONALE ASSOCIATO A BAKER & McKENZIE

PIAZZA MEDA, 3
20121 MILANO

Telephone: +39 02 76 23 14 70
Fax: +39 02 76 23 16 12
E-mail: milan.info@bakernet.com
Website: www.bakernet.com

Languages
English, French, German, Spanish

Other offices
The member firms of Baker & McKenzie International, a Swiss Verein, have 70 offices in 38 countries around the world. For a complete list, please visit www.bakernet.com.

Number of lawyers 3,300+
at this office 75

Contact
Gerardo M Boniello (managing partner)

CATEGORIES OF WORK

Banking and finance

IT/IP (includes media – entertainment)

Telecommunications (includes media – regulatory)

Employment

Dispute resolution

Infrastructure (includes construction, works and projects)

Competition and trade

Tax

Environment and real estate

Pharma regulation

Corporate, M&A (and commercial transactions)

BIN AVVOCATI ASSOCIATI

SALA DEI LONGOBARDI 2
20121 MILAN

Telephone: +39 02 86 39 64 11
Fax: +39 02 86 39 64 22
E-mail: info@binpartners.com
Website: www.binpartners.com

Languages
English, French, German, Italian, Russian, Spanish

Other offices
Turin

Number of lawyers 30

Contacts
Fabio Alberto Regoli, Melinda Geary

CATEGORIES OF WORK

Commercial law

Employment

Mergers and acquisitions

Joint ventures

Company law

Litigation, arbitration, ADR

Administrative law

Domestic and international tenders and works

Planning and environment

Insurance

Restructuring

Immigration

Private equity

Insolvency

Real estate

National and international tax

Intellectual property

Food law

STUDIO LEGALE BERNASCONE & SOCI

PIAZZA SAN BABILA, 3
20122 MILAN

Telephone: +39 02 77 72 15 11
Fax: +39 02 77 72 15 15
E-mail: gbernascone@studiolegale.com
Website: www.studiobernascone.com

Languages
English, French, Italian

Contacts
Gabriele Bernascone, Paola Sangiovanni

CATEGORIES OF WORK	
Corporate and commercial	**Mergers and acquisitions**
Corporate finance	**Power generation, energy**
Data protection	**Privatisation**
Environment	**Project finance**
EU competition	**Reorganisation**
Information technology	**Securities**
Intellectual property	**Telecoms and IT**
Joint ventures	**Venture capital**
Life sciences/biotechnology	

THE FIRM

Clients look to the Milan office Studio Legale Bernascone & Soci, an associated office of Squire, Sanders & Dempsey L.L.P., for creative and forward-looking counsel on a wide variety of legal issues involving energy, corporate law, mergers and acquisitions, e-business and dispute resolution. Originally an office of San Francisco-based Graham & James LLP, Milan joined Squire, Sanders & Dempsey L.L.P. as an associated office in 2000.

The firm has a long history of representing international businesses in Italy's legal capital and second largest city, Milan. Through its association with Squire, Sanders & Dempsey L.L.P., the firm's clients have access to a global law firm with approximately 800 lawyers in 29 offices worldwide.

AREAS OF PRACTICE

The Milan lawyers assist both Italian companies and clients from Asia, Europe and the United States looking to do business in the Italian market.

The Milan lawyers' experience includes mergers and acquisitions, project finance and development, privatisations and energy marketing as well as environmental law. Services range from the formation of corporations and consortiums to the drafting of shareholder agreements. Lawyers also conduct dispute resolution and regulation for large companies and regularly represent clients in both commercial and labour litigation, handling defence work particularly in product liability cases.

The corporate practice serves the transactional needs of public and private companies, emerging companies and financial institutions. Services include participation in complex business transactions including acquisitions and dispositions, joint ventures, commercial loans, asset- and mortgage-backed securitisations, public and private securities offerings, real estate activities, tax matters, secured transactions and creditors' rights. Lawyers represent global investors in their acquisitions of Italian companies in such industries as textiles and fashion accessories, musical instruments, office equipment, home appliances, air conditioners, cars and motorbikes, and food and beverages (including spirits).

Milan lawyers provide counsel on domain rights and jurisdictional issues and have established joint ventures between Milan-based and international technology companies for licensing software. In fact, the office is recognised as a leading law firm in Italy for its representation of Japan-based trading companies particularly in connection with their licensing agreements with Italian primary fashion houses.

The office is also active in the communications arena, advising on Italian and European legislation concerning antitrust, privatisation and liberalisation as it affects the hi-tech and telecoms industries.

Lawyers have significant experience in the life sciences/biotechnology arena. Over the years, the firm's lawyers have provided legal services to numerous clients including biotechnology/biomedical/medical devices companies. A team of Milan lawyers are also founders of The Italian Society for the Study of Biotechnology (SISB), an association involved in the research, study and analysis of the interactions among science, culture, ethics, economy, environmental impact and legislation.

BIRD & BIRD

VIA MONTENAPOLEONE 10
20121 MILANO

Telephone: +39 02 30 35 60 00
Fax: +39 02 30 35 60 11
E-mail: milan@twobirds.com
Website: www.twobirds.com

Languages
English, French, German, Italian

Other offices
Beijing, Brussels, Düsseldorf, Frankfurt, Hong Kong, London, Madrid, Munich, Paris, Rome, Stockholm, The Hague

Number of lawyers 472
at this office 22

Contact
Massimiliano Mostardini

CATEGORIES OF WORK

Advertising/media
Rita Tardiolo

Banking and finance
Raimondo Maggiore

Commercial
Alberto Salvadé

Communications
Claudia Ricciardi, Massimiliano Mostardini

Corporate
Alberto Salvadé

EC competition law
Charlotte de Panafieu

Employment
Caterina Rucci

Information technology
Debora Stella

Intellectual property
Massimiliano Mostardini, Giovanni Galimberti, Paola Frassi

Life sciences
Massimiliano Mostardini, Claudia Ricciardi, Enrico Carlo Bacetti

Litigation
Riccardo Ciampella, Antonio Danile

CMS ADONNINO ASCOLI & CAVASOLA SCAMONI

VIA M. BUONARROTI, 39
20145 MILANO

Telephone: +39 02 48 01 11 71
Fax: +39 02 48 01 29 14
E-mail: info@cms-aacs.com
Website: www.cms-aacs.com

Languages
Bulgarian, Chinese (Cantonese and Mandarin), Dutch, English, French, German, Spanish

Other offices
Rome

Number of lawyers 60+
at this office 10

Contact
Antonella Mameli

Other CMS alliance member firms
CMS Albiñana & Suárez de Lezo, Spain; CMS Bureau Francis Lefebvre, France; CMS Cameron McKenna LLP, UK; CMS DeBacker, Belgium; CMS Derks Star Busmann, Netherlands; CMS von Erlach Henrici, Switzerland; CMS Hasche Sigle, Germany; CMS Reich-Rohrwig Hainz, Austria

CATEGORIES OF WORK

General civil practice

Business and corporate law

International contracts

Foreign investment

Banking

Joint ventures

EU law

Intellectual property

Foreign investment

Mergers and acquisitions

Labour law

Administrative law

Bankruptcy and credit recovery

Property law

Commercial litigation and arbitration

CAJOLA & ASSOCIATI

VIA G ROSSINI, 5
20122 MILANO

Telephone: +39 02 76 00 33 05
Fax: +39 02 78 01 77
E-mail: law@cajola.com
Website: www.cajola.com

Languages
English, French, Spanish

Number of lawyers 10

CATEGORIES OF WORK

Contracts	Intellectual property
Joint ventures	Construction
Mergers and acquisitions	Telecommunication and e-business
Corporate	EU law
Corporate finance	Employment law
Commercial law	Real estate
Banking law	Litigation
Taxation	Aviation law

CHIOMENTI STUDIO LEGALE

VIA G VERDI 2
20121 MILAN

Telephone: +39 02 72 15 71
Fax: +39 02 72 15 72 24
E-mail: milano@chiomenti.net

Languages
English, French, German, Italian, Spanish

Other offices
Brussels, London, New York, Rome

Number of lawyers 210
at this office 80

Member
Lex Mundi

CATEGORIES OF WORK

Corporate and M&A	Litigation and arbitration
Banking and finance	Insolvency and corporate restructuring
Capital markets	Employment
Regulatory and financial services	Telecommunications
Tax	Energy
European law, competition and international law	Real estate
Administrative law	
Intellectual property, media and information technology	

CLEARY GOTTLIEB STEEN & HAMILTON LLP

VIA SAN PAOLO 7
20121 MILAN

Telephone: +39 02 72 60 81
Fax: +39 02 86 98 44 40
Website: www.clearygottlieb.com

Languages
English, French, German, Italian, Spanish

Other offices
Brussels, Cologne, Frankfurt, Hong Kong, London, Moscow, New York, Paris, Rome, Tokyo, Washington DC

Number of lawyers 847
at this office 27

CATEGORIES OF WORK

Banking and finance

Commercial and corporate litigation

Capital markets/securities

EU and competition law

EU litigation

Joint ventures

Mergers and acquisitions

Privatisations

Regulatory issues

Restructuring

Tax

Telecommunications and energy

CURTIS, MALLET-PREVOST, COLT & MOSLE LLP

IN ASSOCIAZIONE CON GILIOLI ALEMANI BOCCHIOLA TAMBURINI E PARTNERS

CORSO VENEZIA 5
20121 MILAN

Telephone: +39 02 76 23 20 01
Fax: +39 02 76 00 90 76
E-mail: info@cm-p.com
Website: www.cm-p.com

Languages
English, French, Italian, Spanish

Other offices
Frankfurt, Houston, London, Mexico City, Muscat, New York, Paris, Stamford, Washington DC

Number of lawyers 187
at this office 18

Contacts
Eric L Gilioli (Milan, New York), Michele Tamburini (Milan)

Member
American Chamber of Commerce in Italy; Union International des Avocats; Rotary International; Italian Chambers of Commerce in the United States and Mexico

CATEGORIES OF WORK

Mergers and acquisitions/ joint ventures
Eric L Gilioli, Elena A Berlucchi

Securities and finance
Maurizio Bocchiola, Elena A Berlucchi

Banking and broker-dealer
Giuseppe Alemani, Fabrizio Vismara

Commercial contracts
Daniel Gilioli, Michele Tamburini

International tax law
Fabrizio Vismara

European Union law
Michele Tamburini

Latin American trade and investment
Antonio M Prida

Investment management, private equity, venture capital
Carl A Ruggiero, Elena A Berlucchi

Infrastructure and public projects
Eric L Gilioli, Michele Tamburini

Arbitration
Maurizio Bocchiola, Enrico Gilioli

Litigation
Maurizio Bocchiola, Enrico Gilioli

Insolvency proceedings
Giuseppe Alemani, Maurizio Bocchiola

Employment law
Enrico Gilioli

Intellectual property
Michele Tamburini

Foundations
Giuseppe Alemani, Fabrizio Vismara

International trusts and estates
Daniel Gilioli

Private client
Giuseppe Alemani, Daniel Gilioli

DLA PIPER RUDNICK GRAY CARY

VIA CORDUSIO 2
20123 MILAN

Telephone: +39 02 80 61 81
Fax: +39 02 80 61 82 02
E-mail: milinfo@dlapiper.com
Website: www.dlapiper.com/italy

Languages
English, French, German, Italian

Other offices
Austria, Belgium, Bosnia-Herzegovina, China, Croatia, Czech Republic, Denmark*, Egypt*, France, Georgia, Germany, Hong Kong, Hungary, Italy, Japan, Netherlands, Norway*, Poland*, Russia, Singapore*, Slovakia, South Africa*, Spain, Sweden*, Thailand, UK, Ukraine, United Arab Emirates, US

Number of lawyers 3,100
at this office 57

Contact
Federico Sutti

Member
DLA Piper Group

CATEGORIES OF WORK

M&A, PFI
Federico Sutti

Corporate
Davide Proverbio

Real estate
Olaf Schmidt

Telecom/technology
Stefano Modenesi

Labour law
Claudio Morpurgo

Tax
Nicola Zeni

Public procurement
Giorgia Romitelli

Energy
Wolf Michael Kühne

Environmental – town planning
Giovanni Landi

Real estate financing
Elisabetta Poltronieri

Banking
Francesco Squerzoni

Litigation
Stefano Modenesi

IP
Giacomo Parmigiani

THE FIRM

DLA Piper Rudnick Gray Cary is a leading global legal services provider with approximately 3,100 lawyers in 58 offices across 22 countries. The organisation is committed to building long-term relationships with its clients and supports their strategic and operational needs both locally and internationally.

In Italy, DLA Piper Rudnick Gray Cary is a full-service, locally led law firm with over ten years' experience and international capability across Europe, Africa, Asia and the US. Lawyers in Milan and Rome specialise in all aspects of business law and regularly advise on cross-border transactions.

While Italy has always been a focus for European trade and investment, the reform of corporate, tax and employment law is set to make Italy an even more attractive environment for both inward investors and national enterprises. The ability to respond quickly to these opportunities is fundamental to all businesses. DLA Piper Rudnick Gray Cary differentiates itself by its speed of response and the desire to put clients first. The organisation invests in its clients to understand what their needs really are and how it can add value to their business. The team will be local lawyers, able to really understand and empathise with clients' commercial needs, both locally and on a broader international level.

DLA Piper is a founding member of an exclusive alliance of full-service legal organisations with a shared vision. DLA Piper Group, established in 1999, has members across Europe, Africa, the Middle East, Asia and the US, which deliver expert local know-how and integrated international solutions.

AREAS OF PRACTICE

Banking and finance – provides legal advice to national and international banks, as well as other financial service providers operating in all areas of banking and finance, including commercial banking and real estate and project finance.

Corporate and M&A – brings extensive experience, both domestically and internationally, on a broad range of matters, including the setting up and structuring of corporate entities, mergers, demergers and acquisitions, the formation of joint ventures and consortia, corporate reorganisations and commercial transactions in general, including all the tax angles thereof.

Human resources – assists in all legal and practical aspects of employment law, as well as the risk assessment of possible disputes.

Litigation – offers global legal assistance before Italian courts to both foreign and Italian clients, handling the full range of international law issues.

Project finance – widely recognised prominence in both private and public finance transactions, plus unique expertise in the field of infrastructure financing. Advises lending institutions involved in PFI transactions, as well as major international real estate developers, primary construction companies and international market leaders in facilities management.

Real estate – assists Italian and international clients in all areas of real estate law, with particular emphasis on acquisition of existing real estate property, development of unbuilt land, construction law and project finance.

Tax – provides clients such as foreign investment funds, international banks and other institutional investors, as well as public and private and multinational companies, with specialist tax advice to develop the best structure for their operations.

Technology, media and communications – provides contentious and non-contentious advice in areas of IT/outsourcing, intellectual property, telecommunications, media, e-commerce, data protection and privacy.

DE BERTI JACCHIA FRANCHINI FORLANI

VIA SAN PAOLO 7
20121 MILANO

Telephone: +39 02 72 55 41
Fax: +39 02 72 55 46 00
E-mail: milan@dejalex.com
Website: www.dejalex.com

Languages
English, French, German, Russian, Spanish, Swedish

Other offices
Brussels, Moscow, Rome

Numbers of lawyers 67
at this office 47

Contact
Gianni Forlani (g.forlani@dejalex.com)

CATEGORIES OF WORK

Administrative and regulatory	European Union law
Arbitration and ADR	Insolvency and restructuring
Automotive	IP and pharmaceutical law
Banking, finance and securities	IT and telecommunications
Competition and antitrust	M&A and private equity
Corporate and commercial	Real estate and planning
Domestic and international litigation	Retail, sport, insurance
Employment and pensions	Successions and trust
Environmental and energy	Tax, transport, shipping, air law

STUDIO LEGALE DELFINO E ASSOCIATI
WILLKIE FARR & GALLAGHER LLP

VIA MICHELE BAROZZI 2
20122 MILAN

Telephone: +39 02 76 36 31
Fax: +39 02 76 36 36 36
Website: www.willkie.com

Languages
English, French, German, Spanish

Other offices
Brussels, Frankfurt, London, Paris, Rome, New York, Washington DC

Number of lawyers 590
at this office 21

Contact
Maurizio Delfino

CATEGORIES OF WORK

Mergers and acquisitions	Tax
Private equity	Antitrust
Capital markets	Litigation
Telecommunication	Arbitration
Energy	

DEWEY BALLANTINE STUDIO LEGALE

VIA FRATELLI GABBA 4
20121 MILAN

Telephone: +39 02 30 30 93 30
Fax: +39 02 30 30 93 40
Website: www.deweyballantine.com

Languages
English, French, German, Italian, Spanish

Other offices
Austin, Beijing, East Palo Alto, Frankfurt, Houston, London, Los Angeles, New York, Rome, Warsaw, Washington DC

Number of lawyers 550+
at this office 26

Contacts
Bruno Gattai (bgattai@deweyballantine.com), Stefano Speroni (ssperoni@deweyballantine.com), Luca Minoli (lminoli@deweyballantine.com)

CATEGORIES OF WORK

Mergers and acquisitions
Nicola Brunetti, Stefano Catenacci, Bruno Gattai, Luca Minoli, Giovan B Santangelo, Stefano Speroni, Adriano Pala, Emanuela Ciaffi

Private equity
Nicola Brunetti, Stefano Catenacci, Bruno Gattai, Giovan B Santangelo, Stefano Speroni

Privatisation
Nicola Brunetti, Bruno Gattai, Adriano Pala, Emanuela Ciaffi

Real estate
Stefano Catenacci, Bruno Gattai, Giovan B Santangelo, Adriano Pala

Energy
Nicola Brunetti, Bruno Gattai, Luca Minoli

Capital markets
Emanuela Ciaffi, Stefano Catenacci Bruno Gattai, Giovan B Santangelo, Stefano Speroni, Adriano Pala, Ugo Giordano, Nicola Brunetti

Securitisation
Stefano Speroni, Ugo Giordano

Derivatives
Ugo Giordano, Giovan B Santangelo, Stefano Speroni

Telecommunications
Stefano Speroni, Giovan B Santangelo

Tax
Luca Dezzani

Litigation
Luca Minoli

DI TANNO E ASSOCIATI

CORSO VENEZIA 36
20121 MILANO

Telephone: +39 02 76 21 31
Fax: +39 02 77 33 12 55
E-mail: ditannoeass@ditanno.it
Website: www.ditanno.it

Languages
English, French

Other offices
Rome, Treviso

Number of lawyers 48
at this office 12

Contacts
Tommaso Di Tanno, Stefano Petrecca

CATEGORIES OF WORK

Tax

Tax litigation

Commercial and company law

Venture capital

Mergers and acquisitions

Corporate finance

Banking and finance

GALGANO

VIALE MAJNO 7
20122 MILAN

Telephone: +39 02 77 72 14 1
Fax: +39 02 76 39 70 91
E-mail: milano@galgano.it
Website: www.galgano.it

Languages
English, French, German, Spanish

Other offices
Bologna

Number of lawyers 40
at this office 24

Contacts
Marco Consonni, Federico Galgano

CATEGORIES OF WORK

Commercial law	**Antitrust**
Company law	**IT, Internet and e-commerce**
Corporate finance, M&A, private equity	**Telecoms**
Banking and finance	**Media and entertainment**
Capital markets	**Intellectual property**
Regulatory and financial services	**Employment**
Project finance	**Administrative**
Real estate	**Litigation and arbitration**

THE FIRM

Galgano was founded in the 1970s by Francesco Galgano, professor of civil law at the University of Bologna. Prof Galgano is a nationally renowned academic and one of the leading Italian practitioners in banking and corporate law. Over the years Galgano has built a loyal following of clients by delivering incisive solutions to practical problems. This has underpinned the firm's steady organic growth: currently the firm is made up of 40 qualified lawyers, including partners and associates, divided between the Bologna and Milan offices.

Galgano is now considered a leading Italian firm with a national and international corporate, commercial and finance practice. The firm concentrates on offering legal services relating to banking and finance, capital markets, M&A and venture capital, TMT and dispute resolution. Clients of the firm include industrial corporations, technology businesses, banks, insurance companies, institutional investors, governmental bodies and other public entities, and private individuals.

The firm is strongly represented in academic circles, with a number of partners holding university professorships in addition to their professional activities. Prof Galgano has also been an active participant in the drafting of new legislation such as the recent reform of corporate law.

The firm's lawyers are qualified to offer legal services across a wide range of industries and practice areas. Galgano is known for an unusually broad experience and versatility which means that it is always able to meet its clients' needs, not only with its day-to-day operations but also in engineering and executing highly innovative transactions or in resolving complex disputes. The firm is appreciated for its pro-active and practical approach and for its 'can do' attitude in solving its clients' problems. Galgano offers its services without undue formality and without over-lawyering.

The Bologna office's details are: 40125 Bologna, Via Santo Stefano 11; tel: +39 051 232622; fax: +39 051 231238; email bologna@galgano.it

AREAS OF PRACTICE

Although the firm's main focus is usually on matters of Italian law, it has substantial experience of working on international transactions, assisting both foreign clients in their Italian operations and Italian corporations in their international affairs or contentious matters.

The firm has a widely recognised expertise in its key areas of banking and finance, capital markets, corporate finance, communications and media and dispute resolution.

Banking, finance and capital markets are one of the key areas of the firm's practice. This group forms part of a wider team of specialists who assist leading domestic and international investment and commercial banks, financial institutions and public and private investors, and provide sector-specific legal services across the full range of financial matters. The firm is also highly regarded for its litigation capability in this area.

Corporate finance, M&A and private equity investments are also a main area of practice. Clients include public and private corporations, investments banks, financial institutions, and private equity providers.

Galgano is also highly regarded for its technology, media and telecoms work. It provides advice on internet law, telecommunications, information technology, media, advertising and audiovisual. The clientele ranges from established companies to emerging businesses and Galgano provides a wide range of services such as start-up financing, help with initial corporate governance, advice on e-commerce strategies and best licensing practice, and litigation.

Galgano is well known for its litigation practice assisting its clients in a wide range of commercial and corporate disputes, such as contentious banking and financial matters, IP litigation, and employment disputes.

Other main areas of practice include: administrative and public law and regulation; antitrust law; commercial law and distribution contracts; employment; IP and competition; projects; real estate and hotel investments; and trust structures.

GILIBERTI PAPPALETTERA TRISCORNIA E ASSOCIATI

VIA VISCONTI DI MODRONE, 21
20122 MILAN

Telephone: +39 02 76 00 15 85
Fax: +39 02 78 08 58
E-mail: studio@giliberti-lex.net

Languages
English, French, German, Italian, Spanish

Number of lawyers 26

Contacts
Carlo Pappalettera, Alessandro Triscornia

CATEGORIES OF WORK

Mergers, acquisitions and corporate law

Joint ventures

International contracts

Banking and finance

Litigation and arbitration

Capital markets

Asset finance/securitisation

Commercial property/real estate

Corporate and commercial

Infrastructure and project finance

Insolvency/corporate restructuring

Privatisation

Private client

JENNY & PARTNERS

VIA DURINI 27
20122 MILAN

Telephone: +39 02 77 80 31
Fax: + 39 02 77 80 32 33
E-mail: mail@jenny.it
Website: www.jenny.it

Languages
English, French, German, Spanish

Number of lawyers 18

Contact
Christoph Jenny

CATEGORIES OF WORK

Corporate
Christoph Jenny

Mergers and acquisitions
Gianmarco Mileni Munari

Banking, finance and insurance
Andrea Polizzi

Commercial
Simona Gallo

Agency, distributionship and franchising
Simona Gallo

Intellectual property
Simona Gallo

Labour
Paulo Soo Invernizzi

Real estate
Luca Pagnotta

Construction
Luca Pagnotta

Energy and utilities
Ruben Pescara

Competition and trade
Christoph Jenny

Litigation and arbitration
Alberto Morgioni

Insolvency and reorganisation
Alberto Morgioni

JONES DAY

VIA TURATI 16-18
20121 MILAN

Telephone: +39 02 76 45 40 01
Fax: +39 02 76 45 44 00
Website: www.jonesday.com

Languages
English, French, German, Spanish

Other offices
Atlanta, Beijing, Brussels, Chicago, Cleveland, Columbus, Dallas, Frankfurt, Hong Kong, Houston, Irvine, London, Los Angeles, Madrid, Menlo Park, Milan, Moscow, Munich, New Delhi, New York, Paris, Pittsburgh, San Diego San Francisco, Shanghai, Singapore, Sydney, Taipei, Tokyo, Washington DC

Number of lawyers 2,200
at this office 30

CATEGORIES OF WORK

Banking and structured finance
Roberto Truffi

Asset finance/securitisation
Ettore Scandale

Mergers and acquisitions
Ettore Scandale, Giovanni M Marini

Tax
Marco Lombardi

Telecoms
Stefano Macchi di Cellere

Private equity
Ettore Scandale, Marco Lombardi

Competition law and distribution
Stefano Macchi di Cellere

Corporate and commercial litigation
Roberto Truffi, Giovanni M Marini

Real estate
Giovanni M Marini, Marco Lombardi, Ettore Scandale

Infrastructure and project finance
Ettore Scandale, Giovanni M Marini

LGV AVVOCATI

VIA PRIVATA C BATTISTI 2
20122 MILANO

Telephone: +39 02 54 06 97 1
Fax: +39 02 54 06 97 30
E-mail: info@lgvavvocati.it
Website: www.lgvavvocati.it

Languages
Italian, English, German, French, Spanish

Number of lawyers 10

CATEGORIES OF WORK

Copyright

Trade marks

Patents

Unfair competition

Advertising

Antitrust and competition

E-commerce, privacy and security information

Commercial law

Corporate law

Mergers and acquisitions

IP procurement services

Arbitration and ADR

Product liability

Trade secrets/know-how

LINKLATERS

VIA PIETRO VERRI, 10
20121 MILAN

Telephone: +39 02 77 88 42 22
Fax: +39 02 77 88 43 33
Website: www.linklaters.com

Languages
All commercial and local languages in the countries where Linklaters operates

Other offices
Amsterdam, Antwerp, Bangkok, Beijing, Berlin, Bratislava, Brussels, Bucharest, Budapest, Cologne, Dubai, Frankfurt am Main, Hong Kong, Lisbon, London, Luxembourg, Madrid, Moscow, Munich, New York, Paris, Prague, Rome, São Paulo, Shanghai, Singapore, Stockholm, Tokyo, Warsaw

Number of lawyers 2,000 worldwide

Contacts
Sarosh Mewawalla (Milan),
Luigi Sensi (Rome)

CATEGORIES OF WORK

Acquisition finance
Sarosh Mewawalla (*Milan*)

Banking
Sarosh Mewawalla (*Milan*)

Capital markets
Luigi Sensi (*Rome*)

Projects
Sarosh Mewawalla (*Milan*)

Securitisations
Sarosh Mewawalla (*Milan*),
Luigi Sensi (*Rome*)

LOIACONO E ASSOCIATI

VIA MANZONI 31
20121 MILANO

Telephone: +39 02 63 61 12 11
Fax: +39 02 63 61 12 22
E-mail: info@loiacono.com
Website: www.loiacono.com

Languages
English, French, German, Spanish

Other offices
London

Number of lawyers 10

Contact
Dario Loiacono

CATEGORIES OF WORK

Banking and financial services

Capital markets

Financial regulatory

Asset management

Mergers and acquisitions

Financial litigation

LOMBARDI MOLINARI E ASSOCIATI

VIA ANDEGARI 4/A
20121 MILAN

Telephone: +39 02 89 62 21
Fax: +39 02 89 62 23 33
E-mail: info@lmlaw.it
Website: www.lmlaw.it

Languages
English, French, German, Italian

Number of lawyers 40

CATEGORIES OF WORK

M&A	**Insolvency and corporate restructuring**
Litigation and arbitration	**Competition**
Banking and finance	**Intellectual property**
Corporate and commercial	**Real estate**

THE FIRM

Lombardi Molinari e Associati is an independent law firm providing legal advice mainly in the areas of corporate and commercial law. The firm has established itself as an important player among law firms in Italy, advising on litigation and arbitration, as well as on corporate and financial transactions.

The firm, founded by Giuseppe Lombardi, who leads it with the other managing partner, Ugo Molinari, has approximately 40 lawyers. The firm maintains strong links with the academic legal community, and members of the firm serve as law professors and young scholars at Italian universities.

Most of the firm's clients are Italian corporations and financial institutions, including banks, insurance companies and private equity funds. The firm's clients are assisted in complex and innovative transactions, as well as in high-profile disputes both within Italy and, increasingly, at an international level. In this context, the firm provides legal assistance also in the English, German and French languages, and has developed far-reaching relations with prominent international law firms, with which the firm works on a regular basis.

The firm has grown steadily, in the belief that a law firm's success depends on the quality of the service it renders rather than its size; thus not on the sheer number of its members, but rather on their skills, passion for their profession and dedication to the clients' needs.

With this perspective, the firm has chosen to restrict its activities to a select number of high-profile matters, with a view to offering the highest possible level of care and attention at any given time. Furthermore, as its partners are directly and personally involved in all aspects of the assistance provided, the firm's clients are always in contact with the partners responsible for handling their cases. This has offered the firm an opportunity to build up and maintain close relationships with its clients over the years.

Another distinctive quality of the firm is its deliberate choice not to be organised into formal departments. The fact that most of the firm's lawyers have worked in a variety of practice areas, on both contentious and non-contentious matters, has significantly helped in training versatile advisers able to develop a deep and broad vision of any legal issues submitted to them. The lawyers' expertise and the current size of the firm make it possible for ad hoc teams of lawyers, led by at least one senior partner, to handle the most complex transactions and cases.

AREAS OF PRACTICE

Since its formation, the firm has been involved in important litigation and arbitration cases in corporate, commercial and general civil law matters. However, the firm has been increasingly active for the last few years in advising and assisting Italian companies, financial institutions and private equity funds in non-contentious matters (mergers and acquisitions, joint ventures, tender offers, and structured finance and banking transactions). Furthermore, the firm has significant experience in business reorganisations, including bankruptcy issues, having assisted various Italian groups in restructuring their activity.

LOVELLS

VIA FRATELLI GABBA 3
20121 MILAN

Telephone: +39 02 72 02 52 1
Fax: +39 02 72 02 52 52
E-mail: information@lovells.com
Website: www.lovells.com

Languages
English, French, German

Other offices
Alicante, Amsterdam, Beijing, Berlin, Brussels, Budapest*, Chicago, Düsseldorf, Frankfurt, Hamburg, Ho Chi Minh City, Hong Kong, London, Madrid, Moscow, Munich, New York, Paris, Prague, Rome, Shanghai, Singapore, Tokyo, Warsaw, Zagreb*

Number of lawyers 1,600
at this office 38

Contact
Paolo Criscione

CATEGORIES OF WORK

Corporate (including M&A, private equity, privatisations)

Antitrust/competition

Tax

Financial services and investment funds

Banking

Capital markets

Project finance

Real estate and construction

Administrative and public law (including town planning, environment, energy)

Pharmaceutical

Insurance

Insolvency

Intellectual property, IT, e-commerce and media

Employment

Litigation and arbitration

Data protection

MACCHI DI CELLERE GANGEMI

VIA G SERBELLONI 4
20122 MILAN

Telephone: +39 02 76 32 81
Fax: +39 02 76 00 16 18
E-mail: milano@macchi-gangemi.com
Website: www.macchi-gangemi.com

Languages
English, French, German, Italian, Portuguese, Spanish

Other offices
Bologna, Paris, Rome, Treviso, Verona, Vicenza

Number of lawyers 95+
at this office 35

CATEGORIES OF WORK

Acquisitions and mergers, corporate reorganisations

Antitrust, competition, EU law

Arbitration and ADR, litigation

Asset-based and structured finance

Banking and investment services

Business organisation, joint ventures

Capital markets and securities

Commercial transactions, investments and trade

Construction, public works, public services

Consumer law and misleading advertising

Corporate governance

E-commerce, telecommunications and media

Energy and natural resources, environment, water

Entertainment

Insolvency, insurance

Intellectual property

Investment companies, mutual funds

Labour and social security

Privacy

Private equity

Project financing

Real estate

Takeovers, privatisations

Tax

STUDIO LEGALE MONDINI-RUSCONI

VIA VISCONTI DI MODRONE 2
20122 MILANO

Telephone: +39 02 77 73 51
Fax: +39 02 77 73 53 33
E-mail: studiolegale@mondinirusconi.it
Website: www.mondinirusconi.it

Languages
English, French, German, Spanish

Number of lawyers 23

CATEGORIES OF WORK

International and EC law
Giorgio Mondini, Anna Carabelli

Company law
Luca Tiberi, Giuseppe Rusconi

Copyright, trade marks and intellectual property
Giorgio Mondini, Anna Carabelli

Media law
Giorgio Mondini, Anna Carabelli

Contracts
Giorgio Mondini, Giuseppe Rusconi

Litigation
Giacomo Bonelli, Alessandro Fano

Telecommunications
Giorgio Mondini, Alessandro Fano

Labour
Giacomo Bonelli, Alessandro Fano

Tax
Giuseppe Rusconi

Construction law
Giuseppe Rusconi, Luca Tiberi

Commercial law – mergers and acquisitions
Giuseppe Rusconi, Luca Tiberi

NCTM – STUDIO LEGALE ASSOCIATO

VIA AGNELLO 12
20121 MILAN

Telephone: +39 02 72 55 11
Fax: +39 02 72 55 15 01
E-mail: info@nctm.it
Website: www.nctm.it

Languages
English, French, German, Spanish

Other offices
Rome, Verona, Vicenza

Number of lawyers 130
at this office 90

Contacts
Filippo Cesaris, Paolo Montironi, Vittorio Noseda, Stefano Padovani, Alberto Toffoletto

CATEGORIES OF WORK

Corporate

Mergers and acquisitions

Private equity

Capital markets and IPOs

Banking and finance

Commercial

Insolvency and debt restructuring

Litigation and arbitration

Antitrust

Real estate

Regulated sectors

Intellectual property

Labour law

Administrative law

Environment and labour security

Tax

NUNZIANTE MAGRONE

FORO BUONAPARTE 70
20121 MILANO

Telephone: +39 02 65 75 18 1
Fax: +39 02 65 70 01 3
E-mail: milano@nmlex.it
Website: www.nmlex.it

Languages
English, French, German, Spanish

Other offices
Bologna, Rome, Turin

Number of lawyers 54
at this office 18

CATEGORIES OF WORK	
Corporate	**Postal**
Banking and finance	**Aviation**
Mergers and acquisitions	**Environmental**
Litigation and arbitration	**Tax**
Intellectual property	**Real Estate**
Administrative	**White-collar crime**
EU and competition	**Immigration**

ORRICK, HERRINGTON & SUTCLIFFE

VIA VISCONTI DI MODRONE, 12
20122 MILAN

Telephone: +39 02 45 41 38 00
Fax: +39 02 45 41 38 01
Website: www.orrick.com

Languages
English, French, German, Spanish

Other offices
Hong Kong, London, Los Angeles, Moscow, New York, Orange County, Pacific Northwest (Portland, Seattle), Paris, Rome, Sacramento, San Francisco, Silicon Valley, Taipei, Tokyo, Washington DC

Number of lawyers 850
at this office 30

Contact
Alessandro De Nicola

CATEGORIES OF WORK

Administrative law	**EU competition law**
Anti-corruption and white-collar crime	**Employment**
Bankruptcy and debt restructuring	**General finance**
Commercial and institutional finance	**Intellectual property and information technology**
Corporate governance	**Litigation**
Corporate, mergers and acquisitions	**Real estate**

THE FIRM

Orrick is an international law firm with more than 850 attorneys located in Asia, Europe and North America. In Europe, Orrick has almost 200 attorneys across five offices, located in London, Milan, Moscow, Paris and Rome. With the firm's European expansion, Orrick now has 16 offices across three continents.

Much of Orrick's client work in Europe involves cross-border transactions and financings that span Europe, the Middle East, Africa, Asia, and the Americas. To support the demands of its clients, Orrick has made seamless client service its number one goal across the firm. As a result, the firm's European lawyers can call on the substantial resources of Orrick's other offices around the world to provide clients with the expertise required to support their transactions.

Above all, Orrick's name stands for excellence in legal services; integrated, responsive client teams throughout the world; innovative leadership and management; and a commitment to the firm's core values, which govern these business standards.

Orrick's highly regarded partners in Milan and Rome rank among Italy's leading lawyers, and also include reputed economists and university professors. Orrick Italy also regularly hosts a forum for general counsels of major Italian companies to discuss the latest legal developments of significance to the Italian business community. In addition to being one of the leaders in the field of white-collar crime and corporate governance programmes, the firm's Italian lawyers focus on cross-border and domestic mergers and acquisitions, antitrust cases, structured finance (with particular emphasis on securitisation transactions), corporate governance and transactions, private equity, debt restructuring, project finance, domestic public finance, administrative law (focusing on public procurements, privatisations, building and town planning), real estate, intellectual property and technology law. Orrick's clients in Italy include many of the world's leading financial institutions, commercial enterprises, both closed-end and public companies, and a number of investment companies.

AREAS OF PRACTICE

Orrick's finance lawyers advise on transactions ranging from credit agreements and public debt issuances to complex cross-border lease financings, including secured and unsecured lending, asset-backed financing, letters of credit, asset-backed commercial paper financing, lease finance and aircraft finance.

Orrick's corporate group advises public and private companies around the globe on all aspects of their businesses and at every stage of their growth and development. The Italian offices represent international companies, both public and private, in a variety of industries and sectors, with extensive experience in mergers and acquisitions, joint ventures and strategic alliances, strategic technology transactions, corporate formations, financings at all stages of company development, restructurings and corporate counselling. Orrick's corporate lawyers draw upon the experience of other practice groups to provide assistance with antitrust, tax, executive compensation and employee benefits, intellectual property, employment, real estate and litigation issues.

The real estate group represents clients in all phases of real estate investment, financing, development, and operations, ranging from traditional purchases, sales, leases, and financings to highly sophisticated and complex portfolio acquisitions and multi-jurisdictional transactions.

The anti-corruption and white-collar crime practice is second to none, its lawyers having experience of advising clients across a range of sectors, from automobile manufacturing and infrastructure development to mail services, insurance and banking.

PAUL, HASTINGS, JANOFSKY & WALKER (EUROPE) LLP

VIA PALESTRO 24
20122 MILAN

Telephone: +39 02 30 41 40 00
Fax: +39 02 30 41 40 05
E-mail: info@paulhastings.com
Website: www.paulhastings.com

Languages
English, French, German

Other offices
Atlanta, Beijing, Brussels, Hong Kong, London, Los Angeles, New York, Orange County, Palo Alto, Paris, San Diego, San Francisco, Shanghai, Stamford, Tokyo, Washington DC

Number of lawyers 15

Contacts
Roberto Cornetta, Bruno Cova

CATEGORIES OF WORK

- **Mergers and acquisitions**
- **Capital markets, securities and privatisations**
- **Project finance**
- **Banking and finance**
- **Real estate**
- **Insolvency and restructuring**
- **Litigation**
- **Corporate investigation and white-collar crime**
- **Employment**
- **Tax**

PEDERSOLI E ASSOCIATI

VIA MONTE DE PIETÁ 15
20121 MILAN

Telephone: +39 02 30 30 51
Fax: +39 02 30 30 53 33
E-mail: contacts@pedersoli.it
Website: www.pedersoli.it

Languages
English, French, German

Number of lawyers 60

Contacts
Carlo Pedersoli, senior partner (c.pedersoli@pedersoli.it),
Enrico Zattoni , international matters (e.zattoni@pedersoli.it)

CATEGORIES OF WORK

- **Mergers and acquisitions**
- **Private equity and venture capital**
- **Corporate and commercial**
- **Capital markets**
- **Securities**
- **Banking**
- **Acquisition finance**
- **Financial sevices**
- **Tax**
- **Litigation and arbitration**
- **Insolvency and restructuring**
- **Pharma and biotech**
- **Antitrust and EU law**
- **Real estate**
- **Project finance**

PIROLA PENNUTO ZEI & ASSOCIATI

VIA VITTOR PISANI 16/19
20124 MILAN

Telephone: +39 02 66 99 51
Fax: +39 02 66 91 80 0
Website: www.pirolapennutozei.it

Languages
English, French, German, Italian, Portuguese, Spanish

Other offices
Bologna, Brescia, Naples, Padua, Parma, Rome, Turin, Verona

Number of lawyers 80
at this office 40

Contacts
Gaetano Arnò, Gabriele Bricchi, Massimo Cremona, Donatella Cungi, Andrea Gottardo, Giuseppe Pirola

CATEGORIES OF WORK

Asset finance/securitisation	**E-commerce**
Aviation	**Employment and labour**
Banking and finance	**Energy and natural resources**
Capital markets	**Environment**
Commercial property/real estate	**Information technology**
Competition and EU	**Infrastructure and project finance**
Corporate and commercial	**Insolvency/corporate restructuring**
Dispute resolution – litigation and arbitration	**Insurance**
	Intellectual property

THE FIRM

Pirola Pennuto Zei & Associati was established in the late 1970s as an association of professionals, by a group of specialists who had been engaged for a number of years in the provision of tax and statutory consulting services to medium- and large-sized companies and multinational groups.

Pirola Pennuto Zei & Associati represents a new approach to tax and legal consulting. The firm consists of 400 professionals, of whom 320 are tax consultants and 80 are lawyers. The firm's lawyers are specialists in particular areas of practice and are business consultants as well as experts in law, dedicated to providing the services that a modern business needs.

AREAS OF PRACTICE

Pirola Pennuto Zei & Associati provides a full range of tax and legal services through specialists, focusing mainly on cross-border M&A transactions, corporate transformation projects and employment law. The firm is a market leader in the design and delivery of complex corporate change, achieved through a focus on strong capabilities with a global outlook, and by ensuring that its implementation skills match its legal ones.

PORTALUPI & PARTNERS

VIA DEI PIATTI 6
20123 MILAN

Telephone: +39 02 89 07 84 50
Fax: +39 02 89 07 84 59
E-mail:
extrelations@portalupiepartners.com
Website: www.portalupiepartners.com

Languages
English, French, German, Italian

Other offices
Rome

Number of lawyers 40

Contacts
Nicoletta Portalupi (managing partner),
Fausto Lanfranchi (senior partner)

Member
Urban Land Institute (ULI);
International Bar Association (IBA);
Interpacific Bar Association (IPBA)

CATEGORIES OF WORK

Real estate

Tax

Mergers and acquisitions

Administrative and antitrust

Banking and finance

Environmental

Corporate

Litigation

STUDIO LEGALE RAPISARDI

VIA SERBELLONI 12
20122 MILAN

Telephone: +39 02 76 30 11
Fax: +39 02 76 30 13 00
E-mail: studio@rapisardi.com
Website: www.rapisardi.com

Languages
English, French, German

Number of lawyers 9

CATEGORIES OF WORK

Trade mark, copyright, patent, utility and design model applications and registrations in Italy and abroad

IP portfolio management (including infringement/ counterfeiting watching, patent and trade mark registrations maintenance, assignments, licensing and technology agreements)

European patents and Euro-PCT patents

Intellectual property dispute resolution (administrative and judicial, including emergency remedies)

Community trade marks, Madrid protocol registrations

Domain name protection and website construction

Searches, watch searches

RINALDI E ASSOCIATI STUDIO LEGALE

VIA CONSERVATORIO 15
20122 MILAN

Telephone: +39 02 76 00 88 60
Fax: +39 02 76 00 69 44
E-mail: mailbox@rinaldilawf.com
Website: www.rinaldilawf.com

Languages
English, French, Portuguese, Spanish

Other offices
Rome

Number of lawyers 20
at this office 17

CATEGORIES OF WORK

- Antitrust and competition
- Banking and finance
- Commercial contracts
- Corporate law
- Employment, labour law
- Insolvency and bankruptcy law
- Intellectual property and information technology law
- Litigation
- Mergers and acquisitions
- Administrative and regulatory law
- Energy and natural resources law
- Environment
- International private law
- Non profit
- Real estate

STUDIO LEGALE RUBINI

CORSO MATTEOTTI 8
20121 MILANO

Telephone: +39 02 76 31 91 96
Fax: +39 02 76 31 91 80
E-mail: info@rubinilaw.it

Languages
English, French, Spanish

Other offices
Rome

Number of lawyers 10
at this office 8

Contacts
Elisabetta Rubini, Cristina Manasse

CATEGORIES OF WORK

- Corporate and commercial law
- Contracts
- EU and competition law
- Intellectual property and IT
- Media law
- Advertising and sponsorship
- Internet
- Art and cultural property
- Charity and not-for-profit organisations
- Insolvency
- Litigation

RUBINO-SAMMARTANO E ASSOCIATI – LAWFED

VIALE CASSIODORO 3
20145 MILANO

Telephone: +39 02 48 19 04 1
Fax: +39 02 48 00 82 77
E-mail: rubinosammartano@lawfed.com
Website:www.lawfed.com

Languages
English, French

Other offices
London*, Paris*, Genoa, Rome, Turin

Number of lawyers 89
at this office 7

Contact
Mauro Rubino-Sammartano

Member
Law Fed, Federation of Law and Tax Law Firms

CATEGORIES OF WORK

Arbitration
Mauro Rubino-Sammartano

Contract law
Francesco Santi

Construction
Mauro Rubino-Sammartano

Commercial law
Francesco Santi

International contracts
Mauro Rubino-Sammartano

Litigation
Marco Bellora, Marco Vouch

Mergers and acquisitions
Mauro Rubino-Sammartano

Joint ventures
Mauro Rubino-Sammartano, Marco Bellora

Administrative law
Riccardo Villata

Employment
Riccardo Musatti, Marco Vouch

SJ BERWIN LLP

CORSO MATTEOTTI 3
20121 MILAN

Telephone: +39 02 36 57 57 01
Fax: +39 02 36 57 57 57
Website: www.sjberwin.com

Other offices
Berlin, Brussels, Frankfurt, London, Madrid, Munich, Paris, Turin

Number of lawyers 550

CATEGORIES OF WORK

Private equity and acquisition finance
Alberto Morano

Corporate finance and securitisation
Arturo Meglio

Corporate and commercial
Massimo Chiaia

Finance
Federico Pavetto

SIMMONS & SIMMONS

CORSO VITTORIO EMANUELE II 1
20122 MILAN

Telephone: +39 02 72 50 51
Fax: +39 02 72 50 55 05
E-mail: enquiries@simmons-simmons.com
Website: www.simmons-simmons.com

Languages
English, French, German, Italian, Spanish

Other offices
Abu Dhabi, Brussels, Dubai, Düsseldorf, Frankfurt, Hong Kong, Lisbon, London, Madeira, Madrid, New York, Oporto, Padua, Paris, Qatar, Rome, Rotterdam, Shanghai, Tokyo,

Number of lawyers 764
at this office 40

Contact
Richard Slater

CATEGORIES OF WORK

Administrative law	**Energy, utilities and infrastructure**
Banking and finance	**Financial institutions**
Capital markets	**IT and telecommunications**
Commercial	**Intellectual property**
Corporate, M&A and private equity	**Life sciences**
Corporate crime	**Projects**
Dispute resolution	**Real estate**
EU and competition	**Restructuring**
Employment and benefits	**Tax**

STUDIO LEGALE SUTTI

VIA MONTENAPOLEONE 8
20121 MILANO

Telephone: +39 02 76 20 41
Fax: +39 02 76 20 48 05
E-mail: maildesk@sutti.com
Website: www.sutti.com

Languages
Bulgarian, Croatian, English, French, German, Italian, Japanese, Portuguese, Romanian, Russian, Serbian, Spanish

Other offices
Belgrade, Bucharest, Genoa, London, Rome, Sofia, Tokyo, Zagreb

Contact
Stefano Sutti

CATEGORIES OF WORK

Company, commercial law	**White-collar crime**
Banking and finance	**EC, competition and antitrust law**
Mergers and acquisitions	**IT and TLC law**
Distribution, agency and franchising	**Litigation and arbitration**
Debt collection and insolvency	**Employment, labour law**
Commercial property law	**Administrative law**
Intellectual property	**Environmental law**
Patent and trade mark agency service	

TOFFOLETTO E SOCI, member of ius laboris

STUDIO LEGALE ASSOCIATO

VIA ROVELLO 12
20121 MILANO

Telephone: +39 02 72 14 41
Fax: +39 02 72 14 45 00
E-mail: sft@toffoletto.it
Website: www.toffoletto.it

Languages
English, French, German, Spanish

Number of lawyers 46

Contacts
Franco Toffoletto (sft@toffoletto.it),
Paola Tradati (spt@toffoletto.it),
Paola Pucci (spp@toffoletto.it),
Aldo Bottini (sab@toffoletto.it),
Elio Cherubini (sec@toffoletto.it),
Emanuela Nespoli (sen@toffoletto.it)

Member
ius laboris, International Employment Law, Pensions and Employee Benefits Alliance

CATEGORIES OF WORK

- Labour and employment law
- Social security
- Human resources
- Contracts
- Restructuring and transfer of undertakings
- Collective labour relations
- Collective dismissals
- European employment law
- Expatriates
- Stock options plans
- Agency and distribution
- Compensation and benefits
- Pensions
- Corporate social responsibility
- Sports law

STUDIO LEGALE TONUCCI

VIA DEI BOSSI 4
20121 MILAN

Telephone: +39 02 85 91 91
Fax: +39 02 86 04 68
E-mail: milano@tonucci.it
Website: www.tonucci.it

Languages
Albanian, English, French, German, Romanian, Spanish,

Other offices
Rome, Padua, Florence, Tirana, Bucharest

Number of lawyers 214
at this office 40

CATEGORIES OF WORK

- Corporate
- M&A and privatisation
- Commercial
- Banking and finance
- Capital markets
- Insurance and pensions funds
- Environment, energy and gas
- Administrative and real estate
- Labour
- Litigation and arbitration
- Taxation
- Telecommunications, IT and media
- Intellectual property
- Competition and antitrust
- Criminal law
- Aviation
- East Europe and developing countries

TREVISAN & CUONZO
AVVOCATI

VIA BRERA 6
20121 MILANO

Telephone: +39 02 86 46 33 13
Fax: +39 02 86 46 38 92
Email: info@trevisancuonzo.com
Website: www.trevisancuonzo.com

Languages
English, French, German, Spanish

Number of lawyers 35

CATEGORIES OF WORK

Copyright	Antitrust and competition
Customs monitoring	Arbitration and ADR
Information technology	Banking
E-commerce	Commercial contracts and litigation
IP procurement services	Corporate litigation
Licensing	Employment
Patent litigation	Franchising
Piracy and anti-counterfeiting	Insolvency
Trade mark litigation	Mergers and acquisitions
Trade secrets and know-how	Product liability
Unfair competition	Property
Utility models and design rights	Tax
Pharmaceutical and biotechnology	Transport

VITA SAMORY, FABBRINI E ASSOCIATI

CORSO G MATTEOTTI, 10
20121 MILANO

Telephone: +39 02 77 42 01
Fax: +39 02 76 39 43 61
E-mail: studio.milano@vita-fabbrini.com
Website: www.vita-fabbrini.com

Languages
English, French

Other offices
Rome

Number of lawyers 45
at this office 40

Contact
Guido Testa

CATEGORIES OF WORK

Antitrust law	Intellectual property
Arbitration	International law
Aviation law	Investment and financial services
Banking and finance law	IPOs
Bankruptcy/insolvency law	Labour law
Civil litigation	Mergers and acquisitions
Commercial law	Private equity
Contracts	Real estate
Corporate law	Software and IT law
Domestic and international taxation	Telecommunications
EU law	Venture capital
Insurance law	

ACLAW – CECCON & ASSOCIATI

GALLERIA BORROMEO 4
35137 PADUA

Telephone: +39 04 98 77 46 30
Fax: +39 04 98 75 02 99
E-mail: lawfirm@aclaw.it
Website: www.aclaw.it

Languages
English, French, German, Hungarian, Spanish

Other offices
Budapest*, Milan*, Pordenone*, Rome*

Number of lawyers 33
at this office 11

Contact
Prof Avv Roberto Ceccon (senior partner)

CATEGORIES OF WORK

General practice	Contracts
International and domestic practice	Bankruptcy
Agency and distributorship	Tax law
Antitrust	Privatisations
Arbitration and ADR	Intellectual property and cyber law
Litigation	Private client
Aviation	Acquisitions and extraordinary transactions
Labour and employment	Business law
EU law	Corporate law
Finance	Real estate investments
Company criminal law	Bankruptcy law
Franchising	

SIMMONS & SIMMONS

LARGO EUROPA 1
35137 PADUA

Telephone: +39 04 98 75 06 72
Fax: +39 04 98 75 36 75
E-mail: enquiries@simmons-simmons.com
Website: www.simmons-simmons.com

Languages
English, French, German, Italian

Other offices
Abu Dhabi, Brussels, Dubai, Düsseldorf, Frankfurt, Hong Kong, Lisbon, London, Madeira, Madrid, Milan, New York, Oporto, Paris, Qatar, Rome, Rotterdam, Shanghai, Tokyo

Number of lawyers 764
at this office 13

Contacts
Paolo Brugnera, Paolo Gnignati

CATEGORIES OF WORK

Administrative law	Energy, utilities and infrastructure
Banking and finance	Financial institutions
Capital markets	IT and telecommunications
Commercial	Intellectual property
Corporate, M&A and private equity	Life sciences
Corporate crime	Projects
Dispute resolution	Real estate
EU and competition	Restructuring
Employment and benefits	Tax

STUDIO LEGALE DI LEGAMI

VIA PRINCIPE DI BELMONTE 90
90139 PALERMO
SICILY

Telephone: +39 09 13 33 64 0
Fax: +39 09 13 33 82 9
E-mail: avv.dilegami@jumpy.it
Website: www.studiodilegami.com

Languages
English

Other offices
Catania-Gela

Number of lawyers 10

Contacts
Rosario Di Legami, Alessandro Di Lello

CATEGORIES OF WORK

Civil litigation

Pollution

Insolvency and restructuring

Company, commercial law

Judiciary administration

Arbitration

Real estate

Intellectual property

IT and telecommunications

Banking and finance

E-commerce

Administrative

Regional law

ALLEN & OVERY – STUDIO LEGALE ASSOCIATO

CORSO VITTORIO EMANUELE II, 284
00186 ROME

Telephone: +39 06 68 42 71
Fax: +39 06 68 42 73 33
E-mail: information@allenovery.com
Website: www.allenovery.com

Languages
English, French, German, Italian, Spanish

Other offices
Amsterdam, Antwerp, Bangkok, Beijing, Bratislava, Brussels, Budapest, Dubai, Frankfurt, Hamburg, Hong Kong, London, Luxembourg, Madrid, Milan, Moscow, New York, Paris, Prague, Shanghai, Singapore, Tokyo, Turin, Warsaw

Number of lawyers 2,304
at this office 70

Contacts
Roberto Casati (senior partner),
G. Massimillano Danusso (managing partner),
Emanuele Borganti (head of operations in Italy)

CATEGORIES OF WORK

Corporate
Paolo Cerina

ICM
G. Massimilliano Danusso

Banking
Giancarlo Castorino

Litigation
Massimo Greco

Tax
Andrea Manganelli

STUDIO PROFESSIONALE ASSOCIATO A BAKER & McKENZIE

VIALE DI VILLA MASSIMO 57
00161 ROMA

Telephone: +39 06 44 06 31
Fax: +39 06 44 06 33 06
E-mail: rome.info@bakernet.com
Website: www.bakernet.com

Languages
English, French, German, Spanish

Other offices
The member firms of Baker & McKenzie International, a Swiss Verein, have 70 offices in 38 countries around the world. For a complete list, please visit www.bakernet.com.

Number of lawyers 3,300+
at this office 32

Contact
Gerardo M Boniello (managing partner)

CATEGORIES OF WORK

Banking and finance

IT/IP (includes media – entertainment)

Telecommunications (includes media – regulatory)

Employment

Dispute resolution

Infrastructure (includes construction, works and projects)

Competition and trade

Tax

Environment and real estate

Pharma regulation

Corporate, M&A (and commercial transactions)

BIRD & BIRD

VIA DI SAN SEBASTIANELLO 9
00187 ROME

Telephone: +39 06 69 66 70 00
Fax: +39 06 69 66 70 11
E-mail: rome@twobirds.com
Website: www.twobirds.com

Languages
English, Italian

Other offices
Beijing, Brussels, Düsseldorf, Frankfurt, Hong Kong, London, Madrid, Milan, Munich, Paris, Stockholm, The Hague

Number of lawyers 472
at this office 5

Contact
Massimiliano Mostardini

CATEGORIES OF WORK

Antitrust
Eutimio Monaco

Communications
Eutimio Monaco

Litigation
Osvaldo Lombardi

CMS ADONNINO ASCOLI & CAVASOLA SCAMONI

VIA A. DEPRETIS, 86
00184 ROMA

Telephone: +39 06 47 81 51
Fax: +39 06 48 37 55
E-mail: info@cms-aacs.com
Website: www.cms-aacs.com

Languages
Bulgarian, Chinese (Cantonese and Mandarin), Dutch, English, French, German, Spanish

Other offices
Milan

Number of lawyers 60+
at this office 39

Contacts
Pietro Cavasola, Giuseppe Ascoli

Other CMS alliance member firms
CMS Albiñana & Suárez de Lezo, Spain; CMS Bureau Francis Lefebvre, France; CMS Cameron McKenna LLP, UK; CMS DeBacker, Belgium; CMS Derks Star Busmann, Netherlands; CMS von Erlach Henrici, Switzerland; CMS Hasche Sigle, Germany; CMS Reich-Rohrwig Hainz, Austria

CATEGORIES OF WORK

- General civil and tax practice
- Business and corporate law
- International contracts
- Joint ventures
- EU law
- Foreign investment
- Mergers and acquisitions
- Labour law
- Administrative law
- Italian and international taxation
- Commercial litigation and arbitration
- Business reorganisation, tax planning
- Transfer pricing policy
- Cost-sharing agreements
- Company evaluations
- Property law
- Intellectual property
- Bankruptcy and credit recovery

CHIOMENTI STUDIO LEGALE

VIA XXIV MAGGIO 43
00187 ROME

Telephone: +39 06 46 62 21
Fax: +39 06 46 62 26 00
E-mail: roma@chiomenti.net

Languages
English, French, German, Italian, Spanish

Other offices
Brussels, London, Milan, New York

Number of lawyers 210
at this office 110

Member
Lex Mundi

CATEGORIES OF WORK

- Corporate and M&A
- Banking and finance
- Capital markets
- Regulatory and financial services
- Tax
- European law, competition and international law
- Administrative law
- Intellectual property, media and information technology
- Litigation and arbitration
- Insolvency and corporate restructuring
- Employment
- Telecommunications
- Energy
- Real estate

STUDIO LEGALE CARNELUTTI

VIA PARIGI, 11
00185 ROMA

Telephone: +39 06 47 39 01
Fax: +39 06 48 19 83 3
E-mail: postmaster@carnelutti.it
Website: www.carnelutti.it

Languages
English, French, German, Spanish

Other offices
Milan, Naples, Paris

Number of lawyers 52
at this office 31

Contacts
Franco L Incutti, Alexandre Carnelutti

Member
Terralex

CATEGORIES OF WORK	
General civil practice	Insurance law
Conflict of laws and international civil procedure	Administrative law, construction
Company law, mergers and acquisitions	International commercial law
EC law	Tax law, banking, economy, finance
Trade marks, patents, copyrights	Litigation
Competition and antitrust	Advertising, unfair competition
International and domestic arbitration	Real estate
	Energy and natural resources

THE FIRM

Carnelutti was originally founded in Venice at the end of the 19th century by Professor Francesco Carnelutti, one of the greatest Italian jurists of all time, who was equally well known for his practice in civil and commercial law, as well as for his practice in criminal law. As the fame of Professor Carnelutti gradually spread throughout Italy and abroad, the firm, through its offices in Rome and Milan, expanded its activities, particularly in civil/commercial matters with a special emphasis on corporate and contractual matters. In recent years, the structure of said offices underwent a series or reorganisations and innovations as a result of a will to expand and improve the services offered to clients. The long-established Carnelutti Rome office continues to carry on its professional activity at the historical address of Via Parigi, 11. Other offices are situated in Milan, Naples and Paris. Through these offices, Carnelutti is able to provide an effective service to commercial institutions of all types and sizes in the new global international economic scenario. The firm also has excellent contacts with lawyers practising in most other commercial centres throughout the world. At the beginning of 1999, Alexandre Carnelutti, professor of international business law in Paris, France, joined the Carnelutti law office in Rome as a partner. The son of the late Tito Carnelutti and grandson of Francesco Carnelutti, Alexandre Carnelutti practises in Paris and has acted in the past as counsel expert in EU law.

AREAS OF PRACTICE

The firm has a broad experience in assisting private clients and public and private corporations in the areas of civil, commercial and administrative law. The firm has particular expertise in the areas of mergers and acquisitions, joint ventures, banking, project finance, securities offering, privatisations, securitisations, litigation and arbitration, EC and antitrust, sports law, contracts, employment, telecommunications, media and entertainment, bankruptcy, real estate, family, insurance, intellectual property and in fiscal and tax planning matters.

CIGLIANO LAW OFFICE

VIA DEGLI SCIPIONI, 132
00192 ROME

Telephone: +39 06 32 43 38 5
Fax: +39 06 32 20 17 9
E-mail: studiocigliano@ciglianolaw.com
Website: www.ciglianolaw.com

Languages
English, French, Italian, Spanish, Tagalog

Other offices
Athens, Brussels, Buenos Aires, Manila, Milan, Naples, New York, San Paulo

Number of lawyers 20
at this office 9

CATEGORIES OF WORK

General corporate
Mariano Cigliano

Banking and finance
Mariano Cigliano

Securities, capital markets and financial services
Mariano Cigliano

Mergers and acquisitions
Mariano Cigliano

Employment and labour laws
Francesco Cigliano

Administrative, energy, telecommunications and environmental law
Francesco Cigliano

Taxation
Francesco Cigliano

Litigation and arbitration
Francesco Cigliano

Real estate
Roberto Cigliano

Intellectual property
Roberto Cigliano

Antitrust
Roberto Cigliano

European Union/ common market law
Roberto Cigliano

CLEARY GOTTLIEB STEEN & HAMILTON LLP

PIAZZA DI SPAGNA 15
00187 ROME

Telephone: +39 06 69 52 21
Fax: +39 06 69 20 06 65
Website: www.clearygottlieb.com

Languages
English, French, German, Italian, Portuguese, Spanish

Other offices
Brussels, Cologne, Frankfurt, Hong Kong, London, Milan, Moscow, New York, Paris, Tokyo, Washington DC

Number of lawyers 847
at this office 47

CATEGORIES OF WORK

Banking and finance

Capital markets/securities

Commercial and corporate litigation

EU and competition law

EU litigation

Joint ventures

Mergers and acquisitions

Privatisations

Regulatory issues

Restructuring

Tax

Telecommunications and energy

COCCIA DE ANGELIS & ASSOCIATI – STUDIO LEGALE E TRIBUTARIO

PIAZZA ADRIANA 15
00193 ROME

Telephone: +39 06 68 80 30 25
Fax: +39 06 68 80 94 16
Website: www.cdaa.it
E-mail: legal@cdaa.it

Languages
English, French, Italian, Romanian, Spanish

Number of lawyers 9

Contact
Massimo Coccia

CATEGORIES OF WORK

Arbitration and ADR
Massimo Coccia, Ana-Maria Fagetan

Banking
Gabriele Bartolucci, Alessandro Gullo

Civil and commercial law
Riccardo La Cognata,
Daniele La Cognata

Competition and antitrust
Massimo Coccia, Riccardo La Cognata

Contracts
Francesca Troilo, Alessandro Gullo

Corporate and finance
Gabriele Bartolucci, Stefano De Angelis

Energy and oil
Francesca Troilo, Riccardo la Cognata

EU and international law
Massimo Coccia, Daniele La Cognata

Litigation
Riccardo la Cognata,
Daniele La Cognata

Intellectual property
Daniele La Cognata

Domestic taxation
Stefano de Angelis

International taxation
Gabriele Bartolucci

Sports law
Massimo Coccia, Riccardo la Cognata

DE BERTI JACCHIA FRANCHINI FORLANI

VIA A BERTOLONI 14
00197 ROMA

Telephone: +39 06 80 91 54 1
Fax: +39 06 80 91 54 44
E-mail: rome@dejalex.com
Website: www.dejalex.com

Languages
English, French, German, Russian, Spanish, Swedish

Other offices
Brussels, Milan, Moscow

Numbers of lawyers 67
at this office 8

Contact
Antonella Terranova (a.terranova@dejalex.com)

CATEGORIES OF WORK

Administrative and regulatory

Arbitration and ADR

Automotive

Banking, finance and securities

Competition and antitrust

Corporate and commercial

Domestic and international litigation

Employment and pensions

Environmental and energy

European Union law

Insolvency and restructuring

IP and pharmaceutical law

IT and telecommunications

M&A and private equity

Real estate and planning

Retail, sport, insurance

Successions and trust

Tax, transport, shipping, air law

DLA PIPER RUDNICK GRAY CARY

VIA DELLA SCROFA 57
00186 ROME

Telephone: +39 06 68 88 01
Fax: +39 06 68 88 02 01
Website: www.dlapiper.com/italy

Languages
Italian, English, French, German

Other offices
Austria, Belgium, Bosnia-Herzegovina, China, Croatia, Czech Republic, Denmark*, Egypt*, France, Georgia, Germany, Hong Kong, Hungary, Italy, Japan, Netherlands, Norway*, Poland*, Russia, Singapore*, Slovakia, South Africa*, Spain, Sweden*, Thailand, UK, Ukraine, United Arab Emirates, US

Number of lawyers 3,100
at this office 11

Contact
Stefano Modenesi

Member
DLA Piper Group

CATEGORIES OF WORK

M&A/PFI
Federico Sutti

Insurance
Francesco Cerasi

Commercial
Roberto Pera

Real estate
Olaf Schmidt

Litigation/IT/TMC
Stefano Modenesi

Energy
Wolf Michael Kühne

Labour
Fabrizio Morelli

Tax
Giulio Azzaretto

Real estate financing
Elisabetta Poltronieri

Public procurement
Giorgia Romitelli

THE FIRM

DLA Piper Rudnick Gray Cary is a leading global legal services provider with approximately 3,100 lawyers in 58 offices across 22 countries. The organisation is committed to building long-term relationships with its clients and supports their strategic and operational needs both locally and internationally.

In Italy, DLA Piper Rudnick Gray Cary is a full-service, locally-led law firm with over ten years' experience and international capability across Europe, Africa, Asia and the US. Lawyers in Milan and Rome specialise in all aspects of business law and regularly advise on cross-border transactions.

While Italy has always been a focus for European trade and investment, the reform of corporate, tax and employment law is set to make Italy an even more attractive environment for both inward investors and national enterprises. The ability to respond quickly to these opportunities is fundamental to all businesses. DLA Piper Rudnick Gray Cary differentiates itself by its speed of response and the desire to put clients first. The organisation invests in its clients to understand what their needs really are and how it can add value to their business. The team will be local lawyers, able to really understand and empathise with clients' commercial needs, both locally and on a broader international level.

DLA Piper is a founding member of an exclusive alliance of full-service legal organisations with a shared vision. DLA Piper Group, established in 1999, has members across Europe, Africa, the Middle East, Asia and the US, which deliver expert local know-how and integrated international solutions.

Further information, as well as a more detailed description of areas of practice, can be found on the website.

AREAS OF PRACTICE

Banking and finance – provides legal advice to national and international banks, as well as other financial service providers operating in all areas of banking and finance, including commercial banking and real estate and project finance.

Corporate and M&A – brings extensive experience, both domestically and internationally, on a broad range of matters, including the setting up and structuring of corporate entities, mergers, demergers and acquisitions, the formation of joint ventures and consortia, corporate reorganisations and commercial transactions in general, including all the tax angles thereof.

Human resources – assists in all legal and practical aspects of employment law, as well as the risk assessment of possible disputes.

Litigation – offer global legal assistance before Italian courts to both foreign and Italian clients, handling the full range of international law issues.

Project finance – widely recognised prominence in both private and public finance transactions, plus unique expertise in the field of infrastructure financing. Advise lending institutions involved in PFI transactions, as well as major international real estate developers, primary construction companies and international market leaders in facilities management.

Real estate – assist Italian and international clients in all areas of real estate law, with particular emphasis on acquisition of existing real estate property, development of unbuilt land, construction law and project finance.

Tax – provides clients such as foreign investment funds, international banks and other institutional investors, as well as public and private and multinational companies with specialist tax advice to develop the best structure for their operations.

Technology, media and communications – provides contentious and non-contentious advice in areas of IT/outsourcing, intellectual property, telecommunications, media, e-commerce, data protection and privacy.

STUDIO LEGALE DELFINO E ASSOCIATI
WILLKIE FARR & GALLAGHER LLP

VIA DI RIPETTA 142
00186 ROME

Telephone: +39 06 68 63 61
Fax: +39 06 68 63 63 63
Website: www.willkie.com

Languages
English, French, German, Spanish

Other offices
Brussels, Frankfurt, London, Milan, New York, Paris, Washington DC

Number of lawyers 590
at this office 8

Contact
Maurizio Delfino

CATEGORIES OF WORK

Mergers and acquisitions

Private equity

Capital markets

Telecommunications

Energy

Tax

Antitrust

Litigation

Arbitration

DEWEY BALLANTINE STUDIO LEGALE

VIA PO 22
00198 ROME

Telephone: +39 06 45 20 62 20
Fax: +39 06 45 20 62 30
Website: www.deweyballantine.com

Languages
English, French, Italian

Other offices
Austin, Beijing, East Palo Alto, Frankfurt, Houston, London, Los Angeles, Milan, New York, Warsaw, Washington DC

Number of lawyers 550+
at this office 6

Contacts
Stefano Speroni (ssperoni@deweyballantine.com);
Giovan Battista Santangelo (gbsantangelo@deweyballantine.com)

CATEGORIES OF WORK

Mergers and acquisitions
Nicola Brunetti, Stefano Catenacci, Bruno Gattai, Luca Minoli, Giovan B Santangelo, Stefano Speroni, Adriano Pala, Emanuela Ciaffi

Private equity
Nicola Brunetti, Stefano Catenacci, Bruno Gattai, Giovan B Santangelo, Stefano Speroni

Privatisation
Nicola Brunetti, Bruno Gattai, Adriano Pala, Emanuela Ciaffi

Real estate
Stefano Catenacci, Bruno Gattai, Giovan B Santangelo, Adriano Pala

Energy
Nicola Brunetti, Bruno Gattai, Luca Minoli

Capital markets
Emanuela Ciaffi, Stefano Catenacci Bruno Gattai, Giovan B Santangelo, Stefano Speroni, Adriano Pala, Ugo Giordano, Nicola Brunetti

Securitisation
Stefano Speroni, Ugo Giordano

Derivatives
Ugo Giordano, Giovan B Santangelo, Stefano Speroni

Telecommunications
Stefano Speroni, Giovan B Santangelo

Tax
Luca Dezzani

Litigation
Luca Minoli

DI TANNO E ASSOCIATI

VIA PAISIELLO 33
00198 ROMA

Telephone: +39 06 84 56 61
Fax: +39 06 84 19 50 0
E-mail: ditannoeass@ditanno.it
Website: www.ditanno.it

Languages
English, French

Other offices
Milan, Treviso

Number of lawyers 48
at this office 36

Contacts
Tommaso Di Tanno, Stefano Petrecca

CATEGORIES OF WORK

Tax	**Mergers and acquisitions**
Tax litigation	**Corporate finance**
Commercial and company law	**Banking and finance**
Venture capital	

THE FIRM

Formed in 1986, the firm has grown slowly through internal expansion, rigorous staff selection and a limited turnover (more than 50% of the professional staff have worked together for over five years). The firm is composed of both lawyers and accountants (almost 50/50) and provides top quality tax and legal advice on a range of issues. Tommaso Di Tanno has acted as tax adviser to several Ministers of Finance. He has been a member of the most prestigious governmental commissions on tax and company law reform and a tax law professor at numerous universities. This professional background helps the firm to provide creative and innovative advice on a range of sophisticated transactions. In particular, the firm specialises in company restructuring and closed-end fund creation. The firm has notably been involved in the Seat (Yellow Pages), Piaggio and Toro acquisition, in the mergers involving Assicurazioni Generali and INA, Wind and Infostrada, Telemom Italia' s real estate spin off and the subsequent partial sale to Starwood, Azimut's acquisition by APAX followed by the listings of the same. The firm has also undertaken work in closed-end funds (Permira Eurofund, Apax Europe V, IPEF IV, S Paolo IMI fund I and II, Investitori Associati III, Beni Stabili real estate fund) and provides a wide range of tax litigation services for high-status individuals. Many of the firm's practice groups are led by highly experienced professionals with training in an array or related fields. For example, the leader of the litigation department (Stefano Petrecca) is a former qualified tax police officer, while a former general counsel of Finmeccanica (Luciano Acciari) now leads the M&A team.

AREAS OF PRACTICE

The firm deals with most multinational companies operating in Italy. These include industrial clients (mainly telecommunications and aerospace) as well as financial clients (mainly banking and insurance). Tommaso Di Tanno is the Chairman of the Statutory Auditors of Banca Nazionale del Lavoro, Vodafone Omnirel and Caltagirone. Di Tanno is an independent director of INA and a member of the European Advisory Board of Aareal Bank; Luciano Acciari is secretary to the board of ST Microelectronics (listed on the Paris Stock Exchange; Fabio Brunelli is the Italian representative on the tax and legal committee of the European Venture Capital Association. Clients include Apax Ventures, Engelhard, Exxon, Lehman Brothers Merrill Lynch, Permira, ST Microelectronics and Vodafone.

GIANNI, ORIGONI, GRIPPO & PARTNERS

VIA DELLE QUATTRO FONTANE, 20
00184 ROMA

Telephone: +39 06 47 87 51
Fax: +39 06 48 71 101
Email: rome@gop.it
Website: www.gop.it

Languages
English, French, German, Spanish

Other offices
Rome, Milan, Padua, Bologna, Naples, Turin
London, New York

Number of lawyers 326
at this office 146

Contacts
Francesco Gianni, Giovanni Nardulli

CATEGORIES OF WORK

Mergers and acquisitions
Francesco Gianni, Filippo Troisi

Banking and finance
Alberto Giampieri, Andrea Giannelli

Capital markets
Bruno Bartocci

Arbitration and litigation
Gian Battista Origoni Della Croce

Antitrust
Alberto Pera

Project finance
Eugenio Grippo

Administrative law and tenders
Antonio Lirosi

Real estate
Domenico Tulli

Intellectual property
Nino Di Bella

Labour law
Matteo Fusillo, Alberto Maggi

Tax
Massimo Agostini

Reorganisation and insolvency
Antonio Auricchio, Aulo Cossu

THE FIRM

Founded in 1988, Gianni, Origoni, Grippo & Partners is an international law firm with 326 professionals, providing legal services and representation to both Italian and international clients in all areas of commercial law.

The firm's capacity to provide comprehensive and creative assistance on all legal aspects of its clients' operations – even for those involving different legal systems – has earned the firm a reputation for providing the highest-quality legal counsel on both a national and international level. In 2004 it twice received the award of 'Law Firm of the Year', from *International Financial Law Review* (in the *IFLR* European Awards) and *Chambers and Partners* (in the *Chambers* Awards).

AREAS OF PRACTICE

Gianni, Origoni, Grippo & Partners provides a comprehensive range of legal services across all areas of practice: mergers and acquisitions, banking and finance, capital markets, litigation and arbitration, antitrust and regulatory, energy and natural resources, real estate, intellectual property, labour, tax and reorganisation and insolvency.

The firm enjoys a formidable reputation for its expertise in M&A, topping all M&A league tables in Italy over the last three years. It is heavily involved in many of the most significant domestic M&A transactions and has assisted international clients in several of the latest large cross-border acquisitions.

In the banking and finance sector, the firm is recognised as a leader, having worked on some of the most complex and high-profile banking and structured finance transactions.

In the capital markets sector, the firm counsels issuers, sellers and underwriters involved in initial and secondary public offerings of equity securities, and advises issuers and underwriters in transactions involving the offering of debentures, convertible and exchangeable bonds as well as other financial instruments.

The firm's litigators represent clients' interests in major legal disputes throughout Italy, including disputes before administrative, trial and appellate courts, as well as the Italian Supreme Court and in some cases before the European Court of Justice.

In only a few years, the firm has built a remarkable team of lawyers dedicated to antitrust and regulatory matters, assisting clients in merger-related disputes, abuses of dominant positions and restrictive agreements. This team is now regarded as one of the leaders in this area.

The firm assists leading foreign and Italian energy companies active in project development in joint venture operations, on regulatory issues and tariffs, physical and financial trading of power and gas, transportation agreements and contracts with regulatory authorities.

The firm's real estate department delivers a full array of legal services to its clients who include construction companies, real estate investors, developers or promoters.

The firm provides a broad range of expertise in the industrial law sector, with an emphasis on patents and trade marks, unfair competition, trade secrets and technology transfers.

The group's labour attorneys work on behalf of industrial, commercial and financial groups. The firm provides assistance in all the main fields of labour law, industrial relations and social security.

In the tax practice, the firm boasts prominent specialists in every area of domestic and international tax, providing its clients with international tax advice and legal expertise integrated with their business transactions, all from one source.

The firm represents debtors and creditors in reorganisation cases as well as other matters and transactions arising from insolvency proceedings. It also represents investment funds and other investors in acquisitions and turnaround transactions of financially troubled companies.

LAURO SOVANI & ASSOCIATI STUDIO LEGALE

VIA LAZIO 6
00187 ROME

Telephone: +39 06 42 01 91 94
Fax: +39 06 47 44 084
Website: www.lauro-sovani.it

Languages
English, French, Italian, Spanish

Other offices
Milan

Number of lawyers 5

International groupings
Global Forum for Cross-Border Human Resource experts (XBHR); European Employment Lawyers Association (EELA)

CATEGORIES OF WORK

Employment law
Rosanna Sovani, Francesca Lauro

Labour law
Rosanna Sovani, Edoardo Ceracchi

Pension law
Francesca Lauro, Edoardo Ceracchi

Litigation
Francesca Lauro, Edoardo Ceracchi, Rosanna Sovani

LOVELLS

VIA DEI DUE MACELLI 66
00187 ROME

Telephone: +39 06 67 58 23 1
Fax: +39 06 67 58 23 23
E-mail: information@lovells.com
Website: www.lovells.com

Languages
English, French, German

Other offices
Alicante, Amsterdam, Beijing, Berlin, Brussels, Budapest*, Chicago, Düsseldorf, Frankfurt, Hamburg, Ho Chi Minh City, Hong Kong, London, Madrid, Milan, Moscow, Munich, New York, Paris, Prague, Shanghai, Singapore, Tokyo, Warsaw, Zagreb*

Number of lawyers 1,600
at this office 39

Contact
Fulvia Astolfi

CATEGORIES OF WORK

Corporate (including M&A, private equity, privatisations)

Antitrust/competition

Tax

Financial services and investment funds

Banking

Capital markets

Project finance

Real estate and construction

Administrative and public law (including town planning, environment, energy)

Pharmaceutical

Insurance

Insolvency

Intellectual property, IT, e-commerce and media

Employment

Litigation and arbitration

Data protection

MACCHI DI CELLERE GANGEMI

VIA G CUBONI 12
00197 ROME

Telephone: +39 06 36 21 41
Fax: +39 06 32 22 15 9
E-mail: roma@macchi-gangemi.com
Website: www.macchi-gangemi.com

Languages
Dutch, English, French, German, Italian, Portuguese, Spanish

Other offices
Bologna, Milan, Paris, Treviso, Verona, Vicenza

Number of lawyers 95+
at this office 40

CATEGORIES OF WORK

Acquisitions and mergers, corporate reorganisations

Antitrust, competition, EU law

Arbitration and ADR, litigation

Asset-based and structured finance

Banking and investment services

Business organisation, joint ventures

Capital markets and securities

Commercial transactions, investments and trade

Construction, public works, public services

Consumer law and misleading advertising

Corporate governance

E-commerce, telecommunications and media

Energy and natural resources, environment, water

Entertainment

Insolvency, insurance

Intellectual property

Investment companies, mutual funds

Labour and social security

Privacy

Private equity

Project financing

Real estate

Takeovers, privatisations

Tax

McDERMOTT WILL & EMERY
STUDIO LEGALE ASSOCIATO

VIA PARIGI 11
00185 ROME

Telephone: +39 06 46 20 24 1
Fax: +39 06 48 90 62 85
Website: www.mwe.com

Languages
All main business languages

Other offices
Boston, Brussels, Chicago, Düsseldorf, London, Los Angeles, Miami, Munich, New York, Orange County, San Diego, Silicon Valley, Washington DC

Number of lawyers 1,000
at this office 11

Contact
Massimo Trentino

CATEGORIES OF WORK

Banking and finance
Massimo Trentino, Marco Pessi

Capital markets
Massimo Trentino, Marco Pessi

Corporate, mergers and acquisitions
Massimo Trentino, Filippo Mazza, Carsten Steinhauer, Marco Pessi

Private equity/venture capital
Filippo Mazza, Carsten Steinhauer

Energy
Filippo Mazza, Carsten Steinhauer

NUNZIANTE MAGRONE

PIAZZA DI PIETRA 26
00186 ROMA

Telephone: +39 06 69 51 81
Fax: +39 06 69 51 83 33
E-mail: roma@nmlex.it
Website: www.nmlex.it

Languages
English, French, German, Spanish

Other offices
Bologna, Milan, Turin

Number of lawyers 54
at this office 23

CATEGORIES OF WORK

Corporate	Postal
Banking and finance	Aviation
Mergers and acquisitions	Environmental
Litigation and arbitration	Tax
Intellectual property	Real estate
Administrative	White-collar crime
EU and competition	Immigration

ORRICK, HERRINGTON & SUTCLIFFE

VIA DEL CONSOLATO, 6
00186 ROME

Telephone: +39 06 45 21 39 00
Fax: +39 06 68 19 23 93
Website: www.orrick.com

Languages
English, French, Spanish

Other offices
Hong Kong, London, Los Angeles, Milan, Moscow, New York, Orange County, Pacific Northwest (Portland, Seattle), Paris, Sacramento, San Francisco, Silicon Valley, Taipei, Tokyo, Washington DC

Number of lawyers 850
at this office 17

Contact
Patrizio Messina

CATEGORIES OF WORK

Administrative law	**Structured finance and securitisation**
General banking and finance	

THE FIRM

Orrick is an international law firm with more than 850 attorneys located in Asia, Europe and North America. In Europe, Orrick has almost 200 attorneys across five offices, located in London, Milan, Moscow, Paris and Rome. With the firm's European expansion, Orrick now has 16 offices across three continents.

Much of Orrick's client work in Europe involves cross-border transactions and financings that span Europe, the Middle East, Africa, Asia and the Americas. To support the demands of its clients, Orrick has made seamless client service its number one goal across the firm. As a result, the firm's European lawyers can call on the substantial resources of other offices around the world to provide clients with the expertise required to support their transactions.

Above all, Orrick's name stands for excellence in legal services; integrated, responsive client teams throughout the world; innovative leadership and management; and a commitment to the firm's core values, which govern these business standards.

Orrick's highly regarded partners in Milan and Rome rank among Italy's leading lawyers and also include reputed economists and university professors. Orrick's Italian offices also regularly host a forum for general counsels of major Italian companies to discuss the latest legal developments of significance to the Italian business community. In addition to being one of the leaders in the field of white-collar crime and corporate governance programmes, the firm's Italian lawyers focus on cross-border and domestic mergers and acquisitions, antitrust matters, structured finance (with particular emphasis on securitisation transactions), private equity, debt restructuring, project finance, domestic public finance, administrative law (focusing on public procurements, privatisations, building and town planning), real estate, intellectual property and technology law. Orrick's clients in Italy include many of the world's leading financial institutions, commercial enterprises, both closed-end and public companies, and a number of investment companies.

AREAS OF PRACTICE

Orrick's Rome office comprises two main groups: the structured finance group and the administrative group, both providing their clients with a comprehensive level of domestic and cross-border legal support. Orrick's Italian structured finance group has extensive experience in both domestic and international finance transactions, providing a broad range of services across the full spectrum of financial products. Areas of experience include derivative products (financial and credit derivatives), financial services regulation and securitisation. Lawyers from the group have extensive experience advising clients on a broad array of asset types and financing techniques, combining their capacity and experience in Italian law with a keen knowledge of the business practices and legal documentation techniques used in the US and UK legal systems. The group's lawyers have represented principal parties in many transactions from the perspective of both arrangers, originators and investors. The Italian structured finance group's areas of focus include transactions involving debentures, convertible and exchangeable bonds, medium-term note programmes, domestic and cross-border leasing, real estate finance, investment funds and aviation finance. The Italian administrative law group is made up of lawyers highly experienced in advising clients from both the public and private sectors. Orrick's practice in Rome includes advising on all aspects of tender processes, from the drafting of financing contracts and the supporting of guarantees, through to the negotiation and drafting of contracts for the supply of works, services and materials, as well as maintenance agreements. Lawyers in the group are frequently called on to assist public institutions, banks and corporations regarding current Italian legislation, and in feasibility studies concerning project finance transactions. In addition, Orrick's administrative law group provides legal advice on specific issues concerning public works, services and supplies, building and town planning, local entities law, privatisations and transportation procedures for companies owned by local municipalities.

PIROLA PENNUTO ZEI & ASSOCIATI

LARGO ANGELO FOCHETTI 28
00154 ROME

Telephone: +39 06 57 02 81
Fax: +39 06 570 28 26 00
Website: www.pirolapennutozei.it

Languages
English, French, Italian, Spanish

Other offices
Bologna, Brescia, MIlan, Naples, Padua, Parma, Turin, Verona

Number of lawyers 80
at this office 30

Contacts
Nicola Antoniozzi, Donald Carrol, Maria Clelia Chinappi, Roberto Padova, Marcello Romano, Andrea Russo

CATEGORIES OF WORK

Asset finance/securitisation	**E-commerce**
Aviation	**Employment and labour**
Banking and finance	**Energy and natural resources**
Capital markets	**Environment**
Commercial property/real estate	**Information technology**
Competition and EU	**Infrastructure and project finance**
Corporate and commercial	**Insolvency/corporate restructuring**
Dispute resolution – litigation and arbitration	**Insurance**
	Intellectual property

THE FIRM

Pirola Pennuto Zei & Associati was established in the late 1970s as an association of professionals, by a group of specialists who had been engaged for a number of years in the provision of tax and statutory consulting services to medium- and large-sized companies and multinational groups.

Pirola Pennuto Zei & Associati represents a new approach to tax and legal consulting. The firm consists of 400 professionals, of whom 320 are tax consultants and 80 are lawyers. The firm's lawyers are specialists in particular areas of practice and are business consultants as well as experts in law, dedicated to providing the services that a modern business needs.

AREAS OF PRACTICE

Pirola Pennuto Zei & Associati provides a full range of tax and legal services through specialists, focusing mainly on cross-border M&A transactions, corporate transformation projects and employment law. The firm is a market leader in the design and delivery of complex corporate change, achieved through a focus on strong capabilities with a global outlook, and by ensuring that its implementation skills match its legal ones.

PGRB - PUOPOLO GEFFERS ROSEN & BOSIN
STUDIO LEGALE

VIA LISBONA,11
00198 ROMA

Telephone: +39 06 88 41 53 5
Fax: +39 06 88 42 09 4
E-mail: info@psglaw.com
Website: www.psglaw.com

Languages
English, French, German, Spanish

Other offices
Milan, Naples

Number of lawyers 43
at this office 23

Contacts
Gianfranco Puopolo, Frank J Geffers, Robert Rosen, Cristiano Bosin, Gianni Emilio Iacobelli

CATEGORIES OF WORK

Banking and finance

Company and commercial

Energy and environmental

Insurance

Mergers and acquisitions

Information technology and communications

Maritime transactions (mega yachts)

Steel and commodities industry

PORTOLANO COLELLA CAVALLO
STUDIO LEGALE

VIA CATONE, 3
00192 ROMA

Telephone: +39 06 39 74 54 37
Fax: +39 06 39 74 54 00
E-mail: info@portolano.it
Website: www.portolano.it

Other offices Milan

Languages
English, French, Spanish

Number of lawyers 12

Contacts
Francesco Portolano, Manuela Cavallo, Domenico Colella

CATEGORIES OF WORK

Television

Broadcasting

Gaming

Media content

Information technology and e-commerce

M&A and venture capital

Corporate

Litigation and arbitration

Real estate

Labour and employment

Aviation

SIMMONS & SIMMONS

VIA BARNABA ORIANI 85
00197 ROME

Telephone: +39 06 80 95 51
Fax: +39 06 80 95 59 55
E-mail: enquiries@simmons-simmons.com
Website: www.simmons-simmons.com

Languages
English, French, German, Italian, Spanish

Other offices
Abu Dhabi, Brussels, Dubai, Düsseldorf, Frankfurt, Hong Kong, Lisbon, London, Madeira, Madrid, Milan, New York, Oporto, Padua, Paris, Qatar, Rotterdam, Shanghai, Tokyo

Number of lawyers 764
at this office 52

Contact
Filippo Pingue

CATEGORIES OF WORK

- Administrative law
- Banking and finance
- Capital markets
- Commercial
- Corporate, M&A and private equity
- Corporate crime
- Dispute resolution
- EU and competition
- Employment and benefits
- Energy, utilities and infrastructure
- Financial institutions
- IT and telecommunications
- Intellectual property
- Life sciences
- Projects
- Real estate
- Restructuring
- Tax

UGHI & NUNZIANTE

VIA VENTI SETTEMBRE, 1
00187 ROMA

Telephone: +39 06 47 48 31
Fax: +39 06 48 70 397
E-mail: un.rome@unlaw.it
Website: www.unlaw.it

Languages
English, French, German, Spanish

Other offices
Milan

Number of lawyers 75
at this office 36

CATEGORIES OF WORK

- Corporate and commercial
- Banking and finance
- Securities
- Insurance
- Litigation
- Labour and employment
- Real estate
- Bankruptcy
- Intellectual property
- EU and competition
- IT and telecommunications
- Transport
- International commercial arbitration
- Taxation
- Media and entertainment
- Energy

WATSON, FARLEY & WILLIAMS

STUDIO LEGALE ASSOCIATO A WATSON, FARLEY & WILLIAMS

VIA VITTORIO VENETO 96
00187 ROME

Telephone: +39 06 48 38 07
Fax: +39 06 42 01 17 89
Website: www.wfw.com

Languages
Afrikaans, Arabic, Cantonese, Danish, Dutch, English, French, German, Greek, Gujarati, Hebrew, Hindi, Italian, Malay, Mandarin, Marathi, Norwegian, Polish, Russian, Spanish, Swahili, Swedish, Thai

Other offices
Bangkok, Hamburg, London, New York, Paris, Piraeus, Singapore

Number of lawyers 198
at this office 10

Contacts
Carlo Galdo, Eugenio Tranchino

CATEGORIES OF WORK

Project finance	Joint ventures
Shipping, aviation and asset finance	Venture capital
Corporate finance	Infrastructure and privatisations
Banking and securities	Debt and corporate restructuring
Debt restructuring	Energy and natural resources
Derivatives	Commercial contracts
Trade finance	EU, competition and antitrust law
Structuring finance and leasing	Intellectual property
Securitisation	General corporate advice
Insolvency matters	Commercial agreements
Mergers and acquisitions	E-business and e-commerce
Private equity	Real estate
Projects	

THE FIRM

Established in 1982, Watson Farley & Williams is an international corporate and commercial law firm recognised for its excellence in banking, structured and asset financing and particularly, in the transport and energy sectors. The firm also advises in a number of specialist areas in corporate law, litigation and tax law. Watson, Farley & Williams opened its office in Rome in 2002.

The Rome office has an excellent reputation in shipping finance, maritime law and project work relating to energy matters. It specialises, in particular, in structured finance, banking and corporate, as well as regulatory matters. In addition, the firm has been involved in complex corporate restructuring, work outs and insolvency transactions.

The firm acts for companies and banks, particularly in the shipping, oil and gas, LNG, power, and telecoms sectors. The firm's clients are banks, shipowners, private equity funds and companies operating in such fields. The firm's finance department deals with general banking finance, structured finance, asset finance and work outs and insolvencies, both in Italy and on a worldwide basis. The firm's corporate department benefits from an established reputation for providing advice in relation to private equity and project finance matters related to renewable energy projects and it is also recognised as one of the leading firms in energy, LNG and gas regulatory matters.

The Rome office has also been handling litigation and competition law matters.

AREAS OF PRACTICE

A key feature is the firm's division into four international practice areas. These groups are not divided by location but work together internationally for the firm's international clients.

International finance group: the firm's lawyers advise all project participants, covering areas such as general banking finance, structured finance, securities and capital markets, derivatives, trade finance, asset finance, project finance, cross-border tax leverage lending and leasing, and work outs and insolvencies. The group has particular expertise and experience in a number of industry sectors heavily dependent on the financing of large capital assets.

International corporate group: the firm's public and private company clients have access to a wide range of domestic and international expertise covering all aspects of international corporate law, including acquisitions, disposals and mergers, public offerings of securities, management buy-outs and buy-ins, business and asset sales, debt structuring, equity financings, corporate restructurings, international privatisations and a wide range of commercial agreements such as distributorship, outsourcing purchase and agency agreements, and joint ventures and partnerships. In addition, the group offers specialist advice on real property, intellectual property, employment, and pensions, service agreements, share option and incentive schemes, executive immigration, and all aspects of European Union competition law.

International litigation group: large-scale litigation, arbitration and dispute resolution matters are handled by the group on a worldwide basis. The firm's lawyers have represented clients involved in international disputes in the areas of banking, construction, offshore oil and gas, power and energy, international trade, shipping (wet and dry) and aviation. The group also advises on the enforcement of security over vessels, marine pollution, marine insurance, shipbuilding, charterparties, and offshore oil and gas contracting.

International tax group: the firm's lawyers advise on domestic and cross-border tax leasing, non-asset-based structured finance, international tax planning, investigations and litigation and indirect tax. They also give advice generally on all types of transactions.

ALLEN & OVERY – BROSIO E ASSOCIATI – STUDIO LEGALE ASSOCIATO

CORSO VITTORIO EMANUELE II, 68
10121 TURIN

Telephone: +39 01 15 11 21
Fax: +39 01 15 11 23 33
Website: www.allenovery.com

Languages
English, French, German, Italian, Spanish

Other offices
Amsterdam, Antwerp, Bangkok, Beijing, Bratislava, Brussels, Budapest, Dubai, Frankfurt, Hamburg, Hong Kong, London, Luxembourg, Madrid, Milan, Moscow, New York, Paris, Prague, Rome, Shanghai, Singapore, Tokyo, Warsaw

Number of lawyers 2,304
at this office 35

Contacts
G. Massimillano Danusso (managing partner), Emanuele Borganti (head of operations in Italy)

CATEGORIES OF WORK

Corporate
Paolo Cerina

Banking
Giancarlo Castorino

Tax
Andrea Manganelli

ICM
G. Massimilliano Danusso

Litigation
Massimo Greco, Alberto Nanni

SJ BERWIN LLP

VIA LAMARMORA 39
10128 TURIN

Telephone: +39 02 36 57 57 01
Fax: +39 02 36 57 57 57
Email: turin@sjberwin.com
Website: www.sjberwin.com

Other offices
Berlin, Brussels, Frankfurt, London, Madrid, Milan, Munich, Paris

Number of lawyers 550

CATEGORIES OF WORK

Corporate finance
Fabio Cigna

Finance
Federico Pavetto

Private equity and acquisition finance
Alberto Morano

JERSEY

Population	85,150
Number of lawyers	182 members of The Jersey Law Society
Professional title	Advocate
Currency	Pound sterling (£)

Index

The Bailiwick of Jersey has the same relationship with the UK and Europe as that enjoyed by Guernsey (although there are in fact no formal links between the two Bailiwicks). As a Crown dependency and a member of the British Isles, though not the United Kingdom, some issues, namely foreign relations and defence, are administered for Jersey by the Crown through the UK government. Otherwise, the Jersey government (the States of Jersey) enjoys a great degree of autonomy. The island is also a member of the OECD.

Business on Jersey continues to boom as the island benefits from its growing reputation as a safe and well-regulated offshore jurisdiction. Its dependence on the UK as a source of business is declining, with more sophisticated forms of business replacing much of the traditional private client work. Jersey has also become a major centre for securitisation as the European industry has acknowledged the value of the island's special purpose vehicle (SPV) structures.

BILLING

Lawyers generally charge by the hour although scale fees still operate for conveyancing work. Fees may vary depending on the lawyer instructed and the job in hand. Clients can expect costs not dissimilar to those charged by City of London firms: around £160 for a newly qualified lawyer, rising to around £350 at partner level.

MARKETING

Jersey advocates may only advertise their services outside Jersey.

THE LEGAL 500

Readers should note that the following is taken from the **Offshore Britain** section of the 2005 edition of *The Legal 500* (UK edition), available at www.legal500.com.

LEGAL MARKET

Lawyers in Jersey are keen to emphasise the regulated nature of the jurisdiction, which means it competes with countries in the Eurozone such as Ireland, as well as its offshore counterparts. A flexible approach by the Jersey States means that legislative, fiscal and regulatory regimes are constantly updated, keeping Jersey at the cutting edge in the fiercely competitive arena of funds. The latest development in this process of change is the introduction of Expert Investor Funds, which has kept law firms busy, although the increased regulation has also meant consolidation in the Jersey trust company client base.

Most law firms also have highly profitable associated trust companies; although the extent to which they are intertwined with the workings of the law firm varies from firm to firm. There is a sharp divide in the market between firms who are committed to a Jersey base and those building a brand across offshore jurisdictions.

Two of the dominant players, **Ogier** and **Mourant du Feu & Jeune**, have both broadened their horizons beyond Jersey. **Mourant du Feu & Jeune** has a presence in Jersey, Cayman and London. **Ogier** also has multiple offshore expertise, establishing a new office in 2004 in Cayman Islands, **Ogier**, created by merger with Cayman firm *Boxalls*. Other locations are Guernsey and London.

Top-tier **Bedell Cristin** is also closely connected with its associated trust company, but has pursued a different strategy for growth, staying firmly on-island (except for its trust company in Dublin and Geneva) and benefits from close relationships with law firms in all the other major offshore centres.

Carey Olsen has to be commended for its rapid rise to the top five, part of a bold strategy which, post-merger in 2003, has made the firm the only fully fledged pan-Channel Islands practice. The firm is the competitor of which the four more established firms are most aware; it houses some first-class lawyers and garners a significant number of quality instructions. It also has a growing London office.

Bailhache Labesse is a leading, full-service firm with a determined Jersey focus. The quality of its practitioners is undisputed, as the firm fields a number of high-flyers. A strategy of measured growth is tangibly demonstrated by the move into a new building on the Waterfront, which houses the entire firm.

The second tier is comprised of two medium-sized firms **Voisin & Co.** and **Crills Advocates**, making seven leading firms in total. Both are commercially orientated and have the resources to undertake decent-sized transactions. **Voisin & Co.** is a two-partner and six-associate practice which attracts quality corporate and commercial work.

The largest firms

1	Carey Olsen	72
2	Ogier	70
3	Mourant du Feu & Jeune	66
4	Bailhache Labesse	46
5	Bedell Cristin	42
6	Crills Advocates	28
7	Nigel Harris & Partners	21
8	Crill Canavan	16
9	Viberts - Jersey Lawyers	15
10	Voisin & Co.	14
11	Le Gallais & Luce	9
12	BakerPlatt (Jersey)	6
13	Jenners	5
	Sinels	5
15	Backhurst Dorey & Crane	4
	Hanson Renouf	4
17	Spoor & Fisher	3
	Steven Slater Legal Service	3
19	Maples and Calder	2

These figures represent the total number of lawyers in this country only, and have been supplied by the firms themselves. The figures should be accurate as at 1 January 2006.

The firm is also focused on ramping up its funds advisory capacity and is looking to develop a niche in innovative products for Islamic financing. **Crills Advocates** continues to build up a dynamic commercial team, recruiting three fee-earners in the past year. The firm is evolving to service international clients, while maintaining its profile with a loyal mid-market client base.

BANKING

Readers are also referred to the **Jersey: Structured finance and securitisation section.**

Peter Byrne heads the four-partner team at **Bedell Cristin**, which is consistently instructed by blue-chip financial institutions on complex financing arrangements, acting for major lenders both on and off the island, such as Barclays, Lloyds TSB and ING BHF-Bank.

Former banker Paul Sugden leads the experienced banking team at **Carey Olsen**. Highlight transactions include developing and implementing an innovative court-sanctioned scheme to allow for the conditional discharge by agreement of Kevin Leech from his £80m bankruptcy, the largest in Jersey's history. Anthony Olsen is a respected litigator with particular expertise in banking and asset recovery work. Major clients include HSBC, Bank of Scotland, ABN Amro and Deutsche Bank.

Mourant du Feu & Jeune's dynamic team is headed by Simon Gould. An impressive list of clients includes Bayerische Hypo und Vereinsbank, Lloyds TSB, Royal Bank of Scotland and Eurohypo. The firm provided Jersey law advice to various Jersey companies involved in the refinancing of the Drax power station in Yorkshire, Europe's largest coal-fired power station, by way of a complex, multi-jurisdictional scheme of arrangement effected simultaneously in three jurisdictions, including Jersey.

Matthew Swan heads the first-class **Ogier** banking practice, which reaps a raft of instructions across the spectrum of commercial lending. Highlight instructions include acting for the Bank of Nova Scotia Channel Islands Ltd on the sale of its Jersey banking and trust business to Barclays Private Bank and Trust Ltd. Marc Yates and Michael Lombardi are recommended.

BANKING

BEDELL CRISTIN ✪
CAREY OLSEN
MOURANT DU FEU & JEUNE ✪
OGIER ✪

BAILHACHE LABESSE

Voisin & Co.

Firms are listed A-Z in tiers which are ranked in order of priority
✪ *Indicates firm displays contact details at the end of this chapter.*

Bailhache Labesse continues to act as sole counsel for Barclays Group, in 2004 advising on the purchase of the Bank of Nova Scotia Group. Another keynote instruction was advising Aberdeen Group on the Jersey Financial Services Commission's investigation into the split-capital sector, Jersey's largest-ever regulatory investigation. Mark Lewis heads the team, while the 'personable' Wendy Benjamin is recommended.

COMMERCIAL LITIGATION

Commercial litigation in Jersey is centred on trust disputes. It is anticipated that mediation will become an increasingly important means of resolving disputes, as changes to the Royal Court procedure were introduced in 2004, enabling the court to stay proceedings to encourage parties to settle.

Bailhache Labesse merits its top-tier status, due to the quality of lawyers and the commitment to litigation. The firm fields one of the largest teams of partner-advocates specialising in litigation, which expanded by two fee-earners in 2004. The 'excellent' Michael O'Connell, Fraser Robertson and Gillian Robinson are all first-rate practitioners. An impressive track record was maintained in 2004 with the firm acting on a number of groundbreaking cases, such as defending insurers in the largest personal injury claim in Jersey, in which liability was estimated as £10m.

Managing partner Anthony Robinson heads the commercial litigation practice at **Bedell Cristin**, which contains insolvency and asset-tracing expert Anthony Dessain and Mark Taylor. High-level trust litigation accounts for a significant proportion of the workload, although the team has advised local institutions on the fallout from split capital trusts and also acts for a number of insolvency practitioners in ongoing tracing and foreign assistance claims.

The excellent Nick Journeaux at **Carey Olsen**, who advised on key case *Re Esteem Settlement*, is now mainly London based. The five-partner team acted on a number of significant cases in 2004, such as advising the Jersey Financial Services Regulator in a groundbreaking case concerning

COMMERCIAL LITIGATION

BAILHACHE LABESSE
BEDELL CRISTIN ✪
CAREY OLSEN
OGIER ✪

CRILL CANAVAN
MOURANT DU FEU & JEUNE ✪

Crills Advocates
Sinels
Voisin & Co.

Firms are listed A-Z in tiers which are ranked in order of priority
✪ *Indicates firm displays contact details at the end of this chapter.*

the multi-million pound collapse of a complex derivatives scheme. The team also acted for HSBC, the major creditor in the Jersey bankruptcy proceedings against multi-millionaire KR Leech. John Kelleher is a leading light of the practice.

Ogier is frequently instructed on high-level disputes. Matthew Thompson is a skilled advocate, in 2004 appearing in the Privy Council in the leading case on solicitors' negligence *Riley v Pickersgill & le Cournu*. Thompson is also well known for his employment expertise. Kerry Lawrence is also highly recommended. In 2004 key cases for the firm included acting for British Home Stores in a lease and rent review dispute, both at trial and in the Court of Appeal. The case established new law for the appointment and challenge of experts.

Crill Canavan's Nuno Santos-Costa is an excellent practitioner, with expertise in high-value trusts disputes, ably assisted by Jane Martin. The team pulled in some chunky litigation cases in 2004, handling trust and commercial litigation as well as personal injury cases, representing insurance companies as well as claimants.

Mourant du Feu & Jeune's commercial litigation team contains several highly rated individuals, such as David Wilson, Alan Binnington, Beverley Lacey and Jonathan Speck. The team acts on high-profile banking and financial services litigation and also has expertise in handling sensitive financial disputes for leading banks. The team advises on trusts disputes and professional negligence claims, complex civil fraud, insolvency and major asset recovery. A sterling client list includes leading domestic and international corporations, global financial institutions, City law firms and high-net-worth individuals.

Senior partner Richard Michel heads **Crills Advocates'** team, which was boosted by the recruitment of David Steenson from **Voisin & Co.** in 2004. The team specialises in high-profile trust and investor action group disputes. Paul Nicholls has a particular focus on asset recovery.

Philip Sinel, the sole partner at **Sinels**, has a formidable reputation for specialist litigation advice and advocacy. The firm is namechecked on landmark Jersey trust cases such as *West v Lazards*, and *Mayo et al v Cantrade Private Bank (Switzerland) CI Ltd et al.*

Voisin & Co. has a solid litigation team, with Ashley Hoy particularly recommended. A steady workload includes high-value asset-freezing cases.

CORPORATE AND COMMERCIAL

The accomplished Peter Byrne heads the successful six-partner practice at **Bedell Cristin**, which has pulled in a steady flow of AIM work, including advising the first Ukrainian business to be listed on the UK junior exchange. The highly regarded team, which includes recommended practitioners Edward Bennett and Martin Paul, handles the full spectrum of corporate and commercial matters.

CORPORATE AND COMMERCIAL

BEDELL CRISTIN ✪
CAREY OLSEN
MOURANT DU FEU & JEUNE ✪
OGIER ✪

BAILHACHE LABESSE

Crills Advocates
Voisin & Co.

Crill Canavan

Firms are listed A-Z in tiers which are ranked in order of priority
✪ Indicates firm displays contact details at the end of this chapter.

Carey Olsen's respected Nicholas Crocker heads the four-partner corporate and commercial team, which expanded by two associate hires in 2004 from **Freshfields Bruckhaus Deringer** and **Allen & Overy LLP**. The team garners a steady flow of referrals from the top-ten City firms, due to its capacity to handle a large volume of complex transactions. A stellar client base includes Allianz, Lendlease and Deutsche Bank. Alex Ohlsson and Edward Quinn are excellent practitioners.

Mourant du Feu & Jeune has a strong corporate and banking team, the leading lights of which are Wendy Malorey and Robert Hickling. High-level instructions are the norm across the board of corporate, regulatory and fund work. Highlight transactions in 2004 included acting for Royal Bank of Scotland International in its acquisition of the residential mortgage portfolio of Bristol & West International in Jersey, Guernsey and the UK.

Ogier's thriving corporate and commercial practice had a busy year. The team acted as Jersey counsel for Randgold Resources Ltd, a London-listed and Nasdaq-listed FTSE 250 company with Southern Africa gold mining interests. Marc Yates leads the team, while Nick Kershaw is recommended. Clive Chaplin specialises in executive remuneration matters and employee benefit trusts.

Bailhache Labesse's Wendy Benjamin is an excellent all-round corporate and commercial lawyer, with niche expertise in IP and sports law. The firm acted in two of the largest banking and corporate transactions on the island in 2004; for Barclays Group on its purchase of the Bank of Nova Scotia Group in the Channel Islands and for Qatar National Bank in the purchase of the Ansbacher Banking Group in the Channel Islands.

Crills Advocates' Peter Harris heads an expanding team of fee-earners, with two more recruits in 2004. The firm handled over £1.5bn-worth of transactions in 2004, among the most notable being advising China Wonder and SovGEM on their AIM listings.

Senior partner Ian Strang heads the two-partner team at **Voisin & Co.**, ably supported by Nigel Pearmain. The firm acts for local trust companies and their clients on innovative corporate and trust structures, acquisitions and disposals; in 2004 advising ED&F Man Holdings Ltd in the multi-million pound acquisition of the Volcafe group.

The corporate and commercial capacity at **Crill Canavan** was diminished by the departure of David Banks, leading to a radical restructuring of the team. The firm undertakes mid-market transactional work for UK and Jersey-based clients. Senior partner Geoffrey Crill currently heads the team.

EMPLOYMENT

With the introduction of new employment legislation in 2005, law firms have been ramping up their employment expertise. The new laws introduce unfair dismissal, a minimum wage, minimum holidays and rest days in Jersey for the first time, creating a raft of work for law firms as they conduct major reviews of employers' terms of employment and alert clients to the implications of the new laws, through training sessions and bulletins. The leading firms also have well-established expertise in advising on employee benefits.

Patrick Jones heads the employee share plans group at **Bailhache Labesse**, which advises on and administers employee incentive arrangements. Plans administered include both UK and global plans with a large number of participants and bespoke incentives. 2004 saw particularly strong growth, with clients ranging from UK FTSE 100/250 companies to private companies. New clients include Barclays Plc and Trinity Mirror Plc.

Bedell Cristin formed an employment law team in 2004 dedicated to advising clients on anticipated changes to employment law practice. Key practitioners in the group are James Campbell, Lisa Springate, David Cadin and James Dickinson. The team handles advisory work on the impact of the new employment laws, as well as providing expertise on taxation, litigation and the employment aspects of corporate transactions.

Carey Olsen's Jersey employment team is led by John Kelleher, ably supported by Siobhan Riley. The team handles both advisory and contentious work, encompassing matters such as immigration advice to employers who wish to take on non-EU

EMPLOYMENT

Bailhache Labesse
Bedell Cristin ✪
Carey Olsen
Mourant du Feu & Jeune ✪
Ogier ✪

Firms are listed alphabetically
✪ Indicates firm displays contact details at the end of this chapter.

nationals and advising employers whether there are good grounds to dismiss a claim of unfair dismissal.

Mourant du Feu & Jeune has a dynamic employment practice under the stewardship of the capable Wendy Malorey, which acts solely for employers; including leading financial institutions and Jersey-based trading entities. Matters undertaken in the past year include compromise agreements, redundancy issues, M&A and general employment advice.

Clive Chaplin heads the skilled employee benefits and pensions team at **Ogier**. The team continues to deliver short and long-term tax-efficient remuneration plans for a number of finance sector employees.

INVESTMENT FUNDS

The funds industry was reinvigorated in 2004 by the introduction of the Expert Investor Funds regime, which positions Jersey as a favourable location for alternative investment funds and family office structures. A notable trend is the growth of property funds, particularly the use of Jersey-based unit trusts in UK real estate acquisitions, in order to mitigate SDLT liability. Hedge funds have also experienced a surge in popularity, while the Channel Islands Stock Exchange is cultivating a good reputation as the place for listing investment funds.

Mourant du Feu & Jeune advises on the full spectrum of funds which use Jersey or Cayman structures: hedge funds, property funds, private equity funds and retail funds. In 2004, a dedicated funds team was created across London and Jersey, built around a core team of eight fee-earners including Jacqueline Richomme and practice area head Cyman Davies. The team has advised on almost half of the new funds established under the Expert Funds regime, including the first-ever fund. Tim Herbert and Robert Hickling are recommended.

Ogier's Nick Kershaw has a high reputation for investment funds work. The team handles a broad range of funds, from property to private equity. Notable instructions in 2004 include advising UBS on five corporate investment funds which will invest in real estate in the UK, Europe, US, Asia and Australasia, and acting for Wellington Advisers on the first successful launch of a German venture capital fund for two years, which is also an expert fund under the new regime.

In response to overwhelming client feedback, **Carey Olsen** moves up a tier this year. Clients particularly rated Edward Quinn, who is instructed by on-island institutions and City firms, as 'fantastic, the best lawyer on the island' for his 'astute commercial advice'. The dynamic Eve Kosofsky heads an expanding ten-fee-earner team, which boasted three new recruits in 2004. In the same year, the team handled a wealth of funds and private equity transactions, including advising on over 70 new investment structures with a total value of around £10bn.

INVESTMENT FUNDS

MOURANT DU FEU & JEUNE ✪
OGIER ✪

CAREY OLSEN

BAILHACHE LABESSE
BEDELL CRISTIN ✪

Crills Advocates
Voisin & Co.

Firms are listed A-Z in tiers which are ranked in order of priority
✪ Indicates firm displays contact details at the end of this chapter.

Simon Howard draws on a wealth of funds-related work at **Bailhache Labesse**. The funds team was involved in the formulation of the Expert Investor Funds policy and non-domicile fund policy, in particular, advising on structuring a new funds classification for institutional, professional and experienced investors in connection with the Expert Investor Funds regime.

Bedell Cristin's investment funds and private equity practice is headed by Martin Paul. In 2004 the three-partner team handled a broad range of funds, including a number of hedge funds and property unit trusts, ranging from expert funds to VPUT and joint venture structures. The team has also dealt with the listing of both Jersey-domiciled and non-domiciled funds on the Channel Islands Stock Exchange. Peter Byrne has input where required, while the skilled Michael Richardson also has a reputation for investment funds work.

In 2004, the team at **Crills Advocates**, headed by Peter Harris, advised on a variety of fund structures with a total value of around £600m.

Bill Gibbon advises **Voisin & Co.**'s institutional client base on the structuring of new funds for clients in Jersey, the UK and Europe. The team has expertise on differing fund structures, including US real estate, umbrella funds and the development of shari'ah-compliant hedge funds.

PERSONAL TAX, TRUSTS AND PROBATE

Ogier has considerable strength in trusts, with Steven Meiklejohn and Julian Clyde-Smith acknowledged by clients and peers as first-class practitioners. Kerry Lawrence is also recommended, while Timothy Le Cocq is one of the island's top trusts litigators.

Bailhache Labesse's Graham Boxall has a solid trusts practice, being frequently instructed by blue-chip trust institutions. The team is acting as sole counsel to Abacus (CI) Ltd, as trustee of a number of discretionary trusts, in its successful attempt to obtain an early discharge from bankruptcy for the beneficiaries of such trusts. The trusts practice benefits from the firm's litigation prowess, as Michael O'Connell has expertise in advising on matrimonial disputes with a trust element.

PERSONAL TAX, TRUSTS AND PROBATE

OGIER ✪

Bailhache Labesse
Bedell Cristin ✪
Carey Olsen
Crills Advocates
Mourant du Feu & Jeune ✪

Backhurst Dorey & Crane
Crill Canavan
Le Gallais & Luce
Voisin & Co.

Firms are listed A-Z in tiers which are ranked in order of priority
✪ Indicates firm displays contact details at the end of this chapter.

Bedell Cristin's six-partner, eight-assistant trust and private capital group is headed by Edward Bennett, while Guy Le Sueur handles the probate side. The talented Alan Dart is also dedicated exclusively to private capital work. A broad client base consists of high-net-worth individuals, trust companies and both local and international banks.

Carey Olsen's three-partner team expanded by two fee-earners in 2004, bringing the total number of fee-earners to ten. Christopher Lakeman has expertise in complex trust litigation and non-contentious applications, while Paul Matthams is one of Jersey's leading trusts and pensions specialists.

Crills Advocates acts for a number of trust companies based in Jersey, advising on all aspects of trusts and administration, including the creation and winding up of trusts, the underlying structures and the activities of trustees.

Formerly of **Ogier**, Giles Corben has moved to **Mourant du Feu & Jeune** to head the private client, trusts and tax team. The team acted on the *Mackinnon v Regent* case, which was key in confirming the validity of a trust instrument and reaffirmed Jersey's position as a leading trust jurisdiction. Litigator Jonathan Speck is viewed by peers and clients alike as 'simply excellent'.

Voisin & Co. has particular expertise in bespoke employee benefit trusts and share option work, and is regularly instructed on private client trust work emanating from the Middle East. Ashley Hoy is recommended for high-value settlement litigation.

REAL ESTATE

Bailhache Labesse's pre-eminent commercial property practice is led by the 'outstanding' John Bisson. The team has established a firm client following, among which are the island's principal developers and major players in the property and leisure market. Timothy Hart acts for financial institutions, governmental agencies, corporate

REAL ESTATE

BAILHACHE LABESSE
OGIER ✪

Bedell Cristin ✪
Carey Olsen
Crill Canavan
Mourant du Feu & Jeune ✪

Crills Advocates
Voisin & Co.

Firms are listed A-Z in tiers which are ranked in order of priority
✪ Indicates firm displays contact details at the end of this chapter.

occupiers and private investors. A raft of quality instructions in 2004 includes acting for the Dandara Group on notable matters, such as advising on the financing and legal structuring of the L'Hermitage Gardens and Spectrum developments and acting for the Waterfront Enterprise Board Ltd.

Ogier's practice head Chris Renouf has a first-class commercial property practice, whose client list includes the leading developers on the island. In 2004 the team was instrumental in advising on the planned changes to the Waterfront area, acting for Harcourt Developments on the £60m development of the Island Site, and for HSBC on the funding of the Harbour Reach development. Peter Bertram has a strong reputation for his expertise in handling complex commercial lease instructions.

Guy Le Sueur of **Bedell Cristin** is an astute commercial property practitioner. The team handles high-value property financing as well as acquisitions, disposals and leases, and in 2004 scooped instruction on the Prudential Investment Managers' £11.8m acquisition of Standard Bank House in St Helier.

Alex Ohlsson is a highly regarded practitioner at **Carey Olsen**. The team combines the international real estate financing expertise of Ohlsson and Nicholas Crocker, with the specialist property know-how of John Kelleher. As well as acting in major Jersey property transactions, the firm acts in UK-based deals involving Jersey corporate owners. Key transactions in 2004 include acting for Legal & General Assurance Society Ltd on its acquisition of 13/14 Esplanade, St Helier, and advising Bristol & West International Ltd on the sale of its mortgage book to The Royal Bank of Scotland International Ltd.

Crill Canavan's Geoffrey Crill has an outstanding reputation for commercial property. The three-partner team acts for most of the national high street retailers trading in the island, commercial and residential developers and investors, as well as substantial commercial tenants.

The forward-thinking Elizabeth Breen heads **Mourant du Feu & Jeune**'s highly specialised team, which handles the full gamut of commercial property work, from sizeable sale and purchase transactions to major financing deals. In 2004 the team acted for Axa Sun Life Plc in acquiring the £14.5m head lease of the Waterfront; and advised Royal Bank of Scotland International on registered security aspects of a £130m overdraft facility to a major Channel Islands trading company. Gio Pollano gets good client feedback.

Julie Melia's team at **Crills Advocates** welcomed Denis Worrall from **Viberts - Jersey Lawyers** in 2004. Major clients of the firm are finance sector names, as well as developers and Jersey businesses. Highlight instructions in 2004 include acting in the acquisition of land for development of 123 houses and in site sales, and acting in various Royal Bank of Scotland International Ltd property finance instructions up to £7.5m.

Voisin & Co. has the capacity to provide the commercial property element to commercial transactions.

STRUCTURED FINANCE AND SECURITISATION

As a jurisdiction focused on financial services, legal expertise in structured finance and securitisation is paramount. The high-level work undertaken by the island's law firms demonstrates that this need is capably fulfilled. 2004 saw growth in the synthetic securitisation sector, reflecting the popularity of this technique in Europe and elsewhere. The credit card-backed sector was also thriving. Jersey is considering whether to introduce netting legalisation, in statutory recognition of limited recourse/contractual subordination arrangements.

Richard Gerwat's team at **Bedell Cristin** has carved a superlative reputation in credit-card securitisation, providing a wealth of experience in establishing MBNA structures for a host of household names, such as Barclaycard, Egg, Morgan Stanley and Capital One. Highlights of 2004 include an innovative transaction advising DZ Bank on a lease-receivables securitisation, involving the issue of €390 million credit-linked notes. Shane Hollywood is recommended.

Mourant du Feu & Jeune's nine-partner capital markets practice is spread across its offices in Jersey and London. The team handled numerous securitisation transactions in 2004 for blue-chip clients including JP Morgan, Credit Suisse First Boston, Lehman Brothers and BNP Paribas. Jonathan Rigby, Simon Felton and Robert Hickling are skilled practitioners in the field.

STRUCTURED FINANCE AND SECURITISATION

BEDELL CRISTIN ✪
MOURANT DU FEU & JEUNE ✪
OGIER ✪

Bailhache Labesse
Carey Olsen

Crills Advocates
Voisin & Co.

Firms are listed A-Z in tiers which are ranked in order of priority
✪ Indicates firm displays contact details at the end of this chapter.

Ogier has significant expertise in all facets of structured finance, and is frequently instructed on Tier 1 fundraisings out of Jersey, including acting for HBOS on a $750m fundraising through the issue of limited partnership interests by a Jersey limited partnership. The team has also handled a raft of complex securitised debt issues in the past year. Chris Byrne leads the experienced team, while Marc Yates and Nick Kershaw are also recommended.

Bailhache Labesse's Mark Lewis is recommended for securitisation matters. In 2004, the team acted as sole Jersey counsel for Nationwide in establishing Cobbler Funding Ltd and Cobbler Funding LC, the first ABC commercial-paper programme established on behalf of a building society.

Carey Olsen's four-partner team includes the 'skilled' Alex Ohlsson, Edward Quinn and former **Linklaters** partner Alan Stevens. Property finance is a significant element of the practice, accounting for over £6bn-worth of transactions in 2004. The team acted for Bradford & Bingley in setting up a £10bn covered-bond programme and, in a ground breaking transaction, advised SVG Diamond Holdings Ltd on the issue of €150 million secured floating and fixed-rate notes for the acquisition of a portfolio of private equity investments.

A new addition to our table this year, **Crills Advocates**, now has the critical mass after a programme of recruitment to advise on significant structured finance transactions, including acting as Jersey counsel to BNP Paribas on the securitisation of certain trade receivables relating to wine and other alcohol products. Peter Harris heads the team.

Voisin & Co. is looking to develop a focus on Islamic funds, building links with its Gulf Co-operation Council investment clients to produce innovative shari'ah-compliant structures. Other key instructions include advising American Express on a number of billion-dollar repackaging transactions. Bill Gibbon, formerly of **Linklaters**, is active in this field.

BAKERPLATT

PO BOX 842
QUEEN'S HOUSE, DON ROAD
ST HELIER

Telephone: +44 1534 613775
Fax: +44 1534 737355
E-mail: admin@bakerplatt.com
Website: www.bakerplatt.com

Languages
English, French

Other offices
Geneva, London

Number of lawyers 5

International groupings
Bedford Row Alliance

CATEGORIES OF WORK

Financial crime
Stephen Baker, Stephen Platt, Emma Jordan

Financial services regulation
Stephen Platt, Emma Jordan

International co-operation in criminal matters
Stephen Baker

Compliance
Stephen Platt, Paul Leary

Confiscation, forfeiture and restitution of the proceeds of crime
Stephen Baker, Stephen Platt, Emma Jordan

Asset recovery
Stephen Baker

THE FIRM

The BakerPlatt group was formed in 2003 out of an alliance between the law firm BakerAssociates and the training and compliance consultancy BakerPlatt ltd.

BakerPlatt is a legal professional services firm specialising in the following fields: financial crime, international asset recovery, financial regulation and compliance issues, money laundering and terrorist financing prevention.

The firm consists of English Counsel, Jersey Advocates and compliance experts who have unparalleled experience in all aspects of fraud, financial regulatory law and asset recovery. This experience is at an international level. The firm's senior partner Stephen Baker is the only lawyer who practises at the Jersey and English Bars advising both onshore and offshore. He had conduct of the investigation of the flow of Abacha's funds through Jersey. This investigation led to the repatriation of US$160m to the Federal Republic of Nigeria.

BakerPlatt has been at the forefront of the leading offshore cases involving money laundering legislation. Stephen Baker prosecuted Jersey's first money laundering trial on behalf of the Attorney General of Jersey. He defended the first prosecution brought under the Money Laundering Order. This was the first prosecution under the Order (or its equivalent legislation) in an offshore or any other common law jurisdiction.

AREAS OF PRACTICE

In the compliance and regulatory arena BakerPlatt is pre-eminent offshore. Stephen Platt drafted the latest of the Jersey Financial Services Commission Anti-Money Laundering and Terrorist Financing Guidance Notes. He also drafted the Mauritius Anti Money Laundering Codes. The firm regularly advises leading financial institutions on the effectiveness of internal control systems and conducts a variety of risk-related reviews.

The principals of the firm are regularly appointed as independent inspectors on behalf of offshore regulators in the investigation of trust company businesses, investment businesses and banks. They have also advised substantial non-European states in anticipation of reviews by the Financial Action Task Force (FATF).

Stephen Platt is the principal author of the UK and international versions of the International Compliance Association Diploma Programs, which are widely recognised as the leading compliance qualifications globally.

All counsel in the firm have significant experience in the investigation of and structures of trusts and the use of offshore financial institutions for illicit purposes. That expertise is utilised in training seminars delivered internationally. In the UK BakerPlatt delivers training seminars in association with the British Bankers Association.

BakerPlatt is also expert in the risks associated with conducting financial business through the United States as a consequence of the provisions of the US Patriot Act. In matters requiring American legal expertise, two attorneys from the New York law firm Rosner Moscow and Napierala, LLP, John Moscow and Jack Blum, co-counsel with counsel from BakerPlatt to represent clients.

BakerPlatt is an alliance partner with the chambers of David Farrer QC, 7 Bedford Row. 7 Bedford Row is one of the leading chambers specialising in financial crime and all aspects of fraud litigation.

BEDELL CRISTIN

PO BOX 75
26 NEW STREET
ST HELIER JE4 8PP

Telephone: +44 1534 814814
Fax: +44 1534 814815
E-mail: enquiries@bedellgroup.com
Website: www.bedellgroup.com

Languages
Afrikaans, English, French, German, Italian, Spanish, Thai

Number of lawyers 42

Contact
Anthony Dessain (senior partner)

CATEGORIES OF WORK

Financial services group including: capital markets and structured finance
Richard Gerwat, Shane Hollywood

Investment funds and private equity
Martin Paul, Michael Richardson

Banking and corporate
Peter Byrne, Martin Paul

Trust and private capital
Edward Bennett, Zillah Howard

Tax
Richard Gerwat, Michael Richardson

Information services
Zillah Howard

Litigation group: trust litigation
Anthony Robinson, Mark Taylor, David Cadin

Asset tracing
Anthony Robinson, Anthony Dessain

Insolvency
Anthony Dessain, Mark Taylor

Private client and local business group, including: private clients
Guy Le Sueur, Anita Regal

Commercial property
Guy Le Sueur

Local business clients
Guy Le Sueur

Employment law
Anthony Robinson, Michael Richardson

Trust and company administration services
Alan Dart, Nick Cawley

Employment benefit trust administration
Michael Richardson, Edward Buckland

THE FIRM

Bedell Cristin is a first-tier law firm, highly rated for the professionalism and technical expertise of its lawyers. With a clear focus on the commercial needs of clients and intermediaries, Bedell Cristin delivers a solution-driven, cost-effective legal service to financial institutions and corporates throughout the world. It has been involved in the establishment of a significant proportion of the banks, investment funds and structured finance vehicles carrying on business from Jersey.

The firm was established in 1939 and was instrumental in the development of Jersey as a finance centre. The firm has excellent contacts with financial institutions and law firms in the world's major financial centres, counting many blue-chip entities amongst its extensive client base, including: ABN Amro, Bank of America, Bank of Nova Scotia, Bank of Scotland, Barclays, Bank of Ireland, Capital One, Chase, Citibank, CSFB, Deutsche Bank, Egg Banking, HSBC, ICI, MBNA, Merrill Lynch/Mercury, Prudential, Rabobank, Rothschild, Royal Bank of Canada, RBS and Schroders.

AREAS OF PRACTICE

Capital markets and structured finance: this group has a strong reputation in asset-backed finance, having acted as Jersey counsel in some of the most innovative transactions in the market. Together with Bedell Cristin Trust and Bedell SPV, the practice area provides a 'one-stop-shop' for establishing SPVs in Jersey.

Investment funds and private equity: this group focuses on the establishment and legal servicing of pooled investment structures qualifying as public collective investment funds or non-public collective investment schemes, private equity funds and pension schemes. Sponsorship and listing services in connection with the Channel Islands Stock Exchange are available through Bedell Channel Islands Limited, which is a category 1 sponsorship member of the Exchange.

Banking and corporate: advice is provided to many banks with a presence in Jersey, and Jersey law advice and legal opinions are provided to banks and multinationals globally. This group also advises on Jersey elements of international M&A transactions, joint venture arrangements, shareholders' agreements/arrangements and acquisitions/disposals of Jersey companies.

Trust and private capital: this group is the largest of its kind on the island, and comprises 14 practitioners, including five partners, who between them provide specialist trust and related corporate law advice to individual and institutional clients on wealth preservation and management, employee and executive share incentive schemes, bespoke trust drafting, the restructuring of assets held in trust and advice to fiduciaries.

Regulatory and compliance: this group is focused on advising local and international clients on the regulatory and compliance issues arising from their operations in Jersey and regularly runs client workshops in this area.

Litigation: the firm's litigation group is one of the largest in Jersey. A full range of litigation and dispute resolution services is provided but particular growth has taken place in contentious trust and regulatory work. Other key work areas include banking, insolvency and asset tracing.

Private client and local business: the firm advises on a wide range of Jersey property and private client matters. The group has particular expertise in IT and telecoms matters (acting for, amongst others, Jersey Telecom).

Bedell Trust Company, a wholly owned subsidiary of the law firm, and one of the leading independent trust companies in Jersey, provides fiduciary and company administration services to institutional and high-net-worth private clients. It is regulated by the Jersey Financial Services Commission under the Financial Services (Jersey) Law 1998 for the purpose of carrying on Trust Company Business. Through Bedell Trust and Bedell SPV, administration services are provided to EBTs, SPVs, private equity structures and limited partnerships. Multi-jurisdictional administration services are provided through Bedell Trust UK, Bedell Trust Ireland and Bedell Trust Suisse.

MOURANT DU FEU & JEUNE

PO BOX 87
22 GRENVILLE STREET
ST HELIER JE4 8PX

Telephone: +44 1534 609000
Fax: +44 1534 609333
E-mail: mdfj@mourant.com
Website: www.mourant.com

Languages
English, French, German, Italian, Portuguese, Spanish

Other offices
London, Cayman Islands, Guernsey

Number of lawyers 80

Member
Lex Mundi

CATEGORIES OF WORK

Capital markets
Robert Hickling

Funds
Jaqueline Richomme

Banking
James Ruane

Property
Elizabeth Breen

Corporate structures
James Ruane

Financial services
Simon Gould

Dispute resolution and litigation
Jonathan Speck

Fund administration
Robert Short

Corporate and commercial
Wendy Malorey

Corporate structures administration
Robert Short

Employment
Wendy Malorey

Property fund administration
Paul Le Marquand

Trusts
Giles Corbin

Private wealth management
Alan Binnington

OGIER

WHITELEY CHAMBERS
DON STREET
ST HELIER JE4 9WG

Telephone: +44 1534 504000
Fax: +44 1534 504444
E-mail: info@ogier.com
Website: www.ogier.com

Languages
French, German, Portuguese, Spanish

Other offices
Cayman Islands, Guernsey, London

Number of lawyers 120
at this office 70

Member
Association of European Lawyers (AEL); STEP; EVCA; BVCA

CATEGORIES OF WORK

Banking
Christopher Byrne, Matthew Swan

Securitisation and structured finance
Christopher Byrne, Michael Lombardi

Capital markets
Christopher Byrne

Investment funds
Nick Kershaw, Richard Thomas

Employee benefits and share plan administration
Clive Chaplin, Phil Norman

Real estate investment
Nick Kershaw, Michael Lombardi

Corporate and commercial
Marc Yates, Richard Thomas

Trust and estate planning
Steve Meiklejohn, Julian Clyde-Smith

Private client
Jonathan White, Steve Meiklejohn

Commercial and residential property
Christopher Renouf, Peter Bertram

Commercial litigation
Matthew Thompson, Kerry Lawrence

Employment law
Matthew Thompson

Regulatory
Matthew Thompson, Steve Meiklejohn

Fiduciary services
Simon Willing, Paul Willing

THE FIRM

Ogier is one of the leading offshore providers of legal and administration services, with approximately 500 employees across offices in Jersey, Guernsey, London and the Cayman Islands.

Ogier has developed an extensive portfolio of international clients and continues to provide legal and administration services for these clients through its dedicated teams.

AREAS OF PRACTICE

Banking: Ogier is widely regarded as a premier firm for banking and international finance. It specialises in advising on all areas of banking, security, structured finance, banking regulation and the establishment of banks.

Corporate and commercial: Ogier's highly experienced and extensive team covers mergers and acquisitions, employment and privacy laws, IT/IP and e-commerce.

Securitisation: Ogier has one of the leading securitisation and capital markets teams, with particular expertise in asset-backed securities, CBOs, ABCP and structured notes.

Structured finance: the structured finance team covers structured equity, asset finance and tax neutral transactions.

Investment funds: Ogier's fund practice comprises one of the largest funds teams in Jersey, Guernsey and the Cayman Islands, and advises on the establishment and strucuturing of funds as well as on regulatory and compliance issues.

Real estate: Ogier Real Estate Services Ltd provides company secretarial, accounting and administration services to a wide range of real estate-related structures. Ogier's real estate team specialises in the establishment and administration of corporate structures in most European jurisdictions.

Employee benefits: the employee benefits team is committed to providing an innovative and flexible approach to assist clients to achieve employee or clients' employee incentive requirements, tailored administration services, comprehensive advice and a quality, efficient and cost-effective service.

Trusts: the trust and estate planning group has one of the largest teams of trust lawyers dedicated to advising trust companies, intermediaries and individuals in matters of trust law.

Private client: Ogier continues to develop and grow its private client practice. The private client team can provide a full range of administration services to trusts, companies and limited partnerships established in the Channel Islands, as well as to entities established elsewhere.

Commercial litigation: Ogier has a specialist and highly regarded trust and commercial litigation group involved in the majority of the leading high-profile Jersey cases. The litigation group is the sole litigation practice in Jersey specialising exclusively in commercial litigation.

Commercial property: one of the largest commercial and residential property law teams in Jersey, Ogier acts in most of Jersey's major property transactions for the buyer, seller or financier.

Fiduciary services: Ogier Fiduciary Services provides professional administration and accounting services to trusts, companies and limited partnerships.

JORDAN

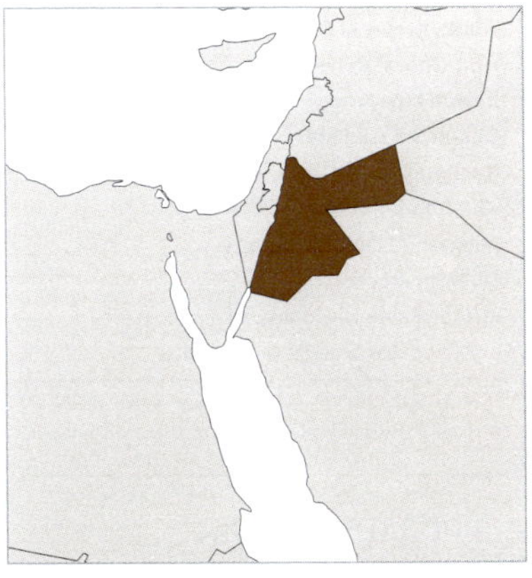

Population	5.7million
Number of lawyers	8,000 (approx)
Professional title	Attorney
Currency	Dinar (JoD)

Index

The Hashemite Kingdom of Jordan emerged as an independent state in 1946, following the termination of British rule and the division of the Middle East by Britain and France. The country is almost entirely surrounded by Syria to the north, Iraq to the northeast, Saudi Arabia to the southeast, and Israel and the West Bank to the west. Its only access to the sea is at Aqaba, some 400km south of the capital, Amman.

Jordan's clashes with Israel over the control of the West Bank were pacified in 1994, when the two countries signed a peace treaty and allowed parts of the West Bank to come under autonomous rule.

The population of Jordan is almost entirely Arab, with half of these being of Palestinian origin. The vast majority of Jordanians are Sunni Muslims, while Christians constitute most of the minority. Although Arabic is the country's official language, English is widely spoken throughout the business community.

Jordan's monarch, King Abdullah II, inherited the throne from his father, King Hussein, in 1999.

BILLING

Billing is normally in US dollars and rates vary considerably depending on the type of work undertaken. However, international clients can expect to pay from €60 an hour for an associate to €230 for the most senior partner.

POLITICAL CLIMATE

Jordan is a constitutional monarchy, and although popular participation in its representative government has been increasing, under the 1952 Constitution, the king's power remains absolute.

The king has frequently reshuffled his cabinet, and on 28 November 2005, he swore in a new 24-member government, appointing a new upper house and fresh advisors to the royal court. This follows the resignation of the former government, and of Prime Minister Adnan Badran, after serving just six months; he had been heavily criticised for his pro-Western reform agenda, which disregarded tribal sensitivities. The new cabinet line-up, overseen by new Prime Minister Marouf Bakheet is set to continue with key IMF-guided reforms, whilst also being encouraged to tighten security after November's deadly terrorist bomb attack on Amman. A former ambassador to Israel, Mr Bakheet had a long career in military intelligence, in significant contrast to Mr Badran, who was an academic.

Despite the upheavals, the political outlook remains positive. King Abdullah's position appears secure and he is generally popular and enjoys strong support from the army.

For years, Jordan has been pivotal to the struggle for power in the Middle East. However, it manages to maintain is close ties with the US, and has made good progress in restoring relations with its neighbours despite the strain caused by the US conflict with Iraq, a country on which Jordan heavily depends for its export market. One of only two Arab countries to have made peace with Israel, the two remain uneasy neighbours, with the ongoing conflict between Israel and the Palestinians sometimes spilling over Jordan's borders. The Jordanian government, steeped in conservative tribal values, remains caught in an awkward diplomatic balance; it seeks to maintain its regional and tribal loyalties, whilst keeping the US as an important ally.

ECONOMY

Despite its limited natural resources and narrow economic base, Jordan has made significant progress in the last twenty years, most recently under King Abdullah II, who continues to drive forward a comprehensive programme of economic reforms. The country faces some key challenges, namely reducing its heavy debt burden and dependence on foreign grants, tackling unemployment and creating investment opportunities. These are made all the more difficult by a rapidly growing population, inadequate supplies of water, a lack of its own oil reserves, and the fact that a large percentage of its land is unsuitable for cultivation.

However, the government has co-operated closely with the IMF, and the combined effort is enabling the country to benefit increasingly from globalisation and developments in ICT. The government began selling off state-owned entities in the early 1990s, and has made considerable progress with its privatisation programme, particularly since the establishment in 1996 of the Executive Privatisation Unit (EPU), which manages the process. Leading the way is the sale of state-owned Jordan Telecom, now almost complete, with the most recent schemes focusing on the privatisation of the electricity sector and Amman's Queen Alia Airport, among others. The government also recently announced the first phase of the privatisation of Aqaba Railway Corporation.

The largest firms

1	Abu-Ghazaleh Legal	30
2	Ali Sharif Zu'bi Advocates & Legal Consultants	21
3	International Business Legal Associates	20
4	Khalifeh & Partners	17
5	Nabeel Law Offices	12
6	Beiruti Law Firm	10
	Khalaf Masa'deh & Partners	10
	Nabulsi & Associates	10
	Petra for Law and Intellectual Property	10
10	Rajai K.W. Dajani & Associates	9
11	Hashem Law Office	8
	Middle Eastern Global Advocates & Legal Consultants	8
13	Marwan Al Hussein & Sons	7
14	A Ghniem & Partners Law Firm	6
	Abdul Karim Al Fauri & Associates	6
16	Saba & Co	2

These figures represent the total number of lawyers in this country only, and have been supplied by the firms themselves. The figures should be accurate as at 1 January 2006.

As the country's markets have opened up, Jordan has liberalised the international trade regime; the country became the fourth Arab member of the WTO in 2000, and signed important free trade agreements with the US and EU the following year. A number of special economic zones, benefiting from low taxes and investor-friendly policies, have been established in the hope of attracting foreign investment and creating job opportunities. The centrepiece of these is the export-orientated Aqaba port.

Jordan suffered a setback with a fall in GDP growth in 2003, largely thanks to the US-led war in Iraq, which is Jordan's biggest export target and key supplier of discounted oil. However, Jordan's economy has recovered well, with the government reaching oil supply agreements with other Gulf states and reviving its tourism industry, which is expected to contribute US$1.4bn to the country's GDP in 2005.

The Amman Stock Exchange is one of the largest and most successful Arab financial markets open to foreign investors. The stock exchange index increased by 64% in 2004, with an average consumer price index inflation of 3.4%, compared with 2.3% in 2003.

LEGAL SYSTEM AND LEGAL MARKET

Jordan's legal system draws upon French civil law traditions as well as Islamic law and custom. The court system comprises three categories of courts: religious, civil, and special. The civil court hierarchy includes magistrates courts, courts of first instance, courts of appeal and, ultimately, the Court of Cassation, Jordan's Supreme Court. All matters concerning the personal status of Muslims are decided by shari'ah courts, while special courts deal with specific matters such as state security, interpretation of the constitution, or judicial review of decisions by government entities.

Lawyers practising in Jordan must join the Jordanian Bar Association. At last count, the country had 19 women judges (up from 11 in 2002), and over 1,000 practising female lawyers registered with the Bar Association.

Until recently the Jordanian legal market was fairly quiet but with economic growth prospects improving, it now looks ripe for expansion. Currently few firms have more than ten lawyers and there is very little specialisation. **Ali Sharif Zu'bi Advocates & Legal Consultants**, with 25 fee-earners, is Jordan's largest firm and is a member of worldwide network *Lex Mundi*. **Khalifeh & Partners**, meanwhile, recently opened an office in Baghdad.

Foreign firms have yet to establish a presence on the ground in Jordan, however several have been involved in work there. **Trowers & Hamlins**, which has five regional offices, and **Clifford Chance** with 36 fee-earners in the Middle East, are probably the most experienced.

CORPORATE AND M&A

ALI SHARIF ZU'BI ADVOCATES & LEGAL CONSULTANTS

International Business Legal Associates
Khalaf Masa'deh & Partners
Nabulsi & Associates
Rajai K.W. Dajani & Associates

A Ghniem & Partners Law Firm
Abdul Karim Al Fauri & Associates
Abu-Ghazaleh Legal ✪
Beiruti Law Firm
Dajani & Associates
Hashem Law Office
Khalifeh & Partners
Marwan Al Hussein & Sons
Obeidat & Freihat
Middle Eastern Global Advocates & Legal Consultants

Firms are listed A-Z in tiers which are ranked in order of priority
✪ *Indicates firm displays contact details at the end of this chapter.*

CORPORATE AND M&A

When commenting on the most active and reliable local practices in Jordan, major foreign firms almost invariably refer to Jordan's largest firm, **Ali Sharif Zu'bi Advocates & Legal Consultants**. Overseen by 'well-connected' managing partner Sharif Ali Zu'Bi, who is also Jordan's current Minister of Trade & Industry, the practice regularly acts in conjunction with major international firms such as **Denton Wilde Sapte**, **Clifford Chance**, **Linklaters** and **Latham & Watkins**. The last year has brought a healthy amount of acquisitions work for clients such as Jordan Phosphate Mines Co, which the team recently assisted in buying a majority share in Indo-Jordan Chemicals Co, and General Electric, which it advised on the purchase of shares in a local business. Finance is also a key strength, with the team recently acting for Calyon in connection with a US$260m facility to Saudi Oger, and advising Aviation Capital Group on an aircraft finance transaction with Royal Jordanian Airlines. 'Commercial and responsive' Khaled Asfour is also highly rated by clients.

Eighteen-strong **International Business Legal Associates** was founded by a former Jordanian Minister of Justice, Dr Salaheddin Al-Bashir. The firm provides a wide range of advice to both local and international clients, including Microsoft, Bureau Veritas, Chemonics International, Bank of Jordan and Century Investment Group. Having assisted the government in the establishment of the Aqaba special economic zone, the practice continues to advise the state-owned Aqaba Development Corporation on operational and procedural issues. 'Open-minded and professional' partner Nancy Dababneh oversees the firm's strong IP department, which acts for a host of multinationals including Philip Morris, DaimlerChrysler and Campero International. The firm's team of litigators counts the establishment of a judicial precedent in respect of an infringement case among its successes.

Established by name partner and former President of the Jordanian Law Society, Khalef Masa'deh, **Khalaf Masa'deh & Partners** is a prominent and reputable firm which acts across a range of practice areas, with particular expertise in foreign investment and WTO law. Clients include Pharmaglobe Ltd, Petra Travel & Tourism Co and Beirut Riyad Bank, as well as a host of Jordanian government entities. Experience includes acting on behalf of a major US-Kuwaiti telecommunications group in connection with setting up business in the Aqaba free zone.

English, French and Arabic-speaking **Nabulsi & Associates** advises a host of local, regional and multinational companies including Motorola and BP Amoco, and financial institutions including the IFC and the World Bank. Managing partner Oman Nabulsi enjoys an excellent reputation and strong links with a variety of governmental bodies, in particular the Ministry of Industry and Trade, where he holds a position on the advisory board. 'On the ball' and 'prompt', Lana Salameh is also highly respected for her skills in IP and telecoms-related matters.

Yousef Khalileh is the managing partner at **Rajai K.W. Dajani & Associates**, which handles the complete range of corporate and commercial work for clients ranging from regulatory authorities and NGOs to international banks, European holding companies and regional software developers. Recent work of note includes drafting proposals in connection with the revisitation of the laws governing NGOs, assisting a telecommunications client in its successful bid for a mobile licence, and advising on the establishment of a new holding company in Jordan on behalf of a group of Iraqi investors. Japan Bank for International Cooperation, General Motors, Hitachi, US Grains Council and Johnson & Johnson are among the firm's clients. Senior partner Rajai Dajani is a former Minister of the Interior.

A Ghniem & Partners Law Firm has six partners and four assistants working across a range of corporate and commercial matters. On its books are regional banks, power companies, hotels and shipowners, as well as international insurance businesses and Asian engineering companies.

New client wins for **Abdul Karim Al Fauri & Associates** include Gymboree Corporation for advice relating to its commercial agreements, including sales and distribution, and Bloomberg International for financial issues such as placement of shares and securities in Jordan. In addition, the firm continues to act for its longstanding clients which include major international banks and corporations as well as Jordanian governmental bodies. The firm's 'impressive, hard-working and highly articulate' managing partner, Abdul Karim, used to work at the Muscat branch of **Trowers & Hamlins**, and the two firms have a solid working relationship.

IP specialists **Abu-Ghazaleh Legal** benefit from a network of regional offices and an impressive roster of multinational clients. In the last twelve months the Amman branch has successfully concluded agreements with the Jordan Customs Department, and the Jordan Institution for Standards and Metrology, which the team is providing with a special database for trade mark anti-counterfeiting.

With ten lawyers and eight assistants, **Beiruti Law Firm** provides an 'exemplary' service advising across a range of issues, which includes shareholder agreements, acquisitions, IPOs, distribution and supply agreements, tax and labour law and construction. Name partner Sabar Beiruti is highly respected by peers, whilst clients recommend 'friendly and knowledgeable' attorneys Mr Mohammed Beiruti, Mr Maher Saber Beiruti, and Ms Huda Attiga. As one client points out, 'the experience they possess allows us to concentrate on our business with confidence and ease of mind'.

The management of two-partner firm **Hashem Law Office** was recently delivered into the hands of Rami H Hashem, the son of establisher Dr Hashim R Hashem who sadly passed away in 2005. Recent work for the team includes advising in relation to an acquisition of a domestic textile business by an Indian company, and acting on behalf of the Jordan National Electricity Company in the drafting of agreements relating to distribution, metering and bill collection. The office has worked with a number of foreign firms such as **Mayer, Brown, Rowe & Maw LLP**, with which it recently teamed up to prepare the defence and counterclaim in an US$140m ICC construction arbitration. Arab Potash Co is a longstanding client.

Established over 100 years ago, family-run **Khalifeh & Partners** has strong relationships with government entities and enjoys good links to the Iraq market, having set up an office in Baghdad in October 2003. Its corporate experience includes assisting clients with registering offshore businesses, both in Jordan and elsewhere in the Gulf region. Senior partner Ziad Khalifeh is the current treasurer of the Jordanian Bar Association.

Commercial and business law is the almost exclusive focus of **Marwan Al Hussein & Sons**, with a particular flair for agency, distribution and franchising. The office has a solid network of associations with international firms, working with names such as **Penningtons Solicitors LLP** in the UK.

Noteworthy for its specialist IP department, **Middle Eastern Global Advocates & Legal Consultants** can also offer broad commercial expertise, representing clients such as Microsoft, Business Software Alliance, Proton Automobile, Kodak and Reckitt Benckiser. The firm had a hand in setting up two major players in Jordan's telecoms market, and it is now also targeting the construction industry. Occupying a position on the legal panel of the British and US embassies, the practice has also worked with a number of international firms, including **DLA Piper Rudnick Gray Cary UK LLP**.

Also recommended for general corporate and commercial matters are **Dajani & Associates** and **Obeidat & Freihat**, both of which enjoy excellent reputations locally.

PROJECTS AND PRIVATISATION

Although there have been few large projects in Jordan for Jordanian firms to gain experience on, some firms do merit mention in the sector. Foremost among these is 'solution-orientated' **Ali Sharif Zu'bi Advocates & Legal Consultants**, which has significant experience in almost all of Jordan's major projects, including acting for the borrowers in the financing of the Khirbet Al Samra wastewater treatment plant, alongside **Freshfields Bruckhaus Deringer**. The team also worked with **Clifford Chance** for the Saudi Oger-led consortium in its bid for the US$750m Disi water pipeline project. Similarly, the 25-lawyer office is heavily involved in privatisation work, advising the government on the ongoing sale of its assets in Jordan Phosphate Mines Co, and advising Goldman Sachs in relation to the privatisation and IPO of Jordan's telecommunications sector. The practice is also representing a bidding consortium in connection with the country's first private sector power project, in eastern Amman.

'Systematic' firm **International Business Legal Associates** can boast considerable involvement in Jordan's privatisation process; the team acted as legal advisor in relation to the privatisation of the management of Aqaba Port terminal, and provides advice to an international consortium in connection with the privatisation of Aqaba Railway Corporation. Recently, the firm won an instruction in respect of the impending

PROJECTS AND PRIVATISATION

ALI SHARIF ZU'BI ADVOCATES & LEGAL CONSULTANTS

International Business Legal Associates
Khalaf Masa'deh & Partners
Nabulsi & Associates

Abdul Karim Al Fauri & Associates
Beiruti Law Firm
Dajani & Associates
Khalifeh & Partners
Obeidat & Freihat
Rajai K. W. Dajani & Associates

Firms are listed A-Z in tiers which are ranked in order of priority.

privatisation of King Hussein Airport in Aqaba. Other matters include acting for the Telecommunications Regulatory Commission in respect of the opening up of the GSM market, and advising the Palestinian Energy Authority in connection with the establishment of a new regulatory body under a World Bank-funded project.

Khalaf Masa'deh & Partners has been involved in many of Jordan's top-drawer energy projects, including the Al Samra IPP and the Wind Plant Power Project. Its experience covers regulatory, structural and commercial issues, in addition to all aspects of project finance. The team played a key role in the privatisation of Jordan's electricity sector as well as the Royal Jordanian Air Academy.

Nabulsi & Associates acted in conjunction with **Pinsent Masons** on the US$264m financing of the Jordanian gas transmission pipeline, which reached financial close in July 2004. The team also acted as local counsel on the Khirbet Al Samra wastewater project, where it advised the lenders alongside **Latham & Watkins**.

Under the 'very able' Abdul Karim, **Abdul Karim Al Fauri & Associates** enjoys a 'considerable presence' in Jordan's projects and ongoing privatisations, working alongside **Trowers & Hamlins** on a number of matters in recent years. These include advising the Ministry of Energy & Natural Resources on the Jordanian gas transportation project, and representing a major US contractor in connection with a proposed EPC contract for the Disi-Amman water project.

Beiruti Law Firm is currently involved in drafting operation and maintenance agreements for the expansion of the Al Fajr project, having represented the sponsors in last year's project financing. The firm is also part of a consortium providing regulatory advice to the Ministry of Energy and Mineral Resources in connection with the removal of barriers for wind farm projects, and is the legal adviser on the construction phase of a free zone industrial estate in the country.

Not to be confused with **Rajai K.W. Dajani & Associates, Dajani & Associates** is recommended for its skills in privatisation and financing deals, and managing partner Rajaie Kamal Dajani is noted for his many years of experience in the sector.

Khalifeh & Partners' experience in the sector includes advising the government on strategies for attracting private finance into infrastructure projects, and advising in connection with the ongoing water sector privatisation programme.

Obeidat & Freihat is a well-regarded firm, and managing partner Thamer Obeidat is considered a 'very capable attorney'.

Alongside **White & Case**, **Rajai K.W. Dajani & Associates** has been advising the government in the privatisation of Jordan's Queen Alia Airport. The firm has also advised in relation to the establishment of free zones in the country.

ABU-GHAZALEH LEGAL

THE ARAB REGIONAL NETWORK FOR GLOBAL LEGAL SERVICES

TAGI HOUSE, QUEEN NOOR STREET
SHMEISANI
PO BOX 921100
AMMAN 11192

Telephone: +962 6 5100 900
Fax: +962 6 5100 901
E-mail: able@tagi.com
Website: www.abughazalehlegal.com
www.tagorg.com

Languages
Arabic, English, French

Other offices
Abu-Dhabi, Algiers, Ankara, Baghdad, Beirut, Cairo, Casablanca, Damascus, Doha, Dubai, Gaza, Jeddah, Khartoum, Kuwait, Manama, Muscat, Nablus, Ramallah, Riyadh, Sana'a, Sharjah, Tripoli, Tehran, Tunis

Number of lawyers 215
at this office 20

Contacts
Samer Pharaon, Tariq Diab

Member
Talal Abu-Ghazaleh Organisation (TAGorg); Associated Firm of Abu-Ghazaleh Intellectual Property (AGIP)

CATEGORIES OF WORK

Intellectual property protection services:

Enforcement of intellectual property rights

IP transfer

IP portfolio management

IP watch service

IP litigation

Online IP

Advice on IP laws and regulations

IP evaluation

Franchising

Corporate and business legal services:

Establishment of companies

Business litigation

E-commerce business legal issues

Dispute resolution

Arbitration

Tax

Real estate

Labour

WTO-related issues

Mergers and acquisitions

KENYA

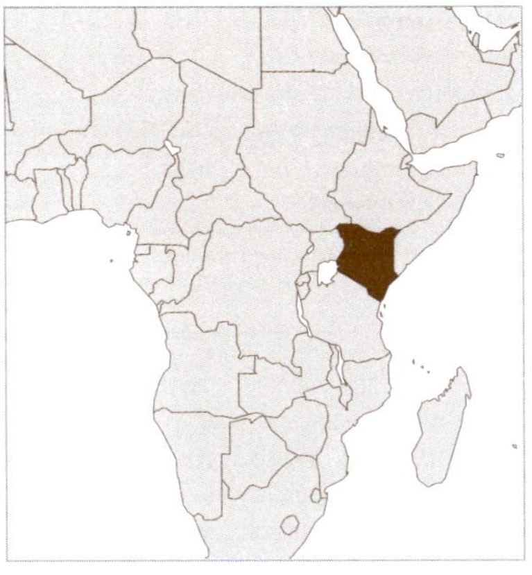

Population	33 million
Number of lawyers	approximately 4,000
Professional title	Advocate
Currency	Kenyan shilling (KES)

Index

The Republic of Kenya straddles the equator. Stepped plateaus and plains rise from the humid, tropical, coastal belt to temperate highlands which cover about a third of the country's 225,000 square miles. Nairobi, the capital, is located in the highlands to the south. Coastal Mombasa is Kenya's second city and a major regional port.

Kenya borders the Indian Ocean and has frontiers with Somalia, Ethiopia, Sudan, Uganda and Tanzania. In 2001 Kenya, Uganda and Tanzania formed the pro-market, pro-liberalisation, East African Community (EAC), which is making some progress towards customs union despite friction between Kenya and Tanzania over tariff rates. Efforts are being made to 'fast-track' longer-term aspirations to political union.

Reliable population statistics are elusive but Kenya's demographic trends are changing. UNICEF estimates total population at 32 million; about half aged 18 or under. UNICEF's estimate of AIDS/HIV sufferers is 1.2 million. Kenya's cities are magnets to the rural poor; the drift to Nairobi, growing at 5% per annum according to UN estimates, has spawned Kibera, Africa's largest shanty town. Kenya's population, comprising some 40 tribal groups and a substantial Muslim minority which could number seven million, has tended to combine ethnic and political loyalties. Kiswahili and English are the official languages although many more indigenous tongues are used.

Kenya's reputation as the most stable of African countries is under threat. Long-term corruption, a major factor in Kenya's failure to fully exploit its position as the 'hub' for East African commerce and finance, has also destroyed trust in political and legal institutions. After gaining independence from Britain in 1963, the ruling KANU party (Kenya African National Union) soon thrust the country into a one-party regime which lasted until 1992. Even then, the multi-party system failed to oust the incumbent president, Daniel arap Moi, until the 2002 elections, when the opposition parties were able to come together as the National Rainbow Coalition (NARC). Mwai Kibaki, with an anti-corruption platform, was elected as president in a landslide victory, and remains in office.

BILLING

The Advocates Remuneration Order sets a statutory scale of charges for certain categories of work including conveyancing and security transactions; proposals to reduce rates are causing concern. For work not covered by the ARO, rates vary widely according to the type of instruction and the client. Pressure on fees since the 2002 election has been fierce; one lawyer estimated a decline of 20-30% in rates over the period, and several lawyers expressed concern about the quality of work emerging from cut-throat tendering for government instructions. Although contingency fees are not permitted, fee caps are common for private client work.

Partners' rates for the firms mentioned in our editorial range from US$120 to US$210; associates are charged at between US$70 and US$150. Kenyan law firms tend to be partner-heavy and this follows through into bills. Professional indemnity insurance is not mandatory in Kenya and uninsured firms may offer lower rates; reputable firms will supply details of cover on request.

POLITICAL CLIMATE

The early hopes for the Kibaki government in 2002 have withered. The anti-corruption Minister, John Githongo, resigned in February 2005, frustrated by impediments to his office. The Transport Minister, a close associate of President Kibaki, was banned from travelling to Britain by the UK government in July 2005 following allegations of involvement in the US$90m *Anglo Leasing* scandal. Despite statements to the contrary, anti-corruption bodies appear to be overwhelmed by their task and the court procedures seem inadequate. A limited amnesty for past corruption offences is now being mooted.

ECONOMY

According to the Central Bank, GDP grew by 4.3% in 2004, an improvement on the 2.8% achieved in 2003. But Kenya's economy is in a poor state. High interest rates, and an exchange rate which remains remarkably firm despite Kenya's inflation rate of 14.4% (year to August 2005) create a difficult climate for business even without the problems caused by corruption. Kenya has slipped towards the bottom of the United Nations Human Development Index, the measure of human poverty.

Some 80% of Kenya's population is dependent on the agricultural sector and some success can be reported here. In 2004 Kenya was the world's largest exporter of tea (up 10.5%); coffee, flowers (up 13.2%), sugarcane and sisal are also important.

Tourism remains a significant foreign currency earner despite security concerns and here too, the earnings generated in 2004 were some 15% up on 2003.

LEGAL SYSTEM AND LEGAL MARKET

The core Kenyan Court system consists of a Court of Appeal, a High Court, and two levels of Magistrates Courts. Although there are no formal tribal courts bound into the core system, customary law within ethnic groups may be used for guidance by the Courts where there is no conflict with Statute. *Kadhis* courts, which have the authority to deal with personal matters in accordance with Islamic law, have, since independence, enjoyed a protection which seems to be threatened by the new constitution.

A recent, radical clear-out of the judiciary has improved the standing of the courts although the judiciary is still not entirely trusted. Lawyers note that the Commercial Court is now working fairly well and that the Chief Justice has established a special court for judicial review matters which is successfully using case management.

The legal profession in Kenya is fused. All lawyers are termed advocates and are members of the Law Society of Kenya, which both represents its members and functions as a force for legal reform. The Law Society is regulated by Act of Parliament. Mr Ahmednasir Abdullahi of **Ahmednasir, Abdikadir & Co** is presently chairman of the Law Society.

In practice, despite the common 'advocate' title, courtroom practitioners tend to specialise and take advocacy instructions from other law firms as well as the public. Most of the larger firms have litigation departments but some of our recommended litigators are niche operators.

Most law firms in Kenya are small; about two thirds of lawyers are in sole practice. The larger firms competent in commerce-related law are concentrated in Nairobi although **Anjarwalla & Khanna** and **Inamdar & Inamdar** both have Mombasa offices. Kenyan lawyers have a regional reputation for excellence and also handle instructions from Tanzania and Uganda; the EAC may allow further development in these markets but current restrictive rules prevent opportunities being fully exploited. There is some competition in Kenya from the larger UK firms, for instance, **Denton Wilde Sapte** has recently advised the Kenya Generation Company Ltd (KENGEN) on a major contract arbitration, but for the most part, local firms maintain links with the UK majors and work in co-operation.

Kaplan & Stratton's Kenyan operation is the largest in East Africa; the firm considered opening branch offices in other East African jurisdictions a few years ago and the earlier negative decision is now under review. **Kaplan & Stratton** is a member of both the *Lex Mundi* and *Lex Africa* associations. Next in size are long-established, **Hamilton Harrison & Matthews**, and **Daly & Figgis**. **Anjarwalla & Khanna** is a founder member of *African Legal Network*, an association of three firms in Kenya, Tanzania and Uganda.

CORPORATE AND M&A

Kaplan & Stratton, indisputably Kenya's leading law firm, offers strong commercial groups in all areas although the litigation specialists have diminished in number because of elevations to the bench. Now fielding 25 lawyers, organised in specialist departments on 'mini-international firm' lines, **Kaplan & Stratton** is the only Kenyan firm with the capacity to draw substantial teams together for large transactional work. The firm has successfully worked alongside major UK firms such as **Clifford Chance**. Oliver Fowler, head of the commercial department, 'is a brand name in himself', universally acknowledged as Kenya's leading corporate lawyer. Richard Harney has 'a jolly good brain' and Peter Hime 'is the best man in town for IP work'. **Kaplan & Stratton**'s recent work includes assisting Nation Media Group (Kenya) in the acquisition of newspaper and radio interests in Tanzania and acting for Canadian Overseas Packaging Corporation on its takeover and subsequent de-listing of East African Packaging Limited. In an interesting and successful tax appeal involving complex transfer pricing issues, Peter Gachuhi appeared for Unilever Kenya Limited against the Commissioners of Income Tax.

Anjarwalla & Khanna has built to 20 lawyers, balanced fairly evenly between Nairobi and Mombasa, where it is the largest firm. **Anjarwalla & Khanna** has adopted the unique, and apparently very successful, strategy of forming an East African 'umbrella': *African Legal Network*, which operates as a cross-border practice with Tanzanian firm **Ringo & Associates**, and in association with a Ugandan firm. **Anjarwalla & Khanna**'s Nairobi office is a corporate boutique, handling M&A and IP work alongside general commercial work. Karim Anjarwalla, Amyn Mussa and Sonal Sejpal (a former City partner) head the Nairobi team, which has handled an impressive range of work for blue-chip clients including Citibank, BAT, and the Rockefeller Foundation. The Mombasa office, headed by highly regarded Atiq Anjarwalla deals with maritime matters, and commodity contract disputes and acts for many of the high-net-worth family businesses operating out of East Africa's busiest port.

Long-established **Daly & Figgis** now boasts 16 lawyers and maintains a strong reputation for high-end corporate, commercial, and property work including M&A, joint ventures and capital markets instructions. 'Very, very, good' head of the commercial department Hamish Keith is in the top rank, as is head of litigation, Zul Alibhai. Commercial partner Ashwini Bhandari is an experienced and popular lawyer and Evans Monari is 'proficient and able' as a commercial litigator. **Daly & Figgis** acts for Woodside, Australia's largest publicly traded oil and gas exploration and production company, handling all legal aspects of its Kenyan operation. The firm also advised long-standing client Lonrho on the sale of its Kenyan hotel interests and for mobile telecoms operator Safaricom in a consortium financing deal worth US$20m.

Nine-partner **Hamilton Harrison & Matthews**, is particularly well connected in the banking and finance sectors and saw a significant increase in regulatory work during 2005. The commercial department is regaining strength after some lawyer losses and now numbers five. Highly respected Richard Omwela heads the corporate and commercial department. Rising star Paras Shah, who is building a strong following, concluded the sale of majority shares in Giro Commercial Bank Limited to the State Bank of India in autumn 2005. **Hamilton Harrison & Matthews** is lead litigation advisor to the Kenya Bankers' Association and Standard Chartered Bank. Ken Fraser, the firm's highly regarded head of litigation, has recently appeared for Guardian Bank and Consolidated Bank of Kenya. Litigation partner Adil Khawaja has impressed some of his senior opponents. The firm is currently handling a large professional negligence claim against one of the major accountancy firms.

Driven forward by the energetic and respected banking lawyer Alexandra Kontos, **Walker Kontos Advocates** now boasts 16 fee-earners and continues to consolidate a reputation for efficient, client-friendly service at reasonable cost. The firm boasts particular strengths in corporate finance, property and corporate recovery. **Walker Kontos Advocates** has excellent contacts within the agricultural, horticultural and hotel businesses which underpin the Kenyan economy as well as an international clientele. The firm recently acted for Celtel Kenya in connection

CORPORATE AND M&A

KAPLAN & STRATTON

Anjarwalla & Khanna ✪
Daly & Figgis
Hamilton Harrison & Matthews
Walker Kontos Advocates

Raffman Dhanji Elms & Virdee

B M Musau & Co
Inamdar & Inamdar
Iseme, Kamau & Maema Advocates
Lumumba, Mumma & Kaluma Advocates
Ochieng', Onyango, Kibet & Ohaga
Oraro & Co Advocates

Firms are listed A-Z in tiers which are ranked in order of priority
✪ Indicates firm displays contact details at the end of this chapter.

with syndicated finance of US$95m and Bank of Africa Benin in the US$1.27m sale of a minority holding in Bank of Africa Kenya. Michael Kontos is 'reliable, he has exactly the right approach,' while Peter Mwangi is an excellent all-round corporate lawyer with useful expertise in employment issues.

Raffman Dhanji Elms & Virdee offers nine lawyers and has a reputation for good quality, mainstream commercial work. The firm is well connected in the horticultural industry and claims several of the major players as clients. The firm has also acted in some substantial deals in the telecoms and insurance sectors. **Raffman Dhanji Elms & Virdee**'s senior partner, Salim Dhanji is 'a smart lawyer' with particular expertise in international law.

B M Musau & Co has grown to a four-partner, ten-assistant firm offering services across the commercial range. The firm has strong banking contacts. **B M Musau & Co**'s commercial clients include Colgate-Palmolive (East Africa) Limited.

Inamdar & Inamdar's Bill Inamdar, 'in the thick of things' since the 1950s, is hugely respected as a litigator and is frequently instructed by other firms; he appeared in the headline *Kenya Telecommunications Investment Group Ltd v Telecommunication Commission of Kenya*. The six-partner firm is a solid performer in the general commercial market and boasts its share of blue-chip clients. Although the level of maritime work in Kenya has diminished, **Inamdar & Inamdar**'s Mombasa office continues to service the dry shipping market and broke East African records for ship mortgage recovery in the US$3m *MV Century Fortuna* case.

James Kamau, managing partner of nine-fee-earner **Iseme, Kamau & Maema Advocates**, is a 'solid guy' in commercial matters. The firm is particularly strong on patents and other IP matters.

Lumumba, Mumma & Kaluma Advocates fields three partners and six associates. The firm's main strengths lie in litigation, with a focus on public and administration law, including environmental law, banking law, and general commercial work, particularly in the construction and utilities sectors. Dr Albert Mumma is well connected and is approved by clients for his pragmatism.

Ochieng', Onyango, Kibet & Ohaga has consolidated well since the three component practices merged in 2002 and established a good reputation as a specialist litigation practice. Five partners, supported by eight associates, take forward the firm's commercial 'court is the last option' approach to dispute resolution. James Ochieng' is a 'brilliant, nicely aggressive, litigator', well experienced in the Court of Appeal.

George Oraro of **Oraro & Co Advocates** is 'a superb corporate litigator', 'one of the top men' and receives wide peer commendation as well as being popular with clients. George Oraro's headline cases during 2005 included: *Econet Systems v Minister of Information and Communication*, a major judicial review matter, and *Standard Chartered Bank v Intercom Services Limited*, a Court of Appeal case concerning banking relationships.

PRIVATISATION AND PROJECTS

Privatisation in Kenya stalled following the 2002 election. The Privatisation Act passed in August 2005 may facilitate the process but lawyers believe that the impediment to further denationalisation is political rather than legal. As we go to press, only two consortia remain in the bidding process for the Kenya and Uganda Railways concession, and the Telkom Kenya privatisation has been shelved until April 2006. The Kenya Electricity Generating Company (KenGen) announced in October 2005 that the appointment of all transaction advisors for the company's IPO had been concluded but the timetable for the offering was not fixed.

PRIVATISATION AND PROJECTS

Kaplan & Stratton

Anjarwalla & Khanna ✪
Daly & Figgis
Hamilton Harrison & Matthews
Walker Kontos Advocates

Lumumba, Mumma & Kaluma Advocates
Oraro & Co Advocates

Firms are listed A-Z in tiers which are ranked in order of priority
✪ Indicates firm displays contact details at the end of this chapter.

Kaplan & Stratton has long experience of project finance and acted for the Brunner Mond Group in the Magadi Pure Soda Ash Expansion Project while **Walker Kontos Advocates**, in conjunction with **Clifford Chance** advised the lenders. **Anjarwalla & Khanna**, with its strong presence in Mombasa, has wide experience of port facility projects, including the US$32.5m Mombasa grain and fertiliser terminal. **Daly & Figgis** boasts an impressive track record of project finance work including work for the World Bank and UK DFID. **Hamilton Harrison & Matthews** handled the record-breaking US$65m syndicated finance package for the Kenyan Ports Authority.

Dr Albert Mumma of **Lumumba, Mumma & Kaluma Advocates** worked with **Wragge & Co LLP** on the railway consolidations preparatory to the concession tendering process.

George Oraro of **Oraro & Co Advocates** was appointed a member of the legal consortium advising on the KenGen IPO in October 2005.

ANJARWALLA & KHANNA

ELDAMA RAVINE GARDENS
OFF ELDAMA RAVINE ROAD
WESTLANDS
PO BOX 200-00606
SARIT CENTRE
NAIROBI

Telephone: +254 20 374 80 89
Fax: +254 20 374 02 42
E-mail: nbi@africalegalnetwork.com
Website: www.africalegalnetwork.com

Languages
English, Kiswahili

Other offices
Mombasa, Dar-Es-Salaam*, Kampala*

Number of lawyers 21
at this office 11

International groupings
Africa Legal Network

CATEGORIES OF WORK

Banking finance and capital markets
Atiq Anjarwalla, Sonal Sejpal

Corporate and commercial
Karim Anjarwalla, Akash Devani

Property
Karim Anjarwalla, Mona Doshi

Civil and commercial litigation
Ushwin Khanna, Samson Okong'o

Arbitration
Ushwin Khanna, Samson Okong'o

Admiralty and maritime law
Ushwin Khanna, Samson Okong'o

Infrastructure projects
Karim Anjarwalla, Amyn Mussa

Private client work
Atiq Anjarwalla, Mona Doshi

Intellectual property
Sonal Sejpal, Samson Okong'o

KUWAIT

Population	2.7 million
Number of lawyers	n/a
Professional title	Advocate
Currency	Kuwaiti Dinar (KD)

In the aftermath of World War Two, Kuwait quickly became one of the first oil super-states in the Persian Gulf. Oil is Kuwait's most precious asset, making it a goldmine for its bigger and one-time more powerful neighbour, Iraq. In 1990, Iraq accused Kuwait of stealing its oil, an accusation that led to a full-blown Iraqi invasion. Civilian lives were lost, the country's infrastructure was devastated, and oil wells and landmark sites torched.

While playing battleground to US-led international military operations against Iraq in 1991 left Kuwait bruised, the country has tenaciously rebuilt itself. Fifteen years on, and there are very few, if any, visible war wounds.

Kuwait is now comfortably positioned and remarkably wealthy, benefiting from oil reserves and a relatively liberal economic market. Kuwait City, the capital, is thriving as home to the headquarters of most Kuwaiti corporations, and is the heart of the country's commercial core.

Ruled by the discreet al-Sabah family, Kuwait is in many ways a more moderate and progressive country than its bigger Gulf neighbours. This is possibly because Kuwait's population is so young (approximately 65% of its population is under the age of 25), and largely forward-looking. For instance, Kuwait was the first Arab country in the region to have a democratically elected parliament, and in June 2005, its first female cabinet minister was sworn in. Parliament granted women full political rights in 2005, including the right to vote and the right to stand for election.

BILLING

Most firms charge on an hourly basis, although the Kuwaiti billing culture is quite flexible and includes fixed fees, annual fees, retainers and contingency fees. Hourly rates vary depending on the seniority of the lawyer. Typically, hourly fees are US$250 for junior lawyers, approximately US$300 for senior lawyers and between US$400-$500 for partners.

MARKETING

Kuwaiti firms have developed good websites to promote their businesses, although they often rely on personal contacts and word-of-mouth recommendations to win work.

ECONOMY

During the Iraqi occupation, Kuwait's economy was annihilated. Most of its wealth was looted and oil production became impossible. But now, oil revenues contribute almost 95% of the country's total export earnings. Kuwait boasts a small but very rich economy, whose oil reserves account for 10% of the world's overall reserves.

But, when it comes to oil, Kuwait, like many Arab oil-states, finds itself in a Catch-22 situation. Despite being so rich in oil, other industries are underdeveloped, meaning sources of national income are limited. Although this doesn't pose a problem for the present or immediate future, it means that the government must plan with considerable foresight for future state income. Kuwaiti law dictates that 10% of all oil revenues must be placed into a special reserve, called 'The Future Generations Fund', to prepare for the time when oil reserves will be exhausted. At present, these funds are estimated to hold between US$50-$80bn.

While larger countries like Saudi Arabia can attempt to diversify their individual economies, this is more problematic for the Kuwaiti economy, not least because it is so small. Even water, an obvious and crucial ingredient for both industrial and agricultural development, is limited and must be imported.

Nevertheless, Kuwait is encouraging foreign direct investment (FDI). In 2000, the Kuwaiti Stock Exchange opened up to foreign investors, and the 2001 Foreign Investment Act restrictions have relaxed. Since 2003, a FDI law has been in place, which permits foreign entities to establish Kuwaiti companies with 100% foreign equity participation and ownership.

Hence multinationals seeking to reap the benefits of post-war reconstruction in Iraq, are creeping into Kuwait, a logical geographical base from which to work. While the new FDI law has attracted some foreign companies into the country, it is thought that many more will follow once the outdated tax system is overhauled.

Unemployment in Kuwait is rising – according to government figures, 35,000 Kuwaitis will be jobless by 2006, although government targets promise 9,000 extra jobs in the private sector by the end of 2006.

LEGAL MARKET

The legal market in Kuwait is buoyant, with firms citing an increase in corporate and commercial activity. Given the small size of Kuwait's legal market, most firms offer across-the-board (rather than specialist) advice.

The largest firms

1	Al Sarraf & Al Ruwayeh in association with Stephenson Harwood	55
2	Al-Twaijri & Partners Law Firm (TLF)	40
3	M M Al-Ghazali & Partners	36
	Mishari Al-Ghazali, Law Offices of	36
5	Al-Essa, Al-Bader & Partners, Law Office of	21
6	Abdullah Kh. Al-Ayoub & Associates	16
7	Alothman & Khalaf	13
8	Al Markaz Law Firm	12
	International Counsel Bureau	12
10	Salman Duaij Al Sabah Law Office	11
11	Anwar Al-Bisher & Partners	10
12	Ali & Partners	9
13	Al Hekook, Advocates & Legal Consultants	8
14	Labeed Abdal, The Law Firm of	6
15	Libra Law Firm	5
16	Al Oudah & Partners	3
17	Abu-Ghazaleh Legal	1
	Mashora Advocates & Legal Consultants (in assoc with Bryan Cave LLP)	1

These figures represent the total number of lawyers in this country only, and have been supplied by the firms themselves. The figures should be accurate as at 1 January 2006.

Kuwaiti law takes its origins from Egyptian and French codes. While Islamic law, or shari'ah, plays an important role, it is not the dominating law. In this respect, the Kuwaiti legal system is quite different from traditional Middle Eastern ones. However, like most Middle Eastern systems, foreign law firms are only permitted to practise in association with a partner Kuwaiti firm. In comparison to the larger legal markets in the region, such as Saudi Arabia, foreign firms are a rare presence in Kuwait, as many Western firms remain cautious about its proximity to Iraq.

Nevertheless, with the economy booming, Kuwait's small legal market is flourishing and attractive. One of the few firms with a long-standing international association is **Al Sarraf & Al Ruwayeh in association with Stephenson Harwood**, one of the strongest and largest firms in Kuwait.

Bryan Cave LLP's Kuwait outfit, **Mashora Advocates & Legal Consultants (in assoc with Bryan Cave LLP)** has a respected presence in the country. Local partners Khalid Al-Neghaimshey and Abdul Rahman Al-Humaidan, (president of the Kuwaiti Bar Association and Law Society), are highly esteemed by the Kuwaiti legal community.

Anwar Al-Bisher & Partners regularly acts as local Kuwaiti counsel for **Baker & McKenzie**'s US offices, and is also a founding member of the *Middle East Legal Alliance*.

Since 2000, **Abdullah Kh. Al-Ayoub & Associates** has been exclusively chosen year-on-year to represent Kuwait in the *Lex Mundi* legal association, while **Salman Duaij Al Sabah Law Office** bears a loose affiliation with **Jones Day**. **M M Al-Ghazali & Partners** is affiliated with **Squire, Sanders & Dempsey**.

Many firms mentioned in this chapter have good connections across the Middle East; **Al-Saleh & Partners** has a particularly long-standing relationship with Saudi Arabian-based **The Law Firm of Salah Al-Hejailan**.

Although it does not have a presence on the ground, **Clifford Chance**'s Middle East team, (largely based in Dubai) is active across the wider Gulf region. In Kuwait, the firm advised the lead arrangers in connection with a US$60m five-year floating rate note issued by the National Industries Group for its listing on the Bahrain Stock Exchange. The National Bank of Kuwait remains a key client.

Pinsent Masons' international arbitration team has advised existing clients in Kuwait on ICC disputes relating to large engineering projects.

BANKING AND FINANCE

Law Office of Al-Essa, Al-Bader & Partners has advised on a number of landmark financial transactions. Its impressive track record includes acting for the issuer of Kuwait's first Eurobond, and advising on the first-ever EMTN programme in Kuwait. Kevin Burke is a respected lawyer, and has represented The Gulf Bank and Gulf Investment Corporation, as well as many other leading financial institutions. The firm has an excellent all-round banking and finance team, which offers advice on all aspects of Islamic financing, project finance, bond issues and syndicated loans.

In 2005, **Al Sarraf & Al Ruwayeh in association with Stephenson Harwood** worked on the establishment of the first branch of a foreign bank in Kuwait for BNP Paribas. Since this, the firm has won instructions from HSBC to similarly advise on the establishment of its foreign operations in Kuwait. Islamic finance is another string to the firm's bow, having recently advised Bahrain Investment Bank on a multi-million-dollar *sukuk*.

Ten-lawyer **Anwar Al-Bisher & Partners** is a sophisticated practice which handles all aspects of general lending, secured and syndicated loan transactions, securitisation and structured finance. Of note, the firm was appointed by Citibank to represent its application for a foreign bank branch licence, and was local counsel to Gulf International Bank in its US$225m loan facility for a publicly traded Kuwaiti company.

Eighteen-lawyer **Abdullah Kh. Al-Ayoub & Associates** has a highly respected banking and finance practice, which wins instructions from global financial institutions and investment banks. Abdullah Khalid Al-Ayoub and Jasmine Kohina are the most prominent lawyers in this department, and recently advised several investment companies in line with their development in Kuwait.

Al-Saleh & Partners has a team of six banking and finance specialists, including the recommended Nazih Hameed. The firm has acted for several banks both in and outside of Kuwait, and was involved in a complex Islamic refinancing structure scheme for a local company.

Al-Twaijri & Partners Law Firm (TLF) is one of the biggest firms in Kuwait, with approximately 40 lawyers. Mohammed Al-Twaijri leads a team of

BANKING AND FINANCE

AL-ESSA, AL-BADER & PARTNERS, LAW OFFICE OF
AL SARRAF & AL RUWAYEH IN ASSOCIATION WITH STEPHENSON HARWOOD ✪
ANWAR AL-BISHER & PARTNERS

Abdullah Kh. Al-Ayoub & Associates
Al-Saleh & Partners
Al-Twaijri & Partners Law Firm (TLF)
Ali & Partners
M M Al-Ghazali & Partners
Mashora Advocates & Legal Consultants (in assoc with Bryan Cave LLP)

Firms are listed A-Z in tiers which are ranked in order of priority
✪ *Indicates firm displays contact details at the end of this chapter.*

seven specialist banking and finance lawyers which largely focuses on domestic or regional work, although it is tapping into the international market. Clients include Burgan Bank, Gulf Bank, Commercial Bank of Kuwait and Kuwait Investment Bank.

Ali & Partners represented US Export-Import Bank in the Kuwait Shuaiba Petrochemical Project and has assisted foreign banks and financial institutions on various transactions and general regional compliance issues.

Mashora Advocates & Legal Consultants (in assoc with Bryan Cave LLP) manages offshore funds on behalf of Kuwaiti clients, and has represented influential members of the Kuwaiti royal family in relation to funds development.

CORPORATE AND M&A

Al Sarraf & Al Ruwayeh in association with Stephenson Harwood has an outstanding corporate presence. There are approximately 50 lawyers, of whom 18 work in the international department, headed by senior partner Sam Habbas. **Al Sarraf & Al Ruwayeh in association with Stephenson Harwood** has acted for Gulf Finance House and Kuwait Finance Investment Corporation as lead managers on the IPO of Bayan Holding Company and is advising Gulf Investment Corporation on its US$2.5bn EMTN programme.

One of the best firms for all-round corporate work is **Mashora Advocates & Legal Consultants (in assoc with Bryan Cave LLP)**. The firm couples solid Western legal knowledge with strong local expertise, and represents major Western defence contractors present in Iraq, such as Halliburton, KBR, DynCorp and Boeing, on all corporate and commercial needs. **Bryan Cave LLP** partner David Pfeiffer and local partners Khalid Al-Neghaimshey and Abdul Rahman Al-Humaidan are the firm's key individuals.

In addition to its top reputation for banking work, **Law Office of Al-Essa, Al-Bader & Partners** has a superb corporate practice, which handles varied transactional work, including capital markets, joint ventures, M&A and tax issues. The firm's name is often mentioned and recommended by its colleagues in the international legal community. Kevin Burke has in-depth experience advising on transactions from the oil and gas sectors.

Senior partner Mary Ann Sharp heads the international department at **Anwar Al-Bisher & Partners**, which advises global companies across the telecommunications, defence, industry and media sectors. According to one client, Sharp 'stands apart from the crowd in terms of her skill level and sensibility.' Indeed, the firm is distinguished by its involvement on some cutting-edge projects, for instance advising Efad Holdings on its US$4bn real estate purchase of the world's largest development of luxury man-made islands off the UAE port, which will be built by 2008. Described as 'invariably excellent', **Anwar Al-Bisher & Partners** also has a solid commercial property practice and offers legal advice on US government contracting legislation to defence contracting clients working in Iraq.

International Counsel Bureau predominantly advises Kuwait Petroleum Company and its subsidiaries, including Petrochemical Industries Company (PIC). The firm has strong ties to the oil and gas sectors – founding senior partner Abdul Rahman Al-Haroun and senior counsel Peter Menting were both legal counsel in Kuwait Petroleum Company, and senior partner Ghazi Al-Qahtani served as head legal counsel of Kuwait Oil Company. The 12-lawyer firm recently conducted a major joint venture for PIC.

Abdullah Kh. Al-Ayoub & Associates works for Arab and international clients. Indian-qualified Jasmine Kohina heads the international department, which advises multinationals on all aspects of corporate and commercial work. The firm has a particular focus on clients from the oil and gas sectors.

Al-Saleh & Partners has advised local financial institutions on acquisitions and advises international clients on corporate and commercial matters. The firm has good experience of working in co-operation with many international law firms.

Ali & Partners advises foreign investors and local clients. It recently acted as sole counsel on a joint venture between a US, regional and a Kuwaiti company. Clients include Credit Agricole, Kadant Lamort and Northrop Grumman.

M M Al-Ghazali & Partners works closely with **Squire, Sanders & Dempsey**, advising companies on matters in post-conflict Iraq. The firm advised the government on potential legal reform.

Eleven-lawyer **Salman Duaij Al Sabah Law Office** advises local banks, embassies and oil giants Texaco and BP.

Abdul Razzaq & Partners Law Firm's clients include Vanguard, Daelim, Osoul, Investment Dar, Subway and Eastern United Petroleum Company.

Nine-lawyer **Al Hekook, Advocates & Legal Consultants** advises international and local clients on all commercial aspects of doing business in Kuwait, such as contractual work and distributorship agreements. Ayyad Al Adwani is the main partner for this work. Clients include Qatar Airways, Rotana Hotels and Al-Jazeera news channel.

Established in 1992, **The Law Firm of Labeed Abdal** advises local and international clients, including Badrutt's Palace Hotel, and US furniture company Perla Lichi Designs.

CORPORATE AND M&A

AL SARRAF & AL RUWAYEH IN ASSOCIATION WITH STEPHENSON HARWOOD ✪
MASHORA ADVOCATES & LEGAL CONSULTANTS (IN ASSOC WITH BRYAN CAVE LLP)

Al-Essa, Al-Bader & Partners, Law Office of
Anwar Al-Bisher & Partners
International Counsel Bureau

Abdullah Kh. Al-Ayoub & Associates
Al-Saleh & Partners
Ali & Partners
M M Al-Ghazali & Partners
Salman Duaij Al Sabah Law Office

Abdul Razzaq & Partners Law Firm
Al Hekook, Advocates & Legal Consultants
Labeed Abdal, The Law Firm of ✪

Firms are listed A-Z in tiers which are ranked in order of priority
✪ Indicates firm displays contact details at the end of this chapter.

DISPUTE RESOLUTION

Law Office of Al-Essa, Al-Bader & Partners has a dedicated litigation practice, and a good reputation in this field for advising both international and local clients in disputes. Of the firm's 18 or so lawyers, six Kuwaiti-qualified advocates support the litigation department.

Of **Al Sarraf & Al Ruwayeh in association with Stephenson Harwood**'s team of around 50 lawyers, about 30 actively participate in litigation work. The solid team is handling a substantial amount of tax-related litigation for *Fortune 50* clients, and is also advising contractors on construction disputes.

Anwar Al-Bisher & Partners has an excellent reputation for litigation success, and obtained several landmark judgments in 2005 in connection with employers' rights and corporate

DISPUTE RESOLUTION

AL-ESSA, AL-BADER & PARTNERS, LAW OFFICE OF
AL SARRAF & AL RUWAYEH IN ASSOCIATION WITH STEPHENSON HARWOOD ✪
ANWAR AL-BISHER & PARTNERS
SALMAN DUAIJ AL SABAH LAW OFFICE

Abdul Razzaq & Partners Law Firm
Abdullah Kh. Al-Ayoub & Associates
Al-Saleh & Partners
Al-Twaijri & Partners Law Firm (TLF)
Al-Wagayan & Al-Awadhi & Al-Saif Law Firm
Labeed Abdal, The Law Firm of ✪
M M Al-Ghazali & Partners
Mashora Advocates & Legal Consultants (in assoc with Bryan Cave LLP)

Firms are listed A-Z in tiers which are ranked in order of priority
✪ Indicates firm displays contact details at the end of this chapter.

governance. The firm represented Coca-Cola in a corporate income tax litigation case against the Kuwait Ministry of Finance.

Salman Duaij Al Sabah Law Office's principal litigator is Fikry Maghrawey, who has a top reputation for winning cases on behalf of his clients. The firm recently won a substantial settlement for a major banking client, and cites an increase in tax-related litigation.

Abdul Razzaq & Partners Law Firm obtained a settlement of over KD200,000 for Vanguard. The firm has represented Daelim and represented members of the Kuwaiti royal family in litigation matters.

Almost half of **Abdullah Kh. Al-Ayoub & Associates**' workload is dispute resolution-related. The firm advises both local and international clients and has appeared regularly before the ICC.

Al-Saleh & Partners has experience in both local and international arbitration and Amar Mansour is a key litigator.

Al-Twaijri & Partners Law Firm (TLF) has a large claims and debt collection division, which handles contentious cases. Clients include Burgan Bank, Gulf Bank and telecoms companies MTC and Wataniya. A team of approximately 40 paralegals handles volume work. **Al-Twaijri & Partners Law Firm (TLF)** is also the Kuwaiti firm of choice for the Commercial Arbitration Centre of the Gulf.

The Law Firm of Labeed Abdal has been representing the former chairman of the Kuwait Oil Tankers Company in its embezzlement case. The case started in 1993, and the firm has been representing its client since 1997 in the commercial, labour, civil and criminal courts.

Name partner Mishari Al-Ghazali at **M M Al-Ghazali & Partners** is a respected litigator.

Mashora Advocates & Legal Consultants (in assoc with Bryan Cave LLP) remains occupied with its on-going representation of the Kuwaiti government in its United Nations Compensation Committee claims worth US$150bn. **Bryan Cave LLP** lawyers Michael Biggers, Robert Van Voorhees and John Lonberg are the key individuals working on this litigation.

INTELLECTUAL PROPERTY

Although Kuwait is a member of the WTO, it is still not fully TRIPS-compliant. However, lawyers cite a rise in the number of instructions received relating to the preservation of intellectual property rights, reflecting increased awareness in trade mark prosecution and registration.

Abu-Ghazaleh Intellectual Property advises on the protection and enforcement of IP rights in relation to joint ownership and technology transferring and licensing. The firm is part of the *Talal Abu Ghazaleh International* network, which has approximately 24 firms in the Middle East, Asia and the Far East.

Law Office of Al-Essa, Al-Bader & Partners has appeared in a number of high-profile IP cases, acting for global clients.

Anwar Al-Bisher & Partners continues to handle trade mark registration for a major global travel corporation.

Abdul Razzaq & Partners Law Firm deals with trade mark protection matters for Subway, and works closely with law firms in Abu Dhabi and Dubai, undertaking trade mark and copyright searches on their behalf.

Abdullah Kh. Al-Ayoub & Associates has represented a number of clients in contentious IP disputes.

Al Sarraf & Al Ruwayeh in association with Stephenson Harwood can competently advise on IP issues, as do **Salman Duaij Al Sabah Law Office** and Iman Hijazi at **Al Hekook, Advocates & Legal Consultants**

As well as handling routine trade mark registration work, **Al-Saleh & Partners** handles the commercial side of IP as well.

INTELLECTUAL PROPERTY

ABU-GHAZALEH INTELLECTUAL PROPERTY
AL-ESSA, AL-BADER & PARTNERS, LAW OFFICE OF
ANWAR AL-BISHER & PARTNERS

Abdul Razzaq & Partners Law Firm
Abdullah Kh. Al-Ayoub & Associates
Al Hekook, Advocates & Legal Consultants
Al-Saleh & Partners
Al Sarraf & Al Ruwayeh in association with Stephenson Harwood ✪
Salman Duaij Al Sabah Law Office

Firms are listed A-Z in tiers which are ranked in order of priority
✪ Indicates firm displays contact details at the end of this chapter.

PRIVATISATION AND PROJECT FINANCE

Privatisation in Kuwait has not been a top priority of late. Since the government is benefiting from the profits of high oil prices, it has not needed to focus on the privatisation of its assets. Projects work is looking more active and, at the time of writing, there were a number of multi-million-dollar projects up for tender, including the North oil field project, and the construction of a new port at Bubiyan Island.

Law Office of Al-Essa, Al-Bader & Partners' outstanding banking and finance practice has impressive project finance experience. Kevin Burke has advised in relation to many large projects in Kuwait, including the US$1.2bn 'Equate' project, Kuwait's largest project financing to date, and the financing of the Sulaibiyah Waste Water Project, Kuwait's first major BOT project valued at US$377m.

Al Sarraf & Al Ruwayeh in association with Stephenson Harwood continues to represent Kuwait Petroleum Corporation on a number of projects in the pipeline. In project finance, the firm is handling a large volume of work for PWC Logistics.

International Counsel Bureau benefits from its extremely strong ties with Kuwait Petroleum Company and Kuwait Oil Company, and most projects work undertaken by the firm is on behalf of these two oil giants. **International Counsel Bureau** recently concluded working on an oil and gas project in Turkey, and has been handling a number of substantial investment projects in the health sector.

Al-Twaijri & Partners Law Firm (TLF) advised the government in relation to its privatisation programme for the gas sector. The firm is at present advising a German company on its tender for a highway project, linking mainland Kuwait to Bubiyan Island.

Ali & Partners has advised on several major oil projects, representing an oil company and financial institutions on oil activities in the Kuwait Neutral Zone area. The firm offers advice to international oil companies on various aspects of the Kuwait oil sector and on procurement procedures.

Anwar Al-Bisher & Partners has solid project finance expertise, and has experience of advising the Kuwaiti government. The firm has represented a number of consortiums, including international and Kuwaiti companies, in governmental tenders for major telecoms, energy and infrastructure projects.

PRIVATISATION AND PROJECT FINANCE

AL-ESSA, AL-BADER & PARTNERS, LAW OFFICE OF
AL SARRAF & AL RUWAYEH IN ASSOCIATION WITH STEPHENSON HARWOOD ✪
INTERNATIONAL COUNSEL BUREAU

Al-Twaijri & Partners Law Firm (TLF)
Ali & Partners
Anwar Al-Bisher & Partners
M M Al-Ghazali & Partners

Firms are listed A-Z in tiers which are ranked in order of priority
✪ Indicates firm displays contact details at the end of this chapter.

AL MARKAZ LAW FIRM

AL-SHARQ, DASMAN COMPLEX
BLOCK 3, 7TH FLOOR
KUWAIT

Telephone: +965 246 4640
Fax: +965 246 4641
E-mail: info@markazlaw.com
Website: www.markazlaw.com

Languages
Arabic, English, French

Number of lawyers 13

Member
Kuwait Bar Association; Egypt Bar Association; American Bar Association; California Bar Association; Arab-American Bar Association; Academy of Political Science; Central Eurasian Studies Society; Southern California Mediation Society; Union of Arab Lawyers

CATEGORIES OF WORK

Corporate and commercial
Fawwaz Al-Saeed, Mary Carmel Byrne, Khairi Ibraheem Hasanen

Litigation and appeals
Osama HI Atteya, Osama S Khadadah

Islamic financing
Fawwaz Al-Saeed, Roupen Avsharian

Agency
Fawwaz Al-Saeed, Hessa A Alfuraih

Construction and real estate
Fawwaz Al-Saeed, Roupen Avsharian

Funds and securities
Fawwaz Al-Saeed, Abdel Karim Abdel Hafez

Franchise and distribution
Fawwaz Al-Saeed, Mary Carmel Byrne

Employment
Fawwaz Al-Saeed, Abdel Karim Abdel Hafez

Intellectual property
Fawwaz Al-Saeed, Osama HI Atteya

Arbitration and mediation
Osama HI Atteya, Osama S Khadadah

Insurance
Fawwaz Al-Saeed, Dr Khaled Alhendiani

Taxation
Roupen Avsharian, Khaldoon Ishaq Rashid

Privatisation and BOT contracts
Roupen Avsharian, Hessa A Alfuraih

E-commerce
Khaldoon Ishaq Rashid, Mary Carmel Byrne

Iraq reconstruction
Fawwaz Al-Saeed, Osama S Khadadah

Oil and gas
Fawwaz Al-Saeed, Roupen Avsharian

THE FIRM

Al Markaz Law Firm was founded in 1983 by Mr Fawwaz Al-Saeed, a prominent attorney who was president of the Kuwait Bar Association in the years 1997 and 1998. Al Markaz Law Firm has experienced sustained growth since its inception. It is a multi-lingual and multi-faceted business law firm based in Kuwait that is committed to providing excellent legal advice, on a consistent basis, to national and international organisations that conduct business in Kuwait. The firm has extensive experience in advising clients on complex legal issues and provides them with innovative solutions to legal problems. Its lawyers are entrepreneurial in their outlook and have extensive negotiating and mediating skills which ensure effective and zealous representation in Kuwait. Al Markaz Law Firm has vast experience in advising clients on sophisticated business transactions and is committed to identifying various approaches to solving legal issues. The lawyers at Al Markaz Law Firm, who come from various parts of the world such as Kuwait, the USA, Egypt, Iraq and Ireland, offer clients strategic thinking to facilitate their businesses in Kuwait.

AREAS OF PRACTICE

The corporate department at Al Markaz Law Firm offers comprehensive legal services to local and foreign companies on their incorporation, capitalisation and re-organisation requirements in Kuwait. It advises business entities on all regulatory requirements, including taxation.

Al Markaz Law Firm advises on all aspects of business law matters. Its team is skilled in drafting and negotiating distribution and franchise agreements and BOT contracts. The firm has particular expertise in every aspect of the oil and gas industries and advises on the registration of commercial agents in Kuwait.

The firm's strong transactional practice is complemented by one of the most dynamic litigation teams in the country. The litigation practice has acquired an excellent reputation in handling difficult cases and has won many cases in the Kuwaiti Supreme and Appellate Courts. In the years 2004 and 2005 the firm has won nine cases in the Kuwaiti Supreme Court. The lawyers at Al Markaz Law Firm have broad experience in dispute resolution and have represented clients in a number of arbitration and mediation venues such as the Cairo Regional Arbitration Centre, the International Chamber of Commerce in Paris, the Arbitration Centre of the Kuwaiti Chamber of Commerce and Industry and the GCC Arbitration Centre.

The firm has developed a niche practice area in advising on the structure and documentation needed for Islamic financing transactions. Al Markaz Law Firm can fully advise on the different Islamic financial structures such as the Murabaha, the Musharaka and other structures and was recently involved in advising on the issue of Islamic Sukuk for a major investment company.

The firm's dedicated employment lawyers can advise clients on all aspects of employment law. Its talented lawyers are experienced in drafting and negotiating employment agreements, policies and procedures in compliance with Kuwaiti laws.

A representative list of the firm's clients can be provided on request.

AL SARRAF & AL RUWAYEH

IN ASSOCIATION WITH STEPHENSON HARWOOD

SALHIYA COMPLEX, GATE 1
3RD FLOOR
PO BOX 1448
SAFAT 13015

Telephone: +965 240 0061
Fax: +965 240 0064
E-mail: asar@asarlegal.com
Website: www.asarlegal.com

Languages
Arabic, French, English

Other offices
Guangzhou, Hong Kong, London, Paris, Piraeus, Shanghai, Singapore

Number of lawyers 55

Contact
Sam Habbas

CATEGORIES OF WORK

Agencies and distributorships	Shipping
Corporate and commercial	Securities
International banking	Taxation
Finance and capital markets	International arbitration
Franchising	Intellectual property
Construction	Oil and gas industry
Government contracts	Projects and privatisation
Foreign investment	Capital markets and securities
Litigation and advocacy	General international trade law
Real estate	Private client services
Insurance	Iraq reconstruction

THE LAW FIRM OF LABEED ABDAL

AL-MUBARAKIYA, ALI AL-SALIM ST
HAMAD COMMERCIAL CENTER
BESIDE COMMERCIAL BANK
(HEAD OFFICE), FIRST FLOOR
PO BOX 29175 SAFAT
KUWAIT 13152

Telephone: +965 240 7020
Fax: +965 243 3757
E-mail: lalaw@qualitynet.net
Website: www.lalaw.com.kw

Languages
English, Arabic

Other offices
Cairo*, Cyprus*, Dubai*, Geneva*, Greece*, Iraq, Lebanon*, London*, Paris*, Riyadh*, USA*

Number of lawyers 6

Contact
Mr Labeed Abdal

CATEGORIES OF WORK

- Admiralty and maritime
- Advertising and marketing
- Art and cultural property
- Banking, financial litigation
- Bankruptcy
- Civil and human rights
- Communications
- Constitutional law and administrative
- Construction
- Corporate and commercial
- Criminal law and traffic offences
- Environmental
- Estate and trust
- Franchising, agency and distribution
- Insurance
- Intellectual property
- International trading
- IT, e-commerce and internet
- Litigation and arbitration
- Labour law
- Real estate
- Patents and trade marks
- Privatisation
- Space law
- Traffic
- White-collar crime

LATVIA

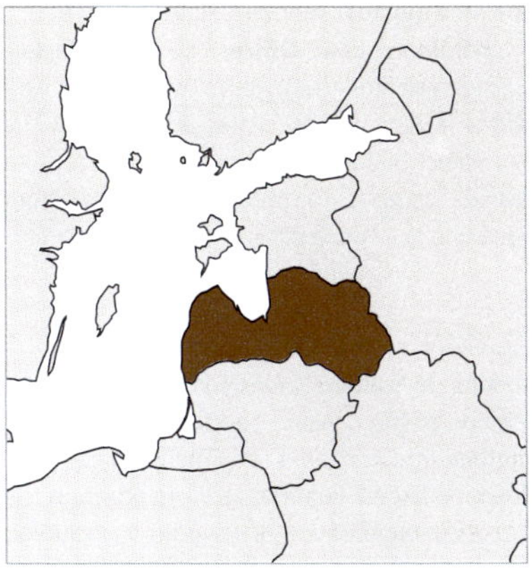

Population	2.4 million
Number of lawyers	833
Professional title	Advokati: advokàts
Currency	Latvian lat (LVL)

Index

Located on the southeastern coast of the Baltic Sea, Latvia shares borders with Estonia, Russia, Belarus and Lithuania. Former tensions with Russia over border issues are a distant memory and Latvia has enjoyed independence for more than ten years, following the break-up of the Soviet Union in 1991. However, although remaining Russian troops left in 1994, the status of the Russian minority (around 30% of the population) remains a concern. Around 19% of the community has Latvian Alien Passports, meaning they are not entitled to vote in elections, work for state institutions or travel within EU borders without a visa.

Since joining Nato in April 2004, and becoming a member of the EU in May 2004, Latvia has experienced a rapid transformation with many positive outcomes. Unfortunately, EU accession gained criticism from various factions who considered the referendum, which received 66.9% of votes in favour of joining, to be unconstitutional and undemocratic due to controversies over government media campaigning and the number of eligible votes received.

BILLING

Hourly rates generally range from €200-€300 depending on the level of experience of the lawyer. Tariffs have been laid down by the Latvian Bar Council but these are not obligatory and are not usually adhered to on account of being unrealistically low.

MARKETING

The Bar Council oversees marketing in Latvia and although aggressive marketing is not permitted, this is not diligently enforced. Most firms now have an English-language website.

IN-HOUSE LAWYERS

Around 50% of large banks and companies retain in-house lawyers but often outsource if specific advice on corporate matters is required. In-house lawyers are not obliged to be members of the Bar.

ECONOMY

The Russian economic crisis in 1996 hit Latvia hard. Fortunately, Latvia overcame the crisis and is back on track towards economic growth and prosperity. This revival was largely due to the government's stringency, gradual reorientation of exports towards EU countries and the lessening of Latvia's trade dependency on Russia.

In 2005, GDP grew by 7.5% and is forecast to increase at 6-8% in the next few years. The increase is attributable to stable domestic demand and an increase in exports. Latvia has one of the highest economic growth rates in the EU and future expectations are extremely positive. The country has, however, felt the impact of gross inflation since accession, affecting every area of the economy.

Trade with EU member states has been consistently expanding since the restoration of independence. Currently more than 70% of Latvian exports are linked to the EU and in 2004 most of the country's foreign trade turnover was made up by commerce with Germany, Lithuania, Sweden, Russia and Estonia.

The country's rapidly expanding banking sector has provided a strong foundation for business growth and macro-economic stability. Construction, manufacturing and tourism are amongst the strongest segments and are seen as promising future development areas. Real estate in particular has emerged as an extremely prosperous market with investors flocking to get involved in this booming industry. Latvia's ports of Riga, Ventspils and Liepaja anchor its vital shipping and transit industry.

Foreign investment is welcomed in Latvia and, according to *The Economist Intelligence Unit*, the country has one of the most attractive transition economies for foreign investors, owing to its dynamic economic growth and progress in structural reforms. Low interest rates and income tax are also encouraging and past obstacles such as corruption, bureaucracy and uncertainties in legislation have become less of a burden for investors. The unemployment rate, at 8.5% in 2005, is reasonably average in comparison with the rest of Europe and is gradually improving.

PPP is beginning to make an appearance in Latvia with the government having introduced guidelines in 2005. However, the practical side of the process is developing slowly with no genuine and successful examples, as yet, due to an underdeveloped legal and political framework.

LEGAL MARKET

The legal market in Latvia has echoed the growth and development of the economy. EU accession in

The largest firms

1	Loze, Grunte & Cers	28
2	Klavins & Slaidins LAWIN	22
	Sorainen Law Offices	22
4	Lejins, Torgans & Partners	16
	Raidla & Partners	16
6	Carrington, Hall & Hamburg Law Office	15
	Glimstedt & Partneri	15
8	Liepa, Skopina / BORENIUS	14
9	Agency Tria Robit	11
	Kronbergs & Cukste	11
11	Valters Gencs, Law Firm of	10
12	Skudra & Udris Law Offices	9
13	Baltmane & Bitans Law Office	8
	Blueger & Plaude	8
	SMA Petrov & Nicolajenko Law Firm	8
16	Kabuce, Punka & Partneri	7
17	"Merkants", Law Office	6
	B2B, Law Office	6
	Spade un Mikelsons Law Office	6
20	Hough, Vilcins, Seppälä & Palubinskas SIA	5
21	E Rubenis & Partners	4
22	Rödl & Partner	3
	Volksons & Petersons	3
24	Rozenfelds & Partners	2

These figures represent the total number of lawyers in this country only, and have been supplied by the firms themselves. The figures should be accurate as at 1 January 2006.

2004 resulted in an influx of international clients and local firms consequently experienced tremendous organic growth. The Latvian legal market is now more active and aggressive and appears to be following the trends of larger European markets. Although foreign growth has been initiated, there is currently not much interest in international firms becoming a permanent presence owing to the existing small market size.

Baltic partnering has become increasingly common in the past year and is likely to persist as the main firms continue to sign up to alliances. Most firms aim to be full-service though very few specialist firms exist as yet.

In May 2005 two of Latvia's leading firms, *Loze & Partners* and *Grunte & Cers*, merged to form **Loze, Grunte & Cers**, Latvia's largest law office with a total of 17 associates and nine partners.

In 2005, well-known **Lejins, Torgans & Partners** partner, Romualds Vonsovics left to set up a litigation boutique. **Lejins, Torgans & Partners** acquired three new associates taking the total number of fee-earners to 16. New recruits include former legal and tax consultant for Deloitte & Touche, Elina Bedanova, and Aldis Gobzems, previously of the Ministry of Justice.

Klavins & Slaidins LAWIN has added six lawyers to its team, due to growth in workload, and further expansion is expected in 2006.

Sorainen Law Offices is in a phase of rapid development and acquired six new lawyers in 2005 including the new head of the tax practice group, Luc Nijs, who boasts over ten years of professional experience in several European countries and a stint at Deloitte & Touche.

LINKS ABROAD

Few foreign firms have a presence in Latvia. However, many leading national firms co-operate closely with international firms such as **Clifford Chance**, **Allen & Overy LLP**, **Pinsent Masons** and **Linklaters**.

Lejins, Torgans & Partners belongs to the structured partnership *RoschierRaidla Fenno-Baltic partnering*. The alliance is the largest of its kind comprising 170 lawyers from **Roschier Holmberg**, Finland, **Raidla & Partners**, Estonia and **Norcous & Partners** Lithuania. A Stockholm office opened at the end of 2005.

Liepa, Skopina/BORENIUS is part of an association with **Luiga Mody Hääl Borenius**, Estonia, **Foigt & Partners/Regija Borenius**, Lithuania and **Borenius & Kemppinen**, Finland, with a view to supplying legal services across the Baltic States and Finland.

Baltmane & Bitans Law Office works closely with **Law Office Ots & Co**, Estonia and **Law Firm Saladzius & Partners**, Lithuania.

Sixty-lawyer, pan-Baltic network *Baltic Legal Solutions* has been referred to as 'one of the most noteworthy developments in the legal field'. **Kronbergs & Cukste**, **Jurevicius, Balciunas & Bartkus**, Lithuania and **Law Firm Teder, Glikman & Partnerid**, Estonia, are members of this grouping.

Klavins & Slaidins LAWIN established the *LAWIN* group together with **Lepik & Luhaäär LAWIN**, Estonia, and **Lideika, Petrauskas, Valiunas ir partneriai LAWIN**, Lithuania. With over 80 lawyers this group is one of the largest legal services providers in the Baltics bringing together three, top-rated firms who have co-operated together informally for over ten years.

Sorainen Law Offices is a full-service business law firm, employing over 65 lawyers, with offices in Riga, Tallinn, Vilnius and Helsinki. The pan-Baltic character of the firm enables it to provide services to multinational companies operating in all three Baltic States.

BANKING AND FINANCE

Klavins & Slaidins LAWIN maintains its top position in the banking and finance table after another triumphant year. The firm advised Norway's largest financial services group in the successful organisation of a syndicate, including five Latvian banks, to provide €120m credit to the largest developer of shopping centres in the Baltic States. The firm also manages legal affairs for UniCredit, HSH Nordbank and Standard Bank of London. Clients find the firm extremely accessible and diligent.

Senior associate Andrejs Lielkalns, **Lejins, Torgans & Partners**, is an expert in banking and finance law and has represented numerous international banks, including world leaders HSBC, Merrill Lynch and Barclays Bank, in complex transactions. In 2005 the firm advised Deutsche Bank on the €120m financing of a major infrastructure project in Riga. Clients say the firm's attorneys 'spare no effort in ensuring prompt and accurate execution of work'.

BANKING AND FINANCE

KLAVINS & SLAIDINS LAWIN ✪
LEJINS, TORGANS & PARTNERS ✪
LOZE, GRUNTE & CERS ✪
SORAINEN LAW OFFICES ✪

Baltmane & Bitans Law Office ✪
Blueger & Plaude
Glimstedt & Partneri ✪
Kronbergs & Cukste ✪
Liepa, Skopina/BORENIUS ✪
Skudra & Udris Law Offices ✪
Valters Gencs, Law Firm of ✪

Carrington, Hall & Hamburg Law Office
Hough, Vilcins, Seppälä & Palubinskas SIA
"Merkants", Law Office

Firms are listed A-Z in tiers which are ranked in order of priority
✪ Indicates firm displays contact details at the end of this chapter.

After the merger of two of Latvia's leading firms, *Loze & Partners* and *Grunte & Cers*, **Loze, Grunte & Cers** is now the largest firm in the country. The firm enjoys a prestigious reputation with over 26 years of combined experience in the legal market ensuring the highest level of expertise and specialisation possible. The banking and finance practice gives in-depth advice on the feasibility of securitisation and consults on all activities in the financial market in Latvia. Big-name clients include the World Bank, Deutsche Bank and Royal Bank of Scotland.

Sorainen Law Offices' celebrated client following matches the firm's A-list reputation and secures it a top-tier position in this year's table. The firm is engaged in equity-related transactions for one of the world's leading banks and advises Barclays Bank and BNP Paribas on various financial matters. Clients praise the firm's 'proactivity, flexibility and availability' and partner, Girts Ruda, comes highly recommended.

In 2005 **Baltmane & Bitans Law Office** considerably expanded its banking and finance-related legal services, earning the law office a promotion in this year's table. The firm advises many of the world's top-ranking companies on complex issues relating to dealings with regulators, development of investment banking services and structuring of derivatives products. The capable lawyers at this firm have been engaged in performing detailed reviews of money-transfer procedures and security rules as set by competent authorities at both the international and national level. Key clients include Big Four accounting firms.

Blueger & Plaude advises banks and individual clients and is instructed by joint stock companies and the EBRD. Clients are impressed with the firm's knowledge of outside legal jurisdictions, enabling it to communicate with utmost efficiency.

Glimstedt & Partneri has a total of 19 lawyers and plans further expansion. The firm represented the Nordic Environment Finance Corporation in its loan facility projects and Swedfund, a risk capital company, in several acquisition and financing projects in Latvia. 'Diligent' Inita Jurka is valued by clients.

'Key attorney', Valters Kronbergs, is responsible for the banking and finance department at **Kronbergs & Cukste**. Last year the firm handled two major bank acquisition due diligence projects, representing at least half of the activity in the market in terms of acquisitions of financial institutions. 'Thorough work and good understanding' are highlighted by content patrons.

The 14-lawyer team at **Liepa, Skopina/BORENIUS** is headed by partners Lauris Liepa and Laine Skopina. Last year the firm represented one of the world's largest banks in a €100m bond issue.

The eight attorneys at **Skudra & Udris Law Offices** pride themselves on their deep knowledge, experience and international education. Banking and finance is a core area of specialisation at this firm, reflected in its enviable client list. Partner, Armands Skudra, is revered in his field of practice and has acted for the World Bank, Morgan Stanley Dean Witter and MasterCard International. In 2005 the firm advised a syndicate of international banks on an €85m loan facility for the Latvian State Mortgage Bank. Strong, worldwide networks are regarded as a key strength by clients.

Law Firm of Valters Gencs moves up a tier in this year's rankings. After expansion in 2005 the firm now has ten lawyers of whom one was chief lawyer at leading Latvian commercial bank, Hansabanka. The firm recently acted for a Swedish hotel chain in a case against a local bank relating to the alleged misappropriation of assets and is also consulted by MasterCard and Société Générale.

Carrington, Hall & Hamburg Law Office counsels banks and financial institutions on investment projects, securities and derivatives. The firm's main client is SIXT, a leading, European vehicle hire service provider. The firm also recently assisted US and UK clients with the release of illegally arrested funds in Latvian commercial banks.

Hough, Vilcins, Seppälä & Palubinskas SIA offers a range of banking services and recently represented a leading UK bank regarding Latvian denominated securities.

CORPORATE AND M&A

Klavins & Slaidins LAWIN retains its top-tier position this year after a succession of unsurpassed M&A transactions. Key focal points include the merger of Lattelekom with Microlink. In association with the other *LAWIN* alliance partners, the firm carried out extensive work on transaction structure, due diligence and the submission of merger notifications to the competition authorities. Born and educated in the UK, Egons Pikelis formerly worked for **Simmons & Simmons** and is respected for his securities and M&A work.

Lejins, Torgans & Partners is highly regarded for its corporate work. Last year the firm represented some of Latvia's largest companies in transactions amounting to hundreds of millions of euro. The 16-lawyer team receives acclaim for its detailed knowledge of Latvian law combined with a practical sense, facilitating transactions. Name partner, Girts Lejins, is recognised for his proficiency.

Rapidly expanding, pan-Baltic **Sorainen Law Offices** has been involved in more than 350 M&A transactions in the last ten years. The firm recently represented a leading, international software company during the acquisition of a PC business and also handled post-transfer activities. The firm has noted a vast increase in cases involving shareholders disputes and assists the world's largest, non-alcoholic beverage producer on its campaign structure. The firm's exceptional reputation and expansive work portfolio earns it a promotion in this year's table.

CORPORATE AND M&A

KLAVINS & SLAIDINS LAWIN ○
LEJINS, TORGANS & PARTNERS ○
SORAINEN LAW OFFICES ○

Baltmane & Bitans Law Office ○
Kronbergs & Cukste ○
Liepa, Skopina/BORENIUS ○
Loze, Grunte & Cers ○

Blueger & Plaude
Glimstedt & Partneri ○
Helena Stanislavska IPZA
O.Cers & J.Jurkans, Law Office
Skudra & Udris Law Offices ○
Valters Gencs, Law Firm of ○

B2B, Law Office
Carrington, Hall & Hamburg Law Office
Hough, Vilcins, Seppälä & Palubinskas SIA
"Merkants", Law Office
Rozenfelds & Partners ○
Spilbridge & Partners

Firms are listed A-Z in tiers which are ranked in order of priority
○ *Indicates firm displays contact details at the end of this chapter.*

Baltmane & Bitans Law Office has seen a boom in M&A-related work in the last 12 months. The firm has handled a number of high-profile, complex transactions and represents companies such as Siemens, Danone and PricewaterhouseCoopers. The firm also specialises in assisting foreign investors in establishing businesses in Latvia. Clients speak highly of partner Maris Vainovskis and commend his 'professionalism, proactivity and efficiency whilst keeping in mind the human aspect of all legal issues'.

Eleven-lawyer **Kronbergs & Cukste** is instructed by several companies on M&A matters and advises on all aspects of corporate law. Clients proclaim lawyers to be adept at handling complex issues and able to apply the law in a 'real' business environment. Name partner, Vineta Cukste, receives acclaim for her profound commercial knowledge.

Dynamic lawyers, Laine Skopina and Sergejs Rudans front the corporate and commercial team at **Liepa, Skopina/BORENIUS**, renowned for its excellent M&A work. The firm demonstrated its abilities lately when representing an international construction company during the sale of its subsidiary in Latvia and also co-operated with **DLA Piper Rudnick Gray Cary UK LLP** during the representation of a global leader in electronic commerce and payment services.

Strengthened by its merger in 2005, **Loze, Grunte & Cers** is a solid and continually evolving full-service firm. The determined corporate department has performed legal due diligence and assisted many prodigious companies in establishing branches in Latvia. The firm has also played a lead role in a number of mergers in Latvia, including Hansabanka and Zemes Bank. Clients comment on the firm's 'professional approach, excellent time management and good customer relations'.

Attorneys at **Blueger & Plaude** are greatly experienced in advising on entrepreneurial activity. Several of them have trained and worked in foreign legal jurisdictions. The firm handles a great deal of M&A, particularly assisting in share acquisitions. Partners Valentin Blueger and Baiba Plaude gain praise for their 'tight relations within the business community'.

Glimstedt & Partneri increased its staff by 25% in 2005, maintaining a high-quality and consistent practice and continuing to improve its reputation in the Latvian legal market. The firm advises TeliaSonera, the premier telecommunications company in the Nordic and Baltic regions, on investment matters. The firm is well regarded for its competent M&A practice.

Helena Stanislavska IPZA, formerly part of *Stanislavska, Lepik & Luhaaar*, is a boutique firm specialising in business law. Clients include Colgate-Palmolive and Pfizer. Clients profess Helena Stanislavska's key strengths include her 'extensive experience and excellent contacts in all business areas'.

Good, open communication is a key strength at six-lawyer **Law Office O.Cers & J.Jurkans**. The firm represents major shareholders in disputes and has advised significant foreign investors. One satisfied client claims the firm 'suggests solutions and carries them through until the end'. Ieva Lenova deserves recognition for the respect gained from clients.

The diverse and extensive corporate and commercial practice at **Skudra & Udris Law Offices** has the ability to provide advice and representation in all phases from the initial 'start-up' of a business, through to obtaining necessary licences and permits. Award-winning managing partner, Ziedonis Udris, is an admired practitioner. Last year the firm was instructed by Wrigley Corporation on the restructuring of its Baltic business operations, and by British Telecom on corporate and regulatory aspects for a new business project in Latvia. Clients praise the firm's 'talented legal expertise, language skills and more-than-adequate resources'.

Full-service, ten-lawyer **Law Firm of Valters Gencs** handles a range of corporate and commercial matters and assisted a German software company on the acquisition of a local business last year.

Law Office B2B co-operates closely with law offices in Lithuania, Estonia, Russia and the Ukraine, allowing it to render clients a wide spectrum of corporate and commercial services, simultaneously in several states. International wood products company, Stora Enso, is amongst the firm's clients.

Carrington, Hall & Hamburg Law Office has seen a boom in M&A-related work recently. In 2005 the firm was responsible for representing global market leader, Stora Enso, in its acquisition of one of the largest companies in Latvia. The firm receives praise for its ability to handle large volumes of work whilst meeting individual demands.

There are six partners at **Hough, Vilcins, Seppälä & Palubinskas SIA** ensuring clients almost always get partner attention. Last year the firm advised a leading Finnish machinery distributor regarding the reorganisation and consolidation of its Baltic operations.

The four lawyers at **Law Office "MERKANTS"** primarily practise commercial law, handling all areas from day-to-day services to the foundation of new companies. Amongst the firm's clients are several of Riga's hospitals.

Spilbridge & Partners offers a small but professional corporate and M&A practice, counting the representation of a large hotel chain during its acquisition of additional premises as a key transaction in 2005. Clients comment on the firm's dedication, claiming 'you get the feeling the firm throws down everything to meet your needs'.

EU AND COMPETITION

The EU and competition department at **Klavins & Slaidins LAWIN** boasts competition expert Liga Hartmane, who publishes and speaks widely on the topic. The firm prepared and managed a merger notification for esteemed client, Lattelekom, in its successful merger with MicroLink. Big-league clients, including Gillette, Heinz and Red Bull, instruct the firm who, last year, assisted Coca-Cola to implement an undertaking to the European Commission. Several competitors have retained **Klavins & Slaidins LAWIN** to provide competition training for their staff in Latvia. Satisfied clients state the firm is 'perfectly up to the task' and available 24 hours a day.

Sorainen Law Offices offers extensive EU and competition advice. Attorneys at the firm have been actively involved in the EU harmonisation process of the Baltics since accession in 2004. Last year the firm represented a major Finnish logistics company regarding international notification issues and advised the world's premier global delivery network on compliance with dawn raid instructions.

The diverse and comprehensive 16-lawyer team at **Lejins, Torgans & Partners** has been increasingly involved in EU and competition issues in 2005. Partner, Dace Silava-Tomsone, is an expert in competition law and regularly advises on intricate legal issues. Last year the firm obtained a merger clearance from the Latvian Competition Council in connection with the acquisition of a leading company for payment card data services in the Baltic States. Clients favour the firm for its 'extremely prompt' turnaround skills.

EU AND COMPETITION

Klavins & Slaidins LAWIN ✪
Sorainen Law Offices ✪

Lejins, Torgans & Partners ✪
Liepa, Skopina/BORENIUS ✪
Loze, Grunte & Cers ✪

B2B, Law Office
Glimstedt & Partneri ✪
Valters Gencs, Law Firm of ✪

Firms are listed A-Z in tiers which are ranked in order of priority
✪ *Indicates firm displays contact details at the end of this chapter.*

Ieva Azanda of **Liepa, Skopina/BORENIUS** has worked at both the European Integration Bureau and the European Central Bank, certifying her reputation in this field of practice. The firm has represented clients before the Competition Council, regarding presumptive misuse of dominant position, and runs competition law compliance training for major clients.

Loze, Grunte & Cers offers extensive experience in competition law matters. Philip Morris, Statoil and Cemex instruct the firm which also maintains a relationship with the Latvian Competition Council regarding issues of merger clearance and antitrust violation.

The EU experts at **Law Office B2B** advise various companies exporting to the EU and make every effort to ensure clients are kept abreast of changes in legislation.

Glimstedt & Partneri is active in the competition arena and last year represented Unibanka in its acquisition of a Latvian insurance company.

In 2005, **Law Firm of Valters Gencs** handled a competition case against a state forestry monopoly on behalf of a Dutch company. The firm recently benefited from the addition of Antis Apsitis, an authority on consumer and competition issues from the Ministry of Economics.

FOREIGN INVESTMENT

Unfaltering, 22-lawyer **Klavins & Slaidins LAWIN**, advised Microsoft on foreign direct investment issues last year, regarding the transfer of operations from Germany to Latvia. The firm is also engaged in negotiations, with the government of Latvia, said to be the largest investment in the country's history.

Leading, full-service firm, **Lejins, Torgans & Partners** has advised numerous foreign entities in connection with setting up subsidiaries, branches, representative offices and joint ventures in Latvia.

FOREIGN INVESTMENT

KLAVINS & SLAIDINS LAWIN ✪
LEJINS, TORGANS & PARTNERS ✪

Kronbergs & Cukste ✪
Loze, Grunte & Cers ✪
Sorainen Law Offices ✪

Baltmane & Bitans Law Office ✪
Blueger & Plaude
Carrington, Hall & Hamburg Law Office
Glimstedt & Partneri ✪
Liepa, Skopina/BORENIUS ✪
Skudra & Udris Law Offices ✪
Valters Gencs, Law Firm of ✪

Hough, Vilcins, Seppälä & Palubinskas SIA
O.Cers & J.Jurkans, Law Office
Rozenfelds & Partners ✪

Firms are listed A-Z in tiers which are ranked in order of priority
✪ *Indicates firm displays contact details at the end of this chapter.*

Last year the firm advised a Danish property group on the acquisition of two major real estate companies. Clients profess the firm to be incredibly helpful and quick to understand individual needs.

Last year **Kronbergs & Cukste** acted on behalf of a prominent international bank in the €50m acquisition of a commercial development site and represented an Icelandic company in due diligence, with a view to acquisition of a large national bank.

Loze, Grunte & Cers is engaged in foreign investment matters for clients such as Statoil, Masterfoods and Kodak. The firm has been actively working on behalf of Neste and Statoil on their ongoing major oil terminal project in the Riga Port.

Sorainen Law Offices has a strong following among international companies and is becoming more attractive to local clients. The firm handles a vast quantity of M&A work for foreign investors and recently provided pan-Baltic advice to a leading, global law firm involved in the acquisition of a business in Latvia.

Baltmane & Bitans Law Office specialises in assisting foreign investors with the establishment of businesses in Latvia and last year aided more than ten investors in a myriad of legal assignments concerning the establishment of subsidiaries in Latvia.

Lawyers at **Blueger & Plaude** have worked as advisors in many foreign investment projects. The firm advised the EBRD on legal matters during the realisation of various projects in Latvia. Academic and top lawyer, Baiba Plaude, lectures on foreign investment law at the University of Latvia. One satisfied international client proclaims: 'I can only recommend other legal entities to benefit from **Blueger & Plaude**'s knowledge, professional skills and attitude.'

The 15 lawyers at **Carrington, Hall & Hamburg Law Office** have advised a number of international clients, including a top financial institution, on foreign direct investment matters. Clients say the firm is 'accessible and ready to respond to questions'.

Glimstedt & Partneri represents big-name clients, including Bosch, on foreign investment matters. The firm has also assisted international companies with the set-up, acquisition and expansion of subsidiaries in Latvia.

Throughout 2005 **Liepa, Skopina/BORENIUS** has advised many international clients regarding investment in Latvia. Amongst clients are regional and international investment funds and property holdings, that the firm aided with the acquisition of real estate and set-up of businesses in Latvia.

Skudra & Udris Law Offices advises several global companies on foreign investment issues in Latvia.

Law Firm of Valters Gencs assists a number of foreign clients in the pan-Baltic establishment of subsidiaries and buying out of local companies. Last year the firm was instructed by a German cosmetics producer on the expansion of a distribution chain in Latvia.

Law Office O.Cers & J.Jurkans recently represented a foreign industrial company.

IP, IT AND TELECOMS

Agency Tria Robit, the only specialist IP firm in the Baltic States, merits a top-tier position in this year's table for its market-leading reputation and expertise. The nine-lawyer firm handles the IP portfolios of many of the world's leading corporations including McDonald's and Ferrari. Last year the firm showcased its capabilities when representing a company in a trade mark case, setting a precedent in Latvia. Satisfied clients praise the firm's excellent communication, prompt turnaround time and claim it to be 'the best firm for IP in Latvia'. Head of office, Vladimir Anohin, is 'reactive, proactive and pre-emptive'.

Loze, Grunte & Cers is one of the only firms in Latvia to have both a licensed trade mark agent and patent agent, ensuring all IP matters are efficiently carried out in-house. The firm recently represented a domestic manufacturer of alcoholic beverages in a dispute settlement concerning the use of trade marks 'Smirnoff' and 'Arsenich'. The firm also experienced success in its telecoms department, representing in co-operation with **White & Case** TeliaSonera in a dispute with the Republic of Latvia regarding a default on the provisions of a shareholder agreement.

The attorneys at **Baltmane & Bitans Law Office** have successfully represented numerous clients in patent, trade mark, copyright protection and other disputes over IP rights, including representing the largest recording company in Latvia. The firm is instructed by the world's largest software company and advises government and

IP, IT AND TELECOMS

AGENCY TRIA ROBIT
LOZE, GRUNTE & CERS ✪

Baltmane & Bitans Law Office ✪
Carrington, Hall & Hamburg Law Office
Glimstedt & Partneri ✪
Klavins & Slaidins LAWIN ✪
Kronbergs & Cukste ✪
Lejins, Torgans & Partners ✪
Liepa, Skopina/BORENIUS ✪
Rozenfelds & Partners ✪
Sorainen Law Offices ✪
Valters Gencs, Law Firm of ✪

B2B, Law Office
"Merkants", Law Office
Skudra & Udris Law Offices ✪

Firms are listed A-Z in tiers which are ranked in order of priority
✪ *Indicates firm displays contact details at the end of this chapter.*

public entities on IT and communications matters. The firm's ability to understand and solve complex issues is a key strength. Partner Agris Bitans is a professor of IP law at the University of Latvia.

At **Carrington, Hall & Hamburg Law Office** the true value of the need to protect IP rights is understood. Noteworthy clients include the Latvian brand of *FHM* and *Cosmopolitan*. The firm is also instructed by cable TV providers and telecoms equipment manufacturers and receives praise for the attorneys' 'advanced education and willingness to provide the best service possible'.

Glimstedt & Partneri counsels the largest telecoms operator in Latvia on legal affairs and handles patent and trade mark matters for various clients.

Klavins & Slaidins LAWIN has a healthy involvement in IP-related work and represented mega-pharmaceutical company, UCB, in complicated administrative matters before the Court of Appeal of the Latvian Patent Board. Trade mark registration matters are conducted on behalf of numerous clients including Coca-Cola.

Kronbergs & Cukste acts as general counsel for the world's largest computer software company, advising it on IP and IT matters in Latvia. The firm also actively represents several national and international telecoms companies. Accessibility and turnaround skills are highlighted by clients.

Last year, all-round firm **Lejins, Torgans & Partners** added three new associates to its team of 13 lawyers. Amongst new arrivals was IP specialist Elina Bedanova. The firm advises Apple Computers on border control issues and also represents large, Latvian wholesale IT companies.

Liepa, Skopina/BORENIUS offers a strong IP and IT practice. Skilled advocate, Ilze Bulkadere, drafted the legal framework for several major IT projects in Latvia and carried out research on the regulation of patents and trade marks in the EU.

Last year the firm assisted in a number of telecoms transactions including bidding for the GSM licence, auctioned by the government, when extensive legal research on the Latvian telecoms market was carried out. The firm provides consultations to a number of international pharmaceutical corporations involving IP matters.

Sorainen Law Offices advises on a full range of IP-related transactions in the Baltic States. A core area of practice is trade mark litigation and the firm has managed trade mark issues for major global and local producers in the Baltic market including EMI and Dior. Senior associate, Brigita Terauda, handles the IP transactions at this firm.

Valters Gencs, **Law Firm of Valters Gencs**, is a European patent and trade mark attorney with an LLM in IP. The firm is instructed by foreign clients, including food and cosmetics companies, in trade mark dispute cases.

The IP team at **Law Office B2B** draws on international resources in order to offer a full range of services for protecting and enhancing clients' IP rights. The firm advises a range of industries including media, IT and industrial producers.

REAL ESTATE AND CONSTRUCTION

BLUEGER & PLAUDE
KLAVINS & SLAIDINS LAWIN ✪
LEJINS, TORGANS & PARTNERS ✪
LIEPA, SKOPINA/BORENIUS ✪

Baltmane & Bitans Law Office ✪
Glimstedt & Partneri ✪
Kronbergs & Cukste ✪
Sorainen Law Offices ✪

Loze, Grunte & Cers ✪
O.Cers & J.Jurkans, Law Office
Valters Gencs, Law Firm of ✪

B2B, Law Office
Carrington, Hall & Hamburg Law Office
Hough, Vilcins, Seppälä & Palubinskas SIA
Skudra & Udris Law Offices ✪
Spilbridge & Partners

Firms are listed A-Z in tiers which are ranked in order of priority
✪ *Indicates firm displays contact details at the end of this chapter.*

REAL ESTATE AND CONSTRUCTION

Renowned in this field, **Blueger & Plaude** handles a large volume of real estate transactions. Last year the firm arbitrated on behalf of one of Latvia's biggest construction companies in a building dispute. The firm is also engaged by shareholders of real estate development projects and investment and trading companies. Clients find the firm 'reliable, serious and competent with excellent local network connections'.

Klavins & Slaidins LAWIN advises Iberdrola, an international, leading private electric utilities company, on its reconstruction and maintenance responsibilities. The firm also represents the owner of Hotel Riga in the project documentation for its reconstruction as a Kempinski Group hotel.

Lejins, Torgans & Partners has a lively real estate and construction department. Last year the firm represented one of the largest development companies in the Baltic States on a holiday and water park development project in Latvia. Distinguished attorney, Martins Aljens, shows 'admirable attention to detail, strong legal knowledge, excellent translation skills and amazing stamina when working long hours'.

Real estate is a key area of practice at **Liepa, Skopina/BORENIUS**. The firm offers veritable expertise in construction, planning, environmental and property litigation. Recently, the firm has been involved in the expansion of a Europe-wide supermarket chain.

Baltmane & Bitans Law Office assists clients in relation to all real estate issues. Last year the firm acted for a large public authority in contract negotiations, valued at over €120m, with a consortium of major national construction companies in Latvia relating to the construction of a bridge over the river Daugava. The firm also advises an international retail company based in Germany on various real estate development issues.

Since the recent real estate boom in Latvia, **Glimstedt & Partneri** has seen this area of practice grow, particularly after the acquisition of partner and real estate expert, Ivars Pommers, who clients proclaim to be an excellent litigator. The firm represents a multitude of well-known companies in their real estate projects, including a global furniture company in its ongoing, multi-million euro expansion in Latvia.

Prominent firm, **Kronbergs & Cukste** not only handles vast quantities of real estate work but also co-publishes guides and handbooks on the area. In the previous 12 months the firm has been involved in large amounts of legal due diligence for several worldwide corporations.

The real estate market in Latvia is in a period of rapid expansion and **Sorainen Law Offices** is equipped to provide extensive advice on this area. The firm's increased showing on real estate-related M&A in recent years has considerably strengthened its position. The firm handled the sale of the largest real estate development project in Latvia and has provided legal assistance to foreign investors regarding the construction of the country's biggest multi-purpose arena.

With 26 lawyers, **Loze, Grunte & Cers** is the largest firm in Latvia. The firm is currently involved in the relocation and restructuring of Riga Port for which it handles the acquisition of real estate and land, environmental aspects and various other business transactions. All partners come highly recommended but the leading personality in clients' opinions is name partner, Janis Loze.

Law Office O.Cers & J.Jurkans is headed by name partners Olavs Cers and Janis Jurkans. In 2005 the firm successfully represented Riga City against private investors regarding the cancellation of a real estate agreement. Clients comment on the firm's 'knowledge, experience and ability to execute work on a timely basis'.

Law Firm of Valters Gencs represents one of Riga's top-class business centres in its real estate matters and has also assisted a number of companies in the purchase of property, in Latvia, for production facilities, agricultural land and energy resources.

Law Office B2B boasts a capable real estate team with a full understanding of this heavily regulated field of practice. The firm acts for developers, local and overseas occupiers, lenders and investors and has assisted in the development of blockhouses for a large Latvian mortgage and land bank.

Partners Bruno Leja and Janis Karklins are renowned for their real estate and construction work at **Carrington, Hall & Hamburg Law Office**. The firm has been markedly active in this field of practice in the past year and has advised on sales, purchases and real estate development projects in Riga, each valued at €3m-€10m. Key strengths include excellent communication skills in several languages.

Hough, Vilcins, Seppälä & Palubinskas SIA recently counselled a leading defence contractor on Latvian construction guidelines.

Highly skilled and experienced attorney, Iveta Berzina, who has a reputation for handling complex and demanding assignments, heads the real estate practice at **Skudra & Udris Law Offices**. The firm was recently engaged by Finnish investors on a major residential development project involving the construction of 35 million houses in Riga. Good contacts in the local community are appreciated by clients.

Daimars Skutans of **Spilbridge & Partners** is something of a PPP expert, having advised a real estate company owned by Riga City Council on social infrastructure under PPP principles last year. Satisfied clients rank this firm on a par with leading firms due to its dedication to client needs.

SHIPPING AND TRANSPORT

Liepa, Skopina/BORENIUS has assisted shipping companies and financial institutions, such as Morgan Stanley and Lloyds Bank, in various matters concerning cargo contracts and ship financing. The firm also provides legal advice to international clients Cargomasters and Cycleon.

Partner, Gints Vilgerts, specialises in shipping law at **Sorainen Law Offices** and has written extensively on the subject. Since joining the EU the firm has experienced growth in its shipping and transport practice with work predominantly emanating from leading worldwide shipping law firms. The firm recently represented a leading

SHIPPING AND TRANSPORT

LIEPA, SKOPINA/BORENIUS ✪
SORAINEN LAW OFFICES ✪

Baltmane & Bitans Law Office ✪
Carrington, Hall & Hamburg Law Office
Kronbergs & Cukste ✪
Lejins, Torgans & Partners ✪
"Merkants", Law Office
Spilbridge & Partners
Valters Gencs, Law Firm of ✪

Firms are listed A-Z in tiers which are ranked in order of priority
✪ Indicates firm displays contact details at the end of this chapter.

Nordic investment bank in the registration of a mortgage and preparation of a legal opinion on a Latvian vessel.

Baltmane & Bitans Law Office raised its profile in the shipping and transport arena in 2005. Clients instructing the firm include one of the largest ferry companies in Europe and the Latvian Ministry of Transport, with whom the firm has joined in order to assist with the development of the country's Maritime Code.

Riga Shipping Company and several of Latvia's biggest yacht owners are represented by **Carrington, Hall & Hamburg Law Office**. Lawyers at this firm are experienced, motivated and apt at dealing with individual claims and class actions involving shipping and transport law. Clients are impressed by the firm's ability to meet deadlines and produce quality results.

Market leader, **Kronbergs & Cukste** boasts some of the world's most widely used airlines in its clientele list. In 2005 the firm advised Latvian Railways on a restructuring project concerning EU legislation.

Lejins, Torgans & Partners offers comprehensive advice and representation in shipping and transport matters. Last year the firm advised a large equipment service provider on the agreement package for the financial lease of transportation equipment and also represented a shipping company in a dispute involving port charges. Attorneys are hailed as 'ethical legal experts'.

Law Office "MERKANTS" handled several cases involving the buying and selling of ships in Latvia in 2005 and provides specialist legal services regarding registration procedure.

Spilbridge & Partners recently accepted engagement in a multi-million euro arbitration concerning export of commodities through Latvia to Western Europe.

Law Firm of Valters Gencs represents Swedish shipowners and obtained the first tax holiday from the tax authorities for shipping companies in Latvia.

TAX

Ilze Baltmane, at **Baltmane & Bitans Law Office**, has over 20 years of experience in tax law. Recent highlights include high-profile cases on behalf of several Latvian and international companies against the State Revenue Service. Clients are impressed by the firm's knowledge in this field and praise its professionalism and enthusiasm.

Kronbergs & Cukste advises on all tax-related issues and acts for several large, Baltic firms on tax litigation. The firm also represents property owners and development and insurance brokerage companies in tax-related matters.

Throughout 2005, **Lejins, Torgans & Partners** counselled numerous investors on tax issues deriving from M&A transactions and rendered specialist international tax planning advice. Highlights included dispensing relevant tax advice to international companies during establishment of cross-border operating units in Latvia. Clients recommend the firm for its speed and ability to understand specific needs.

Comprehensive tax services are on offer at **Law Firm of Valters Gencs**. Specialist lawyers include Valters Gencs and Baiba Abolina, a former employee of the Ministry of Finance. The firm handled the international tax planning for Coca-Cola, General Motors, McDonald's and recently triumphed in a case for a Swedish manufacturer against a VAT claim in the Supreme Court.

Tax expert, Zinta Jansons, is a well-respected, US-qualified attorney at **Klavins & Slaidins LAWIN**. The firm advises Citibank on tax-related matters in Latvia and handles a large volume of tax-structuring work.

The 14-strong team at **Liepa, Skopina/ BORENIUS** has provided tax advice on various cross-border transactions and examined issues relating to the structuring of transactions. The firm advises international and domestic clients on the comparison of tax regimes and provides tax assessment in Latvia.

TAX

BALTMANE & BITANS LAW OFFICE ✪
KRONBERGS & CUKSTE ✪
LEJINS, TORGANS & PARTNERS ✪
VALTERS GENCS, LAW FIRM OF ✪

Klavins & Slaidins LAWIN ✪
Liepa, Skopina/BORENIUS ✪
Loze, Grunte & Cers ✪
Sorainen Law Offices ✪

B2B, Law Office
Blueger & Plaude
Carrington, Hall & Hamburg Law Office
Glimstedt & Partneri ✪

Firms are listed A-Z in tiers which are ranked in order of priority
✪ Indicates firm displays contact details at the end of this chapter.

For affairs involving the design and implementation of tax-efficient structures, corporate and shareholding structure, tax due diligence and all other tax-related disputes, **Loze, Grunte & Cers** provides professional and proficient advice.

The adept tax team at **Sorainen Law Offices** was bolstered by the addition of two tax specialists Janis Tukacs and Luc Nijs. The firm recently advised an international, real estate investment company on pan-Baltic tax planning during the acquisition of several large hotels. The firm also counselled a global investment bank on tax issues related to stock borrowing, lending, repurchase and equity derivatives. Clients proclaim the lawyers to be 'swift, helpful and a pleasure to work with'.

The tax practice at **Law Office B2B** offers broad expertise in all areas of business taxation. Partner and 'tax expert', Valdis Levkans comes highly recommended.

Partners Varis Reinholds and Eugene Manenkov handle tax matters at **Blueger & Plaude**. The capability of staff on all levels is admired by clients.

Carrington, Hall & Hamburg Law Office advises on a full range of tax issues faced by business clients. The 15 lawyers at this firm are highly regarded and clients include major Baltic corporations and government institutions. The firm receives commendation for its accessibility and proficiency with heavy workloads.

BALTMANE & BITANS LAW OFFICE

20A LACPLESA STREET
3RD FLOOR
1011 RIGA

Telephone: +371 728 0102
Fax: +371 750 4566
E-mail: birojs@baltmanebitans.com
Website: www.baltmanebitans.com

Languages
English, German, Latvian, Russian

Number of lawyers 7

Contact
Sarmite Rubene

CATEGORIES OF WORK

Administrative law and procedure
Maris Vainovskis, Kristine Stege

Competition and EU
Maris Vainovskis, Maris Logins

Corporate and commercial
Ilze Baltmane, Dace Cirule

Real estate, commercial property
Kristine Stege, Ilze Baltmane

Construction
Ilze Baltmane, Agris Bitans

Dispute resolution – litigation and arbitraton
Agris Bitans

E-commerce, IT, telecoms
Agris Bitans, Maris Vainovskis

Employment
Ilze Baltmane, Dace Cirule

Insolvency/corporate restructuring
Agris Bitans, Maris Vainovskis

Media and entertainment
Agris Bitans

Foreign direct investment
Ilze Baltmane, Maris Vainovskis

Mergers and acquisitions
Ilze Baltmane, Kristine Stege

Tax
Ilze Baltmane, Maris Vainovskis

Banking and finance
Ilze Baltmane, Maris Vainovskis

GLIMSTEDT & PARTNERS

GERTRUDES 10/12
1010 RIGA

Telephone: +371 780 3380
Fax: +371 780 3381
E-mail: riga@glimstedt.lv
Website: www.glimstedt.lv

Languages
English, French, German, Latvian, Russian, Spanish, Swedish

Other offices
Tallinn, Vilnius

Number of lawyers 63
at this office 18

CATEGORIES OF WORK

Company and commercial
Eriks Blumbergs, Peteris Dalderis

Banking and finance
Inita Jurka, Lauris Zubulis

Mergers and acquisitions
Peteris Dalderis, Agnese Vanaga

Privatisation
Viktors Sadinovs, Baiba Golsta

Competition law
Eriks Blumbergs, Dagnija Libane

Insolvency and business restructuring
Peteris Dalderis, Inita Jurka

Intellectual property
Agnese Vanaga

Telecommunications and information technology law
Aldis Kalinks

Advertising and media
Dagnija Libane

Insurance
Robert Lismanis

Litigation, arbitration, dispute resolution
Peteris Dalderis

Real estate and construction
Ivars Pommers, Liga Mence

International trade and transportation
Robert Lismanis, Lauris Zubulis

Labour law
Ivars Pommers, Marika Rozite

KLAVINS & SLAIDINS LAWIN

ELIZABETES 15
1010 RIGA

Telephone: +371 781 4848
Fax: +371 781 4849
E-mail: advokati@klavinsslaidins.lv
Website: www.klavinsslaidins.lv

Languages
English, German, Latvian, Russian

Number of lawyers 22

Member
Lex Mundi; World Services Group;
International Bar Association;
International Association of Young Lawyers

CATEGORIES OF WORK

Foreign investment in Latvia
Filip Klavins, Raymond Slaidins

Employment, labour
Sanda Lace, Daiga Zivtina

Mergers and acquisitions
Filip Klavins, Raymond Slaidins

European Union
Janis Butkevics

Banking and finance
Egons Pikelis, Zinta Jansons

Competition
Liga Hartmane

Litigation and arbitration
Daiga Zivtina, Ilga Gudrenika-Krebs

Intellectual property
Ilga Gudrenika-Krebs

Real property
Sanda Lace

Securities
Egons Pikelis

Corporate and commercial
Liga Hartmane, Inese Lazdupe

Tax
Zinta Jansons, Elina Girne-Berzina

THE FIRM

Klavins & Slaidins is one of the pre-eminent law firms in Latvia, with a reputation for personal contact and superior legal work that sets it apart from its competitors. Filip Klavins and Raymond Slaidins, both US attorneys of Latvian descent, began practising law in Latvia in 1992. The firm now has 22 lawyers in all and is one of the largest law firms in Latvia. Each of the firm's lawyers is fluent in Latvian and English, and the firm also has fluent Russian and German language capabilities. Four of the lawyers add valuable foreign experience to the firm, having been born and raised, educated and trained in law in the US (three lawyers) and England.

The firm is a member of LAWIN, a group of leading Baltic law firms also including Lepik & Luhaäär LAWIN in Estonia and Lideika, Petrauskas, Valiunas ir partneriai LAWIN in Lithuania.

The firm's lawyers have been at the centre of many of the most important legal matters in Latvia, and the entire team prides itself on maintaining the highest quality in its work product and the strength of its well-established reputation.

The firm is listed in most important law directories, and has the responsibility for preparing and revising the *Martindale-Hubbell Law Directory*, the prominent internationally published digest of Latvian law.

Klavins & Slaidins is concerned about its social environment. The firm donates its time and services to law schools and other worthy non-legal causes. It strives to set a best-practices example in ethics. The firm will not represent a client if the client or the goal of the representation is not completely ethical in substance – form is not enough.

Some of the important areas of activity by members of the firm include: membership of the boards of directors of American and British Chambers of Commerce in Latvia; member of the board and work as arbitrators at the Latvian Chamber of Commerce arbitration tribunal; lecturing at the Riga Graduate School of Law, at the University of Latvia Law Faculty and at the training centre for judges.

Klavins & Slaidins is active in the International Bar Association and the Foreign Investors Council in Latvia.

AREAS OF PRACTICE

Klavins & Slaidins is a specialist in transactions, especially those that are sophisticated or which present unusual circumstances where the firm can use its long years of experience to craft innovative and practical solutions. Klavins & Slaidins is a trusted and reliable outside corporate counsel, helping to fine-tune the daily life of businesses. The firm is a fierce advocate for its clients, whether in negotiations or when formal dispute settlement procedures cannot be avoided and the client is in court or arbitration. The firm is international, with lawyers having practised in, and admitted to, the bars in the US and the UK, adding an additional depth of vision when it provides legal advice about Latvia to clients far beyond Latvia's borders.

Klavins & Slaidins' international practice is enhanced by its membership of the network of leading law firms in jurisdictions all over the world, Lex Mundi.

Klavins & Slaidins' general area of practice is business/commercial law. The firm provides legal consultation and advice to international clients coming to Latvia from all over the world, as well as experienced guidance for local Latvian clients. Klavins & Slaidins specialises in work as outside general counsel for a great many clients, as well as transactional expertise in sophisticated areas of corporate and joint venture structuring, mergers and acquisitions, sale and lease of business and property, loan documentation, all manner of contracts, privatisation, banking and securities, labour law and tax.

KRONBERGS & ČUKSTE

KRONVALDA BULVARIS 3-5
1010 RIGA

Telephone: +371 704 3801
Fax: +371 704 3804
E-mail: advocate@kcadvokati.lv
Website: www.kcadvokati.lv

Languages
English, Latvian, Russian

Number of lawyers 14

Contacts
Valters Kronbergs (valters.kronbergs@kclegal.lv), Vineta Čukste (vineta.cukste@kclegal.lv)

Member
Baltic Legal Solutions, a pan-Baltic legal network including Teder Glikman & Partnerid in Estonia and Jurevicius, Balciunas & Barticus in Lithuania

CATEGORIES OF WORK

- **Energy and utilities**
- **Company law**
- **Corporate law**
- **Competition law**
- **Leases and leasing**
- **Business law**
- **Privatisation**
- **Foreign investment**
- **International commercial law**
- **Intellectual property**
- **Banking law**
- **Securities**
- **Finance**
- **Telecommunications law**
- **Mergers and acquisitions**
- **Real estate**
- **Construction law**
- **Environmental law**
- **Maritime law**
- **Shipping**
- **European Union law**
- **Debt collection**
- **Labour and employment**
- **Tax litigation**
- **Civil litigation**

LEJINS, TORGANS & PARTNERS

20 KR VALDEMARA IELA
1010 RIGA

Telephone: +371 782 1525
Fax: +371 782 1524
E-mail: lt–v@lt–v.lv
Website: www.lt–v.lv

Languages
English, German, Russian

Number of lawyers 16

Member
RoschierRaidla; Meritas; ius laboris, International Employment Law; Pensions and Employee Benefits Alliance

CATEGORIES OF WORK

Banking and finance
Andrejs Lielkalns

Commercial property, real estate
Guntars Zile

Competition
Dace Silava-Tomsone

Commercial
Girts Lejins

Corporate
Toms Sulmanis

Dispute resolution, litigation and arbitration
Martins Aljens

Foreign investments
Girts Lejins

Insolvency, corporate restructuring
Aldis Gobzems

Labour
Toms Sulmanis

Mergers and acquisitions
Dace Silava-Tomsone

Privatisation
Girts Lejins

Intellectual property
Aiga Klimovica

Securities
Andrejs Lielkalns

Tax
Jeva Smilgaine

LOZE, GRUNTE & CERS

BLAUMANA 22
1011 RIGA

Telephone: +371 783 0000
Fax: +371 783 0001
E-mail: lgc@lg-c.lv
Website: www.lg-c.lv

Languages
English, French, German, Latvian, Russian,

Number of lawyers 28

International groupings
TAGLaw (The Appleton Group Legal Network); Interlaw; IBA (International Bar Association); ILN (International Lawyers Network); TerraLex

CATEGORIES OF WORK

Mergers and acquisitions

Structuring and implementation of business transactions

Competition law

Company law

Corporate and commercial law

Real estate transactions

Foreign investments

Intellectual property/trade marks

Litigation and arbitration

Telecommunications and energy law

European Union law

Administrative law

Corporate recovery

Banking and finance

Employment law

Insurance law

Private equity

Building law

THE FIRM

Full service law firm Loze, Grunte & Cers was formed in May 2005 by the merger of two of the leading and most experienced Latvian law firms, who together have more than 13 years' experience in the legal market. The firm comprises 28 lawyers in all, made up of nine partners, one administrative partner and 19 associate lawyers. The specialisation of the professionals and the pre-eminent capacity of the firm allow it to offer the highest quality legal assistance, as well as the implementation of large-scale international projects.

By providing legal advice to clients who operate in Latvia's booming economy, the firm has attained the highest professional level and become one of the leaders in the Latvian legal community.

The firm's lawyers are active members of a number of professional and non-governmental organisations. Some important areas of activity by members of Loze, Grunte & Cers include: the Latvian International Court of Arbitration, the board of directors of WWF Latvia and American, British, Danish and Swedish Chambers of Commerce in Latvia. The firm's lawyers have devoted excessive amounts of time to provide assistance to projects of public importance.

In addition to the Baltic perspective, where Loze, Grunte & Cers collaborates with such well-known and highly valued professionals as Tark & Co in Estonia and Sutkiene, Pilkauskas & Partners in Lithuania, the firm has developed a long track record of successful collaboration with several leading law firms in Scandanavia, Great Britain, the US, Germany and in many other countries worldwide. The firm's wide range of collaboration partners enables the firm to assist clients by obtaining legal services from the best experts of the respective branch abroad as well.

AREAS OF PRACTICE

Loze, Grunte & Cers is a full service law firm, with a general practice area in business and commercial law. It provides legal advice to international clients coming to Latvia from across the world, as well as eperienced guidance for local clients. The firm's practice prioritises work as outside general counsel for many clients, as well as transactional expertise in sophisticated areas of corporate and joint venture structuring, mergers and acquisitions, sale and lease of businesses and property, loan documentation, all manner of contracts, banking and securities, as well as competition, intellectual property and labour law. The firm handles the design and implementation of tax-efficient structures, corporate and shareholding structuring, structuring of business transactions such as sales, purchases, leasing and rent, financing and borrowing, transactions with intangible assets, import and export and repatriation of profits. The firm advises on compliance assurance, tax reviews and tax due diligence and on disputes with authorities and also provides professional advice on financial accounting matters.

The firm's established clients in Latvia include: Severstallat, Cemex, AirBaltic, DDB Latvia, Kesko Food, ICA Baltic AB, MasterFoods, SCA, STatoil, Kodak, Volvo Car Corporation, Skandinaviska Enskilda Banken (SEB), Sampo, Linstow Varner, Philip Morris, Nicon, Michelin and many more prominent international businesses.

LIEPA, SKOPINA/BORENIUS

LACPLESA STR 20A
1011 RIGA

Telephone: +371 7 201 800
Fax: +371 7 201 801
E-mail: advokati@borenius.lv
Website: www.borenius.lv

Languages
English, Finnish, French, German, Russian, Swedish

Number of lawyers 14

Other Borenius group member firms
Borenius & Kemppinen (Helsinki);
Luiga Mody Hääl Borenius (Tallinn);
Foigt & Partners/Regija Borenius (Vilnius)

CATEGORIES OF WORK

Banking and finance

Capital markets

Commercial property

Company and commercial

EU

Electronic commerce

Foreign investments

IP/IT, broadcasting and media law

Labour

Litigation, ADR and arbitration

Maritime, shipping and transport

Mergers and acquisitions

Private equity and venture capital

Privatisation

Real estate

Securities

Tax law

ROZENFELDS & PARTNERS

BLAUMANA STREET 11/13, APT 8
1011 RIGA

Telephone: +371 782 1563
Fax: +371 724 2202
E-mail: law@rozenfelds.lv
Website: www.rozenfelds.lv

Languages
English, Russian

Number of lawyers 2

Contacts
Janis Rozenfelds (partner),
Vadims Mantrovs (associate)

CATEGORIES OF WORK

Intellectual property – trade marks, copyright
Janis Rozenfelds

Real estate
Janis Rozenfelds

Litigation and arbitration
Janis Rozenfelds

Competition law
Janis Rozenfelds

Corporate law
Vadims Mantrovs

Claims of damages
Vadims Mantrovs

Labour disputes
Vadims Mantrovs

Maritime law
Vadims Mantrovs

SKUDRA & UDRIS

MARIJAS IELA 13
1050 RIGA

Telephone: +371 781 2078
Fax: +371 782 8171
E-mail: attorneys@su.lv
Website: www.su.lv

Languages
English, German, Russian

Number of lawyers 9

Contact
Ziedonis Udris

CATEGORIES OF WORK

Banking and finance
A Skudra

Mergers and acquisitions
A Skudra

Corporate finance
A Skudra

Litigation
Z Udris

Arbitration
Z Udris

Real property
Z Udris, I Berzina

Commercial law
Z Udris, M Krumins

Corporate law
A Skudra, Z Udris

EU and competition law
Z Udris

Shipping and transport
Z Udris

Media and entertainment
M Krumins

Energy and infrastructure projects
Z Udris

Intellectual property
M Krumins

Employment law
A Skudra

SORAINEN LAW OFFICES

VALDEMARA CENTRE
KR VALDEMARA STREET 21
1010 RIGA

Telephone: +371 7 365 000
Fax: +371 7 365 001
E-mail: sorainen@sorainen.lv
Website: www.sorainen.com

Languages
English, French, German, Latvian, Russian

Other offices
Tallinn, Vilnius

Number of lawyers 65
at this office 22

CATEGORIES OF WORK

Mergers and acquisitions
Gints Vilgerts, Brigita Terauda

Property and construction law
Girts Ruda, Lelde Lavina

Financial and securities law
Girts Ruda, Rudolfs Engelis

Company law
Brigita Terauda, Evita Gosa

Trade and distribution and services
Julija Jerneva, Brigita Terauda

Insurance law
Gints Vilgerts, Anete Rubene

Employment law
Agris Repss, Andis Burkevics

Taxation law
Janis Taukacs, Edgars Koskins

Competition and public procurement law
Rudolfs Engelis, Debora Pavila

Litigation and arbitration
Agris Repss, Ilze Znotina

Shipping and transport
Gints Vilgerts, Agris Repss

Insolvency and debt collection
Janis Taukacs, Edgars Koskins

Intellectual property
Agris Repss, Brigita Terauda

Energy and environmental law
Julija Jerneva, Evita Gosa

Information technology and telecoms
Agris Repss, Evita Gosa

THE FIRM

Established in 1997 in Riga, today Sorainen Law Offices is one of the largest business law firms operating in Latvia. The firm's affiliated offices in Estonia and Lithuania are part of a fully integrated, pan-Baltic legal practice with a strong international element. Sorainen Law Offices advises the world's leading companies, financial institutions and private investors on their most demanding transactions and assignments.

AREAS OF PRACTICE

The firm's strategic focus is on M&A. Consequently, the firm is involved in most major M&A transactions in Latvia and the Baltic States. Sorainen Law Offices has built its practice through its organic growth and outstanding service. Its corporate and competition team is one of the most experienced in the Baltic States. Being a full-service law firm, Sorainen Law Offices also assists domestic and international clients in the areas of banking and finance, insurance, corporate and commercial, shipping and transport, property, IT and telecoms, IPR, employment, tax, insolvency and restructuring, litigation and arbitration.

LAW FIRM OF VALTERS GENCS

3RD FLOOR
VALDEMARA CENTER
VALDEMARA STREET 21
1010 RIGA

Telephone: +371 724 0090
Fax: +371 724 0091
E-mail: valters.gencs@gencs.lv
Website: www.gencs.lv

Languages
English, Russian, German

Number of lawyers 10

Contact
Valters Gencs (advocate)

Member
International Bar Association; Latvian Bar Association; Licensing Executives Society; International Trade Mark Association

CATEGORIES OF WORK

Business law	**Corporate transactions**
Tax	**Immigration and labour**
Litigation and arbitration	**Intellectual property**
Finance and banking	**Due diligence**
Insolvency	**Real property**
Entertainment law	**Company law**
Competition	**Government contracts**
Mergers and acquisitions	**Shipping**
Art law	

THE FIRM

The Law Firm of Valters Gencs is a full-service, general practice, international business law firm focused on tax, litigation, corporate, immigration, finance and intellectual property law. The firm was established in 2000 by founding partner Valters Gencs, a US and Latvia educated lawyer.

The firm is an active member of the Latvian Bar Association and International Bar Association, as well as foreign chambers of commerce in Latvia. Valters Gencs serves as a board member of the Swedish Chamber of Commerce in Latvia.

The firm's staff comprises a team of ten lawyers and tax advisers. The firm's lawyers have previous experience of working with the Enterprise Register of Latvia, as well as the Ministry of Finance, the Ministry of Foreign Affairs, the Ministry of Economy and the European Integration Bureau and banking sector. Members of the firm have lectured on tax and commercial law issues with the Stockholm School of Economics in Riga.

The firm's representative clients include multinational companies, as well as medium-size companies and entrepreneurial growth companies. The firm has also represented the government of Latvia in an international arbitration case in Denmark and Sweden.

Publicly-disclosed representative clients include: Statoil ASA (Denmark); Nestlé SA (Switzerland); Siemens (Sweden); L'Oreal (France); Wyeth Pharmaceuticals (UK); Firebird Republic Funds (USA); Sony Computer Entertainment (Japan); Mastercard (Belgium); Coca-Cola (USA); McDonalds (USA); General Motors (USA); Infineon technoloiges AG (Germany); Sotheby's (UK).

AREAS OF PRACTICE

Tax: tax planning and optimisation; international cross-border transactions; VAT; social security; corporate income tax; withholding taxes; personal taxation, including filling of annual tax returns for expatriates; representation before tax authorities; appeal of tax assessments; preparation of declarations; arranging residence certificates according to double taxation agreements; property tax; payroll taxes; VAT representations and registration; excise tax; packaging tax; natural resource tax; state dues; land transfer dues; individual clients; tax audits; accounting consulting.

Litigation and arbitration: arbitrating before the Latvian Chamber of Commerce and Industry; representation of clients with all the courts in the Republic of Latvia, including the Supreme Court and arbitrations.

Business law: registrations with a commercial register; company establishments and start-ups; company restructuring and reorganisation; liquidations; mergers and acquisitions; contracts; real estate; mortgages and pledges; security interests; work contracts; registered office services; EU law.

Immigration: arranging visas and residence permits for expatriates in Latvia, arranging work permits for expatriates, appealing decisions of immigration authorities.

Insolvency: representing creditors within company insolvency procedures; purchases of assets from insolvent companies; criminal proceedings against bad-faith debtors.

Finance: EU funds; arranging credit facilities; representing borrowing and lending entities; finance; corporate finance; management consults.

Investments: securing for legal protections of foreign investment in Latvia; application of investment protection treaties to dispute regarding changing of investment climate; securing of financial investments; investments in energy sector and infrastructure.

Intellectual property: registering patents, trade marks, designs and mask works with the Latvian Patent Office and EU Trademark Office; patent and trade mark protection management within the Baltic States and the rest of the former USSR; licensing and franchising of IP; unfair competitors and protection of know-how and trade secrets; valuation of IP; royalties; technology transfer.

Due diligence: tax due diligence before company acquisitions; legal due diligence; post-acquisitions due diligence.

LEBANON

Population	3.8 million
Number of lawyers	n/a
Professional title	Advocate
Currency	Lebanese Pound (LBP)

Index

Lebanon lies at the heart of the Middle East. Its long and often tumultuous history has contributed to a rich, mosaic culture, which is home to both Muslims and Christians.

Once called the 'Paris of the Middle East', the country's capital Beirut remains an important merchant city, strategically placed on traditional trade routes still used today. Although Beirut has been bombed, invaded and occupied during 16 years of civil war, the city has rebuilt itself, both in terms of infrastructure and cultural pride. Tripoli, north of Beirut, is Lebanon's second city and is a major trading centre for northern Lebanon.

Although there is still a long way to go, Lebanon is evolving as a centre of diversity and a home to different traditions, with an Arabic, French and English-speaking population. The potential to create tangible commercial and financial opportunities is already being realised, and the country is steadily attracting tourism, trade and industry.

Lebanon was granted independence from France in 1943. Since the French departed, peace has always been a fragile affair. Upon independence, the Lebanese population grew divided by political power-struggles. Christian groups largely held control of the country and Muslims were excluded from government, resulting in inevitable tensions that lasted nearly two decades.

Simultaneously, Lebanon gradually fell into the fate of Middle Eastern conflict, as displaced Palestinian refugees sought shelter in Lebanon's mountainous terrain, giving rise to the infamous Hizbullah group. From 1975 until the early 1990s, Lebanon was torn by civil war and overtaken by Israeli and Syrian troops and the Palestine Liberation Organisation, all of whom used the country to stage their own conflicts.

Although a peace accord was officially signed in 1989, tensions quite obviously still remain. In 2005, Lebanese Prime Minister Rafik Hariri was assassinated. At the time of writing, Syria remains at the centre of UN investigations into the assassination. Despite the end of civil war nearly 20 years ago, 17,000 Syrian soldiers stayed in Lebanon until 2005 – it was only after considerable international pressure that Syria ended its 29-year military presence in Lebanon.

The Lebanese parliamentary assembly is now dominated by members opposed to Syrian influence in Lebanon, although president General Emile Lahoud enjoys Syrian support. Elected in summer 2005, the new prime minister, Fouad Siniora, spearheading the anti-Syrian coalition, has planned a programme of reform and development.

BILLING

Lebanese billing culture has traditionally been based on monthly or annual retainers, and this remains the preferable billing system for Lebanese clients, although most law firms themselves prefer using hourly fees. International clients are typically charged by the hour, and hourly rates vary from US$100 to US$350 depending on the seniority of the lawyer and the type of work involved.

MARKETING

The Lebanese Bar has a stringent set of rules, which prohibits law firms from actively seeking publicity. Technically, law firms are not permitted websites; a few firms nevertheless do have sites, although they simply display contact details and are not used as marketing tools.

ECONOMY

The legacy of civil war has left a financial scar on the Lebanese government, which now owes almost US$30bn in foreign debt. But the fact that the country has established a liberal economy is an indication of its determination to re-establish its economic infrastructure. Although admittedly the economy is quieter than it was, its potential should not be underestimated.

There was a time when Beirut was a banking and financial centre, for the entire Middle East. When the oil boom of the 60s first kicked off, it was Lebanon, and its banks in Beirut, that stood at the receiving end of the region's petrodollars. Civil war, inevitably, put a hold on all that. Now, Lebanon's commercial banking sector is back with vengeance. Since 1992, Lebanon's banking sphere has seen unprecedented growth, raising billions of US dollars on the international capital, debt and equity markets. The banking and financial services sector now represents about 70% of the nation's total GNP at present.

Meanwhile, Lebanese authorities are planning to diversify the financial sector by creating more private financial institutions, in addition to what already exists in the commercial banking sphere. Several private investment banks have already opened in Beirut.

In some ways, the Lebanese economy is commendably different from other Middle Eastern economies, with a free market which has encouraged the growth of an entrepreneurial private sector. However, observers are cautious

The largest firms

1	Badri and Salim El Meouchi Law Firm	27
2	Raphaël & Associés	26
3	Alem & Associates	23
4	Jamaleddine Law Firm	22
5	Fenianos Law Firm	21
6	Moghaizel Law Offices	20
7	Abousleiman & Partners	19
8	Baroudi & Associates	18
9	George Jabre & Associates	17
10	Tyan & Zgheib	16
11	Abouhamad, Merheb, Nohra, Chamoun, Chedid	15
12	Ibrahim Najjar Law Firm	14
13	Khattar Associates	12
	Lyan & Associés	12
15	Albert and Ziad Najm Law Firm	10
16	Ramzi Joreige and Partners	9
17	Nabil Abdel - Malek's Law Offices	8
	Sami S Nahas Law Offices	8
19	Batonnier Marcel Sioufi, Law Firm of	7
	Berti Law Firm	7
	Ghaleb S Mahmassani Law Firm	7
	Souaiby and Rassi Law Firm	7
23	Walid Nasser & Associates	6
24	Jamil Kanaan Law Office	5
	Obeid Law Firm (OLF)	5
26	Nabil Y Chamas Law Firm	4
	Saba & Co	4

These figures represent the total number of lawyers in this country only, and have been supplied by the firms themselves. The figures should be accurate as at 1 January 2006.

about getting too carried away with the progress that has been made. Those who were once positive about the economy's upturn have been forced to think again, confronted by the blunt reality of the assassination of the late prime minister Hariri in 2005.

Hariri had a positive impact on Lebanon's economy, playing a conspicuous role rebuilding Lebanon's financial prowess. It was, after all, Hariri's government that rebuilt Beirut's old commercial district, a project costing US$30bn. With Hariri no longer in the picture, economists are worried about Lebanon's ability to sustain its economic progress. Privatisation has stopped, and there are fears that the economy will be over-exploited by Syrian interests. Hariri's death has placed the stability of Lebanon's economy in jeopardy and before economic progress can become a priority, Lebanon must first solve its political problems peacefully.

LEGAL SYSTEM AND LEGAL MARKET

The government has ensured that the legal system actively fosters foreign investment and consequently, Lebanon has a well-developed, transparent and sophisticated legal market. Although the domestic market may be small, it is well connected globally via 'best-friends' arrangements with foreign firms, which are not permitted to open in Lebanon.

Abousleiman & Partners has informal ties with the likes of **Dewey Ballantine** and **Norton Rose**, and **Raphaël & Associés** deals closely with **Ernst & Young Global Limited**.

Badri and Salim El Meouchi Law Firm is associated with Paris-based **Baillart & Associés**. **Alem & Associates** has close links with some of the best regional firms in the entire Middle East, such as **Sabbagh & Associates Law Office** in Syria and **Law Offices of Dr Mujahid M. Al-Sawwaf** in Saudi Arabia.

Clifford Chance's large Middle East practice in Dubai regularly advises clients with interests in Lebanon. Similarly, both **Pinsent Masons** and **Freshfields Bruckhaus Deringer** have handled international arbitrations arising from projects in Lebanon. **Dewey Ballantine** first tapped into the Lebanese market in 1994, and has since then been acting as international counsel to the Lebanese Republic and to clients such as Deutsche Bank, Citigroup Global Markets and Banque du Liban.

BANKING AND FINANCE

BANKING AND FINANCE

ABOUSLEIMAN & PARTNERS
BADRI AND SALIM EL MEOUCHI LAW FIRM
NABIL ABDEL – MALEK'S LAW OFFICES

Abouhamad, Merheb, Nohra, Chamoun, Chedid
Alem & Associates
Jamaleddine Law Firm ✪
Lyan & Associés
Moghaizel Law Offices
Nasri Antoine Diab Law Firm
Raphaël & Associés
Tyan & Zgheib ✪

Firms are listed A-Z in tiers which are ranked in order of priority
✪ *Indicates firm displays contact details at the end of this chapter.*

Abousleiman & Partners has represented almost every bank in Lebanon, including big players like Banque de la Méditerranée, First National Bank and Crédit Libanais. The ten-partner firm advised on Banque Audi's acquisition of Banque Saradar, and is one of the few firms in Lebanon with a developed capital markets team. **Abousleiman & Partners** has been involved in the issuance of Eurobonds for the Lebanese Republic and handled numerous financing projects, including one for Phoenicia Intercontinental Hotel valued at over US$100m.

Badri and Salim El Meouchi Law Firm has a sophisticated banking practice, which is often commented upon as 'very professional and very competent'. The 27-lawyer firm offers expert advice on all aspects of banking and financial transactions, and has advised on major acquisitions within this sector.

Nabil Abdel – Malek's Law Offices is one of Beirut's outstanding law firms. The firm is retained by the largest international banks in Lebanon, including Credit Suisse First Boston, Deutsche Bank and ABN Amro. Since 1993, **Nabil Abdel – Malek's Law Offices** has been advising Merrill Lynch and BNP Paribas on their sovereign Eurobonds with the Lebanese government, ranging from US$500m to US$1bn in value.

Abouhamad, Merheb, Nohra, Chamoun, Chedid has a respected banking practice, headed by Antoine Merheb. This firm has been singled out by other players in the Lebanese legal market, for its level of in-depth expertise. **Abouhamad, Merheb, Nohra, Chamoun, Chedid** acts for about six of the biggest and most important banks in Lebanon, including Société de Banque au Liban, and also represents the Association of Lebanese Banks.

Twenty-three-lawyer **Alem & Associates**' banking practice is headed by Ziad Dannaoui. The firm has been involved in some large financial transactions; examples include advising Al Sadafi Group (a major Lebanese holding group) in relation to the structuring of a mezzanine financing facility for the acquisition of an alpha-tier bank in Lebanon, valued at US$165m. **Alem & Associates** also advised Rikaz Development Company and the Shamil Bank of Bahrain on the structuring of the first real estate investment fund to have been regulated by the Bahrain Monetary Agency, valued at US$124m.

Headed by name partner Fady Jamaleddine, **Jamaleddine Law Firm**'s reputation is fast growing. Its most major client in this sector is Jammal Trust Bank, and it also represents some smaller financial corporations on their banking matters on a broad variety of financial regulatory issues, foreign direct investment, infrastructure and project finance.

Eleven-lawyer **Lyan & Associés** advises Gulf International Bank and Arab Banking Corporation on all banking and financial matters. The firm has a small three-lawyer office in Panama to assist on international legal matters.

Other law firms commend **Moghaizel Law Offices** for its 'professionalism and positive attitude'. Of its 20 lawyers, three are specialised in banking law, namely managing partner Fadi Moghaizel, Amine Barsa and Katia Bou Assa. The firm advises a number of banks and financial institutions, including Citigroup, Citibank and HSBC, on all aspects of banking law, including banking litigation, bank contracts, secured lending, loans and securitisation.

Described as 'specialised, professional and very efficient', **Nasri Antoine Diab Law Firm** is developing its banking and finance practice, which advises Lebanese and Middle Eastern clients on complex financial transactions, securitisation and asset finance work. The five-partner firm has represented Demo Securitisation on almost all of its securitisation transactions so far in Lebanon, and has also good experience of Islamic finance.

Raphaël & Associés works closely with **Ernst & Young Global Limited**. The firm represents some Lebanese and international banks, and is 'one of the very few firms that isn't just a one-man show', while another comment was '**Raphaël & Associés** has dependable senior partners, and everyone works together as a team.'

Tyan & Zgheib recently advised on a credit agreement between World Business Capital and a Lebanese company.

CORPORATE AND M&A

ALEM & ASSOCIATES
BADRI AND SALIM EL MEOUCHI LAW FIRM
MOGHAIZEL LAW OFFICES
NABIL ABDEL – MALEK'S LAW OFFICES
TYAN & ZGHEIB ✪

Abouhamad, Merheb, Nohra, Chamoun, Chedid
Abousleiman & Partners
Albert and Ziad Najm Law Firm
Fathallah & Associates
Ibrahim Najjar Law Firm ✪
Jamaleddine Law Firm ✪
Jamil Kanaan Law Office
Lyan & Associés
Nasri Antoine Diab Law Firm
Obeid Law Firm (OLF)
Oussama El Aref Law Office
Raphaël & Associés
Walid Nasser & Associates

Firms are listed A-Z in tiers which are ranked in order of priority
✪ Indicates firm displays contact details at the end of this chapter.

CORPORATE AND M&A

Moving into the top tier on account of its international expertise and high-profile, high-quality work, **Alem & Associates** has an excellent corporate practice led by Rola Tabsh. This well-established 23-lawyer firm has advised Morgan Stanley Dean Witter, Credit Suisse First Boston, Johnson & Johnson, Amazon, the Space Toon Group and Escape Music Channel. Additionally, **Alem & Associates** has advised on several, major, multi-million-dollar real estate development projects in Lebanon, Saudi Arabia and Dubai.

'You only ever hear good things being said about **Badri and Salim El Meouchi Law Firm**' was the praise proffered by one client about this firm. With about 27 lawyers, it is one of the biggest firms in Lebanon, and has a reputation to match, especially when it comes to across-the-board corporate work. Led by Salim El Meouchi, described as 'one of the best lawyers in town', the firm has worked on some hefty M&A work, such as advising Standard Chartered Bank on its acquisition of Metropolitan Bank. Other clients include Virgin Lebanon, L'Oréal, The Coral Oil Company and Star Property.

Moghaizel Law Offices is the go-to firm for transactional work, predominantly advising international buyers on their purchases in the Middle East. It recently advised on a large acquisition of a mineral water production plant on behalf of an international purchaser. About five of **Moghaizel Law Offices**' 20 lawyers work wholly on corporate and commercial matters, and the firm represents a wide range of corporations and *Fortune 500* multinationals, including Hewlett-Packard, IBM and Microsoft. The team also stands apart from the crowd thanks to its structured and dedicated insurance practice, which advises American Life Insurance and Scottish Life. **Moghaizel Law Offices**' lawyers are praised for being 'very thorough and up-to-date – these guys know what they're doing'.

Nabil Abdel – Malek's Law Offices advised on four M&A deals during the course of 2005. The firm represents a wide range of international clients, including EMI Music, Standard Chartered Bank and Caltex, and offers consultancy services on compliance and regulatory matters in addition to its general corporate and commercial expertise. Clients recommend the firm because 'it knows how to handle its international clients well'.

Tyan & Zgheib grew from 11 partners to 16 in the course of 2005. The firm recently advised on Caricorp's acquisition of a Lebanese entity, and remains involved in contractual negotiations between British American Tobacco and its Arab distributors.

Sixteen-lawyer **Abouhamad, Merheb, Nohra, Chamoun, Chedid** represents the Consolidated Contractors Company, a regional construction company, and a key client for the firm. At present, **Abouhamad, Merheb, Nohra, Chamoun, Chedid** is advising the main Lebanese company behind the Sannine Project, one of the largest tourist development projects in the region.

Abousleiman & Partners is distinguished by its securitisation specialisation. The firm handled a major IPO for a Lebanese bank and also for a number of companies within the hotel and leisure sector. Clients include Heineken, Schindler and Libano-Swiss Insurance.

Eleven-lawyer **Albert and Ziad Najm Law Firm** is known as a shipping, maritime and marine insurance firm. It has worked closely with **Clyde & Co** and **Holman Fenwick & Willan** in the past, and most recently collaborated with **Barlow Lyde & Gilbert** on a US$3m livestock mortality insurance claim on behalf of Libano Arabe Insurance.

Fathallah & Associates has won some big-ticket work recently for major European and international companies seeking to enter the Lebanese market. In particular, the firm has carved a niche for itself advising clients from the hotel management sector on contractual work, financing and arbitration.

About 75% of **Ibrahim Najjar Law Firm**'s clients are international, and the firm's corporate team benefits from its close links to international law firms. It has particular experience advising on commercial international distributorship agreements. **Ibrahim Najjar Law Firm** was recently boosted by the arrival of British solicitor Paul Egerton-Vernon, specialised in advising off-shore companies on trusts matters. Vernon worked previously for Rathbones Trust Company in the UK.

Jamaleddine Law Firm represents some of the most popular names in contemporary mainstream style, such as European fashion houses Mango and Zara, which the firm advises on commercial contracts in the Middle East. The firm has acted on behalf of the Council for Development and Reconstruction, and Solidere, the company behind most of the regeneration and reconstruction projects in Beirut.

Nicholas Kanaan is the main English-speaking lawyer at **Jamil Kanaan Law Office**, which focuses almost exclusively on commercial work. The firm represents local, Saudi Arabian and Kuwaiti clients on their investments in Lebanon, and advises a number of banks and insurance companies, such as Fransabank, Groupe Cassar, and the Union Franco-Arabe d'Assurance & de Reassurances.

Lyan & Associés saw US$200m-worth of telecoms-related corporate transactions in 2005. The firm represents about 90% of broadcasting operators in Lebanon, and is assisting the government on its formation of new broadcasting legislation.

Although its predominant focus is on banking and finance work, **Nasri Antoine Diab Law Firm** has a general corporate and commercial division, which advises on contractual work in Lebanon. The firm often works closely with **Jones Day** in Paris.

Three-lawyer **Obeid Law Firm (OLF)** advised several Lebanese companies on contractual arrangements, and has also advised the Lebanese government.

Oussama El Aref Law Office is an eight-lawyer firm, which represents a sizeable proportion of clients from the Gulf. The firm is handling a large volume of hotel projects for high-profile Middle Eastern and international investors. Name partner Oussama El Aref serves on the board of directors for a number of Lebanese companies.

Raphaël & Associés is spoken well of in the Lebanese legal market, described as 'a firm with high standards and determination.' Moussa Raphaël heads an established corporate division which has good international links with firms in Egypt and Saudi Arabia.

Walid Nasser & Associates represents international corporations from the pharmaceutical, software and film industries on general corporate issues. The firm has good links with firms in Dubai.

DISPUTE RESOLUTION

Litigation and arbitration accounts for a significant proportion of **Badri and Salim El Meouchi Law Firm**'s workload. There are 17 lawyers working in the dispute resolution division making it one of the largest disputes teams in Lebanon. **Badri and Salim El Meouchi Law Firm** has also been selected to serve as Lebanon's legal experts on the European Commission's 'Europaid' project for the promotion of international commercial arbitration.

Ibrahim Najjar Law Firm's most important area of practice is arbitration. Ibrahim Najjar, a well-known personality in this field, has good connections with many Western law firms. For the past three years, the firm has worked closely with **Richards Butler** on arbitration and litigation affairs, and has similar links to firms in Switzerland, France and Canada.

Abouhamad, Merheb, Nohra, Chamoun, Chedid has good experience of international commercial arbitration, having represented construction companies on breach of contract disputes.

Abousleiman & Partners represents foreign companies on corporate litigation, most recently representing a major Arab bank based in Bahrain.

Albert and Ziad Najm Law Firm advises on shipping insurance and reinsurance claims on behalf of major terminal operators and insurance companies. Clients include Al Ittihad Al Watani Insurance, Libano Arabe Insurance and SNA Insurance.

Alem & Associates' litigation department is led by partner Nader Obeid. The firm has represented some big names in the past year, including Sabic, the Middle East's largest non-oil industrial company, which it represented in a substantial commercial agency dispute. **Alem & Associates** has also advised Italian furniture company Della Valentina, German client Behringer International, and UK company Cookson Matthey Ceramics.

Around 50% of **Fathallah & Associates**' practice is comprised of major disputes and international arbitration work. **Fathallah & Associates** acted as co-counsel representing a major Arab hotel group in an ICC arbitration with an international hotel chain. It is advising hotel owners in relation to three ongoing construction arbitrations taking place in Cairo and is recommended by one client for its 'superb quality of work, responsiveness and integrity'.

Moghaizel Law Offices' litigation department benefits from its strong name in insurance law, often representing key international insurers on life insurance and injury claims. Almost 30% of the firm's overall disputes workload is insurance related; general commercial disputes make up the remainder of its litigation files. Amine Barsa and Anwar Selwan are the main litigators.

Nabil Abdel-Malek of **Nabil Abdel – Malek's Law Offices** is a respected litigator who has been involved with three major international arbitrations in London and Switzerland. The firm is representing Standard Chartered Bank and the Council of Development & Reconstruction.

Nasri Antoine Diab Law Firm's head partner, Nasri Diab, is a respected name in arbitration, having been involved in ICC arbitrations in Paris.

Obeid Law Firm (OLF)'s lead partner, Dr Nayla Comair-Obeid, has a strong background in international arbitration. The firm advised the Lebanese government in a telecoms dispute with mobile operators, and represented Kuwaiti Airlines in an international arbitration.

DISPUTE RESOLUTION

BADRI AND SALIM EL MEOUCHI LAW FIRM
IBRAHIM NAJJAR LAW FIRM ✪

Abouhamad, Merheb, Nohra, Chamoun, Chedid
Abousleiman & Partners
Albert and Ziad Najm Law Firm
Alem & Associates
Berti Law Firm
Fathallah & Associates
Moghaizel Law Offices
Nabil Abdel – Malek's Law Offices
Nasri Antoine Diab Law Firm
Obeid Law Firm (OLF)
Raphaël & Associés
Tyan & Zgheib ✪
Walid Nasser & Associates

Firms are listed A-Z in tiers which are ranked in order of priority
✪ *Indicates firm displays contact details at the end of this chapter.*

Raphaël & Associés has good experience in both litigation and arbitration, particularly when it comes to advising on disputes within the construction sector.

Tyan & Zgheib's name partner Nady Tyan acted as arbitrator in a case between the largest Lebanese real estate company and a Saudi Arabian prince.

About 85% of **Walid Nasser & Associates**' disputes caseload is intellectual property related, representing international companies in trade mark prosecution cases against pirate operators.

INTELLECTUAL PROPERTY

Lebanon's intellectual property laws remain underdeveloped, although the government has established a parliamentary committee to revise and reform IP legislation in order to tackle piracy.

Leila Laila is the person to go to for all intellectual property matters at **Alem & Associates**, which has a large and impressive IP practice. The firm moves into pole position this year, on account of its broad IP division, which goes beyond bread-and-butter trade mark registration and advises on the full gamut of IP, including technology transfers, licensing and intellectual asset management work. The firm has cross-jurisdictional experience advising international names such as Fashion Bar, the Space Toon Group and Management Recruiters International.

Badri and Salim El Meouchi Law Firm handles a variety of IP work, such as trade mark ownership and litigation. The firm advised a major US software company on its acquisition of codes and software from a regional leading software development company.

Headed by Kamal Berti, **Berti Law Firm** is recommended for its IP practice, and is well known for its trade mark litigation work.

Name partner Walid Nasser of **Walid Nasser & Associates** is a real authority on all things IP-related in Lebanon. The firm stands out from the crowd by its continual lobbying via European and

INTELLECTUAL PROPERTY

ALEM & ASSOCIATES
BADRI AND SALIM EL MEOUCHI LAW FIRM
BERTI LAW FIRM
WALID NASSER & ASSOCIATES

Albert and Ziad Najm Law Firm
Antoine E Henoud Law Firm
Ibrahim Najjar Law Firm ✪
Jamaleddine Law Firm ✪
Moghaizel Law Offices
Oussama El Aref Law Office
Raphaël & Associés

Firms are listed A-Z in tiers which are ranked in order of priority
✪ *Indicates firm displays contact details at the end of this chapter.*

US embassies in Lebanon in order to convince Lebanese authorities to take a stronger stance against piracy prosecution. **Walid Nasser & Associates** advises a Saudi Arabian satellite television company on its rights agreements, and represents well-known international names in the pharmaceutical, software and film industries.

A substantial proportion of **Ibrahim Najjar Law Firm**'s caseload is IP related. The firm represents one of the largest Middle Eastern media houses on its IP litigation matters.

Many other firms advise on trade mark registration and copyright protection. **Albert and Ziad Najm Law Firm** collaborated with **Clyde & Co** on trade mark registration in Lebanon, while **Antoine E Henoud Law Firm** advises multinationals on trade mark infringements and related litigation. **Jamaleddine Law Firm**, **Moghaizel Law Offices** and **Oussama El Aref Law Office** also do similar work regarding trade mark protection and litigation.

PRIVATISATION

Privatisation has more or less stopped at present in Lebanon. The Lebanese government has largely put all of its potential projects on pause; its priorities are to stabilise the political regime. The murder of former Prime Minister Hariri placed the government in a period of uncertainty, which is a turn-off to potential foreign investors. Without the financial input of investors and foreign banks, Lebanon cannot realistically afford to proceed with privatisation plans, which have regardless been pending for the last five years.

There are however some firms who have contributed to paving the way for privatisation, which should make it a smooth process when the ball starts rolling again. **Dewey Ballantine** and **Abousleiman & Partners** have together represented the Higher Council for Privatisation of the Lebanese Republic in connection with all of its privatisation projects. **Dewey Ballantine** is currently collaborating with the new government on reinitiating the overall privatisation scheme for the country.

Badri and Salim El Meouchi Law Firm has a good name for telecommunications privatisation work, having collaborated closely with the Lebanese government on legal reforms surrounding the status of public entities. It is at present advising a major Lebanese bank on the financing of the Libanpost BOT project with the Ministry of Post & Telecommunications.

Nabil Abdel – Malek's Law Offices is another firm with a good background in privatisation. The firm assisted the Ministry of Finance on developing its privatisation law, and has been in discussions for potential privatisation within the tobacco industry.

Nasri Antoine Diab Law Firm advised the Ministry of Economy and Trade on privatisation legislation and **Tyan & Zgheib** participated in the drafting of laws preparing for the privatisation of the electricity sector in Lebanon.

PRIVATISATION

Abousleiman & Partners
Badri and Salim El Meouchi Law Firm
Nabil Abdel – Malek's Law Offices
Nasri Antoine Diab Law Firm
Raphaël & Associés
Tyan & Zgheib ✪
Walid Nasser & Associates

Firms are listed alphabetically
✪ *Indicates firm displays contact details at the end of this chapter.*

IBRAHIM NAJJAR
LAW FIRM

11 MADRASSAT EL-SALAM STREET
PO BOX 116/2270
BEIRUT

Telephone: +961 1 202 100
Fax: +961 1 201 974
E-mail: inajjar@dm.net.lb

Languages
Arabic, English, French, Spanish

Other offices
Paris

Number of lawyers 14

Contacts
Ibrahim Najjar, Nathalie Najjar, Serge Najjar

CATEGORIES OF WORK

International and domestic arbitration
Ibrahim Najjar, Nathalie Najjar

International distribution agreements
Ibrahim Najjar, Nathalie Najjar

Litigation and lawsuits management
Nathalie Najjar

Family law
Ibrahim Najjar

Intellectual property
Ibrahim Najjar, Serge Najjar

Capital markets
Serge Najjar, Paola Khoury

Mergers and acquisitions
Serge Najjar, Paul Egerton-Vernon

Real estate; acquisition of real estate by foreigners
Raïf Akl, Christel Melki

Banking and finance
Serge Najjar

Taxation
Antoine Chneyhi

Corporations and offshore corporations
Paul Egerton-Vernon

Franchise
Nathalie Najjar, Paola Khoury

Trust
Paul Egerton-Vernon

Criminal law
Antoine Khoury, Raïf Akl

JAMALEDDINE LAW FIRM

RAOUCHE-AUSTRALIA STREET
EZZEDDINE BUILDING
1ST AND 2ND FLOORS
PO BOX 13-5113
1102 2010 BEIRUT

Telephone: +961 1 809 999
Fax: +961 1 794 704
E-mail:
lawfirm@jamaleddinelawfirm.com
Website: www.jamaleddinelawfirm.com

Languages
Arabic, English, French, Finnish

Number of lawyers 22

Member
European Association of Lawyers (AEA)

CATEGORIES OF WORK

Commercial and civil law
Fady Jamaleddine

Public and administrative law
Nada Baccar

Litigation and ADR
Hanadi Hajj, Nada Nader

Banking law
Fady Jamaleddine, Chawki Assad

Corporate law
Aed Bouchakra, Hassan Sleiman

Commercial property and real estate law
Sana'a Daakour, Ayman Raad

Aviation
Fady Jamaleddine, Fatima Hussein

Intellectual property
Andre Bouchaaya, Malek Takieddine

Taxation
Fady Jamaleddine, Talal Baz

Criminal law
Hussein Kazan, Kamal Hijazi

Labour law
Andre Bouchaaya, Sana'a Daakour

International law
Fady Jamaleddine, Malek Takieddine

Maritime and admiralty
Malek Takieddine, Lina Sinno

Telecommunication law
Fady Jamaleddine, Nadine Baba

TYAN & ZGHEIB
(FORMERLY TYAN ET ASSOCIÉS)

250 SAMI EL SOLH AVENUE
MANHATTAN BUILDING
3RD FLOOR
BEIRUT

Telephone: +961 1 381 006
Fax: +961 1 381 016
E-mail: tyanasso@dm.net.lb

Languages
Arabic, English, French

Other offices
Paris

Number of lawyers 20
at this office 18

Contacts
Nady Tyan, Romy Rahmeh, Mireille Richa

International groupings
TerraLex

CATEGORIES OF WORK

Corporate and commercial	**Maritime and air transport law**
Mergers and acquisitions	**Insurance law**
Banking and finance	**Taxation**
Intellectual property	**Labour law**
Dispute resolution	**Real estate law**
Distribution and franchise agreements	**Telecommunications**

LIBYA

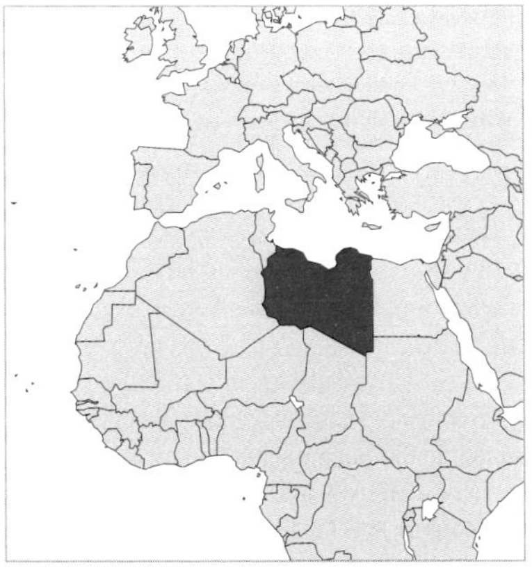

Population	**5.7 million**
Number of lawyers	**n/a**
Professional title	**Advocate**
Currency	**Libyan Dinar**
Index	
Corporate and M&A	834
Country index	**5**

Libya is back on the diplomatic world stage and is slowly regaining international acceptance since leader Mu'ammar al-Qadhafi voluntarily decided to give up his nuclear weapons programme, revealed secrets about the nuclear black market and promised to pay compensation to relatives of the 270 victims of the Lockerbie bombing.

Washington, DC has resumed formal diplomatic ties with the country, and has recently been in discussions with Libya as to the possibility of normalising relations between Libya and the United States.

Libya, (officially named The Socialist People's Libyan Arab Jamahiriya), shares its borders with Egypt, Algeria, Niger and Chad. The language is predominantly Arabic, and the capital and chief port is Tripoli, lying on the Mediterranean coast.

President Mu'ammar al-Qadhafi has been in power since his military coup of 1969 and is internationally famous for his dictatorial control. Although the country is politically stable, Libya still has no democracy or political parties, and little freedom of speech. That said, Qadhafi's control has weakened considerably with the realisation that the only way to quell public dissatisfaction was to allow private businesses to operate. However, very little progress has been made to improve Libya's human rights record, with summary executions and torture still occurring.

BILLING

Various billing methods are employed, including hourly rates, a percentage of transaction or dispute value (result-determined) and lump sums. Hourly rates are approximately €115 and fees are frequently decided by mutual agreement and depend on the nature of the case and the value of the claim.

ECONOMY

Libya's economy is relatively strong, with healthy oil revenues and a robust agricultural sector. The country's potential as an energy market has blossomed since sanctions were lifted: in January 2005 Libya awarded licences for 15 blocks of oil acreage under its exploration and production-sharing formula, with more expected to be issued.

Libya is a major oil producer with untapped reserves. Oil accounts for approximately 94% of Libya's exports and 60% of the government's income, but little revenue passes down to the man on the street: much of the population remains poor and unemployed (the unemployment rate stands at 30%).

Thanks to rising oil prices, oil export revenues have reportedly doubled in the last five years and are expected to continue increasing. Libya is making progress with economic reforms, particularly after UN sanctions were lifted in 2003, followed by the lifting of US unilateral sanctions in April 2004.

Libya's economy under the current prime minister (Ghanem) is currently undergoing an incredible business boom. Many socialist-era, government-run industries are being privatised. The second-largest public company was put up for privatisation in September 2005 – but still has some way to go in liberalising the economy to move to a market-based economy, with plans being hampered by bureaucratic resistance and frequent policy reversals. Libya's application to join the WTO is under consideration but it could take years before a decision is made.

Libya's banking system is highly centralised and transparency in the financial sector is poor. The recent lifting of sanctions is attracting foreign investment and desperately needed technology to Libya: its tourism sector was opened to foreign investors in 2004 and Libya is making concerted efforts to attract foreign investment, particularly in its oil and gas production.

Libya's telecommunications network is undergoing modernisation and an underdeveloped infrastructure is in dire need of upgrading.

LEGAL MARKET

UK firm **Denton Wilde Sapte** is increasing its presence in North Africa and one of its lawyers, Khaled Yassin (based in Cairo) is experienced in Libyan law.

Stéphane Brabant of the Paris office of **Herbert Smith LLP** is an expert in the legal framework in Libya for petroleum activities and is increasingly specialist in this field, advising a number of major clients investing in the country.

Paris-based **Eversheds-Frere Cholmeley** is headed by litigation partner David Sellers who has been involved with Libya for the last 20 years and has a working relationship with **Mukhtar-Kelbash and Elgharabli Attorneys**. The firm has worked on deals including the GPTC (Libyan post office telecoms) and the Libyan-Arab Foreign Bank on participation in and the financing of a pan-African satellite communications project.

Norton Rose has been advising clients on Libyan transactions for many years. The firm currently advises international engineering corporations and oil companies in disputes arising out of the construction of the Great Man Made River Project (GMR Project).

CORPORATE AND M&A

Three-partner firm **MTL Law Office** is large in Libyan terms, and has an associated office in Benghazi, and a liaison office in Canada. Name partner Salah Marghani spends half of his time in Canada. The firm specialises in the petroleum and the energy sectors (the firm acts for two major oil companies) and advises banking, shipping and insurance clients. On the back of the opening up of Libya's economy, the firm has significantly increased its foreign investor practice, both in the oil industry and the service sector, with clients including a major US financial corporation. **MTL Law Office** also has well-regarded commercial litigators, who recently acted for an international bank in litigation against a domestic bank, and acted for an oil operating company in domestic litigation.

Mukhtar-Kelbash and Elgharabli Attorneys leads the roster of Libyan firms specialising in oil and gas work, acting for major foreign oil companies on their negotiations with Libya. The firm also undertakes litigation and arbitration, and has a general corporate and commercial practice, advising Australian resource company Woodside Energy on a major production-sharing agreement and advising a consortium of European companies on a similar matter. The firm has forged contacts with international law firms including **Denton Wilde Sapte**, **Herbert Smith LLP**, and the Paris office of **Eversheds-Frere Cholmeley**.

Five-lawyer firm **Rajab B Bakhnug** acts primarily for Western clients, with a focus on commercial and litigation work. Rajab Bakhnug, a former government legal adviser, counts Daewoo and Hyundai among his clients.

Eight-lawyer **Tumi Law Firm** is one of the largest and most reputable law firms in Tripoli, with a broad-based legal practice incorporating banking and finance, litigation and commercial law, with a particularly strong oil and gas practice, advising clients on the domestic petroleum law. The firm recently advised on the investment and establishment of the first foreign five-star hotel in Libya; and the investment and construction of BAT's cigarette manufacturing plant in Libya. Other clients include AMEC Group, British Airways and Qatar Airways. The firm is a member of the *Arab Society for Intellectual Property*.

Abdelly & Associates is a reputable firm and advises on major real estate, construction and investment projects in Libya, and recently advised, on the establishment and registration of international companies in Libya.

Two-partner **Law Office of Dr. Ben Abderrahmane & Partners in co-operation with Massaoud El-Kanouni**, has a presence in several North African countries as well as having an office in Paris. The firm is particularly busy in the field of international contracts, corporate and commercial law and international arbitration.

El-Atrash Law Firm has been in existence for more than 50 years and has offices in Tripoli and Benghazi, boasting a substantial maritime and shipping practice. The firm acts for major domestic company, Germa Shipping & Stevedoring Company, and has advised Libya Insurance Company. The firm has successfully represented foreign ship owners and protection and indemnity associations.

Law Offices of Ibrahim Legwell has formed an alliance with Middle Eastern firm **Ali & Partners**, a major multi-regional law firm with offices also in Washington, DC and Kuwait. The 11-lawyer Tripoli office specialises in corporate transactions and representative clients include Cisco, BAE, Honeywell, Northrop Grumman, 3M and Ernst & Young. Recently, the firm assisted a large aerospace company, an oil-related service company and the national real estate company (a Libyan government agency) on tourism-related real estate transactions. In addition, it undertakes due diligence work for numerous companies and assists several companies in complying with the government procurement requirements. Dr Legwell served as the head of the defence team for the Lockerbie bombing case.

Maghur And Partners Attorneys at Law is a seven-lawyer corporate and commercial firm most notable for representing the two Libyans accused of the Lockerbie bombing. Senior partner Azza Maghur counts foreign companies among her clients including Volkswagen and Coca-Cola and has a strong litigation practice, recently representing a client in the High Court in London.

Majeri Law Office is a four-lawyer firm specialising in corporate law and banking and finance, and enjoys good relations with international law firms. The firm boasts a roster of international clients including UK companies Moreton Smith International, Pirgon Enterprises Ltd; ETEP SA Greek Co, and Turkish company, Kuryapi Construction and Trading Co Ltd. Local clients include Libya's number one bank, the National Commercial Bank, and shipping company Germa.

CORPORATE AND M&A

MTL Law Office
Mukhtar-Kelbash and Elgharabli Attorneys
Rajab B Bakhnug
Tumi Law Firm

Abdelly & Associates
Ben Abderrahmane in co-operation with Massaoud El-Kanouni (Dr) & Partners, Law Office
El-Atrash Law Firm
Ibrahim Legwell, Law Offices
Maghur And Partners Attorneys at Law
Majeri Law Office

Firms are listed A-Z in tiers which are ranked in order of priority

LIECHTENSTEIN

Population	33,700
Number of lawyers	n/a
Professional title	Rechtsanwalt; Rechtsanwältin
Currency	Swiss Franc (SFr)
Index	
Banking	836
Commercial	837
Country index	5

The Principality of Liechtenstein is one of the world's smallest and richest countries, and one of just two countries that are doubly landlocked. Liechtenstein rests between Switzerland and Austria, situated in the Upper Rhine of the Alps with a river as its western border.

It is the only country with a majority of German-speaking people that does not have Germany as a border. German is spoken with a Swiss and/or Austrian dialect, with English also commonly spoken.

Despite its tiny geographic area and relatively limited natural resources, Liechtenstein is known for its wealth and prosperity and boasts a successful financial services sector and high living standards. The country boasts low tax rates with business rates currently 18%.

Liechtenstein is a constitutional monarchy headed by Prince Hans Adam II, who has been in power since November 1989. In August 2004 he transferred official duties to his son and heir, Prince Alois. Prince Adam, a former banker, is Europe's only monarch with absolute authority to sack the government and to overrule parliament which has caused controversy in recent years.

The head of government is Ottmar Hasler with members of the unicameral Parliament (or Landtag) elected by direct popular vote under proportional representation. The next elections are due in 2009.

BILLING

Complex billing laws are set out in the Liechtenstein Lawyer's Fee Act. The Act establishes a statutory tariff that permits a maximum charge of SFr1,200 (€773) per hour (the tariff depends on the nature of work and the value of the case). Lawyers are not allowed to request a contingency fee for court work. If the lawyer and client prefer, they may discard the tariff and agree to use task-based billing instead. Task-based billing is governed by the Autonomous Fee Guidelines of the Liechtenstein Bar and ranges from SFr300 (€193) to SFr1,000 (€645) per hour. In practice, firms generally charge between SFr350 (€226) and SFr500 (€322) per hour for task-based billing.

For court work the tariff is used most frequently. For other 'out-of-court' services the lawyer may add a flat charge, the value of which must not exceed 40% or 50% of the total value of the 'in-court' charge.

Requesting fees in advance, particularly when dealing with foreign clients or offshore companies, is a standard policy because Liechtenstein court awards cannot be enforced in foreign jurisdictions – the principality is not a signatory to either the Lugano or Brussels conventions on the enforcement of foreign judgments.

ECONOMY

Liechtenstein is small and has limited natural resources but in spite of this, it is prosperous and boasts a highly industrialised economy after a history of a primarily agricultural economy. A boom arrived in the country after the Second World War, sustained by strongly increasing industrial exports and foreigners taking up residence and increasing the population.

Incorporation rules are simply enabling businesses to establish themselves in the country which provides 30% of state revenues.

Liechtenstein is fully integrated with Switzerland, with which it maintains a monetary and customs union. Liechtenstein also entrusts Switzerland with the task of representing it on the international stage. Integration is vital to the sustenance of the success of the economy given its small domestic market, and the government is taking steps to harmonise its economic policies with those of an integrated Europe.

As a member of the European Economic Area (EEA) Liechtenstein is afforded free trade rights with the EU, despite its union to a non-EU country and, in January 2005, the new Financial Market Authority (FMA) Liechtenstein began its tasks including safeguarding the stability of the Liechtenstein financial market, prevention of abuses covering the financial services, implementation of and compliance with recognised international standards and supervision and regulation (on behalf of the government) of the Liechtenstein financial market.

Liechtenstein boasts an extremely high employment rate, depending on employees from Switzerland, Austria and Germany to meet demand. That said, unemployment has doubled since 2002 to 2.4%. The country's industries include electronics and metal manufacturing, dental products and pharmaceuticals, tourism and optical instruments. Industry and manufacturing account for 40% of GDP. One of the government's foremost economy policies is the expansion of Liechtenstein's entrepreneurs by expanding a favourable environment. The country imports 90% of its energy requirements and the bulk of all manufactured goods are exported, primarily to the EU.

The financial services sector has played a major role in boosting the economy. As a low-tax haven, famed for banking discretion, the country attracts significant foreign investment, particularly in the areas of banking, trusts and insurance. Revenues from foreign companies account for 30% of the state's income. But there are also keen plans to change the tax system, and the government has recognised that the introduction of a new tax system is of long-term importance to the country.

Abuse of the finance market in Liechtenstein has been a concern for some time, and the government has recently demonstrated its determination to dispel its reputation as a centre of international money-laundering. Expansion of the financial sector over recent years has triggered the expansion of state authorities and the strengthening of the judicial system.

The revision of the Foundation Law is another step forward (the foundation is the most frequently used legal form in Liechtenstein) and, after years of preparatory work the foundation is now being carefully adjusted to the existing jurisdiction and to European legal standards. Liechtenstein law acknowledges the private law (privatrechtliche) and public law (öffentlichrechtliche) foundation.

MARKETING

The Professional Guidelines of the Liechtenstein Chamber of Lawyers sets out strict guidance restricting advertising. A limited range of passive advertising, for example, a webpage or brochure describing practice areas, is permitted; anything else, including advertising in the printed press, remains forbidden. It is illegal to refer to cases or clients in any advertisement. In-house lawyers are not admitted to the Liechtenstein Bar and readers should note that firms are subject to strict secrecy as to releasing the names of clients.

BANKING

Batliner (Dr Dr) & Dr Gasser
Batliner Wanger Batliner
Holzhacker, Law Office
Müller & Partner Rechtsanwälte
Walch & Schurti

Karlheinz Ritter (Dr iur) Lic iur Cornelia Ritter, Law Office
Lampert Schächle
Marxer (Dr) & Partner, Advokaturbüro
Seeger, Frick & Partner
Sele Frommelt & Partner
Walter Matt (Lic.iur.), Law Office

Firms are listed A-Z in tiers which are ranked in order of priority

BANKING

The banking sector in Liechtenstein has recently grown with the introduction of new regulations, including the statute on investment undertakings.

Dr Dr Batliner & Dr Gasser has a major banking practice including banking litigation. The firm has working relationships with some major international firms including **Clifford Chance**, **Simmons & Simmons** and **Baker & McKenzie**. The bulk of clients comprise Liechtenstein banks and major public and private Swiss banks. The firm has received a royal appointment by the Prince of Liechtenstein to act as his legal counsel on defending constitutional matters.

Four-partner **Batliner Wanger Batliner**'s strong banking practice has expanded rapidly with three new lawyers. Dr Martin Batliner is a member of the board of the Liechtenstein FMA. The firm represents two leading Liechtenstein banks, and international banks, law firms and trusts offices on financial matters. The firm's formidable reputation also derives from now semi-retired name partner Dr Gerard Batliner, a former board member of VP Bank and former head of the Liechtenstein Government.

Law Office Holzhacker & Struth has now ceased practising and Dr Gerhard Holzhacker continues the firm's work under his own name. His new practice, **Law Office Holzhacker** advises a number of banks, including Deutsche Bank, and advises clients on financial matters.

Müller & Partner Rechtsanwälte is a relatively young firm and now has four partners after starting out in 1997. Its reputation is growing and it has a strong banking practice advising foreign banks, financial institutions and insurance companies. The firm has advised LGT bank and its associated trust companies, as well as another large bank in Austria.

Walch & Schurti is large by Liechtenstein standards, with six partners and a total of eleven lawyers and specialises to a large extent in insurance and also undertakes banking work. The firm advises a number of foreign and domestic clients and fiduciaries, and is very strong in the US. Name partner Ernst Walch was foreign minister from 2001 to April 2005.

Law Office Dr iur Karlheinz Ritter Lic iur Cornelia Ritter derives its banking reputation from name partner Cornelia Ritter who is a board member of LLB Bank.

New entrant to the table, **Lampert Schächle** is experienced in financial market regulations and banking.

Advokaturbüro Dr Marxer & Partner is one of the oldest Liechtenstein law firms and has a major banking practice.

Seeger, Frick & Partner maintains relationships with banks such as the New Century Bank, Bank Frick & Co and Bank von Ernst (Liechtenstein).

Sele Frommelt & Partner created a private bank in 1998, which the firm continues to advise.

New entrant to the banking table is the **Law Office Lic.iur. Walter Matt** which undertakes banking and trusts work.

COMMERCIAL

Dr Dr Batliner & Dr Gasser is one of the largest and most reputable law firms in Liechtenstein, with a strong litigation practice comprising about a third of its work. Partner Wolfgang Brandstetter is a professor at the Institute for Criminal Law at the University of Vienna and undertakes major high-value criminal law and civil law cases. In 2004, the firm was appointed by the Prince of Liechtenstein to the selection panel for judges. The firm has increased its IP practice and advises on domestic and international trade marks, patents and copyright law. The firm is in partnership with leading Austrian law firm **Simma Rechtsanwälte Partnerschaft**.

Batliner Wanger Batliner's litigation work has expanded rapidly and is arguably the largest litigation department in Liechtenstein, boasting four partners and four associates. Name partner Dr Gerard Batliner has an impressive political background and is a judge at the country's administrative court and the firm also has specialist arbitration experience. The firm's commercial practice includes advising on the setting up of companies and trusts in Liechtenstein and advises international law firms in this respect.

Advokaturbüro Dr Marxer & Partner is one of the largest firms in the country with

11 partners and 13 associates. Partner Dr Peter Marxer Snr is a member of the International Academy of Estate and Trust Law and is a former party leader in the Liechtenstein parliament. The firm has a general corporate and commercial practice which includes advising on trade marks and copyright law, succession and asset management. Clients range from private individuals to international corporations. The firm is a member of *Lex Mundi* and is associated with trust company Confida.

The expanding six-partner firm of **Walch & Schurti** has a major corporate practice with clients including leading liquor and food companies, and advising on succession matters for famous international families, and trusts and foundation work. The firm also has a major litigation practice particularly in the white-collar crime sector. The firm has lawyers admitted in Liechtenstein as well as Austria, Germany, the UK and the US, from where many of the firm's clients originate. It also undertakes a lot of work for Swiss clients. Both partners, Dr Ernst Walch and Dr Andreas Schurti, are admitted in Liechtenstein and the US. The firm is a member of the *State Capital Globe Law Firm Group* and maintains a number of non-exclusive links to firms in the US.

Batliner & Konrad advises a range of national and international banks and trust companies. Areas of focus include litigation, corporate, public and constitutional law, white-collar crime, due diligence and anti-money-laundering. Karlheinz Konrad also handles real estate contracts, and Andreas Batliner is knowledgeable on foundation law.

Six-lawyer **Harry Gstöhl & Partner** is a full-service law firm advising and representing both local and international clients. Name partner Harry Gstöhl is reputed for his corporate experience and is a past president of the Constitutional Court and was recently nominated Princely Council of Justice. His partner Sabine Mohr-Egger is a litigator with particular expertise in white-collar crime matters, and also has a strong employment practice. The firm is a member of the *Employment Law Alliance*.

Dr Gerhard Holzhacker, under his new firm name of **Law Office Holzhacker** has a reputation as an excellent litigator in fraud and white-collar crime. He has a very busy white-collar crime practice and recently undertook major work on behalf of the government of Trinidad and Tobago in relation to a major fraud. Dr Holzhacker gained his reputation as longstanding counsel in the litigation relating to the Liechtenstein companies of Robert Maxwell. Corporate clients include major international corporations.

COMMERCIAL

BATLINER (DR DR) & DR GASSER
BATLINER WANGER BATLINER
MARXER (DR) & PARTNER, ADVOKATURBÜRO
WALCH & SCHURTI

Batliner & Konrad
Harry Gstöhl & Partner
Holzhacker, Law Office
Karlheinz Ritter (Dr iur) Lic iur Cornelia Ritter, Law Office
Müller & Partner Rechtsanwälte

Sele Frommelt & Partner
Wanger Advokaturbüro ✪

Jelenik & Partners, Advokaturbüro
Kaiser & Kaiser
Lampert Schächle
Meier – Attorneys at Law
Norbert Seeger (Dr jur et lic oec), Advokaturbüro
Ospelt & Partners
Ritter & Wohlwend Advokaturbüro
Seeger, Frick & Partner
Walter Matt (Lic.iur.), Law Office

Firms are listed A-Z in tiers which are ranked in order of priority
✪ *Indicates firm displays contact details at the end of this chapter.*

The two partner firm of **Law Office Dr iur Karlheinz Ritter Lic iur Cornelia Ritter** primarily undertakes trusts and foundation work, including litigation. Corporate, commercial, finance and tax advice are also offered. Partner Cornelia Ritter is a member of the Executive Board of the Liechtenstein Fiduciary Association.

The expanding **Müller & Partner Rechtsanwälte**, based in Schaan, has a particularly strong litigation practice, with senior partner and expert litigator Dr Wolfgang Müller at the helm. The firm also undertakes major trusts work with clients including major Swiss companies. Partner Dr Cornelia Gassner has a political background as a minister in the Liechtenstein government.

Four-partner **Sele Frommelt & Partner** specialises in trusts, litigation and asset management. Much of the firm's work involves trust company Negele Sele Frommelt & Partner Trust Enterprise. The firm has a long-established Swiss and Austrian client base, but is also a good port of call for German, UK and French referrals.

Wanger Advokaturbüro is a four-lawyer general practice with offices in Austria, Belgium, Israel and Brazil and working relationships with international law firms. It acts for major international corporations and fiduciaries, and high-net-worth individuals. The firm has a strong intellectual property practice and advises major international companies on trade mark matters. The firm is a member of the ICC Counterfeiting Intelligence Bureau. Name partner Dr Markus Wanger is a specialist in arbitration and is a judge at the Court of Arbitration for Sport in Lausanne. He is also the managing director of the IP trust company, Patag.

The first of a number of new entrants to the commercial table is **Advokaturbüro Jelenik & Partners** which advises international clients on company matters, and represents litigation clients in criminal and civil proceedings in Liechtenstein and Austria.

A further new entrant to the table, **Lampert Schächle** is a steadily growing two-partner firm. Senior partner Siegbert Lampert is a former secretary general of the Liechtenstein Association of Professional Trustees and a Constitutional Court judge. The firm has a general commercial practice and particular expertise in white-collar crime: name partner Rudolf Schäle recently acted in the defence of a multi-million euro fraud case.

Meier – Attorneys at Law has a general commercial and corporate practice including trusts and foundation law, criminal and administrative law. The firm is associated with one of Liechtenstein's largest trust companies, Allgemeines Treuunternehmen, Vaduz.

Advokaturbüro Dr jur et lic oec Norbert Seeger has a strong general corporate practice. The firm provides legal advice regarding commercial (including contracts) and financial transactions, as well as the establishment of companies. The firm's work includes the protection of intellectual property (trade marks, patents and registered designs) and offers legal representation in criminal, administrative and civil matters.

A third new entrant to the table, **Ospelt & Partners** is a five-partner firm which has a strong white-collar crime practice, acting in the defence on a highly sensitive major worldwide white-collar crime case. The firm also represents major professional organisations in Liechtenstein, and advises international corporations on investments. The firm also represents clients before the European Court of Justice.

Ritter & Wohlwend Advokaturbüro is a four-partner firm acting exclusively within Liechtenstein. The firm has a general corporate practice advising local companies but also represents foreign clients on all aspects of Liechtenstein law. The firm has a special interest in asset recovery in international fraud schemes. In 2005, the firm represented a major Swiss company in an unfair competition case and is dealing with several large-scale disputes.

Partner Dr Mario Frick, a former Liechtenstein prime minister is a partner at **Seeger, Frick & Partner**. The three-lawyer firm advises various trust companies and banks.

Law Office Lic.iur. Walter Matt is a further new entrant to the table and is a general commercial firm with an emphasis on advocacy and trusts, and construction law.

WANGER ®
ADVOKATURBÜRO

AEULESTRASSE 45
9490 VADUZ

Telephone: +423 237 5252
Fax: +423 237 5253
E-mail: wanger@wanger.net
Website: www.wanger.net

Languages
English, French, German

Other offices
Belgium, Switzerland, Austria*

Number of lawyers 5

Contacts
Dr Markus H Wanger (senior partner),
Lic iur Markus Wille (managing partner)

Member
WANGER GROUP represented in Austria, Belgium, Brazil, China, Germany, Israel, Liechtenstein, and Switzerland

CATEGORIES OF WORK

Arbitration
Dr Markus Wanger

Litigation
Dr Johannes Grabher,
Lic iur Markus Wille

EU, conflict of laws
Lic iur Markus Wille,
Dr Johannes Grabher

Banking, finance, capital markets
Dr Markus Wanger

Trusts, charities, non-profit organisations
Dr Markus Wanger

Estate and tax planning
Dr Markus Wanger,
Lic iur Markus Wille

Company
Dr Markus Wanger,
Lic iur Markus Wille

Commercial
Dr Markus Wanger,
Lic iur Markus Wille

IP
Dr Markus Wanger,
Lic iur Markus Wille

IT
Dr Markus Wanger

Art law, media, sport
Dr Markus Wanger

Employment
Dr Johannes Grabher
Lic iur Markus Wille

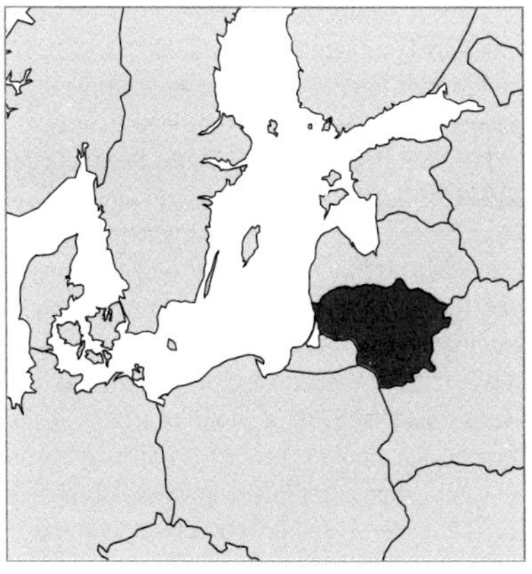

Population	3.4 million
Number of lawyers	1,382
Professional title	Advokatas: juristas
Currency	Litas (LTL))

Index

Lithuania is strategically located as a gateway between the EU and the CIS. It is the largest of the three Baltic States and shares borders with Latvia, Belarus, Poland and Russia. Lithuania was the first Soviet Republic to proclaim independence in 1990, and remaining Russian troops departed in 1993. The country now enjoys a stable political, economic and social environment.

Accession of the Baltic States into the EU in 2004 provoked dramatic, positive developments in Lithuania resulting in its recognition as one of the most reformed countries in the world. The newly acquired European lifestyle has enriched Lithuania's long, intriguing history and strong cultural identity. The country has a complicated and mixed cultural background demonstrating a fusion of colourful traditions, values and influences enhanced by a combination of more than 150 ethnic backgrounds. Lithuania plans to adopt the Euro in 2007.

The country's current president, Valdas Adamkus, is now in his second term following the impeachment and dismissal of previous president Rolandas Paksas on corruption charges in 2004. The political climate appears to have been strengthened since the impeachment. However, the political situation was recently shaken by a government scandal concerning a conflict of interest involving the Prime Minister, Algirdas Brazauskas, and a Russian oil dispute.

BILLING

The Bar Council advises recommended tariffs but generally individual firms set rates ranging from €100-€250 per hour depending on the area of work and seniority of the lawyer.

MARKETING

The Bar prohibits attorneys from advertising. This rule is not rigidly adhered to, with some firms sponsoring events and adopting other indirect marketing activities.

IN-HOUSE LAWYERS

The number of in-house lawyers is growing as it becomes increasingly popular for large corporations to employ in-house council. It is not necessary for in-house lawyers to be members of the Bar.

ECONOMY

Lithuania, a country whose name was until recently only vaguely familiar to the world, has been nicknamed 'The Baltic Tiger' due its strong economic development. In the last decade Lithuania has become an open market economy and a dynamic and competitive state. The European Commission forecast that in the coming three years Lithuania will be the fastest-growing economy among the 25 EU member states. The country has the lowest inflation rate in Europe, a low budget deficit and achieved GDP of 9.7% in 2003, projected to rise annually by 6.5-7.5% in the next three years.

Unemployment was 6.8% in 2004, about average in comparison with the rest of Europe.

Lithuania boasts modern infrastructure, an upgraded road network and the only ice-free seaport in the Baltic States. Living costs are incredibly low, the workforce is highly educated and wages are competitive, making the country an ideal base for taking competitive goods and services to the global market. Furthermore, the country's geographical situation facilitates trade with the East.

The World Bank Group's recent report highlighted Lithuania as one of the top 20 economies in the world for ease of doing business. This may explain why Lithuania has become one of Europe's hubs for foreign direct investment with a turnover of €4.26bn in 2004. The Lithuanian government prioritises financial discipline, currency stability and other business-friendly policies. A favourable investment environment and liberal foreign trade policy provide outside investors with possibilities for expansion nationally and throughout the EU, bridging the gap between Russia, the CIS countries and the West.

Despite the increase in the level of foreign investment, the government still feels growth is insufficient due to the market size and the lack of incentives for investors, unlike in countries such as Poland and the Czech Republic. This is currently being reviewed by the Ministry of Economy with an incentive package likely to be introduced in the near future.

Banking is amongst the strongest sectors of the economy and is a major investment attraction owing to investor-friendly lending rates and government policies providing reduced tax burdens within the EU. Transport and communications are rapidly developing areas and the prosperity brought by entry into the EU has been mirrored in the real property market.

The largest firms

1	Lideika, Petrauskas, Valiunas ir partneriai LAWIN	41
2	Jurevicius, Balciunas & Bartkus	35
3	Bernotas & Dominas Glimstedt, Law Firm	26
4	Vilnius 2nd Law Firm	25
5	Norcous & Partners	20
6	Foigt & Partners/Regija Borenius	19
	Raidla & Partners	19
8	Sorainen Law Offices	18
	Sutkiene, Pilkauskas & Partners	18
	Zabiela, Zabielaite & Partners	18
11	Foresta, Law Firm	16
	Soloveicikas, Markauskas and Aviza, Law Firm	16
13	AAA Baltic Service Company	15
14	Saladzius & Partners, Law Firm	14
15	SPES, Law Firm	13
16	Baublys & Partners	12
	Kazlauskas & Degesys Solvings	12
18	Sarka, Sabaliauskas, Jankauskas	10
19	Budvytis Civilis And Partners, Law Firm	8
	Rödl & Partner	8
21	Gostautas & Partners, Law Firm	6
	Hough, Zulys & Partners	6
	Juridicon Law Office	6
24	Praemissa Teises Firma Law Firm	5
25	Dicsa Baltic	4
	Ramanauskas ir partneriai, Advokatu kontora	4
	Savinijaus Katausko Biuras, Advokato	4

These figures represent the total number of lawyers in this country only, and have been supplied by the firms themselves. The figures should be accurate as at 1 January 2006.

LINKS ABROAD

Baltic partnering continues to be popular amongst the bigger firms in Lithuania due to foreign investors increasingly viewing the three Baltic countries as a unit.

Lideika, Petrauskas, Valiunas ir partneriai LAWIN is a member of the *LAWIN* group, established together with **Lepik & Luhaäär LAWIN**, Estonia and **Klavins & Slaidins LAWIN**, Latvia. *LAWIN* was the first to start the alliance trend in April 2004 and, with more than 80 lawyers this group is one of the largest legal services providers in the Baltics bringing together three, top-rated firms that have co-operated informally for over ten years.

Norcous & Partners belongs to the structured partnership *RoschierRaidla*, a Fenno-Baltic partnering. The grouping is the largest of its kind, comprising 170 lawyers from **Roschier Holmberg**, Finland, **Raidla & Partners**, Estonia and **Lejins, Torgans & Partners**, Latvia. A Stockholm office opened at the end of 2005.

Foigt & Partners/Regija Borenius is a member of an association with **Luiga Mody Hääl Borenius**, Estonia, **Liepa, Skopina / BORENIUS** Latvia and **Borenius & Kemppinen**, Finland. The alliance comprises over 100 lawyers with the aim of supplying legal services across the Baltic States and Finland.

Law Firm Saladžius & Partners works alongside **Law Office Ots & Co**, Estonia and **Baltmane & Bitans Law Office** Latvia.

Sixty-lawyer, pan-Baltic network *Baltic Legal Solutions* has been referred to as 'one of the most noteworthy developments in the legal field'. **Jurevicius, Balciunas & Bartkus**, **Kronbergs & Cukste**, Latvia and **Law Firm Teder, Glikman & Partnerid**, Estonia, are members of this grouping.

Sorainen Law Offices is a full-service business law firm, employing over 65 lawyers, with offices in Riga, Tallinn, Vilnius and Helsinki. The pan-Baltic character of the firm enables it to provide services to multinational companies operating in all three of the Baltic States.

LEGAL MARKET

Echoing the flourishing nature of the economic climate, the legal market has been in a period of rapid growth and development since restoration of independence, and continues to grow.

An influx of international firms is unlikely given the relatively small market and fierce local competition. Some US and UK Magic Circle firms have 'relationships' with Lithuanian firms and Baltic coverage is achieved sufficiently by this method.

The market is based around the legal tradition of continental Europe and principles of substantive law have been codified in recent years. Lithuanian company law reform is under way with amendments of EU and M&A legislation. There have also been significant amendments to the Securities Markets legislation in order to facilitate harmonisation with EU directives.

Following the abolition of Bar exams in 2004, the country witnessed huge growth in the number of Bar members and the legal market experienced an increase in competition in terms of quantity rather than quality of advokatas. This controversy has now been resolved after the reinstatement of mandatory Bar exams.

2005 was a slow year for privatisation, attributable to the fact that 90% of privatisation work was completed between 2001 and 2003. Foreign investment and real estate continue to be increasingly affluent areas of the legal market.

Lideika, Petrauskas, Valiunas ir partneriai LAWIN remains the premier Lithuanian firm. Organisation and good management are key factors behind the firm's strength and it continues to be the only firm with distinct practice groups. Rising stars are cherry picked from other firms, a growth of 20% was achieved in 2005 and the firm is looking to recruit five more attorneys in the coming year due to the consistent increase in work. Education and professional development is a class ahead at **Lideika, Petrauskas, Valiunas ir partneriai LAWIN** with a third of staff holding LLMs from international institutions.

Contemporaries are quick to praise **Law Firm Bernotas & Dominas Glimstedt** where attorneys are said to hold 'extensive experience and professional potential'. The firm recently broke its alliance with *Law Firm Mody Hääl Glimstedt* in August 2005 after the Estonian firm restructured and formed part of the *Borenius* grouping. The arrivals of Povilas Variakojis, former advisor to the Deputy Chairman of the Lithuanian Parliament, and Albertas Stopas, former chief advisor to the Secretary of Judicial Practice Department, have added further weight to the firm.

As a result of regulatory changes **Jurevicius, Balciunas & Bartkus** formally severed its alliance with Ernst & Young in the summer of 2005 and is now a fully independent firm. Clients are still able to benefit from the firm's established relationship with Ernst & Young professionals by request.

BANKING AND FINANCE

Lideika, Petrauskas, Valiunas ir partneriai LAWIN has an excellent track record in banking and finance. The firm boasts a sound portfolio of international banking and investment clients and participated in virtually all major, recent Lithuanian banking and financing transactions. The firm is currently involved in the year's largest banking transaction in the Baltic States regarding the joint venture of a Norwegian financial group and a large Lithuanian bank. The firm has also been advising a top UK firm on the activities of an investment fund client in Lithuania. Head of the firm's finance and tax group, Giedrius Stasevičius leaves clients highly satisfied with the quality of work carried out.

BANKING AND FINANCE

LIDEIKA, PETRAUSKAS, VALIUNAS IR PARTNERIAI LAWIN ✪

Bernotas & Dominas Glimstedt, Law Firm ✪

Baublys & Partners ✪
Foigt & Partners/Regija Borenius ✪
Jurevicius, Balciunas & Bartkus ✪
Norcous & Partners ✪
Saladžius & Partners, Law Firm ✪
Sorainen Law Offices ✪
Sutkiene, Pilkauskas & Partners ✪

Foresta, Law Firm
Juridicon Law Office ✪
Šarka, Sabaliauskas, Jankauskas
Zabiela, Zabielaite & Partners

Firms are listed A-Z in tiers which are ranked in order of priority
✪ *Indicates firm displays contact details at the end of this chapter.*

Law Firm Bernotas & Dominas Glimstedt is active in banking and finance matters. The firm advises on acquisition, asset and project finance and securitisation. Last year the firm instructed the Ministry of Finance on a €600m Eurobond issue. Partner, Gediminas Dominas, is a renowned financing techniques advisor.

Eleven-lawyer **Baublys & Partners** has represented one of Lithuania's largest banks in a variety of civil cases including debt recovery and vitiation of deals.

The 19 lawyers at **Foigt & Partners/Regija Borenius** recently advised Royal Bank of Scotland regarding e-agreements related to the implementation of debt securities sales in Lithuania.

Jurevicius, Balciunas & Bartkus offers international and domestic clients advice on all areas of banking and finance. Last year the firm was engaged by the Lithuanian Mint during the company's restructuring. The firm also advises the World Bank public-private infrastructure advisory facility.

Young but thoroughly capable, 20-lawyer **Norcous & Partners** focuses on banking and finance matters. In March 2005 the team was bolstered by the addition of Ruslanas Bronikovas, formerly a deputy general counsel of SEB Vilnius Bank. Last year the firm advised the EBRD on the disposal of its interest in a Lithuanian company. Irmantas Norkus is highly active in this field and is hailed 'a good, professional lawyer who is very easy to communicate with'.

Law Firm Saladžius & Partners focuses intensively on business law and co-operates with PricewaterhouseCoopers, enabling it to draw upon an excellent set of professional service expertise. Last year attorneys at the firm provided ongoing legal assistance to one of Lithuania's largest banks. Legal assistance was also provided to the country's biggest cosmetics and perfume retailer in raising capital. Clients claim the firm is 'professional, punctual and experienced' and managing partner Jonas Saladžius has established a solid reputation for his knowledge of financial law.

Sorainen Law Offices shows a strong commitment to banking and finance and merits promotion in this year's table after a successful year. The firm is retained by several major financial institutions, including the European Investment Bank, BNP Paribas and JPMorgan Chase. The banking and finance team was recently strengthened by the addition of Algirdas Peksys, former in-house lawyer of the Vilnius Security Exchange and one of the best securities practitioners in Lithuania. Further acclaim is due for partner Kestutis Adamonis. Highlights of the year include preparing a survey on equity derivatives and related transactions for a leading trans-national financial services company.

Sixteen-lawyer **Sutkiene, Pilkauskas & Partners** is a relatively recent addition to the Lithuanian legal market. That said, the firm has already built a distinguished reputation and is comprised of exceptional lawyers. The firm is instructed by several commercial banks and last year advised a major Lithuanian bank on the lease of real property.

Fourteen-lawyer **Law Firm Foresta** has an active banking and finance department. Recent transactions include assisting a large frozen foods producer in securing a loan from the Baltic-American Enterprise Fund. Clients are impressed by the firm's professional approach.

Šarka, Sabaliauskas, Jankauskas is instructed by various foreign and domestic insurance and financial services companies on issues such as the regulatory environment. The firm receives praise for its strong contacts in Germany, including excellent relations with the German Chamber of Commerce.

In 2005 **Zabiela, Zabielaite & Partners** concentrated predominantly on general advisory work, particularly for banks and other financial institutions. A significant transaction involved the representation of a client against Bank of Lithuania before the Supreme Administrative Court of Lithuania.

CORPORATE AND M&A

With 41 lawyers **Lideika, Petrauskas, Valiunas ir partneriai LAWIN** is Lithuania's largest firm and has gained an unrivalled reputation for corporate work through participation in the majority of significant M&A, private equity, joint venture and other corporate transactions in Lithuania. The firm's dazzling client list includes British Airways, Coca-Cola and Nike. Widely involved in corporate and commercial legislation review, the firm is currently preparing a comparative study for the Ministry of Economy on regulation of company law issues within the EU. Four of the eight partners are experts in this sector and clients declare them to be 'reliable, trustworthy and punctual'. Laimonas Skibarka deserves mention for his excellent M&A work and international experience.

CORPORATE AND M&A

LIDEIKA, PETRAUSKAS, VALIUNAS IR PARTNERIAI LAWIN ✪

Bernotas & Dominas Glimstedt, Law Firm ✪
Sorainen Law Offices ✪
Sutkiene, Pilkauskas & Partners ✪

Foigt & Partners/Regija Borenius ✪
Foresta, Law Firm
Jurevicius, Balciunas & Bartkus ✪
Norcous & Partners ✪
Saladžius & Partners, Law Firm ✪
Šarka, Sabaliauskas, Jankauskas
Zabiela, Zabielaite & Partners

AAA Baltic Service Company
Baublys & Partners ✪
Hough, Zulys & Partners
Juridicon Law Office ✪
Kazlauskas & Degesys Solvings
ReLaw
SPES, Law Firm ✪
Tadas Kilmas, Law Office
Vadapalas, Vaitekunas and Partners Eurolex

Firms are listed A-Z in tiers which are ranked in order of priority
✪ *Indicates firm displays contact details at the end of this chapter.*

Twenty-eight-lawyer **Law Firm Bernotas & Dominas Glimstedt** has a reputable corporate practice. The firm advised leading German and Norwegian banks on merger issues in the Baltic States and Scandinavia. Clients commend the firm's ability to provide 'quick, full-service advice in excellent English'. Partner, Kęstutis Jaskutėlis, is a celebrated M&A lawyer.

Pan-Baltic, 16-lawyer **Sorainen Law Offices** has been involved in more than 300 M&A transactions in the last ten years and boasts one of the largest M&A teams in the Baltic States, earning the firm a promotion in the rankings this year. In 2005 the firm advised a client on arguably the largest private equity investment into the second-largest retail chain in Lithuania. Turnover in this department reached over €150m in 2005. The firm also has a strong reputation for its traditional corporate work and lists a number of high-profile corporations amongst its clients. The six lawyers working solely in this department assisted one of the fastest-growing food retailers in Europe on corporate governance requirements and applicable employment terms. Clients are satisfied with the firm's 'proactive attitude, consistent availability and rapid follow-up times'.

'Client-oriented' **Sutkiene, Pilkauskas & Partners** recently represented a major European company engaged in the wholesale and retail trade of pharmaceutical products in connection with the acquisition of a controlling block of shares in several pharmacies operating in Lithuania. Clients claim the firm has a 'professional and pragmatic approach'.

Foigt & Partners/Regija Borenius advises Sony Ericsson Mobile Communications on corporate matters and is a permanent legal advisor to Esso and Hoffman La Roche. A recent high point was the representation of a global leader in electronic commerce and payment services in the acquisition of a major Central and Eastern European card-processing company.

'Highly reliable' **Law Firm Foresta** advises a wide range of national and international businesses on all corporate matters. In 2005, the firm provided a major international medicines producer with regulatory advice concerning the licensing of medicinal products in Lithuania. Tomas Saulenas is described as a 'very talented lawyer with a profound understanding of clients' needs'.

Twenty-three-lawyer **Jurevicius, Balciunas & Bartkus** is well known in the corporate and M&A market. The firm acts for several major global corporations including Microsoft and GlaxoSmithKline. Kaunas City Municipality turns to the firm for advice on PPP.

Norcous & Partners has a strong M&A practice. In 2005 the firm advised the investment-banking arm of a leading Lithuanian bank on the acquisition of a retail business. The firm also represented Kodak on its acquisition of a local photo-services business. Praise is received for the way the firm 'treats every case as if it were the client'.

Law Firm Saladžius & Partners is rapidly expanding in terms of staff and reputation. The firm is particularly well known for its legal due diligence, M&A and corporate restructuring transactions. The firm's team of qualified specialists comprises business-oriented and innovative practitioners. Managing partner Jonas Saladžius is a well-known corporate expert and has advised on large-scale, complex M&A projects. The firm provides legal assistance to Oracle, the world's largest software company, and was involved in the rendering of the company's contract and public procurement advice. The firm also advised Lithuania's largest oil and gas company on the acquisition of the most significant refinery in the Baltics. Clients highlight the firm's 'professional conduct and excellent orientation in local and EU legal issues'.

Šarka, Sabaliauskas, Jankauskas counts corporate matters as a core area of competence. Name partner Linas Sabaliauskas is the chairman of the Corporate/Commercial Law Committee at the Lithuanian Bar Association. Recent transactions include advising a local community on a PPP tender for its district heating services, representing wind energy companies in disputes with Lithuania's main electricity enterprise and advising a newspaper on its reorganisation. The firm has a significant client base in Germany and is well known for its high-quality, German-language services.

Zabiela, Zabielaite & Partners specialises in corporate and M&A, in particular the formation, reorganisation and restructuring of companies. Recent highlights include the foundation and registration of an international Christian charity and sponsorship fund and subsequent advice on regulations related to NGOs in the Baltic States.

Baublys & Partners advises several large corporations on day-to-day corporate and M&A issues including several of Lithuania's oil companies. The firm is particularly strong in arbitration and commercial litigation.

Juridicon Law Office has been involved in large-scale corporate and M&A transactions including the representation of Kaunas Heat Power Plant, an affiliate of energy giant Gazprom, throughout the process of the increase of the company's authorised capital by €13.5m. Clients are impressed by the professional skills demonstrated by Laimonas Marcinkevicius and Andrzej Czajkowski.

Kazlauskas & Degesys Solvings has seen a significant increase in M&A and has advised on several of Lithuania's key deals in the last 12 months. One noteworthy transaction involved rendering advice on all projects-related legal aspects for Lithuania's largest chipboard producer with a project value in excess of €50m. The firm has also carried out due diligence for several large, Lithuanian groups.

ReLaw carried out a due diligence engagement prior to the intended merger of a well-known material-handling business and also advised on the acquisition of real estate valued at over €1.7m. Clients state that 'attorneys are outstanding professionals who really care about the quality of their work.'

Law Firm SPES represented Lithuania's biggest oil-prospecting and extraction company in a dispute with a shareholder and has also acted for various government institutions. Clients state the firm performs 'punctually, efficiently and to a high standard'.

Vadapalas, Vaitekunas and Partners Eurolex's commercial work spills over into real estate and foreign investment. The firm is particularly strong in business matters and clients are fans of the firm's 'willingness to devote time to individuals and deal efficiently with entrepreneurial businesses'.

EU AND COMPETITION

LIDEIKA, PETRAUSKAS, VALIUNAS IR PARTNERIAI LAWIN ✪

Bernotas & Dominas Glimstedt, Law Firm ✪
Sorainen Law Offices ✪

Foigt & Partners/Regija Borenius ✪
Foresta, Law Firm
Juridicon Law Office ✪
Norcous & Partners ✪
Sutkiene, Pilkauskas & Partners ✪
Zabiela, Zabielaite & Partners

Firms are listed A-Z in tiers which are ranked in order of priority
✪ Indicates firm displays contact details at the end of this chapter.

EU AND COMPETITION

Lideika, Petrauskas, Valiunas ir partneriai LAWIN offers a strong team of experienced competition lawyers, amongst them Dr Jaunius Gumbis, Sarunas Keserauskas and Marius Juonys. In 2004 the firm carried out a study for the European Commission regarding private enforcement of European competition rules. The firm is currently handling a record number of cases including the largest-ever investigation regarding abuse of dominant position by competition authorities in the Baltic States.

The competition and EU practice at **Law Firm Bernotas & Dominas Glimstedt** provides a full range of services from assisting in negotiations to filing notifications and complaints. Partner Elijus Burgis is a renowned competition law expert.

Competition and EU law forms a major part of practice at **Sorainen Law Offices**. Since accession, advice on the compliance of Lithuanian law with EU legislation has become extremely important for businesses in the Baltic region, reflected in the firm having handled more than 20 competition law-related assignments in the last 12 months. The firm recently represented a pre-eminent global financial services company during a competition clearance issue before the European Commission. The firm also assisted a UK Magic Circle firm concerning the implementation of EU directives across the Baltic States.

Experts at **Foigt & Partners/Regija Borenius** represented a prominent car manufacturer in a trade mark infringement and unfair competition dispute last year.

Law Firm Foresta advises an international IT company and its Lithuanian subsidiary on EU and local regulations and has provided a major international hygiene products manufacturer with advice on merger control regulation.

Lawyers at **Juridicon Law Office** prepared and filed two separate complaints on behalf of a group of national IT companies against Lithuanian Telecom on the grounds of alleged abuse of dominant position.

Norcous & Partners' EU and competition work is highly rated and clients praise his 'quick response and proficient communication'. The firm advises one of Lithuania's leading retailers on competition compliance matters and represented the Lithuanian National Road Carrier's Association in the dawn raid by Lithuanian competition authorities.

Lina Daruliene of **Sutkiene, Pilkauskas & Partners** is a well-known competition authority and clients commend her competence in technical areas. The firm recently advised Swedbank in connection with Lithuanian competition requirements.

Zabiela, Zabielaite & Partners offers advice on all stages of projects seeking support from EU structural funds. One recent project was within the child and healthcare sector, where targeted funding amounted to €2.5m.

FOREIGN INVESTMENT

Of 25 major foreign investors existing in Lithuania, **Lideika, Petrauskas, Valiunas ir partneriai LAWIN** currently represents 20, reaffirming its premier place in the table this year. The firm actively participates in investment organisations and foreign chambers of commerce, co-operates closely with the Lithuanian Development Agency and publishes an investors guide, 'Investing in Lithuania', in association with the Ministry of Economy.

Law Firm Bernotas & Dominas Glimstedt is a firm with a strong cross-border dimension, having counselled various pan-European companies on investment issues in Lithuania last year.

Foigt & Partners/Regija Borenius advises one of Europe's largest supermarket operators on establishment in the Baltic countries.

In 2005 **Jurevicius, Balciunas & Bartkus** provided legal assistance to a pan-Baltic beer and beverage company regarding the Lithuanian subsidiary's corporate and competition issues.

Up-and-coming **Norcous & Partners** advises large, international companies on potential investment matters in Lithuania. Last year the firm acted for a Latvian investor during the privatisation of a municipal, communal public utilities company.

Law Firm Saladžius & Partners handles legal matters for a broad range of foreign investors including several global corporations. Managing partner Jonas Saladžius is a member of the Corporate Law Committee of the Foreign Investors Forum. The firm represents a number of pharmaceutical companies in their foreign investment ventures and is recognised by clients for its expertise in this arena.

Sorainen Law Offices is known for handling foreign investment emanating from the Scandinavian countries. Last year the firm advised on more than 60 transactions including assisting one of the world's largest life insurance companies with the establishment of a branch in Lithuania. The firm also advised Citigroup on its private equity investment into a major retail chain in Lithuania. The deal involved due diligence, assisting in the negotiation of transaction documents and advising on competition clearance issues.

FOREIGN INVESTMENT

LIDEIKA, PETRAUSKAS, VALIUNAS IR PARTNERIAI LAWIN ✪

Bernotas & Dominas Glimstedt, Law Firm ✪

Foigt & Partners/Regija Borenius ✪
Jurevicius, Balciunas & Bartkus ✪
Norcous & Partners ✪
Saladžius & Partners, Law Firm ✪
Sorainen Law Offices ✪
Sutkiene, Pilkauskas & Partners ✪

Foresta, Law Firm
Juridicon Law Office ✪
Šarka, Sabaliauskas, Jankauskas
SPES, Law Firm ✪
Zabiela, Zabielaite & Partners

Firms are listed A-Z in tiers which are ranked in order of priority
✪ *Indicates firm displays contact details at the end of this chapter.*

Last year **Sutkiene, Pilkauskas & Partners** advised a UK-based medical staff employment intermediary on its activities and related tax issues in Lithuania.

Law Firm Foresta assisted a worldwide IT company in the establishment of a subsidiary in Lithuania in 2005.

Juridicon Law Office recently represented a significant number of international foreign investors from a cross-section of industries with the start-up, development and termination of activities in Lithuania.

Partners at **Šarka, Sabaliauskas, Jankauskas**, together with the German-Baltic Chamber of Commerce, have published a guide on investing in Lithuania. The ten-lawyer firm counsels an array of foreign companies interested in investing in the country.

IT AND TELECOMS

Lideika, Petrauskas, Valiunas ir partneriai LAWIN is exceptionally strong in IT and telecoms. Some 70% of the telecoms market is advised by this firm and Jaunius Gumbis and Aida Raziulyte are highly regarded advokatas. The firm also posts a strong showing in IT, boasting the country's leading specialist, Mindaugas Keskis, advising global giant IBM and having advised on the largest IT acquisition of 2005.

Law Firm Bernotas & Dominas Glimstedt offers a full range of services in the telecoms sector. The firm advises one of Lithuania's biggest mobile telecommunications companies and two commercial television enterprises.

Foigt & Partners/Regija Borenius advises international communications and leading local IT companies on day-to-day matters. Legal due diligence was carried out by the firm for First Data Corporation during the acquisition of a subsidiary.

Last year **Juridicon Law Office** triumphed in court when acting for a client engaged in the creation and administration of a phone number database. The firm also prepared and filed a complaint against Lithuanian Telecom on behalf of a national IT company before the Communications Regulatory Authority.

IT AND TELECOMS

LIDEIKA, PETRAUSKAS, VALIUNAS IR PARTNERIAI LAWIN ✪

Bernotas & Dominas Glimstedt, Law Firm ✪
Foigt & Partners/Regija Borenius ✪
Foresta, Law Firm
Jurevicius, Balciunas & Bartkus ✪
Juridicon Law Office ✪
Norcous & Partners ✪
Saladžius & Partners, Law Firm ✪
Šarka, Sabaliauskas, Jankauskas
Sorainen Law Offices ✪
Sutkiene, Pilkauskas & Partners ✪
Tadas Kilmas, Law Office
Zabiela, Zabielaite & Partners

Firms are listed A-Z in tiers which are ranked in order of priority
✪ *Indicates firm displays contact details at the end of this chapter.*

Norcous & Partners is instructed by a dominant Lithuanian IT company on matters related to the establishment and operation of electronic signature certification. Last year the firm advised a national mobile number portability operator on the establishment and operation of a national numbers database.

Law Firm Saladžius & Partners is retained by several IT and telecoms companies to provide ongoing legal advice. Satisfied clients praise the firm's ability 'to provide solutions to questions, looking from every angle'.

Šarka, Sabaliauskas, Jankauskas handles contract issues for one of Lithuania's most prominent web design companies and advises German and Scandinavian companies on various telecoms issues.

Sorainen Law Offices has experienced growth in the amount of work handled by its IT department. The firm advises a number of prodigious IT and telecoms companies and assisted a well-known mobile telephone company with a trilateral multimedia services agreement involving the largest mobile telecoms company in the Baltic States. Newly acquired attorney, Sergejs Trofimovs specialises.

Zabiela, Zabielaite & Partners demonstrated its skills in several challenging projects in the last 12 months. The firm was consulted by Kaunas University of Technology in the preparation of an IT agreement valued at over €5.5m and provides day-to-day advice to Lithuania's most significant information technology park. The firm also represented telecoms company, Eurocom before the Competition Council of the Republic of Lithuania.

INTELLECTUAL PROPERTY

AAA BALTIC SERVICE COMPANY
LIDEIKA, PETRAUSKAS, VALIUNAS IR PARTNERIAI LAWIN ✪

ReLaw
Sorainen Law Offices ✪

Bernotas & Dominas Glimstedt, Law Firm ✪
Foigt & Partners/Regija Borenius ✪
Foresta, Law Firm
Juridicon Law Office ✪
Norcous & Partners ✪
Saladzius & Partners, Law Firm ✪
Šarka, Sabaliauskas, Jankauskas
Sutkiene, Pilkauskas & Partners ✪
Zabiela, Zabielaite & Partners

Firms are listed A-Z in tiers which are ranked in order of priority
✪ *Indicates firm displays contact details at the end of this chapter.*

INTELLECTUAL PROPERTY

Expert IP firm **AAA Baltic Service Company** remains a leader in the sector. Founder, chairman and senior partner Marius J Jason previously practised in New York for 15 years. He is the founder and president of Lithuania's International Association for the Protection of Intellectual Property and is considered the premier trade mark lawyer in the country. The firm's client list reads like a 'Who's Who' of international corporations and praise is gained for 'quick response times and constant availability'.

A full range of high-quality IP services are on offer at **Lideika, Petrauskas, Valiunas ir partneriai LAWIN**. Associate Gediminas Pranevicius is among the leading Lithuanian IP lawyers. Pranevicius lectures on IP protection at the Lithuanian University of Law and is particularly well known for his expertise in trade mark litigation. A number of Lithuania's dominant corporations proclaim the firm to be 'well staffed, knowledgeable and prompt'.

Well-known for its IP practice, **ReLaw** boasts IP specialists Vytautas Kalmatavicius, who was involved in the harmonisation of Lithuanian IP legislation with EU regulations, and Vilija Viesunaite, a registered patent attorney renowned for her participation in copious highly publicised IP disputes. In 2005 the firm represented a prominent Lithuanian bank in a trade mark infringement case. 'Work is performed and reported on a highly professional level and every matter is regarded with optimum care', declares one content client.

Partner and acclaimed IP practitioner Renata Berzanskiene at **Sorainen Law Offices** has handled a multitude of IP disputes in the past 12 months. Berzanskiene assisted a prominent brewery in a Europe-wide dispute regarding one of the world's best-known beer trade marks. The firm also triumphed in lengthy litigation involving registration of a trade mark.

Law Firm Bernotas & Dominas Glimstedt offers expertise in licensing agreements, registration of trade names and trade marks and claims related to infringement of IP rights. The firm has particular experience in IP matters relating to computer software and IT transactions.

Foigt & Partners/Regija Borenius successfully represented a pharmaceuticals company in concluding a settlement agreement in a dispute over non-performance of a software implementation agreement.

Law Firm Foresta provides a full range of IP services and clients are impressed by the firm's 'accessible, prompt and reliable work'.

In 2005 **Juridicon Law Office** successfully defended a national company seeking to register a trade mark against opposition by IT giant Intel.

Norcous & Partners advises a world-renowned jeans manufacturer on franchising aspects and recently represented a leading Baltic banking and financing group in a trade mark case.

Lawyers at **Law Firm Saladžius & Partners** offer in-depth knowledge and experience in diverse areas of IP. Clients applaud the firm's ability to 'stick to a tight time schedule and uphold promises'.

Šarka, Sabaliauskas, Jankauskas renders advice to a leading European cosmetics company and a Dutch media and print enterprise.

Sutkiene, Pilkauskas & Partners recently defended the interests of a local alcoholic beverages group in the protection of a trade mark.

Zabiela, Zabielaite & Partners advises clients on patent, trade mark and copyright design-related matters. The firm drafted licence agreements for Kaunas University of Technology and an international IT services firm.

PRIVATISATION

LIDEIKA, PETRAUSKAS, VALIUNAS IR PARTNERIAI LAWIN ✪

Bernotas & Dominas Glimstedt, Law Firm ✪
Sutkiene, Pilkauskas & Partners ✪

Foresta, Law Firm
Norcous & Partners ✪
Saladžius & Partners, Law Firm ✪
Šarka, Sabaliauskas, Jankauskas
Sorainen Law Offices ✪
Zabiela, Zabielaite & Partners

Firms are listed A-Z in tiers which are ranked in order of priority
✪ *Indicates firm displays contact details at the end of this chapter.*

PRIVATISATION

2005 was a slow year for privatisation transactions, reflected in most firms' portfolios.

Lideika, Petrauskas, Valiunas ir partneriai LAWIN has an outstanding reputation for privatisation matters and has advised the State Property Fund in virtually all significant privatisation transactions in Lithuania including two of the largest privatisation-related disputes so far. The firm advises the Baltic States' largest oil refinery in the ongoing privatisation of a thermo-electricity plant.

Law Firm Bernotas & Dominas Glimstedt has played a key role in the Lithuanian privatisation process and handled a number of significant transactions. A recent highlight was the firm's involvement in the privatisation of Klaipeda Ship Repair Yard.

In 2005, **Sutkiene, Pilkauskas & Partners** assisted the Government of the Republic of Lithuania on the privatisation of Lithuanian Airlines and also acted for an investor in connection with the privatisation of a printing company. The firm's 'practical and business-minded' approach elicits praise.

Law Firm Foresta represented an investment company during the privatisation of a State-owned airline and also assisted a foreign enterprise in a dispute regarding the privatisation of a local electric power company.

Norcous & Partners provided advice to a Latvian public insurance company during the privatisation of a Lithuanian insurance company last year.

Law Firm Saladžius & Partners recently acted for an Italian wine producer in a privatisation-related dispute with the Lithuanian State Property Fund. The firm represented the client in a special commission before the Lithuanian Parliament relating to the evaluation of the privatisation process.

Sorainen Law Offices provided full-scale legal assistance to the largest greengrocery producer in Estonia during the privatisation of several greenhouses in Lithuania. The firm has also been actively involved in the preparation of several landmark transactions involving PPP structures.

Zabiela, Zabielaite & Partners recently represented a Russian corporation in a case against the State Property Fund concerning privatisation of a European car-parts manufacturer.

REAL ESTATE AND CONSTRUCTION

In the past 12 months leading firm **Lideika, Petrauskas, Valiunas ir partneriai LAWIN** has been advising a major property investment fund on the acquisition of a trade centre, described as the largest investment deal in the real estate market in the Baltics so far. The firm also advised one of Lithuania's premier banks on the planning and development of a new building.

Law Firm Bernotas & Dominas Glimstedt offers skilled services. The firm has carved out a name for itself in advising contractors, developers,

REAL ESTATE AND CONSTRUCTION

LIDEIKA, PETRAUSKAS, VALIUNAS IR PARTNERIAI LAWIN ✪

Bernotas & Dominas Glimstedt, Law Firm ✪
Jurevicius, Balciunas & Bartkus ✪
Sorainen Law Offices ✪
Sutkiene, Pilkauskas & Partner ✪
Zabiela, Zabielaite & Partners

Baublys & Partners ✪
Foigt & Partners/Regija Borenius ✪

Foresta, Law Firm
Hough, Zulys & Partners
Juridicon Law Office ✪
SPES, Law Firm ✪
Saladžius & Partners, Law Firm ✪
Šarka, Sabaliauskas, Jankauskas

AAA Baltic Service Company
Kazlauskas & Degesys Solvings
Soloveicikas, Markauskas and Aviza, Law Firm ✪

Firms are listed A-Z in tiers which are ranked in order of priority
✪ Indicates firm displays contact details at the end of this chapter.

architects and engineers on all civil construction law matters. Last year the firm provided legal support to a local real estate developer regarding the construction and development of two large shopping malls in Vilnius and Kaunas.

The last 12 months have been particularly busy for **Jurevicius, Balciunas & Bartkus** in terms of real estate and construction transactions. The firm demonstrated its capabilities during the development of one of the biggest housing areas in Vilnius. The firm also assisted in a major deal involving the sale of a foreign embassy building and is well known for its advocacy skills. Impressive performance last year sees the firm moving up the table.

Strong in this field, **Sorainen Law Offices** gained further recognition this year due to participation in virtually all key commercial real estate transactions. Partner Kestutis Adamonis gave presentations on the subject at the Baltic Real Estate Investment Forum 2005 and is praised by peers for his expertise. The firm handled more than 20 major deals in 2005 with a value in excess of €100m. Strengths outlined by clients include the 'international focus and experience of the lawyers enabling the firm to provide the quality of service expected from big international firms'.

Sutkiene, Pilkauskas & Partners advised a construction company in connection with the acquisition of shares from a foreign entity.

Last year **Zabiela, Zabielaite & Partners** participated in numerous cases concerning restoration, legalisation and determination of ownership of real estate. The firm also handles financing, building and maintenance projects in the field of construction. A highlight of the year involved representing a Danish retail chain in negotiations with a Lithuanian real estate development company.

Lawyers at **Baublys & Partners** rendered advice to leading real estate developers on competition matters for the construction of several building complexes in Vilnius. Key deals include successfully representing a renowned construction and real estate development company during in a claim for LTL6.4m damages. The firm emphasises its strengths as dedication to clients' needs, responsiveness and reliability.

Foigt & Partners/Regija Borenius advises the leading supermarkets operator in the Baltic States on re-establishment of lease rights and also represented the seller in one of the biggest land transfers in Lithuania in the last year.

Law Firm Foresta represents local companies and international real estate developers in various business operations.

Juridicon Law Office handled a number of contracts involving the construction of petrol stations in a joint venture with Neste, a leading European oil refinery, with a marketing company.

Law Firm SPES recently advised on various real estate projects for the IFC in the execution of the 'Commercialising Energy Efficiency Finance' programme in Lithuania. Clients state the firm 'renders high-quality services promptly and efficiently'.

The real estate and construction team at **Law Firm Saladžius & Partners** recently carried out several due diligence projects for one of the largest European retail chains. The firm assisted an international real estate development company on various matters including joint venture arrangements, project development and PPP projects. Overseas companies in Europe and the US frequently choose this firm to manage their real estate transactions due to its 'excellent communication and time-management skills'.

Šarka, Sabaliauskas, Jankauskas' active real estate department recently handled a transaction on behalf of a German real estate developer for the realisation of a €90m project. Attorneys at the firm performed real estate due diligence for one of the biggest shopping centres in the EU and the firm is advising on the planned €40m development of a new shopping centre.

Kazlauskas & Degesys Solvings is advising on a large development project with the estimated value of more than €31m.

Law Firm Soloveicikas, Markauskas and Aviza is diligent in real estate and construction. In 2005 the firm represented a leading Lithuanian construction company in the €20m sale of an office building to a foreign investor. The firm has also participated in a development project involving the construction of a 26-storey apartment building in Latvia. Clients appreciate the firm's ability to 'always think of the most appropriate outcome for the client'.

SHIPPING AND TRANSPORT

LIDEIKA, PETRAUSKAS, VALIUNAS IR PARTNERIAI LAWIN ✪
RAMANAUSKAS IR PARTNERIAI, ADVOKATU KONTORA

Bernotas & Dominas Glimstedt, Law Firm ✪
Foigt & Partners/Regija Borenius ✪
Hough, Zulys & Partners
Jurevicius, Balciunas & Bartkus ✪
Juridicon Law Office ✪
Saladžius & Partners, Law Firm ✪
Šarka, Sabaliauskas, Jankauskas
Sorainen Law Offices ✪
Sutkiene, Pilkauskas & Partners ✪
Zabiela, Zabielaite & Partners

Firms are listed A-Z in tiers which are ranked in order of priority
✪ Indicates firm displays contact details at the end of this chapter.

SHIPPING AND TRANSPORT

Vilija Vaikute Pavan at **Lideika, Petrauskas, Valiunas ir partneriai LAWIN**, is one of the only lawyers in Lithuania with an LLM in maritime law. The firm advises several of the shipping world's key players on ship registration, arrest, charters, bills of lading and all other aspects of carriage of goods by sea. The firm advised the Government of Lithuania regarding the privatisation of the Klaipeda Transport Fleet.

Advokatu kontora Ramanauskas ir partneriai specialises in shipping matters. Last year the firm handled numerous ship arrest and release matters, repairs and registration disputes. The firm is instructed by Lithuania's second-largest shipping company and also acts for a number of foreign shipowners. According to clients, strengths include 'always acting in accordance with precise wishes and in line with dramatically changing post-communist laws'.

Lawyers at **Law Firm Bernotas & Dominas Glimstedt** advise several municipalities on developing their public transport infrastructure and on renewal of vehicle fleets.

Foigt & Partners/Regija Borenius provides continuous legal services to a Lithuanian national carrier and counsels a number of major road transportation companies. Jurate Rusteikaite is hailed a leading specialist in aviation law.

In 2005 **Law Firm Saladžius & Partners** counselled a client on litigation strategy and process and also litigated against the State Harbour Authorities in relation to the client's major engineering activities.

Partners Arūnas Šarka and Laimutis Jankauskas at **Šarka, Sabaliauskas, Jankauskas** have represented companies in transport disputes before the Lithuanian courts including a leading international transport and logistics services provider on its dealings with Lithuanian Railway.

Sutkiene, Pilkauskas & Partners recently advised one of Lithuania's largest shipbuilders on the acquisition of property.

Last year **Zabiela, Zabielaite & Partners** represented a client in a dispute with Direction of Klaipedos State Seaport concerning the interpretation and non-performance of a lease agreement.

TAX

Giedrius Stasevicius spearheads the tax group at **Lideika, Petrauskas, Valiunas ir partneriai LAWIN** and is assisted by Gintaras Balcius, a former tax service line project manager at PricewaterhouseCoopers. The firm's tax experts are actively involved in the development of tax legislation and handle tax matters for an impressive portfolio of clients who recommend the firm for its 'amiable attitude and punctuality'.

Law Firm Bernotas & Dominas Glimstedt claims to offer tax services which are on a par with those of financial advisors and auditors. The firm represents high-profile companies in disputes against the Public Tax Authorities.

Last year the tax department at **Sorainen Law Offices** benefited from the addition of rising star and international tax lawyer, Luc Nijs. Nijs has extensive experience in representing clients before national administrative institutions, courts and the European Court of Justice. The firm recently handled a number of complicated tax matters including counselling a German electroplating company on options for tax optimisation and risk management. Clients are satisfied with the firm's 'competence and ability to quickly understand and meet needs'.

TAX
LIDEIKA, PETRAUSKAS, VALIUNAS IR PARTNERIAI LAWIN ✪
Bernotas & Dominas Glimstedt, Law Firm ✪
Sorainen Law Offices ✪
Baublys & Partners ✪
Foigt & Partners/Regija Borenius ✪
Foresta, Law Firm
Jurevicius, Balciunas & Bartkus ✪
Juridicon Law Office ✪
Kazlauskas & Degesys Solvings
Saladžius & Partners, Law Firm ✪
AAA Baltic Service Company
Hough, Zulys & Partners
Tadas Kilmas, Law Office
Zabiela, Zabielaite & Partners

Firms are listed A-Z in tiers which are ranked in order of priority

✪ *Indicates firm displays contact details at the end of this chapter.*

Evaldas Rapolas fronts the tax department at **Baublys & Partners.** The firm frequently handles disputes involving expansive, factually and legally complex transactions.

Last year **Foigt & Partners/Regija Borenius** prepared the Lithuanian chapter in the yearly edition of a prestigious book on VAT legislation, and the compliance of such legislation with EU law.

Law Firm Foresta renders tax advice to local and international clients in respect of their business operations. Clients claim to never be disappointed.

Jurevicius, Balciunas & Bartkus offers comprehensive, pan-Baltic tax advice to clients on a day-to-day basis.

Juridicon Law Office handled a high-profile tax dispute last year when representing a US company in a case against the State Tax Inspectorate, claiming current law to be unconstitutional. Laimonas Marcinkevicius and Ingrida Steponaviciene gain credit for their 'speed, professionalism and reliability'.

Norcous & Partners' reputation has grown since its emergence in 2001. The firm recently advised a leading stationery manufacturer on aspects of taxation and the Lithuanian social insurance system. Clients profess the firm to be 'aggressive and loyal whilst being careful to protect clients' interests'.

Law Firm Saladžius & Partners provides advice to numerous local and foreign clients on tax planning and direct and indirect tax issues related to large-scale projects. One client believes this firm to be 'the best in Lithuania'.

Zabiela, Zabielaite & Partners regularly advises foreign and domestic enterprises and individuals on tax issues related to their commercial activities and offers tax advice regarding local and international trade transactions. The firm was recently consulted by an Italian company on import and export levies and other Lithuanian taxation issues.

BAUBLYS & PARTNERS

KONSTITUCIJOS AVE 7
09308 VILNIUS

Telephone: +370 5 248 7388
Fax: +370 5 248 7389
E-mail: vilnius@baublys.lt
Website: www.baublys.lt

Languages
English, German, Russian

Other offices
Kaunas

Number of lawyers 12
at this office 7

Contact
Kęstutis Švirinas (head of Vilnius office)

CATEGORIES OF WORK

- Capital markets
- Commercial property/real estate
- Construction
- Corporate and commercial
- Dispute resolution – litigation and arbitration
- Energy and natural resources
- Environment
- Foreign direct investment
- Insurance
- Tax

BERNOTAS & DOMINAS GLIMSTEDT

JOGAILOS STR 4
01116 VILNIUS

Telephone: +370 5 269 0700
Fax: +370 5 269 0701
E-mail: vilnius@glimstedt.lt
Website: www.glimstedt.lt

Languages
English, French, German, Latvian, Lithuanian, Russian, Swedish

Other offices
Riga, Tallinn

Number of lawyers 63
at this office 27

CATEGORIES OF WORK

- Company and commercial
- Banking and finance
- Mergers and acquisitions
- Privatisation
- Competition law
- Insolvency and business restructuring
- Intellectual property
- Telecommunications and information technology law
- Advertising and media
- Insurance
- Litigation, arbitration, dispute resolution
- Real estate and construction
- International trade and transportation
- Labour law

FOIGT & PARTNERS/REGIJA BORENIUS

J JASINSKIO STR 16A, 8TH FLOOR
01112 VILNIUS

Telephone: +370 5 264 9555
Fax: +370 5 260 8327
E-mail: regija@regija.lt
Website: www.regija.lt

Languages
English, German, Lithuanian, Russian

Number of lawyers 19

Other Borenius group member firms
Borenius & Kemppinen (Helsinki);
Luiga Mody Hääl Borenius (Tallinn);
Liepa, Skopina /Borenius (Riga)

CATEGORIES OF WORK

Banking, finance and securities	Real estate and construction
Commercial law and company law	Litigation
Mergers and acquisitions	Taxation
EU and competition law	Privatisation
Transportation law	Environment
Media, information technology and telecommunications law	Labour law
Arbitration	Corporate finance
Intellectual property	

JUREVIČIUS, BALČIŪNAS & BARTKUS
PROFESSIONAL LAW PARTNERSHIP

SUBAČIAUS 7
01127 VILNIUS

Telephone: +370 5 274 2400
Fax: +370 5 274 2444
E-mail: advocate@jbblegal.lt
Website: www.jbblegal.lt

Languages
English, French, German, Polish, Russian

Number of lawyers 26

Contacts
Raimundas Jurevičius, Gintaras Balčiūnas, Gintautas Bartkus, Gytis Kaminskas

Member
Baltic Legal Solutions

CATEGORIES OF WORK

General practice	Finance
Company law	Telecommunications law
Corporate law	Energy law
Mergers and acquisitions	Environmental law
Competition law	Maritime law
Real estate	Shipping
Leases and leasing	European Union law
Business law	Construction law
Privatisation	Debt collection
Foreign investment	Labour and employment
International commercial law	Tax law
Intellectual property	Civil litigation
Banking law	Sports law
Securities	

JURIDICON LAW OFFICE

TOTORIU STREET 5-7
01121 VILNIUS

Telephone: +370 5 269 1100
Fax: +370 5 269 1010
E-mail: office@juridicon.lt
Website: www.juridicon.lt

Languages
English, German, Polish, Russian

Number of lawyers 6

Contact
Laimonas Marcinkevicius

Member
ILS Group

CATEGORIES OF WORK

Commercial property/real estate
Laimonas Marcinkevicius, Ingrida Steponaviciene

Competition and EU
Andrzej Czajkowski

Corporate and commercial
Laimonas Marcinkevicius, Ingrida Steponaviciene

Dispute resolution, litigation and arbitration
Laimonas Marcinkevicius, Andrzej Czajkowski

E-commerce
Andrzej Czajkowski

Employment
Laimonas Marcinkevicius, Ingrida Steponaviciene

Energy and natural resources
Andrzej Czajkowski

Foreign direct investment
Laimonas Marcinkevicius, Ingrida Steponaviciene

Information technology
Andrzej Czajkowski

Intellectual property
Andrzej Czajkowski

Media and entertainment
Andrzej Czajkowski

Mergers and acquisitions
Laimonas Marcinkevicius, Ingrida Steponaviciene

Private client and trusts
Laimonas Marcinkevicius

Tax
Laimonas Marcinkevicius

Telecommunications
Andrzej Czajkowski

METIDA LAW FIRM OF REDA ŽABOLIENĖ

GEDIMINO AVE 45-6
01109 VILNIUS

Telephone: +370 5 249 0830
Fax: +370 5 249 0833
E-mail: patent@metida.lt
Website: www.metida.lt

Languages
Lithuanian, Russian, English

Number of lawyers 3

Member
AIPPI; FICPI; INTA; CIB; ECTA; Lithuanian Patent Attorneys Association; Lithuanian Bar Association

CATEGORIES OF WORK

Intellectual property

Commercial law

Litigation

Contract law

Company law

LIDEIKA, PETRAUSKAS, VALIŪNAS IR PARTNERIAI LAWIN

JOGAILOS 9/1
01116 VILNIUS

Telephone: +370 5 268 1832
Fax: +370 5 212 5591
E-mail: vilnius@lawin.lt
Website: www.lawin.lt

Languages
English, French, German, Russian

Other offices
Klaipėda

Number of lawyers 41
at this office 40

Contact
Rolandas Valiūnas (managing partner)

CATEGORIES OF WORK

Banking and finance
G Stasevičius, G Rečiūnas

Communications
J Gumbis, A Bičiūnienė

Competition
J Gumbis, M Juonys

Corporate and M&A
R Valiūnas, Ž Zinkevičius

Corporate restructuring, insolvency
M Kiškis, L Skibarka

Dispute resolution
V Vaitkutė Pavan, R Paukštė

Employment and social security
R Petravičius, A Augustinavičius

Energy and natural resources
J Gumbis, A Bičiūnienė

Environment
R Galvėnas, S Gudynas

Information technology
M Kiškis, M Juonys

Insurance
T Kontautas, G Rečiūnas

Intellectual property
M Kiškis, R Pumputiene

Public private partnership
G Stasevičius, D Burgienė

Real estate and construction
R Galvėnas, T Milašauskas

Securities
G Stasevičius, G Rečiūnas

Tax
V Vasiliauskas, G Balčius

Trade
J Gumbis, A Makauskaitė

Transport and maritime
V Vaitkutė Pavan, S Sudintas

THE FIRM

Lideika, Petrauskas, Valiūnas ir partneriai LAWIN is one of the leading and largest law firms in Lithuania and the Baltic States. The firm renders services in all major fields of business and is distinguished by the excellence of services, extensive experience and leading specialists in Lithuania. The firm is a member of LAWIN, a group of the leading Baltic law firms also including Klavins & Slaidins LAWIN in Latvia and Lepik & Luhaäär LAWIN in Estonia. LAWIN currently has over 80 lawyers, making it the largest legal presence working in the Baltics.

The firm's head office is situated in Vilnius and, since 1998, the branch has successfully operated in Klaipeda, a major Lithuanian port. Presently, Lideika, Petrauskas, Valiūnas ir partneriai LAWIN has 41 law professionals. Most of the firm's lawyers have earned postgraduate degrees at US, UK, German and other Western universities. The firm takes an active part in the reform of the Lithuanian legal system, including drafting of the new legislation and other programs.

The firm's clients include multinational corporations, investment banks and international finance institutions as well as leading domestic companies. Cross-border transactions form a significant part of the firm's work and some 80% of the client base are international clients.

The firm has continuously sought specialisation of its lawyers and was probably the first law firm in Lithuania to have effectively introduced practice groups. The firm's lawyers work in five practice groups – corporate and M&A; finance and tax; trade and technologies; property and environment; dispute resolution and transport.

AREAS OF PRACTICE

Lideika, Petrauskas, Valiūnas ir partneriai LAWIN has earned its reputation for being at the heart of the largest and most complex commercial and financial transactions in Lithuania.

The firm has vast experience in the corporate and M&A field gained through participation in major M&A and privatisation transactions, leveraged buy-outs, joint ventures, negotiating and implementing shareholders' agreements and other corporate matters. The firm has an outstanding reputation in privatisation matters – it has been successfully acting in either buyer-side or as adviser of the government (the State Property Fund) in virtually all major privatisation transactions in Lithuania.

The firm has a solid portfolio of international banking clients and regularly advises on debt, equity and derivatives offerings, subordinated and syndicated loans, commercial lending, investment and project financing as well as capital markets and securities.

The firm has a leading competition team which is characterised by diverse subject matter and a combination of legal and economic expertise. The firm assists clients in merger control, joint ventures, regulation of cartels and horizontal co-operation agreements, vertical restrictions, abuse of dominant position, state aid, and sector-specific regulation.

In communications and IT, the firm regularly advises major international and Lithuanian telecom companies, representing them in regulatory matters and litigation with the regulator. The IT team has a strong IT client base including major multinationals and leading Lithuanian IT companies.

The firm's diverse IP practice includes registration of trade marks, drafting of licensing agreements, representing clients before the State Patent Bureau and the Customs Department, and representation in trade mark and other IP-related litigation.

The firm advises a number of leading real estate and construction companies and property investment funds on real estate acquisition and development, lease, planning, and construction as well as property insurance.

The firm is recognised as one of the leading advisers to the shipping and transport industries, counselling on maritime (charterparties, bills of lading, ship registration, ship arrest) and other transport issues, and has leading transport companies among its clients.

NORCOUS & PARTNERS
LAW OFFICES

GOŠTAUTO ST 12 A
01108 VILNIUS

Telephone: +370 5 268 3620
Fax: +370 5 268 3621
E-mail: office@norcous.lt
Website: www.norcous.lt

Languages
English, German, Lithuanian, Polish, Russian

Number of lawyers 20

Member
RoschierRaidla - Fenno-Baltic Partnering; ius laboris, International Employment Law, Pensions and Employee Benefits Alliance

CATEGORIES OF WORK

Mergers and acquisitions
Irmantas Norkus, Aušra Adomaitytė, Žilvinas Kvietkus

Banking and finance
Irmantas Norkus, Ruslanás Bronikovas

Commercial and company law
Aušra Adomaitytė, Lauras Butkevičius, Žilvinas Kvietkus

Competition
Irmantas Norkus, Aušra Adomaitytė

Immigration and expatriates
Arūnas Šidlauskas

Litigation
Arūnas Šidlauskas, Aurimas Brazdeikis, Žilvinas Kvietkus

Privatisation
Irmantas Norkus, Miroslav Nosevič, Žilvinas Kvietkus

EU law
Lauras Butkevičius, Mindaugas Civilka

Real estate
Arūnas Šidlauskas, Aurimas Brazdeikis

Securities
Irmantas Norkus, Aušra Adomaitytė, Eva Suduiko

Tax law and tax disputes
Arūnas Šidlauskas, Aurimas Brazdeikis

IPR and telecommunications
Mindaugas Civilka

LAW FIRM SPES

ZVEJU STR. 14A
09310 VILNIUS

Telephone: +370 5 275 6592
Fax: +370 5 275 6997
E-mail: office@spes.lt
Website: www spes.lt

Languages
English, French, Lithuanian, Polish, Russian

Number of lawyers 13

CATEGORIES OF WORK

Commercial and company law
Zigmas Peciulis, Aivaras Raisutis

Banking and finance
Zigmas Peciulis

Mergers and acquisitions
Zigmas Peciulis, Kornelija Janonyte

Real estate and construction law
Zigmas Peciulis, Kornelija Janonyte

Insurance, securities
Martynas Peciulis, Virgilijus Kaupas

Labour and employment
Martynas Peciulis, Virgilijus Kaupas

Transport law
Martynas Peciulis, Virgilijus Kaupas

Corporate restructuring, insolvency
Virgilijus Kaupas, Kornelija Janonyte

Litigation
Zigmas Peciulis, Martynas Peciulis

Criminal law
Vytautas Sviderskis

SALADŽIUS & PARTNERS

VICTORIA TOWER
J. JASINKSKIO 16B
01112 VILNIUS

Telephone: +370 5 239 2391
Fax: +370 5 239 2390
E-mail: law.firm@splegal.lt
Website: www.splegal.lt

Languages
English, French, German, Lithuanian, Russian

Number of lawyers 14

Contact
Jonas Saladžius (senior partner)

CATEGORIES OF WORK

Commercial and competition
Jonas Saladžius

Company law, corporate structuring
Jonas Saladžius

Dispute resolution
Alvydas Gineitis

Employment and human resources
Max Saveljev

Banking and finance
Jonas Saladžius

EU law
Rimtis Puišys, Andrius Mamontovas

Intellectual property
Rimtis Puišys

Mergers and acquisitions
Jonas Saladžius

Public law
Aušrys Šliavas

Real estate
Jonas Saladžius

Privatisation
Jonas Saladžius

Energy and infrastructure projects
Aušrys Šliavas

Technology, media and communications
Max Saveljev

SOLOVEIČIKAS, MARKAUSKAS AND AVIŽA/SMA

TOTORIU ST 3
01121 VILNIUS

Telephone: +370 5 212 0033
Fax: +370 5 212 1033
E-mail: info@sma.lt
Website: www.sma.lt

Languages
English, German, Latvian, Lithuanian, Russian

Other offices
Riga

Number of lawyers 23
at this office 15

Contact
Dr Deividas Soloveičikas

International groupings
SMA Law Offices

CATEGORIES OF WORK

Project finance
Mr D Soloveičikas, Ms K Alešiūnaitė

Real estate
Mr D Soloveičikas, Ms K Alešiūnaitė

Construction
Mr D Soloveičikas, Ms K Alešiūnaitė

Environment and ecology
Mr L Markauskas

Pharmaceutical and medical
Mr L Markauskas

Corporate and commercial law
Mr L Markauskas, Mr D Kolesnikov

Tax and finance
Mr S Aviža, Mr D Nikolajenko

Intellectual property and media rights
Mr L Markauskas, Mr S Petrovs

International trade
Mr D Soloveičikas

EU law
Mr D Soloveičikas

Litigation
Mr S Aviža, Mr D Soloveičikas, Mr T Bagdanskis

Transportation
Mr S Aviža

Labour and employment
Mr L Markauskas, Mr T Bagdanskis, Mr D Nikolajenko

SORAINEN LAW OFFICES

JOGAILOS G. 4
01116 VILNIUS

Telephone: +370 5 268 5040
Fax: +370 5 268 5041
E-mail: sorainen@sorainen.lt
Website: www.sorainen.com

Languages
English, Estonian, Finnish, French, German, Latvian, Lithuanian, Polish, Russian, Swedish

Other offices
Riga, Tallinn

Number of lawyers 65
at this office 16

CATEGORIES OF WORK

Mergers and acquisitions
Kestutis Adamonis, Raminta Karlonaite

Competition and public procurement law
Raminta Karlonaite, Juhani Siira

Property and construction law
Kestutis Adamonis, Rita Svedaite

Employment law
Mindaugas Lescius, Rita Svedaite

Financial and securities law
Kestutis Adamonis, Algirdas Peksys

Taxation law
Tomas Davidonis, Kestutis Adamonis

Company law
Tomas Davidonis, Algirdas Peksys

Litigation and arbitration
Renata Berzanskiene, Marius Urbelis

Trade, distribution and services
Juhani Siira

Intellectual property and IT law
Renata Berzanskiene, Juhani Siira

Insurance
Mindaugas Lescius

Energy and environmental law
Kestutis Adamonis, Marius Urbelis

THE FIRM

Sorainen Law Offices was established in 1995 in Tallinn, Estonia. The firm expanded into Latvia and Lithuania in 1997 and 1999 respectively. The firm has grown steadily and today is one of the leading Baltic law firms, with 65 lawyers, including 10 partners, in its three offices. Many lawyers of the firm are widely recognised 'experts' in their areas of practice.

The firm's offices in Lithuania, Latvia and Estonia are part of a fully integrated, pan-Baltic legal practice with a strong international element dedicated to providing high-quality legal services to foreign investors and to local businesses in the region.

AREAS OF PRACTICE

The firm's strategic focus is on M&A, with a strong commitment also to property and construction, financial and securities law. Consequently, the firm is constantly involved in most major M&A transactions in the Baltic countries.

Sorainen Law Offices has built its practice through organic growth and outstanding service. Being a full-service business law firm, Sorainen Law Offices assists domestic and international clients in all corporate areas, competition, banking and finance, insurance, corporate and commercial, shipping and transport, property, IT and telecoms, IPR, employment, tax, insolvency and restructuring, litigation and arbitration.

As a truly integrated pan-Baltic law firm, Sorainen Law Offices offers a focused, proactive, business-minded and co-ordinated approach to client service in relation to cross-border transactions.

More detailed information is provided upon request.

SUTKIENE, PILKAUSKAS & PARTNERS

DIDZIOJI STREET 23
01128 VILNIUS

Telephone: +370 5 251 4444
Fax: +370 5 251 4455
E-mail: spp@spp.lt
Website: www.spp.lt

Languages
English, Estonian, French, German, Italian, Lithuanian, Polish, Russian

Number of lawyers 18

Contacts
Eugenija Sutkiene (managing partner), Jonas Pilkauskas (managing partner), Czeslaw Okinczyc (associate partner)

Member
Interlaw; American Chamber of Commerce; British Chamber of Commerce; German and Baltic Chamber of Commerce in Estonia, Latvia and Lithuania; Antitrust Alliance

CATEGORIES OF WORK

Company and corporate law
J Pilkauskas, C Okinczyc

Tax law
L Baikstys, D Zdanavicius

Mergers and acquisitions
J Pilkauskas, E Sutkiene

Intellectual property
N Grazinyte, M Skavronskas

Securities and financial markets
V Drizga, J Pilkauskas

Business financing
V Bernatonis, R Juodka

Real estate and construction
R Juodka, M Matonis

Telecommunications and IT
N Grazinyte, E Sutkiene

Court and commercial arbitration
V Bernatonis, L Daruliene

Labour and immigration law
O Trucinskaite, D Zdanavicius

Competition law
L Daruliene, M Matonis

Public procurement
L Baikstys, V Bernatonis

Insurance law
V Drizga, D Zdanavicius

Corporate restructuring
E Sutkiene, O Trucinskaite

THE FIRM

Sutkiene, Pilkauskas & Partners (SPP) is one of the leading law firms in Lithuania specialising in commercial and business law. SPP works in close co-operation with its partner law firms Tark & Co (Estonia) and Loze, Grunte & Cers (Latvia).

SPP clientele includes the world's largest corporations, as well as small and medium-sized businesses, banks, financial institutions, embassies, non-profit organisations and individuals.

Representing a wide range of clients, either entering or active in Lithuanian and foreign markets, SPP attorneys are also co-operating with specialists from diverse fields, assisting in drafting legal statutes of the Republic of Lithuania.

SPP attorneys are licensed professionals, educated in Lithuania and at institutions in Europe and the US. They have been regular participants in various seminars and courses and have acquired valuable experience and professional relationships during traineeships in distinguished law firms, Lithuanian and international agencies and organisations.

AREAS OF PRACTICE

SPP attorneys handle legal matters pertaining to company law (including privatisation, acquisition, consolidation, merger and transfer, all types of securities transactions), commercial law, finance and tax law, telecommunications and IT law, real estate and real estate property development law, greenfield investments, insurance law, competition law, foreign trade and investments, public procurement, litigation and alternative dispute resolution.

SPP's international experience covers most of its practice areas. The key areas are as follows:

Company law, M&A: SPP's corporate law practice group attorneys provide counsel with in-depth skills, broad experience and a sense of perspective. Following the re-establishment of the independence of the Republic of Lithuania, they pioneered legal aspects of the privatisation process, drafted legislation governing the privatisation of companies, took part in almost every major transaction conducted by Lithuanian and foreign entities, such as Philip Morris, Kraft General Foods, and Coca Cola Bottlers. The services provided include the following: incorporation, liquidation, reorganisation, bankruptcy of legal persons; M&A; representation of potential investors in regard to privatisation procedures; shareholder representation at shareholder meetings, before courts and arbitral tribunals; drafting of all types of documents of a corporate and commercial nature.

Competition law: SPP's antitrust and competition practice group attorneys, having acquired unique expertise through working in the Competition Council of the Republic of Lithuania, are counselling a variety of domestic and foreign investors regarding notification of the Competition Council, concentration control issues, unfair competition, drafting of complaints about competition-restricting actions. They represent before courts and the Competition Council.

Court and commercial arbitration: SPP has extensive experience in successfully preventing and resolving disputes. It represents clients in civil, commercial, labour, tax, competition and administrative cases before courts of all instances, as well as before international and local arbitral tribunals.

Labour law and immigration: SPP represents employers in virtually every industry and counsels both domestic and foreign clients on relevant matters, such as obtainment of work and residence permits, terminations, reductions in force, breaches of conduct, misappropriation of trade secrets and unfair competition.

Real estate and construction: SPP has gained deep expertise in drafting contracts for transfer, acquisition, lease, sublease, holding in trust of real property and corollary contracts. The firm advises on legal aspects of construction and greenfield investments.

LUXEMBOURG

Population	468,600
Number of lawyers	1,000
Professional title	avocat; avocat à la cour
Currency	Euro (€)

Index

Luxembourg is the smallest independent state in the EU. Landlocked, and bordered by Belgium, France and Germany, the geographically tiny country is dominated by its capital, Luxembourg City. The official languages are French and German, with French the main language of the business and legal community. The spoken language of the majority of the population is Luxembourgish, a dialect of German.

The government, led by Prime Minister Jean-Claude Juncker and Deputy President Jean Asselborn, is a coalition of the Luxembourg Socialist Workers' Party and the Christian Social People's Party, and has been in power since 2004. Since Luxembourg's presidency of the Council of Europe ended in mid-2005, the government's popularity has been waning, amid concerns that changes to the tax regime might adversely affect the banking sector. In July 2005, contrary to more prominent EU neighbours such as France, Luxembourg voted in favour of the European Constitution, reiterating its position as one of the strongest advocates of European integration.

BILLING

Billing rates vary between €150 per hour for junior associates, €250 for senior associates, and €300-€450 for partners.

MARKETING

The Luxembourg Bar Association rules prohibit advertising by law firms operating within its jurisdiction. Indirect marketing, including websites and brochures, is permitted.

IN-HOUSE LAWYERS

Large financial institutions operating in Luxembourg often have small in-house teams.

ECONOMY

The basis of Luxembourg's economy is the financial services industry, which accounts for 22% of GDP. Over 170 banks have offices in the country, which also boasts the highest concentration of investment funds in Europe; their number continues to grow, particularly in the field of international private equity. These sectors are driven by a favourable tax and regulatory environment, in a jurisdiction that is often used in international tax planning. The US invests more per capita in Luxembourg than in any other foreign jurisdiction.

Luxembourg's beneficial tax regime – including the lowest VAT rates in the EU and a corporate tax rate of 22.9% – and the attractiveness and flexibility of Luxembourg holding and financing structures, mean that it is an extremely popular jurisdiction through which to structure cross-border M&A and to channel international corporate reorganisations. Many global groups have holding companies in Luxembourg, and over the last two years there has been a surge in transactions of all sizes involving the use of Luxembourg structures, particularly by US companies. The economy appears to be recovering from its 2001 downturn, with 2.3% growth in 2004 and inflation running at around 2.4%.

Leading homegrown companies include media giant RTL (now part of the Bertelsmann group) and internet telephone company Skype Communications, which in September 2005 agreed its US$4.1bn takeover by eBay, in the M&A transaction of the year.

As well as demonstrating an eagerness for European integration, Luxembourg's government has facilitated a strong banking and finance industry by leaving it largely unregulated. It remains to be seen what impact the new government's 15% withholding tax levied on bank accounts held by non-residents, which came into force in July 2005, will have on the flow of money coming into the jurisdiction.

LEGAL SYSTEM AND LEGAL MARKET

Luxembourg City is home to the most important domestic courts, the Court of Cassation and the Court of Appeals, and also houses key EU judicial organs the European Court of Justice (ECJ) and the Court of Justice of the European Free Trade Association.

The Luxembourg legal market is buoyant and law firms are growing, though their development is inhibited by a shortage in the recruitment market; many new hires are currently coming from France and Germany.

The leading independent Luxembourg law firms are **Arendt & Medernach** and **Elvinger, Hoss & Prussen**. The larger of the two, **Arendt & Medernach**, has a Brussels office, a strategic alliance with **Dillon Eustace** in Dublin, and in 2005

The largest firms

1	Arendt & Medernach	158
2	Linklaters Loesch	63
3	Allen & Overy Luxembourg	50
4	Elvinger, Hoss & Prussen	46
5	Bonn Schmitt Steichen	45
	Kremer Associés & Clifford Chance	45
7	Loyens Winandy	42
8	Wildgen & Partners	40
9	Oostvogels Pfister Roemers	39
10	Noble & Scheidecker	28
11	Molitor, Fisch & Associés	18
12	Plottké, Brunel & Associates	15
13	Di Stefano & Sedlo Avocats à la Cour	14
14	AS Avocats	13
15	Schaeffer, Hengel, Geiben & Associés	12
16	Etude Reding - Avocats à la Cour	10
	Le Goueff Avocats	10
	NautaDutilh	10
19	Schiltz et Schiltz	9
20	Wagener, Rukavina & Kettenmeyer	8
21	Adam & Bleser	7
22	Michel - Schanen	6
	Philippe & Partners	6
24	Castegnaro Cabinet d'Avocats, member of ius laboris	5
	De Meester Attorneys at Law	5
	Lutgen & McGaw	5
	Maitland	5
	Wassenich, Étude	5

These figures represent the total number of lawyers in this country only, and have been supplied by the firms themselves. The figures should be accurate as at 1 January 2006.

became the first Luxembourg firm to open an office in New York. **Bonn Schmitt Steichen** is also a major corporate firm, though it is perceived to have lost some ground in recent years. An up-and-coming corporate player, particularly in the field of private equity, is **Oostvogels Pfister Roemers**, which in 2005 became the first Luxembourg firm to open a London office.

Because of Luxembourg's highly developed financial services market, a number of international firms have in recent years established local practices. **Allen & Overy Luxembourg** was the first to enter the market, through a merger with a local firm in 2000. **Kremer Associés & Clifford Chance** has been in operation since 2001, and is seeing a period of considerable expansion. **Linklaters Loesch**, the result of a 2002 merger, is targeting major corporates and asset managers. **Dechert Luxembourg** is the only US-based firm in the country, but is much smaller than the other international firms, with one of its two Luxembourg partners having left at the end of 2005.

Some leading Dutch law firms have established Luxembourg offices as part of their pan-Benelux practices. In 2003, Netherlands-based **Loyens & Loeff** merged its tax practice, established in Luxembourg since 1991, with a local firm with which it had an existing co-operation, to form **Loyens Winandy**. Netherlands-based **NautaDutilh** set up a greenfield Luxembourg office in 2003, and local firm **Molitor, Fisch & Associés** has an official co-operation with Netherlands-based **Houthoff Buruma**.

Noble & Scheidecker used to be associated with PricewaterhouseCoopers under the name of **Landwell**, but is now independent and increasingly developing a presence as a corporate firm.

2005 saw the establishment of two new law firms in Luxembourg. **VandenBulke Avocats** was set up by Denis Van Den Bulke, formerly partner-in-charge of **Dorsey & Whitney LLP**'s Brussels office, while **Brucher & Associés** was established by Jean Brucher, formerly managing partner of **Dechert Luxembourg**.

BANKING AND FINANCE

Luxembourg has a heavily regulated banking sector and flexible banking legislation. It has a strong reputation for active debt capital markets and, following the introduction in 2004 of legislation creating a specific legal and tax framework for securitisation vehicles, the market is now seeing a plethora of securitisations. Until 15 July 2005, the Luxembourg Stock Exchange (LSE) operated only one market, the Bourse de Luxembourg. On 18 July 2005 the LSE also started to operate an alternative market, called the Euro MTF.

Allen & Overy Luxembourg has a strong practice in bank restructuring and mergers. André Marc, who enjoys an outstanding reputation, handles local and regulatory work. Henri Wagener handles international and capital markets work, and advised Barclays Capital, Merrill Lynch & Co and UBS Investment Bank on the restructuring of securities worth US$81m issued by the Republic of Argentina, a large number of which were listed on the LSE.

Arendt & Medernach has a large team that advises around 40% of the banks with offices in Luxembourg. Phillipe Dupont has a strong securitisation practice, and has additionally been handling banking and finance work, including public offerings, for a Luxembourg-based satellite company. Paul Mousel co-heads the banking team and is also recommended. On the equity capital markets, the corporate team recently advised on the Luxembourg aspects of the Frankfurt IPO of a German broadcasting company.

Elvinger, Hoss & Prussen has a leading reputation for banking and finance work and a track record of innovative deals, and is active in national and international securitisations, including for financing small and medium-sized businesses in various EU jurisdictions. The team has been boosted by the lateral hire of partner Andre Hoffmann, formerly head of legal at the Luxembourg arm of Fortis Bank. Pit Reckinger is recommended for regulatory work, and Phillipe Hoss for securitisation and capital markets.

Linklaters Loesch, under Janine Biver, has a high-level practice that is particularly strong on the capital markets side, where it works closely with **Linklaters**' London and Moscow offices. The three offices together advised on the groundbreaking issue of loan participation notes worth US$657m and US$1.2bn by Gazprom, via a

BANKING AND FINANCE

ALLEN & OVERY LUXEMBOURG ✪
ARENDT & MEDERNACH ✪
ELVINGER, HOSS & PRUSSEN
LINKLATERS LOESCH ✪

Bonn Schmitt Steichen ✪
Kremer Associés & Clifford Chance

Dechert Luxembourg ✪
Di Stefano & Sedlo Avocats À La Cour ✪
Le Goueff Avocats
NautaDutilh
Oostvogels Pfister Roemers ✪
Wildgen & Partners

Loyens Winandy
Lutgen & McGaw
Molitor, Fisch & Associés ✪
Noble & Scheidecker ✪
Plottké, Brunel & Associates ✪
VandenBulke Avocats

Firms are listed A-Z in tiers which are ranked in order of priority
✪ Indicates firm displays contact details at the end of this chapter.

Luxembourg SPV. The team is also strong in securitisation, and is advising a mortgage bank on its establishment in Luxembourg. Patrick Geortay is recommended for acquisition finance.

Bonn Schmitt Steichen has been handling a substantial number of securitisation transactions, including advising on a securitisation structure promoted by a major financial institution, which has issued notes worth €10bn over the past two years. Alex Schmitt is recommended.

The bulk of the work at **Kremer Associés & Clifford Chance** involves international acquisitions structured through Luxembourg, and the structuring of financial products. **Clifford Chance** has a leading securitisation practice worldwide, and the Luxembourg office is active on complex securitisations. Christian Kremer focuses on securitisation, regulatory and capital markets work, including acting for leading issuers in the debt capital markets in relation to their Luxembourg programmes. Steve Jacoby handles acquisition finance.

Dechert Luxembourg has a focus on the financial sector and works closely with its offices in the US and the UK. Recent work out of Luxembourg includes advising US clients on the LSE listing of bonds, advising on mezzanine debt investments via Luxembourg, and advising on the launch of a securitisation vehicle. Jean Brucher has now left to establish **Brucher & Associés**; remaining partner Marc Seimetz heads the practice.

DI STEFANO & SEDLO Avocats à la Cour recruited the well-regarded Adrian Sedlo as a partner. He focuses on banking and structured finance, and has recently handled several securitisations worth over €300m. He also acted as Luxembourg counsel on two major CDO transactions arranged by a major US investment bank, and advised on the issue by a Luxembourg SPV of loan participation notes listed on the Irish Stock Exchange.

Le Goueff Avocats recruited a banking associate from **Molitor, Fisch & Associés**, while tax of counsel Olivier Martin, a recent recruit from **Dechert Luxembourg**, also handles banking work, as does name partner Stephan Le Goueff. The team advised a France-based financial institution on a secured financing transaction in the US, and also acted as Luxembourg counsel to a major Canadian bank in relation to a refinancing deal.

The Luxembourg office of Netherlands-based **NautaDutilh** recruited new partner Josée Weydert from **Kremer Associés & Clifford Chance**. She focuses on capital markets and structured finance, and the team as a whole is developing a good reputation for high-level, Anglo-American style advice. It advised Euroclear Finance 2 SA, a Luxembourg securitisation SPV, on the issuance of €300m in fixed/floating-rate securities, and also advised Spain-based gaming company Codere on the Luxembourg aspects of a €335m senior notes issue.

Oostvogels Pfister Roemers has been active in the capital markets, advising on the Luxembourg aspects of an IPO in the financial services sector, and on the LSE listing of Eurobonds. The hire of tax partner Charles Roemers from **Kremer Associés & Clifford Chance** boosted the team's securitisation capability.

Wildgen & Partners' team, headed by Georges Gudenburg, is well versed in advising international financial institutions on regulatory, capital markets (including IPOs) and structured finance matters, including advice on securitisation vehicles.

Loyens Winandy's banking practice is headed by Dirk Leermakers, and focuses on advising some major financial institutions, including on the financing aspects of corporate transactions.

At **Lutgen & McGaw**, Didier McGaw has been working on a €10m financing, and has experience in structured finance. The firm also has a solid banking litigation and secrecy practice.

Molitor, Fisch & Associés partner Paulo Lopes da Silva advises a number of small private banks in Luxembourg, and a handful of global high street banks with Luxembourg operations. The focus is on regulatory matters, banking acquisitions and advice on banking secrecy and anti-money laundering procedures. The firm also handles banking litigation.

At **Noble & Scheidecker**, newly promoted partner Jean-François Trapp heads the finance practice, which focuses on structured finance. The firm has also been advising on the Luxembourg aspects of an IPO in New York.

Plottké, Brunel & Associates has a private banking practice, advising on regulatory matters and litigation. It recently advised a Portuguese bank on the establishment of a branch in Luxembourg, and also advises two significant Luxembourg-based financial institutions.

VandenBulke Avocats is a new firm established by Denis Van Den Bulke, formerly partner-in-charge of **Dorsey & Whitney LLP**'s Brussels office. He has a well-respected banking practice focusing on loan work, and has been advising some major European banks on the issuing of facilities to NYSE-listed groups.

CORPORATE AND M&A

The Luxembourg M&A market is now booming, with a plethora of mainly international transactions involving the use of Luxembourg corporate structures. Most of these transactions come from the private equity market.

Allen & Overy Luxembourg's corporate team has an excellent reputation. It advised General Atlantic Partners and Oakhill Capital Partners on the €850m purchase of General Electric's outsourcing business via the creation of a Luxembourg corporate structure. Marc Feider has a good reputation for efficiency, as does Pierre Schleimer, particularly in relation to regulatory work. The office also has a very strong banking mergers practice.

Arendt & Medernach has a strong private equity practice and has been handling major acquisitions in Europe by US- and France-based funds. The department has been growing at a junior level, and is supported by a small New York office that opened in 2005. Guy Harles heads the team, which has also been advising a major Scandinavian company on a restructuring via Luxembourg.

The corporate team at **Elvinger, Hoss & Prussen** has an outstanding reputation. It acts for numerous international groups and private equity firms, with recent highlights including advising Luxembourg-based IT provider Skype on the Luxembourg aspects of its US$4.1bn sale to eBay. The firm has also been advising Doughty Hanson on real estate and private equity transactions. Philippe Hoss is recommended.

Linklaters Loesch has the leading cross-border M&A practice in Luxembourg. Combining with other **Linklaters** offices, the Luxembourg office led and co-ordinated advice to Dexia Banque Internationale à Luxembourg in 16 jurisdictions, relating to the bringing together of Dexia and Royal Bank of Canada's custody and investor services business, in a joint venture with assets worth US$1.8tr. It also advised on the Luxembourg aspects of the acquisition by a consortium led by Royal Bank of Scotland of a 10% stake in Bank of China. Team head Tom

CORPORATE AND M&A

ALLEN & OVERY LUXEMBOURG ✪
ARENDT & MEDERNACH ✪
ELVINGER, HOSS & PRUSSEN
LINKLATERS LOESCH ✪

Bonn Schmitt Steichen ✪
Kremer Associés & Clifford Chance
Oostvogels Pfister Roemers ✪
Wildgen & Partners

Dechert Luxembourg ✪
Di Stefano & Sedlo Avocats À La Cour ✪
NautaDutilh
Noble & Scheidecker ✪
VandenBulke Avocats

Dupong & Metzler
Jim Penning & Associés
Le Goueff Avocats
Loyens Winandy
Maitland
Molitor, Fisch & Associés ✪
Plottké, Brunel & Associates ✪
Wagener, Rukavina & Kettenmeyer

Firms are listed A-Z in tiers which are ranked in order of priority
✪ *Indicates firm displays contact details at the end of this chapter.*

Loesch is recommended, while the senior associates in the team are also very highly regarded.

Bonn Schmitt Steichen has been advising on the reorganisation of an international group, and the structuring of a US$4bn contribution by the group to another international group in exchange for shares. The private equity team has been growing at junior level, and also worked on the establishment of two private equity structures aimed at investments in international real estate, worth €120m each. Alex Schmitt is recommended.

Kremer Associés & Clifford Chance, together with **Clifford Chance** in London, advised eBay on the acquisition of Skype. The team, led by Christian Kremer, has also been handling a number of private equity transactions structured through Luxembourg and involving the acquisition of German companies.

Oostvogels Pfister Roemers' corporate team has a growing reputation and a strong private equity practice, advising a number of leading private equity clients on European and Asian acquisitions. It also advised on the Luxembourg aspects of Yellow Pages' international restructuring , advised a group on the acquisition of various toll roads in France, and advised a Luxembourg bank on the launch of one of the largest pan-European real estate funds. In 2005, the firm opened a small office in London, with a focus on servicing private equity houses and financial institutions. Stef Oostvogels is recommended.

Wildgen & Partners' team, headed by Pierre Metzler and François Brouxel, is handling an increasing amount of advice to private equity funds investing throughout the world via Luxembourg vehicles. The team has been particularly active in relation to real estate private equity. The team also has good general corporate finance experience.

Dechert Luxembourg partner Marc Seimetz has been advising on the corporate structuring and sale of real estate companies for international investment funds (a deal involving the incorporation of around 15 local companies), and also advising an international group on the corporate aspects of European investments via a Luxembourg securitisation vehicle.

DI STEFANO & SEDLO Avocats à La Cour's highly regarded Mario Di Stefano has an excellent practice that recently advised a NYSE-listed biotechnology group on a US$500m international restructuring via Luxembourg.

NautaDutilh advised Weather Investments, part of the Orascom group, on the Luxembourg aspects of its €12.2bn acquisition and refinancing of Italian telecommunications group Wind, the largest leveraged buy-out in European history. Marc Meyers is recommended.

Noble & Scheidecker's growing corporate team has an excellent reputation and a focus on private equity and real estate. It advised one of the world's leading financial institutions on the implementation of a Luxembourg structure to finance a €400m real estate acquisition in France, and advised a world-leading oilfield services company on a €945m acquisition. Marie-Béatrice Noble is recommended.

At new firm **VandenBulke Avocats**, Denis Van Den Bulke has an excellent reputation for his corporate practice, which is focused on clients from Belgium, France, the UK and the US. He recently advised on the restructuring via Luxembourg of a US company, and advised a Belgian group on a capital increase in the Middle East.

Le Goueff Avocats has been advising a major international car manufacturer on a series of acquisitions in Luxembourg.

Loyens Winandy typically advises on M&A transactions with tax-driven structures, including advice on hybrid instruments involved in corporate matters.

Maitland is a South Africa-based multidisciplinary practice. The lawyers in its Luxembourg office recently advised in relation to the first Luxembourg company to be listed on AIM in London.

Molitor, Fisch & Associés has an official co-operation with one of the major Dutch corporate law firms, **Houthoff Buruma**, which has a particularly strong practice in international restructurings. In Luxembourg, Laurent Fisch handles professional sector acquisitions and corporate finance. The firm has a strong litigation practice, which ties into its corporate advice on directors' and officers' liability and on corporate governance. It also recently advised on a major manufacturing-industry insolvency.

Plottké, Brunel & Associates has a significant international practice with a particular focus on Russian clients, including a NYSE-listed Russian group which it advises on acquisitions and banking ventures relating to Luxembourg.

DISPUTE RESOLUTION

There is a considerable amount of banking litigation in Luxembourg. Arbitration is not common in the jurisdiction, with most arbitrations on Luxembourg matters taking place in Paris. Mediation is also not common.

Allen & Overy Luxembourg has been representing a private equity house in litigation relating to a buy-out, and also advising Gesticom on a VAT dispute. Pier Schliemer is recommended.

Arendt & Medernach's litigation practice, which works mainly for the firm's institutional clients, is headed by senior partner Jean Medernach, while corporate head Guy Harles handles arbitration. The firm also has a property litigation practice, and François Kremer specialises in fraud.

DISPUTE RESOLUTION

ALLEN & OVERY LUXEMBOURG ✪
ARENDT & MEDERNACH ✪
BONN SCHMITT STEICHEN ✪
ELVINGER, HOSS & PRUSSEN
KREMER ASSOCIÉS & CLIFFORD CHANCE
LINKLATERS LOESCH ✪
MOLITOR, FISCH & ASSOCIÉS ✪

Le Goueff Avocats
Welter Wurth Kinsch

Adam & Bleser
Brucher & Associés
Dupong & Metzler
Jim Penning & Associés
Lutgen & McGaw
Michel – Schanen
Schiltz et Schiltz
Wagener, Rukavina & Kettenmeyer

Firms are listed A-Z in tiers which are ranked in order of priority
✪ Indicates firm displays contact details at the end of this chapter.

Bonn Schmitt Steichen has a very strong litigation practice, which has been advising some major international institutional clients. Fabio Trevisan and Guy Arendt head the team.

Elvinger, Hoss & Prussen handles complex arbitration and banking litigation.

Kremer Associés & Clifford Chance's Albert Moro heads a strong and growing team, which recently hired an associate with an in-house banking background. The team has been handling some major arbitration cases, including an arbitration in Paris under ICC rules.

Linklaters Loesch's team, headed by Guy Loesch, has been involved in some high-profile corporate litigation, successfully defending the RTL Group and its directors against an attempted injunction relating to the proposed delisting of the group's shares on the London Stock Exchange.

Molitor, Fisch & Associés is best known as a litigation firm. Paulo Lopes da Silva is very active in banking litigation, particularly matters involving the liability of banks and their directors. His team has also been handling litigation between a major Asian manufacturer of satellite components and its Luxembourg distributor.

Le Goueff Avocats has a focus on IT-related litigation, and has also been handling litigation relating to banking secrecy. The team recruited an associate from **Arendt & Medernach**, and has been representing a Luxembourg-based electronics manufacturer in a €10m dispute with a Taiwanese manufacturer.

Welter Wurth Kinsch is a niche litigation practice, small but very well regarded. The firm is also known for its strong arbitration practice.

Adam & Bleser has a growing practice with particular strength in employment-related litigation.

Brucher & Associés is a new firm established by Jean Brucher, formerly managing partner of **Dechert Luxembourg**. His recent work at his previous firm included successfully advising on an estate liquidation matter at the Court of Cassation.

Lutgen & McGaw has been handling some significant commercial litigation, and **Schiltz et Schiltz** has a strong reputation for insurance litigation, and also handles disputes in the banking sector.

EMPLOYMENT

Luxembourg's 2003 law relating to the transfer of staff in the context of mergers and acquisitions of businesses is now being invoked in many public transfers, and is generating a considerable amount of work for employment lawyers as well as some heated discussion with unions.

Adam & Bleser is a leading employment boutique with a growing team. It has a focus on litigation, but has recently been building up its non-contentious employment practice, where it advises some major financial institutions.

Allen & Overy Luxembourg recently advised Allgemeine Deutsche Direktbank International on the final closing of its Luxembourg activities and the dismissal of its entire staff. André Marc, the firm's co-head of banking, also heads the labour law team, and enjoys an excellent reputation.

Arendt & Medernach's team is headed by Louis Berns and handles a mixture of contentious work, for clients in the financial industry, and non-contentious work, including advising on social plans and pension schemes.

Castegnaro Cabinet d'Avocats, member of ius laboris, another employment boutique, is headed by the highly recommended Guy Castegnaro. It has recently been advising on the dismissal of high-ranking executives in the banking and insurance sectors and organising procedures for placing employees of a client at the disposal of another company. It also has strong recent experience relating to transfers of undertakings and collective dismissals.

Bonn Schmitt Steichen's Anne Morel has an excellent reputation. Her team has been advising on employment litigation, collective dismissals, employee incentive schemes and stock option plans.

Elvinger, Hoss & Prussen's practice is headed by Pierre Elvinger, who leads a team of six fee-earners. It has been advising on a number of negotiations relating to collective dismissals, and handling litigation. Clients include a number of major industrial and banking groups.

Kremer Associés & Clifford Chance's Albert Moros has an active employment litigation practice, which advises major financial institutions on disputes with employees. He also handles collective labour relations and the transfer of undertakings.

Linklaters Loesch recently advised Clerical Medical Europe Financial Services BV on a number of restructuring issues and on individual employee cases. René Diedrich heads the team, and enjoys an excellent reputation.

EMPLOYMENT

ADAM & BLESER
ALLEN & OVERY LUXEMBOURG ✪
ARENDT & MEDERNACH ✪
CASTEGNARO CABINET D'AVOCATS, MEMBER OF IUS LABORIS ✪

Bonn Schmitt Steichen ✪
Elvinger, Hoss & Prussen
Kremer Associés & Clifford Chance
Linklaters Loesch ✪
Molitor, Fisch & Associés ✪
Noble & Scheidecker ✪

Dechert Luxembourg ✪
Decker, Bodry & Braun
Di Stefano & Sedlo Avocats À La Cour ✪
Le Goueff Avocats
Schiltz et Schiltz
Wassenich, Étude

Firms are listed A-Z in tiers which are ranked in order of priority
✪ *Indicates firm displays contact details at the end of this chapter.*

Molitor, Fisch & Associés has a strong client base in the private banking and manufacturing sectors. It advised a major European insurance company on employment matters related to an acquisition process, and also advised a major plastics manufacturer on a restructuring requiring lay-offs. The team, headed by Michel Molitor, has been active in negotiations with trades unions and Luxembourg's Ministry of Labour, relating to the transfer of businesses.

Noble & Scheidecker has a strong practice with a large client base in the IT sector. The team has recently been developing its employment litigation capability through associate-level hires. On the non-contentious side, it advised Skype on the establishment of a stock option plan prior to its merger with eBay, and on the review of this plan in the context of the merger. It also assisted an IT consulting company with the transfer of employees to a new group entity. Marielle Stevenot is recommended.

Dechert Luxembourg advises its clients in the financial services sector on employment matters including, recently, a branch closing.

Decker, Bodry & Braun name partner Andrée Braun focuses on employment law, while **DI STEFANO & SEDLO Avocats à la Cour** has experience in advising on social plans in the financial sector, and, on the contentious side, recently advised in proceedings before the European Court of First Instance.

Schiltz et Schiltz has an employment litigation practice, with clients including various banks and insurance companies.

Étude Wassenich's Marie-Pierre Bezzina has a good reputation for employment matters, and **Le Goueff Avocats** handles employment litigation, particularly for clients in the IT sector.

IP AND IT

Luxembourg is not a particularly active jurisdiction for the enforcement of IP rights or for e-commerce, but the strength of the banking and financial services industry means that IT issues, including data protection, are very important,and there are some excellent IT lawyers in the country.

Arendt & Medernach's Sophie Wagener has a very active practice, and heads a growing team of four fee-earners. It advises some large computer companies on IT matters, including data protection. It also advises jewellery, clothing and car manufacturers on the enforcement of their IP rights in Luxembourg.

Decker, Bodry & Braun is a leading boutique practice with a particular focus on trade mark litigation and copyright. Clients are mainly based in the UK and the US. Nicolas Decker is recommended.

Le Gouëff Avocats' Stephan Le Goueff is renowned for his work in the IT, media and telecommunications sectors, in which areas he has genuine specialism and a very active practice. Associate Gary Cywie, who formerly co-headed the IT practice, left the firm for **Noble & Scheidecker**. However the team has recruited a senior associate from **Molitor, Fisch & Associés** and another associate from **Arendt & Medernach**. IT clients include banks, a large US IT company and some household names in the computer sector, and the work handled includes outsourcing. The firm advises a Luxembourg media group on IP, competition and co-production matters, while in the telecommunications sector, it has been appointed by the Luxembourg

IP AND IT

ARENDT & MEDERNACH ✪
DECKER, BODRY & BRAUN
LE GOUEFF AVOCATS

Allen & Overy Luxembourg ✪
Bonn Schmitt Steichen ✪
Elvinger, Hoss & Prussen
Linklaters Loesch ✪
Noble & Scheidecker ✪
Plottké, Brunel & Associates ✪

Di Stefano & Sedlo Avocats À La Cour ✪
Lutgen & McGaw
Michel – Schanen
Molitor, Fisch & Associés ✪
VandenBulke Avocats

Firms are listed A-Z in tiers which are ranked in order of priority
✪ *Indicates firm displays contact details at the end of this chapter.*

regulatory authority to conduct a major study into the implementation of a telecommunications regulatory package.

Allen & Overy Luxembourg has been representing Recticel and Waterford Wedgewood in trade mark litigation before the ECJ, and also advising Skype on telecommunications issues. Katia Manhaeve is recommended.

Bonn Schmitt Steichen has been advising international clothing companies on trade mark counterfeiting, a financial institution on data protection, and has also been working on a patent sale agreement. Guy Arendt and Véronique Hoffeld head the practice.

At **Elvinger, Hoss & Prussen**, André Elvinger and Yves Prussen focus on IP litigation.

Linklaters Loesch focuses on complex data protection, outsourcing projects and copyright matters, and recently advised InBew on strategic issues relating to data compliance. Team head Emmanuelle Rago handles mediations involving domain names and IP rights.

Noble & Scheidecker recruited associate Gary Cywie, formerly co-head of the IT and IP practice at top-ranking firm **Le Goueff Avocats**, who brings particular experience in trade marks and copyright. The highly recommended Katia Scheidecker heads the team, which has been advising a global e-commerce company on a Luxembourg-related feasibility study and due diligence exercise.

Plottké, Brunel & Associates' Miriam Brunel advises companies in the luxury goods sector on trade marks, and also handles patent litigation; she recently defended two patents before the European Court of First Instance. The firm also has experience in the media sector.

DI STEFANO & SEDLO Avocats à la Cour has been handling IT litigation relating to a failed project, advising on trade mark infringement and domain name litigation, and advising an international group on data protection.

Molitor, Fisch & Associés recently handled litigation relating to international trade mark infringement on behalf of a major international bank, while **VandenBulke Avocats** advises a major telecommunications company on trade mark matters and a bank dealing room on IT issues, as well as advising on data protection.

INSURANCE

Luxembourg is an important centre for insurance companies. Though the insurance market is not as active or aggressive as the banking and financial services markets, there are an increasing number of insurance schemes in the jurisdiction and increasing differentiation between banking and insurance products.

Allen & Overy Luxembourg has been advising the Zurich Insurance Company on outsourcing issues, and also advising Banco BPI SA on the structuring of insurance products and the establishment of operations in Luxembourg. Pierre Schliemer is recommended.

INSURANCE

ALLEN & OVERY LUXEMBOURG ✪
ARENDT & MEDERNACH ✪
BONN SCHMITT STEICHEN ✪
KREMER ASSOCIÉS & CLIFFORD CHANCE
LINKLATERS LOESCH ✪
SCHILTZ ET SCHILTZ

Elvinger, Hoss & Prussen
Le Goueff Avocats
Plottké, Brunel & Associates ✪
Wassenich, Étude
Wildgen & Partners

Firms are listed A-Z in tiers which are ranked in order of priority
✪ *Indicates firm displays contact details at the end of this chapter.*

Arendt & Medernach has a non-contentious regulatory practice in the life insurance sector. Carine Seipel's team, which works within the firm's banking department, also advises on the incorporation of insurance and reinsurance companies in Luxembourg.

Bonn Schmitt Steichen has been advising on the establishment of insurance and reinsurance companies in Luxembourg, and has also been involved in international litigation involving life insurance contracts filed with Luxembourg banks.

Kremer Associés & Clifford Chance's litigation team handles a considerable volume of work in the cross-border life insurance sector. The firm also handles non-contentious insurance work relating to the repackaging of bank products into insurance products.

Linklaters Loesch's team, headed by Mark Loesch, recently advised Clerical Medical Europe Financial Services on a hostile exit from a joint venture with a Luxembourg-based master broker company.

Schiltz et Schiltz is an insurance boutique that is on the panel of some major Luxembourg-based insurance companies, and also has international clients in the sector. It is experienced in insurance litigation and arbitration.

Le Goueff Avocats recently advised a substantial insurance and reinsurance company on fraud-related proceedings in the UK, and regularly handles litigation for a Luxembourg-based insurance company.

Plottké, Brunel & Associates advises Luxembourg-based insurers and self-insured clients. Miriam Brunel has an insurance litigation and regulatory practice, and advises two insurers active in the international capital markets.

Étude Wassenich is experienced in recovery cases and claims adjustments, and receives referrals from Germany and Belgium. Claude Wassenich is recommended.

Wildgen & Partners' Michel Bulach has an active practice, advising international companies on the acquisition and subsequent restructuring of reinsurance companies.

INVESTMENT FUNDS

Luxembourg is the leading centre for fund administration in Europe, and investment fund work was the starting point for the practices of most of the leading local law firms. The largest firms dominate in terms of advising the traditional public funds established by major banks. However, in the booming and relatively new area of international private equity, the legal market is growing and some up-and-coming firms are challenging the dominance of the traditional players. The SICAR (*société d'investissement en capital à risque*) – a new Luxembourg fund structure in existence since 2004 – has given a boost to this side of the market.

Arendt & Medernach has a large team of 45 lawyers, and a large market share of public funds work. The firm has also been very active in advising private equity clients on SICARs. Claude Kremer has a market-leading reputation, and Claude Niedner is also recommended.

Elvinger, Hoss & Prussen has the highest market share of investment fund clients in Luxembourg. The team is led by Jacques Elvinger, who has a leading reputation.

Linklaters Loesch's managing partner, Freddy Brausch, has an outstanding reputation for investment funds work. He heads an excellent team that includes three additional partners and 16 associates, and advises some major investment banks and asset managers. It has a strong structured fund products practice, recently won Morgan Stanley as a new client, and advised Deutsche Bank on the establishment of a series of funds. The corporate team also worked on the establishment of a €41m SICAR for Adara Ventures, the first such fund to secure commitment from the European Investment Fund.

INVESTMENT FUNDS

ARENDT & MEDERNACH ✪
ELVINGER, HOSS & PRUSSEN
LINKLATERS LOESCH ✪

Allen & Overy Luxembourg ✪
Bonn Schmitt Steichen ✪
Kremer Associés & Clifford Chance

Dechert Luxembourg ✪
Di Stefano & Sedlo Avocats À La Cour ✪
Loyens Winandy
Maitland
Oostvogels Pfister Roemers ✪
Wildgen & Partners

Firms are listed A-Z in tiers which are ranked in order of priority
✪ *Indicates firm displays contact details at the end of this chapter.*

Allen & Overy Luxembourg lost Corinne Lamesch to **Kremer Associés & Clifford Chance**, but recruited senior associate Jean-Christian Six, formerly of **Arendt & Medernach** and with a background at Banque Privée Edmond de Rothschild Luxembourg, as its senior dedicated funds lawyer. The team handles some high-level international work, particularly in the area of real estate funds. It recently advised Prudential on the establishment of a pan-European institutional real estate fund.

Bonn Schmitt Steichen acts for a large number of investment funds, representing around US$80m in assets. The team, under Alex Schmitt, established one of the first Luxembourg SICARs and is working on a second on behalf of various leading foreign banks.

Kremer Associés & Clifford Chance has been particularly active in the real estate fund sector, where it acts for a number of German institutional investors. Joëlle Hauser heads the Luxembourg funds practice, which has a focus on complex, structured funds. Christian Kremer is chair of **Clifford Chance**'s global asset management group, and focuses on international work.

Dechert LLP has a very strong reputation in the US for investment funds work, and **Dechert Luxembourg** has an excellent, highly regarded practice. Its clients are mainly large international players, including American Express, Scudder and PIMCO. Marc Seimetz recently advised an international promoter on the incorporation of a fund of funds.

DI STEFANO & SEDLO Avocats à la Cour's new name partner Adrian Sedlo has been advising private sector investment fund clients on compliance issues and the listing of securities on the LSE.

Loyens Winandy partner Gilles Dusemont advises on private equity funds, mostly relating to securitisation vehicles.

Maitland has a well-regarded practice. John Mills recently advised on the establishment and restructuring of a fund which involved the establishment of an offshore mutual fund of a multi-class fund (two hedge fund classes totalling US$500m and US$30m private equity class), including borrowing facilities totalling US$300m.

Oostvogels Pfister Roemers has been advising a major Luxembourg financial institution on the launch of a pan-European investment fund, and is very active in the field of SICARs, hedge funds and real estate funds. Francois Pfister previously worked for Fidelity Investments.

Wildgen & Partners has been advising on the implementation of funds, their listing and the adaptation of their articles and prospectuses to take into account new European regulations.

TAX

Luxembourg's favourable tax environment makes it attractive for tax planning and group structuring, and remains a strong draw for foreign companies.

Allen & Overy Luxembourg's head of tax, Jean Schaffner, has a reputation as a leading player in the market, where he is singled out by many for praise. His six-lawyer team recently advised Lazard on the tax aspects of its IPO, and also advised Goldman Sachs on the establishment of a holding company for investments in Germany.

Arendt & Medernach's team includes two partners, Thierry Lesage and Eric Fort, and nine additional lawyers. It has been advising a global broadcasting company on the tax structuring of a €1.6bn asset sale to a company controlled by funds advised by two leading private equity firms, and also advised a global company on tax structuring relating to a US$6.8bn funding of a Luxembourg holding company as part of a share re-purchase programme. The tax practice is supported by the firm's newly opened New York office.

At **Bonn Schmitt Steichen**, Alain Steichen is a renowned tax specialist. His team, which includes two other partners and four associates, has been active on the tax aspects of private equity and finance transactions, and also handles tax litigation.

TAX

ALLEN & OVERY LUXEMBOURG ✪
ARENDT & MEDERNACH ✪
BONN SCHMITT STEICHEN ✪

Elvinger, Hoss & Prussen
Linklaters Loesch ✪
Loyens Winandy
Oostvogels Pfister Roemers ✪

Kremer Associés & Clifford Chance
Le Goueff Avocats
NautaDutilh

Di Stefano & Sedlo Avocats À La Cour ✪
Plottké, Brunel & Associates ✪
Schaeffer, Hengel, Geiben & Associés ✪
VandenBulke Avocats

Firms are listed A-Z in tiers which are ranked in order of priority
✪ Indicates firm displays contact details at the end of this chapter.

Elvinger, Hoss & Prussen has strong securitisation, transactional and investment fund practices, and its tax team advises on the tax aspects of international work in these areas. André Elvinger, Jean Hoss and Yves Prussen are recommended.

Linklaters Loesch's team is headed by Paul Tulcinsky, who is actively involved in the development of new tax legislation in Luxembourg. He recently advised Vitas Capital Life on the tax aspects of the establishment of a securitisation fund worth US$60-100m for Spanish investors.

Loyens Winandy has a highly regarded, high-level tax team, which is well versed in advising on the establishment of Luxembourg tax structures. Name partner Jean-Pierre Winandy has a focus on tax litigation, and is representing Eurobeton in a high-profile case concerning tax credits for foreign holdings. The team has also recruited Jean-Luc Schaus from **NCR Avocats**.

Oostvogels Pfister Roemers recruited new name partner Charles Roemers from **Kremer Associés & Clifford Chance**. He brings with him a team of five fee-earners, and has a focus on international corporate tax structuring.

Kremer Associés & Clifford Chance lost tax partner Charles Roemers and his team to **Oostvogels Pfister Roemers**, and an associate to **NautaDutilh**, but has also been hiring into its tax practice. Corporate and finance partner Christian Kremer now heads the team, which focuses on capital markets-related work, and also has particular expertise in VAT.

Le Goueff Avocats recruited of-counsel Olivier Martin, formerly of **Dechert Luxembourg**. He has recently been advising on the tax aspects of various banking and M&A transactions.

NautaDutilh's Luxembourg office has a team of five tax lawyers including partner Frédéric Feyten and a recent recruit from **Kremer Associés & Clifford Chance**. The focus is on international corporate and financial products work.

DI STEFANO & SEDLO Avocats à la Cour's Mario Di Stefano has a good reputation for tax advice linked to corporate restructurings and securitisations.

Plottké, Brunel & Associates' recent activity includes advising a major German car manufacturer on tax issues relating to its Luxembourg holding companies, while **VandenBulke Avocats** has been advising leading financial institutions on the tax aspects of the establishment of SICARs.

ALLEN & OVERY LUXEMBOURG

58 RUE CHARLES MARTEL
2134 LUXEMBOURG

Telephone: +352 44 44 551
Fax: +352 44 44 55 222
E-mail: information@allenovery.com
Website: www.allenovery.com

Languages
Dutch, English, French, German, Italian, Spanish

Other offices
Amsterdam, Antwerp, Bangkok, Beijing, Bratislava, Brussels, Budapest, Dubai, Frankfurt, Hamburg, Hong Kong, London, Madrid, Milan, Moscow, New York, Paris, Prague, Rome, Shanghai, Singapore, Tokyo, Turin, Warsaw

Number of lawyers 2,304
at this office 38

Contact
Marc Feider

CATEGORIES OF WORK

Banking
André Marc, Henri Wagner

Company (M&As, formations)
Marc Feider, Pierre Schleimer

Securities and capital markets
Henri Wagner

Contracts
Katia Manhaeve

Distribution
Katia Manhaeve

Labour law
André Marc

EC law
Katia Manhaeve

Offshore investments
Jean Schaffner

Public law
Dominique Bornert

Taxation
Jean Schaffner

Telecoms
Pierre Schleimer

Investment funds
Jean-Christian Six

Intellectual property
Katia Manhaeve

Litigation and insurance
Pierre Schleimer

Real estate
André Marc

ARENDT & MEDERNACH

14 RUE ERASME
PO BOX 39
2010 LUXEMBOURG

Telephone: +352 40 78 78-1
Fax: +352 40 78 04
E-mail: info@arendt-medernach.com
Website: www arendt-medernach.com

Languages
Arabic, Bulgarian, Dutch, English, French, German, Icelandic, Italian, Japanese, Luxembourgish, Portuguese, Russian, Spanish

Other offices
Brussels, New York*

Number of lawyers 163
at this office 158

International groupings
Exclusive alliance with Dillon Eustace, Ireland

CATEGORIES OF WORK

Financial services
Philippe Dupont, Paul Mousel

Corporate tax and intellectual property
Guy Harles

Investment management
Claude Kremer, Claude Niedner

Litigation
Jean Medernach

BONN SCHMITT STEICHEN

44 RUE DE LA VALLÉE
2661 LUXEMBOURG

Telephone: +352 45 58 581
Fax: +352 45 58 59
E-mail: mail@bsslaw.net
Website: www.bsslaw.net

Languages
Dutch, English, German, French, Italian, Spanish

Number of lawyers 45

Member
Lex Mundi

CATEGORIES OF WORK

Banking and finance
Alex Schmitt, Jean Steffen

Securitisation and asset finance
Laurent Lazard, Jean Steffen

Private equity and venture capital
Alex Schmitt, Chantal Keereman

Labour and employment benefits
Guy Arendt, Anne Morel

Taxation and tax planning
Alain Steichen, Jean Steffen

Corporate and commercial law
Chantal Keereman, Jean Steffen

Mergers and acquisitions
Alex Schmitt, Alain Steichen

Intellectual property
Guy Arendt, Véronique Hoffeld

Capital markets
Laurent Lazard, Luc Courtois

Media, IT and e-commerce
Guy Arendt, Véronique Hoffeld

Investment funds
Corinne Philippe, Luc Courtois

Litigation and arbitration
Fabio Trevisan, Guy Arendt

THE FIRM

Bonn Schmitt Steichen is one of Luxembourg's most prominent law firms. Bonn Schmitt Steichen is committed to providing personalised legal services to its clients by working closely with them to understand their business and legal needs. As members of a rapidly growing international and Luxembourg practice, Bonn Schmitt Steichen's attorneys are qualified to practise in Luxembourg, Belgium, France, Italy and New York, US. This unique combination of legal and linguistic experience allows Bonn Schmitt Steichen to deliver legal solutions and advice to clients doing business in one of Europe's leading financial centres.

AREAS OF PRACTICE

The firm's key practice areas include all aspects of banking, corporate, commercial, financial, labour, media, e-commerce and tax law. Bonn Schmitt Steichen is one of the few firms in Luxembourg that enjoys a truly global client base, assisting clients from North America and Asia as well as from Luxembourg and the European Union. The firm represents clients ranging from leading international banks, industrial corporations and national governments to financial service and media companies. The firm also regularly advises Luxembourg state and local authorities and regulatory authorities on a wide range of legal matters.

Bonn Schmitt Steichen is registered with the Luxembourg Bar, and is a member of several international legal organisations, including the International Bar Association and the Union Internationale des Advocats. Members of the firm have published articles in the *Journal of International Banking Law*, the *Stanford Journal of International Law*, *Butterworths' Journal of International Banking and Financial Law*, as well as numerous Belgian, Luxembourg and German journals. Each year, Bonn Schmitt Steichen writes the Luxembourg Law Digest for the *Martindale-Hubbell* Directory.

Bonn Schmitt Steichen's attorneys form a diverse and talented group. The firm's attorneys include law professors and lecturers at law schools around Europe. Over 50% of the firm's lawyers hold Master of Laws (LLM) degrees from law schools in the US and the UK. Bonn Schmitt Steichen also maintains close relationships with leading law firms around Europe, which strengthens the firm's ability to serve its clients in international matters. In addition, Bonn Schmitt Steichen sponsors visiting foreign lawyers and law students as interns in its Luxembourg office, reflecting the firm's global vision and its ongoing relationship with foreign law schools and law firms.

CASTEGNARO CABINET D'AVOCATS, member of ius laboris

33 ALLÉE SCHEFFER
2520 LUXEMBOURG

Telephone: +352 26 86 821
Fax: +352 26 86 82 82
E-mail: contact@castegnaro.lu
Website: www.castegnaro.lu

Languages
English, French, German, Italian, Luxembourgish

Number of lawyers 5

Contacts
Guy Castegnaro (partner)
(guy.castegnaro@castegnaro.lu),
Ariane Claverie (associate)
(ariane.claverie@castegnaro.lu),
Alexandra Castegnaro (associate)
(alexandra.castegnaro@castegnaro.lu),
Erwann Sevellec (trainee)
(erwann.sevellec@castegnaro.lu)

Member
European Employment lawyer's Association (EELA); Institut Européen de Juristes en Droit Social (IES); ius laboris, International Employment Law, Pensions and Employee Benefits Alliance

CATEGORIES OF WORK

Labour law

Social security

Supplementary pensions

Compensation and benefits

Commercial and corporate law

Tax law

Data protection

Labour, social security and commercial litigation

DECHERT LUXEMBOURG

74 RUE DE MERL
BP 709
2017 LUXEMBOURG

Telephone: +352 45 62 62
Fax: +352 45 94 65
E-mail: marc.seimetz@dechert.com
Website: www.dechert.com

Languages
English, French, German, Luxembourgish

Other offices
Austin, Boston, Brussels, Charlotte, Frankfurt, Harrisburg, Hartford, London, Munich, Newport Beach, New York, Palo Alto, Paris, Philadelphia, Princeton, San Francisco, Washington DC

Number of lawyers 900+
at this office 3 (+ 1 counsel)

Contact
Marc Seimetz

Member
Union International des Avocats (UIA); International Bar Association (IBA)

CATEGORIES OF WORK

Banking and finance
Marc Seimetz, Jean-Louis Frognit, Pascal Bouvy

Investment funds
Marc Seimetz, Jean-Louis Frognit, Pascal Bouvy

Corporate and tax
Marc Seimetz, Jean-Louis Frognit, Pascal Bouvy

Litigation
Jean-Louis Frognit

DI STEFANO & SEDLO AVOCATS À LA COUR

24 AVENUE MARIE-THÉRÈSE
BP 2648
1026 LUXEMBOURG

Telephone: +352 26 25 621
Fax: +352 26 25 622
E-mail: contact@mds-legal.com
Website: www.mds-legal.com

Languages
English, French, German, Italian, Luxembourgish, Portuguese, Spanish, Croatian, Dutch

Number of lawyers 12

Member
Alfa International; Association of European lawyers; Union Internationale des Avocats (UIA); IBLC International Business Law Consortium; Ausländischer Anwaltverein Deutschland e V (AAD), State Capital Law Firm Group

CATEGORIES OF WORK

Company and corporate law
Mario Di Stefano, Adrian Sedlo

Contract law
Mario Di Stefano

Tax law
Mario Di Stefano

Antitrust and trade regulations
Mario Di Stefano

Mergers and acquisitions
Mario Di Stefano

European Union law
Mario Di Stefano

Business law
Mario Di Stefano, Adrian Sedlo

Litigation
Mario Di Stefano, Eric Muller

Commercial law
Mario Di Stefano, Adrian Sedlo

Labour and employment
Mario Di Stefano, Eric Muller

Banking and finance
Adrian Sedlo

Investment funds
Adrian Sedlo

IP and IT
Mario Di Stefano

LINKLATERS LOESCH

35 AVENUE JOHN F KENNEDY
1855 LUXEMBOURG

Telephone: +352 26 081
Fax: +352 26 08 88 88
Website: www.linklaters.com

Languages
All commercial and local languages in the countries where Linklaters operates

Other offices
Amsterdam, Antwerp, Bangkok, Beijing, Berlin, Bratislava, Brussels, Bucharest, Budapest, Cologne, Dubai, Frankfurt am Main, Hong Kong, Lisbon, London, Madrid, Milan, Moscow, Munich, New York, Paris, Prague, Rome, São Paulo, Shanghai, Singapore, Stockholm, Tokyo, Warsaw

Number of lawyers 2,000 worldwide

Contact
Freddy Brausch

CATEGORIES OF WORK

Mergers and acquisitions
Jean-Paul Spang

Technology, media and telecommunications
Emmanuelle Ragot

Capital markets
Janine Biver

Employment, pensions and benefits
René Diederich

Banking
Patrick Geortay

Litigation and arbitration
Guy Loesch

Tax
Paul Tulcinsky

Investment management
Freddy Brausch

Real estate
René Diederich

Private equity
Jean-Paul Spang

Asset and structured finance
Tom Loesch

MOLITOR, FISCH & ASSOCIÉS

IN CO-OPERATION WITH HOUTHOFF BURUMA

8 RUE SAINTE ZITHE
PO BOX 690
2016 LUXEMBOURG

Telephone: +352 297 298 1
Fax: +352 297 299
E-mail: mfa@mfa.lu
Website: www.mfa.lu

Languages
English, French, German

Number of lawyers 18

CATEGORIES OF WORK

Arbitration and commercial litigation
Michel Molitor, Paulo Lopes Da Silva

Banking, finance and securities
Michel Molitor, Laurent Fisch

Corporate, mergers and acquisitions
Laurent Fisch, Oliver Huth

Industrial relations and employment
Michel Molitor, Paulo Lopes Da Silva

Information technology and telecoms
Laurent Fisch, Régis Muller

Real estate and construction
Paulo Lopes Da Silva, Laurent Fisch

NOBLE & SCHEIDECKER

398 ROUTE D'ESCH
1471 LUXEMBOURG

Telephone: +352 26 48 42 1
Fax: +352 26 48 42 35 00
E-mail: info@mnks.com
Website: www.mnks.com

Languages
Dutch, English, French, German, Italian, Spanish

Number of lawyers 30

Contacts
Marie-Béatrice Noble, Katia Scheidecker

CATEGORIES OF WORK

Corporate structuring
Jean-François Findling,
Jean-François Trapp

Litigation
Katia Scheidecker,
Patrice Mbonyumutwa

Tax litigation
Vinciane Schandeler,
Catherine Baflast

Employment
Marie-Béatrice Noble,
Marielle Stevenot

Incentive schemes and pension
Marie-Béatrice Noble,
Marielle Stevenot

Private equity and venture capital
Katia Scheidecker,
Marie-Béatrice Noble

Banking and finance
Marie-Béatrice Noble,
Jean-François Trapp

Intellectual property, IT and e-commerce
Katia Scheidecker,
Gary Cywie

Mergers and acquisitions
Marie-Béatrice Noble,
Jean-François Findling

Real estate transactions
Jean-François Findling

OOSTVOGELS PFISTER ROEMERS

20 AVENUE MONTEREY
BP 603
2016 LUXEMBOURG

Telephone: +352 46 83 83
Fax: +352 46 84 84
E-mail: info@oostvogels.com
Website: www.oostvogels.com

Languages
English, French, Dutch, German, Italian, Spanish

Number of lawyers 35

CATEGORIES OF WORK

Corporate law and structures
Stef Oostvogels, François Pfister, Charles Roemers

Mergers, acquisitions and private equity
Stef Oostvogels, François Pfister, Charles Roemers

Banking, finance, investment funds
Stef Oostvogels, François Pfister

Contractual liabilities
Stef Oostvogels, Stéphane Hadet

International private law
François Pfister

Taxation
François Pfister, Stef Oostvogels, Charles Roemers

Audiovisual and new technologies
François Pfister, Stef Oostvogels

Commercial litigation and arbitration
Stef Oostvogels, Stéphane Hadet

PLOTTKÉ, BRUNEL & ASSOCIATES LAWYERLUX

54 RUE D'ANVERS
PO BOX 2038
1020 LUXEMBOURG

Telephone: +352 29 73 15
Fax: +352 29 73 16
E-mail: info@lawyerlux.lu
Website: www.lawyerlux.lu

Languages
English, French, German, Italian

Number of lawyers
12 (+ 3 related lawyers outsourced)

Contacts
Gilles Plottké (managing partner),
Myriam Brunel (litigation, dispute resolution)

Member
Juris Network; AEA; UIA

CATEGORIES OF WORK

Corporate and business law

Intellectual property, media law, telecommunications

Banking and finance

Mergers and acquisitions

Public and administrative

Commercial and civil litigation

EU law, antitrust, unfair competition

Tax law

Real estate

Employment, pensions and benefits

Regulatory law

SCHAEFFER, HENGEL, GEIBEN & ASSOCIÉS

12 AVENUE DE LA PORTE-NEUVE
2227 LUXEMBOURG

Telephone: +352 47 23 72-1
Fax: +352 47 52 73
E-mail: etude@schaeffer.lu

Languages
English, French, German, Italian, Luxembourgish, Spanish

Number of lawyers 13

Member
TTN – Transnational Tax Network

CATEGORIES OF WORK

Corporate law
Nico Schaeffer, Nicolas Schaeffer, Claude Geiben

Business law
Nico Schaeffer, Nicolas Schaeffer, Claude Geiben, Mathis Hengel

Tax law
Nico Schaeffer, Claude Geiben

Shipping and air law
Nico Schaeffer, Nicolas Schaeffer

Civil law
Mathis Hengel

Assistance in litigation matters before tribunals and domestic courts
All partners and assistants

MALTA

Population	400,000
Number of lawyers	800
Professional title	Advocate
Currency	Maltese Lira (LM))

Index

Located in the in the Mediterranean Sea some 90km south of Sicily and 300km north of Africa, the Republic of Malta is home to a population of close to 400,000. The country comprises an archipelago with only the three largest islands (Malta, Ghawdex or Gozo, and Kemmuna or Comino) being inhabited. English and Maltese are both official languages in a country that from 1814 was historically a British territory and a part of the Commonwealth until it became independent in 1964. The chief of state since 4 April 2004 is President Eddie Fenech Adami and the head of government (since 23 March 2004) is Prime Minister Lawrence Gonzi. On the 1 May 2004, Malta became a member of European Union.

There has been much activity transposing EU legislation into national law in the past few years. Legislation imposed by the EU has affected many key industries in Malta, such as shipping, where stricter criteria for registration now apply.

BILLING

For general commercial work, hourly rates range from €60 for assistants to €150 for partners. In contentious matters, the rates litigators charge derive from a complex system of tariffs set by the courts, and depend on the nature of the work undertaken. Commercial property transactions may be charged *ad valorem*, with the fee a percentage of the deal value.

MARKETING

In 2003 the rules on marketing and publicity were somewhat relaxed and constraints in this respect are now not as harsh; previously the Code of Ethics prohibited law firms marketing directly to clients. Firms can now be identified as sponsors of events such as conferences and have greater freedom to be included in listings. More firms also have websites – allowed by the Maltese Chamber of Advocates. Confidentiality regarding names of clients remains obligatory.

IN-HOUSE LAWYERS

There has been an increasing trend in recent years for foreign businesses in Malta to hire in-house lawyers. Most of the work they handle is generally connected with regulatory consultation and administration rather than the practice of law.

ECONOMY

The Maltese economy is largely built on a number of key industries such as manufacturing and ship construction and repair. Accession to European Union membership has stimulated the privatisation of state-controlled businesses and liberalisation of markets. Economic performance, however, hasn't been booming. Tourism, for instance, which accounts for one-third of GDP, has been hard hit since 2001. The National Tourism Authority has, however, been granted a budget to revive the industry.

LEGAL MARKET

EU accession has created a lot of compliance and regulatory work for most law firms. Typically, advocates are versatile and practise in many areas, though specialists can be found in maritime law.

EU law is the area expanding fastest, though IT, including data protection and e-commerce is also growing quickly. There is also a nascent market for alternative dispute resolution (ADR).

FOREIGN FIRMS

Even though EU accession has opened the market to the possibility of foreign firms setting up shop on the island, none of them has yet showed interest in doing so. Being such a small legal market, which is well served by established local outfits, it is unlikely that the coming years will see any influx of foreign firms into the country.

BANKING AND FINANCE

One of the most reputed firms in the banking and finance sector is **Camilleri Preziosi**. Louis de Gabriele and Laragh Cassar head a practice that includes advising on capital markets, corporate finance and investment services. The firm was one of the very early participants in the investment services field, having acted for the promoters of the first fund management company to be set up in Malta. On the general banking and finance side, structured finance transactions by major international banks also generate large amounts of work for the firm.

Fenech & Fenech Advocates is renowned for its top-notch banking practice, which spans a wide range of issues in relation to the obtaining of an investment service licence and the provision of investment services in Malta. The firm acts for a

The largest firms

1	Ganado & Associates	21
2	Mamo TCV Advocates	20
3	Fenech & Fenech Advocates	19
4	Grech Vella Tortell & Hyzler	14
	Sapiano & Associates	14
6	Guido de Marco & Associates	10
7	Ganado Sammut	9
	Muscat Azzopardi & Associates	9
9	Buttigieg & Refalo Advocates	8
	Camilleri Preziosi	8
	Farrugia Schembri Orland Law Firm	8
	Hugh Peralta & Associates	8
13	Dingli & Dingli	7
	Emmanuel Mallia & Associates	7
	Farrugia Gatt & Falzon	7
16	Ellul Mifsud & Debono Advocates	6
	Galea Salomone & Associates	6
18	AVMT Advocates	5
	Cefai & Associates	5
	Gatt Frendo Tufigno Advocates	5
	Patrick J Galea & Associates	5
	R Frendo Randon & Associates	5
	Thake Desira Advocates	5
24	Busuttil & Busuttil	4
	CDF Advocates	4
	Zammit Pace & Co.	4

These figures represent the total number of lawyers in this country only, and have been supplied by the firms themselves. The figures should be accurate as at 1 January 2006.

BANKING AND FINANCE

CAMILLERI PREZIOSI ✪
FENECH & FENECH ADVOCATES
GANADO & ASSOCIATES
MAMO TCV ADVOCATES ✪

AVMT ADVOCATES
CEFAI & ASSOCIATES
GALEA SALOMONE & ASSOCIATES
GRECH VELLA TORTELL & HYZLER

CDF Advocates
R Frendo Randon & Associates

Ellul Mifsud & Debono Advocates
Emmanuel Mallia & Associates
Farrugia Gatt & Falzon
Gatt Frendo Tufigno Advocates ✪
Guido de Marco & Associates
Hugh Peralta & Associates
Rutter Giappone & Associates
Zammit Pace & Co. ✪

Firms are listed A-Z in tiers which are ranked in order of priority
✪ Indicates firm displays contact details at the end of this chapter.

number of Maltese and foreign banks and is also involved in the setting up and licensing of collective investment schemes.

Max Ganado's well-established name as an outstanding practitioner is just one of the reasons for **Ganado & Associates**' leading reputation. The firm advises on a plethora of banking law issues, including loan documentation, syndicated loans, loan participations, collateral and the enforcement of security, confidentiality as well as the provision of banking services on the internet.

Mamo TCV Advocates is going from strength to strength. The firm's banking and finance team, which includes partners David Tonna, Andrew Muscat and Richard Camilleri, advised the IFC on a US$10m loan with a share conversion option to First International Merchant Bank plc. Other highlights include advising foreign clients and financial institutions on the Maltese regulatory structure in the financial industry, following Malta's accession to the EU.

AVMT Advocates acted for an international financial institution in setting up its fully owned subsidiary in Malta and now acts as the Maltese subsidiary's general counsel on legal issues arising from its money lending and money brokering activities.

Cefai & Associates is also recommended, boasting solid expertise in trusts work.

Galea Salomone & Associates' busy financial department has been involved in ongoing work for leading Austrian bank Investkredit and for AFS bank.

Grech Vella Tortell & Hyzler's growing banking and finance practice boasts a team of three lawyers (including name partner partner Simon Tortell). The firm has seen a lot of work coming from abroad in setting up foreign funds locally, especially from the Channel Islands.

CDF Advocates' banking and finance practice is a key focus for the firm. Clients include several banks and financial services companies in Malta, including Bank of Valetta.

R Frendo Randon & Associates has solid trusts expertise, having acted as trustee in various trusts.

Partner Pierre Mifsud is **Ellul Mifsud & Debono Advocates**' head of banking and finance. He led the firm's advice to a London-based consortium of promoters in the setting up of two professional investor funds.

Emmanuel Mallia & Associates' expertise includes setting up and operating trusts, advising on foreign investment and advising Maltese companies on their investments abroad.

Farrugia Gatt & Falzon is also recommended. Its client base includes a number of local banks.

The shipping practice at **Gatt Frendo Tufigno Advocates** generates a fair amount of financial work. Clients of the firm include several foreign banks and international trading companies.

Giannella Caruana Curran spearheads **Guido de Marco & Associates**' banking and finance department. Edward Saliba is also recommended in foreign direct investment and financial services matters. The firm represents a number of financial institutions and insurance companies.

CORPORATE AND M&A

AVMT ADVOCATES
CAMILLERI PREZIOSI ✪
FENECH & FENECH ADVOCATES
GANADO & ASSOCIATES
GATT FRENDO TUFIGNO ADVOCATES ✪
GRECH VELLA TORTELL & HYZLER
MAMO TCV ADVOCATES ✪

Buttigieg & Refalo Advocates
Galea Salomone & Associates
Ganado Sammut ✪
Guido de Marco & Associates
Hugh Peralta & Associates
Muscat Azzopardi & Associates
Sapiano & Associates

CDF Advocates
Camilleri Delia Randon & Associates
Cefai & Associates
Dingli & Dingli
Ellul Mifsud & Debono Advocates
Emmanuel Mallia & Associates
Farrugia Gatt & Falzon
Farrugia Schembri Orland Law Firm
Jos A Schembri & Associates
Patrick J Galea & Associates
R Frendo Randon & Associates
Rutter Giappone & Associates
Thake Desira Advocates
Zammit Pace & Co. ✪

Firms are listed A-Z in tiers which are ranked in order of priority
✪ Indicates firm displays contact details at the end of this chapter.

CORPORATE AND M&A

Anton Micallef is **AVMT Advocates**' head of office, sharing his partnership with Peter Micallef – both highly regarded practitioners in Malta. The firm is one of the leading practices in registration and administration of trusts for international clients and holds a large client base operating International Trading Companies. **AVMT Advocates**' international exposure is also enhanced by its London associated office.

Camilleri Preziosi's highly regarded corporate practice is going from strength to strength. Spearheaded by widely acclaimed experts Louis de Gabriele and Henri Mizzi, the firm acts as legal counsel to the Privatisation Unit on the disposal of the government's 60% stake in Malta Stock Exchange-listed Maltacom plc, one of the largest transactions in 2005. Other highlights include advising Malta International Airport plc in the government's disposal of a 20% stake in the company. The firm also boasts strong expertise in capital markets and EU and competition issues, involving merger proposals and franchise and distribution agreements.

Fenech & Fenech Advocates boasts a strong capital markets and corporate finance practice. The firm has represented clients in the evaluation and negotiation of international derivatives transactions, such as swaps, futures and options, as well as in the evaluation of the best financing options for the particular projects to be undertaken.

Having handled some of the largest mergers and acquisitions in Malta **Ganado & Associates** provides excellent corporate expertise. Spanning a wide range of issues from company law to advising on holding structures, international trading companies, freeport companies, manufacturing companies, listing matters and corporate insolvency, the firm is singled out as an elite practice in Malta.

Gatt Frendo Tufigno Advocates' corporate and commercial practice has had a number of instructions from clients in the telecoms and insurance sectors.

Another of the leading corporate practices in Malta is **Grech Vella Tortell & Hyzler**'s four-strong department, spearheaded by name-partner Albert Grech. The firm has been very busy during 2005, namely setting up captive insurance companies. The firm's client base takes up a lion's share of the corporate market in Malta. Clients include the largest private real estate group and one of the largest multinational telecoms operators.

With three partners dealing with corporate and commercial issues, **Mamo TCV Advocates** is recognised as a leading firm in the field. David Tonna, Andrew Muscat and Richard Camilleri offer extensive experience in a wide range of corporate matters. The firm has been very much involved in privatisations, most notably advising the Maltese government on the privatisation of the public lottery. One of the key clients of the firm is MGI – Malta Government Investments Limited - the government institution that manages state-owned companies.

Eight-lawyer **Buttigieg & Refalo Advocates** has in John Refalo its head of corporate and commercial. The firm's expertise includes drafting and negotiation of agency, distribution and franchise agreements, company law, liquidations, corporate restructuring and joint venture agreements. Clients include leading local industrial and manufacturing companies.

Galea Salomone & Associates is still very much involved in post-merger work following its advice in a major merger in the IT sector. Other highlights include acting for the Maltese seller in the disposal of a large supermarket business, which was acquired by a large Italian supermarket operator.

Ganado Sammut's highly respected corporate team has in Simon Busuttil its best-known personality. With strong expertise in privatisation issues, where highlights include advising on the privatisation of the Maltese lottery and Freeport, the firm also boasts strong expertise in EU law, having been part of the team that negotiated Malta's EU membership.

Guido de Marco & Associates advises several international companies across several industries, including tourism, aviation and telecoms. Mario de Marco is the firm's best-known personality.

Hugh Peralta & Associates receives a large number of instructions from international trading companies and has advised a major European airline and an international bank on corporate-related matters.

One of the key corporate and commercial clients **Sapiano & Associates** has received instruction from is the Maltese government. The firm's corporate practice is highly regarded.

Setting up international trading companies, international holding companies, trusts and companies in general in Malta are a few of the matters **CDF Advocates** deals with, offering solid expertise in the field.

One of the more traditional firms, **Camilleri Delia Randon & Associates** boasts a well-respected corporate and commercial practice.

Dingli & Dingli is also recommended. The firm is well known for its expertise in maritime and financial services matters.

Ellul Mifsud & Debono Advocates' practice has developed strong expertise in the gaming sector. The firm has advised one of the most-established bookmakers in the world in complying with its legal obligations under the Maltese remote control regulations and was also the company's legal advisor in its merger with a London Stock Exchange-listed gaming company. Other highlights include advising a Swedish gaming company with the setting up of its operations in Malta.

R Frendo Randon & Associates acts for a number of international clients mainly from Italy, Russia, the UK and Australia. The firm also represents various important Maltese companies and its commercial work also includes international trading issues and registration of holding companies.

Thake Desira Advocates is very active in corporate and commercial. The firm advises several companies, including one of the largest insurance agencies in Malta. The firm is also concentrating on private client issues including trusts and wealth management.

DISPUTE RESOLUTION

Name partner Professor Ian Refalo, at **Buttigieg & Refalo Advocates**, is regarded as one of the leading authorities in the field in Malta. The firm is often sought out for advice in relation to disputes with most administrative bodies in Malta over a variety of issues, usually concerning the granting of permits or licences.

Fenech & Fenech Advocates' highly regarded litigation practice spans the whole spectrum of civil and commercial disputes with a history and tradition that goes back to the very inception of the firm. The firm set up Malta Dispute Management together with **Ganado Sammut**, an initiative aimed to offer ADR and mediation services to clients.

Leading firm **Ganado & Associates** focuses its practice on commercial and maritime litigation. The firm has assisted a large number of local and foreign clients in lawsuits before Maltese courts as well as in reaching amicable solutions outside court. **Ganado & Associates** has also taken a very prominent role in the arbitration sector and has been involved in several important cases.

Giannella Caruana Curran and Mario de Marco spearhead **Guido de Marco & Associates**' disputes practice – one of the most highly regarded practices in Malta. Its expertise spans a wide range of matters including civil and commercial litigation, arbitration, industrial tribunal cases, family law, debt collection and insurance claims.

Henri Mizzi and Marisa Azzopardi are in charge of **Camilleri Preziosi**'s dispute resolution department, which spans company law matters, construction disputes (often involving arbitration) shipping and competition proceedings.

Emmanuel Mallia & Associates advises a number of local and international clients on various issues, particularly in commercial and insurance claims.

Another strong practice is **Ganado Sammut**. The firm set up Malta Dispute Management, in association with **Fenech & Fenech Advocates**. ADR and debt collection are only two of the firm's strengths.

Gatt Frendo Tufigno Advocates has in partner Michael Frendo its head of practice. He is one of the registered arbitrators in the Malta Arbitration Centre. Besides its arbitration

DISPUTE RESOLUTION

BUTTIGIEG & REFALO ADVOCATES
FENECH & FENECH ADVOCATES
GANADO & ASSOCIATES
GUIDO DE MARCO & ASSOCIATES

Camilleri Preziosi ✪
Emmanuel Mallia & Associates
Farrugia Gatt & Falzon
Ganado Sammut ✪
Gatt Frendo Tufigno Advocates ✪
Grech Vella Tortell & Hyzler
Jos A Schembri & Associates
Mamo TCV Advocates ✪
R Frendo Randon & Associates

AVMT Advocates
Bonello & Bonello
CDF Advocates
Cefai & Associates
Ellul Mifsud & Debono Advocates
Farrugia Schembri Orland Law Firm
Galea Salomone & Associates
Hugh Peralta & Associates
Rutter Giappone & Associates
Sapiano & Associates
Thake Desira Advocates

Firms are listed A-Z in tiers which are ranked in order of priority
✪ *Indicates firm displays contact details at the end of this chapter.*

expertise, the firm also has experience in drafting arbitration clauses into commercial contracts.

Joseph Zammit Maempel spearheads **Grech Vella Tortell & Hyzler**'s five-lawyer litigation practice. Although this is not a core area of the firm, the strength of the corporate department generates a fair amount of spin-off litigation work. Clients include one of the largest multinational telecoms operators which instructs the firm in several proceedings it has against the local regulator. Other highlights include acting for two shareholders of one of the largest Maltese commercial groups, in a claim against its directors for abuse of power.

Jos A Schembri & Associates dedicates a lot of its dispute resolution capabilities to dealing with ADR issues.

Mamo TCV Advocates's main areas of specialisation in litigation are commercial and civil disputes, intellectual property, shipping and aviation, communications and media, employment and insurance credit collection. The firm, led by Franco Vassallo, has most notably advised Pari Mutuel Urbain, an internet betting company, in the protection of its interests, which are run from France.

Also very active in litigation and arbitration is **R Frendo Randon & Associates**, most notably acting for a local newspaper in various libel cases.

Arbitration is a key strength at **AVMT Advocates**. The firm has been very successful in settling disputes out of court, a quality very much appreciated by clients since Malta is a jurisdiction where litigation may be lengthy.

CDF Advocates has successfully represented a number of foreign companies with debt claims against local companies and has also represented clients before the European Court of Human Rights in Strasbourg.

Ellul Mifsud & Debono Advocates partner Tonio Ellul is included in the panel of arbitrators of the Malta Arbitration Centre. He is currently representing a government-owned company in arbitration proceedings related to a commercial dispute.

Name partner Arthur Galea Salomone, at **Galea Salomone & Associates**, has been appointed to act as deputy chairman of the Maltese Arbitration Centre. As such the firm avoids involvement in arbitration issues presently because of conflict situations. The litigation and mediation practices, however, are quite active for clients from various sectors including shipping and tourism.

Thake Desira Advocates boasts strong expertise in litigation, particularly in civil and commercial law issues. The firm also has ADR and mediation capabilities.

INTELLECTUAL PROPERTY

GANADO & ASSOCIATES
GRECH VELLA TORTELL & HYZLER
MAMO TCV ADVOCATES ✪

Dingli & Dingli
Farrugia Gatt & Falzon
Ganado Sammut ✪
Patrick J Galea & Associates
R Frendo Randon & Associates

Buttigieg & Refalo Advocates
CDF Advocates
Camilleri Preziosi ✪
Cefai & Associates
Farrugia Schembri Orland Law Firm
Fenech & Fenech Advocates
Guido de Marco & Associates
Muscat Azzopardi & Associates

AVMT Advocates
Camilleri Delia Randon & Associates
Ellul Mifsud & Debono Advocates
Emmanuel Mallia & Associates
Galea Salomone & Associates
Hugh Peralta & Associates
Rutter Giappone & Associates

Firms are listed A-Z in tiers which are ranked in order of priority
✪ *Indicates firm displays contact details at the end of this chapter.*

Ganado & Associates' IP capability spans trade marks, patents, copyright and IP matters arising from franchising agreements.

Recognised as one of the best practices in Malta, **Grech Vella Tortell & Hyzler** fields an expert name partner Michael Grech, its head of practice. The firm represents some of the largest companies locally, including acting for a large multinational software company in patent matters. It also has litigation capability, especially focused on cases of enforcement and infringement.

Mamo TCV Advocates's busy IP department spans brand registration, cross-border measures, enforcement, anti-counterfeit, trade mark litigation, patents and data protection. Clients of the firm include Nike, adidas, Phillip Morris and Phillips.

Another recommended firm in the field is **Dingli & Dingli**, while **Farrugia Gatt & Falzon** boasts IP capabilities across a wide range of matters.

Ganado Sammut's expertise spans filing and registration of trade marks and patents, and enforcement against infringing parties.

Patrick J Galea & Associates is also recommended, boasting a particular focus on software IP, copyright and trade marks.

R Frendo Randon & Associates has most notably acted for a major international sports company in several IP cases and registration of trade marks.

Buttigieg & Refalo Advocates is recommended for a range of IP issues.

Frank Checuti Dimech, partner in charge of intellectual property at **CDF Advocates** is highly recommended in data protection matters, even though the firm's IP work comes mainly as a spin-off work its busy corporate and finance practices.

Henri Mizzi and Adrian Mallia secure **Camilleri Preziosi**'s intellectual property practice as a spin-off practice from the firm's strong commercial focus.

Trade mark registration and copyright matters are one of **Cefai & Associates**' major strengths. The firm advises a number of international clients.

Farrugia Schembri Orland Law Firm has advised several overseas clients from the US, China and Europe on trade mark registration issues.

Fenech & Fenech Advocates specialises in all fields of IP including registration of patents and trade marks, IP licensing and litigation. In registration issues, the firm also benefits from on-line access to and communication with the Industrial Property Registration Directorate, the Maltese entity responsible for the registration of patents, trade marks and designs.

Muscat Azzopardi & Associates has extensive experience in IP issues connected with the film and entertainment sector. The firm advises on registration, enforcement, technology transfer, disputes and privacy matters.

AVMT Advocates is also recommended in the intellectual property sector.

Ellul Mifsud & Debono Advocates has advised a number of clients in the pharmaceutical sector. The firm is advising a multinational company in the hospitality business in connection with a dispute regarding the infringement of its intellectual property rights by a retail outlet in Malta.

Galea Salomone & Associates' IP practice is mainly a support to its corporate and commercial clients.

REAL ESTATE AND CONSTRUCTION

Regularly involved in major Maltese real estate deals **Camilleri Preziosi** has most notably acted for the vendors on the sale of a major leisure complex in Malta and for the purchasers in another large-scale real estate development. Louis de Gabriele and Henri Mizzi are recommended.

Grech Vella Tortell & Hyzler's real estate and construction team is acknowledged by its peers as one of the leaders in Malta. Name partner Joseph Vella led the firm's advice to one of the acquirers in the Chambray Project, a major development involving the construction and development of 200 holiday apartments and a five-star hotel. Other highlights include acting for one of the leading international hotels in new acquisitions and franchising operations.

Mamo TCV Advocates continues to be one of the best practices all round. The firm is involved in a number of large transactions, namely in the acquisition of the Galaxy tourism complex, where the firm was advising the vendors. Other highlights include representing the seller in the sale of the Germa Palace Hotel. Richard Camilleri, Joseph Caruana Scicluna and Franco Vassallo are highly regarded.

Patrick J Galea & Associates has extensive experience in all types of sale and acquisition of property and particular expertise in construction contracts. Commercial property is one of the firm's core practice areas.

AVMT Advocates successfully concluded a sale of a multi-million dollar five-star tourist resort in Malta to a US international operator. The firm also acts for the purchasers and developers of some of the largest residential and commercial developments in Malta. Other highlights include acting as general counsel to a leading Italian company following its successful tender bid for the reconstruction of roads in Malta.

Buttigieg & Refalo Advocates acts for several established construction companies, engineering firms and contractors, architects and landowners. Its practice spans structuring of property deals, negotiation and drafting of construction agreements and leasehold agreements. The firm is also involved in arbitration both locally and abroad.

Ganado & Associates' property practice also covers permanent resident permits, which have become particularly attractive to high-net-worth individuals from all over the world.

REAL ESTATE AND CONSTRUCTION

CAMILLERI PREZIOSI ✪
GRECH VELLA TORTELL & HYZLER
MAMO TCV ADVOCATES ✪
MUSCAT AZZOPARDI & ASSOCIATES
PATRICK J GALEA & ASSOCIATES

AVMT Advocates
Buttigieg & Refalo Advocates
Cefai & Associates
Emmanuel Mallia & Associates
Farrugia Schembri Orland Law Firm
Fenech & Fenech Advocates
Ganado & Associates
Ganado Sammut ✪
Guido de Marco & Associates
Sapiano & Associates

CDF Advocates
Ellul Mifsud & Debono Advocates
Farrugia Gatt & Falzon
Galea Salomone & Associates
Hugh Peralta & Associates
R Frendo Randon & Associates
Thake Desira Advocates
Zammit Pace & Co. ✪

Firms are listed A-Z in tiers which are ranked in order of priority
✪ *Indicates firm displays contact details at the end of this chapter.*

Guido de Marco & Associates' clients include a number of hotel developers. The firm has solid expertise in both commercial property and construction issues.

Ellul Mifsud & Debono Advocates has assisted one of the largest real estate companies in Malta in establishing its network of foreign partners and regularly assists the company, its property negotiators and clients on matters connected with conveyancing. Other highlights include setting up two investment vehicles holding immovable property in Malta and abroad.

Galea Salomone & Associates acted for a Kuwaiti group and a Maltese group on a €45m (excluding development) joint venture involving the restructuring of a holiday complex turned into a residential area. Arthur Galea Salomone and Andrew Zammit were the key partners involved.

R Frendo Randon & Associates boasts expertise in real estate and commercial property matters.

Thake Desira Advocates is highly active in both real estate and construction. The firm has been involved in some of the largest property developments in Malta and represents owners, developers and contractors.

SHIPPING

Acknowledged as one of the top performers in shipping issues, **Dingli & Dingli** is constantly advising a number of international clients on all aspects of shipping law.

Fenech & Fenech Advocates boasts one of the leading specialists in the field, partner Ann Fenech. She heads a department that is one of the largest on the island and comprises a team of professionals who are highly experienced in the fields of ship registration and finance. The practice spans ship registrations under the Maltese flag, incorporation of shipping companies and registration of mortgages under Maltese law.

Shipping is one of the major strengths at **Ganado & Associates**, having acted for numerous ship financing banks and institutions throughout the world. Its four-strong ship finance division focuses on drafting and review of security documentation and preparation of statutory mortgages for registration. The firm is also active in ship registration, ship arrest, admiralty and marine claims and advising shipping organisations.

Another of the strongest shipping departments in Malta can be found at **Mamo TCV Advocates**, spanning shipping registration and shipping finance. Partner Franco Vassallo regularly acts for the Malta Maritime Authority. Partners David Tonna and Joseph Caruana Scicluna are also leading individuals.

AVMT Advocates is acting for a major international shipping company registered in Malta and providing services in 26 countries around the world.

Camilleri Preziosi acts in the areas of ship registration and renders advice to several international clients in ship finance, charter parties and bills of landing and sales and mortgaging of vessels. The shipping team is often instructed by

SHIPPING

DINGLI & DINGLI
FENECH & FENECH ADVOCATES
GANADO & ASSOCIATES
HUGH PERALTA & ASSOCIATES
MAMO TCV ADVOCATES ✪

AVMT Advocates
Buttigieg & Refalo Advocates
Camilleri Preziosi ✪
Farrugia Schembri Orland Law Firm
Gatt Frendo Tufigno Advocates ✪

Camilleri Delia Randon & Associates
Cefai & Associates
Ellul Mifsud & Debono Advocates
Emmanuel Mallia & Associates
Farrugia Gatt & Falzon
Galea Salomone & Associates
Grech Vella Tortell & Hyzler
Guido de Marco & Associates
Muscat Azzopardi & Associates
R Frendo Randon & Associates
Rutter Giappone & Associates

Firms are listed A-Z in tiers which are ranked in order of priority
✪ *Indicates firm displays contact details at the end of this chapter.*

specialist London firms, P&I clubs and also by owners and operators of vessels.

Farrugia Schembri Orland Law Firm's varied international client base includes important shipping companies from Russia, Ukraine, Canada, the UK, Poland, Turkey and Greece. The firm is active in ship registration matters.

Ship finance is a major strength at **Gatt Frendo Tufigno Advocates**. The firm's client base includes acting for a large bank in Greece and for various international trading companies.

Camilleri Delia Randon & Associates remains focused on dry shipping work, while **Ellul Mifsud & Debono Advocates**' shipping practice spans ship registration, bareboat chartering, ship mortgaging and ship financing. Partner Jeremy DeBono is secretary to the Malta Maritime Authority board of directors.

Emmanuel Mallia & Associates' expertise spans a wide range of areas including registration of ships and shipping companies, mortgages and charters.

Galea Salomone & Associates' shipping practice advises non-resident Maltese companies (namely one of the largest Russian shipowners and Cypriot shipowners) in shipping registration, litigation and financial issues.

Although shipping is not a core area at **Grech Vella Tortell & Hyzler**, the firm still handles financing and registration issues.

Guido de Marco & Associates has received instructions from a number of international shipowners and captains.

CAMILLERI PREZIOSI
ADVOCATES

LEVEL 2
VALLETTA BUILDINGS
SOUTH STREET
VALLETTA VLT 11

Telephone: +356 21 238 989
Fax: +356 21 223 048
Website: www.camilleripreziosi.com

Languages
English, French, Italian

Number of lawyers 8

CATEGORIES OF WORK

Banking and finance, capital markets, corporate finance and investment services
Louis de Gabriele, Laragh Cassar

Company law
Louis de Gabriele, Henri Mizzi

Commercial law
Louis de Gabriele, Henri Mizzi

Commercial property
Louis de Gabriele, Henri Mizzi

Competition law
Henri Mizzi, Adrian Mallia

Dispute resolution
Henri Mizzi, Marisa Azzopardi

EU law
Henri Mizzi, Louis de Gabriele

Franchises
Henri Mizzi, Adrian Mallia

Insurance
Henri Mizzi, Marisa Azzopardi

International business structures, including trusts and taxation
Louis de Gabriele, Henri Mizzi

Maritime law, including ship registration, finance, mortgages, ship arrest and shipping companies
Henri Mizzi

Media and telecommunications, data protection, intellectual property and information technology
Henri Mizzi, Adrian Mallia

Mergers and acquisitions
Louis de Gabriele, Henri Mizzi

GANADO SAMMUT

35-36 ARCHBISHOP STREET
VALLETTA VLT 08

Telephone: +356 21 247 109
Fax: +356 21 247 170
E-mail: info@ganadosammut.com
Website: www.ganadosammut.com

Languages
English, French, Italian, Portuguese

Other offices
Brussels

Number of lawyers 9

CATEGORIES OF WORK

Financial services
Dr Austin Sammut, Dr Celia Mifsud

Company law
Dr Jeannine Giglio, Dr Sarah Galea

Maritime law
Dr Simon Galea Testaferrata, Dr Sarah Galea

European affairs
Dr Simon Busuttil, Dr Mariosa Vella Cardona

Succession and estate management
Dr Peter Fenech, Dr Simon Galea Testaferrata

Property and construction, insurance law
Dr Austin Sammut, Dr Peter Fenech

Intellectual property
Dr Mariosa Vella Cardona, Dr Jeannine Giglio

Trusts and trust management
Dr Austin Sammut, Dr Celia Mifsud

Litigation and debt collecting
Dr Peter Fenech, Dr Simon Galea Testaferrata

Joint ventures and investment
Dr Austin Sammut, Dr Celia Mifsud

Banking and finance
Dr Austin Sammut

Competition law
Dr Mariosa Vella Cardona

Telecommunications and media law
Dr Austin Sammut, Dr Celia Mifsud

GATT FRENDO TUFIGNO ADVOCATES

66 OLD BAKERY STREET
VALLETTA VLT 09

Telephone: +356 21 242 713
Fax: +356 21 242 714
E-mail: info@gftlex.com
Website: www.gftlex.com

Languages
English, French, Italian, Russian, Ukrainian

Number of lawyers 5

Contact
Dr Ivan Gatt

CATEGORIES OF WORK

Company law
Dr Robert Tufigno, Dr Olga Finkel

EU and competition law, EU funding
Dr Olga Finkel, Dr Ian Gauci

Trusts, banking and finance services
Dr Robert Tufigno

Litigation and arbitration
Dr Ivan Gatt, Dr Nikolai Muscat Farrugia

Tourism and hotels
Dr Ivan Gatt, Dr Nikolai Muscat Farrugia

Property and construction law
Dr Ivan Gatt, Dr Nikolai Muscat Farrugia

Energy and infrastructure
Dr Robert Tufigno, Dr Ivan Gatt

Betting and gaming law
Dr Olga Finkel

Telecommunications and IT law
Dr Robert Tufigno, Dr Olga Finkel

Employment
Dr Robert Tufigno, Dr Ian Gauci

Insurance
Dr Ivan Gatt, Dr Nikolai Muscat Farrugia

Registration of ships, ship mortgage and ship finance
Dr Robert Tufigno, Dr Nikolai Muscat Farrugia

IP including trade mark registration
Dr Ivan Gatt

MAMO TCV

PALAZZO PIETRO STIGES
90 STRAIT STREET
VALLETTA VLT 05

Telephone: +356 21 231 345
Fax: +356 21 244 291
E-mail: info@mamotcv.com
Website: www.mamotcv.com

Languages
English, French, Italian

Number of lawyers 20

CATEGORIES OF WORK

Agency distribution and franchise
Dr Franco Vassallo, Dr Richard Camilleri

Aviation
Dr David Tonna, Dr Jesmond Manicaro

Banking, finance and investment
Dr David Tonna, Prof Andrew Muscat

Company law/corporate insolvency
Dr Richard Camilleri, Prof Andrew Muscat

Commercial litigation, civil law practice and arbitration
Dr Joe Caruana Scicluna, Dr Franco Vassallo

EU and competition law
Dr Daniele Cop, Prof Andrew Muscat

Films and media
Dr David Tonna, Dr Daniele Cop

Financial services and international trading companies
Dr David Tonna, Prof Andrew Muscat

Hotel and touristic projects
Dr Joe Caruana Scicluna, Dr Franco Vassallo

Joint ventures
Dr Richard Camilleri, Prof Andrew Muscat

Industrial/manufacturing companies
Dr Joe Borg Bartolo, Dr Franco Vassallo

Insurance
Dr Joe Borg Bartolo, Dr Richard Camilleri

Information law and technology
Dr Richard Camilleri, Dr Antoine Camilleri

Intellectual property law including trade mark and patent registration
Dr Richard Camilleri, Dr David Tonna

Maritime law, registration of ships and ship mortgages
Dr David Tonna

Property and construction law
Dr Joe Borg Bartolo, Dr Richard Camilleri

ZAMMIT PACE & CO.

SUITE 1
215 OLD BAKERY STREET
VALLETTA VLT 11

Telephone: +356 21 222 607
Fax: +356 21 226 087
E-mail: info@zammitpacelaw.com

Languages
English, French, Italian

Number of lawyers 4

Contacts
Roderick Zammit Pace, Remigio Zammit Pace

CATEGORIES OF WORK

Banking and finance

Capital markets

Competition and EU

Corporate and commercial

Insolvency/corporate restructuring

Insurance

Mergers and acquisitions

Private client

Real estate/commercial property/ notarial

Regulatory

MONACO

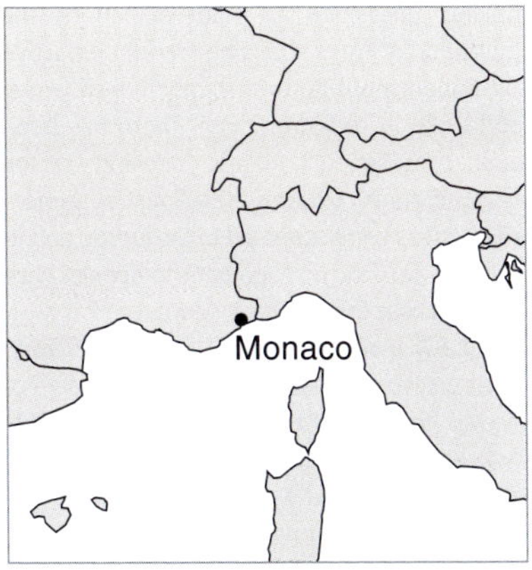

Population	**32,409**
Number of lawyers	**17 Avocats-défenseurs; 8 avocats**
Professional titles	**Avocat-défenseur; Avocat-stagiaire conseiller juridique; notaire**
Currency	**Euro (€)**

Index

The Principality of Monaco is one of Europe's microstates, the second-smallest independent state in the world after the Vatican City. The Monegasque population of 32,000 squeezes into a 2 sq km territory whose only land neighbour is France. To the southeast lies Monaco's famous 4.1 km Mediterranean coastline. Recently, the state's land area has been increased by land reclamation from the Mediterranean to create the new town of Fontvieille, home for over 3,000 people and AS Monaco FC's home ground.

Monaco's long and complex history has resulted in a state whose integrity and independence are guaranteed under a 2002 treaty with France. The Grimaldi family ruled Monaco from 1297, save for one brief period, until the state became a constitutional principality in 1911. A revised constitution was adopted in 1962. Despite the shift to democracy, the Prince or Princess for the time being remains head of state and retains considerable powers exercised through the Council of Government. The judicial and legislative bodies are independent of the Prince's control but the latter remains subject to considerable influence; the democratically elected Conseil National may be dissolved by the Prince at any time. Prince Rainier III, a canny politician, perhaps best known for his marriage to screen-star Grace Kelly, died in April 2005 after a reign of over half a century. He is succeeded by his son Prince Albert II.

Historically Monaco has had strong ties with France, upon which it relies for defence. The Minister of State in Monaco's National Council is a French citizen proposed by the French government. France has also been able to exert considerable pressure on Monaco in financial areas. Monaco's only Double Tax Treaty is with France; this puts French citizens resident in Monaco in much the same position as if they were resident in France. In addition, the Bank of France exerts considerable control over the Monegasque banking system. Monaco is not a member of the EU but, through its treaties with France, which include full customs union, Monaco applies European community laws on VAT (the main rate is tied to the French rate) and enjoys the benefits of the EU free-trade zone. Monaco adopted the euro concurrently with France in January 1999.

BILLING

Billing rates vary widely according to the type of work, the experience of the lawyer and the nature of the client, with international clients attracting higher charges than local ones. Typically major law firms charge €375 to €575 per hour for partners undertaking international instructions.

Avocats range from €200 to €425 per hour depending on seniority, with avocats-défenseurs licensed to appear in the Court of Appeal at the higher end.

Notaires' fees are set according to official scales.

MARKETING

The Monaco Bar Association (Ordre des Avocats) prohibits *avocats* from advertising although international law firms and legal advisers (conseillers juridiques) are not faced with such restrictions and may directly market their services. However, Monaco's strong emphasis on confidentiality and discretion leave legal marketing substantially undeveloped. While some international firms offer websites, most business results from recommendation.

IN-HOUSE LAWYERS

Because of the small size of the domestic legal market, the majority of instructions within the Principality tend to be shared between *avocats* and law firms. A few large commercial organisations have in-house legal support.

ECONOMY

Monaco enjoys a high per capita income, estimated at US$27,000, although no official statistics are published. Government income derives principally from VAT (about 50%) and state-monopolies and semi-monopolies (25%).

The Principality's success was historically based on upmarket tourism, more particularly, the Monte Carlo casino, opened in 1856, which together with other attractions and a benign climate, provided the tax base which allowed Monaco to flourish. Although diminished, tourism remains important; Monaco enjoys excellent communications including direct flights to most major European centres and New York. A major cruise-ship docking facility was opened in 2001.

Since the 1950s, Monaco's economy has diversified, firstly as a tax haven for the super-rich, latterly as a financial centre with particular strength in private banking – there are currently some 70 banks active in Monaco, with a banking turnover in excess of US$1.5bn. Real estate and

The largest firms

1	Lawrence Graham LLP	8
2	A.L.F.A. (Associated Legal & Fiscal Advisors)	4
	Donald Manasse Law Offices	4
4	Berg and Duffy, LLP	3
	Groom Hill Law Offices	3
	Jean-Charles S Gardetto	3
	Pasquier - Ciulla & Zabaldano, Cabinet	3
	Somodeco SAM - Ernst & Young International	3
9	Etude Evelyne Karczag-Mencarelli & Marquet	2
	Georges Blot	2
	Maurizio Cohen	2
	Patrice Lorenzi	2
13	Billon Conseils & Services	1
	Christiane Palmero	1
	Etienne Léandri, Cabinet	1
	Jacques Sbarrato	1
	Jean-Pierre Licari	1
	Richard Mullot	1
	Rémy Brugnetti, Cabinet	1
	Yann Lajoux	1

These figures represent the total number of lawyers in this country only, and have been supplied by the firms themselves. The figures should be accurate as at 1 January 2006.

ship finance have been expanding in recent years. In common with other small jurisdictions, Monaco has been under pressure from the IMF and the EU, as well as France, to prevent money-laundering and tax evasion. Although some French politicians continue to express concerns, international reviews have generally been positive about Monaco's efforts to develop regulatory structures, efforts which were emphasised and approved by Prince Albert II in his July 2005 coronation speech. Monaco is now subject to the EU Savings Directive which requires a 15% witholding tax on interest paid to EU nations from 1 July 2005. The impact of increased regulation on Monaco's banking and investment sector remains to be seen although personal tax rates remain low and seem to guarantee a steady flow of high-net-worth exiles to one of the world's most secure, convenient and glamorous locations.

Under policies promoted by the late Prince Rainier III and which Prince Albert II intends to modernise and extend, tiny Monaco has managed to establish an industrial sector, principally involved in high-value, hi-tech operations such as plastics, cosmetics, electronics and pharmaceuticals. About 30,000 people are employed in industrial concerns, most of whom are 'day-migrants' from France and Italy.

LEGAL SYSTEM AND LEGAL MARKET

The Monegasque civil law system follows the French Napoleonic code and a high proportion of court positions are held by French nationals. There are three categories of legal practitioner in Monaco. Avocats, broadly the equivalent of barristers, normally involved in litigation rather than advising clients, have rights of audience before the courts. As there is no law school in Monaco, intending practitioners must obtain a French law degree before serving a period of apprenticeship with an admitted Monegasque *avocat*. *Avocats* are members of l'Ordre des Avocats-Défenseurs et des Avocats de Monaco, and subject to its disciplinary code. Conseillers-juridiques are authorised to give legal advice by the Government of Monaco. Broadly equivalent to solictors, conseillers-juridiques may be foreign lawyers expert in international matters. Conseillers-juridiques are not regulated in Monaco beyond authorisation but may be subject to 'home-Bar' disciplinary procedures. Notaires have no equivalent in common law systems. Notaires have a monopoly to complete real property transactions, administer estates, deal with marriage contracts and company incorporations.

The Monegasque market for legal services is limited and there are no law firms with more than five fee-earners. The largest local firm is **Lawrence Graham LLP** with five lawyers. Other international firms practising within the jurisdiction are *Lex Mundi* member **Berg and Duffy, LLP**, which also has offices in New York and Mexico City, and **Somodeco SAM – Ernst & Young International** which is part of the Big Four global accountancy partnership.

BANKING AND FINANCE

The healthy banking and finance sector has generated responsive and knowledgeable legal support. The attractions of Monaco as a private banking jurisdiction are underpinned by the application of French banking law and proactive government regulation, which together engender confidence in the jurisdiction. There has been some consolidation in the banking sector, including branch closures. New financial services providers are being attracted to the jurisdiction. In particular, portfolio management companies have started to base themselves in Monaco.

A.L.F.A. (Associated Legal & Fiscal Advisors) boasts a solid reputation and a steady stream of referrals from UK Magic Circle firms. Mireille Chauvet is highly respected and recommended for advice to high-net-worth incomers.

Led by founding partner James P Duffy III , **Berg and Duffy, LLP** specialises in domestic and international banking, representing both institutional clients and high-net-worth individuals.

Donald Manasse Law Offices, practising out of Nice and Monte Carlo, handled the Monegasque end one of the plum deals of 2005, working with **Dundas & Wilson CS LLP** on behalf of Bank of Scotland Joint Ventures in connection with the Monte Carlo Grand Hotel acquisition. Experienced and respected name partner Donald Manasse is qualified in France and the US.

Four-avocat firm **Etude Evelyne Karczag-Mencarelli & Marquet** is highly recommended for banking and finance litigation. *Inter alia*, the firm has acted for CSFB. Name partner Evelyne Karczag-Mencarelli ranks as one of Monaco's most experienced avocats-défenseurs.

Two-partner, three-assistant **Lawrence Graham LLP** is highly praised by banking clients including Coutts and Amex. Local partners William Easun and Peter Walford 'are both extremely competent lawyers who are great to work with'. A

BANKING AND FINANCE

A.L.F.A. (Associated Legal & Fiscal Advisors)
Berg and Duffy, LLP
Donald Manasse Law Offices
Etude Evelyne Karczag-Mencarelli & Marquet
Frank Michel
Jean-Charles S Gardetto
Lawrence Graham LLP
Pasquier – Ciulla & Zabaldano, Cabinet
Somodeco SAM – Ernst & Young International

Firms are listed alphabetically.

comprehensive range of corporate and private banking expertise is offered.

Cabinet Pasquier – Ciulla & Zabaldano's name partners, Christine Pasquier-Ciulla, a member of the National Assembly, and Arnaud Zabaldano are both avocat-défenseurs recommended for banking and finance instructions. Arnaud Zabaldano represents Dryden Wealth Management.

The strength and depth of the **Ernst & Young Global Limited** network of offices, together with the banking and finance expertise of managing partner Francis Ferrari, equip **Somodeco SAM – Ernst & Young International** to serve the needs of institutional and private clients.

CORPORATE AND COMMERCIAL

Private client-centred Monaco has never developed the same importance in private capital, SPV and M&A work as other specialist financial centres. Although there are some international instructions, most corporate work links to local projects or private client work.

Donald Manasse Law Offices is a solid, full-service corporate and commercial office with expertise in trade marks and other IP issues.

Lawrence Graham LLP, 'unusually proactive for members of the legal profession', handles complex cross-border issues with aplomb. During 2005 the firm successfully negotiated an asset management licence on behalf of a banking client. Clients appreciate the support provided by **Lawrence Graham LLP**'s London office.

Somodeco SAM – Ernst & Young International and close associate office **Gordon S Blair Law Offices** both have the capability to advise on corporate and commercial matters.

A.L.F.A. (Associated Legal & Fiscal Advisors) offers a full-service corporate and commercial office.

New York-headquartered **Berg and Duffy, LLP** is the only US firm with a presence in Monaco. **Berg and Duffy, LLP** has acted on behalf of companies, banks and brokerage firms on transactions and boasts particular expertise in servicing small/medium-sized clients in need of international advice.

CORPORATE AND COMMERCIAL

Donald Manasse Law Offices
Gordon S Blair Law Offices
Lawrence Graham LLP
Somodeco SAM – Ernst & Young International

A.L.F.A. (Associated Legal & Fiscal Advisors)
Berg and Duffy, LLP
Etude Evelyne Karczag-Mencarelli & Marquet
Frank Michel
Groom Hill Law Offices
Jean-Charles S Gardetto
Maurizio Cohen

Firms are listed alphabetically.

Three-lawyer **Groom Hill Law Offices**, led by founding partners Simon Groom and James Hill, offers general company and corporate advice, frequently in conjunction with complex personal tax and investment planning matters.

Maurizio Cohen heads into its twentieth year in good form. The downtown, commercial biased, Monte Carlo firm offers advice on international contract negotiation, particularly focusing on distribution, licensing, intellectual property and media. Founding partner Maurizio Cohen has also been appointed as counsel to the Italian Consulate in Monaco and the firm has a useful informal network of associates.

Etude Evelyne Karczag-Mencarelli & Marquet, **Frank Michel** and **Jean-Charles S Gardetto** are recommended for commercial litigation.

PRIVATE CLIENT

Monaco's zero income tax, capital gains tax, and inheritance tax regime continues to attract the global super-rich, including easyJet founder Stelios Haji-Ioannu and billionaire retail entrepreneur Philip Green. Private client legal services are well developed and operate with keen attention to confidentiality.

Berg and Duffy, LLP is fully equipped to handle private clients' needs and particularly addresses the US expatriate market. **Berg and Duffy, LLP** is the Monaco associate of the international *TAGlaw* network.

Donald Manasse Law Offices is well known for private client work, including criminal and defamation instructions. During 2005, Donald Manasse represented cycling champion Lance Armstrong when French sports daily *L'Equipe* published drugs allegations.

Gordon S Blair Law Offices provides legal advice on local and international matters for clients on immigration and residence; English solicitor Simon Huxford is recommended. **Gordon S Blair Law Offices** is backed by the global resources of associate office **Somodeco SAM – Ernst & Young International**.

Small but effective **Groom Hill Law Offices** specialises in private client work particularly where yachts are involved. The firm is also recommended for real estate transactions in Monaco and the south of France.

International executorships, personal tax planning and wealth protection form the foundation of **Lawrence Graham LLP**'s broad private client practice. Celebrity clients include Sir Elton John and Michael Schumacher. The office is recognised as being 'the best of the best' and 'one of the "jewels in the crown" of the Monaco business community'. Andrew Young is client commended as a 'stalwart'.

Maurizio Cohen's private client practice encompasses tax, real estate, trust and estate planning on behalf of high-net-worth individuals.

PRIVATE CLIENT

Berg and Duffy, LLP
Donald Manasse Law Offices
Gordon S Blair Law Offices
Groom Hill Law Offices
Lawrence Graham LLP
Maurizio Cohen
Richard Mullot

Firms are listed alphabetically.

The firm has particular expertise in wealth management provision for sports and entertainment stars.

Richard Mullot is highly recommended as an avocat-défenseur qualified to handle family disputes and other tricky private client work.

DISPUTE RESOLUTION

Avocats fall into two ranks. The avocat qualified and admitted on the basis of a French Maîtrise en Droit, and a three-year apprenticeship with a fully qualified avocat-défenseur, may practise as an avocat, but is not be allowed to submit written pleadings. After five years of independent practice, the avocat gains the status of avocat-défenseur and may practise fully.

Georges Blot is frequently found in high-profile cases. He acted for the defence in the notorious Edmond Safra murder case jointly with Donald Manasse of **Donald Manasse Law Offices**, the American lawyer and French avocat.

Evelyne Karczag-Mencarelli of **Evelyne Karczag-Mencarelli & Marquet** is a well-reputed avocat-défenseur highly competent across the field. She is supported by avocat Alexis Marquet who mainly deals with criminal and labour law.

AVOCATS-DÉFENSEURS

Michel Boeri
Georges Blot
Patrice Lorenzi
Jacques Sbarrato
Evelyne Karczag-Mencarelli
Etienne Léandri
Frédéric Sangiorgio
Rémy Brugnetti
Didier Escaut
Joëlle Pastor-Bensa
Christine Pasquier – Ciulla
Jean-Pierre Licari
Christiane Palmero
Jean-Charles S Gardetto
Frank Michel
Patricia Rey
Richard Mullot

Individuals are listed in order of accession to the Bar

AVOCATS

Géraldine Gazo
Christophe Sosso
Yann Lajoux
Sophie Lavagna-Bouhnik
Déborah Lorenzi
Alexis Marquet
Thomas Giaccardi
Arnaud Zabaldano

Individuals are listed in order of accession to the Bar

Christine Pasquier-Cuilla of **Cabinet Pasquier – Ciulla & Zabaldano**, a member of the Corporation of Avocats-défenseurs attached to the Court of Appeal, is well regarded for her work in the banking and finance sector. The firm also handles construction disputes.

Jean-Charles S Gardetto a graduate of Cornell Law School and Member of the National Council, was head of the Monegasque delegation to Strasbourg which negotiated Monaco's place in the Council of Europe. In addition to EU law, Maitre Gardetto has strong experience in banking and finance litigation.

Frank Michel is recommended for corporate and commercial, banking and employment law; he has represented large banks and financial institutions.

Advocat-défenseur **Richard Mullot**, who gives 'solid legal advice' is supported by Thomas Letailleur. Maitre Mullot is frequently instructed by well-known banks in addition to his private clients.

Géraldine Gazo, highly recommended for banking and criminal defence matters, was also involved in the high-profile Edmond Safra case.

Well-respected avocat **Yann Lajoux** advises on banking and finance, tax, private client matters and also defends serious criminal charges.

MOROCCO

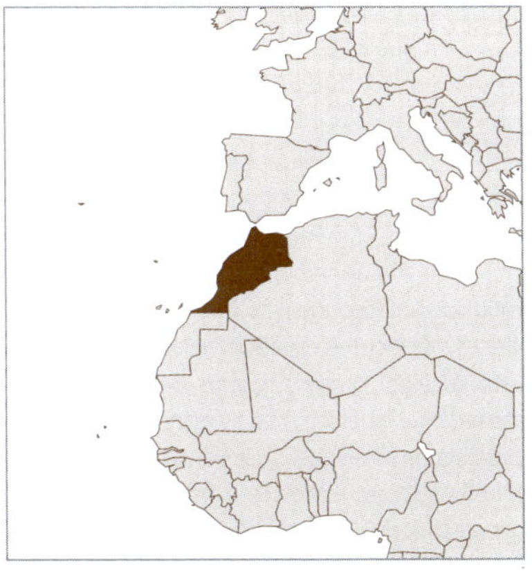

Population	32.2 million
Number of lawyers	n/a
Professional title	avocat/conseil juridique
Currency	Dirham

Index

The Kingdom of Morocco, the second-largest economy in Africa, has seen notable recent economic development, with increased foreign investment, the modernisation of its infrastructure (such as the Tanger Méditerranée port project), privatisations (telecoms, tobacco), and important corporate transactions in the banking, insurance, telecoms and energy sectors. Tourism and projects are two areas where legal work is booming.

At the same time, the country has shown commitment to the WTO and has recently signed a free-trade agreement with the US, following the 1996 Association Agreement with the European Union.

Morocco is increasingly regarded, especially by French and Spanish investors, as a relocation destination for its cheap and qualified workforce, competing directly with Asian and Eastern European countries. As French is spoken in Morocco, there is a demand from French companies for call centres and even technical consultant agencies.

BILLING

Various billing methods are employed, including hourly rates, a percentage of transaction or dispute value (result-determined) and lump sums. The method is agreed in advance.

MARKETING

The Moroccan Bar rules prohibit law firms from local advertising. The major firms do have websites.

LEGAL SYSTEM

Two professions coexist in the Moroccan legal market. Only qualified *avocats* can handle contentious work, while general legal advice is given by *conseils juridiques*. For the latter, there is no monopoly on legal advice or regulation and anyone can practise as a legal adviser. Although only *avocats* can plead in court, a great part of the litigation process is written (usually in Arabic) and *conseils juridiques* can therefore be extensively involved. Firms which have no *avocats* work closely with litigation firms, while in some firms, former *avocats* have developed an advisory practice.

The Moroccan legal system is directly inspired by the French, and many lawyers have studied or worked in France. Many texts pre-date independence from France in 1956, although recent years have seen a modernisation of law with major legal reforms since the 1990s, the most recent being the new labour regulations that came into effect in 2005.

There are some constraints to free growth of the Moroccan legal market: no possible double admission to several bars, prohibition on opening more than one office; only a contractual link can tie a Moroccan firm with a foreign one (as in the case of **Gide Loyrette Nouel – Naciri & Associés**); and marketing is still limited.

LEGAL MARKET

Casablanca remains the economic centre of the Kingdom and all the main firms can be found in the city founded by the French a century ago. Some lawyers mention that the arrival of the French has pulled the market upwards and that it is now nothing like it was some ten years ago.

Three French firms are now active in Morocco – **CMS Bureau Francis Lefebvre**; **Gide Loyrette Nouel – Naciri & Associés**; and **UGGC & Associés**. At the same time, top Spanish law firm **Garrigues** opened an office in Casablanca at the end of 2005.

Some firms developed by offering a mixture of legal, tax, audit and accountancy advice and are known as *fiduciaires*. Since the 1995 law, auditing has been made compulsory in Morocco, which has favoured the development of the Big Four accountancy firms, and in 1997 the audit function was separated by law from advice. *Fiduciaires* are therefore part of the legal Moroccan landscape, notably for tax and, to a lesser extent, legal advice.

Despite these developments, the Moroccan legal market is still small in size and a handful of law firms are active in all the main transactions in the Kingdom. At the same time, the market is growing: **CMS Bureau Francis Lefebvre**, **UGGC & Associés** and **Hajji & Associés** have recruited about three lawyers each in 2005 (nearly doubling in size for some of them), while **Gide Loyrette Nouel – Naciri & Associés** and **Kettani Law Firm** were moving into brand new offices. It is also worth mentioning that some international firms are active from abroad – mainly Paris – as they have the capacity to handle deals from France and no need or desire, so far, to open an office in Casablanca. See the **Foreign firms** at the end of this chapter.

BANKING, FINANCE AND CAPITAL MARKETS
GIDE LOYRETTE NOUEL – NACIRI & ASSOCIÉS ✪
KETTANI LAW FIRM
Hajji & Associés ✪ **Mernissi – FIGES** **SFM**
Firms are listed A-Z in tiers which are ranked in order of priority ✪ *Indicates firm displays contact details at the end of this chapter.*

BANKING, FINANCE AND CAPITAL MARKETS

At **Gide Loyrette Nouel – Naciri & Associés**, the lawyers involved are partner Hicham Naciri and of-counsel Yassir Ghorbal who joined this year after being the head of legal at BMCE Capital. They handle all types of finance, with a number of notable recent highlights. These include advising SFI (Société Financière Internationale – World Bank) in connection with the first bond issue in dirhams for a foreign issuer, the same kind of product was then set up for BAD (Banque Africaine de Développement). The firm was also involved in various financings in the tourism industry (a €200m financing in Al Jadida for South African group Kertzner); handled a €120m local and international financing for Maersk in relation with a port project; and was active in the €50m financing of an interest taken in Meditelecom.

Apart from banking litigation and collection work, **Kettani Law Firm** is involved in transactional finance with partners Azzedine and Nadia Kettani. In 2004/2005, the firm was involved in the €100m bond issue of Lydec; the financing of the €500m acquisition of 16% of Maroc Telecom by Vivendi Universal, advising the lenders; the financing of the Samir refinery project, assisting the Moroccan banks; and the $80m financing for Corral Morocco Holdings, advising the lenders.

A banker initially, Amin Hajji at **Hajji & Associés** handles a great deal of finance. He represented the international banks in the financing of the Samir refinery project and handled derivatives for JPMorgan.

Mernissi – FIGES was active in the 1990s on the first stock market listings for merchant banks and blue chips, and is adviser to the regulatory authority, CDVM (Conseil Déontologique des Valeurs Mobilières).

SFM is traditionally counsel to local institutional banking and insurance clients, and has been working with them for decades. Clients include BMCE, BMCI and Attijariwafa Bank, RMA Alwatania, CAT and ONA.

CORPORATE AND M&A
GIDE LOYRETTE NOUEL – NACIRI & ASSOCIÉS ✪
KETTANI LAW FIRM
UGGC & ASSOCIÉS ✪
CMS Bureau Francis Lefebvre **Hajji & Associés** ✪ **Mernissi – FIGES**
Ernst & Young – Associated Advisers **PricewaterhouseCoopers** **SFM**
Bennani & Associés LLP **Garrigues**
Firms are listed A-Z in tiers which are ranked in order of priority ✪ *Indicates firm displays contact details at the end of this chapter.*

CORPORATE AND M&A

A landmark of the Moroccan legal landscape, *Naciri & Associés* initially developed a contentious practice in the 1990s. Mohamed Naciri is a former chairman of the Casablanca Bar and member of the Constitutional Court. He was joined in 2000 by his son Hicham Naciri who developed the advisory side (now some 70% of the work is for a mixed client base) and sealed the partnership with French heavyweight **Gide Loyrette Nouel** in 2003. The firm now has 25 lawyers and covers the whole range of business law with a focus on M&A, stock exchange law, banking and finance, projects, joint ventures and foreign investment, maritime law and dispute resolution. **Gide Loyrette Nouel** also has offices in Algeria and Tunisia and therefore covers the whole of French-speaking North Africa. Recent deals include the acquisition of CNIA, the fourth insurance company in Morocco, by Saham (advising the buyer); the sale of Somepi to the Akwa Group (advising the seller); and the restructurings of the capitals of Meditelecom (€100m) and Samir ($450m). The firm has also been extensively involved in the constitution of investment funds, for Club Méd and BMCE for instance.

Kettani Law Firm is one of the few major players in Casablanca and founder Azeddine Kettani has developed a 20-lawyer firm dedicated to international business law, now helped by daughters Nadia Kettani and Rita Kettani. The practice is wide and encompasses banking and finance, corporate and commercial law for foreign investors, M&A and privatisation, projects, labour law, IP, maritime law, telecoms, and disputes. Recent deals include acting for BNP Paribas and Merrill Lynch in the €800m IPO of Maroc Télécom; and Roche SA in the disposal of their OTC activities to Bayer in Morocco.

Working with Morocco from Paris since 1996, **UGGC & Associés** opened an office in Casablanca in December 2002, with partner Patrick Larrivé. Seven *conseils juridiques* in Morocco and five *avocats* in Paris (among which name partner Jean-Jacques Uettwiller) work with the Maghreb, mainly Morocco but also Algeria. The firm's scope of activities covers corporate and commercial work, financings and M&A and also public law, real estate, tax, IP and competition. Clients are 40% Moroccan and 60% foreign (half of them being French); they are mainly industrial (construction), banking (funds), insurance and distribution international groups. Recently, the firm was involved in the structuring of four investment funds; assisted the fund Afric Invest in various investments.

CMS Bureau Francis Lefebvre's Frédéric Elbar knows Africa extensively, having worked for five years in Cameroon and opened the Equatorial Guinea and Chad offices for Price Waterhouse (now Landwell). Opening in Casablanca in 1948 as a *fiduciaire*, French firm **CMS Bureau Francis Lefebvre** sold its stake – although still doing Morocco work from Paris – before buying it again in 2001 with the arrival of Elbar. The *cabinet* works alongside an accountancy firm, and can therefore offer clients focused capability in law and tax with a team of eight lawyers. Clients are made up of international investors, mainly in industries such as construction (Bouygues), paint and chemicals (Akzo Nobel), textiles (Lacoste), cars (Renault), parts manufacturers (Valeo), telecoms (Vivendi Universal, Maroc Telecom), and tourism (Thomas Cook). For instance, the firm recently advised Vivendi Universal in the acquisition of an additional 16% stake in Maroc Telecom from the Moroccan State.

Hajji & Associés was founded in 1996 by Amin Hajji, a former international banker, and was from the start dedicated to international work. Both partners (with Myriam Bennani), studied in France and are English-speakers, while associates are Moroccan *avocats* and are dedicated to contentious work. The team comprises nine legal experts with the arrival of two French lawyers in 2005. 80% of the clients come from abroad, the rest being Moroccan multinationals. It handles M&A, concessions and investment projects, including construction and financings. At the same time, contracts, distribution, labour, tax and some IP are dealt with. On the corporate side, the firm acted alongside **Clifford Chance** LLP on some major Moroccan financing operations and M&A. In 2005, **Hajji & Associés** was counsel to Lenovo in Morocco on the acquisition of the IBM Personal Computing division.

Mernissi – FIGES, initially a *fiduciaire*, is now dedicated to business law. Name partner Mohamed El Mernissi is a prominent figure in Moroccan legal life; he is a notable academic and is regularly consulted by the government. He works with daughter Lamya El Mernissi and, even if small in size, the firm is involved in some major cases, working along with **Freshfields Bruckhaus Deringer** on the Tanger seaport project. It covers general company and commercial law, M&A, concession of public services, IPOs, arbitration, insolvency and liquidation. Half the clients are local, with half its foreign client base coming from France. Clients include CMS, ONEP (Office National de l'Eau Potable), Veolia, Lyonnaise des Eaux and Thales.

Lawyers from Arthur Andersen joined Ernst & Young in 2002 to form a single firm, **Ernst & Young – Associated Advisers**, under the leadership of Bachir Tazi. The legal and tax department comprises seven people and is led by Choukry Maghnouj. Its core business is corporate and tax advice for Moroccan and foreign investors, and leading institutions in the banking and insurance industries. The firm is also involved in special projects, mainly infrastructure, for public or private entities, and handles some compliance work.

At **PricewaterhouseCoopers**, Abdelaziz Almechatt is the partner in charge of legal advice. Work is mainly corporate, M&A, restructuring and contracts, although other areas are covered, like labour law, competition and IP. The *conseils juridiques* work in French, English and Arabic. Clients are both local and international.

SFM (Société Fiduciaire du Maroc) was the first *fiduciaire* set up in Morocco in 1929, and is very experienced, especially in the banking and insurance sectors. Joseph Barzilaï, who has also always been close to the Moroccan administration and the Royal Family, advises the French Embassy and is the economic advisor to the French Foreign Affairs Ministry. At the same time, **SFM** acts for foreign investors. Work handled encompasses general corporate and commercial (international contracts and real estate for instance), and tax, working alongside auditing company FIDAROC. Recommended individuals include Jacques Humblé and Moulay Abdallah Lalami. Recently, the firm has been involved in a number of significant mergers such as Royale Marocaine d'Assurances-Al Wataniya; and BMCI (BNP Paribas Group) and ABN-Amro.

Bennani & Associés LLP is a young firm founded in 2004 by two partners, Mehdi Bennani, a New York Bar attorney having previously worked at **Curtis, Mallet-Prevost, Colt & Mosle LLP** and **Bryan Cave LLP**, and Abdellah Moustaid, formerly an associate at **El Andaloussi**. The former is developing an advisory practice as a corporate and finance lawyer, whereas the latter works as a litigator along with six associates. They have started working for clients such as Microsoft, Wafasalaf, CNIA, Axa, and BMCI.

Spanish heavyweight **Garrigues** opened an office in Casablanca at the end of 2005. The team, led by José Ignacio García Muniozguren, is entirely composed of local multilingual legal and tax experts. The firm intends to cash in on an increasing interest towards Morocco among Spanish companies of various sectors (industrial, real estate, hotels and leisure, etc.). The idea is not only to focus on Spanish clients, but also to assist Moroccan companies and clients from other countries.

DISPUTE RESOLUTION

At **Gide Loyrette Nouel – Naciri & Associés**, Mohamed Naciri supervises litigation, white-collar crime and arbitration. The dispute resolution team comprises six lawyers dealing with commercial litigation, employment litigation, administrative litigation in relation with infrastructure projects, national and international arbitration.

DISPUTE RESOLUTION LITIGATION

Gide Loyrette Nouel – Naciri & Associés ✪
Kettani Law Firm

El Andaloussi
Hajji & Associés ✪
Laraqui Fassi Fihri & Kettani ✪
UGGC & Associés ✪

Bennani & Associés LLP

ARBITRATION

El Andaloussi
Gide Loyrette Nouel – Naciri & Associés ✪
Kettani Law Firm
Mernissi – FIGES

Firms are listed A-Z in tiers which are ranked in order of priority
✪ *Indicates firm displays contact details at the end of this chapter.*

Azeddine Kettani, at **Kettani Law Firm**, is a renowned litigator and handles both litigation (including white-collar crime) and arbitration, and the firm also has *avocats* who can handle litigation, for instance in the banking field.

El Andaloussi is renowned in Casablanca among the litigation-focused firms.

Two lawyers at **Hajji & Associés** are Moroccan *avocats* and deal with litigation, in the IP and distribution contracts fields, among others.

Laraqui Fassi Fihri & Kettani is a litigation firm where three partners mainly handle banking recovery.

At **Mernissi – FIGES**, Mohamed El Mernissi is president of the Court of Arbitration of the International Chamber of Commerce of Morocco and regularly acts as an arbitrator. He is also a member of the Competition and Antitrust Authority.

UGGC & Associés handles post-acquisition and procurement contracts litigation in partnership with a Moroccan lawyer for the proceeding aspects.

At **Bennani & Associés LLP**, Abdellah Moustaid handles banking, IP and labour litigation, along with five associates.

INTELLECTUAL PROPERTY

Although the major commercial firms handle some IP work in Morocco, and sometimes from Paris, intellectual property is dealt with by *conseils en propriété industrielle*, the major ones being mentioned in this chapter.

Mehdi Salmouni-Zerhouni's name partner is a patent and trade mark expert. His clients are international groups (90%), about half of them being French. He handles both IP strategic consultations and litigation (infringement and unfair competition). His team is made up of some ten IP specialists and clients include Bic, Moulinex, companies in the chemicals, drugs and mechanical industries, and other firms needing a correspondent in Morocco. Mehdi Salmouni-Zerhouni is also a franchise specialist.

INTELLECTUAL PROPERTY

Mehdi Salmouni-Zerhouni

Abderrazik, Cabinet
Aksiman, Cabinet
Saba & Co
TMP Agents

Firms are listed A-Z in tiers which are ranked in order of priority

We also recommend **Cabinet Aksiman** and **Cabinet Abderrazik** (the latter being a former director of the Office de la Propriété Industrielle); **Saba & Co** and **TMP Agents** which handle patent and trade mark registrations.

PROJECTS AND PUBLIC LAW

Gide Loyrette Nouel – Naciri & Associés advised winning bidders Maersk and consortium Comanav – CMSA – Eurogate on the Tanger Méditerranée project (for the first and second container terminals); the State in the irrigation project of Guerdane; Veolia Water in the concession for the management of water in Tanger and Casablanca; and DIP (Dubai International Property) in the town-planning project of the Bouregreg Valley.

Kettani Law Firm represented Sita El Beïda, a subsidiary of Suez Environnement, in the delegation of domestic waste management for Casablanca, and the local authority in the delegation of urban transport. In the Tanger Méditerranée port project, the firm works alongside CDG (Caisse de Dépôts et de Gestion).

Mernissi – FIGES has been involved in the development of delegation of public services in Morocco since the 1990s, advising Lydec (Lyonnaise des Eaux) and Veolia on the concessions for water, waste and public transport in Casablanca, Rabat, Tetouan and Fès. The firm acts as counsel of Tangier Mediterranean Special Agency (TMSA) in the whole bidding process for the granting of the concessions related to the Tanger seaport.

Prior to joining **CMS Bureau Francis Lefebvre**, Frédéric Elbar advised ExxonMobil on the Chad-Cameroon pipeline project. More recently, the firm advised Bouygues on the Tanger Méditerranée port project; Bourbon – Les Abeilles, successful bidder for the towing concession in the same port project; and the motorway company Salini Italstrade on the Mediterranean circular. It also advises Sogea Vinci on a regular basis.

At **Hajji & Associés**, Myriam Bennani has extensive experience with the privatisation of the Moroccan public sector and works with the

PROJECTS AND PUBLIC LAW

GIDE LOYRETTE NOUEL – NACIRI & ASSOCIÉS ✪
KETTANI LAW FIRM
MERNISSI – FIGES
CMS Bureau Francis Lefebvre **Hajji & Associés** ✪
Ernst & Young – Associated Advisers **UGGC & Associés** ✪

Firms are listed A-Z in tiers which are ranked in order of priority
✪ *Indicates firm displays contact details at the end of this chapter.*

Ministry of Finance and Privatisation on the new concessions law decree. She has been active in various projects recently. For instance, she advised the Moroccan government on the concession for a national zoo in Rabat, and advised an international maritime consortium (Hutchison Port Holdings) for the Tangier Mediterranean Special Agency's terminal container bid. In the bid for the towing concession in the same project, **Hajji & Associés** advised Remolcadores.

Ernst & Young – Associated Advisers is involved in projects led by the Moroccan government in infrastructure development, housing programme implementation, tourism development, and public services concessions.

UGGC & Associés is involved in various infrastructure projects for foreign investors and worked for one of the bidder in the Tanger seaport project.

TAX

CMS Bureau Francis Lefebvre is one of the few firms dedicated to tax advice, and can rely on the outstanding reputation and expertise of the Paris office, arguably the best tax firm in France. Frédéric Elbar is the partner in charge.

A. Saaidi Consultants has well-regarded tax specialist Mohamed Hdid, while Abderrahmane Saaidi is back to business after being the Minister for Privatisations for a few years. Many Moroccan firms without tax departments refer work.

Tax work makes up half of **PricewaterhouseCoopers**' activity, and the department is led by Abdelwaret Kabbaj. Advisory and contentious work are both handled.

Among the *fiduciaires*, **SFM** is active with Joseph Barzilaï and his team.

At **Ernst & Young – Associated Advisers**, Abdelmejid Faiz is the partner in charge.

Rachid Lazrak – Fidumaco is a tax specialist, a university teacher and the author of several books.

Also recommended are **Deloitte & Touche**, **KPMG** (Azzedine Benmoussa), and **Juricom** (Hamad Jouahri).

UGGC & Associés handles tax work from Paris or Casablanca.

TAX

CMS BUREAU FRANCIS LEFEBVRE
A. SAAIDI CONSULTANTS
PricewaterhouseCoopers **SFM**
Deloitte & Touche **Ernst & Young – Associated Advisers** **Juricom** **KPMG** **Rachid Lazrak – Fidumaco** **UGGC & Associés** ✪

Firms are listed A-Z in tiers which are ranked in order of priority
✪ *Indicates firm displays contact details at the end of this chapter.*

TOURISM

CMS Bureau Francis Lefebvre has clients among promoters, hotel and tourism companies. The firm is active in various projects such as the new development of six tourism projects of around 300ha each in Marrakech, a €400m project in the Mogador/Essaouira area and also in the Larache/Lixus area for Accor, Orco and Thomas-Piron.

Gide Loyrette Nouel – Naciri & Associés is also active in the tourism industry and works for Four Seasons on a project in Marrakech ($100m); Kertzner for the development of the seaside resort of Al Jadida; Latsis for the development of a 150ha project in Marrakech; and Club Méd in the constitution of an investment fund.

Hajji & Associés works for foreign investors on projects in Marrakech and Rabat. Clients include Four Seasons and a Saoudi group.

Kettani Law Firm's activities in the tourism industry are on the foreign investors' side. It acts for Accor, Sheraton, Méridien, and Marriott on various Moroccan projects.

UGGC & Associés is advisor to a foreign hotel group in connection with a project in Marrakech; to BEI in the development of a tourist project by Club Méd; and to the Ministry of Tourism in the structuring of the financing of new tourist areas.

FOREIGN FIRMS

Alain Malek has worked for several years in Casablanca, opening an office for French firm *Sokolow Dunaud Mercadier Carreras* in 2000 and then working independently before joining **Norton Rose** in 2004. A great deal of his work is dedicated to Morocco (he also works in Algeria, Lebanon, Egypt, Jordan and Tunisia, assisting French banks and insurance companies in these regions). He mainly handles privatisations and M&A, such as advising ONA and its subsidiaries Maroc Connect and Consumar for, respectively, the successful bid for the third Moroccan fixed telecom licence, and the acquisition of four state-owned Moroccan companies in the sugar industry.

TOURISM

CMS BUREAU FRANCIS LEFEBVRE **GIDE LOYRETTE NOUEL – NACIRI & ASSOCIÉS** ✪
Hajji & Associés ✪ **Kettani Law Firm** **UGGC & Associés** ✪

Firms are listed A-Z in tiers which are ranked in order of priority
✪ *Indicates firm displays contact details at the end of this chapter.*

At **Freshfields Bruckhaus Deringer**, Amir Jahanguiri is active in projects and finance and works closely with **Mernissi – FIGES**. In 2005, he acted for Tangier Mediterranean Special Agency (TMSA) in connection with the award of the concession of the second container terminal of the Tanger-Méd Seaport to a consortium formed by Eurogate, Contship, CMA-CGM, MSC and COMANAV, and of the concession for the operation of tug boats within the perimeter of the new Tanger-Méd seaport to Groupe Bourbon; Holding Marocaine Commerciale et Financière (Holmarcom) in connection with the project of two grain terminals in the Casablanca and Jorf Lasfar seaports.

Clifford Chance advised the government of Morocco on the partial privatisation of Morocco's leading telecommunications operator, Itissalat Al-Maghrib (Maroc Telecom); a group of international banks and financial institutions for financing in connection with a US$1bn de-bottle-necking and environmental upgrade to the Samir refinery; the IFC in connection with the US$1.6bn telecoms project financing of Médi Telecom S.A. (Meditel), a cellular phone company which was awarded the second global systems for mobile communications (GSM) licence in Morocco; and the Moroccan government in connection with the financing of the freight port to be built and run on a BOT basis in Tanger.

Orrick's François Bloch is counsel to the Kingdom of Morocco and the Minister for Finance and Privatisation in deals such as the US$350m sale of four state-owned sugar mills to ONA; the US$1.2bn acquisition by Vivendi Universal of 16% of the share capital of Itissalat al Maghrib/Maroc Telecom; and the €1.3bn acquisition by Altadis of 80% of the share capital of Régie des Tabacs.

FOREIGN FIRMS

NORTON ROSE
Freshfields Bruckhaus Deringer
Clifford Chance **Orrick**

Firms are listed A-Z in tiers which are ranked in order of priority

GIDE LOYRETTE NOUEL – NACIRI & ASSOCIES

63 BOULEVARD MOULAY YOUSSEF
20000 CASABLANCA

Telephone: +212 22 27 46 28
Fax: +212 22 27 30 16
E-mail: gln.casablanca@gide.com
Website: www.gide.com

Other offices
Algiers, Beijing, Belgrade, Brussels, Bucharest, Budapest, Hanoi, Istanbul, London, Moscow, New York, Paris, Prague, Riyadh, Shanghai, Tunis, Warsaw

Number of lawyers 586
at this office 15

Contact
Hicham Naciri (naciri@gide.com)

CATEGORIES OF WORK

Corporate law	Distribution
Mergers and acquisitions	Employment law
Banking and finance law	Intellectual property
Stock exchange, capital markets	Arbitration and dispute resolution
Real estate	Telecommunications law
Tourism, hotels and entertainment	

HAJJI & ASSOCIÉS

28 BLVD. MOULAY YOUSSEF
20000 CASABLANCA

Telephone: +212 22 48 74 74
Fax: +212 22 48 74 75
E-mail: a.hajji@ahlo.ma
Website: www.ahlo.ma

Languages
Arabic, English, French

Number of lawyers 7

CATEGORIES OF WORK

Project financing	Hotel and leisure investment
Aircraft financing	Corporate
Mergers and acquisitions	Securities
Intellectual property	Litigation

LARAQUI FASSI FIHRI & KETTANI

30 RUE MOHAMED BEN BRAHIM
AL MOURRAKOUCHI
20000 CASABLANCA

Telephone: +212 22 26 68 03/06
Fax: +212 22 26 68 07
E-mail: laraquiassocies@menara.ma

Languages
Arabic, English, French

Number of lawyers 20

Contacts
Laraqui Asmar, Fassi-Fihri Bassamat

CATEGORIES OF WORK

Banking, finance and capital markets
Dispute resolution, litigation
Corporate law
Contract law
Commercial law
Bankruptcy and insolvency
Employment law
Mergers and acquisitions
Intellectual property

UGGC & ASSOCIES

93 BOULEVARD MASSIRA
AL KHADRA
CASABLANCA

Telephone: +212 22 77 44 30/40
Fax: +212 22 23 86 66
E-mail: p.larrive@uggcavocats.com
Website: www.uggcavocats.com

Languages
Arabic, Dutch, English, French, German, Italian, Spanish

Other offices
Brussels, Paris

Number of lawyers 95
at this office 4

Contact
Patrick Larrivé

CATEGORIES OF WORK

Corporate law, mergers and acquisitions, privatisations
Bankruptcy/insolvency
Labour law
Tax law
Real estate
Banking and project finance
Competition and property law
Public law

NETHERLANDS

Population	16.4 million
Number of lawyers	11,200
Professional title	Advocaat
Currency	Euro (€)

The Netherlands borders the North Sea to the north and west, Germany to the east and Belgium to the south. With a population of 16.4 million spread out over only 41,500km² (20% of which is water), Holland is one of the world's most densely populated countries. It is also one of the lowest lying (its name literally means low country).

Jan Peter Balkenende is Prime Minister and leads a centre-right coalition government composed of the centrist Christian Democratic Appeal, the right-of-centre Liberals and the centrist Democrats-66. Balkenende's tenure has largely coincided with a period of atypical economic stagnation for a Dutch economy traditionally viewed with envy by other nations. The government has reacted by imposing an austerity package as harsh as any OECD country in recent times, raising taxes, cutting benefits and clamping down on early retirement. Despite being hugely unpopular with the electorate, these draconian measures have had an effect, and have certainly lifted the economy from the doldrums of 2003's recession. Recent figures show that GDP grew by 1.5% in 2005, with further growth of 2% predicted in 2006. Economic problems were, however, undoubtedly one of the key factors in influencing the decision of the voters to reject the EU constitution in a recent referendum

Amsterdam is the key financial centre and houses the majority of national and international blue-chip corporates, financial institutions and law firms. Rotterdam is the second-largest city and home to the largest port in Europe, while The Hague is the administrative centre of the Netherlands and home to the government, and the Supreme Court.

Despite the recent recession, the Netherlands still ranks eighth in the world as an exporter and sixth most popular country for foreign companies to invest in. Dutch companies are indeed world leaders in many fields including banking and finance (ABN Amro, ING, Aegon), oil refining (Shell), and electrical goods (Philips).

BILLING

Although most firms charge on an hourly basis, in an increasingly competitive market lawyers are more inclined to be flexible with their fee structures. Indeed, lawyers and their clients are allowed to come to their own arrangements and agree on mutually acceptable terms of billing. The average hourly billing rate for a corporate partner in Amsterdam is approximately €300, although some will charge in the region of €400. At some international law firms where the corporate work is often of a more international, cross-border nature, fees can be as high as €750.

MARKETING

A highly competitive legal market has stimulated marketing efforts and all of the major firms have their own internal marketing departments. Beauty parades are becoming increasingly common place, and firms are seeking to use their marketing teams to maximum effect. The increase in international law firms has been a major factor in kick-starting these more overt marketing efforts.

IN-HOUSE LAWYERS

Dutch in-house lawyers have full rights of access to the Dutch Bar. All of the large corporates and banks have their own in-house legal teams including the likes of Shell, ABN Amro, ING and Rabobank.

CIVIL LAW NOTARIES

Notaries occupy a unique position amongst fellow legal professionals in the Netherlands. Appointed by the Crown for life, the permanence of the position is designed to safeguard the independence the notary requires to perform his duties. Unlike an advocaat, the notary does not just act for one party. Instead the notary is intended to straddle both parties' interests and to balance both parties' concerns. Essential for commercial property and M&A transactions, most law firms in the Netherlands employ a substantial number of notaries.

LIMITING LIABILITY

Dutch law firms now have a certain level of professional indemnity insurance. Consequently, clients are advised to check the terms and conditions on their contracts and individual firm policies on their website. Most of the major Dutch firms have taken the step of limiting their liability by converting to an NV.

LEGAL MARKET

Despite being a relatively small jurisdiction, the Netherlands supports a number of large firms that

The largest firms

1	Loyens & Loeff	513
2	NautaDutilh	320
3	De Brauw Blackstone Westbroek	310
4	Houthoff Buruma	292
5	CMS Derks Star Busmann	243
6	AKD Prinsen Van Wijmen N.V.	224
7	Allen & Overy LLP	192
8	Holland van Gijzen	185
9	Boekel De Nerée	160
	Pels Rijcken & Droogleever Fortuijn NV	160
11	Stibbe	155
12	Baker & McKenzie	150
13	Clifford Chance	144
14	Van Doorne	135
15	Van Diepen Van der Kroef Advocaten	124
16	Simmons & Simmons	113
17	Dirkzwager advocaten & notarissen	105
18	DLA SchutGrosheide	94
19	Nysingh advocaten - notarissen N.V.	90
20	Kennedy Van der Laan	85
21	Freshfields Bruckhaus Deringer	79
22	Greenberg Traurig LLP	70
	Van Mens & Wisselink	70
24	De Jonge Peters Remmelink	64
25	Lovells	56
26	BarentsKrans	55

These figures represent the total number of lawyers in this country only, and have been supplied by the firms themselves. The figures should be accurate as at 1 January 2006.

are often instructed in sizeable international transactions. The influx of a vast number of international firms is testament to a vibrant and competitive legal market.

Allen & Overy LLP continues to forge an impressive furrow in the Dutch market and has achieved top-tier status in no fewer than 11 of our practice areas. A full-service practice, the firm benefits from the vast scope and reputation of its international network.

De Brauw Blackstone Westbroek remains by some margin the leading independent law firm in the country. With competencies across the board, the firm is the envy of its competitors with its first-rate, blue-chip client base. Despite being independent, the firm benefits from close relationships with a number of leading law firms in other jurisdictions. Through its office in The Hague, the firm has a reputable Supreme Court Practice.

Loyens & Loeff is best known for its Benelux tax practice but is also strong at private equity, securitisation and employment.

NautaDutilh is the largest independent law firm in the Benelux region. Its Dutch practice continues to undergo some upheavals and the firm has suffered a series of partner defections. Nevertheless, the firm remains a major player in the market and has an impressive stable of blue-chip corporate and banking clients.

Stibbe benefits from a formal alliance with Germany-based **Gleiss Lutz** and UK-based **Herbert Smith LLP**, who it acted alongside in the headline-grabbing, TomTom IPO.

Houthoff Buruma is the second-largest Dutch independent firm. Traditionally strong in commercial property, the firm has a growing presence in the M&A and private equity markets.

Clifford Chance excels in banking and finance and offers the stiffest competition to rival UK-based firm, **Allen & Overy LLP**.

Freshfields Bruckhaus Deringer is rapidly becoming known as a firm of the highest quality and offers market-leading capability in intellectual property, corporate and EU and competition. Despite having grown rapidly since its inception in 1999, it still lacks the critical mass necessary to seriously challenge the leading players.

Linklaters is another firm whose star is most assuredly on the ascendency. Richard Levy and Pim Horsten combine to lead a capital markets team that while small, is undeniably of the very highest quality. The strategic recruitment of Martijn Koopal, formerly of **DLA SchutGrosheide**, has bolstered its emerging banking practice.

As a mid-tier firm, **Lovells** offers a 'first-class' service across the full range of disciplines with particular strengths in areas such as IP and employment.

Closely aligned to its international network, **Norton Rose**'s Amsterdam office specialises in key areas such as project finance, energy and construction. Clients are also attracted by its competitive pricing structure.

Simmons & Simmons is the only UK-based firm to be headquartered in Rotterdam. The result of a merger with half of local firm *Trenité Van Doorne*, the firm is progressing well.

US-based **Greenberg Traurig LLP** is still building up its practice in the Netherlands and continues to recruit at partner level. The firm scored a major coup in the M&A market, advising Getronics in its €338m acquisition of PinkRoccade.

The result of a merger with a local firm, **Baker & McKenzie** is beginning to embed itself in the Dutch market. Offering full-service capability, it is particularly strong in tax and employment.

DLA SchutGrosheide offers a full-service practice and garners excellent client feedback.

The Hague-based **Bird & Bird** has a focus on its core areas of IP and IT, while Utrecht-based **CMS Derks Star Busmann** has a focus on the corporate market.

In the independent Dutch mid-market, **AKD Prinsen Van Wijmen N.V.** continues to focus on its core specialities in shipping, insurance, environment, employment and insolvency. The firm also benefits from an alliance with Deloitte.

Boekel De Nerée has an excellent reputation in the market. Philip Paterson and Ferdinand Mason head the firm's impressive Anglo-American advisory group.

Based in The Hague, **Pels Rijcken & Droogleever Fortuijn NV** is best-known as the preferred legal provider to the Dutch government. The firm's Supreme Court practice is revered by its competitors.

The initial teething problems that inevitably followed **Van Doorne**'s merger with **Landwell** appear to be subsiding and the firm is starting to witness substantial growth in revenue and profit.

Founded in 2002, **Faasen & Partners** is a mid-size firm with offices in Rotterdam and Amsterdam.

OFFICES ABROAD

De Brauw Blackstone Westbroek has offices in London and New York, and **Houthoff Buruma** has London and Brussels offices.

Loyens & Loeff is part of a global tax firm with offices in Brussels, Luxembourg, Aruba, Antwerp, Caraçao, Frankfurt, Geneva, London, New York, Paris, Singapore, Tokyo and Zurich.

NautaDutilh has offices in Brussels, London, Luxembourg and New York.

Both **Spigthoff** and **Van Doorne** have offices in Caraçao, and **Van Doorne** also has London and Aruba offices.

Stibbe has offices in London, Brussels and New York, and also benefits from a formal alliance with UK-based **Herbert Smith LLP** and Germany-based **Gleiss Lutz**.

ARBITRATION

DE BRAUW BLACKSTONE WESTBROEK ✪

FRESHFIELDS BRUCKHAUS DERINGER
NAUTADUTILH

Allen & Overy LLP ✪
Boekel De Nerée ✪
CMS Derks Star Busmann ✪
Clifford Chance
Houthoff Buruma ✪
Pels Rijcken & Droogleever Fortuijn NV ✪
Rozemond Van Ramshorst Smit
Simmons & Simmons ✪
Stibbe ✪
Van Doorne ✪

AKD Prinsen Van Wijmen N.V. ✪
Baker & McKenzie ✪
BarentsKrans ✪
Buren van Velzen Guelen ✪
DLA SchutGrosheide ✪
Greenberg Traurig LLP
Loyens & Loeff ✪
Norton Rose
Oostwaard ✪
Spigthoff ✪

Firms are listed A-Z in tiers which are ranked in order of priority
✪ *Indicates firm displays contact details at the end of this chapter.*

ARBITRATION

De Brauw Blackstone Westbroek's arbitration team continues to thrive and reports an increase in international arbitration instructions. Marnix Leijten heads a team that includes Bommel van der Bend. Van der Bend is highly regarded for construction and energy-related arbitrations.

Freshfields Bruckhaus Deringer's 'impressive' arbitration group is equally adept acting for Dutch clients in Dutch-seated arbitrations as it is for international clients in international arbitrations. The firm recently represented ENEL in an ICC arbitration arising out of a contractual dispute with a US company. Brian King is recommended.

NautaDutilh's arbitration group advises a broad range of both domestic and international clients. The firm recently successfully represented Eureko against the Polish State. Bart van Tongeren and Daniella Strik are recommended.

Headed by Willem van Baren, **Allen & Overy LLP**'s arbitration practice continues to pick up a growing share of international commercial arbitration. The team recently represented a Dutch listed company in an ICC arbitration relating to the determination of the purchase price in an asset transaction. At home, the department frequently appears before the Netherlands Arbitration Institute.

Boekel De Nerée's Els Swaab heads a 'proactive and intelligent team' that specialises in handling complex and highly sensitive commercial disputes. The firm recently represented a leading European postal company in arbitration proceedings relating to breach of warranties following the sale of group companies. Lisette Bieleveld often handles IT disputes and is experienced in both domestic and ICC arbitration proceedings.

CMS Derks Star Busmann is representing several major construction companies in the wake of the fraud allegations by government agencies.

Clifford Chance is often involved in arbitrations with an international element. Active in the energy sector, the team recently advised Belgian power generation firm, Electrabel, on stranded costs issues. The team also advised a large oil and energy company in a €1.2bn arbitration. Jeroen Ouwehand is recommended.

Houthoff Buruma's arbitration group has a focus on project development and construction and is instructed by both domestic and international clients at an international, national and local level.

Pels Rijcken & Droogleever Fortuijn NV's René van de Klashorst is handling a major arbitration between the State of the Netherlands and a daughter company of the Dutch Railway Company and KLM, concerning financial aspects of the high-speed rail link between Amsterdam and Brussels.

Construction boutique **Rozemond Van Ramshorst Smit** has an excellent reputation for arbitration. Rob Bleeker is recommended.

Simmons & Simmons' Jan Willem Biter and Gerard Bruyninckx represent clients in both international and domestic commercial arbitrations. Sjoerd Rutten and Jos van de Vijver are both construction lawyers who frequently undertake arbitration proceedings on behalf of their clients.

Stibbe benefits from a close working relationship with leading UK-based dispute resolution firm **Herbert Smith LLP**. Jeroen Fleming is recommended.

Van Doorne's Dries Fransen van de Putte represented Corus in a contractual dispute concerning the delivery of electricity.

In the lower tier, **DLA SchutGrosheide**'s Diederik De Groot has both NAI and ICC arbitration experience, while at **Norton Rose** Arent van Wassenaer continues to develop the practice.

ASSET FINANCE AND STRUCTURED FINANCE

ALLEN & OVERY LLP ✪
CLIFFORD CHANCE
DE BRAUW BLACKSTONE WESTBROEK ✪
NAUTADUTILH

Freshfields Bruckhaus Deringer
Loyens & Loeff ✪
Simmons & Simmons ✪
Stibbe ✪

Baker & McKenzie ✪
Boekel De Nerée ✪
DLA SchutGrosheide ✪
Greenberg Traurig LLP
Houthoff Buruma ✪
Lovells ✪
Norton Rose
Van Doorne ✪

AKD Prinsen Van Wijmen N.V. ✪
CMS Derks Star Busmann ✪
Linklaters ✪

Firms are listed A-Z in tiers which are ranked in order of priority
✪ *Indicates firm displays contact details at the end of this chapter.*

ASSET FINANCE AND STRUCTURED FINANCE

Led by Bart Meesters, **Allen & Overy LLP**'s asset finance practice advised new client, Amsterdam Trade Bank, in relation to the debt financing of a number of aircraft and ships. Niels van de Vijver heads a securitisation team that is praised by clients for 'concentrating on the main issues as opposed to getting bogged down by the details'. The team advises a healthy portfolio of both domestic and international banks including ABN Amro, HBOS, ING and Merrill Lynch. Recent highlights include advising HBOS on its first mortgage receivables securitisation in the Netherlands. Werner Runge is a rising star who has a focus on CMBS securitisations.

Clifford Chance's market-leading securitisation team is often at the forefront of developments in the market and recently advised ABN Amro as arranger in the first-ever Dutch structured covered bonds programme to enter the market. Frank Graaf is highly regarded by his peers and is a recognised leader in CDO transactions. On the asset financing side, the team advised Calyon on the refinancing of four Airbus aircraft for debis Airfinance. Theo Kliebisch has a strong asset finance focus.

Under the strong leadership of Berend Crans, **De Brauw Blackstone Westbroek**'s asset and structured finance team continues to forge an impressive furrow in the competitive Dutch market. On the asset finance side, the team has been active on aircraft finance transactions and recently advised debis AirFinance in the US$125m refinancing of four German leveraged lease transactions. On the structured finance side, it advised Goldman Sachs in its €236m senior facility agreement to refinance an existing debt provided by NIB Capital to QMH.

NautaDutilh is a market leader in RMBS transactions. Led by Willem Ruys and Michaëla Ulrici, the team has advised on the majority of the major domestic RMBS transactions including Arena (acting for ABN Amro) and Delphinus (acting for Fortis). Praised by clients for its innovative approach to transactions, highlights include advising ABN Amro as issuer in the €25bn covered bonds programme. Arend-Jaap van der Lely is recommended for his expertise on tax-driven deals.

Closely integrated with its tax and finance teams, **Freshfields Bruckhaus Deringer** is a market leader in tax and regulatory arbitrage structured finance transactions. The team also continues to advise arrangers in a number of RMBS transactions and has increased its advisory role for Fitch ratings. On the asset finance front, the firm has been involved in a number of aircraft finance transactions, including aircraft operated by KLM, BMI and Denimair. Jeroen Thijssen is recommended for asset finance and Pieter van Welzen for structured finance.

Headed by Mariette van't Westeinde **Loyens & Loeff**'s securitisation practice is recognised as one of the best around. Benefiting from market-leading tax capabilities the firm can really add value to clients in the often tax-driven structured finance deals. The firm has been involved in a number of major RMBS securitisations and recently acted as deal counsel in the €1.22bn SAECURE 5 RMBS. Willem Jarigsma heads the asset finance team that specialises in ship and aircraft finance transactions.

Simmons & Simmons reports an increase in aircraft finance transactions and is advising Sojitz on the financing of 24 aircraft. The team has an outstanding reputation for rail leasing and is exclusive local counsel for Angel Trains. On the structured finance side, Harm van Berkum is advising the Province of Friesland in the monetisation of its €600m equity stake in Nuon. Loet Venrooy is the leading individual in the asset finance practice.

Stibbe's highly regarded securitisation practice is advising KFN on the first-ever conventional Dutch CMBS transaction. Clients include Rabobank, ING and Athlon Group.

Greenberg Traurig LLP's Gérard Moussault is recommended, as is **Baker & McKenzie**'s Boris van Beek.

Leveraging off its pre-eminent reputation for real estate, **Houthoff Buruma**'s property finance team is regularly instructed by ING Real Estate Finance, Fortis and HSH Nordbank. Daphne Brinkhuis has a growing reputation in the securitisation market. She recently advised STATER on the Delta Lloyd Arena 2004-1 transaction. The arrival of senior associate Corinne Schot from **Allen & Overy LLP** has bolstered the team's capabilities in the derivatives market.

Often working closely with the London office, **Norton Rose**'s asset finance practice specialises in complex cross-border work. Gesina van de Wetering is praised for her 'vast legal knowledge'.

BANKING AND FINANCE

Headed by Andrew Thomas, **Allen & Overy LLP**'s banking team offers expertise in both Dutch and English law, and acts for an impressive portfolio of clients including ABN Amro, Bank of Scotland, KLM, TNT and Deutsche Bank. On the acquisition finance side, the group recently advised Bank of Scotland as lead arranger of €235m of senior and mezzanine acquisition facilities for the multi-jurisdictional secondary buyout of IMCD, by ABN Amro Capital. On the global loans side, the firm advised KLM on a €540m standby facility. Under the leadership of Victor de Serière and Niels van de Vijver, the team also offers high-calibre regulatory advice to a number of banking clients.

Clifford Chance's banking team has a global focus and benefits from a number of UK-qualified partners, including the 'outstanding' Mark Huddlestone. Corporate restructurings are a mainstay of the practice and firm was instructed by ING and Rabobank in the respective restructurings of the Bodycare Group and Samas Group. On the loan side, it advised ABN Amro in relation to both the €325m syndicated facility for SBS Broadcasting, and in Getronics' acquisition of PinkRoccade. Frank Graaf and Jan ter Haar have excellent reputations, as does Bas Boris Visser, who is recognised by his peers as a 'rising star in leveraged financings'.

Leveraging off of its impressive blue-chip client base, **De Brauw Blackstone Westbroek**'s banking group has a focus on borrower instructions. On the lender side, the firm is regularly instructed by major domestic banks such as Rabobank International and ING. Highlights include advising Citigroup on a US$550m credit facility to the Acco Group. The team has niche expertise in investment management advice and Paul Klemann heads a dedicated three-partner team that advises a range of retail funds (AXA, Rabobank, Merrill Lynch) and private equity clients (ING Real Estate, Shell Pension Fund and NIB).

NautaDutilh is pre-eminent in banking litigation. New partner Daan Lunsingh Scheurleer is developing a substantial reputation for class actions and was an integral part of the team that recently reached a €1bn settlement on behalf of Dexia. Marc Blom is also recommended for banking litigation. Pim Rank is a market leader in regulatory work and advised the Dutch Central Bank on its documentation for reserve management services. On the loan side, the team has been active in acquisition financing and advised Goldman Sachs Capital Partners on its US$530m acquisition of EURAMAX Group.

Freshfields Bruckhaus Deringer's banking department may be small but in terms of quality it is right up there with the very best. Recent highlights include advising ABN Amro Capital on the €129m senior and mezzanine debt financing of its acquisition of the Roompot leisure group. Jeroen Thijssen and Andrew Petry are recommended.

Backed by strong teams in London and New York, **Loyens & Loeff**'s banking and finance team has a focus on buy-outs and leveraged finance transactions. Recent highlights include advising NIB Capital Bank and ING Real Estate Finance on the €1bn+ financing of the VendexKBB real estate portfolio. Willem Jarigsma and Kitty Lieverse are recommended.

Baker & McKenzie has a niche focus on carbon-trading and advised both Rabobank and Tennet in a JV operation to establish a trading platform for CO2 and other emission rights. On the loan side, the firm advised Bayerishce Hypo-und Vereinsbank and Royal Bank of Scotland on the arrangement of €545m senior and €145m mezzanine facilities for the fashion trade group, CBR Textile. Boris van Beek heads a team that includes Karin Smit, who one client described as a 'great all rounder'.

Led by Jessica Terpstra, **Houthoff Buruma** advised the lenders on the €500m senior and mezzanine facilities for the acquisition financing of the CPI Group. Clients include Bank of Scotland, Citibank, Cristal and Westpac.

Lovells provides 'high-quality advice at competitive rates' to an impressive range of banking clients, both in relation to domestic work and cross-border transactions. Recent highlights include advising Fortis (as leader in an international syndicate) in the provision of €240m credit facilities for DFM. One client said of Ken Bracken: 'He ranks among the best banking and finance lawyers in the Netherlands and he has a great sense of humour.'

BANKING AND FINANCE

ALLEN & OVERY LLP ✪
CLIFFORD CHANCE

DE BRAUW BLACKSTONE WESTBROEK ✪
NAUTADUTILH

Freshfields Bruckhaus Deringer
Loyens & Loeff ✪

Baker & McKenzie ✪
Houthoff Buruma ✪
Lovells ✪
Simmons & Simmons ✪
Stibbe ✪
Van Doorne ✪

AKD Prinsen Van Wijmen N.V. ✪
BarentsKrans ✪
Boekel De Nerée ✪
CMS Derks Star Busmann ✪
DLA SchutGrosheide ✪
Greenberg Traurig LLP
Linklaters ✪
Norton Rose
Spigthoff ✪

Firms are listed A-Z in tiers which are ranked in order of priority
✪ *Indicates firm displays contact details at the end of this chapter.*

Simmons & Simmons has a focus on acquisition and leveraged finance. Recent highlights include representing ABN Amro in the senior debt acquisition financing of Meyn Poultry Processing Solutions by Altor. The firm's strong client base also includes BNP Paribas and Citibank, and has been bolstered by new client wins, Macquarie Bank and Apax. Clients appreciate the firm's 'competitive pricing' and single out Harm van Berkum for particular praise.

Jaap Willeumier heads a seven-partner banking and finance practice at **Stibbe** that benefits from the existence of a fully integrated, Anglo-Dutch finance desk in Amsterdam with **Herbert Smith LLP**. With a focus on borrower instructions, the firm recently advised KFN on a €150m revolving credit facility agreement. Former managing partner Allard Metzelaar is recommended.

Van Doorne's Stefan van Rossum and Roel Botter are recommended for acquisition finance. Recent highlights include advising Merrill Lynch on the €1.375bn acquisition financing of directory and search company, YBR Group. Evert Wiggers specialises in property finance. His clients include UCB and Aareal Bank. Dirk Blaisse is now managing partner of the London office following his departure from **NautaDutilh**.

Under the leadership of Barend Post, **AKD Prinsen Van Wijmen N.V.**'s Amsterdam banking practice continues to do well. Restructurings are an important facet of the practice.

The Hague-based **BarentsKrans** has a focus on banking litigation and is involved in a large number of class actions, and individual civil suits against a number of the country's major financial institutions. The team continues to be involved in the Dexia litigation.

Headed by the 'articulate, innovative and resourceful' Hans Sachse, **Boekel De Nerée**'s banking group is best known for its 'outstanding' litigation practice. However, bolstered by the arrival of associates from both **NautaDutilh** and **Allen & Overy LLP**, the volume of transactional work has increased. Highlights include advising Dutch listed supermarket chain Schuitema on the complete refinancing of the Schuitema and CKK group.

CMS Derks Star Busmann advised Deutsche Bank and others on the refinancing of credit arrangements to a large manufacturer of packaging materials. Utrecht-based Marcel Groenewegen heads the team. The team benefits from its international network and often handles Dutch law aspects of deals driven out of London.

DLA SchutGrosheide's 'reliable, realistic and reasonable' banking practice advised the Nuplex Group, in collaboration with a number of international offices, on its €125m acquisition financing facility. The loss of Martijn Koopal to **Linklaters** was certainly a blow to the practice, however this was largely offset by the arrival of Bart Joosen from **Faasen & Partners**. Joosen has an excellent reputation and advises the Dutch Ministry of Finance on prudential supervision issues for banks and insurance companies.

Greenberg Traurig's banking practice is headed by Wietse de Jong and acts for clients such as Fortis and Robeco.

Linklaters' burgeoning banking practice received a boost with the recent arrival of **DLA SchutGrosheide**'s former head of banking, Martijn Koopal. With expertise in both plain vanilla and complex, highly leveraged deals, Koopal heads a two-partner team that also includes Pim Horsten and associate Onno Bakker. The team advised BNP Paribas in relation to a number of multi-currency revolving credit facilities, including a €1.2bn facility for Atos Origin Group.

At **Norton Rose**, Gijs van Leeuwen heads a department that is praised by clients 'for its flexibility in fees' and 'solution-orientated and pragmatic advice'. The team reports a noticeable increase in the amount of trade financings it is carrying out, for amongst others, Fortis.

Spigthoff has a market-leading banking and securities litigation practice.

CAPITAL MARKETS

Led by Niels van de Vijver, **Allen & Overy LLP**'s first-rate capital markets practice is instructed by an impressive portfolio of clients including ABN Amro, Citigroup, ING and Aegon. The firm has an excellent reputation in the debt markets and advised Aegon on its recent US$925m issuance of Perpetual Capital Securities. In the equity markets, the team recently advised Buhrmann on its €250m rights issue.

At **Clifford Chance**, Frank Graaf heads a team that favours an increasingly integrated approach to both the debt and equity markets. Recent highlights include advising ABN Amro Rothschild and Rabo Securities as joint global coordinators and bookrunners, in a €400m rights issue by Getronics. The firm also advised ABN Amro in a ground-breaking €25bn structured covered bonds programme. The team has detailed knowledge of the regulatory framework of the market and is frequently asked for advice in relation to regulatory issues. Tineke Kothe, Thijs Alexander and Kees Westermann are recommended.

Headed by Jan Marten van Dijk, **De Brauw Blackstone Westbroek** has an excellent track record in both the equity and debt capital markets for both banks, and corporates. In the equity markets, the team advised Goldman Sachs and Lehman Brothers on the €469m IPO of TomTom. Other highlights include advising KPN on a €1bn share buy-back from ABN Amro. Dirk Meerburg has an enviable reputation in the market and is widely admired by his peers. Jan Willem Hoevers and Marnix Somsen have a focus on equity capital markets and financial markets regulation.

Aided by its international network of offices, **Freshfields Bruckhaus Deringer** offers debt and equity capital markets expertise both domestically and in an international setting. The firm has provided Dutch legal advice on a number of IPOs of Dutch companies, or companies with a Dutch asset base, including the IPO of New Skies Satellite. Other highlights include advising Aegon, ING and other institutional investors in the cancellation of ABN Amro's listed preference shares. Other clients include Barclays, JP Morgan and UBS.

Linklaters' 'high-quality and diligent' capital markets team is now a real force in the market, and is increasingly providing stiff competition to the top-tier firms. The lead adviser in some of the years' most notable transactions, clients rave about this developing team. Recent highlights include the €2.52bn equity offering by ABN Amro Holding to fund, in part, its acquisition of Banca Antonveneta. Clients are falling over themselves to praise UK-qualified Richard Levy, who is 'particularly responsive, one of a rare breed conversant in both Dutch law and liability management transactions'. Levy jointly heads the team with 'the experienced and accomplished' Pim Horsten.

NautaDutilh advises a range of corporates, underwriters and lead managers in both debt and equity issues. It advised the Blackstone Group on the acquisition of the business of New Skies Satellites, and the subsequent IPO of that business on the NYSE. The group also advised Mittal Steel Group on its bid for the International Steel Group and subsequent issue and listing of its stock on the Euronext Amsterdam and NYSE. The team benefits from a close working arrangement with New York-based partner, Elizabeth van Schilfgaarde. Petra Zijp is recommended for equity capital markets deals.

Stibbe's 'first-rate' capital markets team was involved in the majority of major equity capital

CAPITAL MARKETS

ALLEN & OVERY LLP ✪
CLIFFORD CHANCE
DE BRAUW BLACKSTONE WESTBROEK ✪

Freshfields Bruckhaus Deringer
Linklaters ✪
NautaDutilh
Stibbe ✪

CMS Derks Star Busmann ✪
DLA SchutGrosheide ✪
Houthoff Buruma ✪
Lovells ✪
Loyens & Loeff ✪
Norton Rose
Simmons & Simmons ✪
Van Doorne ✪

Firms are listed A-Z in tiers which are ranked in order of priority
✪ *Indicates firm displays contact details at the end of this chapter.*

markets transactions in 2005. In collaboration with **Herbert Smith LLP** it advised TomTom on its €470m IPO, the first major IPO in the Netherlands since 2000. Other highlights include advising Laurus on a major equity offering. On the debt side, the firm acted on convertible bond issues for Hagemeyer, Getronics and Draka. 'They are able to react fast when you approach them and the quality is good because they have a pragmatic manner of advising you and that's helpful', said one client. Derk Lemstra stands out in this strong all-round team.

At **CMS Derks Star Busmann**, Reinout Slot heads an equity practice that is involved in listings and hostile takeovers. The firm advised Homburg Invest in its hostile public bid for the share capital of Dutch listed company DIM Vastgoed.

Houthoff Buruma's Alexander Kaarls advised Nell Bidco in its issuance of US$615m 8 3/8% senior notes due 2015 and €500m 8 3/8% senior notes due 2015. Clients include ABN Amro, ING and NIB.

COMMERCIAL LITIGATION

Only specially appointed lawyers based in The Hague can appear before the city's Supreme Court.

With a focus on energy, construction, railways and insurance, **De Brauw Blackstone Westbroek**'s litigation practice is frequently involved in some of the country's highest-profile cases. Recent highlights include advising Royal Dutch Shell in issues regarding its oil reserves incident, and Ahold in a D&O insurance coverage-related dispute. The firm benefits from a huge blue-chip client portfolio and is also frequently instructed in relation to corporate litigation. It advised Unilever in a dispute regarding its preference shares. Berto Winters, Ruud Hermans and Marc Ynzonides are all highly regarded Supreme Court practitioners.

Traditionally strong in insurance law and with a pre-eminent Supreme Court practice, **Houthoff Buruma** has recently acted in connection with a growing number of management liability cases. Led by Hans Londonck Sluijk, the team is representing the directors and officers of the former Dutch listed company, Landis, against claims of mis-management. Whilst in the area of corporate litigation, the firm continues to represent Unilever's shareholders in the high-profile Supreme Court proceedings against the company. Rob Meijer is recommended for Supreme Court work.

The Hague-based **Pels Rijcken & Droogleever Fortuijn NV** has a strong Supreme Court practice that is kept very active by its role as preferred legal counsel of the State of the Netherlands. The team also offers commercial litigation expertise to an impressive list of blue-chip corporates such as Exxon, KPN, ABB and Electrolux. A growing area for the practice is in relation to class actions. Jurjen Lemstra is recommended.

COMMERCIAL LITIGATION

DE BRAUW BLACKSTONE WESTBROEK ✪
HOUTHOFF BURUMA ✪
PELS RIJCKEN & DROOGLEEVER FORTUIJN NV ✪

Allen & Overy LLP ✪
BarentsKrans ✪
Loyens & Loeff ✪
NautaDutilh
Simmons & Simmons ✪
Spigthoff ✪
Stibbe ✪
Van Doorne ✪

AKD Prinsen Van Wijmen N.V. ✪
Baker & McKenzie ✪
Bird & Bird ✪
Boekel De Nerée ✪
Buren van Velzen Guelen ✪
CMS Derks Star Busmann ✪
Clifford Chance
DLA SchutGrosheide ✪
Dirkzwager advocaten & notarissen
Ekelmans & Meijer Advocaten
Freshfields Bruckhaus Deringer
Greenberg Traurig LLP
Höcker Rueb Doeleman Advocaten ✪
Lovells ✪
Nysingh advocaten – notarissen N.V.
Oostwaard ✪
Van Benthem & Keulen ✪
Van Der Wiel Ruitinga Van Noort Felix
Van Diepen Van der Kroef Advocaten ✪
Van Dijk & Van Arnhem Advocaten Apeldoorn
Van Traa Advocaten ✪

Firms are listed A-Z in tiers which are ranked in order of priority
✪ Indicates firm displays contact details at the end of this chapter.

Allen & Overy LLP successfully defended UPC against a US$200m claim by former shareholders of Cignal Communications, in relation to the IPO of Priority Telecom. Clients appreciate the 'excellent litigation and tactical skills' of Arnold Croiset van Uchelen. Marieke van Hooijdonk is also recommended.

BarentsKrans has a fine reputation for commercial liability litigation. Jan Paul Heering is a Supreme Court litigator of some repute. Henk Waling has a focus on international payment-related disputes.

Loyens & Loeff's Winfried van den Muijsenbergh is frequently involved in proceedings at the Enterprise Chamber. He recently represented Lafarge in inquiry proceedings against Carmeuse. Joroen van den Brande is also well known and is often involved in litigation with an international dimension for clients such as Bang & Olufsen, Burger King and Campina.

Headed by Bart Gerretsen, **NautaDutilh**'s corporate litigation practice is instructed by a range of well-known names including ABN Amro, BASF, Sara Lee and Mitsubshi. It advised Chipshol in a €100m dispute with Schiphol Airport over the frustration of property rights. Members of the team regularly appear before the Special Enterprise Chamber of the Court of Appeal in Amsterdam, including the highly regarded Harmen de Mol van Otterloo.

At **Simmons & Simmons**, department head Olaf Trojan recently advised leading Dutch food producer, Peijnenburg, in high-profile litigation against leading Dutch retailer, Albert Heijn. The group has a focus on insolvency-related litigation and continues to represent the trustees in the bankruptcy of Ceteco. Bernard Verbunt specialises in litigation arising out of banking and financial services disputes.

Spigthoff is a leading corporate litigation boutique. Leo Spigt, Jerry Hoff and Jacob Cornegoor are recommended.

Stibbe acts for an impressive roster of clients including ING, Fortis, Hagemeyer and Deloitte. The team boasts an excellent track record for corporate litigation and regularly appears before the Enterprise Chamber. Jeroen Fleming and Toni van Hees are highly regarded by their peers for corporate and banking litigation respectively.

Van Doorne's litigation practice has a focus on D&O and professional liability insurance cases, (the team acts for a number of the leading domestic law firms) and is praised by clients who appreciate its 'accurate and high-quality advice'. Pieter van Regteren Altena and Dries Fransen van de Putte represent Imperial Tobacco in the defence of a class action brought against the Dutch tobacco industry.

Benefiting from its international network of offices, **Baker & McKenzie** is often instructed in relation to multi-jurisdictional disputes. Frank Kroes has a focus on securities litigation and regularly represents Euronext in litigation against various investors. Eduard Ferman heads the team.

Boekel De Nerée is acting for the subsidiary of major state-owned Russian oil-production company, Yuganskneftegas, in proceedings relating to a €1.8bn claim against Yukos Oil Company.

CMS Derks Star Busmann's Dominique van Dijk specialises in agriculture-related litigation.

At **Clifford Chance**, Duco Oranje heads a team whose clients include Citibank, Tele2, Morgan Stanley, Volvo and Vodafone. In collaboration with its London and Moscow offices, it is representing a syndicate of banks in the high-profile recovery of debt from Yukos Oil Company.

Greenberg Traurig LLP's Peter Roorda often handles complex international litigation and arbitration.

Two-partner boutique **Oostwaard** offers commercial litigation expertise across a range of matters, including directors' liability issues, partnership and real estate disputes. Roelof van Holthe tot Echten specialises in art law.

Van Dijk & Van Arnhem Advocaten Apeldoorn represents clients from German-speaking countries as well as their subsidiaries in Netherlands.

CONSTRUCTION

PPPs are occupying a more prominent place as a viable method of funding major projects. Signs are promising for the future and the government is actively promoting further PPP initiatives.

Houthoff Buruma's construction team has a contentious focus. Frank Thunnissen continues to represent BAM in a multi-million Euro claim by the Municipality of The Hague. Jan Michiel Helby is construction and public procurement adviser to a number of public authorities. Clients include Bechtel, Heijmans and Province of North Holland.

At **NautaDutilh**, Lieuwe de Boer heads a construction team that offers contentious, and non-contentious advice to public and private sector clients. The firm is involved in many of the country's leading infrastructure projects and is instructed by the Municipality of Amsterdam on the €1.5bn north-south underground link. On the contentious side, the firm is representing the Municipality of Rotterdam in claims arising out of the delayed extension and renovation of the city's art museum.

Construction boutique **Rozemond Van Ramshorst Smit** has a focus on disputes. The firm has recently been involved in a dispute over a new underground railway and several disputes relating to Betuweroute, the major freight line linking Rotterdam to the German border. Rob Bleeker is recommended.

Headed by the excellent Joop Jansen, **Stibbe**'s construction group has a fine pedigree for PPP work and continues to be instructed by the Municipality of Amsterdam in relation to the €3bn Zuidas development. The team is also instructed by the developer in the €160m Maastricht city centre development. David Orobio de Castro has extensive experience in procurement matters.

Boekel De Nerée's Hans Nicaise heads a group that is frequently involved in some of the largest projects in relation to the construction of utilities and residential buildings. The team continues to advise a syndicate of banks on the prestigious Mahler 4 project.

Headed by Arent van Wassenaer, **Norton Rose**'s construction team has an excellent reputation in the market and is regularly instructed by the majority of major construction companies. Benefiting from the firm's international reputation in the PPP market, the Amsterdam office picks up a lot of work in this area. It is advising the Ministry of Transport in relation to the tendering for the DBFM contract on the second Coentunnel project.

Pels Rijcken & Droogleever Fortuijn NV frequently advises public-sector clients in relation to construction-related disputes. On the non-contentious side, the firm has been increasingly active in PPP transactions.

Jointly headed by Sjoerd Rutten and Jos van de Vijver, **Simmons & Simmons**' construction team has a focus on infrastructure and projects transactions. The firm was appointed as contract lawyer in the €3bn PPP project Meerstad. While on the contentious side, Rutten advised a number of domestic construction companies in relation to recovery claims by the Dutch government, as a result of the fraud investigation.

Van Doorne has a focus on PPP work and has been closely involved in pioneering developments in the area, both in infrastructure and urban renewal. Led by the 'excellent' Mark Moolhuizn, the firm is advising both central and local government bodies in the Meerstad PPP. 'They solve things, instead of making things more complicated. It's a pleasure to work with them', said one client of the practice.

Allen & Overy LLP's Henry van Geen heads a construction team that is developing considerable expertise in the burgeoning area of PPP. It advised the winning consortium in the Netherlands' first PFI school project.

CONSTRUCTION

HOUTHOFF BURUMA ✪
NAUTADUTILH
ROZEMOND VAN RAMSHORST SMIT
STIBBE ✪

Boekel De Nerée ✪
Norton Rose
Pels Rijcken & Droogleever Fortuijn NV ✪
Simmons & Simmons ✪
Van Doorne ✪

AKD Prinsen Van Wijmen N.V. ✪
Allen & Overy LLP ✪
CMS Derks Star Busmann ✪
DLA SchutGrosheide ✪
Lexence ✪
Loyens & Loeff ✪

Firms are listed A-Z in tiers which are ranked in order of priority
✪ *Indicates firm displays contact details at the end of this chapter.*

CORPORATE AND COMMERCIAL

In spite of a closing pack, **De Brauw Blackstone Westbroek** retains its position at the top of the ladder on the basis of its loyal blue-chip corporate client base. Recent highlights include advising Royal Dutch Shell on its high-profile €148.9bn restructuring. Led by Paul Cronheim and Jaap Winter, the team also advised shareholders of PinkRoccade on the frenzied bidding war for the company. Department head Bernard Roelvink and Martin van Olffen, who is dual qualified as a lawyer and a notary, are recommended.

CORPORATE AND COMMERCIAL

DE BRAUW BLACKSTONE WESTBROEK ✪

ALLEN & OVERY LLP ✪
STIBBE ✪

CLIFFORD CHANCE
FRESHFIELDS BRUCKHAUS DERINGER
HOUTHOFF BURUMA ✪
LOYENS & LOEFF ✪
NAUTADUTILH

Baker & McKenzie ✪
Boekel De Nerée ✪
Simmons & Simmons ✪
Van Doorne ✪

AKD Prinsen Van Wijmen N.V. ✪
Bird & Bird ✪
Greenberg Traurig LLP
Lovells ✪
Norton Rose
Pels Rijcken & Droogleever Fortuijn NV ✪

BarentsKrans ✪
CMS Derks Star Busmann ✪
DLA SchutGrosheide ✪
Höcker Rueb Doeleman Advocaten ✪
Hoegen Dijkhof Advocaten
Holland van Gijzen ✪
Kennedy Van der Laan
Lexence ✪
Linklaters ✪
Russell Advocaten ✪
Spigthoff ✪
Van Diepen Van der Kroef Advocaten ✪

Adriaanse & Van der Weel
Borsboom & Hamm N.V.
Buren van Velzen Guelen ✪
De Jonge Peters Remmelink
Dirkzwager advocaten & notarissen
Ekelmans & Meijer Advocaten
Faasen & Partners ✪
Hekkelman Advocaten & Notarissen
Kneppelhout & Korthals ✪
Nysingh advocaten – notarissen N.V.
Ploum Lodder Princen ✪
Rassers Advocaten en Notarissen
Schaap & Partners Advocaten en Notarissen
Udink & De Jong
Van Dijk & Van Arnhem Advocaten Apeldoorn
Van Traa Advocaten ✪
Wieringa Advocaten

Firms are listed A-Z in tiers which are ranked in order of priority
✪ *Indicates firm displays contact details at the end of this chapter.*

Praised for its 'practical advice and client commitment', **Allen & Overy LLP**'s corporate team acts for an impressive list of clients including KLM, UPC, ABN Amro and Aegon. Corporate governance continues to be an active area for Dutch corporate clients following the recent implementation of the Corporate Governance Code and the team is frequently called upon to advise clients as to its far-reaching implications. Clients are effusive in their praise of this 'dynamic and professional team', and single out Gerbrand Visser for his 'profound knowledge of Dutch company law' and Robert Jan Lijdsman, who was described by one client as possessing 'one of the top-ten legal brains in the country'.

At **Stibbe**, Heleen Kersten heads a corporate team that is praised for its 'pragmatic approach and excellent legal knowledge'. Fons Leijten and Egbert Vroom are 'always accessible and offer advice of the highest quality. They are everything that an in-house lawyer needs', opines one client. Leijten has a focus on corporate litigation and frequently represents corporates before the Enterprise Chamber. Clients include Getronics, ING and Versatel.

Clifford Chance's Hector de Beaufort heads a team whose clients include eBay, T-Mobile, Vodafone Group and Carlyle Group. Although best-known for its banking and private equity practice, the firm has developed an increased focus in the outsourcing market and advised ABN Amro in its multi-vendor, multi-jurisdictional five-year IT sourcing initiative. Working in close cooperation with its international network, the transaction was one of the largest and most complex sourcing projects in the financial services sector to date.

Bolstered by the arrival of Robert ten Have from **NautaDutilh**, **Freshfields Bruckhaus Deringer**'s corporate and commercial team is in rude health. As well as benefiting from a strong international network, the firm has a strong domestic corporate client base that includes the likes of ING Group, Essent, Talpa and HMG. The firm advised Atradius and DSB Bank in corporate governance issues. Jan Willem van der Staay and Richard Norbruis are recommended.

Traditionally with a focus on the mid-market, **Houthoff Buruma** is increasingly involved in corporate transactions with a more international flavour. Typical of this is the advice the team is providing for IMS Health in relation to the restructuring of its European holdings. Acting as lead counsel to IMS Health, the firm is also co-ordinating local counsel in the other European jurisdictions. Jan van der Horst and Michiel Wesseling are recommended.

Loyens & Loeff has a strong corporate client base that includes the likes of Aon, Deutsche Bank, JP Morgan, KLM and Heineken. In close collaboration with the firm's tax group, the department has been involved in a number of major restructurings for amongst others, Eni, Intergen and ABN Amro Bouwfonds. Hendrik Portengen advised SITA on its JV with Airbus to develop and commercialise onboard communications services for commercial airlines. Philip van Verschuer, Ruud van Bork and Niek Zaman are recommended.

NautaDutilh advises a wide range of both national and international clients including ABN Amro, Telfort Beheer, Endemol and NIB Capital. Recent highlights include providing corporate governance advice to ABN Amro Capital in relation to its MBO of Loparex Group. It was also instructed by the Dutch State with regard to the proposed restructuring of Gasunie's transport business. Willem Calkoen, Freek Jonkhart and Reinoud Bredius are recommended.

Headed by Mike Jansen, **Baker & McKenzie**'s 'professional and communicative' corporate group works closely with its tax team to provide a seamless service to an impressive client base that includes Specsavers, General Electric and Sony/BMG. The team recently advised the Body Shop on the buy-back of its Benelux franchise operations. Clients praise Marco Wallart's 'legal perspective and commerciality'.

Aided by its Anglo-American and German advisory groups, **Boekel De Nerée** specialises in cross-border matters. Lisette Bieleveld specialises in commercial law and is regularly instructed by clients such as Bausch & Lomb on contractual and distribution issues. Ferdinand Mason recently led the team that carried out a complete corporate review of Royal Ahold.

Simmons & Simmons' Willem de Nijs Bik and Leo Verhoeff are recommended for corporate governance advice. Bik is advising the Municipalities as shareholders in leading energy companies Essent and ENECO, on governance issues relating to the proposed unbundling of the network. Clients include BASF, Allied Domecq and Lazard Freres.

Van Doorne advises both domestic and international companies on a broad spectrum of corporate issues from public bids and joint ventures, to reorganisations and corporate governance. The firm advised Wedge International, one of the major shareholders of Petroplus, on Carlyle Group's public bid for its remaining shares. Author of the first Dutch corporate governance handbook, Hugo Reumkens, is highly regarded in the field. Remkens recently advised both WPG Publishers and Roosdom Tijhuis in relation to governance issues. Managing partner Johan Boeren is recommended.

At **AKD Prinsen Van Wijmen N.V.**, René Stokman heads a department that has a focus on providing day-to-day commercial assistance to a range of national and international clients. The 'highly regarded' Luc Defaix advised Trimoteur in the €40m takeover and refinancing of the Brouwer Group.

Bird & Bird has a focus on the technology-related markets. The firm specialises in commercial contracts and restructurings. Clients include Kawasaki, Orange, and Dun & Bradstreet. Harry Rek is recommended.

Headed by Jan Kees Brandse, **Greenberg Traurig LLP**'s eight-partner department advises an impressive raft of both domestic and multinational clients. Gérard Moussault has a focus on corporate and structured finance.

Lovells has a strong IT client base and was instructed by Ordina in relation to the outsourcing of the back-office activities of domestic bank, Insinger de Beaufort. Clients appreciate the team's 'high level of responsiveness' and single out Johannes Buntjer and Jan de Snaijer for praise.

Norton Rose has a number of important energy clients. Ep Hannema is recommended.

Although it is best known as lead adviser to the Dutch State, **Pels Rijcken & Droogleever Fortuijn NV** also has a presence in the private sector. Work includes restructurings and corporate governance.

BarentsKrans' corporate team offers both contentious and non-contentious advice to a range of domestic and international companies. On the non-contentious side, the firm has been involved in the establishment of a number of large investment funds, including Shopping Parks NV. In an increasingly litigious corporate environment the team has picked up an increasing number of instructions in relation to shareholder, refinancing and investment disputes.

CMS Derks Star Busmann specialises in corporate restructurings. Christian Huiskes, Jelle Timmenga and Eric Vilé are recommended. Clients include Cardinal Health, Armstrong World Industries, Black & Decker and Rabobank.

DLA SchutGrosheide's managing partner, Frans Stibbe – who is praised by clients for his 'excellent advice and approachability' – has been involved in several corporate governance disputes before the Enterprise Section of the Amsterdam Court of Appeal. The firm has long-standing relationships with a number of Dutch listed companies, including Reesink.

Höcker Rueb Doeleman Advocaten has a focus on the media industry, while **Holland van Gijzen** has a fine track record for retail-based transactions.

Kennedy Van Der Laan's Martine de Koning advises Microsoft on a range of commercial matters.

Lexence advised the selling shareholders on the €35m divestment of an online holiday booking company to Holidaybreak Plc. The firm has a strong client base in the construction industry.

Headed by Pieter Riemer, **Linklaters**' corporate team was bolstered by the arrival in September 2005 of leading Dutch corporate lawyer, Peter Goes, formerly of **NautaDutilh**.

Russell Advocaten provides general commercial advice to medium-sized and small companies. The firm has offices in both Amsterdam and The Hague.

Spigthoff is a corporate litigation boutique of some repute. Name partner Jerry Hoff provides general corporate advice to clients.

With three German qualified lawyers at its disposal, **Van Diepen Van der Kroef Advocaten** has a strong Teutonic flavour to its practice. Dr Axel Hagedorn is recommended in particular for his M&A expertise, and his clients include a major reinsurance company.

At **Adriaanse & Van der Weel**, Mike Wolf and René de Groot offer general advice to domestic

CORPORATE AND COMMERCIAL
Eindhoven

AKD PRINSEN VAN WIJMEN N.V.
HOLLAND VAN GIJZEN

Boskamp & Willems
Keizers Poelman Advocaten ✪

Firms are listed A-Z in tiers which are ranked in order of priority
✪ *Indicates firm displays contact details at the end of this chapter.*

corporates, and assist international companies setting up operations in Holland.

Hague-based **Buren van Velzen Guelen** has a particular focus on providing corporate and commercial advice to Central and Eastern European clients.

Faasen & Partners has quickly established itself in the market following its inception in 2002. The firm has been involved in a number of M&A deals in the health, energy and technology sectors.

Rotterdam-based **Kneppelhout & Korthals** has been added this year on account its strategic growth over the past few years. Name partner, Jan Kneppelhout specialises in cross-border joint ventures, and international trade and services.

CORPORATE AND COMMERCIAL Eindhoven

AKD Prinsen Van Wijmen N.V.'s Eindhoven office has a fine reputation in real estate matters. The experienced Bert Heikens offers corporate and commercial support to medium-sized and listed companies.

Holland Van Gijzen's Eindhoven office handles some major construction-related work.

CORPORATE AND COMMERCIAL Utrecht

CMS Derks Star Busmann is the only major corporate law firm with its headquarters in Utrecht. Paulus van den Bos heads the full-service corporate practice in the city.

AKD Prinsen Van Wijmen N.V.'s Luc Defaix offers broad and extensive knowledge of corporate and commercial matters, from advising on M&A deals to advising management and investment companies. Defaix advised Breedenborg Holding and Koop Holding, regarding the participating interest in, and financing of these companies by a consortium of investors.

Van Diepen Van der Kroef Advocaten has strong corporate and employment law teams in its Utrecht office.

CORPORATE AND COMMERCIAL
Utrecht

CMS DERKS STAR BUSMANN ✪

AKD Prinsen Van Wijmen N.V.
Van Diepen Van der Kroef Advocaten

Van Benthem & Keulen ✪
Van Riet en Associees Advocaten B.V.
Wijn & Stael

Firms are listed A-Z in tiers which are ranked in order of priority
✪ *Indicates firm displays contact details at the end of this chapter.*

EU AND COMPETITION

Feeding off its market-leading M&A practice, **Allen & Overy LLP**'s EU and competition group is frequently called upon to file merger notifications. Recent highlights include notifications in relation to the acquisitions of Telfort by KPN, and Versatel by Tele2. The team also frequently appears before the European Commission in infringement matters for amongst others, Kappa Packaging. Department head Tom Ottervanger and Paul Glazener are market leaders.

De Brauw Blackstone Westbroek's four-partner group offers a broad mix of expertise in merger filings, cartel matters and procurement issues. The market-leading competition practice offers strength and depth, and is sufficiently developed to allow sector-specific competencies in energy (Jolling de Pree), telecoms (Martijn Snoep) and seaports (Mark Biesheuvel). Martijn Snoep has been involved in successful merger notifications in the publishing sector (for Wegener and PCM in their newspaper joint venture) and the telecoms sector (KPN's acquisition of Telfort). On the contentious side, the firm represented Dutch supermarket chain, Albert Heijn, in proceedings relating to the well-publicised supermarket price war. Erik Pijnacker Hordijk deserves a name check for his expertise in state aid and public procurement.

Freshfields Bruckhaus Deringer is advising the country's four major energy companies on competition and regulatory issues relating to the proposed unbundling of energy grids. The team recently represented Bombardier and Siemens in a major procurement dispute in which it successfully overturned an injunction obtained by Alstom, relating to the proposed €1bn rolling stock contract with the Dutch Railways. Onno Brouwer and Winfred Knibbeler are well-known members of a team whose clients include Shell, Solvay and Endemol.

Headed by Geert van der Klis, **Clifford Chance**'s practice was involved in some major merger filings for AP Moller Maersk (acquisition of Royal P&ONedlloyd), eBay (acquisition of Skype) and a Macquarie Capital Alliance Group-led consortium (acquisition of TDC Directories). The team has an excellent pedigree in competition law and recently advised Campina in the antitrust aspects of its unsuccessful merger with Arla.

Houthoff Buruma has a focus on cartel cases and continues to defend many leading construction companies against allegations relating to bid-rigging practices. Headed by Weyer Verloren van Themaat the firm is defending leading bicycle manufacturer, Accell Group against allegations of price fixing. Merger notifications are also an important part of the practice and in 2005 the team acted in over a dozen EU and national notifications. The group is developing an interest in the soon-to-be-liberalised health sector.

EU AND COMPETITION

ALLEN & OVERY LLP ✪
DE BRAUW BLACKSTONE WESTBROEK ✪
FRESHFIELDS BRUCKHAUS DERINGER

Clifford Chance
Houthoff Buruma ✪
Loyens & Loeff ✪
NautaDutilh
Pels Rijcken & Droogleever Fortuijn NV ✪
Simmons & Simmons ✪
Stibbe ✪

AKD Prinsen Van Wijmen N.V. ✪
Baker & McKenzie ✪
BarentsKrans ✪
Bird & Bird ✪
Boekel De Nerée ✪
CMS Derks Star Busmann ✪
DLA SchutGrosheide ✪
Greenberg Traurig LLP
Van Doorne ✪

Firms are listed A-Z in tiers which are ranked in order of priority
✪ *Indicates firm displays contact details at the end of this chapter.*

Jointly headed by Maurice Essers and Gert Wim van de Meent, **Loyens & Loeff**'s competition team has a focus on antitrust, public procurement, state aid and merger notifications. The firm acts for an impressively broad spread of clients from a wide range of industries, including, financial (ABN Amro Capital and CVC), energy (Eneco), food (Sligro) and transport (KLM and Arriva).

At **NautaDutilh**, Charles van Sasse van Ysselt heads a practice that offers both non-contentious and contentious advice to clients in both a national and international setting. Merger notifications continue to be a core area for the practice both before the Dutch Competition Authority and the European Commission. Maarten Meulenbelt and Jaap Feenstra are both highly regarded EU law practitioners and offer particular expertise within the life sciences and energy sectors respectively.

Pels Rijcken & Droogleever Fortuijn NV handles European law matters for the State of the Netherlands and competition-related cases on behalf of the Dutch Competition Authority, the NMA.

Headed by the highly regarded Marco Slotboom, **Simmons & Simmons**' Brussels-based practice offers broad-based expertise across a range of matters, including merger control, cartel issues and state aid. The team gained successful merger clearances in the building industry for CRH (following its acquisition of NCD) and in the poultry sector for Cebeco. On the contentious side, the firm successfully defended Peijnenburg against Albert Heijn.

A strong team at **Stibbe** has expertise in both merger control and cartel litigation, and regularly appears before both the domestic courts and the European Commission. Department head Christof Swaak has a focus on complex international cartel disputes and advises high-profile multinationals such as Akzo Nobel. Rein Wesseling has an excellent reputation and scored a major victory on behalf of banana giant, Chiquita, in its recent involvement in the supermarket price war litigation against Albert Heijn. Other clients include Delta Lloyd, Talpa and Campina.

DLA SchutGrosheide successfully defended international seeds producer, Sakata, against allegations of an abuse of a dominant position. Clients appreciate both Léon Korsten and Martijn van Wanroij's 'fast, thorough and accurate service'.

EMPLOYMENT

A strong all-round practice at **Allen & Overy LLP** offers both contentious and non-contentious advice to an impressive range of clients including AFC Ajax, AXA, Ernst & Young and Heineken. The team successfully represented Ajax in a contractual dispute with Tunisian international, Hatem Trabelsi, over the validity of a unilateral option clause. Department head Ferdinand Grapperhaus is one of the leaders in the field and is praised by clients for his 'vast knowledge' and 'willingness to take risks'. Leonard Verburg is also recommended.

Baker & McKenzie has one of the largest employment practices in the Netherlands and offers 'hands-on and proactive' contentious and non-contentious advice to a diverse list of clients including McDonald's, Cisco, Starbucks and Christian Salvesen. Mirjam de Blécourt specialises in collective labour law, Jos van Vlijmen handles employment litigation, and Karin Bodewes specialises in non-compete clauses, golden handshakes and option plans.

Headed by Marian van Eck, **Boekel De Nerée**'s five-partner team advises a wide array of clients, including Merck Sharp & Dohme, Fortis Bank and the Van Gogh Museum. The team recently advised several TV personalities in their transfer to new domestic broadcasting company, Talpa.

Generating stand-alone instructions and leveraging work off the back of its highly impressive blue-chip client base, **De Brauw Blackstone Westbroek**'s employment practice offers contentious and non-contentious advice across a range of issues including collective dismissals, reorganisations, collective labour agreements and pensions law. The team has been involved in some major restructurings for both

EMPLOYMENT

ALLEN & OVERY LLP ✪
BAKER & McKENZIE ✪
BOEKEL DE NERÉE ✪
DE BRAUW BLACKSTONE WESTBROEK ✪
LOYENS & LOEFF ✪
STIBBE ✪

AKD Prinsen Van Wijmen N.V. ✪
BarentsKrans ✪
CMS Derks Star Busmann ✪
Clifford Chance
DLA SchutGrosheide ✪
Holland van Gijzen ✪
Houthoff Buruma ✪
Kennedy Van der Laan
Lovells ✪
NautaDutilh
Pels Rijcken & Droogleever Fortuijn NV ✪
Simmons & Simmons ✪
Van Doorne ✪

Adriaanse & Van der Weel
Bird & Bird ✪
Borsboom & Hamm N.V.
De Jonge Peters Remmelink
Dirkzwager advocaten & notarissen
Ekelmans & Meijer Advocaten
Höcker Rueb Doeleman Advocaten ✪
Ploum Lodder Princen ✪
Russell Advocaten ✪
Van Diepen Van der Kroef Advocaten ✪
Van Gog Van Rijsbergen Advocaten

Firms are listed A-Z in tiers which are ranked in order of priority
✪ *Indicates firm displays contact details at the end of this chapter.*

BGN (a major domestic bookstore chain) and Coca-Cola Enterprises. The Hague-based Rogier Duk is regarded by many of his peers as 'the doyen' of employment law and is known to have, according to one colleague, 'an almost encyclopedic knowledge of all things employment law related'. Evert-Jan Henrichs is also well known and has been involved in the defence of a number of equal-treatment claims for numerous corporates.

Loyens & Loeff's Hermine Voute heads an employment team that specialises in pensions and corporate restructurings. The firm advised Allied Domecq and Pernod Ricard on the integration of their Dutch pension scheme. On the contentious side, the firm advised Arriva in several disputes with its works council. Clients include Campina, Fortis and Polaroid. Frank Doornik and Pavel der Kinderen offer pensions expertise.

Stibbe's clients include KLM and Heineken, whom it has acted for in relation to litigation arising out of the outsourcing of personnel. Jan Trap heads a team that has a particular focus on collective bargaining and discrimination disputes.

Headed by Mark Keuss, **AKD Prinsen Van Wijmen N.V.**'s seven-partner team offers expertise across a range of employment issues, from collective labour agreements and works councils, to reorganisations and disputes. The team is advising GTI NV (part of the Suez Group) on the reorganisation of one of its subsidiaries. Clients include Johnson & Johnson, Accenture and Deloitte.

BarentsKrans' Max Keulaerds and Peter Vas Nunes are experienced practitioners who have been advising employers on a full range of both individual and collective issues since 1983. The group also offers expertise in work permits, equal treatment and pensions matters.

At **CMS Derks Star Busmann**, Jos Pothouf heads a team that advises employers and employees on contentious and non-contentious matters.

Clifford Chance advised ABN Amro on the employment issues related to its €1.8bn multi-vendor IT outsourcing initiative. Ruth van Andel heads the team and has an excellent track-record for representing senior executives of listed companies.

DLA SchutGrosheide offers contentious and non-contentious expertise to an impressive portfolio of clients including Ernst & Young, KPN and KPMG. 'They react very promptly to our requests and they know how to effectively manage our expectations', enthused one client. Department head Saskia Reuling specialises in reorganisations, while Marnix Holtzer has a fine reputation for outsourcing and TUPE issues.

Holland van Gijzen offers contentious and non-contentious advice to employers. The firm has experience in reorganisations and group lay-offs.

Houthoff Buruma offers strength and depth to a client base that includes domestic and multinational blue-chip corporates, local and national authorities, and private individuals. Chairman of the employment group Edward de Bock has been involved in reorganisations for Alstom, Avandis and EMI. Maya Kuyt-Fokkens is experienced in collective and individual dismissals, and negotiations with unions and works councils.

Kennedy Van Der Laan offers 'reliable, trustworthy and transparent advice' to clients as varied as ING, Apple, Nike and Draka. Dirk-Jan Rutgers specialises in health law and advises a number of large hospitals. Gerrard Boot is recommended.

Led by Anita de Jong, **Lovells**' employment team has been active in the area of outsourcing. Recent highlights include advising Stater in the employment issues related to the complex outsourcing agreement with ABN Amro. Clients include Rolls-Royce Energy Systems, Kodak and Ordina.

Working closely with the corporate team, **NautaDutilh**'s employment group offers 'swift and comprehensive advice' on collective labour law issues and employment issues emanating from M&A. The team also offers in-depth pensions knowledge and EU law expertise. Both Simon Tan and Jennifer Willemsen are recommended.

Pels Rijcken & Droogleever Fortuijn NV offers non-contentious and contentious advice to clients such as KPN.

Simmons & Simmons' four-partner team has a strong international focus. An expanding, 20-lawyer practice is testament to an increasing workload from clients such as AON, CSFB and ETNA Group. Alexander Steensma has a focus on works councils' issues and is representing Royal Vopak in a dispute with its works council. Willem Wille is well known for his expertise in pension matters.

Headed by Els de Wind, **Van Doorne**'s employment practice offers 'professional and timely' contentious and non-contentious advice across a broad range of issues, including collective labour matters, individual and collective dismissals, restructurings, and non-compete clauses. The firm has been involved in a number of major reorganisations for clients such as GTI and De Ruiter Seeds. Albert van Marwijk Kooy heads the group's burgeoning pensions team.

A thriving employment group at **Adriaanse & Van der Weel** advises both domestic and multinational companies on a range of issues including corporate restructuring and lay-offs. Nicolaas van Everdingen and Diel Boere are key partners.

Van Diepen Van der Kroef Advocaten's Utrecht office is particularly strong for employment law. The firm is regularly involved in large reorganisations for major companies in the transport and construction industries.

ENERGY

ENERGY
ALLEN & OVERY LLP ✪
DE BRAUW BLACKSTONE WESTBROEK ✪
NAUTADUTILH
NORTON ROSE
Clifford Chance
Freshfields Bruckhaus Deringer
Loyens & Loeff ✪
Stibbe ✪
Baker & McKenzie ✪
Boekel De Nerée ✪
CMS Derks Star Busmann ✪
Houthoff Buruma ✪
Pels Rijcken & Droogleever Fortuijn NV ✪
Simmons & Simmons ✪
Stek Advocaten

Firms are listed A-Z in tiers which are ranked in order of priority
✪ Indicates firm displays contact details at the end of this chapter.

Allen & Overy LLP recorded a landmark victory for Nuon, quashing the forced auctions of generation capacity imposed on it following its acquisition of Reliant Energy Europe. Other highlights include advising Centrica in relation to its acquisition of Oxxio, the fourth-largest energy company in the Netherlands. Paul Glazener heads a team that also includes Henry van Geen. Leading energy regulatory lawyer, Jan Erik Janssen, left to join new corporate boutique, **Stek Advocaten**

De Brauw Blackstone Westbroek advised a number of major energy players including Tenne T, Delta and Electrabel on the implications of the imminent unbundling of the energy networks. On the contentious side, Martijn Snoep successfully overturned the NMA's €1m fine imposed on Texaco for alleged illegal price fixing. Vincent Aarts and Jolling de Pree are widely admired for their regulatory and technical knowledge.

Jointly headed by Charles van Sasse van Ysselt and Harm Kerstholt, **NautaDutilh**'s energy practice focuses on the interface between competition law and energy regulation and offers expertise in relation to alleged cartel behaviour, state aid and access issues. Recent highlights include advising the APX Group in relation to the establishment of a Gas Exchange in the Netherlands and Belgium. The departure of Chris Fonteijn to OPTA was a loss.

Jointly led by Weero Koster and Cecilia van der Weijden, **Norton Rose**'s highly regarded energy practice offers a wide spread of expertise from M&A and privitisations to regulatory and disputes. On the transactional side, the firm advised Danish gas and power company, DONG, on the acquisition of the supply activities of Intergas. The team has been involved in a number of renewable energy projects and successfully completed the NordzeeWind offshore windfarm project. The team acts for an impressive roster of clients including BP, Nuon and Delta.

Jointly headed by Tom de Waard and Tjepco van Voorst Vader, **Clifford Chance**'s energy team offers a broad practice that encompasses regulatory, transactional and competition-led work. Highlights include advising ENECO on the transfer of the power purchase agreement with Intergen in respect of the Rijnmond facility. The team has also been active in the compliance issues relating to the imminent unbundling of the networks.

Freshfields Bruckhaus Deringer's multi-disciplinary team offers contentious and non-contentious advice to an impressive raft of major energy players including Essent, Shell, Total, and Enel. The firm is advising Gaz de France on structuring the €300m equity financing of a majority stake in Romanian State-run gas company, Distrigaz Sud. Jeroen Thijssen is highly regarded by his peers for finance-related energy transactions.

Loyens & Loeff's Max Oosterhuis has a superb reputation and heads a team that acts for an impressive portfolio of clients including Nuon, Eneco, EdF and Electrabel. The firm recently advised the bidders in the sale of the electricity and gas networks of NRE and RWE. The firm also has a niche focus on emissions-trading.

Headed by Martin In de Braekt, **Stibbe**'s energy group has a particular focus on gas and electricity matters. Clients include Air Liquide, Bayer, Norsk Hydro and Nuon.

Headed by Michelle de Rijke, **Houthoff Buruma**'s energy team has a strong regulatory and lobbying practice. Clients include Nuon, Delta, Total and Chevron Texaco.

Pels Rijcken & Droogleever Fortuijn NV handles energy-related disputes on behalf of the State against all the major energy players.

Simmons & Simmons offers expertise in the issues relating to the proposed unbundling on shareholder level of integrated energy distribution companies. Martha Roggenkamp was recently appointed professor of energy law at Groningen University.

ENVIRONMENT AND PLANNING

AKD Prinsen Van Wijmen N.V. advises local and provincial governments across the country on a range of issues including soil, air and water pollution, waste processing, and noise abatement. In the private sector, the firm represents the majority of major producers of herbicides and pesticides, including Monsanto, Bayer Crop Science and Dupont de Nemours. Jos van der Velden heads the group.

De Brauw Blackstone Westbroek provided environmental and zoning advice in a number of major infrastructure projects including the A2 project Maastricht and the Belgzand-Bacton Pipeline project. Godert van der Feltz heads a team that also includes leading emissions-trading expert, Rutger de Witt Wijnen.

Houthoff Buruma has been advising on the planning and zoning regulations in relation to the redevelopment of Noordwijk aan Zee. The group also advised Nuon Energy Sourcing in relation to its CO2 emission rights. Frank Thunnissen, Martin Gelpke, Bowine Meijer, Jaap Hoekstra and Robert Crince Le Roy are recommended.

Jointly headed by Ger Cartigny and Norbert de Munnik, **NautaDutilh** offers both contentious and non-contentious expertise to both public-sector (Amsterdam Municipality) and private-sector clients (PPG Industries Fiber Glass, Mobil and Dupont de Nemours). The team is currently involved in the Hart van Zuid project and is advising Delta Energy on the regulatory and environmental issues attached to the realisation of a new power plant in Zeeland.

As preferred external legal adviser to the Dutch State, **Pels Rijcken & Droogleever Fortuijn NV** is frequently called upon to offer pertinent environmental and planning advice.

Stibbe advised the Ministry of Transport on the planning and zoning issues relating to the port complex in Rotterdam. The team also has expertise in the burgeoning area of CO2 emission rights.

Boekel De Nerée's Anne-Marie Klijn is advising international chemicals and

ENVIRONMENT AND PLANNING

AKD PRINSEN VAN WIJMEN N.V. ✪
DE BRAUW BLACKSTONE WESTBROEK ✪
HOUTHOFF BURUMA ✪
NAUTADUTILH
PELS RIJCKEN & DROOGLEEVER FORTUIJN NV ✪
STIBBE ✪

Boekel De Nerée ✪
CMS Derks Star Busmann ✪
Clifford Chance
Höcker Rueb Doeleman Advocaten ✪
Loyens & Loeff ✪
Simmons & Simmons ✪
Van Diepen Van der Kroef Advocaten ✪

Allen & Overy LLP ✪
Dirkzwager advocaten & notarissen
Greenberg Traurig LLP
Lexence ✪
Russell Advocaten ✪
Van Doorne ✪

DLA SchutGrosheide ✪

Firms are listed A-Z in tiers which are ranked in order of priority
✪ *Indicates firm displays contact details at the end of this chapter.*

pharmaceutical group, Solvay, on environmental matters relating to its Dutch production facilities.

CMS Derks Star Busmann's Frank Leyendeckers advises several major property developers on environmental, planning and zoning issues. Bart van Meer specialises in soil pollution matters.

Clifford Chance advised Emerson on several complex matters in relation to polluted property.

Simmons & Simmons' Jenneke Vijlbrief-van der Schaft has extensive knowledge of planning law and expropriation, and is advising Imca Vastgoed on the major redevelopment of The Hague Central Station. The recent recruitment of environmental and planning specialist, Maayke Maas-Cooymans from **De Brauw Blackstone Westbroek** has bolstered the group.

Van Diepen Van der Kroef Advocaten has particular expertise in waste, where Ron Laan and Bianca Liefting are recommended.

Greenberg Traurig LLP's Lex de Kok is instructed by OVO, a major mutual liability insurer of municipalities, in relation to proceedings relating to administrative and environmental issues.

FRAUD AND WHITE-COLLAR CRIME

CMS Derks Star Busmann's Cees van Bavel and Ruud Verbunt are market-leading experts in EU and tax fraud, and environmental crimes. A growth area for the team has been defending medical practitioners in criminal cases.

FRAUD AND WHITE-COLLAR CRIME

CMS DERKS STAR BUSMANN ✪
NAUTADUTILH
SIMMONS & SIMMONS ✪
SJÖCRONA VAN STIGT
WLADIMIROFF & WALING ADVOCATEN

AKD Prinsen Van Wijmen N.V. ✪
Boekel De Nerée ✪
Hertoghs Tax Lawyers ✪
Stibbe ✪

Allen & Overy LLP ✪
De Brauw Blackstone Westbroek ✪
Loyens & Loeff ✪
Spigthoff ✪
Van Doorne ✪

Firms are listed A-Z in tiers which are ranked in order of priority
✪ *Indicates firm displays contact details at the end of this chapter.*

NautaDutilh's Joost Italianer and Arjen Tillema have excellent reputations in relation to insider trading cases and anti-money laundering.

Simmons & Simmons' corporate criminal defence practice covers a range of white-collar crime issues including insider trading and employee fraud. Ed van Liere is one of the country's leading practitioners and is ably assisted by Marike Bakker.

Specialist criminal defence boutique **Sjöcrona van Stigt** has a focus on fraud and white-collar crime. Well-acquainted with cross-border work, the firm is frequently instructed in relation to extradition matters and mutual legal assistance. Dr Sjöcrona has an excellent reputation, as do Arthur van Stigt and Boudewijn van Eijck.

The Hague-based boutique **Wladimiroff & Waling Advocaten** has an emphasis on corporate criminal law and clients include both corporates and public bodies. Name partners Mischa Wladimiroff and Cornélie Waling are both highly regarded and the latter is one of the country's leading authorities on environmental criminal law. The team was bolstered by the arrival of former fraud specialist prosecutor Aldo Verbruggen.

AKD Prinsen Van Wijmen N.V.'s Peter van Hagen, who leads the tax team, is an expert in tax fraud cases.

Boekel De Nerée is advising the former Director-General of the department of Education in a high-profile fraud case. Carel Raymakers heads the practice.

Stibbe's Daan Doorenbos has a fantastic reputation in the market, particularly with regards to insider trading. Doorenbos was recently appointed as professor of corporate crime at the University of Nijmegen.

INFORMATION TECHNOLOGY

DE BRAUW BLACKSTONE WESTBROEK ✪
KENNEDY VAN DER LAAN

Allen & Overy LLP ✪
Baker & McKenzie ✪
Bird & Bird ✪
Brinkhof
Clifford Chance
Houthoff Buruma ✪
Lovells ✪
Oosterbaan & Van Eeghen
Stibbe ✪

AKD Prinsen Van Wijmen N.V. ✪
Boekel De Nerée ✪
CMS Derks Star Busmann ✪
Freshfields Bruckhaus Deringer
Höcker Rueb Doeleman Advocaten ✪
Holland van Gijzen ✪
Loyens & Loeff ✪
NautaDutilh
Pels Rijcken & Droogleever Fortuijn NV ✪
Van Doorne ✪

Firms are listed A-Z in tiers which are ranked in order of priority
✪ *Indicates firm displays contact details at the end of this chapter.*

INFORMATION TECHNOLOGY

Headed by Bart van Reeken, **De Brauw Blackstone Westbroek**'s IT team advises a range of clients including IT suppliers (IBM, Texas Instruments), corporates (Unilever, Heineken) and ISPs (Planet Internet, Tiscali). Joris van Manen is representing the Dutch press agency, ANP, in relation to the alleged unauthorised access to and use of its database. Lokke Moerel advises multinationals such as Texas Instruments, Heineken and IBM on their international privacy compliance, e-business and e-procurement issues.

Kennedy Van Der Laan continues to advise Microsoft in relation to its pan-EMEA licensing work and domestically for consulting services work. The firm advises ABN Amro in relation to a range of outsourcing deals, and electronic payment issues. Clients enthuse about the 'solution-orientated nature' of the firm's advice, and single out Reinoud Westerdijk, Joost Linnemann and Coen Drion for particular praise.

Headed by the 'proactive and responsive' Herald Jongen, **Allen & Overy LLP**'s IT team provides 'professional and high-quality advice' on a range of matters including outsourcing, software licensing, hosting and system integration. Recent highlights include advising ABN Amro Asset Management on its outsourcing deal with State Street Bank. This was notable for being the first major multinational outsourcing deal in Europe for an asset management company. Other clients include Accenture, EDS and Randstadt.

At **Baker & McKenzie**, Serge Gijrath heads an IT practice that provides contentious and non-contentious advice to service providers, software suppliers and IT users. The team recently advised a large public services company on a major outsourcing deal.

Headed by Jeroen van der Lee, **Bird & Bird**'s fast-growing IT department recently welcomed EDS to an already impressive roster of clients including Ericsson, Toshiba Tec and TPG Post. Highlights include advising Dun & Bradstreet on IT and outsourcing transactions. The team is also increasingly active in data protection law.

Brinkhof advises clients on a range of matters, including the supply and procurement of IT systems, e-commerce and outsourcing contracts, and technology transfer and licensing. Leading partners, Ruprecht Hermans and Eliane de Vilder, regularly act for clients such as Accenture, Apple, Reuters and Wanadoo.

Headed by Joachim Fleury, **Clifford Chance**'s integrated IT team has a focus on cross-border IT and outsourcing transactions. Backed by its international network of offices, the team advised ABN Amro in its €1.8bn multi-vendor, multi-jurisdictional outsourcing arrangement.

Houthoff Buruma's Wolter Wefers Bettink heads an eight-fee-earner IT department that is increasingly instructed in relation to litigation arising out of failed IT projects. The team has a focus on outsourcing and IT procurement and recently advised a large domestic private equity fund in the outsourcing of its IT department. Margaret van Nauta Lemke is recommended.

Headed by Klaas Bisschop, **Lovells**' IT department has a strong reputation for outsourcing. The firm advised Getronics on numerous outsourcing transactions. Clients include Ordina, Delta Lloyd and Ladbrokes.

IT boutique **Oosterbaan & Van Eeghen** ploughs an impressive furrow in a competitive sector, and long-standing clients of the calibre of SAP continue to keep the group busy. The firm advised DBS Business Solutions in a dispute with a UK software owner relating to licensing and distribution rights.

Stibbe's Reinout Rinzema has been advising the Dutch State in relation to outsourcing matters on Project Pay Direct.

In the bottom tier, **Pels Rijcken & Droogleever Fortuijn NV** handles IT disputes on behalf of the Dutch State.

INSURANCE

INSURANCE

HOUTHOFF BURUMA ✪
NAUTADUTILH
VAN DOORNE ✪

Boekel De Nerée ✪
De Brauw Blackstone Westbroek ✪
Ekelmans & Meijer Advocaten
Loyens & Loeff ✪
Stadermann Luiten Advocaten
Van Traa Advocaten ✪

AKD Prinsen Van Wijmen N.V. ✪
Allen & Overy LLP ✪
DLA SchutGrosheide ✪
Dirkzwager advocaten en notarissen
Dolk – Verburg – Diamand
Kennedy Van der Laan
Lovells ✪

Firms are listed A-Z in tiers which are ranked in order of priority
✪ Indicates firm displays contact details at the end of this chapter.

Houthoff Buruma acts for almost all the major international insurance companies operating in the Netherlands including AON, AXA, Zurich and Marsh. With a team of no fewer than 60 lawyers, the firm offers strength and depth in a range of insurance matters including regulatory work, professional indemnity, D&O liability and coverage disputes. The team continues to represent the Dutch insurance industry in an action against the Dutch State, in the aftermath of the Enschede disaster. Willem Hengeveld and Peter Drion are recommended.

NautaDutilh's insurance group advises corporates and insurers on a range of matters, including D&O liability, negligence and environmental damage. Loes Dommering-van Rongen has a focus on product liability matters and heads a team that is advising BAT in a major class action.

Van Doorne has overarching expertise in insurance matters, from contracts with brokers and policy drafting, to policy and coverage disputes. Clients include Legal & General, Hiscox and Delta Lloyd. Dries Fransen van de Putte is recommended.

Boekel De Nerée's insurance team offers expertise in a range of non-contentious and contentious matters, including policy advice, recovery actions, regulation and compliance. Recent highlights include advising the Dutch Bar on policy conditions for professional liability insurance for its Bar members. Joeri Cox represents underwriters in marine insurance, art and valuables insurance and is praised for 'always striving for solutions and working in our best interests'. Jan ter Meer heads the practice.

De Brauw Blackstone Westbroek's Marina de Kort-de Wolde has particular expertise in matters relating to D&O and product liability.

The Hague-based **Ekelmans & Meijer Advocaten** is a well-known specialist insurance and professional liability boutique. Clients include leading domestic insurers, Nationale-Nederlanden and Aegon.

Loyens & Loeff has been involved in D&O liability claims.

Based in Rotterdam, **Stadermann Luiten Advocaten** is an insurance and liability litigation boutique.

Known primarily for its first-rate transport practice, **Van Traa Advocaten** is gaining increasingly favourable reports in relation to its general insurance capabilities.

In the next tier, **DLA SchutGrosheide** has a focus on transport-related insurance, while **Kennedy Van Der Laan**'s impressive insurance group is instructed by Generali, Winterthur and Amev.

INTELLECTUAL PROPERTY

Since its inception at the beginning of 2005, **Brinkhof** has made a considerable impact on the Dutch IP market and has already built up a formidable portfolio of clients including Apple, Canon, Unilever and Novartis. The group has a focus on patent disputes and life sciences, and includes some leading individuals in these fields including former Hague Appeal Court vice-president Jan Brinkhof, US-trained litigator Richard Ebbink and Arnold Versteeg. The firm successfully defended the supermarket chain, Albert Heijn, against high-profile trade mark infringement allegations by Unilever.

In an area of law which has experienced a significant degree of lateral movement, **De Brauw Blackstone Westbroek**'s IP team has remained remarkably stable. Constant van Nispen has 'excellent procedural knowledge and vast experience' and is part of a highly regarded patent litigation team that includes Simon Dack and Jan Pieter Hustinx, both of whom were recently promoted to partner. The firm recently acted for Johnson & Johnson in both its EPO patent litigation and its patent dispute with Schneider. A strong copyright practice is involved in a number of Supreme Court hearings including representing Endemol in a dispute with Bob Geldof's Castaway. Tobias Cohen Jehoram is recommended for trade mark advice.

Freshfields Bruckhaus Deringer's IP group offers contentions and non-contentious expertise across a range of patent, trade mark and copyright issues. The group has reported growth in marketing and trade mark-related litigation. Recent highlights include advising Quicksilver in global trade mark infringement proceedings and Casema in a comparative advertising dispute with rival cable company, KPN. The team has further broadened its scope with the recent launch of a trade mark portfolio management practice. A strong patents practice benefits from close working arrangements with the London and Dusseldorf offices, and frequently coordinates international patent proceedings. Peter Hendrick is a well-known patent litigator.

The Amsterdam office of US-based IP firm, **Howrey LLP** continues to flourish. William Hyung heads the four-partner team that has a strong patent focus. Hyung himself has been involved in several landmark cases and is litigation counsel to several national and multinational pharmaceutical and biotech companies. The firm often works in close collaboration with its US office in multi-jurisdictional litigation.

Klos Morel Vos & Schaap has quickly established a reputation in the market as a soft IP practice of the highest order. Name partner Sven Klos receives plaudits from his peers.

Lovells has a strong pharmaceutical practice and is currently instructed by Merck in relation to a patent infringement case against generic drug manufacturer, TEVA. Klaas Bisschop is representing Philips in a comparative advertising dispute with Dyson, concerning vacuum cleaners. Bert Oosting is highly recommended.

Simmons & Simmons has a more rounded practice following the recent recruitment of trade mark and advertising partner, Willem Leppink. Leppink is instructed by Harley-Davidson on trade mark infringement issues and is advising Wilkinson Sword in its comparative advertising litigation with Gillette. Severin de Wit has an excellent reputation for patent litigation and is frequently involved in disputes with an international dimension. The team works closely with the firm's customs department, to offer clients an invaluable pan-European border-detention service.

Allen & Overy LLP has been involved in high-profile comparative advertising disputes on behalf of KPN, UPC and ANWB. Department head Paul Reeskamp has a contentious focus across a broad range of IP matters including patents and trade marks.

Baker & McKenzie is executing notable anti-counterfeiting operations for two major IT companies. Department head Alexander Odle is 'very hands on and reacts extremely quickly', say clients. Odle is ably assisted by Reina Weening, who offers expertise in trade mark litigation and copyright, design rights and comparative advertising. Weening also heads the burgeoning patents practice.

BarentsKrans has a focus on patent litigation, increasingly with an international flavour. Marleen van den Horst has a strong reputation for patent and regulatory work in the pharmeucitical industry.

At **Bird & Bird**, Wouter Pors heads an IP team, that in unison with its European network, specialises in providing multi-jurisdictional contentious advice, particularly in relation to trade mark and patent disputes. Clients include Honeywell, Richemont and Hoffman-La Roche.

Headed by Willem Hoorneman, **CMS Derks Star Busmann**'s IP team has a focus on trade mark and patent litigation in the pharmaceutical field. Janneke Craaikamp has a strong life sciences practice.

Jeroen Ouwehand heads a team at **Clifford Chance** that has a soft IP focus. Recent highlights include advising Endemol Internaional in relation to multi-jurisdictional litigation over IP infringements of the Big Brother format. Clients include Tele2, AOL and eBay.

INTELLECTUAL PROPERTY

BRINKHOF
DE BRAUW BLACKSTONE WESTBROEK ✪
FRESHFIELDS BRUCKHAUS DERINGER
HOWREY LLP ✪
KLOS MOREL VOS & SCHAAP
LOVELLS ✪

Simmons & Simmons ✪

Allen & Overy LLP ✪
Baker & McKenzie ✪
BarentsKrans ✪
Bird & Bird ✪
CMS Derks Star Busmann ✪
Clifford Chance
Kennedy Van der Laan
NautaDutilh
Steinhauser Hoogenraad, Advocaten

AKD Prinsen Van Wijmen N.V. ✪
Arnold + Siedsma, Attorneys at Law and Patent Attorneys
Boekel De Nerée ✪
Bousie Advocaten
Buren van Velzen Guelen ✪
DLA SchutGrosheide ✪
De Jonge Peters Remmelink
Greenberg Traurig LLP
Höcker Rueb Doeleman Advocaten ✪
Hoens & Souren Advocaten
Holland van Gijzen ✪
Houthoff Buruma ✪
Kneppelhout & Korthals ✪
Loyens & Loeff ✪
Oosterbaan & Van Eeghen
Pels Rijcken & Droogleever Fortuijn NV ✪
Ploum Lodder Princen ✪
Ribbert Van der Kroft Advocaten
Stibbe ✪
Van Benthem & Keulen ✪
Van Doorne ✪

Firms are listed A-Z in tiers which are ranked in order of priority
✪ Indicates firm displays contact details at the end of this chapter.

The 'responsive and pragmatic' **Kennedy Van Der Laan** offers extensive IP knowledge to an impressive range of clients that includes Heinz, Yahoo! and Microsoft. Alfred Meijboom garners respect from clients in particular for his contentious IP and brand protection/anti-counterfeiting work.

NautaDutilh's Charles Gielen has an excellent reputation as a trade mark litigator. Gielen recently succesfully represented DuPont de Nemours in the highly-publicised TEFLON case.

IP boutique **Steinhauser Hoogenraad, Advocaten** has a focus on advertising.

At **AKD Prinsen Van Wijmen N.V.** department head, Ernst Jan-Louwers is representing Texas Instruments in an anti-counterfeit case.

Aided by its international network, **DLA SchutGrosheide** has been involved in a number of anti-counterfeiting matters, including advising the Lance Armstrong Foundation with regard to counterfeit wristbands, LIVESTRONG. The firm also successfully obtained an injunction on behalf of KPN in its comparative advertising dispute with Vodafone.

Greenberg Traurig LLP's Annette Mak has a burgeoning reputation and has been involved in a number of trade mark disputes for multinational clients.

Kneppelhout & Korthals' Kees Capel has a focus in patent law, particularly in the fields of food, beverages and agriculture.

MEDIA AND ENTERTAINMENT

Headed by Erik Keyzer, **Allen & Overy LLP** offers both contentious and non-contentious advice to clients in a wide range of sectors including TV, radio, music, film and sport. The team advised SBS Broadcasting in relation to the protection of programme data, and Eyeworks on the acquisition of two production companies. Time Warner is a major client of the practice.

Boekel De Nerée is involved in television productions, broadcasting and film. Pieter Ariëns Kappers is an expert on film law.

Headed by Kurt Stöpetie, **Brinkhof**'s communications group offers contentious and non-contentious advice to an impressive range of media clients including RTL, the Association of Dutch Commercial Radio Broadcasters and the Netherlands' biggest newspaper publisher, PCM.

De Brauw Blackstone Westbroek advises an impressive array of television and radio broadcasters (RTL, SBS, Sky Radio), publishers (PCM, VNU) and multinational entertainment companies (Universal, AOL Time Warner). Tobias Cohen Jehoram recently successfully represented Gillette in a series of advertising disputes with Wilkinson Sword.

NautaDutilh succesfully represented the Dutch broadcasting foundation, NOS, against allegations of abuse of a dominant position. Piet Sippens Groenewegen heads the group.

Baker & McKenzie's 'fantastic and committed' Alexander Odle heads the department and is handling a high-profile defamation case. Odle advises various Dutch cultural institutions and is a member of the Dutch Advisory Board on Cultural Governance.

Jointly headed by Marjolein Geus and Pauline Kuipers, **Bird & Bird** acts for an impressive mix of media and entertainment clients including the Discovery Channel, De Telefoongids, Dun & Bradstreet and Chello Media.

Media and entertainment boutique **Bousie Advocaten** has rapidly emerged as a serious contender in the market, since its inception in 2003. Name partner, Hans Bousie is a well-known figure in both the music and publishing industry.

MEDIA AND ENTERTAINMENT

ALLEN & OVERY LLP ✪
BOEKEL DE NERÉE ✪
BRINKHOF
DE BRAUW BLACKSTONE WESTBROEK ✪
NAUTADUTILH

Baker & McKenzie ✪
Bird & Bird ✪
Bousie Advocaten
CMS Derks Star Busmann ✪
Clifford Chance
Freshfields Bruckhaus Deringer
Höcker Rueb Doeleman Advocaten ✪
Houthoff Buruma ✪
Kennedy Van der Laan
Klos Morel Vos & Schaap
Lovells ✪
Pels Rijcken & Droogleever Fortuijn NV ✪
Ribbert Van der Kroft Advocaten
Richard Advocaten
Stibbe ✪
Van Diepen Van der Kroef Advocaten ✪

DLA SchutGrosheide ✪
Kalff Katz & Koedooder Media & Entertainment Lawyers
Russell Advocaten ✪
Simmons & Simmons ✪
Steinhauser Hoogenraad, Advocaten
Van Benthem & Keulen ✪

Firms are listed A-Z in tiers which are ranked in order of priority
✪ *Indicates firm displays contact details at the end of this chapter.*

The firm advised the Netherlands' largest retail chain of music stores in its negotiations with the record industry on setting up a download platform.

CMS Derks Star Busmann has a strong sports law focus and advises Dutch National Olympic Committee, the Royal Dutch Skating Union and a number of football clubs. Team head Dolph Segaar is the Chairman of the Audit Commission Doping of the Dutch National Olympic Committee.

Clifford Chance is representing Endemol in a complex cross-border IP infringement matter. The media group has a focus on directories and advised a Macquarie Capital Alliance Group-led consortium on the €1.825bn acquisition of YBR, a pan-European directories business.

Freshfields Bruckhaus Deringer is instructed by Endemol on a range of competition issues. The firm also represented MTV and Quote Media in litigation against SBS Brodcasting.

Höcker Rueb Doeleman Advocaten is involved in a considerable amount of anti-piracy litigation.

Headed by Sebastian Le Poole, **Houthoff Buruma**'s media and entertainment group is instructed by the majority of domestic TV networks including NOS and RTL/UFA. The firm is well known in the publishing industry and advises the publisher of the largest daily newspaper in the Netherlands, *De Telegraaf*.

Kennedy Van Der Laan is instructed by Endemol International in relation to the international licensing of a number of its TV formats, such as Big Brother. Nike is a major client.

IP boutique **Klos Morel Vos & Schaap** has a strong media client base, while **Lovells** continues to advise Philips in a major advertising case.

Pels Rijcken & Droogleever Fortuijn NV represents the Dutch government in relation to media issues.

Ribbert Van der Kroft Advocaten acts for clients in both the broadcasting and music industry.

Established and owned by Theodoor Richard, **Richard Advocaten** is a one-lawyer boutique that specialises in the financing and executive production of feature films and games, often with an Asian flavour. Local Dutch TV station, RNN7, is a major client.

Stibbe advised new media company Talpa in relation to a channel-sharing agreement with MTV Networks and in its acquisition of a Dutch radio station.

Van Diepen Van der Kroef Advocaten's Marco Gerritsen is advising a film production company.

DLA SchutGrosheide is advising Lucas Films on anti-piracy and IP issues, and Bacardi on advertising matters.

Russell Advocaten has an internationally renowned art law practice and advises art dealers, collectors and museums.

Simmons & Simmons is fast developing a respectable media and entertainment practice aided by the recent recruitment of former **DLA SchutGrosheide** partner, Job Rietkerk. Olaf Trojan is instructed by a former soccer great on various IP matters, including the exploitation of his image rights and trade mark issues.

MEDIATION

Boekel De Nerée's Els Swaab is a registered mediator at the National Mediation Institute, and frequently mediates in complex and sensitive commercial disputes.

CMS Derks Star Busmann's John Bosnak is the president of the Dutch Association of Mediators, and the court-annexed mediator to the court of Arnhem.

Clifford Chance is experienced in advising international companies on mediations.

De Brauw Blackstone Westbroek's Bommel van der Bend advises parties on mediations.

A number of lawyers at **Houthoff Buruma** are qualified mediators, including Marry de Gaay Fortman and Freerk Falkena.

NautaDutilh's Bart Gerretsen is a co-founder and board member of ACB Mediation, the mediation organisation that serves the Dutch private sector.

Simmons & Simmons' Jos van de Vijver has an excellent reputation as a mediator in construction and project development disputes.

Van Diepen Van der Kroef Advocaten has a number of mediators on its team.

MEDIATION

Boekel De Nerée ✪
CMS Derks Star Busmann ✪
Clifford Chance
De Brauw Blackstone Westbroek ✪
Houthoff Buruma ✪
NautaDutilh
Simmons & Simmons ✪
Van Diepen Van der Kroef Advocaten ✪

Firms are listed alphabetically
✪ *Indicates firm displays contact details at the end of this chapter.*

MERGERS AND ACQUISITIONS

Allen & Overy LLP is indisputably one of the premier M&A firms in the Netherlands. Jan Louis Burggraaf is praised for his appreciation of both the 'legal and business issues of M&A transactions', and heads a team that includes the 'hard-nosed and deal-driven' Johan Kleyn, and the 'excellent' Justin Steer. Recent highlights include advising KPN on the €980m acquisition of Dutch telecoms operator, Telfort, and Shell Chemicals on the sale of Basell.

At **De Brauw Blackstone Westbroek**, Arne Grimme is advising VNU on its €5.8bn acquisition of IMS Health, while Bernard Roelvink advised DSM on its €515m acquisition of NeoResins. Ernest Meyer Swantée heads an accomplished team that includes Martin van Olffen, Jan Willem de Boer and Ton Schutte.

Clifford Chance advised AP Møller Maersk on its €2.3bn acquisition of Royal P&O Nedlloyd. The biggest acquisition ever in the container shipping sector. The department also advised a consortium of investors, led by J C Flowers & Co in the €1.8bn acquisition of all the outstanding shares in NIB Capital. Hector de Beaufort is described by his peers as 'highly talented' and is backed up by the 'first-rate' Charles Eijsbouts.

Despite being relatively small in size, **Freshfields Bruckhaus Deringer** successfully leverages off the firm's international reputation for M&A and often punches above its weight locally. Highlights include advising Talpa Media in connection with the subscription by Rabobank for a 20% interest in Talpa Media. Richard Norbruis is recommended.

NautaDutilh combines extensive sector knowledge in areas such as energy and telecoms, with an integrated notarial service, to provide a 'first-rate service' to both public and private companies. The team recently advised Ispat

MERGERS AND ACQUISITIONS

ALLEN & OVERY LLP ✪
DE BRAUW BLACKSTONE WESTBROEK ✪

Clifford Chance
Freshfields Bruckhaus Deringer
NautaDutilh
Stibbe ✪

Loyens & Loeff ✪

Baker & McKenzie ✪
Bird & Bird ✪
Boekel De Nerée ✪
Houthoff Buruma ✪
Linklaters ✪
Lovells ✪
Simmons & Simmons ✪
Van Doorne ✪

AKD Prinsen Van Wijmen N.V. ✪
CMS Derks Star Busmann ✪
DLA SchutGrosheide ✪
Lexence ✪

BarentsKrans ✪
Greenberg Traurig LLP
Holland van Gijzen ✪
Kennedy Van der Laan
Ploum Lodder Princen ✪
Van Diepen Van der Kroef Advocaten ✪

Firms are listed A-Z in tiers which are ranked in order of priority
✪ *Indicates firm displays contact details at the end of this chapter.*

International in its acquisition of the entire issued share capital of LNM Holdings and the subsequent acquisition of International Steel Group (resulting in the largest steel company in the world – Mittal Steel Company). The team also advised France Télécom in the sale of all Equant's assets to France Télécom. Hein Hooghoudt and Jeroen Preller are recommended. The departure of the highly regarded Peter Goes to **Linklaters** is a loss.

Headed by Charles Honée, **Stibbe**'s M&A practice reported an increase in deal flow in 2005. Highlights include advising Versatel Telecom International in its proposed merger with Tele2 and Delta Lloyd on its public offer for Euronext-listed company Sarakreek. Marius Josephus Jitta, Paul van den Hoek and Charles Honeé are recommended.

Loyens & Loeff advised Edison Mission Energy on the €2.5bn sale of its non-US assets to International Power and Mitsui. It also advised OTPP and AIG Highstar Capital on the acquisition of Intergen from Shell International. The firm has a focus on cross-border transactions. Philip van Verschuer and Jack Berk are recommended.

Benefiting from its international network, **Baker & McKenzie** is regularly instructed in relation to cross-border M&A. Highlights include advising Sony in its merger with BMG and Oracle in its merger with Peoplesoft. Mike Jansen is recommended.

Bird & Bird's Harry Rek is lead counsel on Dun & Bradstreet's European disposal programme. The firm also advised the Dutch 'yellow pages', Telefoongids, in several acquisitions.

Boekel De Nerée's 'professional and responsive' team advised KPMG Holding on the sale of its certification business, and Zwitzerleven/Swiss Life on the €72m acquisition of the pension fund of Dutch Central Bank. UK-qualified lawyers, Philip Paterson and Ferdinand Mason, head the department's Anglo-American advisory group which has a focus on cross-border M&A.

Houthoff Buruma advised Monsanto on the Dutch elements of its US$1bn acquisition of seed producer, Seminis. On the sale side, Eddie Meijer led the team that advised IHC Caland in the divestment of two shipyards following a complicated pre-transaction restructuring.

Headed by Pieter Riemer, **Linklaters**' burgeoning M&A team was substantially bolstered by the arrival of Peter Goes, formerly of **NautaDutilh**. Certainly one to watch in the future.

At **Lovells**, the 'excellent' Johannes Buntjer heads an M&A group that is praised for its 'thorough and flexible advice'. The firm advised Ordina in its acquisition of Infra Design and Agilent Tchnologies on the sale of its 47% stake in Lumileds Lighting International.

Simmons & Simmons is acting for the Municipality of Rotterdam in the divestment in its sole shareholding in AVR, the leading Dutch waste management company. The firm also advised Alliance Medical in its acquisition of the IHG Group. Jean-Pierre van Leeuwe is recommended.

Van Doorne advised major US chemical company, Albermade Inc, (in collaboration with US firm **Hunton & Williams**) on its €650m acquisition of the Catalyst Division of Akzo Nobel. The team has a focus on the healthcare industry. Onno Boerstra is recommended.

AKD Prinsen Van Wijmen N.V.'s Kris Ruijters advised international transport company, Samskip, in the acquisition of the Dutch intermodal operator, Geest North Sea Line.

CMS Derks Star Busmann advised United Broadcast Facilities in the €35m acquisition of the post-production business of NOB, the largest media production company in the Netherlands. The Dutch offices have been increasingly involved in cross-border transactions. Richard Montijn and Roman Tarlavski are recommended.

DLA SchutGrosheide's Barbara van Hussen, in conjunction with the London office, advised Zez Group Plc on its acquisition of Yul. The arrival of experienced corporate lawyer, Richard Fens, from **Kennedy Van Der Laan** has bolstered the practice.

Lexence advised TCN Property Projects in the purchase of Hilversum Media Park.

Greenberg Traurig LLP joins the rankings courtesy of its high-profile instruction by Getronics, in its €338m acquisition of Pink Roccade. Jan Kees Brandse led this deal and is recommended.

PRIVATE EQUITY

Allen & Overy LLP advised 3i and VSS on the €1.82bn sale of the international telephone directories business, YBR Group. It also advised the management of Deli XL on the divestiture of Deli XL by Ahold. Karine Kodde heads a team that includes the highly recommended Jan Louis Burgraff, and rising star, Justin Steer. Clients include ABN Amro Capital, Gilde and AlpInvest.

Clifford Chance is doing an increasing amount of work for Macquarie Capital Alliance Group, which it advised both on the €650m acquisition of TDC Directories and the €1.82bn acquisition of YBR. It is also advised Warburg Pincus on the acquisition of a majority shareholding in medical diagnostic service provider, Euromedic Interntional. Charles Eijsbouts and Thijs Alexander both have fantastic reputations.

One of the major players in the private equity market, **Loyens & Loeff** is regularly instructed by the major domestic private equity houses including the likes of ABN Amro Capital, AlpInvest Partner, CVC Capital Partners and Rabo Participaties. The firm has advised ABN Amro Capital on a raft of deals including the buy-out of chemicals distributor IMCD Group. Herman Kaemingk is recommended.

De Brauw Blackstone Westbroek's Ernest Meyer Swantée is highly regarded for private

PRIVATE EQUITY

ALLEN & OVERY LLP ✪
CLIFFORD CHANCE
LOYENS & LOEFF ✪

De Brauw Blackstone Westbroek ✪
Freshfields Bruckhaus Deringer
NautaDutilh
Simmons & Simmons ✪

Baker & McKenzie ✪
Bird & Bird ✪
Boekel De Nerée ✪
CMS Derks Star Busmann ✪
Houthoff Buruma ✪
Norton Rose
Stibbe ✪
Van Doorne ✪

AKD Prinsen Van Wijmen N.V. ✪
DLA SchutGrosheide ✪
Lexence ✪
Lovells ✪
Van Benthem & Keulen ✪

Firms are listed A-Z in tiers which are ranked in order of priority
✪ *Indicates firm displays contact details at the end of this chapter.*

equity and venture capital transactions, including de-listings and buy-outs. Swantée advised Dutch private equity firm, NPM, in its divestment of L Konings Beheer.

Freshfields Bruckhaus Deringer continues to make inroads into the Dutch private equity market. Recent highlights include advising CVC Capital Partners and Cinven as joint majority shareholders of Kappa Packaging regarding the merger with the Jefferson Smurfit Group. Other clients include Warburg Pincus, Gilde and Fortis Private Equity.

NautaDutilh's Hein Hooghoudt led the team that advised on the auction sale of NIB Capital to US private equity house, JC Flowers & Co. It also advised Cerberus Capital Management in its acquisition of Debis AirFrance.

Simmons & Simmons advised Rabo Private Equity on its minority stake in Talpa Media. The team has advised private equity firm Gilde Participaties in a number of transactions. Increasingly visible in the market, Jean-Pierre van Leeuwe deserves a name-check.

Baker & McKenzie's private equity group offers tax expertise on cross-border deal structuring. Clients include Life Science Partners, ABN Amro Capital and Advent. Edwin Liem heads a team that advised a group of investors in the largest biotech private placement in the Netherlands in 2005.

Houthoff Buruma advises an impressive portfolio of international and domestic private equity houses including BC Partners, Wagram Equity Partners, NPM Capital and H2 Equity Partners. The team advised CVC Capital Partners in the acquisition of the printing inks and printing plates operations of BASF Printing Systems and ANI Printing Inks.

Norton Rose's Ep Hanema is recommended. Clients include CVC, 3i and Alpinvest.

Van Doorne offers 'first-rate' advice on MBOs and MBIs for both domestic and international private equity houses including Charterhouse, Sun Capital, Pfingsten and Altor. Onno Boerstra advised Scandinavian-based private equity house, Altor Equity Partners in its acquisition of the Meyn Group. Hans van Ramshorst is recommended.

In the bottom tier, **Lexence**'s Michiel van Schooten is recommended.

PROJECT FINANCE

Headed by Bart Meesters, **Allen & Overy LLP** has an overarching presence in both the PFI and commercial project finance markets. In the PFI market, the team can lay claim to the proud boast that it has acted for either the lender or the project company in every completed project in the Netherlands. The team is currently acting for a bidding consortium in the second Coentunnel project. Meesters was instrumental in drafting the standard DBFM contracts for future state-sponsored road PPPs. Werner Runge was instructed by ING, in relation to the €95m project financing of a CO2 gas distribution network.

Freshfields Bruckhaus Deringer is advising a bidding consortium in the second Coentunnel project. The team also continues to advise Infraspeed in the HSL Zuid project. The team also plays a vital support role to the network on non-domestic transactions. Andrew Petry heads the department.

Pooling the resources of strong corporate, real estate and regulatory teams, **Houthoff Buruma**'s project finance group is often found at the sharp end of major financings in the energy, utilities and telecoms sectors. The group has a fine reputation for PFI work, a fact that did not go unnoticed by the Ministry of Finance, which recently instructed the firm on the first Dutch PPP for school buildings. On the private side, the firm is currently instructed by a bidding consortium in the second Coentunnel PPP. Jaap Koster is well known.

De Brauw Blackstone Westbroek is instructed by ISS, one of the participants in the Netherlands' first school PPP.

Instructed by both sponsors and banks, **Norton Rose** has a focus on PPP and energy-related projects. Having drafted the standard infrastructure procurement guidelines for the Ministry of Transport, Arent van Wassenaer is now instructed by the Ministry to assist in the tender for the second Coentunnel project. On the banking side, the team has advised Société Générale on syndicated loans to power-generation projects.

Pels Rijcken & Droogleever Fortuijn NV is involved in a number of major infrastructure projects such as the Harbour of Rotterdam and the HSRL. The firm acts on behalf of the Dutch State.

Leveraging off the back of its market-leading real estate practice, **Boekel De Nerée** 's project finance group has continued to develop its position in the market. Recent highlights include advising DSB on the €40m financing of the AZ stadium in Alkmaar. Headed by the highly regarded Bram Linnartz, the group is picking up a number of new instructions from banks such as Eurohypo and KBC.

Aided by its vast international network, **Clifford Chance**'s Amsterdam office often plays a major role in cross-border project financings. Led by Mark Huddlestone, the team advised Basell Orlen Polyolefins in the €350m project financing for the construction of two production plants in Poland. On the domestic front, the firm has been increasingly active in PPP and has been instructed by sponsors and lenders in relation to the upcoming second Coentunnel project and the Westerscheldetunnel.

At **NautaDutilh**, Erik Geerling heads the project finance team. Under the leadership of New York-based Elizabeth van Schilfgaarde, the team acted as Dutch counsel to a group of lenders on the Indonesian Tuban Petrochemicals project. In the PFI arena, the firm is advising the Dutch Ministry of Finance on the €190m renovation of the Ministry's buildings.

At **Stibbe**, Joop Jansen is frequently instructed by consortia, particularly in relation to infrastructure projects.

PROJECT FINANCE

ALLEN & OVERY LLP ✪
FRESHFIELDS BRUCKHAUS DERINGER

Houthoff Buruma ✪

De Brauw Blackstone Westbroek ✪
Norton Rose
Pels Rijcken & Droogleever Fortuijn NV ✪

Boekel De Nerée ✪
Clifford Chance
NautaDutilh
Stibbe ✪

Firms are listed A-Z in tiers which are ranked in order of priority
✪ Indicates firm displays contact details at the end of this chapter.

REAL ESTATE

Boekel De Nerée's 16-partner department has the strength and depth to handle the most complex transactions for an impressive array of clients including ING Real Estate, Bouwfonds Property Finance, Regus and the Municipality of Amsterdam. Bram Linnartz and David van Dijk (in collaboation with **Clifford Chance**) advised Vendex/KBB on the proposed sale, and lease-back of part of its real estate portfolio in the Netherlands –with a total value of approximately €1.4bn, it is reckoned to be the largest domestic real estate transaction ever. Linnartz also advised a German investor on the €80m acquisition of PwC's head office in Rotterdam. Albert Flesseman is one of the country's foremost authorities on landlord and tenant law as it relates to shopping centres and chain stores. Paul Wanders and Christiaan Toorman are also recommended.

Houthoff Buruma's 19-partner real estate team is involved in the majority of large-scale domestic development projects in the Netherlands. It is advising Fortis Vastgoed on the purchase of five shopping centres and 700 houses from Bouwfonds Projectontwikkeling. Increasingly involved in the corporate finance aspects of real estate, **Houthoff Buruma** advised TKP Investments in Groningen, a subsidiary of Achmea, on its investments in several pan-European real estate funds. Jan Cees Kuiken, Chris Goumans, Aart Barkey Wolf and notary, Onno de Bruijn are recommended. Clients include ING Real Estate, Fortis Bank, ABN/Amro/Bouwfonds, HSH Nordbank, Texaco and Heijmans.

Clifford Chance has a focus on corporate finance real estate-related transactions. Highlights include advising Vendex/KBB on the sale and lease-back of the majority of its Dutch real estate

REAL ESTATE

BOEKEL DE NERÉE
HOUTHOFF BURUMA

Clifford Chance
De Brauw Blackstone Westbroek
Lexence
Stibbe

AKD Prinsen Van Wijmen N.V.
CMS Derks Star Busmann
Loyens & Loeff
NautaDutilh
Simmons & Simmons

Allen & Overy LLP
Baker & McKenzie
BarentsKrans
DLA SchutGrosheide
Greenberg Traurig LLP
Kennedy Van der Laan
Lovells
Pels Rijcken & Droogleever Fortuijn NV
Van Doorne
Van Diepen Van der Kroef Advocaten

Firms are listed A-Z in tiers which are ranked in order of priority
Indicates firm displays contact details at the end of this chapter.

portfolio. The firm also advised Merrill Lynch International on the refinancing of its Dutch property portfolio.

De Brauw Blackstone Westbroek advised ING in the €140m sale of its Rotterdam headquarters. The highly regarded Paul Kerckhoffs has been advising the Municipality of Nieuwegein on the redevelopment of the city centre. The team is well known for its work in real estate portfolio tenders and has been advising, Delta Lloyd and KFN in this area.

Lexence's highly regarded real estate team has been advising property developers in several major projects, including the development of the Anthony Fokker Business park and the Batavia harbour in Lelystad. Stijn Vissers is recommended.

Stibbe advises developers, institutional investors, financial institutions and end-users on sale, and lease transactions in the retail, office and housing markets. The firm continues to advise institutional investors in the €240m Yburg Housing Project. Both Joop Jansen and David Orobio de Castro are recommended.

At **AKD Prinsen Van Wijmen N.V.**, Mark Wintgens led the team that was involved in the Strijp S inner-city redevelopment.

CMS Derks Star Busmann's 13-partner real estate team has specialists in Utrecht, Amsterdam, Arnhem and Hilversum, and advises a wide range of clients including construction companies, developers, financial institutions and municipalities. The firm has been involved in the development of football stadiums for FC Utrecht and Vitesse-Arnhem.

Loyens & Loeff advises municipalities, developers and investors on a range of private and public-funded projects. The firm offers expertise in real estate portfolio matters and recently advised Muermans on the acquisition of the portfolios of Philips Pensioenfonds and ING Real Estate. Hamith Breedveld is highly regarded by clients who appreciate his 'creativity and knowledge'. The firm also has a strong property finance team and is instructed by many leading international banks including Halifax, Bank of Scotland, Allied Irish Banks and Credit Suisse First Boston.

In close co-operation with its banking and tax departments, **NautaDutilh** offers a one-stop-shop to a broad range of clients including local government (Municipalities of Amsterdam and Rotterdam), developers (Achmea Vastgoed), property funds (ING Real Estate) and owners. The firm continues to advise the Municipality of Amsterdam on the South Axis development.

Simmons & Simmons advised the management team on the restructuring and MBO of the largest Dutch project development company. Geert Jansen is recommended.

Allen & Overy LLP's Henry van Geen is praised for his 'responsiveness and ability to explain the issues clearly and concisely'.

DLA SchutGrosheide's Rutger Oranje is instructed by the Rijksmuseum in all aspects of its €300m redevelopment and renovation. Clients include ING Real Estate, BDL Management, Arcadis and UBA.

Kennedy Van Der Laan's Richard-Jan Roks advises Schiphol Airport in relation to construction and commercial property projects.

RESTRUCTURING AND INSOLVENCY

DE BRAUW BLACKSTONE WESTBROEK
HOUTHOFF BURUMA
SIMMONS & SIMMONS
STIBBE

AKD Prinsen Van Wijmen N.V.
Allen & Overy LLP
CMS Derks Star Busmann
Holland van Gijzen
Loyens & Loeff
NautaDutilh
Pels Rijcken & Droogleever Fortuijn NV

Baker & McKenzie
BarentsKrans
Boekel De Nerée
Borsboom & Hamm N.V.
Buren van Velzen Guelen
Clifford Chance
DLA SchutGrosheide
De Jonge Peters Remmelink
Ekelmans & Meijer Advocaten
Höcker Rueb Doeleman Advocaten
Kneppelhout & Korthals
Lovells
Ploum Lodder Princen
Van Benthem & Keulen
Van Diepen Van der Kroef Advocaten
Van Doorne

Firms are listed A-Z in tiers which are ranked in order of priority
Indicates firm displays contact details at the end of this chapter.

RESTRUCTURING AND INSOLVENCY

De Brauw Blackstone Westbroek is instructed by a major domestic pension fund in the restructuring of one of its investment vehicles. The team continues to advise on issues relating to the worldwide Enron restructuring. Sijmen de Ranitz is highly regarded and was recently appointed president of *INSOL International*, a leading international network of insolvency professionals.

Lawyers in **Houthoff Buruma**'s insolvency practice are equally at home acting as court-appointed receivers as they are advising on complex restructurings. Eddie Meijer is one of two trustees in the KPNQwest bankruptcy. The team is often involved in the local law aspects of major international insolvencies.

Headed by Gerhard Gispen, **Simmons & Simmons**' creditor-focused insolvency team has an excellent reputation in the market. Benefiting from its international network of offices, the firm is often involved in multi-jurisdictional insolvency and restructuring matters.

Stibbe's Karen Harmsen is a 'fast-rising star' who heads a small creditor-focused practice that is instructed by a number of major banks including ING and Fortis. The firm also offers litigation experience in relation to D&O liability. The experienced Tony Van Hees also has an excellent reputation.

At **AKD Prinsen Van Wijmen N.V.** Barend de Roy van Zuidewijn is the leading light of an excellent receivership practice. De Roy continues to be involved as a trustee in the KPNQwest Finance insolvency. Georg van Daal heads the department.

Allen & Overy LLP's Amsterdam office is an integral part of the firm's strong global restructuring practice. Rob Abendroth is recommended.

CMS Derks Star Busmann has a receivership practice and is acting as court-appointed trustee in the largest semi-governmental organisation for employability reintegration services. The firm is also advising the largest US bondholder in the bankruptcy of KPNQwest. Utrecht-based Marcel Groenewegen is recommended.

Holland van Gijzen has an excellent receivership practice.

At **Loyens & Loeff** Hendrik van Druten heads a team that has a focus on corporate recovery. Highlights include advising the mezzanine lenders in the international restructuring of the Treofan Group.

NautaDutilh has a good relationship with ABN Amro, advising on issues relating to debtors in financial difficulties. The firm also has a fine reputation for cross-border insolvency issues. It is instructed by Regus on the Dutch law issues of its cross-border restructuring. Robert van Galen heads the practice.

Pels Rijcken & Droogleever Fortuijn NV's Jurjen Lemstra is a recognised expert in insolvency issues and receives a large amount of receivership instructions.

Baker & McKenzie's insolvency team works closely with the international network to provide a cross-border dimension to its insolvency advice.

Lawyers at The Hague-based firm **Buren van Velzen Guelen** are regularly appointed as receivers in insolvencies.

Clifford Chance has acted for the banks on the restructurings of a number of major corporates including Teleplan, Bodycare and Hagemeyer. Aided by its international network, the Amsterdam office is frequently instructed in relation to cross-border restructurings. Alistair McGillivray is recommended.

DLA SchutGrosheide works closely with those parties involved in restructuring, recovery procedures or formal proceedings. Recent highlights include the innovative restructuring of a large road transportation company.

Höcker Rueb Doeleman Advocaten's insolvency department specialises in assisting corporates in financial difficulty.

Kneppelhout & Korthals has a sizeable receivership practice, as does **Van Diepen Van der Kroef Advocaten**, where Reyn Snouckaert van Schauburg is recommended.

SHIPPING, AVIATION AND TRANSPORT

Headed by Leo Boersen, **AKD Prinsen Van Wijmen N.V.**'s Rotterdam-based shipping practice is unquestionably the pre-eminent firm in the market. Offering all-round expertise in both wet and dry shipping, clients include P&O Nedlloyd, Dockwise Shipping and Royal Vopak. Vincent de Brauw has an excellent reputation on the dry side, while on the wet side, Haco van der Houven van Oordt is often involved in major casualties. Francis de Vries Lentsch has developed a niche yacht-building practice.

Boekel De Nerée's Frans Vreede is head of the market-leading logistics and aviation team. His clients include global logistics service providers, as well as foreign entrepreneurs seeking to outsource their logistics operations. On the aviation side, the firm acts in the aftermath of all major aviation accidents involving Dutch passengers or crew, and assists both new and existing airlines in setting up their operations in the Netherlands. Department head Joeri Cox focuses on road transport and represents major underwriters such as Fortis and Delta Lloyd. Jan ter Meer is an expert on maritime law.

Van Traa Advocaten is a boutique providing all-round transport expertise in aviation, road and

SHIPPING, AVIATION AND TRANSPORT

AKD PRINSEN VAN WIJMEN N.V. ✪
BOEKEL DE NERÉE ✪
VAN TRAA ADVOCATEN ✪

Boonk Van Leeuwen
De Brauw Blackstone Westbroek ✪
De Koning & Mulder ✪
NautaDutilh
Simmons & Simmons ✪

Allen & Overy LLP ✪
DLA SchutGrosheide ✪
Dolk – Verburg – Diamand
Wiersma Mendel Prakke Advocaten

Bird & Bird ✪
De Vries Advocaten
Houthoff Buruma ✪
Loyens & Loeff ✪
Kernkamp Advocaten
Koster & Claassen
Russell Advocaten ✪
Smallegange, Van Dam & Van Der Stelt
Van Dunné Witholt Golterman
Van Gog Van Rijsbergen Advocaten
Van Harmelen Beijneveld van Houten

Firms are listed A-Z in tiers which are ranked in order of priority
✪ Indicates firm displays contact details at the end of this chapter.

shipping. In shipping, as well as providing wet expertise, Pieter den Haan also advises shipping companies and high-net-worth individuals in relation to ship-building contracts. Bart Neervoort specialises in road transport law, while Benedict Janssen is recommended for his logistics expertise.

Boonk Van Leeuwen is a niche shipping firm with a focus on the wet side of things.

At **De Brauw Blackstone Westbroek**, Berend Crans heads a cross-practice aviation group that has a strong aircraft lessor client base that includes debis AirFinance, GATX and Pegasus. Drawing in expertise from a number of the firm's practice groups, the team offers expertise on a range of matters from competition and regulatory issues, to asset and structured finance matters. Recent highlights include advising TUI Nederland on the formation of a new airline, ArkeFly.

Previously part of *SchutGrosheide*, **De Koning & Mulder** took the decision to go it alone in the beginning of 2004 and has quickly established itself as a leading player in the transport market. Hinno Postman leads an eight-lawyer practice that offers expertise in shipping (wet and dry), aviation, road transport and international trade. Clients include insurers (Fortis, Erasmus, HDI), port-related companies (APM, Vopak Logistic Services), airlines (Air France) and insurance brokers (Marsh, Aon).

NautaDutilh offers expertise in both wet and dry shipping to a broad range of clients including owners, P&I clubs, and freight forwarders. The team is defending a major Swiss forwarding company accused of alleged undeclared dangerous cargo. The group also has a focus on ship finance. It is advising ABN Amro on the refinancing of the Star Clipper fleet. Based in Rotterdam, Arnold van Steenderen, Gijs Noordam and Erik Geerling are the team's leading lights.

Simmons & Simmons' Jasper Helder is a leader in the field of customs law.

Willem van Baren heads **Allen & Overy LLP**'s strong aviation practice. Highlights include advising Swiss International Airlines in relation to its merger with the Lufthansa Group.

DLA SchutGrosheide's Marc Padberg has a fantastic reputation.

As the only shipping and transport practice based in Amsterdam, **Wiersma Mendel Prakke Advocaten** occupies a unique position in the market. The firm has a specilaism in the collection of trade claims against governments of politically unstable countries.

TAX

The only firm in Benelux that combines tax and legal capabilities of equal size, **Loyens & Loeff** offers a strength and depth that outstrips its rivals. Frequently working alongside other departments in the firm, the tax group offers expertise on M&A, transfer pricing and private equity funds. The firm has a niche strength in VAT and customs law and is often instructed by multinational corporates in setting up sales schemes, and assisting with the planning of the logistical and accounting implications. Guido Derckx, Hessel van der Kolk, Marco de Lignie, Tom van der Meer, Paul Simonis, Arnoud Viersen and Maarten van der Weijden are recommended.

Headed by Olaf van der Donk, **Allen & Overy LLP**'s tax practice recently played a pivotal role in Tele 2's highly tax sensitive public takeover of Versatel. The team was bolstered by the arrival of Erik de Gunst from Ernst & Young.

Baker & McKenzie's 15-partner group has the strength and depth to offer expertise in both direct and indirect tax, including dedicated VAT and transfer pricing teams. Highlights include advising Nova Chemicals on the tax issues in connection with its newly designed pan-European supply chain. Fred de Hosson, Maarten van der Lande and Wouter Paardekooper are recommended.

Clifford Chance has a focus on tax finance and offers expertise in the tax aspects of both securitisation and debt capital markets transactions. Ate van Ijlzinga Veenstra heads the three-partner team and is a market-leader in the growing area of funds, and investment management. The group works closely with the M&A team and provided tax advice in relation to A P Moller-Maersk's acquisition of Royal P&O Nedlloyd. Frank de Vos is recommended for financing and was involved in the structuring of

TAX

LOYENS & LOEFF ✪
Allen & Overy LLP ✪
Baker & McKenzie ✪
Clifford Chance
De Brauw Blackstone Westbroek ✪
Freshfields Bruckhaus Deringer
NautaDutilh
Simmons & Simmons ✪
Spigthoff ✪
Stibbe ✪
AKD Prinsen Van Wijmen N.V. ✪
Buren van Velzen Guelen ✪
CMS Derks Star Busmann ✪
DLA SchutGrosheide ✪
Greenberg Traurig LLP
Houthoff Buruma ✪
Lovells ✪
Norton Rose
Höcker Rueb Doeleman Advocaten ✪

Firms are listed A-Z in tiers which are ranked in order of priority
✪ Indicates firm displays contact details at the end of this chapter.

the first-ever Dutch structured covered bonds programme.

In close co-operation with the M&A, finance and litigation teams, **De Brauw Blackstone Westbroek**'s tax group has a focus on high-value transactions and tax planning. The team has had a key role to play in most of the firm's headline corporate and capital markets transactions, including the TomTom IPO, and VNU's acquisition of IMS Health. Dirk Hofland has an excellent reputation.

Freshfields Bruckhaus Deringer's three-partner tax team has a structured finance focus. The team advised adidas-Salomon on the tax structuring of its takeover of Reebok. Michiel Lambooij has an outstanding reputation in the market.

NautaDutilh's tax practice offers non-contentious and contentious tax advice to an enviable list of clients including NIB Capital Bank, 3i Group plc and Eureko. The group has been kept busy by a noticeable increase in M&A transactions and both Roderik Bouwman and Trudy Perié provided tax advice to the Dutch State in its acquisition of Gasunie. The firm's well-known securitisation practice benefits enormously from the tax input that lawyers of the calibre of Nico Blom can add to the transaction.

Simmons & Simmons advised CSFBi on the Dutch tax aspects of various credit-linked note issues by a number of Dutch programme issuers. Peter de Brock heads the department and is highly regarded by both clients and peers alike.

Corporate boutique **Spigthoff** has a tax litigation focus to its practice. Charles Langereis is recommended.

Headed by Maarten de Bruin, **Stibbe**'s four-partner tax group has an increasing transaction focus to its work. Recent highlights include advising Kantoren Fonds Nederland on its €1.3bn real estate portfolio restructuring and TomTom on its recent IPO. The firm is also active in structured finance transactions. Stef van Weeghel, Martin In de Braekt and Michael Molenaars are recommended. Clients include AIG, Accor, ING and Citibank.

Greenberg Traurig LLP's tax team is praised for its 'professionalism and proactivity'. Erik de Bie is one of the country's foremost customs and VAT lawyers. He represents numerous clients before both the Dutch Tax and Customs Courts.

Norton Rose is strong on the tax structuring of asset finance and securitisation transactions. Gesina van de Wetering receives rave reviews from clients, who appreciate her 'responsiveness and excellent commercial understanding'.

Höcker Rueb Doeleman Advocaten features for the first time in our rankings thanks to its newly formed tax litigation practice. Arnaud Booij heads the group.

TELECOMS

Allen & Overy LLP has been involved in a number of regulatory disputes before the Dutch telecommunications regulator, OPTA, on behalf of KPN Telecom. Paul Glazener advises cable company, UPC, on all of its broadcast-related regulatory and competition work. Quinten Kroes is a highly valued member of the team.

Bird & Bird's market-leading telecommunications practice is headed by Marjolein Geus. The team has a strong track record advising on complex national and international regulatory issues. On the contentious side, the firm is often involved in high-profile cases, involving amongst other things, frequency auctions and mobile terminating access tariffs. Clients include Orange, Tiscali, Qwest and Colt Telecom.

Joachim Fleury splits his time between London and Amsterdam, and heads **Clifford Chance**'s telecoms group. Highlights include advising eBay on its US$2.6bn acquisition of Skype, the global internet communications group. The team has a strong regulatory litigation focus and successfully obtained an injunction on behalf of Tele2 against KPN, regarding its marketing campaign. EU and competition partner Geert van der Klis has a strong telecommunications flavour to his practice. Clients include Vodafone and Tele2.

De Brauw Blackstone Westbroek advises fixed and wireless telecoms companies on a full range of regulatory, competition and transactional issues. The firm has an impressive workload and reports a noticeable increase in instructions from leading telecommunications provider, KPN. Highlights include advising KPN in the OPTA investigation relating to fixed telephony pricing and in its dispute with Wanadoo over a non-compete clause in a reseller agreement. Martijn Snoep is recommended.

TELECOMS

ALLEN & OVERY LLP ✪
BIRD & BIRD ✪
CLIFFORD CHANCE
DE BRAUW BLACKSTONE WESTBROEK ✪
Baker & McKenzie ✪
Houthoff Buruma ✪
Kennedy Van der Laan
NautaDutilh
Stibbe ✪
Boekel De Nerée ✪
Brinkhof
CMS Derks Star Busmann ✪
Freshfields Bruckhaus Deringer
Lovells ✪
Loyens & Loeff ✪
Pels Rijcken & Droogleever Fortuijn NV ✪
Van Doorne ✪

Firms are listed A-Z in tiers which are ranked in order of priority
✪ Indicates firm displays contact details at the end of this chapter.

Baker & McKenzie has been providing the domestic regulatory advice on a telecommunications merger valued in excess of US$1bn. Serge Gijrath heads the team.

Houthoff Buruma is regularly instructed by Dutch mobile operator, T-Mobile. It recently represented it in successfully appealing an OPTA decision relating to network access. Other highlights include advising the City of Amsterdam in the €800m fiber-to-the-home project.

Kennedy Van Der Laan's Patrick Wit is lead counsel to Vodafone and handles all of the company's telecoms matters including the recent responses to the market analysis and litigation against OPTA, regarding mobile terminating tariffs. The firm also advises a number of new entrants in the emerging field of VoIP.

Headed by Piet Sippens Groenewegen, **NautaDutilh** represented Casema before OPTA in a case concernings its fixed telephony tariffs for terminating access. On the transactional side, the team advised the major shareholders of Telfort in relation to its acquisition by KPN.

Stibbe's Reinout Rinzema heads an excellent team whose clients include Talpa, T-Mobile and UPS/Chello Media. Maarten Sanders is a transactional lawyer with a focus on the telecoms sector. Sanders advised UPC in connection with its acquisition of brodacast company AT5.

Brinkhof regularly advises leading carriers including Enertel, Versatel, Scarlet and MCI in disputes before both OPTA and the civil courts. Egbert Dommering is highly regarded.

AKD PRINSEN VAN WIJMEN N.V.

PO BOX 59280
1040 KG AMSTERDAM

Telephone: +31 20 582 5100
Fax: +31 20 582 5150
Website: www.akd.nl

Languages
Chinese, Danish, Dutch, English, French, German, Italian, Norwegian, Portuguese, Spanish, Swedish

Other offices
Breda, Brussels, Eindhoven, Rotterdam, Utrecht

Number of lawyers 230
at this office 39

Contacts
Bert Heikens (bheikens@akd.nl),
Scipio van der Stoel (svanderstoel@akd.nl)

CATEGORIES OF WORK

Corporate and commercial law

Mergers and acquisitions

Shipping, transport and insurance law

Employment law

Administrative and environmental law

Commercial real estate law

European and competition law

Intellectual property and ICT law

Corporate recovery and insolvency law

Tax litigation

Family law

Corporate criminal law

Civil law notaries

Banking and finance

ALLEN & OVERY LLP

APOLLOLAAN 15
PO BOX 75440
1070 AK AMSTERDAM

Telephone: +31 20 674 1000
Fax: +31 20 674 1111
E-mail: information@allenovery.com
Website: www.allenovery.com

Languages
Dutch, English, French, German, Italian

Other offices
Antwerp, Bangkok, Beijing, Bratislava, Brussels, Budapest, Dubai, Frankfurt, Hamburg, Hong Kong, London, Luxembourg, Madrid, Milan, Moscow, New York, Paris, Prague, Rome, Shanghai, Singapore, Tokyo, Turin, Warsaw

Number of lawyers 2,304
at this office 187

Contact
Sietze Hepkema

CATEGORIES OF WORK

Corporate/M&A
Jan Louis Burggraaf

Corporate/notarial
Gerbrand Visser

Private equity
Karine Kodde

Real estate law
Henry van Geen

Project finance
Bart Meesters

Banking
Bart Meesters

Tax
Olaf van der Donk

Competition
Tom Ottervanger

Regulatory, administrative
Hendrik Jan de Ru

International capital markets
Niels van de Vijver

Litigation
Willem van Baren

IP/media and entertainment
Paul Reeskamp, Eric Keyzer

Information technology
Herald Jongen

Restructuring/insolvency
Rob Abendroth

Employment
Ferdinand Grapperhaus

Telecommunications
Peter Eijsvoogel

Energy
Paul Glazener

BAKER & McKENZIE AMSTERDAM N.V.

LEIDSEPLEIN 29
1017 PS AMSTERDAM
PO BOX 2720
1000 CS AMSTERDAM

Telephone: +31 20 551 7555
Fax: +31 20 626 7949
E-mail: info.amsterdam@bakernet.com
Website: www.bakernet.com/amsterdam

Languages
English, French, German, Italian, Japanese, Spanish

Other offices
The member firms of Baker & McKenzie International, a Swiss Verein, have 70 offices in 38 countries around the world. For a complete list, please visit www.bakernet.com.

Number of lawyers 3,300+
at this office 150

Contact
Maarten van der Lande

CATEGORIES OF WORK

Banking and securities law
Boris van Beek, Karin Smit, Piet Schroeder

Commercial litigation practice
Eduard Ferman, Frank Kroes

Corporate and commercial/M&A
Mike Jansen, Edwin Liem, Jeroen Hoekstra

Corporate contracts
Marco Wallart

Corporate notarial/ civil law notaries
Mark Bongard, John Paans

Employment law
Jos van Vlijmen, Karin Bodewes, Mirjam De Blécourt

EU and competition law
Marco Wallart

ICT law/telecommunications law
Serge Gijrath

Intellectual property
Alexander Odle, Reina Weening

Pharmaceuticals and healthcare law
Reina Weening

Real estate, property and projects
Mark Bongard, Olav Andriesse

Tax
Wouter Paardekooper, Erik Scheer

THE FIRM

Baker & McKenzie Amsterdam was established in 1957. The Amsterdam office was the very first in the Netherlands to form part of an international law firm. It now has more than 50 years' experience in international legal practice and is considered as one of the leading providers of legal services and advice in the Netherlands. Baker & McKenzie was also the first law firm in the Netherlands to set up a fully integrated civil law, tax and notarial practice. With 150 attorneys, tax consultants and civil-law notaries, the Dutch office has all the specialist expertise and experience required for a successful national and international legal practice.

Baker & McKenzie Amsterdam is one of the largest offices in the international Baker & McKenzie network which comprises 69 offices in 38 countries worldwide. With offices in every major business and financial centre, Baker & McKenzie offers an unrivalled international network. Baker & McKenzie has more than 620 partners and over 3,300 legal experts worldwide.

Baker & McKenzie focuses on providing legal services to clients in the business community. Baker & McKenzie Amsterdam has specialist expertise and experience in virtually every field of practice, but it offers more than expert legal knowledge alone. Its attorneys immerse themselves in their clients' companies, their needs and the branch of industry in which they operate in order to fully understand their clients' commercial, economic and social backgrounds. The client's interests are the focus of all services. In order to provide the required capacity for large-scale projects immediately, Baker & McKenzie can assign professionals at every level from its offices all over the world to work on specific long-term or short-term projects. Advanced technology, such as extranet, project management tools and intranet, guarantees efficient cross-border collaboration and a global exchange of expertise and know-how.

Baker & McKenzie makes great demands on its legal service professionals: enthusiasm combined with exceptional professional expertise; decisive action combined with a deep understanding of the client's industries and jurisdictions. The firm's dedicated professionals act as trusted advisers adept at offering solutions that are personalised and targeted to its clients priorities, strategies and goals.

The firm was founded on the concept of serving clients' needs across the globe. Baker & McKenzie continues to invest in its clients. Today and in the future. In the Netherlands and worldwide.

Baker & McKenzie International is a Swiss Verein with member law firms around the world.

BOEKEL DE NERÉE

GUSTAV MAHLERPLEIN 2
PO BOX 75510
1070 AM AMSTERDAM

Telephone: +31 20 795 3953
Fax: +31 20 795 3900
E-mail: boekel.de.neree@bdn.nl
Website: www.boekeldeneree.nl

Languages
English, French, German, Italian, Spanish

Number of lawyers 160

Contacts
Philip Paterson, solicitor (philip.paterson@bdn.nl), Ferdinand Mason, advocaat (ferdinand.mason@bdn.nl)

CATEGORIES OF WORK

Mergers and acquisitions
Philip Paterson, Ferdinand Mason

Corporate and commercial law
Lisette Bieleveld, Pieter Ariëns Kappers

Real estate/commercial property, construction law
Christiaan Toorman, Albert Flesseman

Employment/industrial relations law
Marian van Eck

Insurance law/maritime law
Jan ter Meer, Joeri Cox

Transport and aviation
Frans Vreede

Banking, securities and finance
Hans Sachse, Angelique Thiele

EU and competition
Frederieke Leeflang

Environment law/government practice and administrative law
Anne-Marie Klijn

Information and communication technology
Lisette Bieleveld

Intellectual property
Roelien van Neck

Insolvency law
Wouter Jongepier, Jacques Knol

Litigation
Michel Deckers, Wouter Jongepier

Media and entertainment
Pieter Ariëns Kappers, Frederieke Leeflang

Health law
Hester Uhlenbroek

Notarial services
Lex Hartman

THE FIRM

Boekel De Nerée is a leading independent Dutch law firm based in Amsterdam. The firm's 160 lawyers and civil law notaries provide specialist tailor-made services to a wide range of domestic and international clients. The firm's core areas of business are corporate/M&A, real estate, employment and transport and insurance.

Through its in-house foreign lawyers, the firm has very close links with the United Kingdom, the United States and Germany. In addition, Boekel De Nerée has excellent ties with correspondent law firms throughout the world.

AREAS OF PRACTICE

Boekel De Nerée is a full-service business law firm covering all areas of the law, with the emphasis on corporate/M&A, real estate, employment, and transport and insurance.

One of the corporate department's main strengths is the Anglo-American advisory group. This group is specifically geared to serve the special needs of clients from English-speaking parts of the world (in particular the UK and North America) who are embarking on mergers, acquisitions and other corporate transactions in the Netherlands. The group is headed up by two British partners and features a highly experienced cross-border team with an international approach to problem-solving that takes into account global issues within a local market context.

The firm is renowned for having one of the largest and most respected real estate teams in the Netherlands, covering all aspects of real estate law.

The firm has one of the leading employment law practices in the Netherlands, covering the entire spectrum of employment and industrial relations.

The firm's transport and insurance department is highly specialised and provides a full advisory and litigation service at national and international levels.

Each department of the firm deals with its own specific litigation as is customary in the Netherlands. Boekel De Nerée's litigation strength is epitomised by its ability to put together highly specialised cross-departmental litigation teams in complex proceedings.

Boekel De Nerée has a pronounced international character in the strategy and approach it adopts for solving client problems. Great importance is given in international transactions to advising clients from both a cross-cultural and cross-comparative legal perspective, hence the presence of the in-house foreign lawyers to give comfort and international guidance to foreign clients wishing to transact business in the Netherlands.

BRONSGEEST DEUR ADVOCATEN, member of ius laboris

DE LAIRESSESTRAAT 137-143
1075 HJ AMSTERDAM

Telephone: +31 20 305 3333
Fax: +31 20 305 3330
E-mail: e.deur@bd-advocaten.nl
Website: www.bd-advocaten.nl

Languages
Dutch, English, French, German

Number of lawyers 7

Contacts
Erik Deur (e.deur@bd-advocaten.nl),
Henriëtte Bronsgeest
(h.bronsgeest@bd-advocaten.nl)

Member
ius laboris International Employment Law, Pensions and Employee Benefits Alliance

CATEGORIES OF WORK

Labour law (including traditional labour law, collective labour relations, European labour law, criminal aspects of labour law, restructuring and transfer of undertakings, work environment, expatriation, litigation, arbitration)

CMS DERKS STAR BUSMANN

MONDRIAAN TOWER
AMSTELPLEIN 8A
1096 BC AMSTERDAM

Telephone: +31 20 301 6301
Fax: +31 20 301 6333
E-mail: amsterdam@cms-dsb.com
Website: www.cms-dsb.com

Languages
English, French, German, Hebrew, Italian, Russian, Spanish, Turkish

Other offices
Arnhem, Brussels, Hilversum, Utrecht

Number of lawyers 243
at this office 35

Other CMS alliance member firms
CMS Francis Lefebvre, France; CMS Cameron McKenna, UK; CMS von Erlach Henrici, Switzerland; CMS Hasche Sigle, Germany; CMS De Backer, Belgium; CMS Reich-Rohrwig Hainz, Austria; CMS Adonnino Ascoli & Cavasola Scamoni, Italy; CMS Albiñana & Suárez de Lezo, Spain

CATEGORIES OF WORK

Banking and finance
Jelle Timmenga

Capital markets
Reinout Slot, Jelle Timmenga

Corporate law
Martika Jonk, Richard Montijn

Commercial
Christiaan Scholten van Aschat

Mergers and acquisitions
Roman Tarlavski, Jan Peters

Labour law
Marco Meijer

Real estate
Roland Bos

Venture capital and private equity
Reinout Slot, Roman Tarlavski

Notarial law
Roland Bos

DLA SCHUTGROSHEIDE

AMSTELVEENSEWEG 638
1081 JJ AMSTERDAM

Telephone: +31 20 541 9888
Fax: +31 20 541 9999
E-mail: mail@dlapiper.com
Website: www.dlaschutgrosheide.nl

Languages
Dutch, English, French, German

Other offices
Austria, Belgium, Bosnia-Herzegovina, China, Croatia, Czech Republic, Denmark*, Egypt*, France, Georgia, Germany, Hong Kong, Hungary, Italy, Japan, Norway*, Poland*, Russia, Singapore*, Slovakia, South Africa*, Spain, Sweden*, Thailand, UK, Ukraine, United Arab Emirates, US

Number of lawyers 3,100
at this office 90

Contact
Frans Stibbe

Member
DLA Piper Group

CATEGORIES OF WORK

Banking and finance
Bart Joosen

Business support and restructuring
Marc Molhuysen

Civil law notarial service
Monique Laenen

Commercial/technology, media and communications
Niels Mulder

Corporate
Richard Fens

Corporate and commercial litigation
Ellen Soerjatin

Employment and industrial relations
Saskia Reuling

International trade, transport and insurance
Marc Padberg

Real estate, administrative and environmental
Rutger Oranje

Tax
André Jansen

THE FIRM

DLA SchutGrosheide provides top-quality international full-service legal advice tailored to the Dutch market. The firm is part of the global legal organisation DLA Piper Rudnick Gray Cary, which has approximately 3,100 lawyers in 58 offices in 22 countries across Europe, Africa, the Middle East, Asia and the US and helps clients solve their legal problems or prevent them arising in the first place. DLA SchutGrosheide has more than 220 people in Amsterdam and Rotterdam, of which 100 are lawyers.

The firm always offers creative, to-the-point solutions and advice. It is practical, goal-oriented and careful to find the right balance between effort, costs and results. Its working methods are sensible but at the same time personal.

AREAS OF PRACTICE

The DLA SchutGrosheide banking and finance team consists of experienced lawyers who act for both domestic and international financial institutions providing a wide range of banking and finance services. Core specialisms are leveraged and structured finance, asset-based finance, and trade finance. The team furthermore focuses on prudential supervision issues and related transactions, including derivatives and securitisation work.

The business support and restructuring lawyers work with the advisers and managers of underperforming companies and their investors. The Netherlands' insolvency courts regularly appoint the firm's lawyers as administrators in administration and as trustees in a corporate bankruptcy.

The firm's civil law notarial department provides clients with tailor-made services in the fields of corporate law, real estate and family law.

DLA SchutGrosheide's commercial/technology, media and communications lawyers provide contentious and non-contentious advice to clients in the areas of commercial, IT, telecommunications, IP and competition/EU Law.

The firm's corporate lawyers handle all types of transactional and advisory matters in private equity, capital markets, and other M&A work and transactions, as well as advising large and medium-sized (listed and non-listed) companies and institutions on corporate governance, joint ventures, professional associations and (dis)investments.

DLA SchutGrosheide has been a leading law firm in the field of litigation for many years. Its highly experienced corporate and commercial litigation specialists represent clients before the Dutch and European courts in national and international arbitration cases and they provide guidance to their clients in proceedings before foreign courts.

The firm's employment lawyers advise on the full range of employment issues. The group has a strong advice and litigation practice, focusing on a practical approach to often complex legal problems. The majority of the firm's clients are major national and international companies that need advice on local employment matters.

The international trade, transport and insurance group provides legal support for the flow of goods worldwide: from coffee beans to metal ore, chemicals to hi-fi equipment, garlic to currency – by land, sea or air – taking optimal advantage of the Netherlands' strategic role in distribution.

The real estate group provides top-quality, multidisciplinary services to corporate occupiers, developers, the public sector and rapidly changing industry areas such as construction, retail, hotel and leisure.

DLA SchutGrosheide's tax lawyers aim to deliver the highest-quality professional advice and expertise to clients. They have a broad experience of M&A work, corporate restructuring, wage taxes, tax litigation, VAT, customs and excise and anti-dumping duties, as well as tax and estate planning for wealthy individuals.

DE BRAUW BLACKSTONE WESTBROEK

TRIPOLIS 300
BURGERWEESHUISPAD 301
1076 HR AMSTERDAM

Telephone: +31 20 577 1771
Fax: +31 20 577 1775
E-mail: amsterdam@debrauw.com
Website: www.debrauw.com

Languages
Dutch, English, French, German, Italian, Spanish, Swedish

Other offices
London, New York, Rotterdam, The Hague

Number of lawyers 330
at this office 210

CATEGORIES OF WORK

Corporate, M&A
Bernard Roelvink, Lodewijk Hijmans van den Bergh

Corporate governance
Jaap Winter, Martin van Olffen

Corporate litigation
Ruud Hermans, Berto Winters

Banking and capital markets
Jan Marten van Dijk, Jan Willem Hoevers

Asset and structured finance
Berend Crans, Niek Biegman

Corporate restructuring and insolvency
Sijmen de Ranitz, Jako van Hees

Investment management
Paul Klemann, Kees Groffen

Tax
Dick Hofland, Paul Sleurink

Employment and employee benefits
Evert Jan Henrichs, Liesbeth Sneek

Information technology
Bart van Reeken, Lokke Moerel

Intellectual property
Constant van Nispen, Joris van Manen

Real estate
Paul Kerckhoffs, Marja de Leeuw

Aviation
Berend Crans

Energy
Bernard Roelvink, Jaap de Keijzer

Telecommunications
Bart van Reeken, Joris van Manen

Private equity
Arne Grimme, Bernard Roelvink

THE FIRM

De Brauw Blackstone Westbroek is an independent business law firm. De Brauw specialises in providing legal advice in complex business transactions and commercial litigation. Ever since the firm was founded in 1871, it has focused on providing top quality legal services and on developing outstanding lawyers. The firm continuously looks forward to breaking new ground, providing expertise and experience to its clients in their ever-changing markets – year after year; in some cases, for over a century.

Over 40% of the top 100 companies in the Netherlands choose De Brauw Blackstone Westbroek as their lead law firm (KSU, Stand van de Advocatuur, 2005). Many of De Brauw's clients are large international companies or financial institutions and they regularly ask the firm to manage their cross-border corporate or financial transactions. Or they ask the firm to advise or litigate in international commercial disputes which involve a Dutch and/or Netherlands Antilles angle.

The full spectrum of corporate, M&A and finance activities is handled by a team of partners experienced in domestic and international transactions. They are supported by partners in specialist practices, such as EU/competition, tax and employment, who are also leaders in their field. De Brauw's lawyers understand the European and Anglo-American legal cultures and the demands of an international practice. Internationally, the firm maintains close working relationships with the leading firms in the major business jurisdictions.

AREAS OF PRACTICE

De Brauw Blackstone Westbroek offers a combination of a strong corporate and finance practice and a centre of excellence for litigation, believing it provides the ingredients for a unique service to its clients. It also helps the firm to develop innovative legal minds that bring commercial awareness and technical excellence to everything it does.

The firm's practice covers a broad range of Dutch, EU and Netherlands Antilles law. This includes corporate, mergers and acquisitions, private equity, banking, equity and debt capital markets, asset and structured finance, project finance, corporate recovery and insolvency, restructuring, investment management, tax, corporate and commercial litigation, arbitration and mediation, EU/competition, intellectual property, information technology and communication, public law, estate planning, real estate, employment and employee benefits. The firm has cross-practice groups for, among others, energy, pharmaceuticals, telecoms, financial institutions, private equity, public private partnerships, aviation and share plans.

DE KONING & MULDER

DE LAIRESSESTRAAT 151
1075 HK AMSTERDAM

Telephone: +31 20 578 8660
Fax: +31 20 578 8680
E-mail: info@dkm.nl
Website: www.dkm.nl

Languages
Dutch, English, French, German, Italian, Spanish

Other offices
Rotterdam

Number of lawyers 9

CATEGORIES OF WORK

Maritime law (cargo claims, bills of lading, charterparty disputes, ships arrests)
Hinno Postma, Wilbert ten Braak

Collisions and general average
Jurrian Koetsier, Wilbert ten Braak

Aviation (passenger/cargo claims, accidents, insurance)
Jurrian Koetsier, Wilbert ten Braak

Road transport (cargo claims)
Wilbert ten Braak, Jurrian Koetsier

International trade (commodities, chemicals, letter of credit disputes)
Bram Mulder, Hinno Postma

Mediation
Bram Mulder

Insurance law (general commercial liability, fire, transport insurance, professional liability insurance)
Jurrian Koetsier, Harald Ex

Pension law
Harald Ex

Real estate law
Harald Ex

Arbitration
Jurrian Koetsier, Bram Mulder

International debt recoveries
Harald Ex, Hinno Postma

HOWREY LLP

REMBRANDT TOWER, 31ST FLOOR
AMSTELPLEIN 1
1096 HA AMSTERDAM

Telephone: +31 20 592 4411
Fax: +31 20 463 7296
Website: www.howrey.com

Languages
Dutch, English, French, German, Spanish

Other offices
Brussels, Chicago, East Palo Alto, Houston, Irvine, London, Los Angeles, Northern Virginia, Paris, Salt Lake City, San Francisco, Taipei, Washington DC

Number of lawyers 565
at this office 16

Contacts
Willem Hoyng, Bart van den Broek

CATEGORIES OF WORK

Intellectual property litigation and counselling (patents, trade marks, copyright, trade secrets)
Willem Hoyng, Bart van den Broek, Frank Eijsvogels

Information technology
Frank Eijsvogels

National and international litigation and arbitration
Willem Hoyng, Bart van den Broek, Frank Eijsvogels, David Owen

Patent and trade mark prosecution (EU and US)
Koos Rasser, David Owen

Competition (EU and Dutch)
Jean Paul van Marissing

FAASEN & PARTNERS

WIBAUTSTRAAT 224
1097 DN AMSTERDAM

Telephone: +31 20 560 0600
Fax: +31 20 560 0500
E-mail: info@fplaw.nl
Website: www.fplaw.nl

Languages
Dutch, English, French, German, Spanish

Other offices
Rotterdam

Number of lawyers 40
at this office 25

Contact
Michel Chatelin

CATEGORIES OF WORK

Mergers and acquisitions
Claudine Maeijer, Jan ter Horst

Private equity
Marek Kupperman, Claudine Maeijer

Corporate and commercial
Rob Faasen, Marek Kupperman

Corporate finance
Rob Faasen, Judy Oppedijk

Employment
Wouter Hes, Ingrid van Berkel

EU and competition
Michel Chatelin

Energy and utilities
Paul Josephus Jitta, Michel Chatelin

Company law
Claudine Maeijer,
Mick van Waateringe

Notarial
Mick van Waateringe

Distribution, agency, franchising
Michel Chatelin

Public sector
Claudine Maeijer, Michel Chatelin

PPP
Rob Faasen

Securities and financial supervision
Marek Kupperman, Judy Oppedijk

THE FIRM

Faasen & Partners was founded in 2002. The firm has a specific focus on corporate law, employment law and financing law. Within a period of three years Faasen & Partners has been able to position itself, in a difficult economic market, as an independent medium-sized firm running a practice at the level of a large firm. This is explained by the background of the partners – coming from, for example, Loeff (now Allen and Overy), Stibbe, Nauta Dutilh, Trenité Van Doorne (now Simmons & Simmons and Van Doorne), PwC – as well as the nature of their cases and the nature of their clients.

The firm started with five partners and has grown to nine (eight equity partners and one salary partner) and is now one of the largest starting law firms in the Netherlands. Since the beginning of 2002 Faasen & Partners has been the only firm of a certain size which has obtained its market position on its own. Faasen & Partners needed to acquire new clients and new cases on its own and has proved to be successful in that respect. Faasen & Partners attributes this success to the rigorous implementation of its strategy to focus on a limited area of legal expertise and to invest in these practice areas. Furthermore, its forum on certain sectors (energy and other regulated sectors) contributed to the success of the firm.

The lawyers of Faasen & Partners are trained to look beyond the horizon of law and domestic issues. The lawyers often manage multidisciplinary projects with tax lawyers, accountants and consultants. Their experience in international transactions ensures a comprehensive approach that meets the demands of the global environment in which many of their clients operate. The firm applies the best practices to deliver pragmatic and result-orientated advice. Faasen & Partners was elected Best Starting Law Firm of the Netherlands 2002-04 (KSU Awards 2005).

AREAS OF PRACTICE

Faasen & Partners BV is a law firm with a practice directed at medium-sized and large companies, governmental agencies and financial markets participants. With a strong foundation in the Dutch domestic market, Faasen & Partners is a boutique which rivals the big firms in its strategy. Faasen & Partners focuses on business advisory and transaction management, although it also has strongly developed litigation skills in all areas of its practice. Faasen & Partners has a specific focus on transactions, corporate governance, regulated sectors (energy, education, healthcare and housing co-operations), international mobility of workforce and reorganisations.

Faasen & Partners has developed a thorough competence in working together with tax lawyers, accountants and financial-economic experts. When needed, Faasen & Partners offers co-ordination in multidisciplinary projects with tax advisors and financial economic experts chosen by our clients.

Faasen & Partners' practice groups are of a corporate nature. The talented lawyers are specialists in any of the following areas: corporate law, commercial law, M&A, finance, European and competition law, securities law, employment law, and employment participation law.

HÖCKER RUEB DOELEMAN ADVOCATEN

VAN EEGHENSTRAAT 98
1071 GL AMSTERDAM
PO BOX 74654
1070 BR AMSTERDAM

Telephone: +31 20 577 7700
Fax: +31 20 671 9710
E-mail: mail@hrd.nl
Website: www.hrd.nl

Languages
English, French, German, Italian, Russian

Number of lawyers 42

Contact
Leo Sapir (managing partner)

Member
Lexwork International; The Interlex Group

CATEGORIES OF WORK

Company/commercial law
Marc Wolters, Yvette Borrius

Insolvency law
Lucas van Eeghen, Kees van de Meent

Mergers and acquisitions
Antoine Endtz, Marc Wolters

Labour law
Jasper van Hulst, Inge Hofstee

Intellectual property law
Gijsbert Brunt, Eveline Schippers

ICT law
Gijsbert Brunt

Environmental law
Koos van den Berg

Entertainment law
Willem Roos

Family law
Anneke Karsten

Media law
Herman Doeleman, Willem Roos

Property law
Dolf Rueb

Mediation
Anneke Karsten, Herman Doeleman

Tax (litigation)
Arnaud Booy

THE FIRM

Höcker Rueb Doeleman Advocaten is a mid-sized Amsterdam business law firm, which provides a full range of legal services to both domestic and international clients.

The firm offers the best of both worlds to its clients, professional expertise at the highest level and a more personal approach. The firm provides pragmatic advice to achieve top-notch results. Höcker Rueb Doeleman Advocaten is a member of The Interlex Group, Lexwork International and Advertising Law International; enabling the firm to maintain efficient and productive contacts worldwide.

AREAS OF PRACTICE

Höcker Rueb Doeleman Advocaten has a broad practice consisting of: corporate, mergers and acquisitions, tax (litigation), employment, insolvency and restructuring, corporate and commercial litigation, arbitration and mediation, intellectual property, copyrights, trade marks, media, entertainment, information technology, real estate, employment and regulatory.

Höcker Rueb Doeleman Advocaten has specialised industry groups which make prompt to the point advice and assistance standard practice. These groups are aimed at the entertainment, advertising, publishing, care, real estate, travel (aviation) and IT industries and contribute to valuable client-orientated expertise within the firm.

HOUTHOFF BURUMA

GUSTAV MAHLERPLEIN 50
1082 MA AMSTERDAM

Telephone: +31 20 605 6000
Fax: +31 20 605 6700
Website: www.houthoff.com

Languages
English, French, German, Italian, Portuguese, Spanish

Other offices
Brussels, London, Luxembourg*, Rotterdam, The Hague

Number of lawyers 305
at this office 153

Contacts
Jan van der Horst, Robert Tieskens

CATEGORIES OF WORK

Arbitration	Insolvency and restructuring
Automotive	Insurance and reinsurance
Banking, finance and securities	Intellectual property
Capital markets	Media and entertainment
Commercial litigation	Mediation
Construction and real estate	Mergers and acquisitions
Corporate and commercial	Notarial legal services
Employment and pensions	Private equity
Energy and utilities	Professional liability
Environment and planning	Project finance
EU and competition	Tax
Information and communications technology	Telecoms

THE FIRM

Houthoff Buruma is a leading, independent, full-service law firm in the Netherlands with some 750 staff, including over 300 Dutch law specialists. The firm acts for a wide variety of clients, both in the private and public sector. They include listed and non-listed companies, banks and investors, public utilities, healthcare and government authorities. Houthoff Buruma provides its clients with high-level, full-service legal advice, and represents them in litigation. All advice is given in a pragmatic manner which focuses on clients' goals. One of the firm's key strengths is its ability to offer extensive and in-depth knowledge of the Dutch market combined with top-class Dutch law expertise owing to its capacity and the firm's commitment to actively keeping apace with market developments. The firm has offices in Amsterdam, Rotterdam, The Hague, Brussels and London, and is represented in Luxembourg.

For contact details of the firm's offices in London and Brussels, please see the separate entries for these offices. For details of the firm's offices in Rotterdam and The Hague, please refer to the website, at www.houthoff.com.

AREAS OF PRACTICE

Houthoff Buruma's corporate and finance practice is highly regarded. The firm is a leading adviser in mergers and acquisitions, private equity, IPOs and financing, and advises on both domestic and international transactions.

Houthoff Buruma has one of the largest real estate departments of any law firm in the Netherlands. The main areas of work include international cutting-edge transactions, such as major project developments, and major PPP/PFI projects, as well as advising on construction law, public procurement law, environment and planning law, and administrative law.

Houthoff Buruma is widely recognised as one of the leading law firms in the Netherlands when it comes to insurance and insurance-related matters. With a team of over 50 lawyers specialised in advising the insurance sector on every legal aspect of their business, Houthoff Buruma has the largest specialist insurance practice in continental Europe. Whereas litigation remains a cornerstone of the firm's insurance practice, an ever-increasing number of clients call upon it for advice relating to, inter alia, transactions, corporate and regulatory work, reinsurance issues and product development. As a result, Houthoff Buruma has the ability to combine its highly specialised knowledge of the insurance sector with its broad experience in corporate and financial transactions.

Houthoff Buruma has one of the largest and most reputable litigation and arbitration practices in the Netherlands, and is one of the few Dutch law firms with a dedicated corporate and commercial Supreme Court litigation practice.

Other areas in which the firm has an excellent reputation are, among others, automotive, energy, EU and competition, healthcare, insolvency and restructuring, IP, IT, labour law, media, mediation, public law, regulatory, shipping, transport and telecoms.

LEXENCE

PETER VAN ANROOYSTRAAT 7
1076 DA AMSTERDAM

Telephone: +31 20 573 6736
Fax: +31 20 573 6737
Email: info@lexence.com
Website: www.lexence.com

Languages
Bahasa Indonesian, Dutch, English, French, German, Russian, Spanish

Number of lawyers 58

International groupings
Meritas; Counselex

CATEGORIES OF WORK

Mergers and acquisitions
Luc Habets, Michiel van Schooten

Private equity
Michiel van Schooten, Luc Habets, Jeroen Goosens

Corporate and commercial
Joost Houtman

Securities and finance
Joost Houtman

Company law
Henk ten Voorde, Jan Weijenborg, Carolien Bosch

Litigation
Ferry van Schoonhoven, Arthur Kaspers, Erwin van der Wiel

Employment
Bas Westerhout

Arbitration
Ferry van Schoonhoven, Erwin van der Wiel

Real estate (property development)
Stijn Vissers, Menno van Groningen, Erwin van der Wiel, Jan Van Duijvendijk, Taco de Lange, Jan Hockx, René Rietbroek

Real estate (lease)
Ferry van Schoonhoven, Tomas Steenmetser, Erwin van der Wiel

Real estate (transactions)
Stijn Vissers, Menno van Groningen, Jelle Ten Have, Erwin van der Wiel

Administrative law, environment and planning
Arthur Kaspers, Michiel van Driel, Vincent van Oijen

LINKLATERS

WORLD TRADE CENTRE AMSTERDAM
ZUIDPLEIN 180
1077 XV AMSTERDAM

Telephone: +31 20 799 6200
Fax: +31 20 799 6300
Website: www.linklaters.com

Languages
English, Dutch

Other offices
Antwerp, Bangkok, Beijing, Berlin, Brussels, Bratislava, Bucharest, Budapest, Cologne, Dubai, Frankfurt am Main, Hong Kong, Lisbon, London, Luxembourg, Madrid, Milan, Moscow, Munich, New York, Paris, Prague, Rome, São Paulo, Shanghai, Singapore, Stockholm, Tokyo, Warsaw

Number of lawyers 2,000 worldwide

Contacts
Richard Levy, Pim Horsten

CATEGORIES OF WORK

Banking
Martijn Koopal, Onno Bakker

Capital markets
Richard Levy, Pim Horsten

Corporate
Pieter Riemer, Peter Goes

Regulatory and funds
Wim Hazeleger

LOVELLS

FREDERIKSPLEIN 42
1017 XN AMSTERDAM
POSTBUS 545
1000 AM AMSTERDAM

Telephone: +31 20 553 3600
Fax: +31 20 553 3777
E-mail: information@lovells.com
Website: www.lovells.com

Languages
English, French, Spanish

Other offices
Alicante, Beijing, Berlin, Brussels, Budapest*, Chicago, Düsseldorf, Frankfurt, Hamburg, Ho Chi Minh City, Hong Kong, London, Madrid, Milan, Moscow, Munich, New York, Paris, Prague, Rome, Shanghai, Singapore, Tokyo, Warsaw, Zagreb*

Number of lawyers 1,600
at this office 46

Contacts
Jan de Snaijer, Marc Wallheimer

CATEGORIES OF WORK

- Intellectual property and information technology
- Litigation and arbitration
- Corporate, M&A and capital markets
- Banking and finance
- Employment
- Tax

LOYENS & LOEFF

PO BOX 71170
1008 BD AMSTERDAM
FRED ROESKESTRAAT 100
1076 ED AMSTERDAM

Telephone: +31 20 578 5785
Fax: +31 20 578 5888
E-mail: info@loyensloeff.com
Website: www.loyensloeff.com

Languages
Dutch, English, French, German, Italian, Japanese, Malay Indonesian, Portuguese, Russian, Spanish

Other offices
Antwerp (Loyens), Arnhem, Aruba, Brussels (Loyens), Curaçao, Eindhoven, Frankfurt, Geneva, London, Luxembourg (Loyens Winandy), New York, Paris, Rotterdam, Singapore, Tokyo, Zurich

Number of lawyers 710
at this office 267

CATEGORIES OF WORK

- Administrative and regulatory law
- Banking and securities, capital markets, project finance
- Capital markets
- Corporate and financial restructuring
- Corporate/M&A
- Corporate litigation
- Energy
- EU and competition
- Finance
- Financial products/ structured finance
- Employment taxes and labour law
- Private equity
- Real property
- Tax
- Technology, media and litigation
- VAT, customs and international trade

OOSTWAARD

VOORSTRAAT 2
3633BA VREELAND
AMSTERDAM

Telephone: +31 29 421 0333
Fax: +31 29 423 0553
E-mail: info@oostwaard.com
Website: www.oostwaard.com

Languages
Dutch, English, French, German

Number of lawyers 2

Contacts
Roelof van Holthe tot Echten, Rieke Smakman

CATEGORIES OF WORK

- Alternative dispute resolution
- Arbitration
- Art-related disputes
- Asset recovery disputes
- Commercial litigation
- Contractual disputes
- Financing disputes
- Joint venture/partnership disputes
- Mediation

RUSSELL ADVOCATEN

REIMERSBEEK 2
1082 AG AMSTERDAM

Telephone: +31 20 301 5555
Fax: +31 20 301 5678
E-mail: info@russell.nl
Website: www.russell.nl

Languages
Dutch, English, French, German, Spanish

Other offices
The Hague

Number of lawyers 20

Contact
Reiner WL Russell

CATEGORIES OF WORK

- Aviation, shipping and transport
- Arbitration and ADR
- Administrative/environmental law
- Media and entertainment (art law)
- Corporate and commercial law
- Commercial litigation
- Distribution, agency and franchise
- Employment law
- Insurance and (professional) liability
- Restructuring and insolvency
- Intellectual property and information technology
- Family law
- Mediation
- Property/real estate

SPIGTHOFF

DIJSSELHOFPLANTSOEN 14
PO BOX 75546
1070 AM AMSTERDAM

Telephone: +31 20 305 1600
Fax: +31 20 305 1699
E-mail: info@spigthoff.com
Website: www.spigthoff.com

Languages
Dutch, English, French, German

Other offices
Curaçao

Number of lawyers 36
at this office 26

CATEGORIES OF WORK

Corporate litigation
Jacob Cornegoor

Banking
Jerry Hoff

Corporate crime
Leo Spigt

Tax
Charles Langereis

Securities
Karel Frielink

THE FIRM

Spigthoff was established on 1 January 2001 by well-known corporate attorneys Leo Spigt and Jerry Hoff. Other partners in the office are attorney Jacob Cornegoor, tax advisers Arnold van der Smeed and Albert-Jan van Soelen, and attorneys/tax specialists Charles Langereis and Martien Pelinck. Partners at the Curaçao office are attorneys Karel Frielink and Martijn Welten, and tax adviser Xandra Kleine-van Dijk.

Spigthoff's office in Amsterdam employs 26 attorneys, and its Curaçao office has ten attorneys. The firm is also assisted by prominent emeritus attorneys and professors from external sources.

Spigthoff's return to a relatively small group of professionals has set a new trend in the legal profession, as it seldom has to refuse new cases because of conflicts of interest. The firm's offices are staffed by specialist attorneys and tax advisers, predominantly recruited from larger Dutch firms. They specialise in corporate litigation, corporate and securities law and in large, complex matters, which often attract attention in the news.

From the outset, Spigthoff has been developed with a balance between attorneys and tax advisers, who work together as a co-ordinated team. Of the ten partners, six are attorneys and four are tax specialists. The firm maintains a close, personal contact with its clients. It consists of creative deal-makers, noted for their toughness but, at the same time, aiming to solve problems and conflict situations amicably and expeditiously. Spigthoff works under the motto 'make the deal, settle peacefully if possible but go into battle if necessary'. Its lawyers are ready and able to enter into the fray and litigate thoroughly when necessary on their clients' behalf.

AREAS OF PRACTICE

Spigthoff specialises in corporate litigation, corporate law, securities law and tax. It concentrates on (potential) conflict and critical situations. The firm's principal areas of practice are: litigation; restructuring, particularly in cases of insolvency; securities law; mergers, acquisitions and other complex transactions; financial law; and economic criminal law.

STIBBE

STRAWINSKYLAAN 2001
1077 ZZ AMSTERDAM

Telephone: +31 20 546 0606
Fax: +31 20 546 0123
E-mail: info@stibbe.nl
Website: www.stibbe.com

Languages
English, French, German, Italian, Mandarin, Norwegian, Russian, Spanish

Other offices
Brussels, London, New York

Number of lawyers 276
at this office 155

Contact
Joost van Lanschot

CATEGORIES OF WORK

Administrative law and real estate
Niels Koeman

Banking and finance
Jaap Willeumier

Capital markets
Heleen Kersten

Competition and regulation
Christof Swaak

Dispute resolution
Toni van Hees

Insolvency and restructuring
Karen Harmsen

IP/IT communications
Reinout Rinzema

Employment, pensions and social security
Jaap van Slooten

Corporate and M&A
Charles Honée

Notarial practice
Paul Quist

Tax
Maarten de Bruin

VAN DIEPEN VAN DER KROEF ADVOCATEN

DIJSSELHOFPLANTSOEN 16-18
1077 BL AMSTERDAM
PO BOX 76729
1070 KA AMSTERDAM

Telephone: +31 205 74 7474
Fax: +31 205 74 7475
E-mail: amsterdam@vandiepen.com
Website: www.vandiepen.com

Languages
Chinese (Cantonese), Dutch, English, French, German, Greek, Italian, Portuguese, Russian, Spanish

Other offices
Alkmaar, Bussum, Haarlem, Hoorn, The Hague, Utrecht

Number of lawyers 124
at this office 37

Contact
Dr Axel Hagedorn (a.hagedorn@vandiepen.com)

CATEGORIES OF WORK

Administrative and regulatory law

Arbitration

Banking and finance

Commercial property

Competition law

Corporate and commercial

Employment law

Environment/administrative law

German law

Information technology

Insolvency law/restructuring

Intellectual property/ICT

International/European law

Litigation

Media, telecoms and entertainment

Mediation

Mergers and acquisitions

Private equity and venture capital

Property, real estate and construction

Transport and aviation

VAN DOORNE

JACHTHAVENWEG 121
1081 KM AMSTERDAM
PO BOX 75265
1070 AG AMSTERDAM

Telephone: +31 20 678 9123
Fax: +31 20 678 9589
E-mail: info@van-doorne.com
Website: www.van-doorne.com

Languages
English, French, German

Other offices
Aruba*, Curaçao*, London

Number of lawyers 135

CATEGORIES OF WORK

Banking and finance
Roel Botter

Corporate
Onno Boerstra

Employment
Els de Wind

European and competition
Sarah Beeston

Government and property
Michiel Faro

Insolvency
Paul Schaink

Intellectual property/ information technology
Kees Stuurman

Litigation and insurance
Walter Hendriksen

Notarial practice
Saskia Laseur

Tax
Thijs Clement

Healthcare
Willemien Bischot

Media and entertainment
Wouter Seinen

PPP group
Mark Moolhuizen

Sports
Marjolijn Lips

THE FIRM

Van Doorne N.V. is an internationally operating independent Dutch law firm with its principal office in Amsterdam. In addition, it provides advice on Dutch law through its London office and that of the Netherlands Antilles through its associated offices in Curaçao and Aruba. Each office is comprised of lawyers, civil notaries and tax advisers, who work fully integrated in the various practice groups. As an independent Dutch firm servicing the higher end of the commercial market, Van Doorne offers its clients top quality and responsive legal representation.

The firm's independence is valued by clients looking for a well-positioned firm between other (multinational) law firms. The hallmarks of Van Doorne's services include quality, flexibility, partner involvement, goal-oriented and competitive rate structures. The success of the firm's operations is seen in an increase in turnover each year despite some recent slumping of the economy in the Netherlands.

The firm's participation in significant and high-profile cases and transactions demonstrates demonstrates continuing growth over the years. The firm is proud of its Dutch client base, which consists of large and medium-sized companies, banks, insurance companies, (quasi) governmental bodies and Dutch subsidiaries of foreign enterprises. Nonetheless, Van Doorne is well-known for its international practice. Historically, it serves a large number of international clients, particularly from the UK and the US. Moreover, the majority of transactional work carried out by the banking, corporate and tax groups is cross border.

The independent status of Van Doorne provides its clients with a great opportunity to work with the best-equipped law firms for specific matters in other countries. For that purpose, for many years, close working relationships with leading law firms in all important jurisdictions have been maintained. Van Doorne strongly believes in the advantage to be able to instruct in other jurisdictions, or to be instructed for Dutch law as the best possible firm required for the specific (international) subject matters.

AREAS OF PRACTICE

In addition to the categories of work mentioned above, Van Doorne has specialised teams in the following areas: commercial contracting, corporate litigation, employee participation programmes, financial reporting, family-owned business, mediation, outsourcing and offshoring.

VAN MENS & WISSELINK

PIET HEINKADE 55
1019 GM AMSTERDAM

Telephone: +31 20 301 6633
Fax: +31 20 301 6622
E-mail: amsterdam@vmw.nl
Website: www.vmw.nl

Languages
Dutch, English, French, German, Japanese, Russian

Other offices
Rotterdam, Utrecht

Number of lawyers 70
at this office 26

CATEGORIES OF WORK

Mergers and acquisitions
Bart Kastelijn, Ayolt Zoer

Business law/corporate law
Bart Kastelijn, Ayolt Zoer

Real estate
Paul Bavelaar, Michiel de Wit

Administrative law
Elly Koning, Irene Verheijen

Corporate tax law
Harrie van Mens, Frans Duynstee

Criminal law, fraud
David Schreuders, Robin Steenman

Pensions law
Erik Lutjens, Anne-Marie Verweij

Labour law
Wietje de Muink Keizer, Martine Hoogendoorn

Gaming
Paul Bavelaar, Justin Franssen

Notary public
Floris Janse de Jonge

Estate planning
Wouter van Nispen Tot Sevenaer

Energy group
Elly Koning, Ayolt Zoer

German desk
Paul Bavelaar, Ramon Budik

THE FIRM

Van Mens & Wisselink was founded in 1991 by six experienced lawyers, who left an established law firm to combine forces in their new practice in Utrecht. After opening the Amsterdam office in 1998, a Rotterdam office quickly followed in 2000. With a current staff of 160, the firm is one of the few law offices in the Netherlands with a comprehensively integrated legal and tax practice that includes a notarial section. VMW showed the most rapid growth of all law firms in Holland in 2004. The firm has a large international practice and serves clients who operate globally. The clients include large- and medium-sized companies, non-profit organisations, public bodies and high-net-worth individuals. In order to provide the highest standards, VMW is organised into specialist practice groups, regional specialists and industry sector teams. The firm's professionals always consider how a legal structure or transaction may also present complex tax implications and vice versa. For this reason, VMW integrates its legal and tax services to provide clients with seamless legal and tax advice. For more information, visit the website: www.vmw.nl.

AREAS OF PRACTICE

The Amsterdam office opened in 1998 and grew at such a pace that a move was soon needed to accomodate it. Specialisms within this office are: mergers and acquisitions, corporate (tax) law, administrative law, labour law, fiscal law, fraud/white-collar crime, pensions law and the German desk.

Mergers and acquisitions: the mergers group, headed by Bart Kastelijn, advises a vast network of relations, both nationally and internationally. Bart is a renowned and experienced specialist in international company and commercial law. His specialism concerns the gaming and gambling industry and use of the internet in gaming.

Corporate (tax) law: clients at the Amsterdam office consist of medium- and large-sized companies that have to adapt to new rules and regulations or need to restructure parts of their business.

Real estate: commercial real estate is a volatile market in the Netherlands and as most of the business is with Germany, the real estate group, headed by Paul Bavelaar, is mainly concerned with buying, selling and leasing real estate in Holland for German customers and vice versa.

Administrative law: the government is everywhere, legislating, but administrative law is always close by, regulating government activity. Elly Koning points out that the most important development in administrative legislation is the increasing use of private law. Sectors such as healthcare were privatised but the government nevertheless lays down the rules. Clients in this group are chemical and pharmaceutical companies, educational institutions, medical organisations and hospitals.

Criminal law: the client base at the Amsterdam office consists mainly of corporations and their management (corporate criminal law and white-collar crime but also regulatory law). The main practice area is economic and fiscal criminal law in an international context. This practice covers tax, customs and excise, insider trading and other fields of banking and finance, (internet) gaming, money laundering and environmental law. David Schreuders serves his clients both in Europe and in the United States.

Labour law: labour law is a dynamic field of law which deals with the relationship between employer and employee. This section of the law is complex because of the frequent changes in legislation and case law and it is thus of the utmost importance that clients are kept properly and timely upated on the newest developments. Clients include companies in the IT, building, temping, trade and transport sectors.

Pensions law: Professor Erik Lutjens heads the pensions group. He is a gifted specialist in the field. The current situation in pensions is volatile: legislative amendments come in quick succession, following the stock exchange crisis in 2001. Erik advises large pension funds and corporations.

German desk: the provision of legal support to German companies conducting business in Holland and vice versa, is the priority here. Paul Bavelaar is fully conversant with the differences between the two systems.

CMS DERKS STAR BUSMANN

30 JANSBUITENSINGEL
PO BOX 560
6800 AN ARNHEM

Telephone: +31 26 353 8211
Fax: +31 26 443 0943
E-mail: arnhem@cms-dsb.com
Website: www.cms-dsb.com

Languages
English, French, German, Spanish, Russian

Other offices
Amsterdam, Brussels, Hilversum, Utrecht

Number of lawyers 241
at this office 42

Other CMS alliance member firms
CMS Francis Lefebvre, France; CMS Cameron McKenna, UK; CMS von Erlach Henrici, Switzerland; CMS Hasche Sigle, Germany; CMS De Backer, Belgium; CMS Reich-Rohrwig Hainz, Austria; CMS Adonnino Ascoli & Cavasola Scamoni, Italy; CMS Albiñana & Suárez de Lezo, Spain

CATEGORIES OF WORK

Corporate law
Christian Huiskes

Mergers and acquisitions
Christian Huiskes, Sander Drijber

Banking and finance
Sander Drijber

Insolvency law and corporate recovery
Sander Drijber, Piet Gunning

Labour law
Robert Jan Dil, Dirk Jan Bender

International private law
John Bosnak

Property, real estate and construction
Dominique van Dijk, Bart van Meer, Frans Lomans, Bas Martens

Planning, zoning and government
Ivo van Heijst, Conny Delissen

Environment and energy
Bart van Meer, Jos Berenschot

German law
Ton Heebing

HERTOGHS
TAX LAWYERS

PARKSTRAAT 8
PO BOX 4729
4803 ES BREDA

Telephone: +31 76 520 2266
Fax: +31 76 520 2288
E-mail: hertoghs@hertoghsadvocaten.nl
Website: www.hertoghsadvocaten.nl

Languages
English, French, German, Spanish

Number of lawyers 12

Contact
Hans Peek

CATEGORIES OF WORK

Tax litigation
Hans Hertoghs, Roel Kerckhoffs

Criminal tax law, business crime
Hans Peek, Guido de Bont

Unlawful government acts
Hans Hertoghs

Collection law (tax and customs)
Roel Kerckhoffs, Guido de Bont

Tax liability
Hans Peek, Roel Kerckhoffs

KEIZERS POELMAN ADVOCATEN

VESTDIJK 9
GROENE TOREN
POSTBUS 2154
5600 CD EINDHOVEN

Telephone: +31 40 244 5600
Fax: +31 40 244 5411
E-mail: kpa@keizerspoelman.nl
Website: www.keizerspoelman.nl

Languages:
Dutch, English French, German

Number of lawyers 12

Contact
Ton Keizers

CATEGORIES OF WORK

Labour law

Arbitration (national and international)

Banking and financing law (leasing, factoring, refinancing)

Construction law

Commercial contracts

Mergers and acquisitions

In court debt collection

Insolvency law (bankruptcies, suspension of payments)

Management buy-outs

Competition law (Dutch, European)

Litigation

DE BRAUW BLACKSTONE WESTBROEK

BLAAK 34
3011 TA ROTTERDAM

Telephone: +31 10 240 6500
Fax: +31 10 411 3548
E-mail: rotterdam@debrauw.com
Website: www.debrauw.com

Languages
Dutch, English, French, German, Italian, Spanish, Swedish

Other offices
Amsterdam, London, New York, The Hague

Number of lawyers 330
at this office 10

CATEGORIES OF WORK

Corporate
Frederik Buijn, Cees de Monchy

Estate planning
Pieter van Onzenoort

HOLLAND VAN GIJZEN

ATTORNEYS AT LAW AND CIVIL LAW NOTARIES

BOOMPJES 258
3011 XZ ROTTERDAM
PO BOX 2295
3000 CG ROTTERDAM

Telephone: +31 10 406 5453
Fax: +31 10 406 5451
E-mail: gregor.bertens@hollandlaw.nl
Website: www.hollandlaw.nl

Languages
English, German, French, Italian, Russian, Spanish

Other offices
Amsterdam, Chicago, Eindhoven, The Hague, London, New York, Utrecht

Number of lawyers 150

Contact
Gregor Bertens

CATEGORIES OF WORK

Corporate and commercial
Jan Meijerman, Jan Andringa

Mergers and acquisitions
Jan Meijerman, Dick Weiffenbach

Insolvency, corporate restructuring
Louis Deterink, Johan Westerhof

Competition and EU
Dirk Boselie

Banking and finance
Alexander Filius

Employment law and human resources
Marc van Gelder, Hans van Gijzen

Commercial property and real estate
Bart Terhorst, Paul Liesker

Construction
Bart Terhorst, Robert Gebel

Intellectual property and IT
Lidia Ritzema

Media and entertainment
Lidia Ritzema

Dispute resolution – litigation and arbitration
Hugo Nieuwenhuizen

Energy and natural resources
Dick Weiffenbach

Administrative and public law
Huib van Olden

KNEPPELHOUT & KORTHALS

ADVOCATEN

POSTBUS 546
3000 AM ROTTERDAM

Telephone: +31 10 400 5100
Fax: +31 10 400 5111
E-mail: mail@kneppelhout.nl
Website: www.kneppelhout.nl

Languages
English, French, German

Number of lawyers 30

Member
The Parlex Group of European Lawyers (associates in Barcelona, Madrid, Brussels, Copenhagen, Cyprus, Dublin, Edinburgh, Freiburg, Graz, Helsinki, Lisbon, London, Luxembourg, Oslo, Paris, Reykjavik, Stockholm, Thessaloniki, Turin, Milan, Zurich)

CATEGORIES OF WORK

Commercial law
Wibe Reddingius

Commercial property and compulsory purchase
Pieter de Boorder

Construction law
Jan Willem Langeler

Corporate law, M&A
Jan Kneppelhout, Jan Willem Langeler

EU antitrust and competition law
Kees Capel, Jan Willem Langeler

Finance and securities
Jan Kneppelhout, Otto de Witt Wijnen

Franchising, agency and distribution
Jan Kneppelhout, Wibe Reddingius

Insolvency and restructuring
Otto de Witt Wijnen, Joost Vrancken Peeters

Insurance and liability
Wibe Reddingius

Intellectual property
Kees Capel

International trade law
Jan Kneppelhout

Employment law
Arnold Birkhoff

Media and entertainment
Wibe Reddingius

Real estate and tenancy
Pieter de Boorder, Kees Capel

LOYENS & LOEFF

PO BOX 2888
3000 CW ROTTERDAM
WEENA 690
3012 CN ROTTERDAM

Telephone: +31 10 224 6224
Fax: +31 10 412 5839
E-mail: info@loyensloeff.com
Website: www.loyensloeff.com

Languages
Dutch, English, French, German, Italian, Japanese, Malay Indonesian, Portuguese, Russian, Spanish

Other offices
Amsterdam, Antwerp (Loyens), Arnhem, Aruba, Brussels (Loyens), Curaçao, Eindhoven, Frankfurt, Geneva, London, Luxembourg (Loyens Winandy), New York, Paris, Singapore, Tokyo, Zurich

Number of lawyers 710
at this office 187

CATEGORIES OF WORK

Administrative and regulatory law

Banking and securities, project finance

Capital markets

Corporate and financial restructuring

Corporate/M&A

Corporate litigation

Energy

EU and competition

Finance

Financial products/ structured finance

Employment taxes and labour law

Private equity

Real property

Tax

Technology, media and litigation

VAT, customs and international trade

PLOUM LODDER PRINCEN

BLAAK 28
3011 TA ROTTERDAM
PO BOX 711
3000 AS ROTTERDAM

Telephone: +31 10 440 6440
Fax: +31 10 436 4400
E-mail: info@plp.nl
Website: www.plp.nl

Languages
English, French, German, Italian

Number of lawyers 44

Contact
Tom Ensink

Member
Osborne Clarke Alliance

CATEGORIES OF WORK

Asset finance
Stan Commissaris

Commercial contracts
Dorine ten Brink, Dennis Zieren

Commercial litigation and arbitration
Boudewijn Cremers, Maurice Verhoeven, Jeroen Princen

Commercial property
John van Baaren, Stan Commissaris

Competition and EU
Michel Jacobs

Corporate, M&A
Duco Lodder, Tom Ensink

Corporate recovery
Jeroen Princen, Carla Nijhuis

Employment
Rutger Ploum, Peter de Waal, Henriëtte Dekker

Estate planning
Jolande van Loon

Full notarial services
Jolande van Loon, Stan Commissaris

Insolvency
Jeroen Princen, Carla Nijhuis

Intellectual property
Tom Ensink

IT and telecoms
Dorine ten Brink, Tom Ensink, Dennis Zieren

Joint ventures
Duco Lodder

SIMMONS & SIMMONS

WEENA 666
3012 CN ROTTERDAM

Telephone: +31 10 404 2111
Fax: +31 10 404 2333
E-mail: rotterdam@simmons-simmons.com
Website: www.simmons-simmons.com

Languages
Dutch, English, French, German, Italian, Spanish

Other offices
London, Paris, Lisbon, Milan, Rome, Düsseldorf, Frankfurt, Brussels, Madrid, Padua, Oporto, Madeira, Abu Dhabi, Qatar, Hong Kong, Shanghai, Tokyo, New York, Dubai

Number of lawyers 764
at this office 130

Contacts
Gerhard Gispen, Jan van Zuuren (managing partners)

CATEGORIES OF WORK

Corporate
Jean-Pierre van Leeuwe

Banking
Loet Venrooy

Capital markets
Harm van Berkum

Taxation
Peter de Brock

Commercial
Jan Willem Bitter, Jan van Zuuren

EU, competition
Marco Slotboom

Dispute resolution
Michael Gorsira, Jan Willem Bruidegom

Intellectual property
Willem Leppink

Employment
Alexander Steensma

Financial markets
Harm van Berkum

Corporate restructuring
Gerhard Gispen

Energy and utilities
Jos van de Vijver

TMT
Job Rietkerk

Corporate criminal defence
Ed van Liere

Transport and customs
Jasper Helder

Projects, PFI
Jos van de Vijver, Sjoerd Rutten

VAN TRAA ADVOCATEN

MEENT 94
3011 JP ROTTERDAM

Telephone: +31 10 413 7000
Fax: +31 10 414 5719
E-mail: info@vantraa.nl
Website: www.vantraa.nl

Languages
English, French, German, Italian, Polish

Number of lawyers 21

Contacts
Robert de Haan, Benedict Janssen

CATEGORIES OF WORK

Maritime law (cargo claims, bill of lading and charterparty disputes, ship arrests)
Prof Maarten Claringbould, Robert de Haan, Frank Smeele

Hull and machinery (collision, salvage and shipbuilding contracts)
Pieter den Haan

Ship financing (mortgages, registry and auctions)
Pieter den Haan, Robert Pessers

Aviation (aircraft financing, passenger and cargo claims, accidents, insurance, licences and charters)
Marc van Maanen, Robert Pessers

Road transport (cargo claims, logistic contracts)
Jan Teunissen, Benedict Janssen

Insurance (general commercial liability, property and construction)
Jan Teunissen, Bart Neervoort, Robert de Haan

Professional indemnity (lawyers, brokers, contractors and architects)
Bart Neervoort, Marc van Maanen

International trade and commodities
Marc van Maanen

VAN MENS & WISSELINK

HOFPLEIN 20
3032 AC ROTTERDAM

Telephone: +31 10 201 0500
Fax: +31 10 201 0501
E-mail: rotterdam@vmw.nl
Website: www.vmw.nl

Languages
Dutch, English, French, German, Japanese

Other offices
Amsterdam, Utrecht

Number of lawyers 70
at this office 26

CATEGORIES OF WORK

Arbitration
Shawn Conway, Harm Mulder

Litigation
Shawn Conway, Nathan O'Malley

Corporate law
Harm Mulder, Theo Ostermann

Employment
Helma van Dijk, Ankie Smits

Mergers and aquisitions
Johan de Bliek

Mediation
Shawn Conway

Insurance and tort law
Arnold Stendahl, Flip van Huizen

Corporate income tax
Theo Ostermann, Michiel Groenland

Shipping, aviation, transportation
Willem Claassen

THE FIRM

Van Mens & Wisselink was founded in 1991 by six experienced lawyers, who left an established law firm to start a new practice. The Rotterdam office was opened in 2000. With a current staff of 160, the firm is one of the few law offices in the Netherlands with a comprehensively integrated legal and tax practice that includes a notarial section. VMW showed the most rapid growth of all law firms in Holland in 2004. The firm has a large international practice and serves clients who operate globally. In order to provide the highest standards, VMW is organised into specialist practice groups, regional specialists and industry sector teams. The firm's professionals always consider how a legal structure or transaction may also present complex tax implications and vice versa. For this reason, VMW integrates its legal and tax services to provide clients with seamless legal and tax advice. For more information, visit the website: www.vmw.nl.

AREAS OF PRACTICE

Given Rotterdam's prominence as the largest port in the world and one of the main industrial centres in Europe, the client base of this office reflects business sectors such as manufacturing, petro-chemical, heavy industry, transport, logistics, telecoms, insurance and international commerce.

Arbitration: VMW's international arbitration group is dedicated to helping clients handle their commercial disputes. It is led by two partners with extensive experience in international dispute resolution, Shawn Conway and Harm Mulder, and is composed of American and Dutch lawyers. The group is experienced in representing clients at international arbitration tribunals convened under various regimes (ICC, NAI, SCC, AAA and LCIA). The group also represents clients before national courts.

Corporate (tax) law: VMW has a flourishing tax law practice, and many of its clients use the knowledge of the whole firm: attorneys from the Amsterdam and Utrecht offices frequently convene in Rotterdam. This shows the benefits of the integrated tax and civil law approach, as a civil law issue may also present serious tax implications. Clients range from entrepreneurs to international corporations. The group also acts as co-ordinating counsel with colleagues in other jurisdictions for multinationals, in respect of their European activities in the civil and tax law fields.

Insurance and torts: this group represents (Insurance Exchange-listed) insurers, brokers and other intermediaries, as well as insured parties. The practice is divided into two specialisations: torts and insurance. The first deals with liabilities ensuing from business activities, professional liability and functional liability. The insurance specialisation deals with disputes on policy coverage and interpretation. Insurance specialist Flip van Huizen is also a university professor. The group advises clients on the modification or renewal of their policy, as well as the consequences of the new Dutch law, effective from 1 January 2006.

Shipping law: this practice consists of two areas: activities in respect of seagoing vessels registered in the Netherlands or abroad. In this field, the office has the outstanding expertise of three partners who formerly worked together under the name of Koster & Claassen. Services provided include the setting up of foreign companies, assisting in finding financing and advice over special registration or flags for vessels.

Transport law: this practice assists in matters related to carriage of goods by sea, inland waters, road, rail, air and pipeline. The group has expertise in crises like collision, salvage, wreck removal, water pollution, and issues related to the loading, stowage, lashing on board vessels/vehicles (in particular, heavy/abnormal cargoes/dangerous goods). The attorneys have extensive knowledge in advising about auctions and sales. Advice on matters regarding ship purchase, sale, finance and registration is provided in close collaboration with an in-house notarial lawyer.

Mediation: The VMW mediation unit is composed of registered mediators and attorneys with experience of advising clients through mediation processes domestically, internationally and under the recently launched, nationwide, court-annexed mediation programme.

BARENTSKRANS
ADVOCATEN NOTARISSEN

PARKSTRAAT 107
PO BOX 30457
2500 GL THE HAGUE

Telephone: +31 70 376 0606
Fax: +31 70 365 1856
E-mail: info@barentskrans.nl
Website: www.barentskrans.nl

Languages
English, French, German

Number of lawyers 55

CATEGORIES OF WORK

Corporate and commercial law
Henk Waling, Nick Surber, Arie Schaberg

Mergers and acquisitions
Otto de Jong, Nick Surber

EU law
Pierre Bos

Competition, antitrust
Pierre Bos, Harry Ferment

Employment
Peter Vas Nunes, Max Keulaerds

Intellectual property and technology
Marleen van den Horst, Anton Wolf

Banking and finance
William Schonewille

Administrative and environmental law
Joost Huijgen

Distribution, agency and franchise
Harry Ferment

Insolvency
Dirk van den Berg

Insurance and liability
Herman Jansen

Supreme Court litigation
Eric Grabandt, Jan Paul Heering

Pharmaceuticals (patents and regulatory)
Marleen van den Horst, Herman Jansen

Commercial property, real estate
Joost Huijgen, Jacques Buiteman

BIRD & BIRD

PARKSTRAAT 31
2541 JD
PO BOX 30311
2500 GH THE HAGUE

Telephone: +31 70 353 8800
Fax: +31 70 353 8811
E-mail: thehague@twobirds.com
Website: www.twobirds.com

Languages
English, Dutch, French, German

Other offices
Beijing, Brussels, Düsseldorf, Frankfurt, Hong Kong, London, Madrid, Milan, Munich, Paris, Rome, Stockholm

Number of lawyers 472
at this office 44

Contacts
Marjolein Geus, Harry Rek

CATEGORIES OF WORK

Asia desk
Steven van der Waal

Aviation and aerospace
Harry Rek

Communications
Marjolein Geus

Competition
Pauline Kuipers

Corporate
Harry Rek

Employment
Philip Hartman

Information technology
Jeroen van der Lee

Internet and e-commerce
Jeroen van der Lee

Intellectual property
Wouter Pors

Life sciences
Erik Limpens

Media
Marjolein Geus

Notarial practice
Steven van der Waal

Sport
Wouter Pors

Tax
Pieter Camps

BUREN VAN VELZEN GUELEN

ANDRIES BICKERWEG 6
2517 JP DEN HAAG

Telephone: +31 70 318 4200
Fax: +31 70 356 1340
E-mail: info@bvvg.nl

Languages
English, French, German, Spanish

Number of lawyers 30

CATEGORIES OF WORK

Commercial litigation and arbitration
Alfred PJM Guelen, Philip WM ter Burg

Corporate finance
Pieter E van den Berg, Eelko D Smit

Corporate law
Alfred PJM Guelen, Eelko D Smit

Insolvency and bankruptcy
Pieter E van den Berg, Martijn JH Vermeeren

Intellectual property
Philip WM ter Burg

Labour law
Alfred PJM Guelen, Suzan van de Kam

Mergers and acquisitions
Alfred PJM Guelen, Pieter E van den Berg

Real estate
Tom van Velzen, Wim van 't Hoff

Tax
Cees-Frans Greeven

DE BRAUW BLACKSTONE WESTBROEK

ZUID-HOLLANDLAAN 7
2596 AL DEN HAAG

Telephone: +31 70 328 5328
Fax: +31 70 328 5325
E-mail: thehague@debrauw.com
Website: www.debrauw.com

Languages
Dutch, English, French, German, Italian, Spanish, Swedish

Other offices
Amsterdam, London, New York, Rotterdam

Number of lawyers 330
at this office 100

CATEGORIES OF WORK

Litigation and arbitration
Maarten Schenck, Bommel van der Bend

EU, competition
Mark Biesheuvel, Martijn Snoep

Intellectual property
Koen Limperg, Tobias Cohen Jehoram

Public law
Godert van der Feltz, Vincent Aarts

Employment and employee benefits
Rogier Duk, Harro Knijff

Professional liability
Rob Polak, Marina de Kort-de Wolde

Energy
Vincent Aarts, Jolling de Pree

Pharmaceuticals
Constant van Nispen, Martijn Snoep

Telecommunications
Martijn Snoep

PELS RIJCKEN & DROOGLEEVER FORTUIJN NV

PO BOX 11756
2502 AT THE HAGUE

Telephone: +31 70 515 3000
Fax: +31 70 515 3100
E-mail: info@pelsrijcken.nl
Website: www.pelsrijcken.nl

Languages
English, French, German

Other offices
Willemstad (Curaçao)*

Number of lawyers 160

CATEGORIES OF WORK

Administrative law/telecoms
Eric Daalder

Civil litigation
Hans van Wijk

Commercial real estate
Alain de Jonge

Construction and public procurement
Pieter Stuijt

Corporate and insolvencies
Jurjen Lemstra

Environmental and planning
Elisabeth Schippers

European law/competition
Ronald Van den Tweel

Healthcare
Rolf de Groot

ICT and intellectual property
Henk Jan Boukema

Labour
Monique de Witte-van den Haak

Notarial real estate/family law
Rob Gallas

Major projects/public-private partnerships
René Kiers

Supreme Court litigation
Gerbrant Snijders

THE FIRM
Pels Rijcken & Droogleever Fortuijn is based in The Hague, the firm has 42 partners and employs 160 attorneys, (deputy) notaries and paralegals.

Pels Rijcken is a litigation firm by tradition, notwithstanding the fact that a good part of the practice involves advice, transactions and contracts. The firm has an extensive litigation practice in ground-breaking cases before the Dutch Courts and Supreme Court Litigation. Pels Rijcken has a strong public client base, and advises many national and international corporations and institutions.

AREAS OF PRACTICE
Pels Rijcken has a large arbitration practice, and one of the largest Dutch arbitrations ever is currently being handled by the firm. It deals with the proceeds of natural gas mining in The Netherlands and the division of these proceeds between the State of The Netherlands and Shell and ESSO. The firm is also handling a large arbitration between the State of The Netherlands and a daughter company of the Dutch Railway Company and KLM, dealing with financial aspects of the High Speed Rail Link (HSRL) from Amsterdam to Brussels.

Approximately 50% of the firm's work is litigation, it litigates for companies such as Exxon, KPN, ABB, Electrolux and on behalf of many governmental bodies. The corporate litigation practice is growing as is its class action practice; the latter has handled cases on behalf of parties such as the VEB and consumer organisations like the Consumentenbond.

The environment and planning group litigates for public and corporate clients on matters related to environment protection law, pollution and building regulations, zoning plans and nuisance.

The firm handles European law cases for the State of the Netherlands and competition law-related cases for the Dutch Competition Authority. Practice consists of advising ministries, regulators and companies on various EU related matters.

The ICT and IP practice covers all relevant aspects of ICT and IP law. Currently, the firm is involved in large ICT-cases for the Dutch Government. In the intellectual property and media field Pels Rijcken handles cases for, among others, ministers and the prime minister relating to media coverage of these persons.

Another practice area of Pels Rijcken is liability cases for major Dutch insurance companies. The real estate practice acts on behalf of departments of the Dutch Government like Domeinen, Staatsbosbeheer and the Ministry of Finance and on behalf of the city of The Hague.

Pels Rijcken's banking and finance practice is growing, one of the recent developments is its work for ABN Amro.

Most of the work in telecommunications is done for the central government, the telecommunications regulatory authority (OPTA) and the government of Aruba.

The construction practice group is the largest in The Netherlands focused on public clients. The firm acts on behalf of the State of the Netherlands, Rijkswaterstaat, the city of Rotterdam and the city of The Hague. Pels Rijcken is involved in all major infrastructure projects in The Netherlands on the side of the public party. Recently the firm handled an equity transaction between the State of The Netherlands and the city of Rotterdam, regarding the City Harbour Company, which was a deal of €500 million.

Pels Rijcken also handles large project finance infrastructure projects like the High Speed Rail Link, the Harbour of Rotterdam, Main Port Rotterdam and several highway PPP-projects.

CMS DERKS STAR BUSMANN

2 PYTHAGORASLAAN
PO BOX 85250
3508 AG UTRECHT

Telephone: +31 30 212 1111
Fax: +31 30 212 1333
E-mail: utrecht@cms-dsb.com
Website: www.cms-dsb.com

Languages
Danish, English, French, German, Portuguese, Spanish

Other offices
Amsterdam, Arnhem, Brussels, Hilversum

Number of lawyers 243
at this office 122

Other CMS alliance member firms
CMS Adonnino Ascoli & Cavasola Scamoni, Italy; CMS Albiñana & Suárez de Lezo, Spain; CMS Francis Lefebvre, France; CMS Cameron McKenna, UK and CEE; CMS De Backer, Belgium; CMS von Erlach Henrici, Switzerland; CMS Hasche Sigle, Germany and CEE; CMS Reich-Rohrwig Hainz, Austria and CEE

CATEGORIES OF WORK

Corporate law
Dolf Segaar, Jan Willem Schenk

Corporate finance
Dennis Lange, Cees de Tombe

Mergers and acquisitions
Paulus van den Bos, Cees de Tombe

Banking and finance
Reinoud Imhof, Marcel Groenewegen

Property, real estate and construction
Bob Bekker, Arno Moret

Planning and zoning/environment
Frans Otten

EU and competition
Robert Bosman

Health and pharmaceuticals
Janneke van Craaikamp

Franchising
Patricia Hamelberg

Intellectual property, information technology and telecommunications
Willem Hoorneman, Hendrik Struik

Labour law
Madeleine Lamers

Tax law
Jochem de Koning, Dennis Lange

THE FIRM

CMS Derks Star Busmann (CMS DSB) is one of the top ten firms of lawyers, civil law notaries and tax consultants in the Netherlands. It is the result of a number of mergers. These mergers welded together leading firms in Utrecht and Arnhem and combined these with equally high-quality firms in Amsterdam, Hilversum and Brussels .

With more than 550 staff, CMS DSB is among the largest providers of legal services in the Benelux. There are currently some 250 jurists (lawyers, civil law notaries and tax consultants) working in multi-disciplinary teams at all of the firm's offices.

CMS DSB offers legal services in the broadest sense of the word, and represents a diverse client portfolio in various legal fields and industry sectors. Its clientele comprises of national and multinational enterprises and organisations in the public and private sectors. CMS DSB is organised by means of specialised legal departments and industry sector groups, specialising not only in their respective fields of law, but also concentrating on the special requirements in various branches of industry.

Other CMS law firms: CMS Francis Lefebvre (France); CMS Cameron McKenna (UK); CMS von Erlach Henrici (Switzerland); CMS Hasche Sigle (Germany); CMS DeBacker (Belgium); CMS Reich-Rohrwig Hainz (Austria); CMS Adonnino Ascoli & Cavasola Scamoni (Italy); CMS Albiñana & Suárez de Lezo (Spain).

AREAS OF PRACTICE

The firm offers specialist advice and assistance in banking; biotechnology and health and pharmaceuticals; company law; corporate finance; corporate law; EU and competition; franchising; health law; IP, IT and telecommunications; insolvency; labour law; mergers and acquisitions; planning and zoning/environment; property, real estate and construction; private equity; venture capital; and tax law.

VAN BENTHEM & KEULEN

EUCLIDESLAAN 51
POSTBUS 85005
3508 AA UTRECHT

Telephone: +31 30 259 5959
Fax: +31 30 259 5500
E-mail: jkoggink@vbk.nl
Website: www.vbk.nl

Languages
English, French, German, Italian, Russian, Spanish

Number of lawyers 49

Member
State Capital Global Law Firm Group

CATEGORIES OF WORK

Corporate and commercial law
Pim Schermer, Martin Brink

Insolvency
Cees de Jong, Rinke Dulack

Labour
Arno van Beurden

Real estate, administrative
Marlies Muus-de Goede, Wim Vink

Intellectual property, media
Arjan Schuman

Health
John Kopp, Berend Keulen

Insurance
Berend Keulen

Contract law
Pim Schermer

Family
Anke Mulder

Environmental
Marlies Muus-de Goede

Venture capital
Martin Brink

Arbitration, alternative dispute resolution (ADR)
John Kopp

Civil litigation and transport
Marcel Ruygvoorn

Corporate litigation, corporate governance
Martin Brink

THE FIRM

Van Benthem & Keulen is comprised of 49 lawyers in its (sole) office in Utrecht, the Netherlands. Utrecht is the fourth-largest city in the Netherlands, situated in the centre of the country at a 30 minute drive from Amsterdam.

The firm was established in 1939. The firm has not merged with other law firms but grew steadily during the first decades and more rapidly during the 70s, 80s and early 90s to its present size.

The firm's clients are characterised by their diversity: publicly and privately held corporations, venture capital firms, municipalities and healthcare institutions form the backbone of the firm's client base.

One of the firm's top priorities is the recruitment of a qualified and diverse team of attorneys. This objective is ensured by maintaining close contacts with the leading Dutch law schools. Young lawyers are stimulated to specialise in areas of law which are important to the firm, and to publish articles in the leading law journals in the Netherlands. In addition, great attention is paid to improve the fluency of the attorneys in English, German, French, Italian and Russian.

AREAS OF PRACTICE

Van Benthem & Keulen has developed expertise in both the legal advice practice and litigation. The following is representative of the types of cases handled by the firm.

Corporate law: domestic and international mergers and acquisitions, joint ventures, venture capital transactions and reorganisations.

Commercial law: agency, distribution, licensing, computer contracts.

Insolvency law: reorganisations, suspension of payment and bankruptcy.

Health law: mergers and joint ventures between healthcare institutions, disputes between healthcare institutions and medical specialists, personal injury matters.

Competition law: public procurement law, merger control, trade restraints.

Intellectual property law: copyright, trade mark, entertainment and media.

Real estate law: environmental law, zoning and other governmental licensing, construction contracts, turnkey projects.

Labour law: collective labour agreements, collective dismissals, severance payments, workers council.

Family law: domestic and international divorces, estate planning, adoption, inheritance law, marital property law.

Arbitration and alternative dispute resolution: internal disputes within healthcare institution, contractual and corporate conflicts, family law matters.

Transport law: contracts of afreightment, warehousing, distribution and representation.

Litigation: litigation in all fields of law represented above.

Insurance law: assistance in assessing liability and potential liability and in framing or defending claims.

VAN MENS & WISSELINK

WILHELMINAPARK 60-61
3581 NP UTRECHT

Telephone: +31 30 254 7947
Fax: +31 30 252 2552
E-mail: utrecht@vmw.nl
Website: www.vmw.nl

Languages
Dutch, English, French, German, Japanese

Other offices
Amsterdam, Rotterdam

Number of lawyers 70
at this office 18

CATEGORIES OF WORK

Bankruptcy and insolvency
Huan Tan, Oete Schellingerhout

Intellectual property
Gijs van Poppel

Corporate (income) tax
Harrie van Mens, Ingmar Baas

Employment
Barbara Zwezerijnen

Corporate law (restructuring firms)
Bob Conyn, Harrie van Mens

Non-profit and charities
Bob Conyn, Ineke Koele

Inheritance, estate planning
Ineke Koele, Harm Bruggink

Japanese desk
Willem Visser 't Hooft

THE FIRM

Van Mens & Wisselink was founded in 1991 by six experienced lawyers, who left an established law firm to combine forces in their new practice in Utrecht. After opening the Amsterdam office in 1998, a Rotterdam office quickly followed in 2000. With a current staff of 160, the firm is one of the few law offices in the Netherlands with a comprehensively integrated legal and tax practice that includes a notarial section. VMW showed the most rapid growth of all law firms in Holland in 2004. The firm has a large international practice and serves clients who operate globally. The clients include large- and medium-sized companies, non-profit organisations, public bodies and high-net-worth individuals. In order to provide the highest standards, VMW is organised into specialist practice groups, regional specialists and industry sector teams. The firm's professionals always consider how a legal structure or transaction may also present complex tax implications and vice versa. For this reason, VMW integrates its legal and tax services to provide clients with seamless legal and tax advice. For more information, visit the website: www.vmw.nl.

AREAS OF PRACTICE

Van Mens & Wisselink was founded in Utrecht in 1991. VMW now also has offices in Amsterdam and Rotterdam. The current client base of the Utrecht office is drawn from companies and individuals requiring expertise in the fields of estate planning, corporate (tax) law, intellectual property, bankruptcy and insolvency and Japan.

Estate planning: Ineke Koele heads the estate planning and charities practice group and is a specialist in this field. Clients include art collectors, private individuals, executors, trustees and beneficiaries, institutions, including banks, trust companies, professional bodies, cultural and charitable organisations. The group advises on wills, structures involving trusts, foundations and offshore companies. Although the advice focuses on Dutch (tax) law, VMW has experience in co-ordinating international tax strategies and works closely with lawyers in other jurisdictions.

Corporate (tax) law: Harrie van Mens heads the corporate (tax) law practice group. He has an exceptional academic background, is a professor at the University of Utrecht and has published extensively on tax law. He advises wealthy individuals and large and medium-sized companies all over the world. He is also president of a professional organisation and in this capacity works closely with other tax specialists throughout Europe. This group advises mainly on corporate financial structures and assists high-net-worth clients in the structuring and restructuring of their assets.

Intellectual property, information technology and telecommunications: Gijs van Poppel heads this group. He has a wealth of experience in this field, including the protection and purchase/delivery of software and hardware and communication technology. He also has specific experience in providing quick and effective remedies in regard to IP infringements. This group litigates in and advises on trade mark and copyright cases, media and advertising, internet and ICT matters.

Bankruptcy and insolvency: Huan Tan heads a team of six specialists working for the bankruptcy and insolvency group. These specialists act as receivers in bankruptcies or as legal advisers to companies encountering difficulties. Swift and diligent action is required to guide a company or a private individual through involuntary liquidation. The usual problems entail tight cash flow, a decline in trade debtors and an increase in the accounts payable in order to finance working capital. The attorney endeavours to generate revenue and external sources of investment. Time is of the essence, as a struggling company needs time to recover and that is something that creditors are seldom willing to give. A moratorium of payment can, therefore, provide the necessary breathing space.

Japan desk: Willem Visser't Hooft heads the Japan desk, which advises Japanese companies operating in Holland and elsewhere in Europe and Dutch companies doing business in Japan. Willem is fluent in Japanese. The Japanese desk draws on the expertise available at all of the firm's offices.

NIGERIA

Population	123 million
Number of lawyers	45,000
Professional title	Solicitor
Currency	Nigerian Naira (NGN)
Index	
Corporate, commercial and finance	942
Dispute resolution	943
Shipping	944
Country index	5

Since 1999 president Olusegun Obasanjo has striven to transform Nigeria, tackling corruption and poverty, and bringing stability to a country which has endured seven military coups since independence in 1960. In 2003 Obasanjo was re-elected for a further four-year term, but much work remains to be done to modernise the country and prepare for the rest of the twenty-first century. Two-thirds of the population live in absolute poverty, and Nigeria ranks 152nd in the UN's Human development index, out of 175 countries.

In September 2003 Obasanjo announced the National Economic Empowerment and Development Strategy (NEEDS), which seeks to monitor expenditure, reform public services, impose more stringent levels of accountability and promote private investment in the economy. There is no doubt that the economy is making progress, but investment is being deterred by slow reform and a protective trade policy. A major obstacle is the huge level of public debt; interest payments on the US$31bn owed by government consumes one-third of government spending.

Nigeria's best hope for the future lies with prudently exploiting its huge oil and gas reserves. Reserves of 32 billion barrels make it OPEC's sixth-largest oil exporter. Much of the industry is dominated by joint ventures between the national oil company NNPC with oil majors such as Shell, Agip and Total. The country also has the seventh-largest gas reserves in the world and to date nearly US$10bn will have been invested in LNG.

Diversification is also essential, as reliance on oil and gas revenues has clearly so far not paid economic dividends. Infrastructure development, mining and tourism are areas that could be expanded further, if given sufficient backing at government level. Nigeria has ample resources besides oil, as well as impressive human capital.

Berlin-based Transparency International ranks Nigeria as the world's second-most corrupt country. The government is trying to tackle the issue, and the Independent Corrupt Practices Commission (ICPC) has begun proceedings to prosecute several public figures, including members of the senate. The ICPC has a new chairman in former judge Emmanuel Olayinka Ayoola.

The government is increasingly serious about kick-starting the privatisation process. New faces at the Bureau of Public Enterprises shows renewed impetus, and recent debt relief granted by the Paris Club has increased the likelihood that some major assets will be sold in 2006/7. Privatisations were started in 1999 with hotels and insurance companies, and the government is now looking at selling off some of the assets of larger and more complex businesses such as NEPA and NNPC.

Consolidation in the banking sector is another source of lucrative work for many Nigerian firms. In 2004 the Central Bank of Nigeria issued guidelines which substantially increase the minimum capitalisation requirement for commercial banks. The aim is to reduce the number of banks from nearly 100 to about a dozen. United Bank for Africa and Standard Trust Bank have agreed to merge, and about 60 other banks have formed groups that will lead to various complex mergers. South African bank Absa (now owned by Barclays) is interested in investing in the sector. The deadline to meet the new requirements was October 2005, and at least 15 banks look to be in peril after failing to find merger partners.

Nigeria is a federal republic and its capital is Abuja. The legal system is a mixture of English common law and traditional customary courts and in northern states Islamic law is being increasingly used. With more than 400 languages spoken in the country, most high-level business is conducted in English.

BILLING

Much billing amongst the more sophisticated firms is now based on retainers and lump sums, although when hourly rates are used it works out at about €135-€150 for an associate, rising to €250 for a partner.

MARKETING

Conventional restrictions apply to advertising law firms in Nigeria, covering areas such as qualitative claims. Advertising is restricted to journals and certain publications.

LEGAL MARKET

Nigerian law firms tend to be small by international standards, with few having more than a couple of dozen lawyers. Specialisation is therefore quite rare, and few firms possess genuine strength in depth. Having said that, the standard of service from the top-ranking firms listed here is very high, and many of the individual partners are extremely experienced lawyers who comfortably meet the expectations of international clients. Some of the smaller firms regularly appear on headline transactions, largely due to the way work is distributed in Nigeria.

There are few niche firms in Nigeria, but the new **Shipping** section directs readers towards firms with notable experience in that field. For clients seeking specialist intellectual property advice, **Allan & Ogunkeye**, **David Garrick** and **Jackson, Etti & Edu** are all quality firms.

Lagos is the business centre, although firms in Port Harcourt (the major port and centre of the oil industry) are as good as many of the Lagos firms. **Aluko & Oyebode** and **Adepetun Caxton-Martins, Agbor & Segun** both have offices in Port Harcourt as well as in Lagos.

Abuja (the federal capital) is also an important centre, and is easily accessible from Lagos. Kano is the next most important commercial centre, where **Femi Sunmonu & Associates** is a respectable outfit.

Most Nigerian firms do not feel the need to expand internationally. However, **Aluko & Oyebode** also has a small presence in London, while **Olaniwun Ajayi & Co** has an outlet in Johannesburg. **Æ LEX** has an office in Ghana, and **Udo Udoma & Belo-Osagie** also has an associate office in Accra.

The main split in the market is between firms that have historically been known for litigation and those with a more transactional bias, although as in many other countries this distinction is eroding.

The coming years are likely to bring increased consolidation in the Nigerian legal market. In 2004 **Æ LEX** was formed by the merger of four firms: *Anga & Emuwa*, *O Adekoya & Co*, *Victor & Charles* and *Adegbite Adeniji & Co*. Many mid-market players will be considering the viability of their strategies as the market professionalises and develops.

Nigerian firms were generally busier in 2005 than they were in 2004. Historically, much work in the energy sector was kept in-house by the oil majors, but this is gradually changing as more oil companies find local firms they trust. Anti-corruption drives have also created higher standards in corporate governance, which in turn has created more work for local lawyers. Other markets are buoyant at the moment, especially capital markets transactions and work in the telecoms sector.

FOREIGN FIRMS

Much of the work for international firms in Nigeria tends to be energy and infrastructure-related so many larger global firms have some experience in the country. **Allen & Overy LLP**; **Clifford Chance**; **Linklaters**; and **Freshfields Bruckhaus Deringer** regularly appear on headline deals.

Several other UK-based firms have also successfully targeted Nigeria. **Denton Wilde Sapte** has a strong dedicated Africa practice, and recently advised Total on the Obiter Power Project. **Norton Rose** also features on top mandates across the African continent. Fresh from the Nigeria LNG project, the firm is now working on the Brass LNG deal, and is also advising the Nigerian government on its downstream gas strategy.

DLA Piper Rudnick Gray Cary UK LLP has been acting on disputes for Vmobile, as well as for the Nigerian government on recovering money from General Abacha. **Pinsent Masons** has also been active: in 2005 it acted for Dangote on the purchase of a US$300m cement factory and 90km gas pipeline in Nigeria.

Several US firms have also been quick to see Nigeria's potential, usually in the power sector. **Hunton & Williams** continues to advise NEPA and the Ministry of Power & Steel on a variety of projects. **Vinson & Elkins R.L.L.P.** is advising European and US energy companies on multi-billion dollar investments, including the Nigerian blocks in Sao Tome. Having advised the arrangers on the US$1bn Nigeria LNG deal, **White & Case** is now acting for the sponsors on the Brass LNG deal.

South African firms are increasingly interested in Nigerian work. In particular, **Bowman Gilfillan** and **Webber Wentzel Bowens** have been active. **Werksmans Attorneys** is a member of *Lex Africa*, so has a referral relationship with **Giwa-Osagie & Co**.

CORPORATE, COMMERCIAL AND FINANCE

CORPORATE, COMMERCIAL AND FINANCE

ALUKO & OYEBODE
OLANIWUN AJAYI & CO

Adepetun Caxton-Martins, Agbor & Segun
Ajumogobia & Okeke
Banwo & Ighodalo
Templars
Udo Udoma & Belo-Osagie

Æ LEX
F.O. Akinrele & Co
G. Elias & Co.
Giwa-Osagie & Co ✪
Jackson, Etti & Edu
Sofunde, Osakwe, Ogundipe & Belgore
Solola & Akpana ✪
Strachan Partners

Abdulai Taiwo & Co
Chris Ogunbanjo & Co
Siji Soetan & Co

Firms are listed A-Z in tiers which are ranked in order of priority
✪ Indicates firm displays contact details at the end of this chapter.

Nigeria's largest full-service firm, **Aluko & Oyebode** is a first choice for blue-chip multinationals, and international firms looking for local referrals. Managing partner Gbenga Oyebode has extensive international experience. Also highly recommended are Ms Kofo Dosekun for finance, and Ms Olunbumi Fayokun who is 'a practical lawyer who understands the needs of clients'. The firm has genuine depth at associate level compared to other local firms, and banking, insurance and oil and gas are standout areas. Recent headline deals include advising MTN on the Nigeria telecoms deal; advising the lenders on the LNG Plus deal; and the sponsors on the NGL deal.

Lagos-based **Olaniwun Ajayi & Co** also has a small presence in Johannesburg, and is a clear favourite with blue-chip clients and international firms for referrals. Managing partner Konyin Ajayi is often talked of as one of the country's top lawyers, and is described as 'first-class and very good with clients'. Partner Tominiyi Owolabi is also very highly rated, and the firm has a great crop of talented youngsters. Major recent deals include: closing the US$1.2bn NGL/OSO financing for the lenders; advising the lenders on the Obajana Cement Plant deal; and acting for Vmobile on its major financing.

With offices in Lagos, Abuja and Port Harcourt, **Adepetun Caxton-Martins, Agbor & Segun** operates at the upper end of the corporate and energy markets. Now comprised of 25 lawyers, its four partners include the excellent Afolabi Caxton-Martins, who inspires much confidence and 'understands the needs of international clients'. The firm is currently working on projects in the Nigeria Sao Tome and Principe Joint Development Zone.

Interlaw representative **Ajumogobia & Okeke** is a full-service commercial firm of four partners and 32 associates. A solid local and multinational client base covers various sectors, including inward investment, telecoms, energy, intellectual property and shipping. Name partner Chris Okeke has a good name, and partner Ovie Ukiri 'knows what he is doing on oil and gas'. The firm also has good strength in depth at associate level. In 2005 the firm advised the IFC on the Nigeria LNG transaction, and the firm also regularly works for ExxonMobil and Halliburton.

Banwo & Ighodalo is a contender for top corporate and projects instructions, and has few peers for capital markets work. Partner Kenneth Etim in particular gets rave reviews from international clients. Partners Femi Olubanwo and Asue Ighodalo are also well-regarded practitioners, and are supported by 20 associates. Illustrative of the firm's credentials is recent work for the consortium on the Brass LNG deal, with **Norton Rose** as international counsel. The firm is also one of the top commercial practices for intellectual property.

Templars has 27 lawyers across five Nigerian offices covering all commercial work. The firm is well connected and 'knows the oil and gas market very well'. Partner Aghogho Akpata is considered 'highly responsive and adds value, not just technical legal advice'. Recent highlights include advising Norsk Hydro on its bid for a major oil concession and Hutchison Port Holdings on its bid for the US$1.2bn concession to operate various Nigerian ports.

Six partners and 21 other lawyers at **Udo Udoma & Belo-Osagie** are based in Lagos and Port Harcourt, with an associated Ghana office. Much work is for local clients and the Nigerian government, and the firm also worked for the lenders HSBC (with **Norton Rose**) on a US$50m loan to Moni Polu. Partner Dan Agbor specialises in energy and projects; and partner Myma Belo-Osagie is on the oil and gas committee of the IBA.

Æ LEX has settled after its four-way merger in 2004, which created one of the country's largest full-service commercial outfits. The practice covers banking and dispute resolution as well as commercial matters in the telecoms and energy fields. Lawrence Fubara Anga is considered a good finance lawyer (with a niche in aviation), and Adegbite Adeniji is a member of the power law committee of the IBA. For international referrals the firm is affiliated to *Meritas* and *World Services Group*, and also has an office in Ghana.

F.O. Akinrele & Co is not just a firm for disputes, but has a broad commercial workload, including maritime law. Mr F Akinrele SAN is described by a client as 'switched on' and he leads a firm which is considered 'dynamic, impressive and professional' and which 'knows international clients'. The firm is a member of the *West African Law Network*.

One of Lagos's top mid-sized firms, **G. Elias & Co.** undertakes corporate work and finance in the energy sector to the highest standards. Dr Gbolahan Elias has a sterling reputation and is supported by a good crop of seven associates, as well as two other partners. Clients come from a range of sectors, including some notable names in power and oil and gas.

Lex Africa affiliate **Giwa-Osagie & Co** is a solid mid-market player in Nigeria with some impressive clients (such as South Africa's Standard Bank) and good feedback from the market. Teams cover corporate, banking and privatisation work.

Jackson, Etti & Edu is a mid-size firm with a good name for corporate and disputes, and is perhaps one of the country's top IP firms. Highlights in 2005 include some major bank mergers (including MBC International Bank and First Bank of Nigeria); and the firm also had a key role on many aspects of the Oso NGL project and subsequent developments.

Sofunde, Osakwe, Ogundipe & Belgore has four partners based in Lagos covering a range of practice areas. Traditionally known as a litigation firm, the practice has now broadened to include all commercial areas, including insurance and aviation. Ebun Olusegun Sofunde SAN is a respected member of Lagos's business community, as is Gabriel Nkadi Osanugonum Osakwe.

Solola & Akpana has offices in Port Harcourt and Abuja, and plans to open a Lagos office in 2006. Competing with the country's top names in disputes, corporate and energy, the firm also has a separate environment department. Three partners and 18 associates are local counsel to TotalfinaElf and ChevronTexaco, amongst others. In 2005 the firm acted for oil company Moni Pulo on various transactions and disputes in Nigeria.

Strachan Partners is one of a number of reputable litigation firms in Lagos which has successfully branched out into more general corporate and commercial work. Partner Yemi Candide-Johnson has a very good reputation both locally and with international clients.

Abdulai Taiwo & Co has offices in Lagos and Abuja, and a close relationship with **Solola & Akpana** in Port Harcourt. Thirteen lawyers are led by the eminent Chief Ladi Taiwo, and Akin Osinbanjo is Attorney-General for Ogun State. The firm undertakes much finance work for Shelter Afrique as well as Citibank. The client base in predominantly local.

A new entrant this year is **Chris Ogunbanjo & Co**, a small but quality firm run by name partner Chris Ogunbanjo. Covering a broad commercial remit, the firm is highly rated by international firms for referrals.

Lagos-based **Siji Soetan & Co** has nine lawyers covering all commercial areas, including corporate, disputes, IP and energy. Chief Siji Soetan is an eminent name in the Lagos market, and the firm has some impressive clients such as Chevron and Lufthansa.

DISPUTE RESOLUTION

Nigeria has a fused profession, but there is a distinctive pool of lawyers specialising in litigation. Most litigators are sole practitioners, and larger firms often refer court cases to such boutiques and manage the disputes process for major clients. Senior Advocate of Nigeria (SAN) is a similar status to Queen's Counsel in the UK.

Terralex-affiliated **Chief Rotimi Williams' Chambers** is a first port of call for all types of commercial disputes in Nigeria. Name partner Chief Williams is an eminent name and was the country's first QC and first SAN. Apart from general commercial disputes, the team is also experienced in sector-specific disputes in energy, insurance and intellectual property. Arbitration is also covered.

F.O. Akinrele & Co is an excellent choice for all types of disputes: from general commercial to IP, insurance, tax and shipping. Partner Demola Akinrele SAN is a very good litigator, widely respected in the market. He also has extensive ADR experience. The firm is part of the *West Africa Law Network* for referrals.

DISPUTE RESOLUTION

Chief Rotimi Williams' Chambers
F.O. Akinrele & Co
Sofunde, Osakwe, Ogundipe & Belgore
Strachan Partners

Æ LEX
Aina, Blankson & Co ✪
Ajumogobia & Okeke
Akinjide & Co
Akinwunmi & Busari
Aluko & Oyebode
Fidelis Oditah & Co
G. Elias & Co.
Jackson, Etti & Edu
McCarthy Mbadugha & Co
Olaniwun Ajayi & Co

Firms are listed A-Z in tiers which are ranked in order of priority
✪ Indicates firm displays contact details at the end of this chapter.

Sofunde, Osakwe, Ogundipe & Belgore is one of Lagos's most experienced disputes specialists, covering all types of disputes, including arbitration. Partner Ebun Olusegun Sofunde SAN is considered a trustworthy and very capable pair of hands for local and international clientele.

Strachan Partners' litigation practice is up there with the very best in Nigeria, and Yemi Candide-Johnson is a superb practitioner with a strong local following and a good name with international clients. In 2005 the firm continued to act for Econet Nigeria (now Vmobile) on its challenge to the Nigeria Communication Commission's new regulatory regime.

Litigation is central to **Æ LEX**'s full-service offering, where Ms Funke Adekoya SAN has a redoubtable reputation for dispute resolution.

Aina, Blankson & Co is a small firm, which is known to have pioneered ADR in Nigeria.

Ajumogobia & Okeke is a major player on the transactional scene, and also has accomplished capability in all kinds of disputes. Partners H Ajumogobia and Supo Shasore are both well-regarded litigators. Standout recent cases include acting for ExxonMobil on a mass tort oil pollution case, against 4,000 claimants.

Akinjide & Co handles court litigation as well as arbitration, and Chief Richard Akinjide is a well-known and respected practitioner.

Akinwunmi & Busari has a particularly strong name for intellectual property. Tunde Akinwunmi is currently secretary of the Nigerian Chartered Institute of Arbitrators.

Aluko & Oyebode is another premier corporate firm with a solid record on litigation, both for local companies and multinationals. Litigator Tunde Fagbohunlu is experienced and reliable. Besides commercial litigation and arbitration, the firm has experience in IP litigation.

New addition **Fidelis Oditah & Co** is run by Fidelis Oditeh QC, an English-qualified barrister who splits his time between London and Lagos. He is described by clients as 'a very honest and exceptionally intelligent lawyer'. His firm has recently acted in *Chucks Associates v Baker Hughes*; and also *Econet Wireless International v First Bank of Nigeria*. The firm is also building a solid transactional practice.

In 2005, **G. Elias & Co.** acted for Shell on a huge tax case in Nigeria. Other important cases indicative of the firm's standing in the market include advising the Bureau of Public Enterprises (the privatisation agency) on a major dispute concerning an insurance company.

Jackson, Etti & Edu is another new addition this year. In 2005 the firm represented Colgate-Palmolive and major tobacco companies protecting their IP interests in Nigeria. The firm has also represented Vodacom in an action against Vodafone over the use of the name Vodacom.

McCarthy Mbadugha & Co handles disputes as well as commercial work, and is one of the few firms dedicated to maritime matters. Three partners and six other assistants have a solid reputation, and recently acted for the defendants in the *Antonie Reefer* and *Izidher Reefer* litigation.

At **Olaniwun Ajayi & Co**, Konyin Ajayi SAN is not only seen as one of Nigeria's pre-eminent transactional lawyers, but he also has experience in local courts as well as in international disputes. In 2005 the firm represented Vmobile as local counsel on arbitrations, with **DLA Piper Rudnick Gray Cary UK LLP** as international counsel.

As mentioned in the introduction to the **Dispute resolution** section, Nigeria has many other sole practitioners or individuals worthy of mention. Afe Babalola is a leading litigator in Abano, near Lagos, well known as an advisor to the president. Ms Tinuade Oyekunle is a senior arbitrator with extensive international experience; and Dr Alex Izinyo in Abuja and Paul Usoro are also worth a mention.

SHIPPING

Adepetun Caxton-Martins, Agbor & Segun is a serious commercial player, where partner Ms Funke Agbor is experienced in all aspects of maritime law for a diverse client base.

Major commercial firm **Ajumogobia & Okeke** handles all aspects of shipping and international trade for shipowners and P&I clubs, and is one of the safest bets in the country for ship finance. Although based in Lagos, the firm also has a presence in Port Harcourt. Partner Olasupo Shasore is a contact name.

F.O. Akinrele & Co is a popular commercial outfit with capability in all maritime matters, usually on behalf of shipowners and P&I clubs. Examples of clients include the North of England P&I Club; American P&I Club and also the Liverpool and London P&I clubs. The firm also has good referral relationships with the major London specialists.

SHIPPING

Adepetun Caxton-Martins, Agbor & Segun
Ajumogobia & Okeke
F.O. Akinrele & Co
Louis Mbanefo, Law Office of
McCarthy Mbadugha & Co
Paul Usoro & Co

Firms are listed A-Z in tiers which are ranked in order of priority

Law Office of Louis Mbanefo has an office in Lagos and a small presence in London. Louis Mbanefo SAN is vice-president of the Nigerian Maritime Lawyers Association.

Lagos-based **McCarthy Mbadugha & Co** has a notable specialism in shipping. Name partner JN McCarthy Mbadugha is an experienced litigator with good P&I club clients, as well as shipowners and insurance companies. In 2005 the firm acted on the litigation involving the *Antonie Reefer*.

With offices in Lagos, Kaduna and Uyo, **Paul Usoro & Co** has a dedicated maritime and environment practice, headed by partner Mfon Ekong Usoro. The firm has one other partner and 13 solicitors, and covers the full gamut of shipping law. An indication of the firm's stature in the sector is its role assisting in the drafting of the Ports Bill 2004.

ABUKA & PARTNERS

LEGAL PRACTITIONERS

WESTERN HOUSE, 10TH FLOOR
8-10 BROAD STREET
LAGOS

Telephone: +234 1 493 4054
Fax: +234 1 263 1687
E-mail: abukapartners@linkserve.com

Languages
English

Other offices
Abuja, Port Harcourt

Number of lawyers 7

Contact
Patrick C Abuka (managing partner)

CATEGORIES OF WORK

Corporate and commercial (including international joint ventures, foreign direct investment, and international trade)
Patrick Abuka, Queen Uchegbue

Intellectual property (including trade marks, copyrights and patents)
Queen Uchegbue, Peter Affen

Financial law (including banks and banking, capital and money markets, securities, equipment financing and leasing, secured credit transactions and insurance)
Patrick Abuka, Sunday Edward

Natural resources (including petroleum and gas law, solid minerals and environmental law)
Peter Affen, Nathaniel Uchegbue

Shipping (including admiralty and maritime law, law of the sea)
Queen Uchegbue

Government (including government relations, legislative practice, parliamentary lobby, government and defence contracts)
Patrick Abuka, Peter Affen

Privatisation (international bids, public tenders and bids, public procurement, non-profit and charitable organisations (NGO)), real estate, resorts and leisure (hotels) and debt recovery
Patrick Abuka, Peter Affen

Litigation
Peter Affen, Sunday Edward

THE FIRM

Abuka & Partners, Legal Practitioners, had practiced under the name of Abuka Ajegbo Ilogu & Nwaogu, which was founded on 28 March 1979 by the four name partners, who had practiced both individually and separately until that date. The partners had been in the legal profession since 1970.

The firm expanded to Port Harcourt on 1 October 1980, following the increasing needs of clients in commerce and industry in the eastern states of Nigeria.

The Abuja office was set up in the Federal Capital Territory in 1987, initially with a view to effectively providing the complex and sophisiticated legal services required by a major multinational corporate client, with businesses in over 90 countries around the world. As the seat of the Nigerian government has gradually moved from Lagos to Abuja, the firm is in the best position to conduct dealings with government representatives on behalf of its clients from its own office in the new capital. The firm has won the respect of the Nigerian government and of foreign embassies in Nigeria.

Following a restructuring, the firm has now adopted the shorter and simpler name of Abuka & Partners, Legal Practitioners. The firm retains its offices in the three most-important business cities in Nigeria: Lagos, Port Harcourt and Abuja.

The firm represents a large number of international clients, and collaborates with correspondent and associate law firms around the world.

The firm maintains the highest standards of professionalism, ethics and integrity. It recognises that every client is unique and, to that extent, the firm's service to each is personalised as if the individual client were its only client. The firm treats each client's business in strict confidentiality, and details a managing attorney for all the work performed for each client.

The firm is responsive to its clients' enquiries and has a good understanding of the way that US and European companies like to do business. The firm has all Nigerian statutes in case law in its computer database, which is updated regularly in accordance with the developments in Nigerian law to ensure that information is kept current.

Furthermore, the different branches of the law in which the firm specialises are segregated into divisions, stored on the database. The heads of these divisions constantly update their specific area of the database with information gained from seminars, workshops and refresher courses, attended both locally and abroad. These facilitate computer-aided research.

The firm adopts a syndicated approach to the clients' needs. Syndication is the means by which specialists in different fields bring their skills together to bear upon each client's problems. Syndication ensures that the solutions offered by the firm are indepth and comprehensive, addressing all aspects of the matters at hand.

AINA, BLANKSON & CO

133 IGBOSERE ROAD
PO BOX 71263
VICTORIA ISLAND
LAGOS

Telephone: +234 1 264 6020-3
Fax: +234 1 264 7149
E-mail: abc@ainablankson.com
Website: www.ainablankson.com

Languages
English

Other offices
Abuja

Number of lawyers 21

Contact
Folashade Adeloye

CATEGORIES OF WORK

Capital markets, mergers and acquisitions, financing and tax
Oyebimpe Oyetunde

Litigation, commercial arbitration, negotiation and mediation
Ireti B Awofeso

Oil and gas, energy and resources, transport and infrastructure, environment
Emeka Awa Ogwo

Telecommunications, technology, media and entertainment, intellectual property
Oluseye Amusa

Private legal services, corporate services, company secretarial services, small- and medium-scale enterprises
Ayodeji Oladotun-Fasanya

AYODELE, OLUGBENGA & CO

NICON HOUSE, 8TH FLOOR
5 CUSTOMS STREET
LAGOS

Telephone: +234 1 461 3049-50
Fax: +234 1 266 5590

Languages
English

Number of lawyers 10

CATEGORIES OF WORK

General civil litigation
O Onamade, O Fabilola

Admiralty
O Fabilola, O Onamade

Commercial litigation
O Onamade, O Fabilola

Debt recovery
O Fabilola, O Onamade

Arbitration
O Fabilola, A Adejuyigbe

Contract negotiations
O Fabilola, A Adejuyigbe

Loans documentation
A Adejuyigbe, O Fabilola

Real estate
O Fabilola, A Adejuyigbe

Perfection of tranfer instruments
O Fabilola, A Adejuyigbe

General documentation
O Fabilola, O Onamade

Probate practice
O Fabilola, O Onamade

Company formation
O Fabilola, O Onamade

Company secretariat practice
O Fabilola, A Adejuyigbe

DETAIL SOLICITORS

38/39 MARINA, BULL PLAZA
PO BOX 247, MARINA
LAGOS

Telephone: +234 1 461 1098
Fax: +234 1 461 2455
E-mail: info@detail-solicitors.com

Languages
English, French, Yoruba

Other offices
Port Harcourt

Number of lawyers 10
at this office 8

Contact
Ayuli Jemide

CATEGORIES OF WORK

Banking and finance
Ayuli Jemide, Bobajo Omowole

Commercial and company law
Wole Adesola, Dolapo Kukoyi

Mergers and acquisitions
Ayuli Jemide, Charles Nwachukwu

Capital markets
Ayuli Jemide, Bobajo Omowole

Real estate
Bobajo Omowole, Ayuli Jemide

Energy and infrastructure projects
Ayuli Jemide, Nneka Okani

Admiralty solicitors
Dolapo Kukoyi, Ayuli Jemide

Project finance
Ayuli Jemide, Nneka Okani

GIWA-OSAGIE & CO

OLOKE CHAMBERS
4 LALUPON CLOSE
OFF KEFFI STREET
PO BOX 51057, IKOYI
LAGOS

Telephone: +234 1 269 4725/5167
Fax: +234 1 269 3447
+234 1 270 3849
E-mail: giwa-osagie@hyperia.com
Website: www.giwa-osagie.com

Languages
English, French

Number of lawyers 10

Contact
Osayaba Giwa-Osagie

Member
Lex Africa; Networking United States of America (NUSA)

CATEGORIES OF WORK

Corporate finance
Osayaba Giwa-Osagie

Privatisation and commercialisation
Charles Babalola,
Osayaba Giwa-Osagie

Power, energy and natural resources
Osayaba Giwa-Osagie

Commercial and company law
Ronke Bolutayo, Osayaba Giwa-Osagie

Litigation and arbitration
Charles Babalola

SOLOLA & AKPANA

12A IGBODO STREET
OLD G.R.A.
PORT HARCOURT

Telephone: +234 84 231 403
Fax: +234 84 235 595
E-mail: info@sololaakpana.com
Website: www.sololaakpana.com

Languages
English, French, several Nigerian languages

Other offices
Abuja

Number of lawyers 18
at this office 16

CATEGORIES OF WORK

Commercial litigation
Tope Solola, Frank Ahon

Arbitration
Tope Solola, Frank Ahon

Oil and gas law
Tope Solola, Soalabo West

Environmental law
Iboroma Akpana, Soalabo West

Company and investment law
Iboroma Akpana, Tope Solola

Privatisation of public enterprises
Tope Solola, Iboroma Akpana

Securities and capital market issues
Tope Solola, Iboroma Akpana

International joint ventures
Iboroma Akpana, Akunna Nwagha

Banking
Iboroma Akpana, Tope Solola

Corporate finance
Iboroma Akpana, Tope Solola

Mergers and acquisitions
Iboroma Akpana, Tope Solola

Labour and industrial relations
Frank Ahon, Chimele Okezie

Telecommunications law
Iboroma Akpana,
Imomoemi Appah-Ezekiel

Property and real estate law
Iboroma Akpana, Frank Ahon

Commercial law
Tope Solola, Iboroma Akpana

Intellectual property
Tope Solola, Akunna Nwagha

Estate planning
Iboroma Akpana, Akunna Nwagha

THE FIRM

Solola & Akpana was established in 1997 by Tope Solola and Iboroma Akpana and has become one of the fastest-growing commercial law firms in Nigeria. With principal offices situated in Port Harcourt, the heartland of the country's energy belt, the firm has built a demonstrably strong presence in that region. In addition, it has fully functional offices in Abuja, the capital city, to service the regulatory and transactional needs of its clients.

The firm has a broadly based practice with a reputation for quality legal services founded on integrity, professionalism and the best traditions of the Bar. Expertise is provided firm-wide through the emphasis on a strong academic background, including Bar admissions in multiple jurisdictions, continuous learning and specialisation.

The culture of Solola & Akpana is a unique mix, meshing a profound respect for the law and the highest legal standards within a collegial atmosphere. The firm takes pride in its proven legal and business expertise, its entrepreneurial spirit, a recognised ability to find creative solutions to problems and providing clients with the highest level of legal counsel on a timely and cost-effective basis.

AREAS OF PRACTICE

The firm specialises in providing a wide range of both domestic and international commercial work to its clients, which include oil exploration, production and service companies, telecommunications operators, banks and other financial institutions, governmental agencies and private individuals. The principal areas of work are listed above with the lawyers to contact.

The firm is particularly active in the oil and gas industry where, as a result of its deep roots in the Niger Delta region and the considerable expertise acquired through previous involvement, it provides representation for most of the leading multinational and indigenous companies in that industry. The firm represents one of the major private telecommunications operators in Nigeria and has been actively involved in both the commercial and regulatory aspects of the industry.

The firm's commercial litigation and arbitration practice has grown tremendously as a result of its involvement in oil and gas/telecommunications, and is presently one of the firm's strongest practice groups.

Since 2002, the firm has been actively involved in providing legal advisory services in the privatisation of state-owned enterprises and has acted both for the National Council on Privatisation and several core investor groups. The firm is recognised for its ability to walk foreign investors through an entire transaction in a manner that ensures set objectives are met efficiently.

The firm handles real estate and general commercial work, and about 70% of its activity is of a corporate nature, including mergers and acquisitions, restructuring, corporate financing, banking and investment laws.

A brochure providing more detailed information is available on request.

Population	**4.5 million**
Number of lawyers	**5,600**
Professional title	**Advokat**
Currency	**Norwegian Krone (NOK)**

Index

Norway enjoys one of the highest living standards in the world, the result of a fortunate location adjacent to some of the world's largest offshore oil reserves. Norway's oil and gas bonanza is gently waning but is reckoned to have another 20 years to run.

Norway became a constitutional monarchy by the unusual method of having the chosen king confirmed, at his insistence, by popular referendum when union with Sweden ended in 1905. This initial democratic spirit has continued and Norwegians retain a commitment to fairness, openness and community. The Second World War experience of occupation reinforced Norwegians' strong sense of national identity, which still prevails. After the war, Norway adopted a policy of collective security and became a member of Nato in 1949.

The September 2005 general election saw three parties, Labour, the Socialist Left and the Centre party, form the 'Red-Green Coalition' to take power under Prime Minister Jens Stoltenberg. Policy for the next four years is likely to focus on social issues such as education and healthcare and, more controversially, reform of the 'clearly unsustainable' (OECD) pension system.

BILLING

Most firms charge on an hourly basis but admit to fee capping and preferred client arrangements. Prospective clients should consider using regional firms; professional standards for all work except the most complex are similar to those in Oslo and hourly rates are usually lower.

Oslo hourly rates generally fall within the following bands: partners €180 to €325; senior associates €175 to €260; and junior associates €100 to €225. Medium-sized and smaller firms tend to charge lower rates. Insolvency rates are fixed by the Probate Court.

MARKETING

After a period when marketing managers dominated, a considered, lawyer-driven approach to marketing has now been developed by the majority of firms and promotional literature and websites reflect this. Beauty parades are now more common.

IN-HOUSE LAWYERS

Banks and large companies usually have their own legal teams which then instruct law firms as necessary. The increasing number of foreign owners of Norwegian businesses is changing this trend and temporary secondments are more frequent. Litigators frequently start their careers as assistant judges and other government departments recruit law graduates who then move into the profession after three to five years.

ECONOMY

Norway combines a high level of state ownership with free-market capitalism; estimates of the State ownership of economic assets are as high as 90%. The present government is unlikely to extend the privatisation process. After a significant slowdown in 2002-03 the Norwegian economy has recovered strongly as low interest rates and productivity gains take effect. Inflation remains below target due to low import prices rather than weak domestic demand. Norway remains outside the EU but is a member of the European Economic Area (EEA) and subject to EFTA competition rules. Norway's main trading partners are within the EU; 80% of exports and 70% of imports are traded with EU members.

Norway's economy is heavily dependent on oil and gas production and prevailing market prices for petroleum products. Oil exports amount to about 50% of total export revenue. The current high price for oil is certain to flow through into massive visible trade surpluses. Norway took steps in 1990 to prevent 'Dutch disease', the profligate expenditure of the oil windfall, by creating the Government Petroleum Fund, in which central government's net cash flow from petroleum activities is invested. The GPF now stands at approximately US$200bn, which is invested in international markets. The government can use 4% of the market value of the GPF for general budgetary purposes under the 'fiscal rule' but this measure has been exceeded since 2002 and there is pressure from the OECD to get it back in line.

There were fears that the 'Red-Green Coalition' would suspend further development of Norwegian oil and gas reserves but it has been confirmed that the 19th licensing round, will go ahead with awards expected in Spring 2006. This

The largest firms

1	Thommessen Krefting Greve Lund	133
	Wikborg Rein	133
3	Schjødt AS, Advokatfirmaet	125
4	Wiersholm, Mellbye & Bech, advokatfirma AS	115
5	Ernst & Young Tax AS	107
6	Bugge, Arentz-Hansen & Rasmussen	95
	Haavind Vislie AS, Advokatfirmaet	95
8	Deloitte Advokatfirma DA	87
9	Selmer DA, Advokatfirma	86
	Simonsen Føyen Advokatfirma DA	86
11	DLA Nordic	83
12	Steenstrup Stordrange DA, Advokatfirmaet	80
13	Kluge Advokatfirma DA	77
14	Vogt & Wiig AS	70
15	PricewaterhouseCoopers DA, Advokatfirmaet	67
16	Arntzen de Besche Advokatfirma AS	63
17	Hjort DA, Advokatfirmaet	51
18	Grette DA, Advokatfirmaet	46
19	KPMG Law Advokatfirma DA	45
20	Kvale & Co Advokatfirma Ans	36
21	Brækhus Dege Advokatfirma ANS	33
22	Ræder, Advokatfirma	32
23	Bull & Co Advokatfirma AS	22
	Harris, Advokatfirmaet	22
	Torkildsen, Tennøe & Co	22

These figures represent the total number of lawyers in this country only, and have been supplied by the firms themselves. The figures should be accurate as at 1 January 2006.

phase of development, which includes sectors in the Barents Sea, will be characterised by a high level of environmental regulation and co-operation with Russia.

Norway has experienced a huge amount of M&A activity over the past year and this shows few signs of abating. With new owners seeking to rationalise businesses and international competition squeezing high-wage traditional businesses, the present wave of downsizing is also likely to continue through 2006. As the OECD has already expressed concern about state subsidies to early retirement schemes and the high numbers of Norwegians drawing disability pensions 'not directly related to measures of overall health status', unemployment is likely to be a controversial issue for the next decade or more.

LEGAL MARKET

Norway's buoyant economy has kept law firms busy with M&A work and IPOs. Legislative changes to employment and pension law and the tax code have also been demanding. Recruitment has been brisk and there is now a shortage of quality candidates. 'Passed over' senior associates have been taking advantage of the market to make considered career moves and medium and small firms have reaped the benefits.

Norway's legal market remains substantially free of formal international associations although **DLA Nordic** has broken ranks to become fully integrated with **DLA Piper Rudnick Gray Cary UK LLP**. Oslo, the Norwegian capital, is the main legal business centre. Some firms have national networks or branches in other cities. Bergen, a banking centre for the marine and offshore sectors, and Stavanger, 'the petroleum capital', have attracted some very good lawyers and offer potential clients an excellent choice and, in some instances, very competitive pricing.

By consensus, four firms rank as top tier. **Bugge, Arentz-Hansen & Rasmussen**, usually known as BAHR, is *primus inter pares*; the 34-partner firm continues to attract a substantial proportion of the large-scale instructions. **Thommessen Krefting Greve Lund** has grown to 140 fee-earners between offices in Oslo, Bergen, Brussels and London. Oslo-based **Wiersholm, Mellbye & Bech, Advokatfirma AS** remains resolutely independent of international associations while boasting several international 'best friends'. **Wikborg Rein**'s traditional shipping business has promoted an international outlook and the full-service firm now has offices in Oslo, Bergen, London, Singapore and Shanghai.

Advokatfirmaet Schjødt AS, the largest of the second-tier firms, has offices in Oslo, Bergen, Stavanger, Trondheim and Ålesund with a total of 105 fee-earners. In 2005 the firm opened a Brussels office.

Within the following group of law firms of between 70 and 90 lawyers, only **Advokatfirma Selmer DA** seems likely to join the leading four in the shorter term. With 83 fee-earners and a clear strategic plan, **Advokatfirma Selmer DA** has won new business at an impressive rate. **Advokatfirmaet Haavind Vislie AS** made several new appointments during 2005 to meet demand. **Advokatfirmaet Steenstrup Stordrange DA** added a Hammerfest office to its existing four-branch network in 2005. **DLA Nordic**'s integration with the global group provoked an amicable ten-partner exodus as the firm moved to a team-based structure. **Arntzen de Besche Advokatfirma AS**, with 65 lawyers, is known as an extremely competent and commercial firm. **Vogt & Wiig AS**, best known for shipping matters has offices in Oslo and Bergen.

Four-branch, 33-partner **Simonsen Føyen Advokatfirma DA** has comfortably weathered the departmental demerger which created **Føyen Advokatfirma** in early 2005. Both firms offer high standards in their recommended fields.

Kluge Advokatfirma DA still ranks as one of the largest firms in 'home town' Stavanger; the Oslo office houses 34 lawyers. **Kluge Advokatfirma DA** also has a small branch in Bergen. **Advokatfirmaet Hjort DA** tends to be stereotyped by rivals' well-intended accolades that it is the best litigation firm in Norway, although it has a much wider practice.

Brækhus Dege Advokatfirma ANS made several shrewd hirings in the past year which will benefit the partnership age profile. **Advokatfirmaet Grette DA** also made some excellent signings during 2005 in a difficult recruitment market. **Kvale & Co Advokatfirma Ans** is a competent and respected firm with a loyal following. **Bull & Co Advokatfirma AS** had a difficult 2005 when its 2004 expansion unwound and five partners left the firm; the remaining 11 partners deserve credit for refocusing quickly.

Advokatfirma Ræder took in four former **DLA Nordic** partners with effect from January 2006, bringing the partner complement to 22. The Norwegian branch of pan-Scandinavian practice **Advokatfirmaet Nordia DA** doubled partner numbers to 12 during 2005, mainly by recruiting former **Bull & Co Advokatfirma AS** members.

Niche firms include **Torkildsen, Tennøe & Co**, which specialises in estate and construction matters; **Aabø-Evensen & Co Advokatfirma** has shown that a quality M&A boutique can take market share; **Advokatfirmaet Storeng, Beck & Due Lund AS** has an enviable reputation in the employment field; and **Harboe & Co AS** is noted for tax advice.

BANKING AND FINANCE (INCLUDING SHIPPING FINANCE)

Bugge, Arentz-Hansen & Rasmussen's clients include Íslandsbanki and Statkraft. The firm is also advising the Norwegian Public Roads Administration on the high-profile E18 PPP project. Finn Myhre and Rolf Johan Ringdal are highly respected.

BANKING AND FINANCE (INCLUDING SHIPPING FINANCE)

BUGGE, ARENTZ-HANSEN & RASMUSSEN
SCHJØDT AS, ADVOKATFIRMAET ✪
THOMMESSEN KREFTING GREVE LUND ✪
WIERSHOLM, MELLBYE & BECH, ADVOKATFIRMA AS ✪
WIKBORG REIN ✪

Arntzen de Besche Advokatfirma AS ✪
DLA Nordic ✪
Haavind Vislie AS, Advokatfirmaet ✪
Selmer DA, Advokatfirma ✪
Simonsen Føyen Advokatfirma DA ✪
Steenstrup Stordrange DA, Advokatfirmaet ✪
Vogt & Wiig AS ✪

Brækhus Dege Advokatfirma ANS ✪
Grette DA, Advokatfirmaet ✪
Hjort DA, Advokatfirmaet ✪
Kluge Advokatfirma DA ✪

Firms are listed A-Z in tiers which are ranked in order of priority
✪ *Indicates firm displays contact details at the end of this chapter.*

Advokatfirmaet Schjødt AS's Oslo-based banking group, led by experienced Anne Gro Sundby, advises such market-leaders as Nordea Bank and Sparenbanken. The group also handles marine finance. Øystein Horneland is a first port of call for financing in the firm's Bergen office.

Thommessen Krefting Greve Lund's Hans Haugstad handled several major offshore deals including the Ocean Rig refinancing. Experienced Even Bratsberg is recommended in a well-structured team which includes capital markets star Kim Dobrowen.

At **Wiersholm, Mellbye & Bech, Advokatfirma AS** Erik Ramm and Torkel Ernø attracted some high-level corporate finance instructions. During 2005 the firm acted for most banks such as Deutsche Bank and Bank of Nova Scotia, and major corporates including Helly Hansen. Knut Bergo specialises in regulatory matters across the finance sector.

Wikborg Rein's Johan Rasmussen acted for Nordea Bank Norge in a US$210m financing deal for a rig, and for Swedish shipowner Calyon in a four-vessel refinancing. **Wikborg Rein**'s non-shipping deals included the documentation for DnB NOR Bank's NOK1.5bn loan to electricity grid owner Statnett.

Pål Sveinsson's team at **Arntzen de Besche Advokatfirma AS** finalised the November 2005 refinancing of Oslo Børs listed Petroleum Geo-Services in a deal worthUS$1bn, and advised commercial bank BNbank when it was taken over by Ìslandsbanki in a NOK3.3bn deal. Sven Iver Steen is an excellent choice for regulatory matters.

Key players at **DLA Nordic** include Erik Myhr Nilsen for shipping finance and Stein Hegdal for asset-based lending. **DLA Nordic**'s clientele includes Barclays Bank and UBS Warburg. During 2005 the firm restructured CIT Aerospace's Norwegian aircraft financing and acted for Storebrand Bank in enforcing ship mortgages in the Torkenskjold insolvency.

Advokatfirmaet Haavind Vislie AS acts for several large banks including Fortis and Svenska Handelsbanken. Peter Brechan was involved in several projects for KredittBanken after it was acquired by Ìslandsbanki. Børge Krogsrud stepped outside his usual IP specialisation to assist with setting up Norges Bank 2. Harald Arnkværn serves on the board of Nordea AB, Scandinavia's largest financial services group.

Advokatfirma Selmer DA handles some major debt capital transactions. Knut Endre and Einar Grette both bring weight to the practice group which advised DVB Bank AG on the project financing of a US$82m, eight-vessel purchase, including sale and leaseback. Annette Mellbye advised the same bank on US$20m project financing for a jack-up rig.

Simonsen Føyen Advokatfirma DA's Tor Birkeland acted for Oslo-quoted Sparebanken Midt-Norge in its NOK1bn hostile bid for Romsdals Fellesbank. Morten Winther assisted First Securities develop the first Norwegian synthetic securitisation structure, which has been used as a model for subsequent listings on the Oslo Børs.

Advokatfirmaet Steenstrup Stordrange DA's Ian Kenworthy is commended. The firm has recently advised Posten Norge in connection with the provision of banking services. The corporate finance team is working on refinancing Vetco Aibed, the ABB Oil & Gas spin-off. During 2005 **Advokatfirmaet Steenstrup Stordrange DA** recruited Morten Christiansen to develop a specialist loan documentation department.

Vogt & Wiig AS's growing share of the transport and project finance market required four lawyers during 2005. In Oslo, Christine Rødsæther is recommended. In **Vogt & Wiig AS**'s Bergen office, Børge Knustad heads a strong team which is doing well in the city's expanding banking sector. The firm's key clients include DnB and Nordea.

Brækhus Dege Advokatfirma ANS's Christen Mellbye Gjesdahl has immense experience in the banking sector and chairs the Control Committee at Fokus Bank. Pål Berg, a Supreme Court Attorney, acts for Odin Fund founder Petter Goldenheim, on his latest equity fund offering Friggfond.no AS.

Advokatfirmaet Grette DA is recommended for finance leasing; clients include Caterpillar Financial Services and Pitney Bowes Finance Norge. Jacob Sverdup Bjønness-Jacobsen heads the banking department.

Advokatfirmaet Hjort DA's Else Bugge Fougner, chair of local funding agency Kommunalbanken, and Frode Elgesem are retained by KPMG in connection with the US$200m litigation following the collapse of Finance Credit. Kristin Veierød advises the Norwegian development agency NORFUND.

Kluge Advokatfirma DA's Viggo Lange advised pisciculturist Pan Fish in complex loan restructuring which crystallised in Spring 2005.

CORPORATE AND M&A

Bugge, Arentz-Hansen & Rasmussen advised Ericsson when it acquired Axxessit in June 2005; and Compagnie Générale de Géophysique on its acquisition of 60% of Exploration Resources in August 2005. **Bugge, Arentz-Hansen & Rasmussen** also advised Morgan Stanley on the Explora Capital Fund, an open-ended investment company. Arne Tjaum is recommended for capital markets instructions and Gudmund Knudsen for corporate and M&A matters.

Advokatfirmaet Schjødt AS advised on the Oslo Børs listings of Petrojack, Exploration Resources and Aker Seafoods. The firm also handled Swedish TeliaSonera AB's high-profile acquisition of Vollvik Gruppen AS. The firm also advises several of the major Norwegian venture capital funds including Four Seasons, Northzone and Norfund. Erling Christiansen is recommended.

Thommessen Krefting Greve Lund's Hans Cappelen Arnesen, Halvor Sigurdsen and Siri Teigum acted for L-3 Communications Corp in the February 2005 acquisition of the Marine Controls division of CAE. The firm also advised Fugro on its

CORPORATE AND M&A

BUGGE, ARENTZ-HANSEN & RASMUSSEN
SCHJØDT AS, ADVOKATFIRMAET ✪
THOMMESSEN KREFTING GREVE LUND ✪
WIERSHOLM, MELLBYE & BECH, ADVOKATFIRMA AS ✪
WIKBORG REIN ✪

Aabø-Evensen & Co Advokatfirma ✪
Arntzen de Besche Advokatfirma AS ✪
DLA Nordic ✪
Haavind Vislie AS, Advokatfirmaet ✪
Kluge Advokatfirma DA ✪
Selmer DA, Advokatfirma ✪
Simonsen Føyen Advokatfirma DA ✪
Steenstrup Stordrange DA, Advokatfirmaet ✪
Vogt & Wiig AS ✪

Brækhus Dege Advokatfirma ANS ✪
Grette DA, Advokatfirmaet ✪
Harris, Advokatfirmaet ✪
Hjort DA, Advokatfirmaet ✪
Ræder, Advokatfirma ✪

Bull & Co Advokatfirma AS ✪
Kvale & Co Advokatfirma Ans ✪
Nordia DA, Advokatfirmaet
Torkildsen, Tennøe & Co

Firms are listed A-Z in tiers which are ranked in order of priority
✪ *Indicates firm displays contact details at the end of this chapter.*

August 2005 offer for Exploration Resources; and also Rondane Holding AS on the purchase of 59% of the share capital of HÅG in December 2005. The firm also reported a busy year in IPO instructions and private equity matters.

Wiersholm, Mellbye & Bech, Advokatfirma AS's Erik Thyness acted in the Optimera Gruppen sale to Saint-Gobain which closed in August 2005. The top-ranked corporate and commercial team combines legal expertise with a practical, business-based approach in domestic and cross-border matters from contractual issues to start-ups and stock exchange listings.

Wikborg Rein's Arne Didrik Kjørnæs is widely respected as a skilled and experienced corporate lawyer; he recently led on several Oslo Børs listings including Bergesen Worldwide Gas and Revus. Haakon Blaauw handled the listing and IPO of Exploration Resources. Other WR deals included Telia's acquisition of Chess and the sale of Tomra's Brazilian operations.

Recommended to expert investors, M&A boutique **Aabø-Evensen & Co Advokatfirma** delivers big-firm quality in its now established specialist niche. Lead partner Ole Aabø-Evensen brings a focused, approach to due diligence which allows the firm to handle all but the largest cases. The firm represented one of Norway's largest private companies, Umoe Industri AS in the acquisition of Bravida IKT. The firm's international clients include Danish builders' merchant, Danske Trælast.

Arntzen de Besche Advokatfirma AS's corporate group gained from a year of consolidation in the banking sector. The firm acted for SocGen on the acquisition of the equipment financing and factoring business of Elcon Finans AS and for Møre Sparebank in connection with its public offer for Romsdal Fellesbank.

Marius Lysell Andresen heads the **DLA Nordic** commercial team. Major clients include Dun & Bradstreet and Swedish publishing house Bonnier. **DLA Nordic** advised Invitrogen in its NOK2bn acquisition of Dynal Biotech and assisted LSG Sky Chefs Norge acquire SAS Braatens Catering Services, the dominant catering services provider at Oslo and Bergen airports.

Advokatfirmaet Haavind Vislie AS's Amund Fougner Bugge and Tor Wilhelm Seim recently experienced an increase in private equity fund work. The corporate team assisted major timber company Bergene Holm AS with a major acquisition during 2005 and undertook a complex due diligence when Mesta, Norway's state-owned civil engineering giant, was transferred between government departments.

Kluge Advokatfirma DA handled the sale of the Europris retail chain to Industriakapital AB of Sweden and the acquisition of two Scottish fish farming companies by Pan Fish. Stavanger-based Snorre Haukali, team leader of the corporate group, advised Hodne Holding AS on the syndication of hotels in Stavanger and Kristiansand.

Advokatfirma Selmer DA is 'a firm to watch'. In 2005 the team, led by Sverre Tysland, assisted Orkla acquire Collett Pharma AS. Are Herrem was in charge of the group which acted for CapMan AS in its first private equity acquisition in Norway, which led to the formation of Cardinal Foods AS. Thomas G Michelet was partner in charge when **Advokatfirma Selmer DA** advised A-pressen in connection with the reorganisation of two major Russian newspaper companies into a holding structure in which A-pressen took a 25% interest.

Simonsen Føyen Advokatfirma DA's Claus R Flinder, head of the firm's corporate and M&A group, provides ongoing legal advice to private equity leaders Ferd and CapMan. Jørgen Stang Heffermehl advised the principal stockholder in the Wilson Oslo Børs listing.

Advokatfirmaet Steenstrup Stordrange DA has recruited to strengthen its corporate and commercial capacity. Susanne Schneider handled Tandberg Data's acquisition of US target Inostore Corporation in February 2005.

Vogt & Wiig AS's corporate and commercial team attracts some leading national players such as start-up budget airline Norwegian and Lufttransport, the helicopter company.

Brækhus Dege Advokatfirma ANS is a good choice for businesses requiring an experienced team of supportive, hands-on, lawyers with wide-ranging commercial experience. The firm's Sandvika office is located close to Oslo's major industrial and technology parks and benefits accordingly.

Advokatfirmaet Grette DA receives regular instructions from a solid commercial clientele which includes DFDS and Ergo Group. The firm was involved with the €124m acquisition of Hexagon Automation by UK-based Segulah.

Bergen-based **Advokatfirmaet Harris**' 13 partners include five Supreme Court advocates. The competent and friendly firm handles the range of commercial work including high-value domestic and international transactional instructions.

Advokatfirmaet Hjort DA represents a large number of Norwegian and international clients. Sveinung Flaaten acts for the Volvo, Renault and Land Rover Dealerships Association and for paint distributor Fagerike Norway.

Advokatfirma Ræder acted as legal advisor to APL in connection with the offering and application for listing on Oslo Børs in March 2005. Carl Garmann Clausen heads the corporate group.

Bull & Co Advokatfirma AS's key clients include Reichhold, Otis, Simrad and Norsk Stål. The firm is noted for establishing long-term, supportive, full-service relationships with clients. Bjørn Blix is highly respected.

Kvale & Co Advokatfirma Ans offers a solid general practice commercial group and a friendly hands-on approach which SMEs appreciate.

Expanding **Advokatfirmaet Nordia DA** is gradually increasing its profile. The firm now houses previously recommended Bjørn Hanestad and Gunhild Buestad who bring their M&A skills to join an experienced team with a niche practice in retail franchising. Clients include sportswear chain Grevig and Vita AS.

Property specialist **Torkildsen, Tennøe & Co** offers solid corporate and commercial support in shareholder disputes and transactions.

DISPUTE RESOLUTION

Bugge, Arentz-Hansen & Rasmussen's litigation team includes Helge Olav Bugge who is regularly instructed by Volvo Personbiler Norge AS and Sam Harris, whose clients include Telenor.

Advokatfirmaet Haavind Vislie AS's high proportion of Supreme Court attorneys attracts substantial instructions both in number and in value. Helge Jacob Kolrud is, among other things, acting for global oil sector support company Heerema Group in a contractual dispute. **Advokatfirmaet Haavind Vislie AS** has seen an increase in competition law instructions; Ian Anders Tobiassen has appeared in several major cases before the EFTA Court.

Some two-thirds of **Advokatfirmaet Hjort DA**'s 22 partners are Supreme Court attorneys and the firm's strength in litigation is fully acknowledged throughout the legal profession. Erik Keiserud ranks at the very top of litigation; in June 2005 he appeared before a rare hearing by the Supreme Court before all 18 judges in a human rights matter. Keiserud and his colleagues, including Arne Gunnar Aas, frequently act for the defence in major fraud cases and for companies and executives under investigation by Økokrim, the Norwegian investigatory authority for

DISPUTE RESOLUTION

BUGGE, ARENTZ-HANSEN & RASMUSSEN
HAAVIND VISLIE AS, ADVOKATFIRMAET ✪
HJORT DA, ADVOKATFIRMAET ✪
STEENSTRUP STORDRANGE DA, ADVOKATFIRMAET ✪
THOMMESSEN KREFTING GREVE LUND ✪
WIERSHOLM, MELLBYE & BECH, ADVOKATFIRMA AS ✪
WIKBORG REIN ✪

Arntzen de Besche Advokatfirma AS ✪
Brækhus Dege Advokatfirma ANS ✪
DLA Nordic ✪
Grette DA, Advokatfirmaet ✪
Schjødt AS, Advokatfirmaet ✪
Vogt & Wiig AS ✪

Kluge Advokatfirma DA ✪
Kvale & Co Advokatfirma Ans ✪
Selmer DA, Advokatfirma ✪

Firms are listed A-Z in tiers which are ranked in order of priority
✪ Indicates firm displays contact details at the end of this chapter.

economic and environmental crime. Christian B Hjort defended in the largest case of fraud against the State ever to reach the Norwegian courts. Frode Elgesem is acting for the Norwegian Aviation Authority in a precedent-setting case involving the application of EEA legislation to ground-handling fees.

Advokatfirmaet Steenstrup Stordrange DA's dispute resolution practice covers commercial litigation, white-collar crime, and national, and international arbitration. The firm's four Supreme Court attorneys include Bjørn Stordrange who has been acting for Sintef Petroleum MD David Lysne in an alleged corruption investigation. Morten Steenstrup and Hege Ersdal represented ship-fitter Hotech in a major arbitration over a contractual dispute.

Thommessen Krefting Greve Lund, looking to succession and in response to demand, has strengthened the already formidable litigation group led by Carsten Riekeles. The firm represents clients before the EFTA Court as well as at all levels of Norwegian court.

Stephan Jervell heads the litigation and arbitration group at **Wiersholm, Mellbye & Bech, Advokatfirma AS**. Bettina Banoun and Trond Sanfelt successfully acted for Hydro and Hydro Produksjon in the EFTA Court over discriminatory tax rules. Erik Hirsch and Wilhelm Mathesen are representing seven of the banks in the headline claim against KPMG following the Finance Credit collapse.

Wikborg Rein's top-tier litigation group includes Per Ristvedt, who handled a major arbitration for Norwegian GISD during 2005; the case involved complex issues of bankruptcy and contract law. Dag Mjaaland is leading a three-partner team in several confidential gas sales agreement disputes which have massive implications for the gas supply industry. **Wikborg Rein** plans to publish the first Norwegian guide to ADR during 2006.

Arntzen de Besche Advokatfirma AS handled some impressive cases across the field during 2005; including significant employment cases. The reputation of Fred Arne Gade, one of Norway's top commercial litigators, is well established and Terje Granvang is also admired. Kåre Moljord was counsel for KPMG in the headline Finance Credit action. **Arntzen de Besche Advokatfirma AS**'s other clients include Zurich Insurance and Norsk Tipping.

Brækhus Dege Advokatfirma ANS's three Supreme Court attorneys include Jan Krohn who has vast experience in insurance matters both as counsel for Gjensidige Nor and in representing private clients against insurers. The busy firm has a reputation for providing young lawyers with a solid grounding in advocacy.

DLA Nordic's clients include AIG and several Lloyd's syndicates. The firm is involved in a confidential NOK100m insurer/reinsurer dispute which is expected to become public during 2006.

Runar Hansen heads the dispute resolution department. Knud Jacob Knudsen is one of Norway's younger Supreme Court attorneys and a talent to watch.

Advokatfirmaet Grette DA's IP strengths follow through into dispute resolution. Amund Brede Svendsen and Svein Ruud Johansen are leading specialist litigators with a strong following amongst Norway's patent attorneys.

Advokatfirmaet Schjødt AS's Cato Schiøtz remains a key player in a strong practice group. The firm is particularly strong in the telecoms sector.

Vogt & Wiig AS's nine Supreme Court attorneys make a strong group. Morten Lund is highly respected as a litigator and arbitrator. Frithjof Herlofsen is making a name in such matters as ship arrest. High-profile cases in 2005 included *MV Scandinavian Star* and *SS Petrolia*. Jan Vablum in **Vogt & Wiig AS**'s Bergen office is recommended. Arvid Dahm represented Alsvåg Group in Supreme Court litigation.

Kluge Advokatfirma DA's Stig Tufte-Johnsen is a respected and experienced litigator. Much of the firm's work is undertaken on behalf of public entities but advocates are more readily available for ADR and mediation instructions.

Though small, **Kvale & Co Advokatfirma Ans** is handling many of Norway's largest disputes including international arbitrations. Arne Seemann Berg, Christian Stang Våland and Anders Kvale are highly respected.

Advokatfirma Selmer DA's Are Herrem is handling an interesting case, concerning the disputed value of redeemed shares, on behalf of French company Bourbon Maritime. Svein Sulland acted for Rolls-Royce Marine in a protracted dispute with Petroleum Geo-Services which was finally settled by mediation.

EU AND COMPETITION

Bugge, Arentz-Hansen & Rasmussen's Beret Sundet is well known for her work in competition law and has represented Toyota Norge AS and Harald A Møller AS. Helge Stemshaug is 'very capable, one of the best for transactions'.

Thommessen Krefting Greve Lund's Siri Teigum, who serves on the Corporate Assembly of Norsk Hydro, is respected by both corporate and public sector clients as a leader in the competition field. Eivind J Vesterkjær is expert in public procurement regulation.

Anders Ryssdal has stepped down as head of **Wiersholm, Mellbye & Bech, Advokatfirma AS**'s EU and competition law group but remains a force to be reckoned with. Ryssdal, and current head of group Stephan L Jervell, have handled a wide variety of complex competition matters for clients such as expanding power company Sydkraft AB and oil giant Statoil.

Wikborg Rein's broad competition and EU practice continues to grow. Public procurement instructions, for which Morten Goller is recommended, are surging. Øystein Meland continues to advise Odfjell Group over cartel allegations by the European Commission and the US government. Jonas Myrhe is representing Tomra Systems in allegations of abuse of dominant position by the European Commission.

EU AND COMPETITION

BUGGE, ARENTZ-HANSEN & RASMUSSEN
THOMMESSEN KREFTING GREVE LUND ✪
WIERSHOLM, MELLBYE & BECH, ADVOKATFIRMA AS ✪
WIKBORG REIN ✪

Arntzen de Besche Advokatfirma AS ✪
Haavind Vislie AS, Advokatfirmaet ✪
Hjort DA, Advokatfirmaet ✪
Selmer DA, Advokatfirma ✪
Schjødt AS, Advokatfirmaet ✪
Steenstrup Stordrange DA, Advokatfirmaet ✪
Simonsen Føyen Advokatfirma DA ✪

Brækhus Dege Advokatfirma ANS ✪
Bull & Co Advokatfirma AS ✪
DLA Nordic ✪
Føyen Advokatfirma
Vogt & Wiig AS ✪

Firms are listed A-Z in tiers which are ranked in order of priority
✪ *Indicates firm displays contact details at the end of this chapter.*

Arntzen de Besche Advokatfirma AS's Stein Ove Solberg heads the EU and competition group. During 2005 **Arntzen de Besche Advokatfirma AS** acted for Norsk Tipping in an injunction application brought by the Norwegian Gaming Association. Thea Skaug, who has several years' experience as a competition lawyer with the State, 'although young, is one to watch'.

Advokatfirmaet Haavind Vislie AS has been busy with competition matters in court and has handled notifications under the Norwegian Competition Act as well as procurement work and a few 'dawn raids'. Bjørg Ven is head of KOFA, the Norwegian public procurement complaints board.

Advokatfirmaet Hjort DA regularly assists a number of clients, including Telenor and Posten AS, on competition law and procurement issues. Jan Peter Romsås heads the non-contentious group.

Advokatfirma Selmer DA has handled a range of competition and public procurement work from dawn raids to price-fixing allegations and 'Eurodefence' in arbitration on competition covenants. Harald Evensen, head of the group has experience at a senior level in the EFTA Surveillance Authority and the Norwegian Competition Authority. Asbjørn Berg is recommended for distribution and procurement matters.

Several of **Advokatfirmaet Schjødt AS**'s lawyers have worked with the EFTA Surveillance

Authority including former president, the venerable Knut Almestad. Trygve Olavson Laake is recommended in a group that represents Halliburton, Norwegian Airlines and Fesil.

Simonsen Føyen Advokatfirma DA's Espen Tøndel and Mona Søyland acted as legal advisers on TeliaSonera AB's acquisition of mobile service provider Chess Communication AS in a headline transaction combining competition law advice and regulatory matters which received approval from the Norwegian Competition Authority (NCA) in October 2005.

Advokatfirmaet Steenstrup Stordrange DA's Tromsø-based Trond Skogly and Alf I Kirkesæther from the Hammerfest office have co-published a book about competition law. Hildegunn Piro is a promising hire who is building in experience. **Advokatfirmaet Steenstrup Stordrange DA** has represented directory publisher Findexa twice before the High Court in competition and tariff matters.

Legalink member **Brækhus Dege Advokatfirma ANS** has recruited to strengthen competition law skills in the mid-range, while partner Dr Didier Rigault maintains his reputation as a leading practitioner in cross-border contract work.

Bull & Co Advokatfirma AS's EU and competition group, headed by Geir J Kruge, saw growth in public procurement matters and continues to handle proceedings before both Norwegian and EFTA tribunals.

DLA Nordic handled a court-ordered mediation on behalf of Norwegian transport major Linjegoods, which was accused of price-fixing; the State's claim was compromised at 60% of the original demand.

Føyen Advokatfirma's high ranking in construction and real estate flows through into a strong litigation group in the field.

Vogt & Wiig AS's maritime practice extends to connected EU and competition matters.

ELECTRICITY, NUCLEAR AND RENEWABLES

Arntzen de Besche Advokatfirma AS has expanded from its oil expertise into wider energy advice.

Advokatfirmaet Haavind Vislie AS has an extremely strong position in the energy sector, in particular hydro-electric power and grid distribution. The firm acts for many of the leading generating companies and a host of municipalities. Jørgen Monn handled the NOK1.3bn extension to Eikem Saudafaldene's hydro plant, a project involving several large construction contracts and tender procedures.

Advokatfirmaet Hjort DA acts for LVK, the Norwegian association of hydro-electricity producing municipalities, and FSN, which represents 59 electricity transmission companies. Stein Erik Stinessen and Caroline Lund are top lawyers in the field and the firm is a centre of excellence in the area. Lund has recently been advising municipalities on wind-generated electricity issues and drafted standard contracts for the sector. Cross-border electricity matters are handled by Frode Elgeshem.

Advokatfirma Selmer DA has built a strong presence in the energy sector in the liberalising market, with clients including Renewable Energy Corporation AS and Hafslund Nett AS. Jon Vinje and Harald Johannessen were instructed by Statkraft Power Invest to deal with the corporate structure for a major investment in Asia.

Simonsen Føyen Advokatfirma DA is claiming a growing share of the electricity market. Peter Aall Simonsen represents Telfo and KS Bedrift and is expert in framework electricity law and regulation.

Thommessen Krefting Greve Lund's head of the energy group Gunnar Martinsen represents the Norwegian Electricity Industry Association EBL before the Commission considering changes to the legislation on reversion of waterfall rights.

Wiersholm, Mellbye & Bech, Advokatfirma AS is seeing more work in the electricity sector as the industry reshapes. Inge Ekker Bartnes dealt with the NOK1.1m demerger of Nord Trøndelag Elektrisitet FKF's grid and the same company's acquisition of four power stations from Statkraft for NOK1.3m.

Rune Svoren heads the **Bugge, Arentz-Hansen & Rasmussen** energy and renewables team.

DLA Nordic advises several energy companies including Norsk Mlljøkraft SA and Hadeland Energi AS.

Kluge Advokatfirma DA's Marco Lilli advises Statnett SF and several of Norway's district heating companies as well as electricity supplier Lyse.

Advokatfirmaet Schjødt AS acts for energy and communications leader Lyse Energi and has been involved in advice in connection with windmill farm acquisitions.

Wikborg Rein represents Dutch interests in ongoing discussions with Statkraft and Statnett about a power cable between Norway and the Netherlands.

ELECTRICITY, NUCLEAR AND RENEWABLES

Arntzen de Besche Advokatfirma AS ✪
Haavind Vislie AS, Advokatfirmaet ✪
Hjort DA, Advokatfirmaet ✪
Selmer DA, Advokatfirma ✪
Simonsen Føyen Advokatfirma DA ✪
Thommessen Krefting Greve Lund ✪
Wiersholm, Mellbye & Bech, advokatfirma AS ✪

Bugge, Arentz-Hansen & Rasmussen
DLA Nordic ✪
Kluge Advokatfirma DA ✪
Schjødt AS, Advokatfirmaet ✪
Wikborg Rein ✪

Firms are listed A-Z in tiers which are ranked in order of priority
✪ *Indicates firm displays contact details at the end of this chapter.*

EMPLOYMENT

Arntzen de Besche Advokatfirma AS regularly advises Norway's largest companies, including Statoil and SAS Braathens, and has assisted many concerns, including DnB NOR, in complex downsizing programmes. Supreme Court advocate Lars Holo is generally regarded as Norway's finest labour law litigator.

Advokatfirmaet Haavind Vislie AS's Arvid Ødegård is an acknowledged leader in employment law. Associate Kari Gimmingsrud has handled some major downsizing assignments, gaining good client feedback. **Advokatfirmaet Haavind Vislie AS** has wide experience of employment litigation.

Wiersholm, Mellbye & Bech, Advokatfirma AS continues to support clients in need of employment support. Jan Fougner ranks as a leader in the field.

Brækhus Dege Advokatfirma ANS's employment sage Jan Dege's 2004 hiring from **Advokatfirma Selmer DA**, Eva Jarbekk, was made up to partner in January 2006. Ms Jarbekk, within her wider expertise, has developed an interest in the TMT/employment borderline and has advised in some difficult cases involving disloyal employees and access to private emails.

EMPLOYMENT

ARNTZEN DE BESCHE ADVOKATFIRMA AS ✪
HAAVIND VISLIE AS, ADVOKATFIRMAET ✪
WIERSHOLM, MELLBYE & BECH, ADVOKATFIRMA AS ✪

Brækhus Dege Advokatfirma ANS ✪
Bugge, Arentz-Hansen & Rasmussen
DLA Nordic ✪
Hjort DA, Advokatfirmaet ✪
Nordia DA, Advokatfirmaet
Schjødt AS, Advokatfirmaet ✪
Selmer DA, Advokatfirma ✪
Simonsen Føyen Advokatfirma DA ✪
Steenstrup Stordrange DA, Advokatfirmaet ✪
Storeng, Beck & Due Lund AS, Advokatfirmaet

Bull & Co Advokatfirma AS ✪
Føyen Advokatfirma
Grette DA, Advokatfirmaet ✪
Kluge Advokatfirma DA ✪
Kvale & Co Advokatfirma Ans ✪
Ræder, Advokatfirma ✪
Thommessen Krefting Greve Lund ✪
Vogt & Wiig AS ✪
Wikborg Rein ✪

Firms are listed A-Z in tiers which are ranked in order of priority
✪ *Indicates firm displays contact details at the end of this chapter.*

Bugge, Arentz-Hansen & Rasmussen offers competent support to clients in employment matters but does not offer a dedicated team.

Although the loss of previously recommended Elizabeth Ege is a blow, **DLA Nordic** is seeing more cross-border work as international business flows from the wider DLA network.

Advokatfirmaet Hjort DA's litigation expertise extends to employment; the firm also advises on downsizing and contractual matters. Clients include the Norwegian Football Trainers' Association.

Advokatfirmaet Nordia DA's Anne Aanensen heads the employment group which works closely with the commercial group and allows the firm to provide an all-round service to business clients including Reitan Servicehandel AS.

At **Advokatfirmaet Schjødt AS** Trond Stang is highly rated for employment work. The firm's Stavanger office handles good deal of work from the oil sector; clients include Schlumberger and Weatherford.

Advokatfirma Selmer DA handles instructions from employers including Compagnie de Saint-Gobain and Jøtul. Jeppe Normann has a solid reputation for restructuring work and contractual advice in the sports and entertainment sectors.

Simonsen Føyen Advokatfirma DA provides ongoing employment advice to NetCom, Hewlett-Packard Norge and PricewaterhouseCoopers.

Advokatfirmaet Steenstrup Stordrange DA's major clients include Fabricom and Polimoon AS. Hege B Ersdal assisted Priority Telecom in a mass dismissals process.

Three-partner **Advokatfirmaet Storeng, Beck & Due Lund AS**, presently focused on advice and disputes arising from corporate downsizing, provides expert specialist support in the employment field and represents both employers and employees. The firm also authors a series of well-received standard textbooks on employment law.

Bull & Co Advokatfirma AS's Kåre Bjørlo and his team are noted for contentious work across the field. While tending to act for major corporate clients, the firm does handle some cases for employees.

Føyen Advokatfirma's high-value employment work during 2005 flowed from reorganisations, downsizing and outsourcing.

Advokatfirmaet Grette DA's Johan Hveding is highly regarded in the employment field.

Kluge Advokatfirma DA provides a full-service employment practice across three centres. Recent clients include Baker Hughes Group and Universal Sodexho Norway.

Kvale & Co Advokatfirma Ans provides employment advice within its general business service remit.

Advokatfirma Ræder's hiring of employment law specialist Elizabeth Ege from **DLA Nordic** in January 2006 brings the firm into the employment rankings for the first time.

Vogt & Wiig AS's employment group handles both contentious and non-contentious matters.

Wikborg Rein's Tom Knudsen has provided ongoing support to Travel Retail Norway over recruitment and employment issues since start-up in June 2004. Other **Wikborg Rein** clients include NSB, Oracle and Sun.

INSOLVENCY AND CORPORATE RECOVERY

Ro Sommernes Advokatfirma DA continues to rank as the overall leader in the insolvency field. Knut Ro and Ståle Sommernes, both Supreme Court attorneys, and their team mix expertise and a pragmatic approach to the most difficult situations.

Advokatfirma Selmer DA's Thomas Steen Brandi handled the high-profile The 5 Percent Community bankruptcy, in which US$120m has vanished. Brandi and colleague Jon Skjørshammer handled the complex restructuring of Impact Europe Group.

Wikborg Rein's Ketil E Bøe represented the lending banks in the restructuring of Kvaerner Group. Marius M Gisvold handled the complex and long-running efforts to refinance Norsk Lotteridrift on behalf of the lending syndicate, which included DnB and Nordea. Leif Petter Madsen is trustee of the ongoing Finance Credit estate.

At **Arntzen de Besche Advokatfirma AS** Aksel Hillestad receives acclaim for restructuring work.

Brækhus Dege Advokatfirma ANS's recent instructions include retail chain Norsk Sport Invest AS, Samspar Norge, a Christian savings organisation with negligible assets and over a thousand individual creditors and the Thor Tjøheit bankruptcy, which has developed into a NOK88m VAT fraud charge. Bjørn Køhler Thommessen heads the group and is widely respected for cross-border work and asset tracing.

Bugge, Arentz-Hansen & Rasmussen's expertise lies in expert restructuring rather than routine insolvency work.

DLA Nordic's Siv Sandvik, has particular expertise in insurance insolvency. Apart from taking a high proportion of Probate Court appointments, the nine-fee-earner group is involved in a wide variety of recovery situations. **DLA Nordic** is defending Svea Finans against a complex, ten-plaintiff claim. Egil Hatling is administrator of Impact Europe AS.

Advokatfirmaet Grette DA has combined insolvency and corporate departments. The firm advised in over 100 bankruptcies and debt renegotiations during 2005, including the TTB Restaurant Investment AS insolvency.

Advokatfirmaet Haavind Vislie AS handles a steady flow of insolvency work and the firm's excellent banking contacts ensure regular high-value, restructuring instructions.

Kvale & Co Advokatfirma Ans's Tom Hugo Ottesen is an acknowledged leader in insolvency and reconstruction who acts in many of the high-profile cases.

Erling Opdal and Leif Villars-Dahl of **Advokatfirma Ræder** handle a considerable amount of insolvency work.

Thommessen Krefting Greve Lund's constructive and pragmatic Jo Rodin leads a team dedicated to solutions for businesses in financial difficulty.

Wiersholm, Mellbye & Bech, Advokatfirma AS's Leif Moltke-Hansen is frequently lawyer of choice for complex, big-number corporate restructuring; he has recently acted for a number of banks in industry sectors from real estate to shipping.

Advokatfirmaet Hjort DA has proved adept at rescue packages and restructuring.

Five-partner **Rime & Co Advokatfirma DA** has an established reputation in the insolvency field and continues to offer an expert service to private and commercial clients as well as handling Probate Court instructions.

Advokatfirmaet Schjødt AS takes a significant share of the national insolvency market and the corporate team handles some interesting restructuring assignments.

Simonsen Føyen Advokatfirma DA handles a good deal of routine insolvency work but also has the expertise and capacity to address difficult financing arrangements and business rescue work.

Advokatfirmaet Steenstrup Stordrange DA's Frode Finnøy is engaged on a complex debt-to-equity reconstruction on instructions from Geo Global Services.

INSOLVENCY AND CORPORATE RECOVERY

RO SOMMERNES ADVOKATFIRMA DA
SELMER DA, ADVOKATFIRMA ✪
WIKBORG REIN ✪

Arntzen de Besche Advokatfirma AS ✪
Brækhus Dege Advokatfirma ANS ✪
Bugge, Arentz-Hansen & Rasmussen
DLA Nordic ✪
Grette DA, Advokatfirmaet ✪
Haavind Vislie AS, Advokatfirmaet ✪
Kvale & Co Advokatfirma Ans ✪
Ræder, Advokatfirma ✪
Thommessen Krefting Greve Lund ✪
Wahlstrøhm & Thune
Wiersholm, Mellbye & Bech, advokatfirma AS ✪

Hjort DA, Advokatfirmaet ✪
Rime & Co Advokatfirma DA
Schjødt AS, Advokatfirmaet ✪
Simonsen Føyen Advokatfirma DA ✪
Steenstrup Stordrange DA, Advokatfirmaet ✪

Firms are listed A-Z in tiers which are ranked in order of priority
✪ *Indicates firm displays contact details at the end of this chapter.*

INTELLECTUAL PROPERTY

Bull & Co Advokatfirma AS's IP group continues to receive acclaim with Hans Skirstad and Bente Holmvang in particular receiving commendation. The nine-strong team's practice includes trade mark and patent expertise across most industry sectors. Clients include Merck Generics, WM Data, and SAP Norge, as well as publishing houses Glydendhal and Aschehoug. **Bull & Co Advokatfirma AS** remains active in the anti-counterfeit market and has seen a growth in IP valuation work as the M&A market has picked up. Head of team Kristine Madsen continues to impress.

At **Advokatfirmaet Grette DA** copyright expert Astri Lund and her team, which includes acclaimed Amund Brede Svendsen, has been joined by former **DLA Nordic** senior associate, IP specialist, Cecilie Haavik. **Advokatfirmaet Grette DA** is widely admired for its IP work across the field. Patent clients include AstraZeneca and Novartis; the firm's growth in the pharma sector is limited only by conflict issues. Key client for trade mark instructions is Anheuser-Busch.

Advokatfirmaet Schjødt AS's IP star Peter Nitter is particularly strong on litigation. The firm enjoys a good relationship with Bryn Aarflot, the leading patent bureau, which generates a steady flow of instructions.

Thommessen Krefting Greve Lund's Arne Ringnes is one of Norway's top five IP lawyers.

Arntzen de Besche Advokatfirma AS's offers a full-service IP group whose clients include TVNorge, Google and Warner Music. Jan Morten Evertsen is recommended.

Advokatfirmaet Haavind Vislie AS's IP team works closely with the corporate group. Partner Helge Olav Bergan has built expertise in broadcasting issues. Partner Geir Steinberg handles trade mark and patent litigation.

Advokatfirmaet Steenstrup Stordrange DA's IP team is led by Fredny Bade who has considerable experience in patent matters. The firm is representing Scanmar in a know-how case involving employee recruitment which goes to the Appeal Court in Spring 2006.

Wiersholm, Mellbye & Bech, Advokatfirma AS has lost a little ground in IP work due to lawyer losses although the recruitment of Hans Erik Johnsen, former in-house counsel for Telenor, early in 2005, is having a positive impact. Jon Gulbrandsen, head of the firm's large, full-service, 'Infomedia' group, is in the very top rank.

Brækhus Dege Advokatfirma ANS has built a niche in electronic goods and mobile telephone accessories counterfeit instructions.

Bugge, Arentz-Hansen & Rasmussen's Aase Gundersen is highly rated for her IP expertise, particularly pharma and life sciences.

DLA Nordic's reorganisation hit IP capacity more than any other practice area. But capacity is rebuilding in the broad-based IP group. Bård Racin Meltvedt is recommended.

INTELLECTUAL PROPERTY

BULL & CO ADVOKATFIRMA AS ✪
GRETTE DA, ADVOKATFIRMAET ✪
SCHJØDT AS, ADVOKATFIRMAET ✪
THOMMESSEN KREFTING GREVE LUND ✪

Arntzen de Besche Advokatfirma AS ✪
Haavind Vislie AS, Advokatfirmaet ✪
Steenstrup Stordrange DA, Advokatfirmaet ✪
Wiersholm, Mellbye & Bech, advokatfirma AS ✪

Brækhus Dege Advokatfirma ANS ✪
Bugge, Arentz-Hansen & Rasmussen
DLA Nordic ✪
Hjort DA, Advokatfirmaet ✪
Kluge Advokatfirma DA ✪
Ræder, Advokatfirma ✪
Rognlien, Djønne, Galtung, Gandarsson, Marcussen & Hoff
Selmer DA, Advokatfirma ✪
Simonsen Føyen Advokatfirma DA ✪
Stray Vyrje & Co DA Advokatfirmaet
Wikborg Rein ✪

Firms are listed A-Z in tiers which are ranked in order of priority
✪ *Indicates firm displays contact details at the end of this chapter.*

Advokatfirmaet Hjort DA handles a range of trade mark and patent issues for the business sector and, as in other practice areas, excels in contentious matters.

Kluge Advokatfirma DA advises the Central Bank of Norway on IT procurement processes, and, on a more general basis, the National Theatre.

Advokatfirma Ræder acts for clothing concept brand J Lindeberg AB's Norwegian interests and, in particular, trade mark protection and other intellectual property rights issues.

Eirik Djønne of **Rognlien, Djønne, Galtung, Gandarsson, Marcussen & Hoff** is the guru of Norwegian copyright law.

Advokatfirma Selmer DA has a broad-based IP practice linked closely to other transactional and advisory teams.

Simonsen Føyen Advokatfirma DA has a great name for TMT, and also has capability in trade mark issues.

Stray Vyrje & Co DA Advokatfirmaet's Magnus Stray Vyrje is peer nominated as an expert on IP matters.

Wikborg Rein's Gunnar Meyer heads a small but effective group which boasts particular expertise in contentious patent matters.

MARITIME AND OFFSHORE CONSTRUCTION (EXCLUDING FINANCE)

Vogt & Wiig AS recruited four shipping lawyers during 2005 although Anders Færden departed. Clients include major insurers Skuld and Britannia, as well as shipowners and charter parties such as Iver Ships and Grieg-Star Group. Morten Lund is highly regarded and popular.

MARITIME AND OFFSHORE CONSTRUCTION (Excluding finance)

VOGT & WIIG AS ✪
WIKBORG REIN ✪

Bugge, Arentz-Hansen & Rasmussen
DLA Nordic ✪
Selmer DA, Advokatfirma ✪
Steenstrup Stordrange DA, Advokatfirmaet ✪
Thommessen Krefting Greve Lund ✪
Wiersholm, Mellbye & Bech, advokatfirma AS ✪

Firms are listed A-Z in tiers which are ranked in order of priority
✪ *Indicates firm displays contact details at the end of this chapter.*

Wikborg Rein made a key signing in October 2005 when Anders Færden defected from **Vogt & Wiig AS**. **Wikborg Rein**'s senior partner Håkon Stang Lund is an internationally respected authority on shipping law, as is Trond Eilertsen. London office partner Morten Lund Mathisen has seen every type of shipping disaster from total loss to grounding and oil pollution.

Bugge, Arentz-Hansen & Rasmussen's Øystein Ore is recommended for P&I club work.

DLA Nordic's maritime practice is substantially insurance based. The firm acts for several of the leading insurers including AIG Europe and Bluewater. The firm handles worldwide oil shortage and water contamination cases for Gjensidige Forkiskring and their customer Statoil.

Advokatfirma Selmer DA's Nils Bugge acted for Kleven Flore AS in connection with the shipbuilding contracts for two parcel tankers costing US$120m.

Advokatfirmaet Steenstrup Stordrange DA assisted Clavis Impulse technology raise finance for the development of propulsion technology.

Thommessen Krefting Greve Lund brings shipping work within the offshore team. Stephen Knudtzon is a respected lawyer in the discipline.

Wiersholm, Mellbye & Bech, Advokatfirma AS's Erik Blaker appeared on the winning side in the Norsk Viking Supreme Court appeal. The firm is frequently asked to advise in connection with offshore projects as well as ships and rigs.

OIL AND GAS

Arntzen de Besche Advokatfirma AS's internationally renowned oil and gas group has been meeting a changing market. The firm continues to act for most of the major companies operating on the Norwegian Continental Shelf, both through outsourcing arrangements and under specific instructions, and continues to advise the Ministry of Petroleum & Energy. The firm has also managed to acquire several of the oil newcomers to the Norwegian sector and advised in some of the major licensings and acquisitions of 2005. Christian Michelet is outstanding in his field.

OIL AND GAS

ARNTZEN DE BESCHE ADVOKATFIRMA AS ✪
Bugge, Arentz-Hansen & Rasmussen
Kluge Advokatfirma DA ✪
Schjødt AS, Advokatfirmaet ✪
Selmer DA, Advokatfirma ✪
Simonsen Føyen Advokatfirma DA ✪
Wiersholm, Mellbye & Bech, advokatfirma AS ✪
Wikborg Rein ✪
Haavind Vislie AS, Advokatfirmaet ✪
Hjort DA, Advokatfirmaet ✪
Kvale & Co Advokatfirma Ans ✪
Steenstrup Stordrange DA, Advokatfirmaet ✪
Thommessen Krefting Greve Lund ✪

Firms are listed A-Z in tiers which are ranked in order of priority
✪ Indicates firm displays contact details at the end of this chapter.

Bugge, Arentz-Hansen & Rasmussen's Jan Einar Barbo is recommended for onshore and offshore construction contracts. The firm also handles a large proportion of the M&A work in the sector.

Kluge Advokatfirma DA's Stavanger-based Preben Falck leads the oil-biased energy group. **Kluge Advokatfirma DA** now acts for newcomers Marathon, Gaz de France and Paladin as well as long-established clients such as BP Norge and ConocoPhillips.

Advokatfirmaet Schjødt AS notes an increase in pollution and contamination-related framework issues. Non-contentious work in the field is handled by the Stavanger office. Clients include ExxonMobil, BP and Talisman Energy.

Advokatfirma Selmer DA was instructed by Faroe Petroleum plc, Serica Energy plc and other aspirant entrants to the Norwegian Continental Shelf requiring pre-qualification assistance. Mads Iversen in the Trondheim office is a very strong lawyer.

Simonsen Føyen Advokatfirma DA's esteemed Per Seime acts for many of the petroleum players including Premier Oil Norge, and Endeavour Energy Norge. Bjørn-Erik Leerberg is legal consultant to the Norwegian Petroleum Directorate.

Wiersholm, Mellbye & Bech, Advokatfirma AS handled the Awilco offshore tender offer for Petrojack and the incorporation and capitalisation of Sea Drill Limited. Partner Jarle Kvam brought his corporate expertise into the oil sector during 2005 when he handled the DONG AS acquisition of BP Norge AS's interests in the Ormen Lange field and took support services player Bjørge to the Oslo Børs.

Wikborg Rein acted for Talisman on the Petra AS purchase from PGS in Spring 2005 and provides ongoing advice to a number of companies in connection with gas purchase agreements.

Advokatfirmaet Haavind Vislie AS's construction and energy expertise has allowed it to build a presence in the oil sector as the industry has realigned.

Advokatfirmaet Hjort DA's Ulf Larsen is highly rated for oil and offshore contracts although the firm's prestigious contacts in the industry conflict out some instructions.

Kvale & Co Advokatfirma Ans's Anders Kvale is an experienced and highly respected oil and gas lawyer, as is Gunnar Stake-Larsen. The firm continues to act for Statoil.

Advokatfirmaet Steenstrup Stordrange DA's Stavanger-centred oil and gas practice, has grown over the last few years as the 'minnows' have moved into the market. The strategic move into Hammerfest places the firm well for the developing northern sectors. The firm also acts for Maritime GMC.

Thommessen Krefting Greve Lund's energy group is widely respected.

REAL ESTATE AND CONSTRUCTION

Føyen Advokatfirma's recent complex deals include the Warbo-Ava Eiendom divestment of four property companies. **Føyen Advokatfirma** advised on the new Fredrikstad stadium in east Norway and a major contract cancellation dispute in the ten-year NOK3.5bn Kaldnes project.

Advokatfirmaet Haavind Vislie AS has been involved for some 20 years in developing industry standard contracts for Norwegian and international use; partner Helge Jakob Kolrud was lead author on the firm's commentary on Norwegian contract NS 8405. Mikkel Vislie leads the commercial property team, which during 2005 handled its first PPP instruction and dealt with other diverse property-related matters.

Advokatfirma Selmer DA offers strength and depth in property; clients include Aberdeen Property Investors AS and Peab.

Thommessen Krefting Greve Lund's investment in the real estate department has seen transactional market share grow impressively. The property law team, now fields ten full-time lawyers, who worked closely with the corporate and banking groups on two property-based IPOs during 2005; Christian Müller led the projects.

Torkildsen, Tennøe & Co's Andreas Iversen heads a firm noted for expertise in real estate and construction matters and ancillary practice areas. Key clients include Aberdeen Property Investors and Eiendomsspar. Tom Torkildsen is well known and respected, as is Harald Christensen. **Torkildsen, Tennøe & Co** claims to match any other dedicated property department in capacity and expertise.

Wikborg Rein integrates real estate and corporate advice most effectively. The firm is recommended for large project and complex property company work, in which Anne Sofie Bjørkholt excels.

REAL ESTATE AND CONSTRUCTION

FØYEN ADVOKATFIRMA
HAAVIND VISLIE AS, ADVOKATFIRMAET ✪
SELMER DA, ADVOKATFIRMA ✪
THOMMESSEN KREFTING GREVE LUND ✪
TORKILDSEN, TENNØE & CO
WIKBORG REIN ✪
Arntzen de Besche Advokatfirma AS ✪
Brækhus Dege Advokatfirma ANS ✪
Bugge, Arentz-Hansen & Rasmussen
DLA Nordic ✪
Grette DA, Advokatfirmaet ✪
Hjort DA, Advokatfirmaet ✪
Kluge Advokatfirma DA ✪
Schjødt AS, Advokatfirmaet ✪
Sørlie Wilhelmsen, Advokatfirmaet
Steenstrup Stordrange DA, Advokatfirmaet ✪
Vogt & Wiig AS ✪
Bull & Co Advokatfirma AS ✪
Simonsen Føyen Advokatfirma DA ✪
Wiersholm, Mellbye & Bech, advokatfirma AS ✪

Firms are listed A-Z in tiers which are ranked in order of priority
✪ Indicates firm displays contact details at the end of this chapter.

Arntzen de Besche Advokatfirma AS's property team, headed by Hans H Kværne, handles property-related matters on behalf of clients such as Avantor.

Brækhus Dege Advokatfirma ANS's property law practice interacts with its subsidiary Brækhus Dege Eiendom AS, the commercial property management and real estate company. The firm continues its association with the National Federation of House Owners. Embret Støeng, a construction engineer as well as a lawyer, handles planning matters and construction law.

Bugge, Arentz-Hansen & Rasmussen's highly respected Stig Bech is frequently to be found where major construction projects are underway.

DLA Nordic handles high-ticket transactional work and represents major players in the construction sector including developers Skanska Norge and PEAB AS. Espen Moe assisted Veidekke when the construction giant was awarded one of Norway's first PPP contracts.

Advokatfirmaet Grette DA is best known for its superb construction team. The firm hired experienced Anne Cathrine Røed from **Advokatfirmaet Haavind Vislie AS** during 2005 to join Harald Fosse whose 'professional expertise, efficient service and availability' make him a popular choice; clients include Bravida and Olav Thon Gruppen.

Advokatfirmaet Hjort DA is recommended for contentious property, real estate and construction issues. The firm has a strong track record of determined representation in matters as diverse as noise pollution and indigenous people's property rights.

Kluge Advokatfirma DA is strong across the field and boasts planning and expropriation law expertise in addition to a reputation for litigation in the field. Clients include Linstow and Selmer Skanska AS.

Advokatfirmaet Schjødt AS has handled major transactions and development projects such as Fornebu and the new main mail-terminal for Posten Norge. Clients include NCC, Veidekke and KLP Eiendom.

Advokatfirmaet Sørlie Wilhelmsen's Gunnar Sørlie is noted for offshore matters.

Advokatfirmaet Steenstrup Stordrange DA offers comprehensive property and construction advice.

Vogt & Wiig AS's Bjørn Kise represents two of Norway's major property developers, Linstow and NSB, the Norwegian State railway company.

Bull & Co Advokatfirma AS's property team focuses on commercial property.

Simonsen Føyen Advokatfirma DA takes instructions from developers and construction companies, as well as dealing with transactions.

Wiersholm, Mellbye & Bech, Advokatfirma AS acts for several of Norway's major construction companies.

TMT

Føyen Advokatfirma's Arve Føyen leads a strong team, most of whom joined from **Simonsen Føyen Advokatfirma DA** in January 2005. **Føyen Advokatfirma** carries a heavy caseload of high-value ICT procurement work for clients including Eksportsfinans. **Føyen Advokatfirma** assisted the Norwegian Football Association through complex TV rights negotiations and is engaged by Høykim to review broadband legislation.

Simonsen Føyen Advokatfirma DA's charismatic Espen Tøndel has rapidly rebuilt the TMT group and as mentioned elsewhere, handled the headline TeliaSonera AB acquisition of Chess Communications AS which closed in November 2005.

Advokatfirmaet Steenstrup Stordrange DA has added two lawyers and continues to act for telecoms companies Teletopia and Song. The firm assisted UPC in the Smart Call AS acquisition.

Thommessen Krefting Greve Lund's Kai Thøgersen is a leader in telecoms M&A matters. Arne Ringnes heads the strong TMT group.

Arntzen de Besche Advokatfirma AS has experience in most TMT fields including computer hardware and telecoms. Clients include Cisco. The firm is also active in the software anti-piracy market.

Brækhus Dege Advokatfirma ANS's clients include Fujitsu-Siemens Computers AS. The firm is acting in a major software procurement dispute which is at present confidential. Bredo Stabell is recommended.

Bugge, Arentz-Hansen & Rasmussen's Svein Gerhard Simonnæs heads the IT group which advises major players on regulatory matters as well as handling big-ticket transactions.

DLA Nordic made an inspired hiring during 2005 when Alexander Krogstad, an English solicitor and former in-house counsel with Vit, joined the media and rights team.

Advokatfirmaet Grette DA's TMT team handles an impressive array of clients including EDB Business Partners and Song Network. Ulf Samer is highly respected and was joined in 2005 by IT and procurement specialist Erik Bollestad.

Advokatfirmaet Haavind Vislie AS has developed several standard contracts for the IT sector and handled some major procurement and outsourcing instructions; Wilfred Rohde Garder is recommended. Frode Sæter receives acclaim for his expertise.

Wiersholm, Mellbye & Bech, Advokatfirma AS's 'Telemedia' group spans IP and TMT. The firm boasts wide experience of software, hardware and telecoms issues including regulation and licensing.

Wikborg Rein's Torleif Dahl and his team advised Nordisk Mobiltelefon AS/AB in connection with the acquisition of a mobile licence in Sweden, as well as ongoing Norwegian projects.

Bull & Co Advokatfirma AS's TMT expertise is bound to the firm's strength in the IP sector and we expect to see an uplift in rating in the short-term.

Bing & Co is a niche player in the TMT sector, usually in non-contentious or research matters. Jon Bing has an international reputation.

Advokatfirmaet Hjort DA has represented Telenor for over five years in both negotiation and litigation. The team is also expert in media law such as privacy and libel; the firm regularly advises the Norwegian daily newspaper *Dagbladet*.

Kvale & Co Advokatfirma Ans is acting as advisor to the Norwegian Central Bank on IT procurement procedures.

Advokatfirma Ræder advises several TMT companies including FAST.

Advokatfirmaet Schjødt AS's Peter Nitter is a heavyweight in TMT with wide experience across the field as a litigator, arbitrator and mediator.

Advokatfirma Selmer DA's TMT clients include Birdstep Technology, which Nils Kristian Einstabland advised in connection with a partnership agreement with Nokia. Einstabland also handled Fjord Seafood Norway AS's outsourcing of IT, payroll and HR.

TMT

FØYEN ADVOKATFIRMA
SIMONSEN FØYEN ADVOKATFIRMA DA ✪
STEENSTRUP STORDRANGE DA, ADVOKATFIRMAET ✪
THOMMESSEN KREFTING GREVE LUND ✪

Arntzen de Besche Advokatfirma AS ✪
Brækhus Dege Advokatfirma ANS ✪
Bugge, Arentz-Hansen & Rasmussen
DLA Nordic ✪
Grette DA, Advokatfirmaet ✪
Haavind Vislie AS, Advokatfirmaet ✪
Wiersholm, Mellbye & Bech, advokatfirma AS ✪
Wikborg Rein ✪

Bull & Co Advokatfirma AS ✪
Bing & Co
Hjort DA, Advokatfirmaet ✪
Kvale & Co Advokatfirma Ans ✪
Ræder, Advokatfirma ✪
Schjødt AS, Advokatfirmaet ✪
Selmer DA, Advokatfirma ✪

Firms are listed A-Z in tiers which are ranked in order of priority
✪ Indicates firm displays contact details at the end of this chapter.

TAX

Ernst & Young Tax AS's Hans Georg Wille, expert in capital markets, heads a tax team which includes VAT specialist Christin Bøsterud and transfer-pricing leader Einar Brask.

Harboe & Co AS maintains its reputation as a top-tier niche tax practice. Einar Harboe is widely respected for contentious work. Former Esso tax manager Jan Samuelsen adds weight to the firm's petroleum and international tax capacity.

Advokatfirmaet PricewaterhouseCoopers DA's Morten Beck is recommended. The firm's litigation team has successfully represented tax clients as far as the Supreme Court. The firm is well placed to service international tax instructions through the international PwC network and consequently attracts such clients as ExxonMobil and Telenor. Christian Grevstad leads the petroleum tax team which advises Statoil, Talisman and DONG.

Thommessen Krefting Greve Lund's broad-based and expert tax team offers particular

TAX

ERNST & YOUNG TAX AS ✪
HARBOE & CO AS
PRICEWATERHOUSECOOPERS DA, ADVOKATFIRMAET
THOMMESSEN KREFTING GREVE LUND ✪
WIERSHOLM, MELLBYE & BECH, ADVOKATFIRMA AS ✪

Arntzen de Besche Advokatfirma AS ✪
Bugge, Arentz-Hansen & Rasmussen
DLA Nordic ✪
Deloitte Advokatfirma DA ✪
Haavind Vislie AS, Advokatfirmaet ✪
Hjort DA, Advokatfirmaet ✪
KPMG Law Advokatfirma DA
Kluge Advokatfirma DA ✪
Schjødt AS, Advokatfirmaet ✪
Selmer DA, Advokatfirma ✪
Simonsen Føyen Advokatfirma DA ✪
Steenstrup Stordrange DA, Advokatfirmaet ✪
Vogt & Wiig AS ✪
Wikborg Rein ✪

Firms are listed A-Z in tiers which are ranked in order of priority
✪ Indicates firm displays contact details at the end of this chapter.

strength in tax litigation; both Sverre Koch and Morten Fjermeros are highly recommended for complex, high-value, court work. Christian Bruusgaard is widely respected for expertise in international tax.

Wiersholm, Mellbye & Bech, Advokatfirma AS acts for Fokus Bank in a precedent-setting case involving imputation tax credit which has already succeeded before the EFTA Court and which the Norwegian State has appealed for hearing by the Supreme Court. Partner Arvid Aage Skaar won a Supreme Court appeal over depreciation allowances for Baker Hughes (UK).

Arntzen de Besche Advokatfirma AS's comprehensive tax practice, with its unique expertise in petroleum taxation, is recommended for all commercial and international tax planning and disputes, including VAT.

Bugge, Arentz-Hansen & Rasmussen's key tax group includes Frode Talmo who spent a recent two-year secondment with the Ministry of Finance drafting the new tax code.

DLA Nordic's tax group, headed by Sverre Hveding, includes transfer-pricing guru Ulf H Sørdal. **DLA Nordic** acts as tax counsel to several of Norway's medium-size accountancy firms including BDO and InterRevisjon. The firm advised start-up Silver Pensjonsforsikring on structuring and provided ongoing advice to VC fund Telenor Venture.

Deloitte Advokatfirma DA operates from seven offices across Norway and handles tax planning and international tax. Tore Paulshus heads the team, and Rolf Saastad is recommended for M&A and cross-border restructuring.

Advokatfirmaet Haavind Vislie AS's Arne Haavind is an experienced tax counsel, well known in the Supreme Court. Mikael Hellevik strengthened his planning and compliance team by recruiting Trygve H Roald from **Thommessen Krefting Greve Lund**.

Advokatfirmaet Hjort DA offers a sound all-round tax expertise with particular strength in property taxation. Harald G Nyhus, leader of the tax group, is recommended.

KPMG Law Advokatfirma DA's John Killengreen and Anders Liland, noted for transfer-pricing work, are both respected tax experts at the most complex levels.

Eirik Jensen of **Kluge Advokatfirma DA**'s Oslo office is an expert in the field of petroleum law. Jensen advises ConocoPhillips and other oil companies.

Advokatfirmaet Schjødt AS's senior associate Trond Larsen works full time on tax and receives support from M&A expert Wenche Riiser.

Advokatfirma Selmer DA's Einar Bakko is rated as an exceptional corporate tax lawyer. Per Harg specialises in petroleum tax work and notes an increase in instructions as the 'minnows' move into the mature sectors.

Simonsen Føyen Advokatfirma DA's tax group, led by Trond Erik Andersen, provides back-up to other teams and also advises some major insurance companies and public sector bodies.

Advokatfirmaet Steenstrup Stordrange DA's tax-chief Ernst Ravnaas is a well-known name in the tax world, well supported by VAT specialist Eivind Bryne.

Wikborg Rein's Haakon Blaauw and Marianne Iversen are taking a precedent tax case to the Supreme Court on behalf of Westfal-Larsen Shipping AS. Are Zachariassen handled the tax aspects of the repatriation of Eidisva Rederi's shipping business to Singapore, and head of group Arne Didrik Kjornæs restructured Bergesen Worldwide Gas before its October IPO.

ADVOKATFIRMAET HARRIS

DREGGSALMENNING 10-12
POB 4115 DREGGEN
5835 BERGEN

Telephone: +47 55 30 27 00
Fax: +47 55 30 27 01
E-mail: bpost@harris.no
Website: www.harris.no

Languages
English, Norwegian

Other offices
Førde, Nordheimsund, Sogndal

Number of lawyers 22
at this office 18

International groupings
Euroadvocaten

CATEGORIES OF WORK

Corporate and commercial
Knut R Nergaard, Peder Karlsson

Dispute resolution
Frode S Halvorsen, Christian Mathiassen

EU and competition
Paal M Bakka

Employment
Leif Jaeger, Tor Lars Onarheim

Insolvency and corporate recovery
Thomas C Jarning, Peder Karlsson

Intellectual property
Paal M Bakka, Tor Lars Onarheim

Maritime and offshore construction
Tor Lars Onarheim, Frode Risnes

Oil and gas
Tor Lars Oharheim

Real estate
Stig J Harris, Frode Risnes

TMT
Paal M Bakka

Tax
Peder Karlsson, Knut R Nergaard

THOMMESSEN KREFTING GREVE LUND

STRANDGATEN 209
PO BOX 1970 NORDNES
5817 BERGEN

Telephone: +47 55 30 61 00
Fax: +47 55 30 61 01
E-mail: firmapost@thommessen.no
Website: www.thommessen.no

Languages
English, French, German,
the Scandinavian languages

Other offices
Brussels, Hong Kong, London, Oslo, Paris,
Moscow

Number of lawyers 129
at this office 23

Contact
Svein Aage Valen (managing partner)

Member
Lex Mundi; The Scandinavian Law Alliance

CATEGORIES OF WORK

Mergers and acquisitions
Bernt Jacob Pettersen

Banking and finance
Jan J Greve

Tax
Olav Haugland

IT/media
Svein Aage Valen, Pål W Lorentzen

Maritime and transport
Hans Olav Lindal, Jan J Greve

Litigation and arbitration
Pål W Lorentzen, Svein Aage Valen

Energy and natural resources
Vidar Havsgård

Real estate
Dagfinn Heradstveit, Endre Grande

Insurance
Vidar Havsgård

Fishery and marine farming
Bernt Jacob Pettersen

VOGT & WIIG AS

FORTUNEN 1
BOKS 1213
5811 BERGEN

Telephone: +47 55 56 82 00
Fax: +47 55 56 82 01
E-mail: bergen@vogtwiig.no
Website: www.vogtwiig.no

Languages
English, French, German, the Scandinavian languages

Other offices
Oslo, Trondheim

Number of lawyers 70
at this office 20

Contacts
Børge Knustad, Arthur Duus

CATEGORIES OF WORK

Tax
Alf Nielsen, Rolf Husebø

Shipping and ship finance
Børge Knustad, Erik Solheim, Jan Vablum, Katrine Trovik, Gustav Wiig

Maritime and Admiralty
Bjarte Grønlien, Jan Vablum

Companies and corporate
Alf Nielsen, Arthur Duus, Katrine Trovik

Commercial (general)
Gustav Wiig, Erik Solheim, Jan Vablum

Construction
Per Chr Eriksen, Bjarte Grønlien

Labour
Alf Nielsen, Per Chr Eriksen

Mergers and acquisitions
Alf Nielsen, Arthur Duus

Litigation and arbitration
Per Chr Eriksen, Alf Nielsen

Oil and energy
Gustav Wiig, Børge Knustad

International contracts and joint ventures
Arthur Duus, Børge Knustad

Insolvency
Per Chr Eriksen, Egil Horstad

EU and competition
Arthur Duus, Bjarte Grønlien

Securities
Børge Knustad, Kristin Farstad

Fisheries and aquaculture
Arthur Duus, Ole Rieck

Marine insurance
Bjarte Grønlien, Jan Vablum, A Moylan

THE FIRM

Vogt & Wiig is a leading Norwegian law firm. The firm applies a high professional standard and it aims at providing efficient and result-oriented advice to its clients.

Vogt & Wiig AS was established in 2001 when the renowned law firms Vogt & Co in Oslo and Wiig & Co in Bergen merged. Later the firm established an operation in Trondheim, and now has 70 lawyers in Norway's three largest cities. The units that today comprise Vogt & Wiig have more than 100 years of experience in attending to businesses' legal needs.

AREAS OF PRACTICE

Vogt & Wiig's lawyers work in expert groups covering shipping and transport law, commercial litigation and arbitration, corporate/M&A, banking and finance, real estate, general commercial law, EU and competition law, personal injury and environmental law.

Shipping, maritime law and financing have always been a main priority for the firm's practice. Vogt & Wiig is constantly ranked as a leading shipping law firm.

The firm's clients include industrial companies, shipowners and charterers, international and domestic insurers, Norwegian and international banks and several governmental authorities. A large number of its clients are overseas companies.

The firm always ensures that the resources deployed and the fees charged are reasonable, taking into account the complexity of the matter and the amounts at stake.

Vogt & Wiig was the first Norwegian law firm to have implemented a quality assurance system that complies with the ISO standard. The firm obtained ISO 9001 certification in 1997 and upgraded to ISO 9001:2000 in 2003.

WIKBORG REIN

OLAV KYRRESGT. 11
PO BOX 1233 SENTRUM
5811 BERGEN

Telephone: +47 55 21 52 00
Fax: +47 55 21 52 01
E-mail: bergen@wr.no
Website: www.wr.no

Languages
Cantonese, English, French, German, Indonesian, Malay, Mandarin, Russian, the Scandinavian languages, Spanish

Other offices
Kobe, London, Oslo, Shanghai, Singapore

Number of lawyers 158
at this office 31

Member
Den Norske Advokatforening

CATEGORIES OF WORK

Trade and industry
Dag Steinfeld, Peter Frølich

Corporate finance
Haakon Blaauw, Jan Erik Clausen

Energy and natural resources
Per Magne Strandborg

Shipping and offshore
Øystein Meland, Jon Heimset

Banking and finance
Stein Pettersen, Christian Friis

Insolvency and restructuring
Peter Frølich, Knud Lorentzen,

Company law
Jan Erik Clausen, Grunde Bruland

Labour legislation
Per Magne Strandborg, Dag Steinfeld

Litigation and dispute resolution
Dag Steinfeld, Per Magne Strandborg

Competition law (including EU and EEA law)
Øystein Meland, Haakon Blaauw

Stock exchange and securities legislation
Knud Lorentzen, Jan Erik Clausen

Real estate
Peter Frølich, Bjørn Frode Skaar

Energy and petroleum law
Haakon Blaauw

Fisheries and fish farming law
Per Magne Strandborg, Stein Pettersen

Insurance law
Knud Lorentzen, Jon Heimset

Contract and manufacturing
Bjørn Frode Skaar, Jon Heimset

Marine law/transport/marine insurance
Jon Heimset, Øystein Meland

AABØ-EVENSEN & CO ADVOKATFIRMA

FR NANSENS PLASS 2
PO BOX 1789 VIKA
0122 OSLO

Telephone: +47 24 15 90 00
Fax: +47 24 15 90 01
E-mail: law@aaboevensen.com
Website: www.aaboevensen.com

Languages
Danish, English, Norwegian, Swedish

Contacts
Nils Olav Årseth, Ole K Aabø-Evensen

CATEGORIES OF WORK

Mergers and acquisitions	Private equity
Securities and corporations	Fishery and fish farming
Corporate finance	Property finance
Capital markets	Due diligence
Take private and MBOs	Labour and employment
Project finance	Dispute resolution

THE FIRM
Aabø-Evensen & Co was founded in 2002 by four ambitious and experienced commercial lawyers. It is a business law firm with wide knowledge and experience in business law both nationally and internationally. The firm aims to be leading with regard to expertise, personal service, client care and commitment.

The firm's business idea is to be a leading Norwegian business law firm with a focus on M&A and corporate transactions.

Aabø-Evensen & Co's mission statement is to help clients to find the best legal and commercial solutions and to secure their business transactions.

At Aabø-Evensen & Co, all partners and employees are committed to the following base values that shall pervade all their work: quality – the professional quality of the firm's work shall always be pre-eminent; engagement – to be dedicated and committed to clients' businesses; service – the firm will do its utmost to provide clients with swift and effective assistance and close follow-up and walk the extra mile for clients; and creativity – to focus on solutions instead of problems.

The firm has focus and priority on acquiring, maintaining and sharing knowledge and experience. It is currently using some of the top-line software and technology solutions that are available in the market.

Aabø-Evensen & Co is an independent law firm that is not a member of any alliance or network. However, the firm has contacts with some of the best and most well-regarded firms around the globe. Partners have extensive international experience and are proud of the firm's international approach. The firm is able to offer corporate clients the best foreign firm in each jurisdiction.

AREAS OF PRACTICE
Aabø-Evensen & Co specialises mainly in mergers and acquisitions, securities, corporate finance and private equity. The firm's partners have broad experience from some of Norway's largest transactions during the last decade.

The firm also has a strong practice in the Norwegian fishery and fishing industry.

The litigation practice has deployed the latest presentation and investigation technologies for the purpose of preparing and presenting clients' cases before the courts or arbitration tribunals. This enables the firm to take on the most complicated and challenging cases that any client wishes to pursue before a court or panel of arbitrators.

ARNTZEN DE BESCHE ADVOKATFIRMA AS

PO BOX 2734
SOLLI
0204 OSLO

Telephone: +47 23 89 40 00
Fax: +47 23 89 40 01
E-mail: mail@arntzendebesche.no
Website: www.arntzendebesche.no

Languages
English, French, German, Spanish, the Scandinavian languages

Other offices
Stavanger

Number of lawyers 63

CATEGORIES OF WORK

Litigation and arbitration
Fred Arne Gade, Terje Granvang

Oil, gas and energy
Christian Fredrik Michelet, Dag Erlend Henriksen

Banking and finance
Sven Iver Steen, Pål Sveinsson

Securities
Trond Vernegg, Ståle Gjengset

M&A
Trond Vernegg, Ståle Gjengset

Labour, employment
Lars Holo, Ingeborg Moen Borgerud

IT and telecommunications
Knut Glad

IP/media and entertainment
Jan Morten Evertsen

Insurance
Rune Njøs Jacobsen, Sven Iver Steen

Tax
Jan B Jansen, Kåre I Moljord

Company and commercial
Fred Arne Gade, Kåre I Moljord

Real estate
Hans-Henrik Kværne, Erling Høyte

Construction
Christian Fredrik Michelet

Aviation
Jan B Jansen, Ståle Gjengset

EU and competition
Stein Ove Solberg, Jan B Jansen

THE FIRM

Arntzen de Besche has 63 lawyers, including 22 partners. The firm offers legal services within the whole business area, and is a leading law firm in Norway within certain specific areas of practice (see below). A main objective of the firm is to render high-quality legal services in an efficient and problem-solving manner for its clients.

In order to meet the requirements of its clients, considerable resources are put into developing business insight and understanding. Several of the firm's partners have extensive working experience in the energy and finance sectors, as well as in the public area. The firm focuses on developing a modern, knowledge-based company in order to meet the requirements of clients for first-class legal advice and service.

The firm's lawyers have a long tradition of being the authors of legal textbooks and articles, including company and commercial law; oil, gas and energy; insurance; labour; finance; pensions, tax and telecoms. The firm has a strong international orientation, with broad experience in assisting in international transactions and foreign enterprises undertaking business activities in Norway.

The firm's visiting address in Oslo is Bygdøy allé 2, 0257 Oslo. The firm also has an office in Stavanger, the postal address for which is: PO Box 711 Sentrum, 4003 Stavanger, Norway.

AREAS OF PRACTICE

The law firm Arntzen de Besche covers all core business-related areas, and has a leading position in banking/finance/securities and M&A, oil and energy, labour law, commercial real estate, litigation, EU and competition, tax, pensions and regulatory, IT and telecoms, intellectual property rights and aviation. The firm also places emphasis on developing its already extensive litigation practice.

The experience from international projects – typically within finance, M&A and telecoms/e-business – also gives Arntzen de Besche a unique competence as partners in large transaction processes.

BRÆKHUS DEGE ADVOKATFIRMA ANS

HAAKON VII'S GT 5
PB 1369 VIKA
0114 OSLO

Telephone: +47 23 23 90 90
Fax: +47 22 83 60 60
E-mail: advokat@bd.no
Website: www.brakhusdege.no

Languages
English, French, German, Italian, the Scandinavian languages

Other offices
Angers (France), Sandvika (Norway)

Number of lawyers 33
at this office 28

CATEGORIES OF WORK

Commercial law (general)
Bredo Stabell, Stein E Hove

Tax law
Øystein A Sverre, Pål Berg

Mergers and acquisitions
Øystein A Sverre, Pål Berg

VAT law
Petter Jørgen Pettersen

Labour law
Jan Tormod Dege, Espen Rønningen

Computer, communication and information law
Dag Kristen Stadheim, Per Bjørnsen

Banking and finance
Christian Solemslie, Christen Mellbye Gjesdahl

International contracts
Didier Rigault

Competition and EU law
Didier Rigault, Bjørn Køhler Thommessen

Bankruptcy and insolvency
Bjørn Køhler Thommessen, Christian Solemslie

Litigation and negotiations
Fredrik Agerup, Per Bjørnsen

Construction, building
Embret Støeng, Stein E Hove

Real estate
Ivar A Barstad, Embret Støeng

Torts and compensation
Jan Krohn

THE FIRM

Brækhus Dege ANS is a well-established firm founded early in the previous century.

The firm specialises in national and international business law.

The partners of the firm have published several practical books for the business world related to international contract negotiations and drafting, export and taxation, IT, export and import, agents, licensing, European Community law, management of real estate and labour law.

The partners are frequently requested to speak at seminars in Norway and other countries. They are also requested to train professionals in European countries and overseas by multinational undertakings and international organisations.

AREAS OF PRACTICE

The firm's main areas of practice are: international corporate and national law; banking, securities and finance; international contracts (particularly joint venture, agency, distribution, licensing, contract manufacturing, sub-contracting, export/import), litigation and alternative dispute resolution in and outside Norway; tax and VAT law; labour law; computer, communication and information law; EU legislation; bankruptcy and insolvency; real estate and construction law; and personal injury.

The partners own three companies covering the following specialised fields: sale of real estate, management of real estates in Norway and value-added tax (Brækhus Dege Consult AS is the VAT representative in Norway of several foreign companies).

BULL & CO AS

KIRKEGT 2
PB 552 SENTRUM
0105 OSLO

Telephone: +47 23 01 01 01
Fax: +47 23 01 01 11
E-mail: bull@bullco.no
Website: www.bullco.no

Languages
English, French, German, the Scandinavian languages

Number of lawyers 31

Member
Association of European Lawyers; Legal Network International

CATEGORIES OF WORK

Mergers and acquisitions
Bjørn Blix, Bjørn Hanestad

Corporate and commercial
Bjørn Blix, Bjørn Hanestad

Dispute resolution
Hans Olav Heli

Trade marks
Bente Holmvang, Kristine M Madsen

IP and patents
Amund Grimstad, Kristine M Madsen

IT and telecoms
Amund Grimstad

Bankruptcy and insolvency
Stein Inge Spurkland

Contract
Haakon I Haraldsen

EU and competition
Geir J Kruge

Real estate
Roger Vodal, Ole B Gundem

Tax
Morten Wishman, Gunhild Buestad

Franchising
Hans E Skirstad

Labour and employment
Kåre Bjørlo, Geir J Kruge

Electricity
Gunhild Buestad

Family law, wills
Knut Bachke

THE FIRM

Established in 1864, Bull & Co is a full-service law firm comprising 31 lawyers. From its office in Oslo, Bull & Co offers domestic and foreign companies a full range of legal services. The firm is a member of two international networks – the Association of European Lawyers (AEL) and Legal Network International (LNI). These networks provide cross-border legal services for clients.

Bull & Co is strong across a broad range of practice areas and, through the single partner assigned to their business, clients can draw upon a wealth of expertise and experience across the firm. The implementation of a modern, IT-based infrastructure at Bull & Co has resulted in the more cost-efficient management of projects, bringing the firm's services to a higher level of quality.

With the commercial concerns of clients in mind, Bull & Co continually strives to develop its business insight and understanding, and provide legal advice and services that will give clients the competitive edge that they require.

AREAS OF PRACTICE

Bull & Co covers all aspects of commercial law for corporate clients, from day-to-day legal matters to transactions and restructuring. The firm offers broad expertise in commercial IP work and has a leading position in this area. Bull & Co is particularly experienced in the fields of intellectual property, corporate and commercial, labour and employment, insolvency, tax, marketing, competition and EU law, real estate and electricity law. The competence groups in each practice area secure the maintenance of the expertise. The firm's litigation practice is focused on IP, labour, insolvency, tax and real estate disputes.

The demand for legal expertise combined with commercial understanding has led to an internal structure focusing on the trends and development of the following business sectors: industry and trade, innovation, culture and media, real estate and construction.

The firm's client base includes domestic and foreign companies within these sectors.

Lawyers from Bull & Co serve as directors of several Norwegian and foreign-owned entities.

DLA NORDIC

OLAV V'S GATE 4
PO BOX 1364 VIKA
0114 OSLO

Telephone: +47 24 13 15 00
Fax: +47 24 13 15 01
E-mail: info@dlanordic.no
Website: www.dlanordic.com

Languages
English, French, German, the Scandinavian languages

Other offices
Bergen, Copenhagen, Stockholm

Number of lawyers 220
at this office 77

Contacts
Kai Gjesdal Henriksen (CEO), Espen Moe (chairman of the board)

Member
DLA Piper Group

CATEGORIES OF WORK

Corporate
Marius Lysell Andresen

Commercial
Stein Hegdal

Human resources
Per Benonisen

Litigation
Runar Hansen

TMC
Nils Arne Grønlie

IP
Bård R Meltvedt

Tax
Sverre Hveding

Legislative and regulatory
Marius Lysell Andresen

Real estate
Bjørn Slaatta

Insolvency and corporate recovery
Siv Sandvik

Public administrative law
Halfdan Mellbye

THE FIRM

DLA Nordic is the only Nordic law firm with offices in Copenhagen, Oslo, Bergen and Stockholm. The firm ranks among the leading law firms in its respective home markets in Denmark, Norway and Sweden. Each office provides a complete range of integrated legal services across borders, both in the local market and on a global basis.

DLA Nordic is part of DLA Piper Rudnick Gray Cary Group, an exclusive alliance of international full-service law firms with a shared vision. Established in 1999, the group now has members across Europe, Africa, the Middle East, Asia and the US, which deliver expert local know-how and integrated international solutions.

DLA Nordic's vision is to be the leading Nordic law firm, and is based on the observation that many clients have operations in all three countries. DLA Nordic is a modern, growing practice with a distinct client service focus; legal advice is based on a proactive approach and an understanding of the client's business. The firm offers a thorough and cost-effective mode of work, knowledge and insight into the local business environment, seamless Scandinavian and international legal services, and commercially based solutions.

Providing a full service in all major practice areas, the firm is organised into four cross-border legal departments. The departments work together, making sure that legal expertise is exchanged and shared, utilising legal resources fully and providing optimal service to the client.

Clients include public and private companies in a variety of sectors: commerce; industry; manufacturing services; property; construction; finance; IT, telecoms, media and entertainment; transport; shipping; and oil, gas and electricity. The firm also serves a large number of international clients, including large corporations, banks, investment firms and venture capital funds.

AREAS OF PRACTICE

Commercial and company law: extensive experience in company reconstruction; flotations; shareholders/partnership agreements; liquidations and incorporations; and commercial contracts.

Mergers and acquisitions: advice in each phase of mergers and acquisitions; anti-takeover strategies; public and private financing; client due diligence; and competition law.

Banking and finance: DLA Nordic regularly represents lenders, borrowers and other parties in the financial markets – both Scandinavian and international.

TMC: the firm has specialists in law related to technology, media and communications.

Tax: the firm has specialists in both national and international tax law.

Public competition and EU law: DLA Nordic assists in a wide range of questions concerning public law, some of its clients coming from within the municipal authorities.

Litigation: constitutes a central part of DLA Nordic's practice. The firm's integrated work method plays an important role, since litigation skills must often be combined with specialist knowledge.

Construction and property: DLA Nordic has an extensive construction and property law practice. Clients include several major real estate and construction companies in Scandinavia.

Employment: DLA Nordic has years of in-depth experience in labour and employment law and practical industry knowledge.

Oil and gas: specialising in international oil and gas law and electric legislation with experience of offshore construction and service contracts.

Maritime and shipping: DLA Nordic has experts assisting insurance companies and shipowners regarding claims, collisions and adjustment of averages.

Insolvency: DLA Nordic gives advice on insolvency matters to creditors, as well as companies with financial problems.

DELOITTE ADVOKATFIRMA DA

PO BOX 347 SKØYEN
0213 OSLO

Telephone: +47 23 27 96 00
Fax: +47 23 27 96 01
Website: www.deloitte-legal.no

Languages
English, the Scandinavian languages

Other offices
Bergen, Haugesund, Kristiansand, Tønsberg, Trondheim, Stavanger

Number of lawyers 20,000
national 90

Contacts
National/Oslo: Tore Paulshus (managing partner);
Bergen: Håvard Tangen;
Stavanger: Finn Eide;
Trondheim: Bernt Ollestad;
Tønsberg: Bjørn Olav Johansen;
Kristiansand: Oddleif Olsen

Member
International network of Deloitte

CATEGORIES OF WORK

Tax – international (international corporate tax, transfer pricing, expatriate (IAS))

Tax – national (corporate tax, personal tax, succession planning)

VAT, custom

Mergers and acquisitions

Due diligence, tax and legal

Transaction support

International transactions

EU/EEA and competition law

Bankruptcy and insolvency

Labour and employment law

Commercial and company law

Real estate

Intellectual property

THE FIRM

Deloitte Advokatfirma DA is one of the largest business law firms in Norway. The firm currently employs more than 90 lawyers and tax advisers nationwide. Being a full-service law firm and part of a multidisciplinary environment gives the firm the ability to profoundly understand all the aspects of its clients' business. The firm's clients understand that this multidisciplinary service not only resolves their legal problems, but gives added value to their business decisions.

Deloitte Advokatfirma DA has offices in all the major commercial centres in Norway: Oslo, Bergen, Trondheim, Stavanger, Kristiansand, Tønsberg and Haugesund.

Deloitte Advokatfirma DA is an active member of Deloitte Touche Tohmatsu, one of the world's leading multidisciplinary professional services firms delivering services to more than 150 countries. This gives Deloitte Advokatfirma DA the unique ability to deliver seamless, consistent services wherever its clients operate.

AREAS OF PRACTICE

Deloitte Advokatfirma DA provides a full service in all of the legal problems that an international business client can meet. The firm's particular specialities are: tax, VAT, mergers and acquisitions, real estate, corporate law, EU/EEA and competition law, bankruptcy and debt negotiation, restructuring, IP, forensic services, litigation and arbitration.

The firm has a large international client base, as a result of this the firm regularly assists in international transactions.

Deloitte Advokatfirma DA represents and assists both large and medium-sized companies within a variety of businesses such as e-commerce, finance, IT/hi-tech, telecom, media and entertainment, consumer, trade, industry, manufacturing, fish-farming and natural resources, services both public and institutional.

ADVOKATFIRMAET GRETTE DA

HIERONYMUS HEYERDAHLSGT 1
PO BOX 1397 VIKA
0114 OSLO

Telephone: +47 22 34 00 00
Fax: +47 22 34 00 01
E-mail: firmapost@grette.no
Website: www.grette.no

Languages
English, French, German, Italian, the Scandinavian languages

Number of lawyers 48

CATEGORIES OF WORK

Aquaculture, fish farming, fisheries
Cato Myhre

Banking, finance and insurance
Carl R Heber, Petter Albrektsen

Commercial law
Rolf Andreassen, Cato Myhre

Construction and building
Torgeir Myrstad, Harald Fosse

Corporate
J Bjønness-Jacobsen, Johan Mohn

Energy and natural resources
Nils Gulnes

EU and competition law
Amund Brede Svendsen

Food
Felix Reimers, Johan Hveding

IT, e-commerce, telecommunications
Ulf Alex Samer

IP
Amund Brede Svendsen, Astri M Lund

Industrial relations
Johan Hveding, Dag Horsberg Hansen

Life sciences
Svein R Johansen, Felix Reimers

Litigation
Peter Chr Meyer, Lars Jørstad Francke

Mergers and acquisitions
J Bjønness-Jacobsen, Dag H Hansen

Public procurement
Harald Fosse, Anne Catherine Røed

Real estate
Peter Chr Meyer, Kolbjørn Johnsen

Tax law
Tore Karlsson, Jan Ola Hedblad

Unfair competition
Astri M Lund, Cecilie Haavik

THE FIRM

Grette is a full-range commercial law firm with some important areas of specialisation. With 48 lawyers, Grette is among the larger in the medium-size bracket of Norwegian law firms.

Grette's roots date back to 1887. The firm's long traditions and a deliberate and proactive attitude, combined with a commitment to providing services of the highest quality, form the basis of the timely and forward-looking assistance that Grette offers to business and industry. Grette considers professional integrity and independence as prerequisites for providing the assistance that will best serve their clients' interests.

Grette has a reputation for maintaining a consistently high professional standard. Each lawyer specialises in a limited number of areas of the law, enabling the firm to offer clients specialist expertise in all key areas of business law. The firm's practice is international in scope. As well as advising foreign clients in Norway, Grette assists Norwegian clients abroad. Close ties with highly qualified colleagues in many countries are of great assistance in this regard.

When you approach Grette for advice, you will encounter knowledgeable and committed lawyers who will apply their best efforts in helping you to find solutions to the problems and issues that concern you. Grette aims at providing a personal service and to develop a close and trusting relationship with clients.

AREAS OF PRACTICE

Grette represents and advises clients in all areas of business law. The firm is structured around three departments: corporate, contracts and IP. In addition to being a member of one of the departments, each lawyer in Grette is also a member of two or three out of the firm's 15-20 practice area groups, some of which are permanent, and others are task forces set up for specific types of assignment. The practice areas groups include: M&A; corporate; construction; real estate; life sciences; TMT; tax (including inheritance taxation); culture, media and design; aquaculture, fish farming and fisheries; industrial relations; EU and competition; and litigation.

Mergers and acquisitions: Grette advises clients on many types of transactions, including negotiated and non-negotiated acquisitions, asset and share purchase-based transactions related to outsourcing of services, public and private sales, and management buy-outs. Grette provides all-inclusive services in this area.

Corporate law and employment/industrial relations: Grette regularly advises on shareholder agreements and restructuring of businesses and several of the firm's lawyers act as company secretary for companies.

Construction law: Grette has one of the leading practice groups in Norway in this area, and advises many of the most important contractors, both on and offshore (oil and gas). The lawyers in this practice area also represent clients in litigation in court or in arbitration.

Intellectual property: Grette's IP department is a leader in the Norwegian market and offers advice and representation in all areas from patents to copyright. Grette regularly advises Norwegian rights owners' organisations, represents clients in negotiations of both domestic and international technology transfer agreements and joint ventures, and advises on patent prosecutions. Grette's contentious IP work stretches from assisting clients in stopping counterfeited products in the Norwegian market by means of injunctions, to litigating patent infringement and validity cases before all courts, to assisting in cases concerning the statutory compensation owed to employee inventors. Grette's IP lawyers assist clients in all industries and have special competences in the fields of pharmaceuticals and biotechnology, mechanical and oil and gas industry-related inventions. Several of the lawyers in this department are actively involved in the life sciences, aquaculture and M&A practice groups.

IT and telecommunications: Grette has a well-established practice and advises some of the biggest players in the Norwegian IT service provider market in contract negotiations and corporate transactions.

ERNST & YOUNG TAX AS

OSLO ATRIUM
CHRISTIAN FREDERIKS PLASS 6
PO BOX 20
0051 OSLO

Telephone: +47 24 00 24 00
Fax: +47 24 00 29 01
E-mail: adm.tax@no.ey.com
Website: www.ey.no

Languages
English, the Scandinavian languages

Other offices
Bergen, Stavanger, Trondheim

Number of lawyers 107
at this office 59

CATEGORIES OF WORK

Corporate tax
Hans Georg Wille, Bjørgun Jønsberg

Personal tax and employment issues
Johan Killengreen, Antonio Holstad

International tax
Øyvind Hovland, Martin Wikborg

Corporate law
Hans Georg Wille, Einar Brask

Transfer pricing
Marius Leivestad, Lars Haugen

Mergers and acquisitions
Hans Georg Wille, Øyvind Hovland

VAT
Per Oskar Tobiassen, Christin Bøsterud

Accounting Act and related issues
Einar Brask, Hans Georg Wille

Customs and excise
Øystein Arff Gulseth

Tax litigation
Eivind Ludvigsen

EU/EEA Tax
Gjert Melsom

Offshore and oil/gas service industries
Øyvind Eskeland, Eivind Galta

Tax and VAT due diligence
Henning Raa, Christin Bøsterud

Hydro-electricity
Hans Georg Wille

ADVOKATFIRMAET HAAVIND VISLIE AS

BYGDØY ALLÉ 2
POSTBOX 359 SENTRUM
0101 OSLO

Telephone: +47 22 43 30 00
Fax: +47 22 43 30 01
E-mail: post@haavind.no
Website: www.haavind.no

Languages
English, French, German, Italian, the Scandinavian languages

Number of lawyers 95

Contacts
Halfdan Lowzow, Tor Wilhelm Seim, Peter L Brechan

CATEGORIES OF WORK

Natural resources
Johan Fr Remmen, Kristin Bjella

On and offshore construction
Helge J Kolrud, Olav Bergsaker

Banking and finance
Harald Arnkværn, Peter L Brechan

IT and telecommunications
Wilfred Rohde Garder, Børge Krogsrud

M&A, securities
Ketil Hardeng, Amund F Bugge

Intellectual property
Geir Steinberg, Helge Olav Bergan

Insolvency
Hans Otto Meyer

EU and competition
Ian Anders Tobiassen, Trygve Norum

Tax
Ragnar Østensen, Arne Haavind

Labour and employment
Kjell Torkildsen, Arvid R Ødegård

Real estate
Ola Brekken, Mikkel Vislie

Litigation and arbitration
Helge J Kolrud, Bjørg Ven

Public procurement
Tor Wilhelm Seim, Olav Bergsaker

Oil and gas
Ian Anders Tobiassen, Rune Omdahl

ADVOKATFIRMAET HJORT

AKERSGATEN 2
PO BOX 471
SENTRUM
0105 OSLO

Telephone: +47 22 47 18 00
Fax: +47 22 47 18 18
E-mail: advokatfirmaet@hjort.no
Website: www.hjort.no

Languages
English, French, German, Spanish, the Scandinavian languages

Number of lawyers 51

Member
Terralex; Norwegian Bar Association; ius laboris, International Employment Law, Pensions and Employee Benefits Alliance

CATEGORIES OF WORK

Banking and finance
Erik Keiserud, Else Bugge Fougner

Commercial property/real estate
Frode A Innjord, Ola Mæland

Corporate and commercial
Harald Hjort, Armund Fougner

Economic crime
Arne Gunnar Aas, Else Bugge Fougner

Energy and natural resources
Stein Erik Stinessen, Caroline Lund

EU and competition
Frode Elgesem, Jan Petter Romsaas

IT and telecommunications
Kristin Veierød, Jørn Uggerud

Insolvency
Harald G Nyhus, Terje Aakvaag

Intellectual property
Amund Fougner, Rolf Chr T Andersen

Labour and employment
Else Bugge Fougner, Christian B Hjort

Litigation and arbitration
Erik Keiserud, Frode A Innjord

Media
Frode Elgesem, Christian B Hjort

Oil and gas
Erik Keiserud, Arne Jørgensen

Public procurement
Frode A Innjord, Frode Elgesem

Stock exchange and securities
Christian B Hjort, Else Bugge Fougner

Tax
Harald G Nyhus, Caroline Lund

Transactions
Sveinung O Flaaten, Terje Aakvaag

Wills and probate
Elsbeth Bergsland, Annette J Musæus

KLUGE ADVOKATFIRMA DA

FR. NANSENS PL 7
PO BOX 1548
0117 OSLO

Telephone: +47 23 13 92 00
Fax: +47 23 13 92 01
Website: www.kluge.no

Languages
English, French, German, Italian, Nordic languages, Spanish

Other offices
Bergen, Stavanger

Number of lawyers 77
at this office 36

Contact
Viggo Lange
(viggo.lange@kluge.no)

Member
The Law Firm Network

CATEGORIES OF WORK

Corporate and contract law
Viggo Lange, Geir Even Asplin

Banking, finance, shipping and aviation
Ola Bøe, Sverre André Holm

Construction
Odd Tvedt, Pål Grønstad

Intellectual property, technology
Torstein Arendt, Ingvild Mestad

Tax
Geir Even Asplin, Per Sandvik

Aquaculture
Ola Bøe

EU, competition
Marco Lilli

Real estate, planning
Øystein Henriksen, Per Sandvik

Labour and pensions
Harald Kobbe, Marco Lilli,
Ingrid S Sørensen

Oil and gas, offshore
Pål Grønstad, Eirik Jensen

Dispute resolution
Stig Tufte-Johnsen, Wenche E Arntzen

Public procurement
Brynjulf Næss, Arne Scott

Public Law
Wenche E Arntzen, Marco Lilli

KVALE & CO ADVOKATFIRMA ANS

FRIDTJOF NANSENS PLASS 4
PO BOX 1752 VIKA
0122 OSLO

Telephone: +47 22 47 97 00
Fax: +47 22 47 97 01
E-mail: post@kvaleco.no
Website: www.kvaleco.no

Languages
English, German, the Scandinavian languages

Number of lawyers 34

CATEGORIES OF WORK

General corporate and business practice
Gunnar Stake-Larsen, Christian Mevatne

Company and commercial
Thomas S Farhang, Henrik Svane

Oil and energy
Anders Kvale, Jens Brede

Bankruptcy and insolvency
Tom Hugo Ottesen, Arne Seemann Berg

EU and competition
Per T Christoffersen, Henrik Svane

Litigation and arbitration
Anders Kvale, Jens Brede

Mergers and acquisitions
Gunnar Stake-Larsen, Thomas S Farhang

Labour law
Arne Seemann Berg, Laila Myksvoll

Contract
Jens Brede, Per T Christoffersen

Real estate
Christian Sandaker, Espen R Hamar

Employment
Arne Seemann Berg

Agency, distribution
Per T Christoffersen, Henrik Svane

Media
Arne Seemann Berg

Banking and finance
Jens Brede, Christian Stang Valand

Franchise
Per T Christoffersen, Thomas Piro

Telecommunications, media and IT
Anders Kvale, Laila Myksvoll

ADVOKATFIRMA RÆDER

VIKA ATRIUM
MUNKESDAMSVEIEN 45
PO BOX 1600 – VIKA
0119 OSLO

Telephone: +47 23 27 27 00
Fax: +47 23 27 27 01
E-mail: mail@raeder.no
Website: www.raeder.no

Languages
Scandinavian languages, English, French, German

Number of lawyers 28

Member
Eurojuris International

CATEGORIES OF WORK

Commercial property, real estate
Magnus Landmark, Karsten Torkildsen

Corporate and commercial
Carl Garmann Clausen, John Sveinsvold

EU and competition
Carl A Christiansen, Geir Kielland

Agency and distribution
Chr Aasland, Ole Per Solum

Property and construction
Carl A Christiansen, Karsten Torkildsen

Insolvency, corporate restructuring
Leif Villars-Dahl, Erling Opdal

Private clients
Odd Wisløff, Ole Per Solum

Tax
Jens I Kobro, Morten Opstad

Mergers and acquisitions
Carl Garmann Clausen, Joar Heide

Intellectual property
Leif Villars-Dahl, Carl Å Christiansen

Insurance
Joar Heide, Inge Grotli

Employment
Elizabeth Ege, Ole Per Solum

Capital markets, securities
Morten Opstad, Carl Garmann Clausen

Dispute resolution
Joar Heide, Inge Grotli

Municipal and public law
Arve Lønnum, Inge Grotli

Contracts
Carl A Christiansen, Chr Aasland

Arbitrators
Odd Wisløff, Jan Fredrik Ottesen

Trusts and estates
Finn O Eckbo, Morten Opstad

ADVOKATFIRMAET SCHJØDT AS

DRONNING MAUDS GT 11
POSTBOKS 2444 SOLLI
0201 OSLO

Telephone: +47 22 01 88 00
Fax: +47 22 83 17 12
E-mail: schjodt.osl@schjodt.no
Website: www.schjodt.no

Languages
English, French, German, Portuguese, the Scandinavian languages, Spanish

Other offices
Ålesund, Bergen, Brussels, Stavanger, Trondheim

Number of lawyers 130

Contact
Erling Ueland

Member
The Club (European); The World Law Group (Global); World Service Group (WSG); Bech-Bruun Dragsted; Setterwalls

CATEGORIES OF WORK

Capital markets
Thomas Aanmoen

Mergers and acquisitions
Erling Christiansen, Erling Ueland

Oil, gas and energy
Peter A Hiorth, Johs. Faugstad

Tax
Cecilie Amdahl, Jon Rørosgaard

Intellectual property
Peter G Nitter, Halvor Manshaus

Competition and EU
Trygve O Laake,
Jan Magne Juuhl-Langseth

Banking and finance
Anne Gro Sundby, Torbjørn Gjelsvik

Litigation and arbitration
Cato Schiøtz, Ingvald Falch

Labour and employment
Trond Stang, Hans Dale

Venture capital
Morten Foros Krohnstad,
Einar Caspersen

Construction and real estate
Nils-Henrik Pettersson, Geir Frøholm

Maritime, shipping
Per N Sperre, Øystein Horneland

International/ship finance, syndicated loans
Wilhelm Damm, Anne Gro Sundby

Aqua culture/fisheries
Per N Sperre

Telecommunications
Kaare Risung

Information technology
Ola Toftegaard-Hox

THE FIRM

Advokatfirmaet Schjødt is a leading commercial law firm in Norway. The firm, which traces its origins back to the beginning of the 20th century, has grown steadily over the years and now employs 130 lawyers. Headquartered in Oslo, it has offices in Bergen, Trondheim, Stavanger and Ålesund.

The firm has achieved its position by working hard to achieve success for its clients. Business acumen, creativity and perseverance are key elements in the value added legal services the firm provides.

A number of Advokatfirmaet Schjødt's lawyers have spent considerable time practising abroad and the firm regularly assists in international and multinational transactions.

AREAS OF PRACTICE

The firm is organised into departments covering either industries or legal practice areas, the most important of which are:

Capital markets: the firm is a leading law firm in this area in Norway. The clients range from domestic and international investment banks, merchant banks and stock brokerage firms, to listed companies and Norwegian and foreign companies seeking listing or other equity or debt financing.

Mergers and acquisitions: mergers and acquisitions represent a considerable part of the firm's transactional activities. The firm regularly assists foreign buyers in acquiring both public and privately held companies.

Oil, gas and energy: the firm has a very strong practice within the energy sector, and has worked with energy issues from the very start of the petroleum activities on the Norwegian continental shelf. It represents several international oil companies and companies in the electricity sector.

Intellectual property: the firm is at the forefront in the protection of investments in product developments and know-how. It advises on all aspects of commercialisation of intellectual property, including licensing and other intellectual property contracts.

Competition, EU and EEA law: the firm assists in all areas of competition and EU law, including litigation before the EFTA courts and notifications to competition authorities in Norway, in the EU and the EEA.

Banking and finance: the firm assists in all operative aspects of banks and financial institutions as well as organisational matters, including the legal framework for, and statutory regulations of, their establishment and activities.

Litigation: the firm has an important and highly reputable commercial litigation practice and litigates frequently before the Supreme Court. The practice spans all aspects relevant to the business community, such as corporate and securities law, contract disputes, intellectual property, media, competition, agency and distribution, employment disputes and regulatory affairs, including pollution matters.

Venture capital: the firm's venture capital group represents some of the leading investors in Norway as well as a number of exciting start-ups. It assists in setting up venture capital funds as well as their continued funding and investment activities.

Construction/real estate: the firm has one of Norway's premier construction law practices and normally represents contractors, but also receives instructions from developers. The firm advises in connection with contract negotiations and disputes, and litigates a large number of cases before arbitration courts and the ordinary courts.

Telecommunications: the firm has extensive experience in telecommunication projects, both domestic and international.

Employment: the firm assists employers in defining compensation schemes, including options, drafting and employment agreements, and advising non-competition issues and intellectual property. Schjødt's expertise includes collective agreements and individual issues such as reorganisations and termination of employees at all levels.

Media: the firm has amongst its clients a large number of prominent publishers, newspapers and other media.

ADVOKATFIRMA SELAND, BLIKOM & CO DA

KLINGENBERGGT 7 B
PO BOX 1938 VIKA
0125 OSLO

Telephone: +47 24 13 43 40
Fax: +47 24 13 43 41
E-mail: post@sbc-law.no
Website: www.sbc-law.no

Languages
English, German, Scandinavian

Number of lawyers 13

CATEGORIES OF WORK

Company law
Stein Inge Spurkland, Svein Egil Heikvam

Tax law
Einar Heiberg, Audun Gjøstein

Labour law
Per Forsberg, Stein Inge Spurkland

Contract law
Cato R Blikom, Espen Egseth

Computer law
Audun Gjøstein, Anders Utne

Stock exchange law
Johan S Seland

Real estate law
Johan S Seland, Anders Utne

Label law
Per Forsberg

Construction law
Johan S Seland

Litigation
Cato R Blikom, Einar Heiberg

Arbitration
Einar Heiberg, Cato R Blikom

Compensation law
Terje Hensrud, Gustav J Selmer

Corporate and commercial
Einar Heiberg, Audun Gjøstein

Securities law
Per Forsberg, Cato R Blikom

Intellectual property
Terje Hensrud,

Bankruptcy and insolvency
Stein Inge Spurkland

ADVOKATFIRMA SELMER DA

PO BOX 1324 VIKA
0112 OSLO

Telephone: +47 23 11 65 00
Fax: +47 23 11 65 01
E-mail: selmer@selmer.no
Website: www.selmer.no

Languages
Croatian, English, Finnish, French, German, Italian, Mandarin, Polish, Russian, Slovenian, Spanish, the Scandinavian languages

Number of lawyers 86
At this office 84

Other offices
Trondheim

Contacts
Thomas Michelet, Sverre Tysland, Britt Granseth (marketing assistant)

CATEGORIES OF WORK

Banking, finance and insurance
Einar Grette, Knut Endre

Corporate
Dag Erik Rasmussen, Sverre Tysland

EU, EEC and competition
Harald Evensen, Asbjørn Berg

Employment
Pål Kvernaas, André Istad Johansen

Energy and offshore (including shipping)
Anders Rønningen, Nils Bugge, Roy Slettvold

Family law, inheritance and probate
Anne-Blanca Dahl, Mette Stokke Nord

Insolvency and restructuring
Jon Skjørshammer, Thomas S Brandi

Legal procedure and litigation
Jon Vinje, Svein Sulland

Public sector
Knut Endre

Strategy and finance
Anders Rønningen, Halvdr Grov

Russia
Thomas Michelet, Yevgeniy Trequbenko

Real estate
Andreas Rørvik, Svein Sulland

Retail and industry
Are Herrem, Sverre Tysland

Technology, media and culture
Nils Kristian Einstabland, Jeppe Normann

Marine industries
Mads Iversen, Christian Selmer

Tax, duties and accounting
Einar Bakko, Jon Vinje

Transport and tourism
Lars Weyer-Larsen, Asbjørn Berg

SIMONSEN FØYEN ADVOKATFIRMA DA

PO BOX 6641, ST OLAVS PLASS
CJ HAMBROS PLASS 2D
0129 OSLO

Telephone: +47 21 95 55 00
Fax: +47 21 95 55 01
E-mail: post@simonsenfoyen.no
Website: www.simonsenfoyen.no

Other offices
Kristiansand, Stavanger, Tromsø

Languages
English, French, German, the Scandinavian languages

Number of lawyers 80

Contacts
Per Arne Damm (chairman), Terje Rognlien (managing director), Stein Erikstad (Kristiansand), Henning M Stephansen (Stavanger), Kenneth Mikkelsen (Tromsø)

CATEGORIES OF WORK

Technology, media and telecoms
Espen Tøndel, Tor Stokke

Construction and real estate
Peter Simonsen

Offshore construction
Per Kyllingstad, Eirik Høiby

Oil and gas
Per Seime, Bjørn-Erik Leerberg

Petroleum taxation
Jan Syversen

Fisheries and aquaculture
Bjørn Sørgård, Kenneth Mikkelsen

Intellectual property
Espen Tøndel

Shipping
Lars Musæus

Sports law
Sølve Herdal

Public and private health law
Herman Valen

Securities and stock exchange
Tor G Birkeland, Leif Tore Rønning

Banking and finance
Jørgen S Heffermehl, Jan Sindre Egseth

Mergers and acquisitions
Jørgen S Heffermehl, Claus R Flinder

Corporate and commercial
Sigurd Knudtzon, Jørgen S Heffermehl

Tax/VAT
Trond-Erik Andersen, Jan Syversen

Insolvency/restructuring
Claus R Flinder

EU/EEC law
Mona Søyland

Competition
Mona Søyland

Employment
Per Arne Damm

Litigation and dispute resolution
Morten Søvik, Knut Boye

Public acquisitions and PPP
Herman Valen

Electricity
Peter Aall Simonsen

THE FIRM

Simonsen Føyen is one of Norway's largest law firms with 80 lawyers, and a total staff of 110. The firm is leading within the fields of IT and IP, but is also highly regarded within offshore construction, shipping and ship financing, oil and gas, corporate and tax law and real estate and construction. Simonsen Føyen has a substantial international client portfolio, and can also offer global services to its clients through a network of co-operating law firms abroad.

AREAS OF PRACTICE

Simonsen Føyen has extensive expertise in construction law, property law and development, and has also been rated top in several legal publications in these fields. The firm represents some of the country's major builders, contractors and consultants and acts as legal adviser for local regional and national authorities.

Technology, media and telecoms (TMT): Simonsen Føyen has worked extensively with TMT businesses for several years participating in and advising on inter alia contract negotiations, dispute resolutions, data privacy, intellectual and IP law, competition and regulatory issues, licence applications and mergers and acquisitions. In addition, the TMT group has extensive expertise within public procurement. The practice group has prepared several 'packages' on audit procedures within the areas of data privacy, IPR, public and private procurements and competition law; which are offered to the firm's clients. Simonsen Føyen is an innovator in Norway with regard to establishing and making available to clients such standard audit procedures.

The firm's TMT practice group co-operates closely with the corporate/tax group, especially in relation to acquisitions and reorganisations.

Simonsen Føyen is considered to be the leading Norwegian firm within the fields of TMT and IP law. It has been ranked as number one in national and international rating publications. Simonsen Føyen works predominantly with international clients.

The corporate and tax group deals with all legal problems relating to trade and industry, including the establishment and operation of companies. It serves a broad range of national and international clients. The corporate and tax group is the firm's largest, and is divided into practice the areas: corporate and corporate finance, banking and finance, tax and VAT, insolvency and restructuring, securities law, M&A, EU/EEC and competition, litigation, employment, trade and industry and company law. The group has been advising on large national and international transactions, both for acquisitions in Norway and for Norwegian acquisitions abroad; it has been instrumental in establishing national insurance companies and mergers among Norwegian banks, as well as innovative securities schemes.

Petroleum/energy and shipping/ship financing: Simonsen Føyen's highly-regarded shipping practice was founded in 1948. The firm has since established strong capabilities in petroleum and energy law, as well as in defence/aerospace and aquaculture/fishery matters. Petroleum/energy clients include national governments and UN agencies, major independent oil/gas companies, petroleum industry suppliers, owners/operators of drilling rigs/ships and hydroelectric facilities. The firm has in-depth knowledge of the industries, with lawyers who have held senior positions in the Norwegian government and in oil majors. The firm maintains its strong position in offshore construction and services, with six to seven lawyers acting regularly on contract negotiation/drafting/administration and dispute resolution including litigation/arbitration of major claims. Simonsen Føyen continues to be acknowledged as a leading firm in the sector of shipping/ship financing, advising foreign and Norwegian clients on maritime law, financing/building/sale and purchase of ships, corporate law, taxation, marine insurance claims and disputes. The firm enjoys a particularly strong reputation in ship financing, as legal adviser and provider of documentation for the lender banks.

ADVOKATFIRMAET STEENSTRUP STORDRANGE DA

STORTINGSG 22
PO BOX 1829 VIKA
0123 OSLO

Telephone: +47 22 81 45 00
Fax: +47 22 81 45 01
E-mail: lawyers@steenstrup.no
Website: www.steenstrup.no

Languages
English, French, German, Russian, Spanish, the Scandinavian languages

Other offices
Hammerfest, Trondheim, Tromsø, Stavanger

Number of lawyers 81
at this office 60

Member
Interlex Group

CATEGORIES OF WORK

Labour and employment
Thomas Meinich, Magne Mjaaland

Banking, finance and financing
Ian Kenworthy, Ingar Solheim

Stock exchange and securities
Robert Sveen, Susanne Schneider

Tax
Ernst Ravnaas, Ove-Marthin Granlund

VAT
Eivind Bryne, Knut Morten Carlsen

Energy, petroleum and offshore
Ulf-Einar Staalesen, Søren Lous

EU law, competition and marketing
Bjørn Stordrange, Trond Skogly

Company law
Karl-Anders Grønland, Odd Erik Johansen

Intellectual property
Fredny Bade, Søren Lous

Bankruptcy and insolvency
Odd Magne Gjerde, Frode Finnøy

Real property
Dagfinn Strønstad, Ola Strømsmoen

IT and telecommunications
Morten Steenstrup, Jonas Madsø

Litigation and arbitration
Ian Kenworthy, Hege Ersdal

THE FIRM

Advokatfirmaet Steenstrup Stordrange DA is a modern, knowledge-based, full-service business law firm founded in 1989. The firm has concentrated on being able to offer competent legal advice nationally and has four offices throughout Norway. It considers this nationwide competence to be of great advantage to both its domestic and International clients. Of equal importance is the firm's unrivalled commitment to quick, effective, personal and professional assistance in all legal issues. The firm is a member of the Interlex Group, a worldwide association of leading law firms serving international clients.

AREAS OF PRACTICE

The firm's practice covers a full range of commercial work for both domestic and foreign clients. The firm offers first-rate legal, strategic and financial advice covering the full range of commercial work for both domestic and foreign clients. The lawyers act as advisers in all stages of commercial transactions, as well as representing clients in litigation and arbitration. In order to meet a client's legal requirements in any area, the firm has a staff of lawyers with expertise and experience within all legal jurisdictions.

Mergers and acquisitions: the firm's transactions in this area include private acquisition and cross-border takeovers.

Corporate law: Steenstrup Stordrange advises on all aspects of general corporate law, including the drafting of contracts according to Norwegian law.

Stock exchange regulations: the firm handles matters on behalf of investment banks and for listed companies via the stock market and the Oslo Stock Exchange.

Telecommunications and computer law: the firm is very active in this sector. Steenstrup Stordrange advises on contracts, marketing law, intellectual property and employment matters, including CRM-related questions. During the last year the firm has been litigating major cases of principal interest.

Litigation and arbitration: Steenstrup Stordrange deals with commercial litigation, national and international arbitration, and regularly handles cases before the City Courts, the Court of Appeal and the Supreme Court in Norway. The firm also represents international clients in criminal cases, specialising in white-collar crime.

Labour law: the firm handles all matters relating to Norwegian employment law.

The firm also has an extensive practice in the areas of EU law and competition law, both on the national and the EU/EFTA levels.

Strategic counselling: the firm has its own department for strategic counselling, offering a more holistic perspective.

THOMMESSEN KREFTING GREVE LUND

HAAKON VII'S GATE 10
PO BOX 1484 VIKA
0116 OSLO

Telephone: +47 23 11 11 11
Fax: +47 23 11 10 10
E-mail: firmapost@thommessen.no
Website: www.thommessen.no

Languages
Dutch, English, French, German, the Scandinavian languages

Other offices
Bergen, Brussels, Hong Kong, London, Paris, Moscow

Number of lawyers 129
at this office 105

Contact
Kai Thøgersen (managing partner)

Member
Lex Mundi; The Scandinavian Law Alliance

CATEGORIES OF WORK

Banking and finance
Even Bratsberg, Hans Haugstad

Company and commercial
Anders Arnkværn, Baard Bale

Electricity and natural resources
Gunnar Martinsen, Kjersti Ringdal

Employment
Kristine Schei

EU and competition
Siri Teigum, Eivind Vesterkjær

Insolvency
Jo Rodin, Reidar Myhre

Insurance
Berit Stokke

Intellectual property
Kristine Schei, Arne Ringnes

Litigation and arbitration
Pål Lieungh, Erik Samuelsen

Maritime and transport
Olav Vikøren, Stephen Knudtzon

Mergers and acquisitions
Hans Cappelen Arnesen, Kim Dobrowen, Kai Thøgersen

Oil and energy
Gunnar Martinsen, Rune Solberg

Real estate and construction
Christian Müller, Gerhard Holm, Anders Pind

Tax
Morten Fjermeros, Henning Naas

TMT
Arne Ringnes, Kai Thøgersen

THE FIRM

Thommessen Krefting Greve Lund AS is one of the largest law firms in Norway. The firm currently has approximately 220 total staff in Norway.

Of particular importance to the firm is the legal assistance of both Norwegian clients with foreign interests and foreign clients with interests in Norway. It has therefore entered into a corporate agreement with two of the biggest law firms in Denmark and Sweden, respectively Advokatfirmaet Kromann Reumert and Advokatfirman Vinge. The three firms together represent more than 350 lawyers and have foreign branch offices in London, Brussels, Paris, Moscow and Hong Kong. Thommessen Krefting Greve Lund is also a member of Lex Mundi, an international network facilitating co-operation between 158 law firms in 90 countries, which enables it to satisfy its clients' needs for legal services beyond Norway's borders.

The firm actively uses up-to-date information technology, both in daily work throughout the firm, and (subject to restraints arising due to the need for confidentiality) as a means of communication between its offices and with clients.

AREAS OF PRACTICE

The firm concentrates on the business community's legal problems, comprising in particular taxes, corporate law including company takeovers, mergers and split-ups, engineering contracts, contract law, property law, competition law, IT, telecommunications, media, intellectual property law, environmental law, labour law, banking and financing, stock exchange introduction, issues and securities trading, energy, oil and shipping, European Community law, bankruptcy and debt negotiation, litigation and arbitration.

In view of the increasing internationalisation of the business community, it is the objective of Thommessen Krefting Greve Lund to improve still further the possibilities of safeguarding the interests of its clients outside Norway.

One of the firm's partners is qualified both as a Norwegian advokat, and as a solicitor of the Supreme Court of England and Wales.

VOGT & WIIG AS

ROALD AMUNDSENS GATE 6
PO BOX 1503 VIKA
0117 OSLO

Telephone: +47 22 31 32 00
Fax: +47 22 31 32 01
E-mail: oslo@vogtwiig.no
Website: www.vogtwiig.no

Languages
English, German, the Scandinavian languages

Other offices
Bergen, Trondheim

Number of lawyers 70
at this office 35

CATEGORIES OF WORK

Maritime and transportation
Ingar Fuglevåg, Frithjof Herlofsen

Ship finance
Christine Rodsaeter, Knut Erik Westad

Marine insurance
Morten Lund, Frithjof Herlofsen

Real estate
Bjørn H Kise, Per Erik Bergsjø

Tort, personal injury and insurance
Per Erik Bergsjø, Stein Chr Hexeberg

Litigation
Morten Lund, Per Erik Bergsjø

Tax
Arvid Dahm

Aviation
Ingar Fuglevåg, Bjørn H Kise

Securities
Morten Lund,
Christian Ditlev-Simonsen

Mergers and acquisitions
Tor Kielland,
Christian Ditlev-Simonsen

E-commerce
Joakim Marstrander

Environmental law
Morten Lund

General and corporate business
Bjørn H Kise, Knut Erik Westad

Labour
Tor Kielland, Knut Erik Westad

THE FIRM

Vogt & Wiig is a leading Norwegian law firm. The firm applies a high professional standard and it aims at providing efficient and result-oriented advice to its clients.

Vogt & Wiig AS was established in 2001 when the renowned law firms Vogt & Co in Oslo and Wiig & Co in Bergen merged. Later the firm established an operation in Trondheim, and now has 70 lawyers in Norway's three largest cities. The units that today comprise Vogt & Wiig have more than 100 years of experience in attending to businesses' legal needs.

AREAS OF PRACTICE

Vogt & Wiig's lawyers work in expert groups covering shipping and transport law, commercial litigation and arbitration, corporate/M&A, bank and finance, real estate, general commercial law, EU and competition law, personal injury and environmental law.

Shipping, maritime law and financing have always been a main priority for the firm's practice. Vogt & Wiig is constantly ranked as a leading shipping law firm.

The firm's clients include industrial companies, shipowners and charterers, international and domestic insurers, Norwegian and international banks and several governmental authorities. A large number of its clients are overseas companies.

The firm always ensures that the resources deployed and the fees charged are reasonable, taking into account the complexity of the matter and the amounts at stake.

Vogt & Wiig was the first Norwegian law firm to have implemented a quality assurance system that complies with the ISO standard. The firm obtained ISO 9001 certification in 1997 and upgraded to ISO 9001:2000 in 2003.

WIERSHOLM, MELLBYE & BECH, ADVOKATFIRMA AS

RUSELØKKVEIEN 26
PO BOX 1400 VIKA
0115 OSLO

Telephone: +47 21 02 10 00
Fax: +47 21 02 10 01
E-mail: mail@wiersholm.no
Website: www.wiersholm.no

Languages
English, French, German, Spanish, Russian
the Scandinavian languages

Number of lawyers 115

Contact
Arne Engesæth (chairman)

CATEGORIES OF WORK

General and corporate
Erik Thyness, Erling Lind

Corporate finance/banking
Leif Moltke-Hansen, Erik Ramm

Mergers and acquisitions
Erik Thyness, Andreas Mellbye

Litigation
Stephen L Jervell, Jon Tenden

Employment and pensions
Jan Fougner, Eli Aasheim

Tax
Terje Hoffmann, Trond Sanfelt

Intellectual property, copyright, media
John S Gulbrandsen, Kyrre Eggen

Insurance law/maritime insurance
Erik Blaker, Trygve Honne

Securities and stock exchange
Knut Bergo, Tone Østensen

EU and competition law
Wilhelm Matheson, Stephan L Jervell

TMT
John S Gulbrandsen, Kyrre Eggen

Shipping and transportation
Nic Brun-Lie, Erik Blaker

Oil and gas
Inge Ekker Bartnes, Per Raustøl

Electricity
Inge Ekker Bartnes, Jarle Kvam

Property and construction
Helge Morten Svarva, Tom Rune Lian

THE FIRM

Wiersholm, Mellbye & Bech, advokatfirma AS is one of the leading law firms in Norway, founded in 1875. The firm presently has 115 lawyers, comprising 37 partners and 78 associates.

From the office site in Oslo, it serves a national and international client base, and frequently works with lawyers and clients overseas and within Europe.

The firm specialises in commercial practice. By combining its specialist areas, the firm offers its clients a full range of quality services on commercial and corporate transactions.

The firm has several foreign lawyers trained in the US, UK and EU.

AREAS OF PRACTICE

Company and commercial law, including merger and acquisition; takeovers, disposals, equity offerings, flotations, corporate restructuring and management buy-outs; banking law, comprising of advising lenders and borrowers in relation to financial transactions, inter alia asset finance, project finance, lease finance and property finance, and international debt issues.

Additionally, the firm also has a number of specialised practice groups which brings together the skills, expertise and experience of the firm's lawyers. This enables Wiersholm, Mellbye & Bech to offer its clients quality advice in matters such as commercial property, construction, EC and competition law, energy law, corporate, taxation, intellectual property, copyright, media, information technology and telecoms, maritime and transportation law, insurance law, labour law as well as security and stock exchange.

Additionally, Wiersholm, Mellbye & Bech handles litigation and disputes in a wide range of commercial areas.

WIKBORG REIN

KRONPRINSESSE MÄRTHAS PLASS 1, PO BOX 1513 VIKA 0117 OSLO

Telephone: +47 22 82 75 00
Fax: +47 22 82 75 01
E-mail: oslo@wr.no
Website: www.wr.no

Languages
Cantonese, English, French, German, Indonesian, Malay, Mandarin, Russian, the Scandinavian languages, Spanish

Other offices
Bergen, Kobe, London, Shanghai, Singapore

Number of lawyers 158
at this office 109

Member
Den Norske Advokatforening

CATEGORIES OF WORK

Corporate
Susanne Munch Thore, Ketil E Bøe

Trade and industry
Anne Sofie Bjørkholt, Jan L Backer

Shipping/offshore
Trond Eilertsen, Haakon Stang Lund

Energy/natural resources
Jarle Erik Sandvik,
Lars Olav Askheim

Technology, media and telecoms
Torleif P Dahl

Labour legislation
Tom B Knudsen, Jan L Backer

Intellectual property law
Gunnar Meyer, Torleif P Dahl

Competition law (including EU and EEA law)
Morten Goller, Jonas W Myhre

Environmental law
Haakon Blaauw, Trond Eilertsen

Accounting/tax/duties
Marianne Iversen, Are Zachariassen

Company law
Arne Didrik Kjørnæs,
Susanne Munch Thore

Insolvency and restructuring
Leif Petter Madsen, Marius M Gisvold

Banking and finance
Bernhard Haukali, Johan Rasmussen

Real estate
Anne Sofie Bjørkholt,
Leif Petter Madsen

Litigation and dispute resolution
Per Magne Ristvedt

THE FIRM

Wikborg Rein is one of Norway's leading law firms with offices in Oslo, Bergen, London, Singapore, Shanghai and Kobe. The firm's long-standing presence overseas provides extensive international experience and expertise.

A thorough understanding of clients' business, combined with the highest professional standards, ensures that each client recieves the best possible legal assistance.

The firm's traditions complement its modern approach to the management of its resources and the provision of advice and other legal services. (As a leading firm in the area of information technology and management systems, the firm provides services of the highest quality in a cost-efficient manner).

Having a thorough understanding of the client's business, combined with the highest professional standards, the firm ensures that each client receives the best possible legal assistance.

AREAS OF PRACTICE

The firm's practice is broadly based, serving both international clients in Norway, and Norwegian clients domestically and abroad. Wikborg Rein's internal structure is organised for the specific purpose of serving clients in the following areas of business: trade and industry; banking and finance; energy and natural resources; technology, media and telecommunications; shipping, offshore and transport; corporate; real estate; litigation and dispute resolution.

The firm has extensive experience of the application of European law and advises on all aspects relevant to Norway's position as a member of the EEA but not the EU.

Within Norway the firm has pioneered links between business, academic research and the development of relevant legislation. This has enabled it to assist clients in negotiating with and lobbying government authorities and in developing legal practices in rapidly expanding areas of business.

KLUGE ADVOKATFIRMA DA

MASKINVN 32, FORUS
PO BOX 277
4066 STAVANGER

Telephone: +47 51 95 83 00
Fax: +47 51 95 83 01
Website: www.kluge.no

Languages
English, French, German, Italian, Nordic languages, Spanish

Other offices
Bergen, Oslo

Number of lawyers 77
at this office 27

Contact
Snorre Haukali (snorre.haukali@kluge.no)

Member
The Law Firm Network

CATEGORIES OF WORK

Corporate and contract law
Clement Endresen, Egil Willumsen

Banking, finance and shipping
Snorre Haukali, Petter Schmidt, Jostein Sundvor

Construction
Odd-Sverre Rage, Olav Todnem

Technology and media law
Preben Falck, Tore Lunde

Tax
Irene Søreide

Aquaculture
Trond Selvikvåg, Tore Lunde

EU, competition
Marianne H Higson

Public procurement
Gro Amdal

Labour and pensions
Marianne H Higson, Johan Krabbe-Knutsen

Oil and gas, offshore
Clement Endresen, Preben Falck, Per Schøyen

Public law
Trond Selvikvåg

Dispute resolution
Preben Falck, Harald Kobbe

Real estate
Odd-Sverre Rage, Olav Todnem

OMAN

Population	3 million
Number of lawyers	n/a
Professional title	Lawyer
Currency	Omani Rial (OR)

Index

The oldest independent Arab state, the Sultanate of Oman enjoys a strategically important location on the south-east corner of the Arabian peninsula, along the crucial shipping route at the mouth of the Gulf.

Oman's sultan and prime minister, Qaboos Bin-Said Al Said, came to power in 1970 after overthrowing his father in a bloodless coup. His decisions in relation to the finance, defence and foreign policies of the country have largely proven very popular despite the lack of democracy; not least because of his establishment of an ongoing modernisation programme, succoured by moderate, independent policies and good relations with other Gulf states.

The majority of the population is Ibadi Muslim, the rest are largely Shi'a or Sunni. There is also a large expatriate population, which makes up about one quarter of the population.

BILLING

Clients can expect to pay from €150 an hour for an assistant to €300 an hour for a partner. Success or contingency fees for litigation are prohibited.

MARKETING

Advertising is permitted and, although there are no restrictions, it tends to be fairly conservative.

IN-HOUSE LAWYERS

In-house lawyers can appear in court for cases worth less than €5,000. They are employed mainly by the financial, insurance and oil and gas sectors.

ECONOMY

Having joined the WTO in November 2000, Oman sealed its commitment to the expansion of global trade in October 2005 with the conclusion of its long-awaited Free Trade Agreement with the US. The combination of Oman's increasingly free market economy, government incentives such as tax holidays, and the ongoing development of free zones throughout the country, has paved the way for significant amounts of direct foreign investment. This remains crucial to the government's diversification programme, designed to tackle the potential economic crisis that could result from the rapid depletion of the oil reserves on which the country has relied for so long.

Whilst oil refining and export still make up three-quarters of the country's revenue, the non-oil sectors are steadily increasing their contribution to GDP. Oman has a gloriously diverse landscape as well as towns and villages steeped in history, with ancient forts and mosques. The success of tourism in other GCC countries, most notably the UAE, suggests that this is also a viable strategy for Oman, and a number of resorts are now under development. The most significant of these current projects is the US$15bn Blue City development, a self-contained metropolis comprising hotel, residential, education, healthcare and sports facilities situated at the beautiful coastal region of Al Sawaidi.

This increasing focus on tourism also marks (and counterbalances) the government's trend towards Omanisation, whereby expatriate workers are being replaced with Omani nationals in an attempt to combat unemployment and dependency on foreign countries: tourism projects are labour-intensive, and the finished resorts will require heavy staffing.

Oman's many industrial projects also continue apace; to name but two, the Sohar aluminium smelter project is now nearing financial closure, while in the Sur region, the Oman-India Fertiliser Company has almost completed its joint venture for the development of a US$600m fertiliser plant. Furthermore, the government's privatisation process is gathering momentum; the tender and the securing of finance for the Sohar Independent Power and Water Project (IWPP) was important news in the latter part of 2005. Meanwhile, Omantel's loss of its monopoly in the telecoms sector has paved the way for the establishment of the country's second GSM network.

Oil revenues and a trade surplus have allowed the country to develop first-class telecommunications and broadcasting systems, as well as a good network of roads and transport links.

LEGAL MARKET

Oman has a small legal market, although a handful of international firms have opened offices there.

Since acquiring the business of *Fox & Gibbons* in 1998, the Muscat office of **Denton Wilde Sapte** continues to build on its strong relationships with government bodies, as well as advising a host of multinationals and projects companies, under the management of the highly regarded Andrew Watson.

The largest firms

1	Al Alawi Mansoor Jamal & Co	31
2	Trowers & Hamlins	16
3	Denton Wilde Sapte	10
4	Ali Al Jabal Law Office	8
5	Adham & Associates	6
6	Rouhani & Partners	3
7	Gulf Consultants	2
	Said Al-Shahry Law Office in association with Richards Butler	2
9	Abu-Ghazaleh Legal	1
	Curtis, Mallet-Prevost, Colt & Mosle LLP	1

These figures represent the total number of lawyers in this country only, and have been supplied by the firms themselves. The figures should be accurate as at 1 January 2006.

Trowers & Hamlins benefits from a regional network of offices, excellent government relations and formal associations with local firms throughout the region. Sean Angle is the Muscat office's experienced managing partner.

Said Al-Shahry Law Office in association with Richards Butler and **Al Alawi Mansoor Jamal & Co** are highly regarded local firms active in several areas of law including banking and finance, corporate and commercial and dispute resolution. Both are frequently called upon to act as local counsel to international firms doing business in Oman.

Partner Robert Gruendel steers the Oman branch of US firm **Curtis, Mallet-Prevost, Colt & Mosle LLP**. Government work is the firm's primary purpose in the country.

Whilst the day-to-day banking and commercial matters will almost invariably be handled by firms with local offices, a large proportion of work relating to the country's projects and privatisations is handled by international firms based in Dubai, London or New York.

In Dubai, **Clifford Chance**'s pre-eminent reputation for regional projects and privatisation work continues to yield instructions from Oman, whilst under the expert guidance of the highly sought-after Bimal Desai, **Allen & Overy LLP** enjoys a superb project finance presence throughout the Middle East, Oman included.

Experts in banking, **Shearman & Sterling LLP** and **Simmons & Simmons** have a strong project finance presence in Oman and region-wide, from their bases in Abu Dhabi, while the London offices of **Linklaters, Berwin Leighton Paisner** and **White & Case** boast committed Middle East practices, working closely with banks, corporates and project sponsors.

Clyde & Co maintains its formidable shipping and insurance practice throughout the Gulf, whilst demonstrating an increasing capacity for regional projects work.

BANKING AND FINANCE

A first class firm, **Denton Wilde Sapte** maintains a solid reputation in the banking market, under managing partner Andrew Watson. Recent matters for the group include advising Bank Muscat in connection with its global depository receipt issue, which was listed on the stock exchange and is the first of its kind for a GCC entity. The firm has a very robust finance arm, acting in relation to many of the country's most significant projects, representing lenders, borrowers, and a host of governmental entities such as the Ministry of National Economy.

Trowers & Hamlins partners Sean Angle and Andrew Rae are deemed 'most efficient and capable' by their clients, which include lenders such as Bank Muscat, Alliance Housing Bank and International Finance Corporation. A real highlight of 2005 was the group's advice in respect of a US$800m Euro note issue, being the first of its kind in Oman and the largest issue in the country's history. When it comes to banking transactions, the firm has capability across the board, while its heavyweight project finance practice continues to yield lucrative instructions.

BANKING AND FINANCE

DENTON WILDE SAPTE ⭘
TROWERS & HAMLINS

Al Alawi Mansoor Jamal & Co ⭘
Said Al-Shahry Law Office in association with Richards Butler

Curtis, Mallet-Prevost, Colt & Mosle LLP ⭘

Firms are listed A-Z in tiers which are ranked in order of priority
⭘ *Indicates firm displays contact details at the end of this chapter.*

Now with a total of 31 fee-earners, the very respectable **Al Alawi Mansoor Jamal & Co** continues its retainer role for Bank Muscat, National Bank of Oman, and Bank Dhofar, as well as regularly acting for major international banks such as HSBC, in relation to their activities in Oman. Frequently found acting opposite **Trowers & Hamlins** on some of the country's most important transactions, the firm also demonstrates solid project finance ability. The team acted for the lenders in the recently closed Sohar Power Project financing, and is currently representing the financiers in the first phase of the huge Blue City development.

At 'responsive' 14-partner firm **Said Al-Shahry Law Office in association with Richards Butler**, British-qualified Alastair Neale, a former legal adviser to Arab Banking Corporation, is very experienced in banking-related matters, including syndicated loan and securities transactions, investment funds and project finance. He recently oversaw the financing of two LNG carriers for Oman Shipping Company, while colleague Fayyaz Mahmood, also highly recommended, advised ICICI Bank on a facility agreement for the financing of oil rigs. Other recent work includes advising on derivatives transactions for Bank of New York, Standard Chartered and DBS Bank, Singapore.

Although the Muscat branch of **Curtis, Mallet-Prevost, Colt & Mosle LLP** has just one partner and one other fee-earner, it is noteworthy nonetheless for its government finance work, which focuses particularly on shipping-related acquisitions and financing, and other general maritime development schemes.

CORPORATE AND M&A

Denton Wilde Sapte's corporate activity in 2005 included acting in relation to Omantel's US$700m IPO (the largest in Oman's history) where it advised the government. Having acted for ABB

CORPORATE AND M&A

DENTON WILDE SAPTE ✪
TROWERS & HAMLINS

Al Alawi Mansoor Jamal & Co ✪
Said Al-Shahry Law Office in association with Richards Butler

---

Adham & Associates

Firms are listed A-Z in tiers which are ranked in order of priority
✪ Indicates firm displays contact details at the end of this chapter.

Lummas last year on its global pull-out from the Oman polypropylene project, the company has once again sought counsel from the firm in relation to new oil and gas related undertakings. A repeat instruction from Commercial Bank of Qatar has been providing some interesting M&A work, whilst complex negotiations of concession, shareholding and operation agreements between Shell International and the government have also been keeping the team on its toes. Meanwhile, the group continues its routine advice in relation to off-take and supply agreements for oil and gas companies such as PDA and Occidental. 'Professional' managing partner Andrew Watson comes highly recommended.

With ever-growing dominance in the telecoms and tourism markets in Oman, **Trowers & Hamlins** maintains its prowess in all kinds of corporate and commercial matters, from company incorporation to sale and purchase agreements, IPOs, joint ventures, and due diligence exercises. As legal counsel to Oman's second licensed GSM network, Nawras, the team has handled all of its legal work from the point of inception and incorporation, and is advising on many aspects of its operation including logistics contracts, regulatory requirements, and interconnection and distribution agreements. The innovative US$15bn Blue City tourist development is also providing a hefty workload; the team acts as counsel to the project company for concession agreements, corporate structuring and other related matters. Corporate partner Sean Angle is 'always receptive to giving legal shape to creative inputs from clients'.

Al Alawi Mansoor Jamal & Co runs a healthy corporate and commercial practice under 'excellent' managing partner Mansoor Jamal Malik. The group continues to advise Q-Tel on its funding of the Nawras telecommunications project, and is retained general legal adviser to a number of other projects, including the Al Kamil Power Project, and the massive Wave tourist development, where it acts for the government-owned stakeholder, Waterfront Investment Company. For operational issues, Hutchison Port Holdings (the management company of Sohar Industrial Port), is another retained client.

Established in 1992 by name partner Said Al-Shahry, **Said Al-Shahry Law Office in association with Richards Butler** enjoys a sound reputation in the field. Significant instructions of the last twelve months include advising the government in connection with setting up the Salalah Free Zone, among other matters. Other recent matters include advising in relation to corporate issues for Oman India Fertilizer Company, an IPO on behalf of Dhofar Power Company, and employment matters for Oman Refinery Company. Senior legal consultant Alastair Neale is particularly recommended for delivering 'consistently sound advice' on issues such as the formation of joint venture companies, share capital issues, sale and purchase agreements, and distribution agency agreements.

DISPUTE RESOLUTION

In Oman, arbitration remains the preferred way of resolving disputes. Where litigation is required, only Arabic lawyers can appear in court. Most local firms and branches are home to dual-qualified lawyers for this purpose.

With an excellent track record for arbitration, **Denton Wilde Sapte**'s highly regarded litigation department is trusted by many important clients, such as Oman International Bank, Bank Dhofar, Microsoft Corporation, Nokia and Motorola. The firm's English and Arabic-speaking group also acts for a host of insurance companies such as Royal & SunAlliance, American Life Insurance Company, and Al Ahlia Insurance Company, and maintains a strong line in shipping disputes. In 2004, the team successfully represented Oman International Bank in a US$15.5m dispute with Oman National Insurance Company.

Whilst head of litigation Majid Al Toky is on secondment to client Nawras, partner James Harbridge is manning the fort at **Trowers & Hamlins**, overseeing a department which handles all kinds of commercial litigation and arbitration. Housing four UK and Oman-qualified advocates, the firm continues to represent National Bank of Oman for banking-related disputes, in addition to acting on behalf of a number of multinational entities in high-quantum cases involving trade marks, tax issues and agency disputes.

With 17 court advocates, **Al Alawi Mansoor Jamal & Co** has the country's largest team of litigators and an excellent record in the commercial disputes arena, including arbitration. Eight of the firm's Omani-qualified lawyers can appear in the High Court, acting for local and foreign companies across a range of disputes, such as those concerned with construction and insurance, and including debt recovery on behalf of three local banks. The team has also dealt with some high-profile criminal matters.

Said Al-Shahry Law Office in association with Richards Butler has six litigators licensed to appear before all courts in Oman. A member of the Majlis Al Shura and Chairman of its legal committee, name partner Said Al-Shahry is the well-connected principal contact, with experience of handling disputes at all levels including arbitration, an area in which senior legal consultant Alastair Neale is also highly recommended. Recent matters include defending a claim for the termination of a lease on behalf of Kopp International Pipeline Services, acting for Norwich Union Insurance in a claim against Global Insurance, and representing a hotel management company in the execution of a Supreme Court judgment.

DISPUTE RESOLUTION

Denton Wilde Sapte ✪
Trowers & Hamlins

Al Alawi Mansoor Jamal & Co ✪
Said Al-Shahry Law Office in association with Richards Butler

Firms are listed A-Z in tiers which are ranked in order of priority
✪ Indicates firm displays contact details at the end of this chapter.

PROJECTS AND PRIVATISATION

Sohar is Oman's hub of industrial development, with its Independent Power and Water Project being one of the country's most significant current projects. Oman's ongoing process of privatisation means that there is a call for legal advice at every stage. Foreign firms merit attention here for their heavy involvement in the country's major projects.

In the last twelve months, project finance giant **Allen & Overy LLP** has acted on no less than four major projects in the country, two of which were financed at over US$1bn each. The first of these was the Oman LNG project, where the team advised on its US$1.3bn refinancing, and the second was the US$1.2bn Sohar Aluminium Smelter Project, where it acted for the lenders. Bimal Desai is the office's esteemed managing partner, who although based in Dubai has nonetheless garnered 'a very impressive track

PROJECTS AND PRIVATISATION

ALLEN & OVERY LLP
CLIFFORD CHANCE
DENTON WILDE SAPTE ✪
TROWERS & HAMLINS

Al Alawi Mansoor Jamal & Co ✪
Said Al-Shahry Law Office in association with Richards Butler
Shearman & Sterling LLP
Simmons & Simmons
White & Case LLP

Clyde & Co
Curtis, Mallet-Prevost, Colt & Mosle LLP ✪
Freshfields Bruckhaus Deringer
Linklaters

Firms are listed A-Z in tiers which are ranked in order of priority
✪ Indicates firm displays contact details at the end of this chapter.

record' on deals in Oman and is 'highly thought of in the local market'.

The stalwart team at **Clifford Chance**'s Duabi office has been integral to a number of key privatisations and projects in Oman, including the ongoing development and financing of a new MoD military college, where it continues to advise the successful Serco-led consortium. Other current matters include advising Oman Oil Company on the US$300m, Sohar-based polypropylene plant development, and representing the bidders in relation to the government's IPP and IWPP programmes.

Making use of its well-developed relations with Oman's governmental bodies, **Denton Wilde Sapte** stays at the forefront of negotiations relating to Oman's top-drawer projects, including the Sur IWP, the Muscat Solid Waste project, and ongoing matters in connection with the country's electricity and water sector privatisation. The firm recently took on projects and infrastructure expert Mary Allen from the firm's Dubai office. She has been advising the project sponsors in relation to the Sohar fertiliser plant financing, among other matters. Other highlights include acting in the financing of the country's largest road construction project, where Sudanese lawyer Nouraddin Alkheir Ahmed is advising Galfar (a major domestic contractor), and the expansion of Oman Refinery Company, where the team is acting for Gulf International Bank.

Steered by finance expert Andrew Rae, **Trowers & Hamlins** is a prolific force on the Oman projects scene, acting for the lenders in a number of major projects in the country. These include the Sur region's US$600m fertiliser plant, as well as the US$450m fertiliser plant and a US$350m polypropylene plant at Sohar. Having assisted Suez Tractebel in its successful bid for the Sohar IWPP last year, the team continues to advise the company on regulatory matters in connection with the establishment of subsidiaries for the operation of the plant.

In addition to its flourishing project finance practice, **Al Alawi Mansoor Jamal & Co** has played an important role in many of the country's major privatisations. It acted for OmanTel on its de-monopolisation, and in the privatisation of the solid waste services sector where it acted for the government, in conjunction with the financiers and technical experts. Other matters include acting on behalf of the international legal advisers in relation to the privatisation of Salalah Airport, and advising the government in the initial stages of the privatisation of Oman Postal Services.

'Reliable' local firm **Said Al-Shahry Law Office in association with Richards Butler** reaps some noteworthy instructions from both domestic and international clients in connection with project finance and privatisation. Under principal lawyer Said Al-Shahry, the team has been heavily involved in the unbundling of electricity and water sector assets, advising Oman's Electricity Holding Company and its nine subsidiaries in relation to this ongoing process. On the projects and infrastructure side, the team continues its advice in relation to the setting up of the Salalah Free Zone, the establishment of a joint venture of Oman Wastewater Services Company for the operation and maintenance of Muscat Wastewater Project, and phase II of the Barka IWPP project.

From London and Abu Dhabi, **Shearman & Sterling LLP**'s strong interest in the country includes acting as project counsel to Oman Petrochemicals Industries Co, a joint venture between the Oman government and Oman Oil Company set up to design, build and operate a petrochemicals complex in the country. The firm has also been acting in relation to the financing of the Blue City development, and is representing the lenders in the Sohar IWPP.

Simmons & Simmons' Abu Dhabi office has a marvellous reputation for project finance under highly esteemed managing partner and projects specialist Ibrahim Mubaydeen. Recent experience in Oman includes ongoing advice to the sponsors of the Sohar aluminium smelter project, and oil rig acquisition and financing.

Demonstrating its ongoing commitment to projects in the Middle East, **White & Case LLP**'s offices in London and Saudi Arabia co-operated on some significant Omani projects during 2005. These include consulting with the Oman government and other regional governments in connection with the potential integration of the power systems of six GCC countries. Meanwhile, the team has been advising the joint venture company on the project-financed development of Sohar's US$1.6bn aluminium smelter and associated power station.

Representing client Al Ghaith Holdings, **Clyde & Co** has been advising in connection with the establishment, including financing and construction elements, of a steel plant in Oman.

The two-fee-earner Muscat branch of US-based **Curtis, Mallet-Prevost, Colt & Mosle LLP** has a special role in Oman advising the government, as well as various co-operative entities, in relation to government-controlled ventures such as the ongoing development of Oman International Container Terminal at Sohar Industrial Port. Robert Gruendel is the lead partner who splits his time between Oman and New York, with assistant counsel Bruce Mullins carrying the flag in his absence.

Freshfields Bruckhaus Deringer recently opened an office in Dubai, although the firm has been actively participating in the financing and development of Middle East projects since the 1950s. Its current advice to the lenders in connection with the private debt financing of a US$650m chemical fertiliser project in Oman is a recent highlight for the team.

Making full use of its extensive Middle East experience, **Linklaters** has been advising the lenders in connection with a term loan facility to finance the development of Oman's Barr Al Jissah resort, whilst continuing to advise a variety of banks in relation to the US1.2bn Sohar Refinery project financing.

SHIPPING

Oman has been subject to very few major shipping incidents over the last two years. However with its strategic location in the Gulf, it remains an important intermediary for exporting Middle Eastern states.

With its widely acclaimed pre-eminence in the sector, the Dubai office of global shipping giant **Clyde & Co** can usually be found acting in relation to the region's most significant shipping-related matters, and Oman is no exception. Last year the firm acted for the insurers in connection with damage caused by a fire on board a tanker, which followed a collision off the coast of Oman.

Trowers & Hamlins maintains a strong transport finance practice. Salalah Port Services has been a client since its establishment in the mid-1990s, and continues to consult the firm on aspects of its ongoing development, including the recent financing of two new berths as well as the acquisition of cranes and transport-related equipment. The office also advises a Dutch logistics company on its cargo handling activities at Sohar Industrial Port, and in a joint venture with Hutchison for the provision of container-handling facilities.

Al Alawi Mansoor Jamal & Co has a broad shipping practice dealing with ship arrests and vessel acquisition, and also possesses the capability to handle disputes as they arise.

Curtis, Mallet-Prevost, Colt & Mosle LLP retains its distinctive role acting for joint ventures of the government in relation to a variety of maritime matters. These include advising on the acquisition financing of the new Energy Spring LNG carrier, and acting in the preparatory stages of a bid tender package for the construction of four high-speed passenger vessels for a ferry service between points in Oman.

Denton Wilde Sapte handles mostly litigious shipping matters, particularly those concerned with marine insurance, although the firm has also recently been advising Bank Muscat in relation to ship financing.

SHIPPING

Clyde & Co
Trowers & Hamlins

Al Alawi Mansoor Jamal & Co ✪
Curtis, Mallet-Prevost, Colt & Mosle LLP ✪
Denton Wilde Sapte ✪

Firms are listed A-Z in tiers which are ranked in order of priority
✪ *Indicates firm displays contact details at the end of this chapter.*

AL ALAWI, MANSOOR JAMAL & CO

MUSCAT INTERNATIONAL CENTRE
MEZZANINE FLOOR
BAIT AL FALAJ STREET
PO BOX 686
112 MUSCAT

Telephone: +968 2481 44 66
Fax: +968 2481 22 56
E-mail: mj-co@omantel.net.om
Website: www.amjoman.com

Languages
Afrikaans, Arabic, English, French, Hindi, Urdu

Number of lawyers 30

Contacts
Mansoor Jamal Malik, John Alasdair Jeffrey

CATEGORIES OF WORK

Banking

Corporate and project finance

Mergers and acquisitions

Capital markets

Maritime

Energy, oil and gas

Insurance

Commercial and corporate laws of Oman

Privatisations

Litigation and arbitration

Commercial agency

Joint venture

CURTIS, MALLET-PREVOST, COLT & MOSLE LLP

SUITE 46-48, QURUM PLAZA
108 AL WALLAJ STREET
PO BOX 200 JEWEL BEACH
134 MUSCAT

Telephone: +968 564 495
Fax: +968 564 497
E-mail: info@cm-p.com
Website: www.cm-p.com

Languages
English

Other offices
Frankfurt, Houston, London, Mexico City, Milan, New York, Paris, Stamford, Washington DC

Number of lawyers 187
at this office 2

Contacts
Robert J Gruendel, Bruce Mullins

Member
Oman Chamber of Commerce; American Business Council of Oman; Maritime Law Association

CATEGORIES OF WORK

Infrastructure and project finance

Privatisation

Shipping

Port development and operation

Transnational joint ventures

Power generation

Petroleum and petrochemical contracts

Water resource concessions

LNG sales

Construction contracts

Equipment sales and leaseback

Public bidding

Environmental waste concessions

Aviation finance

DENTON WILDE SAPTE

FIRST FLOOR 114, HATAT HOUSE
AL NAHDA STREET
WADI ADAI ROUNDABOUT
PO BOX 3552, 112 RUWI
MUSCAT

Telephone: +968 573 000
Fax: +968 573 097
E-mail: muscat@dentonwildesapte.com
Website: www.dentonwildesapte.com

Languages
Arabic, English, French, German

Other offices
Abu Dhabi, Almaty, Cairo, Dubai, Istanbul, London, Milton Keynes, Moscow, Paris, Tashkent

Number of lawyers 683
at this office 11

Contact
Andrew Watson

CATEGORIES OF WORK

Banking and finance

Commercial litigation and arbitration

Corporate and commercial

Energy

IP and IT

Infrastructure projects

Insurance

International projects

Maritime regulatory

POLAND

Population	39 million
Number of lawyers	7,000 Adwocat; 21,000 Radca prawny
Professional title	Adwocat; Radca prawny
Currency	Polish Zloty (PLN)

Index

Poland came under Soviet influence after WWII, although the government remained relatively tolerant and progressive compared with other Eastern Bloc states. Labor turmoil ultimately led to the formation of the Solidarity trade union that eventually became a political force and swept parliamentary elections in 1990. Polish Pope John-Paul II was an important influence on the movement throughout the 1980s and the Roman Catholic Church remains a potent force in Polish life.

Reforms post-1990 enabled Poland to transform itself into one of Central Europe's strongest economies. Poland joined Nato in 1999 and the EU in 2004.

Between the end of Communism and EU accession, power in Poland switched between centre-right and centre-left governments. Lech Kaczynski, of the conservative Law and Justice Party, has been president since October 2005. Kazimierz Marcinkiewicz, also of Law and Justice, has been prime minister since September 2005. The growing power of the Law and Justice Party has led to some concern in the business community. It is more euro-sceptic and less free-market orientated than its predecessor.

ECONOMY

Centrally planned Poland was a big producer of coal, copper and sulphur, and had a large agricultural sector dominated by peasant farms. The country's industry was generally inefficient and polluting, and the farms, whilst privately owned and run, were uncompetitive in a globalised world.

A policy of economic liberalisation ran throughout the 1990s. Many small and medium-sized state-owned companies were privatised, and new legislation passed to stimulate the development of the private business sector. But much remains to be done. The country sill has a high unemployment rate, whilst legal and bureaucratic obstacles remain. Meanwhile, the restructuring and privatisation of key sectors such as coal, steel, the railroads and energy has been slow and painstaking, and the country's infrastructure is undeveloped. Fortunately, surging exports to the EU contributed to strong growth in 2004, and the country is now enjoying a shift away from traditional heavy industry into services and hi-tech manufacturing. Poland stands to benefit from substantial EU funds and farmers are starting to benefit from EU agricultural subsidies and higher food prices.

On the downside, the continuance of the country's export-led growth is somewhat dependent on the value of the zloty relative to the euro and US dollar. The zloty appreciated almost 20% against the dollar in 2004. Economic growth, which was strong in 2004, has weakened. Growth forecasts for 2005 are in the region of 3-3.5%.

BILLING

For years the market has been oversupplied with law firms, producing downward pressure on fees. Although the amount of work available has been picking up recently, the general result has been an increase in firms' annual billable hours, rather than an increase in fees. There has however, been less need to undercut fees to win deals. It seems that the practice of pursuing specific deals as loss leaders is less common than it was a few years ago.

Headline rates for partners at international firms range between €300 and €400 per hour (occasionally this can be as high as €500, but usually with considerable discounts), whilst associates generally charge in the range of €200 to €300 per hour. At domestic firms €200 per hour seems common for a partner, although many in practice many go lower than this. Capped fees are growing in popularity.

MARKETING

Most firms have websites, although few are prepared to disclose the identity of clients or the specifics of transactions, unless the work was completed a long time ago. Advertising was forbidden for both adwokats and radca prawny until November 2004. However radca prawny have traditionally been a lot less stringent in their interpretation of the rules, and generally domestic firms are more conservative in their approach to advertising than offices attached to international firms.

IN-HOUSE LAWYERS

There are no restrictions on in-house lawyers and they are free to join the Bar Association or association of radca prawny. Large Polish companies tend to have relatively established in-house departments.

LEGAL MARKET

The good news for clients is that Poland is a very competitive jurisdiction, with a wide variety of commercial law firms present. Top international brands such as **Clifford Chance** and **Linklaters**, and leading US firms like **Weil, Gotshal & Manges**

The largest firms

1	Domanski Zakrzewski Palinka	92
2	Soltysinski Kawecki & Szlezak	80
3	CMS Cameron McKenna Pawel Debowski Spólka Komandytowa	65
4	Baker & McKenzie	64
	White & Case - W. Danilowicz, W. Jurcewicz i Wspólnicy Kancelaria Prawna sp.K	64
6	Brockhuis Schnell Jurczak Prusak Sp. k.	59
7	Chalas i Wspolnicy	55
8	Linklaters	52
9	Salans	49
	TGC Corporate Lawyers	49
11	Dewey Ballantine Grzesiak SP.K.	48
12	Grynhoff, Wozny i Wspolnicy sp. kom	47
13	Weil, Gotshal & Manges	44
14	Gide Loyrette Nouel	43
	Wierzbowski Eversheds	43
16	Chadbourne & Parke Polska Sp. z o.o., Wujek, Radzikowski, Szubielska i Wspólnicy. Spólka Komandytowa	40
17	Clifford Chance	39
18	Lukowicz Swierzewski & Partners	38
	Studnicki, Pleszka, Cwiakalski, Górski LLP	38
20	Janusz Kasprzak & Partners	35
	Wardynski & Partners	35
22	Allen & Overy, A. Pedzich sp. k.	34
	Lesnodorski, Slusarek & Partners	34
	Lovells	34
25	Rödl, Korpalski Kancelaria Prawna sp.k.	32

These figures represent the total number of lawyers in this country only, and have been supplied by the firms themselves. The figures should be accurate as at 1 January 2006.

and **Dewey Ballantine LLP** are established. Meanwhile, a number of firms from neighbouring regions that have significant business interests in Poland, such as Germany and Scandinavia, are also active.

The last couple of years have seen comparatively few international firms entering the Polish market. Recent entries, such as **Squire, Sanders & Dempsey L.L.P.**, **Eversheds LLP** and **DLA Piper Rudnick Gray Cary UK LLP** have taken place through mergers with established local firms. In a market that some say is saturated, and with downward pressure on fees, many question whether such new entrants can enjoy much success. But Poland's size as a jurisdiction and its importance as a leading centre in the increasingly attractive Central and Eastern European region mean that a Polish presence is worth fighting for.

Lawyers are divided as to whether or not the future lies in teaming up with international firms. Others question whether it really makes any difference. Even the international firms are almost entirely staffed with Polish lawyers. And the internationals fight with some excellent domestic outfits for business. **Wardynski & Partners**, **Soltysinski Kawecki & Szlezak** and **Domanski Zakrzewski Palinka** are among Poland's largest firms. They are full-service practices and genuine alternatives to the big international firms for cross-border deals. On their own they may not be able to compete with the big international firms on the largest international finance and capital markets-related work, but they are certainly more than capable of handling the Polish side of such transactions, and they get a significant amount of work referred to them by international firms without a presence in Poland. Other notable domestic law firms include **Wiercinski, Kwiecinski, Baehr Sp. k.** and **Chajec, Don-Siemion & Zyto Legal Advisors**. The best domestic firms are also benefiting from a buoyant domestic M&A and capital markets scene. Even lawyers at the international firms concede that the future may lie with advising Polish companies, rather than foreign companies investing in Poland. With their slightly lower fees and established relationships with Polish companies, the best domestic firms may have an edge in this area. As the economy develops and Polish companies invest more outside of Poland into the region and beyond, firms that pursue a strategy of focusing on Polish growth companies stand to benefit.

BANKING AND FINANCE

ALLEN & OVERY, A. PEDZICH SP. K. ○
CLIFFORD CHANCE

BAKER & McKENZIE ○
DEWEY BALLANTINE GRZESIAK SP.K. ○
LINKLATERS ○
LOVELLS ○
WARDYNSKI & PARTNERS ○
WEIL, GOTSHAL & MANGES ○
WHITE & CASE – W. DANILOWICZ, W. JURCEWICZ I WSPÓLNICY KANCELARIA PRAWNA SP.K

CMS Cameron McKenna Pawel Debowski Spólka Komandytowa ○
Chadbourne & Parke Polska Sp. z o.o., Wujek, Radzikowski, Szubielska i Wspólnicy. Spólka Komandytowa
Gide Loyrette Nouel ○
Hogan & Hartson M. Jamka, A. Galos, and Partners, L.L.P. ○
Norton Rose, Piotr Strawa and Partners, Limited Partnership
Soltysinski Kawecki & Szlezak ○

Domanski Zakrzewski Palinka ○
Nörr Stiefenhofer Lutz Sp.z.o.o. Radnoczy Sp.K ○
Salans
Wierzbowski Eversheds ○

BSJP Brockhuis Schnell Jurczak Prusak Sp. k. ○
Beiten Burkhardt K. Rastawicki Sp.K. ○
Chajec, Don-Siemion & Zyto Legal Advisors ○
Czarny & Wadolowski LLP Legal Advisers
GESSEL – Attorneys at Law ○
Gleiss Lutz ○
Kochanski Brudkowski & Partners ○
Laszczuk & Partners ○
Lukowicz Swierzewski & Partners ○
M.Furtek i Wspolnicy Kancelaria Prawnicza ○
Miller, Canfield, W. Babicki i Wspólnicy Sp.k
Rachelski & Wspolnicy
Squire Sanders Wiater sp. k. ○
Urbanski Rucinski, Jarocka, Borkowska s.c.

Firms are listed A-Z in tiers which are ranked in order of priority
○ Indicates firm displays contact details at the end of this chapter.

BANKING AND FINANCE

Allen & Overy, A. Pedzich sp. k.'s world-wide parent has a reputation as a leading global firm for finance transactions. The Warsaw branch is similarly strong. Led by Arkadiusz Pedzich, it has been involved in a wide range of high-value transactions, such as advising Aareal Bank on a €66m financing of ING's Central and Eastern European HQ, Sumitomo Mitsubishi on a €157m guaranteed facility for Telekomunikacja Polka SA, and Sigmakalon on two credit facilities worth €1.769bn. Add some of 2004/2005 leading project financings into the mix, such as advising a consortium of foreign banks on a €226m investment to construct a lignite power plant for Elektrownia Patnów, and another consortium on Poland's first-ever petrochemical sector project financing, and you have a top-tier finance practice.

Peter Deegan and Grzegorz Namiotkiewicz's banking client list at **Clifford Chance** contains numerous leading Polish banks and global financial institutions. Transactional highlights include advising Polskie Górnictwo Naftowe i Gazownictwo SA (Polish Oil and Gas, PGNiG) on its €900m refinancing, and Bank Handlowy and Citibank on the restructuring of all of PGNiG's syndicated and bilateral debt. Key project finance deals include acting for the EBRD and Bank Handlowy on a €150m revenue bond issue for a municipal water company. The banking team also forms the bulk of the office's restructuring and insolvency capability. In recent times it has been involved in several corporate and financial restructurings, advising both lenders and borrowers. A further aspect of the practice includes advising banks on aircraft and ship finance deals.

After a good year in both project and real estate finance transactions, **Baker & McKenzie** advised a banking syndicate on a PLN400m leveraged buy-out recently, and is now working on major bank restructurings, transforming the Polish subsidiaries of foreign banks into branches. The firm's recent transaction list shows a wide variety of both lender and borrower-side work. Jur Gruszczynski is recommended for projects and energy financing, whilst Kryzysztof Korzeniewski runs corporate finance.

Dewey Ballantine Grzesiak SP.K. aims for cutting-edge transactions, often for cash-borrowing energy clients. It worked on the borrower side opposite **Clifford Chance** in the €600m refinancing of PGNiG's bonds. The deal also involved restructuring the company's bank debt, and facilitating additional credit restructuring related to the spin-off of its gas transmission system operator. The complex transaction stands out for the short timescale in which it was necessarily executed.

Linklaters has a new practice head in Jaroslaw Miller, previously head of banking at **CMS Cameron McKenna LLP**. The team also features Adrian Horne, an English associate who has worked in Warsaw for a number of years and is well respected. Notable recent work includes acting as documentation agents for Citibank and Société Générale on a €900m term and revolving facility for PGNiG, and advising on a giant multi-currency and option syndicated facility for a large Polish corporate. Meanwhile, many of the office's banking personnel also have a good deal of project finance experience, whilst real estate finance transactions are picking up at the firm – it advised Eurohypo on a €35m financing of a 15-year office lease recently. One must also remember the finance credentials of the firm's other offices, especially London, so virtually all bases are covered.

Lovells is arguably the market leader in insurance in Poland. Managing partner Beata Balas–Noszczyk helped to draft Poland's Insurance Activity Act, and leads a team that represents a number of insurance companies, notably Sampo and Nationwide Global Holdings. Recently the firm hired three experienced associates from **Linklaters** to boost the banking side of the practice. The firm advised ABN Amro Poland on a PLN410m syndicated loan to Provimi–Rolimpex SA. Partner Jolanta Nowakowska-Zimoch handles real estate and project finance transactions.

Wardynski & Partners has a good domestic banking department headed by Ewa Butkiewicz, formerly head of BRE Bank's legal department. But it is in the project finance field that the firm really shines. It is capable of hybrid projects transactions including limited recourse financing, project bonds and securitisation. It represented the Polish Ministry of Infrastructure on the financing of the A1 motorway recently

Corporate powerhouse **Weil, Gotshal & Manges**' practice is weighted towards the borrower side, notably handling acquisition finance transactions for private equity groups.

Notable recent banking transactions for **White & Case – W. Danilowicz, W. Jurcewicz i Wspólnicy Kancelaria Prawna sp.K** include advising Deutsche Bank on a US$600m certificate of deposit for a major Polish industrial company, and Calyon on a €900m syndicated credit facility for TP SA, Poland's leading teleco. The firm reports another strong year in the project finance field, with its advice to EIB and Nordic Investment Bank on a €640m financing for the A1 motorway PPP of particular note. The practice was strengthened in late 2004 through the recruitment of Lech Giliciński as partner from **Weil, Gotshal & Manges**. He brings with him debt restructuring skills and rare experience with asset-backed securities.

Banking clients of **CMS Cameron McKenna Pawel Debowski Spólka Komandytowa**'s Warsaw office include Eurohypo, Bank BPH and Depfa Bank. The firm mostly acts on real estate finance and project finance transactions, and completed a number of notable deals in 2004/2005, including advising Eurohypo on both a €900m financing of a commercial property portfolio, and on unwinding a securitisation of the Domy Towarowe Centrum department store chain. Following Jaroslaw Miller's departure to **Linklaters** the department is now headed by Wojciech Wadolowski, formerly of **Czarny & Wadolowski LLP Legal Advisers**. Wadolowski brings with him fresh capabilities in debt restructuring and derivatives.

In addition to advising clients such as Credit Agricole, Erste Bank and Invesco Real estate, **Chadbourne & Parke Polska Sp. z o.o., Wujek, Radzikowski, Szubielska i Wspólnicy. Spólka Komandytowa** has an improving project finance practice under the recommended Agnieszka Stankiewicz. In 2005 it represented Zespól Elektrowni Patnów-Adamów-Konin SA (PAK) on the €315m financing of a 460MW lignite-fired facility.

In addition to advising Cetelem SA and Banque PSA Finance on setting up branches in Poland, **Gide Loyrette Nouel** advised on a US$36m refinancing of a construction project. The office strengthened its team with the hire of Agnieszka Kowalska from **Norton Rose** recently, and now benefits from the firm's fledgling London Office.

Hogan & Hartson M. Jamka, A. Galos, and Partners, L.L.P. advised Bank BPH on finance for TVN, Poland's second-largest commercial TV channel. Other notable work recently includes advising a large Polish bank on a major hotel financing, and a private equity fund on restructuring a large financing of one its investments.

Key recent transactions for **Norton Rose, Piotr Strawa and Partners, Limited Partnership** include advising Mezzanine Management on its management buy-out financing for a Polish Bus and Coach manufacturer, and ABN Amro and Rabobank on a €110m loan to PERN, the national oil pipeline system operator. The office is on the panels of HSBC, Citibank and AIG Bank.

Soltysinski Kawecki & Szlezak represented Deutsche Bank in the refinancing of a several-hundred-million euro loan to one of the local mobile network operators in recent years. The practice, led by Andrzej Szlezak counts the Polish operations of ABN Amro and Hypo-Vereinsbank and numerous Polish banks as clients.

Domanski Zakrzewski Palinka's practice, led by Jożef Palinka offers a full banking service, from advising lenders on all types of loan transaction, to obtaining permits for banking operations.

Nörr Stiefenhofer Lutz Sp.z.o.o. Radnoczy Sp.K senior partner Zsolt Radnoczy was formerly CEO of a bank. He has a good deal of experience in multi-jurisdictional leveraged finance and project finance. The firm also handles a lot of real estate finance work. HVB Group is a client.

Four-partner, nine-lawyer **Urbanski Rucinski, Jarocka, Borkowska s.c.** is recommended to Polish clients for banking matters. Specialist banking partners Maciej Urbański and Maciej Ruciński lead a team with experience in handling credit transactions exceeding €20m for domestic banks such as Bank BPH and Bank Gospodarstwa Krajowego. The firm also has an active practice representing companies in disputes against banks.

CAPITAL MARKETS

Liberalisation of investment rules has resulted in a wall of Polish pension fund money becoming available for investment, with the Warsaw Stock Exchange the main beneficiary. In recent years Warsaw has outstripped almost all European exchanges in terms of the number of IPOs, whilst the WIG index of large and mid-sized companies has more than doubled since early 2003. The Exchange benefits from having a comparatively light regulatory regime. Lawyers are optimistic that Warsaw will go on to be the leading equity exchange in the region. The only downside for

CAPITAL MARKETS

DEWEY BALLANTINE GRZESIAK SP.K. ✪

ALLEN & OVERY, A. PEDZICH SP. K. ✪
CLIFFORD CHANCE
LINKLATERS ✪
WEIL, GOTSHAL & MANGES ✪

Chadbourne & Parke Polska Sp. z o.o., Wujek, Radzikowski, Szubielska i Wspólnicy. Spólka Komandytowa
Domanski Zakrzewski Palinka ✪
GESSEL – Attorneys at Law ✪
Norton Rose, Piotr Strawa and Partners, Limited Partnership
White & Case – W. Danilowicz, W. Jurcewicz i Wspólnicy Kancelaria Prawna sp.K

Baker & McKenzie ✪
Gide Loyrette Nouel ✪
Oles & Rodzynkiewicz
Soltysinski Kawecki & Szlezak ✪
Wardynski & Partners ✪

CMS Cameron McKenna Pawel Debowski Spólka Komandytowa ✪
Chajec, Don-Siemion & Zyto Legal Advisors ✪
Czarny & Wadolowski LLP Legal Advisers
Hogan & Hartson M. Jamka, A. Galos, and Partners, L.L.P. ✪
Lovells ✪
Salans
Wierzbowski Eversheds ✪

Firms are listed A-Z in tiers which are ranked in order of priority
✪ Indicates firm displays contact details at the end of this chapter.

lawyers is that the attractiveness of the equity markets has somewhat depressed corporate bond work.

Currently many firms are starting to advise clients in relation to potential securitisations. Although details remain confidential, it looks like this will form the next boom for capital markets lawyers.

After his sabbatical drafting Poland's new Securities Law as vice-chairman of the Polish Securities and Exchange Commission, September 2005 saw Zbigniew Mrowiec returned to take charge of capital markets at **Dewey Ballantine Grzesiak SP.K.**. He re-joins an established practice that continues to feature notable talents such as Jarolsaw Grzesiak and Lejb Fogelman. The firm advises the state treasury in privatisations and capital markets matters, and is notably acting on the up-and-coming privatisation by IPOs of Bank Gospodarki Zywnosciowej and the Warsaw Stock Exchange. Away from equities, the firm is advising both Citigroup and its Polish subsidiary Bank Handlowy on the launch of Citigroup's US$436.5m senior exchangeable notes programme, Poland's first listing of debt securities that are exchangeable for shares. To cap it all, the offices are based in the same building as the Stock Exchange, so they feel like part of the same apparatus.

Under Jacek Jonak **Allen & Overy, A. Pedzich sp. k.** has been involved in the Warsaw IPO boom. It advised PKO Bank Polski on its privatisation by IPO, and acted for Amrest Holding, Poland's fanchisee for KFC and Pizza Hut, on its listing. But it is in high finance that the firm really excels. Its Polish transaction list includes a raft of structured finance and derivatives-related work for major international banks, Polish governmental bodies and global finance-related associations. Critics may point out that the monolithic London office should take credit for this, but you cannot ignore the fact that such resources are available to the Polish office.

Although **Clifford Chance** advised Advent International and Bolix SA on the latter's flotation, and ING Bank on its PLN730m Warsaw offering, the firm was mostly engaged in fixed-income work in 2004/2005. Notable Poland-led deals include acting for Bank BPH on its €3bn EMTN programme, and various banks on the Republic of Poland's own EMTN issue. Also notable is its work for ING Bank on Central European Distribution Corporation's high-yield issue.

Following the departure of Marek Wierzbowski, **Linklaters** consolidated its practice with the hire of Marcin Chyliński from **Weil, Gotshal & Manges**. The firm continues to concentrate on high-value, often complex work. Recently it acted for the loss-marking SkyEurope airlines on its €120m simultaneous IPO on the Warsaw and Vienna exchanges, and is advising a major international bank on an up-and-coming multi-billion dollar privatisation by IPO.

Weil, Gotshal & Manges has worked on many of Poland's biggest IPOs. It acted for CSFB and Bank Gospodarki Zywnosciowej in the €1.765bn Warsaw float of PKO Bank Polski, Europe's second-largest equity offering in 2004. Also noteworthy is its work for PGNiG, the gas distribution monopoly, on its €686m privatisation by IPO, and advising CSFB on its €112m sale of 48% of Opoczno, Poland's leading tile manufacturer, in what was arguably Poland's most significant private equity exit via IPO. All four of the firm's partners are US qualified, whilst Pawel Rymarz and Ania Frankowska both have significant capital markets experience.

Chadbourne & Parke Polska Sp. z o.o., Wujek, Radzikowski, Szubielska i Wspólnicy. Spólka Komandytowa represented Grupa Lotos SA, Poland's second-largest refiner, in its successful IPO. It also worked on a €235m high-yield bond issue. Kazimierz Jeleński and David Dixon are recommended.

Domanski Zakrzewski Palinka has capitalised on the recent surge in IPO work. It also has a good name for debt capital markets transactions. Name partner Grzegorz Domanski was formerly chairman of the Warsaw Stock Exchange, and the firm is acknowledged in the market for its high levels of visible activity.

There is a consensus among rival lawyers that **GESSEL – Attorneys at Law** is carving out a formidable business in handling prospectus preparation and Warsaw IPOs of Polish companies. Leading transactions include the IPOs of Jago SA and Neonet SA. Practice head Leszek Koziorowski has served as an advisor to the chairman of the Polish Securities and Exchange Commission, whilst attorney Tomasz Dragowski also previously worked for the SEC, as deputy chief of the legal department.

Norton Rose, Piotr Strawa and Partners, Limited Partnership has handled a wide variety of capital markets work. Recently the firm advised the underwriters on a proposed second listing in Warsaw of a Euronext-listed company, and acted for a Citigroup subsidiary on both Citibank NA's exchangeable bonds, and IVAX's PLN476m share issue.

White & Case – W. Danilowicz, W. Jurcewicz i Wspólnicy Kancelaria Prawna sp.K has a two-partner team that aims to work on more complicated capital markets work. Its advice to Polimex-Cekop SA during its precedent-setting reverse acquisition by its listed subsidiary is a good example. Other notable work includes advising Eurohypo on a PLN87.5m block sale of 50% of Rheinhyp BRE Bank.

Although less active than many of its peers, **Baker & McKenzie** nevertheless demonstrates capital markets ability through complicated and precedent-setting transactions over the years. It advised MOL on its listing in Warsaw, Poland's biggest-ever dual listing at the time, and Citibank on US$436.5m-worth of bonds exchangeable into the shares of a Polish subsidiary.

Gide Loyrette Nouel's Warsaw office advised Belvedere SA on its Warsaw listing whilst the wider firm worked on a second listing of the company on Euronext. The office handled three other domestic IPOs in with a combined value of around €10m in 2004/2005.

Krakow-based **Oles & Rodzynkiewicz** is a recognised leader for straightforward flotations on the Warsaw Stock Exchange. The firm has handled a very large volume of transactions for small and medium-sized companies in recent years.

Under Andrzej Kawecki, **Soltysinski Kawecki & Szlezak** has participated in numerous equity and debt transactions on both the domestic and foreign securities markets. In the foreign arena the firm has acted for the likes of Merrill Lynch and Daiwa Europe on corporate bonds (including convertibles) and GDRs.

CORPORATE AND M&A

Clients appreciate **Dewey Ballantine Grzesiak SP.K.**'s 'great quality of service at the price', a service that is ' unique in its understanding for the business and its sense of responsibility for the final business result'. Such accolades are borne out by the quality of the firm's recent M&A portfolio. The firm remains active for its strong private

CORPORATE AND M&A

DEWEY BALLANTINE GRZESIAK SP.K. ✪
WEIL, GOTSHAL & MANGES ✪

BAKER & McKENZIE ✪
CMS CAMERON McKENNA PAWEL DEBOWSKI SPÓLKA KOMANDYTOWA ✪
CLIFFORD CHANCE

LINKLATERS ✪
SOLTYSINSKI KAWECKI & SZLEZAK ✪
WARDYNSKI & PARTNERS ✪
WHITE & CASE – W. DANILOWICZ, W. JURCEWICZ I WSPÓLNICY KANCELARIA PRAWNA SP.K

Allen & Overy, A. Pedzich sp. k. ✪
Chadbourne & Parke Polska Sp. z o.o., Wujek, Radzikowski, Szubielska i Wspólnicy. Spólka Komandytowa
Chajec, Don-Siemion & Zyto Legal Advisors ✪
Domanski Zakrzewski Palinka ✪
GESSEL – Attorneys at Law ✪
Gide Loyrette Nouel ✪
Gleiss Lutz ✪
Lovells ✪
Nörr Stiefenhofer Lutz Sp.z.o.o. Radnoczy Sp.K ✪
Salans
Wierzbowski Eversheds ✪

Beiten Burkhardt K. Rastawicki Sp.K. ✪
Drzewiecki, Tomaszek & Wspólnicy Spólka Jawna
Haarmann Hemmelrath ✪
Hogan & Hartson M. Jamka, A. Galos, and Partners, L.L.P. ✪
Kochanski Brudkowski & Partners ✪
Laszczuk & Partners ✪
Norton Rose, Piotr Strawa and Partners, Limited Partnership
Studnicki, Pleszka, Cwiakalski, Górski LLP
TGC Corporate Lawyers
Wiercinski, Kwiecinski, Baehr Sp. k. ✪

BSJP Brockhuis Schnell Jurczak Prusak Sp. k. ✪
Grynhoff, Wozny i Wspolnicy sp. kom
Joachim Hilla, Kancelaria
Kancelaria Prawnicza Magnusson
Lukowicz Swierzewski & Partners ✪
M.Furtek i Wspolnicy Kancelaria Prawnicza ✪
Miller, Canfield, W. Babicki i Wspólnicy Sp.k
Nowakowski i Wspólnicy
Peter Nielsen & Partners Law Office sp. K
Rutkowski Windmill Gasiewski & Roman LP ✪
Siemiatkowski & Davies
Squire Sanders Wiater sp. k. ✪
Stopczyk & Mikulski
Tomczak i Partnerzy Spolka Adwokacka
Zgutka i partnerzy, adwokaci

Continued

equity client base in Poland, representing Enterprise Investors, CA IB Fund Management and Innova Capital in large buy-outs. The trade client base is equally strong, and includes examples of both in-bound and out-bound work, both for Polish, and for international companies. It continued to advise PKN Orlen with respect to its acquisition of the Czech Republic's Unipetrol, Poland's largest-ever corporate investment abroad, successfully representing it before the European Commission in 2005. The eight-partner M&A practice is led by senior partner Lejb Fogelman, a lawyer with a significant profile in the country, and also features Jacek Michalski and Steven Horvath, both of whom enjoy good reputations.

Weil, Gotshal & Manges stands out from the crowd for transactional work, notably for private equity firms. Over the last year the firm advised Enterprise Investors on its exit from Messenger Service Stolica SA. The work involved both handling the sale of the company and conducting litigation in a share conflict. It also represented Bank of America Private Equity on the sale of the frozen food division of one of its portfolio companies, Hortex Holding. On the public company side, the Warsaw office represented Ster-Projekt in a reverse merger with the privately held ABG SA, and acted for Netia SA, Poland's leading fixed-line telco, in a joint venture with Novator Telecom. Around 80% of the Warsaw office's clients are major Polish companies, whilst international clients tend to be world class, such as CSFB, General Electric and Vivendi Universal. Managing Partner Pawel Rymarz is particularly recommended for complicated corporate transactions, and is described as a 'very commercial lawyer'.

Baker & McKenzie's ten-lawyer practice is strong in day-to-day corporate matters, with various members specialising in areas such as commercial contracts, franchising, agreements for sale, distribution or research, and labour law. The Polish subsidiaries of companies such as Hewlet-Packard and Boeing use the firm for ongoing advice. On the transactional side, the office appears to be following the market into mid-sized M&A, advising both the buy and sell-side. For example, it acted for Fresenius Medical Care on its acquisition of the nephrology business of International Nephrology Centres Poland, and Provimi Polska Holding on the sale of part of its farming business to a leading US food producer. Partners Marcin Gmaj and Tomasz Krzyżowski are the firm's leading corporate lights, the latter a private equity and venture capital specialist praised for 'always doing an excellent job' and being 'quite outstanding in terms of price and speed'.

Clients praise the 'high level of satisfaction' they have for the services of **CMS Cameron McKenna Pawel Debowski Spólka Komandytowa**. Its position as a leading firm across the region further solidified in 2005. A recent merger with Central European firm *Hayhurst Robinson* increases its profile in Hungary, Romania and Bulgaria, bolstering its appeal to large cross-border investors, particularly those with significant multi-jurisdictional real estate and projects interests. The Warsaw office is somewhat of a hub within this network. Its 16-lawyer M&A team advises private equity funds on acquisitions, notably Enterprise Investors, whilst a separate team headed by Ian Batty and Malgorzata Surdek is dedicated to driving day-to day commercial advice to companies of the calibre of Diageo, Dixons and GE Group. Managing Partner Andrew Kozlowski has a wealth of experience in energy, project finance and corporate work, and is particularly recommended. 'Possibly the most creative lawyer I have used in Europe,' remarks one client.

Clifford Chance's 23-strong corporate group is headed by Nick Fletcher and Agnieszka Janicka. It is large enough to have dedicated desks for French and German clients on top of its diverse international client base, which features the likes of Kimberly-Clark, Kraft Foods and Advent International, and its local clients, which include leading Polish companies such as PKN Orlen and Energis Polska. The firm reports a move away from privatisation work towards public company M&A. Notable recent work includes advising the EBRD

CORPORATE AND M&A Continued

Chalas i Wspolnicy
Czarny & Wadolowski LLP Legal Advisers
DeBenedetti Majewski Szczesniak Kancelaria Prawnicza Sp. K ✪
Evico sp.j., Kancelaria Prawnicza
Forystek & Partnerzy ✪
I.K. Rokas & Partners Malinowska Kancelaria Prawna sp.k
Kaczor Klimczyk Pucher Wypiór – Advokaci Spólka Partnerska
Kalwas i Wspólnicy s.c.
Karniol Malecki i Wspólnicy Sp. K ✪
Kuczek & Maruta
Kuk, Suszynska, Lachowski & Matecki
Kubas Kos Gaertner
Lesnodorski, Slusarek & Partners ✪
MDDP Michalik Dluska Dziedzic i Partnerzy
Malecki & Rychlowski, Kancelaria Adwokacka
Marcin Maminski, Adwokat ✪
Marek Kacprzak, Kancelaria Radcy Prawnego
Marek Musiol Law Office
Pociej, Dubois & Partners
K Ziemski i Partnerzy spolka komandytowa, Kancelaria Prawna
Rachelski & Wspolnicy
Traple, Konarski, Podrecki s.c.

Firms are listed A-Z in tiers which are ranked in order of priority
✪ *Indicates firm displays contact details at the end of this chapter.*

on its acquisition (alongside Rabobank) of 35% of Bank Gospodarki Zywnosciowej for PLN1.4bn, and advising on the Polish aspects of TEVA's merger with IVAX .

Linklaters' top-tier positions in various key CEE jurisdictions demonstrate why South Korea's Hankook Tyre selected it to advise on the legal issues relating to choosing between Poland, the Czech Republic, Hungary and Slovakia for the development of a €500m tyre manufacturing plant. In Poland the firm is very strong, but perhaps faces greater competition than it does in many other emerging and semi-mature markets. The corporate department is headed by Cezary Wiśniewski, whilst managing partner Tadeusz Komosa is also active. Both specialise in M&A. Key deals for 2004/2005 include advising Rémy Cointreau on its US$270m sale of Bols, Poland's third-largest distiller, and Nordwaggon AB on its formation of a rail transport joint venture with Poland's PS Trans Trade. Also notable is the firm's EU compliance work, particularly for the City of Warsaw with regards to its Metro project, and its competition work, from which advising SIG plc in merger control proceedings in 2004/2005 stands out.

Over the years **Soltysinski Kawecki & Szlezak** has been extensively involved in Poland's privatisation process. The firm is now in a bit of a transition period, with the experienced and respected Stanislaw Soltysinski announcing his intention to step down from full-time practice. He will remain as a part-time consultant however, and the firm has other respected lawyers such as Andrzej Szlezak and Andrzej Kawecki to carry the torch while the firm shifts its attention to domestic and cross-border M&A. Meanwhile, greenfield investments in Poland's Special Economic Zones (SEZs) now play a great part in the firm's corporate workload, with clients such as Gillette, Electrolux and LG Philips using it for investments in manufacturing and distribution facilities in recent years. Also noteworthy are the firm's competition and labour practices, led by Jaroslaw Sroczyński and Bartlomiej Raczkowski respectively. Both are becoming increasingly active as a result of EU compliance work.

Wardynski & Partners made its name in privatisations and has since become a top independent Polish firm for M&A and inward investment. The firm notably advises clients in the manufacturing, telecoms, construction and financial services sectors, and most come from outside of Poland. Cross-border work involving Eastern European jurisdictions is becoming increasingly prominent. In 2004 it signed a co-operation agreement with seven independent CEE law firms, each a leading local firm in their respective jurisdictions. The firm also boasts a Brussels office to represent the firm's clients before EU institutions, often on EU competition law matters, and strengthened in this area recently through the hire of Dorothy Hansberry-Biegunska, an American lawyer with experience of advising the governments of Eastern European countries on competition issues. Pawel Ciećwierz leads the M&A team.

White & Case – W. Danilowicz, W. Jurcewicz i Wspólnicy Kancelaria Prawna sp.K is traditionally strong advising energy and electricity clients on transactions but had a strong transactional year in 2005 in the insurance, construction and private equity sectors. In 2004 the firm advised Polcard SA on its US$6m acquisition of Billbird SA, (in 2003 the firm acted for private equity firm Innova Capital in its US$62.5m acquisition of Polcard). This was one of a number of private equity-related deals handled by private equity specialist Zdzislaw Wieckowski. The four-partner transactional department headed by Wiltold Danilowickz also includes Witold Jurcewickz, who has wide-ranging experience in M&A, privatisation and capital markets, and Dr Janusz Fisher, who combines M&A experience with tax acumen and a specialism in executive compensation and employee benefits. One client with experience of instructing lawyers all over Europe comments that the Warsaw office's service is 'comparable with the best legal firms in Europe'.

Key figures for transactional work at **Allen & Overy, A. Pedzich sp. k.** include practice head Jane Townsend and Partner Jaroslaw Iwanicki. Stand-out transactions include advising HSBC on the sale of its Polish brokerage to PKO BP SA, Société Générale on its acquisition of Euro Bank SA, and Campofrio Alimentación on the de-listing and sale of its Polish meat company to Animex Holding.

Chadbourne & Parke Polska Sp. z o.o., Wujek, Radzikowski, Szubielska i Wspólnicy. Spólka Komandytowa's managing partner Gabriel Wujek is reckoned to be 'among the very best' corporate lawyers in the country, with a wealth of experience in M&A, privatisation and restructurings. The firm notably acts for clients in the automotive, steel and heavy industrial fields, and recently acted for the FSO car plant, which has a licence to produce Daewoo cars, on its sale of a controlling stake to Ukrainian investors.

Chajec, Don-Siemion & Zyto Legal Advisors continues to build a strong brand in M&A work, acting both for trade buyers and private equity funds. The firm appears to be developing a bit of a specialism with confectionery companies. Recent transactions include advising Cadbury Wedel in its acquisition of a distribution network from Leaf Poland, and acting for Jutrzenka in its acquisition of a confectionery plant from Nestlé Poland. Other notable transactions include acting for Enterprise Investors in its acquisition of a majority stake in national cinema chain Kinoplex, and NFI Empik Media on an investment in a national network of language schools. Andrzej Chajec is recommended for M&A and private equity, whilst Ewa Don-Siemion adds significant experience in securities and telecoms. One should also note the firm's labour law practice under Justyna Swiatkowska, which is gaining niche experience of temporary employment matters after it picked up Adecco as a client.

With over 80 lawyers, **Domanski Zakrzewski Palinka** is Poland's largest firm. Its client base is more or less an even spilt between Polish and international clients. The firm is developing an interesting line of business in advising Russian and Ukrainian clients on their investments in Poland, notably advising Awto ZAZ on its purchase of a controlling stake in FSO, a car plant with a licence to produce Daewoo cars in Poland. It was the first-ever takeover of a Polish company by Ukrainian investors. Other stand-out transactions for the firm include advising Getin Bank in its acquisition of Wschondni Bank Cukrownictwa, and Bridgestone on a greenfield investment. Grzegorz Domanski and managing partner Krzysztof Zakrzewski are recommended.

GESSEL – Attorneys at Law boosted its transactional corporate resources in 2004/2005 through the hire of former **Lovells** local managing partner Chrsitian Shmidt. His arrival adds new capabilities to service its German clients such as DB Cargo AG, and Deutsche Telekom AG, and adds additional M&A capacity. The firm continues to be active on the private equity front. It notably acts for AIB WKB Fund Management, Innova Capital and Enterprise Investors, advising the latter on its acquisition of a controlling stake in Zelmer SA. The firm's growing experience of Warsaw-based IPOs furthers its appeal to private equity clients looking to exit Polish investments.

Gide Loyrette Nouel is beginning to diversify away from its French clients towards a more pan-European client base. It is also picking up more Polish clients. For example, it advised DGS on its €95m LBO by Enterprise Investors, one of Poland's largest LBOs to date. M&A remains the firm's staple, but other varied work includes advising the Polish Ministry of the Treasury on the sale of the FSO car manufacturing plant to Ukrainian investors, and representing a major defence contractor in its tender for a €100m contract and offset agreement with the Polish Ministry of Defence.

German firm **Gleiss Lutz** advises clients in media, construction, financial services and retail, notably in M&A and real estate transactions. The firm has a 15-lawyer team in Warsaw under Torsten Bogen.

There is a strong insurance slant to **Lovells**' corporate activities. In addition to providing ongoing advice to insurers, it notably advised on the sale of shares in several Polish insurance subsidiaries, notably those belonging to Citigroup, Nationwide Global Holdings and Sampo. Away from insurance the office's client base is weighted towards banks, investment funds and other financial institutions. Partner Marek Wroniack is recommended for transactional corporate work, and for his funds expertise.

Nörr Stiefenhofer Lutz Sp.z.o.o. Radnoczy Sp.K advises primarily German-speaking clients on their Polish activities. Recently the firm advised ThyssenKrupp, both on restructuring and corporate transactions, and Telenot Electronic GmbH on a joint venture with a Polish distributor. M&A specialist Christoph Spiering is recommended to German private equity clients.

In the corporate sphere **Salans** is recommended to IT, telecoms and pharma clients. The firm is particularly active in regulatory work and reports a good deal of mid-sized M&A activity. Recent transactions of note include advising a French-US telecommunications conglomerate on its investment in a leading Polish mobile phone operator. Thomasz Dabrowski is the office's leader with respect to transactional corporate work. Changes in the Warsaw office recently include the hiring of new partner Wojciech Kozlowski from **Domanski Zakrzewski Palinka** to head up the pharma department. Meanwhile, Warsaw managing partner Dariusz Oleszczuk has been promoted to global managing partner, so the 'excellent' Krzysztof Stafanowicz, a telecoms and IT specialist, now holds the reigns in Warsaw.

After a brief stint as an independent firm in 2004/2005, *Wierzbowski i Wspólnicy*, which was previously part of PwC legal arm **Landwell**, joined with British law firm **Eversheds LLP** to form **Wierzbowski Eversheds**. Many foreign firms entering the market in recent years have found the going tough, but this venture looks sound. There is an excellent fit between the firms. Both focus on day-day corporate advice, and are particularly strong in labour law. With Poland rushing to comply with EU regulations, there are synergies to exploit between the firms. The Polish arm is also notable for its competition practice, and is strong in the telecoms arena – Managing Partner Krzysztof Wierzbowski specialises in the field, and Telekomunikacja Polska SA is a major client. The firm still maintains a close working relationship with PwC.

Hogan & Hartson M. Jamka, A. Galos, and Partners, L.L.P. features a dedicated six-lawyer department under Partner Wladek Rzycki that specialises in public procurement work. It represents Polish and foreign bidders in large public tenders, including world-class Western defence contractors in tenders for defence equipment supplies and offset contracts. A separate M&A team under managing partner Aleksander Galos recently advised Vodafone on its proposed investment in Polkomtel. Clients appreciate the firm's 'good-quality advice delivered through a speedy and reliable response', and its 'balanced approach to problems'.

In 2005 **Kochanski Brudkowski & Partners** made eight up-and-coming associates partner in light of the firm's growing headcount, which now numbers around 22 lawyers. Key areas include corporate work for the firm's automotive, media, IT, banking and pharma clients, which include a number of famous names such as Citibank, Intel and Fiat.

Laszczuk & Partners has carved some successful niches in the Polish market. The firm represents the Polish sales operations of international airlines, notably Lufthansa, SAS and Emirates, is a leading firm for the representation of advertising agencies, such as Oglivy and Mather, and represents direct-selling companies that are active in the Polish and wider European markets. Another aspect is the firm's growing IT practice which numbers Cisco as a client and works in the software development and e-commerce fields. The firm is credited for its 'thorough and pragmatic' advice.

Under managing partner Piotr Strawa, **Norton Rose, Piotr Strawa and Partners, Limited Partnership** continued to advise Nestlé and Lear Corporation, handling the disposal of a major chocolate plant for the former, and advising the latter on the merger of its Polish subsidiaries.

Led by Tomasz Gizbert Studnicki, Krakow-based **Studnicki, Pleszka, Cwiakalski, Górski LLP** enjoys an excellent reputation in the fields of commercial contracts, corporate law, M&A and penal law.

TGC Corporate Lawyers is recommended for employment and tax advice and has a dedicated desk to service German clients.

Two years on from spinning out of **Wardynski & Partners, Wiercinski, Kwiecinski, Baehr Sp. k.** has established a stable, five-partner practice offering a full service, with particular strength in the energy sector. The firm worked on the privatisation and restructuring of the Huta Czestochowa steelworks in 2004/2005, and advised on the merger of two mines and three power plants into a single entity. Andrzej Wierciński is recommended.

Kancelaria Joachim Hilla has a predominantly German-speaking client base and advised on a major privatisation in the energy sector in 2004.

Kancelaria Prawnicza Magnusson straddles the Baltic with offices in Moscow, Copenhagen, Stockholm and Warsaw. The latter provides ongoing advice to Skanska Poland, the Polish subsidiaries of a US electronics manufacturer, and a US software manufacturer on its Polish activities. The office also has a booming real estate practice. With six partners and 22 lawyers under managing partner Andrzej Tokaj, Warsaw is the firm's largest office.

In late 2004 **DLA Piper Rudnick Gray Cary UK LLP** entered the Polish market by adding **Lukowicz Swierzewski & Partners** to its growing network. The domestic firm numbers 25 lawyers and has branches in Krakow, Poznan and Wroclaw. Post-merger, the majority of its clients have been foreign-owned companies, often multinationals in the real estate, retail and banking sectors. Of particular note is the firm's employment practice under Malgorzata Fitrzyk-Barral.

Six-partner **M.Furtek i Wspolnicy Kancelaria Prawnicza** is particularly noted for its work in telecoms and IT. It advised a mobile phone operator in a public tender for a UMTS licence, and Exatel SA as part of a consortium offering to implement a nationwide TETRA mobile system for the Polish Government. IT work includes representing Poland's largest retail bank in IT contracts. Partner Marciej Gawroński combines corporate skills and expertise in the legal aspects of new technologies, such as wireless networks like WAN and VoIP.

US firm **Miller, Canfield, W. Babicki i Wspólnicy Sp.k**, which has offices in Warsaw, Wroclaw and Gdansk, is recommended to clients from the automotive industry. Ford is a notable client.

In 2005 **Nowakowski i Wspólnicy** joined forces with **S. Cetera, M. Wêgrzyn-Wysocka i Wspólnicy** and **Kancelaria Slazak, Zapiór & Partnerzy** to create the *ConsortioLex* consortium in order to compete with the biggest domestic firms. Although not a merger, the consortium creates a group of 110 lawyers in various regional centres including Wroclaw and Katowice. Warsaw-based **Nowakowski i Wspólnicy** led by Adam Krause may be regarded as the lead firm in the group, and has existing strengths in the transportation field, particularly in rail and logistics.

Peter Nielsen & Partners Law Office sp. K has re-branded as an independent firm in Poland. It was formerly the Warsaw office of pan-Scandinavian outfit **MAQS Advokatbyrå**. It has a decent international client base, which notably includes Netto supermarkets. The firm retains a Scandinavian flavour with around 40% of its clients from the region, whilst managing partner Peter Nielsen is Danish born and educated. The firm has a growing labour law practice and has been involved in numerous asbestos-related cases.

Notable clients that **Rutkowski Windmill Gasiewski & Roman LP** provides day-to-day advice to include Poland's leading pharmaceutical company, and its leading TV set manufacturer.

Siemiatkowski & Davies opened for business in 2005 under name partners Andrzej Siemiatkowski and Michael Davies. Both were formerly partners at **Allen & Overy, A. Pedzich sp. k.**. The firm is targeting corporate and projects-related work and appears to have got off to a flying start. In its short life it has advised both a UK-based private equity fund, and a US company, on restructuring, and reports an unexpectedly buoyant real estate practice, notably advising a German real estate fund on a bid for major office block in central Warsaw.

Squire Sanders Wiater sp. k. was created in 2005 through the merger of *Wiater LLP* with **Squire, Sanders & Dempsey L.L.P.**. Critics may claim that Poland lacks room for more international practices, but rather than set up from scratch, **Squire, Sanders & Dempsey L.L.P.** has wisely merged with an established local player. Time will tell whether the venture is successful, but the firm is planning for the long term, and the addition of a Warsaw presence fills a gap for a firm that already has a large presence throughout the region. It seems to have got off to a good start, advising GTS Central Europe in its €60m acquisition of Energis Polska. Managing Partner Krzysztof Wiater has a broad range of commercial experience from running his own firm, including advising major Western defence contractors on offset contracts with the Polish government.

Tomczak i Partnerzy Spolka Adwokacka advises the Polish subsidiaries of a number of famous global companies, including a major international pharmaceutical firm, an iconic clothing brand, and a leading Western European car manufacturer. The firm worked on the Polish aspects of a €1bn-plus acquisition of a health product manufacturer recently.

Two-partner **Zgutka i partnerzy, adwokaci** is advising Obi and Univeg on the construction of a logistics platform to service Obi DIY stores around Poland.

In 2004/2005 **DeBenedetti Majewski Szczesniak Kancelaria Prawnicza Sp. K** advised on the acquisition of five insurance companies on behalf of an EU-based client. The firm's four partners have a wide body of investment fund-related experience. Partner David DeBenedetti has hedge fund experience.

Karniol Malecki i Wspólnicy Sp. K notably advises French and US clients from the publishing, insurance and retail sectors.

Marek Musiol Law Office's client base generally comprises of medium-sized Polish companies and investment funds. The firm advises US venture capital funds on acquisitions of shares in Polish enterprises.

Rachelski & Wspolnicy's 18-fee-earner team has a banking background and experience of corporate transactional work, project finance and restructuring.

DISPUTE RESOLUTION

Wardynski & Partners is a recognised leader for disputes, both in Poland and at EU level, with partners Monika Hartung, Tomasz Wardyński and Marcin Radwan-Rohrenschef all respected practitioners. The firm maintains a relationship with London's **Brick Court Chambers** to train its lawyers in litigation and EU law, and has strengths in IP and competition-related litigation. One recent highlight for the firm involved representing the Law Debenture Trust in a bankruptcy proceeding against Elektrim SA.

Weil, Gotshal & Manges' approach to disputes is somewhat unique in Poland. Opposing lawyers repeatedly use terms like 'aggressive' and 'relentless' in describing it. One even remarked that 'they are not interested in making friends'. But all seem to admire the firm's ability to get results. The Warsaw office represented Vivendi in an arbitration and court proceedings against Deutsche Telekom concerning €2.2bn-worth of property rights to Polska Telefonia Cyfrowa recently.

CMS Cameron McKenna Pawel Debowski Spólka Komandytowa's standalone team represents a range of clients from domestic Polish companies to well-known international brands at all levels of disputes, including international arbitration. Pawel Pietkiewicz's team expanded to three partners and ten assistants last year. It is credited for its 'excellent advice in complicated matters'. The range of cases handled recently includes examples in product liability, tobacco litigation, insolvency proceedings, insurance claims and white-collar crime. The firm's sterling real estate credentials make it particularly recommended for construction disputes.

Soltysinski Kawecki & Szlezak has an excellent track record in disputes. Dariusz Skuza leads a department that is recognised as one of the very best for commercial litigation by rival firms. It has a notable history of representing the Republic of Poland, and is currently representing it in a couple of high-profile arbitrations.

Baker & McKenzie strengthened its ability to represent the interests of public bodies through the hire Michal Kulesz as counsel, who previously ran his own practice in public administrative consulting. Notable work includes representing 40 public hospitals in a case against the State Treasury. The office also represented a Polish company in a multi-million dollar arbitration in Moscow.

Dewey Ballantine Grzesiak SP.K. offers a full range of disputes services, from litigation through to arbitration, both in Poland and abroad. Notable recent work includes successfully acting for SAB Miller in Poland in a case concerning a minority shareholder squeeze-out, and representing Telekomunikacja Polska in arbitration proceedings in Vienna regarding its payment dispute with Danish-Polish Telecommunications Group.

Domanski Zakrzewski Palinka represented Polska Telefonia Cyfrowa in a takeover defence against Deutsche Telekom and Elektrim, and previously advised GlaxoSmithKline and a major US commodities firm in disputes

Drzewiecki, Tomaszek & Wspólnicy Spólka Jawna's Andrzej Tomaszek and Marcin Juszczyk are recommended. The firm is rated for contentious matters by rival law firms. It notably represented clients from the construction industry in proceedings before the Arbitration Court at the National Chamber of Commerce.

Linklaters offers a full-service litigation and arbitration practice through Zbigniew Kruczkowski's stable, eight-strong team. Banking and tax-related disputes dominated the agenda through 2005, including one very high-profile case concerning a shareholding worth a couple of billion euro.

Office leaders such as Krzystof Stefanowicz and Tomasz Dabrowski combine transactional and contentious skills at **Salans**, which moves up the table this year due to its participation in some large, varied and interesting international arbitrations. It represented the Polish State

DISPUTE RESOLUTION

WARDYNSKI & PARTNERS ✪
WEIL, GOTSHAL & MANGES ✪

CMS CAMERON McKENNA PAWEL DEBOWSKI SPÓLKA KOMANDYTOWA ✪
SOLTYSINSKI KAWECKI & SZLEZAK ✪

Baker & McKenzie ✪
Dewey Ballantine Grzesiak SP.K. ✪
Domanski Zakrzewski Palinka ✪
Drzewiecki, Tomaszek & Wspólnicy Spólka Jawna
Linklaters ✪
Salans
Wierzbowski Eversheds ✪

Chadbourne & Parke Polska Sp. z o.o., Wujek, Radzikowski, Szubielska i Wspólnicy. Spólka Komandytowa
Chajec, Don-Siemion & Zyto Legal Advisors ✪
Clifford Chance
Gide Loyrette Nouel ✪
Hogan & Hartson M. Jamka, A. Galos, and Partners, L.L.P. ✪
Joachim Hilla, Kancelaria
Kochanski Brudkowski & Partners ✪
Kubas Kos Gaertner
Laszczuk & Partners ✪
Lovells ✪
M.Furtek i Wspolnicy Kancelaria Prawnicza ✪
Nörr Stiefenhofer Lutz Sp.z.o.o. Radnoczy Sp.K ✪
Rutkowski Windmill Gasiewski & Roman LP ✪
Studnicki, Pleszka, Cwiakalski, Górski LLP
TGC Corporate Lawyers
White & Case – W. Danilowicz, W. Jurcewicz i Wspólnicy Kancelaria Prawna sp.K

Allen & Overy, A. Pedzich sp. k. ✪
Beiten Burkhardt K. Rastawicki Sp.K. ✪
GESSEL – Attorneys at Law ✪
Lesnodorski, Slusarek & Partners ✪
Miller, Canfield, W. Babicki i Wspólnicy Sp.k
Norton Rose, Piotr Strawa and Partners, Limited Partnership
Nowakowski i Wspólnicy
Nowosielski Gotkowicz Kosmus i partnerzy

Firms are listed A-Z in tiers which are ranked in order of priority
✪ Indicates firm displays contact details at the end of this chapter.

Treasury in a case concerning its share of PZU, Poland's largest insurance company, Deutsche Telekom in a case regarding shares in Polska Telefonia, and a shareholding hedge fund in a high-profile arbitration against TP Internet concerning a share sale agreement.

Wierzbowski Eversheds is recommended for disputes in the telecoms field, and for cases before Poland's Office for Protection of Competition and Consumers. The firm's recent merger with **Eversheds LLP** adds a European dimension to the firm, and should help it to exploit its strengths in competition and labour law at EU level. Henryk Romańczuk is recommended.

Chadbourne & Parke Polska Sp. z o.o., Wujek, Radzikowski, Szubielska I Wspólnicy. Spólka Komandytowa is notable for its strong tax department and ability to handle tax-related litigation. Away from tax, the office boasts partner Anna Milosz, who has experience of competition and IP-related litigation, whilst Mariusz Stawiarczyk is recommended for real estate disputes.

Krzysztof Zyto of **Chajec, Don-Siemion & Zyto Legal Advisors** has a ten-year track record as a judge and is recommended for domestic litigation. In recent years he has been involved in an assortment of cases, including advising creditors in several large proceedings concerning money collection, claims against insurance companies, and a claim against an art gallery involving a forged painting.

Clifford Chance has worked on some high-value cases in recent years. Of note is representing bondholders in a dispute regarding the payment of €510m-worth of Elektrim SA's Eurobonds, advising a Polish telecoms company in a range of disputes in both the common and arbitration courts, and winning an arbitration in Switzerland between partners in a media joint venture. Bartosz Kruzewski co-ordinates a seven-strong team.

Gide Loyrette Nouel advises clients at all levels of domestic and international disputes, and has widened its scope in recent years into IP, trade marks, and competition, for which the firm notably advises name-brand cosmetics companies, such as L'Oréal.

Many lawyers in the Polish market rate Krakow-based **Kubas Kos Gaertner** for civil and commercial disputes in Poland.

Laszczuk & Partners is particularly recommended for tax and IP-related disputes, although the firm is also growing in stature in corporate litigation. Maciej Laszczuk is a recognised leader in commercial and tax litigation, including arbitration, and has a growing practice advising the management of large companies facing criminal tax charges.

Marek Furtek of **M.Furtek i Wspolnicy Kancelaria Prawnicza** is recognised by the market as having a good profile in domestic dispute resolution. He represented a Polish bank and a major Polish construction company in arbitrations recently.

Rutkowski Windmill Gasiewski & Roman LP's Karol Rutkowski advises both Polish and international banks, financial institutions and corporations in disputes.

White & Case – W. Danilowicz, W. Jurcewicz i Wspólnicy Kancelaria Prawna sp.K has advised clients in the pharmaceutical, IT, insurance, debt collection and energy sectors. 2004/2005 saw the firm representing investors in disputes concerning the privatisation of state enterprises, trade mark infringements, tax disputes and power-related disputes.

Twenty-six-lawyer **Lesnodorski, Slusarek & Partners** stands out for its services to ventures involving Polish, Russian Ukranian and Belarussian entities. The firm worked on some high-profile litigation in 2005, including acting for the Industrial Union of Donbass in overturning the selection of LNM Holdings (Mittal Steel) as purchaser in the privatisation of the Huta Czestochowa steel business. The firm subsequently advised the Ukrainian steel group on a new and ultimately successful tender for the investment.

INTELLECTUAL PROPERTY

Soltysinski Kawecki & Szlezak's clients include Intel, Silicon Graphics, McDonald's, Rolex, and Microsoft, the latter for which the firm successfully acted in a claim to recover its internet domain name in Poland. Key areas include litigation, licence drafting (particularly software) and trade marks. Stanislaw Soltysinski is a recognised leader in the IP field.

Baker & McKenzie represented some very well-known companies in IP matters recently. Good examples include advising Orange on the re-branding of its Polish mobile operator Idea, handling anti-counterfeiting programmes for both Estée Lauder and Calvin Klein, and representing Best Western Hotels in proceedings concerning the infringement of its trade mark in Poland.

Dewey Ballantine Grzesiak SP.K.'s six-lawyer IP practice under Lukasz Redziniack advises on IT and IP-related matters for media, entertainment, IT and banking clients. Recently it advised PSE Electra in a dispute regarding energy-trading information systems.

At **Hogan & Hartson M. Jamka, A. Galos, and Partners, L.L.P.** Oskar Tulodziecki's team continued to work for its excellent media client base, following up its previous work on unauthorised internet translations of *Harry Potter* with an application for border customs protection of community trade marks for Walt Disney. The firm serves other notable entertainment groups like Warner Bros and Nintendo. In addition to its media clients, the firm is also gaining strength in pharma-related IP. Pharma specialist Bogudar Kordiasiewicz joined the firm recently, and the practice successfully defended Bristol-Myers Squibb in a trade mark infringement case.

Associate Krystyna Szczepanowska Kozlowska's four-strong **Linklaters** team advises both domestic and international companies on IP and provides legal services in the fields of internet domain names, packaging, pharmaceutical data, manufacturing and distribution agreements, franchises, and data protection. Its client base has a bias towards the pharmaceutical, media and financial sectors.

Wlodzimierz Szoszuk of **Wardynski & Partners** has considerable experience. He leads practice with a strong focus on trade mark prosecution work, ably backed up by one of the country's best litigation teams.

Wierzbowski Eversheds' Krzysztof Wierzbowski, Magdalena Orzelska-Bratkowska and Tomasz Zalewski have expertise in IP and IT matters, notably acting for clients in the telecoms and IT sectors.

INTELLECTUAL PROPERTY

SOLTYSINSKI KAWECKI & SZLEZAK

BAKER & McKENZIE ✪
DEWEY BALLANTINE GRZESIAK SP.K. ✪
HOGAN & HARTSON M. JAMKA, A. GALOS, AND PARTNERS, L.L.P. ✪
LINKLATERS ✪
WARDYNSKI & PARTNERS ✪
WIERZBOWSKI EVERSHEDS ✪

CMS Cameron McKenna Pawel Debowski Spólka Komandytowa ✪
Domanski Zakrzewski Palinka ✪
Drzewiecki, Tomaszek & Wspólnicy Spólka Jawna

Gide Loyrette Nouel ✪
Kochanski Brudkowski & Partners ✪
Kuczek & Maruta
Laszczuk & Partners ✪
Traple, Konarski, Podrecki s.c.
White & Case – W. Danilowicz, W. Jurcewicz i Wspólnicy Kancelaria Prawna sp.K

Allen & Overy, A. Pedzich sp. k. ✪
Beiten Burkhardt K. Rastawicki Sp.K. ✪
Chadbourne & Parke Polska Sp. z o.o., Wujek, Radzikowski, Szubielska i Wspólnicy. Spólka Komandytowa
GESSEL – Attorneys at Law ✪
Gleiss Lutz ✪

Clifford Chance
Lovells ✪
Rutkowski Windmill Gasiewski & Roman LP ✪
Salans
Weil, Gotshal & Manges ✪

Firms are listed A-Z in tiers which are ranked in order of priority
✪ Indicates firm displays contact details at the end of this chapter.

At **CMS Cameron McKenna Pawel Debowski Spólka Komandytowa,** senior associate and corporate group member Bogdan Duda is also a qualified patent attorney. His practice is largely concerned with trade marks, advising Bayer AG and Providential Financial recently on trade mark issues.

Domanski Zakrzewski Palinka's more notable IP clients include major pharma groups such as Polpharma, Pfizer and GlaxoSmithKline. The firm offers IP litigation, alongside trade mark, patent and copyright-protection services.

In addition to helping clients acquire and license intellectual property rights, **Drzewiecki, Tomaszek & Wspólnicy Spólka Jawna** works with the Polish customs authorities on the implementation of nationwide anti-piracy actions. Marcjanna Rejman and Andrzej Tomaszek are recommended.

Gide Loyrette Nouel is kept busy by a host of luxury brands such as L'Oréal, Lancôme, LVMH and Giorgio Armani that use the firm for IP-related matters, both in Poland, and elsewhere in Europe.

Tomasz Brudkowski of **Kochanski Brudkowski & Partners** runs a well-regarded IP practice. The firm notably represented ThyssenKrupp in trade mark litigation in recent years.

IT, internet and pharmaceutical clients form a large part of Krakow-based **Kuczek & Maruta**'s client base. The firm has developed a strong IP practice to serve such clients. Founding partner Marcin Maruta specialises in software, internet transactions, and electronic signatures.

Michal Siciarek of **Laszczuk & Partners** runs an IP practice that is held in high regard. The firm's niches in advertising and technology generate a good deal of IP-related work, whilst trade mark and anti-counterfeiting work are an important area for a firm notable for advising Hugo Boss in Poland. The firm's strength in litigation complements the practice.

Elzbieta Traple and Pawel Podrecki of Krakow-based technology and media firm **Traple, Konarski, Podrecki s.c.**, are well regarded among domestic law firms for the quality of their IP advice and reasonable fees.

Under Igor Ostrowski, **White & Case – W. Danilowicz, W. Jurcewicz i Wspólnicy Kancelaria Prawna sp.K** has an IP department that complements the firm's excellent TMT practice. The firm was largely involved with trade mark and anti-piracy issues in 2004/2005. The presence of brand media organisations such as MTV Poland and Columbia Tristar on the firm's client list demonstrate the strength of the department.

GESSEL – Attorneys at Law's Dorota Bryndal specialises in IT, pharmaceutical law and unfair competition. She is also active in IP, advising ComputerLand in an unfair competition dispute against Prokom in the Superior Court in recent years. The firm is currently building a copyright practice for artists.

Rutkowski Windmill Gasiewski & Roman LP advised Poland's leading producer of food seasoning in proceedings against a major rival that had produced a 'lookalike' product.

PROJECTS, ENERGY AND NATURAL RESOURCES

CMS CAMERON McKENNA PAWEL DEBOWSKI SPÓLKA KOMANDYTOWA ✪

BAKER & McKENZIE ✪
DEWEY BALLANTINE GRZESIAK SP.K. ✪
WARDYNSKI & PARTNERS ✪

Allen & Overy, A. Pedzich sp. k. ✪
Chadbourne & Parke Polska Sp. z o.o., Wujek, Radzikowski, Szubielska i Wspólnicy. Spólka Komandytowa
Clifford Chance
Gide Loyrette Nouel ✪
Hogan & Hartson M. Jamka, A. Galos, and Partners, L.L.P. ✪
Linklaters ✪
Salans
Soltysinski Kawecki & Szlezak ✪
Wiercinski, Kwiecinski, Baehr Sp. k. ✪
White & Case – W. Danilowicz, W. Jurcewicz i Wspólnicy Kancelaria Prawna sp.K

Gleiss Lutz ✪
Lovells ✪
M.Furtek i Wspolnicy Kancelaria Prawnicza ✪
Nörr Stiefenhofer Lutz Sp.z.o.o. Radnoczy Sp.K ✪
Norton Rose, Piotr Strawa and Partners, Limited Partnership
Siemiatkowski & Davies
Squire Sanders Wiater sp. k. ✪
Weil, Gotshal & Manges ✪

Firms are listed A-Z in tiers which are ranked in order of priority
✪ Indicates firm displays contact details at the end of this chapter.

PROJECTS, ENERGY AND NATURAL RESOURCES

In addition to its strong project finance practice, **CMS Cameron McKenna Pawel Debowski Spólka Komandytowa** has a lot of experience with project sponsors in the infrastructure and energy sectors. Key infrastructure work in 2004/2005 included advising a foreign consortium on their investment in Poland's first major PPP, the A1 toll motorway project. Recent energy-related work includes advising various clients on oil and gas exploration and development matters, and handling both acquisitions and project financings of powerplants. Key figures in the six-partner teaminclude practice head Dariusz Mioduski, who is recommended for both energy and finance, and office managing partner Andrew Kozlowski, who specialises in PPPs.

Baker & McKenzie continues its involvement in major infrastructure projects, advising Poland's national airports on the development of the second terminal at Warsaw Okecie International Airport, and acting for a couple of clients in negotiations for concessions on €1.7bn-worth of new motorways in Poland. On the energy side, the firm is advising Caterpillar Power Ventures on the acquisition and erection of a power plant, and SGT Europol Gaz SA on the contracts for the Polish section of the Yamal-Western Europe gas pipeline. Jur Gruszczyński is recommended.

Dewey Ballantine Grzesiak SP.K. has an excellent track record in advising energy sector clients on corporate and finance matters. In addition to its sterling work restructuring PGNiG's debt, it continued to represent PSE-Electra SA on the restructuring of its long-term power purchase contracts, and worked on legislation that paves the way for securitisations in the power generation sectors.

Wardynski & Partners has considerable experience with energy companies in Poland, having worked on numerous privatisations in the sector. Tomasz Wardyński has considerable experience of negotiations relating to large public projects. Over the years the firm has been involved in projects for roads, railways, the environment and sewage treatment. The firm's long-running work on the A-1 motorway project also demonstrates a good deal of project finance expertise.

Despite the departure of Michael Davies to set up his own firm, **Allen & Overy, A. Pedzich sp. k.** remains strong for project finance work due to the skills of Arkadiusz Pedzich. In addition, Jane Townsend, who joined the office as joint managing partner in May 2005, has experience of working with energy companies in corporate and reorganisation work.

Igor Muszyński joined **Chadbourne & Parke Polska Sp. z o.o., Wujek, Radzikowski, Szubielska i Wspólnicy. Spólka Komandytowa** in 2005, having previously been head of energy at **White & Case – W. Danilowicz, W. Jurcewicz i Wspólnicy Kancelaria Prawna sp.K.** He has extensive experience of advising both investors and the State Treasury on energy sector privatisations, and now does a good deal of regulatory energy work at his new practice.

Energy companies that have used, or continue to use **Clifford Chance** include Elektrocieplownie Warszawskie, Vattenfall Group, EDF and Energis Polska. The office advised the latter with respect to an investment in the company by Innova in 2004/2005. The firm also advised Energis Polska's shareholders on the €60m sale of 97.5% of the company to GTS. The Poland office also has considerable proficiency in the project finance field.

Gide Loyrette Nouel's Robert Jedrzejczyk specialises in corporate transactions in the energy sector. Recently he advised French investors on the purchase of power plants in Poland, and a large energy company on the privatisation of a Polish electricity distribution company.

Hogan & Hartson M. Jamka, A. Galos, and Partners, L.L.P. has a four-lawyer energy practice under Tomasz Dorowolski. In addition to handling energy-related corporate work, the firm advised on both energy and emissions-trading recently.

Key deals for **Linklaters** in 2004/2005 include advising the City of Warsaw on the Warsaw Metro project's compliance with structural funds, state aid and public procurement rules, and acting for the Polish national grid company on its unbundling and leasing in order to comply with EU laws.

Salans' Arek Krasnodebski is a specialist in energy, infrastructure projects and environmental protection. He has experience of advising on energy-related regulatory matters, and of acting for European and US investors in privatisation and greenfield projects involving energy generation, transmission and trading.

Soltysinski Kawecki & Szlezak has advised SGT EuRoPol GAZ SA in connection with the construction of the US$1bn Polish section of a natural gas transit pipelines linking Siberia to Western Europe.

Name partner Jerzy Baehr of **Wiercinski, Kwiecinski, Baehr Sp. k.** is a specialist energy lawyer with considerable experience in the sector. Much of the firm's corporate work is with energy-related companies. The firm was involved in the unbundling of the country's electricity and gas distribution networks.

White & Case – W. Danilowicz, W. Jurcewicz i Wspólnicy Kancelaria Prawna sp.K's energy sector clients include some of the biggest players on both the Polish and the European scenes. The firm is equally skilled at handling matters as diverse as energy sector privatisations, outbound investments by Polish energy companies, and investments and acquisitions by foreign companies of Polish assets. Strong project finance capabilities and a general strength in energy across the firm's CEE jurisdictions are a further bonus.

M.Furtek i Wspolnicy Kancelaria Prawnicza has experience of telecoms infrastructure work.

Norton Rose, Piotr Strawa and Partners, Limited Partnership advises WKN Windkraft Nord AG, a windfarm developer, on Polish renewable energy projects.

Siemiatkowski & Davies' Michael Davies has a good deal of experience in projects and energy-related work. Wasting no time at his new firm after moving from **Allen & Overy, A. Pedzich sp. k.**, he advised a Dutch company and a UK AIM-listed company on renewable energy projects in Poland.

Squire Sanders Wiater sp. k. features four lawyers experienced in energy matters, most notably Pawel Grzejszczak. Over the years he has advised the Ministry of State Treasury on the privatisation of eight power distribution companies and a national gas supplier on establishing five gas distribution companies.

REAL ESTATE

CMS CAMERON McKENNA PAWEL DEBOWSKI SPÓLKA KOMANDYTOWA ✪

BAKER & McKENZIE ✪
LINKLATERS ✪
SALANS

Chadbourne & Parke Polska Sp. z o.o., Wujek, Radzikowski, Szubielska i Wspólnicy. Spólka Komandytowa
Clifford Chance
Soltysinski Kawecki & Szlezak ✪
Wardynski & Partners ✪
White & Case – W. Danilowicz, W. Jurcewicz i Wspólnicy Kancelaria Prawna sp.K

Allen & Overy, A. Pedzich sp. k. ✪
Dewey Ballantine Grzesiak SP.K. ✪
Domanski Zakrzewski Palinka ✪
Drzewiecki, Tomaszek & Wspólnicy Spólka Jawna
Gide Loyrette Nouel ✪
Hogan & Hartson M. Jamka, A. Galos, and Partners, L.L.P. ✪
Kancelaria Prawnicza Magnusson
Laszczuk & Partners ✪
Lovells ✪
Miller, Canfield, W. Babicki i Wspólnicy Sp.k
TGC Corporate Lawyers
Wierzbowski Eversheds ✪

Chajec, Don-Siemion & Zyto Legal Advisors ✪
GESSEL – Attorneys at Law ✪
Gleiss Lutz ✪
Haarmann Hemmelrath ✪
Malecki & Rychlowski, Kancelaria Adwokacka
Lukowicz Swierzewski & Partners ✪
Nörr Stiefenhofer Lutz Sp.z.o.o. Radnoczy Sp.K ✪
Siemiatkowski & Davies
Squire Sanders Wiater sp. k. ✪
Weil, Gotshal & Manges ✪

Firms are listed A-Z in tiers which are ranked in order of priority
✪ Indicates firm displays contact details at the end of this chapter.

Weil, Gotshal & Manges advised BOT Elektrownia Belchatow on its EPC contract to build a new 833MW lignite-fired power plant, and continues to advise the company on financing.

REAL ESTATE

CMS Cameron McKenna Pawel Debowski Spólka Komandytowa tops the real estate tables in a number of CEE jurisdictions, including Poland, where it is widely recognised by rivals as the leader real in estate and construction matters. Furthermore, practice head Pawel Debowski is acknowledged as one of the country's top practitioners in the field. In addition to serving its significant UK-based clientele, the dedicated four-partner team is sufficiently large to have further desks dedicated German, Spanish and French clients. The group was involved in a number of high-value land purchases and commercial property transactions through 2004/2005, and is ably backed up by a finance team that acts as exclusive counsel to one of Europe's largest mortgage lenders, and a strong projects practice.

Baker & McKenzie is working on some world-class office building projects in Warsaw. It is advising ING Real Estate on the acquisition and development of the €400m Zlote Tarasy Project, and acting for Hochtief Project Development Polska on its construction of the €200m Rondo 1 building. The firm's selection by Warsaw Okecie International Airport to advise it on the construction of its new terminal is further testament to the strengths of Tomasz Kurek and Malgorzata Pietrzak-Paciorek's seven-lawyer practice.

Partner Artur Kulwalski should take credit, for rivals have noticed the growing prominence of **Linklaters** on the Polish real estate scene. The City of Warsaw appears to favour the firm. In addition to the firm's work on the Warsaw Metro, Warsaw handed a couple of €100m real estate PPP projects in 2004/2005, one concerning the redevelopment of historic Warsaw buildings destroyed during WWII. The firm's recent transaction list includes a number of €50m-plus deals, and these alone are varied in nature, including large development projects, complex financings, and portfolio transactions.

Polish real estate lawyers acknowledge that **Salans** is often involved in big property deals, and credit it as one of the leading practices in the country. Marek Grodek, who heads the real estate group and French desk, advises a leading retailer on its development projects in Poland, and has worked on two of Poland's largest city-centre redevelopments. The firm also has a strong property finance practice. One notable transaction involved advising ING Lease Poland on the financing of a multi-million euro logistics centre in Moscow, a deal which demonstrates the firm's ability to handle complex cross-jurisdictional deals within the region.

Chadbourne & Parke Polska Sp. z o.o., Wujek, Radzikowski, Szubielska i Wspólnicy. Spólka Komandytowa represents developers, institutional investors and lenders in office, retail, residential and hotel projects throughout the country. Clients have included Invesco Real Estate, Hyatt Regency Warsaw and Pepsi. The practice features three partners: Mariusz Stawiarczyk, Zbigniew Skórczyński and David Dixon.

Clifford Chance had a good transactional year, notably for hypermarket group Carrefour. The firm advised it on both a US$130m-plus purchase of 13 hypermarkets, and on a €376m sale and leaseback to Aerium of 13 shopping malls and 19 hypermarkets in Poland and elsewhere in Eastern Europe. Meanwhile, the active real estate finance practice advised Eurohypo on a loan facility to purchase Norway House in Warsaw.

Soltysinski Kawecki & Szlezak is active in both transactional real estate work and in greenfield development in SEZs, and has represented a range of foreign investors over the years.

Founding partner Wieslaw Szczepiński runs **Wardynski & Partners**' real estate practice. In addition to acting for both domestic and foreign investors on real estate projects, the firm notably advises on the restitution of properties expropriated during the 1940s.

In 2005 **White & Case – W. Danilowicz, W. Jurcewicz i Wspólnicy Kancelaria Prawna sp.K** expanded its practice to four partners and six associates via several lateral hires, many coming from **Gide Loyrette Nouel**'s real estate team, including Jean Rossi, who joined as practice head. The firm numbers a leading international hotel chain and a top manager of Polish shopping centres as clients. Work for 2004/2005 spanned acquisition, development and construction.

Allen & Overy, A. Pedzich sp. k.'s great strength is the financing side of real estate. The firm continued to advise banks on large property loans in 2005. Particularly noteworthy was its advice to Aareal Bank Ag on a €188m financing for the Silesia City Centre in Katowice.

In addition to advising its corporate clients on real estate matters, **Dewey Ballantine Grzesiak SP.K.** represented fund managers Royalton Partners on its acquisition of 80% of Vratislavia Holdings, a parking and real estate group, and its later restructuring.

Time will tell how **Gide Loyrette Nouel** handles the departures from its real estate team, but it has quickly replenished its numbers, with Bertrand Oldra re-joining from the Paris office, and adding new clients such as Peabody and Pirelli Real Estate.

Pan-Baltic firm **Kancelaria Prawnicza Magnusson** advised a US property developer with respect to a €750m acquisition of a retail chain in Poland, and jointly advised Apollo Rida Developments in its US$75m purchase of Warsaw's tallest office building, the Warsaw Trade Tower. Katarzyna Sawa-Rybaczek heads the real estate team.

TAX

In 2005 **Baker & McKenzie** hired nine tax specialists from the Big Four accountants. The 13-strong team is now led by Miroslaw Barszcz and Slawomir Boruc, both formerly of PwC. It is now the largest tax group at a law firm in Poland. Notable work includes implementing one of Poland's first cross-border commissionaire tax structures, handling the tax implications of converting bank subsidiaries into branches, and working on a couple of multi-million US dollar tax disputes.

Chadbourne & Parke Polska Sp. z o.o., Wujek, Radzikowski, Szubielska i Wspólnicy. Spólka Komandytowa's nine-strong team, which includes three partners, mostly concerns itself with tax and customs-related disputes. Adam Wesolowski is very experienced in representing taxpayers in cases before the Supreme Administrative Court.

Dewey Ballantine Grzesiak SP.K.'s nine-lawyer department under Tomasz Kacymirow is one of the largest among Polish law firms. Notable recent work has involved advising on the tax implications of company restructurings, and handling proceedings before the Polish tax authorities.

Mariusz Aleksandrowicz at **Linklaters** runs a proactive four-strong practice that advises on the tax implications of corporate transactions and investments in addition to more general international tax planning.

Soltysinski Kawecki & Szlezak features a five-lawyer tax, customs and foreign exchange team under Jaroslaw Bieroński that works alongside the corporate department to optimise the tax aspects of the firm's wider transactions, in addition to handling standalone work.

CMS Cameron McKenna Pawel Debowski Spólka Komandytowa's 'professional, creative and available' senior associate Arkadiusz Michaliszyn is the most prominent lawyer in a team that advises clients on post-transactional tax issues, as well as day-to-day taxation matters.

Laszczuk & Partners' well regarded Maciej Laszczuk leads a five-lawyer team that handles the legal aspects of audits, often working alongside Big Four accountants. The firm also works closely with the customs authorities, and is frequently involved in tax-related litigation, often representing the management of large companies facing criminal tax charges.

Lovells' Andrezej Debiec is recognised in the market as an excellent tax lawyer. He recently handled the tax aspects of corporate restructurings and a securitisation.

Founded by former Ernst & Young partners, and comprising mainly of former employees of Big Four accounting firms, **MDDP Michalik Dluska Dziedzic i Partnerzy** is a boutique tax outfit comprising 12 tax advisers and four legal advisers. It offers a full tax service, including litigation, and advises a number of world-class companies.

Wardynski & Partners' team, led by Dariusz Wasylkowski, was strengthened in 2004 with the hire of auditor and tax adviser Krzysztof Szymański and his four-strong team from the Poland office of consultants BDO.

Counsel Robert Krasnodebski of **Weil, Gotshal & Manges** continues to advise many firm-wide clients on tax issues.

TAX

BAKER & McKENZIE ✪

CHADBOURNE & PARKE POLSKA SP. Z O.O., WUJEK, RADZIKOWSKI, SZUBIELSKA I WSPÓLNICY. SPÓLKA KOMANDYTOWA
DEWEY BALLANTINE GRZESIAK SP.K. ✪
LINKLATERS ✪
SOLTYSINSKI KAWECKI & SZLEZAK ✪

Beiten Burkhardt K. Rastawicki Sp.K. ✪
CMS Cameron McKenna Pawel Debowski Spólka Komandytowa ✪
Drzewiecki, Tomaszek & Wspólnicy Spólka Jawna
Gide Loyrette Nouel ✪
Laszczuk & Partners ✪
Lovells ✪
MDDP Michalik Dluska Dziedzic i Partnerzy
Studnicki, Pleszka, Cwiakalski, Górski LLP
TGC Corporate Lawyers
Wardynski & Partners ✪
Weil, Gotshal & Manges ✪
White & Case – W. Danilowicz, W. Jurcewicz i Wspólnicy Kancelaria Prawna sp.K

Allen & Overy, A. Pedzich sp. k. ✪
Gleiss Lutz ✪
Haarmann Hemmelrath ✪
Hogan & Hartson M. Jamka, A. Galos, and Partners, L.L.P. ✪

Clifford Chance
Kochanski Brudkowski & Partners ✪
Nörr Stiefenhofer Lutz Sp.z.o.o. Radnoczy Sp.K ✪
Norton Rose, Piotr Strawa and Partners, Limited Partnership
Nowakowski i Wspólnicy
Ozóg, Stolarek Wolniewicz I Wspólnicy
Salans

Firms are listed A-Z in tiers which are ranked in order of priority
✪ *Indicates firm displays contact details at the end of this chapter.*

White & Case – W. Danilowicz, W. Jurcewicz i Wspólnicy Kancelaria Prawna sp.K notably advises on the tax implications of both structured finance and complicated corporate transactions. Practice head Janusz Fiszer has a great deal of experience in this respect, and is supported by a team of three associates and senior counsel Bernard Lukomski.

As part of *ConsortiaLex*, **Nowakowski i Wspólnicy** beat **Wardynski & Partners** and **Baker & McKenzie** in a tender to represent venture capital fund MCI Management in a major tax case. Time will tell whether the group develops into a major player in tax litigation.

ALLEN & OVERY, A. PÊDZICH SP. K.

SIENNA CENTER
UL ZELAZNA 28/30
00-832 WARSAW

Telephone: +48 22 820 61 00
Fax: +48 22 820 61 99
E-mail: information@allenovery.com
Website: www.allenovery.com

Languages
English, French, German, Russian

Other offices
Amsterdam, Antwerp, Bangkok, Beijing, Bratislava, Brussels, Budapest, Dubai, Frankfurt, Hamburg, Hong Kong, London, Luxembourg, Madrid, Milan, Moscow, New York, Paris, Prague, Rome, Shanghai, Singapore, Tokyo, Turin

Number of lawyers 2,304
at this office 30

Contacts
Jane Townsend, Arkadiusz Pedzich, Jacek Jonak, Jaroslaw Iwanicki

CATEGORIES OF WORK

Arbitration/litigation
Jaroslaw Iwanicki

Banking/finance
Arkadiusz Pedzich

Corporate/commercial
Jaroslaw Iwanicki

Derivatives/securitisations
Jacek Jonak, Arkadiusz Pedzich

Energy
Arkadiusz Pedzich, Jaroslaw Iwanicki, Jane Townsend

Environment
Kamil Jankielewicz, Aleksandra Trzaskowska

EU and competition
Jaroslaw Iwanicki, Agnieszka Soltys

Intellectual property
Jaroslaw Iwanicki

International capital markets
Jacek Jonak, Arkadiusz Pedzich

Investments
Jaroslaw Iwanicki

M&A
Jaroslaw Iwanicki, Jane Townsend

Privatisations
Jaroslaw Iwanicki

Project finance
Arkadiusz Pedzich

Real estate/construction
Arkadiusz Pedzich, Radomil Charzynski

Telecommunications
Jaroslaw Iwanicki

Private equity and venture capital
Jane Townsend, Jaroslaw Iwanicki

BSJP BROCKHUIS SCHNELL JURCZAK PRUSAK

AL ARMII LUDOWEJ 26
FOCUS OFFICE BUILDING
00-609 WARSAW

Telephone: +48 22 579 89 00
Fax: +48 22 579 89 01
E-mail: office@bsjp-chsh.pl
Website: www.bsjp-chsh.pl

Languages
English, German, Italian

Other offices
Gdańsk, Katowice, Poznań, Wroclaw, Bucharest, Budapest, Brussels, Vienna

Number of lawyers 110
at this office 20

Contacts
Joern Brockhuis (joern.brockhuis@bsjp.pl), Christian Schnell (christian.schnell@bsjp.pl)

International groupings
In alliance with CHSH Cerha Hempel Spiegelfeld Hlawati

CATEGORIES OF WORK

Administrative business law, public procurement

Banking and finance, capital markets

Corporate law

Distribution law, franchising

Insolvency law

Intellectual property law

Competition and cartel law

Labour law

Litigation and arbitration

Mergers and acquistions

Privatisations

Real estate and construction law

Tax law, accounting

BAKER & McKENZIE
GRUSZCZYŃSKI & PARTNERS ATTORNEYS AT LAW LP

RONDO ONZ 1
00-124 WARSAW

Telephone: +48 22 445 31 00
Fax: +48 22 445 32 00
E-mail: warsaw@bakernet.com
Website: www.bakernet.com

Languages
English, French, German, Italian, Norwegian, Russian, Spanish, Swedish

Other offices
The member firms of Baker & McKenzie International, a Swiss Verein, have 70 offices in 38 countries around the world. For a complete list, please visit www.bakernet.com.

Number of lawyers 3,300+
at this office 81

Contact
Jur Gruszczyński (managing partner)

CATEGORIES OF WORK

Banking and finance
Krzysztof Korzeniewski

Commercial and competition law
Pawel Świrski, Dr Marta Sendrowicz

Employment law
Piotr Rawski, Sylwia Puzynowska-Sech

Energy
Dr Tomasz Stawecki, Pawel Magierowski

Environment
Jur Gruszczyński

European and public law
Prof Michal Kulesza

IP and IT
Marek Rosiński

Litigation and arbitration
Dr Andrzej Tynel

M&A/privatisation
Marcin Gmaj, Piotr Rawski

Major projects
Jur Gruszczyński

Pharmaceutical law
Paulina Kieszkowska

PE/VC
Tomasz Krzyzowski

Real estate and construction
Malgorzata Pietrzak-Paciorek, Tomasz Kurek

Securities
Konrad Konarski, Dr Jakub Celiński

Taxation
Slawomir Boruc

Telecommunications and media
Wojciech Bialik, Dr Eligiusz Jerzy Krześniak

BEITEN BURKHARDT K. RASTAWICKI SP. K.

UL.KS. IGNACEGO SKORUPKI 5
00-546 WARSAW

Telephone: +48 22 583 71 00
Fax: +48 22 583 71 09
E-mail: bblaw-warschau@bblaw.com
Website: www.bblaw.com

Languages
Cantonese, Czech, English, French, German, Hungarian, Italian, Mandarin, Russian, Slovak, Spanish, Ukrainian

Other offices
Beijing, Berlin, Brussels, Cologne, Düsseldorf, Frankfurt am Main, Hong Kong, Kiev, Leipzig, Moscow, Munich, Nuremberg, St Petersburg, Shanghai

Number of lawyers 249
at this office 17

Contact
Peter Daszkowski

CATEGORIES OF WORK

Company law

Banking and finance

Tax law

European law and cartel law

Foundation, association, societies and sports law

Industrial property rights

Labour law

Procurement law

Public law

Information technology

Estate planning and succession rules

Copyright law

Litigation and arbitration

Telecommunication law

Real estate law

Advertising law

Media law

CMS CAMERON MCKENNA PAWEŁ DĘBOWSKI SPÓLKA KOMANDYTOWA

WARSAW FINANCIAL CENTRE
UL EMILII PLATER 53
00-113 WARSAW

Telephone: +48 22 520 55 55
Fax: +48 22 520 55 56
E-mail: info@cmck.com
Website: www.law-now.com

Languages
English, French, German, Polish

Other offices
Aberdeen, Bristol, Bucharest, Budapest, Edinburgh, Hong Kong, London, Moscow, Prague, Sofia

Number of lawyers 587
at this office 85

Contact
Andrew Kozlowski

International grouping
CMS Cameron McKenna is a member of CMS. CMS is the alliance of major European law firms providing clients with a full range of legal and tax services. CMS's activities are co-ordinated through EEIG, registered in Brussels.

CATEGORIES OF WORK

Arbitration
Pawel Pietkiewicz

Banking and finance
Wojciech Wądołowski

Capital markets
Dariusz Greszta

Commercial
Malgorzata Surdek

Employment
Katarzyna Dulewicz

Energy and projects
Dariusz Mioduski

Environment
Stanislaw Wajda

Financial services
Iain Batty

Insurance and reinsurance
Piotr Czublan

Intellectual property
Bogdan Duda

International pensions and employee benefits
Iain Batty

Inward investment and tax
Arkadiusz Michaliszyn

IT and telecoms
Andrzej Krasuski

Real estate and construction
Pawel Debowski

M&A and private equity
Dariusz Greszta

Pharmaceuticals
Agnieszka Deeg Dabrowska

Dispute resolution
Pawel Pietkiewicz

THE FIRM

CMS Cameron McKenna is a full-service international commercial law partnership, advising businesses, financial institutions and governments in the UK and internationally. Since 1999 the firm has been a member of CMS. CMS is the alliance of major European law firms providing clients with a full range of legal and tax services.

The firm is particularly known for its presence in Central and Eastern Europe, with offices in Warsaw, Budapest, Bucharest, Prague, Sofia and Moscow. These offices are staffed by both local and UK-qualified lawyers and provide a full range of legal services to corporate clients and governments. The Warsaw office was established in 1993.

In 2005, the firm was named Eastern Europe law firm of the year at the *Chambers* Global Awards. The judges said, 'The firm has built on its reputation as a leading player in the region with several major transactions, including the €735m acquisition of the Bulgarian Telecoms company and the sale of Slovenske Elektrarne to Enel, one of the world's largest cross-border electricity deals. In addition, the CEE practice has been consolidated with new offices, joint ventures and associations'.

AREAS OF PRACTICE

CMS Cameron McKenna is one of the largest international law firms in Warsaw and as such is able to support clients in all aspects of their business activity. The firm works with multinational companies and agencies as well as large Polish businesses and organisations.

With the emphasis on quality and best international practice, the firm has attracted clients who have been involved in some of the most high-profile deals in the Polish market. CMS Cameron McKenna is particularly renowned for its work in the energy and real estate sectors. In both these sectors the teams have historically undertaken ground-breaking work. Their credentials include advising in leading PPP assignments and infrastructure projects as well as the creation of the first institutional investment lease.

The firm has also developed a strong reputation in other key practice areas. The corporate and commercial team have concentrated on building knowledge and expertise in several key sectors in order to offer clients a unique understanding of the issues involved. The teams are also becoming known for the creation of innovative products in the private equity market. Integral to the work of the real estate, energy and corporate departments, is the banking team. The banking team's work in project and real estate financing is widely recognised. Should clients come into dispute, CMS Cameron McKenna's significant litigation team has dedicated lawyers that can help. In addition to these core practice areas, the firm has niche competition, environment, insurance, employment, tax, IT and IP practices.

CMS Cameron McKenna runs a legal news service (which can be accessed at www.law-now.com). This service provides regular updates on changes to Polish and EU legislation and is available in English, Polish and French.

CHAJEC, DON-SIEMION & ŻYTO LEGAL ADVISORS

NORWAY HOUSE
UL LWOWSKA 19
00-660 WARSZAWA

Telephone: +48 22 820 07 90
Fax: +48 22 820 07 93
E-mail: kancelaria@cdz.com.pl
Website: www.cdz.com.pl

Languages
Polish, English, French, German, Russian

Number of lawyers 20

CATEGORIES OF WORK

General corporate law
Andrzej Chajec, Krzysztof Żyto

Mergers and acquisitions
Andrzej Chajec, Maciej Kotlicki

Capital markets
Maciej Kotlicki

Litigation
Krzysztof Żyto

Issuing securities on international markets
Ewa Don-Siemion

Investment funds
Andrzej Chajec, Maciej Kotlicki

Venture capital transactions
Andrzej Chajec

Telecommunications and media
Ewa Don-Siemion, Krzysztof Żyto

Energy law
Karol Szymanowski

Public private partnerships
Krzysztof Żyto

Administrative proceedings before the Securities and Exchange Commission
Maciej Kotlicki

Intellectual property law
Justyna Swiatkowska, Piotr Kryczek

Unfair competition and anti-monopoly law
Piotr Kryczek

Real estate and property development
Jakub Pitera, Weronika Kubas

Labour law
Piotr Kryczek

DEBENEDETTI MAJEWSKI SZCZEŚNIAK KANCELARIA PRAWNICZA SP. K.

SASKI POINT
UL. MARSZALKOWSKA 111
00-102 WARSAW

Telephone: +48 22 339 54 00
Fax: +48 22 339 54 01
E-mail: officewarsaw@dms.net.pl
Website: www.dms.net.pl

Languages
English, French, Polish, Russian

Number of lawyers 12

International grouping
Globalaw

CATEGORIES OF WORK

Corporate and business law
Dariusz Szcześniak,
C David DeBenedetti,
Dr hab Marek Michalski

Mergers and acquisitions
Dariusz Szcześniak,
C David DeBenedetti

Securities and capital markets
Dariusz Szcześniak,
Dr hab Marek Michalski

Criminal law
Dr hab Jaroslaw Majewski

Civil litigation
Dr hab Jaroslaw Majewski

Investment funds
Dariusz Szcześniak,
C David DeBenedetti,
Dr hab Marek Michalski

Intellectual property law
C David DeBenedetti

Venture capital transactions
C David DeBenedetti,
Dariusz Szcześniak

Hedge funds
C David DeBenedetti,
Dariusz Szcześniak

DEWEY BALLANTINE GRZESIAK SP.K.

STOCK EXCHANGE BUILDING
UL KSIAZECA 4
00-498 WARSAW

Telephone: +48 22 690 61 00
Fax: +48 22 690 62 22
E-mail: woffice@deweyballantine.com
Website: www.deweyballantine.com

Languages
English, French, German, Polish, Russian

Other offices
Austin, Beijing, East Palo Alto, Frankfurt, Houston, London, Los Angeles, Milan, New York, Rome, Washington DC

Number of lawyers 550+
at this office 50

Contacts
Lejb Fogelman (lfogelman@deweyballantine.com), Jarosław Grzesiak (jgrzesiak@deweyballantine.com)

CATEGORIES OF WORK

Asset finance/securitisation
Jaroslaw Grzesiak, Zbigniew Mrowiec

Banking and finance
Jaroslaw Grzesiak, Lejb Fogelman

Capital markets
Jaroslaw Grzesiak, Zbigniew Mrowiec

Competition
Jacek Michalski, Lukasz Redziniak

Corporate and commercial
Lejb Fogelman, Jaroslaw Grzesiak

Dispute resolution
Lukasz Redziniak

Energy and natural resources
Jaroslaw Grzesiak, Tomasz Kacymirow

Information technology
Lukasz Redziniak

Infrastructure and project finance
Jaroslaw Grzesiak, Tomasz Kacymirow

Intellectual property
Lukasz Redziniak

Insolvency/corporate restructuring
Jacek Michalski, Tomasz Kacymirow

Mergers and acquisitions
Lejb Fogelman, Jacek Michalski

Privatisation
Lejb Fogelman, Jacek Michalski

Real estate
Jacek Michalski

Tax
Tomasz Kacymirow

Telecommunications
Tomasz Kacymirow

e|n|w|c ATTORNEYS AT LAW
EISELSBERG NATLACEN WALDERDORFF CANCOLA

UL KOSZYKOWA 54
00-675 WARSZAWA

Tel: +48 22 584 97 40
Fax: +48 22 584 97 50
Email: warsaw@enwc.com
Website: www.enwc.com

Languages
English, German, Polish

Other offices:
Bratislava, Brno, Budapest, Prague, Vienna

Number of lawyers 47
at this office 4

Contacts
Dr Raimund Cancola, Dr Thomas Brandstätter

CATEGORIES OF WORK

M&A

Joint ventures

Corporate law

Property

Employment and labour law

Competition law

Construction and building

International arbitration and litigation

DOMAŃSKI ZAKRZEWSKI PALINKA

RONDO ONZ 1
00-124 WARSAW

Telephone: +48 22 557 76 00
Fax: +48 22 557 76 01
E-mail: dzp@dzp.pl
Website: www.dzp.pl

Languages
English, French, German, Italian, Japanese, Russian, Spanish

Other offices
Poznan, Wroclaw

Number of lawyers 90+

Contact
Krzysztof A Zakrzewski

CATEGORIES OF WORK

Corporate
Julita Zimoch-Tuchołka, Piotr Andrzejczak

Mergers and acquisitions
Krzysztof A Zakrzewski, Marcin Krakowiak

Banking and finance
Józef Palinka, Andrzej Foltyn

Real estate and property development
Lech Żyżylewski

Regulatory
Grzegorz Domański

Telecommunications
Krzysztof A Zakrzewski, Józef Palinka

Securities and capital markets
Andrzej Foltyn

Private equity funds and venture capital
Andrzej Foltyn, Marcin Krakowiak

Energy
Krzysztof A Zakrzewski

Arbitration/litigation
Grzegorz Domański, Józef Palinka

EU law
Janina Ligner-Zeromska

Intellectual property
Janina Ligner-Zeromska

Employment
Bogusław Kapłon

Antimonopoly law
Janina Ligner-Zeromska

Foreign direct investment
Marcin Krakowiak

Pharmaceuticals
Krzysztof A Zakrzewski

Advertising and media law
Janina Ligner-Zeromska

THE FIRM

Established in 1993, Domański Zakrzewski Palinka is a full-service Polish law firm with 11 partners and about 80 other lawyers, with local offices in Poznan and Wroclaw.

As a professional Polish law firm, Domański Zakrzewski Palinka possesses knowledge of firms' methods of conducting business activities within Poland, which allows the firm to help foreign investors eliminate various obstacles that might be faced when dealing with Polish companies or with state or local government authorities.

The firm offers legal advice regarding all aspects of law connected with business activity. The firm's clients include Polish companies with Polish capital, Polish companies with foreign capital, as well as foreign investors, including large multinationals, operating in various sectors of economy.

AREAS OF PRACTICE

The firm's most developed team advises in the area of corporate issues and M&A. The firm's lawyers represent clients participating in transactions and projects involving sale of businesses, mergers, company divisions and restructuring as well as privatisation transactions. Furthermore, the firm advises foreign clients who wish to establish business in Poland, including advice on formation of companies, all aspects of greenfield investments and relevant employment legislation. The firm's expertise also includes M&A transactions within the public market, IPOs and the establishment of investment funds and brokerage houses. To meet the challenge of dynamically developing e-commerce and IT sectors the firm employs a team of qualified lawyers specialising in these aspects of law. Moreover, the firm has been involved in significant work on antitrust and unfair competition issues. Other important work areas include advice on insurance activities and activities of other financial institutions (investment and pension funds) as well as advice on all aspects of telecommunications law and the media, real estate business and management, and intellectual property law.

Domański Zakrzewski Palinka has teams specially designated to provide services to foreign clients in their own languages, eg German, Spanish, Japanese, Italian.

A brochure providing more details is available upon request.

FORYSTEK & PARTNERZY

UL PULAWSKA 17
02-515 WARSAW

Telephone: +48 12 622 45 11
Fax: +48 12 622 45 10
E-mail: kancelaria@forystek.pl
Website: www.forystek.pl

Languages
English, German, Russian

Other offices
Krakow

Number of lawyers 20

CATEGORIES OF WORK

Mergers and acquisitions
Jozef Forystek, Marek Forystek

Reprivatisation
Jozef Forystek, Marek Forystek

Litigation and arbitration
Jozef Forystek, Marek Forystek

E-commerce
Marek Forystek

Intellectual property
Marek Forystek, Agnieszka Jesiotr

Tax law
Marek Forystek

Corporate and commercial
Jozef Forystek, Marek Forystek

Commercial property
Jozef Forystek, Marcin Pogorzelec

Competition law
Agnieszka Jesiotr, Marcin Pogorzelec

Banking and finance
Jozef Forystek, Marek Forystek

Insurance
Jozef Forystek, Agnieszka Jesiotr

Real estate
Jozef Forystek, Marek Forystek

Employment
Agnieszka Jesiotr, Marcin Pogorzelec

Capital markets, IPO
Marek Forystek, Marta Sajna

GESSEL ATTORNEYS AT LAW

UL SIENNA 39
00-121 WARSZAWA

Telephone: +48 22 318 69 01
Fax: +48 22 318 69 31
E-mail: mail@gessel.com.pl
Website: www.gessel.com.pl

Languages
English, German, Russian

Number of lawyers 25

CATEGORIES OF WORK

M&A, venture capital
B Gessel-Kalinowska vel Kalisz, M Macieszczak

Foreign investment
A Masny, C Schmidt

Corporate and commercial
M Macieszczak, M Fialek

Securities, investment funds
L Koziorowski, A Pietrzak

Labour law, management contracts
D Bryndal, A Nowacka

IP, media and IT
D Bryndal, A Nowacka

Unfair competition
D Bryndal, A Nowacka

Anti-monopoly law
B Kasztelan-Świetlik

Arbitration
B Gessel-Kalinowska vel Kalisz

Court and administrative proceedings
H Gajewska-Kraczkowska, P Matusiak

European law
A Masny

Real estate, construction law
A Dudkiewicz, J Czaiński

Taxes
I Bielińska, A Rzepecka

Energy law
K Sienkiewicz

Pharmaceutical law
D Bryndal

Public trade
T Dragowski

GIDE LOYRETTE NOUEL

STRATOS OFFICE CENTER
UL KS I SKORUPKI 5
00-546 WARSAW

Telephone: +48 (0) 22 583 67 01
Fax: +48 (0) 22 583 67 67
E-mail: gln.warsaw@gide.com
Website: www.gide.com

Other offices
Algiers, Beijing, Belgrade, Brussels, Bucharest, Budapest, Casablanca, Hanoi, Istanbul, London, Moscow, New York, Paris, Prague, Riyadh, Shanghai, Tunis

Number of lawyers 586
at this office 43

Contacts
Dariusz Tokarczuk (tokarczuk@gide.com), Robert Jedrzejczyk (jedrzejczyk@gide.com), Piotr Sadownik (sadownik@gide.com), Rafal Dziedzic (dziedzic@gide.com), Pawel Grzeskowiak (grzeskowiak@gide.com)

CATEGORIES OF WORK

- **Mergers and acquisitions**
- **Securities and capital markets**
- **Banking and finance**
- **Privatisation**
- **Real estate transactions and financing**
- **Construction**
- **Energy and infrastructure**
- **Major projects**
- **Environment**
- **Tax**
- **Labour and employment**
- **Intellectual property**
- **Competition law**
- **Bankruptcy and insolvency**

GLEISS LUTZ

UL SIENNA 39
00-121 WARSAW

Telephone: +48 22 526 55 00
Fax: +48 22 526 55 55
E-mail: info@gleisslutz.com
Website: www.gleisslutz.com

Languages
German, English, French, Polish, Russian

Other offices
Berlin, Frankfurt, Munich, Stuttgart, Brussels, Prague

Number of lawyers 225
at this office 15

Contact
Dr Torsten Bogen

CATEGORIES OF WORK

- **Cross-border joint ventures**
- **General corporate**
- **Real estate, zoning**
- **Trade marks, intellectual property**
- **Antitrust, merger control**
- **Tax**
- **Labour law, employment**
- **General banking law, cross-border finance**
- **Telecommunications**
- **Environment and pollution control**
- **Mergers and acquisitions**

HAARMANN HEMMELRATH

NORWAY HOUSE
UL LWOWSKA 19
00-660 WARSAW

Telephone: +48 22 820 08 00
Fax: +48 22 820 08 88
E-mail: warsaw@haarmannhemmelrath.com
Website: www.haarmannhemmelrath.com

Languages
English, German, Norwegian, Polish, Russian

Other offices
Bielefeld, Bucharest, Budapest, Düsseldorf, Frankfurt, Hamburg, Leipzig, Munich, Moscow, Paris, Prague, Shanghai

Number of lawyers 226

CATEGORIES OF WORK

Corporate and business law	Privatisation
Mergers and acquisitions	Litigation/arbitration
Leasing	Audit and accounting services
Competition law, antitrust	Telecommunications/media
Energy/environmental	Banking and finance
Stock exchange law	Labour law
Real estate transactions	Administrative proceedings
National and international tax law	Construction/projects

HOGAN & HARTSON M. JAMKA, A. GALOS AND PARTNERS LLP

ATRIUM TOWER
AL JANA PAWLA II 25
00-854 WARSAW

Telephone: +48 22 653 42 00
Fax: +48 22 653 42 50
E-mail: agalos@hhlaw.com
Website: www.hoganhartson.pl

Languages
English, French, German, Russian, Spanish

Other offices
Baltimore, Beijing, Berlin, Boulder, Brussels, Budapest, Caracas, Colorado Springs, Denver, Geneva, Hong Kong, London, Los Angeles, Miami, Moscow, Munich, New York, Northern Virginia, Paris, Shanghai, Tokyo, Washington DC

Number of lawyers 1,101
at this office 22

Contact
Aleksander Galos

CATEGORIES OF WORK

- Mergers, acquisitions and divestitures
- Company formation and corporate counselling
- Competition law
- Labour and employment
- Privatisations
- Intellectual property
- Litigation
- Municipal infrastructure projects
- Public/private partnerships
- Offset programmes/ government contracts
- Foreign investment
- Regulations and licensing
- Taxation and customs
- Capital markets
- Financial services (banking, insurance, investment and pension funds)
- Public and private procurement
- European Union law
- Telecommunications and new technology
- Real estate
- Healthcare and drug industry
- Agriculture and food industry
- Automotive industry

KARNIOL MALECKI I WSPOLNICY SP. K

UL SWIETOJERSKA 5/7
00-236 WARSAW

Telephone: +48 22 828 14 60
Fax: +48 22 827 04 63
E-mail: skm@skm.pl
Website: www.skm.pl

Languages
English, French, German, Italian, Polish, Russian

Number of lawyers 74
at this office 15

Member
Group of European Law Firms (NOMOS);
International Bar Association (IBA);
Center for International Legal Studies (CILS);
Competition Society (LIDC)

CATEGORIES OF WORK

Commercial property/real estate

Competition and EU

Construction

Corporate and commercial

Dispute resolution – litigation and arbitration

Labour and employment

Environment

Foreign direct investment

Insurance

Intellectual and industrial property

Media and entertainment

Mergers and acquisitions

Privatisation and reprivatisation

Tax

KOCHANSKI BRUDKOWSKI & PARTNERS

UL CZESKA 22A
03-902 WARSAW

Telephone: +48 22 616 37 61
Fax: +48 22 616 37 62
Website: www.kochanskioffices.com

Languages
English, French, German, Russian

Number of lawyers 22

Contacts
Piotr Kochanski (managing partner),
(p.kochanski@kochanskioffices.com.pl),
Tomasz Brudkowski (managing partner),
(t.brudkowski@kochanskioffices.com.pl)

Member
International Lawyers Network;
International Trademark Association

CATEGORIES OF WORK

Banking and finance
Beata Karas

Commercial property/real estate
Rafal Rapala

Competition and EU
Patrycja Szot

Corporate and commercial
Piotr Kochanski, Rafal Rapala

Dispute resolution/litigation and arbitration
Piotr Kochanski, Tomasz Brudkowski

E-commerce
Tomasz Brudkowski

Information technology
Piotr Banasik, Lukasz Jura

Intellectual property
Piotr Kochanski, Tomasz Brudkowski

Media and entertainment
Robert Sagan

Mergers and acquisitions
Beta Karas, Rafal Rapala

Telecommunications
Piotr Banasik

ŁASZCZUK & PARTNERS

PLAC PIŁSUDSKIEGO 2
00-073 WARSAW

Telephone: +48 22 351 00 67
Fax: +48 22 351 00 68
E-mail: warsaw@laszczuk.pl
Website: www.laszczuk.pl

Languages
English, German

Number of lawyers 17

Contact
Justyna Szpara (justyna.szpara@laszczuk.pl)

CATEGORIES OF WORK

Corporate and commercial
Marek Korcz

Intellectual property and new technologies
Michał Siciarek, Jan Grygo

Dispute resolution, litigation and arbitration
Maciej Łaszczuk, Michał Siciarek

Real estate
Justyna Szpara, Marek Korcz

Tax
Maciej Łaszczuk, Justyna Szpara

LEŚNODORSKI, ŚLUSAREK & PARTNERS

ŁOWICKA STREET 62
02-531 WARSZAWA

Telephone: +48 22 646 42 10
Fax: +48 22 646 28 77
E-mail: kancelaria@lsw.com.pl
Website: www.lsw.com.pl

Languages
English, Russian, German, French

Other offices
Katowice

Number of lawyers 35
at this office 26

International groupings
World Link for Law; Business Centre Club (BCC)

CATEGORIES OF WORK

Intellectual property
Maciej Ślusarek

Media and entertainment
Maciej Ślusarek

Advertisement law
Maciej Ślusarek

Tax law
Dr Piotr Karwat

Corporate and commercial law
Bogusław Leśnodorski, Krzysztof Feluch

Mergers and acquisitions
Bogusław Leśnodorski, Krzysztof Feluch

Capital investment
Bogusław Leśnodorski

Real estate
Marcin Melzacki

Labour law
Anna Sęktas

EU law
Maciej Ślusarek, Katarzyna Czyżewska

Litigation and arbitration
Maciej Ślusarek, Krzysztof Feluch

Competition law
Maciej Ślusarek

Sports law
Bogusław Leśnodorski

Pharmaceutical law
Katarzyna Czyżewska

LINKLATERS

WARSAW TOWERS
UL SIENNA 39
00-121 WARSAW

Telephone: +48 22 526 50 00
Fax: +48 22 526 50 60
Website: www.linklaters.com

Languages
All commercial and local languages in the countries where Linklaters operates

Other offices
Amsterdam, Antwerp, Bangkok, Beijing, Berlin, Bratislava, Brussels, Bucharest, Budapest, Cologne, Dubai, Frankfurt am Main, Hong Kong, Lisbon, London, Luxembourg, Madrid, Milan, Moscow, Munich, New York, Paris, Prague, Rome, São Paulo, Shanghai, Singapore, Stockholm, Tokyo

Number of lawyers 2,000 worldwide

Contact
Tadeusz Komosa

CATEGORIES OF WORK

Corporate/M&A
Cezary Wiśniewski

Privatisation
Jolanta Tropaczyńska

Energy
Krzysztof Golyński

Intellectual property
Krystyna Szczepanowska-Kozlowska

Technology, media and telecommunications
Tadeusz Komosa

Litigation/arbitration
Zbigniew Kruczkowski

Competition/antitrust
Malgorzata Szwaj

Labour law
Agnieszka Lechman-Filipiak

Tax
Mariusz Aleksandrowicz

Real estate
Artur Kulawski

Construction
Artur Kulawski

Banking/finance
Jaroslaw Miller

Capital markets
Marcin Chylinski

EU law
Malgorzata Szwaj

LOVELLS

UL NOWOGRODZKA 50
00-695 WARSZAWA

Telephone: +48 22 529 29 00
Fax: +48 22 529 29 01
E-mail: information@lovells.com
Website: www.lovells.com

Languages
English, German

Other offices
Alicante, Amsterdam, Beijing, Berlin, Brussels, Budapest*, Chicago, Düsseldorf, Frankfurt, Hamburg, Ho Chi Minh City, Hong Kong, London, Madrid, Milan, Moscow, Munich, New York, Paris, Prague, Rome, Shanghai, Singapore, Tokyo, Zagreb*

Number of lawyers 1,600
at this office 38

Contact
Beata Balas-Noszczyk

CATEGORIES OF WORK

Mergers and acquisitions

Banking, securities and finance

Commercial law (general)

Competition, antitrust

Companies, corporations

Pensions

Energy

Environment

Civil law

Insurance

Contract

Construction, building

EC law

Trade marks, intellectual property

Arbitration and litigation

Telecommunications

Projects

Employment

Commercial fraud

Tax

LUKOWICZ SWIERZEWSKI & PARTNERS

UL MAZOWIECKA 13
00-052 WARSAW

Telephone: +48 22 827 33 22
Fax: +48 22 826 83 19
E-mail: office@lukowicz.pl
Website: www.lukowicz.pl

Languages
English, German

Other offices
Poznan, Krakow

Number of lawyers 21
at this office 13

Contacts
Olgierd Swierzewski

Member
DLA Piper Group

CATEGORIES OF WORK

Banking, finance
Krzysztof Weremczuk, Olgierd Swierzewski

Commercial law
Jaroslaw Jankowski

Corporate, mergers and acquisitions
Jolanta Okoniecka, Olgierd Swierzewski

HR and employment
Malgorzata Fitrzyk-Barral, Edyta Jordan

Intellectual property and technology, media and communications
Olgierd Swierzewski, Dariusz Jurkiewicz

Litigation
Alicja Milewska-Gojzewska, Tomasz Mizikowski

Real estate
Dariusz Jurkiewicz, Lukasz Bobel

Tax and customs
Filip Smakowski

Regulatory and public law
Olgierd Swierzewski

THE FIRM

Lukowicz Swierzewski & Partners, Attorneys at Law, Limited Partnership, has been active in the legal services market since 1990.

Since reforms began in Poland, the firm has been involved in numerous privatisation processes and prestigious foreign investments in the country, acting on behalf of both the Polish government and private investors from diverse sectors of the economy.

Currently the firm has a well-established position among Polish law firms.

The firm is a member of DLA Piper Rudnick Gray Cary Group, an exclusive alliance of international full-service legal organisations with a shared vision. Established in 1999, the group now has members across Europe, Africa, the Middle East, Asia and the US, which deliver expert local know-how and integrated international solutions.

Lukowicz Swierzewski & Partners specialises in comprehensive legal services for Polish and foreign companies, relating to business activity in the country.

The firm advises both limited liability and joint-stock companies. The majority of companies currently assisted by the firm were established with its exclusive assistance. Most of them are foreign owned, some of which are large multinational corporations listed on international stock exchanges.

The firm also renders a full range of services to banks and other financial institutions and state-owned enterprises.

AREAS OF PRACTICE

Banking and project finance: the firm is experienced in assisting banks' relations with their clients and in internal relations (banking manuals and procedures); debt recovery and enforcement; and foreign exchange issues.

Commercial law: structuring transactions, drafting a whole range of civil and commercial law contracts; participation in business negotiations.

Corporate, mergers and acquisitions: broad experience in establishing, restructuring, merging, privatising and liquidating companies; advising on the form and structure of transactions; due diligence of the legal status of companies; preparation of related contracts; assistance in listing companies on the Warsaw Stock Exchange.

HR and employment: practical experience in issues arising from employment relations; preparation of employment contracts and company labour by-laws; assistance in labour disputes and relations with trade unions; collective redundancy; and employment of foreigners in Poland.

Intellectual property and technology, media and communications: assistance in registration and transfer of copyright, trade marks, utility/industrial designs; preparation of licence agreements; protection of clients whose IP rights have been violated, including unfair competition. Experience in due diligence of IT businesses and issues related to the publication and use of content on the internet; preparation and negotiation of contracts related to IT services, software and e-commerce.

Litigation: representation of the firm's clients before courts of all instances; negotiations of in- and out-of-court settlements; debt recovery and enforcement; and bankruptcy issues.

Real estate: due diligence of real estate prior to sale/acquisition; preparation of terms and participation in negotiations of real estate acquisitions; assistance to foreign investors in buying or leasing real estate, including drafting relevant contracts; and assistance to foreign investors in obtaining permits for acquisition or construction of real estate in Poland.

Tax and customs: the firm provides tax advice to both Polish and foreign investors in Poland.

Regulatory: experience in obtaining various permits from governmental, regulatory and anti-monopoly authorities.

M. FURTEK I WSPOLNICY

KROLEWSKA 16
00-103 WARSAW

Telephone: +48 22 581 44 00
Fax: +48 22 581 44 10
E-mail: contact@furtek.pl
Website: www.furtek.pl

Languages
English, French, Polish

Number of lawyers 18

CATEGORIES OF WORK

Corporate and commercial
Marek Furtek

Banking, finance and insurance
Magdalena Scibor

IT/hi-tech
Mariusz Grzesiuk, Maciej Gawronski

Telecommunications
Leszek Rydzewski

Mergers and acquisitions (M&A)
Mariusz Grzesiuk

Project finance/corporate finance/ bankruptcy and corporate restructuring
Leszek Rydzewski

Litigation/arbitration/ mediation (ADR)
Marek Furtek, Maciej Gawronski

Labour law
Magdalena Scibor

Project development, competition, anti-monopoly
Mariusz Grzesiuk, Dorota Lempicka

ADWOKAT MARCIN MAMINSKI

7/4 AL ROZ
00-556 WARSAW

Telephone: +48 22 622 99 66
Fax: +48 22 622 99 66
E-mail: recepcja@marcinmaminski.com.pl
Website: www.marcinmaminski.com.pl

Languages
English, French, German

Number of lawyers 5

Contact
Marcin Maminski

Member
Polish-Scandinavian Chamber of Industry; Association of Commercial Lawyers International

CATEGORIES OF WORK

Banking and finance
Marek Kijowski

Dispute resolution – litigation
Marcin Maminski

Arbitration
Marcin Maminski

Corporate and securities
Tomasz Turek

Intellectual property
Zofia Maminska

Information technology
Zofia Maminska

Real estate law
Marcin Maminski

Tax
Pawel Trojanek

Commercial and company law
Marcin Maminski

NÖRR STIEFENHOFER LUTZ Sp.z o.o RADNÓCZY Sp.K KANCELARIA PRAWNA

AL. ARMII LUDOWEJ 26
00-609 WARSAW

Telephone: +48 22 579 3060
Fax: +48 22 579 3070
E-mail: info@noerr.com
Website: www.noerr.com

Languages
English, German, Polish, Russian, Spanish

Other offices
Berlin, Bratislava, Bucharest, Budapest, Dresden, Düsseldorf, Frankfurt, Moscow, Munich, New York, Prague

Number of lawyers 256
(+ 66 tax advisers, public accountants and tax assistants)
at this office 10
(+ 3 tax advisers, public accountants and tax assistants)

Contacts
Dr Christoph Spiering LLM, Krzysztof Sajewski

CATEGORIES OF WORK

- Banking and foreign exchange law
- Commercial law
- Competition and antitrust law
- Corporate law
- Intellectual property and trade mark law
- Labour law
- Law relating to commercial leases
- Privatisation
- Real estate and investment law
- Tax and customs law

RUTKOWSKI WINDMILL GASIEWSKI & ROMAN LP

AL. J. CH. SZUCHA 3/5
00-580 WARSZAWA

Telephone: +48 22 622 26 96
Fax: +48 22 622 26 97
E-mail: karol.rutkowski@rwgr.pl
Website: www.rwgr.pl

Languages
English, French, German, Polish, Russian

Other offices
Gdansk

Number of lawyers 21

Contact
Karol Rutkowski

CATEGORIES OF WORK

- Arbitration and ADR
- Banking and finance
- Capital markets
- Corporate and commercial law
- Employment and labour law
- EU and competition law
- Intellectual property and industrial law
- Legal compliance
- Legislative reforms
- Litigation
- Mergers and acquisitions
- Real estate
- Tax

SOLTYSINSKI KAWECKI & SZLEZAK

UL WAWELSKA 15 B
02-034 WARSZAWA

Telephone: +48 22 608 70 00
Fax: +48 22 608 70 70
E-mail: office@skslegal.pl
Website: www.skslegal.pl

Languages
English, French, German, Russian

Other offices
Katowice, Poznan

Number of lawyers 80
at this office 71

Member
ius laboris, International Employment Law, Pensions and Employee Benefits Alliance

CATEGORIES OF WORK

Administrative law	**Intellectual property law**
Antitrust and competition law	**Litigation**
Banking law	**Media and telecommunications law**
Commercial and commercial law	**Mergers and acquisitions**
Employment law	**Real estate and development**
Environmental law	**Securities law and capital markets law**
European Union law	**Tax, customs and foreign exchange law**
Foreign investments law	

THE FIRM

Soltysinski Kawecki & Szlezak (SK&S) is one of the leading law firms in Poland. Established in 1991, it relies on the unique background and experience of its founders. The firm has 80 attorneys, including 15 partners and three attorneys in an of-counsel capacity. The firm employs a total of over 175 people, including 15 paralegals and a support staff of more than 80.

The firm's main offices are in Warsaw, with smaller, branch offices operating in Poznan and Katowice. SK&S is unique among Polish law firms in at least one respect: many of its attorneys studied and/or practised law in Western countries, especially in the US and the UK. The firm has strong international links, particularly with EU countries. Many of the firm's foreign clients have been referred to it by several renowned law firms with which the firm has maintained excellent working relationships for years.

SK&S is one of the pre-eminent firms in Poland, with a strong reputation for professionalism in legal practice.

AREAS OF PRACTICE

The firm's practice covers most areas of commercial law, with particular emphasis on corporate and commercial law, securities and capital markets, banking and financing, intellectual property, as well as antitrust and unfair competition. The firm also provides legal services related to the acquisition of real estate and land development. It also advises in areas such as tax, customs and foreign exchange law, settlement of disputes, and employment law.

SK&S has represented the government and foreign investors in numerous successful privatisations of the Polish industry. The firm's extensive practice in the area of finance and banking includes local representation of several governmental, private and international financial organisations.

The firm's intellectual property department boasts an impressive practice, representing Business Software Alliance and leading software companies for many years in Poland.

The firm's litigation department has extensive experience in litigation before Polish courts, local and foreign arbitration tribunals, and the Polish Supreme Administrative Court.

SK&S has also been active in the area of securities law and capital market regulation. The firm provides regular advice in this area to several renowned, international investment banks.

The firm's tax lawyers provide strategic tax advice to many large companies and work closely with the firm's corporate attorneys in optimising the tax aspects of all major transactions in which the firm is involved.

The department of antitrust and competition law provides Polish and foreign clients with comprehensive counselling in all areas of Polish anti-monopoly laws, including merger and acquisition notification proceedings.

The employment law department provides comprehensive advice on individual and collective employment law, including, *inter alia*, collective bargaining, as well as employment and non-competition agreements for employees at managerial level.

SQUIRE, SANDERS & DEMPSEY L.L.P.

SQUIRE SANDERS WIATER sp.k.

AL. JANA PAWLA II 25
00-854 WARSAW

Telephone: +48 22 653 43 00
Fax: +48 22 653 43 43
E-mail: kwiater@ssd.com
Website: www.ssd.com

Languages
English, German, Italian, Polish, Russian

Other offices
Beijing, Bratislava, Brussels, Budapest, Caracas, Cincinnati, Cleveland, Columbus, Hong Kong, Houston, London, Los Angeles, Miami, Milan, Moscow, New York, Palo Alto, Phoenix, Prague, Rio de Janeiro, San Francisco, Santa Domingo, Shanghai, Tallahassee, Tampa, Tokyo, Tysons Corner, Washington DC, West Palm Beach, Bucharest*, Buenos Aires*, Dublin*, Kyiv*, Milan*, Santiago*

Number of lawyers 800+
at this office 20

Contact Krzysztof Wiater

CATEGORIES OF WORK

Communications
Pawel Grzejszczak

Corporate transactions and securities regulation
Marta Frackowiak, Jacek Gizinski

Energy
Andrzej Balicki, Pawel Grzejszczak

Government contracts
Katarzyna Radzewicz

Healthcare
Andrzej Balicki

Intellectual property
Andrzej Balicki, Marta Frackowiak

Labour and employment
Malgorzata Grzelak, Edyta Kolkowska

Mergers and acquisitions
Malgorzata Grzelak,
Ewelina Laskowska

Project finance
Grzegorz Kycia, Krzysztof Wiater

Real estate and hospitality
Wojeiech Wachacki

Reorganisation and restructuring
Ewelina Laskowska, Anna Wietrzynska

Taxation
Stanislaw Walenta

THE FIRM

Founded in 1890, Squire, Sanders & Dempsey is a multi-jurisdictional law firm with approximately 800 lawyers practising in offices in Europe, the Americas and Asia. The firm's practice covers most substantive areas of the law, with an emphasis on business and finance matters.

The firm operates as a single global partnership, which ensures client accountability and the seamless delivery of uniformly high-quality legal services throughout the world. The firm's lawyers come from many countries and cultures, are licensed to practise in both common law and civil law jurisdictions, and communicate with clients in their native languages. Today, the firm remains committed to the fundamental principles ordained by its founders: to serve clients effectively and to maintain the professional standards that distinguish both the firm and its people.

AREAS OF PRACTICE

The firm is organised around four major practice areas: advocacy, business, capital markets and regulated industries. Within these practice areas, the firm's work can be divided into numerous areas of specialisation, including banking, bankruptcy and restructuring, biotechnology and pharmaceuticals, communications, competition law, trade law, converging technologies, corporate, energy, environmental, healthcare, intellectual property, international dispute resolution, labour and employment, litigation, mergers and acquisitions, privatisations, project finance, real estate, securities and taxation.

The Warsaw office consists of a team of lawyers experienced in counseling multinational companies in Polish legal matters, bringing global breadth and local depth to its clients' opportunities and challenges. The office takes a dynamic and risk-focused approach to meeting clients' needs for creative and responsive counsel in areas having the most significant impact on business in Central and Eastern Europe.

Lawyers in the Warsaw office have advised large foreign investors on a number of key privatisation and investment opportunities. They advise clients on complex transactions, financings and restructurings in Poland, combining their comprehensive international experience with essential local knowledge in local market practice. Its highly rated state aid team is considered the best in the country.

The firm's practice in Warsaw includes banking and finance, bankruptcy and restructuring, competition law, corporate and commercial law, energy, European Union law, intellectual property, information technology and telecommunications, labour and employment, litigation and alternative dispute resolution, mergers and acquisitions, public procurement and state aid.

Lawyers in the Warsaw office possess a wealth of experience, and several are well recognised as experts in their fields. Collectively, they have served on the faculty of top Polish universities such as the Warsaw School of Economics, lectured at European Union seminars and published articles in their areas of knowledge. They include a co-founder and member of the board of The Polish Association of Law & Economics who has participated in the formation of amendments to Poland's Commercial Companies Code.

WARDYNSKI & PARTNERS

AL UJAZDOWSKIE 10
00-478 WARSAW

Telephone: +48 22 437 82 00
Fax: +48 22 437 82 01
Website: www.wardynski.com.pl

Languages
English, French, German, Russian

Other offices
Brussels, Poznan

Number of lawyers 40
at this office 37

CATEGORIES OF WORK

Mergers and acquisitions

Project financing

Banking and securities law

Real estate and property development

Privatisation/reprivatisation

Restructuring of state enterprises

Insolvency and settlement of debts

Taxation

European Union law

Corporate law

Intellectual property

Unfair competition, anti-monopoly law

Litigation and arbitration

Energy law

Labour law

Media

Pharmaceutical law

Telecommunications and new technologies

WEIL, GOTSHAL & MANGES

WARSAW FINANCIAL CENTER
UL EMILII PLATER 53
00-113 WARSAW

Telephone: +48 22 520 40 00
Fax: +48 22 520 40 01
Website: www.weil.com

Other offices
Austin, Boston, Brussels, Budapest, Dallas, Frankfurt, Houston, London, Miami, Munich, New York, Paris, Prague, Providence, Shanghai, Silicon Valley, Singapore, Washington DC, Wilmington

Number of lawyers 1,200
at this office 36

Contacts
Pawel Rymarz, Anna Frankowska, Roman Rewald, Artur Zawadowski, Piotr Tomaszewski

CATEGORIES OF WORK

Banking and finance	**Mergers and acquisitions**
Capital markets	**Private equity and venture capital**
Corporate	**Privatisation**
Energy	**Property**
Insurance	**Reorganisation and restructuring**
Intellectual property, e-commerce	**Tax**
Litigation and dispute resolution	**Telecoms**

THE FIRM

Weil, Gotshal & Manges is a leader in the marketplace for sophisticated, international legal services. With more than 1,200 lawyers across the US, Europe and Asia, the firm serves many of the most successful companies in the world in their high-stakes matters and transactions. Weil Gotshal has built a world-class team of lawyers by pursuing a strategy of steady, purposeful growth. It continues to build upon a balanced platform of practices and locations without acquiring any debt. The firm's three primary departments – corporate, litigation/regulatory and restructuring – provide healthy diversification in all economic cycles, while its international expansion over the past decade has resulted in a quarter of the firm's lawyers now being in Europe.

AREAS OF PRACTICE

The firm's antitrust/competition practice advises on international M&A regulatory notifications, antitrust distribution counselling, cartels, litigation and government and state competition policy.

The corporate department is the firm's largest, with lawyers in the US and across Europe. The department advises international financial institutions and corporate clients in complex public and private mergers and acquisitions, private equity deals, strategic alliances and other commercial transactions.

The firm's corporate governance practice is recognised as the pre-eminent counsellor of corporate boards, management and institutional investors on the full range of governance issues, including board composition, structure and processes; executive and director compensation; director responsibilities, including in connection with mergers, spin-offs and other extraordinary transactions; internal and governmental investigations of alleged accounting or other corporate misconduct; and shareholder initiatives.

The firm is recognised as a market leader in the handling of complex and innovative finance transactions internationally. The firm advises on a wide range of financing activities and has particular expertise in acquisition finance, asset-based finance, debt restructuring and insolvency, debt and equity capital markets, derivatives, high yield debt, securitisation, structured finance and telecom and multimedia financing.

The firm has a leading intellectual property and technology practice and advises a number of the world's major technology, media and telecommunications companies. It also acts for investors in technology, media and communications entities. The practice handles patent infringement, outsourcing transactions, strategic alliances, cross-border mergers and acquisitions, investments and IPOs. The firm advises on the protection and exploitation of IP and on a wide range of e-commerce matters including data protection. It has expertise in regulatory telecoms matters.

The firm's litigation practice advises international clients on all major areas of the law and has extensive experience in all aspects of dispute resolution. It advises clients in jury trials and appeals, as well as arbitration and alternative dispute forums.

The firm's real estate practice handles complex real estate transactions (including finance, securitisations, development, leasing, sales, acquisitions and debt restructurings) across the US and Europe. It also advises clients on real estate M&A transactions and transactions involving real estate investment trusts.

The firm has one of the largest, most broadly based bankruptcy and business reorganisation practices in the world. The department has been involved in virtually all major chapter 11 reorganisation cases in the US and in major national and international out-of-court debt restructurings.

The tax department provides advice to a broad range of international clients, covering many economic sectors. The department works closely with the firm's other departments to find innovative solutions to problems that present various and competing multidisciplinary considerations.

WIERCIŃSKI, KWIECIŃSKI, BAEHR SP. K.

EMILII PLATER 28
00-688 WARSAW

Telephone: +48 22 630 31 31
Fax: +48 22 630 31 51
E-mail: biuro@wkw.pl
Website: www.wkw.pl

Languages
English, French, German, Italian, Polish, Russian

Other offices
Poznań

Number of lawyers 25

Contacts
Magdalena Kobosko,
Agnieszka Wiercinska-Kruzewska

CATEGORIES OF WORK

Mergers and acquisitions
Andrzej Wierciński

Corporate and commercial
Magdalena Kobosko

Competition and consumer protection law
Jerzy Baehr

Energy and natural resources
Jerzy Baehr

Public procurement
Tomasz Kwieciński

IP, technology, media and telecoms
Agnieszka Wiercińska-Krużewska

Banking and finance
Andrzej Wierciński

Real estate
Krzysztof Zarębski

Labour law
Agnieszka Fedor

Litigation and dispute resolution
Tomasz Kwieciński

Infrastructure projects
Bartłomiej Jankowski

Tax
Anna Łukaszewicz-Obierska

Environmental law
Andrzej Wierciński

Insurance
Tomasz Kwieciński

Pharmaceutical law
Jan Roliński

Insolvency
Andrzej Wierciński

WIERZBOWSKI EVERSHEDS

CENTRUM JASNA
UL JASNA 14/16A
00-041 WARSAW

Telephone: +48 22 505 07 00
Fax: +48 22 505 07 01
E-mail: kancelaria@wierzbowski.pl
Website: www.wierzbowski.pl

Languages
English, French, German, Italian, Spanish

Other offices
Barcelona, Birmingham, Brussels, Budapest, Cambridge, Cardiff, Copenhagen, Doha, Dublin, Ipswich, Kuala Lumpur, Leeds, London, Madrid, Manchester, Milan, Munich, Newcastle, Norwich, Nottingham, Paris, Rome, Sofia, Stockholm, Valladolid, Vienna, Wroclaw

Number of lawyers 2,000
at this office 44

International groupings
Eversheds International

CATEGORIES OF WORK

Commercial and competition
Malgorzata Modzelewska De Raad,
Bozena Ciosek

Corporate structuring
Ewa Lachowska-Brol,
Magdalena Orzelska-Bratkowska

Dispute resolution
Henryk Romanczuk,
Malgorzata Modzelewska De Raad

Employment and human resources
Ewa Lachowska-Brol

Financial services
Wojciech Andrzejczak, Grzegorz Kott

Foreign direct investment
Magdalena Orzelska-Bratkowska,
Daniel Grodzinski

Information technology and intellectual property
Magdalena Orzelska-Bratkowska,
Tomasz Zalewski

Mergers and acquisitions
Michal Kurzynski, Krzysztof Wierzbowski

Personal data protection
Arwid Mednis

Pharmaceuticals
Bozena Ciosek

Real estate
Michal Kurzynski, Wojciech Andrzejczak

Telecommunications
Krzysztof Wierzbowski, Arwid Mednis

German desk
Zbigniew Gaj, Wojciech Andrzejczak

French desk
Arwid Mednis

PORTUGAL

Population	10.2 million
Number of lawyers	23,000
Professional title	Advogado
Currency	Euro (€)

Index

Portugal is set on the Iberian peninsula, which it shares with Spain. The Portuguese language is spoken all around the world in countries such as Brazil, Angola, Macau and East Timor, a legacy of Portugal's seafaring traditions.

In 1974 there was a civil revolution in Portugal, which later brought democracy to the country, and in 1986 Portugal joined the European Union. In 1999 the country joined the European Monetary Union, and substituted the former Portuguese currency (the Portuguese escudo) with the euro.

While debating and preparing for a European constitution, the country has, in the meantime, been going through some political turmoil since the late 1990s. Prime Minister José Sócrates was elected in February 2005 and is now leading Portugal's fourth government in the space of six years.

Lisbon, located north of the river Tagus, is the financial and legal heart of the country. The second-largest city, Oporto, is located in the industrial north.

The archipelagos of Madeira and the Azores are autonomous regions, complete with their own governments. Madeira operates its own offshore centre, and hosts the International Business Centre (IBC).

BILLING

Portuguese legal fees are reasonable, about 20% lower than neighbouring Spain. The Portuguese Bar Association adopts fixed rates for certain procedures, such as standard intellectual property matters. Lawyers generally bill on an hourly basis according to international standards. Contingency fees are not permitted. Average hourly rates range between €80-€250 per associate, and €200-€400 for a partner.

MARKETING

Current Portuguese Bar Association rules, which date from 1984, are very strict on law firms advertising their services or mentioning the names of clients. In practice, the Bar frequently closes its eyes to breaches of regulations following heavy lobbying by lawyers who feel at a distinct competitive disadvantage to their foreign colleagues.

IN-HOUSE LAWYERS

The recruitment of in-house lawyers is not common in Portugal. Corporates, such as banks and large construction and telecoms companies may retain in-house counsel for basic transactions. Those that are employed combine their corporate role with private practice.

ECONOMY

Since joining the European Union in 1986, Portugal's fortunes have been closely linked to the EU; the country is a heavy recipient of EU funding, which can represent as much as 3% of GDP.

Although Portugal joined the European single currency in 1999, it has struggled with its balance of payments deficit for a number of years. In 2001 it became the first European country to have action taken against it by European finance ministers for running an excessive deficit.

Following a period of growth, the country has been hit by an economic slowdown since the end of 2002, in common with many of its European neighbours.

Although Portugal saw significant growth in foreign direct investment at the beginning of the decade, the trend has begun to reverse, and Portugal's competitiveness is currently ranked one of the lowest in the EU. To counter this a raft of new measures have been introduced, which have included reform of labour legislation to raise both productivity and competitiveness with neighbouring countries.

LEGAL MARKET

Following a year of major mergers and growth in 2004, the Portuguese legal market was still vibrant during 2005. After lengthy negotiation, **Morais Leitão, Galvão Teles, Soares Da Silva & Associados** merged with leading Oporto firm *Osório de Castro, Verde Pinho, Vieira Peres, Lobo Xavier e Associados*.

Steady growth has been a common theme for a lot of the leading law firms and already three firms (**Gonçalves Pereira, Castelo Branco & Associados**, **PLMJ – A. M. Pereira, Sáragga Leal, Oliveira Martins, Júdice e Associados Sociedade de Advogados, RL** and **Morais Leitão, Galvão Teles, Soares Da Silva & Associados**) have passed the 100-lawyer barrier.

There are now six large international law firms in the country, five of which have established a leading presence in the market.

Spanish firm **Cuatrecasas** merged with **Gonçalves Pereira, Castelo Branco & Associados** in 2003. Following its merger with *Luiz Gomes &*

The largest firms

1	PLMJ - A. M. Pereira, Sáragga Leal, Oliveira Martins, Júdice e Associados Sociedade de Advogados, RL	200
2	Morais Leitão, Galvão Teles, Soares Da Silva & Associados	126
3	Gonçalves Pereira, Castelo Branco & Associados	125
4	Cuatrecasas	113
5	Vieira de Almeida & Associados	88
6	Simmons & Simmons Rebelo de Sousa	79
7	Uría Menéndez	76
8	Miranda Correia Amendoeira & Associados	70
9	F Castelo Branco & Associados Veiga Gomes, Marques da Cruz, Colmonero	65
10	Barrocas Sarmento Neves	60
11	Abreu, Cardigos & Associados Attorneys at Law	55
12	Almeida Sampaio & Associados	50
13	Garrigues, Leónidas, Matos, SL, Sucursal em Portugal	49
14	Ferreira Pinto & Associados - Sociedade de Advogados	48
15	Franco Caiado Guerreiro & Associados	41
16	Albuquerque & Associates	40
17	Carlos de Sousa e Brito & Associados	38
	Linklaters	38
	Pena, Machete, Botelho Moniz, Nobre Guedes, Ruiz & Associados	38
20	A M Moura & Associados	37
21	Abreu & Marques, Vinhas e Associados	35
22	Belzuz Advogados	34
23	ANBM Advogados Azevedo Neves, Benjamim Mendes & Associados	33
	Sérvulo Correia & Associados	33
25	Jardim, Sampaio, Caldas e Associados	31

These figures represent the total number of lawyers in this country only, and have been supplied by the firms themselves. The figures should be accurate as at 1 January 2006.

Associados, the firm is now one of the three largest firms in the market. **Uría Menéndez**, another Spanish firm, after having initially set up a small office in Lisbon, made a more aggressive move in 2004 and merged with leading firm *Vasconcellos, F Sá Carneiro, Fontes & Associados*. The third Spanish firm to set up offices in Portugal was **Garrigues**. The firm launched a greenfield practice, operating locally as **Garrigues, Leónidas, Matos, SL, Sucursal em Portugal** and is looking to grow further. The last Spanish firm in the market is **Mullerat**, which set up a small practice in Lisbon.

The other two major foreign firms with a leading presence in the Portuguese market are international firms **Linklaters** and **Simmons & Simmons. Linklaters** is the most recent arrival and set up a smaller practice than most, but the firm was soon recognised by market leaders as serious competition. **Simmons & Simmons** was the first to have an office in Portugal. Following an initial phase where the firm had an association with a local Portuguese firm, it decided to merge and set up **Simmons & Simmons Rebelo de Sousa**.

All of these foreign firms have been jostling for position alongside the three largest independent Portuguese firms: **Morais Leitão, Galvão Teles, Soares Da Silva & Associados**; **Vieira de Almeida & Associados**; and **PLMJ – A. M. Pereira, Sáragga Leal, Oliveira Martins, Júdice e Associados Sociedade de Advogados, RL**.

FOREIGN OFFICES AND ASSOCIATIONS

Sérvulo Correia & Associados and **Raposo Bernardo & Associados**, are the only two independent Portuguese firms with an office in Madrid.

Some law firms have established closer links with Brazilian, as well as Spanish, law firms. **Simmons & Simmons Rebelo de Sousa** maintains strong links with leading Brazilian firm **Veirano e Advogados Associados. PLMJ – A. M. Pereira, Sáragga Leal, Oliveira Martins, Júdice e Associados Sociedade de Advogados, RL** is associated with **Tozzini, Freire, Teixeira e Silva**; and **Vieira de Almeida & Associados** with **Pinheiro Neto Advogados**. **Morais Leitão, Galvão Teles, Soares Da Silva & Associados** has very close ties with **Demarest & Almeida Advogados**; while **Gonçalves Pereira, Castelo Branco & Associados** is associated with **Machado, Meyer, Sendacz e Opice – Advogados**. Another Brazilian association combines **Teixeira de Freitas, Rodrigues, e Associados** and **Vieira, Rezende, Barbosa e Guerreiro Advogados**.

A number of firms also have ties with Africa. **Gonçalves Pereira, Castelo Branco & Associados** has an office in Mozambique and **PLMJ – A. M. Pereira, Sáragga Leal, Oliveira Martins, Júdice e Associados Sociedade de Advogados, RL** established an association with two Angolan firms.

But it is **Miranda Correia Amendoeira & Associados** which has, through its 'Miranda Alliance', the strongest and most renowned African presence, with offices in Angola, Mozambique, Sao Tomé e Príncipe, Cape Verde, Guinea Bissau and Equatorial Guinea. The firm also boasts an Asian office in Macao and has most recently opened a US office in Houston, Texas.

Raposo Bernardo & Associados has also set up shop in two African countries, Cape Verde and Mozambique.

Finally, two Portuguese firms boast UK offices: **Neville de Rougemont & Associados** and **PACSA – Henriques da Silva , Paes De Almeida, Corrêa de Sampaio e Associados**.

OPORTO OVERVIEW

Located some 200 miles north of Lisbon, Oporto is Portugal's second biggest and second most important city. Home of the famous port wine and to an important textile industry, the city was European Capital of Culture in 2001.

While local law firms have expanded substantially in the past decade, Lisbon firms keen on establishing national reach and also looking for business opportunities with neighbouring Galicia (in northern Spain), have in recent years started to move in.

LEADING COMMERCIAL FIRMS
Oporto

Having merged with *Osório de Castro, Verde Pinho, Vieira Peres, Lobo Xavier e Associados*, **Morais Leitão, Galvão Teles, Soares Da Silva & Associados** is now at the forefront of the Oporto legal market. Boasting 28 fee-earners (including five partners), the firm also has a hugely successful Lisbon office and is regularly involved in Portugal's major deals. Corporate and commercial, capital markets and tax are three practice areas where the firm collects most plaudits. Oporto clients include one of the biggest national corporations whose business spans the paper, food, retail, real estate, IT and telecoms sectors. Other clients include banks, telecoms companies and natural gas distributors. Carlos Osório de Castro, António Lobo Xavier, Joaquim Vieira Peres, Verde Pinho and António Emílio Vasconcelos are a few of the Oporto office's best known personalities.

Gonçalves Pereira, Castelo Branco & Associados set up its Oporto office in 1989 and is one of the most respected practices in the city. Partner José de Freitas heads the 20-strong office with a particular focus on corporate and commercial and tax, and boasting sound capabilities all-round. The firm was most notably involved in advising FCC, Ramalho Rosa Cobetar and Santa Casa da Misericórdia in its public tender bid for the €1.13bn construction of the Braga hospital.

Another of the best-established names in the market is **Telles de Abreu e Associados –**

LEADING COMMERCIAL FIRMS
Oporto

MORAIS LEITÃO, GALVÃO TELES, SOARES DA SILVA & ASSOCIADOS

GONÇALVES PEREIRA, CASTELO BRANCO & ASSOCIADOS
TELLES DE ABREU E ASSOCIADOS – SOCIEDADE DE ADVOGADOS RL ✪
VIEIRA DE CASTRO, SILVA LOPES, PESSANHA, COSTA LEITE ✪

JPAB – José Pedro Aguiar-Branco & Associados
Joaquim Taveira da Fonseca
Lopes Cardoso & Associados
Miguel Veiga, Neiva Santos & Associados
PLMJ – A. M. Pereira, Sáragga Leal, Oliveira Martins, Júdice e Associados Sociedade de Advogados, RL
Simmons & Simmons Rebelo de Sousa
Uría Menéndez
Vellozo Ferreira, Cavaleiro Brandao, Pinheiro Torres e Associados

Abreu, Cardigos & Associados Attorneys at Law
F Castelo Branco & Associados Veiga Gomes, Marques da Cruz, Colmonero
PACSA – Henriques da Silva , Paes De Almeida, Corrêa de Sampaio e Associados
Raposo Bernardo & Associados ✪

Firms are listed A-Z in tiers which are ranked in order of priority
✪ *Indicates firm displays contact details at the end of this chapter.*

Sociedade de Advogados RL, boasting an impressive local practice with 14 fee-earners (including eight partners). Senior partner Luís Telles de Abreu, Carlos Lucena, Miguel Torres and André Noronha are just a few of the star partners the firm has to offer. The firm advises various national businesses including banks and insurance companies on a wide range of issues including corporate and commercial, tax and employment – the firm's key strengths.

Another force in the Oporto market is **Vieira de Castro, Silva Lopes, Pessanha, Costa Leite** with strong corporate and commercial expertise. The firm is often involved in top-drawer deals as was demonstrated in its advice to Grupo Selenis in its €140m acquisition of La Seda de Barcelona. Pedro Pessanha, José Manuel Silva Lopes and João Vieira de Castro are three of the most reputed lawyers in the country.

JPAB – José Pedro Aguiar-Branco & Associados name partner José Pedro Aguiar-Branco has returned to the firm after having served as Minister of Justice in the previous social-democrat Portuguese government. The firm also boasts a Lisbon office and has its main focus area in corporate and commercial. Clients include banks, insurance companies, food retailers and new technology companies.

Nine-lawyer **Joaquim Taveira da Fonseca** is renowned for being a quality practice and covers corporate and commercial (headed by Joaquim Taveira da Fonseca), banking (Paulo Mendes and Gomes da Mota), public law (Guedes da Costa), civil law (Pinto Ferreira), and insurance (Araújo Correia).

Lopes Cardoso & Associados has a particular focus on public law, even though it offers full-service capability spanning corporate and commercial, civil law, public law and litigation. Tax is also a major strength. The firm boasts a praised team of 12 lawyers, including seven partners.

Name partner Miguel Veiga at **Miguel Veiga, Neiva Santos & Associados** is regarded as a leading practitioner in the market, who, together with name partner Luís Neiva Santos, has built a solid and highly respected practice which covers corporate and commercial, civil law, employment and private client issues. Partners Nuno Aguiar Branco, Adriano Encarnação and Valdemar Pereira da Silva are also leading individuals in the Oporto market.

Another of the Lisbon firms who has gradually been raising its Oporto profile is Portugal's largest firm **PLMJ – A. M. Pereira, Sáragga Leal, Oliveira Martins, Júdice e Associados Sociedade de Advogados, RL**. Partners Fernando Campos Ferreira and Victor Réfega Fernandes jointly head the Oporto practice which had a very successful 2005. The firm has been a major adviser on the construction of four of the main highways in the north and centre of the country.

Litigation is one of the major strengths of **Simmons & Simmons Rebelo de Sousa**'s Oporto practice. Andreia Lima Carneiro leads the firm's well-regarded team of 13 fee-earners. Clients include some of the major Portuguese banks, telecoms companies and renewable energy corporations, namely Casa da Música and Portgás.

One of the youngest and most admired legal teams in Oporto is **Uría Menéndez**'s 12-lawyer practice. Partner João Anacoreta Correia is head of this quality practice, which is the smallest office in the whole of **Uría Menéndez**'s Iberian network. The service spans litigation, corporate and commercial, employment, tax and public law. Highlights include acting for Banco Santander and NYSE-listed company, Smurfit.

Vellozo Ferreira, Cavaleiro Brandao, Pinheiro Torres e Associados is another of the respected firms in Oporto. Partner Damião Vellozo Ferreira (corporate and commercial) has decided to set up his own firm, while partners Manuel Cavaleiro Brandão (public law, employment and arbitration), Carlos Maria Pinheiro Torres (civil law and corporate and commercial) and Luís Cabral will maintain their partnership. All four are highly regarded practitioners and advise on some of the most important cases and deals in the market.

As we were going to press, Lisbon firm **Abreu, Cardigos & Associados Attorneys at Law** announced its merger with leading Oporto firm *Rui Peixoto Duarte & Associados – Sociedade de Advogados*.

Also worthy of mention are the experienced Oporto branches of leading Lisbon firms **F Castelo Branco & Associados Veiga Gomes, Marques da Cruz, Colmonero**, **PACSA – Henriques da Silva , Paes De Almeida, Corrêa de Sampaio e Associados** and **Raposo Bernardo & Associados**.

BANKING AND FINANCE

Linklaters boast an outstanding banking practice with partner António Soares leading a team of four lawyers. In 2005 the firm advised Deutsche Bank in a ground-breaking €257m securitisation of revenues from a pool of four construction contracts. Pedro Siza Vieira also collects high praise from clients in this sector.

One of the most acclaimed specialists in the field is Luís Branco, head of department at **Morais Leitão, Galvão Teles, Soares Da Silva & Associados**. The firm boasts two partners in banking and finance (partner Filipa Arantes Pedroso is also a leading individual) leading a team of eight lawyers. Well known for being the lead advisor to Banco Comercial Português, one of the largest Portuguese banks, **Morais Leitão, Galvão Teles, Soares Da Silva & Associados**' highlights in 2005 include advising the said bank with respect to the granting of credit facilities to Controlinvest, SA for the acquisition of leading Portuguese media group Lusomundo – Serviços, SGPS, SA – a deal worth €184,800m. Senior associates Pedro Gorjão Henriques and Filipe Lowndes Marques are also highly regarded in the sector.

PLMJ – A. M. Pereira, Sáragga Leal, Oliveira Martins, Júdice e Associados Sociedade de Advogados, RL's sensational banking and finance practice is spearheaded by partner Maria Castelos. The firm is regularly involved in real estate finance, advising the lenders.

Uría Menéndez's name in Portugal is synonymous with banking and expert partner Francisco Sá Carneiro is one of the most reputed practitioners in the field in Portugal. The firm has strong relationships with all the major banks and was most notably involved in advising Caixa BI in the restructuring of Parmalat's entire banking debt. Francisco Sá Carneiro also led the firm's advice in the financing of football team Sporting Clube de Portugal's stadium Alvalade XXI. Partner Pedro Malaquias also receives plaudits for his sound expertise.

Vieira de Almeida & Associados' eminence in this sector derives not only from the fact that the firm was originally founded as a banking practice, but also because it boasts the likes of João Vieira de Almeida and Pedro Cassiano Santos. The patronage of almost every leading Portuguese bank outlines the firm's immense credibility and in terms of banking talent it is hard to find a finer team in Portugal.

BANKING AND FINANCE

LINKLATERS ✪
MORAIS LEITÃO, GALVÃO TELES, SOARES DA SILVA & ASSOCIADOS ✪
PLMJ – A. M. PEREIRA, SÁRAGGA LEAL, OLIVEIRA MARTINS, JÚDICE E ASSOCIADOS SOCIEDADE DE ADVOGADOS, RL ✪
URÍA MENÉNDEZ ✪
VIEIRA DE ALMEIDA & ASSOCIADOS ✪

ABREU, CARDIGOS & ASSOCIADOS ATTORNEYS AT LAW ✪
ANTÓNIO FRUTUOSO DE MELO E ASSOCIADOS ✪
GONÇALVES PEREIRA, CASTELO BRANCO & ASSOCIADOS ✪
SÉRVULO CORREIA & ASSOCIADOS ✪
SIMMONS & SIMMONS REBELO DE SOUSA ✪

Abreu & Marques, Vinhas e Associados ✪
Albuquerque & Associates
Baião, Castro, Solla & Associados, RI ✪
Barrocas Sarmento Neves ✪
Barros, Sobral, G Gomes & Associados ✪
Carlos Aguiar, P. Pinto & Associados ✪
F Castelo Branco & Associados Veiga Gomes, Marques da Cruz, Colmonero ✪
Ferreira Pinto & Associados – Sociedade de Advogados ✪
Franco Caiado Guerreiro & Associados ✪
Garrigues, Leónidas, Matos, SL, Sucursal em Portugal ✪
Jardim, Sampaio, Caldas e Associados
Macedo Vitorino e Associados ✪
Marques Bom e Associados Sociedade de Advogados ✪
Marques Mendes & Associados ✪
Miranda Correia Amendoeira & Associados ✪
PACSA – Henriques da Silva , Paes De Almeida, Corrêa de Sampaio e Associados ✪
Serra Lopes, Cortes Martins & Associados ✪
Teixeira de Freitas, Rodrigues, e Associados ✪

Belzuz Advogados ✪
Coelho Ribeiro e Associados ✪
Lebre, Sá, Carvalho & Associados
Lima, Serra, Fernandes & Associados
Lopes Dias & Associados ✪
Lusojurist
Mouteira Guerreiro, Rosa Amaral & Associados – Sociedade de Advogados R.L. ✪
Neville de Rougemont & Associados ✪
Xavier, Bernardes, Bragança

Firms are listed A-Z in tiers which are ranked in order of priority
✪ Indicates firm displays contact details at the end of this chapter.

Abreu, Cardigos & Associados Attorneys at Law boasts a solid banking and finance practice, with name partner Pedro Cardigos at the fore. The firm advised Cable Satisfaction and Catalyst in a €200m refinancing of a major Portuguese cable, internet and telecoms company.

One of the firms that is clearly punching above its weight in this field is **António Frutuoso de Melo e Associados**. António Frutuoso de Melo, one of the most revered partners in the sector, heads this banking boutique, acclaimed as being perhaps the best in Portugal.

2005 was another strong year for **Gonçalves Pereira, Castelo Branco & Associados**, which saw partner Manuel Magalhães advising a major global property company on banking matters in two multi-million euro projects in Portugal. On the finance side, lead partner Maria João Ricou advised Rede Ferroviária Nacional – REFER, EP on a €600m bond issue, on a standalone basis, listed in Euronext Lisbon and in the Luxembourg Stock Exchange. Name partner Manuel Castelo Branco is also a leading name in the finance sector.

Sérvulo Correia & Associados' acquisition finance expertise has been put to practice in connection with its top-drawer public law advice to the Portuguese MOD. José Manuel Sérvulo Correia and Bernardo Diniz de Ayala were the overall coordinators in the firm's advice on the acquisition, financial (Francisco Ferraz de Carvalho) and offset (Lisa Pinto Ferreira) contracts related to the Portuguese Air Force's tactical aircraft programme. The firm also advised the Portuguese MOD on the financial side of the contracts related with the Portuguese Navy and Army's armoured vehicles programme.

Simmons & Simmons Rebelo de Sousa has in name partner Pedro Rebelo de Sousa one of the most reputed banking lawyers in the country. In 2005 the firm closed nine securitisation deals and has advised on approximately 20 structured finance deals for several major international banks.

Baião, Castro, Solla & Associados, RI advised a leading domestic bank on a €110m syndicated loan, one of the largest syndicated loans last year in Portugal. Felipe Baião do Nascimento is the firm's head of department.

Barrocas Sarmento Neves is particularly strong in the banking and finance sector, advising on both complex cross-border transactions and domestic transactions. João Nuno Barrocas led the firm's advice to Fortis Bank and ING Bank on the Portuguese side of a trade financing to a Portuguese/Brazilian group. Jorge Santiago Neves is the firm's head of department. Other clients include MBIA, the largest monoline insurer in Portugal.

Leading corporate and commercial firm **Carlos Aguiar, P. Pinto & Associados** boasts a solid banking and finance practice. The firm advised Dexia Bank on financial operations to several Portuguese municipalities. Clients also include Spanish savings bank Caixa Galicia.

With an increasing presence in the market, **Garrigues, Leónidas, Matos, SL, Sucursal em Portugal** has in well-known name partner Diogo Leónidas Rocha its head of banking, securities and finance. The firm advised a Portuguese listed company on the issue of €50m equity convertible bonds in the international market and also a media company in a €220m IPO and admission to listing made both in the domestic and international markets.

Macedo Vitorino e Associados acted for several international banks on various loan agreements also involving a major domestic bank.

Marques Mendes & Associados also boasts a good banking and finance practice. Recent highlights include acting for a financial subsidiary of a major global corporation.

28-lawyer **PACSA – Henriques da Silva , Paes De Almeida, Corrêa de Sampaio e Associados** advised on a credit securitisation operation for Banco Espírito Santo, the third-largest Portuguese bank.

Luiz Teixeira de Freitas heads **Teixeira de Freitas, Rodrigues, e Associados**' banking and finance practice. The firm's solid client base includes major investment banks such as JP Morgan and Citibank. Highlights include advising JP Morgan's Portuguese branch on the US$2.2bn syndicated loan for the acquisition of Invista by Koch Industries.

CAPITAL MARKETS

Abreu, Cardigos & Associados Attorneys at Law acts in some of the leading deals in the capital markets sector. Miguel Teixeira de Abreu is one of the most highly regarded experts in the market.

Following its merger with boutique firm *Luiz Gomes & Associados*, **Gonçalves Pereira, Castelo Branco & Associados** further enhanced its profile in the capital markets field. Recently arrived expert partner André Luiz Gomes was most notably involved in a €62m structuring of EXPLORER I – Venture Capital Fund for qualified Investors with €62m of subscribed capital. The firm advised Explorer – Capital de Risco.

Linklaters' capital markets department is thoroughly impressive. Boasting a team of four experienced lawyers, António Soares, head of practice, stands out as one of the pre-eminent lawyers in the field. He led the firm's advice to a major Portuguese company in the €313.6m First Look Right and Put Option Agreements in relation to 100% of a major holding structure. Francisco Xavier de Almeida and André Júdice Glória and two of the firm's rising stars.

Morais Leitão, Galvão Teles, Soares Da Silva & Associados is universally acknowledged as being at the top of the capital markets tree. Boasting some of the most highly experienced partners is the field such as name partner João Soares da Silva and Nuno Galvão Teles, the firm was most notably involved in advising Millennium BCP in the €1.5bn securitisation of a mortgage-backed credit portfolio. Following the firm's merger with *Osório de Castro, Verde Pinho, Vieira Peres, Lobo Xavier*

CAPITAL MARKETS

ABREU, CARDIGOS & ASSOCIADOS ATTORNEYS AT LAW ○
GONÇALVES PEREIRA, CASTELO BRANCO & ASSOCIADOS ○
LINKLATERS ○
MORAIS LEITÃO, GALVÃO TELES, SOARES DA SILVA & ASSOCIADOS ○
PLMJ – A. M. PEREIRA, SÁRAGGA LEAL, OLIVEIRA MARTINS, JÚDICE E ASSOCIADOS SOCIEDADE DE ADVOGADOS, RL ○
SIMMONS & SIMMONS REBELO DE SOUSA ○
TEIXEIRA DE FREITAS, RODRIGUES, E ASSOCIADOS ○
URÍA MENÉNDEZ ○
VIEIRA DE ALMEIDA & ASSOCIADOS ○

Abreu & Marques, Vinhas e Associados ○
Baião, Castro, Solla & Associados, Rl ○
Barrocas Sarmento Neves ○
Carlos Aguiar, P. Pinto & Associados ○
F Castelo Branco & Associados Veiga Gomes, Marques da Cruz, Colmonero ○
Ferreira Pinto & Associados – Sociedade de Advogados ○
Franco Caiado Guerreiro & Associados ○
Garrigues, Leónidas, Matos, SL, Sucursal em Portugal ○
Macedo Vitorino e Associados ○
Sérvulo Correia & Associados ○

Albuquerque & Associates
Barros, Sobral, G Gomes & Associados ○
Mouteira Guerreiro, Rosa Amaral & Associados – Sociedade de Advogados R.L. ○
PACSA – Henriques da Silva , Paes De Almeida, Corrêa de Sampaio e Associados ○
Serra Lopes, Cortes Martins & Associados ○

Firms are listed A-Z in tiers which are ranked in order of priority
○ Indicates firm displays contact details at the end of this chapter.

e Associados, the arrival of expert partner Carlos Osório de Castro is one of the most notable ones to **Morais Leitão, Galvão Teles, Soares Da Silva & Associados**' capital markets team.

PLMJ – A. M. Pereira, Sáragga Leal, Oliveira Martins, Júdice e Associados Sociedade de Advogados, RL is another of the leading firms in the capital markets sector, thanks to its impressive team led by Jorge Brito Pereira.

Another leading firm in the capital markets sector in Portugal is **Simmons & Simmons Rebelo de Sousa**. Highlights in 2005 include acting for a major international bank on the first-ever securitisation of SME receivables in Portugal, also the first ever to take advantage of the state securitisation guarantee fund. Name partner Pedro Rebelo de Sousa and local English partner William Smithson are both highly recommended.

Uría Menéndez has an excellent reputation in the capital markets sector. Carlos Costa Andrade is the firm's head of practice. The firm advised Mercapital, N+1 and Explorer on the €105m acquisition of Holmes Place Spain and Portugal.

Vieira de Almeida & Associados' leading credentials in the capital markets arena are demonstrated by its regular work for leading corporates and banks including Merrill Lynch. Client praise continues to support the firm's leading position.

Baião, Castro, Solla & Associados, Rl advised the issuer on a €125m public offer of bonds and was also the advisor to a major bank on a €50m public offer of subordinated bonds.

Barrocas Sarmento Neves has in João Nuno Barrocas its head of department. The firm was involved in a major cross-border debt refinancing, having received one of its most important instructions from Parmalat concerning the re-financing of the company's Portuguese subsidiary.

Carlos Aguiar, P. Pinto & Associados' capital markets expertise includes advising Bloomberg on the implementation of multilateral platforms for negotiating securities and advising Spanish savings banks Caixanova and Caixa Galicia in the issuance of various short-term, medium-term and long-term securities.

Garrigues, Leónidas, Matos, SL, Sucursal em Portugal advised a Portuguese listed media company in a share buy-back programme which allowed an aggregate shareholder remuneration of approximately €90m.

Highlights at **Macedo Vitorino e Associados** include advising several major international banks in connection with a €425m bond issue by a large foreign multinational.

Sérvulo Correia & Associados' clients in the capital markets sector include investment managers Invesco.

CORPORATE AND M&A

Morais Leitão, Galvão Teles, Soares Da Silva & Associados scored a major coup in the market once again by merging with outstanding former second-tier firm *Osório de Castro, Verde Pinho, Vieira Peres, Lobo Xavier e Associados*. The move justifies this year's promotion to a standalone position in first tier, given the unparalleled corporate and commercial team and the quality of clients that were brought together under the same roof. The firm owes its stellar reputation to a thoroughly impressive team of corporate partners which includes name partner João Soares da Silva, Nuno Galvão Teles, Carlos Osório de Castro, António Lobo Xavier, Joaquim Vieira Peres, Eduardo Verde Pinho, Segismundo Pinto Basto and Luísa Soares da Silva. Its expertise in top-drawer deals was confirmed in its advice to EDP (Energias de Portugal) in the negotiation with REN (Rede Eléctrica Nacional) for the termination of a number of power purchase agreements, an operation adding up to €3.2bn. Other highlights include advising the same client in the €81m sale of a 60% stake in the share capital of Edinfor to LogicaCMG.

CORPORATE AND M&A

MORAIS LEITÃO, GALVÃO TELES, SOARES DA SILVA & ASSOCIADOS ○

PLMJ – A. M. PEREIRA, SÁRAGGA LEAL, OLIVEIRA MARTINS, JÚDICE E ASSOCIADOS SOCIEDADE DE ADVOGADOS, RL ○
VIEIRA DE ALMEIDA & ASSOCIADOS ○

GONÇALVES PEREIRA, CASTELO BRANCO & ASSOCIADOS ○
LINKLATERS ○
SIMMONS & SIMMONS REBELO DE SOUSA ○
URÍA MENÉNDEZ ○

Abreu & Marques, Vinhas e Associados ○
Abreu, Cardigos & Associados Attorneys at Law ○
Albuquerque & Associates
Barrocas Sarmento Neves ○
Carlos Aguiar, P. Pinto & Associados ○
F Castelo Branco & Associados Veiga Gomes, Marques da Cruz, Colmonero ○
Ferreira Pinto & Associados – Sociedade de Advogados ○
Garrigues, Leónidas, Matos, SL, Sucursal em Portugal ○
Jardim, Sampaio, Caldas e Associados
Miranda Correia Amendoeira & Associados ○
Serra Lopes, Cortes Martins & Associados ○
Sérvulo Correia & Associados ○
Sousa Machado, Ferreira da Costa & Associados ○

ANBM Advogados Azevedo Neves, Benjamim Mendes & Associados ○
Almeida Sampaio & Associados ○
Azeredo Perdigao & Albuquerque da Fonseca ○
Baião, Castro, Solla & Associados, Rl ○
Barros, Sobral, G Gomes & Associados ○
Belzuz Advogados ○
Coelho Ribeiro e Associados ○
Cruz Martins, Roquette & Associados – Sociedade de Advogados, RL
Espanha & Associados
Franco Caiado Guerreiro & Associados ○
Henrique Abecasis, Andresen Guimaraes & Associados
Jalles Advogados ○
Lebre, Sá, Carvalho & Associados
Lima, Serra, Fernandes & Associados
Lopes Dias & Associados ○
Lusojurist
Macedo Vitorino e Associados ○
Marques Bom e Associados Sociedade de Advogados ○
Marques Mendes & Associados ○
Mouteira Guerreiro, Rosa Amaral & Associados – Sociedade de Advogados R.L. ○
Mullerat ○
Neville de Rougemont & Associados ○
Noronha Advogados
PACSA – Henriques da Silva , Paes De Almeida, Corrêa de Sampaio e Associados ○
Teixeira de Freitas, Rodrigues, e Associados ○

Firms are listed A-Z in tiers which are ranked in order of priority
○ Indicates firm displays contact details at the end of this chapter.

PLMJ – A. M. Pereira, Sáragga Leal, Oliveira Martins, Júdice e Associados Sociedade de Advogados, RL retains some of the most treasured partners in Portugal, personified in names such as Victor Réfega Fernandes, Dulce Franco and Gabriela Rodrigues. The firm has been involved in one of the highest-profile deals of recent years, advising the Portuguese state, through Parpública, in the €1.2bn restructuring of the Portuguese energy sector. Luís Sáragga Leal also collects praise from clients and rivals alike.

Vieira de Almeida & Associados remains at the forefront of Portuguese corporate and commercial law. António Magalhães Cardoso, João Vieira de Almeida and Pedro Cassiano Santos are just three of the 13 partners that provide exceptional advice, following in the path of name partner Vasco Vieira de Almeida.

Making its presence increasingly felt in the Portuguese corporate market **Gonçalves Pereira, Castelo Branco & Associados** is now one of the three largest law firms in Portugal. Advising Tyco International Ltd in the €130m sale of Tyco Group's assets, properties and underlying rights and advising Somague and Sacyr Vallehermoso in the sale of Finerge to Spanish energy giant Endesa are just a few examples that make up a formidable year for the firm. It's second office in Oporto was also most notably involved in the €60m acquisition of Nexannes Portugal, a copper electric wire manufacturer by Superior Essex. The firm was advising the acquirer.

Linklaters remains one of the most respected brands for corporate work in Portugal. The strength of the firm's Lisbon practice was to the fore as it picked up roles advising Semapa on its €1bn takeover of Portucel and Fortis Insurance on its €500m acquisition of Seguros e Pensões. Head of practice and managing partner Jorge Bleck is one of the best-known corporate lawyers in the country.

Advising a wide range of domestic and international clients which benefit from the firm's international network **Simmons & Simmons Rebelo de Sousa** boasts a corporate and commercial team of seven experienced lawyers in its Lisbon office (including expert partner and head of department Octávio Castelo Paulo). The firm advised Sumolis, one of the two winning bidders in the €426m acquisition of Compal. Sumolis, one of the major beverage companies in Portugal was advised by Octávio Castelo Paulo, Paulo Bandeira and Raquel Cuba Martins in its co-acquisition with Caixa Geral de Depósitos of Compal. Other highlights include advising one of the largest Spanish energy companies on both the incorporation and management of several Portuguese energy companies and on the acquisition of Portuguese companies operating wind farms.

One of the most closely watched corporate teams in the market is Spanish leading firm **Uría Menéndez**'s, which seems increasingly closer to being the first firm to break into the tight lock **Morais Leitão, Galvão Teles, Soares da Silva & Associados, PLMJ – A. M. Pereira, Sáragga Leal, Oliveira Martins, Júdice e Associados Sociedade de Advogados, RL** and **Vieira de Almeida & Associados** have had on the top tiers for some years. Duarte Vasconcellos is the firm's head of practice and amongst a plethora of interesting transactions, he led the firm's advice in advising major Spanish company Prisa on its acquisition of Portuguese media conglomerate Media Capital Group, one of the major deals of 2005. Other highlights include advising Svitzer Wijsmuller (AP Moller Group) in the acquisition of Lisbon Tugs, a towage and salvage company with 80% of the Portuguese market share.

Abreu, Cardigos & Associados Attorneys at Law has a highly regarded practice and well-established name in the market. Its reputed corporate team advised Sony on the merger of its record business with BMG in Portugal.

Barrocas Sarmento Neves has one of the largest corporate practices in Portugal. Spear-headed by name partner Manuel Barrocas, the firm advised NYSE-listed Oceaneering International, a major international advanced applied technology company, on Portuguese and Angolan law, concerning several aspects of its core activity.

Even though it has full-service capability, **Carlos Aguiar, P. Pinto & Associados** is best known in the market for its corporate and commercial expertise. Highlights in 2005 include advising Crédit Foncier de France on its entry as a shareholder in the share capital of a Portuguese financial institution. The firm also advised the multinational German pharmaceutical company Stada in its acquisition of a Portuguese pharmaceutical laboratory in the generic drugs sector. Name partners Carlos Aguiar and Pedro Pinto are the firm's best-known personalities.

F Castelo Branco & Associados Veiga Gomes, Marques da Cruz, Colmonero also boasts a highly acclaimed corporate practice and was involved in one of the major deals of 2005. The firm advised LogicaCMG in its €81m acquisition of a 60% stake in Edinfor Sistemas Informáticos. Name partner Miguel Castelo Branco and partner Gonçalo da Cunha are two highly regarded practitioners in this field. Pedro Guimarães and Rodrigo Almeida Dias have been recognised as two of the firm's rising stars.

While Susana Pimenta de Sousa heads **Garrigues, Leónidas, Matos, SL, Sucursal em Portugal**'s general commercial and corporate law department, expert Mário Lino Dias spearheads the firm's M&A practice. Some of the most relevant deals last year were – on the sell side – the firm's advice to a Portuguese listed company in the €300m sale of its media business and also – on the buyer's side – the €150m acquisition of a Portuguese petrochemical complex by a Spanish oil and petrochemical group and subsequent restructuring of the group.

One of the most highly praised mid-sized firms in this field is **Serra Lopes, Cortes Martins & Associados**. 2005 saw the firm involved in two of the major deals of the year. The firm advised Nutrinvest in its €426m sale of Compal and Nutricafés to Sumolis. Acclaimed partner Luís Miguel Cortes Martins also led the firm's advice to Controlinvest in its €300m acquisition of media company Lusomundo. Partner Rafael Lucas Pires is also a highly praised practitioner.

Teresa Serra spearheads **Sérvulo Correia & Associados**'s commercial department. The firm provides ongoing advice to a major Portuguese shipping company on its corporate restructuring and has also been retained for general commercial legal assistance.

Six-lawyer **Azeredo Perdigao & Albuquerque da Fonseca** was most notably involved in the acquisition of Valiant, Lda by Mercury Boats and in the restructuring of Lufthansa's subsidiaries in Portugal. Miguel Azeredo Perdigão is the firm's best-known personality.

Baião, Castro, Solla & Associados, Rl's corporate and commercial department has been involved in various deals through last year, namely advising a major domestic company on a €20m increase of share capital and advising a public infrastructure company on its corporate restructuring. Victor de Castro Nunes is head of department.

Twelve-lawyer **Coelho Ribeiro e Associados** boasts a solid corporate and commercial practice advising premier domestic and international clients. The firm advised EuroZinc and PortuGlobal on a US$128m acquisition of Somincor (one of the largest copper mine companies in Europe) and is, following that operation, dealing with the merger between PortuGlobal and Somincor.

Miguel Cordovil Matos heads **Cruz Martins, Roquette & Associados – Sociedade de Advogados, RL**'s solid corporate and commercial practice. The firm has most notably been advising the Spanish conglomerate El Corte Inglés since its arrival in the Portuguese market, giving advice on the establishment and development of the various companies of the group in Portugal.

Espanha & Associados is a newcomer in the market. The firm was set up in October 2004 following the split of *CERBA & Associados*. Its seven-strong team (which includes three partners) essentially focuses on tax and corporate and commercial. João Espanha is the firm's best-known personality.

Macedo Vitorino e Associados' extensive commercial expertise includes advising international and domestic clients on various corporate issues, most notably a leading software and hardware company, a video games corporation and one of the largest real estate developers in Spain.

Also recomended in this field is **Marques Mendes & Associados**. The firm advised one of the world's largest manufacturers of electronic, electrical and fiber optic interconnection products and systems in the restructuring of its activities in Portugal.

PACSA – Henriques da Silva , Paes De Almeida, Corrêa de Sampaio e Associados advised GMAC Commercial Finance on the Portuguese side of a Master Facilities agreement of over €68m. The firm's best-known personalities in this field are José Henriques da Silva, head of the firm's corporate department, and Maria Antónia Cameira, the firm's London partner and also head of corporate finance and of the international departments.

Teixeira de Freitas, Rodrigues, e Associados' corporate and commercial department is spearheaded by Luiz Augusto Teixeira de Freitas. The firm represented several shipping groups in connection with shipping finance matters.

DISPUTE RESOLUTION

Morais Leitão, Galvão Teles, Soares Da Silva & Associados' formidable capability in litigation is recognised in the market by peers and clients alike. Spearheaded by co-managing partner António Pinto Leite, the deparment boasts eight highly regarded partners and 20 lawyers. Name partner João Morais Leitão (mainly developing his work in arbitration), José Manuel Galvão Teles and Miguel Galvão Teles are just a few of the more senior names. While regularly being involved in some of the leading litigation cases in the country, the firm has also, most notably acted as advocate for the Portuguese government in a case concerning the legality of the use of force before the International Court of Justice (*Serbia and Montenegro v Portugal*). Acting in major arbitrations for EDP – Energias de Portugal are other highlights of 2005.

2005 saw the return of name partner José Miguel Judice to **PLMJ – A. M. Pereira, Sáragga Leal, Oliveira Martins, Júdice e Associados Sociedade de Advogados, RL** after having spent three years as President of the Bar Association. Also back from serving as a Minister in the previous social-democrat Portuguese government is litigation expert partner Nuno Morais Sarmento. The firm's renowned expertise in the field and the return of two of its most prominent partners earn the firm its promotion to the first tier.

One of the most active firms in arbitration is **Barrocas Sarmento Neves**. The firm was involved in one of the largest arbitrations in Portugal, a dispute related to the construction of the Alqueva dam. Partner Carlos Soares leads the firm's practice; 2005 highlights include professional negligence claims involving four major accounting firms.

Cruz Martins, Roquette & Associados – Sociedade de Advogados, RL's is one of the most respected practices in the market. Both name partners Henrique Chaves and Gonçalo Roquette are recommended. Highlights include successfully representing the fine art auctioneers Christie's in a dispute regarding the authenticity of a Picasso painting. The firm also acts regularly for the Spanish conglomerate El Corte Inglés.

Also boasting a leading practice, **Gonçalves Pereira, Castelo Branco & Associados**' credentials were demonstrated, most notably, in a €23.6m arbitration involving the breach of contract of a consortium agreement for the construction works related to the strengthening of a dam. Partner Miguel Esperança Pina was the leading legal counsel representing Somague Engenharia, one of the largest construction companies in Portugal. Other highlights include acting for United Biscuits on a €38.8m arbitration connected with the acquisition of the Triunfo plant to one of the leading Portuguese food groups.

The litigation department at **Linklaters** is a rare example of one that punches above its weight, with its four-lawyer team handling some of the most complex and high-profile cases in Portugal. Partner Miguel Pinto Cardoso, head of the firm's practice, stands out as one of the pre-eminent litigators in the jurisdiction. He successfully led the firm's advice to Normetro, the contractor responsible for the construction of the Oporto light railway system, in a major construction arbitration against Metro do Porto that saw Normetro awarded €94m in compensation and an extension of time to conclude the construction that was worth another €90m.

Proenca de Carvalho – Advogados stands out as one of the most reputed litigation boutiques in Portugal. Name partner Daniel Proença de Carvalho is widely acclaimmed as one of the best practitioners in the country and leads a team of lawyers which focus exclusively on complex and high-profile corporate and private client disputes.

Serra Lopes, Cortes Martins & Associados' considerable know-how in the dispute resolution arena has won numerous accolades particularly in commercial litigation. António Serra Lopes in one of the best-known litigators in the jurisdiction.

Another leading litigation practice is that of **Simmons & Simmons Rebelo de Sousa**. Partner João Caniço Gomes' solid reputation in the market makes the firm one of the most renowned in the field. He led the firm's advice to a major international company in defending a €1m claim presented against it by some of its clients.

Uría Menéndez has continued to impress and can claim to have been one of the leading litigators in one of the highest-profile cases of recent years in Portugal. Tito Arantes Fontes led the firm's extremely successful advice to Uniarme in a highly complex and lengthy claim that involved the alledged liability of Uniarme for a €60m fraud to the Portuguese State. The case also involved the firm's tax and competition department.

DISPUTE RESOLUTION

MORAIS LEITÃO, GALVÃO TELES, SOARES DA SILVA & ASSOCIADOS ✪
PLMJ – A. M. PEREIRA, SÁRAGGA LEAL, OLIVEIRA MARTINS, JÚDICE E ASSOCIADOS SOCIEDADE DE ADVOGADOS, RL ✪

BARROCAS SARMENTO NEVES ✪
CRUZ MARTINS, ROQUETTE & ASSOCIADOS – SOCIEDADE DE ADVOGADOS, RL
GONÇALVES PEREIRA, CASTELO BRANCO & ASSOCIADOS ✪
LINKLATERS ✪
PROENCA DE CARVALHO – ADVOGADOS
SERRA LOPES, CORTES MARTINS & ASSOCIADOS ✪
SÉRVULO CORREIA & ASSOCIADOS ✪
SIMMONS & SIMMONS REBELO DE SOUSA ✪
URÍA MENÉNDEZ ✪
VIEIRA DE ALMEIDA & ASSOCIADOS ✪

Abreu & Marques, Vinhas e Associados ✪
Abreu, Cardigos & Associados Attorneys at Law ✪
Albuquerque & Associates
Carlos Aguiar, P. Pinto & Associados ✪
Carlos Cruz Associados
Coelho Ribeiro e Associados ✪
F Castelo Branco & Associados Veiga Gomes, Marques da Cruz, Colmonero ✪
Ferreira Pinto & Associados – Sociedade de Advogados ✪
Garrigues, Leónidas, Matos, SL, Sucursal em Portugal ✪
Jalles Advogados ✪
Jardim, Sampaio, Caldas e Associados
Lusojurist
Macedo Vitorino e Associados ✪
Marques Bom e Associados Sociedade de Advogados ✪
Miranda Correia Amendoeira & Associados ✪
PACSA – Henriques da Silva , Paes De Almeida, Corrêa de Sampaio e Associados ✪
Sousa Machado, Ferreira da Costa & Associados ✪

ANBM Advogados Azevedo Neves, Benjamim Mendes & Associados ✪
Almeida Sampaio & Associados ✪
Azeredo Perdigao & Albuquerque da Fonseca ✪
Baião, Castro, Solla & Associados, Rl ✪
Barros, Sobral, G Gomes & Associados ✪
Belzuz Advogados ✪
Espanha & Associados
Franco Caiado Guerreiro & Associados ✪
Henrique Abecasis, Andresen Guimaraes & Associados
Lima, Serra, Fernandes & Associados
SCA Advogados

Firms are listed A-Z in tiers which are ranked in order of priority
✪ Indicates firm displays contact details at the end of this chapter.

Vieira de Almeida & Associados offers a powerful arbitration and litigation department thanks in no small part to the expertise of partner Frederico Gonçalves Pereira.

Carlos Aguiar, P. Pinto & Associados' litigation practice spans a wide range of claims connected with its core corporate and commercial focus, from commercial distribution contract claims to construction claims. Clients include Caixanova and Caixa Galicia.

Coelho Ribeiro e Associados has an impressive litigation and arbitration track record. Partner Rui Botica Santos is an official CAS (Court of Arbitration for Sports) arbitrator, the court of appeal for FIFA decisions, based in Lausanne.

Garrigues, Leónidas, Matos, SL, Sucursal em Portugal was the legal adviser to a Portuguese holding company in a €20m claim concerning the violation of a cooperation agreement in the internet sector. Other highlights include representing a Portuguese subsidiary of a Spanish oil company in a claim concerning the violation of a pre-emptive right in the transfer of shareholdings.

Macedo Vitorino e Associados has most notably acted for a Portuguese investment bank in a dispute regarding a €142m credit agreement. The firm also boasts experience in international arbitration.

José Maria Correia de Sampaio led **PACSA – Henriques da Silva , Paes De Almeida, Corrêa de Sampaio e Associados**' advice to a major international investor in a €10m claim related to the construction of a hotel, spa and resort in the Algarve, the southern region of Portugal.

Azeredo Perdigao & Albuquerque da Fonseca's small litigation practice is particularly strong on tax and employment issues.

Baião, Castro, Solla & Associados, Rl has in Ana Paula Matos Martins a solid head of litigation. The firm advised several companies on insolvency and bankrupcy disputes, disputes arising from shareholders' resolutions and most notably a €10m court case based upon a claim in tort.

EU AND COMPETITION

EU AND COMPETITION

LINKLATERS ✪
MARQUES MENDES & ASSOCIADOS ✪
MORAIS LEITÃO, GALVÃO TELES, SOARES DA SILVA & ASSOCIADOS ✪
PLMJ – A. M. PEREIRA, SÁRAGGA LEAL, OLIVEIRA MARTINS, JÚDICE E ASSOCIADOS SOCIEDADE DE ADVOGADOS, RL ✪
SIMMONS & SIMMONS REBELO DE SOUSA ✪
VIEIRA DE ALMEIDA & ASSOCIADOS ✪

Barrocas Sarmento Neves ✪
Gonçalves Pereira, Castelo Branco & Associados ✪
Jalles Advogados ✪
Jardim, Sampaio, Caldas e Associados
Uría Menéndez ✪

Abreu & Marques, Vinhas e Associados ✪
Abreu, Cardigos & Associados Attorneys at Law ✪
Albuquerque & Associates
Azeredo Perdigao & Albuquerque da Fonseca ✪
F Castelo Branco & Associados Veiga Gomes, Marques da Cruz, Colmonero ✪
Ferreira Pinto & Associados – Sociedade de Advogados ✪
Franco Caiado Guerreiro & Associados ✪
Garrigues, Leónidas, Matos, SL, Sucursal em Portugal ✪
Lima, Serra, Fernandes & Associados
Macedo Vitorino e Associados ✪
PACSA – Henriques da Silva , Paes De Almeida, Corrêa de Sampaio e Associados ✪
Sérvulo Correia & Associados ✪

Firms are listed A-Z In tiers which are ranked in order of priority
✪ Indicates firm displays contact details at the end of this chapter.

Linklaters had another successful year across the board, with Carlos Pinto Correia, head of practice, advising Embraer, the fourth-largest commercial aeroplane manufacturer in the world, in a €37.5m complex merger control that was notified in portugal, Italy and Germany. The firm also benefits from its international network, especially its Belgian competition practice, one of the leading practices in Brussels.

One of the few remaining specialist competition firms, **Marques Mendes & Associados** continues to impress with involvement in high-quality instructions across the competition sphere: it has extensive experience in the media sector having represented a major Portuguese media group in a complaint filed against a Portuguese telco. Other highlights include advising a Portuguese regulating authority on complex regulatory implications arising from the launch of a new product and service package in the market. Name partner Mário Marques Mendes one of the most highly regarded and experienced lawyers in the field.

Morais Leitão, Galvão Teles, Soares Da Silva & Associados continues to enhance its reputation with strong merger control capability co-existing alongside a renowned litigation practice, as demonstrated by its representation of BCA (Banco Comercial dos Açores) before the ECJ regarding the annulment of a decision by the Commission on the compatibility of income tax in the Azores with EU state aid rules. Partners Carlos Botelho Moniz and Joaquim Vieira Peres are two of the most reputed lawyers in the field.

Partner José Luìs da Cruz Vilaca at **PLMJ – A. M. Pereira, Sáragga Leal, Oliveira Martins, Júdice e Associados Sociedade de Advogados, RL** is widely acclaimed as one of the best in the field.

With one of the youngest teams in the market, **Simmons & Simmons Rebelo de Sousa** benefits from its international network, namely its presence in Brussels and the solid reputation of both its heads of department name partner Pedro Rebelo de Sousa and Gonçalo Anastácio. Luís Neto Galvão is another reinforcement on the EU litigation side having returned to the office after three years in Luxembourg as referendaire at the Court of First Instance. The firm has worked on one of the most important cartel cases in Portugal.

Vieira de Almeida & Associados has built up a reputation for advising pharmaceutical and telecoms companies on competition law aspects of cartels, abuse of dominant position, mergers and compliance programmes. Nuno Ruiz is the head partner and unanimously acclaimed as one of the country's experts.

Highly regarded corporate partner Frederico Pereira Coutinho and well-respected partner Isabel Gião de Andrade are responsible for **Gonçalves Pereira, Castelo Branco & Associados**' competition practice.

Name partner João Paulo Teixeira de Matos heads the EU and competition department at **Garrigues, Leónidas, Matos, SL, Sucursal em Portugal**. The firm was involved in various concentration filings: in the IT sector concerning a €6m deal; in the solvency information sector regarding a €7m deal; in the handling business on a €30m deal; in the pharmaceutical sector on a €5m deal.

Macedo Vitorino e Associados has generally been involved in state aid issues and giving expert legal opinions on specific EU and competition matters. Clients include domestic and international banks and a telecommunications operator.

Sérvulo Correia & Associados was retained by Spanish energy giant Endesa (also operating in Portugal) to advise the company on competition issues arising from the €22.5bn hostile takeover bid by Gas Natural.

EMPLOYMENT

Within the context of EU integration and harmonisation, especially since the adoption of the single currency in 2002, a growing trend for a number of major international companies is considering Portugal and Spain as one whole economic area. As such, an important part of the work at leading Portuguese law firms' employment teams has concerned corporate restructurings, mainly bringing the Portuguese business in line with a new centralised corporate structure covering the entire Iberian peninsula. Madrid, the Spanish capital, is invariably being chosen as the Iberian decision-making centre while Lisbon will normally host executives who ultimately report to Spain.

EMPLOYMENT

MORAIS LEITÃO, GALVÃO TELES, SOARES DA SILVA & ASSOCIADOS ✪
PLMJ – A. M. PEREIRA, SÁRAGGA LEAL, OLIVEIRA MARTINS, JÚDICE E ASSOCIADOS SOCIEDADE DE ADVOGADOS, RL ✪
SIMMONS & SIMMONS REBELO DE SOUSA ✪

ANBM Advogados Azevedo Neves, Benjamim Mendes & Associados ✪
Abreu & Marques, Vinhas e Associados ✪
Abreu, Cardigos & Associados Attorneys at Law ✪
Albuquerque & Associates
Almeida Sampaio & Associados ✪
Azeredo Perdigao & Albuquerque da Fonseca ✪
Barrocas Sarmento Neves ✪
Belzuz Advogados ✪
Carlos Aguiar, P. Pinto & Associados ✪
Coelho Ribeiro e Associados ✪
Cruz Martins, Roquette & Associados – Sociedade de Advogados, RL
Espanha & Associados
F Castelo Branco & Associados Veiga Gomes, Marques da Cruz, Colmonero ✪
Ferreira Pinto & Associados – Sociedade de Advogados ✪
Franco Caiado Guerreiro & Associados ✪
Garrigues, Leónidas, Matos, SL, Sucursal em Portugal ✪
Gonçalves Pereira, Castelo Branco & Associados ✪
Henrique Abecasis, Andresen Guimaraes & Associados
Lebre, Sá, Carvalho & Associados
Linklaters ✪
Lusojurist
Macedo Vitorino e Associados ✪
Marques Bom e Associados Sociedade de Advogados ✪
Marques Mendes & Associados ✪
Miranda Correia Amendoeira & Associados ✪
Neville de Rougemont & Associados ✪
Oscar Monteiro (Dr)
PACSA – Henriques da Silva , Paes De Almeida, Corrêa de Sampaio e Associados ✪
SCA Advogados
Saraiva e Sousa, Gomes de Almeida & Associados
Sousa Machado, Ferreira da Costa & Associados ✪
Teixeira de Freitas, Rodrigues, e Associados ✪
Uría Menéndez ✪
Vieira de Almeida & Associados ✪

Firms are listed A-Z in tiers which are ranked in order of priority
✪ *Indicates firm displays contact details at the end of this chapter.*

Leading Portuguese law firms have therefore, in recent years, been dealing with a number of high-profile negotiations with company directors in Portugal often aimed at the termination of their post within the local company and subsequent transfer of power to Madrid.

Morais Leitão, Galvão Teles, Soares Da Silva & Associados is legal counsel to some of the most important players in the Portuguese market. The team comprises three partners and is headed by senior associate Luís Miguel Monteiro. Highlights last year include advising BCP (Banco Comercial Português) on the proposed privatisation and acquisition of the majority of the share capital of Banca Comerciale Romana, the largest Romanian bank.

One of the most established names in employment law, **PLMJ – A. M. Pereira, Sáragga Leal, Oliveira Martins, Júdice e Associados Sociedade de Advogados, RL** continues to be at the forefront of this discipline. The ten-lawyer department is led by hugely experienced partner Abel Mesquita and was most notably involved in advising Oporto transport company STCP in designing a new collective employment agreement with the intention of adapting it to the recent Portuguese Employment Code, approved in 2003.

Consistently recognised as one of the best practices in the country, the employment team at **Simmons & Simmons Rebelo de Sousa** is also one of the largest, with ten lawyers (including expert partner César Sá Esteves) fully devoted to employment and immigration matters. César Sá Esteves led the firm's advice in a high-profile and complex negotiation concerning the dismissal of the Portuguese director of a major international company, in which the final sum (close to €2m) has rarely been seen in the Portuguese business environment.

Another of the most experienced and impressive employment practices may be found in managing partner Maria do Carmo Sousa Machado's highly praised team at **Abreu, Cardigos & Associados Attorneys at Law**. The team was involved in advising Sony on the employment side of the merger of its records business with BMG.

Carlos Aguiar, P. Pinto & Associados' employment department is led by Inês Reis. Highlights include advising Procter & Gamble/Gillette in its restructuring and transfer of assets. The firm is a member of the *ius laboris* international alliance.

Garrigues, Leónidas, Matos, SL, Sucursal em Portugal has in associate Rita Nogueira Neto its head of employment. The firm advised on the restructuring of a company in the dredging sector involving a collective dismissal of approximately 65 employees. It also advised a company in the automotive sector on its closure and collective dismissal of approximately 45 employees.

Acknowledged by peers and clients alike as one of the leading practitioners in the field, partner Maria da Glória Leitão at **Gonçalves Pereira, Castelo Branco & Associados** combines her employment skills with an acute commercial awareness, as well as public law expertise.

Also boasting experience in employment, **Marques Mendes & Associados** most notably advised one of the world's largest automakers in the transformation of its Portuguese financial subsidiary into a different type of credit institution covering a wider range of financial activities.

Teixeira de Freitas, Rodrigues, e Associados acted for a major international retail company in the restructuring of its Portuguese HR department and also a Spanish pharmaceutical company in downsizing and restructuring its Portuguese subsidiary.

INTELLECTUAL PROPERTY

Partner César Bessa Monteiro, at **Abreu, Cardigos & Associados Attorneys at Law** is widely acclaimed as being one of the best IP lawyers Portugal has to offer. He has led the firm's advice to several major companies in Portugal in protecting their IP rights (including trade marks, patents, utility models, designs and models and logotypes). Clients include BASF AG, Estée Lauder and Citigroup.

Name partner João Veiga Gomes, at **F Castelo Branco & Associados Veiga Gomes, Marques da Cruz, Colmonero** is another of the leading experts in this field in Portugal.

PLMJ – A. M. Pereira, Sáragga Leal, Oliveira Martins, Júdice e Associados Sociedade de Advogados, RL is also a force in the IP sector with partner José Luís da Cruz Vilaca collecting many plaudits.

Dealing with a wide range of IP matters, **Gonçalves Pereira, Castelo Branco & Associados**' work spans registration of trade marks and patents. The firm also has strong capabilities in IP litigation issues.

Morais Leitão, Galvão Teles, Soares Da Silva & Associados' six-strong team is led by co-managing partner and litigation expert António Pinto Leite and is the adviser of choice for a wide range of international and domestic clients. The firm advised Pernod Ricard Portugal on trade marks in the context of its acquisition of the Allied Domecq Group.

Corporate partner Octávio Castelo Paulo and litigation partner João Caniço Gomes co-head **Simmons & Simmons Rebelo de Sousa**'s IP practice. The firm has provided advice on data protection and establishing the legal regime of a website for clients such as Warner Bros Online and Sony Pictures Entertainment.

Miguel Marques dos Santos is **Garrigues, Leónidas, Matos, SL, Sucursal em Portugal**'s head of department and an acknowledged expert in the market.

António Magalhaes Cardoso at **Vieira de Almeida & Associados** has extensive experience of pharmaceutical IP issues.

INTELLECTUAL PROPERTY

ABREU, CARDIGOS & ASSOCIADOS ATTORNEYS AT LAW ✪
ALBUQUERQUE & ASSOCIATES
F CASTELO BRANCO & ASSOCIADOS VEIGA GOMES, MARQUES DA CRUZ, COLMONERO ✪
FERREIRA PINTO & ASSOCIADOS – SOCIEDADE DE ADVOGADOS ✪
PLMJ – A. M. PEREIRA, SÁRAGGA LEAL, OLIVEIRA MARTINS, JÚDICE E ASSOCIADOS SOCIEDADE DE ADVOGADOS, RL ✪

Barrocas Sarmento Neves ✪
Carlos Cruz Associados
Franco Caiado Guerreiro & Associados ✪
Garrigues, Leónidas, Matos, SL, Sucursal em Portugal ✪
Gonçalves Pereira, Castelo Branco & Associados ✪
Jalles Advogados ✪
Macedo Vitorino e Associados ✪
Morais Leitão, Galvão Teles, Soares Da Silva & Associados ✪
Simmons & Simmons Rebelo de Sousa ✪
Vieira de Almeida & Associados ✪

Abreu & Marques, Vinhas e Associados ✪
Almeida Sampaio & Associados ✪
Barros, Sobral, G Gomes & Associados ✪
Lebre, Sá, Carvalho & Associados
Linklaters ✪
Lopes Dias & Associados ✪
Marques Bom e Associados Sociedade de Advogados ✪
Miranda Correia Amendoeira & Associados ✪
Neville de Rougemont & Associados ✪
Serra Lopes, Cortes Martins & Associados ✪

Firms are listed A-Z in tiers which are ranked in order of priority
✪ Indicates firm displays contact details at the end of this chapter.

PROJECT FINANCE

Linklaters boasts a sound practice with a strong focus on PPP and energy projects. Pedro Siza Vieira is the partner in charge of a highly praised team of ten experienced lawyers (including rising star José Luís Esquível). The firm advised Enerpro Projectos de Energias on a €122m financing of the largest wind farm in Portugal. Other highlights include advising Banco BPI, BBVA and Caja de Ahorros de Madrid on a €452m financing of 22 wind farms, the largest wind farm portfolio in Portugal.

Morais Leitão, Galvão Teles, Soares Da Silva & Associados had another successful year across the board with partners Luís Branco and Filipa Arantes Pedroso spearheading a team whose highlights last year include advising the syndicate of leading Portuguese banks that provided project finance facilities to the Sport Lisboa e Benfica stadium. The work was connected to the €100m restructuring of such facilities by introducing a commercial credits assignment structure. Other major projects the firm was involved in include the €103m Tagus rail link concession and the €36m natural gas concession.

Fernando Campos Ferreira and Maria Castelos at **PLMJ – A. M. Pereira, Sáragga Leal, Oliveira Martins, Júdice e Associados Sociedade de Advogados, RL** are highly regarded practitioners.

Benefiting from its huge expertise in public law, **Sérvulo Correia & Associados** is also a leading performer in the project finance sector in Portugal. The firm acts as legal counsel for the Portuguese government on the ongoing public works concessions of several motorways in the centre and north of Portugal and also on the entire re-negotiation of the railway concession in the Lisbon metropolitan area.

Uría Menéndez's project finance team is going from strength to strength. The firm prides itself on being one of the most experienced firms in the market in wind farm projects. Finance expert partner Francisco Sá Carneiro led the firm's advice to Dexia, BPI, BCP and Caja Madrid in the €242m portfolio of SIIF Wind Farms.

Vieira de Almeida & Associados has a strong track record on energy, transport infrastructure, road network and hospital projects, and maintains an undisputed position in the top bracket of the market. Pedro Cassiano Santos, Manuel Protásio and Margarida Couto all enjoy excellent reputations.

Barrocas Sarmento Neves is going from strength to strength. The firm, led by partner Pedro Madeira de Brito, is advising the Portuguese government on the implementation of its €7bn PPP National Hospital Programme. It is also the lead adviser to RAVE – Rede de Alta Velocidade, for the development and negotiation stages of the €13bn high-speed rail network project that will connect Lisbon to Madrid – Jorge Santiago Neves is the lead partner.

Gonçalves Pereira, Castelo Branco & Associados' emergence in the project finance sector continues. A strong contingent in Oporto, where head of office José de Freitas was involved in a €1.13bn public tender for the construction of the Braga hospital (advising the consortium FCC/Ramalho Rosa Cobetar/Santa Casa da Misericórdia), is augmented by the firm's dominating Lisbon office. Expert partner Diogo Perestrelo was also advising MSF-Moniz da Maia, Serra e Fortunato-Empreiteiros and others in a ground-breaking €1bn cross-border project finance deal connected with the concession of a tolled highway in Bulgaria.

Abreu, Cardigos & Associados Attorneys at Law also boasts a strong parctice in the project finance sector. The firm advised Hydrocontracting Group, producers of hydroelectric energy through mini-hydrics and wind farms, in the refinancing of its Iberian debt through the issuance of a €122m long-term international bond guaranteed by a monline insurer.

Carlos Aguiar, P. Pinto & Associados advised Caixa Galicia in a project finance deal involving the construction of seven motorway service stations. Name partner Carlos Aguiar and Tiago Ferreira Lima are the partners in charge of project finance matters.

PROJECT FINANCE

LINKLATERS ✪
MORAIS LEITÃO, GALVÃO TELES, SOARES DA SILVA & ASSOCIADOS ✪
PLMJ – A. M. PEREIRA, SÁRAGGA LEAL, OLIVEIRA MARTINS, JÚDICE E ASSOCIADOS SOCIEDADE DE ADVOGADOS, RL ✪
SÉRVULO CORREIA & ASSOCIADOS ✪
URÍA MENÉNDEZ ✪
VIEIRA DE ALMEIDA & ASSOCIADOS ✪

BARROCAS SARMENTO NEVES ✪
GONÇALVES PEREIRA, CASTELO BRANCO & ASSOCIADOS ✪
MIRANDA, CORREIA, AMENDOEIRA & ASSOCIADOS ✪
SERRA LOPES, CORTES MARTINS & ASSOCIADOS ✪
SIMMONS & SIMMONS REBELO DE SOUSA ✪

ANBM Advogados Azevedo Neves, Benjamim Mendes & Associados ✪
Abreu & Marques, Vinhas e Associados ✪
Abreu, Cardigos & Associados Attorneys at Law ✪
Albuquerque & Associates
Almeida Sampaio & Associados ✪
Baião, Castro, Solla & Associados, Rl ✪
Barros, Sobral, G Gomes & Associados ✪
Carlos Aguiar, P. Pinto & Associados ✪
F Castelo Branco & Associados Veiga Gomes, Marques da Cruz, Colmonero ✪
Ferreira Pinto & Associados – Sociedade de Advogados ✪
Franco Caiado Guerreiro & Associados ✪
Jardim, Sampaio, Caldas e Associados
Macedo Vitorino e Associados ✪
Xavier, Bernardes, Bragança

Firms are listed A-Z in tiers which are ranked in order of priority
✪ Indicates firm displays contact details at the end of this chapter.

PUBLIC LAW

At the forefront of the public law sector, **Linklaters** boasts hugely impressive expertise in the area, with partner Pedro Siza Vieira and associate José Luís Esquivel two of the firm's best-known personalities.

Morais Leitão, Galvão Teles, Soares Da Silva & Associados offers a high standard of

PUBLIC LAW

LINKLATERS ✪
MORAIS LEITÃO, GALVÃO TELES, SOARES DA SILVA & ASSOCIADOS ✪
SÉRVULO CORREIA & ASSOCIADOS ✪
VIEIRA DE ALMEIDA & ASSOCIADOS ✪

BARROCAS SARMENTO NEVES ✪
GONÇALVES PEREIRA, CASTELO BRANCO & ASSOCIADOS ✪
PLMJ – A. M. PEREIRA, SÁRAGGA LEAL, OLIVEIRA MARTINS, JÚDICE E ASSOCIADOS SOCIEDADE DE ADVOGADOS, RL ✪
SIMMONS & SIMMONS REBELO DE SOUSA ✪
URÍA MENÉNDEZ ✪

ANBM Advogados Azevedo Neves, Benjamim Mendes & Associados ✪
Abreu, Cardigos & Associados Attorneys at Law ✪
Abreu & Marques, Vinhas e Associados ✪
Coelho Ribeiro e Associados ✪
F Castelo Branco & Associados Veiga Gomes, Marques da Cruz, Colmonero ✪
Ferreira Pinto & Associados – Sociedade de Advogados ✪
Garrigues, Leónidas, Matos, SL, Sucursal em Portugal ✪
Henrique Abecasis, Andresen Guimaraes & Associados
Marques Mendes & Associados ✪
Xavier, Bernardes, Bragança

Firms are listed A-Z in tiers which are ranked in order of priority
✪ Indicates firm displays contact details at the end of this chapter.

legal advice and collects praise for its outstanding team. Partner Fernanda Matoso is a leading individual and fellow partners João Serra and João Pereira Reis are also highly regarded practitioners. Some of the firm's main operations include giving legal opinions on public procurement and water legislation issues to ADP (Águas de Portugal), advising concessionaire AGS in matters related to water and sewage concessions, and advising EDP (Electricidade de Portugal) on legal issues concerning electricity tariffs. Senior associate Margarida Olazabal Cabral garners high praise.

The most admired public law practice in Portugal is **Sérvulo Correia & Associados**. The firm's hugely impressive track record in this field was, once again, reaffirmed as the firm was recently retained by the Portuguese state to draft the national Portuguese legislation which will incorporate European directives on public contracting. A new Portuguese Code of Public Contracts is to follow as a result of the firm's advice. Other highlights include advising the Portuguese MOD on the €400m contracts related to the navy and army armoured vehicles procurement programme. Partners José Manuel Sérvulo Correia, Rui Medeiros, João Amaral e Almeida, Bernardo Diniz de Ayala, Lino Torgal and Francisco Ferraz de Carvalho were all involved in both issues. Another key fact was the arrival of highly recognised public law expert partner Sofia Galvão and a team of three lawyers from **PLMJ – A. M. Pereira, Sáragga Leal, Oliveira Martins, Júdice e Associados Sociedade de Advogados, RL** (a major coup for **Sérvulo Correia & Associados** who had seen most of its tax capability move to **PLMJ – A. M. Pereira, Sáragga Leal, Oliveira Martins, Júdice e Associados Sociedade de Advogados, RL** in 2004).

Vieira de Almeida & Associados is thoroughly impressive in public law matters, particularly in public procurement where partners Paulo Pinheiro and Manuel Protásio gain several client recommendations. Partner Margarida Couto is also a leading individual.

Gonçalves Pereira, Castelo Branco & Associados' merger with boutique firm *Luiz Gomes & Associados* also had its benefits in the firm's public law capability. New arrival partner André Luiz Gomes led the firm's advice to a consortium led by NSL in a public tender regarding the €26m first stage of the re-privatisation of energy company EDA (Electricidade dos Açores).

PLMJ – A. M. Pereira, Sáragga Leal, Oliveira Martins, Júdice e Associados Sociedade de Advogados, RL suffered a loss with the departure of expert partner Sofia Galvão and her team. It still boasts a leading practice with Rui Chancerelle de Machete and Teresa Melo Ribeiro as the firm's best-known practitioners.

Simmons & Simmons Rebelo de Sousa not only boasts a team of four lawyers (including head of department José Luís Moreira da Silva) in the general public law practice, but also has an active niche environment practice spearheaded by Mário Melo Rocha (a highly regarded lawyer in this field). Leading clients in the public sector are the Ministry of Transport, the Ministry of the Economy and the port sector, which includes the port of Setúbal and the port of Lisbon, the largest port in the country.

A new arrival in **Uría Menéndez**'s public law department last year was expert partner Cláudio Monteiro, from **Barrocas Sarmento Neves**, following the departure of Mónica Carneiro Pacheco. Duarte Brito de Goes is also a leading individual in this field.

The public law department at **Abreu, Cardigos & Associados Attorneys at Law**, spearheaded by partner Manuel Andrade Neves, has raised its profile with the recent arrival of partner José Eduardo Martins.

REAL ESTATE AND CONSTRUCTION

With particular strength in real estate and construction disputes, **Barrocas Sarmento Neves** was most notably involved in several high-profile arbitrations, representing both public and private entities, whose value surpassed €250m and were related to public construction and concession contracts. Paulo Nogueira da Rocha and Albano Sarmento were the lead partners involved.

Frederico Pereira Coutinho, Diogo Perestrelo and Ana Menéres are the partners involved in the

REAL ESTATE AND CONSTRUCTION

BARROCAS SARMENTO NEVES ✪
GONÇALVES PEREIRA, CASTELO BRANCO & ASSOCIADOS ✪
MORAIS LEITÃO, GALVÃO TELES, SOARES DA SILVA & ASSOCIADOS ✪
PLMJ – A. M. PEREIRA, SÁRAGGA LEAL, OLIVEIRA MARTINS, JÚDICE E ASSOCIADOS SOCIEDADE DE ADVOGADOS, RL ✪
URÍA MENÉNDEZ ✪

Abreu & Marques, Vinhas e Associados ✪
Abreu, Cardigos & Associados Attorneys at Law ✪
Albuquerque & Associates
Azeredo Perdigao & Albuquerque da Fonseca ✪
Baião, Castro, Solla & Associados, Rl ✪
Barros, Sobral, G Gomes & Associados ✪
Carlos Aguiar, P. Pinto & Associados ✪
Coelho Ribeiro e Associados ✪
Cruz Martins, Roquette & Associados – Sociedade de Advogados, RL
F Castelo Branco & Associados Veiga Gomes, Marques da Cruz, Colmonero ✪
Ferreira Pinto & Associados – Sociedade de Advogados ✪
Franco Caiado Guerreiro & Associados ✪
Garrigues, Leónidas, Matos, SL, Sucursal em Portugal ✪
Henrique Abecasis, Andresen Guimaraes & Associados
Jardim, Sampaio, Caldas e Associados
José Osvaldo Gomes e Associados – Sociedade de Advogados
Lebre, Sá, Carvalho & Associados
Lima, Serra, Fernandes & Associados
Linklaters ✪
Macedo Vitorino e Associados ✪
Marques Bom e Associados Sociedade de Advogados ✪
Miranda Correia Amendoeira & Associados ✪
Neville de Rougemont & Associados ✪
Sérvulo Correia & Associados ✪
Simmons & Simmons Rebelo de Sousa ✪
Teixeira de Freitas, Rodrigues, e Associados ✪
Vieira de Almeida & Associados ✪

Firms are listed A-Z in tiers which are ranked in order of priority
✪ Indicates firm displays contact details at the end of this chapter.

highest-profile real estate deals at **Gonçalves Pereira, Castelo Branco & Associados**. The massive expertise they share amongst them was shown in the firm's advice to Deutsche Bank Real Estate in the acquisition of a shopping centre in the Madeira islands, a complex €80m operation carried out through an SPV that had to be adapted to the specialities of the local regulatory environment.

Also recognised as a leading practice, **Morais Leitão, Galvão Teles, Soares Da Silva & Associados** advised Sonae Sierra Group on various issues, namely shopping centres, land use, planning and municipal taxes, and Vilamoura XXI a €350m urban development project in the Algarve. Partner João Pereira Reis led the firm's advice in these transactions. The firm was also advising SAIP on the planning and construction of a €900m tourism real estate venture in the south of Portugal.

Another thoroughly active department at **PLMJ – A. M. Pereira, Sáragga Leal, Oliveira Martins, Júdice e Associados Sociedade de Advogados, RL** is real estate, spearheaded by star partner Pedro Sáragga Leal.

One of the areas where **Uría Menéndez** has an established name and is renowned for having an outstanding capability is real estate. The reputation owes a lot to expert partner Duarte Garin who is praised for being one of the best real estate lawyers in Portugal.

Abreu, Cardigos & Associados Attorneys at Law's busy department has most notably acted for two of the largest Portuguese real estate investment fund managers and has also been involved in the acquisition of real estate and administrative licensing procedures for a client opening a network of supermarkets.

Azeredo Perdigao & Albuquerque da Fonseca's real estate expertise was put to practice in its advice to OPCA (Obras Públicas e Cimento Armado) one of the largest real estate developers in Portugal.

José Castro e Solla heads **Baião, Castro, Solla & Associados, Rl**'s growing real estate and construction practice. The firm has most notably advised the buyers and the promoter in a €20m acquisition of a prime location site in central Lisbon.

Pedro Pinto is in charge of **Carlos Aguiar, P. Pinto & Associados**' real estate practice, which has been very active in turn-key deals for French group Bouygues Immobilier, namely on a project involving the construction, development and commercialisation of a retail park in Braga, in the north of Portugal.

One of **Lima, Serra, Fernandes & Associados**' strongest capabilities is in real estate. All three name partners have acquired extensive experience in field. Clients include major international company TCN Property Projects.

Linklaters' real estate team was most notably involved in advising JP Morgan Chase and Espírito Santo Investment on structuring their joint bid to act as lead arrangers on the €1.2bn outsourcing (sale and leaseback) by the Portuguese government of a large portfolio of commercial property.

Macedo Vitorino e Associados has acted for real estate developers and for buyers in several high-profile deals across the country, including the purchase of a €14m set of properties in the Algarve for the development of a resort.

With the arrival of expert planning partner Sofia Galvão, **Sérvulo Correia & Associados** saw a major boost in its real estate and construction practice. The firm advises several public entities and major private companies on various urban planning and construction law issues.

Simmons & Simmons Rebelo de Sousa has continued to witness a considerable increase in work with both domestic and international complex projects. Partner Maria José Santana is the firm's head of department and has led its advice to a leading Portuguese investment fund in the resale and leasing of several pieces of land.

Teixeira de Freitas, Rodrigues, e Associados' real estate expertise spans planning and infrastructure projects, construction projects (residential and commercial) and legal assistance in maintenance and management of business centres and shopping centres.

Vieira de Almeida & Associados advised on various aspects of a €200m village outlet in Lisbon, including its licensing, financing, construction and lease. The multi-disciplinary deal was a good demonstration of the firm's exceptional capabilities regarding inter-departmental team work having involved partner and head of real estate Pedro Ferreirinha and project finance partners Manuel Protásio and Vanda Cascão.

SHIPPING

The shipping sector is largely dominated by especialist boutiques that are instructed by leading corporate firms in the most complex issues. **Andrade Dias e Associados**; **Armando Henriques, Ana Cristina Pimentel & Associados – Sociedade de Advogados**; and **G Conceicao Silva Advogado** are the three main boutiques in the field. However there are a few larger firms who also boast shipping expertise and are able to advise on a number of shipping issues.

Albuquerque & Associates has extensive experience in the shipping area and has advised some of the most important shipping clients in Portugal.

Also with shipping capability, particularly on the litigation side, **Barrocas Sarmento Neves** is recommended.

Abreu, Cardigos & Associados Attorneys at Law's active shipping practice is spearheaded by partner Miguel Avillez Pereira.

PLMJ – A. M. Pereira, Sáragga Leal, Oliveira Martins, Júdice e Associados Sociedade de Advogados, RL also boasts a first-class shipping practice with partners Nuno Líbano Monteiro and José Felipe Abecassis being the firm's most experienced practitioners in this field.

One of the key shipping clients at **Sérvulo Correia & Associados** is the regional government authorities of the Azores. The firm has advised the Azores government on general transport contracts and also in several shipping contracts regarding fuel transportation between the Azores islands.

Simmons & Simmons Rebelo de Sousa's maritime and shipping practice has seen a significant rise in both clients and issues, most of them connected with the Portuguese islands of Madeira and the Azores. Partner Maria José Santana is the firm's head of department.

Another experienced practice in the shipping sector is that of **Teixeira de Freitas, Rodrigues, e Associados**. The firm advised the Spanish shipbuilder Factorías Vulcano on corporate, finance and tax issues, concerning its €26m acquisition of a bulk.

SHIPPING

ALBUQUERQUE & ASSOCIATES
ANDRADE DIAS E ASSOCIADOS
ARMANDO FELIX PEREIRA (DR)
ARMANDO HENRIQUES, ANA CRISTINA PIMENTEL & ASSOCIADOS – SOCIEDADE DE ADVOGADOS
BARROCAS SARMENTO NEVES ✪
G CONCEICAO SILVA ADVOGADO
MEDEIROS COSME (DR)

Abreu, Cardigos & Associados Attorneys at Law ✪
Barros, Sobral, G Gomes & Associados ✪
Coelho Ribeiro e Associados ✪
Morais Leitão, Galvão Teles, Soares Da Silva & Associados ✪
Neville de Rougemont & Associados ✪
PLMJ – A. M. Pereira, Sáragga Leal, Oliveira Martins, Júdice e Associados Sociedade de Advogados, RL ✪
Serra Lopes, Cortes Martins & Associados ✪
Sérvulo Correia & Associados ✪
Simmons & Simmons Rebelo de Sousa ✪
Teixeira de Freitas, Rodrigues, e Associados ✪

Firms are listed A-Z in tiers which are ranked in order of priority
✪ *Indicates firm displays contact details at the end of this chapter.*

TAX

Gonçalves Pereira, Castelo Branco & Associados' overwhelming tax reputation is on a par with its Spanish practice at **Cuatrecasas**. Expert partner Diogo Ortigão Ramos' credentials are widely acclaimed by clients and rivals alike. He led the firm's advice to domestic energy company

TAX

GONÇALVES PEREIRA, CASTELO BRANCO & ASSOCIADOS ✪
MORAIS LEITÃO, GALVÃO TELES, SOARES DA SILVA & ASSOCIADOS ✪
PLMJ – A. M. PEREIRA, SÁRAGGA LEAL, OLIVEIRA MARTINS, JÚDICE E ASSOCIADOS SOCIEDADE DE ADVOGADOS, RL ✪

Abreu & Marques, Vinhas e Associados ✪
Abreu, Cardigos & Associados Attorneys at Law ✪
Azeredo Perdigao & Albuquerque da Fonseca ✪
F Castelo Branco & Associados Veiga Gomes, Marques da Cruz, Colmonero ✪
Linklaters ✪
Miranda Correia Amendoeira & Associados ✪
Sérvulo Correia & Associados ✪
Simmons & Simmons Rebelo de Sousa ✪
Teixeira de Freitas, Rodrigues, e Associados ✪
Uría Menéndez ✪
Vieira de Almeida & Associados ✪
Xavier, Bernardes, Bragança

Albuquerque & Associates
Barros, Sobral, G Gomes & Associados ✪
Belzuz Advogados ✪
Franco Caiado Guerreiro & Associados ✪
PACSA – Henriques da Silva , Paes De Almeida, Corrêa de Sampaio e Associados ✪

ANBM Advogados Azevedo Neves, Benjamim Mendes & Associados ✪
Barrocas Sarmento Neves ✪
Cruz Martins, Roquette & Associados – Sociedade de Advogados, RL
Espanha & Associados
Henrique Abecasis, Andresen Guimaraes & Associados
Jalles Advogados ✪
Lebre, Sá, Carvalho & Associados
Lima, Serra, Fernandes & Associados
Macedo Vitorino e Associados ✪
Marques Bom e Associados Sociedade de Advogados ✪
Marques Mendes & Associados ✪
Mouteira Guerreiro, Rosa Amaral & Associados – Sociedade de Advogados R.L. ✪
Neville de Rougemont & Associados ✪

Firms are listed A-Z in tiers which are ranked in order of priority
✪ Indicates firm displays contact details at the end of this chapter.

EDP (Electricidade de Portugal) in the reorganisation of its corporate structure in Portugal and Spain, the first-ever Iberian reorganisation of a utility company in the renewable energy sector.

The sheer experience and highly distinguished reputation of partner Francisco de Sousa da Câmara in the market secures **Morais Leitão, Galvão Teles, Soares Da Silva & Associados**' position as a leading practice in the field. In adition, having merged with *Osório de Castro, Verde Pinho, Vieira Peres, Lobo Xavier e Associados*, the firm saw one of the country's most cherished tax experts, António Lobo Xavier, integrate into its astounding team of partners. The firm's capabilities in complex matters were noted in its advice to EDP group, namely in the privatisation of 11% of its share capital. This was a ground-breaking transaction and the largest-ever in Portugal, which was intended to finance the acquisition of a 56.2% stake in Spanish energy company Hidroeléctrica del Cantábrico. Particular tax work was performed in order to have new shareholders benefit from specific tax incentives.

Another hugely impressive tax team is found at **PLMJ – A. M. Pereira, Sáragga Leal, Oliveira Martins, Júdice e Associados Sociedade de Advogados, RL**. The firm boasts some of the finest lawyers in this sector with names such as Diogo Leite Campos and Rogério Fernandes Ferreira.

Often referred to as being among the best especialists in this field, **Abreu, Cardigos & Associados Attorneys at Law**'s tax department owes a lot of its reputation to partner Miguel Teixeira de Abreu. He led the firm's advice to Sony on the tax side of the merger of its record business with BMG. Other highlights include giving tax advice to Hydrocontracting Group in the refinancing of its Portuguese and Spanish operations.

Vítor Félix, at **F Castelo Branco & Associados Veiga Gomes, Marques da Cruz, Colmonero**, is one of the most highly regarded tax practitioners in Portugal.

Sérvulo Correia & Associados' busy tax department is led by partner Ricardo Guimarães.

Senior associate Paula Rosado Pereira has taken over **Simmons & Simmons Rebelo de Sousa**'s well-established tax department following the departure of Vítor Félix in 2004. The firm has advised several major clients such as the Portuguese government, Goldman Sachs and BNP Paribas.

Teixeira de Freitas, Rodrigues, e Associados' tax practice spans mergers and acquisitions, restructuring of enterprises, real estate transactions, tax litigation and also high-net-worth individuals and families on tax issues and estate planning. Clients include Deutsche Bank London.

Pedro Paes de Almeida is **PACSA – Henriques da Silva , Paes De Almeida, Corrêa de Sampaio e Associados**' tax expert and head of department. The practice spans private client and corporate tax issues, with significant expertise on offshore centres – mainly in Madeira Free Trade Zone and Madeira International Business Centre.

Barrocas Sarmento Neves' tax practice spans a wide range of areas including debt and equity market transactions, investment funds, debt finance, investments and exit strategies, mergers and acquisitions transactions and equity offerings. The firm also advises a number of high-net-worth individuals and family businesses.

Gonçalo Roquette is **Cruz Martins, Roquette & Associados – Sociedade de Advogados, RL**'s head of tax, and focuses mainly on advising international clients.

Macedo Vitorino e Associados also has tax capability. Clients span various sectors of the economy including telecoms, automotive, banking and energy.

Marques Mendes & Associados' tax expertise includes advising one of the world's largest car manufacturers in several tax issues.

TELECOMS

VIEIRA DE ALMEIDA & ASSOCIADOS ✪

MACEDO VITORINO E ASSOCIADOS ✪
MORAIS LEITÃO, GALVÃO TELES, SOARES DA SILVA & ASSOCIADOS ✪
PLMJ – A. M. PEREIRA, SÁRAGGA LEAL, OLIVEIRA MARTINS, JÚDICE E ASSOCIADOS SOCIEDADE DE ADVOGADOS, RL ✪
SIMMONS & SIMMONS REBELO DE SOUSA ✪

Abreu & Marques, Vinhas e Associados ✪
Abreu, Cardigos & Associados Attorneys at Law ✪
Albuquerque & Associates
Barrocas Sarmento Neves ✪
Garrigues, Leónidas, Matos, SL, Sucursal em Portugal ✪
Gonçalves Pereira, Castelo Branco & Associados ✪
Marques Mendes & Associados ✪
Uría Menéndez ✪

Coelho Ribeiro e Associados ✪
Franco Caiado Guerreiro & Associados ✪
Henrique Abecasis, Andresen Guimaraes & Associados
Jalles Advogados ✪
Jardim, Sampaio, Caldas e Associados
Linklaters ✪
Marques Bom e Associados Sociedade de Advogados ✪
Mouteira Guerreiro, Rosa Amaral & Associados – Sociedade de Advogados R.L. ✪
Serra Lopes, Cortes Martins & Associados ✪
Sérvulo Correia & Associados ✪
Sousa Machado, Ferreira da Costa & Associados ✪
Teixeira de Freitas, Rodrigues, e Associados ✪
Xavier, Bernardes, Bragança

Firms are listed A-Z in tiers which are ranked in order of priority
✪ Indicates firm displays contact details at the end of this chapter.

TELECOMS

'They will be the top telecoms firm for a long time yet' says one competitor of **Vieira de Almeida & Associados**. The firm has in Margarida Couto one of the most formidable telecoms expert in Portugal who regularly advises Portugal Telecom on a number of complex deals.

Macedo Vitorino e Associados boasts a strong practice in the telecoms sector. The firm has acted for major international providers in various regulatory, competition and licensing issues.

Another of the acclaimed teams in telecoms is headed by Filipa Arantes Pedroso, partner at **Morais Leitão, Galvão Teles, Soares Da Silva & Associados**. She led the firm's advice to ASCOM Holding AG, a Swiss listed telecommunications company in relation to Project Mario, involving the sale of its private branch exchange division to a Danish subsidiary of Aastra Technologies Limited – a €7m transaction that involved a number of share and asset deals across various European countries.

PLMJ – A. M. Pereira, Sáragga Leal, Oliveira Martins, Júdice e Associados Sociedade de Advogados, RL offers a sound practice and has in José Luís da Cruz Vilaca a telecoms expert.

Simmons & Simmons Rebelo de Sousa has felt an increase in the number of consultations and complex deals. The firm has acted for British Telecom, Warner Brothers Online and Sony Pictures Entertainment.

Barrocas Sarmento Neves' telecoms department is led by partner Diogo Lacerda Machado.

Also boasting solid expertise in the sector, **Gonçalves Pereira, Castelo Branco & Associados** has advised international clients on various regulatory issues.

Marques Mendes & Associados' strong expertise as an EU and competition boutique is widely acknowledged with telecoms clients who also instruct the firm on telecoms matters. The firm acted for a subsidiary of a major Portuguese media group also active in the telecoms sector in two complaints against another operator for abuse of dominant position.

Sérvulo Correia & Associados' clients include Portugal Telecom, public television broadcast company RTP and telecoms regulator Anacom.

Teixeira de Freitas, Rodrigues, e Associados acted for a major Portuguese telecoms company on a €10m PLC supply agreement with a major mobile phone network operator.

RAPOSO BERNARDO & ASSOCIADOS

RUA DO ÍNDICO
EDIFÍCIO ALTIS, 1° G
CERRO ALAGOA
8200-139 ALBUFEIRA

Telephone: +351 28 958 64 88
Fax: +351 28 954 13 92
E-mail: albufeira@raposobernardo.com
Website: www.raposobernardo.com

Languages
English, Spanish, French, Italian

Other offices
Cidade da Praia (Cape Verde), Lisbon, Madrid, Maputo (Mozambique), Porto

Number of lawyers 49
at this office 2

CATEGORIES OF WORK

Corporate law, M&A	Litigation, ADR and arbitration
Banking, capital markets and financial law	Health, pharmaceutical law and biotechnology
Commercial law, industrial and intellectual property	Energy and natural resources
Private equity and venture capital	Real estate, construction, planning and environment
Foreign investment	Tourism
Tax law and tax planning	EU and competition law
Employment and social security law	Maritime and aviation law

ANBM ADVOGADOS

AV ANTÓNIO AUGUSTO
DE AGUIAR 27
R/C E 2° DTO
1069-126 LISBON

Telephone: +351 21 358 36 20
Fax: +351 21 315 94 34
E-mail: anbm.advogados@anbm.pt
Website: www anbm.pt

Languages
English, French, German, Italian, Spanish

Number of lawyers 33

Contacts
Benjamin Mendes, Antonio Moura Portugal

CATEGORIES OF WORK

Administrative
Nuno Azvedo Neves

Aviation
Antonio Moura Portugal

Banking and finance
Antonio Moura Portugal

Commercial property/real estate
Luis Filipe Carvalho

Competition and EU
Luis Filipe Carvalho

Corporate and commercial
Benjamin Mendes

Dispute resolution
Joao Nuno Azevedo Neves

Employment
Benjamin Mendes

Foreign direct investment
Benjamin Mendes

Infrastructure and project finance
Benjamin Mendes

Mergers and acquisitions
Benjamin Mendes

Privatisation
Benjamin Mendes

Shipping and transport
Antonio Moura Portugal

Tax
Nuno Azevedo Neves

Environment
Nuno Azevedo Neves

Capital matters
Antonio Moura Portugal

Construction
Luis Filipe Cavalho

Telecommunications
Nuno Azevedo Neves

ATPR – ATHAYDE DE TAVARES & PEREIRA DA ROSA
SOCIEDADE DE ADVOGADOS, RL

RUA JOAQUIN ANTONIO DE AGUIAR 66 5
1070-153 LISBON

Telephone: +351 21 382 75 80
Fax: +351 21 382 75 89
E-mail: atpr@atpr.pt
Website: www.atpr.pt

Languages
English, French, German, Spanish

Number of lawyers 6

Member
American Chamber of Commerce; Portuguese-Brazilian Chamber of Commerce; Alliance of International Business Lawyers (ALLIURIS)

CATEGORIES OF WORK

Arbitration
José de Athayde de Tavares, João Pereira da Rosa

Civil law
Joaó Pereira da Rosa, Paula Lamosa Pinto

Corporate and commercial law
José de Athayde de Tavares, Catarina Morgadinho Barata

EU and competition law
José de Athayde de Tavares

Employment law
José de Athayde de Tavares, Catarina Morgadinho Barata

Tax law
José de Athayde de Tavares, Catarina Morgadinho Barata

Real estate
João Pereira da Rosa

Litigation
João Pereira da Rosa, Cristina Mendona Miguel

ABREU & MARQUES, VINHAS E ASSOCIADOS

RUA FILIPE FOLQUE 2-4º
1069-121 LISBOA

Telephone: +351 21 330 71 00
Fax: +351 21 314 74 91
E-mail: amva@amva.pt

Languages
English, French, Spanish, German

Other offices
Funchal

Number of lawyers 35
at this office 34

CATEGORIES OF WORK

Administrative and environment law
Isabel Garcia, Sofia Amram

Arbitration and litigation
Jorge de Abreu, João Pedro Collares Pereira

Banking and finance, capital markets, investment funds
Afonso Barroso

Corporate and commercial law
Luis Vinhas, Afonso Barroso

EU and competition law
Luis Vinhas, Sofia Amram

Foreign investment
Jorge de Abreu, Luis Vinhas

Intellectual property
Jorge de Abreu

Labour law
Martim Anahory

Investment funds
Afonso Barroso

Madeira free-trade zone
Jorge de Abreu, Afonso Barroso

Mergers and acquisitions
Luís Vinhas, Martim Anahory

Privatisation
Jorge de Abreu, Luís Vinhas

Real estate, construction and tourism
Jorge de Abreu, Henrique Moser

Taxation
Isabel Garcia, Manuel Faustino

ABREU, CARDIGOS & ASSOCIADOS

ATTORNEYS AT LAW

AV. DAS FORÇAS ARMADAS 125
12TH FLOOR
1600-179 LISBOA

Telephone: +351 21 723 18 00
Fax: +351 21 723 18 99
E-mail: general@abreucardigos.com
Website: www.abreucardigos.com

Languages
Danish, English, Finnish, French, German, Italian, Spanish, Swedish

Number of lawyers 68

Other offices Porto

Contact
Carmo Sousa Machado (managing partner)

Member
IBA; International Fiscal Association; AIJA; International Trade Mark Association; International Federation of Industrial Property Consultants; European Communities Trade Mark Association; EVCA; Multilaw Counsel Alliance; International Swaps and Derivatives Association (ISDA)

CATEGORIES OF WORK

M&A, MBOs, MBIs
Miguel Teixeira de Abreu

International taxation and tax planning
Miguel Teixeira de Abreu

EU, antitrust and competition law
Miguel de Avillez Pereira

IP, IT and telecommunications law
Cesar Bessa Monteiro

Environmental law
José Eduardo Martins

Construction law and public works
Manuel de Andrade Neves

Foreign investment
Pedro Cardigos dos Reis

Commercial property, real estate
Armando Martins Ferreira

Employment law
Carmo Sousa Machado

Banking and financial services, swaps and derivatives
Pedro Cardigos dos Reis

Local taxation and tax litigation
Duarte de Athayde

Corporate and commercial
Rui Peixoto Duarte

Capital markets
Miguel Castro Pereira

Sports and leisure law
Nuno Barbosa

Civil and commercial litigation
Miguel Castro Pereira

THE FIRM

Abreu, Cardigos & Associados is a Portuguese law firm that acts, in particular, for corporate entities requiring specialist legal assistance and a range of complementary services. The firm's international experience was initially grounded on the founding partners' experience in major US and UK international law firms. The firm's client base includes some of the largest international companies operating in Portugal. Abreu, Cardigos & Associados is one of the largest law firms in Portugal and is the only one to have been certified by the IPQ, the Portuguese Institute for Quality, with the ISO 9001 norm. NP EN ISO 9001 (issued by SGS ICS International Certification Services) – (Certificate number 9311/35/55200/43201).

AREAS OF PRACTICE

M&A, MBOs, MBIs: the firm provides legal and tax assistance with regard to the purchase or disposal of Portuguese companies. It frequently conducts legal due diligence processes, as well as handling the acquisition and/or disposal structures of Portuguese businesses. It also acts in the execution of restructuring steps, including mergers, split-offs, flotations and asset divisions. Recently, the firm advised Portugal Telecom on the outsourcing of its information systems department.

Banking and financial services: the firm has been selected to advise the Republic of Portugal on operations connected with international financial instruments, including derivatives. The firm advises credit institutions in respect of the securitisation of receivables and mortgage-backed assets of their Portuguese clients.

Local and international taxation and tax planning: the firm provides specialist advice to resident and non-resident corporations, as well as to other law firms in Portugal and abroad. The firm has been involved in the establishment of tax structures regarding financial operations, acquisition of companies, corporate restructuring and international transactions for resident and non-resident corporations. The firm has also been retained in respect of the issuance of tax opinions in context with securitisations transactions in Portugal.

Capital markets: the firm regularly advises resident and non-resident investors on their duties before the Portuguese Capital Markets Regulatory Authorities. The firm has also been involved in the admission and listing of several Portuguese companies on the Lisbon Stock Exchange.

Industrial and intellectual property and IT law: the firm is able to provide prime assistance in the area of industrial and intellectual property law as well as in the field of IT law. Dr Cesar Bessa Monteiro is simultaneously a lawyer and an official industrial property agent. Dr Cesar Bessa Monteiro has been invited to be part of a government commission created to study and review the Portuguese Industrial Property Code. Currently the firm provides assistance to more than 300 international clients on all matters related to industrial and intellectual property law and IT law.

EU, antitrust and competition law: the firm regularly advises Portuguese companies on the implications of EU law. It has represented many multinational companies before the antitrust authorities in connection with mergers and other concentration operations.

Telecommunications: the firm advises resident and non-resident telecoms companies on their entry into the recently liberalised Portuguese telecoms market. The firm is also currently representing a Portuguese telecoms operator on a number of restructuring deals.

Environmental law: members of the firm founded Euronatura, an NGO dedicated to environmental law and policy, and the firm is regularly consulted by its clients on national and European environmental matters.

Labour law: the firm has been increasingly consulted on labour law matters, and represents some of the major international consultancy firms in this area. The firm is also involved in collective negotiation of labour agreements.

Civil and commercial litigation: the firm has extensive experience before Portuguese courts and national and international arbitration.

ALMEIDA SAMPAIO & ASSOCIADOS

AVENIDA DUQUE D'AVILA 66
7° ANDAR
1069-075 LISBON

Telephone: +351 21 353 69 26
Fax: +351 21 353 69 27
E-mail: as.law@asampaio-advogados.pt

Languages
English, French, German, Spanish

Other offices
Porto

Number of lawyers 50
at this office 45

Contact
Carlos de Almeida Sampaio

CATEGORIES OF WORK

Corporate law and contracts	Foreign investment
Taxation	Antitrust and trade regulation
Intellectual property	Mergers and acquisitions
Environmental law	Joint ventures and licensing
Aviation law	E-commerce and cyber law
Energy law	Project finance
Sports law	Litigation
Debt recovery	

THE FIRM

Almeida Sampaio & Associados was established in 1981 as a Portuguese law firm, and is orientated towards a strong corporate practice. Its clients include some of the largest world corporations in the areas of energy, automotive industry, aviation electronics and the media and entertainment industry. In 2005 the firm joined Jardim Sampaio, Caldas e Associados, and CRBA & Associados, becoming one of the leading firms in the Portuguese market and providing its clients with a full range of legal services.

Jardim Sampaio, Caldas e Associados has a strong litigation practice in corporate and commercial issues, as well as in project finance and criminal litigation. Almeida Sampaio e Associados' areas of expertise cover: corporate law and taxation, intellectual property, foreign investment and project finance, antitrust and trade regulation.

The firm also benefits from strong experience and know-how in environmental and energy law, e-commerce, aviation law, entertainment law and media. On an international level, the firm is developing a consistent strategy in order to provide assistance to its clients overseas due to preferential agreements with major law firms in the several relevant jurisdictions.

AREAS OF PRACTICE

Almeida Sampaio & Associados areas of expertise have granted the firm a consistently good reputation, both in domestic and international markets in areas such as intellectual property, foreign investment and project finance, corporate law and taxation.

ALVES PEREIRA ADVOGADOS ASSOCIADOS

AMOREIRAS, TORRE 3
17° ANDAR
1070-274 LISBON

Telephone: +351 21 370 01 90
Fax: +351 21 382 90 03
E-mail: info@alvespereira.com
Website: www.alvespereira.com

Languages
Portuguese, English, French, Spanish

Other offices
Faro

Number of lawyers 10

Member
IAG International

CATEGORIES OF WORK

Corporate law and finance
José Alves Pereira

Insurance
José Alves Pereira, Susana Campos

Real estate and construction
Pedro Osório de Castro, Sara Marques

Hotel and tourism investments
Luis Galvão, Joáo Almeida

Aviation law
José Alves Pereira

Litigation
José Alves Pereira, Joáo Almeida

Arbitration
José Alves Pereira

Advertising and media
Susana Campos

Telecommunications
José Alves Pereira, Sara Marques

Intellectual property
Joáo Almeida

ANTÓNIO FRUTUOSO DE MELO E ASSOCIADOS

AVENIDA DA LIBERDADE, 38-7°
1250-145 LISBOA

Telephone: +351 21 321 86 00
Fax: +351 21 321 86 86
E-mail: afma@afma.pt

Languages
English, French, Portuguese, Spanish

Number of lawyers 22

CATEGORIES OF WORK

Structured finance
António Frutuoso de Melo,
Pedro Porto Dordio

Cross-border leasing
António Frutuoso de Melo,
Pedro Porto Dordio

Securitisation
António Frutuoso de Melo,
António Gaio

Tax
António Frutuoso de Melo,
António Gaio

Mergers and acquisition
António Frutuoso de Melo,
Fernando Magiolo Magarreiro

Commercial and corporate law
António Frutuoso de Melo,
Guilherme Frutuoso de Melo

Banking and finance
António Frutuoso de Melo,
Alda Cabeças

Intellectual property
Guida Vila Nova

Labour, employment, benefits and pensions
Fernando Magiolo Magarreiro, Rita Nina

Food, drugs and health law
Sofia Belard, Rita Nina

Competition and consumer law
Sofia Belard, Rita Nina

Real estate and construction
Fernando Magiolo Magarreiro,
Guilherme Frutuoso de Melo

Litigation
Guida Vila Nova

AZEREDO PERDIGÃO & ALBUQUERQUE DA FONSECA

LAW FIRM

RUA DE SÃO NICOLAU, 23 2°
1100-547 LISBOA

Telephone: +351 21 887 91 42
Fax: +351 21 886 06 33
E-mail:
miguelperdigao@azeredoperdigao.pt

Languages
English, French, Spanish

Other offices
Luanda (Angola)

Contact
Miguel de Azeredo Perdigão
(managing partner)

CATEGORIES OF WORK

Foreign investment and incorporation of companies

Corporate and commercial law

Tax planning, offshore investment and Madeira Free Trade Zone

Banking, capital markets and finance

Tourism, property, construction and real estate

Arbitration, litigation and debt recovery

Agency and distribution agreements

Telecommunications and energy

Intellectual property, trade marks and franchising

EC competition and antitrust law

BAIÃO, CASTRO, SOLLA & ASSOCIADOS, RI

AVENIDA 5 DE OUTUBRO, 17, 9°
1050-047 LISBOA

Telephone: +351 21 319 06 40
Fax: +351 21 319 06 44
E-mail: bcslaw@bcs.pt
Website: www.bcs.pt

Languages
English, French, Italian, Spanish

Number of lawyers 20

CATEGORIES OF WORK

Litigation and arbitration
Ana Paula Martins,
Cláudia de Meneses

Insolvency
Ana Paula Martins,
Cláudia de Meneses

Capital markets
Felipe Baião do Nascimento,
Maria José Campos

Banking and finance
Felipe Baião do Nascimento,
Maria José Campos

Project finance and PPP
Felipe Baião do Nascimento

Corporate and commercial
Victor de Castro Nunes

Mergers and acquisitions
Victor de Castro Nunes

Privatisation
Victor de Castro Nunes

Real estate and construction
José Castro e Solla, Margarida Lima

Public law
Margarida Lima

Information technology
Filipe Viana Lousa

Intellectual property
Filipe Viana Lousa

Tax
Victor de Castro Nunes

BARROCAS SARMENTO NEVES

AMOREIRAS, TORRE 2
16TH FLOOR
1070-274 LISBON

Telephone: +351 21 384 33 00
Fax: +351 21 387 02 65
E-mail: info@barrocas.com.pt
Website: www.barrocas.com.pt

Languages
English, French, Italian, German, Spanish

Other offices
Oporto, Luanda (Angola), Maputo (Mozambique)

Number of lawyers 70
at this office 60

Contacts
Manuel P Barrocas, Albano Sarmento, Jorge Santiago Neves, Pedro Madeira Brito, João Nuno Barrocas

CATEGORIES OF WORK

Banking and finance/projects
Jorge Santiago Neves

Capital markets
João Nuno Barrocas

Construction and public works
Albano Sarmento

Corporate and commercial
Manuel P Barrocas

Dispute resolution and arbitration
Carlos Soares

Employment
Pedro Madeira de Brito

Energy and renewables
Jorge Santiago Neves

Environment, real estate and planning
Paulo Nogueira da Rocha

EU and competition
Margarida P Barrocas

Health and life sciences
Pedro Madeira de Brito

Oil and gas
Albano Sarmento

Tax
Joana Neto

Telecommunications
Diogo Lacerda Machado

Transport, shipping and insurance
Carlos Costa e Silva

THE FIRM

Barrocas Sarmento Neves is one of the leading and most-established law firms in Portugal. The firm delivers a full range of corporate and business services to both Portuguese and international clients. The firm is experienced in a number of global business and financial centres, and regularly advises on a wide range of corporate, commercial and financial matters.

The firm's extensive knowledge and experience spans many jurisdictions and business sectors, both public and private. It regularly advises on cross-border transactions including: international banking and finance transactions; large-scale projects; privatisations; capital markets; joint ventures; energy and telecommunications; mergers and acquisitions; commercial contracts; tax; and insolvency and restructurings. Its lawyers are qualified in both common and civil law jurisdictions.

Barrocas Sarmento Neves is committed to maintaining its long-standing reputation in domestic and international practice. It has particular experience and understanding of working with Portuguese-speaking countries such as Angola, Mozambique, São Tomé e Príncipe and Brazil.

AREAS OF PRACTICE

Banking and finance: Barrocas Sarmento Neves has a leading Portuguese finance practice acting for banks, financial houses and corporations. Its specialist business areas include asset finance, derivatives, leveraged finance, project finance, real estate finance, restructuring, securitisations, telecoms finance and trade finance.

Project finance: the firm's lawyers have significant experience of advising on major projects based on PPP and PFI concepts. The team has advised many different types of clients, including government organisations and other promoters, sponsors and funders across a wide range of industry sectors, with a particular and unrivalled expertise in infrastructure projects. The firm has advised several construction companies and consortiums on all aspects relating to the development and construction of the most significant infrastructure projects in Portugal.

Capital markets: the firm advises on debt, equity, equity-linked and asset-backed securities, derivatives and structured products. The team's experience covers debt issues, international public offerings (IPOs) and other equity offerings, all types of equity-linked issues, securitisations, tiered capital issues and over-the-counter and primary market derivative products.

Corporate and commercial: the firm has one of the largest corporate practices in Portugal and covers transactional and advisory work in M&A, private and public equity, corporate tax, insurance and investment funds. Its team of lawyers specialises in acquisitions, disposals, mergers, flotations, takeovers, security issues, fundraising, private equity, corporate tax and employee incentive arrangements.

Energy: the firm has a solid energy practice in the electricity, oil and gas and water sectors as well as renewable energies. It provides legal services to power producers, oil and gas producers and transporters, power plants, trade associations, energy developers, investors, and lenders involved in and with the energy industry.

Tax: the tax team advises on all aspects of tax in relation to international finance; debt and equity market transactions; investment funds (from establishing and structuring the fund); debt finance; investments and exit strategies; M&A transactions and equity offerings.

Real estate: the firm advises on issues relating to planning, construction, property ownership, real estate litigation, environment and health and safety. It has experience in advising on all aspects of real estate investment projects.

Dispute resolution: the firm provides a full service to its clients, with recognised expertise in all aspects of commercial dispute management. The group has particular expertise in matters relating to international finance and trade, shipping, construction, energy, insurance, technology and telecommunications.

BARROS, SOBRAL, G GOMES & ASSOCIADOS

RUA BRAAMCAMP, NO 40-8º ESQ
1269-013 LISBOA

Telephone: +351 21 387 57 02
Fax: +351 21 387 57 43
E-mail: law@bsgg.pt
Website: www.bsgg.pt

Languages
English, French, Italian, Spanish, German

Other offices
Madeira, Rio de Janeiro, São Paulo, Brasília, Porto Alegre

Number of lawyers 32
at this office 26

Member
Euro American Lawyers Group; European Labour Law Consulting; International Tax Planning Association; Brazilian Entrepreneur Association; several Chambers of Commerce

CATEGORIES OF WORK

Corporate and commercial
João Pedro Gomes, Manuel de Menezes, Sónia Gonçalves Anjo

Banking and finance
João Pedro Gomes, Nuno Telleria, Paula Alcântara Feliciano

Capital markets and project finance
Paula Alcântara Feliciano, Sónia Gonçalves Anjo

International tax planning
João Pedro Gomes, Nuno Telleria, Gisela Xavier Martins

IT and telecoms
Paula Alcântara Feliciano

Privatisation
João Pedro Gomes,Sergio Sobral, João Paulo Ferreira da Conceição

Taxation and planning
Gisela Xavier Martins, Nuno Telleria

Real estate, construction and tourism
João Paulo Ferreira da Conceição, Sónia Gonçalves Anjo

Immigration/nationality
João Paulo Ferreira da Conceição, Inês Oom de Sacadura

Mergers and acquisitions
Paula Alcântara Feliciano, Sónia Gonçalves Anjo

Labour and employment
Manuel de Menezes, Sónia de Magalhães Gonçalves

Dispute resolution
João Pedro Gomes, João Paulo Ferreira da Conceição, Manuel de Menezes

Maritime and shipping
Nuno Telleria, Gisela Xavier Martins

Civil law
João Paulo Ferreira da Conceição

BELZUZ ADVOGADOS

RUA AUREA, 40-48, 2˚ ANDAR
1100-063 LISBON

Telephone: +351 21 324 05 30
Fax: +351 21 347 84 52
E-mail: lisboa@belzuz.com
Website: www.belzuz.com

Languages
English, French, Portuguese, Spanish

Other offices
Madrid, Porto

Number of lawyers 54
at this office 25

International groupings
IGAL (Intercontinental Grouping of Accountants and Lawyers); BILG (benefit Insurance Lawyers Group); AIP (Associação Industrial Portuguesa); CCILE (Câmara de Comércio e Indústria Luso Espanhola)

CATEGORIES OF WORK

Administratlve
Catarina Duarte

Banking and project finance
Nuno Gonçalves da Cunha, Enrique Belzuz Fernández

Corporate and commercial
Nuno Gonçalves da Cunha

Dispute resolution – litigation and arbitration
Paula Campino, Pedro Marques Mantas

Employment
Orlando Santos Silva

Insurance
Teresa Judas Pedrosa

Tax and due diligence
Rui Guerreiro

Family and inheritance
Paula Campino

Debt transactions
Elsa Bayo Tavares

CAETANO DE FREITAS & ASSOCIADOS

AVENIDA DA LIBERDADE
NO 180 A-9º ANDAR
1250-146 LISBOA

Telephone: +351 21 317 06 20
Fax: +351 21 317 06 29
E-mail: geral@caetanodefreitas.com

Languages
English, French, Italian, Spanish

Other offices
Funchal

Number of lawyers 15
at this office 10

Contact
Sofia Almeida Ribeiro
(sofia.ribeiro@caetanodefreitas.com)

Member
Interact Europe; EEIG

CATEGORIES OF WORK

Banking, capital markets and securities

Company and commercial law

Corporate and project finance

Employment, pensions and incentives

EU law, competition and antitrust

Insolvency and business reconstruction

Litigation and arbitration

Mergers, acquisitions and MBOs

Property, planning and environment

Tax law and tax planning

CARLOS AGUIAR, P. PINTO & ASSOCIADOS

AVENIDA DA LIBERDADE
200-4º ESQº
1250-147 LISBON

Telephone: +351 21 355 27 55
Fax: +351 21 355 27 56
E-mail: cappa@mail.telepac.pt
Website: www.cappa.pt

Languages
English, French, Spanish

Number of lawyers 16

Contact
Carlos Aguiar

Member
ius laboris, International Employment Law, Pensions and Employee Benefits Alliance

CATEGORIES OF WORK

Corporate
Carlos Aguiar, Pedro Pinto

M&A
Carlos Aguiar, Tiago Ferreira de Lima

Banking and finance
Manuel Costa Salema, Nuno Galinha

Capital markets
Manuel Costa Salema, Maria Valdez

Real estate/property finance
Pedro Pinto, Carlos Aguiar

Employment
Inês Reis, Bruno Barbosa

Litigation
Inês Reis, Sofia Sousinha

Tax law and planning
Rita Martins

COELHO RIBEIRO E ASSOCIADOS

AV. ENGº DUARTE PACHECO
EMP. AMOREIRAS, TORRE 2-13ºA
1099-042 LISBOA

Telephone: +351 21 383 90 60
Fax: +351 21 385 32 02
E-mail: cra@cralaw.com
Website: www.cralaw.com

Languages
Dutch, English, French, German, Italian, Portuguese, Spanish

Other offices
Dili (East Timor)

Number of lawyers 22
At this office 20

International groupings
PLG, AIJA, IBA, CLA, Ecomlex

CATEGORIES OF WORK

Arbitration and dispute resolution
Rui Botica Santos, Oege De Vries

Aviation
José Carlos Gomes da Silva

Corporate and M&A
Jaíme Medeiros, Nuno Almeida Ribeiro

Intellectual property, media and information technology
Jaíme Medeiros, Mónica Oliveira Costa

Natural resources/ oil and gas
Rui Botica Santos, José Miguel Leitão

Litigation
Isabel Fontelonga Monteiro

Real estate
Rita Amaral

Banking and finance
Nuno Almeida Ribeiro

Labour
Rita Bettencourt, Carla Nunes

Sports
André Mendes

Construction law and public works
Miguel Catela

Cross-border corporate matters with Spain
Virginia Grande

Cross-border corporate matters with Brazil
Carla Nunes

Cross-border corporate matters with Germany and Austria
Wolfgang Stillfried und Rattonitz

FERREIRA PINTO & ASSOCIADOS
SOCIEDADE DE ADVOGADOS RL

EDIFÍCIO MONUMENTAL
AV PRAIA DA VITÓRIA, °71A-7°E
1050-183 LISBOA

Telephone: +351 21 030 31 90
Fax: +351 21 030 31 91
E-mail: mail@lusolegal.pt
Website: www.lusolegal.pt

Languages
English, French, Italian, Spanish

Number of lawyers 48

CATEGORIES OF WORK

Arbitration and litigation
Carlos Costa, José Franqueira Dias

Banking
Fernando A Ferreira Pinto

Corporate, M&A
Fernando A Ferreira Pinto

Corporate and commercial
António Teles

Criminal law
José Lobo Moutinho

EU, antitrust and competition
Fernando A Ferreira Pinto

Energy
Sofia Carreiro

Information technology
Manuel Lopes Rocha

Intellectual property
Manuel Lopes Rocha

Insurance
Armando Pinto Ribeiro

Labour law
Pedro Furtado Martins

Real estate, construction and tourism
Paulo da Silva Almeida

Tax
Pedro Patrício Amorim

F CASTELO BRANCO & ASSOCIADOS VEIGA GOMES, MARQUES DA CRUZ, COLMONERO
SOCIEDADES DE ADVOGADOS

AVENIDA DA LIBERDADE 249-1
1250-143 LISBOA

Telephone: +351 21 358 75 00
Fax: +351 21 358 75 01
E-mail: fcbranco@fcb-legal.com
Website: www.fcb-legal.com

Languages
English, French, Spanish, Portuguese

Other offices
Luanda, (in association with Vitor Felix Advogados), Oporto

Number of lawyers 70
at this office 65

Contacts
Miguel F Castelo Branco (mcb@fcb-legal.com), Vitor Marques da Cruz (vmc@fcb-legal.com)

CATEGORIES OF WORK

Corporate, commercial and M&A

Public/administrative law and public tenders/environmental law

Real estate/property/construction

Dispute resolution

Intellectual property

Employment, benefits and pensions

Banking and capital markets

Energy

Tax

THE FIRM

After a long period of national and international associations, F Castelo Branco & Associados and Veiga Gomes, Marques da Cruz Colmonero are providing their services through the same joint organisation.

F Castelo Branco & Associados was established in 1989, and was the first Portuguese law firm to Establish an EEIG in 1992 with an English, a Spanish and a Brazilian law firm. More than ten years after this change, F Castelo Branco & Associados is now a fully independent law firm. The experience the firm has acquired over the past decade has led to a maturity in its partners and associates, which continues to be shared with its clients and international partners.

Joao Veiga Gomes, Vitor Marques da Cruz and Rui Carlos Colmonero have been working together since 1987. They are well known in Portugal and abroad for their ability to provide a full service to their local and international clients. The decision to set up a joint organisation with F Castelo Branco & Associados was based on the common need to improve specialisation, permanent education and investing in greater and more advanced facilities and infrastructure.

AREAS OF PRACTICE

The firm's partners and associates all have a large amount of international experience, whether directly or indirectly, insofar as the majority of their clients are international companies or groups and their local subsidiaries.

F Castelo Branco & Associados encourage participation in international conferences, seminars and other professional meetings. The firm takes the view that such participation cannot be restricted to a handful of partners and is enthusiastic that its associates also work as ambassadors for the firm. F Castelo Branco and Associados is open to increasing its professional contacts and connections throughout the world, namely in the European Union, and particularly where it has existing contacts such as in the UK and Spain, as well as in Brazil, the USA and the former Portuguese colonies.

FRANCO CAIADO GUERREIRO & ASSOCIADOS
SOCIEDADE DE ADVOGADOS

RUA DUQUE DE PALMELA
Nº 25-2º, 3º, 5º
1250-097 LISBOA

Telephone: +351 21 359 30 50
Fax: +351 21 359 30 51
E-mail: law@fcguerreiro.com
Website: www.fcguerreiro.com

Languages
English, French, German, Spanish

Number of lawyers 41

Contacts
João Caiado Guerreiro, Tiago Caiado Guerreiro

Member
Globalaw; ATTA (Transatlantic Association of Lawyers)

CATEGORIES OF WORK

Banking and finance, M&A
João Caiado Guerreiro, José Pedro Nunes

Tax
Tiago Caiado Guerreiro, Susana Correia Mendes

Competition
João Caiado Guerreiro, Rui Pires Salvado

Corporate and commercial
João Caiado Guerreiro, Ricardo Costa Macedo

Commercial property, real estate
Joana Gomes dos Santos, Ricardo Canossa

Infrastructure and project finance
João Caiado Guerreiro

Capital markets
João Caiado Guerreiro, Ricardo Rodrigues Lopes

Labour law
Ricardo Rodrigues Lopes, Helena Isidoro Cabrita

Media and entertainment
Tiago Caiado Guerreiro, Nuno Jorge Rua

Telecommunications
Ricardo Costa Macedo

Administrative, environmental law
Ana Castro Gonçalves, Tânia Pinheiro

Pharmaceutical law
João Caiado Guerreiro, Helena Isidoro Cabrita

Foreign direct investment
João Caiado Guerreiro, Tiago Caiado Guerreiro

Dispute resolution/litigation
José Saramago, Rui Pires Salvado

Intellectual property
Ricardo Costa Macedo, Catarina Santos Ferreira

GARRIGUES, LEÓNIDAS, MATOS, SL
SUCURSAL EM PORTUGAL

AVª ENGº DUARTE PACHECO
AMOREIRAS
TORRE 1 – 15º
1070-101 LISBON

Telephone: +351 21 382 12 00
Fax: +351 21 382 12 90

Languages
English, Spanish, French

Number of lawyers: 1,300+
At this office: 48

Contacts
João Paulo Teixeira de Matos (joao.teixeira.matos@garrigues.com), Diogo Leónidas Rocha (diogo.leonidas.rocha@garrigues.com)

CATEGORIES OF WORK

Corporate mergers and acquisitions
Diogo Leónidas Rocha, Mário Lino Dias, Susana Pimenta de Sousa

Banking, securities and finance
Diogo Leónidas Rocha, Marta Graça Rodrigues

Labour law
João Paulo Teixeira de Matos, Rita Nogueira Neto

EU and competition law
João Paulo Teixeira de Matos, Ana Ferreira Neues

Telecommunications
Diogo Leónidas Rocha

Real estate law
Miguel Marques dos Santos

Industrial and intellectual property
Miguel Marques dos Santos

Environmental law
Miguel Marques dos Santos

Insurance law
João Paulo Teixeira de Matos

E-business
Diogo Leónidas Rocha, Miguel Marques dos Santos

Arbitration and litigation
João Paulo Teixeira de Matos, João Duarte Sousa

GONÇALVES PEREIRA, CASTELO BRANCO & ASSOCIADOS

PRAÇA MARQUÊS DE POMBAL 1-8º
1250-160 LISBOA

Telephone: +351 21 355 38 00
Fax: +351 21 353 23 62
E-mail: lisboa@gpcb.pt
Website: www.gpcb.pt

Languages
English, French, Portuguese, Spanish

Other offices
Oporto, Maputo (Mozambique), Alicante*, Barcelona*, Bilbao*, Brussels*, Gerona*, Llieda*, London*, Madrid*, New York*, Paris, Santa Cruz de Tenerife*, Seville*, Valencia*, Vigo*, Zaragoza*

Number of lawyers 140
at this office 103

In association with Cuatrecasas

CATEGORIES OF WORK

Company and commercial law
Manuel Castelo Branco, José de Freitas

Joint ventures/mergers and acquisitions
Manuel Castelo Branco, Diogo Perestrelo, José Diogo Horta Osório

Banking and insurance
Manuel Magalhães

Finance and capital markets
Maria João Ricou

Project finance
Diogo Perestrelo

Corporate Finance
André Luiz Gomes

EU/competition
Frederico Pereira Coutinho

Intellectual property
Maria da Glória Leitão

Tax
Diogo Ortigão Ramos

Construction/real estate
Frederico Pereira Coutinho, Diogo Perestrelo

Arbitration and litigation
Manuel Castelo Branco, Miguel Esperança Pina

Administrative and environmental law
Duarte Abecasis

Employment, benefits and pensions
Maria da Glória Leitão

Energy
Frederico Pereira Coutinho, Luis Soares de Sousa

Aviation
Luis Soares de Sousa

JALLES ADVOGADOS

AV ALVARES CABRAL 34
6TH FLOOR
1250-018 LISBON

Telephone: +351 21 388 40 95
Fax: +351 21 388 19 55
E-mail: jalles@jalles.pt
Website: www.jalles.pt

Languages
Dutch, English, French, German, Italian, Portuguese, Spanish

Number of lawyers 10

Contact
Isabel Jalles

CATEGORIES OF WORK

Corporate law

Maritime law

Companies, mergers and acquisitions and taxation

Arbitration and litigation

EC, distribution and competition law

Aviation and transportation law

Telecommunications, media, intellectual property and entertainment

Banking, securities and finance

Privatisation law and administrative law

Family and inheritance

Real estate, construction and leasing law

Personal injury, product liability, and food law

Environment law

LINKLATERS

AV FONTES PEREIRA DE MELO
14-15TH FLOOR
1050-121 LISBON

Telephone: +351 21 864 00 00
Fax: +351 21 864 00 01
Website: www.linklaters.com

Languages
All commercial and local languages in the countries where Linklaters operates

Other offices
Amsterdam, Antwerp, Bankok, Beijing, Berlin, Bratislava, Brussels, Bucharest, Budapest, Cologne, Dubai, Frankfurt am Main, Hong Kong, London, Luxembourg, Madrid, Milan, Moscow, Munich, New York, Paris, Prague, Rome, São Paulo, Shanghai, Singapore, Stockholm, Tokyo, Warsaw

Number of lawyers 2,000 worldwide

Contact
Jorge M Bleck

CATEGORIES OF WORK

Banking and finance
Pedro Siza Vieira

Debt transactions
António Payan Martins

Capital markets
António Soares

Corporate and commercial
Jorge M Bleck

Mergers and acquisitions
Jorge M Bleck

Project/asset finance
Pedro Siza Vieira

Real estate
Jorge Gonçalves

Labour
Nuno Ferreira Lousa

Technology, media and telecommunications
Carlos Pinto Correia

Litigation
Miguel Pinto Cardoso

Private equity
António Soares

EU/competition
Carlos Pinto Correia

Tax
Patrick Dewerbe

LOPES DIAS & ASSOCIADOS

60-2°, AV 24 DE JULHO
1200-869 LISBON

Telephone: +351 21 392 02 90
Fax: +251 21 395 47 66
E-mail: interlaw@netcabo.pt

Languages
Portuguese, English, French, German, Italian Spanish

Number of lawyers 5

International groupings
Intercontinental Grouping of Accountants and Lawyers (IGAL); World IT Lawyers (WITL)

CATEGORIES OF WORK

Corporate, including M&A
Maria L Lopes Dias, Domingos Azevedo

Life sciences
Maria L Lopes Dias, António Borges

International contracts
Maria L Lopes Dias, António Borges

PPP
Maria L Lopes Dias, Domingos Azevedo

IP
Maria L Lopes Dias, António Borges

IT
Maria L Lopes Dias, Domingos Azevedo

Tax law
Domingos Azevedo, Gonçalo d'Avila

Distribution law (agency, franchising)
António Borges, Carla Morais

Property law
Carla Morais, Domingos Azevedo

Labour law
Carla Morais, António Borges

Administrative law
António Borges, Carla Morais.

MACEDO VITORINO E ASSOCIADOS
SOCIEDADE DE ADVOGADOS

RUA GARRETT 12-2°
1200-204 LISBOA

Telephone: +351 21 324 19 00
Fax: +351 21 324 19 29
E-mail: mva@macedovitorino.com
Website: www.macedovitorino.com

Languages
English, French, German, Italian, Spanish

Number of lawyers 23

Contacts
João de Macedo Vitorino,
António de Macedo Vitorino

CATEGORIES OF WORK

- Banking, finance and derivatives
- Capital markets
- Construction and real estate
- Corporate and commercial
- Competition including EU competition law
- Employment
- Energy
- Foreign investment
- Inheritance and family law
- Intellectual property
- International private law
- Litigation and arbitration
- Mergers and acquisitions
- Privatisations
- Project finance
- Regulated industries
- Restructurings
- Securitisation
- Tax
- Technology, media, e-commerce and telecommunications

MARQUES BOM E ASSOCIADOS SOCIEDADE DE ADVOGADOS

AV DUQUE DE LOULÉ, 5°-6°
1050-085 LISBOA

Telephone: +351 21 350 45 10
Fax: +351 21 350 45 20
E-mail: geral@marquesbom.com

Languages
English, French, Spanish

Number of lawyers 12

Contacts
Francisco Marques Bom,
Nuno Borges Alexandrino

CATEGORIES OF WORK

- International contracts, mergers and acquisitions
- Foreign investment
- Banking and finance
- Corporate
- Labour
- Procurement
- Real estate, tourism, construction
- International transport and maritime law
- Tax and administrative law
- Litigation and arbitration

MARQUES MENDES & ASSOCIADOS

AV ENG DUARTE PACHECO, 19-12º
1070-100 LISBOA

Telephone: +351 21 382 63 00
Fax: +351 21 382 63 19
E-mail:
marquesmendes@marquesmendes.pt
Website: www.marquesmendes.com

Languages
English, French, Italian, Spanish

Number of lawyers 12

CATEGORIES OF WORK

Corporate and commercial

Mergers and acquisitions

Finance (including banking, insurance, securities and project financing)

EU law, competition, antitrust

Intellectual property

IT

Telecommunications

Energy

Labour and employment

Entertainment and media

Distribution

Litigation and arbitration

MIRANDA CORREIA AMENDOEIRA & ASSOCIADOS

ATTORNEYS AT LAW

RUA SOEIRO P GOMES, L1-2FL
1600-196 LISBOA

Telephone: +351 21 781 48 00
Fax: +351 21 781 48 02
E-mail: lisbon@mirandalawfirm.com
Website: www.mirandalawfirm.com

Languages
English, French, Italian, Spanish

Number of lawyers 90
at this office 65

Member
Miranda Alliance, with offices in Angola, Cape Verde, Equatorial Guinea, Guinea Bissau, Macao, Mozambique, São Tomé e Príncipe and Houston (Texas)

CATEGORIES OF WORK

Oil and gas
Agostinho Pereira de Miranda

Energy
Rui Amendoeira

Tax
Paulino Brilhante Santos

Real estate
Rita Correia

Commercial law
Diogo Xavier da Cunha

Mining
João Afonso Fialho

Banking and finance
Mafalda Oliveira Monteiro

Technology, media, telecoms and IP
João Luis Traça

M&A/corporate
Catarina Távora

Project finance, PPPs
Alberto Galhardo Simões

Employment
Rui Andrade

Construction and public works
Paulo Trindade Costa

Arbitration
Agostinho Pereira de Miranda

Regulatory
Luis MS Oliveira

MORAIS LEITÃO, GALVÃO TELES, SOARES DA SILVA & ASSOCIADOS

SOCIEDADE DE ADVOGADOS

RUA CASTILHO 75
1250-068 LISBOA

Telephone: +351 21 381 74 00
Fax: +351 21 381 74 99
E-mail: mlgtslisboa@mlgts.pt
Website: www.mlgts.pt

Languages
English, French, Italian, Spanish

Other offices
Funchal, Oporto

Number of lawyers 127
at this office 97

Contact
Nuno Galvão Teles

Member
Lex Mundi

CATEGORIES OF WORK

Arbitration
Miguel Galvão Teles,
António Sampaio Caramelo

Banking and finance
Luís Branco, Filipe Lowndes Marques

Corporate and commercial law
Segismundo Pinto Basto

EU and competition law
Carlos Botelho Moniz

Energy
Nuno Galvão Teles

Mergers and acquisitions
João Soares da Silva,
Nuno Galvão Teles

Litigation
José Manuel Galvão Teles,
António Pinto Leite

Industrial and intellectual property
António Pinto Leite

Capital markets
Luísa Soares da Silva

Project finance
Luís Branco, Filipa Arantes Pedroso

Administrative law and public procurement
João Serra, Margarida Dazabal Cabral

Tax
Francisco de Sousa da Câmara

Telecommunications
Filipa Arantes Pedroso

Labour and employment
Luís Miguel Monteiro

Real estate and urban planning
Fernanda Matoso, João Pereira Reis

Tourism and entertainment
Teresa Morais Leitão, João Pereira Reis

MULLERAT

EDIFICIO AMOREIRAS PLAZA
RUA PROF CARLOS ALBERTO DA MOTA PINTO
NO 9, 5° A-1
1070-374 LISBON

Telephone: +351 21 381 26 20
Fax: +351 21 381 26 21
E-mail: mullerat.lisboa@mullerat.com
Website: www.mullerat.com

Languages
English, French, German, Italian, Portuguese

Other offices
Barcelona, Madrid, Palma de Mallorca

Number of lawyers 70
at this office 8

Contact
Leonor Chastre

CATEGORIES OF WORK

Banking, finance, securities
Rui Nascimento

Corporate/commercial/M&A
Miguel Ascensão

Company law
Miguel Ascensão

Distribution and franchising
Leonor Chastre, Simao Santana

Tax
Rui Nascimento, Pedro Cardoso

Employment
Simao Santana, Joaquim Ferreira

Real estate and zoning law
Miguel Ascensão, Miguel Spínola

Patents and intellectual property
Leonor Chastre

EU and competition
Miguel Spínola

Arbitration and litigation
Leonor Chastre

Criminal law, white-collar crime
Leonor Chastre

Energy and environment
Miguel Spínola

MOUTEIRA GUERREIRO, ROSA AMARAL & ASSOCIADOS
SOCIEDADE DE ADVOGADOS R.L.

AVENIDA MIGUEL BOMBARDA 129
1 ANDAR
1050-164 LISBON

Telephone: +351 21 359 50 90
Fax: +351 21 359 50 99
E-mail: mgra@mgra.pt
Website: www.mgra.pt

Languages
English, French, Portuguese, Spanish

Number of lawyers 15

Contacts
António Mouteira Guerreiro,
Mário da Rosa Amaral

Member
International Lawyers Network (ILN)

CATEGORIES OF WORK	
Banking and finance	Mergers and acquisitions
Tax	Employment and pensions
Capital markets	Aviation and shipping
Corporate and commercial	Public and environmental law
Intellectual property	Telecoms
Project/asset finance	Tourism and leisure
Real estate and construction	Natural resources and energy
Litigation and insolvency	Health and biotechnology
EU and competition	Criminal, inheritance and family law

THE FIRM

Mouteira Guerreiro, Rosa Amaral & Associados (MGRA) is an independent Portuguese law firm, focused on providing legal assistance to companies, investors and the state in critical and complex aspects of their activity in the Iberian market.

MGRA has international practice standards and excellent relationships with leading independent and international law firms around the world, namely through co-operation and know-how sharing agreements, giving its clients a premium and global service.

MGRA legal teams combine technical experience with commercial awareness and were created for attending, with flexibility and innovation, to the pragmatic and tailor-made solutions that international corporations increasingly require in the global economic environment.

MGRA represents high-net-worth individuals and families, public and regulatory bodies, leading national and international companies, banks and financial institutions.

AREAS OF PRACTICE

Being a full-service law firm, MGRA covers all areas of practice.

MGRA is internally split into seven major divisions related to the firm's principal areas of practice: corporate and finance, tax, IT and real estate, administrative and EU, employment and pensions, litigation and insolvency, and public and private.

In addition, MGRA has formed multi-expertise teams for the major industries, providing efficient, practical and timely assistance to its clients, namely in the energy and natural resources, TMT, construction and real estate, transport and infrastructure, tourism and leisure, retail and banking and insurance industries.

MGRA represents a wide range of international clients and its professionals have valuable expertise gained through years of dealing with cross-border transactions, namely in debt and equity issues, securities and derivatives, M&A, corporate restructurings and financings, takeovers, LBOs, MBOs, MBIs and IPOs, strategic alliances, project and asset finance, cross-border leases, concessions, PPP, competition, IT, foreign investment, real estate, tax consultancy, tax planning and tax litigation.

NEVILLE DE ROUGEMONT & ASSOCIADOS

AV. PRAIA DA VITORIA
NO 5 1ST FLOOR
1000-245 LISBON

Telephone: +351 21 319 12 90
Fax: +351 21 352 76 19
E-mail: n.derougemont@ndr.pt
Website: www.nevillederougemont.com

Languages
Afrikaans, English, French, German, Italian, Portuguese, Spanish

Other offices
Cape Verde Islands, Faro (Algarve), Holyport

Number of lawyers 22
at this office 16

CATEGORIES OF WORK

Corporate and insurance
Rosemary de Rougemont, Rui Parente

International
Geoffrey Graham, Vicky Rodrigues

Litigation and arbitration
João Taborda, Claudia Póvoa

Property
Gonçalo Figueira, João Medina

Labour and general commercial
Francisco Salgueiro, Claudia Póvoa

Probate and wills
Geoffrey Graham, Vicky Rodrigues

Aviation
Geoffrey Graham, João Taborda

Planning and tourism
Rosemary de Rougemont, Vicky Rodrigues

Family
Rui Parente, Vicky Rodrigues

Intellectual property
Vicky Rodrigues, Rita Pereira

Tax
Rosemary de Rougemont, Maria Cunha Matos

Immigration
Claudia Póvoa, Rita Pereira

PACSA – HENRIQUES DA SILVA, PAES DE ALMEIDA, CORRÊA DE SAMPAIO E ASSOCIADOS

AV. DA LIBERDADE, 144 – 7° DTO
1250-146 LISBOA

Telephone: +351 21 324 16 00
Fax: +351 21 324 16 16
E-mail: info@pacsa.pt
Website: www.pacsa.pt

Languages
English, French, German, Spanish

Other offices
London, Oporto

Number of lawyers 35
at this office 28

Contacts
José Maria Corrêa de Sampaio (jmcs@pacsa.pt), Pedro Pais de Almeida (ppa@pacsa.pt)

International groupings
CONSULEGIS; AEIE; Commercial Lawyers Group

CATEGORIES OF WORK

Corporate and commercial

Mergers and acquisitions

Taxation

Competition

Capital markets

Corporate finance

Property and construction

Employment

Litigation and arbitration

Insolvency

Environment

Intellectual property

Licensing and franchising

PLMJ – A. M. PEREIRA, SÁRAGGA LEAL, OLIVEIRA MARTINS, JÚDICE E ASSOCIADOS SOCIEDADE DE ADVOGADOS, RL

EDIFICIO EUROLEX
AV DA LIBERDADE 224
1250-148 LISBOA

Telephone: +351 21 319 73 00
Fax: +351 21 319 74 00
E-mail: plmjlaw@plmj.pt
Website: www.plmj.com

Languages
English, French, German, Spanish

Number of lawyers 190

Other offices
Porto, Algarve, Angola*, Brazil*, Macau*
(joint venture with leading local firms)

Contacts
Dr Luís Sáragga Leal,
Dr Francisco Oliveira Martins,
Dr José Miguel Júdice

CATEGORIES OF WORK

Intellectual property
Ana Teresa Pulido

Labour law
Abel Mesquita

Corporate finance
Gabriela Rodrigues Martins

Energy and natural resources
Manuel Santos Vitor

Tax
Diogo Leite de Campos,
Rogério M Fernandes Ferreira

Media law
Vasco Marques Correia

Capital markets
Jorge Brito Pereira

EU and competition law
José Luís da Cruz Vilaça

Administrative law
Teresa Melo Ribeiro

Finance law
Fernando Campos Ferreira,
Maria Castelos

Public law
Rui Chancerelle de Machete

Corporate, M&A
Victor Réfega Fernandes, Dulce Franco,
Gabriela Rodrigues Martins,
Vasco Ataíde Marques

Real estate, construction and tourism
Pedro Sáragga Leal, Maria José Verde

Litigation and arbitration
Nuno L Monteiro, José Miguel Júdice,
Pedro Faria, Nuno Morais Sarmento

Criminal law
João Carlos Medeiros

Pharmaceutical law
Abel Mesquita

Telecommunications and IT
Luís Miguel Pais Antunes

THE FIRM

The foundation of PLMJ was laid down in the late sixties. The internationalisation and specialisation policies, pursued by the firm since its inception led to the continued growth of PLMJ over the following years and to its current position in the Portuguese legal market. PLMJ's sustained growth was achieved both in an organic manner and through an aggressive hiring policy of lawyers with an acknowledged academic background and professional experience in different areas of the law.

PLMJ currently counts 36 senior partners and 44 junior partners in a total of more than 190 lawyers, and has, for many years, been one of the largest Portuguese law firms of acknowledged experience and reputation in all fields of law.

Professional quality, based on the continuous training as well as the academic and professional enhancement of its lawyers, an excellent work environment and human quality have always been fundamental values.

The Porto office is located at: Av da Boavista, Edificio Passeio da Boavista N° 21214, 407, 4100-134 Porto, Tel: 351 22 607 47 00, Fax: 351 22 0747 50. Algarve office: Rua Pinheiro Chagas, 16-2° Dt°, 8000 Faro, Tel: 351 289 804 137, Fax: 351 289 803 588.

AREAS OF PRACTICE

Structured and equipped to meet the growing challenges of modern times, PLMJ is internally organised in departments specially geared to the different fields of law, in particular: corporate, mergers and acquisitions; EU and competition; foreign investment and international contracts; privatisations; financial and capital markets; tax; labour; intellectual property; realty, construction and tourism; constitutional and administrative; public procurement; criminal; environment; maritime and transport; insurances; energy and natural resources; telecommunications; and pharmaceutical. PLMJ also has departments widely experienced in the various areas of litigation and arbitration.

The departments work under the co-ordination of senior partners who directly supervise the quality of the services provided. Whenever the volume or nature of the issues so justify, task forces composed of lawyers from various departments are set up and co-ordinated by one or more senior partners.

As a result of its wide experience, PLMJ has developed its own network of correspondents, both with domestic and foreign law firms, thus being prepared to provide unbounded legal assistance.

RAPOSO BERNARDO & ASSOCIADOS

AV FONTES PEREIRA DE MELO
EDIFÍCIO AVIZ, Nº 35, 18TH FLOOR
1050-118 LISBOA

Telephone: +351 21 312 13 30
Fax: +351 21 356 29 08
E-mail: lisboa@raposobernardo.com
Website: www.raposobernardo.com

Languages
English, French, Italian, Spanish

Other offices
Albufeira, Cidade da Praia (Cape Verde), Madrid, Maputo (Mozambique), Porto

Number of Lawyers 49
at this office 23

CATEGORIES OF WORK

Corporate law, M&A
Nelson Raposo Bernardo,
Sérgio Antunes Teixeira

Banking, capital markets and financial law
Nelson Raposo Bernardo,
João Pateira Ferreira

Commercial law, industrial and intellectual property
Rita Tavares de Almeida

Private equity and venture capital
Nelson Raposo Bernardo,
Alfredo Leite Santos

Foreign investment
Joana Andrade Correia

Tax law and tax planning
Rita Tavares de Almeida

Employment and social security law
Abel Sequeira Ferreira,
Rui Fonseca Machado

Litigation, ADR and arbitration
Ana Luísa Mascate,
Marta Afonso Ferreira,
Marta Pinto Gomes

Health, pharmaceutical law and biotechnology
Sofia Ferreira Enriquez

Energy and natural resources
Abel Sequeira Ferreira

Real estate, construction, planning and environment
Inês Martins Rodrigues

Tourism
Joana Andrade Correia

EU and competition law
João Pateira Ferreira

Maritime and aviation law
Sofia Ferreira Enriquez

THE FIRM

Raposo Bernardo & Associados is an independent law firm, founded in Lisbon, in 1995, by well-known corporate attorney Nelson Raposo Bernardo. Since then the firm has grown steadily to its current size of 49 lawyers, making it one of the largest law firms in Portugal.

With its main offices located in the centre of Lisbon and having achieved a solid position in the Iberian Peninsula market, Raposo Bernardo & Associados decided to spread its practice to other markets, now holding offices in Cape Verde and Mozambique.

Raposo Bernardo & Associados' practice focuses on its clients' needs, providing tailor-made solutions to serve their best interests. For that purpose, the firm has gathered a group of truly 'innovative deal-makers', combining commercial awareness with technical expertise and a practical, proactive and creative approach.

In its Spanish office in Madrid, Raposo Bernardo & Associados provides legal advice in areas such as foreign investment, tax planning and tax law, as well as in corporate and financial law.

The firm's Cape Verdian office, located in Cidade da Praia, provides clients with legal assistance on privatisation matters, foreign investment, law-making processes and on the construction and tourism sectors.

Raposo Bernardo & Associados' Mozabican office regularly provides legal counselling to the agricultural, industrial and financial services areas.

AREAS OF PRACTICE

The firm offers a full-service capability in transactional, corporate and tax matters, covering a wide range of areas for a variety of corporate clients, from multinational companies through the entire range of privately and publicly owned companies and commercial entities, to private individuals.

Corporate law is one of the firm's major fields of practice, providing leading legal advice on M&A, due diligence processes, restructuring operations, private equity, venture capital and corporate financing. The firm's banking, financial law and capital markets department is also responsible for many relevant transactions, involving well-known international companies.

Another important area of practice involves providing advice on tax planning (on a national as well as an international perspective), as well as on tax consequences of various types, and legal assistance on litigation proceedings.

The commercial law department of Raposo Bernardo & Associados handles general commercial work, including the preparation, development and legal advising on contractual negotiations, and the firm's labour and litigation departments provide advice on the relevant employment legislation and the necessary legal assistance on litigation matters and dispute resolutions.

In the above-mentioned areas, Raposo Bernardo & Associados provides services to several national and international top companies, acting in the following sectors: pharmaceutical, tourism, financial services, automotive, construction, utilities, IT and telecoms, transports, food and agricultural industries and sports and leisure.

A brochure providing further details is available upon request.

SERRA LOPES, CORTES MARTINS & ASSOCIADOS

RUE GENERAL FIRMINO MIGUEL
TORRE 2, 12°
1600-100 LISBOA

Telephone: +351 21 723 40 00
Fax: +351 21 723 40 29
E-mail: slcm@slcm-advogados.pt
Website: www.slcm-advogados.pt

Languages
English, French, German, Italian, Spanish

Number of lawyers 21

CATEGORIES OF WORK

Corporate and commercial

Mergers and acquisitions

Banking and finance

Arbitration and dispute resolution

Civil and commercial litigation

Capital markets

Insurance

EU and competition law

Telecommunications and e-commerce

Media and entertainment

Energy and natural resources

Public procurement and administrative law

Shipping and maritime law

Sports law

Tax law

SÉRVULO CORREIA & ASSOCIADOS

RUA ARTILHARIA UM 79-5
1250-038 LISBOA

Telephone: +351 21 383 69 00
Fax: +351 21 383 69 01
E-mail: lisboa@servulo.com
Website: www.servulo.com

Languages
Danish, English, French, German, Italian, Spanish

Number of lawyers 36

Contact
Bernardo Diniz de Ayala

Member
Legalink; Diro

CATEGORIES OF WORK

Administrative law
Sérvulo Correia, Bernardo Ayala

Antitrust and trade regulation
Rui Medeiros, Lino Torgal

Banking and finance
Francisco Ferraz de Carvalho

Capital markets
Francisco Ferraz de Carvalho

Company and commercial
Teresa Serra

Constitutional law
Rui Medeiros, Lino Torgal

Criminal law and corporate liability
Teresa Serra

Utilities
Rui Medeiros, Lisa Pinto Ferreira

Government contracts and public procurement
Sérvulo Correia, João Amaral, Bernardo Ayala

Litigation, arbitration and ADR
Sérvulo Correia, João Amaral

Project finance
Bernardo Ayala, Francisco F de Carvalho

Real estate
Sofia Galvão

Tax law
Ricardo Guimarães

Urban planning and construction law
Sofia Galvão

SIMMONS & SIMMONS REBELO DE SOUSA

RUA D. FRANCISCO
MANUEL DE MELO 21
1070-085 LISBON

Telephone: +351 21 313 20 00
Fax: +351 21 313 20 01
E-mail: enquiries@simmons-simmons.com
Website: www.simmons-simmons.com

Languages
English, French, German, Italian, Portuguese, Spanish

Other offices
Abu Dhabi, Brussels, Dubai, Düsseldorf, Frankfurt, Hong Kong, London, Madeira, Madrid, Milan, New York, Oporto, Padua, Paris, Qatar, Rome, Rotterdam, Shanghai, Tokyo

Number of lawyers 764
at this office 72

Contact
Pedro Rebelo de Sousa

CATEGORIES OF WORK

Corporate and commercial	IT&T and telecoms
EU/competition	Intellectual property
Employment	Litigation and dispute resolution
Energy, utilities and infrastructure	Projects
Financial institutions	Real estate
Financial markets, banking, capital markets, financial services, litigation and insurance, private capital	Taxation
	Technology and life sciences

THE FIRM

Simmons & Simmons is a world-class law firm providing advice to financial institutions, corporates, public and international bodies and private individuals through its international network of offices in Europe, the Middle East and Africa.

Simmons & Simmons has over 210 partners, of which 110 are based in its offices outside the UK, and a total staff worldwide of over 1,900 across 20 offices. It provides a comprehensive range of legal services with strength and depth. It applies considerable expertise to all business sectors but focuses on those key to its clients. These are financial institutions, energy, utilities and infrastructure, and technology and life sciences.

Simmons & Simmons was awarded M&A Team of the Year twice at the *Legal Business* and *The Lawyer* Awards 2004, Projects/ PFI Team of the Year at *The Lawyer* Awards 2003, and Employment Team of the Year at the *Asian Legal Business* Awards in 2003, 2005 and 2005. The pharmaceutical and biotechnology team in Paris won the Healthcare and Pharmaceutical Award at the Trophées du Droit e du Contentieus 2005 (Law and Litigation Awards). Simmons & Simmons also won at the Solicitors' Race Equality Awards 2005 as the best employer – large firms (more than 25 partners) from The Law Society and the Commission for Racial Equality.

Simmons & Simmons is ranked in Global Counsel's 2004 Top 10 world rankings for client service. This ranking is significant as it is based solely on the views of in-house counsel at over 5,000 companies from 80 jurisdictions. Simmons & Simmons is also ranked as the leading UK law firm for client service according to research conducted by *Legal Week Global Media*.

In 2005, the firm celebrated the tenth anniversary of the opening of its Shanghai office. The firm is in the process of establishing its third office in China, in Beijing. The firm opened its third office in the Gulf region, in Dubai, in 2005.

The recruitment of the very best candidates who are interested in a career at a leading international law firm is a priority for Simmons & Simmons. For further information, please see the firm's website, www.simmons-simmons.com.

AREAS OF PRACTICE

Simmons & Simmons has recently advised Telefónica on its proposed £17.7bn acquisition of O2, Azur-GMF on the €5.6bn sale of Gecina SA, Dresdner Kleinwort Wasserstein (together with the other dealers and managers) and The Bank of New York, London Branch (as note trustee) on the establishment of a €5bn covered bond programme for Sampo Housing Loan Bank plc; the £699m public-to-private acquisition of New Look Group PLC, Tata Consultancy Services on the £896m NHS IY outsourcing contract, China Telecom on the $8.2bn acquisition of ten provincial telecommunications networks in China; on the £593m flotation of Halfords; GKN on the £1bn sale of AgustaWestland; Qatar Telecommunications on its successful mobile phone license bid in Oman; PCCW on the HK$7.9bn acquisition of new shares by China Netcom, ADWEA on $2bn aluminium smelter project in Oman, and British Land on £2.1bn refinancing of the Broadgate Estate.

SOUSA MACHADO, FERREIRA DA COSTA & ASSOCIADOS

RUA CASTILHO
Nº 5, 4º ANDAR
1250-066 LISBON

Telephone: +351 21 385 44 69
Fax: +351 21 385 48 15
E-mail: mail@smfcnet.com
Website: www.smfcnet.com

Languages
English, French, Italian, Spanish

Number of lawyers 19

Contacts
Manuel Ferreira da Costa,
Alexandre de Sousa Machado

Member
International Law Firm Association (e-iure)

CATEGORIES OF WORK

Corporate and commercial law
Manuel Ferreira da Costa,
Jorge Fernandes Ferreira

Litigation and arbitration
Manuel Ferreira da Costa,
Alexandre de Sousa Machado

Mergers and acquisitions
Manuel Ferreira da Costa,
Jorge Fernandes Ferreira

Civil law
Alexandre de Sousa Machado,
Manuel Ferreira da Costa

Debt collection and insolvency
Manuel Ferreira da Costa

Inheritance and family law
Alexandre de Sousa Machado

Labour law
Jaime Doria Cortesao,
Nuno Cardoso Ribeiro

Insurance
Manuel Ferreira da Costa

Administrative law
Nuno Cardoso Ribeiro

EU and competition law
Jorge Fernandes Ferreira,
Sérgio Direito

Banking and finance
Manuel Ferreira da Costa,
Sérgio Direito

IP, telecoms and software
Alexandre de Sousa Machado,
Jorge Fernandes Ferreira

TEIXEIRA DE FREITAS, RODRIGUES, E ASSOCIADOS
SOCIEDADE DE ADVOGADOS RL

AVENIDA DA REPUBLICA
N32–4º ESQ
1050–193 LISBON

Telephone: +351 21 781 56 60
Fax: +351 21 781 56 79
E-mail: lawfirm@teixeiradefreitas.pt
Website: www.teixeiradefreitas.pt

Languages
English, French, Italian, Spanish

Other offices
Funchal (Madeira), Luanda*,
Rio de Janeiro*, São Paulo*

Number of lawyers 26
at this office 20

Contacts
Dr Luiz Augusto Teixeira de Freitas,
Dr Rosana Rodrigues, Dr Vasco Carvalho Marques,
Dr Carlos Manuel Silva Gomes

Member
ITPA (International Tax Planning Association);
IFA (International Fiscal Association)

CATEGORIES OF WORK

Corporate

Tax

International tax planning

Commercial

Foreign investment

Shipping

Banking and securities

International contracts

Labour

Real estate

Litigation

Competition

Administrative law

URÍA MENÉNDEZ

RUA CASTILHO, 20-6°
1250-069 LISBON

Telephone: +351 21 030 86 00
Fax: +351 21 030 86 01
E-mail: lisboa@uria.com
Website: www.uria.com

Languages
Catalan, English, Finnish, French, German, Italian, Polish, Portuguese, Russian

Other offices
Barcelona, Bilbao, Brussels, Buenos Aires*, Lima*, London, Madrid, Mexico City*, New York, Porto, Santiago de Chile*, São Paulo*, Valencia

Number of lawyers 485
at this office 68

Contacts
Duarte Garin (dmg@uria.com),
Francisco Sá Carneiro (fsc@uria.com)

In association with
Marval, O'Farrell & Mairal (Buenos Aires); Philippi, Yrarrázaval, Pulido & Brunner (Santiago de Chile); Galicia y Robles, SC (Mexico City); Payet, Rey, Cauvi (Lima); Dias Carneiro Advogados (São Paulo)

CATEGORIES OF WORK

Corporate and commercial
Duarte Vasconcelos

Mergers and acquisitions
Francisco Abreu

Capital markets
Carlos Costa Andrade

Banking and finance
Francisco Sá Carneiro

Project finance
Francisco Sá Carneiro

Real estate
Duarte Garin

Litigation and arbitration
Tito Fontes

Private equity
Pedro Malaquias

Labour
João Dos Santos

Tax
Filipe Romao

Porto
João Anacoreta

VIEIRA DE ALMEIDA & ASSOCIADOS

MOUZINHO DA SILVEIRA 10
1250-167 LISBOA

Telephone: +351 21 311 34 00
Fax: +351 21 311 24 72
E-mail: lisboa@vieiradealmeida.pt
Website: www.vda.pt

Languages
English, French, Spanish

Other offices
Brussels, Madeira (Funchal)

Number of lawyers 96

CATEGORIES OF WORK

Banking and finance
Pedro Cassiano Santos,
João Vieira de Almeida

Pharmaceutical and life sciences
António Magalhães Cardoso,
Paulo Pinheiro

Corporate and commercial
Paulo Olavo Cunha,
António Magalhães Cardoso

Capital markets
Helena Vaz Pinto

Mergers and acquisitions
João Vieira de Almeida,
Helena Vaz Pinto

Real estate and planning
Pedro Ferreirinha

Project finance, energy and natural resources
Manuel Protásio, Vanda Cascão

Litigation and arbitration
Frederico Gonçalves Pereira

EU and competition
Nuno Ruiz

Tax
Tiago Marreiros Moreira

Labour law
Tiago Piló

Telecoms and IT
Margarida Couto,
Fernando Resina da Silva

Corporate governance
Fernando Resina da Silva

Patents and trade marks, IP
António Magalhães Cardoso

Public procurement
Paulo Pinheiro

RAPOSO BERNARDO & ASSOCIADOS

RUA JOÃO DAS REGRAS
N°284-3°, SALAS 7-8
4000-014 PORTO

Telephone: +351 22 201 10 95
Fax: +351 22 204 46 19
E-mail: porto@raposobernardo.com
Website: www.raposobernardo.com

Languages
English, Spanish, French, Italian

Other offices
Albufeira, Cidade da Praia (Cape Verde), Lisbon, Madrid, Maputo (Mozambique)

Number of lawyers 49
at this office 2

CATEGORIES OF WORK

Corporate law, M&A

Banking, capital markets and financial law

Commercial law, industrial and intellectual property

Private equity and venture capital

Foreign investment

Tax law and tax planning

Employment and social security law (pensions and incentives)

Litigation, ADR and arbitration

Health, pharmaceutical law and biotechnology

Energy and natural resources

Real estate, construction, planning and environment

Tourism

EU and competition law

Maritime and aviation law

RUI PEIXOTO DUARTE & ASSOCIADOS
SOCIEDADE DE ADVOGADOS

205 RUA ANTÓNIO PATRÍCIO
4150-100 PORTO

Telephone: +351 22 606 79 08
Fax: +351 22 600 18 16
E-mail: general@abreucardigos.com
Website: www.abreucardigos.com

Languages
English, French, Italian, Spanish, Swedish, Finnish, Danish

Other offices
Lisbon

Number of lawyers 9

Contact
Dr Rui Peixoto Duarte

CATEGORIES OF WORK

As from 1 March, Rui Peixoto Duarte & Associados merged with Abreu, Cardigos & Associados Attorneys at Law. For further information, please refer to the firm's entry under Abreu, Cardigos & Associados Attorneys at Law or visit its website at www.abreucardigos.com

TELLES DE ABREU E ASSOCIADOS
SOCIEDADE DE ADVOGADOS RL

RUA DA RESTAURAÇÃO 348
4050-501 OPORTO

Telephone: +351 22 030 88 00
Fax: +351 22 030 88 98/99
E-mail: ta.advogados@tellesabreu.com
Website: www.tellesabreu.com

Languages
English, French, Portuguese, Spanish

Number of lawyers 30

CATEGORIES OF WORK

Commercial law, insolvency
Dr Luís Telles de Abreu,
Dr Fernando Pizarro Monteiro

Tax law, litigation
Dr Alberto Amorim Pereira

Commercial and financial law
Dr Carlos Lucena

Commercial law and real estate
Dr Pedro Almeida e Sousa

Tax law, real estate and administrative
Dr Miguel Torres

Commercial law
Drª Cristina Ferreira

Litigation
Dr André Navarro de Noronha;
Drª Joana Telles de Abreu

Financial right
Dr Miguel Carvalho

Right of work and competition
Dr Francisco Espregueira Mendes

VIEIRA DE CASTRO, SILVA LOPES, PESSANHA, COSTA LEITE

LARGO DO ADRO 9
4050-016 PORTO

Telephone: +351 22 607 68 00
Fax: +351 22 609 46 88
E-mail: advogados@acrlex.com

Languages
English, French, German, Italian, Spanish

Number of lawyers 8

Member
The Interlex Group

CATEGORIES OF WORK

Administrative
José Manuel Silva Lopes,
Francisco Costa Leite

Banking and finance
João Vieira de Castro

Capital markets
João Vieira de Castro

Commercial property/real estate
João Vieira de Castro, Pedro Pessanha

Competition and EU law
Nuno Castro Marques,
Francisco Costa Leite

Construction
Francisco Costa Leite

Corporate and commercial
Pedro Pessanha

Dispute resolution – litigation and arbitration
João Vieira de Castro,
Francisco Costa Leite

Employment
José Manuel Silva Lopes,
Francisco Costa Leite

Foreign direct investment
Pedro Pessanha, João Vieira de Castro

Fraud and white-collar crime
José Manuel Silva Lopes,
Francisco Costa Leite

Intellectual property
Francisco Costa Leite

Mergers and acquisitions
Pedro Pessanha

QATAR

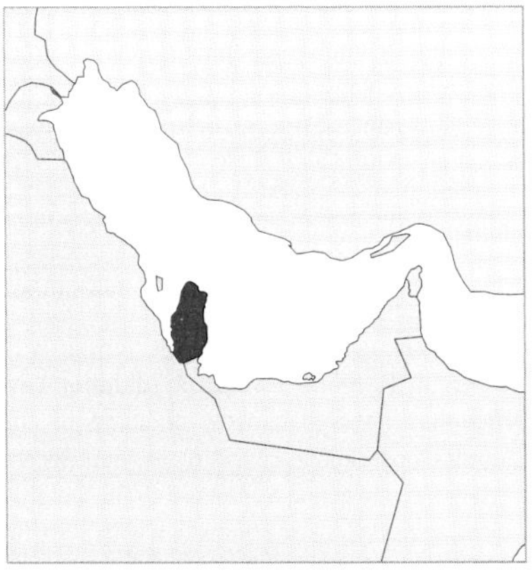

Population	628,000
Number of lawyers	n/a
Professional title	Lawyer
Currency	Qatari Rial (QAR)

Sitting on a peninsula in the Persian Gulf, Qatar shares its borders with Saudi Arabia and the United Arab Emirates (UAE). The country gained independence from Britain in 1971, having declined to join the UAE.

The current Emir, Sheikh Hamad Bin Khalifah Al-Thani, came to power in 1995 after ousting his father in a bloodless coup. His accession marked the beginning of Qatar's transformation from a traditional society that was lagging behind its more prosperous neighbours, to a thriving economic centre for trade and investment. The Emir instigated the beginnings of Qatar's democratisation programme, beginning with the country's first polls in 1999. Approved in 2003, a new, permanent, constitution finally came into effect in June 2005, which, in addition to its clauses covering freedom of expression and religion, provides for a partially elected legislative body. Elections are expected to take place in 2007.

Perhaps to a greater degree than many Gulf states, Qatar strikes a diplomatic balance between co-operating with the West and keeping on good terms with Gulf neighbours.

ECONOMY

Qatar gleaned much of its wealth in the 1950s, when oil was the predominant source of revenue. Such was its success, the country benefits from a well-developed infrastructure and an advantageous welfare sector, with an abundance of free or heavily subsidised services and products. The combination of Qatar's free-market policy, active government investment, and the partial relaxation of the laws governing foreign business, have helped to make it one of the richest per capita GDP countries in the world.

In recent times, the production and export of natural gas has superseded oil as the country's major source of revenue. With over 15% of the world's proven gas reserves, Qatar is set to become the world's largest exporter of LNG; there are already a number of multi-billion-dollar LNG projects underway, with several more in the pipeline. One example is Qatargas II, a joint venture of ExxonMobil and Qatar Petroleum, which reached financial closure in December 2004. The next phase (Qatargas III) is well underway, and there are plans for a further, fourth phase. While ExxonMobil is still the dominant force in Qatar's various LNG projects, Total France has an increasing presence in the sector, while Shell recently signed a US$6bn deal for the supply of LNG to the US and Europe. Annual LNG sales are expected to quadruple by 2011 to more than 70 million tonnes.

In order to maintain its healthy economic status, expansion and diversification has become the strategy of the Qatari government. Ongoing investment in Qatar's tourism industry has led to an abundance of hotel, resort and shopping centre developments. A new US$5bn, three-phase airport is under construction in the capital, Doha, expected to be completed in 2015. The imminent Asian Games tournament has also been a focus of recent years, with various stadia, housing developments and cultural centres cropping up around the capital.

LEGAL SYSTEM

Qatar operates under a 'dual' legal system, whereby the Muslim population is subject to Islamic shari'ah law regarding personal status matters, whilst the increasingly influential adlia court handles all other matters, such as commercial disputes.

Proceedings in Qatari law courts are conducted in Arabic, and clients can only be represented by a Qatari lawyer, although they often consult with expatriate lawyers.

LEGAL MARKET

The legal market in Qatar is small, but as the country yields such lucrative instructions it has attracted the attention of numerous international firms. Foreign firms are, however, only permitted to operate in the country if associated with a Qatari-trained lawyer, or at the special invitation of the government. Currently, the only foreign firms to be granted a licence are **Simmons & Simmons** and **Patton Boggs LLP**, both of which opened their doors in Qatar towards the latter half of 2003.

Long-established firm *Law Offices of Gebran Majdalany*, having formed an association with a Qatari judge, now operates under the auspices of **Ahmed Abdel Latif Al-Mohannadi, managed by Gebran Majdalany**. UAE-based **Al Tamimi & Co** established its presence in Qatar in 2004, when the firm officially affiliated itself with local advocate Mohammed Al-Marri to form **Adv Mohammed Al-Marri in association with Al Tamimi & Co**. **Eversheds LLP** has formally allied itself with A Rahman Mohamed Al-Jufairi, Advocates & Legal Consultants, creating **A Rahman Mohamed Al-**

The largest firms

1	Ahmed Abdel Latif Al-Mohannadi, managed by Gebran Majdalany	17
2	Khalid Al-Attiya, Legal Consultant & Attorney	9
3	Arab Law Bureau	8
	The International Office for Advocacy and Legal Consultations	8
5	Hassan A Alkhater Law Office	6
	Rouhani & Partners	6
7	Adv Mohammed Al-Marri in association with Al Tamimi & Co	5
	Ali bin Nasser Al-Naimi, Law Office of	5
	Patton Boggs LLP	5
10	Simmons & Simmons	4
11	Abu-Ghazaleh Legal	1

These figures represent the total number of lawyers in this country only, and have been supplied by the firms themselves. The figures should be accurate as at 1 January 2006.

Jufairi, Advocates & Legal Consultants in co-operation with Eversheds.

A number of foreign firms have opted for informal co-operative arrangements with local firms rather than attempting to establish a formal presence in Qatar. For example, **Towers & Hamlins** maintains a 'best-friends' relationship with **Hassan A Alkhater Law Office**, while **Clifford Chance** has a steady relationship with **Ahmed Abdel Latif Al-Mohannadi, managed by Gebran Majdalany**.

Several other international firms are noteworthy for their involvement in project finance in Qatar. **Norton Rose**'s extensive work in the country includes advising Hydro Aluminium on the construction of a US$3.6bn aluminium smelter plant, and advising the majority shareholder in the financing of the Q-Chem II project.

A vast Middle East practice at London-based **Linklaters** has secured numerous instructions pertaining to projects in Qatar, including a recent US$700m financing of four new LNG vessels for charter to the RasGas II project. The firm has also been acting for the lenders on the Qatofin project, in which **Milbank, Tweed, Hadley & McCloy LLP** represented the project company, recently closing the US$1.1bn financing deal.

An official adviser to the State of Qatar, from London **Latham & Watkins** has had an assiduous interest in almost all of the country's projects since 1994. In recent months the firm's attentions have been directed towards the financial closure of Qatargas II, where it acted for the export credit agencies, and towards the US$4.6bn first-phase financing of RasGas II/3 where it represented the borrowers.

Allen & Overy LLP has been handling banking and project finance matters in Qatar since the mid-1990s. Recent undertakings include acting for the lenders in the Ras Laffan II project, which closed in the summer of 2005, and representing the export credit agencies in Qatargas III.

From London and New York, **Skadden, Arps, Slate, Meagher & Flom LLP** has advised on some significant corporate and financial matters in connection with a host of major projects in Qatar, such as acting for BNP Paribas in the US$12bn Qatargas II project.

Freshfields Bruckhaus Deringer's new office in Dubai is handling the project finance, corporate and commercial aspects of Total SA's purchase of an equity interest in an LNG facility of Qatargas II.

A number of other foreign firms are worthy of mention: From Dubai, **Vinson & Elkins L.L.P.** is currently acting as counsel to the government in connection with a major IWPP in Qatar. Meanwhile, **Pinsent Masons**' London office advised a joint venture on a US$700m contract for the construction of an oil refinery in Qatar. The Dubai branch of **Clyde & Co** has been acting for a Qatari Insurance Company in relation to marine and non-marine insurance, advising on aspects of Qatari agency law.

Other international firms with significant project experience in the country include **Baker & McKenzie LLP**, **Denton Wilde Sapte** and **White & Case**.

CORPORATE AND COMMERCIAL

Often considered Qatar's pre-eminent firm, **Ahmed Abdel Latif Al-Mohannadi, managed by Gebran Majdalany** has strength in high-end project financing, banking and corporate matters. 'Charming and knowledgeable' managing partner Gebran Majdalany reaps the 'greatest respect', while clients deem associate Greg Englefield to be 'extremely helpful and efficient' and Ed Vink 'very commercial and responsive'. Still first in line for referrals from a number of international firms, the practice handles top-end oil and gas projects and banking work, with an increasing focus on IP.

Maintaining its 'best-friends' relationship with **Towers & Hamlins**, **Hassan A Alkhater Law Office** has handled aspects of some of the country's most significant energy projects. Recent matters include acting as counsel to the Dolphin Project, advising Shell in connection with a gas-to-liquids project, and consulting on the development and financing of a joint venture LNG plant. The practice also has robust corporate and banking arms, with Standard Chartered Bank, Alcatel, Microsoft and Schlumberger being representative clients. Clients have 'extraordinary respect' for senior name partner Hassan Alkhater, whose plaudits include tags such as 'well-connected', 'honest' and 'hard-working'. The firm receives frequent referrals from other top-drawer international firms, and consultant David Silver is a prolific and highly recommended individual.

Having opened an office in Doha towards the end of 2003, **Patton Boggs LLP** is rapidly gaining ground, making use of both its local and international links. The firm, which recently welcomed Leigh Hall, previously of **Ahmed Abdel**

CORPORATE AND COMMERCIAL

AHMED ABDEL LATIF AL-MOHANNADI, MANAGED BY GEBRAN MAJDALANY
HASSAN A ALKHATER LAW OFFICE

Patton Boggs LLP
Simmons & Simmons ✪

A Rahman Mohamed Al-Jufairi, Advocates & Legal Consultants in co-operation with Eversheds
Adv Mohammed Al-Marri in association with Al Tamimi & Co
Arab Law Bureau

M Al-Abdulla (Sultan), The Law Offices of
Sayel Daher, Law Office

Firms are listed A-Z in tiers which are ranked in order of priority
✪ Indicates firm displays contact details at the end of this chapter.

Latif Al-Mohannadi, managed by Gebran Majdalany, has strong links to the Qatari government and is a long-standing adviser to the Emir. In the last year, some lucrative commercial property and real estate transactions have been keeping the team busy, as well as various corporate and energy matters on behalf of Qatar Petroleum and ExxonMobil. Peers report that the firm is also making its presence felt in the project finance arena.

'Solution-orientated' **Simmons & Simmons**, which opened its Doha office in September 2003, has come on in leaps and bounds. The firm recently recruited senior associate and corporate expert Samer Eido from **Adv Mohammed Al-Marri in association with Al Tamimi & Co**, while seasoned consultant David Salt, who joined in 2004 from *Law Offices of Gebran Majdalany*, is considered a 'walk-around library' of legal and commercial knowledge. The team recently advised Al Sabban Real Estate Investment Company on its proposed construction of three towers, and subsequent sale of apartments, in the Pearl of the Gulf project, and is also involved in a significant infrastructure project. Feedback is extremely positive, with clients commenting on the usefulness of the firm's worldwide network, its multi-linguistic aptitude and its strength in assisting international companies setting up business in Qatar.

With two Qatari lawyers and four foreign-qualified lawyers, including **Eversheds LLP** secondee and international trade expert Chris Jobson, **A Rahman Mohamed Al-Jufairi, Advocates & Legal Consultants in co-operation with Eversheds** can offer expertise that stretches across both local and international law. With a client base of government entities, airlines, banks, multinational companies and shipowners, the firm recently garnered several instructions in relation to property development, acquisitions and finance, and is also acting as counsel to Qatar National Olympic Committee in connection with the Oryx Quest Cup 2005.

English, Arabic and French-speaking **Adv Mohammed Al-Marri in association with Al Tamimi & Co** offers expertise in general banking, business incorporations, joint ventures, commercial agreements, IP and telecommunications. Recent highlights include advising a US-based university on setting up business in Qatar's Education City and acting for a large domestic real estate developer in connection with its property issues. A former lawyer at **Clyde & Co** and *Law Offices of Gebran Majdalany*, 'the timely, thorough and practical' Katrina Wilson is recommended for corporate and commercial advice.

Two-partner general commercial firm **Arab Law Bureau** invests large amounts of time in project finance. The team, which draws on experience and qualifications from a number of jurisdictions including the US, Egypt and Jordan, acted as local counsel to the recently closed Qatargas II project. Clients consider partner Ala'a Fathi Hamad to be a 'very important lawyer in Qatar' with excellent connections in the project finance arena. The firm deals with an increasing amount of instructions relating to foreign companies setting up business in Qatar.

The Law Offices of Sultan M Al-Abdulla has a longstanding relationship with **A Rahman Mohamed Al-Jufairi, Advocates & Legal Consultants in co-operation with Eversheds**, and maintains a solid reputation for general corporate, commercial and banking advice. The team recently represented an Asian construction company in connection with a US$100m contract with a Qatari public authority.

Law Office of Sayel Daher's Chris Tingley also comes highly recommended for general commercial matters.

Special mention goes to **Abu-Ghazaleh Legal**, whose regional network of IP experts includes an office in Doha.

DISPUTE RESOLUTION

Only Qatari-qualified lawyers can represent clients in court, meaning that foreign firms have to draft in locally trained advocates where litigation arises. Despite this, a number of foreign lawyers are noted for their in-depth case-preparation skills. Arbitration is sometimes employed as a means of dispute resolution, although many issues settle before they get to this stage.

At **Ahmed Abdel Latif Al-Mohannadi, managed by Gebran Majdalany**, Lebanese name partner Gebran Majdalany's combination of 'experience, charm and intellect' secures his immense reputation as 'the single most outstanding lawyer in Qatar'. He oversees a large team that includes a number of Qatari court representatives, with solid experience in handling a range of commercial disputes such as contract, employment and banking issues. Whilst his Lebanese nationality prevents him from appearing in court himself, Mr Majdalany nonetheless reaps boundless admiration for his technical ability.

Led by 'well-studied' name partner and senior advocate Hassan Alkhater, **Hassan A Alkhater Law Office** comes highly recommended by clients, local peers and international firms for its talents in both commercial and civil litigation and arbitration. In a recent Court of Appeal case pertaining to the alleged unlawful detention of vessels, the team successfully defended the US$14m claim by a foreign power on behalf of the underwriters of a Qatari insurance company. Qatari associate Hassan Noor also handles many cases in the courts.

Lawyers at **The Law Offices of Sultan M Al-Abdulla** can appear before all courts and tribunals in Qatar, and the firm enjoys a sound reputation for its arbitration and litigation practice. Matters handled include building contract disputes, disagreements over payment claims, banking and investment issues and commercial agency disputes.

Qatari name partner Mr Al-Jufairi handles court representation at **A Rahman Mohamed Al-Jufairi, Advocates & Legal Consultants in co-operation with Eversheds**. The practice is experienced in acting for government branches, banks, airlines and commercial businesses, as well as on behalf of private clients. For international disputes, the firm's multi-jurisdictional lawyers come in handy, and the team can call on **Eversheds LLP**'s worldwide legal expertise where necessary. Shipping and international trade disputes are also a speciality.

At **Adv Mohammed Al-Marri in association with Al Tamimi & Co**, Mohammed Al Marri is widely acknowledged for his advocacy skills, and is a former member of Qatar's Public Prosecution Department. UK-trained consultant Katrina Wilson is experienced in pre-litigation advice.

With a team of mediators for ADR, as well as a number of arbitration experts, **Al-Kaabi Law Firm** comes highly recommended for dispute resolution. The firm assists financial institutions and creditors in enforcing their claims against debtors, and handles disputed insurance claims, personal shari'ah matters, and construction disputes among other matters.

Arab Law Bureau's litigation team handles complex contract, banking and civil disputes, and is currently dealing with a groundbreaking agency dispute.

Khalid Al-Attiya, Legal Consultant & Attorney and **The International Office for Advocacy and Legal Consultations** are also recommended for their skills in dispute resolution.

DISPUTE RESOLUTION

AHMED ABDEL LATIF AL-MOHANNADI, MANAGED BY GEBRAN MAJDALANY

Hassan A Alkhater Law Office
M Al-Abdulla (Sultan), The Law Offices of

A Rahman Mohamed Al-Jufairi, Advocates & Legal Consultants in co-operation with Eversheds
Adv Mohammed Al-Marri in association with Al Tamimi & Co
Al-Kaabi Law Firm
Arab Law Bureau
Khalid Al-Attiya, Legal Consultant & Attorney
The International Office for Advocacy and Legal Consultations

---

Firms are listed A-Z in tiers which are ranked in order of priority

SIMMONS & SIMMONS

5TH FLOOR
AL MIRQAB TOWER
AL CORNICHE STREET
PO BOX 23540
DOHA

Telephone: +974 483 9466
Fax: +974 483 9584
Website: www.simmons-simmons.com

Languages
Arabic, English, French

Other offices
London, Rotterdam, Paris, Lisbon, Milan, Rome, Düsseldorf, Frankfurt, Brussels, Madrid, Padua, Oporto, Madeira, Abu Dhabi, Dubai, Hong Kong, Shanghai, Tokyo, New York

Number of lawyers 764
at this office 5

Contacts
Andrew Wingfield, David Salt
(Qatari and international legal advice)

CATEGORIES OF WORK

Corporate	**Employment**
Banking	**Financial markets**
Capital markets	**Pharmaceutical and biotechnology**
Taxation	**Energy and utilities**
Projects, PFI	**TMT**
EU, competition	**Aerospace and defence**
Dispute resolution	**Transport**
Intellectual property	**Consumer goods**
Commercial	**Real estate, construction**

ROMANIA

Population	**22.2 million**
Number of lawyers	**13,000**
Professional title	**Advocate**
Currency	**Leu (lei)**

Index

Romania is in the lower Danube basin, north of the Balkan Peninsula and adjoining the Black Sea. Bordered by Hungary, Moldova, Ukraine, Bulgaria and Serbia and Montenegro, its capital city, Bucharest, is the centre of commercial and legal activity.

A 41-year stretch of communist rule ended in 1989 with the overthrow of Ceaucescu's despotic regime. In parliamentary elections in December 2004, Traian Basescu, leader of the centrist Justice and Truth Alliance was elected, replacing former president Ion Iliescu of the leftist Social Democratic party.

Romania began negotiations for EU accession in 1999 and is making progress in meeting the political, economic, legislative and social accession targets required. In April 2005 Romania signed the EU accession treaty. The earliest joining date will be 2007. Romania became a member of Nato in April 2004.

The country's key industries are steel, agriculture, manufacturing, shipping, aluminium, oil and gas, and automotive.

ECONOMY

Romania has traditionally been dogged by resistance to structural reform from state bureaucracy and industry and unions, which has led to poor competitiveness of exports and large current account deficits. More recently, however, the country has demonstrated positive economic growth, particularly in 2004 and 2005. Key economic drivers include growing export performance, increased intra-regional trade in southeastern Europe, growing real estate investment and an increasing number of bilateral trade agreements. Private consumption and the services sector have both also contributed to economic growth.

GDP in 2004 was 8.3%. Unemployment was 5.7% at the end of April 2005.

Privatisation-related upgrades and increased industrial and agricultural production have also contributed to a growing economy.

BILLING

Minimum rates of billing are enforced by the Romanian Bar Association. Otherwise, all forms of billing familiar to Western business clients are considered. Capped and fixed fees are increasingly being demanded by some clients, with some firms acceding and believed by others to be winning work from those firms that continue to insist on hourly rates.

The hourly rate for a partner is generally between €300 and €600, and can be anything up to €750 for a senior partner. Where local lawyers work in foreign law firms, their rates will tend to be lower than the rates of the foreign lawyers.

Standard rates of billing for junior lawyers are between €100 and €450 for expatriate lawyers, and from as little as €60 up to €400 per hour for local lawyers.

MARKETING

Although the Romanian Bar ostensibly prohibits the advertising of legal services, marketing remains a grey area. Many foreign – and increasingly local – firms advertise in professional directories and the local press. Several have comprehensive websites and sponsorship of high-profile events represents a legitimate way of getting round the ban.

IN-HOUSE LAWYERS

Most major enterprises retain in-house lawyers who are increasingly turning to outside counsel for advice on projects of all sizes. In-house lawyers cannot belong to the Bar, and do not have rights of audience in Romanian courts.

LEGAL MARKET AND FOREIGN FIRMS

Several major international firms, including **Linklaters**, **Salans** and **CMS Cameron McKenna LLP** have longstanding presences in Romania. (**CMS Cameron McKenna LLP** is in the process of finalising a merger with **Hayhurst Robinson** across the region).

Some of the best local law firms in Romania, most notably **Nestor Nestor Diculescu Kingston Petersen**, have teams which compete on an equal footing with the international firms, thanks in part to a long historical presence in the market.

More recently, there has been a trend for lawyers who had previously worked at international firms to form smaller breakaway firms. This trend is expected to continue in the lead up to Romania's EU accession, as the legal market becomes increasingly mature, diverse and sophisticated.

Several firms headquartered in Austria or Germany (including **Nörr Stiefenhofer Lutz**, **Schönherr**, **Haarmann Hemmelrath** and **Wolf**

The largest firms

1	Bostina & Associates	65
	Musat & Asociatii	65
3	Nestor Nestor Diculescu Kingston Petersen	60
4	Tuca Zbarcea & Asociatii	40
5	Sova & Partners	35
	Stefanica, Dutu & Partners	35
7	Linklaters Miculiti Mihai & Asociatii SCA	34
8	Popovici & Asociatii	32
9	Zamfirescu Racoti Predoiu	30
10	Nemoianu & Salcianu Attorneys at Law	25
	Salans - Romania	25
12	Schönherr	24
13	Badea, Georgescu & Asociatii SCA	23
14	Nörr Stiefenhofer Lutz	22
	Stoica & Asociatii Attorneys at Law	22
	Voicu & Filipescu SCA	22
17	Sutti, Studio Legale	21
18	Serban, Mares & Associates	20
	Vilau & Mitel	20
20	D&B David si Baias	19
	Deleanu Vasile - Lawyers	19
22	Gide Loyrette Nouel	18
	Radu Taracila Padurari Retevoescu SCA	18
24	Buzescu Ca	16
	Hayhurst Robinson	16

These figures represent the total number of lawyers in this country only, and have been supplied by the firms themselves. The figures should be accurate as at 1 January 2006.

Theiss, which opened an office in Romania in mid-2005) service a strong German-speaking client base.

French firm **Gide Loyrette Nouel** and Italian firms such as **Studio Legale Sutti** and **SCA Tonucci, Vilaia & Apostol** are also active.

LEGISLATIVE DEVELOPMENTS

Romania's bid to harmonise its legislation with the EU has led to an ongoing host of new regulations, especially in the field of competition law. Nevertheless, commentators predict that a process of widespread active preparation for EU accession (in 2007 at the earliest) over the past few years means that the final stages of accession should be relatively smooth.

The continued opening up of the energy, electricity and telecoms markets led to changes in the legislative framework. New laws to tackle corruption are constantly being introduced.

BANKING, FINANCE AND CAPITAL MARKETS

Nestor Nestor Diculescu Kingston Petersen has an outstanding reputation amongst major Romanian, US and European banks. The firm advised Deutsche Bank in connection a €50m bond issued by Rompetrol Group BV on the Luxembourg Stock Exchange. Other clients include UBS and Raiffeisen Bank.

Badea, Georgescu & Asociatii SCA has an excellent name for a wide range of financing and capital markets work, which is arguably the firm's forte. The firm advised Raiffeisen Bank and Bank Austria on a US$40m (€34m) financing to Telemobil SA and represented JPMorgan and ABN Amro on a €500m bond issue by the City of Bucharest. Daniel Badea is recommended. The firm has a strong following amongst several major banking clients, including JP Morgan, Deutsche Bank, BNP Paribas and ABN Amro.

Linklaters Miculiti Mihai & Asociatii SCA was particularly active in providing advice to its strong institutional banking client base. The team represented the underwriters in relation to the IPO of a Romanian retail store on the Bucharest Stock Exchange. The firm also advised on major financing transactions in the construction and energy industries. Adrian-Cătălin Bulboacă heads the team.

Musat & Asociatii advised Raiffeisen Bank in connection with several multi-million euro loan agreements to Romanian public authorities. The firm also acts for clients such as Standard Chartered and Mizuho Bank.

Salans - Romania was particularly active in financings in the real estate sector. Highlights include advice to Anchor Grup on a €124m real estate portfolio financing for an office centre and shopping mall in Bucharest. Other clients include major Western European banks and private equity funds.

BANKING, FINANCE AND CAPITAL MARKETS

NESTOR NESTOR DICULESCU KINGSTON PETERSEN ✪

Badea, Georgescu & Asociatii SCA ✪
Linklaters Miculiti Mihai & Asociatii SCA ✪
Musat & Asociatii ✪
Salans - Romania
Tuca Zbarcea & Asociatii ✪

CMS Cameron McKenna Cristina Brinzan Law Office ✪
D&B David si Baias ✪
David & Associates SCA
Fruth Oprisan, Popescu & Asociatii ✪
Gide Loyrette Nouel ✪
Gruia Dufaut Law Firm ✪
Haarmann Hemmelrath ✪
McGregor & Partners S.C.A.
Mihaela Grama-Popovici, Law Office
Nemoianu & Salcianu Attorneys at Law ✪
Nörr Stiefenhofer Lutz ✪
Popovici & Asociatii ✪
Radu Taracila Padurari Retevoescu SCA ✪
Rubin Meyer Doru & Trandafir, Spca, in Association with Herzfeld & Rubin, P.C. ✪
Schönherr ✪
Stefanica, Dutu & Partners ✪
Stoica & Asociatii Attorneys at Law ✪
Sutti, Studio Legale ✪
Vilau & Mitel ✪
Zamfirescu Racoti Predoiu ✪

Bostina & Associates ✪
Buzescu Ca ✪
Ciurtin, Brasoveanu & Partners
Danescu, Danescu & Associates ✪
David & Associates SCA
Dorina Dumitrescu Law Office
Grigore Florescu (Dr), Law Office of
PI Partners ✪
Pachiu & Associates ✪
Sova & Partners ✪
Voicu & Filipescu SCA ✪
Wolf Theiss ✪
Wood Lupascu Dumitrescu & Associates SCPA in association with Hall, Dickler

Firms are listed A-Z in tiers which are ranked in order of priority
✪ *Indicates firm displays contact details at the end of this chapter.*

Tuca Zbarcea & Asociatii acts for clients such as Deutsche Bank, BNP Paribas, Raiffeisen and the EBRD. The firm also advised several corporations on loan and debt capital markets transactions.

CMS Cameron McKenna Cristina Brinzan Law Office acts for clients such as Citibank, Erste Bank and OTP Bank.

D&B David si Baias advised ABN Amro on the implementation of complex and groundbreaking derivatives transactions in Romania. Other clients include ING Bank and Société Générale.

Gide Loyrette Nouel advised several French banks and corporations on loan and acquisition financings. Highlights include representing Groupe Soufflet, the malt and barley producer, on a €65m loan facility. Other clients include BRD - Groupe Société Générale.

Haarmann Hemmelrath advised an Austrian bank on its entry into the Romanian market.

McGregor & Partners S.C.A. advised on several ship finance transactions, a key area of focus for the firm.

Nemoianu & Salcianu Attorneys at Law advised banks such as Erste Bank and Banca Romanesca on a range of loan transactions.

Nörr Stiefenhofer Lutz advised on a wide range of real estate and leasing transactions. Clients include banks, real estate companies and shipping companies.

Popovici & Asociatii represented Dexia Bank as lead manager on a €500m international bond issue by the City of Bucharest. The firm also acted for Romania Hypermarkets SA in relation to a €40m credit facility with the EBRD for the construction of a new hypermarket in Bucharest. Other clients include West LB and BNP Paribas.

Radu Taracila Padurari Retevoescu SCA advised the City of Bucharest on a €500m bond issue and acted for Toronto-Dominion Bank on cross-border financings. Royal Bank of Scotland is also a client.

Rubin Meyer Doru & Trandafir, Spca, in Association with Herzfeld & Rubin, P.C. advised Timisoara Municipal Council on one of the largest-ever bond offerings by a municipal authority in Romania. Other clients include Banca Romaneasca.

Schönherr advised several Austrian, German and US banks on multi-million euro loan transactions.

Stefanica, Dutu & Partners advised on several major bond and syndicated loan transactions. The firm represented Cogen Romania on a €75m loan in connection with thermal power plants in Romania.

Vilau & Mitel acted for Raiffeisen Bank on consumer credit agreements in the retail sector and acted for TMCP (a joint venture between GE Aircraft Engines and Turbomecanica SA) in relation to several multi-million euro financings.

Buzescu Ca advises on asset finance and project finance transactions in the shipping and energy sectors.

PI Partners advised Piraeus Bank Romania SA on its potential entry into the Romanian securities market and represented Citibank Romania on the implementation of a new corporate card programme.

Sova & Partners has a special focus on bankruptcy cases.

CORPORATE AND M&A

Linklaters Miculiti Mihai & Asociatii SCA has a strong investment banking and private equity fund client base, acting for clients such as Credit Suisse First Boston, JP Morgan and CVC Capital Partners. Work in the telecoms sector is also a strong focus; recent highlights include advising on two major acquisitions in the telecoms industry in Romania. Other clients come from the pharmaceutical, tobacco, media and consumer goods sectors. Managing partner Michael Tétreault Schilling and Theodore Cominos, who was promoted to partner and head of the corporate department in May 2005, are recommended. Lucian Mihai has a focus on IP matters. The firm works closely with its international offices, especially London and Brussels, and is also active regionally across southeastern Europe.

Nestor Nestor Diculescu Kingston Petersen is the leading firm in the market, with long historical expertise and an extensive list of loyal, blue-chip clients. The firm advised Tenaris SA on the acquisition and subsequent restructuring of several Romanian steel producers and represented Schlumberger on the acquisition of three Romanian oil and gas companies. Other clients include Cargill, MobiFon SA, Gaz de France and Motorola. Partners Ion Nestor, Manuela Nestor and Adriana Gaspar are recommended. The team received a boost when Andrew Kingston returned to the firm in October 2005 after having spent four years in the US.

Salans - Romania boasts an impressive combination of both local Romanian knowledge as well as expertise in structuring cross-border international deals. Highlights include: representing Telesystem International Wireless on Romanian law aspects of the US$3.5bn (€2.9bn) sale of shares in MobiFon (Connex), the Romanian mobile provider, to Vodafone, the UK telecoms company; advising Procter & Gamble on competition law aspects of its acquisition of Gillette in Romania; and acting for a US marketing company on a joint venture in Romania. Other clients include Coca-Cola, Siemens, Aviva and Goodyear. Obie Moore, Anda Todor and Perry Zizzi are recommended. Gabriel Biris has a focus on tax matters. The team is 'business oriented, proactive and understands the issues facing clients'.

Buzescu Ca advised Amer Group plc on its acquisition of Salomon Romania SRL, as part of the company's acquisition of the parent company Salomon France SA, and acted for Estée Lauder in relation to the conversion of its Romanian subsidiary from a limited liability company to a joint stock company. Other clients are Coca-Cola, Bacardi, Monsanto and Qualcomm. The firm also has a strong name for intellectual property matters. Peter Buzescu is a member of the New York and Romanian Bars, and has a strong US client base. The firm often co-operates with major US and UK firms which do not have an office in Romania. Clients appreciate 'clear reports' and 'prompt feedback' from the firm.

McGregor & Partners S.C.A. advised Reconstruction Capital plc, the listed investment fund, on its disposal of the entire issued share capital in Capital Securities SA, the Romanian brokerage house, to EFG Eurobank Ergasias SA, the Greek bank. The firm also represented Siveco SA, the Romanian software company in relation to a US$12m (€9.4m) investment by Enterprise Investors. The firm also acts for several clients from the shipping industry. Neil McGregor heads the team. The firm maintains an association with **Stephenson Harwood** in London and internationally, and is also active regionally in Bulgaria and Serbia.

Musat & Asociatii has long experience of advising blue-chip clients in Romania. The firm advised PepsiAmericas, the manufacturer and distributor of Pepsi-Cola beverages, on its US$51m (€42m) investment in Quadrant-Amroq Bottling Company Limited, in connection with the production, sale and distribution of Pepsi in Romania. Other clients include Intel, SBS Broadcasting and GlaxoSmithKline. Name partner Gheorghe Musat and Catalin Baiculescu are recommended. The team suffered a setback in March 2005 when eight partners left the firm to establish new firm **Tuca Zbarcea & Asociatii**, taking with them several major clients. Since that time, however, **Musat & Asociatii** has been

CORPORATE AND M&A

LINKLATERS MICULITI MIHAI & ASOCIATII SCA ✪
NESTOR NESTOR DICULESCU KINGSTON PETERSEN ✪

SALANS - ROMANIA

Buzescu Ca ✪
McGregor & Partners S.C.A.
Musat & Asociatii ✪
Rubin Meyer Doru & Trandafir, Spca, in Association with Herzfeld & Rubin, P.C. ✪
Tuca Zbarcea & Asociatii ✪
Voicu & Filipescu SCA ✪

Badea, Georgescu & Asociatii SCA ✪
CMS Cameron McKenna Cristina Brinzan Law Office ✪
D&B David si Baias ✪
David & Associates SCA
Gide Loyrette Nouel ✪
Gruia Dufaut Law Firm ✪
Hayhurst Robinson
Nemoianu & Salcianu Attorneys at Law ✪
Nörr Stiefenhofer Lutz ✪
Popovici & Asociatii ✪
Radu Taracila Padurari Retevoescu SCA ✪
Schönherr ✪
Stefanica, Dutu & Partners ✪
Stoica & Asociatii Attorneys at Law ✪
Vilau & Mitel ✪
Zamfirescu Racoti Predoiu ✪

Continued

CORPORATE AND M&A Continued

Andra Musatescu Law & Industrial Property Offices
Bostina & Associates ✪
Burchel & Associates
CHSH Gilescu & Partners Cerha Hempel Spiegelfeld Hlawati
CMS Bureau Francis Lefebvre
Ciurtin, Brasoveanu & Partners
Cobuz & Associates
Cosovanu-Marcu Attorneys-at-Law ✪
Costea & Jalba SCA Law Offices
Danescu, Danescu & Associates ✪
Deleanu Vasile - Lawyers ✪
Dorina Dumitrescu Law Office
Dragomir & Associates
Fruth Oprisan, Popescu & Asociatii ✪
Grigore Florescu (Dr), Law Office of
Gutium si Asociatii SCA
Haarmann Hemmelrath ✪
Hammond, Lāta & Associates
I.K. Rokas & C. Constantinescu SCPA
Magda Volonciu and Associates
Margarit, Florov & Partners
Mihaela Grama-Popovici, Law Office
PI Partners ✪
Pachiu & Associates ✪
Preda & Associates Law Firm
SCA Carnu, Dumitrache, Gherghina & Sebeni
SCA Tonucci, Vilaia & Apostol
Serban, Mares & Associates
Sova & Partners ✪
Sutti, Studio Legale ✪
Virgil Melnic Law Office
Wolf Theiss ✪
Wood Lupascu Dumitrescu & Associates SCPA in association with Hall, Dickler

Firms are listed A-Z in tiers which are ranked in order of priority
✪ Indicates firm displays contact details at the end of this chapter.

actively rebuilding its numbers, especially at associate level, as well as at partner level through the promotion of several associates to the firm's partnership. Clients recommend the firm as 'responsive and accurate'.

Rubin Meyer Doru & Trandafir, Spca, in Association with Herzfeld & Rubin, P.C. advises a range of clients from Romania, the US, Greece, Israel and Germany. The firm advised the National Bank of Greece on a bid for Banca Commerciala Romania. Other clients come from the real estate, manufacturing, energy and media sectors. Well-known partners include Mark Meyer, who divides his time between Romania and the firm's New York office, Lia Doru-Trandafir, Sergiu Doru and Anthony Raftopol.

Tuca Zbarcea & Asociatii was formed in March 2005 when eight partners and a large team of associates left **Musat & Asociatii**. The firm acts for major clients such as Romtelecom, BNP Paribas, IKEA, Volvo and Caterpillar. Transaction highlights in 2005 include advice to Deutsche Bank in relation to the privatisation of Banca Comerciala Romana and representing an international insurance company on an acquisition in Romania. Well-known names include Florentin Tuca, Stefan Damian, Ciprian Dragomir and Cornel Popa. Competition work is also a strong area of focus. Since its inception in March 2005, the firm has continued to expand in number through several lateral hires at associate level. The firm 'understands clients' needs and business perspectives and adapts its advice accordingly'.

Voicu & Filipescu SCA advised on several major M&A transactions, including acting for Liberty Media Inc, the TV cable operator, on its US$400m (€334m) acquisition of Astral Telecom SA and advising Lenovo Group Limited on Romanian law aspects of its acquisition of IBM's production division. The firm has a special focus on private equity work. The firm has an association with **Squire, Sanders & Dempsey L.L.P.**. Clients appreciate the firm's 'speed and quality of response' and 'fees which are reasonable'.

Badea, Georgescu & Asociatii SCA has a strong name for banking and finance work, and acts for several major banks and financial institutions, including Deutsche Bank, Aviva and Warburg Pincus, on a range of corporate matters. Other clients come from the energy, construction and real estate sectors. The firm advised Warburg Pincus on an acquisition in the healthcare sector through a leveraged buyout, and represented a major oil and gas company on restructuring its gas business. The firm often co-operates with several major US and UK firms without a presence in Romania. Daniel Badea and Nadia Georgescu head the team. Clients appreciate 'excellent communication and project management skills' and 'regular reports on a broad range of legal issues'.

At **CMS Cameron McKenna Cristina Brinzan Law Office** work in the private equity industry is a core area of focus. Highlights include advice to Advent International on the acquisition of a paint company in Romania. Other clients come from the banking, energy, transport and retail sectors. Cristina Brinzan and Paul Stallebrass are recommended. The team is described as 'solid, experienced and trustworthy'.

D&B David si Baias is recommended for a range of corporate, M&A, restructuring and tax matters. The firm advised Baxi Group, the heating products group, on its acquisition of a Romanian boiler distribution company. Other clients include Akzo Nobel, Motorola and ING Bank. Name partners Sorin David and Flavius Baias are recommended. The firm often works closely with PwC on transactions. Clients recommend the firm for 'in-depth expertise in the tax sector' and 'always meeting deadlines'.

David & Associates SCA acts for a range of blue-chip clients from the IT, telecoms, pharmaceutical, automotive, energy and banking sectors. US lawyer Charles Vernon and Iulian Patrascanu head a team of 14 assistants. In 2005, the firm advised on several major competition law matters.

Gide Loyrette Nouel advised E.On Rurhgas AG, the utilities group, on a joint venture with a Romanian municipality, and acted for St Gobain Isover, the French insulation company, on a €12m acquisition of shares in a Romanian company. The team works closely with the firm's head office in Paris. The firm has a strong French client base, and also acts for other clients from a range of countries including Italy, Spain, Greece and the US. Bruno Leroy heads a team of 17 associates.

Gruia Dufaut Law Firm advises clients from the construction, insurance, banking and retail sectors. Dana Gruia Dufaut is a member of both the Paris and Bucharest Bars.

Hayhurst Robinson advises on a range of M&A and private equity transactions for clients from the pharmaceutical, IT, telecoms and energy sectors. The team works closely with its network of international offices in Central and South-eastern Europe. At the time of writing, the firm was concluding a merger with **CMS Cameron McKenna LLP**.

Nemoianu & Salcianu Attorneys at Law co-operates closely with KPMG in Romania and internationally. Daniela Nemoianu and Loredana Salcianu head a team recommended for a range of corporate, finance and tax work. The firm advised a Dutch aircraft components manufacturer on a joint venture with a Romanian aircraft producer and acted for a French packaging producer on a transfer of shares. Clients appreciate 'high levels of access to the legal team assigned to projects' and 'comprehensive presentations about the Romanian legal environment'.

Nörr Stiefenhofer Lutz acts for a strong German and Austrian client base. The team advised a major German automotive company on the construction of a greenfield site. Other clients come from the retail, insurance, banking and real estate industries. The firm has a strong focus on tax work. Jörg K Menzer heads a team of 22 fee-earners.

Six-partner, 32-associate **Popovici & Asociatii** advised Apax and Cinven on Romanian aspects of a €2bn acquisition in the telephone directories sector. Other clients include Hewlett-Packard, Orange Romania, Hilton and UPS. The firm also has a particular focus on work for clients in the retail sector (especially hypermarkets) and the oil and gas industry. The firm has broad expertise in a range of other areas, including competition, employment and dispute resolution. Ernest Virgil Popovici and Florian Nitu head the firm. The firm is described as 'clear, efficient, commercial and rigorous' in its work.

Radu Taracila Padurari Retevoescu SCA was particularly active in advising on deals in the private equity sector. In 2005, the firm advised Enterprise Investors, the largest private equity fund in Central and Eastern Europe, in relation to the €17m acquisition (via management buy-in) of Artima Retail Investment Company, one of the largest independent networks of chain supermarkets. The firm also advises clients from the banking, IT, media and energy industries. The team often works closely with major London and Austrian firms that do not have offices in Romania. The firm is 'flexible, efficient and hard working', and is made up of a 'solid team of very good young professionals, with an already impressive track record in M&A and privatisation'. Clients also appreciate competitive billing rates.

Schönherr advises several major Austrian, German and Romanian clients. The firm is also undertaking increasing amounts of work for a range of other European clients. The firm advised Outdoor Akzent in relation to an acquisition in the advertising sector. Other clients come from the hotel, insurance and media sectors. The firm also offers IP and tax advice. Markus Piuk heads a team of 23 lawyers. The firm is ' professional, committed, accurate and timely'.

Stefanica, Dutu & Partners advises on a range of corporate, commercial, employment and M&A matters. The firm advised Amadeus in relation to Romanian law aspects of a proposed global acquisition by Cinven and BC Partners. Other clients come from the retail, energy, banking and insurance sectors. Daniel Stefanica and Florin Dutu head a team of seven partners.

Stoica & Asociatii Attorneys at Law advises on a range of corporate, commercial and employment matters. Dispute resolution is also a strong area of focus. Valeriu Stoica and Cristiana Stoica are recommended.

Vilau & Mitel advised Lear Corporation on the relocation of its businesses in Romania and represented Raiffeisen Bank in connection with a private equity transaction in the retail sector. Other clients include General Electric. Name partners Dragos Vilau and Sorin Mitel head a team of 16 associates. The firm also advises on a growing amount of intellectual property work; highlights include advising on trade mark matters for clients such as Intel, GlaxoSmithKline and UniCredito Italiano.

Zamfirescu Racoti Predoiu was formed in December 2005, following the merger of two well-known local firms, *Racoti - Predoiu, Attorneys at Law* and *Calin Zamfirescu & Associates*. The firm acts for clients from the food and drink, energy, banking and retail sectors. Competition and IP are important areas of focus. Name partners Catalin Predoiu, Ioanna Racoti and Calin Zamfirescu are recommended.

Three-lawyer **Andra Musatescu Law & Industrial Property Offices** is particularly recommended for intellectual property matters. The firm advised on several trade mark and domain name cases in 2005. The firm acts for clients from the telecoms and food and drinks industries. Name partner Andra Musatescu heads the team.

Bostina & Associates advises on a broad range of corporate, employment, IT, real estate and tax matters. Clients include BP, Ikea, Marriott Hotels, Mitsui, BRD - Groupe Société Générale and Raiffeisen Bank. Name partner Doru Catalin Bostina heads a team of ten partners.

Burchel & Associates advises companies such as MTV Europe, Eurosport SA, Microsoft and Agfa Romania. Nicolae Burchel heads the team.

CHSH Gilescu & Partners Cerha Hempel Spiegelfeld Hlawati name partner Radu Gilescu heads a team which advises clients from the forestry, agriculture and alcohol industries from Austria, Germany, the UK and North America.

CMS Bureau Francis Lefebvre advises several French clients, while **Ciurtin, Brasoveanu & Partners** is particularly recommended for real estate work, in addition to a range of corporate and commercial matters. Clients include Raiffeisen Leasing SRL and Target. Adrian Ciurtin was formerly head of the legal department at HVB Leasing Romania SRL. Andrei Brasoveanu is also recommended.

COSOVANU-MARCU Attorneys-at-Law has a special focus on financial and white-collar crime work. Name partners Cornel Cosovanu and Ion Marcu head the team.

Costea & Jalba SCA Law Offices advised Telesport Intermedia SRL on its multi-million euro acquisition of television broadcasting rights from the Romanian Football Association. Other clients include Greek investors in the real estate sector. Clients appreciate 'professional service and commitment'. Daniel Costea and Dan Jalba head a team of four associates.

Danescu, Danescu & Associates advises major European, Japanese and US/multinational clients from the food and drink, retail, real estate, IT and shipping sectors. The firm advises on a range of corporate, employment, real estate and banking matters. Costea Corin Danescu and Alina Danescu head a team of 15 lawyers. The firm 'always meets deadlines' and is described as 'experienced, competent and dedicated'.

Three-partner, 16-associate **Deleanu Vasile - Lawyers** is recommended for commercial, dispute resolution and insolvency matters. Vasile Deleanu heads the team.

Three-partner, six-associate **Dragomir & Associates** advises clients from the electricity, construction and oil and gas sectors. The firm advised Lukoil Downstream SRL on joint ventures and distribution networks in Romania. Dispute resolution work is also an area of focus. Stan Dragomir and Alina Lefter are recommended. The firm is 'realistic and impartial in its advice' and 'keeps clients up to date with ongoing changes in legislation in Romania'.

Fruth Oprisan, Popescu & Asociatii advised Astral Telecom SA on the sale of its shares to a US company. Other clients include Kvaerner Romania NV. Despina Fruth Oprisan heads a team of three partners. The firm 'conducts all its business dealings with the utmost integrity', say clients.

Law Office of Dr Grigore Florescu advises on a range of corporate and commercial work for multinational clients from France, Germany and the US. Grigore Florescu heads the firm.

Gutium si Asociatii SCA advises clients from the oil and gas, telecoms and construction sectors. The firm also advises several government agencies. Eugenia Gutium, who previously worked at **Linklaters Miculiti Mihai & Asociatii SCA** and the legal department of the State Ownership Fund, heads a team of seven lawyers.

Haarmann Hemmelrath acts for several major German, Austrian and Romanian companies on corporate, M&A and tax matters. Catalin Grigorescu became partner and head of the Romanian office in July 2005.

Hammond, Lăta & Associates was formed in October 2005 by name partners Nicholas Hammond and Ariana Lăta. The firm advises clients from the food, energy and private equity sectors.

I.K. Rokas & C. Constantinescu SCPA represents several Greek companies in Romania, working closely with its head office in Athens.

Four-partner **Magda Volonciu and Associates** is well known for its expertise in employment matters. Clients include Coca-Cola. Name partner Magda Volonciu heads the team.

Five-partner **Margarit, Florov & Partners** advises clients in the insurance, banking, construction and shipping sectors. Clients come from Germany, Greece, France and Bulgaria. Catalin Margarit and Tsvetan Florov head the team.

Law Office Mihaela Grama-Popovici's Mihaela Grama-Popovici is also respected.

PI Partners works closely with Big Four accounting firm Ernst & Young in Romania and internationally. The firm advised Wiener Stadtische Versicherung Aktiengesellschaft on the acquisition of Omniasig SA, the Romanian insurance company. Eirinikos Platis heads a team that works closely with the firm's office in Athens in advising several major Greek clients. Other clients include Gillette and Toyota.

Pachiu & Associates advised Emerson Electric on multi-million euro FDI and M&A transactions. The firm also advises on a range of real estate, employment, intellectual property and tax matters. Other clients include WPP and Gruner + Jahr. Laurentiu Pachiu heads the team.

Niche firm **Preda & Associates Law Firm** advises on corporate, commercial, competition and insolvency matters. Clients include Shell and Nobel Romania. Luciana Preda heads a team that is 'flexible, practical, dedicated and experienced'.

SCA Tonucci, Vilaia & Apostol is affiliated with **Studio Legale Tonucci** in Italy. The firm advises several Italian clients from the banking, energy and insurance sectors.

Serban, Mares & Associates advises clients from the household appliances, food and drink, pharmaceuticals, insurance, transport, chemicals and hotel industries. George Serban and Dana Mares are recommended.

Sova & Partners advises a range of clients from the energy, media and IT sectors. Name partner Dan Sova heads a team of 27 associates. The firm advised on a major acquisition in the media sector in 2005. The firm also advises on competition and insolvency matters. Two name partners including Adrian Ratiu left the firm in July 2005.

Studio Legale Sutti advised Daikin Europe on regulatory matters. The firm represents several Italian companies in Romania.

Virgil Melnic Law Office, based in Timisoara, advises clients from the insurance industry.

Wolf Theiss opened an office in Romania in mid-2005 headed by Bryan Jardine, who joined the firm from **Squire, Sanders & Dempsey L.L.P.**. The firm acts for several Austrian clients in Romania.

DISPUTE RESOLUTION

Nestor Nestor Diculescu Kingston Petersen advised Mondial Assurances SA on a major case involving the Romanian insurance regulator and represented Lafarge Romcim SA on a competition case. The team also advised on several major real estate and intellectual property cases.

D&B David si Baias is particularly recommended for complex litigation in the banking, employment, real estate, intellectual property and tax sectors. Clients include Alpha Bank, Pfizer and Romtelecom.

Linklaters Miculiti Mihai & Asociatii SCA's Lucian Mihai heads a team recommended for major litigation and arbitration cases. Clients come from the telecoms, tobacco, consumer goods and mining industries. Many cases handled by the department involve complex issues of intellectual property.

Musat & Asociatii advised the Romanian government in relation to an arbitration brought by a US investor concerning a bilateral investment treaty between Romania and the US. The firm also advised clients such as GlaxoSmithKline, Lotto and Raiffeisen Bank on litigation in Romania.

At **Stoica & Asociatii Attorneys at Law** name partner Valeriu Stoica is one of Romania's best-known litigators.

Tuca Zbarcea & Asociatii advised Colgate Palmolive on litigation concerning competition law. Other clients come from the banking, energy and manufacturing sectors. Cornel Popa is well known.

At **Zamfirescu Racoti Predoiu**, litigation is a core practice area. The firm advised several Romanian banks in relation to debt recovery litigation. The team also undertook IP litigation relating to a well-known trade mark. Name partner Calin Zamfirescu is a well-known litigator.

DISPUTE RESOLUTION

NESTOR NESTOR DICULESCU KINGSTON PETERSEN ✪

D&B David si Baias ✪
Linklaters Miculiti Mihai & Asociatii SCA ✪
Musat & Asociatii ✪
Stoica & Asociatii Attorneys at Law ✪
Tuca Zbarcea & Asociatii ✪
Zamfirescu Racoti Predoiu ✪

Deleanu Vasile - Lawyers ✪
Fruth Oprisan, Popescu & Asociatii ✪
McGregor & Partners S.C.A.
Nemoianu & Salcianu Attorneys at Law ✪
Nörr Stiefenhofer Lutz ✪
Pachiu & Associates ✪
Popovici & Asociatii ✪
Rubin Meyer Doru & Trandafir, Spca, in Association with Herzfeld & Rubin, P.C. ✪
Salans - Romania
Serban, Mares & Associates
Stefanica, Dutu & Partners ✪
Sutti, Studio Legale ✪
Vilau & Mitel ✪

Danescu, Danescu & Associates ✪
David & Associates SCA
Dragomir & Associates
Grigore Florescu (Dr), Law Office of
PI Partners ✪
Preda & Associates Law Firm
Sova & Partners ✪

Firms are listed A-Z in tiers which are ranked in order of priority
✪ Indicates firm displays contact details at the end of this chapter.

Name partner Vasile Deleanu at **Deleanu Vasile - Lawyers** heads a group that advises on insolvency, real estate, debt collection and employment disputes.

McGregor & Partners S.C.A. advised on several shipping, insolvency and liquidation cases.

Nemoianu & Salcianu Attorneys at Law advised Honeywell Garret SRL, the automotive components manufacturer, on tax litigation. Other clients come from the banking, construction and food and drinks sectors.

Nörr Stiefenhofer Lutz acted for a major agricultural company on a dispute with a Romanian bank and represented a pharmaceutical company on an employment dispute.

Popovici & Asociatii acted for clients such as Equant, Shell Gas, Lafarge and Orange SA on complex litigation.

Salans - Romania represented investors in the Rompetrol Group, the oil and natural resources company in relation to a dispute concerning bilateral investment treaties between the Netherlands and Romania. Other clients include Mittal Steel and Abbot Laboratories.

Stefanica, Dutu & Partners advised Noble Ventures, the research and marketing company, on an investment dispute arising out of bilateral economic treaties.

Vilau & Mitel acted for Dasimpex, the Romanian telephone company in connection with a contractual dispute and arbitration against Xerox. The firm also advised on shipping and debt collection disputes.

Danescu, Danescu & Associates advised on a range of commercial, employment and tax disputes.

David & Associates SCA advised a Belgian beverage company on a multi-million euro dispute with the Romanian financial authorities relating to the company's right to receive financial incentives. The firm also represented a telecoms company in a competition case. Dana David is recommended.

At **Dragomir & Associates** name partner Stan Dragomir is an experienced litigator.

PI Partners advised Delta Romania SA on an employment dispute in the Court of Appeal.

Sova & Partners advised on several bankruptcy and debt recovery cases.

ENERGY AND NATURAL RESOURCES

Linklaters Miculiti Mihai & Asociatii SCA advised on several major privatisations in the energy, oil and gas and electricity sectors, including the €311m privatisation of Distrigaz Sud SA, the Romanian national gas distribution company through an the acquisition by Gaz de France. The team is increasingly co-operating with lawyers in the firm's network of international offices, especially in Eastern Europe, on complex, cross-border transactions in the energy sector.

Buzescu Ca acts for several US and European clients from the energy and oil and gas sectors.

D&B David si Baias advised on transactions in the energy and oil and gas sectors.

Gide Loyrette Nouel acted for Nuon, the Dutch energy group, in connection with a thermal energy project in two Romanian cities. Other clients include Schlumberger, the US gas company.

McGregor & Partners S.C.A. acted for financial investors in an energy distribution company.

Musat & Asociatii advised key client Enel SpA on a range of financing and competition matters. Other clients come from the mining and oil and gas industries.

Nestor Nestor Diculescu Kingston Petersen advised Transgaz SA on the Nabucco international gas pipeline project, a natural gas pipeline linking production areas in the Caspian Sea and Middle East to Central and Western Europe. The firm also advises clients such as Gaz de France, Electrica SA and SNP Petrom.

Popovici & Asociatii advised on a range of transactions in the energy, electricity, nuclear and mining sectors. Clients include Shell Gas, Electricité de France and Lafarge.

ENERGY AND NATURAL RESOURCES

LINKLATERS MICULITI MIHAI & ASOCIATII SCA ✪

Buzescu Ca ✪
D&B David si Baias ✪
Gide Loyrette Nouel ✪
Hayhurst Robinson
McGregor & Partners S.C.A.
Musat & Asociatii ✪
Nestor Nestor Diculescu Kingston Petersen ✪
Popovici & Asociatii ✪
Rubin Meyer Doru & Trandafir, Spca, in Association with Herzfeld & Rubin, P.C. ✪
Tuca Zbarcea & Asociatii ✪

Badea, Georgescu & Asociatii SCA ✪
Bostina & Associates ✪
Nemoianu & Salcianu Attorneys at Law ✪
PI Partners ✪
Radu Taracila Padurari Retevoescu SCA ✪
Sova & Partners ✪
Stefanica, Dutu & Partners ✪

Firms are listed A-Z in tiers which are ranked in order of priority
✪ Indicates firm displays contact details at the end of this chapter.

Tuca Zbarcea & Asociatii acted for Petrom SA in relation to competition matters. Other clients include Texaco.

Badea, Georgescu & Asociatii SCA advised Energy AG, the Austrian group, on an acquisition in Romania. Other clients include OMV, the oil and gas company.

Bostina & Associates acts for clients such as BP and Transelectrica SA.

Nemoianu & Salcianu Attorneys at Law advised clients such as the Halliburton Group, the oil and gas company, and Valtec, the automotive oil producer.

Radu Taracila Padurari Retevoescu SCA advised the Romanian government in connection with thermal energy power complexes in Romania.

Sova & Partners advises clients from the energy, minerals and mining industries.

IT, TELECOMS AND MEDIA

Nestor Nestor Diculescu Kingston Petersen acted for Hughes Network Systems, the broadband satellite company on its provision of telecommunications services in Romania. Other clients include Motorola and MobiFon SA.

Salans - Romania acts for clients such as Telesystem International Wireless (TIW), Motion Pictures Association, HBO and Siemens.

David & Associates SCA represents several major clients from the telecoms sector from Scandinavia, southeastern Europe and Romania.

IT, TELECOMS AND MEDIA

NESTOR NESTOR DICULESCU KINGSTON PETERSEN ✪
SALANS - ROMANIA

David & Associates SCA
Linklaters Miculiti Mihai & Asociatii SCA ✪
Musat & Asociatii ✪

D&B David si Baias ✪
Hayhurst Robinson
Nörr Stiefenhofer Lutz ✪
Popovici & Asociatii ✪
Rubin Meyer Doru & Trandafir, Spca, in Association with Herzfeld & Rubin, P.C. ✪
Stefanica, Dutu & Partners ✪
Tuca Zbarcea & Asociatii ✪

Andra Musatescu Law & Industrial Property Offices
Buzescu Ca ✪
Ciurtin, Brasoveanu & Partners
Danescu, Danescu & Associates ✪
Radu Taracila Padurari Retevoescu SCA ✪
Sova & Partners ✪
Sutti, Studio Legale ✪
Voicu & Filipescu SCA ✪
Vilau & Mitel ✪
Zamfirescu Racoti Predoiu ✪

Firms are listed A-Z in tiers which are ranked in order of priority
✪ Indicates firm displays contact details at the end of this chapter.

At **Linklaters Miculiti Mihai & Asociatii SCA**, Simona Delia Pachiu heads a team which advised major Romanian and Western European clients from the telecoms, computing and media sectors. The team also advised several major private equity houses on investments in the TMT sector in Romania and southeastern Europe.

Musat & Asociatii acted for SBS Broadcasting in relation to the €22m acquisition of two radio stations in Romania. The firm also represents IT and software clients such as Intel and Epicor Software Corporation.

D&B David si Baias represented key client Romtelecom on a range of matters. Other clients include Motorola and De Agostini, the publishing company.

Nörr Stiefenhofer Lutz advises several major German publishing and media companies. Other clients include telecoms equipment manufacturers.

Popovici & Asociatii advised clients such as Orange Romania, Hewlett-Packard, Nokia and Equant.

Tuca Zbarcea & Asociatii advised key client Romtelecom on a range of matters. Other clients come from the media and advertising sectors.

Radu Taracila Padurari Retevoescu SCA acted for a shareholder in Orange Romania in relation to its exit from a consortium of regional private equity funds led by AIG-CET. Other clients include United Pan-European Communications (UPC), which the firm advised on a series of acquisitions of Romanian cable operators.

Sova & Partners represents several companies from the publishing, media and TV industries.

PRIVATISATION

Linklaters Miculiti Mihai & Asociatii SCA advised the Romanian government in relation to the privatisation of Distrigaz Sud SA, the Romanian national gas distribution company. The firm also has a wealth of experience of privatisation in the electricity and petroleum industries.

Musat & Asociatii was active in advising on a range of transactions for both the Romanian government and corporations. Highlights include advising Enel SpA in connection with the privatisation of two gas distribution companies in Romania.

PRIVATISATION

LINKLATERS MICULITI MIHAI & ASOCIATII SCA ✪
MUSAT & ASOCIATII ✪
NESTOR NESTOR DICULESCU KINGSTON PETERSEN ✪

Gide Loyrette Nouel ✪
McGregor & Partners S.C.A.
Salans - Romania
Tuca Zbarcea & Asociatii ✪
Zamfirescu Racoti Predoiu ✪

Babiuc, Sulica & Associates
Badea, Georgescu & Asociatii SCA ✪
Bostina & Associates ✪
CMS Cameron McKenna Cristina Brinzan Law Office ✪
David & Associates SCA
Dorina Dumitrescu Law Office
Fruth Oprisan, Popescu & Asociatii ✪
Grigore Florescu (Dr), Law Office of
Gutium si Asociatii SCA
Haarmann Hemmelrath ✪
Hayhurst Robinson
Nemoianu & Salcianu Attorneys at Law ✪
PI Partners ✪
Popovici & Asociatii ✪
Radu Taracila Padurari Retevoescu SCA ✪
Rubin Meyer Doru & Trandafir, Spca, in Association with Herzfeld & Rubin, P.C. ✪
Schönherr ✪
Stoica & Asociatii Attorneys at Law ✪
Sutti, Studio Legale ✪
Vilau & Mitel ✪
Wood Lupascu Dumitrescu & Associates SCPA in association with Hall, Dickler

Firms are listed A-Z in tiers which are ranked in order of priority
✪ Indicates firm displays contact details at the end of this chapter.

Nestor Nestor Diculescu Kingston Petersen advised the Romanian government in connection with the sale of a majority interest in Romania's largest state-owned financial institution. Other clients include Electrica SA.

Gide Loyrette Nouel acted for Nuon, the Dutch energy group, in connection with a thermal energy project in two Romanian cities. Other clients include Schlumberger, the US gas company.

McGregor & Partners S.C.A. advised a Romanian post-privatisation fund on its exit from a Romanian internet and cable company.

Salans - Romania advised an Israeli client on employment matters and post-privatisation obligations relating to the acquisition of a hotel in Bucharest.

Tuca Zbarcea & Asociatii advised on major privatisations in the food and insurance sectors. Clients include corporations, banks and Romanian government agencies.

CMS Cameron McKenna Cristina Brinzan Law Office advised on privatisations in the energy and banking sectors. Highlights include advising Citibank in relation to the €65m privatisation of Distributia Electrica.

Nemoianu & Salcianu Attorneys at Law represented Tenaris, the multinational steel pipe manufacturer, on its acquisition of four state-owned Romanian industrial plants.

Radu Taracila Padurari Retevoescu SCA acted for Banco Commercial Português in relation to the privatisation of Banca Comerciala Romana SA, the largest Romanian bank. The team also undertook work in the energy and electricity sectors.

Vilau & Mitel advised on ongoing privatisations in the banking and electricity sectors.

PROJECT FINANCE

Linklaters Miculiti Mihai & Asociatii SCA has a strong investment banking client base, which the firm advised on projects in the transport, energy and construction industries. The firm also advised the Romanian government on several matters.

Nestor Nestor Diculescu Kingston Petersen was particularly active in advice to lenders. Highlights include representing Nordea Bank on a financing facility for shipbuilding operations. On the sponsor side, the firm advised Mobifon SA on a €200m project in the telecoms sector.

Buzescu Ca advised BNP Paribas on a major project in the chemicals industry.

Musat & Asociatii advised clients such as the EBRD on projects in the oil and gas sector.

Popovici & Asociatii advised Hidroconstructia on the construction of a €500m hydro-energy facility. The firm also advised on projects in the transport sector.

Stefanica, Dutu & Partners acted for Cogen Romania in relation to the construction of thermal power plants in Romania.

Badea, Georgescu & Asociatii SCA advised Bechtel in connection with the financing and construction of a highway in Romania. The firm also has a strong banking client base.

Gutium si Asociatii SCA advised Kampsax, the engineering group, in relation to a PPP project. The firm also advised on projects in the water and motorway sectors.

Tuca Zbarcea & Asociatii advised clients such as the EBRD and Vinci Construction on projects in Romania.

PROJECT FINANCE

LINKLATERS MICULITI MIHAI & ASOCIATII SCA ✪
NESTOR NESTOR DICULESCU KINGSTON PETERSEN ✪

Buzescu Ca ✪
Gide Loyrette Nouel ✪
Musat & Asociatii ✪
Nemoianu & Salcianu Attorneys at Law ✪
Popovici & Asociatii ✪
Rubin Meyer Doru & Trandafir, Spca, in Association with Herzfeld & Rubin, P.C. ✪
Stefanica, Dutu & Partners ✪

Badea, Georgescu & Asociatii SCA ✪
Bostina & Associates ✪
Danescu, Danescu & Associates ✪
David & Associates SCA
Gutium si Asociatii SCA
Tuca Zbarcea & Asociatii ✪

Firms are listed A-Z in tiers which are ranked in order of priority
✪ Indicates firm displays contact details at the end of this chapter.

BADEA, GEORGESCU & ASOCIATII SCA

18 CALEA DOROBANTILOR
SECTOR 1
BUCHAREST

Telephone: +40 21 211 4165
Fax: +40 21 21 211 4168
E-mail: general@brg.ro
Website: www.brg.ro

Languages
English, French

Number of lawyers 23

CATEGORIES OF WORK

Banking and finance
Daniel Badea, Nadia Georgescu

Securities and derivatives
Daniel Badea

Competition
Nadia Georgescu

Corporate and commercial
Nadia Georgescu

Employment and pensions
Nadia Georgescu

Energy and natural resources
Daniel Badea, Nadia Georgescu

IT and telecommunications
Daniel Badea

Mergers and acquisitions
Daniel Badea, Nadia Georgescu

Regulatory
Daniel Badea, Nadia Georgescu

Real estate and construction
Daniel Badea, Nadia Georgescu

Shipping
Daniel Badea

Securitisation and structured finance
Daniel Badea

Privatisation and foreign investments
Daniel Badea, Nadia Georgescu

BOSTINA & ASSOCIATES

12 SILVESTRU STREET
DISTRICT 2
020735 BUCHAREST

Telephone: +40 21 211 4800
Fax: +40 21 211 4723
E-mail: office@scpabostina.ro
Website: www.scpabostina.ro

Languages
English, French, Romanian, Russian

Other offices
Alba Iulia, Chisinau, Constanta, Cyprus (Nicosia), Ramnicu Valcea, Resita, Sibiu, Targu Mures, Timisoara, Zalau

Number of lawyers 65
at this office 11

CATEGORIES OF WORK

Public authorities
Doru Catalin Bostina

Communications and transport
Cristian Costea

Banking and finance
Cezar Gusu

Energy, gas and oil
Dana Dunel

Privatisation
Laura Mocanu

Real estate, construction and utilities
Ciprian Glodeanu

Contracts
Bogdan Paraschiv

Corporate, commercial, M&A
Alexandra Necatu

Fiscal
Ciprian Badea

Litigation and arbitration
Ancuta Elena Man

Intellectual property
Ovidiu-Ionel Mihut

Capital market
Narcisa Galina Fatu

Insurance
Ovidiu Tibuleac

THE FIRM

In 1992, Doru Catalin Bostina laid the foundations of Individual Law Practice Bostina, a law practice registered in 1996. Bostina & Associates is the result of the reorganisation which took place in September 2000.

Bostina & Associates offers a comprehensive range of legal consulting services and representation before all law courts in Romania. It is now one of the most important law firms in the country, having more than 65 lawyers specialising in different legal areas, who carry out business from both the firm's domestic and international offices.

AREAS OF PRACTICE

Telecommunications and IT: assistance with electronic communications field regulations, issue of licences and authorisations, assistance in the privatisation of telecommunications operators, and adoption of regulations in the electronic communications field, as well as involvement in important computerisation projects.

Banking and finance: experience in setting up and authorisation of banking companies and building societies, launching of banking products on the market, preparation of due diligence reports, monitoring of contracts and banking operations with the most important credit institutions.

Energy gas and oil: the team is involved in some of the most important projects, in regard to: privatisation, investment projects, negotiation and signing of commercial contracts and public/private partnership contracts.

Privatisation: B&A provide assistance with most issues regarding the privatisation and postprivatisation processes.

Real estate, construction and utilities: B&A assists foreign and Romanian companies in purchasing properties in Romania, securing mortgage credits, laying claims to real estate, obtaining ownership documents and in representation before law courts.

Corporate and commercial: B&A provides assistance in the establishment and registration of trading companies, associations and foundations, as well as of their branches/subsidiaries, the authorisation of economic activities, the amendment of deeds of incorporation, the registration of entries with the trade register and other competent public authorities, mergers, dissolutions and acquisitions of equity interests.

Fiscal: consultancy and assistance in matters related to the application of tax legislation, the avoidance of double taxation, the obtainment of facilities from the competent authorities, the contesting of debentures, representation before the law courts and the competent authorities, such as the Ministry of Public Finance, the Tax Police and customs authorities.

Litigation and arbitration: the representation of clients, trading companies or parties in civil matters, in litigations of all natures, before the first rank, recourse and supreme courts of justice, as well as before the national or international courts of arbitration, especially in commercial matters but also in financial, civil, contractual and criminal matters.

Intellectual property: the IP department deals with both literary and artistic property (copyright and ancillary author's rights), and the industrial property domain (trade marks, industrial designs and models, inventions, maskworks, know-how).

Capital markets: provides consultancy on and legal assistance in mergers of open companies, the reorganisation of the market institutions according to the new regulations, the establishment of brokerage and financial investment services companies, the regime of investment funds, the acquisition or loss of the status of publicly held companies, major corporate actions, privatisation through specific capital market operations and shareholders rights.

Transport: legal assistance provided to air transport companies, national companies and societies of railway transportation, negotiation and drawing up of various transport contracts and representation in transport litigation.

BUZESCU CA

22 EMANOIL PORUMBARU STREET
SECTOR 1
011421 BUCHAREST

Telephone: +40 21 222 4422
Fax: +40 21 222 2626
E-mail: pbuzescu@buzescu.com
Website: www.buzescu.com

Languages
Romanian, English, French, Spanish

Number of lawyers 16

Contact
Peter Buzescu

CATEGORIES OF WORK	
Corporate and commercial	Competition
M & A and privatisation	Intellectual property
Project finance	Real estate
Joint ventures	Employment
Oil, gas and utilities	Tax

THE FIRM

Buzescu Ca is a corporate law firm which specialises in advising foreign investors operating in Romania. The firm is focused on service and the delivery of pragmatic advice to its clients. Beyond the traditional scope of legal advice Buzescu Ca offers strategies and solutions for viable deals. The firm is managed by Peter Buzescu, who is qualified to practise law in both the US and Romania. After graduating from Bucharest University School of Law and New York University School of Law, Peter was admitted to the Romanian Bar in 1978, and the New York Bar in 1985. He has advised multinationals operating in Romania since 1988. Other members of the firm have studied in England, France, Spain and Switzerland. The firm has English and Romanian drafting capabilities and provides initial transaction documents in English for clients' comments and review. Buzescu Ca co-operates with the Kishinev-based law firm Gorea & Associates on advising multinationals interested in doing business in Moldova.

AREAS OF PRACTICE

Practice areas include: corporate and commercial mergers and acquisitions, privatisations, corporate restructurings, competition, employment, joint ventures, corporate recovery and insolvency, bank lending, acquisition finance, asset finance, equity finance, debt offerings, oil and gas, utilities, real estate, intellectual property.

The firm has been involved with cross-border transactions in several areas, including: negotiating (on behalf of several multinationals) the issuance of Opinion Letters by the Ministry of Finances regarding tax issues relating to oil concession and exploration; negotiating on behalf of foreign investors with the Ministry of Economy and Trade the deregulation of the price of 'newly' produced domestic gas; representing foreign investors and the Petroleum Exploration and Production Operators' Association at negotiations with the Ministry of Finances and the Ministry of Economy and Trade with regard to the amendments of the procurement legislation. The firm has advised some of the world's major companies on long-term land leases and land concessions for greenfield developments and purchase of real estate; advised several multinationals with regard to the restructuring of their subsidiaries in Romania, and sale of their participations in Romanian companies; and advised several international bank syndicates with regard to project finance and secured transactions matters. At the request of several international investment banking firms the firm conducted due diligence investigations of Romanian subsidiaries of multinational companies in connection with IPOs or notes offerings on foreign securities markets. The firm's lawyers advised several multinational companies on successful privatisations of state-owned companies; advised a multinational in connection with a successful bid for supplying trains for the Bucharest underground system; advised several multinationals in connection with tenders for major utilities projects; and successfully advised the subsidiaries of two multinationals investigated by the Competition Council with regard to their distribution practices. The team has also co-ordinated successful campaigns against counterfeiters of well-known trade marks. The firm's lawyers routinely advise clients on employment issues, collective and individual employment contracts, termination of employment contracts, collective dismissals, severance agreements, and notification of employee data transfer. Instead of promoting specialisation in distinct areas the firm encourages its members to develop expertise in multiple fields, which gives them the possibility to offer practical solutions attuned to the clients' business needs.

CHSH GILESCU & PARTENERII
CERHA HEMPEL SPIEGELFELD HLAWATI

STIRBEI VODA STREET 94
SECTOR 1
010118 BUCHAREST

Telephone: +40 21 311 1213
Fax: +40 21 314 2470
E-mail: office@gp-chsh.ro
Website: www.gp-chsh.at

Languages
English, German, Romanian

Other offices
Brussels, Budapest, Vienna

Number of lawyers 76
at this office 11

Contacts
Radu Gilescu, Ovidiu Văleanu,
Alfred Nemetschke, Konrad Koloseus

CATEGORIES OF WORK

Banking, securities and finance
Ovidiu Valeanu

Companies, corporations
Anca Parascan

Mergers and acquisitions
Ovidiu Valeanu

Arbitration and litigation
Vlad Cirjan

Commercial law and contracts
Vlad Cirjan

Information technology
Radu Gilescu

Real estate, construction and buildings
Radu Gilescu

Privatisation and telecommunications
Ovidiu Valeanu

Regulation, administrative and constitutional law
Vlad Cirjan

International and comparative law
Konrad Koloseus

CMS CAMERON McKENNA CRISTINA BRINZAN LAW OFFICE

BULEVARDUL AVIATORILOR 52
SUITE 5, SECTOR 1
BUCHAREST

Telephone: +40 21 316 7491
Fax: +40 21 316 7494/95
E-mail: info@cms-cmck.com
Website: www.law-now.com

Languages
English, French, German, Romanian

Other offices
Aberdeen, Bristol, Budapest, Edinburgh, Hong Kong, London, Moscow, Prague, Sofia, Warsaw

Number of lawyers 587
at this office 11

Contact
Cristina Brinzan

International grouping
CMS Cameron McKenna is a member of CMS. CMS is the alliance of major European law firms providing clients with a full range of legal and tax services. CMS's activities are co-ordinated through EEIG, registered in Brussels.

CATEGORIES OF WORK

Privatisation
Cristina Brinzan, Dan Marez

Banking and international finance
Paul Stallebrass, Ana Radnev

Corporate and commercial
Cristina Brinzan, Loredana Ralea

Projects, utilities, infrastructure
Irina Petre, Helen Rodwell

Real estate
Cristina Brinzan, Dan Mares

Venture capital and M&A
Dan Mares, Ana Radnev

COSOVANU-MARCU ATTORNEYS-AT-LAW

19 DIMITRIE CANTEMIR BOULEVARD
040235 BUCHAREST

Telephone: +40 21 330 2167
Fax: +40 21 330 2167
E-mail: office@cosovanu-marcu.ro
Website: www.cosovanu-marcu.ro

Languages
English, French, Italian, Spanish

Number of lawyers 5

Contacts
Cornel Cosovanu, Ion Marcu

CATEGORIES OF WORK

Fraud and white-collar crime

Civil law – litigation and advice

Commercial property, real estate

Tax law – litigation and advice

D&B DAVID SI BAIAS

OPERA CENTER I, 6TH FLOOR
1-5 COSTACHE NEGRI STREET
BUCHAREST 5

Telephone: +40 21 202 8770
Fax: +40 21 202 8771
E-mail: sorin.david@david-baias.ro
Website: www.pwc.com/ro

Languages
English, French, German, Italian, Russian

Number of lawyers 24

Contacts
Sorin David (sorin.david@david-baias.ro), Flavius Baias (flavius.baias@david-baias.ro)

International groupings
Correspondent law firm of PricewaterhouseCoopers

CATEGORIES OF WORK

Banking and financing
Sorin David, Laura Lupuţi

Commercial and competition
Sorin David, Luiza Tomescu-Dinu

Consumer protection
Sorin David, Laura Lupuţi

Corporate services
Anda Rojanschi, Carmen Medar

Corporate structuring
Sorin David, Laura Lupuţi

Dispute resolution
Flavius Baias, Dan Dascălu

Employment and human resources
Dan Dascălu, Anda Rojanschi

Energy and natural resources
Anda Rojanschi

Intellectual property
Luiza Tomescu-Dinu

Mergers and acquisitions
Sorin David, Flavius Baias

Public procurement; pharmaceutical law
Luiza Tomescu, Livia Constantinescu

Real estate
Flavius Baias, Mădălina Fildan

Securities
Sorin David, Laura Lupuţi

Technology, media and communications
Luiza Tomescu-Dinu, Dan Dascălu

DANESCU, DANESCU & ASSOCIATES

35 ION LUCA CARAGIALE STREET
DISTRICT 2
020043 BUCHAREST

Telephone: +40 21 210 6555
Fax: +40 21 210 6566
E-mail: office@danescu.ro
Website: www.danescu.ro

Languages
English, French

Number of lawyers 15

Contact
Mrs Alina Danescu

CATEGORIES OF WORK

Corporate and commercial Corin Danescu, Alina Danescu	**Mergers and acquisitions** Alina Danescu, Cezar Dragomirescu
Dispute resolution Corin Danescu, Valentin Constantinof	**Competition and EU** Cezar Dragomirescu
Real estate and construction Octavian Raclaru, Oana Nasta	**Intellectual property** Cezar Dragomirescu
Infrastructure and project finance Octavian Raclaru	**Tax** Oana Nasta
Shipping and transport Oana Nasta	**Telecommunications** Octavian Raclaru
Banking and finance Alina Danescu, Oana Nasta	**Bankruptcy and insolvency** Corin Danescu, Valentin Constantinof
Capital markets Alina Danescu	**Property** Corin Danescu, Valentin Constantinof
Insurance, securities Octavian Raclaru, Alina Danescu	**Administrative** Oana Nasta
Labour and employment Octavian Raclaru, Anda Dumitrescu	**Contracts** Corin Danescu, Oana Nasta

THE FIRM

Danescu, Danescu & Associates has developed substantially from the individual practice founded in 1983 by Costea Corin Danescu. Since its establishment, the firm has expanded in size and areas of specialisation, remaining committed to its core values of dignity, style and stability.

Today, the firm is structured into two departments – litigation and legal consultancy – permanently supported by a qualified administrative team. The lawyers in each department work closely together in practice groups to provide full-service legal advice in all major areas of practice. Each legal project is managed by a multi-disciplinary team of specialists, purposely selected to meet the main objectives of the client, under the direct supervision of one of the firm's partners.

Striving to build long-term relationships with its clients, the firm provides practical solutions by combining the solid educational background and expertise of its lawyers with a thorough understanding of the permanently-changing Romanian legislative environment.

AREAS OF PRACTICE

The firm advises both Romanian and international clients, ranging from real estate developers, civil and industrial construction groups, transport carriers, banks and financial institutions, investment funds, insurance companies, IT and telecommunications companies, mass media and publishing groups, advertising agencies, manufacturers, bottlers, retailers, and so on, to government bodies and private individuals.

With a particular focus on corporate and commercial work, the firm provides a comprehensive range of legal services across all areas of practice. The extensive experience of its lawyers ensures that the firm is highly specialised in the following areas.

Corporate and commercial: solid expertise in advising and representing corporate clients on a wide range of issues relating to the incorporation, conduct, dissolution/liquidation, merger or spin-off of companies.

Dispute resolution: the firm has a strong practice in this field and resolves conflicts through negotiation, mediation, arbitration or litigation. Dispute resolution is provided as an integral part of the service across all practice areas.

Real estate and construction: the extensive experience of lawyers in this areas allows the firm to provide complete legal advice to the client on the legal management of the entire beneficiary-contractor-designer-engineer-consultants structure, from the market research and assessment of the ownership rights, to capitalisation of the investment.

Public-private partnership (PPP): the firm has solid practical experience in dealing with the fairly specialised areas of PPP projects, especially in projects related to the rehabilitation and/or construction of domestic traffic infrastructure – highways and national roads.

Competition and EU: providing legal advice and drafting specific documentation regarding the economical outcomes of mergers and acquisitions, exclusive distribution contracts, and individual or main cases of exemption for specific contracts within the state aid domain.

Labour and employment: advising employers and employees on labour-related matters (including drafting collective bargaining agreements; developing human resources policies and strategies; execution, amendment and termination of individual labour agreements; disciplinary aspects, and so on).

Fiscal law: providing clients with advice for the purpose of avoiding negative effects that may occur as a result of misinterpreting legislation, reducing the fiscal obligations; of avoiding double taxation; defending the rights infringed by authorities.

For more details, please visit www.danescu.ro

DELEANU VASILE – LAWYERS

2 MARESAL PILSUDSKI
JOSEF ENTR.
BUCHAREST 1

Telephone: +40 21 211 0414
Fax: +40 21 201 6684
E-mail: office@deleanu.ro
Website: www.deleanu.ro

Languages
English, French, Italian, Spanish

Number of lawyers 18

CATEGORIES OF WORK

Bankruptcy	**Banking and finance**
Debt recovery	**Civil law**
Corporate and commercial law	**Tax law**
Privatisation	**Litigation**
Intellectual property	

THE FIRM

Deleanu Vasile – Lawyers was established in June 1996, with a small staff, a lawyer and several assistants. In time, as the firm's activities, client base and success have increased, the firm has attracted new partners and lawyers.

Although the firm has a solid domestic client base, it has also been quick to recognise the increasing importance and influence of the European Union.

Taking a flexible approach, the firm deals positively with the issues its clients face and enjoys being part of a client's business team, helping to overcome obstacles, accelerating progress and offering effective, economic solutions.

AREAS OF PRACTICE

The main areas of practice are those listed above, from which the emphasis is mainly on corporate and commercial law, and insolvency and debt recovery.

In time, the firm's field of activities has expanded, adapting to the market's and the clients' requests – trade companies with both state (public) and private investments, Romanian and/or foreign.

One major area of work involves consulting on EU-related issues. Given Romania's recent economic adaptation to the EU market, privatisation has been one of the firm's most important forms of activity.

In its extensive international practice, an important aspect is providing advice to foreign clients who wish to establish businesses in Romania, including the formation of companies and the relevant taxation legislation. Given its range of clients, the firm has represented several foreign companies in Romania in litigation as well as in arbitration proceedings.

Other important work areas include providing advice on tax regulations and on contractual negotiations.

Since 2004, Deleanu Vasile – Lawyers has been a member of Warwick Legal Network (formerly known as Moore Stephens Legal Network) an international association of independent law firms.

A brochure providing more information is available on request.

FRUTH OPRISAN, POPESCU & ASOCIATII

3 CORNELIU COPOSU BVD
BLOCK 101, ENTRANCE 3
4TH FLOOR, APT 50
SECTOR 3
030601 BUCHAREST

Telephone: +40 21 323 8341
Fax: +40 21 323 8345
E-mail: fruth@dnt.ro

Languages
English, French, Italian

Number of lawyers 9

Contact
Despina Fruth Oprisan

CATEGORIES OF WORK

Commercial and company
Despina Fruth Oprisan, Alexandra Croitoru

Mergers and acquisition
Despina Fruth Oprisan, Alexandra Croitoru

Intellectual property
Romeo Popescu, Alexandra Croitoru

Litigation
Romeo Popescu, Delia Popescu

Arbitration
Dragos Dumitru

Real estate
Romeo Popescu, Dragos Dumitru

IT, media and entertainment
Despina Fruth Oprisan, Romeo Popescu

Labour and social security law
Dragos Dumitru, Liliana Popa

Public procurement
Romeo Popescu, Liliana Popa

Public-private partnerships
Despina Fruth Oprisan, Liliana Popa

Environment
Despina Fruth Oprisan, Liliana Popa

Competition
Dragos Dumitru

Banking and finance
Despina Fruth Oprisan, Dragos Dumitru

Insurance
Romeo Popescu, Alexandra Croitoru

Privatisation
Despina Fruth Oprisan, Liliana Popa

GIDE LOYRETTE NOUEL

10-12 STRADA MAIOR SONTU
SECTOR 1
BUCHAREST

Telephone: +40 21 223 0310
Fax: +40 21 223 0342
E-mail: gln.bucharest@gide.com
Website: www.gide.com

Other offices
Algiers, Beijing, Belgrade, Brussels, Budapest, Casablanca, Hanoi, Istanbul, London, Moscow, New York, Paris, Prague, Riyadh, Shanghai, Tunis, Warsaw

Number of lawyers 586
at this office 18

Contact
Bruno Leroy (leroyb@gide.com)

CATEGORIES OF WORK

Mergers and acquisitions

Privatisation

Company law

Competition and merger control

State aid

Distribution law

Consumer law

Employment law

Real estate transactions and financing

Banking and finance

Project finance

Concessions

Intellectual property

Arbitration and litigation

GRUIA DUFAUT LAW FIRM

28 HRISTO BOTEV BOULEVARD
3RD DEPARTMENT
030237 BUCHAREST

Telephone: +40 21 305 5757
Fax: +40 21 305 5758
E-mail: bucarest@dgd-conseil.com

Languages
English, French, German, Italian, Romanian

Other offices
Paris

Number of lawyers 15
at this office 14

CATEGORIES OF WORK

Company and commercial	**Contracts**
Privatisation	**Real estate**
Mergers and acquisitions	**Tax and finance**
Competition law	**Intellectual property**
Labour and employment	**Litigation and arbitration**
Capital markets and securities	

THE FIRM

The firm is a thriving French-based law firm with a strong reputation in its field, providing services to Romanian and foreign natural/legal entities, with significant expertise in Romanian law that has built up over more than 12 years. The firm was founded by Dana Gruia Dufaut, a member of both the Paris and Bucharest Bar Associations, and is one of the few local law firms providing Romanian and French legal advice and assistance.

Since 1996, the head of the firm, Dana Gruia Dufaut, has been adviser to the French Embassy in Romania, and she has filled the position of Counsel for the Foreign Trade of France (Conseiller du Commerce Extérieur de la France) since 1998. She relies on qualified professionals with extensive experience in different branches of law, enabling the firm to exceed clients' expectations by providing cost-efficient business solutions, timely and clear advice, as well as aggressive litigation and arbitration services.

The 15-lawyer team is supported by a dynamic and qualified staff of legal advisers, consultants, certified accountants, translators and administrative personnel fluent in French, English and Italian.

AREAS OF PRACTICE

The firm's team provides a full range of legal advice and assistance to both Romanian and foreign companies.

Commercial and corporate: including setting up of new companies; implementing joint ventures; shares sale-purchase transactions; assistance in shares sale-purchase transactions; banking and insolvency proceedings and other practical aspects of doing business in Romania; drafting commercial contracts and all legal documentation; negotiations with business partners, local bodies and ministries involved etc.

Privatisation: including carrying out due diligence assignments for acquisition and privatisation projects; negotiation with different governmental bodies and administrative authorities; bid preparation; negotiating and drafting shares sale-purchase agreements and closing; legal advice on post-control privatisation.

Tax and finance: including double taxation treatment; VAT regulation; withholding taxes and company taxation; tax incentives; transfer pricing; foreign exchange control and customs regulation; different forms of credit and financing.

Competition: including analysis of mergers, acquisitions and joint venture agreements; preparation and registration with the Romanian Competition Council of notifications of economic concentrations; drafting of distribution, supply, franchising, technology and other commercial agreements (and where appropriate, their notification to competent authorities); advice on different aspects of the Romanian competition law.

Capital markets: including legal advice and assistance on mandatory withdrawal of public companies; takeover for the purpose of closing and public purchase offering; admission of companies' shares for trading on a regulated market; legal advice and assistance to public companies to comply with their specific obligations under Romanian capital market legislation; representation of public companies before regulatory/supervisory authorities of the regulated market.

Labour and employment: including negotiation, drafting and registration of individual/collective employment agreements; negotiation with trade unions and employees' representatives; assistance and representation in individual/collective labour conflicts; confidentiality and non-competition agreements; assistance of employers in HR-related issues.

Real estate: including negotiation and drafting of option, sale-purchase and construction agreements; concessions; mortgages; property vindication and nationalised property; obtaining relevant permits and authorisations.

Litigation and arbitration: representation before justice and arbitration courts in a wide range of commercial, fiscal, administrative and civil matters.

HAARMANN HEMMELRATH

STRADA EMANOIL PORUMBARU 77
SECTOR 1
011428 BUCHAREST

Telephone: +40 21 260 0710
Fax: +40 21 260 0711
E-mail:
bucharest@haarmannhemmelrath.com
Website:
www.haarmannhemmelrath.com

Languages
English, French, German, Romanian

Other offices
Bielefeld, Budapest, Düsseldorf, Frankfurt, Hamburg, Leipzig, Moscow, Munich, Paris, Prague, Shanghai, Warsaw

Number of lawyers 226

CATEGORIES OF WORK

Mergers and acquisitions
Catalin Grigorescu

Antitrust and competition law
Catalin Grigorescu, Adriana Duncea

Banking and finance
Catalin Grigorescu, Anca Grigorescu

Corporate
Catalin Grigorescu, Anca Grigorescu

Finance, leasing
Catalin Grigorescu

Privatisation
Adriana Duncea, Anca Grigorescu

Public procurement
Adriana Duncea

Labour law
Anca Grigorescu

Litigation and arbitration
Adriana Duncea

Telecommunications
Anca Grigorescu

Real estate and commercial property
Anca Grigorescu, Adriana Duncea

Tax compliance and tax structuring
Gabriel Sincu

Structuring of inward investments (foreign, domestic)
Anca Grigorescu

Project finance
Catalin Grigorescu

Auditing services
Bogdan Ion, Hubertus Eichler

Customs issues

Financial and advisory services
Hubertus Eichler, Bogdan Ion

LINKLATERS MICULITI MIHAI & ASOCIATII SCA

8 NICOLAE IORGA
SECTOR 1
010434 BUCHAREST

Telephone: +40 21 307 1500
Fax: +40 21 307 1555
Website: www.linklaters.com

Languages
All commercial and local languages in the countries where Linklaters operates

Other offices
Amsterdam, Antwerp, Bangkok, Beijing, Berlin, Bratislava, Brussels, Budapest, Cologne, Dubai, Frankfurt am Main, Hong Kong, Lisbon, London, Luxembourg, Madrid, Milan, Moscow, Munich, New York, Paris, Prague, Rome, São Paulo, Shanghai, Singapore, Stockholm, Tokyo, Warsaw

Number of lawyers 2,000 worldwide

Contact
Michael Tétreault Schilling

CATEGORIES OF WORK

Corporate, M&A
Michael Tétreault Schilling, Theodore H Cominos

Banking and finance, capital markets
Michael Tétreault Schilling (capital markets), Ioan Miculiti (banking), Adrian Catalin Bulboaca (banking)

Energy and natural resources
Simona Delia Pachiu

Technology, media and telecommunications
Simona Delia Pachiu, Theodore H Cominos

Intellectual property
Lucian Mihai

Litigation and arbitration
Lucian Mihai

Real estate
Rodica Constantinovici

Antitrust and EU law
Lucian Bondoc

Tax
Michael Tétreault Schilling, Alexandra Florea

Balkan practice
Michael Tétreault Schilling, Theodore H Cominos

MUSAT & ASOCIATII

43 AVIATORILOR BOULEVARD
1ST DISTRICT
011853 BUCHAREST

Telephone: +40 21 202 5900
Fax: +40 21 223 3957
E-mail: general@musat.ro
Website: www.musat.ro

Languages
English, French, German, Romanian

Number of lawyers 65

Contacts
Gheorghe Musat (managing partner), Catalin Baiculescu, Ion Dragne, Gelu-Titus Maravela, Mona Musat, Ana-Maria Placintescu, Miruna Suciu, Luminita Ivanciu (partners)

Member
Terralex

CATEGORIES OF WORK

Corporate and commercial
Gheorghe Musat, Mona Musat

M&A and privatisations
Gheorghe Musat, Catalin Baiculescu

Banking and finance
Gheorghe Musat, Catalin Baiculescu

Energy and natural resources
Gheorghe Musat, Luminita Ivanciu

IT and communications
Catalin Baiculescu

Competition
Gheorghe Musat, Catalin Baiculescu

Property and construction
Gelu-Titus Maravela, Luminita Ivanciu

Intellectual property
Ion Dragne

Aviation and aerospace
Catalin Baiculescu

Shipping and transport
Mona Musat, Ana-Maria Placintescu

Insurance
Catalin Baiculescu

Employment and pensions
Ana-Maria Placintescu, Miruna Suciu

Capital markets and securities
Gelu Maravela, Miruna Suciu

Taxation
Ana-Maria Placintescu

Litigation
Gheorghe Musat, Ion Dragne

Regulatory legal services
Catalin Baiculescu, Mona Musat

Advertising
Mona Musat, Ana-Maria Placintescu

Technical assistance
Gheorghe Musat, Catalin Baiculescu

THE FIRM

Musat & Asociatii's name stands for extensive expertise in business matters. The firm is reputed for its commercial approach to transactions and its profound understanding of the client's commercial goals. The firm currently has 65 lawyers, all fully admitted to the practice, as well as a further 36 non-legal staff. Over the years, Musat & Asociatii has represented international and domestic clients in all kinds of legal transactions and has gained its reputation by specialisation, efficiency and professional ethics. It is a member of the Romanian Bar Association and has close contacts and alliances with some of the most prestigious law firms in the European Union and the US, enabling the provision of a fully global client service. The firm is the exclusive Romanian representative in Terralex, the worldwide network of independent law firms.

AREAS OF PRACTICE

The firm takes pride in its high-profile portfolio of clients, including international and national private and public companies, operating in the main areas of commerce and industry, individual sectors, government authorities and agencies, major banks, financial institutions and investment funds.

A selective list of representative projects and mandates is available upon request (e-mail general@musat.ro).

Mergers and acquisitions/privatisations: the firm gathered important expertise in privatisations and an extensive M&A expertise in the private sector as many foreign and Romanian companies move to consolidate and expand their operations as the economy diversifies and develops.

Banking and finance: this is one of the firm's main areas of practice. The firm has a substantial practice in the regulatory and advisory field, spanning from the acquisition of banks to international syndicated loans and other facility arrangements to advising on all forms of credit agreements and restructuring. The firm has acted for high-profile international and domestic banks, creditors and debtors and has extensive experience in bilateral and syndicated loans and securitisations.

Energy and natural resources: the firm has an extensive experience that extends across the energy spectrum (gas, oil, both upstream and downstream, electricity and water energy) and had also advised on the Romanian regulatory regime, including the legislative changes necessary for the liberalisation of the gas market.

Corporate/commercial: the firm has advised many international entities on negotiating complex secured and unsecured transactions spanning every form of business. In the corporate area the firm's work is diverse and ranges from incorporations, share capital issues, directors' duties and liabilites, corporate governance issues and the protection of minority shareholders.

Communications and information technology: the firm has represented global and local clients in the communications and information technology field and has advised on all areas of communications, broadcasting, environment, e-commerce and internet providing.

Property and construction: the firm has substantial experience in assisting clients on real estate acquisitions for property development and sales and has advised on greenfield projects from hotels to residential and commercial constructions. The firm also advises on lease agreements and large projects relating to concession of public property.

Litigation: the firm has a broad-based litigation department and its lawyers' experience extends from representation in the lower courts to the Surpeme Court of Justice, as well as in the Constitutional Court and the Court of Audits, to international and domestic arbitration (ICSID, ICC and UNCITRAL procedures).

McGREGOR & PARTNERS S.C.A.
(FORMERLY POPESCU & ASOCIATII S.C.P.A.)

**5TH FLOOR
UNION INTERNATIONAL CENTRE
STR ION CÂMPINEANU 11
010031 BUCHAREST**

Telephone: +40 21 312 2425
Fax: +40 21 312 1646
E-mail: neil.mcgregor@romlegal.com
Website: www.romlegal.com

Languages
Bulgarian, English, French, German, Romanian, Russian

Other offices
Sofia

Number of lawyers 11
at this office 6

Contacts
Neil McGregor (managing partner), Boiana Berchi, Julian Spassov

International groupings
McGregor & Partners S.C.A. maintains an association with Stephenson Harwood, London

CATEGORIES OF WORK

Banking, finance and capital markets
Neil McGregor, Arina Dobrescu

Corporate, commercial and trade
Neil McGregor, Arina Dobrescu

Litigation and dispute resolution
Boiana Berchi, Julian Spassov

Real estate and development
Boiana Berchi, Arina Dobrescu

Information technology, IP, telecommunications and media
Neil McGregor, Julian Spassov

Competition and other regulatory law
Neil McGregor, Arina Dobrescu

Insurance
Neil McGregor, Julian Spassov

Taxation
Julian Spassov, Ioana Enescu

Power, energy, utilities and natural resources
Neil McGregor, Arina Dobrescu

Mergers, acquisitions and privatisation
Neil McGregor, Julian Spassov

Project finance
Neil McGregor, Julian Spassov

Maritime, aviation and transport
Boiana Berchi, Arina Dobrescu

Labour law
Boiana Berchi, Arina Dobrescu

Insolvency
Boiana Berchi, Ioana Enescu

NEMOIANU & SALCIANU ATTORNEYS AT LAW

**CALEA SERBAN VODA NR 133
SECTOR 4
70517 BUCHAREST**

Telephone: +40 21 317 2266
Fax: +40 21 316 1177
Website: www.kpmg.ro

Languages
English, French, Romanian

Number of lawyers 25

CATEGORIES OF WORK

Corporate and commercial

Banking, finance and capital markets

Mergers and acquisitions

Privatisation and investment

Real estate

Energy and natural resources

Competition

Employment

Dispute resolution

Regulatory and compliance

Communications and technology

Intellectual property

Insurance

Infrastructure and public procurement

EU accession

Insolvency, restructuring and recovery

NESTOR NESTOR DICULESCU KINGSTON PETERSEN

BUCHAREST BUSINESS PARK
ENTRANCE A, 4TH FLOOR
1A BUCURESTI-PLOIESTI
NATIONAL ROAD, 1ST DISTRICT
013681 BUCHAREST

Telephone: +40 21 201 1200
Fax: +40 21 201 1210
E-mail: office@nnkp.ro
Website: www.nndkp.com

Languages
English, French

Other offices
Timisoara

Number of lawyers 60

Contacts
Ion Nestor (ion.nestor@nnkp.ro),
Manuela Nestor (manuela.nestor@nnkp.ro)

Member
The South East Europe Legal Group (SEE Legal); Lex Mundi; World Services Group (WSG)

CATEGORIES OF WORK

Banking
Manuela Nestor, Alina Radu

Competition
Carmen Peli, Ilinca Popovici

Consumer products
Alexandru Harsany, Carmen Peli

Corporate/project finance
Manuela Nestor, Adriana Gaspar

Dispute resolution
Ana Diculescu-Sova, Ion Nestor

Energy
Cristina Filip, Adina Chilim

General corporate
Andrew Kingston, Corina Ionescu

Insurance
Alina Radu, Gabriela Cacerea

IP/IT
Alexandru Harsany, Ana-Maria Serban

Labour and employment
Radu Culic, Mihaela Rosca

Mergers and acquisitions
Ion Nestor, Adriana Gaspar

Pharmaceuticals and healthcare
Ana-Maria Serban

Privatisation
Ion Nestor, Cristina Filip

Real estate
Mihaela Rosca, Francisc Eduard Peli

Securities and financial markets
Manuela Nestor, Adriana Gaspar

Telecoms, media and IT
Andrew Kingston, Adina Chilim

THE FIRM

Nestor Nestor Diculescu Kingston Petersen (NNDKP) is one of the largest and most respected law firms in Romania. The firm offers a full range of legal and advisory services. NNDKP assists clients to structure and negotiate corporate transactions, including privatisations, share sales and acquisitions, asset transactions, mergers, reorganisations and liquidations. Lawyers handle corporate formation, administration, financing, legal compliance and regulatory matters, legal due diligence and investigations. In addition to its capabilities in commercial areas, the firm has a premier dispute resolution practice, assisting clients with mediation, arbitration, and trial and appellate litigation.

AREAS OF PRACTICE

General corporate: NNDKP assists clients with entity incorporation, general maintenance, reorganisations of large companies, modifications to capital including capital increases and transfers of shares, as well as legal opinions on specific Romanian corporate law issues. Lawyers also prepare and assist during board, management committee and shareholder meetings.

Mergers and acquisitions: NNDKP advises financial institutions, insurance companies, utilities, telecom operators and technology companies. Expertise includes structuring of mergers, acquisitions, joint ventures, drafting and negotiation, and advice with respect to regulatory, securities competition and labour matters.

Privatisation: NNDKP participated in the first privatisations in Romania and have advised buyers, sellers, lenders and regulators in connection with many of the most important transactions across a range of industries, including banking, energy, steel, telecommunications and consumer products.

Securities and financial markets: NNDKP advises financial institutions, private equity and venture capital funds and the companies in which they invest. The firm's clients have closed many of the largest transactions in Romania involving project finance, revolving and term loans, trade finance, issuance of debt instruments, derivative transactions and public offerings with listings on Romanian and international exchanges.

Competition: NNDKP assists local and foreign companies to meet the requirements of local and international competition legislation. The firm represents clients before the Romanian Competition Council in connection with economic concentration, vertical and horizontal agreement claims, as well as allegations of abuse of dominant position.

Real estate: the firm assists developers, property owners, lenders and investors in connection with greenfield investments, construction agreements, financing and related securities, leasing, exit structuring and dispute resolution. They provide comprehensive advice concerning land use, zoning, title, regulatory and contractual issues.

Intellectual property: NNDKP lawyers and certified intellectual property counsellors advise on protection of IP portfolios, as well as acquisition, development, implementation, integration, use, licensing, financing, marketing, and sale of technology. They have particular expertise dealing with counterfeiting, trade mark infringement and patent litigation.

Dispute resolution: with more experienced litigation lawyers than any other firm in Romania, the dispute resolution group has earned an enviable reputation for delivering positive results. The firm represents clients in administrative proceedings, mediation, local and international arbitration, trial and appellate litigation, and labour matters.

Banking and finance: NNDKP provides legal services in syndicated and bilateral lending, acquisition finance and real estate financings. Banking clients include Romanian and international commercial and investment banks, international finance organisations and government institutions.

NNDKP also provides legal services in the following industry areas: energy, consumer products, telecoms, media and IT, pharmaceuticals and healthcare, and insurance.

NÖRR STIEFENHOFER LUTZ

STR GENERAL CONSTANTIN BUDISTEANU NR 28C, SECTOR 1
010775 BUCHAREST

Telephone: +40 21 312 5888
Fax: +40 21 312 5889
E-mail: info@noerr.com
Website: www.noerr.com

Languages
English, French, German, Italian, Romanian, Spanish

Other offices
Berlin, Bratislava, Budapest, Dresden, Düsseldorf, Frankfurt, Moscow, Munich, New York, Prague, Warsaw

Number of lawyers 256
(+ 66 tax advisers, public accountants and tax assistants)
at this office 22
(+ 6 tax advisers and tax assistants)

Contacts
Zsolt K Radnóczy, Dr Jörg K Menzer

CATEGORIES OF WORK

Banking and finance

Capital markets

Competition and intellectual property

Corporate and commercial law

Energy and environment

EU law

Labour and employment

Litigation and dispute resolution

Media, telecommunications and IT

Mergers and acquisitions

Real estate

Tax, financial and advisory services

PI PARTNERS

FORUM 2000 BUILDING
75 DR N STAICOVICI STREET
4TH FLOOR, SECTOR 5
050557 BUCHAREST

Telephone: +40 21 402 4100
Fax: +40 21 410 6987
E-mail: pi.partners@ro.ey.com
Website: www.eylaw.com/ro

Languages
English, French, German, Greek, Romanian

Other offices
Athens, Istanbul, Sofia, Thessaloniki

Number of lawyers 60
at this office 11

Contact
Eirinikos Platis (eirinikos.platis@ro.ey.com)

International groupings
Ernst & Young

CATEGORIES OF WORK

Banking, finance and securities
Eirinikos Platis

M&A and privatisations
Oana Munteanu

Commercial and corporate
Luana Constantinescu

Human capital services and labour
Cristina Bazilescu

Regulated markets
Raluca Mihalache

Real estate
Eirinikos Platis

PACHIU & ASSOCIATES

36 SPATARULUI STREET
SUITE NO 4
SECTOR 2
BUCHAREST

Telephone: +40 21 212 0023
Fax: +40 21 211 5636
E-mail: office@lp-legal.com
Website: www.lp-legal.com

Languages
English, French, German, Italian, Spanish

Number of lawyers 15

Member
International Bar Asscociation

CATEGORIES OF WORK

Asset finance
Laurenţiu Pachiu

Banking and finance
Andreea Oprisan, Ana-Maria Goga

Capital markets
Laurenţiu Pachiu, Marius Petroiu

Commercial property/real estate
Iulia Ispas, Cristina Bujoreanu

Competition
Andrei Dumitrache, Ramona Ianus

Corporate and commercial
Claudia Oprea-Popa, Alexandru Lefter

Dispute resolution and litigation
Claudia Oprea-Popa, Cristina Stamboli

Energy and natural resources
Claudia Oprea-Popa, Magda Zudor

Government and regulatory
Andreea Oprisan, Ana-Maria Goga

Information technology
Remus Radulescu, Andrei Dumitrache

Infrastructure and project finance
Laurenţiu Pachiu, Iulia Ispas

Insolvency/corporate restructuring
Cristina Stamboli, Magda Zudor

Intellectual property
Marius Petroiu, Claudia Oprea-Popa

Labour law
Andrea Oprisan, Cristina Bujoreanu

Media and entertainment
Marius Petroiu, Claudia Oprea-Popa

Mergers and acquisitions
Laurenţiu Pachiu

Tax
Marius Petroiu, Alexandru Lefter

Telecommunications
Claudia Oprea-Popa, Remus Radulescu

POPOVICI & ASOCIATII

6TH FLOOR
239 CALEA DOROBANTI
1ST DISTRICT
010567 BUCHAREST

Telephone: +40 21 317 7919
Fax: +40 21 317 8500
E-mail: office@popovici-partners.ro
Website: www.popovici-partners.ro

Languages
English, French, German, Italian, Spanish

Number of lawyers 35

CATEGORIES OF WORK

Corporate and commercial
Ernest Virgil Popovici, Florian Nitu

Mergers and acquisitions/ privatisation
Florian Nitu, Cristina Alexe

Real estate, projects/PPP
Ernest Virgil Popovici, Sorin Alazaroaie

Telecommunications and IT
Ernest Virgil Popovici, Florian Nitu

Banking finance and capital markets
Florian Nitu, Bogdan Stoica

Power, energy and natural resources
Irena Tudorie, Vlad Neascu

Insurance
Bogdan Stoica, Irena Tudorie

Employment
Sorin Alazaroaie, Vlad Neacsu

Competition
Cristina Alexe, Silviu Stoica

Intellectual property and copyright
Valentin Creata, Ioana Postelnicu

Litigation and arbitration
Ilinca Stefanescu, Ciprian Dontu

Regulatory
Sorin Alazaroaie, Valentin Creata

THE FIRM

Popovici & Asociatii is one of the first incorporated professional partnerships in Romania. The firm brings together strong local resources, with exceptional credentials, outstanding records and distinguished careers in law, business and academia. The team at the Bucharest office includes 35 lawyers and 20 other fee-earners, involved in a diverse range of complex transactions. Most partners and seniors have completed a double education at national and international schools of law and have handled legal assignments in collaboration with international law firms, located throughout the world.

The firm has acted as outside counsel to a wide spectrum of legal entities, including key players in major industries, financial institutions, public authorities and investment funds. During the last decade, significant investment and acquisition projects on the Romanian market have been managed and carried out with the legal assistance of Popovici & Asociatii.

AREAS OF PRACTICE

Popovici & Asociatii is divided into 12 major practice groups:

Corporate and commercial: the firm is recognised for its corporate and commercial expertise, acting for multinationals and local companies in virtually all legal matters in this field. Client portfolio includes several top ten companies in terms of turnover generated in Romania.

Real estate, projects/PPP: the firm acts for developers, investment funds, institutional financiers and public authorities. Recent deals include water-related utilities and road building projects worth €500m as well as the largest-ever Romanian PPP project worth €1bn.

Mergers and acquisitions/privatisation: M&A is one of the firm's key areas of expertise. It acts in public and private company mergers and acquisitions, corporate restructuring schemes within the entire range of industries and divestiture transactions. The overall value of the M&A/privatisation projects the firm is currently advising on exceeds €4bn.

Telecommunications and IT: acting for key players in the market, including telecom operators, investment funds, financiers and regulatory agencies, and in virtually all their related legal matters has enabled the firm to assist in the most significant deals in these areas to date.

Banking, finance and capital markets: Popovici & Asociatii has widespread knowledge in the field of banking and finance. In the capital markets field, the firm recently advised on the merger of the Bucharest Stock Exchange with Rasdaq, on the creation of the Investor's Compensation Fund and on various listing and de-listing projects.

Power, energy and natural resources: the firm acts for clients involved in electric generation and transmission, gas transportation, electric and gas marketing, oil and gas exploration, production and refining, including assisting in completing environmental impact reviews.

Insurance: Popovici & Asociatii has substantial experience of mergers and acquisitions involving insurance and reinsurance companies, permitting processes and other filling activities and regulatory advice.

Employment: the firm advises on all employment matters, having domestically pioneered outsourcing schemes and related standard service and employment agreements. Mediation of labour disputes and negotiation of collective agreements represent areas of legal excellence.

Competition: the firm has a strong competition counselling and litigation practice in all aspects of antitrust, unfair competition and trade regulations law. It assists within merger control procedures, during investigations or in relation to exclusive distribution or purchase schemes.

Intellectual property and copyright: the firm advises on a broad range of services covering litigation, advisory and commercial support in relation to trade marks. Also counsels on patent licensing and litigation.

Litigation and arbitration: the team has wide-ranging experience in most fields and of civil proceedings.

Regulatory: the firm's experience consists of specific advice in various fields ranging from competition to concession and from energy to gas law.

RADU TĂRĂCILĂ PĂDURARI RETEVOESCU SCA

12 DR PETRE HERESCU ST
050587 BUCHAREST 5

Telephone: +40 31 405 7777
Fax: +40 31 405 7778
E-mail: office@rtpr.ro
Website: www.rtpr.ro

Languages
English, French, Romanian, Russian

Number of lawyers 18

CATEGORIES OF WORK

Corporate, M&A and capital markets
Dragos Radu, Costin Tărăcilă

Privatisation
Dragos Radu, Costin Tărăcilă

Banking and finance
Victor Pădurari, Alexandru Retevoescu

Power, energy and natural resources
Costin Tărăcilă, Alexandru Retevoescu

Real estate
Dragos Radu, Victor Pădurari

Dispute resolution
Costin Tărăcilă, Alexandru Retevoescu

Project finance
Alexandru Retevoescu, Victor Pădurari

Competition
Victor Pădurari, Alexandru Retevoescu

IT and communications
Victor Pădurari, Alexandru Retevoescu

THE FIRM

Radu Tărăcilă Pădurari Retevoescu SCA (RTPR) was established in 2004 by a group of lawyers: Dragos Radu, Costin Tărăcilă, Victor Pădurari and Alexandru Retevoescu. The firm's recognised international experience was initially based on the founding partners' several years of experience in a prestigious international Magic Circle law firm.

RTPR advises on a broad spectrum of projects in Romania, offering services with a special emphasis on business law and mainly to international clients. Its lawyers take and maintain a commercial approach gained from significant experience in corporate and commercial law, major privatisations, capital markets, mergers and acquisitions, and finance.

The two main practice areas of the firm are corporate and commercial (which fall mainly under the co-ordination of Dragos and Costin) and banking and finance (which fall mainly under the leadership of Victor and Alexandru). The other strong practice areas of the firm are real estate, privatisation, and power, energy and natural resources.

AREAS OF PRACTICE

RTPR provides a full service for all the legal problems that an international business client can encounter.

Corporate and commercial is one of RTPR's core practice areas. The firm's lawyers provide expert advice in all industry sectors, and the mandates frequently have a cross-border component. The firm's lawyers also have good expertise in the formation and acquisition of businesses and in advising on licensing requirements and regulatory compliance. They have gained important experience drafting and negotiating various types of commercial agreements such as construction agreements, product supply agreements, distribution agreements, and service agreements.

Banking and finance: the firm has solid experience advising clients on banking and finance activities. The firm advised on the issuance of public debt (both at the national and local government levels), secured transactions and secured lending, drafting financial agreements and conflicts of law-related matters. In 2005 RTPR advised in relation to the first Eurobond issue by a Romanian municipality.

Privatisation: the firm has been involved in some of the largest privatisations in Romania in 2005, one of them considered to be amongst the largest and highest profile in CEE. The firm's assistance includes carrying out due diligence, negotiation with different governmental bodies and administrative authorities, bid preparation, negotiating and drafting share sale-purchase agreements, and post-privatisation issues.

Real estate: the firm has been involved in some of the largest real estate development, investment transactions and infrastructure projects in Romania. It has also acted for the financing parties in relation to loans granted to real estate developers, as well as in relation to relevant security packages. The firm has the experience and expertise to advise on the entire range of real estate issues arising from corporate, banking and project/infrastructure transactions.

Power, energy and natural resources: the firm has advised on regulatory matters relating to the electricity generation and distribution regulatory framework, in the context of the privatisation of three of Romania's largest thermal energy power complexes and various electricity distribution companies. Lawyers at the firm have extensive experience advising clients on regulatory matters and on the EU regulations to be implemented in relation to various sectors such as electricity, oil, natural gas and mining.

RUBIN MEYER DORU & TRANDAFIR, SPCA

IN ASSOCIATION WITH HERZFELD & RUBIN, P.C.

7 PUTUL CU PLOPI STR
SECTOR 1
010177 BUCHAREST

Telephone: +40 21 311 1460
Fax: +40 21 311 1465
E-mail: office@hr.ro
Website: www.hr.ro

Languages
English, French, Italian, Spanish

Other offices
New York, Tel Aviv

Number of lawyers 200
at this office 15

Member
Romanian-American Chamber of Commerce

CATEGORIES OF WORK

Banking and finance
Sergiu Doru, Dana Radulescu

Commercial and company law
Anthony Raftopol, Dana Radulescu

EU and competition law
Corin Trandafir, Roxana Negutu

Mergers and acquisitions
Anthony Raftopol, Corin Trandafir

Securities
Sergiu Doru, Corin Trandafir

Corporate finance
Sergiu Doru, Dana Radulescu

Capital markets
Sergiu Doru, Razvan Popa

Arbitration
Corin Trandafir, Sergiu Doru

Litigation
Sergiu Doru, Lia-Doru Trandafir

Real estate
Lia-Doru Trandafir, Sergiu Doru

Intellectual property
Corin Trandafir, Anthony Raftopol

Construction
Sergiu Doru, Lia-Doru Trandafir

Labour law
Lia-Doru Trandafir, Dana Radulescu

Privatisation
Corin Trandafir, Sergiu Doru

Tax
Sergiu Doru, Razvan Popa

Insurance
Sergiu Doru, Corin Trandafir

Infrastructure and project finance
Corin Trandafir, Anthony Raftopol

Telecommunications
Sergiu Doru, Corin Trandafir

THE FIRM

From its headquarters on New York City's famous Wall Street, Herzfeld & Rubin, P.C. (H&R) has enjoyed a reputation as one of America's leading legal specialists in European business for over 50 years. The attorneys that make up H&R's affiliated Bucharest-based office, known in Romania as Rubin Meyer Doru & Trandsafir, Spca (RMDT), have been working with H&R since 1993 for the purpose of developing an international practice, based in Romania, but designed to capitalise on growth opportunities throughout the region. This team has been joined by another affiliated law firm, Balter, Guth, Aloni & Co (BGA), which is based in Tel Aviv and is one of Israel's largest law firms.

In light of more numerous and complex business transactions in Romania and throughout the Balkans, increased investment interest has further highlighted the need for firms such as H&R to bridge the gap between East and West. Through its international team of Romanian, US and Israeli attorneys, the firm offers sage and timely advice, utilising international standards, to provide value to its clients' business endeavours throughout the Balkans, especially in Romania.

AREAS OF PRACTICE

RMDT provides a wide range of legal services for investors looking to invest in south-eastern Europe. RMDT's attorneys structure some of the largest and most complex multinational corporate, real estate and project finance transactions, while also providing precise and valuable counsel to newly emerging regional and national companies. While a good portion of the firm's practice involves advising large, multinational firms, RMDT also represents smaller businesses looking for assistance in setting up operations in Romania and the region for the first time, or others who require counsel to run existing operations on a day-to-day basis.

On the corporate side, RMDT's attorneys cover virtually all business matters, including M&A, securities, joint ventures, privatisations, project and structured finance, and corporate governance. The firm's experience in banking and financial matters has been acquired through years of working as counsel to some of the world's largest banks with offices in Romania.

The firm's real estate practice handles transactions of all sizes and complexities, whether it is for a local client wishing to purchase a piece of property, or for a multinational corporation involved in a multi-asset transaction spanning various states and foreign jurisdictions. As always, the firm's real estate attorneys have seamless connections to other practice groups and readily rely upon its tax, employment, corporate and international attorneys. In the representation of both foreign and domestic clients, the firm's real estate attorneys have participated in various acquisitions, dispositions, financings, work-outs and restructurings, developments, foreign multi-tiered investments, sale-leasebacks, and all forms of leasing arrangements involving commercial, retail and residential real estate.

Other important work areas include labour law (where the firm advises its clients on labour law matters arising out of a privatisation transaction, as well as post-privatisation restructurings), commercial litigation, intellectual property, tax and government procurement matters.

For further information, please visit www.hr.ro, or contact office@hr.ro for an electronic copy of the firm's brochure.

SCHÖNHERR

PIATA ROMANA 8
010375 BUCHAREST

Telephone: +40 21 319 6790
Fax: +40 21 319 6791
E-mail: office@schoenherr.ro
Website: www.schoenherr.at

Languages
Romanian, German, English, French

Other offices
Belgrade, Brussels, Kyiv Ljubljana, Sofia, Vienna
Zagreb (co-operation office)

Number of lawyers 130
at this office 23

Contacts
Christoph Lindinger
(ch.lindinger@schoenherr.at),
Markus Piuk (m.piuk@schoenherr.at),
Roxana Gologan, Sebastian Gutiu, Matei Florea,
Mihai Radulescu

CATEGORIES OF WORK

International and Romanian practice

International contracts and foreign investment

Banking securities and finance

Project finance

M&A

Privatisations

Public private partnership

Real estate and commercial property

EU law

Competition

SOVA & PARTNERS

19 LOUIS BLANK STREET
SECTOR 1
BUCHAREST

Telephone: +40 31 100 1126
Fax: +40 31 100 1129
E-mail: office@sova-avocati.ro
Website: www.sova-avocati.ro

Languages
English, French, German, Portuguese, Romanian, Russian, Spanish

Number of lawyers 35

CATEGORIES OF WORK

Banking and finance
Dan Sova

Intellectual property
Roxana Eftimie

Tax
Dan Sova

Litigation and abitration
Georgiana Panait

Corporate and commercial
Eugen Pop

Insolvency/corporate restructuring
Irina Marin

Competition
Roxana Eftimie

Energy and natural resources
Bogdan Iacob

Mergers and acquisitions
Bogdan Iacob

Real estate and construction
Roxana Eftimie

Privatisation
Bogdan Iacob

Environment
Eugen Pop

Telecoms, media and IT
Roxana Eftimie

Capital markets and securities
Eugen Pop

THE FIRM

Sova & Partners was founded in 1997 by Mr Dan Sova; it has an unparalleled commitment to excellence and its priority is providing the highest quality service to clients. Since it was founded, Sova & Partners has experienced consistent and dynamic growth and has expanded to cover a range of practices by keeping in line with the latest business trends and developments in the law. The firm now comprises 35 lawyers and a total staff of 44.

The firm has built an integrated, multidisciplinary, business-orientated culture through its entrepreneurial, quality-conscious and partnership-orientated efforts. Sova & Partners has in its portfolio a diverse group of clients, including Romanian and foreign firms and corporations. Furthermore, the firm provides assistance to government agencies and public institutions and to individuals who need high-quality professional advice.

Solid analysis, based on careful examination of all the legal and economic issues, represents the starting point of all of Sova and Partner's activities. The firm's determination to deliver results and expand its clients' opportunities serves as its guiding principle.

Sova & Partners is consistently rated as one of the top national Romanian firms, with strong contracts and a well-defined market position. The firm has a solid network of domestic and international law offices with whom it co-operates to accomplish its clients' goals expeditiously.

AREAS OF PRACTICE

Sova & Partners provides multidisciplinary legal expertise in various sectors, including for industrial, trading and services companies, banks, insurance companies, telecoms, oil and audio-visual media corporations.

The firm is rated as a market leader in tax, financial and banking legal counsel. Dan Sova is a member of the teaching staff at the law faculty of the University of Bucharest, having permanent tenure on Romanian and European tax law courses. Sova & Partners is also regarded as a legal expert in the fields of telecommunications, media and entertainment, intellectual property, competition and real estate.

The general corporate, M&A and privatisation practice provides professional, day-to-day legal advice to clients in ongoing corporate projects. The firm offers assistance in the restructuring of companies in the process of mergers, acquisitions, dissolutions and divisions.

The litigation and insolvency/corporate restructuring division of Sova & Partners currently handles corporate litigation and arbitration work. The firm represents clients before the courts of law or arbitration authorities in complex litigations involving commercial law, corporate law, copyright, tax and administrative law. Clients include major Romanian, as well as foreign companies and multinational corporations. It also provides counsel and assistance on judicial and voluntary insolvency issues, as a number of the firm's lawyers are qualified practitioners in restructuring and liquidation.

Sova & Partner's expertise also provides assistance in law-making projects by appointment of governmental agencies in such fields as telecommunications, EU law, co-operation, large and medium-sized enterprises.

STEFANICA, DUTU & PARTNERS

OPERA CENTER, 7TH FLOOR
1-5 COSTACHE NEGRI STREET
050552 BUCHAREST

Telephone: +40 21 412 00 62
Fax: +40 21 412 00 61
E-mail: avocati@scpa.ro
Website: www.stefanica-partners.ro

Languages
Romanian, English, French, Spanish, Turkish, German, Russian, Italian

Number of lawyers 35

Member
Romanian Bar Association; Romanian Lawyers Association; Trade Network; American Chamber of Commerce

CATEGORIES OF WORK

Commercial and company law
Florin Dutu, Bogdan Vîrjan

Banking, finance and insurance
Omar Asan

M&A and competition
Mihai Guia, Daniel Ştefănică

International and domestic taxation
Daniel Ştefănică, Alexandru Stănoiu

Securities and capital markets
Mihai Guia

Real estate and construction
Bogdan Vîrjan, Omar Asan

Public procurement, concessions, PPP
Ştefania Vieru, Octavian Banu

Intellectual property and media
Alexandru Stanoiu,
Eduard Făgărăşeanu

Arbitration and ICSID
Daniel Ştefănică, Florin Dutu

Litigation
Eduard Făgărăşeanu, Bogdan Vîrjan

Labour law
Florin Dutu, Octavian Banu

Public sector
Daniel Ştefănică, Eduard Făgărăşeanu

THE FIRM

Stefanica, Dutu & Partners was founded in 1997 by Daniel Stefanica and continues to grow and expand, distinguishing itself as an outstanding law firm, offering knowledgeable thinking and continuous improvement.

With 35 lawyers, the firm is one of the largest full-service law firms committed to implementing US and European standards of ethics, professionalism and vision in the practice of law in Romania. Enjoying a well-deserved reputation in the understanding of complex transactions, Stefanica, Dutu & Partners is regularly sought out by international clients. The firms lawyers are fluent in seven European languages.

The firm has extensive experience in corporate law and commercial transactions, with corporate litigation a particularly strong area of practice. Stefanica, Dutu & Partners prides itself on the complex international experience of some of its attorneys in project finance, M&A and in various cross-border transactions involving numerous jurisdictions. The firm has strong banking and tax law capabilities.

The team at Stefanica, Dutu & Partners enjoys challenging work and demanding and innovative clients. The firm knows that every client has different needs, and the firm forms teams appropriate to each situation, providing tailor-made solutions. Its partnership is united through common goals, working practices, and knowledge and information systems, so that it may easily co-ordinate work across borders, providing consistently high-quality services to its clients. From settlements to multiparty negotiations, and client representation in court, the teams react quickly and skilfully to any assignment, large or small and takes clients efficiently towards the achievement of their commercial goals.

AREAS OF PRACTICE

Stefanica, Dutu & Partners provides a wealth of corporate and business services to all types of corporate entities, private or publicly held, foreign or domestic, on a wide range of Romanian and international corporate matters. The firm has a large base of international and domestic clients and a track record of successful cross-border transactions. In addition to the customary areas of expertise, the firm's practice includes a strong legislative drafting and administrative disputes background. During the last year, the company has enriched its experience in banking finance and securities, and it has been substantially involved in the sectors of banking and capital markets, including legal services regarding the procedure for the listing of bonds on the International Stock Market.

The real estate team has structured and finalised transactions for various clients including contractors, developers and commercial landlords, and foreign and domestic investors. Its work includes the full spectrum of issues encountered in successfully closing transactions – negotiating, documenting and drafting contracts.

The firm's banking practice advises credit institutions, underwriters, arrangers and borrowers in financing domestic and cross-border transactions, leveraged buy-outs, and national and international extensions of credit. It has advised in debt and equity financing, public placements and syndicated loans, as well as in securing the optimal financing for clients from various sources.

Finance work covers the drafting of complex specialised agreements, designing and structuring national and international transactions, and customising concepts, all with a view to render value-added key input. The firm provides consistent legal advice in implementing and monitoring security documentation required for the successful completion of transactions in international law.

The firm has an outstanding insurance and reinsurance practice, acting in both disputes and a wide variety of claims. The firm's caseload includes all classes, of professional indemnity, bankers' bonds and financial institutions liability, product liability, directors' and officers' liability, mortgage indemnity, building construction and engineering, contingency risks, and prize insurance for television gameshows.

STOICA & ASOCIATII

OPERA CENTER II
STR DR N STAICOVICI NR 2, ETAJ 2
SECTOR 5
050558 BUCURESTI

Telephone: +40 21 402 0930
Fax: +40 21 402 0931
E-mail: sca@stoica-asociatii.ro
Website: www.stoica-asociatii.ro

Languages
English, French

Number of lawyers 22

CATEGORIES OF WORK

Corporate
Cristiana I Stoica

International contracts
Cristiana I Stoica, Valeriu Stoica

Privatisation
Cristiana I Stoica, Valeriu Stoica

International financing
Cristiana I Stoica, Valeriu Stoica

Foreign investments
Cristiana I Stoica, Valeriu Stoica

Tax
Cristiana I Stoica, Càtàlina Dicu

Mergers and acquisitions
Cristiana I Stoica, Valeriu Stoica

Administrative law
Valeriu Stoica

Competition
Valeriu Stoica

International public law
Cristiana I Stoica, Valeriu Stoica

Civil and commercial litigation
Cristiana I Stoica, Valeriu Stoica

Real estate
Càtàlina Dicu, Valeriu Stoica

Intellectual property
Valeriu Stoica, Càtàlina Dicu

Labour and social law
Cristiana I Stoica, Càtàlina Dicu

Capital markets
Cristiana I Stoica

Human rights
Cristiana I Stoica, Valeriu Stoica

Banking, financial and insurance
Valeriu Stoica

THE FIRM

STOICA & Asociatii was founded in 1995 by Cristiana I Stoica and Valeriu Stoica and has grown steadily since then to its current size of 22 lawyers, of which five are partners and the others are associates and assistants with a total staff of more than 30.

The founding partners have extensive experience of legal practice, co-ordinating the firm's professional activity into two main departments: advising and litigation.

STOICA & Asociatii has developed important professional relationships with lawyers across the Romanian Bar, enabling the firm to practice not only in Bucharest, but also in other jurisdictions within Romania. In the course of time, strong international links have been maintained with law firms from USA, Canada, United Kingdom, France, Italy, Spain, Austria, Belgium, Hungary, Germany, Portugal and others.

AREAS OF PRACTICE

The firm offers a full range of legal services to clients, including international companies, governmental agencies, commercial and financial institutions and private individuals.

The principal areas of work are: business law, international contracts, banking law, taxation, administrative law, competition, international public law, civil and commercial litigation, property law, intellectual property, labour and social law, and capital markets.

STOICA & Asociatii has experience with regard to the establishment and operation of companies, mergers, acquisitions, reorganisation and liquidation and international financing. The firm has specific expertise in taxation, advising on legal issues regarding the withholding of tax and VAT, income tax and various tax-related procedures. Labour law, administrative proceedings and financial law are a permanent activity of the firm, dedicated to both international and Romanian clients.

Finally, STOICA & Asociatii advises on legal matters arising from intellectual property, involving trade mark and copyright law with regard to contracts and registration procedures, especially in the broadcasting, video, entertainment and pharmaceutical industries.

Most of the lawyers also have strong involvement in legal publishing, in Romania and abroad.

Representative clients: Shell Brands International A.G. (Swiss); S.C. MOL RO COMERTS SRL; Shell Gas Romania SA; BRD-GSG; Whirlpool Europe; ING Bank NV; Nordic Investment Bank; BBC World Service; DHL International, Romania; Daimler Chrysler AG; SC Mittal Steel Galati SA; POL AM PACK SA (Poland); ABN-AMRO Bank (Romania).

ȚUCA ZBÂRCEA & ASOCIAȚII

4-8 SOSEAUA NICOLAE TITULESCU
SECTOR 1
011141 BUCHAREST

Telephone: +40 21 204 8890
Fax: +40 21 204 8899
E-mail: office@tuca.ro
Website: www.tuca.ro

Languages
English, French, German, Italian

Number of lawyers 40

Contacts
Florentin Țuca, Gabriel Zbârcea (managing partners), Ștefan Damian (deputy managing partner), Cornel Popa, Andreea Ionescu, Sorin Vlădescu, Dan Borbely, Răzvan Gheorghiu-Testa, Ciprian Dragomir, Robert Roșu (partners)

Member
Bucharest Bar Association

CATEGORIES OF WORK

Taxation
Răzvan Gheorghiu-Testa

Banking and finance
Andreea Ionescu

Capital markets and securities
Ștefan Damian, Cornel Popa

Competition
Ștefan Damian

Corporate and commercial
Florentin Țuca, Răzvan Gheorghiu-Testa

Electronic communications and IT
Sorin Vlădescu

Employment and pensions
Andreea Ionescu

Energy and natural resources
Gabriel Zbârcea, Sorin Vlădescu

Environmental law and permitting
Ciprian Dragomir

PPP, PFI and concessions
Florentin Țuca

Intellectual property
Ciprian Dragomir

Litigation and arbitration
Cornel Popa, Robert Roșu

Real estate
Gabriel Zbârcea, Dan Borbely

Mergers, acquisitions, privatisation
Gabriel Zbârcea, Ștefan Damian

THE FIRM

Țuca Zbârcea & Asociații is one of the major players in the Romanian legal services market. It was founded by eight partners, all of them former partners in a prestigious Romanian law firm. Currently, Țuca Zbârcea & Asociații's team numbers ten partners and over 40 lawyers, who have extensive experience earned in the premier league of the Romanian legal consultancy, as well as more than 20 non-legal staff. The firm's lawyers are 'veterans' in the Romanian legal consultancy business, as they have been active in this market since its emergence. Many of them have managed or have taken part in high-level transactions, both in the private and public sectors. Furthermore, over the past ten years, the firm's lawyers have developed close professional ties with leading law firms throughout the world, enabling them to become familiar with the professional practices of some of the finest minds in the world of legal advice and assistance. These accrued benefits are an integral part of what the firm has to offer its clients.

AREAS OF PRACTICE

Țuca Zbârcea & Asociații uses client-focused teams to serve both private clients and public authorities from many industries. The lawyers' combined expertise covers an extensive range of legal matters, with the aim of providing an integrated business law service.

Listed below are some of the most important deals in which the firm's lawyers have been involved or are currently involved:

Deutsche Bank: assistance with respect to the acquisition/privatisation of Banca Comerciala Romana (BCR), the largest Romanian bank.

Zentiva AS: assistance in connection with a US$200m transaction whereby Zentiva AS acquired Sicomed Bucuresti, one of the largest Romanian drugs producers, including the mandatory public offer on the Bucharest Stock Exchange Market.

Banca Monte dei Paschi di Siena: assistance in connection with the acquisition/privatisation of Casa de Economii si Consemnatiuni (CEC), the largest Romanian savings bank.

CEZ: assistance in connection with (1) the acquisition/privatisation of the largest Romanian electricity distribution subsidiary; (2) the privatisation process of two hydroelectric power plants; (3) the post-privatisation issues of Electrica Oltenia.

International bank: assistance in connection with a secured finance project of US$140m (bond issue).

International bank: assistance in connection with a project finance (8% share acquisition in Petrom, the national oil company).

European Bank for Reconstruction and Development: assistance in connection with a €110m loan granted to a leading family-owned wood panel producer for the financing of a greenfield particle board project in Suceava.

European Bank for Reconstruction and Development: assistance in connection with a €50m loan granted to a Romanian commercial bank for mortgage sub-lending.

Mittal Steel Company NV: assistance in connection with the clearance for the acquisition of the majority stake in Krivorizhsky Ore Mining Company and Steel Works 'Kryvorizhstal', a joint stock Ukrainian company.

Mittal Steel Holdings: assistance in connection with (1) a US$40m successful acquisition of Romportmet, one of the major shipping harbours for iron-ore in Romania; (2) the acquisition of Siderurgica SA Hunedoara, Petrotub SA Roman and Tepro SA Iasi; (3) the acquisition of Sidex, the largest Romanian steel producer.

Petrom SA: assistance during the investigation on the oil and oil products market and also in relation to the investigation regarding the possible abuse of a dominant position by Petrom SA.

STUDIO LEGALE SUTTI

2, UNIRII BLVD, BL 8A, 5TH FLOOR
SUITE 25, SECTOR 4
751012 BUCHAREST

Telephone: +40 21 337 0730
Fax: +40 21 337 3171
E-mail: maildesk@sutti.com
Website: www.sutti.com

Languages
Bulgarian, Croatian, English, French, German, Italian, Japanese, Portuguese, Romanian, Russian, Serbian, Spanish

Other offices
Belgrade, Genoa, London, Milan, Rome, Sofia, Tokyo, Zagreb

Contact
Hugo Vitzman

CATEGORIES OF WORK

Company, commercial law

Banking and finance

Mergers and acquisitions

Distribution, agency and franchising

Debt collection and insolvency

Commercial property law

Intellectual property

Patent and trade mark agency service

White-collar crime

EC, competition and antitrust law

IT and TLC law

Litigation and arbitration

Employment, labour law

Administrative law

Environmental law

VILAU & MITEL

50 AV PETRE CRETU STREET
1ST DISTRICT
012052 BUCHAREST

Telephone: +40 21 224 0052
Fax: +40 21 224 0508
E-mail: office@vilaumitel.ro
Website: www.vilaumitel.ro

Languages
English, French, Italian

Number of lawyers 20

International groupings
INTA

CATEGORIES OF WORK

Aviation and aerospace
Sorin Mitel, Iuliana Bobaru

Banking and finance
Dragos Vilau, Gabriela Anton

Capital markets
Gabriela Anton, Patricia Enache

Communication and IT
Madalina Paisa, Loredana Badea

Competition
Gabriela Anton, Patricia Enache

Corporate and commercial
Madalina Paisa, Gabriela Anton

Dispute resolution and litigation
Ionut Lupsa, Magda Dima

Employment and pensions
Sorin Mitel, Gabriela Anton

Energy, natural resources and utilities
Dragos Vilau, Iuliana Bobaru

Environment, planning and regulatory
Iuliana Bobaru, Laura Stanciu

Intellectual property
Dragos Vilau, Ionut Lupsa

Mergers and acquisitions
Dragos Vilau, Sorin Mitel

Public procurement, PPP and PFI
Sorin Mitel, Madalina Paisa

Real estate and construction
Iuliana Bobaru, Magda Dima

Insurance
Iuliana Bobaru

VOICU & FILIPESCU

UNION INTERNATIONAL CENTER II
26-28 STIRBEI VODA STREET
9TH FLOOR
010113 BUCHAREST 1

Telephone: +40 21 314 0200
Fax: +40 21 314 0290
E-mail: voicud@vf.ro
Website: www.voicufilipescu.ro

Languages
English, French, German, Italian, Portuguese, Spanish, Romanian, Russian

Number of lawyers 22

Contacts
Daniel Voicu, Mugur Filipescu

CATEGORIES OF WORK

Real estate, construction
Daniel Voicu, Marius Rimboaca

Competition
Daniel Voicu, Dan Ciupalá

Energy
Mugur Filipescu

Telecommunications
Mugur Filipescu, Daniel Voicu

Privatisation
Mugur Filipescu, Marta Popa

Banking, finance
Mugur Filipescu, Marta Popa

Corporate, mergers and acquisitions
Daniel Voicu, Mugur Filipescu

Insurance
Mugur Filipescu

Litigation
Daniel Costea

Intellectual property
Laurentiu Popescu

Employment
Marta Popa

THE FIRM

Voicu & Filipescu is a Romanian professional partnership established in 2001 following the acquisition of the Bucharest office of an international law firm. It has 22 lawyers and seven non-legal staff, including a fully dedicated team of two certified English-Romanian translators.

AREAS OF PRACTICE

The relevant experience of Voicu & Filipescu's lawyers covers the entire spectrum of specialised business law and advice to international and Romanian clients in connection with their investments in Romania.

Corporate, M&A: in 2005 the firm advised private (excluding privatisations) M&A transactions exceeding US$1bn in value from the total US$3.4bn at the national level. The firm's attorneys have advised significant foreign investors on all phases of mergers and acquisitions in the Romanian market, including due diligence of target companies, preparation of data rooms, drafting of all necessary transaction documents, negotiation of transaction terms, and post-acquisition/ merger integration issues. Representative transactions in which the firm's attorneys have been involved include the acquisition by the majority shareholder of Orange of 22% shares from the minority shareholders for a price exceeding US$400m. The firm represented Liberty Media Inc in the acquisition of the largest TV cable operator in Romania, Astral Telecom, for a price exceeding US$407m. The firm acted as Romanian counsel for Lenovo Group Limited in the acquisition of the production division of International Business Machines Corporation (IBM) and TBIH Financial Services in the entire process of sale of Omniasig SA to Wiener Staedtische (€70m).

Banking, finance: the firm represented European Bank for Reconstruction and Development as Romanian counsel in negotiation and drafting the finance documents for a loan of €16m to East Point Holdings Limited and a loan of €18m to CNTEE 'Transelectrica' SA to be used for the construction of a 110km overhead electric transmission line. The firm represented Goodyear Dunlop Tires Europe B.V. as Romanian counsel in the process of re-financing the senior secured term loan and revolving credit agreement of €505m.

Competition: the firm's attorneys have advised major investors on economic concentrations and exclusive distribution issues and have represented clients on all issues related to investigation procedures before the Romanian competition authorities. The firm has notified the competition authorities regarding more than 25 major transactions and has advised clients in lobbying for harmonisation of the existing Romanian competition legislation with EU standards.

Energy: the firm has provided regulatory, transactional, project development, policy counselling, and legislative legal services to a diverse range of clients in the electricity, oil and gas sectors.

Telecoms: the firm's attorneys have experience advising clients on various matters in the telecoms sector.

Real estate, construction: the firm's attorneys have extensive experience in a full range of real estate issues, including full examination and appraisal of sites in the private or public domain, and negotiating and drafting various types of contracts.

Litigation: the firm's attorneys represent clients before all Romanian courts and arbitration panels and advise on various litigation issues.

Intellectual property: the firm's attorneys have a strong reputation for success as leading Romanian advisers in all manner of intellectual property issues, including trade mark, copyright and patents, licensing arrangements and related matters, and enforcement of clients' intellectual property rights before the State Office of Patents and Trade Marks and the Romanian Courts.

WOLF THEISS

WORLD TRADE CENTRE
PIATA MONTREAL NR 10
INTRAREA F, ETAJUL 1, SECTOR 1
011496 BUCHAREST

Telephone: +40 21 202 3020
Fax: +40 21 202 3134
E-mail: bucharesti@wolftheiss.com
Website: www.wolftheiss.com

Languages
Romanian, German, English

Other offices
Belgrade, Bratislava, Ljubljana, Prague, Sarajevo, Tirana, Vienna, Zagreb

Number of lawyers 161
at this office 10

Contacts
Horst Ebhardt, Bryan W Jardine, Ancuta Leach, Dorina Dumitrescu

CATEGORIES OF WORK

Arbitration, litigation, mediation	**IT and IP**
Banking, capital markets, securities, project finance, investment funds	**Real estate, construction and leasing**
Corporate and M&A	

THE FIRM

Wolf Theiss was founded in 1957 in Vienna, and today is one of the leading law firms in the CEE/SEE region. Over the past few years the firm has experienced extraordinarily dynamic growth, both domestically and internationally.

Wolf Theiss has established a network of nine offices* in Albania, Austria, Bosnia and Herzegovina, Croatia, the Czech Republic, Romania, Serbia and Montenegro, Slovakia and Slovenia. In 2005 alone, Wolf Theiss opened two new offices, in Bucharest and Sarajevo. The firm also regularly assists its clients with projects in Bulgaria, Hungary, Macedonia, Moldova, Poland, Turkey and Ukraine, in co-operation with local attorneys.

The firm's dynamic growth is also reflected in its increase in personnel. At present, Wolf Theiss employs over 350 individuals at nine locations – compare this to 30 employees in one office, Vienna, ten years ago and the growth is apparent.

*The firm's operations in the various locations are set up in compliance with local law and the Bar rules requirements which include the form of co-operation with independent local attorneys.

ZAMFIRESCU RACOTI PREDOIU

30 BATISTE STREET
020938 BUCHAREST 2

Telephone: +40 21 311 05 17
Fax: +40 21 311 05 18/19
E-mail: office@zrp.ro
Website: www.zrp.ro

Languages
English, French, German, Italian, Romanian, Spanish

Number of lawyers 30

Contact
Cătalin Predoiu Ph D (managing partner)

CATEGORIES OF WORK

Arbitration and dispute resolution
Călin Andrei Zamfirescu Ph D, Mădălin Niculeasa, Cosmin Vasile

Aviation
Anca Danilescu, Raluca Marian

Insolvency and debt recovery
Călin Andrei Zamfirescu Ph D, Stan Tîrnoveanu, Radu Boanță

Banking and finance
Stan Tîrnoveanu, Ioana Racoți

Capital markets
Ioana Racoți, Raluca Marian, Cristina Dinu

Competition
Ioana Racoți, Raluca Marian, Oana Vlădoiu

Corporate and commercial
Ioana Racoți, Lucian Danilescu, Raluca Marian

Energy and natural resources
Ioana Racoți, Marian Nicolae Ph D, Radu Boanță

Mergers and acquisitions
Ioana Racoți, Lucian Danilescu, Anca Danilescu

Project finance and infrastructure
Anca Danilescu, Raluca Marian

Real estate and property
Stan Tîrnoveanu, Radu Boanță

Regulation
Marian Nicolae Ph D, Cătalin Predoiu Ph D, Călin Andrei Zamfirescu Ph D

Tax
Ioana Racoți, Radu Boanță, Mădălin Niculeasa

THE FIRM

ZRP was founded in 2005 by a merger of two law firms, Călin-Andrei Zamfirescu and Partners and Racoți Predoiu. Călin-Andrei Zamfirescu and Partners was founded in 1995 by Călin-Andrei Zamfirescu and Ariana Zamfirescu, two attorneys with over 29 years of experience, and respectively 24 years of experience in the Bucharest Bar Association. Benefiting from the two attorney's experience and reputation, the company quickly became a leader, imposing itself as a specialist in commercial arbitration and civil and commercial litigation. Călin-Andrei Zamfirescu and Partners rapidly developed new services for its clients, such as banking and finance, bankruptcy and reorganisation and bank litigation.

Racoți Predoiu was founded in 1995 by Ioana Racoți and Cătălin Predoiu, at that time two young attorneys who had already gained a good reputation as specialists in commercial transactions. From the outset, the firm rapidly made an impression on the mergers, acquisitions and privatisations niches. Racoți Predoiu has been mandated in several of the most important merger, acquisition and privatisation transactions in Romania between 1997 and 2005. The company gradually extended its services in transactions on the capital market, in acquisitions financing, competition, energy and natural resources fields.

AREAS OF PRACTICE

Corporate and commercial: ZRP offers legal assistance in negotiations of shareholders' agreements; in drafting articles of incorporation; incorporation of new companies and implementation of joint ventures. The firm currently assists clients in corporate governance issues and compliance with the legal requirements pertaining to labour and environmental regulations.

Mergers and acquisitions: ZRP performs thorough legal due diligence of the targeted company, assesses the risks of the transactions and identifies and provides legal solutions for deal-breaker issues. The firm assists the clients in handling transactions for both publicly traded and unlisted companies and provides legal advice on tender offers, unsolicited bids, exchange offers, spin-offs or equity; including representation before the relevant regulatory bodies, when the transactions involve the evaluation of the compliance by the legal criteria pertaining to free competition.

Privatisation and post-privatisation: the firm has been involved in the privatisation of several major state-owned enterprises, providing legal due diligence and making preliminary enquiries, counselling throughout the tendering process, assisting during negotiations, and drafting share sale-purchase agreements and closing.

Capital market: the firm offers legal assistance services to securities issuers and underwriters in cases of sale and purchase, public offerings, company listing and delisting, and private placements. Having in-depth knowledge of the Romanian National Securities Commission's regulations, ZRP provides overall legal assistance throughout, ensuring legal compliance of the transaction structure, and assisting with the drafting of documentation and presentation before the relevant authorities.

Energy and natural resources: ZRP has significant experience in the procedures related to authorising and licensing in the field of natural gas distribution and in the energy sector. The partnership also worked in connection with important privatisation projects in oil and gas fields.

Real estate and property: ZRP provides services and representation in a wide range of matters pertaining to concessions, expropriations, inheritance, mortgages, moveable and immovable property vindication, and nationalised property. Its experience in this area also includes due diligence reports on titles, drafting of agreements, as well as assistance for authorisations and permits.

RUSSIA AND THE CIS

Population	**141 million (Russia)**
Number of lawyers	**19,000**
Professional title	**Advokat**
Currency	**Rouble (Rbl))**

Index

Covering over 17 million sq km and spanning ten time zones from Europe to the very eastern tip of Kamchatka, Russia has the largest landmass in the world. This is reflected in the country's diverse population. While Russians make up over 80% of its 141 million population, there are many other ethnic groups, including the Volga Tatars, the Bashkirs, and the Mongols, to name a few. Orthodox Christianity remains the main religion, though Islam is increasingly prevalent, particularly in the Caucasus region.

After the demise of the age-old Tsarist regime in the revolutions of 1917, Russia (and in turn the Soviet Union) was controlled by the Communist Party. The collapse of the USSR in 1991 presented modern Russia with numerous serious hurdles to overcome, such as the development of a fully democratic political system and a Western-based market economy. There remains a lot of work to be done. President Putin's tenure – since taking over from President Yeltsin in 1999 – can only be considered truly democratic in the loosest sense of the word. Critics point to the brutal war in Chechnya, which has resulted in thousands of deaths, as well as the state's crackdown on the free press.

Nevertheless, the country's recovery from the financial crisis of 1998, boosted in part by the rise in oil prices, has been staggering. The new-found wealth from the energy sector has also gradually trickled down into many other sectors of the economy.

ECONOMY

The Russian economy is heavily influenced by world oil prices, and the continued high price of oil globally in recent times continues to propel the whole Russian economy forward. Exports of oil and gas products grew by over 50% in the first half of 2005 to US$66.9bn (€57bn).

Other sectors, especially manufacturing and retail, have also grown in line with an expanding and more affluent middle class. GDP growth in 2004 was 7.2%.

Economic optimism in Russia is tempered by other factors, however, such as the soaring cost of living and real estate in Moscow.

RUSSIA: BILLING

Clients are likely to pay between €400-€600 per hour for a partner, though more experienced partners at some international firms can cost up to €750 an hour. Assistant charges tend to range between €150 and €415 an hour, depending on experience. Fees at Russian firms are generally lower than those charged by international firms.

RUSSIA: MARKETING

There are no marketing restrictions for law firms in Russia. Most promote themselves through brochures, newsletters, directory listings and websites.

RUSSIA: IN-HOUSE LAWYERS

The largest Russian companies and banks all have experienced in-house legal advisers, who are paid top dollar for their services (much to the chagrin of some law firms, which cannot compete). On domestic M&A, it is not uncommon for the vendor to have no external legal advice, relying almost entirely on its in-house lawyers.

RUSSIA: THE LEGAL MARKET

International firms take different approaches when it comes to their strategy in the Russian legal market. At the very top end firms such as **Linklaters CIS**, **Freshfields Bruckhaus Deringer**, **Leboeuf, Lamb, Greene & MacRae LLP** and **White & Case LLC**, have a longstanding tradition of having at least four or five partners on the ground in Moscow, even during the financial crisis of the late 1990s. All of these were rewarded for their loyalty when things started to pick up again in 2003, and now act for some of the top clients on offer.

Not far behind, firms such as **Allen & Overy Legal Services**, **Clifford Chance**, and **Herbert Smith CIS LLP**, have all invested significantly in their Russian practices, and are getting a good share of the top instructions. **CMS Cameron McKenna LLP**, **Lovells** and **Norton Rose** have also made a strong impression on the market. Several US firms with an interest in the market have taken a different approach, by retaining a minimal partner presence on the ground, and flying in the top partners when necessary. This is certainly the case for firms such as **Akin Gump Strauss Hauer & Feld LLP**, **Cleary, Gottlieb, Steen & Hamilton LLC**, **Latham & Watkins LLP**, **Debevoise & Plimpton LLP** and **Skadden, Arps, Slate, Meagher & Flom LLP**.

Meanwhile, firms such as **Baker & McKenzie** and **Salans** have offices in both Moscow and St Petersburg. Both firms offer excellent commercial services, particularly on the mid-range

The largest firms

1	Pepeliaev, Goltsblat & Partners	102
2	PricewaterhouseCoopers CIS Law Offices BV	84
3	Vegas-Lex Law Firm	73
4	Salans	67
	White & Case LLC	67
6	Clifford Chance	62
7	Linklaters CIS	61
8	Egorov, Puginsky, Afanasiev & Partners LLC	60
9	Baker & McKenzie	59
10	Freshfields Bruckhaus Deringer	55
11	DLA Piper Rudnick Gray Cary	49
12	Iniurcolleguia, Attorneys at Law	45
13	Gorodissky & Partners	41
14	Allen & Overy Legal Services	35
15	Laptev & Partners	34
16	Padva & Partners	33
	YUST Law Firm	33
18	LeBoeuf, Lamb, Greene & MacRae LLP	31
19	CMS Bureau Francis Lefebvre	28
20	Norton Rose	27
21	Nörr Stiefenhofer Lutz	25
22	Denton Wilde Sapte	24
	Reznik, Gagarin, Abushakhmin & Partners	24
24	Alrud Law Firm	22
	Herbert Smith CIS LLP	22

These figures represent the total number of lawyers in this country only, and have been supplied by the firms themselves. The figures should be accurate as at 1 January 2006.

transactions. They are also backed up by a very strong presence throughout the CIS.

Among the Russian firms, few have managed to truly challenge the dominance of the Western interlopers. For corporate matters, the international nature of many of the largest Russian transactions means that most domestic firms cannot compete, as they have no international presence. Nevertheless, several do provide strong advice and are regular referral favourites with Western law firms that do not have a practice on the ground, most notably **Pepeliaev, Goltsblat & Partners** and **Alrud Law Firm**. It is in litigation where Russian firms can level the playing field, and as the rankings indicate, there are several eminently instructable Russians firms.

BANKING AND FINANCE
Russia

Allen & Overy Legal Services is particularly active on the arranger side. The firm advised a syndicate of major Western banks on a US$13.1bn (€11.1bn) loan facility to Gazprom; the transaction was one of the largest-ever corporate loans in Russia. Clients include ABN Amro and Citigroup. Peter Timchur and Andrei Baev head the team.

Clifford Chance has a strong name for finance work in Moscow and internationally. The firm advised on loan and pre-export financing transactions for Russian and Western banks. The firm also advised on several aviation finance transactions. Managing partner Michael Cuthbert heads the team.

Freshfields Bruckhaus Deringer advised on several major acquisitions in the banking sector, including representing Deutsche Bank on the takeover of United Financial Group, the Russian investment bank. The firm is also recommended for banking work for clients such as Société Générale and Raiffeisen Zentralbank Oesterreich. Tobias Müller-Deku relocated to the firm's Munich office in 2005. Mikhail Loktionov, who was promoted to partner in 2005, now heads the team; he has a special focus on transactions in the telecoms and energy sectors.

Herbert Smith CIS LLP's John Balsdon is widely respected by peers and banking clients for advice on major, complex finance transactions. The firm advised on an increasing number of banking transactions in the energy sector. Highlights include advice to ABN Amro and ING in relation to the restructuring of US$1.4bn (€1.2bn) of OAO TNK's secured debt; the transaction was the largest debt restructuring in Russia in 2005. BNP Paribas is also a key client, which the firm advised on several multi-million euro loan transactions. The firm's expertise in dispute resolution matters is brought to bear in many banking transactions.

Linklaters CIS advised a syndicate of Western banks in relation to a US$7.5bn (€6.4bn) acquisition finance facility for Rosneftegaz. Other clients include banks such as Deutsche Bank and Citigroup. Team head Michael Bott is qualified in both New York and the UK.

White & Case LLC advised ABN Amro on a US$1.1bn (€938m) restructuring of several Gazprom financings and acted for Aeroflot on a US$300m (€255m) lease of eight Airbus aircraft. Managing partner Hugh Verrier, and Eric Michailov and Marc Polonsky are recommended. Counsel Maya Melnikas also has an excellent name.

Baker & McKenzie advised the IFC and the Russian government in relation to the legal framework for new banking and securitisation laws. Other clients include Dresdner Bank and Deutsche Bank. David Scott heads the team. Vladimir Dragunov is also recommended.

BANKING AND FINANCE
Russia

ALLEN & OVERY LEGAL SERVICES ✪
CLIFFORD CHANCE
FRESHFIELDS BRUCKHAUS DERINGER
HERBERT SMITH CIS LLP ✪
LINKLATERS CIS ✪
WHITE & CASE LLC

Baker & McKenzie ✪
LeBoeuf, Lamb, Greene & MacRae LLP ✪
Lovells ✪
Norton Rose
Salans
Skadden, Arps, Slate, Meagher & Flom LLP

Akin Gump Strauss Hauer & Feld LLP
CMS Cameron McKenna LLP ✪
Chadbourne & Parke LLP
Cleary, Gottlieb, Steen & Hamilton LLC ✪
DLA Piper Rudnick Gray Cary ✪
Debevoise & Plimpton LLP ✪
Denton Wilde Sapte ✪
Gide Loyrette Nouel ✪
Latham & Watkins LLP
Nörr Stiefenhofer Lutz ✪
Orrick (CIS) LLC ✪

Alrud Law Firm ✪
Beiten Burkhardt ✪
Blishchenko & Partners
CMS Bureau Francis Lefebvre ✪
Egorov, Puginsky, Afanasiev & Partners LLC ✪
Hogan & Hartson L.L.P. ✪
Jurinflot, International Law Office ✪
Laptev & Partners ✪
Macleod Dixon ELP ✪
Monastyrsky, Zyuba, Stepanov & Partners ✪
PricewaterhouseCoopers CIS Law Offices BV ✪
Russin & Vecchi LLC
Vegas-Lex Law Firm ✪

Firms are listed A-Z in tiers which are ranked in order of priority
✪ Indicates firm displays contact details at the end of this chapter.

LeBoeuf, Lamb, Greene & MacRae LLP acted for key client Citigroup on its acquisition of ABN Amro's direct custody business in Russia. The firm also advised on several real estate and project financing transactions.

Lovells advises a broad range of Russian banks, Western banks and corporations. The firm advised JSC Gazprombank in relation to an unsecured syndicated loan to Russian Agricultural Bank and acted for key client Nortel Networks in relation to three separate facilities to three Russian regional telecoms companies. The team suffered a setback when Christopher Owen, previously the managing partner of **Lovells**' Moscow office, left in mid-2005 to join **Chadbourne & Parke**. In addition to the team in Moscow, Andrew Gamble in the London office also has a good name for Russia-related banking work.

Norton Rose advised on several major loan, project finance and leasing transactions. Clients include Russian, UK, Italian and German banks and financial institutions. On the borrower side, the firm acts for several clients from the transport sector (a strength of the firm internationally). Chris Viner and Dmitry Gravin are recommended.

Salans advised a major Russian commercial bank on a US$670m (€567m) trade credit facility for financing the export of natural gas from Russia and acted for a Russian natural resources company in negotiating a US$250m (€211m) loan facility from western European banks. The firm also advised on several transactions for key client the EBRD. London-based team head Mira Davidovski and Mathieu Fabre-Magnan and Timothy Stubbs are recommended.

Skadden, Arps, Slate, Meagher & Flom LLP acts for clients such as UBS, CSFB and Bank of Moscow.

Akin Gump Strauss Hauer & Feld LLP is especially recommended for its advice to borrowers.

CMS Cameron McKenna LLP's David Griston heads a team which advised on a range of loan and debt financing transactions. Other areas of focus include insolvency. Sergei Avramov joined the firm as of-counsel from *Coudert Brothers'* Moscow office in 2005.

Chadbourne & Parke advises clients such as Raiffeisenbank and ING Bank on financing transactions. The firm also advised on several transactions for the IFC and the EBRD.

Well-known for its expertise in capital markets transactions, **Cleary, Gottlieb, Steen & Hamilton LLC** also has a good name for banking work. The firm was particularly active for borrowers; highlights include representing Vnesheconombank on a US$500m (€427m) syndicated loan in July 2005, and acting for Alcoa and its Russian subsidiaries in connection with a US$75m (€64m) EBRD financing.

At **DLA Piper Rudnick Gray Cary** Delphine Nougayrede heads a group which advised RAO UES, the electricity group, in relation to a €80m euro loan agreement with the EBRD and acted for Volvo Leasing on leasing transactions. Eurohypo AG is also a client. The team reports growing involvement with lawyers in the firm's London office for AIM listings-related work.

Debevoise & Plimpton LLP advised Aeroflot-Russian Airlines in a US$150m (€127m) syndicated loan secured by ticket receivables. The team also acts for several investment funds in the private equity sector.

Denton Wilde Sapte acts for both corporations and banks such as ABN Amro, which the firm advised on a US$500m (€423m) syndicated loan facility to Rual Trade Limited. Doran Doeh has a good name.

Gide Loyrette Nouel enjoyed an upsurge in banking work in 2005. The firm advised Evraz Group, the Russian steel producer, in connection with a US$200m (€170m) syndicated pre-export finance facility arranged by ABN Amro, BNP Paribas and Société Générale. New clients in 2005 include Raiffeisen and Gazprombank. The firm is working increasingly closely with its London office for financing matters, where Margaret Boswell enjoys a strong reputation.

Latham & Watkins LLP has a strong name for capital markets work. The firm also advised several Russian borrowers such as Mobile TeleSystems on loan facilities.

Nörr Stiefenhofer Lutz advises borrowers and banks on loans and project finance. The firm advised Bosch Rexroth AG on a tender for renovation of the Bolshoi Theatre in Moscow.

Orrick (CIS) LLC's John Sheedy has a good name.

Alrud Law Firm advised on loan facilities for corporate and banking clients.

CMS Bureau Francis Lefebvre advised Banque Accord on implementing a consumer credit facility. Other clients include Société Générale, Eurohypo and Calyon.

Hogan & Hartson L.L.P. advised ROSBANK in relation to a US$50m (€43m) syndicated loan and represented a fast food chain restaurant in Russia on a US$30m (€25m) loan from Rabobank. Other clients include Macquarie Bank.

Macleod Dixon ELP advises clients such as Standard Bank and Nova Ljubljanska banka, the Slovenian bank. Banking work relating to the mining industry is a core focus.

PricewaterhouseCoopers CIS Law Offices BV advised on banking and asset management matters for several Russian clients.

CAPITAL MARKETS

Russia

Cleary, Gottlieb, Steen & Hamilton LLC has an exceptionally strong name for both equity and debt capital markets transactions. The firm acted for the underwriters on a US$200m (€170m) eurobond on the London Stock Exchange by Promsvyazbank, and represented OAO Gazprom and Blue Stream Pipeline Company on a US$1.869 bn (€1.59bn) bond offering (the first Russian loan participation notes listed on the Irish Stock Exchange). Scott Senecal is well respected.

Latham & Watkins LLP has arguably the strongest name in the market for advice to Russian issuers on IPOs, with a long track record and historical experience of advising on major deals. In July 2005, the firm advised NOVATEK, the largest independent natural gas producer in Russia, on its US$966m (€824m) IPO in London; the transaction was the second-largest Russian IPO to date. Anya Goldin is well respected. The team is described as 'experienced and committed'.

Linklaters CIS is particularly recommended for its work for underwriters in the equity capital markets. The firm advised CSFB and Morgan Stanley in relation to the US$1.56bn (€1.3bn) IPO of AFK Sistema in London. On the debt side, the firm advised the EBRD in relation to major bond issues. The firm is also advising on a growing number of securitisation transactions. Dmitry Dobatkin is recommended.

White & Case LLC has an especially good name for debt capital markets work, particularly amongst a strong investment banking clientele. In a groundbreaking securitisation transaction, the firm advised Merrill Lynch and CSFB on a US$225m (€191m) international bond issue by Rosbank, secured by credit card receivables. On the equity side, the firm advised Lebedyansky Experimental Cannery, the Russian fruit juice producer, on its US$150m (€127m) IPO in March 2005. Sven Krogius heads the team.

Akin Gump Strauss Hauer & Feld LLP is recommended for both equity and debt capital markets transactions, particularly for issuer clients from the energy sector.

Allen & Overy Legal Services was especially active in advising on complex debt capital markets transactions. The firm advised Absolut Bank on its US$100m (€85m) short-term notes issuance programme using a non-Russian SPV. The team also reports a growing amount of securitisation work. Irina Mashlenko and Andrei Baev are recommended.

Clifford Chance advised a banking client in relation to an IPO in the transport sector. The firm also advised several Russian clients on debut eurobond transactions. Other areas of work include the growing securitisation market in Russia. William Knowles transferred from the firm's Prague office in May 2005.

Freshfields Bruckhaus Deringer has a good reputation for equity capital markets transactions. The firm advised Pyaterochka, the Russian retailer, on its listing on the London Stock Exchange in May 2005. The firm also advised on debt transactions including representing Rosbank on its EMTN programme. Mikhail Loktionov heads the group, following Tobias Müller-Deku's relocation to the firm's Munich office in 2005.

Herbert Smith CIS LLP advised on several complex and groundbreaking capital markets

CAPITAL MARKETS
Russia

CLEARY, GOTTLIEB, STEEN & HAMILTON LLC ✪
LATHAM & WATKINS LLP
LINKLATERS CIS ✪
WHITE & CASE LLC

AKIN GUMP STRAUSS HAUER & FELD LLP
ALLEN & OVERY LEGAL SERVICES ✪
CLIFFORD CHANCE
FRESHFIELDS BRUCKHAUS DERINGER
HERBERT SMITH CIS LLP ✪
LEBOEUF, LAMB, GREENE & MACRAE LLP ✪
LINIYA PRAVA ✪
LOVELLS ✪
SKADDEN, ARPS, SLATE, MEAGHER & FLOM LLP

Baker & McKenzie ✪
Debevoise & Plimpton LLP ✪
Hogan & Hartson L.L.P. ✪
Norton Rose
Orrick (CIS) LLC ✪
PricewaterhouseCoopers CIS Law Offices BV ✪
Salans

Firms are listed A-Z in tiers which are ranked in order of priority
✪ Indicates firm displays contact details at the end of this chapter.

transactions, including advising Eco Telecom on a US$350m (€296m) structured equity note issuance involving a pledge over stock in a New York Stock Exchange-listed Russian company. Other highlights include acting for Fitch Ratings in relation to a US$20m (€16m) credit card securitisation by Rosbank. US-qualified partner Allen Hanen heads a team that includes Robin Wittering and finance partner John Balsdon.

LeBoeuf, Lamb, Greene & MacRae LLP advised Rambler Media Limited, the Russian Internet portal and media company on its US$46m (€39m) AIM listing in London. Other clients include Deutsche Bank.

Liniya Prava is the best local Russian firm for capital markets transactions. One client in the banking sector commented: 'The firm can advise on the Russian law components of capital markets transactions as well as – and more cost-effectively than – any international firm.' In 2004, the firm advised on more than 200 debt and securities offerings in Russia. Highlights include advising Open Investments OAO, the Russian commercial and residential real estate construction and development company, on its US$68.8m (€58.7m) IPO and acting for Gazprom OAO on its US$210m (€179m) bond offering. Andrei Novakovskiy and Alexander Timofeev head the team.

Lovells advised Alfa Bank on the update and increase of its EMTN programme.

Skadden, Arps, Slate, Meagher & Flom LLP had a busy year in the equity capital markets, especially on transactions involving advice to underwriters. Highlights include advising Morgan Stanley, UBS and Credit Suisse First Boston as underwriters in an US$966m (€817m) IPO by Novatek, the Russian independent gas producer; the IPO was the second-largest IPO by a Russian company to date. On the issuer side, the firm acted for VimpelCom on a bond offering. Other clients include BNP Paribas, JP Morgan and Bank of Moscow.

Baker & McKenzie advised the lead arrangers in relation to a debut eurobond by a Russian financial institution. The team also advised on several syndicated loan transactions and bond issues in the nascent securitisation market in Russia. David Scott and Vladimir Dragunov are respected.

Debevoise & Plimpton LLP advised Deutsche Telekom on the sale by its subsidiary T-Mobile International of a 15% stake in Mobile TeleSystems, the Russian cellular operator.

Hogan & Hartson L.L.P. provided ongoing advice to Nikoil IBG Bank in relation to a US$150m (€128m) bond issue.

Norton Rose works closely with its London office in advising on Russian law aspects of bond issues and equity placements.

PricewaterhouseCoopers CIS Law Offices BV advised on several AIM placements on the London Stock Exchange.

CORPORATE AND M&A
Moscow

Freshfields Bruckhaus Deringer has longstanding experience of advising major Russian and international clients. The firm advised RUSAL, the Russian aluminium producer, on its acquisition from SUAL of a 50% stake in Komi Aluminium Project. The firm also acts for major brewing companies such as Scottish & Newcastle and Carlsberg. Other clients come from the chemicals, transport, energy and automotive sectors. Managing partner Jacky Baudon heads a team of 36 fee-earners. Kirsten Floss, Michael Schwartz, Dmitry Surikov and Mikhail Loktionov, who was promoted to partner in 2005, are recommended. The firm's finance capabilities suffered a setback when well-known partner Tobias Müller-Deku relocated to the firm's Munich office in 2005. Clients appreciate 'clear, candid and forthright advice'. The firm works closely with its international offices, especially London and Germany.

Leboeuf, Lamb, Greene & MacRae LLP has a particularly strong name for transactions in the energy and oil and gas sector. Highlights include advising China National Petroleum Corporation (CNPC) in connection with investments in Russia and Kazakhstan. Other clients include Statoil and ExxonMobil. The firm also advised Vneshtorgbank, the Russian bank, on its US$1bn (€855m) acquisition of a major Russian industrial company.

Managing partner Brian Zimbler heads a team of four partners, which includes Jonathan Hines, Oleg Berger, Vasilisa Strizh and Mark Banovich. The team is 'commercial' and 'has a good understanding and long experience of the Russian market'.

Despite the transfer of experienced former managing partner Dominic Sanders to the firm's London office in August 2005, **Linklaters CIS** maintains its longstanding expertise and relationships with major corporates and financial institutions in Russia. Managing partner John Goodwin heads a team of six partners and 59 associates. The firm advised key client BP in relation to a reorganisation of TNK-BP group in Russia and represented Gold Fields, the South African gold exploration company, on Russian aspects of its successful defence of an attempted hostile takeover. Russian partner Denis Uvarov is also recommended. The firm reports an increase in work in the retail sector.

White & Case LLC has a long history in Russia and offers an impressive mix of US, English and Russian law capability. The firm advised Deutsche Bank as financial adviser to Gazprom, the Russian national gas company on its US$7.12bn (€6.1bn) sale of shares to the Russian government. Other clients come from the IT, mining, food and drink and energy sectors. Eric Michailov, Igor Ostapets, Marc Polonsky and Hermann Schmitt, who advises several major German clients, are recommended.

Akin Gump Strauss Hauer & Feld LLP's Richard Wilkie heads a team which has a strong name for work in the energy sector. Lukoil is a key client. Other clients come from the US and UK. The team works closely with its London and US offices.

Allen & Overy Legal Services' corporate team works closely with the firm's outstanding banking and capital markets departments. Peter Timchur heads a group which advised Lukoil Finland Oy on an acquisition in the energy sector and represented Heineken on its acquisition of four breweries in Russia.

Baker & McKenzie advised Northgas, the independent gas producer, on a transfer of 51% share in Northgas to Gazprom and represented Orkla Foods, the Scandinavian company, on its acquisition of SladCo, the Russian confectionery group. Sergei Voitishkin, Carol Patterson and Max Gutbrod are recommended. Managing partner Paul Melling has a particular focus on work in the pharmaceutical sector. Other clients include Siemens and Ericsson. The breadth and strength of the firm's expertise in Moscow across a wide range of other practice areas which are complementary to the work the firm's corporate department undertakes, including tax, intellectual property and employment, is rivalled by few other firms. The firm also has an extensive network of offices across the whole of the CIS region which few other firms can match.

CMS Cameron McKenna LLP advised on a multi-million dollar acquisition in the telecoms

CORPORATE AND M&A
Moscow

FRESHFIELDS BRUCKHAUS DERINGER
LEBOEUF, LAMB, GREENE & MACRAE LLP ✪
LINKLATERS CIS ✪
WHITE & CASE LLC

AKIN GUMP STRAUSS HAUER & FELD LLP
ALLEN & OVERY LEGAL SERVICES ✪
BAKER & McKENZIE ✪
CMS CAMERON MCKENNA LLP ✪
CLIFFORD CHANCE
HERBERT SMITH CIS LLP ✪
SALANS
SKADDEN, ARPS, SLATE, MEAGHER & FLOM LLP

Chadbourne & Parke
Cleary, Gottlieb, Steen & Hamilton LLC ✪
Debevoise & Plimpton LLP ✪
Gide Loyrette Nouel ✪
Hogan & Hartson L.L.P. ✪
Latham & Watkins LLP
Lovells ✪
Norton Rose
Orrick (CIS) LLC ✪

Alrud Law Firm ✪
Beiten Burkhardt ✪
CMS Bureau Francis Lefebvre ✪
DLA Piper Rudnick Gray Cary ✪
Denton Wilde Sapte ✪
Jurinflot, International Law Office ✪
Macleod Dixon ELP ✪
Nörr Stiefenhofer Lutz ✪
Pepeliaev, Goltsblat & Partners ✪
Russin & Vecchi LLC

Gorodissky & Partners
Klishin & Partners
Laptev & Partners ✪
Liniya Prava ✪
PricewaterhouseCoopers CIS Law Offices BV ✪
Reznik, Gagarin, Abushakhmin & Partners
Vegas-Lex Law Firm ✪
YUST Law Firm ✪

Barabashev & Partners
Barshchevsky & Partners
Haarmann Hemmelrath ✪
Monastyrsky, Zyuba, Stepanov & Partners ✪
Muranov, Chernyakov & Partners
Squire, Sanders & Dempsey (Moscow) LLC ✪
Vinson & Elkins L.L.P. ✪

AR Consulting Law Firm
Alimirzoev & Trofimov
Baker Botts ✪
Blishchenko & Partners
Clyde & Co ✪
Egorov, Puginsky, Afanasiev & Partners LLC ✪
Yuridicheskaya Firma Magnusson
Ost Legal
Smirnov, Davydov & Susskind Law Offices

Firms are listed A-Z in tiers which are ranked in order of priority
✪ Indicates firm displays contact details at the end of this chapter.

sector. Other clients come from the IT, energy, banking and real estate industries. David Griston heads a team which expanded to welcome five lawyers from *Coudert Brothers'* Moscow office in 2005. Leonid Zubarev has a focus on insurance matters (also a strength of the firm in London and internationally). The firm is based in the same offices as its French and German CMS partners in Moscow.

Clifford Chance's Marc Bartholomy and managing partner Michael Cuthbert head a team which advised on several major acquisitions in the food and drinks, mining and brewing sectors. Competition work and private equity transactions are also areas of focus. The firm advised OAO Gazprom on the US$7.12bn (€6bn) sale of shares to OAO Rosneftegaz, the state-owned holding entity.

Herbert Smith CIS LLP advised on several hostile M&A transactions, a novel and growing trend in Russia. Highlights include advising key client Alfa Telecom on a shareholder dispute with Telenor relating to an expansion in Ukraine by VimpelCom, the mobile phone service provider. The team also advised on several transactions in the brewing and financial services sectors. Robin Wittering and managing partner Allen Hanen are recommended. The corporate group often co-operates closely with lawyers in the firm's outstanding dispute resolution team in Moscow and internationally. The firm is working increasingly closely with its international offices for clients such as Chevron Texaco in the energy sector (a strong client base firm-wide). The team is described as 'responsive, thoughtful, easily accessible and friendly'. The firm often co-operates closely with US firm **Cravath, Swaine & Moore LLP** in Moscow.

Salans benefits from its wide network of offices across the whole of the CIS region. Mathieu Fabre-Magnan and managing partner Jane Tarassova and are recommended. The firm is particularly recommended for mid-market corporate deals, and advised on several transactions in the US$10m-US$50m (€8m-€42m) range, including advising Louis Dreyfus in relation to a US$50m (€42m) merger in the agricultural industry. The firm also advised a consortium of investors led by Fleming Family & Partners on an M&A transaction in the ice cream market. Work for clients in the real estate sector is a particular area of focus. Other clients come from the manufacturing, energy, mining, transport and retail sectors. The firm has had a long historical presence in the Russian market and boasts strong, grass-roots connections with a wide range of clients in Russia. As the Russian legal market continues to evolve and mature rapidly, however, one challenge for the firm in Moscow in seeking to develop and expand its international client base in the coming few years may prove to be the need to compete successfully with several Magic Circle UK law firms and US Wall Street law firms in Moscow which boast strong and deep institutional relationships with a wide range of blue-chip corporations and financial institutions in key international financial centres such as London, New York, Frankfurt and Tokyo, as well as the greater opportunity for those UK and US firms in Moscow to win a significant volume of referral work involving co-operation with lawyers in the international network of offices in those financial centres – both for inbound, as well as, increasingly, for outbound work, in Russia.

Skadden, Arps, Slate, Meagher & Flom LLP advised SUN Trade (International) Ltd on the renegotiation of its agreement to sell its entire stake in Sun Interbrew Limited, the second-largest brewer in Russia, to InBev SA for €600m. The firm has a strong reputation for work in the energy sector and also has a strong name for capital markets work. Other clients include mining companies and Russian and Western financial institutions. Moscow counsel Alexey Kiyashko and Dmitri Kovalenko and partners Pranav Trivedi and Bruce Buck, who divide their time between London and Moscow, are recommended. The team is described as 'efficient and extremely dedicated'.

At **Chadbourne & Parke** managing partner Laura Brank heads a team of 16 lawyers which represented an operating subsidiary of Norilsk Nickel, the gold and minerals company, in connection with its acquisition of a majority stake in a Russian gold company. Other clients come from the telecoms, tobacco, banking, energy and retail sectors. The firm opened an office in St Petersburg in November 2005 and also has an extensive network of other offices across the CIS region. The team received a boost when Christopher Owen, previously the managing partner of **Lovells**' Moscow office, joined the firm in mid-2005.

Cleary, Gottlieb, Steen & Hamilton LLC advised on several high-profile and complex transactions, including acting for Citigroup Venture Capital International on an equity investment in NLC, a Russian warehousing business. The firm also advised the Rostiks Group in its franchising business alliance with Yum! and KFC, the fast food restaurant chains, in Russia. Scott Senecal enjoys an excellent reputation. The team also acts for several clients from the brewing industry and energy sector, including Gazprom and Northgas.

Debevoise & Plimpton LLP advised key client Novolipetsk Steel Group on an acquisition in the ports and shipping sectors. The firm also has a strong focus on work in the aviation industry for clients such as Aeroflot. Other clients include Philip Morris and ExxonMobil. The firm is also active in advising on transactions in the private equity sector; transaction highlights include advice to Baring Vostok Capital Partners Limited on the formation of a US$400m (€341m) private equity fund. Dmitri Nikiforov and international counsel Holly Nielsen head a team of 12 associates.

Gide Loyrette Nouel boasts strong relationships with a wide range of French and

Russian clients, and is increasingly building a strong name amongst a variety of other western European clients. In 2005, the firm advised a major glass producer on the acquisition of two plants and undertook work for a Scandinavian mining company in Russia. BNP Paribas is a key client. Other clients come from the retail, telecoms and transport sectors. David Lasfargue heads a team of 17 associates which works closely with the firm's international network of offices, particularly Paris and London. The firm is 'methodical and efficient'.

Hogan & Hartson L.L.P. advises a strong US clients base, and also acts for a range of other Russian and western European clients. The firm advised EADS on a joint venture to develop telecommunications satellite systems and represented HAVAS/Media Planning Group, the European media and advertising conglomerate, on structuring its Russian operations. Other clients come from the banking, IT, pharmaceutical and retail sectors. The firm works closely with its international offices, especially New York. Managing partner Peter Pettibone, Todd Schafer and Sergey Komolov are recommended.

At **Latham & Watkins LLP** Anya Goldin heads a team which has a strong name for capital markets work. Relationships with Russian corporates which the firm has previously advised on IPO transactions are a strong source of work for the corporate department. The firm advised key client Mechel on the US$870m (€742m) disposal of its stake in MMK, the steel group. The team also reports an increase in private equity transactions across the CIS region.

Lovells advises a broad mix of Russian and Western clients. The firm advised Decathlon, the French sports equipment group, on establishing Russian subsidiaries and represented SABMiller on its acquisition plans in Russia. Oxana Balayan heads the team. Other clients are Mitsubishi, Merrill Lynch and Nortel Networks. The team suffered a setback when Christopher Owen, previously the managing partner of **Lovells**' Moscow office, left in mid-2005 to join **Chadbourne & Parke**. Suren Gortsunyan joined from **White & Case LLC**'s Moscow office in late 2005 as partner.

Norton Rose was particularly active in transactions in the energy sector. Highlights include advising Eni Spa, the Italian energy giant, on a multi-billion dollar joint venture in the oil sector in southern Russia, and representing Valkyries Petroleum Corp, the Canadian oil company, on its acquisition of several oil-producing companies in Russia. Other clients come from the real estate, transport, telecoms, pharmaceutical and banking industries. Chris Viner and Valentina Gluhovskaya are recommended.

Orrick (CIS) LLC opened a Moscow office in June 2005, when three partners and a team of associates joined from *Coudert Brothers'* Moscow office. Managing partner John Sheedy heads the team. The firm advised a major US beverage company on an acquisition of a juice company in Russia; the transaction was one of the largest FDI and M&A transactions in Russia in 2005. Peter O'Driscoll in London also has a good name for Russia-related work.

Alrud Law Firm is one of the very best local independent firms in Russia. The firm acted for Pharmacy Chain 36,6, the Russian pharmaceutical company, on a major acquisition and advised Moody's Investors Service on its activities in Russia. Other clients come from the energy, publishing, manufacturing and automotive sectors. The firm enjoys strong relationships with several leading independent law firms in the UK, US, Germany and other Western jurisdictions which do not have offices in Russia. Vassily Rudomino and Maxim Alekseyev are recommended. Clients describe the firm as 'quick, practical, focused, efficient and impressive'.

Beiten Burkhardt works closely with its extensive network of offices in Germany in advising a long list of respected German clients. Tax work is also an area of focus. The team works closely with its St Petersburg office.

At **CMS Bureau Francis Lefebvre** Jean-Luc Pipon heads a team with long experience in Russia. The firm has a strong French and Russian client base, and works closely with its Paris head office. The firm advised Air Liquide on a US$100m (€85m) joint venture with Severstal, the Russian steel maker. Other clients include Faurecia, the automotive supplier, Société Générale, Cap Gemini, L'Oréal, Clarins and Air Liquide. Tax work is also a strong area of focus (the firm often works closely with **CMS Cameron McKenna LLP** in Moscow in providing tax advice to clients of that firm). The firm 'works with clients to find solutions to problems'.

DLA Piper Rudnick Gray Cary expanded its presence dramatically in Russia in July 2005 when it acquired the lion's share of **EY Law**'s practice and lawyers in Moscow (as well as in St Petersburg and Tbilisi, Georgia). A team of four partners and 31 associates includes managing partner Constantine Lusignan-Rizhinashvili, Delphine Nougayrede and Scott Antel. The firm advised Teich AG, the flexible packaging materials company, on an acquisition in Kuban and represented Stage Holding BV on establishing a US$15m (€12m) theatre production in Moscow. Other clients include Pilkington. The firm advises a wide range of clients from the real estate sector. Tax work is another forte. The firm's dramatic, rapid and aggressive recent expansion both in Russia and internationally is likely to be watched closely by clients and peers alike over the coming few years.

At **Denton Wilde Sapte** work for clients in the banking and energy sector is a core focus. Highlights include acting for Altadis SA on its €201m acquisition of Balkan Star, the Russian tobacco company. Managing partner Doran Doeh heads a team of around 20 lawyers. Consultant Greg Potts is also recommended. Other clients come from the construction, transport and IT sectors. The team is 'practical, available, experienced and friendly'.

Four-partner **Jurinflot, International Law Office** has an excellent name for work in the maritime sector. The firm also advises on corporate and energy transactions. Clients include several mining companies. Alexander Mednikov, managing partner Valery Mandriouc and Vadim Ermolaev are recommended. Name partner Vladimir Mednikov had left the firm in February 2005 to go in-house at a shipping client of the firm.

Macleod Dixon ELP is arguably the leading firm in the market for work in the mining industry. The firm advised Barrick Gold Corporation, the Canadian group, on its investment in the Russian mining industry. Other clients come from the banking and telecoms sectors. Managing partner Anatoly Andriash, Levon Kocharyan and Aydin Jebrailov are recommended. The firm is 'helpful and quick' and 'commercially-minded'.

Nörr Stiefenhofer Lutz advises a strong Russian and German-speaking client base on corporate matters (but lacks a real strength and depth of market share amongst a wider international Western client base in Moscow). The firm advised a major German IT company on joint ventures in Russia and acted for a German logistics company on an acquisition in Moscow. Clients include Volkswagen and Audi. Hans-Peter Zier heads a team of five partners and 26 fee-earners. The firm works closely with its network of offices in Germany and Eastern Europe. The team has a particular focus on tax work. The firm 'meets deadlines' and is 'up-to-date and reliable'.

Pepeliaev, Goltsblat & Partners advised the world's largest restaurant company on its US$100m (€85m) deal with a chain of quick-serve restaurants and acted for Russia's biggest mining company on the US$1.5bn (€1.3bn) spin-off of its gold-mining assets. Other clients come from the media and tobacco sectors. Andrey Goltsblat and Anton Sitnikov are recommended. Sergey Pepeliaev has an excellent name for tax matters. The firm provides 'concise advice' and 'understands the practicalities of providing legal advice to Western companies investing in Russia'.

Russin & Vecchi LLC is especially recommended for its work in the energy sector, working closely with its offices in Vladivostok and Yuzhno-Sakhalinsk. The firm also advised a major Japanese company on its acquisition of shares in a Russian telecoms company. Jonathan Russin heads a team of four partners.

Gorodissky & Partners has an excellent name for IP advice. Managing partner Valery Medvedev heads a team of 11 partners which also has a good name for commercial work.

At **Klishin & Partners** Andrey Fyodorov heads a team which advises a range of clients from Russia, Italy, the UK, Switzerland, Spain, France and Germany. Several clients are from the electricity sector. Name partner Alexander Klishin left the firm in mid-2004 to join the Russian parliament.

Laptev & Partners is recommended for its advice in the energy sector, while **Reznik, Gagarin, Abushakhmin & Partners** partner Nikolay Reznik is also recommended for general corporate and commercial matters.

Liniya Prava has an excellent reputation for capital markets work, and is also recommended for corporate matters. The firm advised Obninsk Milk Factory OAO, the largest Russian milk manufacturer, in relation to its acquisition by Vimm Bill Dann Foodstuffs OAO.

Despite the increasing regulatory hurdles facing many accountancy-tied firms internationally following the Sarbanes-Oxley Act 2002 in the US, **PricewaterhouseCoopers CIS Law Offices BV** maintains an active profile in Russia, especially in the real estate and energy sectors. Other clients include Hitachi, Siemens, Sun International and Gillette. The firm advised Gazprom and its financial advisor DrKW on the US$7.12bn (€6bn) sale of shares to Rosneftegaz. Igor Boldyrev and Igor Makarov lead the team. The firm is 'experienced and professional'.

At **Vegas-Lex Law Firm** a team of seven partners advised two major investment banks on corporate restructuring of regional energy companies. The group also advises on FDI matters for a range of Western clients. Managing partner Albert Eganyan is recommended.

Nine-partner, 38-lawyer **YUST Law Firm** advised a pharmaceutical company on an unfair competition case. Other clients include several energy sector companies. Yury Timokhov advises on corporate and dispute resolution matters. The firm 'renders legal services at a high professional level', say clients.

Barabashev & Partners acts for clients such as Motorola, Corning and Baxter AG, the healthcare company. The firm co-operates closely with US firm **Arnold & Porter LLP**. Alexander Barabashev heads the team.

Vinson & Elkins L.L.P. advised on several transactions in the energy and natural resources sectors. Highlights include representing a Russian steel producer on a US$45m (€38m) acquisition of equipment from German and Swiss manufacturers and acting for a Cypriot company with oil and gas assets in Russia on a US$60m (€50m) acquisition of shares in a medium-sized Russian oil company.

Having closed its Moscow office for several years in the late 1990s and early years of the 21st century, **Baker Botts** is rebuilding its strength in the CIS region. The firm advises a range of clients from the energy and real estate sectors, including Gazpromneft and VimpelCom. Steven Wardlaw and George Goolsby, who divides his time between Russia and the US, are recommended.

Clyde & Co opened a Moscow office in early 2005. Dmitry Zavidov heads a team which advises trade, energy and shipping sector clients. The firm works closely with John Whittaker in the London office.

CORPORATE AND M&A
St Petersburg

The shipping and automotive sectors generate a considerable amount of work for St Petersburg-based law firms.

Baker & McKenzie's Maxim Kalinin heads a team which advises a broad range of clients from the automotive, food and drink, real estate and energy sectors.

DLA Piper Rudnick Gray Cary has a particularly strong focus on work in the real estate sector. The firm acted for Orient-Express Hotels Ltd on its acquisition of the Grand Hotel Europe in St Petersburg; the transaction was one of the largest-ever acquisitions in the Russian real estate sector. Tax work is also a strong point. Olga Litvinova heads a team of over 20 lawyers which significantly expanded its presence in St Petersburg in mid-2005 when a large team of lawyers joined from **EY Law**.

At **Salans** managing partner Mikhail Ivanov and Glenn Kolleeny head a team which works closely with the firm's Moscow office. In addition to corporate matters, real estate work is a key area of focus; highlights include advice to SRV-Okhta, a Russian-Finnish property development joint venture, on a €200m retail shopping, hotel and office centre in St Petersburg. Other practice areas include dispute resolution and intellectual property.

Beiten Burkhardt has a strong German-speaking client base. Clients include several automotive sector companies.

Established in 1994, **Castrén & Snellman St Petersburg Ltd** works closely with its head office in Helsinki. Sergei Lee heads a team which advises a range of Scandinavian and other international clients.

Chadbourne & Parke LLP opened an office in St Petersburg in November 2005 which works closely with its Moscow office.

Clyde & Co advises on asset finance, trade, shipping, insurance and FDI. London-based John Whittaker and Moscow-based Dmitry Zavidov are active. The team works closely with its Moscow office, which opened in 2005.

At **Egorov, Puginsky, Afanasiev & Partners LLC** name parnter Nikolai Egorov advises on corporate and real estate matters. Ilya Nikiforov advises on dispute resolution and IP.

Hough, Mikhailov & Co advises several small and medium-sized companies. William Hough, Vladimir Kuraev and Vadim Malashev are recommended.

Law Firm J.P. Galmond & Co advises several clients from the telecoms sector.

CORPORATE AND M&A
St Petersburg

BAKER & McKENZIE ✪

DLA Piper Rudnick Gray Cary ✪
Salans

Beiten Burkhardt ✪
Castrén & Snellman St Petersburg Ltd ✪
Chadbourne & Parke LLP
Clyde & Co ✪
Egorov, Puginsky, Afanasiev & Partners LLC ✪
Hough, Mikhailov & Co
J.P. Galmond & Co., Law Firm
Mannheimer Swartling ✪
Shcheglov & Partners

Capital Legal Services International LLC
Duvernoix Consulting
Hedman Osborne Clarke Alliance
Pepeliaev, Goltsblat & Partners ✪
PricewaterhouseCoopers CIS Law Offices BV ✪

Firms are listed A-Z in tiers which are ranked in order of priority
✪ Indicates firm displays contact details at the end of this chapter.

Mannheimer Swartling advises a strong Swedish and Scandinavian client base. Corporate, real estate, banking, dispute resolution and insurance work are key practice areas. Other clients come from the pharmaceutical industry. Sven Lexner heads a team of ten lawyers.

Twenty-three-lawyer **Capital Legal Services International LLC** has a special focus on work for clients from the retail and real estate sectors. Clients include a major Scandinavian retailer. Managing partner Vlad Zabrodin has previously worked at **McDermott Will & Emery LLP**. The firm is 'efficient' and 'good at finding creative solutions to complex problems'.

Two-partner, five-lawyer **Duvernoix Consulting** advised a Russian frozen food company on its acquisition of an ice cream company. The firm is also recommended for dispute resolution. Egor Noskov and Igor Guschev head the team. The firm is 'professional, knowledgeable, experienced and able to find the most effective solution for legal matters in different fields of law in a short space of time'.

Hedman Osborne Clarke Alliance advises several UK and Finnish companies, including Finnair. Natalie Neverovskaja heads the team.

At **Pepeliaev, Goltsblat & Partners** US lawyer Tom Stansmore, who has previously worked with a Big Four accounting firm in Russia, heads a team of five lawyers which works closely with the firm's Moscow office in advising on tax, corporate and real estate matters.

DISPUTE RESOLUTION
Russia

BAKER & McKENZIE ✪
CLIFFORD CHANCE
HERBERT SMITH CIS LLP ✪
LINKLATERS CIS ✪
MONASTYRSKY, ZYUBA, STEPANOV & PARTNERS ✪
SALANS

CMS Cameron McKenna LLP ✪
Chadbourne & Parke LLP
Freshfields Bruckhaus Deringer
Jurinflot, International Law Office ✪
Norton Rose
Orrick (CIS) LLC ✪
Padva & Partners
Pepeliaev, Goltsblat & Partners ✪
Reznik, Gagarin, Abushakhmin & Partners
Sikaylo, Gabbasov, Romakhova & Partners (Attorneys at Law) ✪
White & Case LLC

Akin Gump Strauss Hauer & Feld LLP
Alrud Law Firm ✪
CMS Bureau Francis Lefebvre ✪
EY Law
Gowlings International Inc ✪
Haarmann Hemmelrath ✪
Hogan & Hartson L.L.P. ✪
Intellect Ltd
Klishin & Partners
LeBoeuf, Lamb, Greene & MacRae LLP ✪
Lovells ✪
Muranov, Chernyakov & Partners
Nörr Stiefenhofer Lutz ✪
Russin & Vecchi LLC
Tarlo and Partners
Vegas-Lex Law Firm ✪
YUST Law Firm ✪

Firms are listed A-Z in tiers which are ranked in order of priority
✪ *Indicates firm displays contact details at the end of this chapter.*

DISPUTE RESOLUTION Russia

Baker & McKenzie advised major Russian and Western clients on domestic litigation and cross-border disputes in the energy, manufacturing and banking industries. Experienced department head Vladimir Khvalei leads a team of six partners.

Ivan Marisin at **Clifford Chance** heads a group which advised on disputes in the energy, automotive, banking and mining sectors. In a groundbreaking case, the firm also advised on enforcement of the first foreign court judgment in Russia.

Herbert Smith CIS LLP has a strong name for dispute resolution work in Moscow, London and internationally. The firm advised on major disputes in the banking, telecoms, mining and energy industries. The firm advised Alfa Bank and Mikhail Friedman in English High Court defamation proceedings brought by Boris Berezovsky and represented Tajik Aluminium Plant in English High Court proceedings for the recovery of damages and a worldwide freezing injunction order. London-based partner Simon Bushell and Dmitry Kurochkin are recommended.

Linklaters CIS has firm-wide expertise in the energy and natural resources sector in Moscow, and the disputes team acted on several major cases in this sector in 2005, including representing a Russian oil major on a claim for alleged fraudulent misrepresentation. Other clients come from the consumer goods and financial services sectors. Senior associate Alexei Dudko heads the team.

At **Monastyrsky, Zyuba, Stepanov & Partners** dispute resolution work is a core practice area. Yuri Monastyrsky heads a group recommended for both litigation and arbitration. Tax cases are a forte.

Salans partner Sergei Marinich has extensive experience of litigation and arbitration. The firm advised Diageo on a cross-jurisdictional dispute relating to the Smirnoff trade mark in Russia and represented a multinational consumer goods company on a product liability case.

CMS Cameron McKenna LLP advised on disputes in the energy, insolvency and manufacturing sectors. Associate Sergey Yuriev heads the team. Leonid Zubarev advises on insurance and reinsurance disputes. Well-known litigator Vasily Zolotyuk left the firm in late 2004 to work in an oil company.

Chadbourne & Parke LLP advises on disputes in the banking and manufacturing sectors.

Freshfields Bruckhaus Deringer's team advises on both litigation and arbitration cases. The department represented a major Russian ammonia producer in 20 different ongoing litigation proceedings in connection with an attempted hostile takeover of the company. Other cases include representing a major German oil company before the Moscow arbitration court in a dispute involving a media and publishing company. Dmitry Surikov heads the team.

Jurinflot, International Law Office is recommended for dispute resolution work in the transport sector.

Norton Rose advised on litigation and international arbitrations involving government bodies in Russia. Other cases came from the real estate sector. Team head Valentina Gluhovskaya is recommended.

Orrick (CIS) LLC's Olga Anisimova has an excellent reputation for dispute resolution. The firm advised French and Scandinavian clients on disputes in Russia in 2005.

Russian firms **Padva & Partners** and **Reznik, Gagarin, Abushakhmin & Partners** are both active in litigation.

Pepeliaev, Goltsblat & Partners has an outstanding name for disputes in the tax sector.

Sikaylo, Gabbasov, Romakhova & Partners (Attorneys at Law) name partners Alexey Sikaylo and Dimitry Matveev are well-known litigators.

White & Case LLC advised a wide range of clients from the telecoms, energy and banking sectors on litigation and international arbitration. Counsel William Spiegelberger heads the group.

Akin Gump Strauss Hauer & Feld LLP counsel Marina Dumina is recommended for litigation and arbitration cases involving commercial, tax and employment disputes.

At **Alrud Law Firm** Vassily Rudomino and Dmitry Yeremin are recommended for litigation and arbitration.

CMS Bureau Francis Lefebvre advised on debt recovery cases for clients such as the EBRD.

Hogan & Hartson L.L.P. enters the table for the first time. The firm worked closely with its London and New York offices in advising on Russia-related litigation in Russian, UK and US courts.

Leboeuf, Lamb, Greene & MacRae LLP successfully represented Sakhalin Energy Investment Company Ltd in a case concerning an alleged violation of environmental law. Oleg Berger is recommended.

Lovells advised Alfa Eco Group on multi-jurisdictional litigation arising from the purchase of shares in Megafon, the Russian mobile telephone company. Viatcheslav Khorovsky has a focus on banking litigation work. Alexey Kozlov advises on insurance disputes.

Nörr Stiefenhofer Lutz advised an Austrian construction company on a dispute connected with the hostile takeover of its Russian subsidiary in Moscow.

Russin & Vecchi LLC advised an international bank on litigation concerning a marine mortgage. Other clients are media companies and food producers.

At **Tarlo and Partners** litigation is a core practice area. The firm advised on insolvency, real estate and transport sector disputes in 2005. The firm often co-operates with international firms such as **Gide Loyrette Nouel** and **Akin Gump Strauss Hauer & Feld LLP** for litigation cases.

Vegas-Lex Law Firm advised several clients in the energy sector on litigation and arbitration.

YUST Law Firm advises on litigation and arbitration. The firm advised on competition law and white-collar crime cases in 2005. Other highlights include advising a pharmaceutical company on an anti-monopoly case. Yury Timokhov has a good reputation.

EMPLOYMENT Russia

Baker & McKenzie's Evgeny Reyzman heads a highly regarded team which represented clients such as Siemens and Johnson & Johnson on employment disputes in 2005.

Linklaters CIS acts for major banking, energy and IT clients. The firm advised an employer on a

EMPLOYMENT Russia

BAKER & McKENZIE ✪
LINKLATERS CIS ✪

Akin Gump Strauss Hauer & Feld LLP
Freshfields Bruckhaus Deringer
Lovells ✪
Nörr Stiefenhofer Lutz ✪
Salans

CMS Cameron McKenna LLP✪
CMS Bureau Francis Lefebvre ✪
Clifford Chance
DLA Piper Rudnick Gray Cary ✪
PricewaterhouseCoopers CIS Law Offices BV ✪

Firms are listed A-Z in tiers which are ranked in order of priority
✪ Indicates firm displays contact details at the end of this chapter.

complex case involving secondees to nine regions throughout the Russian Federation. Henry Rutstein is well regarded.

Akin Gump Strauss Hauer & Feld LLP counsel Marina Dumina is also recommended.

Freshfields Bruckhaus Deringer advised Alcoa, the aluminium company, on employment matters in Russia. Other clients include Bloomberg.

Lovells advises on employment matters for corporate clients of the firm such as Nortel Networks and Mitsubishi.

Nörr Stiefenhofer Lutz advises several major German-speaking clients. The firm also has a strong tax practice which complements the employment work the firm undertakes.

Salans advised key client Kelly Services, the recruitment company, on a number of matters. The team also advises the firm's corporate clients on a range of employment matters. Associate Marina Ryzhkova is recommended.

DLA Piper Rudnick Gray Cary advised corporate clients of the firm such as Electrolux on employment matters.

PricewaterhouseCoopers CIS Law Offices BV advised several energy clients on employment matters.

ENERGY AND NATURAL RESOURCES Russia

Akin Gump Strauss Hauer & Feld LLP's Richard Wilkie heads a team with a market-leading name for advice to clients such as Lukoil. The firm often works with its international offices in London and the US.

Freshfields Bruckhaus Deringer's Kirsten Floss heads a team which has long experience in the energy sector in Russia. The firm advised ConocoPhillips in relation to its investment in Naryanmarneftegaz JV, a US$500m (€426m) joint venture with Lukoil to develop oil reserves in northern Russia. Other clients include Total and Wintershall, the German oil company.

Leboeuf, Lamb, Greene & MacRae LLP advised key clients Statoil and ExxonMobil on energy projects in Russia. Other clients include MOL, the Hungarian national oil company. Jonathan Hines has a long track record of advising on energy transactions.

Linklaters CIS' work in the energy and oil and gas sector is a mainstay of the firm in Moscow. Daniel Tyrer heads a team which advised key client BP on a range of matters. The firm also advised OAO Gazprom on several major transactions, including the development and financing of a natural gas pipeline linking Russia with western Europe.

White & Case LLC advised a range of major US, UK, German and Russian clients on corporate and financing transactions in the energy sector. Marc Polonsky, managing partner Hugh Verrier and Igor Ostapets are recommended.

Allen & Overy Legal Services advised Lukoil Finland Oy on acquisitions and financings in the energy sector. Other clients include investment banks (a mainstay of the firm's overall client base) such as Barclays and ABN Amro, which the firm advised on transactions in the oil and gas sector.

Baker & McKenzie's Max Gutbrod heads a department recommended for infrastructure projects for energy clients such as Lukoil.

CMS Cameron McKenna LLP was particularly active in advising on transactions in the power, electricity and hydrocarbons industry. Highlights include advising RAO UES on the restructuring of the electricity industry in Russia. Managing partner David Griston and Natalia Kozyrenko are highly recommended.

Chadbourne & Parke represented an operating subsidiary of Norilsk Nickel, the gold and minerals company, in connection with its acquisition of a majority stake in a Russian gold company. The firm also advises several major oil and gas clients.

Denton Wilde Sapte has an excellent name for energy matters in Russia and internationally. The firm advised KBC Bank NV on a US$150m (€126m) pre-export copper financing in Russia to UGMK Group. Doran Doeh head a group which advises other clients such as Shell on upstream and downstream work.

Herbert Smith CIS LLP advised TB Capital Limited on the sale of Oy Teboil Ab and Suomen Petrooli Oy, the petrol station retailers, to Lukoil-Finland and represented Chevron Texaco, Sumitomo Corporation, Lonmin and Mitsui Corporation on several corporate, joint venture and financing transactions. The Moscow team is working increasingly closely with lawyers in the firm's other international offices, especially China, a jurisdiction in which the firm also has a strong name for energy work.

Salans works closely with lawyers in all of its offices in the CIS in advising clients from the oil and gas, minerals and mining sector. The firm was particularly active in its advice to Russian clients in 2005; highlights include representing the City of Moscow on the restructuring of its electricity distribution and advising a major Russian coal producer on distribution matters. Jane Tarassova heads the team.

ENERGY AND NATURAL RESOURCES Russia

AKIN GUMP STRAUSS HAUER & FELD LLP
FRESHFIELDS BRUCKHAUS DERINGER
LEBOEUF, LAMB, GREENE & MACRAE LLP ✪
LINKLATERS CIS ✪
WHITE & CASE LLC

ALLEN & OVERY LEGAL SERVICES ✪
BAKER & McKENZIE ✪
CMS CAMERON MCKENNA LLP✪
CHADBOURNE & PARKE LLP
DENTON WILDE SAPTE ✪
HERBERT SMITH CIS LLP ✪
SALANS

Clifford Chance
Debevoise & Plimpton LLP ✪
Lovells ✪
Macleod Dixon ELP ✪
Norton Rose
Russin & Vecchi LLC
Vinson & Elkins L.L.P. ✪

Baker Botts ✪
Cleary, Gottlieb, Steen & Hamilton LLC ✪
Laptev & Partners ✪
Nörr Stiefenhofer Lutz ✪
PricewaterhouseCoopers CIS Law Offices BV ✪
Vegas-Lex Law Firm ✪
YUST Law Firm ✪

Firms are listed A-Z in tiers which are ranked in order of priority
✪ Indicates firm displays contact details at the end of this chapter.

Clifford Chance advised major Russian and Western mining and oil companies on acquisitions, exploration and financings. Ivan Marisin and Michael Cuthbert head the group.

Debevoise & Plimpton LLP represented Norsk Hydro on negotiations with Gazprom relating to the development of a gas field in the Barentz Sea. ExxonMobil is also a key client. Dmitri Nikiforov heads the team.

Lovells advised Chevron-Texaco on establishing a Russian joint venture with TNK for distribution of retail oil products and subsequently on its exit therefrom following the TNK/BP merger (2002 – 2004). The firm also acts for several major Japanese clients in the energy sector.

Macleod Dixon ELP has a strong client base in the mining industry for clients such as Barrick Gold Corporation, High River Gold and Bema Gold Corporation. The firm also advises on project finance transactions for banking clients. The firm works closely with its office in Almaty.

At **Norton Rose**, energy work is a key area of focus. The firm advised key client Eni SpA, the Italian energy company, on an acquisition in South Russia and represented De Beers on a joint venture in the diamond sector. Other clients include Valkyries Petroleum Corp, the Canadian oil company. Chris Viner and Valentina Gluhovskaya are recommended.

Russin & Vecchi LLC advised two major international oil-producing companies on exploration and joint ventures. The firm works closely with its offices in Vladivostok and Yuzhno-Sakhalinsk.

Vinson & Elkins L.L.P. has a strong name for energy sector work, both in Russia and internationally. The firm represented a shareholder in a Russian gas company in connection with a proposed sale of a stake to a major French oil and gas company. Dirk Walker and Natalya Morozova are recommended. The firm 'represents clients in a balanced matter on complex transactions'.

Baker Botts has a strong name internationally for energy work, especially amongst oil industry clients, including KNOC, the Korean National Oil Corporation, and Gazpromneft.

Nörr Stiefenhofer Lutz acts for one of Russia's biggest oil companies. Igor Budantsev is recommended.

PricewaterhouseCoopers CIS Law Offices BV works closely with its offices in St Petersburg and Yuzhno-Sakhalinsk in advising on energy matters. Clients include Lukoil and Gazprom.

IP/IT Russia

BAKER & McKENZIE ○
GORODISSKY & PARTNERS
GOWLINGS INTERNATIONAL INC ○

Lovells ○
Nörr Stiefenhofer Lutz ○
Salans

ARS-Patent
Beiten Burkhardt ○
Blishchenko & Partners
CMS Bureau Francis Lefebvre ○
CMS Cameron McKenna LLP ○
DLA Piper Rudnick Gray Cary ○
Freshfields Bruckhaus Deringer
Hogan & Hartson L.L.P. ○
Intellect Ltd
Latham & Watkins LLP
LeBoeuf, Lamb, Greene & MacRae LLP ○
Linklaters CIS ○
Norton Rose
Pepeliaev, Goltsblat & Partners ○
PricewaterhouseCoopers CIS Law Offices BV ○
Squire, Sanders & Dempsey (Moscow) LLC ○

Barabashev & Partners
Klishin & Partners
Russin & Vecchi LLC

Firms are listed A-Z in tiers which are ranked in order of priority
○ Indicates firm displays contact details at the end of this chapter.

IP/IT Russia

Baker & McKenzie has a superb reputation for IP work in Moscow and internationally. The firm advised Nike in connection with a police raid against a distributor of counterfeit software. Accenture is also a client. Eugene Arievich enjoys an excellent name for IP work. Max Gutbrod is recommended for IT work.

Gorodissky & Partners is one of Russia's leading firms for IP matters. Valery Medvedev heads a team which advised on a wide range of IP matters for major European, US and Japanese clients.

Canadian firm **Gowlings International Inc** has a strong name for patent prosecution work. The firm also advises on trade mark matters. Vladimir Dementiev and Viacheslav Kliukin are respected. Marina Drel advises on contentious work.

Lovells has a strong reputation for IP both in Russia and internationally. The firm acted for Mattel Inc on a number of trade mark piracy cases. Other clients include Deutsche Telekom and SABMiller, which the firm advised on trade mark matters. Senior associate Natalia Gulyaeva heads the team.

Nörr Stiefenhofer Lutz's Julianna Tabastajewa heads a team which advises on a wide range of IP, IT and media law. The team advised on major IP cases for Volkswagen and Audi.

Salans has a strong team of intellectual property lawyers. The firm successfully represented a major automotive company in a novel trade mark case against an unauthorised dealer. Sergei Marinich and of-counsel Denis Voevodin are recommended.

CMS Bureau Francis Lefebvre advised on several trade mark protection cases and technology transfer contracts.

Leonid Zubarev at **CMS Cameron McKenna LLP** advises several IT and software companies.

DLA Piper Rudnick Gray Cary advised RealNetworks, Inc on negotiations with a Russian subcontractor.

Freshfields Bruckhaus Deringer advised on several trade mark and patent cases. Vitaly Kaliatin has a special focus on Internet cases.

Hogan & Hartson L.L.P. advised Zentiva, the Czech pharmaceutical company, on issues of data protection in Russia. Other clients include US media companies.

Latham & Watkins LLP of-counsel Lev Simkin advised on several anti-piracy cases.

Leboeuf, Lamb, Greene & MacRae LLP associate Veronika Fridman is recommended.

Associate Alexei Dudko at **Linklaters CIS** heads a group which acted for several retail sector clients; highlights include representing Yum!, the restaurant chain, on IP rights relating to an alliance with KFC. Other clients are banks and luxury goods companies.

Russin & Vecchi LLC advised on trade mark and copyright cases for clients such as media and software companies. Other clients include US telecoms companies.

REAL ESTATE Russia

Baker & McKenzie is highly recommended for complex financing, turnkey engineering projects and acquisitions in the real estate sector. The team reports an increase in work involving Asian clients; highlight include advising China Huaming International Investment Co Ltd on its US$300m (€257m) acquisition of land in Moscow for the development of a business centre. Andrei Soukhomlinov heads a team of seven lawyers.

Linklaters CIS' Xavier Hunter heads a team which advised CMI Development on a major business park development in Moscow. The firm also advised on hotel, office and greenfield development projects. Other key clients include Fleming Family & Partners Russian Real Estate Fund. The team suffered a setback when well-known consultant Konstantine Kouzine left the firm in May 2005 to join **PricewaterhouseCoopers CIS Law Offices BV**.

Norton Rose has longstanding and wide-ranging experience in real estate matters. Valentina Gluhovskaya heads a team which represented Capital Group, the Russian real estate developer, on real estate developments and acquisitions in Moscow. IKEA, Samsung, and several banks and foreign investment funds are clients.

Pepeliaev, Goltsblat & Partners has a strong name for real estate work, working closely with its highly-regarded St Petersburg office. The firm advised a global soft drinks producer on its acquisition of a brownfield site in St Petersburg. Other clients include hypermarkets.

CMS Cameron McKenna LLP has a good name for real estate financings and projects for clients such as banks, developers and hotels. Steven Shone leads a team of four assistants.

Marc Bartholomy leads a team at **Clifford Chance** which represented corporates, construction companies and banks on developments and real estate funds work in Moscow and St Petersburg.

At **DLA Piper Rudnick Gray Cary** Scott Antel has an excellent name for advice to real estate and hospitality sector clients. The firm advises several major hotel chains in Moscow, including Marriott, Swissotel and the Ritz, which the firm advsised on the development of a premium luxury hotel in Moscow.

Nörr Stiefenhofer Lutz advises on financing, development and construction. The firm advised on the development of a major business park of skyscrapers in Moscow. The team also advised on

REAL ESTATE Russia

BAKER & McKENZIE ✪
LINKLATERS CIS ✪
NORTON ROSE
PEPELIAEV, GOLTSBLAT & PARTNERS ✪

CMS Cameron McKenna LLP✪
Clifford Chance
DLA Piper Rudnick Gray Cary ✪
Nörr Stiefenhofer Lutz ✪
Salans
White & Case LLC

Alrud Law Firm ✪
Baker Botts ✪
Beiten Burkhardt ✪
CMS Bureau Francis Lefebvre ✪
Freshfields Bruckhaus Deringer
Gide Loyrette Nouel ✪
Hogan & Hartson L.L.P. ✪
LeBoeuf, Lamb, Greene & MacRae LLP ✪
Lovells ✪
Orrick (CIS) LLC ✪
PricewaterhouseCoopers CIS Law Offices BV ✪

Firms are listed A-Z in tiers which are ranked in order of priority
✪ *Indicates firm displays contact details at the end of this chapter.*

several complex greenfield projects in 2005. Clients include Meinl European Land and several Western and Eastern European developers and investment funds.

At **Salans** Anna McDonald heads a team which is recommended for a wide range of real estate development, financing and acquisition work. The firm advised SRV-Okhta, a Russian-Finnish property development joint venture, on a €200m retail shopping, hotel and office centre in St Petersburg.

White & Case LLC advises on a wide range of development, financing and acquisition work. The firm advised Aareal Bank AG on the €50m limited recourse financing of a Marriott hotel in Moscow. Eric Michailov and Hermann Schmitt are recommended.

Alrud Law Firm has good experience in the local market for a range of acquisition, construction and development work. The firm advised Pharmacy Chain 36,6, the Russian pharmacy chain, on purchasing real estate in St Petersburg.

Kirsten Floss at **Freshfields Bruckhaus Deringer** heads a team which advised a Scandinavian hygiene products producer on the development and construction of a plant in the Tula region and represented an Austrian food producer on the development and construction of a plant in Moscow.

Hogan & Hartson L.L.P. counsel Olga Kozyr heads a team which advises on acquisitions, development and leases.

Leboeuf, Lamb, Greene & MacRae LLP advised a major European investment fund on the development of a chain of hypermarkets.

Lovells advises on leasing, development and management agreements for clients such as BMW, Metal One Corporation and Nortel Networks.

Orrick (CIS) LLC represented a Russian real estate developer on a hotel development project.

PricewaterhouseCoopers CIS Law Offices BV enters our table following the recruitment in May 2005 of Konstantine Kouzine, who joined the firm from **Linklaters CIS**. The firm advised on several major industrial and commercial development projects in Moscow.

SHIPPING AND TRANSPORT Russia

Jurinflot, International Law Office has an excellent name for a wide range of both contentious and non-contentious shipping work. Clients include P&I clubs from the UK and Holland. Alexander Mednikov and Vadim Ermolaev are recommended. The firm often co-operates with leading international shipping firms such as **Hill Taylor Dickinson**, **Richards Butler** and **Lawrence Graham LLP**.

Norton Rose has a strong name for a range of shipping and asset finance transactions. Dmitry Gravin heads the team. The firm advised P&O Ports on the expansion of its joint venture operations in Russia.

Denton Wilde Sapte advised UtAir Airlines on a number of matters, including supply of regional turboprop aircraft, charter agreements and an aviation accident.

Linklaters CIS' expertise in the shipping and transport sector is closely connected to its work in other sectors such as energy, banking and infrastructure. The firm acted for Pratt & Whitney on an aircraft lease to a major Russian airline and also advised on several port projects.

At **Salans** Jane Tarassova advises several clients from the aviation sector.

Vegas-Lex Law Firm secured the arrest of a ship in a Bulgarian port on behalf of a Russian client.

Clyde & Co, well known internationally for shipping matters, opened a Moscow office in 2005.

Four-partner **Inmar Legal Co., Ltd.**, based in Vladivostok, has a good name for a wide range of shipping matters.

PricewaterhouseCoopers CIS Law Offices BV advises clients such as Boeing and Emirates Airline.

Russin & Vecchi LLC works closely with its Vladivostok office in advising on a range of shipping matters, including flag registration and fishing quotas.

SHIPPING AND TRANSPORT Russia

JURINFLOT, INTERNATIONAL LAW OFFICE ✪
NORTON ROSE

Denton Wilde Sapte ✪
Linklaters CIS ✪
Salans
Vegas-Lex Law Firm ✪

Clyde & Co ✪
Inmar Legal Co., Ltd.
PricewaterhouseCoopers CIS Law Offices BV ✪
Russin & Vecchi LLC

Firms are listed A-Z in tiers which are ranked in order of priority
✪ *Indicates firm displays contact details at the end of this chapter.*

TAX Russia

Baker & McKenzie's Alexander Chmelev heads a team recommended for expertise in tax issues in the energy sector. The firm also advises clients from the IT, automotive and manufacturing industries.

DLA Piper Rudnick Gray Cary substantially strengthened its tax capability in mid-2005 with the acquisition of several lawyers from **EY Law**. The firm advised several major hotel clients on tax advisory work. Scott Antel heads the team.

Linklaters CIS advised key client BP on tax aspects of its joint venture with TNK. Associate Victor Matchekhin heads a team which advises on a wide range of tax structuring matters for clients of the firm's Moscow office.

Nörr Stiefenhofer Lutz advises on contentious and non-contentious work. The firm advised on tax aspects of several major M&A and restructuring transactions. Ilja Rybalkin has a strong reputation. The firm reports a growing amount of tax due diligence investigations work.

Pepeliaev, Goltsblat & Partners partner Sergey Pepeliaev is one of Russia's best-known tax experts. Clients come from the energy, automotive, publishing and electronics industries.

TAX Russia

BAKER & McKENZIE ✪

DLA Piper Rudnick Gray Cary ✪
Linklaters CIS ✪
Nörr Stiefenhofer Lutz ✪
Pepeliaev, Goltsblat & Partners ✪
Salans
White & Case LLC

Beiten Burkhardt ✪
CMS Bureau Francis Lefebvre ✪
Clifford Chance
Gide Loyrette Nouel ✪
Jurinflot, International Law Office ✪
Macleod Dixon ELP ✪
Vegas-Lex Law Firm ✪

Firms are listed A-Z in tiers which are ranked in order of priority
✪ *Indicates firm displays contact details at the end of this chapter.*

The largest firms

Ajerbaijan

1	Advocate Service	12
2	BM International LLC	11
3	OMNI Consultants	9
4	Ledingham Chalmers	6
	Salans	6
6	Interjurservice Ltd	5
7	Baker & McKenzie - CIS, Limited	4
8	GRATA Law Firm	3
9	Michael Wilson & Partners	2

Belarus

1	Businessconsult Law Firm	14
2	Mikhel and Partners	8
	Vlasova & Partners	8
4	BelJurbureau Attorneys at Law	6
	Dicsa	6
6	Borovtsov & Salei	5
7	Intels - Belarus	2

Georgia

	DLA Piper Rudnick Gray Cary (member firm, Gvinadze & Partners LP)	7

Kazakhstan

1	GRATA Law Firm	55
2	Denton Wilde Sapte	25
3	Salans	22
4	Bracewell & Giuliani, L.L.P.	13
5	Michael Wilson & Partners	10
	Sayat Zholshy & Partners	10
7	Macleod Dixon ELP	9
8	Baker & McKenzie	8
	LeBoeuf, Lamb, Greene & MacRae LLP	8
10	Chadbourne & Parke LLP	7
	McGuireWoods Kazakhstan LLP	7
12	Asia DICSA LexAnalitic	5
13	The Zanger Law Firm	4
	White & Case Kazakhstan LLP	4
15	Zhakenov & Partners in Affiliation with White & Jones LLP	3

These figures represent the total number of lawyers in this country only, and have been supplied by the firms themselves. The figures should be accurate as at 1 January 2006.

Salans advises on a wide range of contentious and non-contentious matters. Oleg Konnov has a very strong reputation.

White & Case LLC's Irina Dmitrieva has been building an excellent reputation since her arrival from **Clifford Chance** in March 2004. The department advises on a broad spectrum of complex tax matters for clients of the Moscow office.

At **CMS Bureau Francis Lefebvre**, tax is a core practice area. The firm advises on a wide range of tax structuring, litigation and government lobbying. The firm often provides tax advice to clients of **CMS Cameron McKenna LLP**, based in the same building in Moscow.

Jurinflot, International Law Office's Alexander Mednikov has a good name for tax work.

Levon Kocharyan at **Macleod Dixon ELP** advises several mining sector clients on tax matters.

Vegas-Lex Law Firm advises clients from the energy and transport sectors on tax matters.

AZERBAIJAN

Baker & McKenzie – CIS, Limited has had an office in Baku since 1998. Daniel Matthews heads an office recommended for a range of corporate, projects, dispute resolution and real estate work. The team advised on a joint venture between Siemens, the State Oil Company of Azerbaijan (SOCAR) and a local company to supply equipment to the oil and gas industry. Other clients include Vitol SA.

Scottish firm **Ledingham Chalmers** was the first foreign law firm to open an office in Baku, in 1992. Work in the oil and gas sector is a particular focus. Other clients include banks and financial services industry clients. Ismail Askerov is recommended.

OMNI Consultants often works closely with several major international firms that do not have a presence in Azerbaijan. The firm advises on corporate, banking, tax and dispute resolution matters. Clients include McDonald's. Jeyhun Bayramov, Roman Alloyarov and Ismayil Zargarli are recommended.

Salans offers a broad range of corporate, employment, property and tax law advice from its Baku office. Managing partner Alum Bati acts for several clients from the oil and gas sector.

AZERBAIJAN

BAKER & McKENZIE – CIS, LIMITED ○
LEDINGHAM CHALMERS ○
OMNI CONSULTANTS ○
SALANS

Azleks International Law Firm
BM International LLC ○
Interjurservice Ltd

Firms are listed A-Z in tiers which are ranked in order of priority
○ Indicates firm displays contact details at the end of this chapter.

At **Azleks International Law Firm** SJ Tagiyev is also recommended, especially for dispute resolution.

Ten-lawyer **BM International LLC** is especially recommended for financing transactions for clients such as the EBRD. Jamal Baghirov heads the firm.

Interjurservice Ltd advises on corporate, banking, IP and dispute resolution matters for clients such as BP, Japan Tobacco and drinks company, Castel Group. Ibrahim Zeynalov heads a team of five lawyers.

BELARUS

Borovtsov & Salei has a strong relationship with **Chadbourne & Parke**. Clients include Coca-Cola, McDonald's and Ford. The firm advised a Western bank on its investment in the telecoms industry in 2005. Vassili Salei and Valentin Borovtsov are recommended.

Vlasova & Partners acts for a long list of blue-chip clients such as Alcatel, Boeing and Japan Tobacco International. In addition to corporate work, dispute resolution is a core practice. Liliya Vlasova and Tatyana Emelianova are recommended. The firm also has an office in Warsaw.

Four-partner **Businessconsult Law Firm** advises on corporate, FDI, banking and dispute resolution. Clients include several blue-chip German corporations such as DaimlerChrysler AG.

At niche firm **Mikhel and Partners** Konstantin Mikhel is also recommended for corporate matters.

Seven-lawyer **DICSA** is recommended for commercial, real estate, debt collection and transport sector work. The firm represents clients from Germany, China and the Middle East. Gennadiy Glinskiy is recommended. The firm provides 'timely, well-researched advice'.

GEORGIA

Gvinadze & Partners LP became part of the **DLA Piper Rudnick Gray Cary** network in mid-2005 and is known locally as **DLA Piper Rudnick Gray Cary (member firm, Gvinadze & Partners LP)** when the firm acquired a large team of

BELARUS

BOROVTSOV & SALEI
VLASOVA & PARTNERS

Businessconsult Law Firm
Mikhel and Partners

DICSA

GEORGIA

DLA Piper Rudnick Gray Cary (member firm Gvinadze & Partners LP) ○

Firms are listed A-Z in tiers which are ranked in order of priority
○ Indicates firm displays contact details at the end of this chapter.

lawyers from **EY Law** both in Moscow and across the whole of the CIS region. The firm works closely with the **DLA Piper Rudnick Gray Cary** Moscow and London offices advising on corporate, FDI, finance and capital markets work.

KAZAKHSTAN

Aequitas works closely with several major international firms that do not have an office in Kazakhstan, especially for banking and capital markets transactions.

Curtis Masters heads **Baker & McKenzie**'s highly respected Almaty office. The firm advises on a wide range of corporate, banking, capital markets, dispute resolution and tax matters. The firm acts for several major clients from the energy sector.

Bracewell & Giuliani, L.L.P.'s Gregory Vojack leads a group which works closely with its US offices in advising on a range of corporate, banking and energy work. One Western banking client described the firm as 'very commercially minded'.

Chadbourne & Parke LLP's Kenneth Mack heads a team of five associates in Almaty. The firm undertakes work in the oil and gas, minerals, and telecoms sectors.

Denton Wilde Sapte partner Marla Valdez has a strong name for oil and gas work. Other clients come from the banking sector. The team expanded to welcome eight lawyers from *Coudert Brothers*' Almaty office, including well-known partner Tom O'Brien, in October 2005.

Grata Law Firm has a strong name for energy work. The firm also advises on corporate and dispute resolution matters. Tlek Baigabulov, Aidar Sarymsakov and Akhmetzhan Abdullayev are recommended. The firm enjoys an excellent relationship with several UK and US law firms that do not have a presence in Almaty.

LeBoeuf, Lamb, Greene & MacRae LLP works closely with its highly regarded Moscow office. The firm has a strong client base in the energy sector.

At **Macleod Dixon ELP** Maxim Telemtayev heads a team which works closely with the firm's Moscow office in advising clients from the mining and energy sectors.

Michael Wilson & Partners has a strong name in the oil and gas and energy sectors. The firm also advises on heavyweight banking and capital markets transactions. The firm reports an increase in advice relating to listings on London's AIM. Strong relationships with Magic Circle UK international firms such as **Linklaters CIS** underscore the firm's pre-eminent reputation in the Almaty legal market. Name partner Michael Wilson and John Emmott are recommended.

Salans managing partner Aigoul Kenjebayeva heads a team of 18 lawyers which works closely with the firm's offices in Moscow and St Petersburg in advising on corporate, FDI, banking and project finance transactions, many of which are in the oil and gas sector. The firm also advised on several international arbitrations.

Sayat Zholshy & Partners is especially recommended for dispute resolution. The firm also advises on corporate, commercial and real estate transactions. Managing partner Aydin Bikebaev heads a team of six partners.

At **White & Case Kazakhstan LLP**, Yuriy Maltsev heads a team which works closely with the firm's highly regarded Moscow office. Clients come from the banking and energy sectors.

Two other local firms with strong commercial practices are **The Zanger Law Firm** and **Zhakenov & Partners in Affiliation with White & Jones LLP**

KAZAKHSTAN

- Aequitas
- Baker & McKenzie ✪
- Bracewell & Giuliani, L.L.P. ✪
- Chadbourne & Parke LLP
- Denton Wilde Sapte ✪
- GRATA Law Firm
- LeBoeuf, Lamb, Greene & MacRae LLP ✪
- Macleod Dixon ELP
- McGuireWoods Kazakhstan LLP
- Michael Wilson & Partners ✪
- Salans
- Sayat Zholshy & Partners ✪
- The Zanger Law Firm
- White & Case Kazakhstan LLP
- Zhakenov & Partners in Affiliation with White & Jones LLP

Firms are listed alphabetically

✪ Indicates firm displays contact details at the end of this chapter.

MOLDOVA

Three-partner **Buruiana & Partners** advises on corporate, IP, telecoms and media sector work. Managing partner Mihail Buruiana heads the team.

At **Levintsa & Associates** Victor Levintsa leads a team which advises on commercial, IT and telecoms matters.

Turcan & Turcan name partner Alexander Turcan heads a firm which advises blue-chip clients from the energy, electricity, banking and retail sectors. The firm regularly co-operates with several major international firms which do not have an office in Moldova.

MOLDOVA

- BURUIANA & PARTNERS
- LEVINTSA & ASSOCIATES
- TURCAN & TURCAN

Firms are listed alphabetically

UKRAINE

At **BC Toms & Co** name partner Bate Toms heads a firm with a long track record of advice in Ukraine. The firm works closely with its London office in advising on corporate, finance, energy, dispute resolution and real estate transactions.

Baker & McKenzie's James Hitch heads a team of four partners which advised a group of European investment funds in connection with the acquisition of Volia Cable, the media and TV group. Other clients include InBev and Flextronics. Partner Olexander Martinenko is also recommended. The firm is also recommended for banking, IP, employment, real estate and tax matters. The firm is described as 'flexible, quick and good at prioritising client requests'.

UKRAINE

- BC TOMS & CO ✪
- BAKER & McKENZIE ✪

- CHADBOURNE & PARKE
- DLA PIPER RUDNICK GRAY CARY
- PRICEWATERHOUSECOOPERS
- SALANS
- SHEVCHENKO DIDKOVSKIY & PARTNERS ✪

- Doubinsky & Osharova
- Frishberg & Partners
- Ilyashev & Partners ✪
- KM Partners
- Magister & Partners ✪
- Sayenko Kharenko
- The Silecky Firm
- Ukrainian Legal Group, L.L.C. ✪
- Vasil Kisil & Partner

- Andreas Neocleous & Co
- Arzinger & Partners ✪
- Astapov Lawyers International Law Group
- Beiten Burkhardt
- Grischenko & Partners ✪
- International Law Offices
- Konnov & Sozanovsky
- Legal Alliance Company
- Pakharenko & Partners ✪
- Proxen
- Salkom ✪

Firms are listed A-Z in tiers which are ranked in order of priority

✪ Indicates firm displays contact details at the end of this chapter.

The largest firms

Kyrgyzstan		
1	GRATA Law Firm	3
Moldova		
1	Brodsky Uskov Looper Reed & Partners	16
2	Turcan & Turcan	6
3	Advocate, LLP	5
	Levintsa & Associates	5
5	Buruiana & Partners	3
6	Bostina & Associates	1
Ukraine		
1	PricewaterhouseCoopers	84
2	Shevchenko Didkovskiy & Partners	46
3	Magister & Partners	45
4	Grischenko & Partners	41
5	Konnov & Sozanovsky	40
6	Salkom	32
7	Baker & McKenzie	25
8	KM Partners	24
9	Vasil Kisil & Partner	22
10	Proxen	21
	Volkov & Partners	21
12	International Law Offices & Veritas Legal Advisers	20
13	BC Toms & Co	18
14	Astapov Lawyers International Law Group	16
	DLA Piper Ukraine LLC	16
16	Ilyashev & Partners	14
17	Ukrainian Legal Group, L.L.C.	13
18	Chadbourne & Parke	12
19	Kravets & Levenets	11
20	Doubinsky & Osharova	10
	Pakharenko & Partners	10
	Salans	10
23	Frishberg & Partners	9
Uzbekistan		
1	Denton Wilde Sapte	4
2	GRATA Law Firm	3
3	Chadbourne & Parke LLP	2

These figures represent the total number of lawyers in this country only, and have been supplied by the firms themselves. The figures should be accurate as at 1 January 2006.

Chadbourne & Parke's Jaroslawa Johnson heads a team which works closely with the firm's Moscow office in advising a range of clients in the telecoms, tobacco, automotive and foods sectors.

At **DLA Piper Rudnick Gray Cary** Margarita Karpenko heads a group which advised Ensto Oy, the Finnish electrical device manufacture, on FDI matters. Other clients include oil and gas, media and real estate companies. The team also has a strong focus on tax work.

PricewaterhouseCoopers has a strong name for tax work, and is also recommended for a range of general corporate work. The firm advised on several M&A transactions in the energy sector. Jorge Intriago leads a team of nine lawyers.

Salans has a good name for corporate, finance, real estate and energy work. The firm acts for several clients in the oil and gas sector. Managing partner Oleg Batyuk and Myron Rabij head a team of 19 lawyers.

Shevchenko Didkovskiy & Partners is recommended for a wide range of corporate, finance and capital markets transactions. The firm also advises several clients from the real estate and energy industries. The firm also has particular expertise in competition matters. Clients include Citibank and Barclays. Managing partner Igor Shevchenko is recommended. The firm enjoys strong relationships with several major US and UK law firms.

Doubinsky & Osharova is arguably the top firm in Ukraine for IP matters. The firm acts for a wide range of blue-chip international clients. Michael Doubinsky heads a team of three partners.

Frishberg & Partners advises a strong client base from the IT, telecoms and software industries. Clients include Hewlett-Packard and Intel. Transaction highlights in 2005 include advising a major US IT company on outsourcing agreements. The firm advises a broad range of other European and US clients from a wide range of sectors, including banking, manufacturing and transport, such as Fiat, Skanska, Commerzbank and KLM. Competition work is also a strong area of focus. Name partner Alexander Frishberg and Scott Brown head a team which works closely with the firm's US office in Portland, Oregon.

Vasil Kisil & Partner has a strong name for dispute resolution matters.

Ilyashev & Partners has a good name for a wide range of corporate, dispute resolution and IP matters. The firm acts for several aviation clients. Mikhail Ilyashev heads a team described as 'dedicated and responsive'.

KM Partners is one of the best firms in the market for tax matters. Alexander Minin is recommended. The firm is 'timely, supportive and good at communicating with clients'.

Magister & Partners is recommended for a wide range of corporate, competition, capital markets, real estate and trade matters. The firm advises several clients from the telecoms sector. The firm also advised on competition matters for clients such as Pernod Ricard. Oleg Riabokon heads the team. Andrew Mac joined as partner in 2005 from **PricewaterhouseCoopers**. The firm is 'responsive' and 'exceeds client expectations'.

Although formed relatively recently in 2004, **Sayenko Kharenko** has been building an excellent reputation, especially for complex finance and capital markets work. The firm also advises on a broad range of corporate and commercial matters. Clients include UBS and Merrill Lynch. The firm provides 'balanced advice', 'dedicates necessary resources to projects' and 'helps us find right solutions', say clients. Michael Kharenko and Vladimir Sayenko are recommended.

The Silecky Firm has a strong name in the market, thanks in part to its association with **Squire, Sanders & Dempsey L.L.P.**. Name partner Markian Silecky is recommended.

Three-partner **Ukrainian Legal Group, L.L.C.** has an excellent and broad-ranging reputation. Particular areas of focus include energy, dispute resolution and IP work. Irina Paliashvili has an excellent name.

Vasil Kisil & Partner has a strong name for dispute resolution.

Three-partner, nine-assistant **Astapov Lawyers International Law Group** has a particular focus on international trade and commodities work. Andrey Astapov heads the team.

Legal Alliance Company has a special focus on advice to clients from the healthcare and pharmaceutical industry.

UZBEKISTAN

Baker & McKenzie's Tashkent office is overseen by Almaty-based Curtis Masters.

Denton Wilde Sapte's niche presence in Tashkent is overseen by Almaty-based partner Marla Valdez.

Chadbourne & Parke LLP also maintains a niche presence in Tashkent.

UZBEKISTAN

BAKER & McKENZIE
DENTON WILDE SAPTE ✪
CHADBOURNE & PARKE LLP

Firms are listed alphabetically

✪ Indicates firm displays contact details at the end of this chapter.

BM INTERNATIONAL LLC

CASPIAN PLAZA BUSINESS CENTER
44 JAFAR JABBARLY STREET
BAKU AZ1065

Telephone: +994 12 497 1914
Fax: +994 12 497 1913
E-mail: info@bmlawaz.com
Website: www.bmlawaz.com

Languages
Azeri, English, French, Russian, Turkish

Other offices
London, Oregon

Number of lawyers 15
at this office 11

Contact
Farhad Aliyev (faliyev@bmlawaz.com)

International groupings
Correspondent law firm of Chadbourne & Parke LLP

CATEGORIES OF WORK

Oil and gas	**IT and telecommunications**
Privatisation	**International private law**
Banking and finance	**Intellectual property**
Security	**Corporate finance**
Aviation	**Real estate**
Tax law	**Mortgage**
Litigation	**Insolvency and bankruptcy**
Labour law	**Family law**
Commercial and company law	

BAKER & McKENZIE – CIS, LIMITED

THE LANDMARK BUILDING
96 NIZAMI STREET
BAKU AZ1010

Telephone: +994 12 497 1801
Fax: +994 12 497 1805
E-mail: baku.office@bakernet.com
Website: www.bakernet.com

Languages
Azerbaijani, English, Russian, Turkish

Other offices
The member firms of Baker & McKenzie International, a Swiss Verein, have 70 offices in 38 countries around the world. For a complete list, please visit www.bakernet.com.

Number of lawyers 3,300+
at this office 6

Contact
Daniel Matthews

CATEGORIES OF WORK

Banking and finance Daniel Matthews	**Mergers and acquisitions** Daniel Matthews
Corporate and commercial Gunduz Karimov	**Major projects and project finance** Daniel Matthews, Aykhan Asadov
Dispute resolution Gunduz Karimov	**Pharmaceuticals** Gunduz Karimov
Employment Aykhan Asadov	**Privatisation** Daniel Matthews
Intellectual property Gunduz Karimov	**Real estate and construction** Natik Mamedov
IT/communications Natik Mamedov	**Tax** Aykhan Asadov

LEDINGHAM CHALMERS

340 NIZAMI STREET
ISR PLAZA, 3RD FLOOR
BAKU AZ1000

Telephone: +994 12 493 2939
Fax: +994 12 498 7132
E-mail: baku@ledinghamchalmers.com
Website: www.ledinghamchalmers.com

Languages
Azeri, English, French, German, Russian, Turkish

Other offices
Aberdeen, Edinburgh, Inverness, Istanbul, London, Port Stanley (Falkland Islands)

Number of lawyers 96
at this office 5

CATEGORIES OF WORK

Banking and finance
Benjamin Paine, Elchin Mammadov

Energy
Ismail Askerov, Elchin Mammadov

Corporate/M&A
Benjamin Paine, Ismail Askerov

Litigation
Elchin Mammadov

Employment
Elchin Mammadov, Ismail Askerov

Real estate
Ismail Askerov, Elchin Mammadov

Natural resources
Benjamin Paine, Elchin Mammadov

Competition
Ismail Askerov

Intellectual property
Ismail Askerov

Tax
Elchin Mammadov

Maritime
Ismail Askerov

Communications
Ismail Askerov

Environment
Ismail Askerov, Elchin Mammadov

MICHAEL WILSON & PARTNERS

4TH FLOOR
340 NIZAMI STREET
ISR PLAZA
BAKU AZ1000

Telephone: +994 12 497 8948
Fax: +994 12 497 8947
E-mail: info@mwp.kz
Website: www.mwp.kz

Languages
English, Russian, Azerbaijani

Other offices
Almaty

Number of lawyers 16

Contact
Mehriban Efendiyeva

CATEGORIES OF WORK

Foreign investments and joint ventures

Corporate, corporate finance and securities

Intellectual property

Arbitration, litigation and dispute resolution

Banking, finance and project finance

Tax and customs

Real estate

Mining and natural resources

Engineering and construction

Privatisation

Power industry (generation, transmission and distribution) and utilities

Labour, employment and work permit matters

Telecommunications

Transportation, shipping and aviation

OMNI CONSULTANTS

CASPIAN PLAZA, 9TH FLOOR
44 JAFAR JABARLY STREET
BAKU AZ1065

Telephone: +994 12 448 0812
Fax: +994 12 499 1256
E-mail: office@omniconsultants.net
Website: www.omniconsultants.net

Languages
English, Azeri, Russian

Number of lawyers 9

CATEGORIES OF WORK

Corporate and commercial
Roman Alloyarov, Ismail Zargarli

Energy and natural resources
Jeyhun Bayramov, Roman Alloyarov

Banking and finance
Roman Alloyarov

Litigation
Ismail Zargarli, Jeyhun Bayramov

Privatisation
Jeyhun Bayramov

IP
Jeyhun Bayramov

Employment
Ismail Zargarli

Telecoms
Jeyhun Bayramov, Roman Alloyarov

Tax
Jeyhun Bayramov

Competition
Jeyhun Bayramov

Real estate
Ismail Zargarli, Roman Alloyarov

THE FIRM

The firm was established in September 2002 by Jeyhun Bayramov, Roman Alloyarov and Ismail Zargarli (all three former associates with the Baku offices of international law firms). The practice has been growing at a rapid pace and today OMNI is a nine-fee-earner firm supported by ten paralegals, administrative and support staff.

The firm consists of local lawyers qualified to practice in Azerbaijan with experience in western law firms having a presence in Azerbaijan. A growing number of the firm's lawyers have completed or currently pursue LLM degrees at US and European law schools. Additionally, Mr Alloyarov is one of only a few Azeri lawyers admitted to the New York Bar (2001). One of the firm's associates has successfully passed the July 2005 New York Bar exam and his application for admission is pending. Mr Zargarli is a member of the Advocates' Chamber of Azerbaijan.

The firm possesses comparative levels of professional qualifications and skills, and maintains the same level of professional ethics as western law firms. Its entire professional and support staff is fluent in English, Azeri and Russian. Lawyers in the firm have significant experience in representing foreign clients in a vast array of Azeri law matters, such as corporate and commercial, in-bound foreign investments, banking and finance, employment, intellectual property, privatisation, real estate, tax, customs and litigation.

OMNI is an independently run firm and is not affiliated or associated with any other firm. It maintains correspondent relations with a number of prominent western law firms and regularly acts upon their instructions.

The clients of the firm include major international companies, joint ventures and prominent Azeri entities in such sectors as energy and natural resources, FMCG, telecoms, banking and financial services, real estate and construction. For further information, please refer to the firm's website, www.omniconsultants.net.

AREAS OF PRACTICE

The firm is a full-service practice and is able to assist on the wide range of Azeri law matters. In 2005, OMNI assumed the role of legal adviser in a number of transactions, which were either inaugural or the largest by value in the Azerbaijan market. Highlights from 2005 include:

Banking and finance: (i) OMNI acted as a local counsel to the State Oil Company of the Azerbaijan Republic and its subsidiary, AzACG (holder of participating interest of the Republic of Azerbaijan in the Azeri-Chirag-Gunashli PSA), in a multi-million-dollar borrowing, which was the largest financing transaction in Azerbaijan in 2005 and was the inaugural transaction for an Azeri company in the international loan market. (ii) OMNI acted as special counsel for a number of lenders, including Black Sea Trade and Development Bank and KfW, in a series of external borrowing of the Micro Finance Bank of Azerbaijan (which counts EBRD and IFC amongs its shareholders).

Corporate/privatisation: (i) the firm is representing the government of Azerbaijan in the privatisation of state shares in the largest domestic mobile operator. This deal is expected to be the largest sale of a state asset in terms of transaction value in the history of Azerbaijan privatisation. In parallel, the firm is also advising the government on the privatisation of the largest fixed line joint venture in the country. (ii) Another coup for the firm was a mandate from an OPIC-backed private equity fund in a first-ever private equity investment into a prominent Azeri company.

Real estate: OMNI acted for a franchise of a global fast food chain in Azerbaijan in connection with expansion of the restaurant chain, including development and leases of new sites.

Dispute resolution: OMNI assisted a prominent South African firm and acted as local counsel in connection with the defence of the Republic of Azerbaijan in the Tigr case, involving a $100m claim against a number of Azeri defendants, brought in the courts of South Africa.

DLA PIPER RUDNICK GRAY CARY
(MEMBER FIRM, GVINADZE & PARTNERS LP)

44 LESELIDZE STREET
TBILISI 0105

Telephone: +995 32 92 11 96/93 64 22
Fax: +995 32 93 27 52
E-mail: ted.jonas@dlapiper.com
Website: www.dlapiper.com/georgia

Languages
Georgian, English, Russian, French

Other offices
Austria, Belgium, Bosnia-Herzegovina, China, Croatia, Czech Republic, Denmark*, Egypt*, France, Germany, Hong Kong, Hungary, Italy, Japan, Netherlands, Norway*, Poland*, Russia, Singapore*, Slovakia, South Africa*, Spain, Sweden*, Thailand, UK, Ukraine, United Arab Emirates, US

Number of lawyers 3,100
at this office 10

Contact
Ted Jonas

Member
DLA Piper Group

CATEGORIES OF WORK

Energy and power

M&A, corporate formation and structuring, joint ventures, contracts

Banking, project and trade finance

Litigation and arbitration

Real estate, property and land

Telecommunications

Employment law

Intellectual property

Tax and customs law

Corporate registrations and incorporation

THE FIRM

DLA Piper Rudnick Gray Cary is a leading global legal services provider with approximately 3,100 lawyers in 58 offices across 22 countries. The organisation is committed to building long-term relationships with its clients and supports their strategic and operational needs both locally and internationally.

DLA Piper in Georgia and the Commonwealth of Independent States (CIS) is staffed by over 100 practising attorneys in Moscow, St Petersburg, Tbilisi and Kyiv, together forming one of the largest legal service providers in the CIS marketplace. The CIS practice is made up of a blend of locally qualified lawyers and expatriates trained in western jurisdictions, all of whom speak at least two languages.

DLA Piper is a founding member of an exclusive alliance of full-service legal organisations with a shared vision. DLA Piper Group, established in 1999, has members across Europe, Africa, the Middle East, Asia and the US, which deliver expert local know-how and integrated international solutions.

AREAS OF PRACTICE

The Georgian member firm of DLA Piper Rudnick Gray Cary, has established itself as one of the highest-quality providers of legal services in Georgia. The firm's reputation for excellence attracts clients in the most high-profile international investment, financing and privatisation transactions in Georgia, as well as the most significant business disputes in local courts and international arbitrations.

Lawyers in this office provide legal advice and representation on a wide range of matters, including corporate and commercial, energy and natural resources law, mergers and acquisitions, real estate, tax and customs law, litigation and arbitration, intellectual property and project finance.

Energy – the office is known as the market leader in the energy sector. Lawyers act on behalf of major petroleum companies in the negotiation and implementation of production sharing agreements, land acquisition, litigation, host government agreements and the creation of special tax regimes for major pipeline projects, and corporate and commercial documentation and land and asset acquisition for tank farms, terminals and on and off-loading facilities.

Power sector – work includes the representation of foreign utilities, developers and lenders, as well as extensive regulatory work relating to the privatisation of energy generation and distribution facilities and regulatory reform in the electricity sector.

Corporate – lawyers in this practice advise numerous clients on the establishment of joint ventures, including advice on the selection of corporate vehicles, drafting and negotiation of complex shareholder agreements and corporate charters, and legal due diligence.

Banking and finance – this practice represents international financial institutions, private commercial lenders, government export-import agencies and project sponsors in over $100m of debt and equity investments in the financial services and industrial sectors, as well as in trade finance.

Litigation – the office is well known for its litigation practice, including contract and commercial matters, privatisation disputes, tort and property damage claims, as well as intellectual property matters. Lawyers in this office also serve as counsel in several international arbitration matters related to Georgia.

Real estate – this practice has extensive experience handling real estate acquisitions, lease arrangements and related property matters for national and foreign clients. Lawyers advise several foreign embassies and numerous commercial and individual clients on the acquisition of real estate, the negotiation and drafting of lease agreements, foreign ownership rights and private ownership of land.

BAKER & McKENZIE – CIS, LIMITED

SAMAL TOWERS, 14TH FLOOR
SAMAL-2
ZHOLDASBEKOV STREET
050051 ALMATY

Telephone: +7 3272 50 99 45
Fax: +7 3272 58 40 00
E-mail: almaty.info@bakernet.com
Website: www.bakernet.com

Languages
English, Kazakh, Russian, Uzbek

Other offices
The member firms of Baker & McKenzie International, a Swiss Verein, have 70 offices in 38 countries around the world. For a complete list, please visit www.bakernet.com.

Number of lawyers 3,300+
at this office 10

Contact
Curtis B Masters

CATEGORIES OF WORK

Banking and finance
Curtis Masters

Capital markets
Curtis Masters

Corporate and commercial
Curtis Masters

Dispute resolution
Azamat Kuatbekov

Employment
Mariya Gekko

IT/C
Alexander Korchagin

Major projects and project finance
Gulmira Utegenova

Mergers and acquisitions
Curtis Masters

Pharmaceuticals
Mariya Gekko, Leila Tashenova

Real estate, construction
Curtis Masters

Tax
Igor Kolupayev

BRACEWELL & GIULIANI LLP

57 AMANGELDY STREET
050012 ALMATY

Telephone: +7 3272 58 14 00
Fax: +7 3272 58 14 44

Languages
English, French, German, Kazakh, Russian, Turkish, Turkmen

Other offices
Astana, Austin, Dallas, Houston, London, New York, San Antonio, Washington DC

Number of lawyers 360
at this office 13

Contact
Greg Vojack

Member
American Chamber of Commerce; Association of Petroleum Negotiators; International Tax and Investment Centre, Washington DC; Chartered Institute of Arbitrators

CATEGORIES OF WORK

Banking and finance
Greg J Vojack

Capital markets
Greg J Vojack

Corporate and securities
Greg J Vojack

Taxation
John A Couch

Commercial and company law
Greg J Vojack

Aviation
John A Couch

Energy and natural resources
John A Couch, Alexey B Yanchenko

Mergers and acquisitions
Greg J Vojack

Privatisations
Greg J Vojack

Litigation and arbitration
Zhanar Kasymbekova

International disputes resolution
Zhanar Kasymbekova

Government relations
Greg J Vojack

Bankruptcy
Greg J Vojack

DENTON WILDE SAPTE

96 BAITURSYNOV STREET
0500022 ALMATY

Telephone: +7 3272 58 19 50
Fax: +7 3272 58 19 05
E-mail: almaty@dentonwildesapte.com
Website: www.dentonwildesapte.com

Languages
English, Kazakh, Russian, Turkish

Other offices
Abu Dhabi, Cairo, Dubai, Istanbul, London, Milton Keynes, Moscow, Muscat, Paris, Tashkent

Number of lawyers 683
at this office 25

Contact
Marla Valdez

CATEGORIES OF WORK

Oil and gas

Mining

Pipelines

Transportation

Construction and infrastructure

Banking and finance

Telecommunications

Corporate

Mergers and acquisitions

Employment

Dispute resolution

LEBOEUF, LAMB, GREENE & MACRAE LLP

PROSPEKT SEYFULLINA, 531
480091 ALMATY

Telephone: +7 3272 50 75 75
Fax: +7 3272 50 75 76
E-mail: info@llgm.kz
Website: www.llgm.com

Languages
English, German, Kazakh, Russian, Turkish

Other offices
Albany, Beijing, Boston, Brussels, Chicago, Hartford, Houston, Jacksonville, Johannesburg, London, Los Angeles, Moscow, New York, Paris, Pittsburg, Riyadh, San Francisco, Washington DC

Number of lawyers 650+
at this office 8

Contacts
Brian Zimbler, Jonathan Hines

CATEGORIES OF WORK

Direct investment
Brian Zimbler, Jonathan Hines

Natural resources
Jonathan Hines, Aset Shyngyssov

Corporate
Aset Shyngyssov, Brian Zimbler

Banking
Brian Zimbler, Aset Shyngyssov

MICHAEL WILSON & PARTNERS

5TH FLOOR
36 SAMAL-1
050059 ALMATY

Telephone: +7 3272 58 48 90
Fax: +7 3272 58 48 94
E-mail: info@mwp.kz
Website: www.mwp.kz

Languages
English, Danish, French, German, Kazakh, Russian, Serbian, Ukrainian

Other offices
Baku

Number of lawyers 16

Contacts
Michael E Wilson, John F Emmott

CATEGORIES OF WORK

- **Foreign investments and joint ventures**
- **Corporate, corporate finance and securities**
- **Intellectual property**
- **Arbitration, litigation and dispute resolution**
- **Banking, finance and project finance**
- **Tax and customs**
- **Real estate**
- **Mining and natural resources**
- **Engineering and construction**
- **Privatisation**
- **Power industry (generation, transmission and distribution) and utilities**
- **Labour, employment and work permit matters**
- **Telecommunications**
- **Transportation, shipping and aviation**

THE FIRM

Michael Wilson & Partners Ltd (MWP) is a full-service law firm in Almaty covering Kazakhstan, the central Asian region and the Caucasus. MWP's founding partner was previously the regional founding partner of a major international law firm with offices in Almaty, Bishkek, Baku, Astana and Tashkent.

As a fully independent law firm, MWP has the ability which international law firms do not have to meet clients' real legal and business needs when approaching and dealing with the most important business opportunities that exist in Kazakhstan and throughout the whole of central Asia.

As of January 2002, John F Emmott joined MWP as a partner, director and shareholder after eight years as an associate and 15 years as a partner in Richards Butler in London.

MWP is not just a law firm, but takes pride in partnering with its clients in relation to their business opportunities, challenges and threats and, in doing so, providing creative, timely and practical solutions specifically tailored to meet its clients' requirements, deadlines and budgets.

AREAS OF PRACTICE

MWP is a unique Kazakhstani firm in today's market, having some of the most experienced lawyers in their chosen fields on staff and can boast over 90 combined years of legal experience within its team. Most of MWP's people are bilingual, and are most sensitive and understanding to the business and cultural needs of the region and its industries.

Operating as a fully autonomous law firm, MWP's focus is on Kazakhstan and the other central Asian Republics of the former Soviet Union including Kyrgyzstan, Uzbekistan, Turkmenistan, Tajikstan, Azerbaijan, Georgia and Armenia. MWP offers a full range of commercial transactional services in the categories detailed above with a strong emphasis on the corporate sector, with a wide range and depth of both international and domestic clients.

The firm is considered one of the regional leaders in the mining and natural resources sector, utilities, and all aspects of foreign investment, joint ventures, financing, privatisations, restructuring, transportation, litigation, intellectual property and general commercial law. Full information on Michael Wilson & Partners Ltd, its staff, and major completed and ongoing projects can be viewed on its website at: www.mwp.kz.

SAYAT ZHOLSHY & PARTNERS

2ND FLOOR, 153A ABAY AVE
050009 ALMATY

Telephone: +7 3272 50 50 83
Fax: +7 3272 50 50 89
E-mail: info@szp.kz
Website: www.szp.kz

Languages
English, German, Kazakh, Polish, Russian

Other offices
Atyrau, Astana

Number of lawyers 23
at this office 18

CATEGORIES OF WORK

Corporate
Aidyn Bikebayev, Rustam Ospanov

Taxation
Daniyar Tenelov, Vitaliy Vodolazkin

Mergers and acquisitions
Arman Berdalin, Rustam Ospanov

Antitrust
Arman Berdalin, Rustam Ospanov

International trade
Aidyn Bikebayev

Project financing
Aidyn Bikebayev, Rustam Ilzhanov

Finance, insurance and securities
Aidyn Bikebayev, Sergey Irzhanov

Natural resources
Rustam Ilzhanov, Daniyar Tenelov

Power industry
Arman Berdalin, Sergey Irzhanov

Litigation and arbitration
Vitaliy Vodolazkin, Dmitriy Vetlugin

Labour, employment and work permits
Daniyar Tenelov, Aydos Kussainov

Licenses and governmental approvals
Rustam Ilzhanov, Kazbek Tanalinov

Criminal
Kazbek Tanalinov

Real estate
Nadezhda Kussaypova,
Assel Sandybaeva

ALLEN & OVERY LEGAL SERVICES

DMITROVSKY PEREULOK 9
107031 MOSCOW

Telephone: +7 501 725 7900
Fax: +7 501 725 7949
E-mail: moscow@allenovery.com
Website: www.allenovery.com

Languages
English, French, German, Mandarin, Russian, Spanish

Other offices
Amsterdam, Antwerp, Bangkok, Beijing, Bratislava, Brussels, Budapest, Dubai, Frankfurt, Hamburg, Hong Kong, London, Luxembourg, Madrid, Milan, New York, Paris, Prague, Rome, Shanghai, Singapore, Tokyo, Turin, Warsaw

Number of lawyers 2,304
at this office 31

Contact
Peter Timchur

CATEGORIES OF WORK

Banking/finance
Peter Timchur, Irina Mashlenko, Dmitry Shiryaev

International capital markets
Irina Mashlenko, Andrei Baev

Corporate/commercial
Peter Timchur, Edwin Tham, Andrei Baev

Energy
Peter Timchur, Irina Mashlenko, Andrei Baev

Investments
Peter Timchur, Edwin Tham

Mergers and acquisitions
Peter Timchur, Edwin Tham, Andrei Baev

Litigation and arbitration
Dmitry Shiryaev, Irina Mashlenko

Privatisations
Edwin Tham, Dmitry Shiryaev

Project finance
Peter Timchur, Andrei Baev

Trade finance
Dmitry Shiryaev, Peter Timchur, Irina Mashlenko

ALRUD LAW FIRM

6TH FLOOR
17 SKAKOVAYA STREET
125040 MOSCOW

Telephone: +7 495 234 9692
Fax: +7 495 956 3718
E-mail: info@alrud.ru
Website: www.alrud.com

Languages
English, French, German, Russian

Number of lawyers 23

Contacts
Vassily Rudomino, Dmitry Yeremin, Irina Anyukhina, Alexander Zharsky, Konstantin Lapshin, Dmitry Ryzhov

CATEGORIES OF WORK

International trade
Dmitry Yeremin, Dmitry Ryzhov

Corporate law
Dmitry Yeremin, Irina Anyukhina

Mergers and acquisitions
Vassily Rudomino, Alexander Zharsky

Corporate finance
Vassily Rudomino, Alexander Zharsky

Due diligence
Irina Anyukhina, Dmitry Ryzhov

Arbitration and commercial litigation
Dmitry Yeremin, Alexander Zharsky

Commercial law
Irina Anyukhina, Dmitry Ryzhov

Real estate and land
Konstantin Lapshin, Vadim Kostenko

Intellectual property
Irina Anyukhina, Dmitry Ryzhov

Competition law, antitrust
Vassily Rudomino, Oksana Vishniakova

Shareholders disputes
Dmitry Yeremin, Oksana Vishniakova

Investments in Russia
Vassily Rudomino, Irina Anyukhina

Currency regulation
Dmitry Yeremin, Oksana Vishniakova

Securities
Vassily Rudomino, Dmitry Yeremin

Tax law
Anna Zvereva, Vadim Kostenko

Labour law
Konstantin Lapshin

ANDREAS NEOCLEOUS & CO

MALIY KOZIHINSKI PER 16/3
APT 2
103001 MOSCOW

Telephone: +7 495 933 8703
Fax: +7 495 510 6421
E-mail: russia@neocleous.com
Website: www.neocleous.ru

Languages
English, French, German, Greek, Russian

Other offices
Brussels, Limassol, Nicosia, Paphos, Budapest, Kiev, Prague

Number of lawyers 75
at this office 6

Contacts
Natalia Tarlo, Andrey Yermakov, Irina Strizhakova, Varvara Knutova, Oleg Ezhov, Andreas Neocleous (visiting partner), Elias Neocleous (visiting partner), Panayiotis Neocleous (visiting partner), Olga Mikhailova (visiting associate)

CATEGORIES OF WORK

Company and commercial law

Mergers and acquisitions

Banking and finance

Tax law and international tax planning

PPP and project finance

Competition law

EU law

Intellectual property

Information technology

Real estate

Admiralty and shipping

BAKER & McKENZIE – CIS, LIMITED

SADOVAYA PLAZA, 11TH FLOOR
7 DOLGORUKOVSKAYA STREET
127006 MOSCOW

Telephone: +7 495 787 2700
Fax: +7 495 787 2701
E-mail: moscow.office@bakernet.com
Website: www.bakernet.com

Languages
Belarussian, English, French, German, Italian, Polish, Portuguese, Spanish, Swedish, Russian, Ukrainian

Other offices
The member firms of Baker & McKenzie International, a Swiss Verein, have 70 offices in 38 countries around the world. For a complete list, please visit www.bakernet.com.

Number of lawyers 3,300+
at this office 68

CATEGORIES OF WORK

Arbitration and litigation
Vladimir Khvalei

Banking and finance
David Scott

Commercial law
Carol Patterson, Max Gutbrod, Paul Melling

Dispute resolution
Vladimir Khvalei

Employment
Evgeny Reyzman

Intellectual property
Eugene Arievich

IT/communications
Max Gutbrod

Major projects and project finance
Max Gutbrod, Carol Patterson, David Scott

Mergers and acquisitions
Carol Patterson, Sergei Voitishkiń

Pharmaceuticals
Paul Melling

Real estate, construction
Andrei Soukhomlinov

Tax
Alexander Chmelev, Alexander Bychkov

Venture capital
Max Gutbrod

BAKER BOTTS LLP

SUITE 450
DUCAT PLACE 11
7 ULITSA GASHEKA
123056 MOSCOW

Telephone: +7 495 545 0777
Fax: +7 495 545 0778
E-mail: steve.wardlaw@bakerbotts.com
Website: www.bakerbotts.com

Languages
Arabic, Azeri, English, French, Kazak, Russian

Other offices
Austin, Dallas, Dubai, Hong Kong, Houston, London, New York, Riyadh, Washington DC

Number of lawyers 700
at this office 11

Contact
Steven Wardlaw

Member
Lex Mundi

CATEGORIES OF WORK

Asset finance	Foreign direct investment
Aviation	Infrastructure and project finance
Banking and finance	Oil and gas, natural resources
Construction	Power
Corporate	Privatisations and restructurings
Dispute resolution	Real estate
Energy	Shipping

BECH-BRUUN

BOLSHOY GNEZDNIKOVSKY PER 1
BUILDING 2, 7TH FLOOR
125009 MOSCOW

Telephone: +7 501 799 5684
Fax: +7 501 799 5687
E-mail: info.moscow@bechbruun.com
Website: www.bechbruun.com

Languages
Danish, English, French, German, Russian, Spanish, the Scandinavian languages

Other offices
Aarhus, Copenhagen

Number of lawyers 254
at this office 4

Contact
Ole Borch (obo@bechbruun.com)

CATEGORIES OF WORK

Construction law	Leases and contracts of sale
Company law	Trade mark law
Joint ventures	Competition law
Mergers and acquisitions	Employment and labour law

BEITEN BURKHARDT

TURCHANINOV PER 6/2
119034 MOSCOW

Telephone: +7 495 232 9635
Fax: +7 495 232 9633
E-mail: bblaw-moskau@bblaw.com
Website: www.bblaw.com

Languages
Cantonese, Czech, English, French, German, Hungarian, Italian, Mandarin, Polish, Russian, Slovak, Spanish, Ukrainian

Other offices
Beijing, Berlin, Brussels, Cologne, Düsseldorf, Frankfurt am Main, Hong Kong, Kiev, Leipzig, Munich, Nuremberg, St Petersburg, Shanghai, Warsaw

Number of lawyers 230
at this office 11

Contacts
Dr Thomas Heidemann,
Dr Christian von Wistinghausen

CATEGORIES OF WORK

Company law
Banking and finance
Tax law
European law and cartel law
Foundation, association, societies and sports law
Industrial property rights
Labour law
Procurement law
Public law
Information technology
Estate planning and succession rules
Copyright law
Litigation and arbitration
Telecommunication law
Real estate law
Advertising law
Media law

CMS BUREAU FRANCIS LEFEBVRE

BUILDING 1A
1 KOROBEYNIKOV PEREOULOK
119034 MOSCOW

Telephone: +7 495 739 3344
Fax: +7 495 739 3355
E-mail: central@cmsbfl.ru
Website: www.cms-bfl.com

Languages
English, French, Russian

Other offices
Brussels, Bucharest, Buenos Aires, Casablanca, Düsseldorf, Lyon, Montevideo, New York, Neuilly-sur-Seine, São Paulo, Shanghai, Strasbourg

Number of lawyers 435
at this office 28

Contact
Jean-Luc Pipon

Member
CMS, the alliance of major independent European law firms

CATEGORIES OF WORK

Investments in the CIS countries
Joint ventures
Mergers and acquisitions
Business law
National and international taxation
Contracts
Intellectual property
Competition law
Employment law
Customs and excise duties
Arbitration law

CMS CAMERON McKENNA LLP

KOROBEYNIKOV PER 1
BUILDING 1A, 3RD FLOOR
119034 MOSCOW

Telephone: +7 495 258 5000
Fax: +7 495 258 5100
E-mail: info@cms-cmck.com
Website: www.law-now.com

Languages
English, Russian

Other offices
Aberdeen, Bristol, Bucharest, Budapest, Edinburgh, Hong Kong, London, Prague, Sofia, Warsaw

Number of lawyers 587
at this office 25+

Contact
David Griston

International grouping
CMS Cameron McKenna is a member of CMS, the alliance of major European law firms providing clients with a full range of legal and tax services. CMS's activities are co-ordinated through EEIG, registered in Brussels. CMS Bureau Francis Lefebvre and CMS Hasche Sigle are also present at this office location in Moscow.

CATEGORIES OF WORK

Finance
Sergei Avramov

Dispute resolution/litigation
Leonid Zubarev, Sergei Yuriev

M&A and private equity
David Griston, Kirill Ratnikov

Energy
Natalia Kozyrenko

Property and construction
Steven Shone

Telecoms and e-commerce
David Griston

Insurance and pensions
Leonid Zubarev

CLEARY GOTTLIEB STEEN & HAMILTON LLP

CGS&H LIMITED LIABILITY COMPANY

PAVELETSKAYA SQUARE 2/3
115054 MOSCOW

Telephone: + 7 501 258 5006
Fax: + 7 501 258 5011
Website: www.clearygottlieb.com

Languages
English, French, German, Russian, Spanish

Other offices
Brussels, Cologne, Frankfurt, Hong Kong, London, Milan, New York, Paris, Rome, Tokyo, Washington DC

Number of lawyers 847
at this office 15

CATEGORIES OF WORK

Banking and finance

Capital markets/securities

Joint ventures

Mergers and acquisitions

CLYDE & CO

SIVTSEV VRAJEK 25/9
BUILDING 1
119002 MOSCOW

Telephone: +7 495 156 5206
Fax: +7 495 156 5205
E-mail: info@clydeco.ru
Website: www.clydeco.com

Languages
English, French, Russian

Other offices
Abu Dhabi, Belgrade, Caracas, Cardiff, Dubai, Guildford, Hong Kong, London, Nantes, Paris, Piraeus, Rio de Janeiro, St Petersburg, Shanghai, Singapore

Number of lawyers 409
at this office 4

Contacts
Dmitry Zavidov, Igor Orlov, John Whittaker, James Varanese, Philip Rogers

CATEGORIES OF WORK

Aviation
Tim Unmack

Construction contracts
Dmitry Zavidov

Corporate law, M&A
Dmitry Zavidov, Philip Rogers

Dispute resolution
Dmitry Zavidov, Igor Orlov

Insolvency law
Igor Orlov

Insurance and reinsurance
John Whittaker

Shipping
Irvine Marr

Trade and energy
John Whittaker, James Varanese

DEBEVOISE & PLIMPTON LLP

BUSINESS CENTRE 'MOKHOVAYA'
ULTISA VOZDVIZHENKA, 4/7
STROYENIYE 2
125009 MOSCOW

Telephone: +7 495 956 3858
Fax: +7 495 956 3868
E-mail: dvnikiforov@debevoise.com
Website: www debevoise.com

Languages
English, German, Russian, Spanish

Other offices
Frankfurt, Hong Kong, London, New York, Paris, Shanghai, Washington DC

Number of lawyers 660+
at this office 15

CATEGORIES OF WORK

Aviation
Dmitri V Nikiforov, Alan Kartashkin

Capital markets
Holly A Nielsen, Alan Kartashkin

Energy
Dmitri V Nikiforov

Private equity
Holly A Nielsen

Project finance
Holly A Nielsen, Alan Kartashkin

M&A
Dmitri V Nikiforov, Holly A Nielsen

DLA PIPER RUDNICK GRAY CARY

SADOVNICHESKAYA UL 82, BLDG 2
115035 MOSCOW

Telephone: +7 495 221 4400
Fax: +7 495 221 4401
E-mail: constantine.lusignan-rizhinashvili@dlapiper.com
Website: www.dlapiper.com/russia

Languages
Armenian, Byelorussian, Danish, English, French, Georgian, German, Italian, Latvian, Russian, Spanish, Ukrainian, Uzbek

Other offices
Austria, Belgium, Bosnia-Herzegovina, China, Croatia, Czech Republic, Denmark*, Egypt*, France, Georgia, Germany, Hong Kong, Hungary, Italy, Japan, Netherlands, Norway*, Poland*, Russia, Singapore*, Slovakia, South Africa*, Spain, Sweden*, Thailand, UK, Ukraine, United Arab Emirates, US

Number of lawyers 3,100
at this office 40

Contact
Constantine Lusignan-Rizhinashvili

CATEGORIES OF WORK

Corporate

Mergers and acquisitions

Restructuring and reorganisation

Banking, finance and capital markets

Energy and natural resources

Real estate and construction

Hospitality

Employment

Intellectual property and information technology

Commercial and project finance

Franchise and distribution

Litigation and arbitration

Tax

Infrastructure and transportation

Shipping, insurance and international trade

THE FIRM

DLA Piper in Russia and the CIS is staffed by over 100 practising attorneys in Moscow, St Petersburg, Tbilisi and Kyiv, together forming one of the largest legal service providers in the CIS marketplace. The CIS practice is made up of a blend of locally qualified lawyers and expatriates trained in western jurisdictions, all of whom speak at least two languages.

AREAS OF PRACTICE

The Moscow office serves as the hub for DLA Piper's growing presence across Russia and the CIS. With over 40 practising attorneys, the office's combined expertise spans all the traditional areas of legal practice, including mergers and acquisitions, restructuring and reorganisation, real estate and construction, general corporate and commercial matters, banking, finance and capital markets, intellectual property, employment, litigation and arbitration, and tax planning.

The Moscow office services a diverse client base, including multinationals and major domestic players, across the consumer goods, construction, hospitality, manufacturing, media, energy, natural resources, transportation and financial services sectors.

The corporate, mergers and acquisitions group makes up the core of the Moscow practice. The group is uniquely multidisciplinary, key service offerings including integrated legal and tax due diligence, and deal structuring advice, as well as full transaction and multi-jurisdictional implementation support.

The energy and natural resources group advises some of the largest energy companies active in Russia and the CIS, as well as lenders, developers, industry associations, transportation companies and multinational consortia. It has advised on the negotiation and drafting of production-sharing agreements and host-government agreements, licensing issues, acquisitions, and major regional infrastructure projects, such as oil and gas pipelines.

The banking and finance group advises corporate borrowers, financial institutions and project sponsors on regulatory, corporate and transactional matters relevant to Russia and the CIS. The office provides the full range of legal services in support of a public offering, including co-ordinated foreign listing assistance, together with specialised teams in London or New York.

The hospitality group represents the majority of western-branded hotels in Russia and the CIS, providing both owners and operators with a full range of legal, taxation and hospitality consulting/strategic advisory services.

The real estate group has negotiated and documented complex construction and urban development projects, such as hotels, diplomatic missions, shopping centres, pipelines and industrial facilities, advising on infrastructure, utilities, mechanical and electrical systems, construction finance, and insurance arrangements.

The litigation and arbitration group handles a wide variety of contentious matters, including tax litigation in local venues and the resolution of commercial and trade disputes through international commercial arbitration.

The tax group advises on tax optimisation and structuring, and provides assistance and representation in negotiations with the tax authorities.

EGOROV, PUGINSKY, AFANASIEV & PARTNERS LLC

40 BOLSHAYA ORDYNKA
BLD 4, 3RD FLOOR
119017 MOSCOW

Telephone: +7 495 935 8010
Fax: +7 495 935 8011
E-mail: mow_office@epam.ru
Website: www.epam.ru

Languages
English, French, Spanish

Other offices
Philadelphia, St Petersburg

Number of lawyers 51
at this office 32

Member
Russian-American Business Council; American Chamber of Commerce in Russia; US-Russia Business Council; Canadian Business Association in Russia; Finnish-Russian Chamber of Commerce; American Bar Association; International Bar Association

CATEGORIES OF WORK

Commercial litigation and arbitration

Corporate transactions: M&A, takeovers, due diligence

Government relations

Securities regulation

Bankruptcy

International trade regulation

Tax and foreign exchange

Real estate and construction

Intellectual property

Maritime and shipping

Certification and standardisation

Insurance

Employment law

THE FIRM

Founded in 1993, Egorov, Puginsky, Afanasiev & Partners is a national law firm specialising in commercial law in Russia and internationally. The firm combines extensive local experience with international professional and ethical standards. It regularly represents foreign companies doing business in Russia and Russian companies internationally. The firm often serves as local counsel to various western law firms.

The firm's partners have distinguished backgrounds in government and academia, and they lecture and publish extensively on Russian commercial law. Many of the firm's lawyers have received additional training in Europe and the US. They enjoy the status of advocates under Russian law, which provides important client protections not available to regular jurists.

AREAS OF PRACTICE

Commercial litigation and arbitration: the firm has handled high-profile commercial cases at all levels of the Russian court system, as well as international commercial arbitration matters in Russia and major western capitals. It has represented clients in some of the largest hostile takeover defences in recent years.

Corporate transactions: the firm regularly represents Russian and foreign clients in acquisitions of shares in Russian and foreign companies, structuring complex corporate transactions, as well as providing ongoing corporate services and due diligence. The firm has extensive expertise in inbound investment regulation in Russia.

Government relations: the firm has developed a sophisticated government relations practice geared toward practical solutions based on an in-depth understanding of client issues and a search for alignment of interests in public policy. Due to the diplomatic experience of the firm's partners, it has advised clients on matters in the US, France, Colombia and certain African countries.

Securities regulation: the firm has represented clients in fund management, broker-dealing, securities placement and investment advisory. It drafted some of the Russian securities regulations in the 1990s.

Bankruptcy: the firm has represented debtors and creditors in major corporate bankruptcies, including some hotly contested cases.

International trade regulation: the firm has represented Russian producers in WTO and market access matters in the US.

Tax and foreign exchange: the firm has provided tax planning and litigation advice to foreign and Russian corporate clients and employs licensed auditors.

Real estate and construction: experience includes a major subway reconstruction, a western hotel development, a dispute between a European bank and a Russian government borrower, the first western-owned office space in St. Petersburg and the largest office tower in Eastern Europe.

Intellectual property: recent work includes designing general IP strategy for production clients, fighting counterfeit products, IP ownership disputes and litigation involving asset stripping through licensing contracts.

Maritime and shipping: the firm has represented maritime creditors and debtors in vessels seizures and other disputes in over 20 countries, as well as in St Petersburg and the Russian Far East.

Certification and standardisation: the firm has organised compliance with local safety, standardisation and hygienic requirements for several consumer products companies and supervised certification procedures.

Insurance: the firm has represented local insurance companies in corporate reorganisations and satellite launch reinsurance, and also advised the largest international insurance broker on product structuring.

Employment law: the firm has advised clients on labour contracts, restrictive covenants, confidentiality agreements and non-compete covenants, and has also represented Russian seafarers' unions against shipowners worldwide.

DENTON WILDE SAPTE

BOLSHAYA DMITROVKA 7/5
6TH FLOOR, BUILDING 2
125009 MOSCOW

Telephone: +7 495 255 7900
Fax: +7 495 255 7901
E-mail: info@dentonwildesapte.ru
Website: www.dentonwildesapte.com

Languages
English, French, German, Russian, Spanish

Other offices
Abu Dhabi, Almaty, Cairo, Dubai, Istanbul, London, Milton Keynes, Muscat, Paris, Tashkent

Number of lawyers 683
at this office 24

Contact
Doran Doeh

CATEGORIES OF WORK

- Banking and finance
- Commercial
- Corporate
- Electricity
- Infrastructure development
- Intellectual property
- Litigation
- Mergers and acquisitions
- Oil and gas
- Real estate
- Privatisation
- Tax
- Telecommunications

GIDE LOYRETTE NOUEL

STOLESHNIKOV PEREULOK 14
107031 MOSCOW

Telephone: +7 495 258 3100
Fax: +7 495 258 3101
E-mail: gln.moscow@gide.com
Website: www.gide.com

Other offices
Algiers, Beijing, Belgrade, Brussels, Bucharest, Budapest, Casablanca, Hanoi, Istanbul, London, New York, Paris, Prague, Riyadh, Shanghai, Tunis, Warsaw

Number of lawyers 586
at this office 14

Contact
David Lasfargue (lasfargue@gide.com)

CATEGORIES OF WORK

- Corporate, M&A
- Banking and finance, pre-financing exports of raw materials
- Joint ventures
- Commercial contracts
- Exchange control
- Competition and antitrust
- Distribution
- Intellectual property
- Customs law
- Arbitration and litigation
- Employment law
- Taxation
- Real estate transactions and financing
- Customs law

GOWLINGS INTERNATIONAL INC

PRECHISTENSKY PEREULOK 14
BUILDING 1, 4TH FLOOR
119034 MOSCOW

Telephone: +7 495 787 2070
Fax: +7 495 787 2071
E-mail: marina.drel@gowlings.com
Website: www.gowlings.com

Other offices
Calgary, Hamilton, Kitchener, Montréal, Ottawa, Toronto, Vancouver

Number of lawyers 12

Contacts
Marina Drel, Viacheslav Kliukin

CATEGORIES OF WORK

Corporate and commercial
Michael Malloy

Litigation
Marina I Drel

Intellectual property
Vladimir N Dementiev, Viacheslav A Kliukin

HAARMANN HEMMELRATH

UL. OSTOSCHENKA 23
119034 MOSCOW

Telephone: +7 501 797 9070
Fax: +7 501 797 9080
E-mail:
moscow@haarmannhemmelrath.com
Website:
www.haarmannhemmelrath.com

Languages
English, French, German, Polish, Russian

Other offices
Bielefeld, Bucharest, Budapest, Düsseldorf, Frankfurt, Hamburg, Leipzig, Munich, Paris, Prague, Shanghai, Warsaw

Number of lawyers 226

CATEGORIES OF WORK

Mergers and acquisitions
Dr Gerd Lenga, Roman Daschko

Company law
Roman Daschko, Michail Borodin

Capital markets
Roman Daschko, Michail Sokolow

Business and trade law
Irene Engel, Kamil Karibow

Real estate and construction law
Eugen Zentner, Anna Minajewa, Kamil Karibow

Lease and finance
Anna Lessowa, Falk Tischendorf

Competition, merger control, antitrust law
Dr Gerd Lenga, Jelena Schigajewa

Intellectual property and IT
Swetlana Turbanowa, Anton Syrow

Labour law
Irene Engel, Wassilij Jermolin

Corporate finance
Marco Koschier

National and international tax
Anna Lessowa, Tatjana Nekrassowa, Dr Anton Wagner

Audit and accounting services
Marco Koschier, Walentina Lewkowitsch

Energy, natural resources
Dr Gerd Lenga, Wassilij Jermolin

Insolvency, litigation and arbitration
Swetlana Turbanowa, Stanislaw Arbenin

Privatisation
Irene Engel, Michail Borodin

HERBERT SMITH CIS LEGAL SERVICES

4TH FLOOR
KOROBEINIKOV 24
119034 MOSCOW

Telephone: +7 495 363 6500
Fax: +7 495 363 6501
E-mail: contact@herbertsmith.com
Website: www.herbertsmith.com

Languages
English, Russian

Other offices
Bangkok, Beijing, Brussels, Hong Kong, London, Paris, Shanghai, Singapore, Tokyo

Number of lawyers 1,089
at this office 23

CATEGORIES OF WORK

Projects
John Balsdon, Robin Wittering

Energy and natural resources
John Balsdon, Robin Wittering

Banking and debt restructuring
John Balsdon

Inward investment
Robin Wittering, Allen Hanen

Litigation
Dmitry Kurochkin

Arbitration
Dmitry Kurochkin

Mergers and acquisitions
Robin Wittering, Allen Hanen

Capital markets
Allen Hanen, Robin Wittering

HOGAN & HARTSON LLP

AMBASSADOR BUILDING
14, PRECHISTENSKIY PEREULOK
119034 MOSCOW

Telephone: +7 495 797 9900
Fax: +7 495 797 9961
E-mail: pjpettibone@hhlaw.com
Website: www.hhlaw.com

Languages
English, German, French,Russian, Spanish

Other offices
Baltimore, Beijing, Berlin, Boulder, Brussels, Budapest, Caracas, Colorado Springs, Denver, Geneva, Hong Kong, London, Los Angeles, Miami, Munich, New York, Northern Virginia, Paris, Shanghai, Tokyo, Warsaw, Washington DC

Number of lawyers 1,101
at this office 14

Contacts
Peter Pettibone, Todd Schafer, Sergey Komolov

CATEGORIES OF WORK

International joint ventures

Private equity

Capital markets

Privatisation

Technology transfers

Mergers and acquisitions

Finance

Energy

Telecommunications

Intellectual property

International trade

Technical service contracts

Regulatory compliance

International litigation

Project finance

Pharmaceuticals

Food and agriculture

Aviation and space

INVIAJURIS LEGAL BUREAU LLC (IVJ)

2 OBOLENSKY PEREULOK
OFFICE 3
119021 MOSCOW

Telephone: +7 495 933 8680
Fax: +7 495 933 8680
E-mail: info@ivj.ru
Website: www.ivj.ru

Languages
English, Russian

Number of lawyers 10

Member
SovereignLaw, UK

CATEGORIES OF WORK

Corporate law
Denis Korolev, Roman Kretov

Commercial and contract law
Nikolay Krenov, Denis Korolev

Mergers and acquisitions
Denis Korolev, Nikolay Krenov

Corporate finance
Nikolay Krenov, Denis Korolev

Project finance
Nikolay Krenov, Denis Korolev

Foreign investment and currency control
Denis Korolev

Securities
Denis Korolev

Capital markets
Denis Korolev

Bankruptcy/insolvency
Denis Korolev, Nikolay Krenov

Commercial and corporate litigation
Nikolay Krenov, Roman Kretov

Arbitration/mediation
Nikolay Krenov, Roman Kretov

JURINFLOT, INTERNATIONAL LAW OFFICE

PO BOX 60
109147 MOSKVA

Telephone: +7 495 792 5701
Fax: +7 495 792 5700
E-mail: jurin@jurinflot.ru
Website: www.jurinflot.ru

Languages
Belarussian, English, French, German, Norwegian, Spanish, Ukrainian

Other offices
Novorossvisk, St Petersburg, Vladivostock

Number of lawyers 12

Member
International Maritime Law Association; International Bar Associaton; Guild of Russian Advocates; Terralex; Juris Consult Alliance

CATEGORIES OF WORK

Company law
VV Mandriouc, KG Ryndin, AV Mednikov

Commercial contracts
VV Mandriouc, IV Panyuk

Transport and trading
VG Ermolaev, TT Mischenko, IV Panyuk

Maritime matters
VG Ermolaev, SS Turusinov

Insurance
IV Panyuk, VG Ermolaev

Asset and project financing
AV Mednikov

Lending and security
AV Mednikov

Foreign investment
AV Mednikov, VV Mandriouc, KG Ryndin

Commercial litigation and arbitration
VG Ermolaev, KG Ryndin, SS Turusinov

Taxation
AV Mednikov

LAPTEV AND PARTNERS

VISHNYAKOVSKY PER. 4
115184 MOSCOW

Telephone: +7 495 953 5686
Fax: +7 495 953 7101
E-mail: laptevandp@mtu-net.ru
Website: www.laptev.ru

Languages
English, Russian

Other offices
Tyumen

Number of lawyers 46
at this office 15

CATEGORIES OF WORK

Administrative
V Akimov, O Kostileva

Banking and finance
A Artyuhov, E Krilova

Commercial property, real estate
N Grigoryeva, A Voznyak

Construction
A Bener, A Pitsakov

Corporate and commercial
V Akimov, T Lapteva

Energy and natural resources
A Bener, N Grigoryeva

Environment
D Toisteva, V Ryabenko

Foreign direct investment
E Krilova

Insurance
V Ryabenko

Media and entertainment
N Grinev

Mergers and acquisitions
D Kostileva

Privatisation
A Voznyak, N Grinev

Tax
N Grigoryeva

LEBOEUF, LAMB, GREENE & MACRAE LLP

NIKITSKY PEREULOK, 5
125009 MOSCOW

Telephone: +7 495 737 5000
Fax: +7 495 737 5050
E-mail: info@llgm.ru
Website: www.llgm.com

Languages
Danish, English, Finnish, French, German, Italian, Norwegian, Portuguese, Russian, Spanish, Turkish

Other offices
Albany, Almaty, Beijing, Boston, Brussels, Chicago, Hartford, Houston, Jacksonville, Johannesburg, London, Los Angeles, New York, Paris, Pittsburg, Riyadh, San Francisco, Washington DC

Number of lawyers 650+
at this office 33

Contacts
Brian Zimbler, Jonathan Hines, Oleg Berger

CATEGORIES OF WORK

International direct investment
Brian Zimbler, Jonathan Hines

Capital markets
Vasilisa Strizh, Mark Banovich

Acquisitions
Oleg Berger, Igor Krivoshekov

Dispute resolution
Leila Litvinova

Energy
Jonathan Hines, Ilia Miniaev

Telecoms/media
Brian Zimbler, Veronica Fridman

Real estate
Dmitri Kounitsa

Project finance
Brian Zimbler

Intellecutal property
Leila Litvinova, Veronica Fridman

Mining
Brian Zimbler, Ilia Miniaev

LINIYA PRAVA

BUILDING 1
UL SCHIPOK 11/28
115054 MOSCOW

Telephone: +7 495 787 7101
Fax: +7 495 787 7102
E-mail: secretary@lp.ru
Website: www.lp.ru

Languages
English, Russian

Other offices
Kiev

Number of lawyers 16

CATEGORIES OF WORK

Securities
Alexander Timofeev

Capital markets
Andrey Novakovskiy

Company and commercial
Tatjana Kachalina

Mergers and acquisitions
Tatjana Kachalina

Corporate finance
Alexander Timofeev

Banking and finance
Alexander Kazakov

Privatisation
Andrey Novakovskiy

Project finance
Tatjana Kachalina

Real estate
Roman Gertsev

Construction
Roman Gertsev

Lititgation
Andrey Novakovskiy

Arbitration
Andrey Novakovskiy

THE FIRM

Liniya Prava is a commercial law firm with offices in Moscow and Kiev. Founded in 2000, Liniya Prava was focused on Russian securities regulation, capital markets and privatisation. Since then it has greatly broadened its professional scope to encompass corporate, M&A, securitisation, financial restructuring, project finance, corporate finance, real estate, and securitisation.

The firm's top-notch practice has won the trust of an extensive and rapidly expanding client base, which includes governmental organisations; oil and gas industry flagships; financial institutions; telecoms companies; heavy industry manufacturers; construction companies; FMCG producers; transportation companies; agricultural producers; and retail chains.

The firm is the leading Russian law firm in the area of equity securities and debt securities issuances. To date, Liniya Prava has acted on over 150 securities issuances with an overall value of US$5bn. As Russian law counsel, Liniya Prava has represented the issuers in nine of the largest initial public offerings, both domestic and international, of leading Russian companies, such as Mechel Steel Group, Open Investments, Severstal-Avto, Vimpelcom, Vimm Bill Dann, Seventh Continent, Concern Kalina, Lukoil, and RBC Information Systems.

Since its formation, Liniya Prava has engaged in high-profile privatisation and M&A deals, especially in the telecoms, heavy machinery and FMCG sector. In 2005, Liniya Prava successfully represented its clients in four multi-million M&A deals.

The experts of the firm have substantial experience representing the Russian authorities and private investors on privatisation deals. The firm has an aggressively developing real estate practice.

Liniya Prava also has a noted project finance practice. The firm's most noteworthy project is representation of the Russian government in the Blue Stream Project, a landmark transaction which provided for the finance and construction of a Russia–Turkey gas transportation system via the Black Sea bay.

Liniya Prava's experts have contributed to a great degree to the creation of the existing mortgage-lending system in the Russian Federation, by drafting the federal legislation in the area of mortgage-backed securities and mortgage lending.

The lawyers of Liniya Prava produce regular professional publications and have a broad lecturing practice.

AREAS OF PRACTICE

The firm provides full-service Russian securities law advice, including structuring deals, drafting of all the necessary filings, drafting of issuance documents and prospectus documents, representing the client before the state authorities and issuance of the regulatory permits and approvals.

Corporate: the firm provides integrated professional support in all aspects of corporate law, including M&A and corporate conflicts.

Finance: the firm provides advice on the full range of financial products, including bank lending, acquisition finance, asset finance, derivatives, project finance, restructuring, and insolvency.

Real estate: the firm provides comprehensive and practical legal advice on all aspects of Russian real estate.

LINKLATERS CIS

PAVELETSKAYA SQUARE 2, BLD 2
115054 MOSCOW

Telephone: +7 495 797 9797
Fax: +7 495 797 9798
Website: www.linklaters.com

Languages
All commercial and local languages in the countries where Linklaters operates

Other offices
Amsterdam, Antwerp, Bangkok, Beijing, Berlin, Bratislava, Brussels, Bucharest, Budapest, Cologne, Dubai, Frankfurt am Main, Hong Kong, Lisbon, London, Luxembourg, Madrid, Milan, Munich, New York, Paris, Prague, Rome, São Paulo, Shanghai, Singapore, Stockholm, Tokyo, Warsaw

Number of lawyers 2,000 worldwide

Contact
John Goodwin

CATEGORIES OF WORK

Corporate/M&A
John Goodwin, Denis Uvarov

Real estate
Xavier Hunter

Capital markets
Dmitry Dobatkin

Employment
Henry Rutstein

Banking and finance
Michael Bott

Litigation and arbitration
Alexei Dudko

Energy
Denis Uvarov, Daniel Tyrer

Tax
Victor Matcheknin

Competition
Denis Uvarov

Intellectual property
Denis Uvarov, Alexei Dudko

LOVELLS

5TH FLOOR, USADBA CENTRE
22 VOZNESENSKY
PEREULOK
125009 MOSCOW

Telephone: +7 495 933 3000
Fax: +7 495 933 3001
E-mail: information@lovells.com
Website: www.lovells.com

Languages
Arabic, English, French, German, Italian, Mandarin, Polish, Russian, Spanish, Swedish, Ukrainian, Vietnamese

Other offices
Alicante, Amsterdam, Beijing, Berlin, Brussels, Budapest*, Chicago, Düsseldorf, Frankfurt, Hamburg, Ho Chi Minh City, Hong Kong, London, Madrid, Milan, Munich, New York, Paris, Prague, Rome, Shanghai, Singapore, Tokyo, Warsaw, Zagreb*

Number of lawyers 1,600
at this office 15

Contact
Oxana Balayan

CATEGORIES OF WORK

Arbitration and litigation

Capital markets

Banking and finance

Corporate and commercial

Corporate finance

Information technology

Energy

Intellectual property

Real estate

MACLEOD DIXON ELP

2ND FLOOR
2/3 PAVELETSKAYA SQUARE
115054 MOSCOW

Telephone: +7 501 931 9905
Fax: +7 501 931 9914
Website: www.macleoddixon.com

Languages
English, French, German, Russian, Swedish, Turkish, Ukrainian

Other offices
Almaty, Calgary, Caracas, Rio de Janeiro, Toronto

Number of lawyers 240
at this office 12

Contact
Jayson Sande

CATEGORIES OF WORK

Corporate and commercial
Anatoly Andriash, Levon Kocharyan

Infrastructure and project finance
Anatoly Andriash, Aydin Jebrailov

Tax
Levon Kocharyan, Yury Kravchenko

Employment, labour law
Olga Pryamostanova, Maria Kadlets

Real estate and construction
Maria Kadlets, Jayson Sande

Energy and natural resources
Levon Kocharyan, Aydin Jebrailov

Intellectual property
Maria Kadlets, Anton Elistratov

Trade
Levon Kocharyan, Dinara Dorizo

Insurance
Aydin Jebrailov

Mergers and acquisitions
Anatoly Andriash, Levon Kocharyan

Regulatory
Levon Kocharyan,
Olga Pryamostanova

Securities law
Aydin Jebrailov, Yury Kravchenko

MONASTYRSKY, ZYUBA, STEPANOV & PARTNERS

3/1 NOVINSKY BOULEVARD
121099 MOSCOW

Telephone: +7 495 231 4222
Fax: +7 495 231 4223
E-mail: moscow@mzs.ru
Website: www.mzs.ru

Languages
English, French, German, Swedish, Ukrainian

Number of lawyers 15

CATEGORIES OF WORK

Corporate law

Mergers and acquisitions

Capital markets

Investments

Securities

Intellectual property

Taxation

Banking regulation

Real estate

Insurance law

Litigation

Arbitration

Oil and gas

Telecommunications

Criminal law

Personal services

Insolvency

Antitrust

Land law

Transportation

Currency

Foreign trade regulation

Mass media

Labour law

Family and succession

Customs regulation

NÖRR STIEFENHOFER LUTZ

ZWETNOJ BOULEVARD 25
BUILDING 3
BUSINESS CENTRE, MOSENKA 2
127051 MOSCOW

Telephone: +7 495 799 5696
Fax: +7 495 799 5697
E-mail: info@noerr.com
Website: www.noerr.com

Languages
English, French, German, Russian, Spanish

Other offices
Berlin, Bratislava, Bucharest, Budapest, Dresden, Düsseldorf, Frankfurt, Munich, New York, Prague, Warsaw

Number of lawyers 256
(+ 66 tax advisers, public accountants and tax assistants)
at this office 26

Contacts
Dr Hans-Peter Zier, Ilja Rybalkin

CATEGORIES OF WORK

Aviation law

Banking, capital investment, project financing

Corporate law (including corporate finance, venture capital, IPO)

Distribution law (including franchising, leasing, agency)

Energy

Environmental law and product liability

Intellectual property and copyright

Insurance

Labour law and restructuring

Law relating to tax offences

Litigation and arbitration

M&A, antitrust law

Media law, IT law and new media

Privatisation

Reorganisation and insolvency

Tax law (national and international)

Zoning, construction and real estate

ORRICK (CIS) LLC

7 GASHEKA STREET
123056 MOSCOW

Telephone: +7 495 775 4805
Fax: +7 495 775 4806
Website: www.orrick.com

Other offices
Hong Kong, London, Los Angeles, Milan, New York, Orange County, Pacific Northwest (Portland, Seattle), Paris, Rome, Sacramento, San Francisco, Silicon Valley, Taipei, Tokyo, Washington DC

Number of lawyers 850
at this office 13

Contact
John Sheedy

CATEGORIES OF WORK

Commercial litigation and arbitration

Energy and natural resources

Finance

Intellectual property

Media and technology

Mergers and acquisitions

Private equity

Property

Securities and capital markets

Tax

Telecommunications

THE FIRM

Orrick is an international law firm with more than 850 attorneys located in Asia, Europe and North America. In Europe, Orrick has almost 200 attorneys across five offices, located in London, Milan, Moscow, Paris and Rome. With the firm's European expansion, Orrick now has 16 offices across three continents.

Much of Orrick's client work in Europe involves cross-border transactions and financings that span Europe, the Middle East, Africa, Asia, and the Americas. To support the demands of its clients, Orrick has made seamless client service its number one goal across the firm. As a result, the firm's European lawyers can call on the substantial resources of Orrick's other offices around the world to provide clients with the expertise required to support their transactions.

Above all, Orrick's name stands for excellence in legal services; integrated, responsive client teams throughout the world; innovative leadership and management; and a commitment to the firm's core values, which govern these business standards.

Orrick opened the Moscow office in June 2005 when the partners in the Moscow office of Coudert Brothers LLP, the first foreign law firm to open an office in Russia, along with a number of the other members of Coudert's Russian practice, joined Orrick.

In almost two decades of practice, its lawyers have developed unparalleled experience in finding solutions to our clients' needs in Russia's challenging and rapidly changing legal and economic environment.

AREAS OF PRACTICE

Orrick's Moscow office comprises both foreign and Russian lawyers who provide a full range of legal services across several industries. Since the late 1980s, when foreign investment in Russia first became possible, lawyers in Orrick's Russia practice group have been at the forefront of legal developments relating to foreign investment in Russia, including the first Russian oil and gas production sharing project, the first project financings, the first proxy fight involving a Russian publicly traded company and the first Russian property development projects.

In energy and natural resources, the firm's lawyers have advised major oil and gas companies on production sharing projects, mineral licensing, M&A transactions and pipeline transportation issues, as well as representing borrowers in the financing of upstream and downstream oil and gas projects in Russia.

In commercial litigation and arbitration, the firm has represented clients in a wide variety of domestic Russian cases in the courts of Moscow, St Petersburg and other cities in the region on various types of disputes involving general commercial clients, such as those active in the oil and gas industry.

The firm is actively involved in international arbitrations in Russia and has handled a variety of disputes involving Russian projects before arbitration panels at the International Arbitration Court of the Russian Chamber of Commerce and Industry in Moscow.

Orrick's Russia practice group also covers a wide range of cases in the Russian courts involving a variety of issues such as legislation, real estate, privatisation, intellectual property, finance, tax, customs, construction and bankruptcy matters, including disputes over production-sharing agreements, share purchase agreements, and disputes over subsoil use and environmental issues.

PEPELIAEV, GOLTSBLAT & PARTNERS

KRASNOPRESNENSKAYA NAB 12
ENTRANCE 7, 15TH FLOOR
WORLD TRADE CENTER-II
123610 MOSCOW

Telephone: +7 495 967 0007
Fax: +7 495 967 0008
E-mail: info@pgplaw.ru
Website: www.pgplaw.ru

Languages
English

Other offices
St Petersburg

Number of lawyers 102

Contacts
Sergei Pepeliaev (managing partner),
Andrey Goltsblat (managing partner),
Svetlana Kleimenicheva (director general)

CATEGORIES OF WORK	
Corporate/M&A/restructuring	Commercial
Tax law and tax litigation	Litigation and arbitration
Intellectual property	Anti-monopoly legislation
Land, real estate and construction	Consumer law
Customs regulations	International private law
Foreign currency transactions	Investment projects
Labour and employment	Environmental issues and regulations
Securities	

THE FIRM

Pepeliaev, Goltsblat & Partners is one of the largest full-service law firms operating in Russia. The firm has eight partners and 102 attorneys based in offices in Moscow and St Petersburg, and offers a full spectrum of legal services providing legal support to clients in all Russian regions and the CIS. Pepeliaev, Goltsblat & Partners often participates in multi-jurisdictional projects and panel work in charge of the Russian part. The firm's lawyers possess an in-depth knowledge of the Russian laws; many have taken an active part in drafting and improving basic Russian laws and are regularly invited as independent experts to share their legal opinion with respect to current legislative initiatives in various spheres.

Being one of the first Russian law firms to provide comprehensive legal support for FDI projects implemented by multinational clients in Russia (setting up industrial production, FMCG manufacturing, retail chains, etc), Pepeliaev, Goltsblat & Partners have accumulated great practical experience based on a deep understanding of Russia's legal realities, social, economic and political processes, local culture, and the mentality and expectations of investors. The firm's lawyers have extensive experience in representing clients in negotiations with authorities at all levels. The firm offers a full range of legal services at all stages of project implementation and continuous post-investment and operational support for the largest multinational companies operating in Russia. Over 60% of the clients are multinational corporations implementing long-term investment projects in the Russian Federation.

AREAS OF PRACTICE

Tax practice is one of the firm's core practice areas. It's lawyers provide comprehensive advice on all complicated tax issues facing business entities in Russia, and represent clients in courts at all levels. The firm has developed its reputation as being on the cutting edge of tax advocacy, the percentage of win cases being over 96%. Many of the decisions reached in court constitute precedents for future decision-making and help in improving the tax legislation.

Corporate practice is one of the firm's key practices, it has played a significant role in consolidating the firms' reputation as one of Russia's premier local law firms. It specialises in: corporate restructuring/M&A, due diligence, corporate governance, securities, competition and antitrust law, joint ventures, corporate finance, corporate dispute resolution, etc.

The land, real estate and construction practice provides comprehensive legal support for land and real estate transactions and construction projects at all stages of their implementation. The firm's expertise in this sphere is unsurpassed. Between 2002 and 2005 more than 250 land, real estate and construction projects in different regions of Russia, predominantly for large multinational investors, were successfully accomplished with the assistance of the firm's lawyers.

Customs and exchange regulations practice provides legal support on a wide range of customs-related issues, mostly dealing with complex cross-border transactions and direct investment projects involving the importation of complex manufacturing equipment into Russia. The firm's lawyers are also experienced in representing clients' in disputes with the customs authorities over transfer pricing, in cases concerning the customs classification of goods, etc.

Commercial practice lawyers advise clients on a wide range of commercial matters, including manufacturing/supply arrangements, distribution, franchising, licensing, e-commerce, advertising law, consumer-related matters, consumer labelling, product liability, certification, etc. The firm has extensive experience in domestic and international litigation and arbitration on investments, contractual disputes, international trade, conflicts of laws, jurisdictional disputes and competition law issues.

The firm offers a full set of IP protection services and advice on all aspects of the creation, exploitation and enforcement of IP rights.

PRICEWATERHOUSECOOPERS CIS LAW OFFICES B.V

KOSMODAMIANSKAYA NAB 52
BUILDING 5
115054 MOSCOW

Telephone: +7 495 967 6000
Fax: +7 495 967 6001
E-mail: law@ru.pwc.com
Website: www.law.pwc.ru

Languages
English, Russian

Other offices
St Petersburg, Yuzhno-Sakhalinsk

Number of lawyers 49
at this office 40

Member
Russian Private Equity and Venture Capital Association; Association of European Businesses; American Chamber of Commerce; Canada Eurasia Russia Business Association; Russo-British Chamber of Commerce

CATEGORIES OF WORK

Aviation
Maxim Kuznechenkov

Banking and finance
Maxim Kandyba

Capital markets
Igor Boldyrev, Georgy Kovalenko

Real estate
Konstantine Kouzine, Maxim Kuznechenkov

Commercial and company law
Igor Makarov, Georgy Kovalenko

Dispute resolution
Igor Makarov, Evgeny Gouk

Employment
Alexei Shinkarenko, Yana Zoloeva

Energy and natural resources
Igor Boldyrev, Yana Zoloeva

Environment
Igor Boldyrev, Evgeny Gouk

Infrastructure and project finance
Igor Makarov, Olga Poleschuk

Intellectual property
Igor Boldyrev, Evgeny Gouk

Mergers and acquisitions
Alexei Shinkarenko, Georgy Kovalenko

Private clients and trusts
Andrei Narutsky

Regulatory
Igor Makarov, Gennady Odarich

Shipping and transport
Evgeny Gouk, Maxim Kuznechenkov

SIKAYLO, GABBASOV, ROMAKHOVA & PARTNERS

ATTORNEYS AT LAW

OFFICE 2
MALAYA BRONNAYA STREET 32
123001 MOSKVA

Telephone: +7 495 202 0167
Fax: +7 495 202 0255
E-mail: office@sikaylo-partners.ru

Languages
English, French

Number of lawyers 10

CATEGORIES OF WORK

Banking and finance
Alexey Afonin, Sergey Zadorogin

Commercial property
Alexey Sikaylo, Viktoriya Sikaylo

Construction
Marat Gabbasov

Corporate law
Alexey Sikaylo, Svetlana Romakhova, Sergey Zadorogin

Foreign investment and joint ventures
Alexey Sikaylo, Svetlana Romakhova

Land law
Marat Gabbasov

Litigationa and arbitration
Alexey Sikaylo, Marat Gabbasov, Svetlana Romakhova, Viktoriya Sikaylo

Natural resources
Marat Gabbasov, Svetlana Romakhova

Real estate
Marrat Gabbasov, Alexey Afonin

Taxation
Alexey Afonin, Sergey Zadorogin

SQUIRE, SANDERS & DEMPSEY (MOSCOW) LLC

2/2 PAVELETSKAYA SQUARE
115054 MOSCOW

Telephone: +7 495 258 5250
Fax: +7 495 258 5251
E-mail: itrifonov@ssd.com
Website: www.ssd.com

Languages
English, French, German, Portuguese, Russian, Spanish, Ukrainian

Other offices
Beijing, Bratislava, Brussels, Budapest, Caracas, Cincinnati, Cleveland, Columbus, Hong Kong, Houston, London, Los Angeles, Miami, New York, Palo Alto, Phoenix, Prague, Rio de Janeiro, San Francisco, Santa Domingo, Shanghai, Tallahassee, Tampa, Tokyo, Tysons Corner, Warsaw, Washington DC, West Palm Beach, Bucharest*, Buenos Aires*, Dublin*, Kyiv*, Milan*, Santiago*

Number of lawyers 800+
at this office 14

Contact Ivan Trifonov

Member
American Chamber of Commerce;
Russo-British Chamber of Commerce;
US-Russian Business Counsel

CATEGORIES OF WORK

Competition law
Ivan Trifonov

Corporate finance, banking, capital markets
David Wack, Sergey Treshchev

Environmental
Ivan Trifonov

Infrastructure, project asset finance
David Wack

Intellectual property
Olga Bezrukova

International transactions
Ivan Trifonov, David Wack

Litigation and arbitration
Sergey Treshchev

Mergers and acquisitions
David Wack, Vladmir Kouznetsov

Oil and gas
Ivan Trifonov

Power generation, energy
David Wack, Ivan Trifonov

Real estate
Ivan Trifonov, Vladmir Kouznetsov

Securities
Sergey Treshchev, David Wack

Telecoms
David Wack

THE FIRM

Founded in 1890, Squire, Sanders & Dempsey is a multi-jurisdictional law firm with approximately 800 lawyers practising in offices in Europe, the Americas and Asia. The firm's practice covers most substantive areas of the law, with an emphasis on business and finance matters.

The firm operates as a single global partnership, which ensures client accountability and the seamless delivery of uniformly high-quality legal services throughout the world. The firm's lawyers come from many countries and cultures, are licensed to practise in both common law and civil law jurisdictions, and communicate with clients in their native languages. Today, the firm remains committed to the fundamental principles ordained by its founders: to serve clients effectively and to maintain the professional standards that distinguish both the firm and its people.

AREAS OF PRACTICE

The firm is organised around four major practice areas: advocacy, business, capital markets and regulated industries. Within these practice areas, the firm's work can be divided into numerous areas of specialisation, including banking, bankruptcy and restructuring, biotechnology and pharmaceuticals, communications, competition law, converging technologies, corporate, energy, environmental, healthcare, intellectual property, international dispute resolution, labour and employment, litigation, mergers and acquisitions, privatisations, project finance, real estate, securities and taxation.

Established in 1992, the Moscow office advises both Russian clients and those doing business in the region on questions arising under corporate, intellectual property, environmental, labour, real property, securities, banking, tax, privatisation, antitrust and currency control laws. The Moscow office is part of Squire Sanders' CIS trade and investment practice.

Lawyers in the Moscow office are actively involved in all phases of the region's growing private sector – from assisting Russian and other CIS policy-makers in the transition to a market economy to structuring new business forms and creating a broad range of new private companies. In November 2001, the office was certified by the Russian Ministry of Justice's State Registration Chamber to register Russian and Western companies establishing operations in Russia.

The Moscow lawyers represent clients in dispute resolution proceedings, including local litigation, international arbitration, insolvency and workout proceedings.

Lawyers provide counsel to industries including aerospace, automotive, commercial and investment banking, energy (including oil, gas and power, as well as providers of equipment and services), engineering, equipment manufacturing, food processing and distribution, pharmaceuticals, mining, radio and television broadcasting, real estate, retail, software development, telecoms and transportation.

The Russia team, including in particular the members resident in Washington DC and London, have participated in the representation of US and other government agencies and international organisations in connection with their activities in Russia.

VEGAS-LEX LAW FIRM

22/25 BLDG 1
BOLSHOY STROCHENOVSKY
PEREULOK
115054 MOSCOW

Telephone: +7 495 933 0800
Fax: +7 495 933 0802
E-mail: vegaslex@vegaslex.ru
Website: www.vegaslex.ru

Languages
English, French, German, Italian, Spanish, Ukranian

Other offices
Krasnodar, London, Samara, Saratov, Volgograd

Number of lawyers 73
at this office 49

Member
Anglo-Russian Law Association (ARLA); International Bar Association (France); Chartered Institute of Arbitrators (UK)

CATEGORIES OF WORK

Mergers and acquisitions
Michael Safarov, Juri Borisenko

Corporate and commercial
Dmitry Orakhelashvili, Michael Safarov

Bankruptcy and corporate recovery
Juri Borisenko

Investment
Albert Eganyan, Roman Domashchenko

Tax and customs
Natalia Postnikova

Litigation and commercial dispute resolution
Anna Khudanova, Alexandra Vasiukhnova, Andrei Korelsky

Arbitration
Ekaterina Galasheva

International trade, anti-dumping
Alexandra Vasiukhnova

Transport and shipping
Ekaterina Galasheva, Aleksandr Koshkin

Mediation
Albert Eganyan

Land law, estate and property
Juri Borisenko

Energy and natural resources
Aleksei Shemonaev, Nikita Nikiforov

Infrastructure and project finance, aviation
Aleksandr Koshkin

THE FIRM

Vegas-Lex was founded in 1995 and since 1999 has ranked either first or second in national surveys on Russian law firms. It has extensive experience in litigation and commercial dispute resolution across Russia, international arbitration, in enforcement of foreign arbitration awards in Russia, in legal support of investments. Corporate and tax consulting form some 40% of the total number of annually carried projects. The firm successfully practices land law, and has a number of precedent-forming estate and property cases. The client base includes major Russian enterprises and a number of multinationals.

Vegas-Lex was founded as a result of a young Russian lawyer's initiative to establish a legal consulting entity of international excellence in Russia. The lawyers of the firm graduated from leading universities across Russia, the UK and the US, and have gained experience with some of the world's largest consulting and law firms such as PricewaterhouseCoopers and White & Case.

Once set, the highest professional standard and strict business rules are scrupulously observed. Vegas-Lex was the first law firm in Russia to offer its clients the InGosStrakh insurance policy, protecting them against any mistakes made by professional lawyers.

Over the years, the firm has expanded dramatically, and has now become a centre of legal advice for multinational, regional and local companies. Dedicated to a practical approach, Vegas-Lex has opened offices in a number of industrial regions in order to be even more flexible to the clients' needs and more efficient in dispute resolution.

In addition to traditional business ethics, the firm has developed the distinctive method of securing confidentiality, which is especially important in dealing with property cases.

The State Duma (Russian Parliament) has chosen Vegas-Lex as its official expert. Co-operation of this kind is constantly explored between the firm and a number of state agencies that have a direct impact upon the strategic planning of major Russian corporations. These include the Ministry of Economic Development and Trade, the Ministry of Finance, the Ministry for State Property, the Ministry for Taxes and Duties, the Ministry of Justice, and the State Customs Committee. Moreover, in 2004 the Russian Union of Industrialists and Entrepreneurs (RSPP) contracted the firm to consult on arbitration matters the members of its board, ie top executive officers of the major Russian enterprises.

Today, Vegas-Lex is regarded as a leading Russian law firm, and services clients from almost every sector of the economy. Recent projects have related to natural resources, agriculture, the chemical and processing industries, banking, aerospace, transport, travel and communications. A number of multinationals refer a wide range of legal issues to Vegas-Lex, including American Express, Ernst & Young, Conoco, and a few major Russian enterprises such as Sibur, Roseenergoatom, Wimm-Bill-Dann, Svyazinvest, RAO UES, Magnitogorsk Metallurgical Complex.

AREAS OF PRACTICE

Recent surveys confirm the sound reputation of the firm. Surveys in the *Expert* analytical magazine (Russia) consistently rank Vegas-Lex either first or second in Russia, and particularly highlight the firm's outstanding experience and efficiency in the field of corporate and commercial legal consulting. In August 2004, a survey in *Izvestia* newspaper ranked Vegas-Lex second to none among the Russian legal consulting firms.

The firm's managing partner Albert Eganyan is one of the most reputable legal advisers to corporate clients and the expert for reference for the Russian legal profession. Being very efficient in establishing business links between European and Russian communities, he has made an impressive commitment to the on-going Russian Legal Reform. The firm's lawyers have extensive experience in litigation across Russia, and in arbitration, as well as enforcement of foreign arbitration awards in Russia.

VINSON & ELKINS LLP

NOVINSKY BULVAR 31
6TH FLOOR
123242 MOSCOW

Telephone: +7 495 544 5800
Fax: +7 495 544 5801
Website: www.velaw.com

Languages
English, Russian

Other offices
Austin, Beijing, Dallas, Dubai, Houston, London, New York, Shanghai, Tokyo

Number of lawyers 781

Contact
Dirk Walker

Member
International Bar Association; International Law Section of the American Bar Association; International Lawyers Group, Moscow

CATEGORIES OF WORK

Banking and finance	Infrastructure and project finance
Capital markets	Labour law
Commercial property/real estate	Media and entertainment
Competition	Mergers and acquisitions
Corporate and commercial	Privatisation
Energy and natural resources	Telecommunications
Foreign direct investment	

WINSTON & STRAWN LLP

4 STASSVOYE STREET
117071 MOSCOW

Telephone: +7 495 975 0623
Fax: +7 495 975 0624
E-mail: nkrylov@winston.com
Website: www.winston.com

Languages
English, French, Russian

Other offices
Chicago, Geneva, London, Los Angeles, New York, Paris, San Francisco, Washington DC

Number of lawyers 850

Contact
Nikolai Krylov (managing partner)

CATEGORIES OF WORK

Corporate	Securities and litigation
Mergers and acquisitions	International arbitration

YUST LAW FIRM

43 SIVTSEV VRAZHEK LANE
119002 MOSCOW

Telephone: +7 495 795 0845
Fax: +7 495 241 1948
E-mail: welcome@yust.ru
Website: www.yust.ru

Languages
English, French, German, Russian

Number of lawyers 33

Contact
Yuri Timokhov

International groupings
American Chamber of Commerce in Russia;
Close co-operation with The European Legal Alliance

CATEGORIES OF WORK

Administrative

Commercial property and real estate

Competition

Construction

Corporate and commercial

Dispute resolution, litigation and arbitration

Employment

Energy and natural resources

Foreign direct investment

Fraud and white-collar crime

Information technology

Infrastructure and project finance

Insolvency and corporate restructuring

Insurance

Intellectual property

Mergers and acquisitions

Privatisation

Tax

Telecommunications

BAKER & McKENZIE – CIS, LIMITED

BOLSHAYA MORSKAYA, 57
190000 ST PETERSBURG

Telephone: +7 812 303 9000
Fax: +7 812 325 6013
E-mail: spb.office@bakernet.com
Website: www.bakernet.com

Languages
English, German, Russian

Other offices
The member firms of Baker & McKenzie International, a Swiss Verein, have 70 offices in 38 countries around the world. For a complete list, please visit www.bakernet.com.

Number of lawyers 3,300+
at this office 8

Contact
Maxim Kalinin (partner)

Member
American Chamber of Commerce in Russia; Baltic Bar Association; Russo-British Chamber of Commerce; Russian Venture Capital Association; St Petersburg International Business Association

CATEGORIES OF WORK

Arbitration and litigation
Maxim Kalinin, Igor Gorchakov

Banking and finance
Igor Gorchakov

Corporate and commercial
Maxim Kalinin

Environment
Maxim Kalinin, Andrey Zhdanov

Intellectual property
Eugene Arievich

Infrastructure and project finance
Maxim Kalinin, Igor Gorchakov

Labour and employment
Maxim Kalinin, Alexander Karpukhin

Mergers and acquisitions
Maxim Kalinin, Igor Gorchakov

Production facilities
Maxim Kalinin, Andrey Zhdanov

Real estate, construction
Maxim Kalinin, Andrey Zhdanov

Tax and customs
Alexander Chmelev

Venture capital
Maxim Kalinin, Igor Gorchakov

DLA PIPER RUDNICK GRAY CARY

NEVSKY PR 62
191023 ST PETERSBURG

Telephone: +7 812 703 7801
Fax: +7 812 703 7802
E-mail: olga.litvinova@dlapiper.com
Website: www.dlapiper.com

Languages
English, French, Georgian, German, Russian, Ukrainian

Other offices
Austria, Belgium, Bosnia-Herzegovina, China, Croatia, Czech Republic, Denmark*, Egypt*, France, Georgia, Germany, Hong Kong, Hungary, Italy, Japan, Netherlands, Norway*, Poland*, Russia, Singapore*, Slovakia, South Africa*, Spain, Sweden*, Thailand, UK, Ukraine, United Arab Emirates, US

Number of lawyers 3,100
at this office 30

Contact
Olga Litvinova (Office Managing Partner)

Member
DLA Piper Group

CATEGORIES OF WORK

Corporate, mergers and acquisitions
Denis Sosedkin

Real estate, construction and utilities
Natalia Diatlova

Tax services
Ruslan Vasutin

Commercial and project finance
Olga Litvinova

Intellectual property and information technology protection
Victor Naumov

Customs and currency control
Wilhelmina Shavshina

Litigation and arbitration
Ivan Smirnov

Employment
Marat Altynbaev

THE FIRM

DLA Piper in St Petersburg is a fully integrated legal and tax consulting practice with a unique multidisciplinary approach to the provision of legal services. With 30 lawyers, the St Petersburg office constitutes the largest legal and tax services provider in Russia's northwest. The firm's professionals have unparalleled experience advising on complex inbound investment projects and have been selected as the preferred tax and legal advisers in most major green and brownfield developments in the region.

AREAS OF PRACTICE

Corporate law, mergers and acquisitions, investment legislation: the group's key areas of expertise comprise of legal support to inbound investment, including green and brownfield developments, joint venture formation, equity and quasi-equity investments, pre-acquisition legal and tax due diligence on behalf of both vendors and purchasers, and full-scope legal support throughout M&A transactions. The group possesses in-depth experience in corporate structuring for outbound investment as well as in providing support to companies by corporate reorganisation and restructuring aiming at IPO, attracting of debt financing or courting a strategic investor.

Real estate, construction and utilities services: the group is a well-known adviser in transactions with commercial and industrial real estate, providing full-scope legal support for the majority of investment projects in the northwest, advising on investing in construction of industrial facilities, demolition, and reconstruction, including green and brownfield developments, as well as on acquisition of real estate property and rights to land. The firm provides comprehensive legal support in all matters relating to utilities connection, including electricity, gas, water and roads.

Litigation: the litigation and dispute resolution group represents clients' interests in arbitration courts, as well as in courts of general jurisdiction and before administrative authorities. The group enjoys a success rate in excess of 95% over the past five years, with a 100% success rate in obtaining emergency injunctions in tax litigation, acting in disputes in the following spheres: antitrust, commercial, customs and currency control, environmental, labour, real estate, tax, technology, media and communications, alternative dispute resolution and international arbitration.

Tax services: the firm possesses the largest tax group in Russian legal practices, comprising 14 tax professionals with both law and accounting degrees. The group provides services which are directly related to tax reporting, including advice on calculation and payment of various taxes, and advice on tax compliance projects. It is also experienced in the application of international tax treaties, tax planning, tax restructuring and optimisation of existing operations; the firm advises on the obtaining of tax concessions and consults on transfer pricing issues. The firm provides full-scope tax due diligence in the context of M&A projects.

Customs and currency control: the firm possesses unique expertise in the field of customs regulation and advises a wide range of industries and geographical areas. The group advises on export-import transactions, assisting with the obtaining of exemptions from customs duties and VAT for in-kind contributions to charter capital, customs clearance procedures, customs rulings and classification decisions.

Intellectual property and information technology protection group: comprises the leading experts in intellectual property and information technology advising on the following areas: IP audit and commercial secrets protection status, development of IP management strategy, creation of IP holdings, IP registration in Russia and abroad, IP and IT taxation, privacy law and data protection, legal support for e-commerce, electronic document flows and electronic financial transactions.

CASTRÉN & SNELLMAN ST PETERSBURG

NEVSKY PROSPECT 24
THIRD FLOOR
191186 ST PETERSBURG

Telephone: +7 812 325 8085
Fax: +7 812 325 8086
Email: firstname.surname@castren.ru
Website: www.castren.fi

Languages
English

Other offices
Helsinki

Number of lawyers 79
at this office 3

Contacts
Heidi Paalanen-Koev, Sergei Lee

CATEGORIES OF WORK

Mergers and acquisitions

Capital markets

Private equity and venture capital: greenfield investments and venture capital arrangements

Banking and finance

Real estate

General corporate

Commercial agreements

Tax

Dispute resolution

Employment

EU and competition

MANNHEIMER SWARTLING

DOM SHVETSII
MALAYA KONYUSHENNAYA 1/3A
191186 ST PETERSBURG

Telephone: +7 812 329 2505
Fax: +7 812 329 2507
Website: www.mannheimerswartling.se

Languages
English, German, Russian, Swedish

Other offices
Berlin, Brussels, Frankfurt, Gothenburg, Helsingborg, Malmö, New York, Stockholm

Number of lawyers 330
at this office 7

Contact
Sven Lexner

CATEGORIES OF WORK

Mergers and acquisitions

Corporate (including establishment of companies, joint venture agreements, etc)

Real estate

Employment

Arbitration

ARZINGER & PARTNERS

43 MOSKOVSKA STREET
3RD FLOOR
01015 KYIV

Telephone: +380 44 494 2350
Fax: +380 44 490 9698
E-mail: mail@arzinger.com.ua
Website: www.arzinger.com.ua

Languages
English, German, Russian, Ukrainian

Other offices
Berlin, Bratislava, Budapest, Moscow, Novosibirsk, Prague

Number of lawyers 26

Member
Interleges; EBA; German-Ukrainian Legal Association; correspondent member: Eurojuris; Eurolaw

CATEGORIES OF WORK

International and domestic litigation
Timur Bondarev, Sergei Schklyar

Securitisation
Wolfram Rehbock

Commercial law
Timur Bondarev, Sergei Schklyar

Foreign investments
Wolfram Rehbock, Timur Bondarev

Joint ventures
Timur Bondarev, Yevgenia Novichkova

Banking and debt finance
Wolfram Rehbock, Anna Pogrebna

Mergers and acquisitions
Timur Bondarev, Sergei Schklyar

Company and corporate transactions
Timur Bondarev, Sergei Schklyar

Tax
Anna Pogrebna

Competition/antitrust
Timur Bondarev, Sergei Schklyar

Privatisation
Timur Bondarev

Restructuring and insolvency
Sergei Schklyar

Intellectual property
Igor Tkach, Wolfram Rehbock

Real estate
Timur Bondarev, Anna Pogrebna

Capital markets
Wolfram Rehbock

Construction
Timur Bondarev, Anna Pogrebna

BAKER & McKENZIE – CIS, LIMITED

MILLENNIUM BUSINESS CENTER
5TH FLOOR
12A VOLODYMYRSKA STREET
01025 KYIV

Telephone: +380 44 490 7070
Fax: +380 44 490 6787
E-mail: kyiv_info@bakernet.com
Website: www.bakernet.com

Languages
English, French, Polish, Russian, Ukrainian

Other offices
The member firms of Baker & McKenzie International, a Swiss Verein, have 70 offices in 38 countries around the world. For a complete list, please visit www.bakernet.com.

Number of lawyers 3,300+
at this office 42

Contact
James T Hitch III

CATEGORIES OF WORK

Banking and finance
Serhiy Chorny

Competition law
Olexander Martinenko

Corporate and commercial
James T Hitch, Olexander Martinenko

Dispute resolution
Olexander Martinenko

Employment
James T Hitch

Intellectual property
James T Hitch

IT/communications
Olexander Martinenko

Major projects and project finance
Serhiy Chorny, Serhiy Piontkovsky

Mergers and acquisitions
James T Hitch

Pharmaceuticals
Olexander Martinenko

Privatisation
Serhiy Piontkovsky

Real estate and construction
Serhiy Piontkovsky

Tax
Serhiy Piontkovsky

Venture capital
James T Hitch

B C TOMS & CO

18 PRORIZNA STREET, APT 1
01034 KYIV

Telephone: +380 44 228 1000
Fax: +380 44 228 6508
E-mail: bt@bctoms.com

Languages
English, French, German, Polish, Russian, Ukrainian

Other offices
London, Odessa

Number of lawyers 17
at this office 14

CATEGORIES OF WORK

Acquisition and privatisation
B Toms, D Svyryd

Banking
B Toms, O Volynets

Company law
S Kheda, T Krivonogikh

Commercial law
I Posypayko, O Prokopovych

Commercial property
S Kheda, R Shepard

Construction
D Korbut, R Shepard

Electricity
B Toms, Z Mylovanova

Insolvency
S Kheda, T Krivonogikh

Intellectual property
O Prokopovych

Labour law
S Kheda

Litigation and arbitration
D Korbut, D Svyryd

Oil and gas
B Toms, T Dumych

Project finance
B Toms, T Dumych

Securities
B Toms, O Volynets

Tax and customs
Z Mylovanova, I Posypayko

Telecommunications
T Dumych, S Kheda

THE FIRM

B C Toms & Co is a law firm of western and Ukrainian lawyers specialising in Ukrainian law. The firm was the first from the West to establish a Ukrainian law practice following Ukrainian independence in 1991. Presently it is among the largest law firms in the Ukraine.

In the last three years alone, the firm has acted for clients in transactions representing in value over $2bn of investments and loans into Ukraine. For example, the firm has handled the legal work for most of the oil and gas and electricity generation projects in Ukraine for western firms and joint ventures with western investment, many of the significant western investments in real estate development, many of the largest international loans to Ukraine, telecommunications projects, greenfield factory developments and many acquisitions of Ukrainian businesses (including through privatisation of state assets).

B C Toms & Co was founded by BC Toms, who was previously a partner in a multinational law firm and has substantial experience practising in the US, and Western as well as Eastern Europe. Toms studied Soviet Studies at university and law at Magdalene College, Cambridge and Yale Law School (where he was an editor of the *Yale Law Journal*).

For the past 14 years, the firm has recruited and trained its Ukrainian lawyers from among the highest-ranked students at Ukraine's leading law schools, most of whom have also studied at US and UK law schools. Based on the firm's practical experience, it has written numerous articles on Ukrainian law, including the legal section of the ICC's book, *Doing Business in Ukraine*.

AREAS OF PRACTICE

As one of the largest law firm's in Ukraine, B C Toms & Co has a general practice. The principal practice areas include project finance and construction, real estate, oil and gas and electricity regulation law, investment and acquisition, securities and corporate law, mining, privatisation, franchising, distribution, telecommunications, trade, banking, labour, bankruptcy and administrative law, as well as lobbying on behalf of clients. In addition, the firm has an active litigation and arbitration practice. The firm also regularly advises on Ukrainian tax law, including from a multinational tax planning perspective.

B C Toms & Co has prepared a wide variety of documentation for clients including joint venture agreements, construction contracts, project financing documentation, production sharing and oil and gas sales agreements, private placement agreements, loan agreements, leases, corporate acquisition, agency, distribution, franchises and licensing contracts. It can also provide practical commercial advice on how to establish and develop a Ukrainian business.

DLA PIPER UKRAINE LLC

77A CHERVONOARMIYSKA VUL
FLOOR 4
03150 KYIV

Telephone: +38 44 490 9575
Fax: +38 44 490 9577
E-mail: ukraine@dlapiper.com
Website: www.dlapiper.com/ukraine

Languages
Ukrainian, Russian, English, German, French, Polish

Other offices
Austria, Belgium, Bosnia-Herzegovina, China, Croatia, Czech Republic, Denmark*, Egypt*, France, Georgia, Germany, Hong Kong, Hungary, Italy, Japan, Netherlands, Norway*, Poland*, Russia, Singapore*, Slovakia, South Africa*, Spain, Sweden*, Thailand, UK, Ukraine, United Arab Emirates, US

Number of lawyers 3,100
at this office 16

Contact
Margarita Karpenko

Member
DLA Piper Group

CATEGORIES OF WORK

Antitrust
Galyna Zagorodniuk

Banking and finance
Oleksandr Kurdydyk

Corporate and M&A
Margarita Karpenko, Olena Bilozor

Intellectual property
Natalia Kochergina

Labour law
Margarita Karpenko

Real estate
Konstantin Gribov

Tax
Valentin Belinsky

THE FIRM
DLA Piper Rudnick Gray Cary is a leading global legal services provider with approximately 3,100 lawyers in 58 offices across 22 countries. The organisation is committed to building long-term relationships with its clients and supports their strategic and operational needs both locally and internationally.

The Kyiv office of DLA Piper focuses on corporate matters, and mergers and acquisitions, as well as banking and finance. It also advises on intellectual property matters, real estate, media, antitrust, communications and tax, as well as project and debt financing. The practice is made up of a blend of locally qualified lawyers trained in western jurisdictions, all of whom speak at least two languages.

DLA Piper is a founding member of an exclusive alliance of full-service legal organisations with a shared vision. DLA Piper Group, established in 1999, has members across Europe, Africa, the Middle East, Asia and the US, which deliver expert local know-how and integrated international solutions.

AREAS OF PRACTICE
Corporate, mergers and acquisitions – advises on complex restructurings and consolidations, representing both buyers and sellers in a variety of M&A transactions across Ukraine. Many of these have included cross-border elements.

Banking, finance and capital markets – covers acquisition and public debt finance; refinancing and recapitalisation; asset-based and leveraged finance; project finance; due diligence and share acquisitions in the financial sector; loans, including syndicated and revolving facilities, and loan participations and assignments; public-private partnerships; Eurobond arrangements; and IPOs.

Commercial and projects – advises on a variety of greenfield and brownfield projects and acts for the full range of project participants, including lenders, sponsors, project and joint venture participants, insurers, contractors and government agencies.

Competition – assists companies to obtain the prerequisite permits from the Antimonopoly Committee for consolidations, mergers and acquisitions, and other business ventures. The firm offers co-ordinated international competition advice with its global network of law offices.

Tax – assists clients to optimise and structure their businesses from a tax-planning perspective, and also provides assistance and representation in negotiations with the tax authorities.

Real estate and construction – advises on the construction and development of hotels, shopping centres, and industrial facilities, including in relation to infrastructure, utilities, mechanical and electrical systems, construction finance, construction insolvencies and construction insurance agreements.

Media law and communications – advice in this area covers the law of publishing and publication risks, digital and cross-jurisdictional publications, mobile and fixed communications, privacy and defamation, freedom of information and data protection, and media projects, amongst other more traditional matters.

Intellectual property and information technology – provides legal support in regard to the registration and protection of patents, models and designs, drafting patent licence agreements, protection of brands, copyright and business know-how, advice on trade marks (including searches), the registration and enforcement of infringements, domain names and cyber squatting, the international protection of intellectual property, intellectual property audit, taxation and management strategy, advertising, anti-piracy and customs law, e-commerce and data privacy.

Employment – assists with all aspects of employment law in Ukraine, including drafting employment contracts and agreements, and structuring and implementing successful employment strategies and policies.

GRISCHENKO & PARTNERS

37-41 ARTEMA STREET
04053 KIEV

Telephone: +380 44 490 3707
Fax: +380 44 490 3709
E-mail: adm@gp.ua
Website: www.gp.ua

Languages
Ukrainian, Russian, English, French, Bulgarian

Other offices
Odessa

Number of lawyers 41
at this office 39

Member
European Business Association; American Chamber of Commerce; OASIS International Club of Lawyers

CATEGORIES OF WORK

Administrative
Yulia Atanasova, Sergei Androschuk

Banking and finance
Savva Poliakov, Rodion Ignatenko

Commercial property/real estate
Savva Poliakov

Construction
Nikolai Atanasov

Corporate and commercial
Igor Kovbasinsky

Dispute resolution – litigation and arbitration
Sergei Voitovich

Foreign direct investment
Savva Poliakov

Infrastructure and project finance
Oleg Vysochinsky, Sergei Voitovich

Intellectual property
Tatiana Demchenko, Tatiana Kozlova

Mergers and acquisitions
Tatiana Kozlova, Oleg Vysochinsky

Privatisation
Dmitri Grischenko, Tatiana Kozlova

Tax
Yulia Atanasova

Corporate and finance
Sergei Voitovich

Litigation and arbitration
Pavlo Kostynchuk, Sergei Androschuk

Securities and stock market
Oleg Vysochinsky

International arbitration
Sergei Voitovich

Competition law
Tatiana Kozlova

ILYASHEV & PARTNERS

4 CHAPAEVA STREET, OFFICE 12
01030 KYIV

Telephone: +380 44 494 1919
Fax: +380 44 494 1999
E-mail: office@attorneys.com.ua
Website: www.attorneys.com.ua

Languages
English, Russian, Ukrainian

Other offices
Kharkov

Number of lawyers 15
at this office 14

CATEGORIES OF WORK

Litigation
Mikhail Ilyashev, Galina Lefor

Arbitration
Mikhail Ilyashev, Roman Marchenko

International arbitration
Mikhail Ilyashev, Roman Marchenko

Real estate, construction
Maksim Kopeichikov, Igor Khasin

Anti-counterfeiting
Mikhail Ilyashev, Evgen Solovyov

Debt collection
Oleg Trokhimchuk, Irina Mishanina

Taxation
Mikhail Ilyashev

Corporate law
Roman Molodetskiy, Evgen Solovyov

Insolvency
Roman Marchenko, Evgen Solovyov

Project finance
Roman Marchenko

Commercial property
Mikhail Ilyashev, Maksim Kopeichikov

MAGISTER & PARTNERS

20 VELYKA ZHYTOMYRSKA
01025 KYIV

Telephone: +380 44 492 8282
Fax: +380 44 492 8272
E-mail: info@magisters.com
Website: www.magisters.com

Languages
English, German, Polish, Russian, Ukrainian

Other offices
Moscow

Number of lawyers 45

Contacts
Oleg Riabokon (trade and commerce),
Eugene Korniychuk (finance, oil and gas),
Oleg Marchenko (tax and corporate),
Serhii Sviriba (arbitration and litigation),
Andrew Mac (corporate and real estate)

CATEGORIES OF WORK

Arbitration and litigation	**Mergers and acquisitions**
Banking and finance	**Oil and gas**
Commercial transactions	**Securities regulation**
Corporate matters	**Taxation**
Foreign investment	**Telecommunications**
International trade	

THE FIRM

Magister & Partners is a well-established, reputable and dynamic firm offering a wide range of services, a wealth of international experience and a qualified legal team. Since 1997, its lawyers have represented foreign companies conducting business in Ukraine, the CIS region, Western Europe and the Americas, as well as domestic blue-chip companies, ten of which lead the list of the 'Top 100 Best Companies in Ukraine'. Most of the firm's associates hold law degrees from the US, Canada or Western European universities, and have worked with leading attorneys in these jurisdictions.

The firm's excellence in the fields of Ukrainian and international law has been widely recognised by the business community and independent research publications, such as the *International Who's Who of Trade and Customs Lawyers* 2005, *Chambers & Partners Global* 2005 and the *International Financial Law Review 1000*, 2006. *Yuridicheskaya Praktika*, the only legal weekly conducting annual ratings of law firms in Ukraine, ranked Magister & Partners second for annual income and third among the 'Top 50 Ukrainian law firms 2005'.

AREAS OF PRACTICE

Magister & Partners provides high-quality services in the field of international trade and customs regulation. Its trade and commercial law practice, headed by managing partner Oleg Riabokon, regularly engages in anti-dumping, countervailing and safeguard proceedings, general defence strategies in trade investigations, customs matters, representation of clients during administrative hearings, negotiation of settlements and undertakings, and foreign market monitoring systems. The firm's lawyers are also heavily involved in all aspects of general commercial practice, including investments, contracts, corporate and intellectual property advice.

The firm's finance practice, led by senior partner Eugene Korniychuk, provides comprehensive legal support to its clients regarding attracting bilateral loans, syndicated loans, and project and structured financing from foreign banks and international financial organisations. Magister & Partners has broad experience in serving major international and national financial institutions, such as World Bank, Deutsche Bank, WestLB, Credit Suisse First Boston, Gazprombank, Vneshekonombank, UkrSibbank, Dresdner Kleinwort Wasserstein, UBS Limited, and ABN AMRO, Bank NV, Citigroup, TuranAlem Bank, Privatbank and Wereximbank.

The oil and gas practice focuses on a wide range of issues related to the energy, oil and gas sectors, and serves as legal adviser to the state joint stock company Naftogaz, the largest oil and gas industry player in Ukraine. The firm has also represented and advised national companies such as Energoatom, Chornomornaftogaz, Ukrnafta, Gas Ukrainy and TNK Ukraine, as well as foreign companies such as Eural Trans Gas, Momentum Energy International, and Petro Santander.

Magister & Partners' arbitration and litigation practice, led by partner Serhii Sviriba, is experienced in representing clients in institutional and ad hoc arbitrations in Ukraine, Europe and the CIS. The firm has won an outstanding reputation for its arbitration and litigation practice using, in addition to judicial actions, alternative dispute resolution methods so as to exploit all possible legal means to satisfy the interests of its clients.

Magister & Partners is well known for its expertise in mergers and acquisitions and corporate matters. The corporate practice is headed by partner Oleg Marchenko, and it represents one of the core areas of the firm. Its corporate clients include ADM, Alfred C Toepfer International, TNK-Ukraine, US Steel Kosice, Interpipe Corporation, Naftogaz of Ukraine, and Sun Interbrew Ukraine. With new partner Andrew Mac the firm has strengthened its real estate practice. Mr Mac's expertise also includes M&A, corporate and commercial law, investment, securities and privatisation.

PAKHARENKO & PARTNERS

72 CHERVONOARMIYSKA STR
ENTRANCE 1, 7TH FLOOR
03150 KYIV
PO BOX 194
01034 KYIV

Telephone: +380 44 451 8340
Fax: +380 44 451 4048
E-mail: pakharenko@pakharenko.kiev.ua
Website: www.pakharenko.com

Languages
English, French, German, Russian, Ukrainian

Other offices
London

Number of lawyers 12
at this offce 10

Contact
Antonia Pakharenko-Anderson,
Elena Shamrina, Alexander Pakharenko

International groupings
AIPPI; INTA; FICPI; LESI; MARQUES; PTMG;
ECTA; ACG; IACC; CIB; IBA

CATEGORIES OF WORK

Intellectual property

Corporate and commercial

E-commerce

Arbitration, litigation and dispute resolution

Customs

Anti-counterfeiting and anti-piracy

Unfair competition

Tax law

Insurance law

Employment and contract law

SALKOM

12 KHRESCHATYK STREET
01001 KYIV

Telephone: +380 44 537 3941
Fax: +380 44 537 3955
E-mail: salkom@salkom.kiev.ua
Website: www.salkom.ua

Languages
English, French, German, Russian, Ukranian

Number of lawyers 32

Contacts
Evgeniy Kubko, Nataliya Kuznetsova,
Valeriy Lukomskiy

Member
IBA (International Bar Association);
EBA (European Business Association); American Chamber of Commerce in Ukraine (ACC);
British-Ukrainian Chamber of Commerce (BUCC)

CATEGORIES OF WORK

Arbitration and litigation
Andrey Kuznetsov, Pavel Lukomskiy

Administrative law
Evgeniy Kubko

Antitrust
Alexey Kot

Banking and finance
Evgeniy Kubko, Nataliya Kuznetsova

Company and commercial
Alexey Kot, Andrey Kuznetsov

Criminal law
Valeriy Lukomskiy

Foreign investments
Nataliya Kuznetsova

EU
Dmitriy Suprun, Evgeniy Kubko

Labour law
Taras Lukash

Mergers and acquisitions
Andrey Kubko

Real estate
Alexey Kot

Privatisation
Nataliya Kuznetsova

Tax
Ludmila Kirilenko

Trade marks, intellectual property
Pavel Lukomskiy

SHEVCHENKO DIDKOVSKIY & PARTNERS

2A KOSTYANTYNIVSKA STREET
04071 KIEV

Telephone: +380 44 230 6000
Fax: +380 44 230 6001
E-mail: lawfirm@shevdid.com
Website: www.shevdid.com

Languages
English, Russian, Ukrainian

Number of lawyers 46

Contact
Igor Shevchenko

International groupings
World Services Group;
European Business Association;
American Chamber of Commerce

CATEGORIES OF WORK

Foreign investment
Igor Shevchenko, Oleksiy Didkovskiy

Corporate and commercial
Oleksandr Padalka, Vadym Samoylenko

Mergers and acquisitions
Igor Shevchenko, Armen Khachaturyan

Antitrust and unfair competition
Oleksandr Padalka

Banking and finance
Armen Khachaturyan,
Oleksiy Didkovskiy

Real estate and construction
Rysbek Toktomushev

Telecommunications
Oleksiy Didkovskiy

Energy and natural resources
Rysbek Toktomushev, Evhen Gusyev

Privatisation
Armen Khachaturyan, Evhen Gusyev

Labour and employment
Oleksandr Padalka

Taxation
Vadym Samoylenko, Oleksandr Padalka

Intellectual property
Oleksandr Padalka

UKRAINIAN LEGAL GROUP, L.L.C.

4-6 PATRISA LUMUMBY ST
BUILDING V, 8TH FLOOR, SUITE 801
01042 KIEV

Telephone: +380 44 502 1024
Fax: +380 44 230 2932
E-mail: general@rulg.com
Website: www.rulg.com

Languages
English, Russian, Ukrainian

Other offices
Washington DC

Number of lawyers 14
at this office 12

Contact
Dr Irina Paliashvili, president (irinap@rulg.com),
Victor Kovalenko, managing partner
(victor.kovalenko@ulg.kiev.ua)

Member
Ukraine-US Business Council; American Chamber of Commerce in Ukraine; EBA; INTA; US-Russia Business Council; Legalink; ABA

CATEGORIES OF WORK

Corporate and commercial

Dispute resolution – litigation, international arbitration and commercial mediation

Foreign direct investment

Energy and natural resources

Mergers and acquisitions

Intellectual property

Competition

Insolvency/corporate restructuring

Asset finance/securitisation

Banking and finance and capital markets

Commercial property/real estate

Construction

Government business/regulatory

Information technology

Infrastructure and project finance

Insurance

Labour law

Media and entertainment

Privatisation

Tax

Telecommunications

Aviation

E-commerce

Environment

Shipping and transport

VOLKOV & PARTNERS

72A CHERVONOARMIYSKA STREET
OLIMPIYSKY BUSINESS CENTER
SUITE 124
03150 KYIV

Telephone: +380 44 207 0270
Fax: +380 44 207 0272
E-mail: office@volkovpartners.com
Website: www.volkovpartners.com

Languages
English, Russian, Ukrainian

Number of lawyers 21

CATEGORIES OF WORK

Corporate
Oleksiy Volkov, Roman Drozhanskyy

Contracts
Alina Plyushch, Olena Teslya

Competition
K Tkachenko, Andrey Karnaukhov

M&A
Oleksiy Volkov, Olena Teslya

Tax
Larissa Kurak, Ihor Martsyn

International finance
Oleksiy Volkov, Larissa Kurak

Real estate, land
Andrey Karnaukhov, Oleksiy Volochay

Banking and financial services
Larissa Kurak, Alina Plyushch

Insolvency, bankruptcy
Ihor Martsyn, Oleksiy Volochay

Intellectual property
K Tkachenko, O Aleksyeyenko

Energy and utilities
Olga Galaka, Oleksiy Volochay

Oil and gas
Oleksiy Volkov, Roman Drozhanskyy

Telecommunications
Oleksiy Volkov, Olena Teslya

Transport and aviation
Ihor Martsyn, O Aleksyeyenko

Labour and employment
Olga Sokol, Kateryna Dorosh

Family and civil law
Olga Sokol, Olga Galaka

Litigation and arbitration
Andrey Karnaukhov, Olga Galaka

Securities and investment markets
Oleksiy Volkov, Alina Plyushch

THE FIRM

Volkov & Partners Law Firm is one of the most dynamically developing and respectable law firms in Ukraine. It offers advice in all aspects relating to business and investment in Ukraine and provides a wide range of legal services. The firm's general practice is concentrated on corporate issues, mergers and acquisitions, oil and gas, taxation, competition and intellectual property law. It also handles major matters involving land law, real estate, transportation and telecommunications.

Volkov & Partners' activities focus on the provision of legal services to international corporate clients in a wide range of matters arising in connection with their business in Ukraine. The firm has successful experience of long-term representation of many brand name corporations protecting their interests in Ukraine as well as Ukrainian companies in Ukrainian and foreign jurisdictions.

AREAS OF PRACTICE

Corporate: the firm provides an extensive range of services in corporate and commercial matters, both nationally and internationally, including bankruptcy, reorganisation, due diligence, and contract drafting. It also handles company incorporations, mergers and acquisitions both in Ukraine and other jurisdictions. The managing partner of the firm, Oleksiy M Volkov, is highly qualified in the sphere of corporate issues and advises a number of Forbes 500 companies.

Taxation: the firm provides comprehensive professional tax services and is active in advising on tax-efficient structures and tax planning. Its expertise covers corporate income taxation, partnership taxation, taxation of investment activity, and tax litigation. Larissa V Kurak, partner, has vast experience in handling finance, tax and related matters.

Competition: the firm has advised clients on general competition and antitrust cases, including merger control, research of markets, and state aid rules. Oleksiy M Volkov has a strong competition practice with advice in antitrust and merger control issues representing clients in competition cases before national courts as well as competition authorities.

Litigation: the practice covers all forms of commercial and civil disputes and provides business-related criminal litigation support. It is active in both domestic and cross-border litigation, including disputes litigated before foreign courts.

Intellectual property: the IP practice encompasses the traditional areas of copyright, trade mark, franchising, and litigation involving infringement of trade marks, copyrights, designs and patents. Andrey L Karnaukhov, partner, handles an increasing amount of commercial, contractual, and other civil disputes.

Transportation: the firm's transportation lawyers work in maritime areas and aviation and represent owners, carriers, forwarders and lenders who finance transportation business. In addition to providing day-to-day services and solutions that affect transportation clients, the firm is also engaged in the regulatory and public policy aspects of transportation law. Andrey L Karnaukhov, partner, has an active maritime and aviation practice and advises a number of foreign and local shipping companies and carriers.

Energy and natural resources: the firm advises on the research and exploitation of natural resources, in particular oil and gas, licensing of special types of activity, commercial operations with energy resources. Oleksiy M Volkov, managing partner, is experienced in providing advice in a variety of legal matters dealing with energy and natural resources.

DENTON WILDE SAPTE

90 ACAD VOSIT VOKHIDOV STREET
YAKKASARAYSKIY DISTRICT
700031 TASHKENT

Telephone: +998 71 120 6946
Fax: +998 71 120 6185
E-mail: tashkent@dentonwildesapte.uz
Website: www.dentonwildesapte.com

Languages
English, French, German, Persian, Russian, Spanish, Uzbek

Other offices
Abu Dhabi, Almaty, Cairo, Dubai, Istanbul, London, Milton Keynes, Moscow, Muscat, Paris

Number of lawyers 683
at this office 4

Contact
Mouborak Kambarova

CATEGORIES OF WORK

Banking and finance

Oil and gas

Telecommunications

Mergers and acquisitions

Corporate

Labour law

Mining

SAUDI ARABIA

Population	26 million
Number of lawyers	n/a
Professional title	Advocate
Currency	Saudi Riyal (SR)

Index

The largest oil-producing country in the world and the birthplace of Islam, the Kingdom of Saudi Arabia is one of the richest and most powerful states in the Middle East.

Hidden amongst the shrouds of uninhabitable desert lie the techno-oases of Jeddah and the capital, Riyadh. Built largely on oil-boom money, both cities (especially Riyadh) are dynamic commercial hubs. Jeddah remains the kingdom's most important seaport, while Riyadh is commonly cited as one of the most prosperous and fastest-growing cities in the world. Here, East literally meets West, as *muttawa* (religious policemen) patrol expensive shopping districts, upholding morality in accordance with Wahhabism, the puritanical branch of Islam popularly followed in Saudi Arabia.

For many commentators, this implied conflict between old and new may contribute to the so-called inevitable decline of the House of Saud, referring to the extravagant ruling Al-Saud dynasty, after whom the country is named.

In August 2005, King Abdullah succeeded his half-brother (the late King Fahd) as ruler, and in turn inherited the increasing problem of terrorism. Ever since Saudi nationals were identified as playing a crucial role in the September 11 attacks, Saudi Arabian administration has been harshly criticised internationally for its allegedly lax attitude towards terror cells. However, under global pressure, King Abdullah, himself openly critical of US foreign policy in the Middle East, and his government are determinedly tackling al-Qaeda-linked groups, especially since the country has itself been victim to militant attacks.

Nevertheless, it remains debatable to what extent authorities will be able to stamp out anti-Western sentiment engendered by the Israel-Palestinian conflict and Iraq war, issues close to Saudi Arabian temperament at large.

BILLING

Saudi Arabian law firms charge by the hour. Local firms usually charge between US$200 to US$300 for partners, and around US$100 for associates. International firms tend to charge higher, going up to about US$600 per hour for partners.

MARKETING

Saudi Arabian firms have no restrictions on marketing, but it remains a muted affair. Many firms win clients on the basis of an established reputation and word-of-mouth recommendations.

IN-HOUSE LAWYERS

Most Saudi banks and major companies have large in-house legal departments, which can easily rival domestic firms in terms of size.

ECONOMY

Despite astronomical levels of economic prosperity as the world's largest oil-producing country, Saudi authorities are already preparing themselves for the inevitable truth that its oil riches will not last forever.

While the economy is more than comfortable at present, claiming 25% of the world's petroleum reserves, Saudi's oil market was on edge when King Fahd passed away in early August 2005. Following news of his death, oil prices peaked to an all-time high, up to US$63.94 a barrel for crude oil in the US. Although oil prices have calmed down, these dramatic fluctuations are one indication of the economy's vulnerability and over-dependency on oil-revenues, which account for about 45% of GDP.

King Abdullah's administration is now focused on diversifying and modernising its financial markets, in a bid to speed economic growth further and wean the economy off oil-dependency. Subsequently, Saudi Arabian officials have been negotiating with US counterparts in order to secure WTO accession (preliminarily planned for the end of 2005).

The Saudi Arabian Stock Exchange is booming, and there has been a surge of IPOs, including that of the National Co-operative Company for Insurance (NCCI), Saudi's largest insurance company, in late 2004. The stock market increased by 70% in 2005 and boasts an average daily turnover of more than US$2bn, making it the biggest emerging stock market in the world.

The new king has also pulled family purse strings tight, putting an end to certain financial privileges of the younger al-Saud generation, such as hugely generous vacation allowances. Such benefits are by no means insignificant- the ruling family's 4,000 princes and princesses' exuberant lifestyles remain a serious drain on national coffers.

Unemployment remains a problem; the official unemployment rate currently stands at 9%, although unofficially, it is thought to be double

The largest firms

1	Salah Al-Hejailan, The Law Firm of	22
2	Abbas F. Ghazzawi & Co. and Hammad & Al-Mehdar, The Alliance of	19
3	Al-Ghazzawi Professional Association	17
4	Majed M Garoub, The Law Firm of	15
5	Al-Jadaan Law Firm in co-operation with Clifford Chance LLP	14
	Toban Law Firm	14
7	Al-Rowaished & Al-Assaf Law Firm	13
8	Hassan Mahassni in association with Trowers & Hamlins, The Law Office of	12
	Legal Advisers in association with Baker & McKenzie	12
	The Alliance	12
11	Al Yaqoub Lawyers and Legal Advisers	10
	Bin Mahfouz International Law Firm	10
	Khalid Alnowaiser (Dr), The Law Firm of	10
14	Audhali Law Firm (Dr)	8
	Nader Law & Translation Offices	8
	The International Law Firm	8
	United Law Firm	8
18	Mujahid M. Al-Sawwaf (Dr), Law Offices of	7
19	Al-Soaib Law Firm	6
	LeBoeuf, Lamb, Greene & MacRae in affiliation with Saud M.A. Shawwaf Law Office	6
21	Abu-Ghazaleh Legal	5
	Abdulaziz H. Fahad (in assoc with Akin Gump Strauss Hauer & Feld), Law Office of	5
23	Mohammed Al-Sharif in association with Johnson & Pump, The Law Firm of	4
24	Mahamed H. Hoshan (Dr), Law Offices of	3
	Mohammed A Al Sheikh (in assoc with White & Case LLP), Law Office of	3
	Mohanned bin Saud Al-Rasheed in association with Baker Botts L.L.P., Law Office	3

These figures represent the total number of lawyers in this country only, and have been supplied by the firms themselves. The figures should be accurate as at 1 January 2006.

that. Each year churns out an increasing number of university graduates, but a limited economy equals limited job opportunities, which implies dangerously rising unemployment levels for the future.

With this in mind, the government launched the 'Saudi-isation' scheme, proposing to increase the number of Saudi employees in the private sector and labour market. During the 1980s, these positions were, and still are, filled by several million foreign workers. But the success of 'Saudi-isation' is yet to be seen. Unemployment seems likely to escalate, and as the government continues its expensive hand-out scheme of £7,250 to every new graduate in the country, young Saudis can afford to wait before entering employment.

LEGAL SYSTEM AND LEGAL MARKET

The Saudi Arabian legal system is based on shari'ah or Islamic law, and the country has over 300 shari'ah courts.

Saudi Arabia has long been criticised for its lack of judicial transparency. There are concerns that the seemingly time-consuming judicial process may eventually test foreign investors' patience. Consequently, the Ministry of Justice is outlining a programme of reform, which includes talk on new commercial laws. Nevertheless, for many, this is just talk, and it remains to be seen when these reforms will be set in motion.

Foreign firms must have an affiliation with a local firm in order to practise, and commitment is the key to survival in Saudi Arabia. Lawyers from Western firms must be genuinely open to a very different cultural and political climate - some firms find it hard to retain Western-qualified lawyers on the ground. Many leading lawyers left the country in 2003 following terrorist attacks, and certain firms are still shifting personnel elsewhere.

But despite the problem of security issues and much-needed reform, foreign investors are still pouring into Saudi Arabia, translating into heavyweight corporate work for lawyers. Couple this with the capital markets boom and national projects work, and the legal market is looking remarkably healthy.

Overall, there are two firms which come up most often when discussing Saudi's legal market. Typically recommended for their international strength, they are: **Al-Jadaan law firm in co-operation with Clifford Chance LLP** and **Legal Advisers in association with Baker & McKenzie**.

Al-Jadaan law firm in co-operation with Clifford Chance LLP has maintained its successful international relationship with **Clifford Chance** for almost ten years now. The 14-lawyer practice is renowned for its privatisation and finance expertise, and maintains expert international and Saudi law capability.

There are typically more US firms than UK firms in Saudi Arabia; **Legal Advisers in association with Baker & McKenzie** remains the longest-standing association in Saudi Arabia, having entered the Kingdom over 25 years ago. The firm boasts some of the best-known lawyers in the market; managing partner John Xefos and Georges Sayen.

Baker Botts, L.L.P. opened in Dubai in April 2005, and at least two associates relocated there from Riyadh's **Law Office of Mohanned bin Saud Al-Rasheed in association with Baker Botts L.L.P.**. A team of approximately five lawyers remains in Riyadh, including two fee-earners from **Baker Botts, L.L.P.**.

In late 205, **Bryan Cave LLP** withdrew from Saudi Arabia. Its Kuwaiti office is now at the centre of its Middle Eastern operations. The local firm initially affiliated with **Bryan Cave LLP** has now entered into an association with US firm **Fulbright & Jaworski LLP**, creating **Kadasah Law Firm (in assoc with Fulbright & Jaworski LLP)**. **LeBoeuf, Lamb, Greene & MacRae in affiliation with Saud M.A. Shawwaf Law Office** also has a respectable presence in Saudi, managed by Khalid Al-Thebity, as does **Law Office of Abdulaziz H. Fahad (in assoc with Akin Gump Strauss Hauer & Feld)**.

Trowers & Hamlins made its official Saudi debut in 2005 and is the only other UK firm besides **Clifford Chance** with a Saudi Arabian presence. The firm joined forces with respected Saudi lawyer, Hassan Mahassni (of *Law Office of Hassan Mahassni (in assoc with White & Case LLP)* in July, forming **The Law Office of Hassan Mahassni in association with Trowers & Hamlins**. Considered by peers to be a legal legend in Saudi Arabia, Hassan Mahassni reached an amicable separation with **White & Case** before **Trowers & Hamlins** joined him in Jeddah.

Meanwhile in Riyadh, **White & Case** teamed up with the 'very capable' Mohammed Al Sheikh, who steps into Mahassni's shoes at the renamed **Law Office of Mohammed A Al Sheikh (in assoc with White & Case LLP)**. Well-liked Al Sheikh worked at *Law Office of Hassan Mahassni (in assoc with White & Case LLP* and although his new role as lead Saudi partner will prove challenging, it is also a natural transition for Al Sheikh, who has worked at **White & Case LLP** in Washington, DC and New York. All eyes are on Al Sheikh, and hopes are high that the firm will continue to carve a stronger position for itself in the Saudi legal market. The firm benefits from the expertise of **White & Case** partner Alexander Kritzalis, who splits base between Riyadh, Abu Dhabi and New York.

Gide Loyrette Nouel is the only French firm in Saudi Arabia, and has a long-standing presence in the country advising international and Saudi clients. Charles-Henri Arminjon and Guillaume de Lalande work closely with local lawyer Shafiq Othman.

Firms do not necessarily need formal international alliances in order to be successful in the market. There are local Saudi Arabian firms (which often employ Western-qualified lawyers as well) with equally excellent reputations, making a good choice for those international firms seeking independent domestic counsel.

Law Offices of Dr Mujahid M. Al-Sawwaf is one such firm, which has a solid and impressive track record in litigation, finance and corporate matters. Name partner Dr Al-Sawwaf and David Wells are well liked and respected individuals.

Similarly, **The Alliance of Abbas F. Ghazzawi & Co. and Hammad & Al-Mehdar** is recommended for its enviable shipping and insurance practice. In early August 2005, the legal community at large regretfully suffered the loss of senior partner, Sheikh Abbas F Ghazzawi, who held a distinguished position in legal and government spheres.

Although it does not have a presence on the ground, **Pinsent Masons**' international arbitration team has advised existing clients in ICC disputes relating to large engineering projects.

BANKING AND FINANCE

Al-Jadaan law firm in co-operation with Clifford Chance LLP's outstanding four-lawyer finance team is fronted by partner Mohammed Al-Jadaan, referred to by one client as 'the best Saudi lawyer in the market.' Finance is the firm's largest area of expertise, and the group advises on all loan facilities, project development agreements, security arrangements, Islamic finance and derivatives work. **Al-Jadaan law firm in co-operation with Clifford Chance LLP** advised the investors in Etisalat International, in the world's largest Islamic finance transaction undertaken in the telecoms sector. Aside from its vast project finance portfolio, the firm has across-the-board banking experience, advising JP Morgan, Samba Financial Group, the Arab National Bank and Saudi Oger.

'If they say they'll do the job, they always do it well' is one way in which **Legal Advisers in association with Baker & McKenzie** has been described. The firm has its hands on some of the biggest deals in Saudi Arabia. It advised Samba Financial Group on a US$600m loan facility, and the Saudi British Bank on a US$650m Euro Medium Term Note (EMTN) programme listed on the Luxembourg Stock Exchange – the first-ever EMTN established by a Saudi company. Key clients include BNP Paribas, Riyad Bank and the Banque Saudi Fransi. The banking team has doubled in size, and now comprises four partners: managing partner Jogn Xefos, Bahrain-based Ian Siddell, recently promoted Julie Alexander, and Harney Shoker, who joined from **Freshfields Bruckhaus Deringer**'s London office.

The Abedi brothers, Ali and Assad, of **The Alliance of Abbas F. Ghazzawi & Co. and Hammad & Al-Mehdar**, make a sturdy banking and finance team. In 2005, the firm advised Credit Suisse, Deutsche Bank and ANZ Investment Bank. Advising the lenders in connection with a term facility to Saudi Arabian Airlines valued at US$480m was another top achievement.

The Law Office of Hassan Mahassni in association with Trowers & Hamlins benefits from Hassan Mahassni's outstanding reputation as 'an excellent lawyer, very reliable and incredibly sharp, who has the rare quality of coming straight to the point'. Described by another client as 'probably one of the best lawyers in Saudi Arabia', Mahassni has strong experience in Islamic banking. Long-standing clients in this field include Dar Al Maal Al Islami, the Islamic Investment Company of the Gulf and Faisal Islamic Bank of Bahrain. **Trowers & Hamlins**' partner Leroy Levy is recommended for project finance.

Under the new lead of Mohammed Al Sheikh, **Law Office of Mohammed A Al Sheikh (in assoc with White & Case LLP)** aims to concentrate on banking, finance and project finance. The firm advised Etisalat on its corporate financing structure and represents some of Saudi's finest banking institutions, including the National Commercial Bank, Riyad Bank, Samba Financial Group and the IFC.

Seven-lawyer **Law Offices of Dr Mujahid M. Al-Sawwaf** has experience advising both sponsors and banks. At present, **Law Offices of Dr Mujahid M. Al-Sawwaf** is working with **Allen & Overy LLP** advising the Japan Bank for International Co-operation on the Saudi law aspects of the Sharq expansion, a US$2.5bn to US$3bn expansion and development project of an existing petrochemical plant. Affable partner David Wells heads the project finance team.

Law Office of Mohanned bin Saud Al-Rasheed in association with Baker Botts L.L.P. concluded the SR142m non-recourse financing of the Equestrian Club's hotel, resorts and sports projects in Jeddah. The transaction took ten years to finalise, after tricky stops and starts which **Law Office of Mohanned bin Saud Al-Rasheed in association with Baker Botts L.L.P.** successfully overcame. Commenting on the firm, one client said 'the work has been thorough and done professionally; the end result was achieved to our total satisfaction.'

Seven-lawyer **The International Law Firm** regularly advises on syndicated transactions, credit and loan facilities, Islamic financing and US Export-Import Bank financing. The firm typically acts on behalf of the lender in financial transactions. Senior legal advisor Vernon Cassin has impressive banking experience.

Law Office of Abdulaziz H. Fahad (in assoc with Akin Gump Strauss Hauer & Feld) acts for a number of Saudi Arabian and foreign banks, as do **LeBoeuf, Lamb, Greene & MacRae in affiliation with Saud M.A. Shawwaf Law Office** and **The Law Firm of Salah Al-Hejailan**.

BANKING AND FINANCE

AL-JADAAN LAW FIRM IN CO-OPERATION WITH CLIFFORD CHANCE LLP
LEGAL ADVISERS IN ASSOCIATION WITH BAKER & McKENZIE ✪

Abbas F. Ghazzawi & Co. and Hammad & Al-Mehdar, The Alliance of ✪
Hassan Mahassni in association with Trowers & Hamlins, The Law Office of
Mohammed A Al Sheikh (in assoc with White & Case LLP), Law Office of
Mujahid M. Al-Sawwaf (Dr), Law Offices of

Mohanned bin Saud Al-Rasheed in association with Baker Botts L.L.P., Law Office ✪
The International Law Firm

Abdulaziz H. Fahad (in assoc with Akin Gump Strauss Hauer & Feld), Law Office of
LeBoeuf, Lamb, Greene & MacRae in affiliation with Saud M.A. Shawwaf Law Office ✪
Salah Al-Hejailan, The Law Firm of

Firms are listed A-Z in tiers which are ranked in order of priority
✪ Indicates firm displays contact details at the end of this chapter.

CORPORATE AND M&A

Al-Jadaan law firm in co-operation with Clifford Chance LLP has an excellent corporate presence. The 'very intelligent' and extremely approachable name partner Mohammed Al-Jadaan works closely with a team of three senior associates who (as one client said) are 'not only good lawyers, but are orientated to finding, wherever at all possible, a solution to their client's issues.' Clients include Saudi Oger, Lucent Technologies, HSBC, ABN Amro and JP Morgan. The team advised the issuer on the Sadafco IPO, the first private company IPO under the new regulations.

Led by partner George Sayen, **Legal Advisers in association with Baker & McKenzie** has been providing ongoing corporate advice to many long-standing, top-quality clients, including Hewlett-Packard, Booz Allen Hamilton, Shell, the Oracle Corporation and Olayan Group. The firm advised the United National Trading Company on the sale of 51% of the United Food Industry Company to Lactalis, and has vast experience advising foreign companies on buyouts of Saudi partners. Capital markets is likewise a thriving area for **Legal Advisers in association with Baker & McKenzie**, which acted on Al-Marai's US$614m IPO and the NCCI's US$380m IPO.

Twenty-one fee-earner **The Alliance of Abbas F. Ghazzawi & Co. and Hammad & Al-Mehdar** has advised on some chunky M&A deals, advising a US specialist energy investment fund on the Saudi aspects of its acquisition of a global oil services company. Clients include insurance companies Norwich Union, Royal & SunAlliance, Swiss Re and BUPA.

Since joining forces with **Trowers & Hamlins** in July 2005, **The Law Office of Hassan Mahassni in association with Trowers & Hamlins** hopes to attract more big-ticket transactional work. The

CORPORATE AND M&A

AL-JADAAN LAW FIRM IN CO-OPERATION WITH CLIFFORD CHANCE LLP
LEGAL ADVISERS IN ASSOCIATION WITH BAKER & McKENZIE ✪

ABBAS F. GHAZZAWI & CO. AND HAMMAD & AL-MEHDAR, THE ALLIANCE OF ✪
HASSAN MAHASSNI IN ASSOCIATION WITH TROWERS & HAMLINS, THE LAW OFFICE OF
MOHAMMED A AL SHEIKH (IN ASSOC WITH WHITE & CASE LLP), LAW OFFICE OF
MUJAHID M. AL-SAWWAF (DR), LAW OFFICES OF

Abdulaziz H. Fahad (in assoc with Akin Gump Strauss Hauer & Feld), Law Office of
Gide Loyrette Nouel ✪
Kadasah Law Firm (in assoc with Fulbright & Jaworski LLP)
LeBoeuf, Lamb, Greene & MacRae in affiliation with Saud M.A. Shawwaf Law Office ✪
Mohanned bin Saud Al-Rasheed in association with Baker Botts L.L.P., Law Office ✪
Salah Al-Hejailan, The Law Firm of
The International Law Firm

Audhali Law Firm (Dr)
Bin Mahfouz International Law Firm
Mohammed Al-Sharif in association with Johnson & Pump, The Law Firm of
Nader Law & Translation Offices

Firms are listed A-Z in tiers which are ranked in order of priority
✪ Indicates firm displays contact details at the end of this chapter.

team advised Saudi American Bank on its merger with United Saudi Bank, and **Trowers & Hamlins** partner Leroy Levy led his 12-lawyer team on the largest IPO in Saudi Arabia to date (worth US$2.7m), for telecoms operator Mobily.

Described as a 'commercial thinker', name partner Mohammed Al Sheikh fronts the corporate practice at **Law Office of Mohammed A Al Sheikh (in assoc with White & Case LLP)**. In line with the wave of capital markets activity hitting Saudi Arabia, the firm is currently representing three major groups on restructuring, part of which will result in three major IPOs planned for 2006. Associate Sami Al-Louzhi is widely tipped as one to watch.

Partner David Wells and senior lawyer John Whitbeck front the corporate practice at **Law Offices of Dr Mujahid M. Al-Sawwaf**. The firm largely advises international companies entering or already existing in Saudi Arabia, such as British Aerospace and General Motors. In 2005, the team advised cement manufacturer Lafarge and Tate & Lyle on significant joint ventures.

Law Office of Abdulaziz H. Fahad (in assoc with Akin Gump Strauss Hauer & Feld) advised Saudi travel company Al-Thayyar on corporate restructuring matters, and Axon is one of the firm's largest clients. The firm also advised on three substantial IPOs for Saudi clients, including Halawani and Al-Rabie's individual stock market debuts.

Charles-Henri Arminjon at **Gide Loyrette Nouel** has extensive M&A experience gleaned from his time at the firm's Paris office. The firm is advising a Swiss company on its acquisition of a minority participation in a Saudi mineral and chemical company, valued at just under SR100m. Clients include Bouygues, Omya Ag and the Al-Shoaibi Group.

Kadasah Law Firm (in assoc with Fulbright & Jaworski LLP) ended its association with **Bryan Cave LLP** in late 2005.

LeBoeuf, Lamb, Greene & MacRae in affiliation with Saud M.A. Shawwaf Law Office has a good reputation and advises clients from both the private and public sectors.

Name partner Mohanned Al-Rasheed and Stephen Matthews lead **Law Office of Mohanned bin Saud Al-Rasheed in association with Baker Botts L.L.P.**'s corporate and commercial practice, although Matthews now splits his time between Riyadh and Dubai. The duo undertake varied corporate work, and the firm is praised for giving 'practical advice that addresses genuine concerns.' Matthews gave lead advice on Wataniya International's acquisition of a 38% stake in a Saudi Arabian public telecommunications company.

The Law Firm of Salah Al-Hejailan has 20 lawyers, and stands as one of the biggest firms in the Kingdom. The full-service firm offers across-the-board corporate advice, and typically advises on joint ventures and foreign investment regulation.

The International Law Firm's good-quality US and Middle East-qualified lawyers advise several *Fortune 500* companies. Partner Ghassan Ibrahim Al Awaji focuses predominantly on corporate transactions.

Seven-lawyer **Dr Audhali Law Firm**'s main area of activity lies in registering joint venture companies. Long-term clients include Bechtel Corporation and Railcorp.

Ten-lawyer **Bin Mahfouz International Law Firm** has experience in M&A, recapitalisation and corporate restructuring. Clients include Bounty, Revlon and the World Trade Centers Association.

Name partner Mohammed Al-Sharif and US-qualified Ronald Pump head **The Law Firm of Mohammed Al-Sharif in association with Johnson & Pump**. United Defense, Hennessy Industries and Century Furniture are examples of the firm's clients.

Led by Dr Mohammed NJ Nader, **Nader Law & Translation Offices** has Shell and British Airways as just two of its many international clients.

DISPUTE RESOLUTION

The Alliance of Abbas F. Ghazzawi & Co. and Hammad & Al-Mehdar is known for its litigation expertise in the banking and insurance sectors. Name partner Adli Hammad is currently acting as arbitrator in Saudi's first-ever banking arbitration. Insurance companies make up a healthy proportion of the firm's clients, and both Hammad and co-partner Mohammed Al-Mehdar have been involved in multi-million US dollar insurance/ reinsurance claims.

2005 has been an excellent year for **Law Office of Abdulaziz H. Fahad (in assoc with Akin Gump Strauss Hauer & Feld)**. The firm has enjoyed a substantial upsurge in its corporate litigation workload, typically advising long-term corporate clients on shareholder disputes. Name partner Abdulaziz H Fahad oversees the dispute resolution division, while senior Saudi lawyers Abdallah Al Habardi and Abdulaziz Al Dukhayyil play significant roles in major disputes.

Name partner Dr Mujahid Al-Sawwaf of **Law Offices of Dr Mujahid M. Al-Sawwaf** is upheld as one of the best litigators in Saudi Arabia, and comes highly recommended. Al-Sawwaf has worked on major litigation, and has represented NCCI, Lucent, General Motors and Lloyd's of London.

The Law Firm of Salah Al-Hejailan has represented clients in contract disputes and claims. The firm's lawyers have sound experience

DISPUTE RESOLUTION

ABBAS F. GHAZZAWI & CO. AND HAMMAD & AL-MEHDAR, THE ALLIANCE OF ✪
ABDULAZIZ H. FAHAD (IN ASSOC WITH AKIN GUMP STRAUSS HAUER & FELD), LAW OFFICE OF
MUJAHID M. AL-SAWWAF (DR), LAW OFFICES OF
SALAH AL-HEJAILAN, THE LAW FIRM OF

Al-Jadaan Law Firm in co-operation with Clifford Chance LLP
Gide Loyrette Nouel ✪
Hassan Mahassni in association with Trowers & Hamlins, The Law Office of
Kadasah Law Firm (in assoc with Fulbright & Jaworski LLP)
LeBoeuf, Lamb, Greene & MacRae in affiliation with Saud M.A. Shawwaf Law Office ✪
Mohanned bin Saud Al-Rasheed in association with Baker Botts L.L.P., Law Office ✪
The International Law Firm

Ahmed Zaki Yamani Lawyers and Legal Consultants, Law Firm of
Audhali Law Firm (Dr)
Bin Mahfouz International Law Firm
Ibrahim Modaimeegh (Dr), The Law Firm of
Legal Advisers in association with Baker & McKenzie ✪
Mohammed A Al Sheikh (in assoc with White & Case LLP), Law Office of
Nader Law & Translation Offices

Firms are listed A-Z in tiers which are ranked in order of priority
✪ Indicates firm displays contact details at the end of this chapter.

of mediation and arbitration. Name partner Salah Al-Hejailan has handled several high-profile criminal cases, and has a good reputation for his defence work.

Al-Jadaan Law Firm in co-operation with Clifford Chance LLP places its emphasis on commercial and corporate litigation. The firm is praised for its 'sincere approach, which gives you the impression that the lawyers have a genuine concern for the client's interest.' Name partner Yousef Al-Jadaan is a respected litigator, with a successful track record representing international corporate clients in shari'ah courts. Senior associates Abdullah Al-Hashim and Abdulaziz Al-Abduljabbar are also key litigation lawyers.

Shafiq Othman at **Gide Loyrette Nouel** has been representing Saudi Fransi in a dispute with investors. The firm handles a wide range of contentious work, including contracting and subcontractor disputes.

The Law Office of Hassan Mahassni in association with Towers & Hamlins has a strong reputation for litigation work; 'Hassan Mahassni is simply in a different class,' comments one client on Mahassni's litigation skills. The firm has represented major clients including BMW, Indo Suez Bank, Hochtief, the Gulf Bank and Cadbury. The firm acted as Saudi Arabian and US counsel to Saudi Cable Company in its cross-jurisdictional dispute with Lucent Technologies, winning a US$100m preliminary arbitration award on behalf of its client.

Partner Nasser Kadasah of **Kadasah Law Firm (in assoc with Fulbright & Jaworski LLP)** has experience in commercial disputes, including shareholder, payment and construction-related cases.

Many of **LeBoeuf, Lamb, Greene & MacRae in affiliation with Saud M.A. Shawwaf Law Office**'s lawyers are licensed to appear before shari'ah courts.

Principal litigator Mohanned Al-Rasheed at **Law Office of Mohanned bin Saud Al-Rasheed in association with Baker Botts L.L.P.** represents one of the biggest Saudi Arabian newspapers on commercial disputes, as well as on more sensitive content issues.

Partner Osama Mohammed Al Sulaim of **The International Law Firm** has wide-ranging litigation experience, acting both in the sha'riah courts and in specialist governmental tribunals. The firm has advised Saudi government agencies on litigation matters in the US and Europe.

Law Firm of Ahmed Zaki Yamani Lawyers and Legal Consultants has advised Saudi Airlines on various matters, and advises many local companies in relation to corporate activity.

Dr Audhali Law Firm has represented a good number of Saudi and international clients in shari'ah courts, including BAE, Saudi American Bank, Zamil Group and national electricity company, SCESCO.

Bin Mahfouz International Law Firm has experience in international commercial arbitration, representing private parties and state trading entities.

The Law Firm of Dr Ibrahim Modaimeegh co-operates with **Legal Advisers in association with Baker & McKenzie** on disputes work. Dr Modaimeegh represents local companies in disputes against the government and governmental agencies.

Since lead litigator Hassan Mahassni left the **White & Case** association, **Law Office of Mohammed A Al Sheikh (in assoc with White & Case LLP)** has downscaled its litigation workload. Nevertheless, the firm retains junior litigation capacity, in the form of Hisham Al-Homoub, while Al Sheikh is at present acting as an arbitrator in a substantial matter.

With many years worth of experience in international arbitration, Dr Mohammed NJ Nader at **Nader Law & Translation Offices** has undertaken substantial amounts of litigation work for Saudi Arabian and international clients, including British Airways.

EMPLOYMENT

Most Saudi Arabian firms have perfectly competent employment expertise, but will not necessarily have a dedicated employment practice, owing to the size and scale of the legal market.

Preserving its exemplary top-tier status for another year, **Law Offices of Dr Mujahid M. Al-Sawwaf** is singled out for its specific employment expertise. Richard Tyner has experience advising on all aspects of employment law, including contractual work for corporate clients like BMI and Sumitomo Chemical. Tyner is also known as an expert on 'Saudi-isation' legal issues. Name partner Dr Mujahid Al-Sawwaf steps in on major employment litigation work.

Al-Jadaan Law Firm in co-operation with Clifford Chance LLP is able to advise its financial and corporate clients on contractual employment matters. Similarly, **Gide Loyrette Nouel** regularly advises its international corporate clients on employment matters, relating to structuring work forces in Saudi Arabia.

The Law Office of Hassan Mahassni in association with Towers & Hamlins offers employment-related advice to existing corporate clients.

Kadasah Law Firm (in assoc with Fulbright & Jaworski LLP) handles a significant volume of employment-related litigation cases, on behalf of employers.

Legal Advisers in association with Baker & McKenzie handles less contentious employment work, but does offer corporate support services on labour law to existing clients. Similar corporate support services are offered by **Law Office of Mohammed A Al Sheikh (in assoc with White & Case LLP)**.

The Law Firm of Salah Al-Hejailan advises clients from the Middle East, the US, the UK and Japan on IP protection and **The International Law Firm** advises on employment agreements.

EMPLOYMENT

MUJAHID M. AL-SAWWAF (DR), LAW OFFICES OF

Al-Jadaan Law Firm in co-operation with Clifford Chance LLP
Gide Loyrette Nouel ✪
Hassan Mahassni in association with Trowers & Hamlins, The Law Office of
Kadasah Law Firm (in assoc with Fulbright & Jaworski LLP)
Legal Advisers in association with Baker & McKenzie ✪
Mohammed A Al Sheikh (in assoc with White & Case LLP), Law Office of
Salah Al-Hejailan, The Law Firm of
The International Law Firm

Firms are listed A-Z in tiers which are ranked in order of priority
✪ Indicates firm displays contact details at the end of this chapter.

INTELLECTUAL PROPERTY

Kadasah Law Firm (in assoc with Fulbright & Jaworski LLP) wins strong recommendations from other law firms, many of which refer specialised trade mark and copyright work on to this firm, owing to its large 30-fee-earner team. The firm handles all IP work, including trade mark and patent registration and actions against counterfeit goods. Nasser Kadasah and Mohammed Jomoa balance an even split between contentious and non-contentious work.

LeBoeuf, Lamb, Greene & MacRae in affiliation with Saud M.A. Shawwaf Law Office has an excellent and well-established trade mark registration practice led by Khalid Al-Thebity.

The International Law Firm offers specialist expertise in IP protection and enforcement, representing major international suppliers of software. Senior lawyer Salah Abdulrahman Al Khudair is recommended.

Law Office of Abdulaziz H. Fahad (in assoc with Akin Gump Strauss Hauer & Feld) has a consistent intake of IP litigation, focusing on trade mark disputes and copyright infringement.

Al-Mohaimeed Law Firm advises on trade mark registration, renewals and IP litigation. Clients include Yves Saint Laurent and Astra Zenica.

Gide Loyrette Nouel continues to advise luxury brand names such as Cartier, Givenchy and Louis Vuitton on IP protection, counterfeit goods and distribution matters.

INTELLECTUAL PROPERTY

KADASAH LAW FIRM (IN ASSOC WITH FULBRIGHT & JAWORSKI LLP)
LEBOEUF, LAMB, GREENE & MACRAE IN AFFILIATION WITH SAUD M.A. SHAWWAF LAW OFFICE ✪
THE INTERNATIONAL LAW FIRM

Abbas F. Ghazzawi & Co. and Hammad & Al-Mehdar, The Alliance of ✪
Abdulaziz H. Fahad (in assoc with Akin Gump Strauss Hauer & Feld), Law Office of
Al-Mohaimeed Law Firm
Gide Loyrette Nouel ✪
Hassan Mahassni in association with Towers & Hamlins, The Law Office of
Legal Advisers in association with Baker & McKenzie ✪
Mohanned bin Saud Al-Rasheed in association with Baker Botts L.L.P., Law Office ✪
Salah Al-Hejailan, The Law Firm of

Firms are listed A-Z in tiers which are ranked in order of priority
✪ Indicates firm displays contact details at the end of this chapter.

The Law Office of Hassan Mahassni in association with Towers & Hamlins is involved with trade mark registration, IP protection and trade mark infringement, often on behalf of international clients. The firm advised a major Saudi Arabian agro-industrial group in connection with its trade mark registration of oil brands and slogans in the US and advised a US entertainment group on its IP protection in Saudi Arabia.

The Alliance of Abbas F. Ghazzawi & Co. and Hammad & Al-Mehdar, **Legal Advisers in association with Baker & McKenzie**, **Law Office of Mohanned bin Saud Al-Rasheed in association with Baker Botts L.L.P.** and **The Law Firm of Salah Al-Hejailan** offer general IP services to clients.

PRIVATISATION

Spurred on by the prospect of WTO accession, the Saudi Arabian government has implemented privatisation in key sector areas.

The Kingdom's Saline Water Conversion Corporation is in the preliminary stages of discussing privatisation, to start around 2008. For now, there has been an increase in independent water and power projects (IWPP), such as the Shoaiba and the Jubail projects. In infrastructure, the new East-West railway land-bridge project to link Jeddah and Dammam has been launched as a BOT private sector operation. Another railway project, the North-South railroad project, has been launched as an independent infrastructure programme. Telecoms remains a strong sector for privatisation. In 2004, the second Saudi Arabian GSM licence was awarded to the private sector telecoms operator Ettihad Etisalat, the parent company of Mobily, and a third GSM licence is likely to be launched in 2006. In transport, Saudi Arabian Airlines is currently focused on privatising its non-core units.

PRIVATISATION

AL-JADAAN LAW FIRM IN CO-OPERATION WITH CLIFFORD CHANCE LLP

Abbas F. Ghazzawi & Co. and Hammad & Al-Mehdar, The Alliance of ✪
Legal Advisers in association with Baker & McKenzie ✪

Abdulaziz H. Fahad (in assoc with Akin Gump Strauss Hauer & Feld), Law Office of
Hassan Mahassni in association with Towers & Hamlins, The Law Office of
Mujahid M. Al-Sawwaf (Dr), Law Offices of

Firms are listed A-Z in tiers which are ranked in order of priority
✪ Indicates firm displays contact details at the end of this chapter.

Unarguably the finest privatisation practice in Saudi Arabia, **Al-Jadaan Law Firm in co-operation with Clifford Chance LLP** retains its top-tier status. Mohammed Al-Jadaan and head of projects, US-qualified Oliver Agha, have been advising the Saudi government on the privatisation of the telecommunications industry and also in connection with the privatisation of certain assets belonging to the Ministry of Water and Electricity. The firm continues to advise on the privatisation of Saudi Arabian Airlines.

Together with **Milbank, Tweed, Hadley & McCloy LLP**, **The Alliance of Abbas F. Ghazzawi & Co. and Hammad & Al-Mehdar** is advising the lenders to the ACWA Power consortium in connection to the Shoaiba IWPP.

Legal Advisers in association with Baker & McKenzie advised mining company Ma'aden on its spin-off gold operations, and acted for the government in the NCCI IPO.

Since winning tender in 2004, **Law Office of Abdulaziz H. Fahad (in assoc with Akin Gump Strauss Hauer & Feld)** continues to advise the Saudi Railways Organization on local law aspects of privatisation of its existing railway, working in co-operation with **Linklaters**.

The Law Office of Hassan Mahassni in association with Towers & Hamlins is advising the project company in the Shoaiba IWPP. Before formalising its association with Hassan Mahassni's practice, **Towers & Hamlins** advised telecoms operator Etisalat (Mobily) as international counsel on its US$3.2bn Islamic financing deal.

Law Offices of Dr Mujahid M. Al-Sawwaf advised British Petroleum on its first joint venture IPO in Saudi Arabia.

PROJECTS AND ENERGY

Projects work constitutes a major part of **Al-Jadaan Law Firm in co-operation with Clifford Chance LLP**'s focus. The firm is easily one of the best in this field, and has worked on some pioneering developments, such as the high-profile establishment of Saudi Chevron Phillips and Jubail Chemical Petrochemical plants. Other deals include advising Saudi International Petrochemical Company as sponsor, and Gulf Advanced Chemical Industries Company, as borrower, in relation to the development and financing of a butanediol plant.

John Xefos and Bahrain-based Ian Siddell's joint reputations as leaders in their field ensures that **Legal Advisers in association with Baker & McKenzie** retains its reputation for projects work. The firm advised Saudi Chevron Phillips on the expansion of an existing petrochemical plant, and the construction of a new integrated facility, at a total value of US$1.1bn. Another major project has been advising a syndicate of financing banks on their provision of US$330m to finance the two-plant expansion of SAFCO's existing fertiliser plant in Jubail.

At present, **The Alliance of Abbas F. Ghazzawi & Co. and Hammad & Al-Mehdar** is advising Marafiq in connection with the construction of an IWPP valued at US$2.5bn. The firm is also advising bidders in connection with the Rabigh IWSPP.

The Law Office of Hassan Mahassni in association with Towers & Hamlins is acting as international counsel to the Saudi/Malaysian consortium in connection with the landmark Shoaiba IWPP project. **Towers & Hamlins**' Leroy Levy is specialised in project finance and infrastructure projects, and up-and-coming project finance lawyers include Zeid Hanania, who joined from the New York branch of **Morrison & Foerster LLP** and Aaron Lee. Both are based in Dubai, but spend significant time in Saudi.

A major highlight for **Law Office of Mohammed A Al Sheikh (in assoc with White & Case LLP)** has been its role advising Saudi Aramco in relation to the Rabigh project, which includes a joint venture with Japanese petrochemical company, Sumitomo Chemical. The project is valued between US$6bn-US$8bn, and includes aspects of both conventional and Islamic financing. The firm is also advising Samba Financial Group on two project finance transactions in Jeddah and Riyadh, and is representing one of the bidders on the Al-Marafiq IWPP project.

David Wells of **Law Offices of Dr Mujahid M. Al-Sawwaf** has worked on the Rabigh project, advising Sumitomo Chemical as the joint venture partner of Saudi Aramco. The firm is also working with **Mayer, Brown, Rowe & Maw LLP** on a US$4.5bn petrochemical project for British Petroleum. In the energy field, the team is advising on the Marafiq project, valued at US$2.5bn, with **Allen & Overy LLP**.

Law Office of Abdulaziz H. Fahad (in assoc with Akin Gump Strauss Hauer & Feld) has experience advising on the corporate side of

PROJECTS AND ENERGY

AL-JADAAN LAW FIRM IN CO-OPERATION WITH CLIFFORD CHANCE LLP
LEGAL ADVISERS IN ASSOCIATION WITH BAKER & McKENZIE ✪

Abbas F. Ghazzawi & Co. and Hammad & Al-Mehdar, The Alliance of ✪
Hassan Mahassni in association with Trowers & Hamlins, The Law Office of
Mohammed A Al Sheikh (in assoc with White & Case LLP), Law Office of
Mujahid M. Al-Sawwaf (Dr), Law Offices of

Abdulaziz H. Fahad (in assoc with Akin Gump Strauss Hauer & Feld), Law Office of
Gide Loyrette Nouel ✪
LeBoeuf, Lamb, Greene & MacRae in affiliation with Saud M.A. Shawwaf Law Office ✪
Mohanned bin Saud Al-Rasheed in association with Baker Botts L.L.P., Law Office ✪
Salah Al-Hejailan, The Law Firm of

Firms are listed A-Z in tiers which are ranked in order of priority
✪ Indicates firm displays contact details at the end of this chapter.

projects work. At present, the firm is offering advice to a consultant engaged on the North-South railroad project.

Gide Loyrette Nouel makes its debut in our projects table, owing to its advisory role to the International Finance Corporation division of the World Bank and the Civil Aviation Authority. The firm advised on both international and local law in relation to two private sector participation projects: the project financing of the construction of a desalination plant at the King Abdulaziz International Airport, and the project financing of the Haj Terminal privatisation.

LeBoeuf, Lamb, Greene & MacRae in affiliation with Saud M.A. Shawwaf Law Office continues to advise the government on its 'Natural Gas' initiative.

Law Office of Mohanned bin Saud Al-Rasheed in association with Baker Botts L.L.P.'s associates Patrick Campos and Nabil Issa, both experienced in project finance, moved to **Baker Botts, L.L.P.** in Dubai. Partners Mohanned Al-Rasheed and Stephen Matthews are representing two international petrochemical companies on their pursuit of cracker projects in Al-Jubail city.

SHIPPING

The Alliance of Abbas F. Ghazzawi & Co. and Hammad & Al-Mehdar's shipping practice is unrivalled in terms of its strength, depth and clients. UK-qualified Andreas Haberbeck is the firm's shipping law expert, and advises members of the International Group of P&I Clubs, including Britannia P&I, North of England P&I, Standard P&I and Steamship Mutual P&I. Haberbeck is currently advising shipowners and liability insurers in marine environmental damages claims.

Although shipping is not one of its main practice areas, **Al-Jadaan Law Firm in co-operation with Clifford Chance LLP** can comfortably advise on aspects of shipping finance and related acquisitions.

Law Offices of Dr Mujahid M. Al-Sawwaf is noted for its experience of handling shipping finance work, as is **The Law Firm of Salah Al-Hejailan**, which advises on ship finance, acquisition and chartering, and also handles marine litigation work.

SHIPPING

ABBAS F. GHAZZAWI & CO. AND HAMMAD & AL-MEHDAR, THE ALLIANCE OF ✪

Al-Jadaan Law Firm in co-operation with Clifford Chance LLP
Mujahid M. Al-Sawwaf (Dr), Law Offices of
Salah Al-Hejailan, The Law Firm of

Firms are listed A-Z in tiers which are ranked in order of priority
✪ Indicates firm displays contact details at the end of this chapter.

AL YAQOUB LAWYERS AND LEGAL ADVISERS

KINGDOM TOWER
LEVEL 21, OROUBA ST
PO BOX 57288
RIYADH 11574

Telephone: +966 1 211 0600
Fax: +966 1 211 0601
Website: www.alyaqoub.com

Languages
Arabic, English

Other offices
Jeddah (KSA), Khober (KSA)

Number of lawyers 16
at this office 8

Contact
Montasir Al Yaqoub

International groupings
Co-operation with Ernst & Young in Gulf area and Middle East and EY Law in Europe

CATEGORIES OF WORK

Corporate and commercial
Mahjoub

Incorporation of companies
Al Fateh

Restructuring and liquidation
Dr AL Sallawi

Mergers and acquisition
Mahjoub

Trade marks
Al Fateh

Joint ventures
Alyaqoub

Real estate
Alyaqoub

Commercial and international contracts
Kalifa

Litigation
Saraha

Shariaa (Islamic law)
Dr Babiker, Saraha

Arbitration
Dr Babiker, Kalifa

Contracts
Dr AL Sallawi

LEGAL ADVISERS IN ASSOCIATION WITH
BAKER AND McKENZIE

PO BOX 4288
RIYADH 11491

Telephone: +966 1 291 5561
Fax: +966 1 291 5571
Website: www.bakernet.com

Languages
Arabic, English, French

Other offices
The member firms of Baker & McKenzie International, a Swiss Verein, have 70 offices in 38 countries around the world. For a complete list, please visit www.bakernet.com.

Number of lawyers 3,300+
at this office 12

Contact
John Xefos (managing partner)

CATEGORIES OF WORK

Aviation, ship and asset finance
Ian Siddell

Bank lending and other extensions of credit
Ian Siddell, John Xefos

Capital markets
John Xefos, Karim Nassar

Corporate and partnership law
George Sayen, John Xefos

Corporate financing (public and private)
John Xefos, Karim Nassar

Franchising, government contracting
Nasser Alfaraj, George Sayen

Labour and employment law
Nasser Alfaraj

Mergers and acquisitions
George Sayen, John Xefos

Project finance
Ian Siddell, John Xefos

Public contracts and utilities
George Sayen, Faisal Khan

Trade (Saudi Arabia, GCC)
Nasser Alfaraj, George Sayen

THE ALLIANCE OF ABBAS F. GHAZZAWI & CO. AND HAMMAD & AL-MEHDAR

POST OFFICE BOX 6387
JEDDAH 21442

Telephone: +966 2 650 4475
Fax: +966 2 657 2007
Website: www.saudilaw.de

Languages
Arabic, English, German

Number of lawyers 19

Contacts
Ali Abedi, Mohammed Al-Mehdar, Majid Ghazzawi, Andreas Haberbeck, Adli Hammad, Asad Abedi

CATEGORIES OF WORK

Administrative law	Environmental
Admiralty and maritime	Government contracts
Banking and finance	Insurance
Bankruptcy	Intellectual property
Commercial	International trade
Construction	Litigation
Corporate	Project finance

THE LAW FIRM OF MAJED M GAROUB

25 OTHMAN IBN AFFAN STREET
PO BOX 18623
JEDDAH 21425

Telephone: +966 2 651 8222
Fax: +966 2 651 8333
E-mail: majed@lawgaroub.com
Website: www.lawgaroub.com

Languages
Arabic, English

Other offices
Riyadh

Number of lawyers 15
at this office 12

Contact
Majed M Garoub (chairman)

CATEGORIES OF WORK

Trade marks	Oil and gas law
Companies law	Contracts
Corporate law	Intellectual property and WTO issues
Banking and finance	Family law
Services law	Insurance law
Alternative dispute resolution	Taxation
Joint ventures	Real estate
Mining	

GIDE LOYRETTE NOUEL

PO BOX 4615
RIYADH 11412

Telephone: +966 1 476 6039
Fax: +966 1 476 1896
E-mail: gln.riyadh@gide.com
Website: www.gide.com

Other offices
Algiers, Beijing, Belgrade, Brussels, Bucharest, Budapest, Casablanca, Hanoi, Istanbul, London, Moscow, New York, Paris, Prague, Shanghai, Tunis, Warsaw

Number of lawyers 586
at this office 2

Contacts
Charles-Henri Arminjon, Guillaume de Lalande

CATEGORIES OF WORK

Foreign investment	**Commercial litigation (agency, distribution and franchise matters)**
Company law	**Arbitration**
Joint ventures	**Intellectual property**
Public and administrative law	**Banking and finance**
Government liaison	**Labour**
Public procurement	**Litigation**
Taxation	

LEBOEUF, LAMB, GREENE & MACRAE LLP

IN AFFILIATION WITH SAUD M.A. SHAWWAF LAW OFFICE

KING FAISAL FOUNDATION BLDG
NORTH TOWER, 13TH FLOOR
KING FAHAD ROAD
PO BOX 2700
RIYADH 11461

Telephone: +966 1 464 8534
Fax: +966 1 464 8480
E-mail: kalthebi@llgm.com
Website: www.llgm.com

Languages
Arabic, English, French

Other offices
Albany, Almaty, Beijing, Boston, Brussels, Chicago, Hartford, Houston, Jacksonville, Johannesburg, London, Los Angeles, Moscow, New York, Paris, Pittsburg, San Francisco, Washington DC

Number of lawyers 650+
at this office 6

Contact
Khalid A Al-Thebity

CATEGORIES OF WORK

International direct investment	**Telecommunications and media**
Energy (oil and gas, electric power)	**Real estate**
Project finance	**Intellectual property**
Dispute resolution	**Banking**

LAW OFFICE OF MOHANNED BIN SAUD AL-RASHEED IN ASSOCIATION WITH BAKER BOTTS L.L.P.

PO BOX 62982
RIYADH 11595

Telephone: +966 1 464 3139
Fax: +966 1 464 9264
E-mail:
stephen.matthews@bakerbotts.com
Website: www.bakerbotts.com

Languages
Arabic, English, Farsi

Other offices
Austin, Dallas, Dubai, Hong Kong, Houston, London, Moscow, New York, Washington DC

Number of lawyers 700
at this office 2

Contact
Stephen Matthews

Member
Lex Mundi

CATEGORIES OF WORK

Arbitration and dispute resolution

Banking

Corporate – general

Corporate – M&A

E-commerce

Energy (power) projects

Oil and gas projects

Project finance

Pipeline projects

Privatisation

Regulatory

Telecommunications projects

SERBIA AND MONTENEGRO

Population	**10.8 million**
Number of lawyers	**(Serbia) 6,000 (Montenegro) 460**
Professional title	**Advokat**
Currency	**(Serbia) New Yugoslav Dinar (Montenegro) Euro**
Index	
Corporate and commercial	**1174**
Country index	**5**

The nation of Yugoslavia terminally dissolved in 1995, as a bloody three-way conflict overwhelmed the land formerly known as the Kingdom of Serbs, Croats, and Slovenes. Though megalomaniac Slobodan Milosevic remained in power after the ethnic cleansing of the Kosovo conflict, which ended following Nato intervention, he was finally arrested and overthrown in October 2000, and shakily the people are rebuilding their country. In 2003 the name Yugoslavia was finally retired, and the State Union of the Republics of Serbia and Montenegro (SiM) was born.

The new state is run as two semi-independent states. Kosovo, though a SiM province, is still under UN authority.

The President of Serbia and Montenegro is elected by the SCG Assembly. However the President of the Assembly and the President of the State Union may not come from the same member state and every four years the member states take over the office of President alternately. The current President of Serbia and Montenegro, Svetozar Marovic comes from Montenegro and the President of the Assembly, Zoran Šami is from Serbia. The stated aim of the nation's leaders is integration into Europe and membership of the EU.

BILLING

Senior lawyers tend to charge between €200 and €250 per hour for international clients. Associates and more junior lawyers seek a more modest €100 to €150 per hour.

MARKETING

Strictly speaking, the Serbian Bar Association prohibits advertising, but all of the leading firms have websites, and there has been an increase in promotion through sponsorship, marketing events, directory listings and contributions to magazines.

IN-HOUSE LAWYERS

Most banks and international companies employ in-house lawyers for internal legal issues, but often turn to larger external firms for corporate expertise.

ECONOMY

The economy was badly damaged by the mismanagement of the Milosevic years, which, combined with the damage caused to infrastructure and industry during the Kosovo war, and a lengthy period of economic sanctions, diminished the economy to only half the size it was in 1990. Since Milosevic's fall in 2000, the Democratic Opposition of Serbia coalition government has worked hard at re-energising the country's economy through aggressive market reform and stabilisation measures. In recent years the country has rejoined the International Monetary Fund, the World Bank, and the European Bank for Reconstruction and Development. Several large debts have been rescheduled and written off, and over €300m has been invested by the EU to aid economic restructuring.

The Republic of Montenegro has a separate and much smaller economy than Serbia, with lower unemployment at about 22%, to Serbia's approximately 30%. The two republics have separate central banks, customs tariffs, and state budgets. They also have different currencies, with Serbia using the Serbian Dinar and Montenegro using the Euro.

The economy's development has been slowed by the complexity of Serbia and Montenegro's political relationships, and ponderous progress in privatisation. Severe unemployment and a high degree of corruption are major problems faced by the current administration. However 2005 has shown some promising signs, with a high degree of foreign interest and investment, an increase in privatisation, and clear indications of greater commercial activity.

LEGAL MARKET

The legal market has not seen dramatic change in the last year. Banking work has been the driving force, with the usual suspects leading the way. **CMS Reich-Rohrwig Hasche Sigle d.o.o**, **Harrisons**, **Jankovic, Popovic & Mitic**, **Joksovic, Stojanovic & Partners**, **Karanovic & Nikolic** and **Prica & Spasic** are the country's leading firms, and they report plenty of privatisation work, and a decent supply of M&A.

Foreign firms seem to be making inroads into the market, with the likes of **Wolf Theiss**, **Gide Loyrette Nouel** and **Schönherr** benefiting from the increase in foreign investment, and continuing their steady expansion.

The most successful law firms in SiM are found in Serbia, with all but one based in Belgrade. **Lalin Radovan Law Office** is found in Serbia's second

The largest firms

1	Karanovic & Nikolic	30
2	Jankovic, Popovic & Mitic	18
3	Harrisons	15
4	Zivkovic & Samardzic Law Office	14
5	IKRP-Prelevic	12
6	Wolf Theiss	11
7	CMS Reich-Rohrwig Hasche Sigle d.o.o	10
8	Joksovic, Stojanovic & Partners	9
	Prica & Spasic	9
	Sutti, Studio Legale	9
11	Ninkovic Law Office	7
	Schönherr	7
	Trifunovic & Cvetkovic	7
14	Mikijelj Jankovic & Bogdanovic	6
	Milosevic, Law Office	6
	Popovic, Popovic, Samardzija & Popovic	6
	Tomic, Stevic Dulic	6
18	Branislav Manic Law Office & Patent Bureau	5
	Gide Loyrette Nouel	5
	Kojovic, Law Office	5
	Lalin Radovan Law Office	5
22	KMN Katarina Nedeljkovic law and patent & trademark office	4
	Milos B Markovic, Slobodan B Markovic	4
24	Djordje Djurisic, Law Office of	2

These figures represent the total number of lawyers in this country only, and have been supplied by the firms themselves. The figures should be accurate as at 1 January 2006.

biggest city, Novi Sad, 40 miles north of Belgrade. Though Serbia and Montenegro have separate legal systems, Serbian lawyers can practise in Montenegro.

LEGISLATIVE DEVELOPMENTS

The Serbian Government has reduced its corporate tax rate to 10%, sending out a clear message that Serbia is open for business. Also litigation reform has taken place in the last year. The Law on Civil Procedure provides a procedural framework that ensures disputes will be heard within a reasonable period of time, and introduces sanctions for failures to comply with procedural requirements. The Law on Enforcement Procedure provides Serbia with a more efficient system for the enforcement of legal rights and remedies. Also registration of pledges and companies has been made easier and the labour laws have been updated. Though it is too early to judge the effects of these new laws, they at least demonstrate that reformers are focused on developing an effective and practical system of litigation. Further evidence of this is the Serbian Government's commitment to adopting a new law on arbitration.

CORPORATE AND COMMERCIAL

Dr Radivoje Petrikic heads the Belgrade office of **CMS Reich-Rohrwig Hasche Sigle d.o.o**. He is ably supported by partners Natasa Zavisin and Stojan Semiz, who is noted for his 'excellent commitment'. In 2005 the firm advised ERSTE Bank Austria on the €90m acquisition of Novosadska Banka, one of the leading banks in Serbia. Other highlights include representing Dutch real estate developer GTC on construction of the largest business centre in Belgrade, and advising Hypo-Alpe-Adria-Bank on financing the leading phone operator in Serbia. At the end of 2005, the firm merged with *Hayhurst Robinson*.

Harrisons' founder Mark Harrison is one of the leading lawyers in the Baltic. He is ably supported by some very experienced partners, including Blanche Sas, an energy expert, Alexsandar Preradovic, a banking and capital markets specialist, and Goran Martinovic, who is Serbia's most active lawyer in the fields of privatisation and foreign investment. Highlights in 2005 include advising on the new Belgrade Railway Station, the largest real estate development in Serbia, and advising a Canadian billionaire on the largest nautical tourism project in Montenegro. Clients include US Steel, British American Tobacco and Pernod Ricard.

Jankovic, Popovic & Mitic has been particularly active in M&A and privatisation. Partner Nenad Popovic led on the acquisition of Delta Banka by Italy's Banca Intesa, and he and fellow partner Nikola Jankovic oversaw the acquisition of Meridian Bank Novi Sad by Credit Agricole of France. Milos Mitic led the privatisation

CORPORATE AND COMMERCIAL

CMS Reich-Rohrwig Hasche Sigle d.o.o ✪
Harrisons
Jankovic, Popovic & Mitic
Joksovic, Stojanovic & Partners UP
Karanovic & Nikolic
Prica & Spasic

Bojović & Dašić
Branislav Manic Law Office & Patent Bureau
Clyde d.o.o. Belgrade
Gide Loyrette Nouel ✪
Mikijelj Jankovic & Bogdanovic
Milos B Markovic, Slobodan B Markovic
Milosevic, Law Office
Ninkovic Law Office
Popovic, Popovic, Samardzija & Popovic
Sutti, Studio Legale ✪
Tomic, Stevic Dulic ✪
Trifunovic & Cvetkovic ✪
Wolf Theiss ✪

Bibic, Law Office
IKRP Rokas & Partners DOO
Lalin Radovan Law Office
Pavlovic, Cabinet
Schönherr ✪
Slobodan A Popovic (Dr) & Branimir A. Popovic, Law Office
Zivkovic & Samardzic Law Office

Firms are listed A-Z in tiers which are ranked in order of priority
✪ Indicates firm displays contact details at the end of this chapter.

of Telecom of Montenegro, on behalf of the government of Montenegro. The firm has an impressive client list of multinationals, international financial organisations and several foreign embassies.

Joksovic, Stojanovic & Partners is the counsel of choice for the German and Austrian embassies in Belgrade. The firm is also counsel to the Privatisation Agency of the Republic of Serbia, with privatisation a real strength of the firm. Senior partners Milan Joksovic and Petar Stojanovic are very experienced and well known lawyers. Clients commend Stojanovic for his 'broad and in-depth knowledge of Serbian law'. The firm's clientele consists mainly of international clients and domestic clients with interests abroad. Due to this the firm has developed a network of relationships with law firms throughout Europe and the US. Work on the Belgrade airport greenfield project is ongoing, and the firm advised on the privatisation of the Aluminium Plant in Podgorica, Montenegro, a transaction worth €150m. Clients praise the firm's service for being 'quick and of outstanding quality'.

Karanovic & Nikolic acted on the Airport City real estate development, and on the ING Bank and Piraeus bank privatisations. The firm also saw significant development in real estate, taxation, and intellectual property in 2005. The firm formally opened an office in Montenegro, and has seen an upturn in property deals in Montenegro as a result. Patricia Gannon comes recommended.

Prica & Spasic is one of the oldest and most prestigious firms in Serbia, formed by the Prica family in 1900 and renowned today for the quality of its work. Led by the politically active Dr Rodoje Prica, the firm offers a wealth of legal experience to mostly foreign clients, generally large multinationals and international financial organisations. The firm is particularly active in banking, M&A, and privatisation, acting for clients such as Xerox and Unilever.

Bojović & Dašić has expanded to eight fee-earners, with plans to recruit one more. The firm acted on EFG Bank's €44m acquisition of the National Savings Bank, and on the restructuring of JAT Airways, the state-owned national carrier. It has also been busy in telecommunications, leading on an aborted takeover bid by a Russian mobile company for a Serbian operator. Marija Bojović and Vladimir Dašić are well respected.

Branislav Manic Law Office & Patent Bureau is a full-service firm specialising in IP. Founded by partner Branislav Manic, who is experienced in corporate law, the firm acts for a number of large international recording companies.

Clyde d.o.o. Belgrade advised a large international bank on the joint venture between a German and a Serbian company. The firm also advised an international metals-trading company and a French agricultural company on foreign investment. The firm has been particularly active in privatisation and in oil and gas represented several major international companies in the Republic of Srpska. Partners Radoje Stefanovic and Boris Baklaja are well-known corporate lawyers, experienced in foreign investments, banking and privatisation.

Gide Loyrette Nouel's Belgrade office is headed by François d'Ornano. The team was joined by Borislav Vicentic from **Prica & Spasic**, and more recently by Ana Marić from **Bojović & Dašić**. Recent work includes advising Société Générale Yoguslav Bank on its takeover of Podgoricka Bank in Montenegro, and acting for Intermarché in the financing of its land acquisition and construction of hypermarkets in Serbia and Bosnia.

Mikijelj Jankovic & Bogdanovic's main strength is in IP and the firm has a very impressive client list mainly generated through this practice area. Clients include Pfizer, Coca-Cola, Guinness, Honda and Shell. The firm also acts for several foreign embassies in Belgrade, has an expanding domain names practice, and has been involved in some ground-breaking Customs & Excise work. Founding partner Dr Jankovic is not only an IP specialist, but also an expert in human rights and criminal law.

Milos B Markovic, Slobodan B Markovic specialises in international legal cases in the civil and commercial fields.

Law Office Milosevic was set up by Radomir Milosevic, an experienced shipping lawyer, who is universally recognised as a leading expert on international company law. The firm provides a full service, particularly to the food, tobacco and telecommunications industries, and often represents professional footballers before FIFA.

Ninkovic Law Office has expanded to five partners, and a total of ten fee-earners, after merging with *Parivodic & Associates* at the beginning of 2005. The two new partners, acquired through the merger, are Milan Samardzic and Milan Parivodic, who is on leave while serving as the Minister for Foreign Economic Relations in the Serbian Government. Recent work includes advising GlaxoSmithKline and Abbott Laboratories on the setting up of Belgrade offices. The firm has also provided Metro Cash & Carry with real estate advice and acted on the acquisition of a Serbian TV channel by a foreign company.

Popovic, Popovic, Samardzija & Popovic is a six-lawyer firm specialising in IP. The firm's main clients include Unilever, Delta and Aventis, for whom the firm has been dealing with trade mark portfolios, including filing and acquisitions, and protecting Pfizer's patents.

Studio Legale Sutti has a strong focus on commercial agreements, particularly those related to leasing, franchising and international trade. The firm acts for several large Italian banks, and is active in privatisations. The office is headed by Dr Dubravka Kosic, who specialises in banking and international trade.

Tomic, Stevic Dulic is headed by partners Ljubica Tomic, Gordana Stevic Dulic and Prof Zoran Tomic. The firm has an international outlook, with real strength in the banking and automotive sectors, and acts for clients such as Mercedes Benz, HVB Bank Yugoslavia, and DaimlerChrysler.

Trifunovic & Cvetkovic is a young firm providing a full service and with the capacity for international commercial arbitration, a rare quality in Serbia. Founding partner Vojin Trifunovic provides a wealth of experience in the structure and management of public and private organisations.

Wolf Theiss now has eight partners and three associates in Belgrade. The Austria-based firm acted on the €50m Bank Austria Creditanstalt acquisition of Eksimbanka, with partners Horst Ehardt and Miroslav Stojanovic leading on the deal. The firm has been active in the employment field, advising ABB, a leader in power and automation technologies, on new contract and labour law issues, and assisting software company SSL in establishing a branch office.

Law Office Bibic is a full service firm, specialising in IP.

Greek firm **IKRP Rokas & Partners DOO** has a broad network across Southern and Eastern Europe. The firm often advises on projects with the aim of restructuring local economies and regenerating economic growth. The five-lawyer office benefits from the firm's list of Greek clients.

Six-lawyer **Lalin Radovan Law Office** offers a broad practice under head of the firm, Lalin Radovan. The firm is well known in the media sector and has been advising Pink TV on its multi-million euro development project for the Serbian film industry, which has involved amendments to existing legislation that are now going through parliament. The firm is also advising on a €3m film, *Shadow – Mileva Maric Einstein*, which is a Serbian/Hungarian co-production and also advised on the Exit 2005 Music festival. The firm is also providing advice on the ongoing privatisation of one of the biggest financial institutions in Serbia.

Cabinet Pavlovic specialises in IP, acting for clients such as Hugo Boss. The firm is managed by Milivoje Pavlovic and Gordana Pavlovic.

Schönherr, led by Markus Piuk advised the OMV group on its €200m investment in Serbia, and acts for this client in all matters in Serbia, Romania and Bulgaria. The firm also advised Hypo-Alpe-Adria Bank on its acquisition of a software company, as well as on a number of international finance transactions.

Law Office Dr Slobodan A. Popovic & Branimir A. Popovic is a family IP outfit consisting of Dr Slobodan Popovic, his son, daughter and brother. Dr Popovic has 50 years of experience in IP, with a particular passion for trade marks and unfair competition. The firm works mainly for the pharmaceutical and agrochemical industries, with Kraft Foods and Colgate-Palmolive as clients, but also advises breweries and machine manufacturers.

Zivkovic & Samardzic Law Office is the Nestlé Goup's new legal adviser in Serbia. The firm also advised the Greek investment bank, Proton on its investment into the First Global Brokers a.d. and on Cypriot TV company Sigma's investment in Serbian broadcaster IBC.

CMS REICH-ROHRWIG HASCHE SIGLE D.O.O.

KNEZ MIHAILOVA 33
11000 BELGRADE

Telephone: +381 11 30 30 136
Fax: +381 11 30 30 137
E-mail: belgrade@cms-rrhs.com
Website: www.cms-rrhs.com

Languages
Croatian, English, French, German, Serbian, Russian

Other offices
Berlin, Bratislava, Brussels, Chemnitz, Dresden, Düsseldorf, Frankfurt am Main, Hamburg, Köln, Leipzig, Munich, Prague, Sofia, Stuttgart, Vienna, Zagreb

Number of lawyers 520
at this office 14

Contact
Radivoje Petrikic

Member
CMS Alliance of major European law firms; World Law Group

CATEGORIES OF WORK

Antitrust and competition

Arbitration and litigation

Banking, capital markets, securities and finance

Construction and real estate

Corporate, M&A, restructuring

Employment, industrial relations, employee benefits and pensions

Government business, regulatory/public procurement

Intellectual property and trade marks

Privatisation

Tax

Telecommunications

GIDE LOYRETTE NOUEL

STUDENTSKI TRG 19
11000 BELGRADE

Telephone: +381 11 30 36 290/291
Fax: +381 11 26 26 236
E-mail: gln.belgrade@gide.com
Website: www.gide.com

Other offices
Algiers, Beijing, Brussels, Bucharest, Budapest, Casablanca, Hanoi, Istanbul, London, Moscow, New York, Paris, Prague, Riyadh, Shanghai, Tunis, Warsaw

Number of lawyers 586
at this office 5

Contact
François d'Ornano (ornano@gide.com)

CATEGORIES OF WORK

Foreign investments

M&A, privatisations

Corporate law

Banking and finance

Tax

Real estate

Employment law

SCHÖNHERR

MIROČKA 1
11000 BELGRADE

Telephone: +381 11 33 42 104
Fax: + 381 11 33 42 105
E-mail: office@schoenherr.co.yu
Website: www.schoenherr.at

Languages
Serbian, German, English, French

Other offices
Brussels, Bucharest, Kyiv, Ljubljana, Sofia, Vienna, Zagreb (co-operation office)

Number of lawyers 130
at this office 8

Contacts
Christoph Lindinger (ch.lindinger@schoenherr.at), Markus Piuk (m.piuk@schoenherr.at)

CATEGORIES OF WORK

International and Serbian practice	Privatisations
International contracts and foreign investments	Public private partnership
Banking securities and finance	Real estate and commercial property
Project finance	EU law
M&A	Competition

STUDIO LEGALE SUTTI

6 DJURE SALAJA STREET
1100 BELGRADE

Telephone: +381 11 33 45 195
Fax: +381 11 33 45 182
E-mail: maildesk@sutti.com
Website: www.sutti.com

Languages
Bulgarian, Croatian, Dutch, English, French, German, Italian, Japanese, Portuguese, Romanian, Russian, Serbian, Spanish

Other offices
Bucharest, Genoa, London, Milan, Rome, Sofia, Tokyo, Zagreb

Contact
Dubravka Kosic

CATEGORIES OF WORK

Company, commercial law	White-collar crime
Banking and finance	EC, competition and antitrust law
Mergers and acquisitions	IT and TLC law
Distribution, agency and franchising	Litigation and arbitration
Debt collection and insolvency	Employment, labour law
Commercial property law	Administrative law
Intellectual property	Environmental law
Patent and trade mark agency service	

TOMIC STEVIC DULIC

CARICE MILICE 3
11000 BELGRADE

Telephone: +381 1 11 32 85 227
Fax: +381 1 11 32 85 153
E-mail: office@tomic-stevic.co.yu
Website: www.tomic-stevic.co.yu

Languages
English, French, German, Russian, Serbian

Number of lawyers 6

Contact
Ljubica Tomic
(ljubica.tomic@tomic-stevic.co.yu)

Member
Serbian Bar Association

CATEGORIES OF WORK

Commercial and company law	Privatisation
Business law and foreign investments	Labour law
Mergers and acquisitions	Administrative Law
Customs and trade regulations	Litigation
Tax law	Construction and real estate
Intellectual property	Distribution and franchising

TRIFUNOVIC & CVETKOVIC

KNEZ MIHAILOVA 7/IV
11000 BELGRADE

Telephone: +381 11 32 81 949
Fax: +381 11 32 81 890
E-mail: office@tclaw.co.yu
Website: www.tclaw.co.yu

Languages
English, French, German, Serbian

Number of lawyers 7

Contacts
Jasna Trifunovic, Goran Cvetkovic

Member
Serbian Bar Association

CATEGORIES OF WORK

Commercial and company law	Employment, pensions and benefits
Banking and finance	IT and communications
Business law and investments	Intellectual property
Mergers and acquisitions	Environment
Major projects and project finance	Privatisation
Corporate restructuring	Venture capital and private equity
EU law	Tax law
Public law	Dispute resolution
Customs and trade regulations	Litigation
Antitrust and trade	Construction and real estate

WOLF THEISS

ČIKA LJUBINA 12
11 000 BELGRADE

Telephone: +381 11 33 02 900
Fax: +381 11 33 02 925
E-mail: beograd@wolftheiss.com
Website: www.wolftheiss.com

Languages
Serbian, German, English

Other offices
Bratislava, Bucharest, Ljubljana, Prague, Sarajevo, Tirana, Vienna, Zagreb

Number of lawyers 161
at this office 11

Contacts
Dieter Spranz, Bojana Bregović, Miroslav Stojanović

CATEGORIES OF WORK

Arbitration	**IT and IP**
Banking, capital markets, securities, project finance, investment funds	**Real estate, construction and leasing**
Corporate and M&A	**Reorganisation and restructuring**

THE FIRM

Wolf Theiss was founded in 1957 in Vienna, and today is one of the leading law firms in the CEE/SEE region. Over the past few years the firm has experienced extraordinarily dynamic growth, both domestically and internationally.

Wolf Theiss has established a network of nine offices* in Albania, Austria, Bosnia and Herzegovina, Croatia, the Czech Republic, Romania, Serbia and Montenegro, Slovakia and Slovenia. In 2005 alone, Wolf Theiss opened two new offices, in Bucharest and Sarajevo. The firm also regularly assists its clients with projects in Bulgaria, Hungary, Macedonia, Moldova, Poland, Turkey and Ukraine, in co-operation with local attorneys.

The firm's dynamic growth is also refelcted in its increase in personnal. At present, Wolf Theiss employs over 350 individuals at nine locations – compare this to 30 employees in one office, Vienna, ten years ago and the growth is apparent.

*The firm's operations in the various locations are set up in compliance with local law and the Bar rules requirements which include the form of co-operation with independent local attorneys.

KMN LAW AND PATENT & TRADEMARK OFFICE

POB 72
7 MAKSIMA GORKOG STREET
21120 NOVI SAD

Telephone: +381 21 662 2691
Fax: +381 21 472 2805
E-mail: knedeljkovic@kmnlegal.com
Website: www.kmnlegal.com

Languages
English, French, Italian, Russian, Serbian

Number of lawyers 4

CATEGORIES OF WORK

Foreign investments
Katarina Nedeljkovic

Corporate law
Mirna Rakic

Privatisation
Katarina Nedeljkovic

M&A
Katarina Nedeljkovic

Commercial law
Katarina Nedeljkovic

Banking law
Katarina Nedeljkovic

Securities and financial law
Srdjana Petronijevic

IP
Katarina Nedeljkovic

Real estate law
Mirna Rakic

International arbitration
Katarina Nedeljkovic

Insurance law
Srdjana Petronijevic

Contracts
Mirna Rakic

Administrative law
Srdjana Petronijevic

Labour law
Srdjana Petronijevic

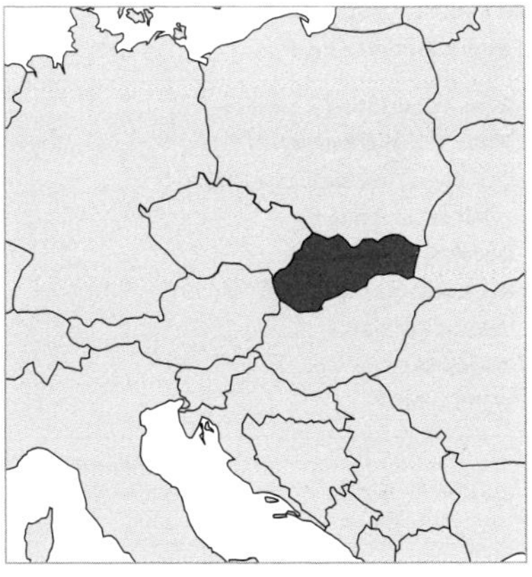

Population	5.4 million
Number of lawyers	1,400
Professional title	Advokát
Currency	Slovak Koruna(SKK)

Index

Like the Czech Republic, Slovakia has been through a dramatic transformation in the last 20 years, and its nascent economic environment remains even less developed than that of its larger neighbour. Czechoslovakia's people pulled off the peaceful Velvet Revolution in 1989, which brought to an end the Soviet and Communist rule that had engulfed the country since World War II. The first free elections were held in June 1990, and then came the so-called Velvet Divorce, when Slovakia separated from the Czech Republic to start out on its own in January 1993. The two countries had combined in 1918.

Slovakia joined both Nato and the EU in April 2004, and in the same month, President Gasparovic was elected leader for a five-year term. The government is a coalition, with the prime minister Mikulas Dzurinda hailing from the Slovak Democratic and Christian Union Party, which shares government with the Party of the Hungarian Coalition, the Christian Democratic Movement and the New Citizens Alliance. Dzurinda has been in power since 1998 and was re-elected in 2002.

Immediately after independence, Slovakia was criticised on the international stage for rejection of economic reform, and the previous prime minister Vladimir Meciar was derided as authoritarian, with a lack of respect for minority rights and the democratic process. He pursued nationalist and populist policies, but was ousted by an alliance of liberals, centrists, left-wingers and ethnic Hungarians in favour of Dzurinda.

Dzurinda has forged ahead with reforms, and economic growth has been strong. The country has mastered much of the difficult transition from a centrally planned economy to a modern market economy, albeit at a slightly slower rate than that of the Czech Republic.

The government has made good progress in macroeconomic stabilisation and structural reform, such that major privatisations are now all-but complete, the banking sector is almost entirely in foreign hands, and the government has helped facilitate a boom in foreign investment with both business-friendly policies and labour-market liberalisation.

ECONOMY

Slovakia's economic growth exceeded expectations between 2001 and 2004, despite the general European slowdown. Unemployment remains the downside, running at an unacceptable 15% for the year 2003-04.

Both heavy industry and agriculture have decreased as a percentage of GDP since the onset of transition, with industry accounting for 26.3% of GDP in 2000 compared to 49% a decade earlier. Services now account for more than 60% of economic output.

The macroeconomic environment suffers from high public finance deficits and structural impediments, owing to a lack of comprehensive public finance reform, meaning budget deficits will remain high in the short term. In 2002 the deficit was 8.2% of GDP, compared to 3.5% in Poland and 6.6% in the Czech Republic.

The country remains vulnerable to external shocks should financing prove difficult to acquire, but the new political stability is widely judged to have had a favourable impact.

Slovakia, like the Czech Republic, is well placed at the heart of the increasingly wealthy European economy. It bridges Western and Eastern Europe and is bordered by the Czech Republic to the west, Poland to the north, Ukraine to the east, Hungary to the south and Austria to the southwest. That means it is in a position to utilise the combined market potential of some 350 million people.

BILLING

Hourly rates are most commonly used, although law firms are becoming increasingly flexible in a competitive market and often offer contingency and fixed fees. Rates vary considerably between the international firms and local firms. Typically, international firms charge an hourly rate of between €300 and €450 for a partner, in contrast to small local firms where partners will typically charge between €100 and €200.

MARKETING

Marketing rules are very restrictive and allow firms only to publicise the barest of details, such as names of lawyers and addresses. Most Slovak commercial law firms, however, possess professional and informative websites.

IN-HOUSE LAWYERS

It remains the case that the vast majority of qualified lawyers choose to work in private practice. However, working in-house is becoming

The largest firms

1	alianciaadvokátov	26
2	Blaha, Erben & Partneri	24
	Valko & Partners	24
4	Detvai Ludik Maly Udvaros, Law Firm	22
5	Dedák & Partners	20
6	Linklaters	19
7	Ruzicka (Dr) Law Office	18
8	Csekes, Világi, Drgonec & Partners spol. s.r.o.	17
	Havlát & Partners Law Office	17
10	Advokátskakancelária	15
11	Allen & Overy Bratislava, s.r.o.	14
12	Weinhold Legal, v.o.s.	13
13	Cechová & Partners	12
14	Nörr Stiefenhofer Lutz	11
	ULC Carnogursky	11
	White & Case	11
17	Cernejová & Hrbek	10
	Peterka & Partners	10
	Squire Sanders s.r.o.	10
20	Freshfields Bruckhaus Deringer	9
	G Lehnert, k.s.	9
	Wolf Theiss	9
23	DLA Weiss-Tessbach/Law Office Milan Cervenka	7
	Marek & Partners	7
	Rödl & Partner S.R.O.	7
	Salans	7

These figures represent the total number of lawyers in this country only, and have been supplied by the firms themselves. The figures should be accurate as at 1 January 2006.

increasingly common amongst the banks, financial institutions and the largest companies, which are in turn becoming more savvy buyers of legal services.

LEGAL MARKET

As a rule, the Slovakian economy is running some two to five years behind its larger neighbour the Czech Republic in terms of development, and the legal market is no exception. Though the country did not benefit to the same extent from an influx of international law firms in the 1990s, it did welcome some on the back of an anticipated boom in privatisation work.

That work is now tailing off, but the legal market remains buoyant. The government has encouraged foreign investment through flat tax rates and cheap labour, and accession to the EU has attracted more companies to a market now perceived as both economically and politically stable. Slovakia is currently one of the most attractive countries for FDI in the region, and law firms are advising inward investors on a glut of projects, with the accompanying real estate work a particular boom area. Advice is also called for on commercial activities and dealings with EU regulators, as the implications of the EU membership throw up competition and harmonisation issues.

US firms **Squire Sanders s.r.o.** and **White & Case** were the first foreign firms to enter Bratislava back in the 1990s, and they remain major players in the market. A run of privatisations in 2000 attracted the UK's international firms to set up in competition, and **Allen & Overy Bratislava, s.r.o.** and **Linklaters** both now have offices.

Real estate work has been thriving for all of the international firms present on the ground, and has played into the hands of regional specialists such as **Salans** and **Dr Ruzicka Law Office**, the local affiliate of **CMS Cameron McKenna v.o.s.**.

Bratislava's proximity to the Austrian capital Vienna attracts a band of law firms that historically hail from Austria, namely **Wolf Theiss**, **Freshfields Bruckhaus Deringer** and **DLA Weiss-Tessbach/Law Office Milan Cervenka**. Also present are German players like **Nörr Stiefenhofer Lutz**, which opened its sixth Central and Eastern European office in Bratislava in 2004.

All of which creates an intensely dynamic and competitive legal market, and as the work levels increase, so local players emerge as budding rivals to the internationalists. Local firms **Cechová & Partners**, **Cernejová & Hrbek** and **Csekes, Világi, Drgonec & Partners spol. s.r.o.** continue to illicit high praise from clients and competitors alike, with a knowledge of the domestic market that is a genuine advantage. Czech firms are also increasingly looking for a toehold in the Slovakian market place.

BANKING, FINANCE AND CAPITAL MARKETS

ALLEN & OVERY BRATISLAVA, S.R.O. ✪
LINKLATERS ✪
WHITE & CASE

Cechová & Partners
Cernejová & Hrbek
Csekes, Világi, Drgonec & Partners spol. s.r.o. ✪
Freshfields Bruckhaus Deringer
Squire Sanders s.r.o. ✪

Avocat Consulting & Services
Blaha, Erben & Partneri
DLA Weiss-Tessbach/Law Office Milan Cervenka ✪
Dedák & Partners ✪
ULC Carnogurský ✪
Valko & Partners
Weinhold Legal, v.o.s.
Wolf Theiss ✪

Firms are listed A-Z in tiers which are ranked in order of priority
✪ Indicates firm displays contact details at the end of this chapter.

BANKING, FINANCE AND CAPITAL MARKETS

In our first tier, **Allen & Overy Bratislava** is home to partner Igor Pálka, who joined the firm in 1999 and is one of the strongest partners working in the region. He is head of the Slovak practice, and handles banking and capital markets work. **Allen & Overy Bratislava,** enhanced its relationship with banks VUB, HVB and HSBC in Slovakia last year, and saw an expansion of its work in aircraft financing following budget airline Sky Europe's expansion in the country. For the firm, the highlight of the year was advising on what is believed to be the largest SKK-denominated financing in the Republic to date, working on the SKK15bn facility for Národná dial'ničná spoločnosť, for a club of banks led by HVB.

Linklaters has one of the strongest capital markets practices in Slovakia, led by the experienced Daniel Torsher. The highlight of 2005 was the culmination of the firm's work on the first Slovakian international IPO, advising Sky Europe Airlines on the issue and offer of ten million new ordinary shares on the Vienna and Warsaw stock exchanges. While the work was led out of London, the pooling of the firm's resources in Bratislava, Warsaw and Budapest showed the value of an international law firm for a Bratislava-headquartered client like Sky Europe.

White & Case partner Ivo Bárta heads the firm's Slovakian banking and finance team, and is advising SLSP, the leading Slovakian bank, on one of the largest real estate financings to be provided to HB Revis, a Slovak real estate developer. The funds, the value of which is not disclosed, are being used to refinance the construction and development of a major administrative and shopping mall in Bratislava. **White & Case** partner Marek Staroň is advising Slovak bank Slovenska Sporitelna in setting up a real estate investment fund in the Netherlands focused on the whole region.

In our second tier are three local firms with solid Slovakian banking practices, all of which come highly recommended and add valuable expertise in the domestic finance market: **Cechová & Partners**; **Cernejová & Hrbek**; and **Csekes, Világi, Drgonec & Partners spol. s.r.o.**.

Of the international firms, **Freshfields Bruckhaus Deringer** has downsized its Bratislava operation, but continues to run it in close co-operation with activities across the border in Vienna. The office is home to five fully qualified Slovak lawyers, and another four associates. The firm's banking and finance clients include Deutsche Bank, Holcim (Slovensko), Caterpillar Financial Services, BNP Paribas and Banque AIG London. **Freshfields Bruckhaus Deringer** represented Deutsche Bank in a securitisation in Slovakia with respect to a receivables portfolio, and worked for Caterpillar on a construction loan facility with a Slovakian shipyard.

At **Squire Sanders s.r.o.**, partner Kevin Connor takes responsibility for both the Bratislava and Budapest offices, though he is not based in Slovakia. His work is largely for Central European corporates on loan facilities, Eurobonds, syndicated financings and domestic bond issues. He has represented such corporations on financings in excess of US$1.5bn.

In the third tier, **Wolf Theiss** is the most active Austrian law firm on the ground in Bratislava, with a sizeable banking client base. The firm works for Raiffeisen International Bank Holding, for Austria's biggest factoring bank, Intermarket Bank, for Slovenska Sporitelna and for Slovenske Cukrovary. The team, led by Lubos Frolkovic, advised on a €4.5m share restructuring for Slovenske Cukrovary, and worked for Intermarket Bank on its expansion into Slovakia.

CORPORATE AND COMMERCIAL, INCLUDING M&A

CORPORATE AND COMMERCIAL, INCLUDING M&A

ALLEN & OVERY BRATISLAVA, S.R.O. ✪
CECHOVÁ & PARTNERS
CERNEJOVÁ & HRBEK
CSEKES, VILÁGI, DRGONEC & PARTNERS SPOL. S.R.O. ✪
LINKLATERS ✪
WHITE & CASE

Avocat Consulting & Services
DLA Weiss-Tessbach/Law Office Milan Cervenka ✪
Detvai Ludik Maly Udvaros, Law Firm
Freshfields Bruckhaus Deringer
Nörr Stiefenhofer Lutz ✪
Peterka & Partners ✪
Ruzicka (Dr) Law Office ✪

Salans
Squire Sanders s.r.o. ✪
Weinhold Legal, v.o.s.

Blaha, Erben & Partneri
Dedák & Partners ✪
Havlát & Partners Law Office
ULC Carnogurský ✪
Valko & Partners
Wolf Theiss ✪

Firms are listed A-Z in tiers which are ranked in order of priority
✪ Indicates firm displays contact details at the end of this chapter.

In our first tier, **Allen & Overy Bratislava, s.r.o.**'s office is renowned in the region for its strong corporate capability, despite its general bank focus elsewhere. Partner Hugh Owen practises as a foreign lawyer, while Martin Magál is an advocate with significant local corporate experience, particularly advising German clients.

In 2005, the office was busy with tender work for the defence industry, and saw an increase in EU-related work. Highlights included advising BAe Systems on various tenders, and advising Slovak Telecom on the acquisition of Zoznam, one of the most significant Slovak internet portals.

Local firm **Cechová & Partners** continues to be a major force in local M&A, acting for numerous large international clients. Partner Katarina Cechová is highly rated by competitors. The firm added Jana Moravčiková to the partnership in 2005, who had previously been an associate in the local office of **White & Case**. The team is well versed in competition issues, restructurings, equity issues and M&A, and has established links with a large number of international law firms.

Cernejová & Hrbek is another leading domestic law firm, with a well-established reputation for corporate work. The three key partners are Alana Cernejová, who is particularly popular for M&A work, plus Milan Hrbek and Peter Stavrovský.

Finally, **Csekes, Világi, Drgonec & Partners spol. s.r.o.** rounds out a triumvirate of Slovak law firms that are highly recommended for corporate and commercial law advice. The practice is led by partner Erica Csekes, who worked in the Bratislava office of **Squire Sanders s.r.o.** before setting up her own firm in 1994. Before that, she served as Slovak counsel in the office of the president of Czechoslovakia.

Linklaters is one of the strongest international law firms to practise in Slovakia, and has an office led by partner Daniel Torsher. He has been based in Bratislava since 1999, and with **Linklaters** since 2000. In the past he advised on the privatisation of Slovenský Plynárenský Priemysel, while more recently the firm's clients in the office have expanded to include Sky Europe Airlines, Provident Financial and Nippon Express.

The two highlights for the **Linklaters** corporate team in 2005 were advising Sky Europe, the Slovak low-cost airline, on its IPO in Vienna and Warsaw, the first time a Slovakian corporate has effectively offered shares in an international IPO, and work for US private equity house Sun Capital on its acquisition of the European branded clothing business of Sara Lee Corporation, which had significant assets in Slovakia.

White & Case is one of the oldest international law firms present in Bratislava, and now has two partners based in its 16-lawyer office, one of the largest teams. Led by practice head Ivo Bárta, the practice added Marek Staroň to the partnership in 2005. The firm's largest corporate clients in Slovakia include Czech energy company CEZ, which the firm represented in its ultimately unsuccessful bid for Slovak energy company Slovenské elektrárne, one of the largest privatisations seen in the country. The firm advised Deloitte as financial advisor on a major Slovak restructuring, and worked for NAY Holding, a consumer electronics retail chain based in the country, on its sale of 48% of its share capital to a fund managed by Enterprise Investors. Other clients of the firm active in Bratislava include Royal Ahold, Johnson Controls, Deutsche Telecom, Electricité de France, RWE Gas and Skanska.

In our second tier, **Avocat Consulting & Services** continues to be involved on many of the major transactions, often working alongside international law firms in need of local law advice.

DLA Weiss-Tessbach/Law Office Milan Cervenka is the local branch of what is now the world's third-largest law firm, and practises in close co-operation with the firm's business in Austria.

Law Firm Detvai Ludik Maly Udvaros is a local firm with established relationships with international players, and is able to provide solid Slovak advice in all corporate and commercial areas.

Freshfields Bruckhaus Deringer's Slovak office continues to have a strong base of German-speaking clients, and is now home to five Slovak-qualified lawyers and four other associates. The firm drafts in further capabilities from the rest of its network when required, particularly from Vienna. Such an approach secured work advising one of the primary bidders in the privatisation of ZSSK Cargo, the largest privatisation of 2005 in the country, and for Gaz de France and Ruhrgas after their successful bid for 49% of Slovak gas company SPP. The firm has a sizeable competition and trade practice in the country, advising clients like HP, Austrian Airlines and Japan Tobacco International on competition matters. On M&A, **Freshfields Bruckhaus Deringer**'s deals include work for Warburg Pincus Ventures International on the acquisition of shares in SL Pharma, which holds shares in publicly listed pharmaceuticals company Slovakofarma, and work for Colas on its acquisition of local construction company Inýubuersje stavby.

Nörr Stiefenhofer Lutz is a German firm which opened its doors in Bratislava in November 2004 in response to demands from some long-standing clients, not least Germany's Volkswagen group. The firm now has six lawyers based in the country, with the office led by partner Jaroslav Melzer, and three further Slovak lawyers practice in Prague and Munich. The firm's major clients active in Bratislava include Credit Suisse Life & Pensions, Commerzbank, RWE/VSE and Saint-Gobain.

Peterka & Partners is a Czech law firm that has opened an office in Bratislava, and is one of very few to have done so. The firm's local presence is headed by partner Ondrej Dusak, and there are a total of 12 lawyers practising in the office. The practice provided commercial advice to Cegelec, which was a member of the consortium on the construction of a factory for Peugeot-Citroen in Slovakia, and to Veolia in the process of the privatisation of the waterworks infrastructure in the country. **Peterka & Partners** also advised international logistics consultant Kühne & Nagel on its Slovak branch, and French logistics group Giraud International on its local work.

Dr Ruzicka Law Office is the local branch of the international alliance of **CMS Cameron McKenna v.o.s.**, and is home to managing partner Jaroslav Ružičká. He is a Slovak advocate who has been practising since 1992, and is one of three partners and 22 fee-earners who spend significant amounts of time in the office. Partner Ian Parker has arrived from **CMS Cameron McKenna v.o.s.** to bring important international client connections and bolster the offering. The firm is now committing additional resources to Slovakia, and the renewed focus has led to a growth in M&A work. The team advised Kia Motors on the acquisition of a local car importer, worked for RWA International in the restructuring of the Slovak part of its holdings, and advised Heros Security buying a local security services provider. The firm also worked for consortiums bidding for both the rail freight and airport privatisations.

Salans has four lawyers and a total of seven fee-earners based in its Bratislava office, which is largely staffed by partners based in the firm's Czech Republic office. The team worked for ABN Amro in seeking approval from the Slovak Antimonopoly Office for a foreign acquisition by a large international industrial conglomerate. It also advised Polish soft drinks and food producer Maspex on its activities in Slovakia, and worked for other global entities looking at Slovakian acquisitions.

Squire Sanders s.r.o. was one of the first international law firms into Slovakia, and partner Kevin Connor continues to act for major global clients doing transactions in the country. Fellow partner Julian Juhasz who, unlike Connor, is based permanently in Bratislava, is now a consultant to the firm.

Weinhold Legal, v.o.s. was founded in 1996, and has some 30 lawyers divided between its offices in Bratislava and Prague. Highly rated by clients and competitors, the firm's clients include Enel, which it advised as winning bidder on the electricity privatisation, Iberdrola, Vivendi Water and Erste Bank.

Finally, in our third tier, **Blaha, Erben & Partneri** is a highly rated local firm capable of providing good commercial and corporate advice, while **Dedák & Partners** is a firm that works in close association with major Czech firm **Havel & Holásek**.

Havlát & Partners Law Office was set up in 1990, and has 11 lawyers, eight of them partners, who offer a full range of corporate and commercial advice to both local and international clients.

ULC Carnogurský was founded in 2000, and in 2004 launched a branch in Italy. With four partners and seven other lawyers, the firm has particular expertise in energy and financial services.

Valko & Partners was set up in 1993 and is home to two locally qualified corporate partners, Ernest Valko and Andrea Tomlainová, and a further five senior legal advisers.

Wolf Theiss is an Austrian law firm that now has eight offices across Central and Eastern Europe, and opened in Bratislava in 2003. The office is headed by partner Erik Steger, who splits his time between Vienna and the firm's Slovak office. The firm's M&A experience in the country includes advising Central European medical laboratories operation Futurelab Holdings on the acquisition of laboratories in the Slovak Republic, advising ABB Holdings on a merger of its Slovakian subsidiaries, and working for ATW Handelsgesellschaft on the sale of its entire Slovak car distribution business for €1.3m.

ALIANCIAADVOKÁTOV

VLČKOVA UL 8/A
81105 BRATISLAVA 1

Telephone: +421 2 5245 3072
Fax: +421 2 5245 3071
E-mail: office@aliancia.sk
Website: www aliancia.sk

Languages
Czech, English, French, German, Italian, Polish, Russian, Slovak

Number of lawyers 26

Member
International Bar Association;
Association of European Lawyers

CATEGORIES OF WORK

Corporate
Gerta Sámelová Flassiková, Jana Tögelová

Banking and tax law
Gerta Sámelová Flassiková, Pavel Hagyari

Privatisation and reprivatisation
Gerta Sámelová Flassiková, Jana Tögelová

Bankruptcy and liquidation
Gerta Sámelová Flassiková, Pavel Hagyari

Securities and capital markets
Gerta Sámelová Flassiková, Pavel Hagyari

Labour and employment
Lucia Kralovičová, Radovan Hrabovecký

Mergers and acquisitions
Gerta Sámelová Flassiková, Pavel Hagyari

Antitrust
Imrich Flassik

Litigation and dispute resolution
Lucia Kralovičová, Marek Ogurčák

Administrative law
Gerta Sámelová Flassiková, Jana Tögelová

Real estate
Gerta Sámelová Flassiková, Jana Tögelová

Intellectual property
Pavel Hagyari, Marián Baláž

THE FIRM

alianciaadvokátov was founded in 1990 and consists of three senior partners, seven junior partners, 16 associates and other employees. It is one of the leading law firms in Slovakia and is based in Bratislava.

The firm consists of several units, each specialising in a particular field of law. The partners, associates and other support staff have an excellent network of local and national co-workers throughout Slovakia, on both private and public levels. The high quality of services provided by alianciaadvokátov is guaranteed by the extensive network of support personnel and some sophisticated technology. The firm's main advantage is the flexibility to adapt to the needs of its clients, reflecting the changing local environment and maintaining a high professional standard.

AREAS OF PRACTICE

alianciaadvokátov offers in-depth expertise and a complex legal service covering numerous business areas. The firm's lawyers possess the qualifications and practical experience to provide individuals and legal entities with a broad range of legal assistance, covering all business activities and legal matters.

alianciaadvokátov has dealt with several large privatisation projects, such as that of a major port and shipping company and a major chemical plant, as well as in the privatisation of the energy sector. The firm's counsel is also crucial for the utility regulator in relation to the privatisation process.

Members of the firm's team have assisted clients with the evaluation of prospective strategic investors, providing legal advisory services, including due diligence within the mergers, joint ventures and changes to the legal form of companies and during acquisitions in large investment projects in the clothing, aviation, building and construction, pharmaceutical, transport, food and chemical industries.

alianciaadvokátov has participated in the establishment of a number of business chambers and assisted in the formation of, among others, large, limited liability companies, joint stock companies, investment funds and investment companies and an affiliate of one of the most important world producers of equipment for commercial chains.

One of the senior partners was the founder of the antitrust agenda in the former Czechoslovakia. alianciaadvokátov represented several clients before the Slovak Antitrust Office, including a major investment company, a chemical plant, a transport company and one of the biggest alternative telecoms operators dealing with market liberalisation in Slovakia.

The firm's real estate lawyers counsel on the acquisition, financing, development, construction, leasing and sale of real estate, as well as contract negotiation during the various phases of construction. The firm's clients are major developers, owners of shopping centres, office buildings and industrial areas, eg a major Danish developer, a member of an internationally renowned developer group and an Israeli developer purchasing real estate for the subsequent development of office premises.

In intellectual property, the firm advises on the registration of patents, trade marks and industrial designs, as well as unfair competition and legal disputes arising therefrom. The firm represented a leading global skylight producer and a leading global beverages producer in an unfair competition dispute, a major Slovak radio station in arranging the transfer of a trade mark and an internationally renowned sport shoes producer.

The firm's clients are public and private companies, private individuals, foreign embassies and chambers of commerce, who seek advice from the firm's specialists. The legal counsel provided to the firm's clients covers the broadest range of the most important legal matters. Major clients include a leading Austrian brick producer, a Danish skylight producer, an American pharmaceutical company, an investment company, a telecoms technology operator, a major beverages producer, leading Slovak newspapers, a large transport company and several state institutions.

The firm also acted as the external legal adviser to the Slovak Republic in drafting several legal acts which were adopted in parliament.

ALLEN & OVERY, BRATISLAVA S.R.O.

CARLTON SAVOY BUILDING
MOSTOVÁ 2, 5TH FLOOR
81102 BRATISLAVA

Telephone: +421 2 5920 2400
Fax: +421 2 5920 2424
E-mail: information@allenovery.com
Website: www.allenovery.com

Languages
Slovak, English, Czech, German, French, Hungarian, Russian

Other offices
Amsterdam, Antwerp, Bangkok, Beijing, Brussels, Budapest, Dubai, Frankfurt, Hamburg, Hong Kong, London, Luxembourg, Madrid, Milan, Moscow, New York, Paris, Prague, Rome, Shanghai, Singapore, Tokyo, Turin, Warsaw

Number of lawyers 2,304
at this office 15

Contacts
Igor Pálka, Hugh Owen

CATEGORIES OF WORK

Acquisition and asset finance
Igor Pálka

Antitrust/competition law
Igor Pálka, Renátus Kollár

Arbitration/litigation
Martin Magál, Igor Pálka

Banking and finance
Igor Pálka, Hugh Owen

Bond and equity issues
Igor Pálka

Capital markets
Igor Pálka, Hugh Owen

Corporate/commercial
Igor Pálka, Martin Magál

Corporate and project finance
Igor Pálka

Employment
Ludmila Borloková

Derivatives and structured financial products
Hugh Owen, Patricia Olšovská

Mergers and acquisitions, syndicated lending
Igor Pálka, Hugh Owen

PFI/PPP
Igor Pálka, Hugh Owen

Private equity
Hugh Owen

Privatisations
Igor Pálka, Hugh Owen

Real estate
Vojtech Pálinkás, Hugh Owen

Telecommunications
Hugh Owen, Igor Pálka

Utilities/energy
Igor Pálka, Hugh Owen

CSEKES, VILÁGI, DRGONEC & PARTNERS SPOL. S R.O.

SASINKOVA 12
81108 BRATISLAVA

Telephone: +421 2 5296 6330
Fax: +421 2 5293 2461
E-mail: office-ba@csekes-vilagi.sk
Website: www.csekes-vilagi.sk

Languages
Czech, English, German, Hungarian

Other offices
Dunajská Streda

Number of lawyers 17
at this office 14

Contacts
Erika Csekes, Peter Michač

Member
The Law Firm Network

CATEGORIES OF WORK

Corporate and commercial law
Beáta Kartíková, Adriana Kovácikavá

Mergers and acquisitions
Erika Csekes, Jana Pagacova

Privatisation
Oszkár Világi, Erika Csekes

Real estate
Ingrid Gyökeresová, Silvia Bernáthová

Securities
Erika Csekes

Civil and commercial litigation
Ingrid Gyökeresová, Silvia Bernáthová

Corporate finance
Erika Csekes, Adriana Kovácikavá

Intellectual property
Erika Csekes

Foreign investments
Erika Csekes, Jana Pagacova

Competition law
Erika Csekes, Beáta Kartíková

Labour law
Beáta Kartíková

Bankruptcy
Patrik Gaal, Ingrid Gyökeresová

Telecommunications
Erika Csekes

DLA WEISS-TESSBACH/LAW OFFICE MILAN CERVENKA

SUCHE MYTO 1
81103 BRATISLAVA

Telephone: +421 2 5920 2123
Fax: +421 2 5443 4585
E-mail: bratislava@dlapiper.com
Website: www.dlapiper.com

Languages
Czech, English, German, Russian, Slovak

Other offices
Austria, Belgium, Bosnia-Herzegovina, China, Croatia, Czech Republic, Denmark*, Egypt*, France, Georgia, Germany, Hong Kong, Hungary, Italy, Japan, Netherlands, Norway*, Poland*, Russia, Singapore*, South Africa*, Spain, Sweden*, Thailand, UK, Ukraine, United Arab Emirates, US

Number of lawyers 3,100
at this office 5

Contact
Stefan Eder (Vienna)

Member
DLA Piper Group

CATEGORIES OF WORK

General corporate	**Banking and finance**
General commercial	**Real estate**
Intellectual property	**EU integration**
Litigation	**Insurance**
Arbitration	**Mergers and acquisitions**

THE FIRM

DLA Weiss-Tessbach was established in 1878 in Austria and is one of the longest-established law firms in the country. Since 1989, the firm has undergone a dynamic expansion across Central and Eastern Europe, growing from 15 to 100 lawyers and from one to seven offices, including Bratislava. DLA Weiss-Tessbach will continue to expand in the Central and Eastern European region as countries adjust to EU membership.

DLA Weiss-Tessbach is part of DLA Piper Rudnick Gray Cary, one of the leading global legal services organisations, with approximately 3,100 lawyers in 58 offices across 22 countries. The organisation is committed to building long-term relationships with its clients and supports their strategic and operational needs both locally and internationally.

AREAS OF PRACTICE

The firm has strengthened its core areas of expertise (commercial and corporate, M&A, banking and finance, general commercial law, real estate) and advises its clients as a full-service firm in all relevant areas of business law, including administrative law, employment law, IT and telecoms, technology, intellectual property, venture capital and capital markets.

DLA Weiss-Tessbach has well-established relations with clients of various backgrounds. The firm advises medium-sized enterprises as well as leading (often publicly listed) international and domestic industrial groups, service providers, banks and other financial institutions and individuals.

DLA Weiss-Tessbach has established a particular reputation for its ability to handle cases in international cross-border contexts. The firm is renowned for its expertise in the structuring and implementation of projects and transactions in Slovakia, as well as in other countries in Central and Eastern Europe. It carefully monitors the ongoing developments in the Central and Eastern European region with the aim of combining the needs of the constantly changing international legal market and industry, whilst also upholding the high standard of service that the firm has always been able to offer to its clients.

DEDÁK & PARTNERS

MLYNSKÉ NIVY 45
APOLLO BUSINESS CENTER
82109 BRATISLAVA

Telephone: +421 2 5828 2828
Fax: +421 2 5828 2829
E-mail: office@dedak.com
Website: www.dedak.com

Languages
Czech, English, French, German, Hungarian, Russian, Slovak, Spanish

Other offices
Kyjov

Number of lawyers 20

Member
IFLR 1000; Martindale-Hubell; TAG law

CATEGORIES OF WORK

Banking and finance
Jiři Budinský, Mária Karcolová

Commercial property/real estate
Marieta Leitnerová, Štefan Dedák

Competition law
Tomáš Kamenec, Pavol Cvik

Corporate and commercial
Reken Lucia, Eduard Winkler

Employment/labour law
Mária Jagelková, Katarína Kordošová

Foreign direct investment
Pavol Blahušiak, Boris Brhlovič

Infrastructure and project finance
Pavol Blahušiak, Boris Brhlovič

Mergers and acquisitions
Pavol Blahušiak, Boris Brhlovič

Privatisation
Pavol Blahušiak, Boris Brhlovič

Due diligence
Pavol Blahušiak, Boris Brhlovič

Copyright law
Tomáš Kamenec, Pavol Cvik

Advertising law
Tomáš Kamenec, Pavol Cvik

Bill of exchange and checks
Jiři Budinský, Mária Karcolová

IT law
Tomáš Kamenec, Pavol Cvik

International law and trade
Pavol Blahušiak, Boris Brhlovič

Trade marks and patents
Tomáš Kamenec, Pavol Cvik

Human rights and personal freedoms
Tomáš Kamenec, Pavol Cvik

Recovery of claims/bankruptcy law
Štefan Dedák, Mária Jagelková

e|n|w|c ATTORNEYS AT LAW

EISELSBERG NATLACEN WALDERDORFF CANCOLA S.R.O.
GRÖSSLINGOVA 4
81109 BRATISLAVA

Telephone: +421 2 5263 2804
Fax: +421 2 5263 2677
E-mail: bratislava@enwc.com
Website: www.enwc.com

Languages
Czech, English, French, German, Hungarian, Slovak

Other offices
Brno, Budapest, Prague, Vienna, Warsaw

Number of lawyers 47
at this office 4

Contacts
Dr Andrej Leontiev, Mgr Radovan Pala

CATEGORIES OF WORK

M&A

Joint ventures

Corporate law

Property

Employment and labour law

Competition law

Construction and building

International arbitration and litigation

KONEČNÁ & ŠAFÁŘ

VENTÚRSKA 12
815 16 BRATISLAVA

Telephone: +421 2 5441 8470
Fax: +421 2 5441 8471
E-mail: bratislava@konecna-safar.com
Website: www.konecna-safar.com

Languages
Czech, English, French, German, Hungarian, Italian, Russian, Spanish

Other offices
Prague

Number of lawyers 8

Contacts
Pavel Šafář, Radka Konečná

Member
American Law Firm Association; Association of European Lawyers; Czech Transportation Law Society; Geneva Group International

CATEGORIES OF WORK

Corporate and commercial law
Dagmar Yoder

Competition law
Dagmar Yoder

Mergers and acquisitions
Pavel Šafář

Project finance
Radka Konečná

Securities
Dagmar Yoder

Restructuring and bankruptcy
Pavel Šafář

Real estate development
Radka Konečná

Commercial litigation
Dagmar Yoder, Martin Repáň

Arbitration
Pavel Šafář

Shipping
Pavel Šafář

Debt collecting
Martin Repáň

Labour and employment
Petr Básti

Intellectual property law
Petr Básti

Telecommunication
Dagmar Yoder

Oil, gas and mining
Pavel Šafář

LINKLATERS

HVIEZDOSLAVOVO NÁMESTIE 13
811 02 BRATISLAVA

Telephone: +421 2 5929 1111
Fax: +421 2 5929 1210
Website: www.linklaters.com

Languages
All commercial and local languages in the countries where Linklaters operates

Other offices
Amsterdam, Antwerp, Bangkok, Beijing, Berlin, Brussels, Bucharest, Budapest, Cologne, Dubai, Frankfurt am Main, Hong Kong, Lisbon, London, Luxembourg, Madrid, Milan, Moscow, Munich, New York, Paris, Prague, Rome, São Paulo, Shanghai, Singapore, Stockholm, Tokyo, Warsaw

Number of lawyers 2,000 worldwide

Contact
Daniel Torsher

CATEGORIES OF WORK

Antitrust
Patrik Bolf

Banking and finance
Daniel Torsher

Company and commercial
Patrik Bolf, Miroslav Németh

Mergers and acquisitions
Patrik Bolf

Corporate finance
Daniel Torsher

Capital markets
Daniel Torsher

Litigation and arbitration
Miroslav Németh

Private equity
Daniel Torsher

Privatisations
Daniel Torsher

Project finance
Daniel Torsher

Real estate/development
Patrik Bolf

Telecoms
Patrik Bolf

Tax
Adam Hodoň

NÖRR STIEFENHOFER LUTZ

AC DIPLOMAT
PALISÁDY 29/A
81106 BRATISLAVA

Telephone: +421 2 5910 1010
Fax: +421 2 5910 1011
E-mail: info@noerr.com
Website: www.noerr.com

Languages
Slovak, German, English, French, Russian, Czech

Other offices
Berlin, Bucharest, Budapest, Dresden, Düsseldorf, Frankfurt, Moscow, Munich, New York, Prague, Warsaw

Number of lawyers 256
(+ 66 tax advisers, public accountants and tax assistants)
at this office 11
(7 locally + 4 in Prague and Munich)

Contact
Zuzana Špániková

CATEGORIES OF WORK

- Arbitration and dispute resolution
- Banking, project finance and capital markets
- Energy
- EU, antitrust and competition
- General commercial practice (agency, franchising, distribution, leasing)
- General corporate practice
- Insurance law
- Intellectual property and unfair competition
- Labour and employment
- Mergers and acquisitions, joint ventures, corporate reorganisations (MBO, MBI)
- Private equity and venture capital
- Privatisation, greenfield investment
- Real estate, commercial property, construction

PETERKA & PARTNERS

KAPITULSKÁ 18/A
81101 BRATISLAVA

Telephone: +421 2 5441 8700
Fax: +421 2 5441 8701
E-mail: office@cabinet.sk
Website: www.cabinet.sk

Languages
Czech, English, French, German, Hungarian, Russian, Slovak

Other offices
Prague

Number of lawyers 39
at this office 10

Contact
Ondřej Dušek

Member
TerraLex®

CATEGORIES OF WORK

- Company and commercial
- Mergers and acquisitions
- Real estate development and construction
- Litigation
- Competition law
- Intellectual property
- Labour law
- International law
- Finance

DR RUZICKA LAW OFFICE

KAPITULSKÁ 15
81101 BRATISLAVA

Telephone: +421 2 5443 3490
Fax: +421 2 5443 5906
E-mail: ruzicka@ccsconsulting.sk

Languages
Croatian, Czech, English, German, Hungarian, Russian, Slovak

Other offices
Prague, Zagreb

Number of lawyers 28
at this office 18

International groupings
In association with CMS Cameron McKenna; CMS Reich-Rohrwig Hainz

CATEGORIES OF WORK

Banking and finance
Mgr L Krechňák, Dr D Nemčíková

Mergers and acquisitions
Ian Parker, Dr D Nemčíková

Securities
Mgr L Krechňák, Dr D Nemčíková

Property finance
Dr J Ružička, Mgr L Krechňák

Capital markets
Mgr L Krechňák, Dr D Nemčíková

Litigation
Dr J Ružička, Mgr K Kováčová

Commercial and company law
Mgr S Szabó, Dr D Nemčíková

Real estate and construction
Dr J Ružička, Mgr S Szabó

Trade marks
Mgr S Szabó

Employment law
Mgr S Szabó, Mgr M Poliaćiková

Competition law
Ian Parker, Mgr L Krechňák

Energy (heating, gas, mining)
Dr D Nemčíková, Mgr S Szabó

Privatisation
Mgr L Krechňák, Ian Parker

SQUIRE SANDERS S.R.O.

ZOCHOVA 5
811 03 BRATISLAVA

Telephone: +421 2 5930 3411
Fax: +421 2 5930 3415
E-mail: kconnor@ssd.com
Website: www.ssd.com

Languages
Czech, English, French, German, Hungarian, Russian, Slovak, Spanish

Other offices
Beijing, Brussels, Budapest, Caracas, Cincinnati, Cleveland, Columbus, Hong Kong, Houston, London, Los Angeles, Miami, Moscow, New York, Palo Alto, Phoenix, Prague, Rio de Janeiro, San Francisco, Santa Domingo, Shanghai, Tallahassee, Tampa, Tokyo, Tysons Corner, Warsaw, Washington DC, West Palm Beach, Bucharest*, Buenos Aires*, Dublin*, Kyiv*, Milan*, Santiago*

Number of lawyers 800+
at this office 10

Contacts
Kevin Connor, Julian Juhasz

Member
American Chamber of Commerce

CATEGORIES OF WORK

Capital markets
Kevin Connor, Michal Luknár

Computer technology, multimedia services
Nataša Nikitinová

Corporate finance, banking
Julian Juhasz, Andrew Sandor

Energy
Roman Prekop

Environmental
Nataša Nikitinová, Roman Prekop

EU competition law
Adrian Barger

Infrastructure, project asset finance
Adrian Barger, Kevin Connor

Intellectual property
Adrian Barger

International transactions, foreign and direct investment
Kevin Connor, Julian Juhasz

Joint ventures
Kevin Connor, Julian Juhasz

Mergers and acquisitions
Andrew Sandor, Julian Juhasz

Privatisations
Kevin Connor, Julian Juhasz

Power generation, energy
Kevin Connor, Roman Prekop

Real estate
Julian Juhasz, Nataša Nikitinová

Securities
Julian Juhasz, Peter Šuba

Telecoms
Peter Šuba, Martina Lapšanská

THE FIRM

Founded in 1890, Squire, Sanders & Dempsey is a multi-jurisdictional law firm with approximately 800 lawyers practising in offices in Europe, the Americas and Asia. The firm's practice covers most substantive areas of the law, with an emphasis on business and finance matters.

The firm operates as a single global partnership, which ensures client accountability and the seamless delivery of uniformly high-quality legal services throughout the world. The firm's lawyers come from many countries and cultures, are licensed to practise in both common law and civil law jurisdictions, and communicate with clients in their native languages. Today, the firm remains committed to the fundamental principles ordained by its founders: to serve clients effectively and to maintain the professional standards that distinguish both the firm and its people.

AREAS OF PRACTICE

The firm is organised around four major practice areas: advocacy, business, capital markets and regulated industries. Within these practice areas, the firm's work can be divided into numerous areas of specialisation, including banking, bankruptcy and restructuring, biotechnology and pharmaceuticals, communications, competition law, converging technologies, corporate, energy, environmental, healthcare, intellectual property, international dispute resolution, labour and employment, litigation, mergers and acquisitions, privatisations, project finance, real estate, securities and taxation.

In 1991, Squire Sanders became the first foreign firm to establish a Bratislava office, and has since been at the forefront of the market economy in the Slovak Republic. The Bratislava lawyers advise a broad range of established and emerging international and domestic clients on a variety of corporate matters including company formation and registration, investment and financing, labour and employment, corporate governance, real estate, environmental and EU competition law. In addition, the lawyers handle a significant number of mergers and acquisitions.

The Bratislava lawyers offer clients a strong combination of international transactional experience and familiarity with the legal infrastructure of Central and Eastern Europe. This combination enables the Bratislava lawyers to advise Slovak and foreign companies on privatisations of state enterprises in the region and in related joint venture, investment, restructuring and financing transactions.

The Bratislava lawyers have significant experience in communications and advise clients on a variety of related matters, including interconnection agreements for the national telecoms company and corporate work for internet and e-commerce startups.

The Bratislava-based finance practice is expansive, handling some of the largest corporate finance transactions in the country.

ULC ČARNOGURSKÝ

JELENIA 4
81499 BRATISLAVA

Telephone: +421 2 5720 1717
Fax: +421 2 5720 1777
E-mail: office@ulclegal.com
Website: www.ulclegal.com

Languages
English, French, German, Italian, Russian

Number of lawyers 12

Contact
Ján Čarnogurský

International grouping
DIRO

CATEGORIES OF WORK

Antitrust and competition
Martin Javorček, Viliam Karas

Arbitration and litigation
Ján Čarnogurský, Andrej Stachovič

Banking, capital markets, securities and finance
Ján Čarnogurský, Martin Javorček

Central and Eastern Europe
Ján Čarnogurský, Viliam Karas

Construction and real estate
Martin Javorček, Ján Čarnogurský

Corporate, M&A, restructuring
Ján Čarnogurský, Martin Javorček

Employment, industrial relations, employee benefits and pensions
Viliam Karas, Rovena Suchánková

Energy law
Silvia Poláková, Martin Javorček

Government business regulatory/public procurement
Viliam Karas, Ján Čarnogurský

Insolvency
Martin Javorček, Silvia Poláková

Intellectual property and trade marks
Silvia Poláková, Ján Korecky

Tax
Ján Čarnogurský, Martin Javorček

Telecommunications
Silvia Poláková, Viliam Karas

White-collar crime
Martin Javorček, Ján Čarnogurský

WOLF THEISS

LAURINSKÁ 3
81101 BRATISLAVA

Telephone: +421 2 5910 1240
Fax: +421 2 5920 4049
E-mail: bratislava@wolftheiss.com
Website: www.wolftheiss.com

Languages
Slovak, Czech, German, English, French, Polish

Other offices
Belgrade, Bucharest, Ljubljana, Prague, Sarajevo, Tirana, Vienna, Zagreb

Number of lawyers 161
at this office 10

Contacts
Erik Steger, L'uboš Frolkovič, Paul Sestak, Dušan Ružič

CATEGORIES OF WORK

Arbitration and litigation

Corporate and M&A

Banking, capital markets, securities, project finance, investment funds

Real estate, construction and leasing

Contracts

THE FIRM

Wolf Theiss was founded in 1957 in Vienna and today is one of the leading law firms in the CEE/SEE region. Over the past few years the firm has experienced extraordinarily dynamic growth, both domestically and internationally.

Wolf Theiss has established a network of nine offices* in Albania, Austria, Bosnia and Herzegovina, Croatia, the Czech Republic, Romania, Serbia and Montenegro, Slovakia and Slovenia. In 2005 alone, Wolf Theiss opened two new offices, in Bucharest and Sarajevo. The firm also regularly assists its clients with projects in Bulgaria, Hungary, Macedonia, Moldova, Poland, Turkey and Ukraine, in co-operation with local attorneys.

The firm's dynamic growth is also reflected in its increase in personnel. At present, Wolf Theiss employs over 350 individuals at nine locations – compare this to 30 employees in one office, Vienna, ten years ago and the growth is apparent.

*The firm's operations in the various locations are set up in compliance with local law and the Bar rules requirements which include the form of co-operation with independent local attorneys.

SLOVENIA

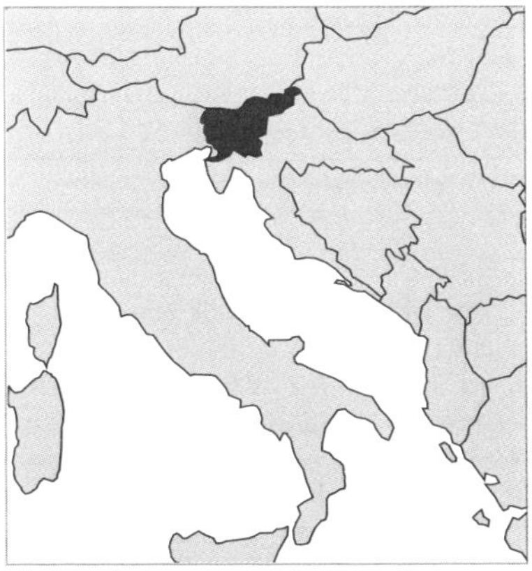

Population	2 million
Number of lawyers	950
Professional title	Odvetnik
Currency	Tolar (SIT)

Index

Slovenia lies to the south-east of the Alps and shares frontiers with Austria, Italy, Croatia and Hungary. Slovenia's valuable 47km of Adriatic coastline boast a thriving tourist industry and the major regional port of Koper. After centuries of subjection to the Austro-Hungarian Empire, and seventy years as a part of Yugoslavia, Slovenia declared independence in 1991. Following referenda, Slovenia joined Nato in March 2004 and the EU in May 2004. Slovenia, with a population of two million, is the fifth-smallest EU member.

Since independence, Slovenia has tended to look to its western neighbours for alliances but, now EU membership has been achieved there are signs that relations with FYR members are improving.

BILLING

Most billing is on an hourly basis although a limited contingency fee scheme is available for litigation. Hourly rates range between €180 and €275 for partners, €160 and €200 for qualified and experienced lawyers, and between €120 and €180 for law graduates in training. Capped fees are sometimes negotiated with established clients. Professional indemnity insurance through the Law Society of Slovenia is obligatory.

MARKETING

Advertising is prohibited by the Law Society of Slovenia although brochures are now of international standard and websites are accepted. Further liberalisation is anticipated in the medium term.

POLITICAL AND ECONOMIC CLIMATE

Slovenia's economy has grown at an average 4% for the last ten years and it ranks as one of the most affluent 'new' EU members. However, there are concerns that growth may fade as higher oil and raw material costs affect the manufacturing sector, which accounts for a quarter of GDP. Inflation is under control, standing at 3.7% in 2004, thanks to sound macro-economic policies. Unemployment rates in August 2005 were 8.6% for men and 12% for women.

Slovenia's last parliamentary elections, held in October 2004, resulted in a narrow victory for the Social Democratic party (SDP) over the Liberal Democrats (LDS). The SDP under Prime Minister Janez Jansa is committed to free-market reform, which is expected to increase inward investment. To date, economic liberalisation has lagged, and some 50% of the economy remains in public ownership. A 'reform blueprint' adopted by Parliament in late November 2005 includes the privatisation of Telekom Slovenije, the telecoms monopoly, in 2006, and the introduction of flat-rate tax by 2007.

Slovenia, a member of the 'mark 2' Exchange Rate Mechanism (ERMII) since mid-2004, intends to adopt the euro in 2007.

LEGAL MARKET

The major law firms, and the smaller firms with commercial expertise, are based in Ljubljana, Slovenia's capital city. **Jadek & Pensa** and **Colja, Rojs & Partnerji op dno**, are the dominant local firms for commercial work, while several competent smaller firms active in the foreign client market offer niche expertise and good service standards.

Practising lawyers are required to be self-employed, which results in a high junior partner ratio in Slovenian firms. Although expert, patent attorneys are not necessarily qualified lawyers. Some 90% of practising lawyers are sole practitioners.

Top-rank Austrian firms **Schönherr** and **Wolf Theiss** have both established Mitteleurop/Balkan networks which include Ljubljana offices and are now 'seen more often' in the high-value mandates. **DLA Weiss-Tessbach** services international companies with a Slovenian presence from its Vienna office.

CORPORATE AND COMMERCIAL

At **Jadek & Pensa** Pavle Pensa and Sreco Jadek continue to attract acclaim and the ten-fee-earner firm seems secure in its top ranking. Noted for expertise in banking, finance and insurance, **Jadek & Pensa** is usually on one side of the major deals. Recent clients include Intergroup and DFDS. The firm is well positioned for the predicted wave of privatisation work in 2006.

Ambitious **Colja, Rojs & Partnerji op dno**, a member of the *JCA International* commercial lawyers network, has grown to six partners. This respected firm services a blue-chip clientele and is recommended for complex commercial work

The largest firms

1	Miro Senica in odvetniki, Attorneys at Law	23
2	Colja, Rojs & Partnerji op dno	14
3	Selih & Partners	11
4	Jadek & Pensa	10
5	Schönherr	6
	Wolf Theiss	6
7	Janko Pucnik, Law Office	5
8	Vidovic & Partnerji o.p. - d.n.o.	4
9	Kuhelj Law Office	3
	Nina Drnovsek, Law & Patent Office	3
	Patentna pisarna d.o.o.	3

These figures represent the total number of lawyers in this country only, and have been supplied by the firms themselves. The figures should be accurate as at 1 January 2006.

across the board. Founding partners Marjan Colja and Alec Rojs head an energetic team of 'good young lawyers who know what they're doing', which has recently been busy with several M&A transactions and a major foodstore chain leaseback deal.

Schönherr's ten-fee-earner practice, the larger of the two foreign firms in Slovenia, has acted, *inter alia* for Mövenpick, Danone and DaimlerChrysler on complex inward investment matters. **Schönherr** offers strength across the board in corporate and commercial work including real estate. The former **Schönherr** Ljubljana chief Ales Lunder left to found a niche international law firm in autumn 2005.

The four partners of **Selih & Partners** came together in autumn of 2005, responding to market changes, which make a partnership structure more effective than the previous association of independent lawyers. Smaller than the two main players, **Selih & Partners**, 'a good practice for foreign clients', has its share of household name clients and offers serious competition in the general corporate and commercial market. Experienced name partner Nina Selih is recommended.

Wolf Theiss's growing Ljubljana office is one of seven located in the capital cities of the FYR and its neighbours. Serviced from the Vienna hub, **Wolf Theiss** boasts blue-chip foreign clients with Slovenian interests, such as Citigroup and Kaertner Sparkasse AG, but has also begun to make inroads into the local market. Markus Brueckmueller heads a team of five with particular strengths in inward investment and cross-border restructuring.

Barbara Kristof-Lucovnik offers a respected niche practice specialising in corporate, real estate and dispute resolution.

CORPORATE AND COMMERCIAL

JADEK & PENSA

COLJA, ROJS & PARTNERJI OP DNO

Schönherr ✪
Selih & Partners
Wolf Theiss ✪

Barbara Kristof-Lucovnik
Janko Pucnik, Law Office ✪
Jurij Dolzan, Law Office
Nina Drnovsek, Law & Patent Office
Vidovic & Partnerji o.p. – d.n.o.

Firms are listed A-Z in tiers which are ranked in order of priority
✪ *Indicates firm displays contact details at the end of this chapter.*

Law Office Janko Pucnik offers five fee-earners concentrating on business law, IP and finance law. Founder Janko Pucnik is highly respected for his work in media, television and telecoms and is also noted for his 'stubborn' stance in litigation against the government.

Law Office Jurij Dolzan's eponymous founder is widely peer-recommended for banking matters.

Lawyer and patent attorney Nina Drnovsek, name partner of five-fee-earner **Law & Patent Office Nina Drnovsek** is 'very good with foreign clients' and, as well as taking direct instructions, works widely with foreign law firms in IP matters.

Vidovic & Partnerji o.p. – d.n.o.'s name partner, Natasha Vidovic receives wide acclaim as Slovenia's top tax lawyer; she is well versed at dealing with cross-border tax issues and inward investment planning. The firm is member of the *Euréseau* lawyers association.

LAW OFFICE JANKO PUČNIK

PODMILŠČAKOVA 25
1001 LJUBLJANA

Telephone: +386 1 430 1115
Fax: +386 1 431 2026
E-mail: odvetnik.janko.pucnik@siol.net

Languages
English, French, Italian, Serbo-Croatian

Number of lawyers 5

CATEGORIES OF WORK

Corporate law

International business law

Business law

Finance law

Intellectual property

Transfer of technology

ATTORNEYS AT LAW MIRO SENICA IN ODVETNIKI

BARJANSKA CESTA 3
PO BOX 1945
1001 LJUBLJANA

Telephone: +386 1 252 8000
Fax: +386 1 252 8080
E-mail: odvetniki.attorneys@senica.si
Website: www.senica.si

Languages
Croatian, English, French, German, Portuguese, Serbian, Slovenian, Spanish

Number of lawyers 23

Contact
Katarina Kresal

International groupings
EuroJuris; Intuitu Attorneys & Business; International Distribution Institute; Advolex; DIRO

CATEGORIES OF WORK

Mergers and acquisitions
Katarina Kresal, Ales Melihen

Securities
Katarina Kresal, Ales Melihen

Commercial and company law
Katarina Kresal, Ales Melihen

Corporate finance
Peter Fasun

Property finance
Peter Fasun

Litigation
Katarina Kresal, Peter Fasun

EU and competition law
Melita Trop, Ales Melihen

Real estate
Peter Fasun, Marko Kosmac

Intellectual property
Katarina Kresal

Administrative law
Matej Podlipnik, Mateja Galic

Constitutional law
Peter Fasun

Public procurement
Mateja Galic

Family law
Matej Podlipnik

Tax issues
Peter Fasun

Telecommunications
Katarina Kresal

Media and entertainment
Peter Fasun, Ales Melihen

Shipping and transport
Marko Kosmac, Matej Podlipnik

Energy and infrastructure projects
Marko Kosmac, Matej Podlipnik

THE FIRM

Attorney at law Miro Senica began his legal practice on 1 April 1986. The office gained its reputation in the field of criminal representation, and has grown and developed from year to year with the most notable cases in the field of commercial law. Today, a team of between 35 and 40 is employed at the office, at least 23 of whom are legal experts.

The foundation of the office is its attorneys at law and other professional associates, who work at building up the respect of clients, thus ensuring the success of the practice. Throughout its work, the firm considers clients' individual needs, demands and rights, and searches for creative approaches to find the best solutions. The firm performs with accuracy, consistency and professionalism. It increases its experience through professional training and by retaining a consistently international focus. This allows the firm to represent clients effectively and successfully.

AREAS OF PRACTICE

Attorneys at Law Miro Senica in odvetniki represents clients including leading companies from Slovenia and abroad, banks, insurance companies, brokerage houses, as well as the most demanding individual clients and numerous institutions of public importance.

The office co-operates on a regular basis with numerous well-known and reputed experts, with individual professors from the faculties of law and economics of Ljubljana, as well as with scientific institutions and faculties. For example, the firm works in co-operation with the Economic Institute at the Faculty of Law of Ljubljana, the Commercial Law Institute at the Faculty of Law of Maribor and others.

SCHÖNHERR

TOMŠICEVA 3
1000 LJUBLJANA

Telephone: +386 1 200 0980
Fax: +386 1 426 0711
E-mail: office@schoenherr.si
Website: www.schoenherr.at

Languages
Slovenian, German, English, Croatian, French, Serbian

Number of lawyers 130
at this office 10

Other offices
Belgrade, Brussels, Bucharest, Kyiv, Sofia, Vienna, Zagreb (co-operation office)

Contacts
Michael Lagler (m.lagler@schoenherr.at), Jani Sorsak (j.sorsak@schoenherr.si)

CATEGORIES OF WORK

International and Slovenian practice

International contracts and foreign investment

Banking securities and finance

Project finance

M&A

Privatisations

Public private partnership

Real estate and commercial property

EU law

Competition

WOLF THEISS

TIVOLSKA 30
1000 LJUBLJANA

Telephone: +386 1 438 0000
Fax: +386 1 438 0025
E-mail: ljubljana@wolftheiss.com
Website: www.wolftheiss.com

Languages
Slovenian, German, English

Other offices
Belgrade, Bratislava, Bucharest, Prague, Sarajevo, Tirana, Vienna, Zagreb

Number of lawyers 161
at this office 7

Contacts
Ralf Peschek, Markus Bruckmüller

CATEGORIES OF WORK

Arbitration	**Employment and labour**
Banking, capital markets, securities, project finance, investment funds	**IP**
Corporate and M&A	**Real estate, construction and leasing**

THE FIRM

Wolf Theiss was founded in 1957 in Vienna, and today is one of the leading law firms in the CEE/SEE region. Over the past few years the firm has experienced extraordinarily dynamic growth, both domestically and internationally.

Wolf Theiss has established a network of nine offices* in Albania, Austria, Bosnia and Herzegovina, Croatia, the Czech Republic, Romania, Serbia and Montenegro, Slovakia and Slovenia. In 2005 alone, Wolf Theiss opened two new offices, in Bucharest and Sarajevo. The firm also regularly assists its clients with projects in Bulgaria, Hungary, Macedonia, Moldova, Poland, Turkey and Ukraine, in co-operation with local attorneys.

The firm's dynamic growth is also reflected in its increase in personnal. At present, Wolf Theiss employs over 350 individuals at nine locations – compare this to 30 employees in one office, Vienna, ten years ago and the growth is apparent.

*The firm's operations in the various locations are set up in compliance with local law and the Bar rules requirements which include the form of co-operation with independent local attorneys.

SOUTH AFRICA

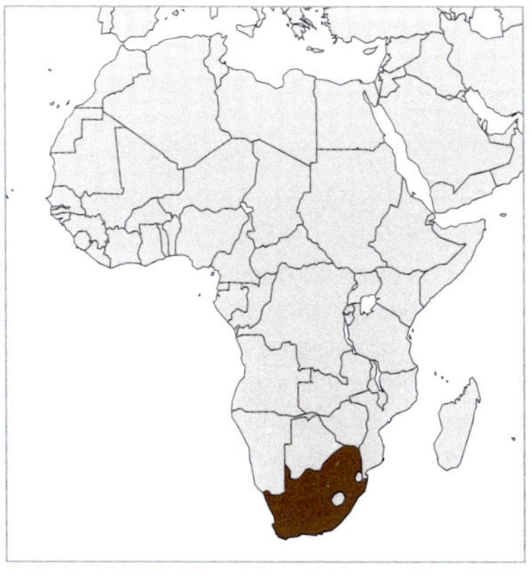

Population	**43.5 million**
Number of lawyers	**n/a**
Professional title	**Lawyer, attorney**
Currency	**Rand**

Index

In the decade since its first full democratic elections, South Africa has enjoyed steady economic growth, substantially reduced its budget deficit, and made significant progress creating a modern liberal welfare state, with a free press and independent judiciary.

The key driver for the economy is mining. South Africa is blessed with unparalleled mineral wealth; being home to nearly half of global gold reserves; and holding significant quantities of other valuable metals and minerals. Such an abundance of commodities offers colossal potential for economic growth. It is estimated that South Africa accounts for about a quarter of Africa's entire wealth.

Serious problems persist: in particular it is the endemic poverty amongst the black and coloured communities which bedevils more progress. Unemployment amongst young black men is very high, crime has proved difficult to bring under control, and the government's handling of the AIDS crisis has attracted extensive criticism. In effect, the economy is split between a first world economy and a third world one, and the country's progress will be determined by how effectively the government can bring those two worlds together.

In order to achieve this, the government has initiated a programme of black economic empowerment (BEE), which seeks to transfer existing wealth from the white community to historically disadvantaged communities.

Black economic empowerment is important to law firms in two ways. Firstly, it has created a surge in instructions from companies operating in South Africa which want to divest shares to black business groups or trusts. The majority of corporate mandates for local firms now involve BEE elements, and such instructions grew by nearly one third in 2004. Some of these deals are very large: the creation of R3.9bn empowered mining company Incwala in 2004 involved **Sonnenberg Hoffmann Galombik**; **Cliffe Dekker Inc**; **Edward Nathan**; **Webber Wentzel Bowens**; **Werksmans Attorneys**; and **Bell, Dewar & Hall Inc.**. Employment advice is increasingly important, so to reflect this we have added an **Employment** section to this chapter.

Secondly, BEE is important to firms because the firms themselves are transforming to reflect the country's ethnic diversity. The government, and increasingly also private companies, restrict instructions to firms that are sufficiently empowered. A firm with up to 25% black partners is termed 'black influenced'; a firm with 25%-50% black partners is 'black empowered'; and with more than 50% black partners is 'black controlled'. This means that good black lawyers are much in demand, and indeed many good black lawyers do leave the big firms to establish their own practices. To reflect this we have a separate **Black controlled firms** section.

LEGAL MARKET

Johannesburg is by far the most important legal centre, followed by Cape Town and then Durban. Many IP boutiques are based in Pretoria.

South Africa has a highly developed legal market, with a good choice of quality firms. Most are general commercial practices, although there are several excellent boutiques in Cape Town. **Winstanley and Cullinana Inc** is a first-class environmental firm, mainly handling litigation. **Walkers** has a history in private client work, and **Michalson's Attorneys** is a niche IT firm of two partners and two associates.

Pretoria-based **Rooth & Wessels Inc** has a substantial property focus. Also in Pretoria, **Consilium Legis** is a transport boutique which often advises the government.

The first foreign firm to open a South African office was **White & Case LLP International Lawyers** in 1995, and on its tenth anniversary demonstrated renewed commitment to its Africa practice by relocating an excellent team from London. **LeBoeuf, Lamb, Greene & MacRae LLP** and **Fasken Martineau DuMoulin LLP** both also have a presence on the ground in Johannesburg, focusing on projects and mining.

In November 2005 **DLA Piper Rudnick Gray Cary UK LLP** entered into an exclusive alliance with **Cliffe Dekker Inc**, which joins the *DLA Piper Group*. **Denton Wilde Sapte** is also rumoured to be interested in link-ups, and continues to advise the Department of Minerals and Energy on the two new IPPs.

Having historically acted for Anglo American and De Beers, **Linklaters** has perhaps the strongest links with corporate South Africa. It has featured on two of the highest-profile recent deals: Gold Fields/Harmony and Absa/Barclays. The firm capped an excellent 2005 with its appointment as lead adviser to the South African government on international capital markets work. **Clifford Chance** advised Barclays on its £2bn takeover of Absa.

Pinsent Masons has a major role advising the government on the Gautrain deal, at R7bn, the largest transport project ever in South Africa. From London, **Freshfields Bruckhaus Deringer** advised Standard Bank and RMB as lead arrangers on the US$1.1bn Gautrain PPP rail project.

Fresh from advising Harmony on its hostile takeover bid for Gold Fields in 2004, **Ashurst** has handled various corporate finance matters for Bidvest; and also for Randgold.

Mayer, Brown, Rowe & Maw LLP has a committed Africa practice and a renowned mining capability, often advising banks. Consultant and environmental expert Michael Hutchinson works from Johannesburg.

BANKING AND FINANCE
BOWMAN GILFILLAN ✪
DENEYS REITZ INC
WEBBER WENTZEL BOWENS
WERKSMANS ATTORNEYS ✪
Bell, Dewar & Hall Inc. ✪
Brink Cohen Le Roux
Cliffe Dekker Inc ✪
Jowell Glyn & Marais
Jurgens Bezuidenhout Attorneys
Sonnenberg Hoffmann Galombik ✪

Firms are listed A-Z in tiers which are ranked in order of priority

✪ *Indicates firm displays contact details at the end of this chapter.*

BLACK CONTROLLED FIRMS
Chuene Kwinana Motsatse Inc
Kathrada Norval Rice Patel Attorneys
Langa Attorneys ✪
Ledwaba & Mazwai
Maponya Inc
Mchunu Koikanyang Attorneys
Mothle Jooma Sabdia
Mukwevho Mkhabela Adekeye Inc
Nalane Manaka Attorneys
Sihlali Molefe Incorporated

Firms are listed alphabetically

✪ *Indicates firm displays contact details at the end of this chapter.*

BILLING

Billing is often based on hourly rates but increasingly sophisticated methods of billing are now being used. Typical rates would be US$65-US$100 for an associate; and up to US$300 for a partner. By international standards, for the quality of lawyers available, this represents excellent value for money, and rates in Cape Town and Durban are even better value.

MARKETING

Each state has its own law society regulating standards, although there are very few restrictions on marketing.

BANKING AND FINANCE

Lex Mundi affiliate **Bowman Gilfillan** has been at the forefront of the finance market for many years, and is trusted by most of the major finance players to handle the most complex transactions. The 31-partner, 71-associate corporate and finance department includes some eminent names, such as Jonathan Schlosberg and Daryn Webb. The firm also has a good Cape Town office and a presence in London.

Deneys Reitz Inc has 21 partners handling finance matters, including partner Lionel Shawe and the very highly thought of head of commercial and banking Kevin Cron. Highlights in 2005 include advising Barclays on its acquisition of Absa Bank for R33bn, South Africa's largest-ever foreign investment; and advising the lenders on the BEE LBO of Afrox Healthcare Limited. Clients include international institutions such as JPMorgan and Deutsche Bank, as well as local names Nedbank and Investec Bank.

In Brigette Baillie, **Webber Wentzel Bowens** has a first-class practitioner, and the firm often attracts major mandates in the banking sector. The firm is advising Absa on its takeover by Barclays; and also advised Citigroup and Liberty on the R7.9bn FirstRand BEE deal. In the more cutting-edge finance areas, such as securitisation and derivatives, the firm has few equals.

Kevin Trudgeon at **Werksmans Attorneys** is considered one of Johannesburg's most accomplished finance lawyers, leading a team with expertise in structured finance, capital markets, securitisation and derivatives. The firm is also active in project finance, regularly gleaning instructions from the South African National Roads Agency.

For mid-market finance transactions, **Bell, Dewar & Hall Inc.** is an excellent choice. Partner Andrew Mitchell also heads one of the country's best project finance practices.

Brink Cohen Le Roux is a solid mid-market player in the finance market. Partner Johan Brink has extensive experience across a range of finance transactions.

Cliffe Dekker Inc is often instructed on major mandates by many foreign banks such as Barclays and ABN Amro, as well as local banks such as Nedbank and Standard Bank. In 2005 the firm acted for the lead arrangers on the inaugural R1bn City of Johannesburg bond issue; and also advised the issuer in the Unitrans note programme.

Jowell Glyn & Marais's name partner Francois Marais is a respected lawyer in Johannesburg. The firm is a mid-sized corporate boutique with acknowledged capability in all types of financing.

Jurgens Bezuidenhout Attorneys is South Africa's only niche finance firm, where Jurgens Bezuidenhout and one other partner handle all types of corporate finance and capital markets transactions.

Sonnenberg Hoffmann Galombik is the only firm with a separate banking department, and acts for all the major banks in South Africa. In addition, premier international institutions such as Deutsche Bank, CSFB, Barclays, and Merrill Lynch are also prominent clients. In 2005 the firm advised Barclays on the huge FirstRand BEE deal.

BLACK CONTROLLED FIRMS

A firm is considered 'black controlled' if more than half its equity is owned by black partners. Many such firms rely on good relations with the public sector, although some are building a more commercial client base. Few black-controlled firms have more than a dozen lawyers so these firms are only offering a high proportion of black partners: many more established non-black firms in fact have higher numbers of black partners. Some of the very best black lawyers have remained at established firms: Mzi Mgudlwa is Johannesburg managing partner of **Sonnenberg Hoffmann Galombik**; and Ezra Davids heads **Bowman Gilfillan**'s corporate department.

For larger transactions the black-controlled firm will usually 'twin' with a more established firm, although the partnerships are not permanent or exclusive. **Chuene Kwinana Motsatse Inc** has made joint bids with **Bowman Gilfillan** on major privatisations and restructurings; **Maponya Inc** often works closely with **Webber Wentzel Bowens**; and **Mothle Jooma Sabdia** has an alliance with **Brink Cohen Le Roux**.

Kathrada Norval Rice Patel Attorneys has six lawyers handling disputes, commercial, regulatory and IT work for a predominantly parastatal client base. In 2005 the firm acted alongside **LeBoeuf, Lamb, Greene & MacRae LLP** advising Eskom on its restructuring. The firm also has a niche in media law.

Langa Attorneys has six lawyers, including the well-respected Themba Langa. Public sector work is the staple, but the firm also advises other types of client such as the soccer team Kaiser Chiefs.

Pretoria-based **Ledwaba & Mazwai** has 17 lawyers, including Metje Ledwaba and Lungile Mazwai. The firm advised the government on toll-way projects and prisons, and continues to advise the government on the Gautrain deal, with **Pinsent Masons** as international counsel.

Johannesburg-based **Mchunu Koikanyang Attorneys** includes Chopologe Koikanyang and former **Werksmans Attorneys**' attorney Titus Mchunu, plus one other partner, five associates and a US-qualified consultant. In 2004 the firm acted on one deal worth more than R500m, and includes amongst its clients South African Airways and Ashanti Goldfields.

From its Johannesburg base **Mukwevho Mkhabela Adekeye Inc** acts for the departments of land affairs and environment on various PPPs. On more general commercial matters the firm also advised the South African Broadcasting Corporation on the Convergence Bill, and Pitsa Ya Setshaba on a joint venture with Russian mining company Renova Group. Justine White is a former **Edward Nathan** lawyer, and partner Leslie Mkhabela is also recommended.

New entry **Nalane Manaka Attorneys** has been involved in some major BEE deals.

Comprising nearly 20 lawyers, including five partners, **Sihlali Molefe Incorporated** is relatively large. Its major recent mandate was advising the Department of Minerals and Energy on new sources of energy, along with **Deneys Reitz Inc** and **Denton Wilde Sapte** as local and international counsel respectively.

CORPORATE AND M&A
Cape Town

While the vast majority of major deals are done from Johannesburg, Cape Town is a centre for shipping, insurance, oil and gas and also asset managers.

Maintaining clear blue water between themselves and Cape rivals, **Sonnenberg Hoffmann Galombik** has more than 120 lawyers in Cape Town, and over 50 in Johannesburg. Executive chairman Piet Faber has created a superb national firm, competing with the top commercial firms in several areas. Tax is a flagship practice area, and the firm is also very strong in the retail sector. A great name internationally is evidenced by its close referral relationships with the likes of **Jones Day**. The firm has a dedicated banking and finance department, and an excellent record on BEE transactions.

With 22 partners, **Bowman Gilfillan**'s Cape Town office is larger than most Johannesburg-based competitors. Commercial work and property are the staples, and the firm's excellent shipping department is also based here. There is further capability in litigation, employment, family and IP.

Cliffe Dekker Inc has 22 partners and nine associates in Cape Town, focusing on property, IP, employment and general commercial. Much work has been done recently for major client Old mutual as well. In 2005 Deputy Chairman Jo Neser acted on a BEE deal for the publishing house Juta & Co; and also for Recaro Seating International (aircraft seat manufacturer) on its acquisition of an interest in Aerodyne Aviation Technology.

Deneys Reitz Inc has developed organically to seven partners and three associates in Cape Town, in contrast to Johannesburg competitors which have grown through merger. The office focuses on insurance and shipping, and has capability across all commercial areas. Highlights in 2005 include advising Aflease Gold and Uranium Resources on several major deals, including its R1.5bn reverse takeover of Southern Cross Resources.

CORPORATE AND M&A
Cape Town

SONNENBERG HOFFMANN GALOMBIK ✪

Bowman Gilfillan ✪
Cliffe Dekker Inc ✪
Deneys Reitz Inc
Jan S De Villiers
Mallinicks Inc
Webber Wentzel Bowens

Fairbridge Arderne & Lawton Inc
Hofmeyr Herbstein & Gihwala Inc
Walkers

Firms are listed A-Z in tiers which are ranked in order of priority
✪ *Indicates firm displays contact details at the end of this chapter.*

Full-service **Jan S De Villiers** historically served the Afrikaner business community, but has successfully diversified its client base of late. Its 28 partners and 20 assistants have a good name for property and insolvency, and major clients include Naspers and Shoprite.

Apart from its premier brand in areas such as property and public law, **Mallinicks Inc** also receives mandates on some of the country's biggest corporate deals. With 18 partners and 40 other lawyers it is one of Cape Town's largest outfits, and in Pierre du Preez has a very good commercial lawyer.

Webber Wentzel Bowens has eight partners in Cape Town focusing on disputes, employment and shipping. Examples of recent work include advising on Standard Chartered's acquisition of the Twenty Twenty division of Saambou Bank; and advising JPMorgan on its acquisition of a subsidiary of Sanlam Bank.

Terralex member **Fairbridge Arderne & Lawton Inc** has 13 partners and 16 other lawyers covering all commercial areas. The firm is well established on the Cape Town scene and has a name for consistent quality.

Building on the old *Herbsteins* brand in Cape Town, **Hofmeyr Herbstein & Gihwala Inc** has since its merger created a truly diverse and original firm. More than 80 lawyers makes it a serious mid-market player, and recent highlights include advising Cape Empowerment Trust on its offer to acquire shares in Cancino Projects.

Walkers is one of oldest firms in the country. It is mainly known for expertise in private client work, but also has a decent general commercial practice.

CORPORATE AND M&A
Johannesburg

M&A activity increased in 2004 and 2005, especially in the context of BEE which continues to provide the bedrock of much corporate work. The largest recent deals include the merger of Sasol and Engen (R12bn); SA Chrome with Xstrata (R8.2bn); and the FirstRand BEE deal (R7.9bn).

CORPORATE AND M&A
Johannesburg

BOWMAN GILFILLAN ✪
CLIFFE DEKKER INC ✪
EDWARD NATHAN
WEBBER WENTZEL BOWENS
WERKSMANS ATTORNEYS ✪

Deneys Reitz Inc
Sonnenberg Hoffmann Galombik ✪

Bell, Dewar & Hall Inc. ✪
Brink Cohen Le Roux
Fluxmans
Hofmeyr Herbstein & Gihwala Inc
Jowell Glyn & Marais
Routledge Modise Moss Morris
Tabacks

Firms are listed A-Z in tiers which are ranked in order of priority
✪ *Indicates firm displays contact details at the end of this chapter.*

Bowman Gilfillan has been at the forefront of the local corporate and commercial market for decades, and is widely considered one of the country's most rounded and reliable full-service firms. A total of 250 lawyers (including 84 partners) receives glowing feedback, often from premier international firms, and the government provides a stream of work too. Jon Schlosberg is the firm's chairman, and head of corporate Ezra Davids has a good name internationally. In 2005 the firm was involved in a range of significant BEE deals, often in the mining sector. Outstanding examples include advising African Rainbow Minerals on its acquisition of a 50% share in Nkomati Nickel Mine by LionOre Mining.

With 31 partners and 13 associates in Johannesburg, **Cliffe Dekker Inc** has experienced strong recent growth and gets excellent feedback for its commitment to client service. Building on its roots in property, the firm now mixes it with the best in corporate: completing more than R13bn in 38 deals in 2004 puts the firm among the corporate elite. Head of corporate Chris Ewing, and Ian Hayes are both very well thought of, handling some epic recent deals: the firm advised Harmony on its hostile £3.5bn takeover bid for Gold Fields; and represented Lonmin on the Incwala BEE deal. **Cliffe Dekker Inc** is the only firm to be appointed by the DTI to advise on BEE good practice.

Making a serious case to be considered South Africa's premier corporate transactional firm, in 2004 **Edward Nathan** for the second successive year took the lion's share of M&A deals: 57 transactions worth in excess of R50bn. This is not surprising given the firm's proximity to dealmaking powerhouse Nedbank, although the firm also excels in other commercial areas such as tax, sports and environmental law. Michael Katz recently advised Gold Fields defending the hostile takeover bid by Harmony, and had a key role on the Sasol/Engen merger. Then in 2005 the firm represented Incwala Group on it award-winning BEE acquisition of interests in Lonmin Group.

Webber Wentzel Bowens is arguably South Africa's premier full-service commercial law firm, offering legal services at the highest level across all practice areas and sectors. Mining is a major strength, as are private equity and financial services. In 2004 the firm acted on more than 40 deals, including some of the country's headline transactions. These included representing Absa on the £2bn takeover by Barclays. Genuine pan-African capability is supplemented by an affiliation with **Maitland**, which has offices in Europe and various offshore jurisdictions.

Werksmans Attorneys is a 100-lawyer firm operating at the apex of the market in its chosen fields: corporate and capital markets; with notable expertise in private equity, property, tax, and litigation. Gareth Driver is head of commercial, and Morné van der Merwe also has a great reputation. Headline deals in 2005 include advising Xstrata on a series of mining deals with Samancor and Merafe worth up to R550m; advising Aspen on the sale of R645m shares to Imithi Investments; and multi-billion rand BEE deals for Mvelaphanda Holdings. **Werksmans Attorneys** also often acts for the government, and although it has only one Johannesburg office, it benefits from membership of the *Lex Africa* network.

With 31 corporate partners, **Deneys Reitz Inc** is an excellent mid-size firm. Traditionally known for mining and insurance, the firm now covers all corporate finance disciplines and project finance to an extremely high standard. As an indication of the firm's stature, Kevin Cron is advising Barclays on its £2bn takeover of 60% of Absa. In 2005 the firm was also acting for a consortium including Ethos Private Equity and Actis Private Equity on an acquisition of parts of Delta Electrical Industries.

Since opening in Johannesburg in 2001, **Sonnenberg Hoffmann Galombik** has made enormous progress, and its involvement in some of the largest corporate finance deals makes it a real player in the national market. Johannesburg head Mzi Mgudlwa leads the team, with clients lavishing praise on the 'legal skills, service, project management skills and general efficiency' of the firm. In almost all commercial areas the firm is equal to the best in South Africa.

Bell, Dewar & Hall Inc. is an excellent mid-tier firm with a great name in projects. In 2004 the firm advised the Lonplats employees on the creation of the empowered mining company Incwala. A further highlight in 2005 was advising the lenders on the Kelvin Power restructuring.

Interlaw member **Brink Cohen Le Roux** has eight partners and eight associates covering general corporate finance and commercial matters. Telkom is a major client.

There are few better option in the mid-market than **Fluxmans**, where head of commercial and CEO Phillip Vallet has moulded an excellent commercial firm. In 2004 the firm acted on 14 deals worth in excess of R24bn, even more in terms of deal value than **Bowman Gilfillan**. In 2005 the firm acted for the scaffolding company Waco International on its JSE listing, with **Linklaters** as global counsel.

Hofmeyr Herbstein & Gihwala Inc is the product of a three-way merger, creating perhaps the most truly diverse South African firm. Ludwig Smith is a good commercially minded lawyer. Examples of important recent work include advising Brimstone on its BEE acquisition of shares in Nedcor and Old Mutual; and advising Makalani Holdings on its R2.5bn JSE listing in 2005.

Jowell Glyn & Marais is a very good, mid-sized corporate firm, consisting of 20 lawyers, including Richard Glyn. The firm handles complex transactions for a predominantly local client base. Investec is the firm's largest client.

Meritas member **Routledge Modise Moss Morris** is a full-service commercial firm, covering areas such as private client and personal injury as well as more mainstream corporate work.

In 2004 **Tabacks** handled corporate deals worth more than R3.5bn. Former **Deneys Reitz Inc** partner Mervyn Taback has built a solid mid-tier corporate firm of about ten lawyers, and in mid-2005 the firm secured something of a coup by tempting corporate partner Chris Stevens from **Deneys Reitz Inc**.

DISPUTE RESOLUTION

Tim Gordon-Grant of **Bowman Gilfillan** is supported by 12 other partners in Johannesburg and Cape Town. The firm is known for its quality and commercially orientated legal advice, and also has notable ADR capability. In 2005 South African Breweries appointed the firm preferred provider of legal services, and the team has extensive experience advising major local names, such as De Beers.

Cliffe Dekker Inc's partner Jonathan Witts-Hewinson is a well-known litigator, admired by peers and clients alike. He is assisted by 15 other lawyers in Johannesburg, and five in the Cape Town office. The team often appears on the most complex and high-profile disputes in various sectors, including banking, construction, mining, insurance and tax.

Deneys Reitz Inc has two of South Africa's finest litigators, and in certain sectors is up there with the best in the country. Jeff Kron is widely admired, and Michael Hart has a great name for insurance and construction disputes. The firm has a good insurance client base of companies such as Eagle Insurance and Mutual & Federal. Examples of recent cases include advising the Ministry of Communication on a major telephone licences dispute; and acting for tobacco manufacturers on product liability.

DISPUTE RESOLUTION

Bowman Gilfillan ✪
Cliffe Dekker Inc ✪
Deneys Reitz Inc
Knowles Husain Lindsay Inc
Sonnenberg Hoffmann Galombik ✪
Webber Wentzel Bowens
Werksmans Attorneys ✪

Firms are listed alphabetically
✪ *Indicates firm displays contact details at the end of this chapter.*

Knowles Husain Lindsay Inc is the litigation arm of corporate powerhouse **Edward Nathan**. Errol Knowles is a well-known and respected litigator. General commercial disputes and property are the key areas. The firm has successfully acted on two major recent hostile takeovers in the courts, appearing successfully in both the Nedcor/Stanbic case, and also in the Gold Fields/Harmony dispute.

Sonnenberg Hoffmann Galombik is a first-class firm for disputes, either in its native Cape Town or in Johannesburg. An experienced team handles all types of commercial disputes in the banking, construction, energy, insurance, and a host of other sectors.

Webber Wentzel Bowens is a top firm for all types of commercial disputes, and in Dairmuid Short has a respected practitioner. The firm also handles politically sensitive cases, and recently acted for Mark Thatcher.

Werksmans Attorneys' litigation department has an outstanding reputation, being instructed on the most important and complex commercial disputes. Des Williams is vice-chairman of the litigation committee of the IBA, and is now the firm's chairman. David Hertz is now head of department, leading 12 directors and 18 other staff. In 2005 the firm is advising Telkom on a major dispute with Telcordia, which is going to the US Court of Appeals.

INTELLECTUAL PROPERTY

With nearly 50 partners and more than 300 total staff, **Adams & Adams** is probably South Africa's largest IP firm. Based in Pretoria, the firm also has offices all around the country, with an impressive client base, and a reputation that is second to none in many areas of IP. Chris Job is chairman, and Colin MacKenzie is head of patents.

Spoor & Fisher is very highly thought of by international clients and firms, especially Charles Webster and Louis Van Wyk, who 'really knows what he's doing'. All IP is covered, and the firm is considered first choice for patents. In 2005 the firm formed an alliance with **Sonnenberg Hoffmann Galombik** for IP-related venture capital transactions. The firm also has a Jersey office.

Bowman Gilfillan has an excellent general intellectual property practice, deriving from the

INTELLECTUAL PROPERTY

ADAMS & ADAMS *Pretoria*
SPOOR & FISHER *Pretoria, Johannesburg*

BOWMAN GILFILLAN ✪ *Johannesburg*
D M KISCH *Johannesburg*
WEBBER WENTZEL BOWENS *Johannesburg*

Burrell's *Johannesburg*
Hahn & Hahn *Pretoria*
McCallum Rademeyer & Friemond *Johannesburg*

Firms are listed A-Z in tiers which are ranked in order of priority
✪ *Indicates firm displays contact details at the end of this chapter.*

LABOUR AND EMPLOYMENT

Bowman Gilfillan ✪
Cheadle Thompson & Haysom Inc
Cliffe Dekker Inc ✪
Deneys Reitz Inc
Perrott, Van Niekerk & Woodhouse Inc
Sonnenberg Hoffmann Galombik ✪
Webber Wentzel Bowens

Firms are listed alphabetically
✪ *Indicates firm displays contact details at the end of this chapter.*

MINING

WEBBER WENTZEL BOWENS

Bell, Dewar & Hall Inc. ✪
Bowman Gilfillan ✪
Cliffe Dekker Inc ✪
Deneys Reitz Inc
Edward Nathan
Fasken Martineau DuMoulin LLP
Tabacks
White & Case LLP International Lawyers

Firms are listed A-Z in tiers which are ranked in order of priority
✪ *Indicates firm displays contact details at the end of this chapter.*

old *John and Kernick* brand. Based in Cape Town, Bastiaan Koster is vice-president of the South African Institute of Intellectual Property Law, and the firm also has capability in Johannesburg. In 2005 the firm acted for Tiger Foods on a successful defence before the appeal committee of the Advertising Standards Authority.

D M Kisch is a decent boutique handling all aspects of intellectual property, and has a particularly good name in the media sector. Although based in Johannesburg the firm also has a Pretoria office.

From Johannesburg, **Webber Wentzel Bowens** handles all aspects of intellectual property for its stellar client base. Partner Ron Wheeldon is a reliable practitioner.

Burrell's is a small niche firm specialising in IP litigation, headed by former **Spoor & Fisher** senior partner Tim Burrell. He is regularly involved in reported cases, and publishes *Burrell's Intellectual Property Law Reports*.

Hahn & Hahn is the intellectual property arm of **Routledge Modise Moss Morris**.

McCallum Rademeyer & Friemond is another firm with solid experience in intellectual property.

LABOUR AND EMPLOYMENT

This is a new section, registering the importance of labour law advice to full-service firms in South Africa. The prominence of BEE deals in recent years has made this an increasingly important area of practice.

Bowman Gilfillan partner John Brand was a pioneer of ADR, and is undoubtedly a leading name. He was a founder of the Independent Mediation Service of South Africa, and has recently facilitated the national wage and working condition negotiation between De Beers and the National Union of Mineworkers. Graham Damant is also a leading practitioner.

Cheadle Thompson & Haysom Inc is well-known for its extensive experience in labour law, with Grant Doble and his team based in Johannesburg, although the firm also has a Cape Town office.

Cliffe Dekker Inc's litigation partner Tim Mills is often involved in reported employment cases. In 2005 the firm advised M-Web on the labour aspects of its acquisition of Tiscali, and subsequent restructuring of the business. The firm is also retained by SAA to act on internal disciplinary hearings.

Deneys Reitz Inc has historically been a leading name in the employment field, and has a reputation for quality, commercially orientated legal advice.

From Johannesburg and Cape Town, employment boutique **Perrott, Van Niekerk & Woodhouse Inc** has seven lawyers advising employers on all aspects of labour law.

Sonnenberg Hoffmann Galombik advises its corporate clients on labour matters in the context of M&A or restructuring. Susan Stelzner is an acting judge in the Labour Court.

With 28 lawyers, **Webber Wentzel Bowens** has one of the country's largest labour departments, mainly acting for employers. The firm also has specialised units for various niches, including health and safety, immigration, and HIV/AIDS.

MINING

Remaining 'unchallenged' at the top of the mining market is **Webber Wentzel Bowens**, which has an awesome corporate practice and clear commitment to the mining sector. Manus Booysen and Peter Leon are both on the IBA's mining law committee, although Bruce Cleaver has left to go in-house at De Beers. The firm has been principal lawyers to De Beers and Anglo American for decades.

Bell, Dewar & Hall Inc. is a new entry for mining. The firm often acts for lenders on major mining deals: a notable recent example was the R1.5bn Palabora Mining Co refinancing. The firm has also recently advised Placer Dome on the South Deep Project.

Bowman Gilfillan has been active on a range of significant BEE deals in the mining sector. The firm is close to African Rainbow Minerals, and recently advised it on its acquisition of a 50% share in Nkomati Nickel Mine by LionOre Mining; and also acted on the sale by Harmony to an empowerment trust of 14% of African Rainbow Minerals, to the value of R800m.

Cliffe Dekker Inc acted on two of the most significant mining deals of the year: representing Harmony on its hostile £3.5bn takeover bid for Gold Fields; and advising Lonmin on the Incwala BEE deal.

Michael Dale at **Deneys Reitz Inc** is a distinguished expert on mining law, and acts for the Chamber of Mines of South Africa. The firm frequently represents major mining houses such as BHP Billiton and AngloPlat on general corporate and commercial matters.

Edward Nathan's powerful corporate department sees it regularly appear on major mining deals. In 2004 the firm advised Gold Fields defending the hostile takeover bid by Harmony; then in 2005 represented Incwala Group on its award-winning BEE acquisition of interests in Lonmin Group. Other mining clients include Falconbridge and Ridge Mining.

Canadian firm **Fasken Martineau DuMoulin LLP** has experience in the global mining market, and mainly acts for Canadian mining companies looking to invest into South Africa; and also for South African entities seeking international finance in the mining sector. Peter Stafford QC is supported by one other associate and a consultant, plus assistance from London when necessary.

Newly recommended is **Tabacks**, which has made a notable push into the mining sector with the recruitment of Chris Stevens from **Deneys Reitz Inc**. The firm undertakes some work for BHP Billiton.

Another new addition is **White & Case LLP International Lawyers**, where Tenneke Heersche is vice-chair of the mining committee of the IBA.

PROJECTS AND INFRASTRUCTURE

The South African government initiated a programme of PPPs in 2000, with more than 50 projects completed or in the pipeline. By far the largest is the Gautrain train deal, which is expected to close late 2005. Now talk is of the two IPPs: a 750MW power station in Eastern Cape, and a 250MW project in Durban.

Bell, Dewar & Hall Inc. has made an indelible mark on the market: clear commitment to projects over some years has produced a mature and

PROJECTS AND INFRASTRUCTURE

Bell, Dewar & Hall Inc. ✪
Bowman Gilfillan ✪
Deneys Reitz Inc
Edward Nathan
LeBoeuf, Lamb, Greene & MacRae LLP ✪
Webber Wentzel Bowens
Werksmans Attorneys ✪
White & Case LLP International Lawyers

Firms are listed alphabetically
✪ *Indicates firm displays contact details at the end of this chapter.*

rounded practice, usually acting for lenders. Andrew Mitchell is a sound practitioner, and has been involved in all but one of the major recent PPPs. Recent deals include advising the borrowers on the R2bn Trac refinancing, and the SARS container scanner project.

Bowman Gilfillan has unparalleled expertise in projects, and in Claire Tucker and Daryn Webb two of Johannesburg's top lawyers, who are, according to clients 'very easy to work with'. 2005 highlights include advising the lenders Standard Bank and RMB on the US$1.1bn Gautrain PPP rail project, with **Freshfields Bruckhaus Deringer**; and advice on the Maloti Drakensburg Transfrontier biodiversity project. The firm will also have a prominent role on the new wave of IPPs.

Deneys Reitz Inc is active on high-profile IPPs for the Department of Minerals and Energy, with **Denton Wilde Sapte** as international counsel. Generally the firm tends to act for concessionaires, and in Kevin Cron and Clair Corke has two widely respected practitioners. More than most firms **Deneys Reitz Inc** is exporting its projects skills all around Africa.

Edward Nathan has a history advising African governments on projects, and in 2005 was instructed by the Kenyan government to advise on the IPO of power utility KenGen. Robyn Stein is a renowned environmental expert; he has often worked in the past for local and national governments all around Africa.

Greg Nott heads **LeBoeuf, Lamb, Greene & MacRae LLP**'s office, aided by three associates. Exploiting the firm's global brand in energy, the firm is working on various African projects, as well as some inward commercial investment. Major deals in recent years have included the Mozambique port project, and advising empowerment group INZA on the Ellis Park Sporting Precinct project. Eksom is an important client.

Webber Wentzel Bowens has one of the country's top projects practices, and in Brigette Baillie an internationally renowned practitioner. The firm has the size and capability to handle projects to the highest international standards, and is seeking to export its expertise around the continent. A continuing highlight is advising the sponsors (the Bombela consortium of Bombardier, Bouyges, Murray & Roberts and RATP) on the US$1.1bn Gautrain PPP rail project.

Werksmans Attorneys represents the South African National Roads Agency on PPPs, including most recently the N3 and N4 toll road projects; and the Platinum Corridor toll road project. The firm is also one of the best bets for complex structured finance.

White & Case LLP International Lawyers partner John Janks continues to advise the government on PPPs, and is currently acting for national power provider Eksom on two new IPPs. In 2005 the firm beefed up its local office, to exploit its potential as a hub for African infrastructure and power deals. Formerly metals and mining co-head in London, Tanneke Heersche relocated to Johannesburg with three associates to make a nine-lawyer office. The firm is currently advising East Coast Energy on the Songo gas-to-electricity project in Tanzania; and is also advising the Mozambique government on the Moatize coal project.

SHIPPING

South Africa is one of the world's favoured jurisdictions for ship arrests, and firms in the ports of Cape Town and Durban are regularly instructed on maritime matters around all of Africa.

From its Durban base, **Garlicke & Bousfield**'s shipping, transport and international trade department includes five partners and one assistant, including Steven Wallace and Tony Norton, who is chair of the South African branch of the Institute of Chartered Shipbrokers. The firm handles all aspects of shipping to the highest international standards. In 2005 the team acted for Fortis Bank as mortgagee on the sale of the vessel *Olympia Countess*.

Shepstone & Wylie is undoubtedly one of South Africa's top maritime practices, acting for a lot of P&I clubs and shipowners on major shipping matters throughout the continent. The 'excellent' Shane Dwyer and Krish Reddy and seven other lawyers in Durban (with another five in Cape Town) receive good feedback from London firms. In recent months the team has acted for P&I clubs and owners in the following casualties: *BBC China*; *High Spirit*; *MSC Katie*; and *MSC Lauren*.

Bowman Gilfillan's Cape Town office has a solid client base of shipowners, P&I clubs and underwriters. Craig Cunningham and Graham Charnock are highly recommended, as is John Dyason, who is now vice-president of the Maritime Law Association of South Africa. The team often acts on casualties (recently on the *Bos 400* case); and also on the collision between *Decurion* and *Giovanna*.

DJ Dickinson & Associates is a niche maritime outfit based in Durban. Name partner Dave Dickinson is a well-known expert on all aspects of shipping law.

Andrew Robinson of **Deneys Reitz Inc** is chairman of the Durban chapter of the Maritime Law Association of South Africa, and the firm also has capability in Cape Town. The firm is renowned for its strong insurance client base, and has a good record on the cargo side. 2005 highlights include advising the owners and underwriters on the loss of *BBC China*; the underwriters on the loss of *Kiperousa*; and the underwriters on the grounding of the *Sealand Express*.

SHIPPING

GARLICKE & BOUSFIELD *Durban*
SHEPSTONE & WYLIE *Durban*

Bowman Gilfillan ✪ *Cape Town*
DJ Dickinson & Associates *Durban*
Deneys Reitz Inc *Cape Town, Durban*
Fairbridge Arderne & Lawton Inc *Cape Town*
Routledge Modise Moss Morris *Durban*
Webber Wentzel Bowens *Cape Town*

Firms are listed A-Z in tiers which are ranked in order of priority
✪ *Indicates firm displays contact details at the end of this chapter.*

Cape Town-based **Fairbridge Arderne & Lawton Inc**'s shipping and international trade department has six partners, including Fiona Stewart and Mike Tucker. Usually representing owners in casualty cases, recent examples include the *Sealand Express* and the *Ouro do Brasil* cases, and for the salvors on the *Cape Africa* salvage. The firm also represents numerous P&I clubs, such as British Marine and Mitsui, as well as local fishing companies.

Routledge Modise Moss Morris's Durban shipping department was poached from **Adams & Adams** in October 2004. The team tends to act on the cargo side, and includes Mike Posemann, who is president of the South African Maritime Law Association. Clients include the London Maritime Arbitrators Association.

From its Cape Town office, **Webber Wentzel Bowens** has three partners and four associates in its maritime and international trade law department. Patrick Holloway is a recognised authority. In 2005 the team acted for the government of Azerbaijan in the *Bos 400* case; and for the owners in the *Juno Trader* case.

TAX

The Big Four accountants take the lion's share of tax work in South Africa, but most law firms also have significant tax capability. Recent years have witnessed a high level of recruitment from the accountants into law firms, and in 2005 a new Tax Court was opened.

With one of the country's top corporate departments and mandates on many of the last year's biggest and most complex deals, **Edward Nathan** fully deserves its top-tier ranking for tax. The firm has two eminent individuals: Emil Brincker is a member of the Special Board for Income Tax Appeals; and Michael Katz is chair of the Tax Advisory Committee to the Minister of Finance.

TAX

EDWARD NATHAN
SONNENBERG HOFFMANN GALOMBIK ✪
WERKSMANS ATTORNEYS ✪
Bowman Gilfillan ✪
Deneys Reitz Inc
Webber Wentzel Bowens

Firms are listed A-Z in tiers which are ranked in order of priority

✪ Indicates firm displays contact details at the end of this chapter.

With more than 40 fee-earners, **Sonnenberg Hoffmann Galombik** has South Africa's biggest tax department, and is arguably the premier tax firm in the country. From Johannesburg, highly recommended partners Bernard du Plessis and Peter Dachs head the department. In 2005 the firm advised on the tax implications of Elephant Consortium's acquisition of R3.5bn shares in Telkom.

Frequently cited as a first-class tax practice, **Werksmans Attorneys** offers tax servicesthrough its subsidiary Werksmans Tax (Proprietary) Limited.The firm has made a big push into tax in recent years, and draws on one of the country's most prestigious corporate brands and enjoys the support of a premier litigation name. Ernest Mazansky and Paul Ferreira are the key contacts.

Bowman Gilfillan inevitably advises on the tax implications of the major M&A transactions it has recently handled, including transactional advice for clients such as Alcatel, SA Chrome and IBM. Alan Keep heads the practice.

Deneys Reitz Inc is a sound choice for all aspects of tax law, both structuring and litigation. Kevin Cron is a very experienced corporate lawyer. Highlights in 2005 include contesting a claim for R13m in taxes in respect of visiting foreign artists for Big Concerts International.

Webber Wentzel Bowens enjoys a superb corporate client base, for which it advises on tax structuring and disputes. Major tax clients include Tiger Brands, De Beers and AngloGold Ashanti. For personal tax matters, the firm is affiliated to **Maitland**.

CLIFFE DEKKER

11TH FLOOR, THE WALDORF
80 ST GEORGE'S MALL
CAPE TOWN 8001

Telephone: +27 21 481 6300
Fax: +27 21 424 5801
E-mail: ctn@cliffe-dekker.com
Website: www.cliffedekker.com

Languages
Afrikaans, English

Other offices
Johannesburg

Number of lawyers 104
at this office 45

Contact
Jo Neser (deputy chairman)

CATEGORIES OF WORK

Corporate and commercial
Jo Neser, David Thompson

Litigation and arbitration
Nick Muller

Mergers and acquisitions
Jo Neser

Employment (labour)
Jacques van Wyk

Competition
David Thompson

Technology and e-commerce
Emma Kingdon

Property/real estate
John Gomes

Black economic empowerment
Brent Williams

Media
Emma Kingdon

SONNENBERG HOFFMANN GALOMBIK

SHG HOUSE
1 NORTH WHARF SQUARE
LOOP STREET
FORESHORE
CAPE TOWN 8001

Telephone: +27 21 410 2500
Fax: +27 21 410 2555
E-mail: info@shg.co.za
Website: www.shg.co.za

Languages
Afrikaans, English, French, German, Indian languages, Portuguese, Shona, Sotho, Spanish, Swazi, Tswana, Xhosa, Zulu

Other offices
Durban, Johannesburg, Mitchells Plain

Number of lawyers 111
at this office 77

Contact
Piet Faber (executive chairman)

CATEGORIES OF WORK

Antitrust and competition
Robert Appelbaum, Wouter Meyer

Banking and finance
Deon de Klerk, Roger Rudolph

Black economic empowerment
Mzi Mgudlwa, Piet Faber

Corporate and commercial/M&A
Koos Pretorious, Lawrence Helman, Robert Appelbaum

Forensics
Steve Powell, Andre Bouwer

Healthcare and pharmaceutical
Lawrence Helman, Robert Appelbaum

Immigration
George van Niekerk, Zahida Ebrahim

Insolvency, business rescue and debt recovery
Leonard Katz, Gary Oertel

Integrated employment solutions
Susan Stelzner, Rod Harper

International trade
Leon Steenkamp, Wally Horak

Litigation/dispute resolution
John Zieff, Brian Biebuyck, Cecil Gelbart

Media, entertainment and sport
Brian Biebuyck, Vivien Chaplin

Real estate/property
Allison Alexander, Deon de Klerk, Charles Smith

Shipping
Janine Lee, Thato Tsautse

Tax (international)
Peter Dachs, Bernard du Plessis, Wally Horak

Transfer pricing
Jens Brodbeck

THE FIRM

Sonnenberg Hoffmann Galombik (SHG) was established in 1936 and is one of the largest corporate law firms in Africa, with 111 lawyers. The firm believes in, and implements, a process of multi-disciplinary teams whereby experts are drawn together from a multitude of disciplines to solve problems. This combination of legal, financial, tax, commercial and forensics skills is one of SHG's key differentiators in the market.

SHG operates from its Johannesburg, Cape Town, Durban and Mitchells Plain offices and services some of Africa's largest companies and institutions, as well as a number of international companies doing business in Africa. SHG is the law firm with the largest and most comprehensive tax department in South Africa and provides a full range of tax advice. SHG is a firm of diverse people and its dedication to transformation has served to further entrench its position as one of the top law firms in the country.

AREAS OF PRACTICE

SHG's main practice areas are antitrust and competition; banking and finance; black economic empowerment; business advisory services; corporate and commercial; fishing and marine resources; forensics; franchising; healthcare and pharmaceutical; immigration; insolvency; business rescue and debt recovery; integrated employment solutions; international trade; JSE/SRP/regulatory; litigation (dispute resolution); media, entertainment and sport; mergers and acquisitions; oil and gas; private client; real estate/property; retail; shipping; swaps and derivatives; tax (corporate, international, personal, VAT and indirect tax); technology; telecommunications; transfer pricing; and transport and logistics.

SHG's client base includes Deutsche Bank, Credit Suisse First Boston, Barclays Bank, Standard Chartered Bank, Merrill Lynch, ArvinMeritor, BP (Southern Africa), SITA, Cargill, Xerox, Toyota, DHL, Estée Lauder, Mvelaphanda, South Africa's national government (Treasury), numerous companies listed on the JSE, including most of South Africa's major retailers, a range of foreign-based merchant banks, investment banks, asset managers and financial services groups, producers and distributors and international oil companies.

Some of SHG's current rankings include being rated first in the large legal firms category of PMR's 2005 survey of South African legal firms; named the top law firm to offer tax advice in South Africa by the *International Tax Review's* World Tax 2005 and 2006 surveys; named as one of the country's top empowerment companies by Impumelelo (Top Empowerment Companies) in 2005/06; described as 'one of the very few law firms to have been successfully transformed' in UK legal publication *In Brief* in April 2005; and described as 'one of the big four law firms in South Africa and one of the '*Magic Circle*' corporate law firms in South Africa' in the *Without Prejudice* legal publication in 2005.

SHG advises corporate clients in relation to their South African and broader African activities. These include advising foreign-based and national corporate companies on their local and cross-border activities, both into Southern Africa and elsewhere in Africa. Recent major transactions include advising: GUS plc and Lewis group Limited in regard to the initial public offering and subsequent listing of certain of the shares in Lewis on the JSE Securities Exchange South Africa; advising the National Treasury and acting as SA counsel to the underwriters in respect of the South African Government US$1 billion Global Note Offering; the South African government on its foreign capital markets activities; BP plc in relation to the sale of a 25% minority interest in its local subsidiary to black economic empowerment investors; a number of foreign-based merchant banks on their South African lending and capital markets activities; the distress debt activities elsewhere in Africa of the Johannesburg branch of a foreign merchant bank; the structuring of a new private equity fund for a leading fund manager; and advising an international merchant bank on its proposed cross-border leasing activities.

BELL, DEWAR & HALL INC.

37 WEST STREET
HOUGHTON
JOHANNESBURG 2001

Telephone: +27 11 710 6000
Fax: +27 11 710 6104
E-mail: bdh@belldewar.co.za
Website: www.belldewar.co.za

Languages
English

Number of lawyers 56

Member
American Law Firms Association (ALFA)

CATEGORIES OF WORK

Financial services
Andrew Mitchell, Blaize Vance

Environment
Christo Reeders, Donovan Smith

Corporate and commercial
David Hoffe, Andrew Leontsinis

Dispute resolution
Duncan Sinclair, Nic Roodt

Competition
Stephen Langbridge, Donovan Smith

Tax
Blaize Vance, Conor McFadden

Employment and pensions
Nigel Carman, Paul Fouche

BOWMAN GILFILLAN

165 WEST STREET
SANDTON
JOHANNESBURG

Telephone: +27 11 669 9000
Fax: +27 11 669 9001
Website: www.bowman.co.za

Other offices
Cape Town, London

Number of lawyers 250

Contacts
Leon Kruger (CEO) (l.kruger@bowman.co.za), Jonathan Schlosberg (Chairman) (j.schlosberg@bowman.co.za)

CATEGORIES OF WORK

Corporate, commercial and financial services

Litigation and arbitration

Dispute resolution

Employment law

Intellectual property

Real estate and conveyancing

Maritime and transport

Family law

THE FIRM

Bowman Gilfillan is a corporate law firm with 83 partners, more than 250 lawyers and a total staff complement of over 500. The firm operates from offices in Johannesburg (Sandton), Cape Town and London. Bowman Gilfillan is widely respected and recognised for its professionalism and for providing legal services of a high quality. It is generally regarded as one of the premier law firms in South Africa and it was voted as the 2003/04 African Corporate Law Firm of the Year by UK legal publishers *Chambers and Partners;* and was a runner up in 2005/06. The firm was also voted as the 'Top Company of the Year' in the support services category for 2004 at the South African Business Awards and as an 'Ideal Employer to work for' in the legal category by a graduate survey in 2005. In addition the firm has won the International Law Office 'Client Choice Award' for South Africa for 2005.

Bowman Gilfillan's strengths lie in the breadth, quality and diversity of its professional staff and its emphasis on the quality of the legal services it renders.

AREAS OF PRACTICE

Corporate, commercial and financial services: Bowman Gilfillan has played a significant role in South Africa's emergence in the global market and has been pivotal in several of the country's groundbreaking corporate and financial services transactions. The firm's expertise covers capital markets (debt and equity) and derivatives; corporate and commercial law; competition (antitrust); privatisations, corporatisations and restructuring of state assets; mergers, acquisitions and takeovers; private equity; banking and finance; project finance and infrastructure development; public private partnership; asset-based finance; insolvency law and security transactions; telecommunications, regulatory, government affairs; environmental, energy and mining; aviation and tax.

Litigation, arbitration and all other forms of dispute resolution are long-established areas of specialisation at Bowman Gilfillan. The firm's approach is to reach a quick, definitive and effective resolution, whether this is achieved through negotiation, mediation, arbitration or litigation.

Employment law: this is probably the largest practice of its kind in South Africa. Collectively this department offers effective, progressive and innovative advice in all aspects of employment and labour law.

Intellectual property: Bowman Gilfillan is the only non-niche law firm in South Africa to have such a large and comprehensive IP department. The department's expertise covers all aspects of patents, trade marks, copyright and designs.

Other areas of expertise include real estate and conveyancing and maritime and transport.

CLIFFE DEKKER

1 PROTEA PLACE
SANDOWN
SANDTON 2196
JOHANNESBURG

Telephone: +27 11 290 7000
Fax: +27 11 290 7300
E-mail: jhb@cliffedekker.com
Website: www cliffedekker.com

Languages
Afrikaans, Dutch, English

Other offices
Cape Town

Number of lawyers 104
at this office 58

Contact
Chris Ewing (chairman)

CATEGORIES OF WORK

Corporate and commercial
Chris Ewing, Ian Hayes

Banking and securities
Hans Evenhuis

Finance
Joz Coetzer

Mergers and acquisitions
Chris Ewing

Telecommunications and media
Janet MacKenzie

Technology and e-commerce
Preeta Bhagattjee

Commercial property/real estate
Hugh Jackson

Litigation and arbitration
Jonathan Witts-Hewinson, Sam Oosthuizen

Competition
Jean Meijer

Black economic empowerment
Kevin Lester

Employment
Tim Mills

Aviation
Sam Oosthuizen

Insolvency and restructuring
Jonathan Witts-Hewinson

THE FIRM

From its beginnings in 1853, Cliffe Dekker has grown to become one of South Africa's (SA's) most prominent, full service commercial law firms. It is, today, a national firm, with regional offices in SA's major financial centres, Johannesburg and Cape Town, and is also one of SA's largest law firms, with 54 directors and 104 lawyers.

Cliffe Dekker is consistently ranked as a first-rate firm in authoritative local and international journals. It is the only law firm in SA to have been voted by corporates as the No 1 Large Law Firm for an unprecedented three years in a row (2004, 2005 and 2006). For two consecutive years (2004 and 2005), Cliffe Dekker was the Legal Advisor on the M&A 'Deal of the Year'. It was the runner-up in the 2005 Chambers Global Law Firm of the Year, Africa awards category.

Cliffe Dekker is the member firm in SA of DLA Piper Group, an alliance of legal practices.

AREAS OF PRACTICE

Cliffe Dekker provides an extensive range of legal services, with a principal focus on corporate and commercial work. It is one of SA's leading M&A practices and has one of the largest corporate practices.

Cliffe Dekker advises corporate clients in domestic and cross-border M&A transactions. The firm has particuar international expertise in private equity transactions and leveraged buy-outs; it has handled international M&A transactions for clients in the mineral and petroleum resources, banking and financial services, pharmaceutical, automotive, media and hospitality and leisure industries. On its website, Cliffe Dekker publishes a comprehensive guide to business and investment in SA.

The firm has significant expertise in banking and finance and acts for most SA banks and most major foreign banks that have local branches. Its competition/antitrust team is the firm's fastest growing specialist department. The litigation department comprises 15 directors, who specialise in diverse fields such as banking, construction law, mining, insurance, administrative law, tax, insolvency and aviation, among others. The TMT unit is made up of specialist telecommunications, IT, e-business and media lawyers, who provide end-to-end legal and business solutions and also assist local and international clients with their intellectual property, trademark and copyright issues.

A constant focus remains to offer pragmatic solutions to help clients deal with the complexities of transacting in SA's increasingly regulated business environment. The firm has developed considerable expertise in the field of black economic empowerment (BEE) – a signifcant factor in all national M&A activity – and its website literature relating to this field has achieved widespread recognition from government and business leaders.

The firm also has acknowledged expertise in employment/labour law and its real estate/property practice serves the needs of developers, investors, corporations and the residential market.

LANGA ATTORNEYS

**423 JAN SMUTS AVENUE
BLAIRGOWRIE
RANDBURG 2125
JOHANNESBURG**

Telephone: +27 11 886 8926/7588
Fax: +27 11 787 7214
E-mail: langa@langaattorneys.co.za
Website: www.langaattorneys.co.za

Languages
English

Number of lawyers 6

Contacts
Themba Langa (langa@langaattorneys.co.za), Jabu Maswanganye (jabu@langaattorneys.co.za), Lydia Shadrach (lydia@langaattorneys.co.za)

CATEGORIES OF WORK

Sports law
Themba Langa, Tshepo Kganane

Commercial law
Themba Langa, Maboi Molepo, Mongezi Ntanga

Corporate law
Themba Langa, Tshepo Kganane

Liquidations
Mmatsatsi Sefalafala, Maboi Molepo

Project finance
Themba Langa, Jabu Maswanganye, Tiledi Kekana

Litigation
MB Mohlahedi, Maboi Molepo, Mmatsatsi Sefalafala

Financial services law
Themba Mohoto, Jabu Maswanganye

Mining law
Themba Langa

Property Law
Themba Langa

LEBOEUF, LAMB, GREENE & MACRAE LLP

**11 ALICE LANE, 2ND FLOOR
WEST WING
STANDARD BANK BUILDING
SANDTON 2196
JOHANNESBURG**

Telephone: +27 11 784 0233
Fax: +27 11 784 2855
E-mail: gnott@llgm.com
Website: www.llgm.com

Languages
Afrikaans, English, French, German, IsiZulu, Kiswahili

Other offices
Albany, Almaty, Beijing, Boston, Brussels, Chicago, Hartford, Houston, Jacksonville, London, Los Angeles, Moscow, New York, Paris, Pittsburg, Riyadh, San Francisco, Washington DC

Number of lawyers 650+
at this office 4

Contact
Gregory A Nott

CATEGORIES OF WORK

Corporate
Rajen Ranchhoojee, Lerato Mokgosi, Mary Chege-Mwangi, Gregory A Nott

Energy
Gregory A Nott

International
Gregory A Nott, Lerato Mokgosi, Mary Chenge-Mwangi

Litigation
Gregory A Nott, Rajen Ranchhoojee

Project and infrastructure finance
Gregory A Nott, Mary Chege-Mwangi

Telecommunications
Gregory A Nott, Mary Chege-Mwangi, Rajen Ranchhoojee

SONNENBERG HOFFMANN GALOMBIK

GROUND FLOOR
ABN AMRO HOUSE
85 MAUDE STREET
SANDTON 2196
JOHANNESBURG

Telephone: +27 11 669 8000
Fax: +27 11 669 8111
E-mail: info@shg.co.za
Website: www.shg.co.za

Languages
Afrikaans, English, French, German, Indian languages, Portuguese, Shona, Sotho, Spanish, Swazi, Tswana, Xhosa, Zulu

Other offices
Cape Town, Durban, Mitchells Plain

Number of lawyers 111
at this office 32

Contact
Piet Faber (executive chairman)

CATEGORIES OF WORK

Antitrust and competition
Robert Appelbaum, Wouter Meyer

Banking and finance
Deon de Klerk, Roger Rudolph

Black economic empowerment
Mzi Mgudlwa, Piet Faber

Corporate and commercial/M&A
Koos Pretorious, Lawrence Helman, Robert Appelbaum

Forensics
Steve Powell, Andre Bouwer

Healthcare and pharmaceutical
Lawrence Helman, Robert Appelbaum

Immigration
George van Niekerk, Zahida Ebrahim

Insolvency, business rescue and debt recovery
Leonard Katz, Gary Oertel

Integrated employment solutions
Susan Stelzner, Rod Harper

International trade
Leon Steenkamp, Wally Horak

Litigation/dispute resolution
John Zieff, Brian Biebuyck, Cecil Gelbart

Media, entertainment and sport
Brian Biebuyck, Vivien Chaplin

Real estate/property
Allison Alexander, Deon de Klerk, Charles Smith

Shipping
Janine Lee, Thato Tsautse

Tax (international)
Peter Dachs, Bernard du Plessis, Wally Horak

Transfer pricing
Jens Brodbeck

THE FIRM

Sonnenberg Hoffmann Galombik (SHG) was established in 1936 and is one of the largest corporate law firms in Africa, with 111 lawyers. The firm believes in, and implements, a process of multi-disciplinary teams whereby experts are drawn together from a multitude of disciplines to solve problems. This combination of legal, financial, tax, commercial and forensics skills is one of SHG's key differentiators in the market.

SHG operates from its Johannesburg, Cape Town, Durban and Mitchells Plain offices and services some of Africa's largest companies and institutions, as well as a number of international companies doing business in Africa. SHG is the law firm with the largest and most comprehensive tax department in South Africa and provides a full range of tax advice. SHG is a firm of diverse people and its dedication to transformation has served to further entrench its position as one of the top law firms in the country.

AREAS OF PRACTICE

SHG's main practice areas are antitrust and competition; banking and finance; black economic empowerment; business advisory services; corporate and commercial; fishing and marine resources; forensics; franchising; healthcare and pharmaceutical; immigration; insolvency; business rescue and debt recovery; integrated employment solutions; international trade; JSE/SRP/regulatory; litigation (dispute resolution); media, entertainment and sport; mergers and acquisitions; oil and gas; private client; real estate/property; retail; shipping; swaps and derivatives; tax (corporate, international, personal, VAT and indirect tax); technology; telecommunications; transfer pricing; and transport and logistics.

SHG's client base includes Deutsche Bank, Credit Suisse First Boston, Barclays Bank, Standard Chartered Bank, Merrill Lynch, ArvinMeritor, BP (Southern Africa), SITA, Cargill, Xerox, Toyota, DHL, Estée Lauder, Mvelaphanda, South Africa's national government (Treasury), numerous companies listed on the JSE, including most of South Africa's major retailers, a range of foreign-based merchant banks, investment banks, asset managers and financial services groups, producers and distributors and international oil companies.

Some of SHG's current rankings include being rated first in the large legal firms category of PMR's 2005 survey of South African legal firms; named the top law firm to offer tax advice in South Africa by the *International Tax Review's* World Tax 2005 and 2006 surveys; named as one of the country's top empowerment companies by Impumelelo (Top Empowerment Companies) in 2005/06; described as 'one of the very few law firms to have been successfully transformed' in UK legal publication *In Brief* in April 2005; and described as 'one of the big four law firms in South Africa and one of the '*Magic Circle*' corporate law firms in South Africa' in the *Without Prejudice* legal publication in 2005.

SHG advises corporate clients in relation to their South African and broader African activities. These include advising foreign-based and national corporate companies on their local and cross-border activities, both into Southern Africa and elsewhere in Africa. Recent major transactions include advising: GUS plc and Lewis group Limited in regard to the initial public offering and subsequent listing of certain of the shares in Lewis on the JSE Securities Exchange South Africa; advising the National Treasury and acting as SA counsel to the underwriters in respect of the South African Government US$1 billion Global Note Offering; the South African government on its foreign capital markets activities; BP plc in relation to the sale of a 25% minority interest in its local subsidiary to black economic empowerment investors; a number of foreign-based merchant banks on their South African lending and capital markets activities; the distress debt activities elsewhere in Africa of the Johannesburg branch of a foreign merchant bank; the structuring of a new private equity fund for a leading fund manager; and advising an international merchant bank on its proposed cross-border leasing activities.

WERKSMANS ATTORNEYS

155 5TH STREET
SANDOWN, SANDTON 2196
PRIVATE BAG 10015
SANDTON 2146
JOHANNESBURG

Telephone: +27 11 535 8000
Fax: +27 11 535 8600
Website: www.werksmans.co.za

Languages
English, Afrikaans, German, French

Number of lawyers 95

CATEGORIES OF WORK

Commercial/M&A
Carl Stein, Gareth Driver

Banking and finance
Wildu du Plessis, Kevin Trudgeon

Litigation
Des Williams, David Hertz

Property
Frans van Hoogstraten, Brian Kew

Tax
Ernest Mazansky

Corporate recoveries
Paul Winer, Eric Levenstein

Liquidation and insolvency
Paul Winer, Eric Levenstein

Competition
Pieter Steyn, Desmond Rudman

Technology
David Walker

Information technology and intellectual property
David Walker, Eric Levenstein

Media law
Amanda Armstrong

Mining law
Hulme Scholes

SPAIN

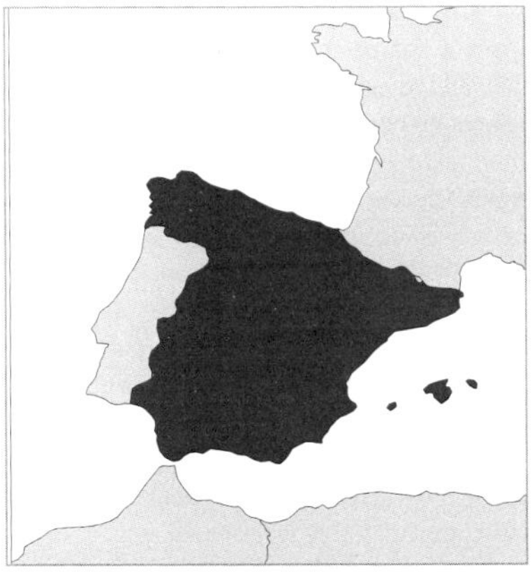

Population	**42.3 million**
Number of lawyers	**105,000**
Professional title	**Abogado**
Currency	**Euro (€)**

Index

Mainland Spain occupies most of the Iberian Peninsula (shared with Portugal and Gibraltar) and the country also includes the Balearic Islands and the Canary Islands, as well as Ceuta and Melilla on the coast of North Africa. It is the second-largest country in the EU after France, and is divided into 17 *comunidades autónomas* (administrative regions) with directly elected authorities.

King Juan Carlos has been Head of State since the death of General Franco in 1975. Prime Minister José Luis Rodríguez Zapatero, of the centre-left Spanish Socialist Workers Party, heads a minority government that won the 2004 election (just days after the Madrid terrorist attacks), following eight years of government under the country's right-of-centre Popular Party. Demands for increased independence from a number of the *comunidades autónomas* are a source of some political instability.

ECONOMY

Spain's economy – driven by Madrid and Barcelona – is the thirteenth largest in the world and the fifth largest in the EU, behind Germany, the UK, France and Italy. GDP for 2004 was just over US$1bn, marking a growth rate of 3.3% for the five-year period from 2000, although growth is forecast to slow to 2.4% by 2007. Unemployment, though falling, is among the highest in the EU at around the 11% mark, and income per capita is around four-fifths of the EU average.

Tourism, financial services, property development and electronics are all key growth sectors in the economy, and vehicle production is a major manufacturing industry. While the country has diversified away from its agricultural roots, it remains an important producer of wine (the third largest in the world), olive oil and fruit among other products.

Spain was one of the group of countries which launched the European single currency in 1999; the euro has been the country's sole currency since January 2002.

BILLING

Competition is such that the pressure on fees remains high, particularly in areas such as capital markets and real estate. Hourly rates range from €300-400 for partners. Some clients pay monthly retainers, and in certain practice areas relatively complex fee arrangements can be introduced as a way of sharing some of the client's transactional risk; private equity is a notable example.

MARKETING

The Spanish Bar has over time relaxed many of the restrictions relating to how law firms can market themselves. Firms increasingly use marketing and business development professionals, and many commercial practices have sophisticated websites. Some of the country's more traditional firms nevertheless remain somewhat reticent about promoting themselves.

IN-HOUSE LAWYERS

Large in-house teams are to be found in the private sector, particularly in the banking, IT and telecoms sectors. The Spanish administration and public bodies also employ a number of lawyers, known as *abogados del estado*.

LEGAL MARKET

2005 was an important year for the rebranded **Uría Menéndez**, with Luis de Carlos and José María Segovia taking over joint management responsibility from Rodrigo Uría, who remains senior partner, and the firm moving from four separate offices into a huge, single building previously occupied by Endesa. The firm is notable both for its stability and its exceptionally high market reputation, in terms of the quality of its client base and the quality of its lawyers across the board.

Garrigues, with its history as part of *Andersen Legal*, is by some distance Spain's largest firm and has a vast geographic spread, with some 23 offices in the country. It is also well known for the quality of its clients, and boasts some of the very best lawyers in the market.

The tax practice is of similarly fundamental importance at **Cuatrecasas**, which began life as a tax boutique in Barcelona. While still thought of by some as a Catalan firm, it now has a roughly equal presence in Madrid and Barcelona as well as ten other offices in Spain.

Leaving aside the two largest audit firms (**Landwell, Abogados y Asesores Fiscales** and **KPMG Abogados**), **Gómez-Acebo & Pombo Abogados** is the fourth-largest firm in the market, and is a regular contender in corporate and

The largest firms

1	Garrigues	1,454
2	Landwell, Abogados y Asesores Fiscales	692
3	Cuatrecasas	654
4	Uría Menéndez	402
5	KPMG Abogados	300
6	Gómez-Acebo & Pombo Abogados	176
7	Roca Junyent	165
8	Ernst & Young Abogados, SL	152
9	Clifford Chance	144
10	Baker & McKenzie	139
11	Legalia Abogados	106
12	Deloitte	90
13	Freshfields Bruckhaus Deringer	87
14	Adarve Corporación Jurídica	81
15	CMS Albiñana & Suárez de Lezo	80
16	Pintó Ruiz & Del Valle	65
	Ramón & Cajal	65
18	Mullerat	62
19	Cremades & Calvo-Sotelo	60
	Jausas	60
21	Perez-Llorca	57
22	Linklaters	56
23	Broseta Abogados	43
24	Maniega & Soler Abogados	42
	Sagardoy Abogados, member of ius laboris	42
26	Ecija Abogados	41
27	Lupicinio Eversheds	40
28	Alza Abogados & Fiscalistas	39
29	Allen & Overy	38
	Lloréns & Díaz de Aguilar	38

These figures represent the total number of lawyers in this country only, and have been supplied by the firms themselves. The figures should be accurate as at 1 January 2006.

finance as well as leading the field for IP and boasting a top-tier real estate practice.

Other domestic firms of note include **PEREZ-LLORCA**, a widely respected nine-partner firm that is a particularly strong choice on the corporate side (including public M&A) and recently took up some impressive new premises in the heart of Madrid.

FOREIGN OFFICES AND ALLIANCES

Cuatrecasas has offices in Brussels, New York, São Paulo, Paris (since mid-2004), Lisbon and Porto. The latter two were gained through the firm's 2003 merger with **Gonçalves Pereira, Castelo Branco & Associados**, which remains the firm's trading name in Portugal; it is now the second-largest firm in the country, following a further merger in March 2005. On the Latin American front, the firm has cooperation agreements with **Machado Associados, Advogados e Consultores** in São Paulo; **Pérez Alati, Grondona, Benites, Arntsen & Martínez De Hoz, Jr** in Buenos Aires; **Creel, García-Cuéllar y Müggenburg SC** in Mexico City; and **Carey** in Santiago, Chile.

Garrigues recently added Shanghai and Casablanca to its list of foreign offices, joining Lisbon, Brussels and New York. The firm also increased its range of Latin American ties, adding alliances with **Gómez-Pinzón Asemarcas** in Colombia and **Barros & Errázuriz** in Chile to those formalised in early 2004, with Argentina's **Bruchou, Fernández Madero, Lombardi & Mitrani**, Brazil's **Barbosa, Müssnich & Aragão**, and Mexico's **Mijares, Angoitia, Cortés y Fuentes SC**. In March 2005, the firm – together with eight other independent firms – founded global tax alliance *Taxand*.

Uría Menéndez has offices in London, Brussels, New York and São Paulo as well as two in Portugal (Lisbon and Porto). The firm is part of **Slaughter and May**'s 'best-friends' network, and has associations with five firms in Latin America, namely **Marval, O'Farrell & Mairal** in Buenos Aires; **Payet, Rey, Cauvi** in Lima; **Galicia y Robles SC** in Mexico City; **Philippi, Yrrázaval, Pulido & Brunner** in Santiago, Chile; and **Dias Carneiro Advogados (in association with Uría Menéndez)** in São Paulo.

Gómez-Acebo & Pombo Abogados has had an office in Brussels since 1985, and has cooperation agreements with firms in Portugal (**Vieira de Almeida & Associados**), Argentina (**Estudio Beccar Varela**), and Brazil (**Pinheiro Neto Advogados**).

Other firms with foreign offices include **Mullerat** (Lisbon); **Roca Junyent** (Moscow); **Fernando Scornik Gerstein** (London); and **Cremades & Calvo-Sotelo** (Buenos Aires).

Firms with alliances in place include: **Adarve Corporación Jurídica**, which is the Spanish member of the *Trans European Law Firms Alliance (TELFA)*; **Pintó Ruiz & Del Valle**, the Spanish member of the *Pannone Law Group*; **Lupicinio Eversheds**, *Lupicinio Abogados* having formalised a strategic alliance with UK-based international law firm **Eversheds LLP** at the start of 2004; and **CMS Albiñana & Suárez de Lezo**, a member of the *CMS* alliance of European law firms.

FOREIGN FIRMS

Clifford Chance has a hard-won reputation in Spain; it has been established in Madrid since 1980 and Barcelona since 1993 with a strategy of competing head-on with the domestic firms, and offers real quality in its corporate, finance and real estate practices among others. It nevertheless saw some well-documented fee-earner departures over 2004/5, the most significant being Javier López Antón and María José Menendez. Finance partner Jaime de San Román and Ignacio Ojanguren in corporate are the joint managing partners.

Freshfields Bruckhaus Deringer appears to be the most stable of the UK Magic Circle firms, and commands very widespread respect in the market for the quality of its fee-earners and its approach on deals. The firm fields 13 equity partners between its offices in Madrid and Barcelona, with John Byrne the managing partner and Fernando Bautista (finance), Joaquin Hervada and Armando Alberrán (both corporate), and Miguel Klingenberg (tax) among the other leading individuals in the firm.

Linklaters saw something of a shake-up on the management side in 2005, with Miles Curley returning to full-time fee-earning, succeeded by the three partners at the head of the firm's corporate, finance and commercial practice streams: Álvaro Sáinz, Iñigo Berrícano, and Miguel Riaño. While not immune to fee-earner departures, and despite its less than organic development since establishing in 2000, the firm is – in the words of one competitor – 'absolutely motoring' in terms of deals; it has also attracted a star capital markets partner, in **Ramón & Cajal**'s Sebastián Albella.

Corporate and finance are the core areas of focus for **Allen & Overy** in Madrid, where banking and finance head Iñigo Gómez-Jordana and projects specialist Graham Donnell are the joint managing partners. The corporate practice took a heavy blow in 2005 with the return to **Cuatrecasas** of Fernando Torrente and a team of five other lawyers. The firm acts for some 14 IBEX 35 companies.

Ashurst has been in Madrid for five years, and is a strong contender in private equity and acquisition finance. The recruitment of María José Menendez from **Clifford Chance** makes for a significant addition to the corporate practice, and the firm also has a new (non-lawyer) director of competition in Julio Pascual y Vicente. Steven Fox is the managing partner.

Baker & McKenzie is a very well-established presence in Spain, having had an office in Madrid since 1965 and Barcelona since 1988. Tax is an area of particular strength, thanks in part to its 2001 incorporation of Madrid's *Briones, Alonso y Martín*; the firm now fields some ten partners in the area. Maite Diez in Madrid and Rafael Jimenez-Gusi in Barcelona are the two managing partners.

SJ Berwin has a two-partner practice in Madrid that is heavily focused on private equity, including tax structuring; Carlos Pazos enjoys a very strong market profile.

Lovells has been in Madrid since September 2004, under the leadership of José María Balaña (a former head of corporate at **Cuatrecasas**), and has been recruiting fast; it now fields a total of six partners, among them banking and finance head Joaquín Sales (ex-**Gómez-Acebo & Pombo Abogados**). The firm also has a well-established European trade mark office in Alicante.

Simmons & Simmons has three Madrid-based partners, most notably managing partner Luis Felipe, who has a strong public-sector background and is known for his rainmaking talents, as evidenced by the instruction to advise Telefónica in its £17.7bn bid for BT spin-out O2 (in conjunction with a host of partners from the firm's London office).

In terms of US firms, the entire team at **Squire, Sanders & Dempsey L.L.P.**'s Madrid office (some ten partners and 15 other fee-earners) was to transfer to **DLA Piper Rudnick Gray Cary** in February 2006, more than doubling the firm's partner numbers and bringing the total number of fee-earners to nearly 60. **Squire, Sanders & Dempsey L.L.P.**'s Madrid office managing partner Juan Picón will take over at the helm of his new firm, with Kenneth Bonavia assuming a more international role.

The development leaves **Jones Day** as the only US firm in Madrid with Spanish law capability; managing partner Juan Tena is very well thought of, and the firm is strong in core areas such as corporate, finance and disputes, although its regulatory capability has taken a significant hit with the departure of competition specialists Juan Jiménez Laiglesia and José María Jiménez Laiglesia (to set up their own firm, **Jiménez-Laiglesia**); they have the distinction of having attracted the mandate to advise Gas Natural on the main competition law aspects of its bid for Endesa.

The only other US firm with a Spanish office is **Davis Polk & Wardwell**, which has a small team offering US law-only capital markets and other corporate advice. Various other US firms are persistently linked to a possible entry in the market (among them **Shearman & Sterling LLP**, **White & Case LLP**, **Cleary Gottlieb Steen & Hamilton LLP** and **Latham & Watkins LLP**), but the consensus is that financial considerations will prevent their appearance for the foreseeable future.

New additions to the legal landscape in Madrid are specialist IT firm **Bird & Bird**, under the leadership of a former **Linklaters** managing associate; and, on the insurance front, **Kennedys**, which took over the practice of *Araúz de Robles y Vélez Abogados*. Both offices opened in October 2005.

BANKING AND FINANCE

Clifford Chance acted for the banks on a host of acquisition finance deals, most notably Permira's acquisition of Ahold's supermarket assets (advising The Royal Bank of Scotland and others) and also CVC's aborted €1.45bn bid for Cortefiel (advising Société Générale), with Stuart Percival the lead partner in each case. In terms of financings and refinancings – where Alberto Manzanares and Carlos Hernández-Canut are among the active partners – highlights included a €1bn-plus refinancing of Sogecable's debt (for HSBC) and a €600m facility to technology company Abengoa SA (for Société Générale), as well as numerous mandates from BBVA.

Freshfields Bruckhaus Deringer has a particularly strong recent record on acquisition finance, including acting for The Royal Bank of Scotland and ING Bank on the €1.3bn financing relating to the bid by PAI and Permira for Cortefiel. On the asset finance side, the firm remains active in the ship and aircraft finance markets and also has experience in structuring transactions involving new assets such as rolling stock, in 2005 advising Caja Madrid on the €100m financing of ten new trains to be operated by Metro de Barcelona. Fernando Bautista heads the practice, with fellow partners John Byrne and Iñaki Gabilondo also recommended.

Uría Menéndez's instructions in 2005 included acting for Goldman Sachs Mezzanine Partners in the €680m mezzanine acquisition finance of Panrico, and for Investcorp in the €250m refinancing of the acquisition of Minimax. In the real estate sector, mandates meanwhile included acting for BBVA and others in the €376m financing for the public tender for Grupo Inmocaral, and a complex mortgage-backed financing for the acquisition of Vodafone's headquarters in Madrid (acting for ING).

Allen & Overy received the mandate to act for the lenders (UBS, Société Générale and La Caixa) on Gas Natural's bid for Endesa, and in asset finance was instructed by Iberia on the award-winning Iberbond 2004 (involving the US$933m financing of its fleet renovation). Key clients of the practice include BBVA (advised on a host of matters in 2004/5 including Service Point Solution's debt restructuring). Iñigo Gómez-Jordana and Eduardo Sebastián de Erice are the two partners in the team.

Cuatrecasas acted for the banks on substantial syndicated facilities to Grupo Ferrovial, Iberdrola and Uralita, among others, while acting for JP Morgan Europe and CIBC World Markets on the financing of CVC's €700m acquisition of the BASF Drucksysteme group was a highlight in the LBO arena. The firm is also active in structured finance, and on the regulatory side has advised the likes of Deutsche Bank, JP MorganChase and Société Générale in relation to national and international structured products. Eduardo Ramírez is the lead partner for banking matters, while Rafael Mínguez heads the finance practice.

Garrigues continues to undertake a full spectrum of banking and finance instructions, from high-end work to more mainstream matters. Headlines in 2005 included the groundbreaking €1.1bn receivables financing of the land concentration works and water network of the Sistema Segarra-Garrigues, and Caja Madrid's jumbo €1.6bn loan to ACS, along with impressive acquisition finance, real estate finance, and finance-sector M&A instructions. Rafael González-Gallarza and José Guardo are the lead partners in Madrid, with Lluis Esquerra the contact partner in Barcelona.

BANKING AND FINANCE

CLIFFORD CHANCE
FRESHFIELDS BRUCKHAUS DERINGER
URÍA MENÉNDEZ ✪

Allen & Overy ✪
Cuatrecasas ✪
Garrigues ✪
Gómez-Acebo & Pombo Abogados ✪
Linklaters ✪

Adarve Corporación Jurídica ✪
Araoz & Rueda ✪
Ashurst ✪
Baker & McKenzie ✪
CMS Albiñana & Suárez de Lezo ✪
Castro, Sueiro & Varela Abogados ✪
DLA Piper Rudnick Gray Cary ✪
M. Vega Penichet, Bufete ✪
Mullerat ✪
Ramón & Cajal
Roca Junyent ✪
SJ Berwin ✪

B Cremades & Asociados
Broseta Abogados ✪
Deloitte
Ernst & Young Abogados, SL ✪
Jones Day ✪
KPMG Abogados ✪
Landwell, Abogados y Asesores Fiscales ✪
Legalia Abogados ✪
Lovells ✪
Lupicinio Eversheds ✪
PEREZ-LLORCA ✪
Rodés & Sala Abogados ✪
Simmons & Simmons ✪
Ventura Garcés & López-Ibor, Abogados ✪

Firms are listed A-Z in tiers which are ranked in order of priority
✪ *Indicates firm displays contact details at the end of this chapter.*

Gómez-Acebo & Pombo Abogados' core banking and finance clients include Ahorro Corporación and BBVA; the firm recently advised the former (along with Banesto) in relation to a €367m receivables transfer for Famosa, and the latter in relation to both the €108m construction financing of a hotel and a €78m facility to Pepe Jeans. Banco Sabadell and EuroHypo AG (for property finance) are recent client gains. Fernando Igartua is one of four Madrid-based partners active in the area.

Linklaters' finance team includes Iñigo Berrícano, Pedro de Rojas and international finance partner Conrado Tenaglia. 2005 saw it advise on the financing of offers for Cortefiel and Recoletos (acting for Permira and the banks, respectively), while other highlights included advising Metrovacesa (in conjunction with lawyers in the firm's Paris office) on the €7.5bn financing of its purchase of a stake in listed French real estate company Gecina, and JP Morgan in a €6bn facility for Telefónica (in part for the purchase of Cesky Telecom).

Araoz & Rueda has a well-regarded finance practice, with areas of expertise including structured and asset finance and debt restructuring. It acted for Bank of Scotland in the €75m senior financing related to Codere's high-yield bond issue, while other recent clients include BBVA and Deutsche Bank. Andrés Lorrio, previously a managing associate in **Linklaters**' finance practice, joined the team as a partner in mid-2005.

Acquisition finance is the core strength of **Ashurst**'s practice; the firm was involved on the financing side of bids for both Cortefiel and Amadeus (advising JP Morgan and others on the bid by Permira and PAI, and CSFB and others on the bid by BC Partners and Cinven, respectively). Gonzalo Jiménez-Blanco heads the international finance practice.

Recent clients of **Baker & McKenzie**'s banking and finance group include Fortis Bank (advised in relation to €175m facilities granted to Belgian film exhibition group Kinepolis), Pepe Jeans (in relation to a substantial syndicated loan, opposite **Gómez-Acebo & Pombo Abogados**), and Commerzbank Atkiengesellschaft (on its acquisition of a Spanish investment services group). The team was also involved on the financing aspects of several worldwide acquisitions over the course of the year. Regulatory expert María Gracia Rubio and José María Sánchez are the key partners in Madrid, while derivatives specialist Claudi Rossell is based in Barcelona.

CMS Albiñana & Suárez de Lezo's practice takes in structured, project and ship finance as well as financial-services sector M&A, through senior partner Gracia Sáinz, José Antonio Rodríguez and Carlos Peña. Clients in 2005 included Banco Espiritu Santo Investment and IXIS Corporate & Investment Bank (the latter advised in relation to the granting of liquidity facilities to various Spanish asset securitisation funds).

Castro, Sueiro & Varela Abogados partners Juan Carlos Castro, Miguel Sueiro and José Ramón Varela all offer banking and finance experience, with structured and ship (and other asset) finance particular areas of strength; the firm's track record includes acting on many of the tax leases of ships built in Spain.

The **Squire, Sanders & Dempsey L.L.P.** Madrid office team to move to **DLA Piper Rudnick Gray Cary** in February 2006 includes Javier López Antón, who transferred to the former firm from **Clifford Chance** in 2005 and has a particular focus on projects and leveraged and structured finance. Juan Díaz Hidalgo meanwhile heads **DLA Piper Rudnick Gray Cary**'s banking and financial services practice, which has recently handled work for Allgemeine Hypothekenbank Rheinboden, Bank of Scotland and ABN Amro Capital.

Mullerat offers a good range of banking and finance experience, including structured, project and asset finance; partners include Miguel Torres, Jorge Adell and Sergio Gimenez, who heads the firm's aviation practice and acts for LTE International Airways among others.

Ramón & Cajal has a very strong record on finance matters, including structured finance and securitisation. Francisco Palá and Javier Menchén co-lead the firm's banking and capital markets practice.

Broseta Abogados' clients include Bankinter, the Valencia Stock Exchange, and the Valencian Finance Institute, with recent work including advising the latter in relation to the restructuring of sports clothes and shoe manufacturer Grupo Kelme.

Jones Day's Luiz Muñoz has many years' experience on financing matters; his key clients include Calyon, recently advised in relation to various construction financings in Latin America (including two electric transmission lines in Brazil). Muñoz works alongside US-qualified of-counsel Richard Puttré, who advises Spanish companies in relation to financing transactions in the US bank market; he has recently acted for Latin American subsidiaries of both Telefónica and Unión Fenosa.

KPMG Abogados handles a range of structured and other finance advice, under Victor Mendoza, while **Legalia Abogados**, under Amalio Miralles, acts for a good range of banks, motor industry finance companies, and other financial institutions, on leasing and mortgage transactions.

Joaquín Sales heads **Lovells**' banking and finance practice; he joined the firm as a partner from **Gómez-Acebo & Pombo Abogados**, with project and property finance, acquisition finance and securitisation among his areas of experience. The Instituto de Crédito Oficial, Spain's AAA finance agency, is a new client.

Lupicinio Eversheds' banking and finance practice is led by Luis Manuel García, while fellow partner Hermenegildo Altozano is notable for his experience in the energy sector (including financing work).

PEREZ-LLORCA handles banking and finance work (mainly acquisition finance and asset finance) as part of its broader corporate and finance practice; 2004/5 deals included the €1.2bn acquisition by Texas Pacific Group and CSFB of the Grohe Group, while Cinebox and Commercial Fasteners are among the firm's recent clients in asset finance. Miguel Temboury Redondo joined the firm as a partner to head the regulatory practice, with areas of experience including the banking and insurance as well as energy and telecoms sectors.

Alvaro Muñoz at **Simmons & Simmons** has a broad practice that takes in some finance work. Recent clients are Barclays Private Bank and Compagnie Plastic Omnium (advised on the establishment of a €100m asset sale programme relating to trade receivables).

Ventura Garcés & López-Ibor, Abogados has a notable aviation finance practice, where clients include Air France (advised in 2004/5 on the leasing of two Boeing 747s to Pullmantur Air). The firm also acted for WestLB and Bayerische Landesbank, in syndicated loan matters.

CAPITAL MARKETS

The IPO market remains very quiet in Spain, with the listings of Telecinco, Cintra, and cosmetic medicine and surgery company Corporación Dermoestética the only three between June 2004 and July 2005. The securitisation market by contrast has for the last few years been sustaining very high levels of activity.

Clifford Chance maintains a very busy debt practice, with José Manuel Cuenca and Stuart Percival the main partners. 2004/5 saw Cuenca advise on numerous major debt issues, among them a €6bn 'obligaciones del estado' issue by the Kingdom of Spain (advising BBVA and others as lead managers) and a €2.25bn issue of floating rate notes by BBVA Senior Finance (advising Calyon and Deutsche Bank). Percival meanwhile led the advice on a host of MTN programmes, most notably Santander Central Hispano's €25bn programme and Telefónica's €15bn programme (advising Morgan Stanley and Barclays Capital respectively). On the securitisation side, highlights included the launch of Spain's first 'second degree' securitisation, acting for Calyon as lead manager and Caja San Fernando as originator.

Freshfields Bruckhaus Deringer acted on the underwriter side of the Corporación Dermoestética IPO (for Morgan Stanley), while other equity instructions included France Télécom's €3bn rights issue (used to finance the company's acquisition of Amena). The firm also has an active securitisation practice, and was instructed on over a dozen transactions in the course of the year (in many cases acting for Fitch

CAPITAL MARKETS

CLIFFORD CHANCE
FRESHFIELDS BRUCKHAUS DERINGER
LINKLATERS ✪
URÍA MENÉNDEZ ✪

Cuatrecasas ✪
Garrigues ✪
Gómez-Acebo & Pombo Abogados ✪
Ramón & Cajal

Allen & Overy ✪
Ashurst ✪
B Cremades & Asociados
Baker & McKenzie ✪
CMS Albiñana & Suárez de Lezo ✪
DLA Piper Rudnick Gray Cary ✪
Davis Polk & Wardwell
M. Vega Penichet, Bufete ✪
Mullerat ✪
PEREZ-LLORCA ✪
Roca Junyent ✪
Simmons & Simmons ✪

Firms are listed A-Z in tiers which are ranked in order of priority
✪ *Indicates firm displays contact details at the end of this chapter.*

Ratings, while other clients included Deutsche Bank, Bank of America Securities and Bank AIG). Fernando Bautista heads the practice, and Armando Alberrán is also active; Monica McConville, who has particular experience on equity offerings, returned to the firm's London office.

Linklaters received a real boost with the arrival from **Ramón & Cajal** of Sebastián Albella, who was a founding partner at his previous firm and is one of the best-known capital markets practitioners in the market. Other key partners are Iñigo Berrícano and Conrado Tenaglia, who recently joined forces on accelerated bookbuilt offerings by Zeltia and Banco Popular (advising HSBC and Goldman Sachs respectively). Debt highlights meanwhile included substantial issues by Jazztel plc (advising Dresdner Kleinwort Wasserstein) and the quasi-sovereign Junta de Comunidades de Castilla-La Mancha.

Uría Menéndez was instructed on the Cintra IPO (acting for the company and Macquarie Infrastructure Group as selling shareholder), and also advised Morgan Stanley on real estate company Metrovacesa's €1bn rights issue in mid-2005 (opposite **Clifford Chance**). Clients on the debt side meanwhile included Caja de Ahorros del Mediterráneo (advised on the creation of, and two issues under, a €2bn EMTN programme) and Caja de Ahorros de Santander y Cantabria. Luis de Carlos and Emilio Díaz are among the best-known names in the market; other partners include David Garcia-Ochoa, who in 2005 led the advice to InterMoney Titulización as managing company on the €2bn 'IM Cédulas 4 FTA' asset securitisation.

Cuatrecasas handled major debt issues for Commerzbank and Caja de Ahorros y Monte de Piedad de Madrid (€4bn and €1.1bn respectively), while other recent capital markets clients include Caja de Ahorros de Castilla La Mancha and Deutsche Bank. The firm was also instructed on the issues of various asset-backed securitisation notes, by Europea de Titulización and Santander de Titulización among others. The practice was boosted by the return in September 2005 of the widely respected Fernando Torrente and a team of five other corporate lawyers, all from **Allen & Overy**.

Garrigues maintains a very strong share of the securitisation market, with recent transactions including the €2bn Cédulas TDA 7 asset securitisation (on which it advised Caja Madrid and managing company Titulización de Activos). Equity highlights in 2005 included acting for Corporación Dermoestética on its IPO, and advising Unión Fenosa on a €750m issue of preferred securities (including a listing on the Luxembourg Stock Exchange). Javier Ybáñez heads the capital markets practice and was the lead partner on all three of these instructions; Fernando Vives is also active.

Gómez-Acebo & Pombo Abogados' capital markets practice is heavily focused on securitisation, with its instructions mainly deriving from leading arranger Ahorro y Titulización; recent examples include two 'cédulas hipotecarias' securitisations (for €5bn and €3.9bn), as well as securitisations of treasury bonds, mortgage certificates and 'cédulas territoriales'. Fernando Igartua is 'one of the very best in the market', according to another client, with Ángel Varela also highly regarded.

Ramón & Cajal has an excellent track record on capital markets work, both debt and equity, although the departure of Sebastián Albella for **Linklaters** is a significant one. Francisco Palá and Javier Menchén jointly lead the capital markets practice, with Alberto Alonso Ureba and Francisco Bauzá among the other individuals with strong corporate finance experience.

Allen & Overy was involved on the Cintra IPO, advising the issuer on the US law side, while on the debt side 2004/5 instructions included acting for Morgan Stanley as underwriter of three major bond issues by BBVA, La Caixa and Banesto and also on innovative Tier 1 preferred securities issues by Banco Pastor and Caixa Terrasa. The capital markets practice is now led solely by Iñigo Gómez-Jordana, following the return of Fernando Torrente to **Cuatrecasas**; the latter's practice was heavily focused on IPOs and other equity work.

Ashurst acted for JP MorganChase on its first Spanish notes programme (for the issue of structured bonds with a limit of €500m), and also advised Bain Capital and Brenntag on the securitisation of the Brenntag Group's European receivables. Gonzalo Jiménez-Blanco heads the international finance practice.

At **Baker & McKenzie**, banking and finance head María Gracia Rubio led the advice to Macquarie Bank in relation to the Cintra IPO, while other work included a US$152m guaranteed senior notes issue for building materials manufacturer Uralita (on which José Mariá Sánchez was the lead partner). Both partners are former in-house counsel for the Spanish Securities and Exchange Commission.

CMS Albiñana & Suárez de Lezo has a good record for capital markets work, through partners such as Rafael Suárez de Lezo, Carlos Peña and Luis Miguel de Dios.

DLA Piper Rudnick Gray Cary is included on the strength of the transfer (set for February 2006) of **Squire, Sanders & Dempsey L.L.P.**'s Madrid office, whose recent clients include SCH Titulización SGFT (advised on a securitisation of loans and assets) and Goodyear Tire & Rubber Company (advised on a pan-European asset securitisation). José Bonilla is among the partners with capital markets experience.

Davis Polk & Wardwell offers US law capability only, on debt and equity capital markets as well as M&A; on the equity side it was instructed on the Rule 144a/Reg S IPOs of both Cintra and Corporación Dermoestética (acting for the underwriters and the issuer respectively). Banco Santander Central Hispano and Codere are recent debt clients, the former advised on a US$4bn offering of senior floating rate notes by a finance subsidiary. Michael Willisch is based full-time in Madrid.

PEREZ-LLORCA, though better known for its public and private M&A and private equity, handles some capital markets work and has boosted its practice with the recruitment of Vicente Conde, a former head of **Uría Menéndez**'s Chilean office with particular expertise on the equity side. 2005 instructions included advising a UK finance provider on the securitisation of the proceeds of a gold mine.

At **Simmons & Simmons**, Alfredo Lorenzo has remained active on various debt-side transactions, for clients such as BBVA and Deutsche Bank; in 2005 the firm acted for the former on the establishment of a rated repackaging programme.

CORPORATE AND M&A

Clifford Chance landed the mandate to act for Endesa in the defence of Gas Natural's hostile takeover bid, with joint managing partner Ignacio Ojanguren leading the advice, while other instructions in 2005 included Air France's sale of its shareholding in Amadeus (also led by Ojanguren), and a number of acquisitions for Red Eléctrica led by José María Fernández-Daza. Javier Amantegui remains focused on private equity work, recently handling work for NMás1, Dinamia, Mercapital and KKR. On the personnel side, María José

CORPORATE AND M&A

CLIFFORD CHANCE
FRESHFIELDS BRUCKHAUS DERINGER
GARRIGUES ✪
URÍA MENÉNDEZ ✪

CUATRECASAS ✪
GÓMEZ-ACEBO & POMBO ABOGADOS ✪
LINKLATERS ✪

Allen & Overy ✪
Araoz & Rueda ✪
Ashurst ✪
Baker & McKenzie ✪
CMS Albiñana & Suárez de Lezo ✪
PEREZ-LLORCA ✪
SJ Berwin ✪

Barrilero & Asociados, Bufete
Castro, Sueiro & Varela Abogados ✪
DLA Piper Rudnick Gray Cary ✪
Jones Day ✪
Landwell, Abogados y Asesores Fiscales ✪
Legalia Abogados ✪
Mullerat ✪
Pintó Ruiz & Del Valle ✪
Ramón & Cajal
Roca Junyent ✪
Simmons & Simmons ✪

Adarve Corporación Jurídica ✪
Brosa
Davis Polk & Wardwell
Deloitte
Ernst & Young Abogados, SL ✪
Giménez Torres, Bufete
Jausas ✪
KPMG Abogados ✪
Lovells ✪
Lupicinio Eversheds ✪
M. Vega Penichet, Bufete ✪

Abogados y Economistas Asociados
Alexander Pitts, Bufete
Alza Abogados & Fiscalistas ✪
B Cremades & Asociados
Belzuz Abogados ✪
Bertrán & Associats, Bufete
Broseta Abogados ✪
Davies Arnold Cooper ✪
De Haan & Mulder SCP Abogados – Advocaten
De Lorenzo Abogados
Díaz-Bastien & Truan ✪
Echecopar Abogados
Ecija Abogados ✪
Iuris Valls Abogados
Maniega & Soler Abogados ✪
Olivencia-Ballester, Abogados ✪
Rodés & Sala Abogados ✪
Roig Aran, Bufete
Ventura Garcés & López-Ibor, Abogados ✪

Firms are listed A-Z in tiers which are ranked in order of priority
✪ Indicates firm displays contact details at the end of this chapter.

Menendez's departure, for **Ashurst**, was an undoubted blow to the practice.

Freshfields Bruckhaus Deringer, under Joaquin Hervada, moves into the top tier on the strength of an outstanding 2005 deal list and its growing stature in the eyes of clients and competitors alike. Public M&A mandates included advising Gas Natural on its bid for Endesa as well as acting for Cinven and BC Partners in the buyout of Amadeus and for former airport concession monopoly Aldeasa in relation to the bids for its share capital. On the private M&A side, meanwhile, highlights included Grupo Mahou-San Miguel's €615m acquisition of Danone's third-share in Mahou (with Danone advised by **Uría Menéndez**). Private equity mandates, aside from numerous instructions from Permira, included KKR's bid for Auna. Armando Albarran enjoys an exceptionally strong individual reputation.

2004/5 saw **Garrigues** act on the seller side of a number of major deals, notably the spin-off of Auna's cable and mobile operations (advising Endesa, Banco Santander Uníon Fenosa as the main shareholders), and the sales of Cortefiel, Panrico and Famosa, and the firm also acted for Terra Networks in its merger with its majority shareholder, Telefónica. Department head Fernando Vives enjoys an outstanding reputation – he is the 'best-in-class for banking, capital markets and M&A', according to one leading financial institution – while other key partners are Javier Urbano and Barcelona-based Ramón Girbau.

Uría Menéndez remains for many Spain's reference firm for M&A and other corporate work. Highlights of 2005 included advising CVC Capital Partners España in relation to the takevoer bid for Cortefiel, with Juan Miguel Goenechea, Christian Hoedl and Eduardo Rodríguez-Rovira the lead corporate partners. The firm was also involved on the public-to-private of Aldeasa and the acquisition of Amadeus (with Hoedl the lead partner in each case, advising Mercapital and others, and the Carlyle Group respectively), as well as acting for Caja de Ahorros del Mediterráneo in the creation of CAMGE Financiera (the second-largest entity devoted to consumer finance in the Spanish market).

The major news for **Cuatrecasas**' corporate group, led by Raimon Segura, was the return in September 2005 of Fernando Torrente and five other lawyers from **Allen & Overy**; Torrente enjoys an excellent reputation among peers in the market, and is described by one institutional client as offering 'the highest possible quality of service: always on call; reachable; provided solutions; high-level contacts'. The firm was instructed by JP Morgan and others in relation to the Auna deal, advising them on the acquisition of a majority stake in Grupo Corporativo ONO and the subsequent purchase of Auna de Telecomunicaciones, while Ferrovial's €646m acquisition of Swissport and Lindsay Goldberg Bessemer's acquisition of the Klöckner group were among the firm's other corporate headlines.

The year saw **Gómez-Acebo & Pombo Abogados** act on €100m-plus acquisitions for Interbrew Belgium, Bridgepoint Capital, Fortune Brands and Gallaher Group, and the firm was also instructed in relation to the buyout of Amadeus, advising Deutsche Lufthansa. Francisco Peña heads a mainly Madrid-based team that includes the 'outstanding' Manuel Martín. 'Service is fast,' according to one client, 'and they try to listen and understand your business before they start legalising'.

Linklaters' corporate team includes Álvaro Sáinz and Alejandro Ortiz along with Miles Curley, who is back to full-time fee-earning following his period as managing partner, and Sebastián Albella, who joined the firm from **Ramón & Cajal** and handles some M&A. The 'remarkably hands-on' Ortiz enjoys a particularly fine individual reputation, and heads the private equity practice; he was the lead partner advising Amadeus and its management team on the company's public-to-private, and also Permira in relation to its offer for Cortefiel. The team also acted for Grupo Corporative ONO on its acquisition of Auna Telecomunicaciones. Antonio Sánchez Pedreño has left the firm for **Baker & McKenzie**.

Allen & Overy's corporate team was seriously reduced by the return of Fernando Torrente and a team of five other lawyers to **Cuatrecasas**, although the firm has been recruiting fast in response; new arrivals include Juan Barona, a senior associate from **Clifford Chance** who joined as a partner in November 2005. Finance and capital markets head Iñigo Gómez-Jordana and highly rated projects specialist Graham Donnell also handle some corporate work. The firm acted for GE Structured Finance and Caisse de Depot et Placement du Quebec on the acquisition of Auna Telecomunicaciones, and, on the private equity side, for Iberia in relation to the Amadeus buyout.

Araoz & Rueda maintains its focus on, and strong reputation for, corporate finance and private equity. In 2005 it acted for Franco-Canadian fund Sagard in its acquisition and financing of Hermès Metal Investissements, while other highlights included acting for longstanding client 3i in the MBO of kitchen furniture company Xey. Francisco Aldavero and Clifford Hendel are among the partners active on corporate work.

Headline private equity and LBO instructions for **Ashurst** in 2004/5 came from Apax Partners España (advised in the acquisition and financing of Panrico, opposite **Garrigues**) and Terra Firma Capital Partners. Jesús Almoguera heads the practice, and now works alongside the widely respected María José Menéndez, who joined as a partner from **Clifford Chance** and has notable experience in the financial services and insurance sectors. The team is praised for its 'Anglo-Saxon approach, ie always available at short notice and willing and able to work to tight deadlines without compromising quality'.

Baker & McKenzie's domestic clients include FCC and Gas Natural, the former advised in 2005 in relation to its €128m acquisition of logistics company Grupo Logistico Santos (opposite **Uría Menéndez**). On the international side the firm has recently handled M&A/private equity instructions from the likes of Abbott, Carglass and Pepe Jeans, and the private equity side of the practice looks set to strengthen with the recruitment of Antonio Sánchez Pedreño from **Linklaters**. The firm's two managing partners in Spain – Maite Diez in Madrid and Rafael Jimenez-Gusi in Barcelona – head the corporate group, while Cecilia Pastor is the key partner in the commercial practice and has recently handled work for Oracle, Sony BMG, and Holcim among others.

Recent highlights for **CMS Albiñana & Suárez de Lezo** include advising Iberdrola in relation to an asset acquisition flowing from the proposed Gas Natural/Endesa takeover, and acting for a group of investors (including Banesto) on their bid for newspaper and media group Recoletos. The team includes well-regarded joint managing partners César Albinaña and Rafael Suárez de Lezo.

PEREZ-LLORCA followed up its 2004/5 role on the Abbey National takeover by Banco Santander with some further impressive mandates, among them the acquisition of Aldeasa (advising Autogrill as joint acquiror with Altadis) and the acquisition of Cortefiel (advising PAI partners as joint acquiror with CVC and Permira). Other recent clients are Cadbury Schweppes, US electricity producer PPL Global and, on the private equity side, MCH. The 13-strong corporate and finance team includes managing partner Pedro Pérez-Llorca and new partner Vicente Conde, a former head of **Uría Menéndez**'s Chilean office.

SJ Berwin has carved a strong niche advising international and domestic private equity funds, particularly on the structuring side. Carlos Pazos has a far-reaching reputation, alongside tax specialist Javier Morera; both are 'top-class professionals'.

Castro, Sueiro & Varela Abogados has acted on M&A transactions across a good range of sectors, with name partners Juan Carlos Castro, Miguel Sueiro, and José Ramón Varela all handling corporate work. The firm recently advised a major domestic pharmaceutical company on its demerger and the sale of its commercial division to an overseas buyer, and also acted on the merger of two construction companies.

DLA Piper Rudnick Gray Cary's corporate finance offering will be greatly boosted by the impending transfer of **Squire, Sanders & Dempsey L.L.P.**'s Madrid team, with Juan Picón, Eduardo Sebastián and Javier Vasserot among the incoming corporate partners. They will be working alongside vastly experienced former managing partner Kenneth Bonavia and also José Antonio Sánchez Dáfos, who joined from **Allen & Overy** and, like Picón and Vasserot, has notable private equity experience. Key clients include ABN Amro Capital and Nazca Capital.

M&A (both industrial and private equity) remains the driver of **Jones Day**'s practice in Madrid. Practice head Juan Tena is a very well-established figure in the market, and co-led the advice – with fellow partner Luis Riesgo – to France Télécom on its acquisition of Amena. Longstanding clients include Suala Capital Partners and Vista Desarrollo; 2004/5 saw the firm act for the former in the sale of Mivisa to CVC, and for the latter in its acquisition of Itevelesa; of-counsel Federico Merino was the lead lawyer in each case.

Landwell, Abogados y Asesores Fiscales' corporate experience includes venture capital deals and securities issues. The firm is associated with PricewaterhouseCoopers.

Legalia Abogados is a well-regarded, mid-size firm whose areas of focus include the health, pharmaceutical and new technologies sectors; generics company Teva Pharmaceuticals Industries, Ibérica de Diagnóstico y Cirugía and Caja Madrid E-Business are among its clients. It has also handled private equity work, for CVC Capital Partners and Talde among others. Celso González heads the corporate and commercial team.

Mullerat maintains its reputation for attracting good-quality M&A and other corporate instructions; key partners include Madrid managing partner Alberto Echarri and, in Barcelona, Jorge Adell, Ramón Mullerat and Miguel Torres, although the departure of Bernat Mullerat for **Cuatrecasas** is a significant one.

Pintó Ruiz & Del Valle is the product of the merger, in 1999, of two long-established firms, namely *Bufete Pintó Ruiz* in Barcelona and *Del Valle Abogados* in Madrid, and offers a range of M&A and other corporate and commercial experience. Sports law is a notable area of strength, through José Juan Pintó Sala.

Ramón & Cajal has a good record on M&A, private equity and joint ventures, aside from the securities work for which it is best known. 2005 saw the firm merge with *Alonso Ureba, Bauzá & Asociados*.

Simmons & Simmons' deal list in 2005 – mainly transactions in the €10-€50m range – was eclipsed by the instruction to act for Telefónica in its £17.7bn bid for BT spin-out O2, one of the UK's largest M&A deals of the year, on which Madrid managing partner Luis Castresana – one of just three partners in Spain – is working in conjunction with various corporate partners in the firm's London office. Castresana is widely known for his strong public-sector connections, and is a former general secretary and chief counsel of SEPI.

Adarve Corporación Jurídica, under Daniel Villar Valero, handles a wide variety of corporate and commercial work for international and domestic clients, including family-owned companies.

Davis Polk & Wardwell in Madrid handles a mix of M&A, capital markets and private equity work, advising on US law only. Clients include numerous Spanish companies listed on the NYSE, among them Telefónica (advised recently in relation to its merger with its internet subsidiary, Terra Networks); acting for BBVA in its proposed €6.5bn acquisition of Italy's BNL was another highlight. Michael Willisch is the lead partner.

KPMG Abogados handles M&A and restructuring work for corporates and private equity funds, with Ramon Pallarés and Fernando Gómez leading the practice. Telefónica and Repsol are recent clients.

Lovells' practice is led by managing partner José Balaña, a former head of corporate and M&A at **Cuatrecasas**. The firm acted for Sacyr Vallehermoso in its €142m acquisition of waste management company Sufi, while other clients advised in 2005 included Cintra and Iberpotash.

Lupicinio Eversheds offers experience across a range of commercial, foreign investment, restructuring and other matters. Luis Manuel García and León Barriola are the two key partners.

Belzuz Abogados has experience of acquisitions in the financial, insurance and optical sectors, with Emilio Pérez Labrador among the partners handling corporate work.

Broseta Abogados recently acted on the MBOs of Marie Claire SA and Nestlé subsidiary Avidesa, while other clients include Ford España, German media group EM.TV, and various private equity funds advised on investments in the Valencia region. Managing partner Manuel Broseta and Antonio Navarro are the lead corporate and commercial partners.

Davies Arnold Cooper has a growing corporate group in Madrid that now includes two corporate partners, with Javier De Dios having been joined by Manuel Rodríguez De Bethencourt (previously at **Ramón & Cajal**). The firm handles corporate and commercial work for a range of insurance, property and other clients.

Recent work for **Ecija Abogados** includes, in the media sector, advising on the merger of Grupo Arbol-Globomedia and Mediapro and handling the corporate, finance, and regulatory aspects of the new 'La Sexta' television channel, a joint venture between GAMP and Televisa. Hugo Ecija is the key partner for corporate finance matters.

Iuris Valls Abogados is a two-partner Barcelona firm established in 2003 that handles corporate finance and commercial advice for a good range of international clients as well as domestic SMEs. Managing partner Carlos Valls is a former head of **Clifford Chance**'s Barcelona office, and works alongside Eusebio Pujol; both are praised by clients for their versatility and responsiveness on M&A work.

Maniega & Soler Abogados handles a range of business law advice, with Carlos Nicolau the lead partner. The firm, whose main office is in Barcelona, is part of **Shearman & Sterling LLP**'s 'best-friends' network.

Rodés & Sala Abogados was initially established in Barcelona, and has recently expanded with the addition of three partners in Madrid. Julio Veloso has a range of corporate experience including private equity work, while Tomas Fornesa focuses on the commercial side. Recent corporate work includes a €165m merger of two European communications groups.

Ventura Garcés & López-Ibor, Abogados – the product of a merger (in March 2004) between Barcelona-based *Ventura Garcés* and a small group of lawyers in Madrid headed by Alfonso López-Ibor – acts for a healthy spread of domestic and international (particularly US, UK and Italian) clients. 2005 deals included Mercapital's €55m acquisition of the Abaco chain of cinemas.

DISPUTE RESOLUTION

Cuatrecasas' disputes practice divides into teams handling commercial, administrative law and tax, criminal and employment litigation, and boasts involvement in a growing number of international as well as domestic arbitrations. The team acted for Bancaja (in relation to a challenge to the validity of a merger, with the amount at stake valued at €108m) and Dragados (in the defence of a substantial construction claim), while BMW, Caterpillar, Hewlett-Packard, Iberpotash and Swatch are other recent clients.

Garrigues has a very sizeable dispute resolution practice, spanning civil and criminal matters, and can point to an array of arbitration experience, advising domestic, Latin American and other international clients. The 'very efficient and sharp' Fernando Pantaleón's recent caseload includes advising an energy producer in an arbitration relating to a €325m dispute arising from the sale of a company in Latin America, while practice head Miguel Moscardó has been advising a finance service provider in a €200m real estate case; other notable partners include José Maria Alsonso, Antonio Fernández and Florentino Orti.

Uría Menéndez's wide-ranging litigation and arbitration practice enjoys an excellent reputation, and takes in civil and commercial, criminal, and public and administrative law disputes. Recommended individuals include Jesús Remón and, for administrative law matters, José Miguel Fatás.

B Cremades & Asociados' areas of strength include arbitration, both national and international; recent cases include acting for a Colombian subsidiary of Dragados in the defence of a €150m claim relating to a subway in Medellín. Aside from civil and administrative proceedings, the firm has also advised in relation to various succession disputes over major Spanish family patrimonies. Bernado Cremades and Ángel Tejada are both well-known practitioners.

Baker & McKenzie's recent highlights include a high-value action to enforce a UK judgement, together with various contractual and other claims in the €10-60m range. Jesús de Alfonso heads the practice in Barcelona and is best known for his contentious IP work, recently leading for Russia's Lukoil in its action to recover its Community Trademark. In Madrid, meanwhile, José Antonio Rodríguez has taken over as practice head from Miguel Pintos, who left to set up his own firm; Rodríguez was previously director of legal at the Sogecable Group.

Clifford Chance has recently been involved in two claims arising from corporate acquisitions, in one acting for a US multinational as defendant and in the other acting for a venture capital firm as plaintiff in an arbitration (seeking nullity of the purchase agreement). It has also been instructed to defend the interests of various clients in enforcement proceedings, notably representing a fund of investors in financial institutions in relation to a €1.1bn judgement against a bank. José Antonio Caínzoz and Íñigo Rodríguez-Sastre are the lead partners in Madrid.

Freshfields Bruckhaus Deringer now has two dispute resolution partners in Madrid, namely practice head Vicente Sierra and Rafael Murillo (promoted in mid-2005). On the arbitration side, the firm continued to act for Total in the CEPSA case (relating to Banco Santander's bid to buy a further stake in the Spanish oil company), and it is also acting for a domestic oil and gas company in a dispute with the government of a Latin American country. Product liability is another area of strength; the firm is one of the four in Spain instructed in the defence of the major tobacco manufacturers (acting for JT International Iberia).

Miguel Ángel Fernández heads the litigation and arbitration practice at **Gómez-Acebo & Pombo Abogados**, which was instructed in some 20 arbitrations over the course of 2004/5. Bacardi, Mercapital, Nike, Tiscali and Unión Fenosa Gas are longstanding clients, while new additions to the list include a consortium comprising Warner, Columbia, Fox and Sony. The firm is also notable for its sizeable criminal law practice, led by Javier Béjar in the Barcelona office; recent clients include a prince of Qatar, advised as the victim of an alleged multi-million-dollar fraud.

Mullerat has a well-regarded litigation practice, with areas of focus including fraud and white-collar crime and contentious IP as well as commercial disputes. Recent activity includes advising the buyer of a substantial portfolio of bad debt from a major domestic bank, on the management and recovery of the debt. Pilar Brindle, in Madrid, is the lead partner.

Pintó Ruiz & Del Valle is particularly notable for its expertise in the sports sector, and has handled a number of cases for the Spanish football league, including actions against Antena 3, Tele 5 and various internet betting companies. It was also instructed in the long-running litigation between sparkling wine producers Freixenet and Codorníu. José Juan Pintó Ruiz is among the individuals specialising in contentious work.

Bufete Ramon Hermosilla is a Madrid-based litigation boutique that commands widespread respect in the market. Ramón Hermosilla Gimeno is the contact for litigation and arbitration, and Javier de Andrés and José Antonio Salgado are also active in those areas. The firm also handles fraud and other criminal work.

Araoz & Rueda recently acted for a Latin American construction company and a European energy company in ICC arbitrations, and, on the domestic front, successfully represented a client in a claim before the Madrid Bar Association. Clifford Hendel and Alejandro Fernández de Araoz are the contact partners.

DISPUTE RESOLUTION

CUATRECASAS ✪
GARRIGUES ✪
URÍA MENÉNDEZ ✪

B Cremades & Asociados
Baker & McKenzie ✪
Clifford Chance
Freshfields Bruckhaus Deringer
Gómez-Acebo & Pombo Abogados ✪
Mullerat ✪
Pintó Ruiz & Del Valle ✪
Ramon Hermosilla, Bufete ✪

Araoz & Rueda ✪
CMS Albiñana & Suárez de Lezo ✪
DLA Piper Rudnick Gray Cary ✪
Davies Arnold Cooper ✪
Ernst & Young Abogados, SL ✪
Jones Day ✪
Linklaters ✪
PEREZ-LLORCA ✪
Roca Junyent ✪

Adarve Corporación Jurídica ✪
Allen & Overy ✪
Alzaga, Caro, G Palencia, Sánchez-Terán y Asociados ✪
Brosa
Broseta Abogados ✪
Cabezuela & Gonzalez. Circulo Legal.
Castro, Sueiro & Varela Abogados ✪
Deloitte
Díaz-Bastien & Truan ✪
Ecija Abogados ✪
Fernando Scornik Gerstein
Hammonds Madrid
Ignacio de Ros
Lovells ✪
Lupicinio Eversheds ✪
Maniega & Soler Abogados ✪
Martínez Lage & Asociados ✪
Olivencia-Ballester, Abogados ✪
Ramos & Arroyo
Simmons & Simmons ✪
Ventura Garcés & López-Ibor, Abogados ✪

Firms are listed A-Z in tiers which are ranked in order of priority
✪ *Indicates firm displays contact details at the end of this chapter.*

CMS Albiñana & Suárez de Lezo, under Carlos Aguilar, has a broad contentious practice that includes insolvency, white-collar crime and arbitration matters. Its 2005 caseload included acting for AON in an unfair competition case involving the Spanish subsidiaries of two major insurance brokers.

DLA Piper Rudnick Gray Cary has experience across a variety of shipping, banking, construction and other disputes, and will be strengthened by the arrival of former **Squire, Sanders & Dempsey L.L.P.** Madrid partners Josep Julià and Gonzalo Aranzabal.

As Spain's leading insurance practice, **Davies Arnold Cooper** has a vast array of experience in the courts, representing both insurance companies and their insureds. The firm handles some banking, commercial and property litigation, and has recently been instructed in two arbitrations in the energy sector.

Jones Day remains involved on behalf of a major Hispanic-Chilean group in a significant arbitration against the Argentine government (concerning the allegedly harmful measures taken by the government in relation to investments in certain Argentine companies, such as the pesification of applicable rates), and it also has an active construction disputes practice. Mercedes Fernández is the lead partner in the team, which includes senior associate Gonzalo Stampa (a former **B Cremades & Asociados** partner).

Linklaters, through Ignacio Díez-Picazo, has been active on a number of international arbitrations – for clients including a Spanish technology company, an international tobacco manufacturer, and an international telecoms company – while other highlights in 2005 included a significant instruction from a Spanish energy company.

PEREZ-LLORCA's recent caseload includes a variety of disputes valued in the €10-€30m bracket, such as multi-jurisdictional proceedings to recuperate embezzled funds, two claims for breach of supply agreements (in the tobacco and gas sectors), and an UNCITRAL arbitration in Geneva relating to a purchase of shares in a Spanish company. David Arias is the partner in the team, and offers a range of domestic and international arbitration experience.

Firms of note in the (newly consolidated) bottom tier include: Valencia's **Broseta Abogados**, which, under Antonia Magdaleno has a good range of experience on insolvency and unfair competition cases and whose clients include Dow Chemical and Bankinter; **Castro, Sueiro & Varela Abogados**, for debt recovery, insolvency and enforcement of foreign judgements, among other matters; **Ecija Abogados**, whose experience includes various e-banking, unfair competition, and debt recovery claims; **Lovells**, where José Luis Huerta has recently provided advice to clients such as Autogrill, Fiat, and France Telecom España; and **Ventura Garcés & López-Ibor, Abogados**, whose recent clients include a Swedish real estate company advised in a €27m claim relating to a land transfer.

EU AND COMPETITION

MARTÍNEZ LAGE & ASOCIADOS ⊙
URÍA MENÉNDEZ ⊙

Cuatrecasas ⊙
Freshfields Bruckhaus Deringer
Garrigues ⊙
Gómez-Acebo & Pombo Abogados ⊙

Allen & Overy ⊙
Araoz & Rueda ⊙
Baker & McKenzie ⊙
CMS Albiñana & Suárez de Lezo ⊙
Clifford Chance
DLA Piper Rudnick Gray Cary ⊙
Jones Day ⊙
Linklaters ⊙
PEREZ-LLORCA ⊙
SJ Berwin ⊙

Alzaga, Caro, G Palencia, Sánchez-Terán y Asociados ⊙
Ashurst ⊙
B Cremades & Asociados
Brosa
Ernst & Young Abogados, SL ⊙
M. Vega Penichet, Bufete ⊙
Mullerat ⊙
Pintó Ruiz & Del Valle ⊙
Roca Junyent ⊙
Ruiz & Veiga Abogados ⊙
Simmons & Simmons ⊙

Firms are listed A-Z in tiers which are ranked in order of priority
⊙ Indicates firm displays contact details at the end of this chapter.

EU AND COMPETITION

Martínez Lage & Asociados is a four-partner market regulatory boutique based in Madrid, with an outstanding reputation for its EU and competition work. Its recent work includes representing Correos before the Spanish competition authorities and national courts in relation to alleged dominant position abuses, and advising ServiRed and Euro 6000 (both licensees of the Visa and MasterCard brands in Spain) in proceedings regarding interchange fees, while other clients in 2005 included Gas Natural, Sogecable and private radio network SER. Managing partner Santiago Martínez Lage has an excellent reputation, and Jaime Pérez-Bustamente is notable for his expertise in the transport and telecoms sectors.

Uría Menéndez has two specialist competition partners based in Spain – practice head Jaime Folguera and the newly promoted Alfonso Gutiérrez – working closely with Edurne Navarro in the firm's Brussels office. Highlights in 2005 included acting for Dimon Inc in merger control proceedings arising from its €670m acquisition of Standard Commercial (creating the world's largest tobacco dealer and processor).

Cuatrecasas' head of EU and competition is Cani Fernandez, who divides her time between Madrid and Brussels. Recent merger control clients include Mecalux and Dräger Medical, while on the anti-trust side the team has been representing a consortium comprising Somague, BCP and others in complaints concerning alleged abuses of dominance by a Portuguese highway concession company during the tender for the Central Coastal Highway linking Lisbon and Porto. Other recent clients – for EU cases – include Industrias Químicas del Vallés, in relation to the withdrawal of a pesticide from the European market.

Freshfields Bruckhaus Deringer, under Franciso Cantos, has been involved in a number of high-profile investigations before the Spanish competition authorities, acting for, among others, Iberia, Sony Pictures Entertainment and Visa. It has also been instructed by Repsol for the first time on antitrust matters (advising it and Gas Natural on their LNG joint venture), while recent clients on the merger clearance side include L'Oréal, Permira and Reed Elsevier. The team, like others at the top end of the market, co-operates extensively with counterparts in Brussels (where the firm has six Spanish associates).

Garrigues has recently provided competition law advice to the likes of Amadeus (on a series of acquisitions), Auna (on divestments to France Télécom and ONO), and Repsol (on its acquisition of a Portuguese subsidiary of Shell), while other clients in 2005 included tobacco company Cetarsa (on an appeal against an article 81 fine) and beer manufacturer CCC. The three-partner practice, led by Marcos Araujo, was enhanced in late 2005 with the hire of José Luis Buendía (previously of the European Commission's Legal Service) to head the firm's Brussels office.

Gómez-Acebo & Pombo Abogados runs an integrated competition practice across its Madrid, Barcelona and Brussels offices, led by Iñigo Igartua; he has succeeded Emiliano Garrayar, whose practice is heavily focused on the regulated sectors. Aside from several heavyweight merger control instructions, the firm has for some while been representing Anged (Spain's largest association of retailers) in an antitrust case relating to multilateral interchange fees, and also advised ASCER in proceedings arising from alleged denial of access to the gas market. The team as a whole is praised for its 'efficiency, responsive assistance and high quality of work'.

Allen & Overy, under associate Pedro Callol, has recently handled M&A-related work for Iberia and CVC Capital Partners, while other clients include Twentieth Century Fox (advised in ongoing antitrust litigation before the Spanish authorities).

At **Araoz & Rueda**, Alejandro Fernández de Araoz and new partner Ainhoa Veiga both handle competition work. The team recently advised Ferroátlantica on its acquisition of France's Péchiney Electométallurgie, while other clients include artists' associations AIE and AISGE.

Baker & McKenzie's key competition specialist in Spain is Ernesto García-Trevijano, whose work in 2005 included, on the merger control side, advising Advent International in relation to the second takeover bid for Aldeasa, as well as coordinating several large-scale, multi-jurisdictional notification assignments. Josep Balcells in Barcelona is also active in the area.

CMS Albiñana & Suárez de Lezo's competition team is led by public law specialist José Giménez, and includes of-counsel Jesús Alfaro. Clients in 2004/5 included (on the merger control side) Iberdrola and also ONO, Heineken, Amena and pharmaceutical wholesaler Cofares (advised in a case relating to Pfizer's distribution of drugs to pharmacies in Spain).

Clifford Chance has recently handled notifications to the Spanish competition authorities for clients of the calibre of Telefónica, Repsol Química, Air France and GE Industrial Systems, while antitrust instructions included representing Standard Commercial in its appeal against its fine in the widely publicised case involving an alleged raw tobacco cartel. Miguel Odriozola is the lead partner.

DLA Piper Rudnick Gray Cary's competition and regulatory practice is led by Antonio Creus, a former **Cuatrecasas** partner who joined the firm at the end of 2004. 2005 saw the team represent Auna Telecomunicaciones in a case concerning football TV rights, while other clients included Amena and Altadis. Josep Julià is to join the firm from **Squire, Sanders & Dempsey L.L.P.**'s Madrid office, and has a range of competition law and EU legislation experience.

Jones Day saw the departure of practice heads Juan Jiménez Laiglesia and José María Jiménez Laiglesia, leaving senior associates Marta Delgado and Raimundo Ortega at the helm. Clients advised in 2004/5 included four trade unions representing tobacco producers (advised in the cartel case before the European Commission), Procter & Gamble, and Repsol. The firm was instructed to act for Gas Natural on the competition law aspects of its bid for Endesa, although the Laiglesia brothers are reportedly continuing to act in this matter following their departure.

Linklaters' competition team handled M&A-related advice on deals such as Capio AB's acquisition of the IDC Group, and has also – for some time – been advising one of Spain's foremost corporate groups in an investigation before the European Commission. The practice is led by senior associate Silvia Pérez-Navarro, and works as an integrated team with counterparts in Brussels.

PEREZ-LLORCA's team, led by Oriol Armengol, receives very strong praise from peers, and has recently advised the likes of Cadbury Schweppes, BAT, Vueling and Camper, while M&A-related highlights include advising on the competition law aspects of PAI Partners' acquisition of a stake in Cortefiel. Miguel Temboury Redondo recently joined the firm as a partner to head the regulatory practice, with areas of experience including the banking and insurance as well as energy and telecoms sectors.

SJ Berwin's recent work includes advising EDP (Portugal's incumbent electricity operator) on its acquisition of joint control (with Eni) over incumbent gas operator GDP, while easyJet, JVC and Universal Music are amongst its other recent clients. The practice is coordinated by Ramón García Gallardo in the firm's Brussels office.

Ashurst has a new director of competition, namely economist Julio Pascual y Vicente, recruited in October 2005 from the Spanish antitrust court (of which he had been a member since 1996). Recent work includes advising Terra Firma Capital on the Spanish competition law aspects of its acquisition of the UCI cinema group.

B Cremades & Asociados has a solid record in competition work; its recent competition activity includes acting for Portugal's Galp in the notification of its acquisition of Shell's Spanish petrol stations.

Pintó Ruiz & Del Valle recently advised in relation to a significant sports-related case before the European Commission. María José Rodríguez, in Barcelona, is the lead competition partner.

At **Ruiz & Veiga Abogados**, Carina Ruiz and Eduardo Veiga both handle some competition advice; recent contentious work includes representing a French liquor manufacturer in unfair competition proceedings for alleged imitation of labelling, while on the advisory side, the firm advised a leading Swiss watchmaking company on reorganisation of its Spanish retail network.

Gonzalo Samaniego's practice at **Simmons & Simmons** includes competition, state aid and public procurement.

EMPLOYMENT

Baker & McKenzie has recently advised on redundancy programmes for the likes of Levi's and Cap Gemini (involving 550 and 300 redundancies respectively), while other clients advised in 2005 included ExxonMobil, EMI Music, and automotive equipment supplier Valeo (in relation to the closure of its two Spanish plants). The five-partner team is led by Eduardo García-Calleja in Madrid and Alex Valls in Barcelona, and is praised by clients for its responsiveness and practical business approach.

Cuatrecasas' 11-partner employment team, under Pilar Cavera, has an excellent reputation. Recent highlights include the defence of a major Spanish group in termination of contract proceedings brought by 300 employees of a shipping company acquired by the group; the team has also been active advising in relation to various significant restructurings and plant closures, for clients such as Coca Cola Spain and Fisipe Barcelona, while clients for collective bargaining advice included Arbora & Ausonia and Nestlé.

Garrigues handles a huge volume of employment law work. The team includes some 17 partners, with specialists based in over half its Spanish offices and has a very strong record on large-scale restructurings. Recommended individuals include practice head Federico Durán, who recently led the advice to El Corte Inglés in a landmark Supreme Court case arising from the dismissal of two union representatives, and Juan José Yago who, together with Paloma Rodríguez de Ravena, led on a restructuring for the Sanofi-Aventis Group that involved over 300 redundancies.

Sagardoy Abogados, Member of Ius Laboris is a hugely respected employment law boutique that handles a full range of advice for

EMPLOYMENT

BAKER & McKENZIE ✪
CUATRECASAS ✪
GARRIGUES ✪
SAGARDOY ABOGADOS, MEMBER OF IUS LABORIS ✪
URÍA MENÉNDEZ ✪

Antras, Bufete
Clifford Chance
Gómez-Acebo & Pombo Abogados ✪

Cremades & Calvo-Sotelo ✪
DLA Piper Rudnick Gray Cary ✪
Ernst & Young Abogados, SL ✪
Freshfields Bruckhaus Deringer
Linklaters ✪
SJ Berwin ✪

Adarve Corporación Jurídica ✪
Allen & Overy ✪
Araoz & Rueda ✪
Bertrán & Associats, Bufete
Brosa
Broseta Abogados ✪
Deloitte
Echecopar Abogados
Fernando Scornik Gerstein
KPMG Abogados ✪
Legalia Abogados ✪
Mullerat ✪
PEREZ-LLORCA ✪
Pintó Ruiz & Del Valle ✪
Roca Junyent ✪
Ventura Garcés & López-Ibor, Abogados ✪

Firms are listed A-Z in tiers which are ranked in order of priority
✪ Indicates firm displays contact details at the end of this chapter.

employers; recent clients include Iberia (advised in relation to its collective negotiation with pilots), Ahold (in relation to its restructuring), and La Caixa (in relation to pensions-related claims). Juan Antonio Sagardoy specialises in contentious matters and enjoys an excellent reputation.

Uría Menéndez maintains a broad and well-respected employment and social security practice, under practice head Ignacio García Perrote. Lourdes Martín and Barcelona-based Mario Ibáñez are the other lead partners.

Bufete Antras in Barcelona is well regarded for its employment work, with name partner José María Antras enjoying a strong individual reputation, while Juan Calvente is the main point of contact at **Clifford Chance** and offers transactional, advisory and contentious experience.

Gómez-Acebo & Pombo Abogados, under sole partner Ignacio Campos, has recently been active on the employment aspects of a number of restructurings, for both domestic and international companies. Established clients include Ahold and Sun Microsystems, while Dell is among the team's recent new clients.

DLA Piper Rudnick Gray Cary's employment group is set to combine in February 2006 with that of **Squire, Sanders & Dempsey L.L.P.**'s Madrid office, whose work (under Pilar Menor) prior to the transfer included advising Technicolor on collective bargaining negotiations. The team includes Angela Toro, who joined **DLA Piper Rudnick Gray Cary** from **Baker & McKenzie**. Luis Peinado has left the firm.

UPS, Warner Bros. Entertainment España, and CIT Newcourt Financial Spain are among **Freshfields Bruckhaus Deringer**'s recent clients for employment advice. Dispute resolution head Vicente Sierra heads the practice, together with Raquel Flórez.

Linklaters' employment practice is headed by senior associate Naiara Rodríguez-Escudero, who has particular experience on M&A- and restructuring-related matters. Transactions in which the team was involved in 2005 included major acquisitions for Capio AB and Nmás1 Private Equity.

SJ Berwin has an active employment practice, with Carlos Gil the main point of contact. Clients include Universal Music International, Michael Page International, and various private equity houses (recently advised on issues such as remuneration structuring systems and executive terminations).

Allen & Overy's employment group is overseen by tax partner Carlos Albiñana and includes specialist senior associate Moira Guitart. Acting for CVC Capital Partners on its acquisition of Mivisa Envases was a highlight on the transactional side, while other clients in 2005 included Twentieth Century Fox, Bank of America and Imperial Tobacco.

Araoz & Rueda recruited Alfonso Suárez from *Bufete Suárez Migoyo* as a partner to head its employment practice. Clients include Sensient Fragrances and various companies in the Tecnipublicaciones group.

Broseta Abogados has advised in relation to numerous collective dismissals, with recent examples including dismissals by Wincanton Trans European España and cinema chain Cinesa.

KPMG Abogados' wide-ranging employment practice is led by the newly recruited Susana Pizarroso (ex-**Garrigues**), while at **Legalia Abogados**, senior associate David Sequera's experience includes various corporate restructurings and collective bargaining matters; Iberica de Diagnóstico (owned by CVC Capital Partners) is a client.

Mullerat has handled contentious and non-contentious employment work for a good variety of international and domestic clients, including advising on numerous collective redundancy procedures. Sonia Cortés heads the practice.

PEREZ-LLORCA, under Javier Fernández Pallarés (ex-**KPMG Abogados**), handles day-to-day employment advice for clients such as Vueling Airlines, Nexity España, UGC Iberia and Bouygues, and also offers a good range of transactional and contentious experience.

Roca Junyent was joined in late 2005 by a team of employment lawyers from **Ernst & Young Abogados, SL**, among them Miguel Ángel Alcaraz, who headed the labour practice at his former firm, and economist Luis Martín, who headed the corporate restructuring department.

Ventura Garcés & López-Ibor, Abogados' clients include Ryanair and easyJet in addition to various senior managers. Alfonso López-Ibor heads the practice.

ENVIRONMENT

Garrigues has a substantial and very well-regarded environmental team, and is praised by clients for its integration of multi-disciplinary teams of consultants and lawyers. Recent work, aside from various M&A- and project finance-related due diligence investigations, includes providing ongoing advice to the Ministry of the Environment about sustainable development, and assisting the environmental authorities of various regional governments on, among other matters, the drafting of regulations. Santiago Garrido and Antonio Baena are the two partners in the team, with associate Jesús de la Morena also very active.

Uría Menéndez offers experience across a full range of environmental matters, including administrative, civil and criminal proceedings, and due diligence and impact audits. Carlos de Miguel in the firm's Madrid office heads the practice.

Baker & McKenzie's key specialists are José Antonio García-Trevijano in Madrid (formerly of leading administrative law boutique *García-Trevijano*, with which the firm merged in 2002) and Xavier Junquera in Barcelona. Recent clients on the advisory side include Holcim (in relation to CO_2 emission rights), Elcogas and ENCE, and the team is also experienced in environmental litigation; in 2005 it represented AMAC in proceedings relating to regulations governing the storage of nuclear waste.

ENVIRONMENT

GARRIGUES ✪
URÍA MENÉNDEZ ✪

Baker & McKenzie ✪
Clifford Chance
Cuatrecasas ✪
DLA Piper Rudnick Gray Cary ✪
Gómez-Acebo & Pombo Abogados ✪
Linklaters ✪
SCHILLER LEXCONSULT Abogados

Broseta Abogados ✪
CMS Albiñana & Suárez de Lezo ✪
Davies Arnold Cooper ✪
Mullerat ✪

Firms are listed A-Z in tiers which are ranked in order of priority
✪ *Indicates firm displays contact details at the end of this chapter.*

At **Clifford Chance**, Juan José Lavilla has a broad administrative law practice that includes environmental work, and has advised on energy emission limits and other matters under Kyoto. On the contentious side, the firm recently acted for a client in a dispute arising from alleged environmental contamination at a combined-cycle plant.

Cuatrecasas has a wide-ranging administrative law, urban planning and environment practice, in which Yolanda Guerra and Albert Raventós are the two partners (both based in Barcelona). The team's experience includes advising on waste management, pollution, health and safety, and contamination matters.

Energy specialist Gonzalo Aranzabal is set to join **DLA Piper Rudnick Gray Cary** in February 2006, as part of the transfer from **Squire, Sanders & Dempsey L.L.P.**'s Madrid office; his track record includes a variety of environmental work, including environmental litigation.

Gómez-Acebo & Pombo Abogados' experience takes in emissions-trading schemes, waste and water management, and noise pollution. Víctor Casarrubios is the lead partner, and now works alongside public law specialists Carlos Vázquez and Pedro Poveda (previously of *AYLA Abogados*, with which the firm merged at the start of 2005). Recent clients include public bodies such as the Consejería de Medio Ambiente del Gobierno de Baleares (advised in relation to draft IPPC legislation), and the Ministerio de Medio Ambiente.

The key individuals at **Linklaters** are administrative and environmental law specialist Miguel Riaño, and managing associate Ignacio Paz, both formerly of **Garrigues**. They continue to handle some good-quality standalone instructions as well as transactional support work, recently acting for the European Recycling Platform (comprising Sony, Hewlett-Packard, Electrolux and others) on the implementation of the Directive on Waste Electrical and Electronic Equipment, and for the Galician Regional Government on the development of IPPC legislation.

SCHILLER LEXCONSULT Abogados has a well-regarded and wide-ranging advisory and contentious environmental practice, with Juan Antonio Loste, based in the firm's Barcelona office, specialising in the area.

Javier Torre de Silva heads the practice at **CMS Albiñana & Suárez de Lezo**, while Ricardo Garrido at **Davies Arnold Cooper** is an environmental liability specialist whose recent work includes advising a client on a US$17m hydrocarbon pollution claim in Mexico; the team also handles advisory work, including drafting environmental liability policies and advising on soil decontamination duties.

IT AND TELECOMS

Clifford Chance has an excellent record on transactions in the telecoms and media sectors. In 2005 the firm acted for Grupo Corporativo ONO on the financing of its €2.25bn purchase of Auna and for Telefónica on the financing of its acquisition of a majority stake in Cesky Telecom (through finance partners Carlos Hernández-Canut and Stuart Percival respectively). Corporate partner José María Fernández-Daza is also experienced in the telecoms sector and led the advice to Red Eléctrica in the sale of its telecoms subsidiary, Albura, to T-Online.

Cremades & Calvo-Sotelo maintains a very strong reputation for telecoms, IT and e-commerce, with key partners including telecoms specialist Javier Cremades and Fernando Pardo Bustillo.

Juan Picón and Josep Julià are among the partners to transfer from **Squire, Sanders & Dempsey L.L.P.**'s Madrid office to **DLA Piper Rudnick Gray Cary** in early 2006, and will take some very strong telecoms experience, both regulatory and transactional, to their new firm. Recent clients include Tele2, advised on the acquisition of Comunitel Global from a Portuguese operator. They will work alongside Jason Flint, who currently heads **DLA Piper Rudnick Gray Cary**'s technology, media and communications practice.

Ecija Abogados is well known for its technology and media expertise, and has been heavily involved in the regulatory and financing aspects of new Spanish television channel 'La Sexta' (with Hugo Ecija leading the advice). The firm also acted for the European Commission on its Euro6IX Project (relating to the implementation of the IPv6 internet protocol), while Colt Telecom, BT, Bearing Point and Vodafone are among the firm's other clients.

IT AND TELECOMS

CLIFFORD CHANCE
CREMADES & CALVO-SOTELO ✪
DLA PIPER RUDNICK GRAY CARY ✪
ECIJA ABOGADOS ✪
GÓMEZ-ACEBO & POMBO ABOGADOS ✪
SÁNCHEZ PINTADO & NÚÑEZ ABOGADOS
URÍA MENÉNDEZ ✪

Ashurst ✪
Baker & McKenzie ✪
Cuatrecasas ✪
Freshfields Bruckhaus Deringer
Garrigues ✪

Abril Abogados, S.L. ✪
Allen & Overy ✪
Bird & Bird ✪
Broseta Abogados ✪
CMS Albiñana & Suárez de Lezo ✪
Castro, Sueiro & Varela Abogados ✪
Deloitte
Jones Day ✪
KPMG Abogados ✪
Legalia Abogados ✪
Linklaters ✪
Lobao Subirats
Lovells ✪
Martínez Lage & Asociados ✪
Mullerat ✪
Pintó Ruiz & Del Valle ✪
Roca Junyent ✪
SJ Berwin ✪
Villar Arregui Abogados

Firms are listed A-Z in tiers which are ranked in order of priority
✪ Indicates firm displays contact details at the end of this chapter.

Gómez-Acebo & Pombo Abogados is best known for its antitrust and regulatory work, and has a strong presence in the audiovisual sector, with 2004/5 work including acting for Axión in various matters relating to broadcasting transmission services. Bloomberg TV and BT Group are among its other recent clients (the latter advised on its acquisition of a Spanish subsidiary of Cable & Wireless). Almudena Arpón de Mendívil heads the communications and audiovisual practice group.

Sánchez Pintado & Núñez Abogados is – with **Cremades & Calvo-Sotelo** and **Ecija Abogados** – the third boutique firm in the top tier, and has a well-established record in the areas of telecoms, new technologies, audiovisual and multimedia. Partners Joaquin Otaola Zamora and Ignacio Núñez are both TMT specialists.

Uría Menéndez is a strong choice for transactional and regulatory advice in the IT, telecoms and broadcasting sectors. 2005 saw Cándido Paz-Ares and Carlos Paredes led the advice to Telefónica on its €3bn merger (by absorption) with Terra Networks, while other clients advised on recent telecoms deals include T-Online, Orange and ING (the latter in relation to the €400m sale of its stake in Auna to Santander Central Hispano).

Ashurst has recently handled a number of corporate transactions for The Carphone Warehouse, among them the acquisition by its Spanish subsidiary (Telechoice España) of telephony services reseller Tecnologías Integrales de Telecomunicaciones. Practice head Gonzalo Jiménez-Blanco is a former head of legal of BT in Spain, and new corporate partner María José Menéndez (ex-**Clifford Chance**) has some strong recent experience in the broadcasting sector.

Maite Diez is head of **Baker & McKenzie**'s communications and IT practice, and specialises on the telecoms side (both transactional and regulatory), recently advising clients such as Tiscali, Iridium, Telecom Italia and Aló Comunicaciones, while Ernesto García-Trevijano's public law practice includes some telecoms regulatory work. Diez is also active on the IT side, and works alongside commercial law partner Cecilia Pastor and José María Méndez, who heads the media, entertainment and IP practice and is particularly highly regarded for his knowledge of the audiovisual sector.

Cuatrecasas acted for JP Morgan Partners, Providence Equity Partners and others in their acquisition of a majority stake in Grupo Corporativo ONO and the subsequent purchase of Auna Telecomunicaciones, while Alcatel, Amena, Terra Networks and Conduit Europe are among the firm's other recent clients on the telecoms side (including regulatory and contentious as well as transactional advice). Jorge Llevat, in Barcelona, meanwhile heads the firm's new technologies law group; IT mandates in the past year included acting for Deutsche Bank Spain in relation to the outsourcing of various services.

Freshfields Bruckhaus Deringer's transactional highlights in 2004/5 included KKR's bid for Grupo Auna and the buyout of Amadeus (advising Cinven and BC Partners), while KPN, Sony Computer Entertainment Europe and Hewlett-Packard were among the firm's clients for regulatory advice. Toni Valverde heads the TMT practice group.

Garrigues has a strong record in telecoms-sector M&A, with Fernando Vives and Javier Marzo in particular recommended; 2005 saw the firm involved on the related sales of Amena and Auna (to Orange and Grupo Corporativo ONO respectively, advising Endesa, Banco Santander and others as selling shareholders), and it also advised Telefónica on its €3.8bn acquisition of a 70% stake in Cesky Telecom (the incumbent operator in the Czech Republic). José María Anguiano meanwhile has a good reputation for e-business and other IT matters.

Abril Abogados, S.L. has a growing IT practice, particularly on the data protection side. Ignacio Temiño Ceniceros is the contact partner.

Allen & Overy was another firm involved on the Auna deal, acting for GE Structured Finance and Caisse de Depot et Placement du Quebec, while other clients in 2004/5 included Cable & Wireless (advised on the sale of CW Business Solutions to BT).

Bird & Bird is a new entrant to the rankings, having opened in Madrid in October 2005 to target – among other areas – specialist multi-jurisdictional work; the partner in charge is Javier Fernández-Samaniego, previously a managing associate and IT and communications practice head at **Linklaters**. Clients include AON Direct Group, business consultancies IMS Health and SOPRA Group, and HCC Financial Group.

Senior associate Juan Carlos Plaza at **Broseta Abogados** specialises in IT and IP, with areas of focus including e-administration and data protection matters, while **Castro, Sueiro & Varela Abogados**' recent transactional track record includes deals for television production, cable TV and internet companies.

CMS Albiñana & Suárez de Lezo's track record includes M&A and other work in the broadcasting and media sectors. José Giménez has some notable telecoms experience.

Jones Day, in conjunction with the firm's Paris office, advised France Télécom on its acquisition of Amena, while other clients – for regulatory, competition and corporate advice – include Colt Telecom España, Tele2 Telecommunications España, Iberbanda and new gain Ya.com (the Spanish internet arm of Deutsche Telekom).

Legalia Abogados' administrative practice includes work in the telecoms as well as other regulated sectors, for clients such as Amena. On the IT side, under senior associate Fernando Ramos, e-commerce and domain name disputes are among the areas of focus.

Linklaters' TMT-sector transactions in 2005 included the public-to-private of Amadeus and ONO Cableuropa's acquisition of Auna's fixed-line telephone and cable broadcasting business, and the firm also advised BP España, on the transfer of data to an India-based outsourcer. Managing associate Carmen Burgos has taken over as head of the IT and communications group following the departure of Javier Fernández-Samaniego for **Bird & Bird**'s new Madrid office.

Lobao Subirats is a new, two-partner firm in Barcelona that is particularly notable for its health and pharmaceutical law practice and also handles data protection and other IT advice. Clients include domestic and international companies, including pharmaceutical laboratories and technology companies. Yolanda Lobao and Margot Subirats are the name partners.

Lovells' TMT group, under Burkhart Goebel, handles a range of e-commerce, IT and entertainment and media advice, and was strengthened by the arrival of senior associate Gonzalo Gallego from **Clifford Chance**.

At **Villar Arregui Abogados**, partners with telecoms expertise include managing partner and state attorney Jose Manuel Villar – 'a very brilliant lawyer', according to one competitor – and Leopoldo Calvo-Sotelo, a former in-house counsel at Vodafone Spain.

INSURANCE

Davies Arnold Cooper has a sizeable insurance team in Madrid; it is led by Pablo Wesolowski and includes five other partners (two of them recent arrivals) and a further 29 fee-earners. It enjoys a strong share of the domestic market as well as acting for many of the international insurers and reinsurers operating in Spain, and has a very broad range of contentious expertise including D&O, employer's liability, insurance brokers PI, medical malpractice and product liability. The team also handles some non-contentious insurance regulatory advice.

Estudio Juridico Sánchez-Calero's insurance practice is very well regarded amongst competitors, with vastly experienced managing partner Professor Fernando Sánchez-Calero enjoying a particularly strong individual reputation. Clients include a host of Spanish and other European insurers and reinsurers.

Albors Galiano & Co Abogados is well known for its marine insurance practice and also offers experience in non-marine matters such as product liability. Zurich and Allianz are among the major insurer clients which the firm has advised.

At **Castro, Sueiro & Varela Abogados**, Miguel Sueiro's broad practice includes insurance work; the firm has experience on a number of M&A transactions involving insurance companies, and recently advised a large US nuclear insurance mutual company in relation to the coverage of risks in Spain, and also a monoline insurer in relation to Spanish projects.

At **Clifford Chance**, disputes partner José Antonio Caínzos has handled some insurance work; his recent track record includes acting for a large British insurer in a series of actions against a former Spanish agent of the company.

Cuatrecasas handles a variety of contentious and non-contentious insurance advice as part of its banking and financial institutions practice. Recent insureds for which the firm has acted include engineering company IDOM (advised in relation to a refusal of cover), while on the insurer side the firm has handled work for Musini, Chubb and various Lloyd's syndicates. Iñigo Quintana is particularly well known for his marine work.

Carlos Pérez heads **DLA Piper Rudnick Gray Cary**'s shipping, transport and insurance department. Aside from its work on the marine side, the firm recently acted for Generali Global in relation to a substantial engineering loss in Mexico, while other clients include a number of leading Irish insurers.

Freshfields Bruckhaus Deringer, under Javier Gómez-Acebo, handles transactional and

INSURANCE

DAVIES ARNOLD COOPER ✪

Sánchez-Calero, Estudio Juridico

Albors Galiano & Co Abogados ✪
Castro, Sueiro & Varela Abogados ✪
Clifford Chance
Cuatrecasas ✪
DLA Piper Rudnick Gray Cary ✪
Deloitte
Freshfields Bruckhaus Deringer
Garrigues ✪
Gómez-Acebo & Pombo Abogados ✪
Kennedys ✪
Uría Menéndez ✪
Velasco & Co Abogados

Adarve Corporación Jurídica ✪
B Cremades & Asociados
Belzuz Abogados ✪
Fernando Scornik Gerstein
Mullerat ✪

Firms are listed A-Z in tiers which are ranked in order of priority
✪ *Indicates firm displays contact details at the end of this chapter.*

complex regulatory advice, including advising on solvency and regulatory capital-related issues. It advised ING Group in relation to the proposed disposal of the insurance operation of ING National-Nederlanden in Spain, and Banque AIG and General Cologne Re Services UK are among its other recent clients.

Garrigues added to its record on insurance-sector M&A by acting for Aegon in the €274m sale of its general insurance subsidiary Seguros Generales to Italy's Group Reale (advised by **Cuatrecasas**), a deal led by Javier Pérez Ardá. Fernando Vives heads the practice, and is leading the advice to Allianz España as one of four defendant insurers in proceedings brought by the Organización de Consumidores y Usuarios relating to allegedly abusive terms and conditions.

Recent work for **Gómez-Acebo & Pombo Abogados** includes advising New York Life Insurance in relation to a substantial bond tranche and acting for Banque PSA Espagne on various brokerage agreements for Peugeot Auto Seguros, while Allianz Ag and MBIA are among the firm's other clients. Fernando Iguarto is the key partner for non-contentious matters.

Specialist insurance firm **Kennedys** opened in Madrid in October 2005, with its sights on a mix of international and Iberian insurance and reinsurance advice, for clients such as AIG and Generali. The firm took over the practice of *Araúz de Robles y Vélez Abogados*, having had an association with it since 2000; Jesús Vélez is the partner in charge.

Uría Menéndez has a particularly strong record on transactional work in the sector, for clients such as MetLife and Cajamar. José María Segovia is the lead partner and has a range of experience including advice on establishment, portfolio transfers, and the distribution of foreign insurers' products.

Belzuz Abogados' specialist areas include product liability and motor claims. It recently acted in the defence of a substantial damages claim arising from the construction of a hospital.

INTELLECTUAL PROPERTY

Gómez-Acebo & Pombo Abogados' IP practice maintains its premium reputation. 2004/5 highlights on the trade mark side included the resolution, for Nike, of a long-running dispute with a former distributor regarding the use of its name, while clients for patent advice included Novartis, Ferring Pharmaceuticals and Nokia (the latter advised in a dispute with Vitelcom relating to GSM technology). Diageo, Microsoft and Lacoste are among the firm's other longstanding clients. Gonzalo Ulloa heads the four-partner team, and enjoys a fine name as a specialist IP litigator, while fellow partner Jesús Muñoz-Delgado is also very highly rated.

A clear highlight for **Baker & McKenzie** was acting for Russian petroleum company Lukoil in the recovery of its Community Trademark, before the sole CTM Spanish Court in Alicante, along with trade mark litigation for Pfizer and anti-counterfeiting disputes for Hewlett-Packard and Lucas Film. Calvin Klein, Ben Sherman, and The Polo Ralph Lauren Company are among the other international brands which the firm represents. The team includes Madrid practice head José María Méndez and Jesús de Alfonso in Barcelona, and was strengthened by the arrival of former **Gómez-Acebo & Pombo Abogados** partner Manuel Lobato.

Clifford Chance is best known for its patent work; in 2004/5 it advised Pfizer in infringement disputes to prevent certain generic products from entering the market, while GlaxoSmithKline, Merck, and Du Pont de Nemours International were among the other clients advised in patent matters. The firm also acted for Philip Morris International in various criminal actions relating to cigarette counterfeiting. Miquel Moñtañá is the key contact, and is based in the firm's Barcelona office.

Elzaburu is a highly rated industrial and intellectual property boutique that is particularly well known for its trade mark registration and prosecution work, and also handles anti-counterfeiting and anti-piracy matters. Alberto de Elzaburu is the managing partner, with fellow partners Antonio Castán and Javier Fernández-Lasquetty also recommended.

Garrigues, under Miguel Moscardó, has been busy on a range of patent and trade mark infringement actions, such as continuing to represent **Lovells** in proceedings relating to the use of its name in Spain. Highlights on the commercial side included advising biotech research centre CIMA in relation to R&D contracts and patent exploitation matters. Carolina Pina is highly recommended, described by one client as 'intelligent, thoughtful, well-prepared and proactive'. The firm has, since 2001, run a dedicated sports and entertainment department, and has its own in-house trade mark and patent agency.

INTELLECTUAL PROPERTY
Barcelona and Madrid

GÓMEZ-ACEBO & POMBO ABOGADOS ✪

Baker & McKenzie ✪
Clifford Chance
Elzaburu
Garrigues ✪
Uría Menéndez ✪

Abril Abogados, S.L. ✪
CMS Albiñana & Suárez de Lezo ✪
Cuatrecasas ✪
DLA Piper Rudnick Gray Cary ✪
Ecija Abogados ✪
Freshfields Bruckhaus Deringer
Grau, Baylos & Angulo ✪
Herrero & Asociados ✪
Mullerat ✪
Pintó Ruiz & Del Valle ✪
Ruiz & Veiga Abogados ✪
Santiago Mediano Abogados ✪

Adarve Corporación Jurídica ✪
Batalla Abogados
Broseta Abogados ✪
Cremades & Calvo-Sotelo ✪
Iuris Valls Abogados
Larrauri & Lopez Ante Abogados ✪
Lovells ✪
Lupicinio Eversheds ✪
M. Vega Penichet, Bufete ✪
SJ Berwin ✪
Sánchez Pintado & Núñez Abogados
Ventura Garcés & López-Ibor, Abogados ✪
Villar Arregui Abogados

Firms are listed A-Z in tiers which are ranked in order of priority
✪ *Indicates firm displays contact details at the end of this chapter.*

Uría Menéndez runs a wide-ranging IP, unfair competition and marketing practice, and is known for having adopted a more selective approach to IP work than some of its competitors. Agustín González is an IP specialist and former head of legal at the Spanish Collecting Society; also active are José Massaguer and, in Barcelona, Montiano Monteagudo.

Abril Abogados, S.L.'s IP practice is focused in its Madrid office, where Carlos Gonzáles Valdes and Ignacio Temiño Ceniceros are both based. 2004/5 saw the firm act for Choice Hotels International, Burger King and Discovery (Channel) Communications in trade mark disputes, and it also represented two mobile telephone content providers in the defence of proceedings brought by Warner Music. ONO is a longstanding client.

CMS Albiñana & Suárez de Lezo's Vicente Arias handles a range of IP, IT and data protection work. Sony-BMG Music and Sony Pictures International are among the firm's clients.

Cuatrecasas has a good reputation for contentious IP, and has been active on trade mark disputes across a range of sectors, for clients such as Pernod Ricard, Bulgari and Ferrero. It also advises a range of media and entertainment clients, on contentious and non-contentious matters. Jorge Llevat is the lead partner.

DLA Piper Rudnick Gray Cary handles some IP work as part of its technology, media and communications practice, led by Jason Flint; its offering will be enhanced by the transfer of **Squire, Sanders & Dempsey L.L.P.**'s Madrid IP practice, which includes privacy and data protection work, for US and other clients.

Ecija Abogados is well known for its copyright expertise, and also handles trade mark and design work. In 2004/5 the firm advised in a trade mark dispute with Telefónica Movistar, and on the non-contentious side acted for Vodafone in relation to its launch of 'Vodafone Life'. Other clients include various ISPs and internet collection societies, as well as media groups, software developers and film producers. Pilár Sánchez-Bleda García is among the individuals specialising in the area.

Freshfields Bruckhaus Deringer, under Antoni Valverde in Barcelona, is advising a major US biotech company in patent litigation against a Spanish pharmaceutical company, while other recent clients include Weight Watchers International, Sony Computer Entertainment Europe, and Adobe Systems Inc.

Grau, Baylos & Angulo is still a young firm, having established in November 2003, but it has a relatively large team of specialist IP litigators, including founding partners Jorge Grau and Alejandro Angulo in Barcelona and María Baylos in Madrid. The firm is instructed in numerous pharmaceutical patent actions and is also acting for an optical technology patent owner in infringement proceedings, as well as handling anti-counterfeiting work for a variety of fashion industry and other brands.

Herrero & Asociados has a good name for its patent and trade mark registration and protection work, and also handles domain name and copyright matters. Recommended individuals include José Antonio Hernández (one of the firm's founding partners) and Patricia Koch.

Mullerat acts for a range of domestic and international brands and is particularly active on the contentious side, advising on trade mark and copyright infringement cases, as well as handling anti-counterfeiting and parallel trade matters. Barcelona managing partner Carles Prat heads the practice.

Pintó Ruiz & Del Valle offers a good range of contentious and non-contentious IP experience, and is notable for its involvement in the long-running dispute between sparkling wine producers Freixenet and Codorníu, which concluded in the Supreme Court in 2005. Javier del Valle and Salvador Ferrandis – both based in the firm's Madrid office – are among the individuals who specialise in the area.

Ruiz & Veiga Abogados partners Carina Ruiz and Eduardo Veiga both handle a mix of IP, competition and commercial work. Recent clients for IPR protection advice include a domestic pharmaceutical company and an Italian golf apparel manufacturer.

Santiago Mediano Abogados has a strong reputation for handling contentious and non-contentious IP and other commercial advice for entertainment, media and technology companies; among them are Hola!/Hello! magazine, Yahoo! and the Stage Entertainment group. Santiago Mediano is, according to one client, 'one of the best, if not the best lawyer for anything related to copyright societies in Spain'; he works alongside fellow founding partners Javier Berrocal, who specialises on the technology side, and Silvia Hernández, who heads the trade mark and patent registration practice.

At **Broseta Abogados**, Juan Carlos Plaza specialises in IP and IT matters. The Valencia-based firm also has an active media, entertainment and sports practice.

Javier Cremades is the key contact for IP at **Cremades & Calvo-Sotelo**, while Kiko Carrión heads the IP (as well as litigation) practice at **Lupicinio Eversheds**.

Carlos Valls at **Iuris Valls Abogados** in Barcelona has some strong IP experience; the firm recently advised a number of US clients on patent infringement matters, and also handles trade mark, passing off and unfair competition advice.

Larrauri & Lopez Ante Abogados is a five-partner, multi-disciplinary firm with offices in Madrid, Bilbao and Malaga. José Manuel Rey and José Luis Chamorro – both Madrid-based – are IP/IT specialists, and count Nintendo and the Spanish NBA among their clients.

Burkhart Goebel heads **Lovells**' Spanish and German IP practice, and transferred to Madrid from the firm's Hamburg office at the end of 2004. The firm is instructed by Anheuser-Busch in a dispute with Czech brewer Budejovicky Budvar, while other clients in 2005 included Deutsche Telekom. The firm also has the leading IP practice in Alicante.

Ventura Garcés & López-Ibor, Abogados' clients include Mattel, which the firm advised in relation to the confiscation of Barbie products in Spain. Andrea Garcés is the lead partner.

Other recommended firms, with offices in Alicante, include: **Landwell, Abogados y Asesores Fiscales**; Germany's **Bardehle Pagenberg Dost Altenburg Geissler** and

INTELLECTUAL PROPERTY
Alicante

LOVELLS ✪

Elzaburu
Landwell, Abogados y Asesores Fiscales ✪

Abril Abogados, S.L. ✪
Bardehle Pagenberg Dost Altenburg Geissler
Boehmert & Boehmert
D.A. Casalonga – Josse, Bureau
Heinonen & Co
LOPEZ GIMENEZ TORRES
Perez Segura, Asociados
Pintó Ruiz & Del Valle ✪
Taylor Wessing
Zeiner & Zeiner

Firms are listed A-Z in tiers which are ranked in order of priority
✪ Indicates firm displays contact details at the end of this chapter.

Boehmert & Boehmert; **Bureau D.A. Casalonga – Josse**; Finland's **Heinonen & Co**; **LOPEZ GIMENEZ TORRES**; **Perez Segura, Asociados**; **Pintó Ruiz & Del Valle**; Anglo-German firm **Taylor Wessing**; and Austria's **Zeiner & Zeiner**.

PROJECT FINANCE

Clifford Chance enjoys a very strong reputation for its work in the energy and infrastructure sectors, with Alberto Manzanares and Carlos Hernández-Canut among the finance partners with specialist projects experience. Javier López Antón has left the firm.

Headline projects for **Garrigues**, under highly rated practice head José Guardo, included the financing of the Consuegra-Tomelloso shadow toll road (Spain's first greenfield road bond), acting for monoline XL Capital Assurance, with **Gómez-Acebo & Pombo Abogados** advising the SPV issuer (Auvisa) and **Clifford Chance** acting for the European Investment Bank. The firm was also instructed on the Perpignan-Figueres High-Speed Rail Link, acting for Royal Bank of Scotland and others as lead arrangers, and is active on a variety of financings in the renewables sector.

Highlights for **Uría Menéndez** in 2005 included acting for Aigües del Segarra Garrigues in a major infrastructure project in Catalunya involving the construction of an irrigation network linked to the Segarra-Garrigues canal, on which Teresa Paz-Ares in Barcelona led the advice. The firm remains particularly active on wind farm projects. Juan Ignacio Gonzáles and Carlos de Cárdenas Smith have very strong individual reputations.

Allen & Overy has been acting for the sponsors on various health sector projects and for Iberdrola on potential renewable energy projects, as well as continuing to act for Unión Fenosa in relation to an LNG project in Damietta, Egypt,

PROJECT FINANCE

CLIFFORD CHANCE
GARRIGUES ✪
URÍA MENÉNDEZ ✪

Allen & Overy ✪
Cuatrecasas ✪
Gómez-Acebo & Pombo Abogados ✪
Jones Day ✪
Linklaters ✪

Ashurst ✪
Baker & McKenzie ✪
Broseta Abogados ✪
Castro, Sueiro & Varela Abogados ✪
DLA Piper Rudnick Gray Cary ✪
Freshfields Bruckhaus Deringer
Legalia Abogados ✪
Lovells ✪
Lupicinio Eversheds ✪
PEREZ-LLORCA ✪
SJ Berwin ✪

Firms are listed A-Z in tiers which are ranked in order of priority
✪ Indicates firm displays contact details at the end of this chapter.

while recent lender-side clients include Lehman Brothers, Royal Bank of Scotland and GESF Finance. Highly rated joint managing partner Graham Donnell heads the practice, and Eduardo Sebastián de Erice – noted for his 'particularly practical style' – has a broad finance practice that includes energy and other projects.

Cuatrecasas continues to advise SCH and others on the €3.3bn financing of the new Line 9 of the Barcelona metro, while other recent work includes various toll road projects (such as the Ocaña-La Rodo road, advising BBVA and others) and two water plant projects in Algeria, advising Aguas de Skikda.

Gómez-Acebo & Pombo Abogados is well known for its expertise in the energy and gas sectors, and has also recently been involved on a variety of toll road financings and refinancings, including advising key client Ahorro Corporación in the €550m financing of the Costa Cálida motorway, and acting for Auvisa in the financing of the Consuegra-Tomelloso shadow toll road. Fernando Igartua and Ángel Varela are both highly experienced.

Jones Day's recent experience includes a number of high-value toll road and hotel projects in Latin America, most notably acting for the developers on the US$672m Americo Vespucio Sur road project in Santiago, Chile. The firm has also handled numerous projects in the renewable energy sector, including recently acting for Caja Madrid in the €123m financing of five windmill plants. Luis Muños heads the practice, combining with US-qualified of counsel Richard Puttré.

Miguel Riaño heads **Linklaters**' projects, public law and regulated sectors practice, working alongside Ignacio Paz, with energy and, increasingly, infrastructure the principal areas of focus. The team continued to advise Sea Energy in relation to wave energy concessions in Galicia and Asturias, and is also instructed by Cobre Las Cruces in relation to a substantial new industrial mining project.

Ashurst was instructed by the TP Ferro Consortium (comprising the ACS, Dragados and Eiffage groups) on the Perpignan to Figueres High-Speed Rail Link project, and has also been advising on the financing side of projects in the rail and health sectors. Gonzalo Jiménez-Blanco heads the firm's international finance practice.

Partners with project finance expertise at **Baker & McKenzie** include José María Sánchez and Ernesto García-Trevijano in Madrid, and Xavier Junquera in Barcelona. The firm has advised on a host of infrastructure, energy and telecoms projects, with recent highlights including a number of hospital projects for Caja Madrid, and the project to build Terminal B of Castellón harbour (advising Banco de Sabadell).

Broseta Abogados offers experience across a variety of infrastructure, energy and other projects. It acted for the successful bidder on the new Castellón international airport project, and has also been advising on the financing of new subway and streetcar lines in Valencia and Alicante.

Castro, Sueiro & Varela Abogados has an active project finance practice; its track record includes advising banks and other financial institutions in a range of motorway, gas pipeline, wind farm and other power projects.

DLA Piper Rudnick Gray Cary is set to be joined by **Squire, Sanders & Dempsey L.L.P.**'s Javier Santos, whose record includes various wind farm and energy plant projects, and also Javier López Antón, who joined the latter firm from **Clifford Chance**. Recent clients include Gobierno Balear, Genesa, and Biocarburantes de Castillo y Léon.

Freshfields Bruckhaus Deringer's practice, under Iñaki Gabilondo, has recently been focused on infrastructure and real estate projects; highlights for 2005 included acting for Goldman Sachs as subordinated lender on the proposed €160m financing for Grupo Ferrovial relating to its bid for the M-30 Madrid ring road project.

Legalia Abogados has advised on the project financing of numerous wind farms and co-generation plants. Clients include wind farm developer Preneal.

Lovells' team includes banking and finance head Joaqín Sales and, for energy and natural resources, Antonio Morales, previously Secretary General of the Nuclear Security Council. European Investment Bank, Iberdrola and water company Canal Isabel II are among the firm's clients.

Hermenegildo Altozano heads **Lupicinio Eversheds**' active energy practice, which was strengthened by the recent arrival of Pedro Mielgo, a former chairman of REE.

Miguel Temboury Redondo, a former state attorney with areas of experience including the energy sector, joined **PEREZ-LLORCA** as partner in charge of the firm's regulatory practice. Recent work includes acting for Endesa and Desarrollos Eólicos in relation to wind farm projects in southern Spain.

REAL ESTATE

Clifford Chance can point to an impressive spread of recent high-value acquisitions, disposals and financings; highlights include advising Hypo Real Estate Bank in providing €155m finance to Arlington for the purchase the 74,000 sq m San Fernando de Henares business park, on which Alfonso Benavides – 'a very good lawyer, and a real gentleman', in the words of one competitor – led the advice, while other clients on €60m-plus deals included LaSalle Investment Management and Credit Suisse Asset Management. Carlos Portocarrero and Barcelona-based Juan Antequera are the two other partners in the team.

Gómez-Acebo & Pombo Abogados has a widely respected real estate practice, whose 2005 highlights included advising Caja Castilla La Mancha on two major projects valued at €100m and €150m, and advising new developer client Agrupación Urbanística de Propietarios del Espacio in relation to various agreements with local authorities. The firm boasts a particularly strong roster of funds clients, among them HypoVereinsbank, Invesco, O'Connor Capital/ Peabody Fund and Standard Life Investments. Victoria Llavero ('experienced, pragmatic, solution-orientated and highly experienced') heads the four-partner team.

Uría Menéndez is particularly well known in the market for acting for international developers, and has an excellent track record on shopping centre, hotel and other development projects. High-value transactions in 2005 included the €115m sale of a Madrid office by Oncisa to an institutional investor, and AM MDC Residential Spain's €107m purchase of a turn-key commercial centre in Oviedo. Department head Ignacio Albinaña and Charles Coward (in Barcelona) are both recommended.

Freshfields Bruckhaus Deringer has just one real estate partner in Spain, in Juan Gómez-Acebo, but his team receives resounding endorsements from clients for the high-end, technical transactions which it targets. Headline deals in 2005 included Permira's acquisition of Ahold Supermercados and the subsequent sale and leaseback of a portfolio of 60 properties, and P&O's sale of the luxury La Manga Club complex, while other clients included two German investment funds advised in relation to shopping centre developments in Gerona and Madrid. Gómez-Acebo is described by one investor client as 'excellent; not aggressive; and very good at maintaining his client relationships'.

REAL ESTATE
CLIFFORD CHANCE GÓMEZ-ACEBO & POMBO ABOGADOS ✪ URÍA MENÉNDEZ ✪
FRESHFIELDS BRUCKHAUS DERINGER GARRIGUES ✪
Baker & McKenzie ✪ Cuatrecasas ✪ DLA Piper Rudnick Gray Cary ✪ Linklaters ✪ PEREZ-LLORCA ✪
Ashurst ✪ Deloitte Díaz-Bastien & Truan ✪ KPMG Abogados ✪ Lupicinio Eversheds ✪
Adarve Corporación Jurídica ✪ Broseta Abogados ✪ CMS Albiñana & Suárez de Lezo ✪ Davies Arnold Cooper ✪ Ecija Abogados ✪ Fernando Scornik Gerstein Legalia Abogados ✪ Lovells ✪ Mullerat ✪ Pintó Ruiz & Del Valle ✪ Roca Junyent ✪

Firms are listed A-Z in tiers which are ranked in order of priority
✪ Indicates firm displays contact details at the end of this chapter.

Garrigues' real estate and planning practice has over 50 lawyers, including five partners; the volume of work handled – spanning acquisition, development, financing and other matters – is accordingly very high, but not to the exclusion of high-quality instructions; clients in 2005 included specialist real estate investment manager AXA REIM (advised in relation to a €140m acquisition of a Madrid office building), and Carrefour (on its €210m disposal of a plot of land in Madrid, for re-acquisition following its development as a shopping centre). Key partners include Felipe Yannone and Lorenzo Clemente.

Baker & McKenzie's lead real estate partners are Isidro del Moral in Madrid and Xavier Junquera in Barcelona. The team has acted for an impressive array of hotel chains, construction companies and investors, with notable examples of the latter including Amancio Ortega's real estate companies; the firm recently advised one such company on the €90m acquisition of an office building in central Madrid, while other clients advised on substantial acquisitions in 2005 included Gadea Restaura and Omega Capital.

Major transactions for **Cuatrecasas** in 2005 included acquisitions for Santander Activos Inmobiliarios, BBVA and Babcock & Brown (the latter relating to two housing developments in

Marbella, valued at €171m). Gerard Hernández heads the real estate and construction practice, and offers a wide range of experience including shopping centre and tourist development projects. The firm also has a good record on property finance work. Bernat Mullerat has joined the firm's M&A practice group as a partner and has particular experience in the real estate sector.

DLA Piper Rudnick Gray Cary maintains an active real estate practice under Javier Ibáñez. In 2005 the team handled significant instructions for, among others, Grupo Lar, Allgemeine Hypothekenbank (advised on a €100m commercial park in Barakaldo), and a BBVA real estate fund (on the €87m sale and leaseback of a Madrid office building). Fernando Rodríguez is now based in the firm's New York office.

Linklaters' investor client base continues to expand, with new gains including AXA Real Estate Investment Managers (advised in the €115m forward acquisition of a 40,000 sq m office building) and IXIS CIB, to add to the likes of MEAG, Henderson and Invesco. Royal Bank of Scotland and Calyon are key real estate finance clients, while on the development side the team has recently handled work for, among others, Harbert Management Corporation (the €35m sale of a shopping centre developed in Madrid, to a German fund). Rafael Molina works alongside finance specialist Jesús Varela, and is widely praised for his negotiation skills and commercialism.

PEREZ-LLORCA continued to act for the developers on three major business park projects (the Las Mercedes, Cristalia and Pegaso parks, advising Nexity, Bouygues Inmobiliaria and Inmobiliaria Urbanitas respectively), while other clients for the Madrid team (led by Luis Zurera) included Klépierre (advised on the €210m purchase of a shopping centre from Carrefour, opposite **Garrigues**). Gerard Serra meanwhile heads the practice in Barcelona, where the team has recently handled several significant transactions for Inmobiliaria Colonial, most notably its €350m acquisition of a portfolio of seven buildings from Mutua Madrileña.

Ashurst's real estate and construction practice is led by Cristina Calvo. The firm acts for a number of US and other investor clients, with transactions in 2005 including offshore property fund Redleaf's disposal of its portfolio of retail centres in Spain. It also advised on the joint venture between Cargill and Stam Europe España for the forward purchase of a retail centre in the Basque Country.

Ángel Lavin is in charge of **Lupicinio Eversheds**' property and planning practices. The firm acts for a variety of financial institutions, corporates and individuals, with areas of expertise including sales and purchases of shopping centres, industrial estates and office buildings, and development work.

Broseta Abogados' recent work includes acting for a firm of architects in relation to the construction of three skyscrapers in Valencia, and for a government body in relation to the expropriation of land for the construction of a high-speed railway. The firm has an active urban planning practice.

CMS Albiñana & Suárez de Lezo's recent clients for real estate advice include Iberdrola (advised in relation to its investment in Media Park, with Antonio Pino among the partners involved). The firm also handles some property finance work.

Davies Arnold Cooper, under Javier de Dios, offers experience across a range of real estate and construction work, including property finance.

Legalia Abogados has a four-fee-earner real estate team, led by partner Pablo Artiñano del Río. Clients include a number of institutional investors, including ONCE.

Lovells' practice is led by Emilio Gómez Delgado, a senior associate who recently joined from **Gómez-Acebo & Pombo Abogados** and handles a mix of real estate, planning and environmental work.

Mullerat's recent activity includes substantial deals in the retail and development sectors, as well as the sale of part of a major real estate portfolio. Jorge Adell heads the department.

Pintó Ruiz & Del Valle's recent work includes acting on various hotel acquisitions in Spain and France, and advising on the restoration of a group of buildings in the centre of Barcelona.

SHIPPING

ALBORS GALIANO & CO ABOGADOS ✪

AMYA, Abogados ✪
DLA Piper Rudnick Gray Cary ✪
Garrigues ✪
Goñi & Co Abogados
Lebrero & Co ✪
MEANA GREEN MAURA & CO ✪
Ruiz Soroa & Zabaleta
San Simón Duch & Co
Uría Menéndez ✪

Actio XXI Abogados
Castro, Sueiro & Varela Abogados ✪
Cuatrecasas ✪
Freshfields Bruckhaus Deringer
Gómez-Acebo & Pombo Abogados ✪
Ignacio de Ros
Mestre Abogados
Ramos & Arroyo
Ruiz-Gálvez Abogados ✪
Velasco & Co Abogados

Firms are listed A-Z in tiers which are ranked in order of priority
✪ *Indicates firm displays contact details at the end of this chapter.*

SHIPPING

Albors Galiano & Co Abogados has offices in Madrid and Bilbao and is particularly well regarded for its admiralty and marine insurance work, with Eduardo Albors, Javier Galiano and Javier Portales all very highly rated individuals. The firm has since mid-2003 had an association with London's **Thomas Cooper & Stibbard**.

José Alcántara at **Abogados AMYA** is a very experienced practitioner and is extremely well known in the market. The firm has experience in a broad range of shipping as well as other transport matters, including ship finance work. Recent examples on the contentious side including the *Sea Promise* collision. The firm has recently formed associations with firms in Cartagena (in Colombia) and Shanghai.

DLA Piper Rudnick Gray Cary, under Carlos Pérez, handles a mix of wet and dry work as well as ship finance, with clients in 2005 including a UK P&I club, a Spanish tanker owner, and Vitalicio Seguros; the latter was advised in relation to a salvage claim brought by the Chinese maritime authorities following the grounding of a tanker in China, with the Spanish team combining with counterparts in the firm's Hong Kong office.

Garrigues' shipping practice is run from the firm's Bilbao office, where practice head Manuel González is based. The firm is active on shipping-related employment matters (advising shipowners and others) and registration and flagging work, as well as wet and dry litigation; recent examples include a case in the Appeal Court of Guipúzcoa relating to the validity of exclusion clauses in towage contracts.

Goñi & Co Abogados is a highly rated Madrid-based shipping boutique, while – also in Madrid – **Lebrero & Co**, under senior partner Rodolfo Gonzales-Lebrero, handles a variety of shipping, as well as aviation and general commercial work; **Lebrero & Co** has some good connections in the Paris and London insurance markets, and handles referral work from various US and other international law firms.

MEANA GREEN MAURA & CO (previously known as *Fernando Meana Green & Co Abogados*) is a well-established specialist shipping firm, and enjoys a very strong reputation amongst competitors in the market. It has offices in Madrid and Bilbao.

Ruiz Soroa & Zabaleta is a Bilbao firm with an excellent market reputation; partners Jose Ruiz Soroa and Santiago Zabaleta are both highly experienced practitioners.

San Simón Duch & Co is a two-partner Madrid firm, with Luis de San Simón and Mercedes Duch handling wet and dry work as well as some ship finance instructions.

Uría Menéndez's broad transport and logistics practice that takes in a range of ship finance and other maritime matters. Tomas Fernández-Quirós enjoys a particularly strong reputation, and works alongside fellow shipping specialists Luis Figaredo and Carlos López-Quiroga. The firm also has some strong experience in shipping-sector M&A.

Actio XXI Abogados has relations with a range of UK and other P&I clubs, and handles a full range of work on the vessel side as well representing cargo insurers against stevedores and hauliers. The firm has a partner in each of its offices in Bilbao, Madrid, Gran Canaria and Vigo; recommended partners include the 'extremely responsive, efficient and reliable' Ernesto Rivera (in Madrid).

Castro, Sueiro & Varela Abogados has a strong record for structured shipbuilding transactions and other ship finance work, advising both banks and borrowers.

Cuatrecasas offers experience on a range of shipping as well as other transport work, both contentious and on the finance side; recent activity includes advising a major maritime agent in relation to a claim for breach of agency agreement. Iñigo Quintana is highly rated.

Freshfields Bruckhaus Deringer maintains an active ship finance practice, advising a range of shipyards, financiers and arrangers; local clients include Caja Madrid and Banesto (the latter recently advised in relation to numerous financings and tax lease structures for new vessels), and the team also acts for HSBC and Barclays. Iñaki Gabilondo heads the practice, with tax specialist Miguel Klingenberg ('very experienced and always innovating') also active.

Gómez-Acebo & Pombo Abogados' practice is similarly focused on the financing side; in 2005 the firm advised in relation to various new builds (mainly acting on the arranger side), and also acted for a syndicate of banks in relation to a substantial facility granted to the Spanish subsidiaries of the Teekay Group. Clients include Ahorro Corporación and Caixanovo.

Mestre Abogados in Barcelona handles a range of maritime work, including collisions, ship arrests, insurance and cargo claims, and yachting matters. Anna Mestre is the sole partner and enjoys a very strong reputation.

TAX

BAKER & MCKENZIE ✪
CUATRECASAS ✪
GARRIGUES ✪

Deloitte
Ernst & Young Abogados, SL ✪
KPMG Abogados ✪
Landwell, Abogados y Asesores Fiscales ✪

CMS Albiñana & Suárez de Lezo ✪
Clifford Chance
Freshfields Bruckhaus Deringer
Gómez-Acebo & Pombo Abogados ✪
Linklaters ✪
Uría Menéndez ✪

Allen & Overy ✪
Araoz & Rueda ✪
Ashurst ✪
Barrilero & Asociados, Bufete
DLA Piper Rudnick Gray Cary ✪
Legalia Abogados ✪
PEREZ-LLORCA ✪
Pintó Ruiz & Del Valle ✪
Roca Junyent ✪
SJ Berwin ✪

Adarve Corporación Jurídica ✪
B Cremades & Asociados
Brosa
Broseta Abogados ✪
Castro, Sueiro & Varela Abogados ✪
Echecopar Abogados
Lovells ✪
Lupicinio Eversheds ✪
M. Vega Penichet, Bufete ✪
Mullerat ✪
Rodés & Sala Abogados ✪
Ventura Garcés & López-Ibor, Abogados ✪

Firms are listed A-Z in tiers which are ranked in order of priority
✪ *Indicates firm displays contact details at the end of this chapter.*

TAX

Baker & McKenzie's widely rated tax group has grown to include ten partners, among them Madrid-based practice heads Luis Briones and Felipe Alonso – former name partners of outstanding tax boutique *Briones, Alonso y Martín*, with which the firm merged in 2001 – and Pedro Aguarón and Esteban Raventós in Barcelona. The team handles a broad range of transactional and standalone advice, including tax audits and tax litigation, for a host of domestic and international companies, wealthy family groups, venture capital funds and others; recent clients on the M&A side include FCC, Occidental Hoteles, Gas Natural, and Sony-BMG. José Luis Prada joined the firm as a partner.

Tax work continues to account for a healthy slice of **Cuatrecasas**' fee income, notwithstanding its successful diversification from a tax firm into a full-service operation; some 35 tax partners are based across its network of Spanish offices (nearly half of them in Barcelona). The practice, led by Carles Puig, spans general and international tax planning, financial taxation, and tax litigation, and enjoys a very high reputation, with recent activity including advice on numerous substantial acquisitions, divestments and group reorganisations.

Garrigues owes the size and extent of its tax practice to its history as part of *Andersen Legal*; the team is comfortably the country's largest, with 48 partners working alongside some 450 other fee-earners, and is held in exceptionally high regard by peers. Transactional highlights in 2005 included Auna's €12.5bn spin-off of its mobile and cable operations, and GE Capital's €1.2bn personal finance joint venture with Caja de Ahorros del Mediterráneo. Ricardo Gómez-Barreda heads the practice, while other leading specialists (also Madrid-based) include Abelardo Delgado, Luis Guerreiro and Enrique Fonseca. 'Their technical knowledge and project management skills, besides the quality of the service and efficiency, keep reaching the utmost level of excellence,' according to one core client in the financial services sector.

The Big Four audit firms all have substantial legal departments advising on tax matters, with international tax, transfer pricing and M&A due diligence and tax structuring among the areas handled.

CMS Albiñana & Suárez de Lezo, under partner Santiago Díez, has a good name for handling both corporate and individual tax advice. The team includes of-counsel César Albiñana Garcia Quintana, a highly experienced professor of law.

José Ignacio Jiménez-Blanco is the principal tax specialist at **Clifford Chance** and offers a range of experience across M&A, capital markets and securitisation transactions.

Freshfields Bruckhaus Deringer is alone among the international law firms in having two full equity partners in its tax group, namely practice head and well-known rainmaker Miguel Klingenberg and Silvia Paternain, who was promoted to partner in 2004. Transactional highlights for 2005 included Gas Natural's bid for Endesa and Goldman Sachs Principal Investment Area's €1.3bn acquisition of Pirelli's cable manufacturing business. The group is also active in equity derivatives, asset and structured finance, and tax lease structures (recently advising Banesto and HSBC in relation to the latter).

Pablo Alarcón and Valencia-based Francisco Fita are the two partners in **Gómez-Acebo & Pombo Abogados**' eight-fee-earner team, whose recent highlights include advising new client Altadis on the tax aspects of its motorcycle Grand Prix sponsorship. Other clients include Losan Hotels (advised on the structuring of its purchase of a London hotel), BT and Brazil's Santista International.

The highly rated Nicolás Martín is the sole partner in **Linklaters**' team, which also includes managing associate Javier García-Pita. The practice remains focused on high-end M&A and finance transactions, including securitisation and tax-based structured finance; Martín is an integral component in the firm's private equity offering, and in 2005 led the tax structuring advice on major acquisitions by, amongst others, Permira, Mercapital, Nmás1 Private Equity, and private healthcare company Capio AB.

Tax work remains a core focus at **Uría Menéndez**, holding a relatively prominent position in the firm's practice as a whole and spanning tax litigation and individual planning advice as well as capital markets, M&A and other transactional support. Jesús Lopez Tello, in Madrid, is the longstanding practice head, while other key partners include Juan Antonio Fernández-Velilla and Luis Viñuales in Barcelona.

Allen & Overy has a dedicated tax partner in Carlos Albinaña, who is highly praised by clients for his efficiency and ability to handle complex transactions. Financing facilities, M&A and corporate reorganisations are among his areas of specialism.

Araoz & Rueda, under Alberto Baeza, handles work for a variety of domestic and international clients, including M&A and restructuring-related advice and international tax planning. The firm recently acted for the Agrimartín Group in actions before the Tax Authority and other claims.

Ashurst's Eduardo Gracia (ex-**Garrigues**) has been active on the tax aspects of M&A, private equity and acquisition finance instructions for the likes of Apax Partners España, JP Morgan and The Carphone Warehouse. Gracia is the sole Spanish member of the EU Joint Transfer Pricing Forum.

The **Squire, Sanders & Dempsey L.L.P.**'s Madrid team set to transfer to **DLA Piper Rudnick Gray Cary** includes specialist tax partner Carlos Rodríguez, whose experience spans M&A support, corporate restructurings and international tax planning work.

Legalia Abogados, under Daniel Riopérez, has a substantial tax team that handles M&A-related and other advice for a good range of medium-to-large domestic companies and financial institutions, among them textile manufacturer Mirto, Mercedes Benz Credit and Caja España.

PEREZ-LLORCA's tax group is active in support of the firm's corporate and real estate practices, where highlight deals included the acquisitions of Aldeasa and Cortefiel and Inmobiliaria Urbanitas' development of the Pegaso Business Park in Madrid. Javier Fernández Cuenca was recently promoted to partner and heads the practice.

Pintó Ruiz & Del Valle offers experience across a range of domestic and international tax work. Ramón Parcerisa, in the firm's Barcelona office, heads the group, and has a practice spanning tax, accounting management and financial investment matters.

The focus of **SJ Berwin**'s tax practice, led by Javier Morera, is planning advice to international and domestic private equity houses, on the establishment of new funds as well as investments and disinvestments. Other recent clients include a Portuguese utility, a German pharmaceutical company, and a major international airline.

Broseta Abogados in Valencia handles procedural and contentious advice, as well as tax planning matters, for – among others – various local companies and public institutions. The group is led by Luis Trigo, a former partner and head of the family business practice at **Baker & McKenzie Madrid S.L.**.

Castro, Sueiro & Varela Abogados offers a good range of corporate and personal tax experience, with name partner Miguel Sueiro particularly active.

Lovells' tax practice is headed by Miguel Ángel Sánchez, who joined shortly after the firm set up in Madrid and has an impressive track record as a former Director General of Taxation. The group counts Banco Pastor, HypovereinsBank, Uni2, Warner Music Spain, and British American Tobacco among its clients.

Mullerat's tax department is led by Juan Alberto Urrengoechea in the firm's Barcelona office, who specialises in the taxation of restructuring procedures; also in Barcelona are **Rodés & Sala Abogados**, where name partner Gonzalo Rodés is one of a number of tax specialists, and **Ventura Garcés & López-Ibor, Abogados**, where Jordi Vilalta heads the practice; the firm's client list includes a variety of domestic and foreign companies, as well as numerous individuals and family businesses.

LOVELLS

BILBAO 1
5º PISO
03001 ALICANTE

Telephone: +34 96 514 41 05
Fax: +34 96 514 43 03
E-mail: information@lovells.com
Website: www.lovells.com

Languages
English, German

Other offices
Amsterdam, Beijing, Berlin, Brussels, Budapest*, Chicago, Düsseldorf, Frankfurt, Hamburg, Ho Chi Minh City, Hong Kong, London, Madrid, Milan, Moscow, Munich, New York, Paris, Prague, Rome, Shanghai, Singapore, Tokyo, Warsaw, Zagreb*

Number of lawyers 1,600
at this office 15

Contact
Dr Verena von Bomhard

CATEGORIES OF WORK

Intellectual property law (representation before the European Trade Mark Office – OHIM)

BAKER & McKENZIE BARCELONA S.L.

AVENIDA DIAGONAL, 652, EDIF D
8TH FLOOR
08034 BARCELONA

Telephone: +34 93 206 08 20
Fax: +34 93 205 49 59
E-mail: info.barcelona@bakernet.com
Website: www.bakernet.com

Languages
Spanish, Catalan, English, French, German, Italian

Other offices
The member firms of Baker & McKenzie International, a Swiss Verein, have 70 offices in 38 countries around the world. For a complete list, please visit www.bakernet.com.

Number of lawyers 3,300+
at this office 47

Contact
Rafael Jimenez-Gusi
(rafael.jimenez-gusi@bakernet.com)

CATEGORIES OF WORK

Commercial and corporate

Tax

Employment

Public

Procedural

European Union, competition and consumer affairs

Pharmaceutical

Family groups and large estates

Real estate, urban development and environmental

Stock market and corporate governance

Industrial and intellectual property, audiovisual media

Financial services

Telecommunications and information technology

CASALS ABOGADOS

AVENIDA DIAGONAL 449, 6º
08036 BARCELONA

Telephone: +34 93 414 41 28
Fax: +34 93 414 00 51
E-mail: casals.advocats@icab.es
Website: www.casalsadvocats.com

Languages
Catalan, English, French, German, Italian, Spanish

Other offices
Madrid

Number of lawyers 34
at this office 26

International groupings
The NOMOS group of law firms

CATEGORIES OF WORK

Commercial law
Xavier Casals, J Mª Alfin

Employment law
S Tudel

Civil law
Oscar Babiloni, Flora Lopez

New technologies and environment
Laura Camacho, Manuel Saez

Litigation, arbitration
Oscar Babiloni, Antoni Freixa

Administrative and town planning
Pilar de Paz, Vicente Fargas

Tax law
Javier Martinez, Esaú Alarcón

Sports law
Pau Pascual, Oscar Sanclimens

CUATRECASAS

PASEO DE GRACIA 111
08008 BARCELONA

Telephone: +34 93 290 55 00
Fax: +34 93 290 55 67
E-mail: info@cuatrecasas.com
Website: www.cuatrecasas.com

Languages
Dutch, English, French, German, Italian, Japanese, Portuguese

Other offices
Alicante, Bilbao, Brussels, Girona, Lisbon, Lleida, Madrid, Paris, New York, Oporto, Palma de Mallorca, San Sebastian, Sao Paulo, Tarragona, Valencia, Vigo, Zaragoza

Number of lawyers 700
at this office 254

In association with
Machado, Meyer, Sendacz e Opice (Brazil); Perez Alati, Grondona, Benites, Artnsen & Martinez de Hoz (Argentina); merged with Gonçalves Pereira, Castelo Branco (Portugal)

CATEGORIES OF WORK

Banking and insurance
Adolfo Rovira

Mergers and acquisitions
José Luis Blanco

Finance
Enric Picanyol

Capital markets
Emilio Coco

Corporate and commercial
Raimon Segura

Arbitration and litigation
Jorge Badía

Employment
Jordi Puigbó, Salvador del Rey

Tax
Carles Puig

Energy and environment
Alberto Raventós, Yolanda Guerra

Intellectual property
Jorge Llevat

EU and competition
Cani Fernández

Pharmaceuticals and life sciences
Jorge Llevat

Insolvency
Javier Castrodeza

Real estate and construction
Gerard Hernández

Administrative law
Alberto Raventós

Telecoms
Alberto Raventós, Juan C Hernanz

GÓMEZ-ACEBO & POMBO ABOGADOS

DIAGONAL 442
08037 BARCELONA

Telephone: +34 93 415 74 00
Fax: +34 93 415 84 00
E-mail: abogados.bcn@gomezacebo-pombo.com
Website: www.gomezacebo-pombo.com

Languages
Basque, Catalan, English, French, German, Italian, Japanese, Portuguese, Spanish

Other offices
Bilbao, Brussels, Las Palmas de Gran Canaria, Madrid, Málaga, Seville, Valencia, Vigo

Number of lawyers 185

Contact
Richard A Silberstein

CATEGORIES OF WORK

M&A
Richard A Silberstein, Íñigo Igartua

Corporate and commercial
Richard A Silberstein, José Ángel Cano

Administrative law, regulation, competition and EC law
Íñigo Igartua

Real estate, planning and environment
José Ángel Cano

Criminal law
Javier Béjar

Civil litigation
Javier Béjar

GRAU, BAYLOS & ANGULO

C/ JOSEP IRLA I BOSCH 5-7
08034 BARCELONA

Telephone: +34 93 202 34 56
Fax: +34 93 240 53 83
E-mail: info@gba-ip.com
Website: www.gba-ip.com

Languages
Catalan, English, French, Italian, Spanish

Other offices
Madrid

Number of lawyers 16
at this office 10

Contacts
Jorge Grau (j.grau@gba-ip.com),
Maria Baylos (m.baylos@gba-ip.com),
Alejandro Angulo (a.angulo@gba-ip.com)

Member
AIPPI; INTA; EPLAW; IPO; MARQUES; APRAM; ACG; IBA

CATEGORIES OF WORK

Intellectual property

Patent litigation

Trade mark litigation

Design litigation

Copyright litigation

Advice on licence agreements

Anti-counterfeiting activities

JAUSAS

PASEO DE GRACIA 103
7TH FLOOR
08008 BARCELONA

Telephone: +34 93 415 00 88
Fax: +34 93 415 20 51
E-mail: law@jausaslegal.com
Website: www.jausaslegal.com

Languages
Catalan, Dutch, English, Finnish, French, German, Italian, Russian, Spanish

Other offices
Madrid

Number of lawyers 60
at this office 40

Member
Conférence Bleue; World IT Lawyers

CATEGORIES OF WORK

Agency and distributorships
Héctor Jausàs, Mercedes Clavell

Commercial property, real estate
Joan Vidal de Llobatera, Juan Sánchez

Construction
Mercedes Caral, Juan Sánchez

Corporate and commercial
Maria Luisa de Alarcón, Dolores Alemany

Company law
Nuria Clemente, Dolores Alemany

EU and competition law
Maria Cedo, Silvia Nebra

E-commerce, IT and data protection
José Manuel Pérez, Gabriel Nadal

Enviromental law
Rafael Muñoz de la Espada

Food law
Silvia Nebra

Foreign direct investment, tax law
M L de Alarcón, Immaculada Sallent

Healthcare, pharmaceutical law
Héctor Jausàs, Remedio Ferreres

Infrastructure and project finance
Gabriel Nadal, Immaculada Salent

Insolvency, corporate restructuring
Agustí Bou

Intellectual property
Rafael Vignoly, José Manuel Pérez

Labour law
Rafael Muñoz de la Espada, August Torà

Litigation and arbitration
Mercedes Caral, Joan Vidal de Llobatera

Mergers and acquisitions
Gabriel Nadal, Agustí Bou

Private client
Mercedes Caral

MANIEGA & SOLER ABOGADOS

AVDA DIAGONAL 618, 5TH FLOOR
THE BEETHOVEN BUILDING
08021 BARCELONA

Telephone: +34 93 414 30 70
Fax: +34 93 414 17 18
E-mail: maniegasoler@maniegasoler.com
Website: www.maniegasoler.com

Languages
Bosnian, Catalan, English, French, Spanish

Other offices
Madrid, Sarajevo, Valencia

Number of lawyers 71

CATEGORIES OF WORK

Civil and administrative
Felipe Cabredo, Mar Santamaria

Criminal law department
Mari Luz Méndez, Miriam Margarit

Maritime, transport and insurance law department
Laura Maniega, Jesús Saavedra

Labour law department
Francisco Godoy, Clara Ollé

Commercial and taxation
Eva Gironés, Alvaro Benejam

LUPICINIO EVERSHEDS

MEMBER OF EVERSHEDS INTERNATIONAL

AVENIDA DIAGONAL 520
08006 BARCELONA

Telephone: +34 93 488 28 02
Fax: +34 93 488 27 33
E-mail: mail.ba@lupicinioeversheds.com
Website: www.lupicinioeversheds.com

Languages
English, French, German

Other offices
Madrid, Valladolid

Number of lawyers 40
at this address 12

Contact
Ángel Valdés
(av@lupicinioeversheds.com)

Associated offices
Gervás & Asociados

CATEGORIES OF WORK

Finance	Tax
Commercial and corporate	Energy
Intellectual and industrial property	Litigation
Labour law	Public law
Telecommunications	Competition law
Real estate	Data protection
Private law	Insurance and reinsurance
Environmental law	

THE FIRM

Lupicinio Eversheds was established in Madrid in 1979 as Lupicinio Rodríguez Abogados. It is a multi-disciplinary law firm with an international outlook. Since 2004, the firm has been part of Eversheds International, a leading international network.

Lupicinio Eversheds currently has a team of 40 lawyers, economists and consultants, all backed by a sizeable support staff. Due to the quality of its lawyers and staff, the volume of cases handled and its excellent client base, Lupicinio Eversheds is one of the most reputable Spanish law firms, with an active international practice.

Lupicinio Eversheds opened its Barcelona office in 1994, enabling it to provide companies based in or with interests in Catalonia with first-rate advice. In 2003, a third office was opened in Valladolid.

Keeping its philosophy of working closely with its clients in mind, in 2005 Lupicinio Eversheds merged with Miró Costart Abogados. Through this merger, Lupicinio Eversheds has strengthened its service capabilities and is able to offer the same high standard of advice to companies with headquarters or interests in Catalonia.

AREAS OF PRACTICE

Lupicinio Eversheds understands the importance of a multi-disciplinary approach: each case, whether of a procedural or transactional nature, has many facets. It is not only about turning to specialists, but also equipping partners and senior lawyers with a broad and resolving approach to the particular legal problem.

Corporate and commercial law: the firm offers a full range of corporate transactional services and specialist skills back up business executive and in-house counsels, providing them top, up-to-date advice and know-how on corporate structures and transactions, including mergers and acquisitions, IPOs, corporate reorganisations, private equity transactions and joint ventures.

Tax: the firm provides specialist tax input to all types of commercial clients, particularly in the areas of corporate finance, banking and financial services. The group provides pragmatic and, where appropriate, innovative advice and solutions, maintaining close contact with clients' objectives.

Litigation and arbitration: the firm is skilled in all forms of dispute management including negotiation, mediation, arbitration, expert determination and adjudication.

Energy and project finance: the firm is part of a select group of law firms with specialist expertise in energy law, and a significant domestic and international energy and utilities practice. It has an in-depth understanding of the industry, of the agenda of the major players, and of the regulatory and competition framework.

Industrial and intellectual property: the firm's expertise in the field of special properties secures its solid position within the market and a sustained growth in the areas of authors law, protection of patents, brands, hardware and software, unfair competition and advertising.

Banking: the firm's expertise encompasses the establishment and regulation of banks, bilateral and syndicated finance, project finance, capital markets, treasury activities, financial markets and regulation, as well as insolvency and corporate reconstruction.

Real estate: the firm's expertise includes land identification, acquisition and appraisal, negotiating contractual terms, as well as obtaining any permit required.

Other areas covered by the firm include: employment law, environmental and town planning law, e-business, data protection, pharmaceutical, telecommunications and media, public law, private law and family business, competition, transport, European law and insurance and reinsurance.

MILINERS ABOGADOS Y ASESORES TRIBUTARIOS

MALLORCA, 270 4º 1ª
08037 BARCELONA

Telephone: +34 93 272 01 80
Fax: +34 93 487 27 21
E-mail: miliners@miliners.com
Website: www.miliners.com

Languages
Catalan, English, French, German, Italian, Spanish

Other offices
Bilbao*, Madrid, Seville*

Number of lawyers 19
at this office 8

International groupings
Computer Law Association; International Bar Association

CATEGORIES OF WORK

Mergers and acquisitions
Rodolfo Fernández, Ignacio Miguel Romero

Tax
Jordi Capelleras

Private client
Jordi Capelleras

Information technology
Rodolfo Fernández

Employment
José Danón, Miguel Albasanz

Corporate arbitration
Rodolfo Fernández

Real estate
Ignacio Miguel Romero

THE FIRM

Miliners Abogados y Ascsores Tributarios was founded in 2004 by three partners with great expertise in the legal profession, focusing particularly on four areas of work: corporate, tax, employment and information technology law. In recent months the firm has also expanded into property law. The firm has relationships with medium-sized law firms around the world, in order to assist both local and international clients in the development of their businesses abroad. When required, the firm accompanies clients to the place where the deal occurs. The firm is expert in helping Spanish companies expand their activities overseas, and also in advising foreign clients about investments in various technology, industrial and service sectors.

The firm is committed to these fundamental principles: serving the client with experienced and specialist lawyers, having direct contact with the client and the issue, and focusing on achieving the goal.

AREAS OF PRACTICE

The firm is organised around four areas of work. In the information technology team the firm advises companies with a high level of intellectual capital and knowledge. This includes companies in hi-tech sectors, as well as companies that render services or sell hi-tech products to the government, and companies which use advanced technology and the internet to do their business and develop their products and services. The firm practices both in litigious and non-litigious matters. Among other things, the firm has advised on copyrights in multimedia and web construction, outsourcing contracts, design and technology, due diligence of web sites and portals, media, image rights and internet content. Software contracts, transfer of intangible assets, and privacy-data protection are also currently part of the firm's work. Some of the department's lawyers have been pioneers of IT law in Spain and teach at the law university.

In corporate law the firm has been successful in merger and acquisition issues (working mainly for medium-sized companies), private equity and project finance. The firm is especially well known in the Spanish market for resolving conflicts between company holders, successfully leading negotiations in order to avoid arbitration or litigation processes. The firm's lawyers also handle corporate restructuring operations by means of joint ventures, spin-offs and contribution of branches. In addition some of the partners in the corporate team teach in law faculties and academic institutions.

The tax department combines prudence and knowledge in its approach to M&A and tax-driven transactions. It advises on mergers, acquisitions and splits in various sectors of business, such as leisure, tourism and resorts, IT, media and the internet, but also advises private clients and international investors acquiring properties or stakes in Spain. The team's advice on tax planning is informed by the most accurate and up-to-date knowledge about tax regulation and administration. The tax team is also very active in the academic world, and some of its professionals are professors in tax planning.

The employment law team is characterised by advice based on the method of anticipating risk, which involves permanent advice of a preventative nature, allowing management teams to make strategic decisions with the greatest possible legal security. The firm's professionals have intervened in relevant restructuring procedures in strategic sectors such as technology. In particular, the firm has been involved in the restructuring of construction companies in Spain, and redefining its system of collective agreements, as well as in the important procedures of mergers and sales of companies in the hotel, consulting and industrial sectors. Likewise the firm has advised and intervened in the negotiation of sector and national collective agreements; in the creation or revision of company collective agreements; as well as in company plans of the most varied scope and importance.

MULLERAT

AVENIDA DIAGONAL 640
4TH FLOOR
08017 BARCELONA

Telephone: +34 93 405 93 00
Fax: +34 93 405 91 76
E-mail: mullerat.barcelona@mullerat.com
Website: www.mullerat.com

Languages
English, French, German, Italian, Portuguese

Other offices
Madrid, Palma de Mallorca, Lisbon

Number of lawyers 70
at this office 40

Contact
Carles Prat

CATEGORIES OF WORK

Banking, finance, securities
Miguel Torres, Jorge Adell

Corporate/commercial/M&A
Jorge Adell, Fernando de la Mata

Company law
Miguel Torres, Felipe Pineda

Distribution and franchising
Sonia Cortés

Tax
Pere M Pons

Employment
Sonia Cortés, Begoña Vilar

Real estate and zoning law
Jorge Adell, Joaquim Sallarès

Patents and intellectual property
Carles Prat, Cristina Duch

EU and competition
Carles Prat, Sonia Cortés

Arbitration and litigation
Carles Prat, Isabel Mateu

Criminal law, white-collar crime
Luis Batlló

Energy and environment
Joaquim Sallarès

Asset finance
Sergio Giménez

Aviation
Sergio Giménez, Gloria Bofill

PINTÓ RUIZ & DEL VALLE

BEETHOVEN 13-7º
08021 BARCELONA

Telephone: +34 93 241 30 20
Fax: +34 93 414 38 85
E-mail: bcn@pintoruizdelvalle.com
Website: www.pintoruizdelvalle.com

Languages
English, French, German, Italian

Other offices
Alicante, Madrid, Palma

Number of lawyers 65
at this office 48

Contact
José Juan Pintó Sala

Member
Pannone Law Group EEIG; International Sport Law Association; Associazione Internazinale Giuristi di Lingua Italiana; International Wine Law Association; Spanish Group of the International Association for the Protection of Industrial Property; French Association of Practitioners of Trade Mark Law; Pharmaceutical Trade Mark Group; European Community Trademark Association International Trademark Association; National Association for the Defence of Trademarks

CATEGORIES OF WORK

Arbitration
José Juan Pintó Ruiz, Miguel Galmés

Banking/finance
Raimundo Clar

Commercial/litigation
Sigrid Martens, Cristina Paloma

Intellectual property
Salvador Ferrandis, Javier del Valle

Labour
Jordi García Viña, María Jesus Yubero

Tax
Ramón María Parcerisa,
Oscar Llandrich

Competition
María José Rodríguez, Antonio Selas

Sport law
José Juan Pintó Sala,
María del Mar Martín

Construction/real estate
Jorge Sánchez, David Peña

Franchising know-how
Fernando Rodríguez, Alfonso Abadía

Corporate
Rafael Abadía, Enrique Martínez

Internet
Jordi López

Mergers/acquisitions
Jorge López, José María Farré

Investments and finance
Javier del Valle Petersfeldt, Delia Clar

Criminal law
Rafael Sánchez, Óscar Farré

IP/litigation
Victoria Ruiz de Velasco, Eva M Ochoa

Bankruptcy
Juan Carlos Noguera

Immigration
Roberto Sánchez, Laura Figuerola

ROCA JUNYENT

ARIBAU 198
08036 BARCELONA

Telephone: +34 93 241 92 00
Fax: + 34 93 414 50 30
E-mail: bcn@rocajunyent.com
Website: www.rocajunyent.com

Languages
Catalan, English, French, German, Italian, Spanish

Other offices
Buenos Aires, Girona, Lleida, Madrid, Palma de Mallorca

Number of lawyers 165

Contact
Miquel Roca Junyent

CATEGORIES OF WORK

Administrative

Advertising and sponsorship

Arbitration

Audiovisual rights

Banking

City planning

Civil

Commercial contracts

Competition

Consumer rights

Corporate product

Court proceedings

E-commerce and electronic signatures

Energy

Environmental

Foundations and sponsorship

Insolvency

Intellectual and industrial property

Investment

Labour and social security

Mergers and acquisitions

Private equity

Property and construction

Tax

Telecommunications

The stock market

RODÉS & SALA ABOGADOS

C/ PAU CASALS 15-3°
08021 BARCELONA

Telephone: +34 93 241 37 40
Fax: +34 93 209 89 96
E-mail: central@rodesysala.com
Website: www.rodesysala.com

Languages
English, French, German, Greek, Italian, Portuguese, Russian, Spanish

Other offices
Madrid

Number of lawyers 33
at this office 26

CATEGORIES OF WORK

Banking, finance and capital markets
Julio Veloso, Núria Vila

Corporate and commercial
Tomás Fornesa, Jaime Fernández

Intellectual property
Javier Sánchez, Jaime Fernández

Labour law and employment
Miguel Queralt, Guillermo Puig

Litigation and arbitration
Jaime Fernández, Katia Garrote

Mergers and acquisitions
Tomás Fornesa, Gonzalo Rodés

Project finance
Julio Veloso, Juan Milagro

Real estate and construction
Rafael Sala, Jose Gómez

Tax
José Herrador, Macarena Llansó

International tax
Gonzalo Rodés

Private equity, MBOs and venture capital
Julio Veloso, Gonzalo Rodés

VENTURA GARCÉS & LÓPEZ-IBOR
ABOGADOS

FREIXA 26-28
08021 BARCELONA

Telephone: +34 93 241 97 40
Fax: +34 93 209 83 91
E-mail:
ventura.garces@ventura-garces.com
Website: www.ventura-garces.com

Languages
English, French, German, Italian, Spanish

Other offices
Madrid

Number of lawyers 25
at this office 16

Contacts
Claudi Garcés
(claudi.garces@ventura-garces.com),
Ricard Gené (ricard.gene@ventura-garces.com)

CATEGORIES OF WORK

Corporate and commercial

Litigation

Finance

Industrial and intellectual property

Tax

Employment

Aviation law

Telecommunications and communication

Private equity

Real estate and construction

Insurance

ABOGADOS AMYA

PRINCESA 61 5º
28008 MADRID

Telephone: +34 91 548 83 28
Fax: +34 91 548 82 56
E-mail: amya@amya.es
Website: www.amya.es

Languages
English, French, German, Greek, Italian, Japanese, Korean, Mandarin, Portuguese

Other offices
Barcelona, Buenos Aires*, Cartagena de Indias*, Las Palmas, Lisbon, Marbella*, Panama, Paris*, Piraeus*, Rome*, Shanghai*, Valencia, Vigo

Number of lawyers 39
at this office 7

Contacts
José M Alcántara, Javier Arias-Camisón

Member
Spanish MLA; CMI; ICC; IMMTA; IIDM, BIMCO

CATEGORIES OF WORK

Shipping and Admiralty
José M Alcántara, Javier Arias-Camisón

Aviation law and road transportation
Esther Zarza, Javier Linaza

Commercial law
Pedro G de Castro Andrews, Javier Arias-Camisón

Arbitration and litigation
José M Alcántara

Foreign investment
Esther Zarza, Javier Arias-Camisón

Insurance
Javier Linaza, Javier Arias-Camisón, José M Alcántara

Finance
Esther Zarza, José M Alcántara

EC law
Macarena Alcántara

Environment law
José M Alcántara, Pedro G de Castro Andrews

Corporate law
Macarena Alcántara, Pedro G de Castro Andrews

Competition and administrative law
Macarena Alcántara, Javier Arias-Camisón

ABRIL ABOGADOS

C/ AMADOR DE LOS RIOS 1-1°
28010 MADRID

Telephone: +34 91 702 03 31
Fax: +34 91 308 37 05
E-mail: abril@abrilabogados.com
Website: www.abrilabogados.com

Languages
English, French, German, Spanish

Other offices
Alicante, Barcelona, Murcia, Valencia, Vigo, Zaragoza

Number of lawyers 20
at this office 12

Member
INTA; ASIPI; AIPPI; LES; IBA; MARQUES; ECTA; IIDA

CATEGORIES OF WORK

Trade mark law
Ignacio Temiño

Distribution and franchising
Ignacio Temiño

Patent and biotechnology
Carlos Gonzalez

Copyright and e-commerce
Clara Bordoy

Unfair competition
Ignacio Temiño

Cross-border litigation
Lara Broschat

Data protection
Alvaro Ramos, Paloma Arribas

Software and internet
Clara Bordoy, Alvaro Ramos

International IP law
Emma Barraclough

Licensing
Salvador Diaz, Ignacio Temiño

Community IP law
Amparo Del Rio

ADARVE CORPORACIÓN JURÍDICA

C/ FRANCISCO DE ROJAS 2
28010 MADRID

Telephone: +34 91 591 30 60
Fax: +34 91 444 53 65
E-mail: info@adarve.com
Website: www.adarve.com

Languages
Catalan, English, French, German, Italian

Other offices
Barcelona, Las Palmas de Gran Canaria, Santiago de Compostela, Seville, Valencia

Number of lawyers 81
at this office 60

Member
TELFA (Trans European Law Firm Alliance)

CATEGORIES OF WORK

Litigation
Juan Jose Garcia

Real estate and construction
Daniel Villalobos

Business and corporate law
Daniel Villar

Family and inheritance
Luis Gutierrez

IT and IP
Daniel Villar

Banking and finance
Juan Jose Garcia

Labour law
Fernando Virseda

Environmental law
Paula Taboada

Tax law
Fernando Virseda

Insurance law
Ana Almendros

ALBORS GALIANO & CO ABOGADOS

VELÁZQUEZ 53
28001 MADRID

Telephone: +34 91 435 66 17
Fax: +34 91 576 74 23
E-mail: madrid@alborsgaliano.com
Website: www.alborsgaliano.com

Languages
English, French, German, Spanish

Other offices
Bilbao, Madrid

Number of lawyers 20

International groupings
International Association for Insurance Law (SEAIDA); International Bar Association; International Maritime Committee; Spanish Maritime Law Association

CATEGORIES OF WORK

Shipping and transport
Eduardo Albors, Javier Galiano, Javier Portales, Luis Souto

Insurance
Eduardo Albors, Javier Portales, Maria González

Litigation
Eduardo Albors, Javier Portales, Javier Galiano

Arbitration
Eduardo Albors, Javier Portales, Javier Galiano

ALLEN & OVERY

PEDRO DE VALDIVIA 10
28006 MADRID

Telephone: +34 91 782 98 00
Fax: +34 91 782 98 99
E-mail: information@allenovery.com
Website: www.allenovery.com

Languages
English, French, German, Portuguese, Dutch

Other offices
Amsterdam, Antwerp, Bangkok, Beijing, Bratislava, Brussels, Budapest, Dubai, Frankfurt, Hamburg, Hong Kong, London, Luxembourg, Milan, Moscow, New York, Paris, Prague, Rome, Shanghai, Singapore, Tokyo, Turin, Warsaw

Number of lawyers 2,304
at this office 36

Contacts
Graham Donnell, Iñigo Gómez-Jordana

CATEGORIES OF WORK

Mergers and acquisitions
Graham Donnell, Juan Barona, Iñigo Gómez-Jordana

General corporate
Juan Barona, Graham Donnell

Private equity
Iñigo Gómez-Jordana, Juan Barona

International capital markets
Iñigo Gómez-Jordana

Banking and asset finance
Iñigo Gómez-Jordana, Eduardo Sebastián de Erice

Project finance, infrastructure and energy
Graham Donnell, Eduardo Sebastián de Erice

Tax
Carlos Albiñana

ALZA ABOGADOS & FISCALISTAS

CALLE CONDE DE PEÑALVER 86
28006 MADRID

Telephone: +34 91 402 74 74
Fax: +34 91 402 24 25
E-mail: alza@alza-sa.com
Website: www.alza-sa.com

Languages
English, French, German

Number of lawyers 39

Contacts
Juan Alonso Zamorano (president), Luis Ortego Castaneda (partner, and general manager), Alfonso Suengas Goenechea (executive manager)

CATEGORIES OF WORK

- Corporate and commercial law
- Mergers and acquisitions
- Patent trade marks and copyright
- Unfair competition
- Distribution, agency, franchise
- Minority shareholders
- Bankruptcy, insolvency/corporate restructuring
- Dispute resolution, litigation and arbitration
- Civil law
- Family, probate, wills and succession
- Consumer goods
- Litigation
- Criminal law
- Banking and finance
- Tax
- Labour and social security law
- Public law
- Licensing
- Real estate and construction
- Intellectual property
- New technologies

ALZAGA, CARO, G PALENCIA, SÁNCHEZ-TERÁN Y ASOCIADOS

MARQUES DE CUBAS 6
28014 MADRID

Telephone: +34 91 360 51 83
Fax: +34 91 521 54 26
E-mail: madrid@iberforo.net
Website: www.iberforo.net

Languages
English, French, German, Italian

Number of lawyers 32

Contacts
Rafael García-Palencia, Miguel López

Member
LG International

CATEGORIES OF WORK

Administrative law
Miguel Angel Sánchez-Terán

Arbitration and litigation
Oscar Alzaga, Miguel López

Civil law
Oscar Alzaga, Miguel López

Commercial and corporate
Oscar Alzaga

EU and competition
Rafael García-Palencia

Distribution, agency and franchise
Rafael García-Palencia

Energy
Rafael García-Palencia

Insurance
Miguel López

Intellectual property
Miguel Angel Sánchez-Terán

IT, e-commerce and data protection
Rafael García-Palencia

Labour law
Rafael García-Palencia

Mergers and acquisitions
Rafael García-Palencia

Real estate
Miguel Angel Sánchez-Terán

Tax law
Aníbal Caro

Telecommunications
Rafael García-Palencia

ARAOZ & RUEDA

CASTELLANA 164
28046 MADRID

Telephone: +34 91 319 02 33
Fax: +34 91 319 13 50
E-mail:
despacho@araozyruedaabogados.es
Website: www.araozyruedaabogados.es

Languages
English, French, German

Number of lawyers 23

CATEGORIES OF WORK

Mergers and acquisitions
Pedro A Rueda, Lourdes Ayala

Private equity
Francisco Aldavero

Banking and finance
Andrés Lorrio

National and international contracting
Lourdes Ayala

Competition
Ainhoa Veiga

Intellectual property
Ainhoa Veiga

Tax
Alberto Baeza

Litigation and arbitration
Clifford J Hendel

Unfair competition
Alejandro Fernández de Araoz

Labour law
Alfonso Suárez

ASHURST

ALCALÁ 44
28014 MADRID

Telephone: +34 91 364 98 00
Fax: +34 91 364 98 01
Website: www.ashurst.com

Languages
Arabic, Catalan, English, French, German, Greek, Italian, Portuguese, Spanish

Other offices
Brussels, Dubai, Frankfurt, London, Milan, Munich, New Delhi*, New York, Paris, Singapore, Tokyo

Number of lawyers 748
at this office 36

Contacts
Steven Fox, Jesús Almoguera

CATEGORIES OF WORK

Mergers and acquisitions
Jesús Almoguera, María José Menéndez

Private equity
Jesús Almoguera

Insolvency and reconstruction
Jesús Almoguera

Telecommunications
Gonzalo Jiménez-Blanco

Media
Jesús Almoguera

Tax
Eduardo Gracia

Banking and finance
Gonzalo Jiménez-Blanco

Project finance
Gonzalo Jiménez-Blanco

Competition
Julio Pascual

Corporate finance
Jesús Almoguera, María José Menéndez

Litigation
Jesús Almoguera

Arbitration
Gonzalo Jiménez-Blanco, J Almoguera

Real estate
Cristina Calvo

Energy, transport and infrastructure
Gonzalo Jiménez-Blanco

BAKER & McKENZIE MADRID S.L.

PASEO DE LA CASTELLANA 92
28046 MADRID

Telephone: +34 91 230 45 00
Fax: +34 91 391 51 49
E-mail: info.madrid@bakernet.com
Website: www.bakernet.com

Languages
Spanish, English, French, German, Italian

Other offices
The member firms of Baker & McKenzie International, a Swiss Verein, have 70 offices in 38 countries around the world. For a complete list, please visit www.bakernet.com

Number of lawyers 3,300+
at this office 92

Contact
Maite Diez (maite.diez@bakernet.com)

CATEGORIES OF WORK

Commercial and corporate

Tax

Employment

Public

Procedural

European Union, competition and consumer affairs

Pharmaceutical

Family groups and large estates

Real estate, urban development and environmental

Stock market and corporate governance

Industrial and intellectual property, audiovisual media

Financial services

Telecommunications and information technology

BELZUZ ABOGADOS

CALLE NÚNEZ DE BALBOA
115 BIS, 1˚C
28006 MADRID

Telephone: +34 91 562 50 76
Fax: +34 91 562 45 40
E-mail: ebf@belzuz.com
Website: www.belzuz.com

Languages
English, French, Italian, Portuguese, Spanish, Swedish

Other offices
Lisbon, Porto

Number of lawyers 54
at this office 20

International groupings
IGAL (Intercontinental Grouping of Accountants and Lawyers); BILG (Benefit Insurance Lawyers Group)

CATEGORIES OF WORK

Administrative
Fernando Moreno de la Santa

Corporate and commercial
Emilio Daniel, Pérez Labrador, Ricardo Rebate Labrandero

Commercial property, real estate
Álvaro Cosmen Fernández

Dispute resolution – litigation and arbitration
Rafael de Andrés Hernández

Employment
José Manuel Martínez Galán

Family
Clara Belzuz Fernández

Insurance
Enrique Belzuz Fernández, José Garzón García

Intellectual property
Julián Plaza García

Tax
Eva Holgado Pascual

BIRD & BIRD

JORGE JUAN 8
1A PLANTA
28001 MADRID

Telephone: +34 91 760 60 00
E-mail: madrid@twobirds.com
Website: www.twobirds.com

Languages
English, French, German, Italian, Spanish

Other offices
Beijing, Brussels, Düsseldorf, Frankfurt, Hong Kong, London, Milan, Munich, Paris, Rome, The Hague

Number of lawyers 472
at this office 5

Contact
Javier Fernández-Samaneigo

CATEGORIES OF WORK

Commercial	**Information technology**
Communications	**Intellectual property**
Corporate	**Life sciences**
Data protection	**Litigation and dispute resolution**
Employment	**Public procurement**

CMS ALBIÑANA & SUÁREZ DE LEZO

C/ GENOVA 27
28004 MADRID

Telephone: +34 91 451 93 00
Fax: +34 91 442 60 45
E-mail: cms-asl@cms-asl.com
Website: www.cms-asl.com

Languages
Arabic, English, French, German, Portuguese

Other offices
Seville, Marbella

Number of lawyers 80
at this office 70

CATEGORIES OF WORK

Corporate law Cesar Albiñana, Rafael Suárez de Lezo	**Labour law** Diana Rodriguez
Mergers and acquisitions Rafael Suárez de Lezo, Antonio Pino	**Administrative law** Javier Torrre de Silva, José Gimenez
Securities market Carlos Peña, Luis Miguel de Dios	**Telecommunications** Cesar Albiñana, José Gimenez
Banking and finance Gracia Sainz, José Antonio Rodriguez	**Distribution, agency, franchise** Mariano Bautista, José R Meléndez
EU, antitrust and competition Diego Crespo, Jesús Alfaro	**Criminal law** Carlos Aguilar, Nuria Serrano
Litigation and arbitration Carlos Aguilar, Juan J Gonzalez	**Real estate** José Miguel Martin-Zamorano
Insolvency, bankruptcy Juan Ignacio Fernández-Aguado	**Intellectual property** Vicente Arias
Taxation Santiago Diez, Ana Jiménez	**Media and information technology** Vicente Arias

CASTRO, SUEIRO & VARELA
ABOGADOS

ALCALÁ 75, 1º
28009 MADRID

Telephone: +34 91 577 50 20
Fax: +34 91 431 59 31
E-mail: csv@csvabogados.com

Languages
English, French, Italian

Number of lawyers 15

Contacts
Juan Carlos Castro, Miguel Sueiro, José Ramón Varela

Member
Globalaw

CATEGORIES OF WORK

- Commercial and corporate
- Banking, securities and capital markets
- Project finance
- Insurance
- Mergers and acquisitions
- Aviation and shipping
- Litigation and arbitration
- Real estate
- Taxation
- Administrative
- Internet
- Employment
- Competition law
- Information technology

COLL-NAVARRO-SANZ-VILLAR
ABOGADOS

ALFONSO XII 32-6º
28014 MADRID

Telephone: +34 91 420 21 08
Fax: +34 91 420 22 35
E-mail: cnsv@cnsvabogados.es

Languages
English, French

Number of lawyers 9

Contact
David Navarro de Palencia

Member
InterAct Europe EEIG (Amsterdam, Athens, Antwerp, Leipzig, Lisbon, London, Madeira, Madrid, Munich, Paris, Porto, Reading, Stockholm, Turku, Vienna)

CATEGORIES OF WORK

- Commercial law
- Corporate law
- Mergers and acquisitions
- Litigation
- Insurance law
- Real estate and construction law
- Labour law, social security
- Insolvency
- Tax
- Competition law

CREMADES & CALVO-SOTELO

JORGE JUAN 30
28001 MADRID

Telephone: +34 91 426 40 50
Fax: +34 91 426 40 52
E-mail: info@cremadescalvosotelo.com
Website: www.cremadescalvosotelo.com

Languages
English, French, German, Italian, Portuguese

Number of lawyers 70

Member
International Telecommunications Advisory Group; Advoc

CATEGORIES OF WORK

Company and commercial law
Juan Ignacio Peinado

Copyright and intellectual property
Javier Cremades

Taxation law
Ignacio Arraez

Labour law
Isabel Conde

Foreign investments law
Ignacio Arráez

Banking and finance law
Santiago Calvo-Sotelo

Litigation and arbitration
Faustino Cordón

Competition and antitrust law
Diego Solana

Licensing
Isabela Crespo Vitorique

Public and administrative law
Jaime Rodriguez Arana

Patents and trade marks
Mariola Ruiz Nuñez

Telecommunications, media and entertainment
Javier Cremades

E-commerce and internet law
Javier Cremades

Mergers and acquisitions
Santiago Calvo-Sotelo

CUATRECASAS

VELÁZQUEZ 63
28001 MADRID

Telephone: +34 91 524 71 00
Fax: +34 91 524 71 24
E-mail: info@cuatrecasas.com
Website: www.cuatrecasas.com

Languages
Dutch, English, French, German, Italian, Japanese, Portuguese

Other offices
Alicante, Barcelona, Bilbao, Brussels, Girona, Lisbon, Lleida, New York, Oporto, Palma de Mallorca, Paris, San Sebastian, São Paulo, Tarragona, Valencia, Vigo, Zaragoza

Number of lawyers 700
at this office 242

In association with
Machado, Meyer, Sendacz e Opice (Brazil); Perez Alati, Grondona, Benites, Artnsen & Martinez de Hoz (Argentina); merged with Gonçalves Pereira, Castelo Branco (Portugal)

CATEGORIES OF WORK

Banking and insurance
Eduardo Ramírez

Finance
Rafael Mínguez

Corporate and commercial
Julián García Rubí

Employment
Pilar Cavero

Energy and environment
Nicolás González-Deleito, Yolanda Guerra

EU and competition
Cani Fernández

Insolvency
Alejo López-Mellado

Administrative law
Nicolás G Deleito, Javier Barnés

Mergers and acquisitions
Javier Villasante

Capital markets
Pere Kirchner, Fernando Torrente

Arbitration and litigation
Antonio Hierro

Tax
Andrés Sánchez

Intellectual property
Enrique Sánchez-Quiñones

Pharmaceuticals and life sciences
Javier Villasante

Real estate and construction
Ricardo Echevarría

Telecoms
Miguel Bravo-Ferrer, Paul A Hitchings

DLA PIPER RUDNICK GRAY CARY

PASEO DE LA CASTELLANA 35
28046 MADRID

Telephone: +34 91 319 12 12
Fax: +34 91 319 19 40
E-mail: juan.picon@dlapiper.com
Website: www.dlapiper.com

Languages
English, French, German, Italian, Spanish

Other offices
Austria, Belgium, Bosnia-Herzegovina, China, Croatia, Czech Republic, Denmark*, Egypt*, France, Georgia, Germany, Hong Kong, Hungary, Italy, Japan, Netherlands, Norway*, Poland*, Russia, Singapore*, Slovakia, South Africa*, Sweden*, Thailand, UK, Ukraine, United Arab Emirates, US

Number of lawyers 3,100
at this office 58

Contact
Juan Picón

Member
DLA Piper Group

CATEGORIES OF WORK

Banking and financial services
Javier López Antón

Capital markets
José Antonio Bonilla

Commercial and projects
Javier Santos

EU and competition law
Antonio Creus

Corporate finance and commercial
Juan Picón

Employment/human resources
Pilar Menor

Infrastructure project finance
Javier López Antón, Javier Santos

Insurance and reinsurance
Carlos Pérez

Litigation and arbitration
Josep Julià

Power generation
Javier Santos

Private equity
José Antonio Sánchez Dafos

Real estate and hospitality
Javier Ibáñez

Shipping, aviation and transport
Carlos Pérez

Tax
Carlos Rodríguez

Technology, media, communications and data protection
Diego Ramos

THE FIRM

DLA Piper Rudnick Gray Cary is a leading global legal services provider with approximately 3,100 lawyers in 58 offices across 22 countries. The organisation is committed to building long-term relationships with its clients and supports their strategic and operational needs both locally and internationally.

Currently 58 lawyers strong, DLA Piper Rudnick Gray Cary's office in Madrid offers a full range of business legal services that combine local expertise with international capability. Lawyers specialise in all aspects of business law and regularly advise on cross-border transactions.

DLA Piper is a founding member of an exclusive alliance of full-service legal organisations with a shared vision. DLA Piper Group, established in 1999, has members across Europe, Africa, the Middle East, Asia and the US, which deliver expert local know-how and integrated international solutions.

AREAS OF PRACTICE

Banking and finance: the banking and financial services practice advises on a full range of international and Spanish finance investment activities and offers full financial support to a range of clients, from lenders developing financing techniques to borrowers identifying the most beneficial financing arrangements.

Commercial and projects: lawyers help Spanish and international clients in both the private and public sectors, with a range of infrastructure financing, structured joint ventures and contractual arrangements designed to minimise risk.

Litigation: the Madrid office provides high-level legal representation and dispute resolution services.

EU and competition: the practice advises on different aspects of competition law and represents companies in proceedings before the national and EU antitrust and regulatory authorities, including the European Court of Justice.

Corporate finance and commercial: the corporate finance and commercial team advises on all corporate matters, including mergers and acquisitions, joint ventures, shareholders' agreements, restructurings, mergers and hive-downs, shareholders' disputes, director's liability, share issues, transfers and asset deals.

Employment: employment law experts advise on due diligence, collective and individual dismissals, employee benefits, compensation and senior executive contracts, pensions and social security.

Insurance: insurance and reinsurance clients are provided with a comprehensive service in every aspect of the industry, both regulatory and private.

Real estate: the team provides cross-border advice to national and international investors, developers, retailers and financers wishing to implement strategies in the Spanish market.

Shipping, aviation and transport: the practice advises on all aspects of Admiralty, aviation, transport, litigation and finance to domestic and international clients.

Tax: the practice is focused on advising on local and international tax planning at all levels, including private client work, and regularly advises on all aspects of Spanish taxation.

Technology, media, communications and data protection: the team has broad experience of the legal and technical issues and advises national and international clients on constantly evolving technology, media, intellectual and industrial property, and communciations issues.

DAVIES ARNOLD COOPER

ABOGADOS

PASEO DE LA CASTELLANA 20
2A PLANTA
28046 MADRID

Telephone: +34 91 781 63 00
Fax: +34 91 576 86 69
E-mail: dacmadrid@dacspain.com
Website: www.dacspain.com

Languages
Catalan, English, French, German

Other offices
London, Manchester, Mexico City

Number of lawyers 148
at this office 35

Contacts
Pablo Weslowski, Paulino Fajardo, Ignacio Figuerol, Javier de Dios, Ricardo Garrido, Enrique Gich, Miguel Roig, Manuel Rodriguez de Bethencourt

CATEGORIES OF WORK	
Insurance	Contingency risks
Reinsurance	Property insurance
D&O	Digital risks
Professional indemnity	Energy
Environmental liability	Arbitration and litigation
Fidelity bonds	Corporate
Product liability	Property and construction
Medical malpractice	Insurance regulatory

THE FIRM

Davies Arnold Cooper started operating back in 1989. The Madrid operation has always focused on the insurance sector and other liability carriers' needs. Benefiting from the reputation and support of Davies Arnold Cooper in the international insurance markets, Davies Arnold Cooper Abogados is involved in the development of the insurance industry in Spain and most jurisdictions in South America, mainly by providing legal services to local and international insurance and reinsurance companies, brokers, Lloyd's syndicates and other liability carriers. Where appropriate, DAC Madrid works closely with DAC London and DAC Mexico City in order to provide a unique seamless service in international insurance and reinsurance matters.

The expertise acquired by being involved in major underwriting projects and developing products within the Spanish market has allowed DAC Madrid to be considered unanimously by Spanish business press as one of the leading insurance law firms in Spain.

In line with its main practice areas, the Spanish office also has a strong capability in property, construction and corporate work. The recent appointment of corporate partner Manuel Rodriguez de Bethencourt further strengthens DAC's capability in these fields.

Currently, DAC Madrid comprises of eight partners and a total team of 35 lawyers.

AREAS OF PRACTICE

DAC Madrid benefits from a notable expertise in insurance law and legal liability matters. From the incorporation of insurance companies in Spain, policy drafting and wording adaptation in accordance with Spanish legislation, to administration of Spanish claims for London and international reinsurers, handling local claims, arbitration and litigation. In this regard, DAC Madrid is involved in some of the largest claims in Spain. DAC Madrid has a strong presence, either directly or through the Mexican office, in South American countries.

Professional liability: DAC Madrid has a leading reputation in directors' and officers' liability and all types of professional liability. These insurance areas developed rapidly in Spain in the early 90s and DAC Madrid having grown simultaneously with the expansion of the local marketplace. DAC Madrid therefore has an incomparable specialist knowledge and expertise in this sector of the insurance business.

Insurance/reinsurance: DAC Madrid is experienced in environmental liability, product liability, property insurance, bankers blanket bond, kidnap and ransom, reinsurance and ART. DAC Madrid's experience in these fields is wide and probably unique.

Corporate/regulatory: DAC has acted in the setting up of the Spanish branches of a number of foreign companies, the firm being experienced in corporate processes (including due diligence procedures, mergers and acquisitions, liquidations, etc). DAC Madrid regularly advises on all the related employment and regulatory aspects. This department continues to grow and currently comprises ten lawyers.

Property and construction: DAC Madrid's expertise extends to all aspects of commercial property, property finance and development. Clients include domestic and international investors and construction companies.

DIAZ-BASTIEN & TRUAN

TORRE PICASSO, PLANTA 35
PLAZA PABLO RUIZ PICASSO, 1
28020 MADRID

Telephone: +34 91 577 36 60
Fax: +34 91 575 54 68
E-mail: dbtmadrid@dbtlex.com
Website: www.dbtlex.com

Languages
English, French, German, Italian

Other offices
London, Marbella

Number of lawyers 32
at this office 16

Managing partner
Conrado Truan

CATEGORIES OF WORK

Litigation/arbitration
Ernesto Díaz-Bastien, Daniel Jiménez

Company and commercial
Rafael Truan, Luis Juega

Real estate law
Héctor Díaz-Bastien, Daniel Rueda

Hotel, leisure and travel
Héctor Díaz-Bastien, Rafael Truan

Agency and distribution
Rafael Truan

EU and competition law
Rosario León

Intellectual property
Eva Ribera

Tax
José María de la Cruz

Insolvency and corporate restructuring
José María de la Cruz, Rafael Truan

Fraud and white-collar crime
Ernesto Díaz-Bastien

Government business/regulatory
José Antonio Magdalena

M&A
Rafael Truan, Luis Juega

Shipping
Marco Coloma

Transport (rail)
José Antonio Magdalena

Data protection
Rosario León

ECIJA ABOGADOS

PLAZA DEL MARQUES DE
SALAMANCA, 3-4
28006 MADRID

Telephone: +34 91 781 61 60
Fax: +34 91 578 38 79
E-mail: buzon@ecija.com
Website: www.ecija.com

Languages
Catalan, English, French, German, Italian, Portuguese, Spanish

Number of lawyers 41

CATEGORIES OF WORK

Banking and finance
Hugo Ecija Bernal

Competition
Juan Salmeron Artero

Corporate and M&A
Hugo Ecija Bernal

Dispute resolution
Jose Pablo Lopez Sanchez

Labour law
Alvaro Ecija Bernal

IT and telecommuncations
Carlos Alberto Saíz Peña

Intellectual property
Hugo Ecija Bernal, Alvaro Ecija Bernal

Media law and entertainment
Hugo Ecija Bernal,
Pilar Sanchez Bleda Garcia

Real estate, inheritance and private client
Juan Salmeron Artero

Tax
Pilar Sanchez Bleda Garcia

ERNST & YOUNG
ABOGADOS

TORRE PICASSO
PLAZA PABLO RUIZ PICASSO, 1
28020 MADRID

Telephone: +34 91 572 73 70
Fax: +34 91 572 72 38
Website: www.ey.com/es

Languages
English, French, German, Italian, Portuguese

Other offices
Barcelona, Bilbao, Las Palmas de Gran Canaria, Malaga, Palma de Mallorca, Pamplona, Santa Cruz de Tenerife, Seville, Valencia, Valladolid, Vigo, Zaragoza

Number of lawyers 335

Contact
Juan Costa (country managing partner)

Member
EY Law Europe; EY Law International

CATEGORIES OF WORK

Administrative law
Sabiniano Medrano

Antitrust, trade regulation and competition
Sabiniano Medrano

Corporate law
Miguel Angel Rodríguez-Sahagún, Nieves Briz

International law
Borja Otero

Real estate
Fernando Delgado

Capital markets and finance
Sabiniano Medrano

Litigation and arbitration
Santiago Nadal

Insurance
Enrique López

International tax
Juan José Terraza

Labour law and employment
Miguel Ángel Rodríguez-Sahagún

Mergers and acquisitions
Miguel Ángel Rodríguez-Sahagún, Nieves Briz

Private wealth
Carlos Carbonell

Tax
Eduardo Sanfrutos, Enrique López

Communications and e-commerce
Ignacio Fernández García

Intellectual property
Santiago Nadal, Ignacio Fernández García

FRORIEP RENGGLI
SWISS LAWYERS

ANTONIO MAURA 10
28014 MADRID

Telephone: +34 91 523 77 90
Fax: +34 91 531 36 62
E-mail: madrid@froriep.es
Website: www.froriep.com

Languages
English, French, German, Spanish

Other offices
Geneva, London, Zug, Zurich

Number of lawyers 62
at this office 3

Contact
Jean-Marie Vulliemin

CATEGORIES OF WORK

Company and commercial

Art

Banking

Sport

Capital markets

Litigation, arbitration

White-collar crime

Wealth management/estate planning

Tax

GARRIGUES
ABOGADOS Y ASESORES TRIBUTARIOS

JOSÉ ABASCAL 45
28003 MADRID

Telephone: +34 91 514 52 00
Fax: +34 91 399 24 08
Website: www.garrigues.com

Languages
Catalonian, English, French, German, Italian, Japanese

Other offices
24 offices in Spain and the following offices worldwide: Bogotá*, Buenos Aires*, Brasilia*, Brussels, Lisbon, Mexico DF*, New York, Rio de Janeiro*, Santiago de Chile*, São Paulo*

Number of lawyers 1,300+

Contacts
José María Alonso, Miguel Gordillo (managing partners)

***In association with**
Mijares Angoitia Cortes y Fuentes, S.C (Mexico); Bruchou, Fernández Madero, Lombardi & Mitrani (Buenos Aires); Barbosa, Müssnich & Aragao (Rio de Janeiro, São Paulo, Brasilia); Barros & Errázuriz (Chile); Gomez-Pinzón (Colombia)

CATEGORIES OF WORK

Commercial and corporate law
Daniel García-Pita, Mónica Martín de Vidales, Jose Manuel Martin, Javier Urbano

Taxation
Ernesto Jiménez, Ricardo Goméz, Enrique Fonseca

Mergers and acquisitions
Ramón Bustillo, Ignacio Urbistondo, Fernando Vives

Banking, securities and insurance
Fernando Vives, Javier Ybáñez, Luis Guerreiro

Labour law
Federico Durán, Juan José Yago

Litigation and arbitration
José María Alonso, Miguel Moscardó

International tax
José Palacios

Administrative law
Pedro García Capdepón

Real estate law
Felipe Yannone

Energy and telecoms (utilities)
Javier Pérez-Ardá, Javier Marzo

Intellectual property
Miguel Moscardó, Carolina Pina

EU general and competition law
Marcos Araujo, Luis Ortiz

Environmental law
Antonio Baena, Santiago Garrido

New technologies
José Maria Anguiano, Rafael Echegoyen

Insolvency
José María Alonso, Antonio Fernández

Sports and entertainment
Julio Senn, Javier Ferrero

GÓMEZ-ACEBO & POMBO ABOGADOS

CASTELLANA 216
28046 MADRID

Telephone: +34 91 582 91 00
Fax: +34 91 582 91 14
E-mail:
abogados@gomezacebo-pombo.com
Website: www.gomezacebo-pombo.com

Languages
Basque, Catalan, English, French, German, Italian, Japanese, Portuguese, Spanish

Other offices
Barcelona, Bilbao, Brussels, Las Palmas de Gran Canaria, Málaga, Seville, Valencia, Vigo

Number of lawyers 185

Contact
Manuel Martín (managing partner)

CATEGORIES OF WORK

M&A
Francisco Peña, Jose María Beneyto

Private equity, restructuring and insolvency
José María Álvarez

Corporate finance
Fernando de las Cuevas

Financial services
Fernando Igartua, Ángel Varela

Corporate and commercial
Francisco Peña, Manuel Martín

Asset finance
Carlos Rueda

Intellectual property and technology
Gonzalo de Ulloa, Jesús Muñoz-Delgado

Labour
Ignacio Campos

Real estate, planning and environmental
Victoria Llavero

International litigation and arbitration
Miguel Ángel Fernández-Ballesteros

Criminal law
Joaquín García-Romanillos

IT and telecoms
Almudena Arpón de Mendívil,

Administrative law, regulation, competition and EC law
Juan Santamaría Pastor, Carlos Vázquez

Tax
Pablo Alarcón, Francisco Fita

HERRERO & ASOCIADOS

C/ALCALÁ 35
28014 MADRID

Telephone: + 34 91 522 74 20
Fax: + 34 91 522 62 49
E-mail: info@herreroasociados.es
Website: www.herreroasociados.es

Languages
English, German, French, Italian, Portuguese

Other offices
Bilbao, Sevilla, Barcelona, Valencia, Alicante, Santiago, Gijoñ, Reus, Lisbon

Number of lawyers 17

Contact
Patricia Koch

Member
INTA; AIPPI; AIPLA; ECTA; FICPI; APPA; EPI; Marques; Agesorpi; ITMA; ASIPI

CATEGORIES OF WORK

Intellectual property (prosecution and litigation)
Patricia Koch, José Antonio Hernández, Jose Luis López, Andrés Gómez, Miguel Aznar

Information technology, internet, e-commerce, data protection
Paz Martin

Unfair competition
Patricia Koch, Juan Casulá, Jose Luis López, Andrés Gómez, Miguel Aznar

Copyright
Alvaro Cabeza, Fernando Ortega

JONES DAY

VELÁZQUEZ 51
28001 MADRID

Telephone: +34 91 520 39 39
Fax: +34 91 520 39 38
Website: www.jonesday.com

Languages
English, French, German, Portuguese, Spanish

Other offices
Atlanta, Beijing, Brussels, Chicago, Cleveland, Columbus, Dallas, Frankfurt, Hong Kong, Houston, Irvine, London, Los Angeles, Menlo Park, Milan, Moscow, Munich, New Delhi*, New York, Paris, Pittsburgh, San Diego, San Francisco, Shanghai, Singapore, Sydney, Taipei, Tokyo, Washington DC

Number of lawyers 2,200
at this office 28

Contact
Juan Tena

*In association with Pathak & Associates

CATEGORIES OF WORK

Banking and structured finance
Luis Muñoz, Richard Puttré

Corporate transactions, M&A
Juan Tena, Federico Merino

Arbitration and litigation
Mercedes Fernández, Gonzalo Stampa

Real estate
Luis Muñoz, Federico Merino

Labour law
Carlos Saldaña

Competition and regulation
Marta Delgado Echevarría, Raimundo Ortega Bueno

Securities and stock exchange regulation
Luis Riesgo, Gregorio Arranz

Private equity
Federico Merino

Tax law
Pablo Baschwitz

TMT
Blanca Escribano Cañas, Paloma Bru Arce

KPMG
ABOGADOS

EDIFICIO TORRE EUROPA
PASEO DE LA CASTELLANA 95
28046 MADRID

Telephone: +34 91 456 34 00
E-mail: kpmglegal@kpmg.es
Website: www.kpmg.es

Languages
Catalan, English, French, German, Japanese, Portuguese

Other offices
A Coruña, Alicante, Barcelona, Bilbao, Girona, Las Palmas de Gran Canaria, Malaga, Oviedo, Pamplona, Seville, Valencia, Vigo, Zaragoza

Number of lawyers 300
at this office 125

Contacts
María José Aguiló, Ramón Pallarés

CATEGORIES OF WORK

Banking and finance
Víctor Mendoza

Commercial and corporate
Ramón Pallarés

Competition
José Manuel Cajigas, Xavier Miravalls

Outsourcing and compliance
Miguel Arias

Indirect taxes
Natalia Pastor, Joaquim Herrera

Fraud
José Manuel Cajigas

Labour
Susana Pizarroso

Mergers and acquisitions
Ramón Pallarés, Fernando Gómez Galicia

Corporate taxation
Javier Múñoz Zapatero, Javier Sabau

EU law
Xavier Miravalls

International tax
Victor Hernán, Federico Linares

Transfer pricing
Juan Rivero, Vincente Durán

LANDWELL
ABOGADOS Y ASESORES FISCALES

PASEO DE LA CASTELLANA 53
28046 MADRID

Telephone: +34 91 568 4400
Fax: +34 91 568 4672
E-mail:
landwellmarketing@es.landwellglobal.com
Website: www.landwellglobal.com/es

Languages
English, French, German, Italian, Swedish, Catalan, Portuguese

Other offices
Alicante, Barcelona, Bilbao, La Coruña, Las Palmas de Gran Canaria, Logroño, Malaga, Oviedo, Palma de Mallorca, Pamplona, San Sebastian, Santa Cruz de Tenerife, Santander, Sevilla, Valencia, Vigo, Vitoria, Zaragoza

Number of lawyers 692

Contacts
Siro A Arias, Antonio Luis Bañón, José Luis Beotas

International groupings
Landwell, law firm associated with PricewaterhouseCoopers

CATEGORIES OF WORK

Competition law
Luis Comas

Corporate structuring/services
Antonio Cañadas

Dispute resolution
Paulino Borrallo

Employment and human resources
Marta Alamán

Energy
José Luis Beotas

EU law
Luis Comas

Financial services
Javier Maceira

E-business
Javier Ribas

Family company
José Luis Martín-Ballestero

Intellectual property
Luis Corno

Mergers and acquisitions/ due diligence
Javier Díaz de Bustamante

Public law
José Luis Beotas

Real estate
Javier García Camacho

Sports law
Juan Ignacio Sanz

Tax
Siro A Arias, Miguel Cruz

Technology, media and communications
Enrique Sanz

Maritime law
Daniel Bosch

Consumer and retail and industrial products
Álvaro Klecker

KENNEDYS

C/MONTALBAN NO 10
2°EXT DCHA
28014 MADRID

Telephone: 34 91 523 72 10
Fax: +34 91 523 72 12
E-mail: j.velez@kennedys-law.com
Website:
www.kennedys-law.com/spain/index.htm

Languages
English, French, Spanish

Other offices
Auckland, Belfast, Cambridge, Chelmsford, Hong Kong, London

Number of lawyers 261
at this office 6

Contact
Jesús Vélez

CATEGORIES OF WORK

Insurance and reinsurance

Shipping and international trade

Commercial law

THE FIRM

Kennedys merged with its Spanish associate firm Araúz de Robles y Vélez Abogados (ARV) in October 2005 to form the Madrid outpost of its international network. It first entered into an association in 2000, two years after the firm's foundation. The merger is a classic example of Kennedys' responsiveness to client needs by increasing its capacity to service clients with interests in Spain and Latin America. The Madrid office works closely with its colleagues in London and both offices have lawyers who are dually qualified in Spain and England. This is helpful to clients who are insuring or reinsuring in London but have a claim arising in Spain or Latin America.

Kennedys, which is based in the UK, has other offices in New Zealand and Hong Kong plus a network of worldwide associates. The firm has a deep understanding of the pressures on the client's bottom line and has developed a reputation for providing straightforward, pragmatic advice cost effectively.

AREAS OF PRACTICE

The Madrid office advises on insurance, reinsurance, commercial law, and shipping and international trade. Its client base includes insurance and reinsurance companies, Lloyd's syndicates, steel and energy companies, manufacturers and distributors, financial institutions and other commercial entities. Kennedys' extensive experience and knowledge of the region has enabled the firm to provide a competitive service to clients who have interests in the Iberian Peninsula and Latin America. Indeed, the merger has provided the opportunity for the firm to take advantage of its combined network of contacts in the Latin American region.

The office advises clients on all aspects of commercial law including commercial contracts; debt management and collection; restructuring and insolvency; bankruptcy law; setting up of companies; contentious and non-contentious employment; mergers and acquisitions and related work; property and regulation.

A wide range of insurance and reinsurance work is handled, including disputes and litigation; policy coverage; professional indemnity and D&O; advising and representing insurers and reinsurers in relation to public bodies.

The maritime and international trade team specialises in international business. This includes commodities, financing, energy, marine and shipping. It also covers all associated insurances.

A brochure providing more details and CVs of individual team members is available on request.

LARRAURI & LOPEZ ANTE ABOGADOS

HERMOSILLA 30
28001 MADRID

Telephone: +34 91 431 10 73
Fax: +34 91 577 07 63
E-mail: info@larraurilopezante.com
Website: www.larraurilopezante.com

Languages
English, French, German, Italian, Portuguese, Spanish

Other offices
Bilbao, Malaga

Number of lawyers 22
at this office 11

Contacts
José Luis Chamorro, José Manuel Rey, Josu Larrauri, Miren Arbulu

Member
ALLIURIS; INTA; LES; ECTA; AIPPI; IPBA; IBA

CATEGORIES OF WORK

Intellectual property

IP and e-commerce law

Patent trade marks and copyright

Anti-counterfeiting activities

Information technology

Unfair competition

Software and telecoms law

Transfer of technology contracts

Licensing

Technology due diligences

Corporate law and legal assistance

General commercial practice

Commercial litigation

Tax law

Real estate law

Labour law and social security

Chapter XI

Acquisitions

Minority shareholders

Competition law

LEBRERO & CO

ALFONSO XII NO 24
28014 MADRID

Telephone: +34 91 531 36 05
Fax: +34 91 531 41 94
E-mail: general@lebreroandco.com
Website: www.lebreroandco.com

Languages
English, French, Italian, Portuguese

Other offices
Barcelona*, Bayonne*, Buenos Aires*, Malaga*, Palma de Majorca*, Las Palmas*, Vigo*

Number of lawyers 12

CATEGORIES OF WORK

Shipping and Admiralty
Rodolfo A Gonzalez-Lebrero, Monica Hervera, Alix Caballero

Aviation
Rodolfo A Gonzalez-Lebrero, Barbara Berreteaga, Alix Caballero

Mediation and arbitration
Rodolfo A Gonzalez-Lebrero, Maria del A De Miranda

Maritime and aviation finance
Rodolfo A Gonzalez-Lebrero, Manuel Arteaga

Competition law
Maria del A De Miranda

Administrative law
Manuel Urraca

Commercial and corporate law
Barbara Berreteaga, Monica Hervera

EU law
Barbara Berreteaga

LEGALIA ABOGADOS

PASEO DE LA CASTELLANA 23-1º
28046 MADRID

Telephone: +34 91 391 20 66
Fax: +34 91 310 22 22
E-mail: legalia@legalia.com
Website: www.legalia.com

Languages
Catalan, English, French, German, Italian

Other offices
Barcelona, Oviedo, Valladolid

Number of lawyers 90
at this office 50

International groupings
Law Firms of America (LFA)

CATEGORIES OF WORK

Banking and finance
Amalio Miralles

Corporate and commercial
Angel Luis Garcia

Mergers and acquisitions
Rafael Montejo

Project finance
Manuel Alvarez-Cienfuegos

Corporate tax
Daniel Riopérez

International
Rafael Montejo

Private equity
Celso Gonzalez

Civil law
Jose Manuel Delgado

Public law
Luis Castro

Labour law
David Sequera

New technologies
Fernando Ramos

Criminal law
Rafael Muriedas

Real estate, urban planning
Luis Castro

LINKLATERS

CALLE ZURBARÁN, 28
28010 MADRID

Telephone: +34 91 399 60 00
Fax: +34 91 399 60 01
Website: www.linklaters.com

Languages
All commercial and local languages in the countries where Linklaters operates

Other offices
Amsterdam, Antwerp, Bangkok, Beijing, Berlin, Bratislava, Brussels, Bucharest, Budapest, Cologne, Dubai, Frankfurt am Main, Hong Kong, Lisbon, London, Luxembourg, Milan, Moscow, Munich, New York, Paris, Prague, Rome, São Paulo, Shanghai, Singapore, Stockholm, Tokyo, Warsaw

Number of lawyers 2,000 worldwide

Contact
Íñigo Berrícano

CATEGORIES OF WORK

Banking and finance
Alejandro Ortiz, Íñigo Berrícano

Debt transactions
Pedro de Rojas

Equity/equity-linked transactions
Íñigo Berrícano

Capital markets
Íñigo Berrícano, Sebastián Albella

Corporate and commercial
Alvaro Sáinz, Alejandro Ortiz, Sebastián Albella

Labour
Naiara Rodríguez-Escudero

International finance
Conrado Tenaglia

Mergers and acquisitions
Alvaro Sáinz, Miles Curley

Project/asset finance
Miguel Riaño

Real estate
Rafael Molina

Regulatory
Íñigo Berrícano

Technology, media and telecoms
Carmen Burgos

Litigation
Ignacio Díez-Picazo

Private equity
Alejandro Ortiz

EU/competition
Silvia Pérez-Navarro

Tax
Nicolás Martín

Utilities and public sector law
Miguel Riaño, Ignacio Paz

LÓPEZ ACOSTA, RIVERO & GUSTAFSON ABOGADOS

AVENIDA DE BURGOS, 17
28036 MADRID

Telephone: +34 91 561 51 01
Fax: +34 91 561 50 66
E-mail: ila@larg-abogados.com

Languages
English, French

Number of lawyers 9

Contact
Ignacio López Acosta

Member
Jurismundi Law Association

CATEGORIES OF WORK

Civil, corporate and commercial	Labour
Mergers and acquisitions	Tax
Litigation and arbitration	Pharmaceuticals
Real estate	Information technology
Licensing, distribution and agency	

LOVELLS

PASEO DE LA CASTELLANA, 51
PLANTA 6A
28046 MADRID

Telephone: +34 91 349 82 00
Fax: +34 91 349 82 01
E-mail: information@lovells.com
Website: www.lovells.com

Languages
Spanish, English, French

Other offices
Alicante, Amsterdam, Beijing, Berlin, Brussels, Budapest*, Chicago, Düsseldorf, Frankfurt, Hamburg, Ho Chi Minh City, Hong Kong, London, Milan, Moscow, Munich, New York, Paris, Prague, Rome, Shanghai, Singapore, Tokyo, Warsaw, Zagreb*

Number of lawyers 1,600
at this office 27

Contact
José Maria Balãna

CATEGORIES OF WORK

Corporate and commercial	Public law
Banking and finance	Competition and EU law
Tax	Employment
Dispute resolution	Real estate
Intellectual property	

LUPICINIO EVERSHEDS

MEMBER OF EVERSHEDS INTERNATIONAL

VILLANUEVA 29
28001 MADRID

Telephone: +34 91 436 00 90
Fax: +34 91 578 44 89
E-mail: mail@lupicinioeversheds.com
Website: www.lupicinioeversheds.com

Languages
English, French, German, Portuguese

Other offices
Barcelona, Valladolid

Number of lawyers 40
at this address 28

Contact
Lupicinio Rodríguez
(lrj@lupicinioeversheds.com)

Associated offices
Gervás & Asociados

CATEGORIES OF WORK

Finance
Hermenegildo Altozano,
Luis Manuel García

Commercial and corporate
Luis Manuel García, León Barriola

Intellectual and industrial property
Kiko Carrión, José Ignacio Martínez

Labour law
José María Aguilera

Telecommunications
Luis Manuel Garcia

Real estate
Ángel Lavín

Private law
Maria del Carmen de Andrés

Tax
León Barriola

Energy
Hermenegildo Altozano

Litigation
Kiko Carrión

Public law
Coral Yáñez

Competition law
Lupicinio Rodríguez, Ángel Valdés

Data protection
Flor Grinberg

Insurance and reinsurance
Alex Grant

Environmental law
Esther Sebastián

THE FIRM

Lupicinio Eversheds was established in Madrid in 1979 as Lupicinio Rodríguez Abogados. It is a multi-disciplinary law firm with an international outlook. Since 2004, the firm has been part of Eversheds International, a leading international network.

Lupicinio Eversheds currently has a team of 40 lawyers, economists and consultants, all backed by a sizeable support staff. Due to the quality of its lawyers and staff, the volume of cases handled and its excellent client base, Lupicinio Eversheds is one of the most reputable Spanish law firms, with an active international practice.

Lupicinio Eversheds opened its Barcelona office in 1994, enabling it to provide companies based in or with interests in Catalonia with first-rate advice. In 2003, a third office was opened in Valladolid.

Keeping its philosophy of working closely with its clients in mind, in 2005 Lupicinio Eversheds merged with Miró Costart Abogados. Through this merger, Lupicinio Eversheds has strengthened its service capabilities and is able to offer the same high standard of advice to companies with headquarters or interests in Catalonia.

AREAS OF PRACTICE

Lupicinio Eversheds understands the importance of a multi-disciplinary approach: each case, whether of a procedural or transactional nature, has many facets. It is not only about turning to specialists, but also equipping partners and senior lawyers with a broad and resolving approach to the particular legal problem.

Corporate and commercial law: the firm offers a full range of corporate transactional services and specialist skills back up business executive and in-house counsels, providing them top, up-to-date advice and know-how on corporate structures and transactions, including mergers and acquisitions, IPOs, corporate reorganisations, private equity transactions and joint ventures.

Tax: the firm provides specialist tax input to all types of commercial clients, particularly in the areas of corporate finance, banking and financial services. The group provides pragmatic and, where appropriate, innovative advice and solutions, maintaining close contact with clients' objectives.

Litigation and arbitration: the firm is skilled in all forms of dispute management including negotiation, mediation, arbitration, expert determination and adjudication.

Energy and project finance: the firm is part of a select group of law firms with specialist expertise in energy law, and a significant domestic and international energy and utilities practice. It has an in-depth understanding of the industry, of the agenda of the major players, and of the regulatory and competition framework.

Industrial and intellectual property: the firm's expertise in the field of special properties secures its solid position within the market and a sustained growth in the areas of authors law, protection of patents, brands, hardware and software, unfair competition and advertising.

Banking: the firm's expertise encompasses the establishment and regulation of banks, bilateral and syndicated finance, project finance, capital markets, treasury activities, financial markets and regulation, as well as insolvency and corporate reconstruction.

Real estate: the firm's expertise includes land identification, acquisition and appraisal, negotiating contractual terms, as well as obtaining any permit required.

Other areas covered by the firm include: employment law, environmental and town planning law, e-business, data protection, pharmaceutical, telecommunications and media, public law, private law and family business, competition, transport, European law and insurance and reinsurance.

BUFETE M. VEGA PENICHET

ALCALÁ 115
28009 MADRID

Telephone: +34 91 431 55 00
Fax: +34 91 431 59 38
E-mail: mvp@mvegapenichet.com
Website: www.mvegapenichet.com

Languages
English, Filipino, French, Spanish

Number of lawyers 18

Contacts
Jorge Vega-Penichet, Pilar Molina, Luis Vega-Penichet

CATEGORIES OF WORK

- Administrative
- Alimentary
- Arbitration, litigation and insolvency
- Aviation
- Banking, finance and capital markets
- Corporate and commercial
- Distribution, agency and franchising
- Energy and natural resources
- Environmental
- EU, competition, unfair competition, publicity
- Intellectual property
- Insurance and reinsurance
- Labour
- Mergers and acquisitions
- New technologies
- Project and asset finance
- Real estate, construction and development
- Tax
- Tourism and hostelry

MARTÍNEZ LAGE & ASOCIADOS

ABOGADOS

CLAUDIO COELLO 37
28001 MADRID

Telephone: +34 91 426 44 70
Fax: +34 91 577 37 74
E-mail: abogados@m-lage.es
Website: www.martinezlage.com

Languages
English, French, German, Italian

Other offices
Brussels*

Number of lawyers 15

CATEGORIES OF WORK

- EU law
- EU and national competition law
- Unfair competition law
- Telecommunications law
- Media law
- Entertainment law
- Intellectual property law
- Mergers and acquisitions
- Dumping
- Utilities
- Pharmaceutical law
- Administrative law
- Company law
- Arbitration and litigation

MEANA GREEN MAURA & CO

VELAZQUEZ 92-2 DCHA
28006 MADRID

Telephone: +34 91 432 38 75
Fax: +34 91 432 38 76
E-mail: info@meanagreenmaura.com

Languages
Spanish, English, French, German, Basque

Other office
Bilbao, Cadiz

Number of lawyers 11
at this office 7

Member
Commercial Arbitration Tribunal of Bilbao; Spanish Maritime Association; ENCR (Euro Arbitration)

CATEGORIES OF WORK

Maritime law (civil, criminal and administrative)

Carriage of goods by sea

Admiralty

Oil pollution

Marine Insurance

Administrative law

Transport (air, road, rail)

Aviation

Fisheries

Personal injury and labour law

EC law

International trade

ADR, litigation and arbitration

Insolvency

Commerce

Company and corporate law

MULLERAT

TORRE PICASSO
PZA PABLO RUIZ PICASSO, 1
28020 MADRID

Telephone: +34 91 399 51 89
Fax: +34 91 399 49 13
E-mail: mullerat.madrid@mullerat.com
Website: www.mullerat.com

Languages
English, French, German, Italian, Portuguese

Other offices
Barcelona, Palma de Mallorca, Lisbon

Number of lawyers 70
at this office 22

Contact
Alberto Echarri

CATEGORIES OF WORK

Banking, finance, securities
Alberto Echarri, Angel Pendás

Corporate/commercial/M&A
Alberto Echarri, César Vázquez

Company law
Angel Pendás, Carmen Esteban

Distribution and franchising
Alberto Echarri, César Vázquez

Tax
Juan Alberto Urrengoechea, Pablo Otero

Employment
Raul García, María Dolores Sánchez

Patents and intellectual property
María Dolores Garayalde

EU and competition
Antonio Bravo

Energy and environment
Angel Pendás

Arbitration and litigation
Pilar Brindle, Antonio Bravo

Criminal law, white-collar crime
Pilar Brindle, Vicente Roldan

Civil rights
María Sánchez

Aviation
Gema Díaz

PEREZ-LLORCA

ALCALÁ 61
28014 MADRID

Telephone: +34 91 436 04 20
Fax: +34 91 436 04 30
E-mail: pll@perezllorca.com
Website: www.perezllorca.com

Languages
Catalan, English, French, German, Italian, Spanish

Other offices
Barcelona

Number of lawyers 58
at this office 53

Contacts
Pedro Pérez-Llorca (Madrid), Gerard Serra (Barcelona)

CATEGORIES OF WORK

Corporate and finance
Pedro Pérez-Llorca, Vicente Conde Viñuelas

Competition and EU
Oriol Armengol

Litigation and arbitration
Jose Pedro Pérez-Llorca, David Arias

Real estate
Luis Zurera, Gerard Serra

Tax
Javier Fernández Cuenca

Labour
Luis Enrique Fernández Pallarés

Administrative and regulatory law
Miguel Temboury

BUFETE RAMÓN HERMOSILLA

CALLE CLAUDIO COELLO 32 1°
28001 MADRID

Telephone: +34 91 431 48 16
Fax: +34 91 435 63 66
E-mail:
hermosilla.abogados@rhermosilla.es

Languages
English, French, German, Italian

Number of lawyers 21

CATEGORIES OF WORK

Companies and corporations
Ramón Hermosilla Gimeno, M Jésús Dehesa

Commercial law
Ramón Hermosilla Gimeno, Carmen Fernández Vadillo

Civil law
Ramón Hermosilla Martin, César Gil de Biedma

Banking law
Ramón Hermosilla Gimeno, M Jésús Dehesa

Litigation
Ramón Hermosilla Gimeno, Javier de Andrés

Mergers and acquisitions
Ramón Hermosilla Gimeno, M Jésús Dehesa

Administrative law
Pedro Rubio Escobar

Criminal law
Eduardo Junco, Juan Casanueva

Business crime
Ramón Hermosilla Gimeno, Eduardo Junco

Family, matrimonial
Elena Garcia Écenarro

Labour law
César Gil de Biedma, Javier de Andrés

Arbitration
Ramón Hermosilla Gimeno, José A Salgado

Environment law
M Jésús Dehesa, Pedro Rubio Escobar

RAPOSO BERNARDO ABOGADOS

PASEO DE LA CASTELLANA
N°140-13°
28046 MADRID

Telephone: +34 91 411 43 27
Fax: +34 91 564 01 41
E-mail: madrid@raposobernardo.com
Website: www.raposobernardo.com

Languages
English, Portuguese, French, Italian

Other offices
Albufeira, Cidade da Praia (Cape Verde), Lisbon, Maputo (Mozambique), Porto

Number of lawyers 49
at this office 4

Contacts
Francisco Silva Carvalho,
Serena Argente Escartín

CATEGORIES OF WORK

Corporate law, M&A

Banking, capital markets and financial law

Commercial law, industrial and intellectual property

Private equity and venture capital, company restructuring

Foreign investment

Tax law, tax planning and tax litigation

Employment and social security law (pensions and incentives)

Litigation, ADR and arbitration

Health, pharmaceutical law and biotechnology

Administrative law, energy and natural resources

Real estate, construction, planning and environment

Tourism

EU and competition law

Maritime and aviation law

RODÉS & SALA ABOGADOS

C/ ALMAGRO 31, 4° DERECHA
28010 MADRID

Telephone: +34 91 391 43 04
Fax: +34 91 319 88 72
E-mail: central@rodesysala.com
Website: www.rodesysala.com

Languages
English, French, German, Greek, Italian, Portuguese, Russian, Spanish

Other offices
Barcelona

Number of lawyers 33
at this office 7

CATEGORIES OF WORK

Banking, finance and capital markets
Julio Veloso, Juan Milagro

Corporate and commercial
Julio Veloso, Teresa Martín

Intellectual property
Javier Sánchez

Labour law and employment
Guillermo Puig

Litigation and arbitration
Jaime Fernández

Mergers and acquisitions
Julio Veloso, Teresa Martín

Project finance
Julio Veloso, Juan Milagro

Real estate and construction
Juan Milagro, Teresa Martín

Tax
Juan Milagro, José Herrador

Private equity, MBOs and venture capital
Julio Veloso, Teresa Martín

RUIZ-GÁLVEZ ABOGADOS

C/ VELAZQUEZ N° 20
4° DCHA
28001 MADRID

Telephone: +34 91 781 21 91
Fax: +34 91 781 21 92

Languages
English, French, Spanish

Other offices
Algeciras*, Barcelona*, Palma de Mallorca*

Number of lawyers 26
at this office 13

Contact
Fernando Ruiz-Gálvez

International groupings
Maritime Law Spanish Association;
Comité Maritime International (CMI)

CATEGORIES OF WORK

Transport and shipping law
Fernando Ruiz-Gálvez Villaverde,
Fernando Ruiz-Gálvez Portanet

Insurance
Félix Ruiz-Gálvez Villaverde,
Gonzalo Ruiz-Gálvez Jiménez

Company
Félix Ruiz-Gálvez Villaverde,
Fernando Ruiz-Gálvez Portanet

Commercial
Fernando Ruiz-Gálvez Villaverde,
Félix Ruiz-Gálvez Villaverde

Litigation
Almudena Jiménez Ruiz-Gálvez,
Teresa Rebollo Mosquera

Civil
Maria Luisa Herrero,
Leticia Ruiz-Gálvez Juzgado

Criminal
Maria Luisa Herrero

New technologies and data protection
Almudena Jiménez Ruiz-Gálvez

Labour
Santiago Moreno Recio

Administrative
Fernando Ruiz-Gálvez Portanet

THE FIRM

Ruiz-Gálvez Abogados was founded in 1928 by Mr Fernando Ruiz-Gálvez López, who was distinguished in 1977 with the Cross of Honour of San Raimundo de Peñafort and appointed titulary member of the International Maritime Committee at the New York conference of 1965; an appointment proudly continued by his son Mr Fernando Ruiz-Gálvez Villaverde at the Sydney conference of 1996.

The firm's current partners, Mr Fernando and Félix Ruiz-Gálvez Villaverde, lead a growing team of 13 lawyers that continues the legal tradition of the family, forming one of the most ancient, experienced and specialised firms in Spain, especially in the maritime, insurance and transport law field, with presence in the most important national and international bodies in the sector.

Since 1973 Mr Fernando Ruiz-Gálvez Villaverde has regularly attended the meetings of the IMO legal committee as legal adviser to the Spanish delegation, and has also participated in several diplomatic conferences. He is a titulary member of the Comité Maritime International (CMI).

Many of the firm's lawyers are involved as lecturers in various masters courses in maritime law.

Today, Ruiz-Gálvez Abogados is much more than a family firm. With associated firms in Algeciras, Barcelona, and Palma de Mallorca, its team of more than 25 lawyers provides tradition, experience, specialisation, dedication, quality, and good, cost-effective results for its clients.

AREAS OF PRACTICE

The firm's traditional areas of expertise are insurance, shipping and transport law.

Transport law comprises road and air transport, and shipping law includes sale and purchase of ships; negotiation and drafting of all kinds of charter parties, maritime arbitration and legal disputes, shipbuilding and financing; registration, modification and cancellation of mortgages and encumbrances; flagging and registration of vessels; arrest of vessels; collisions, passenger and cargo claims; applications for liner routes; marine insurance law; salvage, wreck removals; maritime pollution, competence law in the shipping business, and so on.

Insurance law: this includes analysis and drafting of insurance policies, civil liability insurance, product liability insurance, professional liability insurance, transport insurance, legal defence of the assured, P&I insurance, claims handling, litigation.

Litigation and procedural law: the firm is especially dedicated to civil, administrative, criminal and labour procedures and litigations.

Company and commercial law: this includes legal advisers to BODs, mergers, acquisition and sale of shares, incorporation of companies, drafting of the corporate bye laws, liquidations, bankruptcies, claims against the directors of companies, arrangements before the Merchants Registry, and so on.

Civil law: this includes contracts, family law, and successions.

RUIZ & VEIGA
ABOGADOS

C/RECOLETOS, 14, 1° A
28001 MADRID

Telephone: +34 91 435 28 80
Fax: +34 91 431 88 40
E-mail: info@ruizyveiga.com
Website: www.ruizyveiga.com

Languages
English, French

Number of lawyers 2

Contact
Carina Ruiz

Member
Spanish Group of the International Association for the Protection of Intellectual Property; Association Française des Practiciens du Droit des Marques et des Modèles.

CATEGORIES OF WORK

Industrial property

Intellectual property, copyright

Competition

Antitrust law

Licensing, franchising, distribution

Litigation and arbitration

Commercial law

Consumers law

SJ BERWIN

C/CLAUDIO COELLO 37
1ª PLANTA
28001 MADRID

Telephone: +34 91 426 00 50
Fax: +34 91 426 00 66
E-mail: madrid@sjberwin.com
Website: www.sjberwin.com

Languages
Arabic, Catalan, English, French, Galician, German, Italian, Portuguese

Other offices
Berlin, Brussels, Frankfurt, London, Milan, Munich, Paris, Turin

Number of lawyers 550
at this office 18

Contacts
Carlos Pazos, Javier Morera, Ramon Garcia Gallardo

CATEGORIES OF WORK

Corporate
Carlos Pazos

Banking and finance
Carlos Pazos

Mergers and acquisitions
Carlos Pazos

E-commerce, media and telecommunications
Carlos Pazos

EU/competition
Ramon Garcia Gallardo

Private equity, MBOs, venture capital
Carlos Pazos

Tax
Javier Morera

SAGARDOY ABOGADOS, member of ius laboris

TUTOR 27
28008 MADRID

Telephone: +34 91 542 90 40
Fax: +34 91 542 26 57
E-mail: abogados@sagardoy.com
Website: www.sagardoy.com

Languages
English, French, Spanish

Other offices
Barcelona, Las Palmas de Gran Canarias, Oviedo

Number of lawyers 60
at this office 31

Member
ius laboris; International Employment Law, Pensions and Employee Benefits Alliance

CATEGORIES OF WORK

Labour and employment law
Juan Antonio Sagardoy, José Manuel Martín

Employee benefits and pensions
Iñigo Sagardoy, Martin Godino

International employment contracts
Iñigo Sagardoy

Executive employment contracts
Ana Godino, Martin Godino

Restructuring plans and collective labour law
Antonio Gómez de Enterria, Manuel Codoni, Eduardo Gómez de Enterria

Sports law
Jose Luis Fraile

Immigration
Montserrat Alonso, Ana Garicano

SÉRVULO CORREIA ABOGADOS

C/SERRANO 76-5-I
28006 MADRID

Telephone: +34 91 781 50 40
Fax: +34 91 781 50 41
E-mail: madrid@servulo.es
Website: www.servulo.es

Languages
English, French, German, Portuguese

Other offices
Lisbon

Number of lawyers 8

Contact
Pedro Moreira dos Santos

Member
IBA; Legalink; Diro; TLC

CATEGORIES OF WORK

Company and commercial

Mergers and acquisitions

Public procurement

Banking, securities and financial services

Administrative law

Arbitration and ADR

Project finance

Real estate

Tax

Antitrust and competition law

Labour law

Telecommunications

Transportation, shipping and maritime

Zoning and environmental law

SANTIAGO MEDIANO ABOGADOS

CAMPOAMOR 18 – 4º
28004 MADRID

Telephone: +34 91 310 63 63
Fax: +34 91 310 63 68
E-mail: info@santiagomediano.com
Website: www.santiagomediano.com

Languages
English, French, German, Italian, Russian, Spanish

Other offices
Barcelona

Number of lawyers 25

Contact
Javier Berrocal

CATEGORIES OF WORK

Corporate/commercial, M&A
Javier Berrocal

Criminal law
Dolores Hita

Arbitration and litigation
Arturo Fernández

Employment
Marta González

Tax
Amalia Saavedra

Entertainment and media
Santiago Mediano

International transactions
Chris Cooke

IPRs
Silvia Hernández

Project finance
Maria José Verardini

Public law
Guillermo Izquierdo

Real estate
Juan Amigó-Müller

Technology and data protection
Paula Garcia

THE FIRM

Santiago Mediano Abogados (SMA) is a business law firm offering its clients a comprehensive, prompt and practical legal service in both contentious and non-contentious matters. The firm aims to be an instrumental part of the success of each of its clients, and to bring a high level of added-value to each transaction that it handles.

SMA is a firm with a clear international approach, with a major part of its practice concerning international projects. SMA assists Spanish and foreign clients with their activities in the Spanish market place and in their cross-border transactions.

The firm's international client portfolio includes, among others, leading financial institutions, major international corporations and service companies, major Hollywood studios, real estate developers and investors, and leading IT, entertainment and media companies.

SMA's lawyers have a strong reputation in each area of practice. Six are acknowledged as being among the main Spanish legal experts in the prestigious *European Legal Experts 2006*.

AREAS OF PRACTICE

SMA's core business relates to the following areas of practice.

Corporate/commercial, M&A: SMA handles complex and highly sophisticated operations. The firm provides a wide range of services in these matters, embracing mergers and acquisitions, joint ventures, corporate restructuring, licensing, franchising and distribution agreements, and commercial conflict solving.

Dispute resolution: SMA's litigation group resolves conflicts through negotiation, mediation, arbitration or litigation, both in civil and criminal disputes. The group has a strong reputation in cross-border business disputes and in IP and IT matters.

Real estate: SMA's real estate department provides comprehensive advice in all areas of legal and strategic structuring of commercial real estate projects. Real estate experience spans financing, acquisitions, sales and exchanges, to development, construction, joint ventures, management and leasing.

Tax: the firm's tax group aims to minimise the tax burden of all national and international activities and to assist in the creation of all manner of asset management structures. SMA gives legal advice to clients on a great range of tax matters and transactions within the European Union and with countries outside, taking advantage of relevant double-taxation treaties where applicable.

IPRs, entertainment and media: SMA has a stellar reputation in this area of practice, being at the forefront of IPR developments in Spain. SMA represents some of the world's leading companies where intangible assets are the core business, including TV and film companies, broadcasters, record and music publishers, press and book publishers and video games producers, among others. The firm has its own trade mark and patent registration and prosecution department.

Information technology: the firm also represents leading technology companies, bringing its advice and expertise to transactions relating to all areas of IT, including hardware and software matters, outsourcing, internet and e-commerce, as well as privacy matters. SMA's IT lawyers fully understand the implications, legal issues and arguments surrounding the current emerging communications technologies.

SIMMONS & SIMMONS

MARQUÉS DE VILLAMAGNA
NO 3, 5ª PLANTA
28001 MADRID

Telephone: +34 91 426 26 40
Fax: +34 91 578 21 57
E-mail: enquiries@simmons-simmons.com
Website: www.simmons-simmons.com

Languages
English, French, Italian, Spanish

Other offices
London, Rotterdam, Paris, Lisbon, Milan, Rome, Düsseldorf, Frankfurt, Brussels, Padua, Oporto, Madeira, Abu Dhabi, Qatar, Hong Kong, Shanghai, Tokyo, New York

Number of lawyers 764
at this office 20

Contact
Luis Felipe Castresana

CATEGORIES OF WORK

Corporate	**Employment**
Banking	**Financial markets**
Capital markets	**Pharmaceutical and biotechnology**
Taxation	**Energy and utilities**
Projects, PFI	**TMT**
EU, competition	**Aerospace and defence**
Dispute resolution	**Transport**
Intellectual property	**Consumer goods**

URÍA MENÉNDEZ

PRINCIPE DE VERGARA, 187
28002 MADRID

Telephone: +34 91 586 04 00
Fax: +34 91 586 04 03
E-mail: madrid@uria.com
Website: www.uria.com

Languages
Catalan, English, Finnish, French, German, Italian, Polish, Portuguese, Russian

Other offices
Barcelona, Bilbao, Brussels, Buenos Aires*, Lima*, Lisbon, London, Mexico City*, New York, Porto, Santiago de Chile*, São Paulo*, Valencia

Number of lawyers 485
at this office 267

In association with
Marval, O'Farrell & Mairal (Buenos Aires); Philippi, Yrrázaval, Pulido & Brunner (Santiago de Chile); Galicia y Robles, SC (Mexico City); Payet, Rey, Cauvi (Lima); Dias Carneiro Advogados (São Paulo)

CATEGORIES OF WORK

Administrative
Jose Miguel Fatas

Arbitration and litigation
Jesús Remón

Banking and securities
Salvador Sánchez-Terán, Luis de Carlos

Bankruptcy
Alberto Núnez-Lagos, Rafael Sebastián

Commercial and corporate
Ramiro Rivera, Salvador Sánchez-Terán

Competition
Jaime Folguera, Edurne Navarro

Energy
Luis Pastor, Juan Ignacio González

Environmental
Carlos de Miguel

Intellectual property and copyright
José Massaguer, Agustín González

Labour
Ignacio García-Perrote, Lourdes Martín

Maritime, transport and logistics
Luis Figaredo, Tomás Fernández-Quirós

Mergers and acquisitions
Christian Hoedl, Salvador Sánchez-Terán

Project finance
Carlos de Cárdenas

Real estate
Adolfo Menéndez

Tax
Jesús López Tello, Juan Antonio Fernández-Velilla

Telecommunications
José Pérez Santos, Teresa Paz-Ares

VENTURA GARCÉS & LÓPEZ-IBOR

ABOGADOS

C/JOSE ABASCAL, 55-3° DCHA
28003 MADRID

Telephone: +34 91 521 78 18
Fax: +34 91 524 00 93
E-mail:
ventura.garces.mad@ventura-garces.com
Website: www.ventura-garces.com

Languages
English, French, German, Spanish

Other offices
Barcelona

Number of lawyers 25
at this office 9

Contacts
Alfonso López-Ibor
(alfonso.lopez-ibor@ventura-garces.com),
Marta Gil de Biedma
(marta.gildebiedma@ventura-garces.com)

CATEGORIES OF WORK

Corporate and commercial

Litigation

Finance

Industrial and intellectual property

Tax

Employment

Aviation law

Telecommunications and communications

Private equity

Real estate and construction

Insurance

BCP ABOGADOS & SOLICITORS

AVENIDA RICARDO SORIANO 12
EDIFICIO MARQUÉS DE
SALAMANCA 1-1
29600 MARBELLA

Telephone: +34 952 862 227
Fax: +34 952 861 682
E-mail: info@bcplawfirm.com
Website: www bcplawfirm.com

Languages
English, French, German, Spanish

Other offices
Casablanca*, Edinburgh*, Lago*, Leeds*.
London, Manchester

Number of lawyers 6
at this office 5

Contact
Oscar Abeti

CATEGORIES OF WORK

- Spanish conveyancing
- Solicitors property shop, property finding service, selling, mortgages
- Portuguese conveyancing
- Spanish wills and probate
- Spanish company matters
- Spanish taxation
- Spanish family law
- Spanish debt collection
- Moroccan conveyancing
- Personal injury (Spain)
- Spanish insolvency
- Spanish litigation
- Spanish shipping and yachting
- Spanish planning law

MICHAEL SOUL & ASOCIADOS

ABOGADOS

RAMÓN GÓMEZ DE LA SERNA 5
EDIFICIO MARBELLA AZUL 4º C
29600 MARBELLA
MÁLAGA

Telephone: +34 95 290 0323
Fax: +34 95 286 4261
E-mail: mailbox@spanishlawyers.eu.com
Website: www.spanishlawyers.co.uk

Languages
English, Spanish

Other offices
London, Madrid, Barcelona*,
Palma de Mallorca*, Valencia*

Number of lawyers 12
at this office 3

CATEGORIES OF WORK

- Company and commercial
- Commercial and residential property
- Tax – corporate and VAT
- Foreign investment in Spain
- Construction
- Town and country planning
- Arbitration and litigation
- Enforcement of foreign judgments
- Expert evidence in Spanish law
- Spanish private international law
- Probate, wills and succession
- Tax and cross-border tax planning
- Tax – income wealth and gains
- Tax – inheritance and gifts tax

GÓMEZ VILLARES & ÁLVAREZ (GV&A)
ABOGADOS – CONSULTORES TRIBUTARIOS

SAN JUAN BOSCO 2, 8ºA
29600 MARBELLA
MALAGA

Telephone: +34 95 285 77 19
Fax: +34 95 285 72 07
E-mail: marbella@gvabogados.com
Website: www.gva-abogados.com

Languages
English, French, German, Spanish

Other offices
Madrid, Málaga, Torre del Mar, Javea, Birmingham*, Liverpool*, London*

Number of lawyers 19
at this office 6

Contact
Santiago Gómez

CATEGORIES OF WORK

Banking
Ramón Gómez Villares

Corporate and commercial
Carlos Álvarez, Ramón Gómez Villares

Insurance
Santiago Gómez, Eduardo Ruiz

Litigation
Carlos Álvarez, Andrés Reina

Construction
Miguel González

Private client
Santiago Gómez

Real estate
Cristina Gómez, Vera Matés

Administrative law
Ramón Gómez Pérez-Muñoz

Tax
Eduardo Luque, Nicolás Gómez

Private international
David Posadas

Shipping and transport
Ramón Gómez Villares

THE FIRM

Gómez Villares & Álvarez (GV&A) was founded in 1999 by the merger of two traditional law firms, Gómez Villares (founded 1974) and Álvarez Fernández (founded 1980). Gómez Villares & Álvarez is a traditional practice providing a wide range of services to commercial and private clients. The firm has grown steadily from its original base in Andalucia and now has five offices across Spain at Marbella, Málaga, Madrid, Torre del Mar and Javea.

Whilst the firm maintains a strong domestic client base, it has a large proportion of foreign clients with interests in Spain. Many of the lawyers at the firm have worked in other European countries and some have dual qualification. The firm includes Spanish, English and German lawyers. The firm has a particularly high proportion of English-speaking clients and offers a bilingual service in English and Spanish. The lawyers in the firm know the service that UK clients expect, and can give clear explanations where there are differences between the English and Spanish legal systems.

AREAS OF PRACTICE

The firm's offices on the Costa del Sol and Costa Blanca handle a significant amount of commercial and residential property. The client base includes some of the leading property developers and real estate agents in Spain as well as private individuals. The property and planning specialists in the firm are recognised as experts in the area. The heavyweight litigation team based in the Málaga office supports this sector and has the capacity to pursue construction cases of whatever size.

One major area of work is in banking and finance where the firm advises both foreign and Spanish banks. The expertise offered includes mortgages and investment. The firm acts for overseas lenders with interests in Spain, such as English building societies, and can advise newcomers to the Spanish market on how to comply with regulatory requirements.

The insurance department handles personal injury litigation for some of Spain's leading insurance companies. Expertise includes traffic accidents and claims on household insurance. Plaintiff-based insurance litigation is a growing area within the firm.

The opening of a bigger Málaga office in 2005 has coincided with the expansion of the firm's tax department through collaboration with a leading Spanish specialist on tax regulations. Another important area of work is transport and shipping law.

The firm has developed expertise on private international matters due to the international nature of its client base. With English, German and Spanish lawyers working together in the Spanish jurisdiction, the firm has a genuine understanding of cross-border transactions. The firm can offer practical solutions to the needs of international clients.

Gómez Villares & Álvarez is affiliated with various UK solicitor firms, having representative offices in London, Birmingham and Liverpool. The firm is a member of the Union Internationale des Avocats, Abogados Especializados en Responsibilidasd Civil, and Hispajuris, part of the Jurisnet International Network of Lawyers.

The nature of the practice means that members of the firm travel regularly and can be available for meetings to discuss potential projects in any location.

OLIVENCIA-BALLESTER ABOGADOS

C/FERNÁNDEZ Y GONZALEZ
Nº2 TERCERA PLANTA
41001 SEVILLA

Telephone: +34 95 450 1414
Fax: +34 95 421 2181
E-mail: informacion@olivencia-ballester.com
Website: www.olivencia-ballester.com

Languages
English, French, German, Italian

Other offices
Madrid

Number of lawyers 19
at this office 17

Contact
Luis M Olivencia-Brugger

CATEGORIES OF WORK

Corporate and commercial

Mergers and acquisitions

Privatisation and corporate restructing

Arbitration

Litigation

Insolvency

Environmental, fraud and criminal

Competition and EU law

Intellectual property

Tax

BROSETA ABOGADOS

ESTUDIO JURÍDICO Y TRIBUTARIO

PLAZA TETUAN 8 – 2º
46003 VALENCIA

Telephone: +34 96 392 10 06/07
Fax: +34 96 392 10 88
E-mail: info@broseta.com
Website: www.broseta.com

Languages
English, French, Greek, Italian

Number of lawyers 42

CATEGORIES OF WORK

Company law
Manuel Broseta, Beatriz Montes

Commercial law
Manuel Broseta, Juan Manuel Pérez

Securities, banking and finance
Antonio Navarro, Alejandro Rios

Bankruptcy, litigation and arbitration
Antonia Magdaleno, Patricia Gualde

Taxation
Luis Trigo

Mergers and acquisitions
Manuel Broseta, Juan Manuel Pérez

Urban planning
Jesús Avezuela, Ander Arechavaleta

Foreign investment
Antonio Navarro, Juan Pérez

Real estate and public law
Jesús Avezuela, Ander Arechavaleta

Telecoms, internet law, IP and IT
Juan Carlos Plaza

EU and competition
Fernando Martinez Sanz

Employment and labour law
Isabel Merenciano

IT and e-commerce
Antonio Navarro, Juan Carlos Plaza

Antitrust and trade regulations
Fernando Martinez Sanz

State aids and government subsidies
Miguel Angel Ortega

Sports law
Beatriz Montes

LACASA ABOGADOS, PALACIOS & DIEZ AMORETTI

PLAZA DE LOS SITIOS 12, 2°
50001 ZARAGOZA

Telephone: +34 97 646 8358
Fax: +34 97 646 8359
Website: www.abogados-lacasa.com

Languages
English, French, German, Italian

Number of lawyers 18

CATEGORIES OF WORK

Administrative
Pablo Solá, Daniel Serna

Asset finance, securitisation
Juan I Palacios, Francisco Díez

Banking and finance
Francisco Díez

International trade
Juan I Palacios, Raquel Altolaguirre

Commercial property, real estate
Elena Pastor

Construction
Fernando Lacasa, Cristina Sáenz

Corporate and commercial
Fernando Lacasa, Juan I Palacios

Dispute resolution, litigation and arbitration
Pablo Solá, Miguel Á Palazón

Environment
Idoya Plaza, Celia Peralta

Food law
José R Bonilla

Employment
Sergio A Royo, Lorena Sebastián

Fraud and white-collar crime
Pablo Solá, Miguel Á Palazón

Insolvency, corporate restructuring
Miguel Á Palazón, Diego López

Mergers and acquisitions
Fernando Lacasa

Tax
Francisco Díez, Jorge Aguilella

Infrastructure and project finance
Fernando Lacasa

SWEDEN

Population	8.9 million
Number of lawyers	4,100
Professional title	Advokat
Currency	Swedish Krona (SEK)

Index

Within Western Europe Sweden is only the tenth biggest country by population but the third biggest by land mass, having an area more than 25% larger than Germany. Much of that land is rich, forested and uninhabited providing access to plentiful natural resources that have enabled Sweden to become one of the world's richest countries. It ranks third on the United Nations' Human Development Index, a quality of life measure, closely shadowing leaders Norway and Iceland.

One-sixth of the Swedish population lives in the coastal capital, Stockholm, which is in the southeast of the country. Gothenburg, the second city, is half the size of Stockholm and on the western coast. Malmö, the third city of importance, is at the very foot of the country and is linked to Denmark by a road and rail bridge.

Politically, modern Sweden is a constitutional monarchy characterised by minority and coalition democratic governments. The Social Democratic Party (SAP) is the current incumbent, ruling as a minority single-party government through an uneasy relationship with the Left and Green parties. A general election is due in September 2006.

As with the rest of the Western world an ageing population is a cause for concern in Sweden. Already it has a higher percentage of the population (5.1%) aged over 80 years than any other country in the world. How Sweden's famed social welfare systems will cope with this increasing burden is a question of great political importance.

A fear that adoption of the Euro and greater European integration might damage these systems has often been cited as a cause of popular Swedish ambivalence towards its EU membership. A referendum on the Euro in 2003 famously resulted in Sweden saying 'No'. The prime minister, Goran Persson, and the government remain committed to the single currency.

ECONOMY

Sweden continues to enjoy sound economic growth, with its Treasury presiding over one of the world's largest current account surpluses last year (4.4% of GDP). GDP increased by over 2% in 2005 and this is expected to pick up to approximately 3% in 2006. In line with current OECD trends, unemployment continues to fall gradually and now represents less than 5% of the labour force. A higher percentage of females are employed in Sweden than anywhere else in Western Europe. In both 2003 and 2004 the Swedish economy outperformed the Eurozone, which increased general Swedish uninterest in joining the single currency. The Inflation Rate over the last few years has been under the 2% target set by the government.

Sweden is a net exporter of goods, predominantly machinery and transport, and its trade surplus continues to see positive growth. The US, Norway and Germany remain Sweden's premier export markets with the latter also being the leading source of imports. The country is home to a disproportionately high number of the world's most successful businesses including IT giant Ericsson; telecoms company TeliaSonera; banks, SHB and Nordea; and the clothes retailer Hennes & Mauritz. Volvo, IKEA and SAAB are also significant Swedish companies. Sweden spends a greater percentage of GDP on research and design than any other country in the world.

BILLING

The presence of international firms has pushed hourly billing rates up, particularly amongst the mid-sized firms, and the submission of tenders is increasingly common. However, in reality the market is struggling to function at this elevated level, and firms are resorting to creative billing and sometimes artificially low tenders to secure clients. Hourly rates have remained stable for the past two years, but are now beginning to creep up. Typical rates are in the region SEK950 (€100) to SEK1420 (€150) mark for associates and between SEK2370 (€250) and SEK2840 (€300) for senior associates and junior partners. Rates for senior partners range between SEK3,000 (€315) and SEK4,100 (€430) in Stockholm. Smaller niche firms tend to pitch their services a negotiable 20% lower.

MARKETING

Swedish firms remain wary of Bar Association rules regarding advertising, although these were substantially relaxed in the 1970s. Firms that have recently undertaken relatively bold marketing campaigns include **Setterwalls** and **Lindahl**. The arrival of **Linklaters** in 2001 has spread awareness of more international marketing techniques including road shows and seminars.

The largest firms

1	Mannheimer Swartling	305
2	Vinge	267
3	Lindahl	137
4	Setterwalls	115
5	Linklaters	100
6	Delphi & Co, Advokatfirman	96
7	Wistrand	94
8	Glimstedt, Advokatfirman	89
9	Hamilton Advokatbyrå	87
10	MAQS Advokatbyrå	76
11	LINDHS DLA Nordic	62
12	Cederquist, Advokatfirman	60
13	Gernandt & Danielsson Advokatbyrå	59
14	Gärde Wesslau Advokatbyrå	51
15	Baker & McKenzie	45
	Hammarskiöld & Co	45
17	Fylgia KB, Advokatfirman	41
18	White & Case Advokat AB	40
19	Foyen AB, Advokatfirman	34
	Hellström & Partners Advokatbyrå KB	34
21	Bird & Bird	32
22	Ramberg	29
23	RydinCarlsten Advokatbyrå AB	27
24	Rosengrens Advokatbyrå	23
	Södermark, Advokatfirman	23

These figures represent the total number of lawyers in this country only, and have been supplied by the firms themselves. The figures should be accurate as at 1 January 2006.

IN-HOUSE LAWYERS

In-house counsel are not permitted to become members of the Bar but there is substantial movement between those in private practice and those in in-house positions. When lawyers have had in-house experience their firms are usually keen to emphasise this.

LEGAL MARKET

The Swedish attitude to legal matters remains comparatively liberal. There is no requirement for litigants to employ professional advokats when appearing in court and many contracts, including real estate transactions, can legally be completed without recourse to a lawyer. Any person, regardless of quality or qualification, can offer legal services to the public, although only members of the Bar Association may assume the title 'advokat.' There are a number of niche 'law firms' that are wholly outside the ambit of the Swedish Bar Association but which are nevertheless regarded as leaders within particular areas of law. These include: 25-lawyer tax boutique Skeppsbron Skatt, insolvency practice Akordcentralen, and capital markets niche firm Företagsjuridik Nord & Co.

To become a member of the Bar requires, among other qualities, that a person be domiciled in Sweden or another state within the EU, EEA, or Switzerland. The importance of business law, as opposed to private client work, is becoming evermore attractive to the wider industry and specialisation into one or more areas is increasingly common, if not yet the norm. Given Sweden's reputation as an international arbitration centre, many lawyers at leading firms offer specialist arbitration capabilities in addition to their regular work.

The popularity of Sweden as an international arbitration centre owes something to the plentiful supply of multi-lingual lawyers and the reputation of Sweden as a neutral territory in recent times. Sweden is particularly favoured by parties from Russia and former Communist-bloc countries when in dispute with Western companies and governments. There is no other market in which Sweden enjoys such global renown and consequently it is a highly competitive and lucrative area, with even leading transactional firms claiming that a large arbitration can be more profitable than a multi-billion euro M&A deal.

Mannheimer Swartling and **Vinge** are the biggest firms in Sweden, each having more than double the number of lawyers of the third biggest, **Lindahl**. Until recently, **Linklaters**, which arrived in 2001 by merging with leading firm *Lagerlöf & Leman*, was the third biggest but a strategy of retaining only the most profitable bits of that business has seen it move from being a firm of close to 300 lawyers to one of only 100 lawyers. It is often said, not unreasonably, that were a firm to be founded consisting of all the lawyers that had spent time at *Lagerlöf & Leman* or **Linklaters** then it would be the largest firm in Sweden.

From a business perspective **Linklaters**' strategy has been highly successful and the firm has topped the Scandinavian M&A tables for three years running. It has forced **Mannheimer Swartling** and **Vinge**, both of whom have four domestic offices compared to **Linklaters**' one, to reconsider their own strategies. Rumours abound in the market that **Vinge** will emulate the newcomer's model but it has not yet done so.

If the above three firms lead the market in terms of international reach, reputation and expertise then there is a definite second tier of 40-60-lawyer firms that aim to provide a clear alternative in the largest transactions. Independents **Gernandt & Danielsson Advokatbyrå**, **Advokatfirman Cederquist** and **Hammarskiöld & Co** are Stockholm-only firms, as is the Swedish arm of **White & Case Advokat AB**. All have excellent reputations for quality, though each has a slightly different focus.

Also doing well in a positive transactional market are **Lindahl**, **Setterwalls** and **Wistrand**, a trio of approximately 100-lawyer, multi-office, domestic firms. How these firms differentiate themselves in the future will be a key factor in their continued success going forward.

Other firms to note are **Bird & Bird** and **Roschier Holmberg**. The reputation of the former has come on in 'leaps and bounds' in the past year as it has begun to break out of merely being pigeonholed as an IP and IT firm. It has a unique, UK-style sector focus and is pioneering the concept of absorbing in-house legal teams into its own practice with clients keen to outsource their legal work.

The arrival of **Roschier Holmberg** into the Swedish market was easily the event of the year in the whole of Scandinavia. As Finland's leading transactional firm and also one of its most profitable, there was considerable speculation as to what the firm might achieve in Stockholm. To some observers the fact that it would now undoubtedly lose referrals from Swedish firms, most notably **Mannheimer Swartling**, made the move an odd choice. Others perceived it as being so extraordinarily aggressive and swift that this, coupled with reputation, would make the firm an instant success in a traditional market keen for change. The firm itself spoke of the need to tap into a lucrative stream of Finnish-Swedish trade.

Finally, whilst the top-end of the market has been scrambling to become evermore transaction driven it is noticeable that some lawyers have opted out of the melée in order to found small, multi-talented firms along more traditional lines. Among others, well-known figures Christer Holm and Hans Liljeblad left mid-tier firms to found **Advokatfirman A-Law** and Per Magnusson departed **MAQS Advokatbyrå** for **Magnusson Advokatbyrå**.

INTERNATIONAL LINKS

Mannheimer Swartling and **Vinge** maintain independence, although **Vinge** once toyed with the idea of forming an international network and small offices in London, Paris, Shanghai and Hong Kong are a legacy of that. It is also a member of the *Scandinavian Law Alliance*.

All of the leading independent firms enjoy referrals from notable UK, US and German firms. Lower-tier firms, looking to exploit opportunities in the future, have also been exploring the concept of a pan-Scandinavian/Baltic firm. **MAQS Advokatbyrå** and **LINDHS DLA Nordic** are the two main contenders in this sphere although the latter's global alliance has raised it to a much higher tier.

FOREIGN FIRMS

Until very recently it was quite common to see teams of lawyers from the Magic Circle and US firms residing in Stockholm's hotels in order to carry out work in the country. The arrival of **Linklaters** in 2001 has all but put paid to that practice. International firms continue to take a large slice of work away from the region but also prefer to work with the largest independent Swedish firms and thus present a more competitive challenge to **Linklaters**. Both of Sweden's largest firms **Mannheimer Swartling** and **Vinge** remain staunchly independent.

White & Case Advokat AB was the first foreign firm to venture into Sweden, arriving in 1983. These days it is well liked and largely regarded as a Swedish firm despite the presence of serious international muscle. It is also said to be one of the most profitable businesses in Sweden and this is perhaps due in part to the fact that it has not sought to dominate the market or to grow too large.

Given the excitement surrounding **Roschier Holmberg**, the arrival of UK firm **Eversheds LLP** into the Stockholm market passed almost unnoticed. In autumn 2005, **Eversheds LLP** welcomed ten-lawyer **Andrén Bratt Eversheds Advokatbyrå** – a hitherto little known practice – into its alliance. It now has offices in Copenhagen and Stockholm and is open about its need for bases in Oslo and Helsinki.

LINDHS DLA Nordic, **Baker & McKenzie** and **Bird & Bird** are more recent entrants having absorbed lower-tier local firms. Following the demise of the *Coudert Brothers'* network legacy *Coudert Brothers Advokatbyrå AB* has reverted to its former, independent status as **G Grönberg Advokatbyrå AB**.

Kilpatrick Stockton Advokat KB is largely composed of ex-*Lagerlöf & Leman*/**Linklaters** partners.

BANKING AND FINANCE

There are four leading banks in Sweden: Nordea, Svenska Handelsbanken, SEB and Swedbank. Danske bank is regarded as the fifth leading bank. Personal contacts remain an important factor in a particular firm winning work. International firms are increasingly stealing work from the domestic market and the leading firms are now more likely to meet **Clifford Chance**, **Allen & Overy LLP** or **Shearman & Sterling (London) LLP** than local competitors.

BANKING AND FINANCE

CEDERQUIST, ADVOKATFIRMAN ✪
MANNHEIMER SWARTLING ✪
VINGE ✪

GERNANDT & DANIELSSON ADVOKATBYRÅ ✪
LINKLATERS ✪
WHITE & CASE ADVOKAT AB

HAMMARSKIÖLD & CO ✪
LINDHS DLA NORDIC ✪

Baker & McKenzie ✪
Lindahl ✪
Setterwalls ✪
Wistrand ✪

Bird & Bird ✪
Delphi & Co, Advokatfirman ✪
Gärde Wesslau Advokatbyrå ✪
Hellström & Partners Advokatbyrå KB ✪
Kilpatrick Stockton Advokat KB ✪
MAQS Advokatbyrå
RydinCarlsten Advokatbyrå AB ✪

Firms are listed A-Z in tiers which are ranked in order of priority
✪ Indicates firm displays contact details at the end of this chapter.

Ascension to the top tier this year marks a meteoric rise for **Advokatfirman Cederquist**, which did not possess a banking group prior to the arrival of Svante Hulqvist in 2000. Although the firm is based solely in Stockholm and has no international network from which it can draw expertise, its position in the top tier is not doubted. Other top-tier firms view it as their chief competitor locally and second-tier firms regard Hulqvist's ten-lawyer team as 'the one to beat'. Clients are impressed with the depth of the team 'which is much more than just partners Hulqvist and Martin Rossell and is chock full of rising associates'. All the largest Swedish banks employ the firm, as do a number of international lenders, especially in acquisition finance where it is widely regarded as 'second to none'.

André Andersson heads a 40-fee-earner banking group at **Mannheimer Swartling** which has achieved a measure of dominance in all quarters of the market. Owing to its size it probably has the broadest focus of any firm here, from high-value acquisition finance through to regulatory work and smaller syndicated loans for borrowers. Highlights of 2005 included advice to Svenska Handelsbanken in the financing of a €850m acquisition by Cidron Holding, involving thirteen jurisdictions; and advice to the same bank on a SEK4.3bn (€455m) loan provided to EQT and the Com Hem Group. On the borrower side, **Mannheimer Swartling** advised Swedish Match, Teracom, Securitas and Hilders Anders Group on multi-currency revolving credit and senior facilities agreements worth well over €1.7bn in total. Jan Dernestam is recommended, especially in leasing and aircraft finance, where he is frequenttly active for SAS and GE Capital, among others.

Nordea bank and Svenska Handelsbanken regularly employ **Vinge**'s 30-odd-lawyer banking team, which has traditionally been regarded as a leader in advice to both lenders and borrowers. Hans Wibom, Stefan de Hevesy and Fredrik Wilkens comprise a trio of star names, although none specialises full time in banking work. Wibom in particular is described as 'wonderfully talented' by clients and peers alike. It recently advised Barclays Bank on a joint venture with Föreningssparbank and CVC Capital partners on the €850m leveraged acquisition of sugar confectionary business CSM, in conjunction with Nordic Capital.

Gernandt & Danielsson Advokatbyrå has an 'efficient and thorough' banking capability, although its reputation in pure banking work lags behind its 'exceptional' reputation for capital markets and borrower-side acquisition finance advice. That said, it is not short of work and acted for lender Carnegie on a hybrid debt facility (opposite **Clifford Chance**). It also advised insurer If P&C on two subordinated loans worth €200m (opposite **Allen & Overy LLP**). Hedge funds remain another significant source of work with Dick Lundqvist prominent in this regard.

The return of Jörgen Durban from two years in London to head **Linklaters**' banking and finance team bodes well for the growth of the firm and ill for its competitors. Though referrals from London are still a significant source of work, local lenders now provide over half the revenue generated by a 12-lawyer team. In addition to Durban, Fredrik Rydin is widely regarded as 'a star in the making'. Highlights of 2005 were advice to Nordea and RBS as co-ordinators of a SEK10.5bn (€1.1bn) term facility agreement for Hi3G, and advice to 3i and Bridgepoint on LBOs of Carema Vård och Omsorg and Attendo, respectively. In a purely domestic matter, Svenska Handelsbanken and Handelsbanken Mezzanine Fond 1KB sought the firm's counsel on senior and mezzanine facilities provided to Segulah.

Though smaller than the rest of the top-tier firms, **White & Case Advokat AB** boasts an impressive client following, happy to attest to a 'sophisticated and seamless service'. Nordea, Handelsbanken and Nordic Capital are regular purchasers of the firm's services with the latter employing it twice in 2005; firstly in connection with the leveraged acquisition of Plastel Holding and secondly on the €850m leveraged acquisition of sugar confectionery business CSM. Issuer Toyota Industries Finance instructed the firm on a SEK2bn (€212m) commercial papers programme, and there was a first instruction from GM Acceptance Corporate Commercial Finance in a Scandinavian aircraft leasing transaction. Lars Isacsson was busiest, supported by Göran Åseborn and Clas Romander.

Banking and finance is a core discipline at **Hammarskiöld & Co**, where Per Gustaf Ekbom has a leading name. With the exception of advice to a strong private equity following, **Hammarskiöld & Co** is most often active for lenders such as Nordea Finans, Nordic Mezzanine, Barclays and Intermediate Capital Group, which it advised on the LBO of Carema Vård och Omsorg. It advised EQT on the acquisition financing of its acquisition of Munksjö paper mills, and borrower ICA on a SEK5bn (€500m) multi-currency facility.

Banking and finance is fast becoming a leading strength for **LINDHS DLA Nordic** which ascends one tier for the second year running. The advent of Bengt Kärde, who joins from **Hammarskiöld & Co** will greatly complement Mikael Kövamees' 15-lawyer team by adding a new element of experience at the very highest level. Asset-based finance in the range €75-€250m has been a distinct feature of the firm's work to date, with its global resources also being both an important selling point and source of significant referrals.

Leif Gustafsson and Cecillia Bjelle oversee **Baker & McKenzie**'s banking group, which is most active for lenders in real estate finance, though work for borrowers is also increasing. German banks are a significant source of work with the firm regularly employed by Eurohypo and Hypo Real Estate, as well as Reiten & Co and ABN Amro.

Petra Hendengran heads a banking, finance and reconstruction team at **Lindahl**, active for both borrowers and lenders, and has relatively broad experience of syndicated loans compared to other firms in this tier. In late 2004 it acted for Handelsbanken in a SEK4.05bn (€430m) refinancing of the Perstorp Group.

Finance is a traditional strength for **Setterwalls**, not least ship finance where it completed almost SEK3bn (€320m)-worth of transactions in 2005. 'Multi-talented and poker-faced' Åke J Fors is the highly regarded head of a team that followed up a strong 2004 with advice to a syndicate of banks in a SEK7bn (€740m) refinancing of a Swedish telecoms company. The firm also advised Peab Group and SAFT Group on borrowings worth over €560m.

Tommy Grönberg of **Wistrand** regularly advises HSH Nordbank in Stockholm. Monica Peterson, also Stockholm based, has a borrower-orientated practice and acted for BAE Systems in an aircraft leasing programme.

Peter Sjögren leads a three-lawyer team at **Advokatfirman Delphi & Co**; whilst **Gärde Wesslau Advokatbyrå**'s name partner Hans G Wesslau is regularly active for Svenska Handelsbanken and Nordea banks on smaller transactions, often shipping related.

Kilpatrick Stockton Advokat KB's banking work has grown in stature following the arrival of senior associate Håkon Lindgren from **Linklaters** in 2004.

And **MAQS Advokatbyrå** has an internationally orientated practice undertaking real estate and ship finance for the HSBC, among others.

CAPITAL MARKETS

The wintry chill that had settled over Swedish capital markets in the past two years began to thaw in 2005, as investors, buoyed partly by stock market integration in the region, regained some of their former confidence. There were four IPOs in 2005 and a number of other listings by way of spin-offs or movement from other trading lists. The outlook for 2006 promises many more IPOs.

That **Gernandt & Danielsson Advokatbyrå** should be involved in two of the four IPOs in 2005 and half of the IPOs in 2004 was of little surprise to the market, such is the reputation of Dick Lundqvist. Lundqvist heads a dedicated stock market law group at the firm and advised on the IPO of Indutrade as well as supporting **G Grönberg Advokatbyrå AB** on the Hakon Invest IPO, the largest IPO of the year. This was in addition to advice provided to Ainax on its €1bn sale to Scania, perhaps the most notable transaction of 2005.

Linklaters is firmly aligned towards international capital markets transactions and in this regard it is a 'clear leader' according to clients. Advice provided to a consortium of global banks on a SEK2.1bn (€222m) global offering of shares by Boliden is an example of this. Jörgen S Axelsson is the figurehead, with Svante Johansson providing a 'steadying influence behind the scenes'. **Linklaters** also advised Investment AB Kinnevik on a SEK1.8bn (€190m) spin-off and listing of its subsidiary Invik & Co.

In early 2005, **Vinge** significantly boosted an already strong capital markets team with the hire of Göran Nyström, a leading figure at **Mannheimer Swartling**. Nyström will doubtless continue to see much of his old firm with **Vinge** acting opposite **Mannheimer Swartling** in the merger between OMX and the Copenhagen Stock Exchange (**Vinge** represented CSE) and securities issue by Vattenfall (**Vinge** represented Vattenfall). **Vinge** was counsel to Oriflame, the most significant of the two 2004 IPOs.

In recent years, **Hammarskiöld & Co** has demonstrated consistent ability to attract top-tier capital markets instructions, most notably that of Fisher Scientific International, which was subject to Sweden's largest-ever public takeover in 2003. Name partner Peder Hammarskiöld is the driving force behind the success and no doubt played an instrumental role in the firm's beauty contest victory to advise Scania in its successful €1bn bid for Ainax.

CAPITAL MARKETS

GERNANDT & DANIELSSON ADVOKATBYRÅ ○
LINKLATERS ○
VINGE ○

HAMMARSKIÖLD & CO ○
MANNHEIMER SWARTLING ○

SETTERWALLS ○
WHITE & CASE ADVOKAT AB

Baker & McKenzie ○
Bird & Bird ○
Cederquist, Advokatfirman ○
G Grönberg Advokatbyrå AB ○
Lindahl ○
LINDHS DLA Nordic ○
Wistrand ○

Firms are listed A-Z in tiers which are ranked in order of priority
○ Indicates firm displays contact details at the end of this chapter.

Tom Hård is **Mannheimer Swartling**'s resident capital markets star, attracting the praise of peers and clients. He is well supported by a team that also includes Thomas Wallinder, counsel to the underwriters in a €1bn securities issue by Swedish energy company Vattenfall. Wallinder was also active for buyer OMX in its €164m purchase of the Copenhagen Stock Exchange in late 2004.

The hire of Jan Jensen and Sören Lindström from ABN Amro in 2004 significantly boosted **Setterwalls**' reputation for capital markets work. Jensen was able to put his expertise to immediate use in the €190m Hemtex IPO, advising both Hemtex and Enskilda Securities.

Although no loss to the firm overall, the transfer of upcoming, capital markets star Sven Krogius from **White & Case Advokat AB** in Stockholm to the firm's Moscow office is undoubtedly a loss on a local level. Clas Romander will now resume the reins of a capital markets practice that advised the joint book runners and joint lead managers on the SEK333m (€35m) Orexo IPO.

In common with many of the firms listed here, **Baker & McKenzie** deploys its banking team on capital markets work. There was a strong Danish flavour to work in 2005 with Cecilia Bjelle first taking care of the Swedish aspects of EQT's purchase of all shares in Denmark's ISS and then advising the shareholders of Denmark's Aalborg United on its merger with Karlshamn.

Corporate head Mikael Engqvist is responsible for a growing body of capital markets transactions at **Bird & Bird**. In 2005, this included advice to Swedish mining company ScanMining on a SEK205m (€21.7m) share issue.

Wilhelm Luning is the name to note at **Advokatfirman Cederquist**, which draws on a leading banking capability. In addition to acting for banks and listed companies, **Advokatfirman Cederquist** has a strong regulatory practice and represented VPC, the holder of registers for the Stockholm Stock Exchange, prior to its merger with OMX Exchanges.

G Grönberg Advokatbyrå AB is admitted to the table owing to its leading role in the IPO of Hakon Invest, which was valued at a SEK12.4bn (€1.3bn), making it by far the biggest IPO of 2005. Anders Hedman led.

CONSTRUCTION

This is a narrowing field in which large projects are currently on the wane and specialist firms are becoming evermore prosperous.

Having completed his term as managing partner, Jan Kansmark has been freed up to spend more time leading **Mannheimer Swartling**'s pre-eminent construction team, which has had involvement in every major Swedish construction project of recent years. It continues to advise Botniabanan, the employer, in Sweden's largest project, the SEK13bn (€1.3bn) Botnia high-speed rail link; and the Swedish Rail Authority (the employer) in the second-largest project, namely the construction of a SEK10bn (€1.1bn) railway tunnel underneath Malmö. Increasingly the firm is employed on projects abroad and is advising the Jordanian government on a US$700m water conveyance pipeline project. Tore Wiwen-Nilsson is recommended for his skills on the contentious side.

Lars-Olof Perselius of niche **Andersson & Gustafsson Advokatbyrå KB** is the recipient of peer praise for his contentious work. Thirteen of the firm's 14 lawyers are active in the construction sector and the firm is representing Skanska in the Kista Galleria dispute.

Advokatfirman Foyen AB is best known for its construction expertise, both on the contentious and projects sides. Five partners are active in this sector with Kjell Wikström winning most recognition. Large Swedish consultancy companies, real estate companies, a national road authority, and a rail authority comprise the client base, across offices in Mälmo and Stockholm.

For construction-related litigation and arbitration Clas Zettermarck of **White & Case Advokat AB** has few peers. Beyond Zettermarck, a wider real estate group handles construction advice.

Baker & McKenzie's real estate team also handles a healthy quantity of construction work, including disputes, procurement and lease negotiation. Recent highlights include advice to Jernhusen in a SEK800m (€85m) reconstruction of Stockholm's central station and locality.

Stockholm-based, construction niche **Advokatbyrån Hellgren Linander KB** wins entry on the back of excellent peer recommendations for its construction group.

Drawing on its prominence in the real estate market, **Kilpatrick Stockton Advokat KB** also fields a small construction team headed by Thomas Rajala. It is active for construction companies, developers and owners on both contentious and non-contentious matters. Nicklas Bjorkland is counsel to Kista Galleria in the SEK1.1bn (€116m) arbitration, the largest construction dispute in Sweden.

Johan Söderlund heads **MAQS Advokatbyrå**'s construction group from Gothenburg, where he advises the government on the €800m Hallandsås project in Southern Sweden.

Advokatfirman Engström & Co is a four-lawyer commercial firm in Malmö with a strong construction focus. Carillion is a client.

New entrant **LINDHS DLA Nordic** represents employers and is most active in the housing development sector. Henrik Wollsén and Maria Carlsson are the contacts.

Setterwalls enters the table based on its work for construction company Peab and others in Mälmo.

CONSTRUCTION

MANNHEIMER SWARTLING ✪

ANDERSSON & GUSTAFSSON ADVOKATBYRÅ KB
FOYEN AB, ADVOKATFIRMAN
WHITE & CASE ADVOKAT AB

Baker & McKenzie ✪
Hellgren Linander KB, Advokatbyrån
Kilpatrick Stockton Advokat KB ✪
MAQS Advokatbyrå

Delphi & Co, Advokatfirman ✪
Engström & Co, Advokatfirman
Gärde Wesslau Advokatbyrå ✪
Hellström & Partners Advokatbyrå KB ✪
LINDHS DLA Nordic ✪
Setterwalls ✪
Wistrand ✪

Firms are listed A-Z in tiers which are ranked in order of priority
✪ Indicates firm displays contact details at the end of this chapter.

CORPORATE AND COMMERCIAL

Mannheimer Swartling is a by-word for quality in Sweden, as well as being the country's largest and broadest firm. A traditional reputation for advising the very best of Scandanavia's blue-chip corporates continues to carry weight, with clients insisting that their loyalty is to the firm and not to particular individuals there. Like **Vinge** it maintains four domestic offices. Scandinavian Airlines System (SAS) is a prominent client.

Vinge is poised somewhere between the full-service approach of **Mannheimer Swartling** and the transactions-only strategy employed by **Linklaters**. Peers see the departure of an IP team to **Mannheimer Swartling** and an insolvency team to **Setterwalls** as evidence of a swing to the latter model; but offices in Gothenburg, Malmö and Helsingborg and a headcount more than double that of **Linklaters** suggests that it is still closer to **Mannheimer Swartling** overall. Traditionally, the firm has enjoyed good links to firms across the world and had a strong practice advising new-market companies and inward investors.

Baker & McKenzie enjoys regular instructions from household brands: SpecSavers, Samsung, Jones Lang La Salle and SAS- which the firm advises in tandem with **Mannheimer Swartling**. Despite being relatively small in Stockholm, **Baker & McKenzie** avoids too narrow a focus and offers a full service. It is happy to undertake regular commercial work as well as larger transactions. This is perhaps part of the reason it attracts some of the highest client praise with recent users expressing 'full satisfication' and 'desire to return'. It also boasts a strong franchising group.

CORPORATE AND COMMERCIAL

MANNHEIMER SWARTLING ✪
VINGE ✪

BAKER & McKENZIE ✪
CEDERQUIST, ADVOKATFIRMAN ✪
GERNANDT & DANIELSSON ADVOKATBYRÅ ✪
HAMMARSKIÖLD & CO ✪
LINKLATERS ✪
SETTERWALLS ✪
WHITE & CASE ADVOKAT AB

BIRD & BIRD ✪
DELPHI & CO, ADVOKATFIRMAN ✪
LINDAHL ✪
LINDHS DLA NORDIC ✪
MAQS ADVOKATBYRÅ
WISTRAND ✪

G Grönberg Advokatbyrå AB ✪
Gärde Wesslau Advokatbyrå ✪
Hellström & Partners Advokatbyrå KB ✪
Kilpatrick Stockton Advokat KB ✪
RydinCarlsten Advokatbyrå AB ✪

A-Law, Advokatfirman
AJB Bergh Advokatbyrå AB
Andrén Bratt Eversheds Advokatbyrå
Magnusson Advokatbyrå
Moll Wendén Advokatbyrå AB ✪
Roschier Holmberg

Foyen AB, Advokatfirman
Fylgia KB, Advokatfirman
Glimstedt, Advokatfirman ✪
Hagenfeldt Advokatbyrå
Hamilton Advokatbyrå
Hökerberg & Söderqvist Advokatbyrå KB ✪
Nordia, Advokatfirman
Nova, Advokatfirman

Firms are listed A-Z in tiers which are ranked in order of priority
✪ Indicates firm displays contact details at the end of this chapter.

Full-service **Advokatfirman Cederquist** enjoys a leading reputation in the domestic market, with strengths in a number of disciplines. It has an active client base drawn from various industry sectors and that includes Daimler-Chrysler, Bonnier Group and Segulah. The only serious setback it suffered in 2005 was the departure of two partners to **Roschier Holmberg**'s start-up office.

With approximately 60 lawyers **Gernandt & Danielsson Advokatbyrå** is the largest of the transaction-driven firms, after **Linklaters**. It has enjoyed turnover growth every year since its foundation in 1992 and has one of the highest rates of revenue-per-lawyer. It courts the friendship of a host of international players, including London's Magic Circle, but remains avowedly independent.

A 25% increase in billings in 2004/5 marks a successful year for 45-lawyer **Hammarskiöld & Co**, which shuns the full-service model to deliver 'highly sophisticated services' in it chosen niches: M&A, banking, IT/IP and disputes. Nevertheless a heavy transactional bias does not stop it attracting commercial work and Scania, Skandia and the Swedish alcohol monopoly are regular clients.

Clients are astounded by the transformation that **Linklaters** has undergone in the four years since the Swedish office ceased trading under the *Lagerlöf & Leman* name. Users of **Linklaters** in Stockholm, familiar with the firm's London office, profess that the firm now 'walks, talks and feels just like **Linklaters**'. But this came at a price and an office that began life with 45-equity partners now has only 20. The firm has been stripped down to focus on nothing but the biggest transactions, plus high-value disputes. It will act for Scandanavia's biggest corporates globally but does not pretend to offer a full-service for day-to-day commercial work. For this reason it in the second tier but in terms of global reach and expertise it is without rival.

Setterwalls is Sweden's fourth-biggest firm by turnover and one of its oldest. In recent years it has achieved a remarkable degree of success in creating a younger atmosphere and broadening its reputation beyond traditional redoubts in banking, shipping and insolvency. Young executive partner Richard Åkerman takes a central role in corporate work. A dynamic Malmö office has the ear of the leading firms in Denmark.

White & Case Advokat AB continues to attract the highest respect from clients impressed by the 'consistent standard of its work'. Though small, the firm is rumoured to be one of the most profitable in Sweden and in common with its peers it has focused heavily on transactional work in recent years. That said it offers a broader range of work than some competitors and has a leading shipping practice among other things. BT Industries was a new client win in 2005.

Bird & Bird in Stockholm is an internationally orientated, full-service firm that is going from strength-to-strength. Clients enjoy a 'unique and tailored service' whilst peers are most impressed with the firm's emergence on the transactional side, with the market traditionally perceiving its strengths as IP and media. Corporate all-rounder Mikael Engqvist must take credit for renewed vigour here, heading a group of seven lawyers providing regular advice to the likes of EADs, Serono, Eniro, Michelin and Mandator.

Fresh into new accommodation in Stockholm, **Advokatfirman Delphi & Co** acts for listed and mid-sized domestic companies as well as a number of international companies including Goodyear, Xerox and Reuters. It has a leading name for commercial work in the IT-sector.

Lindahl has six offices in Sweden and is a contender for the largest domestic work. In Stockholm the firm is firmly established in the mid-to-large market with approximately 60 lawyers present on the ground. A core corporate finance group covers M&A, capital markets and regular commercial work. Tyco, Danaher, Concordia, Electronic Arts and Telenor are clients.

Following the rapid growth of the DLA alliance across the globe **LINDHS DLA Nordic** is settling into being a part of the world's second-biggest firm (by headcount). Though it can also draw on expertise from other offices, it offers a full service in Sweden whilst building its strength in core areas, not least finance.

MAQS Advokatbyrå has similar-size offices in Gothenburg and Stockhokm, though it is relatively stronger in the former. A firm with a good influx of foreign referrals, **MAQS Advokatbyrå** has links to **Pinsent Masons**, **Skadden, Arps, Slate, Meagher & Flom LLP**, **Lawrence Graham LLP** and a number of London insurance firms. Financial institutions, energy, franchising and M&A are core areas, as is insurance where corporate head Dan Öwerström is renowned. Torbjörn Claeson is recommended for his energy practice.

Wistrand is regarded as 'having moved forward in 2005'. A traditionally strong Gothenburg presence is these days matched by a dynamic Stockholm office and in the mid-to-large market the firm is an established heavyweight. An impressive clutch of household names also use the firm on commercial matters, including Volvo, Stena, Ericsson and Nokia.

Gärde Wesslau Advokatbyrå is a respected, full-service firm with offices in Stockholm, Helsingborg and Jönköping, Gothenburg and Borås. Sten Gisselberg is recommended.

RydinCarlsten Advokatbyrå AB has hired UK-qualified, senior associate Richard Bird from **Clifford Chance** to form a private equity group at the firm.

Noted corporate finance lawyer Hans Liljeblad and insurance expert Christer A Holm are the main draws at newly-established **Advokatfirman A-Law**, which consists of lawyers from **Hellström & Partners Advokatbyrå KB** and **Advokatfirman Delphi & Co**.

AJB Bergh Advokatbyrå AB is a 17-lawyer transaction-heavy firm that has close but informal links with **Ashurst**. Jonas Bergh is the leading name.

Employment, telecoms, litigation and insolvency comprise a diverse mix of core practices at ten-lawyer **Andrén Bratt Eversheds Advokatbyrå**, which enters the table for the first time this year. Jonas Bratt has a good name in telecoms.

Stockholm office head Per Magnusson has a team of 14-lawyers at **Magnusson Advokatbyrå**, which has smaller offices in Denmark and Russia and a larger one in Poland. Anschutz Entertainment was a new client in 2005 on commercial matters.

Moll Wendén Advokatbyrå AB is a four-partner corporate finance, M&A and real estate boutique in Malmö, established in 2003 by lawyers formerly at **Linklaters**.

Hagenfeldt Advokatbyrå is a four-lawyer commercial practice in Stockholm. Carl Lindstrand and Björn Hagenfeldt are the contacts.

DISPUTE RESOLUTION

Dispute resolution is big business in Sweden. As an international arbitration centre Stockholm is second only to London, Paris and New York. There is no other market in which Stockholm is so highly rated and consequently it is of great importance to nearly all the firms listed here.

Mannheimer Swartling is praised for the breadth of its practice and the 'warm-blooded, cold-headed nature' of its litigators. Claes Lundblad heads a 16-partner group that is best known for international arbitration and that was recently instructed by Russia's Yukos. Kaj Hobér is also recommended.

'Litigation runs through the veins' of **Advokatfirman Södermark**, a name that is synonymous with quality dispute resolution in Sweden. All 23 lawyers at the firm are active in litigation and arbitration, which accounts for over three-quarters of the firm's income. For many years founder Bertil Södermark was the foremost litigator in Sweden, although since 2004 he has only worked in a consultancy capacity. Internally, Södermark's mantle has passed to his 'young, protégé' Torgny Wetterberg who many peers regard as the 'most talented litigator of his generation'. Wetterberg and partner Christer Brantheim represent Lars-Eric Petersson, the former manager of Skandia currently under investigation. Lars Gothlin is also praised.

'Good at whatever he turns his hands to' Claes Zettermarck of **White & Case Advokat AB** has the rare ability to attract praise as a leading corporate lawyer and as a litigator. Within dispute resolution Zettermarck is among the top-three most recognised personalities, recently acting for

DISPUTE RESOLUTION

MANNHEIMER SWARTLING ✪ SÖDERMARK, ADVOKATFIRMAN ✪
WHITE & CASE ADVOKAT AB WISTRAND ✪
BAKER & McKENZIE ✪ BIRD & BIRD ✪ CEDERQUIST, ADVOKATFIRMAN ✪ G GRÖNBERG ADVOKATBYRÅ AB ✪ GERNANDT & DANIELSSON ADVOKATBYRÅ ✪ LINKLATERS ✪ RYDINCARLSTEN ADVOKATBYRÅ AB ✪ VINGE ✪
Delphi & Co, Advokatfirman ✪ Hammarskiöld & Co ✪ LINDHS DLA Nordic ✪ Setterwalls ✪
Andrén Bratt Eversheds Advokatbyrå Dhunér Järvengren Advokatbyrå Gärde Wesslau Advokatbyrå ✪ Kilpatrick Stockton Advokat KB ✪ Lindahl ✪ Magnusson Advokatbyrå MAQS Advokatbyrå

Firms are listed A-Z in tiers which are ranked in order of priority
✪ Indicates firm displays contact details at the end of this chapter.

TeliaSonera in a dispute with other shareholders in a Russian telecoms company. He is supported by Bengt Åke Johnsson and Olof Ragmark, both of whom attract the highest client references.

Dispute resolution is a large part of **Wistrand**'s business, with partner Stefan Lindskog currently serving as chairman of the Swedish Bar Association. The firm had two Supreme Court cases in 2005 (won one, lost one) and three prominent insurance arbitrations (won three), one of which was worth SEK1.8bn; as well as acting as counsel in the first EC-law-based class action against the Swedish government. Lindskog represents auditor Öhrlings PricewaterhouseCoopers in the Prosolvia case, the biggest professional liability case in Sweden ever.

Stefan Bessman of **Baker & McKenzie** attracts the praise of peers for being 'fabulous on his feet'. Bessman is one of two partners in a five-lawyer department devoted exclusively to litigation and arbitration. Insurance sector disputes are an important source of work with the firm instructed in separate matters by insurers in Norway, Finland and Sweden in 2005. It was also counsel to the government of a neighbouring country in a dispute with a major bank, concerning investment.

New riser **Bird & Bird** is identified by top-tier peers as 'a formidable competitor in possession of some sensible brains'. Managing partner Michael Frie is a well-known litigator and one of four partners active in Ulf Mellqvist's disputes team. IT sector clients are a prominent source of work, although by no means all, with Frie and Mellqvist also noted for advice to the estate of insolvent Prosolvia. A Swedish lawyer based in London adds international capacity.

Advokatfirman Cederquist maintains a strong disputes team, visible in both litigation and arbitration. Partner Olof Nilsson works full-time in the area and is counsel for beleaguered plaintiff Skandia Liv in its SEK3bn (€318m) dispute with parent company Skandia. Group head Ola Hansson is prominent in IP and media disputes, where he represents TV3 against Hi3G in a dispute over the trade mark '3'; and Tele2 in a SEK2.5bn dispute with Telia regarding dominant position. Mats Bendrick is also well-known for his work as an international arbitrator.

G Grönberg Advokatbyrå AB, formerly *Coudert Brothers Advokatbyrå*, ascends the tiers for the second year running largely owing to the strength of reputation of arbitrator Einar Wanhainen and leading litigator Lars Edlund, both of whom are regularly name checked by peers. Wanhainen was counsel to supermarket chain ICA in an arbitration against a Norweigian investor valued at over SEK1bn and Edlund continues to sit on the prestigious panel of five arbitrators in the Skandia case.

In addition to excellent transactional capability, **Gernandt & Danielsson Advokatbyrå** has a well-established reputation in high-value litigation and arbitration. Senior partners Karl-Erik Danielsson and Johan Gernandt are the leading names at a firm that is increasingly focusing on domestic and international arbitration, especially East-West.

Senior litigator Henrik Bielenstein is the sole disputes partner at **Linklaters** and draws heavily on the EU and competition, and employment teams for support. Bielenstein enjoys an impressively broad practice that ranges from acting as counsel to the government in cases concerning land rights through to IP, competition, construction law, insurance and telecoms. He acts for Kista Galleria in tandem with Nicklas Bjorkland of **Kilpatrick Stockton Advokat KB**, in its SEK1.1bn construction-related arbitration.

RydinCarlsten Advokatbyrå AB rises one tier on the strength of Bo Nilsson's arbitration expertise, particularly in relation to Russia. Nilsson is described as 'extremely humble but nevertheless the front man for Swedish arbitration everywhere'. The firm is pre-eminent in IP litigation.

Olle Flygt, Christer Söderlund and Hans Bagner comprise a Stockholm disputes group at **Vinge**, which has a large caseload but is perceived by the market to concentrate less on disputes than some of it rivals. It has traditionally undertaken some of the largest East-West arbitrations and Söderlund has a noted Russian practice.

Three partners and five associates comprise a **Hammarskiöld & Co** dispute resolution team, which leans heavily towards the insurance market. Practice head Per Sundin's defence of Folksam Mutual in a SEK 1bn (€106m) suit brought by Commerzbank remains the biggest case of late. The firm's disputes team, though active, lacks the prominence that the firm enjoys in the non-contentious arena.

Henrik Nordensen of **Setterwalls** acts for Skandia in connection with the company's claims for damages against its former CEO and CFO. Nordenson replaced Otto Rydbeck who very tragically passed away. Fred Wennerholm's work for SILEIG, the firm's specialist international and energy disputes group, is also of note.

Magnus Andrén, name partner at **Andrén Bratt Eversheds Advokatbyrå**, is dual US and Swedish-qualified and is one of only a handful of ICC-nominated arbitrators.

Founding partner Per Magnusson of **Magnusson Advokatbyrå** is a noted arbitrator and often acts for US companies. He is supported by litigator Maria Nisell.

EU AND COMPETITION

Despite an avowed aim to focus on only the biggest, international transactions it is clear from the competence of **Linklaters**' competition team in Stockholm that being able to draw on the support of a leading Brussels office is no substitute for having people on the ground. In competition head Kent Karlsson, **Linklaters** possesses one of the most highly regarded specialists in the country, and he is not averse to acting in purely domestic cases, recently winning a case for Flygbussarna Airport Coaches against the Swedish Competition Authority. In more international matters Erik Söderlind acted in two cases against the European Commision, the first for TeliaSonera and the second for AstraZeneca.

It is said of partners Johan Karlsson and Lars Gildéus of **Vinge** that 'they were doing competition work before anyone else'. A cross-office team that is best known for its M&A support capability comprises Karlsson in Stockholm, Gildéus in Malmö and Olle Rislund in Brussels.

Kenny Carlsson, who spent six years as head of the legal secretariat at the Swedish Competition Authority, remains the big-name presence at **Gernandt & Danielsson Advokatbyrå**, which is prominent as an adviser to Vodafone. Carlsson is joined this year by partner-designate Rolf Larsson, a former director at the Swedish Competition Authority. Completing a merger filing in South Korea was a highlight of 2005 and probably a first for a Swedish firm.

Clients of **Mannheimer Swartling** regard Johan Coyet as the 'number one competition lawyer in Sweden' despite the fact that he is currently resident in Brussels. That is expected to change in 2006 with Coyet due to return home and

EU AND COMPETITION

LINKLATERS ✪
VINGE ✪

GERNANDT & DANIELSSON ADVOKATBYRÅ ✪
MANNHEIMER SWARTLING ✪

Baker & McKenzie ✪
Bird & Bird ✪
Dhunér Järvengren Advokatbyrå
Hammarskiöld & Co ✪
Lindahl ✪
Södermark, Advokatfirman ✪
White & Case Advokat AB
Wistrand ✪

Cederquist, Advokatfirman ✪
Delphi & Co, Advokatfirman ✪
LINDHS DLA Nordic ✪
Magnusson Advokatbyrå
Setterwalls ✪

Firms are listed A-Z in tiers which are ranked in order of priority
✪ *Indicates firm displays contact details at the end of this chapter.*

Stefan Perván-Lindeborg is lining up to replace him. Though transactional support is by no means lacking, it is in contentious matters that the firm generates most praise, including representation of Skanska in the alleged asphalt cartel.

Banking head Leif Gustafsson retains responsibility for EU and competition at **Baker & McKenzie** which regularly draws on the support of its European network. Public procurement has been a leading concern of late.

Senior associate Anders Nilsson is the name to note at **Bird & Bird**, although a clutch of partners from various departments lend support in the biggest cases. An example of such a circumstance is advice provided to nine municipalities seeking damages of SEK55m from construction companies in relation to the alleged asphalt cartel.

Dhunér Järvengren Advokatbyrå is a specialist firm with niche overlapping interests in shipping, dispute resolution and EU and competition. It is particularly skilled in logistics and distribution issues. Karl Johan Dhunér is praised for his 'specialist' skills.

EU and competition is assuming growing importance at **Hammarskiöld & Co**. A traditional transactional support capability is now matched by other work, including advice on alleged cartel abuses. Claes Langenius heads a team that acts for the Swedish Civil Aviation Authority and State Alcohol Monopoly and which has seconded a senior associate to **Wilmer Cutler Pickering Hale and Dorr LLP**.

Four lawyers comprise a cross-office **Lindahl** team that is especially active in public procurement, where it has been advising purchaser DMA (Swedish Defence Material Adminsitration) on the RAKEL system case, which went to the Supreme Court. On the transactional side Telenor is a client.

Eric Ericsson is singled out for his talents at **Advokatfirman Södermark**, which is best known for its litigation capability.

White & Case Advokat AB maintains three Swedish lawyers in Brussels, including partner Pontus Lindfelt, and two senior associates in Stockholm. Merger filings, communication with the European Commission and advice on anti-dumping are typical examples of work.

Wistrand's 'tight-knit' competition group boasts involvement in all the major cartel cases in Sweden, not least those involving the petroleum and asphalt industries, where it acts for Shell and Peab, respectively. Ola Wiklund is the primary name to remember in a four-lawyer team that acted for the suppliers in the RAKEL case, and for Unibet in its continued challenge against the Swedish government at the ECJ regarding the state betting monopoly. One to watch.

The departure of **Advokatfirman Cederquist**'s competition head Lars Johansson to **Roschier Holmberg** is a serious blow to a department that was beginning to win work on a stand-alone basis.

EMPLOYMENT

Few competitors complain about employer-focused **Advokatfirman Cederquist**'s top-tier ranking where Jen Tillqvist, Tom Johansson and Olle Jansson form a three-faced team 'at the very pinnacle of its game'. Three associates also provide 'high-quality support' with Erik Danhard attracting considerable praise. In addition to transactional support all of the above are familiar faces before the Labour Court.

Anders Nordström heads an eight-lawyer employment team at **Linklaters** which excels at its primary role of supporting the corporate team, in addition to providing stand-alone specialities such as pensions advice, high-value disputes and matters related to corporate governance. The firm acts exclusively on the employer side and is advising Old Mutual in relation to its bid for Skandia, and Masterfoods and AstraZeneca on pensions matters.

Vinge is commended for the strength of its transactional support capabilities. A ten-lawyer team is split across all three of the firm's domestic offices. In Stockholm Björn Lindskog and Fredrik Dahl are also appointed as arbitrators in employment disputes.

Clients speak highly of 'regular guy and extremely able lawyer' Sten Bauer who heads a **Baker & McKenzie** employment team that is well known in the market. Bauer has particular expertise in the recruitment and termination of top executives in addition to other aspects of work for employers. Bauer advised Flextronics on matters relating to its sale to Telavie, and Carnegie Bank on a redundancy programme involving individual negotiations.

EMPLOYMENT

CEDERQUIST, ADVOKATFIRMAN ✪
LINKLATERS ✪
VINGE ✪

Baker & McKenzie ✪
Elmzell Advokatbyrå HB, member of ius laboris ✪
LINDHS DLA Nordic ✪
Mannheimer Swartling ✪
SJU Advokater

Gernandt & Danielsson Advokatbyrå ✪
Hellström & Partners Advokatbyrå KB ✪
Setterwalls ✪
Wistrand ✪

Andrén Bratt Eversheds Advokatbyrå
Bird & Bird ✪
Delphi & Co, Advokatfirman ✪
Lindahl ✪
MAQS Advokatbyrå
White & Case Advokat AB

Firms are listed A-Z in tiers which are ranked in order of priority
✪ *Indicates firm displays contact details at the end of this chapter.*

Six-lawyer niche employment practice **Elmzell Advokatbyrå HB, member of ius laboris** is the 'boutique *par preference*' among its Stockholm peers . Recommended heads Andus Elmer and Lars Hartzell, have over 50 years' combined experience of the sector. Over 80% of the firm's turnover is derived from instructions from employers, which range from small Swedish companies to a handful of multinational clients; ExxonMobil is a client.

Practice head Mats Borgström is the most highly rated member of a three-partner team at **LINDHS DLA Nordic**, which has traditionally been well known for its employment advice. Competitors like to characterise the firm as being solely active for trade unions, owing to headline work for the ALMEGA union, but, in reality, this work comprises less than a quarter of the practice. 75% of its work is for employers or management-level employees. The firm is frequently present at the Labour Court.

Mannheimer Swartling's cross-office employment group is primarily engaged on transactional support matters, recently assisting EQT in its purchase of Denmark's ISS. Head Magnus Wallander is recommended.

Lars Viklund of niche employment practice **SJU Advokater** is a 'leader in his field' according to top-tier peers, who regularly refer him work.

Wistrand rises one tier on the back of Mats Hilmersson and his team's work for corporates such as Sun Microsystems and National Instruments.

Half of **Andrén Bratt Eversheds Advokatbyrå**'s four partners are employment lawyers. Claes-Göran Westerberg and Fredrik Järund are the names.

Bird & Bird wins entry, having founded a team based around senior associate Patrik

Fallberg, who arrived from an in-house position, and partner Katarina Nordblom, formerly an associate at **Vinge**.

MAQS Advokatbyrå is admitted owing to Stockholm-based Estonian Mango Kask, whose work is well regarded.

ENVIRONMENT

There are 13 lawyers at Stockholm-based environmental niche **Advokatfirman Åberg & Co AB**. In addition to work for public-sector bodies such as the Swedish Railway Construction Agency and Central Government Department of The Environment, it attracts private-sector clients, particularly in relation to large infrastructure projects. Waste disposal is an area of expertise. Mårten Bengtsson is recommended.

'Definitely top tier,' **Alrutz' Advokatbyrå AB** wins its highest commendations for its environment work. Like **Advokatfirman Åberg & Co AB** it is the recipient of instructions from both national and international clients. Thomas Carlberg is recommended.

Environmental law is of increasing importance for **Mannheimer Swartling**, though recommended practice head Per Molander has been active in the field since the 1980s. Molander is assisted by three other partners and has witnessed an increase in instructions to advise on contaminated land. In addition to being able to undertake advice on the biggest and most sensitive matters, such as storage of nuclear material, the firm increasingly sees synergies between work here and its transactional teams. Mikael Hägglöf is also recommended.

Johan Norman is the name to note at **Advokatfirman Delphi & Co**, where he is often the first port of call for other leading firms lacking expertise in this area. A cross-office team of eight environmental lawyers receives regular instruction from Volvo Heavy Trucks, Swedish Airports and the Swedish Flight Authority.

Recommended energy and environment specialists Torbjörn Claeson and Magdalena Persson of **MAQS Advokatbyrå** reside in Stockholm and Gothenburg respectively. Energy is a leading focus of the firm and this often leads to instruction in environmental law. **MAQS Advokatbyrå** assisted the City of Ale on the island of Gotland in a pioneering environmental liability agreement.

Linklaters' environmental team has departed the firm for recommended new environmental niche **Fröberg & Lundholm Advokatbyrå**.

Staffan Michelson of **Hellström & Partners Advokatbyrå KB** has been active in environmental law for over thirty years and consequently enjoys longstanding relationships with a number of key clients.

Environmental advice is provided by corporate all-rounder Thomas Sjöberg at **Vinge**'s Stockholm office and by Ingela Malmborg in Malmö. Malmberg advises cement companies HeidelbergCement and Cementa.

ENVIRONMENT

ÅBERG & CO AB, ADVOKATFIRMAN
ALRUTZ' ADVOKATBYRÅ AB
MANNHEIMER SWARTLING ✪

Delphi & Co, Advokatfirman ✪
MAQS Advokatbyrå

Fröberg & Lundholm Advokatbyrå
Hellström & Partners Advokatbyrå KB ✪
Vinge ✪
Wistrand ✪

Foyen AB, Advokatfirman
Gärde Wesslau Advokatbyrå ✪
Kilpatrick Stockton Advokat KB ✪
Setterwalls ✪

Firms are listed A-Z in tiers which are ranked in order of priority
✪ Indicates firm displays contact details at the end of this chapter.

Kristina Forsbacka of **Wistrand** in Stockholm is a leading name in emissions trading, advising the Swedish Energy Agency, among others. Gothenburg-based Rudolf Laurin boasts a strong energy and environmental practice and, in 2005, advised clients on the establishment of two offshore wind-farms worth SEK400m and SEK1bn, respectively.

Construction-focused **Advokatfirman Foyen AB** hired two senior government water industry lawyers in 2004 in order to build an environmental practice at the firm. Employers and the government are the main sources of work.

New entrant **Gärde Wesslau Advokatbyrå** is increasingly active on the environment scene and now acts for Sweden's two largest airports, Gothenburg-Landvetter and Stockholm-Arlanda. Åke Lewensjö and Roland Adrell, both formerly with **Vinge** in Gothenburg, are the key contacts.

The departure to an in-house position of **Kilpatrick Stockton Advokat KB**'s recommended head Johan Lindberg is a blow to an emerging team. Construction head Thomas Rajala now assumes responsibility for environmental matters.

Malmö is home to a growing environmental group at **Setterwalls**.

Finally, **Baker & McKenzie**'s head of IT Stefan Brandt is also recommended for a niche practice advising on laws and regulations concerning the chemical and paint trades. He acts for KTF (cosmetic, toiletry and household products suppliers association) and SVEFF (paint and ink marketers association).

IT AND TELECOMS

The arrival of recommended IT specialist Stefan Bernhard from **Linklaters** in 2005 helps to elevate **Bird & Bird** to the top tier for the first time. **Bird & Bird** is uniquely capable of justifying its ranking on either the IT or telecoms side. Bernhard now assists Jim Runsten on all aspects of advice to a client list that includes Oracle, Lenovo, Atea and Canon. On the communications side the 'irrepressibly friendly' Johan Tydén is 'a leader in his field,' active for Ericsson, Hi3G and the National Post & Telecom Agency.

IT AND TELECOMS

BIRD & BIRD ✪
DELPHI & CO, ADVOKATFIRMAN ✪
MANNHEIMER SWARTLING ✪

GERNANDT & DANIELSSON ADVOKATBYRÅ ✪
LINDAHL ✪
LINKLATERS ✪
VINGE ✪
WHITE & CASE ADVOKAT AB

Baker & McKenzie ✪
Cederquist, Advokatfirman ✪
Hammarskiöld & Co ✪
LINDHS DLA Nordic ✪
Setterwalls ✪

Danowsky & Partners Advokatbyrå
Foyen AB, Advokatfirman
Gozzo Advokater
Wistrand ✪

Firms are listed A-Z in tiers which are ranked in order of priority
✪ Indicates firm displays contact details at the end of this chapter.

Agne Lindberg of **Advokatfirman Delphi & Co** is the pre-eminent 'out-and-out IT lawyer' in Sweden. Lindberg heads a standalone IT department that, unlike those of some firms, is not just a function of the corporate group. Clients use the firm for its 'technical insights and knowledge of the industry.' The firm's proficiency has been further boosted by the arrival of Peter Nordbeck from **Linklaters**. It is a leader in multi-vendor outsourcing transactions and advice on software matters. Regular work is done for Electronic Arts, Hewlett-Packard, and users in the banking and insurance sectors. It also possesses regulatory telecoms expertise.

Biörn Riese heads a massive nine-partner TMT group at **Mannheimer Swartling** which has a strong transactional focus. It was instructed by key client SAS to advise on outsourcing transactions with CVC and has a history of working with TeliaSonera and Attendo Care.

Steffan de Geer of **Gernandt & Danielsson Advokatbyrå** is a leader in telecoms-sector transactions, as well as outsourcing, licensing and regulatory matters. Tele2 is a prominent client

Staffan Eklöw heads an eight-lawyer TIME (Telecoms, IT, Media, Entertainment) group at **Lindahl**, which attracts the praise of peers. Telenor is the firm's headline client, employing its advice on the €1bn acquisition of Vodafone, Sweden. 'Excellent regulatory and commercial nous' are a significant feature of the firm's work. Erik Bergenstråhle is singled out for telecoms expertise.

Following the departures of Stefan Bernhard and Peter Nordbeck, **Linklaters** fields a very different team to that of a year ago. Competition partner Ingvar Zander has been drafted in to head the ITC team, with former head and M&A star Jörgen Axelsson now playing a supporting role. The new-look team is wholly focused on transactions, especially outsourcing, and regularly acts for leading banks, as well as advising Vodafone in Sweden on its sale to Telenor.

Carl Johan af Petersens and Johan Winnerblad are the leading figures in a **Vinge** telecoms practice that has long been regarded as a leader in this market. It acted for the investors in Bredbandsbolaget during its sale to Telenor in 2005.

Swedish partner Rolf Olofsson heads **White & Case Advokat AB**'s IT group from Brussels where he runs a niche space communications/telecoms practice that acts for the Swedish Space Corporation among others. In Stockholm, Mats Boman holds fort and delivers what is perceived to be a 'very good brand' of IT advice.

Stefan Brandt enjoys a good name for IT at **Baker & McKenzie**, where he acts for Tiscali, Frango and Flextronics, although 2005 saw him advise the latter two on their sale. Instructions from software clients are on the increase, even if the firm remains best known for advice to IT-users. Outsourcing is a traditional strength.

Advokatfirman Cederquist is telecoms- and IT sector focused and offers regulatory, technical and general corporate advice to companies within this field, including Intel, Microsoft and Tele2. No one individual heads the work, although partner Petter Wirell is most closely identified with this field.

Hammarskiöld & Co IP head Thomas Lindqvist is also active in the IT sector for an international client base that includes TietoEnator, SAP, Unisys and Setec Oy. Regulatory, licensing, outsourcing and data protection are some of the services on offer. Jacob Melander adds experience on the telecoms side.

Jan Råssjö heads **LINDHS DLA Nordic**'s TMC group, which is an adviser to the Swedish Governmental Authority on data protection matters. Contentious work is a leading feature of the team's abilities.

SAP is a client of **Setterwalls** in Stockholm, which also acts for Sony Ericsson in Mälmo. Magnus Dahlén, based in Gothenburg, is the contact.

Per Hender, a general counsel at Sony, has joined **Wistrand**'s Gothenburg office; whilst Peter Helle, formerly of legacy *Helle & Westermark* has joined the Stockholm office.

INSOLVENCY

Insolvency in Sweden is not as lucrative a business as it is elsewhere in Europe because of regulations restricting the break-up and sale of bankrupt entities. There have been few new large insolvencies in the last two years.

INSOLVENCY

LINDHS DLA NORDIC ✪
SETTERWALLS ✪
WISTRAND ✪

Delphi & Co, Advokatfirman ✪
Fylgia KB, Advokatfirman
G Grönberg Advokatbyrå AB ✪
Gärde Wesslau Advokatbyrå ✪
Hagenfeldt Advokatbyrå
Hamilton Advokatbyrå
Lindahl ✪
MAQS Advokatbyrå
Vinge ✪

Glimstedt, Advokatfirman ✪
Hellström & Partners Advokatbyrå KB ✪
Hökerberg & Söderqvist Advokatbyrå KB ✪

Firms are listed A-Z in tiers which are ranked in order of priority
✪ Indicates firm displays contact details at the end of this chapter.

In a year in which there was little insolvency work **LINDHS DLA Nordic**'s large insolvency team defied the market by finding 230 new insolvency cases to work on. The most notable of these was its appointment as administrator to the estates of Clinictrac and Strand Interconnect.

Setterwalls' commitment to insolvency work, an area in which it is highly regarded, was again on show in 2005 when it hired a three-lawyer insolvency group from **Vinge**, including partners Leif Baecklund and Thomas Ehrner. Rolf Åbjörnsson is especially worthy of note for his role as liquidator of LUAP (formerly Folksam International), which with debts of SEK2bn (€212m) is Sweden's largest-ever bankruptcy case. Odd Swarting is also recommended for his work in the restructuring of Concordia.

Wistrand is a traditional leader in insolvency work and the reconstruction of companies. Margaretha Andersson and Malmö's Leif Ljungholm are recommended. Ljungholm is trustee for Jomed and PNB Group.

Advokatfirman Delphi & Co has no Stockholm insolvency function but maintains an active team in Gothenburg.

Stockholm's **Advokatfirman Fylgia KB** continues employ one of the largest dedicated insolvency practices in Sweden.

Insolvency continues to be one of the most visible of **G Grönberg Advokatbyrå AB** practices.

Gärde Wesslau Advokatbyrå is also active in Gothenburg as well as Jönköping, Helsingborg and Boras. Peter Thörnwall is the contact.

Insolvency and restructuring are core disciplines for Stockholm's **Hagenfeldt Advokatbyrå** which was founded by Carl Lindstrand of **Wistrand** and lawyers from **Advokatfirman Carler** in 2004. Name partner Björn Hagenfeldt undertook the reconstruction of Sportringen, a sports retail group.

Hamilton Advokatbyrå is traditionally strong in bankruptcy avoidance, dissolution and restructuring.

Three partners comprise an insolvency group at **Lindahl**, which accounts for 25% of business at the firm's Gothenburg office. Felix Körling is recommended.

MAQS Advokatbyrå also has a three-partner insolvency team in Gothenburg.

INSURANCE

On contentious matters Stefan Bessman of **Baker & McKenzie** commands a leading reputation. He was active for over 50 reinsurers, including Swiss Re and Munich Re, in an arbitration against the estate of bankrupt credit insurer Svenska Kredit (**Wistrand**), which saw the plaintiffs win more than €45m. Jonas Benedictsson is also active in claims disputes.

Erik Swartling's 'innovative' insurance team at **Hammarskiöld & Co** remains an important source of business for the firm, which is increasingly marrying work in this sector with that of its banking and finance department. Examples of such cooperation include advice to the securities funds industry and portfolio restructuring. Prudential, Zurich and Trygg are clients, though the departure of Bengt Karde has weakened the firm overall.

Much of **Linklaters**' insurance work is contentious and is therefore handled by Henrik Bielenstein's disputes group. However in tandem with the London office the M&A team is also advising South African insurer Old Mutual on its SEK44.9bn (€4.8bn) bid for Sweden's Skandia, potentially the biggest deal in the region for many years. AIG is another client.

INSURANCE

BAKER & McKENZIE ✪
HAMMARSKIÖLD & CO ✪
LINKLATERS ✪
MAQS ADVOKATBYRÅ
MORSSING & NYCANDER, ADVOKATFIRMAN
WISTRAND ✪

A-Law, Advokatfirman
Kilpatrick Stockton Advokat KB ✪
Mannheimer Swartling ✪
Vinge ✪
White & Case Advokat AB

Delphi & Co, Advokatfirman ✪
Gärde Wesslau Advokatbyrå ✪
Gernandt & Danielsson Advokatbyrå ✪
Setterwalls ✪

Firms are listed A-Z in tiers which are ranked in order of priority
✪ Indicates firm displays contact details at the end of this chapter.

Dan Öwerstrom, board chairman at **MAQS Advokatbyrå** and a former general counsel at Trygg Hansa, is described as 'very much the real thing when it comes to insurance.' His knowledge of both insurance and reinsurance is 'rare and detailed' whilst he also wins praise for an ability to apply insurance knowledge to the pensions market. **MAQS Advokatbyrå** has links with a number of London insurance practices and completed in excess of SEK3bn (€318m) of insurance deals in 2004-05, including portfolio swaps.

Lars Boman of **Advokatfirman Morssing & Nycander** is regularly described by some market watchers as 'clearly the most experienced insurance lawyer in Sweden'. In general, the firm's insurance work leans heavily towards cargo claims and maritime disputes. It also has a product liability practice.

Along with Dan Öwerstrom of **MAQS Advokatbyrå** and Christer Holm **Advokatfirman A-Law**, Rose-Marie Lundström of **Wistrand** is the most frequently cited lawyer for 'technical proficiency and all-round knowledge of the insurance and reinsurance markets'. Lars Olof-Svensson, best known on the insurance insolvency side, also wins plaudits for his adversarial skills and recently acted for an insurer in an arbitration valued at SEK1.8bn (€191m).

Recommended insurance specialist Christer Holm has taken the core of **Advokatfirman Delphi & Co**'s corporate and regulatory practice, including AIG, to three-partner start-up **Advokatfirman A-Law**. There Holm joins former colleague Susanna Norelid, who also has experience of acting for insurers in claims adjustment cases.

Jörgen Eklund is the young star of a **Kilpatrick Stockton Advokat KB** team that belies the office's small size, not least by acting for ACE across the board in Sweden. Half the work is contentious with Nils Sköld also providing policy-structuring advice.

Banking partner Helena Rempler is recommended for corporate insurance matters at **Mannheimer Swartling**, whilst Per Johan Eckerberg is the contact point at **Vinge**.

Bengt Åke Johnsson and 'sidekick' Olof Ragmark build on a 'top-notch' shipping practice at **White & Case Advokat AB** to advise a number of clients in this sector. However, work is by no means limited to shipping and in 2005 the pair were also active for insurers in contentious matters relating to reinsurance contracts and the 9/11 atrocities.

INTELLECTUAL PROPERTY AND MEDIA

INTELLECTUAL PROPERTY AND MEDIA

BIRD & BIRD ✪
DANOWSKY & PARTNERS ADVOKATBYRÅ
GOZZO ADVOKATER
RYDINCARLSTEN ADVOKATBYRÅ AB ✪

CEDERQUIST, ADVOKATFIRMAN ✪
DELPHI & CO, ADVOKATFIRMAN ✪
HAMMARSKIÖLD & CO ✪
LINDAHL ✪
MANNHEIMER SWARTLING ✪
SANDART & PARTNERS ADVOKATBYRÅ

BAKER & McKENZIE ✪
BJÖRKMAN AB, ADVOKATFIRMAN
G GRÖNBERG ADVOKATBYRÅ AB ✪
MAQS ADVOKATBYRÅ
SETTERWALLS ✪
VINGE ✪

A-Law, Advokatfirman
Gärde Wesslau Advokatbyrå ✪
Gernandt & Danielsson Advokatbyrå ✪
Kilpatrick Stockton Advokat KB ✪
Lindberg & Saxon, Advokatfirman
LINDHS DLA Nordic ✪
Linklaters ✪
Wistrand ✪

Firms are listed A-Z in tiers which are ranked in order of priority
✪ Indicates firm displays contact details at the end of this chapter.

Clients and peers alike sing praises of **Bird & Bird**'s Staffan Boström, without doubt the number one music industry lawyer in Sweden. Walo von Greyerz, a former head of legal at Ericsson, also wins plaudits for his work on the IP side. There are great synergies between **Bird & Bird**'s work in this sector and in IT and telecoms and, for the first time, the firm tops the bill in both sections. A strong and internationally focused team also includes international partner and UK solicitor Hubert Best, adviser to events company Jack Morton Worldwide. Life sciences is another core focus area.

Name partner Peter Danowsky of five-partner niche **Danowsky & Partners Advokatbyrå** is 'one of the few lawyers who excels in both IP and media'. The firm continues to punch forcefully above its weight, attracting the praise of the market. In media matters the firm is well known for the strength of its Swedish print client base.

The 2005 merger of two highly-rated IP boutiques, legacy *Grundén & Gozzo Advokater* and *Heidenstam & Nicander Advokatbyrå*, to form **Gozzo Advokater** is considered an 'excellent' decision within the market. The former firm brings the experience and reputation of IP stars Orjan Grunden and Giovanni Gozzo, whilst the latter is younger and in addition to its IP credentials also has a solid media practice. Peter von Heidenstam also has a burgeoning anti-piracy practice. With so many big names now under one roof the new firm ascends to the top tier.

RydinCarlsten Advokatbyrå AB has leading patent litigation capability. Although it is seeking to broaden its reputation the firm remains best known for its 'dominance in all things IP'. It acted for LEGO in a case against Biltema over copyright infringement and also for Atlas Copco in a leading case against Sandvik. Ulf Dahlgren is most highly recommended.

According to peers **Advokatfirman Cederquist** once 'patented quality IP advice', although in recent years the firm has been more prominent on the media side, not least in publishing where the Bonnier Group is a client. Associate Gabrial Lidman is now the head of the team although he draws on the support of partners Lennart Kanter and Per Ugge part time. Warner Music, Sony Music and Microsoft are also clients.

Advokatfirman Delphi & Co wins praise for its trade mark and copyright work, although it is less active in media. A distinct department at the firm handles trade marks and domain name registration. IP litigator Peter Skoglund, was especially busy with infringement and trade secrets litigation in 2005. Electronic Arts is a client.

Hammarskiöld & Co's Claes Langenius is a identified as 'one of the few true media men' and he works closely with Thomas Lindqvist, who heads an IP team. Both are well known in the market and between them both they offer a full range of IP and media advice, including litigation. The Swedish Acadmy is a high-profile client.

Lindahl offers a 'solid' IP and media service, but it is for the latter discipline that the firm attracts superlatives. Staffan Eklöw is 'immersed in the media scene' where he acts for Europe-wide French radio station Radio Energie, TV4, MTV, the Nobel Foundation and Sweden's largest and oldest news agency.

Stefan Widmark's return to **Mannheimer Swartling** following a spell at **Vinge** heralds a change in the market with **Mannheimer Swartling** now poised to offer the most serious competition of any large full-service firm to the traditional leaders on the IP side. Widmark heads a three-partner team that includes Karin Cederlund and Per Josefson and also boasts expertise in the media sector, where he acts for TV4 and Swedish rock icon Ulf Lundell.

Sandart & Partners Advokatbyrå is a niche IP firm of excellent repute. Dag Sandart is frequently cited by peers. It is one of only a handful of firms with patent litigation capability.

Baker & McKenzie is best known on the media side where Mattias Hedwall has a practice that leans heavily to the TV production sector. IT head Stefan Brandt lends support on IP matters.

Legendary, Stockholm, sole practitioner Per Bjorkman of **Advokatfirman Björkman AB** stands out for being 'street smart'. He has a long history of providing advice to the television industry and is also active in all IP matters except patents.

G Grönberg Advokatbyrå AB rises one tier on the strength of its work in the film production sector.

IP is a significant growth area for **MAQS Advokatbyrå** across all its offices. In Stockholm, Monique Wadsted is singled out for her marketing law expertise.

Marc Tullgren continues to head **Setterwalls**' sports and media work from Malmö. Senior associate Kristina Tunkrans is also well known and acts for SKAP (Swedish Composer and Songwriting Group).

The departure of Stefan Widmark to **Mannheimer Swartling** has left **Vinge**'s IP department solely in the hands of 'low-key but effective' partner Per Eric Alvsing, who will firstly concentrate on providing support to the firm's transactional endeavours. Beyond that he offers expertise in IP, life science, sports and media law.

Sole IP partner Peter Nordbeck has departed **Linklaters** for **Advokatfirman Delphi & Co**.

MERGERS AND ACQUISITIONS

MERGERS AND ACQUISITIONS

LINKLATERS ✪
VINGE ✪

GERNANDT & DANIELSSON ADVOKATBYRÅ ✪
HAMMARSKIÖLD & CO ✪
MANNHEIMER SWARTLING ✪

CEDERQUIST, ADVOKATFIRMAN ✪
WHITE & CASE ADVOKAT AB

BAKER & McKENZIE ✪
BIRD & BIRD ✪
LINDAHL ✪
LINDHS DLA NORDIC ✪
ROSCHIER HOLMBERG
SETTERWALLS ✪
WISTRAND ✪

Delphi & Co, Advokatfirman ✪
Hellström & Partners Advokatbyrå KB ✪
Kilpatrick Stockton Advokat KB ✪
MAQS Advokatbyrå
Södermark, Advokatfirman ✪

AJB Bergh Advokatbyrå AB
G Grönberg Advokatbyrå AB ✪
Gärde Wesslau Advokatbyrå ✪
Moll Wendén Advokatbyrå AB ✪
RydinCarlsten Advokatbyrå AB ✪

Firms are listed A-Z in tiers which are ranked in order of priority
✪ Indicates firm displays contact details at the end of this chapter.

Linklaters again dominated proceedings in the Scandinavian M&A market in 2005. In terms of value of deals completed in the first three-quarters, **Linklaters** brooked no rivals, finishing with a total deal value almost 50% larger than second-placed **White & Case Advokat AB**, which was able to draw on two offices in the region. M&A is the overriding focus of the firm in Sweden with almost half of its 20-plus partners active in a department headed by Martin Börresen. Winning the mandate to advise Old Mutual globally on its expected acquisition of Skandia (priced at €4.8bn at the close of 2005) was a big success for the firm as a whole. (Skandia is advised by **Skadden, Arps, Slate, Meagher & Flom (UK) LLP** and Företagsjuridik Nord & Co, a niche firm that does not belong to the Swedish Bar Association). On a smaller Swedish level, advice to Vodafone which was sold to Telenor (**Lindahl**) for €1bn was another highlight, as was **Linklaters**' role as counsel to Jefferson Smurfit in its sale of €500m-worth of shares in Swedish paper business Smurfit Munksjö. Overall, **Linklaters** went from strength to strength in Sweden in 2005.

Vinge is the chief competitor to **Linklaters**. It has streamlined its figure, to give greater prominence to its M&A business. The arrival of Göran Nyström from **Mannheimer Swartling** in early 2005, following an earlier path trodden by Carl Gustaf de Geer and Johan Winnerblad, was billed by many as the most important move of 2005. With Johan Cederland, Stefan de Hevesy and Fredrick von Baumgarten already noted as leaders at the firm, **Vinge** can boast the largest collection of high-profile corporate lawyers under one roof. Although 2005 was not as strong a year as 2004 in relation to its standing against other firms in the region, work was by no means lacking and in the first three-quarters it topped the rankings for independent Swedish firms in terms of value of deals completed. On the buyer side it advised target Bredbandsbolaget on its SEK6bn (€636m) sale to Telenor; and on the sellers side advised BakerCapital and Nordic Capital, CSM, and Denmark's TDC on a trio of acquisitions worth almost €1.8bn in total.

Though less than a quarter the size of **Mannheimer Swartling** and **Vinge**, and therefore not a contender in number of deals done, M&A powerhouse **Gernandt & Danielsson Advokatbyrå** nevertheless continues to get the better of its bigger rivals in terms of average value of deals completed. The high regard in which Dick Lundqvist and Stefan de Geer are held by Sweden's business community is partly responsible for the firm's prowess. Advice to target Ainax in its €1bn acquisition by Scania, by all accounts a highly complex transaction, was the outstanding achievement of 2005. It also acted for Lawson in its €351m purchase of Intentia (**Linklaters**).

Peder Hammarskiöld and the 'excellent' **Hammarskiöld & Co** M&A group received high praise from the market for their successful representation of Scania in its €1bn public offer for Ainax, a deal that generated a great deal of media coverage. Over one half of the firm's income is derived from transactional work, with Hammarskiöld and Jacob Melander routinely recognised as leaders. Other 2005 deals included advice to EQT on its €500m acquisition of Smurfit Munksjö and for Danish-listed Keops on a string of real estate transactions worth approximately €650m in total. It rises one tier.

Over the last decade, **Mannheimer Swartling** has been one of the leading firms in Scandanavia for total value of and number of deals completed in the region. Throughout 2005 the firm consistently completed more deals than any other firm and perhaps has the best reputation internationally of any Swedish firm. However with a broader work profile and more mouths to feed, its average deal value remained lower than **Vinge**'s. It acted for Hexagon in €900m bid for Leica. Tom Hård is the leading figure, although Anders Lindblad was active in an impressive number of deals.

Advokatfirman Cederquist is increasingly noted for the strength of its M&A practice, despite having a broader work profile than some of its competitors. It followed up a strong 2004, in which William Lüning advised Invik & Co AB on its €1.7bn merger with Investment AB Kinnevik, with number of significant deals, not least Lennart Kanter's advice to Sydkraft/E.ON on the €500m purchase of 24 hydroelectric plants. A clutch of smaller deals could be quoted for Segulah and Bonnier groups.

As a global firm with offices in Sweden and Finland, **White & Case Advokat AB** is second only to **Linklaters** in the value of deals it racked up in the Nordic region in 2005. Though the Swedish office was by no means the driver of all those deals, nevertheless it is integral to the firm's success in the region and M&A accounts for over 50% of its business locally. Nordic Capital is a headline client, instructing the firm on two transactions (Plastel and Mölnlyck) in 2005, both for undisclosed values. 'Exceptional' Claes Zettermarck is the undisputed figurehead of the firm and led on both the above deals as well as advising Altor Equity partners on the purchase of Flextronics Network Services. Meanwhile Clas Romander made use of international resources to advise Sweden's Kisel Microelectronics on its US$405m sale to a US buyer.

As in other areas, **Baker & McKenzie** in Stockholm is often involved in the Swedish aspects of global transactions led by the firm's other offices. In this regard, Sweden supported the London office and Denmark's **Gorrissen Federspiel Kierkegaard** in advice to EQT on its €2.97bn purchase of ISS, Denmark's largest deal in 2005. More specific to Sweden was Carl Svernlöv's advice to Flextronics on its US$550m divestiture of its Network Services group and subsequent sale to Telavie.

Bird & Bird rises one tier on the strength of client and peer recommendations, a galloping reputation and, perhaps most importantly, on the strength of work done. It demonstrated the extent of its capabilities in 2005 when advising Eniro on a SEK10.5bn (€1.1bn) acquisition of Norway's Findexa, one of the biggest transactions of the year. Mikael Engqvist, a former in-house counsel at Eniro, led the transaction working closely with

Bird & Bird London and **Gibson, Dunn & Crutcher LLP**. Other deals in the range SEK100m (€11m) to SEK2bn (€212m) could be quoted.

Owing to its enviable position as principal local counsel to Telenor, **Lindahl** was arguably one of the most successful firms in Sweden in M&A in 2005. It first advised Telenor on its SEK6bn (€636m) purchase of Bredbandsbolaget but, most impressively, it worked with **Allen & Overy LLP** and opposite **Linklaters** to advise it on the €1bn acquisition of Vodafone. If it can extend the experience gained here to win other clients in the largest transactions then it can challenge all the above firms. Carl-Olof Bouveng is recommended.

In line with the wider interests of the global firm, **LINDHS DLA Nordic** has an impressive venture capital business which keeps the firm busy in the mid-sized M&A market. 3i Group and Ratos are regular clients.

'A crouching tiger' is how one market watcher perceives **Roschier Holmberg**'s position following its dramatic advent in the Swedish market in 2005, the 'biggest event since **Linklaters** shook Stockholm in 2001'. Axel Calissendorff, for so long 'the face of M&A at **Mannheimer Swartling**', was the first to arrive, quickly adding Ola Åhman of **Advokatfirman Cederquist** and Ulf-Henrik Kull from the firm's Finnish headquarters. Though the firm is included here purely on potential and individual reputation, nevertheless as one of Finland's most profitable firms and one of the strongest brands in the Nordic region, it will doubtless ascend very quickly.

Setterwalls represented TeliaSonera and ABN Amro in the telecoms giant's public offer of approximately €500m for all outstanding shares in Estonian's Eesti Telekom. Jan Jensen led in this deal. Equity funds such as Polaris are an important source of business.

M&A and venture capital transactions account for approximately 35% of **Wistrand**'s business. Robert Kullgren and Lars Hasp are the dominant personalities in a team that is especially active for media company Schibsted, which recently bid SEK4bn (€424m) for Finland's Alma Media Oy.

New entrant **AJB Bergh Advokatbyrå AB** completed over half-a-dozen transactions in 2005, among other things acting for Metrima in its acquisition of Home Solutions from Vattenfall.

REAL ESTATE

Linklaters has a real estate M&A practice headed by recommended partner Per Nyberg and a leading real estate finance group under the auspices of Rolf Johansson. Magnus Lidman is the third partner in a department that is the firm's largest, after M&A/corporate. Over SEK9bn (€954m)-worth of real estate transactions were completed in 2005.

Jesper Prytz heads a 13-partner real estate practice at **Mannheimer Swartling** that has a leading transactional capability in Stockholm and regulatory and transactional capability in Gothenburg. It also draws on leading construction and environment practices. Over €2bn-worth of transactions were completed in 2005 for the likes of Fastighets AB Norrporten and Fastighets AB Tornet. Klas Wennström is prominent.

Although only 20-lawyers in size and therefore not to be compared with the leaders in quantity of work done, nevertheless **Kilpatrick Stockton Advokat KB** deserves a rise of one tier on the back of consistent praise from clients who formerly used the larger firms. Real estate is the flagship discipline of the firm, which is described as providing a 'no-nonsense approach to getting the job done'. Head Pontus Kågerman inspires the most praise, most notably the comment: 'Though he's not Mr Kilpatrick or Mr Stockton, he should be the name partner because he really is that good'. NIAM, Catella, PB Real estate and Merrill Lynch are a selection of the clients.

On the regulatory side of real estate, niche environmental practice **Advokatfirman Åberg & Co AB** is recommended. Infrastructure investment projects are an important source of work for the firm's 13 lawyers.

Mauritz Silfverstolpe and Jan Alexanderson are the partners in a dedicated **Baker & McKenzie** real estate team that completed in excess of SEK6bn (€636m)-worth of real estate transactions in 2005 for Atrium Fastigheter, Norweigian investor Heimstaden, Erik Selin Fastigheter and Visättra Holding.

Some 80% of **Gernandt & Danielsson Advokatbyrå**'s real estate work is transactional with the rest comprising advice on commercial leases. Corporate partner Bob Johanson is noted for the former and Jonas Eklund for the latter.

REAL ESTATE

LINKLATERS ✪
MANNHEIMER SWARTLING ✪

KILPATRICK STOCKTON ADVOKAT KB ✪

Åberg & Co AB, Advokatfirman
Baker & McKenzie ✪
Gernandt & Danielsson Advokatbyrå ✪
MAQS Advokatbyrå
Trägårdh & Falkenborn Advokatbyrå AB
Vinge ✪

AJB Bergh Advokatbyrå AB
Cederquist, Advokatfirman ✪
Delphi & Co, Advokatfirman ✪
Gärde Wesslau Advokatbyrå ✪
Glimstedt, Advokatfirman ✪
LINDHS DLA Nordic ✪
Ramberg
Setterwalls ✪
White & Case Advokat AB
Wistrand ✪

Firms are listed A-Z in tiers which are ranked in order of priority
✪ Indicates firm displays contact details at the end of this chapter.

London & Regional and Steen & Ström are clients of **MAQS Advokatbyrå**, which ascends the table on the back of a stunning year which saw it advise on over €3bn-worth of property deals in the Nordic region.

Stockholm-based Klas Falkenborn of real estate niche **Trägårdh & Falkenborn Advokatbyrå AB** is one of the foremost real estate lawyers in Sweden.

The market acknowledges **Vinge** as 'very strong' in regard to real estate, although it has no distinct department here. In early 2005, Stefan de Hevesy advised the sellers of Nya Stockholm, purchased by Keops for SEK214m (€23m).

SHIPPING

The 'old ship hands' at **Advokatfirman Morssing & Nycander** preserve a strong tradition of quality advice on all aspects of maritime law, including cargo claims, as well as advising on other modes of transport. Lars Boman is the outstanding name in an 'impressively strong' team.

Setterwalls is another firm with an excellent tradition in the shipping sphere, which was the focus of the firm's dominant practice in years gone by. Today Jörgen Almelöv is the younger face of an internationally focused team that is expert in ship finance, disputes and all aspects relating to P&I and hull insurers.

Loyal clients continue to affirm that the combination of Bengt Åke Johnsson and Olaf Ragmark at **White & Case Advokat AB** is 'without parallel in Scandanavia'. Both advise on the whole gamut of maritime law but it is their success on the contentious side that has brought the firm most fame.

Cheddi Liljeström, a former in-house lawyer with SAS, takes charge of aviation matters at **Advokatfirman Delphi & Co**, which also has a small railways practice.

Two-partner **Dhunér Järvengren Advokatbyrå** enjoys 'the strength of reputation

SHIPPING

MORSSING & NYCANDER, ADVOKATFIRMAN
SETTERWALLS ✪
WHITE & CASE ADVOKAT AB

Delphi & Co, Advokatfirman ✪
Dhunér Järvengren Advokatbyrå
Lindahl ✪
Mannheimer Swartling ✪
Vinge ✪
Wistrand ✪

Baker & McKenzie ✪
Gärde Wesslau Advokatbyrå ✪

Firms are listed A-Z in tiers which are ranked in order of priority
✪ Indicates firm displays contact details at the end of this chapter.

that consistent quality brings'. Shipping is one of three core disciplines at the firm (the others being dispute resolution and EU and competition), and both Lennart Jarvengren and Karl Johan Dhunér are active here. Dhunér is especially well-known as a maritime arbitrator. Distribution and logistics matters in the wider transport sector are an interest.

Shipping and transport remain important sources of revenue for **Lindahl**, which acted for Concordia Bus Group in its successful reconstruction in 2005. Erik Linnarsson is the man behind the reputation.

Eight lawyers are active at **Mannheimer Swartling**, primarily in higher-value advice to shipowners including Stena group. SAS is an important corporate client of the firm.

Conversely, **Vinge** is best known for its advice to ship builders and financiers. It also has a solid aviation finance team.

Wistrand has a strong shipping arm in Gothenburg, which is centred on key client Stena Group. Lave Beck-Friis and Anne-Marie Pouteaux comprise a team that 'is not to be overlooked'.

TAX

Accountancy firms dominate the tax market in Sweden, leaving only a small quantity of work for law firms. One firm that has done particularly well is Skeppsbron Skatt, a law-firm-cum-accountancy-practice, which is outside of the ambit of the Swedish Bar Association but which consists solely of lawyers formerly at KPMG.

Peter Nordquist and Brita Munck-Persson are the 'outsanding members of an outstanding team' at **Mannheimer Swartling**, that dominates the legal side of the tax market by dint of its size (seven partners). The team is built around transactional support expertise but also excels in litigation and VAT, where Joachim Agrell is recommended.

TAX

MANNHEIMER SWARTLING ✪

BAKER & McKENZIE ✪
BILL ANDRÉASSON, ADVOKATFIRMAN
LINKLATERS ✪

Cederquist, Advokatfirman ✪
Delphi & Co, Advokatfirman ✪
Kilpatrick Stockton Advokat KB ✪
Wistrand ✪

Bird & Bird ✪
Lindahl ✪
LINDHS DLA Nordic ✪
MAQS Advokatbyrå
Setterwalls ✪
Vinge ✪
Wingqvist AB, Advokatfirman

Gärde Wesslau Advokatbyrå ✪
Södermark, Advokatfirman ✪

Firms are listed A-Z in tiers which are ranked in order of priority
✪ *Indicates firm displays contact details at the end of this chapter.*

According to clients **Baker & McKenzie**'s managing partner Bo Lindqvist is the 'friendliest tax lawyer you will ever meet'. Lindqvist has one of the most recognisable faces at the firm, and tax is a leading strength. In 2005, Lindqvist provided transactional tax support to Jarowskij Holding in a SEK70m (€0.74m) joint venture with MTV and represented Finland's Metso group in two VAT cases worth SEK55m (€0.58m) in total.

'Still on top after all these years,' Bill Andréasson of tax boutique **Advokatfirman Bill Andréasson** is regarded with popular affection in the market having built up a 'highly skilled team' which is especially noted for its litigation capability.

Despite the loss of recommended M&A tax partner Christian Luthman to **Bird & Bird**, **Linklaters** still retains a larger team than most of its competitors. Mats Anderson and Lars Jonsson are the partners in a ten-lawyer team that remains central to the firm's plans in Sweden, though the vast majority of its work is non-contentious.

Advokatfirman Cederquist's four-lawyer tax team has delivered tax advice to a number of government legislative committees and acted for various banks in tax litigation. Olle Stenman heads the group.

Advokatfirman Delphi & Co has a six-lawyer tax department headed by Peter Sjögren, formerly a partner with Ernst & Young. Sjögren has presided over the refurbishment of the tax team since his arrival in 2004 and is gaining a reputation for 'aggressive structuring'.

Managing partner Nils Sköld heads up tax work at **Kilpatrick Stockton Advokat KB**. Skiold has a reputation for VAT work but does much more besides, not least supporting the firm's leading real estate group.

Four lawyers including partner Conny Otteland comprise a recommended corporate support tax group at **Wistrand**'s Stockholm office.

Bird & Bird wins entry following the hire of Christian Luthman from **Linklaters**, which will doubtless see the firm ascend much higher up the table.

Setterwalls demonstrates its greatest tax expertise in Gothenburg and Malmö where it is increasingly winning work from the Big Four accounting firms. It now aims to build a Stockholm practice of similar quality. Björn Odle is the primary figure, recommended for his international knowledge.

Stockholm-based sole practitioner Lennart Wingvist of **Advokatfirman Wingqvist AB** has over 20 years' experience in the tax market. Small Swedish businesses, too small to have their own tax departments, continue to form the bulk of his business.

Advokatfirman Södermark is also admitted on the strength of its tax litigation expertise.

ADVOKATFIRMAN DELPHI & CO

ÖSTRA HAMNGATAN 29
411 10 GÖTEBORG

Telephone: +46 31 10 72 00
Fax: +46 31 13 94 69
E-mail: goteborg@delphilaw.com
Website: www.delphilaw.com

Languages
English, French, German, Spanish

Other offices
Linköping, Malmö, Norrköping, Stockholm

Number of lawyers 96
at this office 15

CATEGORIES OF WORK

Corporate, M&A, capital markets
Vilhelm Nyström, Håkan Wendesten, Olof Myhrman

Commercial law (general)
Rolf Karlsson, Fredrik Emanuel, Ulf Hjelström

Litigation, arbitration
Rolf Karlsson

Environment
Hans L Bergqvist, Leif Ramberg, Patric Lundin

Technology transfer
Vilhelm Nyström, Olof Myhrman

Life sciences
Caroline Ygge

IT, communication, IP
Caroline Ygge

Insolvency, bankruptcy, reconstruction
Hans L Bergqvist, Patric Lundin, Håkan Wendesten, Fredrik Emanuel, Ulf Hjelström

Employment/labour
Leif Ramberg

Commercial property
Rolf Karlsson, Per Håkansson, Ulf Hjelström

Construction
Per Håkansson

Public procurement, EU, competition
Caroline Ygge, Olof Myhrman

THE FIRM

Advokatfirman Delphi & Co is a full-service commercial law firm with offices in Sweden's major business centres, Stockholm, Gothenburg, Malmö and Linköping-Norrköping. Delphi & Co focuses, in particular, on corporate, including M&A, IT and telecoms, EU, banking and finance, competition law, tax, labour law and environmental law.

The firm represents multinational corporations in their activities in Sweden, including cross-border transactions. The firm's clients include a wide range of both publicly traded and privately held Swedish, US and European corporations, banks, financial institutions and others conducting cross-border business. Many of Delphi & Co's clients are Fortune 500 companies but smaller, privately held companies are also on the client list.

AREAS OF PRACTICE

The firm handles all types of financial transactions, such as drafting consortium agreements, loan documentation and performing due diligence processes. In its M&A work, the firm works cross-departmentally, drawing on its lawyers' competence in competition law, corporate finance, venture capital transactions, environment, tax and employment. Recent acquisitions handled by the firm have ranged in value up to €1.5bn.

The firm has one of the largest ITC/IP practice groups in Sweden. In this area, the firm's activities include IT contracts and digital intellectual property rights, e-commerce, IT outsourcing and IT contracts and also telecommunications permits.

Working closely with corporations whose trade marks are well known and respected throughout the world, the firm also specialises in patents, copyrights, trade marks, infringements, etc. The firm's litigators represent enterprises in court proceedings, in arbitration and in mediation, both in Sweden and abroad. Several Delphi lawyers also serve as arbitrators, in Sweden and internationally.

Delphi & Co handles, on an ongoing basis, notifications and filings with DG C in Brussels and with the Swedish Competition Authority. The firm is also one of the major law firms regularly used to review proposed new EU legislation.

Commercial property and insolvency issues, including liquidation and bankruptcies, are other major areas of practice.

MANNHEIMER SWARTLING

PO BOX 2235
403 14 GÖTEBORG

Telephone: +46 31 355 1600
Fax: +46 31 355 1601
Website: www.mannheimerswartling.se

Languages
English, French, German, Polish, Russian, the Scandinavian languages

Other offices
Berlin, Brussels, Frankfurt, Helsingborg, Malmö, New York, St Petersburg, Stockholm

Number of lawyers 330
at this office 53

CATEGORIES OF WORK

Banking and finance
Anders Wikström

Constitutional and administrative law
Claes Beyer

Construction and projects
Torbjörn Molander

Corporate taxation
Martin Nilsson

Employment
Clas Nyberg

EU and competition
Clas Nyberg

Environment
Torbjörn Molander

Insolvency
Henrik Diefke

Insurance
Anders Wikström

Intellectual property
Göran Kraft

Litigation and arbitration
Robin Oldenstam

Maritime and transport
Jerker Sellén

Mergers and acquisitions
Clas Nyberg

Private equity
Jan Holmberg

Real estate
Jesper Prytz

Securities
Anders Wikström

Sport and entertainment
Torbjörn Molander

Telecoms, media and technology
Göran Kraft

SETTERWALLS

KUNGSTORGET 2
PO BOX 11235
404 25 GÖTEBORG

Telephone: +46 31 701 17 00
Fax: +46 31 701 17 01
E-mail:
first name.surname@setterwalls.se
Website: www.setterwalls.se

Languages
English, French, Finnish, German, Spanish

Other offices
Stockholm, Malmö

Number of lawyers 115
at this office 25

CATEGORIES OF WORK

Commercial and corporate law
Torsten Leman

IT and telecommunications law
Magnus Dahlén, Per Furberg

Sports, media and entertainment
Anders Holmgren

Insolvency
Tomas Setterberg

EU and competition law
Dag Fredlund

Banking and finance and securities law
Johan Wilkens

Real estate and construction law
Anders I Bengtsson

Labour law
Dan Bullarbo

Intellectual property
Johan Karlbom

Mergers and acquisitions and corporate finance
Magnus Örtorp

Maritime and transportation law
Max Slotte

Tax law
Björn Ohde, Lars Wessman

Litigation and arbitration
Johan Wilkens

THE FIRM

Setterwalls was founded in Stockholm in 1878 and is one of Sweden's oldest law firms. Its experience and expertise extends to most areas of Swedish and international commercial law.

Setterwalls is a firm possessing significant resources with more than 115 lawyers located at offices in Stockholm, Gothenburg and Malmö working in co-operation with an international network of lawyers.

AREAS OF PRACTICE

IT and telecommunications: provides legal services to all operators within the IT and telecom sectors such as telephone operators, internet suppliers, e-commerce companies, manufacturers of hardware and computer software development companies. Setterwalls also regularly assists clients in other IT-related matters such as procurement of systems solutions, IT services, etc.

Sports, media and entertainment: the department offers legal services to a number of media enterprises, sports associations, event organisers, athletes and artists.

Pharmaceuticals and biotech: provides advice to established and newly-started pharmaceuticals and biotech companies, as well as assistance in matters concerning financing, research and development, patents, licenses and royalties.

Insolvency and restructuring: the group provides clients with advice concerning financial difficulties and the preventing of them. The group consists of specialist lawyers with extensive experience of restructuring and insolvency matters with local as well as international dimensions.

EU and competition: provides legal assistance in matters concerning Swedish and European competition law and other matters in connection with the EU. The firm assists in connection with the filing of various notifications with the Swedish Competition Authority and the European Commission, investigation of competition law aspects in agreements and business concentrations, and assistance in connection with compliance programmes. Setterwalls also represents clients before the Court of Justice of the European Communities and the Market Court.

Banking and finance and securities: has substantial experience in providing legal assistance in matters regarding banking and finance. Work includes matters related to initial public offerings, procurement of capital and new issues of shares, loans and other financing, as well as securities law.

Real estate and construction: assists clients in relation to the purchase, sale and development of real estate and in the procurement of construction contracts. Expertise includes applications for building permits to financing and final leasing or sale, as well as environmental law matters related to real estate. The firm has participated in some of the largest infrastructure projects in Sweden.

Labour law: assists clients in all kinds of labour law matters.

Intellectual property: regularly assists clients in matters relating to trade mark protection, copyright, patents and other intellectual property rights.

Mergers and acquisitions and corporate finance: assists clients in domestic and cross-border business transactions, often in co-operation with banks and investors. Work usually comprises business transfers, investments, mergers, joint venture issues and other matters regarding corporate financing and procurement of capital.

Maritime and transportation law: offers a full range of legal assistance in all areas of maritime and transportation law, including ship financing and transport matters.

Tax law: offers tax law advice to Swedish and international companies, ranging from personal tax advice to cross-border business acquisitions.

Arbitration and litigation: the litigation department represents clients in national and international litigation and arbitration. Several lawyers are regularly appointed as arbitrators.

ADVOKATFIRMAN VINGE

NILS ERICSONSGATAN 17
BOX 11025
404 21 GÖTEBORG

Telephone: +46 31 722 35 00
Fax: +46 31 722 37 00
Website: www.vinge.se

Languages
English, French, German, Italian, Mandarin, Norwegian, Portuguese, Spanish

Other offices
Brussels, Helsingborg, Hong Kong, London, Malmö, Paris, Shanghai, Stockholm

Number of lawyers 300
at this office 60

Contact
Olof Jisland

Member
Scandinavian Law Alliance with Kromann Reumert (Denmark) and Thommessen (Norway); Lex Mundi

CATEGORIES OF WORK

Banking and finance
Fredrik Vinge, Thomas Lakhall

Bankruptcy and liquidation
Fredrik Tengström, Per Settergren

China practice
Björn Aschan

Corporate finance, capital markets
Fredrik Sonander, Michael Sterner

Employment and benefits
Olle Lindén

EU and antitrust
Björn Nicolai

General corporate
Torbjörn Sköld, Göran Petersson

Insurance
Per Olov Skold

Intellectual property
Susann Vahlenbreder Hecht

IT
Olle Linden

Litigation and arbitration
Paulo Fohlin, Lars Jonson

M&A
Michael Sterner, Magnus Pauli

Marketing and media
Olof Jisland,
Susann Vahlenbreder-Hecht

Private equity funds
Fredrik Sonander

Public procurement
Rikard Setterlid

Real estate and environmental
Morgan Hallén, Rikard Setterlid

Tax
Raoul Svensson, Lennart O Larsson

THE FIRM

With some 300 fee-earners, Vinge is one of the largest law firms in Scandinavia. The firm is a member of the Scandinavian Law Alliance together with Kromann Reumert in Denmark and Thommessen in Norway.

Vinge has offices in Stockholm, Gothenburg, Malmö and Helsingborg as well as in London, Paris, Brussels, Hong Kong and Shanghai. The firm's clients include domestic and international commercial enterprises, financial institutions and state and regulatory bodies. Vinge is committed to providing the highest-quality legal advice and experience for all matters in which the firm becomes involved, to the highest professional standards.

Innovation, creativeness and a business-orientated, problem-solving approach are at the core of the practice. The firm's size means that there are resources available to handle large and complex domestic and cross-border transactions within tight time frames. At the same time, there is a strong focus on responsiveness and personal commitments to clients. Vinge's motto is: A good commercial lawyer sees beyond the law.

AREAS OF PRACTICE

Vinge specialises in all aspects of commercial law and is consistently ranked amongst the leading law firms in Scandinavia in a number of key practice areas. Vinge's extensive network of contacts comprises independent law firms, consultants and investment banks with whom the firm works regularly on domestic and cross-border deals and projects.

The firm takes an overall approach as well as providing in-depth knowledge by working together with major foreign law firms. Vinge has developed a wide international network which is available to its clients. The firm's broad experience and expertise means that it is called upon to handle all kinds of commercial law issues. It has learned from experience what resources and services are required in order to find the right solutions to clients' problems.

Vinge does everything it can to help clients to achieve success in their business. The firm sees beyond the problems and seeks the solutions.

WISTRAND

LILLA BOMMEN 1
411 04 GÖTEBORG

Telephone: +46 31 771 21 00
Fax: +46 31 771 21 50
E-mail: gbg@wistrand.se
Website: www.wistrand.se

Languages
Czech, English, Finnish, French, German

Other offices
Malmö, Stockholm

Number of lawyers 94
at this office 35

CATEGORIES OF WORK

Antitrust and EU	Intellectual property
Banking and finance	IT and telecoms
Commercial and corporate law	Labour and employment
Capital markets	Litigation and arbitration
Entertainment and sports law	Media and marketing law
Environmental	Mergers and acquisitions
Insolvency	Shipping and transport
Insurance	Tax law

MANNHEIMER SWARTLING

PO BOX 1384
251 13 HELSINGBORG

Telephone: +46 42 48 92 200
Fax: +46 42 48 92 201
Website: www.mannheimerswartling.se

Languages
English, French, German, Polish, Russian, the Scandinavian languages

Other offices
Berlin, Brussels, Frankfurt, Gothenburg, Malmö, New York, St Petersburg, Stockholm

Number of lawyers 330
at this office 13

CATEGORIES OF WORK

Banking and finance
Göran Miörner

Construction and projects
Jan Kansmark

Corporate taxation
Martin Nilsson

Employment
Madeleine Rydberger

EU and competition
Louise Widén

Environment
Mikael Wärnsby

Insolvency
Niklas Bogefors

Insurance
Göran Miörner

Intellectual property
Pär Andersson

Litigation and arbitration
Pär Andersson

Maritime and transport
Anders Lückander

Mergers and acquisitions
Claes Albinsson

Private Equity
Göran Miörner

Real estate
Lars Kongstad

Securities
Ragnar Lindqvist

Sport and entertainment
Michael Karlsson

Telecoms, media and technology
Niklas Bogefors

ADVOKATFIRMAN VINGE

STALLGATAN 4
BOX 1064
251 10 HELSINGBORG

Telephone: +46 42 24 80 80
Fax: +46 42 24 80 85
Website: www.vinge.se

Languages
English, French, German, Italian, Spanish

Other offices
Brussels, Gothenburg, Hong Kong, London, Malmö, Paris, Shanghai, Stockholm

Number of lawyers 300
at this office 11

Member
Scandinavian Law Alliance with Kromann Reumert (Denmark) and Thommessen (Norway); Lex Mundi

CATEGORIES OF WORK

Corporate finance and capital markets
Sven A Olsson

Employment and benefits
Ingela Malmborg

General corporate
Peter Abrahamsson

Intellectual property
Marcus Palm

IT
Henrik Borna

EU and competition
Pär Remnelid

Litigation and arbitration
Krister Azelius

M&A
Peter Abrahamsson

Public procurement
Peter Abrahamsson

Real estate
Gustav Hintze

Environmental
Ingela Malmborg

THE FIRM

With some 300 fee-earners, Vinge is one of the largest law firms in Scandinavia. The firm is a member of the Scandinavian Law Alliance together with Kromann Reumert in Denmark and Thommessen in Norway.

Vinge has offices in Stockholm, Gothenburg, Malmö and Helsingborg as well as in London, Paris, Brussels, Hong Kong and Shanghai. The firm's clients include domestic and international commercial enterprises, financial institutions and state and regulatory bodies. Vinge is committed to providing the highest-quality legal advice and experience for all matters in which the firm becomes involved, to the highest professional standards.

Innovation, creativeness and a business-orientated, problem-solving approach are at the core of the practice. The firm's size means that there are resources available to handle large and complex domestic and cross-border transactions within tight time frames. At the same time, there is a strong focus on responsiveness and personal commitments to clients. Vinge's motto is: A good commercial lawyer sees beyond the law.

AREAS OF PRACTICE

Vinge specialises in all aspects of commercial law and is consistently ranked amongst the leading law firms in Scandinavia in a number of key practice areas. Vinge's extensive network of contacts comprises independent law firms, consultants and investment banks with whom the firm works regularly on domestic and cross-border deals and projects.

The firm takes an overall approach as well as providing in-depth knowledge by working together with major foreign law firms. Vinge has developed a wide international network which is available to its clients. The firm's broad experience and expertise means that it is called upon to handle all kinds of commercial law issues. It has learned from experience what resources and services are required in order to find the right solutions to clients' problems.

Vinge does everything it can to help clients to achieve success in their business. The firm sees beyond the problems and seeks the solutions.

ADVOKATFIRMAN DELPHI & CO

DJURGÅRDSGATAN 1
PO BOX 465
581 05 LINKÖPING

Telephone: +46 13 35 62 00
Fax: +46 13 35 62 01
E-mail: linkoping@delphilaw.com
Website: www.delphilaw.com

Languages
English, French, German

Other offices
Gothenburg, Malmö, Norrköping, Stockholm

Number of lawyers 96
at this office 13

Contact
Göran M Karlsson

CATEGORIES OF WORK

Corporate, M&A, capital markets
Göran M Karlsson, Bengt Ehrenborg, Stefan Lindh

Commercial law (general)
Torbjörn Ivarsson, Göran M Karlsson, Bengt Ehrenborg, Christopher Bona

Litigation, arbitration
Oscar Brandin, Elisabeth Gustafsson

EU and competition
Torbjörn Ivarsson

Technology transfer and industry
Torbjörn Ivarsson, Christopher Bona, Göran M Karlsson

Banking and finance
Göran M Karlsson

IT, communication, IP
Christopher Bona, Per Magnusson

Insolvency, bankruptcy, reconstruction
Magnus Nedstrand, Oscar Brandin, Johan Andrae, Elisabeth Gustafsson

Employment/labour
Magnus Nedstrand

Commercial property
Bengt Ehrenborg

Tax
Stefan Lindh

THE FIRM

Advokatfirman Delphi & Co is a full-service commercial law firm with offices in Sweden's major business centres, Stockholm, Gothenburg, Malmö and Linköping-Norrköping. Delphi & Co focuses, in particular, on corporate, including M&A, IT and telecoms, EU, banking and finance, competition law, tax, labour law and environmental law.

The firm represents multinational corporations in their activities in Sweden, including cross-border transactions. The firm's clients include a wide range of both publicly traded and privately held Swedish, US and European corporations, banks, financial institutions and others conducting cross-border business. Many of Delphi & Co's clients are Fortune 500 companies but smaller, privately held companies are also on the client list.

AREAS OF PRACTICE

The firm handles all types of financial transactions, such as drafting consortium agreements, loan documentation and performing due diligence processes. In its M&A work, the firm works cross-departmentally, drawing on its lawyers' competence in competition law, corporate finance, venture capital transactions, environment, tax and employment. Recent acquisitions handled by the firm have ranged in value up to €1.5bn.

The firm has one of the largest ITC/IP practice groups in Sweden. In this area, the firm's activities include IT contracts and digital intellectual property rights, e-commerce, IT outsourcing and IT contracts and also telecommunications permits.

Working closely with corporations whose trade marks are well known and respected throughout the world, the firm also specialises in patents, copyrights, trade marks, infringements, etc. The firm's litigators represent enterprises in court proceedings, in arbitration and in mediation, both in Sweden and abroad. Several Delphi lawyers also serve as arbitrators, in Sweden and internationally.

Delphi & Co handles, on an ongoing basis, notifications and filings with DG C in Brussels and with the Swedish Competition Authority. The firm is also one of the major law firms regularly used to review proposed new EU legislation.

Commercial property and insolvency issues, including liquidation and bankruptcies, are other major areas of practice.

ADVOKATFIRMAN DELPHI & CO

STADT HAMBURGSGATAN 9 B
211 38 MALMÖ

Telephone: +46 40 660 79 00
Fax: +46 40 660 79 09
E-mail: malmoe@delphilaw.com
Website: www.delphilaw.com

Languages
English, French, German

Other offices
Gothenburg, Linköping, Norrköping, Stockholm

Number of lawyers 96
at this office 13

Contacts
Per-Ivar Svensson, Hanne Mannheimer

CATEGORIES OF WORK

Corporate, M&A, capital markets
Per-Ivar Svensson, Kent Sangmyr

Commercial law (general)
Per-Ivar Svensson, Kent Sangmyr

Litigation, arbitration
Tomas Eliasson, Mats Engstrand

EU and competition, public procurement
Tomas Eliasson, Anders Jemail

Environment
Hans L Bergqvist *Gothenburg*

Technology transfer
Per-Ivar Svensson, Rebecka Ekberg

IT, communication, IP
Kent Sangmyr, Hanne Mannheimer

Insolvency, bankruptcy, reconstruction

Employment/labour
Hanne Mannheimer

Commercial property, construction
Mats Engstrand

Tax
Thomas Håkansson, Pär Abrahamson

THE FIRM

Advokatfirman Delphi & Co is a full-service commercial law firm with offices in Sweden's major business centres, Stockholm, Gothenburg, Malmö and Linköping-Norrköping. Delphi & Co focuses, in particular, on corporate, including M&A, IT and telecoms, EU, banking and finance, competition law, tax, labour law and environmental law.

The firm represents multinational corporations in their activities in Sweden, including cross-border transactions. The firm's clients include a wide range of both publicly traded and privately held Swedish, US and European corporations, banks, financial institutions and others conducting cross-border business. Many of Delphi & Co's clients are Fortune 500 companies but smaller, privately held companies are also on the client list.

AREAS OF PRACTICE

The firm handles all types of financial transactions, such as drafting consortium agreements, loan documentation and performing due diligence processes. In its M&A work, the firm works cross-departmentally, drawing on its lawyers' competence in competition law, corporate finance, venture capital transactions, environment, tax and employment. Recent acquisitions handled by the firm have ranged in value up to €1.5bn.

The firm has one of the largest ITC/IP practice groups in Sweden. In this area, the firm's activities include IT contracts and digital intellectual property rights, e-commerce, IT outsourcing and IT contracts and also telecommunications permits.

Working closely with corporations whose trade marks are well known and respected throughout the world, the firm also specialises in patents, copyrights, trade marks, infringements, etc. The firm's litigators represent enterprises in court proceedings, in arbitration and in mediation, both in Sweden and abroad. Several Delphi lawyers also serve as arbitrators, in Sweden and internationally.

Delphi & Co handles, on an ongoing basis, notifications and filings with DG C in Brussels and with the Swedish Competition Authority. The firm is also one of the major law firms regularly used to review proposed new EU legislation.

Commercial property and insolvency issues, including liquidation and bankruptcies, are other major areas of practice.

MANNHEIMER SWARTLING

PO BOX 4291
203 14 MALMÖ

Telephone: +46 40 698 58 00
Fax: +46 40 698 58 01
Website: www.mannheimerswartling.se

Languages
English, French, German, Polish, Russian, the Scandinavian languages

Other offices
Berlin, Brussels, Frankfurt, Gothenburg, Helsingborg, New York, St Petersburg, Stockholm

Number of lawyers 330
at this office 42

CATEGORIES OF WORK

Banking and finance
Göran Miörner

Construction and projects
Jan Kansmark

Corporate taxation
Martin Nilsson

Employment
Madeleine Rydberger

EU and competition
Louise Widén

Environment
Mikael Wärnsby

Insolvency
Niklas Bogefors

Insurance
Göran Miörner

Intellectual property
Pär Andersson

Litigation and arbitration
Pär Andersson

Maritime and transport
Anders Lückander

Mergers and acquisitions
Claes Albinsson

Private equity
Göran Miörner

Real estate
Lars Longstad

Securities
Peter Idsäter

Sport and entertainment
Michael Karlsson

Telecoms, media and technology
Niklas Bogefors

MOLL WENDÉN ADVOKATBYRÅ

STORTORGET 8
211 34 MALMÖ

Telephone: +46 40 665 65 00
Fax: +46 40 97 19 17
E-mail: info@mollwenden.se
Website: www.mollwenden.se

Languages
English, German, Spanish,
the Scandinavian languages

Number of lawyers 11

CATEGORIES OF WORK

Corporate and commercial

Mergers and acquisitions

Banking and finance

Information technology and telecommunications

Public procurement

Intellectual property, media and entertainment

Competition and EU

Labour and employment

Commercial property/real estate

Litigation and arbitration

SETTERWALLS

STORTORGET 23
211 34 MALMÖ

Telephone: +46 40 690 04 00
Fax: +46 40 690 04 70
E-mail:
first name.surname@setterwalls.se
Website: www.setterwalls.se

Languages
English, French, German, Italian

Other offices
Stockholm, Gothenburg

Number of lawyers 115
at this office 30

CATEGORIES OF WORK

Commercial and corporate law
Kristian Lundius, Magnus Berlin

IT and telecommunications law
Marc Tullgren, Jonas Frii

Sports, media and entertainment
Marc Tullgren

Pharmaceuticals and biotech
Lennart Arvidson, Hugo Wernbro

Construction
Lennart Iwar, Magnus Berlin

Banking and finance and securities law
Lennart Iwar

Real estate
Kristian Lundius

Labour law
Jörgen Rexö

Intellectual property
Hugo Wernbro, Lennart Arvidson

Mergers and acquisitions and corporate finance
Lennart Arvidson, Lennart Iwar

Environmental law
Martin Jansson

Litigation and arbitration
Magnus Berlin, Gösta Westman

EU and competition law
Karl Olsson

Tax law
Sören Brekell, Pontus Bergman

Insolvency and restructuring
Jörgen Rexö

THE FIRM

Setterwalls was founded in Stockholm in 1878 and is one of Sweden's oldest law firms. Its experience and expertise extends to most areas of Swedish and international commercial law.

Setterwalls is a firm possessing significant resources with more than 115 lawyers located at offices in Stockholm, Gothenburg and Malmö working in co-operation with an international network of lawyers.

AREAS OF PRACTICE

IT and telecommunications: provides legal services to all operators within the IT and telecom sectors such as telephone operators, internet suppliers, e-commerce companies, manufacturers of hardware and computer software development companies. Setterwalls also regularly assists clients in other IT-related matters such as procurement of systems solutions, IT services, etc.

Sports, media and entertainment: the department offers legal services to a number of media enterprises, sports associations, event organisers, athletes and artists.

Pharmaceuticals and biotech: provides advice to established and newly-started pharmaceuticals and biotech companies, as well as assistance in matters concerning financing, research and development, patents, licenses and royalties.

Banking and finance and securities: has substantial experience in providing legal assistance in matters regarding banking and finance. Work includes matters related to initial public offerings, procurement of capital and new issues of shares, loans and other financing, as well as securities law.

Real estate and construction: assists clients in relation to the purchase, sale and development of real estate and in the procurement of construction contracts. Expertise includes applications for building permits to financing and final leasing or sale, as well as environmental law matters related to real estate. Setterwalls has participated in some of the largest infrastructure projects in Sweden.

Labour law: assists clients in all kinds of labour law matters.

Intellectual property: Regularly assists clients in matters relating to trade mark protection, copyright, patents and other intellectual property rights.

Mergers and acquisitions and corporate finance: assists clients in domestic and cross-border business transactions, often in co-operation with banks and investors. Work usually comprises business transfers, investments, mergers, joint venture issues and other matters regarding corporate financing and procurement of capital.

Environmental law: assists clients in all kinds of matters related to environmental law, as well as applications for permits for water operations or environmentally hazardous activities, matters concerning polluted land and environmental damages.

Arbitration and litigation: the litigation department represents clients in national and international litigation and arbitration. Several lawyers are regularly appointed as arbitrators.

EU and competition: provides legal assistance in matters concerning Swedish and European competition law and other matters in connection with the EU, as well as in connection with the filing of various notifications with the Swedish Competition Authority and the European Commission, investigation of competition law aspects in agreements and business concentrations, and assistance in connection with compliance programmes. Setterwalls also represents clients before the Court of Justice of the European Communities and the Market Court.

Tax law: offers tax law advice to Swedish and international companies, ranging from personal tax advice to cross-border business acquisitions.

Insolvency and restructuring: the group provides clients with advice concerning financial difficulties and the preventing of them. The group consists of specialist lawyers with extensive experience of restructuring and insolvency matters with local as well as international dimensions.

ADVOKATFIRMAN VINGE

ÖSTERGATAN 30
BOX 4255
203 13 MALMÖ

Telephone: +46 40 664 55 00
Fax: +46 40 664 55 01
Website: www.vinge.se

Languages
Danish, Dutch, English, German, French, Norwegian, Spanish

Other offices
Brussels, Gothenburg, Helsingborg, Hong Kong, London, Paris, Stockholm, Shanghai

Number of lawyers 300
at this office 42

Contact
Peter Oscarsson

Member
Scandinavian Law Alliance with Kromann Reumert (Denmark) and Thommessen (Norway); Lex Mundi

CATEGORIES OF WORK

Banking and finance
Peter Linderoth, Sofia Olsson

Bankruptcy and liquidation
Lennart Atteryd

Corporate finance, capital markets
Erik Gabrielson, Peter Oscarsson

Employment and benefits
Ingela Malmborg

EU and antitrust
Pär Remnelid, Rikard Azelius

General corporate
Lars Gildéus, Jan Örtenholm

Intellectual property
Anders Forkman, Erik Sjöman

IT
Erik Gabrielson, Jesper Ottergren

Litigation and arbitration
Finn Madsén

M&A
Peter Linderoth, Björn Mullaart

Marketing
Anders Forkman, Erik Sjöman

Media
Anders Forkman, Lars Gildéus

Private equity funds
Jesper Ottergren, Erik Gabrielson

Public procurement
Björn Mullaart

Real estate and environmental
Ingela Malmborg, Peter Bengtsson

THE FIRM

With some 300 fee-earners, Vinge is one of the largest law firms in Scandinavia. The firm is a member of the Scandinavian Law Alliance together with Kromann Reumert in Denmark and Thommessen in Norway.

Vinge has offices in Stockholm, Gothenburg, Malmö and Helsingborg as well as in London, Paris, Brussels, Hong Kong and Shanghai. The firm's clients include domestic and international commercial enterprises, financial institutions and state and regulatory bodies. Vinge is committed to providing the highest-quality legal advice and experience for all matters in which the firm becomes involved, to the highest professional standards.

Innovation, creativeness and a business-orientated, problem-solving approach are at the core of the practice. The firm's size means that there are resources available to handle large and complex domestic and cross-border transactions within tight time frames. At the same time, there is a strong focus on responsiveness and personal commitments to clients. Vinge's motto is: A good commercial lawyer sees beyond the law.

AREAS OF PRACTICE

Vinge specialises in all aspects of commercial law and is consistently ranked amongst the leading law firms in Scandinavia in a number of key practice areas. Vinge's extensive network of contacts comprises independent law firms, consultants and investment banks with whom the firm works regularly on domestic and cross-border deals and projects.

The firm takes an overall approach as well as providing in-depth knowledge by working together with major foreign law firms. Vinge has developed a wide international network which is available to its clients. The firm's broad experience and expertise means that it is called upon to handle all kinds of commercial law issues. It has learned from experience what resources and services are required in order to find the right solutions to clients' problems.

Vinge does everything it can to help clients to achieve success in their business. The firm sees beyond the problems and seeks the solutions.

WISTRAND

BALTZAR CITY, SÖDERGATAN 22
PO BOX 4149
20312 MALMÖ

Telephone: +46 40 669 71 00
Fax: +46 40 669 71 01
E-mail: malmo@wistrand.se
Website: www.wistrand.se

Languages
Czech, English, Finnish, French, German

Other offices
Gothenburg, Stockholm

Number of lawyers 94
at this office 11

CATEGORIES OF WORK

Antitrust and EU	Intellectual property
Banking and finance	IT and telecoms
Commercial and corporate law	Labour and employment
Capital markets	Litigation and arbitration
Entertainment and sports law	Media and marketing law
Environmental	Mergers and acquisitions
Insolvency	Shipping and transport
Insurance	Tax law

ADVOKATFIRMAN BILL ANDRÉASSON

NORRMALMSTORG 14
111 46 STOCKHOLM

Telephone: +46 8 678 05 60
Fax: +46 8 611 46 05
E-mail: info@bill-andreasson.com

Languages
English, German

Number of lawyers 6

Contact
Bill Andréasson

CATEGORIES OF WORK

Tax
Bill Andréasson

BAKER & McKENZIE ADVOKATBYRÅ

LINNÉGATAN 18
PO BOX 5719
114 87 STOCKHOLM

Telephone: +46 8 566 177 00
Fax: +46 8 566 177 99
E-mail: stockholm@bakernet.com
Website: www.bakernet.com

Languages
English, French, German, the Scandinavian languages

Other offices
The member law firms of Baker & McKenzie International, a Swiss Verein, have offices in: Almaty, Amsterdam, Antwerp, Baku, Bangkok, Barcelona, Beijing, Berlin, Bogotá, Bologna, Brasilia, Brussels, Budapest, Buenos Aires, Cairo, Calgary, Cancun, Caracas, Chicago, Chihuahua, Dallas, Düsseldorf, Frankfurt, Geneva, Guadalajara, Hanoi, Ho Chi Minh City, Hong Kong, Houston, Jakarta, Juarez, Kuala Lumpur, Kyiv, London, Madrid, Manama, Manila, Melbourne, Mexico City, Miami, Milan, Monterrey, Moscow, Munich, New York, Palo Alto, Paris, Porto Alegré, Prague, Rio de Janeiro, Riyadh, Rome, St Petersburg, San Diego, San Francisco, Santiago, São Paulo, Shanghai, Singapore, Sydney, Taipei, Tijuana, Tokyo, Toronto, Valencia, Vienna, Warsaw, Washington DC, Zürich

Number of lawyers 3,300+
at this office 45

Contact
Bo Lindquist

CATEGORIES OF WORK

Banking and finance
Leif Gustafsson, Cecilia Bjelle

Commercial agreements
Robert Fröman

Corporate
Johan Widholm, Ingrid Björck

Corporate governance
Carl Svernlöv

Employment
Sten Bauer

EU and competition
Leif Gustafsson, Carl Bökwall

Financial services
Leif Gustafsson, Cecilia Bjelle

Information technology
Stefan Brandt

Insurance
Stefan Bessman

Intellectual property
Stefan Brandt

Litigation, arbitration and insolvency
Jonas Benedictsson, Stefan Bessman

Media and entertainment
Mattias Hedwall

Mergers and acquisitions
Sten Bauer, Carl Svernlöv

Public procurement
Ingrid Björck, Carl Bökwall

Real estate and construction
Mauritz Silfverstolpe, Jan Alexanderson

Securities
Leif Gustafsson, Cecilia Bjelle

Tax
Bo Lindqvist

Telecommunications
Stefan Brandt

Venture capital/private equity
Mattias Hedwall, Anders Fast

BIRD & BIRD

NORRLANDSGATAN 15
BOX 7714
103 95 STOCKHOLM

Telephone: +46 8 506 320 00
Fax: +46 8 506 320 90
E-mail: stockholm@twobirds.com
Website: www.twobirds.se

Languages
English, German, French

Other offices
Beijing, Brussels, Düsseldorf, Frankfurt, Hong Kong, London, Madrid, Milan, Munich, Paris, Rome, The Hague

Number of lawyers 472
at this office 31

Contact
Michael Frie

CATEGORIES OF WORK

Arbitration

Aviation and aerospace

Banking and finance

Commercial

Communications

Competition and regulatory

Corporate

Data protection

Employment

Information technology

Intellectual property

Life sciences

Litigation

Media and entertainment

Outsourcing

Real estate

Sport

Tax

ADVOKATFIRMAN CARLER

NORRLANDSGATAN 11
PO BOX 7557
10393 STOCKHOLM

Telephone: +46 8 545 184 50
Fax: +46 8 545 184 55
E-mail: carler@carler.se
Website: www.carler.se

Languages
English, French, German, the Scandinavian languages

Other offices
Linköping, Paris

Number of lawyers 22
at this office 12

Contact
Karl-Fredrik Björklund

International groupings
Carler EEIG

CATEGORIES OF WORK

Corporate and commercial
Mats Emthén, Jan Holmqvist

Mergers and acquisitions
Mats Olofson, Mats Emthén

Intellectual property
Richard Wessman, Karl-Fredrik Björklund

Distribution, agency and licensing
Mats Olofson, Karl-Fredrik Björklund

IT law
Karl-Fredrik Björklund

Labour law
Karl-Fredrik Björklund

Financial reconstruction
Mats Emthén, Jan Holmqvist

Bankruptcy
Mats Emthén, Jan Holmqvist

Property and real estate
Jan Holmqvist, Sören Birkeland

Arbitration and litigation
Mats Olofson, Mats Emthén

ADVOKATFIRMAN CEDERQUIST

NYBROKAJEN 15
PO BOX 1670
111 96 STOCKHOLM

Telephone: +46 8 522 065 00
Fax: +46 8 522 067 00
Website: www.cederquist.se

Languages
English, French, German

Number of lawyers 60

Contact
Jens Tillqvist (managing partner)

CATEGORIES OF WORK

Capital markets and securities
Wilhelm Lüning

Mergers and acquisitions
Olle Jansson

Banking and finance
Svante Hultqvist

Dispute resolution
Ola Hansson

Intellectual property
Per Ugge

Media and entertainment
Lennart Kanter

Corporate and commercial
Peter Wirell

Telecommunications
Peter Wirell

Information technology
Petter Wirell

Employment/labour law
Jens Tillqvist

EU and competition
Lars Johansson

Tax
Olle Stenman

Real estate
Erika Åslund

EKENBERG & ANDERSSON ADVOKATBYRÅ

PO BOX 7500
103 92 STOCKHOLM

Telephone: +46 8 463 07 50
Fax: +46 8 611 07 60
E-mail: infodesk@ekenbergandersson.se
Website: www.ekenbergandersson.se

Languages
English, Finnish, French, German,
the Scandinavian languages

Number of lawyers 7

Contacts
Thomas Ekenberg, Nils-Evert Andersson

Member
International Lawyers Network (ILN);
Inter-Pacific Bar Association (IPBA)

CATEGORIES OF WORK

Antitrust and EU

Banking and finance

Commercial and corporate law

Capital markets

Entertainment and sports law

Environmental

Insolvency

Insurance

Intellectual property

IT and telecoms

Labour and employment

Litigation and arbitration

Maritime and transport

Mergers and acquisitions

Pharmaceutical law

Tax law

ADVOKATFIRMAN DELPHI & CO

REGERINGSGATAN 30-32
PO BOX 1432
111 84 STOCKHOLM

Telephone: +46 8 677 54 00
Fax: +46 8 20 18 84
E-mail: stockholm@delphilaw.com
Website: www.delphilaw.com

Languages
Chinese, English, French, German, Italian, Polish, Russian

Other offices
Gothenburg, Linköping, Malmö, Norrköping

Number of lawyers 96
at this office 55

Contact
Per Berglöf (managing partner)

CATEGORIES OF WORK

Corporate, M&A, capital markets
Per Berglöf, Örian Odenbro, Anders Björk, Per Granström, Stefan Erhag

Commercial law (general)
Anders Thylin

Litigation, arbitration
Peter Skoglund, Ulf Hårdeman

EU and competition
Peter Skoglund, Elisabeth Legnerfält

Environment
Johan Norman

Public procurement
Anna Ulfsdotter Forssell

IT/C (IT, communication)
Agne Lindberg, Sofia Geilert, Peter Nordbeck

IP (intellectual property)
Ola Wälimaa, Peter Skoglund, Henrik Bengtsson, Richard Lenemark

Life science, biotech
Peter Utterström

Employment law
Fredrik Nordlöf

Commercial property
Cheddi Liljeström, Ulf Hårdeman

Tax
Peter Sjögren, Peter Utterström

THE FIRM

Advokatfirman Delphi & Co is a full-service commercial law firm with offices in Sweden's major business centres, Stockholm, Gothenburg, Malmö and Linköping-Norrköping. Delphi & Co focuses, in particular, on corporate, including M&A, IT and telecoms, EU, banking and finance, competition law, tax, labour law and environmental law.

The firm represents multinational corporations in their activities in Sweden, including cross-border transactions. The firm's clients include a wide range of both publicly traded and privately held Swedish, US and European corporations, banks, financial institutions and others conducting cross-border business. Many of Delphi & Co's clients are Fortune 500 companies but smaller, privately held companies are also on the client list.

AREAS OF PRACTICE

The firm handles all types of financial transactions, such as drafting consortium agreements, loan documentation and performing due diligence processes. In its M&A work, the firm works cross-departmentally, drawing on its lawyers' competence in competition law, corporate finance, venture capital transactions, environment, tax and employment. Recent acquisitions handled by the firm have ranged in value up to €1.5bn.

The firm has one of the largest ITC/IP practice groups in Sweden. In this area, the firm's activities include IT contracts and digital intellectual property rights, e-commerce, IT outsourcing and IT contracts and also telecommunications permits.

Working closely with corporations whose trade marks are well known and respected throughout the world, the firm also specialises in patents, copyrights, trade marks, infringements, etc. The firm's litigators represent enterprises in court proceedings, in arbitration and in mediation, both in Sweden and abroad. Several Delphi lawyers also serve as arbitrators, in Sweden and internationally.

Delphi & Co handles, on an ongoing basis, notifications and filings with DG C in Brussels and with the Swedish Competition Authority. The firm is also one of the major law firms regularly used to review proposed new EU legislation.

Commercial property and insolvency issues, including liquidation and bankruptcies, are other major areas of practice.

ELMZELL ADVOKATBYRÅ HB, member of ius laboris

GAMLA BROGATAN 32
111 20 STOCKHOLM

Telephone: +46 8 21 16 04
Fax: +46 8 21 00 03
E-mail: advokat@elmzell.se
Website: www.elmzell.se

Languages
English, French, German, Swedish

Number of lawyers 5

Contacts
Anders Elmér, Lars Hartzell

Member
ius laboris, International Employment Law, Pensions and Employee Benefits Alliance

CATEGORIES OF WORK	
All aspects of labour law	Employee participation
All aspects of employment law	Pension schemes
Company staff policies	Social security
Compensation and benefits	Tax issues relating to employment law
European labour law	Litigation
Criminal aspects of labour law	Arbitration
Restructuring and transfer of undertakings	Mediation

THE FIRM
Anders Elmér and Lars Hartzell founded Elmzell Advokatbyrå HB in 1988 and the firm is specialised in all aspects of employment and labour law, pensions and employee benefits and all other legal services related to human resources. The firm is one of Sweden's leading law firms within its area of expertise.

Elmzell Advokatbyrå HB is a member of ius laboris, International Employment Law Pensions and Employee Benefits Alliance. The alliance was formed in January 2001 and offers its clients global coverage with over 1,200 lawyers specialised in employment law. In performing projects around the globe, the alliance has also developed a network of firms with which they have worked extensively in those countries where it does not yet have a member, allowing it to provide assistance in most parts of the world.

AREAS OF PRACTICE
The firm deals with all traditional aspects of labour law, such as interpretation and drafting collective bargaining agreements, negotiations with employee organisations, trade union disputes, employee representation and civil liberties, particularly freedom of association.

The firm offers advice and assistance with collective as well as individual aspects in connection with transfer of undertakings, restructuring, redundancies and out-sourcing.

As a result of, for example, the globalisation process, the individual employment law has become more complex thus demanding cutting-edge legal expertise. Elmzell Advokatbyrå HB offers advice and assistance in all aspects of individual employment law: recruitment procedures, employment contracts, renegotiation of employment terms and conditions, severance agreements, post-employment restrictions, trade secrets, discrimination, equal treatment, parental leave and data protection.

In a number of areas within employment law, the company will gain from a well-implemented company policy covering a range of issues from alcohol and drug policies, anti-harassment measures and policies on the usage of information and communications technology. Elmzell Advokatbyrå HB offers advice and often co-operate with the HR department on, for example, drafting company policies, assessment of existing company policies in relation to collective agreements and legislation and possible legal actions as a consequence of non-compliance with company policies.

The firm is highly evaluated for its litigation skills. Elmzell Advokatbyrå HB frequently provides expert advice on and represents clients in all types of employment litigation and other forms of dispute resolution, such as mediation. Anders Elmér and Lars Hartzell are regularly engaged as arbitrators.

G GRÖNBERG ADVOKATBYRÅ AB

KUNGSGATAN 28
PO BOX 7418
103 91 STOCKHOLM

Telephone: +46 8 614 49 00
Fax: +46 8 611 04 04
E-mail: info@gronberg.se
Website: www.gronberg.se

Languages
English, French, German, Spanish

Number of lawyers 20

CATEGORIES OF WORK

Antitrust, competition
Sascha Schaeferdiek

Banking and securities
Alf-Peter Svensson

Construction, real estate, property
Einar Wanhainen, Anders Hedman

Corporate and commercial
Mats Jansson, Anders Hedman

Employment
Mats Jansson

Environmental
Roland Sundqvist

Financial restructuring/insolvency
Roland Sundqvist, Lars Wiking

Intellectual property
Einar Wanhainen

Litigation and arbitration
Einar Wanhainen, Lars Edlund

Media, entertainment
Mats Jansson

Mergers and acquisitions
Lars Wiking, Mats Jansson

Tax
Anders Hedman

Telecoms
Lars Wiking

GÄRDE WESSLAU ADVOKATBYRÅ

NYBROGATAN 34
BOX 5208
102 45 STOCKHOLM

Telephone: +46 8 58 72 40 00
Fax: +46 8 58 72 40 01
E-mail: info@garde.se
Website: www.garde.se

Languages
English, French, German

Other offices
Borås, Gothenburg, Helsingborg, Jönköping

Number of lawyers 51
at this office 17

CATEGORIES OF WORK

Companies, corporations

Mergers and acquisitions

Arbitration and litigation

Insurance

Banking, securities and finance

Competition, antitrust

Trade marks, intellectual property

Maritime and transportation law

Insolvency law

Construction law

GERNANDT & DANIELSSON

ADVOKATBYRÅ

HAMNGATAN 2
BOX 5747
114 87 STOCKHOLM

Telephone: +46 8 670 66 00
Fax: +46 8 662 61 01
E-mail: info@gda.se
Website: www.gda.se

Languages
English, French, German

Number of lawyers 59

Contact
Johan Josjö (managing partner)

CATEGORIES OF WORK

Arbitration
Johan Gernandt, Karl-Erik Danielsson

Litigation
Björn Tude, Christer Danielsson

Banking and finance
Marcus Johansson, Niclas Rockborn

Capital markets
Dick Lundqvist, Manfred Löfvenhaft

Corporate and commercial
Anders Wallén, Maths Heuman

Employment
Manfred Löfvenhaft

EU and competition
Kenny Carlsson

Intellectual property, media, IT and telecommunications
Anders Lundin, Mats Hugoson

Mergers and acquisitions
Stefan De Geer, Tobias Larsson

Public procurement
Björn Tude

Real estate
Jonas Eklund, Bob Johanson

THE FIRM

Gernandt & Danielsson, established in 1992, is one of the leading business law firms in Sweden. Many of the firm's partners had previously worked closely together for many years. Gernandt & Danielsson has been one of the fastest growing firms in recent years, today employing close to 60 lawyers. G&D has well-established contacts with leading law firms in Europe and the US, but is not a member of any alliance or other grouping. As an independent law firm, G&D is free to consult with or recommend the foreign law firm or expert who can best respond to each particular client's needs. Many of the firm's partners and senior associates have been on long-term secondments to UK and US firms.

AREAS OF PRACTICE

Mergers and acquisitions: the firm advises public and private companies, including private equity funds, on all types of mergers and acquisitions, including domestic and cross-border transactions, public and private transactions, public offers and management buy-outs.

Banking and finance: the firm assists Swedish and international banks and financial companies, as well as borrowers and issuers, on areas such as bilateral loans, syndicated loans, securitisation, swaps and derivatives.

Capital markets: the firm advises on a wide range of capital markets matters, including takeovers, listings, public offerings, private placements, redemption and buy back programmes and stock exchange and securities regulations.

Corporate and commercial: the firm regularly handles shareholder and joint venture agreements and acts as adviser in the restructuring of companies and business groups. The firm frequently advises clients on issues concerning board responsibility, changes in capital structure, incentive programmes for employees, annual general meetings of shareholders and other corporate governance issues.

EU and competition: the firm provides advice on all aspects of competition law, including merger clearances and cartel cases. The firm's competition group is headed by Kenny Carlsson, the former legal director of the Swedish Competition Authority.

Public procurement: the firm has advised and counselled authorities and suppliers in a range of matters in this area.

Arbitration and litigation: the firm continuously assists in both international and Swedish arbitral proceedings, including under the Stockholm rules of arbitration, and in litigation proceedings. Several of the firm's lawyers are frequently appointed as arbitrators in international and Swedish arbitration matters.

Telecommunications: the firm's activities range from concessions and competition law matters to infrastructure, joint venture, network procurement, interconnect, supply, and customer agreements.

Employment: the firm handles all matters relating to Swedish employment law.

Real estate: the firm provides advice on general commercial real estate law and real estate transactions, including portfolio acquisitions, as well as real estate finance, securitisation and investments, property management and landlord and tenant law.

ADVOKATFIRMAN GLIMSTEDT

PO BOX 16108
103 22 STOCKHOLM

Telephone: +46 8 566 119 00
Fax: +46 8 566 119 49
E-mail: stockholm@glimstedt.se
Website: www.glimstedt.se

Languages
English, French, German

Other offices
Alingsås, Falun, Göteborg, Helsingborg, Jönköping, Kalmar, Karlskoga, Ludvika, Lund, Norrköping, Örebro, Riga, Stockholm, Tallinn, Vilnius

Number of lawyers 143
at this office 13

International groupings
The Association of European Lawyers

CATEGORIES OF WORK

Arbitration and litigation
Jonas Åberg

Banking and finance
Jonas Gombrii

Commercial law (general)
Bo Ahlenius, Claes Egnell

Construction and projects
Jonas Wahlbom

Employment
Bengt Isman

Environment
Johan Rappman

EU and competition
Michael Lettius

Insolvency
Hans Elliot, Peter Savin

Intellectual property
Håkan Sjöström

IT
Mats Rydh

Mergers and acquisitions, including property
Jan Litborn

Real estate, tenancy
Bengt Ask

HELLSTRÖM & PARTNERS

KUNGSGATAN 33, XV
PO BOX 7305
103 90 STOCKHOLM

Telephone: +46 8 22 09 00
Fax: +46 8 20 40 90
E-mail: info@hpa.se
Website: www.hpa.se

Languages
English, Estonian, French, German, Polish

Number of lawyers 34

Contacts
Mats Hellström, Björn Ulvgården, Staffan Michelson

CATEGORIES OF WORK

Banking and finance
Anders Lundberg, Bengt Olovsson

Commercial and contract law
Björn Ulvgården, Per Winnberg

Competition
Bengt Olovsson, Lennart Melchior

Corporate law
Björn Ulvgården, Anders Lundberg

Dispute resolution
Staffan Michelson, Kim Lindgren

Insolvency and restructuring
Staffan Michelson

Technology, media and telecoms
Mats Hellström, Göran Andersson

Employment and human resources
Mats Hellström

Intellectual property
Jonas Wetterfors, Mats Hellström

Mergers and acquisitions
Björn Ulvgården, Per Winnberg

Real estate
Lennart Melchior, Kim Lindgren

Environment
Staffan Michelson, Kim Lindgren

Insurance
Göran Lundsten

ADVOKATFIRMAN HAMMARSKIÖLD & CO AB

SKEPPSBRON 42
PO BOX 2278
103 17 STOCKHOLM

Telephone: +46 8 578 450 00
Fax: +46 8 578 450 99
E-mail: info@hammarskiold.se
Website: www.hammarskiold.se

Languages
English, French, German, Russian, Finnish

Number of lawyers 45

CATEGORIES OF WORK

Mergers and acquisitions
Peder Hammarskiöld, Jacob Melander

Banking and finance
Per Gustaf Ekbom

Insurance and reinsurance
Erik Swartling, Peter Sarkia

Intellectual property and media
Thomas Lindqvist, Claes Langenius, Ylva Lindquist

IT and telecoms
Thomas Lindqvist, Claes Langenius

Dispute resolution
Per Sundin, Lars Ulrichs

EU and competition law
Claes Langenius, Ylva Lindquist

Corporate and commercial
Jacob Melander, Lars Ulrichs, Ylva Lindquist

Employment
Thomas Lindqvist

Capital markets
Peder Hammarskiöld, Erik Swartling

THE FIRM

Hammarskiöld & Co is one of the leading law firms in Sweden.

Hammarskiöld & Co focuses mainly on the following areas: mergers and acquisitions, banking and finance, insurance and reinsurance, litigation and arbitration, and IT and intellectual property. The firm places special emphasis on client service and even though it has formed a number of specialist groups, the lawyers work in teams that are client centred.

Hammarskiöld & Co has extensive contacts with leading law firms around the world. However, Hammarskiöld & Co remains an independent law firm and is not a member of any alliance or network. Therefore, the firm can link its corporate clients with the very best foreign law firm in each jurisdiction for particular areas of work. All of the firm's lawyers have experience in other jurisdictions and the firm is proud of its international approach. This makes Hammarskiöld & Co a truly Swedish firm.

AREAS OF PRACTICE

Mergers and acquisitions: the firm has participated in several of the most significant M&A transactions in Sweden in recent years. The transactions have ranged from small private acquisitions to very large cross-border takeovers of listed companies.

Banking and finance: the firm represents a wide range of national and international clients, particularly within the banking and finance industries. The practice covers all of the traditional and recently developed areas of banking and finance.

Insurance and reinsurance: important areas of the firm's insurance practice include demutualising and restructuring treaties, and handling insurance and reinsurance litigation.

Intellectual property and media : the firm is highly experienced in all fields of IP law. Copyrights, licensing, media, entertainment, franchising, trade marks and patents are just some of the areas of IP-related expertise. The firm's lawyers have substantial experience in connection with marketing guidelines and in handling consumer disputes before the Swedish Marketing Court. The group also deals with regulatory work and product liability questions.

IT and telecoms: the firm's telecommunications and computer group can advise on all aspects of telecommunications and IT and outsourcing issues.

Dispute resolution: the lawyers within the litigation group have vast experience in commercial litigation, national and international arbitration, and alternative dispute resolution (ADR).

EU and competition law: the firm's competition lawyers have substantial experience in handling antitrust matters and other competition and marketing-related problems that companies face in the Swedish market, as well as public procurement and state aid.

Energy and public utilities: since the deregulation of the Swedish energy sector, this area of law has developed quickly. The firm is at the forefront of such developments.

Corporate and commercial: the firm advises on all aspects of general corporate law. The corporate practice includes drafting and advising on all types of commercial contracts, both international and Swedish.

Employment law: the firm advises on all aspects of Swedish employment law and provides services that range from the employment consequences of corporate acquisitions to employee terminations.

Capital markets: Hammarskiöld & Co plays a major role in the Swedish capital market. The firm regularly advises on some of the largest public takeovers in Sweden. The firm is also experienced in advising on stock market questions and corporate governance issues.

HÖKERBERG & SÖDERQVIST
ADVOKATBYRÅ KB

KUNGSGATAN 36
PO BOX 7836
103 98 STOCKHOLM

Telephone: +46 8 407 88 00
Fax: +46 8 407 88 01
E-mail: mail@hsa.se
Website: www.hsa.se

Languages
English, French, German,
the Scandinavian languages

Number of lawyers 19

Contact
Lars Söderqvist

CATEGORIES OF WORK

Banking, securities and finance

Companies, corporations

Bankruptcy, insolvency

Insurance law, tort, product liability

Arbitration and litigation

Mergers and acquisitions

Commercial law (general) and contract

Intellectual property

KARLERÖ & CO
ADVOKATBYRÅ HB

KUNGSGATAN 26
PO BOX 7330
103 90 STOCKHOLM

Telephone: + 46 8 20 06 10
Fax: + 46 8 20 06 04
E-mail: info@karlero.se
Website: www.karlero.se

Languages
English, German, the Scandinavian languages

Number of lawyers 12

Member
ADVOC

CATEGORIES OF WORK

Corporate and commercial
Lars-Gunnar Karlerö

Technology
Karl Ole Möller

Employment and benefits
Roger Hedlund

Media and entertainment
Karl Ole Möller

Intellectual property
Karl Ole Möller

Real estate and construction
Anne Liverud, Roger Hedlund

Corporate finance, M&A and JVs
Conny Tranberg

Litigation and arbitration
Anders E Bengtsson

Life sciences
Lars-Gunnar Karlerö

Restructuring and insolvency
Anders E Bengtsson

Healthcare
Karl Ole Möller

KILPATRICK STOCKTON ADVOKAT KB

PO BOX 5421
114 84 STOCKHOLM

Telephone: +46 8 505 646 00
Fax: +46 8 505 646 99
E-mail: info@kilpatrickstockton.com
Website: www.kilpatrickstockton.com

Languages
English, the Scandinavian languages

Other offices
Atlanta, Augusta, Charlotte, London, New York, Raleigh, Washington DC, Winston-Salem

Number of lawyers 488
at this office 22

CATEGORIES OF WORK

Banking and finance
Pontus Kågerman, Håkan Lindgren

Information technology
Fredrik Ahlqvist, Johan Gustavsson

Corporate and commercial
Pontus Kågerman, Torbjörn Hultsberg

Construction
Thomas Rajala, Nicklas Björklund

Employment
Jörgen Eklund, Torbjörn Hultsberg

Environment
Thomas Rajala, Johan Gustavsson

Insurance
Jörgen Eklund

Intellectual property
Fredrik Ahlqvist

Dispute resolution
Jörgen Eklund, Nicklas Björklund

Mergers and acquisitions
Pontus Kågerman, Torbjörn Hultsberg

Private equity
Torbjörn Hultsberg, Jörgen Eklund

Real estate
Thomas Rajala, Pontus Kågerman

Tax
Nils Sköld

Media, entertainment and sport
Torbjörn Hultsberg, Fredrik Ahlqvist

Capital markets
Pontus Kågerman, Håkan Lindgren

LINDAHL
LAW OFFICES

SERGELS TORG 12
BOX 14240
104 40 STOCKHOLM

Telephone: +46 8 670 58 00
Fax: +46 8 667 73 80
E-mail: reception.stockholm@lindahl.se
Website: www.lindahl.se

Languages
English, French, German

Other offices
Gothenburg, Helsingborg, Malmö, Örebro, Uppsala

Number of lawyers 130
at this office 60

Contact
Anders Nilsson

CATEGORIES OF WORK

Arbitration and litigation
Bengt Bolin

Banking and finance
Petra Hedengran

Capital markets
Robert Hansson

Corporate and commercial law
Johan Hessius

EC law, competition and antitrust
Eva-Maj Mühlenbock

Insolvency
Håkan Rudström

IT and telecommunications
Anders Christner

Labour law
Cecilia Kindgren-Bengtsson

Media and entertainment
Staffan Eklöw

Mergers and acquisitions
Carl-Olof Bouveng

Real estate
Olof Hallberg

Shipping and transport
Erik Linnarsson

Sports and major events
Staffan Eklöw

Trade marks and intellectual property
Johan Norderyd

Taxation
Jörgen Sandström

Environmental law
Anders Linnerborg

LINDHS DLA NORDIC

KUNGSGATAN 9
PO BOX 7315
103 90 STOCKHOLM

Telephone: +46 8 701 78 00
Fax: +46 8 701 78 99
E-mail: info@dlanordic.se
Website: www.dlanordic.com

Languages
English, French, German, Spanish, the Scandinavian languages

Other offices
Bergen, Copenhagen, Oslo

Number of lawyers 220
at this office 62

Contacts
Per Rönström, Ingrid Eliasson, Kent Hägglund, Gunnar Johansson

Member
DLA Piper Group

CATEGORIES OF WORK

Corporate
Stefan Kamlin, Mikael Kövamees

TMC
Jan Råssjö, Jan Bryme

Tax
Magnus Hagevi

Commercial and litigation
Stefan Sandén, Peter Ihrfelt

Employment
Mats Borgström, Sven Erfors

Construction and real estate
Henrik Wollsén, Peter Kindblom

Energy and transport
Gunnar Johansson, Arthur Csatho

Public, competition and EU law
Peter Orander

Insolvency law
Ulf Mårtensson

THE FIRM

DLA Nordic is the only Nordic law firm with offices in Copenhagen, Oslo, Bergen and Stockholm. The firm ranks among the leading law firms in its respective home markets in Denmark, Norway and Sweden. Each office provides a complete range of integrated legal services across borders, both in the local market and on a global basis.

DLA Nordic is part of DLA Piper Rudnick Gray Cary Group, an exclusive alliance of international full-service law organisations with a shared vision. Established in 1999, the group now has members across Europe, Africa, the Middle East, Asia and the US, which deliver expert local know-how and integrated international solutions.

DLA Nordic's vision is to be the leading Nordic law firm, and is based on the observation that many clients have operations in all three countries. DLA Nordic is a modern, growing practice with distinct client service focus; legal advice is based on a proactive approach and an understanding of the client's business. The firm offers a thorough and cost-effective mode of work, knowledge and insight in the local business environment, seamless Scandinavian and international legal services, and commercially based solutions.

Providing a full service in all major practice areas, the firm is organised into eight cross-border legal departments. The departments work together, making sure that legal expertise is exchanged and shared, utilising legal resources fully and providing optimal service to the client.

Clients include public and private companies in a variety of sectors: commerce; industry; manufacturing services; property; construction; finance; IT, telecoms, media and entertainment; transport; shipping; and oil, gas and electricity. The firm also serves a large number of international clients, including large corporations, banks, investment firms and venture capital funds.

AREAS OF PRACTICE

Commercial and company law: extensive experience in company reconstruction; flotations; shareholders/partnership agreements; liquidations and incorporations; and commercial contracts.

Mergers and acquisitions: advice in each phase of mergers and acquisitions; anti-takeover strategies; public and private financing; client due diligence and competition law.

Banking and finance: DLA Nordic regularly represents lenders, borrowers and other parties in the financial markets – both Scandinavian and international.

TMC: the firm has specialists in law related to technology, media and communications.

Tax: the firm has specialists in both national and international tax law.

Public competition and EU law: DLA Nordic assists in a wide range of questions concerning public law, some of its clients coming from within the municipal authorities.

Litigation: constitutes a central part of DLA Nordic's practice. The firm's integrated work method plays an important role, since litigation skills must often be combined with specialist knowledge.

Construction and property: DLA Nordic has an extensive construction and property law practice. Clients include several major real estate and construction companies in Scandinavia.

Employment: DLA Nordic has years of in-depth experience in labour and employment law and practical industry knowledge.

Oil and gas: specialising in international oil and gas law and electric legislation with experience of offshore construction and service contracts.

Maritime and shipping: DLA Nordic has experts assisting insurance companies and shipowners, regarding claims, collisions and adjustment of averages.

Insolvency: DLA Nordic gives advice on insolvency matters to creditors, as well as companies with financial problems.

LINKLATERS

REGERINGSGATAN 67
BOX 7833
103 98 STOCKHOLM

Telephone: +46 8 665 66 00
Fax: +46 8 667 68 83
Website: www.linklaters.com

Languages
All commercial and local languages in the countries where Linklaters operates

Other offices
Amsterdam, Antwerp, Bangkok, Beijing, Berlin, Bratislava, Brussels, Bucharest, Budapest, Cologne, Dubai, Frankfurt am Main, Hong Kong, Lisbon, London, Luxembourg, Madrid, Milan, Moscow, Munich, New York, Paris, Prague, Rome, São Paulo, Shanghai, Singapore, Tokyo, Warsaw

Number of lawyers 2,000 worldwide

Contact
Jörgen Durban

CATEGORIES OF WORK

M&A, corporate
Martin Börresen

Banking and finance
Jörgen Durban

Tax
Mats Anderson

M&A, real estate
Per Nyberg

Technology, media and telecommunications
Ingvar Zander

EU and competition
Kent Karlsson

Employment
Anders Nordström

Litigation and arbitration
Henrik Bielenstein

MANNHEIMER SWARTLING

PO BOX 1711
111 87 STOCKHOLM

Telephone: +46 8 505 765 00
Fax: +46 8 505 765 01
Website: www.mannheimerswartling.se

Languages
English, Finnish, French, German, Polish, Russian, the Scandinavian languages

Other offices
Berlin, Brussels, Frankfurt, Gothenburg, Helsingborg, Malmö, New York, St Petersburg

Number of lawyers 330
at this office 194

CATEGORIES OF WORK

Banking and finance
André Andersson

Constitutional and administrative law
Sven Unger

Construction and projects
Klas Wennström

Corporate taxation
Martin Nilsson

Employment
Magnus Wallander

EU and competition
Johan Coyet

Environment
Per Molander

Insolvency
Biörn Riese

Insurance
Helena Rempler

Intellectual property
Per Josefson

Litigation and arbitration
Kaj Hobér

Maritime and transport
Sven Unger

Mergers and acquisitions
Biörn Riese

Private equity
Peter Alhanko

Real estate
Klas Wennström

Securities
Eva Hägg

Sport and entertainment
Sven-Åke Bergkvist

Telecoms, media and technology
Biörn Riese

RYDINCARLSTEN ADVOKATBYRÅ AB

NORRMALMSTORG 14
PO BOX 1766
111 87 STOCKHOLM

Telephone: +46 8 463 39 00
Fax: +46 8 611 48 50
E-mail: info@rydincarlsten.se
Website: www.rydincarlsten.se

Languages
English, French, German, Russian

Number of lawyers 25

CATEGORIES OF WORK

Arbitration and litigation

Banking, securities, finance

Corporate and commercial law

Competition, antitrust

Contract law (international projects, sales and distribution)

Intellectual property, patent litigation

IT law

Marketing law

Mergers and acquisitions, joint ventures

Pharmaceutical law

Stock exchange regulations

Corporate governance

ADVOKATFIRMAN SÖDERMARK

STRANDVÄGEN 1
PO BOX 14055
104 40 STOCKHOLM

Telephone: +46 8 670 57 50
Fax: +46 8 663 67 20
E-mail: mail@sodermark.se
Website: www.sodermark.se

Languages
Cantonese, English, French, German, Mandarin

Number of lawyers 23

CATEGORIES OF WORK

Litigation (domestic and international)
Bertil Södermark, Torgny Wetterberg

Maritime and transportation
Peter J Lindskog

General commercial law
Peter Bolmstedt, Christer Brantheim

Corporate law
Ulf Jonsson, Lars Sandberg

Real estate
Magnus Björck

Mergers and acquisitions
Lars Göthlin, Bertil Brinck

Insurance
Peter J Lindskog

Intellectual property, trade marks, copyright
Anders Beck-Friis

EU and competition
Eric Ericsson

Sports and entertainment
Mats Larsson

SETTERWALLS

ARSENALSGATAN 6
111 47 STOCKHOLM

Telephone: +46 8 598 890 00
Fax: +46 8 598 890 90
E-mail:
firstname.surname@setterwalls.se
Website: www.setterwalls.se

Languages
English, French, German, Italian, Finnish

Other offices
Gothenburg, Malmö

Number of lawyers 115
at this office 60

CATEGORIES OF WORK

Commercial and corporate law
Odd Swarting, Anders Söderlind

IT and telecommunications law
Håkan Fohlin, Joacim Johannesson

Sports, media and entertainment
Mats Björkman

Pharmaceuticals and biotechnics
Maria Chambers

EU and competition law
Ulf Djurberg

Banking and finance
Åke J Fors

Securities law
Sören Lindström, Jan Jensen

Real estate and construction law
Karl-Gustav Gripenvik

Labour law
Henrik Larsson

Intellectual property
Owe Hjelmqvist

Mergers and acquisitions and corporate finance
Richard Åkerman

Maritime and transportation law
Jörgen Almelöv

Aircraft financing and aviation law
Mats Waering

Tax law
Emine Lundkvist

Litigation and arbitration
Claes Broman

Insolvency and restructuring
Rolf Åbjörnsson

THE FIRM

Setterwalls was founded in Stockholm in 1878 and is one of Sweden's oldest law firms. Its experience and expertise extends to most areas of Swedish and international commercial law.

Setterwalls is a firm possessing significant resources with more than 115 lawyers located at offices in Stockholm, Gothenburg and Malmö working in co-operation with an international network of lawyers.

AREAS OF PRACTICE

IT and telecommunications: provides legal services to all operators within the IT and telecom sectors such as telephone operators, internet suppliers, e-commerce companies, manufacturers of hardware and computer software development companies. Setterwalls also regularly assists clients in other IT-related matters such as procurement of systems solutions, IT services, etc.

Sports, media and entertainment: the department offers legal services to a number of media enterprises, sports associations, event organisers, athletes and artists.

Pharmaceuticals and biotech: provides advice to established and newly-started pharmaceuticals and biotech companies, as well as assistance in matters concerning financing, research and development, patents, licenses and royalties.

EU and competition: provides legal assistance in matters concerning Swedish and European competition law and other matters in connection with the EU. The firm assists in connection with the filing of various notifications with the Swedish Competition Authority and the European Commission, investigation of competition law aspects in agreements and business concentrations, and assistance in connection with compliance programmes. Setterwalls also represents clients before the Court of Justice of the European Communities and the Market Court.

Banking and finance and securities: has substantial experience in providing legal assistance in matters regarding banking and finance. Work includes matters related to initial public offerings, procurement of capital and new issues of shares, loans and other financing, as well as securities law.

Real estate and construction: assists clients in relation to the purchase, sale and development of real estate and in the procurement of construction contracts. Expertise includes applications for building permits to financing and final leasing or sale, as well as environmental law matters related to real estate. Setterwalls has participated in some of the largest infrastructure projects in Sweden.

Labour law: assists clients in all kinds of labour law matters.

Intellectual property: regularly assists clients in matters relating to trade mark protection, copyright, patents and other intellectual property rights.

Mergers and acquisitions and corporate finance: assists clients in domestic and cross-border business transactions, often in co-operation with banks and investors. Work usually comprises business transfers, investments, mergers, joint venture issues and other matters regarding corporate financing and procurement of capital.

Aircraft financing and aviation law: provides assistance in all matters regarding the purchase, sale, leasing and other forms of financing of aircraft and railway vehicles, as well as all other legal matters related to the operation of airlines and railways.

Tax law: offers tax law advice to Swedish and international companies, ranging from personal tax advice to cross-border business acquisitions.

Insolvency and restructuring: the group provides clients with advice concerning financial difficulties and the preventing of them. The group consists of specialist lawyers with extensive experience of restructuring and insolvency matters with local as well as international dimensions. The group also works within other areas of commercial law.

Arbitration and litigation: the litigation department represents clients in national and international litigation and arbitrations. Several lawyers are regularly appointed as arbitrators.

ADVOKATFIRMAN VINGE

SMÅLANDSGATAN 20
BOX 1703
111 87 STOCKHOLM

Telephone: +46 8 614 30 00
Fax: +46 8 614 31 90
Website: www.vinge.se

Languages
English, French, Italian, Latvian, Russian, Spanish

Other offices
Brussels, Gothenburg, Helsingborg, Hong Kong, London, Malmö, Paris, Shanghai

Number of lawyers 300
at this office 169

Contact
Bertil Hult

Member
Scandinavian Law Alliance with Kromann Reumert (Denmark) and Thommessen (Norway); Lex Mundi

CATEGORIES OF WORK

Banking and finance
Bo Adrianzon, Stefan de Hevesy

Corporate finance, capital markets
Goran Nyström, Johan Cederlund

Employment and benefits
Björn Lindskog, Fredrik Dahl

EU and antitrust
Carl Wetter, Johan Karlsson

Financial services and regulations
Fredrik Wilkens, Per Johan Eckerberg

General corporate
Michael Wigge, Malin Ohlin Åkermark

Insurance
Peter Morawetz, Per Johan Eckerberg

Intellectual property
Per Eric Alvsing

IT
Karin Grauers, Björn Gustavsson

Litigation and arbitration
Olle Flygt, Hans Bagner

M&A
Carl Gustaf De Geer, Bertil Villard

Marketing and media
Per Erik Alvsing

Private equity funds
Christina Kokko, Johan Cederlund

Public procurement
Johan Karlsson

Real estate and environmental
Patrick Forslund, Thomas Sjöberg

Tax
Lennart Larsson, Mattias Schömer

Telecommunications
Carl Johan af Petersens

THE FIRM

With some 300 fee-earners, Vinge is one of the largest law firms in Scandinavia. The firm is a member of the Scandinavian Law Alliance together with Kromann Reumert in Denmark and Thommessen in Norway.

Vinge has offices in Stockholm, Gothenburg, Malmö and Helsingborg as well as in London, Paris, Brussels, Hong Kong and Shanghai. The firm's clients include domestic and international commercial enterprises, financial institutions and state and regulatory bodies. Vinge is committed to providing the highest-quality legal advice and experience for all matters in which the firm becomes involved, to the highest professional standards.

Innovation, creativeness and a business-orientated, problem-solving approach are at the core of the practice. The firm's size means that there are resources available to handle large and complex domestic and cross-border transactions within tight time frames. At the same time, there is a strong focus on responsiveness and personal commitments to clients. Vinge's motto is: A good commercial lawyer sees beyond the law.

AREAS OF PRACTICE

Vinge specialises in all aspects of commercial law and is consistently ranked amongst the leading law firms in Scandinavia in a number of key practice areas. Vinge's extensive network of contacts comprises independent law firms, consultants and investment banks with whom the firm works regularly on domestic and cross-border deals and projects.

The firm takes an overall approach as well as providing in-depth knowledge by working together with major foreign law firms. Vinge has developed a wide international network which is available to its clients. The firm's broad experience and expertise means that it is called upon to handle all kinds of commercial law issues. It has learned from experience what resources and services are required in order to find the right solutions to clients' problems.

Vinge does everything it can to help clients to achieve success in their business. The firm sees beyond the problems and seeks the solutions.

WISTRAND

KLARABERGSVIADUKTEN 70, D:6
PO BOX 70393
107 24 STOCKHOLM

Telephone: +46 8 507 200 00
Fax: +46 8 507 300 00
E-mail: sthlm@wistrand.se
Website: www.wistrand.se

Languages
Czech, English, Finnish, French, German

Other offices
Malmö, Gothenburg

Number of lawyers 94
at this office 48

CATEGORIES OF WORK

Antitrust and EU	**Intellectual property**
Banking and finance	**IT and telecoms**
Commercial and corporate law	**Labour and employment**
Capital markets	**Litigation and arbitration**
Entertainment and sports law	**Media and market law**
Environmental	**Mergers and acquisitions**
Insolvency	**Shipping and transport**
Insurance	**Tax law**

SWITZERLAND

Population	7.48 million
Number of lawyers	7,000
Professional title	Rechtsanwalt; Advokat; Fürsprech; Fürsprecher; avocat; avvocato
Currency	Swiss franc (CHF)

Index

Tracing its origins as a republic back to 1291, Switzerland is a land-locked, historically neutral state bordering France, Germany, Italy, Austria and Liechtenstein. It is split into 26 autonomous states or Cantons, with Bern the capital. The financial centre is in the German-speaking city of Zurich, save for the private banking industry which remains concentrated in the French-speaking city of Geneva.

In 1992 Swiss voters chose to reject joining the EU, though other referendums have entailed it becoming a member of the UN (2002) and a signatory to the Schengen treaty and the Dublin Convention (2005).

Despite continuing to remain outside the EU, in recent years Swiss legislation has been passed generally in line with the laws emanating from Brussels, so that Switzerland may maintain trade with its EU partners, as well as enhance competitiveness. Now listings on the national stock exchange, the SWX, can be EU-compatible, and as a product of an EU-Swiss agreement, a withholding tax is imposed on bank accounts by EU beneficiaries who wish their identities to remain confidential.

As well as a great number of financial services companies and their foreign subsidiaries being based in Zurich and Geneva, Basle is home to a number of global pharmaceutical companies and the chemicals industry, with Bern the administrative heart of Switzerland.

BILLING

The Swiss legal market is cost conscious, with competition on price often a crucial element to successfully winning new business. Fees generally range from €150-€300 per hour for associates, to around €250-€400 per hour for partners.

MARKETING

The publishing of articles remains the traditional way in which a Swiss firm will promote its brand, either by publishing academically to obtain recognition amongst peers, or more direct marketing aimed at a client readership. Gradually firms are appreciating the value of face-to-face contact with potential clients. Accordingly, bespoke presentations are arranged to marketing-friendly clients to raise awareness, indirectly displaying the firm's expertise in a particular field. The Swiss Bar Association adopts a relaxed approach to advertising, providing it is balanced and reflects the public need for information. Mass mailing would be unacceptable.

IN-HOUSE LAWYERS

As Switzerland houses some of the biggest brands in the banking world and in the pharmaceutical and manufacturing industries, in-house legal departments are equally developed, dealing with the day-to-day running of those companies. External legal advice is commonly sought for large, specialised tasks that cannot be handled internally, with the largest players often retaining a panel of lawyers.

ECONOMY

Switzerland has historically been known for its successful market economy, based on international trade and a strong financial services industry, facilitating the highest standard of living in Europe. Switzerland has not been known for economic slumps, though in 2003 this was the case with over 1,000 companies, many house-hold names being declared bankrupt in the first fiscal quarter alone. In 2004 the economy recovered with 1.7% growth, and the economic resurgence continued in 2005, albeit slightly reduced at 1.4%. Compared to the rest of Europe, unemployment remains low at 3.9%, and despite high oil prices inflation is negligible at 1.3%.

Signs that the economy is back on track are evident from increased activity in the international trade and financial services sectors. In the former, Switzerland's traditional strength in exporting manufacturing and chemical/pharmaceutical products remains substantial (US$130bn exports in 2004), together with greater domestic merger activity, as well as a flurry of private equity-driven takeovers. In the financial services sector, the banking industry in particular has seen a great deal of streamlining and restructuring, with many family run private banks being modernised to enhance competitiveness.

LEGAL MARKET

The major firms in Switzerland are generally concentrated in either Zurich being the financial centre, or Geneva the heart of private banking, or in both. In the latter category, the largest Swiss firms **Lenz & Staehelin** and **Schellenberg Wittmer** have evenly proportioned offices, as well

The largest firms

1	Lenz & Staehelin	136
2	Bär & Karrer	113
3	Schellenberg Wittmer	102
4	Pestalozzi Lachenal Patry	100
5	Homburger	85
6	Baker & McKenzie	77
7	Python Schifferli Peter	75
	Vischer	75
9	Niederer Kraft & Frey	65
10	EY Law AG	56
	Walder Wyss & Partners	56
12	Froriep Renggli	50
	Wenger Plattner	50
14	CMS von Erlach Henrici	40
	Wenger & Vieli	40
16	Meyer Lustenberger	38
17	Prager Dreifuss	35
18	Staiger, Schwald & Partner	31
19	Lalive & Partners	30
20	Bratschi Emch Rechtsanwälte	29
21	Borel & Barbey	28
22	Poncet Turrettini Amaudruz Neyroud & Partners	27
23	Badertscher Dörig Poledna	25
24	AMG Attorneys at Law	24
25	Tavernier Tschanz	23

These figures represent the total number of lawyers in this country only, and have been supplied by the firms themselves. The figures should be accurate as at 1 January 2006.

as other heavyweights **Pestalozzi Lachenal Patry** and **Bär & Karrer**. Substantial Zurich-centric practices include **Homburger**, **Niederer Kraft & Frey** and **Walder Wyss & Partners**, whereas in Geneva, **Python Schifferli Peter** and **Borel & Barbey** are the largest local players. The pharmaceutical/ chemical industry capital Basle has also attracted large firms, **VISCHER** and **Wenger Plattner** most notably.

As Switzerland is evenly split between German and French-speaking parts, it is usual for the majority of practitioners to work and communicate in both languages. The Swiss legal market remains relatively unpenetrated by international players, though the largest of which, **Baker & McKenzie** has a strong presence in both Zurich and Geneva. The one significant merger in 2005 that also involved an international firm, was between mid-size practices *CMS von Erlach Klainguti Stettler Wille* and *Henrici, Wicki & Guggisberg*, creating **CMS von Erlach Henrici**.

Though the largest Zurich offices continue to dominate the biggest transactions, the gap between these firms and their smaller rivals is closing. Also, a number of firms are elevating their position in the market by offering niche expertise, including in the areas of intellectual property (**Thomannfischer**), transport (**Benz Attorneys**) and world trade disputes (**Sidley Austin LLP**).

FOREIGN OFFICES

The lack of international firms operating within Swiss borders is mirrored by the lack of presence of Swiss practices on the world stage. Those that have set up abroad are concentrated in London, (**Bär & Karrer** and **Froriep Renggli**), and Brussels **Pestalozzi Lachenal Patry** and **Python Schifferli Peter**. Swiss practices have also been keen to capitalise on the emerging Chinese market, with **Wenger & Vieli**'s Beijing office being well established, as well as an associate office in Shanghai, while **Walder Wyss & Partners** has recently opened a China desk.

FOREIGN FIRMS

As well as **Baker & McKenzie**, other US firms with Swiss offices include **Sidley Austin LLP**, **Hogan & Hartson L.L.P.** and **Winston & Strawn LLP**, which all have offices in Geneva. English firms are gradually realising the potential to offer trusts expertise to Swiss clients, as well as other legal services. Recent additions to the market are **Collyer-Bristow** and **Charles Russell**, both based in Geneva. The former has an office with four fee-earners, representing a major corporation which has its worldwide base in Switzerland, in addition to advising oil clients on refinery issues and also private clients on trusts. **Charles Russell**'s office, comprising of three lawyers opened in January 2006, as an extension of the firm's private client team's international capabilities.

BANKING AND FINANCE
Geneva

LENZ & STAEHELIN ✪

Baker & McKenzie ✪
Froriep Renggli ✪
Notter Mégevand & Partners ✪
Pestalozzi Lachenal Patry ✪
Poncet Turrettini Amaudruz Neyroud & Partners
Schellenberg Wittmer ✪
Tavernier Tschanz

Altenburger
Bär & Karrer ✪
Borel & Barbey ✪
Gillioz Dorsaz & Associés ✪
Lalive & Partners
Python Schifferli Peter ✪

Firms are listed A-Z in tiers which are ranked in order of priority
✪ Indicates firm displays contact details at the end of this chapter.

BANKING AND FINANCE
Geneva

Lenz & Staehelin continues to be instructed by major Swiss and foreign banking names operating within the jurisdiction. The firm advised UBS on a CHF270m (€174.6m) facility for Quadrant. Other instructions from Switzerland's largest bank include an amendment to a syndicated multi-currency loan facility to a SWX-listed borrower, and in conjunction with Credit Suisse, Halifax Plc and Barclays Bank, a syndicated loan to Swiss International airlines Ltd amounting to CHF325m (€210.1m).

Baker & McKenzie was boosted in 2005 with the arrival of Antonio Calvo, who previously worked for UBS in Geneva. Together with senior associate Frédéric Bétrisey's two-year tenure with the Swiss Federal Banking Commission, the team is able to exploit inside knowledge of the Swiss banking industry. Representing major international and local banks in Geneva, the firm is particularly active in public sector financing, real estate financing and commodities. The recent growth of investment fund and hedge fund industries has also translated into instructions in these fields.

Froriep Renggli is able to exploit its network of offices in Geneva, Zurich and Zug for banking and finance matters, and continues to be instructed by the Canton of Geneva in its action against Ernst & Young.

Notter Mégevand & Partners represents one of the top two banks in Switzerland, providing banking and finance expertise together with general legal advice. With a network of offices in Geneva, Berne and Fribourg, the firm is able to serve clients in both the French and German-speaking parts.

Evolving from its strength in private banking, the banking and finance department at

Pestalozzi Lachenal Patry has undertaken two transactions in conjunction with the Zurich office, the mezzanine financing of a new hotel in Geneva for a major financial institution, and advising a consortium on the financing aspects of an acquisition. Partner Gilles Thieffry who joined the firm from BNP Paribas in April 2004 has strengthened the transactional side of the Geneva office.

With over 80 years of practice in Geneva, **Poncet Turrettini Amaudruz Neyroud & Partners** is a ten-partner firm providing banking and finance expertise.

Counting investment fund guru Alain Hirsch amongst its numbers, **Schellenberg Wittmer** has a fully integrated banking and finance group, with 18 lawyers in Zurich and Geneva. Partner Lionel Aeschlimann had a busy year, advising local bank Mirabaud & Cie in its acquisition of Banque Jenni & Cie SA, and also being retained by Banco Santander Group in connection with the cross-border merger of Santander Guernsey and Santander Switzerland. One local banking client commented: 'Personally I find them the best in town.'

Tavernier Tschanz counts major French banks amongst its clients. In the past year the team led by name partner Edmond Tavernier continued to be retained by one bank on an ongoing basis subsequent to its merger with another major French bank, and has also advised a prominent local player on its acquisitions and disposals.

As a product of merging with *Birgit Sambeth Glasner*, which specialised in restructuring and bankruptcy law, **ALTENBURGER** in Geneva has strengthened its team and is seeking to make further hires in 2006.

Bär & Karrer's banking and finance practice represents both local banks and subsidiaries of major foreign banks. The firm advised Goldman Sachs on the offering of 1.625% guaranteed convertible unsubordinated bonds worth CHF350m (€226.3m) in communications company Kudelski SA. The firm is often instructed to produce legal documentation for syndicated loans and financings on behalf of oil clients. Evidence of the firm's repute amongst the banking community, is illustrated by partners such as Cédric Chapuis holding directorial positions at banks.

Counting Merrill Lynch, HSBC, and Mirabaud & Cie amongst its banking clients, **Borel & Barbey** advises on the day-to-day operations of banks, regulatory matters and acquisition finance. With the latter, the firm has been active in 2005, in particular in structuring acquisition finance at the shareholder level.

Gillioz Dorsaz & Associés continues to focus on providing traditional services to Geneva banks. Name partner Pierre Gillioz is also regularly instructed regarding the setting up and registering of investment funds.

Lalive & Partners is able to utilise inside knowledge of the banking industry, as a consequence of several of the firm's partners holding management positions in major Swiss and foreign banks.

The team at **Python Schifferli Peter** has experienced an increase in work stemming from the Federal Act on Merger, Demerger, Conversion and Transfer of Assets and Liabilities 2003, in particular a spin-off on behalf of a bank, where the bank was transformed into a holding company and its banking activities were transferred into a subsidiary. Banking litigation, structuring of clients' capital and general acquisitions comprise the remainder of the year's instructions.

BANKING AND FINANCE
Zurich

Bär & Karrer's team regularly represents banking clients regarding their acquisitions and disposals. The firm advised Bank Hapoalim (Switzerland) Limited on its purchase of Bank of New York-Inter Maritime Bank, and acted for another bank on its sale.

'With an excellent client focus and an exemplary awareness of urgency', **Homburger** advised on some of the most important financing transactions in 2005. In March 2005, the firm advised cement giant Holcim on a £1.6bn multi-currency credit facility. The firm also provided advice to BNP Paribas and Merrill Lynch International on the €671m Mandatory Convertible Securities Issue by Swiss Re, and the team was also active in working with major banks on the issuance of senior notes by Luxembourgish companies to the tune of €290m and €160m respectively. René Bösch is highly reputed in the market.

Offering a fully integrated service between its Zurich and Geneva offices, **Lenz & Staehelin** advised Deutsche Bank in various acquisitions and development loans for the purposes of acquiring/developing Swiss real estate portfolios in the past year. Securisation expertise was also provided to French bank Calyon in relation to a large, pan-European transaction.

'Excellent legal competence, detailed and knowledgeable, solution focussed', **Niederer Kraft & Frey** advised on no less than ten CHF100m-plus financings in 2005, cementing its position as the market leader in this field. Its biggest value deal being acting for JP Morgan on the US$6.6bn acquisition facilities and subscription agreement for mining group Xstrata. Other major deals in which the firm was retained include a €2bn facilities agreement for Ahold Group, a CHF690m (€446.4m) syndicated facility agreement for Synthes Stratec Inc, and CHF100m-plus syndicated facilities in the MBO by Permira of Jet Aviation group. François Bianchi is recommended.

Specialising in acquisition financing and refinancing, **Baker & McKenzie** experienced an upturn in multi-million-dollar instructions in the real estate market in 2005. The firm commonly acts as lead counsel for banking clients, such as advising Credit Suisse on a CHF285m (€185.1m) refinancing of a leasing company. Markus Affentranger who worked on these transactions is recommended along with his team for being 'very attentive to our needs, with good support after transactions'.

Pestalozzi Lachenal Patry has been sought by clients for a number of unique instructions over the past 12 months. The firm was retained by a group of financial advisers on a Shari'ah project finance transaction in Saudi Arabia and the firm set up one of the first insurance derivatives funds in Bermuda. Other traditional transactions include being Swiss counsel to the Swiss originator of a large asset-backed securities transaction, and acting for Credit Suisse on a number of domestic loan transactions. Managing partner Robert Furter is recommended by clients.

Schellenberg Wittmer had a particularly active year in the field of syndicated loans and provision of collateral. Lateral hire from **Homburger**, Mark-Oliver Baumgarten led the team advising ABN Amro on a US$1.6bn syndicated loan to Converium AG, and also for

BANKING AND FINANCE
Zurich

BÄR & KARRER ✪
HOMBURGER ✪
LENZ & STAEHELIN ✪
NIEDERER KRAFT & FREY ✪

Baker & McKenzie ✪
Pestalozzi Lachenal Patry ✪
Schellenberg Wittmer ✪
Vischer ✪
Walder Wyss & Partners ✪

Bratschi Emch Rechtsanwälte ✪
CMS von Erlach Henrici ✪
De Capitani Kronauer Buis ✪
Froriep Renggli ✪
Grüninger Hunziker Roth
Meyer Lustenberger ✪
Staiger, Schwald & Partner ✪
Wenger & Vieli ✪

Altenburger
Blum Attorneys at Law ✪
Hess Dallafior Attorneys at Law ✪
Nobel & Hug
Rinderknecht Klein & Stadelhofer ✪
Suter Howald Attorneys at Law ✪
Umbricht Rechtsanwälte ✪
Wenger Plattner ✪

Firms are listed A-Z in tiers which are ranked in order of priority
✪ *Indicates firm displays contact details at the end of this chapter.*

Bayerische Landesbank, another syndicated loan to the value of €1.75bn to the German KarstadQuelle group. Partners Martin Lanz and Philippe Borens are also recommended, and one banking client enthused:'**Schellenberg Wittmer**'s advice is always impeccable, to the point and in time.'

Experienced in syndicated loans and structured finance, **VISCHER** acted for a major Swiss bank in the arranging of a combined acquisition finance and leasing transaction for a railway company. The transaction encapsulated structured and acquisition finance and necessitated the creation of a unique deal structure. One client remarked: 'I very much appreciated the transparency and loyalty to the client shown by the partners in connection with structured finance transactions.' Representing a publicly listed Swiss concern, a CHF260m (€168.9m) syndicated bank loan was the principal facility advised on by the firm in 2005.

With five partners supported by eight associates, **Walder Wyss & Partners** is pushing to become one of the market leaders in banking and finance, in particular real estate finance. Partner Markus Kroll dominates the market for public securitisations. The firm represented Merrill Lynch International and Deutsche Bank AG on various financings of Swiss real estate acquisitions. Other major banks instructing the firm include Barclays regarding the financing of its acquisition of Iveco and UBS on numerous syndicated loans. One banking client commented:'They are the industry experts in securitisation in Switzerland ... one of the best law firms we have worked with in Europe.'

Bratschi Emch Rechtsanwälte concentrates on anti-money laundering, misdirected investment litigation and international judicial assistance matters for its banking clients. Recent joiner Dr Anton W Blatter who represents a well-known German banking group reinforces the practice.

CMS von Erlach Henrici continues to represent a wide range of foreign and domestic banking interests on regulatory, contractual, and anti-money laundering matters.

The most significant banking-related instruction **De Capitani Kronauer Buis** completed in 2005, was providing legal opinions for a reinsurance company regarding bank guarantees worth CHF1.5bn (€970.4m). The firm regularly advises insurance and reinsurance clients on banking and finance activities. Another reinsurer was advised on pooling and investing insurance premiums valued at CHF50m (€32.5m).

Unlike the majority of Swiss firms, **Froriep Renggli** has the advantage of having an office in London focusing on finance work. One client notes that:'Their lawyers in London are attuned to the requirements of the London market.' The Zurich office was instructed by GE Aviation Capital Services on the US$325m refinancing of the loan to SRT Technics. Whereas in London, 'very responsive and knowledgeable' Dunja Koch advised Citigroup in connection with a complex ECA financing for the importation of Bombardier locomotives into Switzerland.

Grüninger Hunziker Roth frequently gives loan notes advice for its clients. On behalf of the buyer, US$675m of senior notes were publicly offered in connection with an acquisition, and for another buyer, a US$225m accounts receivable securitisation facility was structured. The largest financing advised upon amounted to US$1.9bn of senior debt for a US$4bn acquisition. The name partners are recommended for their 'complete dedication, on-spot, and profound knowledge'.

Meyer Lustenberger has a banking and finance group specialising in a broad range of transaction-oriented work, including security lending transactions and derivatives transactions. The firm works very closely with one of the global Swiss banks, as well as masterminding the worldwide financing structure for a large Mexican corporation. The expertise of the partners is reflected in 15 board directorships that are held by them and one banking client enthused: 'On one side great advice and on the other side timely advice; they never miss a deadline.'

Staiger, Schwald & Partner is often involved in major transactions and restructuring projects. Most notably, the firm was retained in the role of counsel for the financing banks in substantial aircraft financing transactions. Partner Marc Metzger is a specialist in this field.

Wenger & Vieli deals with all the relevant banks in Zurich, offering debt financing advice and particular expertise in bank regulatory work. The firm also has a significant presence in the China market, with two offices (Beijing and Shanghai) staffed by 11 fee-earners. David Hess is recommended and one client commented: 'We rate the firm's overall service "AAA".'

ALTENBURGER regularly advises bank and life insurance companies on restructuring their businesses, and also on the applicability of various banking products in legal markets outside of Switzerland.

Hess Dallafior Attorneys at Law focuses on real estate financings. For one client an innovative leasing-based solution was devised to facilitate the successful completion of a major office building transaction in Zurich.

Rinderknecht Klein & Stadelhofer frequently acts as Swiss transaction counsel for domestic and foreign companies. In the latter capacity, the firm was retained to advise on a US$150m loan from an international development organisation to the Komi project (north-east Russia) of aluminium concern Sual Group. The firm also negotiated financing agreements with ECAs erecting an alumina refinery in the Komi Republic, and represents a major Moscow bank.

Swiss regulatory matters comprise the bulk of banking and finance instructions for **Suter Howald Attorneys at Law**. Approximately ten foreign funds instruct the firm to report on the regulatory aspects of fund registrations. In addition, a foreign banking group received advice as to the restructuring of its Swiss holding structure. 'Excellent work (quality, time, costs, reporting, clear procedures, economic understanding, practical solutions),' reported one client.

Umbricht Rechtsanwälte advises a wide range of banks, in particular on the tax aspects of transactions. Recently the firm was asked to assist on a €230m credit from a bank to a high-net-worth individual. The instruction was complicated by it being multi-jurisdictional, and by the need for a tax-efficient structure to be created.

Wenger Plattner advises on all banking and finance-related matters, encompassing contracts, securities, compliance and regulatory issues.

CAPITAL MARKETS

As the IPO market picked up in 2005, so did the workload at **Baker & McKenzie**. The firm has been highly active in the IPO market, acting as transaction counsel on the CHF108.5m (€70.4m) IPO of dairy group Emmi AG, advisor to Advanced Digital Broadcast Ltd on its CHF100m (€64.9m) IPO, and on behalf of worldwide logistics concern Palpina, an IPO with a value in excess of CHF800m (€519.6m).'I absolutely recommend B & M Zurich,' praised one financial products client.

Acting on the largest capital markets transaction in Switzerland in 2005, **Bär & Karrer** represented the underwriters in the CHF2.5bn (€1.6bn) rights offering of Julius Bär Holding, which was also the first rights issue on the 'EU-compatible' segment of the SWX. Other 'firsts' include the first ever cross border merger under the new Swiss Merger Act for the purposes of an IPO, worth CHF100m (€64.6m) on behalf of Advanced Digital Broadcast SA, and the first reverse merger on the real estate segment of the SWX concerning USI Group Holdings AG for CHF75m (€48.5m). Other sizeable rights offerings undertaken were for Arpida (CHF800m/€517m) and Swiss Prime Site AG (CHF270m/ €174.5m).

Three capital increases dominated the instructions for **Homburger** in 2005. Acting as joint counsel for major investment banks CSFB and JP Morgan, the firm was instructed on the CHF533m (€346m) capital increase of Converium Holding AG. A second capital increase was for Holcim Ltd (CHF454m / €292.8m), and the firm advised Deutsche Bank on the CHF34m (€22m) capital increase of Cytos Biotechnology AG. One banking client recommends partners Daniel Daeniker and Claude Lambert as 'outstanding and reliable professionals who render the services the way we expect it'.

Two pieces of cutting-edge work have been recently completed by **Lenz & Staehelin**. On behalf of Bank Julius Bär the firm acted on a rights

CAPITAL MARKETS

BAKER & McKENZIE ✪
BÄR & KARRER ✪
HOMBURGER ✪
LENZ & STAEHELIN ✪
NIEDERER KRAFT & FREY ✪

Meyer Lustenberger ✪
Schellenberg Wittmer ✪
Vischer ✪
Walder Wyss & Partners ✪

CMS von Erlach Henrici ✪
Froriep Renggli ✪
Grüninger Hunziker Roth
Hess Dallafior Attorneys at Law ✪
Pestalozzi Lachenal Patry ✪
Python Schifferli Peter ✪
Staiger, Schwald & Partner ✪
Tavernier Tschanz
Wyss Wiesli Rechtsanwälte

Firms are listed A-Z in tiers which are ranked in order of priority
✪ *Indicates firm displays contact details at the end of this chapter.*

offering in connection with the acquisition of UBS's private banking business with the approximate value of CHF2.5bn (€1.6bn). The transaction was the first rights offering in Switzerland with a listing on the new EU-compatible segment of the SWX. Secondly, the firm assisted on the first high-yield notes issue on the SWX (US$300m) for Digicel. Also, a CHF90m-plus (€58.2m) IPO was also undertaken for IT company Esmertec, via banking clients UBS and Deutsche Bank.

Niederer Kraft & Frey's most significant capital markets issue in the past twelve months was representing EFG bank on an IPO to the tune of CHF1.39bn (€909m). The team also acted on the aborted CHF2bn (€1.29bn) IPO of Cablecom, and a CHF420m (€301.9m) share buy-back programme of industrial group Givaudan SA. Three out of the four Japanese banks with offices in Zurich retain the firm as local counsel. Partners Hans Niederer and Peter Forstmoser are recognised as corporate giants.

'Strong in the mid-tier market and mid-cap segment', **Meyer Lustenberger** continues to advise longstanding client Allreal, in May 2005 acting as transaction counsel on a CHF160m (€103.9m) share offering. Other significant issues include an undisclosed public offer for handicraft company Pelikan and a CHF200m (€129.8m) share offering for an industrial adhesive concern. One innovative piece of capital markets work involved share lending, in which the shares offered to the new subscribers were temporarily lent by an existing major shareholder.

Schellenberg Wittmer acted on the CHF96.2m (€62.4m) IPO of Winterthur Technologie AG via joint lead runners CSFB and Erste Bank der oesterreichischen Sparkassen. The capital markets team was the first to advise on an authorised capital, rather than conditional capital mandatory convertible securities issue, amounting to CHF70m (€45.4m) on behalf of Züblin Immobilien Holding AG. Martin Lanz, Alexander Jolles and Martin Bernet are valued by clients for their 'excellent work'.

Fast-expanding (seven new lawyers hired 2004-05) Zurich and Basle-based practice **VISCHER** has built upon acting on chemicals giant Clariant's CHF1bn (€645m) share offering in 2004, by representing Lombard Odier (offer manager) on the share offering by electronics company Comet Holding AG. Partners Markus Guggenbühl and Urs Haegi are recommended as being 'business-minded and solution-oriented lawyers'.

Regularly competing with the largest Swiss firms for IPO work, **Walder Wyss & Partners**' banking and finance team led by Enrico Friz is well known in the capital markets field. UBS employed the firm on a rights issue by Holcim AG and Banca del Gottardo was advised on the issue of various structured financial products. 'Their work was overall very professional, always on-time when needed, accurate and to the point.'

CMS von Erlach Henrici remains instructed by General Electric on all its bond issues within Switzerland. Bond issues were also a major facet of *Henrici, Wicki & Guggisberg*'s practice which merged with the firm in October 2005. Former name partner Jürg Guggisberg is the capital markets leading light.

The main capital markets issue for **Froriep Renggli** in 2005, was assisting Vision Capital Partners in connection with the sale of its majority participation in Winterthur Technology AG via an IPO on the SWX. IPO referrals also stem from strong relations between the London office and the City firms there.

Usually the preserve of the largest firms in Switzerland, **Grüninger Hunziker Roth** successfully advised Esmertec in its IPO in 2005, which was worth over CHF90m (€58.2m).

Being able to utilise the resources in its banking and finance group, **Pestalozzi Lachenal Patry** has ample capacity to undertake capital markets work. The firm counts Credit Suisse, Merrill Lynch and Landesbank Baden-Wuerttemberg amongst its clients.

Wyss Wiesli Rechtsanwälte has successfully coordinated the public offering of a financial product worth over €500m.

CORPORATE AND COMMERCIAL
Basle

VISCHER operates a fully integrated practice, with the fee-earners of the firm evenly balanced between the two offices in Basle and Zurich. Significant transactions undertaken in 2005 included a CHF33m (€21.4m) financing round and a CHF97m (€62.9m) IPO for bio/pharmaceutical company Arpida AG. The life sciences sector provides a great deal of work for the Basle office. A further financing totalling CHF24m (€15.6m) was handled for AC Immune AG, and the firm acted on the sale of GlycArt Biotechnology to global player Roche for CHF235m (€152.5m). Matthias Staehelin is commended: 'The level of quality in any aspect (service, efficiency, project management skills etc) was very high on a consistent basis.'

Specialising in all facets of pharmaceutical-related work, **Wenger Plattner** has 20 lawyers in its Basle office. Partners Gerhard Schmid and Alexander Gutmans are able to exploit substantial experience of previously working in-house as legal counsel to large Swiss pharmaceutical companies. The office regularly advises on litigation, reorganisation and admission procedures, as well as acting as an outsourced legal department for medium-sized chemicals and pharmaceuticals concerns.

A six-lawyer team at **Böckli Bodmer & Partners** advises Swiss and international companies as well as high-net-worth individuals. The firm regularly covers shareholder issues including share option plans, dealing with shareholder activism, and representing them on M&A transactions. Founding partner Peter Böckli is highly reputed in corporate circles.

Fifteen-lawyer **Christen Rickli Partner** focuses on representing corporate and individual clients regarding tax and litigation matters. The firm is also qualified to provide notarial services, which is necessary for any real property, inheritance or family matters.

Mathys Schmid Partner is fully equipped to be instructed on transactional work, as well as offering traditional notarial services. Dr Barbara Graham-Siegenthaler was recently appointed lecturer in Swiss and international law at the University of Zurich.

CORPORATE AND COMMERCIAL
Basle

VISCHER ✪
WENGER PLATTNER ✪

Böckli Bodmer & Partners ✪
Christen Rickli Partner
Mathys Schmid Partner
SwissLegal Dürr + Partner
ThomannFischer

Eulau Kaufmann Giavarini & Recher
Joerin Hopf, Advokatur, Notariat, Mediation
Lenz Caemmerer Bender
Simonius Pfrommer & Partner ✪

Firms are listed A-Z in tiers which are ranked in order of priority
✪ *Indicates firm displays contact details at the end of this chapter.*

SwissLegal Dürr + Partner is the umbrella brand under which three firms in Basle, Zurich and Zug operate. The firm offers a full range of corporate and individual legal services.

Six-partner **ThomannFischer** is strong in IP, construction, private client and M&A. In the latter, the firm has acted on a number of sales of companies, including the sale of a retail chain with CHF1bn (€648m) of sales, the sale of a mid-sized pharmaceutical company, and the sale of a leading media publisher on behalf of a media multinational.

Eulau Kaufmann Giavarini & Recher is a corporate boutique and was recently involved in the restructuring of a global financial group. The firm regularly advises on the new Swiss merger law, in particular CHF-multi-million spin-offs. Currently the firm is assisting on a downstream merger between a foreign-owned holding company and an operating company, where the former will be absorbed by its Swiss subsidiary.

Simonius Pfrommer & Partner is a niche dispute resolution practice. Name partner Pascal Simonius regularly appears before the highest courts in Switzerland. Currently he is acting on a high-profile inheritance action, and also a bank liability case involving property funds. Thomas Burckhardt specialises in corporate arbitration, including ongoing disputes over M&A, and the dissolution of joint ventures.

CORPORATE AND COMMERCIAL
Geneva

With 18 partners located in its Geneva office, **Lenz & Staehelin** has extensive expertise to offer to clients seeking corporate and commercial advice. Advice was provided to the founders and management of GlycArt Technology in relation to its sale to Roche. This was the largest European buy-out transaction of a biotech company at a pre-clinical stage. Private equity company Argos Soditic also came to the firm regarding a leveraged management buy-out.

Corporate and commercial work is the core of **Python Schifferli Peter**'s practice, unlike other major Swiss firms who tend to offer clients legal services in a few specialised service areas. The firm has a broad client base comprising SMEs, biotech companies, shoe distributors and a global shipping company.

Schellenberg Wittmer has an enviable client list which includes international and Swiss blue-chips, such as Johnson Controls, Philip Morris International, JC Decaux and Celestica. A major corporate client enthused: 'The work provided was effective, very professional in our field of business and efficient.'

Baker & McKenzie's Geneva team has a strong grounding in private equity, stock option plans and general corporate expertise, working closely with the firm's tax and labour law departments. There has also been an upturn in

CORPORATE AND COMMERCIAL
Geneva

LENZ & STAEHELIN ✪
PYTHON SCHIFFERLI PETER ✪
SCHELLENBERG WITTMER ✪

Baker & McKenzie ✪
Bär & Karrer ✪
Borel & Barbey ✪
Froriep Renggli ✪
Gillioz Dorsaz & Associés ✪
Pestalozzi Lachenal Patry ✪
Tavernier Tschanz

Lalive & Partners
Notter Mégevand & Partners ✪
Poncet Turrettini Amaudruz Neyroud & Partners
Secretan Troyanov

Firms are listed A-Z in tiers which are ranked in order of priority
✪ *Indicates firm displays contact details at the end of this chapter.*

spin-off and merger transactions as a consequence of the 2003 Merger Act coming into force.

The fast-growing Geneva office of **Bär & Karrer** provides bespoke advice to large investment banks, as well as subsidiaries of foreign banks. Outsourcing, biotechnology and private equity clients are also served.

Borel & Barbey expanded its company and commercial team with the hire of two new associates in 2005. The firm is retained regularly by local and international clients to advise on financial and real estate issues. The latter has become more prominent due to the local real estate market booming, and foreign investors favouring Switzerland rather than the US.

Froriep Renggli has seven partners assisted by eight associates in Geneva, concentrating on stock exchange work, asset tracing and international assistance.

Gillioz Dorsaz & Associés specialises in corporate tax, mergers and restructuring. In the latter the firm has been particularly active, advising large public and medium-sized companies.

Pestalozzi Lachenal Patry divides its expertise into three broad areas, general company law, general contract and public and private M&A. The Geneva office is spearheaded by Claude Brechbuhl.

Stemming from its strength in M&A, **Tavernier Tschanz**'s corporate and commercial department is able to deal with all aspects of a client's corporate life, from inception (incorporation, corporate governance) to assisting on important transactions (group restructuring, financing and refinancing), once the company has reached a critical mass.

Start-ups, corporate finance, corporate restructuring, joint ventures and shareholder agreements comprise the legal services offered by the 12 partners at **Lalive & Partners**. In addition to transactional services, the firm also provides contractual support to its clients on all facets of their business.

Notter Mégevand & Partners is instructed by a broad range of clients, including an international sports association and an art foundation. For international brokers active on the various stock and futures markets, advice was provided on investment funds and stock exchange regulations. A leading group in the applied physics industry retained the firm for a broad range of advice, and a real estate investment fund was advised on its CHF80m (€51.7m) transfer to a top Swiss bank.

Secretan Troyanov is an international firm originating in Geneva, with two further offices providing Swiss law advice in London and Moscow. The firm focuses on M&A and corporate restructuring.

CORPORATE AND COMMERCIAL
Zurich

Baker & McKenzie has carved a niche in servicing private equity operators in their investments in Switzerland. The firm advised 3i on acquisitions of minority stakes in Movie-Box Betriebs AG and Pilatus Aircraft Ltd. Various financings have also added to the office's workload, including a Series A financing (for Poly Technos Venture GmbH), a Series B financing (for NumeriX SA) and a Series C financing for The Genetics Company Inc.

Bär & Karrer has undertaken a variety of matters in conjunction with its other teams, including the delisting of SBC from the SWX in connection with the merger with AT&T, and acting as transaction counsel to a private equity fund for its sale to a Swiss banking group.

Homburger has demonstrated its expertise in divestitures, by continuing to be instructed on the most substantial transactions to take place in Switzerland. As lead counsel to UBS, the firm advised on the CHF5.6bn (€3.62bn) divestiture of its private banks and GAM (global asset management) unit to Bank Julius Bär. This follows the CHF3.6bn (€2.33bn) divestiture on behalf of Roche Holding AG in 2004. The firm also acted as lead counsel to Helsana Zusatzversicherungen AG on its acquisition of business portfolios from a Swiss rival. Managing partner Heinz Schärer is a heavyweight in the corporate sector.

Lenz & Staehelin has exploited the need for advising private equity firms in their investments. UBS Capital was represented in its sale of Mister Minit to CVC Capital Partners. Bank Julius Bär also instructed the firm in relation to its capital restructuring to facilitate the creation of a single class of shares. Partners of the firm also sit on the boards of Barclays Bank, JP Morgan, Coutts and BAT.

Corporate and commercial services are at the heart of 'very professional, efficient and practical'

CORPORATE AND COMMERCIAL
Zurich

BAKER & McKENZIE ✪
BÄR & KARRER ✪
HOMBURGER ✪
LENZ & STAEHELIN ✪
PESTALOZZI LACHENAL PATRY ✪

CMS von Erlach Henrici ✪
Froriep Renggli ✪
Niederer Kraft & Frey ✪
Schellenberg Wittmer ✪
Staiger, Schwald & Partner ✪
Vischer ✪
Walder Wyss & Partners ✪
Wenger & Vieli ✪

Badertscher Dörig Poledna ✪
Bill Isenegger Ackermann ✪
Bratschi Emch Rechtsanwälte ✪
Meyer Lustenberger ✪
Rinderknecht Klein & Stadelhofer ✪
Suter Howald Attorneys at Law ✪

Hess Dallafior Attorneys at Law ✪
Nobel & Hug
Prager Dreifuss
Stiffler & Partner ✪
Thouvenin Rechtsanwälte ✪
Umbricht Rechtsanwälte ✪
Wenger Plattner ✪

Altenburger
Blum Attorneys at Law ✪
Bürgi Nägeli Lawyers ✪
Choquard Attorneys
Grüninger Hunziker Roth
Haymann & Baldi ✪
Roesle Frick & Partners
Rohner Rechtsanwälte ✪
Sedgwick, Detert, Moran & Arnold

Firms are listed A-Z in tiers which are ranked in order of priority
✪ Indicates firm displays contact details at the end of this chapter.

Pestalozzi Lachenal Patry. The firm was retained in 2005 to provide legal advice for the (CHF500m/€323.45m) relocation to Switzerland of software corporation Infor Global Solutions, and also acted for CSFB for the equity rights offering of Helvetia Patria amounting to CHF295m (€190.85m). Name partner Peter Pestalozzi is recommended.

CMS von Erlach Henrici has the advantage of the CMS network in providing its clients with a one-stop-shop service across Europe. Typical work varies from day-to-day corporate services to complex divestitures, as well as specialised knowledge in the commodities and energy sectors. Name partner Rudolf von Erlach is known for representing multinational clients.

Froriep Renggli was retained on the restructuring of the entire Swiss and various international entities of logistics concern Thiel. Partner Alessandro Celli also sits on the board.

As well as handling the CHF1.39bn (€909m) IPO, **Niederer Kraft & Frey** advised on the reorganisation of EFG Bank and the creation of a holding structure in anticipation of it. The firm has a strong track record in this field, acting on the capital restructuring of Swisslog Holding AG and UMS Swiss Metals Holding Ltd.

Schellenberg Wittmer's corporate and commercial team often works closely with the capital markets group, a previous example being on the 2004 restructuring of Swiss reinsurer Converium Holding AG. The rights issue was complicated by the share price of the client greatly fluctuating while the company was in turmoil.

Acting as counsel to the largest Swiss manufacturer of rolling stock on public procurement projects, on a corporate transaction worth CHF100m's, **Staiger, Schwald & Partner**'s corporate and commercial department continues to be involved in major transactions and restructuring projects. Name partner Hans-Peter Schwald as well as acting as joint counsel to the company for the transaction, also sits on the board.

The expanding corporate group at **VISCHER** had a varied year, advising Zellweger Luwa AG on a spin-off and sale of its analytics division to US corporation Honeywell International Inc, representing Deutsche Post Ventures GmbH on two private equity transactions, and acting for a Swiss consortium on the acquisition of substantial assets from a German state-owned enterprise. 'The partners I had to deal with were very well skilled and competent,' praised one client.

Walder Wyss & Partners has been active on behalf of insurance clients. Investors were advised on the origination of Glacier Reinsurance, and Allianz Risk Transfer was given compliance advice. In the booming private equity sector, Swiss Life instructed the firm on the sale of its private equity participation. 'Overall we think **Walder Wyss & Partners** is among our top three law firms,' commented a Swiss banking client that uses the firm for its contractual negotiations.

'Very good in all aspects' **Wenger & Vieli** focuses on private equity transactions (buy-outs, distressed investing) and venture capital financing rounds. This commitment has translated into the firm receiving approximately two transactions per month in the past year. Partner Christian Wenger chairs various private equity associations and regularly comments on the sector. The two main venture capital transactions the firm acted on are as counsel to the investors on a CHF34m (€21.9m) transaction involving medical company Precimed, and on behalf of silicon company BridgeCo, a US$15m transaction.

Badertscher Dörig Poledna represents a variety of clients in the automotive, travel, IT, pumps and insurance industries. In the latter, the firm was instructed on the establishment of the largest European credit insurance company in Switzerland.

In 2005 **BILL ISENEGGER ACKERMANN** advised on a tax-sensitive sale of a large real estate company, and was retained by a large foreign group of companies in connection with its entry into the food and non-food market in Switzerland. Corporate restructuring and employment issues were particularly prevalent. Further restructuring advice on an international level was provided to the owners of a group of companies active in the production and sale of agricultural/food machinery. 'The firm is really excellent, and its partners really care about client service – day and night.'

Though historically strong in servicing its banking and financial institutional clients, **Bratschi Emch Rechtsanwälte**'s growth of its pharmaceutical and drugs law practice is evident by the election of Ursula Eggenberger-Stöckli to partnership; she has over 20 years of experience. The firm regularly advises on drug admissions, advertisement issues, competition law and public health.

With an extensive number of board memberships amongst the partnership at **Meyer Lustenberger**, the firm advises corporate clients such as Fujitsu Services AG, Toys R Us AG, and TNT Logistics Switzerland AG on an ongoing basis for all their corporate legal needs.

Rinderknecht Klein & Stadelhofer has an impressive client list, including representing Russian natural resources group Renova and global aluminium group SUAL as both global and lead transaction counsel. The firm advised on the corporate and tax restructuring of the Asian operations of a global trading and marketing group with a turnover of CHF5bn (€3.23bn), and was lead transaction counsel on the purchase of a majority stake in a top-50 airline. Partner Jeanette Wibmer is recommended for being 'very strong in company law'.

'Available at all times, experienced, knowledgeable' **Suter Howald Attorneys at Law** currently represents a major foreign insurer as to the regulatory considerations of setting up its Swiss-based captive reinsurance company. The firm also carved a niche in advising foreign companies on their relocation within Switzerland, including rendering advice for a US-based multinational's transfer of its European headquarters to the jurisdiction, and also setting up Swiss finance branches for foreign multinationals. Name partner Urs Suter, together with Mauro Loosli are recommended by clients.

Hess Dallafior Attorneys at Law has been working on the restructuring of a Swiss subsidiary of a US IT group, and also offers a full range of corporate and commercial services to a number of SME clients.

'**Stiffler & Partner** performed excellent work, in terms of quality and responsiveness,' says one satisfied banking client.

The two most significant transactions **Thouvenin Rechtsanwälte** undertook in 2005 involved complex financing and restructuring expertise. In the former a group of office supply companies was financed and the ownership changed. In the latter, a majority shareholder in a manufacturing company was represented regarding the restructuring and financing on a corporate and private level. Hansjörg Stutzer is recommended and one client enthused: 'I have the highest regard for the work of this firm. They are extremely diligent and knowledgeable in all aspects of Swiss corporate law.'

Umbricht Rechtsanwälte's niche public law team spearheaded by Markus Rüssli is often instructed on high-profile state responsibility cases, two recent examples involved Swiss cantonal banks and a mad cow disease action between a group of farmers and the government. Another niche area is the firm's strength in public procurement, where both private and public clients have been represented as to claims originating from procurement contracts being awarded to particular companies. Markus Hauser is the key contact.

Wenger Plattner focuses on actions of civil responsibility against the management, board members and auditors of investment funds and collective funds, in addition to its core corporate and commercial transactions expertise.

ALTENBURGER has experienced an increase in work for US clients recently, stemming from the American Job Creations Act 2004 (USA) that facilitates the repatriation of foreign earnings by US corporations. The Zurich office also undertakes a great deal of structuring work, and the partnership's reputation has been enhanced by experience at the Commercial Register in Switzerland.

Grüninger Hunziker Roth handles the Swiss corporate affairs of a diverse range of foreign companies, including CEMEX Group a global cement producer, Esmertec AG a leading mobile phone software producer, ResMed Inc a manufacturer of products for the treatment of sleep-disorders, and Magirus Group a German IT company.

Roesle Frick & Partners counts over 40 Swiss companies as clients for the purposes of corporate and commercial matters. Name partner Max Roesle is chairman of a Swiss and a Luxembourgish bank.

DISPUTE RESOLUTION

DISPUTE RESOLUTION

BÄR & KARRER ○
HOMBURGER ○
LENZ & STAEHELIN ○
PESTALOZZI LACHENAL PATRY ○
SCHELLENBERG WITTMER ○

Baker & McKenzie ○
Python Schifferli Peter ○
Vischer ○
Wenger Plattner ○
Winston & Strawn LLP ○

CMS von Erlach Henrici ○
Froriep Renggli ○
Gloor & Sieger
Hogan & Hartson L.L.P. ○
Lalive & Partners
Prager Dreifuss

Meyer Lustenberger ○
Niederer Kraft & Frey ○
Rinderknecht Klein & Stadelhofer ○
Sidley Austin LLP ○
Staiger, Schwald & Partner ○
Tavernier Tschanz
Walder Wyss & Partners ○

Böckli Bodmer & Partners ○
Borel & Barbey ○
De Capitani Kronauer Buis ○
Gillioz Dorsaz & Associés ○
Grüninger Hunziker Roth
Haymann & Baldi ○
Hess Dallafior Attorneys at Law ○

Altenburger
Berger Recordon & de Saugy
Bill Isenegger Ackermann ○
Bratschi Emch Rechtsanwälte ○
Bürgi Nägeli Lawyers ○
Hartmann Müller Partners ○
Poncet Turrettini Amaudruz Neyroud & Partners
Stiffler & Partner ○
Thouvenin Rechtsanwälte ○
Umbricht Rechtsanwälte ○
Wenger & Vieli ○

Firms are listed A-Z in tiers which are ranked in order of priority
○ Indicates firm displays contact details at the end of this chapter.

At **Bär & Karrer**, the two biggest disputes the firm handled in 2005 were both arbitrations involving the enforcement of executing transactions. The first was a CHF500m (€323.1m) construction dispute and the second a multi-billion-dollar mobile phone action. Other significant cases include successfully defending a major private bank in a CHF25m (€16.2m) malpractice claim, and representing a major European business information provider on a CHF65m (€42m) franchise dispute.

Accounting for 40% of the firm's earnings, **Homburger**'s 17-strong dispute resolution team acted on a number of high-profile arbitrations before the ICC and before other forums. In an arbitration arising from a spin-off, partner Markus Wirth acted for Ciba Specialty Chemicals Ltd against Novartis. He also sat as chairman of the arbitration panel on an international arbitration between DaimlerChrysler Ltd and Bombardier Inc over a major M&A transaction. Turkish GSM operators were represented in their actions against US and UK concerns respectively. The team was also active in general litigation matters, particularly in the areas of white-collar crime and mass tort litigation. Most notably, on behalf of a Turkish GSM operator, a landmark decision was successfully obtained from the Swiss Supreme Court, regarding the enforcement of a British freezing order in Switzerland.

Lenz & Staehelin's high repute in dispute resolution is founded upon notable arbitration and litigation specialists in each of its offices in Zurich and Geneva. One of the biggest arbitrations advised on, was a CHF multi-billion case between Dutch Bank ABN Amro and a Turkish telecoms concern, which was handled by Rudolf Tchaeni.

Over the past year, **Pestalozzi Lachenal Patry** was retained on no less than 15 CHF10m-plus litigation and arbitration actions. The biggest-value disputes were a CHF130m–CHF150m (€84m–€96m) inheritance dispute on behalf of a high-net-worth individual, a CHF75m (€48m) claim for damages for a large commodities trader, and representing a large Swiss insurance company, in claims for damages in a pension fund disaster of up to CHF160m (€103.3m).

'Extremely knowledgeable, clear-sighted and capable in the organisation and management of the case', Alexander von Ziegler of **Schellenberg Wittmer** is currently working on one of the highest-profile disputes to take place in Switzerland, the action stemming from the Überlingen air crash; he is leading the team defending the Swiss Air Traffic Control Organisation Skyguide. The firm also represented UBS in recent litigation against a Geneva debtor, in which securing the closure and resale of a luxury hotel was key to completing the action. Other areas of specialisation are white-collar crime, sports disputes and art-related litigation. One client commented: '**Schellenberg Wittmer** did truly outstanding work. They have managed the case to our highest expectations.'

Contentious matters with a cross-border focus are frequently handled by the team at **Baker & McKenzie**. The firm was retained by a leading supplier of transportation systems in a multi-jurisdictional dispute with customers and sub-contractors exceeding US$600m. For a major pharmaceutical concern, a US$20m patent dispute against a former employee was handled, and on behalf of a medical company, litigation relating to the termination of various distribution agreements amounting to US$20m.

With name partners Jacques Python, Pierre Schifferli and Wolfgang Peter all offering significant experience, arbitration is one of the key practice areas for **Python Schifferli Peter**. Recently Thomas Legler acted as chairman of an ICC arbitration in Paris, over a US$32m claim between English and French IT companies. Other arbitrations that the firm is commonly involved in are in the construction, aviation and sports sectors.

The litigation highlight for **VISCHER** in 2005, was on behalf of a Swiss bank obtaining a settlement on responsibility for malpractice in administering assets under management. The firm equally divides its resources between international arbitration and litigation.

International arbitration continues to be a core business of **Wenger Plattner**. Name partner Werner Wenger harnesses a strong reputation in this field, as a consequence of regularly acting as chairman of arbitration panels. International sports arbitration is the preserve of former Olympian Stephan Netzle, in particular anti-doping, football-related disputes and litigation involving international sports organisations.

Winston & Strawn LLP's Geneva office, led by Marc Palay handled some of the most substantial arbirations over the past year. IPOC International Growth Fund Limited (Bermuda) is being represented in two US$800m and one US$600m arbitration. The firm is also retained by Philip Morris International in an ongoing Israeli healthcare cost-recovery claim totalling US$1.7bn. Another high-profile multi-million-dollar claim led by the Geneva office recently started before the Florida District Court, between the Government of Haiti and Telecommunications of Haiti against former president Jean Bertrand Aristide. One client enthused:'The service is highly professional. Would definitely recommend them.'

The dispute resolution group at **CMS von Erlach Henrici** remains instructed on the Yukos Oil litigation, which is being contested before the highest court in Switzerland. Banking litigation is still a staple of the contentious workload, and clients also seek the firm's expertise in international assistance cases.

The arbitration team at **Froriep Renggli** achieved a landmark Court of Arbitration of Sport ruling on behalf of Phonak Cycling, regarding the successful return of its ProTour licence. The case stemmed from anti-doping allegations against its lead rider, Tyler Hamilton. Never before had a decision of the UCI Licensing Committee been successfully challenged. Partners Lucien Valloni and Alessandro Celli spearheaded the team. Another successful sports victory entailed winning back the gold medal for the Endurance Racing World Championship before the FEI Judicial Committee. 'We have used this law firm for many years and we are very happy with the work they do,' praised one client.

'I have worked with Daniel Wehrli of **Gloor & Sieger** on an arbitration matter and I value highly his work.' Wehrli leads the dispute resolution group at **Gloor & Sieger**, and has acted on over 90 international and domestic arbitrations, with a primary focus on disputes emanating from infrastructure projects, joint venture agreements, option agreements and shareholder agreements.

Opening its Geneva office in September 2005, as a consequence of former **Winston & Strawn LLP** partners Charles Adams and Michael Stepek joining the firm, **Hogan & Hartson L.L.P.** has relocated its international arbitration practice for Europe, Asia, the Middle East and Africa there. The firm is currently representing Alsthom Power against BDE Inc in a US$100m dispute, and on behalf of Mehras Co a US$8m international arbitration claim against Dresser DI UK Ltd. The latter is of significance, as Mehras is the first private sector Iranian company to arbitrate before the ICC. One client that instructs the team on large-scale commercial arbitrations remarked: 'Charles Adams is an outstanding lawyer and I would recommend him without reservation.' The office also has a strong international trade practice, assisted by specialist teams in Brussels and Washington, DC. Most notably the Government of Ontario is being represented in the largest countervailing duty subsidy case in the world, with US$5bn of duty deposits at issue.

Regularly going before Swiss and international forums, **Lalive & Partners** specialises in arbitration and international litigation, most notably in the fields of construction, petroleum, telecommunications and intellectual property.

Meyer Lustenberger has boosted its dispute resolution team with the recruitment of Professor Karl Spühler, who previously worked as a judge in the Swiss Federal Supreme Court in Lausanne for 17 years. He has great expertise in bankruptcy law. The firm also handles a number of directors' liability cases, tort liability cases (international insurance groups) and insolvency cases.

The most significant litigation currently being handled by a ten-lawyer team managed by Urs Pulver at **Niederer Kraft & Frey**, involves a dispute over the sale of part of a major Swiss retail company to another Swiss retail company. The firm has also acted on one of the largest ICC arbitrations.

Two multi-million-dollar cases dominated **Rinderknecht Klein & Stadelhofer**'s instructions in 2005. Firstly the firm developed and started implementation of a litigation strategy in a US$1.3bn telecommunications company arbitration. Secondly, in a US$1.5bn corporate litigation the firm was instructed to supervise US local counsel.

Sidley Austin LLP's Geneva office is ideally located next to the WTO's headquarters, and specialises in WTO dispute settlement in tandem with its offices in Brussels and Washington, DC. As counsel to ABRAPA the Brazilian Cotton Association, the team led by Scott Andersen and assisted by Nicholas Lockhart successfully argued that US subsidies adversely affected Brazilian producers. Currently the firm is representing Airbus SAS in the immensely significant EU subsidies dispute involving US rival Boeing, the outcome of which will have significant implications for the global aviation industry.

Staiger, Schwald & Partner has particular strength in directors' liability litigation, defending banks, and IP litigation. The firm regularly receives referrals from other major players due to conflicts issues.

Name partner Pierre-Yves Tschanz fronts the dispute resolution department at **Tavernier Tschanz**. The firm regularly acts as counsel in arbitration cases and is able to utilise indepth knowledge of many international forums.

Walder Wyss & Partners represents various Swiss and international clients in proceedings before Swiss courts and in arbitration proceedings. Managing partner Philipp Habegger has a burgeoning reputation as an arbitrator.

Borel & Barbey remains active in banking litigation and international legal assistance in criminal matters. The practice is headed by former District Court of Geneva judge Patrick Blaser and mutual assistance and criminal specialist Jean-François Ducrest.

De Capitani Kronauer Buis specialises in banking litigation, regularly acting against banks on behalf of high-net-worth individuals. One such case was a CHF8m (€5.2m) asset management malpractice action. The firm also acted on the enforcement of a CHF25m (€16.2m) arbitral award, a CHF12m (€7.8m) dispute over the sale of machinery and textiles, and on behalf of heirs regarding a CHF2m (€1.3m) inheritance claim. The arrival of Paul Bürgi from **Baker & McKenzie** has significantly boosted the team.

Gillioz Dorsaz & Associés via name partner Bernard Dorsaz continues to be active in international arbitration, as well as litigation for banks and major corporations.

Grüninger Hunziker Roth's litigation team successfully represented the receiver in a US$1.1bn bankruptcy liquidation dispute, as well as being counsel to a group of investors in connection with a CHF100m (€64.6m) negligence claim against a foreign financial institution. Judicial assistance (on behalf of the UK Department of Trade and Industry) and arbitration (pharmaceuticals) cases were also handled.

Name partner Roberto Dallafior of **Hess Dallafior Attorneys at Law** is a recognised arbitrator, often receiving referrals from larger firms that are conflicted out.

ALTENBURGER concentrates on international arbitration in its Geneva office. Other litigation expertise offered includes debt enforcement and bankruptcy advice.

BILL ISENEGGER ACKERMANN is representing a large foreign bank in connection with various loans granted to and transactions executed with an airline, which now involves litigation with the liquidator of that airline.

Relying on a number of highly experienced litigators concentrating on banking, commercial and company law disputes, **Bratschi Emch Rechtsanwälte** has been instructed on a number of notable cases, including defending a major telecommunications company in a global case, and acting for the claimant in an action against a global accountancy firm. Partner Daniel Glasl specialises in the liabilities of companies going into bankruptcy.

Best-known for its commercial litigation practice led by Laurent Killias, **Stiffler & Partner** has represented major Swiss banks, Swiss and foreign insurance companies (including one of the largest Japanese players), and is retained by the president of a Swiss bank and the former CFO of a well-known Swiss bank. '**Stiffler & Partner** can certainly be regarded as a top law firm in Switzerland.' commented one client.

Partners Daniel Stoll (banking litigation) and Hansjörg Stutzer (arbitration) of **Thouvenin Rechtsanwälte**, are recommended: '... from the perspective of providing sound legal advice and high-quality legal documentation, as well as being practically oriented in providing advice on legal matters.' Stoll has recently been engaged in an arbitration related to the marketing rights in football, has had his own arbitral award enforced by the Canadian Supreme Court, and is presently sitting on a panel regarding a dispute arising out of a significant infrastructure project in Argentina.

Umbricht Rechtsanwälte has an arbitration specialist in founding partner Robert Umbricht. Construction arbitration cases are regularly handled, as well as more unique actions, including the enforcement of a €30m foreign attachment of assets order, and a rare arbitration victory at the Supreme Court appealing a jurisdiction decision.

Wenger & Vieli has a broad arbitration-oriented team, with the partners experienced in acting as both arbitrators and counsel. The firm counts the ICC, the Swiss Arbitration Association and the Zurich Chamber of Commerce amongst its memberships, and has successfully handled cases before the China International Economic and Trade Arbitration Commission via its Beijing office.

EU AND COMPETITION

Merger control filings (often cross-border) and dominant position actions comprise the majority of the EU and competition instructions for **Baker & McKenzie**. Merger control filings advice was required in relation to the acquisition of Jet Aviation by Permira, on the divestiture of the business communication and transport revenue divisions of Ascom, and also for private equity company EQT concerning its acquisition of services firm ISS/AS. A major airline and an airline parts company have retained the firm in relation to dominant position cases.

Working closely with its tax and TMT groups, **Bär & Karrer**'s competition team focuses on litigating antitrust matters before the courts as well as before the Swiss Competition Commission. For international cases with an EU element, the firm relies on its network of foreign contacts.

EU AND COMPETITION

BAKER & McKENZIE ✪
BÄR & KARRER ✪
HOMBURGER ✪
LENZ & STAEHELIN ✪
PESTALOZZI LACHENAL PATRY ✪

CMS von Erlach Henrici ✪
Froriep Renggli ✪
Hess Dallafior Attorneys at Law ✪
Meyer Lustenberger ✪
Prager Dreifuss
Python Schifferli Peter ✪
Schellenberg Wittmer ✪
Sidley Austin LLP ✪
Staiger, Schwald & Partner ✪
Tavernier Tschanz
Vischer ✪
Walder Wyss & Partners ✪
Wenger Plattner ✪

Firms are listed A-Z in tiers which are ranked in order of priority
✪ Indicates firm displays contact details at the end of this chapter.

Stemming from its strength in M&A and with EU merger control expertise, **Homburger**'s competition department had an active twelve months. For Hoffmann-La Roche antitrust issues arose as a consequence of the disposal of its vitamin division to DSM. Further antitrust advice was provided in relation to the Synthes-Stratec (medical device company) acquisition of Mathys Medizinaltechnik AG, as well as merger control considerations. Feldschlössen Getränke AG was represented before the Swiss Competition Commission, regarding the alleged abuse of a dominant position in the beverage distribution market. The expertise of Marcel Dietrich and Franz Hoffet is acknowledged by peers and clients alike, with one client commenting: 'The lawyers work quickly and thoroughly and they are not satisfied with the obvious solution.'

Lenz & Staehelin acts for blue-chip clients in relation to high-profile competition-related matters. The firm was retained to provide merger control filing expertise regarding the Swisscom and Cinetrade merger, and on Bank Julius Bär Holding's sale to UBS AG. The issue of abuse of dominant position was considered for Ticketcorner and Corner Bank, as well as on the merger between Teleclub and Cablecom. Marcel Meinhardt is recognised by peers as an expert in this field.

Recognised by his peers as being a leading individual, Jürg Borer leads **Pestalozzi Lachenal Patry**'s competition team and was instructed on a number of antitrust matters in 2005. For Telekurs (financial information provider) antitrust expertise was required over credit cards, as well as for Publicitas and Cablecom. For the latter advice was also given on price regulation issues concerning the Swiss price control authority, and for Orange an investigation concerning termination fees.

CMS von Erlach Henrici with an office in Brussels is fully equipped to handle EU-related competition questions. The Swiss team has experienced a surge in instructions resulting from the revised Swiss Cartel Act, and regularly advises on merger control procedures, competition investigations and antitrust compliance.

With two new associate hires in 2005, competition law specialist Alessandro Celli's team at **Froriep Renggli** has boosted its merger control filings capacity and in EU-related competition law matters.

Hess Dallafior Attorneys at Law specialises in antitrust, domestic and competition law matters. Professor Reto Hilty is director at the Max-Planck-Institute for Intellectual Property, Competition and Tax Law.

Meyer Lustenberger's competition team continues to support major clients on issues involving domestic and international merger control, antitrust and distribution and agency agreements.

Being one of the few firms in Switzerland to have an office in Brussels, **Python Schifferli Peter** has international capacity in addition to the network of Swiss offices.

Schellenberg Wittmer offers a wide range of competition law expertise, advising recently on five preliminary and formal investigations by the Swiss Competition Commission, and on four merger control proceedings, all arising under the Swiss Cartel Act. The group also has the capacity to deal with abuse of dominant position allegations, compliance audits, and competition aspects of distribution and licensing agreements.

Sidley Austin LLP has a multi-disciplinary team in its Geneva office, with a senior international trade policy advisor and two trade analysts in addition to the practising lawyers. The former, John Weekes is the former Canadian Ambassador to GATT and the WTO. Multilateral trade negotiations the firm is currently undertaking vary from acting for UPS to improve trade rules on express delivery, to assisting Monsanto in the freeing up of the agricultural biotechnology market. Government departments' interests are also represented. One client stated: 'They make a big effort to understand the sector, they do not just know the law.'

Stemming from name partner Hans-Rudolf Staiger being instructed on the landmark 2003 electricity case between Migros and Watt against EEF, **Staiger, Schwald & Partner** continues to act as counsel for major energy providers in respect of the opening of the energy market in Switzerland in which antitrust issues are important.

Tavernier Tschanz has a highly developed competition practice, advising one of the largest Swiss media groups, the subsidiary of a global drinks company, and a major oil and energy group. 'Their work is of superior quality (even proactive at times); their response is quick and availability is generous.' Partner Silvio Venturi is repeatedly recommended by clients as 'an outstanding and reliable performer in competition matters'.

VISCHER has expanded its EU and competition work group with the lateral hire of senior associate Klaus Neff from **Homburger**, who with Urs Haegi has provided Swiss and EU merger control advice, in particular on the sale of Zellweger Analytics to Honeywell International Inc. Other significant work includes counseling International Henkel Group on its domestic and cross-border competition issues, and Stefan Rechsteiner assisting the Swiss government on legislation to liberalise the energy market. Clients recommend him for rendering services 'of very high quality both in terms of legal quality as well as in terms of client handling.'

Led by the 'excellent' Reto Jacobs **Walder Wyss & Partners**' competition team has been retained to advise on antitrust matters for notable domestic players such as retailer Migros and Swisscom, and for international clients such as Microsoft on general competition issues.

Wenger Plattner is actively involved in drafting and implementing compliance programmes for medium and large-scale corporations. The firm is also instructed to consider antitrust and unfair competition problems and represents clients before the Swiss Competition Commission.

INSOLVENCY AND CORPORATE RECOVERY

Continuing to act on a raft of headline restructurings including Erb Group and Swiss Dairy Food, **Baker & McKenzie** is one of the main players in the insolvency market. One client noted: 'For me it's the most value-adding law firm in Switzerland in business law.' Partners Urs Schenker, Lukas Glanzmann and Richard Gassmann are all highly recommended for their expertise.

Froriep Renggli as well as advising on the restructuring of Thiel, continues to be active in the insolvency field, in particular with Roland Kaufmann in Geneva and Felix Mathis in Zurich. The lawyers regularly act as the creditor-appointed representative, or commissioner in major bankruptcy or debt-restructuring cases.

With expertise in divestitures and debt restructuring, **Homburger** is well equipped to advise companies seeking to avoid financial collapse. The firm advises all parties involved in insolvencies, including individual and corporate creditors, and Swiss and foreign debtors.

The long-running Noga Hilton hotel saga in which **Schellenberg Wittmer** acted for the lending bank in bankrupting the management company of the hotel, came to a successful conclusion in the spring of 2005. Two new additions, Bénédict Foex and Valérie Defago-Gaudin have enhanced the insolvency team fronted by Vincent Jeanneret. He has acted as trustee, commissioner and official liquidator in the Mag-Plastic SA, Bureau genevois d'adresses, Ercal SA, and Cit-Francour SA cases. In the latter, Frantour's assets, trade mark rights and employees were transferred to a subsidiary of the Kuoni group within the tight timeframe of one week.

INSOLVENCY AND CORPORATE RECOVERY

BAKER & McKENZIE ✪
FRORIEP RENGGLI ✪
HOMBURGER ✪
SCHELLENBERG WITTMER ✪
WENGER PLATTNER ✪

Bürgi Nägeli Lawyers ✪
Staiger, Schwald & Partner ✪
Vischer ✪
Walder Wyss & Partners ✪

Bratschi Emch Rechtsanwälte ✪
CMS von Erlach Henrici ✪
Grüninger Hunziker Roth
Hartmann Müller Partners ✪
Lenz & Staehelin ✪
Niederer Kraft & Frey ✪
Python Schifferli Peter ✪
Roesle Frick & Partners
Tavernier Tschanz

Firms are listed A-Z in tiers which are ranked in order of priority
✪ Indicates firm displays contact details at the end of this chapter.

Insolvency and corporate recovery is a key service area offered by **Wenger Plattner**. Few competitors have the capacity to undertake as many claims as the team spearheaded by Karl Wüthrich. He is known as 'Mr Liquidator' and is respected in Switzerland for his independence in acting on the collapses of eminent Swiss corporations such as Swissair, Swiss Dairy Food, Unifina and Big Food. These insolvencies are ongoing and the team's good work has been rewarded by further instructions.

The strength of **Bürgi Nägeli Lawyers**'s insolvency expertise is reflected in it continuing to receive bankruptcy instructions. As well as the ongoing bankruptcy of Energis (Switzerland) AG, the firm is working on the bankruptcy of HMT High Medical Technologies AG and Printoplast AG, a producer of credit cards.

Partners Marc Bernheim and Philipp Känzig of **Staiger, Schwald & Partner** are acting on notable liquidations which are unlikely to conclude any time soon. For Altraxis, a major subsidiary of Swissair, Bernheim is acting as receiver, whereas Känzig is representing the liquidators of the Moore Park Group of companies, which was at the centre of a large investment fund fraud perpetuated in Switzerland.

Recommended partner David Jenny of **VISCHER**'s Basle office acts as court-appointed trustee for Menag Energie AG. Other major projects handled by the firm include acting as a member of the creditors' committee in the breakdown of Erb Group, and advising the private and public shareholders of a regional television broadcasting company on its financial restructuring.

The ongoing Swissair insolvency continues to provide work for 'reliable and efficient' **Walder Wyss & Partners**, along with the majority of the leading firms in Switzerland. The firm represents banks such as Citibank NA, Hypovereinsbank and KfW in composition proceedings relating to the airline insolvency. Enrico Friz is praised in this area for being 'an excellent lawyer, always trying to find practical solutions'.

Bratschi Emch Rechtsanwälte is acting on two of the highest-profile bankruptcies in Switzerland. Partner Professor Jürgen Brönnimann lectures in bankruptcy law, is assisting on the drafting of the new federal civil procedure law, and represents clients in insolvency procedures.

Grüninger Hunziker Roth is involved in the composition proceedings of Swiss Dairy Food AG, acting for a consortium of banks and also as a member of the creditors' committee. For INB Industrias Nucleares do Brazil, a uranium mining company, the firm has been retained on the bankruptcy of Nuexco Exchange AG, and for Newco AG in further composition proceedings amounting to US$250m.

Lenz & Staehelin has advised creditors in the headline insolvency proceedings of Swissair and Erb Group. In the former mainly creditors in the aircraft leasing industry are represented. The firm also advised a bank syndicate in the bankruptcy of the Swiss parent company of an international technology group.

Niederer Kraft & Frey has particular competence in the fields of collection, bankruptcy and financial reorganisations.

Principally acting for its French-speaking clients, **Python Schifferli Peter** undertakes restructuring, insolvency, bankruptcy and asset-tracing instructions.

Roesle Frick & Partners concentrates on insolvency work as a consequence of the established practice of founding partner Max Roesle. He serves on the creditor committee for a major airline, as court-appointed liquidator (internet and voice services provider and property company), and as bankruptcy administrator.

INTELLECTUAL PROPERTY

Focussing on trade mark and IT-related matters, the IP practice group at **Baker & McKenzie** has acted on a number of significant cases, often with an international dimension. The firm advised leading Swiss watch company IWC on complex trade mark litigation in Switzerland and Germany. Further cross-border proceedings were handled

INTELLECTUAL PROPERTY

BAKER & McKENZIE ✪
HOMBURGER ✪
LENZ & STAEHELIN ✪
MEYER LUSTENBERGER ✪
THOMANNFISCHER
WALDER WYSS & PARTNERS ✪

Bär & Karrer ✪
Froriep Renggli ✪
Pestalozzi Lachenal Patry ✪
Schellenberg Wittmer ✪
Troller Hitz Troller & Partners
Vischer ✪

Grüninger Hunziker Roth
Hess Dallafior Attorneys at Law ✪
Junod Guyet Muhlstein & Lévy
Python Schifferli Peter ✪
Rinderknecht Klein & Stadelhofer ✪
Staiger, Schwald & Partner ✪
Wenger Plattner ✪

Firms are listed A-Z in tiers which are ranked in order of priority
✪ Indicates firm displays contact details at the end of this chapter.

for Esprit and pen manufacturer Prodir. Nestlé and Roche also instruct the firm on trade mark and domain name matters. Partner Michael Treis is recommended 'who has often added value by offering proactive advice and possible solutions in order to enhance the strength of our IP'.

Homburger's IP team headed by Werner Stieger is particularly active in IP litigation. For F Hoffmann-La Roche AG Stieger acted against a US patent owner over an alleged infringement of a research tool patent, and for medical manufacturer Aerocrine A/B on a case against a Swiss party. In both cases he was assisted by associate Fritz Blumer. Andri Hess assisted Stieger on other cases, including acting for Swiss private banks in a domain name-grabbing claim against a Swiss consulting firm, and on landmark litigation relating to whether the use of patented technology necessitated obtaining a licence to sell a drug.

Lenz & Staehelin has a comprehensive IP practice serving a broad range of corporate clients. Trade mark and design protection, IP litigation, research and development and licensing arrangements are just some of the services provided.

'Very competent in trade marks in particular and also copyright,' **Meyer Lustenberger**'s IP team is led by Michael Ritscher who is recommended by clients. The department has expanded by three fee-earners in the past year enhancing its capacity to serve noteworthy clients such as Swiss RE, Migros and and IT company CSC. Significant work includes assisting a major company in the finance and insurance sector to reorganise and enforce its trade mark portfolio, and also protecting the copyright and three-dimensional trade marks globally of a leading manufacturer of design furniture classics.

Ideally located in Basle, **Thomannfischer** is able to cater for the IP needs of companies in the IT, e-commerce, chemical and pharmaceutical industries. The firm has represented several multinational pharmaceutical companies in patent litigation involving generics and is acting for international clients in trade mark disputes.

Walder Wyss & Partners advises various Swiss and international clients on patent matters (registering, licensing, franchising, merchandising), and represents them in litigation proceedings to stop those IP rights from being infringed. Copyright and trade mark expertise is also to hand.

Bär & Karrer's six-lawyer IP group has the expertise to facilitate the creation and exploitation of inventions, trade marks, designs and copyright-related products. Contractual advice for artists, producers and distributors in the entertainment industry is also provided.

Froriep Renggli's IP department is run by Roger Staub, who is recommended by clients. The group provides a full range of services, encompassing the IP aspects of joint ventures and arbitration, as well as traditional IP litigation and licensing.

A landmark telecommunications IP case dominated **Pestalozzi Lachenal Patry**'s practice in 2005. The firm acted for a major telecoms provider, where foreign broadcasters sought to prohibit it from re-broadcasting analogue and digital programmes. The litigation is copyright oriented, but also had IT, competition and telecommunications law aspects, with the decision being published in a Swiss IP journal.

Schellenberg Wittmer represents its blue-chip clients regularly on trade mark matters. The sale of Frantour SA to Kuoni group had substantial trade mark implications, and the firm also advised a client on a CHF-multi-million purchase of a very large trade mark portfolio from a leading multinational company. An international airline was represented in a trade mark and unfair competition dispute, and recommended partner Andrea Mondini has served as a panellist on WIPO arbitrations and mediations concerning domain name disputes. One client noted: 'Their work was excellent. Their advice was succinct and practical.'

VISCHER has recently hired biotechnology expert Stefan Kohler who has boosted the firm's practice. Partner Rolf Auf der Maur is instructed by telecommunications and televisual media clients on convergence issues, specifically music distribution and audio-visual content.

Grüninger Hunziker Roth has strengthened its team headed by Daniel Marugg with the appointment of IP specialist Michael Meer. The principal cases in 2005 were advising the Academy of Motion Picture Arts and Sciences regarding infringement of the 'Oscar' statuette copyright/trade mark, establishing an IP holding company for IT player Magirus Group, and acting for a major European pharmaceuticals distributor on parallel imports of patented drugs.

Python Schifferli Peter has strength and depth in its IP department and both the Geneva and Bern offices are busy. Copyright, domain-name litigation and trade mark expertise are all offered.

Rinderknecht Klein & Stadelhofer represents a leading Swiss media company on copyright transactions, is Swiss counsel on licensing restructuring and licensing litigation of an international drug-delivery company, and is general counsel for a leading European classical music agency as to copyright issues. 'They are very responsive and we value their work as being of a high international standard,' reported one media client.

Staiger, Schwald & Partner provides a full range of services to its clients encompassing all of the traditional facets of IP law.

Concentrating on copyright law, **Wenger Plattner**'s Basle office represents a number of global publishers in actions against plagiarists of online content and free riders, as well as being involved in the legislative process for the revision of the Swiss Copyright Act.

MERGERS AND ACQUISITIONS

Its role in advising on one of the largest public takeovers in 2005 underscores **Baker & McKenzie**'s expertise; the firm acted on the CHF1.4bn (€903m) takeover of optical concern Leica by global technology group Hexagon. Other CHF-multi-million deals include acting for Permira on the CHF835m-plus (€538.6m) acquisition of Jet Aviation, for PSP Swiss Property AG on the CHF230m (€148.4m) purchase of GFG Gesellschaft für Grundeigentum, and the CHF160m (€103.2m) sale of Bank of New York to Intermaritime Bank. One client commented that the firm has: 'a professional team able to solve all relevant issues in a professional manner'.

The M&A team at **Bär & Karrer** spearheaded by corporate legend Rolf Watter, acted on two sizeable deals in 2005: for Cablecom on its sale to Liberty Global for CHF4.4bn (€2.8bn); and acting for UBS on its sale of a CHF1.3bn (€839.6m) stake in Motor-Columbus. The firm was also retained to advise on the merger between Swiss Prime Site AG and Maag Holding AG to create Switzerland's second-largest real estate company, and worked on the takeover of Swissair by Lufthansa.

Homburger has acted on one of the most public takeovers in 2005, representing motor system company Johnson Electric in its capacity as preferential 'white-knight' bidder for SWX-listed company Saia Burgess. The latter had been subject to a competing CHF560m (€361.3m) takeover offer from Sumida. The team also acted as transaction counsel in the spin-off of Dottikon ES Holding AG from EMS-Chemie Holding AG, and

MERGERS AND ACQUISITIONS

BAKER & McKENZIE ✪
BÄR & KARRER ✪
HOMBURGER ✪
LENZ & STAEHELIN ✪
NIEDERER KRAFT & FREY ✪
PESTALOZZI LACHENAL PATRY ✪
SCHELLENBERG WITTMER ✪

Froriep Renggli ✪
Meyer Lustenberger ✪
Vischer ✪
Walder Wyss & Partners ✪

CMS von Erlach Henrici ✪
Grüninger Hunziker Roth
Python Schifferli Peter ✪
Rinderknecht Klein & Stadelhofer ✪
Staiger, Schwald & Partner ✪
Tavernier Tschanz
Wenger Plattner ✪
Wenger & Vieli ✪

Badertscher Dörig Poledna ✪
Borel & Barbey ✪
Bratschi Emch Rechtsanwälte ✪
Hess Dallafior Attorneys at Law ✪
Roesle Frick & Partners
Suter Howald Attorneys at Law ✪
Thouvenin Rechtsanwälte ✪

Firms are listed A-Z in tiers which are ranked in order of priority
✪ *Indicates firm displays contact details at the end of this chapter.*

was lead counsel to cement company Holcim on its acquisition of Associated Cement Companies, the second-largest cement manufacturer in India. Partner Daniel Daeniker is respected by clients for being 'bright and aggressive.'

Acquisitions comprise the majority of **Lenz & Staehelin**'s M&A workload, the greatest in value being the CHF6.5bn (€4.19bn) acquisition of UBS's private banking business by Bank Julius Bär. Grupo Ferrovial was represented on its acquisition of Swissport, and CVC capital on its takeover bid for Forbo Holding. The firm also acted for Danaher on a bid for Leica Geosystems. On the sales side, Swisslife instructed the team on its sale of insurance portfolios to Helsana and La Vaudoise.

In the headline-grabbing Saia Burgess takeover, **Niederer Kraft & Frey** acted for the target, defending it from the unwanted advances of Sumida in the proposed CHF560m (€361.3m) transaction. The team has had a high volume of CHF-multi-million deals, in particular representing Bayer Healthcare AG on its purchase of Hoffmann-La Roche's OTC business for €2.2bn, and advising on the merger between Swissfirst AG and Bellevue AG for CHF700m (€451.5m) in the financial services industry.

Completing the triumvirate of advisers in the Saia Burgess takeover is **Pestalozzi Lachenal Patry**, who acted for Sumida in its unsolicited CHF560m (€361.3m) offer for the motor manufacturer. Other high-profile clients in this sector are Glencore, Johnson & Johnson and Coca-Cola.

Currently **Schellenberg Wittmer** is acting for the bidding bank in the massive €20bn potential acquisition of another European bank. The firm also acted for the majority of shareholders of Jet Aviation on the nine-figure sale to Permira Funds. Building materials company Lafarge was represented on the €92m acquisition of Hupfer group, and GE Infrastructure Security, a subsidiary of General Electric sought the firm's expertise on its purchase of Visiowave SA. Partners Lorenzo Olgiati and Martin Weber are recommended, and one banking client stated: 'They have a direct and straightforward approach to legal issues which corresponds to our own business philosophy.'

Froriep Renggli's biggest deal via its London office in the past year was assisting private equity operator Clayton Dubilier & Rice in connection with its €2.4bn acquisition of the Rexel division of Pinault Printemps Redoute. The firm also advised Viseca Card Services SA on the nine-figure purchase of Aduna SA, the Visa and Mastercard credit and debit card business. The latter had complex competition law implications. Beat Barthold is recommended and the firm as a whole 'demonstrates a broad spectrum of service and expertise. All objects were delivered in the highest quality and in time'.

Meyer Lustenberger has been involved in a number of important national and international transactions, often acting as lead counsel, an example being acting for Bauholding/STRABAG in the acquisition of the Egolf group of companies. The firm has also assisted clients seeking to acquire SWX-listed companies Aletsch and Pelikan. Partner Christopher Heiz 'is a proven expert in (public) Swiss capital markets transactions'.

The M&A teams in both the Zurich and Basle offices of **VISCHER** are experiencing growth. Notable deals acted on include representing private equity firm Lindsay Goldberg & Bessemer on the acquisition of Klöckner from WestLB, acting on behalf of ABB on the sale of its building installation business to CapVis, and for Hansa Aktiengesellschaft on a public tender offer for Pelham Investments SA followed by a squeeze-out and delisting. One major rail company client recommends Jürg Luginbühl and Felix Heusler, noting 'efficiency, quality and availability are some of the qualities'.

In 2005, **Walder Wyss & Partners** acted for two blue-chip companies on acquisitions: Microsoft on the acquisition of media-stream.com; and on behalf of Swisscom on its purchase of Cinetrade.

CMS von Erlach Henrici over the past year has advised on a number of SME transactions. The CMS network and previous M&A strength of recent merger partner *Henrici, Wicki & Guggisberg*, are valuable additions.

The biggest value deal for **Grüninger Hunziker Roth** recently was acting as Swiss counsel to the buyer in connection with a US$4.2bn acquisition of INVISTA from DuPont de Nemours; the target is the world's largest integrated fibre, resin and intermediates company. The firm also advised two NYSE-listed companies on deals – firstly for Spirent plc (network technology company) on the divestiture of its interests in Wago Group for £60.7m, and for ResMed Inc (sleep-disordered breathing apparatus producer), on its acquisition of Labhardt AG. Founding partners Marc Grüninger, Bruno Hunziker and Gerhard Roth are all recommended by clients.

Python Schifferli Peter has experienced demand in due diligence instructions, as well as being retained by companies on arbitrations arising out of M&A.

Rinderknecht Klein & Stadelhofer was transaction counsel for a leading Swiss media company on its takeover of an IT company, was special counsel on the refinancing and strategic sale of a pharmaceutical concern to a bigger player, and acted for a US company in the same field on its acquisition of a company together with its European affiliates. One client praised name partner Thomas Rinderknecht for his 'combination of business sense and pragmatism and for being very thorough in financial transactions'.

Stemming from **Staiger, Schwald & Partner** working on the first-ever IPO of a Swiss ice-hockey team, in 2005 the firm acted on one of the biggest sales of a Swiss sports organisation.

Tavernier Tschanz has acted on a plethora of acquisitions and disposals, most notably a world leader in security inks for bank notes retained the firm on the sale of its packaging and inks division. One client enthused: 'They always try to find really practical and pragmatic solutions.'

Wenger Plattner has been advising a number of supply companies in the substantial increase of their share in a utility, advised a US company on its acquisition of a Swiss tool supplier, and has been retained as due diligence counsel on a number of global transactions.

Wenger & Vieli has three partners dedicated to M&A work and joint ventures. Public takeovers are handled and the firm was also instructed on the takeover of Scintilla by Robert Bosch.

In 2005, **Badertscher Dörig Poledna** was instructed on the merger of two SWX-listed IT companies.

Two principal transactions were handled by **Borel & Barbey** in 2005. The firm acted for the buyer on the acquisition of the controlling stake of Banque Baring Brothers (Suisse) SA, and was retained as Swiss counsel for the German ink company Siegwerk Druckfarben AG on its acquisition of Swiss player Sicpa. The latter transaction was complicated by the cross-jurisdictional issues, especially as the target markets its goods in a number of countries. Partners Nicolas Killen and Nicolas Piérard are the most prominent in the M&A field.

Seeking to become one of the leading players in pharmaceutical law, **Bratschi Emch Rechtsanwälte** has broadened its practice by acting on a takeover of a Swiss pharmaceutical company by an Italian rival. Other deals encompass the areas of ground transportation, publishing, sports clubs and the technology sector.

Hess Dallafior Attorneys at Law represented the selling shareholder in the sale of a family enterprise to a private equity investor, one of the largest such transactions in Switzerland in recent times. The firm obtained the instruction as a consequence of its focus on providing a personalised partner-driven service.

Roesle Frick & Partners, led by corporate heavyweight Max Roesle, has represented a real estate company on its sale to a publicly listed rival for €200m.

Handling a number of small and mid-sized transactions, **Suter Howald Attorneys at Law** had a busy year. On the acquisitions side, clients were represented on the purchases of a real estate company and a cosmetics line, as well as representing the management in an MBO. On the disposal side, a foreign corporation was assisted in the sale of assets of its Swiss subsidiary. One client commented: 'Not only did we receive good advice that led to a certain goal, but also they include our needs into their strategy and showed us potential risks and opportunities. Very professional.'

Thouvenin Rechtsanwälte's M&A group is fronted by David Känzig. Domestically, the firm represented a large private equity firm on the sale of its real estate holding to a publicly listed company, and also acted for the sellers of a privately owned telecommunications provider to a European listed company. Internationally, a Chinese company was advised on its Swiss and German textile company acquisitions, and a *Fortune 500* company on its acquisition of a Swiss concern.

PRIVATE BANKING

Located in the heart of Switzerland's private banking market in Geneva, **Baker & McKenzie** has a significant market share in various aspects of private banking work relating to tax and estate planning for individuals and families, as well as advising banks, trust companies and financial intermediaries on the services they provide to clients.

Specialising in acting for high-net-worth individuals, **Bär & Karrer** has a long-standing tradition in advising private clients and their families in personal matters. Estate planning relating to personal and commercial assets, and setting up of legal structures in foreign jurisdictions, are regularly advised on.

PRIVATE BANKING

BAKER & McKENZIE ✪
BÄR & KARRER ✪
NIEDERER KRAFT & FREY ✪
PESTALOZZI LACHENAL PATRY ✪

Borel & Barbey ✪
Lenz & Staehelin ✪
Poncet Turrettini Amaudruz Neyroud & Partners
Python Schifferli Peter ✪
Schellenberg Wittmer ✪
Tavernier Tschanz
Vischer ✪

Altenburger
CMS von Erlach Henrici ✪
Froriep Renggli ✪
Rinderknecht Klein & Stadelhofer ✪
Staiger, Schwald & Partner ✪
Umbricht Rechtsanwälte ✪
Wenger Plattner ✪

Firms are listed A-Z in tiers which are ranked in order of priority
✪ Indicates firm displays contact details at the end of this chapter.

Niederer Kraft & Frey has two partners exclusively dedicated to private banking-related clients. Numerous high-net-worth individuals are represented regarding asset management, inheritance, tax law and tax planning.

Pestalozzi Lachenal Patry primarily advises on complex questions regarding matrimonial property law and succession law for its affluent private clients, as well as assisting with questions on retirement planning and the establishment of foundations and trusts.

Borel & Barbey's private banking team has successfully exploited the booming private wealth management market, serving a number of high-net-worth foreign individuals seeking to invest in the locality. Trust and estate planning is also a strength, and the firm has close relationships with numerous private banks in Geneva.

Lenz & Staehelin offers know-how in setting up and managing trusts, and is able to utilise three in-house English law trust specialists, of which Richard Pease is the most notable. Wealth management and protection services are also offered, together with private bank restructuring expertise.

Python Schifferli Peter is seeking to expand its private banking group, which already represents a number of high-profile artists and sportsmen via partner Thomas Steinmann.

Schellenberg Wittmer has historically focussed on the provision of private banking services, with an international team of lawyers able to exploit expertise acquired in foreign jurisdictions. Clients include a major German industrial trust and Middle Eastern families. The firm also has strong links with private banks, with partners such as Bernard Vischer also sitting on the boards of those banks.

Tavernier Tschanz acts commonly for private banks and private individuals, offering trusts and estates expertise for the latter.

VISCHER is active in the private banking sector, assisting small and medium-sized banks on regulatory and compliance matters. In 2005 the firm was instructed on the complete reorganisation of a family owned private bank, which had regulatory, IT and succession implications. Wealthy private clients are offered banking, asset management, credit security and estate planning advice.

ALTENBURGER's private banking department is closely linked to its tax department, offering compliance and efficiency expertise. The firm also advises on new structures for old family businesses and has experienced an upturn in foreign referrals.

The merger to create **CMS von Erlach Henrici** has enhanced the combined private banking team.

Froriep Renggli advises wealthy individuals, prominent families and private banks regarding holding, preserving and the transfer of assets. With the benefit of contacts in major foreign jurisdictions, the firm is able to offer an integrated, specialised legal service for its international private clients. Tax planning services are also available.

Rinderknecht Klein & Stadelhofer is retained by high-net-worth individuals to advise on transactions, such as negotiating and documenting the purchases of yachts and private jets. The firm also structures and administers family offices and estates for international private clients.

Staiger, Schwald & Partner concentrates on acting for all sizes of Swiss private banks, catering for their civil, regulatory and banking requirements. The strength of the firm's expertise is mirrored by the directorial appointments to the boards of banks of the partners.

Private banking-related work amounts to 40% of **Umbricht Rechtsanwälte**'s banking practice. Around 50% of clients are foreign or have foreign jurisdiction problems. Accordingly the team has a great deal of international experience. Analysis of old tax structures, inheritance problems, and the relocation of high-net-worth individuals and mid-sized corporations to Switzerland are issues regularly handled. Partner Georg Umbricht deals with multi-jurisdictional tax structuring.

Wenger Plattner has a boutique private banking department in its Zurich office, catering for the needs of Swiss and foreign high-net-worth individuals. Estate planning, risk strategies, asset management and tax considerations are on offer.

REAL ESTATE AND CONSTRUCTION

Baker & McKenzie's recent work has been property finance-related. Significant instructions include acting for Eurohypo AG on the acquisition financing of a large commercial property to the tune of CHF73m (€47.4m), and on behalf of Aareal Bank, advising on the acquisition financing of the CHF100m (€64.7m) real estate portfolio of a large Swiss retailer. The team was also instructed by WTF Holdings (Switzerland) Ltd on its CHF100m-plus (€64.7m) divestiture of various Swiss properties. One real estate client noted: '**Baker & McKenzie** approaches the issues from a sound business perspective.'

Acquisitions dominate **Lenz & Staehelin**'s real estate practice. The firm advised Apollo Real Estate Advisors on the sale and partial lease-back transaction amounting to CHF90m (€58.2m), Deutsche Bank and EuroHypo retained the team to advise on various acquisitions and development loans, and foreign investors sought advice on the acquisition of several large commercial projects ranging from CHF35m to CHF680m (€22.6m-€439.8m). The firm also regularly advises retail chains in respect of store leases, and represented two large construction companies regarding the execution of general building contracts worth CHF300m (€194.1m) and CHF220m (€142.3m) respectively.

Schumacher Baur Hürlimann is a real estate specialist, in particular advising on the construction of industrial plants and public construction projects. Both international and domestic clients are assisted with the drafting of construction contracts and joint ventures. The firm also has the capability to undertake construction litigation.

CMS von Erlach Henrici has experienced growth in the real estate sector and is involved in most of the big transactions in the market, commonly representing institutional investors and major real estate players. Former name partner Dietrich Stettler is recognised for advising on Zurich property.

Meyer Lustenberger represents two of the largest Swiss real estate corporations, as well as advising the seller on the sale of a building company, and acting on the merger of two building companies. The firm's strength in this area is reflected in name partner Thomas Lustenberger acting as chairman of the third-largest real estate company in Switzerland.

With a long-standing commitment to real estate, **Schellenberg Wittmer** has structured and negotiated the acquisition (sale and leaseback) of 18 commercial properties previously owned by Coop worth over CHF200m (€129.4m), and represented Chinese investors on their CHF44m (€28.5m) purchase of a landmark commercial building in Geneva. The firm has also been involved in drafting the documents to facilitate the construction and leasing of major new buildings.

Wenger Plattner is able to offer the industry expertise of partners who have sat on the boards of and acted as consultants to publicly listed real estate and construction management companies. Procedures for obtaining building permits for large commercial clients, and litigation concerning public and private disputes are typical services offered.

REAL ESTATE AND CONSTRUCTION

BAKER & McKENZIE ✪
LENZ & STAEHELIN ✪
SCHUMACHER BAUR HÜRLIMANN

CMS von Erlach Henrici ✪
Meyer Lustenberger ✪
Schellenberg Wittmer ✪
Wenger Plattner ✪

Bratschi Emch Rechtsanwälte ✪
Bürgi Nägeli Lawyers ✪
Lalive & Partners
Python Schifferli Peter ✪
Roesle Frick & Partners
Suter Howald Attorneys at Law ✪
Vischer ✪

Firms are listed A-Z in tiers which are ranked in order of priority
✪ Indicates firm displays contact details at the end of this chapter.

Bratschi Emch Rechtsanwälte's real estate department is strong on public law matters, in particular in the representation of public bodies and communities regarding pending new regulations of the Zurich airport operation. In Bern, local construction and planning advice provided.

Bürgi Nägeli Lawyers has been working on various contract portfolios for Zentrum Zürich Nord, an extensive building project of contaminated and polluted sites. Name partner Gudrun Bürgi who specialises in contamination and pollution law annually organises and speaks at the post-graduate convention on contaminated sites in Fribourg. The firm also undertakes restructuring work, and has a network of offices in Zurich, Zug, St Gall, Basle and Bern.

Roesle Frick & Partners acts exclusively for a real estate company holding a CHF300m (€193.9m) property portfolio.

Instructions over the past year for **Suter Howald Attorneys at Law** encompass conducting real estate due diligence on the main property of a Swiss subsidiary in anticipation of an AIM listing, rendering advice for a client on a 20,000 sq m commercial lease, and undertaking traditional real estate transactions.

VISCHER was retained by Deutsche Bank in connection with its successful sale and lease back of parts of its European real estate portfolio, as well as providing an environmental impact assessment of a sizeable parking-lot construction project.

TMT

Baker & McKenzie continues to advise its existing and new clients in connection with regulatory and contractual issues in the telecoms sector, and has also been instructed on several restructuring and litigation assignments.

In 2005 on behalf of parties in a joint venture agreement, **Bär & Karrer** acted as transaction counsel regarding the outsourcing of IT and back office services to banks for an undisclosed amount.

Homburger handles a great deal of contentious TMT work. The firm is advising a sports marketing agency on an international arbitration regarding the termination of a TV broadcast sub-licence agreement, and is lead counsel to a Turkish mobile operator in an ICC arbitration with a UK hardware supplier. Another dispute involves international TV signal overspill. On the non-contentious side, the firm continues to advise a car importation and dealing group on a large IT integration project. One IT product-related client praised the firm as being 'committed, hands on and to the point.'

As a product of publishing frequently on internet law from the mid-1990s **Python Schifferli Peter** has established expertise in this field, and in particular is advising clients on IT arbitrations and the IP implications of voiceover internet protocol software. Partners Thomas Legler and Pierre-Yves Gunter are specialists.

Walder Wyss & Partners is able to exploit its membership of the *TechLaw Group* in serving its TMT clients. Over the past year outsourcing projects for Zurich Financial Services has kept the firm busy.

ALTENBURGER focuses on representing clients in the music industry, with concert organisers, theatres and music clients all instructing the firm.

Bratschi Emch Rechtsanwälte often advises web design and web publishing companies and also litigates on behalf of clients concerning failed IT projects. A case involving a search engine dispute proceeded to the Federal Court of Justice (Switzerland's highest court). The firm also represents media groups, and advises a large international sports and entertainment corporation as to its acquisitions and construction projects.

Hess Dallafior Attorneys at Law acts for one of the few private Swiss TV stations, providing full-service advice on distribution and contracts. The firm has also been instructed to comment upon a new TV Bill.

Lenz & Staehelin has frequently been instructed on IT matters in the banking market, advising Bank Vontobel on its business process insourcing from Raiffeisen Group, on its transaction bank set-up with Avaloq Technology, and representing Sopra Group on its development and licensing of Basel II reporting systems with Zurich Cantonal Bank.

Pestalozzi Lachenal Patry advised a major online auctioneer regarding the responsibility for auctioned goods violating the law, and a major

TMT

BAKER & McKENZIE ✪
BÄR & KARRER ✪
HOMBURGER ✪
PYTHON SCHIFFERLI PETER ✪
WALDER WYSS & PARTNERS ✪

Altenburger
Bratschi Emch Rechtsanwälte ✪
Hess Dallafior Attorneys at Law ✪
Lenz & Staehelin ✪
Pestalozzi Lachenal Patry ✪
Tavernier Tschanz
Vischer ✪
Wenger Plattner ✪
Wiederkehr Forster

Badertscher Dörig Poledna ✪
Bill Isenegger Ackermann ✪
CMS von Erlach Henrici ✪
Meyer Lustenberger ✪
Niederer Kraft & Frey ✪
Prager Dreifuss
Schellenberg Wittmer ✪
Stiffler & Partner ✪
Wyss Wiesli Rechtsanwälte

Firms are listed A-Z in tiers which are ranked in order of priority
✪ *Indicates firm displays contact details at the end of this chapter.*

transport company on a multi-million-dollar outsourcing transaction in India.

Tavernier Tschanz's TMT practice represents technology companies and companies confronted with new technologies law issues. The firm has specific expertise in assisting clients on complex IT projects, such as software development, systems integration, ASP solutions, application management, business process and IT outsourcing.

Partner Rolf Auf der Maur of **VISCHER** advises Swiss and foreign broadcasters including VIVA and Bloomberg. Swisscom internet subsidiary Bluewin AG recently received copyright and regulatory advice. The firm is also regularly retained on outsourcing projects.

Wenger Plattner assists national and foreign companies on IT supply and procurement projects. The firm advised a large supplier of handheld computers on digital rights management issues, and has also experienced a great increase in IT outsourcing advice. In the latter, two large-scale outsourcing projects in the banking sector have been advised on, one involving the migration of 11 banks to a new IT platform.

In the IT and telecoms industry, **Badertscher Dörig Poledna** is experienced in drafting a wide variety of IT agreements, and provides general legal advice to start-ups, portals and ISPs.

BILL ISENEGGER ACKERMANN acted for a Swiss corporation in a technology transfer and licence deal with a large US-listed company in the medical devices field. The transaction was an exclusive licence agreement, with various development agreements connected to it. One IT client who recommends name partners Urs Isenegger and Markus Bill enthused: 'Bill Isenegger Ackermann is really an excellent law firm, and its partners really care about client service – day and night.'

Though the telecoms market is experiencing a period of consolidation, **CMS von Erlach Henrici** still advises clients in this field regarding their day-to-day business.

Four main areas are offered by **Meyer Lustenberger**'s IT and e-commerce team: software licence agreements, IT projects, consumer and data protection laws and domain name protection.

Niederer Kraft & Frey regularly advises banks on their IT issues including outsourcing to other banks and third parties.

Schellenberg Wittmer acts for leading local telecoms company Swisscom AG, as well as a major search engine and a registrar of internet domain names. For the latter, the firm was instructed on an arbitration, and the partners of the team act as panellists on WIPO arbitrations concerning domain name disputes.

Stiffler & Partner specialises in telecommunications law representing clients' interests before Swiss administrative agencies (the Communication Commission, the Federal Office for Communications and the Federal Competition Commission).

Wyss Wiesli Rechtsanwälte advised an investment bank on its worldwide IT outsourcing activities, represented a major financial intermediary on its new €30m-plus IT service location, and coordinated the legal implementation of a technology firm's online platform in over 50 jurisdictions. A leading Swiss web agency also retains the firm on its large-scale projects.

TAX

Baker & McKenzie's Swiss offices deal with a broad range of individual and business tax issues, as well as giving tax planning advice and structuring tax-efficient transactions. Typical tax-related arrangements offered by the firm are shareholder agreements, business succession planning and estate planning.

The tax team at **Homburger** works closely with its corporate lawyers, in particular on joint ventures, cross-border transactions, private equity and international projects. Top executive tax planning, employee share schemes and tax planning for high-net-worth individuals is also undertaken. Eveline Saupper is recommended together with the team, whose work 'demonstrates tremendous depth and breadth of knowledge that gives you tremendous comfort as a client'.

Lenz & Staehelin provides tax planning advice and represents clients in court proceedings and dealings with tax authorities. The firm is sensitive to cross-border aspects, and is able to work with foreign law firms in the provision of such advice.

Oberson & Partners led by recommended name partner Xavier Oberson is a specialist tax firm, offering domestic and international expertise in all of the principal tax fields, encompassing income, corporate, inter-Cantonal and withholding taxes, as well as the taxation of sport, the entertainment business and wealthy individuals.

The strength of **Pestalozzi Lachenal Patry**'s tax department is evident from the fact that four of its fee-earners hold a number of eminent tax positions at Swiss universities (professorships, lectureships), tax boards (Zurich Board of Tax Appeals), and international associations (International Fiscal Association).

Schellenberg Wittmer in 2004 boosted its tax capacity with the hire of Madeleine Simonek a professor of tax law at the University of Lucerne and former partner at **Pestalozzi Lachenal Patry**. Significant tax input on deals in 2005 included to Karstadt Quelle AG, tax advice on a term loan, seasonal and revolving credit agreement and the provision of Swiss collateral totalling US$2.1bn, and advising on the tax aspects of various private placements for Mizuho International plc. Johnson Controls AG instructed the team to comment on the tax structuring of its Swiss operations.

Being one of the first firms to harness international tax expertise, **ALTENBURGER** specialises in tax, regularly giving tax planning and corporate restructuring advice.

The ten-lawyer team at **Bär & Karrer** regularly advises on a wide range of tax issues, as well as working with the firm's corporate lawyers on deals, which have significant tax implications, such as takeovers, mergers and liquidations.

Meyer Lustenberger acts as advisor to the Swiss government and to government-controlled corporations. Major Swiss banks seek the firm's advice as to tax structures relating to their products, and advice is given for the tax planning of international venture capital structures. VAT specialist Manuel Vogel is recommended, together with Adriano Marantelli, 'a first-class expert in Swiss corporate tax law'.

The tax group at **Python Schifferli Peter** has expanded recently and is seeking to further expand over the next 12 months. The firm offers corporate tax advice to banks, in addition to having a specialist team which only deals with SMEs. The Lausanne office mainly deals with high-net-worth individuals from the arts and sports worlds.

Counting a large number of qualified tax experts as members of its tax team, **VISCHER** represents corporate and individual clients in all aspects of taxation in Switzerland, especially on cross-border transactions with Germany, the US and the UK.

TAX

BAKER & McKENZIE ✪
HOMBURGER ✪
LENZ & STAEHELIN ✪
OBERSON & PARTNERS
PESTALOZZI LACHENAL PATRY ✪
SCHELLENBERG WITTMER ✪

Altenburger
Bär & Karrer ✪
Meyer Lustenberger ✪
Python Schifferli Peter ✪
Vischer ✪
Walder Wyss & Partners ✪

Borel & Barbey ✪
Bratschi Emch Rechtsanwälte ✪
CMS von Erlach Henrici ✪
Gillioz Dorsaz & Associés ✪
Grüninger Hunziker Roth
Niederer Kraft & Frey ✪
Rinderknecht Klein & Stadelhofer ✪
Staiger, Schwald & Partner ✪
Umbricht Rechtsanwälte ✪

Firms are listed A-Z in tiers which are ranked in order of priority
✪ *Indicates firm displays contact details at the end of this chapter.*

Walder Wyss & Partners has experienced a 40% increase in revenue deriving from tax work and is retained by Swiss and international clients on various tax matters, including transfer pricing and VAT. Tax structuring of transactions is also often dealt with.

Borel & Barbey's tax group overlaps with the legal services provided by the other groups in the firm, often advising beyond Swiss borders. Recently Middle East investors were advised on the tax implications of private equity placements and sales relating to the acquisition of large commercial properties.

Bratschi Emch Rechtsanwälte has tax partners with previous experience at major accountancy firms, and advises corporations and private clients on a wide range of national and international tax. The group works closely with other teams in the firm and is seeking to grow in 2006.

The importance of the CMS network gives a crucial advantage to **CMS von Erlach Henrici**, as the Swiss office over the past year has received a number of instructions from the French, Italian and German offices in the group.

The three-lawyer tax team at **Gillioz Dorsaz & Associés** is experiencing continued growth, and regularly advises corporate clients on indirect taxes and VAT issues.

Grüninger Hunziker Roth acts as tax counsel in Switzerland for two US corporations, for 3Com a Nasdaq-listed IT company, and ResMed Inc which is listed on the NYSE. Swiss mobile phone software concern Esmertec also instructed the firm in connection with the tax considerations of a CHF33m (€21.3m) convertible notes purchase facility.

Niederer Kraft & Frey has a growing tax team which works closely with the other departments. The firm has experienced an increase in work resulting from gradual harmonisation between Switzerland and the EU. The strength of the tax group is enhanced by two senior fee-earners being certified tax experts, both coming from one of the Big Four accountancy firms.

Rinderknecht Klein & Stadelhofer's tax department has assisted the corporate team by providing tax structuring advice for a joint venture between two Russian aluminium companies, and also acting as general counsel for international tax restructuring of various international estates.

Staiger, Schwald & Partner advises on federal and Cantonal taxes, national and international tax planning, the optimisation of corporate restructuring, and the tax consequences of transactions.

Umbricht Rechtsanwälte's Daniel Holenstein has carved a niche in the market as a criminal tax expert, as well as giving legal assistance advice in connection with white-collar crime cases, and is currently handling a huge German extradition action.

TRANSPORT

Benz Attorneys offers contractual, projects, international litigation and arbitration advice to a diverse range of clients from the transport, logistics, ocean carrier, airlines and cargo fields.

TRANSPORT

BENZ ATTORNEYS
SCHELLENBERG WITTMER ✪

Bratschi Emch Rechtsanwälte ✪
Neupert & Partners ✪
Schiller Denzler Dubs Rechtsanwälte
Thouvenin Rechtsanwälte ✪
Vischer ✪

Firms are listed A-Z in tiers which are ranked in order of priority
✪ *Indicates firm displays contact details at the end of this chapter.*

Eponymous partner Christian Benz specialises and recently acted as an expert on the EU evaluation of an intermodal transport law.

Working closely with its dispute resolution group and with experts in both its Zurich and Geneva offices, **Schellenberg Wittmer**'s trade and transport team represents air traffic controller Skyguide and its insurers Winterthur Insurance Company in the ongoing multi-jurisdictional Überlingen litigation. The same clients were represented in defending claims emanating from the Crossair aircraft accident over Bassersdorf. Further defence expertise was provided to air-cargo client Brink's who were sued over the loss of diamonds.

Bratschi Emch Rechtsanwälte is regularly instructed by one of the largest Swiss road transportation and logistics companies, and also has two aviation specialists, one of which often acts for a foreign airline.

Schiller Denzler Dubs Rechtsanwälte specialises in aviation law and continues to represent parties involved in the major airline disasters in Switzerland in recent years.

The automotive field is catered for by **Thouvenin Rechtsanwälte**, with partner Michael Kneller specialising. Major European and US car manufacturers seek the firm's expertise. Other transport-oriented clients include a major national railway.

VISCHER counts aviation as one of the firm's core practice areas, advising major airlines as to their Swiss activities. Logistics and railway clients are also serviced.

BÖCKLI BODMER & PARTNERS

ST JAKOBS-STRASSE 41
4002 BASLE

Telephone: +41 61 317 94 50
Fax: +41 61 317 94 60
E-mail: bbp@boeckli-bodmer.ch
Website: www.boeckli-bodmer.ch

Languages
English, French, German, Italian

Number of lawyers 6

Contact
Dr Christoph B Bühler LLM
(c.buehler@boeckli-bodmer.ch)

International groupings
Swiss Bar Association; Swiss American Chamber of Commerce; ASA; IFA

CATEGORIES OF WORK

Corporate and commercial
Dr Christoph B Bühler, Jan Bangert

Capital markets
Prof Dr Peter Böckli,
Dr Christoph B Bühler

Banking and finance
Prof Dr Peter Böckli,
Dr Christoph B Bühler

Regulatory
Dr Christoph B Bühler

EU and competition law
Dr Christoph B Bühler

Litigation
Dr Bernhard Bodmer, Jan Bangert

Arbitration
Dr Bernhard Bodmer, Jan Bangert

Dispute resolution
Dr Bernhard Bodmer, Jan Bangert

Construction
Dr Agnes Dormann, Nadine Schneider

Employment
Dr Agnes Dormann, Nadine Schneider

Tax
Prof Dr Peter Böckli,
Dr Christoph B Bühler

Real estate and trusts
Dr Bernhard Bodmer,
Dr Agnes Dormann

Intellectual property
Jan Bangert, Nadine Schneider

SIMONIUS PFROMMER & PARTNER

AESCHENVORSTADT 67
4010 BASLE

Telephone: +41 61 206 45 45
Fax: +41 61 206 45 46
E-mail: simoniuspfrommer@advokaten.ch
Website: www.advokaten.ch

Languages
English, French, German, Italian, Portuguese, Spanish

Other offices
Zurich

Number of lawyers 14

Contact
Dr Thomas Burckhardt

Member
DIRO

CATEGORIES OF WORK

Arbitration
Prof Pascal Simonius,
Dr Thomas Burckhardt

Banking
Prof Pascal Simonius,
Emanuel Wiemken

Commercial and contract law
Dr Heiner Schärrer, Dr Erik Johner

Corporate
Dr Thomas Burckhardt,
Bernhard Simonetti

Criminal law
Dr Urs Beat Pfrommer, Susanna Marti

Estate planning and trusts
Bernhard Simonetti,
Dr Thomas Burckhardt

IT and e-commerce, labour
Dr Erik Johner, Susanna Marti

Insolvency and bankruptcy
Emanuel Wiemken, Philipp Simonius

Insurance
Dr Urs Beat Pfrommer,
Dr Heiner Schärrer

Litigation
Prof Pascal Simonius,
Emanuel Wiemken

Mediation
Dr Urs Beat Pfrommer, Susanna Marti

Notarial services
Bernhard Simonetti,
Prof Pascal Simonius

Real estate
Bernhard Simonetti, David Levin

Social security
Dr Urs Beat Pfrommer,
Dr Annemarie Imhof

Taxation
David Levin

Transport, shipping and aviation
Dr Thomas Burckhardt

VISCHER

AESCHENVORSTADT 4
4010 BASLE

Telephone: +41 61 279 33 00
Fax: +41 61 279 33 10
E-mail: lawyers@vischer.com
Website: www.vischer.com

Languages
English, French, German, Italian, Spanish

Number of lawyers 75
at this office 43

Contact
Dr David Jenny

CATEGORIES OF WORK

Arbitration, ADR
Prof Dr Frank Vischer, Dr Thomas Gelzer

Banking
Felix Heusler

Competition
Dr Sebastian Burckhardt,
Dr Thomas Gelzer

Corporate
Dr Christoph Löw, Dr Michael Pfeifer

Employment law
Ursula Hubschmid

Environment
Prof Dr Beatrice Wagner Pfeifer

Estate planning
Dr Bernhard Christ, Dr Niklaus E Schiess

Corporate finance
Dr Matthias Staehelin

Insolvency, bankruptcy
Dr David Jenny, Dr Roland Müller

Intellectual property
Dr Thomas Gelzer

Litigation
Dr Christian Brückner

Mergers and acquisitions
Dr Sebastian Burckhardt,
Dr David Jenny

Civil law notaries
Dr Roland Müller,
Dr Michael Pfeifer

Project finance
Felix Heusler, Dr Christoph Löw

Tax
Dr Hubertus Ludwig,
Thomas Ziegler

WENGER PLATTNER

AESCHENVORSTADT 55
4010 BASLE

Telephone: +41 61 279 70 00
Fax: +41 61 279 70 01
E-mail: basel@wenger-plattner.ch
Website: www.wenger-plattner.ch

Languages
English, French, German, Italian, Portuguese

Other offices
Zurich, Bern

Number of lawyers 50
at this office 18

CATEGORIES OF WORK

Contract and commercial law
Dr Markus Metz, Dr Bernhard Heusler

Corporate, mergers and acquisitions
Dr Dieter Gränicher,
Dr Peter Mosimann

Arbitration
Dr Werner Wenger, Dr Dieter Gränicher

Commercial litigation
Dr Peter Mosimann,
Dr Dieter Gränicher

Civil law notary services
Stephan Cueni, Dr Alexander Gutmans

Constitutional and administrative law
Prof Dr Gerhard Schmid,
Dr Felix Uhlmann

Intellectual property
Dr Peter Mosimann,
Dr Dieter Gränicher

Media, sports and entertainment
Dr Peter Mosimann,
Dr Bernhard Heusler

Social security and labour
Dr Peter Mosimann, Dr Markus Metz

Real estate and construction
Dr Markus Metz, Stephan Cueni

Competition law
Dr Dieter Gränicher,
Prof Dr Gerhard Schmid

Transportation and shipping
Stephan Cueni

Drug and biotechnology law
Prof Dr Gerhard Schmid
Dr Alexander Gutmans

Trusts and estate planning
Dr Werner Wenger

IT and telecoms
Dr Bernhard Heusler, Roland Mathys

BRATSCHI EMCH RECHTSANWÄLTE

BOLLWERK 15
POSTFACH 5576
3001 BERN

Telephone: +41 31 310 19 19
Fax: +41 31 310 19 20
E-mail: berneoffice@bep.ch
Website: www.bep.ch

Languages
English, French, German, Spanish

Other offices
Zürich

Number of lawyers 27
at this office 15

CATEGORIES OF WORK

Contract and commercial law
Dr P Bratschi, Lukas Wyss

Corporate and mergers and acquisitions
Dr P Bratschi, Mark Ineichen

Commercial litigation and arbitration
Dr P Bratschi, Prof Dr J Brönnimann

Banking and finance
Dr U Emch, Dr P Bratschi

Media and communication
Dr P Bratschi, Mark Ineichen

Taxation
Dr Reto Kuster, Bruno Rieder

Health and drug law
Dr P Bratschi, Ursula Eggenberger Stöckli

Environmental and construction law
Ulrich Keusen

Insolvency law
Prof Dr J Brönnimann, Dr U Emch

Competition
Prof Dr J Brönnimann, Mark Ineichen

International successions
Dr U Emch, Prof Dr J Brönnimann

Administrative law
Dr U Emch, Ulrich Keusen

ADVOKATURBUREAU FRIEDLI UND SCHNIDRIG

BAHNHOFPLATZ 5
POSTFACH 6233
3001 BERN

Telephone: +41 31 326 50 00
Fax: +41 31 326 50 10
E-mail: info@fslaw.ch
Website: www.fslaw.ch

Languages
English, French, German, Spanish

Number of lawyers 6

CATEGORIES OF WORK

Corporate

International legal co-operation in civil, criminal and bankruptcy

Banking law (including secrecy issues)

Family law

Inheritance

Litigation

Commercial and securities laws

National and international arbitration (ICC)

Attorney client privilege

NOTTER MÉGEVAND & PARTNERS

WALDEGGSTRASSE 72
PO BOX 84
3097 BERNE-LIEBEFELD

Telephone: +41 31 979 79 79
Fax: +41 31 979 79 80
E-mail: bern@nomea.ch
Website: www.nomea.ch

Languages
English, French, German

Other offices
Geneva, Fribourg

Number of lawyers 18
at this office 10

CATEGORIES OF WORK

Banking and finance	Construction and real estate
Corporate, capital markets and M&A	Insolvency and restructuring
Arbitration and litigation	Family office
Tax	Art
EU and competition	Sports
Civil law	

STAIGER, SCHWALD & PARTNER

THUNSTRASSE 7
PO BOX 281
3000 BERN 6

Telephone: +41 31 356 48 48
Fax: +41 31 356 48 49
E-mail: ssplaw@ssplaw.ch
Website: www.ssplaw.ch

Languages
English, French, German, Italian

Other offices
Zurich

Number of lawyers 31
at this office 6

Contact
Dr Urs Leu

CATEGORIES OF WORK

Arbitration and litigation	EU law and private international law
Banking, securities, finance	Mergers and acquisitions
Company and commercial law	Tax
Insolvency	Wills, trusts and estate planning
Immigration	Media and entertainment
Competition, antitrust, trade marks and copyright	Energy market law

WENGER PLATTNER

JUNGFRAUSTRASSE 1
3000 BERN 6

Telephone: +41 31 357 00 00
Fax: +41 31 357 00 01
E-mail: bern@wenger-plattner.ch
Website: www.wenger-plattner.ch

Languages
English, French, German, Italian

Other offices
Basle, Zurich

Number of lawyers 50
at this office 7

CATEGORIES OF WORK

Civil, contract and commercial law
Dr Jürg Rieben, Dr Fritz Rothenbühler

Banking law
Dr Fritz Rothenbühler

Corporate, M&A
Dr Jürg Rieben

Arbitration
Dr Christoph Müller, Dr Jürg Rieben

Commercial litigation
Dr Jürg Rieben, Dr Fritz Rothenbühler

Bankruptcy and insolvency
Dr Fritz Rothenbühler, Reto Aschenberger

Competition law
Dr Jürg Rieben, Dr Fritz Rothenbühler

Constitutional and administrative law
Andreas Maeschi, Dr Jürg Rieben

Construction and planning
Andreas Maeschi

Family law
Andreas Maeschi

Inheritance law
Andreas Maeschi

Intellectual property and trade mark law
Dr Fritz Rothenbühler, Reto Aschenberger

International law
Dr Fritz Rothenbühler

Liability law
Dr Fritz Rothenbühler, Dr Christoph Müller

Medical law
Dr Jürg Rieben, Dr Christoph Müller

B.M.G. AVOCATS

8C AVENUE DE CHAMPEL
PO BOX 385
1211 GENEVA 12

Telephone: +41 22 839 4949
Fax: +41 22 839 4950
E-mail: bmglaw@bmglaw.ch
Website: www.bmglaw.ch

Languages
English, French, German, Italian, Spanish

Number of lawyers 17

CATEGORIES OF WORK

Intellectual property and copyright
François Blum, Sylvie Gurry-Veit

Banking and finance
Pierre Louis Manfrini, Guillaume Fatio

Litigation
Louis Gaillard, Pierre Louis Manfrini

Corporate
Manuel Isler, Guillaume Fatio

Arbitration and mediation
Louis Gaillard, François Blum

Bankruptcy and insolvency
Louis Gaillard, Laurent Isenegger

Biotechnology law
Philippe Ducor

Sports and sponsorship
Laurent Isenegger

Mergers and acquisitions
Manuel Isler, Guillaume Fatio

Environmental
Pierre Louis Manfrini, Nicolas Wisard

Commercial and contracts
Sylvie Gurry-Veit, Laurent Isenegger

Real estate and construction
Pierre Louis Manfrini, Nicolas Wisard

Private international law
Louis Gaillard

EC law
Sylvie Gurry-Veit, Dominique Junod Moser

BAKER & McKENZIE GENEVA

CHEMIN DES VERGERS 4
1208 GENÈVE

Telephone: +41 22 707 98 00
Fax: +41 22 707 98 01
E-mail: geneva.info@bakernet.com
Website: www.bakernet.com

Languages
English, French, German, Gujarati, Hindi, Italian, Russian, Spanish, Swedish, Urdu

Other offices
The member firms of Baker & McKenzie International, a Swiss Verein, have 70 offices in 38 countries around the world. For a complete list, please visit www.bakernet.com.

Number of lawyers 3,300+
at this office 24

Contact
Martin Anderson (managing partner)

CATEGORIES OF WORK

Arbitration and litigation
Philippe Preti, Daniel Peregrina

Banking and finance
Martin Anderson, Frédéric Bétrisey

Capital markets
Martin Anderson

Competition, WTO
Serge Pannatier

Corporate and commercial law (general)
Nathalie Sierro, Benjamin Humm

Insolvency, restructuring
Philippe Preti, Daniel Peregrina

Intellectual property
Olivier Ducrey

Labour law and immigration
Daniel Peregrina, Serge Pannatier

Mergers and acquisitions
Martin Anderson, Denis Berdoz

Private clients, trusts and estates
Stephanie Jarrett

Public law, environmental law
Daniel Peregrina

Real estate, property finance
Adrian Moore, Daniel Peregrina

Tax
Denis Berdoz, Per Prod'hom

Telecoms
Daniel Peregrina

BOREL & BARBEY

2 RUE DE JARGONNANT
PO BOX 6045
1211 GENÈVE 6

Telephone: +41 22 707 18 00
Fax: +41 22 707 18 11
E-mail: mail@borel-barbey.ch
Website: www.borel-barbey.ch

Languages
English, French, German, Italian, Norwegian, Spanish

Number of lawyers 28

Contacts
Olivier Dunant, Nicolas Piérard

Other information
Established in 1907

CATEGORIES OF WORK

Commercial law (general) and contracts

Banking, securities and corporate finance

Competition, antitrust

Copyright, industrial property and media law

Mergers and acquisitions, corporate restructuring

Project finance

Tax

Distribution, agency, licensing

International arbitration, banking and commercial litigation

International legal assistance

Bankruptcy, creditors' rights

Wills, trusts and estate planning

Work and residence permits

BYRNE-SUTTON BONNARD LAWSON MEAKIN & ASSOCIÉS

11 RUE DU GENERAL-DUFOUR
1204 GENEVA

Telephone: +41 22 322 25 00
Fax: +41 22 322 25 15
Website: www.ilf.ch

Languages
English, French, German, Hebrew, Italian, Mandarin Chinese, Spanish

Other offices
Lausanne

Number of lawyers 19
at this office 11

Contact
David Lawson

CATEGORIES OF WORK

Dispute resolution

Corporate finance

Intellectual property

Information technology

Construction

Private client services

Shipping and maritime law

Banking law

Asset management and investment funds

Immigration law

International labour law

American law

English law

French law

Chinese law

FRORIEP RENGGLI
SWISS LAWYERS

4 RUE CHARLES-BONNET
1211 GENÈVE 12

Telephone: +41 22 839 63 00
Fax: +41 22 347 71 59
E-mail: geneva@froriep.ch
Website: www.froriep.com

Languages
English, French, German, Italian, Portuguese, Russian, Spanish

Other offices
London, Madrid, Zug, Zurich

Number of lawyers 62
at this office 18

Contact
Jérôme de Montmollin

CATEGORIES OF WORK

Arbitration
Jean-Marie Vulliemin

International judicial assistance
Roland Kaufmann, Philippe Pulfer

Insolvency
Roland Kaufmann

Trusts and estates
Nicolas Junod, Philippe Pulfer

Employment
Roland Kaufmann, Philippe Pulfer

Aviation
Roland Kaufmann

Art
Jean-Marie Vulliemin, Philippe Pulfer

Company and commercial
Jean-Luc Herbez,
Jérôme de Montmollin

Mergers and acquisitions
Alain Gros, Nicolas Junod

Banking and securities
Jean-Luc Herbez,
Jérôme de Montmollin

Private banking
Nicolas Junod, Philippe Pulfer

Sports
Jean-Marie Vulliemin,
Roland Kaufmann

Litigation
Jérôme de Montmollin, Alain Gros

GILLIOZ DORSAZ & ASSOCIÉS

11 RUE DU GÉNÉRAL-DUFOUR
1204 GENÈVE

Telephone: +41 22 702 19 00
Fax: +41 22 702 19 10
E-mail: gdvn@gdlaw.ch
Website: www.gdlaw.ch

Languages
English, French, German, Italian

Number of lawyers 7

CATEGORIES OF WORK

- Commercial law and contracts
- Company law and corporate restructuring
- Tax (Swiss and international)
- Banking and finance
- Commercial litigation
- International arbitration
- Estate planning

HOGAN & HARTSON LLP

3 RUE FRANÇOIS BELLOT
1206 GENEVA

Telephone: +41 22 787 4000
Fax: +41 22 787 4010
E-mail: ccadams@hhlaw.com
Website: www.hhlaw.com

Languages
English, French, German

Other offices
Baltimore, Beijing, Berlin, Boulder, Brussels, Budapest, Caracas,Colorado Springs, Denver, Hong Kong, London, Los Angeles, Miami, Moscow, Munich, New York, Northern Virginia, Paris, Shanghai, Tokyo, Warsaw, Washington DC

Number of lawyers 1,101
at this office 4

Contact
Charlie C Adams Jr

CATEGORIES OF WORK

- International litigation and arbitration
- Business, finance and tax
- Energy
- Infrastructure - construction
- International trade
- Telecommunications, media and entertainment
- Transportation

LENZ & STAEHELIN

ROUTE DE CHÊNE 30
1211 GENEVA 17

Telephone: +41 22 318 70 00
Fax: +41 22 318 70 01
Website: www.lenzstaehelin.com

Languages
English, French, German, Italian, Mandarin, Portuguese, Russian, Spanish

Other offices
Fribourg, Lausanne, Zurich

Number of lawyers 136
at this office 62

Contact
Andreas von Planta
(andreas.vonplanta@lenzstaehelin.com)

CATEGORIES OF WORK

Swiss and international taxation
Henri Torrione, Jean Blaise Eckert

Banking, capital markets
Shelby du Pasquier, Olivier Stahler

Corporate finance
Andreas Rötheli, François Rayroux

Investment trusts, mutual funds
Shelby du Pasquier, Olivier Stahler

International commercial arbitration
Paolo Michele Patocchi,
Xavier Favre-Bulle

Commercial and contract law
Dominique Rochat, Guy Vermeil

Company law, mergers, acquisitions
Andreas von Planta, Andreas Rötheli

International organistations, institutional arbitration
Henri Torrione, Mark Barmes

Residence, work permits, real estate
Olivier Mach

Civil, criminal and administrative litigations, debt and bankruptcy
Benoît Chappuis, Daniel Tunik

Estate planning, trusts
Richard Pease, Caroline Delétra

International private investments
Shelby du Pasquier, Mark Barmes

Copyright, industrial property, unfair competition, media
Mark Barmes, Benoît Merkt

EEC law and antitrust
Olivier Mach, Benoît Merkt

International legal assistance
Benoît Chappuis, Guy Vermeil

Pensions and retirement funds
Olivier Mach, Anne Troillet-Maxwell

NOTTER MÉGEVAND & PARTNERS

PLACE CLAPAREDE 3
1205 GENEVA

Telephone: +41 22 703 47 50
Fax: +41 22 703 47 51
E-mail: geneve@nomea.ch
Website: www.nomea.ch

Languages
English, French, German

Other offices
Berne, Fribourg

Number of lawyers 18
at this office 8

CATEGORIES OF WORK

Banking and finance

Corporate, capital markets and M&A

Arbitration and litigation

Tax

EU and competition

Civil law

Construction and real estate

Insolvency and restructuring

Family office

Art

Sports

PESTALOZZI LACHENAL PATRY

65 RUE DU RHÔNE
1204 GENÈVE

Telephone: +41 22 737 10 00
Fax: +41 22 737 10 01
E-mail: gva@plplaw.ch
Website: www.plplaw.ch

Languages
English, French, German, Italian, Spanish

Other offices
Brussels, Zurich

Number of lawyers 103
at this office 34

Contacts
Jean Patry, Claude Brechbuhl

Member
Lex Mundi

CATEGORIES OF WORK

Commercial law (general)
Jean Patry, Claude Brechbuhl

Companies, corporations
Alain Le Fort, Jean-Charles Roguet

Contract
Claude Brechbuhl, Christophe Emonet

Mergers and acquisitions
Bernard Lachenal, Alain Le Fort

Arbitration and litigation
Guy-Philippe Rubeli, Bernard Lachenal

Construction and environmental law
Philippe Cottier

Sports
Jean-Charles Roguet

Tax
Philippe Cottier

Trade marks, intellectual property
Christophe Rapin

Banking
Alain Le Fort, Serge Calame

Securities, capital markets, finance
Gilles Thieffry, Emmanuel Genequand, Sébastien Roy

Immigration
Guy-Philippe Rubeli

Competition, antitrust
Christophe Rapin

Inheritance, estate planning
Frédéric Cottier

PYTHON SCHIFFERLI PETER

9 RUE MASSOT
1206 GENÈVE

Telephone: +41 22 702 15 15
Fax: +41 22 702 14 14
E-mail: mail@psplaw.ch
Website: www.psplaw.ch

Languages
Dutch, English, French, German, Gujarati, Hebrew, Italian, Japanese, Persian, Portuguese, Spanish, Vietnamese

Other offices
Bern, Brussels, Lausanne, Pully, Sion, Tokyo, Zug

Number of lawyers 79
at this office 53

CATEGORIES OF WORK

Banking and finance

Commercial contracts

Corporate, capital markets and M&A

Venture capital

Arbitration and litigation

Insolvency and restructuring

Intellectual property, IT

Telecom and data protection

Tax

EU and competition

International legal assistance

Construction and real estate

Maritime and transport

Insurance

Private clients

SCHELLENBERG WITTMER

15 BIS RUE DES ALPES
PO BOX 2088
1211 GENÈVE 1

Telephone: +41 22 707 80 00
Fax: +41 22 707 80 01
E-mail: geneva@swlegal.ch
Website: www.swlegal.ch

Languages
English, French, German, Italian, Spanish

Other offices
Zurich

Number of lawyers 102
at this office 52

Contacts
Bernard Vischer, Elliot Geisinger

CATEGORIES OF WORK

Arbitration
Gabrielle Kaufmann-Kohler, Laurent Lévy

Banking and finance
Lionel Aeschlimann

Compliance and white-collar crime
Paul Gully-Hart, Vincent Jeanneret

Corporations, mergers and acquisitions, corporate restructuring
Roy Ryan, Jean Jacques Ah Choon

Employment and immigration
Raphaël Biaggi

Insolvency, bankruptcy
Vincent Jeanneret

Intellectual property and information technology
Fabrizio La Spada

Litigation
Christian Girod

Real estate and construction
Yves Jeanrenaud

Taxation
Pietro Sansonetti, Joëlle Zumoffen

Transport and international trade
Bernard Vischer

Trusts/estate planning
Jacques Wittmer, Bernard Vischer

SIDLEY AUSTIN LLP

RUE DE LAUSANNE 139
SIXTH FLOOR
1202 GENEVA

Telephone: +41 22 908 25 25
Fax: +41 22 908 25 20
Email: sandersen@sidley.com
Website: www.sidley.com

Languages
English, French, German, Hebrew, Spanish

Other offices
Beijing, Brussels, Chicago, Dallas, Frankfurt, Hong Kong, London, Los Angeles, New York, San Francisco, Shanghai, Singapore, Tokyo, Washington DC,

Number of lawyers 1600+
at this office 6

Contacts
Todd J Friedbacher, Scott D Andersen

CATEGORIES OF WORK

WTO litigation

International trade and dispute resolution

International arbitration

Trade regulation

Global trade policy

International intellectual property

WINSTON & STRAWN LLP

43 RUE DU RHONE
1204 GENEVA

Telephone: +41 22 317 75 75
Fax: +41 22 317 75 00
E-mail: mpalay@winston.com
Website: www.winston.com

Languages
English, French, German, Italian, Spanish

Other offices
Chicago, London, Los Angeles, Moscow, New York, Paris, San Francisco, Washington DC

Number of lawyers 850
at this office 8

Contact
Marc S Palay (managing partner)

CATEGORIES OF WORK

International arbitration
Marc S Palay, Nicolas C Ulmer

International judicial assistance
Marc S Palay, Ricardo Ugarte

Product liability
Marc S Palay

Commercial contracts
Nicolas C Ulmer, Franz X Stirnimann

International maritime and Admiralty
Marc S Palay

Mergers and acquisitions
Nicolas C Ulmer, Franz X Stirnimann

International construction law
Marc S Palay

International property law
Marc S Palay, Franz X Stirnimann

Trusts and estates
Nicolas C Ulmer, Franz X Stirnimann

Banking and insurance
Franz X Stirnimann

BYRNE-SUTTON BONNARD LAWSON MEAKIN & ASSOCIÉS

8 RUE DU GRAND-CHÊNE
CP 5463
1002 LAUSANNE

Telephone: +41 21 348 11 88
Fax: +41 21 348 11 89
Website: www.ilf.ch

Languages
English, French, German, Hebrew, Italian, Mandarin Chinese, Spanish

Other offices
Geneva

Number of lawyers 19
at this office 8

Contact
Cyrille Piguet

CATEGORIES OF WORK

Dispute resolution

Corporate finance

Intellectual property

Information technology

Construction

Private client services

Shipping and maritime law

Banking law

Asset management and investment funds

Immigration law

International labour law

American law

English law

French law

Chinese law

RWB ATTORNEYS-AT-LAW

AV. C.-F. RAMUZ 43
CASE POSTALE 1376
1001 LAUSANNE

Telephone: +41 21 711 71 00
Fax: +41 21 711 71 50
E-mail: office@rwblaw.ch
Website: www.rwblaw.ch

Languages
Arabic, English, French, German, Italian

Number of lawyers 14

Contact
Christophe Wilhelm

International grouping
Ledgis Network

CATEGORIES OF WORK

Tax law
Joseph Bechaalany

Litigation
Christophe Wilhelm

Real estate law
Eric Bersier

Corporate governance
Christophe Wilhelm, Joseph Bechaalany, Michael Kenyon

Corporate law and corporate finance
Christophe Wilhelm, Joseph Bechaalany

Labour law
Eric Bersier

Transfer pricing
Joseph Bechaalany

Estate planning
Christophe Wilhelm, Joseph Bechaalany

Bankruptcy litigation and insolvency
Dominique Rigot, Eric Bersier, Christophe Wilhelm

Administrative law
Dominique Rigot

Competition law (Swiss and EU)
Michael Kenyon, Christophe Wilhelm

Contract law
Dominique Rigot, Eric Bersier, Christophe Wilhelm, Michael Kenyon

Intellectual property and technology transfer
Michael Kenyon, Christophe Wilhelm

BADERTSCHER DÖRIG POLEDNA

VIA LODOVICO ARIOSTO 6
PO BOX 5162
6901 LUGANO

Telephone: +41 91 911 80 00
Fax: +41 91 911 80 08
E-mail: bdplaw@bdp.ch
Website: www.bdp.ch

Languages
Czech, English, French, German, Italian, Spanish, Slovak

Other offices
Zurich

Number of lawyers 26
at this office 3

Contact
Stefano Codoni

Member
MSI International; IBA; ALFA International; International Fiscal Association

CATEGORIES OF WORK

Administration and public law
Beat Badertscher, Tomas Poledna

Arbitration, litigation
Markus Dörig, Beat Badertscher

Banking
Beat Badertscher

Company law
Markus Dörig, Beat Badertscher

Commercial law
Beat Badertscher, Markus Dörig

Capital markets
Beat Badertscher, Markus Dörig

Employment
Markus Dörig

Energy
Beat Badertscher

Intellectual property
Stefano Codoni

Information technology
Stefano Codoni

Healthcare
Tomas Poledna

Mergers and acquisitions
Markus Dörig, Jasmin Ghandchi

Privatisations
Tomas Poledna, Stefano Codoni

Telecommunications
Stefano Codoni, Lorenzo Marazzotta

E-commerce
Jasmin Ghandchi, Stefano Codoni

BRUNONI MOLINO MOTTIS ADAMI
LAW OFFICE

VIA PIODA 14
PO BOX 6481
6901 LUGANO

Telephone: +41 91 911 74 11
Fax: +41 91 923 94 68
E-mail: info@legalnotarile.ch
Website: www.legalnotarile.ch

Languages
English, French, German, Italian

Other offices
Locarno

Number of lawyers 19

Contacts
Davide Mottis (dmottis@legalnotarile.ch), Andrea Molino (amolino@legalnotarile.ch)

CATEGORIES OF WORK

Administrative

Corporate and commercial

Commercial property, real estate

Employment

Dispute resolution – litigation and arbitration

Fraud and white-collar crime

Insolvency, corporate restructuring

Foreign direct investment

Intellectual property

Infrastructure and project finance

Private client

Insurance

Notarial services

Mergers and acquisitions

Sports law

Tax

Gambling and gaming

Banking and finance

FRORIEP RENGGLI
SWISS LAWYERS

BAARERSTRASSE 37
6304 ZUG

Telephone: +41 41 710 60 00
Fax: +41 41 710 60 01
E-mail: zug@froriep.ch
Website: www.froriep.com

Languages
English, French, German, Swedish

Other offices
Geneva, London, Madrid, Zurich

Number of lawyers 62
at this office 7

Contact
Hans Stuber

CATEGORIES OF WORK

Notarial services

Commercial litigation, arbitration

Tax

Estate planning

Company and commercial

REICHLIN & HESS

HOFSTRASSE 1A
6300 ZUG

Telephone: +41 41 729 10 70
Fax: +41 41 729 10 80
E-mail: law@reichlin-hess.ch
Website: www.reichlin-hess.ch

Languages
English, French, German

Number of lawyers 10

CATEGORIES OF WORK

Corporate

Intellectual property

Banking and capital markets

Telecoms and media

Contracts

Human resources

Estates

Foreigners

Litigation and arbitration

Public notarisation and legalisation

Real estate, construction and environmental matters

Fiscal matters

BADERTSCHER DÖRIG POLEDNA

MÜHLEBACHSTRASSE 32
PO BOX 769
8024 ZÜRICH

Telephone: +41 44 266 20 66
Fax: +41 44 266 20 70
E-mail: bdplaw@bdp.ch
Website: www.bdp.ch

Languages
Czech, English, French, German, Italian, Slovak, Spanish

Other offices
Lugano

Number of lawyers 26
at this office 23

Contact
Dr Markus Dörig

Member
MSI International; IBA; ALFA International; International Fiscal Association

CATEGORIES OF WORK

Administration and public law
Beat Badertscher, Tomas Poledna

Intellectual property
Martin Kurer, Stefano Codoni

Arbitration, litigation
Markus Dörig, Beat Badertscher

Information technology
Stefano Codoni, Jasmin Ghandchi

Banking
Beat Badertscher, Markus Dörig

Healthcare
Tomas Poledna

Company law
Markus Dörig, Beat Badertscher

Mergers and acquisitions
Martin Kurer, Jasmin Ghandchi

Commercial law
Beat Badertscher, Markus Dörig

Privatisations
Allen Fuchs, Tomas Poledna

Capital markets
Beat Badertscher, Markus Dörig

Telecommunications
Allen Fuchs, Lorenzo Marazzotta

Employment
Markus Dörig

E-commerce
Jasmin Ghandchi, Stefano Codoni

Energy
Beat Badertscher, Allen Fuchs

BAKER & McKENZIE

ZOLLIKERSTRASSE 225
PO BOX
8034 ZÜRICH

Telephone: +41 44 384 14 14
Fax: +41 44 384 12 84
E-mail: zurich.info@bakernet.com
Website: www.bakernet.com

Languages
English, French, German, Italian, Romanian, Spanish, Swedish

Other offices
The member firms of Baker & McKenzie International, a Swiss Verein, have 70 offices in 38 countries around the world. For a complete list, please visit www.bakernet.com.

Number of lawyers 3,300+
at this office 60

Contact
M Treis

CATEGORIES OF WORK

Aircraft financing
J Frick

Arbitration and litigation
F Schenker, U Zenhäusern

Banking and finance
M Affentranger, M Furrer, M Giger

Commercial law (general), contract law
F Schenker, M Berni

Companies, corporations
M Frey, M Berni

Antitrust and EC law
P Reich, P Reinert

Information technology
M Berni, N Passadelis

Insurance
J Frick

Intellectual property
M Treis, U Zenhäusern

Labour law
P Reinert

Mergers and acquisitions
U Schenker, M Frey

Tax
H Koch, P Marcovici, T O'Donnell

Trusts and estates
P Marcovici, R Gassmann

BÄR & KARRER

BRANDSCHENKESTRASSE 90
8027 ZÜRICH

Telephone: +41 58 261 50 00
Fax: +41 58 261 50 01
E-mail: zuerich@baerkarrer.ch
Website: www.baerkarrer.ch

Languages
English, French, German, Italian

Other offices
Geneva, London, Lugano, Zug

Number of lawyers 115

CATEGORIES OF WORK

Financial services
Eric Stupp

Transactional services
Rolf Watter

Listed companies and securities law
Urs Brügger, Ralph Malacrida

Arbitration
Marc Blessing, Michelle Sindler

Litigation
Daniel Hochstrasser,
Andreas Länzlinger

Private clients, trusts and estates
Nedim Peter Vogt,
Christian Steinmann

Corporate and commercial
Felix R Ehrat, Peter J Kienast

Tax
Peter Reinarz, Daniel Lehmann

Intellectual and industrial property and copyright, competition law and cartels, trade marks
Markus Wang, Marc Blessing

IT and telecoms law
Michele Bernasconi

Administrative law and real estate
Peter J Kienast, Daniel Hochstrasser

Construction, insurance, EC law
Marc Blessing

Notarial services
Thomas Stoltz (Zug office),
Cesare Jermini (Lugano office)

BILL • ISENEGGER • ACKERMANN

WITIKONERSTRASSE 61
PO BOX
CH-8032 ZÜRICH

Telephone: +41 44 386 88 88
Fax: +41 44 386 88 99
E-mail: bia@bialaw.ch
Website: www.bialaw.ch

Languages
English, French, German, Italian, Spanish

Number of lawyers 16

Contacts
Dr Urs Isenegger (Urs.Isenegger@bialaw.ch), Peter R Ackermann (Peter.Ackermann@bialaw.ch)

CATEGORIES OF WORK

Contracts

Torts

Corporate law

Mergers and acquisitions

Communications law (including e-commerce, telecoms, internet)

Intellectual property (including technology transfer and exploitation concepts) and competition law

Tax law, insolvency

Banking and securities

Aviation law

Inheritance law (including asset and estate planning)

Litigation and arbitration

Immigration

International private law

BLUM ATTORNEYS AT LAW

USTERISTRASSE 14
8021 ZURICH

Telephone: +41 43 443 88 00
Fax: +41 43 443 88 99
E-mail: info@blumlegal.ch
Website: www.blumlegal.ch

Languages
German, English, French, Dutch, Italian

Number of lawyers 15

Contact
Albrecht Langhart

International groupings
Association of Commercial Lawyers (ACL)

CATEGORIES OF WORK

Banking, securities and finance
Albrecht Langhart

Companies, corporations
Walter H Boss

Commercial, labour and civil
Albrecht Langhart, Adrian Hirzel

Immigration, work and residence permits
Stefan Wehrenberg, Katja Willborn

Mergers and acquisitions
Walter H Boss

Tax, international tax planning
Walter H Boss

Wills, trust and estate planning
Claude Blum, Florian von Meiss

Swiss, European and international public and administrative law
Stefan Wehrenberg, Andreas Ziegler

Arbitration
Albrecht Langhart, Christian Sutter

Litigation
Albrecht Langhart, Christian Sutter

International transactions
André Wahrenberger, Florian von Meiss

Intellectual property and copyright
André Wahrenberger, Christian Sutter

Swiss and European competition law
Albrecht Langhart, André Wahrenberger

E-commerce and IT
Albrecht Langhart, Patrick Dueggelin

Sports and entertainment
André Wahrenberger, Adrian Hirzel

International and European trade and investment law
Stefan Wehrenberg, Andreas Ziegler

BÜRGI NÄGELI LAWYERS

GROSSMÜNSTERPLATZ 9
8001 ZURICH

Telephone: +41 44 268 40 00
Fax: +41 44 268 40 05
E-mail: info@bnlawyers.ch
Website: www.bnlawyers.ch

Languages
German, English, French, Italian, Spanish

Other offices
Bern, Schlieren

Number of lawyers 15
at this office 13

CATEGORIES OF WORK

Company and commercial	**Tax**
Contracts	**Intellectual property**
Real estate and construction	**Communications**
Insolvency and creditors' rights, debt collection	**Matters of public law**
	Arbitration
Inheritance law, trusts, financial and estate planning	**Litigation**
Banking and finance	

THE FIRM

Bürgi Nägeli Lawyers was founded by Urs Bürgi and Dr Catarina Nägeli in 1994; since its inception it has grown steadily. Today the law firm consists of six partners, each of whom has developed specific areas of expertise. The firm counts 15 attorneys in total, who – in co-operation with certified accountants, economists, architects, banking experts – offer a one-stop shop for the firm's clients. The firm places great importance on flexible, efficient, pragmatic and timely solutions, tailored to its clients' individual needs, and therefore generating added value for them. To speed up the implementation of such overall advice, Bürgi Nägeli Lawyers also use products of third parties via existing networks.

The offices are located in the heart of Zurich, directly facing the Grossmünster. The firm also maintains offices in Bern and Schlieren, in order to cater for the specific needs of its clients.

AREAS OF PRACTICE

Bürgi Nägeli Lawyers do not focus exclusively on legal foundations and their interpretation in theory and jurisdiction. Business and economic considerations accompany the legal advice.

Individuals, corporations, authorities and communities avail themselves of the services of Bürgi Nägeli Lawyers.

The business-oriented law firm is active supra-regionally and internationally in an advisory and forensic capacity; Bürgi Nägeli Lawyers apply national, European and international law.

The firm's advisory activity focuses on prevention (compliance), risk management, risk assessment and out-of-court conflict settlement (mediation activity).

Bürgi Nägeli Lawyers regularly advise on: real estate and construction law – building and planning law, contract law in co-operative planning procedures, environmental law/legacies; estate planning, wills and trusts and inheritance law; company law – formation of companies, especially incorporation of companies and advice to foreign companies in matters of opening branch offices in Switzerland and to Swiss companies abroad, location consulting; commercial law; insolvency and creditors rights – debt collection and bankruptcy, company reorganisation, probate proceedings (as counsel for the debtor or as administrator/liquidator, private commissioner in bankruptcy); matters of public law; telecommunications, electronic media, internet; arbitration; probate law, provisions, succession planning, life-cycle-consultancy; banking and securities; and notary support.

BRATSCHI EMCH RECHTSANWÄLTE

BAHNHOFSTRASSE 106
POSTFACH 7689
8023 ZÜRICH

Telephone: +41 44 219 69 69
Fax: +41 44 219 69 99
E-mail: zurichoffice@bep-zh.ch
Website: www.bep.ch

Languages
English, French, German, Italian, Spanish

Other offices
Bern

Number of lawyers 27
at this office 12

CATEGORIES OF WORK

Contract and commercial
Dr C Schmid, Dr AW Blatter

Corporate and M&A
Dr D Glasl, Dr R Arpagaus

Commercial litigation/arbitration
Dr C Schmid, Dr D Glasl

Competition
Dr C Schmid, Dr D Glasl

Banking and finance
Dr R Arpagaus, Dr C Schmid

Media and communication
F Szolansky

Intellectual property
Dr R Arpagaus

Estate and inheritance law
Dr C Schmid, Dr D Glasl

Administrative law
Dr I Häner

Construction and environmental
Dr I Häner

Sports law
F Szolansky, Dr R Arpagaus

Debt enforcement and bankruptcy
F Szolansky, Dr D Glasl

CMS VON ERLACH HENRICI
ATTORNEYS AT LAW

DREIKÖNIGSTRASSE 7
PO BOX 2991
8022 ZÜRICH

Telephone: +41 44 285 11 11
Fax: +41 44 285 11 22
E-mail: info@cms-veh.com
Website: www.cms-veh.com

Languages
English, French, German, Italian, Spanish

Number of lawyers 40

Contact
Patrick Sommer

Member
CMS, the alliance of major European law firms

CATEGORIES OF WORK

Corporate law and transactions

Mergers and acquisitions

Banking and finance

Litigation and arbitration

Tax

Real estate, construction and environment

Competition

Technology

Healthcare and life sciences

Intellectual property

Insurance and reinsurance

Product liability

Labour law and immigration

Estate matters

International legal and administrative assistance

DE CAPITANI, KRONAUER, BUIS

MÜHLEBACHSTRASSE 7/17
PO BOX 672
8024 ZÜRICH

Telephone: +41 44 250 75 25
Fax: +41 44 250 75 26
E-mail: mail@decapitani.ch
Website: www.decapitani.ch

Languages
English, French, German, Italian

Number of lawyers 7

Contacts
Dr M Kronauer, Dr E Buis

CATEGORIES OF WORK

Banking and finance law

Banking litigation

Commercial law

Commercial litigation

Corporate law

FRORIEP RENGGLI
SWISS LAWYERS

BELLERIVESTRASSE 201
8034 ZÜRICH

Telephone: +41 44 386 60 00
Fax: +41 44 383 60 50
E-mail: zurich@froriep.ch
Website: www.froriep.com

Languages
Dutch, English, French, German, Hebrew, Italian, Portuguese, Spanish, Turkish

Other offices
Geneva, London, Madrid, Zug

Number of lawyers 62
at this office 33

Contact
Felix M Mathis

CATEGORIES OF WORK

Company and commercial
Felix M Mathis, Eric Haymann

Mergers and acquisitions
Peter J Merz, Beat M Barthold

Capital markets
Eric Haymann, Beat M Barthold

Banking and finance
Peter J Merz, Beat M Barthold

Telecommunications
Alessandro L Celli

International judicial assistance
Peter J Merz, Marcel C Steinegger

White-collar crime
Marcel C Steinegger

Employment
Marcel C Steinegger

Intellectual property
Roger Staub

Arbitration
Claudia Kälin

Sports
Lucien Valloni

Litigation
Marcel C Steinegger, Lucien Valloni

Trusts and estate
Eric Haymann

Competition
Alessandro L Celli

Insolvency
Felix M Mathis, Beat M Barthold

Aviation
Felix M Mathis

Corporate finance
Beat M Barthold

HARTMANN MÜLLER PARTNERS

ZÜRICHBERGSTRASSE 66
8044 ZÜRICH

Telephone: +41 43 268 83 00
Fax: +41 43 268 83 01
E-mail: contact@hmp.ch
Website: www.hmp.ch

Languages
English, French, German

Other offices
Zug

Number of lawyers 13
at this office 11

International groupings
MULTILAW

CATEGORIES OF WORK

Arbitration
Jürg Hartmann, Niklaus Müller

Banking and finance
Rudolf Schaub, Jürg Burger, Beat Spörri

Competition law
Jürg Hartmann, Beat Spörri

Contracts
Rudolf Schaub, Marco Barbatti, Christoph Martig

Corporate law
Jürg Hartmann, Beat Spörri

E-commerce
Marco Barbatti

Inheritance
Christoph Martig, Marco Barbatti

Insolvency and restructuring
Niklaus Müller, Rudolf Schaub

Intellectual property
Jürg Burger, Niklaus Müller

Litigation
Niklaus Müller, Christoph Martig

Mergers and acquisitions
Jürg Hartmann, Rudolf Schaub

Transportation law (especially shipping)
Christoph Martig

Work permits and immigration
Beat Spörri

HAYMANN & BALDI

ZELTWEG 44
POSTFACH 1622
8032 ZÜRICH

Telephone: +41 44 250 25 25
Fax: +41 44 250 25 00
E-mail: lawyers@hblaw.ch
Website: www.hblaw.ch

Languages
English, French, German, Italian, Portuguese, Spanish

Number of lawyers 9

Contacts
Michel Haymann, Peter Baldi, Michele Caratsch

CATEGORIES OF WORK

Corporate and commercial, mergers and acquisitions

Banking, finance and securities

Initial public offerings and stock exchange law

Corporate taxation and international tax planning

International commercial litigation

International arbitration

Intellectual property

EU law

Estate planning and trusts

Judicial assistance in criminal matters

Antitrust and competition

Labour, employment

Eastern European and CIS privatisations

Project finance in the CIS

HESS DALLAFIOR ATTORNEYS AT LAW

RÄMISTRASSE 5
PO BOX
8024 ZÜRICH

Telephone: +41 44 250 49 49
Fax: +41 44 250 49 00
E-mail: info@hdlegal.ch
Website: www.hdlegal.ch

Languages
English, French, German, Italian

Number of lawyers 15

Contacts
Dr Roberto Dallafior, Dr Mathis Berger

CATEGORIES OF WORK

Commercial law
Dr Daniel Alder, Peter Schatz

Corporate law, mergers and acquisitions
Dr Mathis Berger, Peter Schatz

Banking and financial services
Werner A Schubiger, Dr Markus Hess

Intellectual property, information technology, media
Dr Daniel Alder, Dr Mathis Berger

Competition law
Dr Roberto Dallafior, Dr Mathis Berger

Labour law
Dr Daniel Alder

Litigation and arbitration
Dr Roberto Dallafior,
Dr Florian Baumann

Insolvency
Dr Markus Hess, Peter Schatz

International legal assistance
Dr Florian Baumann

Taxation
Dr Ivo Baumgartner

Private clients
Dr Markus Hess

HOMBURGER

WEINBERGSTRASSE 56/58
8006 ZÜRICH
PO BOX 338
8035 ZÜRICH

Telephone: +41 43 222 10 00
Fax: +41 43 222 15 00
E-mail: lawyers@homburger.ch
Website: www.homburger.ch

Languages
English, French, German, Italian, Spanish

Number of lawyers 85

Contacts
Heinz Schärer (managing partner),
Peter Widmer (senior partner)

CATEGORIES OF WORK

Corporate/M&A
H Schärer, HJ Appenzeller, C Lambert
D Daeniker, F Gerhard, U Huber,
D Gericke, H Grüninger, F Romerio

Financial services
R Bösch, B Maurenbrecher,
D von Schulthess, P Widmer

Competition
F Hoffet, M Dietrich

IP/IT
W Stieger, G Rauber, G Bühler

Litigation and arbitration
T Müller, F Dasser, B Gross, G Naegeli,
M Wirth, G Nater-Bass

Tax
E Saupper, D Grünblatt,
P Riedweg, M Weidmann

LENZ & STAEHELIN

BLEICHERWEG 58
8027 ZÜRICH

Telephone: +41 44 204 12 12
Fax: +41 44 204 12 00
Website: www.lenzstaehelin.com

Languages
English, French, German, Italian, Russian, Spanish

Other offices
Geneva, Lausanne, Fribourg

Number of lawyers 136
at this office 69

Contact
Matthias Oertle
(matthias.oertle@lenzstaehelin.com)

CATEGORIES OF WORK

Arbitration
Rudolf Tschäni, Martin Burkhardt

Banking and capital markets
Stefan Breitenstein, Patrick Schleiffer

Competition
Marcel Meinhardt

Corporate finance
Christoph Reinhardt, Patrick Hünerwadel

Employment and compensation
Urs L Baumgartner

IT, telecoms and media
Lukas Morscher

Intellectual property and copyright law
Thierry Calame, Jürg Simon

Litigation
Martin Burkhardt, Alex Wittmann

Mergers and acquisitions
Rudolf Tschäni, Marcel Meinhardt

Tax
Heini Rüdisühli

Private clients
Peter Max Gutzwiller

Real estate and environment
Urs L Baumgartner

MME – MEYER MÜLLER ECKERT PARTNERS

KREUZSTRASSE 42
8008 ZÜRICH

Telephone: +41 44 254 99 66
Fax: +41 44 254 99 60
E-mail: office@mme-law.ch
Website: www.mme-law.ch

Languages
English, French, German, Italian

Number of lawyers 16

Contact
Dr Balz Hösly

Member
Zurich and Swiss Bar Associations; Chartered Institute of Arbitrators (FCIArb); World IT Lawyers (treasury); Swiss Insurance Broker Association (SIBA) (presidency); Swiss Interactive Media and Software Association (SIMSA) (member of advisory board); Trade and Service Association of the Canton of Zug (HDV) (presidency)

CATEGORIES OF WORK

Corporate and commercial
Dr Martin K Eckert

Compliance work and cross-border assistance
Dr R Luka Müller-Studer

Intellectual property
Dr Sibylle M Wirth-Zubler

IT
Dr Martin K Eckert

Strategic change and crisis management
Dr Balz Hösly

Insurance, liability and financial services
Prof Dr Moritz W Kuhn

Litigation, debt enforcement and bankruptcy law
Dr Dominik Vock

Arbitration
Dr Bernhard F Meyer-Hauser

Dispute resolution and ADR
Dr Andreas Landtwing

Public private partnerships
Dr Balz Hösly

MEYER LUSTENBERGER

FORCHSTRASSE 452
PO BOX 1432
8032 ZÜRICH

Telephone: +41 44 396 91 91
Fax: +41 44 396 91 92
E-mail: zurich@ml-law.ch
Website: www.meyerlustenberger.ch

Languages
English, French, German, Italian, Norwegian, Portuguese, Spanish

Other offices
Geneva, Zug

Number of lawyers 44

Contact
Thomas Lustenberger

CATEGORIES OF WORK

Mergers and acquisitions
Thomas Lustenberger

Banking, capital markets and e-banking
Christoph Heiz

Company, securities, commercial and e-commerce
Alexander Vogel

Tax
Urs Behnisch

Intellectual property
Michael Ritscher

Competition and antitrust, public procurement
Martin Ammann

Media, IT and telecoms
Armin Zucker

Arbitration and litigation, forensic services
Marcel Lustenberger

NEUPERT & PARTNERS

DUFOURSTRASSE 58
8702 ZOLLIKON-ZÜRICH

Telephone: +41 44 396 80 80
Fax: +41 44 396 80 88
E-mail: neupert@nplaw.ch
Website: www.nplaw.ch

Languages
English, French, German, Hebrew, Hungarian, Italian, Russian, Spanish

Other offices
Geneva, Lugano, Zug

Number of lawyers 14
at this office 6

Contact
Dr Dieter W Neupert

Other information
Established 1851

CATEGORIES OF WORK

Business law

Corporate finance

Banking

Taxation

Creditors' rights

Real estate

Employment

Aviation

Litigation

Notarial services

NIEDERER KRAFT & FREY

ATTORNEYS-AT-LAW

BAHNHOFSTRASSE 13
8001 ZÜRICH

Telephone: +41 58 800 80 00
Fax: +41 58 800 80 80
E-mail: nkf@nkf.ch
Website: www.nkf.ch

Languages
Dutch, English, French, German, Italian, Spanish

Number of lawyers 65

CATEGORIES OF WORK

Banking, securities and finance

Company and commercial

Mergers and acquisitions

Competition and antitrust

Tax

EU law

IT and telecommunications

Arbitration, litigation and judicial assistance

Insolvency and restructuring

Insurance

Intellectual property

Project finance (including aircraft finance)

Wills, trusts and estate planning

Environmental and healthcare law

Sports law

PESTALOZZI LACHENAL PATRY

LÖWENSTRASSE 1
8001 ZÜRICH

Telephone: +41 44 217 91 11
Fax: +41 44 217 92 17
E-mail: zrh@plplaw.ch
Website: www.plplaw.ch

Languages
Dutch, English, French, German, Italian, Spanish, Swedish

Other offices
Brussels, Geneva

Number of lawyers 103
at this office 66

Contact
Dr Robert Furter

Member
Lex Mundi

CATEGORIES OF WORK

Commercial law (general)
Christoph R Ramstein, Christian Roos

Companies, corporations
Dr Jakob Höhn, Dr Hans Bollmann

Contract
Dr Jakob Höhn, Dr Peter Straub

Mergers and acquisitions
Dr Hans Bollmann, Dr Jakob Höhn

Arbitration and litigation
Dr Peter Straub, Michael Kramer

Tax
Dr Silvia Zimmermann,
Dr Marcus Desax

Trade marks, intellectual property
Dr Peter Pestalozzi, Dr Robert G Briner

Banking, securities and finance
Gerhard Niggli, Dr Robert Furter

Immigration
Christian Roos, Dr Peter Straub

Competition, antitrust
Dr Jürg Borer, Dr Christoph Lang

Liability
Dr Marcus Desax, Dr Urs Jordi

Employment
Christian Roos, Dr Peter Straub

Insolvency
Michael Kramer, Dr Marc Veit

Telecommunications
Dr Robert G Briner

Inheritance law, estate planning
Dr Urs Jordi, Dr Max Walter

Real estate
Dr Max Walter

RINDERKNECHT KLEIN & STADELHOFER

BEETHOVENSTRASSE 7
PO BOX 2755
8022 ZÜRICH

Telephone: + 41 44 287 24 24
Fax: + 41 44 287 24 00
E-mail: rks@rks.ch
Website: www.rks.ch

Languages
English, French, German, Italian, Portuguese, Russian, Spanish

Other offices
Zug

Number of lawyers 13

Contact
Gerrit Straub

CATEGORIES OF WORK

Litigation, arbitration, international disputes, international legal assistance
Thomas Klein, Gerrit Straub

Banking and finance law, investment funds
Carl Stadelhofer, Thomas Klein

M&A and IPOs
Dr Thomas Rinderknecht, Carl Stadelhofer

Oil, gas, energy and metals contracts and structures
Carl Stadelhofer, Gerrit Straub

International holding and tax structures
Dr Thomas Rinderknecht, Carl Stadelhofer

Estates and wills
Dr Thomas Rinderknecht, Petra-Nicole Marbach

Pharmaceuticals and life sciences law
Dr Thomas Rinderknecht, Dr Jeannette Wibmer

Publishing and media law
Dr Thomas Rinderknecht, Petra-Nicole Marbach

Information technology and e-commerce
Dr Jeannette Wibmer, Mario Ermini

Intellectual property rights, advertising and marketing
Dr Jeannette Wibmer, Mario Ermini

ROHNER RECHTSANWÄLTE

SEESTRASSE 131
8027 ZÜRICH

Telephone: +41 44 281 1000
Fax: +41 44 281 0000
E-mail: mail@rohnerlaw.ch
Website: www.rohnerlaw.ch

Languages
English, French, German, Italian, Spanish

Number of lawyers 3

Contact
Dr Louis Rohner

Member
Interleges

CATEGORIES OF WORK

Business and commercial law

Contract law, internet, contracts

Corporate law, joint ventures

Banking, stock exchange and finance

Securities law

Real property transactions

Intellectual property

Matrimonial and inheritance law

Estate planning, trust and foundations

Product liability, torts

Competition law

Tax law

Employment law

Rents and leases

Immigration law

Insolvency law

Litigation and arbitration

Transportation law

Maritime and aviation law

SCHELLENBERG WITTMER

LÖWENSTRASSE 19
PO BOX 6333
8023 ZÜRICH

Telephone: +41 44 215 52 52
Fax: +41 44 215 52 00
E-mail: zurich@swlegal.ch
Website: www.swlegal.ch

Languages
English, French, German, Italian

Other offices
Geneva

Number of lawyers 102
at this office 50

Contacts
Dr Martin Lanz, Dr Oliver Triebold

CATEGORIES OF WORK

Arbitration
Georg von Segesser, Nathalie Voser

Art law
Georg von Segesser, Alexander Jolles

Banking and finance
Philippe Borens, Mark-Oliver Baumgarten

Capital markets
Martin Lanz, Lorenzo Olgiati

Competition law
Philippe Borens, Martin Weber

Compliance and white-collar crime
Thomas Bolliger, Benno Strub

Corporations, mergers and acquisitions
Martin Weber, Andrea Grimm Widmer

Employment and immigration
Thomas Bolliger, Christine Beusch-Liggenstorfer

Intellectual property
Andrea Mondini

International legal assistance
Peter Burckhardt

IT, telecommunication
Andrea Mondini

Litigation
Martin Bernet, Alexander Jolles

Taxation
Michael Nordin, Madeleine Simonek

Transport and international trade
Alexander von Ziegler

Trusts/estate planning
Georg von Segesser

STAIGER, SCHWALD & PARTNER

GENFERSTRASSE 24
PO BOX 2012
8027 ZÜRICH

Telephone: +41 44 283 86 86
Fax: +41 44 283 87 87
E-mail: ssplaw@ssplaw.ch
Website: www.ssplaw.ch

Languages
English, French, German, Italian

Other offices
Bern

Number of lawyers 31
at this office 25

Contacts
Lic iur HSG Hans-Peter Schwald, Dr Marc Bernheim, Lic iur Philipp Kaenzig

CATEGORIES OF WORK

Arbitration and litigation

Banking, securities, finance

Company and commercial law

Insolvency

Immigration

Competition, antitrust, trade marks and copyright

EU law and private international law

Mergers and acquisitions

Tax

Wills, trusts and estate planning

Media and entertainment

Energy market law

STIFFLER & PARTNER
RECHTSANWÄLTE

DUFOURSTRASSE 101
8034 ZÜRICH

Telephone: +41 44 388 48 48
Fax: +41 44 388 48 00
E-mail: info@stplaw.ch
Website: www.stplaw.ch

Languages
English, French, German, Italian, Norwegian, Portuguese, Spanish

Number of lawyers 9

Member
Lexwork International, an association of mid-sized independent law firms in Europe

CATEGORIES OF WORK

Corporate and business law
Mirko Roš, Heinz Klarer

Commercial litigation
Laurent Killias, Paola Wullschleger

Mergers and acquisitions
Heinz Klarer

Telecommunications
Albert Schmid

Banking
Heinz Klarer

Wills
Mirko Roš, René Strazzer

Civil liability, medical malpractice
Heinz Klarer, Philipp Diederichs

Administrative law
Albert Schmid

Arbitration
Laurent Killias, Paola Wullschleger

Intellectual property
Albert Schmid, Regula Bergsma

White-collar crime
Mirko Roš, Michael Aepli

Bankruptcy
Heinz Klarer

Energy law
Albert Schmid

Tax
Ruedi Bossi, Hans Sulser

Family law
René Strazzer

SUTER HOWALD ATTORNEYS AT LAW

STAMPFENBACHSTRASSE 52
PO BOX 512
8006 ZURICH

Telephone: +41 44 630 48 11
Fax: +41 44 630 48 15
E-mail: info@suterhowald.ch
Website: www.suterhowald.ch

Languages
English, French, German, Italian, Spanish

Number of lawyers 10

Contact
Dr Mauro Loosli

CATEGORIES OF WORK

Corporate and commercial
Urs Suter, Adrian Howald

Mergers and acquisitions
Mauro Loosli, Urs Suter

Banking and finance
Urs Suter, Peter Merz

Employment
Adrian Howald, Romaine Robbiani

Immigration
Eric Kuenzi, Romaine Robbiani

Litigation and arbitration
André Bloch, Mauro Loosli

Insolvency
André Bloch

Information technology and intellectual property
Mauro Loosli, Eric Kuenzi

Competition law
Annette Zimmerli

Real estate and construction
Mauro Loosli

Estate planning, inheritance law
Bettina Rudin

Tax
Urs Suter, Adrian Howald

THOUVENIN RECHTSANWÄLTE

KLAUSSTRASSE 33
8034 ZURICH

Telephone: +41 1 421 45 45
Fax: +41 1 421 45 00
E-mail: info@thouvenin.com
Website: www.thouvenin.com

Languages
English, French, German, Italian

Number of lawyers 18

Contacts
David Känzig, Dr Michael W Kneller

CATEGORIES OF WORK

Arbitration
Hansjörg Stutzer, André Thouvenin

Litigation
Daniel Stoll, Hansjörg Stutzer

Banking and securities
Daniel Stoll, David Känzig

Competition law, automotives
Michael W Kneller

Corporate
Hansjörg Stutzer, Michael W Kneller

Distribution law
André Thouvenin, Michael W Kneller

Employment law
Thomas Rihm, André Thouvenin

Private clients
Michael W Kneller, Thomas Loher

Insolvency law
David Känzig, André Thouvenin

Intellectual property
Thomas Loher, Marc Wenger

Mergers and acquisitions
David Känzig, Thomas Rihm

Railways and transportation law
Michael W Kneller

Telecommunications and new technologies
David Känzig, Hansjörg Stutzer

Turnaround management
Hansjörg Stutzer

Contracts
André Thouvenin, Hansjörg Stutzer

THE FIRM

Founded in 1893, Thouvenin Rechtsanwälte has established itself over recent decades as a reliable and competent partner for high-end legal services in all major areas of commercial law. The combined international expertise of the firm's lawyers and its independent and extensive co-operation with law offices around the globe permits Thouvenin Rechtsanwälte efficiently to co-ordinate and resolve legal issues of an international dimension. The firm is able to provide its clients with seamless all-round support, regardless of whether it be advising or representing the client in all matters relating to commercial and civil law litigation, judicial assistance in criminal, civil and administrative law matters.

Thouvenin Rechtsanwälte strives for a long-term partnership with its clients. The focus of Thouvenin Rechtsanwälte is to achieve the most cost-effective and long-term custom-made solution by combining profound legal expertise and understanding of the various legal systems with a thorough comprehension of the economical backgrounds.

All attorneys at Thouvenin Rechtsanwälte are graduates of Swiss universities and members of both the Zurich and the Swiss Bar Association. Many lawyers successfully completed additional post-graduate studies at leading European or American law schools. All of the lawyers are specialised and bilingual.

The firm's clientele consists of (leading) national and multinational (publicly listed) companies, small and medium-sized enterprises, sports organisations, private (high-net-worth) individuals, as well as several non-profit organisations.

AREAS OF PRACTICE

Thouvenin Rechtsanwälte benefits from a vast expertise in all matters relating to commercial and civil law. The firm has assisted clients in mergers and acquisitions, from small transactions to billion-dollar deals, during the entire process. Besides representing the client's interests before all Swiss courts, Thouvenin Rechtsanwälte acts as counsel in national and international arbitrations under various rules, such as ICC, LCIA, Swiss Rules of International Arbitration and Uncitral. Members of the firm are often appointed as arbitrators.

With regard to telecommunication and new technologies, the firm can look back at a long-standing and profound industry experience. The firm supports fixed-net, mobile and satellite providers on all regulatory and other legal aspects.

In the automotive sector, Thouvenin Rechtsanwälte acts as adviser for several car manufacturers/importing organisations to protect their interests in the distribution and servicing of motor vehicles in Switzerland. In particular the firm advises on competition law issues, distribution and servicing agreements and other legal affairs.

In the banking and securities sector, the firm advises clients on all regulatory issues and the way to conduct business in Switzerland through subsidiary, branch or representative offices. It also advises on issues related to the listing of securities on the Swiss Exchange or with private placements, takeovers and takeover defences. Moreover, the firm is specialised in handling litigation in civil law cases affecting banks and their clients. These areas are all professionally handled by specialists at Thouvenin Rechtsanwälte.

UMBRICHT
RECHTSANWÄLTE

BAHNHOFSTRASSE 22
8022 ZÜRICH

Telephone: +41 44 213 63 63
Fax: +41 44 213 63 99
E-mail: attorneys@umbricht.ch
Website: www.umbricht.ch

Languages
English, French, German, Italian

Number of lawyers 14

Contact
Dr Robert Umbricht

CATEGORIES OF WORK

Commercial law

Banking, securities and finance

Insolvency law

Mergers and acquisitions

Wills, trusts and estate planning

Tax

Companies and corporation

Arbitration and litigation

Constitutional and administrative law

International judicial assistance

WTO law

VISCHER

SCHÜTZENGASSE 1
8023 ZÜRICH

Telephone: +41 44 254 34 00
Fax: +41 44 254 34 10
E-mail: lawyers@vischer.com
Website: www.vischer.com

Languages
English, French, German, Italian, Spanish

Number of lawyers 75
at this office 32

Contact
Dr Christoph M Pestalozzi

CATEGORIES OF WORK

Commercial law, contract law
Dr Felix Egli

Banking and finance
Dr Markus Guggenbühl, Dr Adrian Doerig

Capital markets
Dr Markus Guggenbühl, Dr Jürg Luginbühl

Commercial litigation
Dr Marc Russenberger, Felix C Meier-Dieterle

Arbitration, ADR
Dr Christoph M Pestalozzi

Labour, employment
Urs Haegi

Corporate
Dr Jürg Luginbühl, Dr Robert Bernet

Mergers and acquisitions
Dr Jürg Luginbühl, Dr Markus Guggenbühl

Estate planning
Dr Christoph M Pestalozzi

Insolvency, bankruptcy
Dr Marc Russenberger, Felix C Meier-Dieterle

Competition
Urs Haegi, Dr Rolf Auf der Maur

IT, IP
Dr Rolf Auf der Maur

Tax
Erwin R Griesshammer

Aviation
Dr Christoph M Pestalozzi

Media, entertainment
Dr Rolf Auf der Maur

WALDER WYSS & PARTNERS

MÜNSTERGASSE 2
PO BOX 2990
8022 ZÜRICH

Telephone: +41 44 265 75 11
Fax: +41 44 265 75 50
E-mail: reception@wwp.ch
Website: www.wwp.ch

Languages
English, Chinese, French, German, Italian, Spanish

Number of lawyers 57

Member
Techlaw

CATEGORIES OF WORK

Banking
Enrico Friz, Markus Pfenninger

Capital markets
Enrico Friz, Markus Pfenninger

Structured financial products
Markus J Kroll, Johannes Bürgi

Insurance
Markus Pfenninger, Evan M Spangler

M&A, business reorganisation
Markus Vischer, Christoph Stäubli

Corporate and commercial
Markus Vischer, Christoph Stäubli

EU, competition, environment, energy and utilities
Reto Jacobs, Markus Vischer

Healthcare, life sciences
Reto Jacobs, Daniel Staffelbach

IT, multimedia and telecommunications
Didier Sangiorgio, Mark Reutter

Arts, sports and entertainment
Christoph Stäubli, Mark A Reutter

Intellectual property, copyright and advertising
Magda Streuli-Youssef, Markus Frick

Litigation, international legal assistance
Daniel Wyss, Dieter Hofmann

International arbitration
Daniel Wyss, Philipp Habegger

Venture capital and private equity
Luc Defferrard, Markus Pfenninger

Insolvency and restructuring
Christoph Stäubli, Jörg Witmer

Tax
Martin Busenhart, Thomas Meister

WENGER & VIELI

DUFOURSTRASSE 56
8034 ZÜRICH

Telephone: +41 44 563 33 33
Fax: +41 44 563 33 66
E-mail: mail@wengerlaw.ch
Website: www.wengerlaw.ch

Languages
Croatian, English, French, German, Italian, Mandarin, Spanish

Other offices
Zug, Beijing, Shanghai, Taipei

Number of lawyers 38

Contacts
Dr Christian Wenger, Dr Christoph Schmid

Member
Swiss Bar Association; Meritas

CATEGORIES OF WORK

Corporate, commercial and contract law

Corporate finance

Structured finance and venture law

Regulatory and general banking law

Banking litigation

Litigation

Arbitration

Mergers and acquisitions

Media law

Bankruptcy and insolvency

Employment law and work residence permits

Joint ventures

Life sciences law, antitrust and competition law

IT law

Intellectual property law

International judicial assistance

Estate planning and probate law

Expert opinions

Stock exchange and capital market law

Tax law

WENGER PLATTNER

SEESTRASSE 39
GOLDBACH-CENTER
8700 KÜSNACHT-ZÜRICH

Telephone: +41 43 222 38 00
Fax: +41 43 222 38 01
E-mail: zuerich@wenger-plattner.ch
Website: www.wenger-plattner.ch

Languages
English, French, German, Italian

Other offices
Basle, Bern

Number of lawyers 50
at this office 25

CATEGORIES OF WORK

Contract and commercial law
Dr Jürg Plattner, Filippo Th Beck

Company law
Yves P Meili, Karl Wüthrich

Tax law
Dr Jürg Plattner, Yves P Meili

Arbitration
Dr Jürg Plattner, Dr Stephan Netzle

Litigation
Karl Wüthrich, Yves P Meili

Mergers and acquisitions
Dr Stephan Netzle, Dr Marc Nater

Real estate and construction
Peter Sahli, Dr Thomas Wetzel

Bankruptcy and insolvency
Karl Wüthrich, Peter Sahli

Banking and financial markets
Dr Jürg Plattner, Filippo Th Beck

Trusts and estates
Dr Jürg Plattner, Filippo Th Beck

Technology and telecoms
Yves P Meili, Dr Stephan Netzle

Immigration and employment
Filippo Th Beck

Sports, media and entertainment
Dr Stephan Netzle, Dr Marc Nater

Legal assistance in civil and criminal matters
Filippo Th Beck, Dr Marc Nater

SYRIA

Population	18 million
Number of lawyers	n/a
Professional title	Advocate
Currency	Syrian Pound (SVP)

Index

In 2000, Bashar al-Assad became president, heralding the promise of a new era for Syria. Under al-Assad, Syria enjoyed a momentary period of reform, marked by freedom of expression, political liberalisation, economic reform, modernisation and anti-corruption. However, Syria's ruling Baath party and the military quickly took measures to limit changes which they felt threatened their powers.

The Baath party, the Arab nationalist party known for its authoritarian rule and strong anti-Israeli stance, has been in power since 1963. Syria's relations with Israel are mutually and notoriously violent, and have placed Syria under careful international scrutiny in recent years. Peace talks between Israel and Syria have been almost non-existent for the past five years. In 2003, Israel launched a bombing raid on Syria, following a Syrian suicide bomb attack in the Israeli city of Haifa. Consequently, in 2004, the US imposed upon Syria economic sanctions, accusing it of supporting terror groups and possessing weapons of mass destruction (WMD) on Iraq's behalf.

While Syria has admitted support for Hizbullah, the Lebanese anti-Israeli militia group, and the radical Palestinian faction Hamas, no trace of WMD has been found in Syria. Nevertheless, relations with the US hit a low earlier in 2005, after the assassination of the former Lebanese prime minister Hariri in Beirut. Although it is unclear who was behind the murder, many global commentators are pointing the finger of blame at Syria. Syria is now at the centre of a UN investigation into Hariri's killing.

In compliance with UN demands and bowing to increasing international pressure, Syria has now removed its 17,000 military troops from Lebanon, where they had been stationed for almost 30 years.

Although Syria plays an aloof and largely unstable political role on the Middle Eastern and international stages, hopes for economic reform have not yet been dashed. In June 2005, at the Tenth Congress of the Syrian Baath party, President al-Assad spoke openly of the need to stimulate and liberalise economic reform before political reform. Despite frustrating critics by refusing to prioritise political concerns, the president considers economic reform a crucial step in boosting Syria's status in the international arena.

BILLING

Law firms in Syria have varying approaches towards billing. Some prefer to accept a monthly retainer, while others adopt an hourly rate basis. Hourly rates start from about US$150 to US$250 for international clients.

ECONOMIC CLIMATE

Syrian authorities had high hopes for the economy when Bashar al-Assad stepped into the role of president in 2000. He took office at a positive time, as a result of rising oil prices and increased agricultural output, both key areas of the Syrian economy. Although economic progress has been slow, any progress at all is still an admirable achievement in the light of the stringent political conditions of the Baath party.

Economic reforms have started in the banking sector, namely a new banking law which permits the establishment of private banks with some foreign ownership. Authorities are now seeking to develop the private sector by a series of structured measures, including legislative and regulatory reform. The banking sector in particular has seen the most changes. The Syrian Central Bank opened the country up to foreign bank branches in 2004, and Lebanese banks have been the first to enter Syria, and develop private banking sectors. In the meantime, the government is working on monetary and banking reforms, in order to facilitate private bank ownership.

In 2003, the Syrian authorities announced their plan to establish a stock exchange, as part of the government's seven-year plan for modernisation. In 2005, a stock market regulatory commission was created, which places Syria one step further down the road to establishing its own stock market. This will be a significant boost for the economy, in terms of economic growth, encouraging investment and creating public companies.

Syria is also trying to encourage foreign investment, which is much needed in the country at present, in the light of falling oil output. Syria reportedly needs up to US$9bn worth of foreign investment in order to be able to combat its rising unemployment rate. Under new rules, foreign investors are allowed to establish Syrian operations with 100% ownership, and are similarly permitted to have non-Syrian local managing directors, own real estate and import manufacturing materials without taxation.

Unemployment is extremely high, especially among young adults. Syria must improve and increase its annual economic growth rate in order to absorb some 350,000 people, entering the workforce every year. According to the UNDP, 30% of Syrians live in poverty, two million of them living below the poverty line. President al-Assad cites raising living standards as a key concern.

Like many Middle Eastern states, Syria owes much of its economy to its oil reserves. However, unlike many of its counterparts, Syria has been suffering from a drop in oil production, which does not translate well in the bigger picture of economic growth. Syrian oil production is expected to continue to decline over the coming years. In order to tackle this, the government announced proposals to build new oil refineries in order to enhance its petroleum production, mineral resources and oil refining capacity.

LEGAL MARKET

The Syrian legal market is very small, and by Syrian standards, a firm of six or maybe eight lawyers is considered to be large. Given the size of the market, most lawyers operate as sole practitioners, although a couple of partnerships are emerging. **Al-Kherdaji & Diab Law Firm** is one example of a recently merged firm and new partnership, established between name partners Mr Osama Al-Kherdaji, Dr Sadir Al-Kherdaji and Mr Razi Diab, formerly of *Diab Law Office*.

Given its strategic footing between the Mediterranean Sea, between Turkey and Lebanon, Syria is in some ways a bridge, albeit volatile, between Europe and the Middle East. As a result, many firms listed have good international links with Western firms.

Al-Ahmar & Partners in association with Amereller Rechtsanwälte is the only Syrian firm with a formal international connection. The Syrian firm entered into an association with Munich-based **Amereller Rechtsanwälte** approximately four years ago.

Syrian firms often have good contacts with regional firms, both through informal and formal associations. An example of the latter is the *Arab Law Firm Association*, which was co-founded by **Saleheddin Al Khatib & Co**. This network links law firms in Syria, UAE, Jordan and Lebanon.

Most firms conduct business in Arabic and English. Lawyers mentioned typically have a perfect command of English, and will often also be proficient in French and German.

CORPORATE AND COMMERCIAL

CORPORATE AND COMMERCIAL

AL-AHMAR & PARTNERS IN ASSOCIATION WITH AMERELLER RECHTSANWÄLTE
AL-KHERDAJI & DIAB LAW FIRM
FADI SARKIS ATTORNEY AT LAW
HAKIM LAW FIRM
MAWLA LAW CORPORATION
NAHLAWI LAW OFFICE
SABBAGH & ASSOCIATES LAW OFFICE
SYRIAN ARAB CONSULTANTS LAW OFFICE

Ghazi s. Ghazzi
Kardous Law Office
Mazen Khaddour, Law Offices
Rabie El Solh
S. Nofal (Dr), Law Office of
Saleheddin Al Khatib & Co

Firms are listed A-Z in tiers which are ranked in order of priority

Kanaan Al-Ahmar is the lead partner at **Al-Ahmar & Partners in association with Amereller Rechtsanwälte** The four-lawyer firm advises several Arab governments, and numerous international organisations like Siemens, IBM and BMW. A specialist in IP and trade mark law, Kanaan Al-Ahmar leads a strong practice, which covers all aspects of corporate and commercial law. Partners George Albaba and Antonious Obeid have good experience advising on real estate transactions, and Alissar Al-Ahmar is able to offer legal advice relating to foreign investment matters. The firm benefits from **Amereller Rechtsanwälte**'s network of firms in Germany, Paris, Egypt and the UAE.

Six-lawyer **Al-Kherdaji & Diab Law Firm** advises an impressive mix of local, regional and international clients, such as Sony, SAS Airlines and Italian cosmetics company Mirato. The firm has recently advised several foreign companies such as Canpack and ZTE Corporation on their investments into Syria, and also has a particularly strong name for arbitration, recently handling an arbitration of substantial value before the London Court of International Arbitration. Dr Sadir Al-Kherdaji is a prominent and respected arbitrator, and lectures widely on the subject. He was recently invited by the ICC to advise on a new taskforce relating to complex arbitration procedures. **Al-Kherdaji & Diab Law Firm** has impressive banking law experience, having advised Banque Libano-Française, Credit Libanais Bank and the Bank of Beirut.

Fadi Sarkis Attorney at Law has broad experience advising on international projects in both the private and public sector. In the latter area, name partner Fadi Sarkis is rated for his significant position advising the Syrian government. In 2005, Sarkis was appointed by the State Planning Commission as legal advisor to the Syrian Prime Minister's Office, in order to advise the government on the Euro-Syrian Association Agreement. **Fadi Sarkis Attorney at Law** has sound experience in aspects of insurance law, advising major private insurance companies including Société National d'Assurance, AXA Middle East and Lebanese entity, Arope. Other major clients include Credit Libanais Bank, Bank Audi Syria, GE Energy and the Aga Khan Developing Network.

Hakim Law Firm is extremely respected in the Syrian legal market, and is upheld as one of the oldest firms in the country. Jacques el-Hakim heads the practice and has a strong reputation in the local legal market, having worked with the government on drafting new legislation and reforming the code of commerce. He is also widely respected as an international arbitrator. Youssef el-Hakim is also a prominent lawyer. **Hakim Law Firm** has good contacts with many Western firms including **Baker & McKenzie**, often making it the Syrian firm of choice for international law firms seeking leading domestic counsel, as well as for international clients seeking advice on foreign investment. Many of the firm's clients are multinational companies, including General Motors. **Hakim Law Firm** is also noted for its established intellectual property practice.

Mawla Law Corporation's longest-standing client is the Commercial Bank of Syria, which the firm has been representing since 1970. **Mawla Law Corporation** has good international contacts, with representatives in countries across Europe and the Middle East. Led by Dr Issam Mawla, the firm offers corporate finance, taxation and auditing advice. Clients include Audi, Cisco Systems, Falcon Crest Contracting Co, Volkswagen and Sanyo Electric Co.

Two-lawyer **Nahlawi Law Office** represents the Damascus Chamber of Commerce, and offers across-the-board commercial advice. The firm was founded by Nizar Nahlawi, who has good experience in corporate, banking, finance and investment law.

Six-attorney **Sabbagh & Associates Law Office** handles corporate and business work, advising largely on the establishment of different types of companies. Led by Bassam Sabbagh, the firm is strongly specialised in investment regulations, and has advised on several industrial projects undertaken by major international companies under Syrian investment rules. The firm's international practice advises non-Syrian clients on corporate transactions.

Syrian Arab Consultants Law Office has a good name in telecoms and IP, having advised a number of international mobile and satellite telecommunications companies on service issues in Syria, as well as advising on contract matters for a major local telecoms network. The team includes the extremely well-respected Riad Daoudi and Antoun Jourban, who was the Syrian government's minister of labour and industry for 12 years.

Ghazi s. Ghazzi has good experience advising different UN and World Bank organisations on preparing new laws and conducting feasibility studies. The firm almost exclusively advises international clients on investment projects, international arbitration matters and joint ventures.

Kardous Law Office is coming up trumps and made some key client gains in 2005, adding major names Coca-Cola and Sabic (Saudi Arabia's leading petrochemical and manufacturing company) to its client portfolio. The four-lawyer firm is also in the process of deepening its European ties – it already has associated offices in the UAE and in France, and is likewise entering into association with firms in Italy and Spain. Name partner Fady Kardous has acquired a good reputation for his corporate and commercial expertise, and is regularly called upon by the Ministry of Trade and WTO Unit to provide insight on legislative reform.

Two-partner **Law Offices of Mazen Khaddour** has a solid practice, which has particular expertise in the oil and gas sectors, and has, for example, advised on public tenders and drilling and production contracts. In the corporates sphere, **Law Offices of Mazen Khaddour** has advised Swiss-based Leman Commodities on its transactions with a local Syrian company, and the firm was also involved in a unique project establishing a private university (the Arab European University) in Syria. Inana Group, the telecoms company, remains an important client for **Law Offices of Mazen Khaddour**, which is presently advising on a joint venture agreement between the Inana Group and an Egyptian company.

Long-established **Rabie El Solh** has a niche practice representing engineering and construction companies.

Law Office of Dr S. Nofal opened in 1989, and specialises in civil, commercial, real estate, and international law. The firm predominantly advises European clients on their corporate dealings in both the private and public sector, and also has an established litigation practice. Lawyers Hanaa Makkhul and Jamileh Al-Rifaii work alongside name partner Dr Nofal, and between them, the team can offer advice in Arabic, German, English and French.

Established by Dr Salehaddin Al Khatib, **Saleheddin Al Khatib & Co** has experience advising government organisations, statutory committees, airlines, embassies and multinationals both in and outside of Syria. The firm handles corporate, commercial, banking, finance and insurance law, and is strongly involved in international arbitration.

TUNISIA

Population	10 million
Number of lawyers	n/a
Professional title	Avocat
Currency	Tunisian dinar (TND)
Index	
Banking and finance	1380
Corporate and M&A	1380
Country index	5

Tunisia is located on the North African coast between Algeria and Libya. Tunis is the capital and chief port, and home to all the firms recommended here. The country is 98% Muslim, the official language is Arabic, with French and English also widely spoken.

Tunisia is one of the Arab world's most modern and stable countries boasting a diverse economy including significant agricultural, mining, energy and manufacturing sectors. Its tourist sector is also enjoying significant growth despite recent terrorism threats, and with the cessation of combat operations in Iraq. However, there is a perennial shortage of skilled workers and a high unemployment rate.

Tunisia is making slow progress towards becoming a democratic system, but full political freedom is not yet a luxury enjoyed by its citizens. It has a strong presidential system dominated by one political party: the current president is Zine el-Abedine Ben Ali who, along with his government, is reportedly isolating and intimidating lawyers who do not toe the government's line. Human rights groups label Tunisia a police state, which stifles and regularly beats dissidents. However, Tunisia leads the Arab countries in promoting the legal and social status of women, who enjoy full legal status.

BILLING

Various billing methods are employed, including hourly rates (particularly for foreign clients) or charging a lump sum or percentage of a transaction. Local clients tend to be charged on a case-by-case basis. Hourly rates are on average US$300 depending on the seniority of the lawyer and level of experience.

MARKETING

With a lack of political freedom, there are curbs on the press and freedom of speech which affects the amount of advertising lawyers in Tunisia are permitted to undertake. Very few law firms currently have websites, and those that do are scant in the information and advertising offered.

ECONOMY

Tunisia is enjoying economic reform and liberalisation after many years of state monopoly. But control of the government over economic affairs has lessened over the last ten years, with an increase in privatisation and a simplification of the tax system. The government has completely or partially privatised some 160 state-owned enterprises since its programme started in 1987. However, its success has been marred by a high unemployment rate of more than 14% of the country's workforce.

That said, Tunisia's economic reform programme has been praised as a model by international financial institutions and in June 2005 the World Bank approved a US$150m loan for Tunisia and, in the same month, the central bank sold US$400m of 15-year bonds in the country's longest-dated euro deal.

The country's natural gas sector received a welcome boost in September 2004 when BG Group announced a US$1bn investment for its fields in Tunisia. Another UK company, Petrofac, signed two oilfield development contracts for offshore Tunisia.

Tunisia is slowly removing existing barriers to trade with the EU but future challenges include further liberalisation, increased government efficiency and the reduction of trade deficit. Tunisia is in discussions with Malta as to the commercial exploitation of the continental shelf between the two countries, particularly in relation to oil.

Tunisia boasts one of the best country-risk factors in Africa. It acceded to GATT in 1990 and entered into an Association Agreement with the EU in 1996 (which will remove tariff and other trade barriers on the majority of goods by 2008) and is a member of the WTO, evidence that the country is committed to a free-trade regime and growth in its exports.

The country's telecommunications sector, run by state telecoms company Tunisie Telecom, is strengthening with an increasing capacity thanks to substantial government investment. The mobile phone system is also growing rapidly. Tunisia recently hosted Arabcom 2005, the eighth International Telecom Development Forum and Expo for the Arab world and North Africa.

Expansion of the stock exchange (currently listing nearly 50 companies) continues slowly despite tax incentives offered by the government in a bid to attract companies.

LEGAL MARKET

Over the past 12 months, there has been an upturn in various sectors of legal practice including litigation and privatisation, real estate and investment.

There is comparatively little activity by foreign law firms in Tunisia. Only one foreign law firm, **Gide Loyrette Nouel**, has an office in Tunis (opened in 2001) and is managed by Kamel Ben Salah, a past member of the International Court of Arbitration.

Herbert Smith LLP is the most active foreign firm in Tunisia, and over the past twelve months has become extremely busy in the region, particularly in the oil and gas sectors, representing major domestic and international clients including BG and BG Tunisia. The firm recently advised China National Petroleum Company on its acquisition of interests in an exploration permit in Tunisia. The firm also represents clients from China, India and Japan on investments in Tunisia, and clients include Senoc.

White & Case is active in Tunisia, recently advising Tunisiana, a joint venture between Orascom Telecom and Wataniya in a €330m financing for its Tunisian GSM operation in Tunisia, one of the largest-ever project financings in the region.

Norton Rose enjoys increasing involvement in Tunisian transactions and acts for a wide range of regional and international clients in a variety of sectors, including oil and gas, banking and aviation finance. Noteworthy clients include Nouvelair Tunisie and Calyon SA. The firm recently acted for Maghrab Minerals Ltd on the acquisition of Tunisian zinc assets.

BANKING AND FINANCE

BANKING AND FINANCE

ADLY BELLAGHA & ASSOCIATES

Abdelly & Associates
Donia Hedda Ellouze, Cabinet
El Ajeri & El Ajeri International ✪
Gide Loyrette Nouel ✪
Salaheddine Caid Essebsi and Associates

Firms are listed A-Z in tiers which are ranked in order of priority
✪ *Indicates firm displays contact details at the end of this chapter.*

A series of banking laws has brought about increasing autonomy to Tunisia's banking institutions, bringing them more into line with international standards. Progress is therefore continuing in the banking sector, and the scope of banking business is being widened.

Adly Bellagha & Associates fully deserves its position as Tunisia's premier finance firm. The five-lawyer firm was recently advisor to Telecom Italia in relation to the preparation of its offer for the acquisition of Tunisie Telecom. Other finance clients include Sterling Merchant Finance, Citibank Tunis and Crédit Industriel et Commercial.

Three-partner **Abdelly & Associates**, dating back to 1923, is one of Tunisia's leading law firms with decades of experience in domestic and international banking. Aldine Abdelly is experienced on cross-border transactions, and works with other international firms in multi-jurisdictional projects. The firm handles all aspects of banking and finance including secured and syndicated loan transactions and guarantees, structured finance, project finance and recently advised on a US$150m loan for a major mobile phone company.

Cabinet Donia Hedda Ellouze is a 14-lawyer firm, including five partners, and has an international reputation for its work in foreign investments in Tunisia. Its banking work includes acting in the privatisation of banks.

New entrant to the tables is **El Ajeri & El Ajeri International**, a six-partner firm whose work includes asset finance, banking and finance and capital markets.

Gide Loyrette Nouel has had a Tunisia office since 2001 and is the only foreign law firm in the country. The past 12 months have been particularly busy on the banking and financial front and clients include the Tunisian government. The firm is advising Santander and Attijari on its privatisation bid for Banque du Sud, a leading Tunisian bank; and is legal counsel for a major French bank specialising in consumer credit. Clients include the International Finance Corporation, Merrill Lynch and major African banks.

Salaheddine Caid Essebsi and Associates has a reputable, seven-lawyer banking and corporate finance practice with name partner Salaheddine Caid Essesbi particularly experienced in these areas. The firm benefits from strong political connections – the post of Minister of Justice has been held by various members of the family.

CORPORATE AND M&A

CORPORATE AND M&A

ABDELLY & ASSOCIATES
ADLY BELLAGHA & ASSOCIATES

Donia Hedda Ellouze, Cabinet
El Ajeri & El Ajeri International ✪
Ferchiou & Associés Meziou Knani
Gide Loyrette Nouel ✪
Kallel & Associates
Malouche & Hamouda, Cabinet
Mili & Associates
Salaheddine Caid Essebsi and Associates
Zaanouni Law Firm

Firms are listed A-Z in tiers which are ranked in order of priority
✪ *Indicates firm displays contact details at the end of this chapter.*

The Tunisian Commercial Code is slowly being supplemented by further legislation but further liberalisation of the investment code in order to increase foreign investment is a challenge Tunisia still faces.

Leading firm **Abdelly & Associates** has advised on the partial privatisation of a major oil distribution company, and worked on the development of a new Tunisian airport; advised British Gas in a US$300m deal relating to a Tunisian power plant and also acts for Aurora Metals, a subsidiary of Aurora Gold Corporation. It has a major oil, mining and natural resources practice (name partner Samir Abdelly is a member of the International Association of Petroleum Negotiators), advising mining companies on permits, negotiating with governments and public and private companies and downstream and upstream projects. Recent clients include Maghreb Minerals plc in relation to its admission to AIM – **Norton Rose** advised Maghreb in relation to English law. **Abdelly & Associates** also advises on all aspects of telecommunications and IT law and advised SBC in the bidding for the second GSM licence in Tunisia

Adly Bellagha & Associates has a formidable reputation with both clients and international firms for referrals, and has been appointed as arbitrator in several matters by the ICC. Name partner Adly Bellagha is an experienced M&A lawyer. The firm's recent commercial transactions include acting as negotiator and adviser to the American Cooperative School of Tunis for the loan agreement with Riggs Bank; and on the privatisation front, acting for Cementos de Portugal (Cimpar) on its bid on Sotacib in Tunisia. The firm also advises on insolvencies, and is very strong in the gas and oil sector.

Cabinet Donia Hedda Ellouze is highly recommended for its privatisation work: the firm recently advised on the privatisation of three cement plants for Secil (Portugal), Colacem (Italy) and Prasa (Spain), and the privatisation of theGerman plaster plant, Knauf. The firm also advised in relation to the second licence for GSM Telefónica and acts as legal counsel for a number of multinationals and medium-sized enterprises. The firm also represents Tunisian companies investing abroad.

El Ajeri & El Ajeri International is headed by Mohamed Lotfi El Ajeri, and enjoys strong links with international law firms. The firm undertakes work across a broad spectrum of corporate and commercial issues.

Ferchiou & Associés Meziou Knani is now one of the largest firms in the country, with some 41 lawyers, and headed by name partner Noureddine Ferchiou, with a good reputation in the market. It has a particularly busy practice in the oil sector and is one of the leading commercial law firms in Tunisia. Clients include Merrill Lynch and IBM and the firm advises Orascom on the financing of its operations in Tunisia. The firm has advised in relation to several major privatisation and M&A transactions.

Gide Loyrette Nouel acts for major domestic and foreign companies in corporate matters, and is legal counsel to the government in relation to the construction and operation under a concession agreement of the new Enfidha Airport. It has recently advised a Moroccan company in the virgin oil sector, and advised new investors in Tunisia including in the electronics sector. The firm has enjoyed an upturn in real estate work with an increase in investment in Tunisian real estate contracts from the Far East. **Gide Loyrette Nouel** has a strong practice in M&A; clients include British Gas, United Biscuits and Hilton.

Kallel & Associates is a seven-lawyer firm working for a wide range of individuals andcompanies up to multinational corporations. The firm enjoys affiliations with firms in Europe, the US and the Middle East and is the Tunisian representative of the *Alliance of Arab Lawyers*. The firm has been very active in the government's privatisation programme including its sale of the country's cement producer, and the national energy generator.

Cabinet Malouche & Hamouda is a three-partner firm and is the Tunisian affiliate of *World Services Group*. The firm is active in the communications and banking sectors, and in general clients include major banks including Barclays Bank and Banca di Roma, Club Med, Pepsi Co and Air France.

Three-lawyer firm **Mili & Associates** has enjoyed working relationships with international law firms. Name partner Faouzi Mili has a reputation as one of Tunisia's leading lawyers. The firm specialises in foreign investment, copyright law and competition law, but also has a general corporate practice. It is frequently instructed by major accountancy firms such as PricewaterhouseCoopers and Moore Stephens as local counsel, and acts for a number of multinational corporations including Zeneca Pharmaceuticals (GB), the World Bank, Mitsui and Ayacho & Salaman (Paris).

Salaheddine Caid Essebsi and Associates has a strong corporate practice and expertise in the oil and gas sectors. Name partner Salaheddine Caid Essebsi is an experienced lawyer in international arbitration.

Two-partner firm **Zaanouni Law Firm** has one of the busiest full-service practices in Tunisia. Clients range from individuals to major multinationals.

EL AJERI & EL AJERI

5 RUE DE CHYPRE
MUTUELLE VILLE
1002 TUNIS

Telephone: +216 71 288 251
Fax: +216 71 892 525
Email: lotfi.elajeri@gnet.tn

Languages
Arabic, English, French, Italian

Number of lawyers 15

Contact
Mohamed Lotfi El Ajeri

CATEGORIES OF WORK

Aviation law

Banking and finance

Corporate and commercial

Dispute resolution, litigation and arbitration

E-commerce

Employment

Energy and natural resources

Foreign investment

Defeasance

Information technology

Infrastructure and project finance

Corporate restructuring

Insurance

Intellectual property

Mergers and acquisitions

Privatisation

Shipping and transport

Tax and telecommunications

Mediation

GIDE LOYRETTE NOUEL

21 AVENUE JUGURTHA
LE BELVÉDÈRE
1002 TUNIS

Telephone: +216 71 891 993
Fax: +216 71 893 492
E-mail: gln.tunis@gide.com
Website: www.gide.com

Other offices
Algiers, Beijing, Belgrade, Brussels, Bucharest, Budapest, Casablanca, Hanoi, Istanbul, London, Moscow, New York, Paris, Prague, Riyadh, Shanghai, Warsaw

Number of lawyers 586
at this office 9

Contacts
Kamel Ben Salah (bensalah@gide.com), Amina Larbi-Ezzine (larbi@gide.com)

CATEGORIES OF WORK

Mergers and acquisitions

Banking and finance

Capital markets

Intellectual property

Employment law

Project finance

Distribution and consumer law

Exchange regulations

Energy and natural resources

Arbitration

Real estate

TURKEY

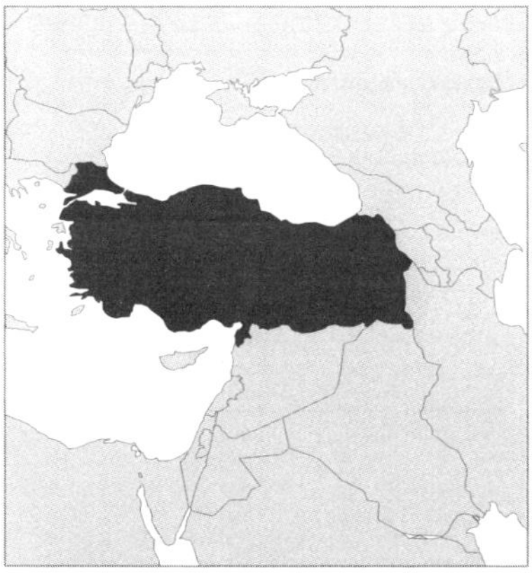

Population	70.3 million
Number of lawyers	35,000
Professional title	Attorney
Currency	Turkish lira (TL)

Index

Turkey has been at the centre of the world's attention in the last year, mainly due to the beginning of negotiations to join the European Union. Strategically important, spanning Europe and Asia, the country has a young demographic in its population of 70 million, a relatively stable and growing economy, and has traditionally aligned itself more closely with Europe following Mustafa Kemal Ataturk's reforms in the 1920s.

Moves towards EU membership have thrown the religious and cultural diversity of this predominantly secular society into sharp relief, and has exposed concerns over perceived human rights abuses, which have bogged down the negotiations. However, now that these talks have begun, greater momentum has built up to harmonise domestic legislation around the Copenhagen Criteria that govern eligibility to join the EU. Accession talks, the ongoing IMF programme, increasing political and economic stability, along with ongoing reform of the legal system, have encouraged foreign investors to enter the Turkish market, and the government's successful programme of major privatisations has led to vastly more foreign capital flowing in during 2005.

Turkey is booming as a place to do business – a far cry from the recession at the start of this decade.

ECONOMY

Foreign direct investment was significantly higher in 2005, with estimates putting it at over US$4bn, up from around US$1bn a year ago. More capital is coming in from Arab countries as well as Europe and the US. This interest has been partly stimulated by the major sales of state-owned assets like Turk Telekom, but many feel that these are simply a catalyst to greater foreign investment into Turkey in the long term.

The Istanbul Stock Exchange was very buoyant in 2005, indicating the solidity in the economy. Furthermore, both inflation and interest rates are down from historical levels. Estimates of gross national income for 2005 suggest an economic growth rate of around 5.5%, which many feel is sustainable in the foreseeable future.

On a technical note, Turkey recently removed the final six zeros from the Lira, bringing it down to more manageable numbers. Following an extended period of high inflation, the TL 20m note, for example, had been worth around US$15. The change is expected to rationalise cross-border transactions, and reflects the country's newly found control of inflation rates.

BILLING

Hourly rates are commonly used across many practice areas, though caps or agreed lump sums are becoming more commonplace. Partner rates vary, and competitive pricing was seen in 2005, though the dramatic increase in the volume of legal work in the market has subdued much price-cutting. Partners charge between US$240 and US$450 per hour, depending on their seniority and the type of work, while rates for associates range from US$180 to around US$220 per hour.

MARKETING

There are strict controls on how firms may advertise their services in Turkey, with legal advice seen as a public rather than a commercial service. Hence, firms are not allowed to advertise on television, in magazines or on the radio, and the naming of clients is largely frowned upon in any public context. As with many other aspects of the legal market, this may change as progress is made towards EU membership.

IN-HOUSE LAWYERS

There is a legal requirement that companies with over US$185,000 in capital must have an in-house legal team. While this means there is a growing number of in-house lawyers, they are nevertheless rarely involved in large projects, and any significant work is usually outsourced to law firms

FOREIGN LAW FIRMS

Restrictions on foreign law firms are extremely tight in Turkey, though many expect them to ease as the transition to EU stipulations on the free movement of services between member states comes into effect in the next few years. Currently, any Turkish lawyer employed directly by a foreign firm is forbidden to practise Turkish law, so very few international firms have a presence in Turkey. Those that do operate on a parallel basis, having a consultancy working in close association with a local firm. **Denton Wilde Sapte** has ties with **Güner Law Office**; **White & Case** works alongside

The largest firms

1	Hergüner Bilgen Özeke	55
2	Pekin & Bayar Law Firm	30
	Yarsuvat Law Firm	30
4	White & Case Mü, Savirlik Ltd. Sirketi	29
5	Derman Ortak Avukat Bürosu	27
	Pekin & Pekin	27
	Çaga & Çaga Law Firm	27
8	Gayret Consultant Services	26
9	CLO - Coskun Law Office	25
10	Akinci Law Office	24
11	Mehmet Gün & Co	22
12	Bener Law Office	21
	Cerrahoglu Law Firm	21
	D & D Law Firm	21
	Esin Lokmanhekim Içtem Gürkaynak	21
	Yamaner & Yamaner Law Offices	21
17	Cosar Avukatlik Bürosu	20
	Paksoy & Co.	20
19	Birsel Law Offices	18
	Postacioglu Law Office	18
	Somay Hukuk Bürosu	18
22	Güner Law Office	17
23	Hidayetoglu & Co	16
24	Gür Law Firm	15
	Ilhan Imik Law Office	15

These figures represent the total number of lawyers in this country only, and have been supplied by the firms themselves. The figures should be accurate as at 1 January 2006.

Derman Ortak Avukat Bürosu in Istanbul and **Çakmak Avukatlik Bürosu** in Ankara; **Salans** has a relationship with **Özel & Özel**; French firm **Gide Loyrette Nouel** works with local partners, and there is also **Senguler & Senguler in association with Ledingham Chalmers**.

Rumours about other international firms entering the market are persistent, but have yet to result in any concrete developments. Many of the large local firms often receive instructions from major international firms, though not necessarily on an exclusive basis.

LEGAL MARKET

Among domestic firms, the prevailing model is still to have a dominant partner, often in a family orientated business, which often leads to younger partners leaving to set up their own firms. However, younger firms like **Hergüner Bilgen Özeke**, which is now Turkey's largest firm, tend towards a more modern, European style of business, giving more opportunity to new partners.

Going forward, the need to have a broader range of specialist practitioners under one roof to handle the growing volume of complex, international legal work in the market may encourage more mergers, as has been seen with the formation of **Esin Lokmanhekim Içtem Gürkaynak** in 2005.

Along with **Hergüner Bilgen Özeke** a number of other domestic firms are seen as highly capable in international transactions, including **Pekin & Pekin**, **Pekin & Bayar Law Firm**, **Paksoy & Co.**, **Birsel Law Offices** and **Cerrahoglu Law Firm**.

BANKING, FINANCE AND CAPITAL MARKETS

BIRSEL LAW OFFICES
DENTON WILDE SAPTE ✪
DERMAN ORTAK AVUKAT BÜROSU
GÜNER LAW OFFICE ✪
HERGÜNER BILGEN ÖZEKE ✪
PAKSOY & CO. ✪
PEKIN & PEKIN ✪
WHITE & CASE LLP MÜ, SAVIRLIK LTD. SIRKETI

Çaga & Çaga Law Firm ✪
Çakmak Avukatlik Bürosu
Cerrahoglu Law Firm
Gide Loyrette Nouel ✪
Pekin & Bayar Law Firm ✪
Reisoglu-Ensari-Budak
Senguler & Senguler in association with Ledingham Chalmers ✪
Tekinalp

CLO – Coskun Law Office ✪
Dogru Law Office ✪
Erdem & Erdem Consultancy ✪
Ersoy Bilgehan Lawyers & Consultants ✪
Esin Lokmanhekim Içtem Gürkaynak ✪
Gökkiliç Law Office
Gürcan Law Offices ✪
Ilhan Imik Law Office ✪
Özel & Özel
Salans
Somay Hukuk Bürosu
Taboglu, Ates & Dermirhan ✪

Firms are listed A-Z in tiers which are ranked in order of priority
✪ Indicates firm displays contact details at the end of this chapter.

BANKING, FINANCE AND CAPITAL MARKETS

Birsel Law Offices comes highly recommended and has widespread respect for its banking, finance and capital markets expertise. Senior partner Mahmut Birsel's firm is seen to have significant capabilities in international transactions and has done well from the growing amount of work in capital markets. Major energy and media companies feature as key clients in this practice area.

Denton Wilde Sapte often works closely with **Güner Law Office** on international transactions, and in 2005 syndicated loans featured strongly. Leading international banks, commodity-trading houses and investment funds including Natexis Banques Populaires, Société Générale and ABN Amro Bank were among its clients. A US$1bn+ distressed debt acquisition was a highlight, as was advising Aviva plc on applications to the Turkish Capital Markets Board.

Derman Ortak Avukat Bürosu has close ties with **White & Case LLP Mü, Savirlik Ltd. Sirketi**, generating large amounts of debt and equity offerings involving foreign investors. Partners Mine H Taygun, Aslı Basgoz and Taylan Bayku have good reputations for handling significant banking matters, as does Aydin Düren in capital markets. Clients praise the firms as accurate, timely, interactive and knowledgeable.

Hergüner Bilgen Özeke is highly regarded and Gokhan Eraksoy was involved in the financing of the Turk Telekom privatisation, even though the firm did not represent the winning bidder. The firm, which added two mid-level associates to its banking team, was involved in Turkey's three largest bank takeovers. It also represents many foreign banks as general counsel in Turkey.

Paksoy & Co. was closely involved in the highly successful public offering of Vakifbank, the largest IPO in Turkey for five years. Serdar Paksoy and Togan Turan in banking, along with Pınar Eryürekli and Ömer Çollak in capital markets, have represented major international banks as underwriters to IPOs in the finance sector, while major retail and property companies have sought the firm's advice on financing and share offerings.

Clients recommend **Pekin & Pekin** highly, and it continues to advise local and foreign brokerage firms, banks, financial institutions and multinational corporations on complex Turkish capital markets law, including structuring and filing of public offerings in Turkey and offerings of Turkish companies in foreign markets. Senior partner Ahmed Pekin, along with M Fethi Pekin, has an outstanding reputation.

Çaga & Çaga Law Firm's wide range of activity in banking and capital markets sees it join the table. Erdem Degerli heads the team, advising clients on option transactions, loan and pledge agreements, collateralisation and securitisation matters, asset-backed financing, hedging mechanisms, bonds and regulatory issues.

Çakmak Avukatlik Bürosu in Ankara enjoys close links with **White & Case LLP Mü, Savirlik Ltd. Sirketi** and clients see it as well informed, proactive and dependable. Clients like HSBC, Limak, Inmet Mining Corporation, and Visa International show the development of its banking and finance practice. Partners Mehtap Yildirim Öztürk and Mesut Çakmak are well regarded.

Cerrahoglu Law Firm remains a high-quality firm with a reputation for handling complex matters for large domestic and international clients. In 2005, it advised a major Turkish holding company in regard to acquisitions in the banking sector.

Gide Loyrette Nouel added junior and mid-level lawyers to handle a good flow of finance deals. It has acted for Turkey's largest bank on a US$1bn securitisation. Bülent Ozdirekcan in Istanbul and newly arrived Güniz Gokçe in London, where she heads the cross-border finance team, have increased the number of international deals, the firm having also acted for German Banks.

Pekin & Bayar Law Firm is also seen as a leading firms in this and many other sectors. Selin Bayar and Sıla Yavuz have handled numerous financings for international banks.

Reisoglu-Ensari-Budak comes highly recommended for its expertise in both banking and capital markets.

The blend of local and international experience at **Senguler & Senguler in association with Ledingham Chalmers** has seen it advise a world-leading credit and debit card company on the launch of new products.

Dr Ünal Tekinalp is well known for his representation of banks, and **Tekinalp** is also favoured for capital markets work. The firm also advised many private companies as purchasers of banks from SDIF.

CLO – Coskun Law Office developed its practice last year, benefiting from is multilingual capability. Mustafa Tokdemir handles capital markets work, while founder Ihsan Coskun is active in banking and finance. Local and international client banks include Akbank, Sekerbank, Finansbank, ABN Amro in Istanbul and Merrill Lynch in London. Germany is a key market for inbound and outbound clients.

Dogru Law Office's Halil Dogru acted on a US$225m bond issue, and was involved in the formation of rules and regulations pertaining to the operation of the Turkish Derivatives Exchange (Turdex), which opened in February 2005.

Zihni Bilgehan heads **Ersoy Bilgehan Lawyers & Consultants**' banking practice, which features Gulistan Baltaci and Semih Sander, as well as its capital markets team, in which Ilknur Peksen and Dogan Eymirlioglu are also active. Much of its financing work is related to its market-leading shipping practice.

Corporate restructuring is key to **Esin Lokmanhekim Içtem Gürkaynak**'s work, the firm having acted for a consortium led by a US investment bank in regard to the sale of non-performing loans. It also represented a Turkish bank in a credit and debit card receivables securitisation deal.

Gökkiliç Law Office's Deniz Gökkılıç acted for a US mutual fund in a deal under the umbrella of the SDIF regarding the establishment of an asset management company, and advised two international banks in relation to Turkish banking regulations.

Cüneyd Gürcan of **Gürcan Law Offices** has been involved in debt restructuring, including transferring the debts of a Turkish company to a banking entity in the Netherlands.

Ilhan Imik Law Office's Ilhan Imik and Baris Oner have advised shareholders in the leading Turkish retail company on the public offering of shares, and also undertake banking-related litigation.

Salans works closely with **Özel & Özel**, and together the firms have maintained an active banking and finance practice, working with Turkish authorities and many parties involved in major privatisations.

Somay Hukuk Bürosu is involved in loans and syndications, leases and corporate financing for Turkish and international companies.

Taboglu, Ates & Dermirhan had an active year, Esin Taboglu acting for many of the Turkish companies listed on NYSE and LSE. The firm has a good reputation for international public offerings and private placements.

COMPETITION

Located in Ankara, **Çakmak Avukatlik Bürosu** is well placed for dealings with the Turkish Competition Authority. The firm works closely with **White & Case LLP Mü, Savirlik Ltd. Sirketi**, which brings in leading international clients, such as Lafarge. Partner Mehtap Yildirim-Özturk is the key player, and the firm is well supported by **Derman Ortak Avukat Bürosu** in Istanbul. Sarp Senol is a Turkish competition law expert and a leading light, advising clients in the finance, steel, petroleum, media, tobacco and food sectors.

Competition law is one of the five key practice areas of **Cerrahoglu Law Firm**, which maintains its strong reputation on the back of a growing stream of corporate work.

Hergüner Bilgen Özeke has added new expertise in the form of lawyers formerly of the Turkish Competition Board, giving the firm a total of three specialists in this area, most notably Mutlu Selçuk. The firm's extensive M&A and privatisation work has driven deals for clients like Peugeot and Roche.

Paksoy & Co.'s Pınar Eryürekli and Togan Turan also saw their workload increase last year, acting for the likes of adidas, Russian steel manufacturer NLMK, POS, Tetra Laval, Dow Chemical and Carlyle Group on filings before the competition authorities.

Aybay & Aybay has also benefited from the growing volume of work generated by M&A activity in Turkey. Major Turkish media clients feature in its client list, and the firm was engaged on a significant application in the airline industry. In the media area, it was also active in preparing for the competition implications of the transition to EU regulations governing the television market.

Cosar Avukatlik Bürosu has represented one of Turkey's leading holding companies before the Council of State, a leading domestic steel company and many other high-quality clients. Partner Utku Çosar is a recognised expert on anti-trust.

Zihni Bilgehan, Ilknur Peksen, Serhat Sayin, Bahar Bircan and Dogan Eymirlioglu at **Ersoy Bilgehan Lawyers & Consultants** have all been busy, the firm advising a leading global listed company in regard to a US$150m acquisition of a

COMPETITION

ÇAKMAK AVUKATLIK BÜROSU
CERRAHOGLU LAW FIRM
DERMAN ORTAK AVUKAT BÜROSU
HERGÜNER BILGEN ÖZEKE ✪
PAKSOY & CO. ✪
WHITE & CASE LLP MÜ, SAVIRLIK LTD. SIRKETI

Aybay & Aybay ✪
Çaga & Çaga Law Firm ✪
Cosar Avukatlik Bürosu ✪
Denton Wilde Sapte ✪
Ersoy Bilgehan Lawyers & Consultants ✪
Esin Lokmanhekim Içtem Gürkaynak ✪
Gide Loyrette Nouel ✪
Gökkiliç Law Office
Güner Law Office ✪
Gürcan Law Offices ✪
Ismen ✪
Mehmet Gün & Co ✪
Pekin & Bayar Law Firm ✪
Pekin & Pekin ✪
Tekinalp
Turunç & Savaşçin ✪

Firms are listed A-Z in tiers which are ranked in order of priority
✪ *Indicates firm displays contact details at the end of this chapter.*

majority stake in a market-leading Turkish company.

Esin Lokmanhekim Içtem Gürkaynak handles work referred by top international law firms. Its strong relationships with banks are key. Formerly *Esin & Co*, the firm expanded with the arrival of new partners Serkan Içtem, who heads the competition and EU regulatory department, and Gönenç Gurkaynak, who is co-head of corporate law.

Gide Loyrette Nouel's Didier Ziya Cailliau became the third partner in the Istanbul office last year. He has a good reputation in competition law, and his promotion reflects the firm's growing expertise in this area.

Gökkiliç Law Office's Ekin Güncan often conducts filings before the Turkish Competition Authority and is currently working for a top-ten Turkish pharmaceutical company and a well-known European telecoms company.

Güner Law Office often works closely with **Denton Wilde Sapte**, with competition issues and filings part of almost all the firm's deals. In 2005, the firm advised a Belgian window profile production company, the Turkish arm of a renowned international food company, and leading Turkish holding companies on competition law.

Gürcan Law Offices' Cüneyd Gürcan and Burcu Aksakoglu were more active last year, as were Nese Tasdemir, Pınar Öztürk, Sevi Bozoglu at **Mehmet Gün & Co**.

Ismen established in late 2004, has clients such as a major US film and entertainment company for competition matters, and last year performed competition law analysis for six state-owned ports. Tolga Ismen, previously at **White & Case LLP Mü, Savirlik Ltd. Sirketi**, has handled investigations and notifications on behalf of major international and domestic companies, as has Özlem Öksün, formerly of **ESC Consulting**.

Pekin & Bayar Law Firm has kept its place among the top firms for competition expertise, following work in acquisitions in the pharmaceutical, finance, technology and industrial chemicals sectors.

Pekin & Pekin has developed an enviable practice in competition matters and antitrust law, acting on behalf of international clients, including many from Europe.

Dr Ünal Tekinalp has written on the subject of competition in relation to EU law, and colleague Mehtap Digili at **Tekinalp** is also an expert in this area.

Turunç & Savasçin's Noyan Turunç and Esin Taylan are leading practitioners of competition law.

CORPORATE AND M&A

CERRAHOGLU LAW FIRM
DERMAN ORTAK AVUKAT BÜROSU
HERGÜNER BILGEN ÖZEKE ✪
PAKSOY & CO. ✪
PEKIN & PEKIN ✪
WHITE & CASE LLP MÜ, SAVIRLIK LTD. SIRKETI

BIRSEL LAW OFFICES
ÇAGA & ÇAGA LAW FIRM ✪
ÇAKMAK AVUKATLIK BÜROSU
CLO – COSKUN LAW OFFICE ✪
COSAR AVUKATLIK BÜROSU ✪
DENTON WILDE SAPTE ✪
GÜNER LAW OFFICE ✪
GÜR LAW FIRM ✪
MEHMET GÜN & CO ✪
PEKIN & BAYAR LAW FIRM ✪
POSTACIOGLU LAW OFFICE ✪

Esin Lokmanhekim Içtem Gürkaynak ✪
Gide Loyrette Nouel ✪
Gürcan Law Offices ✪
Ismen ✪
Özel & Özel
Salans
Somay Hukuk Bürosu
Tekinalp
Turunç & Savasçin ✪

Aksu & Savas & Çaliskan
Aybay & Aybay ✪
Bircanoglu Attorneys at Law ✪
D & D Law Firm ✪
Ersoy Bilgehan Lawyers & Consultants ✪
Gökkiliç Law Office
Inal Law Office ✪
Özkan Law Office
PI Partners ✪
Sakmar & Partners Law Office
Senguler & Senguler in association with Ledingham Chalmers ✪
Serap Zuvin Law Offices ✪
Yarsuvat & Yarsuvat Law Firm

Firms are listed A-Z in tiers which are ranked in order of priority
✪ Indicates firm displays contact details at the end of this chapter.

CORPORATE AND M&A

Cerrahoglu Law Firm is recommended by clients for its high-quality work, with corporate experience that is second to none in Istanbul. The firm advises over 50 multinationals, including leaders in the retail, real estate, aerospace and aviation sectors.

Emre Derman's 'world-class' team at **Derman Ortak Avukat Bürosu** has had its share of the larger volume of work in the market, reflected in Meltem Akol's promotion to partner this year. The M&A team has been busy with new clients such as Esas Holding and Çukurova Holding, as well as existing clients such as TEB and Deutsche Bank, much of the work coming from the banking sector. Current transactions include representing the Çukurova Group in the sale of indirect interest in Turkcell to Russia's largest privately owned financial and industrial conglomerate, Alfa Group. The firm has a close working relationship with **White & Case LLP Mü, Savirlik Ltd. Sirketi**.

Turkey's largest firm and resident heavyweight **Hergüner Bilgen Özeke** has grown further in the last year, adding more corporate lawyers to handle the surge of foreign investment into Turkey. The firm was involved in most of the large M&A deals in 2005, acting for international clients such as Peugeot, BMW and Master Foods. Okan Demirkan is among the key partners.

Paksoy & Co., where Serdar Paksoy, Pınar Eryürekli and Elvan Aziz are the key players, has handled major M&A work for foreign clients, including the representation of NLMK, Russia's third-largest steel manufacturer, in its proposed acquisition of the government's stake in Erdemir, the largest steel manufacturer in Turkey. Other international clients include Polish petroleum company PKN Orlen, Sony Corporation, Carlyle Group and Puma, while leading Turkish clients include Koç Financial Services.

Pekin & Pekin also maintains its strong reputation for advising major international corporations and banking and finance institutions on all aspects of Turkish corporate law, with Ahmed Pekin and M Fethi Pekin seen as key players. Major clients come from the biomedical, technology, banking and pharmaceutical sectors, among others.

Birsel Law Offices is well regarded among the legal community in Turkey for the quality of its work. Senior partner Mahmut Birsel is a leading light.

Çaga & Çaga Law Firm's head of M&A Barbaros Çaga is well known for his long-established presence in the market, and saw his firm grow busier in 2005. It was involved in acquisition bids for high-calibre clients in the telecoms, media, paper, consumer goods and energy sectors. Erdem Degerli also handles corporate and commercial work, which is the mainstay of the firm's activity, representing leading domestic and foreign clients.

Çakmak Avukatlik Bürosu in Ankara has also seen M&A work grow, handling foreign clients through its close ties with **White & Case LLP Mü, Savirlik Ltd. Sirketi**. Instructions came from new clients such as Severstal, SK Telekom, Ineos and Ottoman Energy, as well as transactions for existing clients such as Inmet, Limak, Mineral Technologies and Edison Mission Energy. The firm has particular expertise in energy, mining and petroleum. Clients describe the service as professional, prompt and courteous.

CLO – Coskun Law Office worked on the restructuring of Degirmenci Group, one of the largest producers and exporters of textiles in Turkey, the large and influential media company Sabah Group, and the Yüksel Construction Corporation.

Clients of **Cosar Avukatlik Bürosu** include Italian holding company DeLonghi, which acquired a Turkish firm in 2005; Israeli company Polgat Ltd in a joint venture in the textile sector; and major Turkish companies. Arzu Çosar is seen as a leading lawyer for corporate work.

Güner Law Office work closely with **Denton Wilde Sapte** to bring in foreign clients. Its office is headed by Ece Güner, who specialises in M&A, energy, telecoms and projects work. Major clients include Italcimenti (Ciments Français) on the sale of Rumeli group's cement plants, Shell in the acquisition of state-owned refinery company Tupras, Falconbridge and Rio Tinto.

The corporate department of **Gür Law Firm** is the equal of its market-leading maritime practice, and has extensive experience in share purchase agreements, partnerships and joint ventures, particularly involving foreign investors. It boasts many international clients from the medical, logistics, cargo, textile and finance sectors and has attracted significant M&A work.

Mehmet Gün, Ural Özbek and Eda Okay at **Mehmet Gün & Co** have represented Swedish clients in the purchase of a 50% stake in a Turkish mining company, and acts in founding new businesses and acquiring shareholdings in advertising, industrial and trading sectors. Clients enthuse about the firm's professionalism and its understanding of international legal issues.

Pekin & Bayar Law Firm is still seen as a high-quality firm, Sefika Pekin and Deniz Sorguç being involved in many high-profile company sales.

Postacioglu Law Office has a branch office in Paris as a conduit for both Turkish and French investors. Clients include major players in the medical, finance, insurance, property, leisure and retail sectors.

Esin Lokmanhekim Içtem Gürkaynak, formerly *Esin & Co*, deals with large entities in the retail, port, healthcare and industrial materials sectors. It represented a major Turkish business group in the acquisition of a fast food master franchise in Turkey and advised internationally recognised consumer goods and consultancy businesses on corporate governance matters and commercial contracts.

French firm **Gide Loyrette Nouel**'s Guillaume Rougier-Brierre has gained recognition among Turkish and foreign clients and is one of France's foreign trade advisors in Turkey. He has acted for key French clients including L'Oréal and France Télécom. The firm has also handled the sale of stakes in a joint venture by BNP and Dresdner Bank.

Cüneyd Gürcan, Burku Aksakoglu and Ahu Akin at **Gürcan Law Offices** have acted on many private and public incorporations, due diligence and share acquisitions on behalf of foreign companies.

Tolga Ismen at **Ismen** previously worked for **White & Case LLP Mü, Savirlik Ltd. Sirketi**, and has wide experience in the corporate and commercial sector and was joined this year by Arzu Günalçin, who has 12 years' experience at **Tekinalp**. The firm handled M&A work in the finance, telecoms, mining and FMCG sectors.

Özel & Özel has a close relationship with international firm **Salans**. The firm recently represented a Turkish client in a major purchase in the petroleum distribution sector, involving the purchase of shares from a foreign partner. Haluk Can Özel and Orkun Özel are the key partners.

Somay Hukuk Bürosu is recommended for smaller and mid-market transactions and has long experience in company formations, foreign investment laws, compliance issues and tax matters.

The reputation of **Tekinalp** remains strong in this area, with Dr Ünal Tekinalp widely seen as one of the most famous and capable commercial lawyers in Turkey.

Aksu & Savas & Çaliskan remains active on the incorporation of foreign companies, though advice on corporate governance and M&A-related disputes now feature more strongly.

Ali Kartal's practice at **Aybay & Aybay** is well regarded, as is the team at **Bircanoglu Attorneys at Law**, which is highly recommended. **D & D Law Firm**'s Berna Akkor oversaw a US$1bn loan sale auction by the Turkish government to a potential investor, and performed the relevant due diligence.

Ersoy Bilgehan Lawyers & Consultants' Zihni Bilgehan, Ilknur Peksen, Gulistan Baltaci, Dogan Eymirlioglu and Semih Sander are in demand, with deals including the US$150m acquisition of the majority shares in a leading Turkish company by a foreign entity. An Austrian cement company, and US and European mining companies, typify the quality of clients. It also advised a global leader in the postal services and cargo business.

At **Gökkiliç Law Office**, Ekin Güncan and Deniz Gökkılıç work closely with many foreign law firms. Foreign investors featured strongly as clients in 2005, particularly for M&A work in the packaging, manufacturing and industrial sectors.

Seyma Inal at **Inal Law Office** advises clients on both non-contentious aspects of corporate and commercial matters as well as litigation. She has an impressive background in corporate law, acquisitions and joint ventures. Clients include major Turkish banks.

Özkan Law Office was founded in 2005 by Zeynep Özkan, formerly of **Yamaner & Yamaner Law Offices**, and has already gained a foothold in corporate work.

PI Partners, the Turkish offshoot of a firm based in Greece, is doing well in attracting corporate work, while **Sakmar & Partners Law Office**'s Mine Sakmar and Ata Sakmar are known for handling mainly foreign clients.

Clients are full of praise for **Senguler & Senguler in association with Ledingham Chalmers**, which has further established its presence in Turkey.

Serap Zuvin Law Offices continues to advise on broad aspects of corporate law and deals with a greater inflow of foreign capital.

M&A remains a principal source of work for **Yarsuvat & Yarsuvat Law Firm**, often for international companies.

DISPUTE RESOLUTION

AYBAY & AYBAY ✪
ÇAKMAK AVUKATLIK BÜROSU
COSAR AVUKATLIK BÜROSU ✪
DERMAN ORTAK AVUKAT BÜROSU
HERGÜNER BILGEN ÖZEKE ✪
MEHMET GÜN & CO ✪
PAKSOY & CO. ✪
WHITE & CASE LLP MÜ, SAVIRLIK LTD. SIRKETI

Bircanoglu Attorneys at Law ✪
Birsel Law Offices
Çaga & Çaga Law Firm ✪
Cerrahoglu Law Firm
Denton Wilde Sapte ✪
Gide Loyrette Nouel ✪
Gökkiliç Law Office
Güner Law Office ✪
Okur and Okur
Özel & Özel
Pekin & Bayar Law Firm ✪
Pekin & Pekin ✪
Postacioglu Law Office ✪
Salans
Turunç & Savasçin ✪
Yarsuvat & Yarsuvat Law Firm

CLO – Coskun Law Office ✪
Duman Law Office ✪
Erdem & Erdem Consultancy ✪
Esin Lokmanhekim Içtem Gürkaynak ✪
Gür Law Firm ✪
Gürcan Law Offices ✪
Ilhan Imik Law Office ✪
Sakmar & Partners Law Office
Tekinalp

Firms are listed A-Z in tiers which are ranked in order of priority
✪ *Indicates firm displays contact details at the end of this chapter.*

DISPUTE RESOLUTION

Aybay & Aybay has gained many clients from the insurance sector for litigation work. The firm currently acts for a major surveyor in the oil market, as well as Danish and Italian clients. The spearhead of the litigation practice is Kemal Özturk, who works in a team of six lawyers.

Çakmak Avukatlik Bürosu's location in Ankara means it is well placed for government-related work. Representing Kizilirmak in an ICC arbitration against the Republic of Turkey in relation to an electricity distribution dispute was a highlight, as was an action for Lafarge Beton AS. Partners Mesut Çakmak and Mehtap Yildirim-Özturk are supported by Tugba Bayman, Keskin Çagdas and Evrim Ergun. The firm co-operates closely with **White & Case LLP Mü, Savirlik Ltd. Sirketi**.

Cosar Avukatlik Bürosu ascends the rankings on the back of substantial work in 2005. A strong team, led by Utku Çosar in Ankara, has attracted new clients for international arbitrations and many cases relating to energy disputes, including assisting a Swiss law firm with the defence of the Ministry of Energy & Natural Resources in the Swiss Federal Court. The firm continues to act for Warner Bros in complex licence litigation.

Derman Ortak Avukat Bürosu also works closely with **White & Case LLP Mü, Savirlik Ltd. Sirketi** in handling major foreign clients such as Nestlé. Partner Mutlu Simayli is a key player, supported by good associates.

Hergüner Bilgen Özeke has taken time to build its reputation for litigation, but the addition of more lawyers to handle arbitration work in Murat Karkin's team has placed it firmly in the top tier. It was the first firm to successfully represent a client under Turkey's new international arbitration law.

Mehmet Gün & Co's name partner, along with Rıza Gümbüsoglu and Eda Okay, have maintained a reputation in wider dispute resolution matters, though the firm's strength in intellectual property matters is also a driver of the growing litigation workload.

Serdar Paksoy and Elvan Aziz at **Paksoy & Co.** have maintained high-quality clients including state entities like the Ministry of Energy & Natural Resources, which faced an action from claimants in the US over a power project.

Bircanoglu Attorneys at Law maintains a strong profile for dispute resolution, as does **Birsel Law Offices**, which continues to develop its presence in international commercial arbitration.

Çaga & Çaga Law Firm's litigation department is led by Idil Çaga Degerli and features the well-known Sevda Ar. Currently handling more than 1000 cases, these include complex, high-value tax disputes and shareholder disputes.

Cerrahoglu Law Firm added a new partner in litigation, Selale Kartal, last year, bolstering a team that acts for a world-leading tyre manufacturer and a global brand in the electronics/telecoms sector.

Gide Loyrette Nouel's Nazan Candaner Elver is growing in prominence in Turkish arbitration and she is the youngest lawyer appointed to the shortlist of the Istanbul Chamber of Commerce.

Deniz Gökkılıç of **Gökkiliç Law Office** has seen a growing caseload, working for one of the word's largest pharmaceutical corporations on disputes in Turkey, as well as a major domestic holding company active in seeding capital ventures.

Güner Law Office work closely with **Denton Wilde Sapte**, a relationship that brings in multinational clients for both transactions and litigation. It was involved in the successful enforcement of one of the largest arbitral awards in Turkey's history during 2005, worth around US$1bn. It is currently acting for a Japanese manufacturer on a high-value claim over a distribution agreement.

Okur and Okur comes highly recommended among Turkey's legal community, as does **Pekin & Bayar Law Firm**, whose strong presence in many practice areas also extends to litigation and arbitration.

Senior partner Gökben Erdem is among the respected litigators at **Pekin & Pekin**, where the team comes highly recommended for disputes relating to many practice areas.

Postacioglu Law Office successfully represented one of Turkey's leading sports teams in lawsuits against foreign players, as well as handling disputes for one of Turkey's largest companies and a subsidiary of a major player in the automotive sector.

International firm **Salans** brings its specialisation in international arbitration to its close relationship with **Özel & Özel** in Turkey, the latter currently representing a government body in an ICSID arbitration brought by a leading telecoms company under a clause of the Turkey-US Bilateral Investment Treaty in a claim for US$2bn, plus interest. Haluk Can Özel and Beren Özel are well regarded.

Yarsuvat & Yarsuvat Law Firm has a well-known civil and criminal litigation practice, cross-border expertise and growing experience in alternative dispute resolution.

CLO – Coskun Law Office handles arbitration, mediation and litigation for domestic and international clients, with M Ali Erdogan, prominent in commercial litigation.

Partner Mustafa Duman at **Duman Law Office** is well known. He deals with corporate and commercial disputes, criminal, employment and enforcement lawsuits. Clients include two of Turkey's best-selling newspapers, and he represented a Turkish National Assembly member in a compensation claim against a media company.

Erdem & Erdem Consultancy maintains a presence in litigation, while **Esin Lokmanhekim Içtem Gürkaynak** recently acted for a Turkish holding companies in regard to share-purchase disputes, and foreign entities in cross-border disputes.

Gür Law Firm is active in litigation, arbitration and enforcement of foreign judicial and arbitral awards in Turkey.

Gürcan Law Offices' Mustafa Urganci, Murat Kizilyel and Tarik Erol had another busy year, as has Ilhan Imik at **Ilhan Imik Law Office**.

Sakmar & Partners Law Office's Mine Sakmar and Ata Sakmar are highly regarded, as is Dr Ünal Tekinalp at **Tekinalp**.

IT AND TELECOMS

IT AND TELECOMS

BIRSEL LAW OFFICES
ÇAGA & ÇAGA LAW FIRM ⭘
DENTON WILDE SAPTE ⭘
GÜNER LAW OFFICE ⭘
HERGÜNER BILGEN ÖZEKE ⭘
ÖZEL & ÖZEL
SALANS

Çakmak Avukatlik Bürosu
Derman Ortak Avukat Bürosu
Gide Loyrette Nouel ⭘
Gökkiliç Law Office
Ismen ⭘
Mehmet Gün & Co ⭘
Pekin & Bayar Law Firm ⭘
Pekin & Pekin ⭘
Senguler & Senguler in association with Ledingham Chalmers ⭘
White & Case LLP Mü, Savirlik Ltd. Sirketi

Firms are listed A-Z in tiers which are ranked in order of priority
⭘ Indicates firm displays contact details at the end of this chapter.

Birsel Law Offices has long focused on telecoms, and this remains key to the practice, which was firmly involved in the increasing activity in this field during 2005.

Çaga & Çaga Law Firm's experience in IT and telecoms is extensive after the firm expanded its services to these sectors in recent years. It advised on a merger between major Turkish mobile operators and a state-owned entity, and is active on matters relating to acquisition and telecoms contracts for major domestic companies.

Güner Law Office works closely with **Denton Wilde Sapte**, a relationship that spurred more activity in 2005. Sony and Nokia featured as key clients and Ece Güner's reputation for telecoms work is formidable. She represented a major GSM operator and its Turkish subsidiary in significant transactions, and also advised Hutchison Whampoa Ltd.

Hergüner Bilgen Özeke has contributed to the drafting of Turkey's telecoms laws, and advised a bidder from the UAE and a Turkish holding company in the Turk Telekom deal, though theirs was not the winning bidder. It handles licensing matters for major international telecoms companies, including one that bid for Turkey's second largest GSM operator.

Özel & Özel, which works closely with **Salans**, is part of a consortium assisting the State Planning Organisation on the transition to e-government. Haluk Can Özel and Orkun Güncan are notable lawyers in this field, and last year the firm recruited Sibel Verda Berkarda from the legal department of Turkcell.

Çakmak Avukatlik Bürosu in Ankara has notable individuals in partner Mehtap Yildirim Öztürk and associates Çagdas Evrim Ergün, Sebnem Onder and Tugba Bayman Keskin. The firm advised a major international credit card company on matters of cross-border electronic money transfer and data privacy law is a growing area of the practice. It also advised a party on bids for Turk Telekom, as did **Derman Ortak Avukat Bürosu**, which is currently acting for Orascom in a bid for GSM operator Telsim. Both firms have close links to **White & Case LLP Mü, Savirlik Ltd. Sirketi**.

Gide Loyrette Nouel is advising a party on the auction of a second mobile network licence in Turkey, and **Gökkiliç Law Office** is still strong in IT and telecoms law.

Ismen, established in late 2004 as a two-partner firm has handled the notification for the change of control of a Turkish network operator, and handled the acquisition of a 40% stake in another major operator. Tolga Ismen, previously at **White & Case LLP Mü, Savirlik Ltd. Sirketi**, has wide experience in telecoms work.

Mehmet Gün & Co's IT practice features Ugur Aktekin, Ceylin Beyli and Bilge Saltan and advises foreign clients on e-commerce regulations in Turkey, as well as data protection matters, especially those involving employees' data gathered and processed by the employers.

Pekin & Bayar Law Firm and **Pekin & Pekin** remain active in this practice area.

Senguler & Senguler in association with Ledingham Chalmers advised a major telecoms company from the UK in its partnership with Saudi Oger, the winning bidder in the US$6.55bn Turk Telekom privatisation.

INTELLECTUAL PROPERTY

HERGÜNER BILGEN ÖZEKE ✪
MEHMET GÜN & CO ✪

Arihan & Arihan
Çaga & Çaga Law Firm ✪
Denton Wilde Sapte ✪
Derman Ortak Avukat Bürosu
Gide Loyrette Nouel ✪
Güner Law Office ✪
Istanbul Patent & Trademark Consultancy, Ltd
Postacioglu Law Office ✪
White & Case LLP Mü, Savirlik Ltd. Sirketi

Esref Alacayir Law Office
Gürcan Law Offices ✪
Paksoy & Co. ✪
Pekin & Bayar Law Firm ✪
Pekin & Pekin ✪
Poroy and Özülkü Attorneys At Law
Tekinalp
Turunç & Savasçin ✪

Firms are listed A-Z in tiers which are ranked in order of priority
✪ *Indicates firm displays contact details at the end of this chapter.*

INTELLECTUAL PROPERTY

Hergüner Bilgen Özeke is now in the top tier, having gained major clients from its competitors in the last two years, significantly in the software sector. The firm has a specialist department and has written many of the amendments to IP law as part of the country's ongoing review of legislation. It also trains judges in the application of IP law, and Murat Karkin is well known in this field.

Mehmet Gün & Co has a large roster of major clients, who praise its commercial and strategic style and place it firmly at the top in this field. Many of the firm's lawyers, including Mehmet Gün, Selma Toplu Ünlü, Ugur Aktekin, Ceylin Beyli and Barıs Kalaycı (who is now a partner) handle IP work. The trade mark enforcement department represents many world famous brands and regularly carries out raids and seizures. Leading pharmaceutical companies are key clients, though the firm also acts for entities in the food and beverage, broadcasting, textile, naval construction, computing and mobile content sectors.

Arihan & Arihan specialises in the full range of IP matters, from registration to litigation and enforcement.

Idil Çaga Degerli leads **Çaga & Çaga Law Firm**'s IP division, which has a high volume of high-value actions before Turkey's specialist courts. It is often called upon to consult on licensing and copyright contracts, and last year dealt with major clients in the software, publishing and broadcast sectors.

Derman Ortak Avukat Bürosu's relationship with **White & Case LLP Mü, Savirlik Ltd. Sirketi** is a solid basis for the 'excellent, world-class' work of Mutlu Simayli, Galip M Selcuk and Sezgin Bas, who regularly act for domestic and global clients in the defence of IP rights in Turkey.

Gide Loyrette Nouel's prestigious clients include L'Oréal and the firm has added the experience of Esra Dündar Loiseau as senior associate, previously development manager of the Orangina soft drink for the Turkish market, who has practised in IP in both France and Turkey.

Güner Law Office, which works closely with **Denton Wilde Sapte**, is currently preparing a report for Deceuninck Plastics Industrial in relation to trade mark lawsuit initiated for revocation of a trade mark from the Turkish Trademark Registry, and has advised retailer Marks & Spencer on patent protection.

Istanbul Patent & Trademark Consultancy, Ltd joins this year's list, where head of IP Dilek Ustun handles foreign work, trade marks and copyrights, along with partners Erkan Sevinc, Ibrahim Ekdial and Guven Cali. The firm is also active in internet domain name disputes.

Postacioglu Law Office incorporated its IP team in 1997 and has since developed strong relationships with major international brand names, as well as Turkish listed companies.

MEDIA AND ENTERTAINMENT

ÇAGA & ÇAGA LAW FIRM ✪
DENTON WILDE SAPTE ✪
GÜNER LAW OFFICE ✪

Gide Loyrette Nouel ✪
Mehmet Gün & Co ✪
NSN Law Office
Pekin & Pekin ✪
Taboglu, Ates & Dermirhan ✪

Firms are listed A-Z in tiers which are ranked in order of priority
✪ *Indicates firm displays contact details at the end of this chapter.*

MEDIA AND ENTERTAINMENT

Çaga & Çaga Law Firm is without doubt a top-flight firm in media and entertainment work, its clients including Turkey's premier holding company in this sector and all of its subsidiaries, for which it handles transactions and litigation. It offers regular advice on media-related investments and has a niche in advising broadcasting companies.

The close co-operation between **Denton Wilde Sapte** and **Güner Law Office** has seen it act for one of the world's largest media groups, particularly in regard to its proposed acquisition of Digiturk, the Turkish satellite television transmitter.

Gide Loyrette Nouel recently advised a leading Turkish client in a transaction regarding Star TV, while the team at **Mehmet Gün & Co**, which is driven by Selma Toplu Ünlü and Ceylin Beyli, also remained active.

NSN Law Office joins the rankings, largely due to its involvement last year in the legal contracts for the two largest film productions in Turkey. Nazli Selek and Tugba Unsal were notably involved.

Pekin & Pekin's Can Oguzer, Hasan Caglayan and Selin Bayar were active in this practice area, as was the team at **Taboglu, Ates & Dermirhan**, which advised a leading entertainment company in a merger project with another entity in the media sector.

PRIVATISATION

The relationship between **Çakmak Avukatlik Bürosu** in Ankara, **Derman Ortak Avukat Bürosu** in Istanbul and international firm **White & Case LLP Mü, Savirlik Ltd. Sirketi**, which added a new tax facility that proved key to one finance-sector privatisation, attracts many key instructions. Partner Aslı Basgoz represented a major international steel company in the privatisation of Erdemir and a leading telecoms company in a bid for a stake in Turkcell. Meltem Akol at **Derman Ortak Avukat Bürosu** was also a key player in many deals.

Hergüner Bilgen Özeke was involved in most of the major privatisations during 2005, which was the firm's biggest year in one of its most important practice areas. The firm, still the largest in Turkey, expanded its headcount to cope with the workload in this sector.

Paksoy & Co.'s Serdar Paksoy, Pınar Eryürekli and Togan Turan have advised key clients including a major Russian metals producer interested in the sale of Turkey's state-owned iron and steel company Erdemir. It also advised a Polish company on the sale of refinery corporation

PRIVATISATION

ÇAKMAK AVUKATLIK BÜROSU
DERMAN ORTAK AVUKAT BÜROSU
HERGÜNER BILGEN ÖZEKE ✪
PAKSOY & CO. ✪
PEKIN & BAYAR LAW FIRM ✪
PEKIN & PEKIN ✪
WHITE & CASE LLP MÜ, SAVIRLIK LTD. SIRKETI

Cerrahoglu Law Firm
Cosar Avukatlik Bürosu ✪
Denton Wilde Sapte ✪
Güner Law Office ✪
Ismen ✪
Özel & Özel
Salans

Çaga & Çaga Law Firm ✪
Esin Lokmanhekim Içtem Gürkaynak ✪
Gökkiliç Law Office
Taboglu, Ates & Dermirhan ✪

Firms are listed A-Z in tiers which are ranked in order of priority
✪ *Indicates firm displays contact details at the end of this chapter.*

Tüpras and a US private equity fund in its bid for Turk Telekom. Sales of banks by the SDIF also brought in work.

Pekin & Bayar Law Firm's Selin Bayar, Sefika Pekin, Deniz Sorguç and Muharrem Küçük have been involved for various parties on the sales of Tüpras, Erdemir, Turk Telekom and Telsim, as well as representing bidders in the privatisation of major concerns in the cement industry.

Pekin & Pekin has handled some successful filings for its clients as part of Turkey's privatisation programme and advises lenders as well as bidders. Sales of cement plants, a petroleum distribution company, the state steel producer, an airport handling services concern and numerous banks held by the SDIF featured in its workload.

Cerrahoglu Law Firm has also been involved in some of the major deals, including Turk Telekom, Erdemir, Tüpras and state-owned cement factories.

Cosar Avukatlik Bürosu has acted on behalf of state entities in deals like the Tüpras refinery company sale, as well as the complex Tedas electricity distribution company privatisation. Arzu Çosar in the firm's Istanbul office is the key partner in these and other transactions.

Güner Law Office, working with **Denton Wilde Sapte**, acted on behalf of a major international energy firm that partnered with a large Turkish holding company in its bid for Tüpras, which ultimately proved successful. The firm advised on due diligence, the bid process and the partnership between the two companies.

Though it has a more focused approach on fewer projects than some other firms, new entrant **Ismen** obtained a mandate for port privatisation in early 2005, handling a US$755m 36-year concession for Mersin Port, and an US$80m concession for Iskenderun Port.

Özel & Özel, which works closely with international firm **Salans**, saw privatisations account for a sizeable amount of the its work, having advised a Turkish consortium on its bid for Turk Telekom. Haluk Can Özel, Onur Kordel and Orkun Güncan are prominent in a team that has also been involved in port privatisations, the Tüpras sale and the second tender for the sale of Samsun Fertiliser.

Çaga & Çaga Law Firm currently acts for a German company in the privatisation of vehicle inspection activities in Turkey, both in its dealings with the state and in the contracts with its joint venture partners.

Esin Lokmanhekim Içtem Gürkaynak has acted for state entities in Cyprus in bids (KTHY – Cypriot Turkish Airlines) and represented a consortium bidding in the privatisation of Galataport.

Gökkiliç Law Office's Ekin Güncan heads a team acting for a party involved in the privatisation of the operation rights of a water treatment facility in Kayseri.

Taboglu, Ates & Dermirhan mostly represents potential buyers, notably in the privatisation of petrochemical company Petkim, fertiliser company Igsas and pulp and paper producer Seka.

PROJECT FINANCE

Birsel Law Offices' strengths in banking and finance position it well for involvement in the financing of major projects. Mahmut Birsel has long had a high profile in this area, particularly in regard to energy projects. Arzu Aksaç also has experience.

Çakmak Avukatlik Bürosu in Ankara is advising the owners of Madison Oil on activities in the petroleum sector, and acts for the World Bank in relation to moves in the electricity distribution sector. The firm is also assisting Tractebel with international gas purchase contracts of Botas. Partners Mesut Çakmak, noted by clients for his outstanding work, and Mehtap Yildirim-Özturk have leading roles.

Derman Ortak Avukat Bürosu in Istanbul has close ties with **White & Case LLP Mü, Savirlik Ltd. Sirketi** in the same way as **Çakmak Avukatlik Bürosu**, and Emre Derman, Mine Taygun and Refika Tuzun-Bird are all good practitioners. The firm is working on a US$20m plant expansion for a Turkish company.

Güner Law Office work closely with **Denton Wilde Sapte**, both firms benefiting from Ece Güner's specialisation in M&A, energy, telecoms and projects work. She has acted in deals concerning Tupras and Turcas for a leading global energy company, and handled the sale of an IPP project in the electricity sector.

Hergüner Bilgen Özeke comes highly recommended, advising extensively on BOT and BOR projects. Kemal Mamak and Ender Özeke play prominent roles in this sector.

PROJECT FINANCE

BIRSEL LAW OFFICES
ÇAKMAK AVUKATLIK BÜROSU
DENTON WILDE SAPTE ✪
DERMAN ORTAK AVUKAT BÜROSU
GÜNER LAW OFFICE ✪
HERGÜNER BILGEN ÖZEKE ✪
WHITE & CASE LLP MÜ, SAVIRLIK LTD. SIRKETI

Cosar Avukatlik Bürosu ✪
Özel & Özel
Paksoy & Co. ✪
Pekin & Bayar Law Firm ✪
Pekin & Pekin ✪
Reisoglu-Ensari-Budak
Salans
Senguler & Senguler in association with Ledingham Chalmers ✪
Serap Zuvin Law Offices ✪

Firms are listed A-Z in tiers which are ranked in order of priority
✪ *Indicates firm displays contact details at the end of this chapter.*

Cosar Avukatlik Bürosu's Utku Çosar in Ankara has advised Turkey's major gas entity on matters concerning the transfer of agreements and was involved in the Nabucco Pipeline Project.

Haluk Can Özel at **Özel & Özel**, which works closely with international firm **Salans**, has a reputation in project finance.

Serdar Paksoy and Elvan Aziz at **Paksoy & Co.** have strengths in the projects field, while Selin Bayar and Sıla Yavuz are the leading lights in **Pekin & Bayar Law Firm**'s practice.

Pekin & Pekin has many clients from the power and gas sectors and acts for foreign clients in relation to projects work, which includes advising a German energy service provider on tenders for electricity distribution companies in Turkey.

Reisoglu-Ensari-Budak is another firm that can bring its highly rated expertise in banking and finance to bear on projects work.

Senguler & Senguler in association with Ledingham Chalmers has acted for an Australian oil company in its sale of a natural gas field in the west of Turkey, as well as in its purchase of an oil field.

Serap Zuvin Law Offices is currently acting in two power plant projects and one mining venture for a Turkish holding company.

SHIPPING, AVIATION AND TRANSPORT

Shipping is still the main focus for **Atamer & Karaman Law Firm**, though it has also developed insurance and aviation expertise. It is involved in major collision cases, particularly those that are technically complex and require engineering expertise. All five partners are involved in shipping work, with Mahmut Karaman focusing on dispute

SHIPPING, AVIATION AND TRANSPORT

ATAMER & KARAMAN LAW FIRM ✪
ÇAGA & ÇAGA LAW FIRM ✪
ERSOY BILGEHAN LAWYERS & CONSULTANTS ✪
GÜR LAW FIRM ✪
INAL LAW OFFICE ✪

Aybay & Aybay ✪
Denton Wilde Sapte ✪
Güner Law Office ✪
Hatem Law Office
NSN Law Office
Postacioglu Law Office ✪
Serap Zuvin Law Offices ✪
Tam & Ertan Law Office ✪
Yamaner & Yamaner Law Offices
Yasar Öztürk Law Firm

Firms are listed A-Z in tiers which are ranked in order of priority
✪ *Indicates firm displays contact details at the end of this chapter.*

resolution and Dilek Bektasoglu Sanli handling insurance matters. Feyzi Erçin leads the growing aviation practice. Kerim Atamer has advised the government on shipping regulation.

Çaga & Çaga Law Firm, where Erdem Degerli oversees the transport practice, has a strong tradition in shipping and insurance work, and has also developed aviation expertise. It represents a number of major airlines, several of which are longstanding clients, advising not only on general corporate matters but also on leasing, joint ventures and dispute resolution.

P&I clubs are key clients for **Ersoy Bilgehan Lawyers & Consultants**, which is largely seen as the dominant player in the shipping sector. Zihni Bilgehan, Ergun Ersoy, Ilknur Peksen and Gulistan Baltaci are kept busy with diverse matters, including charter parties, bills of lading, cargo, sale and purchase of ships, plus contractual claims and disputes. Collisions and casualties, salvage and pollution matters in the Turkish Straits featured in 2005.

Gür Law Firm is strong in maritime and shipping law. In 2005 it handled two large salvage cases, including a fire on board a ship at the entrance to the Bosporus. It has two marine claims experts, and partners Serkan Yildirim and Burak Cavus specialise in maritime law and arbitration. New arrival Caglar Coskunsu, who previously worked for a major shipping company, handling cargo claims, personal injury and pollution matters, now supervises the Marine Claims Department.

Seyma Inal at **Inal Law Office** is a leading ship finance lawyer, advising on a range of matters including ship finance. She has extensive experience before the Turkish courts, notably in major collision cases in the Bosporus. The firm is currently acting on numerous fast patrol boat projects. The arrival of Öner Iyigünler in August 2005 balances the departure of Russell Welsh.

Aybay & Aybay has seen more work from the aviation sector recently, including air accident claims. Arzu Aleibek is noted for non-contentious maritime work, though maritime litigation also features.

Güner Law Office, which works closely with **Denton Wilde Sapte**, counts major international shipping and ferry concerns among its clients. It recently acted for parties bidding for Turkey's state-owned shipyard company.

Hatem Law Office is well known in the shipping market and is particularly noted for its litigation expertise.

NSN Law Office joins the rankings on account of its high-quality work. Sevilay Kuru, Nazli Selek and Mehmet Nedret Unlu have been involved in two major collision cases in Turkey, including cleaning operations resulting from pollution, as well as wreck removal.

Postacioglu Law Office has notable Turkish clients in the multi-modal transport and logistics sectors, while **Serap Zuvin Law Offices** has represented an international airline, aerospace and financial entities on aviation financing.

Tam & Ertan Law Office counts major Turkish shipping companies amongst its clients and has a broad shipping practice.

Yamaner & Yamaner Law Offices maintains a strong reputation in aviation, maritime and transportation law, while **Yasar Öztürk Law Firm** is active in ship finance.

ODABAS TAVARES LAW OFFICE

NENEHATUN CADDESI
93-7 GAZIOSMANPASA
06700 ANKARA

Telephone: +90 312 405 6035
Fax: +90 312 405 6036
E-mail: inquiry@odabastavares-law.com

Languages
English, Portuguese, Turkish

Number of lawyers 10
at this office 2

Contact
Mrs Özlem Odabas Tavares

CATEGORIES OF WORK

Project finance	**Government contracts**
Corporate and commercial law	**Mining law**
Defence industry	**Competition law**
Labour law	**Foreign direct investments**
Mergers and acquisitions	**Family law**
International contracts	**Maritime law**
Dispute resolution	**EU law**

AYBAY & AYBAY

SIRASELVILER CAD 87–8
TAKSIM
34433 ISTANBUL

Telephone: + 90 212 293 6744
Fax: + 90 212 245 3949
E-mail: aybay@aybaylaw.com

Languages
English

Number of lawyers 8

Contacts
Ali Kartal, Baris Aybay, Sevin Ozaydin Kartal

CATEGORIES OF WORK

Shipping	**Oil and gas**
Corporate and commercial	**Agencies and distributorships**
Competition	**Dispute resolution and litigation**
Intellectual property	**Insurance**
Aviation and air transport	**Finance and leasing**
Information technology	**Defence procurement**
Criminal law	

AKINCI LAW OFFICE

RUMELI CADDESI
BIRLIK APT. 42/13
34363 NISANTASI ISTANBUL

Telephone: +90 212 296 9888
Fax: +90 212 230 2120
E-mail: info@akincilaw.com
Website: www akinci.av.tr

Languages
Arabic, English, French, German, Italian, Russian, Spanish

Number of lawyers 25

Contact
Prof Dr Ziya Akinci

Member
Arbitration Commission;
IBA (International Bar Association);
ICC Court of Arbitration for 2006-08;
Istanbul Bar Association

CATEGORIES OF WORK

Arbitration
Prof Dr Ziya Akinci, Nesli Agis

International business law
Prof Dr Ziya Akinci, Mert Yalcin

Law relating to foreigners
Mert Yalcin, Cemile Gokyayla

International commercial law
Prof Dr Ziya Akinci, Mert Yalcin

Litigation
Mert Yalcin, Berk Cektir

Construction law
Prof Dr Ziya Akinci, Berk Cektir

Foreign investment
Prof Dr Ziya Akinci, Mert Yalcin

Intellectual property
Mert Yalcin, Berk Cektir

Joint ventures
Prof Dr Ziya Akinci, Berk Cektir

Mergers and acquisitions
Berk Cektir, Hanife Ozturk

Labour law
T Taner Ucar, Serkan Onukar

Transportation law
Prof Dr Ziya Akinci, Mert Yalcin

Telecommunications law
Prof Dr Ziya Akinci, Berk Cektir

Real estate and mortgage
Berk Cektir, Hanife Ozturk

Energy project development
Prof Dr Ziya Akinci, Nesli Agis

Asset management and finance
Berk Cektir, Mert Yalcin,

Family Law
Emre Gokyayla, Serkan Onukar

Administration law
Mert Yalcin, Berk Cektir

THE FIRM
Akinci Law Office is an international law firm which has been committed to providing high-quality legal services in international and domestic practice since 1984. Headquartered in Istanbul, the biggest metropolis in Turkey, Akinci Law Office provides specialised alternative legal services to prominent firms and well-known corporations around the world.

AREAS OF PRACTICE
Arbitration: Prof Akinci is the most frequent arbitrator in Turkey according to the statistics of 2005. As an arbitrator of the ICC, Dr Akinci takes part in domestic and international arbitrations where companies, investors and metropolitan municipalities are parties. Besides these, Akinci Law Office works as counsel in various kinds of arbitrations such as the arbitration between Europe's two leading telecommunications operators, and the arbitration between the European Commission and a Turkish municipality. Dr Akinci also represents investors in investment disputes where the ICSID is determined as the competent authority for settlement.

International business law: the firm provides legal advice for international companies opening businesses in Turkey. Akinci Law Office's services cover legal matters at all stages of the life of a business entity. They include the drafting of formation documents, administrative matters such as obtaining permission papers from the Foreign Capital General Directorate or establishing a branch.

Law relating to foreigners: the office deals with the residence and work permits of foreigners in Turkey, and provides legal services to foreigners for the application of Turkish citizenship.

International commercial law: the services provided in this area include domestic and international sales and trade matters such as commercial manufacturing, service and production agreements.

Litigation: the firm's litigators are experienced in all major fields of litigation at all court levels. Members of the firm act both as counsel to Turkish or non-Turkish corporate claimants. Litigation subject matter includes construction, transportation and trade disputes.

Intellectual property law: Akinci Law Office's wide legal service area also includes intellectual property rights-related disputes. Akinci Law Office assists clients on issues relating to unfair competition, industrial property, copyright, trade mark, trade name, domain names, database, mass media, advertising, consumer protection and customs seizures.

Construction law: the firm drafts and negotiates the construction projects where a dispute has occurred, and provides legal services for litigation or arbitration as the case may be.

Mergers and acquisitions: acting for buyers, sellers, targets and other parties such as financial institutions, the firm provides assistance at all stages of such transactions structuring, offering, negotiating, due diligence, drafting of agreement and other legal documentation, procuring regulatory permits or clearance, and organising signing and closing and post-closing measures.

Labour law: Akinci Law Office assists clients in identifying and avoiding employment-related problems before they occur. One of the attorneys of the firm acts also acts as a court expert. The firm's labour law practice covers the negotiation and drafting of general employment contracts as well as employment contracts for managing editors and board members. It offers advice in labour law matters, in particular on behalf of the employer; negotiation and drafting of severance agreements; obtaining work permits for foreign employees; drafting of internal guidelines and policies; conducting of internal labour law audits or external due diligence; negotiation and enforcement of non-competition agreements; representation in legal proceedings; in particular with respect to termination of employment/dismissals.

Transportation: Akinci Law Office has attorneys who focus on transportation issues, and whose clients include local, regional, national and international transportation companies and/or their insurers.

ASLAN ÇAMLICA TOKSOY PARTNERS & CONSULTANTS

MAYA AKTAR CENTER
100/10 ESENTEPE
34394 ISTANBUL

Telephone: +90 212 211 5011
Fax: +90 212 211 3222
E-mail: info@actistanbul.com

Languages
English, French, German, Turkish

Number of lawyers 10
at this office 6

International groupings
International Bar Association (IBA);
American Bar Association (ABA)

CATEGORIES OF WORK

Competition and EU
Prof Dr Yilmaz Aslan, Fevzi Toksoy

Corporate and commercial
Prof Dr Yilmaz Aslan, Feridun Karakecili

Energy and natural resources
Sahin Ardiyok

Foreign direct investment
Bülent Çamlica, Fevzi Toksoy

Infrastructure and project finance
Bülent Çamlica, Ali Ilicak

Mergers and acquisitions
Fevzi Toksoy, Ali Ilicak

Privatisation
Ali Ilicak, Sahin Ardiyok

Regulatory
Prof Dr Yilmaz Aslan, Sahin Ardiyok

Telecommunications
Prof Dr Yilmaz Aslan, Sahin Ardiyok

THE FIRM

Aslan Çamlica Toksoy Partners & Consultants (ACT) was formed by Prof Dr Yilmaz Aslan, Bülent Çamlica and Fevzi Toksoy. ACT is a leading competition consultancy firm in Turkey, offering advice in line with market structures, its clientele's business needs and the legislative environment, in a key area for Turkey's integration with the global economy. The partners' different backgrounds, in competition law (Prof Dr Yilmaz Aslan), economics and EU law (Fevzi Toksoy) and competition strategy (Bülent Çamlica), help determine the individual needs of their clientele and present services to them based on conditions of privacy, stategy, experience and expertise via the head office in Istanbul, representation in Brussels and a contact office in Beijing. Also, the firm is a member of ABA, IBA, a Turkish Businessmen Association Competition Committee expert member and has associate offices in Beijing, Brussels and Washington DC.

AREAS OF PRACTICE

ACT is a leading competition house in Turkey, offering advice to its clients in line with their individual businesses and the legislative environment. The firm focuses its practice on competition law and competition economics, mergers and acquisitions, privatisation and antidumping, providing a full range of services before administrative bodies such as the Competition Authority and the Undersecretariat of Foreign Trade. The firm is known for its preventative competition advice, Competition Compliance Programs (CCP®) and strategic competition consultancy (Third Eye®). Under the economic consultancy services, it provides independent and objective advice, opinions and testimony to help resolve business disputes and inform judicial, legislative and regulatory decision makers. ACT determines the professional values necessary for achieving its goals according to its priorities in three fields: its clientele, the administrative authorities and its resources. The aim of ACT is to assist its clientele to achieve their goals. Therefore, ACT continuously improves its capabilities to provide, as a long- term solution partner, the expert services required by its clients, many of whom are leaders in their industry sector.

ATAMER & KARAMAN LAW FIRM

CUMHURIYET CADDESI 6A PAK APT D4
TR 34367, ELMADAĞ
ISTANBUL

Telephone: +90 212 219 1818
Fax: +90 212 219 2727
E-mail:
atamerkaraman@superonline.com

Languages
English, French, German

Number of lawyers 11

Contacts
Mahmut Karaman, Feyzi Erçin, Burcu Çelikçapa, Dilek Bektaşoğlu

CATEGORIES OF WORK

Draft commercial code
Dr Kerim Atamer

Administrative
Mahmut Karaman, Feyzi Erçin

Shipping and transport
All partners

Ship finance and shipbuilding
Dilek Bektaşoğlu

Litigation/arbitration
Mahmut Karaman

Project finance and securities
Burcu Çelikçapa, Dilek Bektaşoğlu

Insurance/reinsurance
Dilek Bektaşoğlu

Public procurement
Burcu Çelikçapa

Aviation
Feyzi Erçin

Agents, intermediaries
Burcu Çelikçapa

THE FIRM

Atamer & Karaman is an Istanbul-based law firm established by Dr Kerim Atamer and Mahmut Karaman in 1997. The firm now consists of five partners and six associates, with a varying number of trainees.

The firm's main areas of practice are shipping and transport, insurance and reinsurance and international trade.

During the last few years, Dr Kerim Atamer has been extensively involved in regulatory service for the government. He was appointed to the committee established by the Ministry of Justice, with the task of drafting a new Commercial Code. The draft was submitted to Parliament on 9 November 2005. His contribution to the work of the committee included taking an active role in the drafting of new provisions on maritime, transport and insurance law, drafting the supporting reasons, and editing and research in comparative law. In October 2005, Dr Atamer was instructed to join the Turkish diplomatic delegation attending the tenth assembly of the International Oil Pollution Compensation Fund in London. He also lectures in maritime and insurance law as an assistant professor at Bilgi University Law School, Istanbul.

AREAS OF PRACTICE

Litigation is the firm's priority, representing clients before all courts in Turkey and before various international arbitration ventures.

Shipping has traditionally been the firm's main area of expertise. The firm regularly acts for various British, Danish, Dutch and German P&I clubs and their members, shipowners, charterers, operators, shipbuilders, ports and brokers. The firm also advises various shipyards in the Tuzla area on their shipbuilding and finance projects.

For casualty response, the firm operates on a 24-hour basis and has an excellent reputation for crisis management. The technical expertise of Mahmut Karaman, who worked as a marine chief engineer for ten years, is a significant benefit to the firm. Atamer & Karaman has been involved in all the major casualties in the Straits area. These include collisions, fire and explosions, general average, salvage, towage, wreck removal and marine pollution cases. The firm has successfully defended major P&I clubs, in actions for damages filed by government bodies and third parties. Thereby, the claims have ultimately been dismissed, or clients' exposure has been significantly diminished.

The aviation team has been involved in all local major total losses, accidents and hijackings in recent years. The team also has particular expertise in administrative litigation in respect of aviation-related matters and on debt recovery for airlines and airports.

The firm has historically been active in marine insurance and reinsurance. In 1999, it advised Italian contractors and their local principals on a CAR policy, involving a claim believed to be the highest insurance claim in Turkey. Its expertise and involvement in other areas has since then expanded. The firm has been instructed by the world's leading (re)insurers in significant and high-profile cases involving technical complexity and special expertise. The firm is now involved in both contentious and non-contentious aspects of marine and non-marine insurance, including property damage, liability, business interruption, CAR and BBB policies.

The firm regularly organises seminars for its clients on subjects relating to its areas of practice.

BAŞALAN LAW OFFICE

GIZ 2000 PLAZA
AYAZAGA YOLU NO7 KAT 12
34398 MASLAK ISTANBUL

Telephone: +90 212 290 6277
Fax: +90 212 290 6283
E-mail: attorneys@basalan-law.com.tr
Website: www.basalan-law.com.tr

Languages
English, Turkish

Number of lawyers 8
at this office 7

Contact
Ahmet Başalan

International groupings
Istanbul Bar Association; ABA; IBA; INTA; AIPLA; EPI; PEM; Turkish Patent and Trademark Attorneys Association; British Chamber of Commerce in Turkey (BCCT); Turkish American Businessmen's Association (TABA); Italian Chamber of Commerce in Turkey; Swiss Chamber of Commerce in Turkey

CATEGORIES OF WORK

Intellectual property	**Litigation**
Patents and utility models	**Domain names**
Trade marks	**Dispute resolution**
Industrial designs	**Foreign investment**
Copyrights	**Establishment of business, new companies**
Unfair competition	**Residence and work permits**
Infringement	**Company law**
Prosecution and protection	**Establishment of liaison offices**
Legal proceedings with customs	

THE FIRM

Başalan Law Office, located in the metropolitan city of Istanbul, was founded in 1994 by Ahmet Başalan and Feriha Başalan. Başalan Law Office is redefining the traditional role of law firms by providing innovative legal and consulting services. The firm's lawyers are entrepreneurial creative thinkers, creating a dynamic new definition of a law firm by expanding their services to keep pace with their clients' varied needs.

Başalan Law Office is committed to providing creative solutions to all legal and business problems while adding value to the firm's clients. With experienced attorneys in the fields of establishing new companies and liaison offices, foreign investment law, commercial litigation, unfair competition and infringement, intellectual property law, prosecution and protection and incorporation law; the firm has grown to meet the expanding needs of existing clients and to accommodate the concerns of new ones.

Başalan Law Office is large enough to ensure promptness of service yet personal enough to maintain the firm's established reputation for individual client attention. The firm is committed to providing the highest level of service to clients, while continuing to develop new areas of talent and knowledge.

AREAS OF PRACTICE

Başalan Law Office consists of two main departments: the legal department and the patent and trade mark department, where all the various needs of clients and associates involving intellectual and industrial property protection are satisfied with a professional and specialised service.

With more than 25 staff, the patent and trade mark department is specialised and experienced in all kinds of of IP matters including: trade mark; patent; utility model; industrial design; copyright; domain name applications and registrations with the Turkish Patent Institute, searches related to the mentioned rights, renewals, annuity payments, record of charge name, address, assignment, licence and other formalities.

In addition to this, the legal department is rendering services in Turkey in the fields of intellectual and industrial property protection, which involves all kinds of legal and litigation works including: infringement; unfair competition, cancellation of Turkish Patent Institute Directorates refusal decisions, litigations also related to the cancellation of trade marks, designs, patents and utility models, sending warning letters through Notary Public or Express Mail Service, company law, foreign investments law, commercial litigations, prosecution and protection, the establishment of business and new companies, the establishment of liaison offices, residence and work permits.

BENER LAW OFFICE

YAPI KREDI PLAZA
C BLOK, KAT: 4
34330 LEVENT
ISTANBUL

Telephone: +90 212 270 7050
Fax: +90 212 270 6865
E-mail: inbox@bener.av.tr

Languages
Dutch, English, French, German, Italian, Spanish, Turkish

Number of lawyers 14

CATEGORIES OF WORK

Banking and financing
Burak Okay, Alwin Michaelsen

Corporate and M&A
Erim Bener, Burak Okay

Contracts
Funda Ozsel, Banu Sen

Construction and engineering
Erim Bener, Alwin Michaelsen

Competition law
Serdar Tuncbilek, Funda Ozsel

Customs and free zones
Gokce Ucuzal, Serdar Tuncbilek

Energy law
Erim Bener, Gozde Esen Sakar

IP, patent and trade mark
Feyzal Yildiz, Cenk Kisnisci

Immigration
Maria Celebi

Labour law and employment
Gokce Ucuzal, Deniz Pekgenc

Licensing and distribution
Paul Wouters, Serdar Tuncbilek

Litigation, bankruptcy, winding-up
Feyzal Yildiz, Gozde Esen Sakar

ADR, mediation
Paul Wouters, Feyzal Yildiz

Maritime and shipping arbitration
Paul Wouters

Media and press law
Feyzal Yildiz, Cenk Kisnisci

Privatisation
Erim Bener, Burak Okay

Project finance
Erim Bener, Alwin Michaelsen

Real estate
Funda Ozsel, Gokce Ucuzal

Telecommunications law
Burak Okay, Erim Bener

Transportation law
Paul Wouters, Feyzal Yildiz

BIRCANOGLU ATTORNEYS AT LAW

INONU CAD 69-71, D4
GUMUSSUYU
34437 ISTANBUL

Telephone: +90 212 292 0952
Fax: +90 212 292 1180
E-mail: info@bircanoglu.av.tr
Website: www.bircanoglu.av.tr

Languages
English, German, Greek

Number of lawyers 6

Member
International Law Firms (ILF)

CATEGORIES OF WORK

Banking and capital markets
M Erol Bircanoglu Jr

Intellectual property
M Erol Bircanoglu Jr

Project finance
M Erol Bircanoglu Jr

Corporate law
M Erol Bircanoglu Jr

Mergers and acquisitions
M Erol Bircanoglu Jr

Information technology
M Erol Bircanoglu Jr

Bankruptcy and reorganisation
Senem Gursoy

Real estate
Halit Karabul

Taxation
Sedat Ozkanli

Energy law
M Erol Bircanoglu Jr

Foreign investments
M Erol Bircanoglu Jr

Competition law
M Erol Bircanoglu Jr

Litigation and arbitration
Senem Gursoy

CLO – COSKUN LAW OFFICE

HARMANCI GIZ PLAZA
20TH/21ST FLOOR
LEVENT
80640 ISTANBUL

Telephone: +90 212 280 8661
Fax: +90 212 280 8840
E-mail: law@clolaw.net
Website: www.clolaw.net

Languages
Turkish, English, German

Number of lawyers 25

Contact
Martina Ruhnau (mruhnau@clolaw.net)

Member
International Bar Association

CATEGORIES OF WORK

Asset management
Ihsan Coskun

Banking, finance and capital markets
Ihsan Coskun, Mustafa Tokdemir

Bankruptcy
Devir Bas, Polat Dilli

Construction and real estate
Ihsan Coskun, Mustafa Tokdemir

Contracts
Ihsan Coskun, Polat Dilli

Corporate and commercial law
Ihsan Coskun, Mustafa Tokdemir

Debt settlement
Ihsan Coskun

Foreign direct investment
M Ali Erdogan

Foreign trade and customs
Haydar Yilanli

Intellectual property
Z Erdem Kapluhan, Serdar Arik

Litigation and dispute resolution
Ihsan Coskun, Mustafa Tokdemir

THE FIRM

Attorney Ihsan Coskun founded the Coskun Law Office in 1980, to aid clients in navigating the complexities of the Turkish legal system, and the firm continues to vigorously advocate the rights of clients in order to achieve the best results. Today, CLO is a diversified firm based in Levent, at the heart of the modern commercial and financial district of Istanbul. CLO operates with a base of 25 accomplished lawyers, six trainees, five consultants, 14 support staff and numerous well-connected national and international correspondents and partners from a wide range of disciplines, all chosen on the basis of the highest standards of professional competence and knowledge. Knowing that fast and reliable access to local and international law is today imperative for business success, CLO's multilingual staff has a particular focus on and expertise in advising and representing international clients in their dealings in Turkey.

AREAS OF PRACTICE

The firm focuses on a variety of practice areas, from asset management to litigation and dispute resolution. CLO's client base includes banks and financial institutions, and large- and medium-sized, domestic and international companies and organisations.

One major practice area is banking and finance, and Coskun Law Office represents banks and financial institutions in disputes and provides them with legal solutions fully representing their interests. The firm provides advice on the full spectrum of financial products and procedures, both Turkish and international, including lending, asset and project finance, financial regulations, corporate finance, debt restructuring and insolvency.

Construction is another important practice area of CLO's attorneys. Coskun Law Office represents private individuals or entities involved in construction projects for all of the issues facing clients, whether they are contractors, funders, developers or any other participants. CLO, a law office of good reputation in a number of fields relevant and central to the construction market, ably and reliably provides these services.

Attorneys at CLO assist and provide step-by-step advisory services regarding all aspects of corporate and commercial transactions for both domestic and international clients, including incorporation, organisation, and reorganisation of business activities. As a law firm with a keen focus on international clients with legal needs in Turkey, CLO is in a position to offer advisory services on topics including partnership research, security and management of foreign capital, incorporation issues and M&A.

Dispute resolution (litigation and arbitration) is one of CLO's strongest and most experienced work areas. CLO offers representation and advice to companies and individuals who are, or might become, involved in a lawsuit or appeal, serving as a vigorous advocate in securing the most advantageous terms for its clients. The firm's services include consultation, negotiation, arbitration and litigation in such areas as employment claims, banking, contract disputes, commercial matters, competition, and intellectual property issues. CLO attorneys help clients to resolve disputes in the most efficient and effective manner, whether through arbitration – domestic or international – mediation, litigation, or other means.

Insolvency/corporate restructuring brings challenges not only for the debtor who must wrap up a business, but for creditors and investors who must secure legal representation in order to regain lost investments, and perhaps even take punitive action. It is especially important that international investors and corporations in Turkey know the legalities that may constrain their investments, and that, should those investments fail or be challenged, they have effective recourse. In case of insolvency, Coskun Law Office will help creditors and debtors to achieve the most favourable and expedient discharge of debt and orderly payment. CLO's diverse and detailed knowledge of insolvency, in addition to business operations, sales and purchases, enables its attorneys to maximise asset value for clients in the shortest possible time.

ÇAGA & ÇAGA

SULEYMAN SEBA CAD 48
BJK PLAZA A/88
34357 BESIKTAS
ISTANBUL

Telephone: +90 212 310 3200
Fax: +90 212 310 3232
E-mail: caga@caga.gen.tr
Website: www.caga.gen.tr

Languages
English, French, German, Italian

Number of lawyers 27

Contact
Erdem Degerli

CATEGORIES OF WORK

Aviation, shipping and transport
Erdem Degerli, Sevda Ar

Banking and finance
Barbaros Çaga, Erdem Degerli

Capital markets
Barbaros Çaga

Competition law
Barbaros Çaga, Sevda Ar

Construction law
Barbaros Çaga, Erdem Degerli

Contracts
Erdem Degerli, Idil Çaga Degerli, Omer Yigit Aykan

Corporate law and consultancy
Barbaros Çaga, Erdem Degerli

Dispute resolution
Idil Çaga Degerli, Sevda Ar, Omer Yigit Aykan

E-commerce and consumer protection
Erdem Degerli, Sevda Ar, Idil Çaga Degerli

Employment law
Omer Yigit Aykan, Idil Çaga Degerli

Foreign direct investments
Barbaros Çaga, Erdem Degerli

IT and telecommunications
Erdem Degerli, Idil Çaga Degerli

Intellectual property
Idil Çaga Degerli, T Gökhan Tosun, Omer Yigit Aykan

Media and entertainment
Barbaros Çaga, Idil Çaga Degerli, T Gökhan Tosun

Mergers and acquisitions
Barbaros Çaga, Sevda Ar, Erdem Degerli

Tax law
Barbaros Çaga, Idil Çaga Degerli

THE FIRM

Founded in 1916, Çaga & Çaga is one of the oldest, largest, and most prominent boutique law firms in Turkey; renowned for approaching matters from diverse angles and for preserving discretion and seriousness as well as quality and professional expertise. The firm has an excellent international reputation and a good command of comparative law, especially with regard to the German, Swiss, Italian, French, UK and US legal systems. Current senior partner Barbaros Çaga is a lecturer in law and a member of TUSIAD (Turkish Industrialists and Businessmen Association), the leading NGO of Turkey.

AREAS OF PRACTICE

Aviation and air transport: one of the firm's main areas of practice. Counselling and legal services are rendered to the world's major airlines, airline catering companies, worldwide marketing and ticket sale companies, as well as reservation system firms in all regulatory issues, aircraft leasing contracts, joint ventures and resolution of air transport disputes.

Banking and finance: extensive legal advice is offered on option transactions, loan and pledge agreements, collateralisation and securitisation matters, asset-backed financing, hedging mechanisms, issuing of bonds and debentures, as well as regulatory issues.

Construction: large construction firms are represented in relation to landscaping, gross-market investments, immense land development projects, construction of significant high-rises as well as hotels, holiday villages and golf resorts.

Corporate and commercial: while a major practice area, Çaga & Çaga does not only focus on giving legal advice, it also seeks to approach issues from a business standpoint. The firm assists companies in their establishment stages, daily operations and all of their special investment projects, joint ventures and commercial disputes. Çaga & Çaga also undertakes the management of Turkish affiliates of foreign companies as their trustees, and guides them through the corporate governance maze.

Dispute resolution: another one of the firm's major practice areas, it is exercised to help pave the way for significant precedence creation at the Supreme Court level in the fields of corporate/commercial, tax, intellectual property, employment and air transport laws.

Employment law: the firm represents clients in their collective labour agreement negotiations with Workers' Unions, individual labour disputes and renders legal services related to employment law disputes.

Intellectual property: Çaga & Çaga represents its clients in a number of large volume lawsuits, particularly relating to the infringement of trade marks. The firm offers extensive consultancy services regarding license and copyright contracts.

Media and entertainment: another major field of practice, Çaga & Çaga provides extensive legal consultancy in media-related investments; in special legal restrictions affecting the activities of media; compliance with radio and TV laws; in daily operations of media companies, as well as their management and reorganisations; in advertisement regulations and represents clients in all their media law-related disputes.

Mergers and acquisitions: Çaga & Çaga has always dealt with large volume M&A's in Turkey and has lately represented mobile phone operators, TV and radio companies, tourism firms, industrial entrepreneurs and newspaper publishers in the structuring of their various mergers and acquisitions with a look towards tax planning.

Privatisation: the firm recently represented its clients in two major privatisation projects in Turkey both in relation to their dealings with the state and the contracts with their joint-venture partners.

Tax law: extensive tax and investment planning, consultancy, and tax settlement and litigation services are offered to clients in their multi-million-dollar deals or tax disputes arising out of complicated tax and financing structures.

COŞAR AVUKATLIK BÜROSU

INÖNÜ CAD NO 26/2
34437 TAKSIM
ISTANBUL

Telephone: +90 212 334 6000
Fax: +90 212 334 6090
E-mail: istanbul@cosar.av.tr

Languages
English, German, Turkish

Other offices
Adana, Ankara

Number of lawyers 20
at this office 16

Contact
E Arzu Coşar

CATEGORIES OF WORK	
Commercial law	**Labour law**
Mergers and acquisitions	**Intellectual property**
Joint ventures	**Arbitration**
Foreign investment	**Civil and administrative litigation**
Competition law	**Insolvency and bankruptcy**
Banking and financial law	**Privatisation law**
Capital markets	**Project finance**
Consumer law	**Energy law**
Insurance law	**Administrative law**

THE FIRM

Established in 1969 by Aydın Coşar, Coşar Avukatlık Bürosu acts as legal counsel to a wide range of national and international clients, including financial institutions and some of the largest holding companies in Turkey, as well as governmental agencies. The firm provides professional and high-quality legal service in almost all aspects of Turkish law with special expertise in corporate law, M&As, arbitration, joint ventures, competition law, energy law, IP, privatisation law and civil and administrative litigation.

AREAS OF PRACTICE

Corporate law: Coşar Avukatlık Bürosu provides legal assistance to its clients operating in a diverse range of sectors on general corporate matters, as well as on drafting and negotiating commercial transactions, including mergers and acquisitions and joint venture arrangements.

The firm's recent corporate work includes acting as legal counsel to a multinational company in its transfer of shares held in a joint venture company to its Turkish partner. Also in 2005 Coşar acted as legal counsel to an Italian industrial company in a complex share purchase transaction where the firm was responsible for drafting and negotiating all documents.

Arbitration and civil and administrative litigation: Coşar has great experience in this practice area. The firm's expertise in litigation includes debt restructuring, execution, and bankruptcy proceedings, the collection of receivables, as well as alternative dispute resolution.

In the last two years Coşar's attorneys represented the Ministry of Energy and Natural Resources of the Republic of Turkey in two multi-hundred-million-dollar compensation claims before the ICC Court of Arbitration in Geneva with respect to disputes arising from the transfer of operating rights of various power plants in Turkey. Coşar is currently representing a claimant state entity in a dispute involving a foreign state entity at the ICC in Geneva. Other recent work includes representing a Turkish financial entity in an intellectual property lawsuit, acting for a major multinational company in a series of zoning-law related lawsuits, and working on behalf of a client in a major capital markets law-related case. In 2005 Coşar also successfully represented a US-based entertainment company in a US$5m claim in a complex commercial law case.

Energy law: Coşar provides legal assistance in relation to various transactions in the energy sector involving sales, supply, purchase and transmission agreements. Coşar has provided legal advice to private energy companies in co-generation projects, and in relation to the financing and establishment of a power project.

Coşar currently acts as legal counsel to a consortium of companies involved in one of the leading projects of the Turkish energy sector. This involves advising the client in all Turkish law aspects of the transaction.

Privatisation: Coşar is currently acting as legal counsel to the Turkish Privatisation Administration in two separate projects. Coşar lawyers are involved in the privatisation of TÜPRAS, Turkey's largest petroleum refining company. The tender process for 51% of TÜPRAS has been completed in the amount of US$4.1bn. Coşar also represents the Privatisation Administration regarding the privatisation of TEDAS, Turkey's Electricity Distribution Company, with the aim of privatising 20 distribution regions in Turkey.

Competition law: Coşar provides legal assistance to a wide range of national and international companies in relation to Turkish competition law, particularly that relating to mergers and acquisitions and distributorship agreements. The firm's lawyers also have experience in competition litigation.

In 2005 Coşar represented a motor vehicle distributor in receipt of an exemption before the Turkish Competition Authority, and in a merger notification filed in Turkey for a worldwide merger of two major aluminium companies. Coşar currently provides legal advice to a leading iron and steel company, as well as two major cement companies.

D & D LAW FIRM

CUMHURIYET CAD NO 18/9
ELMADAG
TAKSIM
ISTANBUL

Telephone: +90 212 291 0710
Fax: +90 212 291 0713
E-mail: bakkor@dved.net
Website: www.dved.net

Languages
English, French, Turkish

Other offices
Ankara, Izmir

Number of lawyers 21
at this office 10

Contact
Berna Akkor

Member
World Jurist Association; International Bar Association; UNCITRAL; European Network of Correspondent Law Firms; ICC (Paris); Counsel-Alliance; GESICA

CATEGORIES OF WORK

- Corporate law, mergers and acquisitions
- Joint ventures
- Banking law
- Litigation
- Foreign investment
- Intellectual property law
- Criminal law
- Arbitration
- Labour law
- Tax law
- Licensing and franchising
- Contract law
- Energy and telecommunications
- Maritime and aviation law
- Competition law
- Insolvency and bankruptcy law
- BO and BOT projects
- Commercial dispute resolution
- Public auctions

DENTON WILDE SAPTE

LEVENT CADDESI,
ALT ZEREN SOKAK
NO:7 DAIRE 1
LEVENT 34330
ISTANBUL

Telephone: +90 212 284 6091
Fax: +90 212 284 6096
E-mail: istanbul@dentonwildesapte.com
Website: www.dentonwildesapte.com

Languages
English, French, German, Turkish

Other offices
Abu Dhabi, Almaty, Cairo, Dubai, London, Milton Keynes, Moscow, Muscat, Paris, Tashkent

Number of lawyers 683
at this office 20

Contact
David Nanson

CATEGORIES OF WORK

- Banking and finance
- Capital markets
- Competition
- Corporate and commerical
- Dispute resolution
- Employment
- Energy-infrastructure projects
- Insurance
- Intellectual property
- Joint ventures
- M&A
- Media and telecoms
- Mining
- Projects
- Real estate
- Telecommunications

DOGRU LAW OFFICE

TEVFIK ERDONMEZ SOKAK NO 22/4
YAYLA PALAS APT.
ESENTEPE
ISTANBUL

Telephone: +90 212 212 8882
Fax: +90 212 212 8805
E-mail: info@dogru.com.tr

Languages
English

Number of lawyers 5

Contact
Halil Dogru

CATEGORIES OF WORK

Banking and finance

Capital markets and securities

Litigation

Corporate

Arbitration

Mergers and acquisitions

Tax

DUMAN LAW OFFICE

HALASKARGAZI CD BÜLBÜL AP
289 B KAT: 8 D: 18-19 OSMANBEY
ISTANBUL

Telephone: +90 212 219 7720
Fax: +90 21 212 219 7723
E-mail: info@dumanlawoffice.com
Website: www.duman.av.tr

Languages
English, Turkish, Russian

Number of lawyers 6

Contact
Mustafa Duman

Member
International Bar Association (IBA);
Council of the Bars and Law Societies of the European Union (CCBE); Russian and Turkish Businessman's Union (RTIB)

CATEGORIES OF WORK

Corporate finance
Sibel Sevinç

Due diligences
Sibel Sevinç, Elif Erocak

Mergers and acquisitions
Mustafa Duman, Sibel Sevinç

Labour/employment law
Elif Erocak, Hilal Demirelli

Intellectual and industrial property rights
Mustafa Duman

Media law
Mustafa Duman

Maritime law
Mustafa Duman

Business law
Mustafa Duman

ESC CONSULTING

S SEBA CAD AKARETLER SIRAEVLERI NO 35, BESIKTAS 34357 ISTANBUL

Telephone: +90 212 236 9656
Fax: +90 212 261 4196
E-mail: esc@escrc.com
Website: www.escrc.com

Languages
English, French, Turkish

Number of lawyers 14

International groupings
IBA; Istanbul Bar; AAA (Attendees and Alumny of The Hague Academy of International Law)

CATEGORIES OF WORK

Competition and EU
Prof Arif Esin

Corporate and commercial law
Kemal Cavusoglu, Gozde Ruscuk

Dispute resolution – litigation and arbitration
Kemal Cavusoglu

Foreign direct investments
Prof Arif Esin, Kemal Cavusoglu

Administrative
Prof Gursel Ongoren

Infrastructure and project finance
Kemal Cavusoglu

Regulatory
Prof Asif Esin

Intellectual property law
Kemal Cavusoglu, Prof Gursel Ongoren

Mergers and acquisitions
Prof Arif Esin, Kemal Cavusoglu

Privatisation
Prof Arif Esin, Kemal Cavusoglu

Dumping
Prof Arif Esin

Construction law
Kemal Cavusoglu

E-commerce
Kemal Cavusoglu

Energy and natural resources
Kemal Cavusoglu

Private client and trusts
Gozde Ruscuk

ERSOY BILGEHAN LAWYERS & CONSULTANTS

MAYA AKAR CENTER BUYUKDERE CAD 100-102 KAT 26, 34394 ESENTEPE SISLI, ISTANBUL

Telephone: +90 212 213 2300
Fax: +90 212 213 3600
E-mail: ersoybilgehan@superonline.com
Website: www.ersoybilgehan.com

Languages
English, French, German, Italian

Other offices
Famagusta*

Number of lawyers 12

Contacts
Ergun Ersoy, Zihni Bilgehan

CATEGORIES OF WORK

Company and commercial
Zihni Bilgehan, Ilknur Peksen

Banking and finance
Gulistan Baltaci, Semih Sander

Mergers and acquisitions
Ilknur Peksen, Dogan Eymirlioglu

Insurance/reinsurance
Ilknur Peksen, Ergun Ersoy

Maritime
Ergun Ersoy, Zihni Bilgehan

Capital markets
Ilknur Peksen, Dogan Eymirlioglu

Ship finance/project finance
Gulistan Baltaci, Zihni Bilgehan

Arbitration
Ergun Ersoy

Litigation
Ergun Ersoy

Telecommunications/IT
Gulistan Baltaci

Industrial property rights
Serhat Sayin

Competition
Ilknur Peksen, Serhat Sayin

Intellectual property
Ilknur Peksen, Gulistan Baltaci

Privatisation
Ilknur Peksen, Dogan Eymirlioglu

ERGENÇ LAW GROUP

CUMHURIYET CAD SEYHAN
APT 12/3
ELMADAG
80200 ISTANBUL

Telephone: +90 212 296 2136
Fax: +90 212 233 3953
E-mail: emre@ergenc.av.tr
Website: www.ergenc.av.tr

Languages
English, German, Turkish

Other offices
Ankara, Izmir

Number of lawyers 15
at this office 10

Contacts
M Nida Ergenç (nida@ergenc.av.tr),
Emre Ergenç (emre@ergenc.av.tr)

Member
International Bar Association

CATEGORIES OF WORK

Banking and finance
M Nida Ergenç

Litigation
Safiye Aytekin

Dispute resolution
A Emre Ergenç

Commercial law
Hülya Ózer

Consultancy for foreign investors
Ayten Eren

Intellectual property
A Emre Ergenç, Deniz Saribas

Patent/trade mark registration
Safiye Aytekin

Contracts
M Nida Ergenç

Debt
M Nida Ergenç

Energy law
Firdevs Uzun, Gülden Turan

THE FIRM

Ergenç Law Firm was established by Mustafa Nida Ergenç almost 35 years ago. The firm has grown rapidly since, and its success has been founded on its ability to attract and retain exceptionally difficult, challenging and resourceful cases. The firm hopes to sustain this level of success.

The firm endeavours to keep its lawyers abreast of all legal developments that may affect their practice, especially those regarding the rapid amendments to Turkish law.

The firm may not be the largest in Turkey in terms of lawyer numbers, but it considers itself to be the 'tailor-made law firm' for current and prospective clients. Its goal is to be the firm of choice for clients with the most challenging transactions and cases. The firm has more than ten affiliate offices around Turkey in addition to its branches in Ankara and Ìzmir.

Ergenç Law Firm forever tries to retain a focus on its clients' interests and needs, combining high levels of professionalism with a keen understanding of clients' businesses. This enables the firm to help solve its clients' problems in the most effective manner possible.

AREAS OF PRACTICE

Ergenç Law Firm specialises in a diverse range of legal services, and considers itself to be particularly accomplished in handling litigation matters. All members of the firm are true experts in this field. In addition to its litigation expertise, the firm also excels in the areas of insolvency and financial reconstructing, bankruptcy, intellectual property disputes, auditing, tax law, administrative law, civil law, all areas of commercial law and also capital markets-related matters. The firm specialises in all matters that require special attention and precedent-setting experience.

ERYUREKLI & FIDAN

CUMHURIYET CAD 315/5
HARBIYE
34367 ISTANBUL

Telephone: +90 212 343 9270
Fax: +90 212 343 9275
E-mail: admin@ef-law.com
Website: www.ef-law.com

Languages
English, French, German

Number of lawyers 9

Contacts
Murat Eryurekli, Erdoğan Fidan

CATEGORIES OF WORK

Banking and finance	**Competition**
Capital markets	**Telecommunications**
Project finance	**Privatisations**
Real estate and construction	**Intellectual property**
Foreign investment	**E-commerce**
Mergers and acquisition	**Labour law**
General corporate matters	

THE FIRM

Eryurekli & Fidan was founded in 2004 by Murat Eryurekli and Erdoğan Fidan, two former partners of Pekin & Pekin. Despite the firm's young history, given the partners' extensive background, expertise and experience in international and domestic business transactions, the firm has grown steadily, in terms of both size and its broad range of services.

Mr Murat Eryurekli began his career as a legal expert and consultant at the Capital Markets Board of Turkey, the highest regulatory and supervisory authority in Turkish capital markets, where he served for five years. Upon his departure, Mr Eryurekli joined Pekin & Pekin where he advised major European and American banks, financial institutions and multinational corporations with respect to their numerous investments in the Turkish business sector, in particular in capital markets and banking.

Mr Erdoğan Fidan gained his experience at Pekin & Pekin where he worked for seven years. During this period, Mr Fidan was involved in numerous privatisation, telecommunication and project finance transactions and gained a reputation as a leading adviser in these practice areas.

AREAS OF PRACTICE

The firm aims to provide high-quality services to Turkish and international clients by focusing on all aspects of business law, particularly capital markets and securities, banking and finance, project finance, privatisation, real estate and construction business, general corporate matters, labour law, foreign investment, mergers and acquisitions, telecommunications and e-commerce.

Recent transactions undertaken by Eryurekli & Fidan include rendering advice on the acquisition of the shares of a major Turkish brokerage firm by a leading German bank. Moreover, the firm advised on various capital markets transactions of the German bank in Turkish capital markets.

The firm advised a US-based international wheel company in the merger of two multinational corporations in Turkey in the form of a joint venture structure.

The firm provided legal advice to an international car manufacturer based in Germany in relation to its various financing and distribution arrangements in the Turkish market.

The firm has been involved in major project financing transactions, acting mainly for developers and lenders. Project financing of several international hotel chains, shopping centres, Istanbul Atatürk, Izmir Adnan Menderes airports and the financing of various real property investments are only a few examples of the firm's practice in 2005.

Eryurekli & Fidan has also been involved in the privatisation of vehicle inspection stations, one of the largest privatisation projects in Turkey in 2005, and advised the lenders in the financing thereof.

In addition to these specific transactions, the firm renders extensive legal counselling and comprehensive service to foreign companies investing in Turkey, and to major local banks and brokerage firms in all aspects of business law.

Through its professional team of nine, the firm currently represents leading international banks and financial institutions, as well as domestic and international corporations.

For additional information about the firm's areas of practice please see www.ef-law.com.

ESIN LOKMANHEKIM ICTEM GURKAYNAK

CITLENBIK SOKAK NO: 12
YILDIZ MAH, BESIKTAS
34349 ISTANBUL

Telephone: +90 212 327 1724
Fax: +90 212 327 1725
E-mail: info@eliglegal.com
Website: www.eliglegal.com

Languages
English, French, German

Number of lawyers 21

Contact
Dr Ismail G Esin

International groupings
ICC; DIS; LCIA; IBA; ASA

CATEGORIES OF WORK

Mergers and acquisitions
Dr Ismail G Esin, S Tunc Lokmanhekim

Corporate and commercial
S Tunc Lokmanhekim,
Gonenc Gurkaynak

Banking and finance
Serkan Ictem

Competition and EU law
Gonenc Gurkaynak

Dispute resolution and arbitration
Dr Ismail G Esin

Telecommunications
Dr Ismail G Esin, Gonenc Gurkaynak

Litigation
Sedat Yilmaz, Dr Murat Canyürek

Administrative law
Dr iur Burak Oder

Securities
Serkan Ictem

Intellectual property
Serkan Ictem

THE FIRM

ELIG is an eminent, independent Istanbul law firm. The firm has 21 lawyers in its offices, including five partners and two counsels. Dr Ismail G Esin and Mr Tunc Lokmanhekim founded the firm in 2002 as a result of a de-merger from their previous firm. The firm grew and changed its name to Esin Lokmanhekim Ictem Gurkaynak (ELIG), adding two new name partners: Mr Serkan Ictem and Mr Gonenc Gurkaynak.

ELIG strives to combine its academic perspective with a business-mined approach and serve its clients with the diligence of an academician but also with the flexibility of a practitioner. All lawyers at the firm continue their advanced legal studies to improve their capabilities.

The firm has established close relations with a number of international law firms and has served mutual clients on numerous M&A transactions, competition law matters, commercial arbitration and other projects. It also has formal alliances with two local law firms in Ankara and Izmir, that assist ELIG in any assignments within those cities.

The firm is a member of several international accredited associations or chambers, such as the International Chamber of Commerce, the German Institution of Arbitration, the Swiss Arbitration Association, the London Court of International Arbitration, and the International Bar Association. It has been a contributor to the Turkish sections of 'Getting The Deal Through Merger Control' and 'Mergers & Acquisitions' for the last three years.

The members of ELIG are fluent in either English, German or French; some are fluent in all three.

AREAS OF PRACTICE

ELIG specialises in a wide variety of domestic and international commercial work such as M&A transactions, banking and finance, competition law, corporate law, international arbitration, litigation, securities, commercial law, labour law, intellectual property, property law, privatisations, telecommunications law, transportation law and tax law.

The firm is divided into seven main practice groups, although its partners do not work exclusively in these groups.

The firm's main focus area is commercial and corporate law with an emphasis on M&A transactions. Dr Esin and Mr Lokmanhekim recently co-edited a book on M&A transactions entitled 'M&A Transactions Under Turkish Law', authored jointly by members of the firm and available in Turkish and English. This is the first book in Turkish legal literature on how to structure M&A transactions under Turkish law.

ELIG has represented several multinational companies in M&A and joint venture projects. The firm's M&A team, supervised by the firm's name partners, has vast experience in advising sellers and purchasers. The firm acted in 26 sizeable transactions during 2005. Moreover, the firm's corporate team has a solid practice in advising foreign clients, providing numerous commercial and corporate services.

Besides this main focus, the firm also focuses on bank finance, with an emphasis on leveraged finance transactions, led by Mr Serkan Ictem. He represented agent banks in providing senior and subordinated financing to a large number of borrowers operating in a variety of industries.

Competition law is one of ELIG's key areas of practice. Led by Mr Gonenc Gurkaynak, a lawyer with many years' competition law experience in Turkey, Brussels and the US, ELIG's competition law team was, in 2005 only, involved in more than 20 merger notifications to the Competition Authority, more than ten written and oral defenses before the Competition Board, and regular competition law counselling.

The firm also renders a wide variety of litigation and arbitration services, led by Mr Sedat Yilmaz and Dr Murat Canyürek (litigation) and Dr Esin (arbitration). The firm specialises in unfair competition and trade mark lawsuits, and also offers tax advice led by Dr Canyürek.

ELIG also has a strong practice in administrative law. Dr iur Burak Oder heads the practice, which has significantly grown in 2005 due to representations in numerous appeals.

GIDE LOYRETTE NOUEL

**BÜYÜKDERE CAD.
YAPI KREDI PLAZA
C BLOK KAT 3, LEVENT
34330 ISTANBUL**

Telephone: +90 212 325 3581
Fax: +90 212 325 3587
E-mail: gln.istanbul@gide.com
Website: www.gide.com

Other offices
Algiers, Beijing, Belgrade, Brussels, Bucharest, Budapest, Casablanca, Hanoi, London, Moscow, New York, Paris, Prague, Riyadh, Shanghai, Tunis, Warsaw

Number of lawyers 586
at this office 13

Contact
Guillaume Rougier-Brierre (rougier@gide.com)

CATEGORIES OF WORK

- Corporate law, mergers and acquisitions
- Privatisation
- Joint ventures
- Banking and finance, project finance
- Restructuring
- Tax, customs and exchange controls
- Media, IT and telecommunications
- Real estate transactions and financing
- Litigation and arbitration
- Intellectual property
- Employment law and social security
- Competition
- State aid
- Public procurement
- Insurance

GÜNER LAW OFFICE

**LEVENT CADDESI
ALT ZEREN SOKAK
NO 7, DAIRE 2, LEVENT
34330 ISTANBUL**

Telephone: +90 212 282 4385
Fax: +90 212 282 4305
E-mail: guner@guner.av.tr

Languages
English, French, German, Turkish

Number of lawyers 20

Contact
Ece Güner

CATEGORIES OF WORK

- Banking and finance
- Capital markets
- Commercial
- Competition
- Corporate
- Dispute resolution
- Energy and infrastructure
- Employment
- Insurance
- Intellectual property
- Joint ventures
- Media technology
- Mergers and acquisitions
- Mining
- Projects
- Real estate
- Telecommunications

GUR LAW FIRM

HACI ADIL SOKAK NO 44
LEVENT
34330 ISTANBUL

Telephone: +90 212 325 9020
Fax: +90 212 325 9023
E-mail: info@gurlaw.com
Website: www.gurlaw.com

Languages
English, French, German, Greek, Italian, Portuguese, Turkish

Number of lawyers 15

Contact
Tevfik Gur (tevfik@gurlaw.com)

International groupings
Turkish-American Chamber of Commerce; London Maritime Arbitration Association; Mondaq

CATEGORIES OF WORK	
Corporate	**Personal injury/death**
Commercial	**Banking/debt recovery**
Maritime/Admiralty	**Real property**
Mergers and acquisitions	**Energy**
Employment law/contracts	**Finance**
Arbitration/enforcement of foreign judgments and arbitration awards	**Intellectual property rights/patent and trade mark registration**

THE FIRM

The firm was originally established by Tevfik Gur in Mersin in 1984 where he dealt with a range cases and achieved considerable success. He has been pursuing his career in Istanbul since 1993. Being one of the leading Turkish law firms, Gur Law Firm has an outstanding reputation with broad expertise and experience in many areas of law. The firm is well known for its substantial international practice. Gur Law Firm's lawyers are distinguished by their ability to combine imagination with perspectives.

AREAS OF PRACTICE

Gur Law Firm offers a full range of legal services as listed below.

Corporate: Gur Law Firm has an established corporate practice advising on a complete range of corporate and equity-based transactions, share purchase, partnership and joint venture agreements. The firm advises clients on structuring their corporate investments in Turkey.

Commercial: Gur Law Firm represents many commercial clients in sectors ranging from the fast moving world of IT to the more traditional commercial areas such as debt collection and contract enforcement. It handles all forms of commercial work in the contentious and non-contentious fields. The firm aims to achieve dispute resolution for its clients whether it be through arbitration, litigation or other means, but always consistent with the client's commercial objectives.

Maritime: the firm's maritime practice includes providing advice to shipyards, ship owners and banks in preparing, negotiating and drafting contracts for the construction, purchase and sale of vessels, and in contracts to finance such operations. The firm provides advice on charter contracts, maritime insurance, P&I, and all types of maritime proceedings and litigation. The firm is also an established collision handler.

Mergers and acquisitions: Gur Law Firm provides assistance to its clients in transactional structures, mergers and demergers, restructuring of companies, due diligence, acquisition funding. The firm provides assistance in the establishment and registration of legal entities, drafts articles of associations, charters, foundation and shareholders agreements. The firm also drafts joint venture and consortium and pre-bid agreements.

Employment law/contracts: Gur Law Firm has the necessary experience in labour law/business law and the legal regulations in this area. The firm frequently engages in the preparation of business contracts for mutual clients as well as the settlement of disputes.

Personal injury/death: the firm represent its clients in cases of personal injury and death, and conducts negotiations with the opposition and also finalises the necessary legal procedures.

Arbitration/enforcement of foreign judgments and arbitration awards: the arbitration practice includes advising on the drafting of arbitration clauses, representing domestic and international clients as claimants and respondents in institutional and ad hoc arbitral proceedings, and conducting litigation to enforce arbitration awards.

Banking/debt recovery: the firm has the experience necessary for examining and preparing all contracts relating to loans and securities granted by foreign and domestic banks.

Energy, oil and gas: the firm provides its clients with specialised service and advice in designing the legal framework, and drafting contracts for foreign and Turkish joint ventures, consortiums and companies.

Gur Law Firm has established a special IPR department which gives legal advice to multinational pharmaceutical producers in Turkey.

Finance: Gur Law Firm advises on domestic and cross-border transactions on asset finance, project finance, capital markets, derivatives, convertible bonds, bond issues debt trading, global loans, leveraged finance, real estate finance, restructuring, mergers and acquisitions, securitisation, telecoms, energy and infrastructure finance.

GÜRCAN LAW OFFICES

MAÇKA CADDESI
NO 23/1, KAT: 4, DAIRE: 5
34367 MAÇKA
ISTANBUL

Telephone: +90 212 231 2115
Fax: +90 212 241 3490
E-mail: gurcan@gurcanlaw.com
Website: www.gurcanlaw.com

Languages
English, French

Other offices
Izmir

Number of lawyers 9
at this office 7

Member
The International Project Finance Association

CATEGORIES OF WORK

Banking and finance

Project finance

Ship finance

Privatisation

Corporate law

Mergers and acquisitions

Capital markets

Securities

Commercial law

Intellectual property law

Arbitration and litigation

Energy

E-commerce

ILHAN IMIK LAW OFFICE

BAHCELIEVLER MAH,
ZUBEYDE HN CAD NO 43
NATO YOLU ÇENGELKÖY
ISTANBUL

Telephone: +90 216 308 7100
Fax: +90 216 308 7112
E-mail: iimik@superonline.com
Website: www.ilhanimik.av.tr

Languages
English, German

Number of lawyers 15

Contact
Derya Icoz

CATEGORIES OF WORK

Contracts
I Imik, F Esen

Developing strategies on media and public relations
I Imik, F Esen

Competition law
I Imik, F Esen

Commercial law
I Imik, O Saglam

Political counselling
I Imik, B Oner

Litigation and arbitration
I Imik, O Saglam

Debt collection and insolvency
F Esen, D Icoz

Business law
O Akinci, N Boz

Real property law
I Imik, F Boldag

Establishment of foreign investments
I Imik, B Oner

Licensing for foreign investments
B Oner, Y Unal

Maritime law
O Akinci, A Tok

Banking law
F Esen, I Imik

Financial disputes
I Imik, N Boz

HERGÜNER BİLGEN ÖZEKE

SÜLEYMAN SEBA CAD 55-57
AKARETLER SIRAEVLER
34357 BEŞİKTAŞ
ISTANBUL

Telephone: +90 212 310 1800
Fax: +90 212 310 1899
E-mail: info@herguner.av.tr
Website: www.herguner.av.tr

Languages
English, French, German, Japanese

Number of lawyers 55+

Contacts
Ümit Hergüner (managing partner), Ender Özeke, Gökhan Eraksoy, Tolga Danısman

Member
International Attorneys Club; International Bar Association; American Bar Association

CATEGORIES OF WORK

Corporate practice
Ayşe Bilgen, Tolga Danısman

Oil, gas and energy
Ümit Hergüner, Cüneyt Yüksel

Employment
Ayşe Bilgen, Okan Gündüz

Telecommunications
Itır Sevim Çiftçi, Senem İşmen

Joint ventures, M&A
Ümit Hergüner, Itır Sevim Çiftçi

Competition
Ilmutluhan Selçuk, Deniz Polat

Litigation, execution and bankruptcy
Ayşe Bilgen, Tolga Danısman, Okan Gündüz

Privatisation
Itır Sevim Çiftçi, Hakkı Gedik, Senem İşmen

Banking and finance
Gökhan Eraksoy, Hakkı Gedik

Arbitration
Ender Özeke, Cüneyt Yüksel

Securities and capital markets
Gökhan Eraksoy, Hakkı Gedik

Intellectual property
Cüneyt Yüksel, Zaman Ozer

Project finance
Ender Özeke, Kemal Mamak, S İşmen

Real property
Tolga Danısman, Serkan Gül

THE FIRM

Hergüner Bilgen Özeke is one of the largest law firms in Turkey, representing international and Turkish clients in a variety of sectors on all aspects of business law.

AREAS OF PRACTICE

Corporate practice: Hergüner renders general legal advice to numerous national and multinational companies. Clients are from a wide range of sectors including telecoms, pharmaceuticals, transportation, energy, textiles, cement, construction, food, consultancy and banking and finance. Work includes all aspects of corporate, contracts, property, employment and compliance matters.

Joint ventures, M&A: in 2005 the firm represented a major Turkish bank in the sale of its shares to a Belgian bank and was involved in at least four M&A deals involving electricity generating companies. The firm also advised a leading international port operator in its acquisition of a Turkish company for building an international container port; and an international commodities group in its acquisition of another worldwide cosmetics company.

Privatisation: the firm was heavily involved in every major privatisation deal in 2005, including Türk Telecom, Erdemir and TÜPRAS, as well as Mersin Port, Eti Aluminum and Basak Sigorta. The firm is currently advising an Italian group in the privatisation of Milli Piyango (state lottery) and an American company in the privatisation of the state's electricity distribution facilities.

Banking and finance: Hergüner has acted for numerous multinational financial institutions and international banks and borrowers, in connection with their financing activities and transactions in Turkey. In 2005, Hergüner acted as Turkish counsel to the arranging financial institutions in relation to the financing of the acquisition of Türk Telekom for the amount of US$1.4bn and is also involved in the financing of a major airport project.

Project finance: the firm has been involved in a number of infrastructure projects in the transportation sector, as well as local distribution companies for different utility services, in addition to some of the largest project financings to date in Turkey.

Oil and gas: Hergüner provides legal assistance to the consortium of oil companies in the multi-billion-dollar Baku-Ceyhan-Tbilisi pipeline project. The firm was involved in deals concerning the acquisition of a major Turkish oil company by a multinational petrol group; and the transfer of petrol licenses. Since mid-2005, Hergüner has been advising a major energy group in connection with the proposed petrol pipeline between the northern and southern coasts of Turkey.

Telecoms: the firm's lawyers have played a key role in restructuring the regulatory framework of the telecoms sector in Turkey. In 2005 the firm advised a consortium in the privatisation of Türk Telekom. Currently the firm is advising the winning bidder for the acquisition of Turkey's second largest GSM company.

Competition: the firm saw a substantial increase in its work concerning investigations and judicial review of competition board decisions, particularly in automotive, energy/mining and pharmaceuticals sectors. Hergüner has provided legal services for clearance of M&A transactions by the competition board, some involving the Turkish leg of global M&A transactions.

Dispute resolution: the firm has a strong litigation and arbitration practice, and represents a number of Turkish and international companies in legal proceedings before courts, execution offices and arbitral tribunals. The firm has been successfully representing the subsidiary of a multinational water services company in an arbitration concerning a development project sponsored by the World Bank.

Intellectual property: Hergüner's IP practice has developed significantly over the past three years. The firm has been representing an alliance of international software companies in Turkey since 2002.

Real property: the firm has been extensively involved in real estate-related projects, disputes, zoning legislation, and inheritance-related issues in Turkey. Since 2004 the firm has rendered legal advice to a UK-based retail giant.

INAL LAW OFFICE

BUYUKDERE CADDESI
EREN TALU BINASI KAT:7
LEVENT 34330
ISTANBUL

Telephone: +90 212 339 0797
Fax: +90 212 339 0790
E-mail: office@inal-law.com
Website: www.inal-law.com

Languages
English, Portuguese, Turkish

Number of lawyers 6

Contacts
Seyma Inal, Ebru Akbudok Sozer

Member
British Chamber of Commerce in Turkey (BCCT); International Bar Association; Turkish American Business Association (TABA); Turkish Maritime Law Association

CATEGORIES OF WORK

Asset finance/securitisation

Banking, finance

Corporate and commercial

Competition

Construction

Dispute resolution, litigation

Employment

European community

Energy

Foreign investment

Information technology

Insurance

Intellectual property

Mergers and acquisitions

Shipping, ship finance

Telecommunications

Death, personal injury

Real estate

ISMEN

BUYUKDERE CADDESI
MAYA AKAR CENTER
NO: 100-102, 19TH FLOOR
34394 ESENTEPE, ISTANBUL

Telephone: +90 212 272 6364
Fax: +90 212 272 6365
E-mail: tolga.ismen@ismen-law.com
Website: www.ismen-law.com

Languages
English, French, German, Turkish

Number of lawyers 10

Contact
Tolga Ismen

CATEGORIES OF WORK

Corporate and commercial
Tolga Ismen, Arzum Gunalcin

Mergers and acquisitions
Tolga Ismen, Arzum Gunalcin

Competition law, EU
Tolga Ismen, Ozlem Oksun

Telecommunications law
Tolga Ismen

Privatisations
Tolga Ismen, Arzum Gunalcin

Banking and finance
Arzum Gunalcin, Tolga Ismen

Securities
Tolga Ismen

KORTUN & ONUR

CUMHURIYET CAD 211/1
HARBIYE
80230 ISTANBUL

Telephone: +90 212 230 0011
Fax: +90 212 241 4220
E-mail: onur@kobhukuk.com
Website: www.kobhukuk.com

Languages
English, Turkish

Number of lawyers 9

Contact
Ms Sitare Önür

International groupings
Association of Independent European Lawyers; Turkish-British Chamber of Commerce and Industry

CATEGORIES OF WORK

- Commerce
- Maritime
- Company
- Real estate
- Taxation
- Banking and finance
- Foreign capital investment
- Insolvency and company restructuring
- Mergers and acquisitions
- Joint ventures
- Transport
- Project finance
- Intellectual property rights

PI PARTNERS

BÜYÜKDERE CADDECI, NO. 22
BEYTEM PLAZA, FLOOR 3
34360 ŞIŞLI
ISTANBUL

Telephone: +90 212 315 3000
Fax: +90 212 233 5360
E-mail: pi.partners@tr.ey.com
Website: www.eylaw.com/tr

Languages
Dutch, English, French, German, Greek, Turkish

Other offices
Athens, Bucharest, Sofia, Thessaloniki

Number of lawyers 60
at this office 8

Contact
Solita Saltiel (solita.saltiel@tr.ey.com)

International groupings
Ernst & Young

CATEGORIES OF WORK

- Company and commercial
- Labour
- Mergers and acquisitions

MEHMET GÜN & CO

KORESEHITLERÌ CAD
Nº 32 ZINCIRLIKUYU
ISTANBUL 34394

Telephone: +90 212 275 9003
Fax: +90 212 274 2095
E-mail: gun@mehmetgun.com.tr
Website: www.mehmetgun.com.tr

Languages
English, French, German

Other offices
Ankara, Izmir
(and correspondents in each EU country)

Number of lawyers 22
at this office 19

Contacts
Mehmet Gün, Selma Toplu Ûnlû

Member
TELFA (Trans European Law Firms Alliance); IBA; INTA; ECTA; PTMG; EALA; GALA

CATEGORIES OF WORK

Commercial law	**Employment law**
Company law	**Energy law**
Banking law	**Insurance law**
Competition – antitrust law	**Litigation (commercial, administrative and intellectual property)**
Foreign investments	**Privatisation**
Intellectual property law (copyrights, trade marks, patent and designs)	**Pharmaceutical law**
Computer law	**Telecommunications law**
E-commerce	

THE FIRM

Mehmet Gün & Co was established in 1986 to provide full legal services for corporate clients, including intellectual property law services. Since then, the firm has gained a reputation for professionalism and has become one of the leading law firms in Turkey. The firm's philosophy is to understand the client's commercial objectives; keeping them at the forefront and to provide quality legal services.

Mehmet Gün & Co is based in the financial centre of Istanbul, it has working offices in Ankara and Izmir with correspondents in Adana, Antalya, Bursa and Trabzon covering approximately 70% of Turkey.

AREAS OF PRACTICE

The firm has an outstanding reputation in intellectual property, unfair competition, corporate and commercial practice, antitrust law and litigation. The firm is unique for its full range of intellectual property services, ranging from copyrights, trade marks, patents to industrial designs from advisory services to prosecution and protection, including the investigation department for the clients needs for IP investigation.

Mehmet Gün & Co operates an extensive in-house training scheme for new graduates, sharing its expertise and experience in order to develop its future associates and partners. The firm has grown with its own trained attorneys and continously invests in their further education and training. The firm's lawyers enter the firm as an apprentice and remain to become partners.

Most of the firm's lawyers have degrees from European legal institutions, and are familiar with other cultures. Thus the firm is often called upon to liaise between foreign clients and their local counterparts.

In addition to its correspondents in countries across Europe, the firm co-operates and works closely with major UK and US law firms, and has contacts with law firms all over the world.

The firm's clientele is a blend of foreign and local small, medium and large corporations from all over the world. The majority of clients, mostly referred by satisfied clients, are from the UK, the US, and from European and Far Eastern countries.

Mehmet Gün & Co aims to provide a highly personal service to its clients in the most cost-efficient manner and to add value to its clients' businesses. It provides detailed billing accounts, and always respects clients' queries.

Mehmet Gün & Co is fully committed to professionalism and to the professional rules of the Istanbul Bar Association and the Union of Turkish Bar Associations.

PAKSOY & CO.

BEYBI GIZ PLAZA
MEYDAN SK NO 28 KAT 10
MASLAK
34398 ISTANBUL

Telephone: +90 212 290 2350
Fax: +90 212 290 2355
E-mail: admin@paksoy.av.tr
Website: www.paksoy.av.tr

Languages
English, French, German, Swedish

Number of lawyers 20

CATEGORIES OF WORK

Banking and finance
Serdar Paksoy, Togan Turan

Capital markets
Serdar Paksoy, Omer Collak

Competition
Pinar Eryùrekli, Togan Turan

Corporate
Elvan Aziz, Pinar Eryùrekli

Energy
Serdar Paksoy, Deger Boden

Mergers and acquisitions
Serdar Paksoy, Pinar Eryùrekli

Privatisation
Serdar Paksoy, Togan Turan

Project finance
Serdar Paksoy, Elvan Aziz

Telecommunications
Serdar Paksoy, Deger Boden

IT law
Serdar Paksoy

Arbitration
Serdar Paksoy, Deger Boden

Litigation
Serdar Paksoy, Deger Boden

Labour and employment
Elvan Aziz

Real estate
Serdar Paksoy, Omer Collak

THE FIRM

Paksoy & Co. is a full-service law firm based in Istanbul. The firm provides a comprehensive service to domestic and international corporations, government and institutional clients.

AREAS OF PRACTICE

Paksoy & Co. offers a full range of legal services to domestic and international business and financial organisations, with its work highly regarded in the areas of banking and finance, mergers and acquisitions, corporate, competition, project finance, privatisation, telecommunications, real estate, litigation and arbitration.

Paksoy & Co.'s practice covers all aspects of financing transactions, including international lending transactions and advising on new issues, IPOs, listings on the stock exchanges, eurobonds, banking and securities transactions. Paksoy & Co. advised the largest Turkish IPO to date with a mobile phone operator's flotation on the New York and Istanbul Stock Exchanges, raising a total of $1.9bn.

In 2005, Paksoy & Co. advised JPMorgan and UBS Investment Bank in the IPO of VakifBank, one of the largest banks in Turkey, which was quoted by *The Financial Times* as the largest in the last five years. The firm also advised underwriters Merrill Lynch and CSFB in an offering of shares in equity stock of BIM, the largest retailer supermarket chain in Turkey.

Paksoy & Co. has extensive experience in cross-border M&A transactions. The firm advised CA IB in relation to a lending transaction involving a European-style call option in Sabanci Holding shares.

The firm advised Koc Holding and its Italian partner UniCredito in the acquisition of 57.4% of shares in Yapı Kredi Bank, one of the landmark deals of 2005. The firm advised the Savings Deposit Insurance Fund of the Republic of Turkey regarding the sale to Vodafone of Turkey's second largest GSM operator, Telsim.

Paksoy & Co. is also involved in almost all major privatisations. In 2005, the firm advised The Carlyle Group in relation to its joint bid with Koc Holding in Turk Telekom; NLMK, the Russian iron-steel manufacturer, in the privatisation of Erdemir, Turkey's leading state-owned iron-steel company; and PKN Orlen, the Polish oil refineries, in the privatisations of Tupras, Turkey's leading petroleum refinery.

The firm handles matters for clients involved in BOT and BOO types of infrastructure projects, ranging from construction of power stations and container terminals to development of water treatment facilities and transportation networks, representing project sponsors, export credit agencies and commercial banks.

Paksoy & Co. also advises international net operators, software and hi-tech companies operating in Turkey. The firm's experience in telecommunications goes back a decade to when the Turkish government took steps to decentralise the mobile communications sector.

The firm provides competition law advice to domestic and international clients, including regulatory filings with the Turkish Competition Authority. Last year the firm sucessfully represented companies such as Dimon, Standard, Finmeccanica, IBM, Tetra Laval, Doosan, Puma, TPV, Adidas and Actavis on the competition law aspects of their transactions in Turkey.

The firm represents a variety of clients in all major real estate matters, including real estate developments, mortgage finance, commercial property and purchase of property by foreigners. The firm's representation of clients in relation to REICs is significant.

The firm's practice covers domestic and international dispute resolution over a wide area, ranging from commercial disputes, insolvency and debt restructurings, and construction law conflicts to enforcement actions of foreign arbitral awards and court judgments. Paksoy & Co.'s representation of the Turkish government's interests in a major international dispute in arbitration before the ICSID in Washington is noteworthy.

PEKIN & BAYAR LAW FIRM

AHULAR SOK, NO 15
ETILER
34337 ISTANBUL

Telephone: +90 212 359 5700
Fax: +90 212 359 5757
E-mail: pekin@pekin.com.tr
Website: www.pekin-bayar.av.tr

Languages
English, French, German, Turkish

Other offices
Ankara, Izmir, Adana

Number of lawyers 30
at this office 23

Contact
Mrs Sefika Pekin (s.pekin@pekin.com)

Member
World Services Groups; ISDA

CATEGORIES OF WORK

Banking and finance
Selin Bayar, Sila Yavuz

Capital markets
Selin Bayar

Corporate, commercial and M&A
Sefika Pekin, Sila Yavuz

Dispute resolution
Can Oguzer

Infrastructure
Muharrem Kücük

Project finance
Selin Bayar

Intellectual property
Deniz Sorguc, Can Oguzer

Labour and employment
Hasan Caglayan

Real estate
Can Oguzer, Hasan Caglayan

Shipping and civil aviation
Deniz Sorguc

Tax
Selin Bayar

Privatisation
Selin Bayar, Muharrem Kücük

Energy
Sefika Pekin, Muharrem Kücük

Telecoms
Selin Bayar

Competition
Deniz Sorguc

SENGULER & SENGULER
IN ASSOCIATION WITH LEDINGHAM CHALMERS

CUMHURIYET CAD, NO 47/1, KAT 4
TAKSIM
34437 ISTANBUL

Telephone: +90 212 361 5066
Fax: +90 212 361 5067
E-mail: info@senguler.av.tr
Website: www senguler.av.tr
www.ledinghamchalmers.com

Languages
English, Turkish

Other offices
Aberdeen, Baku, Edinburgh, Inverness, Port Stanley (Falkland Islands)

Number of lawyers 81
at this office 7

Contacts
Jonathan Blythe, Selcuk Senguler

CATEGORIES OF WORK

Banking and finance

Energy

Corporate

Commercial

Taxation

Intellectual property

Competition

Property

Employment

Projects

Joint ventures

Litigation

M&A

PEKIN & PEKIN

LAMARTINE CADDESI 10
TAKSIM
34437 ISTANBUL

Telephone: +90 212 313 3500
Fax: +90 212 313 3535
E-mail: postmaster@pekin-pekin.com
Website: www.pekin-pekin.com

Languages
Dutch, English, French, German, Turkish

Number of lawyers 29

Contacts
Ahmed Pekin (senior partner),
Fethi Pekin (managing partner)

Member
Lex Mundi; Terralex; The Association of European Lawyers; The Futures and Options Association (FOA); International Swaps & Derivatives Association (ISDA); International Project Finance Association

CATEGORIES OF WORK	
Anti-dumping and environment	Foreign exchange and investment
Banking and finance	Insolvency and bankruptcy
Business and privatisation law	IP: trade marks, patents, know-how
Capital markets law	Labour law
Civil aviation and maritime law	Litigation
Commercial and competition law	Mergers and acquisitions
Communications, media, IT	Mining law
Construction and real estate	Securities law
Consumer law	Sports law (FIFA/UEFA)
EU law	Tax law
Financial leasing law	Telecommunications

THE FIRM

Established in 1971, Pekin & Pekin is one of the largest law firms in Turkey. Pekin & Pekin has an outstanding reputation for its high-quality service to clients in Europe, Asia, North America, the Middle East, Russia and the former Russian republics, as well as within Turkey itself. The firm employs 29 attorneys and a support staff of 30. The main office is based in Taksim, in the centre of Istanbul.

Clients are represented on both a retainer and case-by-case basis. The firm has represented numerous Fortune Global 500 companies, including approximately 70% of the international banks listed, as well as several American Fortune 500 corporations and other smaller companies, major European companies and others, and major Japanese corporations. Additionally, the firm acts as counsel to a diverse group of major Turkish corporations and joint venture companies organised under the laws of the Republic of Türkiye.

AREAS OF PRACTICE

Build-operate-transfer projects: Pekin & Pekin has provided and is currently providing legal advice for major BOT projects in various domains, including hotel projects, power plant projects, dam and water projects, and electricity generation projects.

Debt financing: international and local commercial paper, bond issuance and other securities; international and local securitisation.

Money markets: currency and interest repurchase agreements, forward agreements, future derivatives and loan agreements.

Privatisation projects: Turkey has an active privatisation administration, with many state-owned agencies at various stages of privatisation. Pekin & Pekin has been involved in numerous high-profile transactions under the Republic of Turkey's privatisation program, including the privatisation of several state-owned banks, cement plants, a petroleum distribution company, an LPG company, an airport handling services company, an airline catering company and a major telecommunication equipment company. Pekin & Pekin has extensive knowledge in all aspects of privatisation as the firm's representation has encompassed both the privatisation administration and the private sector, including the purchasers, the lenders, as well as the bidders, in relation to these various transactions.

Structured finance: guarantees and other securities, loan agreements, project finance, syndicated loan agreements.

International and/or local IPOs: issues related to the Capital Markets Board and stock exchanges, due diligence, letters of intent, obtaining necessary permissions, offering circulars, underwriting agreements, share purchase and sale agreements, and shareholders agreements.

Incorporation of financial and non-financial companies: banks, brokerage institutions, factoring companies, financial leasing companies, insurance companies, non-financial companies.

License: license agreements, know-how agreements, technical assistance agreements, management agreements.

Mergers and acquisitions: environmental law due diligence, joint ventures (preparation of articles of incorporation and incorporation of joint venture companies), legal due diligence, share purchase and sale agreements, and shareholders' agreements.

POSTACIOĞLU LAW OFFICE

ABDI IPEKÇI CADDESI NO 65
NAZEM APT KAT 2 NO 2
MAÇKA ISTANBUL

Telephone: +90 212 232 2202
Fax: +90 212 232 2730
E-mail: contactist@postacioglu.av.tr
Website: www.postacioglu.av.tr

Languages
English, French, Italian

Other offices
Izmir, Paris

Number of lawyers 20
at this office 9

CATEGORIES OF WORK	
Domestic/international litigation	Intellectual property
International arbitration	Competition law
Labour law	Construction
Tax law	Law of execution and bankruptcy
Banking and finance	Transportation law
Contract law	Capital markets
Corporate and commercial law	Insurance
International joint ventures	Privatisation
Mergers and acquisitions	Commercial property and real estate

THE FIRM

Postacioğlu Law Office was founded in 1907 by Ibrahim Etem Postacioğlu, and administrated by him until 1958. It was then headed by his eldest son, Sukru Postacioğlu, a professor in commercial law, until 1988. Since 1980, the grandson of the firm's founder, Etem Postacioğlu, has increased the dimensions of the offices in Izmir and Istanbul to an international level. In addition to the offices in Turkey, the firm is now represented in Paris.

The firm's lawyers' philosophy is to think simultaneously as lawyers and businessmen.

AREAS OF PRACTICE

The firm's main areas of practice can be divided up as follows:

Domestic and international litigation and arbitration: Postacioğlu Law Office has an intensive litigation and arbitration practice covering all aspects of civil law, property law, maritime law, private international law, international commercial law and law of contracts. The department works with clients to resolve disputes in a timely and effective manner through prompt assistance and sound legal advice. The firm has the capability to handle complex and urgent litigation thanks to its experience in a wide variety of claims and disputes.

Labour law: the firm offers a comprehensive service to its regular clients regarding labour law. Postacioğlu Law Office advises and represents companies on individual and collective labour claims of employees, for example on terms of employment, working rules and conditions, obligations under social security systems and so on. Services provided for clients include: drafting and negotiation of employment contracts; litigation in matters of dismissal and termination of employment contracts; work-related accidents and illness; interpretation and application of the laws and regulations regarding health and security in the workplace.

Tax law: the firm has significant experience in advising and assisting clients with regard to taxes on business activities. Its service includes submissions of enquiries to take authorities and advocacy to the courts concerning tax-related disputes.

Banking and finance: Postacioğlu Law Office advises and acts on behalf of borrowers and lenders in this field. Among its clients are local and international banks, and local and foreign companies and investors. The department concentrates on various aspects of banking law, loans, and finance of international trade (including letters of credit, counter-guarantees, accredits, etc).

Commercial law: Postacioğlu Law Office offers its clients extensive experience in various aspects of commercial law. The firm assists and represents a wide range of corporations and partnerships, as well as individuals, on regular business affairs and/or specific projects and undertakings. Advice to corporations covers matters such as: incorporations of companies in Turkey and abroad; shareholder agreements and corporate governance; capital-raising transactions; takeovers, mergers and acquisitions; and the establishment and dissolution of joint ventures, partnerships and limited-liability companies.

Intellectual property law: IPP is a company established within the organisational structure of Postacioğlu Law Office. IPP deals with all aspects of intellectual property law, for example: patent and trade mark protection; design registration; copyright and licensing of technology and related agreements on the transfer of such rights, etc. The firm's specialist intellectual property lawyers assist its clients on every single detail, and give worldwide service from consultation and registration steps through to acting in the courts in such cases as unfair competition, piracy and so on.

SERAP ZUVIN LAW OFFICES

BUYUKDERE CADDESI
EMLAK KREDI BLOKLARI
A-1 BLOK K:7 D:30
34 330 1. LEVENT
ISTANBUL

Telephone: +90 212 280 7433
Fax: +90 212 278 1911
E-mail: office@zuvinlaw.com.tr
Website: www.zuvinlaw.com.tr

Languages
English, French, German, Turkish

Other offices
Ankara

Number of lawyers 8
at this office 6

Member
Global 3000; International Bar Association

CATEGORIES OF WORK

Aviation	Foreign direct investment
Asset finance and securisation	Infrastructure and project finance
Banking and finance	Intellectual property
Bankruptcy and repossession procedure	Mergers and acquisitions
Capital markets	Patent and trademark registration
Corporate and commercial	Telecommunications
Commercial property and real estate	Labour law
Commercial mortgages	Pharmaceuticals
Energy law	International arbitration and litigation

THE FIRM

Serap Zuvin Law Office was founded in Istanbul in 2001 by Ms Serap Zuvin. The firm provides sophisticated legal advice and services to many of the world's most dynamic and global organisations and has an international commercial niche practice, employing a young and dynamic team. The firm has the knowledge and resources to deliver the broad scope of quality legal services required to respond effectively to both international and local needs – consistently, confidently and with a sensitivity for cultural, social and legal practice differences.

Since its formation, the firm has advised its clients on all questions of international, industrial and commercial law; with particular emphasis on cross-border and multinational transactions.

Serap Zuvin Law Office prides itself on maintaining a fresh and friendly approach with its clients while striving to provide expert and efficient professional advice. The firm is based in Levent, at the heart of the commercial and financial district of Istanbul. With its associated office in Ankara, the firm liaises with the civil servants in the higher echelons of Ankara to ensure that all bureaucratic procedures are fulfilled promptly and in impeccable order. The firm is a leading niche practice, which undertakes high-profile and quality work comprising both contentious and non-contentious matters. Clients include a number of blue-chip names, among whom are global financial insitutions and world leading aircraft manufacturers. The firm contributes from time to time to the publications of international legal publishers, including IBA, JURIS, Asset Finance International, Euromoney Publications and World Bank.

AREAS OF PRACTICE

Serap Zuvin Law Office is experienced in a broad range of legal services and is a full-service commercial law firm. The firm regularly handles matters relating to aircraft purchase, finance, lease, registration and maintenance contracts.

The firm has established a strong reputation as an international deals firm and acts for clients ranging major multinational business corporations and financial insitutions. It is especially favoured by entrepreneurial business clients who find the firm particularly well atuned to their outlook and needs.

Cross-border and cross-sector knowledge in combination with a deep understanding of business reasoning enables service to clients with the broadest possible support in all their negotiations and business decisions.

Serap Zuvin Law Office is actively involved with its clients in providing regulatory counselling in all areas of commercial law, as well as assisting them through the fields of M&A transactions in Turkey, throughout Europe and internationally.

In addition, the firm serves multinational telecommunications and informaiton technology companies, and has advised on matters including telecommunications, contract and commercial law.

The firm has extensive experience in various aspects of local and international law and is well organized to provide a range of essential business legal advice including: foreign investment law; aviation law; pharmaceuticals and healthcare; labour law; telecommunications; commercial property and real estate; project finance and structured finance; international arbitration and litigation; cross-border transactions, mergers and acquisitions, joint ventures, divestitures and commercial mortgages.

The firm also has a substantial practice in capital markets by representing clients in asset securutisation and advising them on serious issues in solving Turkish capital markets law. In view of the increasing internationalisation of the business community, it is the objective of Serap Zuvin Law Office to improve still further the possibilities of safeguarding the interests of its clients in and outside Turkey.

TABOGLU, ATES & DEMIRHAN ATTORNEYS-AT-LAW

LEVENT CADDESI
NO 9 LEVENT
34330 ISTANBUL

Telephone: +90 212 339 8800
Fax: +90 212 339 8899
E-mail: enquiries@taboglu.av.tr
Website: www.taboglu.av.tr

Languages
English, French, Turkish

Number of lawyers 15

Contacts
Esin Taboglu, Elif Ates, Ebru Demirhan

International Groupings
Istanbul Bar Association; Association of Fellows and Legal Scholars of the CFIL (honourary member); International Bar Association; Turkish Women Entrepreneurs Association (founding member); Harvard Alumni Club (Istanbul); Turkish Women Fund (board member), Corporate Governance Association of Turkey

CATEGORIES OF WORK

Asset finance	**Energy and natural resources**
Aviation	**Environment**
Banking and finance	**Foreign direct investment**
Capital markets	**Information technology**
Commercial property	**Intellectual property**
Competition	**Mergers and acquisitions**
Corporate and commercial	**Project finance**
Corporate governance	**Privatisation**
Employment	**Telecommunications**

THE FIRM

The firm was founded in 2002 by Esin Taboglu, who is a former partner of one of the major Turkish law firms. Esin Taboglu has offered legal services to numerous international financial and commercial organisations during her 16-year professional career.

In 2005, Elif Ates joined the firm as a partner. Elif Ates started her career in 1993. After becoming partner in a major Turkish law firm in 2000, she acted as corporate counsel and corporate governance secretary to the board of Turkcell Iletişim Hizmetleri A.Ş., the leading Turkish GSM operator, from 2001-05.

In 2006, Ebru Demirhan became a partner. She has been with the firm from the beginning.

The firm has three partners, twelve associates and five support staff.

AREAS OF PRACTICE

Taboglu, Ates & Demirhan is one of the leading Turkish law firms, with an extensive international practice and experience. The firm has a team of lawyers who have developed a practice with a proven record for high-quality work, serving both Turkish and international clients. The firm's clients include international financial institutions, local and multinational companies and state entities. The firm advises its clients on corporate and foreign investment, mergers and acquisitions, joint ventures, contracts, securitites and capital markets, banking, privatisation, project finance, telecommunications, real estate, competition, intellectual property, environmental law and labour law.

Taboglu, Ates & Demirhan has an excellent reputation and experience in privatisation matters. Members of the firm have participated in many privatisation projects, including the privatisation of telecommunications, airlines, petroleum distribution, steel, fertiliser, petrochemical, tobacco, alcohol and cement production companies, advising either the state entity in charge of privatisation or the investors.

The firm is involved in public and private mergers and acquisitions, as well as in joint ventures between local and foreign investors. The practice area covers business acquisitions, private equity, public takeovers, mergers, demergers, spin-offs or reorganisations and joint ventures.

The firm has been actively involved in representing issuers, selling shareholders and underwriters in the full range of securities offerings. These include initial public offerings, private placements of securities, global equity offerings for Turkish issuers, listings in major exchanges, including NYSE and LSE, convertible bonds and asset-backed offerings.

TAM & ERTAN LAW OFFICE

FINDIKLI BILEZIK SOK
GUNES IS MERKEZI
NO 3, KAT 4-5, BEYOGLU
ISTANBUL

Telephone: +90 212 244 2009
Fax: +90 212 243 3081
E-mail: t.ertanlawoffice@superonline.com

Languages
English, French, Turkish

Number of lawyers 6

CATEGORIES OF WORK

Shipping (wet)	**Arbitration**
Shipping (dry)	**International trade**
Ship sale and purchase	**Marine insurance**
Shipbuilding contracts	**General average**
Litigation	

TURUNÇ & SAVASÇIN

MAÇKA CADDESİ 32/2
TESVİKİYE
80200 ISTANBUL

Telephone: +90 212 259 4536
Fax: +90 212 259 4538
E-mail: ts-info@turunc-savascin.com.tr
Website: www.turunc-savascin.com.tr

Languages
English, French

Other offices
Izmir, Ankara

Number of lawyers 14
at this office 5

Contact
Noyan Turunç

CATEGORIES OF WORK

Banking and finance
Noyan Turunç, Demir Savasçın

Capital markets and securities
Simhan Savasçın, Dr Esin Taylan

EU and competition law
Noyan Turunç, Dr Esin Taylan

Insolvency, bankruptcy
Demir Savasçın, Selen Egeli

Construction
Buket Onelge, Pinar Çulha

Labour
Demet Cengiz

Litigation
Demir Savasçın, Yücel Ezberci

Foreign investment, commercial and corporate
Lerzan Nalbantoğlu, Selen Egeli

Mergers and acquisitions, joint ventures
Simhan Savasçın, Lerzan Nalbantoğlu

Intellectual property
Lerzan Nalbantoğlu

Oil and gas, energy
Noyan Turunç, Simhan Savasçın

Tax and customs
Buket Onelge, Selen Egeli

Insurance
Adnan Töre

Arbitration
Noyan Turunç, Dr Esin Taylan

Maritime
Pinar Çulha

THE FIRM

Turunç & Savasçın was established in 1990 and offers services in all areas of business law.

AREAS OF PRACTICE

The firm renders services on corporate law to domestic and international corporate clients, including: establishing companies covering preparation of all documents, submissions for approvals, registration with official agencies, producing necessary certificates; corporate governance issues, mergers and acquisitions, assisting in the management of companies, liabilities under tax and non-tax laws; and joint ventures including investment and conducting business in Turkey and abroad.

Mergers and acquisitions work represents a significant portion of Turunç & Savasçın's corporate law activities. The firm is highly experienced in business acquisitions, private takeovers, mergers/reorganisations and joint ventures. The firm's clients include domestic and international corporations. The firm advises on all aspects relating to M&A transactions, including due diligence, warranties, organisation of transaction, management and documentation, regulatory and financing issues, tax structuring, environmental issues, employment, submissions, approvals, registrations, and clearance from the Competition Board. The firm makes contributions to international publications on M&A.

Competition work for domestic and international clients also represents a significant portion of the firm's corporate law practice. The firm has great experience in all aspects of competition transactions, including preventive advice, contract drafting, assistance in the event of an investigation, submissions for individual exemption and negative clearances, notifications for pre-merger and pre-acquisition, and litigating competition cases.

Financial matters: Turunç & Savasçın acts as the Turkish legal counsel for multinational financial institutions and banks with respect to all or any of their interests in Turkey; and advises industrial enterprises and commercial and trading companies in their relationship with financial institutions and banks. Such work includes compliance with banking legislation, including corporate governance, credit facilities, securitisation, guarantees, public debt legislation, government guarantees, assignment of privileges and rights, and security interests; advice on banking and financial requirements and deals, agreements of financial nature, such as loans and guarantees assignment. The firm has vast experience in bankruptcy and insolvency. The firm contributes to international publications on financial matters.

Turunç & Savasçın advises on trade and related regulatory issues including, licensing and distribution, intellectual property, leasing, franchises, product liability, anti-dumping and trade. The firm has a substantial litigation practice on trade cases.

The firm's dispute resolution practice encompasses resolving disputes by litigation and arbitration, and offers clients an unrivalled array of services in litigation and arbitration. Turunç & Savasçın's work includes a broad range of commercial disputes, and work in specialist areas such as indemnification, product liability, intellectual property and insolvency.

With respect to employment, pensions and benefits, Turunç & Savasçın advises on all aspects of labour and employment law. The work includes advising on individual and collective employment, including such aspects as mergers and acquisitions.

Turunç & Savasçın's intellectual property practice includes IP transactional work, litigation, and combating trade mark infringements.

The firm is well-versed in Turkey's tax and customs regimes. The firm's practice includes: corporate tax, international tax planning, value-added tax, customs rules and procedures including the importation regime, customs tax, and tax and customs disputes.

Turunç & Savasçın provides an integrated service to clients in the automotive industry, from manufacturing/importation to distribution, retail and aftermarket services. The firm has considerable experience in consumer claims, product liability issues and IP litigations.

ERDEM & ERDEM LAW OFFICE

SEHIT NEVRES BULVARI NO. 10/7
35210 MONTRÖ IZMIR

Telephone: +90 232 441 6100
Fax: +90 232 466 2121
E-mail: izmir@erdem-erdem.com
Website: www.erdem-erdem.com

Languages
English, French, German, Turkish

Other offices
Istanbul

Contacts
Prof Dr H Ercüment Erdem, Piraye Erdem

CATEGORIES OF WORK

- Administrative law
- Agency and distributorships
- ADR and international arbitration
- Antitrust and trade regulation
- Aviation law
- Banking and finance law
- Business and commercial law
- Capital markets
- Civil law
- Competition law
- Construction law
- Corporate law
- Energy and mining law
- Environmental law
- Execution and bankruptcy law
- Foreign investment law
- Franchising and leasing
- Insurance law
- Intellectual property
- International contracts
- Joint ventures
- Litigation
- Maritime and transportation law
- Mergers and acquisitions
- Privatisation and project finance
- Tax law

UNITED ARAB EMIRATES

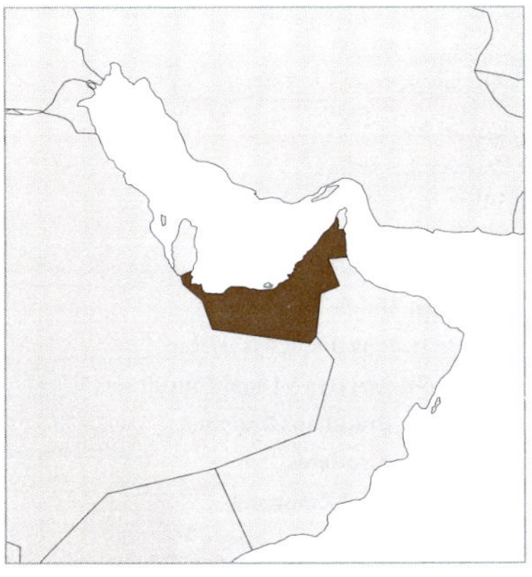

Population	3.1 million
Number of lawyers	n/a
Professional title	Advocate
Currency	UAE Dirham (AED)

The UAE is a federation of seven emirates, formed when independence was achieved in 1971. The most liberal and Westernised of all Middle East countries, foreign workers and expatriates comprise three quarters of its population, while its rich, diverse economy continues to attract a wealth of inward investment.

Abu Dhabi and Dubai are the two principal centres of the country. Historically, Abu Dhabi is the capital and political centre, the source of most oil wealth and instigator of legislation, while Dubai has focused heavily on making itself into a hub for regional commercial business. In 2004, the country suffered the death of much-loved president, Sheikh Zayed Bin Sultan Al Nahyan. His son, Crown Prince of Abu Dhabi Sheikh Khalifa bin Zayed Al Nahyan, was appointed as the new president in November 2004. With the aim of continuing his father's work in terms of diversifying and maximising the economy, he is also taking steps to draw attention back to Abu Dhabi, particularly in terms of developing its real estate and tourism sectors.

BILLING

Clients can expect to pay an hourly rate of up to €400 for a senior partner and €200 and above for an associate or junior partner, although a higher fee may be charged for particularly complex matters such as top-end government work.

Capped fees and fixed arrangements are often preferable for the largest transactions - mainly those in the project finance area.

MARKETING

The UAE relies on the reputation and connections of individuals as much as it does on marketing, which is unrestricted. Client confidentiality will be the only consideration preventing lawyers from disclosing the names of clients or projects.

IN-HOUSE LAWYERS

In-house lawyers are commonly found within companies dealing with particularly complex transactions, such as the leading banks and oil companies.

ECONOMY

The UAE is cash-rich, dynamic, and increasingly diverse. Having become a business hub for the region, Dubai continues to develop at a phenomenal rate, aided by government initiatives designed to encourage inward investment, such as the numerous 'free zones' that have been set up around the country. These provide a haven for foreign investors, which benefit from 100% business ownership and certain tax concessions in these areas.

The world has been holding its breath for the opening of the Dubai International Financial Centre (DIFC), and its associated stock market (DIFX) and independent, world-standard regulatory body (DFSA). These finally came into being in September 2005. The activity surrounding the DIFC has caused a great buzz of excitement throughout the region and a host of foreign companies, including financial institutions, are making moves to set up business in this zone. However, the legislative matters involved are complex, ongoing, and will undoubtedly take time to fully implement.

Almost without exception, every business sector in the country is booming, and Dubai (aptly nicknamed 'Crane City') is awash with construction projects for hotels, residential complexes, commercial business centres, shopping malls and tourist attractions. Correspondingly, there is also a huge demand for infrastructure and energy projects, with many of these also underway.

LEGAL MARKET

Arguably, the UAE has the most important legal market in the Middle East, being a favourable and safe living environment with a range of quality firms. The booming energy and property markets and the recent opening of the DIFC have fuelled a 'gold rush' of firms looking to take advantage by opening offices in the country. A significant recent addition is Magic Circle firm **Linklaters**, whose establishment of an office in the DIFC consolidates a long history of top-drawer project finance work in the Middle East. In early 2006, the ubiquitous **DLA Piper Rudnick Gray Cary** opened its Dubai branch, which from April 2006 will be managed by Jayshree Gupta, formerly head of corporate and commercial at **Denton Wilde Sapte**. **Freshfields Bruckhaus Deringer** and **Baker Botts L.L.P.** cemented their profiles in the region when they opened offices in Dubai in mid-2005. **Simmons & Simmons** recently unveiled a new Dubai office to complement its Abu Dhabi practice, while **Ashurst**, **Akin Gump Strauss Hauer & Feld LLP** and Cayman Islands firm **Walkers** have also established offices in the financial centre. **Berwin**

The largest firms

1	Al Tamimi & Co	64
2	Hadef Al Dhahiri & Associates	41
3	Denton Wilde Sapte	32
4	Masons Galadari	31
5	Clyde & Co	30
6	Clifford Chance	28
7	Bin Shabib & Associates (BSA), Advocates & Legal Consultants	23
8	Trowers & Hamlins	21
9	Afridi & Angell	20
10	Habib Al Mulla & Company	18
11	Allen & Overy LLP	17
12	Norton Rose	14
13	Al Sharif Advocates & Legal Consultants	12
	Rouse & Co. International	12
15	Key & Dixon	10
16	Emirates International Law Firm	9
	Simmons & Simmons	9
18	Al-Suwaidi & Company	8
	Amereller Legal Consultants	8
	Shearman & Sterling LLP	8
21	AlRaya Advocates and Legal Consultants	7
	Greenwald & Van De Kraats	7
23	Abu-Ghazaleh Legal	6
	Al-Sayegh Richards Butler	6
	Baker Botts, L.L.P.	6
	Rights Lawyers, The	6

These figures represent the total number of lawyers in this country only, and have been supplied by the firms themselves. The figures should be accurate as at 1 January 2006.

Leighton Paisner LLP is tipped as a possible next contender.

The federal capital Abu Dhabi is largely concerned with governmental matters, oil and energy work, whereas Dubai is much more varied, commercially focused and entrepreneurial. This makes for quite different legal environments in each. **Shearman & Sterling LLP** undertakes a lot of work for the Abu Dhabi government on energy and infrastructure, as does **Simmons & Simmons**. Work relating to IT and IP is now frequently directed to new branches in the ever-growing Dubai Media City (DMC), and Dubai Internet City (DIC), where **Denton Wilde Sapte** has an additional office to its Dubai and Abu Dhabi branches. **Clyde & Co**, however, has closed it DMC branch, preferring instead to focus matters around the Dubai office and its newly opened Abu Dhabi office.

Both **Allen & Overy LLP** and **Clifford Chance** have worked extensively in the Middle East for over twenty years, and are widely regarded as giants of the region's commercial, banking and project finance markets. Meanwhile, two-office **Trowers & Hamlins** continues to grow in reputation, working in conjunction with its other offices in the GCC and in London. **Norton Rose** continues to build up its banking and corporate practice since opening in Dubai in 2003.

With its myriad commercial, residential and hotel developments, infrastructure and energy projects, construction has become a very important focus for law firms in the UAE. Many firms handle such matters as those relating to contracts, indemnity and disputes over delay. Increasingly visible on sector issues is specialist construction practice **Masons Galadari**, a joint venture between local firm **Galadari & Associates** and UK-based **Pinsent Masons**.

Due to the laws on representation in court, foreign firms tend to draft in qualified nationals for contentious matters, whereas local firms will often have their own UAE-trained lawyers. However, arbitration is the area that attracts most work/value and can be handled by either type of firm. Local firms such as **Al Tamimi & Co** and **Habib Al Mulla & Company** have strong litigation practices, but also deal increasingly with corporate and commercial work. Other local firms of note are **Galadari & Associates** and **Hadef Al Dhahiri & Associates**, which have excellent reputations both in their own right and for taking on referrals from larger, international firms.

The country has a small number of niche firms, particularly in intellectual property where **Rouse & Co. International** and **The Rights Lawyers** deal specifically with this area of law. **Donald H. Bunker and Associates** is noteworthy for specialist aviation financing.

BANKING AND FINANCE

The newly opened DIFC continues to attract interest from large international finance players. The banks are cash-rich, and an abundance of real estate and industrial projects means that there is continued need for heavy finance. The transactions keep getting bigger and more complex, and a raft of investment funds ensures that the legal market maintains its buoyancy in this area. In a significant amount of current projects, Islamic finance is now used alongside conventional financing techniques, and is becoming increasingly sophisticated.

Allen & Overy LLP's celebrated global banking practice, in addition to a long-established presence in Dubai, keeps it securely in the top tier. Finance expert Bimal Desai is a prominent figure in the arena who garners praise from far and wide; one client declared him 'one of the finest legal counsels that I have come across in my career'. One regularly sees the firm acting on the most important financial transactions in the region; in the last year, the firm advised Emirates Airlines on its successful US$500m sukuk issue, and acted for the lead managers on the debut bond issue of Abu Dhabi Commercial Bank.

The 12-lawyer banking and finance department at **Clifford Chance** is headed up by Malcolm Turner, who recently moved to Dubai from Singapore, and Robin Abraham who was recently made up to partner. The firm has had a Dubai office for 30 years, providing regulatory advice to leading financial institutions such as Barclays, Morgan Stanley, Merrill Lynch, Goldman Sachs, HSBC and Deutsche Bank. 'Experienced and professional', the team's advice stretches across

BANKING AND FINANCE

ALLEN & OVERY LLP ✪
CLIFFORD CHANCE
DENTON WILDE SAPTE ✪
SIMMONS & SIMMONS ✪

NORTON ROSE
SHEARMAN & STERLING LLP

Al-Sayegh Richards Butler
Al Tamimi & Co ✪
Clyde & Co ✪
Linklaters
Trowers & Hamlins

Afridi & Angell
Baker Botts, L.L.P. ✪
DLA Piper Middle East LLP
Donald H. Bunker and Associates
Emirates Advocates & Legal Consultants ✪
Freshfields Bruckhaus Deringer
Galadari & Associates
Habib Al Mulla & Company
Hadef Al Dhahiri & Associates ✪
Key & Dixon
Vinson & Elkins L.L.P. ✪

Firms are listed A-Z in tiers which are ranked in order of priority
✪ Indicates firm displays contact details at the end of this chapter.

financial products, asset and structured finance, and aviation finance and leasing. Regional telecoms giant Etisalat recently consulted the firm in relation to the world's largest-ever Islamic financing, while the team has also been advising the Islamic financiers on the US$2.1bn acquisition of shares in Pakistan Telecommunications Company Limited.

In addition to its experience in advising on massive conventional syndicated financings, the expanding practice at **Denton Wilde Sapte** can also boast one of the most advanced Islamic finance practices in the region for corporate, project and real estate transactions. Partners Richard de Belder and Farmida Bi come highly recommended, with clients particularly noting 'can-do' lawyer Rahail Ali in the area of shari'ah-compliant finance and capital markets. Recent matters of note include advising on the huge US$500m Emirates Airlines sukuk, which combines a number of Islamic techniques. The team also recently advised the underwriters, Standard Chartered Bank and Dubai Islamic Bank on a first-of-its-kind, international joint venture rated Islamic bond for Dubai Metals & Commodities Centre.

Ibrahim Mubaydeen is the highly respected managing partner at **Simmons & Simmons**. From its Abu Dhabi base and its new Dubai office, the group continues to act in many significant corporate and project financing deals throughout the Gulf region. Its experience in the sector includes advising Emirates Power Company on its US$540m refinancing, and advising National Bank of Abu Dhabi on both the financing of Al Jazirah Towers and a US$400m term loan facility for Union Water and Electricity Company. The team has also been acting in relation to the financing of the Capital Plaza residential, commercial and shopping complex in Abu Dhabi.

'A great firm with excellent resources', **Norton Rose**'s Dubai office continues to gather pace since opening in 2003. A full range of banking-related advice includes project finance, aircraft finance and leasing, and asset and structured finance. The firm stands at the forefront of Islamic transactions, bonds and financial products, and its big-ticket project finance practice regularly employs innovative shari'ah elements, with the team recently winning instructions from Etisalat in connection with its US$3bn shari'ah-compliant financing. Highly recommended are 'knowledgeable and approachable' Islamic finance expert Nadim Khan, and the 'diligent and proactive' Zubair Mir, described by one client as 'one of the best finance lawyers I have worked with'.

From its office in Abu Dhabi, **Shearman & Sterling LLP** is ideally placed to advise government-owned investment companies on finance. The firm acted on approximately US$6bn-worth of financing deals in 2005, including the US$3.4bn refinancing of a bridge loan, complete with Islamic tranche, for Dolphin Energy. It also advised key client International Petroleum Investment Company, firstly on a bridge fund, then on permanent financing, for a €590m facility.

Although it acts mainly for borrowers, **Al-Sayegh Richards Butler** also regularly acts for Abu Dhabi Commercial Bank, recently assisting the bank as issuer under a US$2.5bn EMTN programme. Aviation finance remains a core strength.

Al Tamimi & Co's Husam Hourani has been described by clients as 'the most knowledgeable banking lawyer in Dubai, insofar as the local market is concerned' and is noted for his expertise in relation to the newly established DIFC. The team's 'solid understanding and very good experience' in respect of Islamic finance is also a feature that goes down well with clients, who add that 'turnaround times and efficiency are the best in Dubai'.

With its strong regulatory experience, **Clyde & Co**'s involvement in the creation of the DIFX, and the subsequent development of Dubai's capital market, has been keeping the team busy. Stock exchange listings, many of which are dual listings on both the Dubai and the London exchanges, have been a particular focus of recent months.

Under banking head Tim Ross, newly opened **Linklaters** will be focusing on the burgeoning areas of capital markets and project finance, and it will be interesting to see what impact this global giant will have on our top tiers over the next year or two. Luma Saqqaf, formerly of **Allen & Overy**, joins the team to lead the Islamic finance arm. The firm also benefits from a very strong record in asset finance in the region.

The Abu Dhabi team of **Trowers & Hamlins** has been advising Etisalat on mobile operation and licensing issues in Saudi Arabia, including bridge financing arrangements which put in place US$2.8bn of security, and subsequently, a US$1.6bn Islamic financing. The office also recently consulted on the finance aspects of new terminal facilities at Cairo International Airport. The Dubai group's clients include Travelex, which recently called on the team for help with establishing its business in the country.

Afridi & Angell has three offices in the UAE, as well as two in Pakistan and one in New York. The firm is an important player in the regional market with good banking connections, advising international and domestic financial institutions on matters such as credit facilities, syndicated loans, Islamic finance and regulatory matters.

With its links to the Saudi banking sector, **Baker Botts, L.L.P.**'s new Dubai office is acting for the lenders in its financing agreements with a Saudi automobile finance company, and also represents Emirates Bank International on branch activities in Saudi Arabia.

The banking and funds practice at **DLA Piper Middle East LLP**'s new Dubai office is one to keep an eye on.

Dubai-based **Donald H. Bunker and Associates** is noteworthy for its specialist aviation finance practice, while local firm **Emirates Advocates & Legal Consultants** has a good reputation and is regionally well-connected, acting for banking clients such as Citibank and Dubai National Bank.

Freshfields Bruckhaus Deringer's new office in Dubai is off to a strong start. The team has been acting on a number of region-wide finance deals such as the debt financing for the development of a US$650m chemical fertiliser complex in Oman, and advising on an aircraft financing in Lebanon. Within the UAE itself, the practice recently advised Dubai Metals and Commodities Centre in connection with the issue of a US200m Islamic sukuk, and Etihad Airways on lease financing.

Galadari & Associates' Dubai team handles bond issues and other capital markets instruments, equity securities, derivative and structured securities, syndicated lending, acquisition finance and international financial services regulation, among a host of other matters. With a number of high-profile clients in the field, including major domestic and international banks, the team recently advised the Dubai Civil Aviation Authority on the US$1bn Ijara Al Sukkuk for the Dubai International Airport.

Acting for both borrowers and lenders, **Hadef Al Dhahiri & Associates**' clients include ANZ Investment Bank, CSFB, HSBC, Standard Chartered and Emirates Bank International. Recent work includes advising National Bank of Abu Dhabi on the creation of an Islamic fund, and advising the borrowers in the US$3bn bid for the Taweelah B IWPP. Clients particularly note the team's effectiveness in the area of setting up new funds and its 'unrivalled' experience in representing companies in IPOs.

Key & Dixon has experience of syndicated finance, debt restructuring and Islamic finance. In the last year, the team has been handling a number of corporate finance and marine finance matters.

Also recommended are **Vinson & Elkins L.L.P.**, where associate Ayman Khaleq is deemed to be 'very strong in corporate finance, funds, capital markets and Islamic finance,' and local firm **Habib Al Mulla & Company**, which has a formal association with **Kennedys** and enjoys a good reputation.

CORPORATE AND M&A

The opening of the DIFC has further paved the way for international companies, and firms can take advantage of the need for advice on setting up, expanding and restructuring their businesses in the country.

Allen & Overy LLP provides 'solid legal technicians who are able to meld sound legal advice with an understanding of the commercial and technical deal drivers'. Led by seasoned experts

CORPORATE AND M&A

ALLEN & OVERY LLP ✪
CLIFFORD CHANCE
CLYDE & CO ✪

AL-SAYEGH RICHARDS BUTLER
DENTON WILDE SAPTE ✪
NORTON ROSE
SIMMONS & SIMMONS ✪
TROWERS & HAMLINS

Afridi & Angell
Al Tamimi & Co ✪
Habib Al Mulla & Company
Hadef Al Dhahiri & Associates ✪
Key & Dixon
Linklaters
Vinson & Elkins L.L.P. ✪

Al-Mehairi Legal Consultants in Association with Fulbright & Jaworski LLP
Al Sharif Advocates & Legal Consultants
Baker Botts, L.L.P. ✪
Bin Shabib & Associates ✪
Freshfields Bruckhaus Deringer
Galadari & Associates
Holman Fenwick & Willan ✪
James Berry & Associates Legal Consultants
Trench & Associates

Firms are listed A-Z in tiers which are ranked in order of priority
✪ *Indicates firm displays contact details at the end of this chapter.*

Simon Roderick, Duncan Macnab and Khalid Garousha, the firm continues to focus on emerging markets such as lucrative telecommunications deals and private equity; an area where Mr Garousha is particularly noted for his capability. From an international corporate and M&A perspective, the firm stays at the top of its game, recently advising the government of Pakistan on a US$2.6bn sale of shares in Pakistan Telecommunications Company.

From its new, state-of-the-art offices in the DIFC, **Clifford Chance**'s globally recognised expertise in telecoms, M&A, private equity, privatisation and capital markets continues to impress big-name clients. The firm's involvement in establishing the legislation behind the DIFC and associated Dubai Financial Services Authority (DFSA) demonstrates its key position in the market. Meanwhile, its advice to Saudi Oger on its recent acquisition of a stake in Turk Telekom, and its current assistance on the first private company IPO unders Saudi Arabia's new Capital Markets Law, exemplifies its international reputation. One client comments, 'we have found them willing to go the extra mile in terms of ensuring that we have their support as we need it and when we need it'.

'Professional, organised and focused', **Clyde & Co** maintains its reputation for having one of the most expansive and mature practices in the UAE. In the firm's Dubai office, experienced corporate head Jonathan Silver is widely acknowledged as 'one of the best corporate lawyers in the GCC'. Meanwhile, spearheading the commercial arm is Anthony Garrod, the 'preferred choice of counsel' for numerous market players. Manager of the Abu Dhabi office, Niall O'Toole is noted for being an 'excellent and practical lawyer', and a 'very good thinker'. The team is handling a significant number of IPOs, which are a big focus for firm now that the DIFX has come into being. Telecoms is another area where the firm has securely established itself, while an expanding Indian subcontinent practice demonstrates how its regional reach is now stretching beyond GCC countries alone.

Based in Abu Dhabi, **Al-Sayegh Richards Butler** has 'very good contacts throughout the Middle East', and an impressive corporate client list, representing international companies such as BAE Systems, Chevron Texaco, Hyundai and Umbro across a range of general corporate and commercial issues. Under 'consummate professional' Peter Michelmore, the team recently advised Nike on a distributorship in Saudi Arabia, where many of its key regional clients are based, and advised De La Rue on commercial contracts in the UAE and Qatar. On the corporate side, the team recently assisted Abu Dhabi Commercial Bank in a joint venture to establish a treasury and risk management business. Clients are 'very impressed by the firm's customer care skills', adding 'one gets first-class legal opinion coupled with the personal touch'.

With offices in Abu Dhabi, Dubai and Dubai Internet City, the team at **Denton Wilde Sapte** is increasingly focused on IPOs and other issues relating to the DIFC and DIFX, such as advice to companies opening offices in the complex. The team demonstrates its ability to juggle local and international law in its advice to Dubai Islamic Bank in connection with the Dubai Waterfront project, one of the largest property developments in the world. Corporate expert and department head Tom Deegan comes highly recommended for his international commercial perspective.

Building on its strength in private equity, investment funds and corporate finance, in 2003 **Norton Rose** consolidated an already strong Middle East practice with the opening of its Dubai office, which now serves as its regional base under managing partner Graeme Muir. A 'well-rounded' team focuses on top-end corporate work, recently securing Etisalat for its US$2.5bn acquisition of Pakistan Telecommunications Company, and acting for AXA in connection with its acquisition of Norwich Union's insurance business in the Middle East. Clients appreciate the firm's global capability, adding, 'the fact that they are a worldwide law firm coupled with a local presence here in Dubai gives us the best of both worlds'. The firm is also dealing with an increasing amount of privatisation throughout the region.

According to clients, Abu Dhabi-based **Simmons & Simmons** 'helps us get to where we want via the shortest route'. Managing partner Ibrahim Mubaydeen enjoys an extremely good reputation, not least for his 'very good relations' with key government departments such as the Ministry of Economy & Trade in Abu Dhabi. Significantly bolstered by the opening of a new office in Dubai, which has been staffed with three partners and nine other legal staff, the firm handles major acquisitions, corporate restructurings, privatisations and IPOs, and commercial contract issues.

Trowers & Hamlins' long-established network of Middle East offices, coupled with its presence in London, 'provides a unique level of service', according to clients. Dubai's Jennifer Bibbings is described as 'personable and thorough', and her team as 'extremely dedicated and efficient'. Edward Rose, who oversees the Abu Dhabi office, is also an experienced and reputable lawyer. In addition to handling the financing aspects of Etisalat's bid for Saudi Arabia's second GSM mobile phone network licence in 2005, the team also dealt with all the corporate aspects, including restructuring. Other matters include helping to establish the regional retail operations of a large Hong Kong subsidiary, and acting in connection with a US$1.4bn acquisition by T&F Informa plc.

Offering 'sensible and helpful' advice, **Al Tamimi & Co** has the capability to handle corporate matters such as foreign direct investment, acquisitions, joint ventures, regulatory advice and a variety of commercial matters under head of department, Walid Chiniara. Recent matters for the group include advising a large Japanese advertising company on its entry into the UAE market, and representing Morgan Stanley and Goldman Sachs in connection with a major IPO. Telecoms is also a strong focus.

Under the Dubai office's 'very competent and dependable' managing partner Sadiq Jafar, the team at **Hadef Al Dhahiri & Associates** has 'the knowledge, experience, & skills' to manage complex corporate, commercial and financial transactions. In Abu Dhabi, the 'experienced' Dr Faraj Ahnish and team have handled IPOs on behalf of Abu Dhabi Islamic Bank and Abu Dhabi Ship Building Company. The firm has been involved in the creation and licensing of a number of prominent corporate entities in the UAE, including Union Water and Electricity Company, Arabtec and Dolphin Energy.

With four partners in Dubai, **Key & Dixon** advises on a wide range of commercial matters, including agency and distribution agreements, hotel purchases and operations, and e-business. On the corporate side, the team deals with public offerings, M&A, and restructuring. Clients of Christopher Dixon find him to be 'an effective and hands-on' managing partner, who is 'ably supported by his team'.

With few peers globally in the corporate field, **Linklaters** has pulled off a great coup by securing corporate guru Ewan Cameron from **Clifford**

Chance. The firm is certainly one to keep an eye on as its new office in the DIFC gathers pace.

Already with a well-established presence in Saudi Arabia, **Baker Botts, L.L.P.** opened its Dubai branch in April 2005, and the office now serves as the regional base for this international firm. A fast-expanding and 'innovative' team is seeing an increasing number of instructions relating to corporate, commercial, banking and project finance, under partner Stephen Matthews, whose 'quick grasp of the major issues' and 'sound negotiating skills' go down very well with clients. In the area of corporate and M&A, the oilfield services sector is a current focus, with the firm handling the acquisition and sale of a number of drilling rigs.

Led by corporate partner Joseph Huse, **Freshfields Bruckhaus Deringer** recently opened an office in Dubai, as a base for its regional undertakings. With an expanding client base of government entities, international financial institutions and local and international corporations, the branch is one to watch as it builds on its UAE and wider Middle East presence.

Mohammed Abdul Karim and Simon Taylor oversee the practice at **Galadari & Associates**, which has long-established offices in both Dubai and Abu-Dhabi. A team of 50 legal staff covers the full range of corporate and commercial matters, retaining a number of large UAE-based businesses for advice on share acquisitions, mergers, disposals, corporate restructuring and consolidation. Working in conjunction with the banking and finance department, the group recently acted for the government of Dubai in its first-ever bond issue, subsequently listed on the Dubai Financial Market.

The entire business and staff of **Hill Taylor Dickinson** in Dubai has transferred to become the regional office of **Holman Fenwick & Willan**. The team recently handled the various corporate restructurings of a leading ship operator.

Former *Fox & Gibbons* lawyer Cynthia Trench heads up a small but capable team at **Trench & Associates**, which advises in relation to business start-ups, M&A and joint ventures, among other matters. Al Bawardi Enterprises is a key client.

DISPUTE RESOLUTION

In the UAE arbitration is often much more complex and of higher value than court litigation. Rights of audience are reserved for UAE nationals, whom the international firms will draft in as necessary. A big step forward was taken when the Dubai International Arbitration Centre was set up in 2003, while the development of the DIFC's independent commercial court has caused a great deal of anticipation for the future of international dispute resolution.

Led by head of department Hassan Arab, **Al Tamimi & Co** has an excellent record for dispute resolution, with a number of UAE-qualified advocates who also benefit from their experience in other jurisdictions such as the US and UK. As well as being experienced arbitrators, the firm's lawyers have wide expertise in litigation, where typical matters include enforcement of contracts, damages suits, and marine and international trade disputes. The judicial enforcement of intellectual property rights is a particular area of strength.

Recent successes for **Allen & Overy LLP** include acting for the government in a high-profile claim brought under a bilateral investment treaty by a wealthy individual, and obtaining a favourable settlement for the claimant in a US$300m ICC arbitration concerning a recent bank merger. In line with the UAE's vast number of construction projects, the firm is seeing an increasing amount of disputes arising in this area, and is being approached by numerous international and domestic contractors. Simon Roderick is an experienced international commercial arbitrator, with the firm maintaining an impressive track record in this field.

Clifford Chance is experienced in handling disputes relating to banking and finance, insurance, construction, shipping and general commercial matters, and has acted for innumerable high-profile clients in these sectors. Seasoned international arbitrator Graham Lovett heads up the group.

In line with its ever-growing telecommunications practice, the 'timely, efficient and professional' team at **Clyde & Co** recently handled a US$400m ICC arbitration on a telecoms-related investment issue, whilst locally the team conducted an arbitration dealing with a disputed hospital management contract. Department head Alec Emmerson is an 'efficient and skilful' lawyer, whose 'effective and pragmatic approach' has clients singing his praises. The firm maintains an immense reputation in international trade, and its expertise in related trade and shipping disputes is, arguably, unparalleled.

Habib Al Mulla & Company is a strong contender when it comes to referrals from larger firms without advocates of their own. Led by name partner Dr Habib Al Mulla, the team has an excellent litigation and ICC arbitration portfolio, acting on behalf of major corporates and regional joint ventures.

Dubai-based **Al-Mehairi Legal Consultants in Association with Fulbright & Jaworski LLP** has garnered a solid reputation for its capability in all kinds of commercial dispute, while local firm **Al Sharif Advocates & Legal Consultants** has acted in cross-border business disputes and has a particular flair for issues concerning shari'ah law.

Senior construction lawyer Paul D Taylor, who joined **Berrymans Lace Mawer** in 2005, is an experienced hand when it comes to construction and engineering contract disputes.

Ziad Abdullah Galadari, a UAE national and senior advocate at **Galadari & Associates**, is an experienced arbitrator and a member of the Tribunal Panel of the Dubai Technology Media

DISPUTE RESOLUTION

AL TAMIMI & CO ✪
ALLEN & OVERY LLP ✪
CLIFFORD CHANCE
CLYDE & CO ✪
HABIB AL MULLA & COMPANY

Al-Mehairi Legal Consultants in Association with Fulbright & Jaworski LLP
Al Sharif Advocates & Legal Consultants
Berrymans Lace Mawer
Galadari & Associates
Hadef Al Dhahiri & Associates ✪
Holman Fenwick & Willan ✪
Towers & Hamlins

Afridi & Angell
Al-Sayegh Richards Butler
Bin Shabib & Associates ✪
Denton Wilde Sapte ✪
Hilal & Associates
Key & Dixon
Lutfi Al Bahar & Co.
Masons Galadari ✪

Firms are listed A-Z in tiers which are ranked in order of priority
✪ *Indicates firm displays contact details at the end of this chapter.*

Free Zone. Ahmed Abdullah Galadari spearheads the solid litigation team, which handles cases from those in the local High Courts to the UAE Federal Supreme Court. The team recently acted on behalf of a subsidiary of one of the world's biggest *Fortune 500* technology sector groups in a major auditor's liability claim.

Hadef Al Dhahiri & Associates has a large dispute resolution team, spanning the firm's offices in both Dubai and Abu Dhabi. The firm boasts a number of 'reliable, responsive and technically excellent' Federal Court advocates, including managing partner Dr Faraj A Ahnish and senior partner and Supreme Court advocate Dr Hadef Al Dhahiri. Local counsel to a swathe of large foreign firms, the team has acted for some noteworthy international client banks including Standard Chartered and HSBC. 'Experienced, approachable and commercial', new partner Richard Briggs co-ordinates the provision of advice for clients in the maritime, trade and insurance fields.

Holman Fenwick & Willan's expertise lies in shipping and insurance-related disputes. Richard Jowett and team receive a significant number of instructions from dredging companies on a variety of issues in the region, is currently acting in a US$500m non-marine insurance claim, and retains a domestic petroleum company for litigation and international arbitration.

The team at **Towers & Hamlins** is described as 'very good and responsive', and 'easy to work with'. Led by client favourite Jennifer Bibbings, the firms handles the preparatory work for litigation, working closely with top-drawer local advocates for court representation.

Afridi & Angell handles all kinds of litigation and arbitration and enjoys a strong local reputation, although its growing capacity for multi-jurisdictional disputes is also worthy of mention.

Overseen by Peter Michelmore, **Al-Sayegh Richards Butler** also has one assistant and a consultant handling dispute resolution. With the assistance of local advocates for court representation, the team is the first point of call for many of its corporate clients, and continues to represent a Korean contractor in long-running litigation.

The dispute resolution team at **Denton Wilde Sapte** has benefited from the thriving UAE construction market, and from the addition of expert arbitrator Michael Kerr, who joins the team from London. In the last year the firm has advised Mowlem, Longulf, Reckitt Benckiser Arabia and Itochu Corporation in arbitrations and court proceedings.

Key & Dixon provides a 'personal and immediate support service' to clients, recently acting in a dispute between a high-profile domestic industrial company and a Japanese contractor, in respect of a US$110m turnkey project in the UAE. The firm is also currently conducting an appeal in the Court of Arbitration for Sport.

Based in Dubai, specialist construction firm **Masons Galadari** successfully defended a high-profile health and safety prosecution on behalf of employees of an international contractor, following the recent collapse of a retaining wall at Dubai Airport. Other significant matters include acting for a major UAE contractor in arbitration proceedings arising out of problems with the flooring works in a prestigious shopping mall in Dubai. The firm is also increasing its capability in representing oil and gas companies and projects in contract and employment disputes.

INFORMATION TECHNOLOGY

The UAE is the most advanced of the Middle Eastern countries in terms of IT. Due to a federal decree, local service provider Etisalat is losing its monopoly on internet and mobile services, paving the way for competition from outside investors. Elsewhere in the Gulf, the telecoms market has opened up considerably, and the UAE serves as the hub for a host of lucrative telecommunications deals throughout the region.

Maintaining its top-of-the-league ranking, **Clyde & Co**'s resources in the sector continue to impress, and the firm has established itself as synonymous with the region's top-end technological advancements. The practice is largely focused on the telecommunications sector, as well as systems integration and software agreements and licensing, with department head Anthony Garrod remaining the 'preferred choice of counsel' on a number of major IT and telecoms-related projects. One example of the group's enormous capacity in the sector is its management of a detailed command and control network being developed and implemented for a regional police force.

INFORMATION TECHNOLOGY

CLYDE & CO ✪

Al-Mehairi Legal Consultants in Association with Fulbright & Jaworski LLP
Al Tamimi & Co ✪
Allen & Overy LLP ✪
Clifford Chance
DLA Piper Middle East LLP
Denton Wilde Sapte ✪
Rights Lawyers, The
Simmons & Simmons ✪
Trowers & Hamlins

Firms are listed A-Z in tiers which are ranked in order of priority
✪ *Indicates firm displays contact details at the end of this chapter.*

Al Tamimi & Co's specialist IT team benefits from the combination of local and international experience. Clients include Microsoft, IBM, and Business Software alliance as well as a number of local entities for advice on such matters as software agreements and licensing.

Former **Linklaters** IT specialist Matthew Glynn heads up **DLA Piper Middle East LLP**'s IT and telecoms practice.

Led by technology expert Mark Hill in Dubai, **The Rights Lawyers**' recent highlights in the field include advising on the Oyoon Project, a content portal and multimedia business for Dubai's lands-based government department. The team is also handling all the legal matters of a world-leading software solutions provider to the real estate market. Clients describe the team as 'extremely efficient, helpful and effective'.

With an eye on the expanding telecoms market, **Simmons & Simmons** also handles technology-related matters such as IT outsourcing and interconnection for clients ranging from finance houses to government entities.

In the last year, **Trowers & Hamlins**' Abu Dhabi office has been handling IT contracts, including specialised turnkey procurement contracts, and IT outsourcing agreements on behalf of two major governmental entities.

Also recommended for their strong IT practices are **Al-Mehairi Legal Consultants in Association with Fulbright & Jaworski LLP**, **Allen & Overy LLP**, **Denton Wilde Sapte** and **Clifford Chance**.

INSURANCE

Noted for his 'excellent and very proactive' management of difficult liability cases, insurance expert Alex Emmerson and the rest of the team at **Clyde & Co** have a well-deserved reputation for their expertise in contentious and non-contentious insurance. The practice handles insurance-related issues arising out of power projects, shipping and medical schemes among other matters. The firm's involvement with the establishment of the DIFC has included a significant amount of insurance-related regulatory work, while Islamic insurance and reinsurance is also an indisputable strength. Clients particularly comment on the team's marine insurance and litigation capability, with Chris Mills coming highly recommended.

INSURANCE

CLYDE & CO ✪
HOLMAN FENWICK & WILLAN ✪

Afridi & Angell
Berrymans Lace Mawer
Clifford Chance
Hadef Al Dhahiri & Associates ✪

Firms are listed A-Z in tiers which are ranked in order of priority
✪ *Indicates firm displays contact details at the end of this chapter.*

Holman Fenwick & Willan has an excellent insurance practice. Between them, Richard Jowett and Edward Newitt handle cargo insurance, personal injury and professional indemnity, while on the non-marine side, the team has plenty of capability in advising on energy and construction insurance and reinsurance. Drafting, regulatory work and litigation are also well within its remit. The firm was formerly the Dubai office of **Hill Taylor Dickinson**.

Afridi & Angell handles insurance coverage disputes, and advises on problem investments, permitted insurance activities, and D&O liability. The firm also represents a number of maritime indemnity clubs and underwriters.

Berrymans Lace Mawer's construction and development practice includes professional indemnity matters on behalf of the building trade, and the team also manages construction-related insurance disputes.

Clifford Chance acts for a number of leading insurance and reinsurance companies, which includes resolving disputes, including professional negligence claims.

Hadef Al Dhahiri & Associates' new addition to the team, partner Richard Briggs (formerly of **Clifford Chance** and, more recently, **Al Tamimi & Co**) has a reputation as 'one of the most experienced and reputable lawyers in Dubai'. The firm's clients in the sector include Oman Insurance Co, Adamjee Insurance Co and Boeing Corporation.

INTELLECTUAL PROPERTY

Over the last three years or so, the government has been active in enforcing intellectual property rights in order to increase the attractiveness of the country as a business centre. IP and related

INTELLECTUAL PROPERTY

AL TAMIMI & CO ✪
ROUSE & CO. INTERNATIONAL

Clyde & Co ✪
Denton Wilde Sapte ✪
Rights Lawyers, The

Al-Sayegh Richards Butler
Amereller Legal Consultants
Clifford Chance
Emirates Advocates & Legal Consultants ✪
Hadef Al Dhahiri & Associates ✪
James Berry & Associates Legal Consultants
Trench & Associates

Firms are listed A-Z in tiers which are ranked in order of priority
✪ *Indicates firm displays contact details at the end of this chapter.*

legislation has become increasingly sophisticated and international in its standards.

Dubai-based **Al Tamimi & Co**'s Hoda Barakat is an undoubted 'leader in her field'. Clients include Microsoft and Business Software Alliance for litigation, an area in which the team has a fantastic track record, while for general IP advice, it represents Philip Morris, Sony, Nokia and BMW, among others. Usefully, the firm also has three IP lawyers in its office in Dubai Internet City, and maintains excellent relationships with a variety of government entities for regulatory work. The team also acts for a variety of regional media and television companies.

Led by Edward Hardcastle, **Rouse & Co. International** is a pure IP boutique with a network of international offices and a team of experienced individuals including specialist trade mark agents and dedicated private investigators. Its Dubai office serves the Middle East region and beyond, with the capability to provide a complete IP service to its clients. Long-standing client adidas recently made use of the firm's skills for matters relating to the design, implementation and management of an annual retail level raid campaign, as part of its region-wide anti-counterfeiting activities. Currently, the team is involved in a groundbreaking piece of litigation relating to rights enforcement on behalf of a well-known Japanese manufacturer. Other clients include Harley-Davidson, GlaxoSmithKline, Kodak, Shell and Unilever.

Led by Rob Deans, the IP team at **Clyde & Co** undertakes high-end, complex work in the sector, from franchise arrangements for local and multinational retail outlets to anti-counterfeiting programmes for international clients, also handling tricky, cutting-edge commercial IP disputes as they arise. One corporate client recently sought advice in respect of rationalising and maximising its local and global intellectual property as part of its international expansion programme. The firm also handles the commercial and intellectual property aspects of Middle Eastern media broadcasters and various sporting bodies.

Clients of **Denton Wilde Sapte**'s new senior IP specialist Elizabeth Spong describe her as 'clear, concise and business-focused'. In addition to handling the usual trade mark and patent registrations, the team advised on some significant matters in 2005. These include acting for THE One on strategic global trade mark protection throughout the GCC, supervising anti-counterfeiting raids on behalf of Pfizer, and advising Dubai International Holdings Company in relation to brand architecture, contentious cross-border issues, co-existence arrangements and other matters relating to its global IP portfolio. Other clients include Singapore Airlines, Reckitt Benckiser and CNBC Arabia.

Based in Dubai Media City, **The Rights Lawyers** is a well-connected, international IP, IT and media and entertainment specialist offering 'invaluable and thorough' support and advice to the creative industries, including music, television and advertising. Led by former **Clyde & Co** partner Mark Hill, the team was recently called upon to advise on franchising issues for a new international enterprise, and to handle the worldwide patenting of new video technology on behalf of Photint Venture Group. Appreciating the firm's 'superb network of contacts and partners', clients include Bavaria Hotels, Execujet, Vespa and Yardley.

Whilst IP is not a main focus for the team at **Al-Sayegh Richards Butler**, the firm nonetheless has plenty of capability when it comes to trade mark registrations, infringement issues and other related matters.

Amereller Legal Consultants represents leading IT companies and software companies, and acts as regional counsel for one of the world's leading copyright associations. Led by Nasser Ali Khasawneh, the team also handles trade mark registrations and infringements.

Consultant Deepak Devades is recommended for 'consistent and professional' advice on Arabic trade mark matters at **Emirates Advocates & Legal Consultants**, whilst clients of **Hadef Al Dhahiri & Associates** consider the firm to be 'responsive and knowledgeable' for registration and infringement advice.

Although small in numbers, staff at **James Berry & Associates Legal Consultants** is a recommended outfit for technology-related advice, which covers all aspects from trade mark protection and registration, to patenting and design.

Trench & Associates is highly recommended for its IP capability, which includes anti-counterfeiting.

PROJECTS AND ENERGY

A high volume of ongoing projects keeps the UAE economy busy. The country was once heavily dependent on oil and gas projects, but much more significant now is the super-abundance of high-value construction and real estate deals, industrial facilities developments, and tourist resorts. The country is also used as a base for project development and finance throughout the Gulf.

PROJECTS AND ENERGY

ALLEN & OVERY LLP ✪
CLIFFORD CHANCE

DENTON WILDE SAPTE ✪
SHEARMAN & STERLING LLP
TROWERS & HAMLINS

Linklaters
Norton Rose
Simmons & Simmons ✪
Vinson & Elkins L.L.P. ✪

Afridi & Angell
Baker Botts, L.L.P. ✪
Clyde & Co ✪
Freshfields Bruckhaus Deringer
Hadef Al Dhahiri & Associates ✪
Key & Dixon

Firms are listed A-Z in tiers which are ranked in order of priority
✪ *Indicates firm displays contact details at the end of this chapter.*

In line with its globally renowned projects experience, **Allen & Overy LLP**'s Dubai branch has a huge project finance presence throughout the Middle East. Partners Bimal Desai and Duncan Macnab maintain glorious reputations in the field, overseeing a 'receptive team' which recently concluded the US$700m financing of the Qalhat LNG project, and is currently working on the US$700m Acetyls Complex project in Saudi Arabia. Domestically, the firm has been working on the recently closed Fujairah wastewater project, and on a university PFI project in Abu Dhabi. Clients comment that the firm 'focuses on finding solutions that facilitate the deal, rather than point scoring'.

Clifford Chance's projects team continues to expand with the arrival of Malcolm Turner from the London office, Robin Abraham's promotion to partner and the arrival of three further lawyers. The firm has undeniable strength in depth when it comes to regional oil and gas, power and water projects and related financial transactions, and now the UAE office is increasingly being called upon to service clients outside the GCC region, including those in China and North Africa. Currently the team is advising on the QASCO financing in Qatar, and on the financing of the Palm's Atlantis project, which is the largest non-oil and gas financing in the UAE.

'Efficient' **Denton Wilde Sapte** boasts a standalone energy and natural resources department. Here, energy expert Sean Korney works alongside esteemed Middle East head Neil Cuthbert to provide 'a very good service' in high-value projects, as well as joint venture agreements, bids, service contracts and other issues. The client base includes major multinationals such as Shell, Occidental and Sumitomo Corporation. In addition to its advice on the financing aspects of the massive Atlantis project, the firm is also being consulted by the government of Oman in relation to the region's first IWP, and is representing the project company in the restructuring of the Ajman sewerage project.

In Abu Dhabi, the two-partner office of **Shearman & Sterling LLP** which has worked on some of the region's most significant high-value projects, is starting work on a US$3bn project financing for the Borouge petrochemicals joint venture in Abu Dhabi. New partner Timothy Pick is an experienced power and energy counsel, while managing partner Philip Dundas can always be relied upon to provide sound advice to clients, which now include Qatar Water & Electricity Company.

Led by oil and gas expert Edward Rose, **Trowers & Hamlins**' Abu Dhabi office has advised on a number of significant projects throughout the region, including the development of a US$312m polypropylene plant in Oman, where the group acted on behalf of Oman Refinery Company. Belying its relatively small international size, the firm has handled a number of key projects in Abu Dhabi, including the US$1.2bn Borouge petrochemicals project, which, following its successful establishment, retained the team for other matters including shareholder agreements, construction contracts and further financing arrangements. The team is now advising on Borouge's Step II project and on the expansion of the original plant. Following its involvement with Taweelah A2, Umm Al Nar and other IWPP programmes, the group is now being instructed in relation to the pre-bid stage of the Abu Dhabi IWPP project.

With an already strong profile in Middle East project finance, newcomer **Linklaters** will no doubt be making full use of its solid relationships with international and regional banks to secure further top-drawer projects work for its new office in the DIFC.

Norton Rose's excellent banking practice gives it strong capability in the project finance arena, and the firm is more than capable of meeting the demand for Islamic project finance, one example being its involvement in the QatarGas II offshore liquefaction project. The team also recently advised the Liquidity Management Centre BSC on the US$134m sukuk to finance aspects of the Bahrain Financial Harbour Project.

'Well-connected' and with excellent relations with government authorities, Abu Dhabi-based **Simmons & Simmons** has made its presence felt in some of the region's most prominent projects, from Abu Dhabi's Taweelah B project, to a major aluminium project in Oman. It is also no stranger to advising on large petrochemicals projects, and is seeing an increasing amount of work in the property development arena.

With four partners and three assistants, the Dubai branch of **Vinson & Elkins L.L.P.** is small, but has a powerful brand and very good lawyers. Under office head Jeffrey Eldredge, the firm has carved a great reputation for projects work throughout the Gulf region. Matters handled include representing Chevron Phillips in the development and financing of Qatar's Q-Chem II project, and Saudi Arabia's Jubail Chevron Phillips project, and representing an international energy company in connection with its successful bid for the Saudi upstream gas offering.

A new and expanding Dubai office for **Baker Botts, L.L.P.** benefits from the experience of lawyers previously housed in Saudi Arabia, which has a good record for project finance. Currently the new office is representing one of the bidders on the Saudi Land Bridge project.

Clyde & Co is advising the arrangers in a proposed US$1.5bn real estate and leisure project in Dubai, and is assisting a major Middle Eastern construction company on its proposed investment in respect of an oil and gas pipeline in Sudan. The firm is heavily involved in the Palm Island project, advising on a six-lane tunnel through the island and on a monorail system.

Although its Dubai office is still in its infancy, **Freshfields Bruckhaus Deringer** has been working on projects throughout the region for decades, and expectations are that the new office will be quick to gain ground. The Dubai team is already advising on a number of key projects in countries such as Oman, Bahrain and Qatar.

'Technically excellent' **Hadef Al Dhahiri & Associates** has been involved in some important projects such as Taweelah B, and is advising Omnix Group on the conventional and Islamic financing of the multi-billion dirham development at the Pearl, Dubai. Dubai-based partner Sadiq Jafar is highly estimated by clients, whilst associate Alan Rodgers has a reputation as a 'solid, experienced and efficient lawyer'. One client comments that 'very few local and international firms in Dubai can count on having such consummate professional and efficient lawyers in their ranks'.

Key & Dixon has a 'professional team with depth, international qualifications and experience', with clients also appreciating the team's 'local knowledge and contacts'.

REAL ESTATE AND CONSTRUCTION

Currently, the construction sector is one of the most important for firms in the UAE. Not only are they riding the wave of a huge residential and commercial property boom in Dubai; Abu Dhabi is now starting to take off in this area too. In addition, there is an enormous requirement for infrastructure and energy developments.

The highly regarded Michael Grose oversees **Clyde & Co**'s construction and engineering department. The firm gets involved with almost all of the country's major construction and development projects; one example of its presence in the market is the Palm Jumeirah project, where the team is advising an Australian joint venture on the creation of the huge Atlantis water park. The team is also currently assisting a Kuwaiti developer in a large residential development, and is being consulted on significant aspects of the Dubai airport expansion. Contentious issues also benefit from the firm's excellent dispute resolution team.

REAL ESTATE AND CONSTRUCTION

CLYDE & CO ✪
DENTON WILDE SAPTE ✪

Allen & Overy LLP ✪
Al-Sayegh Richards Butler
Masons Galadari ✪
Trowers & Hamlins

Al Tamimi & Co ✪
Berrymans Lace Mawer
Bin Shabib & Associates ✪
Clifford Chance
Hadef Al Dhahiri & Associates ✪
Key & Dixon
Norton Rose
Simmons & Simmons ✪

Firms are listed A-Z in tiers which are ranked in order of priority
✪ *Indicates firm displays contact details at the end of this chapter.*

Construction is a cornerstone practice area for **Denton Wilde Sapte**. David Courtney-Hatcher, a construction and engineering specialist with 25 years of experience in the field, has moved from London. Meanwhile, new arbitration expert Michael Kerr bolsters the contentious arm. Together, they bring more than the necessary expertise to carry the flag in the many high-value construction projects that the team continues to be instructed in. These include the Dubai Light Rail project and the Atlantis project.

With its host of project company clients, **Allen & Overy LLP** regularly advises on significant commercial and industrial construction contracts, such as those for the International Airport expansion and a university PFI project in Abu Dhabi.

In 2004 **Al-Sayegh Richards Butler** closed a major IWPP project in Iran, and now the firm has switched its attentions to a similar project in Bahrain. In addition, the firm has been advising English project management and construction companies on contractual disputes with local employers and on management documentation.

'Extremely capable' three-partner **Masons Galadari** is a joint venture between UK-based **Pinsent Masons** and local firm **Galadari & Associates**. Since its inception, the firm has been steadily building a reputation for contentious and non-contentious construction matters, and is now developing a noteworthy presence in the infrastructure, power and energy sectors. Recent transactions include advising the contractors in connection with the Dubai Light Rail project, and TECOM on the US$1.4bn Jumeirah Beach Residence project.

Trowers & Hamlins has a strong focus on big-ticket commercial property and real estate work, dealing with all aspects in the field including construction, where recent arrival Nigel Truscott from **Denton Wilde Sapte** brings significant experience. Under Nick White, the team continues to act for Arcapita Bank of Bahrain in connection with its US$150m 'Victory Heights' project joint venture with Dubai Sports Land. Clients claim to be 'very satisfied with the quality of work and their responsiveness', one adding that the team was 'extremely helpful in helping us navigate difficult legal issues in UAE real estate'.

Al Tamimi & Co has a good name in the region for construction and commercial property matters. Although the firm recently said goodbye to partner Lisa Dale, who headed up the department, it still has plenty of capability in Tara Marlow and Greg Peebles, both well-regarded UK lawyers with solid experience.

With the recent recruitment of two further construction specialists, **Berrymans Lace Mawer**'s presence in the construction and project development arena is growing ever more dominant. Commercial law specialist Jeremy Cama oversees the team, which was bolstered recently by new additions Dennis Brand, who has experience of development and construction law throughout the Middle East and North Africa, and Paul D Taylor, who was previously head of **Beachcroft Wansbroughs**' Manchester construction team. Together, they have the know-how to provide advice on projects from start to finish, acting for public and private developers and contractors.

Bin Shabib & Associates is advising on the development of a number of projects within the tourist attraction, Dubailand, and on the legal structuring of a multi-billion dollar real estate development at Umm Al Quwan.

Clifford Chance is currently advising on a US$450m hotel and residential complex being built on Palm Island, and is heavily involved in various aspects of the US$1.2bn Atlantis hotel and leisure park project, including construction elements.

Noted for its 'bilingual ability, Western approach and good connections', **Hadef Al Dhahiri & Associates** has advised on a number of major construction projects, from commercial property developments to hotels and residential complexes. Recently, the firm has been advising the developer in relation to the Al Reem Island project in Abu Dhabi, and is assisting with the development of the Australasia continent within 'The World' development, offshore in Dubai.

Key & Dixon has been busy advising a major UAE developer on its concession arrangements for the development of mixed-use space next to stations of the planned Dubai Metro System. Clients of Peter Shaw, seconded from associate firm **Taylor Wessing** describe him as 'very competent'.

With support from partners in the London office, **Norton Rose**'s recent new addition and former **Nabarro Nathanson** lawyer, senior associate Martin Preston, now oversees the department. The team supports a client base of property developers, energy projects and real estate companies in some key construction projects in the country, including the US$260m Hexagon development in Dubai, and the Dubai Metro project where its advises Jumeirah Capital on concession agreements.

Simmons & Simmons is also highly recommended for its real estate and construction practice.

SHIPPING

According to clients, **Clyde & Co**'s Chris Mills is 'without a doubt the best marine lawyer in the UAE market'. The firm will regularly be found acting on many of the largest shipping-related issues in the region, including ongoing claims arising out of the Dubai Drydocks incident. The firm's corporate team recently helped to establish the country's first-ever Islamic shipping fund, whilst the group is particularly active in lucrative oil rig sales and purchases.

Al Tamimi & Co has an excellent reputation for its shipping practice, covering shipbuilding, operations, chartering, collisions, insurance, disputes and marine environmental issues. The majority of its clients are shipowners, although one will also find a variety of insurance companies, compensation funds and port authorities on the firm's books.

In early 2006 **Holman Fenwick & Willan** took over the Dubai office of **Hill Taylor Dickinson**. The firm can often be seen acting in relation to the region's most significant marine accidents, and the team has widened its practice over the last few years to include advice relating to such matters as ship finance, corporate structuring, IT contracts, and ship management agreements. Recent matters of note include handling legal aspects of the recent collision between the *Yasa Aysa* and the *USS Philadelphia* off Bahrain, and the ongoing claims surrounding the Dubai Drydocks incident. For marine insurance, Edward Newitt maintains a strong reputation.

Galadari & Associates has a client base of shipowners, charterers, cargo owners, P&I clubs, brokers, freight forwarders and logistics companies. The team regularly represents clients in the Court of Cassation in cases concerned with such issues as unsafe ports and seaworthiness, loss of cargo due to fire, and shipbuilding and repair disputes.

Hadef Al Dhahiri & Associates' advice is 'prompt, accurate and to the point', according to clients, and the firm's recent addition of seasoned expert Richard Briggs has no doubt boosted its reputation and capacity in the field.

Also recommended are **Afridi & Angell**, **Clifford Chance** and **Habib Al Mulla & Company**.

SHIPPING

CLYDE & CO ✪

Al Tamimi & Co ✪
Holman Fenwick & Willan ✪

Afridi & Angell
Clifford Chance
Galadari & Associates
Habib Al Mulla & Company
Hadef Al Dhahiri & Associates ✪

Firms are listed A-Z in tiers which are ranked in order of priority
✪ Indicates firm displays contact details at the end of this chapter.

CLYDE & CO

7TH FLOOR WEST TOWER
ABU DHABI MALL
PO BOX 54204
ABU DHABI

Telephone: +971 2 644 6633
Fax: +971 2 644 2422
E-mail: mero@clydeco.ae
Website: www.clydeco.com

Languages
Afrikaans, Arabic, English, French, German, Italian, Japanese, Latvian, Polish, Punjabi, Russian, Spanish, Urdu

Other offices
Belgrade, Caracas, Cardiff, Dubai, Guildford, Hong Kong, London, Moscow, Nantes, Paris, Piraeus, Rio de Janeiro, St Petersburg, Shanghai, Singapore

Number of lawyers 409
at this office 5

Contacts
Niall O'Toole, Wayne Jones

CATEGORIES OF WORK

Corporate
Niall O'Toole, Amrik Sangha

IP/IT
Rola Madi

Aviation
Niall O'Toole

Dispute resolution
Wayne Jones, Mareejoseph Gittany

Insurance and reinsurance
Wayne Jones, Mareejoseph Gittany

Construction and engineering
Niall O'Toole

Inward investment
Niall O'Toole

DENTON WILDE SAPTE

SUITE 1204
AL GHAITH TOWER
HAMDAN STREET
PO BOX 47656
ABU DHABI

Telephone: +971 2 626 6180
Fax: +971 2 626 6175
E-mail: abudhabi@dentonwildesapte.com
Website: www.dentonwildesapte.com

Languages
Arabic, Bengali, English, French, Urdu

Other offices
Almaty, Cairo, Dubai, Istanbul, London, Milton Keynes, Moscow, Muscat, Paris, Tashkent

Number of lawyers 683
at this office 6

Contact
Richard de Belder

CATEGORIES OF WORK

Arbitration

Aviation

Banking and finance

Corporate and commercial

Commercial litigation

Construction

Corporate finance

Energy and utilities

Environment

Hotels and leisure

Intellectual property

Islamic finance

Mergers and acquisitions

Project finance

Telecoms

EMIRATES INTERNATIONAL LAW FIRM

FLOOR 3, GIBCA TOWER
KHALIFA STREET
PO BOX 469
ABU DHABI

Telephone: +971 2 626 5600
Fax: +971 2 626 5123
E-mail: lawyers@emirates.net.ae
Website: www.eilf.com

Languages
Arabic, English, French

Number of lawyers 9

Contact
Dr AbdulRahman Al Shaikh

CATEGORIES OF WORK

Business and corporate law	**Insurance and reinsurance law**
Banking and financial institutions law	**Employment law**
Oil and gas law	**Maritime law**
Construction	**Sports law**
Real estate law	**Litigation**
Intellectual property (IP) law	**Arbitration**
Constitutional law	**Alternative dispute resolution**
Administrative law	

THE FIRM

EILF was formed in 1996 (by merger of AlQasimi and AlShaikh firms) to serve the legal needs of local and international businesses in the UAE. It is staffed by experienced advocates, legal consultants and internationally-trained lawyers, offering high-calibre advice on the law of the UAE and other member states of the Gulf Co-operation Council (GCC). The founders of the firm are HE Shaikh Fahim Bin Sultan Al Qasimi, the Minister of Supreme Council and GCC Affairs and Dr AbdulRahman Al Shaikh, a practitioner and professor of law at the UAE University School of Law.

EILF's mission is to meet the needs of its clients throughout the UAE, whether those clients are operating locally or globally.

EILF is currently advising on matters with underlying values in the billions of dirhams. The firm's clients include local and foreign corporations, industries, governmental bodies, sovereign and private individuals.

AREAS OF PRACTICE

EILF specialises in all aspects of UAE laws and in representing clients before the courts in all the Emirates The main practice areas of EILF are:

Business and corporate law: EILF handles all issues pertaining to corporate creations, such as establishing public and private joint stock companies and all other legal forms of companies, governance, mergers and acquisitions, joint ventures, project finance, bankruptcy, securities issues, white-collar crimes and the emerging offset programmes.

Banking and financial institutions law: EILF advises banks and financial holdings companies in their own corporate transactions, including internal and administrative operations, formation of bank holding companies, M&A, equity offerings and administrative actions by regulatory agencies.

Oil and gas law: EILF provides counsel to a variety of clients in connection with natural gas and crude oil engineering and construction issues, transportation, refining and marketing regulations and agreements and general practice related to the energy field.

Construction: EILF offers a full range of services in matters involving breach of contract variations and claims for delay, disruption and loss of productivity. The firm also has extensive experience in drafting contracts at every stage of the construction project, from conception to completion.

IP law: EILF lawyers apply to obtain IP rights in the UAE. Globally, the firm operates through associated firms. EILF also registers, protects, litigates and obtains legal enforcement against violations of IP rights for a range of foreign and domestic clients. The firm represents the clients in all proceedings, in identifying, registering and protecting their rights.

Arbitration: EILF lawyers have participated in many UAE and international arbitrations, including ADNOC group (Abu Dhabi National Oil Company) arbitrations. If a UAE decision is not honoured, EILF has the expertise to enforce the decision through the courts. The firm is also conversant with the rules of the International Chamber of Commerce, the American Arbitration Association and UNCITRAL.

Insurance and reinsurance law: EILF represents a variety of clients, including carriers, reinsurers, holding companies and individual clients. EILF's lawyers have substantial litigation experience in representing both sides of the insurance claims or disputes. The firm also acts as private counsel to organisations related to the insurance industry.

Litigation: EILF's litigation group has a reputation for providing high-quality representation in litigation matters. This department devotes itself exclusively to litigation and is frequently involved in civil and criminal disputes, commercial and insurance claims, intellectual property, construction, employment and personal injury litigation.

Constitutional law: EILF advises on issues related to the UAE constitution, including the interplay between commercial activites and the Federal Constitution. EILF lawyers, with former members of the judiciary who are of-counsel to the firm, provide in-depth analysis.

Maritime law: EILF represents ship owners, charterers, insurers and shippers in a wide range of maritime disputes.

HADEF AL DHAHIRI & ASSOCIATES

PO BOX 3727
ABU DHABI

Telephone: +971 2 627 6622
Fax: +971 2 627 6556
E-mail: contact@hadalaw.ae
Website: www hadalaw.com

Languages
Arabic, English, French

Other offices
Dubai

Number of lawyers 39
at this office 14

Contact
Dr Faraj A Ahnish

CATEGORIES OF WORK

Corporate affairs
Michael Dark, Tarik El Bakri

Commercial transactions
Michael Dark, Tarik El Bakri

Banking and finance
Alan Rodgers

Energy, water and power
Michael Webb

Shipping and maritime
Basil Siddiqi

Construction and engineering
Roger Morris

Intellectual property
Tarik El Bakri

Information technology
Dr Faraj A Ahnish

Real estate
Roger Morris

Government regulation
Dr Faraj A Ahnish

Environmental
Dr Faraj A Ahnish

WTO/GATT
Tarik El Bakri

UAE offset operations
Dr Faraj A Ahnish

Litigation and arbitration
Saleh Ahnaish

SIMMONS & SIMMONS

THE ADNIC BUILDING
KHALIFA STREET
PO BOX 5931
ABU DHABI

Telephone: +971 2 627 5568
Fax: +971 2 627 5223
E-mail: enquiries@simmons-simmons.com
Website: www.simmons-simmons.com

Languages
Arabic, English, French

Other offices
Brussels, Dubai, Düsseldorf, Frankfurt, Hong Kong, Lisbon, London, Madeira, Madrid, Milan, New York, Oporto, Padua, Paris, Rome, Rotterdam, Qatar, Shanghai, Tokyo

Number of lawyers 764
at this office 11

Contact
Ibrahim Mubaydeen

CATEGORIES OF WORK

Corporate

Banking

Capital markets

Taxation

Projects, PFI

EU, competition

Dispute resolution

Intellectual property

Employment

Financial markets

Pharmaceutical and biotechnology

Energy and utilities

TMT

Aerospace and defence

Transport

Consumer goods

AL TAMIMI & CO

DUBAI INTERNATIONAL FINANCIAL CENTRE
SHEIKH ZAYED ROAD
PO BOX 9275
DUBAI

Telephone: +971 4 331 7090
Fax: +971 4 331 3177
E-mail: info@tamimi.com
Website: www.tamimi.com

Other offices
Abu Dhabi, Baghdad*, Dubai Internet City, Doha*, Sharjah

Number of lawyers 45

Contacts
Essam Al Tamimi, Hoda Barakat

CATEGORIES OF WORK

Banking and finance	**Litigation**
Corporate and commercial	**Arbitration and alternative dispute resolution**
Family business governance	**Maritime, trade and insurance**
Telecommunications	**Construction**
Information technology and media	**Property law**
Intellectual property	

THE FIRM

Al Tamimi & Company, originally established in 1989, is today one of the leading law firms in the Arabian Gulf region. It is one of the largest local, non-affiliated law firm in the United Arab Emirates with offices in Dubai, Abu Dhabi, Sharjah and associated offices in Baghdad and Doha.

An international team of high-calibre lawyers ably serves clients from the United Kingdom, North America, Europe, Africa, the United Arab Emirates and several other Arab countries. Each member of the team of professionals and qualified administrative staff is fully committed to providing clients with accurate, thorough and cost-effective advice.

Al Tamimi & Company prides itself on complete knowledge of the laws and regulations applicable to home jurisdiction and the commercial community abroad. Within the UAE, it regularly confers with government ministries during the introduction of new legislation and the ongoing amendment of internal regulations, relying on long-established contacts in all government departments.

The firm can assist multinational companies to establish operations in the UAE. independently, or in association with local partners. Both local clients, many of whom have business interests outside the United Arab Emirates, and international companies, rely on our global perpective. The firm publishes a monthly magazine *Law Update*. The company subscribes to the belief that the world of opportunity does not recognise national boundaries.

AREAS OF PRACTICE

Al Tamimi & Company is among the leading law firms in the UAE and the banking and finance department reflects this position by advising a number of prominent local and international banks in relation to the finance operations in the UAE and GCC. The department advises both lenders and borrowers on all aspects of structuring, negotiating, documenting financing transactions and has represented local and international banks and financial institutions in both conventional and Islamic transactions.

Company and commercial law are two of Al Tamimi & Company's most important specialisations. It facilitates company formations, be it the creation of a purely local enterprise or helping a mutlinational to establish a corporate presence in the UAE. In the commercial non-company context, we regulatly draft and review commercial contracts, at all times striving to help our clients to identify hidden opportunities or pitfalls and find creative, cost-effective solutions.

As a regionally recognised force in telecommunications law, Al Tamimi & Company has been closely involved in the deregulation and liberalisation of telecommunications markets throughout the Gulf region.

Al Tamimi & Company has rapidly become one of the leading law firms with a specialist intellectual property practice in the Gulf region. Clients know that they can confidently rely on a comprehensive range of in-house legal services to establish, protect and defend their intellectual property rights, in the UAE and throughout the world.

The information technology law practice emphasises electronic business and internet law, as well as software amd computer law. It advises clients on legal aspects of technolgy transfer and e-business, including issues of commercial and licensing laws, electronic contracting, privacy and data protection, domain name registration and cyber squatting, software protection, digital signatures and certificates, and website legal and privacy policy statements.

The media team acts for leading players in the Gulf market. Experience covers the full spectrum of requirements from defamation to competition and regulation to corporate advisory work, including where media meets technology and telecommunications.

ALLEN & OVERY LLP

1603 API WORLD TOWER
SHEIKH ZAYED ROAD
PO BOX 3251, DUBAI

Telephone: + 971 4 332 3190
Fax: +971 4 332 3192
E-mail: information@allenovery.com
Website: www.allenovery.com

Languages
English, Urdu, Arabic, French, German, Spanish, Korean, Japanese

Other offices
Amsterdam, Antwerp, Bangkok, Beijing, Bratislava, Brussels, Budapest, Frankfurt, Hamburg, Hong Kong, London, Luxembourg, Madrid, Milan, Moscow, New York, Paris, Prague, Rome, Shanghai, Singapore, Tokyo, Turin, Warsaw

Number of lawyers 2,304
at this office 16

Contacts
Bimal Desai, Duncan Macnab, Simon Roderick, Kahlid Garousha

CATEGORIES OF WORK

Banking and finance
Bimal Desai, Ian Ingram-Johnson

Commercial
Simon Roderick, Khalid Garousha

Project finance
Ian Ingram-Johnson, Bimal Desai

Construction
Duncan Macnab

M&A
Khalid Garousha, Simon Roderick

Aviation
Simon Roderick, Duncan Macnab

Capital markets
Bimal Desai, Luma Saqqaf

Litigation and arbitration
Simon Roderick

Corporate
Simon Roderick, Khalid Garousha

IP
Simon Roderick

ASHURST

LEVEL 42 EMIRATES TOWERS
SHEIKH ZAYED ROAD
PO BOX 119974
DUBAI

Telephone: +971 4 319 7530
Fax: +971 4 319 7474
Website: www.ashurst.com

Languages
Arabic, English, German

Other offices
Brussels, Frankfurt, London, Madrid, Milan, Munich, New Delhi*, New York, Paris, Singapore, Tokyo

Number of lawyers 748
at this office 4

Contact
Paul de Cordova

CATEGORIES OF WORK

Energy, transport and infrastructure

Company/commercial

International finance

Employment

Private equity

Litigation

Investment banks

BAKER BOTTS L.L.P.

ART TOWER, 1ST FLOOR
AL-MINA ROAD, AL-RAFFA
PO BOX 119210
DUBAI

Telephone: +971 4 311 9515
Fax: +971 4 311 9525
E-mail:
stephen.matthews@bakerbotts.com
Website: www.bakerbotts.com

Languages
Arabic, English, Spanish, Farsi, German, French, Urdu

Other offices
Austin, Dallas, Hong Kong, Houston, London, Moscow, New York, Riyadh, Washington DC

Number of lawyers 700
at this office 6

Contact
Stephen Matthews

Member
Lex Mundi

CATEGORIES OF WORK

- Arbitration and dispute resolution
- Banking
- Corporate
- Energy (power) and projects
- Project finance
- Oil and gas projects
- Pipeline projects
- Infrastructure projects
- Privatisation
- Regulatory
- Telecommunications projects

BIN SHABIB & ASSOCIATES

19TH FLOOR
WORLD TRADE CENTER
PO BOX 262
DUBAI

Telephone: +971 4 331 8888
Fax: +971 4 331 8883
Website: www.binshabib.com

Languages
Various international languages

Other offices
Abu Dhabi

Number of lawyers 23
at this office 21

International groupings
UAE Ministry of Justice (court practice);
Dubai Chamber of Commerce;
Bar Associations in a variety of countries

CATEGORIES OF WORK

- Aviation
- Banking and finance
- Commercial property and real estate
- Construction
- Corporate and commercial
- Corporate restructuring
- Dispute resolution – litigation and arbitration
- Energy and natural resources
- Foreign direct investment
- IT
- Infrastructure and project finance
- Insurance
- Intellectual property
- Mergers and acquisitions
- Private clients and trusts
- Public offerings and securities law
- Shari'ah law
- Shipping and transport
- Telecommunications

CLYDE & CO

CITY TOWER 2
SHEIKH ZAYED ROAD
PO BOX 7001
DUBAI

Telephone: +971 4 331 1102
Fax: +971 4 331 9920
E-mail: mero@clydeco.ae
Website: www.clydeco.com

Languages
Afrikaans, Arabic, English, French, German, Italian, Japanese, Latvian, Polish, Punjabi, Russian, Spanish, Urdu

Other offices
Abu Dhabi, Belgrade, Caracas, Cardiff, Guildford, Hong Kong, London, Moscow, Nantes, Paris, Piraeus, Rio de Janeiro, St Petersburg, Shanghai, Singapore

Number of lawyers 409
at this office 40

Contacts
Anthony Garrod, Alec Emmerson, Jonathan Silver

CATEGORIES OF WORK

Inward investment
Simon Adams

Corporate
Jonathan Silver, Simon Adams

Commercial, agency and distribution, franchising
Simon Adams, Anthony Garrod

Banking and financial services
Jonathan Silver, Abhi Jalan

Establishment, government liaison
Karam Gayed, Raafat Hares

Employment
Simon Adams, Philip O'Riordan

Oil, gas and energy
Jonathan Silver, Simon Adams

Construction and engineering
Jonathan Silver, Michael Grose

International trade
Alec Emmerson, Patrick Murphy

Shipping and transport
Christopher Mills, Brian Nash

Insurance and reinsurance
Alec Emmerson, Wayne Jones

Dispute resolution
Alec Emmerson, Christopher Mills

Debt recovery and insolvency
Alec Emmerson, Christopher Mills

E-commerce, IT and telecoms
Anthony Garrod

IP and trade marks
Rob Deans

Media, advertising and sport
Rob Deans

DENTON WILDE SAPTE

26TH FLOOR, API WORLD TOWER
SHEIKH ZAYED ROAD
PO BOX 1756
DUBAI

Telephone: +971 4 331 0220
Fax: +971 4 331 0201
E-mail: dubai@dentonwildesapte.com
Website: www.dentonwildesapte.com

Languages
Afrikaans, Arabic, Dutch, English, French, Gujerati, Hindi, Spanish, Urdu

Other offices
Abu Dhabi, Almaty, Cairo, Istanbul, London, Milton Keynes, Moscow, Muscat, Paris, Tashkent

Number of lawyers 683
at this office 26

Contacts
Neil Cuthbert, Jayshree Gupta, Mathew Kidwell, Rahail Ali, Thomas Deegan, Sean Korney, David Courtney-Hatcher, Michael Kerr, Mary Allan

CATEGORIES OF WORK

Banking and finance
Neil Cuthbert, Rahail Ali

Corporate and commercial
Tom Deegan, Jayshree Gupta

Construction
David Courtney-Hatcher, Bernard Hau

Energy
Sean Korney, Mathew Kidwell

IT, media
Marc Oufi, Elizabeth Spong

Infrastructure projects
Neil Cuthbert, Mary Allan

Intellectual property
Elizabeth Spong

Islamic finance
Rahail Ali, Rustum Shah

Litigation and arbitration
Michael Kerr, Ravinder Bhullar

Mergers and acquisitions
Jonathan Dawe, Jayshree Gupta

EMIRATES ADVOCATES & LEGAL CONSULTANTS

14TH FLOOR
EMIRATES TOWERS
SHEIKH ZAYED ROAD
PO BOX 9055
DUBAI

Telephone: +971 4 330 4343
Fax: +971 4 330 3993
24-hour call centre: + 971 50 328 9999
E-mail: contact@emiratesadvocates.com
Website: www.emiratesadvocates.com

Languages
Arabic, Chinese, English, French, Hindi, Tagalog

Other offices
Abu Dhabi, Dubai, Sharjah

Number of lawyers 120
at this office 30

Member
International Chamber of Commerce;
International Bar Association; AEA International

CATEGORIES OF WORK

Banking and finance

Real estate and property

Corporate and commercial

ADR and litigation

Construction

Debt recovery

Government regulation

Healthcare

Employment and labour

Intellectual property

Maritime

Information technology

Insurance and reinsurance

Telecommunications

Offshore incorporation

HADEF AL DHAHIRI & ASSOCIATES

PO BOX 37172
DUBAI

Telephone: +971 4 332 3222
Fax: +971 4 332 3300
E-mail: s.jafar@hadalaw-dubai.ae
Website: www hadalaw.com

Languages
Arabic, English

Other offices
Abu Dhabi

Number of lawyers 39
at this office 25

Contact
Sadiq Jafar

CATEGORIES OF WORK

Corporate affairs
Sadiq Jafar

Commercial transactions
Sadiq Jafar

Banking and finance
Sadiq Jafar

Energy, water and power
Sadiq Jafar

Shipping and maritime
Richard Briggs

Construction and engineering
Richard Briggs

Intellectual property
Sadiq Jafar

Information technology
Sadiq Jafar

Real estate
Richard Briggs

Government regulation
Sadiq Jafar

Environmental
Sadiq Jafar

WTO/GATT
Richard Briggs

UAE offset operations
Sadiq Jafar

Litigation and arbitration
Richard Briggs

HOLMAN FENWICK & WILLAN

COMMERCIAL TOWER
HOLIDAY CENTRE
SHEIKH ZAYED ROAD
PO BOX 53934
DUBAI

Telephone: +971 4 331 7788
Fax: +971 4 331 9988
E-mail: holmans@hfw.ae
Website: www.hfw.com

Languages
Afrikaans, Arabic, English, Greek

Other offices
Hong Kong, London, Melbourne, Paris, Piraeus, Rouen, Shanghai, Singapore

Number of lawyers 209
at this office 10

CATEGORIES OF WORK

Admiralty and maritime law
Edward Newitt, Richard Jowett

Alternative dispute resolution
Edward Newitt, Richard Jowett

Aviation
Rula Dajani

Commercial litigation
Edward Newitt, Richard Jowett

Company and commercial
Rula Dajani

Company setup/restructuring
Rula Dajani

Information technology
Richard Jowett

Insurance
Edward Newitt, Richard Jowett

Property
Rula Dajani

Reinsurance
Richard Jowett

Ship finance
Edward Newitt, Rula Dajani

THE FIRM

Holman Fenwick & Willan is an international law firm specialising in shipping and transport, trade and energy, insurance and reinsurance and commercial law. The firm has a reputation worldwide for excellence and innovation. It has one of the largest international arbitration and dispute resolution practices of its kind, with offices in Europe, the Middle East and Asia Pacific.

The firm's international practice is founded upon its principal offices in London, Paris, Piraeus, Dubai, Hong Kong, Shanghai, Singapore and Melbourne and over 120 years' experience of working with other law firms in jurisdictions throughout the world.

Opened in February 2006, the Middle East office in Dubai is staffed by nine lawyers and the combined regional experience of the three resident partners is more than 30 years. The office handles a broad range of non-contentious and contentious work for international and multinational clients, and for major regional and local entities, in their commercial and corporate activities. The property investment and development practice is also a significant part of the work undertaken by the office.

AREAS OF PRACTICE

Admiralty and maritime law; aircraft registration; alternative dispute resolution; commercial law; commercial litigation; company law; computers and software; company setup/restructuring; insurance law; property; reinsurance and ship finance.

MASONS GALADARI

AL GHUBAIBA ROAD
BUR DUBAI
PO BOX 115580
DUBAI

Telephone: +971 439 37001
Fax: +971 439 37764
E-mail: mblanksby@masonsgaladari.com
Website: www.masonsgaladari.com

Languages
Arabic, English, French, Spanish

Other offices
Abu Dhabi, Birmingham*, Bristol*, Brussels*, Dubai*, Edinburgh*, Glasgow*, Hong Kong*, Leeds*, London*, Manchester*, Shanghai*

Number of lawyers 900
in this country 35
at this office 6

Contacts
Steven Hunt, Mark Blanksby

CATEGORIES OF WORK

Construction and engineering
Mark Blanksby, Steven Hunt

Arbitration
Mark Blanksby, Michelle Nelson

Litigation
Ziad Galadari, Michelle Nelson

Infrastructure projects
Sachin Kerur, Sofia Parra

Energy and natural resources
Sachin Kerur, Sofia Parra

Project finance
Sachin Kerur

SIMMONS & SIMMONS

14TH FLOOR
DUBAI WORLD TRADE CENTRE
SHEIKH ZAYED ROAD
PO BOX 9521
DUBAI

Telephone: +971 4 332 0140
Fax: +971 4 332 0141
Website: www.simmons-simmons.com

Languages
English

Other offices
Abu Dhabi, Brussels, Düsseldorf, Frankfurt, Hong Kong, Lisbon, London, Madeira, Madrid, Milan, New York, Oporto, Padua, Paris, Qatar, Rome, Rotterdam, Shanghai, Tokyo

Number of lawyers 764
at this office 2

Contacts
Rober Leigh, Ibrahim Mubaydeen

CATEGORIES OF WORK

Corporate

Banking

Capital markets

Taxation

Projects, PFI

EU, competition

Dispute resolution

Intellectual property

Employment

Financial markets

Pharmaceutical and biotechnology

Energy and utilities

TMT

Aerospace and defence

Transport

Consumer goods

VINSON & ELKINS LLP

11TH FLOOR
EMIRATES TOWERS OFFICE
SHEIKH ZAYED ROAD
DUBAI

Telephone: +971 4 330 1800
Fax: +971 4 330 1300
Website: www.velaw.com

Languages
Arabic, English, French

Other offices
Austin, Beijing, Dallas, Houston, London, Moscow, New York, Shanghai, Tokyo, Washington DC

Number of lawyers 781
at this office 4

Member
International Bar Association; Union International des Avocats; Arab International Forum; American Business Council of Dubai and the Northern Emirates; Business Law, Corporate Counsel and International Law Sections, State Bar of Texas

CATEGORIES OF WORK

Mergers and acquisitions

Project finance and development

Business law

Telecommunications

Corporate law

Energy

Corporate finance

Construction law

Privatisation transactions

UNITED KINGDOM
ENGLAND AND WALES

Population	**52.5 million**
Number of lawyers	**solicitors 116,110 barristers 13,985**
Professional title	**Solicitor, barrister**
Currency	**Pound sterling (£)**

Index

The last year has not been particularly kind to lawyers. UK firms across the board reported that corporate work, particularly M&A and capital markets, was slow. For many firms, however, litigation, restructurings, regulatory and employment remained relatively busy.

For a more detailed view of the UK legal market see *The Legal 500* – 2005 edition at www.legal500.com.

BILLING

Solicitors' charges dropped in 2003 by as much as 20%-25% at the top end of the market. Hourly rates for partners in a large City firm range from £250 to £375 for commercial property work; £250 to £425 for corporate/finance; and £250 to £400 for litigation work. Partners in large regional firms typically charge an hourly rate of between £195 and £240 depending on the geographical region rather than the type of work. Assistant solicitors' rates are approximately 50%-60% of partners' fees.

MARKETING

Law firms and barristers' chambers can freely advertise both in print and online as the UK marketing regulations are among the most relaxed in the world. Details of specific deals can be disclosed as long as the client's permission is granted beforehand.

THE PROFESSION

In the UK the profession is split into solicitors and barristers. The solicitor is usually a client's first port of call while barristers concentrate on in-court advocacy. There have been developments in recent years designed to improve the efficiency of the litigation process.

IN-HOUSE LAWYERS

There are over 10,000 legal professionals working in business in the UK. In recent years there has been an increase in lawyers choosing an in-house career due to the salary increases and general buoyancy in the in-house market.

LEGAL MARKET

Recent times have seen a number of mergers, most notably the merger of *Theodore Goddard* with *Addleshaw Booth & Co*, to create **Addleshaw Goddard**. The biggest surprise, however, was the merger that initially created *Jones Day Gouldens*. In December 2003, the firm renamed as **Jones Day** after the US powerhouse. *Gouldens* was one of the UK's most profitable corporate finance boutiques and most observers would have thought the firm could have thrived as an independent. Still, the merger gives *Gouldens* access to **Jones Day**'s enormous corporate client base across the globe.

Altheimer & Gray dissolved in August 2003 with a fair amount of its 50+ London-based lawyers moving to **Kilpatrick Stockton LLP**.

However, several top American firms have expanded the breadth of their UK practices and appear in high tiers of our tables. This trend looks set to continue. A number of US firms in London are proving serious competitors to the UK firms.

We cover specialist boutiques as well as providing details of the major commercial firms outside London.

ACQUISITION FINANCE

Allen & Overy LLP's team is led by Tony Keal. The firm advised Apax and Cinven on the financing of their €2.1bn acquisition of VNU World Directories. On the bank side, the firm continues to act for all the major players across both London and Europe.

At **Clifford Chance**, the team led by James Johnson and Mark Stewart is consistently praised. The firm's strength on the equity side gives the banking team access to a huge volume and spread of work: the team advised CVC and Permira on their £1.75bn acquisition of the Automobile Association, and Citigroup and Goldman Sachs on the $6bn financing of Cemex's acquisition of RMC.

Linklaters is now truly established in third place, with the depth of resources to challenge the top two. This is in no small part down to its hire of Adam Freeman and Stephen Lucas. The team acted for ABN Amro and ING on the €600m Vendex buyout, and for JP Morgan, CSFB, Goldman Sachs and Bank of America on the €2.1bn VNU deal.

At **Ashurst**, the team is led by partner Nigel Ward. The firm is strong for both borrowers and banks.

Freshfields Bruckhaus Deringer is increasingly making headway with the banks, thanks to the efforts of partners Brian Gray and Sean Pierce 194. Regular bank mandates come from Barclays Capital, Goldman Sachs, CSFB, ING, ABN Amro and Deutsche Bank.

The largest firms

1	Eversheds LLP	1,813
2	Clifford Chance	1,141
3	Allen & Overy LLP	1,128
4	Linklaters	1,050
5	DLA Piper Rudnick Gray Cary UK LLP	1,030
6	Freshfields Bruckhaus Deringer	906
7	Beachcroft Wansbroughs	821
	Pinsent Masons	821
9	Herbert Smith LLP	796
10	Lovells	750
11	Addleshaw Goddard	658
12	Wragge & Co LLP	575
13	Norton Rose	573
14	Hammonds	552
15	Denton Wilde Sapte	512
16	Ashurst	485
17	Slaughter and May	484
18	Nabarro Nathanson	468
19	Berwin Leighton Paisner LLP	467
20	CMS Cameron McKenna LLP	460
21	Cobbetts	446
22	Dickinson Dees	435
23	SJ Berwin LLP	393
24	Walker Morris	362
25	Hill Dickinson LLP	355

These figures represent the total number of lawyers in this country only, and have been supplied by the firms themselves. The figures should be accurate as at 1 January 2006.

ACQUISITION FINANCE

ALLEN & OVERY LLP ✪
CLIFFORD CHANCE

LINKLATERS ✪

Ashurst ✪
Freshfields Bruckhaus Deringer
Shearman & Sterling (London) LLP
White & Case ✪

CMS Cameron McKenna LLP
DLA Piper Rudnick Gray Cary UK LLP ✪
Denton Wilde Sapte ✪
Lovells ✪
Macfarlanes ✪

Cleary, Gottlieb, Steen & Hamilton LLP ✪
Dickson Minto WS
Simpson Thacher & Bartlett LLP
Slaughter and May ✪
Weil, Gotshal & Manges ✪

Addleshaw Goddard
Baker & McKenzie LLP ✪
Berwin Leighton Paisner LLP
Debevoise & Plimpton LLP ✪
Eversheds LLP
Herbert Smith LLP ✪
SJ Berwin LLP ✪
Skadden, Arps, Slate, Meagher & Flom (UK) LLP
Travers Smith

Firms are listed A-Z in tiers which are ranked in order of priority
✪ Indicates firm displays contact details at the end of this chapter.

At **Shearman & Sterling (London) LLP**, a team led by Anthony Ward is able to provide integrated senior and high yield debt advice. It offered this one-stop-shop service to the banks – Hypovereinsbank and Mizuho – on the €1.2bn buyout of ATU by KKR.

White & Case's London team is headed by Mike Goetz and Maurice Allen. The team has increased the penetration of its banking client base, advising CIBC, Citigroup, CSFB, Deutsche Bank, JP Morgan and Deutsche and Morgan Stanley on their €3.1bn financing of Blackstone's acquisition of Celanese.

CMS Cameron McKenna LLP partners John Naccarato and Will Meredith are popular with clients, who include Lloyds TSB, Royal Bank of Scotland, ABN Amro and HSBC.

DLA Piper Rudnick Gray Cary UK LLP regularly advises HBOS, RBS, Barclays, and increasingly Lloyds TSB.

Denton Wilde Sapte's team, led by partner Chris Fanner, is praised by clients. Clients include RBS and Bank of Scotland.

Lovells group head Matthew Cottis continued to advise Barclays, Bank of Scotland, Mizuho, Nomura and CIBC.

Macfarlanes has grown with the addition of Tom Speechley and Bronwen Jones. Their arrivals have dramatically increased the team's deal volumes, and brought in key clients RBS, NIB Capital, Mizuho and Barclays.

ARBITRATION

Increasingly firms are structuring their departments to include a standalone specialist arbitration group.

Clifford Chance still has the most admired arbitration practice in London. Recent examples of numerous matters include representing the offshore lenders to the Dabhol power station project; and the Republic of Hungary in ICSID arbitration proceedings.

Allen & Overy LLP's arbitration practice that has recently dealt with many cutting-edge cases. Recently the group handled more than 15 cases where the amount at stake exceeded $100m.

Freshfields Bruckhaus Deringer which trades on its international network, moves up a tier this year. Geoff Nicholas, who heads the group, 'has a deep understanding of business and is particularly impressive.'

Larry Shore leads the group at **Herbert Smith LLP**. The firm recently acted on the Laura Ashley ICC arbitration, and for Telekom Malaysia in disputes arising from its foreign investment in Ghana.

Lovells recently acted on an ICSID/Energy Charter Treaty arbitration, and an ICC arbitration for a major Singaporean corporation. Phillip Capper, Andrew Foyle and Patrick Sherrington have all recently been appointed as arbitrators.

Linklaters boasts six partners as arbitration specialists. The past year has seen the group handle around 100 arbitrations around the world with a cumulative value of almost $8bn.

White & Case is a firm that has a stellar international arbitration reputation, particularly in the United States. The firm deals with a steady flow of high-value cross-border and domestic industry-based arbitrations.

Wilmer Cutler Pickering Hale and Dorr LLP, known for the expertise of Gary Born, has recently been involved in approximately 50 arbitration matters, a significant number of which involved amounts in dispute exceeding $50m.

Ashurst continues to provide a full arbitration package to its clients. Recently the firm has acted in relation to a $38m insurance claim, and a £25m power station dispute. The Japanese market in Europe remains one of the firms' strongholds.

Peter Griffin 's arrival at **Baker Botts** in London has made quite an impact on the market. The fantastic experience he gained at his previous firm has certainly set him in good stead in his new location.

Although a firm famed for its US arbitration capability, **Debevoise & Plimpton LLP** rises a

ARBITRATION

CLIFFORD CHANCE

ALLEN & OVERY LLP ✪
FRESHFIELDS BRUCKHAUS DERINGER
HERBERT SMITH LLP ✪
LOVELLS ✪

LINKLATERS ✪
WHITE & CASE ✪
WILMER CUTLER PICKERING HALE AND DORR LLP ✪

Ashurst ✪
Baker Botts ✪
Debevoise & Plimpton LLP ✪
Norton Rose ✪
Skadden, Arps, Slate, Meagher & Flom (UK) LLP

Baker & McKenzie LLP ✪
CMS Cameron McKenna LLP
Latham & Watkins
Pinsent Masons ✪
SJ Berwin LLP ✪
Shearman & Sterling (London) LLP
Simmons & Simmons ✪
Slaughter and May ✪

Clyde & Co ✪
Eversheds LLP
Holman Fenwick & Willan ✪
Ince & Co ✪

Davies Arnold Cooper
Denton Wilde Sapte ✪
Hammonds
Mayer, Brown, Rowe & Maw LLP
Richards Butler
Vinson & Elkins R.L.L.P. ✪
Watson, Farley & Williams LLP

Barlow Lyde & Gilbert
Bryan Cave
Covington & Burling ✪
Hunton & Williams
Kennedys
Kilpatrick Stockton LLP ✪
Kirkpatrick & Lockhart Nicholson Graham LLP
McDermott Will & Emery UK LLP ✪
Olswang
Osborne Clarke
Stephenson Harwood
Steptoe & Johnson ✪
Taylor Wessing ✪
Weil, Gotshal & Manges ✪

Firms are listed A-Z in tiers which are ranked in order of priority
✪ *Indicates firm displays contact details at the end of this chapter.*

tier this year in recognition of the ongoing work of its London office.

Norton Rose has recently handled arbitrations valued in excess of $1.5bn. Peter Rees, who leads the arbitration group is recommended.

Skadden, Arps, Slate, Meagher & Flom (UK) LLP rises two tiers this year, largely due to the continued efforts of Karyl Nairn:

Baker & McKenzie LLP draws great strength from its global reach. The firm has particular expertise in construction and engineering arbitrations, as well as arbitrations in the Middle East, in Central and Eastern Europe and Central Asia.

Neil Aitken is head of **CMS Cameron McKenna LLP**'s international arbitration group. The firm specialises in arbitrations arising out of insurance/reinsurance, construction, energy, and technology disputes.

Up the table this year, **Latham & Watkins** has recently acted on an ICC arbitration valued at $1.5bn and a multi-million-dollar UNCITRAL arbitration. Philip Clifford heads up the arbitration team.

Gordon Bell is the key arbitration contact at **Pinsent Masons**. The merger bought together the construction and projects arbitration practice of *Masons* with the commercial arbitration practice of *Pinsents*.

SJ Berwin LLP has considerably boosted its international arbitration capability with the formation of a specialist group within its dispute department and the hire of David Goldberg.

Shearman & Sterling (London) LLP relies on its Paris office, where Emmanuel Gaillard is a prominent arbitrator.

At **Simmons & Simmons**, Simon Morgan and David Sandy spend 100% of their time on arbitration-related matters. The firm has recently worked on arbitrations arising out of financial services, bond, IT, joint venture, insurance, agency agreement and political risk insurance disputes.

Slaughter and May recently acted for a Wall Street investment bank defending a claim of damages in excess of $2.8bn.

ASSET FINANCE AND LEASING

ALLEN & OVERY LLP ✪
CLIFFORD CHANCE
FRESHFIELDS BRUCKHAUS DERINGER
NORTON ROSE ✪

DENTON WILDE SAPTE
LINKLATERS ✪
SLAUGHTER AND MAY ✪

CMS Cameron McKenna LLP
Lovells ✪
Simmons & Simmons ✪
Watson, Farley & Williams LLP
White & Case ✪

Addleshaw Goddard
Berwin Leighton Paisner LLP
Clyde & Co ✪
DLA Piper Rudnick Gray Cary UK LLP ✪
Herbert Smith LLP ✪
Stephenson Harwood

Bryan Cave
Clark Ricketts
Eversheds LLP
Harbottle & Lewis LLP
Hogan & Hartson ✪
Osborne Clarke
Richards Butler
Travers Smith
Wragge & Co LLP ✪

Field Fisher Waterhouse
Hill Taylor Dickinson
LeBoeuf, Lamb, Greene & MacRae ✪
Salans

Firms are listed A-Z in tiers which are ranked in order of priority
✪ *Indicates firm displays contact details at the end of this chapter.*

ASSET FINANCE AND LEASING

Allen & Overy LLP has considerable expertise around the globe, recently handling Iberia's latest ground-breaking 'Iberbond'. Another highlight was advising ABN Amro on a $900m financing for Qatar airways. The firm's appointment to the ECA panel has already paid dividends, and its appointment to the GE UK Panel is also likely to bring in further big-ticket aviation work.

Clifford Chance's London team is led by Geoffrey White. It is notably strong in the aviation sector but is also well-versed in ship and rail finance. The firm acted on Iberia's 2004 Iberbond. A recent highlight was acting for the European ECAs, Lloyds TSB and Natexis on the award-winning structured operating leases of three A340-300Es to South African Airways.

An extremely strong London tax department supports **Freshfields Bruckhaus Deringer**'s eight-partner team. Recent key deals included acting for three European ECAs, KfW and a syndicate of banks on the finance restructuring of 38 Airbus aircraft for Air Canada. Tim Lintott heads the team.

Norton Rose has a large London team under leading lawyer Peter Thorne. It concentrates on high-value, complex structured transactions, usually involving a cross-border element. Instructions have included advising easyJet on a $3.6bn simultaneous financing of 82 Airbus A319s and Royal Bank of Scotland on £400m-worth of receivables financing for UK retailers.

Denton Wilde Sapte is now the only firm on both the ECA and Airbus panels and acted for BNP Paribas in a widely admired $160m ECA financing for five Airbus A320s to EgyptAir. On the rail side it advised Serco-NedRailways on the mobilisation of its Northern Rail Franchise, and it has also been active in receivables financing.

Linklaters' practice under Ron Gibbs is active at the upper end of the aviation, rail, and plant and equipment markets. It continues to work for Emirates, setting precedents with the first Japanese operating lease of an A340-500 and the first financing of spare engines in a $110m sale and leaseback.

Although **Slaughter and May** does not have a large practice, the firm's strengths in tax and structured finance, and the versatility of its finance lawyers, ensure that it remains a serious player in the sector. Recent activity includes a variety of big-ticket aviation work.

CMS Cameron McKenna LLP continues to act for GATX on a number of aircraft purchases, new operating leases and existing lease restructurings. It has also advised a major financial institution in relation to the purchases of asset-rich leasing companies.

Lovells continues to receive notable instructions, particularly from finance providers in the aviation arena. It recently advised a German bank on a UK tax structured off-balance sheet financing of a state-owned carrier, and acted for a federal institution in relation to a Japanese operating lease of an Airbus A340 for another state-owned carrier. On the rail side, the firm gained experience advising borrowers in connection with loan financing for new rolling stock.

Kim Walkling, practice head at **Simmons & Simmons**, is renowned for his financing work for the MoD and continues to advise on its £13bn Future Strategic Tanker Aircraft programme. The firm has won new clients such as Mitsubishi and Gulf Air.

Watson, Farley & Williams LLP has particular experience acting on behalf of lessees, notably in the shipping and oil and gas sectors. It is also active in the aviation market and recently acted for a major international carrier in the sale of four 747s. The nine-partner team, led by Michael Vernell, has good multi-jurisdictional capability.

White & Case is both admitted to the ECA panel for Airbus financings, and has worked on $2bn-worth of aviation deals. Acting for a bank on the restructuring of a major airline was a highlight, as was advising KfW on the $37m EIB supported financing of two Embraer aircraft for Polish LOT Airlines. The two-partner practice is led by Justin Benson.

Addleshaw Goddard recently acted for Dart Group/Channel Express on the purchase and financing of five Boeing 737-300 aircraft. Aside from aviation it has been advising Singer & Friedlander Leasing in connection with incorporating an operating lease in a PFI Project.

Berwin Leighton Paisner LLP is particularly strong in the rail sector and recently advised Porterbrook Leasing Company on the leasing of 15 fleets of rolling stock to various UK rail franchises. It also has a good deal of PFI and project finance experience and has handled asset financings within this context and runs a consumer credit leasing and asset receivable financing.

Clyde & Co's aviation practice continues to develop under Gavin Hill. The firm advised on $750m-worth of aviation deals in 2004, including an ECA-supported financing of three A340s for a major European airline. The firm has merged with niche aviation firm *Beaumont and Son*.

DLA Piper Rudnick Gray Cary UK LLP had an active year in aviation finance and handled a number of big-ticket transactions, notably a sale and leaseback of nine A319s for South African Airways, and an acquisition and finance leasing of 26 new A340s for Virgin Atlantic.

Clive Barnard at **Herbert Smith LLP** has experience in asset finance, as well as PFI/PPP and project finance transactions, and is adept at delivering tax-efficient solutions to clients. The firm has advised Eurotunnel on a number of project finance and leasing projects.

Stephenson Harwood has a growing aircraft finance department and notably handled aircraft leases for Bank of Scotland and Kingfisher Airlines.

AVIATION: AIRLINES, AIRPORTS AND REGULATORY

A highly specialised area, aviation law demands commercial, international and EU and UK regulatory specialisms for airlines and airports. Expertise tends to lie with individual lawyers.

DLA Piper Rudnick Gray Cary UK LLP advises on a broad range of regulatory and competition matters for clients such as Globespan Group plc, Virgin Atlantic and Qatar Airways. Highlights include advising Virgin Atlantic Airways on the establishment of a new Nigerian carrier. Department head Mark Franklin receives able back-up from a team that includes rising star Elizabeth Hichens.

Headed by Nick Chandler, **Denton Wilde Sapte**'s aviation team advises on a broad range of regulatory, commercial and competition matters for clients such as Airbus, Qatar Airways and Turkish Airlines. Carolle Blackshaw has been instructed by a number of leading airlines in the revision of their conditions of carriage and carrier's regulations in light of EU and UK legislation.

Lane & Partners LLP advises clients across the aviation spectrum. The firm advised BMI British Midland on the landmark hearing and subsequent appeal before the Civil Aviation Authority on the allocation of scarce capacity on air routes between UK and India. Industry legend Richard Venables commands enormous respect for his regulatory knowledge.

Norton Rose's aviation team advised clients on the Single European Sky initiative and the ECJ's 'open skies' decisions. The firm acts for a diverse range of clients, including airlines (easyJet, SAS), airports (TBI), regulatory bodies (European Commission) and tour operators (TUI). Patrick Farrell and John Cook are highly regarded.

Wilmer Cutler Pickering Hale and Dorr LLP 'has a real understanding of the regulatory and aeropolitical environment in which the industry operates'. The team advised both United Airlines and Air France on high-value slot exchange transactions at Heathrow airport and represented Lufthansa in relation to its strategic investment in bmi British Midland. Michael Holter is highly regarded and heads a team that includes well-known partners Dieter Lange and Paul Von Hehn.

AVIATION: AIRLINES, AIRPORTS AND REGULATORY

DLA PIPER RUDNICK GRAY CARY UK LLP ⊙
DENTON WILDE SAPTE ⊙
LANE & PARTNERS LLP
NORTON ROSE ⊙
WILMER CUTLER PICKERING HALE AND DORR LLP ⊙

Addleshaw Goddard
Barlow Lyde & Gilbert
Beaumont & Son – Aviation at Clyde & Co
Field Fisher Waterhouse
Freshfields Bruckhaus Deringer
Harbottle & Lewis LLP
Linklaters ⊙

Simmons & Simmons ⊙
Slaughter and May ⊙
Wragge & Co LLP ⊙

Baker & McKenzie LLP ⊙
Clark Ricketts
Hogan & Hartson ⊙
Howard Kennedy
Ince & Co ⊙
LeBoeuf, Lamb, Greene & MacRae ⊙
Pinsent Masons ⊙
Thomas Cooper & Stibbard

Bird & Bird ⊙
Bryan Cave
Fladgate Fielder ⊙
Hammonds
Holman Fenwick & Willan ⊙
Latham & Watkins
Travers Smith

Firms are listed A-Z in tiers which are ranked in order of priority
⊙ *Indicates firm displays contact details at the end of this chapter.*

Headed by Rory MacCarthy, **Addleshaw Goddard** advises airlines, manufacturers, banks and leasing companies on a range of transactional, regulatory and contentious issues. Susannah Sheppard specialises in competition and regulatory matters.

Barlow Lyde & Gilbert offers diverse expertise that spans competition, regulatory and commercial advice. Recent highlights include providing safety-related regulatory advice to BAE Systems. Generating substantial regulatory work from its first-rate insurance practice, the firm was appointed to handle all regulatory matters on behalf of new clients, Air Hong Kong, Cathay Pacific Airways and Dragonair. Richard Gimblett, and Sue Barham are singled out for praise.

The merger with **Clyde & Co** that created **Beaumont & Son – Aviation at Clyde & Co** has given the firm a substantial presence in the market. John Balfour is highly recommended.

Field Fisher Waterhouse's aviation team offers an all-round service that encompasses general commercial advice, route licensing and other regulatory work. Simon Chamberlain is an expert in the aviation industry.

Freshfields Bruckhaus Deringer are recognised providers of heavyweight competition and regulatory advice. Highlights include advising several European airlines on their alliance arrangements with British Airways and successfully representing a fractional ownership operator in a competition investigation by the OFT. John Davies, Alan Ryan and Rex Rosales are highly regarded.

Harbottle & Lewis LLP's impressive team offers broad ranging advice to aviation clients on matters including start-up issues, engine leasing, and sale and leaseback agreements. Headed by Douglas Lochhead, the team also includes aviation experts, Dermot Scully and Colin Howes.

Headed by Ron Gibbs, **Linklaters**' cross-practice aviation group has the international reach, corporate clout and regulatory capacity to excel in the cross-financing of major assets. The firm continues to advise Air France on the regulatory matters arising out of the merger with KLM, and received new instructions from private equity fund Terra Firma in relation to its acquisition of debis Airfinance.

Headed by Kim Walkling, **Simmons & Simmons**' aviation team advised key client, the Ministry of Defence, on the regulatory aspects of the £13bn Future Strategic Tanker Aircraft Project. The department continues to thrive in the area of fractional ownership programmes. Christopher Boresjo is recommended.

Despite the absence of a stand-alone aviation team, **Slaughter and May**'s corporate, tax and competition teams offer a 'seamless service' to numerous aviation clients, including British Airways. Bertrand Louveaux, Malcolm Nicholson and Philippe Chappatte offer first-rate competition law advice.

Led by David Lowe, **Wragge & Co LLP**'s aviation team continues to provide commercial, IT, regulatory and contentious advice to key client, British Airways. The firm's cross-practice group advised new client, SITA, on the OnAir enterprise to allow passengers to use mobile phones and the internet on commercial flights.

Baker & McKenzie LLP is ideally placed to deal with multi-jurisdictional aviation projects. Headed by the experienced Mark Henrick, the firm advised a Tunisian airline on the acquisition and leasing of aircraft.

Jointly headed by name partners Ian Clark and Robert Ricketts, **Clark Ricketts**' niche practice offers 'a pragmatic, knowledgeable and sensibly priced' service. The firm also has a niche expertise in advising helicopter clients.

Hogan & Hartson offers commercial and regulatory expertise to a range of aviation clients, with a particular focus on serving executive airline operators and cargo airlines. Austen Hall has a substantial portfolio of aviation clients from both Switzerland and US.

At **Howard Kennedy**, Chris Gooding heads a team that understands the aviation industry both from a strategic and commercial perspective. Recent highlights include advising a Middle Eastern airline on its formation and the regulatory requirements for its operations.

At **Ince & Co**, Anthony Fitzsimmons heads an aviation team whose increasing caseload has included advising clients on international treaty negotiations regarding liability for terrorism in the air. Chris Walsh has greatly enhanced **Ince & Co**'s presence in the market, particularly in the Middle East.

LeBoeuf, Lamb, Greene & MacRae is in the enviable position of having strong practices in both London and New York. Mitri Najjar heads the aviation team and Peter Sharp is also highly recommended.

Pinsent Masons' projects-focused aviation team is increasingly instructed by governments to develop PPP-style contracts in relation to the procurement or development of airports. As well as advising the Cypriot government in the development of two airports, the firm represents London Luton airport on the letting of a 30-year concession. Andrew Dewsnap is recommended.

Thomas Cooper & Stibbard advises airlines and business jet owners and operators on EU, competition and regulatory matters. Alfred Merckx has a particular focus on the energy markets and Eastern Europe.

BANK LENDING

Allen & Overy LLP recently acted on more than 100 investment grade transactions, with standouts including acting for the lead arrangers on France Telecom's €10bn corporate facility. Key acquisition finance deals included the €2.1bn buy-out of VNU (advising Apax and Cinven) and the £896m bid for Chelsfield plc by Duelguide plc (advising Bank of Scotland and others on the senior and mezzanine debt financing). Mike Duncan, Trevor Borthwick, Stephen Gillespie, Tony Humphrey, Tony Keal, Stephen Kensell and George Link are recommended.

Clifford Chance has a comparable track record and market reputation. Recent syndicated work includes acting for Citibank and others on the $4.4bn loan facility financing the acquisition by Bacardi of the Grey Goose Vodka brand. On the acquisition finance side, the firm was instructed by the lenders on the acquisitions of the AA, Brenntag, Cemex and the New Look Group, while other highlights included advising RBS on the senior debt package for Findexa's issue of high yield dividend shares. The emerging markets and telecoms sectors remain significant areas of focus. Mark Campbell is the firm's global head of finance; James Johnson, Alan Inglis, Mark Stewart and Malcolm Sweeting are among the team's other core partners.

BANK LENDING

ALLEN & OVERY LLP ✪
CLIFFORD CHANCE

LINKLATERS ✪

ASHURST ✪
FRESHFIELDS BRUCKHAUS DERINGER
SHEARMAN & STERLING (LONDON) LLP

LOVELLS ✪
WHITE & CASE ✪

Herbert Smith LLP ✪
Latham & Watkins
Norton Rose ✪
Slaughter and May ✪

Baker & McKenzie LLP ✪
CMS Cameron McKenna LLP
DLA Piper Rudnick Gray Cary UK LLP ✪
Denton Wilde Sapte ✪
Macfarlanes ✪

Berwin Leighton Paisner LLP
SJ Berwin LLP ✪
Simmons & Simmons ✪
Taylor Wessing ✪
Travers Smith
Weil, Gotshal & Manges ✪

Cleary, Gottlieb, Steen & Hamilton LLP ✪
Jones Day ✪
Simpson Thacher & Bartlett LLP
Skadden, Arps, Slate, Meagher & Flom (UK) LLP

Addleshaw Goddard
Bird & Bird ✪
Cadwalader, Wickersham & Taft LLP ✪
Dechert LLP
Eversheds LLP
Field Fisher Waterhouse
Hammonds
LeBoeuf, Lamb, Greene & MacRae ✪
Mayer, Brown, Rowe & Maw LLP
McDermott Will & Emery UK LLP ✪
Middleton Potts
Nabarro Nathanson
Olswang
Osborne Clarke
Pinsent Masons ✪
Stephenson Harwood
Watson, Farley & Williams LLP
Winston & Strawn London ✪

Firms are listed A-Z in tiers which are ranked in order of priority
✪ Indicates firm displays contact details at the end of this chapter.

Linklaters' advised Goldman Sachs and Deutsche Bank on the financing of the proposed acquisition of the LSE by Deutsche Börse, and, on the leveraged side, acted for JP Morgan and others on the €1.8bn financing for the acquisition of VNU. Telecoms work included acting for a consortium of private equity funds on the leveraged €650m acquisition of Bulgaria's MobilTel. John Tucker, Robert Elliott, Benedict

James, Gideon Moore, Nick Syson and Giles White are recommended.

Ashurst acted for the lenders on two of the UK's highest-profile deals recently, namely Centrica's sale of the AA to CVC and Permira (on which it advised Barclays Capital on its provision of £1.35bn financing), and Charterhouse's successful £1.35bn bid for Saga (on which it advised Bank of Scotland and others). Nigel Ward heads the international finance group.

Freshfields Bruckhaus Deringer has an excellent reputation for corporate borrower work, with acquisition finance, restructuring and the telecoms sector core areas of focus. Edward Evans led the advice to Invensys on its £2.7bn recapitalisation, while other headline deals included the €1.75bn restructuring of German retail group KarstadtQuelle's bilateral facilities. Chris Howard, David Ereira, Sean Pierce, Brian Gray and Presley Warner have excellent reputations.

At **Shearman & Sterling (London) LLP** Anthony Ward led the advice to Morgan Stanley, JP Morgan and others on the €2.4bn financing of the acquisition of Rexel SA. Caroline Leeds Ruby, Clifford Atkins and Kenneth MacRitchie are recommended.

Lovells advised the lead debt arrangers on 30 acquisition finance deals recently with a total value of over £3.3bn. Other areas of strength include structured property finance, where key clients include Nomura and ING, and project finance and restructuring. Matthew Cottis heads the London finance practice, while David Hudd has taken over as head of international.

White & Case, under Maurice Allen and Mike Goetz, continues to run a fast-expanding and very successful practice. Deutsche Bank, Morgan Stanley and BNP Paribas are among its key clients, and recent headlines include acting for the lead arrangers on the £1.8bn refinancing of Telewest. Moscow Narodny and Standard Bank London are new client gains for mainstream lending work.

Herbert Smith LLP, under Jason Fox, acts for an even balance of banks and borrowers. Transaction highlights include acting for SocGen on a €215m funding package for Luxembourg-based mobile telecoms company MACH Sarl, while recent panel appointments include Citibank and Hypo. Clive Barnard has returned to full-time fee-earning, and Peter Long is also recommended, for his work in the property sector.

James Chesterman and Christopher Hall are the core partners in **Latham & Watkins**' London banking and leveraged finance practice. Recent headlines included acting for Apax Partners on the restructuring of financing arrangements to Damovo, and for Cablecom GmbH on its major bank/bond financing. The team is increasingly active on asset-backed lending work, recently acting for GE Commercial Finance and Bank of America among others.

Norton Rose's practice, under Jeffery Barratt, spans three core areas of general finance, project finance and asset finance, with longstanding relationships including RBS, HBOS and a number of European banks. The firm has remained active in the telecoms sector. Stephen Parish heads the UK banking group. Areas targeted for growth include Islamic finance.

Slaughter and May maintains its reputation for complex, high-quality transactions and comparatively generalist partners. On the borrower side, it recently advised Old Mutual and Post Office Limited on major loans, while arranger side work has included advising JP Morgan Europe on a €6.5bn facility for Telecom Italia. On acquisition finance, the firm advised Morgan Stanley on the recommended offer for Canary Wharf by Songbird. Andrew Balfour is head of the finance stream.

Baker & McKenzie LLP continues to major on pan-European acquisition financings, with partners Ian Jack and Bernard Sharp both very active. The firm recently acted for The Royal Bank of Scotland on the senior and mezzanine facilities for the €234m leveraged recapitalisation of the Tetra Group. Chris Hogan leads the team.

CMS Cameron McKenna LLP has a very well-regarded acquisition finance team, led by John Naccarato. Key clients include RBS, ABN Amro, and Lloyds TSB. The team includes Will Meredith and Douglas Colliver. Andrew Ivison specialises in project finance and heads the firm's transactional banking practice.

DLA Piper Rudnick Gray Cary UK LLP remains dominant in the sub-£100m deal bracket as well as continuing to gain ground on higher-value work, for HBOS, RBS and others. Philip Butler and John Cutler are both well known, as is Simon Woolley. Asset finance and real estate finance are other core areas for the firm.

Denton Wilde Sapte, under Ian Roberts, continues to handle a good volume of leveraged work, both mid-market and higher value; recent highlights include acting for ABN Amro on the financing of the £1.75bn facility offer for shares of Safeway by Wm Morrison.

Macfarlanes has been busy on a range of acquisition and mezzanine finance work, increasingly acting on the lender side. It handled a number of deals for RBS recently, while clients for mezzanine finance included GSC Partners Europe. Julian Howard heads the team, which includes Tom Speechley.

Berwin Leighton Paisner LLP is well known for the strength of its property finance practice, and runs a separate, banking and capital markets practice under Marc Palley. Recent work includes advising South Africa's Absa Bank (as borrower) on a $320m syndicated facility. Mark Daley and Jennifer Mackerras are recommended.

SJ Berwin LLP, under Gillian Smith, handles a variety of acquisition, property and trade finance work, and continues to develop the lender side of its practice. It acted for new client Landsbanki Íslands on facilities relating to the £326m takeover of Big Food, while longstanding clients include RBS, for which it handles a broad range of instructions.

Mark Norris now heads **Simmons & Simmons**' banking. Norris specialises in cross-border structured and acquisition finance, while other areas of focus for the team include property finance, and structured trade financings. Headlines included advising ABN Amro and others on the $300m acquisition financing of the De Dietrich Thermique Group.

Taylor Wessing is well established on the property finance side, and continues in its efforts to develop a European debt finance practice, with structured finance and projects core areas of focus. Clients include GMAC-RFC, which the firm has recently advised on numerous mortgage portfolio sales. Rodney Dukes heads the finance and projects group, which includes recent partner hires Akmal Ghauri, from **Osborne Clarke**, and Emma Menzies, from **DLA Piper Rudnick Gray Cary UK LLP**.

Under Neil Murray **Travers Smith** maintains a strong profile for property finance work as well as continuing to handle a variety of corporate banking, acquisition finance and other matters. It acted for Allied Irish and others on the £425m financing provided for the acquisition of The Savoy Group.

Weil, Gotshal & Manges is well known for its work for private equity clients such as Apax Partners and Hicks, Muse, Tate & Furst. Its core London finance partners are Chris Harrison and Richard Ginsburg, who is dual UK- and US-qualified.

Key individuals in **Cleary, Gottlieb, Steen & Hamilton LLP**'s banking and financial institutions practice include Andrew Shutter, who led the advice to Goldman Sachs on the £225m mezzanine financing for the bid for Canary Wharf. Glen Scarcliffe is also recommended.

Jones Day's finance group team includes partners Ed Nalbantian and Marc Isaacs, as well as Liz Saxton on the property and acquisition finance side. Citigroup, RBS and Standard Bank London are key clients.

Simpson Thacher & Bartlett LLP has two recently recruited UK-qualified partners handling acquisition and other leveraged finance work, namely Euan Gorrie and Stephen Short. Clients include The Blackstone Group and JP Morgan.

Mark Darley remains the sole partner in **Skadden, Arps, Slate, Meagher & Flom (UK) LLP**'s banking and leveraged finance group, which is heavily focused on higher margin work, predominantly acting for corporates. Clients included Doughty Hanson and Ashtead Group.

CONSTRUCTION: CONTENTIOUS

Pinsent Masons' construction team continues to brand itself as an 'industry adviser', an assertion reinforced by its representation of 18 out of the top 20 UK contractors. The firm's presence in several Asian outposts, means that a strong international arbitration practice co-exists

CONSTRUCTION: CONTENTIOUS

PINSENT MASONS ✪

BERWIN LEIGHTON PAISNER LLP
CMS CAMERON McKENNA LLP
CLIFFORD CHANCE
FENWICK ELLIOTT LLP
HERBERT SMITH LLP ✪
LOVELLS ✪
MAYER, BROWN, ROWE & MAW LLP
SHADBOLT & CO LLP

Ashurst ✪
Freshfields Bruckhaus Deringer
Hammonds
Kirkpatrick & Lockhart Nicholson Graham LLP
Linklaters ✪
Macfarlanes ✪
Nabarro Nathanson
Norton Rose ✪
Taylor Wessing ✪
Trowers & Hamlins ✪

Firms are listed A-Z in tiers which are ranked in order of priority
✪ Indicates firm displays contact details at the end of this chapter.

alongside heavyweight domestic capabilities. Andrew Hibbert and Mark Roe have taken over the UK and international groups respectively.

For **Berwin Leighton Paisner LLP** complex multi-party litigation is a particular forte, and the firm's appointment to London Underground's panel to advise on issues arising out of the PPP agreements for the upgrading and refurbishment of the tube network is a significant fillip. Julian Holloway leads a department that includes Terry de Souza, Caroline Pope and Bob Maynard.

CMS Cameron McKenna LLP's continued progress was marked by some terrific disputes work, such as advising Metronet, the PPP service provider for the majority of London Underground's tube lines, on a range of claims relating to the concession. Prudential, AMEC and Kier are also regular sources of work for a group which includes Henry Sherman and Caroline Cummins.

Clifford Chance's international credentials were reinforced by the arrival of Emerson Holmes and the representation of a Russian company in a dispute with an American entity concerning a major engineering project in Siberia. Domestically, Nicholas Fletcher and John Beechey are recommended.

Fenwick Elliott LLP recently acted for the Great Eastern Hotel in its successful, and much publicised, action against Laing as construction manager. Alongside a much-vaunted adjudication capability the practice reports an increase in international arbitration work. Simon Tolson and Anthony Francis are the key partners.

Herbert Smith LLP gains considerable leverage from cross-fertilisation with the firm's litigation, projects and international arbitration practices. Clients include developers, financiers, NHS trusts and government bodies spread across a broad range of industry sectors. Michael Davis heads the department.

Lovells has a strong relationship with a number of Japanese contractors, and recently acted for one on matters arising from the construction of a state-of-the-art pharmaceutical plant in Ireland. Phillip Capper heads a terrific outfit.

Mayer, Brown, Rowe & Maw LLP has recently been involved in an ICC arbitration in Jordan, and represented Halcrow Gilbert Associates in claims brought by the London Fire and Emergency Planning Authority arising out of the design and construction of a fire training centre. The group also undertakes the firm's professional indemnity construction work on behalf of insurers.

Shadbolt & Co LLP has recently handled a number of international arbitrations and high-profile multi-party TCC claims. It successfully defended Elga against Yorkshire Water, demonstrating that it can turn its hand to cases dealing with complex scientific and technical issues. Anthony Albertini leads the department.

Ashurst has developed a particular niche advising on PFI/PPP-related disputes, but also receives a healthy amount of plain vanilla instructions such as representing P&O on issues arising from the construction of new berthing facilities. Chris Vigrass leads the department.

Freshfields Bruckhaus Deringer operates a multidisciplinary cross-border practice that is able to advise on complex and high-value matters throughout Europe and beyond. Domestically, the firm has been particularly active on disputes over tendering procedures. Sally Roe heads the team.

Hammonds' is currently acting for a claimant in an arbitration relating to the construction and commissioning of an oil refinery and petrochemical plant in India, and counts numerous local authorities as clients.

Kevin Greene leads the team at **Kirkpatrick & Lockhart Nicholson Graham LLP** which over the past year has been busy acting for Costain and Skanska in disputes arising out of the refurbishment of the Great Western Royal Hotel, and for Haden Young in a TCC matter against Bovis Lend Lease in relation to mechanical works at the BBC White City project.

Linklaters acts for Petrobras in the ongoing Commercial Court actions concerning the construction of the world's largest oil production platform.

Macfarlanes continues to be involved in substantial matters for key clients, such as advising Sir Robert McAlpine in relation to the Emcor Drake and Scull Dudley Hospitals dispute. International and significant private client matters provide a steady stream of instructions for Patrick Holmes 'team.

Nabarro Nathanson's work for developers and property owners reflects the traditional strength of its real estate practice, though the firm's construction group attracts a significant amount of standalone instructions.

At **Norton Rose**, Christopher Hill is the key contact in a team where all litigators are trained for higher rights of audience, and international arbitration is a particular focus.

With three accredited mediators and the regular appointment of Peter Shaw as an international conciliator, **Taylor Wessing** is well placed to handle domestic and overseas mediation. The firm continues to advise Ballast following the withdrawal of financial support by its parent company.

Trowers & Hamlins contentious practice is part of the firm's projects and construction department, undertaking private sector as well as a significant amount of public sector work.

CONSTRUCTION: NON-CONTENTIOUS

Berwin Leighton Paisner LLP enters the top tier on the back of its work for developers on high-profile projects, such as the 'Shard of Glass' for Sellar Property. The firm also remains the sole provider of construction legal services to Tesco, and, on the finance side, assisted Royal Bank of Scotland on the funding of the next phases of the More London development. John Hughes-D'Aeth is recommended.

Clifford Chance advises on the largest and most complex UK and international construction projects. Working closely with the firm's highly rated project finance, real estate and PFI/PPP

CONSTRUCTION: NON-CONTENTIOUS

BERWIN LEIGHTON PAISNER LLP
CLIFFORD CHANCE
LINKLATERS ✪

CMS CAMERON McKENNA LLP
FRESHFIELDS BRUCKHAUS DERINGER
HERBERT SMITH LLP ✪
LOVELLS ✪
PINSENT MASONS ✪

Ashurst ✪
Denton Wilde Sapte ✪
Fenwick Elliott LLP
Hammonds
Kirkpatrick & Lockhart Nicholson Graham LLP
Macfarlanes ✪
Mayer, Brown, Rowe & Maw LLP
Nabarro Nathanson
Norton Rose ✪
Shadbolt & Co LLP
Taylor Wessing ✪
Trowers & Hamlins ✪

Firms are listed A-Z in tiers which are ranked in order of priority
✪ Indicates firm displays contact details at the end of this chapter.

groups, recent highlights include acting for the funders on the redevelopment of Ascot Racecourse, advising the Guardian Media Group on the construction of its new headquarters, and assisting Multiplex on the White City development. Tim Steadman leads the team.

Ann Minogue heads a formidable practice at **Linklaters** which is consistently involved in landmark projects. The firm recently provided preliminary advice to Chelsfield and Stanhope regarding the £3bn Stratford City regeneration project, acted for Stanhope in the refurbishment of Unilever House, and is engaged by the Royal Festival Hall on its refurbishment including the construction of an extension.

Marc Hanson leads a team at **CMS Cameron McKenna LLP** that receives a high volume of domestic development mandates as well as spin-off work from the firm's PFI/PPP and project finance practices. The group advises White City General Partner Limited on its £1.4bn redevelopment of White City.

Freshfields Bruckhaus Deringer is heavily involved in project finance and PFI/PPP work, and is currently advising the iNavSat consortium, on construction and procurement issues. The firm continues to be active on major office development projects.

Nicholas Downing is the key contact at **Herbert Smith LLP**. The firm recently secured the London Development Agency as a client, which received advice on the construction of bridges at Wembley Stadium. Acting for Minerva on the construction aspects of Minerva Tower is another noteworthy instruction.

Lovells is a key player in domestic and international projects, and recent highlights include advising Mercury Health on the largest independent sector treatment centre scheme to reach financial close, and a major UK utility in relation to the world's largest automated material handling centre. Gillian Thomas is recommended.

Though contentious work was very much the force behind *Masons'* construction reputation, **Pinsent Masons** continues to operate an integrated practice. Domestically, the PFI/PPP sector supplies a healthy amount of front-end instructions, and further afield acted for the Dangote Group in the procurement of a cement factory, power plant and gas pipeline in Nigeria.

Ashurst is involved in a broad range of activities from PFI projects to retail developments, and has been appointed by Sheffield University to provide all procurement and construction advice for its residential accommodation programme.

Denton Wilde Sapte's practice is split between London, where infrastructure, transport and energy project work is the focus, and Milton Keynes, where UK real estate and retail instructions are to the fore.

At **Fenwick Elliott LLP** the education sector is a particular focus, with University College London, the LSE and the Open University regularly instructing the firm. Julian Critchlow and Victoria Russell are recommended.

Rupert Cowen heads **Hammonds**' department, which has been appointed by English Partnerships to its panels for regeneration work in the South East and Thames Gateway regions.

Kirkpatrick & Lockhart Nicholson Graham LLP is likely to benefit from a strong US construction practice with links to Halliburton and Kellogg Brown & Root.

Patrick Holmes leads **Macfarlanes**' non-contentious team, which is advising London Bridge Development on the high-profile More London scheme.

John Rushton at **Mayer, Brown, Rowe & Maw LLP** advised St Mowden Developments on the redevelopment of Edmonton Shopping Centre.

Nabarro Nathanson's construction capability has considerable range, embracing office, retail, urban regeneration and infrastructure work. Terry Fleet leads a department which is currently acting for a funding consortium on all construction aspects of Liverpool's Paradise Street development.

Christopher Hill at **Norton Rose** is currently advising Kerzner International in relation to the redevelopment of the Millennium Dome and Sport City Manchester. The firm has a good mix of developers, funders and project companies as clients.

Shadbolt & Co LLP's non-contentious group can call upon the skills of 15 lawyers including recent arrivals Robert Meakin and Cecily Davis.

Taylor Wessing continues to impress with quality instructions in projects, finance and development related work. The firm is currently advising Academy Land on the proposed redevelopment of Blackpool retail centre. Helen Garthwaite is recommended.

Towers & Hamlins has added new developer and corporate clients such as the Berkeley Group and De Vere Hotels to an enviable local government and housing association base. The firm was recently appointed to advise the London Borough of Ealing on the regeneration of South Acton Estate. David Mosey is highly recommended.

CONSTRUCTION: OTHER RECOMMENDED FIRMS

The core of **Allen & Overy LLP**'s construction capability is located within its projects group, which over the past year has been highly active in the Middle East. Lending instructions constitute a large slice of the domestic practice, and Nomura Properties recently engaged the firm.

Baker & McKenzie LLP's projects team undertakes a significant amount of Middle Eastern construction work. On the contentious side, Jeremy Winter is something of an authority on delay claims.

Campbell Hooper currently acts for Taylor Woodrow in a TCC dispute concerning a major shopping centre. A creditable front-end capability undertakes good quality domestic and international work Annette Fritze-Shanks is recommended.

At **Davies Arnold Cooper** the majority of partners handle contentious instructions, such as acting for Midland Expressway in connection with disputes arising out of the construction, maintenance and operation of the M6 toll road.

CONSTRUCTION: OTHER RECOMMENDED FIRMS

Allen & Overy LLP ✪
Baker & McKenzie LLP ✪
Campbell Hooper
Davies Arnold Cooper
Glovers
Lawrence Graham LLP
Lewis Silkin ✪
Reynolds Porter Chamberlain
Simmons & Simmons ✪
Speechly Bircham
White & Case ✪
Wragge & Co LLP ✪

Addleshaw Goddard
Beachcroft Wansbroughs
Berrymans Lace Mawer
Boodle Hatfield
Clyde & Co ✪
DLA Piper Rudnick Gray Cary UK LLP ✪
Eversheds LLP
Field Fisher Waterhouse
Howard Kennedy
Kendall Freeman
Kennedys
Manches LLP
Richards Butler
Stephenson Harwood
Travers Smith
Winward Fearon

Barlow Lyde & Gilbert
Beale and Company Solicitors LLP
Bircham Dyson Bell
Corbett & Co
Dechert LLP
Dundas & Wilson LLP
Finers Stephens Innocent LLP
Fladgate Fielder ✪
Forsters LLP
Kingsley Napley
Lane & Partners LLP
Maples Teesdale
McGrigors London
Olswang
Reed Smith ✪
SJ Berwin LLP ✪
Slaughter and May ✪
Wedlake Bell

Firms are listed A-Z in tiers which are ranked in order of priority
✪ Indicates firm displays contact details at the end of this chapter.

The firm's experience also covers international arbitration. David Weare leads the department.

Glovers typically advises on multi-party actions involving claims for defects, extensions of time for payment and the performance of construction professionals, and specialises in disputes between residential occupiers and builders.

Lawrence Graham LLP recently advised Sainsbury's on the development and construction of retail units and car parking at London Colney. Town centre regeneration is a particular specialism on the non-contentious side, whereas the Far East is a regular source of contentious instructions.

Lewis Silkin has recently completed a number of regeneration schemes for Wandle Housing Association. The firm also advises several sponsors of the government's academies programme. Involvement in a project relating to a 1,500 year-old monastery in Sinai, together with niche focuses on advertising and IT clients, indicate the range of skills the firm offers.

At **Reynolds Porter Chamberlain** the arrival of Michael Blackburne and Ron Nobbs has significantly strengthened the firm's pure construction capacity. Carillion and the Veolia Group are key clients.

Simmons & Simmons acted for Earls Terrace in relation to its claims against an architect arising out of a development in Kensington, where the TCC decided a number of preliminary issues that set important precedents regarding the law on damages and interest.

Speechly Bircham over the past year has represented the likes of Sainsbury's, Jacobs Engineering and P&O on disputes, the latter also instructing the firm in relation to the redevelopment of Drake Circus in Plymouth.

White & Case's Ellis Baker is involved in some of the biggest infrastructure projects in the Middle East, including Qatargas II. The firm's international punch leads to large arbitration instructions, with Latin America a notable centre of activity.

Acting for the joint venture developers on the £100m redevelopment of Coventry city centre is illustrative of **Wragge & Co LLP**'s regeneration expertise, and the firm also has strong links with house builders such as Cala Homes and Taylor Woodrow. Adjudications are the staple on the contentious side, though the practice is no stranger to big-ticket litigation.

CORPORATE TAX

Freshfields Bruckhaus Deringer's complex cross-border finance work is a forte, thanks to the firm's well-integrated international tax offering. Sue Porter; David Taylor; Roger Berner; Murray Clayson; Richard Ballard; and Colin Hargreaves are all recommended. Contentious work includes advising on the 3G mobile phone licence litigation.

Linklaters continues to warrant its top-tier position. Tax structured finance, corporate matters and capital markets are all areas of strength. The contentious practice is busy, with tax head Guy Brannan advising a group of phone companies on 3G VAT litigation before the ECJ. Charles Hellier, Mike Hardwick, Andrew Beverley and Yash Rupal are recommended.

Slaughter and May has a superlative reputation for tax. The team's depth of expertise and breadth of experience is virtually unrivalled in M&A and restructuring. Group head Steve Edge is arguably London's pre-eminent tax lawyer. Tony Beare, Graham Air and Sara Luder also win praise.

Allen & Overy LLP is best known for its tax structured finance expertise, though it has strengths across the board including international capital markets and restructuring work. Patrick Mears, Brenda Coleman, David Lewis, Miles Walton, Mark Brailsford and David Hughes are all highly recommended.

Clifford Chance advised on the tax-intensive £8.9bn Banco Santander bid for Abbey National. The team's capabilities in tax-critical real estate, securitisation, structured finance and private equity remain first class. Douglas French heads the firm's 220-strong global practice. David Harkness, Stephen Shea, Sarah Squires, Richard McIlwee and Michael Wistow are all excellent.

John Watson heads **Ashurst**'s team supported by one of the finest crops of tax associates in London. Private equity and funds are the firm's speciality, though it covers the full range of work. Nicholas Gardner recently advised Blackstone Group International on a £162m acquisition, and Patricia Allen continues to impress.

Baker & McKenzie LLP attracts an impressive number of multinational clients including BP and Sony Corporation of America. The team is particularly rated for cross-border group restructuring and tax planning. James MacLachlan, Geoffrey Kay and John Fairley all warrant mention.

CMS Cameron McKenna LLP's wide-ranging practice consolidated its market standing over the last year, in particular developing its work in the private equity and hotels sectors and growing its profile in central Europe. Mark Nichols and Richard Croker are recommended for SDLT structuring, while Keith Gregory and Simon Meredith specialise in structured finance.

Recent highlights for **Herbert Smith LLP** include advising Roger de Haan on the £1.35bn sale of Saga; and Hollinger International Group on *The Telegraph* sale. Heather Gething, Neil Warriner, Ross Fraser and Isaac Zailer are all excellent, while Derek Hill is up-and-coming.

Lovells enjoys an exceptionally strong reputation for tax in London, and benefits from a global network of tax practitioners. Highlighting two particular areas of strength for the team, Karen Hughes recently advised Tube Lines on its

CORPORATE TAX

FRESHFIELDS BRUCKHAUS DERINGER
LINKLATERS ✪
SLAUGHTER AND MAY ✪

ALLEN & OVERY LLP ✪
CLIFFORD CHANCE

ASHURST ✪
BAKER & McKENZIE LLP ✪
CMS CAMERON MCKENNA LLP
HERBERT SMITH LLP ✪
LOVELLS ✪
MACFARLANES ✪
NORTON ROSE ✪
SIMMONS & SIMMONS ✪
TRAVERS SMITH

ADDLESHAW GODDARD
BERWIN LEIGHTON PAISNER LLP
FIELD FISHER WATERHOUSE
McDERMOTT WILL & EMERY UK LLP ✪
NABARRO NATHANSON
OLSWANG
SJ BERWIN LLP ✪
SIDLEY AUSTIN
WEIL, GOTSHAL & MANGES ✪

Cleary, Gottlieb, Steen & Hamilton LLP ✪
DLA Piper Rudnick Gray Cary UK LLP ✪
Dechert LLP
Denton Wilde Sapte ✪
Dorsey & Whitney ✪
Eversheds LLP
Fried, Frank, Harris, Shriver & Jacobson (London) LLP
Hogan & Hartson ✪
Jones Day ✪
Kirkpatrick & Lockhart Nicholson Graham LLP
Mayer, Brown, Rowe & Maw LLP
Milbank, Tweed, Hadley & McCloy LLP ✪
Shearman & Sterling (London) LLP
Skadden, Arps, Slate, Meagher & Flom (UK) LLP
Taylor Wessing ✪
Watson, Farley & Williams LLP
White & Case ✪

Barlow Lyde & Gilbert
Beachcroft Wansbroughs
Bird & Bird ✪
Bristows
Charles Russell
Clyde & Co ✪
Debevoise & Plimpton LLP ✪
Dewey Ballantine ✪
Hammonds
Lawrence Graham LLP
Manches LLP
McGrigors London
Osborne Clarke
Pinsent Masons ✪
Richards Butler
Speechly Bircham
Stephenson Harwood
Wilmer Cutler Pickering Hale and Dorr LLP ✪

Firms are listed A-Z in tiers which are ranked in order of priority
✪ Indicates firm displays contact details at the end of this chapter.

£2.1bn refinancing, while Kevin Ashman acted for Slough Estates on is £700m property swap with Land Securities. Another highlight was advising the Barclay brothers on their purchase of *The Daily Telegraph*.

Macfarlanes is a firm to watch. Mark Baldwin is increasingly well regarded, and Elizabeth Sherwood wins numerous plaudits. Core areas are tax structuring of all types and corporate transactional advice, though property and private equity also feature. Despite being a single-office firm, work often has an international element.

Norton Rose enjoys solid reputation, particularly for leasing and asset finance work. Louise Higginbottom heads the team and Dominic Stuttaford shows increasing market presence. Clients include major corporates and banks.

Simmons & Simmons' tax team is part of a growing international network and commands respect. M&A tax structuring and private equity are growing areas. The team recently advised CSFB on a $300m structured finance transaction. Nick Cronkshaw is the team's M&A guru, while Paul Hale concentrates on funds and indirect tax matters.

Travers Smith had a busy year advising on a high volume of corporate finance and private equity deals. Top-tier firms acknowledge the firm's wide-ranging capabilities. Alasdair Douglas is extremely experienced and respected, as is Richard Stratton.

Addleshaw Goddard predominantly advises on banking, corporate and property matters, though it also boasts media tax expertise. A recent highlight was advising Bayerische Landesbank on a £373m refinancing of 78 Marks & Spencer stores. The firm also regularly provides London-based US law firms with tax advice. Ed Jenkins and Peter Sayer are highly regarded.

Moving up the table is the expanding department at **Berwin Leighton Paisner LLP** which has worked hard to increase its breadth. Property and urban regeneration work remain key areas and key client is Tesco. Practice head John Overs is a sound generalist, Cathryn Vanderspar and Gary Richards are both recommended.

Field Fisher Waterhouse's high-calibre team has an enviable client list and genuine strengths in four key areas. Tax head Nicholas Noble has finance expertise; Graeme Nuttall specialises in M&A and restructuring; Nick Beecham is the resident indirect tax expert; and Michael Stirling handles transfer pricing.

McDermott Will & Emery UK LLP is primarily known for its eminent transfer pricing expertise, forming part of its sophisticated cross-border transactional practice. Though a number of the team's blue-chip clients are referrals from the US, a large proportion are 'home grown' including Eli Lilly, Heinz and Shell. US partner David Ryder recently joined the team headed by Peter Nias.

Nabarro Nathanson's stock has risen in the last year on the back of a growing reputation for the quality of its advice. Property is the department's strongest suit, with practice head Michael Cant singled out. A recent highlight was advising Land Securities on the tax structuring of a series of acquisitions.

Kay Butler is head of tax at **Olswang**, whose clients are drawn from a broad range of sectors. Recent work includes advising on the establishment of funds, admissions to AIM and cross-border financing. Graham Chase is recommended.

SJ Berwin LLP's 'flexible' team, headed by Heather Corben, has had a successful year. Pat Dugdale, John Skoulding, Dominic Adams and Michael Trask are all recommended.

Sidley Austin is experienced in finance and securitisation, restructuring and insolvency, and capital markets work. Tax litigation is also undertaken. Clients include Federal Mogul, HBOS, JP Morgan and Fitch Ratings. Drew Scott heads the practice.

The high calibre of work at **Weil, Gotshal & Manges** pushes it up a tier. Recent highlights include the highly complex take-private of Warner Chilcott and the pan-European sale of Six Flags European division. Partners Sarah Priestley and John Baldry are both highly regarded. Andrew Norwood leads a team of dedicated securitisation tax specialists.

DISPUTE RESOLUTION

Herbert Smith LLP commitment to high-profile, high-value commercial litigation remains unbeaten. The firm's quite astonishing client base continues to grow, with recent additions including Zurich Financial Services, Petrobras Limited, AXA General Insurance Hong Kong and Arriva plc. Work highlights include advising BSkyB, Cambridge Antibody Technology Limited, TXU, Rabobank and Equitable Life. It has strengthened its relationships with investment banks, developing in particular its regulatory and compliance capability. Sonya Leydecker is now head of dispute resolution.

Allen & Overy LLP's cross-border practice continues to blossom. The firm continues to act for an investment bank on the fall-out of Parmalat, and represented the United Arab Emirates in defending claims for damages in excess of $600m. There are specialist litigation teams with expertise in particular industry sectors, such as real estate, contentious regulatory and energy in addition to the firm's well-known core areas of expertise, namely, banking and finance, IP and employment law. Peter Watson manages the group.

Clifford Chance's commercial disputes specialists place great emphasis on their ability to avoid disputes and resolve issues should they arise, with minimal disruption to the client, and not necessarily by means of litigation firepower. Highlights include working on the split capital investment trusts investigation, the British Energy litigation and the Sumitomo trial. Jeremy Sandelson leads the team in London.

Jo Rickard leads the dispute resolution group at **Freshfields Bruckhaus Deringer**. The group holds itself out to be a first port of call for clients whose cases are critical, and prides itself on its quality of service. It has a strong international network, which is particularly impressive in Europe. As well as acting for the Bank of England in the long-running BCCI trial, the firm has also advised Marsh UK on allegations made in New York by Eliot Spitzer; Apple Computer against the Beatles' record label; and Legal & General in the first FSMA tribunal.

Lovells is regularly involved in major disputes and is led by Patrick Sherrington. Of particular note,

DISPUTE RESOLUTION

HERBERT SMITH LLP ✪

ALLEN & OVERY LLP ✪
CLIFFORD CHANCE
FRESHFIELDS BRUCKHAUS DERINGER
LOVELLS ✪

LINKLATERS ✪
SLAUGHTER AND MAY ✪

ASHURST ✪
NORTON ROSE ✪
RICHARDS BUTLER
SIMMONS & SIMMONS ✪

BAKER & McKENZIE LLP ✪
BARLOW LYDE & GILBERT
CMS CAMERON McKENNA LLP
CLYDE & CO ✪
SJ BERWIN LLP ✪

Berwin Leighton Paisner LLP
Eversheds LLP
Holman Fenwick & Willan ✪
Ince & Co ✪
Kirkpatrick & Lockhart Nicholson Graham LLP
Mayer, Brown, Rowe & Maw LLP
Stephenson Harwood
Watson, Farley & Williams LLP

Addleshaw Goddard
Cadwalader, Wickersham & Taft LLP ✪
Charles Russell
DLA Piper Rudnick Gray Cary UK LLP ✪
Denton Wilde Sapte ✪
Jones Day ✪
Kendall Freeman
Olswang
Reynolds Porter Chamberlain
Taylor Wessing ✪
Travers Smith
Weil, Gotshal & Manges ✪
White & Case ✪

Continued

the firm acted in privilege matters that included the ongoing Three Rivers and Philip Morris tobacco cases. It also worked on the largest recall of a prescription drug in history with its continued representation of Merck & Co, and dealt with a highly complex section 75 consumer credit dispute.

Linklaters represented Ernst & Young in the £350m Western Star litigation. The firm's litigators also defended a claim challenging the privatisation of a Russian oil company, and were involved in a multi-billion-pound telecoms dispute. John Turnbull's group has also been increasingly acting on complex regulatory investigations.

Slaughter and May move up a tier this year. The quality of the work the firm has undertaken, and the feedback from its clients is truly impressive. Elizabeth Barrett leads the dispute resolution team. The group represented Mahonia Ltd and JP Morgan Chase Bank in a $165m letter of credit dispute against West LB, and were instructed by BAT in relation to a dispute with Philip Morris, and MyTravel on its proposed £800m restructuring plan.

At **Ashurst**, Edward Sparrow leads a strong litigation group, with a growing commercial practice across Europe. Each partner has expertise in specialist fields such as product liability, energy, investment banking and property litigation. New clients include Equitable Life and RHM whilst the firm secured settlements in the Barings and Sumitomo cases.

Norton Rose is the only City law firm accredited by the Law Society to run its own higher rights advocacy training. Sector expertise is in fraud, financial services, banking and insurance, with specialist experience in areas such as competition litigation and professional negligence. Val Davies is singled out for praise.

Charles Hewetson and Belinda Paisley co-head the commercial disputes group at **Richards Butler**. The group specialises in multi-jurisdictional matters, with clients that include Barclays Bank, BBC Worldwide Limited, Direct Line, Expedia, SmithKline Beecham and Xerox.

Simmons & Simmons is currently handling six disputes worth over £100m. The dispute group, which is led by Colin Passmore, has expertise in the finance, energy, transport and pharmaceuticals sectors. A broad range of work is covered, including pensions, professional liability and IT disputes.

Baker & McKenzie LLP prides itself on its international expertise and cross-border capability. In particular, the London dispute group, led by Andrew Keltie has focused on competition litigation recently, with the establishment of a specialist unit. Recent highlights include continued representation of Gruppo Torras and acting for Roy Ranson in relation to the proceedings brought by Equitable Life. Disclosable clients include O2, Federal Express, Siemens and Sony. Nick Pearson is head of the firm's global dispute resolution group.

DISPUTE RESOLUTION
Continued

Hammonds
Lawrence Graham LLP
Lewis Silkin ✪
Macfarlanes ✪
Manches LLP
McDermott Will & Emery UK LLP ✪
Nabarro Nathanson
Pinsent Masons ✪
Speechly Bircham

Bird & Bird ✪
Byrne and Partners
Covington & Burling ✪
Davies Arnold Cooper
Dechert LLP
Field Fisher Waterhouse
Finers Stephens Innocent LLP
Harbottle & Lewis LLP
Howard Kennedy
Irwin Mitchell
LeBoeuf, Lamb, Greene & MacRae ✪
Mishcon de Reya
Morgan Lewis ✪
Osborne Clarke
Payne Hicks Beach
Withers LLP
Wragge & Co LLP ✪

Firms are listed A-Z in tiers which are ranked in order of priority
✪ *Indicates firm displays contact details at the end of this chapter.*

Clare Canning heads up the commercial litigation practice at **Barlow Lyde & Gilbert** which now includes an accountancy team. She continues to represent Ernst & Young in the high-profile £2.6bn claim brought by Equitable Life. Other clients include Shell, Winterthur Life UK, Mohamed Al Fayed, and Deutsche Bank.

CMS Cameron McKenna LLP's group leader is Tim Hardy. The firm's international network provides the group with complex cross-border work, particularly from eastern and central Europe.

Clyde & Co fields over 60 commercial litigation partners. Last year the group was formally appointed to both the Legal & General and BP panels and two of the General Electric legal panels. The firm recently contributed to the resolution of the $100m Aon 77 Energy Cover case. Other clients include AXA, Chevron Texaco, Nokia, Royal & SunAlliance, Hewlett Packard and the Turkish Government.

Fourteen partners, led by Craig Pollack make up the commercial litigation department at **SJ Berwin LLP**.

Up a tier this year, **Berwin Leighton Paisner LLP** has secured a plethora of new clients. They include Investec Asset Management Limited, Moto Hospitality Ltd and Compass Group Plc. The group, headed by David Parkin, has recently represented West LB, Homebase, Hollinger International and Messinger Insurance PCC Limited.

Eversheds LLP benefits from a network of regional offices. Recently it advised Apple Corps Ltd in the high-profile dispute over iTunes, and Spectris Plc over an international supply agreement.

Up a tier this year, **Holman Fenwick & Willan** has been dealing with increasingly high-value claims across its four core practice areas of commercial, trade and energy, insurance and re-insurance and shipping and transport. Recently the firm was involved in 24 contested hearings, of which 11 were reported. The firm appeared on nine occasions before the Court of Appeal.

Also up a tier this year, **Ince & Co**'s sector expertise remains in shipping and trade, insurance and reinsurance, professional indemnity, energy and aviation. Recent highlights have included work on the Equitable Life litigation, Arrows F1, an aerospace financial reinsurance claim, and involvement in the high-profile split capital trust claims. Senior partner Peter Rogan and Steven Fox are recommended.

Kirkpatrick & Lockhart Nicholson Graham LLP acted for Mercer Human Resource Consulting and the trustees of Wasps rugby club. John Magnin leads a team that is recommended for 'its dedication and courage in really difficult litigation'.

At **Mayer, Brown, Rowe & Maw LLP** David Allen and Sean Connolly head up the team that recently secured a number of new clients including GE, Reuters, HBOS, and BDO Stoy Hayward.

John Fordham heads up the commercial litigation group at **Stephenson Harwood**, and has dealt with the extremely high-profile Dame Shirley Porter case. The firm has predominantly retail banking expertise, but is gaining a reputation amongst both multinationals and large UK corporations. Major clients include Cadbury Schweppes, Christie's International plc, London Underground Limited and the Royal College of Art.

Maritime and banking specialist **Watson, Farley & Williams LLP** has worked for Calyon, Nordea, Teekay and Maersk. The commercial litigation group also has an increasing reputation for construction and offshore oil and gas disputes. David Kavanagh 's group regularly deals with complex, multi-million-dollar disputes.

Addleshaw Goddard has a mixed client base that includes media and technology clients and financial institutions and manufacturing companies. Notwithstanding the firm's lack of overseas offices, the disputes practice is international. Existing clients of the group, led by Simon Twigden, include GSK, Diageo plc, Associated British Foods and Smiths Industries plc..

At **Cadwalader, Wickersham & Taft LLP**, Michelle Duncan heads the small but extremely effective commercial litigation group. Work that deserves special mention includes representing

British Energy in its restructuring, acting for TXU's administration team.

Charles Russell's commercial litigation department continues to go from strength to strength. Recently the firm successfully resolved a major public service IT dispute and worked on a multi-million-pound telecom traffic dispute.

Iannis Alexopoulos continues to head the London commercial litigation group of **DLA Piper Rudnick Gray Cary UK LLP**, with Julian Stait leading the global group out of London. The group acted on a £320m IT dispute, represented Bottin (International) Investments Limited and Vee Networks Limited. Panel memberships include Barclays Bank plc, Merrill Lynch and MCI.

Denton Wilde Sapte acted on reported cases which ranged in subject matter from insolvency and banking to pensions, tax and directors' duties. Of note, the firm specialises in insurance and insolvency-related litigation, but has seen an increase in both banking and regulatory disputes.

At **Jones Day**'s London office, Craig Shuttleworth leads the group, whose clients include Motorola, Dell, Intercontinental Hotels Corp and Occidental Petroleum. The office is now an integral part of one of the world's largest litigation firms. Recent highlighted work includes acting for TUI Northern Europe Limited, and the Waste Recycling Group plc.

Clients are impressed with **Kendall Freeman**'s commercial litigators, particularly because they make a real effort to understand clients' business, economic model and strategy: Practice head Kevin Perry is particularly highly rated.

David Stewart leads the commercial litigation department at **Olswang**. Recent work includes acting for a defendant in a claim for fraudulent misrepresentation arising out of AWG's acquisition of Morrison Plc.

Reynolds Porter Chamberlain moves up a tier this year. Recently the firm's insurance and non-insurance litigation partners have acted on a raft of high-profile matters, including football club insolvencies, the World Trade Center and Enron. An area of increasing expertise is both indirect and direct tax litigation. Stephen Mayer is head of this practice area.

Although renowned for its expertise in the TMT sector, **Taylor Wessing**'s commercial litigators also deal with trusts and estates, fraud and insolvency disputes. The firm provides 'in-depth, reliable and timely service with results to match'.

John Kingston heads up the commercial litigation group at **Travers Smith**. The firm deals with all kinds of commercial work, with an emphasis on cross-border disputes. Recently the firm's practice has expanded to include areas such as banking, professional negligence and pensions litigation.

Weil, Gotshal & Manges uses a trial lawyer approach to litigation, holding itself out as a pioneering one-stop-shop for the firm's clientele. Michael Jones heads up the group. The firm majors in high-stakes, high-profile international dispute resolution and crisis management.

White & Case has recently advised a group of banks in a high-profile bid to obtain control of the Formula One business.

EU AND COMPETITION

Freshfields Bruckhaus Deringer's London team is almost double the size of any rival. It has the resources across Europe and well-reputed partners to match its stellar reputation. Though the firm's strong corporate client base is an obvious boon, the competition team has time and again won and retained clients on its own merit. Deirdre Trapp's reputation continues to rocket upwards. John Davis' six-year mandate to advise PepsiCo on highlighting alleged abuses of a dominant position by Coca-Cola should be noted.

Herbert Smith LLP continues to improve its business with new clients such as Yell, Provident Financial, Rio Tinto and BHP Billiton. The firm worked on 30 significant mergers including Securicor's £3.8bn merger with Group 4 Falck to form Group 4 Securicor, encompassing major competition issues. The firm has a broadly based practice and is well regarded in the utilities arena, in particular Dorothy Livingston in the rail sector and James Quinney for water.

Linklaters boasts muscle in merger control, behavioural and contentious issues, and has one of the foremost regulatory practices in Europe. Senior figure Bill Allan is one of London's top five competition law practitioners. When it comes to utilities, Michael Cutting has a wealth of experience. Gavin Robert has impressive merger control and behavioural experience, having spent a significant spell in Brussels. Diana Good is a litigator with experience of key competition cases and a familiarity with Brussels. The team advised Microsoft on the EC merger clearance required for its joint acquisition with Time Warner of ContentGuard.

Slaughter and May marked yet another good year with a raft of high-quality mandates. Though its merger control work remains a key part of the business, the team tends to gain instructions for the most challenging behavioural and contentious issues. With the City's most celebrated competition lawyer at the helm Malcolm Nicholson, an assertive figure with a strong handle on economic fundamentals, and strong support from Philippe Chappatte and Bertrand Louveaux, **Slaughter and May** arguably has the strongest practice in the UK for its size.

SJ Berwin LLP remains the surprise inclusion in the upper echelons of the competition rankings, relying less on instructions emanating out of large corporate practices, but on its long track record in antitrust thanks to the presence of pre-eminent names such as Stephen Kon. Simon Holmes, Elaine Gibson-Bolton and Ralph Cohen have a tight grip on the nuances of competition and regulatory law, but deliver advice in a pleasant and pragmatic manner. Complex litigation, challenging behavioural instructions and an increasingly prestigious register of clients, such as newer names 02 and Expedia, outlines its leading credentials.

Allen & Overy LLP retains exceptional credibility due to the presence of strong partners

EU AND COMPETITION

FRESHFIELDS BRUCKHAUS DERINGER
HERBERT SMITH LLP ✪
LINKLATERS ✪
SLAUGHTER AND MAY ✪

SJ BERWIN LLP ✪

ALLEN & OVERY LLP ✪
ASHURST ✪
BAKER & McKENZIE LLP ✪
CLIFFORD CHANCE
LOVELLS ✪
SIMMONS & SIMMONS ✪

CMS Cameron McKenna LLP
Latham & Watkins
Macfarlanes ✪
Mayer, Brown, Rowe & Maw LLP
Norton Rose ✪
Shearman & Sterling (London) LLP

Addleshaw Goddard
DLA Piper Rudnick Gray Cary UK LLP ✪
McDermott Will & Emery UK LLP ✪
Richards Butler

Arnold & Porter (UK) LLP ✪
Berwin Leighton Paisner LLP
Bird & Bird ✪
Bristows
Burges Salmon LLP *Bristol*
Charles Russell
Dechert LLP
Denton Wilde Sapte ✪
Eversheds LLP
Hammonds
Jones Day ✪
Kirkpatrick & Lockhart Nicholson Graham LLP
Lawrence Graham LLP
Nabarro Nathanson
Olswang
Pinsent Masons ✪
Sullivan & Cromwell LLP
Taylor Wessing ✪
Travers Smith
Watson, Farley & Williams LLP
Weil, Gotshal & Manges ✪
Wilmer Cutler Pickering Hale and Dorr LLP ✪
Wragge & Co LLP ✪

Firms are listed A-Z in tiers which are ranked in order of priority
✪ *Indicates firm displays contact details at the end of this chapter.*

Mark Friend and Alistair Lindsay. According to clients and economic consultants, the team remains effective thanks in particular to John Wotton. The firm worked on the impressive instruction to advise Sun Microsystems as the only official complainant in the European Commission case against Microsoft. The relocation of Philip Mansfield to the London office from Brussels has enhanced the team's behavioural credibility, particularly with regard to cartels in the technology sector.

Ashurst's formidable practice includes the City's most sophisticated group of economists at a law firm, led by Mat Hughes. It is these innovations that have brought the firm to prominence in the antitrust area, thanks in no small part to the efforts of the exceptionally bright Nigel Parr. Clients such as RBS now instruct the competition team on a regular basis, while Intel, Ford, Coors and P&O mandate the practice on a standalone basis. Furthermore, its presence in the contentious arena was demonstrated by the five cases in front of the Competition Appeal Tribunal (CAT).

With strength across the competition, regulatory and trade sectors, **Baker & McKenzie LLP** remains a true force in the market. Cartel cases are a real forte for the team, thanks to the efforts of department head Samantha Mobley. Former partner Lynda Martin-Alegi provides further gravitas on a consultancy basis, but key clients have not seen her as any less responsive and regard her as especially commercial. Robbie Downing is gaining further prominence in the competition market and clients pick out senior associate Keith Jones for exceptional work in regulated technology sectors. Ross Denton heads the leading trade practice.

It's **Clifford Chance**'s Brussels practice that is gaining prominence with Thomas Vinje and Simon Baxter working on a throng of notable mandates. The London group is headed by Alex Nourry.. Names such as contentious specialist Elizabeth Morony and Oliver Bretz are regularly commended. The latter is praised for his commercial understanding of competition law. Bretz is certainly forging a reputation as one of the brightest young antitrust advisers. The team also boasts a strong utilities practice.'

John Pheasant has taken over as head of **Lovells**' London competition practice and is one of the finest litigators in the competition arena. With the Brussels practice gaining further credibility, London achieved another stellar year, acting notably for the Barclay brothers in their successful bid for The Telegraph Group. This was the first major transaction under the new UK merger control regime for newspaper acquisitions. Brussels partner Philip Collins became chair of the OFT in 2005.

A strong standalone competition practice at **Simmons & Simmons** continues to gain credibility. New clients for the team include HMV and New Look, and the group is often brought in to advise on antitrust issues of transactions where another firm deals with the corporate aspects. **Simmons & Simmons** advises leading players in every regulated sector including postal, rail, water, power and telecoms. Martin Smith heads the group, with Charles Bankes known in particular for his regulatory expertise and Tony Woodgate for litigation.

With the firm's business in Central and Eastern Europe blossoming, **CMS Cameron McKenna LLP**'s London competition team has got to grips with a range of quality mandates in the region. The London team also has a fine record in the regulated industries, with David Marks on electricity and telecoms, and Sue Hankey on oil and gas. The team represented the whistleblower in the headline soccer replica kits case.

Latham & Watkins is a renowned adviser on state aid and cartel issues and boasts the presence of esteemed individuals Marc Hansen, John Kallaugher and John Colahan. Clients such as Brittany Ferries, Cisco Systems and Fujitsu are symptomatic of a practice with strong international credentials. Recent instructions include advice to Brittany Ferries in the UK merger clearance of the acquisition of certain P&O assets.

Macfarlanes' Marc Israel has a blossoming reputation in the competition arena. Israel has augmented a team led by the experienced and astute Jane Whittaker which made a name for itself with a pivotal role in the *IBA Health* case, the first challenge to a merger under Article 120 of the Enterprise Act.

Frances Murphy leads the team at **Mayer, Brown, Rowe & Maw LLP**. The firm has consolidated some impressive client relationships including AstraZeneca and is regularly called upon to give a second opinion following advice provided by firms in the higher ranks. The firm also employs several economists.

Norton Rose's strong competition and regulatory practice (particularly in the rail sector) continues to win accolades. Martin Coleman is an experienced individual, ably supported by Michael Grenfell and Mark Jones. New clients include Asda Stores.

Chris Bright 's part-time appointment at the Competition Commission limits his involvement with the team at **Shearman & Sterling (London) LLP**. Nonetheless he has built a $5m business, which he will continue to lead with counsel John Schmidt. The London team was instructed by Ispat International (now Mittal Steel) on the two-stage transaction to form the world's largest steel group. Gas utilities continue to be an important business area.

Addleshaw Goddard's fine team, led by Guy Leigh, warrants a promotion up the rankings thanks to its excellent London group enhanced by a serious national practice. The team is also strong in the regulated industries sector, recently acting for the Royal Bank of Scotland in relation to the postal services sector.

DLA Piper Rudnick Gray Cary UK LLP's record in competition law is becoming ever more impressive thanks to involvement in pivotal cases such as the replica soccer kit price fixing investigation by the OFT. Martin Rees and Mike Pullen have affirmed their antitrust acumen in the last two years. This has been recognised by new clients such as Virgin Atlantic and Emirates Airlines.

McDermott Will & Emery UK LLP's impressive London practice was augmented by the acquisition of a team in Brussels led by Clive Stanbrook QC. Scott Megregian and Ian Rose combine to form a fine London practice with a burgeoning reputation.

Richards Butler has a solid reputation for behavioural work and is regularly involved in notable OFT investigations. Katherine Holmes and Stephen Sayer lead a small but weighty team.

Arnold & Porter (UK) LLP's London practice is headed by Tim Frazer. The firm has an outstanding antitrust brand in the US and thus gains impressive mandates for high-profile clients such as Philip Morris.

Berwin Leighton Paisner LLP is acknowledged for its competition work in the leisure and rail sectors. Adrian Magnus leads the practice.

Bird & Bird's Richard Eccles is a real intellectual who has also demonstrated client-winning skills beyond the firm's technology focus.

Bristows' Pat Treacy has leveraged off the firm's strong IP brand and built a notable competition practice in the technology sector. Clients include Telewest Communications.

Bristol-based **Burges Salmon LLP** has invested serious resources into its competition team, with three partners leading and a wealth of top-quality clients endorse the practice with their custom. Laura Claydon has an excellent reputation.

Charles Russell enhanced its practice through the recruitment of Emanuela Lecchi as a partner. Lecchi has substantial experience working with the telecoms industry, including for Cable & Wireless. She links up with the experienced Angus Murray, who provided counsel to the Jockey Club during the OFT's investigation into horseracing.

Dechert LLP's Edward Kling and Peter Crockford are two vastly experienced competition practitioners with strong reputations, particularly in the behavioural domain.

Denton Wilde Sapte remains a name in the market, but it has haemorrhaged partners in recent years. Nevertheless, ex-litigator Jonathan Tatten is lauded by clients and has enormous gravitas.

Eversheds LLP has one of the most prolific dawn raid practices in the UK and is ably led by Ros Kellaway. Kellaway recently acted for the Association of British Insurers in its successful appeal against an OFT decision relating to credit hire claims. Stephen Rose is also commended.

Hammonds' Alasdair Bell is a strong name with a history of acting for UEFA. Though it has a small competition presence in London, the firm has an established business in Brussels.

Jones Day has a strong record in telecoms, but the UK practice is successfully leveraging off the prestigious client contacts of the Brussels office. Mastercard, O2 and the International Steel Group have all instructed the London department which is led by Greg Olsen.

Kirkpatrick & Lockhart Nicholson Graham LLP is particularly strong in the sports sector. Department head Neil Baylis is also developing the department's business in the beverages sector.

Lawrence Graham LLP's record in contentious proceedings is gathering pace thanks to the efforts of the excellent Anthony Woolich. Like the firm, the competition practice is particularly strong in the leisure sector.

Cyrus Mehta heads the competition practice at **Nabarro Nathanson**, a team with considerable standalone business. Public sector, public procurement and state aid work is an increasing source of business, but private sector clients have recognised Mehta's expertise.

Olswang is recommended for TMT and sport sector competition work under the auspices of partner Howard Cartlidge.

A period of substantial investment has given **Pinsent Masons**' strength in London and Birmingham in particular, with Alan Davis to the fore.

Led by US partner Bob Osgood, **Sullivan & Cromwell LLP** boasts an impressive presence, particularly in merger clearance.

Taylor Wessing's competition team excels in the technology sectors, including life sciences and telecoms. The firm has also demonstrated its rigour in regulated industries, particularly in postal and telecoms services. Martin Baker and Peter Willis are solid professionals.

Travers Smith partner Margaret Moore 's reputation is growing and is regularly referred work from leading firms in London that do not have a competition capability.

Watson, Farley & Williams LLP' Stephen Tupper leads a small London team with a strong record in behavioural issues and in the utilities sector, particularly water.

Weil, Gotshal & Manges' Doug Nave represents Coca-Cola Enterprises and has represented the company in relation to the long-running European Commission investigation into its distribution practices.

Wilmer Cutler Pickering Hale and Dorr LLP's London competition team has made a stunning start since the hire of Suyong Kim. Kim has continued to advise long-term client Liberty Media at her new firm, while the team has demonstrated its utilities expertise by advising Welsh Water before the Competition Appeal Tribunal.

Wragge & Co LLP's hire of the experienced Simon Taylor gives it credibility in London, augmented by Bernadine Adkins and her team in Birmingham.

EMPLOYMENT

Allen & Overy LLP is home to some of the market's most incisive legal minds, and this is borne out in its esteemed client base. Innovations in HR and the softer side of employment advice continue to win the faith of many. Mark Mansel, Julie Quinn, Stefan Martin and Karen Seward are highly regarded.

Led by Christine O'Brien, the **Baker & McKenzie LLP** team acts exclusively for employers, particularly City institutions and blue-chip companies. Clients appreciate the partners' specialisms, with Ellen Temperton leading on dispute resolution and privacy; and Sarah Gregory heading up equal opportunities. Immensely well-regarded new partner Monica Kurnatowska has joined John Evason in the collective rights group. The practice's international capability is illustrated by its co-ordinating employment advice in over 50 countries for Sony Music in its joint venture with Bertelsmann.

Simmons & Simmons' employment practice has won major financial and corporate clients, including Visa International Service Association. Half its work is non-UK, and it now acts for nine of the 11 international divisions of General Electric, as well as advising UBS on cross-border employee relocation. William Dawson, Simon Watson, Julian Taylor and Philip Bartlett are highly regarded.

Financial services work dominates at **Eversheds LLP**, with Elaine Aarons, Helga Breen and Roger Steel particularly in demand. Client wins include Schroders, which the practice has helped set up a cutting-edge staff forum. The team advised almost 40 other organisations on the new information and consultation requirements, aided by its in-house HR consultants.

Herbert Smith LLP is building on its contentious expertise by establishing a dedicated advocacy unit, and the appointment of Ian Gatt QC, formerly of **Littleton Chambers**, added significant employment law capability. The employment group itself, offers robust, well-founded advice through John Farr and Peter Frost. Four new associates have joined the team, which has won an array of high-profile new clients including Capital One, Coca-Cola, HBOS and Vodafone.

Employment is one of **Lewis Silkin**'s core areas and accounts for one third of its revenues. A unique new team in Oxford, led by the respected Russell Brimelow, solely handles employment work, operating as 'one practice' with the London office. Collaboration is also close with member firms of the international employment and pensions alliance, *ius laboris*. Despite high-profile work for individuals in investment banking, most notably Stephanie Villalba in her sex discrimination claim against Merrill Lynch, about 70% of the department's work continues to be for employers.

Lovells showed off its contentious prowess last year with its headline-grabbing defence of Merrill Lynch in the claim by its former employee, Stephanie Villalba. Up and coming discrimination specialist Lisa Mayhew led on the case, keeping control of an enormous disclosure exercise and witness statement effort. The practice's skill in industrial relations issues was demonstrated by work for Trinity Mirror in successfully opposing an NUJ recognition bid.

Mayer, Brown, Rowe & Maw LLP's practice works closely with its European and US offices, and is experiencing an increasing international dimension to its work. Finance and retail are key areas, but the Football Association, which the team advised on 'Svengate', is a new client. The longstanding combination of the excellent Julian Roskill and widely admired Nicholas Robertson, is

EMPLOYMENT

ALLEN & OVERY LLP ✪
BAKER & McKENZIE LLP ✪
SIMMONS & SIMMONS ✪

EVERSHEDS LLP
HERBERT SMITH LLP ✪
LEWIS SILKIN ✪
LOVELLS ✪
MAYER, BROWN, ROWE & MAW LLP
McDERMOTT WILL & EMERY UK LLP ✪
PINSENT MASONS ✪

Beachcroft Wansbroughs
CMS Cameron McKenna LLP
Charles Russell
Clifford Chance
DLA Piper Rudnick Gray Cary UK LLP ✪
Fox Williams
Linklaters ✪
Olswang
Taylor Wessing ✪

Addleshaw Goddard
Berwin Leighton Paisner LLP
Dechert LLP
Denton Wilde Sapte ✪
Farrer & Co
Freshfields Bruckhaus Deringer
Macfarlanes ✪
Nabarro Nathanson
Norton Rose ✪
Osborne Clarke
SJ Berwin LLP ✪
Travers Smith

Continued

complemented by two newer partners, Christopher Fisher and Louise Hobbs.

Clients consistently commend the partner quality at **McDermott Will & Emery UK LLP**. The team has advised over 20 companies on the new information and consultation regulations, which is a testament to Fraser Younson 's pre-eminence in this area. David Dalgarno is a financial sector expert and Alison Wetherfield specialises in discrimination. The group's reputation for dealing with collective and multi-jurisdictional issues has been enhanced by a ground-breaking 25-country European Works Council negotiation, the first involving all ten new member states.

Newly merged **Pinsent Masons** looks set to become a formidable force, led by Tom Flanagan, one of the most established names in employment. The team now combines *Pinsents'* strength in financial services and TUPE with *Masons'* brand in construction and IT, and has enhanced its national capability. On behalf of ASDA, the practice has successfully rebuffed a TGWU application for union recognition.

Despite **Beachcroft Wansbroughs**' health sector roots, 70% of the team's work is now for commercial clients, with new wins including Citigroup, McAlpine and L'Oréal. Nick Chronias acted for the fire authorities defending the largest test case in employment tribunal history, brought by 16,000 part-time firefighters. Elizabeth Adams heads the national employment practice, while Rachel Dinely leads the discrimination unit. Stephen Gummer and TUPE specialist Charles Newman also deserve recognition.

CMS Cameron McKenna LLP boasts two highly experienced partners in Simon Jeffreys and Anthony Fincham. Key work has included creating a framework for staff transfers in the first academy schools project, advising Royal Mail on potential industrial action, and, thanks to the firm's international coverage, work on a landmark Central European telecoms privatisation. The team also defended Metronet Rail against high-profile unfair dismissal claims by track maintenance workers.

Charles Russell's growing team has broken free of the firm's commercial department to become a standalone employment service group, with offices in Guildford and Cheltenham as well as London. Drawing on the respected David Green's mediation skills, and reflecting the rise of internal disputes within companies, the team is launching a mediation service for large financial institutions.

Clifford Chance has taken on several new assistants, reflecting a growth in instructions. On the contentious side, group head Chris Goodwill secured over £2m in damages for football manager Jean Tigana after his dismissal from Fulham FC, while Bruce Hedley successfully acted for Brook Street Bureau in a landmark agency worker case. The non-contentious practice saw significant PFI and TUPE work, plus projects for new clients Debenhams, Royal & SunAlliance and Gucci.

DLA Piper Rudnick Gray Cary UK LLP successfully acted for Botes Building in a key TUPE outsourcing case, and advised ITV on the HR aspects of its Carlton merger. Team head Tim Marshall is 'very approachable and professional'. Makbool Javaid has a burgeoning discrimination practice and is 'a good man to have on your side'.

The employment department at **Fox Williams** is the firm's largest. The team has an eclectic mix of employer clients, including public schools, US law firms and the GMB union, as well as a leading practice representing senior executives and partnerships. Jane Mann was appointed by new client Chelsea Football Club to defend it in litigation brought by former chairman Ken Bates. Ronnie Fox and Anne Nicholson are highly regarded.

EMPLOYMENT Continued

Ashurst ✪
Barlow Lyde & Gilbert
Bates Wells & Braithwaite
Bird & Bird ✪
Field Fisher Waterhouse
Hammonds
Jones Day ✪
Richards Butler
Salans
Slaughter and May ✪
Speechly Bircham
Stephenson Harwood
Wragge & Co LLP ✪

Aldridge Parker
Archon Solicitors
Bevan Brittan LLP
Campbell Hooper
Capsticks
Clyde & Co ✪
Davenport Lyons
Finers Stephens Innocent LLP
Harbottle & Lewis LLP
Kemp Little LLP
Kilpatrick Stockton LLP ✪
Kingsley Napley
Lawrence Graham LLP
Manches LLP
McGrigors London
Mishcon de Reya
Morrison & Foerster MNP
Reed Smith ✪
Reynolds Porter Chamberlain
Tarlo Lyons
Trowers & Hamlins ✪
Watson, Farley & Williams LLP
Wedlake Bell
Withers LLP

Firms are listed A-Z in tiers which are ranked in order of priority
✪ *Indicates firm displays contact details at the end of this chapter.*

Linklaters has the international spread and resources to advise on large-scale corporate transactions, with examples including Centrica's disposal of AA, and JP Morgan Chase in its joint venture with Cazenove. The team has also represented some of the biggest outsourcers such as Barclays and BT, and advised on PFI and PPP initiatives..

Key instructions for **Olswang**'s 'pragmatic' team included advising on the employment aspects of M&C Saatchi's float and the outsourcing of Five News Services to BSkyB. Praised for his 'superb' guidance on difficult TUPE issues and 'sensible, commercial advice', Daniel Aherne has been chosen as exclusive employment law adviser to ITN.

The energetic Sean Nesbitt is the new employment head at **Taylor Wessing**, with Andrew Granger becoming international integration partner. Technology companies and other inward investors are key clients, with new wins including German computer company Maxdata AG and US software house Adobe. EasyJet and Club Med are major clients, and the group also acts for high-net-worth city individuals and teams.

A high-profile project for the Department of Health and increasingly high-quality instructions from J Sainsbury are two highlights of **Addleshaw Goddard**'s current workload. New wins include two retail giants; Travelodge; pub and restaurant owner Spirit Group; and Swiss Re; adding to a list of household names and FTSE 100 clients. Michael Leftley is a good negotiator, while Alasdair Simpson is one of the foremost advisers of executive directors and senior management.

Berwin Leighton Paisner LLP has won a slew of new clients, including French Connection, Waterstones, Schroders, for which it has reviewed worldwide bonus arrangements, eBay and Google. The team also took over the defence of a whistleblowing case from another leading firm. Alexandra Davidson has a strong leisure and retail practice, while team head Rob Eldridge focuses on the financial sector.

The team at **Dechert LLP**, led by the highly regarded Charles Wynn-Evans, are seeing greater volumes of work from their major corporate clients. Mellon Bank, Etam and Saatchi & Saatchi are key clients. The firm's US offices enable the practice to advise on cross-jurisdictional issues.

Denton Wilde Sapte has an impressive array of clients in the finance, transport, retail and media sectors. These include GE Capital, and new client Kia Motors. Guy Fifield advised J Sainsbury on its new chief executive's service agreement, while Gilla Harris is known for advising film companies such as Universal Pictures. Pauline McArdle and Richard Nicolle have acted on the employment aspects of major insolvencies and on PFI/PPP projects in schools, hospitals and central government.

Clients consistently rate **Farrer & Co**'s David Smellie as a leading practitioner, and the young team had a high-profile year defending Eton College in the 'Harrygate' affair, and the Prince of Wales in the tribunal claim brought by Elaine Day. The firm has also been appointed to Imperial College's panel of legal advisers, and offers a sound educational practice, as well as advising media, charity and public sector clients.

The team at **Freshfields Bruckhaus Deringer** derives much strength from its integration with the firm's global employment, pensions and benefits practice. Close links with the firm's banking and dispute resolution groups allows the team to focus increasingly on employment issues arising from FSA regulatory investigations. Nicholas Squire is recommended for his understanding of difficult issues and ability to develop a strategy to take clients through complex transactions.

Macfarlanes has a busy contentious practice, with contested team moves featuring prominently. Dan Lavender specialises on this side, while department head Seán Lavin leads the non-contentious practice, having advised Carlton TV on its merger with Granada and Logicom on a TUPE-related dispute with Fujitsu, involving hundreds of staff. KFC and Reebok are other household-name corporate clients, while Tony Thompson is particularly well known for representing senior executives.

Nabarro Nathanson has a high profile in the not-for-profit sector, and has recently secured major new commercial clients Harrods and Apple UK; the latter was advised on the employment law aspects of setting up its flagship UK store. The team's pro bono work for a group of British Airways stewardesses pursuing sex discrimination claims illustrates its equal opportunities expertise and contentious capacity. Sue Ashtiany and Susan Gordon are both commended.

The practice at **Norton Rose** has grown in stature under Peter Talibart 's confident lead. Talibart has advised a sovereign Middle Eastern state on restructuring its labour law system, and acted on the reorganisation of a major metals producer in a deal reported to have saved 1,700 jobs. He has been joined as a partner by Paul Griffin, who has successfully defended a household name client against a multi-million-pound claim by 2,400 employees. New clients include Nestlé, Orange and HSBC Holdings.

Osborne Clarke's London office is now concentrating heavily on financial services, on which David Cubitt is the main adviser. On media and advertising Victoria Parry leads. The Bristol and Thames Valley offices have different sector focuses, but lend strength to the City practice, praised for its quick advice. New financial clients include Citigroup and Lazard, while technology wins include Microsoft Global Outsourcing and DHL. Four new lawyers have boosted the team's lower ranks.

Partners Nicola Kerr and Hilary O'Connor of **SJ Berwin LLP** are an enthusiastic and likeable pairing, offering added value to clients through their popular workshops and user-friendly approach. Restructuring and executive moves are strengths, and the team has a substantial list of media and leisure clients.

Acting almost entirely for employers, **Travers Smith** has a growing and varied set of clients won largely on the strength of the department's own merits. Clients highlight the team's non-textbook approach and opportunities given to junior staff. Dorothy Henderson, Si?n Keall and Andrew Lilley are recommended

ENVIRONMENT

Allen & Overy LLP's Owen Lomas heads a very strong team which never fails to impress new and long-standing clients. Renewables and waste are key areas of the firm's practice. On the renewables side, the firm advised a syndicate of banks to provide a debt facility to Beaufort Wind to acquire a wind farm portfolio with an estimated capacity of 430 megawatts. One highlight for its waste practice was advising a waste management company on its proposed acquisition of a major landfill business.

Freshfields Bruckhaus Deringer is applauded for its top-quality and pan-European work, as well as the breadth of its practice. Highlights for the firm included advising mobile telephone network operators on legal challenges brought against them regarding telephone masts. On the non-contentious side, in addition to transactional work the firm provides advice on the Equator Principles to a variety of lenders.

Ashurst's capability for waste issues is evidenced by its work for Shanks Group Plc on the sale of its £227.5m landfill business. Other strings to the team's bow are its projects and renewables expertise. It advised Kent Enviropower Ltd on one of the largest energy-from-waste projects in the UK.

CMS Cameron McKenna LLP's Paul Sheridan, is described by numerous environmental professionals as being one of the best environmental lawyers in the UK. Significantly the firm advised the Brett Group on the sale of Brett Waste Management.

Clifford Chance continues to ride high in the table thanks to a host of excellent instructions and a significant number of client wins. Of note, the firm advised on the restructuring of long-standing client British Energy. The team's leading lights include Brian Hall, Michael Redman and Nigel Howorth.

Vanessa Havard-Williams is the lead partner of **Linklaters**' environmental practice. The group's position in the table was consolidated by a raft of quality instructions recently, ranging from major contaminated land transactions, to advising on the financing of a large renewable energy portfolio.

At **Addleshaw Goddard** Claire Sheppard is well regarded for her contaminated land expertise. The diversity of the expertise is evidenced by its impressive standalone work, and its involvement in the South Hook Terminal LNG project.

ENVIRONMENT

ALLEN & OVERY LLP ✪
FRESHFIELDS BRUCKHAUS DERINGER

ASHURST ✪
CMS CAMERON McKENNA LLP
CLIFFORD CHANCE
LINKLATERS ✪

Addleshaw Goddard
Baker & McKenzie LLP ✪
Berwin Leighton Paisner LLP
Denton Wilde Sapte ✪
Herbert Smith LLP ✪
Jones Day ✪
Kirkpatrick & Lockhart Nicholson Graham LLP
Leigh, Day & Co
Lovells ✪
Macfarlanes ✪
Mayer, Brown, Rowe & Maw LLP
Norton Rose ✪
Simmons & Simmons ✪
Slaughter and May ✪

Barlow Lyde & Gilbert
Dundas & Wilson LLP
Hammonds
Lawrence Graham LLP
Nabarro Nathanson
SJ Berwin LLP ✪
Trowers & Hamlins ✪

Berrymans Lace Mawer
Bircham Dyson Bell
Burges Salmon LLP Bristol
Davies Arnold Cooper
Eversheds LLP
Field Fisher Waterhouse
Lewis Silkin ✪
Pinsent Masons ✪
Richard Buxton *Cambridge*
Stephenson Harwood
Taylor Wessing ✪

Firms are listed A-Z in tiers which are ranked in order of priority
✪ Indicates firm displays contact details at the end of this chapter.

For climate change issues **Baker & McKenzie LLP**'s senior associate Anthony Hobley is the first lawyer mentioned by all competitors. Partner Christopher Norton's team also deals with the whole gamut of environmental issues and advised BP Chemicals on two major transactions.

At **Berwin Leighton Paisner LLP** recent highlights include advising new client Northumbrian Water on a major reservoir project. The practice's Northern Ireland capability is a distinguishing factor.

Denton Wilde Sapte's group is best known for its waste-related expertise and it has advised at least three major clients on the definition of waste. In addition, the firm advised Kroll, the administrators of Federal Mogul (the automotive company) on UK administration. which included asbestos-related issues.

Dual US/UK qualified senior assistant Maria Cull at **Herbert Smith LLP** is extremely well regarded. The firm has a first-rate track record for waste management issues.

At **Jones Day** Chris Papanicolaou and senior associate Steven McNab are described as 'very professional and commercial' and 'excellent', respectively. Along with partner Clare Deanesly the department has a broad range of expertise.

Elisa de Wit has built up an excellent reputation for her waste expertise since she joined **Kirkpatrick & Lockhart Nicholson Graham LLP**. Clients confirm that she and her team 'rise to the challenge' whenever necessary. John Garbutt acts as consultant to the firm.

For claimant litigation **Leigh, Day & Co** is the leading light. Managing partner Martyn Day is extremely well thought of. The firm has acted for clients in claims brought against the National Environmental Research Council, the Ministry of Defence and the Environment Agency.

Transactional work is a key strength for Louise Moore and her team at **Lovells**. In addition, the group advises on waste and oil spillages. The firm was boosted by the arrival of Valerie Fogleman as a consultant. She is a leading environmental insurance practitioner. Competitors readily acknowledge her acumen and point to her involvement in the Sevonoaks District Council appeal as evidence of her prowess.

No environmental lawyer receives more plaudits from clients and competitors than **Macfarlanes**' Paul Davies. With department head Andrew Jackson he secured a significant amount of work for the firm, and increasingly focuses on environmental insurance.

Mayer, Brown, Rowe & Maw LLP's Cate Sharp is praised by clients for her enviable knowledge of this area. Although he is set to relocate to South Africa, Michael Hutchinson has been retained as a consultant. A large amount of the group's work is transactional support, but it also deals with a significant proportion of regulatory work too.

Brian Greenwood at **Norton Rose** has a superb reputation. The firm boasts a multitude of high-profile clients including Crown Castle International and Associated Ports. It advised the former on the environmental aspects of the £1.1bn sale of Crown Castle (UK) Ltd.

Mike Nash now heads the team at **Simmons & Simmons**. The firm has recently won new clients including BP and the Housebuilders Federation.

Slaughter and May's Ed Keeble is regarded as an outstanding lawyer in a transaction-focused practice. The firm acted for Terra Firma on the financing of the Waste Recycling Group, and for United Utilities Green Energy on the disposal of its renewable energy business.

Barlow Lyde & Gilbert's Aidan Thomson defended two major prosecutions relating to water pollution and waste management.

Mark Brumwell 's arrival ensures **Dundas & Wilson LLP**'s appearance in the table this year. Brumwell has an excellent reputation and is acting for the Environment Agency and Southern Water on a variety of matters.

Caroline May at **Hammonds** leads the firm's impressive environment group. The team is described as 'effective' and its clients include National Grid Transco, EDF Energy Plc and RWE NPower.

At **Lawrence Graham LLP** Paul Rice is described as 'very professional' and is lauded for his ability to produce 'concise analysis'. Significantly the firm has seen growth in its waste practice.

Anna Marshall heads **Nabarro Nathanson**'s London team. Much of the group's work stems from its investment and developer clients, including Quintain Estates and Costco UK Ltd. The group also has experience of advising on environmental risk issues arising from landlord and tenant relationships.

Following the departure of Mark Brumwell, **SJ Berwin LLP** lacks a dedicated environmental partner. However, senior assistant Sue Davidson has taken over the day-to-day management of the group. The firm advised Unilever on environmental aspects of its science and research park near Bedford.

Trowers & Hamlins moves up a tier this year thanks to the reputation of its department head Andrew Wiseman. The firm advised a plethora of local authorities on contaminated land issues.

At **Berrymans Lace Mawer** Paul Taylor and Philip Vallance QC are recommended. Construction partner Michael Salau is noted for his knowledge of waste matters and is described as 'commercially driven'.

Bircham Dyson Bell advised the Environment Agency on, among others, dredging consents on the River Dee.

Burges Salmon LLP is included in the London table this year thanks to its growing national reputation. The firm boasts two extremely able practitioners: Ian Salter and Ross Fairley.

Davies Arnold Cooper's environment team forms part of the firm's regulatory group, with strengths in brownfield development. Notable practitioners include Tim Johnson and Fiona Gill. The firm is also developing its waste practice.

Eversheds LLP is featured in the table for the first time thanks largely to Manchester-based partner Elizabeth Shepherd 's national reputation. Highlights for the London office include advising on the sale of Kuwait Petroleum's UK assets.

Richard Webber is **Field Fisher Waterhouse**'s best known environmental lawyer, who also spends part of his time on planning matters. The department's clients include ICI, BP and Bank of Scotland.

Historically **Lewis Silkin**'s group was best known for its contaminated land work, but increasingly it has seen a broadening of its practice. Of note partner Neil Toner advised Wandle Housing Association on the translocation of slow worms (a protected species).

At **Pinsent Masons** Peter Stockdale heads the environment group, which was boosted when Richard Ford joined the firm. He splits his time between Birmingham and London.

Cambridge's **Richard Buxton** name partner Richard Buxton boasts considerable expertise in environmental claimant litigation. In particular the firm is commended in the marketplace for its conservation-related work.

Consultant David Cuckson of **Stephenson Harwood** is commended by clients for his 'effectiveness and efficiency'. In addition to wide-ranging work, the firm advised Clean Air Capital on proposed participation in the EU Emissions Trading Scheme.

Alison Askwith of **Taylor Wessing** divides her time between planning and environment work. On the environment side the firm advised venture capital clients on the purchase of a power station. It also advised a bank on environmental warranties in a property transaction worth more than £10m.

INFORMATION TECHNOLOGY

Ian Ferguson, heads the CMT group at **Allen & Overy LLP** focusing mainly on corporate matters. Jane Finlayson-Brown is recommended for commercial aspects. Clients include financial institutions such as Commerzbank and supplier Sun Microsystems, which it advised on its battle with Microsoft.

Michael Hart and Harry Small jointly head **Baker & McKenzie LLP**'s IT and e-commerce practice. The firm was short-listed for a *Legal Business* award in 2005 for its advice on the European launch of iTunes. Robbie Downing continues to showcase his regulatory expertise acting for Wanadoo broadband on pricing matters.

Bird & Bird's IT practice is headed by Hamish Sandison and Roger Bickerstaff. Sandison advised on the re-tender of the DWP's £1bn medical services contract with ATOS Origin. Bickerstaff, meanwhile, advised the Department of Health of the implementation of NHS Direct digital TV. Other notable clients include Mitsui..

Julian Stait jointly leads **DLA Piper Rudnick Gray Cary UK LLP**'s formidable IT practice with Danelle Dinsdale. Dinsdale acted for Barclays on a £400m IT outsourcing. George Wheeler-Carmichael led advice to the OGC on its new guidance on public sector IT procurement. Other notable clients include ITV.

Pinsent Masons' outsourcing and technology group, headed by Clive Seddon, retains a reputation as one of the best in the country, with particular strength in disputes. Seddon and Rob McCallough are highly recommended for contentious matters.

INFORMATION TECHNOLOGY

ALLEN & OVERY LLP ✪
BAKER & McKENZIE LLP ✪
BIRD & BIRD ✪
DLA PIPER RUDNICK GRAY CARY UK LLP ✪
PINSENT MASONS ✪

BARLOW LYDE & GILBERT
BRISTOWS
DENTON WILDE SAPTE ✪
FIELD FISHER WATERHOUSE
HERBERT SMITH LLP ✪
KEMP LITTLE LLP
LINKLATERS ✪
TAYLOR WESSING ✪

Ashurst ✪
Berwin Leighton Paisner LLP
Clifford Chance
Freshfields Bruckhaus Deringer
Lawrence Graham LLP
Lovells ✪
Olswang
Osborne Clarke
Simmons & Simmons ✪

Addleshaw Goddard
Beachcroft Wansbroughs
CMS Cameron McKenna LLP
Charles Russell
Clyde & Co ✪
Eversheds LLP
Harbottle & Lewis LLP
Kirkpatrick & Lockhart Nicholson Graham LLP
Latham & Watkins
Mayer, Brown, Rowe & Maw LLP
McGrigors London
Nabarro Nathanson
Norton Rose ✪
Pillsbury Winthrop Shaw Pittman LLP
Slaughter and May ✪
Stephenson Harwood
Steptoe & Johnson ✪
Tarlo Lyons
Technology Law Alliance
Weil, Gotshal & Manges ✪
Wragge & Co LLP ✪

Firms are listed A-Z in tiers which are ranked in order of priority
✪ Indicates firm displays contact details at the end of this chapter.

David Isaac has been successful in winning clients. New instructions came from Lloyds TSB and HSBC.

Barlow Lyde & Gilbert has an excellent commercial and technology group. Highly rated Simon Shooter is the primary partner for key clients such as PwC, UBS and Hutchison 3G.

Bristows' practice, headed by Philip Westmacott, has acted for six of the top ten suppliers over the past three years, including NEC, Cisco, and IBM. Mark Watts ' arrival from IBM has strengthened links with the latter.

Denton Wilde Sapte's ranking in this section owes much to its considerable work in outsourcing.

Field Fisher Waterhouse has a strong reputation in this area. This is due in no small part to Michael Chissick. The firm acts for big-name suppliers such as Accenture. It is also extremely active for customers on a range of public sector and private sector IT projects.

Christopher Rees heads **Herbert Smith LLP**'s thriving IT and communications team. Bill Moodie handles contentious matters and defended easyJet in its three-year dispute with Navitaire. Complex work for some impressive new customer clients such as Coca-Cola and Société Générale mean it is pushing for a place in the top tier.

Technology boutique **Kemp Little LLP** continues to thrive in the shadow of the bigger City firms. Managing partner Richard Kemp and a coterie of dynamic young talent, including David Meredith and Paul O'Hare, are establishing reputations acting for the biggest suppliers such as Microsoft and EDS.

Christopher Millard heads **Linklaters**' team. John Crozier, who focuses largely on outsourcing, and Marly Didizian, who has been active for the Big Four on compliance issues, are talented technology specialists. Clients include institutions such as Barclays and suppliers such as Microsoft.

Taylor Wessing's team, led by Glyn Morgan, retains its position at the forefront of the European market for technology advisers. The Cambridge office, headed by corporate and technology specialist Simon Walker, continues to perform well, particularly on the venture capital and licensing fronts. The team has distinguished itself acting on complex projects for both suppliers and customers such as British Airways.

Chris Coulter and Mark Lubbock jointly head **Ashurst**'s strong all-round team. It advised on an impressive range of international outsourcing, UK procurement, and IT/media matters for big name clients.

Adam Rose leads **Berwin Leighton Paisner LLP**'s increasingly successful communications group. It has won places on notable panels: Accenture and Legal & General. It also continues to expand its involvement with Tesco's burgeoning business. Simon Harper is recommended. for e-commerce matters.

David Griffiths at **Clifford Chance** maintains an outstanding reputation despite the firm's somewhat diminishing emphasis on TMT. Its global offering is impressive and institutional clients such as Barclays and suppliers including Accenture are testament to the firm's strength.

Freshfields Bruckhaus Deringer regularly advises leading suppliers such as HP and IBM. The team, led by Avril Martindale, also acts for major customers, particularly financial institutions such as JP Morgan and the Bank of England.

The combined strength of the existing **Lawrence Graham LLP** team headed by Jonathan Riley, and the arrival of the former *Tite & Lewis* team, wins a ranking in the third tier this year.

Quentin Archer leads **Lovells**' small but formidable team. He and Conor Ward have outstanding reputations. The team is capable of regularly winning prestigious instructions. Along with Christopher Thomas it acted for Novell in its European Commission proceedings against Microsoft.

Olswang's practice, headed by Simon Briskman, leads the way in e-commerce. The firm's contentious capability led by Steven Baker is also impressive and wins instructions from suppliers and customers alike. Key clients include Avis Europe. John Enser is recommended for convergence matters.

At **Osborne Clarke** Simon Rendell has returned from his stint in-house at Vodafone to head the commercial department. The firm is better placed than most to take full advantage of the normalisation of the technology market. Adrian Lifely is among the leading contentious IT partners in London. Clients include Adobe and Yahoo!.

David Barrett leads **Simmons & Simmons**' activities in this area. He and Michael Sinclair have a strong reputation, particularly for technology outsourcing. The team was strengthened by the arrival of one of London's outstanding TMT generalists, Jonathan Little. Clients include Tata Consultancy Services and Dubai International Financial Centre.

IP: CONTENTIOUS

Morag Macdonald and Trevor Cook jointly head **Bird & Bird**'s IP team. Their reputations precede them. The firm has considerable strength in depth: note rising star partners Katharine Stephens and Robert Williams. Stephens has been active for clients involving Nestlé, while Williams acted alongside Macdonald in the precedent-setting passing off case *Sir Robert McAlpine v Alfred McAlpine*.

Bristows' Paul Walsh concentrates primarily upon trade mark litigation. David Wilkinson handles mainly copyright and design matters. Highly rated partner Simon Ayrton also distinguished himself with sterling work for Sony Computer Entertainment.

Charles Lloyd leads **Taylor Wessing**'s team. Highly enthusiastic young partner Niri Shanmuganathan wins widespread plaudits from clients. As well as big-name commercial clients such as PepsiCo and Christian Dior, the firm has an impressive client base in music and publishing, including BMG and Routledge.

Managing partner of **Addleshaw Goddard**'s commercial division, Hamish Porter leads the firm's IP group in London. The group benefits from firm-wide strengths in sport, entertainment, media and retail. Disputes work is abundant and flows from

IP: CONTENTIOUS

BIRD & BIRD ✪
BRISTOWS
TAYLOR WESSING ✪

ADDLESHAW GODDARD
BAKER & McKENZIE LLP ✪
DLA PIPER RUDNICK GRAY CARY UK LLP ✪
FIELD FISHER WATERHOUSE
HERBERT SMITH LLP ✪
HOWREY LLP ✪
LINKLATERS ✪
OLSWANG
SIMMONS & SIMMONS ✪
WILLOUGHBY & PARTNERS IN ASSOC WITH ROUSE & CO. INTERNATIONAL

Allen & Overy LLP ✪
Arnold & Porter (UK) LLP ✪
Ashurst ✪
Briffa
Clifford Chance
Denton Wilde Sapte ✪
Freshfields Bruckhaus Deringer
Hammonds
Kilpatrick Stockton LLP ✪
Lovells ✪
Macfarlanes ✪
Marks & Clerk Solicitors
Mayer, Brown, Rowe & Maw LLP
McDermott Will & Emery UK LLP ✪
Redd
Richards Butler
SJ Berwin LLP ✪
Slaughter and May ✪

Berwin Leighton Paisner LLP
Charles Russell
Collyer-Bristow
Davenport Lyons
Dechert LLP
Dorsey & Whitney ✪
Eversheds LLP
Harbottle & Lewis LLP
Kirkpatrick & Lockhart Nicholson Graham LLP
Lewis Silkin ✪
Manches LLP
McGrigors London
Mishcon de Reya
Norton Rose ✪
Reynolds Porter Chamberlain
Stephenson Harwood
Wedlake Bell
White & Case ✪
Withers LLP
Wragge & Co LLP ✪

Firms are listed A-Z in tiers which are ranked in order of priority
✪ *Indicates firm displays contact details at the end of this chapter.*

these areas. Clients include the British Horseracing Board and JVC. The firm wins promotion to the second tier in our rankings this year.

Baker & McKenzie LLP move up a tier, with Harry Small, Paul Rawlinson and Michael Hart recommended. Rawlinson is chair of the global IP practice and continues to distinguish himself with advice to big-name clients such as L'Oréal. Small's reputation for advising on disputes involving technology sector clients is second to none. Other notable clients include BAT and Apple.

DLA Piper Rudnick Gray Cary UK LLP make a meteoric leap in our tables this year, due mainly to the arrival of a team who moved en masse from **Denton Wilde Sapte**. Simon Levine wins praise from clients. His team has joined existing rated partners Jeremy Dickerson and Richard Penfold, who act for the likes of easyGroup and Harrods.

Highly rated partner Nick Rose leads **Field Fisher Waterhouse**'s activities in this area. He manages enforcement programmes for clients such as Ordnance Survey and Capital One. Simon Chapman has won a reputation, particularly through acting for Remington in its battle with Philips. Jonathan Radcliffe is recommended for trade mark matters. Though more of a patent expert, David Knight also undertakes contentious work on soft IP.

Nick Gardner took up the reins from Bill Moodie as head of **Herbert Smith LLP**'s impressive practices, and the firm moves up a tier. Moodie continues to practice at the highest level, acting for easyJet in complex litigation against Navitaire. Joel Smith has done sterling work for leading leisure brand Quiksilver on parallel imports. Mark Shillito, meanwhile, has showcased his considerable trade mark expertise for Yell against BT.

In Isabel Davies, **Howrey LLP** has without doubt one of Europe's leading contentious IP specialists. She acts for some of the top brands in the world, such as Intel, on protection of their trade mark portfolio in Europe. Partners Richard Willoughby and James Irvine are also recommended.

Nigel Jones heads **Linklaters**' team. There have been several departures in recent years, but talk of the firm's reduced firepower in this area is misleading. With partners such as Roland Mallinson, Robert Swift, and Benedict Bird still plying their trade at Silk Street, the firm's prominent place in the market is assured.

Paul Stevens and Michael Burdon jointly head **Olswang**'s core IP function. Stevens was particularly active for clients such as eBay, Amazon, and Tate & Lyle. Joel Barry acts for a string of big-name media clients such as M&C Saatchi, *The Guardian*, and ITV Plc. Burdon is recommended for litigation in the copyright field.

Richard Binns has taken over as head of the group at **Simmons & Simmons**. He is particularly well regarded for trade mark litigation. Jeremy Morton, meanwhile, is recommended for copyright matters across the TMT sector. Talented new partner Adrian Smith leads the firm's brands group. Clients include Bacardi-Martini and Reebok.

Willoughby & Partners in association with Rouse & Co. International's senior partner Tony Willoughby is one of the biggest names in the IP world. He has an unrivalled reputation, particularly for trade mark matters, passing off, copyright and confidential information. He also has particular experience of parallel imports/grey market and anti-counterfeiting litigation. Younger partner Shireen Peermohamed is establishing a reputation for handling passing off, as well as copyright and trade mark infringement. Clients include Getty Images and GlaxoSmithKline.

Catriona Smith leads **Allen & Overy LLP**'s activities in this area. The firm successfully distinguished itself recently with involvement in both William Hill's battle with the BHB and the *Harry Potter* copyright litigation.

Arnold & Porter (UK) LLP enters our rankings in the third tier. This is largely due to the arrival of IP specialist partner Clive Thorne. His reputation for contentious matters precedes him. In addition, the firm undertakes impressive trade mark and copyright work for market-leading clients such as Random House, IPC Media, and Sony.

Ashurst has a strong track record in this area. Ian Starr leads the team. Clients include big-name media companies such as BSkyB and leading brands, including Rolex. Jeremy Drew is also recommended.

Briffa is winning a reputation for its highly focused IP advice. Name partner Margaret Briffa is known for cutting-edge assignments. One such saw her acting for 321 Studios in its copyright battle with Warner Studios. Partner Ralph Wehrle is winning a reputation, particularly for his work for Teddy Smith in its battle with Lambretta over design rights.

Clifford Chance has three IP generalist partners who turn their hand to contentious matters in soft IP for a roster of major global companies. John Hornby is recommended for his trade mark expertise. Peter Taylor 's activities also encompass copyright and design. Clients include Mars, Reuters, and Coca-Cola.

Denton Wilde Sapte is in rebuilding mode following the departure of Simon Levine and his team. The swift recruitment of excellent partner John Linneker bodes well for the future.

Freshfields Bruckhaus Deringer can point to a raft of big-name clients such as Microsoft and Sony Computer Entertainment. Partners Dinah Nissen and Justin Watts have won loyal clients.

Hammonds has done a good job of consolidating its place in the market since the arrival of Paul Harris and Carl Rohsler. It acts on numerous disputes for high-profile clients. Notable among them is Black & Decker.

Kilpatrick Stockton LLP's practice enters the tables due to the arrival of the formidable Helen Newman. She is among the City's leading experts on the protection, enforcement and management of brands. Virginia Taylor is recommended for trade mark matters.

Dusseldorf partner Andreas von Falck now heads **Lovells**' IP practice. Michael Golding was kept busy acting for Prudential in trade mark disputes. Other notable clients include adidas and Royal Mail.

Geoff Steward leads **Macfarlanes**' activities in this area. The firm offers a genuine one-stop-shop for the full range of contentious soft IP expertise. It has been kept busy on a continuing basis by Kangol. Early Learning Centre was a good client win last year.

Since converting from *Blair & Co* to become **Marks & Clerk Solicitors**, the firm has gone from strength to strength. Not least, given the arrival of one of the country's leading IP practitioners Gregor Grant. Mark Blair is also highly experienced and has acted for Czech brewers Budejovicky Budvar in its battle with Anheuser-Busch. Other big name clients include BMW and HBOS.

Stephen Gare leads **Mayer, Brown, Rowe & Maw LLP**'s strong practice. The firm won repeated instructions from Cadburys on trade mark issues. Ian Wood is recommended.

Larry Cohen leads **McDermott Will & Emery UK LLP**'s small but impressive team. The firm undertakes the full range of contentious soft IP matters for clients such as Interlotto, which it advised on its battle with Camelot.

Since establishing their own firm, **Redd**, partners Charters Macdonald-Brown and Simon Chalkley have found no difficulty in claiming a prosperous niche in the market. Major clients include GSK, for which the firm acted on trade mark litigation and parallel imports.

Richards Butler's team undertakes a good level of work for the firm's roster of media, banking, and insurance clients. Michael Skrein is recommended.

In Ray Black and David Rose, **SJ Berwin LLP** has two outstanding IP practitioners. The firm won notable profile acting for William Hill against the BHB in the dispute over database rights.

Slaughter and May's team, led by Susie Middlemiss, undertakes a range of high-level work. The firm advised Arsenal FC on trade mark and copyright issues. It also acts for major financial institutions and recognised brands such as Marks & Spencer.

Wragge & Co LLP's head of department Gordon Harris has strong support from his team in Birmingham and London. Clients include Cadbury Schweppes and easyGroup.

IP: NON-CONTENTIOUS

Christina Demetriades and Michael Hart continue to drive **Baker & McKenzie LLP**'s practice. Recently, the firm undertook a balance of heavyweight corporate support and stand-alone matters. Demetriades assisted Apple on its European launch of iTunes.

Morag Macdonald leads **Bird & Bird**'s activities in this area alongside commercial and corporate IP focused partner John Wilkinson. Wilkinson has been active for major clients such as AstraZeneca on complex agreements. Headline-winning deals include Chelsea FC's record-breaking sponsorship agreement.

IP: NON-CONTENTIOUS

BAKER & McKENZIE LLP ✪
BIRD & BIRD ✪
BRISTOWS
DLA PIPER RUDNICK GRAY CARY UK LLP ✪
FRESHFIELDS BRUCKHAUS DERINGER
HERBERT SMITH LLP ✪
LINKLATERS ✪
SIMMONS & SIMMONS ✪
TAYLOR WESSING ✪

Allen & Overy LLP ✪
Ashurst ✪
Berwin Leighton Paisner LLP
Field Fisher Waterhouse
Hammonds
Harbottle & Lewis LLP
Macfarlanes ✪
Norton Rose ✪
Olswang
Osborne Clarke
Redd
Reynolds Porter Chamberlain
Slaughter and May ✪

Addleshaw Goddard
Arnold & Porter (UK) LLP ✪
Briffa
CMS Cameron McKenna LLP
Campbell Hooper
Charles Russell
Clifford Chance
Davenport Lyons
Denton Wilde Sapte ✪
Dechert LLP
Dorsey & Whitney ✪
Eversheds LLP
Finers Stephens Innocent LLP
Jones Day ✪
Kilpatrick Stockton LLP ✪
Kirkpatrick & Lockhart Nicholson Graham LLP
Lawrence Graham LLP
Lewis Silkin ✪
M Law
Marks & Clerk Solicitors
Mayer, Brown, Rowe & Maw LLP
McDermott Will & Emery UK LLP ✪
Mishcon de Reya
Nabarro Nathanson
Pinsent Masons ✪
Richards Butler
SJ Berwin LLP ✪
Tarlo Lyons
Wragge & Co LLP ✪

Firms are listed A-Z in tiers which are ranked in order of priority
✪ *Indicates firm displays contact details at the end of this chapter.*

Matthew Warren leads **Bristows**' activities in this area. The firm wins promotion in this year's rankings in recognition of its true IP specialism and significant technical knowledge.

Simon Levine has taken his team to **DLA Piper Rudnick Gray Cary UK LLP**. Specialists such as Bonella Ramsay have considerably strengthened the firm's offering in this area. Levine has a loyal following including big-name clients such as Honda. Richard Penfold undertakes impressive work for Zurich Financial Services. Recently, Jeremy Dickerson advised Barclays on various sponsorship and commercial agreements.

Avril Martindale is joint head of **Freshfields Bruckhaus Deringer**'s IP/IT practice worldwide. Richard Lister leads the firm's push on the international outsourcing front. Dinah Nisser has an outstanding reputation, particularly for trade mark expertise. Clients include 3 and AstraZeneca.

Nick Gardner replaced Bill Moodie as head of **Herbert Smith LLP**'s practice. Moodie continues to act at the highest level. He advised Hollinger International on the sale of the Telegraph Group. Highly rated partner Mark Shillito was active for Virgin Mobile on its IPO.

Linklaters' practice is among the best in the UK. It is headed by Nigel Jones, who gets strong support from partners, Benedict Bird and Ian Karet. Jones acts on a swathe of the firm's most impressive deals, such as UCB's acquisition of Celltech. Karet was active on the IPO of Cambridge Silicon Radio. Bird, meanwhile, acts for De Beers and JPMorgan.

Simmons & Simmons has a longstanding and well-deserved reputation for its IP, led by Richard Binns. Big name clients include Barclays and the MoD.

Boasting one of the largest IP departments in London, **Taylor Wessing** also offers considerable niche strength relating to the panoply of TMT areas from publishing to pharmaceuticals. Clients of the standing of Macmillan in the former sector, and Eli Lilly in the latter, speak volumes. Big-name clients that newly instructed the firm in 2004 include Christian Dior and Guerlain.

In Colleen Keck and Colin Pearson, **Allen & Overy LLP** offers clients the benefit of two of the City's outstanding non-contentious IP specialists. Both work as an integral part of the firm's CMT group. The firm is active for some of the biggest names across the sector, such as pharmaceutical company Pfizer and media giant News International. In addition, it provides high-level advice across the full range of corporate and finance.

Mark Lubbock heads **Ashurst**'s excellent team. It has been active for a wide range of clients from well-known brands such as Dunlop Slazenger to major private equity houses such as Apax Partners.

Since the arrival of Simon Clark, **Berwin Leighton Paisner LLP**'s practice has gone from strength to strength. Clients include Tesco and Bliss.

Mark Abell heads **Field Fisher Waterhouse**'s extremely strong BTMT practice. The group's talented individuals who include Jonathan Radcliffe and John Olsen – act on a wide range of media and brand-related matters as well as high level technology and pharmaceuticals clients. The firm also continues to act for Petronas superbike team.

Recent recruits Paul Harris and Carl Rohsler have boosted **Hammonds**' team considerably. The firm undertakes impressive work for media clients such as WPP and technology clients such as Matsushita.

As one would expect of one of the country's foremost media and entertainment-focused firms, **Harbottle & Lewis LLP** offers a wealth of IP expertise. Mark Owen is particularly highly rated. A glittering client base flows from the firm's leading film and theatre practices.

Jeremy Courtenay-Stamp leads a strong group of non-contentious IP experts at **Macfarlanes**. Clients include Red Bull Racing and Virgin.

Kim Walker leads **Olswang**'s team. Walker was particularly active for ITN and the Hustler Hollywood brand. John Enser is regarded as one of London's leading IP generalist partners. Other clients include the BBC and Whitbread.

Having returned from his stint in-house at Vodafone, Simon Rendell again leads **Osborne Clarke**'s excellent collection of media-oriented IP specialists. Clients of the standing of Vodafone and Yahoo! speak largely for themselves.

Redd was formed by three highly rated former **Jones Day** lawyers: Charters Macdonald-Brown, Simon Chalkley, and Sara Ashby. Though small, the firm undertakes an impressive level of work for big name clients such as Eidos and well-known consumer brands.

Reynolds Porter Chamberlain enters the rankings in the second tier this year in recognition of its broadly based IP practice. The firm undertakes an impressive range of work for media clients such as Associated Newspapers and HMV Group. Andrew Hobson and Maddie Mogford lead the firm's activities in this area.

Susie Middlemiss leads **Slaughter and May**'s non-contentious practice. The three-partner team acts for an incomparable roster of heavyweight corporate names and blue-chip sport and media clients. Examples include Cazenove, Marks & Spencer and Arsenal FC.

IP: PATENT LITIGATION

In this section, *The Legal 500* reviews firms purely on their ability to act for clients on contentious matters relating to hard IP. Major disputes often relate to patents in the mechanical, electronic and chemical industries. However, disputes in the pharmaceutical and life sciences sector generally dominate the headlines and the courts, and generate the biggest fees. Teams with prominent roles in these win high rankings. For strength in other areas relevant to the Pharmaceutical and Biotechnology see the section later in this chapter.

IP: PATENT LITIGATION

BRISTOWS

BIRD & BIRD ✪
LINKLATERS ✪
SIMMONS & SIMMONS ✪
TAYLOR WESSING ✪

Hammonds
Herbert Smith LLP ✪
Lovells ✪

Baker & McKenzie LLP ✪
Clifford Chance
DLA Piper Rudnick Gray Cary UK LLP ✪
Field Fisher Waterhouse
Marks & Clerk Solicitors
McDermott Will & Emery UK LLP ✪
Olswang
Redd
SJ Berwin LLP ✪
Wragge & Co LLP ✪

Addleshaw Goddard
Allen & Overy LLP ✪
Ashurst ✪
Freshfields Bruckhaus Deringer
Roiter Zucker
White & Case ✪
Willoughby & Partners in association with Rouse & Co. International

---

Arnold & Porter (UK) LLP ✪
Briffa
CMS Cameron McKenna LLP
Eversheds LLP
Jones Day ✪
Norton Rose ✪
Stringer Saul LLP

Firms are listed A-Z in tiers which are ranked in order of priority
✪ Indicates firm displays contact details at the end of this chapter.

Philip Westmacott leads **Bristows**' outstanding patent practice. Senior partner David Brown has almost 40 years' experience. In 2005, he led the team in *Halliburton v Smith*. Sally Field is also extremely highly rated and acted for Kimberly-Clark in its international battle with Procter & Gamble. Penny Gilbert undertakes high-level arbitration.

As long as Morag Macdonald and Trevor Cook continue at the top of their game, **Bird & Bird**'s standing in this areas is assured. The firm won a *Legal Business* award for its advice to Aventis & TKT in 2005 for its advice on the successful battle against Kirin-Amgen.

Nigel Jones leads **Linklaters**' activities in this area. Rivals regularly refer to the downsizing of the team, but there is no denying the quality of the client base. Names such as Johnson & Johnson, GlaxoSmithKline, and Wyeth speak volumes and the firm wins promotion as a result.

In Rowan Freeland and Kevin Mooney, **Simmons & Simmons** has two of the leaders in the field. The firm's headline client is GlaxoSmithKline, which it advised on two big-selling products – Seroxat and Seretide. Outside the pharmaceuticals sector the firm has been remarkably active for LG Philips LCD on disputes over patents on LCD monitors.

Taylor Wessing was strengthened by the return of former managing partner Gary Moss to fee-earning. Moss and Simon Cohen acted for Amgen in its five-year battle with Aventis & TKT. Mark Hodgson acted in the Lilly/Viagra technical board of appeal hearing in the EPO.

Hammonds' team has gone from strength to strength since the arrival of IP litigation specialist Paul Harris. He continues to undertake significant work for headline client Black & Decker.

Bill Moodie stood down as head of the **Herbert Smith LLP** team and Nick Gardner has taken up the reins. He focuses mainly on disputes in the technology sector. Moodie continues to undertake high-level cases. Joint head of the firm's pharmaceuticals group, Andrew Rich acted for Cambridge Antibody Trust in its high-value dispute with Abbott.

Lovells' Robert Anderson acted for longstanding client DSM, a leading Dutch pharmaceuticals manufacturer, in its battle with GSK. Nicholas Macfarlane, meanwhile, acted for Statoil in a dispute with Southampton University. Other key clients include Centoor, the biotech wing of Johnson & Johnson.

Baker & McKenzie LLP has two leading IP specialists, in Stephen Jones and consultant Don Jerrard. The pair lead a strong team that acts for numerous big name pharmaceutical clients such as Abbott and Pfizer as well as institutions such as Lloyds TSB and technology clients such as Sony.

Clifford Chance's John Hornby has established a strong reputation acting for major pharmaceutical clients such as Elan and Pfizer. Peter Taylor, meanwhile, undertakes a considerable amount of contentious patent work for the likes of Coflexip and Hitachi.

DLA Piper Rudnick Gray Cary UK LLP's, practice has been significantly boosted by the arrival of Simon Levine from. He wins glowing praise from clients who appreciate his 'focused and responsive' approach.

Jonathan Radcliffe leads **Field Fisher Waterhouse**'s team, acting for Sabaf on its precedent setting House of Lords appeal.

Gregor Grant 's arrival at **Marks & Clerk Solicitors** has been a significant boost. Grant and partners Mike Gilbert and Mark Blair act for a range of clients including British Technology Group and TT Electronics. It successfully defended

MedImmune in its long-running litigation with Celltech.

McDermott Will & Emery UK LLP's Larry Cohen, is well known as one of the leading patent litigators in London. Recently he has been busy for Hitachi Data Systems.

Michael Burdon jointly heads **Olswang**'s IP team alongside Paul Stevens. Burdon acted for University of California in its battle with Dendron over medical devices.

Redd is the firm formed by the former **Jones Day** lawyers Charters Macdonald-Brown, Simon Chalkley and Sara Ashby. Since setting up, the firm has acted for ERICO International on its dispute with Gripple Ltd.

Ray Black and David Rose, lead **SJ Berwin LLP**'s activities in this area. Recently Black was busy acting for Ranbaxy in its battle with Abbott. Competition and regulatory specialist Stephen Kon is also active for leading pharmaceutical sector clients such as AstraZeneca.

Despite the departure of Gregor Grant, **Wragge & Co LLP** retains strength in this area. Adam Cooke is recommended.

Several individuals in the fifth tier merit particular mention. **Allen & Overy LLP**'s Catriona Smith for example and **Ashurst**'s Ian Starr have strong reputations. At **Freshfields Bruckhaus Deringer** partner Justin Watts and Chris Forsyth who acted for Abbott against Ranbaxy, are also recommended. Claire Turnstall at **Roiter Zucker** has a burgeoning reputation.

IP: TRADE MARK FILING AND OPPOSITION

Field Fisher Waterhouse's commitment to this area in London outstrips all other firms. John Olsen heads the trade mark and brand protection group. Recently the team distinguished itself acting for the owners for the Chinawhite nightclub in the Court of Appeal, a case that established new law on the meaning of 'bad faith' in the filing of trade mark applications. The firm also advised well-known brands such as Lonsdale, Dunlop, and Slazenger on the rollout of their multi-million-pound trade mark licensing programmes. The firm's recent headline client is Apple.

Stephen Jones and Paul Rawlinson lead **Baker & McKenzie LLP**'s activities in this area. The firm organises its trade mark offering in an integrated way, with trade mark agents and solicitors conducting prosecution and filing matters for big name clients. The team has been kept busy by Frito-Lay, part of the PepsiCo Group.

Bristows' Paul Walsh heads the firm's excellent trade marks practice. It acts for leading clients such as BBC and Georgia-Pacific. Walsh and Sally Field also act for Diageo. Brian Cordery 's headline client is Sara Lee, for which he coordinated filing strategies in relation to body care brands.

IP: TRADE MARK FILING AND OPPOSITION

FIELD FISHER WATERHOUSE

BAKER & McKENZIE LLP ✪
BRISTOWS
CLIFFORD CHANCE
DECHERT LLP
LINKLATERS ✪
SJ BERWIN LLP ✪

Berwin Leighton Paisner LLP
Briffa
Davenport Lyons
Lewis Silkin ✪
Manches LLP
Mayer, Brown, Rowe & Maw LLP
McDermott Will & Emery UK LLP ✪
Nabarro Nathanson
Olswang
Pinsent Masons *Leeds*
Simmons & Simmons ✪
Wragge & Co LLP ✪

Firms are listed A-Z in tiers which are ranked in order of priority
✪ Indicates firm displays contact details at the end of this chapter.

Vanessa Marsland manages **Clifford Chance**'s group. The emphasis is on strategic portfolio management and conducting large-scale filing programmes. The firm handles such work for numerous household names, including Gap, Rolex and Weightwatchers.

Paul Kavanagh heads **Dechert LLP**'s business IP group. He has a wealth of experience advising on the full range of soft IP issues for US, European, and international clients. The firm has been active for well-known brands such as Campbell Soup and Travelex Financial Services.

Linklaters' team is led by Roland Mallinson. Benedict Bird acts for De Beers on prosecution of its non-industrial diamond trade mark portfolio. Mallinson acts for Granada. The firm's international reach is also impressive.

SJ Berwin LLP's team is spearheaded by Ray Black and David Rose. Outstanding senior assistant Barry Gerber is responsible for the day-to-day management of the trade mark and design practice. The firm acts for some big-name clients such as Apax Partners and Japanese toy company Bandai.

In the third tier there are several firms that have smaller teams with highly rated individuals. One such is **Berwin Leighton Paisner LLP**, where Simon Clark has an outstanding reputation. He leads the group, which acts for major portfolios such as Tie Rack and, following a successful pitch, won the advisory work for *The Financial Times*. David Marchese and Niall Tierney at **Davenport Lyons** have strong reputations. Tierney advised Federation of Hong Kong Industries. The arrival of Alex Carter-Silk at **Manches LLP** has significantly boosted its practice. Gordon Harris has assembled a strong team at **Wragge & Co LLP**.

INSOLVENCY AND CORPORATE RECOVERY

ALLEN & OVERY LLP ✪
CLIFFORD CHANCE
DENTON WILDE SAPTE ✪
LINKLATERS ✪

BINGHAM McCUTCHEN LLP
CADWALADER, WICKERSHAM & TAFT LLP ✪
FRESHFIELDS BRUCKHAUS DERINGER
HERBERT SMITH LLP ✪
LOVELLS ✪
SLAUGHTER AND MAY ✪
WEIL, GOTSHAL & MANGES ✪

ASHURST ✪
BERWIN LEIGHTON PAISNER LLP
CMS CAMERON McKENNA LLP
DLA PIPER RUDNICK GRAY CARY UK LLP ✪
LAWRENCE GRAHAM LLP
NORTON ROSE ✪
SIDLEY AUSTIN

Kirkland & Ellis International LLP ✪
Latham & Watkins
Mayer, Brown, Rowe & Maw LLP
Nabarro Nathanson
White & Case ✪

Akin Gump Strauss Hauer & Feld
Baker & McKenzie LLP ✪
Debevoise & Plimpton LLP ✪
Jones Day ✪
Orrick, Herrington & Sutcliffe ✪
Richards Butler
SJ Berwin LLP ✪
Shearman & Sterling (London) LLP
Simmons & Simmons ✪
Stephenson Harwood
Taylor Wessing ✪
Travers Smith

Continued

INSOLVENCY AND CORPORATE RECOVERY

Allen & Overy LLP's Gordon Stewart is widely considered to be the finest restructuring lawyer in the City and is supported by a fine group of partners.. The firm's pre-eminent banking practice is the basis from which this leading team has emerged; its banking contacts have brought the firm roles in Drax and Cordiant in recent years.

Clifford Chance's outstanding work on British Energy's financial restructuring was sanctioned by the court in January 2005 and enabled the firm to win the *Legal Business* award for corporate/restructuring in 2005. Philip Hertz and Mark Hyde led the restructuring team that allowed British Energy's shares to relist on the London Stock Exchange. On the formal insolvency front, the firm has roles in both Parmalat and Federal-Mogul and is advising Swissport

International in connection with the administration of its UK subsidiary.

Denton Wilde Sapte boasts a massive team with a reputation to match. Its links to Kroll brought it into major mandates such as Federal-Mogul's giant cross-border bankruptcy, on which the Mark Andrews is leading the team. The Federal-Mogul instruction represents just one example of the firm's standing with administrators and liquidators such as PwC, KPMG and Ernst & Young. Its former close connection with NatWest, prior to its takeover by RBS, has continued to blossom with the latter name.

Linklaters' credentials as a leading City and global practice were enhanced by its advice to Welcome Break Finance and its administrative receivers Deloitte in the restructuring of Welcome Break, incorporating the first whole business securitisation structured in the UK. The firm also advised the ad hoc committee on Eurotunnel and the banks on Jarvis. Robert Elliott heads the dynamic practice.

Bingham McCutchen LLP and **Cadwalader, Wickersham & Taft LLP** have carved out considerable market share as advisers to bondholders and noteholders. **Bingham McCutchen LLP** acted for the lending steering committee on the restructuring of Queens Moat Houses. At **Cadwalader, Wickersham & Taft LLP**, Andrew Wilkinson is one of London's most prominent practitioners thanks to his eminent bondholder work.

Freshfields Bruckhaus Deringer's role as counsel to Telewest on its gargantuan restructuring showed its pan-European strength and power in this area. Sandy Shandro leads a practice that is widely acknowledged for its work on the debtor side, but has also developed its connections with banks and creditors such as ABN Amro, Barclays, HSBC and RBS

Herbert Smith LLP's headline work for Ernst & Young as administrators and liquidators on the TXU European group's company voluntary arrangement (CVA), was another complex cross-border mandate for the firm. Partner Stephen Gale enjoys an outstanding reputation, and Laurence Elliott and Kevin Pullen are also recommended individuals.

In terms of bank-led restructurings there are few practices with a greater profile than **Lovells**. However, the firm's increasing prominence in bondholder work and its sustained activity in formal insolvency should be noted. It continues to advise the Asbestos Committee on the UK aspects of the Federal-Mogul bankruptcy. Robin Spencer leads the team, which includes strong players such as Joe Bannister and the Matthew French.

Slaughter and May is more involved in restructurings thanks to its outstanding corporate portfolio. Its stellar work on Jarvis (an instruction referral to the firm by the accountants involved) and MyTravel deserves further recognition. It is also developing a greater profile with lending banks such as Lazard, Rothschild and Deutsche Bank.

INSOLVENCY AND CORPORATE RECOVERY Continued

- Addleshaw Goddard
- Bird & Bird ✪
- Clyde & Co ✪
- Eversheds LLP
- Field Fisher Waterhouse
- Halliwells LLP
- Holman Fenwick & Willan ✪
- Kennedys
- Moon Beever ✪
- Olswang
- Salans
- Skadden, Arps, Slate, Meagher & Flom (UK) LLP

- Beachcroft Wansbroughs
- Bryan Cave
- Charles Russell
- Cleary, Gottlieb, Steen & Hamilton LLP ✪
- Collyer-Bristow
- Davenport Lyons
- Davies Arnold Cooper
- Dechert LLP
- Fladgate Fielder ✪
- Hammonds
- Kirkpatrick & Lockhart Nicholson Graham LLP
- Manches LLP
- Mishcon de Reya
- Osborne Clarke
- RadcliffesLeBrasseur
- Reynolds Porter Chamberlain
- Speechly Bircham
- Wedlake Bell
- Withers LLP

Firms are listed A-Z in tiers which are ranked in order of priority
✪ Indicates firm displays contact details at the end of this chapter.

Weil, Gotshal & Manges' outstanding record over the last two years – warranting a promotion to the second tier – is thanks in part to the efforts of the formidable Chris Mallon. The firm's global profile has played a significant role, with Mallon and New York partner Marcia Goldstein being brought in by the investment banks to advise Parmalat on its restructuring, working alongside Italian firm **Gianni, Origoni, Grippo & Partners**.

Ashurst's practice is debtor led with the partners in the main coming from a corporate deal-making background. The exception is Ben Tidswell, an insolvency litigation specialist who advised the liquidators of Baring Futures (Singapore) on their action against its auditors, which settled in May prior to consideration by the Court of Appeal. The firm receives frequent referrals from Magic Circle practices, much to the credit of the highly respected Nick Angel.

Berwin Leighton Paisner LLP's role on Henlys' restructuring (involving over £700m of debt) shows its credibility with financial institutions and company doctors. Though the team has a strong standalone reputation, the firm's efforts to build a leading finance practice are enhancing its offering. Like most of the top-tier firms it concentrates on major restructuring mandates, but also has a vibrant formal insolvency business, with David Leibowitz to the fore in the latter.

CMS Cameron McKenna LLP's Rita Lowe has an outstanding reputation amongst peers and Duncan Aldred is a fine leader of the team. The practice retains a notable mid-to-large market business, with a healthy flow of formal insolvency work.

DLA Piper Rudnick Gray Cary UK LLP's success with the banks, including RBS, Barclays and Bank of Scotland, has encouraged yet more progress for the firm in this sector. It has a broad mid-to-upper range generated by a throng of clearing banks.

Lawrence Graham LLP's IP-led practice operates largely in the mid-market sector with single bank lends in the range of £1m to £40m. Instructions from Grant Thornton have been prevalent over the years, including a role in the Wimbledon FC administration. The team has also worked for Bank of Scotland on the Noble House refinancing, while not being on the bank's panel for insolvency and restructuring. As such it is pushing its credentials in the restructuring market.

Norton Rose's strong finance practice has enabled it to gain a solid business in restructurings and insolvencies. Restructuring partner Richard Calnan is considered an exceptionally bright individual, while contentious insolvency specialist Val Davies is also widely admired. Hamish Anderson has a prominent reputation in formal cross-border insolvency work. The firm also represents IPs such as Grant Thornton, Kroll and BDO.

When it comes to cross-border and international mandates there are few firms with as prestigious a business as **Sidley Austin**. The London team continues to play a key role in Federal-Mogul's insolvency, as well as the headline bankruptcies of Parmalat and Budget Rent-A-Car. The firm's connections to Bank of America and its excellent restructuring brand in the US has served London well.

Kirkland & Ellis International LLP and **Latham & Watkins** are moving closer to the major cross-border mandates that their American counterparts **Sidley Austin** and **Weil, Gotshal & Manges** have found so lucrative. **Kirkland & Ellis International LLP** is developing this through Lyndon Norley, while at **Latham & Watkins** John Houghton is particularly noted on the private placement side and is prominent with the distressed debt trading desks at leading banks.

Mayer, Brown, Rowe & Maw LLP's now sizeable team offers significant strength in this area and has won the recognition of important clients such as PwC, BDO Stoy Howard and Begbies Traynor. The arrival of Richard Gregorian has played a part in this, but David Allen, Ian McDonald and David Morrison are all gaining recognition. The firm should also be noted for its distressed debt work throughout Europe.

Nabarro Nathanson has an established practice with excellent credentials, much to the credit of the astute Patricia Godfrey. More restructuring work has resulted from the firm's reputation amongst US firms in London with no insolvency and restructuring department. The firm's excellent property practice has also been a significant source of business. Godfrey recently acted for SwissAir Finance, as the unsecured creditors of the Flightlease group.

White & Case's strong banking brand has brought considerable success to the restructuring practice led by the excellent Dan Hamilton. European cross-border instructions form the bulk of the business. The firm is recommended in particular for restructurings of high yield and leveraged financings.

Akin Gump Strauss Hauer & Feld is known for its representation of bondholders in the US, but has yet to achieve the same heights in the UK. The team includes Jeff Drew and is well placed to build on the firm's immense US standing.

Baker & McKenzie LLP is an acknowledged leader in the technology, retail and manufacturing sectors, and in Jeremy Goldring it has one of the most experienced recovery and insolvency specialists in the City. The firm is building its hedge fund connections, whilst augmenting its IP links that include KPMG, Grant Thornton and Kroll.

Debevoise & Plimpton LLP's has a notable record on multinational restructurings, with recent roles including acting for the bondholders of Parmalat Dairy and Bakery Inc In relation to the CND$610m (£287m) refinancing of its senior debt. The team has also been mandated to advise a debtholder on the restructuring of Eurotunnel.

Jones Day is making considerable progress under Adam Plainer, who is consolidating the firm's links to investment banks and accountants such as RBS and Grant Thornton. With more work coming from IPs, the firm has the basis of a broad insolvency and restructuring practice. Sion Richards provides the contentious expertise.

Orrick, Herrington & Sutcliffe has yet to make a significant impact on the European market, but it has made progress on bondholder and secured lender work, on the back of its reputation in the US.

Richards Butler focuses on formal insolvency work and has well-established connections with leading IPs. Jonathan Yorke is frequently touted as a favourite for IPs and clearing banks, while Michael McCarthy provides the contentious insolvency skills.

SJ Berwin LLP's Stephen Maffey leads a respectable team on the debtor side, but is also using the firm's private equity connections to good effect. The arrival of Michael Woollard is a welcome boost.

Simmons & Simmons acts for Barclays on major restructurings and also advises RBS on a regular basis. The firm is also known for mid-market insolvencies. Peter Manning leads the practice, which remains involved in MyTravel, Box Clever and British Energy.

Stephenson Harwood has outstanding insolvency and restructuring experience. It continues to effectively bridge the mid-market work with the occasional large mandate. Paul Gordon-Saker leads the small practice.

Taylor Wessing's Alison Goldthorp and Nick Moser are viewed as strong niche insolvency players with excellent reputations according to clients.

Travers Smith's burgeoning turnaround business for distressed corporates, turnaround practitioners and private equity houses is thanks to the efforts of the immensely respected Keith Bordell and Jeremy Walsh. Headline instructions include working with turnaround practitioner Martin May to assist Cape plc and PlaneStation Group.

MERGERS AND ACQUISITIONS

Freshfields Bruckhaus Deringer's M&A department is consistently lauded for its technical mastery and sound commercial advice delivered on a stream of highly complex deals. The firm acted for the Brascan consortium on its ultimately failed bid for Canary Wharf, and for Novar on the defence of a bid from AIM-listed shell company Melrose and the recommended £960m offer from Honeywell. Tim Jones continues to head the corporate department in London supported by Barry O'Brien, Edward Braham, James Davis, William Lawes and Mark Rawlinson.

Linklaters' impressive stable of FTSE 100 clients allows its corporate partners the kind of high-level deal-making experience so prized by clients. The firm advised National Grid Transco on the £1.1bn acquisition of Crown Castle UK, and for Centrica on its £1.75bn disposal of the AA. David Barnes recently took over as head of corporate. Further leading advisers in the department include Matthew Middleditch, Charlie Jacobs, Richard Godden, Jeremy Parr and Derek McMenamin.

Few firms have the same level of access to the boardrooms of corporate Britain as **Slaughter and May**. In one of the M&A performances of the year the firm advised Marks & Spencer on the defence of Philip Green's approaches and then picked up the *Legal Business* award for M&A team of the year for its advice to the victorious consortium on the £5.2bn acquisition of Canary Wharf. In a partner team of considerable strength we would highlight department heads Stephen Cooke and Christopher Saul, leading rainmaker Nigel Boardman, Frances Murphy, Andy Ryde, William Underhill and Padraig Cronin.

MERGERS AND ACQUISITIONS

FRESHFIELDS BRUCKHAUS DERINGER
LINKLATERS ✪
SLAUGHTER AND MAY ✪

ALLEN & OVERY LLP ✪
CLIFFORD CHANCE
HERBERT SMITH LLP ✪

ASHURST ✪

LOVELLS ✪

MACFARLANES ✪
NORTON ROSE ✪

CMS Cameron McKenna LLP
SJ Berwin LLP ✪
Shearman & Sterling (London) LLP
Simmons & Simmons ✪
Skadden, Arps, Slate, Meagher & Flom (UK) LLP
Travers Smith
Weil, Gotshal & Manges ✪

Baker & McKenzie LLP ✪
Berwin Leighton Paisner LLP
Cleary, Gottlieb, Steen & Hamilton LLP ✪
Denton Wilde Sapte ✪
Jones Day ✪
Latham & Watkins
Mayer, Brown, Rowe & Maw LLP

Addleshaw Goddard
DLA Piper Rudnick Gray Cary UK LLP ✪
Eversheds LLP
Milbank, Tweed, Hadley & McCloy LLP ✪
Taylor Wessing ✪
White & Case ✪

Barlow Lyde & Gilbert
Dechert LLP
LeBoeuf, Lamb, Greene & MacRae ✪
McDermott Will & Emery UK LLP ✪
Nabarro Nathanson
Olswang
Pinsent Masons ✪
Wragge & Co LLP ✪ *Birmingham*

Hammonds
Lawrence Graham LLP
Mishcon de Reya
Osborne Clarke
Reed Smith ✪
Richards Butler
Stephenson Harwood
Watson, Farley & Williams LLP

Firms are listed A-Z in tiers which are ranked in order of priority
✪ Indicates firm displays contact details at the end of this chapter.

Allen & Overy LLP has maintained its position as one of the leading M&A practices in the market. The team picked up a succession of high-profile instructions including HBOS on its bid for Abbey National, Malcom Glazer on his ultimately successful pursuit of Manchester United, and Standard Chartered on its $3.3bn acquisition of Korea First Bank. In addition, it secured appointments to the panels of Accenture, National Australia Bank, GE, HSBC and Lehman Brothers. Clients praise the technical expertise of global head of corporate Richard Cranfield while they also highlight Alan Paul 's experience on both public and private deals Alistair Asher, Mark Gearing, Susan Howard, Mark Dizhero and departmental managing partner Mark Wippell are also recommended.

Clifford Chance enjoyed one of its best years for UK M&A. The year saw the firm pick up instructions from the likes of Canary Wharf, on the long-running battle for the iconic Docklands development, for Banco Santander in its £8.9bn acquisition of Abbey, and for Multiplex, as part of a consortium on the £2.2bn offer for Duelguide. Leading individuals in the London team include David Pearson, Daniel Kossoff whose tireless efforts on the restructuring of British Energy finally reached a conclusion, lead partner on the Abbey deal David Pudge, all-rounder Adam Signy and Kathy Honeywood.

Herbert Smith LLP is one of the City's class performers in M&A. The firm boasts a host of top corporate clients and leading connections with the investment banking community. In an impressive portfolio of deals the firm acted for Hollinger International on the sale of the Telegraph Group, in one of the most fiercely contested auctions of the year, and for the majority shareholder in the £1.35bn disposal of Saga. Michael Walter now heads the practice. Further specialists include Anthony Macaulay, James Palmer, Stephen Hancock and Ben Ward.

Ashurst has forged a reputation as one of the City's finest M&A outfits. The firm's deal-making credentials were augmented after it was instructed to advise retail tycoon Philip Green on his bid for Marks & Spencer. Chris Ashworth led on that deal and remains one of the firm's go-to partners on public bids although Adrian Clark has replaced him as head of corporate. The firm was also to the fore for Deutsche Börse on its offer for the London Stock Exchange, and for Taylor & Francis on its £1.5bn merger with Informa. Charlie Geffen, Paul Gadd, Nigel Stacey, David Kershaw, Jeffrey Sultoon and Graeme Ward are also recommended.

Lovells remains a key adviser to clients on high-profile and complex M&A. The firm boasts an impressive corporate client list but it is with the investment banking community where it is making most progress in developing the practice. Illustrative of this was the firm's role advising JPMorgan, joint financial adviser to Banco Santander on its acquisition of Abbey National. Nigel Read led on that deal. The firm remains a key player in a number of sectors including energy where a team led by John Cooper acted for Petro-Canada on its $980m acquisition of Intrepid Energy North Sea. Hugh Nineham and John Davidson both stand out for their deal-making expertise and Steven Bryan recently joined the firm.

Macfarlanes close links with a number of top-tier investment banks is indicative of the esteem in which the practice is held in the City. In a range of deals the team picked up the mandate to advise Goldman Sachs on France Telecom's acquisition of shares in Orange for €6bn and followed that by acting for France Telecom in its €6bn purchase of shares in Wanadoo. Senior partner Robert Sutton is one of the most respected deal doers in the City. Further expertise is offered by Robert Boyle, Charles Martin, John Dodsworth and Tim Lewis.

Norton Rose combines a tight sector focus with what is still one of the strongest corporate brands in the City. The firm's M&A profile in the financial institutions sector stands out in particular. HSBC remains a trophy client for the firm; in 2004 **Norton Rose** advised the banking giant on its acquisition of Marks & Spencer's retail financial services. The firm also acted for ISIS Asset Management on its £1bn merger with F&C Group to form F&C Asset Management. Tim Marsden heads the global corporate finance practice. Further specialists of note include Margaret Coltman, Martin Scott, Laurence Levy, Simon Sackman and Mauro Mattiuzzo

CMS Cameron McKenna LLP possesses first-class M&A expertise across a range of sectors. Energy is a particular strength where the firm's links with the likes of BP and National Grid Transco are commensurate with a leading City practice. The practice is also building an impressive track record acting for financial institutions including the likes of HSBC and Barclays. In one of the sale mandates of the year the firm was on board for National Grid Transco on the £5.8bn disposal of four of its regional gas distribution networks. Sean Watson led on the deal and Andrew Sheach and Louise Wallace also impress.

SJ Berwin LLP moves up a tier this year on the back of 12 months of undoubted progress for its M&A team. In the course of the year, new instructions were received from Associated British Foods, Goldman Sachs, Hicks Muse Tate & Furst and Macquarie Bank joining the likes of British Land, Hilton and the Royal Bank of Scotland as clients. In a range of deals the practice acted for Morgan Grenfell private equity and Mid-Ocean Partners on their phased exit from the Laurel Pub Company, and Musgrave on its purchase of Londis. Steven Davis, Robert Burrow, Rob Day, Peter Anderson and Michael Goldberg all impress.

Shearman & Sterling (London) LLP's decision to build up its UK corporate practice is clearly proving a success. The practice's profile with major corporates and institutions in the City continues to grow and with the firm's impressive international client list the corporate team is well placed to add value in complex, multi-jurisdictional deals. Deals of note included advising Viacom and Vivendi on their disposal of United Cinemas International and acting for the Berkeley Group in its £1.45bn return to shareholders. Adrian Knight, Jonathan Coppin and Peter King are all recommended.

Simmons & Simmons enjoys a considerable reputation for its corporate work in the City. On the deals front the firm advised GKN on the £1.06bn disposal of its 50% shareholding in AgustaWestland to Finmeccanica, and acted for Shell on the disposal of the oil giant's oil products businesses in the West Indies. Damon Le Maitre-George continues to head the practice with key support from Mark Curtis, Stuart Evans, Tim Field and Charles Mayo.

Skadden, Arps, Slate, Meagher & Flom (UK) LLP maintains a small but top-quality English-qualified M&A team in London. Practice head Michael Hatchard is regularly singled out, while John Adebiyi is the firm's other key specialist on English M&A. Highlight deals for the practice included acting for Honeywell International on the $2.4bn acquisition of Novar, and for Westfield group on its bid for Duelguide.

Travers Smith remains one of the most admired players in the mid-market while also boasting a track record advising on multi-billion-pound deals. It remains a key adviser to NTL and, under corporate finance head Spencer Summerfield advised the cable company on the £1.27bn disposal of its broadcast division. The firm's credentials on innovative deals was also confirmed by its role advising Numis and Centaur on the accelerated IPO of Centaur. Oliver Barnes, Chris Hale and Charles Barter are all leading specialists and Phil Sanderson and Richard Skelton command growing deal-making reputations.

Weil, Gotshal & Manges' English M&A practice continues to thrive. A list of high-quality instructions and the breadth of the partner team confirms that the firm's profile continues to grow in the domestic market. Mike Francies remains the undoubted lead performer in the practice but there is a growing band of specialists alongside him. Among them, Ian Hamilton confirmed his credentials in the take private of Warner Chilcott and the turbulent battle for Canary Wharf. Will Rosen also enjoys a growing profile.

Baker & McKenzie LLP's M&A team enjoyed an impressive year. Among a range of deals it picked up the mandate to advise Kidde on its defence of a £1.4bn hostile approach and subsequent recommended offer from UTC. The firm retains a key sector focus fielding teams in the TMT, public companies and industrial and resources, energy, chemicals and pharmaceuticals sectors. Tim Gee and Bernd Ratzke are both recommended by clients and peers alike.

Berwin Leighton Paisner LLP is one of the standout advisers in the mid-market. Andrew Sherratt has added considerable experience on both M&A and capital markets. In one deal of note the firm advised Barchester Healthcare on the £525m purchase of Westminster Health Care. David Collins heads the practice with key support from Keith Stella and Antony Grossman.

Cleary, Gottlieb, Steen & Hamilton LLP's English M&A team comprises partners Andrew Curran and Simon Jay. The practice is regularly instructed on complex, cross-border deals and offers clients access to a top-tier global network. Among the standout deals in 2004, the firm advised LNM Holdings on its $13.3bn disposal to Ispat International to form Mittal Steel. William Groll is the firm's lead US-qualified M&A adviser in London.

Denton Wilde Sapte remains noteworthy for M&A work in its chosen sectors: TMT; energy, transport and infrastructure; financial institutions; and real estate. On the TMT front Virgin Mobile, Nokia and Liberty Media are all key clients while on the finance side the firm has close links with GE, RBS and MBNA. Among a range of deals in the energy sector the firm advised ONGC, the state-owned Indian oil company, on a series of cross-border acquisitions. Philip Goodwin heads the practice and Richard Macklin is also recommended.

Jones Day combines the connections of a global legal giant with the City background of legacy *Gouldens*. While the legacy English firm's connections in the corporate finance mid-market are still extant it is **Jones Day**'s growing track record handling complex multi-jurisdictional deals out of London that impresses most. Department head John Phillips has been among those to benefit and advised Alfa Group and Access Renova on the $1.35bn disposal of a 49.5% interest in Slavneft. Further specialists of note include Simon Allport, Peter Roberts and the up-and-coming Giles Elliott.

Latham & Watkins remains a global heavyweight for M&A. Its City practice is a key component of this worldwide footprint with an English-qualified partner team of considerable strength in depth. Complex cross-border transactions with a significant financing element play particularly to the firm's strengths. Highlight deals included advising the Carlyle Group in its joint acquisition of Dunlop Aerospace Group. Michael Bond, Nigel Campion-Smith, Charles Fuller and Martin Saywell are all respected.

Mayer, Brown, Rowe & Maw LLP offers clients a leading City practice with considerable global coverage. The firm's impressive client list includes ICI, Marconi and Reuters. On the deals front an undoubted highlight was the firm's role advising Danske Bank on its £2bn acquisition of Northern Bank and National Irish Bank. Senior partner and head of department Paul Maher remains the firm's heavyweight corporate specialist with Andrew Copley, Mark Uhrynuk, Stephen Bottomley and Peter Dickinson also recommended.

M&A: SMALLER DEALS

Bird & Bird ✪
Charles Russell
Debevoise & Plimpton LLP ✪
Dewey Ballantine ✪
Faegre & Benson LLP
Field Fisher Waterhouse
Fox Williams
Gibson, Dunn & Crutcher LLP
Kilpatrick Stockton LLP ✪
Kirkland & Ellis International LLP ✪
Kirkpatrick & Lockhart Nicholson Graham LLP
Lewis Silkin ✪
Morrison & Foerster MNP
Reynolds Porter Chamberlain
Speechly Bircham
Wilmer Cutler Pickering Hale and Dorr LLP ✪

Bircham Dyson Bell
Bristows
Collyer-Bristow
Covington & Burling ✪
Dorsey & Whitney ✪
Dundas & Wilson LLP
Finers Stephens Innocent LLP
Howard Kennedy
Maclay Murray & Spens
Manches LLP
Marriott Harrison
Middleton Potts

Continued

M&A: SMALLER DEALS

Jointly led by Chris Barrett and Neil Blundell, **Bird & Bird**'s excellent M&A team was further buoyed by the arrival of cross-border specialist Mark Pinder. BT remains **Bird & Bird**'s biggest client and whilst predominantly focused on TMT transactions, the team is broadening its clientele. **Bird & Bird** recently advised Spanish oil company Disa on its multi-million-euro acquisition of Shell's Spanish fuel business, opposite **Clifford Chance**.

Charles Russell's outstanding team was boosted by the arrival of John Fletcher and the return of Peter Elliott. The firm tallied 34 total deals in the past year and has a rapidly growing client portfolio. **Charles Russell** is more than credible in cross-border deals and advised on a substantial international acquisition in the telecommunications industry, valued at over €150m.

Led by James Kiernan, **Debevoise & Plimpton LLP** recruited English-qualified partner Jeremy Hill. The move brings extensive insurance-related M&A experience into the firm's classy corporate practice. **Debevoise & Plimpton LLP** is impressively advising on the year's largest European LBO, acting for a consortium which includes Merrill Lynch Global Private Equity and Eurazeo, in the pending €3.7bn acquisition of Rexel.

Dewey Ballantine is increasingly focusing on transactions in Central and Eastern Europe and the group comprises an even split of UK- and US-qualified lawyers. Successes include acting for the financial advisers in the €77m Sanofi–Aventis merger and representing Citigroup in Interbrew's acquisition of a South American brewery.

Faegre & Benson LLP has been thriving since its merger. The firm is attracting bigger international clients, and the M&A department boasts an enviable client portfolio, including The Hearst Corporation and its UK subsidiary, The National Magazine Company. Paul Taylor elicits praise.

Clinching major deals for top names in the technology and fashion industries reinforces **Fox Williams**' excellence in M&A. Tina Williams advised the shareholders of long-term client Karen Millen on its £120m sale to Icelandic group Baugur. Williams also acted for *Kirkpatrick & Lockhart LLP* on its merger with *Nicholson Graham & Jones*. Mark Tasker is also recommended.

Gibson, Dunn & Crutcher LLP stands out for its private equity M&A transactions. Judith Shepherd and Kenneth Lamb played pivotal advisory roles to US company Serena Software in its rare share-for-share takeover of UK-based Merant, opposite **Macfarlanes**.

Despite losing two partners **Kilpatrick Stockton LLP** upholds its status in M&A, thanks to its sector specialised focus on TMT and IP-related acquisitions. **Kilpatrick Stockton LLP** counts Jimmy Choo, Premiere Global Services and National Property Solutions amongst its clients. Led by Ken Boehner, the department has top experience in public company acquisitions in the telecommunications sector and wins glowing recommendations from clients.

Rated for its private equity know-how, **Kirkland & Ellis International LLP**'s slick M&A practice handles leveraged buy-outs and multi-jurisdictional transactions predominantly for private equity funds active in Europe. The firm advised Bain Capital on the €1.4b LBO of Brenntag and Interfer. Stuart Mills and Nigel Dunmore standout in the London practice.

Kirkpatrick & Lockhart Nicholson Graham LLP headline deals include advising the investment vehicle of Russian billionaire Alisher Usmanov in his £250m investment in Corus Group, led by Alex Woodfield. Owen Waft is also recommended.

Lewis Silkin appointed Joanne Evans to the helm of its corporate team. The group is renowned for its cutting-edge, media-focused expertise. **Lewis Silkin** advises some of the most innovative names in the media industry, such as Delaney Lund Knox Warren and Partners. Nigel Edwards and associate Sean Ashley led advertising giant Havas on a series of disposals.

Morrison & Foerster MNP's team was joined by James Gubbins, Ed Lukins and Paul Claydon.

Tim Anderson leads **Reynolds Porter Chamberlain**'s superb corporate team which

M&A: SMALLER DEALS Continued

- Arnold & Porter (UK) LLP ✪
- Baker Botts ✪
- Bates Wells & Braithwaite
- Boodle Hatfield
- Campbell Hooper
- Chadbourne & Parke
- Clyde & Co ✪
- Davenport Lyons
- Davies Arnold Cooper
- Dawsons
- Dickson Minto WS
- Farrer & Co
- Fladgate Fielder ✪
- Goodman Derrick
- Halliwells LLP
- Harbottle & Lewis LLP
- Hogan & Hartson ✪
- Holman Fenwick & Willan ✪
- Hunton & Williams
- Ince & Co ✪
- Kemp Little LLP
- Kendall Freeman
- Lane & Partners LLP
- McGrigors London
- Pritchard Englefield
- RadcliffesLeBrasseur
- Rooks Rider
- Rosenblatt Solicitors
- Salans
- Trowers & Hamlins ✪
- Vinson & Elkins R.L.L.P. ✪
- Wallace LLP
- Wedlake Bell
- Withers LLP

Firms are listed A-Z in tiers which are ranked in order of priority

✪ *Indicates firm displays contact details at the end of this chapter.*

boasts top-class expertise in mid-market M&A transactions. Of note, Barry Stimpson advised on the £115m acquisition of a number of offshore property companies on behalf of Hanson Capital Management Group. The team is increasingly active in cross-border transactions.

Jointly led by Michael Lingens and Nick Janmohamed, **Speechly Bircham** has a unique focus on transactions in the private health sector, advising private care home operators on buy-outs. Valued by clients, the M&A team handled one of the largest UK MBOs of 2004, advising long-standing vending and food services client Autobar on its acquisition from the Kuwaiti Investment Office by Charterhouse Development Capital.

Wilmer Cutler Pickering Hale and Dorr LLP's focused London practice acts principally on mid-market deals in the hi-tech and communications market. Five partners are English qualified, and the corporate team is well placed to conduct cross-border transactions across the US, the UK and Europe. David Gent and Robert Bough are commended.

Bircham Dyson Bell's burgeoning M&A unit now acts for a total of 13 AIM-quoted clients, having won Falkland Islands Holdings as a new key client. Of note, Carol Martin advised an AIM-listed client on three simultaneous acquisitions, of an aggregate value of £10.4m.

Bristows' superb M&A team benefits from the firm's market-leading might in IP and technology. The division acts for a vast client portfolio, including entrepreneurial clients and multinationals, such as global marketing group Taylor Nelson Sofres. The group's biggest success of the year was advising Gowrings Plc, one of the largest Burger King franchises, on its recommended public takeover by Caspian, valued at £9.7m.

Establishing its first overseas office in Geneva enabled **Collyer-Bristow** to hone in on a growing international corporate client base. Paul Sillis and newly promoted partner Silvia Fazio merit praise.

Steadily making an impression in the London market, **Covington & Burling** is acquiring a notable European clientele. On the private equity scene, **Covington & Burling** recently advised on the huge acquisition of a private equity funds portfolio in excess of $600m.

M&A transaction specialist Ewan Robertson of **Dundas & Wilson LLP** relocated to London. Known for its energy and utility expertise, **Dundas & Wilson LLP**'s biggest success in the year was advising Scottish and Southern Energy plc on the joint acquisition of national gas distribution networks from National Grid Transco. Valued at £3.2bn, this was one of the largest M&A deals that the firm has yet been involved in.

Finers Stephens Innocent LLP handled three major deals each worth over £50m recently. Of these, advising the shareholders of Tragus Holding in its £100m sale of 157 Bella Italia and Café Rouge restaurants was the group's headline transaction, led by Paul Millett and Brian Slater.

Four new recruits at varying levels of seniority joined **Howard Kennedy**, including former in-house corporate financier from Credo Corporate Finance, Andrew Woolf. Led by Alan Banes, the team's forte is advising on hotels and property-related transactions. Jason Lewis and James Stewart are both praised by clients.

Maclay Murray & Spens merged with *The City Law Partnership* and the corporate department now comprises seven partners.

Christopher Owen heads the corporate department at **Manches LLP**, which reports increased involvement in sizeable cross-border deals in North Europe, the US and Canada. The group is focused on sector-specialised transactions, notably within property and retail, representing Karen Millen, Liberty and Marks & Spencer.

Headed by Jon Sweet, **Marriott Harrison**'s tight-knit corporate team was joined by three new partners, including Jonathan Bor. The group excels in mid-market, domestic deals in the sub-£20m bracket. Simon Vivian wins recommendations from clients.

Middleton Potts clinched at least ten new clients including HSH Nordbank and Nomatica. Led by David Godfrey, the team has a strong European outlook. **Middleton Potts**' client portfolio comprises long-standing Italian, German and French clients, including Europe's third-largest insurer, Assicurazioni Generali Group.

PENSIONS

At **Freshfields Bruckhaus Deringer**, the large pensions team is directed by David Pollard, Ken Dierden and Dan Schaffer. This year the firm focused heavily on several special projects, including for MFI, E.ON and Western Power Distribution. The firm, along with other strong corporate firms, has benefited recently from the increasing importance of pensions issues in corporate transactions. Investment and funding issues are also on the increase, and the team acts for clients Cinven and Morgan Stanley, providing advice on 'moral hazard' provisions. Advice on scheme mergers and restructuring has been provided to BAE Systems 2000 Plan Trustees, IBM and Ofcom.

Linklaters has a very large pensions practice, which benefits from a specialist pensions litigation team. The firm acts for a large number of FTSE 100 company pensions, and has an international presence, particularly in Europe. Although the team benefits from the strength of the firm's corporate practice, the pensions team is a standalone practice, consistently winning new clients such as the GUS group and the United Biscuits Group schemes. The firm has undertaken high-profile work for WH Smith plc, JP Morgan and Marks & Spencer. Ruth Goldman leads the team and Tim Cox has an outstanding reputation.

The highly regarded **Mayer, Brown, Rowe & Maw LLP** pensions practice continues to provide an excellent service. A large team ensures clients receive plenty of partner contact and expert advice. The team is led by Andrew White, who is ably supported by Anna Rogers and Philippa James. The firm acts for National Grid Transco, P&O Pensions Funds Investments Ltd and The BOC Group plc. Recently the team advised the trustees of the Henlys Group pension scheme on restructuring proposals, following the employer going into administration.

Sacker & Partners LLP is a unique boutique pensions firm. Ian Pittaway has taken over as senior partner, and is ably supported by a plethora of talent, including Fiona Franklin, Peter Docking, Jonathan Seres and Paul Phillips. Recently the firm won ten new clients by tender and dealt with a wide range of complex issues, including 'moral hazard' anti-avoidance provisions, funding and deficit challenges, and merger issues. The firm provides an individually customised trustees

PENSIONS

FRESHFIELDS BRUCKHAUS DERINGER
LINKLATERS ✪
MAYER, BROWN, ROWE & MAW LLP
SACKER & PARTNERS LLP ✪

ALLEN & OVERY LLP ✪
BAKER & McKENZIE LLP ✪
CMS CAMERON McKENNA LLP
LOVELLS ✪
PINSENT MASONS ✪
SLAUGHTER AND MAY ✪
TRAVERS SMITH

Clifford Chance
DLA Piper Rudnick Gray Cary UK LLP ✪
Eversheds LLP
Hammonds
Herbert Smith LLP ✪
Macfarlanes ✪
Taylor Wessing ✪
Wragge & Co LLP ✪

Denton Wilde Sapte ✪
Field Fisher Waterhouse
McDermott Will & Emery UK LLP ✪
Nabarro Nathanson
Norton Rose ✪
Richards Butler
Simmons & Simmons ✪

Berwin Leighton Paisner LLP
Jones Day ✪
Lawrence Graham LLP
SJ Berwin LLP ✪
Speechly Bircham
Stephenson Harwood

Firms are listed A-Z in tiers which are ranked in order of priority
✪ Indicates firm displays contact details at the end of this chapter.

training programme. The UK firm is a member of the global employment and pensions alliance *ius laboris*, and its web-site is extremely popular in the pensions world.

Allen & Overy LLP's growing team is led by Derek Sloan. This year the team has handled complex work for the trustees of the T&N Retirement Benefits Scheme, and the ICI Pension Fund. New clients include Macquarie UK Broadcast Ltd, the Trustees of Standex Holdings Pension Scheme and the BCA.

The very experienced Robert West leads the accomplished team at **Baker & McKenzie LLP**. The team has attracted new clients, KONE plc, and Quest plc, among others. The practice provides a full service, but has particular expertise in restructuring schemes, mergers, scheme funding, public sector transfers and multinational transactions.

CMS Cameron McKenna LLP receives regular referrals from the other big players, a sign of its standing in the market. The firm's views on the Pensions Bill 2004 were quoted in Parliament recently, and the team contributed much to the well-received web-based *Plain English Guide to the Pensions Act 2004*. Major work in the past year was for Big Food Group pension fund, Lazard and Parsons Corporation. Nigel Moore heads the team, which includes partners Mark Atkinson and Mark Grant.

Lovells has an excellent pensions practice, led by Russell Strachan and starring partner Jane Samsworth. The team acts for an impressive client list, with recent highlights including pensions advice on the sale of the Automobile Association. It also acted for Equitable Life Assurance Society, Unitised Common Investment Fund, and was instructed to advise the asbestos creditors' committee of Federal Mogul in the T&N Retirement Benefits Scheme.

Chris Mullen leads the team at **Pinsent Masons**, which includes well-known pensions lawyer Robin Ellison. The firm attracts a broad range of clients, such as Bayer Group, Textron, and Wagon plc.

Slaughter and May's pension team boasts Philip Bennett, Charles Cameron and Jonathan Fenn. The firm was involved in the pensions aspects of high-profile corporate transactions, including for Marks & Spencer plc. For Akzo Nobel Uk Ltd the firm advised on benefit changes to reduce its deficit.

Travers Smith's team advised the Akzo Nobel trustees on benefit changes, and the trustees of Deloitte Pension Scheme on its scheme merger. Department head Paul Stannard is supported by fellow partner Peter Esam.

Clifford Chance's highlights include advising on pension scheme wind-ups, restructuring benefits, investment issues, for clients who include Norwich Union, Accenture and HSBC. Clients recommend Nick Sherwin and Imogen Clark.

The **DLA Piper Rudnick Gray Cary UK LLP** pensions practice has a huge national profile, leading the market in regions such as the North West. Yet the London practice is also on the rise, led by Michael Cowley. National department head David Wright is highly regarded by his peers and clients. Partners Jonathan Fenton and Michael Forkin also come highly recommended.

Eversheds LLP has an experienced national team which acts for big-name clients. Recent work includes National Grid Transco, setting up four 'mirror image' schemes, the Electricity Supply's £17bn scheme, and for the Department of Transport. The highly experienced expert Harold Lewis heads the London practice.

Hammonds boasts a 20-strong team in London, led by Jay Doraisamy which collaborates with the firm's national group and its international benefits practice, led by London partner Jane Marshall. With an international perspective, the firm acts for clients such as Vodafone, General Motors and Halliburton.

Ian Gault heads the team at **Herbert Smith LLP**. Major work includes advising the Institute of Actuaries on conflicts of interest, Macquarie Bank on pensions aspects of an acquisition, and Securicor on the pensions aspects of its merger. Clients praise partner Alison Brown, and the firm continues to advise clients such as Time Warner and KPMG.

Team leader Hugh Arthur at **Macfarlanes** is highly regarded. The firm is praised by clients. Recent highlights include working on the Deloitte pension scheme merger.

Taylor Wessing has an experienced team, led by Carolyn Saunders. The firm receives a lot of referrals from other solicitors and barristers and has recently gained Remploy Ltd, Sun Chemical Europe Ltd, and Smas-Groep NV as clients.

Though predominantly Birmingham-based, **Wragge & Co LLP** now has five lawyers based in London. Birmingham-based department head Peter Shave is highly recommended and the firm impresses clients. The team continues to act for THK Ltd and Shell International Ltd, and has added Baird Group, Philips Pension Fund, and Equity to its client list.

The **Denton Wilde Sapte** team is led by partner Alan Jarvis, and continues to act for two of the largest pension funds in the UK: J Sainsbury and The Royal Bank of Scotland. The firm has worked on a wide range of issues, including advising the administrators of Federal-Mogul UK/T&N Ltd, Mayflower plc, and acting for DuPont and Fuji in relation to the winding-up of the Crosfield Pension Fund.

Field Fisher Waterhouse has gained many new clients confirming it as a major player in the pensions market. The firm has a reputation for regulatory work, and an increased focus on the public sector, providing advice to the Foreign & Commonwealth Office and the Home Office. Belinda Benney leads the team.

McDermott Will & Emery UK LLP provides a truly international service, with clients including Land Securities Plc, Dresdner Kleinwort Wasserstein and Mizuho Corporate Bank. Recent highlights include the highly pressured pension plan mergers carried out for Tyco International, and the complex pensions-led restructuring for Aker Kvaerner.

Nabarro Nathanson has brought in Carol Jones and Ian Greenstreet to fill the void caused by Mario Conti's retirement. The practice is trustee focused, and has a strong public sector focus. Complex, innovative work was completed this year for IBM trustees.

Peter Ford and Lesley Browning lead the expanding team at **Norton Rose** which regularly acts on the pensions issues on corporate transactions. New clients won include RMC, Colgate-Palmolive, and SG UK Ltd, acting for the trustees of the pension schemes in each case.

Simon Hartley and consultant Keith Wallace at **Richards Butler** provide a full range of pension law expertise, but with a clear focus on trustee advice. Currently the firm's major work is for the trustees of the Civil Aviation Authority Pension Scheme, and the trustee of the HHG Staff Pension Scheme, as well as establishing the Henderson Group Pension Scheme.

Simmons & Simmons had a busy year. Led by Michael Wyman, the firm advised the trustees of the SmithKline Beecham Common Investment Fund on its merger into the Glaxo Common Investment Fund. The team also provided pensions advice to Collins Stewart, and Channel House Trustees Limited, in both instances taking advantage of the firm's international capabilities.

PRIVATE EQUITY

Ashurst acts for more than 30 major private equity firms, and added to that list with first instructions from Terra Firma Capital Partners, Blackstone Group and Lazard European Equity Partners. The team is led by Charlie Geffen. Also recommended are partners Simon Beddow, Bruce Hanton and Graeme Ward.

The biggest leveraged buyout recently was Permira and CVC's acquisition of the AA for £1.7bn, on which **Clifford Chance** partners James Baird and Simon Tinkler advised. Three other partners also spend 100% of their time in private equity: Matthew Layton, new partner Ian Bagshaw and David Walker.

Freshfields Bruckhaus Deringer has significantly increased its profile in this market, with 12 partners in London charged by leader Christopher Bown with targeting a broad range of clients. The practice joined the Apax panel and attracted new clients Allianz Capital Partners, Fox Paine, KKR, Thomas H Lee and Bain Capital to a list that already included Cinven, Goldman Sachs and Warburg Pincus.

At **Linklaters**, partners Graham White and Raymond McKeeve act for Candover, JP Morgan Partners, CVC, Graphite Capital and Montagu Private Equity.

Lovells' major clients include Advent International, Hg Capital, Terra Firma, Doughty Hanson and Charterhouse, which it advised on its £535m buyout of Autobar last year. Partners Marco Compagnoni and Derek Baird are recommended.

Macfarlanes and **Travers Smith** advise on UK mid-market buyouts, though both occasionally 'punch above their weight' on bigger deals.

Macfarlanes has been busy for key client Alchemy, which it advised on both its £775m disposal of Four Seasons Healthcare to Allianz and its £313m buyout of Swift Advances, plus five other deals.

Travers Smith's team advises Bridgepoint Capital, Phoenix Equity Partners, 3i and Exponent Private Equity. Partner Chris Hale is praised.

At **Dickson Minto WS**, partner Alastair Dickson is recommended. He advised

PRIVATE EQUITY Buy-outs

ASHURST ✪
CLIFFORD CHANCE

FRESHFIELDS BRUCKHAUS DERINGER
LINKLATERS ✪
LOVELLS ✪
MACFARLANES ✪
TRAVERS SMITH

Dickson Minto WS
SJ Berwin LLP ✪
Weil, Gotshal & Manges ✪

Allen & Overy LLP ✪
CMS Cameron McKenna LLP
DLA Piper Rudnick Gray Cary UK LLP ✪
Latham & Watkins
Olswang
Slaughter and May ✪
Taylor Wessing ✪

Cleary, Gottlieb, Steen & Hamilton LLP ✪
Debevoise & Plimpton LLP ✪
Kirkland & Ellis International LLP ✪
O'Melveny & Myers LLP ✪
Skadden, Arps, Slate, Meagher & Flom (UK) LLP

Addleshaw Goddard
Baker & McKenzie LLP ✪
Berwin Leighton Paisner LLP
Eversheds LLP
Herbert Smith LLP ✪
McDermott Will & Emery UK LLP ✪
Osborne Clarke
Pinsent Masons ✪
White & Case ✪
Wragge & Co LLP ✪

Firms are listed A-Z in tiers which are ranked in order of priority
✪ Indicates firm displays contact details at the end of this chapter.

Charterhouse on the £1.35bn buyout of Saga, one of only two UK deals that exceeded £1bn last year.

SJ Berwin LLP remains best known for its funds practice, but recently advised on 70 disclosable deals worth a total of £11.3bn. The firm won Hicks Muse Europe as a buyout client, advising on its £101m acquisition of Jimmy Choo.

The London office of **Weil, Gotshal & Manges** was boosted by the arrival of Mark Soundy to work alongside frenetic deal-doer Mike Francies. The office advised on 28 deals with a total value of more than €30bn, for clients including Advent International, Apax, Blackstone, Change Capital and Hicks Muse.

Allen & Overy LLP acts for clients including Nikko Principal Investments, Charterhouse, Electra and PAI Partners. Partner Alison is highly commended.

CMS Cameron McKenna LLP partner Andrew Sheach advises Global Innovation Partners, Legal & General Ventures, ABN Amro Capital and Advent International.

PRIVATE EQUITY Funds

SJ BERWIN LLP ✪

CLIFFORD CHANCE

Ashurst ✪
Macfarlanes ✪

Debevoise & Plimpton LLP ✪
Linklaters ✪
O'Melveny & Myers LLP ✪

Allen & Overy LLP ✪
Freshfields Bruckhaus Deringer
Travers Smith

Firms are listed A-Z in tiers which are ranked in order of priority
✪ Indicates firm displays contact details at the end of this chapter.

At **DLA Piper Rudnick Gray Cary UK LLP**, partner Andrew Holt has relocated to London to head the team, and Andrew Harris has joined the firm. New clients include Englefield Capital, Granville Baird and Blackstone.

Latham & Watkins in London, led by Michael Bond and Charles Fuller, advises Carlyle, Charterhouse, Indigo Partners and Providence Equity Partners.

Olswang partners Fabrizio Carpanini and Chris Mackie last year advised on 29 deals totalling £650m in value, and won Blackstone as a client on its £130m acquisition of Cine-UK.

Slaughter and May advised on 50 private equity transactions recently, compared to 30 the year before, and strengthened relationships with Permira, Goldman Sachs, Palomon Capital and Francisco Partners.

Taylor Wessing partner Martin Winter is popular with clients including Legal & General Ventures.

We also draw attention to five US firms whose London offices include English-qualified private equity practitioners and boast strong US client bases.

At **Cleary, Gottlieb, Steen & Hamilton LLP**, UK-qualified partners Andrew Curran and Simon Jay advise Texas Pacific Group.

Debevoise & Plimpton LLP's English partner Colin Bogie works on deals for Clayton, Dubilier & Rice and Oaktree Capital Partners.

The UK partners of **Kirkland & Ellis International LLP** act for Bain Capital, Change Capital Partners, and CapVest.

O'Melveny & Myers LLP significantly enhanced its London buyout capability last year with the hire of Matthew Hudson from Coller Capital, and Andrew Carpenter. They act for Apollo and JP Morgan Partners.

Skadden, Arps, Slate, Meagher & Flom (UK) LLP UK partner Allan Murray-Jones acts for Doughty Hanson, and advised them on three major acquisitions.

Addleshaw Goddard's UK-wide practice is run by Sean Lippell while **Baker & McKenzie LLP**'s

London partner Charles Whitefoord shows 'enormous commitment' on deals.

Berwin Leighton Paisner LLP has added Daljit Singh to lead the group. **Eversheds LLP**'s team is led by Mark Spinner and was last year appointed to act for Royal London Private Equity and Montagu. **Herbert Smith LLP** now advises Blackstone Group, Cabot Square Capital, TDR Capital and Ripplewood Holdings.

McDermott Will & Emery UK LLP's William Charnley advised Aldersgate Investments as a member of the consortium on the £896m acquisition of Duelguide.

Osborne Clarke's London private equity partners are Roma Linton and Julian Gamble. **Pinsent Masons** acts for ISIS Equity Partners and Bridgepoint Capital.

White & Case partner Alan Greenough advises Nikko Principal Investments, NGBI Private Equity, Royal London Private Equity and Montagu Private Equity.

Wragge & Co LLP's London partners Maurice Dwyer and Andy Stylianou are also recommended.

PROJECT FINANCE

For sheer breadth and depth, **Allen & Overy LLP**'s project finance practice is second to none. Under the unrivalled leadership of Graham Vinter, the team ticks every possible sector box, acting for both sponsors and lenders, be it in oil, gas, petrochemicals, power, natural resources or infrastructure. Key projects include advising Qalhat LNG on the building of a third liquefaction train for its Qalhat LNG project. In the power sector it advised JBIC and the commercial lenders on the $2bn Taweelah B IWPP in Abu Dhabi. The group boasts an array of heavy-hitting partners including Timothy Arnheim, Andrew Castle, Anne Baldock and Gareth Price.

Clifford Chance's first-class London-based project finance team, headed by Peter Blake, works hand-in-hand with the firm's unrivalled global practice, which is led by Rodney Short. The firm advises across the full range of sectors for a healthy mix of sponsor and lender clients. Major instructions include advising International Power and Saudi Oger on the 1075MW Saudi Aramco natural gas fired captive co-generation plant in Saudi Arabia. The group also advised IPM Eagle on its innovative $2bn acquisition of Edison Mission Energy's portfolio of ten power generation projects.

Linklaters' top-notch global projects group underwent changes recently when Bruce White replaced Alan Black as practice head. The presence of global energy head Stuart Salt will also be missed in London, following his move to the firm's Hong Kong office. The practice as a whole continues to work at the cutting edge of the market, as demonstrated when it advised Deutsche Bank on the unique securitisation of receivables from four Portuguese road PPP construction contracts. On the oil and gas side, continuing work for sponsors on the epic Sakhalin II project in Russia shows how the group has the capacity to work on the very largest, most complex projects on offer. Clive Ransome is recommended

Few can dispute the quality of **White & Case**'s practice, which is headed by Philip Stopford, one of the UK's best-known project finance lawyers. The firm recently advised the sponsor on the $11.2bn Qatargas II project, and has since been instructed by the sponsors to work on the even larger Qatargas III, which will ship gas to the US. As well as advising lenders on Sakhalin II, it is acting for the project sponsors on the $1.9bn Sohar aluminium smelter project in Oman. Craig Nethercott, Peter Finlay, Jason Kerr and Doug Peel are all highly recommended.

Nick Bliss and Kent Rowey jointly head **Freshfields Bruckhaus Deringer**'s quality project finance team. 2004 was another capital year for the firm, which advised seven export credit agencies on the massive $3.6bn Baku-Tbilisi-Ceyhan (BTC) pipeline project, which finally completed in February of that year. Other key deals include advising the sponsors on the €360m Zagreb-Macelj toll motorway project in Croatia.

Milbank, Tweed, Hadley & McCloy LLP should be one of the very first choices for international power and oil and gas projects. Headed by Phillip Fletcher, one of the market's best-known practitioners, the group has acted on a high volume of major projects. Recent highlights include advising the lenders on the $1.2bn financing of OPIC's NGL II natural gas liquids project in Nigeria. In the power sector, the group advised El Ezzel Power Company on the $495m financing of Bahrain's first IPP, in Manama. Highly rated partners Cathy Marsh and John Dewar are both very active in the area.

Norton Rose's project finance team is headed by Jeffery Barratt and receives excellent feedback from its clients. The firm handles a range of energy, power, natural resources and infrastructure projects, and recently advised the sponsors on the Taweelah B IWPP in Abu Dhabi. Martin McCann is recommended, as are Jon Ellis, Chris Brown and Simon Currie. John Inglis is singled out.

Under Nick Buckworth 's guidance, **Shearman & Sterling (London) LLP** maintains its superb reputation for project finance work. It advised the consortium of lenders on the financing of IPM Eagle's purchase of ten power projects from Edison Mission Energy. The group is best known for its oil, gas and power work, especially in the Middle East, but is also strengthening its domestic infrastructure capabilities, as demonstrated by the recruitment of rail expert John Ellard as of-counsel from **Linklaters**. Partner Kenneth MacRitchie also enjoys an excellent reputation.

Herbert Smith LLP's 'very high standard' projects team is comfortable in a wide range of areas, and is becoming increasingly popular with lender clients. The firm advised Sumitomo Chemical on its $4.5bn project to redevelop the Rabigh refinery and petrochemical complex in Saudi Arabia. The team has also become key legal adviser to the London Underground on all its existing and future projects. Infrastructure guru Nick Tott jointly heads the team with energy expert Paul Griffin. Finance head Jason Fox is also highly recommended.

Latham & Watkins' top-quality projects group moves up a tier on the back of its excellent

PROJECT FINANCE

ALLEN & OVERY LLP ✪
CLIFFORD CHANCE
LINKLATERS ✪
WHITE & CASE ✪

FRESHFIELDS BRUCKHAUS DERINGER
MILBANK, TWEED, HADLEY & McCLOY LLP ✪
NORTON ROSE ✪
SHEARMAN & STERLING (LONDON) LLP

HERBERT SMITH LLP ✪
LATHAM & WATKINS
LOVELLS ✪
SLAUGHTER AND MAY ✪

Ashurst ✪
Baker & McKenzie LLP ✪
CMS Cameron McKenna LLP
LeBoeuf, Lamb, Greene & MacRae ✪

Berwin Leighton Paisner LLP
Chadbourne & Parke
Denton Wilde Sapte ✪
Dewey Ballantine ✪
Pinsent Masons ✪
Simmons & Simmons ✪
Skadden, Arps, Slate, Meagher & Flom (UK) LLP
Sullivan & Cromwell LLP
Trowers & Hamlins ✪

Cadwalader, Wickersham & Taft LLP ✪
Clyde & Co ✪
DLA Piper Rudnick Gray Cary UK LLP ✪
Debevoise & Plimpton LLP ✪
Gibson, Dunn & Crutcher LLP
Hogan & Hartson ✪
Mayer, Brown, Rowe & Maw LLP
McDermott Will & Emery UK LLP ✪
Ogilvy Renault LLP
Taylor Wessing ✪
Vinson & Elkins R.L.L.P. ✪
Watson, Farley & Williams LLP

Firms are listed A-Z in tiers which are ranked in order of priority
✪ *Indicates firm displays contact details at the end of this chapter.*

reputation and experience. Headed by Joseph Blum, the firm advised ABN AMRO and Lehman Brothers on the $4.4bn financing of Tengizchevroil's massive upstream oil field project in Kazakhstan. David Miles and Dennis Nordstrom both enjoy excellent reputations.

Few can rival **Lovells** for its expertise in infrastructure projects. The firm's experience was recognised when it was instructed by Galileo Joint Undertaking to act on its massive €3.3bn satellite project, which will be the basis for Europe's very own satellite navigation system. Other highlights include advising the Brisa consortium on the €795m Litoral Centro road project in Portugal. The group is also comfortable at the cutting edge of the secondary market, and advised Tube Lines on the complex refinancing of its London Underground PPP. Gavin McQuater heads the team, which includes several star names including Mike Matheou, Jason Radford, Charles Robson and Shibeer Ahmed.

Slaughter and May boasts an excellent projects practice headed by Christopher Saunders. Unsurprisingly the firm advises numerous blue chips on the sponsor side, including Shell and Alcatel, as well as Arsenal on the £357m financing of its new football stadium. On the lender side it can also match its largest rivals, acting for the European Investment Bank on two Irish road projects. Helen Griffiths and Steven Galbraith are both highly recommended by clients.

Headed by Mark Elsey, **Ashurst**'s impressive projects team has experience across a broad range of sectors. Recent highlights include advising Petrochemical Industries Company on the highly structured $2.5bn expansion of its Equate petrochemicals project in Kuwait. Huw Thomas and Nick Avery are both recommended.

On top of its highly rated projects work in the oil and gas sector, **Baker & McKenzie LLP** is fast developing a strong reputation for infrastructure work, particularly in Eastern Europe. Recently the firm advised Autostrada Wielkopolska on Phase II of the A2 toll motorway in Poland. Group heads Mike Webster Annie Williams, and partner Neil Donoghue are all recommended.

CMS Cameron McKenna LLP continues to be first choice for major rail projects. The practice is very strong on the lender side and advised Sumitomo Mitsui Banking Corporation on the funding of the Chiltern Railways London to Birmingham line. The group, which is headed by the esteemed Andrew Ivison, is also recommended for power projects.

LeBoeuf, Lamb, Greene & MacRae's project finance team operates across Africa, the CIS and Europe. The firm advised ExxonMobil on the $4.4bn financing of the TengizChevroil oil field project in Kazakhstan. In Europe the group acted for Hochtief and Dragados on the £800m submerged tunnel project in Thessaloniki, Greece. Bruce Johnston heads the top-notch practice.

REAL ESTATE

BERWIN LEIGHTON PAISNER LLP
CLIFFORD CHANCE
LOVELLS ✪

FRESHFIELDS BRUCKHAUS DERINGER
HERBERT SMITH LLP ✪
LINKLATERS ✪
NABARRO NATHANSON
SJ BERWIN LLP ✪

Allen & Overy LLP ✪
Ashurst ✪
DLA Piper Rudnick Gray Cary UK LLP ✪
Dechert LLP
Denton Wilde Sapte ✪
Eversheds LLP
Jones Day ✪
Lawrence Graham LLP
Macfarlanes ✪
Taylor Wessing ✪
Wragge & Co LLP ✪

Addleshaw Goddard
CMS Cameron McKenna LLP
Field Fisher Waterhouse
Mayer, Brown, Rowe & Maw LLP
Norton Rose ✪
Olswang
Richards Butler
Simmons & Simmons ✪
Slaughter and May ✪
Stephenson Harwood

Fladgate Fielder ✪
Forsters LLP
Hammonds
Howard Kennedy
Kirkpatrick & Lockhart Nicholson Graham LLP
Lewis Silkin ✪
Maples Teesdale
Mishcon de Reya
Osborne Clarke
Pinsent Masons ✪
Speechly Bircham
Travers Smith
Trowers & Hamlins ✪

Continued

REAL ESTATE

Berwin Leighton Paisner LLP is arguably the most ambitious firm in the real estate market. The hire of Robert MacGregor to head the department should herald a more international approach, along with a new relationship with German firm **Beiten Burkhardt**. The firm's commitment to the sector is reflected in strength and experience in all areas. David Battiscombe 's arrival beefs up the development and regeneration side, bringing client Beetham to the firm. His added experience in the hotels sector offsets the departure of former department head Daniel Braham. Partner Catherine Cook brings experience on the corporate side. Claire Milton is another extremely impressive figure. Tesco remains a key client, with instructions including various site acquisitions and redevelopments. Other regeneration mandates were Paradise Street in Liverpool, Wood Wharf and Victoria Square, Belfast. Strategic thinking, attention to detail, project management and resourcing are identified by clients as areas of strength.

The select property practice at **Clifford Chance** welcomed back Iain Morpeth from sabbatical to further bolster an already impressive team. New clients include Shangri-La Hotels, which was advised on the lease of 18 floors of the 'Shard of Glass' building, and Legal & General. Of note is the firm's development capability in Jonathan Soloman and Tony Briam, showcased advising Hammerson and the Corporation of London on the Shoreditch and Spitalfields redevelopment. The firm also excels in securitisation work, having advised Land Securities and RBS on such matters, as well as the securitised bond issue secured on a Tesco sale and leaseback portfolio transaction.

Lovells combines excellent penetration of the market, outstanding individuals and a dynamic business focus to ensure a top spot. The firm's expertise in property outsourcing has seen it score key instructions in recent years, including of late from Barclays Bank. The Mexican Wave has seen it remarkably active, notching up its 3,000th mandate, in a buoyant retail sector through the Prudential's activities. The firm has a knack for some innovative deals including its sale of a 50% interest in Bluewater Shopping Centre worth £1bn. Other matters of note included advising Slough Estates on a 'land swap' of 23 industrial estates with Land Securities, and the BBC's recquisition of its White City Estate. On the funds side, the firm enjoys a good relationship with Henderson. Department head Robert Kidby is enormously popular with clients, as is Michael Stancombe.

The sheer diversity of deals handled by **Freshfields Bruckhaus Deringer** is perhaps the department's most impressive statistic. It scored heavily from its longstanding relationship with Scottish Widows, advising on nine-figure acquisitions and disposals as well as a £211.4m investment in the Thornfield Redditch Limited Partnership. New client WestInvest was advised on a £44m City investment, while P&O was advised on the sale of Immogolf SA, the holding company of La Manga Club. The firm has showcased its pan-European capability before in Deutsche Bank's portfolio sale and leaseback, and did so again in 2004 with various international transactions. On the retail side the firm advised CVC Capital Partners on the Debenhams' refinancing before overseeing a sale and leaseback PropCo/OpCo structure for Debenhams. Land Securities Trillium was advised on the outsourcing of the DWP Employment Services Estate.

Herbert Smith LLP continues to impress at all levels. In development, the firm advises Southwark Borough Council on the £1.5bn regeneration of Elephant & Castle. Standard Life, one of the largest real estate investors in 2004, was a key client, instructing the firm on deals with an aggregate value of £800m during the year. James Barnes heads a department packed with talent, including Chris de Pury, Neil Warriner and Jeremy Walden which has attracted a client list to die for, including Helical Bar, AMEC, Minerva, British Land and House of Fraser.

At the top end of the market, there are few better operations than at **Linklaters**. A commendable front-end construction practice has contributed to the firm's reputation in development, receiving instructions from British Land on the proposed tower at 122 Leadenhall Street. Patrick Plant 's team boasts expertise across the sector despite a streamlining of numbers over the past few years. Areas of particular strength are on the financing and development sides, providing a bespoke service for high-value, highly complex projects such as the pre-let at ALP's Spinningfields scheme.

Nabarro Nathanson can safely be regarded as one of the pre-eminent operators in the field, with outstanding expertise and experience in development and investment. The firm recently acted on shopping centre transactions valued at over £3bn. The Mall, among others, instructed the firm on several high-value acquisitions during the year. Clients such as Threadneedle, Hammerson and Land Securities give an indication of how highly the firm is regarded in the industry, while the firm's large team allows it to multi-task effectively. A full-service provider, the firm showed versatility in advising Land Securities on the due diligence exercise of £6.2bn worth of refinancing work, and the £700m assets swap with Slough Estates. Graham Lust and John Cumpson have been particularly active on various mandates. Nick Collins heads a team which has a longstanding real estate presence.

SJ Berwin LLP has had a superb year. The *Legal Business* Real Estate Team of the Year was notably busy towards the end of the year when Jon Vivian advised on almost £2bn worth of deals including Brixton plc's £675m acquisition of Industrious Holdings Limited, and a subsequent disposal worth £250m, as well as other noteworthy transactions for Delancey and Prestbury. Bryan Pickup heads a practice that scored highly with instructions from the other sides of transactions, and consistent high levels of service ensure a longstanding client base which includes British Land and The Crown Estate. The loss of Sally Pinkerton failed to slow the firm's momentum.

Allen & Overy LLP made huge progress in the funds market, recruiting the superb Robert Porter and his team, and securing new instructions from Tishman Speyer, Quinlan and Brixton plc on high-value acquisitions, and JP Morgan and Prudential on pan-European fund structuring. There are few firms in the market with financial expertise on a level with the firm, giving it a market-leading position on complex, tax-driven structures. On the development side, the firm picked up work from Lend Lease. Adam Cleal heads a very impressive outfit. Hotels and leisure continues to be a strong area, with the acquisition of the Savoy Group for Quinlan among deals valued at €8.45bn (£5.8bn) during the year, a higher figure than any other firm, and a reflection of the diversity of the client base, which encompasses lenders and investors.

Ashurst has a profitable relationship with Cinven. A strong development practice advised BT in relation to a 2,000 acre regeneration project in the Midlands; Sheffield University on its residential accommodation programme; and Bristol City Council on a huge retail-led project. A strong relationship with Canary Wharf Group led to instructions on the letting of new headquarters to Reuters. David Evans is active in structuring opportunity funds, including the EHI Fund which is geared towards investment across Europe and has utilised the firm's significant European network.

DLA Piper Rudnick Gray Cary UK LLP is spreading its wings internationally, with more real estate lawyers than any other firm around the world, and the London office is an increasingly successful fulcrum. The entrepreneurial approach of new group head David Taylor has seen the arrival of the revered Howard Bassford, which more than addresses a previous shortfall in planning, while junior recruitments have been geared towards building a funds practice. New clients AMEC and Ropemaker Properties Limited have engaged the firm on significant redevelopment projects. Philip Perry advised Blackstone on the sale of the Savoy Group for £750m in one of the highlight deals of the year. A regional network of high repute allows the firm to serve national clients with a flexible cost structure and a consistency of service. Richard Parker is commended.

Ciaran Carvalho heads the department at **Dechert LLP** and has been involved in major retail and leisure schemes at White City and Merry Hill. Clients such as GMAC, Land Securities and ING Real Estate keep the firm active in the acquisitions market, while the firm boasts a strong presence among retail occupiers. AXA REIM was advised on several purchases around Europe. On the development side, Helical Retail was advised on the acquisition and pre-letting of a mixed-use scheme in Nottingham. The firm was also appointed by Kroll as administrators of Allders to handle the real estate assets of the retailer. Patrick Gloyens remains a key figure.

Denton Wilde Sapte was notably active in the development field during the past year, advising both local authorities and developers on schemes including the huge mixed-use regeneration scheme of Feltham Town Centre, in which it is advising Thornfield plc. Other major projects are located in Surrey, the North East and across the country for Sainsbury's. London and Regional Properties plc was advised on the acquisition and leaseback of three hotels based around Europe from Accor, while closer to home Reuters was advised on its office move to Canary Wharf. The firm retained its place on the English Partnerships panel, a significant success which is generating work in Milton Keynes and the East Midlands.

Genuine excellence across the regions at **Eversheds LLP** is a major aspect of the firm's real estate offering, but the London office is carving a reputation for itself for work at the very top of the market. William Naunton won Equitable Life as a new client, which is advised alongside other life

REAL ESTATE Continued

Baker & McKenzie LLP ✪
Bircham Dyson Bell
Boodle Hatfield
Campbell Hooper
Charles Russell
Clyde & Co ✪
Davenport Lyons
Davies Arnold Cooper
Dundas & Wilson LLP
Finers Stephens Innocent LLP
Gibson, Dunn & Crutcher LLP
Halliwells LLP
Manches LLP
Maxwell Batley
McGrigors London
Paul, Hastings, Janofsky & Walker (Europe) LLP ✪
Penningtons Solicitors LLP
RadcliffesLeBrasseur
Wedlake Bell
White & Case ✪

Beachcroft Wansbroughs
Beauchamps
Bevan Brittan LLP
Bristows
Collyer-Bristow
Dawsons
Kingsley Napley
Maclay Murray & Spens
Morgan Cole
Payne Hicks Beach
Reed Smith ✪
Reynolds Porter Chamberlain
Russell-Cooke
Tarlo Lyons
Thomas Eggar
Wallace LLP
Weil, Gotshal & Manges ✪

Continued

funds Henderson and Legal & General, while Bruce Dear advised on over £1bn of shopping centre portfolio deals in 2004, a showcase for the national network. The firm is also now on the panel for English Partnerships, with a focus on London. US company Sunrise Senior Living is being advised on the proposed development of 25 care homes. The firm's celebrated planning team advised the LDA on the London 2012 Olympic bid, which included the acquisition of the site. The arrival of Oliver Emanuel is yet another boost to a team growing in stature and numbers.

Jones Day remains commendably active despite the departure of former head of finance Tom Budd. David Roberts' team has access to US funds such as Highcross, while UK funds such as Hercules Unit Trust and Arlington Business Parks Partnership are also clients. The firm showed well in the transactional market, with the sale of a £132.7m portfolio for Ashtenne Holdings a particular highlight.

Lawrence Graham LLP is a fixture in the upper echelons of the property market. Among new clients was Multiplex, which instructed the firm on a proposed £3bn regeneration project in Cricklewood. Longstanding client Legal & General continues to instruct the firm on major transactions. Retail was a major area, with Sainsbury's again providing a significant part of the firm's work, including a mixed-use village scheme and the disposal of nine development projects for J Sainsbury Developments Ltd. David Hayward is known in the market for sensible, pragmatic thinking.

Macfarlanes improves year on year. Retail clients such as Comet, Harvey Nichols and J Sainsbury Plc were all advised during the past year. Alongside development funding for AXA REIM, More London, Carillion Richardson Partnership and ING Real Estate Developments, an area in which Chris Field excels, the firm broke into the lucrative casino field with first instructions from Caesars Entertainment. On the funds side Pinder, Fry & Benjamin, Dunedin Property and Legal & General Industrial Property were active clients. The huge private client base engages the firm's top-notch residential and leasehold enfranchisement practice. David Sanders is noted for exceptional performance on complex matters, while the firm is universally praised for its commercial approach.

Taylor Wessing impresses across the board. The firm advised Prestbury in a joint venture acquisition and leaseback of the Spirit pub portfolio, an endorsement of the firm's strength in leisure and finance, and Canada Life on sales and acquisitions across the country. Keith Barnett 's practice advised Stannifer Developments on the development and letting of its town centre scheme in High Wycombe. A major car manufacturer instructs the firm on the acquisition of property and development of purpose-built dealerships. The firm's hotel practice is another important element, linking up with the German arms of the practice in some development work across Europe; Marriott is a key client. On the investment side, the firm is active with clients such as Merrill Lynch and Derwent Valley Holdings. Adam Marks heads a distinguished team.

The arrival of the dynamic Sally Pinkerton at **Wragge & Co LLP** is key to the firm establishing a top-notch London practice to accompany the outstanding Birmingham office, especially following the retirement of Gerald Bland from the partnership, though he remains as a consultant. Peter Thorne has relocated to London to head the team. The launch of a regeneration team paid immediate dividends with its appointment by Sanctuary Housing Association on a seven-year development programme, and various London schemes including work in connection with the London 2012 Olympics bid for Greater London Authority. A solid year for the hotels teams saw instructions from Atlantic Hotels Limited on a refinancing mandate, while on the leisure side, the firm advised Nomura on its £245m joint venture acquisition of Earls Court. The investment practice is endorsed by clients such as Schroders and LaSalle UK Commercial Property Fund.

REAL ESTATE Continued

Barlow Lyde & Gilbert
Bates Wells & Braithwaite
Bird & Bird ✪
Bowling & Co.
Faegre & Benson LLP
Farrer & Co
Fox Williams
Glovers
Hamlins
Hempsons
KSB Law LLP
Laytons
Middleton Potts
Pemberton Greenish
Pritchard Englefield
Rooks Rider
Rosling King
Steptoe & Johnson ✪

Dorsey & Whitney ✪
Goodman Derrick
Harbottle & Lewis LLP
Kilpatrick Stockton LLP ✪
Latham & Watkins
Lee & Pembertons
Rochman Landau
Rosenblatt Solicitors
Russell Jones & Walker
Salans
Shearman & Sterling (London) LLP
Stepien Lake Gilbert & Paling
Withers LLP

Firms are listed A-Z in tiers which are ranked in order of priority
✪ Indicates firm displays contact details at the end of this chapter.

Addleshaw Goddard's real estate offering goes from strength to strength. Although headed from the Leeds office by Michael Reevey, the London practice showed an increasing presence in the market with the appointment to the English Partnerships panel for the South, a strategically significant appointment in line with the firm's focus on development and urban regeneration. The firm also boasts a number of retail occupier clients, and advised Travelodge on a major sale and leaseback recently.

CMS Cameron McKenna LLP boasts a huge property manager and developer client base, with a healthy level of indirect investment driving the practice. Taylor Woodrow continues to be the firm's biggest client, with the sale of St Katharine's Estate and adjoining property for £283.3m a typically high-profile mandate. In development, the firm advised Crest Nicholson on the £300m mixed-use redevelopment of Bristol Harbourside. The arrival of Daniel Braham takes the Hotels group to another level, while the firm's unmatched real estate expertise in central and eastern Europe means it is in pole position to take advantage of the potential investment hotspot.

Field Fisher Waterhouse built on a terrific existing practice with three high-profile recruits in construction, property litigation and property finance, and with three significant client gains in GE Capital, BP Group and Deutsche Asset Management. Whitbread Group plc remains a key client, engaging the firm on the sale of the Marriott chain to Marriott International for over £1bn, as well as other portfolio disposals. Leisure and retail clients cross over, with David Lloyd Leisure and House of Fraser instructing the firm. Edward Bannister is praised.

Mayer, Brown, Rowe & Maw LLP took first instructions from GE Capital Real Estate last year, adding to a list of active clients which already includes St Modwen and Quintain. A major highlight was the development and forward sale of Unilever's London headquarters to SloaneCap, a complex and worthy deal for a team which is on the up. Backed by a superb property finance practice, and with increasing penetration in the German market, Jeremy Clay 's team, including the excellent Peter Sugden, goes from strength to strength.

Norton Rose boasts one of the top all-round real estate lawyers in the market in Robin Mitchell, whose work on the £1.3bn forward funding of the White City retail centre for CGI was one of the most impressive deals of the year. The practice is heavily ingrained in development work, with other projects including the regeneration of London Gateway in Thurrock, Essex, while housebuilders Persimmon Plc are also new clients to the firm.

Olswang beefed up its property finance capability with two lateral partner hires, adding another string to its impressive bow. UBS was advised on £350m worth of acquisitions, while key client Prestbury was advised on the £268m portfolio sale to Hermes. Delancey is another top-end client, and first instructions from Paddington Development Corporation Limited on two sales indicate the firm's prestige.

Richards Butler has an array of Middle Eastern investment and banking clients which provide the firm with considerable instructions, and the io Group has been particularly active for the firm in 2004, with portfolio sales of warehouse and development sites, acquisitions for The Industrial Investment Partnership, managed by the io Group. Oppenheim Immobilien is proving a profitable client, being advised on the purchase of several properties around the UK. On the development side, few projects enjoy as high a profile as Battersea Power Station, while retail management and development remains an area of strength. On the leisure side, Mecca Bingo and Grosvenor Casinos were advised on new premises. Graham Reid and Mark Hargreaves stand out in the team.

Simmons & Simmons scored a notable coup in securing instructions from ING Real Estate Investment Management, advising on the acquisition of a £380m shopping centre portfolio for a new fund. Overseas investors continue to furnish the firm with quality instructions, including several disposals in London during the year, particularly for funds managed by established client Henderson. Alan Butler is the stand-out figure. The Ministry of Defence remains a key client, with property aspects of PFI/PPP projects accounting for much of the firm's work.

Slaughter and May has been notably active in the leisure sector, advising Spirit Group on the sale of Premier Lodge to Whitbread for over £536m and the sale and leaseback by the same client of 220 pubs to Prestbury. The firm also advised Punch Taverns on major sale and acquisition mandates. In development financing, major redevelopments such as White City for London Underground and Paradise Street, Liverpool for Grosvenor, continue to keep the firm at the top of the market. On the retail side, House of Fraser is a high-profile client. Graham White heads the team.

Stephenson Harwood is becoming increasingly noticeable in the market. The firm was appointed by new joint venture HelioSlough on the purchase of a development site ahead of more established rivals, while St Martins Property Group was advised on the phased development of the £100m 'Centrale' shopping centre in Croydon, which includes construction, development and retail letting issues. A strong hotels group is another asset to the firm, where Robert Newman and Stephen Laud are praised for being highly responsive and customer focused.

Fladgate Fielder boasts some very experienced practitioners, who were joined by Adrian Leavey. Much work is generated from a wealthy private client base, especially from the Middle East, so the firm's competence in shari'ah-compliant financing is heavily utilised. Anthony Vaughan's hotel practice has been involved in high-value, innovative structures in the West Indies for private investors.

At **Forsters LLP** Clerical Medical provided some significant instructions in the past year, including the transfer of 51 properties into Insight Investment's new listed Foundation Property Trust, and the subsequent acquisition of the McKenzie portfolio for over £150m. The arrival of Guy Jordan from *Masons* brings a variety of clients to the firm, including Fujitsu and Enterprise Inns. Redevelopment work is being undertaken for Chester City Council, while Irish investors have also been a notable feature of the year for the firm. A highly regarded leasehold enfranchisement practice completes the picture.

Hammonds' Jonathan Morshead retains an excellent reputation, and clients including Morley Fund Management and HBoS are indications of a highly regarded practice. The past year saw several shopping centre mandates incorporating development, investment and management issues handled for various institutional clients.

Howard Kennedy's assertion of 'if it's real estate, we'll do it', was popular enough with clients to bring in transactions worth over £2.8bn, and has not restricted the firm to smaller deals. It advised Canary Wharf and Ballymore on a joint venture acquisition of Wood Wharf, and various purchasers of high-value property in London including hotels and retail sites for development purposes. Paul Springall heads a growing team.

The arrival of Neil Rainey at **Kirkpatrick & Lockhart Nicholson Graham LLP** brings vast experience in property development, having worked on various large-scale shopping centre schemes. The US merger has brought Merrill Lynch to the firm, while Fidelity is another key client. The firm is strong in funds, having advised Henderson UK Retail Warehouse Fund on acquisitions valued over £180m in total.

Lewis Silkin's combined strengths in planning and the public sector, including social housing, has given it a platform to build an excellent commercial real estate practice. The firm has been advising developers on some major mixed-use schemes, while Hewlett-Packard instructed the firm on a site development in Bristol. Residential development remains an area of strength, while Jonathan Barnes has increased the investment side of the practice over the last three years, with the Minton Group's sale of the Cavendish portfolio for £40m a highlight.

Niche firm **Maples Teesdale** welcomed Roger Thornton, bringing investment expertise into the firm. An array of charity clients includes Cancer Research, while BMG instructed the firm for the first time on the development of new headquarters, a recognised area of expertise at the firm.

Mishcon de Reya boosted its investment side with the recruitment of Daniel Lipman, while the arrival of Oliver Goodwin is a huge asset to the firm's planning team. The appointment to the UBS Triton Property Fund alongside some major players shows the progress the firm has made in the market in recent years, while Helical Bar plc was advised on various acquisitions and disposals.

Osborne Clarke boasts a good all-round practice. Colin Kearney enjoyed a particularly impressive year, advising Topland Group Holdings Limited alongside finance expert Nadine Strahl on a £675m joint venture with Tesco, among other relocation deals. The firm is strong in the retail sector, regularly advising Marks & Spencer, Somerfield, Dixons and Asda Stores. On the development side, it advised Barratt Homes Limited and Bowmere Estates Limited on the purchase of various sites for residential development, while Charles Gait has been active on the development, letting and disposal of several sites. The firm also has a strong presence in the leisure sector, where Punch Taverns is a key client.

Following the merger, **Pinsent Masons** now boasts teams around the country, and regional strength is certainly the major asset of the new firm, which will be especially advantageous to a wide housebuilding client base that includes The Berkeley Group, Bellway, Wates, Goldcrest Homes and Furlong Homes.

Speechly Bircham houses several veterans of the real estate market, including department head Charles Palmer and Mark Hodgkinson, while the recruitment of Susan Lewis adds expertise to the development practice. The firm has a longstanding relationship with RBS, handling a significant amount of the firm's portfolio work, including the disposal of 20 freehold and leasehold interests in Manchester. Anne Magill is recommended.

Travers Smith was involved in some heavyweight transactions in the past year, most notably the sale of ntl's broadcast towers and transmission division, requiring investigation of title to over 3,000 properties, and the sale of Earls Court for £245m. A strong year in retail included advising John Lewis plc in connection with the acquisition and development of a new department store in Portsmouth, and Violet Investments on the acquisition and development of a Sainsbury's supermarket.

Trowers & Hamlins' significant presence in the Middle East attracts clients such as Kuwait Finance House and Gulf Finance House, and the firm's international network is of great importance to the firm. A market-leading presence in social housing is obviously an asset, and regeneration projects for local authorities is becoming a specialism, while the firm is increasing its funds work. Commercial understanding impresses clients, as does promptness and efficiency.

SHIPPING: DRY

CLYDE & CO ✪
HOLMAN FENWICK & WILLAN ✪
INCE & CO ✪

RICHARDS BUTLER

HILL TAYLOR DICKINSON
STEPHENSON HARWOOD

Barlow Lyde & Gilbert
Bentleys, Stokes & Lowless
Clifford Chance
MFB
Norton Rose ✪

Lawrence Graham LLP
Middleton Potts
Shaw and Croft
Thomas Cooper & Stibbard
Watson, Farley & Williams LLP

Curtis Davis Garrard
Davies Arnold Cooper
Elborne Mitchell
Jackson Parton
Waterson Hicks
Winter Scott

Constant & Constant
Davis & Co
E G Arghyrakis & Co
Eversheds LLP *Newcastle*
Hill Dickinson LLP *Liverpool*
Holmes Hardingham
Howe & Keates
Mills & Co *Newcastle*
Rayfield Mills *Newcastle*
Ross & Co
Taylor Wessing ✪
Waltons & Morse

Firms are listed A-Z in tiers which are ranked in order of priority
✪ *Indicates firm displays contact details at the end of this chapter.*

SHIPPING DRY

'Dry' shipping encompasses advice on charterparties, bills of lading and cargo claims.

With a strong reputation amongst cargo clients, **Clyde & Co** has sought to diversify its client base and has picked up increased instructions from charterers, owners and P&I clubs. Often at the cutting edge of legal developments within the shipping market, the firm successfully represented cargo interests in the *Rafaela S* case before the House of Lords. Other major cases include *Snow Crystal* and *Silversea Cruises*. The firm continues to have a strong trader client base and has attracted new instructions from oil majors BP and TNK. Department head Derek Hodgson and Irvine Marr are singled out for particular praise.

Holman Fenwick & Willan is instructed by shipowners and their P&I clubs on a variety of matters. Highlights include advising several shipowners on substantial claims arising from irregularities in the Chinese steel market and representing hull and machinery underwriters in the *Kastor Too* case before the Court of Appeal. Praised for the strength and depth of its team, Hugh Livingstone, Richard Crump and James Gosling receive special mention.

Ince & Co's strength in depth and network of offices means it is frequently called upon to advise on big-ticket, multi-jurisdictional work. Headline cases include the *Hanjin Pennsylvania*, *Kriti Akti* and *Spring Glory*. Bob Deering heads the department and receives able support from a team that includes Charles Foster, Paul Herring and Jonathan Lux.

Richards Butler's heavyweight litigation team is often instructed in high-profile and complex litigation, including the *Nelson* and *Easy Rider* cases. Working closely with its trade and commodities group, the shipping team has picked up new energy-related instructions from clients such as Koch group and SBM. The arrival of Chris Zavos has strengthened the marine insurance practice. Clients praise the firm and single out Charles Weller, Stephen Kirkpatrick, Lindsay East and Andrew Taylor for praise.

Often working closely with its offices in Piraeus and Dubai, **Hill Taylor Dickinson** regularly handles shipping disputes in multiple jurisdictions. As well as representing shipping clients on traditional dry matters, the team also has a focus on freight and commodities. Andrew Johnson has a fine reputation for international disputes.

Stephenson Harwood's Duncan McDonald heads a team that has altered its practice in line with a changing market. While the firm still picks up a large share of low-value cases from the P&I clubs, it has seen a marked increase in instructions in developing areas such as LNG transportation and shipping competition law cases. Valued team members include Stuart Beadnall who focuses on shipbuilding dispute resolution, and Paolo Ghirardani, who advises on some of the more substantial P&I claims. Rising star Ingolf Kaiser successfully advised major trading house Vitol in a charterparty dispute before the Court of Appeal.

Headed by Nigel Wagland, **Barlow Lyde & Gilbert**'s shipping team offers first-rate litigation experience to clients from the insurance industry and P&I clubs. Tim Taylor and Patrick Foss are highly regarded for their expertise in energy-related matters and are currently advising BP Amoco in major ongoing coverage-related litigation.

Bentleys, Stokes & Lowless advises a core base of shipowners and their P&I clubs with a particular focus on the Greek, Italian and Scandinavian markets. Involved in a number of reported cases, including the *Kastor Too* and the *Casco*, the firm's department offers sensible advice to clients. Paul Griffiths, Vernon Sewell and Joanna Steele are recommended.

Clifford Chance successfully represented the owners of a fleet of gas carriers in a claim regarding the payment of freight and is advising Petrobras in a $500m floating production storage and offloading facility (FPSO) dispute. Mark Morrison heads a team that is also active in the luxury-yacht market.

MFB advises a broad range of shipowners, charterers and insurance industry clients. Led by Stuart Blaxell and Andrew Wright the firm successfully acted for the owners in the important House of Lords decision, *The Jordan II*.

Norton Rose advises leading players in the shipping market including major shipowners, P&I clubs, international shipbuilders and energy companies. Led by Roger Heward, the firm currently acts for the owners and insurers in a claim in excess of $100m for damages caused to a container ship. Bruce Macaulay is a fine litigator and, as well as being involved in arbitrations, is frequently called upon to make emergency applications before the High Court. Helen Graham has a particular focus on shipbuilding contracts and disputes.

Headed by Mike Lax, **Lawrence Graham LLP**'s shipping group advises clients on a range of issues including international trade litigation, charterparty disputes, cargo claims and marine insurance. The team was bolstered by the arrival of Christopher Tite and Louise Gowman following the firm's merger with *Tite & Lewis*. Both have extensive ports expertise and industry contacts.

Middleton Potts advises shipowners, operators, charterers and P&I clubs on a range of issues. Recognised as one of the leading firms in the market for commodities and international trade, the firm has an enviable list of clients that includes the Louis Dreyfus Group and Cargill. Senior partner David Lucas has extensive shipping and commodities knowledge and is ably backed by lawyers of the calibre of Andrew Meads and Haris Zografakis.

Shaw and Croft advises P&I clubs, shipowners, shipyards and charterers on a range of matters including charterparty, demurrage and shipbuilding disputes. The firm has a niche expertise in disputes regarding tankers and liquid cargoes and acts for a number of the largest tanker owners and oil majors. Ben Browne and Michael Moon are recommended.

Thomas Cooper & Stibbard advises on a range of cargo claims including LNG cargoes. Tim Kelleher is highly recommended and has a particular knowledge of container trade.

Leveraging off its world-class ship financing department, **Watson, Farley & Williams LLP** has a particular specialisation in shipbuilding and repair and offshore oil and gas disputes. Led by Andrew Hutcheon and assisted by EU and competition expert Stephen Tupper, the firm advised a Middle Eastern shipowner in a dispute with an international pool operator. Peter Flint and Charles Buss are recommended.

Headed by Simon Curtis and Ian Garrard, niche firm **Curtis Davis Garrard** specialises in high-value shipbuilding and marine construction work. As well as acting for Kuwait Oil Tanker in its fleet renewal programmes, the firm continues to act in the long-running *Solitaire* arbitration.

Davies Arnold Cooper's Marjorie Holmes heads a team that advises P&I clubs and shipping lines and consortia on a range of EU and competition matters.

As well as providing all-round contentious and non-contentious advice to a host of shipping industry clients, **Elborne Mitchell**'s shipping team, in close co-operation with its insurance and reinsurance groups, provides specialist advice on marine risks.

Jackson Parton advises a broad range of national and international shipowners and P&I clubs, including a number of prestigious Japanese owners. The firm is increasingly active in the Commercial Court and Nick Parton has performed the advocacy on behalf of P&I clubs and owners in a number of anti-suit and mareva injunctions.

Niche firm **Waterson Hicks** advises a range of major shipping, commodities and oil industry clients. Mark Aspinall, Andrew Ridings and John Hicks are recommended.

Headed by Glenn Winter, **Winter Scott** has quickly established itself as a force in the market. The firm successfully represented the buyers of a $180m vessel in their dispute with the shipbuilders.

SHIPPING: WET

'Wet' or admiralty lawyers advise on cases arising out of collisions, salvages, total loss and pollution.

SHIPPING: WET
HOLMAN FENWICK & WILLAN ✪
INCE & CO ✪
CLYDE & CO ✪
HILL TAYLOR DICKINSON
RICHARDS BUTLER
Bentleys, Stokes & Lowless
Shaw and Croft
Stephenson Harwood
Barlow Lyde & Gilbert
Clifford Chance
MFB
Norton Rose ✪
Waltons & Morse
Winter Scott
Eversheds LLP *Newcastle*
Holmes Hardingham
Jackson Parton
Middleton Potts
Waterson Hicks
Bryan Cave
Constant & Constant
Curtis Davis Garrard
DLA Piper Rudnick Gray Cary UK LLP ✪
Davies Arnold Cooper
Elborne Mitchell
Howe & Keates
Lawrence Graham LLP
Thomas Cooper & Stibbard

Firms are listed A-Z in tiers which are ranked in order of priority
✪ *Indicates firm displays contact details at the end of this chapter.*

With no fewer than 11 former mariners amongst its ranks, **Holman Fenwick & Willan** is on the casualty response panel of several shipowners, and recently received a notable instruction from one owner following a major oil spill in China. Other headline cases include the grounding of the *Iran Ardebil* and the *Athos 1*. Offering strength in depth and benefiting from an extensive network of offices, James Gosling and Hugh Brown are recommended.

Acting for shipowners and P&I clubs, **Ince & Co** works closely with its extensive network of offices and has been involved in a large proportion of the major casualties around the world. Jointly headed by James Wilson and Faz Peermohamed, the team was instructed by owners and insurers of both the *Tropic Brilliance* and the *Kaminesan* (in its collision with the *Hyundai 105*). The firm is increasingly involved in the regulatory aspects of the industry and, as well as advising intergovernmental bodies, it is instructed by the main industry bodies to assist in addressing current political concerns. Colin de la Rue is a recognised expert in oil pollution matters.

Clyde & Co remains the pre-eminent cargo practice in the UK and recently acted for the cargo insurers in *Hyundai No 105* and *Cape Africa*. On the salvage side, the firm continues to be instructed by leading salvors Tsavliris International and Les Abeilles International. Simon Fletcher leads a team in Guildford that includes the highly recommended Stephen Pink.

Hill Taylor Dickinson has extensive international wet experience and represents clients' interests in relation to collisions, salvage, groundings and oil pollution. In a team that includes four legally qualified master mariners, including the vastly experienced Mike Mallin, the firm has the practical experience to match its legal acumen.

Headed by Richard Harvey, **Richards Butler** receives top-quality instructions from both owners and salvors, including key client Svitzer Wijsmuller. Piraeus-based John Reece and Hong Kong-based Paul Apostolis give the firm an enviable capability in Europe and Asia. Highlights include acting for owners of the *Kariba* in its collision with the *Tricolor* and the major salvage case *Iran Ardebil*.

Thanks to a team that includes four master mariners, three of whom are qualified solicitors, **Bentleys, Stokes & Lowless** is able to offer practical experience to a client base that includes German, Norwegian and French hull underwriters. Highlights include advising the owners and underwriters on the *Rocknes* and the *Al Samidoon*. Joe Quain, Vernon Sewell and Simon Tatham are recommended.

Shaw and Croft acts for a range of clients including shipowners, P&I clubs, salvors and harbour authorities. With a focus on representing salvors and cargo owners, the team has acted in a number of high-profile cases including the *Tricolor* litigation. The firm has good links with the Middle East and North Africa and acts for a number of state-owned shipping companies. Ben Browne, Hamish Edgar and Jonathan Kenyon are recommended.

Headed by Joe Atkinson and Ron Clark, **Stephenson Harwood**'s admiralty practice acts for a wide range of shipowners, charterers and their P&I clubs in casualty-related incidents. Highlights include advising charterers in the salvage of a serious marine casualty arising out of the recent tsunami tragedy and representing owners in respect of a serious grounding in South America.

Barlow Lyde & Gilbert's Simon Chumas has vast experience in marine insurance matters and is ably supported by both Tim Taylor and Patrick Foss. Highlights include advising the liability insurers in relation to the potential claims following the total loss of the *Ythan*.

Clifford Chance advises a diverse range of clients including shipowners, financial institutions and salvors. Highlights include advising a salvage company following the grounding of the *Cristoforo Colombo* and representing tug owners in the *Tasman Spirit*.

At **MFB**, master mariner Michael Mitchell heads a team that has the practical experience to deal with all issues arising out of casualties.

Headed by Paul Williams, **Norton Rose**'s wet team provides excellent support to a busy admiralty practice in Piraeus. The firm is written in to the emergency plans of a number of major passenger ship operators, and provides a dedicated round-the-clock emergency response team. Neil Q Miller and Philip Roche also specialise in the offshore energy sector and both have the OPTIO certification that allows them to investigate incidents offshore.

Waltons & Morse is a highly regarded cargo practice and in 2004 represented cargo insurers in significant casualties including *NYK Argus* and *Iran Ardebil*.

Headed by the highly rated Ken Scott and ably assisted by former Royal Navy lawyer Michael Ellis, **Winter Scott** has quickly established itself as a first-rate salvage practice. The firm also advises P&I clubs and shipowners on a range of marine casualty work.

TELECOMMUNICATIONS

BIRD & BIRD ✪

ALLEN & OVERY LLP ✪
BAKER & McKENZIE LLP ✪
CLIFFORD CHANCE
FIELD FISHER WATERHOUSE
LINKLATERS ✪

DLA Piper Rudnick Gray Cary UK LLP ✪
Freshfields Bruckhaus Deringer
Lovells ✪
Mayer, Brown, Rowe & Maw LLP
Olswang
Simmons & Simmons ✪

Ashurst ✪
Charles Russell
Denton Wilde Sapte ✪
Osborne Clarke
White & Case ✪
Wilmer Cutler Pickering Hale and Dorr LLP ✪

Addleshaw Goddard
Arnold & Porter (UK) LLP ✪
Berwin Leighton Paisner LLP
Eversheds LLP
Herbert Smith LLP ✪
Kemp Little LLP
Lawrence Graham LLP
Norton Rose ✪
Richards Butler
Slaughter and May ✪
Taylor Wessing ✪
Towerhouse Consulting
Travers Smith
Weil, Gotshal & Manges ✪

Firms are listed A-Z in tiers which are ranked in order of priority
✪ Indicates firm displays contact details at the end of this chapter.

TELECOMMUNICATIONS

Bird & Bird's chief executive David Kerr and Paris managing partner Frédérique Dupuis-Toubol are joint-heads of this outstandingly strong practice. New arrivals, Rhys Williams and Graeme Maguire, are testament to the firm's continuing success and apparently limitless ambition. Both Williams and Dominic Cook have won plaudits for the consummate ease with which they have handled advice to BT on the NHS NPfIT procurement. Gill Andrews is also recommended. Other clients include O2 and T-Mobile.

Allen & Overy LLP wins promotion to the second tier this year. The team, led by the firm's head of international communications, media and technology, Ian Ferguson, consists of three core partners: Ferguson, regulatory guru Chris Watson and Claire Wright, who offer a broad range of experience on regulation, acquisition, and network agreements. The firm acted for BT on its $965m acquisition of Infonet, one of the world's leading providers of international managed voice and data network services. Other active clients include Cable & Wireless and Virgin Mobile.

Peter Strivens heads **Baker & McKenzie LLP**'s formidable team. He advised the Turkish government on privatisation matters. Clients describe him as 'a guru, strong on regulatory matters. You wouldn't make a big decision without consulting him first.' Robbie Downing continues to showcase his considerable regulatory expertise, acting for Wanadoo on the Oftel decision relating to the pricing of broadband. The team was further strengthened by the arrival of James Burdett. Other clients include 3.

Joachim Fleury leads **Clifford Chance**'s somewhat downsized but, nevertheless, talented team. Fleury wins praise for his private equity experience. Daniel Sandelson, too, has a well-deserved reputation as one the City's leading communications specialists. Elizabeth Hiester is recommended for regulatory matters.

Tony Ballard leads **Field Fisher Waterhouse**'s telecoms group. He is, without doubt, one of the foremost experts in the sector. Andrew Blankfield is gaining an ever-greater profile for telecoms-related corporate advice. The team provides cutting-edge advice to some of the leading media companies in the world, notably the BBC. Other telecoms-specific clients include Orange and Level 3 Communications, which the firm advised on regulatory issues relating to VOIP.

Linklaters' recently reinvigorated practice continues to thrive despite the loss of Graeme Maguire. Tim Schwarz heads the team and has a redoubtable reputation, particularly for major international telecoms projects. Clients of the standing of Vodafone and BT speak largely for the quality.

DLA Piper Rudnick Gray Cary UK LLP wins promotion in the rankings this year. The newly formed global firm gives litigation and regulatory expert Julian Stait and his team a much-enhanced platform. The practice already boasts big-name clients such as Cable & Wireless and COLT and looks set to go from strength to strength. Purvi Parekh is recommended.

Simon Marchant and Rachel Brandenburger co-head **Freshfields Bruckhaus Deringer**'s TMT sector group. It applies the firm's formidable strength in corporate and regulatory matters to the communications industry with some élan. Headline clients include Hutchison, mmo2, and MCI. David Aitman is recommended.

Following the retirement of former practice head, Heather Rowe, the highly experienced Quentin Archer leads **Lovells**' outstanding telecoms practice. In Archer and Conor Ward the firm has two of the leading TMT specialist partners in the City. Both act for big-name clients on impressively high-level deals. This strength in London is matched by considerable strength in key markets from Brussels to Beijing.

Peter Dickinson leads **Mayer, Brown, Rowe & Maw LLP**'s activities in this area. He has a particularly strong relationship with Cable & Wireless. Richard Page, meanwhile, continues to distinguish himself, most recently acting for Easynet Group on acquisitions. Support from corporate finance star Paul Maher makes this firm an excellent choice for corporate-related telecoms instructions.

Colin Long leads **Olswang**'s activities in this area. The practice is undertaking high-level work for some of the leading players in the industry and wins promotion in our rankings as a result. The team acted for Viatel on its transatlantic and pan-European $52m financing. Affable TMT generalist partner John Enser is recommended for commercial matters.

Simmons & Simmons' team, headed by David Barrett, had a strong year. The departure of Rhys Williams was counterbalanced by the arrival of Jonathan Little. The firm won impressive new instructions from Orange, TeliaSonera and IDT.

Clive Tucker heads **Ashurst**'s seven-partner team. It is recommended for complex multi-jurisdictional matters. Clients include NEC, Arabsat, which Tucker advised on licensing issues, and Kingston Communications.

Mark Moncreiffe heads **Charles Russell**'s strong telecoms group. He is also client partner for headline clients Cable & Wireless and ntl. The group is one of the few to have expanded in recent years. The arrival of Danny Preiskel, who joined the firm as a consultant was a boost. Sue Cozens is also recommended for corporate-related telecoms matters.

Denton Wilde Sapte lost numerous TMT lawyers in the course of the year. Despite this, the firm offers considerable telecoms expertise. The team, led by sector head John Worthy, acts for big-name clients such as Virgin Mobile and Nokia.

Simon Rendell returned from his stint in-house at Vodafone to lead a resurgent **Osborne Clarke**. The firm advised Vodafone on one of the largest telecoms projects of the year: the MVNO with BT. James Mullock also distinguished himself advising major US VOIP company Vosage on setting up in Europe.

Both **White & Case** and **Wilmer Cutler Pickering Hale and Dorr LLP** offer highly respected telecoms specialists in David Eisenberg and Robert Bratby, respectively.

FOREIGN LAW FIRMS IN LONDON – US FIRMS

The year was a mixed one for the US firms in London, with the majority dropping headcount. There are eight firms with more than 100 fee-earners in the City, including **Kirkpatrick & Lockhart Nicholson Graham LLP**, which was formed out of the merger of London's *Nicholson Graham & Jones* and Pittsburgh's *Kirkpatrick & Lockhart*.

Interestingly, the transatlantic merged firms no longer dominate these tables as they once did. Organic growth has elevated **White & Case** to third by size, with 250 lawyers and 10% headcount growth last year, proving that American firms with commitment can indeed build an English practice to compete with the established players.

Many of the US firms in London now combine significant US law capability with an even larger English law resource. What follows here is a brief description of the practices of the 50 largest US firms in London: readers should refer to the relevant London practice area sections for more detail, where the American firms are ranked alongside their English competitors.

TRANSATLANTIC MERGERS

DLA Piper Rudnick Gray Cary UK LLP was formed in January 2005 as the result of the three-way link-up of UK firm *DLA* with US firms *Piper Rudnick* and *Gray Cary Ware & Friedenrich*. The combination is the first attempt at a merger of equals, as the firm now has 2,800 lawyers spread across 18 countries and 49 offices worldwide. The firm is full-service in London.

Dechert LLP is the oldest of the transatlantic mergers, formed in 2000. Of its 36 London partners, just three are US-qualified. Key practice areas are corporate, financial services and real estate. The firm hired Mark Davis in private equity from **Ashurst**.

Faegre & Benson LLP merged in 2003, and now boasts 12 partners in London, 11 of them UK-qualified. The largest practice areas are disputes and real estate, and the City office is well known for corporate finance. Last year the firm hired Greg Campbell from Tite & Lewis to boost employment.

The London office of **Jones Day** now boasts 178 lawyers, down from 235 last year. Of these, just five are US-qualified. The largest practice areas remain M&A and real estate, and key clients are Pillar Property, Arlington, and Edison Mission Energy. Last year the firm transferred energy partner Peter Roberts to London from Hong Kong.

The second of the new transatlantic tie-ups, **Kirkpatrick & Lockhart Nicholson Graham LLP** was formed in January 2005. In London the combined firm boasts 134 lawyers, all English-qualified. Key practice areas are dispute resolution, M&A and real estate, while UK clients include Henderson Global Investors and Anglo Irish Bank.

Mayer, Brown, Rowe & Maw LLP is the second-largest of the transatlantic firms operating in the City, with nearly 300 lawyers, just seven of them American partners. Last year the London office hired construction partner Jonathan Hosie from **Hammonds**, and litigators Richard Gregorian from **Cadwalader, Wickersham & Taft LLP** and Andrew Legg from **Linklaters**.

Reed Smith's London office is home to one US corporate partner, and one US banking partner regularly works out of the office. Beyond that, the practice is UK-centric, for clients including Nations Healthcare, Siemens, Sara Lee and Tate & Lyle. Top practice areas are disputes, financial service and real estate.

Steptoe & Johnson is the smallest of the merged firms in London, with 25 lawyers, most of them partners. The practice is dominated by disputes and M&A, for clients including Motorola and Swiss Re. The office hired Raymond Werbicki from *Masons* and insurance partner Neil Ellis from *DLA*.

PREDOMINANTLY US LAW CAPABILITY

The group of American firms doing purely US law in London gets smaller every year.

Cravath, Swaine & Moore LLP is one of only two firms in London, alongside **Davis Polk & Wardwell**, that employs not a single English lawyer. The firm has 19 lawyers here, practising in M&A, capital markets and finance.

Davis Polk & Wardwell has 36 American lawyers based in London. As well as the three core practice areas of M&A, capital markets and finance, the office practices in energy, restructuring, insurance, life sciences, TMT and tax.

The London office of **Simpson Thacher & Bartlett LLP** is home to two UK-qualified acquisition finance partners: Euan Gorrie and Stephen Short. The office has also added four English assistants, supporting its practice in capital markets, finance and M&A. Major clients are private equity firms Blackstone and Kohlberg Kravis Roberts & Co, and JP Morgan and Deutsche Bank.

Sullivan & Cromwell LLP boasts 56 lawyers in London, including one English project finance partner, Jamieson Logie. The largest practice areas are capital markets, M&A and project finance, employing 45 lawyers.

PREDOMINANTLY US LAW CAPABILITY

CRAVATH, SWAINE & MOORE LLP
DAVIS POLK & WARDWELL
SIMPSON THACHER & BARTLETT LLP
SULLIVAN & CROMWELL LLP

Firms are listed alphabetically

DUAL US/UK LAW CAPABILITY: OVER 100 FEE-EARNERS

SHEARMAN & STERLING (LONDON) LLP
WEIL, GOTSHAL & MANGES ✪
WHITE & CASE ✪

Firms are listed alphabetically
✪ Indicates firm displays contact details at the end of this chapter.

DUAL US/UK LAW CAPABILITY: OVER 100 FEE-EARNERS

Shearman & Sterling (London) LLP now boasts 27 partners in London, nine of them US-qualified. Key practice areas are finance, capital markets, insurance and M&A, and the firm added real estate capability with the hire of Ian Nisse from **Ashurst**. London's top clients include Anglo American, BG Group on its Egyptian LNG project financing, and Stelmar Shipping.

Weil, Gotshal & Manges boosted its London M&A practice with the hire of the highly rated Mark Soundy from **Travers Smith**. He adds to the already strong private equity team, while other major practices include capital markets, disputes, finance, securitisation and restructuring. Top clients include General Electric and Parmalat.

White & Case has topped 250 lawyers in London this year through steady growth, making it the largest organically grown practice in headcount terms. Major hires included Alan Greenough from Pinsents in private equity, Tom Winsor, the former UK Rail Regulator, and John Higham QC from **Stephenson Harwood** in disputes.

DUAL US/UK LAW CAPABILITY: 50-100 FEE-EARNERS

Cadwalader, Wickersham & Taft LLP has 13 partners in London, five US-qualified. Major practice areas are restructuring and insolvency, capital markets, and finance. Restructuring clients include British Energy, Telewest Communications, Energis, MyTravel and Parmalat.

DUAL US/UK LAW CAPABILITY: 50-100 FEE-EARNERS

Cadwalader, Wickersham & Taft LLP ✪
Cleary, Gottlieb, Steen & Hamilton LLP ✪
Covington & Burling ✪
Debevoise & Plimpton LLP ✪
Latham & Watkins
LeBoeuf, Lamb, Greene & MacRae ✪
McDermott Will & Emery UK LLP ✪
Orrick, Herrington & Sutcliffe ✪
Sidley Austin
Skadden, Arps, Slate, Meagher & Flom (UK) LLP
Wilmer Cutler Pickering Hale and Dorr LLP ✪

Firms are listed alphabetically
✪ Indicates firm displays contact details at the end of this chapter.

Cleary, Gottlieb, Steen & Hamilton LLP in London has 15 partners, ten of them American. The UK contingent was boosted with the hire of Simon Ovenden, a finance partner from **Linklaters**.

Covington & Burling has built a 50-plus London office, with an 11-partner team split 50-50 between US and English law. Major practice areas are life sciences, corporate, regulatory services and disputes.

Debevoise & Plimpton LLP's London office focuses on private equity and M&A, capital markets, restructuring, insurance and dispute resolution. The office added Richard Ward from **Bird & Bird** in tax, and Jeremy Hill from **Ashurst** in insurance.

Latham & Watkins has 28 partners in London, 13 of them UK-qualified. The largest practice areas are capital markets, finance and projects. The firm hired Ian Clark from **White & Case** in capital markets, Robert Volterra from **Herbert Smith LLP** in dispute resolution, and John Hull from **Richards Butler** in litigation.

LeBoeuf, Lamb, Greene & MacRae's London office remains focused on two key sectors: insurance and energy. For those clients the firm does capital markets, disputes, finance and M&A work, and it hired four partners, including IP partner Marija Danilunas from **Hammonds**.

McDermott Will & Emery UK LLP added three corporate partners last year, two from **Allen & Overy LLP**: Andrew Caunt and Andrew Croxford; and Michael McFall from **Dorsey & Whitney**. Other major practice areas are capital markets, finance and employment.

Orrick, Herrington & Sutcliffe made significant strides in London in 2005 with the hire of several partners from *Coudert Brothers*.

The London office of **Sidley Austin** is home to 31 partners, 24 of them English qualified. The largest practice area, employing more than half of the office, is finance, with capital markets, insolvency and M&A all growing. Key hires were John Woodhall from **Clifford Chance**, Matthew Dening from **Baker & McKenzie LLP** and Richard Hughes from **Linklaters**, all of whom do structured finance.

Skadden, Arps, Slate, Meagher & Flom (UK) LLP has 16 partners in London, seven of them UK-qualified. The firm enhanced its continental European offering with a private equity team in Germany. The London office remains focused on M&A and capital markets.

Wilmer Cutler Pickering Hale and Dorr LLP is the result of a domestic US merger last year, between *Wilmer, Cutler & Pickering* and *Hale and Dorr*, both of which had sizeable London offices. The combined offering boasts 19 partners, three of them American. Major practice areas are M&A and disputes, and the office maintains a TMT bias.

DUAL US/UK LAW CAPABILITY: 25-50 FEE-EARNERS

- Arnold & Porter (UK) LLP ✪
- Bingham McCutchen LLP
- Bryan Cave
- Dewey Ballantine ✪
- Dorsey & Whitney ✪
- Fried, Frank, Harris, Shriver & Jacobson (London) LLP
- Gibson, Dunn & Crutcher LLP
- Hogan & Hartson ✪
- Hunton & Williams
- Kilpatrick Stockton LLP ✪
- Kirkland & Ellis International LLP ✪
- Milbank, Tweed, Hadley & McCloy LLP ✪
- Morgan Lewis ✪
- Morrison & Foerster MNP
- O'Melveny & Myers LLP ✪

Firms are listed alphabetically

✪ Indicates firm displays contact details at the end of this chapter.

DUAL US/UK LAW CAPABILITY: 25-50 FEE-EARNERS

Arnold & Porter (UK) LLP's London office has a focus on life sciences and TMT, and clients include GlaxoSmithKline and Sanofi. Last year IP partner Clive Thorne joined from **Denton Wilde Sapte**.

In London, half of **Bingham McCutchen LLP**'s work is in insolvency and restructuring. The team added Neil Micklethwaite last year in disputes, from *DLA*.

Bryan Cave's largest practice areas in London are M&A and dispute resolution, and the office has a strong private client team.

Dewey Ballantine is one of the leading New York M&A firms, and London clients include General Electric, ABN Amro and Total. Other major practice areas are project finance and capital markets.

In all, 85% of **Dorsey & Whitney**'s London lawyers are UK-qualified. The office added US securities partner Richard Baumann from **Norton Rose** and Peter Bond in competition from **Bryan Cave** last year.

Fried, Frank, Harris, Shriver & Jacobson (London) LLP significantly expanded its London offering in the past year. The office now has 14 partners, four of them UK-qualified. Major additions were Justin Spendlove from **Ashurst**, who is now firmwide managing partner, and Siân Withey in capital markets, also from **Ashurst**. On M&A, Jerry Walter joined from **Simmons & Simmons**, while in early 2005 a tax team joined from **Jones Day**.

Gibson, Dunn & Crutcher LLP added three London partners in the past year, though its dominant practice area remains M&A. In competition, James Ashe-Taylor joined from **Crowell & Moring**. In US capital markets, Alan Bannister joined from **Clifford Chance**, and in finance, Tom Budd was added from **Jones Day**.

Hogan & Hartson has nearly 40 lawyers in London, with major practices in M&A, energy, real estate and project finance. Clients include Finartis Group and Henderson Global Investors.

Hunton & Williams' four major practices in London are capital markets, finance, M&A and project finance. The office hired three partners from **Hammonds** in the past year: Martin Thomas in corporate finance, John Deacon in construction, and Jonathan Marsh in financial services.

Kilpatrick Stockton LLP has major London teams covering dispute resolution and finance, for clients such as Serco Group, Carillion and Hyder Business Services.

Kirkland & Ellis International LLP is focused on private equity in London, for clients including Bain Capital, Vestar Capital Partners and CapVest.

Milbank, Tweed, Hadley & McCloy LLP has significant London teams in project finance, capital markets and M&A, and last year hired Laurence Jacobs to cover IT outsourcing from **Allen & Overy LLP**.

Morgan Lewis has 13 London partners, three of them US-qualified. Major practices are dispute resolution and M&A, and the team added partners in TMT and insurance last year.

Morrison & Foerster MNP expanded significantly in London last year, with a team of three outsourcing partners from **Pillsbury Winthrop Shaw Pittman LLP**, two corporate life sciences partners from **Weil, Gotshal & Manges**, and a corporate partner from **Simmons & Simmons**.

O'Melveny & Myers LLP has added five English partners, and has quickly put in place a team focused on private equity. Clients include Apollo Management, JP Morgan and Bear Sterns.

DUAL US/UK LAW CAPABILITY: UNDER 25 FEE-EARNERS

Akin Gump Strauss Hauer & Feld added three UK-based energy partners in the past year, so now 12 of its 23 London lawyers focus on that market.

Baker Botts is a Houston firm, and its London office mirrors its US energy focus, acting for clients like Halliburton and Petrocon India.

Chadbourne & Parke started 2005 with the hire of a five-partner insurance team from **Denton Wilde Sapte**. The office is also strong in energy, product liability, and finance work.

King & Spalding International LLP's major clients in London include Choice Point, General Electric and SUN Interbrew.

Orrick, Herrington & Sutcliffe is focused on finance in London, including securitisation, and hired two structured finance partners from **Jones Day** in the past year.

The largest practice area at **Paul, Hastings, Janofsky & Walker (Europe) LLP** in London is real estate, which employs eight of the office's 15 lawyers.

Squire, Sanders & Dempsey's major London practice areas are TMT and M&A. The firm began

DUAL US/UK LAW CAPABILITY: UNDER 25 FEE-EARNERS

Akin Gump Strauss Hauer & Feld
Baker Botts ✪
Chadbourne & Parke
King & Spalding International LLP
Paul, Hastings, Janofsky & Walker (Europe) LLP ✪
Pillsbury Winthrop Shaw Pittman LLP
Squire, Sanders & Dempsey ✪
Vinson & Elkins R.L.L.P. ✪
Winston & Strawn London ✪

Firms are listed alphabetically
✪ *Indicates firm displays contact details at the end of this chapter.*

2005 with the hire of MCI's chief international counsel Ann LaFrance.

Vinson & Elkins R.L.L.P. continues to focus on corporate finance work for energy clients in London, working for Hudson Advisors, Hg Capital and Cairn.

Winston & Strawn London boosted its finance practice in London in past year, with the hire of Graham Wedlake and Neil James from **Barlow Lyde & Gilbert**.

BENELUX FIRMS

De Brauw Blackstone Westbroek partners Pierre Nijnens and Niek Biegman head a team recommended for a broad range of corporate, finance, capital markets and tax matters. The firm was the first Dutch firm to open an office in London in 1990. Highlights include acting for JP Morgan and ING in relation to a €125m convertible bond issue. Other clients include ABN Amro.

Houthoff Buruma's London office works closely with its Dutch head office in advising on corporate, securities and banking and finance matters. Albert Dreese and M&A specialist Alexander Kaarls are recommended. Senior associate Jessica Terpstra is recommended for banking and project finance transactions. Clients include EMI, Monsanto, Morgan Stanley and GE Capital.

Loyens & Loeff has a strong name for both standalone tax work, as well as tax planning aspects of M&A, joint venture and corporate restructuring. Clients include several major US multinational companies and private equity houses. Marc Klerks and Bas Vletter are recommended.

NautaDutilh boasts a team of three partners in London, including managing partner Gijs Gerretsen, recommended for M&A, corporate finance

and private equity. Tax partner Pieter Elias is also recommended. Recent transaction highlights include advising Deutsche Bank and Allied Irish Banks in relation to the buyout of Candover by Warburg Pincus as private equity contributor in Clondalkin.

BENELUX FIRMS

De Brauw Blackstone Westbroek *Netherlands*
Houthoff Buruma ✪ *Netherlands*
Loyens & Loeff ✪ *Netherlands*
NautaDutilh *Netherlands*
Stibbe ✪ *Belgium/Netherlands*
Van Doorne *Netherlands*

Firms are listed alphabetically
✪ *Indicates firm displays contact details at the end of this chapter.*

At **Stibbe** Michael Molenaars heads a London office especially recommended for tax advice, working closely with the firm's Brussels and Amsterdam offices. The team also advises on corporate, M&A and banking matters. The firm has alliances with German firm **Gleiss Lutz** and UK firm **Herbert Smith LLP**. Partner Gerhardt Vels is recommended for corporate transactions. Clients include Barclays, ABN Amro and Mitsui, which the team advised on a joint venture with Shell in relation to an LNG terminal in Mexico.

Van Doorne's London office has a focus on banking and capital markets work for clients such as HSBC, Barclays and JP Morgan. Hans van Ramshorst divides his time between Amsterdam and London, where he is supported by a team of two associates.

For a detailed review of the Benelux legal market, see *The Legal 500 – Europe, Middle East & Africa* at www.legal500.com

FRENCH FIRMS

Gide Loyrette Nouel MNP's London office is particularly recommended for heavyweight banking and capital markets transactions. A team of six partners and around 30 associates also advises on corporate and commercial transactions, working closely with its Paris head office. Clients include Deutsche Bank, Morgan Stanley, General Electric company and new clients such as UBS and Nomura. Key personalities include: New York-qualified capital markets partners Christopher Mead and Scott Cameron ; Colin Mercer who focuses on banking, securitisation and project finance; Margaret Boswell, recommended for banking and securitisation transactions; Michael Doran, recommended for capital markets work; and finance and capital markets partner Arnaud Duhamel, who divides his time between London and Paris.

Alexen Avocats' niche presence in London is maintained by partner Remi Turcon, who divides his time Paris and London. The firm handles domestic and international work for corporate clients and private individuals.

Castaldi Mourre Sprague in London is recommended for its work for clients from the

FRENCH FIRMS

Gide Loyrette Nouel MNP ✪

Alexen Avocats
Castaldi Mourre Sprague
DS London
Ginestié Magellan Paley-Vincent
JP Karsenty & Associés
Triplet & Associés

Firms are listed A-Z in tiers which are ranked in order of priority
✪ *Indicates firm displays contact details at the end of this chapter.*

energy sector, including the purchase and sale of power generation plants in the UK, advising investors on the acquisition of UK energy companies, and advising on the contractual arrangements for UK and foreign energy markets. A team of two partners includes Steven Sprague, who has over 15 years' experience in the energy sector, and Sally Barrett-Williams. A further four lawyers divide their time between London, Paris and Milan.

DS London is run in close co-operation with associate firm **Browne Jacobson LLP** and operates out of its London office. London is one of the firm's network of ten offices in Europe and the Far East.

At **Ginestié Magellan Paley-Vincent** Marcus Rebuck heads a team of two associates in London which works closely with its Paris office in advising on corporate transactions for a strong SME client base. The team advised a French call centre provider on several acquisitions in the UK and represented a Chicago-based Fortune 500 IT company on acquisitions of private UK companies.

JP Karsenty & Associés offers its clients French law advice and has associated offices with **Beachcroft Wansbroughs** in London and Brussels.

The London office of Lille-based **Triplet & Associés** has a strong focus on employment law. Part-time partners Philip Jenkinson and Didier Lebon advise on French corporate, IP, banking and residential property matters for a range of clients from the UK, Ireland and the US. The firm is a member of TAGLaw and also has offices in Paris and Marseille.

For a detailed review of the French legal market, see *The Legal 500 – Europe, Middle East & Africa* at www.legal500.com

GERMAN FIRMS

Commercial lawyer Hans Hartwig at **Hartwig** leads a team of around ten dual-qualified lawyers in London and Croydon which offers legal and notary services in English, German, Spanish, French and Italian. The firm advises on a range of personal matters, in addition to corporate work, competition and litigation. Manfred Kuhn is

GERMAN FIRMS

Hartwig
Haarmann Hemmelrath LLP ✪
Hoffmann.Eitle
Redeker Sellner Dahs & Widmaier

Firms are listed alphabetically
✪ *Indicates firm displays contact details at the end of this chapter.*

IRISH FIRMS

A&L Goodbody ✪
Arthur Cox ✪
Matheson Ormsby Prentice ✪
McCann FitzGerald

Firms are listed alphabetically
✪ *Indicates firm displays contact details at the end of this chapter.*

ITALIAN FIRMS

Chiomenti Studio Legale ✪
LCA Legal Limited
Sutti, Studio Legale

Firms are listed alphabetically
✪ *Indicates firm displays contact details at the end of this chapter.*

recommended for IP matters. The firm has associate offices in Zeebrugge, Frankfurt and Hamburg.

At **Haarmann Hemmelrath LLP** a team of English and German lawyers advise on corporate, banking, insolvency, dispute resolution and tax matters, working closely with the firm's network of offices in Germany and continental Europe. Clients include several major US and European investment banks. Philip Newhouse is recommended for corporate transactions.

Hoffmann.Eitle is one of the largest patent law firms in Germany. A team of 11 European and British chartered patent attorneys advise major US, Japanese and European clients on patent prosecution work in the European Patent Office. Managing partner Stephen Avery heads a team of two partners.

Redeker Sellner Dahs & Widmaier is recommended for corporate, capital markets, EU and competition, dispute resolution and IP matters. The team also reports an increase in private equity work in the past year. Christiane Gursch and Dr Peter-Andreas Brand advise purely on German law.

For a detailed review of the German legal market, see *The Legal 500 – Europe, Middle East & Africa* at www.legal500.com

IRISH FIRMS

A&L Goodbody works closely with its Dublin head office in advising a wide range of international clients on corporate, banking and capital markets transactions. London office managing partner Julian Yarr heads the team. Geraldine East also advises several clients from the entertainment industry. Transaction highlights include advising eircom on its €1.2bn flotation on the Irish and London Stock Exchanges. The firm also advised on several major private equity transactions.

Arthur Cox advises on corporate, banking, capital markets and structured finance transactions. Resident corporate partner John Matson heads the London and New York offices. Structured finance partner Cormac Kissane and capital markets partner Glenn Butt divide their time between Dublin and London.

Matheson Ormsby Prentice provides Irish law advice to multinational corporates and financial institutions doing business in Ireland, as well as handling referral work for a wide range of London-based international law firms. Corporate partner Andrew Doyle heads a team of ten lawyers in London which received a boost when Leanne Robson joined as partner in London from **Freshfields Bruckhaus Deringer**. Senior banking and finance partner Michael Jackson advises on investment funds and structured finance.

McCann FitzGerald has maintained a presence in London for around 20 years. Hugh Beattie heads a team especially recommended for banking, capital markets and securitisation transactions. Highlights in the past year include advising Credit Suisse First Boston in relation to 'Titan Europe', a commercial mortgage-backed securitisation conduit; the transaction was the first European securitisation to replicate a US-style capital structure.

For a detailed review of the Irish legal market, see *The Legal 500 – Europe, Middle East & Africa* at www.legal500.com

ITALIAN FIRMS

Chiomenti Studio Legale is recommended for expertise in banking, project finance and real estate finance transactions. Other areas of expertise include capital markets and tax. Highlights in the past year include acting as Italian counsel to HSBC in connection with a project financing in Qatar. Three partners, including senior partner Luigi Bendi, spend time in London. The firm has offices in Rome, Milan, Turin, New York and Brussels, and also has a 'best friends' relationship with **Skadden, Arps, Slate, Meagher & Flom LLP**.

LCA Legal Limited advises on corporate, banking, IT and real estate matters. The firm advised on the creation of an Italian finance vehicle and acted for an Italian company in relation to a concession agreement with a major UK department store. London office resident partner Roberta Crivellaro heads a team of three Italian lawyers. The firm also has offices in Venice, Padua, Milan, and Munich.

Studio Legale Sutti's London office has a strong name for IP work. The firm also advises on competition and tax matters. Livia Oglio heads the team. The London team reports an increase in work involving co-operation with the firm's network of offices in Bulgaria, Romania and Serbia and Montenegro.

For a detailed review of the Italian legal market, see *The Legal 500 – Europe, Middle East & Africa* at www.legal500.com.

PORTUGUESE FIRMS

At Portuguese firm **Neville de Rougemont & Associados**, Rosemary de Rougemont heads a team which advises on corporate, commercial, labour, immigration, property and tax law. The firm bases its UK operations in Maidenhead. The three-lawyer office includes two dual-qualified lawyers who are qualified in both English and Portuguese law.

For a detailed review of the Portuguese legal market, see *The Legal 500 – Europe, Middle East & Africa* at www.legal500.com.

SCANDINAVIAN FIRMS

Of the Scandinavian firms present in London, *Lex Mundi* members **Kromann Reumert** of Denmark, Norway's **Thommessen Krefting Greve Lund** and Swedish firm **Vinge** share an office in the City and operate as the *Scandinavian Law Alliance*, as is the case in Brussels.

The London office of **Hamilton Advokatbyrå** advises on commercial, banking and litigation matters. Partners Christoffer Hamilton and Dag di Meo, who divide their time between London and Stockholm, head a team whose clients include UK clients doing business in Sweden, as well as Swedish banks with a UK presence.

Kromann Reumert offers finance and corporate law advice to a strong investment banking clientele. Associate Jakob Bernhoft heads

PORTUGUESE FIRMS

Neville de Rougemont & Associados

SCANDINAVIAN FIRMS

Hamilton Advokatbyrå *Sweden*
Kromann Reumert *Denmark*
Thommessen Krefting Greve Lund ✪ *Norway*
Vinge ✪ *Sweden*
Wikborg Rein ✪ *Norway*

Firms are listed alphabetically
✪ *Indicates firm displays contact details at the end of this chapter.*

the London office. The firm also has offices in Copenhagen and Aarhus.

Thommessen Krefting Greve Lund offers Norwegian law advice in relation to shipping, finance, corporate and cross-border M&A matters. Clients include several major multinational companies from the oil and gas sector. Resident partner Halvor Mansaker heads a team of two lawyers.

Vinge advises on corporate, banking, syndicated loan and structured finance transactions. Corporate finance partner Maria-Pia Midenbäck-Hope heads a team of two associates in London which worked closely with the firm's Stockholm head office in advising Macquarie Bank on a major project financing.

Norwegian firm **Wikborg Rein** is particularly well known for its work for clients from the shipping and oil and gas sectors. The firm is also recommended for corporate, securities and M&A advice. Morten Lund Mathisen heads the London office.

For a detailed review of the Scandinavian legal market, see *The Legal 500 – Europe, Middle East & Africa* at www.legal500.com.

SPANISH FIRMS

Spanish heavyweight firm **Uría Menéndez** maintains a London office headed by Juan Francisco Falcón. The department works closely with the firm's Madrid office in advising both Spanish and UK clients on a wide range of corporate, M&A, finance, capital markets and real estate transactions.

At **Díaz-Bastien & Truan** Rafael Truan Blanco heads a one-partner London office which focuses purely on Spanish law advice. The firm works closely with its offices in Madrid and Marbella in advising UK clients on investment in Spain as well as on cross-border litigation.

Fernando Scornik Gerstein advises on property and conveyancing, litigation, insurance, tax and personal injury matters for a range of UK companies and private clients. The team in London advises on Spanish, English and Argentinean law. The London office works closely with its network of Spanish offices in Barcelona, Madrid, Tenerife, Gran Canaria and Lanzarote.

At **Hector Diaz & Co**, managing partner Hector Diaz heads a three-lawyer office which is particularly active in advising on property-related work. The firm also advises on commercial, banking and family law. The firm is able to provide English law advice through its association with **KSB Law LLP**.

Dual-qualified senior partner Michael Soul at **Michael Soul & Asociados – Abogados** heads a team of Anglo-Spanish lawyers which advises on commercial, property, insolvency and litigation matters. The London office works closely with the firm's network of Spanish offices in Madrid, Malaga and Marbella, and a network of associated offices, including the Balearic and Canary Islands.

SPANISH FIRMS

Uría Menéndez

Díaz-Bastien & Truan
Fernando Scornik Gerstein
Hector Diaz & Co
Michael Soul & Asociados – Abogados

SWISS FIRMS

Bär & Karrer
Froriep Renggli ✪
Secretan Troyanov

Firms are listed A-Z in tiers which are ranked in order of priority
✪ *Indicates firm displays contact details at the end of this chapter.*

For a detailed review of the Spanish legal market, see *The Legal 500 – Europe, Middle East & Africa* at www.legal500.com.

SWISS FIRMS

Bär & Karrer advises on corporate, M&A and capital markets transactions. The firm offers services in German, French, English and Italian. Resident London partner Gianpaolo Arrigoni is recommended.

Froriep Renggli was the first Swiss firm to set up in London, 20 years ago, and has established a solid client base of blue-chip international clients, including Airbus, Barclays Bank, RBS, Clayton Dubilier & Rice and XL Capital. Bruno Boesch heads a team which advises UK clients on Swiss law, for a range of corporate and commercial, M&A, private equity, securities, banking and aviation, international wealth transfer and international litigation and commercial arbitration matters. Partner Dunja Koch advises on aviation and financing transactions.

Secretan Troyanov offers Swiss law advice to multinational and mid-sized companies, as well as high-net-worth individuals. The London office has broad experience of finance, capital markets, investment funds, international arbitration, employment and estate planning matters. Resident partner Eva Stormann heads the team.

For a detailed review of the Swiss legal market, see *The Legal 500 – Europe, Middle East & Africa* at www.legal500.com.

UKRAINIAN FIRMS

BC Toms & Co is one of the largest firms in Ukraine. The London office fields a team of five lawyers, including founding partner Bate Toms. Banking work relating to heavyweight corporate and project finance transactions (especially in the power, oil and gas and telecoms sectors) in the Ukraine is a key focus of work in the firm's London office. The firm also advises on real estate, IP, competition, and litigation.

For a detailed review of the Ukraine legal market, see *The Legal 500 – Europe, Middle East & Africa* at www.legal500.com.

UKRANIAN FIRMS

BC Toms & Co

OFFSHORE FIRMS

Carey Olsen is the largest firm in the Channel Islands. London-based corporate partner Fiona Fleming advises on a broad range of Guernsey corporate, M&A, private equity and collective investment scheme matters. The team received a boost when Nicolas Journeaux and Nicole Langlois, two Jersey litigation partners, moved full-time to the London office to focus on complex commercial and trust litigation, contract disputes and asset recovery.

Mourant du Feu & Jeune was the first Jersey firm to open an office in London in 2000 to offer Jersey law advice to UK-based clients. Jonathan Rigby heads the Jersey team, which advises on a wide range of corporate, banking, capital markets and fund structure matters. The London office received a boost when Stacey Overholt, who is qualified to practise law in Cayman, New York, England and Wales and Ontario, Canada, joined the firm from **Maples and Calder** to head the London-based Cayman Islands team. Overholt's move now enables the nine-lawyer London office to advise on both Jersey and Cayman law. Examples in the past year include advising a major investment bank on both Jersey and Cayman law elements of CDO and hedge fund repackaging transactions.

Jersey-based **Ogier** fields a two-lawyer office which opened in London in 2003. The office offers advice on structured finance, investment funds,

OFFSHORE FIRMS

Appleby Spurling Hunter *Cayman Islands, Bermuda*
Arias, Fábrega & Fábrega *Panama*
Carey Olsen *Guernsey, Jersey*
Conyers Dill & Pearman *Bermuda*
Harney Westwood & Riegels LLP ✪ *BVI*
Lennox Paton ✪ *Bahamas*
Maples and Calder *Cayman Islands*
Mourant du Feu & Jeune *Jersey*
Ogier ✪ *Jersey*
Patton, Moreno & Asvat *Panama*
Quijano & Associates *Panama*
Simcocks *Isle of Man*
Vallarino, Vallarino y Rivera *Panama*
Walkers *Cayman Islands*

Firms are listed alphabetically
✪ *Indicates firm displays contact details at the end of this chapter.*

real estate investment and trusts. Through Ogier Fiduciary Services, the office also provides administration and accounting services to trusts and commercial clients. Aaron DeLacey and Brian Lee are the key contacts in London.

Maples and Calder is the largest law firm in the Cayman Islands. A three-partner, ten-associate team in London advises on banking, capital markets, structured debt, international equity offerings, mutual and hedge funds, private trusts and litigation. Clients include international and domestic law firms and high-net-worth individuals.

Walkers was the second Cayman Islands firm to arrive in London. Partners Ann Nealon, Susan Harper and David Whittome head a team of four associates. The firm advises on general finance and banking, including hedge funds and structured finance for several major London institutions. The team also advises on BVI law.

Appleby Spurling Hunter was created by the merger of Bermuda-based *Appleby Spurling & Kempe* with Cayman Islands firm *Hunter & Hunter*. Resident partner Warren Cabral, Deborah Poole and senior counsel Rory Todd head a team which advises on both Bermuda and Cayman law. The London office acts for blue-chip clients on a wide range of corporate, banking, capital markets and funds advice.

Bermuda-headquartered **Conyers Dill & Pearman** boasts a five-lawyer team in London headed by Martin Lane which advises on Bermuda, BVI and Cayman Islands law. Kieran Loughran and Christopher Johnson-Gilbert advise on funds in Cayman, Bermuda and BVI. Stephen Pollard, who advises on BVI law, joined from **Allen & Overy LLP**. Roger Burgess advises on Bermuda corporate matters, with a special focus on insurance and derivatives law.

Bahamas-based **Lennox Paton** has a niche presence in London which advises on banking, asset finance and shipping law, often working closely with leading shipping law firms in London, Norway and Greece for shipping law.

At BVI firm **Harney Westwood & Riegels LLP**, Leonard Birmingham heads a team of three lawyers in London. Associate Wendy Walker focuses on investment funds work.

Leading Panama firm **Arias, Fábrega & Fábrega** advises on corporate, banking, tax and private client matters. The team also advises on shipping matters such as the flagging of vessels and yachts in Panama. The London office works closely with its offices in the BVI, Luxembourg and Hong Kong. Enrique Sibauste heads the two-lawyer office.

Quijano & Associates' Daphne Quijano heads a niche practice in London which advises on Panamanian corporate and maritime law.

Panama-based **Patton, Moreno & Asvat** and **Vallarino, Vallarino y Rivera** are recommended for corporate and shipping law.

Isle of Man firm **Simcocks** has a part-time London presence.

MIDDLE EASTERN FIRMS

A K Anvari & Associates (Dr)
Sabi and Associates

Firms are listed alphabetically

MIDDLE EASTERN FIRMS

Dr A K Anvari & Associates advises UK firms and private clients in the areas of commercial, finance, family and shipping. Name partner Dr Anvari has been practising Iranian law for more than 40 years. The firm has offices in London, Tehran and Isfahan.

Niche firm **Sabi and Associates** advises on Iranian law for European, Middle Eastern and US clients. International arbitration and litigation, primarily pursued against Iranian government agencies, is a key area of focus. Hamid Sabi heads the team.

For a detailed review of the Middle Eastern legal markets, see *The Legal 500 – Europe, Middle East & Africa* at www.legal500.com.

AUSTRALIAN FIRMS

Mallesons Stephen Jaques' London office is headed by Rowan Russell, who transferred from the firm's Sydney office, and has a focus on financial services and capital markets work. Russell heads a team of eight associates, which includes a mixture of lawyers qualified to practise in both England and Australia. The firm acted for AMP Bank on UK and Australian aspects of the sale of its £400m portfolio of UK residential mortgages. Other clients include ANZ Banking Group, Deutsche Bank, Royal Bank of Scotland, National Australia Bank and Telstra Corporation. The firm is 'commercial and realistic' in its advice, say clients.

Minter Ellison was the first antipodean firm to set up an office in London, over 30 years ago. Robert Hanley and Michael Whalley, who has been practising in London for 29 years, head a team of six associates offering both Australian and English law advice on a range of corporate, securities, finance and capital markets transactions. The firm advised Lloyds TSB in relation to acquisition financing of airlines by Qantas. One London-based client with Australian subsidiaries perceives the firm's strong employment practice in Australia to be a notable asset.

For a detailed review of the Australian legal market, see *The Asia Pacific Legal 500* at www.legal500.com.

AUSTRALIAN FIRMS

Mallesons Stephen Jaques
Minter Ellison

Firms are listed alphabetically

BRAZILIAN FIRMS

Noronha Advogados

BRAZILIAN FIRMS

Brazilian firm **Noronha Advogados** has had a presence in London since 1988. Partners Eliana Maria Filippozzi and Vera Helena de Moraes Dantas head a team which advises on banking and international trade, working closely with the firm's offices in Brazil and Portugal.

For a detailed review of the Brazilian legal market see www.legal500.com

CANADIAN FIRMS

At **Blake, Cassels & Graydon LLP** a London-based team of two partners and one associate advises on corporate, M&A and finance transactions. David Glennie, who has been based in London since 1992, and Carlos Cerqueira, who transferred from Canada in the past year, are recommended. The firm acted as Canadian counsel to Vodafone Group plc in relation to the Canadian aspects of its US$3.5bn acquisition of the European telecoms business of Telesystem International Wireless Inc. The group also has a special focus on transactions in the natural resources sector.

Fasken Martineau DuMoulin LLP advises on corporate, M&A, capital markets and project finance transactions. London office managing partner John Elias heads the team. In addition to co-operating with the firm's network of offices in Canada, the London office also often works together with lawyers in the firm's Johannesburg office. Clients include Barclays, Citigroup and UBS.

At **McCarthy Tétrault** Robert Brant heads a two-partner, four-assistant team in London. The group has a strong focus on capital markets work, and has advised on several major AIM flotations. Other areas of work include corporate and project finance transactions, especially in the oil and gas and telecom sectors. The team reports an increase in work relating to the Middle East in the past year. Clients include CIBC, CSFB and LionOre International Mining.

Ogilvy Renault LLP's Peter Noble heads a team in London which advises on corporate, capital markets and project finance transactions. Debt capital markets transactions are a key area of

CANADIAN FIRMS

Blake, Cassels & Graydon LLP
Fasken Martineau DuMoulin LLP
McCarthy Tétrault
Ogilvy Renault LLP
Stikeman Elliott LLP

Firms are listed alphabetically

work. Clients include Canadian corporates and financial institutions such as Royal Bank of Canada and Bombardier, as well as major UK and European clients.

Stikeman Elliott LLP has one of the largest presences of any Canadian firm in London. Derek Linfield heads a team which grew from 11 lawyers to 13 recently. The team advised on several AIM listings and project finance transactions for clients in the natural resources sector. Shawna Miller is recommended for debt capital markets and securitisation transactions. Richard Hay advises on private client matters. Martin Byatt joined the team as of counsel from *Coudert Brothers* to focus on work for clients in the energy and natural resources sector.

SOUTH AFRICAN FIRMS

At **Bowman Gilfillan** Heather Duffey heads a team in London which works closely with the firm's offices in South Africa in advising both European and multinational corporates in relation to M&A transactions and joint ventures in South Africa, as well as South African corporates doing business in London.

Maitland is a European multi-disciplinary firm affiliated to South African firms **Webber Wentzel Bowens** and **Shepstone & Wylie**. Key focus areas include corporate, banking and investment funds, private client matters, tax and estate planning and international arbitration. Senior principal Eric Pfaff and corporate lawyer Michael Solomon are recommended. The firm acts for major South African blue-chip companies such as Anglo American and De Beers. **Maitland** has a network of European offices in Dublin, the Isle of Man, Luxembourg and Paris.

For a detailed review of the South African legal market, see *The Legal 500 – Europe, The Middle East and Africa* at www.legal500.com.

SOUTH AFRICAN FIRMS

Bowman Gilfillan
Maitland

Firms are listed alphabetically

INDIAN FIRMS

At **ALMT Legal** partners Shalini Agarwal and Sakate Khaitan head a team of three lawyers in London which advises on Indian law matters for major US and European clients. Areas of focus include corporate, banking, dispute resolution and tax law. The team works closely with its offices in Mumbai and Bangalore.

INDIAN FIRMS

ALMT Legal
Lexindia
Singhania & Co

Firms are listed alphabetically

Lexindia's Tony Khindria heads a team in London which advises on both Indian and English law for a range of multinational and SME clients. Clients come from the automotive, banking, construction, defence, pharmaceutical and telecoms sectors. The firm also has offices in New Delhi and Paris.

Singhania & Co is one of the largest firms on the Indian sub-continent, and was the first to set up an office in London, in 1990. The firm advises on corporate and dispute resolution matters for European clients active in India. IP is also a key area of work, for clients such as banks and telecoms, software and IT companies. Vijay Goel and Raja Murugan head a team of six lawyers. The firm has a network of seven offices in India.

For a detailed review of the Indian legal market, see *The Asia Pacific Legal 500* at www.legal500.com.

OUTSIDE LONDON: THE REGIONS

The main legal centre for the UK is London but there are a good number of firms with strong commercial practices in the regions. International clients could find that one of the leading regional firms perfectly fits their requirements; generally at a much lower cost.

EAST ANGLIA

East Anglia comprises the counties of Cambridgeshire, Norfolk and Suffolk. Agriculture is a major industry, and there is a hi-tech cluster around Cambridge, with some large companies (though few plcs) based in the area. Nearby Peterborough is home to a number of bigger corporates, particularly in the food industry. Suffolk is dominated by Ipswich and the port of Felixstowe. In Norfolk, the city of Norwich is the historical business centre of East Anglia, and a notable seat of old money. Many prominent London individuals own property in Norfolk, making private client work an important practice stream for local firms.

CORPORATE AND COMMERCIAL CAMBRIDGE

Eversheds LLP's team has decreased in size but lead corporate partner Anthony McGurk has been working on one of the largest recent deals in the east of England, the £135m acquisition of an international group for Astron Group Ltd, and also on the complex £2m acquisition of the Flagship Food Group for Tulip Ltd, a subsidiary of Danish Crown. Glynne Stanfield has been focusing on the education sector, including university mergers. The former head of the separate Cambridge-based commercial services department, Paul Hughes, has now left for an academic position, and Cambridge-based senior associate Liz Fitzsimons now leads the East of England commercial services team.

Hewitsons has a strong, four-partner corporate team that often acts for technology companies rather than investors. The team recently advised locally based software company Amino Technologies plc on its AIM flotation, after winning a competitive tender against City firms. The highly regarded John Dix is now the firm's managing partner, but still spends a good portion of his time on client work. James Lawrence and Jason Williams are also much liked by clients, who say that the practice has 'the experience of a large City firm, but without the arrogance or assumed superiority that is often encountered'. Another client commented: 'Our London-based corporate finance advisers and brokers were pleasantly surprised by the quality of this firm, and would recommend it to others of their clients'.

Mills & Reeve's recent corporate finance work includes acting for the shareholders of Primagraphics Holdings Ltd on the US$21m sale of the company to the UK subsidiary of a NYSE-listed company. Brian Marshall who led this work, is well liked by clients – they describe him as 'user friendly' – as is team head Claire Clarke who is described as 'very knowledgeable and an absolute pleasure to work with'. Tom Pickthorn is also highly regarded.

Taylor Wessing has a small but high-powered Cambridge office that focuses on advising VCs and other investors in the technology sector. Cambridge corporate partner David Mardle and Simon Walker who splits his time between London and Cambridge, are praised by clients for working well together and being 'excellent without exception'. One client added: 'Many firms claim to want to work with start-up companies, but few deliver on this claim. **Taylor Wessing** is one of them.' Cambridge clients include Trigenix Ltd and Broadcom Europe Ltd.

The departure of **Taylor Vinters**' TMT partner Simon Smith to **Blake Lapthorn Linnell** has resulted in corporate partner Quentin Golder 's move to head the TMT team. The main corporate partner is now John Short whom clients praise for his 'excellent understanding of restructuring matters' and for 'always driving the job forward'. Banking partner James Allen also handles corporate finance work including, recently, the £5m refinancing of UTM Holdings Ltd via a debt-to-equity swap.

Dorsey & Whitney's year-old Cambridge office is still small but is performing well, with two senior associates focusing on technology start-up and VC work and dividing their time between Cambridge and London. Clients include Cambridge Consultants and various Cambridge University spin-outs. The office also offers access to the firm's offices in the US and Far East.

Kester Cunningham John's Cambridge-based corporate partner, Fiona Roberts recently advised Icefresh Food Ltd, one of the UK's leading frozen food groups, on an acquisition. One client said: 'It is in the company commercial field that this firm is making greatest strides and challenging the established four firms'. The firm is also increasingly handling bank lending work.

Clients say that they are 'very satisfied' with the commercial advice given by **Barr Ellison**.

CORPORATE AND COMMERCIAL Cambridge

EVERSHEDS LLP

Hewitsons
Mills & Reeve
Taylor Wessing

Taylor Vinters

Dorsey & Whitney
Kester Cunningham John

Barr Ellison

Firms are listed A-Z in tiers which are ranked in order of priority

CORPORATE AND COMMERCIAL Ipswich

BIRKETTS

Ashton Graham
Prettys

Gotelee & Goldsmith Solicitors

Blocks
Kerseys

Firms are listed A-Z in tiers which are ranked in order of priority

IPSWICH

Birketts' five-partner team, led by James Austin is described by Suffolk clients as 'the law firm of first choice for corporate matters'. Adrian Seagers a recent addition to the firm from **Eversheds LLP**, advised an MBI team on the acquisition of Caterham Cars, while the highly regarded Annette Whybrow advised Anglian Crown Ltd on a £16m divestment.

Ashton Graham recently acted on the £4.2m MBO of a local construction company. Ipswich-based corporate finance partner Paul Whittingham is praised by clients as being 'technically very capable and pleasant', and clients also appreciate the firm's competitive pricing. Complaints that Whittingham lacked back-up in Ipswich have been addressed by the recruitment of an assistant from **Clifford Chance**.

Prettys now has a two-partner team following the promotion of Keith Vincent to the partnership. One client said: 'The single best decision we made in our management buy-out process was to appoint Keith and his team.' The practice focuses on advising owner-managed businesses in Suffolk, and is particularly strong in the healthcare and transport sectors, where it acts for a number of national clients. The team, headed by Ian Waine has recently been appointed to the RBS panel.

NORWICH

Mills & Reeve is set to recruit (in the summer of 2005) **Eversheds LLP**'s entire Norwich corporate team, comprising three partners and a team of 13 additional lawyers and support staff and including Terry Gould who is widely regarded as the leading corporate finance lawyer in East Anglia. At the time of going to press, it was not known which of his prestigious local clients would follow him to his new firm. The new recruits will also include partner Craig Hodgson who has been been developing an increasingly strong reputation. The existing team is led by Nick Fischl who is described by clients as 'every bit a match' for counterparts at Magic Circle firms. James Hunter is also extremely highly regarded by clients. Bryony Falkus retired in May 2005.

CORPORATE AND COMMERCIAL Norwich
MILLS & REEVE
Birketts
Howes Percival
steeles (law) llp
Leathes Prior
Greenland Houchen
Hansells
Kester Cunningham John
Cozens-Hardy & Jewson
Fosters
Hatch Brenner
Rogers and Norton

Firms are listed A-Z in tiers which are ranked in order of priority

Birketts' new Norwich office, made up of ex-**Eversheds LLP** lawyers, is increasingly competing on price with **Mills & Reeve**. Adrian Seagers who spends part of his time at the Ipswich office, is supported by a full-time assistant in Norwich, and recently advised the Norfolk-based Acteon Group on its acquisition of a US company. Clients describe the team as 'a tremendous resource'.

Howes Percival has been advising a Norwich-based company on an international merger and its intended AIM listing, and National Carpets on a £4m disposal. Clients praise Jon Baskerville for his sound advice and focus, and say he is 'reliable and effective'. Fellow partner Andrew Wood is also well liked and described as 'excellent in his grasp of international law'.

steeles (law) llp has a three-partner team and a focus on public sector clients. In the private sector, Nigel Lubbock – whom clients describe as 'very understanding' – has been advising NYSE-listed Ionics Inc on the restructuring of its UK-based businesses as part of an international acquisition.

Leathes Prior's Paul Warman recently advised the management team on the MBO of local company Hadley & Ottaway Ltd, and has growing experience in insurance-sector acquisitions. Corporate head Jonathan Chadd is known for his franchising practice.

PETERBOROUGH

Buckles Solicitors LLP has a strong local and Cambridgeshire practice led by Nigel Moore whom clients describe as 'market-minded' and 'an excellent corporate lawyer'. Martin Lewis has particular experience in internet retailing, and recently advised an East Anglia company in the food industry on a £6m acquisition, and Austin Blackburn is now focusing on corporate rather than employment work.

CORPORATE AND COMMERCIAL Peterborough
BUCKLES SOLICITORS LLP
GREENWOODS SOLICITORS LLP
Hegarty & Co
Hunt & Coombs

Firms are listed A-Z in tiers which are ranked in order of priority

Greenwoods Solicitors LLP has a smaller team but handles some high-level national work including, recently, corporate finance projects in the food sector. David Woods – whom clients say is high-quality and 'good value for money' – is the full-time corporate partner, while managing partner Shelagh Smith spends 20% of her time on client work. The corporate governance capability of the firm has been significantly boosted by the arrival of new business defence partner Kathryn Gilbertson from **Dechert LLP**.

Hegarty & Co's corporate associate Andrew Heeler is much liked by clients, one of whom described him as 'the best lawyer I've dealt with'. Heeler's recent work includes advising the local development hall on a substantial refinancing. Senior partner Richard Hegarty also spends a proportion of his time on corporate work.

Hunt & Coombs managing partner Paul Tate spends half of his client time on corporate work, and has a focus on the retail sector. Clients say that they are 'extremely pleased' with his work. Personal injury partner John Bates handles some commercial work, including advising on franchise agreements.

ELSEWHERE IN EAST ANGLIA

Clients say that **Ashton Graham**'s Bury St Edmunds-based commercial partner David Barnes has 'a gift for getting to the heart of an issue'.

Suffolk firm **Greene & Greene** has a solid corporate practice that handles some sizeable deals for the mid-Anglia region, with partners Chris Thomson and David Medcalf highly regarded by clients.

Kester Cunningham John has a strong mid-Anglia practice. Bury St Edmunds-based Anna Soroko – formerly in-house with TXU – has the leading energy practice in the region and a strong M&A background. Clients describe her as 'constructive, proactive and prompt'. She has been advising the DTI on a national energy project which is being run out of East Anglia. Thetford-based Clive Wadham-Smith is now focusing increasingly on commercial rather than real estate work.

CORPORATE AND COMMERCIAL Elsewhere in East Anglia
ASHTON GRAHAM *Bury St Edmunds*
GREENE & GREENE *Bury St Edmunds*
KESTER CUNNINGHAM JOHN *Bury St Edmunds, Thetford*
Leeds Day *Huntingdon*
Bates Wells & Braithwaite *Sudbury*
Blocks *Felixstowe*
Gross & Co *Bury St Edmunds*
Nicholsons *Lowestoft*
Rustons & Lloyd *Newmarket*

Firms are listed A-Z in tiers which are ranked in order of priority

COMMERCIAL LITIGATION CAMBRIDGE

Mills & Reeve's head of commercial litigation, Graeme Menzies is described by clients as 'well informed, pleasant and helpful' and 'thorough and easy to work with'. Fellow partner Jamie Wheatley who is best known for his insolvency work but also offers general commercial litigation experience, is also well liked. One client involved in major litigation said: 'I appreciated the wisdom offered by Jamie, aimed at helping me get through the emotional pressure of it all.' The team has significant experience in representing public sector clients.

Jane Lichtenstein is the Cambridge-based commercial litigation partner in **Eversheds LLP**'s London-led team. She is the lead partner for new client the General Medical Council in London and the South East, and has also recently acted for Incos Ltd in two High Court actions against major perfume houses.

Hewitsons' Simon Biggin who handles insolvency matters in addition to general commercial litigation, is praised by clients for offering 'practical, common sense, commercial, realistic advice'. He heads a three-partner team that recently advised a major German bank on an international debt recovery matter.

Taylor Vinters' Edward Perrott has been handling some groundbreaking competition litigation. Clients says that he is 'competent, thorough and practical', and that fellow partner Christopher Falvey offers 'sound guidance'. Sarah Sharratt has now retired.

COMMERCIAL LITIGATION Cambridge
MILLS & REEVE
Eversheds LLP
Hewitsons
Taylor Vinters
Kester Cunningham John
Barr Ellison

Firms are listed A-Z in tiers which are ranked in order of priority

Kester Cunningham John's Michael Frape is described by clients as 'excellent, and a breath of fresh air in Cambridge', while Martin Kemp is noted as 'well known in Cambridge and clever'. These partners have recently been handling two majority shareholder actions.

IPSWICH

Birketts' Ipswich team head Bob Wright has been working on a competition appeals tribunal case involving cartel allegations against vitamin suppliers, with several million pounds in dispute. IP partner Matthew Atkins also has a good reputation for general commercial litigation.

Commercial litigation clients describe **Prettys** as 'an excellent provincial firm'. The team, headed by Peter Blake handles disputes for clients including Ipswich Town Football Club, Norfolkline and the SEH Group.

Ashton Graham has been acting for Suffolk-based Jack Brand Ltd in multiple challenges relating to the Food Safety Act against the Food Standards Agency. Mark Merriam who is also the firm's managing partner, heads the team, and Rob Adam who is based in Bury St Edmunds but also handles work in Ipswich, is praised by clients for his communication skills and accessibility.

Gotelee & Goldsmith Solicitors' Jonathan Ripman has a strong practice with a focus on the transport industry. He also handles general contractual disputes.

COMMERCIAL LITIGATION Ipswich
BIRKETTS
Prettys
Ashton Graham
Gotelee & Goldsmith Solicitors
Kerseys

COMMERCIAL LITIGATION Norwich
BIRKETTS
MILLS & REEVE
Howes Percival
steeles (law) llp
Fosters
Kester Cunningham John
Leathes Prior
Cozens-Hardy & Jewson
Greenland Houchen
Hansells
Rogers and Norton

Firms are listed A-Z in tiers which are ranked in order of priority

Kerseys wins its place in the tables on the strength of the reputation of Anthony Wooding Clients praise his case management skills, saying that he 'works very hard and diligently'.

NORWICH

Birketts' team is led by **Eversheds LLP**'s former Norwich-based dispute resolution partner Paul Matthews whom clients describe as having been 'excellent through many difficult litigations'. He is currently acting for Ransomes plc in two connected Commercial Court actions, involving £1m claims. Max Roessler also has a very good reputation.

Rachel Higgs at **Mills & Reeve**'s Norwich office has a market-leading reputation. She is currently acting for the majority shareholders in a complex and high-value shareholder dispute, and has considerable experience of settling these types of disputes by mediation. Clients describe her as 'well-balanced' and 'professional'.

Howes Percival has particular expertise in handling professional negligence work, including claims against solicitors. Highly experienced department head Andrew Barnes has recently been dealing with an increasing amount of work in the motor industry, for clients such as the Polar Motor Company Ltd.

steeles (law) llp's department head Peter Hastings is praised by clients for 'taking time to develop a sound understanding of our business'. Clients also speak highly of his skill in advising parties to commercial mediation. One said: 'Peter was streets ahead of his opponent, realistic, on the ball, perceptive and sensible.'

Fosters has two partners who handle commercial mediation, with Alison Kirby notably handling some substantial partnership disputes.

Kester Cunningham John's Chris Gilbert specialises in construction-related disputes, and also handles general commercial litigation.

Leathes Prior's Mike Barlow has a good reputation for franchising disputes, and has recently been acting in arbitration against a major overseas franchisor. Martin Plowman has been developing the firm's commercial mediation practice.

ELSEWHERE IN EAST ANGLIA

Buckles Solicitors LLP's team is headed by James Maxey whom clients describe as 'very competent'. He has been handling a high-profile dispute over land sale contamination issues. He and fellow partner Paul Branch sit as commercial mediators; one mediation client said that they were 'very personable, and kept the momentum going'.

At **Greenwoods Solicitors LLP**, senior associate Darren Morgan heads a team whose recent activity includes a major motor industry dispute involving four defendants, and an embezzlement freezing injunction involving a £1.5m claim.

COMMERCIAL LITIGATION Elsewhere in East Anglia
BUCKLES SOLICITORS LLP *Peterborough*
Greenwoods Solicitors LLP *Peterborough*
Hegarty & Co *Peterborough*
Hunt & Coombs *Peterborough*
Ashton Graham *Bury St Edmunds*
Bates Wells & Braithwaite *Sudbury*
Kenneth Bush *King's Lynn*
Kester Cunningham John *Thetford*
Leeds Day *Huntingdon*
Nicholsons *Lowestoft*
Ward Gethin *King's Lynn*

Firms are listed A-Z in tiers which are ranked in order of priority

One client described the litigation practice at **Hegarty & Co** as 'better than the London firms I've used'. Partner Matthew Sidebottom enjoys a good reputation in Peterborough, and recently defeated a challenge to a local authority's plan for the allocation of housing in the Administrative Court.

Hunt & Coombs' Julie McQuoid has been handling commercial disputes for the Anglia Regional Cooperative Society's retail operation, for which the firm is the sole legal adviser.

EAST MIDLANDS

The East Midlands is bounded by Birmingham to the west; Yorkshire and the Peak District to the north; the Home Counties to the south; and the North Sea to the east. It is a region of diverse character, with large swathes of rural landscape in the east giving way to big business and major cities in the centre and west.

Comprising Derbyshire, Lincolnshire, Leicestershire, Northamptonshire and Nottinghamshire, the five principal cities of the East Midlands are also the five capitals of these counties. Nottingham is often seen as the leading city (although this is hotly disputed elsewhere in the region) and the biggest corporates, including Experian, Rolls Royce, Capital One and Boots, cluster around this city.

CORPORATE AND COMMERCIAL NOTTINGHAM AND DERBY

Eversheds LLP now operates a corporate team across an expanded 'Central Region' which includes Cardiff as well as Nottingham and Birmingham. Although the changes have resulted in the departure of partners Ben Johnson and David Tilly for **Geldards LLP**, the firm nevertheless retains the heaviest corporate muscle on the ground and is praised 'for a very high standard of service'. In addition to being regular corporate advisers to Rolls-Royce, the firm was also instructed by 3i on the £92m sale of Reeves

CORPORATE AND COMMERCIAL
Nottingham and Derby

EVERSHEDS LLP *Nottingham*

BROWNE JACOBSON LLP *Nottingham*
FREETH CARTWRIGHT LLP *Nottingham, Derby*
GELDARDS LLP *Nottingham, Derby*
SHOOSMITHS *Nottingham*

HBJ Gateley Wareing LLP *Nottingham*

Berryman *Nottingham*
Nelsons *Nottingham, Derby*

Actons *Nottingham*
Flint Bishop & Barnett *Derby*

Firms are listed A-Z in tiers which are ranked in order of priority

Oilfield Services, and had a significant role on the Britton Group MBO. Nottingham-based Stephen Kitts who now heads the Central Region group, led the advice on the latter transaction.

Browne Jacobson LLP is regarded as the primary competitor to **Eversheds LLP** for the bigger deals. It is also far happier than its rival to advise on smaller local deals, with a seven-partner team active in 100 deals recently worth a total of £800m. Highlights included acting for Advantage Capital on its acquisition of Charcol, and for backer LDC on the £46m MBO of Britton, the region's largest private equity deal. Department head Gavin Cummings is the most highly regarded star, with Robert Metcalfe and Nigel Blackwell also winning praise.

Nottingham-based John Heaphy is the 'most prominent personality corporate-wise' at **Freeth Cartwright LLP**, which is 'prospering' in the East Midlands following advice on 75 transactions in the past year, worth a total of £700m. One highlight was acting for GW Padley Holdings on its sale of a £200m-turnover poultry business to a US food company, with Karl Jansen leading the advice.

Geldards LLP 'has made a cracking start to raising its game' following the arrival of 'impressive' duo Ben Johnson and David Tilly from **Eversheds LLP**. Johnson and Tilly link arms with the 'excellent' Andrew Borkowski and will doubtless seek to surpass the recent convincing haul of over 100 deals averaging £6m each. Specialist German and US teams particularly impress clients as 'a powerful tool and exceptional marketing strategy'.

Shoosmiths retains some of the best corporate talent in the market under the guidance of head Peter Seary but appears less in the local market than many others. The reason lies partly in the fact that the firm aims to compete in the £10m to £20m deal bracket which is too seldom available in Nottingham; the firm therefore feeds a substantial quantity of its national plc work through Nottingham, including a lucrative stream of commercial due diligence work for a major US firm. National corporate head Oliver Brookshaw is often Nottingham-based, and Andrew Pickin heads an impressive EU and competition team. Recent activity includes acting for Reeves Oilfield Services on its £92m sale to Precision Drilling.

Corporate heavyweight Austin Moore at 'top-notch' **HBJ Gateley Wareing LLP** (following *Gateley Wareing's* merger with Scottish firm *Henderson Boyd Jackson*) enjoys the 'run of some deeply entrenched networks'. Owner-managed and technology sector businesses are a core focus of the office. Moore is supported by Mark Rutherford who also has a strong following.

Predominantly active in the £1m to £5m deal market, **Berryman**'s corporate offering is enjoying good times, as evidenced by a 40% rise in fee income. Duncan James led a team that advised Orion Trent on its sale to SIG for a value in the region of £20m.

Also active in the £1m to £5m market, **Nelsons** continues to grow. Nottingham head Duncan Taylor led the advice to Femcare, a medical equipment company, on its multi-million-pound MBO. In Derby, Clare Vickers is well regarded for her corporate acquisition prowess.

Adrian Forster heads **Actons**' corporate and commercial team, which continues to be a leading player in the owner-managed market, with deals typically in the region of £1m.

Flint Bishop & Barnett acted on over 20 transactions in the past year, with an aggregate value of £10m. One highlight was acting, under David Kaplan for Dutch company Falco BV on its acquisition of UK company Arunhithe.

ELSEWHERE IN EAST MIDLANDS

Harvey Ingram LLP typically completes about 50 transactions annually, many of which are in the £1m to £2m range. Following the hire of partner Rhys Lewis from **Al-Sayegh Richards Butler** there are now five partners in the team. John Stobart and Roy Botterill are headline names.

Jit Singh heads **Howes Percival**'s Leicester corporate department, which is going from strength to strength, having acted in 55 deals in the past year worth a total of £600m. Foremost among these was the instruction from Travelsphere Holdings to act on its acquisition of Page & Moy Travel Group (advised by **Eversheds LLP**). Gerald Couldrake heads a smaller Northampton team that recently advised EasyCar on its high-profile restructuring.

Clients cannot fault the team at **EMW Law LLP**, a transaction-focused firm that 'looks and feels comfortable from the word go' and leaps up the rankings this year. Ian Zant-Boer and Ian Morris are the leading names.

CORPORATE AND COMMERCIAL
Elsewhere in East Midlands

HARVEY INGRAM LLP *Leicester*
HOWES PERCIVAL *Leicester, Northampton*

EMW Law LLP *Northampton*
Freeth Cartwright LLP *Leicester*
HBJ Gateley Wareing LLP *Leicester*
Hewitsons *Northampton*
Shoosmiths *Northampton*

Spearing Waite *Leicester*
Wilkin Chapman *Grimsby, Lincoln*

Nelsons *Leicester*
Sills & Betteridge *Lincoln*

Firms are listed A-Z in tiers which are ranked in order of priority

Freeth Cartwright LLP has benefited from the arrival of corporate partner David West from **Eversheds LLP**. West is well versed in corporate finance and joins department head Robert Rowley.

Gareth John is responsible for corporate matters at **HBJ Gateley Wareing LLP** in Leicester. John often acts alongside Nottingham-based Mark Rutherford and together they attract some sizeable deals across the region; recent examples include acting for DCC plc on its £20m acquisition of the business of Shell Direct UK.

Clients of **Hewitsons** range from plcs through to local owner-managed businesses, with respected team head Richard Ingram handling corporate matters and partner Kevin Fletcher focusing on the commercial side. In the past year, the firm advised on some 50 transactions with an aggregate value of £100m.

Shoosmiths has 'excellent corporate credentials' throughout the East Midlands, although corporate is less of a focus in the Northampton office than in Nottingham or Milton Keynes. Nevertheless, the firm's clients include some of Northampton's leading names, for example DaimlerChrysler.

Spearing Waite enjoys a good reputation among its Leicester owner-managed business client following. It acted for the Blenheim consortium in its purchase of Notts County Football Club from its administrators.

Lincolnshire firm **Wilkin Chapman** advised on some 50 transactions in the past year, including advice to the management team on the multi-million-pound MBO of Cardsave backed by Royal London Private Equity. The team is strengthened by the return of associate Anna Hillman after four years with **Eversheds LLP**.

Pip Dawkins is active at SME-focused **Nelsons**, which specialises in corporate finance. Dawkins is supported by Melanie Oswin who advises on corporate recovery and lending matters.

Lincoln's **Sills & Betteridge** is recommended for general corporate and commercial matters. The firm stands out for its energy sector experience.

COMMERCIAL LITIGATION NOTTINGHAM AND DERBY

Paul Worth **Eversheds LLP**'s leading disputes partner in Nottingham, is 'making a real impact in the Midlands'. Worth works closely with Ian Gray who heads a wider Midlands litigation practice and is also based in Nottingham. The firm is alone in the region in being able to lay claim to a truly local, national and international client base; clients include locally based Rolls-Royce, national client DEFRA, and Joy Mining, an international company that recently instructed the firm on a £100m arbitration with a significant Siberian element.

Browne Jacobson LLP's commercial disputes group was restructured recently to include other teams practising litigation within the firm. The new team includes three full-time partners: Peter Ellis Paul Southby and Fiona Carter Carter was instructed by Express, now part of Arla Foods, in the defence of pollution claims brought by the Environment Agency.

Freeth Cartwright LLP operates three separate Nottingham commercial litigation teams headed by Philippa Dempster Charles Powell and Graham Greenfield as well as a Derby team. Clients include HMV, Coors and Nottinghamshire County Council. Alternative dispute resolution is a key selling point of the group, with three partners active as mediators.

Nino Simone heads a diverse practice at **Geldards LLP**, which has a strong rail sector following. Simone is supported by three other partners, including media law specialist Paul Hackney.

Approximately 15% of **Nelsons**' revenue is derived from its six-partner commercial disputes group. Three lawyers are higher courts advocates and group head Chris Adams is an accredited mediator.

The arrival at **Actons** of partner Chris Murratt from **Freeth Cartwright LLP** will boost the litigation credentials of his new firm, which is a leader in the field of insolvency litigation.

Berryman Shacklock combines the talents of IP litigator Steven Skiba construction head Richard Brackenbury and property litigator Clare Brady to form a broad disputes team.

'Private client focused' and acknowledged 'king of the freight industry' **Rothera Dowson** is a regular visitor to the High Court, Court of Appeal and European Court of Human Rights thanks to its niche transport expertise. Jane George is the name to note.

Flint Bishop & Barnett continues to boast the talents and experience of Andrew Cochrane whilst **Smith Partnership** is home to the highly regarded Russell Davies.

COMMERCIAL LITIGATION
Nottingham and Derby

EVERSHEDS LLP *Nottingham*

BROWNE JACOBSON LLP *Nottingham*
FREETH CARTWRIGHT LLP *Nottingham, Derby*

Geldards LLP *Derby, Nottingham*
Nelsons *Nottingham, Leicester, Derby*

Actons *Nottingham*
Berryman *Nottingham*
Rothera Dowson *Nottingham*

Flint Bishop & Barnett *Derby*
Smith Partnership *Derby*

Firms are listed A-Z in tiers which are ranked in order of priority

ELSEWHERE IN THE EAST MIDLANDS

Clients of Chris Saul at **Harvey Ingram LLP** assert that he is 'down to earth and good at what he does'. Employment head John Simon also stands tall in a seven-partner team, by far the biggest in Leicester and responsible for almost one-quarter of the firm's total revenue.

Litigation for financial institutions is a traditional strength for **Shoosmiths** and the number of fee-earners active in this area has recently swollen to 20. Disputes arising from commercial property matters are increasing. Practice head John Hill is recommended.

The Leicester arm of **Freeth Cartwright LLP**'s commercial disputes group is headed by Julian Middleton who also undertakes employment and professional negligence work.

Hewitsons wins the recommendation of top-tier peers for the quality of its globetrotting disputes practice; recent work has included cross-border collaborations with French, Dutch, German, US, Polish and Irish law firms. Dominic Hopkins heads the practice.

Few enjoy such unalloyed client praise as Geraint Davies, head of litigation at **Howes Percival**. Davies is widely regarded as 'helpful and hardworking' and 'at his best in demanding times', and as a 'provider of a real service'. Ashwin Mody heads the Northampton team.

EMW Law LLP's department spans general commercial, property and TMT-related litigation. Katharine Summers and founding partner Michael Eyton-Jones are the partners in charge.

Chattertons has a partner specialising in litigation in each of its Horncastle, Boston and Grantham offices, whilst **HBJ Gateley Wareing LLP**'s disputes team is led by senior associate Mukesh Patel.

Other recommendations include Andrew Argyle of **Langleys Solicitors** in Lincoln; Peter Bennett of **Roythornes** in Spalding; and **Wilkin Chapman** in Grimsby.

COMMERCIAL LITIGATION
Elsewhere in East Midlands

HARVEY INGRAM LLP *Leicester*
SHOOSMITHS *Northampton*

Freeth Cartwright LLP *Leicester*
Hewitsons *Northampton*
Howes Percival *Leicester, Northampton*

EMW Law LLP *Northampton*

Chattertons *Boston, Horncastle, Grantham*
HBJ Gateley Wareing LLP *Leicester*
Langleys Solicitors *Lincoln*
Roythornes *Spalding*
Wilkin Chapman *Grimsby*

Firms are listed A-Z in tiers which are ranked in order of priority

NORTH

Newcastle is the largest legal and business centre north of Leeds and dominates the North. The region also includes Cumbria, Durham, Northumberland and Tyne and Wear.

The main drivers of the North's economy are manufacturing, transport and insurance, and major corporations in the region include Nike, Sage Group, Arriva and Nissan. The North East in particular is fast becoming a haven for businesses and industries, who are increasingly realising the potential of the area.

CORPORATE AND COMMERCIAL NEWCASTLE

Offering a strength in depth that is unparalleled in the region, **Dickinson Dees**' 27-partner department goes from strength to strength. One of only a handful of firms in the region that can offer true specialisation, leading individuals include M&A experts John Flynn and department head Jamie Pass private equity specialist Chris Harker and Jonathan Hewitt who specialises in listings work. Major highlights included advising Helen McArdle Care Limited on its £100m sale to Bondcare Group and Bell Stores Limited on its sale to J Sainsbury (the firm is now instructed by J Sainsbury). The firm has a strong technology client base and advised Business Serve plc and Monstermob Group plc on several acquisitions. Whilst being instructed by a large number of plcs, the lifeblood of the firm is its long-established, grass-roots ties with the region's SMEs.

Headed by David Bowcock **Eversheds LLP**'s corporate and commercial department had a strong year and advised on 109 transactions with a total deal value in excess of £403m. Highlights included advising 3i on the £47m sale of Jaycare Holdings, and also acting on the MBO of the Cramlington division of BASF's fine chemicals

CORPORATE AND COMMERCIAL
Newcastle

DICKINSON DEES
EVERSHEDS LLP **ROBERT MUCKLE** **WARD HADAWAY** **WATSON BURTON LLP**
Hay & Kilner
Mincoffs Solicitors LLP **Sintons**

Firms are listed A-Z in tiers which are ranked in order of priority

group. The recent arrival of the focused and well-connected Alan Fletcher from **Robert Muckle** and Paul Cato who previously worked in-house at Nissan, bodes well for the future.

With a focus on serving the owner-managed business sector and offering a dedicated service to SMEs, **Robert Muckle**'s six-partner department continues to go from strength to strength. Offering a full range of corporate and commercial services, the firm has been particularly busy in M&A, advising both Longhirst Group and Dickinsons Furnishers on £1m-plus acquisitions. Clients appreciate the firm's commercial approach, adaptability and 'excellent grasp of the issues', and single out Hugh Welch Ian Gilthorpe Robert Phillips and Peter Robinson for particular praise. Recent arrival Andrew Davison garners enormous respect from both clients and peers, and is viewed by many as one of the best corporate lawyers in the region.

Headed by Martin Hulls **Ward Hadaway**'s 32-fee-earner department is second only to **Dickinson Dees**' in terms of size. Offering real strength in depth, the department specialises in plc, private equity and MBO work. Dispensing with its corporate finance advisory practice has given the department more focus, and 70 deals at a total of over £300m tells its own story. Highlights on the buy-out side including acting for the management team of Jaycare in its £47m buy-out by Phoenix Equity Partners. Private equity specialist Duncan Reid joined from **Pinsent Masons** and bolstered a strong department that includes Colin Hewitt Robert Thompson David Crone and Matt Collen all of whom have excellent followings.

Watson Burton LLP's eight-partner department offers 'clear and effective advice' to a range of corporate clients that includes Albany Group and Fairs Plc. Transaction highlights include advising the Co-operative Group Pharmacy on its acquisition of 11 pharmacies in South Wales, and acting on the MBO of a well-known local fashion brand. Department head Gillian Hall is highly regarded by clients for her commercial and pragmatic advice. Andrew Hoyle offers both experience and expertise and clients appreciate his ability to 'see the bigger picture'.

Headed by the 'outstanding' Nick James **Hay & Kilner**'s six-partner corporate and commercial department receives instructions from owner-managed businesses on a range of issues including M&A, corporate re-organisation and MBOs. The department is also instructed by clients in the US and Italy, and frequently receives referrals from other law firms and accountants.

Mincoffs Solicitors LLP advised on 50 transactions in the past year with a combined value in excess of £200m. The three-partner department had a particularly good year in M&A, advising Moulton Park Investments in the substantial acquisition of 13 SPV companies holding a number of district shopping centres, and also acting on the £40m sale of Factory Shop Group to Barclays Private Equity. Paul Hughes and John Nicholson are singled out for praise, particularly for their ability to work to tight deadlines.

With a focus on SMEs and owner-managed businesses, **Sintons**' corporate department had a strong year and the acquisition of Technology Services Group as a new client was a major coup. A niche area of expertise is partnership law; the team provides high-quality advice to a raft of clients that include law firms and medical practices. Karen Simms heads the practice that includes the 'highly capable' Chris Welch

CUMBRIA

Baines Wilson Solicitors acted for M-Sport on its new contractual arrangements with Ford, and for the management on the MBO of Capital Aluminium Extrusions. John Wilson is highly regarded and clients appreciate his 'efficient and expert advice' and 'ability to identify and tackle the pertinent commercial issues'.

Burnetts advised on several disposals and acquisitions in the financial services sector. Headed by John Noctor and ably supported by Vaughan Jones the department advises clients from the education, local government and transport sectors.

With five offices in the region, **Cartmell Shepherd** is well placed to serve its predominantly owner-managed clients.

Livingstons Solicitors provides commercial support to clients in south Cumbria.

CORPORATE AND COMMERCIAL
Cumbria

BAINES WILSON SOLICITORS *Carlisle* **BURNETTS** *Carlisle*
Cartmell Shepherd *Carlisle*
Livingstons Solicitors *Carlisle*

Firms are listed A-Z in tiers which are ranked in order of priority

CORPORATE AND COMMERCIAL
Elsewhere in the North

Archers Law LLP *Stockton-on-Tees* **Dickinson Dees** *Tees Valley* **Jacksons Commercial & Private Law LLP** *Stockton-on-Tees* **The Endeavour Partnership LLP** *Stockton-on-Tees*
Blackett Hart & Pratt *Darlington* **Latimer Hinks** *Darlington* **Tilly Bailey & Irvine** *Stockton-on-Tees*
Dobermans (a Division of Crutes Law Firm) *Middlesbrough* **Merritt & Co** *Yarm* **Punch Robson** *Middlesbrough* **Smith & Graham** *Hartlepool*

Firms are listed A-Z in tiers which are ranked in order of priority

ELSEWHERE IN THE NORTH

Archers Law LLP's John Richardson has a considerable reputation in the Tees Valley region and advises owner-managed businesses on a range of issues including M&A and commercial contracts.

Headed by the 'excellent' Nigel Williams **Dickinson Dees**' department had a busy year and advised on the sales of Bells Stores (to J Sainsbury) and Reg Boyle (to Corals). The office has since handled a number of instructions for J Sainsbury.

Led by Tony Wentworth **Jacksons Commercial & Private Law LLP** has experience across a variety of M&A, start-up and restructuring work. The firm advises clients from the manufacturing sector and places an increasing emphasis on providing corporate support in addition to offering heavyweight transactional strength.

With a focus on providing a range of services to indigenous Teesside businesses, **The Endeavour Partnership LLP** offers a breadth of expertise including MBOs and stock market flotations. Paul Bury heads a department that also includes the vastly experienced and accomplished Toby Tilly In the past year, the firm advised on 27 corporate transactions with a total deal value of more than £110m.

Blackett Hart & Pratt's Gary Copeland was recently promoted to partner and he now heads an accomplished team whose clients include numerous engineering and manufacturing businesses. Neil Hilton and Michael Winskell are valued members of the team.

At **Latimer Hinks**, Nick Poole has an excellent reputation for commercial and M&A work, and advises on non-contentious employment issues.

Headed out of the Tees Valley office by John Walters **Tilly Bailey & Irvine** provides all-round corporate support to the region's business community.

Dobermans (a Division of Crutes Law Firm) (formerly *Doberman Horsman*) and **Punch Robson** both have good reputations in Middlesbrough, while Noel Coward at Yarm-based firm **Merritt & Co** has a high profile.

Smith & Graham is well known in Hartlepool and also has offices in Durham, Peterlee and Darlington.

COMMERCIAL LITIGATION NEWCASTLE

Dickinson Dees advises corporate clients on a broad range of matters including shareholder disputes, complex contractual claims, and breach of warranty and property disputes, with Guy Harvey and John Marshall both receiving plaudits from their peers. The firm is also instructed by numerous public authorities on litigation matters.

Headed by Elizabeth Speed **Eversheds LLP**'s commercial litigation team advised the Argo Fund in its US$29.5m claim in relation to a disputed transfer of loan participations. The department is praised by clients as being 'responsive and helpful' and being able to offer excellent value for money. The arrival of the 'top-notch' Claire Frater from **Fox Williams** has strengthened a team that also includes the 'efficient and diligent' Susan Howe.

Headed by the 'energetic and dynamic' Ian Collinson **Ward Hadaway**'s six-partner department has experience across a range of complex, high-value litigation. The loss of Bob Elliott to **Baines Wilson Solicitors** was undoubtedly a blow, although the recent hire of IP expert Tim Toomey from **V-Lex Limited** was a notable one.

Led by Allan Henderson **Watson Burton LLP**'s 15-strong team advises clients on issues including shareholder and partnership disputes and white-collar crime. A leading practice in commercial fraud, Mark Heath has particular experience in NHS-related work and is frequently instructed by health authorities and primary care trusts throughout the country. Tristan Meears-White 's arrival from the Leeds office of **DLA Piper Rudnick Gray Cary UK LLP** has given the firm a regulatory capability.

Boasting a superb reputation for litigation particularly in the insurance sector, **Crutes Law Firm** also has considerable experience in partnership disputes. Helen Ager heads the department and firm chairman Tim Wallis has a high profile amongst clients in the insurance industry.

Hay & Kilner has a broad capability, with particular expertise in professional partnership disputes, railway litigation, judicial review and minority shareholder claims. Responding to the increasing recourse to mediation as a means of settling a dispute, the department has been proactive in proposing both formal ADR and CEDR mediations, and more informal meetings between the respective parties. Martin Soloman is particularly active in this area and is himself a mediator.

COMMERCIAL LITIGATION
Newcastle

DICKINSON DEES
EVERSHEDS LLP

WARD HADAWAY
WATSON BURTON LLP

Crutes Law Firm
Hay & Kilner
Robert Muckle

Blackett Hart & Pratt
Short Richardson & Forth

Gibson & Co
Sintons

Mincoffs Solicitors LLP

Firms are listed A-Z in tiers which are ranked in order of priority

Tony McPhillips heads **Robert Muckle**'s young but ambitious commercial litigation team. Working closely with colleagues in the firm's highly acclaimed property services group, the team is increasingly picking up a substantial number of quality property dispute instructions. Recent highlights include advising a majority shareholder in a multi-million-pound breach of trust dispute, and successfully obtaining an injunction preventing a union from industrial action. Mary Anne Roff has left the firm.

Blackett Hart & Pratt's team advises on a wide range of issues including contract, construction, partnership and product liability disputes. David Hunter Graeme Ritzema and Robin Winskell are recommended. Chris Judd left the firm in 2005.

Seasoned practitioners with a wealth of City experience behind them, Toby Gibson and Jane Gibson of **Gibson & Co** have successfully attracted instructions from numerous high-profile clients including Northern Rock and ANZ Bank.

Headed by David Dobbin **Sintons**' commercial litigation team works closely with the firm's other departments to provide a full-service package to companies and partnerships.

Mincoffs Solicitors LLP's small practice largely acts as a support service to existing corporate clients, predominantly in the leisure and property sectors.

ELSEWHERE IN THE NORTH

Burnetts advises a broad spectrum of commercial clients. Patricia Hall has particular expertise in professional negligence cases and inheritance disputes, and Michael Cousins is also recommended.

Crutes Mounseys Law Firm's Michael Robson offers expert litigation advice to an impressive list of commercial clients. Recommended by clients for his approachability, Paul Forster has a focus on housing disputes.

COMMERCIAL LITIGATION
Elsewhere in the North

Burnetts *Carlisle*
Crutes Mounseys Law Firm *Carlisle*
Dickinson Dees *Tees Valley*
Jacksons Commercial & Private Law LLP *Stockton-on-Tees*

Baines Wilson Solicitors *Carlisle*
Blackett Hart & Pratt *Durham*
Cartmell Shepherd *Carlisle*
Hayton Winkley Kendal *Kendal*
Latimer Hinks *Darlington*
The Endeavour Partnership LLP *Teesdale*
Tilly Bailey & Irvine *Stockton-on-Tees*

Firms are listed A-Z in tiers which are ranked in order of priority

Dickinson Dees' Craig Monty has particular expertise in pensions disputes and since joining from **Lovells** has built up a strong client base both in the region and nationally. Monty heads a team acting for an independent trustees company and its insurers in a breach of trust action following the winding-up of an occupational pension scheme.

Jacksons Commercial & Private Law LLP's department head, Nigel Kidwell is recommended for his contract and fraud work, particularly in the technology sector.

The arrival of Bob Elliott has given **Baines Wilson Solicitors** a presence in the market; he joined from **Ward Hadaway**.

Latimer Hinks advises on commercial, partnership, shareholder and insolvency disputes. Ken Wiper and Mark Gardner are both recommended.

Paul Bennett heads **The Endeavour Partnership LLP**'s team and recently gained higher rights of audience in the civil courts. Advising on a mix of commercial disputes, often with an international element, the firm receives frequent referrals from solicitors and accountants.

NORTH WEST

This chapter covers the practices of law firms in Greater Manchester, Merseyside, Lancashire and Cheshire. Several regional firms have offices in both Manchester and Liverpool, and sometimes beyond, while the national firms tend to favour Manchester and Leeds for their northern outposts; see also the **Yorkshire and the Humber** chapter. Multi-site firms can serve national clients across the regions, and expertise and personnel can be drawn upon from elsewhere in the network as the client requires. Satellite Lancashire towns host plenty of firms willing and able to handle commercial matters.

CORPORATE AND COMMERCIAL MANCHESTER

Addleshaw Goddard's sterling reputation in the market is evidenced by the calibre of new clients engaging the firm recently: Interflora was advised on its proposed demutualisation and protracted sale to 3i, while PZ Cussons was advised on the £37m acquisition of Charles Worthington Hair & Beauty Company. The eight-partner team boasts enviable expertise in the likes of Tim Hamilton and Paul Devitt, and increasing exposure to national FTSE 350 clients, thanks in part to the thriving London office, has not diluted the firm's presence in the local upper mid-market. Clients include BT plc and ten of the 11 Manchester VCs. Darryl Cooke, who departed for **DLA Piper Rudnick Gray Cary UK LLP** recently, has yet to be replaced.

Eversheds LLP's trio of Edward Pysden, Danny Hall and Peter Halpin spearhead a very impressive corporate practice, 'excellent in all areas', that advised Montagu Private Equity on its buyout of Maplin Electronics Limited for £244m. The merger of UMIST and the University of Manchester was an unusual deal which saw the firm's education group come into play. The firm also houses a distinct commercial services team, which focuses on all aspects of commercial contracts and has enjoyed particular penetration in the public sector under Alison Brearey, while Sean Caldwell recently advised Centrica on facilities management issues. Matthew Baker arrived from **Cobbetts** to head up the company secretarial unit. 'They are people I like and trust, and they take time to understand the deal,' said one client.

'Consistently excellent' **DLA Piper Rudnick Gray Cary UK LLP** enjoyed success across the corporate spectrum: SSL International plc was advised on the sale of its medical division, involving the multi-jurisdictional disposal of three businesses for a total of £247m; Northern Trust was advised on the purchase of the Brannigans pub chain; and the firm also acted for longstanding client Enterprise plc on its transfer from AIM to the Official List. Private equity was also a lucrative market for the renowned and experienced team, and the arrival from **Addleshaw Goddard** of Darryl Cooke, a genuine regional star, is a real boost to the firm's capability in the area. Jonathan Watkins is also singled out for praise.

Halliwells LLP is particularly active in the AIM market, where it has advised more companies on flotations than any other firm in the region, and also in private equity, where Tim Jackson-Smith is a recognised expert. Recent highlights include acting on the tertiary buyout of Morris Group for £170m.

Hammonds' corporate team continues to be involved in deals at the highest level, with recent work for Stephen Levy 's team including advising Montagu Private Equity on its £146m acquisition of Survitec Group. On the commercial side, Tom Bridgford is a regional leader in franchising matters, with household names such as Müller UK, Michelin, Marriott Inc and Allied Domecq instructing the firm in the past year. The Co-operative Group was advised on various commercial matters including a multi-million-pound deal with Glasgow Rangers FC, RBS was advised on an outsourcing contract, and chemicals giant Ineos Group – a client gain from 2003 – continues to furnish the firm with quality work.

The corporate and commercial practice at **Brabners Chaffe Street** is the success story of the Manchester office, accounting for 60% of the office's turnover. The seven-partner team is expected to grow by two more, while overseas and local OMBs are swelling a traditional industrial and manufacturing client base, which praises the firm for providing a value-for-money, partner-led service. The National Bank of Australia now engages the firm across its three offices on smaller corporate finance matters.

Cobbetts continues to be involved in some of the more interesting corporate activity the region has to offer. AIM work has increased; the firm has advised on companies' dual listing on the UK and Australian stock exchanges; and it secured the instruction to act on the first UK listing for a Ukrainian company in history. On the domestic side, the firm has advised on several take-privates. Primary care trusts have also provided significant instructions as the firm continues to impress in its work with foundation hospitals. Matthew Baker left for **Eversheds LLP**.

DWF continues to reap the benefits of close relationships with clients in the food sector, including Inter Link Foods, thanks to a specific sector focus. New client Prologic plc was advised on its admission to AIM, an area which has provided a good volume of work for the firm of late. Andrew Needham heads a Manchester practice that advises a number of entrepreneurial clients impressed with its response times and professionalism.

Pinsent Masons continues to secure instructions from management on MBOs, acting in this capacity on most of the larger buyouts of the year. Public Recruitment Group plc proved an important client, instructing the firm on several acquisitions and its admission to AIM, with AIM work a notable area of strength for the firm. Sean Fitzgerald receives excellent feedback from clients in the financial sector.

Kuit Steinart Levy continued in the successful vein of 2003 with notable activity in MBOs (including for Airline Services Ltd) and MBIs. New partner Rob Buckley has good experience in sports-related commercial matters, which is utilised in advice to clients such as Manchester City FC. A focus on AIM work garnered the instruction to act on the admission of a Chinese company to the market.

Mace & Jones Solicitors made up its previous shortfall in commercial capability with the recruitment of David Clinch from **Halliwells LLP**. The firm does well out of its real estate presence, recently advising Pochin on the acquisition of a Balfour Beatty subsidiary, and is developing a niche in telecoms work.

Philip Treanor and Simon Wallwork continue to develop **Pannone** into one of the more impressive single-site Manchester firms in the market. The firm held a solid mid-market position in a difficult year through a successful public sector practice that shows strongly in regeneration matters, while corporate activity included acting on an AIM listing and several local acquisitions and disposals.

Paul Ellaby heads the corporate and commercial practice at **Hill Dickinson LLP**'s Manchester operation, where SMEs are the client focus.

Five-partner firm **nexus Solicitors** was initially established as a commercial boutique focusing on a local OMB client base, but has branched out into the media and sports world on the back of clients from those sectors. Clients are impressed with the accessible, 'first-rate' one-to-one service of Tony Brook.

Beachcroft Wansbroughs is achieving notable successes in the AIM market. Key to this are the arrivals of Mark Broadhead, from an in-house position at Royal London Life, and the

CORPORATE AND COMMERCIAL Manchester
ADDLESHAW GODDARD
EVERSHEDS LLP
DLA PIPER RUDNICK GRAY CARY UK LLP
HALLIWELLS LLP
HAMMONDS
Brabners Chaffe Street
Cobbetts
DWF
Pinsent Masons
Kuit Steinart Levy
Mace & Jones Solicitors
Pannone
Hill Dickinson LLP
nexus Solicitors
Beachcroft Wansbroughs
Laytons
Wacks Caller
Berg Legal
George Davies Solicitors
Ricksons
Stephensons
turner parkinson LLP
Weightmans

Firms are listed A-Z in tiers which are ranked in order of priority

'immensely capable' Leila Porter from **Eversheds LLP**, whose interpersonal skills and ability to handle complex matters have brought several new clients to the firm.

Laytons' recent move into Manchester provides a vehicle to expand the firm's existing SME and venture capital contacts. David Sefton has an eye on technology start-ups and other new business ventures.

Wacks Caller boasts a large local entrepreneurial client base, and name partner Martin Caller retains a position of some respect in the market. The firm has suffered departures on the corporate side, while recruitment has been made in employment and commercial litigation.

Berg Legal is carving itself out a decent reputation advising smaller local companies in substantial transactions opposite much larger corporations and their advisers.

George Davies Solicitors advised on two AIM listings during the past year. The firm also advises the NHS on general commercial matters, and the arrival of Chris Wilkinson, formerly head of corporate at *Bullivant Jones*, is a further boost to a strong niche practice, praised for offering an 'efficient service for a reasonable fee'.

Ricksons made serious strides recently, adding to the *Elliotts* commercial legacy with the recruitment of Joe Glass from **Wacks Caller**, corporate finance expert Keith Melling from **Addleshaw Goddard**, and sponsorship and advertising expert Robert Stoker from an in-house position at adidas. An impressive list of mergers and acquisitionswas a fine start in the Manchester market, with clients finding the firm to be 'completely and utterly professional throughout'. A new commercial presence in Leeds is a further boost to the firm's overall capability.

Stephensons opened an office in Manchester in 2005, effectively relocating its Salford office. It is aiming to build on a decent SME client base and make inroads into the major commercial market on the back of a close working relationship with the city council. The firm acted on several MBOs in the past year. Nick Yates is described as the 'ultimate professional'.

Weightmans' ambitions in the corporate sector took a knock with the departure of three partners. However the firm is aiming to refocus on the market with new recruits.

LIVERPOOL

DLA Piper Rudnick Gray Cary UK LLP remains a peerless force in Liverpool's corporate arena, and close co-operation with the Manchester office gives it unsurpassed regional strength; the firm's four biggest deals of the year were handled by both offices in tandem, with each office generating two. Though dealing with national clients, the Liverpool presence is strong, with clients including Park Group, Mersey Waste Holdings and Liverpool FC keeping the firm on the local map.

CORPORATE AND COMMERCIAL
Liverpool

DLA PIPER RUDNICK GRAY CARY UK LLP

BRABNERS CHAFFE STREET
DWF

Hill Dickinson LLP
Mace & Jones Solicitors

Halliwells LLP
Lees Lloyd Whitley
O'Connors LLP
Weightmans

Firms are listed A-Z in tiers which are ranked in order of priority

Brabners Chaffe Street gained new client Tower Group recently, indicative of the firm's commitment to the city's SME businesses. A recognised player in the mid-market, Denise Walker's team acted on the disposal of the insulation division of Icopal Ltd to SIAE Electronica recently. The firm continues to receive instructions from James Hall & Co.

DWF is the third of Liverpool's leading commercial firms. Although the Manchester office has a larger commercial team than its Liverpool sister, David Clay's team showed strength in the food sector, acting on several acquisitions and disposals for Edward Billington & Son. The firm also advised Princes Foods on the acquisition of Well Well Well (UK) Limited.

Hill Dickinson LLP's corporate workflow leverages heavily off its successful real estate practice. Glyn Dale-Jones advised FLS Industries on its £100m sale to Swiss company SRT Technics, while new client Peacock Group plc instructed the firm on the £15m acquisition of The Fragrance Shop. The firm is heavily involved in the Greater Merseyside Enterprises Objective One scheme.

Mace & Jones Solicitors boasts Welsh-speaking capability at associate level, one of many unusual attributes which ensure the firm's continued popularity with clients.

Halliwells LLP now advises Everton FC, a legacy *Cuff Roberts* client, on commercial matters, with recent mandates including advising on the sponsorship agreement with Chang Beer and the sale of Wayne Rooney to Manchester United FC. The entrepreneurial approach of the firm strikes a positive chord with clients.

Lees Lloyd Whitley continues to secure work in the SME and OMB markets through a strong referral relationship with the Greater Merseyside Enterprises Objective One scheme.

Weightmans' Liverpool office has good commercial exposure in the retail sector.

ELSEWHERE IN THE NORTH WEST

The consistently impressive **Aaron & Partners LLP** continues to advise The Associated Octel Corporation on general commercial matters, and handled a £10.5m investment in Kimmel Park for Italian client Tecnoplast, one of several inward investment mandates in Wales for the firm. Although Ben Quirk left during the year, the experienced Elizabeth Delgado remains. Clients commend the firm's 'thoroughness and accuracy' and levels of communication.

Daniel Milnes at **Forbes** continues to impress in an increasingly sophisticated Lancashire market, recently acting on a number of MBOs and the formation of a company for the purposes of a sale and leaseback. Burnley FC instructs the firm on commercial matters. The firm's eight offices across the region give it enviable penetration and resources.

Tim Dennis heads **Gorvins**' well-regarded corporate and commercial practice, which has particular expertise in IP/IT matters. The firm advised on several seven-figure acquisitions and disposals recently, and its all-round capability – which now incorporates insolvency advice – is a plus point for SMEs.

Hill Dickinson LLP is targeting the North Wales market from its Chester office. It advises private clients on commercial services and represents several manufacturing companies.

Keoghs made ambitious strides in the past year, luring M&A and corporate finance specialist Melanie Yeomans from **Clifford Chance**. The firm advised North Manchester Enterprises on a £6m joint venture with Bolton Metro.

Kippax Beaumont Lewis made an entry into the regional corporate market in 2005, hiring Jonathan Shorrock from **Weightmans**.

Neil Myerson Solicitors drew on its reputation in the motor trade to secure the seller's mandate on TVR's sale to a Russian multi-millionaire. The firm also advised a local agricultural supplier on its admission to AIM. Carl Newton and name partner Neil Myerson continue to impress in the regional SME market.

Splitting her time between **Ricksons**' Preston and Manchester offices, asset finance specialist Katharine Mellor led on several local seven-figure M&A transactions during the past year. John

CORPORATE AND COMMERCIAL
Elsewhere in the North West

Aaron & Partners LLP *Chester*
Brabners Chaffe Street *Preston*
Forbes *Blackburn*
Gorvins *Stockport*
Hill Dickinson LLP *Chester*
Keoghs *Bolton*
Kippax Beaumont Lewis *Bolton*
Neil Myerson Solicitors *Altrincham*
Ricksons *Preston*
Stephensons *Wigan*

Firms are listed A-Z alphabetically

Hartup heads the regional team from Preston, while former **Addleshaw Goddard** senior associate and new partner Keith Melling is active in both the Preston and Manchester offices.

'Professional, efficient and incredibly responsive' **Stephensons** opened a new Manchester office in 2005, to add to its offices in Wigan, St. Helens and Leigh. It closed its Salford office in 2005, relocating personnel to Manchester. The firm enjoys close links with Wigan Borough Chamber of Commerce.

COMMERCIAL LITIGATION MANCHESTER:

Addleshaw Goddard's superb litigation group was strengthened by the arrival from the firm's London office of 'innovative lateral thinker' Ian Hargreaves, a specialist in insolvency, IT and sports disputes. Leeds-based Simon Kamstra heads the trans-Pennine team, whose focus is weighted towards IT, outsourcing and banking litigation for an enviable blue-chip client base. Individuals garnering plaudits from clients include Mark Amsden, deemed 'the lawyer to have on your side in any dispute'.

Stewart Plant 's impressive six-partner litigation team at **DLA Piper Rudnick Gray Cary UK LLP** focuses on risk management and mediation between parties. The team advises a predominantly FTSE 350 client base on multi-party, high-value corporate and finance disputes, and recently represented Zurich Insurance in a significant product liability claim.

Eversheds LLP maintains its top-tier status with increased growth in specialist dispute sectors, including international competition infringements and financial services. Led by Michael Clavell-Bate, the team is experienced in directors' disqualification proceedings, with a record that includes successfully defending former directors of the Uno Group.

DWF concentrates on corporate and contractual litigation. Headed by Ian Titchmarsh, the department has been involved in numerous significant high-value cases of late, notably representing property developers in local and national disputes valued at around the £5m mark.

Halliwells LLP's merger with *Cuff Roberts* reinforced partner levels amongst the 'efficient and expert' commercial litigation team, bringing Ron Farrell, and Liverpool-based Anne Heseltine and David Rawlinson to the ranks. The firm's successes include advising a high-net-worth individual on a complex multi-jurisdictional asset case.

Hammonds maintains its respectable position due to its continued presence in substantial disputes, such as representing the Royal Bank of Scotland in a landmark case taken to the House of Lords. The team expanded under the leadership of Lucci Dammone, with two fee-earners recruited in the past year, and remains active in ADR. Michael Shepherd, Paul Bratt and Rob Elvin are prominent litigators.

COMMERCIAL LITIGATION
Manchester

ADDLESHAW GODDARD
DLA PIPER RUDNICK GRAY CARY UK LLP
EVERSHEDS LLP

DWF
HALLIWELLS LLP
HAMMONDS
PANNONE
PINSENT MASONS

Cobbetts

Beachcroft Wansbroughs
Berg Legal
Berrymans Lace Mawer
Brabners Chaffe Street
Davies Arnold Cooper
Gorvins
Hill Dickinson LLP
Kuit Steinart Levy
Laytons
Ricksons
Rowe Cohen
Wacks Caller

Firms are listed A-Z in tiers which are ranked in order of priority

The massive, 32-strong litigation team at **Pannone** remains a powerful force in the disputes market and has clinched a number of new commercial clients. The retirement of Vincent O' Farrell was compensated for by the lateral hires of Stuart Irons from **DWF** and Paul Jonson from **Robert Muckle**. Paul Jonson has a top-class reputation and Alex Megaw is identified as 'very tenacious'. Longstanding clients include Manchester Airport and Urban Splash.

Pinsent Masons' robust commercial disputes team was enhanced twofold as a result of the firm's merger and the transfer of joint managing partner Carl Garvie from the Birmingham office. Praised for its 'positive attitude', the team is competitive in the contentious and regulatory arena, with substantial experience on OFT and FSA work. Recent highlights include successfully defending a FTSE 250 company before the FSA.

Internal reorganisation at **Cobbetts** saw Joel Heap promoted to partner. The group is advising the Department of Trade and Industry on disqualification disputes, and counts a growing number of local authorities as clients. Recent highlights include participation in the Zahid Mubarek inquiry. Team head Mark Whittell is experienced in banking litigation.

Commercial litigation accounts for around 35% of **Berg Legal**'s workload. The firm positions itself as offering a bespoke service, able to handle complicated shareholder and boardroom disputes for SMEs.

Although **Hill Dickinson LLP** is traditionally viewed as a Liverpool player, the firm has successfully entered Manchester after lateral hires and internal partner moves, namely the arrival of partner Tim Stone and transfer of Andrew Bogle, experienced in pensions and banking litigation respectively.

The highly experienced Daniel Izza left **Pannone** in 2003 in order to develop a litigation practice at **Laytons**, which focuses on insolvency-related work. Despite its relatively small size, the disputes team represented Blackburn Rovers in a £7m settlement against four separate insurance companies, and has advised numerous Italian clients as a result of being on a panel of Italian-speaking solicitors.

LIVERPOOL

Although smaller than its counterpart litigation group in Manchester, **DLA Piper Rudnick Gray Cary UK LLP** in Liverpool remains well placed to advise corporate clients in heavyweight disputes. Mark Goodwin is applauded for being 'approachable and understanding'. The team is working in conjunction with the firm's Moscow office, representing a Belarussian company in an international arbitration.

Jacqui Lloyd heads one of the largest commercial litigation teams in the region at **Brabners Chaffe Street**. The successful defence of the *Liverpool Daily Post* and *Liverpool Echo* against the Cream Group was a landmark win. The litigation team has expertise in construction, IP, media and property disputes. Rachel Jones is commended for her 'practical and thoughtful advice'.

David Blaquière and Paul Berry of **DWF** are active in commercial insurance litigation.

A shrewd banking litigator, Noel Fagan continues his leadership of the commercial disputes group at **Hill Dickinson LLP**, which recently won a major confidentiality case against a merchant bank.

Weightmans has developed a good regulatory and representative practice, and has recently advised in various inquests around the UK.

COMMERCIAL LITIGATION
Liverpool

DLA PIPER RUDNICK GRAY CARY UK LLP

Brabners Chaffe Street
DWF
Hill Dickinson LLP
Weightmans

Bermans
Halliwells LLP
Lees Lloyd Whitley
Mace & Jones Solicitors

Firms are listed A-Z in tiers which are ranked in order of priority

Merging with *Cuff Roberts* has given **Halliwells LLP** a considerable disputes base in Liverpool, with expertise in property and construction.

Lees Lloyd Whitley reports steady growth and offers litigation advice relating to construction and engineering contracts amongst other matters.

Mace & Jones Solicitors' general commercial litigation practice includes contentious insolvency, contentious probate matters, and property and IP disputes. Highlights include representing Liverpool FC in a £6.5m claim for damages by Middlesbrough FC, which was concluded recently.

ELSEWHERE IN THE NORTH WEST:

The 'timely and professional' group led by John Devoy at **Aaron & Partners LLP** has across-the-board experience in banking, retail and construction litigation.

Alexander Harris benefits from a spill-over of work from its key insurance areas, and focuses on high-profile product liability disputes.

Brabners Chaffe Street's Preston office is distinguished by its contentious environmental practice; the firm has advised numerous commercial clients in relation to Environment Agency and health and safety investigations.

Hill Dickinson LLP in Chester advises a number of higher education institutions on contentious and regulatory matters.

Non-personal injury related litigation work for insurance companies forms the backbone of **Keoghs**' commercial disputes caseload. The firm advises on policy matters, property damage and engineering and construction disputes.

Michael Slater is the new head of commercial litigation at **Kippax Beaumont Lewis**. The firm is active in contractual, construction and landlord and tenant disputes.

Ricksons' expanding commercial litigation team now consists of five partners and six associates. Chris Scott has particular skill representing clients from the construction industry on a wide range of contract disputes.

COMMERCIAL LITIGATION
Elsewhere in the North West

Aaron & Partners LLP *Chester*
Alexander Harris *Altrincham*
Brabners Chaffe Street *Preston*
Hill Dickinson LLP *Chester*
Keoghs *Bolton*
Kippax Beaumont Lewis *Bolton*
Maxwell Gillott *Lancaster*
Ricksons *Preston*
Taylors *Blackburn*
Walker Smith Way *Chester*

Firms are listed alphabetically

SOUTH EAST

This region comprises the south east of England excluding London. With such a broad spread of counties, the area includes several distinct legal communities rather than comprising a single market. The chapter is therefore divided into five sub-regions: Thames Valley, Berks, Oxon, M4/M40; Kent, Surrey, Sussex; Hampshire; Beds, Bucks, Herts, Middx; and Essex.

Proximity to London, lower fees and a generation of sophisticated consumers comfortable with instructing advisers on a 'horses for courses' basis are all factors which have worked in favour of local firms, many of which are able to field City-trained lawyers who have moved away from the capital in search of a better work : life balance. Moreover, as the London elite increasingly eschew smaller domestic deals to pursue their global ambitions, regional and national firms have been all too willing to fill the vacuum. A related phenomenon is the successful assault that US practices have made on the European transactional stage, which has led to several South East firms offering 'bolt-on' corporate support in specialist areas such as employment and IP.

CORPORATE AND COMMERCIAL THAMES VALLEY, BERKS, OXON, M4/M40

As the major corporate and commercial player in Oxford, **Manches LLP** attracts many of the city's premium instructions, and in Peter Angel the firm boasts a true Thames Valley heavyweight. Local publishers are a key source of work, with recent acquisitions completed for both Blackwell Publishing and Oxford University Press. Patrick Baddeley, Rob Jonckheer and David Tighe complete a four-partner line-up.

By no means the region's largest firm, **Osborne Clarke** has a powerful Thames Valley presence that is driven by an impressive array of transactional lawyers. Head of corporate Greg Leyshon is the lead relationship partner for local private equity clients Barclays Private Equity and 3i, and technology specialist Russell Bowyer spearheads the commercial offering. The completion of a staggering 120 deals in the past year illustrates the practice's current strength, and the recent recruitment of Moray Macpherson, with his 20 years of experience of the south coast at **Bond Pearce LLP** amongst other firms, is a bold statement of future intent.

'They provide me with exactly what I need: competent, efficient, swift and moderately priced no-frills work,' says one client of **Shoosmiths**, whose Thames Valley and Solent teams were recently merged in a bid to become the dominant South East player. By advising the majority shareholders of Reeves Oilfield Services on the company's £92.4m sale, the department, led by the outstanding Nigel Thorne, took a significant step towards achieving that goal last year.

CORPORATE AND COMMERCIAL
Thames Valley, Berks, Oxon, M4/M40

MANCHES LLP *Oxford*
OSBORNE CLARKE *Reading*
SHOOSMITHS *Reading*

Boyes Turner *Reading*
Clarkslegal LLP *Reading*
Morgan Cole *Oxford, Reading*
Olswang *Reading*
Pitmans *Reading*

Blake Lapthorn Linnell *Oxford*
Blandy & Blandy *Reading*
Darbys *Oxford*
Field Seymour Parkes *Reading*
Penningtons Solicitors LLP *Newbury*
Wilmer Cutler Pickering Hale and Dorr LLP ✪ *Oxford*

BrookStreet Des Roches *Witney*
Charles Lucas & Marshall *Newbury*
Clifton Ingram *Wokingham*
Henmans *Oxford*
Horsey Lightly Fynn *Newbury*
Key2Law (Thames Valley) LLP *Reading*

Firms are listed A-Z in tiers which are ranked in order of priority
✪ Indicates firm displays contact details at the end of this chapter.

The steady increase in European work from UK and multinational clients is a factor in **Boyes Turner**'s continued upward mobility. Philip Tranter leads the corporate group, which last year notched up acquisition mandates for both Biomol International and Steer Holdings, while on the commercial side Bill Gornall-King is a renowned technology expert.

Richard Lee heads up **Clarkslegal LLP**'s department, which claims a healthy mix of local businesses, FTSE 250 companies and international outfits amongst its clients. The past year saw the firm handle three acquisitions in the pharmaceutical IT sector for Cegedim SA, while client gains included Alliance Unichem, which it acted for on the disposal of Crest Medical for £7m. The arrival of partner Adam Dowdney from **Charles Russell** has added gravitas to the corporate side.

Morgan Cole's longstanding relationship with key clients BP and Castrol is demonstrated by the fact that several members of the department have been seconded to both. The firm also provides ongoing commercial advice to one of the region's Formula One teams. Bruce Potter leads a practice that has acted for Canadian listed company Vanguard Response Systems on its £15.3m acquisition of PW Allen Holdings.

In a solid but unspectacular year for Marshall Leopold 's team at **Olswang**, highlights included acting on the sale by the majority shareholders of Resonance Instruments Ltd to Oxford Instruments plc, and advising Direct Image and its shareholders in relation to the company's merger with Hendy Banks.

John Hutchinson is the key contact at **Pitmans**, which has recently been strengthened by the arrival of Janice Wall as a partner from **Dechert LLP**'s London office. Another year of intense transactional activity saw the firm advise the shareholders of Prime Business Solutions in the company's £22m sale to 2e2 Holdings, and Prologic on its AIM flotation.

Mark Hepworth and Edward Lee are the leading lights at **Blake Lapthorn Linnell**'s Oxford office, the former singled out for having 'commercial knowledge and an ability to deal with challenging situations'. Notable activity in the past year included advising on the defence of a hostile takeover bid, and assisting Surrenda-link Mortgage Holdings in obtaining a substantial ring-fenced asset funding line from an international banking syndicate.

The last year has seen **Blandy & Blandy** move up a gear in terms of profile and instructions. The recruitment of Simon Lovegrove from **Stephenson Harwood** has added City experience to one of Reading's more established departments, which is led by the well-respected David Few. The firm acted for the management on Healthcall Optical Services' recent MBO.

Formerly legal counsel at 3i, Phil Riman heads up a team at **Darbys** that is steadily establishing itself as a serious competitor to Oxford stalwarts **Manches LLP** and **Blake Lapthorn Linnell**. Thirty corporate transactions in the course of the past year, together with numerous restructurings and refinancings, bears witness to the team's upward trajectory.

Field Seymour Parkes enjoys a lot of respect amongst local competitors. Mary Winter leads a department that recently advised the vendors in the £200m sale of a group of eight companies owning a property portfolio.

Corporate partner John Riddick has established himself as a leading Newbury player at **Penningtons Solicitors LLP**, and his seven-strong team continues to develop at a steady pace with a healthy stream of acquisition work handled in the past year. The Frontiers Group was a key client gain; the firm advised it in relation to the marketing of England cricketer Andrew Flintoff and recording artist Robbie Williams.

Wilmer Cutler Pickering Hale and Dorr LLP has seen solid progress in the development of its technology practice and its international reach, and the firm's involvement on behalf of Logistics Technology Group in its $43m sale to US publisher RedPrairie Inc demonstrates the practice's value when dealing with American companies.

KENT, SURREY, SUSSEX

Clyde & Co advised on transactions valued at over £2.5bn in the past year for a strong plc and international client base, including Securicor plc and Hachette Livre SA, underscoring the firm's ability to handle heavyweight corporate transactions from its Guildford office. Andrew Holderness and head of commercial Matthew Cowan are recommended. Simon Bickerdike left the firm in to join **Penningtons Solicitors LLP** in Godalming. Clients appreciate a 'thorough, commercial' approach.

Cripps Harries Hall LLP acts for clients from the technology, mining, banking, higher education and property sectors, with recent highlights including advising European Nickel plc in relation to a mining joint venture with BHP Billiton plc. Larry Leporte heads a team of three partners described by clients as 'exemplary in its commitment and service'. Experienced partner Trevor Carney left to join **Vertex Law LLP**.

Stevens & Bolton LLP acts for a number of the region's plcs and major financial institutions, including Hays plc and Sanofi-Aventis. Transaction highlights include advising Caspian UK (Camberley) Limited on its acquisition of Gowrings plc to create the largest privately owned UK Burger King franchise business. Clients praise the firm's 'strong technical and commercial advice' and its ability to deal with large workloads efficiently and cost-effectively, with its lawyers described as 'open, personable and entrepreneurial'. Richard Baxter and Ken Woffenden (ex **Simmons & Simmons**) are recommended.

DMH recently merged with London practice *Stallard Solicitors* to form **DMH Stallard**, with offices in Crawley, Brighton and London. The new firm's regional clients are likely to benefit from a City presence, especially for FSA and banking-related matters. Clients include GE Life, P&O Ferries and EDF Energy Group. The department provides 'pragmatic, sensible business advice'. Dual-qualified US lawyer Vincent O'Brien heads the team.

asb law advised on transactions worth in excess of £250m in the past year, including acting for key client First Choice Holidays plc on the purchase of The Adventure Company from ebookers plc. Clients find that the firm is 'responsive' and provides 'good turnaround time on transactions'. Jonathan Grant and Alina Nosek are well respected, and Matthew Newman's arrival as a partner from **Davies Lavery** was a significant lateral hire.

Mundays LLP has a very strong name in the pharmaceutical and healthcare industries, though clients also come from the IT and travel sectors. Peter Munday and head of commercial David Irving are recommended. Clients laud the firm's 'sharp, commercial' advice, its 'hard-working, flexible approach' and its good connections with a variety of European practices.

Rawlison Butler acts for a selection of SMEs from the automotive, engineering, travel and IT sectors, with partners Tim Sadka and James Chatfield heading a six-fee-earner team. Clients include several major international companies. The firm is praised for being professional, responsive and reasonable on fees.

CORPORATE AND COMMERCIAL
Kent, Surrey, Sussex

CLYDE & CO *Guildford*
CRIPPS HARRIES HALL LLP *Tunbridge Wells*
STEVENS & BOLTON LLP *Guildford*

DMH Stallard *Brighton, Crawley*

---

asb law *Crawley, Croydon*
Mundays LLP *Cobham*
Rawlison Butler *Crawley*
Shadbolt & Co LLP *Reigate*
Thomas Eggar *Chichester, Crawley, Reigate, Worthing*

Charles Russell *Guildford*
Laytons *Guildford*
Penningtons Solicitors LLP *Godalming*
Thomson Snell & Passmore *Tunbridge Wells*

Barlow Robbins *Guildford, Woking*
Furley Page *Canterbury*
Mackrell Turner Garrett *Woking*
Paul Davidson Taylor *Horsham*
Vertex Law LLP *Maidstone*

Adams & Remers *Lewes*
Clarkson Wright & Jakes *Orpington*
Hart Brown *Guildford*
T G Baynes *Bexleyheath, Dartford, Orpington*
TWM Solicitors LLP *Guildford*

Firms are listed A-Z in tiers which are ranked in order of priority

Shadbolt & Co LLP boasts an unrivalled reputation for construction work, but is also recommended for its excellent corporate department, which acts for a growing number of standalone clients. Andrew Trotter heads a group that advised the management team of RCG Moody International on a $55m buyout from its US parent company.

Thomas Eggar has been busy building up its presence in Crawley, a commercial centre that is a key strategic location for the practice's corporate work. Nick Rutter, Neil Hart and Daniel Bastide are recommended. The department acts for several major clients from the pharmaceutical industry.

Charles Russell is building an increasingly visible and active profile in the region, especially amongst Guildford-based corporates and financial institutions. Geoffrey Sparks heads the team, and Catherine Drew's arrival from **Olswang**'s Reading office has started to attract some quality instructions. The firm advised on 30 deals in the past year, six of which were in the £1m-£5m range. One Guildford-based accountant views the practice as a 'safe pair of hands' for small to medium-sized corporate deals, with other clients appreciating its 'detailed, thorough advice in clear English and with a minimum of legalese'.

At **Laytons**, Neale Andrews joined from the firm's London office and heads a team that advised on 12 M&A transactions valued at a total of around £30m. The department acts for several clients from the TMT sector, including Samsung, which receives guidance on a variety of commercial matters.

Penningtons Solicitors LLP has recently acted on several major deals in the IT sector, including representing Diagonal plc on its acquisition of Egility Solutions Ltd. Simon Bickerdike joined the Godalming office from **Clyde & Co**.

Thomson Snell & Passmore has substantial experience of corporate and M&A transactions, with recent highlights including advising William Ransom & Son plc on its £8m acquisition of Health Perception UK Ltd. The firm's strong name for private client work creates many opportunities for advising its strong owner-managed business client base on corporate transactions.

Furley Page recently advised an international freight transport company in connection with an MBI into the business. Other clients include several regional banks and corporates based in and around Canterbury.

Paul Davidson Taylor's Noel Ruddy heads an entrepreneurial team that advises several small to mid-size clients. The firm is especially known for its factoring practice.

Headed by Stuart Butler-Gallie, formerly of **Davies Lavery**, **Vertex Law LLP** is a new entrant to the market. The firm acts for a range of clients from the property development and technology sectors, with several of its leading partners enjoying a strong reputation and following.

Adams & Remers advised on ten deals in the past year with a total value of over £18m. Highlights include advising a South East motor dealer group on the acquisition of a cluster of VW and Audi franchises.

Clarkson Wright & Jakes advises a broad mix of SMEs and owner-managed businesses, many of which instruct the firm as a one-stop shop for a range of commercial, employment and property law matters. The practice provides 'quality, timely advice' and is 'hardworking and very commercial'. John Bowden and Andrew Wright head the team.

T G Baynes acts for several local companies in the property industry on a range of commercial and company matters.

HAMPSHIRE

Simon Treherne heads **Blake Lapthorn Linnell**'s department, which advises a broad mix of the region's plc and financial services sector clients. The firm also represents several major players in the transport sector. Mark Shepherd led a team that advised Kerry Group plc on its £238m purchase of the multinational Quest Foods Ingredients division of ICI. Clients appreciate a combination of 'commercial advice' and lawyers who are 'personable and easy to work with'. Commercial partner Mary Chant is also recommended.

CORPORATE AND COMMERCIAL
Hampshire

BLAKE LAPTHORN LINNELL *Southampton*
BOND PEARCE LLP *Southampton*

Coffin Mew & Clover *Southampton*
Moore & Blatch *Southampton*
Paris Smith & Randall LLP *Southampton*
Penningtons Solicitors LLP *Basingstoke*
Shoosmiths *Fareham*

Clarke Willmott *Southampton*
Lamport Bassitt *Southampton*

Dutton Gregory *Winchester*
Lester Aldridge *Southampton*
Trethowans *Southampton*
White & Bowker *Winchester*

Firms are listed A-Z in tiers which are ranked in order of priority

Bond Pearce LLP's Stephen Pierce heads a group that is universally acknowledged by peers and clients as one of the south coast's pre-eminent corporate teams. Highlights of the past year include advising RWE npower on the £400m financing of a wind farm project. Other clients come from the retail and IT sectors. The firm 'takes time to understand our business' and provides 'practical, sound, deal-facilitating advice' characterised by 'quick response times' and 'reasonable fees'. Nick Page is also recommended for competition matters.

Coffin Mew & Clover is particularly recommended for transactions around the £5m mark. Bank of Scotland is a key source of work, with other clients coming from the transport and IT sectors. Amanda Brockwell and Nick Gross head a team that provides 'accurate, timely advice' and 'dedicates large teams of lawyers to a transaction where necessary'. Malcolm Padgett has niche expertise in FSA-related matters.

Moore & Blatch advised on over a dozen transactions in the £1m-£10m range in the past year, including acting for Bestinvest (Holdings) Limited on its £5.5m acquisition of a firm of City brokers. Roger Bailey and Peter Jeffery head the team, which is appreciated for its 'commitment and dedication' on major corporate transactions.

Southampton's **Paris Smith & Randall LLP** has a solid reputation as a premier, single-office firm. The practice boasts strong ties with many of the region's owner-managed businesses, thanks in no small part to the strength of its private client team, which is often a source of cross-referral work for the corporate group. Andrew Heathcock is 'personable' and 'communicates issues clearly' to clients, and is especially well regarded for his expertise in banking law aspects of corporate transactions.

At **Penningtons Solicitors LLP**'s Basingstoke office, managing partner Franco Bosi heads a team that advises a solid SME client base, along with several plcs from the IT, transport and real estate sectors. The firm is 'easy to work with' and 'inspires confidence' on transactions.

Shoosmiths has been building up its presence with entrepreneurial zeal and aggression over the past year. Following the recruitment of Sean Wright from **Blake Lapthorn Linnell**, the team also expanded to welcome John Jackson from **DLA Piper Rudnick Gray Cary UK LLP**'s London office. Transaction highlights include advising a subsidiary of Cobham plc on the £21.1m acquisition of Spectronic Denmark A/S. The firm provides advice which is 'practical, straightforward and problem-solving'.

At **Clarke Willmott**, Sally Norcross-Webb has been building an increasingly visible profile in the market since her arrival from **Shoosmiths**, especially amongst the region's banking and accountancy clients. Highlights include advising a major UK bank on its £36m financing of the acquisition of American Golf (UK) Limited. The firm's Southampton office has a strong focus on real estate work, with many of the corporate transactions having a property flavour to them.

Lamport Bassitt rises in the table on the strength of its involvement in several major corporate transactions, including advising ebookers plc on the sale of The Adventure Company to First Choice, and acting for the management team on the £102m MBO of the Red Funnel Group. Experienced partner Sean Kelly heads a team of three partners recommended by clients for 'hands-on, partner-led' advice.

Lester Aldridge has recently acted on several transactions in the £5m-£10m range for clients in the manufacturing, automotive and real estate sectors, while **White & Bowker** has handled various deals in the £1m-£4m range, including acting for a tour operating company on a £3.8m share sale.

BEDS, BUCKS, HERTS, MIDDX

EMW Law LLP now boasts five partners and 12 other fee-earners, making it one of the largest corporate teams in the area. Arrivals include Uzma Khan from **Simmons & Simmons**, and Simon Arkell from **Shoosmiths**. With specialist corporate, commercial and leveraged finance units, the firm handles work for several major banks and plcs. Managing partner Ian Morris and his team are praised by clients for their 'pragmatism, efficiency and effectiveness'.

Howes Percival continues to impress under the stewardship of Brandon Ransley, and has recently acted on a number of disposals including that of Wealdstone Engineering Ltd to Caterpillar. The department's specialist automotive industry unit deserves special mention, competing with national firms for a variety of motor trade clients.

CORPORATE AND COMMERCIAL Beds, Bucks, Herts, Middx
EMW LAW LLP *Milton Keynes*
HOWES PERCIVAL *Milton Keynes*
KIMBELLS LLP *Milton Keynes*
MATTHEW ARNOLD & BALDWIN *Watford*
SHOOSMITHS *Milton Keynes*
Moorcrofts LLP *Marlow*
SA Law LLP *St Albans*
Taylor Walton *Luton*
B P Collins *Gerrards Cross*
Fennemores *Milton Keynes*
Iliffes Booth Bennett (IBB) *Uxbridge*
Geoffrey Leaver Solicitors *Milton Keynes*
Machins *Luton*
Sherrards *St Albans*
Stanley Tee *Bishops Stortford*
Turbervilles with Nelson Cuff *Uxbridge*
Woodfine Batcheldor *Bedford*

Firms are listed A-Z in tiers which are ranked in order of priority

Kimbells LLP acted on more than 40 transactions in the past year, most significantly the £100m sale of Midland Medical Technologies to US-based Smith & Nephew. One client praises Jonathan Hambleton for being 'the most effective corporate resource this company has ever encountered'. The practice features a specialist 'brewing services' unit that handles a range of commercial advice for clients such as Scottish & Newcastle and The Spirit Group.

Peers praise **Matthew Arnold & Baldwin** for its corporate capabilities, and the firm enters the top tier in recognition of its continued growth under Richard Phillips. A strong client base includes Europcar, which the team advises on concession agreements and franchising operations. The practice also has experience across a range of transactions, including acquisitions, disposals and MBOs.

Shoosmiths' Oliver Brookshaw is a highly experienced corporate lawyer, and recently advised a technology plc on a £14.2m acquisition. Department head Sebastian Price and partner Keith Lewington are also recommended, with a number of high-profile clients between them. The firm recently gained a place on the corporate and commercial panel of DaimlerChrysler.

Moorcrofts LLP has come on in leaps and bounds since its inception in 2000. The corporate arm continues to develop under the guidance of ex-*Garretts* expert Adrian Philips, and the team now deals with a substantial volume of venture capital fund raising and restructuring work. Andrew Katz leads on the commercial side, with a particular focus on the healthcare sector.

SA Law LLP launched in June 2005 and is the former commercial department of **Pictons Solicitors LLP**. Led by Christopher Wilks, the team offers 'friendly, no-nonsense' advice on sales, refinancings and corporate reorganisations among other matters, with an increasing focus on deals with an international element.

Led by Clive Borthwick, **Taylor Walton** is strong in M&A, restructuring and construction-related work. Recently promoted to partner, Patrick McGrath has secured a number of banking clients including Barclays, while Mike Pettit nurtures the firm's technology client base.

Enviable clients at **B P Collins** include Systemax Europe Ltd, Datasat Communications Ltd and Continental Tyre Group, with David Stanning overseeing matters.

Led by Chris Robinson, **Fennemores** is renowned for its work in relation to the transformation of Wimbledon FC into Milton Keynes Dons.

Under the stewardship of David Jackson, **Iliffes Booth Bennett (IBB)** continues to build expertise in financial services, onshore and offshore company structures, technology and property support work. Anila Preston is noteworthy for her advice on shari'ah insurance and reinsurance.

ESSEX

Wollastons is the clear market leader for commercial work in Essex, bolstered by the recent appointment of former **Ashurst** lawyer Karl Taylor, who has particular expertise in private equity, share and business purchases and joint ventures. Under the guidance of name partner Richard Wollaston, the firm is seeing an increase in work in the automotive sector; a notable highlight was a joint venture between a number of vehicle retail groups with a total turnover of £1bn.

Birkett Long continues to make ground on **Wollastons**, with recent instructions including the sale of E2V Technologies. Whilst the team's core business comes from local owner-managed businesses, it demonstrates an increasing capability for cross-border transactions. David Wisbey heads the Chelmsford group, while Philip George keeps matters ticking over smoothly in Colchester.

CORPORATE AND COMMERCIAL Essex
WOLLASTONS *Chelmsford*
Birkett Long *Chelmsford, Colchester*
Tolhurst Fisher *Chelmsford*
Wortley Byers LLP *Brentwood*
Ellisons *Colchester*
Thompson Smith & Puxon *Colchester*

Firms are listed A-Z in tiers which are ranked in order of priority

Tolhurst Fisher offers general corporate advice on matters such as business start-ups, venture capital funding and flotations, while on the commercial side the firm has advised on a variety of international trade, lending and insolvency matters. Senior partner Philip Tolhurst is an experienced practitioner.

Brentwood's **Wortley Byers LLP** offers a range of business advice from commercial agreements to corporate ventures.

COMMERCIAL LITIGATION THAMES VALLEY, BERKS, OXON, M4/M40

Antony Morris leads an impressive line-up at **Clarkslegal LLP**, which over the past year has represented a public body in a high-value engineering project dispute, defended a multi-million-pound ICC arbitration for a US client, and undertaken several instructions involving issues of competition law. David Rintoul is the construction expert in a team that has taken on a further two assistants.

Consistent with the firm's reputation **Olswang** deals with a significant volume of IT disputes. Departmental head Tim Clark recently led a team acting for TTPCom in connection with an application for an urgent injunction against it and a $53m damages claim, which saw the injunction successfully defended, costs awarded and the claim discontinued. Assistant Katrina Mulligan won the 2004 CEDR National Junior Award for Excellence in ADR.

The Oxford office of **Blake Lapthorn Linnell** is rated for construction and property litigation, with Richard Wade and Carol Oster Warriner respectively recommended. Jonathan Lloyd-Jones is active in the mediation arena.

Since his arrival in 2003 Geoff Mendelsohn has added further substance to **Boyes Turner** through his expertise in contentious IT; his clients include EDS, the world's second-largest supplier of computer services.

'They make it a pleasure to deal with what can be daunting issues,' says one client of **Henmans**, which can call upon solid City experience in the shape of Tony Nurse-Marsh and Francis Dingwall. The team deals with complex and high-value litigation for a wide variety of clients. Acting for a large foreign publishing company in a multi-jurisdictional suit arising out of over 100 disputed licensing agreements was a notable recent highlight.

Manches LLP is well versed in managing large-scale actions, as demonstrated by its longstanding involvement on behalf of the British Geological Survey in a claim where Bangladeshi citizens are alleging negligence in failing to identify naturally occurring arsenic contamination in drinking water. Julie Bond heads a department that also handles trusts and estate cases, property litigation and negligence claims.

COMMERCIAL LITIGATION
Thames Valley, Berks, Oxon, M4/M40

CLARKSLEGAL LLP *Reading*
OLSWANG *Reading*

Blake Lapthorn Linnell *Oxford*
Boyes Turner *Reading*
Henmans *Oxford*
Manches LLP *Oxford*
Morgan Cole *Oxford, Reading*
Pitmans *Reading*
Shoosmiths *Reading*

Blandy & Blandy *Reading*
BrookStreet Des Roches *Witney*
Clifton Ingram *Wokingham*
Darbys *Oxford*
Field Seymour Parkes *Reading*

Firms are listed A-Z in tiers which are ranked in order of priority

Working across its Oxford and Reading offices, **Morgan Cole** has a hard-earned reputation for dealing with heavyweight disputes in the commercial and public sectors. Stephanie Walls leads a team that has specialist expertise in contentious public law applications, energy, education and Chancery proceedings.

Pitmans' Sue O'Brien has a good name in Reading, where over the past year she has been active in various complex contractual disputes, insurance policy disputes, financial services claims, and injunctions relating to the protection of assets outside the jurisdiction. The department boasts an excellent success rate in mediation.

Clients praise **Shoosmiths** for having 'a streamlined and efficient way of dealing with things'. Claire Rowe leads the firm's national dispute resolution team from Reading. The practice takes on instructions from significant IT and motor industry clients.

KENT, SURREY, SUSSEX

Clyde & Co is one of the South East's top commercial litigation outfits, and is particularly recommended for heavyweight finance, insurance and international trade disputes. The firm recently acted for financiers in relation to proceedings before the Turkish courts, while other highlights include new appointments to Legal & General's and BP's panels. Jonathan Wood and Michael Parker are respected names.

Charles Russell has advised on several major insolvency, product liability and contested probate cases, with highlights in the international arena including successfully acting for two Balinese companies in a High Court case against an English timeshare company relating to foreign ownership of land in Indonesia. Guildford office managing partner Duncan Elson heads the team.

COMMERCIAL LITIGATION
Kent, Surrey, Sussex

CLYDE & CO *Guildford*

Charles Russell *Guildford*
Cripps Harries Hall LLP *Tunbridge Wells*
DMH Stallard *Brighton, Crawley*
Stevens & Bolton LLP *Guildford*

---

asb law *Crawley*
Rawlison Butler *Crawley*
Shadbolt & Co LLP *Reigate*
Thomas Eggar *Chichester, Reigate, Worthing*
Thomson Snell & Passmore *Tunbridge Wells*

Barlow Robbins *Guildford*
Brachers *Maidstone*
Clarkson Wright & Jakes *Orpington*
Furley Page *Canterbury*
Mundays LLP *Cobham*
Paul Davidson Taylor *Horsham*
stevensdrake *Crawley*
T G Baynes *Bexleyheath, Dartford, Orpington*

Firms are listed A-Z in tiers which are ranked in order of priority

Peter Ashford heads a line-up at **Cripps Harries Hall LLP** that has advised on several heavyweight international cases including recently representing an Indian steel producer in a dispute with an international banking syndicate involving proceedings in London and Singapore. Ed Weeks and Peter Garry, who is an authority on partnership disputes, are also recommended.

DMH Stallard advises clients from the hi-tech, banking, insurance and retail sectors. A heightened presence in London following the firm's merger and expansion in January 2005 is likely to complement the dispute resolution capability of the firm's Crawley and Brighton offices.

Stevens & Bolton LLP recently advised Compass Management Consulting Limited in relation to a high-profile, £160m claim involving IBM and Cable & Wireless. Other clients include several FTSE 250 companies. Richard King heads an experienced five-partner, 11-associate team.

Andrew Clinton of **asb law** oversees a three-partner team whose recent work included advising key client First Choice Holidays plc on a £2.8m breach of contract claim against a major UK insurer. Having joined the firm in July 2003, Richard Mumford, formerly of **CMS Cameron McKenna LLP** and the Financial Services Authority, has now been admitted to the partnership and focuses on litigation for banking and financial services sector clients.

Rawlison Butler's Clive Lee heads a team that advises a broad range of UK companies, not to mention a growing number of international clients from Europe, the US and Japan.

In addition to **Shadbolt & Co LLP**'s celebrated contentious construction capability, the firm also handles general commercial litigation for clients such as Group 4 Securicor. Kate Matthews is recommended.

Thomas Eggar has advised on a wide range of complex financial, shareholder and transport-sector disputes. The team received a leg-up when Vicky Brackett, who has expertise in insurance litigation, joined as a partner from **Freshfields Bruckhaus Deringer**. Jonathan Hood is singled out for praise.

At **Thomson Snell & Passmore**, Peter Radula-Scott heads a team of five partners that has advised on several heavyweight disputes for clients including local councils, banks and insurance brokers.

We also recommend Peter Hawkes at **Furley Page**, Fiona McAllister at **Mundays LLP**, and Ian Price at **Stevensdrake**.

HAMPSHIRE

The Fareham office of **Blake Lapthorn Linnell** is home to more litigators than any of the firm's other branches. Stephen Murfitt heads a team that acts for blue-chip companies from the construction, IT, banking and manufacturing sectors. Susan Dryden is a mediation specialist.

Bond Pearce LLP is Hampshire's other heavyweight dispute resolution practice, and has a special focus on clients from the TMT, retail and energy sectors. The firm recently acted for a Norwegian oil company in litigation arising from a multi-billion-dollar pipeline project in the North Sea. Gavin Matthews is recommended.

Clarke Willmott's Philip Tebbatt heads a two-partner, four-assistant team that works closely with the firm's Bristol and Taunton offices advising on commercial disputes. Trevor Watkins acts for several sports clients.

Penningtons Solicitors LLP rises a tier following the recruitment from **Laytons**' Guildford office of Simon Emmerson, who has a

COMMERCIAL LITIGATION
Hampshire

BLAKE LAPTHORN LINNELL *Fareham*
BOND PEARCE LLP *Southampton*

Clarke Willmott *Southampton*
Penningtons Solicitors LLP *Basingstoke*
Shoosmiths *Fareham*

Coffin Mew & Clover *Southampton*
Lamport Bassitt *Southampton*
Moore & Blatch *Southampton*
Paris Smith & Randall LLP *Southampton*
Trethowans *Southampton*
White & Bowker *Chandler's Ford*

Firms are listed A-Z in tiers which are ranked in order of priority

special focus on disputes in the IT sector. Michael Felce heads the three-partner team, which advises high-calibre clients such as Allianz Cornhill.

Shoosmiths recently advised an aviation client on a major dispute in the defence industry. Richard Cook heads the practice.

Also recommended are **Lamport Bassitt**'s Rick Munro, **Moore & Blatch**'s Paul Whitaker, and Clive Thomson at **Paris Smith & Randall LLP**.

BEDS, BUCKS, HERTS & MIDDX

Spearheaded by James Fairbairn, **Denton Wilde Sapte**'s Milton Keynes practice is split between construction-related disputes and corporate matters. The team represents a wide range of clients including banks, airports and local authorities.

Since the arrival of arbitration expert Louis Flannery from **SJ Berwin LLP**, **Howes Percival** has continued to develop skills in cross-border litigation. Recent successes include an anti-suit injunction and a High Court *quantum meruit* claim against the British Museum. Led by Andrew Myers, the team is described as 'responsive and strategic'.

Matthew Arnold & Baldwin advises a number of corporates and banks, and is retained on the litigation panel of Barclays Bank. Partner Mark Tudor is recommended for IP-related work, while Clare Stothard is singled out for being 'knowledgeable and creative'.

B P Collins is highly rated by one client for its 'professionalism and commerciality'. Whilst committed to resolving issues through mediation, the department has also been involved in a number of groundbreaking reported cases. Team head Nick Hallchurch is a standing mediator to the Central London County Court.

Through Katharine Summers and Northampton-based Michael Eyton-Jones, **EMW Law LLP** handles general litigation of all kinds, with specialist expertise in property, IP/IT and contentious insolvency matters.

At **Fennemores**, department head Guy Brooks has a flair for professional negligence work, and with an increasingly international focus, construction litigation is also something of a strength.

Partner Paul Kite leads the line at **Iliffes Booth Bennett (IBB)**, which has recently appointed two further senior solicitors. Renault UK is a noteworthy client, and in the past year the team received a new instruction from Slush Puppie. Andrew Olins heads a dedicated property litigation team.

Kimbells LLP specialises in commercial and property litigation for the brewing and pub company sector, led by the 'very professional and thorough' Richard Brown. Contentious competition, misrepresentation and disputes over trading ties make up a large part of the group's workload.

Andrew Knight and the four-partner team at **Taylor Walton** handle some high-profile cases in the northern home counties. Professional negligence and contentious probate are real strengths, as are software disputes and employment cases.

Also recommended are **SA Law LLP** for professional negligence, construction and pensions claims; **Stanley Tee** for environmental disputes; and **Turbervilles with Nelson Cuff** for property and debt recovery claims.

COMMERCIAL LITIGATION
Beds, Bucks, Herts, Middx

WILDE SAPTE *Milton Keynes*
HOWES PERCIVAL *Milton Keynes*
MATTHEW ARNOLD & BALDWIN *Watford*

B P Collins *Gerrards Cross*
EMW Law LLP *Milton Keynes*
Fennemores *Milton Keynes*
Iliffes Booth Bennett (IBB) *Chesham, Uxbridge*
Kimbells LLP *Milton Keynes*
Taylor Walton *Luton*

SA Law LLP *St Alban*
Stanley Tee *Bishop's Stortford*
Turbervilles with Nelson Cuff *Uxbridge*

Geoffrey Leaver Solicitors *Milton Keynes*
Harold Benjamin *Harrow*
Hawkins Russell Jones *Hitchin*
Machins *Luton*
Pictons Solicitors LLP *Luton*
Woodfine Leeds Smith *Sandy*

Firms are listed A-Z in tiers which are ranked in order of priority

ESSEX

Headed by Peter Allen, **Birkett Long** in Chelmsford maintains a solid practice dealing with disputes relating to property, construction, professional negligence and insolvency. At the Colchester branch, Simon Loome has been promoted to partner and Adrian Livesley is recommended for his ADR work.

COMMERCIAL LITIGATION
Essex

BIRKETT LONG *Chelmsford, Colchester*
WOLLASTONS *Chelmsford*

Davies Lavery *Chelmsford*
Ellisons *Colchester*
Thompson Smith & Puxon *Colchester*
Tolhurst Fisher *Southend*
Wortley Byers LLP *Brentwood*

Firms are listed A-Z in tiers which are ranked in order of priority

Bruce Bowler heads up a pre-eminent litigation practice at **Wollastons** that spans environmental, administrative and public law as well as corporate and property disputes. The firm also has a dedicated IT/IP dispute resolution practice, which deals with numerous multi-million-pound disputes. New partner Jon Legorburu, formerly of **Slaughter and May**, bolsters the team's expertise in this area.

SOUTH WEST

The South West is divided into four areas: Bristol; Dorset and South Wiltshire; M4 Corridor and Gloucestershire; and the West Country. The leading practices in the region are comparable to those in the West Midlands, Yorkshire and the Humber, and the North West, and certain firms can boast national reputations in particular areas of practice.

CORPORATE AND COMMERCIAL BRISTOL

At **Burges Salmon LLP**, Andrew Dunlop and associate Martin Cuell are both 'very knowledgable, attentive, and professional negotiators', who ensure that 'work is always turned around in a timely fashion', while Chris Seaton's commercial advice is described as 'practical and knowledgable'. The firm is generally highly praised by the many clients who have moved work from City firms.

Osborne Clarke's Bristol head of corporate Alisdair Livingstone, Patrick Graves and Paul Cooper 'demonstrate outstanding commitment to the task in hand', employing excellent project management skills to serve a genuinely national client base that includes private equity houses and the sort of plc clients that rarely used to take advice from outside the City. Partner Lara Burch has built an excellent commercial practice, providing strategic advice to FTSE 250 companies.

TLT Solicitors' managing partner David Pester and department head Robin Staunton have built a practice with a reputation for high-quality work and excellent partner contact and service levels. Other stars in the department include corporate finance head John Wood – 'Young Dealmaker of the Year' in the *Western Daily Press Awards* – and well-respected outsourcing supply agreement lawyer Bill Hull. The firm's commercial practice was boosted by the arrival of highly regarded partner Perran Jervis and three assistants from **Thring Townsend**.

Veale Wasbrough Lawyers' David Emanuel heads a department that is praised for its timely responses and focused commercial advice. The firm is particularly recommended for management buyout work, and has taken steps to boost its weight on the banking and tax support it is able to offer on deals.

CORPORATE AND COMMERCIAL Bristol
BURGES SALMON LLP
OSBORNE CLARKE
TLT SOLICITORS
VEALE WASBROUGH LAWYERS
Bevan Brittan LLP
Bond Pearce LLP
Lyons Davidson
Clarke Willmott
Thring Townsend
Firms are listed A-Z in tiers which are ranked in order of priority

CORPORATE AND COMMERCIAL M4 Corridor and Gloucestershire
CHARLES RUSSELL *Cheltenham*
CLARK HOLT *Swindon*
BPE *Cheltenham*
Rickerbys Solicitors *Cheltenham*
Thring Townsend *Bath, Swindon*
Wiggin LLP *Cheltenham*
Withy King *Bath, Swindon*
Davies and Partners *Gloucester*
Willans *Cheltenham*
Firms are listed A-Z in tiers which are ranked in order of priority

CORPORATE AND COMMERCIAL The West Country
ASHFORDS *Exeter*
BOND PEARCE LLP *Exeter, Plymouth*
FOOT ANSTEY *Exeter, Plymouth*
MICHELMORES *Exeter*
STEPHENS & SCOWN *Exeter, Plymouth*
Stones *Taunton*
The Stokes Partnership *Crewkerne*
Firms are listed A-Z in tiers which are ranked in order of priority

At **Bevan Brittan LLP**, John Townsend is recommended for advice on joint venture and private equity transactions.

On the commercial side, Julian Kinsey at **Bond Pearce LLP** offers advice that is 'professional and practical', while **Lyons Davidson**'s Richard Squire and Roger Acock are good choices for commercial advice as well as SME transactions.

Clarke Willmott is recognised for its work in the food and drink sector, and has built on its reputation in the sports sector with the arrival of Adam Shore from motor sport practice *Rivers & Co.* Department head Paul Hardman is praised as 'prompt, logical and thorough', and Nigel Lindsay is applauded for his dedication as a contact partner, ensuring that deals in the £1m-£10m range are well supported. Clients include Burger King.

For its entrepreneurial client base, **Thring Townsend**'s managing partner Tony Harris is an excellent choice on SME mergers, acquisitions and joint ventures.

DORSET AND SOUTH WILTSHIRE

Lester Aldridge is praised for its excellent corporate finance advice. The department has been boosted by the firm's merger with *Park Nelson.*

Steele Raymond LLP wins plaudits from an extremely loyal local client base, which turns to partner Paul Longland for the full range of commercial, M&A and restructuring advice.

CORPORATE AND COMMERCIAL Dorset and South Wiltshire
LESTER ALDRIDGE *Bournemouth*
STEELE RAYMOND LLP *Bournemouth*
Coles Miller *Bournemouth*
Parker Bullen *Salisbury*
Firms are listed A-Z in tiers which are ranked in order of priority

M4 CORRIDOR AND GLOUCESTERSHIRE

Charles Russell impresses clients with its 'professional service and speed of response across the board', with Richard Norton singled out as 'knowledgable and impressive'.

Clark Holt has reported its strongest year to date for corporate transactions. Richard Clark and Philip Humphreys have an excellent reputation for handling SME corporate deals, especially IT-related transactions. The recruitment of **Morgan Cole** partner Jeff Jenkins has strengthened the firm's AIM practice.

Clients praise **BPE**'s lawyers as 'very committed at all levels' and note that 'the service levels and quality of support is excellent'.

Rickerbys Solicitors offers a 'truly excellent' service for management buyouts. Richard Knight combines 'friendliness' with 'total professionalism'.

Thring Townsend partner Simon Holdsworth is an excellent transactional lawyer and brings a 'capable and commercial' approach to any SME deal, while at **Wiggin LLP**, Mike Turner is praised as an 'excellent' and 'proactive' lawyer with a reputation for moving quickly to an agreement.

Withy King is recommended for its thorough and commercial approach to corporate work in the £1m-£5m range.

THE WEST COUNTRY

Ashfords' managing partner Simon Rous is recommended for complex corporate work. The firm is praised for 'always looking to add value' and for keeping clients up to date on the progress of instructions.

Experienced corporate finance lawyer Tim Jackman leads **Bond Pearce LLP**'s practice, which is particularly recommended for private equity deals, own share purchases and mid- to high-value restructuring work.

At **Foot Anstey**, Richard Coombs and Mark Lewis are praised for running 'an effective, well-disciplined and cost-conscious operation', 'highly recommended for the £1m-to-£5m deal'.

Michelmores partners Malcolm Dickinson, Stephen Morse and Samantha Billingham are recommended for corporate work that mostly falls in the £1m-£30m range. As one comments, 'the firm's deals are well run, well supported, and show a close attention to the details that matter'.

Perceived for a while as having lost ground to other Exeter practices, **Stephens & Scown** deserves credit for closing the gap. The deal size handled by the firm has broken through the £5m mark on more than 20 occasions in the past year, and on acquisitions, management buyouts and company law advice partners James Keliher, Guy Curry and Tony Welford are praised as capable, commercial and responsive.

COMMERCIAL LITIGATION BRISTOL

Bevan Brittan LLP's strengths in insurance and construction make it a popular choice for major professional negligence, fraud and asset recovery claims. The 'tenacious and commercially astute' Patricia Mitchell impresses the firm's insurance and finance practice clients on the largest cases. Partners Robin Neill and Tom Ellis are excellent choices for fraud cases, arbitrations and financial services disputes. Ellis is also recommended for IT and IP disputes.

Aside from the excellent contentious work handled by **Burges Salmon LLP** in construction, competition, health and safety and IP, Paul Haggett and David Hall are highly recommended for 'good strategic thinking' on heavyweight corporate and banking and finance disputes. Adrian Llewelyn-Evans is a good choice for disputes with an international element. The construction and engineering group sits within the commercial litigation team.

At **Osborne Clarke**, Peter Clough is 'user-friendly and accessible, with a good strategic mind'. Clients – who include energy and natural resources groups, engineering companies and food manufacturers – are impressed with the 'practical nature of his advice'. Clare Robinson is also recommended for bringing a pragmatic eye

COMMERCIAL LITIGATION Bristol
BEVAN BRITTAN LLP
BURGES SALMON LLP
OSBORNE CLARKE
CLARKE WILLMOTT
TLT SOLICITORS
VEALE WASBROUGH LAWYERS
Beachcroft Wansbroughs
Bevans
Bond Pearce LLP
Lyons Davidson
Thring Townsend

Firms are listed A-Z in tiers which are ranked in order of priority

to complex disputes for clients from the financial services, manufacturing and utilities sectors.

Robert Morfee at **Clarke Willmott** is a particularly strong choice for financial services-related litigation; his track record includes handling claims on behalf of Equitable Life policy-holders. Head of department William Whiteley acts mainly for developers and local authorities.

TLT Solicitors' head of department Chris Owen, Philip May and Richard Flowerdew are 'technically excellent' and bring 'solid strategic judgement' to shareholder, partnership and contract disputes. Loyal clients include Imperial Tobacco and Hanson.

At **Veale Wasbrough Lawyers**, managing partner Simon Pizzey and Vicky Ward are praised for the high standard of their work, their promptness of response, and their appreciation of clients' business agendas.

Clients of **Beachcroft Wansbroughs** appreciate the firm's ability to take a 'hard-line stance'. Associate Travis Toemoe is singled out for his 'tenacious and proactive' approach to defending claims. Another client adds: 'They display an amazing technical knowledge of the law and its unique application to our needs as a client.'

Bevans is well respected for claims against financial institutions on behalf of customers and other stakeholders.

Bond Pearce LLP Bristol partner Stephen Lister has handled a growing volume of complex cases, including work for International Power. Recently Lister added two senior associates to the team.

Martin Bastow at **Lyons Davidson** is a good choice for most types of SME disputes.

Thring Townsend's Bill Brydon is praised for an 'effective and commercially focused' service for clients including Somerfield Stores Ltd.

DORSET AND SOUTH WILTSHIRE

Lester Aldridge's banking clients praise Rachel Small 's ability to remain steadfast whilst showing 'empathy and consideration'. Department head Jon Kelly is recommended for cases with an insolvency element.

Andrew Breckenridge at **Parker Bullen** has an excellent reputation for banking litigation for major retail banks.

At **Steele Raymond LLP**, Peter Rolph impresses with his work on high-value construction disputes. Robert Bajaj provides a good service to national retail and leisure clients, and the experienced Simon Outten is an excellent choice for disputes with an employment law element.

M4 CORRIDOR AND GLOUCESTERSHIRE

Charles Russell's head of department Peter Scandrett is one of the best individual litigators outside the City, and in addition to a wide range of commercial experience is recommended for several niche specialisms, including professional negligence, media, employment and aviation.

At **Maitland Walker** Rupert Croft's excellent track record includes the landmark case *Crehan v Inntrepreneur*. He is also well regarded for anti-trust, shareholder, and property disputes. Julian Maitland-Walker and Hilary Coles also have an excellent record on contentious competition cases and IP disputes.

Wiggin LLP partners Caroline Kean and Simon Baggs have an excellent reputation for heavyweight defamation work and music-industry litigation, and Philip Radford and Joanne Davis at **BPE** offer a 'professional and friendly service' with a good grasp of business needs.

THE WEST COUNTRY

Ashfords' head of department Ian Daniells brings broad experience and a 'business-like approach' to partnership and shareholder disputes, and fiduciary duty claims. Partner David Beadel is a particularly strong choice for media-related disputes, including defamation claims.

At **Bond Pearce LLP**, Andrew Tobey is praised by clients as 'professional, practical' and for 'understanding the commercial impact of disputes' on their business, while banks recommend Robin Brown at **Foot Anstey** for his 'calm conduct' and 'reasoned review' of complex cases.

Tim Richards and Simon Barnett at **Michelmores** are described by clients as 'extremely professional, courteous and a great asset to the firm'. The firm has undertaken an impressive range of disputes, and is a strong choice for judicial review or IP litigation.

Stephens & Scown partner Chris Harper offers wide experience of commercial disputes, including endowment misselling cases.

COMMERCIAL LITIGATION Dorset and South Wiltshire
LESTER ALDRIDGE *Bournemouth*
PARKER BULLEN *Salisbury*
STEELE RAYMOND LLP *Bournemouth*

COMMERCIAL LITIGATION M4 Corridor and Gloucestershire
CHARLES RUSSELL *Cheltenham*
MAITLAND WALKER *Cheltenham, Minehead*
WIGGIN LLP *Cheltenham*
BPE *Cheltenham*
Rickerbys Solicitors *Cheltenham*
Stone King LLP *Bath*
Thring Townsend *Bath, Swindon*

COMMERCIAL LITIGATION The West Country
ASHFORDS EXETER, PLYMOUTH
BOND PEARCE LLP EXETER, PLYMOUTH
FOOT ANSTEY EXETER, PLYMOUTH
MICHELMORES EXETER
Stephens & Scown Exeter, Truro
Nash & Co Plymouth
Stones Exeter
The Stokes Partnership Crewkerne

Firms are listed A-Z in tiers which are ranked in order of priority

WEST MIDLANDS

The West Midlands comprises Birmingham and the surrounding counties of Herefordshire and Worcestershire, Warwickshire, Shropshire and Staffordshire.

CORPORATE AND COMMERCIAL BIRMINGHAM

Wragge & Co LLP's corporate group, led by Jeremy Millington, has over a dozen Birmingham-based partners, and reports having completed some 95 transactions with an aggregate value of just over £3bn in the past year. Foremost among them were Nomura's £245m acquisition of Earls Court and Olympia, which was the first deal the firm has completed for the bank, and Safestore Acquisition's £209m takeover of Mentmore plc (acting for the purchaser and its funder, with Andrew Smith leading). The team includes Ian Metcalfe, who has particular experience in the technology sector. Stuart Young has joined highly rated private equity specialists Maurice Dwyer and Andy Stylianou in the firm's London office, while Nick Smith, the lead partner on the Nomura deal, has moved in-house to the Japanese bank.

CORPORATE AND COMMERCIAL
Birmingham

WRAGGE & CO LLP ✪

DLA PIPER RUDNICK GRAY CARY UK LLP
EVERSHEDS LLP
PINSENT MASONS

HBJ Gateley Wareing LLP
Hammonds

Browne Jacobson LLP
Cobbetts
Heatons LLP
Martineau Johnson

Bevan Brittan LLP
Mills & Reeve
Putsmans
The Wilkes Partnership

Cartwright & Lewis
Shakespeares

Firms are listed A-Z in tiers which are ranked in order of priority
✪ *Indicates firm displays contact details at the end of this chapter.*

Russell Orme heads **DLA Piper Rudnick Gray Cary UK LLP**'s seven-partner Birmingham corporate team, which includes managing partner Chris Rawstron. It has real strength on the private equity side, with Jim Lavery a leading specialist, and recently handled significant instructions for ISIS, Barclays Private Equity and LDC among others, while capital markets highlights included Dignity plc's £172m flotation, working alongside the firm's securitisation team in London. David Glover heads an expanding five-partner commercial and projects group, which has recently handled work for Barclays and GNER.

Eversheds LLP has a team of six Birmingham-based corporate partners operating under regional corporate head Stephen Kitts (based in Nottingham). It has continued to attract some excellent transactions, most notably the £160m flotation of longstanding client Jessops plc and the £110m secondary buyout of Goldsmiths Group plc (acting for the management vendors, with Mike Seabrook the lead partner), while other clients advised on substantial deals included MG Rover, Centrica and Austria's Wienerberger AG. Sue Lewis is highly rated and, on the commercial side, Anne Harris has a strong reputation for her rail-sector work.

Pinsent Masons' eight-partner corporate team is led by private equity specialist Andrew Hornigold, with Gary Laitner now charged (along with Paul Finlan) with an international role following the firm's merger. Recent public company transactions include the £10m-take private of West Bromwich Albion plc, while on the private equity side the firm acted on the £51m sale of Dennis Eagle Limited, a Bridgepoint investment, to an ABN Amro-backed newco. Simon Pigden remains the firm's national head of commercial; his team has recently handled major instructions from National Grid Transco and AXA among others.

HBJ Gateley Wareing LLP (following its merger with Scottish firm *Henderson Boyd Jackson*) maintains its exceptional profile in the local corporate market; the last year was a year of consolidation that saw the firm handle some 200 corporate and private equity transactions, among them the £70m MBO of Denby Group (advising the management) and the sale of Brownsword to The Capita Group. The six-partner team includes Paul Hayward on the private equity side, senior partner Michael Ward, and Paul Cliff and Katie Silvester together spearheading the plc practice.

Hammonds' highlights included advising the shareholders (including Bridgepoint as majority shareholder) on the £135m disposal of Western Wines, while National Grid Transco and ProLogis are among its key clients. Head of corporate Patrick Somers was set to leave for **Berwin Leighton Paisner LLP** in the summer of 2005, leaving a five-partner corporate team that includes M&A specialist Martin Letza – an important and much talked about recent hire from **Eversheds LLP** – and Amanda Allen, whose specialisms include automotive and industrial M&A.

Browne Jacobson LLP's widely rated corporate practice is focused on M&A and private equity, with former **Hammonds** partners Roger Birchall and Joanne Bligh the two partners in the team. They have been attracting some impressive instructions of late, such as advising the management on the £89m secondary buy-out of Nightfreight and acting for SP Group on the £33m exit of a Bridgepoint-backed MBO.

Cobbetts' corporate work included acting for AIM-listed Highland Gold on a US$100m share placing, and advising the vendors in the £25m disposal of Mason Richards Partnership. The corporate team – which includes national head Stephen Gilmore and Graham Muth – has been invigorated on the public company side by the arrival from **Freshfields Bruckhaus Deringer** of new partner Charles Bond, while Simon Bates' commercial team has expanded with the arrival of German-qualifed partner Jan Becher.

Private company work remains the core of **Heatons LLP**'s well-regarded corporate practice. The firm is best known in the market for the succession of high-value deals it has handled for Icelandic venture capital group Baugur, such as its recent £110m acquisition of Goldsmiths. But the departure in March 2005 of managing partner (and Baugur relationship partner) David Beech, to investment house Arev, is a significant loss. He leaves behind head of department Paul Wakefield and Rob Parry on the corporate finance side, while Mark Beech is the lead partner for commercial matters.

Martineau Johnson's corporate practice remains split into two core areas: funds work (including advice to venture capital trusts providing private equity for the mid-market, and financial services regulatory advice), and M&A (to a range of corporates, local and national). Roger Blears heads the funds team, which now acts for 12 VCTs including Foresight Technology and Matrix Ventures, with Enid Armstrong leading on the financial services side. Recent M&A work, under Richard Wrigley, includes the acquisition of Blackpool airport and a string of deals for Homeserve plc.

Bevan Brittan LLP runs an integrated corporate practice across its offices in Bristol, Birmingham and London, with Geoff Perry still the sole Birmingham-based corporate finance partner. Birmingham-led work in the past year included acting for the management team on the £12.5m MBO of Mitie Generation Limited. The scope of the practice has broadened with the arrival from **Pinsent Masons** of Christine McElroy on the tax side.

Mills & Reeve, under the 'first-class' Tim Winn, handles corporate and commercial work for a broad public and private sector client base, with recent additions including Stanhope Leisure, Beaumont Pubs, and Imperial College London (advised in relation to an overseas joint venture relating to diabetes). The firm's commercial contracts group, in which Peter Manford is the key figure, has been restructured to include health and public sector expertise.

Putsmans' team, under Gareth Griffiths, expanded in early 2005 with the addition of two new partners: Keith Spedding was previously a senior associate at **Wragge & Co LLP** and brings extensive public company experience, while Gary Davie is a former **Martineau Johnson** partner with a mainstream private company practice. Recent work included advising on the £70m acquisition of a property holding company with a brownfield site for development.

The Wilkes Partnership has a four-partner team led by Gareth O'Hara offering a full range of corporate and commercial experience, including AIM and other listing work. Recent M&A instructions include acting for Stadco Limited on its purchase of the business of Mayflower Vehicle Systems plc, with former *Pinsents* partner Jeremy Parkin leading. On the commercial side, clients include National Grid Transco.

ELSEWHERE IN WEST MIDLANDS

George Green enjoyed a strong year for corporate work, acting on some 60 transactions with a total value of more than £60m, with the secondary buyout of Minivator Limited (advising the purchaser) a standout deal. Joining the Lloyds TSB panel was another highlight; other panel appointments include Venture Finance and Bank of Scotland. Richard Cliff and Paul Bennett are the two partners.

KJD maintains a four-partner corporate team that includes senior partner Anthony Reeves and

CORPORATE AND COMMERCIAL
Elsewhere in West Midlands

GEORGE GREEN *Cradley Heath*
KJD *Stoke-on-Trent*
KNIGHT & SONS *Newcastle-under-Lyme*
MANBY & STEWARD *Wolverhampton*
REED SMITH *Coventry*
WRIGHT HASSALL *Leamington Spa*

Alsters Kelley *Leamington Spa*
fbc *Wolverhampton*
Grindeys LLP *Stoke-on-Trent*
Higgs & Sons *Brierley Hill*
Keelys *Lichfield*
Lanyon Bowdler *Shrewsbury*
Martin Kaye Solicitors *Telford*
ORJ Solicitors LLP *Stafford*

Blythe Liggins *Leamington Spa*
Brindley Twist Tafft & James *Coventry*
Goodger Auden *Burton-upon-Trent*
Hacking Ashton LLP *Newcastle-under-Lyme*
Hadens *Walsal*
Harrison Clark LLP *Worcester*
Thursfields *Kidderminster*
Varley Hibbs LLP *Coventry*

Firms are listed A-Z in tiers which are ranked in order of priority

practice head Peter Ellis. Recent activity includes a good variety of M&A, restructuring, and joint venture advice. JCB Group and Britannia Building Society are among the firm's longstanding clients. Dr Michael Servian heads up the firm's commercial practice.

Derek Miller leads a sizeable team at **Knight & Sons** that includes one other partner, Susan Honeyands. Recent M&A work included advising Abnormal Load Engineering on its acquisition of Alsthom's road haulage division, while other clients include University of Keele, The Tussauds Group, and Bet 365 Group.

Manby & Steward has two Wolverhampton-based corporate partners – department head Gavin Southall and James Knight – handling work for a variety of medium to large owner-managed businesses, other SMEs and some plcs. They work alongside consultant David Hughes, a former *Pinsents* partner who joined the firm at the end of 2002, while Telford-based Stuart Rea is the third partner in team.

The focus of **Reed Smith**'s corporate practice is increasingly international; as well as handling general M&A and corporate finance advice for UK, US and other clients, the firm offers notable niche expertise, with managing partner Chris Hill specialising in offshore structures and trusts. David Cranfield is the second partner in the team.

Wright Hassall's corporate and commercial practice is a key engine of growth for the firm. Department head Keith Ainsworth handles a mix of corporate and banking work, and recently advised on a £20m multi-option mezzanine note issue facility. Other recent work includes acting for the Royal Agricultural Society in a joint venture (by way of LLP) relating to The Royal Show, with Mark Lewis leading the advice.

COMMERCIAL LITIGATION BIRMINGHAM

Pinsent Masons' disputes group, under managing partner Greg Lowson continues to advise on a variety of complex and high-value litigation, handling some 11 cases worth over £10m in the past year and representing Defra in disputes arising from the foot and mouth outbreak with a total value of around £55m. The team includes the 'proactive and accomodating' Jim Richards, whose specialisms include contractual disputes involving the public sector, and also a forensic accountant in Kevin Hills.

Wragge & Co LLP has by some distance the largest team of litigators in Birmingham, and handles significant amounts of volume litigation as well as national and international cases at the complex end of the spectrum. The team includes department head Andrew Manning Cox, Nicola Mumford, whose specialisms include the automotive sector, and Andrew Smith, whose recent activity includes leading the advice to Chase Midland plc in the defence of a claim for commission by property consultants. The service provided is, according to one client, 'very good: very helpful, co-operative and cost-effective.'

Recent activity at **DLA Piper Rudnick Gray Cary UK LLP** included acting for a major US-based multinational in the successful defence of a US$74m claim in the High Court relating to a joint venture in Shanghai, while other recent clients include Ansbacher Group Legal and Sendo Holdings (the latter advised in relation to UK litigation with Microsoft, with Fran Davie the lead partner). The team is praised as 'cost effective and efficient when dealing with both straightforward disputes and highly complex, high-value disputes'. Neil Bowker took over from Jim Sharkey as practice head in March 2005.

Eversheds LLP operates an integrated commercial litigation team under Ian Gray across its Birmingham, Nottingham and Cardiff offices. Stephen Barker is the lead partner of the Birmingham team, which includes three other partners and has grown significantly at sub-partner level, and reported impressive turnover growth in the past year. A team led by Gray won appointment to the National Grid Transco panel for commercial litigation in November 2004.

Commercial dispute resolution is one **Cobbetts**' fastest growing practice areas, with turnover reported as having increased by around 18% for each of the last two years. Richard Whittingham heads what is now a four-partner team whose recent workload includes acting in a substantial shareholders dispute involving BVI, Vietnamese and English law issues, and a high-profile contested probate action. Whittingham offers significant experience as a mediator.

COMMERCIAL LITIGATION
Birmingham

PINSENT MASONS
WRAGGE & CO LLP ✪

DLA PIPER RUDNICK GRAY CARY UK LLP
EVERSHEDS LLP

COBBETTS
HAMMONDS
MARTINEAU JOHNSON

Anthony Collins Solicitors LLP
HBJ Gateley Wareing LLP
Putsmans
The Wilkes Partnership

Blakemores
Challinors Lyon Clark
Ferdinand Kelly
Irwin Mitchell
Mills & Reeve
Shakespeares

Firms are listed A-Z in tiers which are ranked in order of priority
✪ *Indicates firm displays contact details at the end of this chapter.*

Ann Benzimra has taken over as head of **Hammonds**' department following the retirement of Digby Rose, and enjoys an excellent reputation. She has particular expertise in the food and drink sector, and has handled a variety of commercial disputes, including sizeable IT disputes and corporate warranty claims. Sarah Watson has left the firm.

Martineau Johnson's wide-ranging commercial disputes management group is now led by Andrew Adams, who is a specialist in the energy sector, while other partners in the team include Stuart Farr and, on the contentious education side, Smita Jamdar. Recent activity includes advising on a significant product liability dispute. Former practice head Andrew Spooner left the firm in 2005 to become director of litigation at **Heatons LLP**.

At **Anthony Collins Solicitors LLP**, Andrew Lancaster heads the commercial litigation department and has been leading on a major dispute in the automotive sector, while Nick Carter specialises on contentious regulatory work. Clients include Ofsted Early Years and various charitable organisations.

Stephen Goodrham heads **HBJ Gateley Wareing LLP**'s commercial dispute resolution practice, and is the sole partner in the team. He continues to lead the advice to a longstanding pharmaceutical client on £55m breach of contract claim in the International Court of Arbitration.

Department head Peter Adkins remains the key individual at **Putsmans** for commercial litigation; his experience spans manufacturing, product liability and motor sport-related disputes.

Nick Briggs has been a valuable addition on the contentious IP side.

The Wilkes Partnership has a good range of commercial litigation experience, with senior partner Nigel Wood the main point of contact.

Steve Allen, previously a senior associate at **Wragge & Co LLP**, joined **Mills & Reeve** to head its new commercial litigation practice in Birmingham. His recent work includes acting for Budget Inc's main UK franchisee in a US$4.5m claim against Budget Rent A Car in the US.

ELSEWHERE IN WEST MIDLANDS

KJD has a broad-based contentious practice and offers some solid experience on commercial litigation, with the 'sharp, practical and pragmatic' Stephen Hadley, newly promoted partner Stephen Taylor and department head Graham Neyt all active. Adrian Ross left the firm, moving in-house to longstanding client JCB Group; other clients include British Energy, Severn Trent Water Authority and Britannic Assurance.

The Coventry office of US-based **Reed Smith** has handled an array of high-level litigation for US, UK and other European clients. Jonathan Hofstetter's practice is focused on complex international litigation and arbitration, including IP and IT-related disputes, while Larry Coltman's specialisms include international agency and insurance contract law. Darren Smith is the third partner in the team, and majors on product liability work, including group litigation.

Sarah Perry has taken over as head of **Wright Hassall**'s commercial litigation team, which also includes Richard Lane (former head, now deputy managing partner) and Rhys Jarman on the contentious IP side. The firm is increasingly attracting instructions from banks and other financial institutions, while other clients include WH Smith, British Waterways Board and P&O.

George Green offers wide-ranging commercial disputes experience, with former *Pinsents* partner Neil Williams leading the team. Recent work included acting for insurance brokerage firm Commercial Express Quotes in a relatively substantial four-party dispute and mediation. Both Williams and associate Mark Elder are trained mediators.

Tim Wolley heads **Grindeys LLP**'s commercial litigation practice, while **Harrison Clark LLP**'s wide-ranging litigation department is led by Andrew James and acts for clients such as Tarmac and Cox Homes.

Knight & Sons' recent caseload includes advising on the mediation of a £1m-plus claim by a supplier of safety devices to a national cable telecoms network. Andrew Davidson heads the department, which includes one other partner and a full-time consultant.

Manby & Steward recently acted for a construction company in a claim against HM Inspector of Tax relating to its refusal to renew a tax certificate. Peter Taylor heads the commercial litigation team, which was bolstered by the recent arrival of contentious insolvency specialist Brian Aikman from **Martineau Johnson**; both are based in the firm's Wolverhampton office.

Martin Kaye Solicitors has continued to handle a range of commercial disputes, under partner Graham Davies, while **ORJ Solicitors LLP**, under Patrick Tedstone, has recently been active on an assortment of £1m-plus manufacturing-related claims.

John Sullivan at **Sullivan & Co** is a former head of international litigation and insolvency at *Edge & Ellison*, and continues to undertake a mix of complex commercial litigation and contentious insolvency work.

COMMERCIAL LITIGATION
Elsewhere in West Midlands

KJD *Stoke-on-Trent*
REED SMITH *Coventry*
WRIGHT HASSALL *Leamington Spa*

George Green *Cradley Heath*
Grindeys LLP *Stoke-on-Trent*
Harrison Clark LLP *Worcester*
Knight & Sons *Newcastle-under-Lyme*
mfg Solicitors *Halesowen*
Manby & Steward *Wolverhampton, Bridgnorth, Telford*
Martin Kaye Solicitors *Telford*
ORJ Solicitors LLP *Stafford*
Sullivan & Co *Malvern*

Alsters Kelley *Leamington Spa*
fbc *Wolverhampton*
Hadens *Walsall*
Higgs & Sons *Brierley Hill*
Lanyon Bowdler *Telford, Shrewsbury*
Thursfields *Kidderminster*
Tinsdills *Stoke-on-Trent*

Firms are listed A-Z in tiers which are ranked in order of priority

YORKSHIRE AND THE HUMBER

Yorkshire and Humber includes the highly competitive legal market of Leeds at its heart with further key commercial legal centres in Sheffield, Hull and York. Clients seeking to instruct a lawyer in the region can choose from a range of full-service practices, from the multi-site national giants to some of the finest single-site outfits in the UK.

CORPORATE AND COMMERCIAL LEEDS AND WEST YORKSHIRE

Addleshaw Goddard offers clients a broad corporate offering from its Leeds office. Private equity is a particular strength, with Yunus Seedat and Simon Pilling, who splits his time between London and Leeds, two of the most respected buyout specialists in the market. The firm has prove particularly adept at strengthening its relationships to key corporates such as J Sainsbury. Ian McIntosh is widely admired for his public M&A track record while Adam Bennett and David Heffron have established leading reputations in the financial services sector.

With Alastair Da Costa becoming national head of corporate, Jonathan Procter has taken over as **DLA Piper Rudnick Gray Cary UK LLP**'s department head in Leeds. M&A remains the mainstay of the practice with a steady flow of private equity deals, but the firm also enjoys an excellent reputation for corporate finance work. Highlights include advising (together with the Sheffield office) on the £20m AIM flotation of Sanderson Group, and acting for Brewin Dolphin on placings for Nord Anglia, Haveaux and Acquito. Wendy Harrison and Stephen Atkinson both win client praise for their dealmaking skills.

In Keith Froud and Robin Johnson **Eversheds LLP** has two of the most prolific dealmakers in the Leeds market. The ebullient Johnson handles a growing number of international instructions and is undoubtedly the practice's big-hitter, handling work for clients such as Next and Richmond Foods. New clients include Babcock International Group and Colson, while key deals include acting for Wolseley on the £120m acquisition of Brooks Group. On the private equity side Robin Skelton wins praise as one of the go-to buyout specialists in the market.

CORPORATE AND COMMERCIAL
Leeds and West Yorkshire

ADDLESHAW GODDARD *Leeds*
DLA PIPER RUDNICK GRAY CARY UK LLP *Leeds*
EVERSHEDS LLP *Leeds*

HAMMONDS *Leeds*
PINSENT MASONS *Leeds*
WALKER MORRIS *Leeds*

Cobbetts *Leeds*
Gordons *Leeds*

Brooke North *Leeds*
Ford & Warren *Leeds*
Irwin Mitchell *Leeds*
Lupton Fawcett *Leeds*
McCormicks *Leeds*

Denison Till *York*
Fox Hayes *Leeds*
Keeble Hawson *Leeds*
Last Cawthra Feather LLP *Bradford, Shipley, Ilkley*
Lee & Priestley *Leeds*

Firms are listed A-Z in tiers which are ranked in order of priority

Hammonds' corporate practice boasts a growing international profile with a solid base of Yorkshire plc work and close ties with key intermediaries. Ian Greenfield combines his role as head of the Leeds office with that of practice head, and is noted for his down-to-earth approach to dealmaking. On the private equity side Jonathan Jones is one of the most active deal-doers around although his position as national head of private equity has led some clients to comment that he is less visible in the local market. Transaction highlights include acting for Vane Holdings on its £17m AIM flotation, and for Automotive Products Group on the $36m disposal of its US business.

At **Pinsent Masons** Martin Shaw heads the team and enjoys a first-rate reputation for M&A and securities work. In one particularly noteworthy instruction the firm advised Countrywide Assured Group on its demerger and on the subsequent relisting of Countrywide and Chesnara. New partners Philip Goldsborough and Peter Wood are both recognised as rising stars in the department. On the commercial side Vincent King heads a team that acts for both public and private sector clients.

The corporate team at **Walker Morris** remains one of the most admired in the market with clients commenting that the six-partner group punches well above its weight and is particularly flexible on fees. While the firm enjoys excellent links with the local corporate and intermediary market, it also picks up key instructions further afield from major corporates. Witness its work for Caterpillar Logistics on the £105m acquisition of MG Rover's parts business. Ian Gilbert and department head Peter Smart both enjoy excellent reputations.

Cobbetts continues to grow its corporate and commercial offering, which now includes five corporate partners and three commercial specialists. In a deal portfolio of impressive breadth the firm acted on the £10m BIMBO of Multigraphics, and on a placing of shares and acquisition of Navigator Sports for Real Affinity. Guy Jackson heads the corporate practice while Mark Green leads on the commercial side.

Gordons has one of the most vibrant corporate practices in the market. Wm Morrison remains the firm's leading client and partner John Holden continues to win praise for his work for the supermarket giant. The firm's recent merger with *Nelson & Co* has brought extra resource to the corporate team, with Andrew Jordan particularly prominent on the private equity side. In a range of deals Jordan led the team that advised management on the £115m secondary buyout of Hillarys Blinds.

Brooke North is noted for the quality of its corporate offering advising on deals up to £50m in the owner-managed sector. Hugh Middlemass heads the practice with key support from partner Nigel Hoyle. The expanding team includes four partners supported by three assistants.

Ford & Warren acts for clients across a range of sectors including transport and leisure. The respected Peter Reeve heads the team.

Kevin Cunningham heads **Irwin Mitchell**'s corporate practice, which operates as a combined unit across the firm's Leeds and Sheffield offices. The team has been significantly strengthened with the hire of partner Helena Jones from **Pinsent Masons**. Deal highlights include advising Van Leeuwen Pipe & Tube Group on the acquisition of MK Wheeler from US-owned company the Marmon Group.

Lupton Fawcett's corporate practice is headed by the vastly experienced Bob Harrap. In the course of the past year the practice handled over 40 transactions with a value in excess of £160m. Key clients include ICM Computer Group, Shepley Window System and Real Affinity. The firm also has a standalone commercial team made up of seven fee-earners.

McCormicks combines a considerable deal-doing track record with an enviable reputation for commercial work in the media and sport sectors. Richard Moran heads the corporate team, which has undergone considerable growth in recent years. In one notable instruction the firm acted on the formation and operation of the Viking Fund, a new venture capital investment company.

Denison Till boasts the leading corporate practice in York, regularly competing for work against larger firms from across the region. Andrew Lindsay and Alistair Duncan are the firm's principal corporate partners in a department that in the past year advised on 38 deals worth just over £90m.

Fox Hayes managing partner Philip Drazen heads the firm's corporate and commercial practice. Among a range of transactions corporate partner Malcolm Jones acted for the shareholders of Blue Beck on the company's merger with MFORMA.

Keeble Hawson's corporate team is particularly active on deals below £25m, and handled over 130 transactions in the past year. Jim Gervasio is the sole Leeds-based partner following the departure of Sharon Needle.

Last Cawthra Feather LLP's Bradford-based corporate practice includes four partners and is headed by Susan Clark. The firm is best known for its work in the owner-managed business sector and continues to strengthen its corporate offering.

Lee & Priestley has bolstered its corporate practice with the hire of partner Jonathan Priestley from **Addleshaw Goddard**. Morgan Williams heads the team, which also includes Jonathan Oxley as a deal-doer of note.

SHEFFIELD AND SOUTH YORKSHIRE

DLA Piper Rudnick Gray Cary UK LLP's corporate practice remains the market leader in Sheffield, with no other firm able to match the breadth of instructions that the four-partner team continues to pick up; recent examples include acting for Bridgepoint Capital and management on the €347m sale of Anglo-Dutch laboratory business Alcontrol Holdings. Neil Thompson, one of the most established advisers in the market, heads the practice.

Clive Lightburn heads the two-partner team at **Nabarro Nathanson**, which has a strong reputation for transport-related work for the likes of Siemens AG, Jarvis and Triumph Motorcycles. The firm acted for Albion Chemicals on the acquisition of a chemical storage plant in Liverpool, and for IFI Limited on the disposal of Roofpax.

HLW's respected corporate team is particularly active in the SME and owner-managed business sectors. Senior partner Andrew Hartley is one of the most experienced deal-makers in the market, with fellow partner Roger Dyson another specialist of note.

Irwin Mitchell's corporate team operates across the firm's Sheffield and Leeds offices with Michael Jelly the firm's principal specialist in Sheffield. The firm acted for Kleinwort Capital Trust on the disposal of Baldwin Francis Limited. On the commercial side the firm is establishing a solid track record acting in the higher education and insurance fields.

Keeble Hawson has a four-partner corporate team based in Sheffield including practice head Andrew Coombe. The firm is particularly noted for its venture capital work, acting for YFM Group and the East Midlands Regional Venture Capital fund via its fund manager Capital Venture Managers.

Wake Smith continues to build on its corporate standing in the Sheffield and South Yorkshire markets. The firm boasts a five-partner team of considerable depth with Jonathan Hunt, David Ware and John Baddeley forming a trio of respected specialists. Ware led a team that advised on the sale of the entire share capital of a nursing home group for £5m.

CORPORATE AND COMMERCIAL
Sheffield and South Yorkshire

DLA PIPER RUDNICK GRAY CARY UK LLP *Sheffield*

Nabarro Nathanson *Sheffield*

HLW *Sheffield*
Irwin Mitchell *Sheffield*
Keeble Hawson *Sheffield*
Wake Smith *Sheffield*

Ashton Morton Slack *Sheffield*

Richmonds *Doncaster*
Taylor & Emmet *Sheffield*

Firms are listed A-Z in tiers which are ranked in order of priority

CORPORATE AND COMMERCIAL
East Yorkshire and The Humber

Gosschalks *Hull*
Rollits *Hull*

Andrew M Jackson *Hull*

Stamp Jackson and Procter *Hull*

Firms are listed A-Z in tiers which are ranked in order of priority

EAST YORKSHIRE AND THE HUMBER

Gosschalks' five-partner corporate team includes senior partner and practice head Simon Lunt. Recently the firm advised William Hill on several corporate acquisitions, and acted for the shareholders of Strategic Information Technology Services Group on its £14m disposal to Tribal Group.

Rollits' corporate practice is particularly recommended for deals with a value of £2m to £80m. The department includes practice head Richard Field, managing partner Stephen Trynka and Neil Jenneson as leading players in the local market. Among a range of deals the firm acted on the MBO of Macfarlane Transport, and on the merger of tour operators Inntravel and Great Rail Journey.

Andrew M Jackson handles corporate work for a range of public and private clients. While **Stamp Jackson and Procter** is also recommended.

COMMERCIAL LITIGATION LEEDS, WEST YORKSHIRE

Addleshaw Goddard boasts an impressive three-partner litigation team including Mark Amsden, Susan Garrett and Simon Kamstra. Practice head Kamstra, in particular, is forging a considerable reputation offering litigation advice to blue-chip corporates. The practice is developing a growing name advising on disputes arising out of outsourcing and PFI/PPP deals, and also has a high-profile niche acting on sports-related disputes.

DLA Piper Rudnick Gray Cary UK LLP's litigation team handles a broad range of work for both private companies and public bodies. It enjoys a growing international profile, handling work for multinationals such as Cendant Corporation and MCI, while its reputation in IT and telecoms litigation has seen it play a key role offering contract management and dispute resolution support for the NHS National IT Programme in respect of eight major IT contracts. Damian Crosse heads the practice and is one of the most widely admired litigators in the market.

Eversheds LLP's litigation team continues to pick up work from major new clients including Honda, HJ Heinz, Energis and Abbeycrest. Key partners include regional practice head Gary Pellow, national commercial litigation supremo

COMMERCIAL LITIGATION
Leeds and West Yorkshire

ADDLESHAW GODDARD *Leeds*
DLA PIPER RUDNICK GRAY CARY UK LLP *Leeds*
EVERSHEDS LLP *Leeds*
HAMMONDS *Leeds*
PINSENT MASONS *Leeds*
WALKER MORRIS *Leeds*

Brooke North *Leeds*
Gordons *Leeds*
Irwin Mitchell *Leeds*
Keeble Hawson *Leeds*
Lupton Fawcett *Leeds*
McCormicks *Leeds*

Cobbetts *Leeds*
Denison Till *York*
Ford & Warren *Leeds*
Langleys Solicitors *York*

Firms are listed A-Z in tiers which are ranked in order of priority

Jonathan Sinclair and Richard Matthews, with overall national head of litigation and dispute management John Heaps also based in Leeds. Key instructions of late include acting for Abbeycrest in a major contractual dispute with a Far East supplier.

Hammonds' dispute resolution team enjoys a strong reputation particularly for its mediation and advocacy expertise. David Williams heads the Leeds practice with support from fellow partners Simon Miller and qualified barrister Patrick Walker. The firm handles a range of work for large multinationals, financial institutions and high-net-worth individuals. Former practice head Peter Crossley is now **Hammonds**' national managing partner.

Pinsent Masons' innovative approach to litigation has led to the firm picking up new clients of the calibre of Marshalls, LogicaCMG and DaimlerChrysler. A team of impressive breadth includes practice head Stuart Chapman, who enjoys an excellent reputation advising on high-value technology disputes, Andrew Masterson and Pauline Munro (both noted for their product liability expertise), forensic accounting expert Tony Chapman and health and safety specialist Peter Atkinson.

Walker Morris has doubled the size of its commercial litigation practice in the past four years. The 18-fee-earner team has impressive strength and depth and includes three partners, practice head Gwendoline Davies, Malcolm Simpson and Nick Bates. The practice enjoys a growing national reputation acting for the likes of HBOS, Lloyds TSB and Caterpillar.

Brooke North partner Nigel Middlemass has been representing the administrator of a group of four companies in connection with possible fraud in the insurance industry involving a claim in excess of £100m. The firm has a growing profile for professional negligence work with Richard Stockdale being appointed to the professional negligence panel of the Law Society.

Gordons offers clients a broad litigation service. John Singleton heads the practice and specialises in property litigation. Other specialists of note include Victoria Davey who heads the interventions department, contentious IP/IT and media partner Matthew Howarth, Paul Lewis for property litigation and general commercial disputes, and mediation specialist Richard Nolan.

Irwin Mitchell's two-partner litigation team has a growing reputation for its ADR practice. The practice is led by Peter Bell with further support from corporate recovery and insolvency specialist Richard Hughes.

Keeble Hawson's litigation team is on something of a roll picking up more complex and higher profile instructions. Charles Rothwell heads a three-partner team that is spread across the firm's Leeds and Sheffield offices. Mediation is a particularly buoyant area for the practice, with the firm acting on 23 mediations in the course of the past year.

The quality of **Lupton Fawcett**'s litigation practice continues to improve. The firm has picked up instructions from high-quality clients such as BAT, Federal-Mogul and TI Automotive and has increased its workload from Barclays Bank.

McCormicks handles a broad range of contentious instructions, including high-profile IP and sports-related matters. Simon Young heads the commercial disputes team while Neil Goodrum heads the ADR practice. Among a range of instructions the firm advised Jemella on several passing-off, copyright and trade mark infringement disputes.

SHEFFIELD AND SOUTH YORKSHIRE

DLA Piper Rudnick Gray Cary UK LLP's commercial litigation team remains strong across the board. Ashley Mott heads the team, which includes Stephen Sly, one of the savviest specialists in the market. The practice has a particular niche acting on contentious IT and telecoms work, advising the likes of Cable & Wireless, Colt Telecommunications and MCI with new partner Richard Norman enjoying a growing profile in the sector.

Irwin Mitchell boasts one of the largest contentious teams in the region and continues to lead the way in the development of commercial group actions. The team counts BOC, Doncaster MBC and Esso as key clients. In one highlight instruction, the firm advised Esso on a group litigation order in connection with claims brought by 100 former retailers. Peter Bellamy has left the firm.

Nabarro Nathanson acts on a broad range of contentious cases for public and private sector

COMMERCIAL LITIGATION Sheffield and South Yorkshire
DLA PIPER RUDNICK GRAY CARY UK LLP *Sheffield*
Irwin Mitchell *Sheffield*
Nabarro Nathanson *Sheffield*
Ashton Morton Slack *Sheffield*
HLW *Sheffield*
Keeble Hawson *Sheffield*
Taylor & Emmet *Sheffield*
Wake Smith *Sheffield*
Firms are listed A-Z in tiers which are ranked in order of priority

clients including ICI, Travelex, Network Rail and Siemens. Practice head Gerard Khoshnaw is an experienced mediator as well as a general commercial litigator. In one standout instruction the firm advised Kellogg's in relation to the recovery of €1m-plus losses following the supply of faulty ingredients.

At **Ashton Morton Slack** Robert Bryars heads the civil and commercial litigation practice with key support from two assistants.

Keeble Hawson's principal Sheffield-based litigator is Stuart Ward, who specialises in commercial disputes, property litigation, professional negligence and probate litigation. The local team combines with the Leeds practice and offers clients credible expertise in ADR including mediation.

Wake Smith's litigation team comprises three partners and four assistants. Partner Mark Serby heads the practice, which advises clients on a range of disputes including contentious IP cases, professional negligence claims and property-related disputes.

EAST YORKSHIRE AND THE HUMBER

The sheer depth of **Rollits**' litigation team marks it out as the market leader in the region. The experienced George Coyle heads the practice and is also a member of the firm's regulatory law group. Fellow partner Ralph Gilbert is one of the best-known insolvency lawyers in the market as well as handling a significant volume of property litigation work.

COMMERCIAL LITIGATION East Yorkshire and the Humber
Rollits *Hull*
Andrew M Jackson *Hull*
Gosschalks *Hull*
Stamp Jackson and Procter *Hull*
Firms are listed A-Z in tiers which are ranked in order of priority

Andrew M Jackson's litigation team is headed by Hugh Smith, who has a particular niche advising on professional negligence and food law litigation. The firm boasts expertise across a range of specialisms including contentious property work, construction and insolvency litigation.

At **Gosschalks** Bruce Wilkie heads the litigation practice with key support from Nick Dean and Ian Brown. The firm is particularly noted for its commercial approach to disputes and has one of the most buoyant contentious practices in the region.

WALES

Wales is made up of many regions and many markets, each with its own unique character. Cardiff is the main commercial hub and, with Swansea a short distance away, the main hive of activity is in the south west of the country.

The regeneration funding enjoyed by Cardiff in recent years is now moving along the M4 motorway, with Swansea benefiting from major projects such as the SA1 Waterfront development. Newport is also targeted for significant regeneration work.

Some areas further north, however, do not share the same affluence, after the demise of the coal and steel industries, but funding has been flowing into these areas, largely through the Welsh Development Agency (WDA).

Agriculture and estates work is a significant area of practice, and the country is also home to a number of high-net-worth individuals, while commercial activity is largely concentrated on SMEs. The infrastructure linking Wales to the north west and south west of England, combined with a very low cost base, makes it an attractive location for businesses, as well as for clients seeking legal advice at competitive rates.

CORPORATE AND COMMERCIAL CARDIFF AND SOUTH WALES

Eversheds LLP has many strands to its corporate and commercial practice in Cardiff, and handles larger regional and national deals. The three-partner commercial services division, led by Bridgette Wilcox and including ex-**Morgan Cole** partner Alun Cole, handles central government work, while Paul Lowe and Michelle Thomas are the key individuals on the corporate finance side.

Some competitors speak of Alan Whiteley at specialist corporate, commercial and property firm **M & A Solicitors** as the most accomplished practitioner in Cardiff, with Stephen Berry also coming highly recommended. Recently the team advised Celtic Inns Ltd on its refinancing and Buy as You View Ltd on an MBO funded by 3i.

Recent restructuring means that half of **Morgan Cole**'s corporate team is now in Cardiff.

CORPORATE AND COMMERCIAL Cardiff and South Wales
EVERSHEDS LLP *Cardiff*
M & A SOLICITORS *Cardiff*
MORGAN COLE *Cardiff*
Berry Smith *Cardiff*
Capital Law *Cardiff*
Dolmans Solicitors *Cardiff*
Geldards LLP *Cardiff*
Hugh James *Cardiff*
MLM *Cardiff*
Harding Evans LLP *Newport*
Leo Abse & Cohen *Cardiff*
Robertsons *Cardiff*
Firms are listed A-Z in tiers which are ranked in order of priority

The city is also home to the firm's commercial team, which has three experienced partners in Peter Jones, Chris Williams and Emyr Lewis. Both the commercial team and Rob Cherry 's corporate team have acted for significant clients such as the PHS Group, the National Assembly of Wales, British Energy and Finance Wales.

At **Berry Smith**, Andrew Bound – described as 'attentive, easily accessible and diligent' by clients – and Nigel Greenaway are part of a six-lawyer team that handled over £100m in deals in the past year. Key clients include BBI, Project Wren and Invacare.

Capital Law advises on all aspects of corporate law, from debt and equity financing to MBOs, MBIs and reorganisations. The team, headed by Duncan Macintosh, handles work for many SME clients and private equity funds. Rebecca Mansfield-Fellowes, Nicola McNeely and Iorwen Brooks-Jones are praised for their keenness to deliver high-quality service and their ability to help clients feel involved in the legal process.

Jonathan Rees at **Dolmans Solicitors** completed eight deals with a combined value of more than £15m recently, among them the raising of equity capital for design company Xternal Dimensions and the acquisition by Midland Oil Refinery of Lanstar.

Geldards LLP had another solid year, with the corporate team handling 47 M&A deals with an aggregate value of over £1bn. Highlights included advising WM Wrigley on its purchase of food businesses from Kraft.

As well as transactional work **Hugh James** is seeing more demand for constitutional advice, largely from key client Welsh Rugby Union. Though Bill Snowdon left recently, Geoffrey Adams and Alun Jones 'group still advise Cardiff City Council and the Environment Agency procurement team.

Managing partner Jon Fernandez Lewis heads the **MLM** team, working with associate

Aled Walters. Key work of late includes acting on the sale by Brittons Holdings of assets to Travis Perkins, and acting for Swansea technology company Enfis Ltd on a £900,000 financing.

Harding Evans LLP in Newport is the only Gwent firm to boast a specialist corporate and commercial department. The highly respected Mike Jenkins advises on acquisitions and disposals, most notably in the transport and haulage industry. Bill Morris has retired.

The bulk of **Leo Abse & Cohen**'s clients are SMEs, on the back of which the practice has grown. Commercial law specialist Sian Elvis is seeing the team's turnover increase.

SWANSEA

Swansea has an even lower cost base than Cardiff, and cheaper fees are a powerful draw to some businesses.

Morgan Cole has half of its corporate team in Swansea. Partner Rob Cherry 's team, which acts for both public and private companies, has completed some 95 transactions to date for PHS Group, with other clients including BP Chemicals, HSBC, HBOS and many AIM-listed companies.

The commercial division at **JCP Solicitors (John Collins & Partners LLP)**, reorganised and relocated two years ago, has continued to raise its profile among private and public sector organisations across Wales. Stephen Penny, described by clients as efficient, prompt and very responsive, heads the corporate and commercial team, which acted for Swansea City AFC on the Swansea Stadium project and has picked up new clients such as Castell Howell Foods and Celtic Technologies.

William Barletta at **Morgan LaRoche Limited** is well known in the Welsh legal community, and recently his team surpassed the previous year in terms of deal flow, much of it acquisition, disposal and reorganisation work. Formed by key partners from **Morgan Cole** three years ago, the firm prides itself on partner-led work, which is much desired among clients.

Kenneth Morgan and Michael Snowdon have seen the team at **Douglas-Jones Mercer** handle more transactions, many from new clients from South and West Wales, often on recommendation from banks, accountants and other solicitors. Some new clients wins from outside Wales have given the practice an optimistic outlook on future growth.

NORTH AND MID WALES

Gabb and Co, the oldest firm in Wales, acts for an established private and agricultural client base, but prides itself on the personal service on offer from its corporate and commercial team, where partners Mike Stock and Abergavenny-based John Price and David Vaughan have broad expertise.

CORPORATE AND COMMERCIAL
Swansea

MORGAN COLE

JCP Solicitors (John Collins & Partners LLP)
Morgan LaRoche Limited

Douglas-Jones Mercer

CORPORATE AND COMMERCIAL
North and Mid Wales

Gabb and Co *Abergavenny, Crickhowell*
Gamlins *Rhyl, Holywell*

Aaron & Partners LLP *Chester*
Clement Jones Limited *Holywell*
Gabbs *Hereford*

Firms are listed A-Z in tiers which are ranked in order of priority

Gamlins in Rhyl gives advice on financing and leasing matters and acquisitions and disposals, mainly to SMEs and, increasingly, decent-sized plcs, some of which are attracted by a lower cost base than can be found in other parts of the country.

Elizabeth Delgado 's commercial team at **Aaron & Partners LLP** recently grew with the addition from **Addleshaw Goddard** in Manchester of Clare Gray (née Lillistone), who focuses on M&A, private equity and joint ventures.

Clement Jones Limited has also built a reputation for handling transactional work to a high standard.

COMMERCIAL LITIGATION

Senior appointments Gerallt Owen from **Orchard** and Nicola Williams from **Slaughter and May** to Peter Jones' team have increased **Eversheds LLP**'s capacity to service national clients, many of which are from the public sector and the financial services industry. New clients appreciate the dedication to personal attention at a practice where ADR is also a key focus.

Geldards LLP had a busy and profitable year, with Paul Hopkins ' commercial dispute resolution team advising the likes of Citibank and HM Inspector of Education and Training. Hopkins is well regarded by his peers. The team includes Kempton Rees.

Well regarded by his peers, **Hugh James**' Ian Herbert leads a group of 12 partners, many of whom are regularly engaged in work for new client Royal Mail, though the firm has a number of other large clients that provide a steady stream of instructions.

ADR is also important at **Morgan Cole**. Partner Phillip Howell-Richardson has a UK-wide reputation as a mediator and leads the firm's cross-office, seven-partner dispute management group, which acts for many NHS trusts and government bodies as well as manufacturers and plcs. Amanda Wooding in Swansea and Alex Pay and Allan Wilson in Cardiff are the disputes partners based in Wales, and associate Lee Fisher is building a reputation as a capable litigator.

COMMERCIAL LITIGATION

EVERSHEDS LLP *Cardiff*
GELDARDS LLP *Cardiff*
HUGH JAMES *Cardiff*
MORGAN COLE *Cardiff, Swansea*

Berry Smith *Cardiff*
Capital Law *Cardiff*
Dolmans Solicitors *Cardiff*
Douglas-Jones Mercer *Swansea*
JCP Solicitors (John Collins & Partners LLP) *Swansea*
Morgan LaRoche Limited *Swansea*

Aaron & Partners LLP *Chester*
Harding Evans LLP *Newport*
Leo Abse & Cohen *Cardiff*
Loosemores *Cardiff*
MLM *Cardiff*

Firms are listed A-Z in tiers which are ranked in order of priority

Though Christopher Nott, joint managing partner of **Capital Law**, is active in many areas of the firm's work, he specialises in commercial litigation, particularly complex, sensitive or high-value cases. With his team of Andrew Brown and John O'Sullivan, he has acted for clients such as Bellway Homes and Deanminster.

With John Wilkins moving to a consultancy role at **Dolmans Solicitors**, associate Alison Henders-Green has arrived from **Eversheds LLP** and hit the ground running. This has helped to maintain the firm's momentum in acting for a growing client base of major local firms.

With Hugh Hitchcock at its head, **Douglas-Jones Mercer**'s team of two partners and four assistants has seen a growing caseload from existing clients, most notably the National Children's Home charity and two large local employers, Alberto-Culver UK and Travel City Ltd.

Clients describe Kevin O'Brien, lead partner in **JCP Solicitors (John Collins & Partners LLP)**'s team, as very responsive and providing a high quality of service at good value. Managing partner Paul Newman is part of the group, which has grown with the addition of assistant Osian Llyr Davies from **Douglas-Jones Mercer**.

Morgan LaRoche Limited welcomed Jason Williams from **Morgan Cole** and has since added another assistant and a paralegal to handle a growing caseload. Stephen Mundy is an experienced construction litigator, while Timothy Jones brings employment litigation expertise to a broad practice.

Aaron & Partners LLP in Chester prides itself on aggressive representation and the commercial acumen of its litigators.

Managing partner Zep Bellavia oversees the newly formed dispute resolution team at **Harding Evans LLP** and has experience of major commercial, industrial, financial services and pensions disputes. Pauline Kent also has extensive experience from her time as a senior litigator for British Rail.

Leo Abse & Cohen mostly handles work for SME clients, and a number of **Loosemores** partners are experienced in negotiation, ADR and advocacy.

MLM has Chris Mayers in charge of litigation and employment, mainly advising local SMEs.

WRAGGE & CO LLP

55 COLMORE ROW
BIRMINGHAM B3 2AS

Telephone: +44 870 903 1000
Fax: +44 870 904 1099
E-mail: mail@wragge.com
Website: www.wragge.com

Languages
Afrikaans, Arabic, Bengal, Cantonese, Cypriot, Danish, Dutch, Farsi, French, German, Gujarati, Hindi, Italian, Japanese, Malay, Maltese, Portuguese, Punjabi, Spanish, Urdu, Welsh

Other offices
London, Brussels

Member
Individual partners are members of the International Bar Association and various committees of the International Chamber of Commerce. World Bank accredited.

CATEGORIES OF WORK

Banking and insolvency
Julian Pallett

Competition, public and regulatory
Bernardine Adkins, Simon Taylor

Construction
Simon Baylis

Corporate and private equity
David Vaughan, Maurice Dwyer

Dispute resolution
Eddie Breen

E-commerce and advertising
Rafi Azim-Khan

Employment, pensions
Martin Chitty, Glyn Ryland

Energy
Derek Goodban

Franchising
Michael Luckman

Information technology
Bill Jones

Intellectual property
Gordon Harris, David Barron

Outsourcing
David Hamlett

PFI
Stephen Kenny

Property litigation
Suzanne Lloyd Holt

Public sector
Mark Greenburgh

Real estate
Adrian Bland, Peter Thorne

Tax
Kevin Lowe

Transport
Michael Whitehouse

THE FIRM

Wragge Co LLP is a major UK law firm providing a full range of legal services to businesses worldwide. It advises more than 30 FTSE 100 companies, including British Airways, GlaxoSmithKline, HSBC, Vodafone and Marks & Spencer, as well as international blue chip businesses like BUPA, ADP and EON.

Wragge & Co is different from many law firms in the way that it delivers its services and in the advice that it provides. With 105 partners and more than 450 lawyers, Wragge & Co has the resources and expertise to handle the largest instructions in the UK and beyond. Around one quarter of its work is international and the firm has a formal association with leading German independent law firm Graf von Westphalen Bappert & Modest.

What really makes the firm stand out is its commitment to client relationships, leading to tailored, commercial solutions for the organisations it works with. Clients know Wragge & Co provides a quality service, technically excellent lawyers and a dedicated team. Its lawyers make sure their advice is relevant, and add real value by understanding clients' objectives, business and market. Award-winning IT systems support this approach.

As one of the UK's largest firms with a main base outside London, Wragge & Co LLP operates on a lower cost base than almost any other corporate firm with equivalent strengths and resources. Many Wragge & Co LLP teams are acknowledged to be among the best in the UK, including: intellectual property; EU and competition; e-marketing; outsourcing; pensions; private equity; real estate and construction. Many of the firm's lawyers have earned excellent reputations in their specialist areas and appear in the lists of the UK's leading legal experts. *The Sunday Times* ranked it in their list of the best companies for which to work, while *The Financial Times* placed the firm in its list of the 50 best workplaces in the UK and the 100 best in the EU.

Wragge & Co LLP is proud of its approach to corporate responsibility, which brings together its commitment to diversity, the environment, pro bono and community investment, and professional dealings with external partners.

AREAS OF PRACTICE

Wragge & Co LLP is a full-service firm with core work areas of corporate, real estate, human resources, dispute resolution and litigation, and finance projects and technology.

The firm has 18 specialist and dedicated sector teams, including aerospace, automotive, food and drink, healthcare, retail and public sector.

A&L GOODBODY

AUGUSTINE HOUSE
AUSTIN FRIARS
LONDON EC2N 2HA

Telephone: +44 20 7382 0800
Fax: +44 20 7382 0810
E-mail: info@algoodbody.com
Website: www.algoodbody.ie

Languages
Dutch, French, German

Other offices
Boston, Dublin, New York

Number of lawyers 215
at this office 5

CATEGORIES OF WORK

Inward investment
John Coman

General corporate and commercial
Julian Yarr, Paul White

Mergers and acquisitions
Julian Yarr, John Given

EU and competition
Vincent Power

Capital markets
John Olden

Banking and finance
Julian Yarr, Catherine Duffy

Funds
Brian McDermott

Insurance
James Grennan

Intellectual property
John Whelan

Entertainment law
Geraldine East

Litigation and dispute resolution
Peter Law

Project finance
Kevin Feeney

Technology law, e-commerce
Liam Kennedy, Mark Ward

Corporate tax
Peter Maher

Commercial property
Mairead Sherlock

ALLEN & OVERY LLP

ONE NEW CHANGE
LONDON EC4M 9QQ

Telephone: +44 20 7330 3000
Fax: +44 20 7330 9999
E-mail: information@allenovery.com
Website: www.allenovery.com

Languages
Arabic, Bengali, Cantonese, Czech, Danish, Dutch, Finnish, French, German, Greek, Hebrew, Hindi, Hungarian, Italian, Japanese, Korean, Malay, Mandarin, Persian, Polish, Portuguese, Punjabi, Russian, Spanish, Swedish, Urdu

Other offices
Amsterdam, Antwerp, Bangkok, Beijing, Bratislava, Brussels, Budapest, Dubai, Frankfurt, Hamburg, Hong Kong, Luxembourg, Madrid, Milan, Moscow, New York, Paris, Prague, Rome, Shanghai, Singapore, Tokyo, Turin, Warsaw

Number of lawyers 2,304
at this office 1,090

CATEGORIES OF WORK

Company and commercial law and equity capital markets
Richard Cranfield

Mergers, acquisitions and MBOs
Richard Cranfield, Alan Paul

EU and competition
John Wotton

Corporate tax (including VAT)
Patrick Mears

Real estate
Adam Cleal

Banking
Jonathan Brayne

Projects/PPP
Graham Vinter, Anne Baldock

Insolvency and business reconstruction
Gordon Stewart

International capital markets
Boyan Wells

Commercial litigation
Andrew Clark

Employment, pensions and incentives
Derek Sloan, Mark Mansell, Paul McCarthy

Private client
Clare Maurice

Information technology, intellectual property
Ian Ferguson, Colleen Keck

Environmental
Owen Lomas

Energy
Ian Elder, Stuart Harray

THE FIRM

Allen & Overy is an international legal practice comprising Allen & Overy LLP and its affiliated undertakings (collectively described below as 'Allen & Overy'). Founded in 1930, it has over 4,800 staff, including some 450 partners, working in 25 major centres worldwide serving businesses, financiers and governments wherever there is a need for decisive legal advice on complex transactions.

Through its network of offices and close contacts with local law firms around the globe, the practice is well placed to respond quickly and effectively on a co-ordinated, worldwide basis.

AREAS OF PRACTICE

The main areas of work in which the practice is involved are: company and commercial law including takeovers, mergers and acquisitions, disposals, flotations, international equity offerings, joint ventures and strategic alliances, corporate restructurings and management buyouts; banking law covering all types of financing transactions both in the UK and overseas, including projects and project finance, real estate finance, trade finance, asset finance and lease finance, insolvency and reconstruction; international capital markets law covering international debt and equity issues including funding through derivatives and securitisation; litigation handling all forms of commercial dispute, including alternative dispute resolution, and national and international arbitration; and, uniquely amongst City legal practices, Allen & Overy has a private client department advising wealthy individuals, trustees, families, museums, universities, charities and national and international partnerships. In addition, Allen & Overy has a number of specialist practice groups, which bring together the skills and experience of lawyers from different departments to advise clients on building societies, communications, construction, corporate and indirect taxation, derivative products, EU and competition law, employment, pensions and incentives, energy law, environmental law, financial services, housing associations, information technology, insurance law, intellectual property, media and entertainment, pharmaceuticals and medical products, the Public Private Partnerships, Private Finance Initiative (PFI), projects, privatisations, and real estate.

ARNOLD & PORTER (UK) LLP

TOWER 42
25 OLD BROAD STREET
LONDON EC2N 1HQ

Telephone: +44 20 7786 6100
Fax: +44 20 7786 6299
Website: www.arnoldporter.com

Languages
Arabic, Bengali, Chinese, Ebrou, Estonian, Farsi, Filipino, French, German, Greek, Hebrew, Hindustani/Punjabi/Urdu, Hungarian, Italian, Japanese, Konkani (Indian), Latin, Marathi, Portuguese, Russian, Sesotho, Spanish, Turkish, Vietnamese

Other offices
Brussels, Denver, Los Angeles, McLean (Virginia), New York, San Francisco, Washington DC

Number of lawyers 633
at this office 26

Member
The World Law Group

CATEGORIES OF WORK

Antitrust, competition and trade regulation
Tim Frazer (London), Bill Baer (DC)

Bankruptcy
Brian Leitch (Denver)

Corporate and commercial
Jeremy Willcocks (London), Steve Kaplan (DC)

Environmental
Thomas Milch (DC)

EU regulatory
Ian Dodds-Smith (London)

Financial institutions
Patrick Doyle (DC)

Food, drug and medical devices
Daniel Kracov (DC), Dara Corrigan (DC), Ian Dodds-Smith (London)

Intellectual property and technology
Joel Freed (DC), David Apatoff (DC)

International arbitration
Jean Kalicki (DC)

International trade
Larry Schneider (DC)

Life sciences, biotech
Richard Johnson (DC), Lincoln Tsang (London)

Litigation
Robert Weiner (DC)

Product liability
Ian Dodds-Smith (London)

Tax
Dick Hubbard (DC)

Telecoms/media and internet
Michael Ryan (London), Patrick J Grant (DC)

Real estate
Gary Humes (DC), Lee Narrow (London)

ARTHUR COX

29 LUDGATE HILL
LONDON EC4M 7JE

Telephone: +44 20 7213 0450
Fax: +44 20 7213 0455
E-mail: london@arthurcox.com
Website: www.arthurcox.com

Languages
French, German, Italian, Spanish

Other offices
Belfast, Dublin, New York

Number of lawyers 223
at this office 3

CATEGORIES OF WORK

Corporate and commercial
Mark Saunders, Ciarán Bolger

Inward investment
Declan Drislane, John Matson

Mergers and acquisitions
Mark Saunders, Colm Duggan

EU and competition
John Meade, Patrick O'Brien

Project finance
Grainne Hennessy, Liam Carney

Capital markets
Glenn Butt, Cormac Kissane

Banking and finance
Mark Saunders, Fiona O'Neill

Structured finance
Cormac Kissane, Glenn Butt

Funds
Carl O'Sullivan, Sarah Cunniff

Listing
Helen Berrill

Litigation
Conor McDonnell, Isabel Foley

Property
John Walsh, Mark Barr

Technology
John Menton, Rob Corbet

Projects
Patrick McGovern

Energy
Alex McLean, Patrick McGovern

ASHURST

BROADWALK HOUSE
5 APPOLD STREET
LONDON EC2A 2HA

Telephone: +44 20 7638 1111
Fax: +44 20 7638 1112
E-mail: enquiries@ashurst.com
Website: www.ashurst.com

Languages
Bulgarian, Chinese, Dutch, English, Finnish, French, German, Greek, Gujurati, Hindi, Icelandic, Italian, Latvian, Malay, Mandarin, Polish, Romanian, Russian, Spanish, Swahili, Urdu, Welsh

Other offices
Brussels, Dubai, Frankfurt, Madrid, Milan, Munich, New Delhi*, New York, Paris, Singapore, Tokyo

Number of lawyers 748
at this office 485

CATEGORIES OF WORK

International finance
Nigel Ward

Employment, incentives, pensions
C Carter, P Randall, S Hull

Private equity and buy-outs
Charlie Geffen

Investment funds
Jeremy N Sheldon, Paul Gadd

Corporate/commercial (inc IP)
Adrian Clark, Ian Starr

Litigation
Michael Madden

EU and competition law
Nigel Parr, Julian Ellison

Real estate
Simon Cookson

Investment banking
Adrian Clark

Tax
John Watson

Energy, transport and infrastructure
Mark Elsey

IT, telecoms, betting and gaming
C Coulter, C Tucker, M Lubbock

Financial institutions
James Perry, David Page

Biotechnology/pharmaceuticals
Mark Lubbock

THE FIRM

Ashurst is an international law firm with offices in Brussels, Dubai, Frankfurt, London, Madrid, Milan, Munich, New York, Paris, Tokyo and Singapore, as well as a liaison office in New Delhi. The firm has developed a top-class, international M&A, corporate and structured finance practice, principally in Europe but also on a wider, international stage, where its skills and expertise can benefit clients and the market. The firm provides a comprehensive range of complementary integrated practices in areas including antitrust, real estate, tax, litigation, energy, transport and infrastructure.

AREAS OF PRACTICE

Commercial contracts; communications; employee benefits and incentives; employment; environmental and health and safety; healthcare; information technology; intellectual property; outsourcing; pensions; corporate advice; financial institutions; investment funds; M&A and corporate finance; private equity and buy-outs; restructuring and insolvency; sport; US securities and M&A; energy; PFI/PPP; public international law; transport; EU and competition; world trade; leveraged finance; project finance; real estate finance; securities and structured finance; banking and finance litigation; commercial litigation; contentious and non-contentious construction; energy, transport and infrastructure litigation; EU and competition litigation; financial regulatory litigation; international arbitration; IP and IT litigation; product liability and environmental litigation; real estate litigation; restructuring and insolvency litigation; planning and public sector; real estate finance; real estate tax; tax.

BAKER & McKENZIE LLP

100 NEW BRIDGE STREET
LONDON EC4V 6JA

Telephone: +44 20 7919 1000
Fax: +44 20 7919 1999
E-mail: london.info@bakernet.com
Website: www.bakernet.com

Languages
Afrikaans, Bulgarian, Chinese, Czech, French, German, Hebrew, Hindi, Italian, Japanese, Kiswahili, Korean, Portuguese, Russian, Spanish, Swedish

Other offices
The member firms of Baker & McKenzie International, a Swiss Verein, have 70 offices in 38 countries around the world. For a complete list, please visit www.bakernet.com.

Number of lawyers 3,300+
at this office 290

Contact
Gary Senior

CATEGORIES OF WORK

Banking and finance
Christopher Hogan

Civil fraud and insolvency
Nick Pearson, Jeremy Goldring

Commercial
Ilana Saltzman

Corporate
Michael Caro

Dispute resolution/insurance
Andrew Keltie, Peter Schwartz

EC competition and trade
Samantha Mobley

Employment and pensions
Christine O'Brien, Robert West

Intellectual property and media
Michael Hart, Paul Rawlinson

Information technology, e-commerce
Harry Small, Robbie Downing

Pharmaceutical and healthcare
Beatriz Araujo

Privatisations and securities
Tim Gee, Michael Caro

Projects and construction
Mike Webster, Jeremy Winter

Property and environment
Michael Smith, Christopher Norton

Structured and project finance
Annie Williams, Mike Webster

Tax and private client
Alex Chadwick, Paul Stibbard

Telecommunications
Peter Strivens

BAKER BOTTS

41 LOTHBURY
LONDON EC2R 7HF

Telephone: +44 20 7726 3636
Fax: +44 20 7726 3637
E-mail:
katie.harrington@bakerbotts.com
Website: www.bakerbotts.com

Languages
Arabic, French, Hindi, Mandarin, Russian, Spanish, Urdu

Other offices
Austin, Dallas, Dubai, Hong Kong, Houston, Moscow, New York, Riyadh, Washington DC

Number of lawyers 700
at this office 20

Contact
Antony Higginson

Member
Lex Mundi

CATEGORIES OF WORK

Asset finance

Aviation

Banking

Chemicals

Corporate, M&A

Energy

International arbitration

Litigation

Oil and gas

Project finance

TMT

Shipping

BIRD & BIRD

90 FETTER LANE
LONDON EC4A 1JP

Telephone: +44 20 7415 6000
Fax: +44 20 7415 6111
E-mail: london@twobirds.com
Website: www.twobirds.com

Languages
Dutch, Flemish, French, German, Italian, Mandarin, Spanish, Swedish

Other offices
Beijing, Brussels, Düsseldorf, Frankfurt, Hong Kong, Madrid, Milan, Munich, Paris, Rome, Stockholm, The Hague

Number of lawyers 472
at this office 176

CATEGORIES OF WORK

Aviation and aerospace
Catherine Erkelens, Paul Briggs

Banking and financial services
Trystan Tether, Brett Israel

Commercial
Dominic Cook

Communications
David Kerr,
Frédérique Dupuis-Toubol

Corporate
Neil Blundell, Chris Barrett, Mark Pinder

Data protection
Ruth Boardman, Hazel Grant

Dispute resolution
Jane Player

E-commerce
Felicity Reeve, Nick Perry

Employment
Ian Hunter, Warren Wayne

EU and competition
Richard Eccles, Olivier Fréget

Information technology
Hamish Sandison, Roger Bickerstaff

Intellectual property
Morag Macdonald,
Wolfgang von Meibom

Life sciences
Gerry Kamstra, Trevor Cook

Media
Justin Walkey

Outsourcing
Gill Andrews, Stéphane Lemarchand

Real estate
Jonathan Baker

Sport
Justin Walkey, Felicity Reeve

Tax
Peter Fisher

THE FIRM

Bird & Bird is a full-service international commercial law firm with a reputation for excellence in key industry sectors and areas of legal practice. The firm focuses on aviation and aerospace, communications, e-commerce, information technology, life sciences, media, sport and banking and financial services. Bird & Bird has more than 450 lawyers spread across key business centres in Europe and Asia.

AREAS OF PRACTICE

Aviation and aerospace: the firm works with a variety of companies ranging from airlines to ground-handlers and air traffic control service providers.

Banking and financial services: the firm advises on a full range of banking issues including e-banking, project finance, PFI, secured and syndicated lending, insolvency, corporate reconstruction and litigation.

Communications: the firm has one of the largest multi-jurisdiction teams of lawyers dedicated to the communications sector of any law firm in the world. Clients include a wide range of companies.

E-commerce: the firm has an unparalleled reputation as a leader in the field of e-commerce and the internet. Its expertise encompasses every aspect of e-commerce including dot-com start-ups.

IT: the firm's lawyers advise both IT users and suppliers from the public, private and utilities sectors on a variety of major projects.

Life sciences: the firm offers wide-ranging advice on IP, corporate and commercial issues to a range of companies from those spun out from universities through to large multinational biosciences and pharmaceutical companies.

Media: the firm's expertise spans all areas of media with a particular focus on negotiating and drafting finance and distribution agreements, publishing deals and issues of digital convergence.

Sport: the firm's sports lawyers have extensive experience of advising governing bodies, rights purchasers, broadcasters, sponsors and leading sportsmen and women.

Commercial: providing practical professional advice and assistance on a wide range of commercial arrangements – from strategic planning of transactions – to deal implementation and contract management.

Corporate: offering a comprehensive range of corporate services, the firm's lawyers undertake a wide variety of work spanning M&A, joint ventures, strategic alliances, investment, equity financing, venture capital and public offerings.

Data protection: the firm provides a range of advice including compliance on particular matters to data protection compliance reviews.

Dispute resolution: the firm is experienced in running both national and complex multi-jurisdictional disputes as well as providing strategic advice on the pros and cons of resolving a dispute.

Employment: the firm advises on both contentious and non-contentious issues, ranging from employee contracts and termination agreements to changes in employment legislation.

EU and competition: the firm has a significant EU and competition capability, concentrating on anti-trust enforcement and legislative developments. It provides advice on EC and national competition law.

Finance: the firm provides advice on a wide range of finance-related issues including contentious matters.

IP: the firm offers one of the most comprehensive IP law services in Europe – covering all aspects of IP and related EU legal issues.

Outsourcing: the firm advises its clients on all types of outsourcing transactions from 'traditional' IT and telecoms outsourcings to innovative deals.

Real estate: the firm's expertise ranges from PFI structures and commercial agreements to pan-European regulatory issues.

Tax: advice on a wide range of tax matters including transaction related issues and internal restructuring.

CADWALADER, WICKERSHAM & TAFT LLP

265 STRAND
LONDON WC2R 1BH

Telephone: +44 20 7170 8700
Fax: +44 20 7170 8600
E-mail: cwtinfo@cwt.com
Website: www.cadwalader.com

Other offices
New York, Charlotte (North Carolina), Washington DC, Beijing

Number of lawyers 653

Contacts
Robert O Link Jr, Andrew Wilkinson

CATEGORIES OF WORK

Capital markets
Neil Weidner, Charles Roberts, Angus Duncan, Christian Parker, Conor Downey

Corporate and M&A
Richard Nevins, Andrew Lucas, Peter Baldwin

Financial restructuring
Andrew Wilkinson, Tony Horspool

Litigation
Michelle Duncan, James Douglas

Global finance
Paul Biggs, Justin Jowitt

THE FIRM

Cadwalader Wickersham & Taft LLP has sought to meet clients' changing legal needs for 200 years, and has a reputation for developing innovative business and financial solutions and precedent-setting legal strategies.

Established in 1997, the London office is staffed with UK and US lawyers, and serves clients interested in capitalising on European and worldwide markets, and those seeking US-style services and access to American capital markets.

AREAS OF PRACTICE

With a focus on international transactions, the firm represents the world's leading commercial and investment banks, multinational corporate groups and high-net-worth clients.

Global finance: includes layered debt structures, secured and unsecured acquisition finance, leveraged finance, high-yield bonds and structured finance. Counsels private equity and venture capital funds, multilateral financing organisations, export credit agencies and parties engaged in infrastructure and privatisation financings. Real estate experience spans financing, acquisitions sales and exchanges to development, construction, joint ventures, management and leasing.

Capital markets: has assisted in over US$1 trillion in residential and commercial mortgages, and asset-backed deals. Includes traditional fixed income and equity capital markets, structured finance, synthetic products, hybrid products, and derivatives. A broad asset-backed commercial paper practice counsels on commercial paper conduits, transactions, bond and note issues, swaps, options leasing deals and tax-driven products and other OTC derivatives.

Corporate, mergers and acquisitions: handles complex mergers and acquisitions, joint ventures, corporate reconstructions, high-yield and other financings, and advises on corporate governance, securities law and disclosure issues. Advises on UK Companies Act provisions and other statutory matters, and US SEC disclosure issues and the potential impact of new legislation, including Sarbanes-Oxley Act of 2002.

Financial restructuring: handles complex cross-border insolvencies, corporate turnarounds (including debt restructurings), work-outs and disposal programmes. Advice extends to directors of troubled companies and counsel on solvent reconstructions, using insolvency law techniques to release capital and structure transactions. Regularly retained by leading US distressed debt investors, the firm is well known for insurance company insolvency.

Litigation: resolves conflicts through negotiation, mediation, arbitration or litigation, as well as in proceedings before administrative and regulatory agencies and international tribunals. Expertise is in domestic and cross-border disputes involving financial institutions and instruments, such as loans, bonds and derivatives, and disputes and investigations arising out of corporate insolvency.

Project finance: a multidisciplinary practice with experience across 50 jurisdictions, advising developers of, and lenders to, transactions in the power, oil and gas, telecoms and new technologies, energy trading, infrastructure and transport, privatisation and water sectors, among others.

Tax: pioneers innovative tax structures that drive complex, tax-advantaged transactions, many of which involve cross-border components. Following the firm's ground-breaking work to develop the US federal regime for taxing asset-backed securities, Cadwalader remains a leader in formulating tax advantaged securitisation.

CHIOMENTI STUDIO LEGALE

20 BERKELEY SQUARE
LONDON W1J 6HF

Telephone: +44 20 7569 1500
Fax: +44 20 7569 1501
E-mail: london@chiomenti.net

Languages
English, French, German, Italian, Spanish

Other offices
Brussels, Milan, New York, Rome

Number of lawyers 210
at this office 16

Member
Lex Mundi

CATEGORIES OF WORK

- Corporate and M&A
- Banking and finance
- Capital markets
- Regulatory and financial services
- Tax
- European law, competition and international law
- Administrative law
- Intellectual property, media and information technology
- Litigation and arbitration
- Insolvency and corporate restructuring
- Employment
- Telecommunications
- Energy
- Real estate

CLEARY GOTTLIEB STEEN & HAMILTON LLP

CITY PLACE HOUSE
55 BASINGHALL STREET
LONDON EC2V 5EH

Telephone: +44 20 7614 2200
Fax: +44 20 7600 1698
Website: www.clearygottlieb.com

Languages
Dutch, English, Farsi, French, German, Gujarati, Italian, Japanese, Korean, Mandarin, Polish, Russian, Spanish, Swedish, Urdu

Other offices
Brussels, Cologne, Frankfurt, Hong Kong, Milan, Moscow, New York, Paris, Rome, Tokyo, Washington DC

Number of lawyers 847
at this office 73

CATEGORIES OF WORK

- Banking and finance
- Capital markets/securities
- Commercial
- Competition law
- Corporate
- Financial services
- Intellectual property
- Joint ventures
- Mergers and acquisitions
- US, UK and international tax

CLYDE & CO

51 EASTCHEAP
LONDON EC3M 1JP

Telephone: +44 20 7623 1244
Fax: +44 20 7623 5427
E-mail: info@clydeco.com
Website: www.clydeco.com

Languages
Arabic, Cantonese, Danish, Finnish, French, German, Greek, Gujarati, Hebrew, Italian, Japanese, Malay, Mandarin, Norwegian, Portuguese, Punjabi, Russian, Spanish, Swedish, Turkish

Other offices
Abu Dhabi, Belgrade, Caracas, Cardiff, Dubai, Guildford, Hong Kong, Moscow, Nantes, Paris, Piraeus, Rio de Janeiro, St Petersburg, Shanghai, Singapore

Number of lawyers 409
at this office 312

Contact
Adrian Desoutter

CATEGORIES OF WORK

ADR
Jane Andrewartha

Aviation
Tim Brymer, John Balfour

Banking
Paul Friedman

Dispute resolution
Jonathan Wood, Paul Friedman

Corporate and commercial
James O'Shea, Andrew Holderness

EU, WTO and competition law
John Milligan, Philippe Ruttley

Employment
Paul Newdick, Steve Blunt

Energy
David Reynolds, Andrew Wells

Immigration
Jonathan Chaimovic

Insolvency
Juliette Stevens

Insurance and reinsurance
Nigel Brook, Nigel Chapman

International trade
John Whittaker, Andrew Wells

IP/IT and telecoms
Philip Hooley, Matthew Cowan

Property
Robert Pilcher, Paul Berry

Shipping and transport
Derek Hodgson, Irvine Marr

Tax
Susan Ball

THE FIRM

Clyde & Co's roots are in global commerce and transportation. It has expanded rapidly in recent years and is a dominant player in the insurance, reinsurance, international litigation, shipping, aviation, transport, international trade, energy and commodities sectors. Clyde & Co has one of the largest litigation practices in the UK. Through its network of foreign offices and correspondents, the firm services the needs of clients worldwide.

AREAS OF PRACTICE

Clyde & Co undertakes a wide variety of commercial work nationally and internationally. It has extensive experience in handling complex multi-party international actions. Its client base includes multinational companies, banks, insurance and trading companies.

Insurance and reinsurance: the firm advises on a range of areas including aviation, general liability, insolvency and recovery, marine and energy, political and credit risks, professional indemnity, property and construction. There is also a dedicated corporate insurance group that specialises in insurance-related corporate transactions and regulatory work.

Shipping and transport: the firm's expertise in this field is second to none. It advises all sectors of the maritime industry on an international basis on a wide range of work, including wet and dry, shipbuilding, ship repair and shipping finance.

Aviation: the firm has the world's leading aviation practice and advises on aviation insurance, liability cases, aviation finance and non-contentious aviation work to the airline/aviation/aerospace industry and their insureds.

Corporate and commercial: company and commercial law is a cornerstone of the firm extending beyond insurance transactions. Principal areas of expertise span company formation and joint ventures through MBOs, venture capital, M&A rights issues, OFEX and AIM listings, IPOs and placings. Specialist subjects include corporate tax, real estate, employment and immigration, IP/IT, e-commerce, EU competition and WTO.

Dispute resolution: the firm has one of the largest commercial dispute resolution practices of any international law firm, offering comprehensive litigation, arbitration and mediation services. The firm's expertise spans all major jurisdictions.

Energy and natural resources: the firm's energy team has considerable experience and industry knowledge. The firm's practice is consulted by some of the world's leading oil, gas and power multinationals, as well as governments, banks, finance houses, traders, minerals, metals and mining companies.

Property: the firm's property and construction team offers a fully comprehensive service. With wide-ranging expertise spanning investment, development, funding, retail, leisure, landlord and tenant and energy-related transactions, the breadth of resources enables the firm to handle projects of any magnitude.

Employment and immigration: the firm's experience in these areas is extensive.

COVINGTON & BURLING

265 STRAND
LONDON WC2R 1BH

Telephone: +44 20 7067 2000
Fax: +44 20 7067 2222
E-mail: infolondon@cov.com
Website: www.cov.com

Languages
Azerbaijani, Hebrew, Hindi, Ukrainian, all European languages

Other offices
Brussels, New York, San Francisco, Washington DC

Number of lawyers 550+
at this office 45

International groupings
Please see www.cov.com for firm affiliations

CATEGORIES OF WORK

Arbitration
Robert Pietrowski

Litigation
Richard Mattick, Anne Ware

Corporate and M&A
Edward Britton

Life sciences
Richard Kingham

Private equity and investment funds
Simon Goodworth

Tax
David Hinds

EU and competition
David Hull

Employment
Hilary Prescott

Intellectual property
Lisa Peets

Financial services regulation
Simon Currie

IT and e-commerce
Louise Nash, Robert Stankey

Financial services
Lodewijk van Setten

Data protection
Dan Cooper

THE FIRM

Covington & Burling is a leading international law firm with over 550 lawyers and offices in London, Washington DC, New York, San Francisco and Brussels.

AREAS OF PRACTICE

Corporate: the firm's corporate lawyers in London have particular expertise in mergers and acquisitions, venture capital and private equity, securities and finance, private equity and investment funds, financial services regulation, and joint ventures, licensing and other strategic alliances. The London corporate group acts for major public and private US and European companies (many of them multinationals), investment and commercial banks, private equity firms, investment managers, emerging companies, investment funds and other financial institutions on transactions and other matters ranging in value from several million pounds to several billion dollars. Most of the transactions on which the corporate group in London advises are international in nature, including cross-border acquisitions, investments and securities placements.

IT, IP and e-commerce: the London office works with the Brussels office on issues relating to technology law reform throughout the EU. From London, the firm oversees IP reform and enforcement in 40 countries in Europe, the Middle East and Africa. It routinely advises multinational clients on cross-border internet jurisdictional issues and strategic, regulatory and other issues raised by efforts to enter the UK and European markets. In addition, the firm provides commercially oriented and forward-looking advice to clients involved in corporate, licensing and content-sharing transactions. The London office also advises US and European companies on issues relating to information transfer across borders, data storage and processing, and mobile location privacy. It works with the firm's Washington office to provide co-ordinated advice on 'safe harbour' issues and the impact of US state and federal privacy schemes on European companies.

Life sciences: the London office advises biotechnology and pharmaceutical clients on regulatory, commercial, corporate and tax issues. The firm's life sciences regulatory practice is one of the largest and most comprehensive in the EU and the US. It has advised many of the major multinational pharmaceutical manufacturers, biotechnology companies, and medical devices, cosmetics, food, food packaging, pesticide, speciality chemicals and consumer product companies. The London office also advises life sciences clients on a range of commercial transactions, including standard research collaboration and licensing agreements and complex joint ventures. It also advises on transactions including evaluation and option agreements, co-marketing agreements and clinical site agreements.

Tax: the London office's tax practice covers a wide range of transactional and advisory work and includes advising private companies and multinational corporations on the tax-effective structuring of cross-border transactions. The firm also assists multinational companies to plan and implement tax-efficient corporate and operational structures, and advises high-net-worth individuals in respect of their international tax and estate planning. The firm has particular expertise in transfer pricing associated with high-value intangible property, with new modes of business operations and sophisticated trading structures.

Litigation and arbitration: the London office represents clients before virtually all major international arbitral tribunals and the English courts. Lawyers handle a broad range of disputes, including disputes involving complex corporate transactions or commercial contracts, IP, life sciences, product liability, wrongful denials of insurance coverage, competition law, environmental torts and sovereign states.

Employment: the firm's UK and European labour and employment practice is co-ordinated from its London office. The employment group advises corporate clients on strategic and transaction-specific issues in the context of acquisitions and other corporate matters. The group also advises on day-to-day contentious and non-contentious employment matters.

CURTIS, MALLET-PREVOST, COLT & MOSLE LLP

53 NEW BROAD STREET
LONDON EC2M 1BB

Telephone: +44 20 7011 9500
Fax: +44 20 7011 9501
E-mail: info@cm-p.com
Website: www.cm-p.com

Languages
Arabic, English, French, Spanish

Other offices
Frankfurt, Houston, Mexico City, Milan, Muscat, New York, Paris, Stamford, Washington DC

Number of lawyers 187
at this office 6

Contacts
Charles LO Buderi, Tom Mackay, Bruce Palmer, Eero Rautalahti

Member
The Law Society; Quoted Companies Alliance; British Institute of International and Comparative Law; United Kingdom Middle East Association; American Society of International Law

CATEGORIES OF WORK

Infrastructure and project finance

Petroleum and petrochemicals

Power generation

Privatisation

Construction

General corporate and commercial

Mergers and acquisitions

Financial services law

Venture capital

Private equity

Joint ventures

Sales and distribution arrangements

Arbitration

DLA PIPER RUDNICK GRAY CARY UK LLP

3 NOBLE STREET
LONDON EC2V 7EE

Telephone: +44 8700 111 111
Fax: +44 20 7796 6666
E-mail: info@dlapiper.com
Website: www.dlapiper.com

Languages
English, Cantonese, Danish, Dutch, French, German, Gujarati, Hungarian, Italian, Mandarin, Polish, Portuguese, Punjabi, Russian, Spanish, Swedish

Other offices
Austria, Belgium, Bosnia-Herzegovina, China, Croatia, Czech Republic, Denmark*, Egypt*, France, Georgia, Germany, Hong Kong, Hungary, Italy, Japan, Netherlands, Norway*, Poland*, Russia, Singapore*, Slovakia, South Africa*, Spain, Sweden*, Thailand, Ukraine, United Arab Emirates, US

Number of lawyers 3,100
at this office 470

Contact
Nigel Knowles (Co-CEO UK, Europe and Asia)

Member
DLA Piper Group

CATEGORIES OF WORK

Banking
Michael Burton

Business support and restructuring
Simon Neilson-Clark

Commercial and projects
Mark Swindell

Corporate
Alastair Da Costa

Human resources
David Bradley

Insurance
Mike Tinker

Litigation
David Gray

Marine, aviation and reinsurance
Nigel Montgomery

Real estate
David Taylor

Regulation
Neil Gerrard

Technology, media and communications
Simon Levine

THE FIRM

DLA Piper Rudnick Gray Cary is a leading global legal services provider with approximately 3,100 lawyers in 58 offices across 22 countries. The organisation is committed to building long-term relationships with its clients.

In the UK, DLA Piper Rudnick Gray Cary provides a full range of integrated legal services throughout the country and supports its clients with their strategic and operational needs both locally and internationally.

DLA Piper is a founding member of an exclusive alliance of full-service legal organisations with a shared vision. DLA Piper Group, established in 1999, has members across Europe, Africa, the Middle East, Asia and the US, which deliver expert local know-how and integrated international solutions.

AREAS OF PRACTICE

The banking group represents major financial institutions, including clearing and investment banks, building societies, monoline insurers, issuers, borrowers and institutional investors. The group works closely with real estate and corporate, and specialises in asset-based finance, infrastructure and project finance, leveraged finance, real estate finance, securitisation and capital markets.

The corporate group handles all types of transactional and advisory matters. The group advises mid-sized Plcs and top FTSE companies, combining the strength of its City and UK teams together with an international reputation to create a substantial presence in the corporate market.

The commercial and projects group delivers services related to infrastructure and project finance and structured joint ventures, working with specialist lawyers from a number of disciplines, including finance, construction and competition. The group has over 100 lawyers across the UK, backed by international capability across the world.

The human resources group works with clients on a strategic and operational level to help mould their people strategies and work practices in order to support wider business objectives. The team comprises over 90 lawyers and consultants.

The insurance group is one of the largest in the country, and acts for insurers, reinsurers, self-insured corporates and public sector clients in the management of pre-litigation and litigated claims.

The litigation group's approach is to minimise risk and maximise certainty in commercial disputes. Over 400 lawyers, experienced in all aspects of commercial dispute management, work in partnership with clients to manage the litigation process.

The real estate group provides top-quality, multi-disciplinary services, not only to institutions and property companies, but also to those businesses for which real estate is merely a resource required to deliver their main commercial output. The team works with corporate occupiers, developers, the public sector and rapidly changing industry areas, such as construction, retail, hotel and leisure.

The technology, media and communications group provides contentious and non-contentious advice to clients in the areas of IT, telecommunications and IP.

Other types of work include: business support, corporate recovery and restructuring, EU and competition, marine, aviation and regulatory.

DEBEVOISE & PLIMPTON LLP

TOWER 42
OLD BROAD STREET
LONDON EC2N 1HQ

Telephone: +44 20 7786 9000
Fax: +44 20 7588 4180
E-mail: jcscoville@debevoise.com
Website: www.debevoise.com

Languages
Arabic, Dutch, Finnish, French, German, Hurgarian, Italian, Mandarin, Portuguese, Russian, Spanish, Swedish

Other offices
Hong Kong, Frankfurt, Moscow, New York, Paris, Shanghai, Washington DC

Number of lawyers 660+
at this office 61

CATEGORIES OF WORK

Mergers and acquisitions
James A Kiernan, Jeremy Hill

Capital markets
James C Scoville, Jeremy Hill

Financing
Peter Hockless, Katherine Ashton

International dispute resolution
Mark W Friedman

Private equity buyouts
James A Kiernan, Geoffrey P Burgess

Insurance
Jeremy Hill, James C Scoville

Private equity funds
Marwan Al-Turki, Geoffrey Kittredge

Restructuring
Katherine Ashton, Peter Hockless

Corporate tax
Richard Ward, Peter FG Schuur

Litigation
Mark W Friedman

DEWEY BALLANTINE

ONE LONDON WALL
LONDON EC2Y 5EZ

Telephone: +44 20 7456 6000
Fax: +44 20 7456 6001
Website: www.deweyballantine.com

Languages
French, German, Italian, Polish, Spanish, Russian, Ukrainian

Other offices
Austin, Beijing, East Palo Alto, Frankfurt, Houston, Los Angeles, Milan, New York, Rome, Warsaw, Washington DC

Number of lawyers 550+
at this office 40

Contact
Fred Gander
(fgander@deweyballantine.com)

CATEGORIES OF WORK

Capital markets
Camille Abousleiman, Louise Roman Bernstein

Central and Eastern Europe
Stephen Horvath, James Simpson

Energy
James Simpson

International tax
Fred Gander, David Blumenthal

Italy
Ugo Giordano

Mergers and acquisitions
Stephen Horvath

Middle East and North Africa
Camille Abousleiman

Private equity
James Simpson

Project finance
James Simpson, Jane Da Vall

Securitisation
Louise Roman Bernstein, Ugo Giordano

Structured finance
Fred Gander

International arbitration/litigation
Robert De By, Andrei Yakovlev

Germany
Kai-Uwe Steck

DENTON WILDE SAPTE

FIVE CHANCERY LANE
CLIFFORD'S INN
LONDON EC4A 1BU

Telephone: +44 20 7242 1212
Fax: +44 20 7404 0087
E-mail: info@dentonwildesapte.com
Website: www.dentonwildesapte.com

Languages
Afrikaans, Arabic, Bulgarian, Cantonese, Chinese, Czech, Danish, Dutch, Flemish, French, German, Greek, Hebrew, Hindi, Italian, Japanese, Korean, Mandarin, Norwegian, Portuguese, Punjabi, Romanian, Russian, Spanish, Swedish, Urdu

Other offices
Abu Dhabi, Almaty, Cairo, Dubai, Istanbul, Milton Keynes, Moscow, Muscat, Paris, Tashkent

Number of lawyers 683
at this office 512

Contact
Howard Morris

CATEGORIES OF WORK

Banking and finance
Matthew Jones

Corporate
Philip Goodwin

Dispute resolution
Liz Tout

Employment and pensions
Alan Jarvis

Energy and infrastructure and transport
Christopher McGee-Osborne

EU and competition
Jonathan Tatten

Technology, media and telecommunications
John Worthy

Real estate and retail
Stephen Ashworth

Tax
Charlotte Sallabank

THE FIRM

Denton Wilde Sapte is a leading international law firm based in the City of London offering a comprehensive range of the highest quality and affordable commercial legal advice. Denton Wilde Sapte has 13 offices across Europe, the Middle East and Asia.

AREAS OF PRACTICE

Denton Wilde Sapte offers a comprehensive range of commercial legal advice and is particularly known for its strengths in the financial institutions, energy, transport and infrastructure, TMT and real estate sectors. The network of offices enables the firm to serve clients in a number of different locations and to support them wherever their businesses take them. The firm works alongside its clients, to help them achieve their business objectives. To do this, it is essential that the firm understands their business and the environment in which they operate. With a combination of locally trained lawyers and sector specialists, all the firm's offices are able to provide this level of expertise.

The firm's international work is not just restricted to the private sector. Denton Wilde Sapte has worked with a large number of governments and government agencies, particularly in drafting and reworking of local legislation and regulations.

The firm's international clients include: Hitachi, Shell, Statoil, Total, United Airlines, Sony, Standard Chartered Bank, BNP Paribas, Royal Bank of Scotland, MBNA, Barclays Bank, Microsoft, AOL Time Warner, Pearson Plc, BBC, Virgin and the UK Government.

DORSEY & WHITNEY

21 WILSON STREET
LONDON
EC2M 2TD

Telephone: +44 20 7588 0800
Fax: +44 20 7588 0555
E-mail: klaas.paul@dorsey.com
Website: www.dorsey.com

Languages
Afrikaans, Dutch, English, French, German, Norwegian, Spanish

Other offices
Anchorage, Cambridge, Denver, Des Moines, Fargo, Great Falls, Hong Kong, Minneapolis, Missoula, New York, Palo Alto, Salt Lake City, San Fransisco, Seattle, Shanghai, Southern California, Toronto, Vancouver, Washington DC

Number of lawyers 600+
at this office 40+

Contact
Paul Klass (klass.paul@dorsey.com)

CATEGORIES OF WORK

Arbitration
Paul Klaas

Capital markets
John Chrisman, Richard Baumann

Corporate
Barry Glazer

Direct tax
Simon Whitehead

Employment
Steve Milne

Indirect tax
Leslie Allen

Intellectual property
Ian Craig

Litigation
Simon Whitehead, Nick Burkill

Mergers and acquisitions
Andrew Rimmington

Real estate
Nadeem Khan

THE FIRM

Dorsey and Whitney LLP is among the largest law firms in the world. The firm offers a full range of business-related services through its 19 offices in the United States, Canada, Asia and Europe. The firm is particularly strong in litigation, intellectual property and corporate law. By harnessing its resources throughout its offices worldwide, the firm delivers cost-effective, high-quality legal services to its international business clients.

AREAS OF PRACTICE

Dorsey's London office reflects the full-service strength of the firm as a whole, with specialists in corporate, litigation, UK real estate, employment and intellectual property. The office includes both UK and US qualified lawyers.

Dorsey's corporate lawyers in the United States have completed more M&A transactions than any other firm during the past ten years. The London office's active M&A practice specialises in cross-border transactions, and frequently advises on pan-European corporate issues utilising its own multi-qualified staff and its network of correspondent counsel. Dorsey's corporate expertise in London extends to US and UK capital markets, emerging companies, and general corporate and commercial transactions.

While the office acts for UK clients as well as clients from a number of countries, the office has substantial experience in representing clients from the United states, Scandinavia, South Africa and India in connection with their outbound transactions.

In 2005 Dorsey's London Trial group was nominated by a UK legal magazine as 'Litigation Team of the Year'. Dorsey's litigation and arbitration group is one of the largest such groups in a US-originating firm in London. With offices in London, the United States, Canada and Asia, Dorsey provides clients with obvious advantages in the management of disputes worldwide. The London office provides advice and representation on a range of national and international disputes using both litigation and arbitration. Dorsey's sophisticated London-based contentious practice advises on disputes arising out of the direct and indirect tax treatment of international companies, the protection of international property rights, fraud and other important disputes in a range of sectors, including the banking and finance sector, as well as providing support for clients in conducting internal investigations. Dorsey lawyers are leading several high-profile group litigation cases. The group has a highly regarded general commercial team advising on a full range of disputes.

FLADGATE FIELDER

25 NORTH ROW
LONDON W1K 6DJ

Telephone: +44 20 7323 4747
Fax: +44 20 7629 4414

Languages
Cantonese, French, German, Gujarati, Hebrew, Hindi, Italian, Spanish, Urdu

Number of lawyers 88

Member
International Lawyers Network

CATEGORIES OF WORK

Corporate finance
Anthony Vaughan

Anglo-German
Andrew Kaufman

Anglo-Middle East
Ella Leonard

Anglo-India
Sunil Sheth

Anglo-Asia
Simon Ekins

Anglo-Israel
Avram Kelman

Commercial
David Robinson

Commercial litigation and professional indemnity
Simon Ekins

Employment and pensions
Andrew Kaufman

Commercial property
Allen Cohen

Institutional investment and development group
Robert Muir

Taxation and shares schemes
Andrew McKenzie

Corporate recovery and insolvency
Rupert Connell

Sports, media and technology
Mark Buckley

Intellectual property
Eddie Powell

Technology
Anthony Lee

THE FIRM

Fladgate Fielder is one of the leading business law practices in central London providing legal advice of the highest quality for a diverse portfolio of clients. The firm's client base has a strong commercial focus, comprising leading public and private companies, financial institutions and entrepreneurs in the UK and overseas.

The firm provides a pro-active and efficient service for clients with international business through specialist teams which serve continental Europe (with an emphasis on the Germanic countries), Israel, India, the US, Asia Pacific, the Gulf states and the wider Middle East. Operating from London and comprising multilingual and multi-qualified lawyers, these groups facilitate cross-border activities for a diverse range of companies.

The firm is a member of the International Lawyers Network, a worldwide non-exclusive association of high-quality full-service law firms based in 61 countries.

The firm's fee-earners have an in-depth knowledge of the industries in which they practise and extensive experience of delivering advice that is both commercial and technically expert.

AREAS OF PRACTICE

There are currently 88 fee-earners and some 180 staff in the firm and its principal departments comprise corporate (which includes tax and employment groups), litigation and property (which includes separate planning, construction, property litigation and environmental teams). Cross-departmental teams also focus on areas of sector specialisation, including real estate, hotels and leisure, insurance, media, sports, intellectual property and technology, finance and lending, trusts and professional practices.

FROERIEP RENGGLI

SWISS LAWYERS

1 KNIGHTRIDER COURT
LONDON EC4V 5JP

Telephone: +44 20 7236 60 00
Fax: +44 20 7248 02 09
E-mail: london@froriep.ch
Website: www.froriep.com

Languages
English, French, German, Italian, Swedish

Other offices
Geneva, Madrid, Zug, Zurich

Number of lawyers 62
at this office 5

Contact
Bruno W Boesch

CATEGORIES OF WORK

Company and commercial
Dunja Koch

Mergers and acquisitions
Dunja Koch

Securities
Dunja Koch

Banking
Bruno W Boesch

Aviation
Dunja Koch

Litigation, arbitration
Bruno W Boesch

White-collar crime
Bruno W Boesch

Wealth management/estate planning
Bruno W Boesch

GIDE LOYRETTE NOUEL

CITY POINT
1 ROPEMAKER STREET
LONDON EC2Y 9HT

Telephone: +44 20 7826 9700
Fax: +44 20 7826 9701
E-mail: gln.london@gide.com
Website: www.gide.com

Other offices
Algiers, Beijing, Belgrade, Brussels, Bucharest, Budapest, Casablanca, Hanoi, Istanbul, Moscow, New York, Paris, Prague, Riyadh, Shanghai, Tunis, Warsaw

Number of lawyers 586
at this office 36

Contacts
Margaret Boswell (mboswell@gide.com),
Scott PF Cameron (scameron@gide.com),
Anthony Davis (adavis@gide.com),
Michael Doran (mdoran@gide.com),
Arnaud Duhamel (duhamel@gide.com),
Christopher B Mead (cmead@gide.com),
Colin Mercer (cmercer@gide.com)

CATEGORIES OF WORK

Banking and finance

Securitisation

Structured finance

International capital markets

Taxation

Project finance

HARNEY WESTWOOD & RIEGELS LLP

7 LUDGATE BROADWAY
LONDON
EC4V 6DX

Telephone: +44 20 7332 5620
Fax: +44 20 7332 5621
E-mail: london@harneys.com
Website: www.harneys.com

Languages
French, German, Spanish, Russian, Japanese

Other offices
Anguilla, British Virgin Islands, Hong Kong

Numbers of lawyers 44
at this office 4

CATEGORIES OF WORK

Admiralty and shipping
Sheila George

Banking and finance
Peter Tarn

Corporate and commercial
Peter Tarn, Leonard Birmingham

Insolvency
Leonard Birmingham, Phillip Kite

Intellectual property
Peter Tarn

Litigation
Phillip Kite

Local business, property and tax
Sheila George

Investment funds and regulatory
Kieron O'Rourke

Corporate and fiduciary services
Richard Parsons

Trusts, wills and estates
Sheila George

THE FIRM

Harney Westwood & Riegels is a premier offshore legal practice and is the oldest and largest law firm in the British Virgin Islands. It was established in 1960 and now has over 160 lawyers and staff, providing services from offices in the British Virgin Islands, Anguilla, London and Hong Kong.

The firm's focus is British Virgin Islands and Anguillan law, and its team of legal experts, many of whom have been recruited from top City law firms and international financial centres, have an in-depth understanding of the commercial environment in which their clients operate. The firm's client base ranges from leading international businesses and banks to private individuals, and the firm's London and Hong Kong offices offer European and Far East-based clients time-zone sensitive advice on all aspects of British Virgin Islands and Anguillan law.

Members of the firm are active in a number of government advisory committees dedicated to the development of the BVI's financial services industry and related legislative developments.

AREAS OF PRACTICE

Practice areas include: banking and finance; corporate and commercial; investment funds and regulatory; corporate and trust litigation; insolvency; trusts, wills and estates; intellectual property; admiralty and shipping; captive insurance; and local business, property and tax.

The firm offers expertise in a broad range of transactions, including: syndicated and bilateral loans; bond issues; derivatives; securitisations and other structured finance; project finance; initial public offerings; joint ventures; mergers and takeovers; private placements; corporate restructurings; continuations; sale and purchase of shares; special purpose vehicles; copyrights; trade marks; patents; intellectual property disputes; high-profile multi-jurisdictional disputes, as well as fraud, trusts, insolvency and shareholder disputes; and offshore collective investment schemes, with particular emphasis on hedge funds.

The firm's close affiliation with Harneys Corporate Services Limited and Harneys Insurance Management Services Limited also allows for the seamless provision of related corporate services, including company formation and administration, trust administration and captive insurance management services.

HERBERT SMITH LLP

EXCHANGE HOUSE
PRIMROSE STREET
LONDON EC2A 2HS

Telephone: +44 20 7374 8000
Fax: +44 20 7374 0888
E-mail: contact@herbertsmith.com
Website: www.herbertsmith.com

Languages
Afrikaans, Cantonese, Czech, Dutch, French, German, Greek, Gujarati, Hindu, Indonesian, Italian, Japanese, Malaysian, Mandarin, Portuguese, Punjabi, Russian, Spanish, Urdu

Other offices
Bangkok, Beijing, Brussels, Hong Kong, Moscow, Paris, Shanghai, Singapore, Tokyo

Number of lawyers 1,089
at this office 812

CATEGORIES OF WORK

Arbitration
Laurence Shore

EU and competition
Jonathan Scott

Corporate
Michael Walter

Corporate recovery and insolvency
Kevin Pullen

Employment and trusts
Colin Chamberlain

Energy, natural resources and utilities
Paul Griffin

Finance and banking
Jason Fox

Financial institutions
David Willis, Christa Band

Intellectual property and information technology
Nick Gardner

Mergers and acquisitions
Caroline Goodall

Litigation
Sonya Leydecker

Project finance
David Wyles

Real estate
James Barnes

Tax
Heather Gething

THE FIRM

Herbert Smith is a leading international law firm with offices in Europe and Asia. Through its network of over 1,000 lawyers, the firm advises its clients on corporate, dispute resolution, finance and banking matters, and also offers a range of specialist services.

A significant proportion of the firm's work is international, involving the co-ordination and management of clients' commercial activities across many jurisdictions. The firm's capability is resourced from offices in London, Brussels, Moscow and Paris and in Asia through offices in Bangkok, Beijing, Hong Kong, Shanghai, Singapore and Tokyo.

In January 2002, Herbert Smith established a three-way alliance with German firm Gleiss Lutz (with offices in Berlin, Brussels, Frankfurt, Munich, Prague, Stuttgart and Warsaw) and Dutch and Belgian firm Stibbe (with offices in Amsterdam, Brussels, London and New York). The firm's formal association with Hiswara Bunjamin & Tandjung in Jakarta and Bangkok provides further expertise in Asia.

AREAS OF PRACTICE

The London office offers a leading full-service capability in transactional and contentious matters, covering all areas of commercial law. It is organised into three divisions – corporate, dispute resolution, and finance and banking – and five specialist departments – employment and trusts, EU and competition, IP/IT, real estate and tax. The firm also has top-class US law advisory capabilities.

The majority of matters handled in London have an international aspect. They frequently involve other offices in the global network and other firms with which Herbert Smith has an association including Gleiss Lutz and Stibbe. The office acts as a hub of knowledge and expertise for the worldwide firm and its clients, enabling its offices around the world to call on the support and input of specialist teams with specific regional, sector and language skills.

HOGAN & HARTSON

SOLICITORS AND REGISTERED FOREIGN LAWYERS

ONE ANGEL COURT
LONDON EC2R 7HJ

Telephone: +44 20 7367 0200
Fax: +44 20 7367 0220
E-mail: gjpegg@hhlaw.com
Website: www.hhlaw.com

Languages
Czech, French, German, Korean, Polish

Other offices
Baltimore, Beijing, Berlin, Boulder, Brussels, Budapest, Caracas, Colorado Springs, Denver, Geneva, Hong Kong, Los Angeles, Miami, Moscow, Munich, New York, Northern Virginia, Paris, Shanghai, Tokyo, Warsaw, Washington DC

Number of lawyers 1,101
at this office 55

Contact
Garry Pegg

CATEGORIES OF WORK

Capital markets

Corporate finance

Competition

E-commerce

Energy

IP/IT

Insurance

Joint ventures and strategic alliances

Labour and employment

Life sciences

Litigation

Mergers, acquisitions and divestitures

Privatisation

Project finance

Real estate

Tax

Telecommunications

Venture capital, private equity and strategic investments

HOLMAN FENWICK & WILLAN

MARLOW HOUSE
LLOYDS AVENUE
LONDON EC3N 3AL

Telephone: +44 20 7488 2300
Fax: +44 20 7481 0316
E-mail: holmans@hfw.co.uk
Website: www.hfw.com

Languages
Afrikaans, Arabic, Bengali, Cantonese, Castillian, Czech, Dutch, Farsi, Flemish, French, German, Greek, Hebrew, Hindi, Hungarian, Indonesian, Italian, Japanese, Malay, Mandarin, Norwegian, Polish, Portuguese, Punjabi, Russian, Sinhalese, Spanish, Swedish, Urdu

Other offices
Dubai, Hong Kong, Melbourne, Paris, Piraeus, Rouen, Shanghai, Singapore

Number of lawyers 209
at this office 133

Founding patron and member
European Maritime Law Organisation (EMLO)

CATEGORIES OF WORK

Admiralty and crisis management
James Gosling, Hugh Brown

Commercial arbitration/litigation
Peter Bennett, Steven Paull

Corporate and financial
Nick Hutton, Jay Tooker

EC and competition law
Philip Wareham

Employment
Andrew Dekany

Energy
Robin Byron, Diana France

Environmental
James Gosling, Hugh Brown

Information technology
Craig Neame

Insolvency/fraud/asset recovery
Noel Campbell

Insurance
John Duff, Paul Wordley

International trade and commodities
Chris Swart, Simon Blows

Marine litigation
Hugh Livingstone, Richard Crump

Marine non-contentious
Stephen Drury, Jay Tooker

Personal injury
Paul Dean

Professional negligence
David Robinson

Property
Nick Barr

Reinsurance
John Duff, Andrew Bandurka

Transport: air, rail and road
Glenn Moore

THE FIRM

Holman Fenwick & Willan is an international law firm specialising in shipping and transport, trade and energy, insurance and reinsurance and commercial law. The firm has a reputation worldwide for excellence and innovation. It has one of the largest international arbitration and dispute resolution practices of its kind, with offices in Europe, the Middle East and Asia Pacific.

The firm's international practice is founded upon its principal offices in London, Paris, Piraeus, Hong Kong, Shanghai, Singapore and Melbourne and over 120 years' experience of working with other law firms in jurisdictions throughout the world.

AREAS OF PRACTICE

The firm is pre-eminent in maritime work and has one of the world's largest Admiralty and marine litigation practices. It is a recognised leader in dry shipping work including charter parties, bills of lading, other carriage contracts, marine insurance and related disputes. Renowned as leaders in Admiralty and crisis management and operates a 24-hour emergency service geared to providing an immediate response to maritime casualties worldwide. Specialists deal with all forms of contractual disputes, marine insurance claims, collisions, fire and explosions, salvage, towage, wreck removal and recovery, personal injury, damage to oil terminals, rigs and offshore structures, pollution, environmental damage and clean up.

The international trade and commodity practice provides the international trading and financial community with services including advising on sale, purchase and futures contracts, quality claims, damage and shortfall disputes, swaps and barter trade, trade finance, EU law and transportation agreements.

Energy is another specialist work area covering power generation, oil and gas, coal and liquid natural gas.

The firm's insurance and reinsurance practice is recognised internationally as an industry leader. It advises on contentious and non-contentious matters including: facultative insurance and reinsurance coverage issues and policy interpretation; captive insurance and reinsurance; errors and omissions and professional negligence; property damage, business interruption and liability insurance; insolvency and schemes of arrangement; contract drafting and regulatory issues.

Areas of considerable strength are commercial litigation, arbitration and disputes in the areas of financial disputes, technology, coal, oil and gas, environmental claims, professional negligence, sovereign debt and fraud and asset recovery.

The fraud and asset recovery work focuses on the civil side with an emphasis on asset tracing and recovery in overseas jurisdictions. Other methods of recovery are also pursued.

The full spread of insolvency work is undertaken including voluntary arrangements, receiverships, provisional liquidations, liquidations and administrations. Much of the work focuses on international aspects, fraud-related insolvency and the insurance industry.

The firm's company and finance practice advises some of the world's largest shipowners and operators on a wide variety of contractual issues, ranging from shipbuilding, and other offshore and construction contracts, financing documentation, the raising of capital, corporate finance and acquisitions, project and asset finance and joint ventures, as well as advising banks and financial institutions. It also advises on EC and competition law, intellectual property and commercial property matters. All aspects of employment law are covered.

Advice is given on every aspect of e-commerce and information technology.

The firm advises a range of clients in the travel and leisure industry on all legal aspects, both litigious and non-litigious.

Holman Fenwick & Willan has extensive experience of air, road and rail, advising operators, financiers and underwriters on transactions, litigation and regulatory issues.

HOUTHOFF BURUMA

33 SUN STREET
LONDON EC2M 2PY

Telephone: +44 20 7422 5050
Fax: +44 20 7422 5055
Website: www.houthoff.com

Languages
Dutch, English

Other offices
Amsterdam, Brussels, Luxembourg*, Rotterdam, The Hague

Number of lawyers 305
at this office 6

Contacts
Albert Dreese, Jessica Terpstra

CATEGORIES OF WORK

Asset finance and structured finance

Banking and finance

Capital markets

Corporate and commercial

Mergers and acquisitions

Private equity

Project finance

HOWREY LLP

22 TUDOR STREET
LONDON EC4Y 0AY

Telephone: +44 20 7628 3303
Fax: +44 20 7065 6650
Website: www.howrey.com

Languages
Dutch, French, German, Spanish

Other offices
Amsterdam, Brussels, Chicago, East Palo Alto, Houston, Irvine, London, Los Angeles, Northern Virginia, Paris, Salt Lake City, San Francisco, Taipei, Washington DC

Number of lawyers 565
at this office 22

Contacts
Isabel Davies (head of intellectual property), Peter Fitzpatrick (head of litigation)

CATEGORIES OF WORK

Global counselling

Global litigation, dispute resolution and arbitration

Medical negligence

Intellectual property and information technology covering: litigation and dispute resolution; patent, trade marks and designs; trade mark prosecution

INCE & CO

INTERNATIONAL HOUSE
1 ST KATHARINE'S WAY
LONDON E1W 1UN

Telephone: +44 20 7481 0010
Fax: +44 20 7481 4968
E-mail: firstname.lastname@incelaw.com
Website: www.incelaw.com

Languages
Arabic, Cantonese, French, German, Greek, Gujarah, Hindi, Iranian (Farsi), Italian, Japanese, Korean, Mandarin, Norwegian, Portuguese, Romanian, Russian, Spanish, Urdu, Welsh, Yoruba

Other offices
Hamburg, Hong Kong, Le Havre, Paris, Piraeus, Shanghai, Singapore

Number of lawyers 228
at this office 150

Contact
David Steward (business development partner)

CATEGORIES OF WORK

Aviation
Anthony Fitzsimmons, Chris Walsh, Ian Cranston

Business and finance
Nick Gould, David Coupe, Stephen Jarvis

Commercial disputes
Denys Hickey, Ben Ogden

Energy
Denys Hickey, Jeremy Farr

Insurance and reinsurance
Peter Rogan, Jan Heuvels, Simon Todd

Shipping and trade
Bob Deering, Faz Peermohamed, James Wilson, Stuart Shephard

THE FIRM

Ince & Co is an international law firm, with offices in Hamburg, Hong Kong, Le Havre, London, Paris, Piraeus, Shanghai and Singapore. The firm practises English, French, German and Hong Kong law, in six main business strands. Underpinning the firm's expertise is a clear grasp of clients' commercial needs. Ince & Co provides non-contentious business and finance advice for clients in a wide range of industries, and also deploys all methods of dispute resolution.

AREAS OF PRACTICE

Aviation: with a team that 'really understands the aviation business' (*The Legal 500*, 2005) and with in-depth market knowledge, Ince & Co has the flexibility to handle any kind of aviation matter anywhere in the world – from aircraft purchase to major incidents and lesser accidents worldwide. The firm often deploys legal tools to solve problems that appear to be mainly commercial in nature. For crises or disasters, the Ince Worldwide Emergency Response Service is only a phone call away.

Business and finance: the firm's team of specialist commercial lawyers works with clients to find the answers that help drive their businesses forward. With the combination of high levels of commercial nous and a capacity for hard work, the firm can help clients achieve their goals – whether acquisition, disposal, joint venture or conclusion of a complex commercial contract. Ince & Co's experience ranges from management buy-outs, through the resolution of shareholder disputes to difficult employment issues.

Commercial disputes: once described in the press as 'brutal litigators', the firm also has a lighter touch. Ince & Co's expertise covers all forms of dispute resolution, ranging from dialogue, through ADR to arbitration and court proceedings. Where litigation is judged to be in a client's interests, or is unavoidable, the firm draws on immense experience in the commercial courts of the countries where it has offices, and a worldwide network of correspondent lawyers. The firm's cases come from many sectors, including sport, entertainment and financial services.

Energy: the firm has been in the oil and gas business for as long as many of its clients. Since the early days of North Sea development, the firm's energy practice has spread all around the world, both onshore and off, from exploration and drilling to FPSOs and refineries. It now extends to renewable sources such as wind.

Insurance and reinsurance: Ince & Co's team serves clients who provide coverage, those who broke it and those who purchase it. Whether the case is contentious or non-contentious and however straightforward or complex the subject matter insured, the firm offers all the legal services required in these industries. The firm's direct insurance practice covers all manner of insurance claims, including marine and energy insurance, political contingent and credit risk, and coverage disputes. Reinsurance is also a strong area of focus for the firm. The team advises on, among other things, every aspect of run-off business.

Shipping and trade: from shipyard to scrapyard, from factory to receiver, from finance to flotation, the firm provides all the legal services required by the shipping and commodities industries. The firm counts among its clients many of the world's leading shipowners, charterers, shipbuilders, traders, banks and insurers. *The Legal 500* refers to the firm's 'unrivalled knowledge of the market' and its 'strength in depth'.

Emergency Response: Ince & Co operates a 24-hour emergency response service, 365 days a year. It has vast experience of the practical and legal problems following a major emergency, disaster or crisis. Its teams can respond immediately to a wide range of incidents, from accidents in the aviation, shipping, energy, hotel and rail sectors, including pollution and contamination, through natural disasters and outbreaks of disease, to terrorist acts. Tel: +44 20 7283 6999.

JONES DAY

21 TUDOR STREET
LONDON EC4Y 0DJ

Telephone: +44 20 7039 5959
Fax: +44 20 7039 5999
Website: www.jonesday.com

Other offices
Atlanta, Beijing, Brussels, Chicago, Cleveland, Columbus, Dallas, Frankfurt, Hong Kong, Houston, Irvine, London, Los Angeles, Madrid, Menlo Park, Milan, Moscow, Munich, New Delhi*, New York, Paris, Pittsburgh, San Diego, San Francisco, Shanghai, Singapore, Sydney, Taipei, Tokyo, Washington DC

Number of lawyers 2,200
at this office 183

*In association with Pathak & Associates

CATEGORIES OF WORK

Corporate, M&A
John Phillips, Russell Carmedy

Capital markets
Giles Elliott

Litigation
Craig Shuttleworth

Lending and structured finance
Edward Nalbantian

Real estate
David Roberts

Private equity
Adam Greaves

Intellectual property
Alastair McCulloch

Energy
Peter Roberts

Environmental
Clare Deanesly

Labour and employment
Martin Piers, Richard Martin

Pensions
John Papadakis

UK tax
Blaise Marin-Curtoud

Banking and finance
Edward Nalbantian

Competition, EU
Greg Olsen

Business restructuring and reorganisation
Adam Plainer

KILPATRICK STOCKTON LLP

ONE CANADA SQUARE
39TH FLOOR
LONDON E14 5NZ

Telephone: +44 20 7154 6000
Fax: +44 20 7154 6100
E-mail: kboehner@kilpatrickstockton.com
Website: www.kilpatrickstockton.com

Languages
Arabic, English, French, Serbo-Croatian, Spanish

Other offices
Atlanta, Augusta, Charlotte, New York, Raleigh, Stockholm, Washington DC, Winston-Salem

Number of lawyers 488
at this office 17

Contact
R Kenneth Boehner

CATEGORIES OF WORK

Arbitration
Mary O'Connor

Dispute resolution
Patricia Martin, Mary O'Connor

Intellectual property
Helen Newman

Labour and employment
Tim Johnson

Mergers and acquisitions
R Kenneth Boehner

Private equity
R Kenneth Boehner

Trade marks
Helen Newman

KIRKLAND & ELLIS INTERNATIONAL LLP

TOWER 42
25 OLD BROAD STREET
LONDON EC2N 1HQ

Telephone: +44 20 7816 8700
Fax: +44 20 7816 8800
E-mail: bwooster@kirkland.com
Website: www.kirkland.com

Languages
French, German, Italian, Spanish, Mandarin

Other offices
Chicago, Los Angeles, Munich, New York, San Francisco, Washington DC

Number of lawyers 1,110
at this office 45

Contact
Brigitte C Wooster (office administrator)

CATEGORIES OF WORK

Mergers and acquisitions, capital markets
Stuart Mills

Restructuring
Lyndon Norley

Intellectual property, IP litigation, competition
Pierre-André Dubois

Arbitration/litigation
Christopher Colbridge

Acquisition finance
John Markland

Private equity
James Learner

Corporate
Dr Nigel Dunmore

Tax
Ian Taplin

THE FIRM

For nearly 100 years, Kirkland & Ellis, a premier law firm, has handled complicated transactional, intellectual property, litigation and counselling matters for major US and international clients.

The London office, with more than 45 attorneys focusing on private equity, mergers and acquisitions, capital markets, acquisition finance, arbitration, intellectual property and financial restructuring matters, has been serving UK, European and US clients since 1994.

AREAS OF PRACTICE

Kirkland & Ellis is known for its ability to negotiate and close highly sophisticated transactions, representing private equity investors and public and private companies in mergers and acquisitions, securities, spin-offs and split-offs, and private equity transactions. The firm has a premier private equity practice, having represented private investment funds, the private equity groups at several major money centre banks and other participants in this industry for more than 25 years. During the last five years, Kirkland & Ellis' private equity practice has represented more than 50 different clients in leveraged acquisitions and other transactions and has been principal counsel in over US$80bn in fund formations. In the M&A and securities area, Kirkland & Ellis has represented clients including a number of the world's largest corporations, major banks and investment banks in some of the world's largest and most complex M&A transactions and securities offerings.

On the litigation and arbitration side, Kirkland & Ellis' attorneys have a stellar reputation as trial lawyers (not just 'litigators') by successfully defending companies with business-threatening lawsuits and class actions in diverse legal areas such as commercial, intellectual property, product liability, insurance coverage, and many others, handling the trial, appellate, and other US Supreme Court phases. This trial-ready reputation has been the impetus for favourable and prompt results for the firm's clients through settlements as well as through the various alternative dispute resolution mechanisms (ADRs) employed whenever practicable and desired by the client.

Kirkland & Ellis also represents some of the world's leading technology companies and brings its expertise to all areas of intellectual property, patent litigation, trade mark matters, outsourcing, computer software licensing, distributions, joint venture agreements, biotechnology, data protection and e-commerce issues, as well as competition law-related matters. With a dedicated practice dating from 1925, Kirkland & Ellis has always been at the forefront of IP developments. Kirkland & Ellis has adopted and adapted to the internet and e-commerce, and its 200 intellectual property lawyers understand fully the intricacies, implications, legal issues and arguments surrounding today's and tomorrow's communication and emerging technologies.

On the financial restructuring side, Kirkland & Ellis has in excess of 75 insolvency specialists providing a broad range of advice on international insolvency matters to a varied client base. Representation of clients includes complex financial restructurings, corporate insolvencies, liquidation of troubled businesses, debtor-in-possession financings, litigation of all contentious issues arising out of insolvency-related situatons, and equitable subordination of claims.

Kirkland & Ellis bases its commitment to client service on developing an intimate knowledge of each client's needs and objectives. The firm seeks long-term relationships with clients, ensuring the best total solution to the client's multi-disciplined and industry-specific legal service needs. The firm 's goal is to be an instrumental part of each client's success.

LEBOEUF, LAMB, GREENE & MACRAE

NO 1 MINSTER COURT
MINCING LANE
LONDON EC3R 7YL

Telephone: +44 20 7459 5000
Fax: +44 20 7459 5099
E-mail: londoninfo@llgm.com
Website: www.llgm.com

Languages
Arabic, Cantonese, Danish, French, German, Hindi, Hungarian, Italian, Malay, Polish, Portuguese, Punjabi, Russian, Spanish, Ukrainian, Vietnamese

Other offices
Albany, Almaty, Beijing, Boston, Brussels, Chicago, Hartford, Houston, Jacksonville, Johannesburg, Los Angeles, Moscow, New York, Paris, Pittsburg, Riyadh, San Francisco, Washington DC

Number of lawyers 650+
at this office 70

Contact
Peter J Sharp

CATEGORIES OF WORK

Aviation
Mitri J Najjar

Capital markets
Joseph D Ferraro

Commercial litigation
David Waldron

Competition
Peter Crowther

Corporate finance/M&A
Lynn McCaw, Brian Zimbler

Employment
Peter Holt

Energy/utilities
L Keith Hughes, Christopher Prior

Finance
Bruce Johnston, Anthony Richmond

Intellectual property
Marija Danilunas

Insolvency
Peter J Sharp

Insurance corporate
James Lewis, Joseph D Ferraro

Insurance regulatory
William C Marcoux, Nicholas JR Bugler

Insurance/reinsurance litigation
Nicholas D Rochez, David Wilkinson

Private equity
Lynn McCaw

Project finance
Bruce Johnston

Real estate
Nick Shepherd

Shipping and marine
Andrew Bickley

Tax
Andrew Terry

LENNOX PATON

NO 1 CORNHILL
LONDON
EC3V 3ND

Telephone: +44 20 7743 6490
Fax: +44 20 7743 6491
Website: www.lennoxpaton.com

Languages
English

Other offices
Nassau

Number of lawyers 23
at this office 1

Contact
Laura Harris

CATEGORIES OF WORK

Financial services (collective investment schemes, securitisation, investment holding structures, financial institutions, financial products, financial advisory services)
Michael L Paton

Private client (trust, investment holding structures, real estate, immigration)
David R Johnstone

Litigation and dispute resolution (asset tracing and recovery, trust litigation, insolvency, enforcement of foreign judgments, commercial litigation, Admiralty litigation)
Brian C Simms

Shipping
David R Johnstone

LEWIS SILKIN, member of ius laboris

12 GOUGH SQUARE
LONDON EC4A 3DW

Telephone: +44 20 7074 8000
Fax: +44 20 7832 1200
E-mail: info@lewissilkin.com
Website: www.lewissilkin.com

Languages
All principal European languages

Other offices
Oxford

Number of lawyers 117

Member
ius laboris, International Employment Law, Pensions and Employee Benefits Alliance; EALA (European Advertising Lawyers' Alliance); GALA (Global Advertising Lawyers' Alliance); International Chamber of Commerce

CATEGORIES OF WORK

Advertising and marketing services
Roger Alexander, Brinsley Dresden

Company commercial
Trevor Watkins

Construction
Clare Reddy, James Levy

Corporate finance
Jo Evans

Defamation
Rod Dadak

Employment
Michael Burd, James Davies, Russell Brimelow

Information technology
Gillian Cordall

Intellectual property
Ian Jeffery, Dr Thomas Hays

Employee incentives

Litigation and dispute resolution
Tom Coates, Clive Greenwood

Housing and project finance
Gillian Bastow, Lynne Murray

Property, planning, construction and regeneration
Len Goodrich, Jonathan Barnes

Partnership law
Fergus Payne, Clive Greenwood

Sports
Dominic Farnsworth, Duncan Sandlant

THE FIRM

This distinctive commercial law firm, with 38 partners and 230 total staff, has developed a successful profile in 11 key areas: employment and incentives; marketing services; corporate services; litigation and dispute resolution; property; construction; housing and project finance; sports; defamation; media, brands and technology; and partnership law. Clients range from large corporations and plcs to entrepreneurs, and are in such diverse sectors as advertising, publishing, newspapers, IT, retail, government services, utilities, social housing and property development. Lewis Silkin has a reputation for excellence and expertise which belies its size. The emphasis is on client service and delivering relevant and commercial solutions. The firm has strong links with a variety of other European and overseas firms, which are specialist and expert in similar areas of practice such as advertising, employment, corporate advice or dispute resolution.

AREAS OF PRACTICE

Lewis Silkin's corporate finance team undertakes work including M&A, flotations, MBOs, employee benefits, shareholders' agreements and regulatory advice, acting on behalf of company clients, venture capitalists and sponsors. Much of this work has a European dimension.

The firm is an acknowledged leader in providing a comprehensive service to the advertising and marketing services industry, with an increasing emphasis on new media and brands. Good European connections through EALA are valuable to advise on pan-European or international advertising issues. Brinsley Dresden is currently the managing director of EALA.

The employment and incentives team is highly regarded, with a reputation for providing straightforward practical advice when a sensitive and commercial approach is needed. The team also specialises in international work.

Other important areas of work are litigation and dispute resolution, property, construction, media and technology, and housing and project finance.

Please visit our website for a further flavour of the firm: www.lewissilkin.com.

LINKLATERS

ONE SILK STREET
LONDON EC2Y 8HQ

Telephone: +44 20 7456 2000
Fax: +44 20 7456 2222
Website: www.linklaters.com

Languages
All commercial and local languages in the countries where Linklaters operates

Other offices
Amsterdam, Antwerp, Bangkok, Beijing, Berlin, Bratislava, Brussels, Bucharest, Budapest, Cologne, Dubai, Frankfurt am Main, Hong Kong, Lisbon, Luxembourg, Madrid, Milan, Moscow, Munich, New York, Paris, Prague, Rome, São Paulo, Shanghai, Singapore, Stockholm, Tokyo, Warsaw

Number of lawyers 2,000 worldwide

CATEGORIES OF WORK

Asset finance
Robert Fugard

Banking
John Tucker

Capital markets
Nick Eastwell

Corporate/M&A
David Barnes

Employment
Raymond Jeffers

Pensions and incentives
Ruth Goldman (pensions), Janet Cooper (incentives)

Environment and planning
Vanessa Havard-Williams

EU and competition
Alec Burnside, Gerwin van Gerven

Financial markets
Paul Nelson

Intellectual property
Nigel Jones

Investment management
Tim Shipton

TMT
Christopher Millard

Litigation and arbitration
John Turnbull

Projects
Bruce White

Real estate and construction
Patrick Plant

Restructuring and insolvency
Robert Elliott

Tax
Guy Brannan

THE FIRM

Linklaters advises the world's leading companies, financial institutions and governments on their most challenging transactions and assignments. With 2,000 lawyers, including 500 partners, and offices in major business and financial centres, its clients choose the firm for its distinctive combination of technical skill, commercial experience and outstanding service.

Linklaters has built a formidable global practice through organic growth and a series of mergers, joint ventures and co-operations with other respected law firms. In April 2005, Linklaters completed its merger with leading Japanese lawyers Mitsuhiro Yasuda and Akihiro Wani and their team, allowing Linklaters to offer Japanese legal advice alongside English and US advice in Tokyo. In February 2006, Linklaters opened its first office in the Middle East in Dubai.

In 2001, Linklaters merged with three of Europe's leading law firms to form Linklaters Oppenhoff & Rädler in Germany, Linklaters in Sweden, Linklaters De Bandt in Belgium and Linklaters Loesch in Luxembourg. In the same year, the firm formed a co-operation with Brazilian firm Lefosse Advogados, combining Linklaters' international capability with Lefosse Advogados' extensive knowledge of the Brazilian market. In Singapore the firm practises as Linklaters Allen & Gledhill, a joint venture with the premier Singapore practice Allen & Gledhill.

AREAS OF PRACTICE

Linklaters offers a rare combination of market-leading corporate, finance and commercial capability. As would be expected of a global firm of its size, it offers strong experience across a wealth of practice areas, including asset finance, banking, capital markets, competition, corporate/M&A, employee incentives, employment, environment and planning, financial markets, intellectual property, investment management, litigation and arbitration, pensions and incentives, private equity, projects, real estate and construction, restructuring and insolvency, tax, and technology, media and telecommunications.

Understanding a client's business environment and strategic aims is key to providing first-class legal and commercial support. Linklaters' sector groups bring together lawyers with particular business sector experience from different disciplines and jurisdictions. The sector groups include aerospace and defence, automotive, aviation and shipping, chemicals, energy and utilities, food and beverages, forestry, paper and packaging, healthcare, IT and business services, infrastructure and construction, insurance, investment management, leisure and hotels, media and entertainment, mining, real estate, retail and telecommunications.

LOVELLS

ATLANTIC HOUSE
HOLBORN VIADUCT
LONDON EC1A 2FG

Telephone: +44 20 7296 2000
Fax: +44 20 7296 2001
E-mail: information@lovells.com
Website: www.lovells.com

Languages
Chinese, Czech, Dutch, French, German, Italian, Japanese, Russian

Other offices
Alicante, Amsterdam, Beijing, Berlin, Brussels, Budapest*, Chicago, Düsseldorf, Frankfurt, Hamburg, Ho Chi Minh City, Hong Kong, Madrid, Moscow, Milan, Munich, New York, Paris, Prague, Rome, Shanghai, Singapore, Tokyo, Warsaw, Zagreb*

Number of lawyers 1,600
at this office 724

CATEGORIES OF WORK

Banking
Andrew Gamble, Matthew Cottis

Business restructuring/insolvency
Robin Spencer

Capital markets
David Hudd

Commercial and trading law
Andrew Skipper

Competition, EU and trade
John Pheasant

Corporate (including private equity)
Hugh Nineham, Marco Campagnoni

Dispute resolution
Patrick Sherrington

Employment
David Harper

Energy
David Moss, John Cooper

Financial services
Richard Stones

Insurance (corporate)
John Young

Insurance and reinsurance
John Powell

Intellectual property
Andreas von Falck

International arbitration
Andrew Foyle

Pensions
Russell Strachan, Jane Samsworth

Project finance
Gavin McQuater

Projects/engineering/construction
Philip Capper, Nicholas Gould

Real estate
Robert Kidby

Tax
Daniel Friel, Kevin Ashman

Technology, media and telecoms
Quentin Archer, Conor Ward

THE FIRM

With over 3,000 people operating from 26 offices in Asia, Europe and the US, Lovells is one of a small number of truly international law firms.

The firm has a strong presence in every major European jurisdiction offering a wide range of legal advisory expertise to its clients.

In the US, the New York and Chicago offices have flourished thanks to the firm's market-leading expertise in insurance and reinsurance and the development of its banking, capital markets and restructuring practices.

In Asia, with the emergence of China as a global business player, the firm has developed capabilities in Beijing and Shanghai, complementing the well established offices in Hong Kong, Tokyo and Singapore.

The firm advises many of the world's largest corporations, financial institutions and governmental organisations. It regularly acts on complex, international transactions, as well as some of the most high-profile commercial disputes.

AREAS OF PRACTICE

The firm has major strengths in its corporate, banking, project finance and capital markets practices. Equally, one of the firm's strongest suits is its formidable dispute resolution practice.

For a firm of the size and global presence of Lovells, it offers its clients an unusually rich and well-balanced range of legal expertise. This includes intellectual property, real estate, construction and engineering, EU, competition and trade law, telecommunications, media and technology, labour law, employee share incentives and pensions, together with industry-specific practices such as financial services and insurance and reinsurance.

Each of these are free-standing practices in their own right, rather than – as with some firms – adjuncts to corporate finance activities. The firm acts for its own clients on issues of significant commercial importance, often multi-jurisdictionally.

Lovells operates a number of multi-disciplinary industry sector groups comprising partners with an impressive track record of advice and a deep understanding of the way these sectors operate. Lovells sector groups include life sciences, financial services, energy and utilities and consumer services.

LOYENS & LOEFF

26 THROGMORTON STREET
LONDON EC2N 2AN

Telephone: +44 20 7826 3070
Fax: +44 20 7826 3080
E-mail: marc.klerks@loyensloeff.com, bas.vletter@loyensloeff.com
Website: www.loyensloeff.com

Languages
Dutch, English, French, German, Italian, Japanese, Malay Indonesian, Portuguese, Russian, Spanish

Other offices
Amsterdam, Antwerp (Loyens), Arnhem, Aruba, Brussels (Loyens), Curaçao, Eindhoven, Frankfurt, Geneva, Luxembourg (Loyens Winandy), New York, Paris, Rotterdam, Singapore, Tokyo, Zurich

Number of lawyers 710
at this office 8

CATEGORIES OF WORK

- **Administrative and regulatory law**
- **Banking and securities, capital markets, project finance**
- **Capital markets**
- **Corporate and financial restructuring**
- **Corporate/M&A**
- **Corporate litigation**
- **Energy**
- **EU and competition**
- **Finance**
- **Financial products/ structured finance**
- **Employment taxes and labour law**
- **Private equity**
- **Real property**
- **Tax**
- **Technology, media and litigation**
- **VAT, customs and international trade**

MACFARLANES

10 NORWICH STREET
LONDON EC4A 1BD

Telephone: +44 20 7831 9222
Fax: +44 20 7831 9607
Website: www.macfarlanes.com

Languages
Cantonese, Dutch/Flemish, French, German, Greek, Gujarati, Hebrew, Italian, Japanese, Portuguese, Punjabi, Spanish, Swedish, Urdu, Welsh, Yoruba

Number of lawyers 255

CATEGORIES OF WORK

Advertising and marketing
Jeremy Courtenay-Stamp

Banking and debt finance
Julian Howard

Buy-outs/private equity
Charles Martin

Construction
Patrick Holmes

Corporate tax
Mark Baldwin

Employment/benefits
Seán Lavin

Pensions
Hugh Arthur

EU/competition
Jane Whittaker

Financial services and investment funds
Bridget Barker

Intellectual property
Geoff Steward

Litigation and dispute resolution
Willie Manners

M&A/corporate finance
Robert Sutton

Company law
Simon Martin

Securities
Tim Lewis

Private client
Jonathan Conder

Property
Chris Field

THE FIRM

Macfarlanes' client base ranges from multinationals to private individuals. The firm provides a comprehensive service in its chosen areas of expertise, handling work of a quality and scale that places the firm amongst the leading law firms in the City.

Macfarlanes takes a partner-led approach towards client service and relationships. This promotes continuity, communication, working efficiency and intelligent cost management. The firm's simple business model means that internal management distractions do not get in the way. Nowhere is personal connection more important than in the international arena. Clients rely on their lawyers to interpret the law and much more when they are operating away from the jurisdictions that they know best. Much of the firm's practice is international in nature, involving continental European and US corporate clients and investors in the UK, outbound M&A and private equity, cross-border litigation, and wealthy international families. This work is driven by the firm's excellent relationships with leading independent law firms outside the UK. Macfarlanes invests heavily in building these relationships through secondments and technical know-how sharing to give clients a first class and seamless service.

AREAS OF PRACTICE

Corporate: Macfarlanes is particularly highly regarded for its work in the areas of corporate finance and mergers and acquisitions, including private equity and takeovers. The firm's specialist practice areas, such as intellectual property, corporate tax and employee benefits enable Macfarlanes to provide its broad range of commercial clients with high-quality legal services, both in relation to corporate transactional work and at the clients' operational level. The firm has a particularly strong reputation for advertising and marketing work, as well as for its investment funds and financial services practice. Acquisition and property finance for lenders and borrowers are the core areas of the firm's rapidly expanding debt finance group, and non UK financing under English law is an important part of the practice.

Property: by City standards, Macfarlanes' property practice is substantial. Property work accounts for a quarter of the firm's work. Work for the property sector covers all transactions involving the ownership, development, investment in and financing of real estate. Commercial property investment and development transactions are at the core of the firm's property practice.

Litigation and dispute resolution: Macfarlanes' business litigation and dispute resolution practice is well regarded and has a strong record in all aspects of corporate and transactional dispute resolution. Work includes: advising on disputes arising out of corporate acquisitions, shareholder and minority/unfair prejudice issues; employment matters; advertising and intellectual property cases; marketing disputes; property litigation; disputes over computer hardware and software; financial services and regulatory issues and investigations; trust and probate litigation; judicial review; breach of contract and professional negligence claims; major construction arbitrations and jurisdictional disputes.

Private client: Macfarlanes has a long-standing reputation for first class private client work and the practice continues to grow and flourish. Combined with the firm's corporate and property capability, this means that Macfarlanes is in a particularly strong position to advise high-net-worth entrepreneurs. The firm's reputation is for advising private clients and their family trusts, both domestically and internationally. Tax planning, including the creation and administration of trusts, the preparation of wills and the administration of estates, are central to this work. The international element is a significant part of the work of the department both for UK-based families and for overseas taxpayers seeking advice on tax and trust law. The firm also advises on tax investigations, charity, immigration and Lloyd's related matters.

MATHESON ORMSBY PRENTICE

PINNACLE HOUSE
23-26 ST DUNSTANS HILL
EC3R 8HN
LONDON

Telephone: +44 20 7618 6750
Fax: +44 20 7618 6790

Other offices
Dublin, New York, Palo Alto (CA)

Number of lawyers 230
at this office: 6

CATEGORIES OF WORK

Asset management
Michael Jackson, James Scanlon

Banking
Patrick Molloy, William Prentice

Capital markets
Michael Jackson, Tim Scanlon

Commercial litigation and dispute resolution
Stuart Margetson, Michael Tyrrell

Commercial property/real estate
Cara O'Hagan, Patrick Sweetman

Corporate and commercial
Andrew Doyle, Leanne Robson

EC, competition and regulatory
Helen Kelly

Employment, pensions and benefits
Brian Buggy, Paul Glenfield

Insurance
Sharon Daly, Liam Flynn

Information technology and intellectual property
Don McAleese, Alistair Payne

Inward investment
Robert O'Shea, John Ryan

Life sciences
Karen Holmes, Stuart Margetson

Mergers and acquisitions
Andrew Doyle, Patrick Spicer

Private equity
Edward Miller, Stanley Watson

Projects and construction
Damien Keogh, Michael O'Connor

Retail and leisure
Lorraine Compton, Nicola Palmer

Structured finance, securitisation and repacking
Tara Doyle, Turlough Galvin

Tax
Liam Quirke, John Ryan

McDERMOTT WILL & EMERY UK LLP

7 BISHOPSGATE
LONDON
EC2N 3AR

Telephone: +44 20 7577 6900
Fax: +44 20 7577 6950
Website: www.mwe.com

Languages
All main business languages

Other offices
Boston, Brussels, Chicago, Düsseldorf, Los Angeles, Miami, Munich, New York, Orange County, Rome, San Diego, Silicon Valley, Washington DC

Number of lawyers 1,000
at this office 74

CATEGORIES OF WORK

Banking and finance
Graham Rowbotham

Corporate and corporate finance
William Charnley

Employment
Fraser Younson

Energy
Graham Rowbotham

Equity capital markets
Andrew Caunt, Andrew Croxford

EU and competition
Scott Megregian

Financial services and funds
William Yonge

Insolvency and restructuring
Graham Rowbotham, Rick Mitchell

Intellectual property, media and technology
Larry Cohen

International dispute resolution
John Reynolds

Mergers and acquisitions
William Charnley

Pensions and incentives
Danny Tsang, David Dalgarno

Private equity
Michael McFall

Project finance
Andrew Watson

Taxation
Peter Nias

US securities
Rick Mitchell

MILBANK, TWEED, HADLEY & McCLOY LLP

DASHWOOD HOUSE
69 OLD BROAD STREET
LONDON EC2M 1QS

Telephone: +44 20 7448 3000
Fax: +44 20 7448 3029
E-mail: info@milbank.com
Website: www.milbankeurope.com

Other offices
Frankfurt, Hong Kong, Los Angeles, Munich, New York, Singapore, Tokyo, Washington DC

Number of lawyers 520
at this office 50

Contact
Phillip Fletcher

CATEGORIES OF WORK

Acquisition finance
Kevin Muzilla

Private equity
Michael Goroff

Banking
Patrick Holmes

Outsourcing
Laurence Jacobs

Capital markets
Tom Siebens

Project finance
John Dewar

IP litigation
David Perkins

M&A
Tim Emmerson

Structured finance
John Walker

Tax
Russell Jacobs

THE FIRM

Milbank is committed to providing high-quality legal services wherever the firm practices. The firm recruits from among the most promising lawyers and is committed to their training as well as providing opportunities for promotion. Milbank draws on its strengths globally to ensure that it can address the needs of its clients wherever they are.

AREAS OF PRACTICE

Capital markets: international securities offerings represent a very substantial portion of Milbank's capital markets practice including initial public offerings, high-yield bond offerings, project bonds, securitisations and other types of highly structured cross-border offerings.

Corporate: the firm represents buyers and sellers, private equity investors, strategic partners and financial advisors in the full range of M&A transactions throughout Europe.

Outsourcing: Milbank is recognised as a global leader in information technology and outsourcing law and has played a significant role in many of the largest and most complex international and domestic business process outsourcing transactions completed to date.

Intellectual property: Milbank has developed a leading intellectual property practice, encompassing both contentious and non-contentious matters, with experience ranging across patents and trade marks.

Leveraged finance: the firm's leveraged finance practice in Europe includes high yield, acquisition finance and mezzanine finance, and is widely recognised for its depth and breadth of experience.

Project and asset finance: Milbank has a leading project finance practice involving diverse industries such as independent power; mining and metals; petroleum and natural gas; petrochemicals; aerospace; telecommunications; satellites; timber and paper processing; pipelines, toll roads, airports and other types of infrastructure.

Structured finance: the firm's lawyers have acted on numerous transactions where the application of capital markets instruments and derivative product techniques have created tax or balance sheet advantage, reprofiled existing cash flows or maximised arbitrage opportunities.

Tax: Milbank's tax group supports M&A and private equity transactions by providing international investment banking and corporate clients with co-ordinated structuring capability, bringing to bear tax planning techniques and general advisory support for the providers of equity and debt alike.

MOON BEEVER SOLICITORS

24-25 BLOOMSBURY SQUARE
LONDON
WC1A 2PL

Telephone: +44 20 7637 0661
Fax: +44 20 7436 4663
E-mail: info@moonbeever.com
Website: www.moonbeever.com

Languages
English, French, German, Gujerati, Hindi

Other offices
Brussels, Washington DC

Number of lawyers 28

Contact
Frances Coulson (managing partner)

CATEGORIES OF WORK

Insolvency	**IT law**
Corporate and commercial	**Property**
Civil fraud	**Employment**
Litigation/dispute resolution	**Private client**
Wealth management and tax planning	**Intellectual property**
Estate planning	**Debt recovery**

THE FIRM

Moon Beever practices from offices in Bloomsbury, London, where it was established in 1851, close to both the Royal Courts of Justice and the City. Moon Beever is a founder member of ShawnCoulson International Lawyers, with offices, associates and contacts worldwide. Through its international experience, the firm is able to provide a wide range of international support, assistance and advice.

The practice acts for a wide range of commercial clients and has notable strengths in litigation, including IT disputes, insolvency and intellectual property which are also specialist areas. A broad spectrum of corporate/commercial work and property services are undertaken. Advice for private clients includes trusts, tax and probate work. The insolvency and business recovery department has built a strong reputation with insolvency practitioners and creditor clients alike. Recent years have seen the department act in some of the most significant UK cases.

By bringing together some of the best people in the legal profession and sustaining high-quality services, the firm maintains its commitment to provide creative solutions for its clients that will promote the growth of the business.

The firm and its lawyers have been acknowledged by leading directories including the UK 2005 edition of *The Legal 500* and 2006 *Chambers UK*.

AREAS OF PRACTICE

Moon Beever offers a comprehensive range of legal advice, its principal departments are: insolvency, debt recovery, corporate/commercial, property, litigation and private client.

Insolvency: niche expertise in insolvency and recovery services including bankruptcy and individual voluntary agreements, retention of title claims, liquidations, receiverships, corporate voluntary arrangements, administrations and director's responsibilities. The firm enjoys a good reputation in insolvency and business recovery and has built a strong reputation for resolving complex problems quickly and efficiently.

Debt recovery: the firm has a large and well-respected debt recovery department that can professionally manage any volume of instruction, from substantial debt portfolios to one off cases.

Employment litigation: includes dismissal claims, redundancy and restrictive covenant actions.

Corporate/commercial: the firm advises and acts for diverse businesses, which range in size from international corporations to small partnerships and sole traders. Services include acquisitions and disposals of companies and businesses, company and business formation, administration of companies, joint ventures, shareholders' agreements, management buy-outs and intellectual property. Advice is also given on EU law.

Commercial and residential property: the firm advises on property developments and funding, acquisitions and sales, landlord and tenant law, planning matters, auctions and tenders, building contracts and property taxation.

Litigation: the firm has extensive trial experience in courts and tribunals throughout the UK and also provides a seamless service through their partnership with ShawnCoulson International Lawyers. The firm's approach is to reach a quick, definitive and effective resolution, whether it is achieved through negotiation, mediation, arbitration or litigation.

Private clients: service includes trusts, settlements and wills, financial advice, tax planning and all matters including separation and divorce.

MORGAN LEWIS

2 GRESHAM STREET
LONDON EC2V 7PE

Telephone: +44 20 7710 5500
Fax: +44 20 7710 5600
E-mail: info@morganlewis.com
Website: www.morganlewis.com

Languages
Afrikaans, English, French, German, Spanish

Other offices
Boston, Brussels, Chicago, Dallas, Frankfurt, Harrisburg, Irvine, Los Angeles, Miami, New York, Palo Alto, Paris, Philadelphia, Pittsburgh, Princeton, San Francisco, Tokyo, Washington DC

Number of lawyers 1,200+
at this office 30

CATEGORIES OF WORK

Corporate, acquisition finance, M&A, private equity, US securities
Keith Black, Rachel Gonzalez

General commercial litigation, international arbitration, fraud, securities
Robert Goldspink, Robert Falkner, Neville Byford

Banking litigation, regulatory investigations and gaming
Robert Falkner

Insurance and reinsurance litigation, pensions litigation
Peter Hardy

Life sciences
Anthony Warnock-Smith, Keith Black

Commercial
Richard Barratt

Outsourcing, IP and IT, sport, licensing
Richard Barratt

Labour and employment
Simeon Spencer

US and international tax, and inward investments
Charles Lubar, Michael Cashman

THE FIRM

Morgan Lewis, with more than 1,200 lawyers in 19 offices in the US, Europe and Asia, is one of the largest law firms in the world.

Morgan Lewis represents clients across the globe, from mergers and acquisitions and joint ventures to technology and outsourcing; from fraud and money laundering to employment and property. With its international reach, Morgan Lewis can resolve differing and conflicting laws in a number of jurisdictions to produce optimum results for its clients. The firm's lawyers understand the problems and complexities of transactional litigation and cross-border negotiation and can advise on US and EU regulatory matters.

The firm's clients are diverse and include Fortune 250 companies, leading financial services and investment banking organisations, as well as pioneers in the e-commerce and internet sector. The firm also represents high-net-worth individuals. All clients receive the same high level of care and benefit from the firm's local presence in a global market.

The firm handles a vast diversity of legal work including antitrust, business and commercial litigation, business and finance, corporate transactions, employment, labour and benefits, energy and utilities, insurance, intellectual property, international arbitration, investment management, life sciences, mergers and acquisitions, real estate, outsourcing, securities, sport, tax, and technology.

AREAS OF PRACTICE

Morgan Lewis, London is fully integrated with the firm's 18 other offices and offers a strong pan-European service in combination with the Brussels, Frankfurt and Paris lawyers.

The London office opened 25 years ago and incorporates a fully dual US/UK corporate, commercial and financing capability advising major US, UK, European and International corporate clients on M&A and joint venture transactions as well as capital-raising transactions.

Robert Goldspink heads the London office and oversees a highly ranked (*Chambers* and *Legal 500* 2005 editions) English law litigation and international arbitration practice, which has acted for clients in several high-profile matters. These include the biggest Commercial Court case of 1999 and, more recently, Court of Appeal cases and one House of Lords case. The team have strong fraud and asset recovery specialists and the litigation team has been further boosted by the addition of Peter Hardy from the prestigious Norton Rose insurance team and Robert Falkner from Cantor Fitzgerald joining the global securities, financial services litigation and regulatory enforcement group in 2004.

The life sciences practice in London is headed by Anthony Warnock-Smith, ranked as a leading individual in the *Chambers* 2005 edition for his contribution to this sector. Working with Keith Black the team covers regulatory and corporate work in the biotech, medtech and pharmaceutical markets.

Richard Barratt joined Morgan Lewis from his post as global head of IP at Norton Rose in 2004 to spearhead the firm's outsourcing team in Europe. Working closely with the Paris and New York team's Richard has brought energy and high-profile work to Morgan Lewis in outsourcing, sport and licensing.

Simeon Spencer recently joined the London team from Morrison & Foerster to set up the labour and employment practice in the UK for Morgan Lewis.

NORTON ROSE

KEMPSON HOUSE
CAMOMILE STREET
LONDON EC3A 7AN

Telephone: +44 20 7283 6000
Fax: +44 20 7283 6500
Website: www.nortonrose.com

Languages
Afrikaans, Arabic, Bahasa Malay, Cantonese, Czech, Danish, Dutch, Flemish, English, French, German, Greek, Hebrew, Hindi, Italian, Japanese, Maltese, Mandarin, Norwegian, Polish, Russian, Shona, Spanish, Swahili, Swedish, Thai

Other offices
Amsterdam, Athens, Bahrain, Bangkok, Beijing, Brussels, Dubai, Frankfurt, Hong Kong, Jakarta*, Milan, Moscow, Munich, Paris, Piraeus, Prague, Rome, Singapore, Warsaw

Number of lawyers 1,018
at this office 595

Contacts
Peter Martyr (chief executive),
Paul Giles (chairman)

CATEGORIES OF WORK

Aviation
Jeremy Edwards

Banking
Jeffery Barratt

Competition and EC
Martin Coleman

Corporate finance
Tim Marsden

Dispute resolution
James Bagge

Energy and natural resources
Richard Metcalf

Employment, pensions and incentives
Peter Talibart, Peter Ford, David Cohen

Communications, media and technology
Mike Rebeiro

Insurance
James Bateson

Rail
Gordon Hall

Real property, planning and environmental
Lindsay Morgan

Shipping
Harry Theochari

Tax
Louise Higginbottom

THE FIRM

International law firm Norton Rose has more than 1,000 lawyers providing an integrated business law service from a network of offices across Europe, Asia and the Middle East. Norton Rose was one of the first firms to organise itself into international industry groups. This reflects the firm's traditional emphasis on industry expertise and allows it to share industry knowledge across the network. Norton Rose focuses on five key areas: international corporate finance, financial institutions, transport, energy and infrastructure, and technology.

AREAS OF PRACTICE

The global nature of the firm's client base of international corporates and financial institutions, and its strength in project, asset and Islamic finance, international M&A and international dispute resolution, means that much of its work is conducted across jurisdictions.

The firm's major clients include: ABN AMRO, AIG, AXA, BMW, BNP Paribas, Citigroup, Calyon, Corus, Eni, ExxonMobil, France Télécom, GE, HBOS, HVB Group, HSBC, ING, Nestlé, Société Générale, Siemens, Stena and Sumitomo.

The firm is an acknowledged leader in international corporate finance, where specialisations include cross-border M&A, public offerings, private equity, investment funds, financial services and US corporate finance. Major deals on which the firm worked recently include: the listing of Drax on the London Stock Exchange involving a complex £1bn restructuring and M&A auction process in parallel; advising HSBC and UBS on the listing of China COSCO Holding Company Limited by way of Hong Kong Public Offer and international offer raising US$1.22bn; AXA Asia Pacific Holdings Limited's joint venture with Bharti Enterprises in Indian life insurance business, Bharti AXA Life Insurance Company Limited; advising Telekom Malaysia on several transactions including its bid for the privatisation of Pakistan Telecommunication Company Limited and acquisition of Multinet Pakistan.

The strong banking and finance practice includes top teams in bank lending, acquisition finance, Islamic finance, asset, structured and project finance and capital markets. Recent major transactions include: the €230m Mestre PPP hospital development in Italy; the Shari'ah compliant Sukuk issue for the financing of the Bahrain Financial Harbour; advising Marubeni Corporation and its consortium partners on its successful bid to acquire, expand and operate the ground-breaking Taweelah B power and desalination plant in Abu Dhabi; acting for Standard Chartered Bank on the financing of five UK wind farms for Fenland Windfarms Limited.

Norton Rose has one of the largest and most varied dispute resolution practices of any international law firm. The firm has extensive experience in resolving disputes worldwide through litigation, arbitration, mediation, adjudication and other forms of dispute resolution.

The competition lawyers provide excellent capability in competition and regulation; their relationships with, and understanding of, regulatory bodies are outstanding. The team advises on high-profile merger filings, cartel investigations, public procurement, state aids, trade and regulatory work.

The leading employment, pensions and incentives team covers the full range of contentious and non-contentious work. The firm also offers first-class technical tax expertise with a team experienced in the tax structuring aspects of corporate and finance transactions and dispute resolution cases.

The international communications, media and technology team offers a full-service practice in relation to intellectual property, e-commerce/m-commerce, media and communications.

The real estate, planning and environmental team attracts considerable recognition on an international level for its involvement in some of the largest and most high-profile projects and transactions.

O'MELVENY & MYERS LLP

WARWICK COURT
5 PATERNOSTER SQUARE
LONDON EC4M 7DX

Telephone: +44 20 7088 0000
Fax: +44 20 7088 0001
E-mail: lwoodward@omm.com
Website: www.omm.com

Languages
Cantonese, Danish, English, French, German, Gujarati, Hindi, Japanese, Mandarin, Mirpuri, Portuguese, Punjabi, Spanish, Turkish

Other offices
Beijing, Brussels, Century City, Hong Kong, Los Angeles, Newport Beach, New York, San Fran, Shanghai, Silicon Valley, Tokyo, Washington DC

Number of lawyers 1,049
at this office 41

Contact
Matthew Hudson

Member
BVCA; BABI; CBBC; EVCA; AIMA

CATEGORIES OF WORK

Acquisition finance
Stuart Hills, Michael Crosby

Corporate finance
Matthew Hudson, Chris Ashworth

Employment
Blair Adams, Helen Samuel

Funds
John Daghlian, Solomon Wifa

IP/IT
Matthew Harrison

IPOs
John Daghlian, Andrew Carpenter

Outsourcing
Matthew Harrison

Private equity M&A
Matthew Hudson, Andrew Carpenter

Real estate
Victoria Forrest, Jo Brass

Regulatory
Alasdair Gordon

Strategic M&A
Matthew Hudson, Chris Ashworth

Structured finance
Stuart Hills

Tax
Jan Birtwell, Guy Dingley

Venture capital
Matthew Hudson, James Ford

THE FIRM

O'Melveny & Myers LLP is a top-ten global law firm with a presence in three continents, embracing key locations including London, New York, Los Angeles, Silicon Valley, Shanghai and Beijing.

In January 2005, O'Melveny celebrated its 120th anniversary. While over a century of continuous service gives name recognition and stability, the firm is far from centenarian in outlook. With a strong foundation in the US and Asia, O'Melveny has turned to building a pre-eminent private equity, M&A and corporate finance and banking practice in London.

The London office, headed by Matthew Hudson, was formed by hiring the very best lawyers recognised for their skills and creative approach in their respective fields to service the firm's workflow. O'Melveny's clients, which include many of the world's largest financial institutions, leading private equity houses, investment banks and corporates, generally require geographical reach and a large enough stock of specialists to handle the most difficult assignments at a moment's notice, anywhere in the world. O'Melveny & Myers LLP London is staffed for this, having grown from four to over 40 fee-earners in 20 months and with further growth of up to 60 lawyers by the end of 2006. With all of its lawyers UK qualified, the London office's local expertise is enhanced by being able to draw on the huge reservoir of know-how and experience from the firm's offices around the world, allowing it to provide its clients with the very best local and international advice.

Recognition of the London office's achievements (including advising on over £8bn of deals in 2005) has been highlighted by O'Melveny & Myers being named 'Best US Law Firm in London' at the 2005 *Legal Business* Awards.

O'Melveny & Myers LLP's European presence has been further strengthened by the formation of its Brussels office, headed by Riccardo Celli who leads the European antitrust/competition practice. The firm's lawyers in Brussels focus on EU and member country competition and regulatory law, including mergers and acquisitions and joint ventures, anti-competitive agreements and concerted practices, cartel investigations, abuse of monopoly positions and state aid.

AREAS OF PRACTICE

Globally, O'Melveny & Myers' capabilities span virtually every area of legal practice, including antitrust/competition, capital markets, corporate finance, entertainment and media, global enforcement and criminal defence, intellectual property and technology, labour and employment, litigation, mergers and acquisitions, private equity, project development and real estate, restructuring and insolvency, securities, tax, and trade and international law. O'Melveny & Myers LLP regularly handles domestic, cross-border and multi-jurisdictional transactions involving senior and/or mezzanine loans (secured and unsecured) and/or bonds (including high yield).

Over the past few years O'Melveny & Myers has committed to build a global transaction practice. The organic growth of its Asian practice, its combination in New York City with O'Sullivan LLP in 2002, its acquisition of part of Brobeck's VC practice in Silicon Valley in 2003 and now its significant investments in London and Brussels, have given rise to one of the legal profession's premier corporate and private equity practices. For example, the firm now has a team of 250 lawyers worldwide dedicated to private equity.

The London office divides into private equity, corporate finance and M&A, finance and banking. It also has experts in the fields of tax, regulatory, employment, property and intellectual property. The Brussels office is focused exclusively on competition/antitrust.

Within the legal industry, it is unusual to have a firm that offers seamless private equity and international venture capital experience in the UK, US and Asia. O'Melveny is one of the very few, if not the only global law firm, who has developed this infrastructure.

OGIER

2 ROYAL EXCHANGE BUILDINGS
LONDON EC3V 31F

Telephone: +44 20 7220 1170
Fax: +44 20 7220 1199
E-mail: info@ogier.com
Website: www.ogier.com

Languages
English, French

Other offices
Cayman Islands, Guernsey, Jersey

Number of lawyers 120
at this office 4

Member
Association of European Lawyers (AEL); STEP; EVCA; BVCA

CATEGORIES OF WORK

Banking
Gray Smith, Aaron DeLacey

Capital markets: securitisation, derivatives, CBOs/CLOs/CDOs, repackagings and structured finance
Gray Smith, Aaron DeLacey

Corporate and commercial: joint ventures, mergers and acquisitions
Gray Smith, Aaron DeLacey

Investment funds
Gray Smith

Trust and estate planning
Brian Lee

Private client
Brian Lee

Employee benefits and share plan administration
Brian Lee

Fiduciary services
Brian Lee

THE FIRM

Ogier is one of the leading offshore providers of legal and administration services with approximately 500 employees across offices in Jersey, Guernsey, London and the Cayman Islands.

Ogier has developed an extensive portfolio of international clients and continues to provide legal and administration services to them through its dedicated teams.

A large proportion of the firm's qualified lawyers have worked in some of the world's leading financial centres and bring to the firm exceptional experience and expertise. The firm places great importance and value on its relationships with intermediaries and professional advisers in other jurisdictions. It seeks to work more closely with those advisers to deliver added value and commerical advantages to their clients' businesses.

Ogier's London office provides its clients and intermediaries with easier access to Ogier's offshore legal and administration services across three of the world's leading offshore centres: Jersey, Guernsey and the Cayman Islands.

AREAS OF PRACTICE

Banking: Ogier is widely regarded as a premier firm for banking and international finance. It specialises in advising on all areas of banking, security, structured finance, banking regulation and the establishment of banks.

Corporate and commercial: Ogier's highly experienced and extensive team covers mergers and acquisitions, employment and privacy laws, IT/IP and e-commerce.

Securitisation: Ogier has one of the leading securitisation teams, with particular expertise in asset-backed securities, CBOs, ABCP and structured notes.

Structured finance: the structured finance team covers structured equity, asset finance and tax neutral transactions.

Employee benefits: the employees benefits team is committed to providing an innovative and flexible approach to assist clients to achieve employee or clients' employee incentive requirements, tailored administration services, comprehensive advice and a quality, efficient and cost-effective service.

Trusts: the trust and estate planning group has one of the largest teams of trust lawyers dedicated to advising trust companies, intermediaries and individuals in matters of trust law.

Private client: Ogier continues to develop and grow its private client practice. The private client team can provide a full range of administration services to trusts, companies and limited partnerships established in the Channel Islands, as well as to entities established elsewhere.

Fiduciary services: Ogier Fiduciary Services provides professional administration and accounting services to trusts, companies and limited partnerships.

ORRICK, HERRINGTON & SUTCLIFFE

TOWER 42, LEVEL 35
25 OLD BROAD STREET
LONDON EC2N 1HQ

Telephone: +44 20 7562 5000
Fax: +44 20 7628 0078
Website: www.orrick.com

Other offices
Hong Kong, Moscow, Los Angeles, Milan, New York, Orange County, Pacific Northwest (Portland, Seattle), Paris, Rome, Sacramento, San Francisco, Silicon Valley, Taipei, Tokyo, Washington DC

Number of lawyers 850
at this office 43

Contact
Martin Bartlam

CATEGORIES OF WORK

- **Bankruptcy and global debt restructuring**
- **Energy and project finance**
- **Commercial and institutional finance**
- **Employment**
- **General corporate**
- **International arbitration**
- **Litigation**
- **Mergers and acquisitions**
- **Private equity**
- **Property**
- **Tax**

THE FIRM

Orrick is an international law firm with more than 850 lawyers located in Asia, Europe and North America. In Europe, Orrick has almost 200 lawyers, located in London, Paris, Milan, Rome and Moscow. Much of Orrick's work in Europe involves cross-border transactions and financings that span Europe, the Middle East, Africa, Asia and the Americas. To support the demands of its clients, Orrick has made seamless client service its number one goal across the firm. As a result, the firm's European lawyers can call on the substantial resources of Orrick's other offices around the world to provide clients with the expertise required to support their transactions. Above all, Orrick's name stands for excellence in legal services; integrated, responsive client teams throughout the world; innovative leadership and management; and a commitment to the firm's core values, which govern these business standards. London's importance to global markets makes it a critical business centre for the firm's clients, many of whom have major operations in the UK. Established in 1998, the London office comprises of a talented team of US and UK lawyers with substantial experience in structured finance, project finance, general finance, bankruptcy and debt restructuring, employment, litigation and dispute resolution, private equity, mergers and acquisitions, tax and general corporate matters. Orrick's London office represents many of the leading international commercial and investment banks and multinational corporations.

AREAS OF PRACTICE

Orrick boasts a global team of professionals, comprising lawyers from the US, the UK and the rest of continental Europe (qualified in English, US, French and German law, among others). Orrick's London finance lawyers advise on transactions ranging from traditional credit agreements and public debt issuances to complex cross-border lease financings, including secured and unsecured lending, asset-backed financing, letters of credit, asset-backed commercial paper financing, lease finance and aircraft finance. In structured finance, the firm's London lawyers represent issuers, arrangers, trustees and investors in structured finance and capital markets transactions, including privately placed debt and equity securities under European and US law. Orrick also has experience in the full range of swaps and derivates instruments, particularly in cross-border structured financing. The firm's energy and project finance lawyers in London serve the needs of clients in the energy, communications and other key infrastructure sectors. Orrick acts as counsel to banks, sponsors, developers and other clients in these sectors, providing practical legal advice under US, English, French, German, Italian and EU law. Lawyers in the firm's London bankruptcy and debt restructuring group represent formal and ad hoc bondholder committees; unsecured creditor committees; lenders syndicates, secured and unsecured creditors, and insolvency practitioners from leading accounting firms. Orrick's London corporate practice represents European, North American, Asian and African companies, both public and private, in a variety of industries and sectors. The firm's expertise includes mergers and acquisitions, joint ventures, technology transactions, corporate formations, financings, restructurings, and general corporate matters. Orrick's property lawyers advise clients on all phases of real estate investment, development, financing and operations. The firm is pre-eminent in the area of real estate investments and representing pension funds and other institutional investors, public and private real estate investment trusts (REITs), and offshore investors. The employment law practice encompasses both contentious and non-contentious matters and has extensive experience advising and representing both private and public sector employers. Orrick litigators represent employers and employee benefits professionals in complex, highly sensitive employee disputes and focus on high-stakes litigation and arbitration, including class and mass tort actions and high-dollar compensation and benefits cases.

PAUL, HASTINGS, JANOFSKY & WALKER (EUROPE) LLP

88 WOOD STREET
LONDON EC2V 7AJ

Telephone: +44 20 7710 2000
Fax: +44 20 7796 2233
E-mail: info@paulhastings.com
Website: www.paulhastings.com

Languages
English, German, Spanish, Hebrew, Hindi, Punjabi

Other offices
Atlanta, Beijing, Brussels, Hong Kong, Los Angeles, Milan, New York, Orange County, Palo Alto, Paris, San Diego, San Francisco, Shanghai, Stamford, Tokyo, Washington DC

Number of lawyers 25

Contact
Mark J Eagan

CATEGORIES OF WORK

- Mergers and acquisitions
- Private equity
- Banking and finance
- Capital markets
- Project finance
- Real estate
- Dispute resolution and arbitration
- Litigation
- Tax
- Employment

PINSENT MASONS

DASHWOOD HOUSE
69 OLD BROAD STREET
LONDON EC2M 1NR

Telephone: +44 20 7418 7000
Fax: +44 20 7418 7050
E-mail: enquiries@pinsentmasons.com
Website: www.pinsentmasons.com

Languages
All major European languages, several Indian languages, Arabic, Cantonese, Hebrew, Japanese, Malay, Shanghainese

Other offices
Birmingham, Bristol, Edinburgh, Glasgow, Leeds, Manchester, Brussels, Dubai, Hong Kong, Shanghai

Number of lawyers 900+
at this office 320+

Contacts
Chris Mullen, Tony Bunch

CATEGORIES OF WORK

Banking and finance
Stephen Miles

Corporate
Gareth Edwards

Dispute resolution and litigation
Nigel Kissack

Employment, pensions and tax
Judith Greaves

Insurance and reinsurance
Tim Burton

International construction and energy
Mark Roe

Outsourcing, technology and commercial
Clive Seddon

Projects
Patrick Twist

Property
Adrian Barlow

UK construction and engineering
Andrew Hibbert

THE FIRM

Pinsent Masons is a full-service commercial law firm, distinguished by its depth of knowledge, experience and commitment to specialist market sectors. The firm is ranked in the top 15 in the UK, and internationally ranks in the Global 100 of law firms. The firm has over 260 partners, a total legal team of around 900 and more than 1,500 staff in the UK and internationally.

With a fundamental commitment to good client service, the firm has invested in building a practice which is strong in all areas of law that are key to business. This bedrock of expertise is overlaid with significant experience in a number of market sectors where Pinsent Masons has concentrated its development.

AREAS OF PRACTICE

It is Pinsent Masons' depth of sector knowledge and commitment to sector growth which singles out the firm. Through this approach, the firm's lawyers have first-hand knowledge of different industries both in the UK and overseas, and can give advice appropriate to the sector, the circumstances and the jurisdiction. In several cases, the firm's lawyers have other professional qualifications as engineers, surveyors or doctors, further deepening their sector insight.

Pinsent Masons' chosen markets are: energy and utilities, financial services and insurance, government, infrastructure and construction services, manufacturing and engineering, services, technology.

Activity in each of the firm's sectors is underpinned by its expertise and experience in the areas of practice highlighted under 'Categories of Work'. Within these groups, the firm further specialises with dedicated teams for areas such as competition and EU work, data protection, health and safety, international arbitration and trade marks.

In all areas of practice, the firm has lawyers who are independently rated for their expertise.

REED SMITH

MINERVA HOUSE
5 MONTAGUE CLOSE
LONDON SE1 9BB

Telephone: +44 20 7403 2900
Fax: +44 20 7403 4221
E-mail:
firstinitialsurname@reedsmith.com
Website: www.reedsmith.com

Languages
English, French, German

Other offices
Century City, Coventry, Los Angeles, Munich, New York, Newark, Northern VA, Oakland, Paris, Philadelphia, Pittsburgh, Princeton, San Francisco, Washington DC, Wilmington

Number of lawyers 1,078
at this office 74

Contact
Timothy G Foster

CATEGORIES OF WORK

Banking and finance, insurance and reinsurance
Ian Fagelson, David Heard

Life sciences
John Wilkinson

Technology
Jeff Rodwell

Intellectual property
Rajita Sharma

Employment
Mark Hunt

Real estate
Richard Perkins

Property litigation
Lesley Webber

Planning
Lesley Webber

Litigation
Marcus Rutherford

Immigration
Caron Pope

Pensions
Michael Calvert

Corporate/M&A
Peter Borrowdale

Project finance
Vinay Ganga

Product liability
Paul Llewellyn

Corporate finance
Giles Bede

THE FIRM

Reed Smith is a leading international law firm. The firm has grown rapidly over the past few years through a series of strategic mergers and lateral additions and it now has over 1,000 lawyers across 14 US and four European cities. A strong presence on both coasts of the US makes the firm ideally positioned to offer clients a transatlantic capability. It continues to invest in key markets to meet clients' needs and, in 2005, opened its first offices in mainland Europe, in Munich and Paris. In the UK the firm now has 95 lawyers based across two offices in London and the Midlands.

Reed Smith represents clients, large and small, across a great number of legal disciplines and many industry sectors. In Europe, its key industries are financial services and life sciences. Its firmwide clients include financial institutions, pharmaceutical companies, manufacturers, healthcare providers and insurers, communications and media companies and real estate developers and government bodies.

AREAS OF PRACTICE

Reed Smith's core services in Europe are corporate, life sciences, financial services, litigation, employment, real estate and TMT.

Corporate: the firm's largest department handles a wide variety of corporate and commercial transactions for, in particular, US and European clients. The department's expertise includes mergers and acquisitions, corporate finance, competition and corporate tax. It enjoys a strong track record in alternative investment market–related work.

Life sciences: the department supports leading-edge companies in pharmaceuticals, biotechnology, diagnostics, medical devices and healthcare. The firm advises life sciences companies on debt and equity financing and partners with clients through all phases of development, production, marketing and distribution of products. It is also widely acknowledged for its work defending clients in high-profile, multi-jurisdictional product liability claims.

Financial services: the financial services group advises on capital market products, consumer financial services, regulatory advice (Financial Services and Market Act 2000) and transactions (acquisitions, divestitures, restructurings). It also has a transatlantic project finance team.

Commercial litigation: the firm handles substantial commercial disputes and is particularly well known for its work in international asset recovery, financial regulation and multi-jurisdictional claims. Specific areas of expertise include product liability claims, insolvency and corporate restructuring, intellectual property and domestic and international arbitration. It has a dedicated team of French-speaking advocates.

Employment: the team provides a full service to employers and HR professionals encompassing service agreements and employment contracts, employee benefits, business transfers, dismissals, redundancies, discrimination and trade union law. It also advises on all EU aspects of employment law and offers transactional and non-transactional pensions advice. In addition, the UK business immigration team is recognised as one of the leading practices in the country and provides corporate clients and individual foreign investors with advice in connection with residence and working in the UK.

Real estate: the real estate group advises on high-value acquisitions and disposals for corporate clients in the retail, financial, services, media and manufacturing industries. High-level property litigation, contentious and non-contentious planning and infrastructure expertise is an additional strength of the team.

TMT and IP/IT: the firm represents a variety of media and entertainment, technology and telecommunications companies on all contractual, commercial, intellectual property and regulatory aspects. The firm works closely with broadcast clients and cable companies on all issues relating to broadcasting and the convergence of communication technologies. It advises on outsourcing and licensing, as well as other technology transactions.

SJ BERWIN LLP

10 QUEEN STREET PLACE
LONDON EC4R 1BE

Telephone: +44 20 7111 2222
Fax: +44 20 7111 2000
E-mail: info@sjberwin.com
Website: www.sjberwin.com

Languages
All principal languages are spoken

Other offices
Berlin, Brussels, Frankfurt, Madrid, Milan, Munich, Paris, Turin

Number of lawyers 550
at this office 404

Contacts
Jonathan Blake, Ralph Cohen

Member
Interlaw – a worldwide association of independent law firms

CATEGORIES OF WORK

Banking and financial services
Gillian Smith, Bruce Gardner

Corporate finance, M&A
Robert Burrow, Steven Davis

IT and e-commerce
Andrew Shindler, Martin Bowen

EU, competition
Stephen Kon, Ralph Cohen

Employment, pensions
Nicola Kerr, Wyn Derbyshire

Insolvency and reconstruction
Stephen Maffey

Intellectual property
Ray Black, Jeremy Schrire

Leisure and sport
Perry Yam

Litigation, ADR, advocacy, public law
Tim Taylor, David Shapiro

Media and communications
Nigel Palmer, Tim Johnson

Pharmaceuticals and biotechnology
Jeremy Schrire, Stephen Kon

Private equity, MBOs, venture capital
Jonathan Blake, Steven Davis

Real estate, real estate funds, property litigation, construction, planning and environment
Bryan Pickup

Tax, VAT
Michael Trask, Heather Corben

THE FIRM

SJ Berwin LLP is a leading corporate and commercial legal practice providing bright solutions, specialist advice and legal services to the UK and international business community.

As business demands have changed, so SJ Berwin has rapidly adapted, expanded, grown its client base and, at the same time, sought to maintain its individuality and commitment to excellence.

AREAS OF PRACTICE

SJ Berwin has established a strong reputation among the leading corporate and commercial law firms as a European deals firm and acts for clients ranging from major multinational business corporations and financial institutions to high-net-worth individuals. SJ Berwin is especially favoured by entrepreneurial business clients who find the firm particularly well attuned to their outlook and needs. The firm's clients also include foreign governments, banks and institutional clients, particularly in highly specialised practice areas.

Increasingly, the firm is focusing on industry sectors including pharmaceuticals and biotechnology, fisheries and agrochemicals, e-commerce, telecommunications and IT, retailing, sport, leisure and media, publishing, and music. Specialist cross-departmental teams have been established to address the needs of these industry sectors.

The firm offers a full range of corporate finance services including mergers and acquisitions, capital markets, private equity, management buy-outs and venture capital and securities regulation, coupled with active international banking, financial services and insolvency and reconstruction practices.

The EU and competition department is highly regarded and advises on all aspects of EU and UK competition law especially in industry sectors highly regulated at community and domestic levels. These include: pharmaceuticals, chemicals and agrochemicals, music and media; telecommunications; information technology; transport; banking and financial services, packaging and fishery law.

International trade mark, copyright and patent litigation, licensing and international trade mark registration is undertaken by a specialist intellectual property group.

Other significant areas of commercial work include media and communications, international commercial contracts, information technology and communications.

The real estate division provides a comprehensive service for UK and international public and private companies, including investors, developers, financial institutions, retailers, banks and local and health authorities. Specialist groups advise on real estate funds, property litigation, planning and environmental law and construction.

Taxation advice including the fiscal and financial structuring of international transactions and groups of companies is provided by the tax department. Estate planning and asset protection advice is given to private clients in the UK and abroad.

The firm's litigation and dispute resolution practice handles a broad range of international and domestic commercial litigation, arbitration and mediation.

The insolvency specialists deal with corporate insolvency, bankruptcy or reconstructions.

All aspects of employment law including employee benefits and pensions are handled.

SACKER & PARTNERS LLP, member of ius laboris

29 LUDGATE HILL
LONDON EC4M 7NX

Telephone: +44 20 7329 6699
Fax: +44 20 7248 0552
E-mail: enquiries@sackers.com
Website: www.sackers.com

Languages
French, German, Spanish

Number of lawyers 46

Contacts
Peter Docking (ius laboris co-ordinating partner), Joanna Matthews (partner), Paul Phillips (partner)

Member
ius laboris, International Employment Law, Pensions and Employee Benefits Alliance; IPEBLA, Association of Pension Lawyers International Committee

CATEGORIES OF WORK

Pensions	**Pensions litigation**

THE FIRM

Sacker & Partners is one of the largest specialist pensions law practices under one roof in the UK. The firm comprises 21 partners and a total complement of 46 fee-earners who specialise solely in pensions law and its related areas.

The firm is the UK pensions member of ius laboris, the highly regarded international alliance of independent law firms providing specialist services in employment, pensions and employee benefits primarily for employers.

Peter Docking co-chairs the International Pensions Group within ius laboris and Joanna Matthews is an active member of the group and chairs its External Marketing Sub-Committee. Members of the International Pensions Group work closely together and meet regularly to discuss legal developments at national and international levels.

Sacker & Partners acts for a wide variety of clients including trustee boards, independent trustees, employers, members, trade unions, life offices, firms of consulting actuaries and benefit consultants. The firm is retained by over 800 pension schemes. Over 20 of its clients are FTSE-100 companies.

Specialist units exist within the firm to deal with key areas of pensions law. These include the firm's international unit, dispute resolution, investment unit, services to other law firms unit and schemes in transition unit.

AREAS OF PRACTICE

The firm provides pro-active advice on all aspects of pension law including: pensions advice relating to the UK, including national compliance issues; setting up global pensions programs; pension provision for expatriates; pensions aspects of multinational transactions; new and forthcoming legislation; Pan-European pension funds; international investment pooling arrangements.

As a member of the ius laboris International Pensions Group of leading practitioners from each ius laboris member firm, Sacker & Partners has access to a unique pool of resources and specialist skills in other jurisdictions around the globe.

Clients can be reassured that the lawyers they are dealing with within ius laboris are all highly regarded in their own right.

Both Sacker & Partners and ius laboris are committed to adding value to their clients and provide additional services such as newsletters on the latest international developments, and organise seminars on hot topics and in-house training for clients.

SIMMONS & SIMMONS

CITYPOINT
ONE ROPEMAKER STREET
LONDON EC2Y 9SS

Telephone: +44 20 7628 2020
Fax: +44 20 7628 2070
E-mail: enquiries@simmons-simmons.com
Website: www.simmons-simmons.com

Languages
Afrikaans, Arabic, Cantonese, Czech, Dutch, English, French, German, Greek, Hindi, Hungarian, Italian, Japanese, Latvian, Mandarin, Polish, Portuguese, Russian, Slovakian, Spanish, Swedish, Vietnamese

Other offices
Abu Dhabi, Brussels, Dubai, Düsseldorf, Frankfurt, Hong Kong, Lisbon, Madeira, Madrid, Milan, New York, Oporto, Padua, Paris, Qatar, Rome, Rotterdam, Shanghai, Tokyo

Number of lawyers 764
at this office 346

CATEGORIES OF WORK

Corporate and commercial
Damon Le Maître-George

EU/competition
Martin Smith

Employment
Simon Watson

Energy, utilities and infrastructure
David Shasha

Financial institutions
Jeremy Hoyland

Financial markets, banking, capital markets, financial services, litigation and insurance, private capital
Jeremy Hoyland

IT&T and telecoms
David Barrett

Intellectual property
Richard Binns

Litigation and dispute resolution
Ian Hammond

Projects
Richard Armitage

Real estate
John Sirs

Taxation
Nick Cronkshaw

Technology and life sciences
David Barrett

THE FIRM

Simmons & Simmons is a world-class law firm providing advice to financial institutions, corporates, public and international bodies and private individuals through its international network of offices in Europe, the Middle East and Africa.

Simmons & Simmons has over 210 partners, of which 110 are based in its offices outside the UK, and a total staff worldwide of over 1,900 across 20 offices. It provides a comprehensive range of legal services with strength and depth. It applies considerable expertise to all business sectors but focuses on those key to its clients. These are financial institutions; energy, utilities and infrastructure; and technology and life sciences.

Simmons & Simmons was awarded M&A Team of the Year twice at the *Legal Business* and *The Lawyer* Awards 2004, Projects/ PFI Team of the Year at *The Lawyer* Awards 2003, and Employment Team of the Year at the *Asian Legal Business* Awards in 2003, 2004 and 2005. The pharmaceutical and biotechnology team in Paris won the Healthcare and Pharmaceutical Award at the Trophées du Droit e du Contentieus 2005 (Law and Litigation Awards). Simmons & Simmons also won at the Solicitors' Race Equality Awards 2005 as the best employer – large firms (more than 25 partners) from The Law Society and the Commission for Racial Equality.

Simmons & Simmons is ranked in Global Counsel's 2004 Top 10 world rankings for client service. This ranking is significant as it is based solely on the views of in-house counsel at over 5,000 companies from 80 jurisdictions. Simmons & Simmons is also ranked as the leading UK law firm for client service according to research conducted by *Legal Week Global Media*.

In 2005, the firm celebrated the tenth anniversary of the opening of its Shanghai office. The firm is in the process of establishing its third office in China, in Beijing. The firm opened its third office in the Gulf region, in Dubai, in 2005.

The recruitment of the very best candidates who are interested in a career at a leading international law firm is a priority for Simmons & Simmons. For further information, please see the firm's website, www.simmons-simmons.com.

AREAS OF PRACTICE

Simmons & Simmons has recently advised Telefónica on its proposed £17.7bn acquisition of O2, Azur-GMF on the €5.6bn sale of Gecina SA, Dresdner Kleinwort Wasserstein (together with the other dealers and managers) and The Bank of New York, London Branch (as note trustee) on the establishment of a €5bn covered bond programme for Sampo Housing Loan Bank plc; the £699m public-to-private acquisition of New Look Group PLC, Tata Consultancy Services on the £896m NHS IT outsourcing contract, China Telecom on the US$8.2bn acquisition of ten provincial telecommunications networks in China; on the £593m flotation of Halfords; GKN on the £1bn sale of AgustaWestland; Qatar Telecommunications on its successful mobile phone licence bid in Oman; PCCW on the HK$7.9bn acquisition of new shares by China Netcom, ADWEA on US$2bn aluminium smelter project in Oman, and British Land on £2.1bn refinancing of the Broadgate Estate.

SLAUGHTER AND MAY

ONE BUNHILL ROW
LONDON EC1Y 8YY

Telephone: +44 20 7600 1200
Fax: +44 20 7090 5000
Website: www.slaughterandmay.com

Other offices
Paris, Brussels, Hong Kong

Number of lawyers 566
at this office 484

CATEGORIES OF WORK

Mergers and acquisitions
Stephen Cooke

Corporate and commercial
Christopher Saul

Financing, financial regulation
Andrew Balfour, Ruth Fox

Capital markets
Peter Brien (equity),
Marc Hutchinson (debt)

Tax
Tony Beare

Competition
Malcolm Nicholson

IP and IT
Susie Middlemiss

Technology, media and telecoms
William Underhill

Real estate, commercial real estate
James Featherby, Graham White

Environment
Ed Keeble

Dispute resolution
Elizabeth Barrett

Pensions and employment
Eddie Codrington

Asset management
James Cripps

Corporate recovery and insolvency
Jonathan Rushworth

Energy and natural resources
Charles Randall, Steven Galbraith

Insurance
Glen James

Outsourcing, sport
Robert Sumroy

Pharmaceuticals/biotechnology
Frances Murphy, Susie Middlemiss

Private equity
Mark Horton, Jeffrey Twentyman

Projects and project finance
Christopher Saunders, Steven Galbraith

THE FIRM

Slaughter and May is a leading international law firm with a worldwide corporate, commercial and financing practice comprising 566 partners and associates. The firm provides its clients with a professional service of the highest calibre, combining technical excellence with commercial awareness and a practical, constructive approach to legal issues. The firm's lawyers are encouraged to handle a broad range of work in each of the firm's main practice areas.

International work is central to the firm's practice. Slaughter and May has a diverse and extensive international practice, advising on a wide range of corporate, commercial and financing matters for UK and international clients. The firm has close working relationships with leading independent law firms around the world, which enables it to provide clients with first-class and seamless legal advice worldwide.

AREAS OF PRACTICE

Slaughter and May provides a comprehensive range of legal services. Its main practice groups are corporate and financing (advising on mergers and acquisitions, other corporate and commercial transactions, capital markets, private equity, bank lending, acquisition and leveraged financing, derivatives, leasing and asset finance, projects, project finance, securitisation and structured finance); financial regulation; dispute resolution; technology, media and telecoms; intellectual property and information technology; commercial real estate; environment; corporate tax; competition; and pensions and employment. Rather than developing single specialisms, lawyers in the core practice areas are encouraged to adopt a multidisciplinary approach and the firm is well known for its innovative work.

SQUIRE, SANDERS & DEMPSEY

A MULTINATIONAL PARTNERSHIP OF FOREIGN LAWYERS AND SOLICITORS REGULATED BY THE LAW SOCIETY

60 CANNON STREET
LONDON EC4N 6NP

Telephone: +44 20 7189 8000
Fax: +44 20 7189 8111
E-mail: mbabin@ssd.com
Website: www.ssd.com

Languages
Croatian, English, French, German, Hungarian, Russian, Spanish

Other offices
Beijing, Bratislava, Brussels, Budapest, Caracas, Cincinnati, Cleveland, Columbus, Hong Kong, Houston, Los Angeles, Miami, Moscow, New York, Palo Alto, Phoenix, Prague, Rio de Janeiro, San Francisco, Santo Domingo, Shanghai, Tallahassee, Tampa, Tokyo, Tysons Corner, Warsaw, Washington DC, West Palm Beach, Bucharest*, Buenos Aires*, Dublin*, Kyiv*, Milan*, Santiago*

Number of lawyers 800+
at this office 16

Contact Mara Babin

Member
American Chamber of Commerce

CATEGORIES OF WORK

Banking
Stephen Nelson

Capital markets
Martin Walsh

Computer technology, multimedia services
Andrew Wilkinson

Employment
Rebecca Emmett

EU competition law
Ann LeFrance, Andrew Wilkinson

Hospitality
Daniel Larkin, Stephen Nelson

Insolvency, corporate restructurings
Stephen Nelson, Paul Lewis

Intellectual property
Andrew Wilkinson

International dispute resolution
Carol Welu

International transactions
Mark Cusick, Mara Babin

Joint ventures
Mara Babin, Paul Lewis

Mergers and acquisitions
Mara Babin, Stephen Nelson

Private equity
Mara Babin, Daniel Larkin

Privatisations
Mark Cusick

Project finance
Daniel Larkin

Real estate
Daniel Larkin

Telecoms
Ann LeFrance, Mark Cusick

THE FIRM

Founded in 1890, Squire, Sanders & Dempsey is a multi-jurisdictional law firm with approximately 800 lawyers practising in offices in Europe, the Americas and Asia. The firm's practice covers most substantive areas of the law, with an emphasis on business and finance matters.

The firm operates as a single global partnership, which ensures client accountability and the seamless delivery of uniformly high-quality legal services throughout the world. The firm's lawyers come from many countries and cultures, are licensed to practise in both common law and civil law jurisdictions, and communicate with clients in their native languages. Today, the firm remains committed to the fundamental principles ordained by its founders: to serve clients effectively and to maintain the professional standards that distinguish both the firm and its people.

AREAS OF PRACTICE

The firm is organised around four major practice areas: advocacy, business, capital markets and regulated industries. Within these practice areas, the firm's work can be divided into numerous areas of specialisation, including banking, bankruptcy and restructuring, biotechnology and pharmaceuticals, communications, competition law, converging technologies, corporate, energy, environmental, healthcare, intellectual property, international dispute resolution, labour and employment, litigation, mergers and acquisitions, privatisations, project finance, real estate, securities and taxation.

The London office advises clients on complex international and UK transactions in the communications, technology, real estate, transport, hospitality and leisure, private equity, energy and manufacturing sectors.

Opened in 1992, the London office offers a full set of services to clients investing or doing business in the UK, Europe or globally.

The London lawyers advise corporate and investment banking clients on transactional and commercial matters including cross-border international M&A, privatisations, joint ventures, project finance, real estate, securitisations, international capital markets, due diligence, management buy-outs, company restructuring, reorganisations, infrastructure, international dispute resolution and employment – often in multiple jurisdictions across the world.

An important centre of the firm's international practice, the London office serves the needs of clients with global businesses. Transactions with an international element are often centred in London and frequently require English or US law to govern key contractual relationships. Utilising experienced and sophisticated UK solicitors and US lawyers, the office is well positioned substantively and geographically to respond to the needs of the most complex and significant transactions in which globally-oriented clients engage.

The communications group provides advice on transactional and regulatory matters to cable broadband and telephony, satellite service providers, GSM and other wireless operators, data service and network companies, internet service providers, private equity investors, investment banks, government agencies and multinational development organisations.

The London office has a particular focus on IT and e-business and handles cross-border IT M&A as well as all other IT and e-business-related contracts and arrangements, systems integration, network management and project outsourcing and facilities management contracts.

The property and tourism group represents global corporate and financial groups, private equity investors and governments in a wide variety of multi-jurisdictional transactions. The group is active with joint ventures, secured financings, acquisitions, disposals, privatisations, mergers and listings, as well as acting on pure real estate transactions involving single assets, new developments and property portfolios.

The employment group counsels clients on all aspects of UK and European employment law. Areas of particular advancement include domestic and international employment contracts, company handbooks, TUPE issues, secondment arrangements, large-scale redundancy programs, stock options and pensions.

STEPTOE & JOHNSON

CLEMENTS HOUSE
14-18 GRESHAM STREET
LONDON EC2V 7JE

Telephone: +44 20 7367 8000
Fax: +44 20 7367 8001
E-mail: london@steptoe.com
Website: www.steptoe.com

Languages
French, German, Italian, Malay, Mandarin, Norwegian, Russian, Spanish, Urdu

Other offices
Brussels, Los Angeles, New York, Phoenix, Washington DC

Number of lawyers 439
at this office 31

CATEGORIES OF WORK

Commercial property
Brendan Patterson

Corporate/commercial
Michael Thompson

Employment
Alison Wallace

Insurance/reinsurance
Angus Rodger

International dispute resolution
Raymond Werbicki

International trade/EU law
Iain MacVay

Technology/telecommunications
Maury Shenk

STIBBE

EXCHANGE HOUSE
PRIMROSE STREET
LONDON EC2A 2ST

Telephone: +44 20 7466 63 00
Fax: +44 20 7466 63 11
E-mail: info@stibbe.co.uk
Website: www.stibbe.com

Languages
English, Dutch

Other offices
Amsterdam, Brussels, New York

Number of lawyers 276
at this office 6

Contact
Michael Molenaars

CATEGORIES OF WORK

Administrative law/ real estate

Banking and finance

Capital markets

Competition and regulation

Dispute resolution

Insolvency and restructuring

IP/IT communications

Employment, pensions and social security

Corporate and M&A

Notarial practice

Tax

TAYLOR WESSING

CARMELITE
50 VICTORIA EMBANKMENT
BLACKFRIARS
LONDON EC4Y 0DX

Telephone: +44 20 7300 7000
Fax: +44 20 7300 7100
E-mail: london@taylorwessing.com
Website: www.taylorwessing.com

Languages
Arabic, English, French, German, Greek, Gujarati, Hebrew, Indonesian, Italian, Malay, Portuguese, Punjabi, Spanish, Romanian, Russian

Number of lawyers 598
at this office 278

Contacts
Michael Frawley (UK managing partner), Martin Winter (senior partner)

Member
Interlex; Unilaw

CATEGORIES OF WORK

Banking and finance
Rodney Dukes

Construction and engineering
Christopher Bourgeois

Corporate
David Roberts

Corporate tax
Peter Jackson

Litigation and dispute resolution
Lawrence Cobb

Defamation
Niri Shan

Employment/pensions
Sean Nesbitt, Carolyn Saunders

Publishing
Paul Mitchell

Media and entertainment
Richard Pertwee, Tony Ghee

Insolvency
Alison Goldthorp

Infrastructure projects and PFI
Dominic FitzPatrick, Hamid Yunis

Private equity/venture capital
Martin Winter, Simon Walker

Real estate
Adam Marks

Securities
Tim Stocks

Intellectual property (patents)
Richard Price

Intellectual property (trade marks)
Charles Lloyd

Inward investment
David Kent

IT/telecoms
Glyn Morgan, Ted Mercer

Leisure
David Roberts, Richard Bursby

Life sciences/biotechnology
Mark Hodgson

THE FIRM

Taylor Wessing is a powerful source of legal support for organisations doing business in or with Europe and is based primarily in the UK, Germany, France and Belgium, with further offices in Dubai, Shanghai and Alicante. A market leader in advising IP and technology-rich industries, Taylor Wessing boasts a strong reputation in the corporate, finance and real estate sectors alongside in-depth experience across the full range of legal services including tax, commercial disputes and employment.

Taylor Wessing has offices in Berlin, Brussels, Cambridge, Düsseldorf, Frankfurt, Hamburg, London, Munich and Paris, alongside representative offices in Alicante and Shanghai and an associated office in Dubai.

AREAS OF PRACTICE

Taylor Wessing offers a comprehensive list of legal services. Client matters are dealt with by specialist practice groups, which bring together expertise from a number of disciplines to speed response, explore opportunities, and reduce time and expense.

The firm operates through seven core areas, including:

Corporate/commercial, which places particular emphasis on corporate finance, M&A, environmental law, EC/EU law and corporate tax.

Intellectual property, one of the largest practices in Europe, where its highly regarded team includes specialists in entertainment, media, life sciences, telecoms, e-commerce, sports and information technology.

Finance and projects, which has particular expertise in project finance (advising leading sponsors and finance providers on project and structured finance in a wide range of sectors), energy, PFI, property finance, banking, capital markets and derivatives, and bank lending.

Commercial litigation, with specialist groups advising on fraud, construction and engineering, professional negligence, shipping, banking and corporate recoveries, advising clearing, merchant and foreign banks.

Employment and pensions, dealing with related contracts and disputes, pensions and employee benefits.

Real estate, including development and finance, incorporating specialist planning, property management and environmental teams.

Private client, providing advice on taxation, wills and settlements (including trusts and estates), matrimonial law and residential property.

TROWERS & HAMLINS

SCEPTRE COURT
40 TOWER HILL
LONDON EC3N 4DX

Telephone: +44 20 7423 8000
Fax: +44 20 7423 8001
E-mail: enquiries@trowers.com
Website: www.trowers.com

Languages
Arabic, French, German, Italian, Russian

Other offices
Abu Dhabi, Bahrain, Cairo, Dubai, Exeter, Manchester, Muscat

Number of lawyers 246
at this office 177

CATEGORIES OF WORK

Aviation
Roger Clarke, Andrew Rae

Banking and finance
Andrew Rae, Neale Downes

Capital markets
Sean Angle, Adrian Jones

Commercial agencies and distribution
Jennifer Bibbings, Nick White

Commercial law
Sara Hinton, Adrian Jones

Islamic finance
Sarah Gooden, Neale Downes

IT law
Adrian Creed, Majid Al Toky

Litigation, arbitration
Nigel Truscott, James Harbridge

Oil, gas and petrochemicals
Edward Rose, Martin Amison

Power and water
Adrian Creed, Leroy Levy

Private equity
Dominic O'Neil

Privatisation
Martin Amison, Leroy Levy

Project finance
Andrew Rae, Leroy Levy

Public international
John McHugo

Tax
Nicholas Edmondes

Trade marks
Majid Al Toky

Telecoms
Abdullah Mutowi, Majid Al Toky

Construction
Martin Amison, Nigel Truscott

THE FIRM

Trowers & Hamlins is an international law firm with its head office in the City of London and offices in the UK and overseas. Over the last 45 years it has developed a substantial international practice, with five offices in the Middle East, in Abu Dhabi, Bahrain, Cairo, Dubai and Oman (all of which provide advice on local law), as well as an extensive network of correspondent relationships with respected local counsel in most states of the MENA region. The firm has been working in the Middle East region since 1959 and currently has 60 lawyers (including 18 partners) working in its dedicated Middle East team. It has contacts in the USA and Europe and works with Ledingham Chalmers in Azerbaijan and Istanbul. The firm's head office in London acts as the nucleus for the network of international offices and for the international projects, public international and private finance practices.

AREAS OF PRACTICE

Trowers & Hamlins has been involved in a number of high-profile projects. Work handled includes a significant number of major projects, banking and finance (including Islamic finance), capital markets and commercial transactions. The firm has a substantial telecoms practice in the region. In Oman the firm has been heavily involved in the establishment and roll-out of new operator Nawras. The firm advised Etihad Etisalat, the mobile telecoms company on the world's largest ever Islamic financing: a US$1.6bn Murabaha financing to fund the winning US$3.5bn bid for Saudi Arabia's new GSM and 3G mobile telecoms licenses. The financing was completed in October 2004. Trowers & Hamlins is also advising the Bahrain government on the privatisation of its ports and has substantially advised new Abu Dhabi airline Etihad Airways throughout its establishment phase.

The firm advised the government of Jordan on its master plan for energy and on a large-scale cross-border gas pipeline project. It continues to lead in the Middle East region in its participation in independent power and water projects; recently advising the developer of the Shuaibah IWPP the first of the Saudi Goevernment's programme of IWPP projects. The firm adds this first deal in Saudi Arabia to its firsts in Abu Dhabi (Taweelah A2) and Oman (Manah); the firm acting for the developer in each instance. In Abu Dhabi the firm also acted as sole external counsel to the developers of Umm Al Nar and the Shuweihat S1 IWPP (CMS Energy of the US and International Power of the UK). In Oman, the firm advised on IPP/IWPPs at Manah (two phases), Barka, Al Kamil and Salalah. Now also advising in the ports sector in Abu Dhabi and Bahrain, the firm advised Salalah Port Services Company SAOG (SPS) on the original concession agreement and related project financing for the development of a strategic container transhipment terminal in the south of Oman. The initial private sector operated and financed project has been enhanced by a further 30-year concession agreement for the operation and management of the port's conventional cargo facilities. The firm is currently advising SPS on a major expansion which will more than double the size of the port. Trowers & Hamlins acted as lead counsel (international and local) for Borealis A/S in all aspects of the development, financing and current expansion of the Abu Dhabi Polymers Company (Borouge), a global-scale petrochemicals joint venture with ADNOC valued in excess of US$1.5bn. The firm has acted for the lenders on the US$1bn Oman India Fertiliser Plant (OMIFCO) and on a considerable number of aircraft financings for regional carriers. Trowers & Hamlins also advises two of the region's central banks and has considerable work for investment funds and institutions employing both Islamic and conventional finance. During 2005 the firm has advised a number of developers of high-profile real estate projects in the leisure and financial services sectors. These developers include both investors from conventional groups and Islamic institutions investing in accordance with Shari'ah principles. The firm has considerably increased its business in the Middle East during 2005 and has expanded its complement of lawyers within the international department to 60.

THOMMESSEN KREFTING GREVE LUND

42 NEW BROAD STREET
LONDON EC2M 1JD

Telephone: +44 20 7920 3000
Fax: +44 20 7920 3099
E-mail: hma@thommessen.no
Website: www.thommessen.no

Languages
English, French, German, the Scandinavian languages

Other offices
Bergen, Brussels, Hong Kong, Oslo, Paris, Moscow

Number of lawyers 129
at this office 1

Contact
Halvor Mansaker (resident partner)

Member
Lex Mundi; The Scandinavian Law Alliance

CATEGORIES OF WORK

General corporate law	Banking and finance
Private equity	Securities offering
M&A	Shipping

VINSON & ELKINS RLLP

CITY POINT 33RD FLOOR
ONE ROPEMAKER STREET
LONDON EC2Y 9UE

Telephone: +44 20 7065 6000
Fax: +44 20 7065 6001
Website: www.velaw.com

Languages
French, German, Spanish

Other offices
Austin, Beijing, Dallas, Dubai, Houston, Moscow, New York, Shanghai, Tokyo, Washington DC

Number of lawyers 781
At this office 21

Member
International Bar Association; International Law Section of the American Bar Association; International Lawyers Group, Moscow; Law Society of England and Wales; The Bar of England and Wales; The State Bar of Texas International Law Section

CATEGORIES OF WORK

Asset finance/securitisation	Energy and natural resources
Banking and finance	Infrastructure/project finance
Capital markets	Labour law
Construction	Mergers and acquisitions
Corporate and commercial	Privatisation
Dispute resolution	Telecommunications

ADVOKATFIRMAN VINGE

42 NEW BROAD STREET
LONDON EC2M 1JD

Telephone: +44 20 7920 3000
Fax: +44 20 7920 3099
Website: www.vinge.se

Languages
Spanish, Swedish

Other Offices
Brussels, Gothenburg, Helsingborg, Hong Kong, Malmö, Paris, Shanghai, Stockholm

Number of lawyers 300
at this office 3

Contact
Maria-Pia Midenbäck-Hope

Member
Scandinavian Law Alliance with Kromann & Reumert (Denmark) and Thommessen (Norway); Lex Mundi

CATEGORIES OF WORK

Banking and finance	**Litigation and arbitration**
Bankruptcy and liquidation	**M&A**
China practice	**Marketing**
Corporate finance, capital markets	**Media**
Employment and benefits	**Private equity funds**
EU and antitrust	**Public procurement**
Financial services and regulations	**Real estate and environmental**
General corporate	**Tax**
Insurance	**Telecommunications**
Intellectual property	**Transport**
IT	

THE FIRM

With some 300 fee-earners, Vinge is one of the largest law firms in Scandinavia. The firm is a member of the Scandinavian Law Alliance together with Kromann Reumert in Denmark and Thommessen in Norway.

Vinge has offices in Stockholm, Gothenburg, Malmö and Helsingborg as well as in London, Paris, Brussels, Hong Kong and Shanghai. The firm's clients include domestic and international commercial enterprises, financial institutions and state and regulatory bodies. Vinge is committed to providing the highest quality legal advice and experience for all matters in which the firm becomes involved, to the highest professional standards.

Innovation, creativeness and a business-orientated, problem-solving approach are at the core of the practice. The firm's size means that there are resources available to handle large and complex domestic and cross-border transactions within tight time frames. At the same time, there is a strong focus on responsiveness and personal commitments to clients. Vinge's motto is: A good commercial lawyer sees beyond the law.

AREAS OF PRACTICE

Vinge specialises in all aspects of commercial law and is consistently ranked amongst the leading law firms in Scandinavia in a number of key practice areas. Vinge's extensive network of contacts comprises independent law firms, consultants and investment banks with whom the firm works regularly on domestic and cross-border deals and projects.

The firm takes an overall approach as well as providing in-depth knowledge by working together with major foreign law firms. Vinge has developed a wide international network which is available to its clients. The firm's broad experience and expertise means that it is called upon to handle all kinds of commercial law issues. It has learned from experience what resources and services are required in order to find the right solutions to clients' problems.

Vinge does everything it can to help clients to achieve success in their business. The firm sees beyond the problems and seeks the solutions.

WEIL, GOTSHAL & MANGES

ONE SOUTH PLACE
LONDON EC2M 2WG

Telephone: + 44 20 7903 1000
Fax: + 44 20 7903 0990
E-mail: weil.london@weil.com
Website: www.weil.com

Other offices
Austin, Boston, Brussels, Budapest, Dallas, Frankfurt, Houston, Miami, Munich, New York, Paris, Prague, Providence, Shanghai, Silicon Valley, Singapore, Warsaw, Washington DC, Wilmington

Number of lawyers 1,200
at this office 130

Contact
Mike Francies (managing partner)

CATEGORIES OF WORK

Acquisition finance	**Litigation, arbitration**
Banking	**Private equity**
Competition	**Property**
Consumer finance	**Restructuring**
Corporate finance and M&A	**Securitisation**
Debt and equity capital markets	**Taxation**
IP, technology and communications	

THE FIRM

Weil, Gotshal & Manges is a leader in the marketplace for sophisticated, international legal services. With more than 1,200 lawyers across the US, Europe and Asia, the firm serves many of the most successful companies in the world in their high-stakes matters and transactions. Weil Gotshal has built a world-class team of lawyers by pursuing a strategy of steady, purposeful growth. It continues to build upon a balanced platform of practices and locations without acquiring any debt. The firm's three primary departments – corporate, litigation/regulatory and restructuring – provide healthy diversification in all economic cycles, while its international expansion over the past decade has resulted in a quarter of the firm's lawyers now being in Europe.

AREAS OF PRACTICE

The firm's antitrust/competition practice advises on international M&A regulatory notifications, antitrust distribution counselling, cartels, litigation and government and state competition policy.

The corporate department is the firm's largest, with lawyers in the US and across Europe. The department advises international financial institutions and corporate clients in complex public and private mergers and acquisitions, private equity deals, strategic alliances and other commercial transactions.

The firm's corporate governance practice is recognised as the pre-eminent counsellor of corporate boards, management and institutional investors on the full range of governance issues, including board composition, structure and processes; executive and director compensation; director responsibilities, including in connection with mergers, spin-offs and other extraordinary transactions; internal and governmental investigations of alleged accounting or other corporate misconduct; and shareholder initiatives.

The firm is recognised as a market leader in the handling of complex and innovative finance transactions internationally. The firm advises on a wide range of financing activities and has particular expertise in acquisition finance, asset-based finance, debt restructuring and insolvency, debt and equity capital markets, derivatives, high yield debt, securitisation, structured finance and telecom and multimedia financing.

The firm has a leading intellectual property and technology practice and advises a number of the world's major technology, media and telecommunications companies. It also acts for investors in technology, media and communications entities. The practice handles patent infringement, outsourcing transactions, strategic alliances, cross-border mergers and acquisitions, investments and IPOs. The firm advises on the protection and exploitation of IP and on a wide range of e-commerce matters including data protection. It has expertise in regulatory telecoms matters.

The firm's litigation practice advises international clients on all major areas of the law and has extensive experience in all aspects of dispute resolution. It advises clients in jury trials and appeals, as well as arbitration and alternative dispute forums.

The firm's real estate practice handles complex real estate transactions (including finance, securitisations, development, leasing, sales, acquisitions and debt restructurings) across the US and Europe. It also advises clients on real estate M&A transactions and transactions involving real estate investment trusts.

The firm has one of the largest, most broadly based bankruptcy and business reorganisation practices in the world. The department has been involved in virtually all major chapter 11 reorganisation cases in the US and in major national and international out of court debt restructurings.

The tax department provides advice to a broad range of international clients, covering many economic sectors. The department works closely with the firm's other departments to find innovative solutions to problems that present various and competing multidisciplinary considerations.

WHITE & CASE

5 OLD BROAD STREET
LONDON EC2N 1DW

Telephone: + 44 20 7532 1000
Fax: +44 20 7532 1001
Website: www.whitecase.com

Languages
Extensive language capabilities

Other offices
Almaty, Ankara, Bangkok, Beijing, Berlin, Bratislava, Brussels, Budapest, Dresden, Düsseldorf, Frankfurt, Hamburg, Helsinki, Ho Chi Minh City, Hong Kong, Istanbul, Johannesburg, Los Angeles, Mexico City, Miami, Milan, Moscow, Mumbai, Munich, New York, Palo Alto, Paris, Prague, Riyadh, San Francisco, São Paulo, Shanghai, Singapore, Stockholm, Tokyo, Warsaw, Washington DC

Number of lawyers 1,976
at this office 213

CATEGORIES OF WORK

Arbitration
J Bellhouse, S Bond (Paris)

Asset financing and leasing
J Benson, T McDonald (Paris)

Bank finance
Maurice Allen, Gilles Peigney (Paris)

Bankruptcy and workouts
D Hamilton, K Pannen (Hamburg)

Capital markets
J Kiernan, P Haussila (Helsinki)

Commercial litigation
A Graham, E Rosenfield (Paris)

Construction
E Baker, C Seppala (Paris)

Corporate, M&A
P Finlay, A Stilcken (Frankfurt)

Energy, infrastructure and project finance
P Stopford, P Biensan (Paris)

Employment
O Brettle, S Odeurs (Brussels)

EU and competition
P Lindfelt (Brussels), J MacLennan (Brussels)

IP
D Llewelyn, C Rohnke (Hamburg)

Private equity
A Greenough, F Leloup (Paris)

Privatisation
J Matejcek (Prague), D Eisenberg

Real estate
L Ufland, E Lettau (Berlin)

Structured finance
D Barwise, U Kreppel(Frankfurt)

Tax
N Woodgate, J Große Honebrink (Frankfurt)

Telecoms and technology
D Eisenberg, R Olofsson (Brussels)

THE FIRM

To be of use to its clients a law firm must be able to readily co-ordinate efforts and share knowledge across multiple jurisdictions. White & Case is not an affiliation of individual units; it is a single unified partnership working across offices with a consistency of quality, philosophy and ethical standards. Located in the world's major financial centres and key emerging markets, the firm's global team of almost 2,000 lawyers is adept at working within myriad legal systems, distinguishing subtle, cultural nuances and identifying local concerns while simultaneously managing larger multi-jurisdictional issues. As a result the firm is able to detect and address the countless factors, both common and unusual, that make or break deals, or win or lose cases.

AREAS OF PRACTICE

Antitrust: the firm has successfully defended mergers before the US Department of Justice, the Federal Trade Commission and the European Commission, as well as various regulatory bodies across Asia.

Arbitration: the firm has long-standing experience of arbitrations worldwide (including, in particular, ICC arbitrations), and has successfully concluded disputes in most arbitration forums around the globe.

Asset financing and leasing: White & Case has one of the strongest global asset finance practices of any law firm, with highly regarded teams across Europe, the Americas and Asia.

Bank finance: the firm is acknowledged as a world leader in the field of bank finance, with a unique US, English, European and Asian legal capability.

Bankruptcy and workouts: the firm has wide experience in multinational insolvencies and a strong practice in restructurings.

Capital markets: White & Case has a formidable reputation in the field on international securities and finance.

Commercial litigation: most of the firm's 38 offices offer leading commercial litigators who excel at both local and cross-border work.

Construction: White & Case has an international practice advising on all aspects of engineering, procurement and construction projects including the resolution of construction-related disputes.

Employment: the firm has an experienced employment practice group with particular expertise in employee benefits law.

Energy, infrastructure and project finance: the firm is recognised as one of the world's leading providers of project finance, energy and infrastructure law advice in all the major jurisdictions.

EU and competition: the firm's EU law team is renowned for its expert handling of matters before the European Commission involving the full range of industry sectors.

IP: White & Case acts to protect the IP rights of its clients through the work of its IP law teams across the globe.

Corporate, M&A: the firm has taken the lead in devising creative deal structures and acquisition programmes in the full range of domestic and cross-border transactions.

Privatisation: the global privatisation practice group has acted for governments, state-owned enterprises, multilateral institutions, international banks and investors.

Real estate: the firm advises on the assemblage, acquisition, development, ownership, operation and financing of all types of real estate assets.

Securitisation and structured finance: the firm continues to be a market leader in CDOs and is building a strong reputation in the securitisation market place.

Sovereign: White & Case has represented an extremely large number of countries in sovereign-related projects.

Tax: the firm acts on a wide range of corporate and financial transactions, develops tax-advantaged financial products and helps multinational clients achieve worldwide tax efficiency.

Telecoms and technology: the firm offers a full service to clients in the e-commerce, media and technology sectors.

WIKBORG REIN

ONE KNIGHTRIDER COURT
LONDON EC4V 5JP

Telephone: +44 20 7236 4598
Fax: +44 20 7236 4599
E-mail: london@wr.no
Website: www.wr.no

Languages
English, the Scandinavian languages

Other offices
Bergen, Kobe, Oslo, Shanghai, Singapore

Number of lawyers 158
at this office 6

Contacts
Morten Lund Mathisen, Stephen N Lamb, Lars Gunnar Aas

CATEGORIES OF WORK

Shipping/offshore (maritime law, transport, maritime insurance, ship financing, banking)

Trade and industry (labour legislation, contract manufacturing, competition law, EU/EEA law)

Natural resources (energy and petroleum law)

Corporate (company law, M&A, accounting, tax, duties)

WILLKIE FARR & GALLAGHER LLP

1 ANGEL COURT
LONDON EC2R 7HJ

Telephone: +44 20 7696 5454
Fax: +44 20 7696 5455
Website: www.willkie.com

Other offices
Brussels, Frankfurt, Milan, New York, Paris, Rome, Washington DC

Number of lawyers 590
at this office 3

Contact
Gregory Astrachan

CATEGORIES OF WORK

Corporate and financial services
Gregory Astrachan

WILMER CUTLER PICKERING HALE AND DORR LLP

ALDER CASTLE
NOBLE STREET
LONDON EC2V 7QJ

Telephone: +44 20 7645 2400
Fax: +44 20 7645 2424
Website: www.wilmerhale.com

Languages
Afrikaans, Czech, Farsi, French, German, Hindi Italian, Russian, Sindhi, Spanish, Swedish

Other offices
Baltimore, Beijing, Berlin, Boston, Brussels, Munich, New York, Northern Virginia, Oxford, Palo Alto, Waltham, Washington DC

Number of lawyers 1,100
at this office 60

CATEGORIES OF WORK

Aviation
Michael Holter, Dieter Lange

Competition, merger control and EU law
Suyong Kim

Communications
Michael Holter, Paul von Hehn

Corporate transactions
Richard Eaton

Employee share plans
Christopher Prout

Labour and employment
Henry Clinton-Davis

Financial services and investment funds
David Gent, James Greig

Intellectual property
Mark Haftke

International arbitration and litigation
Gary Born, Robert Barry

Private equity and venture capital
Chris Grew, Struan Penwarden

Tax
Simon Court

THE FIRM

WilmerHale offers unparalleled legal representation across a comprehensive range of practice areas that are critical to the success of its clients. The firm has over 1,000 lawyers operating in five countries and practices at the very top of the legal profession. The depth and scope of the practice give it the ability to anticipate obstacles, seize opportunities and get the case resolved or the deal done – and the experience and know-how to prevent it from being undone.

Over 70 lawyers are based in the UK in London and Oxford. The London office was established more than 30 years ago and offers an extensive range of legal services to private and public companies at all stages of the growth cycle. The firm combines comprehensive local knowledge with first class cross-border and multi-jurisdictional capabilities.

The London practice (also located at 4 Carlton Gardens, London SW1Y 5AA, tel +44 20 7872 1000, fax +44 20 7839 3537) comprises 60 lawyers who offer advice in antitrust and competition, aviation, corporate, corporate tax, financial services, intellectual property (IP), patent litigation, international arbitration and labour and employment law. The Oxford office has considerable experience in M&A and venture capital transactions, as well as advising university spin-out companies, both during and beyond the spin-out process. The office also handles international transactions for non-UK clients operating in Europe and for UK clients developing their businesses outside the UK.

AREAS OF PRACTICE

The London office has one of the world's leading arbitration and dispute resolution practices. Experience includes international civil litigation, ADR and complex matters in technical fields, (eg construction, energy, financial services, communications). The group has specialised IP litigators.

The corporate group is a premier provider of legal services to UK and European technology companies and venture capital firms, representing clients throughout their financing lifecycle. It has wide experience of international corporate and commercial transactions, including M&A, equity and debt financing and franchise and distribution arrangements.

The competition group advises clients from a range of industries on UK and EU competition law, including merger control, joint ventures and other commercial arrangements, cartels and abuse of market power inquiries.

The IP group focuses on a broad range of work across three main sectors: pharma/biotech licensing, university spin-outs and IT.

The communications practice focuses on commercial, corporate and regulatory matters, both contentious and non-contentious, with a particular strength in international competition issues. Clients include companies from the fixed, mobile and broadband sectors.

The labour and employment team offers a full range of employment and business immigration services. The UK-qualified employment lawyers have been trained in US and German law and have particular experience in advising US clients on their operations in the EU and further afield.

The aviation team offers a full range of experience, including transactional services, competition law and regulatory and aeropolitical issues. It acts for airlines, airports, governments and international agencies.

The financial services team advises investment businesses on all aspects of regulation by the Financial Services Authority and on EU financial services legislation. Work is carried out for retail and wholesale banks, asset managers, securities and derivatives broker dealers, commodity traders, private equity advisers and corporate financiers.

The tax team advises clients on the tax implications of international and domestic business transactions, M&A, corporate reorganisations, corporate finance and venture capital. The practice also includes taxation of IP licensing, e-commerce and fund formations.

The firm also advises public and private companies on a wide variety of employee incentive arrangements, ranging from advising multinational corporations to UK-based venture-backed companies.

WINSTON & STRAWN LLP

BUCKLESBURY HOUSE
3 QUEEN VICTORIA STREET
LONDON EC4N 8NH

Telephone: +44 20 7429 0000
Fax: +44 20 7429 0100
E-mail: info@winston.com
Website: www.winston.com

Languages
English, French, German, Greek

Other offices
Chicago, Geneva, Los Angeles, Moscow, New York, Paris, San Francisco, Washington DC

Number of lawyers 850
at this office 18

Contact
Tom Benz

CATEGORIES OF WORK

Corporate UK and cross-border M&A and transactional

International capital markets: debt and equity

Bank lending

Private equity

Employment

UK and cross-border dispute resolution

WILMER CUTLER PICKERING HALE AND DORR LLP

PARK GATE
25 MILTON PARK
OXFORD OX14 4SH

Telephone: +44 1235 823000
Fax: +44 1235 823030
Website: www.wilmerhale.com

Languages
Afrikaans, Czech, Farsi, French, German, Hindi Italian, Russian, Sindhi, Spanish, Swedish

Other offices
Baltimore, Beijing, Berlin, Boston, Brussels, London, Munich, New York, Northern Virginia, Palo Alto, Waltham, Washington DC

Number of lawyers 1,100
at this office 11

CATEGORIES OF WORK

Corporate transactions
Joe Pillman, Kate Eavis

Employee share plans
Christopher Prout

Employment
David Andrews

Intellectual property
Emily Beswick

Private equity and venture capital
Kate Eavis, Jonathan Loake

Tax
Simon Court

THE FIRM

WilmerHale offers unparalleled legal representation across a comprehensive range of practice areas that are critical to the success of its clients. The firm has over 1,000 lawyers operating in five countries and practices at the very top of the legal profession. The depth and scope of the practice give it the ability to anticipate obstacles, seize opportunities and get the case resolved or the deal done – and the experience and know-how to prevent it from being undone.

Over 70 lawyers are based in the UK offices in London and Oxford. The London office was established more than 30 years ago and offers an extensive range of legal services to private and public companies at all stages of the growth cycle. The firm's approach is to combine comprehensive and detailed local knowledge with first class cross-border and multi-jurisdictional capabilities.

The London practice (also located at 4 Carlton Gardens, London SW1Y 5AA, tel +44 20 7872 1000, fax +44 20 7839 3537) comprises 60 lawyers who offer advice in antitrust and competition, aviation, corporate, corporate tax, financial services, intellectual property, patent litigation, international arbitration and labour and employment law.

The Oxford office opened in 2000 to serve the technology and life sciences community in Oxford and the Thames Valley area which is recognised as one of the UK's leading centres for technology and life sciences. With 11 lawyers based in Oxford, this office has experience in M&A and venture capital transactions, as well as advising university spin-out companies, both during and beyond the spin-out process. The office also handles international transactions for non-UK clients operating in Europe and for UK clients developing their businesses outside the UK.

AREAS OF PRACTICE

The corporate group is a premier provider of legal services to UK and European technology companies and venture capital firms, representing clients throughout their financing lifecycle, from seed stage to initial public offering. The group has deep experience in international corporate and commercial transactions, including M&A, equity and debt financing and franchise and distribution arrangements.

The labour and employment team offers a full range of employment and business immigration services. The UK-qualified employment lawyers have been trained in both US and German law and have particular experience in advising US clients regarding their operations throughout the EU and further afield. Members of the UK team are working out of both the Oxford office and the London office. Working across offices on matters is positively encouraged by the firm. All team members frequently work out of the Oxford office and on matters for clients who are based in the Thames Valley. The strength of the Thames Valley practice is the large volume of work undertaken for clients based there and in the South East.

The intellectual property practice combines the legal and technical skills often associated with boutique IP firms with the capabilities of a general practice firm. The group focuses on a broad range of work across three main sectors and across jurisdictional borders: pharma/biotech licensing (both within the UK and globally); university spin-outs; and IT. Worldwide, more than 120 of the firm's lawyers and technology specialists hold degrees in technological and scientific disciplines.

The firm's tax team advises clients on the tax implications of domestic and international business transactions, M&A, corporate reorganisations, corporate finance and venture capital. The practice also includes taxation of IP licensing, e-commerce and fund formations.

The firm also advises public and private UK, European and US companies in connection with a wide variety of employee incentive arrangements, ranging from advising large multinational publicly-traded corporations in relation to option and restricted stock arrangements in Europe and the Far East to establishing enterprise management incentive option schemes for UK-based venture backed companies.

UNITED KINGDOM: NORTHERN IRELAND

Population	1.7 million
Number of lawyers	2,420 (1,850 solicitors, 570 barristers)
Professional title	Barrister; solicitor
Currency	Pound sterling (£))

Index

Northern Ireland is part of the United Kingdom and consists of six counties: Tyrone and Fermanagh in the west, Down and Armagh in the southeast, and Londonderry and Antrim in the north. The most densely populated area of the Province is that surrounding its capital, Belfast.

ECONOMY

In 1921 the North was partitioned from the rest of Ireland. Fifty years of Unionist rule followed, ending in 1972 when the British government imposed direct rule from London. The bloody conflict from the late 1960s to the mid-1990s, known as the 'Troubles', is well documented. The 1998 Good Friday Agreement, which led to a new Assembly and devolved powers, brought optimism and renewed hopes of peace to the Province. The road to peace has been protracted and difficult, however. The Northern Ireland Assembly has been suspended since 2002, after allegations of IRA information-gathering, and so far the DUP and Sinn Fein have been unable to reach a deal which would make a power-sharing executive a reality. A major breakthrough occurred in summer 2005 when the IRA announced an end to its armed campaign. All eyes are now on Ulster.

Peace has helped to stabilise the economy. After decades in the doldrums following the decline of traditional industries such as shipbuilding, prospects are brighter. The Province is strong in manufacturing, textiles and construction. New industries are coming to the fore: biotech, pharma, hospitality and retail. Tourism is up, and unemployment levels are at an all time low. The government is one of the largest employers, as jobs linked either directly or indirectly to public sector account for a considerable number of employees.

BILLING

The predominant billing structure is still the hourly rate, which varies widely between firms. The top rate for a partner is around £220 per hour. Tenders are becoming increasingly common, as are fixed fees and capped fees.

MARKETING

Due to the size of the jurisdiction personal recommendations count for more than a targeted marketing strategy. Beauty parades are becoming more common. Most firms produce brochures and have websites.

IN-HOUSE LAWYERS

Most in-house lawyers in Northern Ireland work in the public sector; but they are not a particular feature of the Northern Irish legal market.

LEGAL SYSTEM

Northern Ireland is a separate legal jurisdiction from the UK with its own legislation. Much of this is based on that in England and Wales, although there are differences in the property, environment, planning, probate and employment sectors. There has been no radical overhaul of the legal system akin to the Woolf reforms in the UK, although the prospect is one under discussion.

LEGAL MARKET

Most law firms in the Province consist of sole practitioners. Of the larger firms, some have formed alliances with Dublin firms to work on 'all island' projects. **L'Estrange & Brett** has had links with one of the top five firms in the Republic **McCann FitzGerald** since 1999, called the *North South Legal Alliance*. **Tughans** has teamed up with **William Fry**, while **Cleaver Fulton Rankin** and **Matheson Ormsby Prentice** together form the *All Island Law Alliance*. **Arthur Cox** is the only Irish firm to have a presence up and down the country, with **Arthur Cox Northern Ireland** in the North, which has integrated office systems with its Dublin counterpart. **Arthur Cox Northern Ireland** also has a formal preferred partnership arrangement with **Pinsent Masons**, which exited the Republic in 2004. **C & H Jefferson** is 'best friends' with mid-sized firm **Eugene F. Collins**, while **Carson McDowell** and **Mason Hayes+Curran** are allies in the *i-law alliance*. **A&L Goodbody** has a presence in PPP work in the Province, running the work from its Dublin office.

City firm **Travers Smith** has a Northern Ireland-qualified commercial property team, which regularly jets in from London, while **Berwin Leighton Paisner LLP** is also active on large-scale construction projects. Regional firm **Dickinson Dees** also has an itinerant presence in the Province. Niche insurance practice **Kennedys** has a Belfast office, while personal injury specialist

The largest firms

1	L'Estrange & Brett	44
2	Tughans	42
3	Carson McDowell	34
4	Cleaver Fulton Rankin	30
5	Arthur Cox Northern Ireland	27
6	C & H Jefferson	26
	Elliott Duffy Garrett	26
8	Mills Selig	18
9	John McKee & Son	15
	McKinty and Wright	15
11	Diamond Heron	13
	Wilson Nesbitt	13
13	Babington & Croasdaile	12
	McCartan Turkington Breen	12
	O'Reilly Stewart Solicitors	12
16	Hewitt & Gilpin	11
17	Johns Elliot	10
18	Kearney Sefton	8
19	Bigger & Strahan	7
	Francis Hanna & Co	7
	McGrigors Belfast	7
	Napier and Sons	7
	Thompsons McClure	7
24	Comerton Hill	6
25	Kennedys	5

These figures represent the total number of lawyers in this country only, and have been supplied by the firms themselves. The figures should be accurate as at 1 January 2006.

Thompsons is represented in the Province by **Thompsons McClure**. Scottish firm **McGrigors Belfast** has had a Belfast presence since 2000, which concentrates chiefly on PPP work, combined with growing corporate and commercial capability.

BANKING AND FINANCE

'Most-respected adversary' Angus Creed heads the banking and finance department at **Arthur Cox Northern Ireland**, which had a busy 2005. The firm acted for a syndicate of banks led by Bank of America on the refinancing of a group of US companies through substantial Northern Irish subsidiaries, involving facilities of US$350m. The team also acted for Ulster Bank, arranging facilities of £59m granted to a major Northern Irish group of companies.

Lex Ross and Avril McCammon are 'astute and adept' banking practitioners at **John McKee & Son**, winning praise from clients and peers alike. The team's reputation continues to grow, as the firm has seen an increase in instructions over the past year, in particular arranging secured lending for Northern Ireland's main clearing banks. The team also advises on the financing of PFI/PPP projects.

L'Estrange & Brett has a superb reputation for high-quality banking work. Brian Henderson heads the firm's banking unit, which acts on the full spectrum of banking and secured lending work, including acting for both originators and funders on securitisation programmes involving Northern Irish assets. Highlights for 2005 include acting for SHS Group in negotiating the debt-funding package for its takeover of Merrydown Plc, a listed English company. As well as Brian Henderson, Richard Gray and Adrian Eakin 'pack a punch'.

C & H Jefferson has a strong corporate finance and banking practice, which acts for top-drawer clients such as Ulster Bank, Bank of Ireland and First Trust Bank.

Carson McDowell maintains its reputation for fielding a solid banking and finance practice, which also acts for the main financial players in the Northern Irish market, including Bank of Ireland, Ulster Bank and First Trust Bank. Thomas Adair has an excellent reputation.

Stephen Cross is viewed as a banking aficionado at **Cleaver Fulton Rankin**. The banking team has mature expertise in banking and finance, advising on securisations, refinancings and the funding of energy projects.

Elliott Duffy Garrett has considerable expertise in corporate lending, as well as a good all-round practice. Kevin McVeigh is a highly regarded practitioner.

The banking and finance team at **Tughans** regularly advises on secured and unsecured lending for household-name financial institutions. John Mills is the best-known personality for banking and finance at the firm.

BANKING AND FINANCE

ARTHUR COX NORTHERN IRELAND ✪
JOHN McKEE & SON ✪
L'ESTRANGE & BRETT ✪

C & H Jefferson
Carson McDowell
Cleaver Fulton Rankin ✪
Elliott Duffy Garrett
Tughans

Babington & Croasdaile
Johns Elliot
McGrigors Belfast
McKinty and Wright
Mills Selig

McManus Kearney

Firms are listed A-Z in tiers which are ranked in order of priority
✪ Indicates firm displays contact details at the end of this chapter.

In 2005 **McManus Kearney** recruited former **Norton Rose** practitioner Andrew McCluggage from the banking team at **Tughans** to build up its banking and finance team. One to watch.

CORPORATE AND M&A

Key practitioners in **Carson McDowell**'s corporate practice are Michael Johnston and David Jamison. The firm has an excellent reputation in the Northern Irish market, and regularly scoops referral work from City firms. Clients find the team 'responsive and attentive to client needs'. A broad mix of work includes both high-level domestic M&A and the Northern Irish elements of large international transactions.

L'Estrange & Brett fields an array of skilled practitioners in M&A, including Paul McBride, Richard Gray and Adrian Eakin. In 2005 the firm advised Danske Bank on all the Northern Irish aspects of the acquisition of Northern Bank from NAB, a landmark transaction in terms of size in the Northern Irish market. The team also advised SHS Group Ltd in the funding and corporate aspects of the recommended acquisition by SHS of listed company Merrydown Group Plc, by means of a scheme of arrangement.

The corporate group at **Arthur Cox Northern Ireland** dealt with a high turnover of M&A and other corporate transactional work in 2005. The 'superlative' Kerry Canavan heads the practice. Highlights include advising Diageo on the Northern Ireland aspects of its £100m acquisition of The Old Bushmills Distillery Company Ltd, and acting for Northern Ireland Energy Holdings Ltd on its merger with Moyle Holdings Ltd.

Cleaver Fulton Rankin fields two experienced corporate partners with excellent reputations: head of department Jennifer Ebbage and Stephen Cross. In 2005, the firm continued to make high-value acquisitions for BT in Northern Ireland and advised

CORPORATE AND M&A

CARSON McDOWELL
L'ESTRANGE & BRETT ✪

ARTHUR COX NORTHERN IRELAND ✪
CLEAVER FULTON RANKIN ✪
MILLS SELIG
TUGHANS

C & H JEFFERSON
ELLIOTT DUFFY GARRETT

JOHN McKEE & SON ✪
JOHNS ELLIOT
McGRIGORS BELFAST
McKINTY AND WRIGHT

Babington & Croasdaile
Dickson & McNulty
McCartan Turkington Breen
Napier and Sons
R M Cullen & Son
Wilson Nesbitt

Bigger & Strahan
Comerton Hill
Fisher & Fisher
O'Reilly Stewart Solicitors
Thompson Mitchell

Firms are listed A-Z in tiers which are ranked in order of priority
✪ *Indicates firm displays contact details at the end of this chapter.*

Airtricity Group on a corporate restructuring. The firm is on the panel of solicitors for Invest Northern Ireland, which advises on equity investments in Northern Irish companies.

Mills Selig has capacity across a wide remit of corporate work, from M&A and MBOs to equity investments and joint ventures. The firm is also experienced in advising on private equity, a growing sector in Northern Ireland. Richard Fulton has considerable corporate expertise.

Tughans scooped a raft of high-value corporate deals in 2004 and 2005, including advising JP Morgan on the Northern Irish aspects of its acquisition of Warner Chilcott for US$3.1bn, and advising Bank of Ireland on the corporate aspects of the acquisition by UTV of The Wireless Group, for £98m. An expanding team (which increased by two fee-earners in 2005) is headed by the 'highly capable' John-George Willis.

C & H Jefferson is developing a quality corporate and commercial client base which includes Shorts, Harland & Wolff and well-known high street banks and retailers. Mark Tinman heads the corporate practice.

Elliott Duffy Garrett acts for a varied client base of local and international companies, including many foreign corporations recently established in Northern Ireland. Michael Wilson is an active practitioner in the department.

Lex Ross and Avril McCammon are active corporate practitioners at **John McKee & Son**; both boast first-class reputations in the market.

Johns Elliot's corporate focus is on M&A, MBOs and company reconstructions. Managing partner, the 'focused and committed' Maurice Butler heads the corporate department

McGrigors Belfast first established itself in Belfast in 2000 to reap the PFI/PPP work, but has also built up notable corporate capability.

Frederick Boyd is a key partner in **McKinty and Wright**'s corporate practice which deals with the full remit of corporate matters.

DISPUTE RESOLUTION

Our top-tier firms win their places through either strength across the board or for exceptional expertise in one field; most are there for the merits of an insurance litigation practice.

C & H Jefferson is 'very strong' in dispute resolution, fielding a large team with five partners and nine other fee-earners. The practice is focused on insurance defence work, for which the firm has a first-class reputation. Clients include international insurance companies, Lloyd's syndicates and composite insurers. The 'able and assured' Gareth Jones handles commercial litigation, professional negligence and insurance law.

Peter Davison at **Carson McDowell** is a skilled dispute resolution practitioner. The firm continues to act in a high-profile matter relating to the collapse of a development at Rossorry Quay. 'Excellent' head of department Brian Turtle has a good reputation for employment and professional negligence work.

Michael Lynch heads the dispute resolution team at **Elliott Duffy Garrett**. The firm has extensive experience handling complex litigation on a range of specialisms, from professional negligence to insurance and shipping law.

Insurance-focused English firm **Kennedys**' Belfast team has a strong following in the Northern Irish market. Seán Craig attracts praise from clients and peers alike as 'someone you can do business with'. The practice focuses on insurance litigation but also covers general commercial disputes and professional negligence claims for professionals such as engineers, architects, accountants and brokers.

L'Estrange & Brett boasts a number of experienced and esteemed practitioners, namely Sam Beckett, Adam Brett and David Kirkpatrick. The team was reinforced in 2005 by the arrival of Peter Hopkins from **Jones Day**. Expertise across a range of specialisms ranges from agency and distributorship disputes to breach of contract, intellectual property and professional negligence disputes.

McKinty and Wright has a ten-partner litigation team, which although known for its insurance defence work, also handles the full range of commercial litigation. Senior partner John Cross leads the dispute resolution practice.

Defamation expert Paul Spring heads a compact but effective team at **Mills Selig**.

DISPUTE RESOLUTION

C & H JEFFERSON
CARSON MCDOWELL
ELLIOTT DUFFY GARRETT
KENNEDYS
L'ESTRANGE & BRETT ✪
McKINTY AND WRIGHT
MILLS SELIG
TUGHANS

Arthur Cox Northern Ireland ✪
Cleaver Fulton Rankin ✪
Johns Elliot

Babington & Croasdaile
Fisher & Fisher
Napier and Sons
O'Reilly Stewart Solicitors
Thompsons McClure

Firms are listed A-Z in tiers which are ranked in order of priority
✪ *Indicates firm displays contact details at the end of this chapter.*

The firm handles all aspects of commercial litigation, from general commercial litigation to defamation and product liability and planning disputes.

Tughans has two separate litigation units, one unit focuses on general litigation such as insurance defence work; the other concentrates on commercial litigation, such as building contract disputes, landlord and tenant and shareholder disputes. Michael Gibson has retired and is now acting as a consultant. Managing partner Grahame Loughlin has a first-class reputation for defence litigation.

Arthur Cox Northern Ireland acquired two significant new client gains this year. The firm negotiated a settlement for a marine insurance client in respect of a serious personal injury claim, initially valued over £600,000. The team also continues to act in a raft of commercial cases relating to allegedly defective upvc profiles for two manufacturing clients. The 'skilled' Peter Martin heads the department.

William Cross heads **Cleaver Fulton Rankin**'s general commercial litigation practice, which has specialisms in construction, property, IP, insolvency and professional indemnity disputes. Clients find Brendan Fox 'a commercial, pragmatic individual, with a robust, no-nonsense approach' who is '"streetwise" in his tactics'. The team has considerable expertise in construction disputes. High-profile cases include acting for residents in the Rossorry Quay dispute against Anglia Water.

Johns Elliot has experience in land disputes, mortgage repossessions, judicial reviews, copyright infringements and commercial litigation. The firm is carving a strong reputation for defamation defence work, while also covering debt recovery and accident and personal injury advice. Ronald Robertson is recommended.

EMPLOYMENT

The 'adept and commonsensical' Brian Turtle leads the team at **Carson McDowell**. The team has a well-established practice in the Industrial and Fair Employment Tribunals and in the mainstream court system, as well as providing transactional support advising on redundancy and TUPE issues.

Elliott Duffy Garrett has a dedicated employment law unit that regularly acts in major industrial disputes and advises on the implementation of anti-discrimination legislation. Managing partner Harry Coll heads the practice.

L'Estrange & Brett's 'versatile' Adam Brett heads the employment unit, which boasts an impressive client list including Queen's University of Belfast, J Sainsbury Plc and a wide range of semi-public, financial, commercial, retail and manufacturing clients. Associate Hilary Griffith covers the full range of employment issues, from advice on terms and conditions, discrimination, equal pay and TUPE aspects of mergers.

Eugene O'Loan's employment practice at **Tughans** moves up a tier this year in recognition of its strength on both contentious and advisory employment issues. The firm has three full-time partners dedicated to employment, who regularly advise on religious discrimination and unfair dismissal claims, as well as providing corporate support.

Highlights for **Arthur Cox Northern Ireland** in 2005 include advising on the employment aspects of Conexant Systems Inc's acquisition of Amphion SemiConductor Ltd, and acting for Kirk McClure Morton on an asset sale to RPS Group Plc. As well as corporate support, the firm handles both advisory and contentious employment matters to a high standard. Anna Beggan heads the employment team.

At **Cleaver Fulton Rankin**, Alyn Hicks is now head of department following Rosalie Prytherch's appointment as a magistrate. Clients find Hicks 'extremely helpful, supportive and knowledgable', and his advice 'meticulous.' The firm advised Desmond & Sons Ltd on major restructuring at board level, and advised one of the Big Four accountants on employment and other litigation related to a major liquidation.

Jones & Cassidy is a niche practice with a reputation for being 'very strong for plaintiff work'. The three-partner team handles human rights law, anti-discrimination and employment work. Beverley Jones is an able practitioner.

Mills Selig has a quality client list of manufacturers and UK retailers, who regularly consult the firm on employment matters. Adam Curry heads the practice.

At **Napier and Sons**, major clients for the employment team include Local Press Ltd, the Post Office and BT. 'Orlagh O'Neill is an exceptional lawyer with a great following,' comments one client. The other half of the duo is John Gordon, who is a 'capable and experienced' practitioner.

ENVIRONMENT AND PLANNING

Cleaver Fulton Rankin move up to the top tier in recognition of the firm's dedication to this practice area. Karen Blair is unusual in being a planning specialist rather than a commercial property partner. The team has two full-time fee-earners in its mixed environment and planning practice. Highlights include acting for Belfast City Airport on the renegotiation of its planning agreement, and advising AES Kilroot Power Ltd on its proposed flue gas de-sulphurisation development, which resulted in a successful planning appeal in September 2005.

Carson McDowell regularly advises on planning inquiries, in 2005 acting for Sainsbury's at Londonderry, Stewart Superstore at Newcastle and Tesco at Knocknagoney and Bentrim Road, Lisburn. The team, led by commercial property partner Rosemary Carson, regularly advises on environmental audits and is also a first port of call for US investors in the Province.

L'Estrange & Brett's environmental and planning law unit comprises three partners: Sam Beckett, Ian Huddleston and Donna Matchett. Sam Beckett has acted in a number of high-profile planning inquiries for retail heavyweights such as Sainsbury's throughout the Province. The firm also advises a score of large-scale developers, which include Bord Gáis Éireann and DOE Water Service.

Tughans' Deirdre Magill has focused expertise on planning inquiries while Tracey Schofield advises on environmental issues, in particular in relation to corporate transactions.

IP AND IT

The IT and IP team at **L'Estrange & Brett** focuses on information technology, e-commerce, communications, intellectual property, bio-technology and banking and financial services. A raft of biotech and pharma companies is included in its impressive client list. Highlights include advising Randox Laboratories Ltd on a wide range of biotechnology matters, and Grafton Recruitment, Ulster Bank and the Association of Northern Ireland Colleges on a range of large-scale IT procurement and outsourcing issues. Paul McBride heads a quality team, while David Kirkpatrick deals with IP/IT disputes.

Carson McDowell's Alan Taylor and his team provide the full range of advice to IT and e-commerce-based industries. The team advises some of the largest Northern Ireland information technology companies as well as acting for overseas clients on investments in IT and e-commerce companies in the Province. A quality client list includes two universities involved in setting up spin-off companies.

Cleaver Fulton Rankin is active on patent disputes and acts for a number of well-known brands. Highlights of 2005 include advising Hewlett-Packard Ltd on large-scale projects in Northern Ireland. Jennifer Ebbage leads the team.

EMPLOYMENT

CARSON McDOWELL
ELLIOTT DUFFY GARRETT
L'ESTRANGE & BRETT ✪
TUGHANS

Arthur Cox Northern Ireland ✪
Cleaver Fulton Rankin ✪
Jones & Cassidy
Mills Selig
Napier and Sons

C & H Jefferson
John McKee & Son ✪
Johns Elliot
McKinty and Wright

Firms are listed A-Z in tiers which are ranked in order of priority
✪ Indicates firm displays contact details at the end of this chapter.

ENVIRONMENT AND PLANNING

CLEAVER FULTON RANKIN ✪

CARSON McDOWELL
L'ESTRANGE & BRETT ✪
TUGHANS

Arthur Cox Northern Ireland ✪
C & H Jefferson
Elliott Duffy Garrett
Johns Elliot
McKinty and Wright
Mills Selig
Napier and Sons

Firms are listed A-Z in tiers which are ranked in order of priority
✪ Indicates firm displays contact details at the end of this chapter.

IP AND IT

L'ESTRANGE & BRETT ✪

CARSON McDOWELL
CLEAVER FULTON RANKIN ✪
TUGHANS

Arthur Cox Northern Ireland ✪
Elliott Duffy Garrett

C & H Jefferson
John McKee & Son ✪
Johns Elliot
Mills Selig
Napier and Sons
Wilson Nesbitt

Firms are listed A-Z in tiers which are ranked in order of priority
✪ Indicates firm displays contact details at the end of this chapter.

Tughans fields two capable practitioners: Adrian O'Connell, a dedicated IT expert, and Ian Coulter, who is a capable practitioner on the transactional side. Major clients include Fujitsu, Kainos Software Ltd and IIB Bank Ltd.

The workload at **Arthur Cox Northern Ireland** is focused on the IP and technology issues arising in M&A and corporate transactions. The 'experienced' Kerry Canavan heads the team.

Elliott Duffy Garrett has a wide-ranging practice advising on the full scope of IP, IT and e-commerce.

INSOLVENCY

The Enterprise Act 2002 is not yet in force in Northern Ireland, so there has not been the same upsurge in personal bankruptcy as seen in England and Wales. There is still a plentiful supply of corporate insolvency work, some of it cross-border.

Corporate and commercial expert David Jamison heads **Carson McDowell**'s insolvency and corporate restructuring team, which has a solid client list of liquidators, administrators and receivers. Peter Davison also acts in insolvency matters.

Newly made-up partner Michael Neill leads **Cleaver Fulton Rankin**'s dynamic insolvency practice, which regularly deals with cross-border insolvency work, as well as asset-tracing and fraud. The firm is the lead adviser to Invest Northern Ireland on corporate recovery and acts for the major accountancy firms, for liquidators, receivers as well as administrators.

Elliott Duffy Garrett's insolvency practice is headed by the experienced Michael Wilson, while at **John McKee & Son** partner Lex Ross specialises in corporate receiverships.

'**L'Estrange & Brett** fields a three-fee-earner corporate recovery and insolvency unit headed by ex-**Eversheds LLP** lawyer Kieran McGarrigle. Peter Hopkins, who joined the firm from **Jones Day** in 2005, adds contentious capability. An impressive client list includes numerous insolvency practitioners and lending institutions.

Napier and Sons has an established reputation for its insolvency expertise. John Gordon is the chief expert. Fiona McCarthy has left to act as an insolvency master in the High Court. The firm deals principally with personal bankruptcy but also has experience in corporate insolvency matters.

Angus Creed and Peter Martin advise on insolvency matters at **Arthur Cox Northern Ireland**. The firm also has debt recovery expertise.

C & H Jefferson's insolvency practice covers both corporate and personal insolvency, with a focus on the manufacturing sector. Ken Rutherford deals with the bulk of insolvency instructions.

James Pringle at **Johns Elliot**, together with David Leitch, advises on company reconstructions as well as general insolvency matters.

John Kearns heads a busy insolvency practice at **Mills Selig**, which, like the other firms, benefits from a good relationship with the small and medium-sized accountancy firms.

INSOLVENCY

CARSON McDOWELL
CLEAVER FULTON RANKIN ✪
ELLIOTT DUFFY GARRETT
JOHN McKEE & SON ✪
L'ESTRANGE & BRETT ✪
NAPIER AND SONS
Arthur Cox Northern Ireland ✪
C & H Jefferson
Johns Elliot
Mills Selig
Babington & Croasdaile
Tughans
Wilson Nesbitt

Firms are listed A-Z in tiers which are ranked in order of priority
✪ Indicates firm displays contact details at the end of this chapter.

PROJECT FINANCE AND PFI

L'Estrange & Brett has an established PPP focus, with three partners active in the area: Adrian Eakin, Richard Gray and the 'excellent' Ian Huddleston. The firm acts on the largest projects in Northern Ireland for both public and private sector clients. Recent accomplishments include closing the Strategic Investment Board's first PPP in Northern Ireland, the firm's lead role in the £500m Belfast Schools PPP scheme, and being selected by Northgate Plc to advise on its first pathfinder Building Schools for the Future ICT scheme in Bristol.

A&L Goodbody's team, led by Kevin Feeney, makes frequent forays into Northern Ireland to advise on choice projects. The firm acts on PPPs throughout Ireland, including Invest Northern Ireland's new headquarters in Belfast and on the M3: Clonee/Kells motorway project.

Arthur Cox Northern Ireland has a formal preferred partnership arrangement with **Pinsent Masons** in projects and construction, acting in conjunction on the upcoming roll-out of significant projects in water, energy, education, health and transport. Peter Stafford is recommended.

Carson McDowell has had a role on a number of major PFI projects, acting both for the funder and for public bodies such as the Water Service and the Roads Service. Michael Johnston leads the projects and infrastructure team.

Kevin McVeigh is an experienced practitioner at **Elliott Duffy Garrett**, while Lex Ross is recommended at **John McKee & Son**.

McGrigors Belfast's local presence means the firm is well positioned to scoop work on major PFI projects in both the public and private sectors. Gregor Hamilton is an experienced practitioner, while associate Cathy Lagan is considered an 'up-and-coming' star.

Tughans' John-George Willis is highly recommended, spearheading the firm's increasing PFI workload. Highlights include advising Bilfinger, alongside **Allen & Overy LLP**, on the £90m Westlink roads project in which Bilfinger is the preferred bidder.

Partner Ken Rutherford is the main contact for PFI work at **C & H Jefferson**.

Cleaver Fulton Rankin advised a project company on compliance with Northern Irish law for the development of a laboratory and pharmacy services at Altnagelvin Hospital, which reached financial close in April 2005. Jennifer Ebbage has PFI experience.

Mills Selig has also some expertise in project finance.

PROJECT FINANCE AND PFI

L'ESTRANGE & BRETT ✪
A&L Goodbody
Arthur Cox Northern Ireland ✪
Carson McDowell
Elliott Duffy Garrett
John McKee & Son ✪
McGrigors Belfast
Tughans
C & H Jefferson
Cleaver Fulton Rankin ✪
Mills Selig

Firms are listed A-Z in tiers which are ranked in order of priority
✪ Indicates firm displays contact details at the end of this chapter.

REAL ESTATE

There have been some exciting developments in Northern Ireland over the past few years, such as the Victoria Square Shopping Centre, anchored by House of Fraser, and the development of the cathedral quarter in Belfast. In the pipeline is the sale of almost all of the government's civil service buildings with leaseback in a PFI initiative. At the time of writing, the project was at tender stage, but the move will generate quality work for Northern Irish and City of London law firms.

Carson McDowell has a reputation for being 'very good at property', particularly in the retail sector in which the firm acts for both landlords and tenants, with heavy-hitters such as Tesco and Debenhams on the client list. In the past year the team has also had an additional focus on site-development work. Alan Reilly, Jeremy Hill and Rosemary Carson are all 'adept and commercially focused' practitioners.

Kathryn Collie heads the team of two partners and six other fee-earners at **Cleaver Fulton Rankin**. The firm has a good reputation for its work for retailers but has recently seen an increase in advising on developments. Highlights include acting for Whitestar Science Park in putting an agreement-for-lease in place with a major financial institution, and advising Abbey National

Plc in the sale of Scottish Provident Buildings in Belfast as part of the disposal of a UK-wide portfolio of investment properties.

L'Estrange & Brett's team was boosted by three new solicitors, adding strength to an already 'first-rate' commercial property practice headed by Brian Henderson. The firm acted for Baronsgate (Antrim) Ltd on the sale of a shopping centre to Active Retail Fund, and also advised on the property aspects of the share sale of the Bairds chemist group to Alliance Unichem Plc in May 2005.

Tughans has a thriving commercial property practice, fielding respected property experts Phyllis Agnew and John Mills. The team has a strong reputation acting for developers, but also acts for significant retailers, such as Tesco. A varied workload includes the development of business, leisure and retail parks.

Rowan White leads **Arthur Cox Northern Ireland**'s practice, which in 2005 advised Musgrave Group, which owns the SuperValu and Centra retail franchises, on its ongoing programme of acquisitions, disposals and franchising of supermarkets and convenience stores. As well as retailers, the two-partner team acts for developers and institutional clients. Patricia Johnston is recommended.

C & H Jefferson has strong relationships with property developers, which bring in a raft of work. Mark Tinman has a good reputation in the market.

Elliott Duffy Garrett's clients include major property developers, retailers, funders, private and institutional investors both in the UK and Ireland. A snapshot of work includes commercial housing developments, property acquisition and financing, and landlord and tenant. Laurence Mahood heads the department.

London corporate firm **Travers Smith** utilises its expertise of working on sizeable UK property projects to its advantage in the Province. Andrew Barrow heads a team of three, dual-qualified lawyers, who advised AM Development on the landmark £200m Victoria Square project, as well as having an active presence in the tender processes for future large-scale projects.

John McKee & Son has expertise in the financing of property transactions, while **McGrigors Belfast**'s Alan McAlister advises on development work.

Clients report that David Leitch, head of the property practice at **Johns Elliot**, is 'very good at clear, property advice'. A varied client list includes buyers, developers, landlords, lenders, borrowers and tenants for all types of commercial property.

Brian Ham heads the team at **Mills Selig**, which regularly advises contractors and property development companies. Melanie McKelvey is 'very professional', and 'great to deal with.'

REAL ESTATE

CARSON McDOWELL
CLEAVER FULTON RANKIN ✪
L'ESTRANGE & BRETT ✪
TUGHANS

ARTHUR COX NORTHERN IRELAND ✪
C & H JEFFERSON
ELLIOTT DUFFY GARRETT
TRAVERS SMITH

John McKee & Son ✪
Johns Elliot
McGrigors Belfast
Mills Selig

Babington & Croasdaile
Bigger & Strahan
Fisher & Fisher
Kearney Sefton
McKinty and Wright
Napier and Sons
R M Cullen & Son
Wilson Nesbitt

Firms are listed A-Z in tiers which are ranked in order of priority
✪ *Indicates firm displays contact details at the end of this chapter.*

ARTHUR COX
NORTHERN IRELAND

CAPITAL HOUSE
3 UPPER QUEEN STREET
BELFAST BT1 6PU

Telephone: +44 28 9023 0007
Fax: +44 28 9023 3464
E-mail: belfast@arthurcox.com
Website: www.arthurcox.com

Languages
French, German, Italian, Spanish

Other offices
Dublin, London, New York

Number of lawyers 223
at this office 24

CATEGORIES OF WORK

Corporate and commercial
Mark Thompson, Peter Stafford

Banking
Angus Creed, Judith Brown

Commercial property
Rowan White, Patricia Johnston

Financial services
Angus Creed, Kerry Canavan

Energy
MarkThompson, David Finn

Projects
Peter Stafford

Litigation
Peter Martin, Amanda Wylie

Employment
Peter Martin, Anna Beggan

EU and competition
John Meade

IP/IT
Mark Thompson, Kerry Canavan

Transport
Peter Martin (shipping),
Amanda Wylie (roads)

CLEAVER FULTON RANKIN

50 BEDFORD STREET
BELFAST BT2 7FW

Telephone: +44 28 9024 3141
Fax: +44 28 9024 9096
E-mail: info@cfrlaw.co.uk
Website: www.cfrlawonline.com

Number of lawyers 28

Member
International Lawyers Network;
International Bar Association

CATEGORIES OF WORK

Corporate
Stephen Cross

Commercial property
Kathryn Collie

Commercial litigation
Michael Neill

Banking
Stephen Cross

Intellectual property
Brendan Fox

Environment and planning
Karen Blair

Employment
Alyn Hicks

Projects
Patrick Fleming

Insolvency
Michael Neill

Private client
Alastair Rankin

Construction
Brendan Fox

Licensing
Karen Blair

IT
Jennifer Ebbage

Energy
Stephen Cross

JOHN McKEE & SON

HAMPDEN HOUSE
55 ROYAL AVENUE
BELFAST BT1 1FD

Telephone: +44 28 9023 2303
Fax: +44 28 9023 00 81
E-mail: info@jmckee.co.uk
Website: www.jmckee.co.uk

Number of lawyers 15

CATEGORIES OF WORK

Banking and finance
Lex Ross, Avril McCammon

Project finance/PFI
Lex Ross, Avril McCammon

Corporate
Sarah Burrows

Litigation
Leonard Edgar, Chris Ross

Property
Gerard Small

Insolvency
Lex Ross

Employment
Andrea McCann

L'ESTRANGE & BRETT

ARNOTT HOUSE
12-16 BRIDGE STREET
BELFAST BT1 1LS

Telephone: +44 28 9023 0426
Fax: +44 28 9024 6396
E-mail: law@lestrangeandbrett.com
Website: www.lestrangeandbrett.com

Languages
French, German, Italian, Spanish

Number of lawyers 45

Member
North South Legal Alliance with McCann FitzGerald (Dublin)

CATEGORIES OF WORK

Companies, corporations
Richard Gray, Paul McBride

Commercial and competition law
Richard Gray, Paul McBride

Mergers and acquisitions
Richard Gray, Paul McBride

Commercial property
Graham Pierce, Ian Huddleston

Bankruptcy, insolvency
Paul McBride, Kieran McGarrigle

Banking, securities and finance
Brian Henderson, Richard Gray

Projects, public private partnerships
Adrian Eakin, Richard Gray

Employment, labour
Adam Brett

Commercial litigation, intellectual property, maritime and shipping
Adam Brett, Samuel Beckett

Environment
Ian Huddleston, David Kirkpatrick

Wills, trusts, estate planning, financial services and private client
Ian Huddleston, Alan Hewitt

Construction and planning
Samuel Beckett, Andrea McIlroy-Rose

Technology/biotechnology
Paul McBride

UNITED KINGDOM: SCOTLAND

Population	5.06 million
Number of lawyers	8,768
Professional title	Solicitor, advocate
Currency	Pound sterling (£)

Index

Scotland's central belt, which stretches between Edinburgh and Glasgow, is the engine room of the country's banking and corporate markets. Aberdeen, some 120 miles to the north, is an almost entirely separate market, focused heavily on the North Sea oil and gas industries.

BILLING

Clients are charged between £185 and £210 (€312 and €355) per hour for partners undertaking corporate/finance and litigation work and between £155 and £160 (€262 and €270) per hour for assistant solicitors. The Law Society of Scotland provides guidance on billing.

MARKETING

There are no restrictions on lawyers advertising in Scotland. Most of the major firms have websites and produce brochures for clients. Details of transactions can be disclosed, provided clients' prior permission has been given.

IN-HOUSE LAWYERS

The Law Society of Scotland supports a specialist group which represents the interests of in-house lawyers. In-house lawyers are employed in all areas of industry and are particularly prevalent in the public sector.

THE LEGAL 500

For additional information on the law firms and legal practice in Scotland, see *The Legal 500 2005* (UK edition) at www.legal500.com.

LEGAL MARKET

The start of 2006 saw the merger of full-service firm *Henderson Boyd Jackson* with Midlands firm *Gateley Wareing*, to form **HBJ Gateley Wareing**. This is the first cross-border merger of Scottish and English firms since **McGrigors**' ill-fated alliance with *KLegal*.

The legal market in Edinburgh and Glasgow is dominated by the 'Big Four'. **Dundas & Wilson**, under the guidance of managing partner Chris Campbell, consolidated its position at the top of the market making several major lateral hires. Apart from private client work, there are few areas where the firm is not at or near the top of the market. **McGrigors** dissolved its ill-fated marriage with accountancy firm KPMG. However, with its strong infrastructure, top-notch lawyers and offices in London and Northern Ireland, the firm is expected to make a full recovery. Scotland senior partner Shonaig MacPherson retired in October 2004, and was replaced by Kirk Murdoch. **Maclay Murray & Spens** opened an office in Aberdeen and merged with London property boutique *Fenners*, which gives it a solid foothold in the capital. The firm has superb practices across the board. **Shepherd+ Wedderburn** is widely regarded as the most conservative of Scotland's Big Four, although this is no bad thing. While its rivals have gone through peaks and troughs, the firm has continued to grow at a steady pace, with turnover increasing by 13.4% in 2004. This full-service firm has strengths in all areas and has now opened an office in Aberdeen.

Elsewhere, Aberdeen-based **Paull & Williamsons** has a sterling reputation for corporate and oil and gas work. The firm benefited from the arrival of partner Bruce McLeod who joined from an in-house role at BP. **Ledingham Chalmers** is building a name in commercial litigation, insolvency and general corporate work. The Edinburgh office is starting to make an impression and the firm also has offices in Turkey, Azerbaijan and the Falklands.

BANKING AND FINANCE

Dickson Minto WS's first-class banking practice is almost entirely focused on acquisition and structured finance. Acting mostly for lenders, it recently advised Bank of Scotland on the debt financing of the acquisition of the Early Learning Centre. Partner Colin McHale comes highly recommended, as does name partner Bruce Minto.

Dundas & Wilson CS LLP's Stephen Phillips heads the group, which acts for the very largest banking clients, including RBS, Bank of Scotland and Lloyds TSB. Recently, the firm advised Bank of Scotland on the £105m syndicated financing of Edinburgh Oil and Gas' acquisition of the Buzzard Field in the North Sea.

Maclay Murray & Spens' banking practice is headed by acquisition finance expert Susan Kelly. The firm advised a range of borrowers and lenders on debt transactions totalling £10bn, with highlights including advising Bank of Scotland on Philip Green's proposed bid for Marks & Spencer, as well as on the secondary buy-out of the Antler luggage group.

The largest firms

1	Dundas & Wilson CS LLP	256
2	Shepherd+ Wedderburn	247
3	Maclay Murray & Spens	229
4	McGrigors	162
5	MacRoberts	158
6	Tods Murray LLP	141
7	Biggart Baillie	137
8	Anderson Strathern	131
9	Brodies LLP	112
10	Burness	102
11	DLA Piper Rudnick Gray Cary Scotland LLP	94
12	HBJ Gateley Wareing LLP	93
13	Morton Fraser	85
14	Harper Macleod LLP	80
	Ledingham Chalmers	80
16	Paull & Williamsons	79
17	McClure Naismith	78
18	Thorntons	70
19	Turcan Connell	67
20	Simpson & Marwick	65
21	Brechin Tindal Oatts	62
22	Semple Fraser LLP	60
23	Balfour & Manson	57
24	Wright, Johnston & Mackenzie LLP	54

These figures represent the total number of lawyers in this country only, and have been supplied by the firms themselves. The figures should be accurate as at 1 January 2006.

McGrigors' broad-based banking practice covers the whole gamut of finance work, including property – for which practice head Michael Watson comes highly recommended – acquisition, structured, and project finance. The firm acts for borrowers and lenders, recently advising new client Cairn Energy on $240m-worth of bilateral loan facilities with five banks, including the IFC. Major institutional clients include RBS, Bank of Scotland and Lloyds TSB

Scott Wilson's team at **Burness** has a strong lender-based following, and is recommended for project, property and structured finance. The firm's largest banking client is Bank of Scotland, which it advised, alongside Bank of Ireland, on the provision of £54m of syndicated debt to Stannifer Group Holdings. Other major clients include RBS, Standard Life and Anglo Irish Bank

Shepherd+ Wedderburn's well-regarded banking and finance group regularly acts for borrowers and lenders on major transactions, particularly in the arenas of property, project and acquisition finance. Major clients include the AIB Group, Halifax Bank of Scotland, and HSBC.

Tods Murray LLP is undoubtedly one of the best firms to go to for asset-backed finance and securitisation, where group head Graham Burnside enjoys a superb reputation. The firm advised Bank of Scotland on its £58m loan to Dundee Student Villages, for the development of halls of residence. It also advised on the Scottish aspects of Barclays Capital's £129m funding and securitisation of the BBC's Scottish headquarters.

Biggart Baillie's solid banking and finance practice advised on over 100 transactions, with a total value of £1bn. Lender clients include RBS, Bank of Scotland and Bank of Ireland. Alasdair Peacock heads the team

DLA Piper Rudnick Gray Cary Scotland LLP's expanding banking and finance team is starting to attract some impressive instructions. Bank of Scotland is a major client and was recently advised on the £70m financing of Tonstate Edinburgh's purchase of the Omni Centre. Other major clients include Citigroup Global Markets and the Anglo Irish Bank. Jack Gardiner and John Maciver jointly head the practice, from Glasgow and Edinburgh respectively.

Banking and finance clients praise **McClure Naismith**. Headed by John Blackwood, the expanding team has several first-class practitioners. The firm regularly advises Bank of Scotland on property finance transactions.

Brodies LLP comes highly recommended, particularly for its retail banking expertise. Here it recently advised RBS on the preparation of the RBS/Nat West offset product, designed to comply with new mortgage regulations. The practice, which is also strong in acquisition finance, is headed Bruce Stephen. The firm has gained several impressive new clients, including Goldman Sachs International and GE Life Equity Release.

BANKING AND FINANCE

DICKSON MINTO WS *Edinburgh, Glasgow*
DUNDAS & WILSON CS LLP ✪ *Edinburgh, Glasgow*
MACLAY MURRAY & SPENS *Glasgow, Edinburgh*
McGRIGORS *Glasgow, Edinburgh*

BURNESS *Edinburgh*
SHEPHERD+ WEDDERBURN *Edinburgh, Glasgow*
TODS MURRAY LLP *Edinburgh, Glasgow*

Biggart Baillie *Glasgow, Edinburgh*
DLA Piper Rudnick Gray Cary Scotland LLP *Glasgow, Edinburgh*
McClure Naismith *Glasgow, Edinburgh*

Brodies LLP *Edinburgh*
Golds *Glasgow*
Harper Macleod LLP *Glasgow*
MacRoberts *Glasgow, Edinburgh*
Morton Fraser *Edinburgh*
Semple Fraser LLP *Edinburgh*

Anderson Strathern *Edinburgh*
Archibald Campbell & Harley WS *Edinburgh*
HBJ Gateley Wareing LLP *Edinburgh, Glasgow*
Ledingham Chalmers *Aberdeen*
Paull & Williamsons *Aberdeen*

Firms are listed A-Z in tiers which are ranked in order of priority
✪ *Indicates firm displays contact details at the end of this chapter.*

Golds has carved itself a highly lucrative and innovate niche in high-volume property finance, re-mortgage and security work. The firm acts for a string of first-class banks and building societies on transactions usually ranging between the £1m and £10m mark.

Harper Macleod LLP acts for a range of lenders on small to mid-size loans, with particularly strong experience of housing association finance. In 2004, the firm gained several new clients, including the Scottish Executive, and Interbrew UK. Other clients include Dunfermline Building Society, Barclays Bank and Bank of Scotland. Managing partner Professor Lorne Crerar heads the group.

Norman Martin heads the team at **MacRoberts**. The group is particularly recommended for property and project finance, and advised Sumitomo Mitsui Bank on a £60m facility to Crawley Schools. Other clients include RBS and Depfa Bank.

Morton Fraser has made a strong push into banking and finance in recent years. The group acts for borrowers and lenders, and recently advised the management team on the Schuh MBO on its £20m financing. Susan Younger 's team acts for a range of impressive clients, including Lloyds TSB, Bank of Scotland and Clydesdale Bank.

CONSTRUCTION
MACROBERTS *Glasgow, Edinburgh*
PINSENT MASONS *Glasgow, Edinburgh*
DUNDAS & WILSON CS LLP ✪ *Edinburgh, Glasgow*
McGRIGORS *Glasgow, Edinburgh*
Maclay Murray & Spens *Glasgow, Edinburgh*
Shepherd+ Wedderburn *Edinburgh, Glasgow*
Biggart Baillie *Glasgow, Edinburgh*
Burness *Edinburgh, Glasgow*
DLA Piper Rudnick Gray Cary Scotland LLP *Glasgow, Edinburgh*
Morton Fraser *Edinburgh, Glasgow*
Tods Murray LLP *Edinburgh, Glasgow*
Anderson Strathern *Edinburgh*
Brodies LLP *Edinburgh*
McClure Naismith *Glasgow, Edinburgh*
Semple Fraser LLP *Glasgow, Edinburgh*
Bell & Scott *Edinburgh*
Bishops Solicitors LLP *Glasgow, Edinburgh*
HBJ Gateley Wareing LLP *Edinburgh, Glasgow*
Harper Macleod LLP *Glasgow*
Ledingham Chalmers *Aberdeen*
Paull & Williamsons *Aberdeen*

Firms are listed A-Z in tiers which are ranked in order of priority
✪ Indicates firm displays contact details at the end of this chapter.

Semple Fraser LLP's banking and finance team has a heavy property bent. The firm recently advised Bank of Ireland in connection with a £50m office development in central Leeds. Other clients include Bank of Scotland, Dunfermline Building Society and Dunbar Bank. Alex Innes heads the team.

CONSTRUCTION

MacRoberts has consolidated its position as a leader in the market, maintaining a very high profile in both non-contentious and contentious construction work. The team acted for John Doyle Construction in the landmark case *John Doyle Construction v Laing Management*. Neil Kelly is the department head.

The top-quality construction practice at **Pinsent Masons** is led by Fraser McMillan. It recently saw impressive expansion, with new wins including Miller Construction, Morrison and Byzak Contractors.

Lindy Patterson's team at **Dundas & Wilson CS LLP** handles a steady flow of big-ticket work for a broad client base , enjoying accelerated growth in contentious and non-contentious work from both sides of the border. It was involved in the extensive redevelopment of the Royal Museum in Edinburgh, and was appointed to the AWG/Morrison panel. The team is also penetrating the specialist insurance market, receiving instructions from Zurich, Gerlings and ACE Europe.

McGrigors reinforced its place as a market leader in construction, demonstrating real capability in both contentious matters and procurement, and represented AWG Residential in Northern Ireland's largest construction dispute. Top-class clients include Morrison Construction, Miller Construction and Sir Robert McAlpine.

Maclay Murray & Spens' construction department has a strong developer focus. Department head Mark Macaulay is a specialist in procurement. Over the past 12 months the department was involved in several high-profile developments, including the second phase of the Aberdeenshire Schools project for the refurbishment and construction of six schools.

Led by Kevin Taylor, **Shepherd+ Wedderburn** boasts an experienced team that is known for its high-quality work. Major highlights include acting for the developer in the £400m mixed-use redevelopment of the old Royal Infirmary site in Edinburgh. Lynne Mendelsohn continues to advise the Scottish Parliamentary corporate body on ongoing issues relating to the construction of the new parliament building.

Biggart Baillie's commercial and proactive construction department advised a number of retailers including Homebase, Marks & Spencer and Next on the protections provided by the construction packages offered in connection with prospective leases. It also acted in a number of complex adjudications.

Burness' construction department heads Gavin Paton and James Forbes bring expertise to the firm's property and contractor client base. The team was particularly active in contentious matters, acting successfully for Scrabster Harbour Trust in one of Scotland's largest and longest adjudications, valued at around £15m.

Fenella Mason leads **DLA Piper Rudnick Gray Cary Scotland LLP**'s impressive construction practice. Significant instructions include acting for Dignity Funerals in the development of an innovative PPP for crematoria for North and South Lanarkshire councils. The firm also has a hard-hitting presence in contentious matters.

Ross Campbell heads the team at **Tods Murray LLP**, which boasts Balfour Beatty Group and the Kenmore Group as key clients. The contentious arm dealt with a variety of adjudications, and the team also outlined its advisory credentials by offering expertise on the construction aspects of a newly developed cinema, office and supermarket complex by Hermes Property Unit Trust.

CORPORATE AND COMMERCIAL

Premier firms: With offices in Edinburgh and London, corporate boutique **Dickson Minto WS** leads the pack for private equity and M&A work. Recent highlights include advising on the sale of Jenners, Edinburgh's most prestigious department store, to House of Fraser. Name

CORPORATE AND COMMERCIAL Premier Firms
DICKSON MINTO WS *Edinburgh, Glasgow*
DUNDAS & WILSON CS LLP ✪ *Edinburgh, Glasgow*
MACLAY MURRAY & SPENS *Edinburgh, Glasgow*
SHEPHERD+ WEDDERBURN *Edinburgh, Glasgow*
McGRIGORS *Edinburgh, Glasgow*

Firms are listed A-Z in tiers which are ranked in order of priority
✪ Indicates firm displays contact details at the end of this chapter.

partner Bruce Minto is undoubtedly one of Scotland's best-known corporate lawyers, with a strong line in investment fund work to boot.

Dundas & Wilson CS LLP's high-quality corporate team, headed by Michael Polson, acted on several keynote transactions that would leave most major City firms flushing with envy. An undoubted highlight was advising Scottish and Southern Energy on its £3.2bn acquisition of National Grid Transco's Scotland and South of England gas distribution networks. Further corporate work for Standard Life, Bank of Scotland, Voxar, and Babtie Group cements the firm's position at the top end of the Scottish corporate market.

Kenneth Shand heads **Maclay Murray & Spens**' highly rated corporate team. The group acted on several major transactions, including Blavod Black Vodka's acquisition of the Tennessee-based Extreme Beverage Company. Other highlights included the sale of the Scotch Malt Whisky Society to Glenmorangie, and Prudential's sale of Premier Mortgage Service. Despite its extrication from Glasgow, 3i remains a key client, and provides plenty of energy-related work for the Aberdeen office. The firm's recent merger with *The City Law Partnership* in London will also provide added capabilities in the financial services and investment funds arena.

Led by James Will, **Shepherd+ Wedderburn**'s practice is particularly strong in equity capital markets; it recently acted on 28 listings, for major clients including Collins Stewart and Numis Securities, which it advised on a £100m placing by Augean. The firm also acted for Cairn Energy in its £102.9m placing of ordinary shares. The firm was recently instructed by ProStrakan Group to act on the UK aspects of its £180m merger with Proskelia.

McGrigors' corporate practice is commended by clients. Glasgow-based partner Paul Davidson heads the team, which acts for a string of top-quality clients, including ScottishPower, Forth Ports and West Coast Capital. A recent highlight was advising CanArgo Energy Corporation on its $40m global listing on the US and Norwegian stock exchanges.

CORPORATE AND COMMERCIAL
Edinburgh and Glasgow

BIGGART BAILLIE *Glasgow, Edinburgh*
BRODIES LLP *Edinburgh*
BURNESS *Edinburgh, Glasgow*
MACROBERTS *Glasgow, Edinburgh*
TODS MURRAY LLP *Edinburgh, Glasgow*

DLA Piper Rudnick Gray Cary Scotland LLP *Glasgow*
Harper Macleod LLP *Glasgow, Edinburgh*
McClure Naismith *Glasgow, Edinburgh*

Anderson Strathern *Edinburgh*
HBJ Gateley Wareing LLP *Edinburgh, Glasgow*
Morton Fraser *Edinburgh*
Semple Fraser LLP *Edinburgh*

Bell & Scott *Edinburgh*
Boyds Solicitors LLP *Edinburgh*
Fyfe Ireland *Edinburgh*
Pinsent Masons *Glasgow*
Wright, Johnston & Mackenzie LLP *Glasgow*

Firms are listed A-Z in tiers which are ranked in order of priority

Edinburgh and Glasgow: David Allan 's commercial team at **Biggart Baillie** enjoyed almost 50% revenue growth, despite a relatively slow market. A major transaction was acting for Kenmore Property Group on the formation of a £200m joint venture with Uberior Ventures in the commercial property sector, involving intricate corporate and banking advice.

Brodies LLP enjoyed a banner year on the corporate front. Headed by Charles Smith the team advised the Strategic Rail Authority on the £1.9bn re-let of the ScotRail franchise was an obvious highlight, and the firm also acted for Vladimir Romanov on his high-profile acquisition of a 29.9% interest in Heart of Midlothian FC, Scotland's third-largest football club.

Burness' corporate practice is headed by Alan. A notable recent mandate was from UA Group, on the £52m takeover offer by Elphinstone Land, and the firm also advised SMG in the £90.5m off-market disposal of its 27.8% shareholding in Scottish Radio Holdings to Emap.

MacRoberts has acted swiftly in getting its house back in order. Partners Robert Burns and Alan Kelly were both recently made up, and the firm advised on several key instructions, including work for British Energy on the Scottish aspects of its massive restructuring. On the transactional front it advised Fishers Holdings' management team in its high-profile £30m MBO. Ian Dickson heads the team.

Under David Dunsire's guidance, **Tods Murray LLP**'s corporate finance practice is developing a good reputation. It advised private shareholders on the £300m sale of Glenmorangie to Moët Hennessy Investissements, and also acted for the Maclay Group on its purchase of the whole issued share capital of the Thistle Pub Company.

Bruce Westbrook heads **DLA Piper Rudnick Gray Cary Scotland LLP**'s impressive three-partner group. A major highlight was advising Stolt Sea Farms on the UK aspects of its global merger with Nutreco Holdings, to create Marine Harvest.

Donald Munro heads **Harper Macleod LLP**'s increasingly busy corporate practice. The firm recently advised Optical Express on its purchase of Boots' dental and laser eye correction business. It also acted for Thus Plc on the disposal of its call centre business across the UK. Other major clients include Tulloch and Arriva Trains.

McClure Naismith's corporate finance practice has developed a good track record for mid-cap listings on AIM. Most notably it advised Goals Soccer Centres on its £26m listing, and it also acted for Bowleven on its pre-IPO placing and admission to AIM, raising £31m. Dr Kenneth Chrystie heads the team.

Anderson Strathern's popular corporate group head Simon Brown generates positive feedback from clients. The firm enjoyed an active year, advising Stannifer Group on its £60m sale to Chelsfield and also acting for Scotmid on its acquisition of the Morning, Noon & Night chain.

HBJ Gateley Wareing LLP's young corporate team acted on a string of acquisitions and MBOs in 2004. Clients of Fraser Jackson's group include BUE Marine, Heart of Midlothian FC, Scottish & Newcastle and BT.

Morton Fraser's increasingly active corporate group is headed by Christian Hook. A transactional highlight was advising the management team on the MBO of Schuh. The firm has also seen an increase in property fund work, setting up separate funds for Dundas Commercial Property Fund II and Salamanca Capital Investment.

Semple Fraser LLP acted on several significant deals recently, such as advising Metron Technology on the UK aspects of the £100m sale of its worldwide business. The firm also represented BLGGI on its £29m sale of Tay Properties. Dawn Davidson heads the team.

CORPORATE AND COMMERCIAL
Elsewhere in Scotland

LEDINGHAM CHALMERS *Aberdeen*
PAULL & WILLIAMSONS *Aberdeen*

Iain Smith & Co *Aberdeen*
Stronachs *Aberdeen*

Raeburn Christie Clark & Wallace *Aberdeen*
The Commercial Law Practice *Aberdeen*
Thorntons *Dundee*

Firms are listed A-Z in tiers which are ranked in order of priority

Elsewhere in Scotland : Ledingham Chalmers' top-notch corporate practice is headed by Malcolm Laing. Much of the work resides, unsurprisingly, in the oil and gas sector; the firm recently advised Energy North Sea on its $200m acquisition of some of Shell's non-core assets in the North Sea, and later advised the company on its eventual sale to Marubeni North Sea.

Paull & Williamsons' 'excellent' corporate practice compares favourably with almost all those in the central belt, and the 'very attentive and extremely dedicated' Kenneth Gordon is highly recommended. The firm acts for a range of major clients, including FirstGroup, Lime Rock Partners and the John Wood Group.

Roy Roxburgh 's group at **Iain Smith & Co** has a very strong track record for corporate work in the agricultural sector. **Stronachs** of Aberdeen and Inverness also has a good reputation for corporate work, with Ewan Neilson heading the team.

CORPORATE TAX

Maclay Murray & Spens boasts one of the very best corporate tax teams in Scotland. Gwen Souter heads the group, which regularly advises on acquisitions and disposals, MBOs, restructurings and property work. Clients include 3i, Stagecoach and Alfred McAlpine.

MacRoberts' director of corporate tax, Isobel d'Inverno , commands immense respect within the market. The group provides excellent support to the firm's corporate and real estate teams, and recently advised A McLelland & Son, the UK's third-largest cheese producer, on the tax aspects of its sale to Lactalis.

Ian Gordon heads the corporate tax group at **McGrigors**, which provides excellent support on corporate and property-related matters. The firm recently advised West Coast Capital on issues concerning interest funding bonds for the Birthday Group.

Brodies LLP's tax practice is led by Alan Barr. Says one client: 'They give us the impression that we are an important client and have the ability to

CORPORATE TAX

MACLAY MURRAY & SPENS *Glasgow, Edinburgh*
MACROBERTS *Edinburgh*
McGRIGORS *Glasgow, Edinburgh*

Brodies LLP *Edinburgh*
Burness *Glasgow, Edinburgh*
Dickson Minto WS *Edinburgh, Glasgow*
Dundas & Wilson CS LLP ✪ *Edinburgh, Glasgow*
Shepherd+ Wedderburn *Edinburgh, Glasgow*

Biggart Baillie *Glasgow, Edinburgh*
McClure Naismith *Glasgow*

Firms are listed A-Z in tiers which are ranked in order of priority
✪ *Indicates firm displays contact details at the end of this chapter.*

coordinate with other departments in their firm to provide a single and overall view.'

Burness is recommended for corporate and real estate taxation issues, with the tax practice also working closely with the firm's employment and pensions group. The group recently advised Kosaido on tax issues relating to the £38m sale of St Andrews golf course and hotel. John Rafferty heads the team.

Dickson Minto WS's superb corporate finance practice is backed up by resident tax expert Nial Tosh , who enjoys a very strong reputation.

Susan Hoyle heads the tax group at **Dundas & Wilson CS LLP**, which provides ample support to the firm's pre-eminent corporate finance practice. The firm's overall capabilities were given a boost by the recruitment of tax expert Jim Hillan into its London office.

Shepherd+ Wedderburn's practice is very good for property-related tax advice, and Malcolm Rust is well versed in stamp duty land tax and trust structures. The team was boosted by the arrival of new group head Jenny.

DISPUTE RESOLUTION

Brodies LLP remains one of the top destinations for litigation in Scotland. Chairman Joyce Cullen heads the team, which recently represented RBS in a groundbreaking Court of Session action against Bannerman Johnstone Maclay, involving an auditor's duties to a lender The disputes practice continues to grow, with the recent arrival of contentious shipping specialist Duncan.

Headed by Lorna Sibbald, **Dundas & Wilson CS LLP**'s litigation team offers its clients top-notch disputes advice across a range of sectors. For advice on construction disputes, Lindy Patterson is one of Scotland's best-known litigators. A recent highlight was successfully defending Anchor International against the Inland Revenue in the Court of Session.

Maclay Murray & Spens' high-quality dispute resolution team regularly advises clients across the UK, from its offices in Glasgow, Edinburgh and London. The firm continues to act for Mohammed Al Fayed and the Harrods group of companies on its dispute with the Inland Revenue over revoked forward tax agreements; the case is currently on appeal in the House of Lords.

McGrigors' commercial litigation team is headed by solicitor advocate Craig Connal QC. Proving that the firm has more cases on its books than just the epic Imperial Tobacco litigation, it recently represented UGC Estates in the Court of Session, over a £5m breach of contract claim.

Burness' litigation team saw a recent change of management, with David Morgan replacing the new chairman, Philip Rodney , as group head. The firm garners glowing reviews from clients. Notable instructions include defending Artech SRL against pan-European claims brought by a Scottish distributor.

DISPUTE RESOLUTION

BRODIES LLP *Edinburgh*
DUNDAS & WILSON CS LLP ✪ *Edinburgh, Glasgow*
MACLAY MURRAY & SPENS *Glasgow, Edinburgh*
McGRIGORS *Glasgow, Edinburgh*

BURNESS *Edinburgh, Glasgow*
MACROBERTS *Glasgow, Edinburgh*
SHEPHERD+ WEDDERBURN *Edinburgh, Glasgow*

Anderson Strathern *Edinburgh*
Biggart Baillie *Edinburgh*
Harper Macleod LLP *Glasgow*
Morton Fraser *Edinburgh*
Simpson & Marwick *Edinburgh*

DLA Piper Rudnick Gray Cary Scotland LLP *Glasgow, Edinburgh*
HBJ Gateley Wareing LLP *Edinburgh, Glasgow*
McClure Naismith *Glasgow, Edinburgh*
Ross Harper *Glasgow*
Semple Fraser LLP *Glasgow, Edinburgh*
Tods Murray LLP *Edinburgh, Glasgow*

Archibald Campbell & Harley WS *Edinburgh*
Balfour & Manson *Edinburgh*
Bishops Solicitors LLP *Glasgow, Edinburgh*
Boyds Solicitors LLP *Glasgow, Edinburgh*
Fyfe Ireland *Edinburgh*
Golds *Glasgow*
Iain Smith & Co *Aberdeen*
Lawford Kidd *Edinburgh*
Ledingham Chalmers *Aberdeen, Edinburgh*
Miller Samuel LLP *Glasgow*
Morisons *Edinburgh*
Paull & Williamsons *Aberdeen, Edinburgh*

Firms are listed A-Z in tiers which are ranked in order of priority
✪ *Indicates firm displays contact details at the end of this chapter.*

David Arnott heads a strong litigation team at **MacRoberts**. The firm's involvement in the British Energy restructuring has thrown up its fair share of court work, including three separate petitions to the Court of Session. The firm also boasts a superb reputation for construction disputes. Regular clients include Network Rail, Scottish Equitable and Honda.

Headed by Kenny Cumming, **Shepherd+ Wedderburn**'s commercial litigation team represents English and Scottish clients across a range of disciplines and sectors, including property, transport, energy and insolvency. One of the firm's largest cases is for West Castle Properties in the Court of Session, seeking dilapidation costs against its former tenants, The Scottish Ministers

Anderson Strathern's dispute resolution practice is strong for regular commercial cases, but has become particularly adept at complex banking disputes. Ruari MacNeill heads a team that regularly acts for Bank of Scotland, RBS, Chelsea Building Society and Clydesdale Bank, among others. The firm is also very strong in insurance disputes work.

Brent Haywood has taken over as head of **Biggart Baillie**'s rapidly improving litigation team. Recently the firm achieved a successful settlement for Marine Harvest in a major action against a supplier. It also acts for ScottishPower, BASF and BBC Scotland.

Harper Macleod LLP's highly rated disputes practice is headed by Rod McKenzie, one of Scotland's best-known litigators. The firm's Edinburgh office enjoyed a 40% increase in caseload in the past year. One of its major recent cases was for Credential Bath Street in the Court of Session, on the recovery of rent and dilapidations in excess of £1m from tenant Callpoint Europe. Other clients included William Hill, Alba Life and Britannic.

Ewan McIntyre 's litigation team at **Morton Fraser** covers a broad range of areas. The firm acts for the Ministry of Defence on all its Scottish disputes, and was recently appointed by the Scottish Executive to advise on defender reparation. Another high point was advising the liquidator, Tenon, on the liquidation of *Boyd Napier LLP*, the first liquidation of a law firm LLP in Scotland..

Simpson & Marwick is Scotland's best known litigation boutique. The firm has over 50 dedicated litigators and focuses largely on defending insurance-related civil claims, where it is second to none. The firm has some of Scotland's best-known litigators.

DLA Piper Rudnick Gray Cary Scotland LLP's disputes team is recommended for both general commercial litigation and insurance-related disputes. Gordon Hollerin heads the commercial side, which has acted on several major disputes of late, most notably for Rangers Football Club, which it represented in three court actions against sellers of unlicensed merchandise.

Margaret Moodie heads **HBJ Gateley Wareing LLP**'s litigation practice. A highlight for the practice was successfully defending Alba Diagnostics in the House of Lords, against a claim concerning the rights to a patent brake fluid tester. The firm is recommended for property litigation.

McClure Naismith's disputes team is notable in that it has two disputes partners working out of London. Headed by Jeffrey Hutcheson the group covers a diverse range of specialisms and recently advised an animal feed producer in a major product liability claim.

Semple Fraser LLP's impressive litigation team focuses largely on insolvency, employment and planning-related disputes. Highlights include advising Standard Life Investments and Land Securities in two challenges concerning a new town centre on the site of the former Ravenscraig Steelworks. Kenneth Carruthers heads the team.

Michael Simpson heads **Tods Murray LLP**'s solid disputes team. The firm acted for the Scottish

Environment Protection Agency (SEPA) on a judicial review relating to the definition of waste. Other clients include Balfour Beatty, the Forestry Commission and Co-operative Insurance Society.

EU AND COMPETITION

EU and competition expert Tom Usher has settled in well at **Dundas & Wilson CS LLP**. It is testament to his reputation that several major clients followed him north of the border. The practice is by no means a one-man show, and the junior fee-earners are described as 'unfailingly professional and good-humoured, and often impressively shrewd for their years'.

Michael Dean at **Maclay Murray & Spens** remains one of Scotland's foremost EU and competition experts. The firm regularly represents clients before the EU Commission in Brussels, and recently responded to two Commission Statements of Objection, in separate inquiries. The group has strong experience in OFT inquiries and dawn raids, and benefits greatly from the firm's Brussels office.

Headed by James McLean, **Burness**' competition team comes highly recommended by clients. 'The response times of James McLean are the best I have ever encountered,' comments one client. 'I appreciated his almost exclusive use of email and links to relevant EU case law.'

MacRoberts' competition group is headed by David Flint, who sits on the CBI competition panel. Clients include British Energy, Coca-Cola, Johnston Press and Western Ferries.

McGrigors climbs a rung, following the recruitment of competition specialist Rod Lambert. Lambert works closely with both the corporate and litigation teams, and advised West Coast Capital on the competition aspects of its disposal of the Birthday Group to Clinton Cards.

EU AND COMPETITION

DUNDAS & WILSON CS LLP ✪ *Edinburgh, Glasgow*
MACLAY MURRAY & SPENS *Glasgow, Edinburgh*

BURNESS *Edinburgh, Glasgow*
MACROBERTS *Glasgow, Edinburgh*
McGRIGORS *Glasgow, Edinburgh*
SHEPHERD+ WEDDERBURN *Edinburgh, Glasgow*

Anderson Strathern *Edinburgh*
Biggart Baillie *Glasgow, Edinburgh*
Brodies LLP *Edinburgh*
McClure Naismith *Glasgow, Edinburgh*

Firms are listed A-Z in tiers which are ranked in order of priority
✪ *Indicates firm displays contact details at the end of this chapter.*

Gordon Downie and Richard Cockburn are the main points of contact for competition advice at **Shepherd+ Wedderburn**. The group recently advised a leading UK independent school on an OFT investigation into allegations of price fixing.

EMPLOYMENT

Brodies LLP undoubtedly fields one of the most innovative practices in Scotland. It boasts a top-class litigation portfolio and solid ties with the Scottish finance sector. A recent highlight was designing and producing a modular training programme for the RBS HR advisory centre. Led by department head Joan Cradden, the team has extensive experience in high-volume litigation and tribunal work, representing clients in the EAT and the Court of Appeal..

Eilidh Wisemen heads the employment practice at **Dundas & Wilson CS LLP**. Highlights include advising The Standard Life Assurance Company on complex employment issues relating to the restructuring programme prior to its planned demutualisation. Partner David Walker heads a sound immigration practice.

The team at **Maclay Murray & Spens** distinguishes itself across the board, offering expertise on a full range of employment issues. Recent instructions include advising several police forces on matters relating to conduct. The highly respected Malcolm Mackay moved to head up the firm's international consultancy business, Law at Work.

Raymond Williamson leads the exemplary department at **MacRoberts**, which is admired by competitors and clients alike. Recent impressive work includes devising a five-module management development programme for the Student Loans Company. The highly respected Stephen Miller also successfully represented Glasgow City Council before the EAT against race discrimination and victimisation claims.

Under the leadership of Alun Thomas, **Anderson Strathern**'s employment unit has an impressive market share. Jill Bell heads Spectrum, the firm's dedicated discrimination law service.

DLA Piper Rudnick Gray Cary Scotland LLP saw significant growth in its employment practice recently. The department was instructed by PricewaterhouseCoopers to defend an action by 170 employees of an insolvent company, and new clients include Telewest, Abbey, and Tesco. Russell Bradley leads the practice.

Harper Macleod LLP has consolidated its expertise and launched its employment, pensions and incentives practice group. The arrival of Scott Moncur from Scottish Widows strengthened the firm's non-contentious capacity, and the team added to its impressive client list Enable Scotland, Strathclyde Fire Brigade and Gordonstoun School.

McGrigors' employment team has gone from strength to strength. Significant instructions include a complex and high-profile employment dispute for Reid Furniture. BP, Marks & Spencer, and HarperCollins are all clients.

EMPLOYMENT

BRODIES LLP *Edinburgh*
DUNDAS & WILSON CS LLP ✪ *Edinburgh, Glasgow*
MACLAY MURRAY & SPENS *Glasgow, Edinburgh*
MACROBERTS *Glasgow, Edinburgh*

ANDERSON STRATHERN *Edinburgh*
DLA PIPER RUDNICK GRAY CARY SCOTLAND LLP *Edinburgh*
HARPER MACLEOD LLP *Glasgow*
McGRIGORS *Glasgow, Edinburgh*
MORTON FRASER *Edinburgh*

BURNESS *Edinburgh*
SHEPHERD+ WEDDERBURN *Edinburgh, Glasgow*

Brechin Tindal Oatts *Glasgow*
McClure Naismith *Glasgow*
Semple Fraser LLP *Glasgow*

Biggart Baillie *Glasgow*

Blackadders *Dundee*
HBJ Gateley Wareing LLP *Edinburgh*
Kidstons & Co *Glasgow*
Ledingham Chalmers *Aberdeen*
Paull & Williamsons *Aberdeen*
Simpson & Marwick *Aberdeen*
The Anderson Partnership *Glasgow*
Tods Murray LLP *Edinburgh*
Turcan Connell *Edinburgh*
Wright, Johnston & Mackenzie LLP *Glasgow*

Firms are listed A-Z in tiers which are ranked in order of priority
✪ *Indicates firm displays contact details at the end of this chapter.*

David Stewart heads the department at **Morton Fraser**. It is advising the MoD in relation to employment issues in Scotland, with Stewart involved in ongoing cases in the Court of Session in which ex-service personnel are claiming breaches of their human rights.

Burness' employment unit forms an integral part of the firm's dispute resolution department. Practice head Ronald Mackay successfully acted for the Baxters Food Group in defending multiple applications of unfair dismissal, and new clients include Adam & Company, Highland Spring and the Scottish Football Association.

Shepherd+ Wedderburn continues to impress, with acting department head John Griffiths at the helm. The team advised Scottish Courage in relation to an alleged failure to consult under TUPE regulations on an acquisition in northern England. It also provides non-contentious advice to ScottishPower, the Scottish Environment Agency and Endura.

Caroline Carr heads the employment practice at **Brechin Tindal Oatts** which is strong in contentious matters, especially discrimination claims.

McClure Naismith handles both advisory and contentious work. Significant matters for the year included a complex discrimination case, and advising Whyte and Mackay on employment and agency contracts. Department head Alan Thomson leads the department.

ENERGY

ENERGY
SHEPHERD+ WEDDERBURN *Edinburgh, Glasgow*
CMS CAMERON McKENNA LLP (SCOTLAND) *Aberdeen*
LEDINGHAM CHALMERS ABERDEEN
BIGGART BAILLIE *Glasgow, Edinburgh*
DUNDAS & WILSON CS LLP ✪ *Edinburgh, Glasgow*
MACLAY MURRAY & SPENS *Glasgow, Aberdeen*
PAULL & WILLIAMSONS *Aberdeen*
MacRoberts *Glasgow, Edinburgh*
McGrigors *Glasgow, Edinburgh*
Pinsent Masons *Glasgow*
Anderson Strathern *Edinburgh*
Brodies LLP *Edinburgh*
Burness *Edinburgh, Glasgow*
DLA Piper Rudnick Gray Cary Scotland LLP *Edinburgh*
Harper Macleod LLP *Edinburgh, Glasgow*
McClure Naismith *Glasgow, Edinburgh*
Tods Murray LLP *Edinburgh*
Wright, Johnston & Mackenzie LLP *Glasgow*

Firms are listed A-Z in tiers which are ranked in order of priority
✪ Indicates firm displays contact details at the end of this chapter.

Shepherd+ Wedderburn maintains the pace in the Scottish energy market. Led by James Saunders, the team advises a range of clients including ScottishPower, Talisman Energy, Cairn Energy and InterGen, on a healthy mix of corporate, development and regulatory issues. It acted for CRE Energy, a subsidiary of ScottishPower, on the development of the 62-turbine Blacklaw wind farm in Lanarkshire, the largest onshore windfarm approved to date. The firm also advised Cairn Energy on its $50m acquisition of Shell's interests in the Sangu gas field in Bangladesh.

Penelope Warne's superb oil and gas practice at **CMS Cameron McKenna LLP (Scotland)** is a force to be reckoned with, offering its clients the local advantage of an Aberdeen office as well as the heavyweight back-up of London. The firm's client list is a veritable who's who of the energy industry, including BP, Shell, Talisman, ExxonMobil and ConocoPhillips. In addition to the firm's transactional and regulatory capabilites, the office also has a vital health and safety practice headed by Alexander Green.

Ledingham Chalmers' group head Robert Ruddiman is one of the UK's best-known lawyers working in the upstream oil and gas industry. His practice was significantly enhanced by the arrival of partner Clare Munro from BP. A highlight was advising Energy North Sea on its $200m acquisition of some of Shell's non-core assets in the North Sea, and the firm later advised the company on its eventual sale to Marubeni North Sea.

Through its strong relationship with ScottishPower, **Biggart Baillie** has plenty of expertise in the energy sector. Advising SP Dataserve and ScottishPower Energy Retail on the implementation of the Ofgem-driven review of gas metering arrangements took up much of firm's time in the past year. Other major clients include the Association of Independent Gas Transporters and ECO European. David Ross heads the highly rated team.

Andrew Renton heads **Dundas & Wilson CS LLP**'s increasingly active energy group. The department regularly acts for Scottish and Southern Energy, its largest sector client, including recently on its £3.2bn purchase of gas distribution networks from National Grid Transco. The team also boasts plenty of experience in renewables, and advised Centrica on its acquisition of the Glens of Foundland Wind Farm.

Maclay Murray & Spens' oil and gas capabilities were enhanced significantly by the recruitment of partner Uisdean Vass , who now heads the Aberdeen-based oil and gas practice. Michael Dean heads the overall energy group, which acts for a number of major clients, including Ofgem. It also advises 3i on its numerous interests in the sector, and has strong experience in renewables.

Gordon Buchan 's impressive team at **Paull & Williamsons** is commended, with highly rated partner Bruce McLeod being singled out by clients. The firm acts for a range of majors, senior and junior independent oil companies, financiers and contractors. Significant instructions include advising Talisman on its Tweedsmuir gas transportation arrangements, and the firm also acted for Challenger Minerals and Sterling Resources on their interests in Mauritania and Romania respectively.

MacRoberts' energy practice is run by corporate head Ian Dickson. The firm recently advised the equity investors on the Scottish aspects of RWE Innogy's groundbreaking financing deal for Beaufort Wind. The group is also providing Scottish legal advice to British Energy on its massive restructuring.

McGrigors' energy practice, headed by Murdo Maclean, is making a considerable impression on the Scottish market. The group has experience in oil and gas, electricity and renewables, and comes highly recommended in related PFI work. Most recently it advised BP on the restructuring of its power and supply arrangements at the Sullom Voe oil terminal in Shetland. Major clients include CanArgo Energy, ScottishPower, Cairn Energy and InterGen.

Pinsent Masons has a number of major clients in the oil and gas, power and renewables sectors. The firm advised AMEC Wind on the Ardkinglas wind farm in Argyll, and also acted for ScottishPower on the £100m construction and maintenance of the Black Law wind farm. Highly rated partner Alastair Morrison heads the impressive practice.

Anderson Strathern's energy practice is recommended for its expertise in renewables, where it regularly acts for landowners and developers on offshore and onshore wind farms. Planning partner Alastair McKie heads the team.

Brodies LLP has developed a strong niche advising on the provision of heat and electricity to local councils. It is advising Caithness Heat and Power on the development of an innovative CHP plant for the community, to be fired by wood chip biomass, and is handling similar advice for Plymouth City Council. Charles Smith heads the active team.

Burness' energy group, headed by Nick Jones focuses largely on renewables. It regularly advises North British Windpower on its wind farm developments throughout Scotland.

DLA Piper Rudnick Gray Cary Scotland LLP has strong experience in renewables, and advised Boyndie Wind Energy and Falck Renewables on the development of the Boyndie wind farm in Aberdeenshire. Andrew Fitchie heads the group.

Pamela Todd is the main point of contact for energy work at **Harper Macleod LLP**, which has strong experience in the coal sector, where it is sole adviser to the Scottish Coal Company. The firm also acts for Airtricity in the renewables sector.

One of **McClure Naismith**'s largest energy clients is Bowleven, which it advised on a £30m capital raising and listing on AIM. It is also advising Npower on three hydro schemes. Steven Brown is the key contact in this sector.

Ian McPake is the main point of contact for energy work at **Tods Murray LLP**. The firm is currently advising the States of Guernsey on its waste to energy projects.

David Bone at **Wright, Johnston & Mackenzie LLP** has established a good track record for wind farm and renewable energy work.

ENVIRONMENT

Under the stewardship of Charles Smith, **Brodies LLP** provides its clients with superb environmental advice. The team advised Clackmannanshire Council in relation to a possible contaminated land issue at a housing development in Alloa, and also advised on the

ENVIRONMENT

BRODIES LLP *Edinburgh*
SEMPLE FRASER LLP *Glasgow, Edinburgh*

DUNDAS & WILSON CS LLP ✪ *Edinburgh, Glasgow*
MACLAY MURRAY & SPENS *Glasgow, Edinburgh*
SHEPHERD+ WEDDERBURN *Edinburgh, Glasgow*

Biggart Baillie *Glasgow, Edinburgh*
MacRoberts *Glasgow, Edinburgh*
McGrigors *Glasgow, Edinburgh*
Morton Fraser *Edinburgh, Glasgow*
Tods Murray LLP *Edinburgh, Glasgow*

Anderson Strathern *Edinburgh*
Archibald Campbell & Harley WS *Edinburgh*
Bishops Solicitors LLP *Glasgow*
Burness *Edinburgh, Glasgow*
DLA Piper Rudnick Gray Cary Scotland LLP *Glasgow, Edinburgh*
HBJ Gateley Wareing LLP *Edinburgh, Glasgow*
Harper Macleod LLP *Edinburgh*
Ledingham Chalmers *Aberdeen*
Pinsent Masons *Glasgow, Edinburgh*
McClure Naismith *Glasgow, Edinburgh*
Paull & Williamsons *Aberdeen*
Thorntons *Dundee*

Firms are listed A-Z in tiers which are ranked in order of priority
✪ *Indicates firm displays contact details at the end of this chapter.*

Scottish law aspects of Terra Firma's acquisition of a landfill and waste disposal site. New client wins include SEPA and Danaher Corporation.

Semple Fraser LLP's team is led by the first-class Vincent Brown. The team continues to receive top-quality instructions from impressive clients, acting on both advisory and contentious matters. It advised Marathon Oil on international and EU law issues associated with offshore oil exploration and production, and also assisted the WWF with the preparation of draft marine legislation.

Mark Brumwell joined **Dundas & Wilson CS LLP** as new department head, bringing several high-calibre clients including Southern Water and the Environment Agency. Significant instructions included acting for Scottish and Southern Energy on the £3.2bn acquisition from National Grid Transco of two gas distribution networks.

Under the leadership of Chris Smylie, **Maclay Murray & Spens**' team handles complex stand-alone matters. The team advised Schlumberger on the formation of its water services and solutions division.

Environmental and planning specialist Colin Innes leads the environment practice at **Shepherd+ Wedderburn**. The firm advised Waterfront Edinburgh on contaminated land issues relating to the regeneration of the Granton Waterfront, and also acted for Viridor on the Scottish aspects of its proposed acquisition of a part of the Shanks Group.

Biggart Baillie continues to build on its solid environment practice. Led by Neil Amner , the department advised National Express on contamination and remediation liabilities at railway maintenance depots, and also acted for Marine Harvest in respect of a multi-million-pound claim arising from an ISA infection of stock in various fish farms.

Jamie Grant leads the team at **MacRoberts**. Recent work includes advising Network Rail on noise abatement notice appeals, while other clients include the Shanks Group and British Energy.

Jennifer Ballantyne is the department head of **McGrigors**' practice. Recently the team saw an increase in instructions from the renewable energy sector, acting for Lewis Windpower and Renewable Energy Systems amongst others. Major clients also include BP and Tarmac. Edinburgh-based partner Michael Spence is an expert in regeneration and contaminated land issues.

Morton Fraser's environmental unit is headed up by Nick Atkins . In the past year the team flexed its muscles in a range of issues, including advising on the decommissioning of a former nuclear plant, and on contaminated land issues for private and public sector clients.

Tods Murray LLP's environmental team is a significant player in the market. Highlights have included advising Aberdeen Environmental Services on issues related to its PFI wastewater treatment concession. The department also provides SEPA with advice on a range of contentious matters.

INFORMATION TECHNOLOGY AND INTELLECTUAL PROPERTY

Dundas & Wilson CS LLP continues to impress with some weighty instructions and top-notch clients. The firm was re-appointed by the University of Glasgow to act exclusively on its IP commercialisation transactions, and it also provided an IP audit and advised on a strategic commercialisation model review for ePoint. Other impressive clients include ITN. Laurence Ward receives high praise from clients.

Gill Grassie heads the practice at **Maclay Murray & Spens**. The team has a strong presence in contentious IP, and acted on behalf of Technip in a landmark patent infringement appeal in the Court of Session. Other highlights include acting for Scottish Enterprise and the University of Paisley in the disposal of the Scottish Property Network. Edinburgh-based Caroline Rollestone-Brown heads the corporate technology practice.

Joanna Boag-Thomson leads **Shepherd+ Wedderburn**'s team, bringing expertise in IP and life science matters. Recent highlights include acting for ITI Scotland, and advising MicroEmissive Displays Group on aspects of its admission to AIM.

INFORMATION TECHNOLOGY AND INTELLECTUAL PROPERTY

DUNDAS & WILSON CS LLP ✪ *Edinburgh*
MACLAY MURRAY & SPENS *Glasgow*
SHEPHERD+ WEDDERBURN *Edinburgh*

PINSENT MASONS *Glasgow*

BIGGART BAILLIE *Glasgow*
MACROBERTS *Glasgow*
McGRIGORS *Glasgow*
MORTON FRASER *Edinburgh*
TODS MURRAY LLP *Edinburgh*

Brechin Tindal Oatts *Glasgow*
Brodies LLP *Edinburgh*
Burness *Edinburgh*
DLA Piper Rudnick Gray Cary Scotland LLP *Glasgow*
Lindsays WS *Edinburgh*
Wright, Johnston & Mackenzie LLP *Glasgow*

Anderson Strathern *Edinburgh*
HBJ Gateley Wareing LLP *Edinburgh, Glasgow*
Harper Macleod LLP *Glasgow*
Ledingham Chalmers *Aberdeen*
McClure Naismith *Glasgow*
Semple Fraser LLP *Glasgow*
Thorntons *Dundee*

Firms are listed A-Z in tiers which are ranked in order of priority
✪ *Indicates firm displays contact details at the end of this chapter.*

Telecoms specialist Paul Carlyle advised Scottish Enterprise in relation to the creation of a wholesale broadband network.

John Salmon heads **Pinsent Masons**' respected practice. It was appointed by the Office to the Solicitor of the Scottish Executive to provide specialist telecoms advice in respect of Broadband for Scotland.

Biggart Baillie's IP/IT team continues to increase its profile and win quality instructions, with strategic expansion in the areas of telecoms, e-commerce, data protection and litigation. Department head Colin Miller is acting for an individual who is pursuing a claim against a tabloid newspaper for breach of privacy. New client wins include WWAV Rapp Collins and Clinical Informatics.

David Flint heads **MacRoberts**' technology and media department. The team advises on a range of IP issues, including data protection, licensing and copyright disputes.

McGrigors had an active and successful year, acting for the Registers of Scotland in relation to its appointment of a strategic IT/IS partner. It also saw an increased level of instructions from KPMG, Royal Bank of Scotland and Caledonian McBrayne. Seona Burnett heads the highly regarded IP practice, which advised Maxxium UK on a logistics services agreement. Matthew Godfrey-Faussett took over as head of IT.

Lorne Byatt heads the department at **Morton Fraser**. Ewan McIntyre has recently advised in a number of significant patent infringement cases, and the team also offers data protection and outsourcing advice to various charities and educational and financial services organisations. National Australia Group, Ice Robotics and Voxar are all clients.

Tods Murray LLP's team advised MacDonald Resorts in its negotiations with a large US software company in connection with a database and customer management ASP contract. The team has been appointed to SEPA's legal panel for IP work.

Pauline McBride heads the IP department at **Brechin Tindal Oatts**, which is instructed by a broad client base. Recent highlights include acting for a software supplier in a dispute with a major software company.

Grant Campbell leads **Brodies LLP**'s technology practice, which is taking on increasingly prominent work. Weighty instructions include acting for Siemens in the negotiation of an outsourcing agreement, while other significant clients include Channel 4 and BAe Systems.

Burness' IP and IT team is a key adviser to Scottish Enterprise on IT and high-profile business projects. David Goodbrand 's team has strengthened its focus in technology outsourcing and procurement, with clients such as SMG plc, GE Capital and the Scottish Arts Council.

DLA Piper Rudnick Gray Cary Scotland LLP acts for several leading IT providers and customers in the private and public sectors, with John McKinlay leading the practice. Recent high-profile instructions include being appointed to advise on the digitisation of the entire archive of the *Scotsman* newspaper.

Lindsays WS was significantly strengthened by the arrivalof partner David Wood, who is an expert in non-contentious IP. The team acts for a variety of clients in negotiating cross-border ventures and technology-led investments. It also acts for a wide range of SME software and technology companies, as well as equity investors. The University of Edinburgh and the University of St. Andrews are key clients. David Reith heads the IT/IP department.

Wright, Johnston & Mackenzie LLP is experienced in IT and e-commerce matters, and is respected for its life science work.

Simon Brown heads the solid IP practice at **Anderson Strathern**. The team advised Kwik-Fit on a complete joint branding agreement with a large UK bank relating to a customer card loyalty scheme. Napier University and the Mental Welfare Commission for Scotland are also clients.

HBJ Gateley Wareing LLP' sister business Demys continues to develop, advising large corporates on domain name strategy, management and disputes. Andrew Walker leads a practice that boasts clients such as Chartered Brands and United International Pictures.

Harper Macleod LLP boasts a sound IP and IT practice that saw its quality of instructions grow. Lead partner Tom Thomas is the principal adviser to the Scottish Premier League on IP/IT matters, while other clients include Arriva, Student Loans Company and Thus.

McClure Naismith offers a comprehensive range of advice on IP and IT matters. The team advises Bank of Scotland on its sponsorship of the Scottish Premier League, and is also acting for Chivas Brothers on passing off and trade mark issues. Kenneth Chrystie leads the practice.

INSOLVENCY AND CORPORATE RECOVERY

Dundas & Wilson CS LLP's insolvency and corporate recovery group remains in a league of its own. Partners Yvonne Brady, David Gibson and group head Ian Cuthbertson are all at the top of their game. Recently the firm advised the main lenders in the £120m restructuring and refinancing of ASCO, and major clients include Ernst & Young, KPMG, Deloitte and Kroll.

Andrew Sleigh heads **Burness**' well-regarded insolvency group. The firm acted on several significant receiverships, for example advising RBS on pre-insolvency matters and Deloitte on the subsequent receivership of the J D Crane Group.

DLA Piper Rudnick Gray Cary Scotland LLP's highly rated insolvency practice is headed by experienced partner Gordon Hollerin . The firm advised Kroll on the receivership of property investment company Parkcross. Other clients include Deloitte, PricewaterhouseCoopers and KPMG.

Michael Hughes heads **Maclay Murray & Spens**' well-regarded practice, which has strong expertise across the full range of insolvency and corporate recovery matters. The firm recently advised Barr Group on the restructuring of its subsidiaries.

McGrigors' commendable restructuring and insolvency practice is headed by litigation partner Jim Cormack. The group advised Lloyds TSB and subsequently Deloitte on the Caithness Glass insolvency. Other clients include Pricewaterhouse-Coopers, KPMG and Grant Thornton.

Semple Fraser LLP enjoys a strong reputation for insolvency work and continues to act for the DTI's Insolvency Service's Directors Disqualification Unit in Scotland. A major highlight has been advising Citibank on the Scottish aspects of the British Energy restructuring. Rachel Grant heads the team.

Former chief executive and insolvency expert Paul Hally now heads **Shepherd+ Wedderburn**'s active practice. The firm recently acted for the Assets Recovery Agency in its first Scottish proceedings to enforce provisions in the Proceeds of Crime legislation. Major clients include Bank of Scotland, KPMG, Deloitte and Kroll.

Corporate partner John Kerr heads **Anderson Strathern**'s solid insolvency team, which regularly acts for banks, including the Bank of Scotland. The firm advised sportscotland as creditor in the high-profile insolvencies of Ratho Climbing Centre and Dundee Football Club.

Led by Brent Haywood, **Biggart Baillie** stands out as one of only two firms to be on the DTI's panel for directors' disqualification cases, the other being **Semple Fraser LLP**. The firm acts for several accountancy firms, including KPMG, Tenon and Grant Thornton, on small to medium-sized liquidations.

Robin Macpherson's practice at **Brodies LLP** acts for a range of impressive clients, including Grant Thornton, Haines Watts, KPMG and PricewaterhouseCoopers.

Harper Macleod LLP has a solid insolvency practice, which advised the administrator and the directors in the creditors voluntary arrangement for Motherwell FC. James Lloyd heads the group.

The largest instruction on **MacRoberts**' books is advising British Energy on the Scottish aspects of its restructuring. The group is headed by David Flint.

George Frier is the main insolvency partner at **McClure Naismith**, which recently acted for Grant Thornton and Barclays Bank on the receivership and sale of Forth Tool & Valve.

INSOLVENCY AND CORPORATE RECOVERY

DUNDAS & WILSON CS LLP ✪ *Edinburgh, Glasgow*

BURNESS *Edinburgh, Glasgow*
DLA PIPER RUDNICK GRAY CARY SCOTLAND LLP *Glasgow, Edinburgh*
MACLAY MURRAY & SPENS *Glasgow, Edinburgh*
McGRIGORS *Glasgow, Edinburgh*
SEMPLE FRASER LLP *Glasgow*
SHEPHERD+ WEDDERBURN *Edinburgh, Glasgow*

Anderson Strathern *Edinburgh*
Biggart Baillie *Glasgow, Edinburgh*
Brodies LLP *Edinburgh*
Harper Macleod LLP *Glasgow*
Iain Smith & Co *Aberdeen*
MacRoberts *Glasgow, Edinburgh*
McClure Naismith *Glasgow, Edinburgh*
Tods Murray LLP *Edinburgh, Glasgow*

Blackadders *Dundee*
Boyds Solicitors LLP *Glasgow*
Gillespie Macandrew WS *Edinburgh*
HBJ Gateley Wareing LLP *Edinburgh, Glasgow*
Ledingham Chalmers *Aberdeen*
Morton Fraser *Edinburgh*
Paull & Williamsons *Aberdeen*

Firms are listed A-Z in tiers which are ranked in order of priority
✪ Indicates firm displays contact details at the end of this chapter.

Glasgow-based corporate partner Alastair Burrow heads **Tods Murray LLP**'s solid insolvency practice, which has experience across a range of matters. Clients include Baker Tilly, Citigroup and Kroll.

PENSIONS

Shepherd+Wedderburn remains in pole position, offering expertise to large commercial clients and trustees of their pension schemes. Highlights of the year included advising AWG on strategic provision for pension arrangements, and advising the trustees of three AWG schemes, while other clients include ScottishPower and Stagecoach. Andrew Holehouse heads the market-leading practice.

Biggart Baillie's pension department continues to build on its strong reputation. New clients of note include the Standard Life Staff Pension Scheme, ASCO Final Salary Plan and Richmond Fellowship Scotland. Iain Talman heads the group.

Steven Dunn leads **Burness**' pensions team, which operates as part of the firm's wider employment, pensions and benefits practice. It advised Kosaido on the pensions issues arising from the £38m sale of the St Andrews Old Course Hotel and Dukes golf course to Kohler.

Dundas & Wilson CS LLP's flourishing department was bolstered significantly by the arrival of pensions expert David Knox. Top-quality instructions included advising Chicago-based VC specialist Code Hennessey & Simmons on the pensions aspects of the $40m sale of certain UK subsidiaries of AMF Bowling.

Maclay Murray & Spens' pensions department acts for a number of employers and trustees on the strategic planning of final salary schemes. Clients include BPI plc, Communities Scotland, and Malcolm Group. Department head Jane Fraser is highly recommended.

Peter Trotter heads **MacRoberts**' team. Highlights have included being appointed independent trustee of the ASCO Final Salary Plan, and new clients include Compass Investment Trust and Eadie Brothers Pension Scheme.

PENSIONS

SHEPHERD+ WEDDERBURN *Edinburgh*

BIGGART BAILLIE *Glasgow*
BURNESS *Edinburgh*
DUNDAS & WILSON CS LLP ✪ *Edinburgh*
MACLAY MURRAY & SPENS *Glasgow*
MACROBERTS *Glasgow*

McGrigors *Glasgow*
Tods Murray LLP *Edinburgh*

Firms are listed A-Z in tiers which are ranked in order of priority
✪ Indicates firm displays contact details at the end of this chapter.

McGrigors had an exceptionally strong year advising companies and scheme trustees with pension scheme deficits.

Martin Thurston Smith brings 20 years' experience to the department at **Tods Murray LLP**. The team has been advising the Bank of Scotland Pension Scheme in connection with a variety of issues arising from property-related investment transactions.

REAL ESTATE

Edinburgh and Glasgow: Brodies LLP moves into the top tier, thanks to superb clients wins including Moorfield Group, Ediston Properties and Palmer Capital Partners. Highlights have included advising the Old Torry Partnership on the £60m redevelopment of the Old Torry Waterfront area of Aberdeen. The team also advised Land Securities Trillium on the Scottish aspects of the development agreement for the new BBC headquarters at Pacific Quay in Glasgow. The department has a solid retail practice representing top-notch clients such as Zara, Co-op and Debenhams. Denis Garrity heads the impressive practice.

Dundas & Wilson CS LLP receives top-quality instructions from top-quality clients. The team was recently appointed by Land Securities to handle the disposal and acquisition of three shopping centres, and also acted for News International in relation to its proposed development of a major new printing facility at the Eurocentral site, a 650-acre business development park located in the M8/A8 corridor. Leading environmental lawyer Mark Brumwell recently joined the firm.

Maclay Murray & Spens' sizeable team, under Norman Smith, acts across the board for a variety of clients, including retailers, developers and property companies, and has been involved in a raft of sizeable transactions of late. Highlights include acting for the Tonstate Group in the £70m acquisition of the Omni Centre.

McGrigors' commercial property department boasts impressive strength in depth. Alison Newton worked on the largest property deal in Scotland, the £270m sale of the St Enoch Centre in Glasgow on behalf of Deka Immobilien Investment Gmbh. The team also recently advised Clydeport on the disposal of a portfolio of 19 properties in Glasgow and Edinburgh. Retail and development specialist Richard Linton receives instructions from several major clients including Co-operative Group (CWS), Farrow and Ball, and Ottakar's.

Dorothy Boyd heads **Shepherd+Wedderburn**'s team, which has received a marked increase in cross-border instructions. Significant work includes acting on behalf of the Auchinlea Partnership in relation to the letting of Glasgow Fort Retail Park, as well as its £194m sale. The firm acts for SEPA and has been re-appointed to the Scottish Enterprise panel.

Burness' commercial property team saw impressive recent growth. The team advised The Carlyle Group on property issues arising from its joint venture with the Halladale Group, and acted on the acquisition and development of a £100m production and retail park in Cumbernauld. Caroline Drummond leads the quality outfit.

REAL ESTATE
Edinburgh and Glasgow

BRODIES LLP *Edinburgh*
DUNDAS & WILSON CS LLP ✪ *Edinburgh, Glasgow*
MACLAY MURRAY & SPENS *Glasgow, Edinburgh*
McGRIGORS *Glasgow, Edinburgh*
SHEPHERD+ WEDDERBURN *Edinburgh, Glasgow*

BURNESS *Edinburgh, Glasgow*
DLA PIPER RUDNICK GRAY CARY SCOTLAND LLP *Glasgow, Edinburgh*
MACROBERTS *Glasgow, Edinburgh*
SEMPLE FRASER LLP *Glasgow, Edinburgh*

BIGGART BAILLIE *Glasgow, Edinburgh*
MORTON FRASER *Edinburgh, Glasgow*
TODS MURRAY LLP *Edinburgh, Glasgow*

Anderson Strathern *Edinburgh*
Bell & Scott *Edinburgh*
Boyds Solicitors LLP *Glasgow, Edinburgh*
Fyfe Ireland *Edinburgh*
Harper Macleod LLP *Glasgow*
Lindsays WS *Edinburgh*
McClure Naismith *Glasgow, Edinburgh*
Pinsent Masons *Glasgow*

Archibald Campbell & Harley WS *Edinburgh*
Bishops Solicitors LLP *Glasgow*
Brechin Tindal Oatts *Glasgow*
Golds *Glasgow*
HBJ Gateley Wareing LLP *Edinburgh, Glasgow*
Ledingham Chalmers *Aberdeen*
Leslie Wolfson & Co *Glasgow*
Miller Samuel LLP *Glasgow*
Morisons *Edinburgh*
Paull & Williamsons *Aberdeen*
Wright, Johnston & Mackenzie LLP *Glasgow, Edinburgh*

Firms are listed A-Z in tiers which are ranked in order of priority
✪ Indicates firm displays contact details at the end of this chapter.

Drew Wallace heads the team at **DLA Piper Rudnick Gray Cary Scotland LLP**, which is taking an increasing share of the market. Highlights include acting on the acquisition of a portfolio of properties from Norwich Union via of a Jersey unit trust. Top-drawer clients include Ashtenne Holdings, Abbey, and Cannon Capital. Sandy Telfer joined the team, bringing significant planning expertise. Graeme Sunter is department head at the Glasgow office.

MacRoberts continues to impress with top-quality instructions. Recent highlights include acting for ISIS Waterside Regeneration in a joint-venture between AMEC and British Waterways on a major urban regeneration scheme in Glasgow. Laurence Fraser and Allan MacKenzie head the department.

Elspeth Carson is the department head at **Semple Fraser LLP**'s sound practice, which acts on big-ticket property deals for high-profile clients. Highlights of the year included acting for British Land in the £500m retail partnership between British Land and Land Securities.

Biggart Baillie boasts a sizeable commercial property team. Iain McLean 's group acted for an impressive list of blue-chip multinationals on a variety of transactions. Retail clients include the Arcadia Group, Gap and Starbucks. Peter Cruickshank is experienced in asset-backed cross-border financings.

Craig Bowman is the department head at **Morton Fraser**, which recently advised Volkswagen Financial Services on the development and forward leasing of the Audi Regional Headquarters at Braehead. The firm recruited Brian Hutcheson to its Glasgow office to develop its nascent practice in the city.

The property department at **Tods Murray LLP** has continued to grow. The team acted for Insight Investment Management in the Scottish property aspects of the acquisition of McKenzie LP's property portfolio, and added Clerical Medical Investment Group and Travelodge Hotels to an already impressive client list.

Anderson Strathern's commercial property team has seen steady expansion following the recruitment of Neil Farrell and Ian Moffett. Quality instructions included advising Scottish Midland Co-Operative Society in the acquisition of Morning Noon and Night. Alan Menzies heads the department.

Bell & Scott's commercial property practice was bolstered by the arrival of the experienced Heather O'Neill. Paul Jennings heads the team, which acts for its extensive clientele on a range of property matters. New client wins include Unilever, Compass Group, and Chiquitos.

Boyds Solicitors LLP fields a solid commercial property practice under David Boyce . The department has acted for Reg Vardy Group and Miller Homes.

Fyfe Ireland has a solid practice headed by James Roscoe. The department has a strong focus on commercial leasing and secured lending work.

McClure Naismith boasts a comprehensive commercial property practice. The firm recently acted for Coal Pension Properties on the Scottish aspects of the disposal of a property portfolio. Wilson Aitken's team acts for several major high-street names.

Pinsent Masons' commercial property department is led by Hugh Bruce-Watt. The team recently advised on FM Developments' acquisition of a residential site from Forth Ports in Granton. It also advises Barr Group, Interserve, and Honda Finance Europe.

REAL ESTATE
Elsewhere in Scotland

PAULL & WILLIAMSONS *Aberdeen*

LEDINGHAM CHALMERS *Aberdeen*

Iain Smith & Co *Aberdeen*
Raeburn Christie Clark & Wallace *Aberdeen*
Stronachs *Aberdeen, Inverness*
Thorntons *Dundee*

Blackadders *Dundee*

Firms are listed A-Z in tiers which are ranked in order of priority

Elsewhere in Scotland: Paull & Williamsons continues to be the market leader outside the central belt. The department has received instructions to act on various land acquisitions for the Stewart Milne Group, and it is also advising BP on its proposed new headquarters in Aberdeen, as well as a number of other oil majors on similar projects. Former practice head Leslie Delgano has taken a new client development role for the property group and the firm.

John Curran 's team at **Ledingham Chalmers** had another busy year. Highlights included acting for GSS Development on the intended world headquarters for First Group. The team also acted for Graham Cooper on its acquisition of Newton Trading Estate in Ayr.

Iain Smith & Co of Aberdeen has a strong commercial property team. The firm also has a Stonehaven office.

Recently merged **Raeburn Christie Clark & Wallace** provides solid commercial property advice to corporate entities from a variety of sectors.

Under the stewardship of Duncan Campbell , **Stronachs**' team continues to act for Highlands and Islands Enterprise. The firm also has an Inverness office.

Thorntons' commercial property team provides secured lending advice to several major banks. The team was recently appointed to the Bank of Scotland corporate panel.

TRANSPORT

HBJ Gateley Wareing LLP remains a market leader in both maritime and admiralty matters, and acts for numerous ship owners and P&I clubs.

Aberdeen-based **Mackinnons** has a stellar reputation for all aspects of marine law, with Keith MacRae particularly highly regarded.

TRANSPORT

HBJ GATELEY WAREING LLP *Edinburgh, Glasgow*
MACKINNONS *Aberdeen*
MACLAY MURRAY & SPENS *Glasgow, Edinburgh*

BRODIES LLP *Edinburgh*
DUNDAS & WILSON CS LLP ✪ *Edinburgh, Glasgow*
MORTON FRASER *Glasgow, Edinburgh*

Biggart Baillie *Edinburgh, Glasgow*
Tods Murray LLP *Edinburgh, Glasgow*

Firms are listed A-Z in tiers which are ranked in order of priority
✪ Indicates firm displays contact details at the end of this chapter.

Maclay Murray & Spens' department is impressively strong and offers a breadth of expertise in litigation and financing. Enviable clients include Lithgow's, Clyde Marine, and SEPA. Andrew Meakin heads the practice.

Brodies LLP continues to increase its market share in the transport sector. The team completed the re-let of the £1.9bn ScotRail franchise. The arrival of shipping expert Duncan MacLean was a significant boost.

Dundas & Wilson CS LLP acted for TIE in respect to the public inquiry into the Edinburgh congestion charging scheme, and for Edinburgh City Council on the extension of the city's controlled parking zone. The firm also handles a broad range of maritime issues.

Morton Fraser is a new entry in the table this year, on the strength of its recruitment of aviation and shipping specialist Alexia Henriksen , formerly of Norway's **Wiersholm, Mellbye & Bech, advokatfirma AS**. Recent work includes undertaking a review of Ferguson Shipbuilders' shipbuilding contracts. The department has also been appointed to the shipping and aviation panel of the National Australia Group.

Neil Amner heads **Biggart Baillie**'s transport team. It provides specialist advice to ScotRail in relation to railway contracts and franchise and regulatory agreements concerning the Scottish Passenger Rail Franchise. New clients include the British Transport Police Authority.

Tods Murray LLP partner Alastair Burrow is experienced in non-contentious shipping matters.

DUNDAS & WILSON

SALTIRE COURT
20 CASTLE TERRACE
EDINBURGH EH1 2EN

Telephone: +44 131 228 8000
Fax: +44 131 228 8888
E-mail: dw-enquiries@dundas-wilson.com
Website: www.dundas-wilson.com

Languages
French, German, Italian, Spanish

Other offices
Glasgow, London

Number of lawyers 330
at this office 172

CATEGORIES OF WORK

Banking
Stephen Phillips

Construction and engineering
Lindy Patterson

Corporate
Michael Polson

Corporate recovery
Ian Cuthbertson

Dispute resolution
Colin Macleod

Employment
Eilidh Wiseman

Environment
Mark Brumwell

EU and competition
Graeme Young

IP/IT
Laurence Ward

Pensions
David Knox

Planning and transportation
Ann Faulds

Projects
Alan Campbell

Property
Iain Doran

Tax
Susan Hoyle

WHO'S WHO IN THE LAW

Professional contacts

AUSTRIA

ANGERMAIR, Thomas

Dorda Brugger Jordis
Phone: Vienna (+43 1 533 47 95 24)
E-mail: thomas.angermair@dbj.at
Labour and employment; litigation and arbitration.
Position: Thomas Angermair heads the firm's employment team. His practice also focuses on private trusts, litigation and arbitration. His client base covers a wide range of industry sectors (including cultural industries), banking and international organisations. Thomas Angermair's main areas of practice are Austrian and EU employment law. He advises on employment contracts, dismissals, termination agreements, employment issues arising from mergers and acquisitions as well as from corporate restructuring and reorganisation. He also focuses on incentive schemes, company pension and stock option plans. The work with international clients includes the employment of foreign employees in Austria. Having specialised in arbitration and litigation for many years, Thomas Angermair has extensive expertise with major legal disputes, representing his clients before arbitral tribunals as well as public courts.
Career: Associate Dorda Brugger Jordis 1987; partner since 1992. In addition to his law practice, he gives lectures and runs specialised seminars on employment law. He has published numerous articles in Austrian and international professional journals. Thomas Angermair is a member of supervisory boards and of several boards of trustees at Austrian private trusts.
Languages: German, English.
Member: IBA; UIA; Austrian Arbitration Association.
Education: University of Vienna (1986 JD).
Personal: Born 1964.

ARTNER, Stefan, MMag

Dorda Brugger Jordis
Phone: Vienna (+43 1 533 47 95 103)
E-mail: stefan.artner@dbj.at
Real estate law; M&A and corporate restructurings.
Position: Partner; head of the firm's real estate desk. His practice focuses on real estate law and M&A. His expertise includes acquisition of real estate, privatisation of real estate portfolios, corporate and private leases and due diligence. Transactions include the representation of Bundesimmobiliengesellschaft, the Austrian privatisation agency for real estate. He has also advised on a wide range of M&A transactions and major Austrian and multinational corporate restructurings.
Career: Associate at different Vienna-based law firms; associate at Dorda Brugger Jordis; international trainee at Shearman & Sterling, New York; admitted to the Austrian Bar in 2000; partner Dorda Brugger Jordis since 2000. Publications: author of numerous articles on real estate and corporate law; presentations at specialised seminars and conferences in Austria on topics such as 'Real Estate Due Diligence' and 'Purchase of Real Estate in Eastern Europe'.
Languages: German, English.
Member: IBA; AIJA (Association Internationale des Jeunes Avocats).
Education: University of Vienna (1993 JD); Vienna University of Economics and Business Administration (1996 Master in Economic Studies).
Personal: Born 1968.

BRODEY, Martin, Dr

Dorda Brugger Jordis
Phone: Vienna (+43 1 533 47 95 38)
E-mail: martin.brodey@dbj.at
Corporate; national and international M&A; competition; liberalised markets; life sciences.
Position: Partner specialising in corporate law and M&A. He has advised numerous international clients on sizeable acquisition projects in Austria and CEE, in particular, privatisation projects such as the acquisition (and later sale) of a strategic interest in the Austrian incumbent mobile and fixed telecom operators by Telecom Italia. The main industries covered are the 'liberalised markets' (such as energy and telecom), wood and paper industry, construction as well as the chemical, pharmaceutical and health industries (life sciences).
Career: Traineeships with Sidley & Austin, Washington DC and White & Case, New York; admitted to the Austrian Bar 1994. Publication of numerous articles (with special attention to telecommunications law) in Austrian and international professional journals; presentations at specialised seminars and conferences in Austria and abroad.
Languages: German, English, French.
Member: IBA; UIA; Austrian Association of Lawyers (Juristenverband).
Education: University of Virginia (1989 LLM); University of Vienna (1992 JD); law studies at the University Paris II 'Assass'.
Personal: Born 1963.

BROGYÁNYI, Christoph, Mag

Dorda Brugger Jordis
Phone: Vienna (+43 1 533 47 95 480)
E-mail: christoph.brogyanyi@dbj.at
Corporate law; capital markets law; restructurings; M&A.
Position: Partner specialising in corporate law, corporate finance, capital markets, privatisations and M&A (including corporate restructurings). He co-heads the firm's corporate and tax law team. Christoph Brogyányi advises corporate clients, investment and corporate banks and private equity houses in national and international corporate finance and capital market transactions (equity and debt) as well as privatisations and M&A transactions (including corporate restructurings).
Career: Associate Dorda Brugger Jordis; admitted to the Austrian Bar in 2002; partner Dorda Brugger Jordis since 2002; lecturer at various seminars on corporate law.
Languages: German, English.
Education: University of Vienna (1996 JD); Bar exam 2001.
Personal: Born 1970.

BRUGGER, Walter, Dr

Dorda Brugger Jordis
Phone: Vienna (+43 1 533 47 95 13)
E-mail: walter.brugger@dbj.at
Corporate and competition law.
Position: Founding partner of Dorda Brugger Jordis, specialising in corporate restructurings and competition and cartel law. He has advised numerous national and international clients on corporate restructurings (including the squeeze-out of minority shareholders), and on merger and de-merger projects including listed companies. His practice in the area of competition law extends to all aspects of Austrian and European antitrust law. Services provided range from out-of-court advice to representation before antitrust authorities and litigation.
Career: Admitted to the Austrian Bar in 1983. Publications: book on 'Unternehmenserwerb - Acquisition of Business Enterprises'; lecturer on competition and corporate law at the Vienna University of Technology; presentations at specialised seminars; numerous articles in Austrian and international professional journals on corporate law.
Languages: German, English, Spanish.
Member: Austrian Banking Society; UNION Lawyers' Association.
Education: University of Vienna (1978 JD).
Personal: Born 1954.

DESKOVIC, Ivo

DLA Weiss-Tessbach
Phone: Vienna (+43 1 531 78 1701)
E-mail: ivo.deskovic@dlapiper.com
Commercial practice group.
Position: Heads the commercial practice group of DLA Weiss-Tessbach in CEE, which comprises all the full-service elements required for advising clients in the region, including general commercial law, telecommunications law, employment law, litigation, public law and IP. Particular expertise includes general commercial law, banking regulatory law, litigation and telecommunications law.
Career: Trained at Weiss-Tessbach, Vienna, Linklaters, London, and Creditanstalt Bank, Vienna, London and New York; qualified as Austrian attorney 1993; partner DLA Weiss-Tessbach 1993.
Languages: German, English.
Member: Austrian Bar Association; International Bar Association; International Chamber of Commerce; Commission on Environment.
Education: Law Faculty University of Vienna (1988 Mag Iuris - LLB).
Personal: Born 1962; resides Vienna.

DORDA, Christian, Dr

Dorda Brugger Jordis
Phone: Vienna (+43 1 533 47 95 14)
E-mail: christian.dorda@dbj.at

M&A; corporate law; financial law; arbitration.
Position: Founding partner of Dorda Brugger Jordis specialising in M&A, corporate restructurings and corporate finance. His work includes the sale of business enterprises, joint ventures, privatisations, capital-market transactions and private equity. He is experienced in cross-border transactions, with a focus on Austria's neighbouring CEE region where he co-operates with local counsels of leading law firms. In international arbitration, he is regularly sought after as both a party counsel and an arbitrator.
Career: Admitted to the Austrian Bar 1976. Author of various articles on corporate and commercial law and numerous conference papers.
Languages: German, English, French.
Member: Board of Trustees of the American Chamber of Commerce in Austria; permanent legal counsel to the French-Austrian Chamber of Commerce; editorial board of the 'European Lawyer'; alternate member of the ICC International Court of Arbitration; chairman of the M&A Commission of the Union Internationale des Avocats; Austrian Bar; IBA; supervisory board of various Austrian corporations and of the management board of private foundations.
Education: University of Vienna (1976 JD).
Personal: Born 1947.

EBNER, Martin

Schönherr
Phone: Vienna (+43 1 534 37 193)
E-mail: m.ebner@schoenherr.at
Position: Junior partner specialising in banking, structured finance, project finance, capital markets, derivative financial instruments.
Career: Admitted to the Austrian Bar 2002; co-author 'Co-operation and investment handbook: Czech and Slovak Republics'; country correspondent of 'IFLR'; lecturer at the University of Salzburg and the McGeorge School of Law, University of the Pacific; gives seminars on cross-border and structured finance.
Languages: German, English.
Education: University of Salzburg (1995 Mag iur); Pallas Consortium, Nijmegen, The Netherlands (1997 LLM).
Personal: Born 1972.

EDER, Stefan, Dr

DLA Weiss-Tessbach
Phone: Vienna (+43 1 531 78 1601)
E-mail: stefan.eder@dlapiper.com
Projects and finance practice group.
Position: Regional managing partner CEE; head of practice group projects and finance CEE. Advises clients on all types of project and finance matters, real estate development projects and cross-border M&A and finance transactions in Central and Eastern Europe. Expertise includes in particular public-private partnerships and other public-private financing models, as well as (cross-border) debt recovery and related insolvency issues. As regional managing partner for CEE, oversees co-ordination and development of legal services offered by the firm's offices in Austria and Central and Eastern Europe.
Career: Trained Weiss-Tessbach, Vienna, and Clifford Chance, London; qualified as Austrian attorney 1992; qualified as foreign attorney in Czech Republic 1997 and Hungary 1999; partner DLA Weiss-Tessbach since 1992. Author of several articles and books in areas of expertise, including the Austrian chapter of the 'European Insolvency and Restructuring Guide 2005/2006' (2005, Global White Page, together with Miklos Revay) and the 'Co-operation and Investment Handbook' (1998, ecoplus Niederösterreichs Regionale Entwicklungsagentur Gesellschaft mbH). Currently giving lectures on 'Project Development in Central and Eastern Europe' at the Vienna University of Technology's Masters Program for Real Estate Development and Evaluation.
Languages: German, English.
Member: Austrian Bar Association; International Bar Association; Gesellschaft für Informatik; Austrian Computer Society; International Fiscal Association.
Education: Law Faculty University of Vienna (1984 Dr Iuris - PhD); Economics and Informatics Faculty University of Vienna (1987 Magister Iuris - LLB).
Personal: Born 1962; resides Vienna.

FEHRINGER, Sabine, MMag

Fellner Wratzfeld & Partner Rechtsanwälte GmbH
Phone: Vienna (+43 1 537 70)
E-mail: sabine.fehringer@fwp.at
Corporate, IP, IT, telecoms, media and competition law, distribution law.
Position: Partner.
Career: Joined Fellner Wratzfeld & Partners as a partner in 2000; author of various articles in the field of e-commerce.
Languages: English, German, French.
Member: Austrian Bar.
Education: University of Vienna; Vienna University of Business Administration; London School of Economics and Business Administration.
Personal: Born 1965; resides Vienna.
Leisure: Literature, music, tennis.

FEYL, Peter, Dr

Schönherr
Phone: Vienna (+43 1 53 43 70)
E-mail: p.feyl@schoenherr.at
Position: Partner dealing with banking, capital markets, corporate law, trusts, mergers and acquisitions.
Career: Admitted to the Austrian Bar 1990.
Languages: English, French, German.
Education: University of Vienna (1984 Dr iur); University of Virginia (1986 LLM).
Personal: Born 1961.

FROTZ, Stephan, Dr

Schönherr
Phone: Vienna (+43 1 53 43 70)
E-mail: s.frotz@schoenherr.at
Position: Partner dealing with banking law, corporate restructurings, mergers and acquisitions, tax.
Career: Admitted to the Austrian Bar 1987.
Languages: English, French, German.
Education: University of Vienna (1981 Dr iur); research scholar, Max Planck-Institute for Foreign and International Patent.
Personal: Born 1957.

GRAF, Ferdinand, Dr

Graf, Maxl & Pitkowitz Rechtsanwälte GMBH
Phone: Vienna (+43 1 401 17 0)
E-mail: graf@gmp.at
Competition and commercial.
Position: Partner dealing with mergers and acquisitions, cartel and competition law, corporate law, general trade law, media law, telecommunications law.
Career: Assistant professor at University of Vienna, Institute of Civil Law 1988-89; internship at Arent, Fox, Kintner, Plotkin & Kahn, Washington DC 1991; associate Dr Ferdinand Graf and Preslmayr & Partners 1990-94; admitted to New York Bar 1993; admitted to Austrian Bar 1994; founding partner Graf, Maxl & Pitkowitz 1994.
Languages: English, German.
Member: Austrian Bar; American, New York State and International Bar Associations; Center for International Legal Studies, Salzburg.
Education: University of Vienna (1990 JD); New York University (1991 Master of Laws).
Personal: Born 1965; resides Vienna.

GÜNTHER, Stefan, MMag Dr

Dorda Brugger Jordis
Phone: Vienna (+43 1 533 47 95 57)
E-mail: stefan.guenther@dbj.at
Corporate restructurings; constitutional, administrative and community law.
Position: Partner specialising in corporate restructurings and acquisition of business enterprises; constitutional and administrative law; community and public procurement law.
Career: University assistant at the Institute of Public Law and Political Science, University of Innsbruck; member of the scientific staff at the Constitutional Court in Vienna; admitted to the Austrian Bar 1999; associate Dorda Brugger Jordis; partner Dorda Brugger Jordis since 2000; lecturer at the University of Vienna since 2001. Publications: author of numerous articles in professional journals and books on constitutional and community law including 'Constitution and Social Insurance' (1994), 'EC Competition Rules in National Courts - Austria' (2001), and 'Government Liability in case of denial to refund taxes' (2005).
Languages: German, English, French.
Member: Austrian Commission of Legal Experts (Österreichische Juristenkommission); IBA.
Education: University of Innsbruck (1992 JD; 1996 Master of Political Science); College of Europe, Hamburg (supplementary studies on 'European Integration and International Business Relations').
Personal: Born 1968.

HAUER, Christian, Dr

Schönherr
Phone: Vienna (+43 1 53 43 70)
E-mail: ch.hauer@schoenherr.at
Position: Partner dealing with unfair competition law, trade marks, pharmaceuticals, food and drug law.

Career: Admitted to the Austrian Bar 1976.
Languages: English, French, German.
Member: Examining board for candidates for judgeship.
Education: University of Vienna (1967 Dr iur).
Personal: Born 1942.

HECHT, Michael, Dr
Fellner Wratzfeld & Partner Rechtsanwälte GmbH
Phone: Vienna (+43 2 537 70)
E-mail: michael.hecht@fwp.at
Infrastructure and real estate, environment, public administrative law and corporate law.
Position: Partner.
Career: Former associate professor and lecturer at Vienna University law school, author of various books and articles on public andministrative and corporate law, joined Fellner Wratzfeld & Partners as partner in 2000.
Languages: English, German.
Member: Austrian Bar; Vienna Law Society.
Education: University of Vienna.
Personal: Born 1965; resides Vienna.
Leisure: Culture, sports.

HERBST, Christian, Dr
Schönherr
Phone: Vienna (+43 1 53 43 70)
E-mail: ch.herbst@schoenherr.at
Position: Partner dealing with (international) mergers and acquisitions, takeovers, corporate law and arbitration.
Career: Admitted to the Bar 1988; foreign associate with a New York City law firm 1984. Lecturer on international M&A and business transactions at the University of Economics and Business Administration (since 2003), Vienna, and on the MBL program at Salzburg University (since 2000).
Languages: English, German.
Member: IBA; UIA; Forum Kartellrecht.
Education: Salzburg University (1982 Dr iur); School of Advanced International Studies JHU, Bologna (1983 Diploma); Harvard University (1984 LLM).
Personal: Born 1959.

HÖDL, Sascha Oliver
Schönherr
Phone: Vienna (+43 1 53 43 7266)
E-mail: s.hoedl@schoenherr.at
Position: Partner dealing with (cross-border) mergers and acquisitions, public takeovers, acquisition finance, equity capital markets, private equity and venture capital.
Career: Legal service of the European Commission, Brussels (1995-96); associate with international law firm, Vienna and Brussels (1997-99); admitted to the bar in Austria in 2001. Lecturer on international mergers and acquisitions, Vienna University of Economics and Business Administration (since 2003), and at the MBL programme, University of Salzburg Business School (since 2000).
Languages: German, English.
Education: University of Graz (1993 Mag iur; 1996 Dr iur); Harvard Law School (2000 LLM).
Personal: Born 1970.

ISOLA, Alexander
Graf, Maxl & Pitkowitz Rechtsanwälte GMBH
Phone: Graz (+43 316 833 777)
E-mail: isola@gmp.at
Insolvency and corporate restructuring; banking.
Position: Partner.
Career: Partner Rae Hofstätter & Isola Kommandipartnerschaft, Graz, until 1998; partner Schönherr Rechtsanwälte OEG, until mid-2002; partner Graf, Maxl & Pitkowitz, Vienna and Graz, since mid-2002. Co-author of 'The Handbook for Receivership' ('Handbuch des Masseverwalters'); author of several articles on bankruptcy law and corporate restructuring. Teaching positions, seminars in the field of corporate restructuring and insolvency law.
Languages: English, German.
Member: EIPA European Insolvency Practitioners Association; AIJA International Association of Young Lawyers; advisory board Zeitschrift für Insolvenzrecht und Kreditschutz (ZIK).
Education: University of Graz (1981 Dr iuris); traineeship European Council (1981); New York University (M1984 CJ).
Personal: Born 1957; resides in Graz and Vienna.
Leisure: Collecting modern art.

JORDIS, Theresa, Dr
Dorda Brugger Jordis
Phone: Vienna (+43 1 533 47 95 15)
E-mail: theresa.jordis@dbj.at
Corporate law; contract law; private companies and trusts.
Position: Founding partner, focusing mainly on large and medium-sized Austrian clients who are major shareholders of companies with strong industrial interests. Her practice centres on both domestic and cross-border transactions, mergers and acquisitions, joint ventures and general corporate matters. Her clients include companies in the automotive, paper and textile industry. She has advised on the privatisation and restructuring of several major state-owned companies on behalf of the purchasing party.
Career: Admitted to the Austrian Bar 1981. Author of various articles in professional periodicals and holds a position as legal program manager in academies for legal training of company staff, for which she holds specialised seminars.
Languages: German, English, French.
Member: IBA; UIA; chairperson of the non-executive board of the Medical University of Vienna; supervisory board chairperson and member of major listed Austrian stock corporations (bank, insurance, paper, metal and textile industries); member of the management board of numerous private trusts.
Education: University of Vienna (1971 JD).
Personal: Born 1949.

KAJABA, Markus, Mag
Fellner Wratzfeld & Partner Rechtsanwälte GmbH
Phone: Vienna (+43 2 537 70)
E-mail: markus.kajaba@fwp.at
Public law, spatial planning law, public procurement, real estate, commmercial law, bankruptcy law and unfair competition.
Position: Partner.
Career: Joined Fellner Wratzfeld & Partners 2002; author of various articles in the fields of commercial law, unfair competition, civil and tax law.
Languages: German, English.
Member: Austrian Bar; Vienna Law Society.
Education: University of Vienna.
Personal: Born 1965; resides Vienna.
Leisure: Literature, sports.

KONWITSCHKA, Peter, Dr
Schönherr
Phone: Vienna (+43 1 53 43 70)
E-mail: p.konwitschka@schoenherr.at
Position: Partner dealing with commercial law, corporate, banking, M&A.
Career: Admitted to the Austrian Bar 1999.
Languages: English, French, German, Russian.
Education: University of Vienna (1991 Mag iur; 1998 Dr iur).
Personal: Born 1969.

KREMSLEHNER, Florian, Dr
Dorda Brugger Jordis
Phone: Vienna (+43 1 533 47 95 18)
E-mail: florian.kremslehner@dbj.at
Banking law; civil litigation; arbitration; business crime; international enforcement.
Position: Partner; heads the litigation and arbitration desk and is a member of the firm's banking and finance team. He advises a wide range of banking and industry clients, governments and international organisations. His practice as an arbitrator and party counsel includes telecom disputes, business crime and insurance cases, as well as banking and finance transactions.
Career: Associate at law firms in Vienna; admitted to the Austrian Bar 1990; partner Dorda Brugger Jordis 1992. In addition to his law practice, Florian Kremslehner gives lectures and runs specialised seminars. His recent publications include articles on money laundering, the legal aspects of cash pooling and on directors' and officers' liability.
Languages: German, English, Italian, French.
Member: IBA; UIA; Associazione Internazionale Guiristi di Lingua Italiana; Austrian Banking Society (Österreichische Bankwissenschaftliche Gesellschaft).
Education: University of Vienna (1988 JD); Harvard's Program of Instruction for Lawyers.
Personal: Born 1960.
Leisure: Golf, rowing and ski mountaineering. Member of the Sovereign Order of Malta.

KUCSKO, Guido, Dr
Schönherr
Phone: Vienna (+43 1 53 43 70)
E-mail: g.kucsko@schoenherr.at

Position: Partner dealing with unfair competition law, trade marks, copyright and information technology.
Career: Admitted to the Austrian Bar 1984. Adjunct professor in IP law, University of Vienna.
Languages: English, German.
Member: Executive Council of the Vienna Bar.
Education: University of Vienna (1979 Dr iur); university assistant, University of Vienna (1979-80); scholar, Max Planck Institute for Foreign and International Patent, Copyright and Competition Law, Munich (1979).
Personal: Born 1954, Austria.

LAGLER, Michael F

Schönherr
Phone: Vienna (+43 1 53 43 7142)
E-mail: m.lagler@schoenherr.at
Position: Partner dealing with mergers and acquisitions with special focus on Central Eastern Europe real estate, Central Eastern Europe business law.
Career: Admitted to the Austrian Bar 2001; assistant at the University of Salzburg 1992-95; lecturer on transnational business practice, collaborative LLM programme, law faculties of the University of Salzburg and the McGeorge School of Law, University of the Pacifics.
Languages: German, English.
Education: University of Salzburg (1994 Mag iur; 1996 Dr iur). Master in European Business Law, Nijmegen, The Netherlands (1997 LLM).
Personal: Born 1970.

LINDINGER, Christoph, Dr

Schönherr
Phone: Vienna (+43 1 53 43 70)
E-mail: ch.hindinger@schoenherr.at
Position: Partner dealing with EU law, mergers and acquisitions, banking and antitrust.
Career: Admitted to the Austrian Bar 1991.
Languages: English, German.
Education: University of Salzburg (1984 Dr iur).
Personal: Born 1962.

MADL, Peter, Dr

Schönherr
Phone: Vienna (+43 1 53 43 70)
E-mail: p.madl@schoenherr.at
Position: Partner dealing with corporate law, construction, litigation and arbitration.
Career: Admitted to the Austrian Bar 1990.
Languages: English, German.
Education: University of Vienna (1983 Dr iur); University of Economics, Vienna (1987 Mag rer soc oec); university assistant at University of Vienna (1983-86).
Personal: Born 1960.

MARKUS, Fellner, MMag Dr

Fellner Wratzfeld & Partner Rechtsanwälte GmbH
Phone: Vienna (+43 1 537 70)
E-mail: markus.fellner@fwp.at
Mergers and acquisitions, banking and finance, corporate finance, competition law, restructuring and reorganisation.
Position: Partner.
Career: Founded Fellner Wratzfeld & Partners, together with Kurt Wratzfeld, in 1999; author of various books and many articles in the field of corporate law and M&A.
Languages: English, German.
Member: Austrian Bar; IBA; Vienna Law Society; International Bar Assocation.
Education: University of Vienna; Vienna University of Business Administration.
Personal: Born 1967; resides Vienna.
Leisure: Sports.

MAXL, Martin, Dr

Graf, Maxl & Pitkowitz Rechtsanwälte GMBH
Phone: Vienna (+43 1 401 17 0)
E-mail: maxl@gmp.at
Corporate.
Position: Partner dealing with mergers and acquisitions, reorganisations, corporate and media law, antitrust.
Career: Trained Weiss-Tessbach and Zeiner & Zeiner; Coca-Cola East Central Europe Division; admitted 1994; founding partner Graf, Maxl & Pitkowitz 1994.
Languages: English, French, German.
Member: Austrian Bar; IBA.
Education: University of Graz (1988 Mag iur; 1989 JD).
Personal: Born 1961; resides Vienna.
Leisure: Sports (running, cycling and skiing), collecting fine art and photography.

MAYR, Andreas W, Dr

Dorda Brugger Jordis
Phone: Vienna (+43 1 533 47 95 64)
E-mail: andreas.mayr@dbj.at
Co-head of the banking and finance team.
Position: Partner specialising in corporate mergers and acquisitions as well as banking and finance law. His client base includes major Austrian banks, international and commercial investment banks and private equity houses. He also represents a significant number of large and mid-sized companies listed on the Vienna Stock Exchange, Nasdaq, on the Frankfurt Stock Exchange and the New York Stock Exchange.
Career: Skadden, Arps, Slate, Meagher & Flom, LLP in Frankfurt and Vienna; Heller Löber Bahn & Partners (now Freshfields Bruckhaus Deringer) in Vienna; CMS Strommer Reich-Rohrwig Karasek Hainz in Vienna; admitted to the New York Bar 1993; admitted to the Austrian Bar 1998; Publications: numerous articles on banking and finance, as well as securities and capital markets law in Austrian and international professional journals; presentations at specialised seminars and conferences in Austria and abroad.
Languages: German, English.
Member: IBA; New York Bar Association; EASD Legal and Regular Committee.
Education: University of Salzburg (1995 Dr iur); Columbia University, School of Law (1991 LLM).
Personal: Born 1966.

PITKOWITZ, Nikolaus, Dr

Graf, Maxl & Pitkowitz Rechtsanwälte GMBH
Phone: Vienna (+43 1 401 17 0)
E-mail: pitkowitz@gmp.at
Real estate, arbitration and litigation.
Position: Partner dealing with corporate law, real estate law, arbitration and litigation, central and eastern Europe.
Career: Admitted to Austrian Bar 1990; partner with a major Austrian law firm 1990-94; university lecturer in Czech business law 1993-99; founding partner Graf, Maxl & Pitkowitz 1994; permanent arbitrator at Austrian Chamber of Commerce; permanent arbitrator at ICC; registered mediator.
Languages: English, German.
Member: Austrian Bar; IBA; American Foreign Lawyers Association.
Education: University of Vienna (1984 JD); Georgetown University (1991 Orientation in the US Legal System); University St Gallen (1999 MA European and International Business Law).
Personal: Born 1961; resides Vienna.

POLSTER, Stephan, Dr

Dorda Brugger Jordis
Phone: Vienna (+43 1 533 47 95 35)
E-mail: stephan.polster@dbj.at
Telecommunications law, energy law, competition and antitrust law, corporate law.
Position: Partner specialising in telecommunications law, energy law, competition and antitrust law, acquisitions of business enterprises, and corporate law. He has recently represented the biggest Austrian electricity producer in its merger with five regional electricity suppliers in the merger control proceedings before the European Commission. He regularly advises two of the major Austrian mobile operators and a number of foreign telecommunications providers in regulatory and commercial law matters.
Career: Associate at Dorda Brugger Jordis; Stagiaire at the European Commission, DG XIII (Telecommunications), Brussels, Belgium; Stagiaire at Kilpatrick Stockton LLP, Brussels; admitted to the Austrian Bar in 1999; partner Dorda Brugger Jordis since 1999. Publications: author of books including 'Das Telekommunikationsrecht der Europäischen Gemeinschaft' (Telecommunications law of the European Community); 'Kommentar zum TKG 2003' (Commentary on the new Austrian Telecommunications Act 2003), 'Cash Pooling, Praxis, Recht und Steuern' (Cash Pooling, Tax and Legal Issues); numerous articles in Austrian and international journals on e-commerce, telecommunications law, energy law and corporate law; he has given presentations at specialised seminars and conferences in Austria and abroad.
Languages: German, English.
Member: IBA; AIJA.
Education: University of Wolverhampton (1994 MA); University of Vienna (1998 JD).
Personal: Born 1968.

SCHETT, Gregor, Dr

Fellner Wratzfeld & Partner Rechtsanwälte GmbH
Phone: Vienna (+43 1 537 70)
E-mail: gregor.schett@fwp.at

Banking, finance, corporate and corporate restructuring, litigation and arbitration.
Position: Partner.
Career: Started his career as assistant at the University of Salzburg. He joined Fellner, Wratzfeld & Partner as partner in 2004; former partner of Haarmann Hemmelrath; author of several articles in professional journals.
Languages: English, German.
Member: Austrian Bar; Cantab Law Masters.
Education: University of Vienna; University of Cambridge (Law Masters).
Personal: Born 1968; resides Vienna.
Leisure: Culture, sports.

SCHMELZ, Christian, Dr
Schönherr
Phone: Vienna (+43 1 53 43 70)
E-mail: ch.schmelz@schoenherr.at
Position: Partner dealing with public law including environmental law, licensing, telecoms and information technology.
Career: University assistant, University of Vienna (1980-85); lecturer, University of Vienna (since 1982); admitted to the Austrian Bar 1987.
Languages: English, German.
Education: University of Vienna (1979 Dr iur).
Personal: Born 1955.

STIPPL, Christoph, Dr
Dorda Brugger Jordis
Phone: Vienna (+43 1 533 47 95 102)
E-mail: christoph.stippl@dbj.at
Co-head arbitration and litigation.
Position: Partner specialising in international commercial arbitration, mergers and acquisitions, and international transactions. Mr Stippl has appeared in numerous ad-hoc arbitrations and in proceedings before major arbitration institutions. He is experienced in handling multi-jurisdictional disputes; the disputes relate in particular to CEE jurisdictions and involve amounts exceeding €100m. His industry experience focuses on corporate law, joint ventures, M&A (including privatisation), telecommunications, construction and distributorship/commercial agency disputes. Mr Stippl is recommended in Euromoney's 'Guide to the World's Leading Experts in Commercial Arbitration' (2005). In addition to his arbitration practice, Mr Stippl has broad M&A and privatisation experience in Austria and in the new EU accession countries.
Career: Internship at ASA Avocats Associés, Paris; Hausmaninger Herbst Rechtsanwälte, Vienna; partner at Dorda Brugger Jordis, Vienna since 2003; admitted to the New York Bar 1997 and to the Austrian Bar 2001. Publications: author of publications on commercial arbitration, including a doctor thesis on multi-party arbitration.
Languages: German, English, French.
Member: Chartered Institute of Arbitrators (MCIArb); International Bar Association; ICDR Young and International (of the American Arbitration Association); Austrian Arbitration Association; Young Austrian Arbitration Practitioners (YAAP); LCIA Young International Arbitration Group.
Education: Columbia University School of Law (1996 LLM); University of Vienna School of Law (2000 Dr iur).
Personal: Born 1969.

TORGGLER, Hellwig, Dr
Schönherr
Phone: Vienna (+43 1 53 43 70)
E-mail: h.torggler@schoenherr.at
Position: Partner dealing with corporate law, mergers and acquisitions, arbitration and tax.
Career: Admitted to the Austrian Bar 1969; adjunct professor, commercial law and taxation, University of Graz; visiting professor and lecturer, University of Economics, Vienna; arbitrator, ICC, International Arbitral Centre of the Austrian Federal Economic Chamber, and other institutional and ad hoc Courts of Arbitration.
Languages: English, French, German, Italian.
Member: Vice-chairman ICC, Austria; ICC International Court of Arbitration; Examining Board for the Austrian Bar Examination.
Education: Universities of Vienna, Graz, and St Gallen (1961 Dr iur; 1962 Dr rer pol); Southern Methodist University, Dallas (1963 LLM).
Personal: Born 1938.

VARGA, Tibor, Dr
Dorda Brugger Jordis
Phone: Vienna (+43 1 533 47 95 28)
E-mail: tibor.varga@dbj.at
Finance, banking, corporate and tax law.
Position: Partner specialising in corporate finance, banking and capital markets law, restructurings, M&A and corresponding tax law. He has advised on a wide range of corporate transactions, including acquisitions linked with public tender offers (takeover law) and corporate restructurings (including the squeeze-out of minority shareholders). In the area of banking and finance, he has advised domestic and foreign clients on syndicated loans, acquisition, mezzanine and project finance as well as cross-border lease transactions.
Career: Internship at the Council of Europe in Strasbourg, France; KPMG Austria Wirtschafts- und Steuerberatungs GmbH in Vienna; associate at Dorda Brugger Jordis; internship at Hunton & Williams in Brussels, Belgium; admitted to the Austrian Bar in 1999; partner Dorda Brugger Jordis since 1999. Publications: articles in Austrian and international professional journals on takeover and general corporate law; he has given presentations at specialised seminars and conferences in Austria and abroad.
Languages: German, English, Hungarian.
Member: IBA; AIJA.
Education: University of Vienna (1992; 1998 JD).
Personal: Born 1970.

WÄCHTER, Otto, Dr
Graf, Maxl & Pitkowitz Rechtsanwälte GMBH
Phone: Vienna (+43 1 401 17 0)
E-mail: waechter@gmp.at
Banking and finance.
Position: Partner dealing with project finance, infrastructure, corporate, securities (telecommunications and postal law), arbitration.
Career: Admitted Austria 1994, New York 1995, California 1996; worked at law firms in Austria, New York and Adelaide, Australia; partner Gabler & Gabler in Vienna 1996-99; partner Graf, Maxl & Pitkowitz since 1999.
Languages: English, German.
Member: Austrian Bar; Australian Law Society; New York State and Californian Bar Associations.
Education: University of Vienna (1987 Dr); NYU School of Law (1994 LLM Corporate Law); University St Gallen (1998 Master of European and International Business Law).
Personal: Born 1961; resides Vienna.

WENGER, Thomas, Dr
Schönherr
Phone: Vienna (+43 1 53 43 70)
E-mail: t.wenger@schoenherr.at
Position: Partner dealing with corporate law, mergers and acquisitions, construction and litigation.
Career: Admitted to the Austrian Bar 1992.
Languages: English, German.
Education: University of Vienna (1983 Dr iur); University of Economics, Vienna (1987 Mag rer soc oec).
Personal: Born 1960.

WIDNER, Jakob
Graf, Maxl & Pitkowitz Rechtsanwälte GMBH
Phone: Vienna (+43 1 401 17 0)
E-mail: widner@gmp.at
Labour and employment law.
Position: Partner dealing with employment and executive contracts, pension schemes, bonus and stock option agreements, redundancy measures (social plans) and collective bargaining on behalf of corporate clients.
Career: Admitted in Austria 1999; New York 2002. Partner at Graf, Maxl & Pitkowitz since 1999.
Languages: English, German.
Member: Austrian Bar; New York State Bar Association.
Education: University of Vienna (1992 Mag iur); NYU School of Law (2001 LLM corporate law).
Personal: Born 1967; resides Vienna.

WOLLMANN, Hanno, Dr
Schönherr
Phone: Vienna (+43 1 53 43 70)
E-mail: h.wollmann@schoenherr.at
Position: Partner dealing with EU law, antitrust and corporate law.
Career: Admitted to the Austrian Bar 1995.
Languages: English, French, German.
Education: University of Vienna (1991 Dr iur); University of Economics, Vienna (1991 Mag rer soc oec); University of Exeter (1992 LLM).
Personal: Born 1964.

WRATZFELD, Kurt, Dr
Fellner Wratzfeld & Partner Rechtsanwälte GmbH
Phone: Vienna (+43 1 537 70)

E-mail: kurt.wratzfeld@fwp.at
Labour law, corporate, litigation, insolvency and civil law.
Position: Partner.
Career: Founded Fellner Wratzfeld & Partners, together with Markus Fellner, in 1999; author of articles on insolvency and labour law.
Languages: English, German.
Member: Austrian Bar; Vienna Law Society.
Education: University of Vienna.
Personal: Born 1967; resides Vienna.
Leisure: Sports, culture, history.

ZAHRADNIK, Andreas, Dr
Dorda Brugger Jordis
Phone: Vienna (+43 1 533 47 95 42)
E-mail: andreas.zahradnik@dbj.at
Banking and capital markets.
Position: Partner specialising in banking law (with emphasis on regulatory aspects), capital markets and financial services. He mainly advises international banks, investment firms, venture capital and investment funds. His advice also covers cross-border activities and the establishment of branches and subsidiaries.
Career: Admitted to the Austrian Bar 1996; associate Dorda Brugger Jordis; partner since 1997. Lecturer on capital markets and regulatory banking law, University of Vienna; presentations at various specialised seminars and conferences. Publications: books on financial services and community law; numerous articles in Austrian and international professional journals on banking, capital markets and community law.
Languages: German, English.
Member: IBA; UIA; EVCA's Tax and Legal Committee.
Education: University of Vienna (1991 JD).
Personal: Born 1968.

ZEILER, Gerold, Dr
Schönherr
Phone: Vienna (+43 1 53 43 70)
E-mail: g.zeiler@schoenherr.at
Position: Partner dealing with employment law, litigation and arbitration.
Career: Admitted to the Austrian Bar 1993.
Languages: English, German, Italian.
Education: University of Vienna (1988 Mag iur; 1996 Dr iur).
Personal: Born 1964.

BELGIUM

BELLIS, Jean-François
Van Bael & Bellis
Phone: Brussels (+32 2 647 73 50)
E-mail: jfbellis@vanbaelbellis.com
Position: Managing partner, specialising in competition and trade law; in the field of competition law, Jean-François Bellis has advised international clients in numerous cases at EC and national level, involving a broad range of antitrust issues, including price-fixing, abuses of a dominant position, mergers, distribution and licensing; in the field of trade law, he has advised international clients in countless EC anti-dumping cases, as well as in many of the less frequently used EC countervailing, safeguard and 'trade barriers' proceedings; he has been appointed by the WTO director-general as a member of a WTO panel; he has extensive litigation experience in EC competition and trade cases; he has been involved in a large number of the major competition and trade cases in front of the Court of First Instance and the Court of Justice of the European Communities; he has written numerous books and articles in the field of competition and trade law and has spoken on these two subjects at many international conferences and seminars.
Career: Started to practice law in Brussels 1975; legal secretary to Lord Mackenzie Stuart at the Court of Justice of the European Communities in Luxembourg 1979-80; founded Van Bael & Bellis with Ivo Van Bael 1986; lectures on EC competition law at the University of Brussels and taught WTO and EC trade remedy law at the University of Liège (Ulg) 1990-2004.
Member: Brussels Bar.
Education: University of Brussels (ULB) (1972 Law); University of Michigan Law School (1974 LLM).

BERG, Werner
Crowell & Moring
Phone: Brussels (+32 2 282 4082)
E-mail: wberg@crowell.com
EU and German antitrust law, general EU law, international trade law.
Position: Partner.
Career: Gleiss Lutz (Stuttgart and Brussels) 1997-2005; partner since 2002; partner at Crowell and Moring since 2005.
Languages: German, English, French.
Member: IBA, Studienvereinigung Kartellrecht (Antitrust Law Study Group), Wissenschaftliche Gesellschaft für Europarecht.
Education: University of Trier (1991, law degree); University of East Anglia, UK (1992, LLM); University of Trier (1997, Dr. iur.); Land Berlin (1997 bar exam).
Personal: Born 1965, resides Brussels.

DE BAERE, Philippe
Van Bael & Bellis
Phone: Brussels (+32 2 647 73 50)
E-mail: phdebaere@vanbaelbellis.com
Position: Partner specialising in EC and WTO trade law, with a particular emphasis on anti-dumping and anti-subsidy law, as well as on EC customs law; he has been involved in most major EC anti-dumping, anti-circumvention and anti-subsidy proceedings since 1990 and has represented clients before the EC Commission, the European Court of Justice and the WTO Appellate Body; he also acts for EC exporters in anti-dumping proceedings initiated by third countries; he has assisted governments during their WTO accession negotiations, as well as during the Uruguay Round negotiations; in recent years, he has represented several large manufacturers of high-technology products in disputes concerning customs classification, valuation and origin, both before the European Commission and the European Court of Justice; Philippe De Baere is a regular speaker at trade seminars and has contributed to several leading publications on EC anti-dumping and other trade protection laws; he was a co-author of the 'Business Guide to Trade Remedies in the European Community', (ITC, Geneva 2004).
Languages: Dutch, English, French, Spanish.
Member: Brussels Bar.
Education: University of Antwerp and University of Leuven (1984 Law); University of Leuven - research Fellow, international trade law.

DE KEYSER, Steven
DLA Piper Rudnick Gray Cary
Phone: Brussels (+32 2 500 15 05)
E-mail: steven.de.keyser@dlapiper.com
Technology, media and communications.
Position: Managing Director Continental Europe. Practices in the field of information technology contracts, including outsourcing. Further active in the broader government sector and in particular assists with the reorganisation of government-owned entities and structures forms of public-private partnerships and structured joint ventures.
Career: Lawyer De Bandt, van Hecke, Lagae (now Linklaters) 1988-91; assistant professor KU Leuven - Institute of Company Law 1988-93; partner and general counsel Europe Andlinger & Company, Brussels 1991-94; structured finance executive Banque Indosuez London 1994-95; senior legal counsel EMEA Andersen Paris 1995-97; managing partner Belgium and member executive team Andersen Legal Europe, Caestecker & Partners (Andersen Legal Belgium), Brussels 1997-2002; member Excom of Andersen BeLux (as of 2000) and responsible for Andersen Legal Luxembourg (as of 2000); KU Leuven - Lector IT contracts 1998-2003; managing partner Belgium DLA Piper Rudnick Gray Cary 2002-05; Managing Director Continental Europe and member executive management team for Europe and Asia since 2005; regular speaker at conferences and seminars covering mostly outsourcing and IT-related topics, as well as public-private partnerships.
Languages: Dutch, French, English.
Member: Board member American Chamber of Commerce.
Education: Universities of Antwerp and Leuven (1987 Law); University of Chicago (1988 Master of Laws); Ecole de Commerce Solvay, Brussels (1991 Executive MBA); courses at the London School of Economics and Harvard Business School.

DE MEESE, Thomas
Crowell & Moring
Phone: Brussels (+32 2 282 1842)
E-mail: tdemeese@crowell.com
EU regulatory, competition, communications. Partner dealing with EC and Belgian competition, EU regulatory law and Belgian and EU communications law.

Position: Partner.
Career: Associate, Price & Partners 1993-96; associate, de Bauw & Maeyaert 1996-2000; partner, De Bauw & Maeyaert Brussels 2001; partner, Crowell & Moring 2001 to date; member of the editorial board of the Revue de Droit Intellectuels.
Languages: Dutch, French, English.
Member: Avocat of the Dutch Order of the Brussels Bar 1993. Registered foreign lawyer with the Law Society of England and Wales 2001. Member of the International Bar Association 1996; Ligue Internationale du Droit de la Concurrence.
Education: University of Antwerp (Licence en Droit 1992); College of Europe (Master of Advanced European Studies, 1993).
Personal: Born 1969, resides Grimbergen.

DE SCHRIJVER, Steven

Van Bael & Bellis
Phone: Brussels (+32 2 647 73 50)
E-mail: sdeschrijver@vanbaelbellis.com
Position: Partner specialising in corporate transactions, including mergers and acquisitions, joint ventures, corporate restructuring, financing of acquisitions, private equity and venture capital; his work in the area of corporate transactions has involved him in several cross-border transactions in the telecoms, IT, biotech, petrochemical and cement sectors; Steven De Schrijver has also handled numerous complex commercial agreements and projects dealing with new technologies (e-commerce, software licensing, website development and hosting, privacy law, technology transfer, digital signature, IT-outsourcing etc); for instance, he has handled several pan-European data protection compliance programmes; Steven De Schrijver is a regular speaker at conferences; he was also one of the editors of Van Bael & Bellis' 'Business Law Guide to Belgium' (2nd ed) and frequently publishes articles on selected topics relating to company law and IT law; he is also a member of the editorial board of Computerrecht, the only Dutch-language IT law magazine.
Languages: Dutch, English, French, German, Spanish.
Member: Brussels Bar; national representative of AIJA (l'Association Internationale des Jeunes Avocats - www.aija.org - in Belgium; secretary of the Computers and Telecommunications Commission of the UIA (l'Union Internationale des Avocats - www.uianet.org; and the Belgian member of EuroITCounsel, a quality circle of independent IT lawyers - www.euroitcounsel.com.
Education: University of Antwerp (1992 Law magna cum laude); University of Virginia (1993 LLM); University of Antwerp (1995 Diploma in Business Law magna cum laude); EHSAL (1997 Diploma in Corporate Law magna cum laude); King's College, London (1999 post-graduate diploma EC Competition Law).

DELTOUR, Eric

Dechert LLP
Phone: Brussels (+32 2 535 54 11)
E-mail: eric.deltour@dechert.com
Position: Partner in the Brussels office dealing with corporate and securities, and mergers and acquisitions. Main areas of practice include commercial law, corporate law, mergers and acquisitions, joint ventures, and arbitration. Represents and advises clients in private equity transactions such as takeover bids, shareholders' agreements and shareholders' disputes, joint venture structures, and venture capital investments for Belgian, US, and European clients. Recommended as a leading lawyer in M&A and corporate finance in 'European Counsel 3000' (1999); for matters relating to joint ventures in 'Global Counsel 3000' (2000, 2001); for company and commercial law in 'The European Legal 500' (1999, 2000) and 'European Legal Experts' (2001, 2002); and for M&A in 'Global Counsel Mergers and Acquisitions Handbook' (2001, 2002) and 'Chambers Global' (2002).
Member: International Bar Association.
Education: Université Catholique de Louvain, Belgium (1982 JD cum laude); Columbia-Leiden-Amsterdam Summer Program in American Law (1984).

DI GIANNI, Fabrizio

Van Bael & Bellis
Phone: Brussels (+32 2 647 73 50)
E-mail: fdigianni@vanbaelbellis.com
Position: Partner focusing on two main areas: international and European trade law and EC and Italian competition law; in international and European trade law, Fabrizio Di Gianni assists a wide range of clients (governments, industry associations, associations of companies, producers and importers) in trade-related matters involving WTO, EC and third countries' trade legislation; he has represented clients involved in major EC trade investigations; his activities focus on representing the interests of clients in all stages of the procedure before the European Commission; he also advises companies on other EC trade-related matters, such as marks of origin and customs investigations; he advises and assists governments and associations in regard to WTO law and has represented companies involved in trade investigations initiated by countries outside the EU; in the field of EC and Italian competition law, Fabrizio Di Gianni advises clients in connection with EC and Italian antitrust law; he has represented companies in cartel cases before the European Commission and the Italian Antitrust Authority; he has also been involved in state aid cases before the European Commission and the European Courts; he was a contributor to 'Il Diritto della Concorrenza nella Comunità Europea', Van Bael & Bellis (1995) and to 'Anti-Dumping and Other Trade Protection Laws of the EC' (4th ed 2004); he is a regular speaker at conferences and has recently published 'Le recouvrement a posteriori de la dette douanière à la lumière de la jurisprudence des juridictions communautaires et la position des importeurs communautaires' in the Revue du Droit de l'Union européen (editions Clément Juglar, vol3-2003).
Career: Van Bael & Bellis 1990 to date; partner 1998; qualified to plead before the Italian Supreme Court.
Languages: Italian, English, French, Spanish.
Member: Rome Bar.
Education: University Federico II, Naples, Italy (1987 Law magna cum laude); College of Europe, Bruges, Belgium (1989 post-graduate EC law); Georgetown University, Washington DC, USA (1995 MA Common Law, Thomas Bradbury Chetwood, SJ prize).

ELLIOTT, Porter

Van Bael & Bellis
Phone: Brussels (+32 2 647 73 50)
E-mail: pelliott@vanbaelbellis.com
Position: Partner specialising in competition law, with particular experience in merger control proceedings, having successfully represented clients in numerous complex cases before the European Commission, as well as national competition authorities in Europe and elsewhere; he also regularly counsels clients on all other aspects of competition law, including cartels, abuses of dominant market position, distribution agreements and state aid; Porter Elliott regularly speaks and publishes on issues of EC competition and merger control law; he was a key contributor to Van Bael & Bellis' 'Competition Law of the European Community' (4th ed 2004) and is the editor of the newsletter 'Van Bael & Bellis on Competition Law'; he served as editor-in-chief of the 'Georgia Journal of International and Comparative Law 1995-96; he has lectured on merger control issues at conferences and has conducted training sessions on merger control issues for the Turkish competition authorities; he also regularly participates as a dissertation and case study adviser for law students at the Vrije Universiteit Brussels' Programme on International Legal Co-operation and is a regular speaker at the Brussels Seminar on Law and Institutions of the European Community.
Career: Van Bael & Bellis 1997 to date; partner 2005.
Member: State Bar of Georgia.
Education: University of Maryland, USA (1992 BS); University of Georgia School of Law, USA (1996 JD); Vrije Universiteit Brussels, Belgium (1997 LLM Program on International Legal Co-operation (PILC)).

FAES, Pascal

Van Bael & Bellis
Phone: Brussels (+32 2 647 73 50)
E-mail: pfaes@vanbaelbellis.com
Position: Partner specialising in corporate transactions (mergers and acquisitions, joint ventures), including corporate and tax structuring; publications include: 'Abuse of Law in Tax Matters' (Gent, Mys & Breesch 1994) (in Dutch); 'Belgian Income Tax Law. Principles and Practice' (Chicester, Wiley 1995); 'Tax Management Portfolio - Business Operations in Belgium' (Washington DC, Tax Management Inc 2005, co-authored with Jaques Malherbe); and various contributions on corporate and tax issues in both Belgian and international law reviews; Pascal Faes is the editor of the newsletter 'VBB on Belgian Business Law'; he is special consultant to 'Tax Management', Washington DC and is also a regular speaker at conferences.
Career: Professor of tax law at Vlekho, Brussels until 2003.
Languages: Dutch, English, French.

Member: Brussels Bar; International Fiscal Association; American Bar Association.
Education: University of Ghent (RUG) (1984 Law); University of Brussels (VUB) (1987 special degree in economics); University of Brussels (ULB) (1990 MA Tax Law).

FAVART, Martin

Van Bael & Bellis
Phone: Brussels (+32 2 647 73 50)
E-mail: mfavart@vanbaelbellis.com
Position: Partner specialising in European and Belgian competition law and Belgian commercial and corporate law; as a Belgian business lawyer, he handles both advisory files and litigation cases in a wide range of commercial matters, with a special emphasis on competition, contracts, distribution, trade practices and marketing; as regards EU law, Martin Favart focuses on competition law, with a particular emphasis on abuses of dominance and cartels; his competition law experience covers a wide variety of sectors (basic industries, beverages and foodstuffs, automobiles, building materials, chemicals, electronics, information and communications technology) and includes notifications, litigation before community and national courts and counselling.
Career: Van Bael & Bellis 1997 to date; partner 2006.
Member: Brussels Bar.
Education: Facultés Universitaires Saint-Louis, Belgium (1993 Cand Jur); Université Catholique de Louvain, Belgium (1986 Lic Jur); University of Oxford, UK (1997 M Jur).

FORBES, Reshad

Van Bael & Bellis
Phone: Brussels (+32 2 647 73 50)
E-mail: rforbes@vanbaelbellis.com
Position: Partner specialising in various aspects of the European Community's regulatory laws, in particular, EC environmental law, consumer protection laws and policy, product safety, standards and CE marking, food safety and chemicals; as regards environmental law, Reshad Forbes manages a team of lawyers specialising in all its aspects, from the rules relating to cadmium and other dangerous substances to producers' responsibilities under the directives on end-of-life products; in addition, he advises clients on all aspects of the 'new approach' directives (concerning, among others, electrical equipment, machinery, toys, construction products and personal protective equipment), CE markings and the harmonised standards which are frequently adopted under these directives; Reshad Forbes regularly works on behalf of multinationals, trade associations and SMEs in Europe, the United States and Asia; he is in constant contact with the Community Institutions (Commission, Parliament and Council) and member states' regulatory authorities; he is in charge of the firm's fortnightly newsletter 'The European Monitor', which analyses the EC's latest newsworthy events in the trade, internal market, competition and enlargement fields.
Career: Van Bael & Bellis 1997 to date; partner 2005.
Member: Solicitor, England and Wales.
Education: University of Mumbai, India (1988 BA English Literature); London School of Economics, UK (1991 LLB); Guildhall University, UK (1993 Law Society Finals).

GONNE, René H

Dechert LLP
Phone: Brussels (+32 2 535 54 11)
E-mail: rene.gonne@dechert.com
Position: Partner in the Brussels office, dealing with corporate and securities, and mergers and acquisitions. Focuses on corporate law, corporate finance, mergers and acquisitions, company restructuring, and contracts. Has advised on a variety of joint ventures, shareholder agreements, private transactions, and capital restructurings of publicly listed and unlisted companies. Has also developed a domestic and international expertise in the area of takeover bids and public bids of exchange, including hostile defence. Has participated in some of the largest takeovers in Belgium since 1988. Recommended as a leading lawyer for corporate and M&A in 'Chambers and Partners Global'. Is also recommended for M&A (since 2002), insolvency and restructuring (since 2002) and dispute resolution (since 2004) in PLC 'Which Lawyer?' (former Global Counsel 3000) and for corporate and commercial law (since 2002) in 'European Legal Experts'.
Career: Assistant professor Université Catholique de Louvain, Belgium 1982-85.
Member: International Bar Association; Conférence du Jeune Barreau de Bruxelles.
Education: Université Catholique de Louvain, Belgium (1979 JD magna cum laude).

GYBELS, Emmanuel

Crowell & Moring
Phone: Brussels (+32 2 282 1837)
E-mail: egybels@crowell.com
Litigation and corporate department. Deals with all areas of corporate and transactional law and litigation, including international arbitration.
Position: Managing partner of Crowell & Moring's Brussels office.
Career: Trainee and associate at Liederkerke, Wolters, Waelbroeck & Kirkpatrick 1988-91; associate at Covington & Burling 1991-96; partner of De Bauw & Maeyaert Brussels, 1998-2001; partner of Crowell & Moring January 2001 to date.
Languages: Dutch, English, French.
Member: Avocat of the Dutch Order of the Brussels Bar 1988; registered foreign lawyer with the Law Society of England and Wales 2001. Member of the Association Internationale des Jeunes Avocats 1999.
Education: University of Leuven (1998); University of Brussels (DES Droit Economique, 1990).
Personal: Born 1964, resides Brussels.

KMIECIK, Andrzej

Van Bael & Bellis
Phone: Brussels (+32 2 647 73 50)
E-mail: akmiecik@vanbaelbellis.com
Position: Partner, specialising in all aspects of competition law, with considerable experience in merger control proceedings and cartel cases, as well as distribution, pricing and intellectual property matters; represents clients before the European Commission and the EU courts, as well as in national competition law proceedings; his practice covers a wide range of industrial sectors, including aerospace, automobiles, pharmaceuticals, forest products, office equipment, petro-chemicals, clothing and footwear; Andrzej Kmiecik is a contributor to Van Bael & Bellis' 'Competition Law of the European Community' (4th ed 2004) and he lectures and speaks frequently at conferences on competition law topics.
Member: Solicitor, England and Wales.
Education: Merton College, Oxford University, UK (1985 MA); College of Law, London, UK (1988); College of Europe, Bruges, Belgium (1990 Diploma in European Law).

KUILWIJK, Kees, Dr

Steptoe & Johnson LLP
Phone: Brussels (+32 2 626 0500)
E-mail: kkuilwijk@steptoe.com
IT and competition.
Position: Dr Kuilwijk is a partner in the firm's Brussels office. Dr Kuilwijk has extensive experience in relation to legal and regulatory issues associated with electronic businesses and the internet. He advises clients on all legal aspects of conducting businesses on-line, in particular issues regarding data protection, intellectual property, competition and liability in the on-line environment. In addition, Dr Kuilwijk assists telecommunications and internet companies with a variety of commercial matters ranging from licensing and distribution agreements to purchase and lease of equipment and property. Dr Kuilwijk has considerable experience in all areas of competition law, including merger control. He regularly deals with the European Commission and national competition authorities on behalf of companies under investigation, as well as complainants. He has advised on horizontal agreements, licence agreements, vertical distribution and supply agreements, and has designed and implemented general competition law compliance programs for many clients. This has included extensively advising clients on fining and leniency procedures and making leniency applications.
Career: Qualified 1986; Lovells 1996-98; Herbert Smith 1998-2000; Steptoe & Johnson LLP 2000-present, made partner 2002. Member of the International Bar Association (IBA) and Brussels Bar.
Languages: English, French, German.
Education: Leyden University, the Netherlands (1986 JD); European University Institute, Florence, Italy (1996 PhD cum laude).
Personal: Born 1963; resides Brussels.
Leisure: Tennis.

L'ECLUSE, Peter

Van Bael & Bellis
Phone: Brussels (+32 2 647 73 50)
E-mail: plecluse@vanbaelbellis.com

Position: Partner specialising in competition law, intellectual property, pharmaceutical law and litigation; Peter L'Ecluse's litigation practice focuses on complex matters involving both EU and Belgian law, eg representing a US directories publisher in over 30 cases before the Belgian courts, the European courts, the European Commission and the telecommunications regulator against Belgium's incumbent telecommunications operator; he was successful in defending and later helping to expand the client's business franchise; the cases raised delicate issues of market liberalisation, market regulation, competition and IP rights; he also acts for a number of the world's largest pharmaceutical companies in reimbursement matters, commercial litigation and intellectual property disputes; he has written a number of articles about competition law and intellectual property; was a contributor to Van Bael & Bellis''Business Law Guide to Belgium' (2003 ed Kluwer Law International/Bruylant) and 'Competition Law of the European Community (2004 ed Kluwer Law International) and he is also a regular speaker at conferences.
Languages: Dutch, English, French.
Member: Brussels Bar.
Education: Katholieke Universiteit Leuven (KUL), Belgium (1985 Philosophy); Katholieke Universiteit Leuven (KUL), Belgium (1986 Law); The George Washington University, Washington DC, USA (1987 MA Comparative Law).

LONGEVAL, Catherine

Van Bael & Bellis
Phone: Brussels (+32 2 647 73 50)
E-mail: clongeval@vanbaelbellis.com
Position: Partner specialising in litigation before the Belgian courts, with a particular emphasis on unfair trade practices, collective and individual employment law, pharmaceutical law and intellectual property law; she also advises clients on a wide range of issues in these and other areas, including distribution law, product liability, competition law and general commercial law; she was a contributor to Van Bael & Bellis''Business Law Guide to Belgium' (2003 ed Kluwer Law International/Bruylant) and has published articles on procedural law and pharmaceutical law.
Career: Associate with a leading Brussels law firm 1989-94; Van Bael & Bellis 1994 to date; partner 1997.
Languages: Dutch, English, French.
Member: Brussels Bar.
Education: Katholieke Universiteit Leuven (KUL), Belgium (1987 Law); Université Libre de Bruxelles (ULB), Belgium (1989 MA European Law).

LOUIS, Pierre-M

Dechert LLP
Phone: Brussels (+32 2 535 54 11)
E-mail: pierre.louis@dechert.com
Position: Partner in the Brussels office specialising in competition, energy, and general EC law. Often represents clients before the EC Commission, the Belgian competition authorities, and the EC courts and in litigation before the Belgian courts. Areas of expertise include vertical and horizontal restraints, the liberalisation of the energy sector, abuses of dominant positions, the essential facilities doctrine, and the private law consequences of competition infringements. As a former clerk to the president of the Court of Justice of the European Communities, also has experience in general EC law, including the free movement of goods, services and persons, all aspects of the implementation process for directives, the liability of member states for breaches of EC law, and several areas of sector-specific secondary legislation.
Career: Accredited lobbyist to the European Parliament; tutor at the Institut d'études européennes (Université Libre de Bruxelles).
Education: Université Libre de Bruxelles (1987 JD magna cum laude; 1988 Masters in Economic Law magna cum laude).

LUFF, Richard

Van Bael & Bellis
Phone: Brussels (+32 2 647 73 50)
E-mail: rluff@vanbaelbellis.com
Position: Partner specialising in international trade law, in particular, anti-dumping and anti-subsidy law, who has represented clients before the EC Commission, the European Court of Justice and the WTO; he has personally handled in excess of 100 anti-dumping cases for clients from around the world, including the USA, China, Russia, Korea, Taiwan, the Middle East, South East Asia and Mexico, in a wide variety of industries, for example steel, textiles, chemical products and electronics; Richard Luff also advises governments, other public institutions and international clients on market access issues and other WTO-related matters; he is also asked on a regular basis by governments to run training programmes for their anti-dumping and anti-subsidy units; Richard Luff is a regular speaker at trade conferences and seminars.
Career: Van Bael & Bellis 1990 to date; partner 1996.
Languages: English, French, Italian, Spanish.
Member: Brussels Bar.
Education: University of Brussels (ULB), Belgium (1986 Law; 1987 post-graduate economic law; 1989 MA EC law); London School of Economins, UK (1990 LLM International Business Law).

MACLEAN, Robert, Dr

Crowell & Moring
Phone: Brussels (+32 2 286 1168)
E-mail: rmaclean@crowell.com
Dealing with all areas of EU law and international trade law, including EU litigation and WTO law.
Position: Partner.
Career: Intern, European Parliament 1990; intern, European Commission 1992-93; trainee and associate, Wright Johnston & MacKenzie 1991-94; associate, Stanbrook & Hooper 1995-98; partner CMS McKenna Brussels 2000-03; partner, Crowell & Moring, January 2004 to date. Publications include 'EU Trade Barrier Regulation' (Second Edition, Sweet & Maxwell, 2005).
Languages: English, French.
Member: Solicitor of the Law Society of Scotland 1994; Advocate of the French Order of the Brussels Bar - List E 2002; registered foreign lawyer with the Law Society of England and Wales 2001; Member of the International Bar Association 2002.
Education: University of Glasgow (1985 LLB); University of Glasgow (1986 DipLP); University of Alberta (1988 LLM); University of Glasgow (1995 PhD).
Personal: Born 1963, resides Brussels.

MINJAUW, Harold IG

Dechert LLP
Phone: Brussels (+32 2 535 54 11)
E-mail: harold.minjauw@dechert.com
Position: Partner in the Brussels office dealing with corporate and securities, and mergers and acquisitions. Main areas of expertise are mergers and acquisitions and corporate law, as well as agency and exclusive distributorship law. Regularly advises clients in Belgian or cross-border acquisitions, cross-border corporate restructurings, joint ventures, venture capital investments, and MBOs in Europe. Practice also includes general corporate advice, as well as corporate and commercial litigation for clients involved in a wide variety of sectors, including entertainment, banking, venture capital investments, and advertising.
Career: Legal adviser in the financial, corporate and international law department of a major Belgian bank; admitted to Brussels Bar.
Education: Katholieke Universiteit Keuven, Belgium (1992 JD cum laude); Bayerische Julius-Maximilians-Universität Würzburg, Germany; Université Libre de Bruxelles, Belgium (1994 Masters in Economic Law magna cum laude).

MOURLON BEERNAERT, Fabrice

Dechert LLP
Phone: Brussels (+32 2 535 54 11)
E-mail: fabrice.mourlonbeernaert@dechert.com
Position: Partner is the Brussels office dealing with bankruptcy/corporate recovery and insolvency, corporate and securities, financial services and securities litigation, and mergers and acquisitions. Main areas of practice are corporate and securities law, capital markets and corporate finance, and mergers and acquisitions. Regularly represents clients in the acquisition and sale of Belgian companies, as well as in private equity transactions and corporate restructurings. Also advises clients on public offerings for stock purchase and on general corporate matters.
Career: Deputy judge of the Commercial Court of Brussels; lecturer-assistant professor at the Université Libre de Bruxelles; lecturer on corporate law for the preparatory course of the (Brussels) Bar Exam. Has authored and co-authored a number of publications on corporate and financial law, mergers and acquisitions and bankruptcy proceedings. In 1994, won first prize in the national legal service competition.
Education: Université Libre de Bruxelles, Belgium (1992 JD magna cum laude; 1994 Masters in Economic Law magna cum laude).

RAHMAN, Isabelle M

Dechert LLP
Phone: Brussels (+32 2 535 5445)

E-mail: isabelle.rahman@dechert.com
Position: Litigation partner and a member of the antitrust/competition group, dealing with antitrust/competition and EU law. Focuses practice on EC competition and telecommunications law and serves European and international clients in Brussels. Has substantial experience in the application of EC competition rules. Drafts notifications and complaints, handles cartel investigations, and advises on possible leniency applications. Also regularly advises on EC merger control and has made merger filings on behalf of clients who are active in a wide range of industries. Also experienced in dealing with national competition authorities in Europe and in other foreign jurisdictions and regularly co-ordinates multiple national filings in these jurisdictions. In addition, advises telecommunications industry clients on EU regulatory issues in the telecommunications sector and on competition-related matters. Also represents telecommunications clients in their dealings with national telecommunications authorities on licensing, interconnection, and pricing issues.
Career: Admitted to the English Bar in 1988.
Languages: English, French.
Education: University of Paris II (1985 Licence en droit, with distinction); University of Oxford (1987 BA jurisprudence).

REINART, Stephanie
Van Bael & Bellis
Phone: Brussels (+32 2 647 73 50)
E-mail: sreinart@vanbaelbellis.com
Position: Partner specialising in EC competition law and German competition law; she has secured merger clearance from the German Federal Cartel Office (Bundeskartellamt) in numerous cases; in the field of EC competition law, she has handled several international cartel cases in which she defended companies in antitrust investigations by the European Commission (in particular, regarding patent licensing); she regularly advises clients on how to structure various types of agreements (including strategic alliances, co-operation and supply agreements) to ensure compliance with competition law requirements; she frequently counsels companies with a dominant market position on their commercial conduct, so as to avoid abusive behaviour (such as through pricing policies); in order to train company employees in the field of competition law, Stephanie Reinart has prepared several antitrust compliance programmes and assisted companies with their implementation; Stephanie Reinart is a regular speaker at conferences on EC competition law; she has co-authored several publications on competition law, such as Van Bael & Bellis' 'Competition Law of the European Community (4th ed 2004) and an article on the treatment of cartels under EC competition law, published in the Antitrust & Competition Review 2004.
Career: Legal traineeship in Germany; qualified as a German lawyer 1995; in-house legal adviser at a major European trade association in Brussels; Van Bael & Bellis 1998 to date.
Member: Koblenz Bar, Germany.
Education: University of Trier, Germany (1993 Law).

ROOX, Kristof
Crowell & Moring
Phone: Brussels (+32 2 282 1843)
E-mail: kroox@crowell.com
Intellectual property and life sciences departments. Deals with all areas of IP law, litigation and private international law, with a focus on patent litigation.
Position: Partner.
Career: Associate, Price Blanpain Quagebeur & Maeyaert 1994-96; associate, De Bauw & Maeyaert 1996-2001; counsel/associate, Crowell & Moring September 2001-03; partner, Crowel & Moring January 2004 to date; assistant professor private international law, University of Gent 1998-2002. Publications: Various publications in the field of IP and private international law.
Languages: Dutch, English, French.
Member: Avocat of the Dutch Order of the Brussels Bar 1994; registered foreign lawyer with the Law Society of England and Wales 2004. Member: editorial board of IRDI; INTA; BVBA; LES; BMM; AIPPI.
Education: University of Brussels (1994 Lic Jur); University of London, Queen Mary & Westfield College (1996 LLM intellectual property law).
Personal: Born 1971, resides Brussels.

RUSSOTTO, Jean
Steptoe & Johnson LLP
Phone: Brussels (+32 2 646 0500)
E-mail: jrussotto@steptoe.com
Financial services, EU competition law.
Position: Jean Russotto is senior and managing partner of the Brussels office of Steptoe & Johnson LLP. His practice focuses primarily on competition law, trade and legal issues encountered by EU technology industries. He advises on policy and strategic representation before various directorates of the EU Commission. Mr Russotto also has expertise in financial services, especially banking.
Career: Counsel for the department of Justice, Canton of Vaud, Switzerland. Counsel for Nestlé. Chair of EC Competition Policy subcommittee of American Chambers of Commerce, Brussels 1982-95. Partner, Oppenheimer Wolff & Donnelly 1972-2003. Chair of Swiss EU committee of Swiss Chamber of Commerce in Brussels. Partner of Steptoe & Johnson LLP 2004.
Languages: French, English.
Member: Member of the Brussels Bar.
Education: University of Lausanne (1962 Doctorate of Law); Harvard Law School (1965 LLM); College of Europe, Bruges, Belgium.

SEARLES, James
Steptoe & Johnson LLP
Phone: Brussels (+32 2 626 0500)
E-mail: jsearles@steptoe.com
International trade, EU competition and environment law.
Position: James Searles is a partner in the Brussels office of Steptoe & Johnson LLP. His practice focuses on international trade and EU law. James advises on EU external trade measures, intra-EU trade obstacles, WTO law and international market access issues in general. Outside of the EU, he has significant international trade experience relating to China and Japan.
Career: Qualified, 1979; Oppenheimer Wolff & Donnelly (Brussels) 1986-2003; partner 1990; partner Steptoe & Johnson LLP 2004.
Languages: English and French.
Member: Brussels Bar; Ohio Bar; International Bar Association; American Chamber of Commerce to the European Union.
Education: University of Toledo Law School (1979 JD); University of Wisconsin-Madison (1974 BA with distinction).
Personal: Born 1952; resides Brussels.
Leisure: Travel, tennis.

SERVAIS, Benoît
Van Bael & Bellis
Phone: Brussels (+32 2 647 73 50)
E-mail: bservais@vanbaelbellis.com
Position: Partner, specialising in all aspects of EC and WTO trade law, with a particular emphasis on anti-dumping and anti-subsidy laws, as well as customs law; he has been involved in most major EC anti-dumping, anti-circumvention and anti-subsidy proceedings since 1992 and has represented clients before the EC Commission, the European Court of Justice and the European Court of First Instance; he also acts for EC exporters in anti-dumping proceedings initiated by third countries; he was the main contributor to 'Anti-Dumping and Other Trade Protection Laws of the EC' (4th ed 2004) and is a regular speaker at trade conferences and seminars.
Languages: English, French.
Member: Brussels Bar.
Education: University of Liège, Belgium (1989 Law); College of Europe, Bruges, Belgium (1990 post-graduate EC law).

TAVERNIER, Yves
DLA Piper Rudnick Gray Cary
Phone: Brussels (+32 2 500 15 90)
E-mail: yves.tavernier@dlapiper.com
Commercial and projects.
Position: Managing partner dealing with corporate law, mergers and acquisitions, joint ventures, general commercial law and distribution law, as well as banking litigation.
Career: Admitted to the Bar 1973; trustee in bankruptcy 1979-97; deputy justice of the peace 1980-90; deputy judge Court of Commerce, Ghent 1990-2005; founding partner of the firm Schrans, Verhegge, Tavernier & Mertens 1979; founder of the firm Tavernier & Coppens, later named Tavernier & Partners (a founding member of Law Europe EEIG in 1991), 1990; chairman 1993-99; partner and member of the board Coppens, Van Ommeslaghe & Faurès 1999; partner and member of management committee Coudert Brothers LLP 2000; partner DLA Piper Rudnick Gray Cary UK LLP 2005; Managing Partner, Belgium 2006.
Languages: Dutch, French, English, German.
Member: Section of business law IBA; American European Community Association.

Education: University of Ghent (1973 Law); University of Brussels (1974 Maritime and Aviation Law); University of Ghent (1974 European Law).

TEMKO, Richard J

Dechert LLP
Phone: Brussels (+32 2 535 5411)
E-mail: richard.temko@dechert.com
Position: Business partner dealing with alternative investment funds, bank financing and securitisation, bankruptcy/corporate recovery and insolvency, corporate and securities, domestic and international tax, finance and real estate, financial services, mergers and acquisitions, private equity, and venture capital. Work involves commercial, corporate, tax, and banking matters, including mergers and acquisitions, corporate reorganisations, venture capital, joint ventures, licensing, and a significant amount of international asset-based financing and cross-border leasing work.
Career: Business partner, has practised in Brussels since 1976; managing partner of Dechert's Brussels office since 1983; member of the New York and District of Columbia Bars; associate member of the Brussels Bar; writes and lectures frequently on financing and tax matters.
Languages: French.
Member: Legal and Taxation Committee of the American Chamber of Commerce in Belgium.
Education: Williams College (1972 BA); Columbia Law School (1974 JD).

VAN BAEL, Ivo

Van Bael & Bellis
Phone: Brussels (+32 2 647 73 50)
E-mail: ivanbael@vanbaelbellis.com
Position: Founding partner specialising in EC competition/antitrust law and EC and WTO trade law; he has been involved in a large number of the most significant competition cases over many years.
Career: Started practicing in a Wall Street firm in New York 1963; later worked in its offices in Paris and Brussels; co-founded Van Bael & Bellis with Jean-François Bellis 1986; professor of law at the College of Europe in Bruges, Belgium and at the University of Amsterdam; past visiting lecturer/professor at the University of Tokyo.
Languages: Dutch, English, French, Italian.
Member: Brussels Bar; has been active in the American Bar Association (ABA) and the International Bar Association (IBA); chairman of the Antitrust and Trade Law Committee of the IBA's section on business law 1987-89.
Education: University of Louvain (1961 Law); University of Bologna Law School; the Bologna Center of the John Hopkins University; University of Michigan Law School (MA Comparative Law).

VAN HOVE, Kris

Van Bael & Bellis
Phone: Brussels (+32 2 647 73 50)
E-mail: kvanhove@vanbaelbellis.com
Position: Partner specialising in competition law (cartels, dominant positions, merger control, joint ventures, distribution, technology transfer and state aid) and regulatory affairs (aviation law and energy law); his competition law experience covers a wide variety of sectors (basic industries, energy, construction equipment, building materials, chemicals, electronics, information and communications technology and aviation) and includes notifications, litigation before Community and national courts and counselling; his regulatory affairs experience includes representation of clients before the Community institutions (Commission, Council and European Parliament); he was a contributor to Van Bael & Bellis''Competition Law of the European Community' (4th ed 2004) and to the only comprehensive guide to Belgian business law in English to date: Van Bael & Bellis''Business Law Guide to Belgium' (2nd ed 2003); he is also a regular speaker at seminars on EU competition law and EU aviation law.
Languages: Dutch, English, French.
Member: Brussels Bar.
Education: University of Leuven (1989 Law); Sorbonne (Paris II) (1990 post-graduate European Law); Duke University, North Carolina (1992 MA Law).

WELLINGER, Markus

Van Bael & Bellis
Phone: Brussels (+32 2 647 73 50)
E-mail: mwellinger@vanbaelbellis.com
Position: Partner; Markus Wellinger has represented clients before the European and national courts, the European Commission and national competition authorities in several member states; in the field of competition law, his practice focuses on advising and representing clients in areas including merger control cases, compliance programmes and cartel investigations, strategic alliances and other commercial arrangements (such as distribution, R&D and technology licensing), issues related to abuse of dominant position and EC state aid rules; he has secured merger antitrust clearance from a large number of national competition authorities within and outside the European Union; he has also published an article on 'Managing a multi-jurisdictional filing' in the International Comparative Legal Guide to Merger Control 2006; Markus Wellinger is a contributor to Van Bael & Bellis''Competition Law of the European Community (4th ed 2004); he has written articles on various competition and internal market issues and has also spoken on these subjects at seminars; Markus Wellinger has played a key role in the development of a competition compliance training DVD entitled 'Complying with EU competition law, a practical training tool' which is part of a more complete practical compliance programme offered to clients.
Career: Van Bael & Bellis 1993 to date; partner 2001 to date; prior to this, worked at a leading Belgian bank.
Languages: Dutch, English, French, German and Swiss German.
Member: Brussels Bar.
Education: University of Brussels (ULB) (1989 Law magna cum laude); Institut d'Etudes Europeénnes, Brussels (1991 LLM European Law magna cum laude); University of Keele (1992 MA Diplomatic Studies).

WOOLFSON, Philip

Steptoe & Johnson LLP
Phone: Brussels (+32 2 626 0500)
E-mail: pwoolfson@steptoe.com
Insurance and financial services.
Position: Philip Woolfson is a partner in the Brussels office of Steptoe & Johnson LLP. His practice area focuses on insurance and financial services. He is particularly well known for his experience in cross-border insurance regulation. He is a regular speaker at conferences on financial services and is a frequent contributor to European and international journals.
Career: Trained at AJ & A Graham, Solicitors, Glasgow; qualified 1981; Theodore Goddard, Conseils Juridiques, Paris, France; qualified 1987; partner, Steptoe & Johnson LLP, 2004. Publications of note: joint editor, Sweet & Maxwell, special edition, January 1999, 'Millennium Bug: Aspects of Banking, Computer, Insurance and Company Law'; member of, and EU contributor to, editorial board of Sweet & Maxwell publication 'Encyclopaedia of Insurance Law'; Sweet & Maxwell 'Special Report on Cross-Frontier Insolvency of Insurance Companies' (2001), author of chapter on France and joint-author on Belgium.
Languages: English, French.
Member: Financial services sub-committee, American Chamber of Commerce, Brussels; EU liaison officer for the Association of International Life Offices.
Education: High School of Glasgow, Glasgow, Scotland; University of Glasgow (1976 MA; 1979 LLB Hons 2(1)); College of Europe, Bruges, Belgium (1982 Certificate of Advanced European Studies).
Personal: Born 1955; resides Brussels.
Leisure: Skiing; reading; music; food.

BULGARIA

ATANASSOV, Stoyan

Atanassov & Ivanov Law Firm
Phone: Sofia (+359 2 981 43 31)
E-mail: atanassov@atanassovivanov.com
Position: Partner specialising in M&A, corporate and commercial litigation, tax advice, private and international law, sports law, currency regimes and foreign investments.
Career: Labour union, legal assistant; employment and social security law consulting 1993-95; legal consultant 'Temida' project; various consultancy services in the field of legal information science, organisation of legal databases; commercial law consulting; various investment and international projects 1996-98; judicial trainee Sofia City Court/Bulgarian Ministry of Justice, Sofia; internship at all levels of the Bulgarian judicial system: courts, County Prosecutors' Office, Regional Prosecutors' Office, Public Notary Office 1998-99; legal adviser for PassConsult; legal advisory services in respect of various clients and projects; negotiations support; commercial, civil litigation and real estate, as

well as compliance with local regulations and drafting of contracts 1999-2000; attorney at law for PricewaterhouseCoopers, Bulgaria; various tax and legal services related to tobacco sector issues; foreign investments, incorporation and restructuring of businesses and compliance with local regulations, tax compliance, contracts, corporate and commercial; various tax and legal services related to tobacco sector issues; banking and private pension funds regulations; foreign investment and currency regime regulations; legal and tax due diligence, due diligence reviews of companies targeted for acquisition or privatisation; dispute resolution, negotiations 2000-02; senior associate at Atanassov & Ivanov (previously Totev & Ivanov), focusing on advisory services in respect of foreign investments, incorporation and restructuring of local businesses, litigation and compliance with local regulations; legal due diligence reviews of companies targeted for acquisition or privatisation, tax advice and tax planning to international clients, tax compliance, contracts, corporate and commercial; foreign investment and currency regime regulations 2002-04; partner Atanassov & Ivanov, specialising in M&A, corporate and commercial litigation, tax advice, private and international law, sports law, currency regimes and foreign investment 2004 to date.
Languages: English, Russian, Bulgarian.
Member: Sofia Bar Association 2000; AAA Lawyers' Intergroup (International Organisation of Lawyers acting in co-operation with the Hague Academy of International Law) 2003 to date.
Education: St Kliment Ohridsky University Law School (1998 LLM); scholarship student of Open Society Foundation, Bulgaria (1995-97); e-business course, Brussels (2001); specialist course on Creating Values for Multinational Companies, Evian, France (2002); specialist course on Private International Law at the Hague Academy of International Law, Netherlands (2003).
Personal: Born 1974; resides Sofia.

IVANOV, Ilian

Atanassov & Ivanov Law Firm
Phone: Sofia (+359 2 981 43 31)
E-mail: ivanov@atanassovivanov.com
Position: Partner specialising in tax planning, labour law, social security levies, energy law, currency regime and litigation.
Career: Lawyer advising domestic and international clients, including Henkel Ecolab, Reemtsma and Sofregaz 1995-98; PricewaterhouseCoopers Bulgaria; tax advice and tax planning to international clients, including Philip Morris, Kraft Foods, Socotab and The Coca-Cola Company; advice on real estates and construction matters to a tobacco manufacturer in relation to the construction of a tobacco processing facility in Bulgaria; transaction support to a multinational bank in the acquisition of a Bulgarian pension administrator company; due diligence and transactions support to a pension insurance company 1998-2001; partner, Atanassov & Ivanov, focusing on project finance and construction, energy, oil and gas law; within the firm, Ilian specialises in tax advice and litigation, employment and regulatory regimes; local adviser to Entergy in relation to a successful project finance deal at a total cost of $650m for the acquisition, operation and rehabilitation of the Maritza East III power plant; advice and representation of Enel S.p.A. in relation to the privatisation of the country's seven electricity distribution companies; legal advisor to a US oil and gas company in their successful natural gas exploration activities in Bulgaria 2001 to date. Publications: 'Deficiencies in Article 109 of the Tax Procedure Code' in Bulgarian Business, August 2001; 'Bulgarian Double Tax Treaties - Introduction' in Tax Practice, September 2001.
Languages: English, French, Serbian.
Member: Sofia Bar Association 1999.
Education: St Kliment Ohridsky University Law School (1997 LLM); Bulgarian Academy of Science (2001 PhD Energy Law).
Personal: Born 1971; resides Sofia.

PENKOV, Vladimir

LIC-Penkov, Markov & Partners
Phone: Sofia (+359 2 971 3935)
E-mail: lega@bg400.bg
Executive managing partner.
Position: Specialises in commercial and company law, foreign investments, licences and know-how, privatisation, mergers and acquisitions, concessions, taxation and customs law, international commercial arbitration. Has handled numerous acquisitions and joint venture establishment in breweries, banking, insurance, construction, electronics, telecommunications, soft beverages etc. Represented Domaine Boyar AD for debt and equity financing by EBRD and Baring Central European Investments; TBI Holding for acquisition of BULSTRAD and privatisation of DZI insurance; Gallagher Ltd in the bid for privatisation of Bulgartabac; Strabag AG for investment in construction; Koehne Group on infrastructure project for investment in railroad construction. Recently represented Titan Cement for investment in cement plant; Chipita International for investment in confectionery industry; the Bulgarian government for privatisation of Navibulgar (Bulgarian sea commercial fleet) and the Bulgarian River commercial fleet; Advent International in the bid for privatisation of Bulgarian Telecommunications Company (BTC); Salini Costruttori S.p.A in acquisition of concession rights for a motorway; Ealing Studios in the bid for privatisation of Boyana Film; the acquisition of Bankya Mineral Waters; the acquisition of Eurobank.
Career: Qualified 1977; legal counsel and senior counsel Bulgarian Ministry of Foreign Economic Relations 1977-87 and 1989-90; chief legal counsel Technica Foreign Trade Organisation 1987-89; founder and managing partner Lega InterConsult and LIC-Penkov, Markov & Partners 1990 to date. Publications include: 'The Promotion and Protection of Foreign Investments in Bulgaria: some legal aspects' in 'International Relationships' magazine; articles in 'Foreign Trade', 'Bulgarisches Wirtschaftsblatt' and 'Business Opportunities in Bulgaria'; 'Rechtliche Grundlagen für ausländische Investoren in Bulgarien' in 'Südeuropa Mitteilungen'; 'Legal Aspects' and 'Legal Privatization Issues in Bulgaria' in 'International Privatization Review' (Euromoney); 'Richtige Partnerauswahl hilft Vorteile zu gewinnen', interview in 'Bulgarisches Wirtschaftsblatt'; 2005 presented the topic of 'Small and middle enterprises - macroeconomic environment and development strategy' in Vienna.
Languages: Bulgarian, English, German.
Member: Vice-president Bulgarian Chamber of Commerce and Industry (BCCI); former member of the Managing Board of Bulgarian International Business Association; arbitrator Arbitration Court at BCCI; Consultative Committee of International Association for Industrial Property Protection (AIPPI); member of the board and former CEO Zagorka Brewery AD, Stara Zagora; chartered member and former president First Lions Club, Bulgaria. Member of the Barons 500, subject to biographical record in Who's Who of the World 1999-2000 Global Edition and International Who's Who of Professionals 2005.
Education: Economy University, Berlin (1970-72); Sofia University St Clement Ohridsky (1976 LLM).
Personal: Born 1952.

CYPRUS

DEMETRIOU, Andrew

Law Office of Andrew Demetriou & Co
Phone: Nicosia (+357 22 67 50 90)
E-mail: ad@ademetriou.com
Position: Senior partner of Cyprus law firm Law Office of Andrew Demetriou & Co, barrister and chartered arbitrator (international panel member of Chartered Institute of Arbitrators), specialising in commercial litigation, arbitration, construction law, energy law, competition, procurement and BOT. Legal adviser to the Electricity Authority of Cyprus and a number of local and commercial entities. Has served as chairman of the Cyprus branch of the Chartered Institute of Arbitrators and is the current chairman of the Cyprus Arbitration Club. Has represented the Republic of Cyprus by special appointment by the Attorney General of the Republic and the Ministry of Defence of the UK by special appointment by the Attorney General of the Sovereign Base Area Administration on Cyprus.
Career: Called to Bar of England and Wales 1982; internal legal adviser DG Jones & Partners International Construction Consultants (now main board director and group general counsel of DG Jones International) 1983-85; called to the Cyprus Bar 1985; founded Law Office of Andrew Demetriou & Co 1985.
Languages: English, Greek.
Member: Honourable Society of Gray's Inn; Cyprus Bar Association; International Bar Association; Chartered Institute of Arbitrators; Institute of Directors.
Education: University of Liverpool (1980 LLB Hons); Inns of Court School of Law, Gray's Inn.
Personal: Born Manchester, England, 1959; resides Nicosia, Cyprus.

CZECH REPUBLIC

CERMÁK, Karel, Dr

Cermak Horejs Myslil a spol
Phone: Prague (+42 02 96 167 111)
E-mail: info@apk.cz
Position: Senior partner - main area of practice includes IP law, trade marks, arbitration, international law, contracts, foreign investments, advice and consulting in international licensing and unfair competition. Represents in patent and trade mark matters including disputes in the Czech Republic for a number of international companies. Takes active part in the legislative process in the field of intellectual property.
Career: Practised law since 1959; specialising in IP, arbitration and private international law 1961; president of the Bar 1968; president of the Czech Bar Association 1990; re-elected 1996-2001; arbitrator of the Arbitration Court with the Czech Chamber of Commerce and the Czech Chamber of Agriculture; the Arbitration Court with the Federal Chamber of Commerce in Vienna and of the World Intellectual property Arbitration Center in Geneva. In 1994 obtained 'The Award for Merits for the Republic of Austria', granted by the president of the Republic of Austria.
Languages: Czech, English, French, German.
Member: AIPPI; International League of Competition Law and many other international organisations in the IP field.
Education: Academic Grammar School (Gymnasium), Prague; Faculty of Law of Charles University (1965 Dr Juris).
Personal: Born 1934; resides Prague.

CERMÁK JR, Karel, Dr

Cermak Horejs Myslil a spol
Phone: Prague (+42 02 96 167 444)
E-mail: kcermak@apk.cz
Position: Partner, specialising in intellectual property, private international law, unfair competition, pharmaceuticals, trade marks, business law, mergers and acquisitions. Represents a number of national and international companies in proceedings before the Czech Industrial Property Office as well as in court litigation proceedings, in particular patent litigation matters. He has successfully dealt with a number of trade mark, patent and domain name infringement cases and provided legal support for a number of mergers and acquisitions by foreign companies in the Czech Republic (particulars on clients and cases may not be disclosed by virtue of local deontological rules).
Career: Legal trainee in Cermák Horejs Vrba 1996-99; traineeship with other domestic and foreign law firms, including Gaedertz Rechtsanwälte, Cologne 1997; admitted to Bar 1999; partner in Cermák Horejs Myslil Lawyers and Patent Attorneys 2000. Publications: 'The Problems of Conflict of Law in the Anglo-American Legal Orbit and Some Continental Jurisdictions'; publishes in a number of legal journals, in the field of industrial property among others. Co-author of 'Legal aspects of Domain Names', Linde Praha 2000 (in Czech); chapters on company law and contract law in 'Handbuch für Wirtschaft und Recht in Osteuropa' (Handbook on Economy and Law in Eastren Europe), CH Beck, Munich 2002 (in German).
Languages: English, French, German.
Member: Vice-president of the Czech National Group of AIPPI; committee member of the Czech National Group of International League of Competition Law (LIDC).
Education: Grammar School (Gymnasium) Sladkovského in Prague; Faculty of Law of the Charles University 1991-96 (1998 PhD); Université de Provence (Aix-en-Provence) 1994-95; European Academy of Legal Theory, Brussels (2000 LLM).
Personal: Born 1973; resides Prague.

MATEJKA, Jan, Dr

Cermak Horejs Myslil a spol
Phone: Prague (+42 02 96 167 501)
E-mail: jmatejka@apk.cz
Patents, trade marks.
Position: Partner dealing with intellectual property law, patents, trade marks, commercial, corporate law, contracts, international law, unfair competition, arbitration. Represents in patent and trade mark matters including disputes in the Czech Republic. Takes an active part in the legislative process, namely in the field of intellectual property. Publishes in a number of legal journals.
Career: Legal trainee, Legal Consultancy in Pelhrimov 1971-75; attorney-at-law (advocate), head of law office in Pelhrimov 1975-83; Chairman of regional committee - Ceské Budejovice 1983-90; partner in Cermák Horejs Vrba 1991-2000; partner in Cermák Horejs Myslil Law and Patent Offices since 2000.
Languages: English, German, Russian.
Member: Czech National LES Committee; Bar Exams Board member; discipline commission of the Czech Bar Association; INTA.
Education: Academic Grammar School (Gymnasium) in Pelhrimov (1962-65); faculty of law, Charles University (1974 Dr Juris); University of California, School of Law - Orientation in American Law 1993.
Personal: Born 1946; resides Prague.

MYSLIL, Richard, Dr Ing

Cermak Horejs Myslil a spol
Phone: Prague (+42 02 96 167 609)
E-mail: intelprop@apk.cz
Position: Partner, specialising in commercial law, acquisitions, companies, competition law, agreements.
Career: Legal trainee, Bubník & Myslil 1995-97; partly practised in Coudert Brothers in New York 1996; Herbert Smith in London 1995; Laffili van Crombrugghe, Brussels 1995; management practice in chemical and pharmaceutical industry (1984-95); admitted to Bar 1997. Partner in Bubník & Myslil 1997; partner in Cermák Horejs Myslil 2001.
Languages: English, French.
Education: University of Chemistry Technology in Prague, specialisation economy and management (1980-84); Faculty of Law of Charles University (1990-95). Post-graduate studies at the University of Birmingham (1995).
Personal: Born 1962.

MYSLIL, Stanislav, Dr

Cermak Horejs Myslil a spol
Phone: Prague (+42 02 96 167 520)
E-mail: smyslil@apk.cz
Commercial law.
Position: Partner dealing with all areas of commercial/corporate law including mergers and acquisitions, investments, formation and restructuring of commercial companies and related fields.
Career: Former chief of section, legal department, Ministry for Foreign Affairs; United Nations legal staff; attorney at Law Office No 1, Prague; partner Bubnik Myslil 1991-2000; arbitrator, Arbitration Court, Prague; author of two books and many articles on international public and private law.
Languages: English, French, German, some Russian.
Member: Czech Bar; honorary member of Center for International Legal Studies, Salzburg.
Education: Charles University Prague (postgraduate studies); Charles University Prague (partly London University).
Personal: Born 1930; resides Prague.

NÜRNBERGER, Jörg

DLA Weiss-Tessbach
Phone: Prague (+420 224 234 413)
E-mail: joerg.nuernberger@dlapiper.com
Corporate and M&A.
Position: Head of DLA Weiss-Tessbach's Prague office. With more than 11 years' experience in Central and Eastern Europe, Jörg Nürnberger is an expert in international M&A deals and finance transactions in the region. Has acted on behalf of international clients in the acquisition of existing local or international businesses in the Czech Republic and the establishment of new businesses. Advises clients in many sectors and industries and has significant experience in the area of banking and finance.
Career: Trained Weiss-Tessbach, Prague; qualified as German attorney 1997; admitted in Czech Republic 1997; partner DLA Weiss-Tessbach 1999; admitted in Austria 2003. Lecturer in Czech labour law. Publications of note: 'The Bar Laws in the Accession Countries' (Czech country report, together with Martina Dokoupilova), December 2003, Prof Dr Dieter Kolonowitz, Vienna; 'Company Law in Europe' (Czech Republic division, with Lucie Brejskova), December 2002, Butterworth; 'International Encyclopedia of Agency and Distribution Agreements' (Czech Republic chapter), December 2002, IBA Series, Agustin Jausàs, Kluwer Law International; 'Unternehmerische Tätigkeit von Ausländern in der Tschechischen Republik - Erfahrungen aus der anwaltlichen Praxis' ('Doing business as a foreigner in the Czech Republic - experiences from the legal practice') in 'Tschechien, Deutschland und die EU', Karel Simka, Westböhmische Universität, Pilsen, 2001.

Languages: German, Czech, English.
Member: German, Czech, Austrian Bar Associations; Euregio Egrensis.
Education: University of Bayreuth, Germany (1993 First State Examination; 1995 Second State Examination); Charles University, Prague (1998 postgraduate studies in Czech environmental law).
Personal: Born 1967; resides Prague.

DENMARK

BUGGE, Jens Jakob

DLA Nordic
Phone: Copenhagen (+45 77 30 42 60)
E-mail: jens.jakob.bugge@dlanordic.dk
Technology, media and communications.
Position: Managing partner, previously head of TMC, specialising in intellectual property/IT, trade mark and patent litigation, parallel imports, design and copyright.
Career: Trained Horton & Partners (DLA); qualified 1990; admitted Supreme Court; partner DLA Nordic 1998; managing partner; board member Müller Martini A/S; board member Erik Bagger A/S. Author 'Requirement of Use' (EIPR 2004).
Languages: English, Scandinavian.
Member: Danish Bar Association.
Education: University of Copenhagen (1990 Law).
Personal: Born 1964; resides Copenhagen.
Leisure: Tennis, football.

ØKSNEBJERG, Jim

DLA Nordic
Phone: Copenhagen (+45 77 30 40 50)
E-mail: jim.oksnebjerg@dlanordic.dk
Corporate.
Position: Partner in the corporate department of DLA Nordic. Practice focuses on mergers and acquisitions, securities law, private equity investments, company law and foundation law. Also highly experienced within public-to-private and cross-border transactions. Has lead DLA Nordic teams advising on a number of transactions, including the Municipality of Copenhagen/Copenhagen Energy's approx €1.4bn sale of its electricity business to DONG A/S, including a 34 per cent share holding in Energy E2 (total enterprise value approx €3bn) conducted as an auction process following the more than €2.7bn restructuring of all the utility businesses of Copenhagen Energy.
Career: Trained Copenhagen; qualified 1993; Danish Commerce and Companies Agency within the Ministry of Industry 1993-97; DLA Nordic 1997; partner DLA Nordic 2001; lecturer on property, contract and tort law University of Copenhagen 1994-2000; assistant professor of company law University of Copenhagen since 2003; has conducted a number of courses on mergers and acquisitions, company law and share incentive schemes. Editor of the 'Company Document Guide' (CD-rom) published by Magnus Informatik A/S, Wolters Kluwer, yearly up-dating (a collection of form agreements within company law and interactive guidance); co-author of 'Aktiebaseret aflønning' (2003) concerning the legal matters of share incentive schemes.
Languages: Fluent in the Scandinavian languages and English.
Member: Legal committee Danish Venture Capital Association; Danish Bar and Law Society.
Education: University of Copenhagen (1993 Law).
Personal: Born 1966; resides Copenhagen.

EGYPT

BASSIOUNY, Omar Salah

DLA Matouk Bassiouny
Phone: Cairo (+20 2 792 0075)
E-mail: omar.bassiouny@dlamatoukbassiouny.com
Position: Executive partner, specialising in mergers and acquisitions within Egypt, securities-related transactions involving the Stock Exchange and the Capital Market Authority, including bonds issuing, funds' management, dual securities listing, and has strong experience in project finance. Also has substantial experience in the field of Egyptian privatisation: has advised a variety of multinationals and local investors on the privatisation of public sectors banks, fertiliser and cement factories. Advises as well on all aspects of corporate compliance in relation to labour, social insurance, corporate and capital markets laws.
Career: Ibrachy & Dermarkar Law Firm 1998-99; Shalakany Law Office 1999; White & Case, Federssen 1999-2000; Ibrachy & Dermarkar Law Firm 2000-02; Denton Wilde Sapte 2002-05; managing partner Bassiouny & Associates 2002-05; executive partner DLA Matouk Bassiouny 2005. Publications: 'Venture Capital Investment in Egypt - Legal and Regulatory Issues' in 'International Mergers & Acquisitions Review' 2004/2005 (Euromoney Publications, 2004); 'An Insight on Doing Business in Egypt' (BCA, November 2004 issue); 'Five Fundamental Steps to Perfect Your Title' (BCA, October 2004 issue); 'Equity Transactions in Egypt - Legal and Regulatory Issues Faced by Inward Investors' in 'International Mergers & Acquisitions Review' 2003/2004 (Euromoney Publications, 2003).
Languages: Fluent English, French, Arabic.
Member: American Chamber of Commerce in Egypt; Club D' Affaires Franco-Egyptian; Egyptian Bar Association.
Education: American University in Cairo (1998 BA); Cairo Faculty of Law (1999 License de Droit).

MATOUK, F John

DLA Matouk Bassiouny
Phone: Cairo (+20 2 792 0075)
E-mail: john.matouk@dlamatoukbassiouny.com
Position: Managing partner. Heads the office's corporate, capital markets, commercial and aviation departments (all of which are recognised as premier practices in the market). Experienced in advising on all aspects of investing and doing business in Egypt and has significant experience in the field of Egyptian privatisation: has advised the Government of Egypt on the privatisation of its water and telecommunication sectors and has advised major US, Canadian, UK, French and Asian multinationals on a broad range of privatisation issues, including tendering, BOOT projects, and private sector participation in public sector companies. Referred to as 'highly regarded' in 'The European Legal 500' (2004 edition). Selected as a legal expert in Egyptian banking and finance (Legal Business 2003 publications).
Career: Qualified in State of New York; Denton Wilde Sapte, London and Cairo, liaison with Paris office 1998-2005; partner 2003; managing partner DLA Matouk Bassiouny 2005. Publications: 'Venture Capital Investment in Egypt - Legal and Regulatory Issues' in 'International Mergers & Acquisitions Review' 2004/2005 (Euromoney Publications, 2004); 'Equity Transactions in Egypt - Legal and Regulatory Issues Faced by Inward Investors' in 'International Mergers & Acquisitions Review' 2003/2004 (Euromoney Publications, 2003); 'Gas Regulation in Egypt' in 'Global Competition Review' (2003); 'The Regulatory Regime for Public Utilities Concessions in Egypt' in 'International Power Finance Review' 1999/2000 (Euromoney Publications, 1999); 'Egypt Amends Companies law' in 'Middle East Executive Reports' (MEER, May 1998).
Languages: Fluent English, French, Arabic.
Member: International Bar Association; New York State Bar Association; English Law Society (foreign registered lawyer); American Chamber of Commerce in Egypt; Centre D'Affaires Franco-Égyptien (CAFÉ).
Education: George Washington University, (1997 JD with honours); Yale University (1993 BA Double Thesis, International Relations/Literary Theory, with high honors).

ESTONIA

VARUL, Paul

Advokaadibüroo Paul Varul
Phone: Tartu (+372 6 264 300)
E-mail: tallinn@varul.ee
Position: Partner dealing with all areas of corporate law, commercial law and insolvency; author of over 70 academic publications.
Career: Partner Advokaadibüroo Paul Varul 1994 to date; Minister of Justice of the Republic of Estonia 1995-99; civil law professor at the University of Tartu 1992 to date; a member of the head commission in the development of the European Civil Code 2003 to date.
Languages: English, Estonian, Russian.
Member: Estonian Bar Association.
Education: University of Tartu (1975); St Petersburg University (1985 PhD).

FINLAND

ALANEN, Jouni
Hammarström Puhakka Partners, Attorneys Ltd
Phone: Helsinki (+358 9 474 2280)
E-mail: jouni.alanen@hpplaw.fi
Position: Partner specialising in EC law, competition law, antitrust, trade regulations, market law, public procurement and energy law.
Career: Ministry of Trade and Industry, commercial secretary 1990-91; Environment and Business Lawyers Ltd, partner 1993-2001; Attorneys' House ANPR Ltd, partner 2001-04; Hammarström Puhakka Partners, Attorneys Ltd, partner 2004 to date.
Languages: Finnish, Swedish, English, German.
Member: Finnish Competition Law Association; Finnish Society for European Law (board member).
Education: Attorney-at-law 2001; master of European law, University of Saarland (1995 LLM Eur); University of Helsinki (1995 LLLic); University of Helsinki (1990 LLM).
Personal: Born 1963.

ALHO, Jari-Pekka
Krogerus Attorneys Ltd
Phone: Helsinki (+358 9 622 6520)
E-mail: jp.alho@krogerus.com
Corporate advisory and dispute resolution (CAD).
Position: Partner and head of corporate advisory and dispute resolution (CAD) group; specialises in litigation and arbitration, labour law, insolvency law, IT, telecommunications, and contract law; work consists mainly of advising major companies on their operative legal issues, representing companies in arbitration or litigation and assisting companies in establishing in Finland; additionally active in legal and technology policy. Co-author of 'Toimitusjohtajasopimukset', a book on directorship contracts and liability.
Career: Legal counsel, Law Office Aaltonen, Alho & Untamala Oy 1995-98; legal counsel, Helsinki Chamber of Commerce 1998-2000; policy manager (IT, telecommunication and e-commerce), International Chamber of Commerce (ICC), Paris, 2000-01; associate, Matti Oksala Attorneys-at-Law 2001-02; associate, Krogerus Attorneys Ltd 2002-03; partner 2003.
Languages: English, Finnish, Swedish, Spanish.
Member: Finnish Bar Association; International Bar Association; ICC Commission E-Business, IT and Telecom; Helsinki Chamber of Commerce Legal and Tax Committee.
Education: University of Helsinki (1996 LLM; 1998 Postgraduate Degree).
Personal: Born 1970; resides Espoo.
Leisure: Golf, sailing.

EEROLA, Mikko
Waselius & Wist
Phone: Helsinki (+358 9 668 9520)
E-mail: ww@ww.fi
EU and competition, mergers and acquisitions, and corporate and commercial.
Position: Partner whose principal practice areas are: EU and competition, mergers and acquisitions, and corporate and commercial law.
Career: Trainee European Commission, Brussels 1997-98; secondment Lovells, Brussels 2003; partner Waselius & Wist 2004. Numerous articles in Finnish and international professional publications in the field of EU and competition law, M&A and energy law.
Languages: Finnish, Swedish, English, German.
Member: Finnish Bar Association; Legal Society of Finland; International Bar Association; Finnish Society of Competition Law.
Education: University of Helsinki (1998 LLM); King's College (2002 postgraduate diploma in EC Competition Law).
Personal: Born 1972.

HAMMARSTRÖM, Jörgen
Hammarström Puhakka Partners, Attorneys Ltd
Phone: Helsinki (+358 9 474 2220)
E-mail: jorgen.hammarstrom@hpplaw.fi
Position: Partner and managing director specialising in business law, company and corporate law, mergers and acquisitions, contracts and arbitration and litigation.
Career: Ministry of Transport and Communications, deputy researcher; Nenonen & Rantasila Attorneys-at-Law, associate lawyer 1985-88; Nenonen & Rantasila Attorneys-at-Law, partner 1988-89; Ahola, Nenonen, Pokela & Rantasila Attorneys-at-Law, partner 1989-93; Attorneys' House ANPR Ltd, partner 1993-2004; Attorneys' House ANPR Ltd, managing director 2002-04; Hammarström Puhakka Partners, Attorneys Ltd, managing director and partner 2004 to date.
Languages: Swedish, Finnish, English.
Member: Juridical Society of Finland; International Bar Association; Alumni Association of the Academy of American and International Law (the Comparative Law Center of the Southwestern Legal Foundation, Dallas, USA).
Education: Attorney-at-law 1988; deputy judge (trained on the bench) 1985; University of Helsinki (1984 LLM).
Personal: Born 1957.

JÄRVINEN, Marja-Liisa
Krogerus Attorneys Ltd
Phone: Jyväskylä (+358 14 333 0800)
E-mail: marja-liisa.jarvinen@krogerus.com
Jyväskylä office.
Position: Partner specialising in public procurements, EU projects and legal services for small- and medium-sized companies.
Career: Lawyer, Chamber of Commerce of Central Finland 1987-91; associate Attorneys-at-Law Hirvonen & Raivio 1991-93; partner, Attorneys-at-Law Marja Liisa Järvinen Oy 1993-2002; partner Krogerus Attorneys Ltd 2003.
Languages: Finnish, English.
Member: Finnish Bar Association.
Education: University of Turku (1987 LLM); trained at the Bench 1990.
Personal: Born 1961; resides Jyväskylä.
Leisure: Motorcycling, gym.

JOENPOLVI, Katri
Krogerus Attorneys Ltd
Phone: Helsinki (+358 9 622 6520)
E-mail: katri.joenpolvi@krogerus.com
EU and competition.
Position: Heads the firm's competition law practice group. Advises and represents clients in I.A. litigation on competition and communication law issues, merger control cases (including remedy negotiations), antitrust compliance programs and exemption regulations. Co-author of studies and surveys concerning significant market power and dominant position in the area of telecommunications and the merger control guidelines of the FCA articles on merger control.
Career: Associate, Procopé & Hornborg Attorneys-at-Law 1994-95; senior research officer, deputy head of division Finnish Competition Authority 1996-2000; legal counsel, manager, Klegal Oy 2000-01; senior associate Krogerus Attorneys Ltd 2001-03; partner 2003.
Languages: Finnish, English, Swedish.
Member: Finnish Bar Association.
Education: University of Edinburgh (1993-94); University of Helsinki (1994 LLM); trained at the Bench 1996.
Personal: Born 1969; resides Helsinki.
Leisure: Reading, jogging, skiing.

JUUTILAINEN, Jaana
Mäkitalo Rämö Juutilainen Oy, Attorneys-at-Law
Phone: Helsinki (+358 50 2860)
E-mail: jaana.juutilainen@mrjlaw.fi
Position: Partner dealing with all areas of corporate law including franchise, litigation, arbitration and environment law.
Career: Trained on the Bench (District Court of Pirkkara); partner at Mäkitalo Rämö Juutilainen 1996 to date.
Languages: Finnish, Swedish, English.
Member: Finnish Bar Association.
Education: University of Helsinki (1991 LLM).
Personal: Born 1965, resides Espoo.

KAPANEN, Pasi
Krogerus Attorneys Ltd
Phone: Jyväskylä (+358 14 333 0800)
E-mail: pasi.kapanen@krogerus.com
Jyväskylä office.
Position: Partner and head of Jyväskylä office; specialises in mergers and acquisitions, contract law and commercial law.
Career: Associate at Krogerus Attorneys Ltd from 1994; partner since 1999.
Languages: Finnish, English.
Member: Finnish Bar Association; International Bar Association.
Education: University of Lapland (1990 LLM); trained at the Bench 1993.
Personal: Born 1966; resides Laukaa.
Leisure: Cross-country skiing, motorcycling.

KATAINEN, Juha Pekka
Krogerus Attorneys Ltd
Phone: Helsinki (+358 9 622 6520)
E-mail: jp.katainen@krogerus.com
Corporate advisory and dispute resolution (CAD).
Position: Partner and head of technology, media and telecommunications group; dealing with IT, technology and telecommunications law, contract law, outsourcing arrangements, IT, technology, and telecommunications and dispute resolution.
Career: Partner, Law Office Katainen & Co from 1997 to 2001; partner, Krogerus Attorneys Ltd 2001; frequently lectures on IT law.
Languages: Finnish, English, Swedish.
Member: Finnish Bar Association; International Bar Association.
Education: University of Helsinki (1997 LLM).
Personal: Born 1969; resides Helsinki.
Leisure: Golf, literature.

KROGERUS, Hannu
Krogerus Attorneys Ltd
Phone: Helsinki (+358 9 622 6520)
E-mail: hannu.krogerus@krogerus.com
Transactions.
Position: Senior partner and head of corporate advisory practice group, specialising in company law, corporate law, commercial law, contracts, mergers and acquisitions, corporate restructuring, banking and finance, and commercial litigation and arbitration. Advises major companies in their global transactions, business development, legal risk management and corporate governance.
Career: Legal counsel, Finnish Export Credit Ltd, Kansallis-Osake-Pankki, and Lohja Oy Ab 1971-87; administrative director and general counsel, Lohja Oy Ab 1987-91; senior vice-president, Oy Metra Ab 1991-92; partner, Krogerus Attorneys Ltd since 1992.
Languages: Finnish, English, Swedish.
Member: Finnish Bar Association; International Bar Association.
Education: University of Helsinki (LLM 1971); trained at the Bench 1975.
Personal: Born in 1949; resides Helsinki.
Leisure: Classic opera, music, boating, Australia.

LATOLA, Antti
Krogerus Attorneys Ltd
Phone: Oulu (+358 8 534 4400)
E-mail: antti.latola@krogerus.com
Oulu office.
Position: Partner and member of the board of Krogerus Attorneys Ltd. Mr Latola is highly experienced in corporate law and financing, and he specialises in M&A, venture capital, and other financing transactions. He acts as an expert member on company boards, which operate, for example, in the retail trade, electronics, investment, as well as other industries.
Career: Trained at the Bench 1985; bank manager of Corporate Bank, OKO Bank, Oulu 1990-93; attorney-at-law since 1994; attorney-at-law, partner Helevä & Hollmén Oy Attorneys-at-law 1993-2005; partner Krogerus Attorneys Ltd 2005 to date.
Languages: Finnish, English, German and Swedish.
Member: Finnish Bar Association.
Education: University of Helsinki (1983 LLM).
Personal: Born 1959; resides Oulu.
Leisure: Golf, downhill skiing.

LATOLA, Mirja
Krogerus Attorneys Ltd
Phone: Oulu (+358 8 534 4400)
E-mail: mirja.latola@krogerus.com
Oulu office.
Position: Partner specialising in construction and real estate law issues, as well as on labour law. Ms Latola has extensive experience, for example, in contractual issues relating to construction companies and contractors, as well as construction-related litigation.
Career: Associate Asianajotoimisto Haaksiluoto ja Vesala Oy Attorneys-at-law 1987-88; trained at the Bench 1989; lawyer, Service Sector Employer's Association, North Finland office 1989-95; attorney-at-law Helevä & Hollmén Oy Attorneys-at-law 1995-2000; partner Helevä & Hollmén Oy Attorneys-at-law 2000-05; partner Krogerus Attorneys Ltd 2005 to date.
Languages: Finnish, English.
Member: Finnish Bar Association.
Education: University of Lapland (1987 LLM).
Personal: Born 1961; resides Oulu.
Leisure: Downhill skiing, dogs.

LENNI-TAATTOLA, Juho
Hammarström Puhakka Partners, Attorneys Ltd
Phone: Helsinki (+358 9 474 2210)
E-mail: juho.lenni-taattola@hpplaw.fi
Position: Partner specialising in finance and business law, mergers and acquisitions, and insolvency.
Career: Central Pension Security Institute, associate lawyer 1991-93; Garantia Insurance Company Ltd, lawyer 1993-99; Attorneys' House ANPR Ltd, associate lawyer 1999-2003; Attorneys' House ANPR Ltd, partner 2003-04; Hammarström Puhakka Partners, Attorneys Ltd, partner 2004 to date.
Languages: Finnish, Swedish, English.
Education: Attorney-at-law 2001; deputy judge (trained on the bench) 1990; University of Turku (1989 LLM); Turku School of Economics (1986 Econ.Mag).
Personal: Born 1960.

MÄKITALO, Juha
Mäkitalo Rämö Juutilainen Oy, Attorneys-at-Law
Phone: Helsinki (+358 50 2840)
E-mail: juha.makitalo@mrjlaw.fi
Position: Senior partner dealing with all areas of contract and corporate law including IPR and competition law, European law, and international and domestic arbitration.
Career: Trained on the Bench (District Court of Kauhajoki, 1978); partner Mäkitalo Rämö Juutilainen 1990 to date.
Languages: Finnish, Swedish, English.
Member: Finnish Bar Association.
Education: University of Turku (1976 LLM); Vrije Universiteit Brussels (1980 LLM).
Personal: Born 1951: resides Espoo.
Leisure: History, hunting, golf.

MAKKONEN, Jarmo
Krogerus Attorneys Ltd
Phone: Kuopio (+358 17 368 1800)
E-mail: jarmo.makkonen@krogerus.com
Kuopio office.
Position: Partner dealing with company law, contract law, mergers and acquisitions, capital markets, litigation, insolvency and general practice.
Career: Lawyer, Finnvera Oyj 1990-96; partner, Attorneys-at-Law Karvinen, Kuosmanen & Makkonen Ky 1996-2003; partner, Krogerus Attorneys Ltd 2003.
Languages: Finnish, English.
Member: Finnish Bar Association; the Association of Finnish Lawyers.
Education: University of Lapland (1989 LLM).
Personal: Born 1966; resides Kuopio.
Leisure: Jogging, slalom skiing, badminton.

MALI, Mikko
Krogerus Attorneys Ltd
Phone: Helsinki (+358 9 622 6520)
E-mail: mikko.mali@krogerus.com
Transactions.
Position: Partner, heads the transactions practice group; specialising in M&A and capital markets transactions such as venture capital investments, private placements and IPOs; work in 2005 has included advising in several multi-million euro M&A transactions, public offerings, as well as capital market transactions with venture capital investors.
Career: Lawyer, Helsinki Money Market Center Ltd 1990-94; associate, at Castrén & Snellman Attorneys-at-Law 1994-2001; partner, Krogerus Attorneys Ltd since 2001.
Languages: Finnish, English, Swedish.
Member: Finnish Bar Association; The Association of Finnish Lawyers; International Bar Association.
Education: University of Helsinki (1990 LLM); trained at the Bench 1991.
Personal: Born 1964; resides Espoo.
Leisure: Basketball, sailing.

MARTTINEN, Kari
Hammarström Puhakka Partners, Attorneys Ltd
Phone: Helsinki (+358 9 474 2260)
E-mail: kari.marttinen@hpplaw.fi
Position: Partner specialising in environmental law of Finland and the EU, real estate and property law, planning and zoning, construction law, pollution and environmental damages, environmental liabilities and environmental protection law.
Career: University of Helsinki, assistant in real estate and water law 1991-93; Helsinki University of Technology, researcher and deputy professor in economic law 1994, 1996, 1998-99 (several periods); Environment and Business Lawyers Ltd, partner 1994-2001; Attorneys' House ANPR Ltd, partner 2001-04; Hammarström Puhakka Partners, Attorneys Ltd, partner 2004 to date.
Languages: Finnish, Swedish, English.

Member: Association of Finnish Lawyers; Finnish Society for Environmental Law.
Education: Attorney-at-law 2001; University of Helsinki (1995 LLLic); University of Helsinki (1991 LLM).
Personal: Born 1966.

OKKONEN, Vesa

Krogerus Attorneys Ltd
Phone: Kuopio (+358 17 368 1800)
E-mail: vesa.okkonen@krogerus.com
Kuopio office.
Position: Partner dealing with company law, contract law, tax law and labour law.
Career: Lawyer and bank manager, OKO Bank Kuopio 1982-92; partner, Aatos Sarvi Oy 1992-99; vice-president and president Oy Karelia Parketti Ltd 1999-2002; vice-president, Karelia Corporation 2002-03; partner, Krogerus Attorneys Ltd 2003.
Languages: Finnish, English.
Member: Finnish Bar Association.
Education: University of Turku (1981 LLM); trained at the Bench 1986.
Personal: Born 1954; resides Kuopio.
Leisure: Motorcycling, downhill skiing, Finnish design.

PALSOLA, Hannu

Krogerus Attorneys Ltd
Phone: Kuopio (+358 17 368 1800)
E-mail: hannu.palsola@krogerus.com
Kuopio office.
Position: Partner dealing with corporate law, mergers and acquisitions, litigation, arbitration, mediation, company law, contracts, sports law and general practice.
Career: Attorney, Procopé & Hornborg Attorneys-at-Law; partner, Kolari, Heikinheimo & Palsola Oy; partner, Kolari, Heikinheimo, Palsola & Reinikainen Oy; partner, Krogerus Attorneys Ltd 2003.
Languages: Finnish, English, Swedish.
Member: Finnish Bar Association.
Education: University of Turku (1983 LLM).
Personal: Born 1956; resides Kuopio.
Leisure: Golf, ice hockey.

PELTOLA, Lauri

Waselius & Wist
Phone: Helsinki (+358 9 668 9520)
E-mail: ww@ww.fi
Corporate and banking.
Position: Partner dealing with mergers and acquisitions, finance law, capital markets, banking law, securities law.
Career: Admitted 1978. Ministry of Trade and Industry 1975-76; Procope & Hornborg 1976-92 (partner 1980, head of London branch 1984, secondment SG Archibald, Paris 1980); Roschier-Holmberg 1993-2002 (head of London branch 1993, partner 1995). Waselius & Wist, partner 2002. Numerous articles in Finnish and international professional publications in the fields of corporate and financial law.
Languages: Finnish, Swedish, English, German.
Member: Finnish Bar Association; Legal Society of Finland; International Bar Association.
Education: University of Helsinki (1974 LLM); trained at the Bench (1977).
Personal: Born 1950.

PENTTILÄ, Kimmo

Krogerus Attorneys Ltd
Phone: Oulu (+358 8 534 4400)
E-mail: kimmo.penttila@krogerus.com
Oulu office.
Position: Partner and head of Oulu office, main fields of activities include technology law, M&A, litigation, general business law, environmental law and real estate law.
Career: Associate, Procopé & Hornborg Attorneys-at-Law, Helsinki 1989-94; partner, Jouko Penttilä Attorneys-at-Law, Oulu 1995-99; partner, Krogerus Attorneys Ltd, Oulu, since 1999.
Languages: Finnish, English, Swedish.
Member: Finnish Bar Association; International Bar Association.
Education: University of Helsinki (1988 LLM); Master of Laws Diploma 1994.
Personal: Born 1963; resides Oulu.

PUHAKKA, Pekka

Hammarström Puhakka Partners, Attorneys Ltd
Phone: Helsinki (+358 9 474 2270)
E-mail: pekka.puhakka@hpplaw.fi
Position: Partner specialising in arbitration and litigation, mergers and acquisitions, intellectual property and employment law.
Career: National Board of Patents and Registrations, Trade Register, lawyer 1981-82; Nenonen & Rantasila Attorneys-at-Law, lawyer 1983-88; Nenonen & Rantasila Attorneys-at-Law, partner 1988; Ahola, Nenonen, Pokela & Rantasila Attorneys-at-Law, partner 1988-93; Attorneys' House ANPR Ltd, partner 1993-2004; Hammarström Puhakka Partners, Attorneys Ltd, partner 2004 to date.
Languages: Finnish, English, Swedish, French, German.
Member: Finnish Arbitration Association; Chartered Institute of Arbitrators, London Court of International Arbitration; Finnish Copyright Association; Finnish Association for Industrial and Property Rights; Finnish Labour Law Society. Many domestic and international positions of trust: member of the ICC Commission on Arbitration 1999 to date; Young Lawyers' International Association (AIJA), member of the Executive Committee 1988-92, national vice-president 1992-98, honorary vice-president 2001 to date; vice chairman of the Task Force on Arbitrating Competition Law Issues of ICC Commission on Arbitration 2003; member of the Task Force on Small Claims Arbitration of ICC Commission on Arbitration 2002-03; member of the Committee on Mediation of the Finnish Bar Association 2002 to date; member of the European Advisory Council of the Defence Research Institute 2001; member of a working group preparing recommendations on mediation for the European Commission/Project Marc 2000, 2000-02; Magazine of legal development, editorial council, chairman 1997-2001; auditor of the Finnish Bar Association 1992 to date; member of the Committee of International Affairs of the Finnish Bar Association 1991-98; secretary of the Helsinki Bar Association 1987-92.
Education: Attorney-at-law 1984; deputy judge (trained on the bench) 1983; University of Helsinki (1981 LLM).
Personal: Born 1956.

RAMM-SCHMIDT, Marja

Krogerus Attorneys Ltd
Phone: Helsinki (+358 9 622 6520)
E-mail: marja.ramm-schmidt@krogerus.com
Corporate advisory and dispute resolution (CAD).
Position: Partner specialising in corporate and commercial law, arbitration and mediation, inheritance and property law.
Career: Associate at Juhani Salmenkylä Ky, Attorneys-at-law 1974-78; Hannes Snellman Oy, Attorneys-at-law 1978-93, partner 1984-93; Ramm-Schmidt & Co. Oy, Attorneys-at-law 1993-2001; Krogerus Attorneys Ltd from 2001, partner.
Languages: English, Finnish, German, Swedish.
Member: Member of the Finnish Bar Association since 1977; member International Bar Association; certified mediator Finnish Bar Association; member Commission on Arbitration of ICC; member Board of Arbitration of the Central Chamber of Commerce 2002-04; member Finnish Sports' Arbitration Panel since 1991; President of the Helsinki Bar 1992-96; AIJA Honorary Vice President 1996; AIJA Executive Committee 1987-90; member delegation of the Finnish Bar 1992-98; member Professional Board of the Finnish Bar 1998-2001; member Ethical Board of the Finnish Bar 1988-92; chairman Young Lawyers Board of the Finnish Bar 1998-2001; member Ethical Board of Advokaatti (magazine of the Finnish Bar) since 1996, chairman 1999-2004; member Association of Finnish Lawyers since 1974; member Juridiska Föreningen; member Deutsch-Nordische Juristenvereinigung; founding member Sports Law Federation, member of the Board 1994-99; member Medical Commission of International Orienteering Federation since 1998; member Board of Sports Institute Kisakallio 1994 to date, chairman 2001 to date.
Education: University of Helsinki (1974 LLM); trained at the Bench 1977.
Personal: Born 1949; resides Espoo.
Leisure: Cross-country skiing, sailing, orienteering.

RISTO, Rämö

Mäkitalo Rämö Juutilainen Oy, Attorneys-at-Law
Phone: Helsinki (+358 400 411 936)
E-mail: risto.ramo@mrjlaw.fi
Position: Senior partner dealing with all areas of corporate law including company restructuring, contract and IPR law, and finance.
Career: Partner at Mäkitalo Rämö Juutilainen 1999 to date.
Languages: Finnish, Swedish, English, German, Spanish.
Member: Finnish Bar Association.
Education: University of Turku (1968 LLM).
Personal: Born 1943, resides Espoo.
Leisure: Golf.

ROSENLEW, Nina

Waselius & Wist
Phone: Helsinki (+358 9 668 9520)
E-mail: nina.rosenlew@ww.fi
Banking and finance law, capital markets, and mergers and acquisitions.
Position: Partner dealing with banking and finance law; capital markets; corporate and commercial law; and mergers and acquisitions.
Career: Trainee Clyde & Co, London 1993; trainee Charles Russell Solicitors, London 1993; referendary Western Finland Water Rights Court, Helsinki 1995-96; bench training Parainen District Court 1996-97; Waselius & Wist 1997. Published articles in international professional publications in the field of banking and finance law, capital markets and mergers and acquisitions.
Languages: Swedish, English, Finnish.
Member: Finnish Bar Association; Association of Finnish Lawyers; Finnish Law Society; Association Internationale des Jeunes Avocats; International Bar Association.
Education: University of Helsinki (1995 LLM).
Personal: Born 1967.

SARASTE, Tuomas

Hammarström Puhakka Partners, Attorneys Ltd
Phone: Helsinki (+358 9 474 2200)
E-mail: tuomas.saraste@hpplaw.fi
Position: Partner specialising in competition law, mergers and acquisitions, contract law and public procurement.
Career: Ministry of Education of Hungary/OECD-Phare co-ordinating office, visiting researcher 1993; Charles University (Prague), visiting researcher 1994-95; Attorneys' House ANPR Ltd, lawyer 1996-2001; Attorneys' House ANPR Ltd, partner 2001-04; Hammarström Puhakka Partners, Attorneys Ltd, partner 2004 to date.
Languages: Finnish, Swedish, English, French.
Member: Ius Gentium Finland; Central Eastern European Countries Trade Association.
Education: Attorney-at-law 1999; University of Helsinki (1996 LLLic); deputy judge (trained on the bench) 1994; University of Helsinki (1991 LLM).
Personal: Born 1966.

SILASKIVI, Vesa

Hammarström Puhakka Partners, Attorneys Ltd
Phone: Helsinki (+358 9 474 2290)
E-mail: vesa.silaskivi@hpplaw.fi
Position: Partner specialising in competition law and mergers and acquisitions.
Career: Helsinki City Court, interim judge (deputy) 1990; the Finnish Defence Forces, purchasing section, legal counsel 1990-91; Valio International, Valio Ltd, Legal Counsel 1991-93; EC Commission (Brussels), exchange programme 1993; Valio Ltd, corporate counsel, secretary of board, adviser 1993-95; Valio Ltd (Brussels), vice-president, EU affairs 1995-97; Valio Ltd, senior vice-president, corporate planning 1997-2000; Elisa Communications Plc, senior vice-president, corporate planning 2000-01; Elisa Corporation, chief financial officer 2001-03; Attorneys' House ANPR Ltd, senior adviser 2004; Hammarström Puhakka Partners, Attorneys Ltd, senior adviser 2004 to date.
Languages: Finnish, Swedish, English, French, German.
Member: Association of Board Professionals.
Education: University of Helsinki (2004 PhD Jur); Helsinki School of Economics (1993 LicBA Econ); University of Helsinki (1989 LLM).
Personal: Born 1966.

STÅHLBERG, Mika

Krogerus Attorneys Ltd
Phone: Helsinki (+358 9 622 6520)
E-mail: mika.stahlberg@krogerus.com
Transactions.
Position: Co-heads firm's M&A practice with special emphasis on private equity and venture capital. Specialises in M&A, venture capital and private equity, capital markets and transaction financing. Acts continuously for a number of private equity and venture capital investors in making investments (including MBO/MBI/LBO). Advises major corporations and other trade buyers in their M&A activities in Finland. Has also advised corporations and investment banks in relation to several IPOs, share issues and mergers.
Career: Legal Counsel at Okobank and Skandinaviska Enskilda Banken; associate at Krogerus Attorneys Ltd from 1997; partner since 2000.
Languages: Finnish, English, Swedish.
Member: Finnish Bar Association; International Bar Association.
Education: University of Helsinki (1995 LLM).
Personal: Born 1969; resides Helsinki.

TAIPALE, Juha

Krogerus Attorneys Ltd
Phone: Helsinki (+358 9 622 6520)
E-mail: juha.taipale@korgerus.com
Corporate advisory and dispute resolution (CAD).
Position: Partner in the corporate advisory and dispute resolution (CAD) group; specialises in technology, media and telecommunications. Expert in international commercial transactions, M&A and technology contracting.
Career: International banking, Kansallis-Osake-Pankki 1985-90; trained at the Bench 1987; legal counsel and assistant general counsel, KONE Corporation 1990-96; managing partner, Gilbert, Segall and Young, Attorneys at Law 1996-2000; managing director and CEO, Bitboys Oy 2000-03; Krogerus Attorneys Ltd since 2003; partner 2005.
Languages: Finnish, English, Swedish.
Member: Finnish Bar Association; Computer Law Association.
Education: University of Turku (1985 LLM).
Personal: Born 1960; resides Espoo.
Leisure: Music, sports and technology.

WASELIUS, Jan

Waselius & Wist
Phone: Helsinki (+358 9 668 9520)
E-mail: ww@ww.fi
Mergers and acquisitions, contracts, corporate law, finance law, banking law, capital markets, labour law, arbitration and litigation.
Position: Partner practising in corporate law; finance law; banking law; mergers and acquisitions; commercial law; industrial property rights; labour law; litigation and arbitration; securities law.
Career: Admitted 1972, Finland, Roschier-Holmberg & Waselius 1968-97 (partner 1970-95, senior partner 1986-95, of-counsel 1996-97); numerous articles in Finnish and international professional publications in the field of corporate and financial law.
Languages: Finnish, Swedish, English.
Member: OBE, Knight of Dannebrogen; member Order of Oranje-Nassau; Officer First Class of The Royal Order of the Polar Star; Finnish honorary legal adviser to several foreign governments; board member of several Anglo-American and European corporations in Finland and abroad; Finnish Bar Association; Legal Society of Finland; International Bar Association; International Fiscal Association.
Education: University of Helsinki (1968 LLM); trained at the Bench 1972.
Personal: Born 1944.

WESSMAN, Juha

Krogerus Attorneys Ltd
Phone: Helsinki (+358 9 622 6520)
E-mail: juha.wessman@krogerus.com
Transactions.
Position: Leads the finance group of the firm and co-heads the real estate practice group; expertise includes (i) project and infrastructure finance, public-private-partnerships (PPP), credit facilities and security arrangements and international finance projects as well as equipment and real estate leasing and financing, and (ii) real estate transactions; continuously advises both domestic and international banks and other financing institutions and companies in project financing transactions, PPP projects, credit facilities and real estate transactions, being accustomed to drafting, reviewing and negotiating documentation relating to such transactions (including term sheets, sale and purchase agreements, shareholders' agreements, sponsor undertakings, financing and security documentations and legal opinions). He also posses experience in dealing with governmental and multinational financial institutions and organisations in relation to project financing, as well as multilateral development banks.
Career: Legal counsel at Finnish Fund for Industrial Cooperation Ltd (FINNFUND) and Kansallis Finance Ltd; senior associate at Krogerus Attorneys Ltd from 1998, partner since 2000.
Languages: Finnish, English, Swedish.
Member: Finnish Bar Association; International Bar Association.
Education: University of Helsinki (1987 LLM); trained at the Bench 1991.
Personal: Born 1962; resides Kerava.

WIST, Tarja

Waselius & Wist
Phone: Helsinki (+358 9 668 9520)
E-mail: ww@ww.fi
Capital markets, finance law, mergers and acquisitions.
Position: Partner whose principal practice areas are: banking and finance law; capital markets; corporate law; mergers and acquisitions.
Career: Admitted 1994; trainee at Rechtsanwaltskanzlei Schmidt, Wiederman und Hintermayer, Nürnberg, Germany 1988; Roschier-Holmberg & Waselius 1989-97; secretary to the Legislative Commission for Securities Market Legislation 1990-93; member of the legislative working group for implementation of the Takeover Directive 2004-05. Publications: numerous articles in Finnish and international professional publications in the field of corporate and financial law.
Languages: Finnish, Swedish, English, German.
Member: Finnish Bar Association; Association of Finnish Lawyers; International Bar Association; co-chair of the Innovations in Financing Sub-Committee.
Education: University of Helsinki (1989 LLM).
Personal: Born 1965.

FRANCE

ALBERTINI, Marie

Reed Smith Rambaud Charot LLP
Phone: Paris (+33 1 76 70 4000)
E-mail: malbertini@reedsmith.com
Litigation.
Position: Marie is a partner in the Paris office. Her practice focuses on commercial law and liability matters. Her litigation practice in commercial law includes both breach of contract and other business torts. She has court as well as arbitration experience. Marie also specialises in liability law and insurance law, in particular toxic product risks, such as asbestos, solvents and so on (for example, industrial risks and occupational diseases). In addition, Marie is experienced in professional liability matters such as liability of banks (granting of credits, stock exchange transactions and so on). Marie's practice includes class action as well as individual cases filed across the country. In addition to litigating, Marie provides business counselling to clients on a wide range of issues including plant varieties and biotechnologies. She has worked with clients operating in a number of business sectors such as construction materials, glazing, aluminium and manufactured goods, arable crop seeds, plant biotechnologies, banking and financial services.
Career: Qualified 1989; partner Rambaud Martel 1996-2005; joined Reed Smith Rambaud Charot LLP as partner 2005.
Languages: French, English.
Member: Cercle Olympe; Interbiotech.
Education: Université Paris II (MA business law); Université Paris X (DEA).
Personal: Born 1964.
Leisure: Visiting art exhibitions and museums; antiques and flea markets.

ARAGONÉS, Joseph J

Dechert
Phone: Paris (+33 1 53 65 05 00)
E-mail: joseph.aragones@dechert.com
Position: Partner in the mergers and acquisitions and corporate groups dealing with corporate and securities, and mergers and acquisitions. Specialises in international mergers and acquisitions, including European cross-border acquisitions, joint ventures, and restructurings. During career, has also handled matters involving acquisitions, privatisations, and energy-related project finance in Latin America.
Career: Admitted to practice in New York, and England and Wales.
Languages: English, French, Spanish.
Education: University of Chicago (1984 Economics); University of Paris I - Sorbonne (1986 Political Science); Fordham Law School (1992 JD).

CARADET, Bertrand

Dechert
Phone: Paris (+33 1 53 65 05 06)
E-mail: bertrand.caradet@dechert.com
Position: Deals with bank financing and securitisation, corporate and securities, financial services, mergers and acquisitions, and private equity. Focuses on M&A, banking, securities, and financial transactions. Advises French and international asset management companies, private banks and hedge funds; private equity and venture capital funds; banks; and issuers and underwriters of IPOs. Dechert has one of the leading investment management practices in the world, and the firm's clients include leading mutual funds, investment managers and hedge funds. Advises asset managers as well as private banks who are managing their clients' assets on establishing their operations in France or other appropriate domiciles. Also advises them on the highly regulated aspects of product development, distribution and marketing, and in acquiring other asset management companies, funds or private banks. Works extensively with private equity funds and venture capital funds in developing their auction strategies, making investments in portfolio companies, refinancing and restructuring portfolio companies, and in developing exit strategies that maximise the return on their investments. A skilled negotiator, Mr Caradet is known for working to bring parties to transactions together so that deals are successfully and timely closed. In the highly technical area of structured finance, he represents banks as issuers of collateralised debt obligations, including mortgaged- and other asset-backed offerings. A securities lawyer, Mr Caradet represents issuers and underwriters of securities of large and mid-cap French companies who are listing on the French markets, making an international private placement, or making an IPO in the US.
Career: Admitted to the Paris Bar.
Languages: French, English.
Education: University of Paris II (Assas) (1982 LLM Corporate Law; 1982 LLM European and International Law; 1984 DEA corporate law); University of Paris V (René Descartes - Malakoff) (1984 DESS international taxation).

CARIDDI, Alan F

DLA Piper Rudnick Gray Cary US LLP, correspondents of CARIDDI, MEE, RUE, association d'avocats au barreau de Paris
Phone: Paris (+33 1 40 15 24 00)
E-mail: alan.cariddi@dlapiper.com
Corporate, mergers and acquisitions.
Position: Founded the Paris office and has served as its managing partner since 1982. Corporate and commercial lawyer whose practice focuses principally on French and international (including US) mergers and acquisitions, joint ventures and strategic alliances and commercial transactions. Has represented numerous corporate entities, including large and medium-sized American, French and Japanese companies engaged in a wide variety of commercial, industrial and other activities.
Career: Associate Dewey, Ballantine, New York 1973-75 and 1980-81; Paris 1975-80; associate then partner Mudge Rose Guthrie Alexander & Ferdon, New York 1981-82; managing partner and head of Paris office 1982-95; managing partner and head of Paris office Hogan & Hartson 1995-2004. Admitted to New York, DC, and Paris Bars.
Languages: English, French, Portuguese.
Member: American Bar Association; International Bar Association; New York Bar Association.
Education: Georgetown University (1970 AB, magna cum laude, Phi Beta Kappa); Columbia University (1973 JD).
Leisure: Member of Racing Club de France; golf.

CHAROT, Benoit

Reed Smith Rambaud Charot LLP
Phone: Paris (+33 1 76 70 4000)
E-mail: bcharot@reedsmith.com
Litigation.
Position: Benoit specialises in civil and criminal liability (specifically product liability, including asbestos-related claims); insurance; professional negligence; health care and pharma; white-collar crime; M&A and transactional.
Career: Admitted to the Bar 1985; partner Rambaud Martel 1990; joined Reed Smith Raumbaud Charot LLP as partner 2005.
Languages: French, English.
Education: Institut d'Etudes Judiciaires (Faculty of Rennes).

CLARET, Kathie D

Dechert
Phone: Paris (+33 1 53 65 05 15)
E-mail: kathie.claret@dechert.com
Position: Partner dealing with antitrust/competition, brand integrity/counterfeit, commercial litigation, construction, corporate and securities, intellectual property, intellectual property litigation, international

disputes, international trade, labour and employment, mass torts and product liability, media, mergers and acquisitions and focusing on advisory services and dispute resolution relating to commercial transactions, product liability, and labour and employment. Advises French and multinational companies on structuring mergers and acquisitions, sales, joint ventures, strategic alliances, licensing and distribution arrangements, and with regard to their ongoing business operations. Handles the corporate aspects as well as related issues, such as intellectual property and employment. Has particular experience in working with companies in the construction and life sciences industries. Also a litigator, and represents parties in commercial disputes, for example, those involving post-acquisition valuation issues, disputes regarding the assumption of liability, interpretation of intellectual property rights, and other contractual matters. Dechert is renowned for defending clients in product liability suits. Ms Claret advises manufacturers, including those in the life sciences sector, on avoiding liability for product failure, and defends them in French courts when they are sued for allegedly causing bodily injury or property damage. In a recent case that went twice to the French Supreme Court, she obtained a decision of 'no defect' for a client and a damage award that was fully offset by counterclaims. The labour and employment laws of France are challenging for employers, and Ms Claret advises companies on their compliance obligations and on approaches for achieving essential business reorganisations and restructurings.
Career: Has practised law in France since 1976; has written numerous articles in the fields of product liability, intellectual property, and trade secrets, including 'Product Liability in France', 'Product Liability: European Laws and Practice' (1993, Sweet & Maxwell, London), 'French Intellectual Property Law', 'International Protection of Intellectual Property' (1995, FT Law and Tax, London), 'Trade Secrets in France', 'Worldwide Trade Secrets Law' (1993, Clark Boardman Callaghan, Deerfield, Illinois), and 'Media Liability in France' (1997, John Wiley & Sons, Ltd, West Sussex, England). Admitted to the bars of Paris and New York.
Languages: Fluent English, French; conversant Russian, German, Italian.
Education: Harvard University (1972 AB magna cum laude); New York University School of Law (1975 JD).

DE KERGOS, Yann

Dechert
Phone: Paris (+33 1 53 65 05 00)
E-mail: yann.dekergos@dechert.com
Position: Partner in the tax department dealing with domestic and international tax. Provides advice on a range of tax services, including corporate acquisitions, reorganisations, and transfer pricing. Has also been involved with numerous studies and implementations of transfer pricing policies for major French companies in several different economic sectors, including the software and pharmaceutical industries. Also works closely with the life sciences and mergers and acquisitions teams.
Career: Partner Dechert; served as national reporter on 'Tax treatment of computer software' (Amsterdam Congress - 1988) and on 'Practical issues in the application of double tax conventions' (London Congress - 1998). Lecturer at the University of Paris V-René Descartes and author of 'Information Technology, Taxation and Accounting' (Delmas 1987) and 'Taxation of Mergers and Business Transfers' (EFE 1994). In addition, has written many articles on taxation in different publications and newspapers.
Member: International Fiscal Association; Institute of Tax French Lawyers; former member of the Bar Council of the Hauts de Seine (1996-98 and 2001-04).
Education: University of Paris X (Predoctorate - DES); Fondation Nationale pour le Droit et l'Entreprise (Masters in Private Law and a Degree in Tax Studies).

DECOMBE, Alain

Dechert
Phone: Paris (+33 1 53 65 05 00)
E-mail: alain.decombe@dechert.com
Position: Partner focusing on mergers and acquisitions and life sciences matters. Extensive experience in international corporate transactions, including acquisitions and group reorganisations among multinationals. Has worked with clients in the food and highly engineered products industries, as well as healthcare clients, such as pharmaceutical and biotech companies, medical device manufacturers, and private clinic networks.
Career: Admitted to the Paris Bar.
Member: Treasurer of the Association for the Promotion of Innovation and the Biotechnologies.
Education: University of Paris II - Assas (1985 Advanced Specialised Studies in Business and Tax Law); University of California Los Angeles School of Law (1988 LLM).

DESCROZAILLE, Marie-Agnès

Kuntz & Associés
Phone: Paris (+33 1 44 94 95 00)
E-mail: madescrozaille@kuntz-avocats.com
Litigation, commercial law, competition law, contracts.
Position: Specialises in commercial litigation, relating more particularly to the automotive industry (and sub-contracting in that area), IT and telecommunications, and has acquired a well-respected degree of expertise in those fields. Also specialises in the drafting of commercial contracts, both in French and English.
Career: Admitted in France 1995; has worked with Jean-Emmanuel Kuntz for over ten years.
Languages: French, English.
Education: University of Paris II Pantheon-Assas (1993 DEA de Droit International Prive (mention bien)).
Personal: Born 1970.

DUNHAM, Philip

Dechert
Phone: Paris (+33 1 53 65 05 00)
E-mail: philip.dunham@dechert.com
Position: Partner at the Paris office of Dechert LLP dealing with commercial litigation and international disputes. Has specialised in international commercial arbitration since 1992, having previously worked in London (1992-95) and Paris (2005-). Principal activity has been acting as counsel in over 40 international commercial disputes, whether ad hoc (including under the UNCITRAL Rules), or under the rules of the International Chamber of Commerce (ICC), the London Court of International Arbitration (LCIA), or the Arbitration Institute of the Stockholm Chamber of Commerce. Practice covers a wide range of matters specialising in general corporate, licence, joint venture, oil and gas energy, and construction disputes, in respect of which he has regularly acted for or against state entities. Listed in Euromoney Legal Group's 'Guide to World's Leading Experts in Commercial Arbitration' (2004), 'European Legal Experts 2005' and the Parker School Guides to 'International Arbitration: The Roster of International Arbitrators'.
Career: Head of commercial arbitration practice Coudert Frères, Paris; Dechert, Paris; solicitor of the Supreme Court in England and Wales 1994; registered as a foreign lawyer with the Paris Bar 2004.
Member: London Court of International Arbitration; Young International Arbitration Group; International Bar Association; Franco-British Lawyers Society.
Education: Université Robert Schuman de Strasbourg (1989 Diplôme d'Etudes Juridique); London School of Economics (1990 LLB French and English Law Degree); College of Law (1992 Law Society Finals).

FELDMAN, Reid

Kramer Levin Naftalis & Frankel LLP
Phone: Paris (+33 1 44 09 46 00)
E-mail: rfeldman@kramerlevin.com
Corporate, insurance, banking and finance, real estate.
Position: Partner. Mr Feldman has broad experience in general corporate matters (including numerous French and cross-border mergers, acquisitions and restructurings, in a variety of business sectors); insurance/reinsurance (including regulatory issues, transfers of businesses, structuring insurance/reinsurance products and ART transactions); banking and finance (including corporate acquisition, aircraft and real estate finance); commercial matters (including licensing and distribution); and real estate. He also has significant litigation experience (including insolvency) and has handled numerous international arbitrations (ICC and AAA) and insurance/reinsurance disputes.
Career: Admitted to the District of Columbia Bar 1971; admitted to the Paris Bar 1979.
Languages: French, English.
Member: American Bar Association; American Chamber of Commerce in France; Comite Français de l'Arbitage Board of Advisors; Yale Law School Center for Study of Corporate Law.
Education: Columbia University (1968 BA); Yale Law School (1971 JD); Oxford University (1981 M Litt).

KUNTZ, Jean-Emmanuel

Kuntz & Associés
Phone: Paris (+33 1 44 94 95 00)
E-mail: jekuntz@kuntz-avocats.com

Business law, bankruptcy, business restructuring, insolvency; litigation; mergers and acquisitions.
Position: Well-known commercial litigator and insolvency and company reorganisation law practitioner. During time at the Bar, was involved in commercial litigation and arbitration matters, LBO and LMBO operations (in particular during the 'Internet Buble') insolvency cases, reorganisations, asset purchase plans, and has acted both for solvent and insolvent organisations, as well as for trustees in bankruptcy.
Career: Admitted in France 1993; partner at Foucaud Tchekhoff Pochet, Bartfeld Destremau Kuntz and Poulain & Associés over a period of nine years; 13 years at the Bar.
Languages: French, English, German.
Education: Institut d'Etudes Politiques de Paris (1988 Sciences Po); Univerity of Paris II Pantheon-Assas (DESS de Droit des Affaires et Fiscalite (mention bien); 1992 Magistère de Juriste d'Affaires (mention Bien, major de promotion)).
Personal: Born 1966.
Leisure: Opera, paintings.

LECLER, Philippe

Reed Smith Rambaud Charot LLP
Phone: Paris (+33 1 76 70 4000)
E-mail: plecler@reedsmith.com
Corporate.
Position: Philippe specialises in corporate law, M&A, securities law (including litigation) and privatisation.
Career: Student teacher at Paris University (corporate law and commercial law) 1994; in charge of studies (legal adviser) in the litigation department of the French Ministry of Defence 1994; trainee Stibbe Simont 1996; associate Galexia 1997; associate Rambaud Martel 1998; partner Rambaud Martel 2004; partner Reed Smith Rambaud Charot LLP 2005.
Languages: French, English.
Education: Maitrise carrières judicaires; maitrise droit des affaires; DEA de droit des affaires (LLM); Paris University (DESS banque et finance (MA)); Paris Bar School (1996).
Leisure: Travel.

LEMAIRE, Gillian

Dechert
Phone: Paris (+33 1 53 65 05 18)
E-mail: gillian.lemaire@dechert.com
Position: Partner dealing with commercial litigation, construction, energy, finance and real estate, international disputes, international trade, mass torts and product liability, and mergers and acquisitions. Practice centres on representing French and multinational companies in international commercial transactions and dispute resolution, notably international arbitration. A broad client base ranges from construction and engineering, utilities and infrastructure, energy, real estate and hotels through to heavy and light manufacturing, information technology and distribution sectors. In the area of dispute resolution, represents clients in international arbitrations, counsels them in arbitration-related matters and handles enforcement procedures. Has served as counsel in International Chamber of Commerce, ad hoc and trade association arbitrations involving issues ranging from joint venture disputes to project finance. Has extensive experience across different cultures and jurisdictions and has handled cases involving common, civil and Islamic law systems. Part of a highly rated global outfit, works in concert with lawyers in other Dechert offices and other foreign counsel to bring together the right team for resolution of an international dispute. Also represents parties in commercial disputes before national courts. Recently brought together a European/US Dechert team that was successful in achieving the early dismissal of a high-value litigation from a US court on behalf of a French corporation. Also has significant transactional experience, advising companies in relation to French and international bids and contracts, notably long-term contracts between private parties and public authorities. In addition to advising in French projects, has assisted clients in the utilities and infrastructure sectors in relation to projects in south-east Asia, North Africa and Europe.
Career: Has practised law in France for over 15 years; published a number of articles in the UK and France on dispute resolution and infrastructure topics. Member of the Paris Bar and a solicitor in Scotland.
Languages: English, French.
Member: Comité français de l'arbitrage; French National Committee of the International Chamber of Commerce; International Arbitration Institute.
Education: University of Strathclyde (1982 LLB).

MARQUARDT, Alexander

Kramer Levin Naftalis & Frankel LLP
Phone: Paris (+33 1 44 09 46 40)
E-mail: amarquardt@kramerlevin.com
Corporate, mergers and acquisitions, alternative dispute resolution, banking and finance, capital markets, financial services, international dispute resolution.
Position: Mr Marquardt is the managing partner of Kramer Levin Naftalis & Frankel LLP's Paris office. His general corporate practice includes mergers and acquisitions, structured finance, construction projects and arbitrations. Mr Marquardt has been involved in financings and corporate acquisitions in more than a dozen countries. His primary area of focus includes M&A, private equity and securitisations for multinational financial service clients. Additionally, Mr Marquardt frequently serves as an arbitrator or counsel in arbitrations. He is an author and speaker on the topics of corporate and structured finance and arbitration.
Career: Admitted to the Paris Bar 1974; admitted to the New York Bar 1976; has published a series of articles in the 'International Financial Law Review' and other law reviews discussing French and international corporate and capital markets issues.
Languages: French, English, German.
Member: American Bar Association; International Bar Association; Union Internationale des Avocats; Inter-Pacific Bar Association; Commission on Arbitration of the International Chamber of Commerce.
Education: University of Munich; University of Paris; University of Vienna (JD 1969); Columbia Law School (1970 LLM).

MATTOUT, Jean-Pierre

Kramer Levin Naftalis & Frankel LLP
Phone: Paris (+33 1 44 09 46 40)
E-mail: jpmattout@kramerlevin.com
Corporate, banking and finance, financial services, mergers and acquisitions, corporate governance.
Position: Partner. Mr Mattout's practice primarily focuses on national and international banking and financial transactions, mergers and acquisitions, company law and corporate governance issues. He has been involved in all types of banking and financial transactions, national and international. As former general counsel of the Paribas Group, a position held for more than ten years, he participated directly in the formulation and implementation of many strategic operations, including large mergers and acquisitions. From 2002 until 2004, he was the general counsel of the France Telecom Group. Additionally, based upon his experience as the chief legal officer of an international bank and one of Europe's largest business corporations, he has a wealth of knowledge in corporate governance issues. Mr Mattout teaches international banking law, financial and monetary law at Paris II University.
Career: Admitted to the Paris Bar.
Languages: French, English.
Member: European Society for Banking and Financial Law; International Chamber of Commerce; Association Nationale des Societés par Action; International Law Association; International Arbitration Institute; Comité Français de Droit International Privé.
Education: Diplome d'études supérieures en droit privé et en sciences criminelles (1974); Panthéon-Sorbonne (PhD 1990).

NYSSEN, Xavier

Dechert
Phone: Paris (+33 1 53 65 05 00)
E-mail: xavier.nyssen@dechert.com
Position: Partner in charge of the litigation department of Dechert Paris, dealing with commercial litigation, and international disputes. Specialised in litigation and international arbitration since 1988. Acts as counsel of international companies, especially in the energy, pharmaceutical and electronics sectors. Also represents clients in French courts in product liability, unfair competition, and post-acquisition matters. Listed in 'The Legal 500 Paris''Décideurs Juridiques et Financiers', and Martindale Hubbell.
Career: Loeff Claeys, Brussels; Coudert, Paris; Dechert, Paris; admitted to practice in Brussels, Paris and New York.
Education: University of Liege, Belgium (MA Law); Columbia University (LLM).

ORENGO, Christian

Kramer Levin Naftalis & Frankel LLP
Phone: Paris (+33 1 44 09 46 40)
E-mail: corengo@kramerlevin.com
Litigation, white-collar defence.

Position: Partner. Mr Orengo is the head of the litigation department in the Paris office. His practice focuses on civil and commercial litigation as well as white-collar criminal law. Mr Orengo has vast trial experience before French courts, specialising in bankruptcy litigation and lenders' liability defence. He represents a large number of international financial institutions and factoring companies before the French courts and in arbitration proceedings. He was a winner of the Moot Court Competition before the Supreme Court in 1971 (Conference du Stage des Avocats au Conseil d'Etat et à la Cour de Cassation) and of the Moot Court Competition before the Court of Appeals in 1973 (Conference du Stage des Avocats à la Cour d'Appel).
Career: Admitted to the Paris Bar 1970.
Languages: English, French.
Member: Council for the Paris Bar.
Education: University of Paris-Panthéon (1968 LLB private law; 1969 LLM business law).

PASZKIEWICZ, Antoine

Kramer Levin Naftalis & Frankel LLP
Phone: Paris (+33 1 44 09 46 00)
E-mail: apaszkiewicz@kramerlevin.com
Corporate, mergers and acquisitions, real estate, tax, cross-border transactions.
Position: Partner. Mr Paszkiewicz practises corporate and tax law with an emphasis on mergers and acquisitions. A specialist in French corporate law and taxation, Mr Paszkiewicz has represented both public and private clients. He acted for the government of France and local political entities in the transactional and financial aspects of a multi-million-dollar project near Paris involving a recreational park and concessions to be constructed over a 30-year period. For corporate clients active in a wide range of industrial, financial, media and real estate sectors, Mr Paszkiewicz has been involved in acquisitions, divestitures and reorganisations in France, and also in the United States, Australia, New Zealand and many European countries including Belgium, the Netherlands, Germany, Greece, Denmark, Spain and Poland. Principally he has represented buyers, sellers and investors, especially in connection with legal and tax problems encountered when foreign-based companies make acquisitions in Europe. Mr Paszkiewicz has also been active in structuring foreign-owned real estate holdings in France.
Career: Admitted Paris Bar 1977; New York Bar 1980.
Languages: English, French, Polish.
Member: World Trade Executive International; New York State Bar Association.
Education: Institution N.D. de Sainte Croix (1972); University of Paris (1976 JD; 1977 DESS (Tax)); Columbia Law School (1979 LLM).

RAMBAUD, Mathieu

Reed Smith Rambaud Charot LLP
Phone: Paris (+33 1 76 70 4000)
E-mail: mrambaud@reedsmith.com
Corporate.
Position: Mathieu specialises in mergers and acquisitions, company restructuring, company law, securities, stock exchange, regulation, privatisation, negotiations of agreements and director's liability.
Career: Qualified 1988; associate Rambaud Martel 1988, partner 1992; joined Reed Smith Rambaud Charot LLP as partner 2005.
Languages: French, English.
Education: Institute of Legal Studies, Paris University (carrières judiciaires (MA)).
Personal: Born 1960; resides Paris.
Leisure: Tennis, sailing, diving.

ROTKOPF, Sabine

Kuntz & Associés
Phone: Paris (+33 1 44 94 95 00)
E-mail: srotkopf@kuntz-avocats.com
Litigation; social law; commercial law; bankruptcy; civil law; family law.
Position: Specialises in employment law, commercial and bankruptcy law, and crime law. Has acquired a high level of expertise in employment law, particularly with respect to redundancy plans adopted in the course of insolvency proceedings, as well as in white-collar crime cases.
Career: Admitted in France 1995.
Languages: French, English.
Education: University of Paris I Pantheon-Sorbonne (1991 Maitrise de Droit des Affaires); University of Paris XII Creteil (1987 Certificat d'Anglais Juridique).
Personal: Born 1965.
Leisure: Paintings, travelling.

SCHUR, Jonathan

Dechert
Phone: Paris (+33 1 53 65 05 10)
E-mail: jonathan.schur@dechert.com
Position: Partner dealing with commercial litigation, corporate and securities, health, international disputes, life sciences/pharmaceutical, mergers and acquisitions, privacy law, and technology. Represents technology-based companies in structuring transactions and financings, regulatory matters, and dispute resolution. Particular focus is on working with French and multinational companies in the pharmaceutical, medical device, and healthcare sectors. Has been based in Paris for more than 25 years. Advises companies in structuring mergers and acquisitions, divestitures, licensing and distribution arrangements, joint ventures, and co-operative development and marketing relationships. For example, recently advised a multinational company on a successful strategy for acquiring a product of a French company that was the subject of a Federal Trade Commission divestiture agreement, where knowledge of FTC procedures was critical to the acquisition strategy. Has advised many strategic buyers making acquisitions in France on the focus of their due diligence, and drafts agreements to resolve potential problems that are unique to France. Particularly known for ability to bring parties to transactions together so that the structural, legal, and cultural gulfs between French and US companies can be bridged effectively. Working in concert with Dechert securities lawyers in the US, for example, he recently restructured a French biotechnology company and successfully prepared it for its debut in the US capital markets. Also works with clients to arrange venture and later-stage financing, as well as representing them pre-IPO and at the IPO stage. US companies intent upon entering the market in France are likewise counselled on both legal and management structures that are necessary to achieve regulatory compliance in the French marketplace. This includes the French regulatory aspects of product and pricing authorisations, clinical trials, agreements with hospitals and physicians, privacy, and marketing practices in the life sciences sector. In the area of dispute resolution, also represents clients in litigation before the French courts and in international arbitrations involving commercial, licensing, marketing and distribution, and related issues. Experience includes representing a multinational manufacturer with potentially hundreds of millions of dollars at risk to terminate a development agreement with a French licensor.
Career: Administrative director of the Union Internationale des Avocats 1987-89; trustee of American Library in Paris; admitted to the Bars of Paris and New York.
Languages: English, French.
Education: Harvard College (1975 AB cum laude); Harvard Law School (1978 JD cum laude).

SILVA ROMERO, Eduardo

Dechert
Phone: Paris (+33 1 53 65 05 00)
E-mail: eduardo.silvaromero@dechert.com
Position: Partner dealing with international disputes and focusing on litigation and arbitration matters. Focuses particularly on international disputes involving state entities, as well as Spanish and Latin American parties. Over the course of career, has served as assistant counsel, counsel, and deputy secretary general of the ICC International Court of Arbitration. In these roles, he supervised thousands of arbitration cases, spanning all industry sectors and held all over the world. During his tenure as deputy secretary general, reviewed all draft awards submitted by the ICC arbitral tribunals for approval by the ICC International Court of Arbitration. Has also acted as counsel in ICC, ad-hoc (UNCITRAL), and Bogota Chamber of Commerce arbitrations. Experience includes matters involving international sales and distribution contracts, construction, oil, and electricity-related disputes.
Career: Member of the foreign editorial board of the 'Revista Brasilera de Arbitragem'; member of the editorial board of the 'Revista Colombia de Arbitraje'; also speaks at conferences and seminars on international commercial arbitration in Latin America, the US, and Europe.
Member: Institute for International Arbitration of the French Committee for Arbitration; Academic Council of the Institute for Transnational Arbitration; Groupe de Travail Contrats Internationaux; founding member of the Brazilian Committee for Arbitration; founding member and first secretary of the Colombian Committee for Arbitration; International Council of the Brazilian Revista de Arbitragem e Medicao.

Education: Universidad del Rosario (1993 Law Degree first in class); The Hague Academy of International Law (1995 Private International Law); University of Paris II (1995 LLM Private International Law first in class; 1996 DEA Philosophy of Law first in class; 2000 PhD Docteur en Droit summa cum laude).

SMALLHOOVER, Joseph

Dechert
Phone: Paris (+33 1 5365 0517)
E-mail: joseph.smallhoover@dechert.com
Position: Partner who has practiced in France since 1985. Focuses on investment management and hedge fund regulation, international and French banking and financial law, French securities regulation, general corporate law and M&A, corporate restructuring and insolvency. Has extensive experience across the full range of legal matters relating to the products and services that international financial institutions offer to both the public and specific investors. Investment management is a key area of expertise, especially in relation to the formation, operation, licensing, marketing and distribution of both public and private funds, including hedge funds, mutual funds, offshore funds, and non-US investment funds, including funds organised as SICAV and unit trusts. In addition, advises on the development of procedures for compliance with specific regulatory requirements such as those covered by the European Union's UCITS directives and the 2002 US Sarbanes-Oxley act. Also provides first-class advice to the firm's clients in the arena of corporate law, including mergers and acquisitions (for both financial buyers as well as strategic buyers), including on the financing of acquisitions, initial public offerings (IPOs), public takeover bids, corporate restructurings and insolvency matters. Other areas of expertise include French and international tax law and real estate transactions.
Career: Adjunct professor at the McGeorge School of Law, Salzburg Institute on International Legal Studies in Austria since 1989; taught at l'Institut d'Etudes Politiques de Paris (1992-95) and l'Universite de Paris X (Nanterre, 1986-92); admitted to the Paris, California, and Pennsylvania Bars; registered foreign lawyer in Frankfurt am Main and in England and Wales; bilingual editor of 'Revue de Droit des Affaires Internationales'/'International Business Law Journal' since 1986 and publishes articles regularly on financial and corporate law matters; has written extensively on a wide range of legal topics, including for such prestigious French business and legal publications as 'L'Agefi', 'Les Echos', 'Option Finance', 'Marchés et Techniques Financières', and 'La Semaine Juridique'; major publications include 'The Economic and Commercial Benefit of Corporate Guarantees - An International Comparison' (Butterworths), 'Fund and Asset Management in France' (IFLR), 'Gestion de Tresorerie Centralisee ou Decentralisee?' ('Centralized or Decentralized Cash Management?') (Revue de Droit des Affaires Internationales) and 'The Euro: The Practical Implications for Its Introduction' (The National Law Journal); also the bilingual editor of 'Revue de Droit des Affaires Internationales/International Business Law Journal' (Paris) since 1986.
Languages: English, French, German, Spanish.
Member: American Bar Association; International Bar Association; Duke University Alumni Club of France; American Chamber of Commerce in France; American Council on Germany; secretary of the Rheinischer Internationaler Juristenverein (Düsseldorf, Germany).
Education: Duke University (1975 AB magna cum laude); University of Virginia (1976 MA); University of Pittsburgh School of Law (1980 JD).

STEVENSON, John A

Kramer Levin Naftalis & Frankel LLP
Phone: Paris (+33 1 44 09 46 40)
E-mail: jstevenson@kramerlevin.com
Corporate, banking and finance, litigation, capital markets, mergers and acquisitions, cross-border transactions.
Position: Partner. Mr Stevenson practises international corporate law, focusing on the areas of banking, financial services, structured finance and capital markets. He has served as counsel to European and US companies in a wide variety of international financial and business transactions, including cross-border and structured financings, securitisations, debt trading, mutual fund offerings, outsourcing transactions, initial public offerings, project finance, joint ventures and corporate acquisitions and investments. He also has substantial experience in international commercial arbitration. Mr Stevenson is a frequent author and speaker on topics implicated by his practice, including foreign investment regulations, French securities laws, mutual fund regulation and European banking/financial services regulation.
Career: Admitted New York Bar 1988; Paris Bar 1993.
Languages: English, French.
Education: Princeton University (1984 BA magna cum laude); Harvard Law School (1987 JD cum laude).

GERMANY

FASSHAUER, Olaf, Dr

Dechert LLP
Phone: Munich (+49 89 21 21 63 21)
E-mail: olaf.fasshauer@dechert.com
Position: Partner working out of the Munich office dealing with corporate and securities, employee benefits and executive compensation, labour and employment, and mergers and acquisitions. Concentrates practice on domestic and cross-border M&A transactions, as well as general corporate and corporate finance work. Has been involved in buy-outs, joint ventures and structured finance matters. Also advises on employment-related aspects of corporate transactions. Work covers the contentious and non-contentious aspects of labour law, including measures of redundancy, unfair dismissal, wrongful dismissal, agreed terminations, tax issues, social security issues and employment-related litigation.
Career: Coudert Brothers LLP; Dechert LLP.
Languages: Fluent German, English.
Education: University of Göttingen, Germany (1990); University of Geneva, Switzerland (1991); and the University of Munich, Germany (1994).

FISCHER, Michael I

Reed Smith LLP
Phone: Munich (+49 89 20 304 10)
E-mail: mfischer@reedsmith.com
Corporate.
Position: Michael has over 16 years' experience in German and international transactions and legal matters. His practice encompasses all aspects of German corporate law, including M&A, venture capital transactions and partnership matters. He has advised a large number of German and foreign clients, and has experience working with companies in traditional industries as well as hi-tech and media companies. He is experienced in handling the engagements of corporate clients and private equity houses.
Career: Assistant lecturer at University of Tübingen (corporate and commercial law department) 1988; legal clerkship Court of Appeal, Stuttgart, including stages at the District Court of Tübingen, the Criminal Court of Calw, the Administrative Court of Sigmaringen, the Office of the District Attorney of Tübingen, the regional authority of South Wuerttemberg-Hohenzollern and the law firm Heck & Kollegen, all in 1988; Linklaters Oppenhoff & Rädler/Rädler Raupach Bezzenberger 1992; EY Law Luther Menold/Andersen Legal (Andersen Luther) 2000; partner Reed Smith 2005.
Languages: English, German.
Member: Association of the Bar at the Court of Appeals of Munich; German-American Lawyers Association.
Education: Universities of Tübingen and Würzburg (1982); First State Exam (1988 JD equivalent); University of Kostanz (1990); Second State Exam, Stuttgart (1991); University of Tübingen (2000 PhD corporate law).
Leisure: Golf, cycling, hiking, reading, enjoying time with his family.

HAFT, Klaus

Reimann Osterrieth Köhler Haft Rechtsanwälte
Phone: Düsseldorf (+49 211 550 22 340)
E-mail: Klaus.Haft@rokh-ip.com
Position: Klaus Haft advises on patent infringement litigation and subsequent litigation regarding damages in the area of intellectual property law, namely patent, know-how, design and trade mark law.
Career: IP experience since 1990; partner Reimann Osterrieth Köhler Haft 2004. Publications of note: co-author with Köhler, Birde, Butler and Sigworth 'The damages test - comparing damages for infringement in the US and Germany' in 'Patentworld' (issue 77, 2005); co-author with Donle, Ehlers and Nack 'Punitive damages as a contentious issue of IP rights', AIPPI report on Q 186 (2005) (http://www.aippiorg/reports/q186/q186_germany.pd) in 'GRUR Int 2005', 403; co-author with Osterrieth 'Cross-

border patent litigation in Europe' in 'Festschrift 50 Jahre VPP' p372 (2005); co-author with Reimann 'The calculation of infringer's profits following the 'overhead share' - decision of the German Federal Supreme Court (BGH) of 2 November 2000, in 'Mitt' 2003 p437-445; co-author with Whittington 'Spin-off technology transfer and intellectual property rights in the field of fundamental research, CERN as a case', 'Law Journal of the University of the Philippines' (1997).
Languages: German, English.
Member: AIPPI; Deutsche Physikalische Gesellschaft (German Physics Society); GRUR; IPO; VPP; LES.
Education: Universities of Würzburg and Munich (1990); European Center for Particle Physics, Geneva (1997 diploma degree in physics).
Personal: Born 1970; resides Düsseldorf.

KANZ, Christine, Dr

Reimann Osterrieth Köhler Haft Rechtsanwälte
Phone: Düsseldorf (+49 211 550 22 320)
E-mail: Christine.Kanz@rokh-ip.com
Position: Christine Kanz advises German and international clients in all intellectual property matters, especially in patent law. Her further main focus is the drafting of intellectual property agreements, co-operation agreements, research and development agreements, and so on.
Career: Qualified 1998; associate with a global law firm 2000; associate Reimann Osterrieth Köhler Haft 2002; partner 2006. Publications of note: co-author with Kay N Kasper 'Management of US discovery in continental Europe: a practice report from Germany' in 'The IP Litigator' (September/October 2005); 'Schutz von Medizinprodukten durch technische Schutzrechte' in Anhalt and Dieners 'Handbuch des Medizinprodukterechts' (2003); 'Zum Kennzeichenrecht im Internet' (Düsseldorf 2002); 'Haftungsrechtliche Aspekte von Fahrerassistenzsysteme' (ZfAW, 38 ff).
Languages: German, English.
Member: AIPLA; GRUR; IPO; LES; VPP.
Education: Universities of Bonn and Passau (1990); University of Sydney (1998); University of Düsseldorf (2002 Dr iur).
Personal: Born 1971; resides Düsseldorf.

KASPER, Kay N

Reimann Osterrieth Köhler Haft Rechtsanwälte
Phone: Düsseldorf (+49 211 550 22 350)
E-mail: Kay.Kasper@rokh-ip.com
Position: Kay N Kasper acts primarily in national and multinational patent litigation and advises on all matters related to intellectual property rights, especially designs. He advises clients in many technical areas and also in transactional matters. He has significant experience in negotiating license and co-operation agreements and co-ordinating with US and English patent proceedings.
Career: Qualified 2002; associate with a global law firm 2002; Reimann Osterrieth Köhler Haft 2004; lecturer in patent law at the University of Applied Science, Darmstadt since 2004. Publications of note: 'Urteilsanmerkung zu BGH X ZR 152/03 - Gummielastische Masse II' in 'Mitt', 488 (2005); co-author with Kanz 'Management of US discovery in continental Europe: a practice report from Germany' in 'The IP Litigator' (September/October 2005).
Languages: German, English, Danish.
Member: AIPPI; GRUR; IPO; VPP.
Education: University of Frankfurt (1994); Keele University (1996).
Personal: Born 1964; resides Düsseldorf.

KÖHLER, Martin, Dr

Reimann Osterrieth Köhler Haft Rechtsanwälte
Phone: Düsseldorf (+49 211 550 22 350)
E-mail: Martin.Koehler@rokh-ip.com
Position: Founding partner specialising in patent litigation, co-ordination of multinational patent litigation and the preparation of opinions on patent infringement. He also represents clients in trade mark, design and unfair competition litigation. He advises on license, research and development agreements as well as on employee invention law.
Career: Qualified 1998; patent litigation partner at an international law firm; founding partner of Reimann Osterrieth, Köhler Haft 2004. Publications of note: comment on BGH 5/7/2005 - Abgasreinigungsvorrichtung in Mitt (2005) s505 f; co-author with Haft, Birde, Butler and Sigworth 'The damages test - comparing damages for infringement in the US and Germany' in 'Patentworld' (issue 77, 2005); 'Standard related patents: between fast-track litigation and competition dead end' in 'Patentworld' (July/August 2005); comment on BGH - 'Staubsaugerrohr' in 'Mitt' (2005) s281 and 283; co-author with Cohen 'Disclosure in European patent litigation: towards an efficient protection of patent owners' in 'IP Litigator' vol 11, 2 (2005); member of editorial board 'IP Litigator' and 'Patent World'.
Languages: German, French, English, Italian.
Member: AIPLA; AIPPI; EPLAW; GRUR; IPO; LES; VPP.
Education: University of Saarbrücken (1991; 2002 Dr jur); Trinity College, Dublin (1991); University of Toulouse (1995 DESS).
Personal: Born 1969; resides Düsseldorf.

KUGLER, Stefan

Reed Smith LLP
Phone: Munich (+49 89 20 304 10)
E-mail: skugler@reedsmith.com
Corporate.
Position: With over 12 years' professional experience, Stefan has substantial knowledge and extensive experience in German and international transactions and legal matters, particularly in the areas of asset management (mutual funds, hedge funds, mezzanine funds, real estate funds), regulatory and internet (electronic) banking laws and finance. He regularly advises on financial transactions such as structured finance, acquisition finance, asset-backed securities finance, factoring, as well as cross-border and domestic lease finance agreements. In the area of asset management, he advises on all industry issues, including the setting up of new investment funds in Germany and abroad, registration of foreign investment funds with the Federal Supervisory Authority for Finance (BaFin), as well as on all aspects of custody, transfer agency, distribution, marketing and outsourcing related thereto.
Career: Legal clerkship with the Court of Appeals in Munich, 1989; internship with HypoVereinsbank, New York 1990; Rogers & Wells (now Clifford Chance) 1994; EY Law Luther Menold (previously Andersen Legal) 1998; partner Reed Smith 2005.
Languages: English, German, French.
Member: Association of the Bar at the Court of Appeals of Munich; German-American Lawyers Association.
Education: Hans-Carossa Gymnasium (1982); School of Law, University of Munich (1985); University of Lausanne, Switzerland (including a course in comparative law in Strasbourg 1986); University of Hamburg (1987); University of Munich (1988); First State Exam (JD equivalent), Munich (1989); Second State Exam (bar admission equivalent), Munich (1992); Southern Methodist University, Dallas (1993 LLM international and comparative law); University of Konstanz (1996 PhD Law).
Leisure: Tennis, mountain biking, hiking, reading, art, enjoying time with his family.

OSTERRIETH, Christian, Dr

Reimann Osterrieth Köhler Haft Rechtsanwälte
Phone: Düsseldorf (+49 211 550 22 310)
E-mail: Christian.Osterrieth@rokh-ip.com
Position: Founding partner practising in the field of national, European and international intellectual property law (technology law, trade mark law and unfair competition law) since 1986. Specialises in patent and trade mark litigation.
Career: Qualified 1984; partner at one of the world's largest law firms; founding partner of Reimann Osterrieth Köhler Haft; lecturer at the Universities of Konstanz and Düsseldorf; former president LES, Germany. Publications of note: 'Patent law' (CH Beck, NJW-Schriftenreihe, 2nd edition 2004); 'Part B treatise by standard-forms, patent license agreements, Part A III antitrust law' in Pfaff and Osterrieth 'License agreements - treatise by standard-forms' (CH Beck, 2nd edition 2004); co-author in Fezer 'UWG, Lauterkeitsrecht' (München 2005, 4th edition - special unfair competition issue 'Allgemeine Marktbehinderung'; articles 78 and 79 EPC in Benkard 'EPÜ Europäisches Patentübereinkommen' (CH Beck, 2002); 'The possibilities to protect dishwashing and detergent tabs according to the case law established by the European Court of Justice', 'European Law Report' 6, 251; co-author with Haft 'Cross-border patent litigation in Europe' in 'Festschrift 50 Jahre VPP' (2005).
Languages: German, English, French.
Member: AIPPI; GRUR; INTA; IPO; VPP.
Education: University of Paris II (1982); University of Konstanz (1986 Dr jur).
Personal: Born 1957; resides Düsseldorf.

PAPPALARDO, Federico G

Dechert LLP
Phone: Munich (+49 89 21 21 63 11)
E-mail: federico.pappalardo@dechert.com

Position: Partner in the corporate group, dealing with bank financing and securitisation, mergers and acquisitions, private equity, and venture capital, and concentrating practice on private equity, venture capital investments, and buy-outs. Advises private equity companies and management teams on all stages of financing and buy-out transactions, as well as on corporate restructurings. Top-tier private equity and venture capital funds regularly call on Mr Pappalardo to advise them in a wide range of German and international transactions. Whether it be a Series A financing or a significant leveraged buy-out, Mr Pappalardo evaluates, structures, negotiates, and consummates transactions with a constant focus on accomplishing successful exits. Several publications, including 'JUVE', 'Chambers Global', and 'The Legal 500', recognise Mr Pappalardo as a leading lawyer in the private equity industry. Recent highlight transactions include advising Citigroup Venture Capital Equity Partners, LP on its €1.2bn sale of the Flender Holding GmbH to Siemens, Buchanan Industrial Technologies in the management buy-out of automotive supplier Erwin Behr Automotive GmbH and the management of Berliner Verlag on Veronis Suhler Stevenson (VSS) and Mecom Group PLC's acquisition of Berliner Verlag from Verlagsgruppe Georg von Holtzbrinck. In addition, advises both German and foreign clients on all aspects of corporate law, corporate transactions, and financing law. Also provides advice to both banking and corporate clients on a wide range of financial transactions, including acquisition finance and structured finance.
Career: Prior to joining Dechert, was with another large international law firm; two years with the world's leading CAD/CAM software company. Frequently acts as moderator and panelist at corporate finance-related seminars; has written a number of articles on legal issues relating to private equity transactions.
Education: University of Mainz; University of Dijon (1984-90).

REIMANN, Thomas, Dr

Reimann Osterrieth Köhler Haft Rechtsanwälte
Phone: Düsseldorf (+49 211 550 22 300)
E-mail: Thomas.Reimann@rokh-ip.com
Position: Founding partner of Reimann Osterrieth Köhler Haft, dealing with all areas relating to intellectual property. Specialises in patent litigation in all technical fields, acts before the national German courts and plans and co-ordinates multi-jurisdictional litigation. Takes part in oppositions and nullity proceedings on a national level and with the European Patent Office.
Career: Qualified 1973; former European head of IP of one of the world's largest law firms; founding partner of Reimann Osterrieth Köhler Haft. Recent publications include: co-author with Haft 'The calculation of infringer's profits following the 'overhead share' - decision of the German Federal Supreme Court (BGH) of 2 November 2000' in 'Mitt' (2003, p437-445); co-author with Kreye 'More on staying the procedure in patent litigation' in Keller (Hrsg) 'Festschrift für Winfried Tilmann', Köln 2003, p587-597; co-author with Köhler 'The scope of protection of European patents between appropriateness and legal certainty' in 'GRUR' (2002, p931-935); 'Brand management - country analysis: Germany' in 'Intellectual Property Handbook' (2000, p95-103).
Languages: German, English.
Member: AIPPI; AIPLA; EPLA; chairman of the patent committee of GRUR (German Intellectual Property Organisation); IPO; IBA; LES.
Education: University of Munich (1963); University of Bonn (1970 Dr jur).
Personal: Born 1943; resides Düsseldorf.

RIPPERT, Stephan

Reed Smith LLP
Phone: Munich (+49 89 20 304 10)
E-mail: srippert@reedsmith.com
TMT.
Position: Stephan is the head of the German technology, media and telecommunications (TMT) group and a commercial lawyer with international expertise in a wide range of sophisticated and complex transactions. Stephan regularly advises on all commercial and regulatory TMT matters including content distribution via various technical means, licensing and syndication, affiliation and alliance agreements, IT outsourcing and business process outsourcing, software, e-commerce, intellectual property, R&D agreements and telecommunication regulations, among others. His practice also encompasses joint ventures, mergers and acquisitions and strategic alliances. Stephan has advised on several major transactions in Germany with respect to the purchase of German broadband and digital platform operations. His clients include major international broadcasters, US film studios, cable companies, software and IT companies and an international medical technology company.
Career: Fiedler & Forster, Frankfurt 1992; State Bar Exam, New York 1995; senior counsel Viacom International, New York 1996; Freshfields Bruckhaus Deringer, Frankfurt 2000; Haarmann Hemmelrath & Partner, Frankfurt 2004; Reed Smith 2006.
Languages: English, German.
Member: New York State Bar Association; Munich Bar Association.
Education: University of Munich (1982); University of Mainz (1983); First State Bar Examination, Mainz (1987); Second State Bar Examination (Frankfurt); University of Mainz (1993 PhD Law); McGeorge School of Law, California (1993 LLM International Business Transactions.
Leisure: Tennis, golf, piano, spending time with family.

SCHMITZ, Thomas H

Reimann Osterrieth Köhler Haft Rechtsanwälte
Phone: Düsseldorf (+49 211 550 22 330)
E-mail: Thomas.Schmitz@rokh-ip.com
Position: For some years Thomas Schmitz has focused on various fields of intellectual property law, in particular trade marks, unfair competition and copyrights. He is highly experienced not only in litigation, but also in drafting license and co-operation agreements. Another focus is the worldwide development and support of trade mark portfolios.
Career: Qualified 1998; associate with a speciality law firm 2000; Reimann Osterrieth Köhler Haft 2005.
Languages: German, English, French.
Member: AIPPI; GRUR; IPO.
Education: University of Cologne (1990); University of Lausanne (1993).
Personal: Born 1971; resides Düsseldorf.

TRIMBORN, Michael, Dr

Reimann Osterrieth Köhler Haft Rechtsanwälte
Phone: Dusseldorf (+49 211 550 220)
E-mail: michael.trimborn@rokh-ip.com
Position: Dr Michael Trimborn litigates and advises on all intellectual property matters, with a special focus on employee invention law and patent law. In the area of employee invention law, the emphasis is on the calculation of remuneration, lump-sum compensation models with clauses regulating the purchase of inventors rights and the treatment of inventions in cases of restructuring and long-term secondments of employees. His patent practice is especially focused on complex national and multi-national patent infringement cases. He concentrates, in particular, on the technical fields of electrical and mechanical engineering, including automotive and general mechanics.
Career: Qualified 1993; Dr Trimborn has been working in intellectual property law since 1993, first with a specialty firm in Cologne, before co-heading the patent department of a general practice firm in Stuttgart.
Languages: German, English.
Member: German-British Law Association; GRUR; IPO; VPP.
Education: University of Cologne.
Personal: Born 1963; resides Düsseldorf.

GHANA

ANKOMAH, Ace Anan

Bentsi-Enchill & Letsa
Phone: Accra (+233 21 224 612)
E-mail: ace.anan.ankomah@belonline.org
Litigation.
Position: Partner, head of litigation team. Important cases include corporate litigation involving Kasapa Telecom, the Ghanian subsidiary of Hutchison Whampoa, and debt recovery litigation involving the International Finance Corporation and the United States Exim Bank.
Career: Trained in Ghana and admitted 1992; made partner in present firm in 2000. Senior lecturer in civil procedure, Ghana School of Law; lecturer in company law, Faculty of Law and School of Administration. General manager, Data Centa Ltd. Research assistant, Faculty of Law, Queen's University in Canada.

Publications of note: 'The Responsiveness of the Companies Code to Business Environments' (2004).
Languages: English, Twi and Fanti.
Member: Ghana Bar Association.
Education: Mfantsipim School; University of Ghana, Legon (1990, LLB); Ghana School of Law (1992, QCL); Queens University, Kingston, Ontario, Canada (1994, LLM).
Personal: Born 1967; resides Accra.
Leisure: Music, reading, tennis.

ASANTE, Seth Kwasi

Bentsi-Enchill & Letsa
Phone: Accra (+233 21 221 171)
E-mail: seth.asante@belonline.org
Corporate department.
Position: Partner: corporate department. Representative cases: corporate finance, Ghana Telecom, US$40m Bond Issue and US$60m syndicated loan; trade finance, Ghana Telecom, US$68m syndicated loan; mining finance, Red Back Mining, US$48m loan from Macquarie Bank; capital markets, merger of Guiness Ghana Limited and Ghana Breweries Limited.
Career: Qualified in 1999; made partner in present firm 2004; district registrar, Judicial Service; lecturer in company law, Ghana School of Law.
Languages: English and Twi.
Member: Ghana Bar Association.
Education: Sunyani Secondary School; University of Ghana (1997, LLB); Ghana Law School (1998, QCL); London School of Economics (2001, MSc in law and accounting).
Personal: Born 1969; resides Accra.
Leisure: Music, football, reading fiction.

BENTSI-ENCHILL, Kojo

Bentsi-Enchill & Letsa
Phone: Accra (+233 21 221 171)
E-mail: kojo.bentsi-enchill@belonline.org
Corporate team.
Position: Partner, head of corporate team. Notable cases: telecoms, $190m, arbitration of Western Wireless Corporation versus Government of Ghana; bank finance, $60m, Government Receivable Agreement for SCB; petroleum, $50m, Facility for Bost (Bulk Oil Storage Transport Ltd); project finance, Mesma Holdings, International Hotel Resort in Ghana.
Career: Qualified in 1975 and made partner in present firm in 1990. Positions of note: assistant programme officer, Ford Foundation, New York; foreign associate, Shearman & Sterling, New York; member, Technical Committee of Energy Commission on Electricity and Natural Gas.
Languages: English, French, Fanti and Ga.
Member: Ghana Bar Association.
Education: Leighton Park School; University of Ghana, Legon (1973, LLB); Ghana Law School (1975, QCL); Magdalene College, Cambridge.
Personal: Born 1950; resides Accra.
Leisure: Listening to music, playing piano, chess.

DARKO, Joyce

JLD Legal Consultancy Services
Phone: Accra (+233 21 78 3890)
E-mail: joyce@jldlaw.net
Position: Partner, dealing with corporate and commercial law, mergers and acquisitions, building and engineering contracts, minerals and mining law, and alternative dispute resolution. Has for many years represented major international companies, banks and institutions investing and working in Ghana and West Africa and has obtained considerable experience in advising in all fields of corporate and commercial practice. Has been associated with the highest-profile corporate transactions in Ghana involving major international acquisitions and cross-border mergers. As national president of the Ghana-France Chamber of Commerce, Industry and Agriculture (GFCCIA), has been a major liaison for Franco-Ghanaian business. Has been executive member of board of American Chamber of Commerce (AMCHAM), Ghana (as mediator, co-ordinated and partnered that body to establish the Commercial Conciliation Centre - the first of its kind in the country). From position as national treasurer, became the national president of the Ghana-France Chamber of Commerce and is now charter president of the organisation. As president of the chamber, was a major champion of the OHADA initiative, organising many fora and seminars aimed at sensitising Ghanaian professionals on OHADA and culminating in the establishment of the OHADA Documentation Centre in Accra. As local representative, of DIAGNOS (European Union), assisted the Ministry of Justice in the national legal reform program. As member of the national committee on OHADA, shares in the task of administrating the process of harmonisation of business laws in Africa.
Career: Called to Bar of England and Wales 1978; worked in City of London until 1980; called to Ghana Bar with special mention 1980; associate in legal chambers; legal manager of private company in Accra; executive director in charge of legal and administrative affairs; founded JLD Legal Consultancy Services.
Member: Ghana Bar Association; Honourable Society of Lincoln's Inn; charter president GFCCIA; Ghana Arbitration Centre; Ghana National Committee on OHADA.
Education: London School of Economics and Political Science (1977).

KUDOADZI, Rosalind Awovi

Bentsi-Enchill & Letsa
Phone: Accra (+233 21 227 187)
E-mail: rosa.kudoadzi@belonline.org
Corporate law.
Position: Partner, corporate team. Notable transactions: cocoa - US$550m trade finance for Ghana Cocoa Board; energy - US$170m corporate finance for Tema Oil Refinery; telecoms - US$40m corporate finance for Scancom Limited; capital markets - merger of Guinness Ghana Limited and Ghana Breweries Limited.
Career: Qualified in 1993 and made partner of present firm in 2004. Senior associate and associate at Bentsi-Enchill & Letsa (1997-2004); associate at Kudjawu & Co (1995-97); junior counsel, Ama Harding Chambers (1993-95).
Languages: English, French (working knowledge), Ewe, Twi, Ga.
Member: Ghana Bar Association; Ghana Arbitration Centre.
Education: OLA Secondary School; University of Ghana (1991, LLB); Ghana Law School (1993, QCL); University of London (2001, LLM International Business Law).
Personal: Born 1968; resides Accra.
Leisure: Reading, music, walking, tennis, golf, aerobics, and gardening.

LETSA, Divine Kwaku Duwose

Bentsi-Enchill & Letsa
Phone: Accra (+233 21 227 187)
E-mail: d.k.d.letsa@belonline.org
Commercial and property team.
Position: Partner, head of commercial and property team. Cases of note include Ghana Airway (in liquidation): acting for CDH, secured credit in enforcing securities; Ghana Urban Water Project: local counsel for World Bank/Gide Loyrette Nouel; international trade commodity finance: advice on Master Discount Agreement; Acquisition of immovable property by West African Pipeline Company.
Career: Trained in Accra, Ghana, and admitted in 1975. Made partner in present firm 1990. Positions of note: legal officer, State Insurance Corporation; private legal practice, Sekyere Chambers, Kumasi; lecturer, University of Cross River State, Nigeria; assistant director, civil litigation and advice; director of Laryx Farms, Oil & Lubricants.
Languages: English, Twi, Ewe, and Ga.
Member: Ghana Bar Association.
Education: Mawuli School, Ho; University of Ghana, Legon (1973, LLB); Ghana Law School (1975, QCL).
Personal: Born 1950; resides Accra.
Leisure: Football, walking, preaching and teaching.

GREECE

ANAGNOSTOPOULOS, Ilias G

Anagnostopoulos Bazinas Fifis
Phone: Athens (+30 210 729 2010)
E-mail: i.anagnostopoulos@abf.gr
Criminal law and litigation.
Position: Has appeared as lead counsel in most significant cases in Greece during the past 15 years, including business and financial fraud, tax and customs fraud, medical malpractice, product and environmental liability, money laundering, corruption practices, anti-terrorism, extradition and mutual assistance. Regularly instructed to advise and represent international and domestic corporations from the energy, defence, aviation, financial services, raw materials, pharmaceuticals, food, healthcare, telecommunications and media sectors, as well as

foreign governments and governmental organisations. As a legal expert, regularly offers opinions in Greek and foreign jurisdictions.
Career: Admitted to Athens Bar 1981; assistant professor of criminal law and criminal procedure at the School of Law, University of Athens. Has published extensively in Greek, English and German on matters of Hellenic, European and international criminal law, business crimes, securities fraud and insider trading, reform of criminal procedure and human rights; some publications are: co-author with K Magliveras 'Criminal Law in Greece' (Kluwer Law International 2000); editor 'Internationalisierung des Strafrechts' (Nomos 2003); 'Mutual Assistance in Criminal Matters in the European Union' (IELR 2002); 'Ne bis in idem in a European Context' (IELR 2000).
Member: Secretary General Hellenic Criminal Bar Association; Criminal Law Experts Committee of the Hellenic Ministry of Justice; the Criminal Law Committee of the Council of Bars and Law Societies of the European Union; Fraudnet of the International Chamber of Commerce; advisory board of European Criminal Bar Association; the International Association of Penal Law; the International Criminal Law Association; International Society for the Reform of Criminal Law.
Education: School of Law, University of Athens (1978); University of Frankfurt am Main (1983 Dr juris).
Personal: Born 1956.

BAZINAS, George V

Anagnostopoulos Bazinas Fifis
Phone: Athens (+30 210 725 4800)
E-mail: g.bazinas@abf.gr
Commercial law and litigation.
Position: Specialises in complex civil and commercial litigation and arbitration, involving all types of business disputes, banking and finance law, and is actively engaged in the domain of insolvency and reorganisation law and practice. Has extensive experience of cross-border disputes and proceedings, and acts mainly for international clients from a wide array of sectors, including banking and financial services, aviation, automobiles, media, energy, and industrial production, as well as foreign governmental organisations.
Career: Admitted to Athens Bar 1981, before the Court of Appeals 1986 and before the Supreme Court 1990; founded independent practice, subsequently merged into current firm Anagnostopoulos Bazinas Fifis, 1988; head of commercial law and litigation department Anagnostopoulos Bazinis Fifis. Publications: chapter on Greece in 'Collier International Business Insolvency Guide' (Matthew Bender/LexisNexis 2004); chapter on Greece in legal section of 'The European Restructuring and Insolvency Guide' (White Page 2002); 'Insolvency, Re-organisation, and the new EC Regulation on Insolvency Proceedings: Perspectives of Greek Law and Process' in 'Norton Annual Survey of Bankruptcy Law' 2003; has also written on security interests, including the chapter on Greek law in the Centre of Commercial Law Studies' book on European laws (to be published 2005).
Member: International Insolvency Institute; the American Hellenic Institute; the International Bar Association; Hellenic Commercial Lawyers Association.
Education: School of Law, University of Athens (1978); King's College, London (1981 LLM).
Personal: Born 1955.

BERNITSAS, Panayotis M, Prof

M & P Bernitsas
Phone: Athens (+30 210 36 15 395)
E-mail: bernitsas@bernitsaslawoffices.gr
Position: Managing partner, head of the telecommunications and media department and joint head of the litigation, arbitration and dispute resolution department. Also deals with aviation, banking and finance, capital markets, EU and competition, internet, mergers and acquisitions, privatisations, project finance, public procurement and tax.
Career: Admitted 1974 Athens Bar; Athens Court of Appeal and Supreme Court of Greece; Professional Representative before the European Patent Office; Associate Professor of International Economic Law and Law of International Business Transactions and European Community Law, University of Thrace; Counsel, Ministry of National Economy during negotiations for Greece's accession to European Communities (EEC) 1977-82; Legal Counsel, Hellenic Banks Association 1980-90; Counsel to Greek Commissioner for Common Market Transport Matters, Brussels 1983-84; Special Secretary for Public Investments, Regional Policy and Integrated Mediterranean Programmes, Ministry of National Economy 1989; Counsel to Greek Prime Minister Zolotas on EEC matters 1989-90; Counsel to Minister of Foreign Affairs 1989-90; Counsel to the Minister of National Economy on illegal state aids and privatisation issues 1990-91; Secretary-General of the Hellenic Centre for European Studies 1990-93; Ad Hoc Counsel to the Minister of National Economy on EEC matters; Ad Hoc Counsel to the Ministry of National Economy on the privatisation of state-owned enterprises (National Telecommunications Organisation (OTE) and Refineries) 1991-93; is or has been an active arbitrator in various ICC arbitrations. Has published numerous articles and contributed extensively to national and international legal publications on a wide range of topics. Recent publications include 'European Cross-Border Insolvency: A Guide to Insolvency Procedures Across the European Union', Greek section (Sweet and Maxwell 2005); 'Evaluation of the Application of the National Control on Concentrations of Enterprises' (chapter entitled 'Merger Control in the Context of Free Competition Legislation'), Nomiki Vivliothiki, Athens (1998); 'Telecommunications in Greece: the Current Regulatory Framework', magazine of the American-Hellenic Chamber of Commerce (May-June 1998); 'European Union Telecommunications Liberalisation - Regulatory Handbook' (sections on Greece of report concerning the extent of liberalisation of the telecommunications sector in European Union member states under the direction of SJ Berwin & Co), Phillips Tarifica (March 1998); and 'Merger Control in the Member States of the European Economic Area, Switzerland and the United States of America' (chapter on Greece of survey on the procedures and the substantial laws conducted by the Brussels office of Globalex, the international alliance of Foley and Lardner, Nicholson Graham and Jones, Setterwalls and Thümmel, Schütze and Partner) (October 1997).
Languages: English, French, German, Greek, Italian.
Member: Athens Bar Association; International Bar Association (IBA); International Fiscal Association (IFA), Greek section; Hellenic Society for International Law and Relations; International Law Association (ILA); American-Hellenic Chamber of Commerce; British-Hellenic Chamber of Commerce; Hellenic Society for Private International Law; Union des Avocats Europeens (UAE); Association des Juristes Europeens.
Education: University of Athens Law School (Degree in Law); University of Paris (1973 DES in Public Law); Hague International Law Academy (1973); Institute of Advanced Legal Studies, London (1975 Research); University of Thessaloniki (1979 PhD).

BERSIS, George

PI Partners
Phone: Athens (+30 210 28 86 550)
E-mail: giorgos.bersis@gr.eylaw.com
Banking, finance, capital markets.
Position: Partner dealing with securities, derivatives, syndicated loans, IPOs, investment services, banking and corporate transactions.
Career: Mr Bersis drafted the CSD rulebook for dematerialised securities in Greece, and participated in the listing of Bank of Cyprus (the first foreign company) in ATHEX. He is a lecturer at the ATHEX training center on securities and derivatives issues, and on corporate governance issues in the MSc in business for lawyers programme; has advised a great number of IPOs, public offerings and share capital increases.
Languages: Greek, English, French, Spanish.
Member: New York Bar; Athens Bar.
Education: University of Athens (1994 LLB); School of Law, New York University (1996 LLM).
Personal: Born 1970; resides Athens.

DINOVA, Anelia

PI Partners
Phone: Athens (359 2 81 77 301)
E-mail: anelia.dinova@bg.eylaw.com
M&A and privatisations.
Position: Partner, dealing with investment services, banking, M&A and privatisations and corporate transactions.
Career: Specialises in corporate law and mergers and acquisitions, with a primary focus on assisting inward investments. Experience covers greenfield start ups, privatisations, acquisitions, disposals and various other company reorganisations. Has worked with McDonalds, General Chemical, Scancem, Barlo Group, Standard Commercial Tobacco Company, Chupa Chups, British Wireless, Intercontinental Hotels Company, Sheraton, Societe Generale, Hypovereinsbank, OTP, ING, IntesaBci, EnBW, Connex,

Holcim, Efes Breweries, Eko, Elda and many other major international companies in relation to their acquisitions/investments in Bulgaria, Russia and the Slovak Republic.
Languages: Bulgarian, English, Russian, Slovak.
Member: Sofia Bar.
Education: Sofia University (1998 LLM); University of Limerick, Ireland (1993 Master of Arts, European Integration).
Personal: Born 1964; resides Sofia.

DRYLLERAKIS, John C

Dryllerakis & Associates
Phone: Athens (+30 2 10 362 8159)
E-mail: jcd@dryllerakis.gr
Position: Senior partner dealing with all business matters, including specialisation in tax matters, both as consultation and litigation. Representative international clients of the firm: Barilla, Beiersdorf, Danone, Exxon, Hollister, Hyatt, Lectra, Leo Burnett, Metsa Serla, Nintendo, Pechiney, Rahyteon, SCA, Shell, TVX Gold.
Career: Practising since 1962. Senior partner of Dryllerakis & Associates Law Firm (established 1972); made partner 1972. General counsel and general tax counsel for ten years of the Exxon affiliates in Greece and subsequently of Shell Hallas; member of their management teams. Long experience in management and in decision-taking processes, in international transactions and in financial matters, results in an excellent combination of legal culture and entrepreneurial orientation. Author of many legal books (financial and tax analysis of the corporations law, investment (tax) incentives, liberalisation of capital movement, competition law) and of numerous publications in legal magazines and in the financial press. Has lectured on Greek tax law in the summer courses of the Temple University and has also delivered many speeches in seminars.
Languages: Greek, fluent English, reading level French.
Member: Athens Bar Association; International Bar Association; International Fiscal Association; Independent Competition Committee and Capital Markets Committee; Griechische Gesellschaft für Gesetzgebung; director, Competition Law Society, the Hellenic Society of Tax Law and of Fiscal Studies; special secretary, board of the Hellenic Society of European Law.
Education: Athens University Law School (Law and Economics).
Personal: Born 1937; resides Athens.

ECONOMOU, George

G. C. Economou & Associates
Phone: Athens (+210 364 0030)
E-mail: economou@gce-associates.gr
Position: Senior partner; specialist areas of practice are shipping and ship finance; arbitration; international company law; tax planning; corporate structuring and trusts.
Career: Trained England, Greece and Cyprus; qualified 1965; member of the English and Greek Bars; member of the Cyprus Bar until 2005. Publications of note: chapter on Greece in 'Maritime Law Handbook: enforced sale of ships' (IBA); chapter on Greece in 'International execution against judgement debtors' (Sweet and Maxwell); chapter on Greece in 'Dispute resolution methods' (Graham & Trotman). Holds a large number of directorships.
Languages: Greek, English, French.
Member: FCI Arb; IBA; IFA; on the panel of arbitrators of many professional bodies.
Education: Famagusta and Athens; Council of Legal Education; Greek Bar Examinations.
Personal: Born 1940; resides Athens.

ILIADOU, Efstathia

PI Partners
Phone: Athens (+30 210 28 86 512)
E-mail: tati.iliadou@gr.eylaw.com
Corporate and labour law.
Position: Partner dealing with corporate, commercial and labour law.
Career: Previously associated with the law firm of Karatzas & Perakis in Athens 1989-92; in-house counsel to Ernst & Young (Hellas)1992-95.
Languages: Greek, English, French.
Member: Athens Bar.
Education: University of Athens (1987 LLB); University of Paris I and II (1989 DEA Banking and Public Law).
Personal: Born 1964; resides Athens.

LYMPEROPOULOS, John

G. C. Economou & Associates
Phone: Athens (+210 364 0030)
E-mail: john@gce-associates.gr
Position: Real property transactions; acquisition and takeover of companies; setting up new businesses in Greece.
Career: Trained Athens; qualified 1995; partner G.C.Economou & Associates 2006; non-executive director in a number of companies.
Languages: Greek, English.
Education: The American College of Greece; University of Athens; University of Canterbury, Kent (LLB; LLM).
Personal: Born 1972; resides Athens.

PAPACONSTANTINOU, Helen

Law Offices Papaconstantinou
Phone: Athens (+30 210 729 57 50)
E-mail: hpaplaw@ath.forthnet.gr
Position: Partner.
Career: Admitted 1982, Athens; 1982, New York; legal associate Phillips, Nizer, Benjamin, Krim and Ballon, New York 1980-81; 'The Extraterritorial effects of EEC Antitrust Law', 1981, Stagiaire at the European Commission in Brussels (Directorate-General of Competition) 1983; author of publications including 'Is the Greek State Monopoly of Petrol Consistent with EEC Laws?' Economikos Tahidromos, (Financial Courrier) 11.8.83; 'Is the Greek Policy on Public Supplies Consistent with EEC Laws?' Economikos Tahidromos, 12.1.84 English Translation in Greece's Weekly, 10.3.84; 'Greek Foreign Exchange Controls and Community Law' Economikos Tahidromos, 14.6.84; 'Is the Marketing Compaign "Buy Greek" consistent with EEC Laws?' Economikos Tahidromos, 9.8.84; 'Is it possible to protect the national interest without contravening EEC Laws?' Economikos Tahidromos, 26.12.85; 'Free Trade and Competition in the EEC: Law, Policy and Practice', 1988, published by Routledge; 'Corporate Law Recent Developments - Greece', International Business Lawyer 1988, 89, 90, 91; also contributor to the following publications: 'Commercial Agency and Distribution Agreements - Law and Practice in the Member States of the European Community' (Chapter on Greek law), published by Graham and Trotman on behalf of the Association Internationale des Jeunes Avocats; 'Mergers and Acquisitions in Europe' (Chapter on Greek Law), published by Professional Publishing Limited in conjunction with S.G. Warburg Group as editors; 'European Franchising - Law and Procedure in the European Community' (Chapter on Greek Law), published by Waterlow's Publishers; 'Acquisition of shares in a foreign country - Substantive law and legal opinions' published by Graham and Trotman and International Bar Association; 'International Corporate Procedures', Chapter on Greek law, published by Jordans.
Languages: Greek, English, French.
Member: Association of European Lawyers (Greek branch) for the protection of the financial interests of the community; Association Internationale de Jeunes Avocats; American Bar Association; Greek Team Europe; Harvard Alumni Association of Greece (president of the Association); Hellenic Association for European Law; International Bar Association; Union Internationale des Avocats; Union des Avocats Européens.
Education: London School of Economics and Political Science (1979 LLB); Harvard Law School (1980 LLM); Université Libre de Bruxelles (1985 PhD).
Personal: Married to Symeon Sikiaridis; two children, 16 and 14 years old.

PAPARRIGOPOULOS, Xenophon

PI Partners
Phone: Athens (+30 210 28 86 550)
E-mail: xenophon.paparrigopoulos@gr.eylaw.com
Litigation and arbitration, EU Law and intellectual property law.
Position: Partner dealing with dispute resolution, competition and intellectual property.
Career: Legal counsel to the Greek Parliament 1989 to present; assistant professor of Law and Philosophy at the University of Thessalia 1995 to present. Author of 'Unger's System of Rights: A Defence, European Journal of Law, Philosophy and Computer Science', 1995, The Scientific Department of the Greek Parliament in Makridimitri's book 'Issues of Administrative Transformation', 1995, 'The John Rawls theory on justice' in K Beys book 1994.
Languages: Greek, English, French, Italian, German.
Member: Athens Bar.
Education: University of Athens (1980 LLB); Harvard Law School (1981 LLM; 1984 SJD).
Personal: Born 1956; resides Athens.

POTAMITIS, Stathis
PI Partners
Phone: Athens (+30 210 28 86 550)
E-mail: stathis.potamitis@gr.eylaw.com
Banking, finance and M&A.
Position: Managing partner; recognised expert in securities, investment services, banking and corporate transactions.
Career: Previously associated with the New York law firm of Paul, Weiss, Rifkind, Wharton & Garrison (1986-91); general counsel of Egnatia Bank (1991-94); deputy chairman of the Athens Derivatives Exchange (1998-99). Author: 'A Synopsis of Securities Exchange Legislation', Athens Stock Exchange 1996. Member of the committee for the codification of securities exchange legislation; has drafted the Code of Conduct for Investment Services Firms, regulations for licensing and reporting by investment services firms as well as several laws.
Languages: Greek, English, French.
Member: New York Bar; Athens Bar.
Education: University of Toronto (1979 BA; 1982 MA; 1986 LLB); Eleve Titulaire, University of Paris IV (1983).
Personal: Born 1956; resides Athens.

SARRIS, Lydia
G. C. Economou & Associates
Phone: Athens (+210 364 0030)
E-mail: lsarris@lexconsult.gr
Position: Partner; specialises in shipping and ship finance; sale and purchase of ships.
Career: Trained England, Cyprus and Greece; qualified 1964; holds several non-executive directorships.
Languages: Greek, English, French.
Member: Cyprus Bar.
Education: Nicosia; Council of Legal Education.
Personal: Born 1943; resides Athens.

SPYROPOULOS, Philippos C
Dryllerakis & Associates
Phone: Athens (+30 2 10 362 8159)
E-mail: ps@dryllerakis.gr
Position: Specialises in litigation at the Supreme Administrative Court, consultations and legal opinions mainly in matters of public law; contracts.
Career: Qualified and joined Athens Bar 1976; licensed to practice before all courts, including the Supreme Court. Ex general secretary of the Ministry of Justice. Regular member of the independent authority Telecommunications and Posts Committee. Professor of public law at the Law School of the Athens University.
Languages: English, French.
Member: Athens Bar Association; Association of Greek Constitutionalists; Legal Counsel of the Church of Greece; National Telecommunications Committee 2000 to present day; Greek Human Rights Committee 2000 to present day.
Education: Law School of Athens University (1974 LLM); University of London LSE (1979 Dr iur); University of Freiburg (i Br).
Personal: Born 1952; resides Athens.

TOMPROS, Elias
G. C. Economou & Associates
Phone: Athens (+210 364 0030)
E-mail: economou@gce-associates.gr
Position: Senior associate; specialises in civil cases both in the Court of First Instance and in the appeal courts.
Career: Trained Athens; qualified 1991.
Languages: Greek, English.
Education: The American College of Greece; The Aristotelian University of Thessaloniki; University of Kent, Canterbury (LLB; LLM).
Personal: Born 1968; resides Athens.

VEKRIS, Johnny
PI Partners
Phone: Athens (+30 210 28 86 549)
E-mail: ioannis.vekris@gr.eylaw.com
Corporate and commercial, M&A, shipping, and real estate.
Position: Partner dealing with corporate and commercial law, arbitrations, shipping law and real estate.
Career: Previously associated with major shipping operators in Greece and with the Boston law firm of Bingham Dana & Gould 1985-86. Co-authored encyclopedia entitled 'Modern Legal Systems', chapter on Greece, edited by Prof Kenneth R Redden of the University of Virginia 1985.
Languages: Greek, English, French.
Member: New York Bar; Athens Bar.
Education: University of Athens (1983 LLB); University College, London (1984 LLM); Harvard Law School (1985 LLM).
Personal: Born 1960; resides Athens.

HUNGARY

BUDAI, Judit, Dr
Szecskay - Attorneys at Law
Phone: Budapest (+36 1 472 3000)
E-mail: judit.budai@szecskay.com
Position: Partner dealing with corporate/M&A, competition law, project finance, capital markets, banking and IP law. Advised ÁPV Rt in the course of the privatisation of Antenna Hungária Rt, one of the largest Hungarian Telecom companies; the value of the transaction was €46m. Represented Láng Group, one of Hungary's main printing and publishing companies, as purchaser in the successful privatisation of Nemzeti Tankönyvkiadó Rt, the publisher of study books by ÁPV Rt; the value of the transaction was €13m. Advised Állami Nyomda (State Printing) Private Company Limited and its shareholders, including Royalton Capital Investors, in connection with the acquisition of shares from the exiting venture capital investor Bazille Investments Limited; the value of the transaction was €13m. Also advised shareholders of Állami Nyomda (State Printing) Plc in selling their shareholding in a real property holding company - separated from Állami Nyomda (State Printing) Plc, holding and leasing the printing sited to State Printing Company - to leasing companies belonging to the HVB/Bank Austria Group; the value of the transaction was €10m. Advised Állami Nyomda (State Printing) Plc and its majority private person shareholders and Royalton Capital Investors Three Limited in the introduction of the shares of Állami Nyomda (State Printing) Plc at the Budapest Stock Exchange and sale of shares via public offerings and private placements; the value of the transaction was €22m. Advised the Hungarian Development Bank (MFB) in connection with the acquisition of Körte-Organica Limited (a company delivering waste-water purification system services by ecotechnology) with respect to assessing legal risks of the acquisition. Advised Ferro in a cartel proceeding in connection with a cartel agreement with Bayer AG and applying for leniency. Advised Tessenerlo in a cartel proceeding in connection with a cartel agreement with Kemira and applying for leniency. Advised the Zwack Group and Zwack Unicum Public Company Limited, the leading spirit manufacturer and trading company, in renegotiating a Zwack and Unicum trade mark license agreement.
Career: Admitted to the Budapest Bar 1994; made partner 2002. Publications of note: article on merger control in 'Competition Law' (Global Counsel Handbook 2005), several articles on capital markets, banking, e-commerce and IP in the 'International Law Office' (Practical Law, Global Counsel Handbooks and Euromoney publications).
Languages: English, Hungarian.
Member: UIA/standing member for Hungary of the M&A and the corporate committees; ethics committee member of the Hungarian Venture Capital Association; LIDC; IBA; AIPPI.
Education: Eötvös Loránd Faculty of State and Legal Science, Budapest (1991, JD); Budapest Economic University (BEU), London Business School programme (1996, MBA).
Personal: Born 1967; resides Budapest.

GYÖRFI-TÓTH, Péter
Horváth & Partners DLA Weiss-Tessbach
Phone: Budapest (+36 1 325 30 20)
E-mail: peter.gyorfi-toth@dlapiper.com
Projects and finance.
Position: Partner. With more than ten years' experience, has been advising clients in numerous major local and cross-border transactions in the fields of banking, projects and finance, real estate development, regulatory law, insurance, real estate development, liquidation, litigation and arbitration. Areas of practice: banking, project and corporate finance, real estate, (international) commercial law and arbitration, insolvency and restructuring, EU internal markets and competition law. Major project finance transactions: Hungary - bank consortium led by Erste Bank Hungary Rt. Advised bank on restructuring an international five-star hotel, Radisson, in Bük, Hungary. Transaction value: ca HUF4.7bn; Hungary/Austria - international bank consortium led by the Immorent Group. Advice on the

structured financing of the supermarket chain Tempo (by means of operating leasing) and on the syndicated refinancing thereof. Transaction value: HUF6bn; Hungary/Austria - IMMORENT AG. Advice on the structured financing of five four-star and three-star ACCOR hotels by means of operating leasing. Transaction value: €88m; Hungary - Immorent Group and Erste Bank Hungary Rt. Advice on the financing of the development of a four-star hotel in Balatonalmádi by means of operating leasing. Transaction value: HUF1.5bn; Hungary - Magyarországi Volksbank Rt. Advice on diverse infrastructural (public utilities - water supply network) developments in Hungary. Average transaction value: HUF1bn. Major finance/refinance transactions: Hungary - international consortium led by Erste Bank der Österreichischen Sparkassen AG. Advised bank on restructuring and refinancing an international four-star hotel, Marriott/Millennium Court and Centre, in Budapest, Hungary. Transaction value: €28m; Hungary - Erste Bank Hungary Rt. Advice on financing the acquisition of a company for the purposes of acquiring an office building located in Budapest. Transaction value: €4.75m; Hungary - Erste Bank Hungary Rt. Advised bank on financing purchase of an office building and industrial area in Budapest. Transaction value: €3.8m; Hungary/Austria - Bank Austria/Creditanstalt. Advised bank on restructuring and refinancing of office buildings Arpád and Globe in Budapest, Hungary. Transaction value: €27.5m; Hungary - Magyarországi Volksbank Rt. Advice on diverse financial transactions. Average transaction value: HUF500m; Hungary - IMMORENT Group. Advice on diverse financial leasing (mostly sale and lease back) transactions on the side of the lessor. Average transaction value: HUF300m. Miscellaneous major transactions: Hungary - Magyarországi Volksbank Rt. Advice on the takeover of two branch offices of BNP Paribas in Budapest along with the total client portfolio thereof. Transaction value: ca HUF4.5bn; Hungary - Magyarországi Volksbank Rt. Advice on the local government financing and review of the pertaining documentation; Hungary/Austria - Kommunalkredit AG. Survey in respect of the legal background of local government financing in Hungary. Major clients include: Erste Bank AG, Erste Bank Rt, CIB Bank Rt, Hungarian Volksbank Rt, Eurohypo AG, Immorent AG, CEE Property Group.

Career: Associate at Horváth and Partners, Weiss-Tessbach, Budapest 1994-97; qualified 1995; attorney-at-law at Horváth and Partners, Weiss-Tessbach, Budapest 1997-2000; partner with Horváth and Partners, Weiss-Tessbach, Budapest since 2000; participation in the codification of the Hungarian Civil Code (reform of securitisation) since 1999; appointed as an arbitrator of the Financial and Capital Market Court of Arbitration in Budapest; arbitrator at the Money and Capital Market Court of Arbitration in Hungary. Lecturer at the Eötvös Loránd University Faculty of Law on comparative corporate law 1997 to date; has given seminars on collaterals and security and comparative corporate law Eötvös Loránd University, Budapest since 1998; lecturer at the Eötvös Loránd University Faculty of Law on security 2000 to date; lecturer on enforcement of claims at the IIR Seminar, Vienna 2001 to date. Publications: regularly publishes in Hungarian and international legal publications; 'The Stand-Alone Mortgage' (1997 Budapest); 'Changes in the Regulation of Mortgages in the Hungarian Civil Code' (Budapest, 'Notary Journal', 2002).

Languages: Hungarian, German, English.

Education: Eötvös Loránd University, Budapest (1994; 1997 Diploma in Company Law); Karl-Ruprecht University (1996 LLM).

Personal: Born 1971; resides Budapest.

NIDDAM, Laurent

Szecskay - Attorneys at Law

Phone: Budapest (+36 1 472 3000)

E-mail: laurent.niddam@szecskay.com

Position: Partner dealing with domestic and cross-border M&A, corporate finance, dispute resolution and international arbitration. Provides ongoing assistance to the owners of a market leader company in Romania in connection with the staged acquisition of a stake in that company by a foreign strategic investor. Provides ongoing assistance to a foreign utility company in a dispute with public authorities regarding an investment in Hungary. Currently advises the Ministry of Economic Development of Azerbaijan in connection with that country's development of a legal and economic framework for the encouragement of foreign investments in the non oil and gas sectors. Provides ongoing assistance to the Auchan Hypermarket Group in connection with its investment program to build and develop commercial centres in Hungary. Advises various foreign investors in acquiring stakes in local enterprises and managing the relationship with the local partner. Represented a producer of tobacco products in dispute settlement proceedings with an equipment manufacturer in connection with the unsatisfactory performance of purchased equipment. Advised various global international companies on dawn-raid procedures and strategy. Regularly advises large international and Central European corporations in acquisitions (including cross-border) joint ventures and other corporate and commercial transactions. Advised on various venture capital transactions, underwritings of securities, project financing and real estate development.

Career: Qualified in New York (1994) and Paris (1995); made partner in present firm in 2003. Regular contributor to various publications on international arbitration and international commercial transactions. Publications of note: 'Dispute Resolution', 2005/6 Global Counsel Handbook 95-100; 'Unilateral Arbitration Clauses', The Arbitration and Dispute Resolution Law Journal 147 (1996); 'L'arbitrabilité des Dommages et Intérêts Punitifs en droit Américain' (Arbitrability of Punitive Damages Under US Law), Revue de l'Arbitrage 295 (1995); 'L'exécution des Sentences Arbitrales Internationales aux Etats-Unis' (Enforcement of International Arbitral Awards in the US), Revue de l'Arbitrage 13-62 (1993).

Languages: English, French.

Member: Member of the board of the French-Hungarian Chamber of Commerce and Industry; IBA; Comité Français de l'Arbitrage.

Education: Université Paris II, Panthéon Assas (1991 LLB Hons, 1992 LLM Hons); Columbia Law School (1994 LLM Hons, Harlan Fiske Stone Scholar).

Personal: Born 1960; resides Budapest.

Leisure: Horsemanship, long distance riding, music, literature.

POSZTL, András

Horváth & Partners DLA Weiss-Tessbach

Phone: Budapest (+36 1 325 30 20)

E-mail: andras.posztl@dlapiper.com

PG corporate, M&A.

Position: Partner. Has been involved in numerous international cross-border and domestic corporate, financing and other commercial transactions. With more than seven years' experience, has been involved in major international M&A and corporate financing transactions (including the largest Hungarian takeover bid so far) covering also the competition law aspects (merger clearance procedure), corporate housekeeping, due-diligence exercises, and public and private acquisitions advising the sellers, the purchasers, the target companies and their financial advisors. Areas of practice: drafting and negotiating private M&A transactions, including asset deals and share deals, private merger agreements and accompanying transaction documents, advising clients on structuring and financing the transactions; advising clients on structuring public issue of stocks; due diligence exercises, including advising the seller and/or the purchaser, preparation of due diligence reports, risk assessment; advising clients on merger control approval issues; drafting and negotiating project agreements, including shareholder and participation agreements, financing agreements; advising clients on specific regulatory issues in the energy sector, public utilities sector (water and waste water treatment), concession contracts; drafting and advising clients on capital market transactions and public takeovers. Major transactions: (client - Austrian investor) advice and representation in successful public takeover bid for the listed company BorsodChem, the second biggest petrochemical company in Hungary and the biggest isocyanides producer in CEE. Representation at the Hungarian Antitrust Authority for the licencing of the acquisition; (client - Austrian investor) advised on the acquisition of concession right in the public utilities sector (water and sewage supply). Activity included advice and representation on the financing, and corporate matters (establishment of the concession company), such as drafting and negotiating the concession contract; (client - multinational telecommunications company) advised on a joint venture relating to a Hungarian cable television company. Advised on the corporate structure, the competition law aspects of the transaction and the legal due diligence on the Hungarian subsidiaries; (client - several foreign investors and multinational companies) represented in the establishment of their Hungarian subsidiaries, and acted for Hungarian and foreign clients on corporate restructuring, general corporate housekeeping and the implementation of

stock award plans; (client - Austrian investor) advised on the acquisition of shareholdings in KÖGÁZ gas distribution company from the State Privatisation and Property Holding Ltd. Activity included the legal due diligence of the company, advising on the transaction documents, legal assistance during negotiations, providing ongoing legal advice in the course of the privatisation; (client - German Land Mortgage Bank) advised on the financing (sale and lease back) of the headquarter building of a major Hungarian Bank; (client - German Bank consortium led by Eurohypo AG Europaeische Hypothekenbank der Deutschen Bank) advised on the refinancing of Mammut I Retail Centre and advised on the financing and refinancing of the new Mammut II Retail Centre development. Major clients include: VCP-Group, BorsodChem Rt, Eurohypo AG, ITW-Group, EVN Energieversorgung Niederösterreich.
Career: Junior and senior associate at Horváth and Partners, Weiss-Tessbach, Budapest 1994-2000; qualified Hungarian solicitor 1997; secondment with Gaedertz Rechtanwälte, Frankfurt am Main 1997-2000; partner with Horváth and Partners, Weiss-Tessbach, Budapest since 2000; working with Central and Eastern European desk of DLA, London since 2004.
Languages: Hungarian, German, English.
Member: Budapest Bar; Hungarian Bar Association.
Education: Eötvös Loránd University, Budapest (1994); Universität Trier (1994 Dr iuris summa cum laude EU law studies); corporate legal adviser postgraduate studies (2002).
Personal: Born 1970; resides Budapest.

SZECSKAY, András, Dr
Szecskay - Attorneys at Law
Phone: Budapest (+36 1 472 3000)
E-mail: andras.szecskay@szecskay.com
Position: Founding and managing partner dealing with M&A, corporate and project finance, litigation/arbitration and IP law. Counsel to Richter Gedeon Rt in the €639m transaction, tantamount to privatisation, where ÁPV Rt issued bonds exchangeable into Richter Gedeon Rt shares. Adviser to ÁPV Rt in the course of the privatisation of Antenna Hungária Rt, one of the largest Hungarian Telecom companies; the value of the transaction was €46m. Involved in the privatisation of Budapest Airport: ÁPV Rt announced a privatisation tender in two rounds in June 2005 which was halted due to insufficient consultation with workers. As a result, a new procedure started and, after the evaluation of the bids and the necessary consultation with the employees' representatives, the transaction was closed in Decemeber 2005 by selecting a successful bidder. Represented Láng Group, one of Hungary's main printing and publishing companies, as purchaser in the successful privatisation of Nemzeti Tankönyvkiadó Rt, the publisher of study books by ÁPV Rt; the value of the transaction was €13m. Advised Állami Nyomda (State Printing) Private Company Limited and its shareholders, including Royalton Capital Investors, in connection with the acquisition of shares from the exiting venture capital investor Bazille Investments Limited; the value of the transaction was €13m. Advised Auchan Hypermarket Group with respect to the purchase of various real properties, and the establishment of various commercial centres in Hungary; the total value of the ongoing transactions is in the order of €330m.
Career: Founded Szecskay - Attorneys at Law 1992. Managing partner of Szecskay - Attorneys at Law from 1992; resident partner of Szecskay - Moquet Borde et Associés 1992-2004; partner of SBG&K Patent and Law Office 1975-92. Admitted to the Budapest Bar 1975. Publications of note: co-author of the Hungarian section of the 'Digest of Commercial Laws of the World' (edited by N Stephan Kinsella and Paul E Comeaux); 'Competition Law' and 'International Banking Law & Regulation' (Oceana Publications, Inc); 'Dispute Resolution 2005/06' (Global Counsel Handbooks).
Languages: English, Hungarian.
Member: Vice president of the Budapest Bar; member of IBA, UIA, UAE, HVCA, LIDC, AIPPI, LES, MIE.
Education: József Katona Gimnázium; Szeged University Law School (1973, JD summa cum laude).
Personal: Born 1948; resides Budapest.
Leisure: Music, literature, skiing, trekking, cycling.

VARGA, Ildikó, Dr
Nagy és Trócsányi
Phone: Budapest (+36 1 487 8700)
E-mail: varga.ildiko@nt.hu
Corporate transactions group.
Position: Head of the corporate transactions group with significant experience and practice in M&A, structuring foreign direct investments and transnational transactions.
Career: Eötvös Lorànd Tudomànyegyetem qualified 1988. Joined White & Case, New York (1990) as foreign attorney; moved to Arent Fox, Washington (1991); Joined Nagy és Trócsànyi as partner in 1993. Publications: 'Comparative Study of Constitutional Courts of Europe and the USA' Vol I and II, published by the Law Institute of the Hungarian Academy of Sciences (1988).
Languages: English, Hungarian.
Member: New York Bar; Budapest Bar.
Education: Eötvös Lorànd Tudomànyegyetem, Faculty of Law (1985), Faculty of Arts (1986); Université de Strasbourg (1987); NYU, Graduate School of Arts and Sciences in New York (1989-90).
Personal: Born 1957; resides Budapest.

INTERNATIONAL

CAYMAN ISLANDS

CATER, Roisin
Mourant du Feu & Jeune
Phone: Grand Cayman (+1 345 946 2212)
E-mail: roisin.cater@mourant.com
Partner, Cayman office.
Position: Advises on investment funds, private equity and general corporate.
Career: Trained at Linklaters, London, articled clerk 1991-93, assistant solicitor 1993-96, qualified in 1993. Attorney at Hunter & Hunter, Cayman Islands 1996-98, senior listing executive, Cayman Islands Stock Exchange 1998-2000, attorney at law, Boxalls, Cayman Islands 2000-05. Made partner of Mourant du Feu & Jeune 2005.
Languages: French, Spanish.
Member: Law societies of England and Wales and the Cayman Islands.
Education: St Annes School, Windermere; Nottingham University (1990 LLB Hons).
Personal: Born 1968, resides Grand Cayman.

JONES, Owen
Mourant du Feu & Jeune
Phone: Grand Cayman (+1 345 946 1206)
E-mail: owen.jones@mourant.com
Capital markets, corporate and banking, asset and project finance, funds.
Position: Partner specialising in capital markets, asset finance, with particular experience in all aspects of aircraft finance and project finance. Owen is qualified in four jurisdictions: England and Wales, Cayman, New York and the British Virgin Islands.
Career: Trained Freshfields; admitted New York 1994, England 1996, Cayman 1997 and the British Virgin Islands 2004. Made partner Mourant de Feu & Jeune 2004 to date.
Education: Cheltenham College; London School of Economics (LLB first class Hons); Trinity Hall, Cambridge (LLM first class Hons).
Personal: Born 1966; resides Cayman Islands.

IRELAND

CALDWELL, Jennifer
Maples and Calder
Phone: Dublin (+353 1 667 9800)
E-mail: jennifer.caldwell@maplesandcalder.com
Position: Managing partner and partner in the commercial department specialising in corporate finance, in particular, IPOs, fundraisings, venture capital investments, take-overs and mergers and acquisitions; her client base includes listed companies, substantial private companies, venture capitalists and individual investors; she has acted as legal adviser in relation to a number of high-profile listings and fundraisings; she has experience working in a variety of markets, including NASDAQ, the Official List of the London Stock Exchange, the Irish Stock Exchange, AIM and the IEX.
Career: Qualified in the UK 1980; in Ireland 1982.
Languages: English.

CHARLTON, Gerard

Reddy Charlton McKnight
Phone: Dublin (+353 1 66 19 500)
E-mail: n.shorton@rcmck.com
Commercial litigation.
Position: Senior partner.
Career: With over 30 year's experience as a senior partner of the firm; he has vast experience as a commercial lawyer in both transactional and litigation matters; and has been successfully involved in many major cases.
Education: Graduated in economics from University College, Dublin and qualified as a solicitor in 1956.

KEANE, Paul

Reddy Charlton McKnight
Phone: Dublin (+353 1 66 19 500)
E-mail: p.keane@rcmck.com
Commercial.
Position: Managing partner, also acts as business adviser and director for a number of companies.
Career: Has distinguished experience in commercial and taxation matters, main areas of interest are: corporate law, contracting and taxation. He has on numerous occasions been a consultant to the Law School of the Law Society and its continuing legal education programme. In 2004, was nominated by the Law Society to join the network of experts on contract law, which was established by the Comission of the European Union as part of its project on European contract law. He has lectured widely in Ireland and abroad.
Languages: Holds a diploma in Legal French.
Member: Associate of the Institute of Taxation in Ireland and a member of the Society of Trust and Estate Practitioners; a member of the Business Law Committee of the Law Society of Ireland and is chairperson of the Probate and Taxation Law Committee of the Dublin Solicitors Bar Association.
Education: Read for his primary degree in law at Trinity College, Dublin and took his masters degree in law at the London School of Economics, qualified as a solicitor in 1979.

MARREN, Tom

Reddy Charlton McKnight
Phone: Dublin (+353 1 66 19 500)
E-mail: tmarren@rcmck.com
Commercial property.
Position: Partner, with a strong background in commercial litigation and arbitration, now specialises in commercial property development and related commercial work, and has extensive experience in acting in all property-related transactions. He has a special interest in construction law and landlord and tenant law, and acts as legal adviser to a number of property-related companies.
Career: Partner, Reddy Charlton McKnight for over 20 years.
Education: Qualified as a solicitor in 1978.

McAULIFFE, Lorna

Reddy Charlton McKnight
Phone: Dublin (+353 1 66 19 500)
E-mail: lmcauliffe@rcmck.com
Partner and head of the litigation department.
Position: Has a wide-ranging depth of experience acting for plaintiffs and defendants from district to Supreme Court level, initially specialised in the area of criminal law and personal injury litigation then progressed to work on landmark product liability cases which had far-reaching ramifications in the state. Lorna has dealt with a wide range of commercial litigation disputes and has considerable experience in the following: media law; intellectual property disputes; construction law; property disputes; arbitration and employment disputes (including injunctions and EAT actions).
Career: Lorna McAuliffe is a partner in the firm and head of the litigation department. She has represented very high profile clients before the Moriarty and Flood tribunals. Lorna has gained considerable experience in sports administrative law, acting for both professional players and European clubs, which included injunctive challenges against administrative rules of European sports bodies. Since her appointment as head of the litigation department, she has successfully defended the GAA against actions, which had serious implications for the organisation and has advised on many issues through these challenging times.
Education: University College, Cork (BCL; LLB).

McEVOY, Bernard

McEvoy Partners
Phone: Dublin (+353 1 415 5900)
E-mail: bmce@mcevoypartners.ie
Corporate department.
Position: Partner, providing corporate legal services to national and international clients. Bernard's particular area of expertise is mergers and acquisitions, equity and debt fundraisings.
Career: Qualified in 1982, Bernard was a partner in two other law firms before establishing McEvoy Partners in 2002.
Languages: English.
Member: Incorporated Law Society of Ireland; Law Society of England and Wales.
Education: University College, Dublin (1978 BCL).
Personal: Born 1958; resides Dublin.
Leisure: Running and cycling.

O'BRIEN, Orlaith

McEvoy Partners
Phone: Dublin (00 353 1 415 5900)
E-mail: oob@mcevoypartners.ie
Corporate department.
Position: Partner, providing corporate legal services to national and international clients. Orlaith has extensive experience in advising Irish companies on domestic and international corporate law issues. She has guided a number of Irish and UK companies through the process required to achieve a listing on the Alternative Investment Market of the London Stock Exchange and works with clients on their fundraisings and acquisitions.
Career: Qualified 1999, a founding partner of McEvoy Partners.
Languages: English.
Member: Incorporated Law Society of Ireland; Institute of Taxation in Ireland.
Education: Trinity College, Dublin (1993 BBS).
Personal: Born 1971; resides Dublin.

ISRAEL

ALTER, Avi, Dr

Dr Avi Alter & Co Law Offices
Phone: Tel Aviv (+972 3 696 6633)
E-mail: avi@altertax.co.il
Position: Senior partner at Dr Avi Alter & Co, Israel's leading firm on taxation matters. Specialist areas of expertise include: international tax planning and tax solutions, taxation of mergers and acquisitions, taxation of public offerings, ESOPs and ESPPs; taxation of hi-tech companies. Also handles taxation of corporations and individuals, direct and indirect taxation, tax litigations and arbitrations, betterment tax, trust taxation and management, tax treaties, offshore companies, capital gains tax, real estate, non-profit organisations, and obtaining taxation pre-rulings from Israel tax authorities. Initiator of tax legislation and provider of legal opinions.
Career: Former Deputy Income Tax Commissioner and chief legal counsel to the national Income Tax Commission of Israel (1986); former chairman of IFA-Israel; Israel's representative on the IFA Scientific Committee; chairman of the Tax Committee of the Israel Bar Association; chairman of tax committee, the Chamber for Co-Ordination, Economic Organisations in Israel; co-ordinator of taxation subjects at the Business Administration Faculty of T.A.U.; lecturer in Business Administration and Law Faculties at Tel Aviv University, Bar Ilan and Hebrow (Jerusalem) Universities and several academic colleges. Author of official explanations of I.R.S. Circulars (Collection of Instructions and Practices of the Income Tax Commission). Served in ten public committees on taxation: Bank's Bad Debts (Givoli 1989); Mergers and Acquisitions (Agron 1992); Tax reform in Real Estate (Rabinovitz 2001); Encouragement of Capital Investments Law in Israel (Dalia Ytsick, Minister of Trade and Industry and Silvan Shalom, Ministerof Finance, 2002); Reform of Personal and International Taxation (Rabinovitz 2002); and more. Author and editor of 11 books on taxation, including: 'The VAT Book' (with Prof Gross), 'Reform in the Real Estate Taxation' (50th amendment, 2002); 'Reform in Capital Market Taxation' (2002); 'Reform in International Taxation' (2003); 'Tax Treaties' (2004) encyclopedia (vol 1-2) with O Kalif; Book of 111 Tables of Tax Treaties (2004); 'Stamp Duty Law' (2005). Active lecturer and organiser of public lectures

at the C.P.A. Israeli Institution and other public organisations.
Languages: English, Hebrew, Russian.
Member: Israel Bar Association; IFA - Israel.
Education: Tel Aviv University (1981 BA magna cum laude; 1985 doctorate - direct track bypassing master's degree).
Personal: Born 1953; resides Tel-Aviv.
Leisure: Spending time with family and friends.

BAND, Tal

S. Horowitz & Co
Phone: Tel Aviv (+972 3 567 0604)
E-mail: talb@s-horowitz.co.il
Intellectual property group.
Position: Partner whose practice focuses on litigation and rendering advice in relation to various areas of intellectual property law, including patents, trade marks, trade secrets and copyright. Litigation experience includes the civil courts as well as the Israeli Patents and Trade Marks Office. Particular emphasis is placed on the pharmaceutical industry, with that group of the firm's clientele comprising pharmaceutical companies receiving representation and advice on issues of particular interest to that industry, not only with respect to IP law, but on regulatory matters and commercial law as well.
Career: Trained at the Supreme Court and S. Horowitz & Co; qualified 1984; partner 1990. Lecturer on intellectual property, Law Faculties of Tel-Aviv, Haifa and Hebrew Universities. Editor of 'Mishpatim' Hebrew University Law Review (1981-83); author Israeli chapter in 'International Intellectual Property Litigation' (FT 1997); and 'Intellectual Property World Desk Reference (Kluwer). Ranked as a leading lawyer and expert for intellectual property matters in Israel by 'Global Counsel 3000' and 'European Legal Experts'. Secretary Israeli Group of Association Internationale pour la protection de la Propriete Industrielle (AIPPI) 1998-2004; chairman Intellectual Property Committee Lex Mundi 1997-2001.
Languages: English, Hebrew.
Member: Israel Bar; Law Revision Committees (patents, trade marks, TRIPS, Patent Office practice, standards); president Israeli Group of Association Internationale pour la protection de la Propriete Industrielle (AIPPI); International Trade Mark Association (INTA); ALAI; AIPPI.
Education: Law School, Hebrew University (1983 LLB cum laude).
Personal: Born 1957; resides Tel-Aviv.

BLOCH, Anthony

S. Horowitz & Co
Phone: Tel Aviv (+972 3 567 0631)
E-mail: anthonyb@s-horowitz.co.il
Corporate and banking group.
Position: Partner dealing with all matters relating to cross-border and domestic corporate and banking law, including syndicated and non-syndicated bank financings, technology transfers and intellectual property commercialisation, joint ventures, mergers and acquisitions, IPOs, and advising international clients on operating, conducting and developing their business and trading activities in Israel.
Career: Trained Mallinick & Associate, South Africa; qualified as South African lawyer 1988; partner Mallinick & Associate London 1988; trained and qualified S. Horowitz & Co 1992; partner 1999. Ranked as a leading lawyer and expert for corporate/M&A, projects, banking and finance matters in Israel by 'Global Counsel 3000', and banking and finance and corporate and commercial by 'European Legal Experts' and 'Chambers Global'.
Languages: English, Hebrew.
Member: Israel Bar.
Education: University of Cape Town, South Africa (1983 BA; 1985 LLB cum laude; 1990 LLM cum laude).
Personal: Born 1962; resides Raanana.

COHEN, David

Cohen Legal Partners
Phone: Herzliya Pituach (+972 9 957 5011)
E-mail: david.cohen@clplegal.com
Position: Senior partner and founder of the firm. David has been very active during the past few years in AIM-related and UK public investment work in respect of Israeli companies, including the listings of Servision PLC and Dori Media Ltd on the AIM market. He is currently in the process of establishing a technology investment fund for clients which is intended to commence activities during 2006. In addition to his public offering work, David has advised on international mergers, joint ventures, transactions with distributors and agents, software-related matters and others. He has been involved in a number of investment structures, including private offering of shares through English entities and offerings on the London Capital Markets including the TechMark (LSE) and AIM. He has also respresented technological companies in offerings on NASDAQ in their corporate and commercial dealings and in labour matters and has acted for the commercial arm of the Weizmann Institute and that of Hadassa Hospital in commercial transactions. David specialises in local and international aspects of corporate and commercial law, real estate, property, international trade, business transactions and international project finance. He maintains close ties to the UK and many commercial spheres.
Career: Articled Denton Hall (now Denton Wilde Sapte); admitted as a solicitor of the Supreme Court of England and Wales 1992; made aliyah to Israel 1992; admitted to the Israel Bar 1995; worked in two prominent law firms in Israel before establishing Cohen Legal Partners; editor of 'Israel-British Trade' (quarterly journal of the Israel British Chamber of Commerce).
Languages: Fluent in English, Hebrew, French, Russian, Spanish and Italian.
Member: Managing committee member IBLA (Israel-British Law Assocation); board member Israel British Chamber of Commerce; tax committee International Bar Assocation; STEP (Society of Trust and Estate Practitioners).
Education: Cambridge University (1988 Hons Law).

DANZIGER, Yoram, Dr

Danziger, Klagsbald & Co
Phone: Ramat Gan (+972 3 611 0700)
E-mail: yoram@danklaw.co.il
Heads the corporate department of the firm and specialises in corporate law.
Position: Managing partner and co-founder specialising in all areas of business law, with vast experience in corporate reconstructions, joint ventures and M&A activity. He often serves as legal counsel to international corporations operating in Israel and gained a considerable reputation in the representation of Israeli companies operating worldwide. He frequently uses his expertise to serve as an arbitrator and mediator resolving a wide variety of disputes.
Career: Awarded the Israeli Association for Parliamentarism's prize; appointed by the Minister of Justice to the official committee to review the structure and operations of the Official Receiver and General Custodian. Former member of Board of Editors, Tel Aviv University Law Review; vice-editor, Israeli Bar Law Review; author of a book entitled 'The Right to Information about the Company' (2000), as well as a wealth of other legal articles both in Israel and UK, focusing mainly on corporate law; lecturer in law, Tel Aviv University Faculty of Law from 1981 to date; co-chairman of the Institute of Continuing Legal Studies of the Israeli Bar Association.
Languages: English, Hebrew.
Member: Israeli Bar Association since 1980.
Education: University of Tel Aviv Faculty of Law (LLB and LLM); London School of Economics (1983, PhD in law), specialising in take-over bids (tender offers).
Personal: Born 1953.

DAVIS, Clifford

S. Horowitz & Co
Phone: Tel Aviv (+972 3 567 0633)
E-mail: cliffordd@s-horowitz.co.il
Corporate and banking group.
Position: Partner dealing with all matters relating to cross-border and domestic corporate and banking law, including mergers and acquisitions, joint ventures, IPOs, syndicated and non-syndicated bank financings, securities law, intellectual property licensing, and advising international clients on operating, conducting and developing their business and trading activities in Israel.
Career: Trained Gouldens (now part of Jones Day) City of London; qualified as English solicitor 1989; associate corporate department Gouldens 1989-95; trained and qualified S. Horowitz & Co 1996; partner 2002. Contributor World Bank's 'Corporate Governance Project' and author of articles in 'International Financial Law Review' and 'Global Counsel 3000'. Ranked as a leading Israeli lawyer and expert for corporate/M&A by 'European Legal Experts', 'Chambers Global' and 'IFLR 1000', and for corporate/M&A, projects, banking and finance, and telecoms by 'Global Counsel 3000'.
Languages: English, Hebrew.
Member: Israel Bar; Law Society of England and Wales; City of London Law Society; associate member

American Bar Association; committee member of: The Israel-British Law Association; Task Force on International Acquisition Transactions (sub-committee of the Section of Business Law, American Bar Association); Negotiated Acquisitions (a committee of American Bar Association).
Education: Bristol University (1986 LLB Hons); College of Law, Guildford (1987).
Personal: Born 1964; resides Tel-Aviv.
Leisure: Family life, travelling, history; Chelsea Football Club.

EFRAT, Zvi
Gornitzky & Co
Phone: Tel Aviv (+972 3 710 9191)
E-mail: efrat@gornitzky.co.il
Corporate and commercial.
Position: Senior partner specialising in banking and finance, mergers and acquisitions, international trade and transactions. His clients range from multinational public companies to private family-owned companies. Mr Ephrat is able to draw on his years of experience in international law and banking to assist his clients both as a business adviser and as a lawyer. A significant part of his practice involves serving as legal counsellor for personal and commercial matters to one of Israel's leading business families. In this capacity, Mr Ephrat provides both legal and business advice to the companies and shareholders of this major conglomerate. He also represents and helps to structure the conglomerate's various subsidiaries and has also assisted its related companies in shipping, regulatory and antitrust matters, technology investments, corporate finance, manufacturing and energy, amongst others. He has regularly advised various public Israeli companies. Since 1987, Mr Ephrat has been in private practice, where significant transactions include: the privatisation by acquisition of one of the largest shipping companies from the Israeli government; investments in public semiconductor company and the subsequent financings and refinancing of its growth; acquisition of a public cable manufacturing company and the subsequent sale of its activities to an international competitor; established venture capital funds.
Career: Admitted 1972; senior partner Gornitzky & Co since 2001 when the firm he founded and led, Ephrat Smith & Co merged with Gornitzky. Mr Ephrat has also served as a director of the following companies: Granite Hacarmel (Israeli public company) and its subsidiary Sonol 1982-87 - as senior representative of Bank Hapoalim; Ampal (US public company) 1983-87 - as senior representative of Bank Hapoalim; Bank Hapoalim, Switzerland 1982-87, and also served as a director of two other Bank Hapoalim subsidiaries; Bank Mizrachi 1995 to present, and also serves as a member of the executive committee, audit committee and credit committee; chairman of the daily newspaper Davar Rishon 1995-97.
Languages: Hebrew, English.
Member: Israel Bar Association.
Education: Hebrew University of Jerusalem (1966 LLB).

FELIX, Martyn
Cohen Legal Partners
Phone: Herzliya Pituach (+972 9 957 5011)
E-mail: martyn.felix@clplegal.com
Position: A senior associate, Martyn has experience in corporate finance, general corporate and commercial work. In particular, he acts for financial and industry clients and advises on mergers and acquisitions, joint ventures, reorganisations and capital market transactions. As a member of CLP's venture capital team, Martyn acts for a number of venture capital funds in portfolio investments both in Israel and abroad. He specialises in local and international aspects of corporate and commercial law, real estate, property, international trade, business transactions and international project finance and maintains close ties to the UK and in many commercial spheres.
Career: Admitted to practice in Israel 2001; prior to joining Cohen Legal Partners 2006, worked for prominent Israeli law firms as well as acquiring additional professional experience in the Ministry of Justice and the Judge Advocate General Department.
Languages: Fluent in Hebrew and English.
Education: Queen Mary & Westfield College, London (1998 LLB).
Personal: Born 1976.

HACMUN, Amos
Heskia-Hacmun Law Firm
Phone: Tel Aviv (+972 3 608 1122)
E-mail: amos.hacmun@hh-law.co.il
Commercial, corporate, banking and international transactions.
Position: Managing partner.
Career: Negotiated and represented a European banking group in the sale of a 40% controlling interest in an Israeli bank. He was also nominated by an international banking group to serve as a board member at the Israel Continental Bank. Regularly consults for financial institutions in corporate, regulatory and credit matters. Headed a purchase transaction of a local company by an international group of companies specialising in the manufacture of hardware for the telecommunications industry, and also led the licensing of technology and know-how essential for the establishment of a semiconductor Fab project in northern Israel, at a cost of US$1.5bn. Handled the representation of a publicly traded German company active in the field of advanced technology. Handled the Israeli aspects of a credit facility exceeding US$300m extended by a consortium of banks. Represented investors in a financing and acquisition agreement of an Israeli company which is a market leader in the field of remote meter readings. Represented a group of investors in the acquisition of a company with innovative technology for the food and agricultural industries. Has published various articles in the legal sections and on the internet.
Languages: English, German, Hebrew.
Member: Board member of the German-Israeli lawyers association.
Education: Bar-Ilan University (1997 LLB).
Personal: Born 1972; resides Tel Aviv.

HERTMAN, Alex
S. Horowitz & Co
Phone: Tel Aviv (+972 3 567 0629)
E-mail: alexh@s-horowitz.co.il
Dispute resolution group.
Position: Partner dealing with all matters relating to litigation with particular emphasis on commercial litigation, hostile takeovers, shareholders' disputes, banking litigation, commercial administrative law litigation and arbitration.
Career: Trained S. Horowitz & Co; qualified 1982; partner 1988. Lecturer on lawyer's professional ethics at the Hebrew University until 2002, and at the Administrative College 2001-03. Ranked as an Israeli leading lawyer and expert for litigation and arbitration by 'European Legal Experts', for dispute resolution by 'Global Counsel 3000', and for general commercial litigation by 'Chambers Global'. Chairman Ethics Committee of Tel-Aviv and Central District of the Israel Bar Association and member of the District Committee 1995-99; member board of directors of the international association of law firms, Lex Mundi 1996-2000; chairman National Ethics Committee of the Israel Bar Association, chairman of the Committee for the Revision of the Ethics Rules, member of the Central Committee of the Israel Bar 1999-2003.
Languages: English, Hebrew.
Member: Israel Bar; president International Association of Jewish Lawyers and Jurists; member Appointing Committee of the Attorney General of the State of Israel.
Education: The Hebrew Univeristy of Jerusalem (1981 LLB cum laude).
Personal: Born 1956; resides Tel Aviv.

HESKIA, Dor
Heskia-Hacmun Law Firm
Phone: Tel Aviv (+972 3 608 1122)
E-mail: dor.heskia@hh-law.co.il
Corporate and litigation.
Position: Managing partner in charge of commercial and litigation matters.
Career: Has an impressive track record in lawsuits concerning the various aspects of foreign companies with their Israeli partners, distributors and commercial agents. Has been nominated to represent a well-known European bank in its defence against a derivative lawsuit involving a claim for the amount of NIS152m from former directors and officers at a local bank. He won an appeal against an Israeli bank concerning the issue of banking secrecy and client information. Was appointed by a well-known German telecom company to head its representation in a complex dispute with its Israeli partners. The dispute included a series of lawsuits, one of which involved a derivative lawsuit against the major shareholder and its board members. Mr Heskia's defence was successful, and the ruling set a precedent as it was the first time such a lawsuit was rejected on grounds of lack of good faith. Mr Heskia

also represented a prominent singer, and former winner of The Eurovision Song Contest, in a lawsuit against the Israeli telecommunications company Bezek International. Mr Heskia claimed that the rights of his client, especially the right to publicity, were being compromised by the telecommunications company. The infringement was confirmed, and the parties came to a settlement, which included an apology from Bezek International before the singer. Mr Heskia is active in liquidation and insolvency proceedings. He was nominated as liquidator of a number of companies and successfully obtained protection from the court (stay of proceedings) for clients that aimed to restructure their businesses to avoid bankruptcy. Represented former steel industry leader before the District and Supreme Courts in matters concerning bankruptcy and white-collar crime. Represented the leading Israeli file sharing website in a lawsuit that was brought against it by the music and film industries. Was nominated to defend an internationally well-known manufacturer of fragrance and cosmetics products in a claim brought against it by its former Israeli distributor.
Languages: English, Hebrew.
Education: Beer Sheva University (1989, BSc Electrical and Computer Engineering); Haifa University (1991, Advanced Management Studies); Bar Ilan University, Tel Aviv (1997, LLB).
Personal: Born 1964; resides Tel Aviv.

HORESH, Yehoshua

S. Horowitz & Co
Phone: Tel Aviv (+972 3 567 0618)
E-mail: yehoshuah@s-horowitz.co.il
Dispute resolution group.
Position: Partner dealing with all matters relating to litigation with particular emphasis on commercial litigation (specialising in energy and infrastructure), antitrust, tenders' law, administrative law, planning and building law, arbitration and public enquiry committees.
Career: Trained S. Horowitz & Co; qualified 1976; partner 1982. Ranked as an Israeli leading lawyer and expert for litigation and arbitration and real estate by 'European Legal Experts', and for general commercial litigation by 'Chambers Global'.
Languages: English, Hebrew, Hungarian.
Member: Israel Bar.
Education: Tel-Aviv University (1975 LLB).
Personal: Born 1949; resides Moshav Bnei-Tzion.

KLAGSBALD, Avigdor, Dr

Danziger, Klagsbald & Co
Phone: Ramat Gan (+972 3 611 0700)
E-mail: dori@danklaw.co.il
Litigation department.
Position: Co-founder and head of litigation department; has vast experience handling high-profile and precedent-setting cases; has represented domestic and international individuals and business enterprises of all sizes, and has argued numerous cases before the Israeli Supreme Court, lower courts, and other judicial and administrative tribunals. He has set several notable precedents in the areas of corporate law, constitutional law, bids and tenders, antitrust, white-collar and economic criminal law.
Career: Former member of Board of Editors, Tel Aviv University Law Review; author of a book entitled 'Tribunals of Enquiry' (2001), as well as a variety of legal articles in both Israel and the UK focusing mainly on constitutional law and administrative law; lecturer in law in the Inter-disciplinary Center for the Studies of Business, Law and Technology, teaching courses in constitutional and administrative law.
Languages: English, Hebrew.
Member: Israeli Bar Association since 1981.
Education: University of Tel Aviv Faculty of Law (LLB and LLM); University of Tel Aviv (1988, PhD in law), specialising in tribunals of inquiry.
Personal: Born 1953.

MATALON, Moriel

Gornitzky & Co
Phone: Tel Aviv (+972 3 710 9191)
E-mail: matalon@gornitzky.co.il
Corporate and commercial.
Position: Managing partner specialising in infrastructure and energy projects, international trade and transactions, real estate, corporate and commercial transactions, hi-tech and communications, mergers and acquisitions, hotels. Mr Matalon has had significant experience in large infrastructure projects and in this capacity has represented the firm, inter alia, in the following matters: serving as the leading lawyer on behalf of the government of Israel in the Cross-Israel Highway Project; serving as the leading lawyer on behalf of the government of Israel on the Tel Aviv Light Railway Project; leading an international consortium for the world's largest sea-water desalination project at in Ashkelon, with an estimated investment value of $300m. As one of the leading commercial lawyers at Gornitzky & Co, Mr Matalon represented clients in significant commercial matters, including: involvement in the launching of Israel's first satellite TV company, by representing the group awarded the license to establish and broadcast satellite television, including receipt of license from the government and regulatory and legislative aspects up until appeals to the Israeli Supreme Court; representing the government of Israel in the privatisation and IPO of the government-owned company, Shekem 1990-93; acting on behalf of the government of Israel in the privatisation and sale of the Paz oil company 1984-87. Significant aspects of general practice have included involvement in hotels and tourism, where he represents leading international and Israeli hotel chains in industry related matters as well as in day to day legal matters; acting as a director of Bank Hapoalim Swiss; investments, where he has acted on behalf of leading local and foreign investors.
Career: Admitted 1975; served as an assistant to an Israeli government minister 1969-70; served at the Military Advocate-General Unit of the Israel Defense Forces, first as a military prosecutor, and later as the deputy head of the International Law department of the Israel Defense Forces 1970-75; associate Amen, Weissman and Butler, New York 1975-78; joined Gornitzky & Co 1978; partner 1981.
Languages: Hebrew, English.
Member: Israel Bar Association.
Education: Hebrew University (1970 LLB; 1974 LLM cum laude).

ORDO, Avi

S. Horowitz & Co
Phone: Tel Aviv (+972 3 567 0601)
E-mail: avio@s-horowitz.co.il
Intellectual property and dispute resolution groups.
Position: Partner whose practice focuses on commercial litigation and commercial disputes, with specific emphasis on all contentious matters relating to intellectual property law; litigation experience includes the civil courts as well as the Israeli Patents and Trade Marks Office; partner responsible for the patents and trade marks prosecution department of S. Horowitz & Co.
Career: Trained at Tel-Aviv District Court and S. Horowitz & Co; qualified 1993; partner 2000. Member editorial board of 'Iunei Mishpat' Tel-Aviv University Law Review 1989-91; assistant teacher Law Faculty, Tel-Aviv University 1991-93. Described as 'highly recommended' in the area of intellectual property by the 2004 edition of 'European Legal 500'.
Languages: English, Hebrew.
Member: Israel Bar.
Education: Faculty of Law Tel-Aviv University (1992 LLB cum laude); Tel-Aviv University (1992 BA post-graduate economics).
Personal: Born 1966; resides Rishon-Lezion.

RUBIN, Pinhas

Gornitzky & Co
Phone: Tel Aviv (+972 3 710 9191)
E-mail: rubin@gornitzky.co.il
Corporate and commercial.
Position: Chairman and senior partner specialising in taxation; antitrust; capital markets; banking and finance; litigation; international trade and transactions; class actions; white-collar crime; insolvency and liquidations. Acting across a broad range of legal fields, Mr Rubin has extensive involvement in the firm's - and in Israel's - most significant transactions. Recent transactions include: mergers, acquisitions and reorganisations of leading Israeli companies including Israel's largest energy companies; the structuring of a three-way merger of three publicly-traded Israeli insurance companies; structuring of a merger between Israel's two largest food manufacturers; acting on behalf of Israel's largest banks in mergers and acquisitions; representation of Israel's largest bank, in its share offering by prospectus to accredited foreign investors; representation of Israel's major companies in IPOs; assisting Israel's largest commercial groups in tax planning; representation of high-profile corporate leaders in white-collar criminal activities; involvement in taxation matters on behalf of leading international telecommunications, hi-tech, financial services and banking companies in Israel; litigation, including representation of the leading Israeli industrial and

commercial holding companies, Israeli banks and insurance companies, foreign reinsures and the Tel Aviv Stock Exchange, in class action suits; acting on behalf of US and Israeli investors in the acquisition of a controlling interest in Israel's largest bank; regular representation of Israel's largest banks on various corporate and tax issues; advising and litigation on behalf of the Israel's leading insurance companies on various corporate, tax and commercial matters; representation of the CEO of a leading company, traded both in the US and Israel, in the appeal of a criminal tax violation in the Israeli Supreme Court which overturned the lower courts decision; representation of three former high-ranking government ministers in the governmental investigation committee regarding the collapse of bank securities on the Tel Aviv Stock Exchange; representation of a significant private shareholder in the sale of their interest in one of Israel's largest insurance companies; serving as a liquidator of a large international insurance company, including devising a plan for liquidation and negotiation with international creditors for an international 'scheme of arrangement'; representation of one of Israel's leading commercial families in their personal and commercial affairs, including their purchase of significant banking and insurance interests.
Career: Admitted 1974; recently appointed as the chairman of the advisory committee of one of the largest private real estate company in Canada; lecturer in tax, business and commercial law at Tel Aviv University and regularly lectures for the Bar Association's continuing legal education for both judges and attorneys and at legal, accounting and business conferences. Mr Rubin has been consistently ranked by local and international legal guides as one of Israel's top lawyers; he has been chosen in each of the past four years as one of the most influential people in the Israeli economy by the financial magazine 'The Marker'; rated as Israel's premier taxation lawyer and as one of the top five commercial lawyers in Israel in a poll among Israeli lawyers conducted by one of Israel's major daily newspapers and ranked as the most successful lawyer of 2003, by 'Globes', Israel's leading economical newspaper. Mr Rubin is considered by the Israeli economical press to be a 'key position' holder and was listed therein as on of the people who will 'open any door for you'.
Languages: Hebrew, English.
Member: Former member National Advisory Committee on Reform of the Israeli Court System; chairman Israel Bar Association's taxation committee 1985-99; member National Committee on Reform of Taxation (known as the 'Rabinovitz Committee') 2002.
Education: Tel Aviv University (1974 LLB).

SHENHAV, Ayal, Dr

Danziger, Klagsbald & Co
Phone: Ramat Gan (+972 3 611 0700)
E-mail: ayal@danklaw.co.il
Heads the hi-tech and tax practice groups of the firm. These practice groups are consistently ranked as among the best in Israel.
Position: Dr. Shenhav represents a large number of venture capital and private equity funds, advising them with respect to formation, tax structure and operations. He has also been involved in dozens of financing transactions representing investors, companies and founders. Dr. Shenhav also provides Israeli and international tax advice to a wide range of clients. In addition he represents many hi-tech companies, providing them with ongoing advice in areas such as financing rounds, technology transactions, mergers and acquisitions and more.
Career: Dr. Shenhav practiced law for several years at the New York office of Davis Polk and Wardwell LLP. He was previously the vice dean of the Radziner School of Law at the Inter-Disciplinary Center for the Studies of Business, Law and Techology, and was the founder of Ayal Shenhav & Co, which in January 2005 merged with Danziger, Klagsbald & Co. Dr. Shenhav is also an adjunct professor at Tel Aviv University, Bar Ilan University and the Inter-disciplinary Center for the Studies of Business, Law and Technology.
Languages: English, Hebrew.
Member: Israel Bar Association since 1991; New York Bar Association since 1992.
Education: Tel Aviv University Faculty of Law (LLB cum laude); New York University School of Law (LLM in taxation, and a Doctor of Juridical Science degree).
Personal: Born 1964.

SOFER, Ilan

S. Horowitz & Co
Phone: Tel Aviv (+972 3 567 0614)
E-mail: ilans@s-horowitz.co.il
Litigation group; commercial litigation, white-collar crime, antitrust and environmental department.
Position: Partner dealing with all matters relating to litigation with a focus on white-collar crime, antitrust, environmental, securities, fraud and insurance.
Career: Trained at the National Labour Court (with the president of the court) and S. Horowitz & Co; qualified 1994; partner 2000. Ranked as one of the top ten lawyers under the age of 40 in a survey carried out by 'Forbes' magazine of 100 leading Israeli law firms.
Languages: English, Hebrew.
Member: Israel Bar.
Education: Tell-Aviv University (1993 LLB).
Personal: Born 1965; resides Tel-Aviv.

STERN, Asgad

S. Horowitz & Co
Phone: Tel Aviv (+972 3 567 0604)
E-mail: asgads@s-horowitz.co.il
Dispute resolution and antitrust group.
Position: Partner dealing with all matters relating to commercial litigation, white-collar crime and dispute resolution, with a particular emphasis on antitrust and class actions.
Career: Trained S. Horowitz & Co; qualified 1974; partner 1980. Lecturer in legal procedure, antitrust and health insurance at various institutions. Ranked as a leading lawyer and expert for competition in Israel by 'European Legal Experts' and 'Global Counsel 3000'. Member management board Bar-Ilan University.
Languages: English, German, Herbrew.
Member: Israel Bar.
Education: Tel-Aviv University (1973 LLB).
Personal: Born 1947; resides Tel-Aviv.

WEINROTH, Avraham, Dr

Dr J Weinroth & Co
Phone: Tel Aviv (+972 3 718 1111)
E-mail: avi@weinrothlaw.com
Litigation, commercial.
Position: Senior partner; has developed an impressive career in the fields of commercial litigation, corporate law, banking law, administrative law, and many others. Deals with a variety of clients - personal, corporate and official bodies.
Career: Admitted to the Israeli Bar 1989; senior partner Dr J Weinroth & Co; lecturer at Tel Aviv University Law School (governmental companies, banking law, Jewish law); has published numerous books and articles on the subjects of governmental corporations, interest, lending, unlawful linking of bank services, taxation of not-for-profit organisations and more.
Languages: Hebrew, English, German.
Education: Bar Ilan University (1988 cum laude).
Personal: Born 1963.

WEINROTH, Jacob

Dr J Weinroth & Co
Phone: Tel Aviv (+972 3 718 1111)
E-mail: jacob@weinrothlaw.com
Litigation.
Position: Areas of practice include: general practice, civil and criminal litigation, corporate and commercial law. Handles a wide range of litigation work, including commercial cases, securities law, company liquidations, client-bank relations, family law and personal status. Has built up a reputation in the field of white-collar offences. Has represented two prime ministers, Ariel Sharon and Benjamin Netanyahu, a former president, Ezer Weizman, many government ministers, police chiefs and other notable figures.
Career: Admitted to Israeli Bar 1973; founder and senior partner Dr J Weinroth & Co since 1974. Currently lectures at Tel Aviv University in: insolvency and corporate law, Jewish law, white-collar crime, and philosophy. Publications include: 'The Law of Corporate Insolvency' (1978).
Languages: Hebrew, English, German.
Education: Tel Aviv University (1973 LLB; 1975 LLM; 1982 Doctor of Law).
Personal: Born 1947.
Leisure: Music, chess.

ZELICHOV, Ariel

Gornitzky & Co
Phone: Tel Aviv (+972 3 710 9191)
E-mail: zelichov@gornitzky.co.il
Corporate and commercial.
Position: Mr Zelichov is a transactional lawyer specialising in infrastructure and energy projects; real estate; capital markets; banking and finance. Over the last 20 years he has developed an expertise in advising companies on all forms of financing and securities

options and M&A strategy. His client base includes large corporations, infrastructure and project finance groups and large real estate development companies. Significant transactions in which Mr Zelichov has been involved include: acting as a legal adviser to Israel's largest land and property development group, first representing the purchasers of control of the company and then representing the company and its major subsidiary in its reorganisation and listing on the stock exchange; acting as legal adviser to a private company in the purchase of control of one of Israel's major banks; advising the state of Israel and private consortiums in some of Israel's largest BOTs including the Cross-Israel Highway project and light railways; managing the sale and acquisition of large companies in industry, finance and others; representing foreign investors in banking and trade projects in Israel; acting on behalf of UK-based investors in Israeli real estate investments; serving as the legal adviser to some of Israel's largest real estate, construction and land development companies, and other significant investors in real estate; representation of Israel's major companies in IPOs; broad commercial involvement on behalf of large public and private companies in matters of securities law, reorganisations and purchase offers, and so on; serving as an arbitrator and mediator of various controversies. Mr Zelichov has been recognised as an expert in the respected legal guides in the fields of project finance and banking.
Career: Admitted 1982.
Languages: Hebrew, English.
Member: Israel Bar Association.
Education: Hebrew University (1981 LLB).

ITALY

ACCIARI, Luciano, Avv
Di Tanno e Associati
Phone: Rome (+39 06 845661)
E-mail: l.acciari@ditanno.it
Position: Partner.
Career: Finmeccanica S.p.A. (large multiutility State owned company) in the legal, corporate and tax department until September 1996. Co-ordinated the major M&A transactions of the group as regards legal, corporate and tax matters.
Languages: English, French.
Education: Università La Sapienza (Rome).
Personal: Born 1945, resides Rome.

ADONNINO, Pietro
CMS Adonnino Ascoli & Cavasola Scamoni
Phone: Rome (+39 06 47815305-306)
E-mail: pietro.adonnino@cms-aacs.com
Domestic and international business taxation.
Position: Partner.
Career: Has broad experience in tax litigation. Represents clients before the Supreme Court and Court of Justice of EC. Professor of tax law at La Sapienza University of Rome. Has published more than 100 national and international specialised publications.
Languages: Italian, English, French and German.
Member: He has been a member of the Superior Finance Council of the Italian Ministry of Finance and of the ad hoc committee delivering advice on anti-avoidance rules following tax-payers ruling procedures. Former president of International Fiscal Association (IFA); now honorary president of it and president of IFA's Italian branch. Member of International Bar Association. He is member or chairman of the board of auditors of various major Italian companies. From 1979 to 1984 he has been member of the European Parliament and from 1984-85 chairman of the EU ad hoc committe of personal representatives of chiefs of state or governments of member states. He is a member of the Rome Bar and registered in the list of certified auditors.
Education: Law degree from 'La Sapienza' University, Rome (1953).

AMADIO, Renzo, Dott
Di Tanno e Associati
Phone: Rome (+39 06 845661)
E-mail: r.amadio@ditanno.it
Position: Partner. Certified public accountant. He focuses mainly on income taxes and VAT, merger and acquisitions, and company restructuring.
Career: Teaches specialised matters in tax law at a number of business schools and school of Ordine Dottori Commercialisti.
Languages: English.
Education: Università La Sapienza (Rome, 1982).
Personal: Born 1958, resides Rome.

ASCOLI, Giuseppe
CMS Adonnino Ascoli & Cavasola Scamoni
Phone: Rome (+39 06 47815305-306)
E-mail: giuseppe.ascoli@cms-aacs.com
Specialises in corporate tax and extraordinary operations.
Position: Partner.
Career: In 1978 he co-operated with an international audit firm; in 1979 he was in the financial police army department as an officer; in the same year on the register of the Dottori Commercialisti of Rome. Since 1988 he has been on the register of the Consulenti Tecnici at the Civil Court of Rome; since 1995 (the year of the registry's establishment) he has been on the register of Revisori Contabili. In 2003/4 he was appointed president of the Commissione Consultiva per la Fiscalità Internazionale del Consiglio dell' Ordine dei Dottori Commercialisti. He is used to carrying out various eminent tasks, committed to him by pubic and private institutions, such as company evaluations, tax and corporate assistance. He is currently co-operating with specialised magazines dealing with taxation topics through the publication of some articles.
Languages: Italian and English.
Member: A member of the International Fiscal Association (IFA) and is one of the members of the General Council.
Education: Law degree in economics from La Sapienza University of Rome in 1977. Also attended a graduate course in the US in 1980.

BRUNELLI, Fabio, Dott
Di Tanno e Associati
Phone: Rome (+39 06 845661)
E-mail: f.brunelli@ditanno.it
Position: Partner dealing in particular with investment funds structuring, private equity, M&A and financial investments.
Career: With the firm since 1989. Lecturer at the Central Tax Police School and at the Master in Private Equity of Politecnico of Milano - Borsa Italiana. Frequent speaker at national and international seminars and work-shops. Author of articles on tax matters.
Languages: English.
Member: IFA.
Education: Università La Sapienza (Rome).
Personal: Born 1963, resides Rome.

CANTAMAGLIA, Paolo, Dott
Di Tanno e Associati
Phone: Rome (+39 06 845661)
E-mail: p.cantamaglia@ditanno.it
Position: Partner with the firm since 1987.
Career: Certified public accountant, dealing in particular with insurances tax regime, M&A, private equity and company restructuring. Member of the board of inspection for insurances liquidation at the Ministry of Industry.
Languages: English.
Member: IFA (International Fiscal Association).
Education: Università La Sapienza (Rome).
Personal: Born 1954, resides Rome.

CAVASOLA, Pietro
CMS Adonnino Ascoli & Cavasola Scamoni
Phone: Rome (+39 06 478151)
E-mail: pietro.cavasola@cms-aacs.com
His areas of specialisation include corporate law, mergers and acquisitions, banking and finance, oil and gas, publishing law, joint ventures, international contracts, and antitrust.
Position: Partner.
Career: Admitted to Bar, Italy, 1977; partner of Studio Legale Cavasola, 1981; qualified to act in the Supreme Courts (Court of Cassation and State Council), 1991; registered auditor, 1994; member of CMS Executive committee, 2001. He has far-reaching international experience; his clients include several important national and multinational enterprises, operating in industries ranging from oil and gas, publishing and printing, construction, steel, automotive, car rental, transportation, pharmaceuticals and electronics, to general and credit insurance, brokerage and banking. He also represents a number of public entities and private individuals. He sits on the board of directors/auditors of several major Italian and international companies; has been appointed by the Bank of Italy to the boards of banks in special administration.

Languages: Italian, English, French and German.
Member: IBA; UIA; UAE; ABA; IGAL.
Education: In 1975 he graduated with honours in law, University of Rome, 1975; legal training at the EU in Bruxelles, 1976; assistant to civil law professor Stefano Rodotà at the University of Rome.

CECCON, Roberto

ACLAW - Ceccon & Associati
Phone: Padua (+39 049 87 74 630)
E-mail: r.ceccon@aclaw.it
Aviation law, international trade law, international contracts, joint ventures mergers and acquisitions, privatisations, finance, company law, arbitration, private clients.
Position: Founder partner.
Career: Admitted 1983, Italy; admitted to plead before the Supreme Court of Cassation, 1998. Arbitrator, American Arbitration Association, World Intellectual Property Organisation. Fellowship Chartered Institute of Arbitrators, London. Former Secretary General, Venice Chamber of National and International Arbitration. Professor, international arbitration, University of Trento, Faculty of Law. Author of publications on international arbitration. Speaker in numerous domestic and international conferences.
Languages: Italian, English and French.
Member: International Bar Association; European Lawyers Association; Italian Bar Association (Padua).
Education: University of Padua (1979 JD).
Personal: Born 1954.
Leisure: Golf.

DI TANNO, Tommaso

Di Tanno e Associati
Phone: Rome (+39 06 845661)
E-mail: t.ditanno@ditanno.it
Position: Founding partner. Full professor of international tax law at Cassino University; editor-in-chief of 'Bollettino Tributario'. Board member of INA; chairman of Statutory Auditors of Vodafone (Italian subsidiary), and of Caltagirone. He focuses on international affairs, mergers and acquisitions, LBO and MBO, investments vehicles and structures.
Career: Until 1979 at Studio Fantozzi-Biscozzi (Milan); until 1982 Arthur Andersen (Rome); 1986 created Di Tanno e Associati. Member of EVCA tax and legal committee 1992-2000; tax adviser to the Minister of Finance 1996-2000; member of several commissions of study appointed by the Treasury or the Justice Ministers on tax and companies laws 1993-2002. Visiting professor of tax law at central school of tax police 1980-2000. Numerous works on fiscal topics (about 100), 'la Dual Income Tax', Giuffrè (1998); 'Plusvalenze patrimoniali', Ipsoa (1984); 'l'Iva nei rapporti con l'estero', Ipsoa (1981).
Languages: English.
Member: International Fiscal Association (speaker at several conventions).
Education: Degree in political science (administrative law branch) cum laude, La Sapienza University of Rome; public accountant, registered auditor.

FIORELLI, Andrea

Di Tanno e Associati
Phone: Rome (+39 06 845661)
E-mail: a.fiorelli@ditanno.it
Position: Partner. He focuses on international affairs, M&A, investment vehicles, private equity, customs duties and excises and tax litigation.
Career: Until 1994, officer in the Italian financial and fiscal police (Guardia di Finanza); European Union Anti-Fraud Office OLAF 1995-96; admitted to the Bar in 1993 and enrolled in the Rome Bar since 1996.
Languages: English, French.
Member: International Bar Association; International Fiscal Association.
Education: University of Urbino, law degree (cum laude); University La Sapienza, Rome, PhD in legislation of international institutions and markets; University Tor Vergata, Rome, degree in economic and financial security sciences.
Personal: Born 1965; resides Rome.

LAURO, Francesca

Lauro Sovani & Associati Studio Legale
Phone: Rome (+39 06 42 01 91 94)
E-mail: francesca.lauro@lauro-sovani.it
Employment and labour law.
Position: Partner of the firm. Specialises in labour and employment law since 1993. Assists national and multinational companies in relation to all aspects of employment law encompassing proceedings before employment tribunals.
Career: After gaining significant experience in corporate law as in-house counsel of several major multinational companies, Francesca specialised in employment law at Pavia e Ansaldo Law Firm. She then moved to the international law firm Lovells, where she was head of the employment team for four years. In 2004 she founded Lauro Sovani & Associates Law Firm.
Languages: Italian and English.
Member: Global Forum for Cross-Border Human Resources experts (XBHR).
Education: JD degree from University of Milan law faculty, 1987. Admitted to Rome Bar in 1997.
Personal: Born 1963; resides Rome.
Leisure: Sailing.

MODENESI, Stefano

DLA Piper Rudnick Gray Cary
Phone: Rome (+39 06 688 801)
E-mail: stefano.modenesi@dlapiper.com
Litigation.
Position: Office managing partner of the Rome office.
Career: Qualified 1994; trainee Studio Bianchi & Associati; admitted to Milan Bar 1999.
Languages: Italian, French, English.
Member: Board of directors Permanente Museum of Fine Arts of Milan; board of directors of UGIVI; Milan Bar Association.
Education: Liceo Classico Manzoni (secondary school); University of Milan.
Personal: Born 1970; resides Rome.

PETRECCA, Stefano, Avv

Di Tanno e Associati
Phone: Rome (+39 06 845661)
E-mail: s.petrecca@ditanno.it
Position: Partner since 1989. He focuses mainly on M&A, company restructuring and tax litigation.
Career: Admitted to the Rome Bar in 1986 and to the Superior Court in 1996. Professor at the Tax Administration Superior School. Registered auditor.
Languages: English.
Member: IBA (International Bar Association) and ITPA (International Tax Planning Association).
Education: Università La Sapienza (Rome) (1982 degree cum laude).
Personal: Born 1958, resides Rome.

PORTALUPI, Nicoletta

Portalupi & Partners
Phone: Milan (+39 02 8907 8450)
E-mail: milano@portalupiepartners.com
Position: Managing partner specialising in real estate, and mergers and acquisitions. Clients include some of the major banks, merchant banks and developers.
Career: Admitted to Bar 1981; a founder and head of real estate department of Gianni Origoni & Partners; founder of Portalupi & Partners.
Languages: Italian, English, French, German.
Member: ULI; IBA; IPBA; Association des Femmes Chefs d'Entreprise.
Education: University of Milan (1976 JD magna cum laude).
Leisure: Collecting antique books.

ROMITA, Eugenio, Dott

Di Tanno e Associati
Phone: Milan (+39 02 762131)
E-mail: e.romita@ditanno.it
Position: Partner.
Career: Chartered accountant since 1992, lecturer at University of Cassino 1991-97, Direct Tax Working Party member at Fédération des Experts Comptables Européens (Brussels) 1997-99, partner Di Tanno e Associati since 2002. Author of articles on tax matters in Italian and international journals, speaker at tax seminars and conferences, lecturer at Tax High School of Ministry of Finance.
Languages: English.
Member: IFA.
Education: University of Cassino.
Personal: Born 1965, resides Milan.

SOVANI, Rosanna

Lauro Sovani & Associati Studio Legale
Phone: Rome (+39 06 42 01 91 94)
E-mail: rosanna.sovani@lauro-sovani.it
Employment and labour law.
Position: Partner of the firm. Specialises in labour and employment law and has in particular accrued skills in relation to those employment aspects linked to reorganisation and restructuring processes, M&A, agency relationships, outsourcing, transfer of business and draft of employment contracts for senior managers.

Career: Following her JD degree Rosanna Sovani worked for the Attorney General, then attended a stage (apprenticeship) at the EU office of Telecom Italia SpA. She then practiced as attorney at a well-known Rome boutique firm; she specialised in telecommunication and criminal law and consolidated her skills in labour law with Lovells from 2001. In 2004 she founded Lauro Savani and Associati Law Firm.
Languages: Italian and English.
Member: European Employment Lawyer Association (EELA).
Education: Attained her JD degree at LUISS of Rome in 1999. Admitted to the Italian Bar Association of Rome in 2002.
Personal: Born 1975; resides in Rome.
Leisure: Horse riding.

SUTTI, Federico

DLA Piper Rudnick Gray Cary
Phone: Milan (+39 02 80 61 81)
E-mail: federico.sutti@dlapiper.com
M&A/corporate/PFI.
Position: Regional managing partner of the Italian offices, dealing with all areas of corporate law, mergers and acquisitions and project finance.
Career: Qualified in 1989; trainee at Pavia e Ansaldo; admitted to Milan Bar 1992; admitted to Supreme Court 2005.
Languages: Italian, English.
Member: Milan Bar Association; ANIMP.
Education: Liceo Classico Leone XIII; University of Milan (law degree magna cum laude).
Personal: Born 1965; resides Milan.

TOGNONI, Marianna

Di Tanno e Associati
Phone: Rome (+39 06 845661)
E-mail: m.tognoni@ditanno.it
Position: Partner.
Career: Certified public accountant. Previously in the tax department of the Italian subsidiary of a multinational group, she has been with the firm since 1996. Her practice focuses on domestic and international tax law and includes corporate tax, VAT, tax planning, M&A, and taxation of non-profit entities. Author of articles in tax magazines and speaker at conferences and workshops.
Languages: English.
Member: International Fiscal Association (IFA).
Education: Università La Sapienza, Rome.
Personal: Born 1965; resides Rome.

JERSEY

BAKER, Stephen

BakerPlatt (Jersey)
Phone: St Helier (+44 1534 766 254)
E-mail: stephenbaker@bakerplatt.com
Senior partner, dealing with litigation.
Position: Senior partner specialising in the recovery of assets, the proceeds of fraud and corruption, financial crime, international investigation into co-operation and financial regulation. Important cases include the Government of Pakistan's asset recovery, Abacha recovery and Bank Cantrade C.I Ltd. He advised a notable state on FATF requirments.
Career: Manchester University (1987 LLB), Cambridge University (1989 LLM), Sidney Susssex College.
Languages: English.
Member: English Bar, Jersey Bar.
Education: Qualified 1989, 1989-90 joined Fraser Milner Casgrain Barristers and Solicitors (Toronto); 1990-99 door tennant, 7 Bedford Row, London; 1999-2003 worked as a senior adviser to the Attorney General of Jersey and in 2003 became an ad hoc expert to United Nations on matters of confiscation.
Personal: Born 1965; resides Jersey.
Leisure: Sport, rugby union in particular.

BINNINGTON, Alan

Mourant du Feu & Jeune
Phone: St Helier (+44 1534 609 380)
E-mail: alan.binnington@mourant.com
Mourant private wealth.
Position: Partner and advocate; advises on private wealth structures.
Career: Admitted 1981 to English Bar (Middle Temple); Jersey Bar 1984; joined Mourant du Feu & Jeune 1981; partner 1985; editorial board of the Jersey Law Review; one of Jersey's Law Commissoners.
Languages: English, French.
Member: Honorary Consul for Belgium in the Channel Islands; Association of Contentious Trust and Probate Specialists; Society of Trust and Estate Practitioners; International Academy of Estate and Trust Law.
Education: Victoria College; St Catharine's College, Cambridge (1980 MA).
Personal: Born 1958.

BIRTWISTLE, Daniel

Mourant du Feu & Jeune
Phone: St Helier (+44 1534 609 339)
E-mail: daniel.birtwistle@mourant.com
Funds, business affairs.
Position: Partner specialising in funds and mergers and acquisitions work.
Career: Admitted Jersey solicitor 1998; Jersey advocate 1999; partner Mourant du Feu & Jeune 2004.
Languages: English.
Member: Jersey Law Society.
Education: Victoria College, Jersey; Cardiff University (1994 Hons Law); BVC; 1995 ICSL.
Personal: Born 1972.

BREEN, Elizabeth

Mourant du Feu & Jeune
Phone: St Helier (+44 1534 609 240)
E-mail: liz.breen@mourant.com
Property, financial services.
Position: Partner and head of the property practice area which deals with commercial leases, development and joint venture agreements and associated documents, mortgages, corporate and private relocation, property management and all Jersey conveyancing-related matters.
Career: Admitted 1986 as Jersey solicitor; partner Mourant du Feu & Jeune 1993.
Languages: English, French.
Member: Society of Trust and Estate Practitioners; Whitely 90; Jersey Law Society.
Education: Southampton University (1976-79).
Personal: Born 1953.

CHAPMAN, Julia

Mourant du Feu & Jeune
Phone: St Helier (+44 1534 609 547)
E-mail: julia.chapman@mourant.com
Mourant international finance administration.
Position: Partner specialising primarily in the field of specialist collective investment structures and capital markets structures.
Career: Trained Simmons & Simmons, London; qualified England and Wales 1990; qualified Jersey 1995; Ogier & Le Cornu, Jersey 1990-94; joined Mourant du Feu & Jeune 1994; partner 1999; regularly makes contributions to professional publications; speaks at conferences and seminars.
Languages: English, French, Spanish.
Education: St Mary's Convent, Ascot; Queens' College, Cambridge (1986 BA Hons).
Personal: Born 1965.

CHAPMAN, Nicholas

Mourant du Feu & Jeune
Phone: St Helier (+44 1534 609 392)
E-mail: nicholas.chapman@mourant.com
Litigation.
Position: Associate specialising in general litigation.
Career: Trained Simmons & Simmons; English solicitor 1988; qualified Jersey advocate 1995; joined Mourant du Feu & Jeune 1997.
Languages: English, French.
Education: Dragon School, Oxford; Sherborne School, Dorset; University of East Anglia; University de Caen.
Personal: Born 1961.

CORBIN, Giles

Mourant du Feu & Jeune
Phone: St Helier (+44 1534 609 521)
E-mail: giles.corbin@mourant.com
Trusts.
Position: Head of trusts practice area since September 2004, currently practising in all areas of non-contentious trusts, advising leading Jersey corporate trustees on high and ultra high (over US$1bn net value) private trusts. Clients include Allen & Overy, JP Morgan, Kleinwort Benson, Royal Bank of Canada, BNP Paribas, Coutts, Equity Trust, UBS, Deutsche Bank and SG Hambros. Advice on creation, termination and power use with purpose, charitable and hybrid trusts. Interest in settlor reserve, power trusts, Guernsey and Cayman trust laws and indemnity issues. Contributor to statutory reform think tank on Trusts (Jersey) Law.

Career: Trained Ogier & Le Masurier; qualified Jersey solicitor 1999; Jersey advocate 2000; made partner Mourant de Feu & Jeune January 2005.
Languages: English, French.
Member: Jersey Law Society, Society of Trusts and Estate Practitioners.
Education: Victoria College, Jersey; Southampton University (1993 joint honours politics and law 2(1)); College of Law, Guildford (1995 LPC).
Personal: Born 1972; resides Jersey.
Leisure: Jersey Long Distance Swimming Club - swam to France from Jersey in August 2004; Jersey Triathlon Club; Jersey representative in Europa Truck Trials 2004; member of Royal Jersey Golf Club (12 handicap); PADI Nitrox certified diver.

COUTANCHE, Conrad

Mourant du Feu & Jeune
Phone: St Helier (+44 1534 609 203)
E-mail: conrad.coutanche@mourant.com
Private wealth management.
Position: Senior partner specialising in the needs of the private clients primarily in the fields of independent wealth management, cross-border estate work, estate planning including wills and trusts, and immigration.
Career: Admitted 1979, Jersey solicitor; partner Mourant du Feu & Jeune 1981.
Languages: French.
Education: Victoria College, Jersey.
Personal: Born 1946.

DAVIES, Claire

Mourant du Feu & Jeune
Phone: St Helier (+44 1534 609 336)
E-mail: claire.deacon@mourant.com
Private client litigation.
Position: Associate specialising in all areas of private client litigation.
Career: Jersey solicitor and advocate 1997.
Languages: English.
Education: Coventry University (Business law).
Personal: Born 1970.

DAVIES, Cyman

Mourant du Feu & Jeune
Phone: St Helier (+44 1534 609 346)
E-mail: cyman.davies@mourant.com
Funds.
Position: Partner leading the funds practice area and specialising in trust and mutual fund work, including retail and private equity funds.
Career: Admitted 1987 to English Bar (Middle Temple); 1989 Jersey Bar; partner Mourant du Feu & Jeune 1993; frequent speaker at conferences and contributor of articles including 'Financial & Commercial Handbook of the Channel Islands'; editorial panel of 'Trusts & Trustees'; assisting formulating amendments to both the Trusts (Jersey) Law 1994 and the Companies (Jersey) Law 1991; contributor of articles to legal journals.
Languages: English, French.
Member: Law society; Society of Trust and Estate Practitioners; International Tax Planning Association.
Education: University College, Oxford (1983-86).
Personal: Born 1965.

DAVIES, Nicola

Mourant du Feu & Jeune
Phone: St Helier (+44 1534 609 606)
E-mail: nicola.davies@mourant.com
Position: Chief executive.
Career: Admitted English Bar (Middle Temple) 1989; Jersey Bar 1991; joined Mourant du Feu & Jeune 1988 in commercial department; also worked for Mourant International Finance Administration; partner Mourant du Feu & Jeune 1995; deputy managing partner 2002-03; chief executive 2003; has spoken at numerous conferences across Europe and the USA; contributed to a number of professional journals.
Languages: English, French.
Member: Jersey Law Society; Jersey Capital Markets Working Group.
Education: Queen Elizabeth High School; St Hilda's College, Oxford (1988).
Personal: Born 1967; two children.
Leisure: Scuba diving, cooking, sailing.

DEVENPORT, Edward

Mourant du Feu & Jeune
Phone: St Helier (+44 1534 609 243)
E-mail: edward.devenport@mourant.com
Trusts, financial services, funds.
Position: Partner specialising in collective investment funds and trusts.
Career: Admitted English Bar (Middle Temple) 1988; admitted as Jersey solicitor 1993; joined Mourant du Feu & Jeune 1990; partner 1996.
Languages: English, French.
Member: Society of Trust and Estate Practitioners.
Education: Birmingham University (1986 LLB Hons).
Personal: Born 1965.

GOULD, Simon M

Mourant du Feu & Jeune
Phone: St Helier (+44 1534 609 367)
E-mail: simon.gould@mourant.com
Financial services, corporate and banking.
Position: Partner leading the financial services practice area and specialising in banking, financial services and corporate law.
Career: Pupillage 2 Gray's Inn Square, London 1992; joined Mourant du Feu & Jeune, 1992; associate 1997; partner 2000; regularly contributes to professional publications and speaks at conferences and seminars; member of Jersey Finance Industry working groups in relation to banking, financial services and anti-money laundering procedures.
Languages: English, French.
Member: Law Society of Jersey; Society of Trust and Estate Practitioners.
Education: LLB Hons (1990); Inns of Court School of Law (1991); Jersey law professional exams (1994).
Personal: Born 1966.

GUILLAUME, Marc

Mourant du Feu & Jeune
Phone: St Helier (+44 1534 609245)
E-mail: marc.guillaume@mourant.com
Corporate and banking, trusts.
Position: Associate specialising in offshore structures, trusts, pensions and employee share plans.
Career: Admitted English Bar 1993; Jersey Bar 1998.
Languages: English.
Education: Balliol College, Oxford.
Personal: Born 1968.

HAMEL, Nicole

Mourant du Feu & Jeune
Phone: St Helier (+44 1534 609579)
E-mail: nicole.hamel@mourant.com
Trusts.
Position: Associate specialising in legal advice on the creation and administration of trusts.
Career: Trained Mourant du Feu & Jeune, Jersey; qualified 1990; associate 1992.
Languages: English.
Member: Society of Trust and Estate Practitioners; Jersey Law Society.
Education: Convent FCJ, Jersey.
Personal: Born 1959.

HAMILTON, Michaela L

Mourant du Feu & Jeune
Phone: St Helier (+44 1534 609427)
E-mail: michaela.hamilton@mourant.com
Funds, corporate and banking.
Position: Partner specialising in investment funds, securitisations and structured finance.
Career: Trained Bond Pearce, Plymouth; qualified 1997; admitted England and Wales 1997; Jersey advocate 2001; associate Mourant du Feu & Jeune 2003.
Languages: English, French.
Member: Law Society of England and Wales; Law Society of Jersey.
Education: Beaulieu Convent School, Jersey; Exeter University (1993 BA French); College of Law, London (1994 Dip Law; 1995 Dip LP).
Personal: Born 1970; resides Jersey.

HERBERT, Tim

Mourant du Feu & Jeune
Phone: St Helier (+44 1534 609339)
E-mail: tim.herbert@mourant.com
Position: Managing partner, but client involved, maintained through specialisation in investment fund work, corporate affairs and mergers and acquisitions.
Career: Admitted 1982 to English Bar; Middle Temple; 1985 to Jersey Bar; joined Mourant du Feu & Jeune 1983; partner 1987; managing partner 2004; has spoken at conferences in the UK, US and Jersey and contributes to a number of professional journals. Director Channel Islands Stock Exchange.
Languages: English, French.
Member: International Bar Association; Institute of Directors; Honorary Consul for Finland.
Education: Trinity College, Oxford (1981).
Personal: Born 1959.

HICKLING, Robert

Mourant du Feu & Jeune
Phone: St Helier (+44 1534 609396)
E-mail: robert.hickling@mourant.com
Capital markets, corporate and banking.
Position: Partner leading the capital markets practice area and specialising in capital markets, investment funds, banking and structured finance, securitisation.
Career: Admitted as English solicitor 1987; Jersey solicitor 1998; partner 2000.
Languages: English, French.
Education: Birmingham University (1983).
Personal: Born 1962.

JAMES, Ian

Mourant du Feu & Jeune
Phone: St Helier (+44 1534 609335)
E-mail: ian.james@mourant.com
Capital markets, corporate and banking.
Position: Chairman.
Career: English solicitor 1976; Jersey solicitor 1986; joined Mourant du Feu & Jeune 1981; partner 1986.
Languages: English.
Member: International Bar Association.
Education: Queen's College, Oxford (1969-73).
Personal: Born 1950.

LACEY, Beverley

Mourant du Feu & Jeune
Phone: St Helier (+44 1534 609 371)
E-mail: beverley.lacey@mourant.com
Dispute resolution, financial services.
Position: Partner and crown advocate, specialising in commercial litigation, with particular specialism in shareholder disputes and company reorganisations, insolvency, regulatory compliance and investigations.
Career: Admitted English Bar; Inner Temple; 1985; Chambers of NP Valios QC 1985-90 (general common and commercial law); admitted Jersey Bar 1994; joined Mourant du Feu & Jeune 1990; partner 1996.
Languages: English, French, German.
Education: Eastwood Hall Park School; Leeds University (1984 LLB Hons).
Personal: Born 1962.
Leisure: Sailing, family.

MALOREY, Wendy

Mourant du Feu & Jeune
Phone: St Helier (+44 1534 609349)
E-mail: wendy.malorey@mourant.com
Business affairs.
Position: Partner leading the business affairs practice area and specialising in employment law, mergers and acquisitions, and all aspects of local business advice, including regulatory and corporate matters.
Career: Admitted as Jersey solicitor 1993; associate Mourant du Feu & Jeune 1995; partner 2000; regularly contributes to professional publications and speaker at conferences and seminars on employment law issues; chair of the Employment Forum (a statutory body set up to publicly consult and advise the Employment and Social Security Committee on employment legislation in Jersey).
Languages: English, French.
Member: Employment Forum; Employment Lawyers Association.
Education: University of London (1990 LLB).
Personal: Born 1967.
Leisure: Family, horse riding.

MILLAR, Elaine

Mourant du Feu & Jeune
Phone: St Helier (+44 1534 609129)
E-mail: elaine.millar@mourant.com
Business affairs, financial services.
Position: Associate and head of the M&A team; member of the corporate and commercial and data protection teams specialising in financial services, banking and financial services regulation.
Career: Qualified 1987; private practice in Glasgow, Bird Semple Fyfe Ireland and McGrigor Donald 1987-93; The Royal Bank Of Scotland Group 1993-2002, latterly director, Legal and Regulatory Services of Royal Bank of Scotland International Group; associate Mourant de Feu Jeune 2002 to date. Admitted as Jersey advocate in 2005. Co-authored chapter on Jersey law for publication on International Secured Transactions (Centre for International Legal Studies).
Languages: English.
Education: Greenfaulds High Scool, Cumbernauld; Edinburgh University (1984 LLB Hons; 1985 Diploma in Legal Practice).
Personal: Born 1962; resides Jersey.

PLATT, Stephen

BakerPlatt (Jersey)
Phone: St Helier (44 1534 613775)
E-mail: stephenplatt@bakerplatt.com
Managing partner.
Position: Managing partner, specialising in financial services regulation and the criminal abuse of financial services.
Career: Trained at Essex Court London and qualified 1995, became a partner of Bakerplatt in 2000. Mr Platt is the professional director of the International Compliance Association and a visiting lecturer at the University of Manchester Business School and is a door tenant at the chambers of David Farrer QC, 7 Bedford Row, London. His publications of note include: International Compliance Association Compliance and diploma programs and the 'MLRO Reference Guide'.
Languages: English.
Education: Lan (1993 hons), English barrister from 1995.
Personal: Born 1979.

RAINER, John

Mourant du Feu & Jeune
Phone: St Helier (+44 1534 609679)
E-mail: john.rainer@mourant.com
Funds, corporate and banking.
Position: Associate specialising in offshore structures, funds and corporate/commercial work.
Career: Trained Gouldens; qualified 2000; Mourant du Feu & Jeune 2000; qualified in Jersey 2003; associate 2004.
Languages: English, Spanish.
Member: Law Society of England and Wales; Jersey Law Society.
Education: Wellington College; University of Bristol (1996 LLB).
Personal: Born 1973; resides Jersey.
Leisure: Reading and tavel.

ROBINS, Ben

Mourant du Feu & Jeune
Phone: St Helier (+44 1534 609475)
E-mail: ben.robins@mourant.com
Capital markets, funds, corporate and banking.
Position: Partner specialising in structured finance, capital markets, private equity and property funds.
Career: Trained Speechly Bircham; qualified english solicitor 1996; Jersey solicitor 2000; joined Mourant du Feu & Jeune 1997; associate 2001; partner 2002.
Languages: English, French.
Member: Jersey Law Society.
Education: Victoria College, Jersey; University of Reading (1992 English Degree); College of Law, Guildford (1994 CPE and LPC legal exams).
Personal: Born 1971; resides Jersey.

SCHOLFIELD, W Brian

Mourant du Feu & Jeune
Phone: St Helier (+44 1534 609 601)
E-mail: brian.scholfield@mourant.com
Corporate and banking, capital markets, funds.
Position: Specialises in capital markets; structured finance; securitisations, investment funds and limited partnerships.
Career: Qualified as an Ontario, Canada barrister and solicitor 1986; Hong Kong solicitor 1997; English solicitor 1999; associate Goodmans, Toronto 1986; partner Goodmans 1993; co-managing partner Goodmans, Hong Kong 1995-99; joined Mourant du Feu & Jeune 1999. Currently a director of CVC Capital Partners Asia Limited and CVC Capital Partners Asim II Limited.
Languages: English.
Member: Law Society of England and Wales; Law Society of Upper Canada; Law Society of Hong Kong; Canadian Bar Association.
Education: University of Toronto (Juris Doctor; BA).
Personal: Born 1959.

SCOTT, Emma

Mourant du Feu & Jeune
Phone: St Helier (+44 1534 609188)
E-mail: emma.scott@mourant.com
Capital markets.
Position: Associate specialising in capital markets, securitisation and structured finance transactions.
Career: Articled Vaudreys (now Beachcroft Wansbroughs); qualified England and Wales 1996; Jersey advocate 1999; associate Mourant du Feu & Jeune 2003.
Languages: English, French.
Member: Law Society of England and Wales; Jersey Law Society.
Education: Jersey College for Girls; University of Bath (1992 BSc Hons 2(1) Business Administration); College

of Law, York (1993 CPE commendation; 1994 LPC distinction).
Personal: Born 1969; resides Jersey.

WESTON, Nigel
Mourant du Feu & Jeune
Phone: St Helier (+44 1534 609278)
E-mail: nigel.weston@mourant.com
Funds, corporate and banking.
Position: Partner specialising in investment funds, corporate, commercial, finance and regulatory law.
Career: Admitted English solicitor 1992; Jersey solicitor and advocate 1999.
Languages: English, French, Spanish.
Member: Law Society England and Wales; Jersey Law Society; Committee of Jersey Funds Association and chairman of legal sub-committee; Society of Trust and Estate Practitioners; Institute of Directors.
Education: Charterhouse, King's College London; College of Law, Guildford.
Personal: Born 1966.

WILSON, David
Mourant du Feu & Jeune
Phone: St Helier (+44 1534 609257)
E-mail: david.wilson@mourant.com
Dispute resolution, financial services, trusts.
Position: Partner specialising in commercial litigation, with expertise in complex fraud, asset tracing, insolvency, financial services regulation and trust, banking, corporate, professional negligence disputes.
Career: Cameron McKenna 1989-93; English solicitor 1991; joined Mourant du Feu & Jeune 1993; Jersey solicitor 1996; Jersey advocate 1997; associate 1997; partner 2000.
Languages: English, French, German.
Member: The Law Society; Jersey Law Society; Society of Trust and Estate Practitioners; Association of Contentious Trust and Probate Specialists; honorary member Commercial Bar Association.
Education: Gillotts' School, Henley on Thames; King James' College, Henley; King's College, University of London (1987 LLB Hons).
Personal: Born 1965.
Leisure: Family, sports, reading, piano.

LATVIA

KLAVINS, Filip K
Klavins & Slaidins LAWIN
Phone: Riga (+371 781 48 48)
E-mail: filips.klavins@klavinsslaidins.lv
Position: Founding partner of Klavins & Slaidins specialising in corporate and commercial law, mergers and acquisitions, corporate finance, securities and real estate.
Career: Attorney at Finley, Kumble, Wagner, Heine, Underberg, Manley, Myerson & Casey, New York; attorney Baker & McKenzie, New York; worked as lecturer in contract law, University of Latvia Law Faculty and Latvian Ministry of Foreign Affairs prior to beginning private practice in Latvia; founding partner Klavins & Slaidins 1992; has lectured on legal ethics, Stockholm School of Economics in Riga and University of Latvia Law Faculty; frequent speaker at numerous business and law conferences and events. Directorships: Arbitration of the Latvian Chamber of Commerce and Industry; Latvian National Opera Foundation; New Theatre of Riga Foundation.
Languages: English, Latvian.
Member: Latvian Bar; New York Bar; Connecticut Bar; International Bar Association; American Bar Association.
Education: Tufts University, Massachusetts (1983 BA cum laude); Duke University School of Law, North Carolina (1986 JD).

SLAIDINS, Raymond L
Klavins & Slaidins LAWIN
Phone: Riga (+371 781 48 48)
E-mail: raimonds.slaidins@klavinsslaidins.lv
Position: Founding partner of Klavins & Slaidins specialising in corporate and commercial law, mergers and acquisitions, corporate finance, securities and real estate.
Career: Attorney Carroll, Burdick & McDonough, San Francisco; senior corporate counsel Ingres Corporation, Alameda, California; worked as counsellor to the Foreign Minister of Latvia prior to beginning private practice in Latvia; founding partner Klavins & Slaidins 1992; registered trade mark agent in Latvia; has lectured on legal ethics, Riga Graduate School of Law and Stockholm School of Economics in Riga; frequent speaker at numerous business and law conferences and events, including IBA conferences.
Languages: English, Latvian.
Member: Latvian Bar; California Bar; International Bar Association; president American Chamber of Commerce in Latvia (board of directors since 1996).
Education: University of California at Berkeley (1980 BA); Santa Clara University, California (1984 JD).

LITHUANIA

OKINCZYC, Czeslaw
Sutkiene, Pilkauskas & Partners
Phone: Vilnius (+370 5 212 1192)
E-mail: czokinczyc@spp.lt
Corporate law practice group; real estate and real estate development practice group.
Position: Dealing with all areas of corporate law (including mergers and acquisitions, privatisation), commercial law, business financing, real estate and real estate development.
Career: Attorney-at-law, Law Office No 1 of the City of Vilnius 1982-90; elected to the Supreme Council (The Reconstituting Seimas of the Republic of Lithuania), signatory to the Act of Independence of the Republic of Lithuania, a member and deputy chairman of the Foreign Affairs Committee of Parliament 1990; founder of law firm Anicas, Okincic & Partners 1996; adviser to the President of the Republic of Lithuania 1998; title of Ambassador Extraordinary and Plenipotentiary of the Republic of Lithuania bestowed 2001; associated partner of Sutkiene, Pilkauskas & Partners 2005. Has participated in the following major deals: represented a Polish company, Opoczno SA, in connection with the due diligence on a major manufacturer in Lithuania, AB Dvarcioniu keramika - advised on matters pertaining to the acquisition of the company; represented Warsaw Stock Exchange and Securities Depository of Poland in connection with the due diligence on National Stock Exchange of Lithuania (AB Nacionaline vertybiniu popieriu birza) and Central Securities Depository of Lithuania (AB Lietuvos centrinis vertybiniu popieriu depozitoriumas) - advised on matters pertaining to the privatisation of the above stock companies; represented AB Vilniaus bankas in connection with the acquisition of the shares of a major commercial bank in the Ukraine, AGIO AB; represented and advised AXA Assistance Polska SA on investments in Lithuania, Latvia and Estonia; counselled Viessmann regarding the contruction of its plant in Russia and investments in Lithuania, Latvia, Estonia, Russia, Ukraine and Kazakhstan; counselled an IT company, EMAX SA, regarding investments in Lithuania; counselled Elektrim Megadex SA in connection with the tender for the building of a boiler in Ignalina Nuclear Power Plant; counselled SNC Lavalin Group Inc regarding the completion of construction works at the Ignalina Nuclear Power Plant; advised a foreign investor, Pumped Storage Power Plants Co, in connection with the privatisation of a major electricty distributor, AB Rytu skirstomieji tinklai; counselled Enterprise Investors on acquisitions of companies in Lithuania; represented Reiffeisen Bank Polska SA in connection with the establishment of its representative office in Lithuania; counselled Krakowskie Centrum Inwestycyjne SA in connection with the dredging of the harbour entrance contracted out by the Klaipeda State Sea Port; advised a major Polish company, Computerland, on the establishment of its subsidiaries in Lithuania, Latvia and Estonia; advised WARTA SA on the restructuring of its subsidiary, AB Panevezio stiklas; assisted a major Polish life insurance company, Commercial Union Polska (Aviva group) in establishing its subsidiary, Commercial Union Lietuva gyvybes draudimas; represented television channel POLSAT SA in connection with its acquisition of television channels in Lithuania, Latvia and Estonia; advised PBG SA on its tender for the construction of a gas pipeline in Lithuania; represented Kredyt Bank SA in connection with the establishment of its first foreign branch in Lithuania. Awards: Comandor's Cross of the Order of Poland's Revival 1996; Grand Cross with a Star 1999; Order of the Lithuanian Grand Duke Gediminas (Comandor's Cross) 2000; Golden Medal awarded by Polish Success Academy for vast input and immense

participation in developing relations between Poland and Lithuania 2001.
Languages: English, Lithuanian, Polish, Russian.
Member: Lithuanian Bar Association.
Education: Vilnius University, Faculty of Law (1982 diploma).
Personal: Born 1955; resides Vilnius.
Leisure: Travelling, reading, sports, theatre; member of Vilnius University Council.

PILKAUSKAS, Jonas

Sutkiene, Pilkauskas & Partners
Phone: Vilnius (+370 5 251 44 44)
E-mail: jpilkauskas@spp.lt
Corporate law practice group; finance and securities practice group.
Position: Dealing with all areas of business law (including mergers and acquisitions, privatisation), competition law, international trade and foreign investments, business financing and banking.
Career: Attorney at Vilnius office of US law firm McDermott, Will & Emery 1994-2001; partner of law firm Jaskutelis, Sutkiene & Masiokas 2001-03; co-founder of law firm Sutkiene, Pilkauskas & Partners 2003. Has participated in many major deals, including: advised YIT Corporation, a Finnish company, in connection with its acquisition of a major construction company in Lithuania, AB Kausta; advised on the merger of AB Vilniaus bankas and AB bankas Hermis, two major commercial banks in Lithuania; advised AB Siauliu bankas on EBRD's investments, prepared transaction documents and issued relevant legal opinion; represented foreign clients in connection with the lease of aircraft and sale of spare parts to the Lithuanian Airlines, AB Lietuvos avialinijos; represented International Monetary Fund (IMF) in connection with the conclusion of contracts for the lease of real property; provided advice concerning the public offering of shares (IPO) in a major pharmaceutical company in Lithuania (AB Sanitas); advised Lithuanian Telecom (AB Lietuvos telekomas) on the offering of shares and depository receipts through stock exchanges in Lithuania and in London (the second phase of the privatisation); represented a major meat products producer in Europe in connection with its recovery of debts; advised UAB Nemuno bangos grupe, a major PET packaging manufacturer in Lithuania on the construction of its plant in Lithuania; represented a foreign investor in connection with the privatisation of Lithuanian Gas, AB Lietuvos dujos; provided consultations to a major international bank, Euroclear Bank SA, regarding the procedure for the enforcement of security interests and agreements under Lithuanian law; represented Tamro Corporation, a major Scandinavian wholesaler of pharmaceuticals, in connection with its acquisition of major distributors of pharmaceuticals in Lithuania; represented AB Hansabankas in its acquisition of a life insurance company in Lithuania, UAB Lietuvos draudimo gyvybes draudimas; represented a Swedish post office in connection with its acquisition of a business in Lithuania; together with Bank Paribas Consortium, advised the government on the privatisation of strategic objects in and the reorganisation of the oil sector of Lithuania; advised on the acquisition of real estate for the Finnish Embassy in Lithuania; assisted numerous major western banks (including EBRD, Nordic Investment Bank, ABN Amro Bank, Overseas Private Investment Corporation, Bankers Trust Company (Trust and Security Services, Global Security Services), Deutsche Bank AG) in connection with their financing projects.
Languages: English, Lithuanian and Russian.
Member: Lithuanian Bar Association; International Bar Association (IBA).
Education: Vilnius University, Faculty of Law (1997 diploma); University of Swansea, Wales (UK); John Marshall Law School, Chicago (USA).
Personal: Born 1974; resides Vilnius.
Leisure: Travelling, reading, sports, theatre.

SALADŽIUS, Jonas

Law Firm Saladžius & Partners
Phone: Vilnius (+370 5239 2391)
E-mail: jonas.saladzius@splegal.lt
Corporate law, mergers & acquisitions, corporate restructuring, finance law, foreign investment, real estate, privatisation, dispute resolution.
Position: Managing partner of the firm, attorney-at-law. Has led numerous complex and large-scale legal projects in the spheres of privatisation, private investment, mergers and acquisitions and corporate restructuring. Has extensive experience in transaction support and drafting of commercial contracts as well as in-depth knowledge of the finance and banking sector.
Career: Head of tax and legal services of PricewaterhouseCoopers in Lithuania 1995-1998; leader of legal services of PricewaterhouseCoopers in Lithuania 1998-1999; managing partner of Saladzius & Partners from 2000. Lecturer of EU finance law at the Law University of Lithuania; lecturer of international treaties at the Institute of International Relations and Political Science (Vilnius University); lecturer of EU finance law at the International Business School (Vilnius University). Co-editor of the magazine of the Lithuanian Bar Association; co-author of the books 'International Organisations' and 'International Business Law'.
Languages: Lithuanian, English, Russian.
Member: International Bar Association (committees on banking law, business organisations, mediation and conciliation of the section on legal practice, and member of the European and capital markets forums); Lithuanian Bar Association (member of the disciplinary committee and the commission on the attorney qualification examination, and head of the LBA delegation to CCBE from 2005); board member, Junior Achievement in Lithuania; board member, American Chamber of Commerce in Lithuania.
Education: Vilnius University, Lithuania (LLM). Diploma in International and EU Law from Gröningen University, the Netherlands.
Personal: Born 1973, resides Vilnius.
Leisure: Member of the Lion's Club.

SUTKIENE, Eugenija

Sutkiene, Pilkauskas & Partners
Phone: Vilnius (+370 5 251 4444)
E-mail: esutkiene@spp.lt
Corporate law practice group, litigation practice group.
Position: Dealing with all areas of business law (including mergers and acquisitions, privatisation), competition law, international trade and foreign investments, energy and natural resources, biotechnology, telecommunications and media law, litigation.
Career: Trained at foreign law firms McDermott, Will & Emery (USA) and Paisner & Co (UK); head of legal department of Lithuanian State Wholesale Enterprise 1984-89; head of legal department of Ministry of Trade of the Republic of Lithuania in charge of Commercial Arbitration 1989-91; founder of Vilnius office of US law firm McDermott, Will & Emery 1991; head of Vilnius office of US law firm McDermott, Will & Emery 1991-99; partner of law firm Jaskutelis, Sutkiene & Masiokas 1999-2003; co-founder of law firm Sutkiene, Pilkauskas & Partners 2003. Has participated in many major deals, including: represented a prospective buyer of shares in the single oil refinery in the Baltic States, AB Mazeikiu nafta; advised Coca Cola Bottlers in connection with its investment into the construction of a factory for the bottling of soft drinks in Lithuania; assisted a major US consumer products company, Mars, Masterfoods, in connection with the construction of its modern petfood factory in Lithuania; advised a major US tobacco manufacturer, Philip Morris, in connection with the acquisition of the State Tobacco Factory in Klaipeda; represented a major US food company, Kraft General Foods, in connection with the acquisition (through public tender) of the Kaunas Confectionery Factory; in co-operation with UBS and CIBS (CIBC Wood Gundy), handled all in-country legal aspects of the privatisation of state-owned shares in the Lithuanian Telecom (AB Lietuvos telekomas) for the Government of Lithuania; together with Bank Paribas Consortium, advised the government on the privatisation of strategic objects in and the reorganisation of the oil sector of Lithuania; assisted Balcans Investment Bank A.D. in connection with the privatisation of the shares of BRAC ZDP Zvornik (Serbia, Bosnia and Herzegovina), a factory owned by Energoinsvest MDP; advised in connection with the financing by the European Bank for Reconstruction and Development of the renovation of Kaunas Water Company (SP UAB Kauno vandenys); in co-operation with CAIB (Corporate Finance Ltd), advised the government of the Republic of Lithuania on the privatisation of major power supply and distribution companies; advised Inditex SA on the conclusion of franchise agreements (for the use of the trademark Zara); in co-operation with the Lovells Law Firm, assisted CIBC (Canadian Imperial Bank of Commerce) in connection with the acquisition of the Finnish company FinVass Acquisition Oy (formerly Aplisole Oy), together with its subsidiaries in the Baltic States; assisted Svenska Lantmannen Energi AB, a Swedish company in connection with its long-term investment into a major chemical products manufacturer in Lithuania; advised the government of

the Republic of Lithuania regarding the privatisation of the Lithuanian Airlines, AB Lietuvos avialinijos; represented AB Kauno tiekimas in connection with the settlement of disputes with Samsung; assisted numerous major western banks (including EBRD, Nordic Investment Bank, ABN Amro Bank, Overseas Private Investment Corporation, Bankers Trust Company (Trust and Security Services, Global Security Services), Deutsche Bank AG) in connection with their financing projects. Publications: International Law Office, corporate chapter (1999-2002); Privatisation & Public/Private Partnership Review 2002-03 Lithuanian Privatisation; The EU Parliament Magazine Agriculture Chapter: Homework for Lithuania, No 146, September 30, 2003; The American Bar Association's magazine International Lawyer Comparative Law Essay (vol No 36, p 751).
Languages: English, Lithuanian, Polish and Russian.
Member: Lithuanian Bar Association; International Bar Association (IBA).
Education: Vilnius University, Faculty of Law (1984, diploma); University of Krakow, Poland.
Personal: Born 1956; resides Vilnius.
Leisure: Travelling, reading, theatre.

LUXEMBOURG

DI STEFANO, Mario
DI STEFANO & SEDLO Avocats à la Cour
Phone: Luxembourg (+352 262 5621)
E-mail: mdistefano@mds-legal.com
Company law, corporate law, taxation, business law, antitrust and trade regulation, mergers and acquisitions, European Union law, labour and employment.
Career: Admitted to the Luxembourg bar 1996; trainee lawyer (Rechtsreferendar) in Germany; passed second state examination, 1990. Previous positions: Luxembourg Bank, through 1980; in-house lawyer, 1991-96 and managing director, 1993-96, Luxembourg Trust Company.
Languages: English, French, German, Italian and Luxembourgish.
Member: Union Internationale des Avocats (UIA); Ausländischer Anwaltverein Deutschland e.V. (AAVD).
Education: Bachelor's degree (1979); University of Trier, Germany (1987 Law).
Personal: Born Stuttgart, Germany, 1960.

SEDLO, Adrian
DI STEFANO & SEDLO Avocats à la Cour
Phone: Luxembourg (+352 262 5621)
E-mail: asedlo@mds-legal.com
Position: Main areas of practice are banking and finance, securitisation, derivatives, capital markets, corporate law.
Career: Admitted 1999, Luxembourg; professional football player 1987-94; associate and senior associate in major English and Luxembourg law firms.
Languages: English, French, German, Croatian.
Education: Bachelor's degree (1987); University of Strasbourg (1998 Law); MA business law (DEA Droit des Affaires) (2003).
Personal: Born 1969, Frankfurt/Main, Germany.

SEIMETZ, Marc
Dechert Luxembourg
Phone: Luxembourg (+352 45 62 62 23)
E-mail: marc.seimetz@dechert.com
Position: Partner and member of the firm's financial services practice group dealing with alternative investment funds, corporate and securities, financial services, and international disputes. Focuses on financial law (including investment funds), company and commercial law, and contract law, advising clients on the incorporation of investment funds and companies, regulatory approvals, corporate documents, contracts, listings, offering of securities, mergers, and liquidations. Also provides advice on labour law to corporations.
Career: Designated by the Grand Duchy of Luxembourg for a six-year term as a conciliator and arbitrator on the list held by the International Centre for Settlement of Investment Disputes (ICSID) in Washington (2002). Regularly speaks at conferences and has published articles on investment fund law and company law. Also an arbitrator for the Luxembourg Sports Arbitration Commission. Has been an attorney and member of the Luxembourg Bar Association since 1990.
Education: University of Paris I Panthéon-Sorbonne (1989 Masters degree Business Law); University of London (1993 LLM).

MALTA

DE GABRIELE, Louis
Camilleri Preziosi
Phone: Valletta (+356 2123 8989)
E-mail: louis.degabriele@camilleripreziosi.com
Position: Partner responsible for banking and finance, investment services and capital markets. Main area of work is banking, corporate finance and commercial law.
Career: Qualified 1989; in-house legal counsel Bank of Valletta Plc 1989-92; joined Camilleri Preziosi 1993; partner 1995.
Languages: English, Maltese, Italian.
Member: Chamber of Advocates, Malta.
Education: University of Malta (1988 LLD); London School of Economics (1989 LLM).
Personal: Born 1964; resides Balzan, Malta.
Leisure: Football and tennis.

MIZZI, Henri
Camilleri Preziosi
Phone: Valletta (+356 2123 8989)
E-mail: henri.mizzi@camilleripreziosi.com
Position: Partner responsible for corporate and commercial law, litigation, competition law, media and telecommunications law and maritime law.
Career: Qualified 1989; joined Camilleri Preziosi 1989; partner 1995.
Languages: English, Maltese, Italian.
Member: Chamber of Advocates, Malta.
Education: University of Malta (1988 LLD); University of Cambridge (1988 LLM).
Personal: Born 1965; resides Swieqi (Malta).
Leisure: Reading.

NETHERLANDS

REULING, Saskia
DLA SchutGrosheide
Phone: Amsterdam (+31 20 541 98 78)
E-mail: saskia.reuling@dlapiper.com
Employment and industrial relations.
Position: Head of the DLA SchutGrosheide employment practice group. Has an internationally acclaimed reputation in the field of reorganisations, collective dismissals and employee consultation. Has recently been involved in one of the country's most prestigious reorganisation exercises and subsequent litigation. Advice led to the development of new ways of successfully retaining valuable staff by the creative application of the 'last in, first out' principle, which has instigated new legislation on this issue. Has assisted many listed and non-listed companies in strategic employment advice and collective labour law issues. Also an expert on alternative dispute resolution. As a certified mediator in labour relations, focuses on alternative approaches to resolving complex tactical issues. Working closely with the tax law practice group, has assisted large clients in risk management exercises on employee benefit and tax law schemes.
Career: Qualified 1982; partner DLA SchutGrosheide 1991; certified mediator (NMI) 2005.
Languages: Dutch, English.
Member: Local board Association of Amsterdam Labour Lawyers (VAA).
Education: University of Amsterdam (1982 Dutch Law); New York University School of Law (1983 Master of Comparative Jurisprudence); Grotius Academy (2000 Employment Law).
Personal: Born 1956; resides Amsterdam.

STIBBE, Frans
DLA SchutGrosheide
Phone: Amsterdam (+31 20 541 98 07)
E-mail: frans.stibbe@dlapiper.com
Corporate.
Position: Experienced corporate lawyer who is being recognised in the market place as an expert on corporate governance and corporate litigation matters. Account manager of major Dutch listed clients of DLA SchutGrosheide. Frans' practice focuses on corporate transactions, general corporate governance and corporate litigation matters. Acts as general corporate

counsel to Dutch companies. Heads the Dutch DLA offices as a managing partner.
Career: Vos, Seilder & Plas 1985-89; Nysingh advocaten, Arnhem 1989-91; DLA SchutGrosheide 1991 to date; partner 1993; regional managing partner 2003.
Languages: Dutch, English.
Member: Corporate Litigation Association; Securities Law Association.
Education: University of Groningen (1985 Dutch Law); Grotius Academy (2000 Corporate Law).
Personal: Born 1959; resides Amsterdam.

NIGERIA

AKPANA, Iboroma
Solola & Akpana
Phone: Port Harcourt (+234 84 231 403)
E-mail: iakpana@sololaakpana.com
Position: Managing partner and partner dealing with all aspects of commercial law, including mergers and acquisitions, corporate finance, banking and securities, and privatisation of public enterprises.
Career: Admitted Nigeria 1993, New York 2004, England and Wales 2005; appointed notary public of Nigeria; associate Banwo & Ighodalo 1993; partner Solola & Akpana 1997.
Languages: English, local languages.
Member: Nigerian Bar Association; International Bar Association; American Bar Association; Bar Association of the State of New York; Law Society of England and Wales.
Education: University of Jos, Nigeria (1992 LLB 2(1)); Nigerian Law School (1993 BL 2(1)); Harvard Law School (2002 LLM).
Personal: Born 1964.
Leisure: Soccer, chess, cycling.

GIWA-OSAGIE, Osayaba
Giwa-Osagie & Co
Phone: Lagos (+234 1 267 1513)
E-mail: giwa-osagie@hyperia.com
Corporate.
Position: Managing partner dealing with all areas of corporate law including banking, finance, securities, foreign trade, investment laws, mergers and acquisitions, telecommunications, arbitration and mining laws. Advised Lafarge/Blue Circle Industries Plc in the acquisition of majority shares in West African Portland Cement Company (WAPCO). Currently advising Telecom SA on its bid for acquisition of shares in NITEL Plc.
Career: Trained Abayomi Sogbesan & Co (SAN) and G.O.K. Ajayi & Co (SAN) 1986-89; managing partner Giwa-Osagie & Co since 1990; honorary legal adviser to the Nigerian-South African Chamber of Commerce; notary public and a consultant to the African Development Bank (ADB). Publications of note: co-author 'Privatisation in Nigeria' in the 'International Privatisation Review' (Euromoney 2000-01); 'Credit risk, securitisation and loan guarantees in Nigeria: appropriate legal and fiscal framework for exploration and mining' in 'Traders' magazine.
Languages: English, Edo.
Member: Nigerian Bar Association; International Bar Association; Nigerian Maritime Law Association; the Nigerian Institute of International Affairs, Africa.
Education: University of Warwick (1985); Nigerian Law School (1986).
Personal: Born 1957; resides Lagos.
Leisure: Listening to music, sports, travelling.

JEMIDE, Ayuli
Detail Solicitors
Phone: Lagos (+234 1 4610098)
E-mail: ayuli@detail-solicitors.com
Partner in charge of corporate and commercial law, commercial arbitration, real estate, oil and gas, foreign investment and Admiralty practice.
Position: Lead partner.
Career: Qualified in 1988; solicitor at GM Ibru & Co 1989; legal counsel for DEUTAG Drilling Group; managing partner of Jemide & Associates 1993; lead partner at Detail Solicitors 2004.
Languages: English.
Member: Chartered Institute of Arbitrators (London); International Bar Association; Nigerian Bar Association; Association of International Petroleum Negotiators; Nigerian-Swiss Chamber of Commerce; Business Law Section, Nigerian Bar Association.
Education: University of Benin, Nigeria; Nigerian Law School.
Personal: Born 1966, resides Lagos.
Leisure: Swimming, golf, travelling.

SOLOLA, Tope
Solola & Akpana
Phone: Port Harcourt (+234 84 231 403)
E-mail: tsolola@sololaakpana.com
Position: Partner dealing with all areas of commercial litigation, arbitration, oil and gas law, energy and natural resources law.
Career: Admitted 1988; associate at C. Kunle Oyero & Co 1988; assistant company secretary Municorp Limited 1991; head of chambers Banwo & Ighodalo 1993; partner Solola & Akpana 1997.
Languages: English, Yoruba.
Member: Nigerian Bar Association; International Bar Association; Chartered Institute of Arbitrators UK (MCI Arb); and an associate of the Chartered Institute of Arbitrators of Nigeria (ACI Arb Nig).
Education: University of Lagos (1987 LLB); Nigerian Law School (1988 BL); University of Dundee, UK (2003 LLM with distinction).
Personal: Born 1965.
Leisure: Cricket, soccer, photography.

WOLE, Adesola
Detail Solicitors
Phone: Lagos (+234 1 264 2667)
E-mail: wole@detail-solicitors.com
Practices in project finance, commercial transactions, industrial and labour relations, international trade, and real property.
Career: Qualified in 1986; counsel at Abdulahi Ibrahim, San & Co, Lagos; legal counsel for Wema Bank PLC, Lagos, 1991; head of legal department at Nigerian Bottling Company PLC (the authorised Coca-Cola bottler in Nigeria), 1993-2005.
Languages: English.
Member: Nigerian Bar Association; International Bar Association; Nigerian Institute of Public Relations.
Education: University of Ife, Nigeria; Nigerian Law School.
Personal: Born 1963, resides Lagos.
Leisure: Travelling, reading and dancing.

NORWAY

AABØ-EVENSEN, Ole Kristian
Aabø-Evensen & Co Advokatfirma
Phone: Oslo (+47 2415 9010)
E-mail: oka@aaboevensen.com
M&A, corporate finance, capital markets and securities, private equity, dispute resolution.
Position: Specialising in counseling and representation of clients, both corporate and individual, in connection with M&A, corporate reorganisations, international transactions, private equity, securitisation of assets, banking, securities and structured financing work and general legal services; also an experienced advocate, particularly within the fields of director's liability and white-collar crime.
Career: Attorney and associated partner, de Besche & Co, Oslo 1988-94; trainee at Sinclair Roche & Temperley (solicitors) and Four Essex Court (barristers, now Essex Court Chambers), London 1992; partner and head of Corporate Legal Services KPMG, Oslo 1995-2002; mentioned in the 'Guide to the World's leading White-Collar Crime Lawyer's'.
Languages: English, the Scandinavian languages.
Member: IBA; Norwegian Bar Association; International Fiscal Association; Honorably Member Center for International Legal Studies.
Education: University of Oslo (1988); King's College, London (1992 English Law and International Finance).
Personal: Born 1964.

ÅRSETH, Nils Olav
Aabø-Evensen & Co Advokatfirma
Phone: Oslo (+47 2415 9020)
E-mail: noa@aaboevensen.com
M&A, corporate finance, capital markets, property finance.
Position: Partner specialising in international M&A, take private and MBO's, private equity and capital markets, reorganisations, contracts and contract negotiations, international transactions, agency and distribution; also experienced within legal issues

relating to real estate, hereunder tenancy and construction law.
Career: Associated partner, Wiersholm, Mellbye & Bech; head of legal services, Unitor ASA; general manager, Unitor (Italy).
Languages: English, the Scandinavian languages.
Member: Norwegian Bar Association.
Education: University of Bergen (1988).
Personal: Born 1963.

BERG, Arne Seemann
Kvale & Co Advokatfirma Ans
Phone: Oslo (+47 22 47 97 00)
E-mail: seemann.berg@kvaleco.no
Media, intellectual property law, labour law, company law, acquisition and sale of business, negotiations and litigation.
Position: Partner.
Career: Admitted Norway 1982; legal officer, Defence Construction Directorate 1979-80; associate/salaried partner, de Bosche & Thune 1980-86; partner, Brokhus & Alo 1986-92; partner, Kvale & Co since 1992; lecturer Norwegian Law Society.
Languages: English, the Scandinavian languages.
Member: Norwegian Bar Association.
Education: University of Oslo (1979 Candidate in Jurisprudence).
Personal: Born 1953; resides Oslo.

BREDE, Jens
Kvale & Co Advokatfirma Ans
Phone: Oslo (+47 22 47 97 00)
E-mail: brede@kvaleco.no
Petroleum and energy law, contracting law, company law, financing, aviation, capital markets, negotiations and litigation.
Position: Partner.
Career: Admitted Norway 1986; assistant judge Lofoten District Court 1984-86; associate Wikborg Rein & Co 1986-88; partner Kvale & Brede 1988-92; partner Kvale & Co since 1992.
Languages: English, the Scandinavian languages.
Member: Norwegian Bar Association.
Education: University of Oslo (1984 Candidate in Jurisprudence).
Personal: Born 1958; resides Oslo.

CHRISTOFFERSEN, Per Torp
Kvale & Co Advokatfirma Ans
Phone: Oslo (+47 22 47 97 00)
E-mail: christoffersen@kvaleco.no
Agency distribution/competition, company law, contract and marketing law, insurance and compensation law, labour law, telecommunications, media and IT.
Position: Partner.
Career: Admitted Norway 1986; legal adviser Ministry of Justice 1981-84; associate judge 1984-85; associate Nergaard, Mellbye, Schjoldager & Sejersted 1985-88; partner Langseth, Mår & Stake-Larsen; partner Kvale & Co, since 1992.
Languages: English, German, the Scandinavian languages.
Member: Norwegian Bar Association.
Education: University of Oslo (1981 Candidate in Jurisprudence).
Personal: Born 1955; resides Oslo.

FARHANG, Thomas S
Kvale & Co Advokatfirma Ans
Phone: Oslo (+47 22 47 97 00)
E-mail: farhang@kvaleco.no
Company law, acquisitions and sale of business, negotiations and litigation.
Position: Partner.
Career: Admitted Norway 1998; legal officer Headquarters Defence Command Norway 1996; associate Kvale & Co 1996-98; salaried partner Kvale & Co 1998-2000; partner Kvale & Co since 2001.
Languages: English, Farsi, the Scandinavian languages.
Member: Norwegian Bar Association.
Education: University of Oslo (1995 Candidate of Jurisprudence).
Personal: Born 1970; resides Oslo.

HAMAR, Espen R
Kvale & Co Advokatfirma Ans
Phone: Oslo (+47 22 47 97 00)
E-mail: hamar@kvaleco.no
Contracting law, property, restructuring, insolvency proceedings and credit security, contract and marketing law, negotiations and litigation, wills and probate, inheritance planning.
Position: Partner.
Career: Admitted Norway 1993; Supreme Court of Norway 1998; legal officer Directorate of Prices 1990-92; associate Kvale & Co 1992-94; assistant/acting judge Vardø District Court 1994-95; partner Hegg & Hamar 1995-99; partner Kvale & Co since 1999.
Languages: English, the Scandinavian languages.
Member: Norwegian Bar Association.
Education: University of Oslo (1989 Candidate in Jurisprudence).
Personal: Born 1964; resides Oslo.

JENSSEN, Lars Trygve
Kvale & Co Advokatfirma Ans
Phone: Oslo (47 22 47 97 00)
E-mail: jenssen@kvaleco.no
Telecommunications, media and IT, competition and marketing law, intellectual property law, corporate and commercial.
Position: Partner.
Career: Admitted Norway 1999; associate Lindh Stabell Horten 1997-2000; salaried partner Lindh Stabell Horten 2001-04; partner Kvale & Co since 2005.
Languages: English, the Scandinavian languages.
Member: Norwegian Bar Association.
Education: University of Oslo (1996 Candidate in Jurisprudence).
Personal: Born 1967; resides Oslo.

KVALE, Anders
Kvale & Co Advokatfirma Ans
Phone: Oslo (+47 22 47 97 00)
E-mail: kvale@kvaleco.no
Petroleum and energy law, telecommunications, media and IT, company law, negotiations and litigation.
Position: Partner.
Career: Admitted Norway 1977; executive officer The Industrial Bank 1971-72, business manager 1972-76; lawyer in private practice 1976-83; lawyer Norsk Hydro 1983-85; own law practice 1985-88; partner Kvale & Brede 1988-92; partner Kvale & Co since 1992.
Languages: English, the Scandinavian languages.
Member: Norwegian Bar Association.
Education: Norwegian School of Economics and Business administration (1970 MBA); University of Oslo (1977 Candidate in Jurisprudence).
Personal: Born 1947; resides Oslo.

MEVATNE, Christian
Kvale & Co Advokatfirma Ans
Phone: Oslo (47 22 47 97 00)
E-mail: mevatne@kvaleco.no
Corporate law, mergers and acquisitions, competition law, labour law, agency law.
Position: Partner.
Career: Admitted Norway 1975, assistant judge Karmsund district court 1973-74, legal council Oslo tax office 1974-75, partner Martens law firm, Bergen 1976-83, president Vesta American Insurance Co New York 1984-88, president Bretvin Finne & Partners 1988-89, partner Lindh Stabell Horgen 1989-04, partner Kvale & Co since 2004.
Languages: English, Scandinavian languages.
Member: Norwegian Bar Association.
Education: MBA from IMEDE, (CEI) in Switzerland in 1976 University of Oslo (1972 Candidate in Jurisprudence).
Personal: Born 1944; resides Oslo.

MYKSVOLL, Laila
Kvale & Co Advokatfirma Ans
Phone: Oslo (+47 22 47 97 00)
E-mail: myksvoll@kvaleco.no
Telecommunications, media and IT, contract and marketing law, company law, wills and probate, inheritance planning, labour law.
Position: Partner.
Career: Admitted Norway 1998; legal officer Sør-Trøndelag County Tax Office 1995-96; associate Giæver & Helge, Trondheim 1996-97; associate Kvale & Co 1997-99; salaried partner Kvale & Co 1999-2002; partner Kvale & Co since 2003.
Languages: English, the Scandinavian languages.
Member: Norwegian Bar Association.
Education: University of Bergen (1995 Candidate in Jurispudence).
Personal: Born 1964; resides Oslo.

NILSEN, Geir Johan
Aabø-Evensen & Co Advokatfirma
Phone: Oslo (+47 2415 9030)
E-mail: gin@aaboevensen.com
M&A, labour and employment, due diligence, dispute resolution.
Position: Partner specialising in M&A, labour law, reorganisations, contracts and contract negotiations,

international transactions, director's liability, arbitration and negotiations.
Career: Nine years with the law firm Flod & Co; attorney and partner, KPMG Law Advokatfirma 1997-2002; lecturer in jurisprudence, University of Oslo.
Languages: English, the Scandinavian languages.
Member: Norwegian Bar Association; Norwegian Chartered Engineer's Group for Hearing of Legal Reforms on Business and Corporate law.
Education: University of Oslo (1987 company law, tax law).
Personal: Born 1960.

OEGLAEND, Henning
DLA Nordic
Phone: Oslo (+47 24 13 16 21)
E-mail: henning.ogland@dlanordic.no
Corporate, banking and finance.
Position: Partner and chairman in DLA Nordic EEIG. Active within the private equity and investment community and serves with the board of an number of investment companies. Country representative for the Nordic private equity company Ratos.
Career: Qualified 1983; Mobil Exploration Norway Inc; partner Strøm Sandaker & Øglænd 1987; active in establishing and chairman of the first pan-Scandinavian law firm Lindh, Stabel, Horten; brought that firm (now DLA Nordic) into global law firm group DLA Piper Rudnick Gray Cary LLP. Former chairman ResidenSea Ltd 'The World' (the first residential cruise ship ever built); board member of a number of large Norwegian companies, such as Møllergruppen, Arcus and Bluegarden.
Languages: The Scandinavian languages, English, German.
Member: Norwegian Bar Association.
Education: University of Oslo (1983).
Personal: Born 1957; resides Oslo.
Leisure: Golf, tennis, boating, travelling.

OTTESEN, Tom Hugo
Kvale & Co Advokatfirma Ans
Phone: Oslo (+47 22 47 97 00)
E-mail: ottesen@kvaleco.no
Restructuring, insolvency proceedings and credit security, wills and probate, inheritance planning.
Position: Partner specialising in descendant estates, insolvency.
Career: Admitted Norway 1986; associate Thune & Co 1984-89; partner Thune & Co 1989-96; partner Kvale & Co since 1996; lecturer Norwegian Law Society.
Languages: English, the Scandinavian languages.
Member: Norwegian Bar Association; International Bar Association.
Education: University of Oslo (1984 Candidate in Jurisprudence).
Personal: Born 1957; resides Oslo.

PIRO, Thomas
Kvale & Co Advokatfirma Ans
Phone: Oslo (47 22 47 97 00)
E-mail: piro@kvaleco.no
Restructuring, insolvency proceedings and credit security, company law, acquisition and sale of businesses, competition and marketing law.
Position: Partner.
Career: Admitted Norway 2000, associate Kvale & Co 1998-01, salaried partner, 2001-04, partner since 2004.
Languages: English, Scandinavian languages.
Member: Norwegian Bar Association.
Education: University of Oslo (1998 Candidate in Jurisprudence).
Personal: Born 1972; resides Oslo.

REVHEIM, Magne
DLA Nordic
Phone: Bergen (+47 55 30 10 33)
E-mail: magne.revheim@dlanordic.no
Commercial, real estate, energy, principal contract and law of torts.
Position: Partner in DLA Nordic and serves as a strategic adviser on the board of a number of companies.
Career: Qualified 1978; associate Secher & Co; partner Secher & Co (became Lindh, Stabell Horten, then DLA Nordic); admitted to the Supreme Court 1993. Chairman of the football club Brann, a top Norwegian league club. Lecturer on construction law and negotiating skills.
Languages: The Scandinavian languages, English.
Member: Norwegian Bar Association.
Education: University of Bergen (1978).
Personal: Born 1950; resides Bergen.
Leisure: Boating/yachting, fishing, mountain walks, travel.

ROMANSKY, Robert
Kvale & Co Advokatfirma Ans
Phone: Oslo (47 22 47 97 00)
E-mail: romansky@kvaleco.no
Company law, acquisition and sale of business, capital markets, financing.
Position: Partner.
Career: Admitted Norway 2001; associate Bugge, Arentz-Hansen & Rasmussen 1999-2001; associate Kvale & Co 2001-02; salaried partner Kvale & Co 2002-05; partner Kvale & Co since 2005.
Languages: English, the Scandinavian languages.
Member: Norwegian Bar Association.
Education: University of Oslo (1999 Candidate of Jurisprudence).
Personal: Born 1972; resides Oslo.

SANDAKER, Christian
Kvale & Co Advokatfirma Ans
Phone: Oslo (+47 22 47 97 00)
E-mail: sandaker@kvaleco.no
Negotiations and litigations, property, acquisition and sale of businesses, wills and probate, inheritance planning, leasehold, company law.
Position: Partner.
Career: Admitted to Norway 1976, associate Strøm Flod og Strøm 1974-79, partner Strøm, Sanaker, Øglænd & Fossum 1986-91, partner Lindh Stabell Horten 1991-04, partner Kvale & Co.
Languages: English, Scandinavian languages.
Member: Norwegian Bar Association.
Education: University of Oslo (1973 Candidate of Jurisprudence).
Personal: Born 1948; resides Oslo.

STAKE-LARSEN, Gunnar
Kvale & Co Advokatfirma Ans
Phone: Oslo (+47 22 47 97 00)
E-mail: stake-larsen@kvaleco.no
Acquisitions and sale of businesses, company law, capital markets, contract and marketing law, negotiation and litigation.
Position: Partner.
Career: Research assistant University of Oslo 1978-79; associate judge Sandnes 1980-81; assistant judge 1980-81; admitted Norway 1982; Supreme Court of Norway 1988; associate Nergaard, Mellbye, Schjoldager & Sejersted 1982-85; partner Langseth, Mår & Stake-Larsen 1985-1992; partner Kvale & Co since 1992.
Languages: English, German, the Scandinavian languages.
Member: Norwegian Bar Association; Norwegian Association for Protection of Industrial Property.
Education: University of Oslo (1980 Candidate in Jurisprudence).
Personal: Born 1953; resides Oslo.

SVANE, Henrik
Kvale & Co Advokatfirma Ans
Phone: Oslo (+47 22 47 97 00)
E-mail: svane@kvaleco.no
Competition and antitrust law, EU law, intellectual property, agency and distributorship.
Position: Partner.
Career: Admitted 1995; associate in legal department in Københavns Telefon Aktieselskab 1987-88; executive officer the Price Directorate (The Norwegian Competition Authority) 1988-91; attorney-at-law and partner Wiersholm, Mellbye & Beth 1991-2002; partner Kvale & Co since 2003.
Languages: English, the Scandinavian languages.
Member: Norwegian Bar Association.
Education: University of København (1987 Candidate of Jurispudence).
Personal: Born 1970; resides Oslo.

VALAND, Christian Stang
Kvale & Co Advokatfirma Ans
Phone: Oslo (+47 22 47 97 00)
E-mail: vaaland@kvaleco.no
Financing and capital markets, petroleum and energy law, adviser in the public sector.
Position: Partner.
Career: Admitted Norway 1994, research assistant, Institute for public law University of Oslo 1990, assistant judge Eiker, Modum and Sigdal County Court 1992-93, associate law firm Stabell Tellmann Strøm 1993-94, associate Stabell 1994-97, partner Stabell Horten 1998-04, partner Kvale & Co since 2004.
Languages: English, Scandinavian languages.
Member: Norwegian Bar Association.
Education: Univeristy of Oslo (1991 Candidate in Jurisprudence).
Personal: Born 1944; resides Oslo.

POLAND

BAEHR, Jerzy, Dr

Wierciński, Kwieciński, Baehr Sp. k.
Phone: Poznań (+48 61 855 32 20)
E-mail: j.baehr@wkw.pl
Energy; public procurement, anti-monopoly law.
Position: Specialises in providing legal services to businesses in the energy industry and is an expert on energy law, public procurement law and anti-monopoly law.
Career: Partner of Domański, Zakrzewski, Palinka; co-founding partner of Wierciński, Kwieciński, Baehr Sp. k; author of many articles on energy law, co-author of commentary on public procurement law and commentary on energy law; participated, as an expert, in the parliamentary legislation process aimed at EU directives implementation regarding energy law and public procurement. For many years he was an expert at the Ownership Transformation Council, an advisory body to the Prime Minister, as well as a Supervisory Board member in such companies as Zaklady Chemiczne Police S.A., XI NFI S.A. or Huta Szkla Ujscie S.A.
Languages: English, Polish.
Member: District Chamber of Legal Counsels in Poznań.
Education: Faculty of Law and Administration at Adam Mickiewicz University (1992 PhD dissertation on privatisation); studied in Oxford, Leyden and Trident.
Personal: Born 1961; resides Poznań.
Leisure: Family, swimming.

BRYNDAL, Dorota

GESSEL - Attorneys at Law
Phone: Warsaw (+48 22 318 6901)
E-mail: d.bryndal@gessel.com.pl
Legal adviser, partner.
Position: Partner. Experienced in copyright, media, and computer law, competition, trade mark protection, transfer of intellectual property, labour law, pharmaceutical law, new technologies, digital data transmission and internet.
Career: Admitted to practise as a legal adviser in 2001. With GESSEL Attorneys at Law since 1999. Previously: lawyer at White & Case (Poland) Ltd 1998-99; lawyer/in-house counsel at Canal+ Polska 1995-98; lawyer at Film Plus Ltd; free legal aid at Polis Community Center (Toronto, Canada). Author of numerous publications on the intellectual property, trade mark protection and copyright and media law.
Languages: English, Polish, Russian.
Member: Polish Bar Association.
Education: Nicolaus Copernicus University, Torún (Poland). Postgraduate: study on Antimonoploy Law and Study on Copyright Law and Media Law at The Institute of Inventiveness and Protection of Intellectual Property (part of the Jagiellonian University in Kraków).
Personal: Born 1964, resides Warsaw.
Leisure: Classic music, travel, sport (skiing).

DEBENEDETTI, C. David

DeBenedetti Majewski Michalski Szczesniak Kancelaria Prawnicza Sp. K.
Phone: Warsaw (+48 22 339 54 07)
E-mail: ddebenedetti@dms.net.pl
NY Attorney, solicitor in England and Wales.
Position: Partner, specialising in investment funds and hedge funds, law and arbitrage opportunity investments, as well as commercial law and intellectual property. He advises in cross-border aspects of litigation, and has worked extensively in venture capital transactions and general corporate mergers and acquisitions.
Career: In 1997 Mr DeBenedetti began as an associate at the Warsaw office of an international law firm. In 2001, he moved to the New York office and from 2003 onwards has split his time between New York and Warsaw. Most recently in 2004, he co-authored a White Paper published by the Polish Association of Financial Investors on the structuring of leveraged buyouts in Poland. Was admitted as a solicitor in England and Wales after passing the QLTT (Qualified Lawyers Transfer Test).
Languages: English (native) and Polish.
Member: New York State Bar Association, American Chamber of Commerce in Poland.
Education: University of Toledo (BA 1991); Georgetown University Law Centre (JP 1996); admitted to practice in the state of Ohio in 1997 (currently inactive) and New York in 2001; law clerk to the Honorable James G Carr (US District Court, Northern Ohio) 1996-97.
Personal: Born 1969; married with three children.
Leisure: Travel, local history and international relations.

GASIEWSKI, Mariusz

Rutkowski Windmill Gasiewski & Roman LP
Phone: Warsaw (+48 58 305 85 99)
E-mail: mariusz.gasiewski@rwgr.pl
Position: Partner at Rutkowski WIndmill Gasiewski & Roman LP, who deals with corporate, IT/IP/media, real estate and tax law.
Career: Qualified as judge 1993; as legal counselor 1994; legal adviser of Doradca Consultants Sp. zo. o in Gdynia, responsible for complex legal servicing of restructuring processes involving communes; took part in privatisation processes in Poland and Belarussia as a consultant with IFC; head of legal department Ernst & Young, Gdansk office; partner Gasiewski & Roman since 1996; Gasiewski & Roman was the sole representative of CMS Cameron McKenna in the Pomeranian region of Gdansk 1997-99; co-author of 'The Law in Sea Harbours'.
Languages: English, Russian.
Member: Chamber of Legal Counselors in Gdansk.
Education: Law Faculty, University of Gdansk (1991).
Leisure: Horse riding, skiing.

GESSEL KALINOWSKA VEL KALISZ, Beata

GESSEL - Attorneys at Law
Phone: Warsaw (+48 22 318 6901)
E-mail: beata@gessel.com.pl
Legal adviser, managing partner.
Position: Managing partner, arbitrator in the Arbitration Court of the Domestic Chamber of Commerce. Her practice concentrates on the public securities market, equity transactions, mergers, and arbitration proceedings.
Career: Admitted to practise as a legal adviser 1992. Listed as an arbitrator at the Arbitration Court at the Polish Chamber of Commerce 1999. Has an experience with other law entities: Arthur Andersen, Weil, Gotshal & Manges, the Parliamentary Commission for Foreign Economic Development, Polski Dom Aukcyjny Sp. z.o.o. Lectured on the areas of her specialisation for Euroforum and for the Business Development Institute of the Privatisation Centre Foundation. Her publications include 'Aircraft Finance: Registration, Security and Enforcement', the 'Poland' chapter (Longman, London 1991); 'Environmental Liabilities and Regulation in Europe', the 'Poland' chapter (International Business Publishing, The Hague 1993); 'Securing the object of the claim' (International Bar Association Committee D News, February 2003), and numerous contributions to Polish dailies and periodicals, including 'Rzeczpospolita', 'Businessman Magazine', and 'Parkiet'.
Languages: English.
Member: International Bar Association; Polish Business Bar Association; Council of the Foundation for Development of Equity Market Standards.
Education: Graduated from the Department of Law and Administration at Warsaw University (1989).
Personal: Born 1964, resides Warsaw.
Leisure: Modern art.

KOZIOROWSKI, Leszek

GESSEL - Attorneys at Law
Phone: Warsaw (+48 22 318 6901)
E-mail: l.koziorowski@gessel.com.pl
Legal adviser, partner.
Position: Partner. Experienced in securities law, management options, share and bond issues, the procedural rules of the SEC and legal issues relating to brokerage offices and investment funds. Involved in drafting legislation regulating bonds and investment funds.
Career: Admitted to practise as a legal adviser 1998. With GESSEL since 1999 (partner since 2002). Previously vice chairman of the Examination Board for Investment Advisors, chief expert in the Securities Exchange Commission, Department of Brokerage Houses and Investment Funds. Adviser to the chairman of SEC since 1997. Lecturer since 1995, he teaches courses for investment advisers, brokers and auditors. Author of numerous publications on the capital market and securities ('Prawo Papierów Wartosciowych', 'Przeglad Prawa Handlowego', 'Radca Prawny', 'Rzeczpospolita').
Languages: Polish, English.
Member: Polish Bar Association.
Education: Department of Law and Administration at Warsaw University (1994).
Personal: Born 1970, Warsaw.
Leisure: Collecting old securities, climbing and mountain hiking. Member of the International Bond and Share Society and Collectors of Historic Securities Society.

KWIECIŃSKI, Tomasz

Wiercinski, Kwieciński, Baehr Sp. k.
Phone: Warsaw (+48 22 630 31 31)
E-mail: t.kwiecinski@wkw.pl
Dispute resolution; public procurement; telecoms.
Position: Experience covers company law, civil law, law of public procurement and telecommunications. Involved in numerous privatization and restructurings projects. Wide experience in litigation (including arbitration); provides ongoing legal assistance to corporate clients.
Career: Partner of Wardyński & Partners; co-founding partner of Wiercinski, Kwieciński, Baehr Sp. k.; author and co-author of more than 50 legal publications, including the commentary on the public procurement law and the commentary on the municipal property management law. Member of an expert think-tank advising the Polish Public Procurement Office on the reform of public procurement system in Poland; member of the Ownership Transformation Council; member of an advisory body for the Prime Minister for privatization matters.
Languages: English, Polish.
Member: District Chamber of Legal Counsels in Poznań.
Education: Faculty of Law and Administration at Adam Mickiewicz University (1978 PhD in insurance law).
Personal: Born 1950; resides Warsaw.
Leisure: Reading, skiing.

MAJEWSKI, Jaroslaw, Dr. hab., Professor

DeBenedetti Majewski Michalski Szczesniak Kancelaria Prawnicza Sp. K.
Phone: Warsaw (+48 22 339 54 06)
E-mail: jmajewski@dms.net.pl
Advocate/legal adviser.
Position: Litigation partner, specialising in litigation, banking law, criminal law, commercial law and consumer law.
Career: Professor Majewski qualified as a judge in 1993 and qualified as a legal adviser in 1994; since 1995 he has practised law as a legal adviser. He was the associate director of the legal department at PKO BP SA (1995-97); director of the legal department at BGZ SA (1999-2003); he has been inter alia and a member of the Commission for Ethical Banking as part of the Polish Union of Banks. He is also the author of many legal treatises prepared for, among others, at the request of Parliament, and became an advocate in 2005. Professor Majewski is the author or co-author of over 90 publications in different fields of law, has written treatises, commentaries and articles including a well-received commentary on criminal code, and has been quoted by colleagues in Poland and abroad. Since 2003 Mr Majewski has been a professor of criminal law theory and criminal law at Cardinal Wyszynski's University law department in Warsaw.
Languages: Polish, English and German.
Member: Advocate's (Barrister) Bar.
Education: Law faculty at Jagiellonian University in Krakow (1991); Doctorate in law (1996); Post Doctorate (2002 Dr hab).
Personal: Born 1967; married with one child.
Leisure: Antiques, history.

MICHALSKI, Marek, Dr. hab., Professor

DeBenedetti Majewski Michalski Szczesniak Kancelaria Prawnicza Sp. K.
Phone: Warsaw (+48 22 339 54 05)
E-mail: mmichalski@dms.net.pl
Partner.
Position: Partner, specialising in securities law, secured transactions and banking law, commercial and bankruptcy law as well as investment fund law.
Career: Professor Michalski is an associate Professor of Law in the commercial law department at the Jagiellonian University in Kraków, he also received a scholarship to the L'Universite Panteon-Assas (Paris II) in Paris. He is currently a lecturer at the Legal Advisers Bar Association in Kraków; and has been an expert on investment funds at the Polish Development Bank in the investment fund management department (1995-96); director of the legal department at the National Depository of Securities (1996-2000); adviser to the Ministry of the State Treasury on the draft reprivatisation law (2000-01); associate and then in 2004, counsel to the Warsaw office of the international law firm Salans (2000-04) and an expert for the Studies and Expertise Office of Polish Parliament regarding the draft investment fund law, the law on public trade in securities, banking law and other related laws. Since June 2004, he has been an arbiter at the Arbitration Tribunal of the National Depository of Securities; and an arbiter of the Arbitration Court at the Polish Confederation of Private Employers, 'Lewiatan'. Professor Michalski is the author or co-author of approximately 80 publications regarding securities, public trading, banking law, capital markets law, commercial law and joint stock companies; the author or co-author of commentaries to laws, including the law on public trade in securities, banking law, investment fund law and mortgage bank law.
Languages: Polish, English and French.
Education: Law Faculty at Jagiellonian University in Kraków (1991); Doctorate in law (1996); Post-Doctorate (2005 Dr hab).
Personal: Born 1966.
Leisure: Ancient history, history of French revolution, architecture and fitness.

MIZIKOWSKI, Tomasz

Lukowicz Swierzewski & Partners
Phone: Warsaw (+48 22 8 27 33 22)
E-mail: tmizikowski@lukowicz.pl
Litigation.
Position: Partner and legal adviser with 33 years of professional experience; litigation, bankruptcy law, arrangement law, arbitration and enforcement; leadership of litigation practice group; arbitrator at Arbitration Court of the Polish Chamber of Commerce, Warsaw; arbiter in commercial arbitrage (20 years in judging commercial trials).
Career: Partner Lukowicz & Partners 2005; commercial judge of the District (Wojewódzki) Court in Warsaw.
Languages: Polish, Russian.
Member: District Chamber of Legal Advisers in Warsaw.
Education: Warsaw University (1970 Mag Jur).
Personal: Born 1949; resides Warsaw.

ROMAN, Zygmunt

Rutkowski Windmill Gasiewski & Roman LP
Phone: Warsaw (+48 58 305 85 99)
E-mail: zygmunt.roman@rwgr.pl
Position: Partner at Rutkowski Windmill Gasiewski Roman LP, dealing with litigation and employment.
Career: Qualified as a judge 1993; as a legal adviser 1994; he has been a legal adviser to Bank Gdanski since 1993, involved in development projects run by highly-qualified specialists, one of them concerning the creation of a consortium to finance the building of The Bank and Finance Centre, Pulawska Street, Warsaw; specialises in fusions and mergers of companies and banks; partner Gasiewski & Roman since 1996; Gasiewski & Roman was the sole representative of CMS Cameron McKenna in the Pomeranian region of Gdansk 1997-99.
Languages: English.
Member: Chamber of Legal Advisors, Gdansk.
Education: Faculty of Law, Gdansk (1991).
Leisure: Tennis, diving.

RUTKOWSKI, Karol

Rutkowski Windmill Gasiewski & Roman LP
Phone: Warsaw (48 22 622 26 96)
E-mail: karol.rutkowski@rwgr.pl
Position: Senior partner of Rutkowski Windmill Gasiewski & Roman LP, which deals with litigation and arbitration, banking, capital markets and corporate matters. Mr Rutkowski has significant experience in Polish securities law, banking law and litigation, including civil and criminal cases. He is an arbitrator of the Court of Arbitration at the National Chamber of Commerce in Warsaw. He is the author of many articles on dispute resolutions, banking and capital markets, and has participated in the drafting of the Polish 'Accounting Law', the 'Chartered Auditors Law' and the 'Act on the Organisation and Operation of Pension Funds'.
Career: Qualified as a prosecutor and judge 1988, as a legal adviser (solicitor) 1993, and as an advocate (barrister) 1996; head of financial crimes department, Regional Public Prosecutor's Office 1988; legal adviser, Bank Gospodarki Zywnosciowej 1992; vice-president, Coopers & Lybrand 1994; partner, Cameron McKenna, Warsaw 1996; partner London 1997; partner, Lovells 2001; founded Karol Rutkowski Law Office LP 2003; senior partner Rutkowski Windmill Gasiewski & Roman LP 2005. During his professional life, Karol Rutkowski has been responsible for the preparation and submission to the Polish Securities and Stock Exchange Commission of nine prospectuses for public offerings of shares, including the privatisation of one of the major commercial banks and two other banks listed on the Stock Exchange. He was also in charge of a team of lawyers which conducted a due diligence exercise on five leading Polish commercial banks, and led the team which carried out the separation of the National

Depository of Securities from the Warsaw Stock Exchange. He also led the legal team which put together the agreement establishing the only banking group in Poland during the consolidation of the Polish banking sector and which prepared a comprehensive report on the legal issues associated with this venture.
Languages: Polish, English.
Member: District Chamber of Barristers, Warsaw; District Chamber of Legal Advisers, Warsaw; Court of Arbitration, National Chamber of Commerce, Warsaw; Law Society of England and Wales.
Education: Faculty of Law, University of Gdansk; Faculty of Law and Administration, Warsaw University (1986 MA Law); Law Institute, Polish Academy of Sciences PAN (doctoral studies).
Leisure: Natural philosophy, sport.

SCHMIDT, Christian

GESSEL - Attorneys at Law
Phone: Warsaw (+48 22 318 6901)
E-mail: c.schmidt@gessel.com.pl
Partner responsible for German desk.
Position: Partner and rechtsanwalt, focusing on foreign investment in Poland, either through mergers and acquisitions with Polish companies or through direct investment in various sectors of industry, including: steel, engineering, automotive, food, pharmaceuticals, transport, media, real estate, banking and insurance. He also advises German banks and financial institutions granting finance to Polish borrowers or dedicated to projects in Poland.
Career: Legal consultant in Central and Eastern Europe 1990-94; associate at Boesebeck, Barz & Partner 1995-97; associate at the Warsaw office of Boesebeck Droste 1997-99; managing partner at Lovells Warsaw 2000-05. Author of many publications on legal issues and legal aspects of the developing economies of Central and Eastern Europe.
Languages: German, English, Polish, Spanish, Russian, French.
Member: Polish Bar Association; Rechtsanwaltskammer, Frankfurt am Main.
Education: Hamburg University, Law Faculty and Slavonic languages studies; St Petersburg University, Law Faculty (postgraduate studies); The Hague Academy of International Law; Max Planck Institute, foreign and international private law, Eastern Europe; Johann Wolfgang Goethe University, Frankfurt.
Personal: Born 1957; resides Warsaw.
Leisure: Literature, art, music.

SWIERZEWSKI, Olgierd

Lukowicz Swierzewski & Partners
Phone: Warsaw (+48 22 827 33 22)
E-mail: oswierzewski@lukowicz.pl
Banking, finance; corporate, mergers and acquisitions; intellectual property and technology, media and communications; regulatory and public law.
Position: Partner and legal adviser, specialising in regulatory, competition, commercial and civil law and intellectual property law. Has extensive experience in regulatory risk management, as well as in performing regulatory impact assessment analysis for the Polish Government, the Organisation for Economic Co-operation and Development and private companies. Has led many projects for Ernst & Young Legal and Ernst & Young Transaction Advisory Services connected with legal risk forecasting and assessing the impact of new regulatory acts for the business. Has extensive expertise in preparation of regulatory strategies, legal risk management (including legal risk audit), disputes with regulatory bodies, harmonisation of Polish law with European law (an expert of the Polish Parliament and the Polish Government), legal screening, restructuring, privatisation agreements, reorganisation of processes (concepts and legal implementation). Moreover, Olgierd Swierzewski has extensive experience in intellectual property management, as well as in performing cross-border transactions with reference to trade mark and patents, and analysis for the Polish Government concerning new legislation - industrial property law and intellectual property law. Has led many projects connected with legal protection of intangible assets and intellectual capital. Has extensive expertise in preparation of IP management strategies (including IP risk audit), disputes with regulatory bodies, and harmonisation of Polish law with European law in the area of patents, trade marks and protection of design.
Career: Trained District Bar Association of Legal Advisers in Warsaw; qualified 2005; partner 2006; former lecturer at the District Bar of Legal Advisers in Warsaw (European intellectual property law).
Languages: Fluent Polish and English; basic Russian and French.
Member: Member District Bar Association of Legal Advisers in Warsaw.
Education: Faculty of Law and Administration, Warsaw University (1995); European Law Academy, Trier (1998 supplementary studies); Warsaw School of Economics (2000 postgraduate management study); Scuola di Managemento, Guido Carli University, Rome (2002 course on structural fund management).
Personal: Born 1971; resides Warsaw.

SZCZEŚNIAK, Dariusz

DeBenedetti Majewski Michalski Szczesniak Kancelaria Prawnicza Sp. K.
Phone: Warsaw (+48 22 339 54 04)
E-mail: dszczesniak@dms.net.pl
Legal adviser.
Position: Managing partner, specialising in pensions funds, investment funds, insurance law, securities law and corporate law; as well as administrative proceedings.
Career: Mr Szcześniak has been a legal adviser since 1996, and qualified as a judge in the same year. He was a member and then head of the legal team of the fund management branch of Polski Bank Rozwoju SA (1995-97); has been a legal adviser and director of the legal department of PBK ATUT Investment Fund (1997-98); an associate at CMS Cameron McKenna, Warsaw (1998-2000) and was in charge of the capital markets department of Salans Warsaw office (2000-04). In 2003, Euromoney Legal Media Group in the Guide to the World's Leading Capital Markets Lawyers recommended Mr Szcześniak as a legal expert on capital markets in Poland.
Languages: Polish, English and Russian.
Member: Warsaw Chamber of Legal Advisers.
Education: Law Faculty at Warsaw University (1993).
Personal: Born 1969; married with three children.
Leisure: Skiing and windsurfing.

WIERCIŃSKI, Andrzej, Dr

Wierciński, Kwieciński, Baehr Sp. k.
Phone: Warsaw (+48 22 630 31 31)
E-mail: a.wiercinski@wkw.pl
Mergers and acquisitions, insolvency law, restructuring law.
Position: Extensive experience in corporate mergers and acquisitions; headed and advised on most complex projects in this area in Poland. Took part in the privatization of the first five state enterprises as well as the first two state-owned banks and has advised on the creation of the first Polish joint ventures. Has gained substantial experience in insolvency law (sale of insolvent shipyard, composition proceedings of major Polish private telecom holding company, including security arrangements) and in energy law (privatization and consolidation of the energy distribution sector).
Career: Co-founding partner of Wardyński & Partners; co-founder of Wierciński, Kwieciński, Baehr Sp. k. For the last few years he has been a regular correspondent for Global Competition Review. Recommended as a leading counsel in Poland (in the field of corporate law and mergers & acquisitions) by inter alia: (i) The Global Counsel Handbooks, Mergers and Acquisitions 2004/05, (ii) The Chambers Global The World's Leading Lawyers 2003, (iii) The Chambers & Partners Global The World's Leading Lawyers 2003-2004, (iv) The European Legal 500 (2003).
Languages: English, Polish, Russian.
Member: Warsaw Bar Association; International Bar Association; Association of Competition Law.
Education: Faculty of Law and Administration at Adam Mickiewicz University (1973 PhD, 1982 advanced doctorate in legal studies).
Personal: Born 1947; resides Warsaw.
Leisure: Tennis, history, cooking.

WINDMILL, Robert

Rutkowski Windmill Gasiewski & Roman LP
Phone: Warsaw (+48 22 622 26 96)
E-mail: robert.windmill@rwgr.pl
Position: Partner at Rutkowski Windmill & Roman LP.
Career: 40 year's legal experience, specialising in mergers and acquisitions; partner in CMS Cameron McKenna for 25 years; head of the London-based Japan group, representing Japanese investors in in-bound acquisitions in Europe; acted on behalf of Fuji Bank in several transactions for their clients, Nomura International plc, in conjunction with the privatisation of the Danubius hotel chain in Hungary and for numerous Japanese companies in the UK; until its closure in 1995, he wrote regular columns reporting on European mergers and acquisitions in Keizaikai M&A, then the leading Japanese M&A journal; founded and headed up the Central European group of CMS

Cameron McKenna, opening offices in Budapest, Prague, Warsaw, Moscow and Bucharest 1989-2001; has been active in transactions arising out of the privatisation programmes in Poland, Hungary, Russia, the Czech Republic, Romania, Bulgaria and the Baltic States and has had extensive contact with the relevant privatisation ministries; in the mid-1990s, he co-founded, with partners from Swedish and Danish law firms, a group of law firms in the Baltic region (the Hansa Law Group); largely responsible for bringing the Swedish and Danish firms in the Baltic grouping into the CMS group; a partner of the firm became the CMS chief executive; joined Haarmann Hemmelrath as a partner 2001; focused on the Central and Eastern European practice of the firm in Poland, Hungary, the Czech Republic and Romania; specifically managed the Warsaw and Budapest offices and the legal group in their Bucharest office; managed the practice of Haarmann Hemmelrath in central Europe 2001-04; currently, Robert is a partner in Rutkowski Windmill Gasiewski & Roman Law Office and leads its M&A practice, as well as co-ordinating international contacts.
Languages: English, French.
Member: The Law Society of England and Wales.
Leisure: Fishing, shooting.

PORTUGAL

BAIÃO DO NASCIMENTO, Felipe

Baião, Castro, Solla & Associados, RI
Phone: Lisbon (351 21 319 0646)
E-mail: fbn@bcs.pt
Banking and capital markets, project finance, PPP.
Position: Partner.
Career: Qualified 1994; in-house lawyer BCP Investimento; Committee for the Reform of the Law on Portuguese Public Debt; lecturer University of Lisbon Faculty of Law (tax law and public finance); partner Baião, Castro, Solla & Associados, RI 1997 to date. Publications include 'Reforma da Dívida Pública - Legislação Anotada' (co-authored).
Languages: Portuguese, English, Italian, Spanish.
Member: Portuguese Bar Association; International Bar Association; Portuguese Securities Institute.
Education: University of Lisbon Faculty of Law (1992).
Personal: Born 1969; resides Lisbon.

CANIÇO GOMES, João

Simmons & Simmons Rebelo de Sousa
Phone: Lisbon (+351 21 313 20 00)
E-mail: joao.canico@prs.pt
Litigation, arbitration, dispute resolution, insolvency/corporate restructuring and real estate.
Position: Head of litigation and disputes resolution departments, with expertise in dealing with commercial and civil arbitration. 'Chambers Global' quotes João's team as offering 'matchless technical know-how in the litigation domain.' Moreover, according to 'Chambers Global', he is distinguished for his trial and arbitration practice on such topics as unfair competition and general commercial disputes, and his clients and peers state that they admire his 'deep knowledge on the technical side'.
Career: Qualified 1991; partner JA Pereira da Silva, Rui Afonso & Associados, Lisbon; Simmons & Simmons Rebelo de Sousa, Lisbon 1993; partner, Lisbon 2001 to date. João has contributed a variety of articles on dispute resolution to various publications, including the Bar Association Journal and the 'Diário Económico'. He is a regular speaker at seminars and public conferences on his practice areas.
Languages: Portuguese, English, Spanish, French.
Member: Elected member of the Portuguese Bar Association (1998-2001); chairman of the Disciplinary Council of the Lisbon Bar Association (1999-2001).
Education: Faculdade de Direito da Universidade Lusíada.

CARNEIRO, Andreia Lima

Simmons & Simmons Rebelo de Sousa
Phone: Oporto (+351 22 543 2613)
E-mail: andreia.carneiro@prs.pt
Dispute resolution.
Position: Andreia is head of the dispute resolution practice in the Oporto office. She has extensive experience in all areas of civil and commercial litigation and arbitration, and has advised Portuguese clients on various contentious issues. Andreia leads a team of lawyers with particular expertise in corporate, labour and administrative law issues.
Languages: English, Portuguese, Spanish.
Member: Portuguese Legal Bar Association (since 1994).
Education: Católica University (1992 law degree); Portucalense University (2003 post-graduate law degree).
Leisure: Reading, cinema.

CASTELO PAULO, Octávio

Simmons & Simmons Rebelo de Sousa
Phone: Lisbon (+351 21 313 20 00)
E-mail: octavio.paulo@prs.pt
Position: Partner of the firm and head of the corporate commercial department and the telecommunications, media and technology practices. Octávio deals in particular with M&A matters, agency and distribution agreements, telecommunications regulatory issues and with technology and related IP issues.
Career: Legal adviser of several Portuguese Government Secretaries of State in late 1980s and early 1990s; lawyer at CTT - Correios de Portugal (postal incumbent) and later at Portugal Telecom; joined Simmons & Simmons in 1993 and became partner in 1999. Octávio lectures on commercial and corporate law in the Lusíada Lisbon University and writes on the subjects of his speciality. He contributes to various legal publications and speaks at international and national conferences and seminars.
Languages: Portuguese, English, Spanish, French.
Member: Portuguese Bar; Lusíada Lisbon University and APDC - Portuguese Association for the Development of Communications.
Education: Graduated in law from the law faculty of the Lusíada Lisbon University.
Personal: Born 1964; resides Lisbon.
Leisure: Literature, music, European history of the 20th Century and travelling.

CASTRO E SOLLA, José

Baião, Castro, Solla & Associados, RI
Phone: Lisbon (351 21 319 0640)
E-mail: jcs@bcs.pt
Real estate and construction.
Position: Partner.
Career: Qualified 1993; in-house lawyer Tabaqueira; senior in-house lawyer Nutrinveste, SGPS; senior in-house lawyer Finibanco; partner Baião, Castro, Solla & Associados, RI 1997 to date.
Languages: Portuguese, English, Spanish.
Member: Portuguese Bar Association.
Education: University of Lisbon Faculty of Law (2004-05 postgraduate studies on construction, administrative and environmental laws); Portuguese Catholic University Faculty of Law (1990).
Personal: Born 1967; resides Lisbon.

CASTRO NUNES, Victor

Baião, Castro, Solla & Associados, RI
Phone: Lisbon (351 21 319 0647)
E-mail: vcn@bcs.pt
Mergers and acquisitions, corporate and commercial, privatisation, tax.
Position: Partner.
Career: Qualified 1993; senior in-house lawyer BCP Investimento; lawyer Miguel Galvão Teles, João Soares da Silva & Associados; lecturer University of Lisbon Faculty of Law (Tax Law and the Law of Economy); partner Baião, Castro, Solla & Associados, RI 1997 to date.
Languages: Portuguese, English, French, Spanish.
Member: Portuguese Bar Association; International Bar Association; Portuguese Fiscal Association; International Fiscal Association.
Education: University of Lisbon Faculty of Law (1990); Queen Mary University of London (1994 LLM).
Personal: Born 1968; resides Lisbon.

DA SILVA, José Moreira

Simmons & Simmons Rebelo de Sousa
Phone: Lisbon (+351 21 313 20 00)
E-mail: moreira.silva@prs.pt
Public/administrative law.
Position: Local partner and head of public and administrative law. José is highly regarded in the fields of public law, licensing, concessions, public procurement and administrative litigation. He advises multinational companies, banks and the public and private sector on general public law issues and other related work. In 2004, he was recognised as a specialist in administrative law by the Portuguese Bar Association.
Career: Lawyer since 1986; cabinet member of the Portuguese Secretary of State for Transportation 1986-90; assistant professor of public law at Lisbon University

1990-2004; in-house lawyer State Savings Bank Caixa Geral de Depósitos 1993-2000; cabinet member of the Ministry of Employment and Social Security 1994-95; member of the Portuguese Parliament 1996-99. Author of several works and scientific articles and regularly contributes to various legal publications; speaker at international and national conferences and seminars.
Languages: English, Spanish, French, German.
Member: Portuguese Law Society; several legal associations of public and regulatory law.
Education: Universidade Católica Portuguesa (masters degree); Faculdade de Direito de Lisboa (doctorate).

ESTEVES, César Sá

Simmons & Simmons Rebelo de Sousa
Phone: Lisbon (+351 21 313 2000)
E-mail: cesar.esteves@prs.pt
Employment/pharmaceutical.
Position: Partner and head of the employment department at Simmons & Simmons Rebelo de Sousa & Associados (SSRS). Also responsible for the pharmaceutical and biotechnology practice, the insurance practice and the immigration practice.
Career: Called to the Portuguese Bar 1994; author of several publications on European and Portuguese employment law and currently a co-author and co-ordinator of the Portuguese 'Practical Guide to Labour Procedures' (Verlag Dashöfer, 2004 to date); regular speaker at seminars and public conferences on his practice areas.
Languages: English, Portuguese, French, Spanish.
Member: Portuguese representative on the Executive Board of the European Employment Lawyers Association (EELA) since 2001; member, European Immigration Lawyers Network (EILN) 2002 to date; vice president of Portuguese Young Lawyers Association 2000-02.
Education: Universidade Católica de Lisboa (1992 law degree); Instituto Superior de Gestão, Lisbon (1996 post-graduate course in business law); Universidade de Coimbra (2002 post-graduation course in pharmaceutical law).
Leisure: Cinema, reading, theatre.

MARQUES MENDES, Mário

Marques Mendes & Associados
Phone: Lisbon (+351 21 382 63 00)
E-mail: mmm@marquesmendes.pt
Position: Mário Marques Mendes is a senior partner at Marques Mendes & Associados, whose practice covers a wide spectrum of business and commercial law, with emphasis on corporate, banking/finance and all areas of EU law, in particular competition/antitrust and regulatory matters, as well as litigation and arbitration. The firm is also strongly involved in the information technology, telecommunications, energy and media areas. Focusing his practice on EU and international trade law, notably competition/antitrust, M&A, intellectual property, state aid and public procurement, Mário Marques Mendes has advised and represented public and private sector clients in significant cases at both national and EC levels, handling important litigation before national and EC courts.
Career: After graduating, Mário Marques Mendes became assistant professor of law at the University of Lisbon Law School, and lectured on international trade law at the Centre for European Studies of the Portuguese Catholic University, Lisbon, while resuming private practice. He served as vice-president of the Lisbon Council of the Portuguese Bar Association (1996-98). He is a frequent speaker and has written extensively on various subjects of international trade law and EU law, notably competition/antitrust.
Member: Portuguese Bar Association; Portuguese Association of European Law; European Association of Lawyers; International Bar Association.
Education: Law graduate of the University of Lisbon Law School (1976); EC law graduate of the College of Europe, Bruges (1981); and as a Fulbright Scholar, a law graduate of the University of Michigan Law School (1984, LLM).
Personal: Born 1954.

MATOS MARTINS, Ana Paula

Baião, Castro, Solla & Associados, RI
Phone: Lisbon (351 21 319 0640)
E-mail: apmm@bcs.pt
Litigation, arbitration and insolvency.
Position: Partner.
Career: Qualified 1994; lawyer José Miranda Dias (Law Office); partner Baião, Castro, Solla & Associados, RI 2001 to date.
Languages: Portuguese, English, Spanish.
Member: Portuguese Bar Association; Portuguese Bar Association Examinations Board.
Education: University of Lisbon Faculty of Law (1992).
Personal: Born 1969; resides Lisbon.

MOUTEIRA GUERREIRO, António

Mouteira Guerreiro, Rosa Amaral & Associados - Sociedade de Advogados R.L.
Phone: Lisbon (+351 21 359 50 90)
E-mail: amg@mgra.pt
Corporate and finance division.
Position: Co-founding partner of MGRA and head of its corporate and finance division. Main areas of expertise are corporate and finance, including M&A and corporate restructurings; LBOs, MBOs, MBIs and IPOs; capital markets; takeovers; project, asset and lease finance (including cross-border leasing); telecoms; banking and insurance; real estate and construction.
Career: Legal consultant Portuguese Securities Market Commission (CMVM) until 1998; senior lawyer banking and finance division Gonçalves Pereira, Castelo Branco & Associados until 2004; co-founding and co-managing partner MGRA. Publications: author of several works in the corporate and finance area, including: 'New Portuguese Securities Code' (IFLR); 'Banking Law in Portugal' (BM); 'Naked Warrants' (JN). Speaker at several lectures, including: 'Leasing, Renting and ALD' (IFIR, Lisbon); and 'Legal Advisory Roundtable Across Europe' (Big Ticket Leasing Convention - Asset Finance/Euromoney, London, 2004). Participant in several national and international seminars and congresses related with area of expertise.
Languages: English, Portuguese, Spanish.
Member: Portuguese Bar Association.
Education: University of Lisbon (Law; 1998 Securities Law).
Personal: Resides Lisbon; married.

PRATA, Nuno Miguel

Simmons & Simmons Rebelo de Sousa
Phone: Madeira (+351 291 20 22 60)
E-mail: nuno.prata@prs.pt
Commercial and corporate.
Position: Local partner and head of the Madeira office since its opening in 1999; main areas of activity include commercial and corporate law.
Career: Trained Simmons & Simmons Rebelo de Sousa, Lisbon; qualified 1996; partner and head of Madeira office 1999 to date. Contributes to various legal publications; speaker at international and national conferences and seminars.
Languages: English, Portuguese, Spanish.
Member: Portuguese Bar Association (since 1996).
Education: Universidade Católica Portuguesa do Porto; University College London (1994 LLM in international trade and European law).
Leisure: Tennis, photography.

REBELO DE SOUSA, Pedro

Simmons & Simmons Rebelo de Sousa
Phone: Lisbon (+351 21 313 20 00)
E-mail: pedro.rebelosousa@prs.pt
Mergers and acquisitions and corporate finance, energy.
Position: Managing partner of Simmons & Simmons Rebelo de Sousa, regarded as a specialist in finance law by the Portuguese Bar Association.
Career: In-house lawyer Citibank NA, Latin America, Brazil 1977-81; vice president and international general counsel 1982-84; vice president, LDC and deputy department and country unit head Citicorp Investment Bank, New York 1985-87; vice president, international corporate finance division Citibank NA, New York 1988-90; president and chief executive office (responsible for the privatisation process) Banco Fonsecas & Burnay, SA, Lisbon 1990-92; managing partner Simmons & Simmons Rebelo de Sousa in Lisbon, Oporto and Madeira 1993 to date. Author of several works and scientific articles and regularly contributes to various legal publications; speaker at international and domestic conferences and seminars; visiting professor at business and law schools. Board member of Simmons & Simmons and supervisory/advisory board member of several companies: Galp, PT Intal, Sumol, Nova Base, Banif Invest, Alcatel Portugal.
Languages: English, Portuguese, French, Spanish.
Member: Bars of Portugal, Brazil and England and Wales.
Education: Faculdade de Direito da Universidade de Lisboa (1976); Catholic Law University, Sao Paulo, Brazil (1979 post-graduate course); Getúlio Vargas Business School, Sao Paulo (1981 masters in international business administration).
Leisure: Swimming, travelling, music, reading.

ROCHA, Mário Melo

Simmons & Simmons Rebelo de Sousa
Phone: Lisbon (+351 21 313 20 00)
E-mail: melo.rocha@prs.pt
Environment.
Position: Head of environment and renewable energies department, advising on the construction of several wind farms and a photovoltaic power plant. Also advising companies on the assessment of environmental impact matter, water and waste matters, contaminated lands matters and biofuels matters.
Career: ENERNOVA (EDP group); ENERSIS; AMPER; RENATURA; several municipalities. Professor of environmental law at the Catholic Portuguese University; author of several works and scientific articles and regularly contributes to various legal publications; speaker at international and national conferences and seminars.
Languages: English, Spanish, French, Italian.
Member: SEDES Association; TEAM EUROPE Association.
Education: Faculdade de Direito de Coimbra: Universidade Católica Portuguesa (masters); Faculdade de Direito da UCP de Lisboa (doctorate preparation).
Leisure: Reading.

ROSA AMARAL, Mário da

Mouteira Guerreiro, Rosa Amaral & Associados - Sociedade de Advogados R.L.
Phone: Lisbon (+351 21 359 50 90)
E-mail: mra@mgra.pt
Tax division.
Position: Co-founding partner of MGRA and head of the tax division. Main area of expertise is tax, including tax litigation and tax infractions, and national and international tax consultancy and planning, namely finance and real estate structured operations and Madeira free zone.
Career: Tax lawyer Morais Leitão, Galvão Teles & Associados until 2000; senior tax lawyer Gonçalves Pereira, Castelo Branco & Associados until 2004; co-founding and co-managing partner MGRA.
Publications: author of several works in the area of taxation, including 'Portugal: Transition from Escudo to Euro' (JIBL); 'Taxation of Wealth Manifestations' (JN); co-author of various specialised articles published by the International Bureau of Fiscal Documentation and by the American Bar Association; co-author of various tax guides. Participant in several lectures and seminars related with area of expertise.
Languages: English, Portuguese, Spanish.
Member: Portuguese Bar Association; Portuguese Fiscal Association; Portuguese Tax Consultants Association.
Education: University of Lisbon (Law); Superior Institute of Administration (1999 Tax Law).
Personal: Resides Lisbon.

SANTANA, Maria José

Simmons & Simmons Rebelo de Sousa
Phone: Lisbon (+351 21 313 2000)
E-mail: maria.santana@prs.pt
Real estate.
Position: Local partner and head of real estate department. Has experience in dealing with tourism and hotels, construction and travel agencies; M&A, LBO and MBO transactions; joint ventures; public-to-private deals representing domestic and foreign investors (debt and equity investors), public tenders and privatisations, government concession contracts, LDD, maritimr transport, port operations and insurance.
Career: Legal adviser CII - Consultoria International de Investimentos, SA; associate lawyer Corrêa Mandes e Associados - Sociedade de Advogados; partner Oliveira, Martins, Moura, Esteves & Associados - Sociedade de Advogados (a Landwell law firm); real estate DH Simmons & Simmons Rebelo de Sousa - Sociedade de Advogados.
Languages: Portuguese, English, French.
Member: Portuguese Bar Association since 1988.
Education: Graduate of the law faculty of the University of Lisbon (1985).
Personal: Born 1961; resides Cascais.
Leisure: Reading, cinema, theatre.

SMITHSON, William

Simmons & Simmons Rebelo de Sousa
Phone: Lisbon (+351 21 313 2000)
E-mail: william.smithson@simmons-simmons.com
Head of finance markets practice, Lisbon office.
Position: William is highly regarded in the fields of corporate finance, banking and capital markets. He advises investment banks and companies on public and private mergers and acquisitions, joint and other related work. William has built up an extensive securitisation practice having worked on 40 ABS and RMBS transactions by Portuguese originators. He also advises on debt and equity capital markets transactions and has established an active structured securities practice. Recent work includes: advising international investment banks (including Deutsche Bank, BNP Paribas, CSFB and HSBC), as well as Portuguese originators, on over 40 securitisations (ABS, RMBS and trade receivables) by Portuguese entities; advising Sociéété Générale on the Douro securtsation of SME Loans by Banco BPI, the first securitisation of SME Loans in Portugal and the first securitisation by Banco BPI; advising the arranger on the first-ever debt private placement in the US by a Portuguese company (CIMPOR); advising Goldman Sachs on the first-ever acquisition of a non-performing loan portfolio in Portugal; advising Scottish and Newcastle on the acquisition of Centralcer; advising Warner Brothers on its disposal of 50% of Warner Lusomundo; advising ENI on its participation in GALP; advising Alenia/Finmeccanica on the privatisation of OGMA.
Career: Trained Simmons & Simmons, London; qualifed 1989; banking and capital markets lawyer Simmons & Simmons, London 1989-92; banking, capital markets and corporate finance lawyer Simmons & Simmons, Lisbon 1992-2000; partner Simmons & Simmons, Lisbon 2001 to date.
Languages: English, Portuguese, Spanish (working knowledge).
Member: England and Wales Law Society.

QATAR

SALT, David

Simmons & Simmons
Phone: Doha (+974 483 9466)
E-mail: david.salt@simmons-simmons.com
Business law.
Position: Consultant. Involved in corporate and commercial, banking, project finance, mergers and acquisitions, insurance, oil and gas, aviation and construction. Advised the two main lenders on the Dolphin Pipeline Project; advised on the first-ever debt-equity swap in Qatar; advised on the first insurance portfolio transfer in Qatar; advised Oryx GTL Limited QSC in relation to gas-to-liquids project between Qatar Petroleum (QP) and Sasol.
Career: Trained Slaughter & May; qualified 1981; partner Clyde & Co 1990-2001; head of English langguage department law offices at Gebran Majdalany, Qatar 2001-04.
Languages: English, Russian, French, German (written); learning classical Arabic (spoken and written) and Persian.
Member: Law Society.
Education: Keble College, Oxford (MA); College of Law, Chester.
Personal: Born 1954; resides Doha.
Leisure: Travel, bird watching, opera.

WINGFIELD, Andrew

Simmons & Simmons
Phone: Doha (+974 483 9466)
E-mail: andrew.wingfield@simmons-simmons.com
Business law.
Position: Managing partner. Deals with all areas of corporate, commercial and financial services law.
Career: Trained Simmons & Simmons; qualified England and Wales 1985; qualified Hong Kong 1986; head of corporate department Hong Kong office; managing partner New York office 1999-2005; moved to Doha 2005.
Languages: English.
Member: Law Society of England and Wales; Law Society of Hong Kong; licensed Foreign Legal Consultant in New York; New York City Bar Association; IBA; IPBA; ABA.
Education: University of Bristol; College of Law, London.
Personal: Born 1959; resides Doha.
Leisure: Tennis, sailing, skiing and travel.

ROMANIA

BAICULESCU, Catalin
Musat & Asociatii
Phone: Bucharest (40 21 202 59 04)
E-mail: catalin@musat.ro
Position: Partner. Mr Baiculescu's expertise in banking and finance spans all aspects of general finance and banking law, including securities law, contractual relationships, syndicated loans and compliance, with a focus on financing transactions, bank restructuring/privatisation, electronic banking and insurance law. He has advised financial institutions in the financing of complex transactions, has represented international banks in negotiating consortium agreements, takeovers, debt restructuring and asset finance transactions. Mr Baiculescu has acted on a number of high-profile mergers and acquisitions and Romanian banking privatisations, having a wide and considerable experience of the due diligence process and the negotiation of privatisation agreements. Further areas of experience include aviation, communications, media and information technology.
Languages: Romanian, English, French.
Member: Bucharest and Romanian Bar Associations.
Education: Law degree RO.

BUZESCU, Peter
Buzescu Ca
Phone: Bucharest (+40 21 222 4422)
E-mail: pbuzescu@buzescu.com
Position: Managing partner.
Career: In-house counsel, Midia Petrochemicals 1977-78; private practice, 1978-81; senior legal specialist, European Law Division, US Library of Congress, 1984-88 - in such capacity he provided advice and legal opinions on international matters to the US Justice Department, and members of the US Congress; private practice 1988-to present; Administrative Law Judge, Environmental Control Board of the City of New York, 1990-91; publications: 'What to Expect from Joint Ventures in Moscow' (The 'Wall Street Journal', Europe edition, 6 January 1987); 'Foreign Investment and Taxation of Foreign Enterprises and Individuals in Romania' (Library of Congress, ed 1986); 'Foreign Bank Operations in Switzerland: New Regulations and Some Practical Considerations' (19 The International Lawyer 897, 1985); 'Joint Ventures in Eastern Europe' (the American Journal of Comparative Law 407, 1984).
Languages: English, French, Romanian.
Member: New York State Bar; Bucharest Bar; past vice-president of the American Chamber of Commerce in Romania; International Bar Association; International Trademark Association.
Education: Bucharest University School of Law (LLB magna cum laude, 1975); New York University School of Law (LLM, 1984).
Personal: Born 1951; resides Bucharest.
Leisure: Egyptology, arts of Renaissance, reading.

CHILIM, Adina
Nestor Nestor Diculescu Kingston Petersen
Phone: Bucharest (+40 21 20 11 200)
E-mail: adina.chilim@nnkp.ro
Position: Partner dealing with projects related to gas distribution, project finance, mergers and acquisitions and telecommunications.
Career: Joined Nestor Nestor Diculescu Kingston Petersen 1997; partner 2004.
Languages: English.
Member: Bucharest Bar Association.
Education: University of Bucharest, Law Faculty (1997, magna cum laude).
Personal: Born 1974; resides Bucharest.
Leisure: Climbing, reading, music, cinema.

DAMIAN, Ştefan
Ţuca Zbârcea & Asociaţii
Phone: Bucharest (+40 21 204 88 93)
E-mail: stefan.damian@tuca.ro
Mergers, acquisitions and privatisations; competition.
Position: Ştefan is the deputy managing partner at Ţuca Zbârcea & Asociaţii; he has built up a wealth of experience in high-profile privatisation/mergers and acquisitions transactions, including the post-acquisition/privatisation period; one of the most significant cases handled by Ştefan, as a co-ordinator, was the privatisation of the largest steel plant in Eastern Europe; he has presented many cases to the Romanian Competition Council and advised on the full range of competition issues (mergers, antitrust, state aid), including assistance to obtain merger clearances, individual and block exemptions; he has also assisted in investigations and dawn raids, as well as in litigation involving all aspects of competition law; other areas of practice include corporate/commercial, securities law and project finance; he has recently advised, or is currently advising, Deutsche Bank AG, Mittal Steel Group, Petrom SA, Merrill Lynch, Visa International, Citigroup, France Telecom, GlaxoSmithKline, Friesland, Tetra Laval, General Electric, BNP Paribas, Raiffeisen Bank, Astaldi SpA, Alcoa Fujikura GmbH, the Authority for State Assets Recovery (AVAS), OPSPI, the Romanian Ministry of Economy and the Romanian Ministry of Finances; author of various articles to financial and legal publications, such as: 'Merger and acquisition - What Should Be Taken Into Account' in Merger & Acquisition Yearbook 2001; 'Global Merger Notification Handbook 2002-05' - Romanian chapter; 'Squeeze-out/Delisting Procedure under the New Capital Market Regulation'; 'Considerations on the Joint Liability Existing within Some Groups of Companies.'.
Career: Trained Musat & Asociatii; qualified 1999; partner 2001-05; deputy managing partner Ţuca Zbârcea & Asociaţii 2005 to date.
Languages: English, Romanian.
Member: Bucharest Bar Association.
Education: Romanian-American University (1997 Law).
Personal: Born 1974; resides Bucharest.

DANESCU, Alina
Danescu, Danescu & Associates
Phone: Bucharest (+40 21 210 65 55)
E-mail: alina.danescu@danescu.ro
Head of the legal consultancy department.
Position: Managing partner, coordinating the firm's activities; advising on a broad range of practice areas, with a particular focus on corporate. Project coordinator, managing the legal accounts of the firm's foreign and international clients. Broad expertise in the field of capital markets. Main areas of specialisation include commercial, mergers and acquisitions, competition, banking and finance, contracts.
Career: One of the first Romanian lawyers to specialise in the legal aspects of capital markets, Mrs Alina Danescu was involved in the establishment of organisations such as RASDAQ and UNOPC, as well as in drafting and implementing the capital market regulations. She organised seminars, in collaboration with the American Bar Association, relating to this area of practice, for the judges of the Courts of Appeal, and for students.
Languages: English.
Member: Bucharest Bar Association since 1990.
Education: University of Bucharest, Faculty of Law (1990); awarded 'Best Young Jurist' diploma 1993.
Personal: Born 1967; resides Bucharest.

DANESCU, Costea Corin
Danescu, Danescu & Associates
Phone: Bucharest (+40 21 210 65 55)
E-mail: corin.danescu@danescu.ro
Head of the litigation department.
Position: Senior partner highly specialised in dispute resolution, dealing with all aspects of litigation and arbitration. Particular expertise in recovering properties nationalised under the communist regime, Mr Costea Corin Danescu has successfully settled an impressive number of legal cases in this area, as adviser to long-established Romanian families. His main areas of expertise cover: civil and commercial law, real estate and construction, banking, taxation, labour, bankruptcy and insolvency, contracts, administrative law.
Career: Founded the private practice which later became Danescu, Danescu & Associates in 1983; tutor with the Romanian Institute for the Training and Development of Lawyers.
Languages: English, French.
Member: Bucharest Bar Association since 1983; arbiter with the UNSAR Insurance Arbitration Commission.
Education: University of Bucharest, Faculty of Law (1983); National School for Administration, Paris (1990).
Personal: Born 1958; resides Bucharest.

DICULESCU-SOVA, Ana
Nestor Nestor Diculescu Kingston Petersen
Phone: Bucharest (+40 21 20 11 200)
E-mail: ana.diculescu@nnkp.ro
Position: Senior partner dealing with all aspects of the dispute resolution practice, including civil, commercial, competition and fiscal law.
Career: Private practice in civil and commercial litigation from 1977; vice-president, Romanian International Union of Lawyers 1996; ad hoc judge, European Court for Human Rights 1999; partner Nestor Nestor Diculescu Kingston Petersen 2001.

Languages: French.
Member: Bucharest Bar Association.
Education: University of Bucharest, Law Faculty (1976 magna cum laude; 1988 PhD).
Personal: Born 1954; resides Bucharest.
Leisure: Reading, theatre.

EFTIMIE, Roxana

Sova & Partners
Phone: Bucharest (+40 311 001 126)
E-mail: roxana.eftimie@sova-avocati.ro
Competition law, telecommunications, media and IT, intellectual property, real estate and construction.
Position: Partner specialising in competition, dealing with complex matters covering a wide range of projects in antitrust law, economic concentration, unfair competition and state aid; she has expertise in the telecommunications and IT sectors due to participation in legislative projects, along with the pertinent public authorities; one of her most significant projects was in 2003-04 on behalf of the National Regulatory Authority for Communications: 'Assistance for Drafting and Promoting Regulations and Ongoing Technology Transfer for Enforcing the Legislative and Regulatory Framework, Training and Assistance for Training Strategy, Curriculum and Training Material, Development of the Training Centre, Romania'; she also has experience in the media and advertising sectors, having rendered general consultancy for major companies in the market, such as: Grafitti BBDO, Lowe Lintas GGK, Amerom Television etc; co-ordinated important projects regarding trading companies in collaboration with Ministry of Small- and Medium-sized Enterprises and Co-operation; publications include: Competition Strategy of Romania magazine 'Profile: Competition'; Romanian Business Law Magazine.
Career: Associate lawyer Cerveni & Cerveni Law Office and Ciubutariu Teodor Law Office, responsible for representation in courts in the fields of civil and commercial law 1999-2001; legal counsellor Romanian Competition Council, responsible for harmonising the provisions of Romanian competition law with those in the European legislation 2001-02; associate lawyer Sova & Partners, responsible for providing consultancy in the fields of competition law, mergers and acquisitions, governmental projects on trading companies, communication, media and IT, intellectual property 2002-04; partner and head of the consultancy department 2005.
Languages: English, French, Romanian.
Member: Bucharest Bar Association; Romanian Bar Association.
Education: University of Bucharest (1998 Faculty of Law; postgraduate courses, competition law 2001).
Personal: Born 1976; resides Bucharest.

FILIP, Cristina

Nestor Nestor Diculescu Kingston Petersen
Phone: Bucharest (+40 21 20 11 200)
E-mail: cristina.filip@nnkp.ro
Position: Partner dealing with projects related to electricity distribution and power generation, mergers and acquisitions and cross-border finance transactions.
Career: Joined Nestor Nestor Diculescu Kingston Petersen 1998; partner 2004.
Languages: English.
Member: Bucharest Bar Association.
Education: University of Bucharest, Law Faculty (1998, magna cum laude).
Personal: Born 1975; resides Bucharest.
Leisure: Reading, interior design.

GASPAR, Adriana

Nestor Nestor Diculescu Kingston Petersen
Phone: Bucharest (+40 21 20 11 200)
E-mail: adriana.gaspar@nnkp.ro
Position: Senior partner dealing with securities and capital markets, mergers and acquisitions and infrastructure development and financing.
Career: Judge, Bucharest Court - Sector 1 1993; associate professor, Bucharest University Law Faculty 1997; partner, Nestor Nestor Diculescu Kingston Petersen 2001.
Languages: English.
Member: Bucharest Bar Association.
Education: University of Bucharest, Law Faculty (1993 magna cum laude); Romanian Judicial College for Judges and Magistrates (1994 honours graduate).
Personal: Born 1970; resides Bucharest.
Leisure: Sport, theatre.

MUSAT, George

Musat & Asociatii
Phone: Bucharest (+40 21 202 59 01)
E-mail: musat@musat.ro
Managing partner.
Position: Apart from heading the management committee and overseeing the direction of the firm, George Musat is still heavily involved in the practice. He has practised for over 25 years and counts a substantial amount of Supreme Court hearings. He has an extensive wealth of experience from the foreign investors' perspective in Romania and a deep knowledge of the local market both in the private and state-owned sectors. He numbers important achievements as legal adviser in the privatisation and reorganisation of state-owned companies in Romania. He has been involved as team leader in various successful mergers and acquisitions, as well as in most of the major privatisation deals in Romania, acting either on the side of the Romanian government or the buyer's side. His experience specialises on corporate and commercial law, mergers and acquisitions/privatisation, project and corporate finance, banking and foreign investment law.
Languages: Romanian, English, French.
Member: Bucharest and Romanian Bar Associations.
Education: Law degree (RO).

NESTOR, Ion

Nestor Nestor Diculescu Kingston Petersen
Phone: Bucharest (+40 21 20 11 200)
E-mail: ion.nestor@nnkp.ro
Position: Senior partner dealing with cross-border finance transactions, mergers and acquisitions, securities and capital markets.
Career: Legal adviser and chief legal counsel, Romanian Consulting Institute 1976; legal consultant Institute of Legal Research, Romanian Academy in Bucharest 1983; private practitioner 1984; partner Nestor Nestor Diculescu Kingston Petersen since formation in 1990.
Languages: English, French.
Member: Bucharest Bar Association.
Education: University of Bucharest, Law Faculty (1976 magna cum laude).
Personal: Born 1953; resides Bucharest.
Leisure: Tennis, music, history.

NESTOR, Manuela

Nestor Nestor Diculescu Kingston Petersen
Phone: Bucharest (+40 21 20 11 200)
E-mail: manuela.nestor@nnkp.ro
Position: Senior partner dealing with cross-border finance transactions, mergers and acquisitions, securities and capital markets.
Career: Legal adviser and general counsel, Romanian Consulting Institute 1976; general counsel, University of Bucharest 1987; partner Nestor Nestor Diculescu Kingston Petersen since formation in 1990.
Languages: English, French.
Member: Bucharest Bar Association.
Education: University of Bucharest, Law Faculty (1976 magna cum laude).
Personal: Born 1953; resides Bucharest.
Leisure: Sport, music, reading.

RADU, Alina

Nestor Nestor Diculescu Kingston Petersen
Phone: Bucharest (+ 40 21 20 11 200)
E-mail: alina.radu@nnkp.ro
Position: Partner dealing with banking, project finance, mergers and acquisitions and real estate.
Career: Joined Nestor Nestor Diculescu Kingston Petersen 1997; partner 2004.
Languages: English.
Member: Bucharest Bar Association.
Education: Bucharest University, Law Faculty (1997 magna cum laude).
Personal: Born 1974; resides Bucharest.
Leisure: Reading, art.

SOVA, Dan

Sova & Partners
Phone: Bucharest (+40 311 001 126)
E-mail: dan.sova@sova-avocati.ro
Tax law, corporate law, M&A, commercial law, privatisations, project finance and infrastructure, judicial and judiciary restructuring, oil and gas, media, telecommunications.
Position: Founding and managing partner of Sova & Partners; directly and constantly involved with the firm's clients, serving as principal adviser on a wide variety of matters; has co-ordinated high-profile privatisation projects, as well as mergers and acquisitions projects, representing major players in the oil industry (Vitol) and the banking and finance sector (BRD-Groupe Société Générale), among others; he has supervised and co-ordinated major projects as a

certified practitioner in restructuring and liquidation; as a specialist in tax law, Mr Sova successfully led complex litigation matters with public institutions and government agencies, such as the Ministry of Public Finance and the National Authority for Tax Administration, before the courts of law; publications include: Tax Law Textbook, co-author Dan Drosu Saguna, work in progress; 'Public Financial Law Textbook', co-author Dan Drosu Saguna, All Beck Publishing House (2005); 'The Tax Code', revised edition, Rosetti Publishing House (2004); 'Tax Procedure', co-authors Simona Iliescu, Dan Drosu Saguna, Oscar Print Publishing House (1996); Romanian Law Business Magazine; University of Bucharest Annals; Commercial Law Magazine.
Career: Founded Sova & Partners 1997; director of the Business Law Magazine, one of the most respected magazines in Romania's business and law sector, 2002 to date; tenured lecturer on Romanian and European tax law at the Law School of the University of Bucharest; holds a seminar on tax procedures at the National Institute for Magistracy; has published extensively, including several books, textbooks and numerous articles in law magazines.
Languages: English, French, Romanian.
Member: Bucharest Bar Association; Romanian Bar Association; Romanian Union of Practitioners in Restructuring and Liquidation; Academic Staff Association of the University of Bucharest.
Education: University of Bucharest (1995 Faculty of Law; 2001 Faculty of History; MA in Public International Law and Public Politics 1996; PhD in Tax Law 2005); Ecole de Formation du Barreau de Paris, France (1996).
Personal: Born 1973; resides Bucharest.

ŢUCA, Florentin

Ţuca Zbârcea & Asociaţii
Phone: Bucharest (+40 21 204 88 91)
E-mail: florentin.tuca@tuca.ro
PPP, PFI and concessions; corporate and commercial.
Position: Florentin Ţuca is the managing partner at Ţuca Zbârcea & Asociaţii; having practised for 14 years, he has a wealth of experience in project finance, concessions and other forms of PPP/PFI projects, notably in infrastructure and energy; he has also handled, as co-ordinator, numerous privatisations, joint ventures, mergers and acquisitions, as well as corporate restructuring projects; he has gained a good reputation in handling complex domestic and international arbitration, particularly in relation to privatisation and cross-border disputes; in the first international arbitration case brought before the ICSID recently, he co-ordinated the team of lawyers who competently and successfully defended the Romanian Government against the claim of Noble Ventures Inc for $447m; other areas of practice include banking, secured transactions and corporate law; Florentin is also highly skilled in drafting laws and regulations, being involved in the development and implementation of the legal framework relate to privatisation, concessions, banking and other areas; he has recently advised, or is currently advising, Deutsche Bank AG, Mittal Steel Group, Monte dei Pachi di Siena, Vinci Concessions, Romtelecom, Petrom, Société Générale, CEZ, EBRD, Eximbank, the Romanian Government, the Romanian Ministry of Finance and the Romanian Ministry of Economy; author of many articles, books and legal considerations on topics relating, especially, to corporate law, PPP and concessions, including: 'Consequences of the Shares Transfer on the Quality of Creditor of the Dividends' in Juridica no1/2000; 'Civil Responsibility of Building Contractors' in Studia January-March 1/2002, issued by Babes-Bolyai University of Cluj-Napoca; 'The Present Interest of Building Contracts' in Commercial Law magazine no4/2002, edited by Lumina Lex; 'New Rules for Public-Private Partnerships', article published by World Markets Regulatory Analysis April 2002, available in electronic format at www.worldmarketsanalysis.com; 'The Public-Private Partnerships, a New Perspective' in Bucharest Business Week magazine April 22-28 2002; 'The Public-Private Partnerships - Romanian Outstanding Legal Issues' in Privatisation & Public-Private Partnership Review 2002/2003, edited by Euromoney.
Career: Trained Musat & Asociatii 1993; qualified 1995; partner Musat & Asociatii 1995-2000; managing partner 2000-05; managing partner Ţuca Zbârcea & Asociaţii 2005 to date.
Languages: English, French.
Member: Bucharest Bar Association, founding member and general secretary of the French-Romanian Chamber of Commerce.
Education: University of Bucharest (1993 Law); assistant professor to the Law School of Bucharest University (1996-99); PhD candidate.
Personal: Born 1969; resides Bucharest.

ZBÂRCEA, Gabriel

Ţuca Zbârcea & Asociaţii
Phone: Bucharest (+40 21 204 88 92)
E-mail: gabriel.zbarcea@tuca.ro
Energy and natural resources; real estate; mergers, acquisitions and privatisations.
Position: Gabriel Zbârcea is a managing partner at Ţuca Zbârcea & Asociaţii; his practice focuses on corporate and commercial law, mergers and acquisitions/privatisations, energy and natural resources; he has considerable experience in assisting Romanian and foreign companies in international joint ventures and corporate restructuring; he has acted, as co-ordinator, in major industry mergers and acquisitions and privatisations deals, as well as in complex energy projects in the oil, gas and mining sectors; he also specialises in property law and financial and security aspects of real estate transactions; Gabriel was the president of the Authority for State Assets Recovery and was in charge of the recovery of banking assets, the implementation of the Government's strategy to conclude the privatisation process of all companies in which the Romanian state holds interests and which are in the Authority's portfolio, the management of the state's interests in such companies, the sale of the state's shares in companies in the Authority's portfolio, the monitoring of the compliance with clauses of the privatisation contracts; he was also the president of the Privatisation Commission for Banca Comerciala Romana and the co-ordinator of the Inter-ministerial Committee for chapter 6 on competition; the privatisation of Banca Comerciala Romana, the largest Romanian commercial bank, was one of the most important organised under his mandate; further to his activity with the Inter-ministerial Committee on competition, the issue became less sensitive, as proven by the recent EU Commission's report concerning Romania's progress towards EU accession, according to which the 'safeguard clause' in case of insufficient progress in competition, will no longer be triggered; Gabriel has advised governmental institutions, as well as important Romanian and foreign companies, including General Electric, General Motors Corporation, Enel SpA, France Telecom, BKW FMB Energie AG, Raiffeisen Bank, Bank Hapoalim, BNP Paribas and ABN AMRO bank; he has published various articles on banking, oil and gas and mergers and acquisitions, including 'Report on the Banking Regulations in Romania' in The Regulation of Banking in Central and Eastern Europe, edited by the International Research Center on Business Law; 'Romania - The New Investment Regime' in Impact - Identifying opportunities and risks on global markets; 'Labour Law, Taxation and Customs Law in Romania' in The Business Transaction in Eastern Europe, edited by The Center for International Legal Studies (3rd and 4th eds); 'Regulation of the Oil and Gas Sector in Romania' in International Oil & Gas - Finance Review 2001, edited by Euromoney.
Career: Trained Musat & Asociatii 1995-97; qualified 1997; partner 1997-2002; deputy managing partner 2002-05; managing partner Ţuca Zbârcea & Asociaţii 2006 to date.
Languages: English.
Member: Bucharest Bar Association; honorary member of the Association of Fellows and Legal Scholars of the Center for International Legal Studies; Junior Chamber International (JCI); former president of the Youth Promotion Association (APT); former president of the Students' League; former secretary general of the European Law Student Association (ELSA).
Education: University of Bucharest (1995 Law).
Personal: Born 1973; resides Bucharest.

RUSSIA AND THE CIS

GEORGIA

GVINADZE, Nick

DLA Piper Rudnick Gray Cary (member firm, Gvinadze & Partners LP)
Phone: Tbilisi (+995 32 93 64 22)
E-mail: nick.gvinadze@dlapiper.com
Commercial and projects.
Position: Partner with considerable experience in both Georgian and cross-border commercial law and

focuses on energy, tax and customs law, and litigation and dispute resolution. Has advised on a number of key foreign investment projects in Georgia, including major oil and gas transportation projects in the Caspian.
Career: Head of Ernst & Young's legal practice in Georgia; partner at Georgian law firm GCG Law Office; served as attorney to financial department of Georgian Parliament; acted as local counsel to Clyde & Co, UK; former chairman of the Arbitration Court of the Georgian Chamber of Commerce and Industry (during which, authored the Court's arbitration rules); partner Gvinadze & Partners LP.
Languages: Fluent Georgian, Russian, English.
Member: Founding member of the Georgian Bar; founding member Georgian Young Lawyers Association; member International Bar Association.
Education: Tbilisi State University (Diploma in Jurisprudence with High Honours); Centre for Commercial Law Studies at the University of London (Diploma); London School of Economics (LLM).

JONAS, Theodore C

DLA Piper Rudnick Gray Cary (member firm, Gvinadze & Partners LP)
Phone: Tbilisi (+995 32 93 6422)
E-mail: ted.jonas@dlapiper.com
Corporate, commercial and projects.
Position: Managing partner of DLA Piper's Tbilisi office. Advises clients on international business transactions, energy and infrastructure projects, government relations, and dispute resolution. Practice involves the negotiation and documentation of company formations, joint ventures, privatisations, financings, oil and gas production sharing agreements, and private equity funds; the negotiation and resolution of complex disputes; public policy consulting work, and representation of clients in negotiations with government agencies. A US-trained and educated lawyer licensed in Washington, DC, he has worked on cross-border transactions and disputes in the US, the EU, Russia, Turkey, Kazakhstan, Azerbaijan and Georgia. Significant transactions include: acquisition by international investment funds of a US public corporation with telecommunications assets in the Republic of Georgia; acquisition by a Russian mining conglomerate of a 51 per cent interest in a publicly traded US mining company; due diligence and negotiations advice in merger of Franco-German pharmaceutical company's subsidiary with the US subsidiary of a German pharmaceutical company; formation and co-sponsorship of two investment limited partnerships by a Russian and a US capital management firm, and a series of other investments by the Russian firm in US private equity funds; investigation of state and state oil company claims against international oil company investors in Central Asian production sharing agreement; numerous project finance, credit line, export finance, and equity investment transactions in Georgia; negotiation and documentation of international oil and gas pipeline projects transiting Georgia; Black Sea terminal and transit projects for crude oil, petroleum products and freight; negotiation and arbitration of a complex dispute with a Georgian government-owned mining company; detailed legal analysis and advice on restructuring state-owned railway of a former Soviet country; advice and representation regarding the treaty relations of a multilateral development bank and a former Soviet republic; advice and training on election laws and other public policy matters.
Career: Legislative aide in US House of Representatives 1985-88; lead articles editor 'Cornell International Law Journal' 1990-91; qualified 1991; law clerk for the Honorable Joseph W Hatchett, US Court of Appeals for the 11th Circuit 1991-92; one of the founders of GCG Law Office, Tbilisi (the legacy firm on which DLA Piper's Georgia practice is based) 1996-99; of-counsel Baker Botts, L.L.P., Washington, DC 1999-2004; partner DLA Piper Rudnick Gray Cary International LLP and Gvinadze & Partners LP 2005-present. Publications: 'International Fugitive Snatching in US Law' in 24 'Cornell International Law Journal' (1991); 'Georgia Country Review' in 'Privatisation International Yearbook 2001' (Thomson Financial, London, January 2001; Jonathan S Hale, co-author); 'Georgian Civil Code' (English; translation editor and author of commentary, USAID/IRIS, Tbilisi, 2001); 'Parting the Sea: Caspian Littoral States Seek Boundary Disputes Resolution' in 'Oil & Gas Journal' (May 2001).
Languages: Fluent English and Georgian; proficient French.
Member: Admissions and Bar memberships: District of Columbia; State of Georgia (inactive status); Law Society of England and Wales (registered foreign lawyer); American Bar Association; US District Court for the Northern District of Georgia; Superior Courts of Georgia.
Education: Cornell University (1984 History BA); Cornell Law School (1991 JD cum laude).
Personal: Born 1962; resides Tbilisi.
Leisure: Hiking, cycling, skiing, reading.

KAZAKHSTAN

EMMOTT, John F

Michael Wilson & Partners
Phone: Almaty (+7 3272 58 48 90)
E-mail: john.emmott@mwp.kz
Oil and gas (upstream and downstream), foreign investments and joint ventures, international trade, banking and finance, litigation and arbitration.
Position: Partner. John has worked in many countries throughout the world and in the last five years has spent much of his time working within the CIS, in particular Kazakhstan, Azerbaijan, Uzbekistan, Ukraine and Russia. John has acted as adviser to many companies and foreign investors in a wide variety of sectors of the economy, as well as state agencies of the Government of Kazakhstan and the Russian Parliament on dispute and investment matters. Experience of note includes: advising the governments of Georgia and Azerbaijan on the Energy Charter Treaty under a TACIS programme; advising the State Duma of Russia on securities legislation; advising the Supreme Economic Court of Uzbekistan on issues of international arbitration; advising the Ministry of Justice of Kazakhstan on energy issues; advising on many international investment disputes both in the energy sector and in general.
Career: Qualified 1977; lawyer at Johnson Stokes & Master, Hong Kong 1981-83; associate Richards Butler, UK 1983-86, partner 1986-2002; partner Michael Wilson & Partners Ltd since 2002.
Languages: English.
Member: Law Society of England and Wales; International Bar Association; admitted as a solicitor of the Supreme Court of England and Wales 1985; admitted as a solicitor, proctor and attorney of the Supreme Court of New South Wales and a solicitor of the High Court of Australia 1978.
Education: University of Sydney (1974 BA; 1977 LLB).
Personal: Born 1953; resides Almaty.
Leisure: Golf, classical music.

WILSON, Michael Earl

Michael Wilson & Partners
Phone: Almaty (+7 32 72 58 48 90)
E-mail: michael.wilson@mwp.kz
Corporate, commercial, major projects.
Position: Michael has initiated and led many of the major privatisations and other projects to date in Kazakhstan and has been involved in many of the largest projects in Uzbekistan and Kyrgyzstan. He has more than 13 years of experience in London and Sydney and has practised law in central Asia for over nine years.
Career: Admitted as a solicitor of the Supreme Court of England and Wales 1984; barrister and solicitor of the Supreme Court, Victoria, Australia 1988; solicitor, proctor and attorney of the Supreme Court of New South Wales, Australia 1988; founding partner of an international law firm with a large presence in the CIS; founding partner of an international law firm in Almaty 1994-95, Tashkent 1995, Bishkek and Astana 1997, and Baku 1998; founding partner of Michael Wilson & Partners Limited in Almaty 1998 and Baku 2003.
Languages: English.
Member: Law Society of England and Wales; Law Society of Victoria, Australia; Law Society of New South Wales; UK-based Major Projects Association; founding member, treasurer and chairman, European Business Association of Kazakhstan (1998-2004); founding member Business Lawyers Association of Kazakhstan; member American Chamber of Commerce in Kazakhstan; selected by the EBRD as a member of the Foreign Investors Council in 1998 under the president of the Republic of Kazakhstan, as the leading foreign lawyer practising in Central Asia.
Education: Manchester University (1980); Chester Law School (1981).
Personal: Born 1958; resides Almaty since 1995; married with three children.
Leisure: Skiing, running, swimming, tennis, horse riding (Director of the Department of Show Jumping of the Equestrian Federation of the Republic of Kazakhstan).

RUSSIA

AFONIN, Alexey Vladimirovich
Sikaylo, Gabbasov, Romakhova & Partners (Attorneys at Law)
Phone: Moscow (+7 495 202 0167)
E-mail: afonin@sikaylo-partners.ru
Position: Member dealing with bankruptcy, EU law, int private law, litigation.
Career: Admitted 2005, Russia.
Languages: Russian, English.
Education: Moscow State Institute of Foreign Affairs (University) (BL, 2003).
Personal: Born 1978; resides Moscow.

ANYUKHINA, Irina
Alrud Law Firm
Phone: Moscow (+7 495 234 9692)
E-mail: ianyukhina@alrud.ru
Position: Senior associate dealing with foreign investments, international business and trade, mergers and acquisitions, real estate. Experienced in consulting on private international law, corporate law, contract law, intellectual property law, labour law, insurance, telecommunications, aerospace.
Career: Legal consultant RusOTIS JV; lawyer Dr Eckstein & Partners LLC; senior associate InSpace Consulting (Russia) LLC; joined Alrud Law Firm 2002.
Languages: Russian, English, French.
Education: Moscow State Institute of International Relations under Russian Ministry of Foreign Affairs, International Law Faculty (1994).
Personal: Born 1970; resides Moscow.

GABBASOV, Marat Nazimovich
Sikaylo, Gabbasov, Romakhova & Partners (Attorneys at Law)
Phone: Moscow (+7 495 202 01 67)
E-mail: gabbasov@sikaylo-partners.ru
Position: Partner dealing with land, real estate, construction, natural resources, and litigation.
Career: Partner Klishin & Partners 1992; partner Sikaylo, Gabbasov, Romakhova & Partners (Attorneys at Law), formerly Sikaylo, Matveev, Gabbasov & Partners, 1999.
Languages: German.
Education: State University of VI Lenin (1982).
Personal: Born 1959; resides Moscow.

GOLTSBLAT, Andrey
Pepeliaev, Goltsblat & Partners
Phone: Moscow (+7 495 967 0007)
E-mail: a.goltsblat@pgplaw.ru
Senior partner, managing partner of corporate and commercial department.
Position: Managing partner and senior partner of the firm's corporate department; concentrates primarily on mergers and acquisitions; restructuring; joint ventures; as well as counseling boards of directors and senior management on domestic and overseas companies in connection with investment projects and deal structuring in Russia and the CIS.
Career: Recognised as a leading authority on establishing businesses, offering clients representation before government authorities at all levels. Also has extensive experience in acting as legal counsel for a number of foreign Fortune 500 companies in Russia and the CIS. Mr Goltsblat headed a group of experts on the Constitutional Commission engaged in drafting the Russian Constitution; he has acted as chief adviser to the legal department of the State Duma (the lower house of the Russian Parliament); responsible for legislative drafting; examining draft laws and providing advice to MPs on legal matters and technical aspects of legislation.
Languages: English.
Member: International Bar Association.
Education: Law School, Interior Ministry of the USSR (with honours 1987; JD 1994).
Personal: Born 1962; resides Moscow.

LAPSHIN, Konstantin
Alrud Law Firm
Phone: Moscow (+7 495 234 9692)
E-mail: klapshin@alrud.ru
Position: Associate specialising in Russian labour law, real estate and land, corporate law, commercial law, intellectual property as well as telecommunications.
Career: Attorney Andrey Gagarin and Partners Law Firm; senior attorney Norman DL Associates Law Firm; joined Alrud Law Firm 2002; author of analytical and theoretical articles on key legal issues.
Languages: Russian, English.
Education: Moscow State Academy of Law, Institute of State and Law of the Russian Academy of Sciences (postgraduate course).
Personal: Born 1967; resides Moscow.

LITVINOVA, Olga
DLA Piper Rudnick Gray Cary
Phone: St Petersburg (+7 812 703 7801)
E-mail: olga.litvinova@dlapiper.com
Corporate and commercial.
Position: Office managing partner dealing with all areas of corporate and commercial law, mergers and acquisitions, corporate reorganisations, IPO, structuring of inbound investments, and projects accomplished under PPP schemes.Co-ordinated legal assistance for numerous major regional investment projects, including the negotiation of tax and other investment incentives. Was involved in a number of M&A projects, including the largest real estate acquisition in Russia. Has led numerous legislative initiatives aimed at improving the investment climate and drafted and negotiated much of the regional concession legislation.
Career: Began career at Andersen (became first Russian woman to achieve partner status at the firm). Author of a number of publications on corporate and commercial matters; often gives comments to the federal and regional business press.
Languages: Fluent English.
Member: Co-chair Advisory Board of SPIBA (St Petersburg International Business Association); St Petersburg Bar.
Education: St Petersburg State University (1995 Law; 1997 postgraduate studies).

PEPELIAEV, Sergey
Pepeliaev, Goltsblat & Partners
Phone: Moscow (+7 495 967 0007)
E-mail: s.pepeliaev@pgplaw.ru
Managing partner.
Position: Specialises in financial law, including budget law, tax law, banking law, exchange regulation and securities. His practice areas also include arbitration proceedings.
Career: Has vast experience in providing legal support for big projects, in drafting legislation and handling tax disputes in arbitration courts, courts of general jurisdiction, the Supreme Arbitration Court and the Constitutional Court of the Russian Federation. He has participated in Supreme Arbitration Court conferences concerning taxation and financial issues and was invited by the Russian Constitutional Court to act as a tax expert. Has also acted as adviser to the State Duma Budget and Finance Committee; was involved in the discussion and finalisation of the draft Russian Tax Code; participated in projects aimed at improving Russian tax legislation, including TACIS projects. Mr Pepeliaev is a member of the Panel of Experts of the Federation Council Committee for legal and judicial matters; he is also a laureate of the 'Femida' prize and has written books which made a major contribution to the basis for modern Russian tax law. Mr Pepeliaev has headed groups of lawyers involved in large-scale auditing and legal consulting projects, some carried out by order of major Russian and foreign companies operating in different industries, others - within the framework of World Bank programmes. Extensive project work has included auditing procedures; assessment of current and potential corporate liabilities; development and improvement of cash flow control procedures; advice on book-keeping and taxation; assessment of possibilities for debt restructuring and debt reduction etc.
Member: Presidium of the Russian Tax Law Association and the Federation Counsel Committee's panel of experts for legal and judicial matters.
Education: Moscow State University, law department (1987; JD 1991).
Personal: Born 1964; resides Moscow.

ROMAKHOVA, Svetlana Jurievna
Sikaylo, Gabbasov, Romakhova & Partners (Attorneys at Law)
Phone: Moscow (+7 495 202 0167)
E-mail: romakhova@sikaylo-partners.ru
Position: Partner dealing with corporate law, registration of entities, arbitration litigation, bankruptcy.
Career: Lawyer Klishin & Partners 1993; partner Sikaylo, Gabbasov, Romakhova & Partners (Attorneys at Law), formerly Sikaylo, Matveev, Gabbasov & Partners, 1999.
Languages: English.

Education: Moscow State University of MV Lomonosov (1989).
Personal: Born 1964; resides Moscow.

RUDOMINO, Vassily
Alrud Law Firm
Phone: Moscow (+7 495 234 9692)
E-mail: vrudomino@alrud.ru
Position: Senior partner; leads projects dealing with both the Russian and foreign parties within the territory of Russia and abroad; experienced in investment projects in all stages of their implementation; expert in corporate law; garnered unique experience in company M&A transactions, anti-trust legislation, the pharmaceutical industry and real estate.
Career: Co-founder Alrud Law Firm.
Languages: Russian, English.
Member: International Bar Association (IBA); Moscow Advocate Chamber.
Education: Moscow State Institute of International Relations under Russian Ministry of Foreign Affairs, International Law Faculty, International Commercial Law Department (1993).
Personal: Born 1969; resides Moscow.

RYZHOV, Dmitry
Alrud Law Firm
Phone: Moscow (+7 495 234 9692)
E-mail: dryzhov@alrud.ru
Position: Associate specialising in commercial law, M&A, general corporate law, arbitration and civil procedure, legal aspects of bankruptcy procedure, international private law, civil law, currency control.
Career: In-house lawyer RINCO Holding (oil and gas, real estate); attorney Gazprom (media business); attorney Legal Technologies Center (legal consulting); senior lawyer D'Arcy, Masius, Benton & Bowles (advertising agency); senior lawyer Law Firm A.R. Consulting and Co.
Languages: Russian, English, German.
Education: Moscow State University for International Relations (MGIMO) (1999 LLB international trade law; 1999 LLM international trade law in the European Union; currently studying for course in external trade and international economics).
Personal: Born 1976; resides Moscow.

SIKAYLO, Alexey Vadimovich
Sikaylo, Gabbasov, Romakhova & Partners (Attorneys at Law)
Phone: Moscow (+7 495 202 01 67)
E-mail: sikaylo@sikaylo-partners.ru
Position: Partner dealing with litigation, corporate law, investment law and property.
Career: Trained with Allen & Overy, London; qualified 1991; partner Klishin & Partners 1992; partner Sikaylo, Gabbasov, Romakhova & Partners (Attorneys at Law), formerly Sikaylo, Matveev, Gabbasov & Partners, 1999.
Languages: English.
Education: Moscow State University (1991).
Personal: Born 1966; resides Moscow.
Leisure: Sport.

SIKAYLO, Victoria Petrovna
Sikaylo, Gabbasov, Romakhova & Partners (Attorneys at Law)
Phone: Moscow (+7 495 202 0167)
E-mail: v.sikaylo@sikaylo-partners.ru
Position: Member dealing with civil law, copyright law, litigation.
Career: Admitted 2005, Russia.
Languages: Russian, English, French.
Education: Moscow State University of M.V. Lomonosov (BL, 2003).
Personal: Born 1973; resides Moscow.

VASUTIN, Ruslan
DLA Piper Rudnick Gray Cary
Phone: St Petersburg (+7 812 703 78 01)
E-mail: ruslan.vasutin@dlapiper.com
Tax.
Position: Tax partner leading the St Petersburg tax practice and dealing with transaction structuring and reorganisation, developing efficient cross-border fund remittance techniques, and co-ordinating tax dispute procedures. Has developed considerable experience in the areas of due diligence reviews and related tax planning advice.
Career: Andersen; senior tax and legal manager Ernst & Young (when Andersen and Ernst & Young combined their operations in Russia) 2002; partner 2005; co-chairman of taxation committee of American Chamber of Commerce, St Petersburg for several years. Frequent contributor to technical journals on various legal issues; US CPA (certified public accountant).
Languages: Fluent English.
Education: St Petersburg State University (1995 Law); St Petersburg State University of Economics and Finance (1997 certificate in accounting); University of Economics and Finance (1999 postgraduate study).

YEREMIIN, Dmitry
Alrud Law Firm
Phone: Moscow (+7 495 234 9692)
E-mail: dyeremin@alrud.ru
Position: Senior associate specialising in international commercial arbitration, dispute resolution, litigation, general commercial law, currency regulation and exchange control, investments, corporate law, contracts, real estate, international private law.
Career: Legal counsel International Tobacco Corporation; legal counsel New Technologies and Investments; attorney Group Krona, Ivanov and partners law firm; assistant to the president of the raw materials department, ALFA-Eco; joined Alrud Law Firm 1998; author of numerous articles on dispute resolution, insolvency and other questions of contemporary Russian and international legislation.
Languages: Russian, English.
Member: Moscow Advocate Chamber.
Education: Moscow State Institute of International Relations under Russian Ministry of Foreign Affairs, International Law Faculty, International Commercial Law Department (1993).
Personal: Born 1969; resides Moscow.

ZADOROGIN, Sergey Igorevich
Sikaylo, Gabbasov, Romakhova & Partners (Attorneys at Law)
Phone: Moscow (+7 495 202 0167)
E-mail: zadorogin@sikaylo-partners.ru
Position: Member dealing with corporate law, labour law, litigation, taxation.
Career: Admitted 2005, Russia.
Languages: Russian, English.
Education: Academy of Labour and Social Affairs (BL, 2001); Moscow Humanitarian University (PhD).
Personal: Born 1979; resides Moscow.

ZHARSKY, Alexander
Alrud Law Firm
Phone: Moscow (+7 495 234 9692)
E-mail: azharsky@alrud.ru
Position: Associate specialising in corporate and financial transactions, mergers and acquisitions, arbitration and litigation.
Career: Associate BSP Legal, Moscow; associate Alrud Law Firm from 2004; author of more than ten articles on international public and private law).
Languages: Russian, English, Belarussian.
Education: Belarussian State University, Minsk (1998 law with hons; 2001 SJD); Moscow School of Social and Economic Sciences (1999 LLM hons - validated by the University of Manchester); TMC Asser Institute, Asser College Europe, The Netherlands (2000 postgraduate course in international trade and business law).
Personal: Born 1976; resides Moscow.

UKRAINE

GRISCHENKO, Dmitri
Grischenko & Partners
Phone: Kiev (+38 044 490 37 07)
E-mail: dig@gp.ua
Corporate law, securities, intellectual property, litigation and arbitration, export/import operations, privatisation.
Position: Managing partner and attorney-at-law, specialising in international business transactions, Ukrainian corporate law, banking, security and insurance regulations, privatisation, agriculture and land, due diligence, and restructuring agricultural entities. Represented foreign clients in Ukraine and represented clients in domestic and international courts and arbitrations. Drafted commercial agreements, export/import contracts, joint venture agreements, etc. Prize-winner in the Ukrainian contest 'The Lawyer of the Year 2000' in the category of 'Practising Lawyer'. In 2004, by decree of the President of Ukraine, was given the honorary title 'Distinguished Lawyer of Ukraine'.
Career: Junior Researcher Institute of State and Law of the Ukrainian Academy of Sciences, Kiev 1980-87; senior legal council, head of legal department Ukrainian Foreign Trade Association (UKRIMPEX), Kiev

1987-91; legal intern (Soviet Lawyers Internship Program sponsored by ABA and Soros Foundation) international practice group Kilpatrick & Cody, Atlanta, US 1991; licensed by Ukrainian Ministry of Justice to practise law in Ukraine 1991; partner, attorney-at-law Grischenko & Partners, Kiev 1992; legal intern in the corporate group Chadbourne & Parke, New York 1995; legal intern in the corporate and CIS practice groups Debevoise & Plimpton, New York 1995. Contemporaneous activity: lecturer Ukrainian School of International Business (Conbiz) 1990-92; sub-contractor on reforming and drafting laws of Ukraine on foreign investments and on oil and gas industry Tacis 1993-94; consultant and co-author of law of Ukraine on foreign economic activities and foreign investment law of Ukraine, sub-commission on foreign economic relations Ukrainian Parliament 1990-94; consultant drafting electricity law, sub-commission on nuclear policy and nuclear energy Ukrainian Parliament 1995-96; consultant, commission on science and technology Ukrainian Parliament 1996-2000; member of supervisory board The State Export-Import Bank of Ukraine 2005 to present. Publications: 'International Centre on Investment Disputes Regulation: Some Questions on Jurisdiction and Arbitrational Production' (June 2005); co-author of OECD 'Investment Guide on Ukraine' (1993).

Languages: Fluent English, Ukrainian, Russian.

Member: Kiev City Branch of the Ukrainian Bar (since 1994); International Bar Association; OASIS International Club of Lawyers; American Chamber; European Business Association.

Education: Shevchenko Kiev State University (1980 Diploma - international lawyer and interpreter of English, qualified to practice law in the former Soviet Union); Institute of International Law, Washington, DC (1991 training program in American legal system); New York University (1995 LLM).

Personal: Born 1958; resides Kiev.

Leisure: Boxing, skiing, hill walking.

KARPENKO, Margarita E

DLA Piper Ukraine LLC

Phone: Kyiv (+380 44 490 9565)

E-mail: margarita.karpenko@dlapiper.com

Corporate.

Position: Partner experienced in corporate law, M&A, antitrust legislation, intellectual property and labour law; has advised extensively in the consumer products, oil and gas, media, real estate and hospitality sectors. Major transactions under her supervision include: number of due diligences for clients from various industry sectors (real estate, communications, food and food processing, RCP, etc); legal support to the largest Russian oil extracting and refining company on creation of a joint venture with a Ukrainian petrochemical and refining company; legal support of acquisition of a Ukrainian real estate company by a Russian developer; legal advice to a number of Ukrainian media companies on their structuring in Ukraine; legal support in process of acquisition of a Ukrainian plant by a well-known international company (food sector); assistance to a Hungarian oil and gas company in reviewing tax and legal issues of the storage of Ukrainian gas; assistance to a major Polish oil and gas company in its initiative to acquire a major stake in a Ukrainian company of oil and gas sector (due diligence, full preparation of the transaction, assistance to the client on various legal issues); support and investigation of the possible entrance into the Ukrainian market of the world's leading oil and gas company (legal research, drafting documents, assistance in negotiations, co-ordination of the legal issues); legal support of acquisition of the majority stake in a Ukrainian glass factory by a worldwide glass manufacturer; legal support of international hotel chain with regard to entering the Ukrainian market.

Career: Head of EY Law (legal practice of Ernst & Young in Kyiv 2002-05; managing partner DLA Piper Ukraine since 2005. Author of many publications in Ukrainian business press, including: 'The Ukrainian Journal of Business Law' and 'The Business Weekly'.

Languages: Russian, Ukrainian, English.

Member: Kyiv City Bar Association (2000); legal committee European Business Association.

Education: Moscow State University (1991 MA Law).

Personal: Born 1967; resides Kyiv.

Leisure: Swimming, skiing, cycling.

VOITOVICH, Sergei

Grischenko & Partners

Phone: Kiev (+38 044 490 37 07)

E-mail: sav@gp.ua

Investment, financial, corporate, contractual, real estate and international law and arbitration.

Position: Partner and attorney-at-law. In 2003, honoured by the Cabinet of Ministers of Ukraine for considerable contribution to Ukraine's victory in the arbitration case initiated by the American company Generation Ukraine Ltd at the ICSID. Between 1998-2004, represented Ukraine as a legal councillor in three arbitration cases at the ICSID (Washington).

Career: Partner Grischenko & Partners 1993; adviser to Organisation for Economic Development (OECD) 1993-94; participant Annual Session of American and International Law, Dallas, Texas 1995; four-month internship at Dickson Minto W.S., London 1996; participated in four panels Chamber of Independent Experts on Foreign Investment under the President of Ukraine 1997-2001; associate professor Kyiv University School of International Law for a number of years. Author of monograph 'International Economic Organisations in the International Legal Process' (Martinus Nijhoff 1994) and more than 50 minor professional publications, including the book 'International Centre on Investment Disputes Regulation: Some Questions on Jurisdiction and Arbitrational Production' (June 2005).

Languages: Ukrainian, Russian, English; working knowledge of Italian.

Member: Kyiv Bar; International Bar Association; OASIS International Club of Lawyers; American Chamber; European Business Association.

Education: Kyiv International Law School (1981; 1984 Candidate of Science (International Law) degree); European University Institute, Florence (1990 LLM International and Comparative Law; 1993 PhD International and Comparative Law).

Personal: Born 1959; resides Kiev.

Leisure: Tennis, billiards, art lover.

VOLKOV, Oleksiy M

Volkov & Partners

Phone: Kiev (+380 44 207 0270)

E-mail: volkov@volkovpartners.com

Position: Managing partner whose practice covers contracts, corporate law, M&A, partnerships, privatisation, securities, mineral rights and concessions, joint ventures, international litigation, competition, and corporate finance.

Career: Senior legal adviser, director of foreign trade firm, 'Electron' production amalgamation, Sumy, 1987; legal adviser at Yurvneshservice Law Firm, 1991; partner and managing partner at Vasil Kisil & Partners Law Firm, 1992; managing partner, Volkov & Partners Law Firm, 2005.

Languages: Ukrainian, Russian, English.

Education: International Law School of Kyiv State University; International Law Institute, Washington DC (1987, LLM); Welborn Dufford Brown & Tooley, PC, Denver Colorado (internship).

Personal: Born 1962; resides in Kiev.

Leisure: Sailing, antique legal literature, photography.

VYSOCHINSKY, Oleg

Grischenko & Partners

Phone: Kiev (+38 044 490 37 07)

E-mail: oiv@gp.ua

International commercial law, project finance, corporate, investment, tax and securities law.

Position: Partner and attorney-at-law.

Career: Lawyer at representative office of Smith Lyonnes, Ukraine 1995-96; Grischenko & Partners 1996; senior lawyer 2002.

Languages: Ukrainian, Russian, English.

Member: European Business Association.

Education: Ukrainian Institute of International Relations (1995 Master of International Private Law).

Personal: Born 1973; resides Kiev.

Leisure: Swimming, studying languages.

SAUDI ARABIA

SADIG ALYAQOUB, Montasir

Al Yaqoub Lawyers and Legal Advisers

Phone: Riyadh (+966 1 211 0600)

E-mail: msalyaqoub@alyaqoub.com

Corporate, commercial and business law.

Position: Managing partner.

Career: Specialises in incorporation, restructuring and liquidation of companies. Joint venture contracts, including national and international companies. Started the practice working in association with Arthur

Andersen 1992. Became junior partner when the office converted to a firm 1994. Senior partner 1996 and managing partner 2000. Worked in association with the defunct Arthur Andersen (Saudia) and Ernst & Young (Saudia, Gulf and Middle East). Attorney for top royals and business tycoons and conglomerates.
Languages: Arabic, English.
Member: IBA; Saudi Bar.
Education: University of King Saud - Riyadh Faculty of Law and Administration (LLB).
Personal: Born 1967; resides Riyadh.

SERBIA AND MONTENEGRO

ALEKSIC, Nenad
Tomic, Stevic Dulic
Phone: Belgrade (+381 11 3285 227)
E-mail: nenad.aleksic@tomic-stevic.co.yu
Head of intellectual property department.
Position: Fields of expertise include intellectual property, commercial law, litigation, civil law and real estate.
Career: Bogicevic Law Office 1999-2003; Alexopoulos - Chaldoupis Law Office 2003-04; Tomic Stevic Dulic Law Office 2004 to date.
Languages: Serbian, English, German.
Member: Bar Association of Belgrade.
Education: Faculty of Law Belgrade (Judicial State Examination of the Republic of Serbia); International Patent Attorney Examination.
Personal: Born 1973; resides Belgrade.

NEDELJKOVIC, Katarina
KMN Katarina Nedeljkovic law and patent & trademark office
Phone: Novi Sad (+381 21 662 2691)
E-mail: knedeljkovic@kmnlegal.com
Position: Katarina specialises in foreign investments, corporate law, privatisation, M&A, IP, international commercial arbitration and banking; she has over 10 years' experience in legal consulting and advises high-profile clients in the benchmarking transactions in Serbia and Montenegro, including privatisations, M&A and IP; she is regularly consulted on various EU and World Bank projects, including the Serbian Real Estate and Registration Project and is author of a book and numerous articles.
Career: Admitted to practice in Serbia and Montenegro 1999; and in New York 2002; registered patent and trade mark agent with the Intellectual Property Office in Belgrade 2001 to date; standing court interpreter in English, Russian, French and Italian 1997 to date.
Languages: English, Russian, French, Italian.
Member: Bar Association of Vojvodina; The New York State Bar Association; American Bar Association; American Society for International Law; member of the management board of the AIPPI National Chapter for Serbia and Montenegro; Association of Scientific and Technical Translators of Vojvodina; secretary general and founding member of the Harvard Club of Serbia and Montenegro; member of the management board of the Fulbright Alumni Association of Serbia and Montenegro.
Education: University of Belgrade (1994 LLB); Moscow State University (1994 LLB, MA International Law); University of Cambridge (1995 LLM Commercial Law); University of Turin (2000 UNCITRAL post-graduate course in International Trade Law); Harvard Law School (2002 LLM).

STEVIC DULIC, Gordana
Tomic, Stevic Dulic
Phone: Belgrade (+381 11 3285 227)
E-mail: gordana.stevic@tomic-stevic.co.yu
Head of litigation department.
Position: Fields of expertise include litigation, real estate, labour law, corporate law and mergers and acquisitions.
Career: Cvetkovic-Markovic-Trajs Law Office 1994-96; Stevic Law Office 1996-99; founder and partner Tomic Stevic Dulic Law Office 2000.
Languages: Serbian, English.
Member: Bar Association of Serbia.
Education: Faculty of Law Belgrade (Judicial State Examination Republic of Serbia).
Personal: Born 1971; resides Belgrade.

TOMIC, Ljubica
Tomic, Stevic Dulic
Phone: Belgrade (+381 11 3285 227)
E-mail: ljubica.tomic@tomic-stevic.co.yu
Head of corporate department.
Position: Fields of expertise include corporate law, business law, M&A, international contracts, and administrative law.
Career: Legal department of the bank Jugobanka AD 1994-95; Djurdjevic Law Office 1995-99; founder and partner Tomic Stevic Dulic Law Office 2000. Author of published articles in the fields of constitutional law and labour law.
Languages: Serbian, German, English.
Member: Bar Association of Serbia.
Education: Faculty of Law Belgrade (Judicial State Examination Republic of Serbia; specialised in international contracts).
Personal: Born 1970; resides Belgrade.

SOUTH AFRICA

EWING, Chris
Cliffe Dekker Inc
Phone: Sandton (+27 11 290 7120)
E-mail: ewing@cliffedekker.com
Corporate and commercial.
Position: Chairman; head of the corporate and commercial department; principal practice areas are mergers and acquisitions, particularly private equity and black economic empowerment transactions and the formation and initial structuring of new business entities, particularly joint ventures; recognised internationally as a leader in his field, Chris has assisted numerous international clients establish businesses in South Africa and counselled many merchant banks in major leveraged buy-out transactions; he has been involved in a number of South Africa's largest and most complex M&A transactions.
Career: Trained at Cliffe Dekker; qualified 1976; partner 1979; apppointed national chairman 2002.
Languages: Afrikaans, English.
Education: University of the Witwatersrand (1975 B Com LLB).
Personal: Born 1949; resides Johannesburg.

SPAIN

AMIGÓ-MÜLLER, Juan
Santiago Mediano Advocats
Phone: Barcelona (+34 93 481 7997)
E-mail: jamigo-mueller@santiagomediano.com
Real estate department.
Position: Senior partner responsible for the real estate department as well as the 'German desk' at the firm. His practice areas are real estate, corporate and international private law. He specialises in any kind of commercial real estate-related work such as: the sale and purchase of any kind of commercial premises (office buildings, hotels, industrial, shopping centres, for example), advice on the execution of real estate developments such as office buildings, industrial premises, parks, shopping centres; commercial leases and construction-related work of any kind; 'in rem' guarantees related to real estate finance work; all manner of real estate-related corporate issues (such as joint ventures, shareholders agreements, company law and commercial agreements of any kind).
Career: Has worked as a lawyer for the past 14 years, in well-recognised international and national firms in Spain, as well as being seconded to practise law in Germany for over a year.
Languages: English, German, Spanish.
Member: Society of German-Speaking Directors in Spain; Spanish-German Lawyers Association; Barcelona Bar Association.
Education: University of Barcelona (1992 Law Degree; 1997 MBA management and higher business skills (in the faculty of business science)).
Personal: Born 1968.

BERROCAL, Javier
Santiago Mediano Abogados
Phone: Madrid (+34 91 310 6363)
E-mail: jberrocal@santiagomediano.com
Corporate and commercial department.

Position: Managing partner and head of the corporate and commercial department; an experienced lawyer dealing with both local and international clients, including major textile and lodging corporations and leading IT (hardware, software, e-commerce and the internet), entertainment and media companies; he has extensive experience as general legal adviser in corporate and commercial law; deals with complex transactions/operations including M&A, MBOs, alliances and joint ventures, takeovers, licensing, franchising and distribution, corporate restructuring, commercial conflict-solving and developing intellectual property rights protection and exploitation strategies.
Career: Joined Santiago Mediano Abogados after working at leading Spanish, US and UK international law firms. He also worked in the copyright legal department of the Motion Picture Association (MPA).
Languages: English, Spanish.
Member: Madrid Bar Association; Salamanca Bar Association.
Education: University of Salamanca (1996 Law Degree).
Personal: Born 1973.

BROSETA, Manuel

Broseta Abogados
Phone: Valencia (+34 96 392 1006)
E-mail: mbroseta@broseta.com
Corporate.
Position: Partner since 1993 specialising in, among others, corporate law; mergers and acquisitions; company law; securities; arbitration.
Career: Qualified in 1991; former associate at Uria & Menéndez 1991-93, associate professor of Business Law at the University of Valencia 1996-2000; regular lecturer on different masters courses and conferences. Patron of the International Fair of Valencia; Protector of the Investor in Valencia's Stock Exchange since 2000; Special Counsellor of the Local Government of Valencia for the high-speed Madrid-Valencia train (1999-2000).
Languages: English, French.
Member: Valencia and Madrid Bar Association; Valencia Court of Arbitration; Chamber of Commerce of France.
Education: University of Valencia (1990 Law degree Hons; Extraordinary Graduation Prize); Kings College London (1990 EEC Law); College of Europe, Bruges (1991 Master in European Law); Harvard Law School (1992 Negotiation Workshop); Georgetown University (1992 US Legal System).
Personal: Born 1967; resides Valencia.
Leisure: Golf.

COOKE, Chris

Santiago Mediano Abogados
Phone: Madrid (+34 91 310 6363)
E-mail: ccooke@santiagomediano.com
International operations department.
Position: Senior associate specialising in all manner of international entertainment-related commercial deals, including, by way of example, audio-visual finance, production, sales and distribution agreements, complex chain-of-title and rights acquisition issues, magazine format publishing agreements, logo and product clearances, technology development agreements, anti-piracy matters and dispute resolution.
Career: Admitted to the Bar of England and Wales 1993; before joining the firm he worked in the UK for some of the most important film production companies and studios; also has experience as practising barrister, including appearances in the Court of Appeal; ten years' experience working in the entertainment and media area.
Languages: English, Spanish.
Member: Honourable Society of the Inner Temple in London.
Education: Bristol University (1991 LLB).
Personal: Born 1969.

FERNANDEZ, Arturo

Santiago Mediano Abogados
Phone: Madrid (+34 91 310 6363)
E-mail: afernandez@santiagomediano.com
Dispute resolution and litigation department.
Position: Senior partner providing legal advice and representing national and international clients in all matters concerning civil and criminal law, especially in the non-fulfilment of agreements, claims for damages, intellectual property, copyright and related rights.
Career: Has a broad professional career regarding conflict-solving both before Spanish courts and arbitration bodies on a national, European and international basis with regard to trade marks, parallel imports and designs; has lately offered his services on real property to a wide range of companies. Lectures on procedural and civil law in different relevant institutions.
Languages: English, Italian, Spanish.
Member: Madrid Bar Association; BLACA (London); Institute of Advanced Legal Studies.
Education: University of Navarra (1994 Law); Universidad Complutense of Madrid (1996 MA Corporate Legal Advice); University of London (2001 LLM Intellectual and Industrial Property field).
Personal: Born 1970.

HERNANDEZ, Silvia

Santiago Mediano Abogados
Phone: Madrid (+34 91 310 6363)
E-mail: shernandez@santiagomediano.com
Industrial property department.
Position: Senior partner, represents domestic and foreign companies belonging to different industries (such as shipping, textile, food, telecommunications, entertainment, and so on); renders professional advice on matters regarding registration, infringement, protection and exploitation strategies of industrial property rights and on the drafting of, amongst others, assignment, license and settlement agreements; she is the head of the intangible assets unit which deals with any proceedings related to the registration of intellectual and industrial property rights (inventions, designs and marks) both in Spain and abroad; one of her main professional activities is the auditing of intangible assets.
Career: Has developed her professional career at highly prestigious and recognised national and international law firms; registered Industrial Property Agent and a European Agent of Trademarks and Designs.
Languages: English, French, Spanish.
Member: Colegio Oficial de Doctores y Licenciados de Madrid; Colegio Oficial de agentes de la propiedad insustrial.
Education: Universidad Complutense, Madrid (1993 Spanish and English studies).

MAGDALENO, Antonia

Broseta Abogados
Phone: Valencia (+34 96 391 60 68)
E-mail: amagdaleno@broseta.com
Litigation department.
Position: Partner specialising in litigation, alternative dispute resolution, criminal law, torts, white-collar crime, and bankruptcy. She is currently a trustee in bankruptcy, appointed by the Commercial Courts of Valencia as well as a lecturer at the University of Valencia in litigation law.
Career: Partner Broseta Abogados 2005 to date. Has written many articles for specialised magazines.
Languages: English, French, Spanish.
Education: University of Valencia (law degree).
Personal: Born 1968; resides Valencia.
Leisure: Travelling.

MEDIANO, Santiago

Santiago Mediano Abogados
Phone: Madrid (+34 91 310 6363)
E-mail: smediano@santiagomediano.com
Intellectual property department.
Position: Senior partner, expert in media and intellectual property; leads a team of experts dealing with all areas of intellectual property and information technology.
Career: Was responsible for general advice in the legal department of the Spanish Authors and Publishers Society (SGAE); was the head of the IP department of international and national law firms in Spain; professor of civil law at the Complutense University of Madrid and professor of private law at the Ramon Carande University of Madrid; regular collaborator in courses, conferences and master programmes on intellectual property, at the Madrid Bar Association and the Carlos III University of Madrid; author of several publications on this subject.
Languages: English, German, French, Italian, Spanish.
Member: MMRC (Multimedia Rights Clearance System) Group of Experts; ALADDA (Literary and Artistic Association for the Defence of the Author); Madrid Bar Association.
Education: Universidad Autónoma de Madrid (1991 law).
Personal: Born 1968.

NAVARRO, Antonio

Broseta Abogados
Phone: Valencia (+34 96 392 10 06)
E-mail: ajnavarro@broseta.com
Commercial law department.
Position: Partner dealing with business law, commercial law, agency and distribution, international

trade and finance.
Career: Qualified in 1992; former associate Uria & Menendez, Madrid and Barcelona; former associate Fox & Horan, New York.
Languages: English, Italian.
Member: Madrid and New York Bar Associations.
Education: University of Murcia (1991 Law Degree); Institute de Empresa, Madrid (1992 Master in Business Law); University of Edinburgh (1993 English Law); New York University (1995 Master of Laws LLM).
Personal: Born 1968; resides Valencia.
Leisure: Fishing.

PICÓN, Juan

DLA Piper Rudnick Gray Cary
Phone: Madrid (+34 91 319 12 12)
E-mail: juan.picon@dlapiper.com
Corporate mergers and acquisitions.
Position: Managing partner of the Madrid office. A highly experienced mergers and acquisitions lawyer with a special focus on cross-border transactions and on representing multinational clients doing business in Spain. Also regularly involved in private equity transactions (LBOs, MBOs and other corporate structures). Has been involved in a number of major telecommunication projects, including the privatisation of Spain's second network operator on behalf of a bidding consortium, as well as representation of national and international companies with respect to cable telecommunications matters, fixed and mobile services, broadcasting and media and the internet.
Career: Qualified 1987; managing partner Squire Sanders & Dempsey, Spain 1997-2005; partner DLA Piper Rudnick Gray Cary 2005; regional managing partner.
Languages: Spanish, English, French.
Member: Board of directors Spanish Association of Telecommunications Law; Madrid Bar Association.
Education: Universidad Pontificia Comillas de Madrid (1987 JD); Université Libre de Bruxelles (1989 LLM European Union Law).
Personal: Born 1964; resides Madrid.
Leisure: Marathon running, skiing, reading.

RUIZ-GÁLVEZ VILLAVERDE, Félix

Ruiz-Gálvez Abogados
Phone: Madrid (+34 91 781 21 91)
E-mail: fx@ruizgalvezabogados.com
Insurance law department.
Position: Founding partner dealing with all areas of insurance and company law.
Career: In-house legal adviser of CÍA Transmediterránea, SA for over nine years. Legal adviser of the in-house legal department of GAN, and secretary general of this insurance company until deciding to dedicate his full time to Ruiz-Gálvez Abogados. Founding member of the Instituto Iberoamericano de Derecho Marítimo Español (IME-ICADE); and at the masters course (LLM) organised by the Foundation Valencia Port. Author of many articles on insurance law and frequent lecturer on insurance law matters.
Languages: Spanish, French and English.
Member: Madrid Bar Association; Spanish Maritime Law Association; founding member of the Instituto Iberoamericano de Derecho Marítimo (IIDM).
Education: Law degree at the Universidad Complutense de Madrid (UCM), 1973.
Personal: Born 1951. Resides Monte-Rozas, Madrid.
Leisure: Sailing, golf, skiing, tennis, canoeing.

RUIZ-GÁLVEZ VILLAVERDE, Fernando

Ruiz-Gálvez Abogados
Phone: Madrid (+34 91 781 21 91)
E-mail: fernando@ruizgalvezabogados.com
Maritime law department.
Position: Founding partner dealing with all areas of maritime law.
Career: Legal adviser of CÍA Transmediterránea, SA for more than 27 years. Head of the in-house legal department and general secretary of the company until deciding to dedicate his full time to Ruiz-Gálvez Abogados. Legal adviser of the Spanish delegation at the legal committee of IMO. Teacher for the masters course (LLM) organised by the Instituto Marítimo Español (IME-ICADE); and for the masters course (LLM) organised by the Foundation Valencia Port. Author of many articles on maritime law and frequent lecturer on maritime law matters, especially on pollution.
Languages: Spanish, English and French.
Member: Madrid Bar Association; Spanish Maritime Law Association; titulary member of the International Maritime Committee (CMI).
Education: Law degree at the Universidad Complutense de Madrid (UCM), 1964.
Personal: Born 1941; resides Madrid.
Leisure: All sports, walking, classical music, travelling, theatre.

SAAVEDRA, Amalia

Santiago Mediano Abogados
Phone: Madrid (+34 91 310 6363)
E-mail: asaavedra@santiagomediano.com
Tax and accountancy department.
Position: Senior associate focusing her work on direct taxation, dealing with international restructurings, including mergers, branches and subsidiaries incorporations and day-to-day work, expatriates and transnational operations among others. With regard to indirect taxation, she advises on VAT and on double tax conventions.
Career: Has practised in well-known international consulting groups, representing the interests of national and multinational companies before the Spanish Tax Administration; has dealt with tax inspections and appeals before the Spanish authorities for both domestic and international operations; also works for the Industrial Organisation School in Madrid as tax professor for small and medium-sized entrepreneurs.
Languages: English, French, Spanish.
Member: Madrid Bar Association.
Education: Comillas Pontificial University (1992 Law; diploma in business administration); Instituto de Empresa, Madrid (1993 MA tax law for corporations).
Personal: Born 1968.

TRIGO, Luis

Broseta Abogados
Phone: Valencia (+34 96 392 10 07)
E-mail: ltrigo@broseta.com
Tax department.
Position: Partner specialising in corporate income tax, due diligence, fiscal law, inheritance law, international estate taxation, capital gains tax, corporate taxation and non-profit corporations.
Career: Tax adviser Companie Español de Petroles 1987-97; lecturer, Universidad Rey Juan Carlos de Madrid in tax law 1994-2002; partner Baker & McKenzie Madrid office 2000-04; partner Broseta Abogados 2005 to date. He has dictated numerous conferences relative to tributary law and has written many articles for specialised magazines on tributary law and accounting.
Languages: English.
Member: Madrid Bar Association.
Education: University Complutense of Madrid; University San Pablo CEU (graduated in law).
Personal: Born 1962; resides Valencia.
Leisure: Travelling.

VERARDINI, María José

Santiago Mediano Abogados
Phone: Madrid (+34 91 310 6363)
E-mail: mjverardini@santiagomediano.com
Corporate and commercial department.
Position: Senior associate; as part of her legal assessment, Mariá José is in charge of the analysis, negotiation, preparation, wording, complaint, termination, and so on of any commercial letter of intention, pre-contract, or contract, including but not limited to: shareholders' agreements, companies' sale, sale contracts in general, commercial representation and distribution contracts (agency, mediation, franchising, distribution, etc); contracts of an associative nature, such as joint ventures, commercial renting contracts (contract of works, services, engineering, technology transfer, outsourcing collaboration, consultancy contracts, merchandising, etc); advertising contracts, contracts of funding and confidentiality agreements. She works as general legal adviser in commercial law and, in particular, corporate law, commercial trading and contractual guarantees, international trading, law of exchange, mergers and acquisitions, MBOs, joint ventures, financial restructuring and corporate reorganisation as well as structured funding (project finance). Among other services, her work on due diligence is of utmost importance, considered as an initial step to an acquisition, in order to foresee and correct potential legal anomalies in whichever companies, or regarding the optimisation of resources from a legal point of view.
Career: Over the last 14 years, has developed her professional career in international law firms of great prestige, as well as in the legal department of international companies.
Languages: English, French, German, Russian, Spanish.
Member: Madrid Bar Association.
Education: University of Comillas (1991 Law, diploma in business law).
Personal: Born 1968.

SWEDEN

ELIASSON, Ingrid
LINDHS DLA Nordic
Phone: Stockholm (+46 8 701 78 75)
E-mail: ingrid.eliasson@dlanordic.se
Technology, media and communications.
Position: Partner in the Stockholm office specialising in banking, finance, telecommunications and media law. Has extensive experience in cross-border asset finance transactions, primarily representing international lenders, as well as in regulatory work in the banking and finance sector. Also has in-depth knowledge of the TV and telecoms sectors and particular expertise in respect of mergers and acquisitions in the telecom/media sectors, as well as telecommunications and cable TV infrastructure. In banking and finance expertise is in asset-based financing, structured financing, leasing and lending and regulatory (authorisations to conduct various kinds of financial operations, and compliance). In media and telecommunications, expertise is in all aspects of TV distribution, including procurement of equipment, transmission capacity, programme services, sports and other content, as well as international co-operation on technical standards and media competition law; telecommunication infrastructure contracts and regulatory aspects on infrastructure, as well as consumer contracts; payments and financial services via the internet and mobile telephone networks; and commercial contracts regarding telecommunications, joint ventures, mergers and acquisitions within the telecom sectors.
Career: Judicial clerk Stockholm District Court 1986-89; associate Advokatfirman Lagerlöf 1989-91; associate Advokatfirma Lindhs DLA Nordic KB 1991-95; partner Advokatfirma Lindhs DLA Nordic KB 1996 to date.
Languages: Swedish and English.
Member: Swedish Bar Association (1992).
Education: University of Uppsala (1986 LLM).
Personal: Born 1953.

HÄGGLUND, Kent
LINDHS DLA Nordic
Phone: Stockholm (+46 8 701 78 04)
E-mail: kent.hagglund@dlanordic.se
Commercial and litigation.
Position: Senior partner in Stockholm office with considerable experience in general corporate law, mergers and acquisitions, insolvency law, intellectual property, banking and litigation. For many years, has worked advising companies, including guiding companies to the Stock Exchange and advising in Stock Exchange regulations. Also has considerable experience in mergers and acquisitions, including cross-border transactions of both public and private companies within EU, Central and Eastern Europe. A 'prominent' practitioner enthusiastically recommended for long experience in the field of insolvency 'Chambers & Partners 2004-05'. Has more than 25 years' experience of IP litigations (trade marks and company names).
Career: Legal counsel National Patent and Registration Office 1974-76; judicial clerk Stockholm District Court 1976-78; associate Law Firm Rindborg 1978-82; admitted Swedish Bar 1981; partner Hägglund & Ramm-Ericson 1983-2001; partner Lindhs DLA Nordic 2001; secretary to the board of Resco AB, quoted on the O-list of the Stockholm Stock Exchange; secretary to the board of TMG International AB (publ), quoted on the Nordic Growth Market (NGM), an Exchange under the supervision of the Swedish Financial Supervisory Authority.
Languages: Swedish and English.
Member: Swedish Bar Association (1981).
Education: University of Stockholm (1975 LLM).
Personal: Born 1947.

SWITZERLAND

BAJAN, Björn
Haymann & Baldi
Phone: Zurich (+41 44 250 25 25)
E-mail: bbajan@hblaw.ch
Position: Partner dealing with international commercial litigation and arbitration, compulsory enforcement and bankruptcy law, reconstructions, corporate and commercial, banking, contracts, employment, trusts and wills.
Career: Admitted 1986; advocacy 1989; publications: co-author contribution on Switzerland in Park & Cromie 'International Commercial Litigation', Butterworths (1997); co-author 'Dilemmas of a Withholding Agent' (June 1995); 'Handling a Tax Appeal' (March 1995) in 'Forum' (Tax Management International); co-author 'Dispute Resolution Methods in Switzerland' ('Comparative Law Yearbook of International Business', 1994).
Languages: English, German, French.
Member: Zürich Bar Association; member of various cantonal bars; Institute for Civil Procedure; Swiss Arbitration Association; Chartered Institute of Arbitrators (ACIArb) London.
Education: Zürich University (1986 lic iur, cum laude); Queen Mary and Westfield College, London (1994 LLM).
Personal: Born 1960; Biel.

BALDI, Peter
Haymann & Baldi
Phone: Zurich (+41 44 250 25 25)
E-mail: pbaldi@hblaw.ch
Position: Partner dealing with business law, banking law, arbitration, competition law, international civil procedure, international commercial litigation, intellectual property law, wills and trusts.
Career: Admitted 1977, Zürich Bar; previously corporate lawyer with bank; in advocacy since 1980, for own account since 1985; partner Haymann & Baldi; publications: 'Über die Gewährleistungspflicht des Verkäufers von Aktien, insbesondere beim Verkauf aller Aktien einer Gesellschaft' (1975); contribution on Switzerland in Park & Cromie 'International Commercial Litigation', Butterworths (1997); 'Switzerland, Double Taxation Treaties' (1992).
Languages: English, French, German, Italian.
Member: International Bar Association (sections on business and banking law); Swiss Bar Association; member of various cantonal bars; German Society for Banking Law.
Education: University of Zürich (1971 Lic iur magna cum laude; 1974 Dr iur summa cum laude).
Personal: Born 1946; Brunnen.

CARATSCH, Michele
Haymann & Baldi
Phone: Zurich (+41 44 250 25 25)
E-mail: mcaratsch@hblaw.ch
Position: Partner dealing with commercial and corporate law, Eastern European and CIS M&A, project finance and privatisations, Swiss and US securities law, initial public offerings, unfair competition law, intellectual property law, international commercial litigation and international arbitration.
Career: Admitted 1991, Zürich; admitted 1996, New York Bar; partner Haymann & Baldi, previously associate lawyer, Winston & Strawn, New York; publications: contribution on Switzerland in 'Worldwide Injunctions', in 'International Commercial Litigation' (June 1999); contribution on Tajikstan in 'International Privatisation Review' (2001-02); contribution on Uzbekistan in 'Privatisation & Public Private Partnership' (2005-06); contribution on Switzerland in 'Client Guide', in 'IFLR' (March 2004); contribution on Switzerland in 'IFLR - Guide to Corporate Governance' (2005).
Languages: English, German, Italian, Portuguese, Spanish.
Member: Zürich Bar Association; American Bar Association; Aigli Associazione Internazionale Giuristi di Lingua Italiana; ICC Fraudnet Network.
Education: New York University (1995 LLM Corporate Law); University of Zürich (1988 lic iur cum laude).
Personal: Born 1963; St Gall.

ECKERT, Martin K, Dr
MME - Meyer Müller Eckert Partners
Phone: Zurich (+41 44 254 99 66)
E-mail: eckert@mme-law.ch
Business and corporate law; international trade law; information technology; company foundations; intellectual property rights; trade names; trade marks; insurance law; litigation; arbitration.
Position: Partner specialising in business and corporate law, international trade law, information technology, intellectual property rights, trade names and trade marks.
Career: High Court secretary at the Commercial Court of the Canton of Zurich 1991; qualified 1994; associate Carrard Paschoud Heim et Associés, Lausanne 1994-95; associate Hartmann, Meyer and Partner 1995-99; partner Meyer Müller Eckert 1999 to date. Judge at the Swiss Federal Appeal Commission of Intellectual Property (since 2002).
Languages: English, French, German.

Member: Swiss and Zurich Bar Associations; World IT Lawyers; INGRES (Swiss Intellectual Property Institute); Swiss Interactive Media and Software Association (simsa); Licensing Executives Society; AIPPI ;Computer Law Association; ASA (Swiss Arbitration Association); Ordre des Avocats Vaudois (membre honoraire); International Bar Association.
Education: University of Zurich (1992 Dr iur).
Personal: Born 1963; resides Zurich.

FAVRE, Raphaëlle

Rohner Rechtsanwälte
Phone: Zurich (+41 44 281 1000)
E-mail: raphaelle.favre@rohnerlaw.ch
Transportation law, trade law, banking and commercial law, litigation and arbitration.
Position: Partner dealing with all areas of maritime and aviation law, transportation, trade and commercial law, banking and finance, contracts, insurance and reinsurance law.
Career: Qualified 1997; admitted to the Bar 1997; partner Rohner Rechtsanwälte 2006.
Languages: English, French, German, Italian.
Member: Zurich Bar Association; Swiss Bar Association; Association Internationale des Jeunes Avocats (AIJA); Swiss Commission on Sea Navigation; Swiss Maritime Law Association.
Education: University of Fribourg (1994 JD); Tulane University School of Law (2002 LLM).
Personal: Born 1970; resides Zurich.
Leisure: Skiing, swimming, scuba diving.

FRIEDLI, Georg

Advokaturbureau Friedli und Schnidrig
Phone: Bern (+41 31 326 50 00)
E-mail: g.friedli@fslaw.ch
Position: Partner dealing with bankruptcy, international insolvency, banking law, international banking law, international business law, commercial dispute resolution, commercial litigation, corporate contracts, criminal litigation, international criminal law, money laundering, and Hague Convention proceedings.
Career: Justice Department Canton of Bern 1978-80; Legal Department Swiss Bank Corporation, General Managers, Basle 1981-83; private practice in Bern since 1983. Author of various publications on banking issues.
Languages: German, English, French, Spanish.
Member: Bernese and Swiss Bar Associations.
Education: University of Bern (Fürsprecher); George Washington University (1981 MCL).
Personal: Born 1952; resides Burgdorf, Switzerland.
Leisure: Rock climbing, hiking, sports.

HAYMANN, Michel

Haymann & Baldi
Phone: Zurich (+41 44 250 25 25)
E-mail: mhaymann@hblaw.ch
Position: Partner dealing with business law, banking and securities, mergers and acquisitions, EC law, arbitration, competition law, international civil procedure, and international commercial litigation, wills and trusts.
Career: Admitted 1975, Zürich Bar; in advocacy since 1974; for own account since 1977; partner Haymann & Baldi; publications: 'Extraterritoriale Wirkung des EWG-Wettbewerbsrechtes' (1973); 'Extraterritorial Application of Antitrust Law, The Swiss Approach' in: 12 Revue Suisse du Droit International de la Concurrence (May 1981); 'Swiss to Outlaw Insider Trading' in: International Financial Law Review (October 1987); 'Contract Drafting Problems in the Light of the Lugano Convention' in: Bar European News, No 27; 'The Lugano Convention and the European Communities (May 1990)' in: Current ED Legal Developments Series, The Lugano and San Sebastian Conventions, Butterworths (1990); 'Joint Ventures and Mergers as a Test-Mark for a European Competition Law between EEC and EFTA: Switzerland as an Example' in: World Competition Law and Economics Review Vol 14 No. 1 (September 1990); 'Contribution on Switzerland' in: Cromie, Merger Control in Europe, IFR Publishing Limited (1991); 'Approaching Europe: Swiss Prospectives and Dilemmas' in: Legal Issues of European Integration (1992-1); contribution on Switzerland in: Stamp/Welsh (ed), 'International Insider Dealing', FT Law and Tax (1996); contribution on Switzerland in: Park & Cromie, 'International Commercial Litigation', second edition, Butterworths (1997); contribution on Switzerland in: 'Guide to Corporate Governance 2004', IFLR Supplement (2004).
Languages: English, French, German, Italian.
Member: American Society for International Law; International Bar Association (Antitrust and Banking Law Section); Swiss Association for International Law; Swiss Bar Association; member of various cantonal bars; Swiss Jurists Association; Union Internationale des Avocats (EEC Law Section); Association Suisse de l'Arbitrage.
Education: University of Zurich (1968 Lic iur magna cum laude; 1973 Dr iur summa cum laude).
Personal: Born 1942; Zürich.

HÖSLY, Balz, Dr

MME - Meyer Müller Eckert Partners
Phone: Zurich (+41 44 254 99 66)
E-mail: hoesly@mme-law.ch
Contract and corporate law; strategic change; crisis management; competition law; public-private partnerships; intellectual property; international trade; insurance and financial services; arbitration.
Position: Partner specialising in strategic change; crisis management; competition law and public-private partnerships.
Career: Qualified 1987; Winterthur Insurance Group/Credit Suisse Group (member of senior management) 1987-99; Osec Business Network Switzerland (Swiss Trade Promotion) (CEO) 2000-04. Living and working experience in the UK and Belgium; working experience in Denmark, the emerging markets in Eastern Europe and Asia, Austria, Poland as well as with the Swiss Federal Administration (State Secretariat for Economy, (seco) foreign ministry, (EDA) and the administration of the Canton Zurich.
Languages: German, English, French.
Member: Swiss and Zurich Bar Associations; member of the advisory board of the Swiss Interactive Media Society (SIMSA); Rotary Club Zurich-Turicum (president 2005-06); Swiss Management; Chevalier dans l'Ordre National du Mérite (France).
Education: University of Zurich (1987 Dr iur); International Institute for Management Development (IMD), Lausanne (1991 Program for Executive Development (PED); Malik Institute, St Gallen (2001 system-oriented management).
Personal: Born 1958; resides Zurich.

KUHN, Moritz W, Prof

MME - Meyer Müller Eckert Partners
Phone: Zurich (+41 44 254 99 66)
E-mail: kuhn@mme-law.ch
Insurance law; finance; banking law; capital markets; business law; corporate law; money laundering; gaming law; medical liability; medical malpractice agency and distributorships; unfair competition; litigation; arbitration; insurance litigation; mergers and acquisitions.
Position: Partner specialising in private and public insurance law, commercial law EEC law, medical law, medical malpractice, mandate law, arbitration.
Career: Qualified 1972; Swiss Life (general counsel and head of legal and tax services to the board) 1973-99; professor for private and insurance law, University of Zurich; president of the Supreme Court of the State (Canton) Zurich (Kassationsgericht); president Swiss Insurance Brokers' Association (SIBA); judge at the Swiss Federal Appeal Commission of Private Insurance Law.
Languages: English, French, German.
Member: Swiss and Zurich Bar Associations; Swiss Association of Insurance and Liability Law; Presidential Council of AIDA (International Association of Insurance Law); Swiss Arbitration Association since 1987.
Education: University of Zurich (1970 Dr iur).

LANDTWING, Andreas, Dr

MME - Meyer Müller Eckert Partners
Phone: Zurich (+41 44 254 99 66)
E-mail: landtwing@mme-law.ch
Business law; contract law; international trade; corporate law; agency and distributorships; international litigation; mediation; administrative law; notarial services.
Position: Partner specialising in business, administrative law, ADR and social security.
Career: Qualified 1999; London School of Economics and Political Science, London (LLM in Tax Law, 2000/2001); Legal Clerk of the Penal Court of the State (Canton) Zug. Certified Social Insurance Specialist (2002); Mediator by approval of the Swiss Bar Association (2003).
Languages: German, English and French.
Member: Swiss, Zurich and Zug Bar Associations.
Education: University of Zurich (1998 Dr iur); London School of Economics (2001 LLM); University of Zurich (2005 MA Applied Ethics).
Personal: Born 1966; resides Zug.

MEYER-HAUSER, Bernhard F, Dr
MME - Meyer Müller Eckert Partners
Phone: Zurich (+41 44 254 99 66)
E-mail: meyer-hauser@mme-law.ch
International litigation and arbitration; mergers and acquisitions; banking; licensing, agency and distribution law; intellectual property; joint ventures; unfair competition.
Position: Partner specialising in arbitration, litigation and contracts.
Career: Qualified 1975; associate Baker & McKenzie 1978-82; partner Hartmann, Meyer and Partner 1983-99; partner Meyer Müller Eckert Partners 1999 to date; living and working experience in the US.
Languages: English, French, German, Italian.
Member: Co-chairman Zurich Chamber of Commerce Arbitration Court; chairman Arbitration Specialist Group of Zurich Bar Association; chairman Zurich Local Group of Swiss Arbitration Association (ASA); chairman emeritus [international sales section] of the International Bar Association (IBA); member Swiss Arbitration Commission of International Chamber of Commerce (ICC); member German Institution for Arbitration; member Austrian Arbitration Association; Swiss and Zurich Bar Associations; International Bar Association (IBA); Inter-Pacific Bar Association (IPBA); American Bar Association (ABA). Arbitration Panels: ICC (International Chamber of Commerce), Paris; ICDR/AAA (American Arbitration Association), New York WIPO (World Intellectual Property Organization), Geneva; LCIA (London Court of International Arbitration), London; International Arbitral Centre of the Austrian Federal Economic Chamber, Vienna; CIDRA (Chicago International Dispute Resolution Association), Chicago; HKIAC (Hong Kong International Arbitration Centre), Hong Kong; SIAC (Singapore International Arbitration Centre), Singapore.
Education: University of Zurich (1979 Dr iur); Northwestern University School of Law, Chicago (1977 LLM); Chartered Institute for Arbitrators (1999 FCIArb).
Personal: Born 1946; resides Zurich.

MÜLLER-STUDER, R Luka, Dr
MME - Meyer Müller Eckert Partners
Phone: Zug (+41 41 726 99 66)
E-mail: muller@mme-law.ch
Business and corporate law; money laundering law; cross border assistance; compliance and forensic services; gaming law; agency and distribution law; competition law international litigation; international debt collection.
Position: Partner, specialising in legal compliance for the financial sector.
Career: Qualified 1992; public prosecutor in 1993; associate at a Zurich law firm 1995-99; member of several working groups of different Federal departments in the field of enforcement of money laundering control legislation 1997-98; member of task force to set up self-regulating organisations to control money laundering (SRO) 1997-98; partner Meyer Müller Eckert 1999 to date; member of an advisory board of an SRO.
Languages: English, French, German.
Member: Swiss, Zurich and Zug Bar Associations; President of the Trade and Service Association of the Canton of Zug (HDV); Institute of Advanced Legal Studies, London.
Education: University of Zurich (1990 lic iur); London School of Economics and Political Science, London (1994 LLM); University of Basel (1999 Dr iur).
Personal: Born 1964; resides Zurich.

RAUCH, Men, Dr
Rohner Rechtsanwälte
Phone: Zurich (+41 44 281 1000)
E-mail: men.rauch@rohnerlaw.ch
Tax and corporate; litigation.
Position: Attorney-at-law dealing with all areas of tax contract and corporate law including mergers and acquisitions, succession planning.
Career: Qualified 1980; admitted to the Bar 1983; attorney-at-law Rohner Rechtsanwälte 1995; author and co-author of several commentaries on tax law.
Languages: English, French, German, Italian.
Member: Zurich Bar Association; Swiss Bar Association; IPBA.
Education: University of Zurich (1985 JD).
Personal: Born 1954; resides Zurich.
Leisure: Mountaineering, biking, skiing, piano.

ROHNER, Louis, Dr
Rohner Rechtsanwälte
Phone: Zurich (+41 44 281 1000)
E-mail: louis.rohner@rohnerlaw.ch
Banking and finance; trusts and estates.
Position: Partner dealing with all areas of banking and finance including trusts.
Career: Qualified 1974; admitted to the Bar 1977; partner Rohner & Partner 1982; author of several publications on computer law.
Languages: English, French, German, Italian, Spanish.
Member: Zurich Bar Association; Swiss Bar Association; IBA; Swiss Arbitration Association; International Fiscal Association; AIPPI.
Education: University of Zurich (1976 JD); Harvard Law School (1978 LLM).
Personal: Born 1949; resides Zurich.
Leisure: Golf, tennis, skiing.

VOCK, Dominik, Dr
MME - Meyer Müller Eckert Partners
Phone: Zurich (+41 44 254 99 66)
E-mail: vock@mme-law.ch
Civil procedure law; judicial commercial disputes and liability litigations; debt enforcement and bankruptcy law; international arbitration; contract and corporate law.
Position: Partner specialising in litigation and debt enforcement and bankruptcy law.
Career: Judicial clerk at the disrict court of Andelfingen 1994; research assistant at the chair for civil procedure law, debt enforcement and bankruptcy law and private law at the University of Zurich law school 1996-2000; lecturer at the law faculty of the University of Zurich for civil procedure law 1999-2000; associate with two business law firms 2005.
Languages: English, French, German.
Member: Swiss and Zurich Bar Associations.
Education: University of Zurich (2000 Dr iur); University of Pennsylvania Law School (2003 LLM).
Personal: Born 1966; resides Zurich.

WIRTH ZUBLER, Sibylle, Dr
MME - Meyer Müller Eckert Partners
Phone: Zurich (+41 44 254 99 66)
E-mail: wirth_zubler@mme-law.ch
Business law; corporate law; agency and distributorships; information technology; intellectual property; unfair competition; advertising law; employment law; international trade; litigation; arbitration.
Position: Partner specialising in contracts, international trade, intellectual property, unfair competition and advertising law.
Career: Qualified 1994; Legal Counsel in a multinational life science corporation (1997-2000); research experience in the US and Germany; lecturer on advertising law 1995-96; lecturer on contract law since 2000.
Languages: German, English and French.
Member: Swiss and Zurich Bar Associations; INGRES (Swiss Intellectual Property Institute).
Education: University of Zurich (1993 Dr iur).
Personal: Born 1964; resides Zurich.

TURKEY

ÇAGA, Barbaros
Çaga & Çaga Law Firm
Phone: Istanbul (+90 212 310 32 00)
E-mail: barbaros@caga.gen.tr
Head of firm.
Position: Head of firm specialising in all aspects of business law including corporate law, mergers and acquisitions, competition law, tax law and employment law. Also focuses on media and aviation law, capital markets law, construction law, foreign direct investments, as well as banking and finance.
Career: Qualified 1973; took over family firm in 1978. Has lectured on corporate governance, mergers and acquisitions and consumer law at Yeditepe University Law School, Istanbul.
Languages: Turkish, German, English.
Member: Istanbul Bar; chairman of ethics committee and member of the social security and labour law committee of TUSIAD, Turkish Industrialists and Businessmen Association; German High School Alumni Association; Cultural and Educational Foundation of German High School Graduates (founding member); Çaga Law Foundation (founder and chairman).
Education: German High School (1960); Ludwig Maximilians University Law School, Munich; Istanbul University Law School (1972 lic iur).
Personal: Born 1941; resides Istanbul.

ÇAGA DEGERLI, Idil
Çaga & Çaga Law Firm
Phone: Istanbul (+90 212 310 32 00)
E-mail: idil@caga.gen.tr
Corporate law, contracts and employment.
Position: Partner specialising in dispute resolution, tax law, corporate law, contracts and employment law. Also specialises in intellectual property matters and media and entertainment law, with a particular focus on advertising law, e-commerce and consumer protection, and IT and telecommunications.
Career: Apprentice Çaga & Çaga; qualified 1998; Çaga & Çaga 1998 to date.
Languages: Turkish, German, English, French.
Member: Istanbul Bar; German High School Alumni Association; Çaga Law Foundation (founder and secretary).
Education: German High School (1992); Istanbul University Law School (lic iur 1996); Ludwig Maximilians University Law School, Munich (1998 LLM).
Personal: Born 1973; resides Istanbul.
Leisure: Member, Protection of Natural Life Association.

CAVUSOGLU, Kemal
ESC Consulting
Phone: Istanbul (+90 212 236 9656)
E-mail: kcavusoglu@kcavusoglu.av.tr
Corporate, construction, mergers and acquisitions, litigation.
Position: Partner dealing with corporate and commercial, international private, insolvency and corporate restructuring, mergers and acquisitions, arbitration, debt settlements, intellectual property and media, trade mark privatisation and e-commerce law.
Career: Qualified 1993; junior and senior lawyer Pekin & Pekin Law Firm 1993-2000; head of legal department Calik Holding 2001-04; partner ESC Consulting 2004 to date.
Languages: English, Turkish.
Member: Istanbul Bar; IBA; AAA (The Hague Academy of International Law).
Education: University of Istanbul, Faculty of Law; University of California at Riverside; The Hague Academy of International Law; University of Bern (World Trade Institute).
Personal: Born 1967; resides Istanbul.
Leisure: Yachting, scuba diving, music.

CETINER, Gündüz
CLO - Coskun Law Office
Phone: Istanbul (+90 212 280 86 61)
E-mail: gcetiner@clolaw.net
Position: General manager.
Career: Assistant auditor Esbank 1982-85; auditor Esbank 1985-90; assistant credit manager Esbank 1990-92; manager Esbank 1992-95; assistant general manager at a private textile company 2000-02; general manager Coskun Law Office 2002.
Languages: English, Turkish.
Education: Gazi University, Ankara (1979 Business Administration); University of Toledo, Ohio (1998).
Personal: Born 1955; resides Istanbul.
Leisure: Swimming, music, literature, cats.

COSKUN, Ihsan
CLO - Coskun Law Office
Phone: Istanbul (+90 212 280 86 61)
E-mail: icoskun@clolaw.net
Asset management, banking, finance and capital markets, construction and real estate, corporate and commercial law, debt settlement, litigation and dispute resolution.
Position: Founder.
Career: Qualified 1979; founder and partner Coskun Law Office 1980.
Languages: Turkish.
Member: Turkish and Istanbul Bar Association.
Education: Istanbul University Law School (1979 LLB).
Personal: Born 1955; resides Istanbul.
Leisure: Golf, travel.

DEGERLI, Erdem
Çaga & Çaga Law Firm
Phone: Istanbul (+90 212 310 32 00)
E-mail: erdem@caga.gen.tr
Corporate, construction, transport and shipping, aviation, e-commerce and consumer protection, foreign direct investments, mergers and acquisitions, banking and finance, IT and telecommunications, as well as contracts.
Position: Partner concentrating on corporate law and consultancy, mergers and acquisitions, construction law, banking and finance, aviation, shipping and transport, e-commerce and consumer protection, foreign direct investments, IT and telecommunications, as well as contracts.
Career: Apprentice Güreli & Sanver Law Office; qualified 1995; associate Güreli & Sanver 1995; Çaga & Çaga 1995 to date; internship Altheimer & Gray, Chicago 1998.
Languages: Turkish, English, German.
Member: Istanbul Bar; Robert College Alumni Association; Çaga Law Foundation (member of board of directors).
Education: American Robert College, Istanbul (1988); Istanbul University Law School (1993 lic iur); Boston University Law School (1998 LLM in Banking and Finance).
Personal: Born 1970; resides Istanbul.

ERYUREKLI, Murat
Eryurekli & Fidan
Phone: Istanbul (+90 212 343 9270)
E-mail: meryurekli@ef-law.com
Position: Managing partner of Eryurekli & Fidan specialising in capital markets, banking, mergers and acquisitions and e-commerce. He has particular expertise in capital markets activities and derivatives.
Career: Qualified 1993; legal counsel Capital Markets Board of Turkey 1994-98; partner Pekin & Pekin Law Firm 1998-2004; managing partner Eryurekli & Fidan 2004 to date; authorised arbitrator for capital markets disputes; licensed expert on capital markets and derivatives; author of article on 'Corporate governance standards in Turkey' in 'IFLR' (ed 1000, 2004).
Languages: English.
Member: Istanbul Bar Association; International Bar Association.
Education: Istanbul University School of Law (1992 law diploma).
Personal: Born 1969; resides Istanbul.

ESIN, Arif, Prof
ESC Consulting
Phone: Istanbul (+90 212 236 9656)
E-mail: esc@escrc.com
Competition department.
Position: Professor Arif Esin heads the firm's competition group, which provides legal services in antitrust and merger control law, which entail the filing of notification to the Competition Authority and to the European Commission. Major cases defended include a Turkish cement case, Turkish pharmaceutical case, fertilizer case, wood industry case, RWE, AGI/Thames Water merger operation, Metro, TNT Forwarding.
Career: Qualified 1979; partner ESC Consulting 1989. Publications include Competition Law and State Aid Law, as well as many books on competition and EU law.
Languages: French, English.
Member: President of the Competition Lawyers Association.
Education: Saint Benoît College; University of Paris, Faculty of Law; University of Istanbul, department of EU law (professor 1992).
Personal: Born 1956; resides Istanbul.
Leisure: Chess, painting.

ESIN, Ismail G, Dr
Esin Lokmanhekim Içtem Gürkaynak
Phone: Istanbul (+90 212 327 1724)
E-mail: ismail.esin@eliglegal.com
Corporate law, mergers and acquisitions, arbitration.
Position: Partner dealing with all areas of corporate law, mergers and acquisitions and arbitration.
Career: Teaching assistant, Marmara University, School of Law 1992-96; Lecturer, civil law and obligations 1992-2004; admitted to Istanbul Bar 1998; partner Canyurek, Akman & Esin Law Office 1998-2000; partner Sanver, Esin & Co 2000-02; lecturer, mergers and acquisitions, Bilgi University 2001 to date; partner ELIG 2002 to date; masters classes for economical law, Galatasaray University 2004 to date. Publications: 'The Abuse of the Right to File a Lawsuit Against General Meeting Resolutions of a Joint Stock Company and Liability of the Plaintiff's Counsel' (in Turkish), Hayri Domanic'e Armagan, Istanbul 1995; 'Liability of the Seller in Business Enterprise Acquisition', Frankfurt 1997; 'Contradiction of the Legal Restrictions on Immovable Ownership Arising from Law and Agreement' (in Turkish), Prof Dr Selahattin Tekinay'in Hatirasina Armagan, Istanbul 1999; 'Materials on International Arbitration', Istanbul, March 2003; 'Mergers and Acquisitions in Practice', Istanbul, November 2003.
Languages: German, English.
Member: ICC Turkish National Committee; London Court of International Arbitration (LCIA); DIS (German Arbitration Committee); AHK (German-Turkish Trade and Industry Chamber).

Education: Istanbul University School of Law (1990 LLB); Tübingen University School of Law (1991 LLM, the abuse of the right to file an annulment lawsuit against general assembly resolutions of a joint stock company (in German); 1997 PhD, Sachmänglhaftung beim Unternehmenskauf - liability of the seller in business enterprise acquisition).
Personal: Born 1967; resides Istanbul.

FIDAN, Erdoğan

Eryurekli & Fidan
Phone: Istanbul (+90 212 343 9270)
E-mail: efidan@ef-law.com
Position: Partner specialising in project finance, real estate and construction business, privatisation and telecommunication projects.
Career: Qualifiied 1997; partner Pekin & Pekin 1998-2004; partner Eryurekli & Fidan 2004 to date.
Languages: English.
Member: Istanbul Bar Association; International Bar Association.
Education: Marmara University School of Law (1997 law diploma).
Personal: Born 1971; resides Istanbul.

GURKAYNAK, Gonenc

Esin Lokmanhekim Içtem Gürkaynak
Phone: Istanbul (+90 212 327 1724)
E-mail: gonenc.gurkaynak@eliglegal.com
Competition and EU law, corporate and commercial.
Position: Partner dealing with competition law and EU law, corporate and commercial law and telecommunications.
Career: Trained Istanbul; qualified 1998; admitted to Istanbul Bar 1998; associate Derman Ortak Avukat Burosu (White & Case Istanbul) 1997-2000 and September 2004-February 2005; associate White & Case LLP, New York 2001-03; admitted to New York State Bar 2002; associate White & Case LLP, Brussels January 2003-August 2004; admitted to the Law Society of England and Wales as a solicitor (currently non-practising); lecturer on Anglo-American law in Bilkent University, 2004 to date; lecturer on the Economics of Antitrust law in Bogazîcí University, 2005 to date. Publications include: 'Foundations of Merger Control: Thoughts on Why? and How?' (The Turkish Competition Authority Press, September 2004); 'A Discussion on the Prime Objective of the Turkish Competition Law from a Law and Economics Perspective' (The Turkish Competition Authority Press, September 2003); 'Some Essential Issues of the Turkish Merger Control Regime' (White & Case Woldwide Merger Survey, 2003 ed, pp 28-32); 'Shifting the Burden of Proof in the Turkish Competition Law' (Global Competition Review, February-March 2002); 'The Problem with Turkey's Competition Regime' (International Finance Law Review, January 2002).
Languages: English, French.
Member: American Bar Association, New York Bar, Istanbul Bar, Law Society of England and Wales (non-practising).
Education: Ankara University School of Law (1997 LLB); Harvard Law School (2001 LLM).
Personal: Born 1976; resides Istanbul.

ICTEM, Serkan

Esin Lokmanhekim Içtem Gürkaynak
Phone: Istanbul (+90 212 327 1724)
E-mail: serkan.ictem@eliglegal.com
Banking and finance, securities, intellectual property.
Position: Partner dealing with banking and finance, securities matters, and intellectual property-related litigation.
Career: Associate Derman Ortak Avukat Bürosu (White & Case Istanbul) 1997-99 and 2003-04 (trade mark attorney); associate White & Case LLP, New York 2000-03; partner ELIG 2004 to date. Publications: 'Turkish Law Gives Personal Liability From Corporate Public Debts to LLC Members', Tax Notes International, March 2003; 'Underwriting Methodology', Turkish Capital Markets Magazine 2004; 'Analysis of Joint Stock Company Share Transfer Restriction Provisions' (in Turkish), Istanbul Bar Association Journal 2004/2; 'Thin Capitalisation Rules under Turkish Corporate Tax Law', Global Tax Report, July 2004, Tax Notes International, July 2004.
Languages: English.
Member: Istanbul Bar Association (1997), New York State Bar (2001), American Bar Association (2001).
Education: Istanbul University Law School (1996 LLB); New York University Law School (2000 LLM).
Personal: Born 1974; resides Istanbul.

LOKMANHEKIM, S Tunc

Esin Lokmanhekim Içtem Gürkaynak
Phone: Istanbul (+90 212 327 1724)
E-mail: tunc.lokmanhekim@eliglegal.com
Corporate, mergers and acquisitions.
Position: Partner dealing with all areas of corporate law and mergers and acquisitions.
Career: Associate Derman Ortak Avukat Bürosu (White & case Istanbul) 1997-98; admitted to Istanbul Bar 1998; associate, Sanver, Esin & Co 1998-2002; partner ELIG 2002 to date. Publications: 'Mergers and Acquisitions in Practice', Istanbul 2003; 'Mergers and Acquisitions in Turkey', Getting The Deal Through 2003, London 2003.
Languages: English.
Member: International Bar Association.
Education: Istanbul University School of Law (1996 LLB); University of Marmara (LLM).
Personal: Born 1974; resides Istanbul.

ODABAS TAVARES, Ozlem

Odabas Tavares Law Office
Phone: Ankara (90312 405 6035)
E-mail: oot@odabastavares.com
Corporate.
Position: Partner dealing with all areas of practice.
Career: Trained in Metin Baran Law Office and qualified 1993; visiting foreign lawyer for Sinclair, Roche & Temperley and Ince & Co Solicitors in London, 1995; associate at the Gur&Inal Law Office in Istanbul, 1996; counsel, White & Case LLP, Ankara Office, 1998; senior associate at Cakmak Avokatlik Bürosu, Ankara, 2003; partner at Odabas Tavares Law Office, Ankara, present.
Languages: English, Portuguese, Turkish.
Member: Ankara Bar.
Education: University of Istanbul (1992 LLB); University of Nottingham (1994 LLM).
Personal: Born 1970; resides Ankara.

RUHNAU, Martina

CLO - Coskun Law Office
Phone: Istanbul (+90 212 280 86 61)
E-mail: mruhnau@clolaw.net
Position: Legal consultant.
Career: Qualified 1992; joined Coskun Law Office 2005.
Languages: English, German, Turkish.
Member: Turkish-German Chamber of Commerce in Istanbul.
Education: Justus-Liebig University Law School, Giessen, Germany.
Personal: Born 1962; resides Istanbul.
Leisure: Slow food, modern art.

YILANLI, Haydar

CLO - Coskun Law Office
Phone: Istanbul (+90 212 280 86 61)
E-mail: hyilanli@clolaw.net
Foreign trade and customs law.
Position: Lawyer.
Career: Qualified 1980; joined Coskun Law Office 2005.
Languages: English, Turkish.
Member: Turkish and Bursa Bar Association.
Education: Ankara University Law School.
Personal: Born 1950; resides Istanbul.

UNITED ARAB EMIRATES

AL TAMIMI, Essam

Al Tamimi & Co
Phone: Dubai (+971 4 331 7090)
E-mail: e.tamimi@tamimi.com
Commercial law; domestic and international law.
Position: Founder and senior partner.
Career: Qualified 1983; founded Al Tamimi & Co 1989. Publications include: 'Labour Law in the United Arba Emirates' (1995); 'Arbitration Law in the United Arab Emirates' (1997); 'Setting Up in Dubai' (2002); 'Setting Up in Abu Dhabi' (2002); 'The Practical Guide to Litigation and Arbitration in the UAE' (2003); 'United Arab Emirates Court of Cassation Judgments 1989-1997' (2003); 'United Arab Emirates Court of Cassation Judgments 1998-2003' (2005). Contributor to firm's monthly magazine 'Law Update' (www.tamimi.com).
Member: LCIA Court.
Education: UAE University Al Ain (1983 LLB) Harvard Law School (LLM).
Personal: United Arab Emirates national.

ALSHAIKH, Dr AbdulRahman, Dr

Emirates International Law Firm
Phone: Abu Dhabi (+971 2 6265 600)
E-mail: lawyers@emirates.net.ae
Position: Managing partner of EILF.
Career: Legal consultant in commercial law, in particular finance, banking, commercial companies, international contracts and intellectual property; professor of law at the UAE University School of Law; former head of the private law department and provost assistant, in charge of faculty members' development at the UAE University; has participated in drafting various UAE laws and contributed in negotiating intergovernmental and international agreements; practices as an advocate at the UAE Federal Supreme Court and Dubai Court of Cassation.
Languages: Arabic, English, French.
Member: International Association for the Advancement of Teaching and Research in Intellectual Property (ATRIP), Association Litteraire et Artistique Internationale (ALIA) and IBA.
Education: University of Azhar, Egypt (1971 License in Sharia and Law); French National School for the Judiciary (1979 distinction); University of Paris for Law and Economics (1986 MA Business Law; PhD (Doctorat d'Etat) distinction).

ARAB, Hassan

Al Tamimi & Co
Phone: Dubai (+971 4 331 7090)
E-mail: h.arab@tamimi.com
Litigation.
Position: Partner and head of department.
Career: Al Tamimi & Company 1997; admitted 1998. Published extensively in the local press on matters related to commercial and corporate law and arbitration.
Languages: Arabic, English, Urdu.
Education: Beirut University, Alexandria (1996 LLB).

BABAISH, Jassim

Al Tamimi & Co
Phone: Dubai (+971 4 331 7090)
E-mail: j.abdullah@tamimi.com
Litigation.
Position: Partner whose area of practice includes litigation, civil, commercial and sharia law.
Career: Admitted UAE 1994; joined Al Tamimi & Company 1995; partner 1997.
Languages: Arabic.
Education: UAE University Al Ain (License of Law 1987).

BARAKAT, Hoda T

Al Tamimi & Co
Phone: Dubai (+971 4 331 7090)
E-mail: h.barakat@tamimi.com
Position: Managing partner, head of IP/IT department. Specialises mainly in intellectual property.
Career: Formerly worked as a qualified trade mark attorney in the UK. Joined Al Tamimi 1995. Initiated the information technology practice in the firm 2002.
Languages: Arabic, English.
Member: International Bar Association; Institute of Trade Mark Attorneys; International Trademark Association; Marques; Pharmaceutical Trade Mark Group; British Business Group.
Education: Cambridge University (Hons 1991); (MA Law 1995).
Personal: British national.

CHINIARA, Walid S.

Al Tamimi & Co
Phone: Dubai (+971 4 331 7090)
E-mail: w.chiniara@tamimi.com
Position: Legal consultant, acting head corporate and commercial department.
Career: Deputy general counsel, Paris; special counsel, ALJ, Jeddah; private practice, USA and Canada.
Languages: Arabic, English, French.
Member: Quebec Bar; Family Firm Institute.
Education: Saint Joseph University, Beirut (BA Law); New York University (Master of Comparitive Jurisprudence).

HOURANI, Husam

Al Tamimi & Co
Phone: Dubai (+971 4 331 7090)
E-mail: h.hourani@tamimi.com
Banking and finance.
Position: Partner and head of department.
Member: Law and Society Association; International Insitution for the Sociology of Law; Jordan Bar Association; International Bar Association.
Education: Kent University (1992 Hons Law); IISL Spain (1993 MA Law). Supplementary postgraduate courses in syndication of loans, Islamic finance, fraud prevention, documentary credits and project finance.

MOWAFAQ AL-SAOUDI, Yazan

Al Tamimi & Co
Phone: Dubai (+971 4 331 7090)
E-mail: y.saoudi@tamimi
Maritime, transport and insurance.
Position: Partner and head of department specialising in maritime and trade disputes.
Career: Legal advisor for Arthur Andersen, Jordan (1992); joined Al Tamimi 1997.
Languages: Arabic, English.
Member: Jordanian Bar Association.
Education: University of Jordan (1992).

SHIRI, Hussain Eisa

Al Tamimi & Co
Phone: Dubai (+971 2 674 4535)
E-mail: h.shira@tamimi.com
Litigation, intellectual property and trade mark law.
Position: Partner.
Career: UAE Military 1989-1997; joined Al Tamimi 1998; partner 2002.
Languages: Arabic, English.
Education: Beirut University, Alexandria (1996 LLB).

WAHIDALULAMA, Abdul

Al Tamimi & Co
Phone: Dubai (+971 4 331 7090)
E-mail: a.alulama.com
Banking and finance.
Position: Partner.
Career: Trainee Al Tamimi & Company 1999; admitted 2000.
Languages: Arabic, English, Persian, Urdu.
Education: UAE University (1999 LLB); University College London (2001 Maritime Law and International Trade LLM).

UNITED KINGDOM

ENGLAND AND WALES

ASHWORTH, Chris

O'Melveny & Myers LLP
Phone: London (+44 20 7558 4890)
E-mail: cashworth@omm.com
Transactions.
Position: Chris Ashworth is a partner in O'Melveny & Myers' London office specialising in mergers and acquisitions, equity capital markets, corporate finance, reconstruction and insolvency. Clients include a number of UK FTSE 250 and European listed companies. Recent transactions include: the sale of Channel 5 for £270m by United Business Media plc to RTL (2005); the proposed £9bn offer for Marks and Spencers by Philip Green (2004); the investment trust bid by PIGIT for Securities Trust of Scotland plc (2005); the £1.5bn bid by Deutsche Börse AG for the London Stock Exchange (2005); the recommended offer for Redbus Interhouse plc (2005/6). Notable transactions include: acting for Railtrack Group Plc following the administration of its subsidiary, the subsequent restructuring, disposal of assets including the Channel Tunnel Raillink for £8.8bn and its subsequent solvent liquidation; advising BT Group on its bid for the 3G Mobile Telecom UK licence; advising on the UK and European aspects of the SunGuard Data US$11.3bn buyout; acting for Henlys Group on its restructuring and subsequent reappearance as Bluebird; acting for AMVESCAP on its acquisitions of Perpetual Plc, UK asset management and Trimark, Canadian asset management and sale of its private client business, Atlantic Wealth; acting for MGPE on the acquisition of Formula One and subsequent sale; acting on the demergers of Garban Plc and Express Dairies; acting for Andersen Worldwide in relation to the Andersen Partnerships following ENRON; acting on the £8.4bn purchase of One2One by Deutsche Telekom; acting for Finmeccanica on its joint venture with EADS and BAE Systems.
Career: Chris Ashworth was formerly head of the corporate department at Ashurst, London, as well as previously being head of M&A, investment banking and telecoms, and a member of the board. Chris is

included in the Who's Who of International Corporate Governance Lawyers and International M&A Lawyers as well as specifically recommended by 'The Legal 500', 'Chambers UK' and 'Global Directories'. He speaks regularly at conferences, including the IBA, and contributes to various publications.
Member: Law Society of England and Wales.
Education: University of Southampton (LLB First).

BAILEY-HARRIS, Rebecca

Chambers of Bruce Blair QC
Phone: London (+44 20 7797 7070)
E-mail: bailey-harris@1hc.com
Position: Barrister specialising in family law.
Career: Called 2000.

BIRTWELL, Jan

O'Melveny & Myers LLP
Phone: London (+44 20 7088 4874)
E-mail: jbirtwell@omm.com
Specialises in tax law.
Position: Partner in O'Melveny & Myers' London office. Jan has advised on the tax aspects of upstream (fundraising) as well as downstream (buy-out) private equity business, including the structuring of management incentive arrangements for the funds and investee companies. Jan has extensive experience advising on the UK and international tax aspects of corporate finance, M&A and private equity transactions and on the tax structuring of investment funds and asset based finance. Her professional experience includes acting for JP Morgan Partners in connection with its leveraged buyout of IMO Car Wash Group Limited; acting for MidOcean Partners in relation to the spin-out of the private equity management team from Deutsche Bank and the concurrent fundraising by that team both to fund an acquisition of an 80% interest in the existing portfolio of investments under management and to raise new money for future investment; acting for MidOcean Partners on its exit from its investment in CenterParcs, firstly in Continental Europe by a sale to Pierre et Vacances and subsequently from the UK by way of accelerated IPO; the leveraged buyout of the Linpac group by Montagu Private Equity; acting for HSBC in connection with the spin-out of its private equity management team to form Montagu Private Equity and the concurrent fundraising by that team; acting for Terra Firma in connection with the spin-out of the private equity management team from Nomura headed by Guy Hands and the concurrent formation of funds, one to hold the existing portfolio and a separate fund to raise monies for future investment; advising on the spin-out of ISIS Equity Partners from F&C Asset Management.
Career: Admitted as a solicitor to the Supreme Court of England and Wales in 1986. Joined O'Melveny in March 2005 from the UK London law firm of Linklaters where she had been a tax partner since May 2001.
Education: University of Bristol (1983, LLB Hons); College of Law (Guildford), Law Society Final Examinations Part II (1984).

CARPENTER, Andrew

O'Melveny & Myers LLP
Phone: London (+44 20 7088 4820)
E-mail: acarpenter@omm.com
Works in the European private equity practice. Andrew is also responsible for the China Desk of O'Melveny & Myers' London office.
Position: Partner in O'Melveny & Myers' London office. Has acted on a wide range of international and domestic private equity led transactions, follow on investments and acquisitions as well as successful exits of private equity investments through IPOs and refinancings including securitisation. Recent transactions include the secondary buyout of Southern Cross Healthcare Holdings Limited backed by the Blackstone Group; the secondary buyout of Kaye Office Supplies Limited backed by Legal and General Ventures; the disposal of Atlantic Waste Holdings Limited to Augean plc; acting for JP Morgan Partners LLC on their participation in the take private of Warner Chilcott Plc; acting for Francisco Partners LP on its acquisition of RedPrairie Corporation through the merger with Francisco's wholly owned subsidiary Giants Holding Inc; acting for the directors and the non-institutional shareholders on the merger of Southern Cross Healthcare Holdings Limited with NHP plc and subsequent opco/propco re-organisation; representing Oji Paper Co, Ltd of Japan on its acquisition of Ilford Imaging Switzerland GmbH from Ilford International Holdings BV; acting for Stonebridge Partners Equity Fund III, LP on the acquisition of Dorbyl UK (Holdings) Limited from Dorbyl Limited; acting for Takara Bio Inc on its acquisition of Clontech Laboratories Inc from Beckton Dickson & Company.
Career: Admitted as a solicitor to the Supreme Court of England and Wales in 1991. Former contributing author of Tolleys Company Law. Before joining O'Melveny & Myers in July 2004 Andrew was the head of private equity with the London office of DLA Group and acts for a number of leading UK private equity firms.
Education: Liverpool University, BSc (first class honours) and PhD; Nottingham Trent University, Law Society Finals (first class honours).

DAGHLIAN, John

O'Melveny & Myers LLP
Phone: London (+44 20 7088 4862)
E-mail: jdaghlian@omm.com
Position: Partner in O'Melveny & Myers' London office. John has acted on a large range of international and domestic private equity driven transactions, including the establishment of private equity funds, private equity portfolio transactions, management buyouts, domestic flotations and M&A. He has also advised on over 20 public offerings of shares by publicly traded private equity funds (including the first ever share issue by a venture capital trust). His professional experience includes advising Apax Partners on the establishment of the Apax Europe V Fund (over €4.4bn), and previously advising on the establishment of its predecessor funds); advising the Bridgepoint management team on its management buyout of Bridgepoint (previously NatWest Equity Partners) from NatWest Bank, against the background of the hostile takeover of NatWest Bank, and the related transfer of NatWest's private equity portfolio to a syndicate of investors led by Coller Capital. At over US$1bn this was then the biggest placing of interests in a private equity portfolio; advising Nomura on the establishment by Guy Hands and former members of the Nomura Principal Finance Group of Terra Firma Capital Partners, and the arrangements for continuing management by Terra Firma of Nomura's very substantial private equity portfolio; acting for Coller Capital on the separate acquisitions of a substantial interest in BT's Brightstart venture portfolio and of Abbey National's private equity portfolio (which comprised some US$1.33bn of commitments). Since joining O'Melveny & Myers in 2004, John has advised general partners establishing funds for investment in various sectors and countries including Germany, China, Africa, the renewable energy sector, technology and real estate; investors investing over US$2bn in private equity funds; European development finance institutions on the establishment of a €90m co-investment arrangement with the European Investment Bank to invest in Africa and the Caribbean; five secondary transactions; the IPO of Spectrum Interactive PLC (the second largest provider of payphones in Germany and the UK); ISIS on its spin-out from F&C Asset Management; other private equity teams on the establishment of a number of co-investment and management incentive schemes.
Career: Admitted as a solicitor to the Supreme Court of England and Wales in 1991. Co-author of 'AIM and EASDAQ - The New Enterprise Markets'.
Education: St John's College, Cambridge (awarded an Exhibition on entry).

FELTON, Simon

Mourant du Feu & Jeune
Phone: London (020 7073 7877)
E-mail: simon.felton@mourant.com
Corporate and banking, capital markets, funds.
Career: Made an associate of the firm in 2005.
Languages: English.
Personal: Resides in London.

HILLS, Stuart

O'Melveny & Myers LLP
Phone: London (+44 20 7088 4872)
E-mail: shills@omm.com
Banking and finance lawyer who represents financial buyers, private equity houses, borrowers and lenders on a broad range of international and domestic transactions.
Position: Partner in O'Melveny & Myers' London office. Stuart has represented many of the UK's largest corporate borrowers and private equity houses on the financing aspects of various multi-juridictional acquisitions, both public and private. Stuart has also acted as lender counsel on a number of private and public acquistion financings.

Career: Admitted as a solicitor 1995. Stuart began his career at Standard Chartered Bank working in their UK corporate lending team which focused on property finance and leveraged finance transactions. After 5 years with Standard Chartered Bank, Stuart requalified as a lawyer and joined Freshfields Bruckhaus Deringer in 1993. In 2004 Stuart became a partner at O'Melveny & Myers.
Education: Durham University (1992, BA Honours in Law).

HUDSON, Matthew

O'Melveny & Myers LLP
Phone: London (+44 20 7088 4801)
E-mail: mhudson@omm.com
Position: Head of O'Melveny & Myers' London office and chair of the firm's European corporate finance and private equity practices. Within corporate finance, Matthew has acted for sellers, buyers and advisers on all aspects of M&A (both private and public), on IPOs and capital markets. Within private equity, he has advised private equity houses on fund formation, carried interest structures, LBOs, MBOs and venture capital. In addition, he has represented management teams, as well as portfolio companies, throughout their financing, exit and M&A activity. He has also spent six years within the private equity industry, undertaking LBOs for a fund established by a global investment bank, venture capital at an early stage investment group, and secondary fund and asset acquisitions at a large secondaries house. His management and entrepreneurial experience has involved helping to found the largest European legal group in private equity, founding and acting as CEO of a venture capital group, helping found a boutique investment bank and establishing his own legal and commercial advisory firm. His professional experience includes acting for a private equity house on the MBO of a software group, and its subsequent IPO on NASDAQ/EASDAQ (the first joint listing on the two exchanges); acting on a public to private LBO by way of scheme of arrangement; acting for private equity investors on leveraged acquisitions of non-core divisions from large quoted groups and their subsequent disposals; acquisition of a mortgage group and its subsequent securitisations; acting for a secondary private equity house on the acquisition of fund positions, co-investments and a series of directs from a large UK financial services group; acting on the establishment of a private equity group and the raising of its first fund.
Member: IMRO (Investment Management); FSA (Financial Services Authority - Investment Management and Corporate Finance).
Education: University of East Anglia (1983, LLB).

O'MEARA, Ian

Mourant du Feu & Jeune
Phone: London (+44 20 7073 7867)
E-mail: ian.omeara@mourant.com
Corporate and banking, capital markets.
Position: Associate of the firm practicing in the capital markets and corporate and banking practice areas. Based in the City of London office, Ian undertakes a range of work but specialises in securitisations, CDOs, tier/capital issues, repackagings and other structured finance work.
Career: Trained Travers Smith Braithwaite; qualified 1992 (England and Wales); Travers Smith Braithwaite 1990-95; Standard Chartered Bank 1995-99; Merrill Lynch Investment Managers 1999-2001; associate Mourant de Feu Jeune 2004.
Member: Law Society of England and Wales.
Education: Elizabeth College, Guernsey; Balliol College, Oxford (1988 BA Hons jurisprudence 2(1)); College of Law, Guildford (1989 Law Society Finals).
Personal: Born 1966; resides London.

NORTHERN IRELAND

BECKETT, Samuel R

L'Estrange & Brett
Phone: Belfast (+44 2890 230 426)
E-mail: sam.beckett@lestrangeandbrett.com
Commercial litigation, including construction and professional indemnity.
Position: Partner in the firm's litigation department. Deals with commercial disputes including construction and professional indemnity cases. Also concerned with liquor licensing applications.
Career: Qualified 1980. John Johnson & Son 1980; L'Estrange & Brett 1984; made partner 1986; served on the Contentious Business Committee of the Incorporated Law Society of Northern Ireland.
Member: Chancery Division Liaison Committee; Commercial Court Liaison Committee.
Education: Bangor Grammar School; Queen's University of Belfast (1979 LLB); Certificate of Professional Legal Studies (1980).
Personal: Born 1957; resides Holywood, County Down.
Leisure: Cricket, rugby, golf and music.

BRETT, Adam TG

L'Estrange & Brett
Phone: Belfast (+44 2890 230 426)
E-mail: adam.brett@lestrangeandbrett.com
Litigation, including employment law, administrative law, professional negligence and intellectual property.
Position: Jointly heads litigation department; responsible for a wide range of commercial litigation including professional negligence, administrative law and judicial review, injunctive relief and intellectual property cases. Principal area of work is in relation to employment law and employee reward schemes. Involved in many claims brought in Northern Ireland alleging discrimination on grounds of religious belief/political opinion. Deals with a wide range of claims on other discriminatory grounds, including equal pay claims, disability claims and race claims. Has been involved in formal investigations undertaken by the Equal Opportunities Commission. Advises on the terms and conditions of employment, disciplinary and grievance procedures and issues relating to employee reward including bonus schemes and pensions. Advises in relation to restrictive covenants, European directives affecting employment law, trade union/strike action matters and cross-border employment issues. Deals with exit agreements/compromise agreements for senior management, for both employers and employees.
Career: Qualified 1981; partner at L'Estrange & Brett 1984. Contributor on Employment Law in Northern Ireland to Encyclopaedia of 'Employment Law and Practice' (Gee) and 'Employment Forms and Precedents'.
Member: Chairman of the Employment Lawyers Group for Northern Ireland 2002-5. Member of the Employment Lawyers Association.
Education: Rugby School; Oxford University (MA); Queen's University of Belfast (Certificate of Professional Legal Studies).
Personal: Born 1957; resides Belfast.
Leisure: Council member, the Royal Society for the Protection of Birds; Chairman of the Society's Northern Ireland Committee.

EAKIN, Adrian

L'Estrange & Brett
Phone: Belfast (+44 2890 230 426)
E-mail: adrian.eakin@lestrangeandbrett.com
Corporate department (projects unit).
Position: Partner in the corporate department specialising in infrastructure and project finance.
Career: Goldman Sachs International, London 1995-96; Allen & Overy, London 1996-98; admitted 1998; L'Estrange & Brett, Belfast 1998-2003, partner 2003 to date.
Member: Law Societies of England, Wales and Northern Ireland.
Education: Coleraine Academical Institution, University of Dundee (1993 LLB Hons); College of Law, York (1995 LPC).
Personal: Born 1970; resides Belfast.
Leisure: Sporting interests.

GRAY, Richard

L'Estrange & Brett
Phone: Belfast (+44 2890 230 426)
E-mail: richard.gray@lestrangeandbrett.com
Corporate department, including corporate finance and banking work. Also project finance, PFI and inward investment work.
Position: Partner in the corporate and commercial department. Main areas of practice are in company, commercial and banking law, particularly in the areas of PFI/PPP and project finance.
Career: Called to the Northern Ireland Bar 1989; admitted as a solicitor in England and Wales and Northern Ireland 1992; joined the firm in 1992, having spent a number of years working with Cameron, Markby Hewitt (now CMS Cameron McKenna, London); course adviser and tutor at the Institute of Professional Legal Studies in Belfast (company law).
Member: Law societies of Northern Ireland and England and Wales.

Education: Methodist College, Belfast; Queen's University of Belfast, (1993 LLB).
Personal: Born 1966; resides in Belfast.
Leisure: Football, walking.

HENDERSON, Brian

L'Estrange & Brett
Phone: Belfast (+44 2890 230 426)
E-mail: brian.henderson@lestrangeandbrett.com
Commercial property - banking.
Position: Senior partner and head of banking unit, advising on all aspects of banking and secured lending work; advises generally on commercial property matters.
Career: Administrative trainee in the European Commission 1978; qualified in 1976; partner L'Estrange & Brett 1979.
Languages: English, German.
Member: Non-Contentious Business Committee of the Law Society of Northern Ireland; Solicitor's European Group.
Education: Campbell College, Belfast; Trinity College, Dublin (1973 BA Mod; 1973 LLB).
Personal: Born 1951; resides Belfast.
Leisure: Tennis.

HUDDLESTON, Ian W

L'Estrange & Brett
Phone: Belfast (+44 2890 230 426)
E-mail: ian.huddleston@lestrangeandbrett.com
Commercial property.
Position: Partner in commercial property department and advises in relation to all aspects of commercial property law, with emphasis on development work and the property aspects of PFI/PPP transactions.
Career: Qualified 1991; partner L'Estrange & Brett 1994. Part-time lecturer and course facilitator at Queen's University, Belfast (commercial conveyancing).
Member: Land Registry E-Conveyancing Working Group; Environmental and Planning Law Association for Northern Ireland; Society of Trust and Estate Practitioners.
Education: Down High School, Downpatrick; Queen's University of Belfast (1988 LLB); Bristol University (1989 LLM).
Personal: Born 1965; resides Belfast.
Leisure: Hill walking, cycling and farming.

KIRKPATRICK, David J

L'Estrange & Brett
Phone: Belfast (+44 2890 230 426)
E-mail: david.kirkpatrick@lestrangeandbrett.com
Litigation including agency/distributorship, contract, construction, insurance, insolvency and personal injury.
Position: Partner in the litigation department; specialises in commercial litigation including agency/distributorship, construction, contract, insurance and insolvency.
Career: Qualified 1990; partner 2001; worked with the European Commission in Brussels 1992-93.
Member: Association of Personal Injury Lawyers.
Education: Wallace High School, Lisburn; Queen's University of Belfast (1988 LLB); University of Edinburgh (1991 LLM).
Personal: Born 1965; resides Belfast.

MATCHETT, Donna D

L'Estrange & Brett
Phone: Belfast (+44 28 9023 0426)
E-mail: donna.matchett@lestrangeandbrett.com
Commercial property and environment.
Position: Partner in the firm's commercial property department. Advises on all related transactions but with a particular emphasis on landlord and tenant and environmental matters.
Career: SJ Berwin 1993-96; qualified 1995; Francis Hanna & Co 1996-98; T M Heron & Sons 1998-99; L'Estrange & Brett 1999 to date; partner 2005.
Member: Law Society of England & Wales; Law Society of Northern Ireland; Environmental & Planning Law Association Northern Ireland.
Education: Methodist College, Belfast; Oxford University; Guildford College of Law (1997 MA Hons Jurisprudence).
Leisure: Reading, painting, theatre and rambling.

McBRIDE, Paul M

L'Estrange & Brett
Phone: Belfast (+44 2890 230 426)
E-mail: paul.mcbride@lestrangeandbrett.com
Corporate department, including corporate and commercial, project finance and inward investment.
Position: Partner in the corporate department. Advised in a number of significant mergers and acquisitions, management buy-outs and venture capital projects in Northern Ireland; experience in PFI and project finance transactions, advising both public and private sector clients; advised on a number of substantial inward investment projects.
Career: Called to the Bar 1990; admitted as a solicitor in Northern Ireland 1993; trained McKinty and Wright, Belfast; partner L'Estrange & Brett 1998.
Member: Law Society of Northern Ireland.
Education: Queen's University of Belfast (1989 LLB); Sidney Sussex College, University of Cambridge (1991 corporate law and finance).

McGRATH, Sinéad

L'Estrange & Brett
Phone: Belfast (+44 2890 230 426)
E-mail: sinead.mcgrath@lestrangeandbrett.com
Banking unit.
Position: Advises on a broad range of banking transactions but with a particular emphasis on secured lending.
Career: McKinty & Wright 1994-99; L'Estrange & Brett 1999 to date; associate in 2001 and partner in 2005.
Member: Law Society of Northern Ireland.
Education: Dominician College, Belfast; Queen's University of Belfast; Institute of Professional Legal Studies, Belfast (1994 LLB Hons, 1996 CPLS).
Leisure: Walking, yoga and cinema.

McILROY-ROSE, Andrea

L'Estrange & Brett
Phone: Belfast (+44 2890 230 426)
E-mail: andrea.mcilroy-rose@lestrangeandbrett.com
Commercial property and construction.
Position: Partner in the commercial property department; specialises in commercial leases and retail, investment and development work, and in particular shopping centres. Member of the construction group; with particular experience of PFI projects, advising on both property and construction matters.
Career: Qualified in England 1991; spent eight years working for Mayer, Brown, Rowe & Maw, (City of London firm); partner at L'Estrange & Brett 2000. Retains a practising certificate for England and Wales as well as Northern Ireland and acts for clients in both jurisdictions.
Member: Law Society of England and Wales; Law Society of Northern Ireland; Society of Construction Law.
Education: Victoria College, Belfast; University of Reading; The College of Law, Guildford (1987 LLB).
Personal: Born 1965; resides Belfast.

PIERCE, I Graham L

L'Estrange & Brett
Phone: Belfast (+44 2890 230 426)
E-mail: graham.pierce@lestrangeandbrett.com
Commercial property.
Position: Partner in commercial property department and advises on all aspects of commercial property work with particular emphasis on retail development and institutional investment; advises landlords and tenants on the impact of Business Tenancies legislation in Northern Ireland and writes on the subject. Sits on the firm's construction unit; advises developers, contractors and consultants on construction contracts, professional appointments and collateral warranties.
Career: Qualified 1988; partner 1992; sits on the firm's training committee, and construction practice committee.
Member: Law Society of Northern Ireland.
Education: Portora Royal School, County Fermanagh; De Montfort University (1986 LLB Hons).
Personal: Born 1965; resides Belfast.